Funk & Wagnalls

STANDARD DESK

DICTIONARY

Funk & Wagnalls

STANDARD DESK

DICTIONARY

Funk & Wagnalls

a company of
The Dun & Bradstreet Corporation

1980

TABLE OF CONTENTS

PREFACE

EDITORIAL STAFF

GUIDE TO THIS DICTIONARY

Pronunciations *by James B. McMillan*   xv

Level and Style Labels *by Frederic G. Cassidy*   xix

Etymologies *by Albert H. Marckwardt*   xxii

Synonyms *by S. I. Hayakawa*   xxiv

Weights and Measures   xxvi

Table of English Spellings   xxvii

Special Signs and Symbols   xxviii

Pronunciation Key   xxix

Abbreviations Used in This Book   xxxii

A DICTIONARY OF THE ENGLISH LANGUAGE   **1–800**

Gazetteer (with ZIP Code numbers)   801

Abbreviations   842

Biographies   857

Secretarial Handbook *by Alice Ottun*   866

Manuscript Preparation   866

Word Usage and Word Relationships   867

Punctuation   867

Capitalization   870

Spelling   871

Confusing Words   872

Consistency of Tense and Person of Verbs   872

Business Correspondence   873

Forms of Address   875

PREFACE

This dictionary contains over 100,000 entries, offering comprehensive coverage of the general vocabulary and including many scientific and technical terms seldom found in dictionaries of comparable size. Based upon the considerably larger Standard College Dictionary, it represents an up-to-date survey of the English language, and includes, apart from the main body of vocabulary words, a wide selection of idioms and figurative expressions, as well as many common slang terms and meanings. It also includes a large number of usage notes, marked off in the dictionary proper by this symbol [◆], which give helpful information and counsel on a variety of traditionally troublesome words, such as *can* and *may, lay* and *lie, infer* and *imply.*

Following the main vocabulary section is the *Gazetteer*, including all major localities in the United States and Canada, as well as all the countries of the world and the major foreign cities, and indicating political status, location, and, if appropriate, ZIP Code number. A separate section, *Abbreviations*, is a comprehensive list of abbreviations and acronyms that one is most likely to encounter, whether in business practice or in everyday affairs. *Biographies*, which immediately follows the abbreviations section, lists and pronounces the names of, and gives information about, people of the past and present who have distinguished themselves in the arts and sciences, in world affairs, or in other areas of endeavor.

Finally, the *Secretarial Handbook* includes sections on usage, punctuation, business correspondence, and forms of address that should be of considerable help not only to secretaries but to anyone who is sometimes puzzled by the complexities of English grammar and usage, or who is called upon to write an important business letter.

For a more complete account of these sections as well as other features of this book, and for valuable discussions of pronunciation, restrictive labels, etymologies, and synonyms and antonyms, the reader is urged to read the *Guide to This Dictionary* beginning on p. viii.

The Editors

EDITORIAL STAFF

Funk & Wagnalls' Editorial Board for Dictionaries consists of Albert H. Marckwardt, Chairman, Professor of English and Linguistics, Princeton University; Frederic G. Cassidy, Professor of English, University of Wisconsin; S. I. Hayakawa, Professor of English, San Francisco State College; and James B. McMillan, Professor of English, University of Alabama. Each of these scholars has contributed an essay in his field of special competence to the *Guide to This Dictionary*. In addition, many other authorities in a variety of fields have given us the benefit of their specialized knowledge and advice in formulating the definitions that appear in this book.

GUIDE TO THE USE OF FUNK & WAGNALLS STANDARD DESK DICTIONARY

The following explanatory material deals with the different kinds of information given in this dictionary and with their arrangement within each entry. A careful reading of the fourteen items discussed below, and of the essays on **Pronunciations, Level and Style Labels, Etymologies,** and **Synonyms** that begin on page xv, will help the reader use this dictionary effectively. Items 1–14 are listed in roughly the same order in which the information they describe appears in most individual entries:

1. The Main Entry
2. Pronunciations
3. Parts of Speech
4. Inflected Forms
5. Definitions
6. Restrictive Labels
7. Collateral Adjectives

8. Variant Forms
9. Cross-references
10. Etymologies
11. Run-on Derivatives
12. Usage Notes
13. Synonyms and Antonyms
14. Geographical Entries

1. The Main Entry

The main entry word or words have been printed in large, boldface type, set slightly into the left-hand margin so as to be easily found. General vocabulary words and phrases, prefixes and suffixes, foreign terms, biographical and geographical entries, etc., are arranged in one alphabetic list. Thus, the entry for **harlequin** precedes that for **Harlequin.** Biographical entries, geographical entries, and abbreviations appear in separate alphabetical lists following the main vocabulary section.

A center period is used to indicate division in main entry words, as **par·ti·cip·i·al.** In other boldface entries, such as run-on derivatives and variant forms, the center period is eliminated wherever the primary and secondary syllable stresses are marked, as **par′ti· cip′i·al·ly.** Phrasal entries, as **intelligence quotient,** are not divided when the elements are individually entered elsewhere.

2. Pronunciations

Pronunciations are shown in parentheses immediately following the boldface main entry, as **di·chot·o·my** (dī·kot′ə·mē). The pronunciation system used in this dictionary utilizes, with a few exceptions, the letters of the alphabet, combined with certain standard diacritical marks, such as the macron for the so-called "long vowels" (ā, ē, ī, ō, yōō). The "short vowels" have no diacritical marks. The breve is retained in the one symbol (o͝o), the vowel in *book*, to avoid confusion with the vowel in *pool*, for which the macron is used (ōō). The dieresis is used for one symbol (ä), and the circumflex for three (â, ô, û). The schwa (ə) is used for the unstressed neutral vowel, however spelled. This pronunciation key is based on phonemic principles to the extent that each symbol represents a single sound or closely associated cluster of sounds, and no sound is transcribed with more than one symbol.

The pronunciation key appears in full on p. xxix; an abbreviated key is given at the foot of every odd-numbered page in the main vocabulary section. For a fuller discussion of the treatment given pronunciation in this dictionary, see p. xv.

3. Parts of Speech

These are shown in italics following the pronunciation for main entries, and are abbreviated as follows: *n.* (noun), *v.* (verb), *pron.* (pronoun), *adj.* (adjective), *adv.* (adverb), *prep.* (preposition), *conj.* (conjunction), *interj.* (interjection). When more than one part of speech is entered under a main entry, the additional designations are run in and preceded by a boldface dash, as **cor·ner** (kôr′nər) *n.* . . . — *v.t.* . . . — *v.i.* . . . — *adj.* . . .

Verbs used transitively are identified as *v.t.*, those intransitively as *v.i.*; those used both transitively and intransitively in all senses are designated *v.t. & v.i.*

4. Inflected Forms

These include the past tense, past participle, and present participle of verbs, the plural of nouns, and the comparative and superlative of adjectives and adverbs. Inflected forms are entered wherever there is some irregularity in spelling or form. They are shown in boldface type, with syllabication, immediately after the part-of-speech designation. Only the syllable affected is shown, unless ambiguity may occur, as **com·pute** (kəm·pyo͞ot′) *v.t. & v.i.* **·put·ed, ·put·ing.** An inflected form that requires pronunciation or is alphabetically distant from the main entry will also be separately entered and pronounced in its proper vocabulary place.

Principal parts of verbs The order in which the principal parts are shown is past tense, past participle, and present participle, as **come** (kum) *v.i.* **came, come, com·ing.** Where the past tense and past participle are identical, only two forms are entered, as **bake** (bāk) *v.* **baked, bak·ing.** When alternative forms are given, the first form indicated is usually the one preferred, as **grov·el** (gruv′əl, grov′-) *v.i.* **grov·eled** or **·elled, grov·el·ing** or **·el·ling.** Principal parts entirely regular in formation — those that add *-ed* and *-ing* directly to the infinitive without spelling modification — are not shown.

Plurals of nouns Irregular forms are here preceded by the designation *pl.*, as **a·lum·nus** (ə·lum′nəs) *n. pl.* **·ni** (-nī); **co·dex** (kō′deks) *n. pl.* **co·di·ces** (kō′də·sēz, kod′ə-); **deer** (dir) *n. pl.* **deer.** When alternative plurals are given, the first shown is the preferred form, as **buf·fa·lo** (buf′ə·lō) *n. pl.* **·loes** or **·los; chrys·a·lis** (kris′ə·lis) *n. pl.* **chrys·a·lis·es** or **chry·sal·i·des** (kri·sal′ə·dēz).

Comparison of adjectives and adverbs The comparatives and superlatives of adjectives and adverbs are shown immediately after the part of speech when there is some spelling modification or a complete change of form, as **mer·ry** (mer'ē) *adj.* **·ri·er, ·ri·est; bad**[1] (bad) *adj.* **worse, worst; well**[2] (wel) *adv.* **bet·ter, best.**

5. Definitions

In entries for words having several senses, the definition appearing first is the one most frequently used. Successive definitions are listed, wherever possible, in order of declining frequency of use rather than according to semantic evolution. Each such definition is distinguished by a boldface numeral, the numbering starting anew after each part-of-speech designation when more than one sense follows. Closely related meanings, especially those within a specific field or area of study, are defined under the same number and set apart by boldface letters.

6. Restrictive Labels

No restrictive label is required for those general-purpose words and meanings, usable in any context, which make up the bulk of the English language as it is spoken and written throughout the world. Words or particular senses of words, however, which have any restriction of use are labeled. A number of different types of labels are used in this dictionary to indicate where, by whom, or in what context a particular word or expression is most commonly used. For a full discussion of **Level and Style Labels,** including the labels *Informal, Dial.* (for *dialectal*), *Slang,* and *Illit.* (for *illiterate*), see p. xix. The following are other types of labels found in this dictionary:

Currency Labels Both standard and nonstandard words may be in less than general currency. If these are included they are labeled *Rare, Archaic,* or *Obs.* (obsolete). (See the definitions of these words in the body of the dictionary.)

Locality Labels These identify the geographical region of the English-speaking world in which a word or meaning, either standard or nonstandard, is used exclusively or more characteristically than it is in other regions. (For example, *elevator* is labeled *U.S.,* while the synonymous *lift* is labeled *Brit.*)

Field Labels These identify the field of learning or of activity in which a word or sense belongs. (Some common examples are *Bot., Chem., Mil., Photog.* — see the list of abbreviations.) Because of the frequent overlapping between fields, however, these labels can be applied only broadly.

Foreign-language Labels These identify the source of words or phrases not fully naturalized into English. Because these retain the foreign spelling and pronunciation, though used in English context, they should be italicized when written. (Examples are *joie de vivre* labeled *French, Weltschmerz* labeled *German.*)

7. Collateral Adjectives

Because of extensive borrowing in English from Norman French and Medieval Latin, we find a good many English nouns which have adjectives closely connected with them in meaning, but not in form, such as *arm* and *brachial, horse* and *equine, dog* and *canine, day* and *diurnal,* etc. These functionally related adjectives are defined in this dictionary in their alphabetic place, but as an added convenience many of them are also shown with their associated nouns. Collateral adjectives follow the sense or senses of the noun to which they apply, and are introduced with a diamond symbol:

> **arm** (ärm) *n.* **1.** *Anat.* **a** The upper limb of the human body.... ◆ Collateral adjective: *brachial.*

8. Variant Forms

Some words have more than one standard spelling or form, as *center, centre; algebraic, algebraical.* Sometimes, completely different forms have the same meaning, as *bachelor's-button* and *cornflower.* These variants are listed in two ways: (1) When the variant form is alphabetically close to the commoner form, it is entered with the main entry in boldface type, syllabicated, stressed, and, where necessary, pronounced; (2) When the variant is alphabetically distant, it is shown in italic print under the main entry, and is also listed in its proper alphabetic place with a cross-reference to the main entry.

> **bach·e·lor** (bach′ə·lər, bach′lər) *n.*..... **3.** A young knight serving under another's banner: also **bach′e·lor-at-arms′** ....
> **bas-re·lief** (bä′ri·lēf′, bas′-) *n.* That type of sculpture in which the figures project ...: also called *low relief.*

Forms that have some restricted usage are labeled accordingly, as **hon·or** .... Also *Brit.* **hon′our.**

9. Cross-references

Cross-references are directions to see another entry for additional information. The entry to be sought is generally indicated in small capital letters, as **car·a·cul** ... See KARAKUL; **cor·po·ra** ... Plural of CORPUS; **Vulgar Latin** See under LATIN.

Some entries are defined by citing another form:

cach·a·lot (kash′ə·lot, -lō) *n.* The sperm whale.
cou·gar (kōō′gər) *n.* The puma.
fog chamber *Physics* A cloud chamber.

Complete information will be found under the word or term used in the definition.

Cross-references are also used to indicate where more information may be found, or when an important semantic distinction might otherwise be missed, as **petit mal** ...: distinguished from *grand mal*; **Brunhild.** ... Compare BRUNNHILDE.

For information about cross-references used in the etymologies, see p. xxii.

10. Etymologies

Etymologies are given in brackets at the end of each entry. For a full discussion of the treatment given etymology in this dictionary, see p. xxii.

11. Run-on Derivatives

Words that are actually or apparently derived from other words by the addition or replacement of a suffix, and whose sense can be inferred from the meaning of the main word, are run on, in smaller boldface type, at the end of the appropriate main entries. The run-on entries are preceded by a heavy dash and followed by a part-of-speech designation. They are syllabicated and stressed, and, when necessary, a full or partial pronunciation is indicated:

in·sip·id (in·sip′id) *adj.* .... — **in·si·pid·i·ty** (in′si·pid′ə·tē), **in·sip′id·ness** *n.* — **in·sip′id·ly** *adv.*

12. Usage Notes

Special points of grammar and idiom, when essential to correct usage, are included, following a colon, after the particular sense of a word to which they apply, as **anx·ious** ... **3.** Intent; eagerly desirous: with *for* or the infinitive. ... More extensive notes consisting of supplementary information on grammar, accepted usage, the relative status of variant forms, etc., are entered at the end of the relevant entries and prefaced with the symbol ◆. Examples may be found under the entries **Asiatic, gotten,** and **me.**

13. Synonyms and Antonyms

Extended discussions of the differentiation in shades of meaning within a group of related words are given at the end of relevant entries in paragraphed form. They are introduced by the abbreviation **Syn.** Since a word may have distinct synonyms for each of several senses, the discussions are numbered, where necessary, to accord with the numbering of relevant definitions in the preceding entry. In addition to the discussions, lists of synonyms and antonyms are entered in cases where the distinctions between the words in question are easily ascertained from the definitions. For a full discussion of the treatment given synonyms in this dictionary, see p. xxiv.

14. Geographical Entries

Population figures for places in the United States are based on the 1970 census, and those for Canada and Australia on the 1971 censuses. Population figures for foreign places are based on the latest available census or estimate.

PRONUNCIATIONS by James B. McMillan

A pronunciation is correct when it is normally and unaffectedly used by cultivated people. Strictly, any pronunciation is correct when it serves the purposes of communication and does not call unfavorable attention to the speaker, but the user of a desk dictionary does not need or expect to find every pronunciation of every word that may be heard in the smallest, most isolated communities. He expects to find the pronunciations that he can use comfortably before educated audiences.

We do not have in the English-speaking world a standard of pronunciation like the standard specimens of meters, liters, feet, and gallons that national bureaus of standards keep to preserve and enforce uniformity. It would be technically simple to have a professional speaker record on magnetic tape his pronunciation of every word in a dictionary and to store the tapes in libraries where they could be heard, even in distant cities, by dialing the telephone number of a computer that would select and play back the pronunciation of any desired word. But choosing the model speaker would not be simple. Should he pronounce *forest* as it sounds in Boston? Or Chicago? Or Atlanta? Or Spokane? If he pronounced *dew* and *do* differently, would educated people who pronounce the two words alike change to conform? Or if he pronounced both (do͞o), would educated people who distinguish the two words be willing to give up their distinction? Simple inanimate quart jars and foot rulers can easily be taken to a government bureau and compared with a standard measure, but pronunciations are articulations of sounds by individual human vocal organs, with all the diversity of human beings. One standard of correctness is impractical, unenforceable, impossible.

Correctness in pronunciation is so flexible and pronunciations are so varied that a desk dictionary cannot list nearly all the acceptable forms of even common words; for this reason the absence of a pronunciation, for example *said* as (sād), rhyming with *laid*, does not mean that the pronunciation is necessarily "incorrect," but simply that there is not space to record every minority practice. The editors do not include (bûr′ē) for *bury* (rhyming with *hurry*) because they have heard it very rarely, and not usually in cultivated speech. On the other hand, when a pronunciation is listed the dictionary user can be confident that the pronunciation is in actual use among educated people. Disagreements that arise because two people do not pronounce the key words alike cannot be settled; the fact that every user has to interpret the pronunciation symbols in terms of his own pronunciation of the key words makes each one, in a sense, his own standard.

Because words are listed in a dictionary as separate items, not as segments of a flow of speech, the pronunciations given are for words pronounced in isolation; for example the pronunciation (fāt) is what one would say in answering "How do you pronounce the word spelled *f-e-t-e*?" In the stream of speech, many words, particularly pronouns, articles, and auxiliaries, occur in shortened or changed form when they are weakly stressed. Thus the words (tel), (him), (hē), (haz), (tōō), (sē), (hûr) may appear in sentence form as (tel·im·ē·has·tə·sē·ər). The changed pronunciations that actual utterance produces are not normally listed.

Syllabication in pronunciation follows, in general, the breaks heard in speech, rather than the conventional division of the boldface entry, as **hid·ing** (hī'ding), **lat·er** (lā'tər), **of·fi·cial** (ə·fish'əl). Syllable boundaries are sometimes impossible to set with certainty and are sometimes variable. Thus words like **met·ric** (met'rik) and **cad·re** (kad'rē) are divided between the consonants, although many people pronounce both consonants in the second syllable (me'trik) and (ka'drē), as the contrast between *metric* and *met Rick* will show.

Three levels of stress are indicated in the pronunciations. Syllables with weakest stress are not marked; every word with two or more syllables has one primary stress marked, as *editor* (ed'it·ər); and words with three or more syllables frequently have a secondary stress marked by a light symbol, as *acceleration* (ak·sel'ə·rā'·shən), or a secondary stress indicated simply by a vowel, as in the final syllable of *ameliorate* (ə·mēl'yə·rāt). These three levels correspond to the primary, tertiary (*not* secondary), and weak levels in the four-stress system commonly used by linguists. The secondary level of the four-stress system is not used here because it occurs only in phrases or other word groups, not in single words.

Because a dictionary records and reports the pronunciations of educated people, and all educated people do not pronounce identically, a dictionary must list variant forms of thousands of words. When two or more pronunciations are indicated for a word, the one that the editors believe must frequent in the northern and western sections of the United States is listed first, but other pronunciations are equally reputable. (The dictionary does not list socially substandard pronunciations, no matter how common they may be.)

Pronunciation differences are of seven principal kinds:

(1) Different consonants may be used in the same word; e.g. some people pronounce *exit* (ek'sit), others (eg'zit); some pronounce *blouse* (blous), others (blouz).

(2) Different vowels may be used in the same word; e.g. for some people the word *lever* rhymes with *clever*

(klev′ər), for others it rhymes with *beaver* (bē′vər); the
first syllable of *economics* may rhyme with *peck* (ek·ə·
nom′iks) or with *peak* (ē·kə·nom′iks).

(3) A word may have different syllables stressed; e.g.
altimeter (al·tim′ə·tər) or (al′tə·mē′tər), and *abdomen*
(ab′də·mən) or (ab·dō′mən).

(4) The same consonant may be used in a word, but it
may be articulated very differently; e.g. the /t/* in *metal*,
or *writer*, or *winter*, or the /r/ in *very* (sometimes humorously written *veddy*).

(5) The same vowel may be used in a word, but it may
be articulated very differently; e.g. the /ô/ in *raw*, the
/ou/ in *house*, the /ī/ in *ice*, and the /ä/ in *park*, which
have wide regional variations.

(6) Although all dialects of American English seem to
have the same twenty-four consonants, some have fewer
vowels than others; e.g., the contrasts made in some regions between *morning* and *mourning*, *cot* and *caught*,
burred and *bird*, and *Cary*, *Kerry*, and *Carrie* are not
made in other regions.

(7) The same vowel or consonant may not occur in
the same positions in all varieties; e.g., some speakers
pronounce /y/ before /o͞o/ in *cute* (kyo͞ot) but not in
new (no͞o) or *due* (do͞o) or *tune* (to͞on), while others of
equal education pronounce these words (nyo͞o), (dyo͞o),
and (tyo͞on). Some speakers have /zh/ normally between vowels, as in *pleasure* (plezh′ər) and *vision* (vizh′·
ən) but not at the ends of words, so that *garage* is both
(gə·räzh′) and (gə·raj′).

Some differences in pronunciation can be correlated
with geography, and others are purely personal. No
dictionary can pick one pronunciation of *dog*, or *either*,
or *room* and ignore other pronunciations of equal repute.
The principal variants must be acknowledged. For rare
words, such as terms in the arts and sciences that are not
learned vernacularly, analogy and the pattern of source
languages provide the pronunciations listed.

Two methods of providing variants are used, (1)
multiple pronunciations, as *fog* (fog, fôg), and (2) variable symbols keyed to common words, such as /â/ as in
dare, fair; it is assumed that when a dictionary user looks
up *parterre* and finds (pär·târ′) he will pronounce the
first syllable to rhyme with *bar* and the second syllable
to rhyme with *dare, air*, since /ä/ is keyed to the word
father, and /â/ is keyed to the words *dare, air*. The dictionary does not tell the user how to pronounce the key
words, assuming that they represent stable basic patterns.

*The symbols printed between virgules represent phonemes.

When a variant pronunciation differs only in part from the first pronunciation recorded, only the differing syllable or syllables are shown, provided there is no possibility of misinterpretation, as **eq·ua·ble** (ek′wə· bəl, ē′kwə-).

Phrasal entries of two or more words are not pronounced if the individual elements are separately entered in proper alphabetic place.

Sometimes a word will differ in its pronunciation depending on its use as a noun, verb, etc., or in some particular sense. The differing pronunciations are shown immediately after the entry word, with the applications clearly indicated, as follows:

ad·dress (ə·dres′; *for n. defs. 2, 3, also* ad′res)
re·ject (*v.* ri·jekt′; *n.* rē′jekt)

A few foreign words occur with sufficient frequency in English to require dictionary entry; as their use increases they usually become adapted to English pronunciation patterns. For the dictionary user who speaks the language from which a word is imported, no pronunciation is necessary; he recognizes the word or can pronounce it from his knowledge of the spelling of the foreign language. However, the dictionary user who does not speak the foreign language may wish to pronounce a word in a recognizable approximation of its native form. Such words are respelled with the English vowels and consonants that are closest to the foreign phonemes, plus a handful of symbols for French and German sounds that have no counterparts in English. Thus the French word *chef-d'oeuvre* is respelled (she· doe′vr′), which warns that a non-English vowel occurs in the second syllable and that the /r/ at the end is voiceless. It is assumed that the consonants /sh/, /d/, and /v/, and the vowel /e/ will be reasonably similar to the corresponding (but not identical) French sounds, and that the stress on the second syllable will be lighter than English primary stress.

LEVEL AND STYLE LABELS   by Frederic G. Cassidy

The language is often thought of as existing on two "levels of usage," the standard and the nonstandard. This distinction rests on the fact that, though there is nothing intrinsically higher or lower, better or worse in one word than in another *considered as words* (language signals), every speech community nevertheless responds more or less favorably toward individual words and senses on the basis of association, habit, imposed value judgments, and the like. The language of cultivation, being that normally used by the leading part of the community, and that most widely understood within the English-speaking world, has high prestige and is considered to be of the "upper" level. This is *Standard English*. In contrast, the language of limited, local, or uncultivated use is nonstandard and of "lower" level. The following scheme represents the relative positions of various types of discourse and the corresponding labels used in this dictionary.

Standard English
{
Throughout the English-speaking world (No label)
Characteristic of a national division of English
  Labels: *U.S., Brit., Scot., Austral.,* etc.
Characteristic of a broad region of a national division
  Labels: *Southern U.S., SW U.S.,* etc.
Characteristic of general informal use
  Label: *Informal*
}

Nonstandard English
{
Used within a small geographical area, and often rural and traditional
  Label: *Dial.*
Used to express a humorous, racy, and irreverent attitude, often within a particular group
  Label: *Slang*
Used within a group in connection with a common activity, trade, or profession
  (No label or a field label)
Used by the least educated, and considered incorrect by most users of Standard English
  Label: *Illit.*
}

The dictionary concentrates on standard words and meanings; only those nonstandard ones are included which have wide currency or which deserve notice for some other reason (e.g., their relationship to standard words). Lines of distinction cannot always be sharply drawn between the various types of nonstandard words or meanings. It is sometimes necessary also to combine the labels (e.g., *Brit. Dial., U.S. Slang*) for precise discriminations.

In addition, since the response to words depends in part upon the stylistic context in which they are used, the dictionary maker must take this response into consideration in applying labels. Two distinct styles are generally recognized: Formal and Informal.*

Formal style is that appropriate to all public and serious expression; to spoken use in legislative assemblies, in courts, in the pulpit; to "belles lettres" or artistic literature; to legal and scientific writing. Because its users belong to the cultivated and literate part of the public it tends to be more deliberate, precise, discriminating, and orderly than the casual usage normal to everyday discourse, even that carried on by this same cultivated group.

Informal style, that employed by most people a great part of the time in both speaking and writing, differs from the formal in being less consciously controlled, less precise, less complex and compact, less careful in diction — though quite acceptable within its sphere, and more appropriate to relaxed situations than formal style would be.

In pronunciation the formal style is more controlled, with conscious use of prosodic features (pitch, pause, stress) and with clear articulation and syllabication (though without restressing, spelling-pronunciation, or other distortions). In grammar it is conservative; in sentence form it has more variety and range than everyday discourse has. Its vocabulary is far broader and richer, demanding sharper distinctions and more sensitive choice. In overall structure it is orderly, consciously articulated, intellectually directed.

In pronunciation the informal style is easy, relaxed; it admits a degree of slurring and ellipsis, though not to the point of becoming unclear. It makes fuller use of voice qualifiers (indicating emotional attitudes) than does formal style; it is therefore far more personal. In grammar it is less conservative, reflecting contemporary tendencies in the development of the language. In sentence form it is less complex and varied, and in vocabulary less discriminating, than is formal style: it experiments with neologisms, slang, and the livelier words of current vogue. It is given to abbreviation and contraction. In overall structure it is likely to be casual, not closely knit, additive rather than integral.

New scientific and literary words are apt to enter the sphere of standard usage at once; new popular words, by contrast, tend to remain nonstandard for a time — perhaps always; but they may and sometimes do rapidly gain status and enter the standard sphere.

Since "formal" and "informal" properly describe *styles* of discourse, the application of one of these terms

*The label *Colloq.* (colloquial — see its definition in the body of the dictionary) is now so widely misunderstood by the public as to be no longer serviceable and is therefore not used in this dictionary.

to an individual word or meaning indicates only that such an item is appropriate to the one style or the other. If a word of one style is employed in a context not its own, it will give some effect of its own style to that context. Further, since no meaning is irrevocably fixed, the connotation of a word repeatedly used in a stylistic context not its own may change.

A word or meaning labeled *Informal* is therefore one which, though as well known as any other standard one, is less acceptable (i.e., less accepted at any given time) for formal use than for informal. The actual usage of cultivated writers and speakers is the only valid test of such status. Words not labeled are appropriate to formal use.

The "levels" and "styles" do not coincide exactly. Their relationship may best be expressed by the following diagram, in which the sphere of Standard English is represented by a circle, the nonstandard lying outside it.

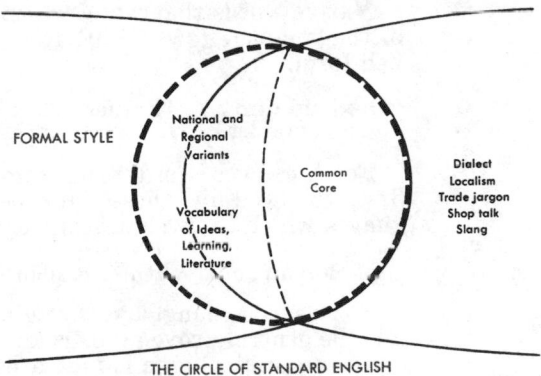

THE CIRCLE OF STANDARD ENGLISH

The circle is broken to indicate that nonstandard usages sometimes enter and become standard, and that formerly standard words also drop out into nonstandard usage or disappear altogether. Elliptical lines to left and right, drawn through the circle of Standard English, set off those parts that are appropriate respectively to formal and informal style. The Common Core comprises those words and senses which are used in all types of English.

Distinctions within the levels of language can be made nowadays with a considerable degree of objectivity. Distinctions of style, on the other hand, are partly esthetic and subjective. In every case an accurate application of labels must rest on the investigation of the situations in which any word or sense is actually used, the kind of people who do or do not use it, and the kind of response (apart from that of its denotative meaning) which it is likely to elicit in any linguistic community. Ultimately, however, it must also depend to some extent upon the judgment of the lexicographer.

ETYMOLOGIES   by Albert H. Marckwardt

Etymology is the systematic study of word origins, or in a particular sense the facts relating to the derivation or formation of a word. To illustrate, *etymology* is a borrowing of French *étymologie*, which developed from Latin *etymologia*, itself a borrowing from the Greek. The Greek form may be divided into two parts, *etymon* a form of the adjective "true" and *logos* "word, study, account." Thus we have the elements which entered into the formation of this word and the languages through which it passed into English.

The etymology of a word is given after the definition. It appears in square brackets, and precedes the boldface listing of derivative forms. The following three symbols are used: < "derived from"; + "and" or "combined with"; ? "possible."

Native words that were present in the earliest period of the language (450–1050) are shown in their Old English form.

bed·rid·den ... [Earlier *bedrid* < OE *bedrida* < *bed* bed + *rida* rider]

For borrowed words, the immediate source is given first, followed by those intermediate forms and languages which show significant changes.

pi·ra·nha ... [< Pg. (Brazilian) < Tupi, toothed fish]

If the specific language of origin cannot be determined but the general provenance is known, a linguistic family or a geographical area is indicated as the source.

ba·nan·a ... [< Sp. < native African name]

Words of unknown or uncertain origin are so marked. If there is a Middle English form for a word of obscure origin, it is cited. Even though the origin of a word cannot be determined, it is sometimes possible to give cognate forms from related languages. Be careful to note the difference between the mark < which means "derived from" and the abbreviation *cf.* which indicates a cognate relationship but not a derivation.

bud ... [ME *budde*; origin uncertain]
gloat ... [Cf. ON *glotta* to grin]

In order to avoid repetition and to present as much information as possible within a limited space, cross-references are occasionally used to direct attention to main entries where detailed information may be found.

de·cep·tion ... [See DECEIVE.]
de·ceive ... [< OF < L < *de-* away, down + *capere* to take]

The etymologies of words representing various types of combinations of free and bound forms (*wildcat, prejudge, goodness*) may be found under the main entries for *wild, cat; pre-, judge; good, -ness*.

Etymologies of a somewhat unusual character, especially those connecting words with particular people, places, or events are recorded with additional notes explaining the historic background of the word. For examples of this see *buncombe, gerrymander, knickerbocker*. Acronyms and blends are shown by placing the portions of the source words which have survived in the new formation in distinctive type. Back formations and instances of folk etymology are so labeled. See *donate, legislate, woodchuck*.

A knowledge of etymology can be useful in many ways. If, for example, those words which have come into English from any one language are considered as a group, they often reveal much about the nature of the cultural impact of that language and the people who speak it upon English. The fact that so many of our mineralogical terms come from German suggests the preeminence of that nation in the development of the science and our indebtedness to its scientists. The same might be said with respect to the Italian origin of our musical terminology. The common and intimate character of many of the Scandinavian borrowings in English tells us something of the nature of the relationship between the Norse and the English during the tenth and eleventh centuries.

It may also be true that in certain instances a knowledge of the etymology of a word may give the individual speaker or writer a surer sense of its meaning and use. A word like *supercilious* would seem, at least, to be more vivid to someone who can connect it with raised eyebrows than to the person for whom it is merely a polysyllable with a general implication of superiority of attitude. The word *equinox* will be employed with a greater feeling of certainty by one who connects the component parts of the word with the simple facts behind them.

A note of warning is called for, however. Etymology, informative and interesting though it may be, is not a valid criterion of present meaning or determiner of use. Meaning is determined by present usage; the meanings assigned to the words included in this dictionary were determined by a careful and systematic examination of their use in actual context.

The fact that *dilapidated* contains a form of *lapis* "stone" does not signify that this word can be applied only to stone structures. The word *etymology* itself is an excellent illustration of this point. Despite the fact that its first element is the neuter form of *etymos* "true," the etymology of a word is not the sole determiner of a single "true" or correct meaning, however much light it may shed upon aspects of its significance.

SYNONYMS   by S. I. Hayakawa

The English language is unusually rich in synonyms and near-synonyms. This richness is due to the fact that the vocabulary of English, a language especially hospitable to loan-words, is drawn from many sources. The vocabulary of Anglo-Saxon, already containing loan-words from Celtic, Latin, and Scandinavian, was just about doubled after the Norman Conquest by borrowings from French, to form the Middle English vocabulary. From the sixteenth century on, with the revival of classical learning, there was vast borrowing from Latin and Greek. Wherever English-speaking people have subsequently gone, in war, travel, or colonization, they have added new words to the language, and they continue to do so today. Thus, one may give a *speech* or *talk* (Anglo-Saxon words), a *lecture* or *address* or *harangue* (French words), an *oration* (Latin), or a *homily* (Greek). One may live on a wide and open *plain* (Old French), *steppe* (Russian), *prairie* (French), *tundra* (Lapp), *pampas* (South American Indian), or *savanna* (Spanish). A person may adhere to a *teaching* (Anglo-Saxon), a *doctrine* (French), a *tenet* (Latin), a *dogma* (Greek). Some words were borrowed more than once, at different times and in different forms, like *warden* and *warranty* (Norman French) as compared with *guardian* and *guarantee* (Central French); like *loyal* and *legal*, *royal* and *regal*, *fancy* and *fantasy*, *count* and *compute*, *gentle* and *genteel*, *priest* and *presbyter*. Some of these "doublets" are alike in meaning, some are quite different.

Often the borrowings were in a strict sense unnecessary; many that remain today are simply relics of the sixteenth-century fad of embellishing one's speech and writing with Latinisms. Certainly it is possible to talk about *kissing* without using the word *osculatory*, about *day* without *diurnal*. Nevertheless, the availability of foreign and learned vocabularies, even if they partly duplicate the native vocabulary, is a tremendous asset to any language. An advanced civilization needs, in addition to a language of everyday life (from which emerges the language of poetry), a language for law and social organization and the discussion of policy, and an even more abstract language for scientific and philosophical discourse. These many distinct needs are more easily met by a language that has had a long history of borrowing than by a language (like Gaelic) whose speakers insist on a fanatical "purity" of vocabulary, such as can only result in a poverty of things to talk about.

Are there any *exact* synonyms? The general semanticists, who assert that "no word ever has exactly the same meaning twice," would seem to assert that a word cannot even be synonymous with itself. What they mean is that the word *apple*, for example, cannot be applied twice to *exactly* the same referent, because every apple is different from every other apple, and because each apple is itself changing from moment to moment. However, in a dictionary we are concerned not so much with referents as with *verbal* equivalences: what word or phrase or circumlocution can serve as an equivalent for the word defined. Thus, *entire* means "having no part missing; whole; complete." Insofar as certain words can be substituted for others without affecting the meaning of a sentence, one can indeed speak of exact synonyms. "The *entire* (*whole, complete*) cast was invited to the party." The test for exact synonymy, then, is interchangeability. Despite Hilaire Belloc's haughty distinction, "what Anglo-Saxons call a *foreword*, but gentlemen a *preface*," these terms are also genuinely interchangeable in most contexts. But interchangeability in certain contexts does not mean interchangeability in all. "The cast is now *complete*" — not *whole*, or *entire*. A skirmish may be a *preface* to a battle, but not a *foreword*.

Hence interchangeability is by no means the whole story on synonyms. What are treated as synonyms in this dictionary are more often words that point to the same facts but convey different attitudes on the part of the speaker. An individual's regard for himself may be termed *egotism*, *conceit*, or *self-esteem*, depending on whether or not the speaker approves of it. Other synonyms point to similar actions or events, but in different contexts or applications: a *journey* is usually by land, a *voyage* by water; a short journey, whether by land or water, is a *trip*; an *excursion* is a short trip (usually for pleasure) from which one soon returns to a starting point; a military excursion is a *sortie*. We *accompany* our equals, *attend* those whom we serve, *conduct* those whom we guide, *escort* those whom we protect, except for merchant ships, which we *convoy*. It would be simpler if *go with* could be used in all these contexts. But the language would be infinitely poorer if these shades of meaning, expressive of innumerable nuances of human relationships, attitudes, and perceptions, were to be lost.

Occupational and regional differences also account for many synonyms. Is a *loch* a *lake*? Is an *arroyo* a *dry wash*? Is a *billabong* the same as an *oxbow*? What is the difference between the *headmaster* of a school and a *principal*, between a *dining room* and a *mess*, between being *cashiered*, *disbarred*, *unfrocked*, and *drummed out*? Words not only point to things and events and ideas; they also advertise our social affiliations and reinforce our self-concepts. It is as important for a sailor to refer to a privy as a *head* as it is for him to wear his uniform; indeed, his nautical vocabulary is part of his uniform. The richness of English synonymy attests to the variety of adventures of both body and mind encountered by speakers of English in many climes over many centuries.

WEIGHTS AND MEASURES

METRIC SYSTEM

LENGTH

Unit		Metric Equivalent	U.S. Equivalent
millimeter	(mm)	0.001 meter	0.03937 inch
centimeter	(cm)	0.01 meter	0.3937 inch
decimeter	(dm)	0.1 meter	3.937 inches
METER	(m)	1.0 meter	39.37 inches
dekameter	(dkm)	10.0 meters	10.93 yards
hectometer	(hm)	100.0 meters	328.08 feet
kilometer	(km)	1000.0 meters	0.6214 mile

WEIGHT OR MASS

Unit		Metric Equivalent	U.S. Equivalent
milligram	(mg)	0.001 gram	0.0154 grain
centigram	(cg)	0.01 gram	0.1543 grain
decigram	(dg)	0.1 gram	1.543 grains
GRAM	(g)	1.0 gram	15.43 grains
dekagram	(dkg)	10.0 grams	0.3527 ounce avoirdupois
hectogram	(hg)	100.0 grams	3.527 ounces avoirdupois
kilogram	(kg)	1000.0 grams	2.2 pounds avoirdupois

CAPACITY

Unit		Metric Equivalent	U.S. Equivalent
milliliter	(ml)	0.001 liter	0.034 fluid ounce
centiliter	(cl)	0.01 liter	0.338 fluid ounce
deciliter	(dl)	0.1 liter	3.38 fluid ounces
LITER	(l)	1.0 liter	1.05 liquid quarts
dekaliter	(dkl)	10.0 liters	0.284 bushel
hectoliter	(hl)	100.0 liters	2.837 bushels
kiloliter	(kl)	1000.0 liters	264.18 gallons

AREA

Unit		Metric Equivalent	U.S. Equivalent
square millimeter	(mm²)	0.000001 centare	0.00155 square inch
square centimeter	(cm²)	0.0001 centare	0.155 square inch
square decimeter	(dm²)	0.01 centare	15.5 square inches
CENTARE also	(ca)	1.0 centare	10.76 square feet
square meter	(m²)		
are also	(a)	100.0 centares	0.0247 acre
square dekameter	(dkm²)		
hectare also	(ha)	10,000.0 centares	2.47 acres
square hectometer	(hm²)		
square kilometer	(km²)	1,000,000.0 centares	0.386 square mile

VOLUME

Unit		Metric Equivalent	U.S. Equivalent
cubic millimeter	(mm³)	0.001 cubic centimeter	0.016 minim
cubic centimeter	(cc, cm³)	0.001 cubic decimeter	0.061 cubic inch
cubic decimeter	(dm³)	0.001 cubic meter	61.023 cubic inches
STERE also	(s)	1.0 cubic meter	1.308 cubic yards
cubic meter	(m³)		
cubic dekameter	(dkm³)	1000.0 cubic meters	1307.943 cubic yards
cubic hectometer	(hm³)	1,000,000.0 cubic meters	1,307,942.8 cubic yards
cubic kilometer	(km³)	1,000,000,000.0 cubic meters	0.25 cubic mile

SYMBOLS

g	10^9 times (a unit); giga-
m	10^6 times (a unit); mega-
k	10^3 times (a unit); kilo-
h	10^2 times (a unit); hecto-
dk	10 times (a unit); deka-
d	10^{-1} times (a unit); deci-
c	10^{-2} times (a unit); centi-
m	10^{-3} times (a unit); milli-
μ	10^{-6} times (a unit); micro-
n	10^{-9} times (a unit); nano-
μμ	10^{-12} times (a unit); micromicro-
Å, λ	Angstrom unit
μμ	micromicron
μ	micron

U.S. SYSTEM

LIQUID MEASURE

4	gills	= 1 pint (pt.)
2	pints	= 1 quart (qt.)
4	quarts	= 1 gallon (gal.)
31.5	gallons	= 1 barrel (bbl.)
2	barrels	= 1 hogshead
60	minims	= 1 fluid dram (fl. dr.)
8	fluid drams	= 1 fluid ounce (fl. oz.)
16	fluid ounces	= 1 pint

LINEAR MEASURE

1	mil	= 0.001 inch (in.)
12	inches	= 1 foot (ft.)
3	feet	= 1 yard (yd.)
6	feet	= 1 fathom
5.5	yards	= 1 rod (rd.)
40	rods	= 1 furlong
5280	feet	= 1 mile (mi.)
1760	yards	= 1 mile

SQUARE MEASURE

144	square inches (sq. in.)	= 1 square foot (sq. ft.)
9	square feet	= 1 square yard (sq. yd.)
30.25	square yards	= 1 square rod (sq. rd.)
160	square rods	= 1 acre (A.)
640	acres	= 1 square mile (sq. mi.)

APOTHECARIES' WEIGHT

20 grains (gr.)	= 1 scruple
3 scruples	= 1 dram (dr.)
8 drams	= 1 ounce (oz.)
12 ounces	= 1 pound (lb.)

AVOIRDUPOIS WEIGHT

27.34	grains (gr.)	= 1 dram (dr. av.)
16	drams	= 1 ounce (oz. av.)
16	ounces	= 1 pound (lb. av.)
2000	pounds	= 1 short ton (sh. tn.)
2240	pounds	= 1 long ton (l. tn.)

TROY WEIGHT

24 grains	= 1 pennyweight (dwt.)
20 pennyweight	= 1 ounce (oz. t.)
12 ounces	= 1 pound (lb. t.)

CUBIC MEASURE

144 cubic inches (cu. in.)	= 1 board foot (bd. ft.)
1728 cubic inches	= 1 cubic foot (cu. ft.)
27 cubic feet	= 1 cubic yard (cu. yd.)
128 cubic feet	= 1 cord (cd.)

DRY MEASURE

2	pints	= 1 quart (q.
8	quarts	= 1 peck (pk.,
4	pecks	= 1 bushel (bu./
3.28	bushels	= 1 barrel (bbl.)

SYMBOLS

lb., #	pound(s)
'	foot, feet
"	inch(es)

Apothecaries' Measure

℔	pound(s)
ʒ	dram(s)
℥	ounce(s)
Ə	scruple(s)
ℳ, ℞, ℳ	minim
i, j	one: used as a coefficient
ÿ	two
	one half
iss	one and one half

TABLE OF ENGLISH SPELLINGS

FOLLOWING is a list of words exemplifying the possible spellings for the sounds of English. The sounds represented by these spellings are shown in the pronunciation symbols used in this dictionary, followed by their equivalents in the International Phonetic Alphabet.

DICTIONARY KEY	IPA SYMBOL	EXAMPLES
a	æ	*c*at, pl*ai*d, c*a*lf, l*au*gh
ā	eɪ,e	m*a*te, b*ai*t, g*ao*l, g*au*ge, p*ay*, st*ea*k, sk*ei*n, w*ei*gh, pr*ey*
â(r)	ɛ,ɛr	d*a*re, f*ai*r, pr*ay*er, wh*e*re, b*ea*r, th*ei*r
à	a	b*a*r, *a*sk, c*o*t (a vowel midway in quality between [æ] and [ɑ], used in some regional American speech)
ä	ɑ	d*a*rt, *ah*, s*e*rgeant, h*ea*rt
b	b	*b*oy, rub*b*er
ch	tʃ	*ch*ip, ba*tch*, righ*te*ous, bas*ti*on, struc*tu*re
d	d	*d*ay, lad*d*er, calle*d*
e	ɛ	m*a*ny, a*e*sthete, s*ai*d, s*ay*s, b*e*t, st*ea*dy, h*ei*fer, l*eo*pard, fri*e*nd, f*oe*tid
ē	i	C*ae*sar, qu*ay*, sc*e*ne, m*ea*t, s*ee*, s*ei*ze, p*eo*ple, k*ey*, rav*i*ne, gr*ie*f, ph*oe*be, cit*y*
f	f	*f*ake, co*ff*in, cou*gh*, hal*f*, *ph*ase
g	g	*g*ate, be*g*gar, *gh*oul, *g*uard, va*gue*
h	h	*h*ot, *wh*om
hw	hw,ʍ	*wh*ale
i	ɪ	pr*e*tty, b*ee*n, t*i*n, s*ie*ve, w*o*men, b*u*sy, g*ui*lt, l*y*nch
ī	aɪ	*ai*sle, *ay*e, sl*ei*ght, *ey*e, d*i*me, p*ie*, s*i*gh, g*ui*le, b*uy*, tr*y*, l*y*e
j	dʒ	*e*dge, sol*d*ier, mo*d*ulate, ra*g*e, exa*gg*erate, *j*oy
k	k	*c*an, a*cc*ost, sa*cch*arine, *ch*ord, ta*ck*, a*c*quit, *k*ing, tal*k*, li*qu*or
l	l	*l*et, ga*ll*
m	m	dra*chm*, phle*gm*, pal*m*, *m*ake, li*mb*, gra*mm*ar, conde*mn*
n	n	*gn*ome, *kn*ow, *mn*emonic, *n*ote, ba*nn*er, *pn*eumatic
ng	ŋ	si*n*k, ri*ng*, meri*ngue*
o	ɑ, ɒ	w*a*tch, p*o*t
ō	ou,o	b*eau*, y*eo*man, s*ew*, *o*ver, s*oa*p, r*oe*, *oh*, br*oo*ch, s*ou*l, th*ou*gh, gr*ow*
ô	ɔ	b*a*ll, b*a*lk, f*au*lt, d*aw*n, c*o*rd, br*oa*d, *ou*ght
oi	ɔɪ	p*oi*son, t*oy*
ou	aʊ	*ou*t, b*ou*gh, c*ow*
o͞o	u	rh*eu*m, dr*ew*, m*o*ve, can*oe*, m*oo*d, gr*ou*p, thr*ou*gh, fl*u*ke, s*ue*, fr*ui*t
o͝o	ʊ	w*o*lf, f*oo*t, c*ou*ld, p*u*ll
p	p	ma*p*, ha*pp*en
r	r	*r*ose, *rh*ubarb, ma*rr*y, dia*rrh*ea, *wr*iggle
s	s	*c*ite, di*ce*, *ps*yche, *s*aw, *sc*ene, *sch*ism, ma*ss*
sh	ʃ	o*ce*an, *ch*ivalry, vi*ci*ous, *psh*aw, *s*ure, *sch*ist, pre*sci*ence, nau*se*ous, *sh*all, pen*si*on, ti*ss*ue, fi*ssi*on, po*ti*on
t	t	walke*d*, thou*gh*t, *ph*thisic, *p*tarmigan, *t*one, *Th*omas, bu*tt*er
th	θ	*th*ick
th	ð	*th*is, ba*th*e
u	ʌ	s*o*me, d*oe*s, bl*oo*d, y*ou*ng, s*u*n
yo͞o	ju,ɪu	b*eau*ty, *eu*logy, q*ueue*, p*ew*, *ewe*, ad*ieu*, v*iew*, f*u*se, c*ue*, *you*th, *yu*le
û(r)	ɜr, ɝ	y*ea*rn, f*e*rn, *e*rr, g*i*rl, w*o*rm, j*ou*rnal, b*u*rn, g*ue*rdon, m*y*rtle
v	v	o*f*, Ste*ph*en, *v*ise, fli*vv*er
w	w	*ch*oir, q*u*ilt, *w*ill
y	j	on*i*on, halle*lu*jah, *y*et
z	z	wa*s*, s*c*issors, *x*ylophone, *z*oo, mu*zz*le
zh	ʒ	rou*g*e, plea*s*ure, inci*si*on, sei*z*ure, gla*z*ier
ə	ə	*a*bove, fount*ai*n, dark*e*n, clar*i*ty, parl*ia*ment, cann*o*n, porp*oi*se, vici*ou*s, loc*u*s
ər	ər, ɚ	mort*ar*, broth*er*, elix*ir*, don*or*, glam*our*, aug*ur*, natu*re*, zeph*yr*

SPECIAL SIGNS AND SYMBOLS

ASTRONOMY

Astronomical Bodies

☉ **1.** the sun **2.** Sunday
☿ **1.** Mercury **2.** Wednesday
♀ **1.** Venus **2.** Friday
⊕, ♁, ⊖ the earth
☾, ☽, ◐ **1.** the moon **2.** Monday
○, ◉ full moon
☽, ◐,), ◑, ☽ the moon, first quarter
☾, ◑, (, ☾, ☾ the moon, last quarter
● new moon
♂ **1.** Mars **2.** Tuesday
①, ②, ③, etc. asteroids: in order of discovery, as ① Ceres, ② Pallas, etc.
♃ **1.** Jupiter **2.** Thursday
♄ **1.** Saturn **2.** Saturday
♅, ♅, ♅ Uranus
♆ Neptune
♇, P Pluto
☄ comet
✳, ✶ star; fixed star
α, β, γ, etc. stars (of a constellation): in order of brightness, the Greek letter followed by the Latin genitive of the name of the constellation, as α Centauri

Position and Notation

☌ in conjunction; having the same longitude or right ascension
⚹ sextile; 60° apart in longitude or right ascension
□ quadrature; 90° apart in longitude or right ascension
△ trine; 120° apart in longitude or right ascension
☍ opposition; 180° apart in longitude or right ascension
☊ ascending node
☋ descending node
♈ vernal equinox
♎ autumnal equinox
α right ascension
β celestial latitude
δ declination
λ celestial or geographical longitude
Δ distance
θ sidereal time
a mean distance
υ, ☊ longitude of ascending node
ϕ **1.** angle of eccentricity **2.** geographical latitude

Signs of the Zodiac

♈ Aries, the Ram ♉ Taurus, the Bull ♊, Π Gemini, the Twins	Spring Signs
♋, ⊗ Cancer, the Crab ♌ Leo, the Lion ♍ Virgo, the Virgin	Summer Signs
♎ Libra, the Balance ♏ Scorpio, the Scorpion ♐, ↗ Sagittarius, the Archer	Autumn Signs
♑, ♑ Capricorn, the Goat ♒ Aquarius, the Water Bearer ♓, ♓ Pisces, the Fishes	Winter Signs

BIOLOGY

○, ⊙, ① annual plant
⊙, ⊙, ♂ biennial plant
♃ perennial herb
△ evergreen plant
⊙ monocarpic plant
|w plant useful to wildlife
♂, ♁ **1.** male organism or cell **2.** staminate plant or flower
♀ **1.** female organism or cell **2.** pistillate plant or flower
☿ hermaphroditic or perfect plant or flower
⚲ neuter organism or cell
○ individual organism, especially female
□ individual organism, especially male
∞ indefinite number
P parental generation
F filial generation
F_1, F_2, F_3, etc. first, second, third, etc., filial generation

BOOKS

f°	folio
4mo, 4°	quarto
8vo, 8°	octavo
12mo, 12°	duodecimo
18mo, 18°	octodecimo
32mo, 32°	thirty-twomo

CHEMISTRY

Elements

See table of ELEMENTS.

Compounds

Compounds are represented by the symbols for their constituent elements, each element followed by a subscript numeral if the number of atoms of it appearing in the compound is greater than one, as NaCl, H_2O, H_2SO_4, etc. If a radical appears more than once in a compound, the radical is enclosed in parentheses followed by a subscript numeral, as $Ca(OCl)_2$, $Al_2(SO_4)_3$, etc. Molecules consisting entirely of one element are represented by the symbol for the element followed by a subscript numeral indicating the number of atoms in the molecule, as H_2, O_2, O_3, etc. In addition:
· denotes water of crystallization or hydration, as $CaSO_4{\cdot}5H_2O$.
α, β, γ, etc., *or* 1, 2, 3, etc. (in names of compounds), indicate different positions of substituted atoms or radicals.
\+ denotes dextrorotation, as + 120°.
− denotes levorotation, as − 113°.
[ ] include parentheses if one radical contains another, as $Fe_3[Fe(CN)_6]_2$.
In structural formulas:
—, =, ≡, etc., *or* ., :, ⁝, etc., denotes a single, double, or triple bond, etc.
R— denotes any alkyl radical.
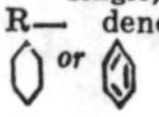 denotes a benzene ring.

Ions

Ions are represented by the symbols for their respective elements or by the symbols for the elements composing them, followed by a superscript symbol indicating the electric charge, as H^+, Cl^-, SO_4^{--}, etc. Thus:
$^-$, $^{--}$, $^{---}$, etc., *or* $^{-1}$, $^{-2}$, $^{-3}$, etc., denote a single, double, triple, etc., negative charge.
$^+$, $^{++}$, $^{+++}$, etc., *or* $^{+1}$, $^{+2}$, $^{+3}$, etc., denote a single, double, triple, etc., positive charge.
′, ″, ‴, etc., denote single, double, triple, etc., valence or charge (especially negative), as S″.

Chemical Reactions

Chemical reactions are written in a form resembling equations, with reactants on the left and products on the right. If more than one equivalent of a compound appears, it is preceded by a coefficient. Conditions of temperature, pressure, catalysis, etc., are indicated above the arrow that shows direction. The following symbols are used:
→ *or* ← denotes "yields"; also indicates the direction of the reaction.
⇌ indicates a reversible reaction.
\+ denotes "added to; together with."
↓ (written after a compound) denotes appearance as a precipitate.
↑ (written after a compound) denotes appearance as a gas.
△ denotes the presence of heat.
= *or* ⇌ denotes equivalence of amounts in a quantitative equation.

COMMERCE AND FINANCE

@ **1.** at: peaches @ $.39 per pound **2.** to: nails per pound $.50 @ $.60
$, $ dollar(s); peso(s): $100
¢ cent(s): 37¢
₱ peso(s) (Philippines)
/ shilling(s) (British): 3/
£ pound(s): £25
d penny, pence (British): 4d
¥, Y yen
₨, R rupee(s)
Rs rupees
℔ per: 50¢ ℔ dozen
\# number: #60 thread

MATHEMATICS

See table at MATHEMATICS.

MISCELLANEOUS

&, & and See AMPERSAND.
&c et cetera
7ber, 8ber, etc. September, October, etc.
† died
% percent
× by: used in expressing dimensions, as a sheet of paper 8½″ × 11″
© copyright; copyrighted
♠ spade
♥ heart
♦ diamond
♣ club

MUSIC

Music is generally written on one or more staves. The pitch of each staff is indicated by a clef. The forms of the various notes and their corresponding rests indicate relative duration. In addition the following are used:

♭ flat
♯ sharp
♭♭ double flat
※ double sharp
♮ natural
𝄴 common time; 4/4 meter
𝄵 alla breve; 2/2 or 4/2 meter
∾ turn
∽ inverted turn
𝆗 mordent
〰 inverted mordent
>, <, ∧ accent
· ' staccato
— tenuto
tr trill
⌒, ‿ slur or tie
' phrase or breath mark
𝆔 grace note
𝆒 crescendo
𝆓 diminuendo; decrescendo
⊓ down-bow
V up-bow
8va all' ottava; at the octave (raises the pitch of a staff one octave when written above it, lowers it when written below)
𝄐, 𝄑 hold

PHYSICS

α alpha particle
β beta particle
c velocity of light
g acceleration due to gravity
h Planck's constant
λ wavelength
ν frequency
j square root of minus one
∽ cycles (of alternating current or voltage)

RELIGION

✠, + **1.** a sign of the cross used by bishops before their names **2.** in some service books, an indication that the sign of the cross is to be made
* in some service books, a mark used to divide psalm verses into two parts
℟ response
℣, V', V, versicle
☧, ☧, ☧ a monogram for Christ [Gk. Χρ(ιστός)]

PRONUNCIATION KEY

The primary stress mark (ʹ) is placed after the syllable bearing the heavier stress or accent; the secondary stress mark (ʹ) follows a syllable having a somewhat lighter stress, as in **com·men·da·tion** (kom′ən·dā′shən).

a	add, map	m	move, seem	u	up, done
ā	ace, rate	n	nice, tin	û(r)	urn, term
â(r)	care, air	ng	ring, song	yoo͞	use, few
ä	palm, father				
b	bat, rub	o	odd, hot	v	vain, eve
ch	check, catch	ō	open, so	w	win, away
d	dog, rod	ô	order, jaw	y	yet, yearn
e	end, pet	oi	oil, boy	z	zest, muse
ē	even, tree	ou	out, now	zh	vision, pleasure
f	fit, half	oo͞	pool, food		
g	go, log	oo͝	took, full	ə	the schwa, an un-
h	hope, hate				stressed vowel
		p	pit, stop		representing the
i	it, give	r	run, poor		sound spelled
ī	ice, write	s	see, pass		*a* in *above*
		sh	sure, rush		*e* in *sicken*
j	joy, ledge	t	talk, sit		*i* in *clarity*
k	cool, take	th	thin, both		*o* in *melon*
l	look, rule	th	this, bathe		*u* in *focus*

The schwa (ə) varies widely in quality from a sound close to the (u) in *up* to a sound close to the (i) in *it* as heard in pronunciations of such words as *ballot, custom, landed, horses*.

The (r) in final position as in *star* (stär) and before a consonant as in *heart* (härt) is regularly indicated in the respellings, but pronunciations without (r) are unquestionably reputable. Standard British is much like the speech of Eastern New England and the Lower South in this feature.

In a few words, such as *button* (but′n) and *sudden* (sud′n), no vowel appears in the unstressed syllable because the (n) constitutes the whole syllable.

FOREIGN SOUNDS

à   as in French *ami, patte*. This is a vowel midway in quality between (a) and (ä).

œ   as in French *peu*, German *schön*. Round the lips for (ō) and pronounce (ā).

ü   as in French *vue*, German *grün*. Round the lips for (oo͞) and pronounce (ē).

kh   as in German *ach*, Scottish *loch*. Pronounce a strongly aspirated (h) with the tongue in position for (k) as in *cool* or *keep*.

ṅ   This symbol indicates that the preceding vowel is nasal. The nasal vowels in French are œṅ (*brun*), aṅ (*main*), äṅ (*chambre*), ôṅ (*dont*).

ʼ   This symbol indicates that a preceding (l) or (r) is voiceless, as in French *fin-de-siècle* (faṅ·de·sye′kl′) or *fiacre* (fyà′kr′); that a preceding (y) is pronounced consonantly in a separate syllable followed by a slight schwa sound, as in French *fille* (fē′y′); or that a consonant preceding a (y) is palatalized, as in Russian *oblast* (ô′bləsty′).

NOTE ON THE ACCENTUATION OF FOREIGN WORDS

Many languages do not employ stress in the manner of English; only an approximation can be given of the actual situation in such languages. As it is not possible to reproduce the tones of Chinese in a work of this kind, Chinese names have been here recorded with primary stress on each syllable and may be so pronounced. Japanese and Korean have been shown without stress and may be pronounced with a level accent throughout. French words are shown conventionally with a primary stress on the last syllable; however, this stress tends to be evenly divided among the syllables (except for those that are completely unstressed), with slightly more force and higher pitch on the last syllable.

Funk & Wagnalls

STANDARD DESK

DICTIONARY

ABBREVIATIONS USED IN THIS BOOK

A.D.	year of our Lord
adj.	adjective
adv.	adverb
Aeron.	Aeronautics
AF	Anglo-French
Agric.	Agriculture
Alg.	Algebra
alter.	alteration
Am. Ind.	American Indian
Anat.	Anatomy
Ant.	Antonyms
Anthropol.	Anthropology
appar.	apparently
Archeol.	Archeology
Archit.	Architecture
assoc.	association
Astron.	Astronomy
aug.	augmentative
Austral.	Australian
Bacteriol.	Bacteriology
B.C.	Before Christ
Biochem.	Biochemistry
Biol.	Biology
Bot.	Botany
Brit.	British
c.	century
cap.	capitalized
cf.	compare
Chem.	Chemistry
Chron.	Chronicles
Col.	Colossians
compar.	comparative
conj.	conjunction
contr.	contraction
Cor.	Corinthians
Crystall.	Crystallography
Dan.	Daniel, Danish
def.	definition
Dent.	Dentistry
Deut.	Deuteronomy
Dial.	Dialect, Dialectal
dim.	diminutive
Du.	Dutch
E	English
Eccl.	Ecclesiastical
Eccles.	Ecclesiastes
Ecclus.	Ecclesiasticus
Ecol.	Ecology
Econ.	Economics
Electr.	Electricity
Engin.	Engineering
Entomol.	Entomology
Eph.	Ephesians
esp.	especially
est.	estimate
Esth.	Esther
Ex.	Exodus
Ezek.	Ezekiel
F, Fr.	French
fem.	feminine
freq.	frequentative
G, Ger.	German
Gal.	Galatians
Gen.	Genesis
Geog.	Geography
Geol.	Geology
Geom.	Geometry
Gk.	Greek (Homer — A.D. 200)
Gmc.	Germanic
Govt.	Government
Gram.	Grammar
Hab.	Habakkuk
Hag.	Haggai
Heb.	Hebrews
HG	High German
Hind.	Hindustani

Hos.	Hosea
Hung.	Hungarian
Icel.	Icelandic
Illit.	Illiterate
imit.	imitative
infl.	influence, influenced
intens.	intensive
interj.	interjection
Isa.	Isaiah
Ital.	Italian
Jas.	James
Jer.	Jeremiah
Jon.	Jonah
Josh.	Joshua
Judg.	Judges
L, Lat.	Latin (Classical, 80 B.C.– A.D. 200)
Lam.	Lamentations
Lev.	Leviticus
LG	Low German
LGk.	Late Greek (200– 600)
Ling.	Linguistics
lit.	literally
LL	Late Latin (200– 600)
M	Middle
Mal.	Malachi
masc.	masculine
Math.	Mathematics
Matt.	Matthew
MDu.	Middle Dutch
ME	Middle English (1050–1475)
Mech.	Mechanics
Med.	Medicine, Medieval
Med. Gk.	Medieval Greek (600–1500)
Med. L	Medieval Latin (600–1500)
Metall.	Metallurgy
Meteorol.	Meteorology
MF	Middle French (1400–1600)
MHG	Middle High German (1100– 1450)
Mic.	Micah
Mil.	Military
Mineral.	Mineralogy
MLG	Middle Low German (1100– 1450)
n.	noun
Nah.	Nahum
N. Am. Ind.	North American Indian
Naut.	Nautical
NE	Northeast
Neh.	Nehemiah
neut.	neuter
NL	New Latin (after 1500)
Norw.	Norwegian
Num.	Numbers
NW	Northwest
O	Old
Obad.	Obadiah
Obs.	Obsolete
OE	Old English (before 1050)
OF	Old French (before 1400)

OHG	Old High German (before 1100)
OIrish	Old Irish
ON	Old Norse (before 1500)
orig.	original, originally
Ornithol.	Ornithology
OS	Old Saxon (before 1100)
Paleontol.	Paleontology
Pathol.	Pathology
Pet.	Peter
Pg.	Portuguese
Phil.	Philippians
Philem.	Philemon
Philos.	Philosophy
Phonet.	Phonetics
Photog.	Photography
Physiol.	Physiology
pl.	plural
pop.	population
pp.	past participle, pages
ppr.	present participle
prep.	preposition
prob.	probably
pron.	pronoun
pronun.	pronunciation
Prov.	Proverbs
Ps.	Psalms
Psychoanal.	Psychoanalysis
Psychol.	Psychology
pt.	preterit
ref.	reference
Rev.	Revelation
Rom.	Romans
Russ.	Russian
Sam.	Samuel
S. Am. Ind.	South American Indian
Scand.	Scandinavian
Scot.	Scottish
SE	Southeast
sing.	singular
Skt.	Sanskrit
Sociol.	Sociology
S. of Sol.	Song of Solomon
Sp.	Spanish
Stat.	Statistics
superl.	superlative
Surg.	Surgery
Sw.	Swedish
SW	Southwest
Syn.	Synonyms
Telecom.	Telecommunication
Theol.	Theology
Thess.	Thessalonians
Tim.	Timothy
Tit.	Titus
trans.	translation
Trig.	Trigonometry
ult.	ultimate, ultimately
U.S.	American (adj.)
v.	verb
var.	variant
Vet.	Veterinary medicine
v.i.	intransitive verb
v.t.	transitive verb
WGmc.	West Germanic
Zech.	Zechariah
Zeph.	Zephaniah
Zool.	Zoology

< from   + plus   ? possibly

A

a, A (ā) *n.* *pl.* **a's** or **as, A's** or **As, aes** (āz) **1.** The first letter of the English alphabet. **2.** Any sound represented by the letter *a.* — *symbol* **1.** Primacy in class. **2.** A substitute for the numeral 1. **3.** *Music* **a** One of a series of tones, the sixth in the natural diatonic scale of C, or the first note in the related minor scale. **b** A written note representing this tone. **c** The scale built upon A. **4.** *Chem.* Argon (symbol A).

a¹ (ə, *stressed* ā) *indefinite article* or *adj.* In each; to each; for each: one dollar *a* bushel. [OE *on, an* in, on, at]

a² (ə, *stressed* ā) *indefinite article* or *adj.* One; any; some; each: expressing singleness, unity, etc., more or less indefinitely. It is used: **1.** Before a noun expressing an individual object or idea: *a* bird; *a* hope. **2.** Before an abstract noun used concretely: to show *a* kindness. **3.** Before a collective noun: *a* crowd. **4.** Before a proper noun denoting a type: He is *a* Hercules in strength. **5.** Before plural nouns with *few, great many,* or *good many*: *a* few books. **6.** After *on, at,* or *of,* denoting oneness, sameness: birds of *a* feather. ◆ Before vowel sounds the form becomes *an.* See note under AN¹. [Reduced form of AN¹ used before consonant sounds]

a-¹ *prefix* In; on; at: *aboard, asleep, agog, agoing.* [OE *on, an* in, on, at]

a-² *prefix* Up; on; away: *arise, abide.* [OE *ā-* up, on, away]

a-³ *prefix* Of; from: *athirst, akin, anew.* [OE *of-* off, of]

a-⁴ *prefix* Without; not: *achromatic.* **2.** Apart from; unconcerned with: *amoral.* [Reduced form of AN-¹]

a-⁵ Reduced var. of AB-¹.

a-⁶ Reduced var. of AD-.

aard·vark (ärd′värk′) *n.* A burrowing, ant-eating African mammal. [< Afrikaans < Du. *aarde* earth + *vark* pig]

aard·wolf (ärd′wŏŏlf′) *n.* A hyenalike mammal of Africa. [< Afrikaans < Du. *aarde* earth + *wolf* wolf]

Aar·on (âr′ən, ar′ən) The first high priest of the Hebrews, older brother of Moses. *Ex.* xxviii 1–4.

ab-¹ *prefix* Off; from; away: *absolve, abduct, abrogate.* Also: *a-* before *m, p, v,* as in *avocation; abs-* before *c, t,* as in *abscess, abstract.* [< L < *ab* from]

ab-² Var. of AD-.

Ab (ab, äb) *n.* The eleventh month of the Hebrew year. See (Hebrew) CALENDAR.

ab·a·ca (ab′ə-kä, ä′bə-kä′) *n.* **1.** A banana plant of the Philippines. **2.** The inner fiber of this plant, used for cordage. Also **ab′a·ka.** [< Tagalog]

a·back (ə-bak′) *adv.* *Naut.* Back against the mast: said of sails so blown by the wind. — **taken aback** Disconcerted, as by a sudden check. [OE *on bæc* on or to the back]

ab·a·cus (ab′ə-kəs) *n.* *pl.* **·cus·es** or **·ci** (-sī) **1.** A calculator with sliding counters. **2.** *Archit.* A slab forming the top of a capital. [< L < Gk. *abax* counting table]

a·baft (ə-baft′, ə-bäft′) *Naut. adv.* Toward the stern; aft. — *prep.* Further aft than; astern of. [OE < *on* on, at + *be* by + *æftan* behind, back]

ab·a·lo·ne (ab′ə-lō′nē) *n.* An edible shellfish having a shell lined with mother-of-pearl. [< Am. Sp.]

a·ban·don (ə-ban′dən) *v.t.* **1.** To give up wholly; desert; forsake. **2.** To surrender or give over: with *to.* **3.** To yield (oneself) without restraint, as to an emotion. — *n.* Utter surrender to one's feelings or natural impulses. [< OF *abandoner* < *a bandon* under one's control] — **a·ban′don·er** *n.* — **a·ban′don·ment** *n.*

a·ban·doned (ə-ban′dənd) *adj.* **1.** Deserted; forsaken. **2.** Unrestrained. **3.** Profligate; shameless.

a·base (ə-bās′) *v.t.* **a·based, a·bas·ing** To lower in position, rank, prestige, or estimation; cast down; humble. [< OF < LL *abassare* to lower] — **a·bas′ed·ly** (ə-bā′sid·lē) *adv.* — **a·bas′ed·ness** *n.* — **a·base′ment** *n.* — **a·bas′er** *n.*

a·bash (ə-bash′) *v.t.* To deprive of self-possession; disconcert; make ashamed or confused. [< AF < OF *esbaïr* to astonish] — **a·bash·ed·ly** (ə-bash′id·lē) *adv.* — **a·bash′·ment** *n.*

a·bate (ə-bāt′) *v.* **a·bat·ed, a·bat·ing** *v.t.* **1.** To make less; reduce in quantity, value, force, or intensity. **2.** To deduct. **3.** *Law* To do away with (a nuisance); annul (a writ). — *v.i.* **4.** To become less, as in strength or degree. **5.** *Law* To fail; become void. — **Syn.** See ANNUL, DECREASE. [< OF *abatre* to beat down] — **a·bat·a·ble** (ə-bā′tə-bəl) *adj.* — **a·bat′er** *n.* — **a·bate′ment** *n.*

ab·ba·cy (ab′ə-sē) *n.* *pl.* **·cies** The office, term of office, dignity, or jurisdiction of an abbot.

ab·bé (ab′ā, *Fr.* à·bā′) *n.* **1.** In France, a title given to a priest or other cleric. **2.** An abbot. [< F]

ab·bess (ab′is) *n.* The female superior of a community of nuns connected with an abbey. [ME < OF *abbesse*]

ab·bey (ab′ē) *n.* *pl.* **·beys** **1.** A monastery or convent under the jurisdiction of an abbot or abbess. **2.** A church or building attached to an abbey. [ME < OF < LL < Gk. < Aramaic *abbā* father]

ab·bot (ab′ət) *n.* The superior of a community of monks. [OE < LL < Gk. < Aramaic *abbā* father] — **ab′bot·cy, ab′bot·ship** *n.*

ab·bre·vi·ate (ə-brē′vē·āt) *v.t.* **·at·ed, ·at·ing** **1.** To condense or make briefer. **2.** To shorten, as a word or expression, esp. by omission or contraction. [< L < *ad-* to + *breviare* to shorten] — **ab·bre′vi·a·tor** *n.* — **Syn.** shorten, curtail, abridge, contract.

ab·bre·vi·a·tion (ə-brē′vē·ā′shən) *n.* **1.** A shortened form of a word or phrase, used to represent the full form: Mr. is an *abbreviation* of Mister. **2.** The act of abbreviating, or the state of being abbreviated.

— **Syn.** **1.** An *abbreviation* is a shortening by any method. A *contraction* is made by omitting certain medial elements (whether sounds or letters) and bringing together the first and last elements. *Rec't* for *receipt* is a written *contraction* as well as *abbreviation; Am.* for *American* is a written *abbreviation,* but not a *contraction.*

ABC (ā′bē′sē′) *pl.* **ABC's** **1.** *Usually pl.* The alphabet. **2.** The rudiments, elements, or basic facts (of a subject).

Ab·di·as (ab-dī′əs) The Douai Bible name for OBADIAH.

ab·di·cate (ab′də-kāt) *v.* **·cat·ed, ·cat·ing** *v.t.* **1.** To give up formally; renounce, as a throne, power, or rights. — *v.i.* **2.** To relinquish power, sovereignty, or rights. [< L *abdicare* to renounce] — **ab·di·ca·ble** (ab′di-kə-bəl) *adj.* — **ab′di·ca′tion** *n.* — **ab′di·ca′tive** *adj.* — **ab′di·ca′tor** *n.*

ab·do·men (ab′də-mən, ab-dō′mən) *n.* **1.** In mammals, the body cavity between the diaphragm and the pelvic floor containing the viscera. **2.** In other vertebrates, the region or cavity that contains the viscera. **3.** In insects and other arthropods, the hindmost of the main body divisions. [< L] — **ab·dom·i·nal** (ab-dom′ə-nəl) — **ab·dom′i·nal·ly** *adv.*

ab·duct (ab-dukt′) *v.t.* **1.** To carry away wrongfully, as by force or fraud; kidnap. **2.** *Physiol.* To draw aside or away from the original position. [< L < *ab-* away + *ducere* to lead] — **ab·duc′tion** *n.* — **ab·duc′tor** *n.*

a·beam (ə-bēm′) *adv.* *Naut.* **1.** At right angles to the keel of a vessel. **2.** At or off the side of a vessel: with *of.*

a·bed (ə-bed′) *adv.* In bed; on a bed; to bed.

A·bel (ā′bəl) Second son of Adam. *Gen.* iv 2.

ab·er·rant (ab-er′ənt, ab′ər·ent) *adj.* **1.** Straying from the right way or usual course; wandering. **2.** Varying from type; abnormal; exceptional. [< L < *ab-* from + *errare* to wander] — **ab·er′rance, ab·er′ran·cy** *n.*

ab·er·ra·tion (ab′ə·rā′shən) *n.* **1.** Deviation from a right, customary, prescribed, or natural course or condition. **2.** Partial mental derangement.

a·bet (ə-bet′) *v.t.* **a·bet·ted, a·bet·ting** To encourage and support; esp., to support wrongdoing or a wrongdoer. [< OF < *a-* to + *beter* to tease, bait] — **a·bet′ment, a·bet′tal** *n.*

a·bet·tor (ə-bet′ər) *n.* One who abets. Also **a·bet′ter.**

a·bey·ance (ə-bā′əns) *n.* **1.** Suspension or temporary inaction. **2.** *Law* An undetermined condition, as of an estate not legally assigned. Also **a·bey′an·cy.** [< AF < OF < *a-* to, at + *bair* to gape] — **a·bey′ant** *adj.*

ab·hor (ab-hôr′) *v.t.* **·horred, ·hor·ring** To regard with re-

CHINESE ABACUS
The counters in the upper compartment have five times the value of those below.

pugnance; detest; loathe. — **Syn.** See HATE. [< L *ab*- from + *horrere* to shudder] — **ab·hor′rer** *n.*

ab·hor·rence (ab-hôr′əns, -hor′-) *n.* **1.** A feeling of utter loathing. **2.** Something loathsome or repugnant.

ab·hor·rent (ab-hôr′ənt, -hor′-) *adj.* **1.** Repugnant or detestable. **2.** Opposed: with *to*. **3.** Feeling repulsion. — **ab·hor′rent·ly** *adv.*

a·bide (ə-bīd′) *v.* **a·bode** or **a·bid·ed, a·bid·ing** *v.i.* **1.** To continue in a place; remain. — *v.t.* **2.** To look for; wait for. **3.** To endure; put up with. — **to abide by 1.** To behave in accordance with; adhere to, as a promise or rule. **2.** To accept the consequences of; submit to. [OE *ābīdan*] — **a·bi′dance** *n.* — **a·bid′er** *n.* — **a·bid′ing·ly** *adv.*

a·bil·i·ty (ə-bil′ə-tē) *n.*, *pl.* **·ties 1.** The state or quality of being able; capacity. **2.** *pl.* Talents. **3.** Competence or skill. [< OF < L < *habilis* suitable < *habere* to have, hold]

ab·ir·ri·tant (ab-ir′ə-tənt) *n.* A soothing agent; medicine that eases irritation. — *adj.* Relieving irritation; soothing.

ab·ir·ri·tate (ab-ir′ə-tāt) *v.t.* **·tat·ed, ·tat·ing** *Med.* To diminish sensibility or irritation in. — **ab·ir′ri·ta′tion** *n.*

ab·ject (ab′jekt, ab-jekt′) *adj.* **1.** Sunk to a low condition; groveling; mean; despicable. **2.** Hopelessly low; disheartening. [< L < *ab*- away + *jacere* to throw] — **ab·jec′tive** *adj.* — **ab′ject·ly** *adv.* — **ab′ject·ness, ab·jec′tion** *n.*

ab·jure (ab-jŏŏr′) *v.t.* **·jured, ·jur·ing 1.** To renounce under oath; forswear. **2.** To retract or recant, as an opinion. — **Syn.** See RENOUNCE. [< L < *ab*- away + *jurare* to swear] **ab′ju·ra′tion** *n.* — **ab·jur·a·to·ry** (ab-jŏŏr′ə-tôr′ē, -tō′rē) *adj.* — **ab·jur′er** *n.*

ab·la·tive (ab′lə-tiv) *adj. Gram.* In some inflected languages, as Latin and Sanskrit, pertaining to a case expressing separation, position, motion from, instrumentality, etc. — *n.* **1.** The ablative case. **2.** A word in this case. [< L, *ablatus*, pp. of *aufferre* < *ab*- away + *ferre* to carry]

a·blaze (ə-blāz′) *adv.* On fire. — *adj.* **1.** Flaming. **2.** Zealous; ardent.

a·ble (ā′bəl) *adj.* **a·bler** (ā′blər), **a·blest** (ā′blist) **1.** Having adequate power. **2.** Having or exhibiting superior abilities; skillful: an *able* writer. [< OF < L *habilis* suitable, fit < *habere* to have, hold] — **a′bly** *adv.*

-able *suffix* **1.** Given to; tending to; likely to: *changeable.* **2.** Fit to; able to; capable of; worthy of: *eatable, solvable.* Also spelled *-ble, -ible.* [< F < L *-abilis, -ibilis, -bilis*]

a·ble-bod·ied (ā′bəl-bod′ēd) *adj.* Having a sound, strong body; competent for physical service; robust.

able-bodied seaman An experienced and skilled seaman.

able seaman *pl.* **·men 1.** In the Royal Canadian Navy the fourth lowest grade. **2.** One who holds this grade.

a·bloom (ə-blōōm′) *adj. & adv.* Blooming; in blossom.

ab·lu·tion (ab-lōō′shən) *n.* **1.** A washing or cleansing of the body; a bath. **2.** *Eccl.* **a** A ceremonial washing of the priest's hands or of the chalice and paten during the Eucharist. **b** The liquid used for this. [< L < *ab*- away + *luere* to wash] — **ab·lu′tion·ar′y** *adj.*

-ably *suffix* Like; in the manner of: *peaceably*: used to form adverbs from adjectives ending in *-able.*

ab·ne·gate (ab′nə-gāt) *v.t.* **·gat·ed, ·gat·ing** To deny; renounce. [< L < *ab*- away + *negare* to deny] — **ab′ne·ga′tion** *n.* — **ab′ne·ga′tor** *n.*

ab·nor·mal (ab-nôr′məl) *adj.* Not according to rule; different from the average; unusual; irregular. [< F < Med.L < L < *ab*- from + *norma* rule] — **ab·nor′mal·ly** *adv.*

ab·nor·mal·i·ty (ab′nôr-mal′ə-tē) *n.*, *pl.* **·ties 1.** The state of being abnormal. **2.** An abnormal thing.

a·board (ə-bôrd′, ə-bōrd′) *adv.* **1.** On board; into, in, or on a ship, train, etc. **2.** Alongside. — **all aboard!** Get on board! Get in!: a warning to passengers. — *prep.* **1.** On board of; upon or within. **2.** Alongside of.

a·bode (ə-bōd′) Past tense and past participle of ABIDE. — *n.* **1.** A place of abiding; dwelling; home. **2.** The state or act of abiding; sojourn; stay. [OE *ābād*]

a·bol·ish (ə-bol′ish) *v.t.* To do away with; put an end to; annul; destroy. [< F < L *abolere* to destroy] — **a·bol′ish·a·ble** *adj.* — **a·bol′ish·er** *n.* — **a·bol′ish·ment** *n.*

ab·o·li·tion (ab′ə-lish′ən) *n.* **1.** The act of abolishing, or the state of being abolished. **2.** *Sometimes cap.* The abolishing of slavery in the United States. — **ab′o·li′tion·al, ab′o·li′tion·ar′y** *adj.* — **ab′o·li′tion·ism** *n.* — **ab′o·li′tion·ist** *n.*

ab·o·ma·sum (ab′ə-mā′səm) *n.*, *pl.* **·sa** (-sə) The fourth or true digestive stomach of a ruminant: also called *reed.* Also **ab·o·ma·sus** (ab′ə-mā′səs). [< NL < L *ab*- away from + *omasum* bullock's tripe]

A-bomb (ā′bom′) *n.* An atomic bomb.

a·bom·i·na·ble (ə-bom′in-ə-bəl) *adj.* **1.** Very hateful; loathsome. **2.** Extremely disagreeable; bad. — **a·bom′i·na·ble·ness** *n.* — **a·bom′i·na·bly** *adv.*

a·bom·i·nate (ə-bom′ə-nāt) *v.t.* **·nat·ed, ·nat·ing 1.** To regard with loathing; abhor. **2.** To dislike strongly. — **Syn.** See HATE. [< L *abominari* to abhor as an ill omen] — **a·bom′i·na′tion** *n.* — **a·bom′i·na·tor** *n.*

ab·o·rig·i·nal (ab′ə-rij′ə-nəl) *adj.* **1.** Of or pertaining to aborigines. **2.** Native; indigenous. — *n. Austral.* An aborigine. — **ab′o·rig′i·nal·ly** *adv.*

ab·o·rig·i·ne (ab′ə-rij′ə-nē) *n.* **1.** One of the original native inhabitants of a country. **2.** *pl.* Flora and fauna indigenous to a geographical area. [< L *ab origine* from the beginning]

a·bort (ə-bôrt′) *v.i.* **1.** To bring forth young prematurely; miscarry. **2.** To fail of complete development. — *v.t.* **3.** To cause to have a miscarriage. **4.** To bring to a premature or unsuccessful conclusion. [< L *aboriri* to miscarry]

a·bor·tion (ə-bôr′shən) *n.* **1.** *Law* A miscarriage produced artificially, esp. as an illegal operation. **2.** The expulsion of a fetus prematurely; miscarriage. **3.** The defective result of a premature birth. **4.** Partial or complete arrest of development in anything. — **a·bor′tion·al** *adj.*

a·bor·tion·ist (ə-bôr′shən·ist) *n.* One who causes abortion.

a·bor·tive (ə-bôr′tiv) *adj.* **1.** Coming to naught; failing. **2.** Brought forth or born prematurely. **3.** Imperfectly developed; rudimentary. **4.** *Med.* Causing abortion. — **Syn.** See FUTILE. — **a·bor′tive·ly** *adv.* — **a·bor′tive·ness** *n.*

a·bound (ə-bound′) *v.i.* **1.** To be in abundance; be plentiful. **2.** To have plenty; be rich. **3.** To be full; teem. [< OF < L < *ab*- from + *undare* to flow in waves]

a·bout (ə-bout′) *adv.* **1.** Approximately; nearly. **2.** *Informal* Almost; not quite. **3.** Nearby; in the vicinity. **4.** To a reversed position; around. **5.** In rotation; around and around. **6.** In every direction; to all sides. **7.** Here and there, as without direction. **8.** Astir; in motion; active. **9.** On every side; around. — *prep.* **1.** On every side of; encircling. **2.** Near; within; on some side of. **3.** Here and there in or upon. **4.** Near; close to. **5.** Engaged in. **6.** Concerning; in reference to. **7.** In one's possession. **8.** Attached to (a person) as an attribute. **9.** On the point of; ready to. [OE < *on, a* on + *būtan* outside]

a·bout-face (*n.* ə-bout′fās′; *v.* ə-bout′fās′) *n.* **1.** *Mil.* A pivoting turn to the rear executed when halted. **2.** Any turning around or reversal, as of opinion or point of view. — *v.i.* **-faced, -fac·ing** To perform an about-face.

a·bove (ə-buv′) *adv.* **1.** In or to a higher place; overhead; up. **2.** Superior in rank or position. **3.** In an earlier section of something written. **4.** In heaven. — *adj.* Given, said, named, etc., in what is above; preceding: The *above* men were acquitted. — *n.* That which is higher up or just before: preceded by *the.* — *prep.* **1.** Directly over; on top of. **2.** Higher than; rising beyond. **3.** Farther north than. **4.** More than, in number, quantity, degree, etc.; beyond. **5.** Superior to in authority or power. **6.** Beyond the influence or reach of. [ME *aboven* < OE *onbufan*]

a·bove·board (ə-buv′bôrd′, -bōrd′) *adj. & adv.* In open sight; without concealment, fraud, or trickery.

ab·ra·ca·dab·ra (ab′rə-kə-dab′rə) *n.* **1.** Any spell or incantation. **2.** Jargon or nonsensical words. [< L]

a·brade (ə-brād′) *v.t.* **a·brad·ed, a·brad·ing** To rub or wear off by friction; scrape away. [< L < *ab*- away + *radere* to scrape] — **a·bra′dant** *adj. & n.* — **a·brad′er** *n.*

A·bra·ham (ā′brə-ham) The progenitor of the Hebrews; first called **A·bram** (ā′brəm). *Gen.* xvii 5.

a·bran·chi·al (ā-brang′kē-əl) *adj. Zool.* Without gills. Also **a·bran·chi·ate** (ā-brang′kē-it, -āt). [< A-⁴ without + Gk. *branchia* gills]

a·bra·sion (ə-brā′zhən) *n.* **1.** A wearing or rubbing away, as of rocks by glaciers. **2.** An abraded area, as on the skin.

a·bra·sive (ə-brā′siv, -ziv) *adj.* Abrading or tending to abrade. — *n.* An abrading substance, as emery or sand.

a·breast (ə-brest′) *adv. & adj.* Side by side. — **abreast of (or with)** Side by side with.

a·bridge (ə-brij′) *v.t.* **a·bridged, a·bridg·ing 1.** To give the substance of in fewer words; condense. **2.** To shorten, as in time. **3.** To curtail or lessen, as rights. **4.** To deprive. [< OF < L *abbreviare* < *ad*- to + *brevis* short] — **a·bridg′a·ble** or **a·bridge′a·ble** *adj.* — **a·bridg′er** *n.*

a·bridg·ment (ə-brij′mənt) *n.* **1.** The act of abridging, or the state of being abridged. **2.** A condensation, as of a book; epitome; abstract. Also **a·bridge′ment.**
— **Syn. 2.** An *abridgment* gives the most important portions of a work substantially as they stand. An *abstract, digest,* or *précis* is an independent statement of what a book or an article contains; the *abstract* closely following the main heads, the *digest* or *précis* giving careful consideration of all the contents.

a·broad (ə-brôd′) *adv.* **1.** Out of one's home or abode; out-of-doors. **2.** In or to foreign lands. **3.** At large; in circulation. **4.** Broadly; widely. **5.** Wide of the mark. [ME]

ab·ro·gate (ab′rə-gāt) *v.t.* **·gat·ed, ·gat·ing** To annul by authority, as a law; abolish; repeal. — **Syn.** See ANNUL. [< L < *ab*- away + *rogare* to propose a law] — **ab·ro·ga·ble** (ab′rə-gə-bəl) *adj.* — **ab′ro·ga′tion** *n.* — **ab′ro·ga′tive** *adj.* — **ab′ro·ga′tor** *n.*

a·brupt (ə-brupt′) *adj.* **1.** Beginning, ending, or changing suddenly; unexpected. **2.** Unceremonious; rude, as in speech or departure. **3.** Unconnected, as literary style. **4.** Steep, as a cliff. — **Syn.** See BLUNT. [< L < *ab*- off + *rumpere* to break] — **a·brupt′ly** *adv.* — **a·brupt′ness** *n.*

abs- Var. of AB-¹.
Ab·sa·lom (ab′sə-ləm) The favorite and rebellious son of David. II *Sam.* xiii–xix.
ab·scess (ab′ses) *Pathol. n.* A collection of pus in any part of the body, often inflamed —*v.i.* To form an abscess. [< L < *ab-* away + *cedere* to go] — **ab′scessed** *adj.*
ab·scis·sa (ab-sis′ə) *n. pl.* **ab·scis·sas** or **ab·scis·sae** (-sis′ē) *Math.* The distance of any point from the vertical or Y-axis in a coordinate system, measured on a line parallel to the horizontal or X-axis. [< L (*linea*) *abscissa* (line) cut off < *ab-* off + *scindere* to cut]
ab·scis·sion (ab-sizh′ən, -sish′ən) *n.* **1.** The act of cutting off or removing. **2.** In rhetoric, an abrupt breaking off for effect, as in the middle of a sentence. [< L < *ab-* off + *scindere* to cut]

ABSCISSA
AB: x axis.
AC: y axis.
Ae abscissa of point *f.*

ab·scond (ab-skond′) *v.i.* To depart suddenly and secretly, esp. to escape the law. [< L < *ab-* away + *condere* to store away, conceal] — **ab·scond′er** *n.*
ab·sence (ab′səns) *n.* **1.** The state of being absent. **2.** The period of being away. **3.** Lack.
ab·sent (*adj.* ab′sənt; *v.* ab-sent′) *adj.* **1.** Not present; away. **2.** Lacking; nonexistent. **3.** Inattentive; absent-minded. —*v.t.* To take or keep (oneself) away. [< L < *ab-* away + *esse* to be] — **ab·sent′er** *n.* — **ab′sent·ly** *adv.* — **ab′sent·ness** *n.*
ab·sen·tee (ab′sən-tē′) *n.* One who is absent, as from a job. — *adj.* Temporarily absent. — **ab′sen·tee′ism** *n.*
ab·sent-mind·ed (ab′sənt-mīn′did) *adj.* Inattentive to one's immediate surroundings or business because of preoccupation of the mind; forgetful. — **ab′sent-mind′ed·ly** *adv.* — **ab′sent-mind′ed·ness** *n.*
absent without leave *Mil.* Absent without authorization but not intending to desert. Abbr. *a.w.o.l.*, *A.W.O.L.*
ab·sinthe (ab′sinth) *n.* **1.** A green, bitter liqueur having the flavor of licorice and wormwood. **2.** Wormwood. Also **ab′sinth.** [< F < L *absinthium* wormwood]
ab·so·lute (ab′sə-lōōt) *adj.* **1.** Free from restriction; unlimited; unconditional. **2.** Complete; perfect. **3.** Unadulterated; pure. **4.** Not relative to anything else; independent. **5.** Positive; certain. **6.** *Gram.* **a** Free from the usual relations of syntax or construction with other words in the sentence, as *It being late* in *It being late, we started home.* **b** Of a transitive verb, having no object expressed, as *That professor inspires and stimulates.* **c** Of an adjective standing without a noun, as *the brave and the fair.* — *n.* That which is absolute or perfect. — **the Absolute** *Philos.* The ultimate basis of all thought, reasoning, or being. [< L < *ab-* from + *solvere* to loosen] — **ab′so·lute·ness** *n.*
ab·so·lute·ly (ab′sə-lōōt′lē, *emphatic* ab′sə-lōōt′lē) *adv.* **1.** Completely; unconditionally. **2.** Positively. **3.** *Gram.* So as not to take an object: to use a verb *absolutely.*
absolute pitch *Music* The ability to produce or name the pitch of any note sounded or asked for: also *perfect pitch.*
absolute zero That temperature at which a body contains no heat, and at which a perfect gas exerts no pressure, equivalent to about $-273.16°$ C. or $-459.7°$ F.
ab·so·lu·tion (ab′sə-lōō′shən) *n.* **1.** The act of absolving, as from guilt. **2.** *Eccl.* **a** A remission of sin and its penalties pronounced by a priest. **b** A formula declaring the forgiveness of sin. [< L < *ab-* from + *solvere* to loosen]
ab·so·lut·ism (ab′sə-lōō-tiz′əm) *n.* In government, the doctrine or practice of unlimited authority and control; despotism. — **ab′so·lut′ist** *n.* — **ab′so·lu·tis′tic** *adj.*
ab·solve (ab-solv′, -zolv′, əb-) *v.t.* **·solved, ·solv·ing 1.** To free from the penalties or consequences of an action. **2.** To release, as from an obligation. **3.** *Eccl.* To grant a remission of sin. [< L < *ab-* from + *solvere* to loosen.] — **ab·solv′a·ble** *adj.* — **ab·sol′vent** *adj. & n.* — **ab·solv′er** *n.*
ab·sorb (ab-sôrb′, -zôrb′) *v.t.* **1.** To drink in or suck up, as through or into pores. **2.** To engross completely. **3.** To take up or in by chemical or molecular action, as gases, heat, liquid, light, etc.: distinguished from *adsorb.* **4.** To take in and incorporate. **5.** To receive the force or action of; intercept. [< L < *ab-* from + *sorbere* to suck in] — **ab·sorb′a·bil′i·ty** *n.* — **ab·sorb′a·ble** *adj.* — **ab·sorb′er** *n.* — **ab·sorb′ing** *adj.* — **ab·sorb′ing·ly** *adv.*
ab·sor·bent (ab-sôr′bənt, -zôr′-) *adj.* Absorbing or tending to absorb. — *n.* A substance, duct, etc., that absorbs. — **ab·sor′ben·cy** *n.*
absorbent cotton Cotton from which all fatty matter has been removed, used in surgical dressings, etc.
ab·sorp·tion (ab-sôrp′shən, -zôrp′-) *n.* **1.** The act of absorbing, or the condition of being absorbed. **2.** Assimilation, as by the digestive process. **3.** Preoccupation of the mind. — **ab·sorp′tive** *adj.* — **ab·sorp′tive·ness, ab′sorp·tiv′i·ty** *n.*

ab·stain (ab-stān′) *v.i.* To keep oneself back; refrain voluntarily: with *from.* [< OF < L *abstinere* to hold back < *ab-* from + *tenere* to hold] — **ab·stain′er** *n.*
ab·ste·mi·ous (ab-stē′mē-əs) *adj.* Eating and drinking sparingly; abstinent; temperate. [< L < *ab-* from + root of *temetum* intoxicating drink] — **ab·ste′mi·ous·ly** *adv.* — **ab·ste′mi·ous·ness** *n.*
ab·sten·tion (ab-sten′shən) *n.* An abstaining. — **ab·sten′·tious** *adj.*
ab·sti·nence (ab′stə-nəns) *n.* **1.** The act or practice of abstaining, as from food, pleasure, etc. **2.** Abstention from alcoholic beverages. [< F < L *abstinere* < *ab-* from + *tenere* to hold] — **ab′sti·nent** *adj.* — **ab′sti·nent·ly** *adv.*
ab·stract (*adj.* ab·strakt′, ab′strakt; *n.* ab′strakt; *v.* ab-strakt′) *adj.* **1.** Considered apart from matter or from specific examples; not concrete. **2.** Theoretical; ideal, as opposed to practical. **3.** Abstruse. **4.** Considered or expressed without reference to particular example, as numbers, attributes, or qualities. **5.** In art, generalized or universal, as opposed to concrete, specific, or representational. — *n.* **1.** A summary or epitome, as of a document. **2.** The essence of some larger object or whole. **3.** An abstract idea or term. Abbr. *abs.* — **Syn.** See ABRIDGMENT. — **in the abstract** Apart from concrete relation or embodiment; abstractly. — *v.t.* **1.** To take away; remove. **2.** To take away secretly; purloin. **3.** To withdraw or disengage (the attention, interest, etc.). **4.** To consider apart from particular or material instances. **5.** To make an abstract of; summarize. [< L < *ab-* away + *trahere* to draw] — **ab·stract′er** *n.* — **ab·stract′ly** *adv.* — **ab·stract′ness** *n.*
ab·stract·ed (ab-strak′tid) *adj.* **1.** Lost in thought; absentminded. **2.** Separated from all else; apart. — **ab·stract′·ed·ly** *adv.* — **ab·stract′ed·ness** *n.*
ab·strac·tion (ab-strak′shən) *n.* **1.** The process of abstracting. **2.** A product of this process; a concept. **3.** A visionary or impractical theory. **4.** The act of withdrawing; separation. **5.** Absence of mind; preoccupation. **6.** An art form or work of art in which the qualities are abstract.
ab·strac·tive (ab-strak′tiv) *adj.* **1.** Of, pertaining to, or tending to abstraction. **2.** Having the power of abstraction; epitomizing. — **ab·strac′tive·ly** *adv.* — **ab·strac′tive·ness** *n.*
abstract noun *Gram.* A noun that names a quality, idea, etc., as *goodness, democracy, reputation.*
ab·struse (ab-strōōs′) *adj.* Hard to understand. — **Syn.** See COMPLEX, MYSTERIOUS. [< L < *ab-* away + *trudere* to thrust] — **ab·struse′ly** *adv.* — **ab·struse′ness** *n.*
ab·surd (ab-sûrd′, -zûrd′) *adj.* Irrational; ridiculous. [< F < L < *ab-* completely + *surdus* deaf, dull] — **ab·surd′ly** *adv.* — **ab·surd′ness** *n.*
ab·surd·i·ty (ab-sûr′də-tē, -zûr′-) *n. pl.* **·ties 1.** The quality of being absurd. **2.** Something absurd.
a·bun·dance (ə-bun′dəns) *n.* **1.** A plentiful or overflowing supply. **2.** Wealth; affluence.
a·bun·dant (ə-bun′dənt) *adj.* **1.** Existing in plentiful supply; ample. **2.** Abounding. — **Syn.** See PLENTIFUL. [< OF < L *abundare.* See ABOUND.] — **a·bun′dant·ly** *adv.*
a·buse (*v.* ə-byōōz′; *n.* ə-byōōs′) *v.t.* **a·bused, a·bus·ing 1.** To use improperly or injuriously; misuse. **2.** To hurt by treating wrongly; injure. **3.** To speak in coarse or bad terms of or to; revile. — *n.* **1.** Improper or injurious use; misuse. **2.** Ill-treatment; injury. **3.** Vicious conduct, practice, or action. **4.** Abusive language; slander. [< F < L < *ab-* away + *uti* to use] — **a·bus′er** *n.*
a·bu·sive (ə-byōō′siv) *adj.* **1.** Mistreating. **2.** Insulting; vituperative. — **a·bu′sive·ly** *adv.* — **a·bu′sive·ness** *n.*
a·but (ə-but′) *v.i.* **a·but·ted, a·but·ting** To touch, join, or adjoin at the end or side; border: with *on, upon,* or *against.* [< OF < *a-* to + *bout* end] — **a·but′ter** *n.*
a·but·ment (ə-but′mənt) *n.* **1.** The act of abutting. **2.** Something that abuts, the thing abutted upon, or the point of junction. **3.** A supporting or buttressing structure.
a·bys·mal (ə-biz′məl) *adj.* Unfathomable; immeasurable; extreme: an *abysmal* ignorance. — **a·bys′mal·ly** *adv.*
a·byss (ə-bis′) *n.* **1.** A bottomless gulf; chasm. **2.** Any profound depth or void. **3.** The depths of the sea. [< L < Gk. < *a-* without + *byssos* bottom] — **a·bys′sal** *adj.*
Ab·ys·sin·i·an (ab′ə-sin′ē-ən) *adj. & n.* Ethiopian.
ac- Assimilated var. of AD-.
-ac *suffix* **1.** Having; affected by: *demoniac.* **2.** Pertaining to; of: *cardiac.* [< Gk. -*akos* or L -*acus* or F -*aque*]
a·ca·cia (ə-kā′shə) *n.* **1.** Any of various flowering, leguminous trees and shrubs of the tropics and warm temperate regions. **2.** The locust tree. **3.** Gum arabic. [< L < Gk. *akakia,* a thorny tree < *akē* point]
ac·a·dem·ic (ak′ə-dem′ik) *adj.* **1.** Pertaining to an academy, college, or university; scholarly. **2.** *U.S.* Offering or having to do with liberal rather than vocational or technical

studies. **3.** Theoretical, as opposed to practical. **4.** Pedantic. Also **ac·a·dem′i·cal.** — *n.* A college or university student or faculty member. — **ac′a·dem′i·cal·ly** *adv.*

a·cad·e·mi·cian (ə·kad′ə·mish′ən, ak′ə·də-) *n.* A member of an academy of art, science, or literature.

ac·a·dem·i·cism (ak′ə·dem′ə·siz′əm) *n.* Pedantic formalism, as in art. Also **a·cad·e·mism** (ə·kad′ə·miz′əm).

a·cad·e·my (ə·kad′ə·mē) *n. pl.* **·mies 1.** A secondary school, usually a private one. **2.** A school giving instruction in some science or art. **3.** A learned society for the advancement of arts or sciences. [< F < L < Gk. *Akadēmeia* the grove where Plato taught]

A·ca·di·a (ə·kā′dē·ə) A former name for a region in eastern Canada, including Nova Scotia and New Brunswick.

A·ca·di·an (ə·kā′dē·ən) *adj.* Of or pertaining to Acadia or Nova Scotia. — *n.* One of the early French settlers of Acadia or their descendants. See CAJUN.

acantho- *combining form* Thorn or thorny; spine, point. Also, before vowels, **acanth-.** [< Gk. *akantha* thorn]

a·can·thus (ə·kan′thəs) *n. pl.* **·thus·es** or **·thi** (-thī) **1.** A plant having large spiny leaves, common in the Mediterranean region. **2.** *Archit.* A decorative representation of its leaf, characteristic of the Corinthian capital. [< L < Gk. *akē* thorn] — **a·can′thine** (-thin) *adj.*

a cap·pel·la (ä′ kə·pel′ə, *Ital.* ä′ käp·pel′lä) *Music* Sung without accompaniment. [< Ital., in chapel style]

ac·cede (ak·sēd′) *v.i.* **·ced·ed, ·ced·ing 1.** To give one's consent or adherence; agree; assent: with *to.* **2.** To come into or enter upon an office or dignity: with *to.* [< L < *ad-* to + *cedere* to yield]

ac·cel·er·an·do (ak·sel′ə·ran′dō, *Ital.* ät·chā′lä·rän′dō) *Music adj.* Gradually quickening in time. — *adv.* In gradually quickening tempo. [< Ital.]

ac·cel·er·ant (ak·sel′ər·ənt) *n.* That which accelerates.

ac·cel·er·ate (ak·sel′ə·rāt) *v.* **·at·ed, ·at·ing** *v.t.* **1.** To cause to act or move faster. **2.** To hasten the natural or usual course of. **3.** To cause to happen ahead of time. — *v.i.* **4.** To move or become faster. [< L < *ad-* to + *celerare* to hasten] — **ac·cel′er·a·ble** *adj.* — **ac·cel′er·a′tive** *adj.*

ac·cel·er·a·tion (ak·sel′ə·rā′shən) *n.* **1.** The act of accelerating or being accelerated. **2.** *Physics* The rate at which the velocity of a body increases per unit of time.

ac·cel·er·a·tor (ak·sel′ə·rā′tər) *n.* **1.** One who or that which accelerates. **2.** *Physics* Any of various devices for accelerating the velocity of atomic particles: also called *atom smasher.* **3.** *Mech.* The foot throttle of an automobile.

ac·cent (*n.* ak′sent; *v.* ak′sent, ak·sent′) *n.* **1.** The prominence given in speech to a particular sound, syllable, or word. **2.** A mark used to indicate the place of accent in a word. The **primary accent** notes the chief stress, and the **secondary accent** a somewhat weaker stress. **3.** A mark used in some languages to show the quality of a vowel. In French, the accents are acute (´), grave (`), and circumflex (^). **4.** A modulation of the voice. **5.** Mode of utterance; pronunciation: a Southern *accent.* **6.** In prosody, the stress determining the rhythm of poetry. **7.** *Music* An emphasis given to one tone or chord. **8.** *pl.* Speech; words. — *v.t.* **1.** To speak, pronounce, play, or sing with an accent; stress. **2.** To write a mark indicating accent. **3.** To accentuate or emphasize. [< L < *ad-* to + *cantus* a singing]

ac·cen·tu·al (ak·sen′chōō·əl) *adj.* **1.** Of or pertaining to accent. **2.** In prosody, having a stress accent. — **ac·cen′tu·al·ly** *adv.*

ac·cen·tu·ate (ak·sen′chōō·āt) *v.t.* **·at·ed, ·at·ing 1.** To strengthen or heighten the effect of; emphasize. **2.** To mark or pronounce with an accent. — **ac·cen′tu·a′tion** *n.*

ac·cept (ak·sept′) *v.t.* **1.** To receive with favor, willingness, or consent. **2.** To give an affirmative answer to. **3.** To receive as satisfactory or sufficient. **4.** To take with good grace; submit to. **5.** In commerce, to agree to pay, as a draft. **6.** To believe in. [< L < *ad-* to + *capere* to take] — **ac·cept′er** *n.*

ac·cept·a·ble (ak·sep′tə·bəl) *adj.* Worthy of acceptance. — **ac·cept′a·ble·ness, ac·cept′a·bil′i·ty** *n.* — **ac·cept′a·bly** *adv.*

ac·cep·tance (ak·sep′təns) *n.* **1.** The act of accepting. **2.** The state of being accepted or acceptable. **3.** Favorable reception; approval. **4.** Assent; belief. **5.** In commerce, an agreement to pay a bill of exchange, etc.; also, the paper showing this. Also **ac·cep′tan·cy.** — **ac·cep′tant** *adj.*

ac·cep·ta·tion (ak′sep·tā′shən) *n.* The accepted meaning of a word or expression.

ac·cept·ed (ak·sep′tid) *adj.* Commonly recognized, believed, or approved; popular.

ac·cess (ak′ses) *n.* **1.** The act of coming to or near. **2.** A passage; path. **3.** The state or quality of being approachable; accessibility. **4.** A sudden attack of a disease. **5.** An outburst of emotion, etc. [< L *accedere* to yield]

ac·ces·si·ble (ak·ses′ə·bəl) *adj.* **1.** Easy of access; approachable. **2.** Attainable; obtainable. **3.** Open to the influence of. — **ac·ces′si·bil′i·ty** *n.* — **ac·ces′si·bly** *adv.*

ac·ces·sion (ak·sesh′ən) *n.* **1.** The act of attaining an office, dignity, or right. **2.** An increase by something added. **3.** Assent; agreement. — *v.t.* To record, as additions to a library or museum. — **ac·ces′sion·al** *adj.*

ac·ces·so·ry (ak·ses′ər·ē) *n. pl.* **·ries 1.** Something added for convenience, display, etc., as to an automobile or to one's attire. **2.** *Law* A person who, though absent during the perpetration of a felony, instigates, aids, or encourages another to commit the felony (**accessory before the fact**), or knowingly comforts, conceals, or assists the felon (**accessory after the fact**). — *adj.* **1.** Aiding the principal design, or assisting subordinately the chief agent, as in the commission of a crime. **2.** Contributory; supplemental; additional. Also **ac·ces′sa·ry.** [< LL < L *accedere* to yield] — **ac′ces·so′ri·al** *adj.* — **ac·ces′so·ri·ly** *adv.* — **ac·ces′so·ri·ness** *n.*
— **Syn.** (noun) **2.** In law, an *accessory* assists in planning or concealing a crime, though he is not present when it is committed. An *accomplice* is actively or constructively present during the act itself. *Confederate* is a general term for one who assists another.

ac·ci·dent (ak′sə·dənt) *n.* **1.** Anything occurring unexpectedly, or without known cause. **2.** Any unpleasant or unfortunate occurrence involving injury, loss, or death. **3.** Chance; fortune. **4.** Any nonessential attribute. [< L < *ad-* upon + *cadere* to fall]

ac·ci·den·tal (ak′sə·den′tal) *adj.* **1.** Happening or coming by chance. **2.** Nonessential; subordinate; incidental. **3.** *Music* Pertaining to or indicating a sharp, natural, flat, etc., elsewhere than in the signature. — **ac′ci·den′tal·ly** *adv.*

ac·claim (ə·klām′) *v.t.* **1.** To proclaim with applause; hail: They *acclaimed* him victor. **2.** To shout approval of. — *v.i.* **3.** To applaud; shout approval. — *n.* A shout of applause. — **Syn.** See PRAISE. [< L < *ad-* to + *clamare* to shout] — **ac·claim′a·ble** *adj.* — **ac·claim′er** *n.*

ac·cla·ma·tion (ak′lə·mā′shən) *n.* **1.** The act of acclaiming or of being acclaimed. **2.** A shout of applause or welcome. **3.** An oral vote, as in public assembly. **4.** *Canadian* Election without opposition. — **ac·clam·a·to·ry** (ə·klam′ə·tôr′ē, -tō′rē) *adj.*

ac·cli·mate (ə·klī′mit, ak′lə·māt) *v.t. & v.i.* **·mat·ed, ·mat·ing** *Chiefly U.S.* To adapt or become adapted to a new climate or environment. [< F < à- to + *climat* climate] — **ac·cli·ma·ta·ble** (ə·klī′mə·tə·bəl) *adj.* — **ac·cli·ma·tion** (ak′lə·mā′shən), **ac·cli·ma·ta·tion** (ə·klī′mə·tā′shən) *n.*

ac·cli·ma·tize (ə·klī′mə·tīz) *v.t. & v.i.* **·tized, ·tiz·ing** To acclimate. — **ac·cli·ma·ti·za′tion** *n.*

ac·cliv·i·ty (ə·kliv′ə·tē) *n. pl.* **·ties** An upward slope: opposed to *declivity.* [< L < *ad-* to + *clivus* hill] — **ac·cliv′i·tous, ac·cli·vous** (ə·klī′vəs) *adj.*

ac·co·lade (ak′ə·lād′, -läd′) *n.* **1.** The salutation (at first an embrace, now a light blow with a sword) in conferring knighthood. **2.** A conferring of praise; an honor. [< F < Ital. *accollare* to embrace about the neck]

ac·com·mo·date (ə·kom′ə·dāt) *v.* **·dat·ed, ·dat·ing** *v.t.* **1.** To do a favor for; oblige; help. **2.** To provide for; give lodging to. **3.** To be suitable for; contain comfortably. **4.** To adapt or modify, as to new conditions. **5.** To reconcile or settle, as conflicting opinions. — *v.i.* **6.** To be or become adjusted, as the eye to distance. [< L < *ad-* to + *commodare* to make fit, suit] — **ac·com′mo·da′tive** *adj.* — **ac·com′mo·da′tive·ness** *n.*

ac·com·mo·dat·ing (ə·kom′ə·dā′ting) *adj.* Disposed to make adjustment; obliging. — **ac·com′mo·dat′ing·ly** *adv.*

ac·com·mo·da·tion (ə·kom′ə·dā′shən) *n.* **1.** The act of accommodating, or the state of being accommodated; adjustment; adaptation. **2.** Reconciliation; compromise. **3.** Anything that supplies a need; convenience. **4.** *Usu. pl. U.S.* Lodging, board, etc. **5.** Willingness to please or help.

ac·com·pa·ni·ment (ə·kum′pə·ni·mənt, ə·kump′ni-) *n.* **1.** Anything that accompanies something. **2.** *Music* A subordinate part supporting a leading part.

ac·com·pa·nist (ə·kum′pə·nist, ə·kump′nist) *n.* One who plays or sings the accompaniment. Also **ac·com′pa·ny·ist.**

ac·com·pa·ny (ə·kum′pə·nē) *v.t.* **·nied, ·ny·ing 1.** To go with; attend; escort. **2.** To be or coexist with. **3.** To supplement. **4.** To play a musical accompaniment to or for. [< F < à- to + *compagne* companion]

ac·com·plice (ə·kom′plis) *n.* An associate in wrongdoing; partner in crime. — **Syn.** See ACCESSORY. [< *a,* indefinite article + F *complice* accomplice]

ac·com·plish (ə·kom′plish) *v.t.* To bring to pass or to completion. [< OF < LL < L *ad-* to + *complere* to fill up, complete] — **ac·com′plish·a·ble** *adj.*

ac·com·plished (ə·kom′plisht) *adj.* **1.** Completed; done. **2.** Proficient; skilled. **3.** Trained in the social graces.

ac·com·plish·ment (ə·kom′plish·mənt) *n.* **1.** The act of accomplishing. **2.** Something accomplished; achievement. **3.** An acquirement or attainment, esp. a social skill. — **Syn.** See ATTAINMENT.

ac·cord (ə·kôrd′) *v.t.* **1.** To render as due; grant. **2.** To make harmonize or agree. — *v.i.* **3.** To agree; harmonize. — *n.* **1.** Harmony, as of sentiment, colors, sounds, etc.; agreement. **2.** A settlement of any difference, as between governments. — **Syn.** See HARMONY. — **of one's own ac-cord** By one's own choice. [< OF < LL < L < *ad-* to + *cor* heart] — **ac·cord′a·ble** *adj.* — **ac·cord′er** *n.*

ac·cord·ance (ə-kôr′dəns) *n.* Agreement; conformity. — **ac·cord′ant** *adj.* — **ac·cord′ant·ly** *adv.*

ac·cord·ing (ə-kôr′ding) *adj.* Being in accordance or agreement; harmonizing. — *adv.* Accordingly. — **according as 1.** In proportion as; just as. **2.** Depending on whether. — **according to 1.** In accordance with. **2.** As stated by; on the authority of. **3.** In proportion to.

ac·cord·ing·ly (ə-kôr′ding-lē) *adv.* **1.** In accord; correspondingly. **2.** Consequently; so.

ac·cor·di·on (ə-kôr′dē·ən) *n.* A portable musical wind instrument with metallic reeds and a keyboard, the air for which is furnished by a bellows operated by the performer. [< Ital. *accordare* to harmonize] — **ac·cor′di·on·ist** *n.*

ac·cost (ə-kôst′, ə-kost′) *v.t.* To speak to first; address; greet. [< F < L < *ad-* to + *costa* rib]

ac·couche·ment (ə-kōōsh′mənt, *Fr.* à-kōōsh-män′) *n.* Confinement; childbirth. [< F *accoucher* to put to bed]

ac·count (ə-kount′) *v.t.* **1.** To hold to be; consider; estimate. — *v.i.* **2.** To provide a reckoning, as of funds paid or received: with *to* or *with* (someone), *for* (something). **3.** To give a rational explanation: with *for.* **4.** To be responsible; answer: with *for.* **5.** To cause death, capture, or incapacitation: with *for.* — *n.* **1.** A record of events; narrative; description. **2.** A statement of causes; explanation. **3.** A record of monetary transactions. **4.** Worth; importance. **5.** Judgment; estimation. **6.** Profit; advantage. — **on account of** Because of. — **on no account** Under no circumstances. [< OF < LL < L *ad-* to + *computare* to reckon together]

ac·count·a·ble (ə-koun′tə·bəl) *adj.* **1.** Liable to be called to account; responsible. **2.** Capable of being explained. — **ac·count′a·bil′i·ty** *n.* — **ac·count′a·bly** *adv.*

ac·count·ant (ə-koun′tənt) *n.* One whose business is to keep or examine books, as of a mercantile or banking house. — **ac·count′an·cy** *n.*

ac·count·ing (ə-koun′ting) *n.* The art or system of recording, classifying, and summarizing commercial transactions.

ac·cou·ter (ə-kōō′tər) *v.t.* To furnish with dress or trappings; equip, as for military service. Also *Brit.* **ac·cou′tre.** [< F *accoutrer*; ult. origin uncertain]

ac·cou·ter·ment (ə-kōō′tər·mənt) *n.* **1.** *pl.* Equipment; trappings; especially, the equipment of a soldier other than arms and dress. **2.** The act of accoutering.

ac·cred·it (ə-kred′it) *v.t.* **1.** To give credit to as the owner, author, or creator of; attribute to: with *with.* **2.** To accept as true; believe. **3.** To bring into credit; vouch for. **4.** To furnish or send with credentials. **5.** To certify as fulfilling official requirements. [< F < L < *ad-* to + *credere* to believe, trust]

ac·cred·i·ta·tion (ə-kred′ə·tā′shən) *n. U.S.* The granting of approved status to an academic institution.

ac·cre·tion (ə-krē′shən) *n.* **1.** Growth by external additions or by adhesion or inclusion. **2.** An external addition; something added. **3.** Increase by natural growth.

ac·crue (ə-krōō′) *v.i.* ·**crued,** ·**cru·ing 1.** To come as a natural result or increment, as by growth: with *to.* **2.** To accumulate, as the interest on money: with *from.* [< F < L < *ad-* to + *crescere* to grow] — **ac·cru′al, ac·crue′ment** *n.*

ac·cu·mu·late (ə-kyōōm′yə·lāt) *v.* ·**lat·ed,** ·**lat·ing** *v.t.* **1.** To heap or pile up; amass; collect. — *v.i.* **2.** To become greater in quantity or number; increase. [< L < *ad-* to + *cumulare* to heap] — **ac·cu′mu·la·ble** (-lə-bəl) *adj.*

ac·cu·mu·la·tion (ə-kyōōm′yə·lā′shən) *n.* **1.** The act or process of accumulating. **2.** That which is accumulated. **3.** The addition of earnings or profits to capital.

ac·cu·mu·la·tive (ə-kyōōm′yə·lā′tiv, -lə·tiv) *adj.* **1.** Tending to accumulate. **2.** Arising from accumulation. — **ac·cu′mu·la′tive·ly** *adv.* — **ac·cu′mu·la′tive·ness** *n.*

ac·cu·mu·la·tor (ə-kyōōm′yə·lā′tər) *n.* **1.** A person or thing that accumulates. **2.** *Brit.* A storage battery.

ac·cu·ra·cy (ak′yər·ə·sē) *n.* The condition or quality of being accurate; exactness; precision; correctness.

ac·cu·rate (ak′yər·it) *adj.* Conforming exactly to truth or to a standard; without error; precise; exact. [< L < *ad-* to + *cura* care] — **ac′cu·rate·ly** *adv.* — **ac′cu·rate·ness** *n.*

ac·curs·ed (ə-kûr′sid, ə·kûrst′) *adj.* **1.** Lying under a curse; doomed. **2.** Deserving a curse; detestable. Also **ac·curst′.** — **ac·curs′ed·ly** *adv.* — **ac·curs′ed·ness** *n.*

ac·cu·sa·tion (ak′yōō·zā′shən) *n.* **1.** The act of accusing or the state of being accused. **2.** The crime or act charged. Also **ac·cu·sal** (ə-kyōō′zəl). — **ac·cu·sa·to·ry** (ə-kyōō′zə·tôr′ē, -tō′rē) *adj.*

ac·cu·sa·tive (ə-kyōō′zə·tiv) *Gram. adj.* Denoting, in inflected languages, the case or relation of the direct object of a verb or preposition, or the goal toward which an action is directed; objective. Also **ac·cu·sa·ti·val** (ə-kyōō′zə·tī′vəl). — *n.* **1.** The case of Latin and Greek nouns corresponding to the English objective. **2.** A word in this case. [< L *accusativus,* trans. of Gk. (*ptōsis*) *aitiatikē* (the case) of the effect < *aitiatos* effected] — **ac·cu′sa·tive·ly** *adv.*

ac·cuse (ə-kyōōz′) *v.* ·**cused,** ·**cus·ing** *v.t.* **1.** To charge with fault or error; blame; censure. **2.** To bring charges against: with *of.* — *v.i.* **3.** To make accusation; utter charges. [< OF < L < *ad-* to + *causa* a cause, lawsuit] — **ac·cus′er** *n.* — **ac·cus′ing·ly** *adv.*

— **Syn. 2.** *Accuse* is a general word for declaring a person guilty of a fault; *charge* is more formal and stresses the serious or criminal nature of an act: to *accuse* a man of lying, to *charge* him with perjury. An *accused* man is *indicted* by a grand jury, and *arraigned* before a court to answer the indictment. *Incriminate* implies involvement in a serious crime.

ac·cused (ə-kyōōzd′) *n. Law* The defendant or defendants in a criminal case: preceded by *the.*

ac·cus·tom (ə-kus′təm) *v.t.* To familiarize by custom or use; habituate or inure: with *to:* to *accustom* oneself to noise.

ac·cus·tomed (ə-kus′təmd) *adj.* **1.** Habitual; usual. **2.** Wont; used: *accustomed* to hard work.

ace (ās) *n.* **1.** A playing card, die, etc., having a single spot. **2.** A very small amount, distance, or degree: within an *ace* of death. **3.** One who excels in a particular field, especially a combat flyer. **4.** In tennis and similar games, a point won by a single stroke, as upon the service. — **ace in the hole** *U.S. Slang* A hidden advantage. — *v.t.* **aced** (āst), **ac·ing** To score a point against in a single stroke, as in tennis. [< OF < L *as* unity, unit]

-acea *suffix Zool.* Used in forming names of classes and orders of animals. [< L, neut. pl. of *-aceus*]

-aceae *suffix Bot.* Used in forming names of families of plants. [< L, fem. pl. of *-aceus*]

a·ce·di·a (ə-sē′dē·ə) *n.* **1.** Extreme mental or spiritual torpor. **2.** Sloth regarded as one of the seven deadly sins. [< LL < Gk. < *a-* without + *kēdos* care]

a·cen·tric (ā-sen′trik) *adj.* Without a center; off center.

-aceous *suffix* Of the nature of; belonging or pertaining to; like: used to form adjectives corresponding to nouns in *-acea, -aceae.* [< L *-aceus* of the nature of]

ac·er·bate (as′ər·bāt) *v.t.* ·**bat·ed,** ·**bat·ing 1.** To make sour; embitter. **2.** To exasperate. [< L *acerbus* sharp]

a·cer·bi·ty (ə-sûr′bə·tē) *n. pl.* ·**ties 1.** Sourness, bitterness, as that of unripe fruit. **2.** Severity, as of temper, etc.; harshness. Also **a·cer·bi·tude** (ə-sûr′bə·tōōd, -tyōōd).

acet- Var. of ACETO-.

ac·e·tab·u·lum (as′ə·tab′yə·ləm) *n. pl.* ·**la** (-lə) *Anat.* The socket in the hip in which the head of the femur rests and revolves. [< L, a vinegar cup < *acetum* vinegar]

ac·e·tal (as′ə·tal) *n. Med.* A volatile, colorless liquid, $C_6H_{14}O_2$, having hypnotic properties.

ac·et·an·i·lide (as′ə·tan′ə·līd, -lid) *n. Chem.* A derivative of aniline, C_8H_9ON, used as a sedative and antipyretic.

ac·e·tate (as′ə·tāt) *n. Chem.* A salt or ester of acetic acid.

a·ce·tic (ə-sē′tik, ə·set′ik) *adj.* Pertaining to or like vinegar; sour. [< L *acetum* vinegar + -IC]

acetic acid *Chem.* A colorless, pungent liquid, $C_2H_4O_2$, occurring in a dilute form in vinegar.

a·cet·i·fy (ə-set′ə·fī) *v.t. & v.i.* ·**fied,** ·**fy·ing** To change into acid or vinegar. — **a·cet′i·fi·ca′tion** *n.* — **a·cet′i·fi′er** *n.*

aceto- *combining form* Of, pertaining to, or from acetic acid or acetyl. Also, before vowels, *acet-.* [< L *acetum* vinegar]

ac·e·tone (as′ə·tōn) *n. Chem.* A clear, flammable liquid, C_3H_6O, used as a solvent for fats, camphor, and resins. — **ac·e·ton·ic** (as′ə·ton′ik) *adj.*

a·cet·y·lene (ə-set′ə·lēn) *n. Chem.* A colorless hydrocarbon gas, C_2H_2, used as an illuminant and for cutting metals.

ac·e·tyl·sal·i·cyl·ic acid (as′ə·til-sal′ə-sil′ik, ə·sē′təl-) Aspirin.

ace·y-deuc·y (ā′sē·dōō′sē, -dyōō′sē) *n.* A variety of backgammon.

A·chae·an (ə-kē′ən) *adj.* Pertaining to Achaea, its people, or their culture. — *n.* **1.** A member of one of the four major tribes of ancient Greece. **2.** A Greek. Also **A·cha·ian** (ə-kā′ən, -kī-).

ache (āk) *v.i.* **ached** (ākt), **ach·ing 1.** To suffer dull, continued pain; be in pain or distress. **2.** *Informal* To yearn; be eager; with *for* or the infinitive. — *n.* A local, dull, and protracted pain. [OE *acan*] — **ach′ing·ly** *adv.*

a·chene (ā-kēn′) *n. Bot.* A small, dry, one-seeded pericarp, as in the dandelion, buttercup, etc.: also spelled *akene.* [< NL < A-⁴ not + Gk. *chainein* to gape] — **a·che′ni·al** *adj.*

Ach·e·ron (ak′ə·ron) **1.** In Greek and Roman mythology, the river of woe, one of the rivers surrounding Hades. **2.** Hades. [< L < Gk. *Acherōn*]

a·chieve (ə·chēv′) *v.* **a·chieved, a·chiev·ing** *v.t.* **1.** To accomplish; do successfully. **2.** To win or attain, as by effort or skill. — *v.i.* **3.** To accomplish something. [< OF < LL *ad caput* (*venire*) (to come) to a head, finish] — **a·chiev′a·ble** *adj.* — **a·chiev′er** *n.*

a·chieve·ment (ə·chēv′mənt) *n.* **1.** Something accomplished. **2.** The act of achieving. — **Syn.** See ACT.

A·chil·les (ə·kil′ēz) In the *Iliad*, the foremost Greek hero of the Trojan War, who killed Hector and was killed by an arrow Paris shot into his right heel, his only vulnerable spot. — **Ach·il·le·an** (ak′ə·lē′ən) *adj.*

Achilles′ heel A vulnerable point.

Achilles′ tendon *Anat.* The tendon connecting the calf muscles to the heel bone.

ach·ro·mat·ic (ak′rə·mat′ik) *adj.* **1.** *Optics* Free from color or iridescence; transmitting light without separating it into its constituent colors, as a lens. **2.** *Music* Diatonic; without accidentals. [< Gk. < *a-* without + *chrōma* color] — **ach′ro·mat′i·cal·ly** *adv.* — **a·chro·ma·tism** (ā·krō′mə·tiz′əm), **a·chro·ma·tic·i·ty** (ā·krō′mə·tis′ə·tē) *n.*

a·chro·ma·tin (ā·krō′mə·tin) *n. Biol.* The substance in the cell nucleus that does not readily take color from stains.

a·chro·ma·tize (ā·krō′mə·tīz) *v.t.* **·tized, ·tiz·ing** To make achromatic.

a·chro·mic (ā·krō′mik) *adj.* Colorless. Also **a·chro′mous.**

ac·id (as′id) *adj.* **1.** Sharp and biting to the taste, as vinegar; sour. **2.** *Chem.* Pertaining to or like an acid. **3.** *Geol.* Acidic. **4.** Sharp-tempered; biting. — *n.* **1.** Any sour substance. **2.** *Chem.* A compound containing hydrogen in which all or a part of the hydrogen may be exchanged for a metal or a basic radical, forming a salt. Aqueous solutions of acids are sour, and redden litmus. — **Syn.** See SOUR. [< L *acidus*] — **ac′id·ly** *adv.* — **ac′id·ness** *n.*

ac·id-fast (as′id-fast′, -fäst′) *adj.* Not readily decolorized by acids when stained: said of bacteria, epithelial tissue, etc.

a·cid·ic (ə·sid′ik) *adj.* **1.** *Geol.* Containing a high percentage of silica: said of rocks. **2.** *Chem.* Acid.

a·cid·i·fy (ə·sid′ə·fī) *v.t. & v.i.* **·fied, ·fy·ing** To make or become acid; change into an acid. — **a·cid′i·fi′a·ble** *adj.* — **a·cid′i·fi·ca′tion** *n.* — **a·cid′i·fi′er** *n.*

a·cid·i·ty (ə·sid′ə·tē) *n.* **1.** The state or quality of being acid. **2.** Degree of acid strength. **3.** *Chem.* The combining power of a base with reference to an acid. **4.** Hyperacidity.

ac·i·do·sis (as′ə·dō′sis) *n. Pathol.* Acid intoxication due to faulty metabolism. — **ac·i·dot·ic** (as′ə·dot′ik) *adj.*

acid test A final, decisive test, as of worth or integrity.

a·cid·u·late (ə·sij′ōō·lāt) *v.t.* **·lat·ed, ·lat·ing** To make somewhat acid or sour. — **u·cid′u·la′tion** *n.*

a·cid·u·lous (ə·sij′ōō·ləs) *adj.* Slightly acid; sour. Also **a·cid′u·lent.** [< L *acidulus* slightly sour]

a·ci·nus (as′ə·nəs) *n. pl.* **·ni** (-nī) **1.** *Bot.* One of the small parts of a fruit, as of the raspberry. **2.** A berry, as a grape, growing in bunches; a bunch of such berries. [< L *grape*]

-acious *suffix of adjectives* Abounding in; characterized by; given to: *pugnacious, vivacious.* [< L *-ax, -acis* + -OUS]

-acity *suffix* Quality or state of: used to form abstract nouns corresponding to adjectives in *-acious.* [< L *-acitas*]

ack-ack (ak′ak′) *n.* Antiaircraft fire. [British radio operator's code for *A.A.* (antiaircraft)]

ac·knowl·edge (ak·nol′ij) *v.t.* **·edged, ·edg·ing** **1.** To admit the truth or fact of; confess. **2.** To recognize as or avow to be. **3.** To admit the validity of, as a claim or right. **4.** To show appreciation of or admit obligation for; express thanks for. **5.** To report receipt or arrival of. — **Syn.** See CONFESS. [Earlier *aknowledge* < obs. *aknow* to admit, confess] — **ac·knowl′edge·a·ble** *adj.* — **ac·knowl′edg·er** *n.*

ac·knowl·edg·ment (ak·nol′ij·mənt) *n.* **1.** The act of admitting; confession. **2.** Recognition of the existence or truth of something. **3.** Something done or given in return. **4.** *Law* A formal certificate. Also **ac·knowl′edge·ment.**

ac·me (ak′mē) *n.* The highest point. [< Gk. *akmē* point]

ac·ne (ak′nē) *n. Pathol.* A skin disease marked by pimples, chiefly on the face. [? Alter. of Gk. *akmē* point]

ac·o·lyte (ak′ə·līt) *n.* **1.** An attendant or assistant. **2.** An altar boy. **3.** In the Roman Catholic Church, a member of the highest minor order. [< Med.L < Gk. *akolouthos* follower, attendant]

ac·o·nite (ak′ə·nīt) *n.* **1.** The monkshood, or any similar plant. **2.** An extract of this plant, used as a sedative. Also **ac·o·ni·tum** (ak′ə·nī′təm). [< F < L < Gk. *akoniton*]

a·corn (ā′kôrn, ā′kərn) *n.* The fruit of the oak, a one-seeded nut, fixed in a woody cup. [OE *æcern*]

a·cous·tic (ə·kōōs′tik) *adj.* **1.** Pertaining to the act or sense of hearing, heard sound, or the science of sound. **2.** Adapted for conveying sound or aiding hearing. Also **a·cous′ti·cal.** [< F < Gk. *akouein* to hear] — **a·cous′ti·cal·ly** *adv.*

a·cous·tics (ə·kōōs′tiks) *n.pl.* (*construed as sing. in def. 1*) **1.** The branch of physics that treats of sound. **2.** The sound-transmitting qualities of an auditorium, room, etc.

ac·quaint (ə·kwānt′) *v.t.* **1.** To make familiar or conversant. **2.** To cause to know; inform. [< OF < LL < L *ad-* to + *cognitus,* pp. of *cognoscere* to know]

ac·quain·tance (ə·kwān′təns) *n.* **1.** Knowledge of any person or thing. **2.** A person or persons with whom one is acquainted. — **ac·quain′tance·ship** *n.*

ac·quaint·ed (ə·kwān′tid) *adj.* Having acquaintance; having personal knowledge: with *with.*

ac·qui·esce (ak′wē·es′) *v.i.* **·esced** (-est′), **·esc·ing** To consent or concur tacitly; assent; comply. [< MF < L < *ad-* to + *quiescere* to rest] — **ac′qui·esc′ing·ly** *adv.*

ac·qui·es·cence (ak′wē·es′əns) *n.* Quiet submission; passive consent. — **ac′qui·es′cent** *adj.* — **ac′qui·es′cent·ly** *adv.*

ac·quire (ə·kwīr′) *v.t.* **·quired, ·quir·ing** **1.** To obtain by one's own endeavor or action. **2.** To come to possess; receive. — **Syn.** See GET, RECEIVE. [< L < *ad-* to + *quaerere* to seek] — **ac·quir′a·ble** *adj.* — **ac·quir′er** *n.*

acquired character *Biol.* A noninheritable change in an organism resulting from environmental influences.

ac·quire·ment (ə·kwīr′mənt) *n.* **1.** The act of acquiring. **2.** Something acquired, as a skill; an attainment.

ac·qui·si·tion (ak′wə·zish′ən) *n.* **1.** The act of acquiring. **2.** Anything gained or acquired.

ac·quis·i·tive (ə·kwiz′ə·tiv) *adj.* Able or inclined to acquire (money, property, etc.); grasping. — **ac·quis′i·tive·ly** *adv.* — **ac·quis′i·tive·ness** *n.*

ac·quit (ə·kwit′) *v.t.* **·quit·ted, ·quit·ting** **1.** To free or clear, as from an accusation. **2.** To relieve, as of an obligation. **3.** To repay or return. **4.** To conduct (oneself); behave. [< OF < L *ad-* to + *quietare* to settle, quiet] — **ac·quit′tal** *n.* — **ac·quit′ter** *n.*

ac·quit·tance (ə·kwit′ns) *n.* **1.** A release, as from a debt. **2.** Satisfaction of indebtedness or obligation. **3.** A receipt.

a·cre (ā′kər) *n.* **1.** A measure of land, equal to 43,560 square feet. **2.** *pl.* Lands; estate. [OE *æcer* field]

a·cre·age (ā′kər·ij, -krij) *n.* Area in acres; acres collectively.

a·cred (ā′kərd) *adj.* Comprising or owning acres of land.

ac·rid (ak′rid) *adj.* **1.** Cutting or burning to the taste or smell. **2.** Sharp and satirical, as speech. [< L *acer, acris*] — **a·crid·i·ty** (ə·krid′ə·tē), **ac′rid·ness** *n.* — **ac′rid·ly** *adv.*

ac·ri·mo·ny (ak′rə·mō′nē) *n. pl.* **·nies** Sharpness or bitterness of speech or temper; acridity. [< L < *acer* sharp] — **ac·ri·mo·ni·ous** (ak′rə·mō′nē·əs) *adj.* — **ac′ri·mo′ni·ous·ly** *adv.* — **ac′ri·mo′ni·ous·ness** *n.*

acro- *combining form* **1.** At the tip or end of. **2.** *Med.* Pertaining to the extremities. [< Gk. *akros* at the end]

ac·ro·bat (ak′rə·bat) *n.* One skilled in feats requiring muscular coordination, as in tightrope walking, tumbling, trapeze performing, etc.; a gymnast. [< F < Gk. *akrobatos* walking on tiptoe < *akros* at the tip + *bainein* to walk, go] — **ac′ro·bat′ic** or **·i·cal** *adj.* — **ac′ro·bat′i·cal·ly** *adv.*

ac·ro·bat·ics (ak′rə·bat′iks) *n.pl.* The skills or activities of an acrobat, as in gymnastics.

ac·ro·gen (ak′rə·jən) *n. Bot.* A plant growing at the tip only, as ferns, mosses, etc. — **ac·ro·gen·ic** (ak′rə·jen′ik), **a·crog·e·nous** (ə·kroj′ə·nəs) *adj.* — **a·crog′e·nous·ly** *adv.*

ac·ro·meg·a·ly (ak′rō·meg′ə·lē) *n. Pathol.* A disorder of the pituitary gland characterized by an enlargement of the extremities, thorax, and face, including both soft and bony parts. [< F < Gk. *akros* at the tip + *megas, megalou* big] — **ac·ro·me·gal·ic** (ak′rō·mi·gal′ik) *adj. & n.*

ac·ro·nym (ak′rə·nim) *n.* A word formed by combining initial letters (*Eniac, UNESCO*) or syllables and letters (*radar, sonar*) of a series of words or a compound term. [< ACRO- + -*nym* name, as in *homonym*]

a·crop·o·lis (ə·krop′ə·lis) *n.* The citadel of an ancient Greek city. — **the Acropolis** The citadel of Athens. [< Gk. < *akros* at the top + *polis* city]

a·cross (ə·krôs′, ə·kros′) *adv.* **1.** From one side to the other. **2.** On or at the other side. **3.** Crosswise; crossed, as arms. — *prep.* **1.** On or from the other side of; beyond; over. **2.** Through or over the surface of. **3.** From side to side of. [< A-[1] on, in + CROSS]

a·cros·tic (ə·krôs′tik, ə·kros′-) *n.* A poem or other composition in which initial or other letters, taken in order, form a word or phrase. — *adj.* Of or resembling an acrostic. [< Gk. < *akros* at the end + *stichos* line of verse] — **a·cros′ti·cal·ly** *adv.*

A·crux (ā′kruks) *n.* One of the 20 brightest stars, 1.05 magnitude; Alpha in the constellation Crux.

a·cryl·ic acid (ə·kril′ik) *Chem.* Any of a series of acids having a sharp, acrid odor, and used in plastics.

act (akt) *v.t.* **1.** To play the part of; impersonate, as in a drama. **2.** To perform on the stage, as a play. **3.** To perform as if on a stage; feign the character of. **4.** To behave as suitable to. — *v.i.* **5.** To behave or conduct oneself. **6.** To carry out a purpose or function; perform. **7.** To produce an effect: often with *on.* **8.** To serve temporarily or as a substitute, as in some office or capacity. **9.** To perform on the stage; be an actor. **10.** To pretend, play a part so as to appear. **11.** To serve for theatrical performance or use: This

scene *acts* well. **— to act on** (or **upon**) To order one's conduct in accordance with; obey: to *act on* someone's advice. **— to act up** *Informal* To behave mischievously; appear troublesome. **—** *n.* **1.** The exertion of mental or physical power; the performance of a function or process; a doing: taken in the very *act*. **2.** Something done; a deed; action. **3.** An enactment or edict, as of a legislative body. **4.** *Often pl.* A formal written record or statement of a transaction, action taken, etc. **5.** One of the main divisions of a play or opera. **6.** A short theatrical performance. **7.** *Informal* Something feigned; a pose. [< L *actum* a thing done]
— Syn. (noun) **2.** *Act* and *deed* are both used for something done, while *action* refers more to the doing of it. *Acts* and *deeds* may be good or bad, but a *deed* is commonly great or notable. A *feat* requires daring and skill, and usually involves physical *action*. *Achievement* is usually notable and distinguished.
act·a·ble (ak′tə·bəl) *adj.* That can be acted, as a role in a play. **— act′a·bil′i·ty** *n.*
ACTH A pituitary hormone that stimulates the secretion of cortisone by the adrenal cortex.
act·ing (ak′ting) *adj.* **1.** Operating or officiating, especially in place of another: *acting* secretary. **2.** Functioning; working. **—** *n.* **1.** The occupation of an actor. **2.** Pretense or simulation.
ac·tin·i·a (ak·tin′ē·ə) *n.* A sea anemone. Also **ac·tin′i·an.** [< NL < Gk. *aktis, aktinos* ray]
ac·tin·ic (ak·tin′ik) *adj.* Of, pertaining to, or having actinism. Also **ac·tin′i·cal.** **— ac·tin′i·cal·ly** *adv.*
actinic rays Those wavelengths of violet and ultraviolet light capable of effecting chemical changes.
ac·ti·nide series (ak′ti·nīd) *Physics* A series of radioactive elements beginning with actinium, atomic number 89, and ending with lawrencium, atomic number 103.
ac·tin·ism (ak′tin·iz′əm) *n.* **1.** The property of radiant energy that effects chemical changes. **2.** The production of such change.
ac·tin·i·um (ak·tin′ē·əm) *n.* A radioactive element (symbol Ac), isolated from pitchblende, and having a half life of about 13 years. See ELEMENT.
ac·ti·noid (ak′ti·noid) *adj.* Having the form of rays; radiate, as a starfish.
ac·ti·non (ak′ti·non) *n. Chem.* A radioactive isotope of radon, with a half life of nearly four seconds. [< NL]
ac·ti·no·zo·an (ak′ti·nə·zō′ən) *n. Zool.* An anthozoan. [< Gk. *aktis* ray + *zōion* animal] **— ac′ti·no·zo′al** *adj.*
ac·tion (ak′shən) *n.* **1.** The process of acting, doing, or working; operation. **2.** The result of putting forth power; a deed; act. **3.** *pl.* Habitual behavior; conduct. **4.** Activity, energy. **5.** The exertion of power; influence. **6.** *Physiol.* The performance by an organ of its proper function. **7.** *Mech.* **a** The mechanism by which a machine operates. **b** The movement of the parts of a machine. **8.** *Mil.* A battle; combat. **9.** *Law* A lawsuit. **10.** The posture and gestures of an actor or orator. **11.** In literature, the series of connected events that form the plot in a story or play. **12.** In sculpture or painting, gesture or attitude intended to express passion or sentiment. **— Syn.** See ACT, BATTLE. [< F < L < *agere* to do]
ac·tion·a·ble (ak′shən·ə·bəl) *adj.* Affording ground for prosecution, as a trespass or a libel. **— ac′tion·a·bly** *adv.*
ac·ti·vate (ak′tə·vāt) *v.t.* **·vat·ed, ·vat·ing 1.** To make active. **2.** To organize (a military unit) for its assigned function. **3.** *Physics* To make radioactive. **4.** *Chem.* To promote or hasten a reaction in, as by heat. **5.** To purify by aeration, as sewage. **— ac′ti·va′tion** *n.* **— ac′ti·va′tor** *n.*
ac·tive (ak′tiv) *adj.* **1.** Abounding in or exhibiting action; busy. **2.** Being in or pertaining to a state of action; not extinct or quiescent. **3.** Agile; quick; nimble. **4.** Characterized by much activity; brisk; lively. **5.** Causing or promoting action or change; not contemplative. **6.** Bearing interest: *active* investments. **7.** In business, busy; productive: *active* accounts. **8.** *Gram.* Designating a voice of the verb that indicates that the subject of the sentence is performing the action. **—** *n. Gram.* The active voice. Abbr. *a.* [< F < L *activus* < *agere* to do] **— ac′tive·ly** *adv.* **— ac′tive·ness** *n.*
ac·tiv·i·ty (ak·tiv′ə·tē) *n. pl.* **·ties 1.** The state of being active; action. **2.** Brisk or vigorous movement or action; liveliness; energy. **3.** A particular action or sphere of action.
act of God *Law* An event caused by the operations of nature unmixed with human agency or human negligence.
ac·tor (ak′tər) *n.* **1.** A player on the stage, in motion pictures, etc. **2.** One who does something.
ac·tress (ak′tris) *n.* A woman or girl who acts, as on the stage.
Acts of the Apostles The fifth book of the New Testament. Also **Acts.**
ac·tu·al (ak′chōō·əl) *adj.* **1.** Existing in fact; real. **2.** Be-

ing in existence or action now; existent; present. [< F < LL < L *actus* a doing] **— ac′tu·al·ness** *n.*
ac·tu·al·i·ty (ak′chōō·al′ə·tē) *n. pl.* **·ties 1.** The state or quality of being actual; reality; realism. **2.** *pl.* Actual circumstances or conditions.
ac·tu·al·ize (ak′chōō·əl·īz′) *v.t.* **·ized, ·iz·ing 1.** To make real; realize in action, as a possibility. **2.** To make seem real; represent realistically. **— ac′tu·al·i·za′tion** *n.*
ac·tu·al·ly (ak′chōō·əl·ē) *adv.* As a matter of fact; really.
ac·tu·ar·y (ak′chōō·er′ē) *n. pl.* **·ar·ies** A statistician who calculates and states risks, premiums, etc., for insurance purposes. [< L *actuarius* clerk] **— ac·tu·ar·i·al** (ak′chōō·âr′ē·əl) *adj.* **— ac·tu·ar′i·al·ly** *adv.*
ac·tu·ate (ak′chōō·āt) *v.t.* **·at·ed, ·at·ing 1.** To set into action or motion, as a mechanism. **2.** To incite or influence to action: *actuated* by motives of kindness. [< Med.L < L *actus* a doing] **— ac′tu·a′tion** *n.* **— ac′tu·a′tor** *n.*
— Syn. *Actuate* and *impel* both imply mental or moral reasons for acting, while *urge* more often involves persuasion by others or from without.
acu- *combining form* Needle; point. [< L *acus*]
a·cu·i·ty (ə·kyōō·al′ə·tē) *n.* Acuteness; sharpness. [< MF < Med.L < L *acus* needle]
ac·u·men (ə·kyōō′mən,ak′yōō·mən) *n.* Quickness of insight or discernment. [< L < *acuere* to sharpen]
— Syn. 1. *Sharpness, acuteness,* and *insight,* however keen, and *perception,* however deep, fall short of the meaning of *acumen,* which belongs to an astute and discriminating mind.
a·cu·mi·nate (ə·kyōō′mə·nāt; *for adj., also* ə·kyōō′mə·nit) *v.t.* **·nat·ed, ·nat·ing** To sharpen; make pointed. **—** *adj.* Ending in a long, tapering point, as a leaf, feather, fin, etc.: also **a·cu′mi·nat′ed** [< L *acuminatus,* pp. of *acuminare* to point, sharpen] **— a·cu′mi·na′tion** *n.*
a·cute (ə·kyōōt′) *adj.* **1.** Coming to a crisis quickly; violent: said of a disease: opposed to *chronic.* **2.** Of the greatest importance; crucial. **3.** Affecting keenly; poignant; intense. **4.** Keenly discerning or sensitive. **5.** *Music* High in pitch; shrill. [< L *acutus,* pp. of *acuere* to sharpen] **— a·cute′ly** *adv.* **— a·cute′ness** *n.*
acute accent See ACCENT (def. 3).
acute angle *Geom.* An angle less than a right angle.
-acy *suffix of nouns* Forming nouns of quality, state, or condition from adjectives in *-acious,* and nouns and adjectives in *-ate: fallacy, celibacy, curacy.* [< F *-atie* < L *-acia, -atia* < Gk. *-ateia;* or directly < L or < Gk.]
ad (ad) *n.* **1.** *Informal* An advertisement. **2.** In tennis, advantage.
ad- *prefix* To; toward; near: *adhere:* also spelled *a-, ab-, ac-, af-, ag-, al-, an-, ap-, ar-* before various consonants. [< L *ad-* < *ad* to]
-ad *suffix of nouns* Of or pertaining to; used to form: **a** Collective numerals: *triad.* **b** Names of poems: *Iliad.* [< Gk. *-as, -ados*]
ad·age (ad′ij) *n.* A maxim; proverb. **— Syn.** See PROVERB. [< F < L < *ad-* to + root of *aio* I say]
a·da·gio (ə·dä′jō, -zhē·ō, -zhō) *Music adj.* Slow. **—** *adv.* Slowly. **—** *n.* A composition in adagio time. [< Ital.]
Ad·am (ad′əm) In the Bible, the first man, progenitor of the human race. *Gen.* ii 7. **—** *n.* Mankind collectively. **— the old Adam** Unregenerate human nature.
ad·a·mant (ad′ə·mant, -mənt) *n.* A very hard legendary mineral, later identified with the diamond or lodestone. **—** *adj.* **1.** Immovable; unyielding. **2.** Very hard. [< OF < L < Gk. < *a-* not + *damaein* to conquer] **— ad·a·man·tine** (ad′ə·man′tin, -tēn, -tīn) *adj.*
Adam's apple The prominence made by the thyroid cartilage at the front of the human throat, conspicuous in males.
a·dapt (ə·dapt′) *v.t.* **1.** To fit for a new use; make suitable: with *for.* **2.** To adjust (oneself or itself) to a new situation or environment. **—** *v.i.* **3.** To become adjusted to a circumstance or environment. [< F < L *ad* to + *aptare* to fit]
a·dapt·a·ble (ə·dap′tə·bəl) *adj.* **1.** Capable of being adapted. **2.** Able to change easily to meet new circumstances. **— a·dapt′a·bil′i·ty, a·dapt′a·ble·ness** *n.*
ad·ap·ta·tion (ad′əp·tā′shən) *n.* **1.** The act of adapting or the state of being adapted. **2.** Anything produced by adapting. **— ad′ap·ta′tion·al** *adj.* **— ad′ap·ta′tion·al·ly** *adv.*
a·dapt·er (ə·dap′tər) *n.* **1.** A person or thing that adapts. **2.** *Mech.* **a** A device that connects parts not designed to fit together. **b** A device that extends or alters the function of an apparatus. Also **a·dap′tor.** Abbr. *ad.*
a·dap·tive (ə·dap′tiv) *adj.* Capable of, fit for, or manifesting adaptation. **— a·dap′tive·ly** *adv.* **— a·dap′tive·ness** *n.*
A·dar (ə·där′, ä′där) *n.* The sixth month of the Hebrew year. See (Hebrew) CALENDAR.
add (ad) *v.t.* **1.** To join or unite, so as to increase the importance, size, quantity, or scope: with *to.* **2.** To find the sum of, as a column of figures. **3.** To say or write further.

— *v.i.* 4. To make or be an addition: with *to*. 5. To perform the arithmetical process of addition. — **to add up** 1. To accumulate to a total. 2. *Informal* To make sense. [< L *ad-* to + *dare* to give, put] — **add′a·ble** or **add′i·ble** *adj.* — **Syn.** 1. *Add* denotes the joining of one thing to another to increase it. To *append* is to add something supplemental; *annex* indicates that the addition is subordinate, and often remains distinct. Compare INCREASE.

ad·dend (ad′end, ə·dend′) *n. Math.* A quantity or number that is to be added to another.

ad·den·dum (ə·den′dəm) *n. pl.* **·da** (-də) 1. A thing added, or to be added. 2. A supplement, as to a book; appendix. [< L, neut. gerundive of *addere* to add]

ad·der (ad′ər) *n.* 1. A viper, esp. the common European viper. 2. Any of various other snakes, as the puff adder. [OE *nǣdre* (a *nadder* in ME becoming *an adder*)]

ad·der's-tongue (ad′ərz-tung′) *n.* 1. A fern with a narrow spike. 2. The dogtooth violet.

ad·dict (v. ə·dikt′; n. ad′ikt) *v.t.* To apply or devote (oneself) habitually: with *to*. — *n.* One who is given to some habit, esp. to the use of narcotic drugs. [< L *ad-* to + *dicere* to say] — **ad·dic′tion, ad·dict′ed·ness** *n.*

ad·dict·ed (ə·dik′tid) *adj.* Given over to a pursuit, practice, or habit: with *to: addicted to drugs*. — **Syn.** *Addicted* suggests a pathological weakness; *given*, a tendency or usual practice. Both words may apply to good or bad things, but usually to bad: *addicted* to alcohol, *given* to lying.

ad·di·tion (ə·dish′ən) *n.* 1. The act of adding. 2. That which is added. 3. The uniting of two or more quantities in one sum. — **ad·di′tion·al** *adj.* — **ad·di′tion·al·ly** *adv.*

ad·di·tive (ad′ə·tiv) *n.* Something added or to be added to a product or device. — *adj.* That is to be added; serving or tending to increase. — **ad′di·tive·ly** *adv.*

ad·dle (ad′l) *v.t. & v.i.* **·dled, ·dling** 1. To become or cause to become confused. 2. To spoil, as eggs. — *adj.* 1. Confused; mixed up: now generally in compounds: *addlepated*. 2. Spoiled, as eggs; rotten. [OE *adela* liquid filth]

ad·dle-brained (ad′l·brānd′) *adj.* Confused; mixed up. Also **ad′dle·head′ed, ad′dle·pat′ed, ad′dle·wit′ted.**

ad·dress (ə·dres′; *for n. defs. 2, 3, also* ad′res) *v.t.* **·dressed, ·dress·ing** 1. To speak to. 2. To deliver a set discourse to. 3. To direct, as spoken or written words, to the attention of: with *to: address* prayers to God. 4. To devote the energy or force of (oneself): with *to: address* oneself to a task. 5. To mark with a destination, as a letter. 6. To consign, as a cargo to a merchant. 7. To aim or direct. 8. To pay court to, as a lover; woo. 9. To assume a preparatory stance toward (a golf ball, etc.). — *n.* 1. A set or formal discourse. 2. The writing on an envelope, etc., indicating its destination. 3. The name, place, residence, etc., of a person. 4. The manner of a person; bearing. 5. *Chiefly pl.* Any courteous or devoted attention; wooing. 6. Adroitness; tact. [< OF < L *ad-* to + *directus* straight] — **ad·dress′er, ad·dress′or** *n.*

ad·dress·ee (ad′res·ē′, ə·dres′ē′) *n.* One to whom mail, etc., is addressed.

ad·duce (ə·dōōs′, ə·dyōōs′) *v.t.* **·duced, ·duc·ing** To present for proof or consideration, as an example; cite; allege. [< L *ad-* to + *ducere* to lead] — **ad·duce′a·ble** or **ad·duc′i·ble** *adj.*

ad·duct (ə·dukt′) *v.t. Physiol.* To draw toward the axis: said of muscles. — **ad·duc′tion** *n.* — **ad·duc′tive** *adj.*

ad·duc·tor (ə·duk′tər) *n.* An adducting muscle.

-ade¹ *suffix of nouns* 1. Act or action: *cannonade*. 2. A person or group concerned in an action or process: *cavalcade*. 3. That which is produced by an action or process: *pomade*. 4. A beverage made with or containing a fruit juice: *lemonade*. [< F < L *-ata*, fem. pp. ending]

-ade² *suffix of nouns* Relating to; pertaining to: *decade*. See -AD¹. [< F *-ade* < Gk. *-as*, *-ados*]

adeno- *combining form* Gland. Also, before vowels, **aden-**. [< Gk. *adēn* gland]

ad·e·noid (ad′ə·noid) *adj.* Of or like a gland; glandular. Also **ad′e·noi′dal.** — *n. Usually pl. Pathol.* An enlarged lymphoid growth behind the pharynx.

ad·e·no·ma (ad′ə·nō′mə) *n. Pathol.* A tumor of glandular origin or structure. — **ad·e·nom·a·tous** (ad′ə·nom′ə·təs) *adj.*

a·dept (ə·dept′; *for n., also* ad′ept) *adj.* Highly skilled; proficient: an *adept* worker. — *n.* One fully skilled in any art; an expert. [< L < *ad-* to + *apisci* to get] — **a·dept′ly** *adv.* — **a·dept′ness** *n.*

ad·e·quate (ad′ə·kwit) *adj.* 1. Equal to what is required; fully sufficient. 2. Barely sufficient. [< L < *ad-* to + *aequus* equal] — **ad′e·qua·cy** *n.* — **ad′e·quate·ness** *n.* — **ad′e·quate·ly** *adv.* — **Syn.** 1. *Adequate* is applied to ability or power; *sufficient*, to quantity or number. A man is *adequate* to a situation; a supply is *sufficient* for a need. A thing is *satisfactory* if it measures up, more or less; it is *equal* if it is exactly commensurate. The connotation of these terms varies widely in contexts. An actor called *adequate* is usually regarded as mediocre. A *sufficient* reason may range from

ADENOIDS
(a)

the flimsiest pretext to the surest demonstration. *Satisfactory* is a term in many grading systems, varying from passing to good.

ad·here (ad·hir′) *v.i.* **·hered, ·her·ing** 1. To stick fast or together. 2. To be attached or devoted to a party or faith. 3. To follow closely or without deviation. [< L < *ad-* to + *haerere* to stick] — **ad·her′ence** *n.* — **ad·her′er** *n.*

ad·her·ent (ad·hir′ənt) *adj.* Clinging or sticking fast. — *n.* One who is devoted or attached, as to a cause or leader; a follower. — **ad·her′ent·ly** *adv.* — **Syn.** (noun) *Adherent* is the weakest term. A *follower* is more fervid in his attachment. A *disciple* has a pupil-teacher relationship with the one he follows. A *supporter* is one who aids in any way, while a *partisan* is militant in his support.

ad·he·sion (ad·hē′zhən) *n.* 1. The act of adhering, or the state of being joined. 2. Firm attachment, as to a cause; fidelity. 3. *Physics* The binding force exerted by molecules of unlike substances in contact: distinguished from *cohesion*. 4. *Med.* Abnormal surface union of dissimilar tissues as a result of inflammation, etc. [See ADHERE.]

ad·he·sive (ad·hē′siv) *adj.* 1. Tending to adhere; sticky. 2. Prepared to adhere; gummed. — *n.* A substance that causes adhesion. — **ad·he′sive·ly** *adv.* — **ad·he′sive·ness** *n.*

adhesive tape A piece or strip of fabric coated with adhesive material, used for bandages, dressings, etc.

ad hoc (ad hok′) *Latin* For this purpose.

ad·i·a·bat·ic (ad′ē·ə·bat′ik, ā′dē·ə-) *adj. Physics* Pertaining to a thermodynamic system in which changes are effected without gain or loss of heat. [< Gk. < *a-* not + *dia-* through + *bainein* to go + -IC]

a·dieu (ə·dōō′, ə·dyōō′; *Fr.* à·dyœ′) *n. pl.* **a·dieus,** *Fr.* **a·dieux** (à·dyœ′) A farewell. — *interj.* Good-by; farewell: literally, to God (I commend you). [< F]

ad in·fi·ni·tum (ad in′fə·nī′təm) *Latin* Endlessly; forever.

ad in·ter·im (ad in′tə·rim) *Latin* In the meantime.

a·di·os (ä′dē·ōs′, ad′ē·ōs′; *Sp.* ä·thyōs′) *interj.* Farewell; good-by: literally, to God (I commend you). [< Sp.]

ad·i·pose (ad′ə·pōs) *adj.* Of or pertaining to fat; fatty: also **ad·i·pous** (ad′ə·pəs). — *n.* Fat. [< NL < L *adeps, adipis* fat] — **ad·i·pose′ness, ad·i·pos·i·ty** (ad′ə·pos′ə·tē) *n.*

ad·ja·cen·cy (ə·jā′sən·sē) *n. pl.* **·cies** 1. The state of being adjacent; contiguity. 2. That which is adjacent.

ad·ja·cent (ə·jā′sənt) *adj.* Lying near or close at hand; adjoining; contiguous. Abbr. *adj.* [< L < *ad-* near + *jacere* to lie] — **ad·ja′cent·ly** *adv.*

adjacent angle *Geom.* An angle having a common side with another angle and the same vertex.

ad·jec·tive (aj′ik·tiv) *n. Gram.* Any of a class of words used to limit or qualify a noun: one of the eight traditional parts of speech. — *adj. Gram.* Functioning as an adjective; depending upon or standing in adjunct relation to a noun. Abbr. *a., adj.* [< L *adjicere* to add to < *ad-* to + *jacere* to throw] — **ad·jec·ti·val** (aj′ik·tī′vəl, aj′ik·ti·vəl) *adj.* — **ad′jec·ti′val·ly** *adv.*

adjective clause *Gram.* A dependent clause usually introduced by a relative pronoun and qualifying its antecedent, as *who painted my house* in *the man who painted my house*: also called *relative clause*. Also **adjectival clause.**

ad·join (ə·join′) *v.t.* 1. To be next to; border upon. 2. To join to; append; unite: with *to*. — *v.i.* 3. To lie close together; be in contact. [< OF < L < *ad-* to + *jungere* to join]

ad·join·ing (ə·joi′ning) *adj.* Lying next; contiguous.

ad·journ (ə·jûrn′) *v.t.* 1. To put off to another day or place, as a meeting or session; postpone. — *v.i.* 2. To postpone or suspend proceedings for a specified time. 3. *Informal* To move or go to another place. — **Syn.** See POSTPONE. [< OF < LL < L *ad-* to + *diurnus* daily < *dies* day] — **ad·journ′ment** *n.*

ad·judge (ə·juj′) *v.t.* **·judged, ·judg·ing** 1. To determine or decide judicially, as a case. 2. To pronounce or order by law: His testimony was *adjudged* perjury. 3. To condemn or sentence: with *to*. 4. To award by law, as damages. [< OF < L < *ad-* to + *judicare* to judge]

ad·ju·di·cate (ə·jōō′də·kāt) *v.* **·cat·ed, ·cat·ing** *v.t.* 1. To determine judicially, as a case; adjudge. — *v.i.* 2. To act as a judge. — **ad·ju′di·ca′tion** *n.* — **ad·ju′di·ca′tor** *n.*

ad·junct (aj′ungkt) *n.* 1. Something joined to something else, but in an auxiliary or subordinate position. 2. A helper; assistant. 3. *Gram.* A modifier. 4. *Logic* Any nonessential quality of a thing. — *adj.* Joined subordinately; auxiliary. [See ADJOIN.] — **ad·junc·tive** (ə·jungk′tiv) *adj.* — **ad·junc′tive·ly** *adv.*

ad·jure (ə·jŏŏr′) *v.t.* **·jured, ·jur·ing** 1. To charge or entreat solemnly, as under oath or penalty. 2. To appeal to earnestly. [< L < *ad-* to + *jurare* to swear] — **ad·ju·ra·tion** (aj′ŏŏ·rā′shən) *n.* — **ad·jur·a·to·ry** (ə·jŏŏr′ə·tôr′ē, -tō′rē) *adj.* — **ad·jur′er** or **ad·ju′ror** *n.*

ad·just (ə·just′) *v.t.* 1. To arrange so as to fit or match. 2. To harmonize or compose, as differences. 3. To regulate or make accurate. 4. To determine the amount to be paid in settlement of (an insurance claim). 5. To arrange in order. — *v.i.* 6. To adapt oneself; conform, as to a new environment. [< OF < L ad- to + juxta near; refashioned on F juste right < L justus] — ad·jus′ta·ble adj. — ad·just′er or ad·jus′tor n. — ad·jus′tive adj.

ad·just·ment (ə·just′mənt) n. **1.** The act of adjusting or the state of being adjusted. **2.** An instrument or means of adjusting. **3.** The amount to be paid in settling a claim.

ad·ju·tant (aj′ŏŏ·tənt) n. **1.** Mil. A staff officer who assists a commanding officer in administrative duties. Abbr. adj. **2.** A carrion-eating East Indian stork: also called marabou: also **adjutant stork, adjutant crane.** [< L adjutare to assist] — ad′ju·tan·cy, ad′ju·tant·ship n.

adjutant general pl. **adjutants general** The adjutant of a military unit having a general staff. — **The Adjutant General** The major general in charge of the administrative branch of the United States Army.

ad-lib (ad′lib′) Informal v.t. & v.i. **-libbed, -lib·bing** To improvise, as words or gestures not called for in the script. — n. An instance of this. [< AD LIBITUM]

ad lib·i·tum (ad lib′ə·təm) **1.** Latin As one pleases. **2.** Music Freely: a direction indicating that a section may be played as the performer wishes.

ad·meas·ure (ad·mezh′ər) v.t. **·ured, ·ur·ing** To apportion. [< OF < LL < ad- to + mensurare to measure] — ad·meas′ur·er n. — ad·meas′ure·ment n.

ad·min·is·ter (ad·min′is·tər) v.t. **1.** To have the charge or direction of; manage. **2.** To supply or provide with; apply, as medicine or treatment. **3.** To inflict; mete out; dispense. **4.** Law To act as executor or trustee of. **5.** To tender, as an oath. — v.i. **6.** To contribute help; minister: with to. **7.** To carry out the functions of an administrator. [< OF < L < ad- to + ministrare to serve] — ad·min·is·te·ri·al (ad·min′is·tir′ē·əl) adj. — ad·min′is·tra·ble adj.

ad·min·is·trate (ad·min′is·trāt) v.t. **·trat·ed, ·trat·ing** To administer.

ad·min·is·tra·tion (ad·min′is·trā′shən) n. **1.** The act of administering, or the state of being administered. **2.** The executive personnel of a government, institution, etc.: also, their policies. **3.** The term of office of such a government. **4.** Law The legal management of an estate.

ad·min·is·tra·tive (ad·min′is·trā′tiv) adj. Pertaining to administration; executive. — ad·min′is·tra′tive·ly adv.

ad·min·is·tra·tor (ad·min′is·trā′tər) n. **1.** One who administers something; an executive. **2.** Law One commissioned by a competent court to administer the personal property of a deceased or incompetent person. [< L] — ad·min′is·tra′tor·ship n.

ad·min·is·tra·trix (ad·min′is·trā′triks) n. pl. **·tra·trix·es** or **·tra·tri·ces** (-trā′trə·sēz, -trə·trī′sēz) A woman administrator. Also **ad·min·is·tra′tress.**

ad·mi·ra·ble (ad′mər·ə·bəl) adj. Worthy of admiration; excellent. — ad′mi·ra·ble·ness, ad′mi·ra·bil′i·ty n. — ad′mi·ra·bly adv.

ad·mi·ral (ad′mər·əl) n. **1.** The supreme commander of a navy or fleet. **2.** In the U.S. Navy and Royal Canadian Navy, an officer of the next to highest rank, equivalent to a general; also, loosely, a rear admiral or a vice admiral. [< OF < Arabic amīr-al commander of the]

Admiral of the Fleet The highest rank in the U.S. and Royal Canadian Navies, corresponding to General of the Army or Field Marshal. Also **Fleet Admiral.**

ad·mi·ral·ty (ad′mər·əl·tē) n. pl. **·ties 1.** The office or functions of an admiral. **2.** Law Maritime law or courts.

Ad·mi·ral·ty (ad′mər·əl·tē) n. **1.** A department of the British government having charge of naval affairs. **2.** The building in London housing this department.

ad·mi·ra·tion (ad′mə·rā′shən) n. **1.** A feeling of wonder and approbation, as at the sight of anything rare, excellent, or sublime. **2.** High esteem. **3.** That which is admired.

ad·mire (ad·mīr′) v. **·mired, ·mir·ing** v.t. **1.** To regard with wonder, pleasure, and approbation. **2.** To have respect or esteem for. — v.i. **3.** To feel or express admiration. [< F < L < ad- at + mirari to wonder] — ad·mir′er n. — ad·mir′ing adj. — ad·mir′ing·ly adv.

ad·mis·si·ble (ad·mis′ə·bəl) adj. **1.** Worthy of being considered; allowable. **2.** Such as may be admitted. — ad·mis′si·bil′i·ty, ad·mis′si·ble·ness n. — ad·mis′si·bly adv.

ad·mis·sion (ad·mish′ən) n. **1.** The act of admitting, or the state of being admitted. **2.** Authority to enter. **3.** An entrance fee. **4.** A confession. **5.** Anything conceded.

ad·mis·sive (ad·mis′iv) adj. Characterized by, implying, or granting admission. Also **ad·mis·so·ry** (ad·mis′ər·ē).

ad·mit (ad·mit′) v. **·mit·ted, ·mit·ting** v.t. **1.** To allow to enter. **2.** To be the means or channel of admission to; let in. **3.** To allow to join. **4.** To have room for; contain. **5.** To leave room for; permit: His impatience admits no delay. **6.** To concede or grant as valid. **7.** To acknowledge or avow. — v.i. **8.** To afford possibility or opportunity: This problem admits of several solutions. **9.** To afford entrance; open on:

with to: This gate admits to the garden. — **Syn.** See CONFESS. [< OF < L < ad- to + mittere to send]

ad·mit·tance (ad·mit′ns) n. **1.** The act of admitting, or the state or fact of being admitted; entrance. **2.** Right or permission to enter. **3.** Actual entrance; admission. **4.** Electr. The ability of a circuit to carry an alternating current, combining the effects of conductance and susceptance.

ad·mit·ted·ly (ad·mit′id·lē) adv. By admission; confessedly.

ad·mix (ad·miks′) v.t. & v.i. **·mixed** or **·mixt, ·mix·ing** To mingle or mix with something else. [ME < L ad- to + miscere to mix]

ad·mix·ture (ad·miks′chər) n. **1.** The act of mixing, or the state of being mixed. **2.** Anything added in mixing.

ad·mon·ish (ad·mon′ish) v.t. **1.** To administer mild reproof to. **2.** To caution against danger or error; warn. **3.** To charge authoritatively; exhort; urge. [< OF < LL < L < ad- to + monere to warn] — ad·mon′ish·er n.

ad·mo·ni·tion (ad′mə·nish′ən) n. **1.** The act of admonishing. **2.** A gentle reproof. Also **ad·mon′ish·ment.**

ad·mon·i·tor (ad·mon′ə·tər) n. One who admonishes. [< L] — **ad·mon·i·to·ry** (ad·mon′ə·tôr′ē, -tō′rē) adj.

ad nau·se·am (ad nô′zē·əm, -sē-, -zhē-, -shē-; äd) Latin To the point of nausea or disgust.

a·do (ə·dōō′) n. Activity; bustle; fuss. [ME at do to do]

a·do·be (ə·dō′bē) n. **1.** An unburnt, sun-dried brick. **2.** The mixed earth or sandy, calcareous clay of which such bricks are made. **3.** A structure made of such bricks. [< Sp.]

ad·o·les·cence (ad′ə·les′əns) n. **1.** The period of growth from puberty to adulthood. **2.** The quality or condition of being adolescent. Also **ad′o·les′cen·cy.**

ad·o·les·cent (ad′ə·les′ənt) adj. **1.** Approaching adulthood. **2.** Characteristic of or pertaining to youth. — n. A person in the period of adolescence. — **Syn.** See YOUTHFUL. [< L < ad- to + alescere to grow]

A·don·is (ə·don′is, ə·dō′nis) In Greek mythology, a youth beloved by Aphrodite for his beauty and killed by a wild boar. — n. Any man of rare beauty.

a·dopt (ə·dopt′) v.t. **1.** To take into some new relationship, as that of son, heir, etc. **2.** To take into one's family or as one's child by legal measures. **3.** To take and follow as one's own, as a course of action. **4.** To take up from someone else and use as one's own. **5.** To vote to accept, as a motion. [< MF < L < ad- to + optare to choose] — a·dopt′a·ble adj. — a·dopt′er n. — a·dop′tion n.

a·dop·tive (ə·dop′tiv) adj. **1.** Of or characterized by adoption. **2.** Related by adoption. — a·dop′tive·ly adv.

a·dor·a·ble (ə·dôr′ə·bəl, ə·dōr′-) adj. **1.** Worthy of adoration. **2.** Informal Delightful; lovable. — a·dor′a·ble·ness, a·dor′a·bil′i·ty n. — a·dor′a·bly adv.

ad·o·ra·tion (ad′ə·rā′shən) n. **1.** The act of adoring, as in worship. **2.** A feeling of profound admiration and devotion. **3.** An act of homage to a person or object.

a·dore (ə·dôr′, ə·dōr′) v. **a·dored, a·dor·ing** v.t. **1.** To render divine honors to; worship as divine. **2.** To love or honor with intense devotion. **3.** Informal To like especially. — v.i. **4.** To worship. — **Syn.** See VENERATE. [< OF < L < ad- to + orare to speak, pray] — a·dor′er n.

a·dorn (ə·dôrn′) v.t. **1.** To increase the beauty of; enhance. **2.** To furnish or decorate with or as with ornaments. [< OF < L < ad- to + ornare to deck out] — a·dorn′er n. — a·dorn′ment n.

ad·re·nal (ə·drē′nəl) Physiol. n. An adrenal gland. — adj. **1.** Near or upon the kidneys. **2.** Of or from the adrenal glands. [< AD- + L renes kidneys + -AL³]

adrenal gland One of a pair of small ductless glands situated on the kidneys of most vertebrates, in man secreting epinephrine and cortin: also called suprarenal gland.

Ad·ren·a·lin (ə·dren′ə·lin) n. Proprietary name for a brand of epinephrine. Also **ad·ren·a·lin** (ə·dren′ə·lin).

ad·re·no·cor·ti·co·tro·pic hormone (ə·drē′nō·kôr′ti·kō·trō′pik) Physiol. ACTH.

A·dri·at·ic (ā′drē·at′ik) adj. Of or pertaining to the Adriatic Sea or to the inhabitants of its coastal regions.

a·drift (ə·drift′) adv. & adj. Without moorings; drifting.

a·droit (ə·droit′) adj. Skillful; expert. [< F < ð to + droit right] — a·droit′ly adv. — a·droit′ness n.

ad·sorb (ad·sôrb′, -zôrb′) v.t. Chem. To condense and hold by adsorption: distinguished from absorb. [< AD- + L sorbere to suck in] — ad·sor′bent n. & adj.

ad·sorp·tion (ad·sôrp′shən, -zôrp′-) n. Chem. The action of a body, as charcoal, in condensing and holding a gas or soluble substance upon its surface. — ad·sorp′tive adj.

ad·u·late (aj′ŏŏ·lāt) v.t. **·lat·ed, ·lat·ing** To flatter or praise extravagantly. [< L adulari to fawn] — ad′u·la′tion n. — ad′u·la′tor n. — ad·u·la·to·ry (aj′ŏŏ·lə·tôr′ē, -tō′rē) adj.

a·dult (ə·dult′, ad′ult) n. **1.** A person who has attained the age of maturity or legal majority. **2.** Biol. A fully developed animal or plant. — adj. **1.** Pertaining to mature life;

full-grown. **2.** Of or for mature people. [< L < *ad-* to + *alescere* to grow] **— a·dul′ness** *n.* **— a·dul′hood** *n.*

a·dul·ter·ant (ə·dul′tər·ənt) *n.* An adulterating substance. *— adj.* Adulterating.

a·dul·ter·ate (ə·dul′tə·rāt; *for adj., also* ə·dul′tər·it) *v.t.* **·at·ed, ·at·ing** To make impure or inferior by admixture of other ingredients; corrupt. *— adj.* Corrupted; debased. [< L < *ad-* to + *alter* other, different] **— a·dul′ter·a′tion** *n.* **— a·dul′ter·a′tor** *n.*

a·dul·ter·er (ə·dul′tər·ər) *n.* One who commits adultery. **— a·dul′ter·ess** (-tər·is, -tris) *n. fem.*

a·dul·ter·ous (ə·dul′tər·əs) *adj.* Of, pertaining to, or given to adultery; illicit. **— a·dul′ter·ous·ly** *adv.*

a·dul·ter·y (ə·dul′tər·ē) *n.* *pl.* **·ter·ies** The voluntary sexual intercourse of a married person with someone not the spouse; unfaithfulness. [< L *adulterium*]

ad·um·brate (ad·um′brāt, ə·dum′-) *v.t.* **·brat·ed, ·brat·ing** **1.** To represent the mere shadow of; outline sketchily. **2.** To overshadow; darken. [< L < *ad-* to + *umbrare* to shade] **— ad′um·bra′tion** *n.* **— ad·um′bra·tive** *adj.*

ad va·lo·rem (ad və·lôr′əm, -lō′rəm) *Latin* According or in proportion to the value. *Abbr.* **adv., ad val.**

ad·vance (ad·vans′, -väns′) *v.* **·vanced, ·vanc·ing** *v.t.* **1.** To move or cause to go forward or upward. **2.** To offer; propose. **3.** To further; promote. **4.** To put in a better or more advantageous rank, position, or situation. **5.** To make occur earlier; accelerate. **6.** To raise (a rate, price, etc.). **7.** To pay, as money or interest, before legally due. **8.** To lend, as money. **9.** *Law* To provide an advancement for. *— v.i.* **10.** To move or go forward. **11.** To make progress; rise or improve. *— adj.* **1.** Being before in time; early. **2.** Being or going before; in front. *— n.* **1.** The act of going forward; progress. **2.** Improvement; promotion. **3.** An increase or rise, as of prices. **4.** *pl.* Personal approaches; overtures. **5.** The supplying of goods, money, etc., on credit. **6.** The goods or money so supplied; a loan. **7.** The payment of money before it is legally due. **8.** *U.S.* The front or foremost part. *Abbr.* **adv. — in advance 1.** In front. **2.** Before due; beforehand. [ME < OF *avancier* < L < *ab-* away + *ante* before] **— ad·vanc′er** *n.*

ad·vanced (ad·vanst′, -vänst′) *adj.* **1.** In advance of others, as in progress or thought. **2.** In front; moved forward. **3.** At a late or forward stage, as of life, time, etc.

ad·vance·ment (ad·vans′mənt, -väns′-) *n.* **1.** The act of advancing, or the state of being advanced. **2.** Progression; promotion; preferment. **3.** An advance of property or money.

ad·van·tage (ad·van′tij, -vän′-) *n.* **1.** Any circumstance, state, or condition favoring success. **2.** Benefit or gain; profit. **3.** A better state or position; superiority. **4.** In tennis, the first point scored after deuce. **— to advantage** To good effect; favorably. **— to take advantage of 1.** To avail oneself of. **2.** To impose upon; use selfishly. *— v.t.* **·taged, ·tag·ing** To give advantage or profit to. [< OF < *avant* before < L *ab ante* from before]

ad·van·ta·geous (ad′vən·tā′jəs) *adj.* Affording advantage; profitable; favorable; beneficial. **— ad′van·ta′geous·ly** *adv.* **— ad′van·ta′geous·ness** *n.*

ad·vec·tion (ad·vek′shən) *n.* *Meteorol.* Heat transfer by the horizontal motion of air. [< L < *ad-* to + *vehere* to carry] **— ad·vec′tive** *adj.*

ad·vent (ad′vent) *n.* A coming or arrival. [< L < *ad-* to + *venire* to come]

Ad·vent (ad′vent) *n.* **1.** The birth of Christ. **2.** The Second Advent. **3.** The season prior to Christmas.

Ad·vent·ist (ad′ven·tist, ad·ven′-) *n.* A member of a denomination that believes the Second Advent is imminent. The largest U.S. Adventist bodies are the **Advent Christian Church** and the **Seventh-Day Adventists.**

ad·ven·ti·tious (ad′ven·tish′əs) *adj.* Not inherent; accidentally acquired; extrinsic. **— ad′ven·ti′tious·ly** *adv.* **— ad′ven·ti′tious·ness** *n.*

ad·ven·tive (ad·ven′tiv) *adj.* Occurring away from the natural habitat; exotic.

ad·ven·ture (ad·ven′chər) *n.* **1.** A hazardous or perilous undertaking. **2.** A stirring or thrilling experience. **3.** Risky or exciting activity. **4.** A commercial venture; speculation. *— v.* **·tured, ·tur·ing** *v.t.* **1.** To venture upon; take the chance of. *— v.i.* **2.** To venture upon daring or dangerous undertakings. [< OF < L *adventura* about to happen]

ad·ven·tur·er (ad·ven′chər·ər) *n.* **1.** One who seeks after or takes part in adventures. **2.** One who seeks his fortune in war; a soldier of fortune. **3.** A speculator in commerce. **4.** A person who seeks advancement by questionable means. **— ad·ven′tur·ess** *n. fem.*

ad·ven·tur·ous (ad·ven′chər·əs) *adj.* **1.** Disposed to seek adventures or take risks; venturesome. Also **ad·ven′ture·some** (-səm). **2.** Attended with risk; hazardous. **— ad·ven′tur·ous·ly** *adv.* **— ad·ven′tur·ous·ness** *n.*

ad·verb (ad′vûrb) *n.* *Gram.* Any of a class of words used to modify the meaning of a verb, adjective, or other adverb, in regard to time, place, manner, cause, degree, etc. [<

L < *ad-* to + *verbum* verb] **— ad·ver′bi·al** *adj.* **— ad·ver′bi·al·ly** *adv.*

adverb clause *Gram.* A dependent clause that functions as an adverb in a sentence, as *when the guests arrive* in *We will eat when the guests arrive:* also **adverbial clause.**

ad·ver·sar·y (ad′vər·ser′ē) *n.* *pl.* **·sar·ies** One actively hostile to another; an opponent; enemy. **— Syn.** See ENEMY.

ad·ver·sa·tive (ad·vûr′sə·tiv) *adj.* Expressing opposition or antithesis. *— n.* An antithetic word or proposition. [< L *adversativus* opposite] **— ad·ver′sa·tive·ly** *adv.*

ad·verse (ad·vûrs′, ad′vûrs) *adj.* **1.** Opposed; antagonistic. **2.** Unpropitious; detrimental. **3.** Opposite. [< L < *ad-* to + *vertere* to turn] **— ad·verse′ly** *adv.* **— ad·verse′ness** *n.*

ad·ver·si·ty (ad·vûr′sə·tē) *n.* *pl.* **·ties 1.** A condition of hardship or affliction. **2.** *Often pl.* A misfortune.

ad·vert (ad·vûrt′) *v.i.* To call attention; refer: with *to.* [< L *advertere* < *ad-* to + *vertere* to turn]

ad·vert·ent (ad·vûr′tənt) *adj.* Giving attention; heedful. **— ad·ver′tence, ad·ver′ten·cy** *n.* **— ad·ver′tent·ly** *adv.*

ad·ver·tise (ad′vər·tīz, ad′vər·tīz′) *v.* **·tised, ·tis·ing** *v.t.* **1.** To make known by public notice; proclaim the qualities of, as by publication or broadcasting, generally in order to sell. *— v.i.* **2.** To inquire by public notice, as in a newspaper: to *advertise* for a house. **3.** To distribute or publish advertisements. Also **ad′ver·tize.** [< MF < L *adverter* to direct one's attention to] **— ad′ver·tis′er** *n.*

ad·ver·tise·ment (ad′vər·tīz′mənt, ad·vûr′tis·mənt, -tiz-) *n.* A public notice, as in a newspaper or on a radio program. Also **ad′ver·tize′ment.** *Abbr.* **ad., adv., advt.**

ad·ver·tis·ing (ad′vər·tī′zing) *n.* **1.** Advertisements collectively. **2.** The business of writing and publicizing advertisements. Also **ad′ver·tiz′ing.**

ad·vice (ad·vīs′) *n.* **1.** Counsel given to encourage or dissuade; suggestion. **2.** *Often pl.* Information; notification. [< OF < LL < L *ad-* to + *videre* to see]

ad·vis·a·ble (ad·vī′zə·bəl) *adj.* Proper to be advised or recommended; sensible. **— Syn.** See EXPEDIENT. **— ad·vis′a·bil′i·ty, ad·vis′a·ble·ness** *n.* **— ad·vis′a·bly** *adv.*

ad·vise (ad·vīz′) *v.* **·vised, ·vis·ing** *v.t.* **1.** To give advice to; counsel. **2.** To recommend. **3.** To notify; inform, as of a transaction: with *of.* *— v.i.* **4.** To take counsel: with *with:* **5.** To give advice. *Abbr.* **adv.** [< OF < LL < L *ad-* to + *videre* to see]

ad·vised (ad·vīzd′) *adj.* **1.** Planned; deliberate: chiefly in *ill-advised, well-advised.*

ad·vis·ed·ly (ad·vī′zid·lē) *adv.* With forethought or advice.

ad·vise·ment (ad·vīz′mənt) *n.* Consultation; deliberation.

ad·vis·er (ad·vī′zər) *n.* **1.** One who advises. **2.** A teacher in a school or college who counsels students about their studies, careers, etc. Also **ad·vi′sor.**

ad·vi·so·ry (ad·vī′zər·ē) *adj.* **1.** Having power to advise. **2.** Containing or given as advice; not mandatory.

ad·vo·ca·cy (ad′və·kə·sē) *n.* The act of advocating or pleading a cause; vindication; defense.

ad·vo·cate (*v.* ad′və·kāt; *n.* ad′və·kit, -kāt) *v.t.* **·cat·ed, ·cat·ing** To speak or write in favor of; defend; recommend. *— n.* **1.** One who pleads the cause of another; an intercessor. **2.** One who espouses or defends a cause by argument: an *advocate* of slavery. [< OF < L < *ad-* to + *vocare* to call] **— ad′vo·ca′tor** *n.* **— ad·voc·a·to·ry** (ad·vok′ə·tôr′ē, -tō′rē) *adj.*

adz (adz) *n.* A hand cutting tool with its blade at right angles to its handle and usually curved inward, used for dressing timber, etc. Also **adze.** [OE *adesa*]

ae- For those words not entered below see under E-.

æ 1. A ligature of Latin origin, equivalent to Greek *ai:* usually printed *ae.* It is sometimes retained in the spelling of Greek and Latin proper names and in certain scientific terms, but, in modern use, is generally reduced to *e.* **2.** A character in Old English, representing the sound of *a* in modern *hat.*

ADZES
a Sculptor's.
b Cooper's.
c Carpenter's.

a·e·des (ā·ē′dēz) *n.* A mosquito that carries yellow fever: formerly called *stegomyia.* [< NL < Gk. < *a-* not + *hēdys* sweet]

Ae·ge·an (i·jē′ən) *adj.* Of or pertaining to the Aegean Islands or the Aegean Sea.

Æ·gir (ā′jər, ā′jər) The Norse god of the sea. Also **Æ′ger.**

ae·gis (ē′jis) *n.* **1.** In Greek mythology, the breastplate of Zeus and Athena. **2.** Any shield or armor. **3.** A protecting influence. Also spelled *egis.* [< Gk. *aigis* goatskin]

-aemia See -EMIA.

Ae·ne·as (i·nē′əs) In classical legend, a Trojan warrior and hero of the *Aeneid.* After the sack of Troy he wandered for seven years before reaching Latium.

Ae·ne·id (i·nē′id) *n.* A Latin epic poem by Vergil, narrating the adventures of Aeneas.

ae·o·li·an (ē·ō′lē·ən) *adj.* Pertaining to or caused by the winds; wind-borne: also spelled *eolian.*

Aeolian harp A stringed instrument so constructed as to produce musical sounds when exposed to a current of air.
Ae·o·lus (ē′ə·ləs) In Greek mythology, the god of the winds.
ae·on (ē′ən, ē′on), **ae·o·ni·an** (ē·ō′nē·ən) See EON, etc.
aer- Var. of AERO-.
aer·ate (âr′āt, ā′ər·āt) *v.t.* **·at·ed, ·at·ing** 1. To supply or charge with air or gas. 2. To purify by exposure to air. — **aer·a′tion** *n.* — **aer′a·tor** *n.*
aeri- Var. of AERO-.
aer·i·al (âr′ē·əl, ā·ir′ē·əl) *adj.* 1. Of or in the air. 2. Living or moving in the air. 3. Extending into the air; lofty. 4. Light as air; airy. 5. Unsubstantial; intangible; imaginary. 6. Of, by, or pertaining to aircraft, or to flying. — *n.* An antenna, as in television. [< L *aer* air] — **aer′i·al·ly** *adv.*
aer·i·al·ist (âr′ē·əl·ist, ā·ir′ē·əl-) *n.* One who performs on a tightrope, trapeze, etc.
aer·ie (âr′ē, ir′ē) *n.* 1. The nest of a predatory bird, as the eagle, on a crag. 2. The brood or young of such a bird. 3. A house or stronghold situated on a height. Also spelled *aery, eyrie, eyry.* [< Med.L < OF < L *area* open space]
aer·i·fy (âr′ə·fī, ā′ər·ə·fī) *v.t.* **·fied, ·fy·ing** 1. To aerate. 2. To change into a gaseous form. — **aer′i·fi·ca′tion** *n.*
aero- *combining form* 1. Air; of the air. 2. Of aircraft or flying. 3. Gas; of gases. Also *aer-, aeri-.* [< Gk. *aēr* air]
aer·obe (âr′ōb, ā′ər·ōb) *n.* A microorganism that can live only in air or free oxygen. [< AERO- + Gk. *bios* life] — **aer·o′bic** *adj.*
aer·o·drome (âr′ə·drōm, ā′ər·ə-) *n.* An airdrome.
aer·o·dy·nam·ics (âr′ō·dī·nam′iks, ā′ər·ō-) *n.pl.* (*construed as sing.*) The branch of physics that treats of the laws of motion of gases, under the influence of gravity and other forces. — **aer′o·dy·nam′ic** *adj.*
aér·o·gramme (âr′ə·gram, ā′ər·ə-) *n.* An international airmail letter consisting of a single folded sheet. [< Fr.]
aer·o·lite (âr′ə·līt, ā′ər·ə-) *n.* A meteorite containing more stone than iron. Also **aer′o·lith** (-lith). [< AERO- + Gk. *lithos* stone] — **aer·o·lit′ic** (-lit′ik) *adj.*
aer·ol·o·gy (âr·ol′ə·jē, ā′ər·ol′-) *n.* *pl.* **·gies** The scientific study of the atmosphere and its phenomena. — **aer·o·log′ic** (âr′ə·loj′ik, ā′ər·ə-) or **·i·cal** *adj.* — **aer·ol′o·gist** *n.*
aer·o·me·chan·ics (âr′ō·mə·kan′iks, ā′ər·ō-) *n.pl.* (*construed as sing.*) The science that treats of equilibrium and motion of air and gases. — **aer·o·me·chan′ic** *adj.* & *n.*
aer·o·naut (âr′ə·nôt, ā′ər·ə-) *n.* One who pilots a balloon or dirigible. [< F < Gk. *aēr* air + *nautēs* sailor]
aer·o·nau·tics (âr′ə·nô′tiks, ā′ər·ə-) *n.pl.* (*construed as sing.*) 1. The science or art of navigating aircraft. 2. That branch of engineering that deals with the design, construction, operation, and performance of aircraft. — **aer′o·nau′tic**, **aer′o·nau′ti·cal** *adj.*
aer·o·pause (âr′ə·pôz, ā′ər·ə-) *n.* *Meteorol.* The region of the atmosphere near outer space.
aer·o·phyte (âr′ə·fīt, ā′ər·ə-) *n.* An epiphyte.
aer·o·plane (âr′ə·plān, ā′ər·ə-) *n.* *Brit.* Airplane.
aer·o·sol (âr′ə·sōl, -sol, ā′ər·ə-) *n.* A suspension of solid or liquid particles in a gas.
aerosol bomb A small spraying can holding a liquid, as an insecticide, etc., under gas pressure.
aer·o·space (âr′ō·spās, ā′ər·ō-) *n.* 1. The earth's atmosphere and outer space, considered as a single region in the operation of spacecraft. 2. The study of this region.
aerospace medicine The branch of medicine that deals with conditions and disorders associated with space flight.
aer·o·sphere (âr′ə·sfir, ā′ər·ə-) *n.* The entire atmosphere considered as a single gaseous shell surrounding the earth.
aer·o·stat (âr′ə·stat, ā′ər·ə-) *n.* Any lighter-than-air craft, as a balloon or dirigible. [< F < Gk. *aēr* air + *statos* standing] — **aer′o·stat′ic** or **·i·cal** *adj.*
aer·o·stat·ics (âr′ə·stat′iks, ā′ər·ə-) *n.pl.* (*construed as sing.*) The branch of physics that treats of the mechanical properties of air and gases in equilibrium.
aer·y (âr′ē, ir′ē) See AERIE.
Aes·cu·la·pi·us (es′kyə·lā′pē·əs) In Roman mythology, the god of medicine: identified with the Greek *Asclepius.* — **Aes′cu·la′pi·an** *adj.* & *n.*
Æ·sir (ā′sir, ē′-) *n.* *pl.* of **As** (äs) The gods of the Norse pantheon collectively.
aes·thete (es′thēt), **aes·thet·ic** (es·thet′ik), etc. See ESTHETE, etc.
aes·ti·val (es′tə·vəl, es·tī′-), **aes·ti·vate** (es′tə·vāt), etc. See ESTIVAL, etc.
ae·ther (ē′thər) See ETHER (defs. 3 and 4).
ae·ti·ol·o·gy (ē′tē·ol′ə·jē) See ETIOLOGY.
af- Assimilated var. of AD-.
a·far (ə·fär′) *adv.* At, from, or to a distance; remotely.
af·fa·ble (af′ə·bəl) *adj.* Easy to approach and speak to; friendly; courteous. [< F < L < *ad-* to + *fari* to speak] — **af′fa·bil′i·ty**, **af′fa·ble·ness** *n.* — **af′fa·bly** *adv.*

af·fair (ə·fâr′) *n.* 1. Anything done or to be done; business; concern. 2. *pl.* Matters of business or concern. 3. A thing or occurrence. 4. A love affair. [< OF < L *ad* to + *facere* to do]
af·fect¹ (*v.* ə·fekt′; *n.* af′ekt) *v.t.* 1. To act upon or have an effect upon; influence. 2. To touch or move emotionally. 3. To attack or attaint, as a part of the body. — *n.* *Psychol.* Emotion; feeling. [< L < *ad-* to + *facere* to do; noun < G *affekt*]
af·fect² (ə·fekt′) *v.t.* 1. To show a preference for by wearing, using, etc.; fancy: to *affect* large hats. 2. To imitate or assume: to *affect* a British accent. [< F < L *affectare* to aim at. See AFFECT¹.] — **af·fect′er** *n.*
af·fec·ta·tion (af′ek·tā′shən) *n.* 1. A studied pretense; display: with *of.* 2. Artificiality of manner or behavior.
af·fect·ed¹ (ə·fek′tid) *adj.* 1. Acted upon, as by a drug. 2. Moved emotionally. 3. Attacked, as by disease.
af·fect·ed² (ə·fek′tid) *adj.* 1. Artificial; feigned. 2. Showing affectation. [pp. of AFFECT²] — **af·fect′ed·ly** *adv.* — **af·fect′ed·ness** *n.*
af·fect·ing (ə·fek′ting) *adj.* Having power to move the feelings; touching; pathetic. — **af·fect′ing·ly** *adv.*
af·fec·tion (ə·fek′shən) *n.* 1. Fond attachment or kind feeling. 2. *Often pl.* A mental state brought about by any influence; an emotion or feeling. 3. An abnormal state of the body; disease. 4. The act of affecting or the state of being affected.
af·fec·tion·ate (ə·fek′shən·it) *adj.* Having or expressing affection; loving; fond. — **af·fec′tion·ate·ly** *adv.* — **af·fec′tion·ate·ness** *n.*
af·fer·ent (af′ər·ənt) *adj.* *Physiol.* Conducting inward, or toward the center, as nerves that transmit sensory stimuli to the central nervous system: opposed to *efferent.* [< L < *ad-* to + *ferre* to bear]
af·fi·ance (ə·fī′əns) *v.t.* **·anced, ·anc·ing** To promise in marriage; betroth. — *n.* A betrothal; pledge of faith. [< OF *afiance* trust, confidence] — **af·fi′an·cer** *n.*
af·fi·da·vit (af′ə·dā′vit) *n. Law* A sworn, written declaration, made before competent authority. — **Syn.** See TESTIMONY. [< Med.L, he has stated on oath]
af·fil·i·ate (*v.* ə·fil′ē·āt; *n.* ə·fil′ē·it) *v.* **·at·ed, ·at·ing** *v.t.* 1. To associate or unite, as a member or branch to a larger or principal body: with *to* or *with.* 2. To join or associate (oneself): with *with.* 3. To determine the source or relations of. — *v.i.* 4. To associate or ally oneself: with *with.* — *n.* An affiliated person, company, etc. [< L *affiliare* to adopt < *ad-* to + *filius* son] — **af·fil′i·a′tion** *n.*
af·fin·i·ty (ə·fin′ə·tē) *n.* *pl.* **·ties** 1. A natural attraction or inclination. 2. Any close relation or agreement; kinship in general; similarity. 3. Relationship by marriage. 4. An attraction between certain persons, esp. of opposite sexes; also, the person exerting such attraction. 5. *Chem.* The property by which differing chemical elements or groups of elements unite to form a new compound. [< L *affinis* adjacent, related < *ad-* to + *finis* end]
af·firm (ə·fûrm′) *v.t.* 1. To declare or state positively. 2. To confirm or ratify. — *v.i.* 3. *Law* To make a formal judicial declaration, but not under oath. [< OF < L < *ad-* to + *firmare* to make firm] — **af·firm′a·ble** *adj.* — **af·firm′a·bly** *adv.* — **af·firm′ance** *n.* — **af·firm′ant** *adj.* & *n.* — **af·firm′er** *n.*
af·fir·ma·tion (af′ər·mā′shən) *n.* 1. The act of affirming; assertion. 2. That which is affirmed or asserted. 3. A solemn declaration made before a competent officer, in place of a judicial oath. — **Syn.** See OATH.
af·firm·a·tive (ə·fûr′mə·tiv) *adj.* 1. Characterized by affirmation; asserting that the fact is so. 2. Positive. Also **af·firm·a·to·ry** (ə·fûr′mə·tôr′ē, -tō′rē). — *adv.* Yes; that is so: a military usage. — *n.* 1. A word or expression of affirmation or assent. 2. The side in a debate that affirms the proposition debated. — **af·firm′a·tive·ly** *adv.*
af·fix (*v.* ə·fiks′; *n.* af′iks) *v.t.* 1. To fix or attach; fasten; append. 2. To connect with or lay upon, as blame, responsibility, etc. — *n.* 1. That which is attached, appended, or added. 2. A prefix, suffix, or infix. [< L *affigere* < *ad-* to + *figere* to fasten]
af·fla·tus (ə·flā′təs) *n.* Any creative inspiration or impulse. [< L < *ad-* to + *flare* to blow]
af·flict (ə·flikt′) *v.t.* To distress with continued suffering; trouble greatly. [< L < *ad-* to + *fligere* to dash, strike] — **af·flict′er** *n.* — **af·flic′tive** *adj.* — **af·flic′tive·ly** *adv.*
af·flic·tion (ə·flik′shən) *n.* 1. The state of being afflicted; sore distress of body or mind. 2. A misfortune; calamity.
af·flu·ence (af′lōō·əns) *n.* Riches; wealth.
af·flu·ent (af′lōō·ənt) *adj.* 1. Abounding; abundant. 2. Wealthy; opulent. — *n.* A stream that flows into another. [< L < *ad-* to + *fluere* to flow] — **af′flu·ent·ly** *adv.*
af·ford (ə·fôrd′, ə·fōrd′) *v.t.* 1. To have sufficient means for;

be able to meet the expense of. **2.** To incur without detriment. **3.** To spare. **4.** To provide, yield, or furnish. [OE *geforthian* to further, promote] — **af·ford/a·ble** *adj.*

af·fray (ə-frā/) *n.* A public brawl or fight; a disturbance of the peace. [< OF, *effrei, esfrei*]

af·fri·cate (af/ri·kit) *n. Phonet.* A sound consisting of a stop followed by the fricative release of breath at the point of contact, as *ch* in *match*. [< L < *ad-* against + *fricare* to rub] — **af·fric·a·tive** (ə-frik/ə·tiv) *n. & adj.*

af·front (ə-frunt/) *v.t.* **1.** To insult openly; treat with insolence. **2.** To confront in defiance; accost. — *n.* An open insult or indignity. — **Syn.** See OFFEND. [< OF < LL *affrontare* to strike against] — **af·front/er** *n.* — **af·fron/·tive** *adj.*

af·ghan (af/gən, -gan) *n.* A soft wool coverlet, knitted or crocheted, often in many-colored geometrical patterns.

Af·ghan (af/gən, -gan) *n.* A native of Afghanistan. — *adj.* Of or pertaining to Afghanistan, its inhabitants, etc.

a·field (ə-fēld/) *adv.* **1.** In or to the field; abroad. **2.** Off the track; astray.

a·fire (ə-fīr/) *adv. & adj.* On fire. [ME]

a·flame (ə-flām/) *adv. & adj.* Flaming; glowing.

a·float (ə-flōt/) *adv. & adj.* **1.** Floating. **2.** Not aground or ashore; at sea. **3.** In circulation: Rumors were *afloat*. **4.** Overflowed; flooded, as the deck of a ship. **5.** Adrift.

a·foot (ə-fo͝ot/) *adv.* **1.** On foot. **2.** In motion or progress; on the move; astir. [ME *on flote*]

a·fore·men·tioned (ə-fôr/men/shənd, ə-fōr/-) *adj.* Mentioned previously.

a·fore·said (ə-fôr/sed/, ə-fōr/-) *adj.* Mentioned before.

a·fore·thought (ə-fôr/thôt/, ə-fōr/-) *adj.* Intended beforehand: now chiefly in the phrase *malice aforethought*.

a·fore·time (ə-fôr/tīm/, ə-fōr/-) *adv.* At a previous time.

a·foul (ə-foul/) *adv. & adj.* In entanglement or collision; entangled. — **to run (or fall) afoul of** To become entangled with; get into difficulties with.

a·fraid (ə-frād/) *adj.* Filled with fear or apprehension; apprehensive; fearful: often used to soften an unpleasant statement: I'm *afraid* you're wrong. [Orig. pp. of AFFRAY]

a·fresh (ə-fresh/) *adv.* Once more; anew; again.

Af·ri·can (af/ri·kən) *adj.* Of or pertaining to Africa, or its inhabitants. — *n.* **1.** A native inhabitant of Africa. **2.** A member of one of the African peoples; a Negro or Negrito.

Af·ri·kaans (af/ri·käns/, -känz/) *n.* The Dutch dialect spoken in South Africa.

Af·ri·ka·ner (af/ri·kä/nər) *n.* An Afrikaans-speaking South African of Dutch ancestry. Also **Af/ri·kan/der** (-kan/dər).

Afro- *combining form* African; African.

Af·ro-A·mer·i·can (af/rō-ə-mer/ə·kən) *adj.* Of or pertaining to Americans of black African descent. — *n.* An Afro-American person.

aft (aft, äft) *Naut. adj.* Of or near the stern of a vessel. — *adv.* At, toward, or near the stern. [OE *æftan* behind]

af·ter (af/tər, äf/-) *prep.* **1.** In the rear of; farther back than; following: He came *after* me. **2.** In search or pursuit of: Strive *after* wisdom. **3.** In relation to; concerning: to inquire *after* one's health. **4.** Subsequently to; at a later period than. **5.** In succession to; following repeatedly: day *after* day. **6.** As a result of; subsequently to and because of. **7.** Notwithstanding; subsequently to and in spite of: *After* the best endeavors, one may fail. **8.** Next below in order or importance: *after* the king in power. **9.** According to the nature, wishes, or customs of; in conformity with: a man *after* my own heart. **10.** In imitation of; in the manner of. **11.** In honor, remembrance, or observance of. **12.** *U.S.* Of time by the clock, past. — *adv.* **1.** In the rear; behind. **2.** At a later time; subsequently. — *adj.* **1.** Following in time or place; later; subsequent: In *after* years they lived as friends. **2.** *Naut.* Toward the stern; farther aft. — *conj.* Following the time that: *After* I went home, I ate. [OE *æfter*]

af·ter·birth (af/tər·bûrth/, äf/-) *n.* The placenta and fetal membranes expelled from the uterus after childbirth.

af·ter·bod·y (af/tər·bod/ē, äf/-) *n. Aerospace* A section of a rocket or missile that continues to trail the nose cone or satellite from which it was separated in flight.

af·ter·brain (af/tər·brān/, äf/-) *n. Anat.* The metencephalon.

af·ter·burn·er (af/tər·bûr/nər, äf/-) *n. Aeron.* A device for injecting extra fuel into the exhaust system of a jet engine as a means of increasing the thrust. — **af/ter·burn/ing** *n.*

af·ter·damp (af/tər·damp/, äf/-) *n. Mining* A mixture of dangerous gases resulting from a fire or explosion in a mine.

af·ter·deck (af/tər·dek/, äf/-) *n. Naut.* That part of a deck aft of amidships.

af·ter·ef·fect (af/tər·ə·fekt/, äf/-) *n.* An effect succeeding its cause after an interval.

af·ter·glow (af/tər·glō/, äf/-) *n.* A glow after a light has disappeared, as in the western sky after sunset.

af·ter·im·age (af/tər·im/ij, äf/-) *n. Physiol.* The persistence or renewal of the image of an object after the direct stimulation has been withdrawn.

af·ter·math (af/tər·math, äf/-) *n.* Result; consequence.

af·ter·most (af/tər·mōst, äf/-) *adj.* **1.** *Naut.* Nearest the stern: also **aft/most. 2.** Last.

af·ter·noon (af/tər·nōōn/, äf/-) *n.* **1.** The part of the day between noon and sunset. **2.** The closing part: the *afternoon* of life. — *adj.* Of, for, or occurring in the afternoon.

af·ter·taste (af/tər·tāst/, äf/-) *n.* A taste persisting in the mouth, as after a meal.

af·ter·thought (af/tər·thôt/, äf/-) *n.* **1.** An expedient, explanation, etc., that occurs to one after decision or action. **2.** A subsequent or second thought.

af·ter·ward (af/tər·wərd, äf/-) *adv.* In time following; subsequently. Also **af/ter·wards.** [OE *æfterweard*]

ag- Assimilated var. of AD-.

a·gain (ə-gen/, *esp. Brit.* ə-gān/) *adv.* **1.** Another time; once more; anew. **2.** Once repeated. **3.** To the same place or over the same course; back, as in a previous condition. **4.** Further; moreover. **5.** On the other hand. [OE *ongegn*]

a·gainst (ə-genst/, *esp. Brit.* ə-gänst/) *prep.* **1.** In the opposite direction to; counter to. **2.** In contact or collision with; upon. **3.** In contact with and pressing upon. **4.** In opposition to; contrary to. **5.** In contrast or comparison with. **6.** In preparation for. **7.** In hostility to. **8.** In resistance to. **9.** To the debit of. **10.** Directly opposite; facing: now usu. *over against*. [OE *ongegn* + -*es*, adverbial suffix]

Ag·a·mem·non (ag/ə·mem/non, -nən) In Greek legend, king of Mycenae and chief of the Greek army in the Trojan War.

a·gape (ə-gāp/, ə-gap/) *adv. & adj.* In a gaping state; gaping.

a·gar-a·gar (ä/gär·ä/gär, ä/gor-, ä/gär-, ag/ər-) *n.* A gelatinous substance obtained from seaweeds, used as a laxative and in the cultivation of bacteria. Also **a/gar.** [< Malay]

ag·a·ric (ag/ə·rik, ə·gar/ik) *n.* Any of several mushrooms, esp. the common edible variety. [< L < Gk. *Agaria*, a town in Sarmatia] — **a·gar·i·ca·ceous** (ə·gar/i·kā/shəs) *adj.*

ag·ate (ag/it) *n.* **1.** A variegated waxy quartz or chalcedony, in which the colors are usually in bands. **2.** A child's playing marble. **3.** *Printing* A size of type, 5½ points. [< F < L < Gk. *Achatēs*, a river in Sicily]

a·ga·ve (ə-gä/vē) *n.* Any desert plant of the amaryllis family, as the century plant. [< Gk. *Agauē*, a proper name]

a·gaze (ə-gāz/) *adv.* Gazing.

age (āj) *n.* **1.** The period of existence of a person, thing, nation, etc., particularly as measured by the time past. **2.** The entire span of life of any being or thing. **3.** The time of life marked by maturity and discretion; adulthood; esp., that age when full civil rights or certain personal rights can be legally exercised, usually 18 or 21 years: also called *legal age*. **4.** Any period of life which, by reason of natural development or custom, fits or unfits for anything. **5.** Any distinct stage of life. **6.** The closing period of life; the state of being old. **7.** Any great period of time in the history of man, of the earth, etc., marked off by certain distinctive features or characters. **8.** The people alive at a given time; a generation. **9.** *Informal* A long time. — **mental age** *Psychol.* The level of mental development as measured against the chronological age at which this level is reached by the average child. Abbr. *MA, M.A.* — *v.* **aged, ag·ing** or **age·ing** *v.t.* **1.** To make or cause to grow mature or old. — *v.i.* **2.** To assume or show some characteristics of **age**; ripen. [< OF < L *aetas* age, a span of life]

-age *suffix of nouns* **1.** Collection or aggregate of: *leafage*. **2.** Condition, office, service, or other relation or connection of: *haulage*. [< OF < L *-aticum*, neut. adj. suffix]

a·ged (ā/jid *for defs. 1 & 2*; ājd *for def. 3*) *adj.* **1.** Advanced in years; old. **2.** Of, like, or characteristic of old age. **3.** Of or at the age of: a child, *aged* six. — **Syn.** See OLD. — **the aged** Those who are old. — **a/ged·ly** *adv.* — **a/ged·ness** *n.*

age·ing (ā/jing) See AGING.

age·less (āj/lis) *adj.* **1.** Not seeming to grow old. **2.** Having no limits of duration; eternal.

age·long (āj/lông/, -long/) *adj.* Lasting for a long time.

a·gen·cy (ā/jən·sē) *n. pl.* **·cies 1.** Active power or operation; activity. **2.** Means; instrumentality. **3.** A firm or establishment where business is done for others. **4.** The office or function of an agent. [< L < *agere* to do]

a·gen·da (ə-jen/də) *n. pl.* of **a·gen·dum** (ə-jen/dəm) (*usu.* construed as *sing.*) A list of things to be done; esp., a program of business at a meeting. [< L *agere* to do]
  ◆ *Agenda*, originally the plural of the Latin *agendum*, now has a regular English plural *agendas*.

a·gent (ā/jənt) *n.* **1.** One who or that which acts or has power to act; an efficient cause of anything. **2.** One who acts for or by the authority of a government, company, etc. **3.** Any force, substance, or organism that causes a material change. **4.** A means by which something is done; instrument. **5.** *Informal* A traveling salesman. [< L *agens, agentis*, ppr. of *agere* to do] — **a·gen·tial** (ā·jen/shəl) *adj.*

a·gent pro·vo·ca·teur (ȧ·zhäṅ/ prô·vô·kȧ·tœr/) *pl.* **a·gents pro·vo·ca·teurs** (ȧ·zhäṅ/ prô·vô·kȧ·tœr/) *French* A secret agent planted in a trade union, political party, etc., to incite actions or declarations that will incur punishment.

Ag·ge·us (ə-gē'us) The Douai Bible name for HAGGAI.
ag·glom·er·ate (ə-glom'ə-rāt; *for adj. & n., also* -ər-it) *v.t. & v.i.* **·at·ed, ·at·ing** To gather, form, or grow into a ball or rounded mass. — *adj.* Gathered into a mass or heap; clustered densely. — *n.* A heap or mass of things thrown together indiscriminately. [< L < *ad-* to + *glomerare* to gather into a ball] — **ag·glom'er·a'tion** *n.* — **ag·glom'er·a'tive** *adj.*
ag·glu·ti·nant (ə-gloō'tə-nənt) *adj.* Tending to cause adhesion; uniting. — *n.* Any sticky substance.
ag·glu·ti·nate (ə-gloō'tə-nāt; *for adj., also* -nit) *v.t. & v.i.* **·nat·ed, ·nat·ing** 1. To unite, as with glue; join by adhesion. 2. *Ling.* To form (words) by agglutination. 3. *Physiol.* To mass together, as bacteria. — *adj.* Joined by adhesion. [< L < *ad-* to + *glutinare* to glue] — **ag·glu'ti·na·tive** *adj.*
ag·glu·ti·na·tion (ə-gloō'tə-nā'shən) *n.* 1. Adhesion of distinct parts; also, a mass formed by adhesion. 2. *Ling.* A combining of words into compounds in which the constituent elements retain their characteristic forms.
ag·glu·ti·nin (ə-gloō'tə-nin) *n. Biochem.* An antibody in blood serum that causes the red corpuscles or any bacteria it touches to coalesce into floccules.
ag·gran·dize (ə-gran'dīz, ag'rən-dīz) *v.t.* **·dized, ·diz·ing** 1. To make great or greater; enlarge or intensify. 2. To make appear greater; exalt. [< F < L *ad-* to + *grandire* to make great] — **ag·gran·dize·ment** (ə-gran'diz-mənt) *n.* — **ag·gran'diz·er** *n.*
ag·gra·vate (ag'rə-vāt) *v.t.* **·vat·ed, ·vat·ing** 1. To make worse; intensify, as an illness. 2. To make heavier or more burdensome, as a duty. 3. *Informal* To provoke or exasperate. [< L < *ad-* to + *gravare* to make heavy] — **ag'gra·vat'ing** *adj.* — **ag'gra·vat'ing·ly** *adv.* — **ag·gra·va'tion** (ag'rə-vā'shən) *n.* — **ag'gra·va'tive** *adj.*
ag·gre·gate (*v.* ag'rə-gāt; *adj. & n.* -git) *v.t.* **·gat·ed, ·gat·ing** 1. To bring or gather together, as into a mass, sum, or body. 2. To amount to; form a total of. — *adj.* Collected into a sum or mass; gathered into a whole. — *n.* The entire number, mass, or quantity of anything; amount; total. — **in the aggregate** Collectively; as a whole. [< L < *ad-* to + *gregare* to collect] — **ag·gre·ga·tion** (ag'rə-gā'shən) *n.* — **ag'gre·ga'tive** *adj.* — **ag'gre·ga'tor** *n.*
ag·gress (ə-gres') *v.i.* To undertake an attack; begin a quarrel. [< L < *ad-* to + *gradi* to step, go]
ag·gres·sion (ə-gresh'ən) *n.* 1. An unprovoked attack or encroachment. 2. Habitual aggressive action or practices.
ag·gres·sive (ə-gres'iv) *adj.* 1. Of or characterized by aggression or attack. 2. Disposed to vigorous activity; assertive. — **ag·gres'sive·ly** *adv.* — **ag·gres'sive·ness** *n.*
ag·gres·sor (ə-gres'ər) *n.* One who commits an aggression.
ag·grieve (ə-grēv') *v.t.* **·grieved, ·griev·ing** 1. To cause sorrow to; distress or afflict. 2. To give cause for just complaint, as by injustice. [< OF < L *aggravare*]
a·ghast (ə-gast', ə-gäst') *adj.* Struck dumb with horror. [ME < OE *ā* + *gǣstan* to terrify; spelling infl. by *ghost*]
ag·ile (aj'əl, aj'īl) *adj.* Able to move or act quickly and easily; active. [< F < L *agere* to move] — **ag'ile·ly** *adv.*
a·gil·i·ty (ə-jil'ə-tē) *n.* Quickness in movement.
ag·ing (ā'jing) *n.* 1. The process or the effects of growing mature or old. 2. Any artificial process for producing the effects of age. Also, *Brit., ageing.*
ag·i·tate (aj'ə-tāt) *v.* **·tat·ed, ·tat·ing** *v.t.* 1. To disturb or shake irregularly. 2. To set or keep moving. 3. To excite or stir up; perturb. 4. To keep before the public, as a controversial issue. — *v.i.* 5. To excite, or endeavor to excite, public interest and action. [< L *agitare* to set in motion]
ag·i·ta·tion (aj'ə-tā'shən) *n.* 1. Violent motion; commotion. 2. Strong emotional disturbance.
ag·i·ta·tor (aj'ə-tā'tər) *n.* One who or that which agitates; esp., one who persists in political or social agitation.
a·gleam (ə-glēm') *adv. & adj.* Bright; gleaming.
a·glit·ter (ə-glit'ər) *adv. & adj.* Glittering.
a·glow (ə-glō') *adv. & adj.* In a glow; glowing.
ag·no·men (ag-nō'mən) *n. pl.* **ag·nom·i·na** (ag-nom'ə-nə) A nickname. [< L < *ad-* to + (g)*nomen* name] — **ag·nom'i·nal** *adj.*
ag·nos·tic (ag-nos'tik) *adj.* Of or pertaining to agnostics or agnosticism. — *n.* One who holds the theory of agnosticism. — **Syn.** See SKEPTIC. [< Gk. < *a-* not + *gignōskein* to know]
ag·nos·ti·cism (ag-nos'tə-siz'əm) *n.* The doctrine and philosophical theory that man cannot know God, first truths, or anything beyond material phenomena.
Ag·nus De·i (ag'nəs dē'ī, dä'ē) 1. *Eccl.* A figure of a lamb, as an emblem of Christ, often bearing a cross and banner. 2. *Eccl.* **a** A Eucharistic prayer beginning with *Agnus Dei.* **b** Its music. [< LL, Lamb of God. See *John* i 29.]
a·go (ə-gō') *adv.* In the past; since: long *ago.* — *adj.* Gone by; past: a year *ago.* [OE *āgān* past, gone away]

a·gog (ə-gog') *adv. & adj.* In a state of eager curiosity; excited; expectant. [< MF *en gogues* in a merry mood]
-agogue *combining form* Leading, promoting, or inciting: *demagogue, pedagogue.* Also **-agog.** [< Gk. *agein* to lead]
ag·o·nize (ag'ə-nīz) *v.* **·nized, ·niz·ing** *v.i.* 1. To be in or suffer extreme pain or anguish. 2. To make convulsive efforts; strive. — *v.t.* 3. To subject to agony; torture. [< F < Med.L < Gk. *agōnizesthai* to contend, strive]
ag·o·ny (ag'ə-nē) *n. pl.* **·nies** 1. Intense suffering of body or mind; anguish. 2. Any intense or sudden emotion. 3. The suffering that precedes death. 4. Violent striving. [< L < Gk. *agōn* contest]
ag·o·ra (ag'ər-ə) *n. pl.* **ag·o·rae** (-ər-ē) or **ag·o·ras** 1. In ancient Greece, a popular assembly. 2. Any place of popular assembly, esp. a market place. [< Gk.]
a·gou·ti (ə-goō'tē) *n. pl.* **·tis** or **·ties** A tropical American rodent of grayish color, with slender limbs and three hind toes. Also **a·gou'ty.** [< F < Sp. *aguti* < Tupi]
a·grar·i·an (ə-grâr'ē-ən) *adj.* 1. Pertaining to land or the distribution of lands. 2. Organizing or furthering agricultural interests. — *n.* One who advocates equal distribution of lands or equalizing farm income. [< L < *ager* field] — **a·grar'i·an·ism** *n.*
a·gree (ə-grē') *v.* **a·greed, a·gree·ing** *v.i.* 1. To give consent; accede: with *to* or the infinitive. 2. To come into or be in harmony. 3. To be of one mind; concur: often with *with.* 4. To come to terms, as in the details of a transaction: with *about* or *on.* 5. To be acceptable; suit: with *with.* 6. *Gram.* To correspond in person, number, case, or gender. — *v.t.* 7. To grant as a concession: with a noun clause. [< OF < L *ad* to + *gratus* pleasing]
a·gree·a·ble (ə-grē'ə-bəl) *adj.* 1. Pleasant to the mind or senses. 2. Being in accordance or conformity. 3. Ready or willing to agree. — **a·gree'a·bil'i·ty, a·gree'a·ble·ness** *n.* — **a·gree'a·bly** *adv.*
a·greed (ə-grēd') *adj.* 1. In agreement. 2. Settled by consent, bargain, or contract. 3. Granted: used as a rejoinder.
a·gree·ment (ə-grē'mənt) *n.* 1. The act of coming into accord. 2. The state of being in accord; conformity. 3. A contract. 4. *Gram.* Correspondence in person, number, case, or gender.
ag·ri·cul·ture (ag'rə-kul'chər) *n.* The science and art of the cultivation of the soil, the breeding and raising of livestock, etc.; tillage; farming. Abbr. *agr., agric.* — **Department of Agriculture** An executive department of the U.S. government headed by the Secretary of Agriculture, that administers loans and grants in aid to farmers and assists in production, irrigation, etc. [< F < L *ager* field + *cultura* cultivation] — **ag'ri·cul'tur·al** *adj.* — **ag'ri·cul'tur·al·ly** *adv.*
ag·ri·cul·tur·ist (ag'rə-kul'chər·ist) *n.* 1. An expert in agriculture. 2. A farmer: also **ag'ri·cul'tur·al·ist.**
agro- *combining form* Of or pertaining to fields or agriculture: *agronomy.* [< Gk. < *agros* field]
ag·ro·bi·ol·o·gy (ag'rō-bī-ol'ə-jē) *n.* The quantitative study of plant life, esp. in relation to the cultivation of cultivated plants. — **ag'ro·bi·o·log·ic** (ag'rō-bī'ə-loj'ik) or **·i·cal** *adj.* — **ag'ro·bi·o·log'i·cal·ly** *adv.* — **ag'ro·bi·ol'o·gist** *n.*
ag·ro·nom·ics (ag'rə-nom'iks) *n.pl.* (*construed as sing.*) Agronomy.
a·gron·o·my (ə-gron'ə-mē) *n.* The application of scientific principles to the cultivation of land. [< Gk. < *agros* field + *nemein* to distribute, manage] — **ag·ro·nom·ic** (ag'rə-nom'ik) or **·i·cal** *adj.* — **a·gron'o·mist** *n.*
a·ground (ə-ground') *adv. & adj.* On the shore or bottom, as a vessel; stranded.
a·gue (ā'gyoō) *n.* 1. *Pathol.* A periodic malarial fever marked by intermittent chills. 2. A chill or paroxysm. [< OF < L (*febris*) *acuta* acute (fever)] — **a'gu·ish** *adj.*
ah (ä) *interj.* An exclamation expressive of various emotions, as surprise, triumph, satisfaction, contempt, etc. [ME]
a·ha (ä-hä') *interj.* An exclamation expressing surprise, triumph, or mockery. [ME]
a·head (ə-hed') *adv.* 1. At the head or front. 2. In advance. 3. Onward; forward. — **ahead of** In advance of, as in time, rank, achievement, etc. — **to be ahead** *U.S. Informal* To have as profit or advantage; be winning. — **to get ahead** To make one's way socially, financially, etc.
a·hem (ə-hem') *interj.* An exclamation similar to the sound of clearing the throat, made to attract attention.
a·hoy (ə-hoi') *interj.* Ho there!: a call used in hailing.
aid (ād) *v.t. & v.i.* To render assistance (to); help. — *n.* 1. Assistance; help. 2. A person or thing that affords assistance. 3. An aide. [< OF < L < *ad-* to + *juvare* to help] — **aid'er** *n.*
aide (ād) *n.* 1. An aide de camp. 2. An assistant. [< F]
aide-de-camp (ād'də-kamp') *n. pl.* **aides-de-camp** A military or naval officer on the personal staff of a superior officer

in a high command as his confidential assistant and secretary: also *aide.* Also *U.S.* **aid'-de-camp'.** [< F *aide de camp,* lit., field assistant]

ai·grette (ā'gret, ā·gret') *n.* **1.** The tail plume of the egret. **2.** A tuft of feathers or gems, worn on a helmet, headdress, etc. Also **ai'gret.** [< F', a heron]

ail (āl) *v.t.* **1.** To cause uneasiness or pain to; trouble; make ill. — *v.i.* **2.** To be somewhat ill; feel pain. [OE *eglan*]

ai·lan·thus (ā·lan'thəs) *n.* A large, deciduous tree of the quassia family, having malodorous, greenish flowers. [< NL, genus name] — **ai·lan'thic** *adj.*

ai·le·ron (ā'lə·ron) *n. Aeron.* Any of several movable surfaces of an airplane wing, used to bank the airplane. [< F]

ail·ing (ā'ling) *adj.* Sick; ill. — **Syn.** See SICK.

ail·ment (āl'mənt) *n.* A slight illness.

aim (ām) *v.t.* **1.** To direct, as a weapon, remark, or act, toward or against some object or person. — *v.i.* **2.** To have a purpose; try: with the infinitive. **3.** To direct a missile, weapon, etc. — *n.* **1.** The act of aiming. **2.** The line or direction of anything aimed. **3.** Design; purpose. [< OF < L *aestimare* to estimate]

aim·less (ām'lis) *adj.* Wanting in aim or purpose. — **aim'·less·ly** *adv.* — **aim'less·ness** *n.*

ain't (ānt) *Illit. & Dial.* Am not: also used for *are not, is not, has not,* and *have not.*
◆ **ain't, aren't I?** *Ain't* is now nonstandard, although users of standard English sometimes say or write it for amusing effect when they are sure it will not be taken as their normal usage. *Aren't I?* is an ungrammatical locution used to avoid *Ain't I?* when one means *Am I not?*

air (âr) *n.* **1.** The mixture of gases that forms the atmosphere of the earth, consisting chiefly of oxygen and nitrogen very nearly in the proportions one to four. **2.** The open space around and above the earth; sky. **3.** An atmospheric movement or current; wind; breeze. **4.** Utterance abroad; publicity: to give *air* to one's feelings. **5.** Peculiar or characteristic appearance; mien; manner: an honest *air.* **6.** *pl.* Assumed manner; affectation: to put on *airs.* **7.** *Music* A melody; tune. **8.** The medium through which radio signals are sent. — **in the air 1.** Prevalent; abroad, as gossip. **2.** In the making, as plans. — **on the air** Now broadcasting or transmitting, as by radio; being broadcast. — **up in the air** *Informal* Undecided. — *v.t.* **1.** To expose to the air; admit air into so as to purify or dry; ventilate. **2.** To make public; display; exhibit. [< OF < L < Gk. *aēr* air, mist]

air base A base for operations by aircraft.

air bladder 1. *Zool.* In fishes, a sac filled with air, aiding them to maintain an equilibrium in the water: also called *sound, swimming bladder.* **2.** Any vesicle filled with air.

air·borne (âr'bôrn', -bōrn') *adj.* **1.** Carried through the air, as bacteria, pollen, etc. **2.** Transported in aircraft: *airborne* infantry. **3.** In flight; flying.

air brake A brake operated by compressed air.

air·brush (âr'brush') *n.* A kind of atomizer for spraying paint or other liquids by compressed air. Also **air brush.**

air·bus (âr'bus') *n.* A large passenger airplane designed to accommodate hundreds of people. [< AIR (PLANE) + BUS]

air castle A visionary project; a daydream.

air chamber An enclosed space containing, or designed to contain, air, esp. in hydraulics.

air chief marshal In the Royal, Royal Canadian, and other Commonwealth air forces, an officer of the next to highest rank. See table at GRADE.

air coach *U.S.* The second-best and cheaper class of accommodations in commercial aircraft. Also **air·coach** (âr'cōch').

air commodore In the Royal, Royal Canadian, and other Commonwealth air forces, an officer ranking next above group captain. See table at GRADE.

air·con·di·tion (âr'kən·dish'ən) *v.t.* To equip with or ventilate by air conditioning. — **air'·con·di'tioned** *adj.*

air conditioner Any of various air-conditioning devices.

air conditioning A system for treating air in buildings, etc., so as to maintain those conditions of temperature, humidity, and purity best adapted to personal comfort, etc.

air·cool (âr'kōōl') *v.t.* To cool, as the cylinders of an engine, with a flow of air instead of liquid. — **air'-cooled'** *adj.*

air·craft (âr'kraft', -kräft') *n. pl.* **·craft** Any form of craft designed for flight through or navigation in the air.

aircraft carrier *Naval* A large ship designed to carry aircraft, having a flight deck for landing and taking off.

air·craft·man (âr'kraft'mən, kräft'-) *n. pl.* **·men** *Brit.* Any of the four lower grades in the Royal or Royal Canadian Air Force. See table at GRADE.

air·drome (âr'drōm') *n. Chiefly Brit.* An airport.

air·drop (âr'drop') *n.* Aerial delivery of supplies and equipment from an aircraft in flight. — *v.t. & v.i.* **·dropped, ·drop·ping** To drop (supplies, etc.) from an aircraft.

Aire·dale (âr'dāl) *n.* A large terrier with a wiry tan coat. [after *Airedale,* the Aire river valley, England]

air·field (âr'fēld') *n.* An airport.

air·foil (âr'foil') *n. Aeron.* A surface, as a wing, aileron, etc., designed to provide the maximum aerodynamic advantage for an airplane in flight.

air force The air arm of a country's defense forces. — **United States Air Force** The air force of the United States.

air gun A gun impelling a charge by compressed air.

AIREDALE
(About 23 inches high at shoulder)

air hole 1. A hole containing, or made by or for, gas or air. **2.** A flaw in a casting. **3.** An opening in the ice over a body of water. **4.** *Aeron.* An air pocket.

air·i·ly (âr'ə·lē) *adv.* In a light or airy manner; jauntily.

air·ing (âr'ing) *n.* **1.** An exposure to air, as for drying. **2.** Public exposure or discussion. **3.** Exercise in the air.

air lane A route regularly used by airplanes.

air·less (âr'lis) *adj.* Destitute of air or of fresh air.

air letter 1. An airmail letter. **2.** A sheet of lightweight paper for airmail letters. **3.** *Brit.* An aérogramme.

air·lift (âr'lift') *n.* The transporting of passengers and cargo by aircraft. — *v.t. & v.i.* To transport by airplane.

air·line (âr'līn') *n.* A business organization that transports passengers and freight by air. — **air'lin'er** *n.*

air lock An airtight antechamber, as of a caisson, for maintaining the air pressure.

air mail 1. Mail carried by airplane. **2.** A system of carrying mail by airplane. — **air'-mail', air'mail'** *adj.*

air·man (âr'mən) *n. pl.* **·men** (-mən) An aviator; flyer.

air marshal In the Royal, Royal Canadian, and other Commonwealth air forces, an officer ranking next below air chief marshal. See table at GRADE.

air mass *Meteorol.* A body of air having essentially uniform conditions of temperature, humidity, etc.

Air Medal A decoration awarded by the U.S. Air Force for meritorious achievement during flight. See DECORATION.

air·plane (âr'plān') *n.* A heavier-than-air, powered flying craft having fixed wings. Also, *Brit., aeroplane.*

air pocket *Aeron.* A sinking mass of cooled air.

air·port (âr'pôrt', -pōrt') *n.* A field laid out as a base for aircraft, including all structures and appurtenances necessary for operation, housing, storage, and maintenance.

air power The strength of a nation in terms of its command of the air in peace and war.

air·proof (âr'prōōf') *adj.* Impenetrable by air. — *v.t.* To make airproof.

air raid An attack by military aircraft, esp. by bombers.

air-raid shelter A place set aside and equipped for the protection of people during an air raid.

air sac *Ornithol.* One of the membranous sacs filled with air in different parts of the body in birds and communicating with the lungs.

air shaft An open shaft intended to provide ventilation.

air·ship (âr'ship') *n.* A lighter-than-air, powered flying craft.

air·sick·ness (âr'sik'nis) *n.* Motion sickness caused by air travel. — **air'sick'** *adj.*

air·space (âr'spās') *n.* That portion of the atmosphere overlying a designated area, considered as subject to territorial jurisdiction or international law.

air speed The speed of an airplane with relation to the air.

air·strip (âr'strip') *n.* A flat surface used as an airfield.

air·tight (âr'tīt') *adj.* **1.** Not allowing air to escape or enter. **2.** Having no weak places; flawless: an *airtight* case.

air vice-marshal (vīs'mär'shəl) In the Royal, Royal Canadian, and other Commonwealth air forces, an officer ranking next below air marshal. See table at GRADE.

air·way (âr'wā') *n.* **1.** Any passageway for air, as the ventilating passage of a mine. **2.** *Aeron.* An air lane.

air·wor·thy (âr'wûr'thē) *adj.* Being in fit condition to fly: said of aircraft. — **air'wor'thi·ness** *n.*

air·y (âr'ē) *adj.* **air·i·er, air·i·est 1.** Of or pertaining to the air. **2.** Like or resembling air; immaterial. **3.** Thin or light as air; delicate. **4.** Light or buoyant in manner; lively; gay. **5.** Unsubstantial as air; unreal; empty. **6.** Dealing with fancies; visionary; speculative. **7.** Open to the air; breezy. **8.** Performed in the air; aerial. **9.** *Informal* Giving oneself airs; affected. — **air'i·ness** *n.*

aisle (īl) *n.* **1.** A passageway between rows of seats. **2.** A division of a church, usu. divided from the nave by a range of columns or piers. [< MF < L *ala* wing]

a·jar[1] (ə·jär') *adv. & adj.* Partly open, as a door. [ME *a-on + char,* OE *cerr* turn]

a·jar[2] (ə·jär') *adv. & adj.* Not in harmony.

a·kim·bo (ə·kim'bō) *adv. & adj.* With hands on hips and elbows outward. [ME *in kenebowe* in a sharp bow]

a·kin (ə·kin') *adj. & adv.* **1.** Of the same kin; related by blood. **2.** Of similar nature or qualities. [< A-[3] + KIN]

al-[1] *prefix* The Arabic definite article, seen in words of Arabic origin, as *Alkoran, algebra.*

al-² Assimilated var. of AD-.

-al¹ *suffix of adjectives and nouns* Of or pertaining to; characterized by: *personal, musical.* [< L *-alis*]

-al² *suffix of nouns* The act or process of, used in nouns formed from verbs: *betrayal, refusal.* [< OF < L *-alis*]

-al³ *suffix Chem.* Denoting a compound having the properties of or derived from an aldehyde: *chloral.* [< AL(DEHYDE)]

a·la (ā'lə)   *n.   pl.* **a·lae** (ā'lē)   A wing or a winglike part. [< L, wing]

à la (ä' lä, ä' lə; *Fr.* à lä)   After the manner or in the style of. Also **a la.** [< F]

al·a·bam·ine (al'ə·bam'ēn, -in)   *n.* A hypothetical element of atomic number 85; replaced by astatine. [*Alabama*]

al·a·bas·ter (al'ə·bas'tər, -bäs'-)   *n.* **1.** A white or tinted fine-grained gypsum. **2.** A banded variety of calcite. — *adj.* Made of or like alabaster; smooth and white: also **al·a·bas'trine** (-trin). [< L < Gk. *alabast(r)os* alabaster box]

à la carte (ä' lə kärt')   By the bill of fare; each item having a separate price. Compare TABLE D'HÔTE. [< F]

a·lac·ri·ty (ə·lak'rə·tē)   *n.* Cheerful willingness and promptitude; liveliness. [< L *alacer* lively] — **a·lac'ri·tous** *adj.*

A·lad·din (ə·lad'n)   In the *Arabian Nights*, a boy who can summon a jinni by rubbing a magic lamp or a magic ring.

à la king (ä' lə king')   Cooked in a cream sauce, with pimiento or green pepper, mushrooms, etc.

Al·a·mo (al'ə·mō)   A Franciscan mission building, San Antonio, Texas; besieged and taken by Mexicans, 1836.

à la mode (ä' lə mōd', al' ə mōd')   **1.** In style; fashionable. **2.** In cookery: **a** Served with ice cream: said of pie. **b** Braised with vegetables and served in a rich gravy. [< F]

à la New·burg (ä' lə nōō'bûrg, nyōō'bûrg)   Cooked with a sauce made of egg yolks, cream, sherry, and butter.

a·lar (ā'lər)   *adj.* Having or pertaining to an ala or wing; wing-shaped. [< L *ala* wing]

a·larm (ə·lärm')   *n.* **1.** Sudden fear or apprehension caused by awareness of danger. **2.** Any sound or signal intended to awaken or apprise of danger; a warning. **3.** Any device, as a bell, for giving such a signal. **4.** A call to arms, to meet danger or attack. — *v.t.* **1.** To strike with sudden fear. **2.** To arouse to a sense of danger; give warning to. [< OF < Ital. *all' arme* to arms] — **a·larm'a·ble** *adj.*

alarm clock A clock fitted with a device to sound a bell or buzzer when the hands reach a predetermined hour.

a·larm·ing (ə·lär'ming)   *adj.* Exciting alarm; causing fear and apprehension; disturbing. — **a·larm'ing·ly** *adv.*

a·larm·ist (ə·lär'mist)   *n.* **1.** One who needlessly excites or tries to excite alarm. **2.** One who is easily alarmed.

a·las (ə·las', ə·läs')   *interj.* An exclamation of regret, sorrow, etc. [< OF a ah! + *las* wretched]

a·late (ā'lāt)   *adj. Bot.* Winged, as a stem, petiole, or fruit. Also **a'lat·ed.** [< L *ala* wing]

alb (alb)   *n. Eccl.* A white linen eucharistic vestment reaching to the ankles, close-sleeved and girded at the waist. [OE < L *alba* (*vestis*) white garment]

al·ba·core (al'bə·kôr, -kōr)   *n.* Any of various tunas or large related fishes of the Atlantic. [< Pg. < Arabic *al* the + *bukr* young camel]

Al·ba·ni·an (al·bā'nē·ən, -bān'yən)   *adj.* Of or pertaining to Albania, its people, or their language. — *n.* **1.** A native or inhabitant of Albania. **2.** The language of Albania.

al·ba·tross (al'bə·trôs, -tros)   *n.   pl.* **·tross·es** or **tross** A large, web-footed sea bird, with long, narrow wings and a hooked beak. [Orig. *alcatras* frigate bird < Sp., < Pg. *alcatraz*]

al·be·it (ôl·bē'it)   *conj.* Even though; although. [ME *al be it* although it be]

al·bes·cent (al·bes'ənt)   *adj.* Growing white or moderately white; becoming whitish. [< L *albescens, -entis*, ppr. of *albescere* to become white] — **al·bes'cence** *n.*

Al·bi·gen·ses (al'bə·jen'sēz)   *n.pl.* A sect of religious reformers during the 11th to 13th centuries in the south of France, suppressed as heretics. [< Med.L, after *Albi*, a town in southern France] — **Al'bi·gen'si·an** (-sē·ən, -shən) *adj. & n.*

al·bi·no (al·bī'no)   *n.   pl.* **·nos 1.** A person lacking pigment in the skin, hair, and eyes. **2.** Any plant or animal lacking normal pigmentation. [< Pg. < L *albus* white] — **al·bin·ic** (al·bin'ik) *adj.* — **al·bin·ism** (al'bə·niz'əm) *n.*

al·bum (al'bəm)   *n.* **1.** A booklike container for stamps, pictures, phonograph records, etc. **2.** A set of phonograph records stored in such a container. [< L, blank tablet]

al·bu·men (al·byōō'mən)   *n.* **1.** The white of an egg. **2.** *Bot.* The nutritive material in a seed between the embryo and the seed coats. **3.** Albumin. [< L < *albus* white]

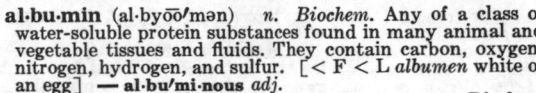

ALBATROSS
(About 40 inches long; wingspread 10 to 12 feet)

al·bu·min (al·byōō'mən)   *n. Biochem.* Any of a class of water-soluble protein substances found in many animal and vegetable tissues and fluids. They contain carbon, oxygen, nitrogen, hydrogen, and sulfur. [< F < L *albumen* white of an egg] — **al·bu'mi·nous** *adj.*

al·bu·min·ize (al·byōō'mən·īz)   *v.t.* **·ized, ·iz·ing** *Biochem.* To convert into or coat with albumin.

al·caz·ar (al'kə·zär; *Sp.* äl·kä'thär)   *n.* A Moorish castle in Spain. — **the Alcazar** A Moorish palace in Seville, later used by the Spanish kings. [< Sp. < Arabic *al-qasr* the castle]

al·che·mist (al'kə·mist)   *n.* One skilled in or practicing alchemy. — **al'che·mis'tic** or **·ti·cal** *adj.*

al·che·mize (al'kə·mīz)   *v.t.* **·mized, ·miz·ing** To transmute by or as by alchemy.

al·che·my (al'kə·mē)   *n.* **1.** The chemistry of the Middle Ages, concerned primarily with the transmutation of base metals into gold. **2.** Any power or process of transmutation. Also **al'chy·my.** [< OF < Med.L *alchimia* < Gk. *cheein* to pour] — **al·chem·ic** (al·kem'ik) *adj.* — **al·chem'i·cal·ly** *adv.*

al·co·hol (al'kə·hôl, -hol)   *n.* **1.** Either of two volatile, flammable, pungent liquids, ethanol, the intoxicating principle of wines and liquors, and methanol, or wood alcohol. **2.** Any drink containing alcohol. **3.** *Chem.* Any of a group of organic compounds derived from the alkanes by the substitution of one hydroxyl radical for one hydrogen atom. [< Med.L < Arabic *al-kohl* the fine powder (of antimony)]

al·co·hol·ic (al'kə·hôl'ik, -hol'-)   *adj.* **1.** Containing or using alcohol. **2.** Caused by alcohol or alcoholism. **3.** Suffering from alcoholism. — *n.* One who suffers from alcoholism.

al·co·hol·ism (al'kə·hôl'iz·əm, -hol'-)   *n. Pathol.* A diseased condition resulting from the excessive or persistent use of alcoholic beverages.

al·co·hol·ize (al'kə·hôl·īz', -hol-)   *v.t.* **·ized, ·iz·ing 1.** To change into alcohol. **2.** To mix or saturate with alcohol. — **al'co·hol·i·za'tion** *n.*

Al·co·ran (al'kō·rän', -ran')   *n.* The Koran.

al·cove (al'kōv)   *n.* **1.** A recess at the side of a larger room. **2.** Any secluded spot. [< F < Sp. < Arabic *al-qobbah* the vaulted chamber]

Al·deb·a·ran (al·deb'ə·rən)   *n.* A red star, one of the 20 brightest, 1.06 magnitude, Alpha in the constellation Taurus.

al·de·hyde (al'də·hīd)   *n.* **1.** *Chem.* Any of a group of compounds derived from the alcohols, and intermediate between the alcohols and the acids. **2.** Acetaldehyde.

al·der (ôl'dər)   *n.* A shrub or small tree of the birch family, growing in wet ground and bearing small catkins. [OE *alor*]

al·der·man (ôl'dər·mən)   *n.   pl.* **·men 1.** *U.S.* In many municipalities, a member of the governing body. **2.** In England and Ireland a member of the higher branch of a municipal or borough council. [OE *eald* old, senior + *man*] — **al'der·man·ship'** *n.* — **al'der·man'ic** (-man'ik) *adj.*

Al·der·ney (ôl'dər·nē)   *n.* One of a breed of cattle originally peculiar to the island of Alderney.

ale (āl)   *n.* A fermented malt flavored with hops, resembling beer but generally having more body. [OE *ealu*]

a·le·a·to·ry (ā'lē·ə·tôr'ē, -tō'rē)   *adj.* Dependent on gambling or luck. [< L *aleator* gambler]

a·lee (ə·lē')   *adv. Naut.* At, on, or to the lee side. [< ON]

ale·house (āl'hous')   *n.* A public place where ale is sold.

a·lem·bic (ə·lem'bik)   *n.* **1.** An apparatus of glass or metal formerly used in distilling. **2.** Anything that tests, purifies, or transforms. [< OF ult. < Arabic < Gk. *ambix* a cup]

A·len·çon lace (ə·len'sən, *Fr.* ä·län·sôn')   A fine needlepoint lace. [after *Alençon*, France]

a·lert (ə·lûrt')   *adj.* **1.** Keenly watchful; ready for sudden action; vigilant. **2.** Lively; nimble. **3.** Intelligent; bright. — *n.* **1.** A warning against attack; esp., a signal to prepare for an air raid. **2.** The time during which such a warning is in effect. — **on the alert** On the lookout; vigilant. — *v.t.* To warn, as of a threatened attack or raid. [< Ital. *all'erta* on the watch] — **a·lert'ly** *adv.* — **a·lert'ness** *n.*

-ales *suffix Bot.* A feminine plural used to form the scientific names of plant orders. [< L, pl. of *-alis*]

A·le·ut (al'ē·ōōt)   *n.   pl.* **Al·e·uts** or **Al·e·ut 1.** A native of the Aleutian Islands. **2.** The language of the Aleuts. — **A·leu·tian** (ə·lōō'shən), **A·leu'tic** *adj.*

ale·wife (āl'wīf')   *n.   pl.* **·wives** A small North American herring-like fish. [Origin unknown]

Al·ex·an·dri·an (al'ig·zan'drē·ən, -zän'-)   *adj.* **1.** Of Alexandria in Egypt. **2.** Of Alexander the Great, his reign, or his conquests. **3.** In prosody, Alexandrine. — *n.* **1.** An inhabitant of Alexandria. **2.** An Alexandrine verse.

Al·ex·an·drine (al'ig·zan'drin, -drēn, -zän'-)   *n.* In prosody, a line of verse having six iambic feet with the caesura generally after the third. — *adj.* Of, composed of, or characterized by Alexandrines. Also *Alexandrian.*

al·fal·fa (al·fal'fə)   *n.* A cloverlike plant of the bean family,

---

PRONUNCIATION KEY: add, āce, câre, pälm; end, ēven; it, īce; odd, ōpen, ôrder; tōōk, pōōl; up, bûrn; ə = a in *above*, e in *sicken*, i in *flexible*, o in *melon*, u in *focus*; yōō = u in *fuse*; oil; pout; check; go; ring; thin; this; zh, vision.

used as forage. Also, *Brit., lucerne.* [< Sp. < Arabic *alfasfasah*, the best kind of fodder]

al·fres·co (al-fres′kō) *adv.* In the open air. — *adj.* Occurring outdoors, as a meal. Also **al fresco.** [< Ital.]

al·ga (al′gə) *n. pl.* **·gae** (-jē) Any of various primitive, chlorophyll-bearing plants widely distributed in fresh and salt water and moist lands, including the seaweeds and kelps. [< L, seaweed] — **al·gal** (al′gəl) *adj.*

al·ge·bra (al′jə-brə) *n.* The branch of mathematics that treats of quantity and the relations of numbers in the abstract, and in which calculations are performed by means of letters and symbols. [< Ital. < Arabic *al-jebr* the reunion of broken parts, bonesetting] — **al·ge·bra·ic** (al′jə-brā′ik) or **·i·cal** *adj.* — **al′ge·bra′i·cal·ly** *adv.* — **al′ge·bra′ist** *n.*

Al·ge·ri·an (al-jē′ri-an) *adj.* Of or pertaining to Algeria or its people. — *n.* A citizen or inhabitant of Algeria.

-algia *suffix* Pain: *neuralgia.* [< Gk. *algos* pain]

al·gid (al′jid) *adj.* Cold. [< F < L *algere* to be cold]

al·gin (al′jin) *n.* The dried, gelatinous form of various seaweeds, used as an emulsifier, etc. [< ALGA]

Al·gon·ki·an (al-gong′kē-ən) *adj. & n.* Algonquian.

Al·gon·kin (al-gong′kin) *n. pl.* **·kin** or **·kins** Algonquin.

Al·gon·qui·an (al-gong′kē-ən, -kwē-ən) *n. pl.* **·qui·an** or **·qui·ans** 1. A family of North American Indian languages, including Arapaho, Blackfoot, Cheyenne, Cree, Ojibwa, Micmac, Delaware, and Massachusett. 2. A member of an Algonquian-speaking tribe. — *adj.* Of or pertaining to the Algonquian family of languages.

Al·gon·quin (al-gong′kin, -kwin) *n. pl.* **·quin** or **·quins** 1. A member of certain Algonquian tribes formerly living along the Ottawa River. 2. The Algonquian language.

Al·ham·bra (al-ham′brə) The palace of the Moorish kings at Granada, Spain, built in the 13th and 14th centuries. [< Sp. < Arabic *al-hamrā′* the red (house)]

a·li·as (ā′lē-əs) *n. pl.* **a·li·as·es** An assumed name. — **Syn.** See PSEUDONYM. — *adv.* Called by an assumed name: Miller, *alias* Brown. [< L, at another time]

al·i·bi (al′ə-bī) *n. pl.* **·bis** 1. *Law* A form of defense by which an accused person attempts to show that he was elsewhere when the crime was committed. 2. *U.S. Informal* An excuse. — *v.i.* **·bied, ·bi·ing** *U.S. Informal* To make excuses for oneself. [< L, elsewhere]

al·ien (āl′yən, ā′lē-ən) *adj.* 1. Owing allegiance to another country; unnaturalized; foreign. 2. Of or related to aliens. 3. Not one's own; strange. 4. Not consistent with; incongruous; opposed: with *to*. — *n.* 1. An unnaturalized foreign resident. 2. A member of a foreign nation, tribe, people, etc. 3. One estranged or excluded. [< L *alius* another] — **Syn.** (adj.) 4. extrinsic, extraneous, irrelevant. — (noun) 1. An *alien* is not a citizen of the country in which he resides. A *foreigner* is not a native of the country where he lives, but he may become a naturalized citizen.

al·ien·a·ble (āl′yən-ə-bəl, ā′lē-ən-) *adj. Law* Capable of being transferred in ownership. — **al′ien·a·bil′i·ty** *n.*

al·ien·ate (āl′yən-āt, ā′lē-ən-) *v.t.* **·at·ed, ·at·ing** 1. To make indifferent or unfriendly; estrange. 2. To cause to feel estranged or withdrawn from society. 3. To turn away: to *alienate* the affections. 4. *Law* To transfer, as property. [< L *alienare* to estrange] — **al′ien·a′tor** *n.*

al·ien·a·tion (āl′yən-ā′shən, ā′lē-ən-) *n.* 1. The act of alienating, or the state of being alienated; estrangement: the growing *alienation* of students. 2. Insanity.

al·ien·ee (āl′yən-ā′, ā′lē-ən-ē′) *n. Law* One to whom property is transferred.

al·ien·ist (āl′yən-ist, ā′lē-ən-) *n.* A doctor skilled in the treatment of mental disorders; used chiefly in medical jurisprudence. [< F < L *alienus* insane] — **al′ien·ism** *n.*

al·ien·or (āl′yən-ər, ā′lē-ən-ôr′) *n. Law* One who alienates property to another; a vendor. Also **alien·er.** [< AF]

al·i·form (al′ə-fôrm, ā′lə-fôrm) *adj.* Wing-shaped; alar. [< F *ala* wing + -FORM]

a·light[1] (ə-līt′) *v.i.* **a·light·ed** or **a·lit, a·light·ing** 1. To descend and come to rest; settle, as after flight. 2. To dismount. 3. To come by accident: with *on* or *upon*. [OE *ālihtan* < *ā-* out, off + *lihtan* to alight]

a·light[2] (ə-līt′) *adj. & adv.* Lighted; burning.

a·lign (ə-līn′) *v.t.* 1. To bring into a straight line. 2. To put (oneself, one's party, etc.) on one side of an issue, controversy, etc. — *v.i.* 3. To fall into line. Also spelled *aline*. [< F *aligner* < *a-* to + *ligner* to place in line]

a·lign·ment (ə-līn′mənt) *n.* 1. Position, place, or arrangement in a straight line. 2. A line or lines so made. 3. The state of being on one side of an issue, controversy, etc.

a·like (ə-līk′) *adj.* Having resemblance; like one another: used predicatively: The family are all *alike*. — *adv.* In the same or like manner; equally. [Fusion of ON *ālīkr* and OE *gelīc, anlīc*] — **a·like′ness** *n.*

al·i·ment (al′ə-mənt) *n.* 1. Food for body or mind; nutriment. 2. That which sustains or supports. — *v.t.* To furnish with food; nourish. [< L *alere* to nourish] — **al·i·men·tal** (al′ə-men′təl) *adj.* — **al′i·men′tal·ly** *adv.*

al·i·men·ta·ry (al′ə-men′trē, -tə-rē) *adj.* 1. Supplying nourishment. 2. Connected with food or the function of nutrition. 3. Providing support; sustaining.

alimentary canal The food canal between the mouth and the anus, including esophagus, stomach, and intestines.

al·i·men·ta·tion (al′ə-men-tā′shən) *n.* 1. The act or process of supplying or receiving nourishment. 2. Maintenance; support. — **al·i·men·ta·tive** (al′ə-men′tə-tiv) *adj.*

al·i·mo·ny (al′ə-mō′nē) *n. Law* The allowance made to a woman from her husband's estate or income after a divorce or legal separation. [< L < *alere* to nourish]

a·line (ə-līn′), **a·line·ment** (ə-līn′mənt) See ALIGN, etc.

al·i·quant (al′ə-kwənt) *adj. Math.* Not dividing evenly into another number: 4 is an *aliquant* part of 11. [< L *alius* other + *quantus* how large, how much]

al·i·quot (al′ə-kwot) *adj. Math.* Dividing evenly into another number: 4 is an *aliquot* part of 12. [< L *alius* other + *quot* how many]

a·lit (ə-lit′) Alternative past tense and past participle of ALIGHT[1].

a·live (ə-līv′) *adj.* 1. In a living or functioning state; having life. 2. In existence or operation: to keep hope *alive*. 3. In lively action; animated: *alive* with enthusiasm. 4. Aware; sensitive: with *to*. 5. Abounding. [OE *on līfe* in life]

a·liz·a·rin (ə-liz′ə-rin) *n. Chem.* An orange-red compound, $C_{14}H_8O_4$, formerly prepared from madder, used as a dye. Also **a·liz·a·rine** (ə-liz′ə-rin, -rēn). [< F < Arabic *al-asārah* juice]

al·ka·li (al′kə-lī) *n. pl.* **·lis** or **·lies** *Chem.* 1. A hydroxide of any of the alkali metals, soluble in water and capable of neutralizing acids and of turning red litmus paper blue. 2. Any compound that will neutralize an acid, as lime, magnesia, etc. [< MF < Arabic *al-galiy* the ashes of saltwort]

al·ka·li·fy (al′kə-lə-fī′, al·kal′ə-fī) *v.t. & v.i.* **·fied, ·fy·ing** To change into or become alkaline or an alkali.

alkali metals *Chem.* A group of elements including lithium, sodium, potassium, rubidium, cesium, and francium.

al·ka·line (al′kə-lin, -līn) *adj. Chem.* Of, like, or containing an alkali. Also **al′ka·lin.** — **al′ka·lin′i·ty** *n.*

alkaline earths *Chem.* The oxides of calcium, strontium, barium, and sometimes magnesium.

al·ka·lize (al′kə-līz) *v.t. & v.i.* **·lized, ·liz·ing** To convert into or become alkali or alkaline. — **al′ka·li·za′tion** *n.*

al·ka·loid (al′kə-loid) *n. Chem.* Any of a class of nitrogenous organic bases, especially one of vegetable origin, having a physiological effect on animals and man, as strychnine or morphine. — **al′ka·loi′dal** *adj.*

Al·ko·ran (al′kō-rän′, -ran′) *n.* The Koran. — **Al′ko·ran′ic** (-ran′ik) *adj.* [< Arabic *al-qurān* the reading]

al·kyl (al′kil) *n. Chem.* A univalent radical obtained by removing one hydrogen atom from an aliphatic compound.

al·kyl·a·tion (al′kə-lā′shən) *n. Chem.* The introduction of an alkyl group into an organic compound.

all (ôl) *adj.* 1. The entire substance or extent of: *all* Europe. 2. The entire number of: known to *all* men. 3. The greatest possible: in *all* haste. 4. Any whatever: beyond *all* doubt. 5. Every: used in phrases with *manner, sorts*, and *kinds*: *all* manner of men. 6. Nothing except: He was *all* skin and bones. — *n.* 1. Everything that one has: to give one's *all*. 2. Whole being; totality. — *pron.* 1. Everyone: *All* are condemned. 2. Everything: *All* is lost. 3. Every part, as of a whole: *All* of it is gone. — **above all** Primarily. — **after all** Everything else being considered; nevertheless. — **all in all** Taken as a whole. — **at all** 1. In any way: I can't come *at all*. 2. To any degree or extent: no luck *at all*. — **for all** To the degree that: *For all* I care, you can go alone. — **for all of** As for: You can leave now, *for all of* me. — **in all** Including everything; all told: ten books *in all*. — *adv.* 1. Wholly; entirely: fallen *all* to bits. 2. Exclusively; only: This desk is *all* for me. 3. For each; on each side: a score of three *all*. — **all but** 1. Almost; on the verge of. 2. Every one except. — **all in** *Informal* Wearied. — **all out** Making every effort: *all out* for victory. — **all the (better, more,** etc.**)** So much the (better, more, etc.). [OE]

Al·lah (al′ə, ä′lə) In Islam, the one supreme being; God. [< Arabic]

all-A·mer·i·can (ôl′ə-mer′ə-kən) *adj.* 1. Composed of the best in the United States: an *all-American* football team. 2. Of or composed of Americans or American products exclusively. — *n.* A player selected for an all-American team.

all-a·round (ôl′ə-round′) *adj.* All-round.

al·lay (ə-lā′) *v.t.* **·layed, ·lay·ing** 1. To lessen the violence or reduce the intensity of. 2. To lay to rest, as fears; pacify; calm. [OE < *ā-* away + *lecgan* to lay] — **al·lay′er** *n.*

all clear The signal indicating that an air raid is over.

al·le·ga·tion (al′ə-gā′shən) *n.* 1. The act of alleging. 2. That which is alleged. 3. Something alleged without proof. 4. *Law* The assertion that a party to a suit undertakes to prove. [< L < *ad-* to + *legare* to commission]

al·lege (ə-lej′) *v.t.* **·leged, ·leg·ing** 1. To assert to be true without proving; affirm. 2. To plead as an excuse, in support of or in opposition to a claim or accusation. [< AF < OF < L *ex-* out + *litigare* to sue] — **al·lege′a·ble** *adj.* — **al·leged′** (ə·lejd′, ə·lej′id) *adj.* — **al·leg′er** *n.*

al·leg·ed·ly (ə·lej′id·lē) *adv.* According to allegation.

al·le·giance (ə·lē′jəns) *n.* **1.** Fidelity, or an obligation of fidelity, to a government or sovereign. **2.** Fidelity in general, as to a principle. [ME < *a-* to + OF *liege* liege]

al·le·gor·ic (al′ə·gôr′ik, -gor′-) *adj.* Pertaining to, appearing in, or containing allegory; figurative. Also **al′le·gor′i·cal.** — **al′le·gor′i·cal·ly** *adv.*

al·le·go·rist (al′ə·gôr′ist, -gō′rist, al′ə·gər·ist) *n.* One who composes or uses allegories.

al·le·go·ris·tic (al′ə·gə·ris′tik) *adj.* Allegorizing.

al·le·go·rize (al′ə·gə·rīz′) *v.* **·rized, ·riz·ing** *v.t.* **1.** To turn into an allegory; relate in the manner of an allegory. **2.** To explain or interpret as an allegory. — *v.i.* **3.** To make or use allegory. — **al·le·go·ri·za·tion** (al′ə·gôr′ə·zā′shən, -gor′-) *n.* — **al′le·go·riz′er** *n.*

al·le·go·ry (al′ə·gôr′ē, -gō′rē) *n.* *pl.* **·ries 1.** A story or narrative, as a fable, in which a moral principle or truth is presented by means of fictional characters, events, etc. **2.** The presentation of a truth or moral by such stories. **3.** Loosely, any symbolic representation in literature or art. [< L < Gk. *allos* other + *agoreuein* to speak publicly]

al·le·gret·to (al′ə·gret′ō, *Ital.* äl′lä·gret′tō) *Music adj. & adv.* Rather fast. — *n.* *pl.* **·tos** A composition, movement, etc., in such tempo. [< Ital., dim. of *allegro* lively]

al·le·gro (ə·lā′grō, ə·leg′rō; *Ital.* äl·lä′grō) *Music adj. & adv.* Lively. — *n.* *pl.* **·gros** A composition, movement, etc., in such tempo. [< Ital.]

al·lele (ə·lēl′) *n.* *Genetics* One of a series of hereditary characters alternative to each other. Also **al·le·lo·morph** (ə·lē′lə·môrf, ə·lel′ə-). [< Gk. *allēlōn* of one another + *morphē* form] — **al·le·lo·mor′phic** *adj.* — **al·le·lo·mor′phism** *n.*

al·le·lu·ia (al′ə·lōō′yə) *n. & interj.* Hallelujah: the Latin spelling and more common liturgic form. Also **al′le·lu′iah.**

al·ler·gen (al′ər·jən) *n.* Any substance capable of producing allergy. Also **al′ler·gin.** — **al·ler·gen·ic** (al′ər·jen′ik) *adj.*

al·ler·gic (ə·lûr′jik) *adj.* **1.** Of, pertaining to, or having an allergy. **2.** *Informal* Having an aversion: *allergic* to work.

al·ler·gist (al′ər·jist) *n.* A specialist in the diagnosis and treatment of allergies.

al·ler·gy (al′ər·jē) *n.* *pl.* **·gies** *Med.* A condition of heightened sensitivity to a substance, as food, pollen, dust, etc. [< NL < Gk. *allos* other + *ergon* work]

al·le·vi·ate (ə·lē′vē·āt) *v.t.* **·at·ed, ·at·ing** To make lighter or easier to bear. [< L. < *ad-* to + *levis* light, not heavy]

al·le·vi·a·tive (ə·lē′vē·ā′tiv, ə·lē′vē·ə·tiv) *adj.* Tending to alleviate. Also **al·le·vi·a·to·ry** (ə·lē′vē·ə·tôr′ē, -tō′rē), — *n.* Anything that alleviates.

al·ley (al′ē) *n.* **1.** A narrow passageway; esp., a narrow way between or behind city buildings. **2.** A bowling alley. **3.** A walk bordered with trees or shrubbery. [< OF *alee* a going, passage < *aler* to go]

al·ley·way (al′ē·wā′) *n.* A passageway between buildings.

All Fools′ Day The first of April, a day on which jokes and tricks are commonly practiced: also *April Fools′ Day.*

all fours The four legs of a quadruped, or the arms and legs of a person. — **to go** (or **be**) **on all fours** To rest or crawl on all four limbs.

All·hal·low·mas (ôl′hal′ō·məs) *n.* All Saints′ Day. Also **All·hal·lows** (ôl′hal′ōz).

al·li·ance (ə·lī′əns) *n.* **1.** The state or condition of being allied. **2.** The relationship or union brought about by marriage. **3.** Any union, coalition, or agreement between parties, sovereigns, nations, etc., in their common interest. **4.** Relationship in qualities or characteristics; affinity. [< OF < L < *ad-* to + *ligare* to bind]

al·lied (ə·līd′, al′īd) *adj.* **1.** United, confederated, or leagued. **2.** Closely related: *allied* interests.

Al·lies (al′īz, ə·līz′) *n.pl.* **1.** The twenty-seven nations allied against the Central Powers in World War I; esp., Russia, France, Great Britain, Italy, and the United States. **2.** The nations and governments—in-exile known as the United Nations in World War II. — **Al·lied** (ə·līd′, al′īd) *adj.*

al·li·ga·tor (al′ə·gā′tər) *n.* **1.** A large crocodilian reptile found only in the southern United States and in the Yangtze river, China, having a shorter, blunter snout than the crocodile. **2.** Leather made from the skin of the alligator. [< Sp. *el lagarto* < L *lacertus* lizard]

ALLIGATOR
(To 16 feet long)

alligator pear The fruit of the avocado.

all-im·por·tant (ôl′im·pôr′tənt) *adj.* Very important.

all-in·clu·sive (ôl′in·klōō′siv) *adj.* Including everything.

al·lit·er·ate (ə·lit′ə·rāt) *v.* **·at·ed, ·at·ing** *v.i.* **1.** To use alliteration. **2.** To contain alliteration. — *v.t.* **3.** To make alliterative. [< AL-² to + L *littera* a letter (of the alphabet)]

al·lit·er·a·tion (ə·lit′ə·rā′shən) *n.* The occurrence, in a phrase or line, of two or more words having the same initial sound or sound cluster, as in "A fair field full of folk."

al·lit·er·a·tive (ə·lit′ə·rā′tiv, -ər·ə·tiv) *adj.* Of or like alliteration. — **al·lit′er·a′tive·ly** *adv.* — **al·lit′er·a′tive·ness** *n.*

allo- *combining form* **1.** Other; alien. **2.** Extraneousness; difference from or opposition to the normal: *allopathy.* [< Gk. *allos* other]

al·lo·cate (al′ə·kāt) *v.t.* **·cat·ed, ·cat·ing 1.** To set apart for a special purpose, as funds. **2.** To apportion; assign as a share or in shares. **3.** To locate or localize, as a person or event. [< Med.L < L *ad-* to + *locare* to place] — **al·lo·ca·ble** (al′ə·kə·bəl) *adj.* — **al′lo·ca′tion** *n.*

al·lom·er·ism (ə·lom′ər·iz′əm) *n. Crystall.* Constancy of crystalline form with variation in chemical constitution. [< ALLO- + Gk. *meros* a part] — **al·lom′er·ous** *adj.*

al·lo·path (al′ə·path) *n.* One who practices or favors allopathy. Also **al·lop·a·thist** (ə·lop′ə·thist).

al·lop·a·thy (ə·lop′ə·thē) *n.* A system of treatment that seeks to cure a disease by producing a condition different from the effects of the disease. — **al·lo·path·ic** (al′ə·path′ik) *adj.* — **al′lo·path′i·cal·ly** *adv.*

al·lot (ə·lot′) *v.t.* **·lot·ted, ·lot·ting 1.** To assign by lot; distribute. **2.** To apportion or assign: with *to.* [< OF < *a-* to + *loter* to apportion]

al·lot·ment (ə·lot′mənt) *n.* **1.** The act of allotting, or that which is allotted. **2.** *U.S. Mil.* A portion of a serviceman's pay regularly assigned, as to a member of his family.

al·lo·trope (al′ə·trōp) *n. Chem.* One of the forms assumed by an allotropic substance.

al·lot·ro·py (ə·lot′rə·pē) *n. Chem.* The variation in properties shown by elements or their compounds without change of chemical composition. Also **al·lot·ro·pism** (ə·lot′rə·piz′əm). [< Gk. *allos* other + *tropos* turn, manner] — **al·lo·trop·ic** (al′ə·trop′ik) or **·i·cal** *adj.* — **al′lo·trop′i·cal·ly** *adv.*

al·lot·tee (ə·lot′ē) *n.* One to whom anything is allotted.

all-out (ôl′out′) *adj.* Complete and entire; total.

all·o·ver (*adj.* ôl′ō′vər; *n.* ôl′ō′vər) *adj.* Extending over the whole or surface of anything: the *allover* effect. — *n.* A fabric or other substance having an allover pattern.

al·low (ə·lou′) *v.t.* **1.** To permit to occur or do. **2.** To concede; admit. **3.** To make allowance or provision for: to *allow* an hour for lunch. **4.** To make concession of: to *allow* a month to pay. **5.** To grant; allot. **6.** *U.S. Dial* To say; declare. — *v.i.* **7.** To permit or admit: with *of:* Your remark *allows* of several interpretations. **8.** To make concession or due allowance: with *for.* [< OF *alouer* to place, use, assign < Med.L < L < *ad-* to + *laudare* to praise]

al·low·a·ble (ə·lou′ə·bəl) *adj.* Permissible; admissible. — **al·low′a·ble·ness** *n.* — **al·low′a·bly** *adv.*

al·low·ance (ə·lou′əns) *n.* **1.** That which is allowed. **2.** A definite sum of money given at regular intervals. **3.** A discount, as for a purchase in volume, a trade-in, etc. **4.** The act of allowing; toleration; sanction. **5.** Admission; acceptance. — **to make allowance(s) for** To take into account or to excuse because of modifying circumstances. — *v.t.* **·anced, ·anc·ing 1.** To put on an allowance; limit to a regular amount. **2.** To supply in limited quantities.

al·low·ed·ly (ə·lou′id·lē) *adv.* Admittedly.

al·loy (*n.* al′oi, ə·loi′; *v.* ə·loi′) *n.* **1.** *Metall.* **a** A mixture or combination formed by the fusion of two or more metals or of a metal and a nonmetal. **b** A baser metal mixed or combined with a finer one. **2.** Anything that reduces purity. — *v.t.* **1.** To reduce the purity of, as a metal, by mixing with an alloy. **2.** To mix (metals) so as to form into an alloy. **3.** To modify or debase, as by mixture with something inferior. [< F < OF < L < *ad-* to + *ligare* to bind]

all-pur·pose (ôl′pûr′pəs) *adj.* Generally useful.

all-right (ôl′rīt′) *adj. Slang* **1.** Dependable; honest; loyal. **2.** Good; excellent.

all right 1. Satisfactory. **2.** Correct, as a sum in addition. **3.** Uninjured. **4.** Certainly. **5.** Yes. See ALRIGHT.

all-round (ôl′round′) *adj.* **1.** *U.S.* Of comprehensive range or scope; complete in action or effect. **2.** Excelling in all or many aspects; many-sided; versatile. Also *all-around.*

All Saints′ Day *Eccl.* November 1, a festival commemorative of all saints and martyrs. Also **All Saints.**

All Souls′ Day *Eccl.* November 2, a day of commemoration on which intercession is made for the souls of all the faithful departed. Also **All Souls.**

all·spice (ôl′spīs′) *n.* **1.** The aromatic dried berry of the pimento. **2.** The sharply flavored spice made from it.

al·lude (ə·lōōd′) *v.i.* **·lud·ed, ·lud·ing** To refer without express mention; make indirect or casual reference: with *to.* [< L < *ad-* to + *ludere* to play]

al·lure (ə-lŏŏr′) *v.t. & v.i.* **·lured, ·lur·ing** To draw with or as with a lure; attract; entice. — *n.* That which allures. [< OF < *a-* to + *leurre* lure] — **al·lure′ment** *n.* — **al·lur′er** *n.*

al·lur·ing (ə-lŏŏr′ing) *adj.* Attractive; fascinating. — **al·lur′ing·ly** *adv.* — **al·lur′ing·ness** *n.*

al·lu·sion (ə-lŏŏ′zhən) *n.* The act of alluding; indirect reference; suggestion. [< L *alludere* to play with, joke]

al·lu·sive (ə-lŏŏ′siv) *adj.* Making allusion; suggestive. — **al·lu′sive·ly** *adv.* — **al·lu′sive·ness** *n.*

al·lu·vi·al (ə-lŏŏ′vē-əl) *adj.* Pertaining to or composed of earth deposited by water. — *n.* Alluvial soil.

al·lu·vi·um (ə-lŏŏ′vē-əm) *n.* *pl.* **·vi·a** (-vē-ə) or **·vi·ums** A deposit, as of sand or mud, transported and laid down by flowing water in river beds, flood plains, lakes, etc. [< L]

al·ly (ə-lī′, al′ī) *v.* **·lied, ·ly·ing** *v.t.* **1.** To connect by some relationship or bond: with *to* or *with*. — *v.i.* **2.** To enter into alliance; become allied. — *n.* *pl.* **·lies 1.** A person or country connected with another, as by treaty or common action. **2.** Any friendly associate or helper. **3.** An organism or substance associated with another by similarity. [< OF < L < *ad-* to + *ligare* to bind]

al·ma ma·ter (al′mə mä′tər, al′mə mā′tər, äl′mə mä′tər) The institution of learning that one has attended. Also **Al′ma Ma′ter.** [< L, fostering mother]

al·ma·nac (ôl′mə·nak) *n.* A yearly calendar giving weather forecasts, astronomical information, times of high and low tides, etc. [< Med.L < Sp. < Arabic *al-manākh*]

al·might·y (ôl-mīt′ē) *adj.* **1.** Able to do all things; omnipotent. **2.** *U.S. Informal* Great; extreme: an *almighty* noise. — *adv.* *U.S. Informal* Exceedingly: *almighty* mad. — **the Almighty** God; the Supreme Being. [OE *eal* all + *mihtig* mighty] — **al·might′i·ly** *adv.* — **al·might′i·ness** *n.*

al·mond (ä′mənd, am′ənd) *n.* **1.** A small tree of the rose family, widely cultivated in the warmer temperate regions. **2.** The kernel of the fruit of the almond tree. **3.** Anything having the pointed, oval shape of an almond. [< OF < LL < L < Gk. *amygdalē*]

al·mon·er (al′mən·ər, ä′mən-) *n.* An official dispenser of alms. Also **alm·ner** (alm′nər, äm′nər). [< OF < LL < L < Gk. *eleēmosynē* alms < *eleos* pity]

al·most (ôl′mōst, ôl-mōst′) *adv.* Approximately; very nearly; all but: *almost* complete. [OE *ealmǣst*]

alms (ämz) *n. sing. & pl.* A gift or gifts for the poor. ◆ Collateral adjective: *eleemosynary.* Some self-explanatory compounds have *alms* as their first element: **almsgiver, almsgiving, almsmoney,** etc. [OE < LL < Gk. *eleēmosynē* alms < *eleos* pity]

alms·house (ämz′hous′) *n.* A poorhouse.

al·oe (al′ō) *n.* *pl.* **·oes 1.** An Old World plant of the lily family, some species of which furnish a drug, and others valuable fiber. **2.** *pl.* (*construed as sing.*) A cathartic made from the juice of certain aloes. [OE < L < Gk. *aloē*] — **al·o·et·ic** (al′ō·et′ik) or **·i·cal** *adj.*

a·loft (ə-lôft′, ə-loft′) *adv.* **1.** In or to a high or higher place; on high; high up. **2.** *Naut.* In or to the higher parts of a ship's rigging. [< ON *ā lopt* in (the) air]

a·lo·ha (ə-lō′ə, ä·lō′hä) *n. & interj. Hawaiian* Love: used as a salutation and a farewell.

Aloha State Nickname of HAWAII.

a·lone (ə-lōn′) *adv. & adj.* **1.** Without company; solitary. **2.** Excluding all others; only: He *alone* survived. **3.** Without equal; unique; unparalleled: As an artist, he stands *alone.* [ME *al one* solitary]

a·long (ə-lông′, ə-long′) *adv.* **1.** Following the length or course of; lengthwise: usually with *by.* **2.** Progressively onward in a course; forward: The years roll *along* quickly. **3.** In company or association; together: usually with *with.* **4.** *U.S.* As a companion: Bring a friend *along.* **5.** *U.S. Informal* Advanced in its natural course. **6.** *U.S. Informal* Approaching a time, age, number, etc.: usually with *about.* — **all along** From the outset; throughout. — **to be along** *U.S. Informal* To arrive at a place; come. — **right along** *U.S. Informal* Without interruption. — *prep.* Throughout or over the length or course of. [OE *andlang* continuous]

a·long·shore (ə-lông′shôr′, ə-long′-, -shōr′) *adv.* Along the shore, either on the water or on the land.

a·long·side (ə-lông′sīd′, ə-long′-) *adv.* Close to or along the side. — *prep.* Side by side with; at the side of.

a·loof (ə-lōōf′) *adj.* Distant, esp. in manner; unsympathetic. — *adv.* At a distance; apart: to stand *aloof.* [< A-¹ + *loof* < Du. *loef* windward] — **a·loof′ly** *adv.* — **a·loof′ness** *n.*

a·loud (ə-loud′) *adv.* Loudly or audibly.

alp (alp) *n.* **1.** A lofty mountain. **2.** Any peak of the Alps. [Back formation < L *Alpes* the Alps]

al·pac·a (al·pak′ə) *n.* **1.** A domesticated ruminant of South America, related to the llama and vicuña. **2.** Its long silky wool. **3.** A thin cloth made of or containing this wool. **4.** A glossy black fabric of cotton and wool. [< Sp. < Arabic *al* the + Peruvian *paco,* name of the animal]

al·pen·horn (al′pən·hôrn′) *n.* A long, slightly curved horn, made of wood and used in the Alps for signaling over long distances. Also **alp′horn′.** [< G]

al·pen·stock (al′pən·stok′) *n.* A long, iron-pointed staff used by mountain climbers. [< G]

al·pha (al′fə) *n.* **1.** The first letter in the Greek alphabet (A, α), corresponding to English *a.* See table for ALPHABET. **2.** The first of anything. [< Gk. < Hebrew *āleph* ox]

al·pha·bet (al′fə·bet) *n.* **1.** The letters that form the elements of written language, in an order fixed by usage. **2.** Any system of characters or symbols representing the sounds of speech. **3.** The simplest elements of anything. [< L < Gk. < Hebrew *āleph* ox + *beth* house]

al·pha·bet·i·cal (al′fə·bet′i·kəl) *adj.* **1.** Arranged in the order of the alphabet. **2.** Pertaining to or designated by an alphabet. Also **al′pha·bet′ic.** — **al′pha·bet′i·cal·ly** *adv.*

al·pha·bet·ize (al′fə·bə·tīz′) *v.t.* **·ized, ·iz·ing 1.** To put in alphabetical order. **2.** To express by or furnish with an alphabet or alphabetic symbols. — **al·pha·bet·i·za·tion** (al′fə·bet′ə·zā′shən) *n.* — **al′pha·bet·iz′er** *n.*

alpha particle *Physics* The positively charged nucleus of the helium atom.

alpha ray *Physics* A stream of alpha particles.

alpha rhythm *Physiol.* The recurring cycles of electrical change in the brain, each cycle known as an **alpha wave.**

al·pine (al′pīn, -pin) *adj.* **1.** Like an alp; lofty and towering. **2.** *Biol.* Inhabiting or growing in mountain regions.

Al·pine (al′pīn, -pin) *adj.* Pertaining to or characteristic of the Alps. [< L *Alpes* the Alps]

al·pi·nist (al′pə·nist) *n.* A climber of alps; a mountaineer. Also **Al′pi·nist.** — **al′pi·nism, Al′pi·nism** *n.*

al·read·y (ôl·red′ē) *adv.* Before or by the time mentioned.

al·right (ôl·rīt′) *adv.* All right: a spelling not yet considered acceptable.

Al·sa·tian (al·sā′shən) *adj.* **1.** Of or pertaining to Alsace. **2.** Of or pertaining to Alsatia. — *n.* **1.** A native or inhabitant of Alsace. **2.** A German shepherd dog.

al·so (ôl′sō) *adv.* In addition; besides; likewise. [OE *alswā, ealswā* all (wholly) so]

al·so·ran (ôl′sō·ran′) *n. U.S. Informal* **1.** A horse that fails to win, place, or show in a race. **2.** Any unsuccessful competitor.

Al·ta·ic (al·tā′ik) *adj.* Of the Altai Mountains or the languages spoken there. Also **Al·tai·an** (al·tā′ən, -tī′-) *adj.*

al·tar (ôl′tər) *n.* **1.** Any raised place or structure on which sacrifices may be offered or incense burned as an act of worship. **2.** *Eccl.* The structure of wood or stone on which the elements are consecrated in the Eucharist. [OE < L *altus* high]

altar boy An attendant at the altar; acolyte.

al·tar·piece (ôl′tər·pēs′) *n.* A painting, mosaic, or bas-relief over and behind the altar; a reredos.

al·ter (ôl′tər) *v.t.* **1.** To cause to be different. **2.** *U.S.* To castrate or spay. — *v.i.* **3.** To change. [< MF < Med.L < L *alter* other]

al·ter·a·ble (ôl′tər·ə·bəl) *adj.* Capable of alteration. — **al′ter·a·bil′i·ty, al′ter·a·ble·ness** *n.* — **al′ter·a·bly** *adv.*

al·ter·a·tion (ôl′tə·rā′shən) *n.* **1.** The act or process of altering. **2.** Any change. [< MF < Med.L < L *alter* other]

al·ter·a·tive (ôl′tə·rā′tiv) *adj.* **1.** Tending to produce change. **2.** *Med.* Tending to change gradually the bodily condition to a normal state. — *n. Med.* An alterative medicine or treatment. Also **al·ter·ant** (ôl′tər·ənt).

al·ter·cate (ôl′tər·kāt, al′-) *v.i.* **·cat·ed, ·cat·ing** To dispute vehemently. [< L *alter* other]

al·ter·ca·tion (ôl′tər·kā′shən, al′-) *n.* A heated dispute.

al·ter e·go (ôl′tər ē′gō, al′tər eg′ō) **1.** Another self; a double. **2.** An intimate friend. [< L, lit., other I]

al·ter·nant (ôl·tûr′nənt, ôl′tər·nənt, al-) *adj.* Alternating.

al·ter·nate (*v.* ôl′tər·nāt, al′-; *adj. & n.* ôl′tər·nit, al′-) *v.* **·nat·ed, ·nat·ing** *v.i.* **1.** To follow one another by turns. **2.** To change from one place, condition, etc., to another and back again repeatedly. **3.** *Electr.* To reverse direction of flow repeatedly: said of a current. — *v.t.* **4.** To do or perform by turns. **5.** To cause to follow one another by turns. — *adj.* **1.** Existing, occurring, or following by turns. **2.** Referring or pertaining to every other of a series. **3.** Alternative: *alternate* plans. — *n.* A substitute or second. [< L *alternus* every second one] — **al′ter·nate·ly** (-nit·lē) *adv.* — **al′ter·nate·ness** *n.*

alternate angle *Geom.* Either of two nonadjacent interior or exterior angles formed on opposite sides of a line that crosses two other lines.

al·ter·na·tion (ôl′tər·nā′shən, al′-) *n.* Occurrence or action of two things in turn; passage from one place or state to another and back again.

al·ter·na·tive (ôl·tûr′nə·tiv, al-) *n.* **1.** A choice between two things: often loosely applied to more than two. **2.** Either of the two or more things to be chosen. **3.** The remaining choice. — *adj.* Affording or implying a choice between two (or sometimes more) things. — **al·ter′na·tive·ly** *adv.* — **al·ter′na·tive·ness** *n.* [< Med.L *alternativus*]

al·ter·na·tor (ôl′tər·nā′tər, al′-) *n. Electr.* A generator giving an alternating current. Also **al′ter·nat′er.**

al·the·a (al·thē′ə) *n.* Any of several plants of the mallow family, including the rose of Sharon. Also **al·thae′a.** [< Gk. *althainein* to heal]

alt·horn (alt′hôrn′) *n.* An alto flügelhorn or saxhorn.

al·though (ôl·thō′) *conj.* Notwithstanding the fact that; supposing that; though. Also **al·tho′.**

alti- *combining form* High. Also *alto-.* [< L < *altus* high]

al·tim·e·ter (al·tim′ə·tər, al′tə·mē′tər) *n.* **1.** An aneroid barometer for determining altitudes. **2.** Any instrument for determining altitude. **— al·tim·e·try** (al·tim′ə·trē) *n.*

al·ti·tude (al′tə·tōōd, -tyōōd) *n.* **1.** Elevation above any given point, esp. above mean sea level; height. **2.** *Astron.* Angular elevation above the horizon. **3.** *Geom.* The vertical distance from the base of a figure to its highest point. **4.** A high place or rank. [< L *altus* high] **— al′ti·tu′di·nal** *adj.*

al·to (al′tō) *Music n. pl. ·tos* **1.** The lowest female voice; contralto. **2.** The highest male voice; countertenor. **3.** A singer who has an alto voice. **4.** A musical part for this voice. **— adj.** Of or for the alto. [< Ital. < L *altus* high]

alto- Var. of ALTI-.

al·to·geth·er (ôl′tə·geth′ər, ôl′tə·geth′ər) *adv.* **1.** Completely; wholly; entirely. **2.** With everything included. **— n.** A whole. **— in the altogether** *Informal* Nude.

al·tru·ism (al′trōō·iz′əm) *n.* Selfless devotion to the welfare of others. [< F < L *alter* other] **— al′tru·ist** *n.* **— al·tru·is·tic** (al′trōō·is′tik) *adj.* **— al′tru·is′ti·cal·ly** *adv.*

al·um (al′əm) *n. Chem.* An astringent, crystalline, double sulfate of aluminum and potassium, $K_2SO_4Al_2(SO_4)_3·24H_2O$, used in medicine and industry. [< OF < L *alumen* alum]

a·lu·mi·na (ə·lōō′mə·nə) *n. Chem.* Aluminum oxide, Al_2O_3, occurring in the silicate minerals and as corundum in the sapphire and ruby. Also **al·u·min** (al′yə·min), **al·u·mine** (al′yə·mēn, -min). [< NL < L *alumen* alum]

a·lu·mi·nize (ə·lōō′mə·nīz) *v.t.* **·nized, ·niz·ing** To cover or treat with aluminum. Also **a·lu·me·tize** (ə·lōō′mə·tīz).

a·lu·mi·num (ə·lōō′mə·nəm) *n.* A light, bluish white, malleable and ductile metallic element (symbol Al) found only in combination. It is widely used in alloys. Also *Brit.* **al·u·min·i·um** (al′yə·min′ē·əm). See ELEMENT. [< NL < L *alumen* alum] **— a·lu′mi·nous** *adj.*

a·lum·na (ə·lum′nə) *n. pl. ·nae* (-nē) *U.S.* A female graduate or former student of a college or school. [< L]

a·lum·nus (ə·lum′nəs) *n. pl. ·ni* (-nī) *Chiefly U.S.* A male graduate or former student of a college or school. [< L, foster son, pupil < *alere* to nourish]

al·ve·o·lar (al·vē′ə·lər) *adj.* **1.** *Anat.* Denoting that part of the jaws in which the teeth are set. **2.** *Phonet.* Formed with the tongue tip touching or near the alveolar ridge, as (t), (d), and (s) in English. **— n.** *Phonet.* A sound so produced.

al·ve·o·late (al·vē′ə·lit, al′vē·ə-) *adj.* Having alveoli arranged like the cells of a honeycomb; deeply pitted. Also **al·ve·o·lat·ed** (al·vē′ə·lā′tid). **— al·ve·o·la′tion** *n.*

al·ve·o·lus (al·vē′ə·ləs) *n. pl. ·li* (-lī) *Anat.* **1.** A small cavity or pit, as an air cell of the lung. **2.** The socket in which a tooth is set. **3.** *pl.* The bony ridge holding the upper front teeth. [< L, dim. of *alveus* a hollow]

TABLE OF FOREIGN ALPHABETS

(1) ARABIC			(2) HEBREW			(3) GREEK			(4) RUSSIAN			(5) GERMAN		
ا	alif	—[1]	א	aleph	—[6]	A α	alpha	ä	А а	ä	ä	𝔄 a	ä	A a
ب	ba	b	בּ, ב	beth	b, v	B β	beta	b	Б б	be	b	𝔄 ä	e[21]	Ä ä
ت	ta	t	גּ, ג	gimel	g, gh[3]	Γ γ	gamma	g	В в	ve	v	𝔅 b	bā	B b
ث	sa	th				Δ δ	delta	d	Г г	ge	g	ℭ c	tsā	C c
ج	jim	j	דּ, ד	daleth	d, dh	E ε	epsilon	e	Д д	de	d	𝔇 d	dā	D d
ح	ha	h	ה	he	h	Z ζ	zeta	z	Е е	ye	ye, e[12]	𝔈 e	ā[22]	E e
خ	kha	kh	ו	vav	v	Η η	eta	ā	Ё ё	yŏ	yŏ, ŏ[12, 13]	𝔉 f	ef	F f
د	dal	d	ז	zayin	z	Θ θ	theta	th[3]	Ж ж	zhe	zh[14]	𝔊 g	gā	G g
ذ	zal	dh	ח	ḥeth	ḥ	I ι	iota	ē	З з	ze	z	ℌ h	hä	H h
ر	ra	r	ט	ṭeth	t	K κ	kappa	k	И и	ē krät′. kə·yə	ē[15]	ℑ i	ē	I i
ز	za	z	י	yod	y	Λ λ	lambda	l	Й й	ē krät′.	ē[16]	𝔍 i	yŏt	J j
س	sin	s	כ, ך[8]	kaph	k[5], kh	M μ	mu	m	К к	kä	k	𝔎 f	kä	K k
ش	shin	sh	ל	lamed	l	N ν	nu	n	Л л	el	l	𝔏 l	el	L l
ص	sad	s	מ, ם[8]	mem	m	Ξ ξ	xi	ks	М м	em	m	𝔐 m	em	M m
ض	dad	d	נ, ן[8]	nun	n	O o	omicron	o	Н н	en	n	𝔑 n	en	N n
ط	ta	t	ס	samek	s	Π π	pi	p	О о	ŏ	ŏ	𝔒 o	ō[22]	O o
ظ	za	z	ע	ayin	—[7]	P ρ	rho	r	П п	pe	p	𝔒 ö	œ[21]	Ö ö
ع	ain	—[2]	פ, ף[8]	pe	p, f	Σ σ, ς[8]	sigma	s	Р р	er	r	𝔓 p	pā	P p
غ	ghain	gh[3]	צ, ץ[8]	sade	s	T τ	tau	t	С с	es	s	𝔔 q	kōō	Q q
ف	fa	f	ק	ḳoph	k[4]	Υ υ	upsilon	ü, ōō	Т т	te	t	𝔑 r	er	R r
ق	qaf	k[4]	ר	resh	r	Φ φ	phi	f[10]	У у	ōō	ōō	𝔖 ſ, ß[8]	es	S s
ك	kaf	k[5]	שׂ, שׁ	sin, shin	s, sh	X χ	chi	kh[11]	Ф ф	ef	f	—	es′tset	— ß[23], ss
ل	lam	l	תּ, ת	tav	t, th	Ψ ψ	psi	ps	Х х	khä	kh	𝔗 t	tā	T t
م	mim	m				Ω ω	omega	ō	Ц ц	tse	ts[14]	𝔘 u	ōō	U u
ن	nun	n							Ч ч	che	ch[17]	𝔘 ü	ü[21]	Ü ü
ه	ha	h							Ш ш	shä	sh[14]	𝔙 v	fou	V v
و	waw	w							Щ щ	shchä	shch[17]	𝔚 w	vā	W w
ي	ya	y							Ъ ъ	tvyŏr′dē znäk	—[18]	𝔛 x	iks	X x
									Ы ы	ē[19]	i[19]	𝔜 y	üp′si·lŏn	Y y
									Ь ь	myäkh′. kyē znäk	—[20]	𝔷 z	tset	Z z
									Э э	e	e			
									Ю ю	yōō	yōō, ōō[12]			
									Я я	yä	yä, ä[12]			

In each column the characters of the alphabet are given first, followed by their names. In columns 4 (Russian) and 5 (German) the names are printed in the phonetic system used in this dictionary. The last rows of columns 1 through 4 show the approximate sound represented by each character. Columns 3 through 5 show the upper- and lower-case forms.

The Arabic characters are given in their final, unconnected forms. The German style letter, called *fraktur*, has been gradually replaced by the Latin letter. The last row of column 5 gives the Latin equivalents.

[1] Functions as the bearer of *hamza* (the glottal stop), or as a lengthener of short *a*. [2] A voiced pharyngeal fricative. [3] A voiced velar fricative. [4] A uvular stop. [5] A voiceless velar stop. [6] A glottal stop, now usually silent, or pronounced according to the accompanying vowel points. [7] A pharyngeal fricative, now usually silent, or pronounced according to the accompanying vowel points. [8] The alternate form is restricted to the ends of words. [9, 10, 11] In classical Greek these were pronounced as aspirated stops similar to the sounds in *foothill*, *haphazard*, and *blockhouse*. [12] Preceded by a *y* glide when initial, following a vowel, or following a previously palatalized consonant. The glide is otherwise omitted and the preceding consonant palatalized. [13] The diacritical mark is most often omitted. [14] Never palatalized. [15] Palatalizes the preceding consonant. [16] A short vowel, as *y* in *boy*, used only as the second element of diphthongs. [17] Always palatalized. [18] No phonetic value, used to separate parts of compounds and indicate that the consonant preceding it is not palatalized; a hard sign. [19] No English equivalent, similar to *i* as in *kick* with the tongue drawn back. [20] Indicates that the preceding consonant is to be palatalized. [21] See UMLAUT in vocabulary section. [22] In German this vowel is not a diphthong. [23] Restricted to the ends of words.

al·ways (ôl'wāz, -wiz) *adv.* **1.** Perpetually; for all time; ceaselessly. **2.** At every time; on all occasions. [ME *alles weyes* < OE *aelne weg*]

a·lys·sum (ə·lis'əm) *n.* **1.** Any plant of the mustard family, bearing white or yellow flowers. **2.** The sweet alyssum. [< NL < Gk. < *a-* not + *lyssa* madness]

am (am, *unstressed* əm) Present indicative, first person singular, of BE. [OE *eom, am*]

a·mah (ä'mə, am'ə) *n.* In India and the Orient, a female attendant for children; esp., a wet nurse. Also **a'ma.** [< Anglo-Indian < Pg. *ama* nurse]

a·mal·gam (ə·mal'gəm) *n.* **1.** An alloy or union of mercury with another metal. **2.** A silver-white, brittle compound of mercury and silver. **3.** Any combination of two or more things. [< MF < Med.L < Gk. *malagma* an emollient < *malassein* to soften]

a·mal·ga·mate (ə·mal'gə·māt) *v.t. & v.i.* **·mat·ed, ·mat·ing** **1.** To form an amalgam. **2.** To unite or combine. — **a·mal'ga·ma·ble** (ə·mal'gə·mə·bəl) *adj.* — **a·mal·ga·ma·tive** (ə·mal'gə·mā'tiv) *adj.* — **a·mal'ga·ma'tor** or **a·mal'ga·mat'er** *n.* — **a·mal'ga·ma'tion** *n.*

a·man·u·en·sis (ə·man'yōō·en'sis) *n. pl.* **·ses** (-sēz) One who copies manuscript or takes dictation; a secretary. [< L < (*servus*) *a manu* hand (servant), secretary]

am·a·ranth (am'ə·ranth) *n.* **1.** Any of various allied plants, as the love-lies-bleeding. **2.** *Poetic* An imaginary nonfading flower. [< L < Gk. < *a-* not + *marainein* to wither] — **am'a·ran'thine** *adj.*

am·a·ryl·lis (am'ə·ril'is) *n.* A bulbous plant, producing large, lily-like flowers. [< L < Gk. *Amaryllis*, fem. personal name]

a·mass (ə·mas') *v.t.* To heap up, esp. wealth or possessions for oneself. [< OF < *a-* to + *masser* to pile up] — **a·mass'a·ble** *adj.* — **a·mass'er** *n.* — **a·mass'ment** *n.*

am·a·teur (am'ə·chŏor, -tŏor, -tyŏor, am'ə·tûr') *n.* **1.** One who practices an art or science for his own pleasure, rather than as a profession. **2.** An athlete who has not engaged in contests for money. **3.** One who does something without professional skill or ease. — *adj.* **1.** Of, pertaining to, or done by an amateur. **2.** Not expert. [< F < L *amare* to love] — **am'a·teur·ism** *n.*

— **Syn.** (noun) **1.** In present usage, *amateur* is often used to indicate lack of skill, while *connoisseur* implies the ability to make discriminating judgments. A *dilettante* loves the arts, and often possesses great esthetic sensitivity, but lacks technical mastery.

am·a·teur·ish (am'ə·chŏor'ish, -tŏor'-, -tyŏor'-, -tûr'-) *adj.* Lacking the skill or perfection of an expert or professional. — **am'a·teur'ish·ly** *adv.* — **am'a·teur'ish·ness** *n.*

am·a·to·ry (am'ə·tôr'ē, -tō'rē) *adj.* Pertaining to, expressing, or exciting love, especially sexual love. — **Syn.** See AMOROUS. [< L *amare* to love]

a·maze (ə·māz') *v.t.* **a·mazed, a·maz·ing** To overwhelm, as by wonder or surprise; astonish greatly. [OE *āmasian* to confuse] — **a·maz·ed·ly** (ə·mā'zid·lē) *adv.* — **a·maz'ed·ness** *n.*

a·maze·ment (ə·māz'mənt) *n.* Extreme wonder or surprise; astonishment.

a·maz·ing (ə·mā'zing) *adj.* Causing amazement; astonishing; wonderful. — **a·maz'ing·ly** *adv.*

Am·a·zon (am'ə·zon, -zən) *n.* **1.** In Greek mythology, one of a race of female warriors. **2.** Any large, strong or athletic woman or girl: also **am'a·zon.** [< L < Gk. *Amazōn* < Gk. *a-* without + *mazōs* breast, because of the fable that they cut off the right breast to facilitate the use of the bow] — **Am'a·zo'ni·an** (-zō'nē·ən) *adj.*

am·bas·sa·dor (am·bas'ə·dər, -dôr) *n.* **1.** An accredited diplomatic agent of the highest rank, appointed as the representative of one government to another. **2.** Any personal representative or messenger. — **ambassador-at-large** An ambassador accredited to no specific government. [< F, ult. < LL *ambactus* servant, goer about, prob. < Celtic] — **am·bas·sa·do·ri·al** (am·bas'ə·dôr'ē·əl, -dō'rē·əl) *adj.* — **am·bas'sa·dress** (-dris) *n.fem.* — **am·bas'sa·dor·ship** *n.*

— **Syn. 1.** A diplomatic representative of highest rank is an *ambassador*; one of lower rank is a *minister.* A *minister* sent on a special mission is called an *envoy.* A *nuncio* is a papal *ambassador*; a papal *envoy* is a *legate.*

am·ber (am'bər) *n.* **1.** A yellow or brownish-yellow fossilized vegetable resin, hard, brittle, and translucent, used in jewelry, etc. **2.** The color of amber. — *adj.* Pertaining to or like amber. [< OF < Arabic *anbar* ambergris]

am·ber·gris (am'bər·grēs, -gris) *n.* An opaque, grayish secretion of the sperm whale, sometimes found floating on the ocean, used in perfumery. [< F *ambre gris* gray amber]

ambi- *combining form* Both: *ambidextrous.* [< L *ambo* both]

am·bi·dex·trous (am'bə·dek'strəs) *adj.* **1.** Able to use both hands equally well. **2.** Very dexterous or skillful. **3.** Dissembling; double-dealing. — **am'bi·dex'trous·ly** *adv.* — **am·bi·dex·ter'i·ty** (-dek·ster'ə·tē), **am'bi·dex'trous·ness** *n.*

am·bi·ent (am'bē·ənt) *adj.* **1.** Surrounding; encircling; encompassing. **2.** Circulating. [< L < *ambi-* around + *ire* to go] — **am'bi·ence** *n.*

am·bi·gu·i·ty (am'bə·gyōō'ə·tē) *n. pl.* **·ties 1.** The quality of being ambiguous; doubtfulness. **2.** An expression, statement, situation, etc., that can be variously interpreted.

am·big·u·ous (am·big'yōō·əs) *adj.* **1.** Capable of being understood in more senses than one; having a double meaning. **2.** Doubtful or uncertain. [< L < *ambi-* around + *agere* to go] — **am·big'u·ous·ly** *adv.* — **am·big'u·ous·ness** *n.*

am·bi·tion (am·bish'ən) *n.* **1.** Eager desire to succeed, to achieve power, wealth, fame, etc. **2.** The object of aspiration or desire. — *v.t.* To desire and seek eagerly. [< L *ambitio, -onis* a going about (to solicit votes) < *ambi-* around + *ire* to go]

am·bi·tious (am·bish'əs) *adj.* **1.** Actuated or characterized by ambition. **2.** Greatly desiring; eager for: with *of* or the infinitive. **3.** Challenging; difficult: an *ambitious* project. — **am·bi'tious·ly** *adv.* — **am·bi'tious·ness** *n.*

am·biv·a·lent (am·biv'ə·lənt) *adj.* **1.** Uncertain or changeful, esp. because affected by contradictory emotions. **2.** *Psychol.* Experiencing contradictory emotions, as love and hate, toward the same object. [< AMBI- + L *valens, -entis,* ppr. of *valere* to be strong, be worth] — **am·biv'a·lence** *n.*

am·ble (am'bəl) *v.i.* **·bled** (-bəld), **·bling 1.** To move, as a horse, by lifting the two feet on one side together, alternately with the two feet on the other. **2.** To walk or proceed leisurely. — *n.* **1.** The gait of a horse when ambling. **2.** Any movement resembling this. [< OF < L *ambulare* to walk] — **am'bler** *n.* — **am'bling·ly** *adv.*

am·bro·sia (am·brō'zhə, -zhē·ə) *n.* **1.** In classical mythology, the food of the gods, giving immortality. **2.** Any very delicious food or drink. [< L < Gk. < *a-* not + *brotos* mortal]

am·bro·sial (am·brō'zhəl, -zhē·əl) *adj.* **1.** Of or like ambrosia; fragrant; delicious. **2.** Worthy of the gods; heavenly. Also **am·bro·sian** (am·brō'zhən, -zhē·ən) — **am·bro'sial·ly** *adv.*

am·bu·lance (am'byə·ləns) *n.* **1.** A special vehicle equipped for conveying the sick and wounded. **2.** A moving or field hospital. [< F < L *ambulare* to walk]

am·bu·lant (am'byə·lənt) *adj.* Walking or moving about.

am·bu·late (am'byə·lāt) *v.i.* **·lat·ed, ·lat·ing** To walk about; move from place to place. [< L *ambulare* to walk] — **am·bu·la'tion** *n.*

am·bu·la·to·ry (am'byə·lə·tôr'ē, -tō'rē) *adj.* **1.** Of or for walking. **2.** Able to walk, as an invalid. **3.** Shifting; not fixed or stationary. **4.** *Law* Alterable; changeable. — *n.pl.* **·ries** A sheltered place for walking, as a cloister.

am·bus·cade (am'bəs·kād') *n.* An ambush. — *v.t.* **·cad·ed, ·cad·ing** To ambush. [See AMBUSH.] — **am'bus·cad'er** *n.*

am·bush (am'bŏosh) *n.* **1.** A lying in wait to attack unawares; also, the attackers. **2.** Any unseen peril or snare. **3.** A secret position for surprise attack. Also **am'bush·ment.** — *v.t.* To attack from a hidden place; waylay. [< OF < Ital. < L *in-* in + *boscus* a wood] — **am'bush·er** *n.*

a·me·ba (ə·mē'bə) *n. pl.* **·bas** or **·bae** (-bē) A unicellular protozoan found in stagnant water or as a parasite, of indefinite shape, and reproducing by simple division: also spelled *amoeba.* [< NL < Gk. *amoibē* change] — **a·me·bic** (ə·mē'bik) *adj.*

a·me·boid (ə·mē'boid) *adj.* Resembling an ameba, as in its change of form: also spelled *amoeboid.*

a·meer (ə·mir') See AMIR.

a·mel·io·rate (ə·mēl'yə·rāt) *v.t. & v.i.* **·rat·ed, ·rat·ing** To make or become better; meliorate; improve. [< F < L *ad-* to + *meliorare* to better] — **a·mel·io·ra·ble** (ə·mēl'yər·ə·bəl) *adj.* — **a·mel'io·rant** (-rənt) *n.* — **a·mel'io·ra'tion** *n.* — **a·mel·io·ra·tive** (ə·mēl'yə·rā'tiv, -rə·tiv) *adj.* — **a·mel'io·ra'tor** *n.*

a·men (ā'men', ä'-) *interj.* So it is; so be it: used at the end of a prayer or statement to express agreement. — *n.* The word *amen* or any use of it. — *adv.* Verily; truly. [< L < Gk. < Hebrew *āmēn* verily]

a·me·na·ble (ə·mē'nə·bəl, ə·men'ə-) *adj.* **1.** Capable of being persuaded; submissive. **2.** Liable to be called to account; responsible to authority. **3.** Capable of being tested or judged by rule or law. [< AF < *a-* to + *mener* to lead < L *minare* to drive (with threats)] — **a·me'na·bil'i·ty, a·me'na·ble·ness** *n.* — **a·me'na·bly** *adv.*

a·mend (ə·mend') *v.t.* **1.** To change for the better; improve; correct. **2.** To change or alter by authority. — *v.i.* **3.** To become better in conduct. [< OF < L *emendare* to free from faults] — **a·mend'a·ble** *adj.* — **a·mend'a·ble·ness** *n.* — **a·mend'er** *n.*

a·mend·a·to·ry (ə·men'də·tôr'ē, -tō'rē) *adj.* Tending to amend; corrective.

a·mend·ment (ə·mend'mənt) *n.* **1.** Change for the better. **2.** A removal of faults; correction. **3.** The changing, as of a law, bill, or motion. **4.** The statement of such a change.

a·mends (ə·mendz') *n.pl.* Reparation, as in satisfaction or compensation for loss, etc. [< OF < L *mendum* fault]

AMBROSIA (*def.* 4)

Common ragweed (3 to 6 feet high)

a·men·i·ty (ə-men′ə-tē) *n. pl.* **·ties 1.** Agreeableness; pleasantness. **2.** *Usu. pl.* An act or expression of courtesy; civility. [< L *amoenitas, -tatis* < *amoenus* pleasant]

a·merce (ə-mûrs′) *v.t.* **a·merced, a·merc·ing 1.** To punish by an assessment or arbitrary fine. **2.** To punish, as by deprivation. [< AF < *a merci* at the mercy of] — **a·merce′·a·ble** *adj.* — **a·merce′ment** *n.* — **a·merc′er** *n.*

A·mer·i·can (ə-mer′ə-kən) *adj.* **1.** Pertaining to the United States of America, its history, government, people, etc. **2.** Pertaining to the continent or people of North or South America, or of the Western Hemisphere. — *n.* **1.** A citizen of the United States. **2.** An inhabitant of America.

A·mer·i·ca·na (ə-mer′ə-kä′nə, -kan′ə, -kā′nə) *n.pl.* Any collection of American literary papers, sayings, etc., that relate to America.

American eagle The bald eagle. See under EAGLE.

American English The English language as used or spoken in the United States.

American Expeditionary Forces United States troops sent to Europe in World War I.

American Federation of Labor A federation of trade unions, founded in 1886, in 1955 merged with the Congress of Industrial Organizations. Abbr. *AFL, A.F.L., A.F. of L.*

A·mer·i·can·ism (ə-mer′ə-kən-iz′əm) *n.* **1.** A trait, custom, or tradition especially characteristic of the people of the United States or of some of them. **2.** A word, phrase, or usage especially characteristic of American English. **3.** Devotion to the United States, its institutions, etc.

A·mer·i·can·ize (ə-mer′ə-kən-īz′) *v.t. & v.i.* **·ized, ·iz·ing** To make or become American in spirit, methods, speech, etc. — **A·mer′i·can·i·za′tion** *n.*

American League See under MAJOR LEAGUE.

American Revolution See under REVOLUTION.

American Standard Version or **American Revised Version** See under KING JAMES BIBLE.

am·er·ic·i·um (am′ə-rish′ē-əm) *n.* An unstable radioactive element (symbol Am), resulting from the bombardment of uranium and plutonium by high-energy helium ions. See ELEMENT. [< NL, after *America*]

Am·er·in·di·an (am′ə-rin′dē-ən) *adj.* Of or pertaining to the American Indians or the Eskimos. Also **Am′er·in′dic.** — *n.* An American Indian or Eskimo. Also **Am·er·ind** (am′ə-rind).

am·e·thyst (am′ə-thist) *n.* **1.** Quartz with clear purple or violet color, a semiprecious stone. **2.** A purple variety of sapphire or corundum used as a gem: also called *Oriental amethyst.* **3.** A purplish violet. [< OF < L < Gk. < *a-* not + *methystos* drunken < *methy* wine; from the ancient belief that a wearer of the stone would be unaffected by wine]

am·e·thys·tine (am′ə-this′tin, -tīn) *adj.* Violet; purple.

a·mi (à·mē′) *n.masc. pl.* **a·mis** (à·mē′) *French* A friend. — **a·mie** (à·mē′) *n.fem.*

a·mi·a·ble (ā′mē·ə-bəl) *adj.* **1.** Pleasing in disposition; kindly. **2.** Free from irritation; friendly: an *amiable* rivalry. [< OF < L *amicabilis* friendly < *amicus* friend] — **a′mi·a·bil′i·ty, a′mi·a·ble·ness** *n.* — **a′mi·a·bly** *adv.*

am·i·ca·ble (am′i·kə-bəl) *adj.* Friendly; peaceable. [< L *amicabilis* friendly] — **am·i·ca·bil·i·ty** (am′i·kə-bil′ə-tē), **am′i·ca·ble·ness** *n.* — **am′i·ca·bly** *adv.*

a·mi·cus cu·ri·ae (ə-mē′kəs kyoor′ē-ī) *Law* One who advises or is asked to advise a court upon a pending cause to which he is not a party. [< L, friend of the court]

a·mid (ə-mid′) *prep.* In the midst of; among. Also *amidst, midst.* [ME < OE *on middan* in the middle]

am·ide (am′īd, -id) *n. Chem.* **1.** Any compound of the type formula RCONH₂. **2.** A derivative of ammonia in which a metal replaces a hydrogen atom. Also **am·id** (am′id). — **a·mid·ic** (ə·mid′ik) *adj.*

amido- *combining form Chem.* **1.** Pertaining to or containing both the NH₂ radical and an acid radical. **2.** Less frequently, amino-. [< AMIDE]

am·i·dol (am′ə·dol, -dōl) *n.* A white crystalline powder, C₆H₈N₂O·2HCl, used in photography as a developer.

a·mid·ships (ə·mid′ships′) *adv. Naut.* Halfway between bow and stern; toward the middle of a ship: also *midships.*

a·midst (ə·midst′) *prep.* Amid. [ME *amidde* + *-s³* + *t*]

a·mi·go (ə·mē′gō) *n. pl.* **·gos** A friend; comrade. [< Sp.]

a·mine (ə·mēn′, am′in) *n. Chem.* One of a class of organic compounds derived from ammonia by replacement of one or more of its hydrogen atoms by an alkyl radical. Also **am′in.**

a·mi·no (ə·mē′nō, am′ə-nō) *adj. Chem.* Of or pertaining to the NH₂ group combined with a nonacid radical. [< AMINE]

amino acid *Biochem.* Any of a group of organic compounds containing the amino group combined with the carboxyl radical and forming an essential part of the protein molecule.

a·mir (ə·mir′) *n.* **1.** A sovereign of Afghanistan. **2.** A Moslem prince or governor. Also spelled *ameer.* [< Arabic *amīr*]

Am·ish (am′ish, ä′mish) *adj.* Relating to or designating the adherents of Jacob Ammann, a 17th-century Mennonite. — *n.pl.* A sect of Mennonites, founded by Jacob Ammann.

a·miss (ə·mis′) *adj.* Out of order or relation; wrong; improper: used predicatively: Something is *amiss.* — *adv.* In a wrong or defective way; erroneously. — **to take amiss** To take offense at. [ME < *a-* at + *mis* failure]

am·i·to·sis (am′ə·tō′sis) *n. Biol.* Cell division without the formation and splitting of chromosomes; direct division. [< NL < A⁻⁴ without + MITOSIS] — **am·i·tot·ic** (am′ə-tot′ik) *adj.* — **am′i·tot′i·cal·ly** *adv.*

am·i·ty (am′ə-tē) *n. pl.* **·ties** Peaceful relations, as between nations; friendship. [< MF < L *amicus* friend]

am·me·ter (am′mē′tər) *n. Electr.* An instrument for measuring amperage.

am·mo·ni·a (ə·mōn′yə, ə·mō′nē·ə) *n.* **1.** A colorless, pungent, suffocating gas, NH₃, obtained chiefly by the synthesis of nitrogen and hydrogen. **2.** Spirits of hartshorn. [< NL < SAL AMMONIAC] — **am·mo′ni·ac** *adj.*

am·mo·ni·ac (ə·mō′nē·ak) *n.* The resinous gum of a tree found in Persia and western India, used in medicine: also *gum ammoniac.* [< F < L < Gk. *ammōniakon,* a resinous gum]

am·mo·ni·ate (*v.* ə·mō′nē·āt; *n.* ə·mō′nē·it) *v.t.* **·at·ed, ·at·ing** To treat or combine with ammonia.

am·mon·ite (am′ən·īt) *n. Paleontol* A curved or spiral fossil cephalopod shell, commonly found in Mesozoic rocks. [< NL *ammonites* < L (*cornu*) *Ammonis* (horn) of Ammon]

am·mo·ni·um (ə·mō′nē·əm) *n. Chem.* The univalent radical NH₄, that in compounds formed from ammonia acts as an alkali metal.

ammonium hydroxide *Chem.* A compound, NH₄OH, formed in ordinary aqueous or caustic ammonia.

am·mu·ni·tion (am′yə·nish′ən) *n.* **1.** Any one of various articles used in the discharge of firearms and ordnance, as cartridges, shells, rockets, etc. **2.** Any resources for attack or defense. [< F < L *munire* to fortify]

am·ne·sia (am·nē′zhə, -zhē·ə) *n. Psychiatry* Partial or total loss or impairment of memory. [< NL < Gk. < *a-* not + *mnasthai* to remember] — **am·ne·sic** (am·nē′sik, -zik), **am·nes·tic** (am·nes′tik) *adj.*

am·nes·ty (am′nəs·tē) *n. pl.* **·ties 1.** A general pardon by which a government absolves offenders. **2.** Intentional overlooking, esp. of wrongdoing; forgetfulness. — *v.t.* **·tied, ·ty·ing** To pardon; grant amnesty to. [< F < L < Gk. < *a-* not + *mnasthai* to remember]

am·ni·on (am′nē-ən) *n. pl.* **·ni·ons** or **·ni·a** (-nē·ə) *Biol.* A membranous sac enclosing the embryo and fetus in mammals, birds, and reptiles. [< Gk. *amnion* the fetal envelope] — **am·ni·ot·ic** (am′nē·ot′ik), **am·ni·on·ic** (am′nē·on′ik) *adj.*

a·moe·ba (ə·mē′bə), **a·moe·bic** (ə·mē′bik), **a·moe·boid** (ə·mē′boid), etc. See AMEBA, etc.

am·oe·bae·an, am·oe·be·an (am′ə·bē′ən) See AMEBEAN.

amok (ə·muk′, ə·mok′) See AMUCK.

a·mong (ə·mung′) *prep.* **1.** In the midst of. **2.** In the class or number of: He was *among* the dead. **3.** Within or by the group of: a practice *among* the French. **4.** By the joint or concerted action of: *Among* us, we can build the wall. **5.** In portions for each of: to distribute money *among* the poor. **6.** Reciprocally between: disputes *among* friends. Also **a·mongst′.** ◆ See note under BETWEEN. [OE *on gemonge* in the crowd]

a·mon·til·la·do (ə·mon′tə·lä′dō, *Sp.* ä·môn′tē·lyä′tho) *n.* A pale dry sherry. [< Sp., after *Montilla,* a town in Spain]

a·mor·al (ā·môr′əl, ā·mor′əl) *adj.* **1.** Not subject to or concerned with moral or ethical distinctions. **2.** Lacking a sense of right and wrong. — **Syn.** See IMMORAL. — **a·mo·ral·i·ty** (ā′mə·ral′ə·tē) *n.* — **a·mor′al·ly** *adv.*

am·o·rous (am′ər·əs) *adj.* **1.** Tending to fall in love; affectionate; loving. **2.** Of or related to love. **3.** Showing or arising from love or sexual desire; ardent. **4.** In love; enamored: often with *of: amorous* of the truth. [< OF < LL < L *amor* love] — **am′o·rous·ly** *adv.* — **am′o·rous·ness** *n.* — **Syn. 1, 2.** *Amorous* is applied to persons and emotions; *amatory* refers to literature and other things that deal with love.

a·mor·phous (ə·môr′fəs) *adj.* **1.** Without definite form or shape. **2.** Of no fixed character; anomalous; unorganized. **3.** *Chem.* Uncrystallized. [< Gk. < *a-* without + *morphē* form] — **a·mor′phism** *n.* — **a·mor′phous·ly** *adv.* — **a·mor′phous·ness** *n.*

am·or·tize (am′ər·tīz, ə·môr′tīz) *v.t.* **·tized, ·tiz·ing** To extinguish gradually, as a debt or liability, by installment payments or by a sinking fund. Also *Brit.* **am′or·tise.** [< OF < *amortir* to extinguish < L *ad-* to + *mors, mortis* death] — **am·or·tiz·a·ble** (am′ər·tīz′ə·bəl, ə·môr′tīz·ə·bəl) *adj.* — **am′or·ti·za′tion, a·mor·tize·ment** (ə·môr′tiz·mənt) *n.*

A·mos (ā′məs) Eighth-century B.C. Hebrew minor prophet. — *n.* A book of the Old Testament containing his prophecies.

a·mount (ə·mount′) *n.* **1.** A sum total of two or more quantities. **2.** The value of the principal with the interest upon it, as in a loan. **3.** The entire significance, value, or effect. **4.** Quantity: a considerable *amount* of discussion. *— v.i.* **1.** To reach in number or quantity: with *to:* to *amount* to ten dollars. **2.** To be equivalent in effect or importance: with *to:* It *amounts* to treason. [< OF < L *ad* to + *mons, montis* mountain]

a·mour (ə-mŏŏr′) *n.* A love affair, esp. an illicit one. [< F]

a·mour-pro·pre (à-mŏŏr′prôpr′) *n. French* Self-respect.

am·per·age (am-pir′ij, am′pər·ij) *n. Electr.* The strength of a current in amperes.

am·pere (am′pir, am-pir′) *n. Electr.* The practical unit of current strength; such a current as would be given by one volt through a wire having a resistance of one ohm. [after A. M. *Ampère,* 1775-1836, French physicist]

am·per·sand (am′pər·sand, am′pər·sand′) *n.* The character & or & or &′ meaning *and.* [< *and per se and,* lit., & by itself = and]

am·phet·a·mine (am-fet′a·mēn, -min) *n.* An acrid liquid compound, C₉H₁₃N, used as a nasal spray. [< *a(lpha)-m(ethyl)-ph(enyl)-et(hyl)-amine*]

amphi- *prefix* **1.** On both or all sides; at both ends. **2.** Around: *amphitheater.* **3.** Of both kinds; in two ways. [< Gk. < *amphi* around]

am·phib·i·an (am-fib′ē·ən) *adj.* **1.** *Zool.* Of or pertaining to a class of cold-blooded, chiefly egg-laying vertebrates adapted for life both on land and in water, as frogs, newts, salamanders, etc. **2.** Amphibious. *— n.* **1.** An amphibian animal or plant. **2.** An airplane constructed to rise from and alight on either land or water. **3.** A vehicle capable of self-propulsion upon land and upon water.

am·phib·i·ous (am-fib′ē·əs) *adj.* **1.** Living or adapted to life on land or in water. **2.** Capable of operating or landing on land or water. **3.** Of a mixed nature. [< Gk. < *amphi-* of two kinds + *bios* life] **— am·phib′i·ous·ly** *adv.* **— am·phib′i·ous·ness** *n.*

am·phi·bole (am′fə·bōl) *n. Mineral.* Any of a class of variously colored hydrous silicates, consisting chiefly of calcium, magnesium, iron, aluminum, and sodium, as asbestos. [< F < L < Gk. < *amphi-* around + *ballein* to throw]

am·phi·bol·ic (am′fə·bol′ik) *adj.* Ambiguous; equivocal.

am·phi·ox·us (am′fē·ok′səs) *n. Zool.* The most primitive of the chordates, a lancelet. [< AMPHI- + Gk. *oxys* sharp]

am·phi·the·a·ter (am′fə·thē′ə·tər) *n.* **1.** An oval structure having tiers of seats built around an open space or arena. **2.** A level area surrounded by slopes. **3.** A place of contest. Also *Brit.* **am′phi·the′a·tre.** [< L < Gk. < *amphi-* around + *theatron* theater]

am·pho·ra (am′fə·rə) *n.* *pl.* **·rae** (-rē) In ancient Greece and Rome, a tall, two-handled earthenware jar for wine or oil, narrow at the neck and the base. [< L < Gk. < *amphi-* on both sides + *phoreus* bearer] **— am′pho·ral** *adj.*

AMPHORAE

am·pho·ter·ic (am′fə·ter′ik) *adj. Chem.* Exhibiting the characteristics of both an acid and a base. [< Gk. *amphoteros* both]

am·ple (am′pəl) *adj.* **1.** Of great dimension, capacity, amount, degree, etc.; large. **2.** More than enough; abundant. **3.** Fully sufficient; adequate. **— Syn.** See PLENTIFUL. [< F < L *amplus* large, abundant] **— am′ple·ness** *n.* **— am·ply** (am′plē) *adv.*

am·pli·fi·ca·tion (am′plə·fi·kā′shən) *n.* **1.** The act of extending or enlarging; also, that which is added. **2.** An extended statement, phrase, etc.

am·pli·fi·er (am′plə·fī′ər) *n.* **1.** One who or that which amplifies or increases. **2.** *Electronics* Any of a class of devices for reinforcing a signal by means of power supplied to the output from a source other than the input.

am·pli·fy (am′plə·fī) *v.* **·fied, ·fy·ing** *v.t.* **1.** To enlarge or increase in scope, significance, or power. **2.** To add to so as to make more complete, as by illustrations. **3.** To exaggerate; magnify. **4.** *Electronics* To increase the strength or amplitude of, as electromagnetic impulses. *— v.i.* **5.** To make additional remarks. [< F < L < *amplus* large + *facere* to make] **— am·pli·fi·ca·tive** (am′plə·fi·kā′tiv, am·plif′i·kə·tiv), am·plif·i·ca·to·ry** (am·plif′i·kə·tôr′ē, -tō′rē) *adj.*

am·pli·tude (am′plə·tōōd, -tyōōd) *n.* **1.** Greatness of extent; largeness; breadth. **2.** Fullness; abundance. **3.** Scope or range, as of mind. **4.** *Physics* **a** The extent of the swing of a vibrating body on each side of the mean position. **b** The peak value attained by a wave or an alternating current during one complete cycle. [< L *amplus* large]

amplitude modulation *Telecom.* That form of radio transmission in which the carrier wave is modulated by varying the amplitude above and below a standard value in accordance with the signals to be transmitted. Compare FREQUENCY MODULATION. Abbr. *AM, am, a.m., A.M.*

am·pule (am′pyōōl) *n. Med.* A sealed glass vial used as a container for one dose of a hypodermic solution. Also **am·poule** (am′pōōl), **am·pul** (am′pul, am′pōōl). [< F < L *ampulla* ampulla (def. 1)]

am·pul·la (am-pul′ə) *n.* *pl.* **·pul·lae** (-pul′ē) **1.** An ancient Roman bottle or vase with slender neck and flattened mouth, used for oil, wine, or perfume. **2.** *Eccl.* **a** A cruet for wine or water at the Eucharist. [< L, dim. of *amphora* jar]

am·pu·tate (am′pyōō·tāt) *v.t. & v.i.* **·tat·ed, ·tat·ing** To cut off (a limb, etc.) by surgical means. [< L < *ambi-* around + *putare* to trim] **— am′pu·ta′tion** *n.* **— am′pu·ta′tor** *n.*

am·pu·tee (am′pyōō·tē′) *n.* One who has had a limb or limbs removed by amputation.

a·muck (ə-muk′) *adv.* In a murderous or frenzied manner: only in the phrase **to run amuck.** Also **amok.** [< Malay *amoq* engaging furiously in battle]

am·u·let (am′yə·lit) *n.* Anything worn about the person as protection against accident, evil, etc.; a charm. [< L *amuletum* charm; ult. origin unknown]

a·muse (ə-myōōz′) *v.t.* **a·mused, a·mus·ing** **1.** To occupy pleasingly. **2.** To cause to laugh or smile. [< MF < *d* at + OF *muser* to stare] **— a·mus′a·ble** *adj.* **— a·mus′er** *n.*

a·muse·ment (ə-myōōz′mənt) *n.* **1.** The state of being amused. **2.** That which diverts or entertains.

amusement park A park having various devices for entertainment, as roller coasters, shooting galleries, etc.

a·mus·ing (ə-myōō′zing) *adj.* **1.** Entertaining, or diverting. **2.** Arousing laughter or mirth. **— a·mus′ing·ly** *adv.*

a·myg·da·la (ə-mig′də·lə) *n.* *pl.* **·lae** (-lē) **1.** *Anat.* Any almond-shaped structure or part; esp., a tonsil. **2.** An almond. [< L < Gk. *amygdalē* almond] **— a·myg′de·late** (-lit, -lāt), **a·myg′da·line** (-lin, -līn) *adj.*

am·yl (am′il) *n. Chem.* The univalent alcohol radical, C₅H₁₁, derived from pentane. [< Gk. *amylon* starch + -YL] **— a·myl′ic** (ə·mil′ik) *adj.*

am·y·la·ceous (am′ə·lā′shəs) *adj.* Of or like starch.

am·y·lase (am′ə·lās) *n. Biochem.* An enzyme, found in plant and animal tissue, that promotes the conversion of starch and glycogen into maltose.

am·y·loid (am′ə·loid) *n.* **1.** A gummy or starchlike substance formed in certain diseased plant and animal tissues. *— adj.* Like or containing starch: also **am′y·loi′dal.**

am·y·lum (am′ə·ləm) *n.* Starch (def. 1). [< L < Gk.]

Am·y·tal (am′ə·tal, -tôl) *n.* Proprietary name for a colorless, crystalline compound, C₁₁H₁₈N₂O₃, used as a sedative. [< AMYL + -AL]

an (an, *unstressed* ən) *indefinite article* or *adj.* Equivalent to the article *a,* but used before words beginning with a vowel, as *an* eagle and sometimes before words beginning with *h* in an unstressed syllable, as *an* hotel. [OE *ān* one]

an-¹ *prefix* Without; not: *anarchy.* Also, before consonants (except *h*) *a-.* [< Gk.]

an-² Var. of ANA-.

an-³ Assimilated var. of AD-.

-an *suffix* Used to form adjectives and nouns denoting connection with a country, person, group, doctrine, etc., as follows: **1.** Originating in; belonging to: *human, sylvan.* **2.** Originating in; living in: *Italian.* **3.** Adhering to; following: *Lutheran.* **4.** *Zool.* Belonging to a class or order: *amphibian.* See -IAN. [< L *-anus*]

ana- *prefix* **1.** Up; upward: *anadromous.* **2.** Back; backward: *anapest.* **3.** Anew: sometimes capable of being rendered *re-,* as *anabaptism,* rebaptism. **4.** Thoroughly: *analysis.* Also, before vowels or *h, an-.* [< Gk. < *ana* up, back]

-ana *suffix* Pertaining to: added to the names of notable persons, places, etc., to indicate a collection of materials, such as writings or anecdotes, about the subject: *Americana.* Also *-iana.* [< L, neut. pl. of *-anus.* See -AN.]

An·a·bap·tist (an′ə·bap′tist) *n.* One of a sect that arose in Switzerland about 1520, who rejected infant baptism and limited church membership to adults baptized after a confession of faith. [< NL < LL < Gk. < *ana-* new + *baptizein* to baptize] **— An′a·bap′tism** *n.*

an·a·bi·o·sis (an′ə·bī·ō′sis) *n.* A return to life; resuscitation. [< NL < ANA- + Gk. *bios* life] **— an·a·bi·ot·ic** (an′-ə·bī·ot′ik) *adj.*

a·nab·o·lism (ə·nab′ə·liz′əm) *n. Biol.* The process by which food is built up into protoplasm: opposed to *catabolism.* [< Gk. *anabolē* a heaping up] **— an·a·bol·ic** (an′ə·bol′ik) *adj.*

a·nach·ro·nism (ə·nak′rə·niz′əm) *n.* **1.** The assigning of an event, person, etc., to a wrong, esp. an earlier, date. **2.** Something out of its proper time. [< F < L < Gk. < *ana-* against + *chronos* time] **— a·nach′ro·nis′tic, a·nach′ro·nis′ti·cal, a·nach′ro·nous** *adj.*

an·a·con·da (an′ə·kon′də) *n.* **1.** A very large, nonvenomous tropical serpent that crushes its prey in its coils. **2.** Any boa constrictor. [? < Singhalese]

a·nad·ro·mous (ə·nad′rə·məs) *adj. Zool.* Of fishes, as the salmon, going from the sea up rivers to spawn. [< Gk. < *ana-* up + *dromos* a running, course]

a·nae·mi·a (ə·nē′mē·ə), **a·nae·mic** (ə·nē′mik), etc. See ANEMIA, etc.

an·aer·obe (an·âr′ōb, an·ā′ə·rōb) *n.* An anaerobic organism. [See ANAEROBIC]

an·aer·o·bic (an′âr·ō′bik, -ob′ik) *adj.* Living or functioning in the absence of free oxygen. [< NL < AN-¹ without + AERO- + Gk. *bios* life] — **an·aer·o′bi·cal·ly** *adv.*

an·aes·the·sia (an′is·thē′zhə, -zhē·ə), **an·aes·thet·ic** (an′·is·thet′ik), etc. See ANESTHESIA, etc.

an·a·gram (an′ə·gram) *n.* **1.** A word or phrase formed by transposing the letters of another word or phrase. **2.** *pl.* (*construed as sing.*) A game in which the players make words by transposing or adding letters. [< MF < LGk < Gk. < *ana*-backwards + *gramma* letter] — **an·a·gram·mat·ic** (an′·ə·grə·mat′ik) or **·i·cal** *adj.* — **an′a·gram·mat′i·cal·ly** *adv.*

an·a·gram·ma·tize (an′ə·gram′ə·tīz) *v.t.* **·tized, ·tiz·ing** To arrange as an anagram.

a·nal (ā′nəl) *adj. Anat.* Of, pertaining to, or situated in the region of the anus. [< L *anus* + -AL¹]

an·a·lects (an′ə·lekts) *n.pl.* Selections or fragments from a literary work or group of works. Also **an·a·lec·ta** (an′ə·lek′·tə) [< L < Gk. < *ana-* up + *legein* to gather]

an·al·ge·si·a (an′al·jē′zē·ə, -sē·ə) *n. Pathol.* Inability to feel pain. Also **an·al·gi·a** (an·al′jē·ə). [< NL < Gk. < *an-* without + *algos* pain]

an·al·ge·sic (an′əl·jē′zik, -sik) *Med. n.* A drug for the alleviation of pain. — *adj.* Promoting analgesia.

analog computer A computer that solves problems by substituting analogous quantities, as voltage, etc., for the variables of the problems. Compare DIGITAL COMPUTER.

a·nal·o·gous (ə·nal′ə·gəs) *adj.* **1.** Resembling or comparable in certain respects. **2.** *Biol.* Having a similar function but differing in origin and structure, as the wings of birds and insects: distinguished from *homologous*. — **a·nal′o·gous·ly** *adv.* — **a·nal′o·gous·ness** *n.*

an·a·logue (an′ə·lôg, -log) *n.* Anything analogous to something else. Also **an′a·log.**

a·nal·o·gy (ə·nal′ə·jē) *n. pl.* **·gies 1.** Agreement or resemblance in certain aspects. **2.** *Biol.* A similarity in function and appearance, but not in origin. **4.** *Logic* Reasoning in which relations or resemblances are inferred from others that are known or observed. Abbr. *anal.* [< L < Gk. < *ana-* according to + *logos* proportion]
— **Syn. 1, 2.** In careful usage, an *analogy* is drawn only between things clearly unlike in kind, form, or appearance, and refers to their similar properties, relations, behavior, etc. A *resemblance* is almost always a likeness in appearance, while *similarity* is usually a likeness in some external or superficial aspect or characteristic.

a·nal·y·sis (ə·nal′ə·sis) *n. pl.* **·ses** (-sēz) **1.** The separation of a whole into its parts or elements: opposed to *synthesis.* **2.** A statement of the results of this; logical synopsis. **3.** A method of determining or describing the nature of a thing by separating it into its parts. **4.** *Chem.* The determination of the kind, quantity, and proportions of constituents forming a compound or substance. **5.** Psychoanalysis. [< Med.L. < Gk. < *ana-* throughout + *lyein* to loosen]

an·a·lyst (an′ə·list) *n.* **1.** One who analyzes or is skilled in analysis. **2.** A psychoanalyst.

an·a·lyt·ic (an′ə·lit′ik) *adj.* **1.** Pertaining to or proceeding by analysis. **2.** Separating into constituent parts or first principles. Also **an′a·lyt′i·cal.** — **an′a·lyt′i·cal·ly** *adv.*

an·a·lyt·ics (an′ə·lit′iks) *n.pl.* (*construed as sing.*) **1.** The science or use of analysis. **2.** The part of logic concerned with analysis.

an·a·lyze (an′ə·līz) *v.t.* **·lyzed, ·lyz·ing 1.** To separate into constituent parts or elements, especially so as to determine the nature, form, etc., of the whole by examination of the parts. **2.** To examine critically or minutely. **3.** To psychoanalyze. Also, *Brit.,* **analyse.** See ANALYSIS. — **an′a·lyz′a·ble** *adj.* — **an′a·ly·za′tion** *n.* — **an′a·lyz′er** *n.*

an·a·pest (an′ə·pest) *n.* **1.** In prosody, a metrical foot consisting of two short or unaccented syllables followed by one long or accented syllable (˘ ˘ ´). **2.** A line of verse made up of such feet: Then the **rāin** | **ănd thĕ trēē** | **wēre ălōne.** Also **an′a·paest.** [< L < Gk. < *ana-* back + *paiein* to strike, so called because it is a reversed dactyl] — **an′a·pes′tic** *adj.*

an·ar·chic (an·är′kik) *adj.* **1.** Pertaining to or like anarchy. **2.** Advocating anarchy. **3.** Inducing anarchy; lawless. Also **an·ar′chi·cal.** — **an·ar′chi·cal·ly** *adv.*

an·ar·chism (an′ər·kiz′əm) *n.* **1.** The theory that all forms of government are incompatible with individual and social liberty and should be abolished. **2.** The methods of anarchists. — **an·ar·chis·tic** (an′ər·kis′tik) *adj.*

an·ar·chist (an′ər·kist) *n.* **1.** One who believes in and advocates anarchism. **2.** One who encourages or furthers anarchy. Also **an·arch** (an′ärk).

an·ar·chy (an′ər·kē) *n.* **1.** Absence of government. **2.** Lawless confusion and political disorder. **3.** General disorder. [< Gk. < *an-* without + *archos* leader]

an·as·tig·mat·ic (an·as′tig·mat′ik) *adj. Optics* Not astigmatic; esp., corrected for astigmatism, as a lens.

a·nas·to·mose (ə·nas′tə·mōz) *v.i.* **·mosed, ·mos·ing** To connect by anastomosis.

a·nas·to·mo·sis (ə·nas′tə·mō′sis) *n. pl.* **·ses** (-sēz) **1.** *Physiol.* A union, interlacing, or running together, as of veins, nerves, or canals of animal bodies. **2.** Any intercommunication, as of two or more rivers. [< NL < Gk. *anastomōsis* opening] — **a·nas′to·mot′ic** (-mot′ik) *adj.*

a·nath·e·ma (ə·nath′ə·mə) *n. pl.* **·mas** or **·ma·ta** (-mə·tə) **1.** A formal ecclesiastical ban or curse, excommunicating a person or damning something, as a book or doctrine. **2.** Any curse or imprecation. **3.** One who or that which is excommunicated or damned. **4.** One who or that which is greatly disliked. [< L < Gk. *anathema* a thing devoted (to evil)]

a·nath·e·ma·tize (ə·nath′ə·mə·tīz′) *v.* **·tized, ·tiz·ing** *v.t.* **1.** To pronounce an anathema against. — *v.i.* **2.** To utter or express anathemas. — **a·nath′e·ma·ti·za′tion** *n.*

an·a·tom·i·cal (an′ə·tom′i·kəl) *adj.* Of or pertaining to anatomy. Also **an·a·tom′ic.** — **an′a·tom′i·cal·ly** *adv.*

a·nat·o·mist (ə·nat′ə·mist) *n.* One skilled in anatomy.

a·nat·o·mize (ə·nat′ə·mīz) *v.t.* **·mized, ·miz·ing 1.** To dissect (an animal or plant) for the purpose of investigating the structure, position, and interrelationships of its parts. **2.** To examine minutely; analyze. **a·nat′o·mi·za′tion** *n.*

a·nat·o·my (ə·nat′ə·mē) *n. pl.* **·mies 1.** The structure of a plant or animal, or of any of its parts. **2.** The science of the structure of plants or animals. **3.** The art or practice of anatomizing. [< F < L < Gk. < *ana-* up + *temnein* to cut]

-ance *suffix of nouns* Used to form nouns of action, quality, state, or condition from adjectives in *-ant*, and also directly from verbs, as in *abundance, forbearance.* Compare -ANCY. [< F *-ance* < L *-antia, -entia*, a suffix used to form nouns]

an·ces·tor (an′ses·tər) *n.* **1.** One from whom a person is descended; progenitor; forbear. **2.** *Biol.* An organism from which later organisms have been derived. [< OF < L < *ante-* before + *cedere* to go] — **an·ces·tress** (an′ses·tris) *n.fem.*

an·ces·tral (an·ses′trəl) *adj.* Of, pertaining to, or descending from an ancestor. Also **an·ces·to·ri·al** (an′ses·tôr′ē·əl, -tō′rē-). — **an·ces′tral·ly** *adv.*

an·ces·try (an′ses·trē) *n. pl.* **·tries 1.** A line or body of ancestors; ancestors collectively. **2.** Ancestral lineage.

an·chor (ang′kər) *n.* **1.** A heavy implement, usu. of iron or steel, with hooks or flukes to grip the bottom, attached to a cable and dropped from a ship or boat to hold it in place. **2.** Any object used for a similar purpose. **3.** Anything that makes stable or secure. — **at anchor** Anchored, as a ship. — **to drop** (or **cast**) **anchor** To put down the anchor in order to hold fast a vessel. — **to ride at anchor** To be anchored, as a ship. — **to weigh anchor** To take up the anchor so as to sail away. — *v.t.* **1.** To secure or make secure by an anchor. **2.** To fix firmly. — *v.i.* **3.** To lie at anchor, as a ship. [OE < L < Gk. *ankyra*]

an·chor·age (ang′kər·ij) *n.* **1.** A place for anchoring. **2.** A coming to or lying at anchor. **3.** A source or place of stability or security. **4.** A fee charged for anchoring.

an·cho·rite (ang′kə·rit) *n.* One who has withdrawn from the world for religious reasons; hermit. Also **an′cho·ret** (-rit, -ret). [< L < Gk. < *ana-* back + *chōreein* to withdraw] — **an′cho·rit′ic** (-rit′ik) *adj.*

an·cho·vy (an′chō·vē, -chə·vē, an·chō′vē) *n. pl.* **·vies** or **·vy 1.** A very small, herringlike fish inhabiting warm seas, valued as a delicacy. **2.** *U.S.* Smelt. [< Sp., Pg. *anchova*]

an·chy·lose (ang′kə·lōs), **an·chy·lo·sis** (ang′kə·lō′sis) See ANKYLOSE, etc.

an·cien ré·gime (äṅ·syaṅ′rā·zhēm′) *French* A former political and social system; esp., the system in France before the revolution of 1789. Also **Ancient Regime.**

an·cient (ān′shənt) *adj.* **1.** Existing or occurring in times long past, esp. before the fall of the Western RomanEmpire, in A.D. 476. **2.** Having existed from remote antiquity; of great age. **3.** Very old: said of persons. Abbr. *anc.* — *n.* **1.** One who lived in ancient times. **2.** An aged or venerable person. — **the ancients 1.** The ancient Greeks, Romans, Hebrews, or other civilized nations of antiquity. **2.** The ancient authors of Greece and Rome. [< OF < LL < L *ante* before] — **an′cient·ness** *n.* — **an′cient·ly** *adv.*

an·cil·lar·y (an′sə·ler′ē) *adj.* Subordinate; auxiliary. [< L *ancilla* maid]

an·con (ang′kon) *n. pl.* **an·co·nes** (ang·kō′nēz) **1.** *Anat.* The point of the elbow. **2.** *Archit.* An elbow-shaped projection, as for an ornament on a keystone. Also **an·cone** (ang′·kōn). [< L < Gk. *ankōn* a bend, the elbow] — **an·co·nal** (ang′kə·nəl), **an·co·ne·al** (ang·kō′nē·əl) *adj.*

-ancy *suffix of nouns* A modern variant of -ANCE: used to form new words expressing quality, state, or condition (*infancy, vacancy*), or to refashion older nouns of quality in *-ance* (*constancy*). [< L *-antia*]

an·cy·los·to·mi·a·sis (an′sə·lōs′tə·mī′ə·sis) *n.* A progressive anemia caused by nematode worms that suck the blood from the small intestine. Also called *hookworm disease.* [< NL < Gk. *ankylos* crooked + *stoma* mouth + -IASIS]

---

and (and, *unstressed* ənd, ən, 'n) *conj.* **1.** Also; added to; as well as: a particle denoting addition, emphasis, or union, used as a connective between words, phrases, clauses, and sentences: shoes *and* ships *and* sealing wax. **2.** As a result or consequence: Make one move *and* you are dead! **3.** To: with *come, go, try,* etc.: Try *and* stop me. [OE *ond, and*]

an·dan·te (an·dan′tē, än·dän′tā) *Music adj. & adv.* Moderately slow; slower than allegretto but faster than larghetto. — *n.* An andante movement or passage. [< Ital., walking]

an·dan·ti·no (an′dan·tē′nō, än′dän-) *Music adj. & adv.* Slightly quicker than andante; originally, slower than andante. — *n.* An andantino movement or passage. [< Ital., dim. of *andante*]

An·de·an (an·dē′ən, an′dē·ən) *adj.* Of the Andes.

and·i·ron (and′ī′ərn) *n.* One of two metal supports for holding wood in an open fireplace: also called *firedog.* [< OF *andier*; infl. by *iron*]

and/or Either *and* or *or,* according to the meaning intended.

andro- *combining form* **1.** Man in general. **2.** The male sex. **3.** *Bot.* Stamen; anther. [< Gk. *anēr, andros* man]

an·droe·ci·um (an·drē′shē·əm, -sē·əm) *n. pl.* **·ci·a** (-shē·ə, -sē·ə) *Bot.* The stamens of a flower collectively. [< NL < ANDRO- + Gk. *oikos* house] — **an·droe′cial** (-shəl) *adj.*

an·dro·gen (an′drə·jən) *n. Biochem.* Any of various hormones that control the development of masculine characteristics. — **an·dro·gen·ic** (an′drə·jen′ik) *adj.*

an·drog·y·nous (an·droj′ə·nəs) *adj.* **1.** Uniting the characteristics of both sexes; hermaphroditic. **2.** *Bot.* Having the male and female flowers in the same cluster. Also **an·drog′y·nal** (an·droj′ə·nəl), **an·dro·gyn·ic** (an′drə·jin′ik). [< Gk. < *anēr,* man + *gynē* woman] — **an·drog′y·ny** *n.*

An·drom·a·che (an′drəm′ə·kē) In Greek legend, the wife of Hector, taken captive to Greece after the fall of Troy.

An·drom·e·da (an·drom′ə·də) In Greek mythology, a princess rescued from a sea monster by Perseus, who then married her. — *n.* A constellation containing the bright star Alpheratz.

an·dros·ter·one (an·dros′tə·rōn) *n. Biochem.* A male sex hormone, $C_{19}H_{30}O_2$.

-androus *suffix* **1.** *Bot.* Having a (specified) number or kind of stamens. **2.** Having a (given) number of husbands. [< Gk. *anēr, andros* man]

-ane¹ *suffix* Used primarily to differentiate words that have a corresponding form in -AN, as *human, humane.* [< L *-anus*]

-ane² *suffix Chem.* Denoting a hydrocarbon compound of the methane series: *pentane.* [An arbitrary formation]

an·ec·do·tal (an′ik·dōt′l) *adj.* Pertaining to, characterized by, or consisting of anecdotes.

an·ec·dote (an′ik·dōt) *n.* A brief account of an interesting or entertaining nature. [< Med.L < Gk. < *an-* not + *ekdotos* published < *ekdidonai* to give out, publish]

an·ec·dot·ic (an′ik·dot′ik) *adj.* **1.** Anecdotal. **2.** Habitually telling or given to anecdotes. Also **an′ec·dot′i·cal.**

an·ec·dot·ist (an′ik·dō′tist) *n.* One who collects, publishes, or is given to telling anecdotes.

a·ne·mi·a (ə·nē′mē·ə) *n. Pathol.* A deficiency in hemoglobin or the number of red corpuscles in the bood, characterized by pallor, loss of energy, etc. [< NL < Gk. < *an-* without + *haima* blood] — **a·ne′mic** *adj.*

a·nem·o·graph (ə·nem′ə·graf, -gräf) *n. Meteorol.* An instrument that makes a record of the velocity and direction of the wind. — **a·nem′o·graph′ic** *adj.*

an·e·mom·e·ter (an′ə·mom′ə·tər) *n. Meteorol.* An instrument for measuring the velocity of the wind. — **an·e·mo·met·ric** (an′ə·mō·met′rik) or **·ri·cal** *adj.*

an·e·mom·e·try (an′ə·mom′ə·trē) *n. Meteorol.* The technique of determining the velocity of the wind.

a·nem·o·ne (ə·nem′ə·nē) *n.* **1.** A plant having flowers with no petals but showy, multicolored sepals: also called *windflower.* **2.** *Zool.* The sea anemone. [< Gk. *anemos* wind]

ANEMOMETER

an·er·oid (an′ə·roid) *adj.* Not using liquid. — *n.* An aneroid barometer. [< F < Gk. *a-* not + *nēros* wet + -OID]

aneroid barometer An instrument for measuring atmospheric pressure through its effect upon the flexible top of a partially evacuated chamber.

an·es·the·sia (an′is·thē′zhə, -zhē·ə) *n.* Partial or total loss of physical sensation, particularly of pain, due to disease or certain drugs. Also **an·es·the·sis** (an′is·thē′sis). [< NL < Gk. < *an-* without + *aisthēsis* sensation]

an·es·thet·ic (an′is·thet′ik) *n.* A drug, gas, etc., that causes anesthesia. — *adj.* **1.** Pertaining to or like anesthesia. **2.** Producing anesthesia. Also spelled *anaesthetic.*

an·es·the·tist (ə·nes′thə·tist) *n.* A person trained to administer anesthetics: also spelled *anaesthetist.*

an·es·the·tize (ə·nes′thə·tīz) *v.t.* **·tized, ·tiz·ing** To render insensible, esp. to pain, by means of an anesthetic: also spelled *anaesthetize.* — **an·es′the·ti·za·tion** *n.*

an·eu·rysm (an′yə·riz′əm) *n. Pathol.* A dilatation of the wall of an artery, forming a sac. Also **an′eu·rism.** [< Gk. < *ana-* up + *eurys* wide] — **an·eu·rys·mal** (an′yə·riz′məl) or **·ris′mal** *adj.*

a·new (ə·nōō′, ə·nyōō′) *adv.* **1.** Again. **2.** Over again in a different way. [OE *of niwe*]

an·ga·ry (ang′gə·rē) *n.* In international law, the right of a belligerent, in case of need, to seize, use, or destroy neutral property, esp. ships, subject to claim for full compensation. [< F < LL < Gk. *angaros* courier]

an·gel (ān′jəl) *n.* **1.** *Theol.* **a** A spiritual being attendant upon the Deity; a heavenly messenger. **b** A fallen spiritual being, also immortal. **2.** A conventional representation of an angel, usually a youthful winged human figure in white robes and with a halo. **3.** A person of real or fancied angelic qualities, as of character or beauty. **4.** *Informal* The financial backer of a play, etc. **5.** A former English gold coin. [OE < L < Gk. *angelos* messenger]

an·gel·fish (ān′jəl·fish′) *n. pl.* **·fish** or **·fish·es** **1.** A raylike shark having very large, winglike pectoral fins. **2.** A fish of warm seas having brilliant coloration, as the porgy.

angel food cake A delicate, spongy cake made without shortening or egg yolks. Also **angel cake.**

an·gel·ic (an·jel′ik) *adj.* **1.** Pertaining to, of, or consisting of angels; celestial. **2.** Like an angel; pure; beautiful. Also **an·gel′i·cal.** — **an·gel′i·cal·ly** *adv.*

an·gel·i·ca (an·jel′i·kə) *n.* **1.** A fragrant plant of the parsley family. **2.** The stalks of one species of this plant, often candied and used as a flavoring and an aromatic. [< Med.L (*herba*) *angelica* the angelic (herb)]

an·ge·lus (an′jə·ləs) *n. Eccl.* **1.** A devotional prayer used to commemorate the Annunciation. **2.** A bell rung at morning, noon, and night as a call to recite this prayer: also called **angelus bell.** Also **An′ge·lus.** [< L]

an·ger (ang′gər) *n.* A feeling of sudden and strong displeasure and antagonism directed against the cause of an assumed wrong or injury; wrath; ire. — *v.t.* To make angry; enrage. [< ON *angr* grief]

An·ge·vin (an′jə·vin) *adj.* **1.** Of or from Anjou. **2.** Of or pertaining to the Plantagenet kings of England. — *n.* **1.** A native or inhabitant of Anjou. **2.** A member of the royal house of Anjou. Also **An′ge·vine** (-vin, -vīn). [< F]

an·gi·na (an·jī′nə, an′jə·nə) *n. Pathol.* **1.** Any disease characterized by spasmodic suffocation, as croup. **2.** Angina pectoris. [< L, quinsy < *angere* to choke]

angina pec·to·ris (pek′tə·ris) *Pathol.* A defect of coronary circulation, characterized by paroxysmal pain below the sternum. [< NL, angina of the chest]

angio- *combining form* **1.** *Bot.* Seed vessel. **2.** *Med.* Blood vessel; lymph vessel. Also, before vowels, **angi-.** [< Gk. *angeion* case, vessel, capsule]

an·gi·o·ma (an′jē·ō′mə) *n. pl.* **·mas** or **·ma·ta** (-mə·tə) *Pathol.* A tumor consisting of dilated blood or lymph vessels. — **an·gi·om·a·tous** (an′jē·om′ə·təs) *adj.*

an·gi·o·sperm (an′jē·ə·spûrm′) *n.* Any of a class of plants having the seeds in a closed seed vessel. — **an′gi·o·sper′mal, an′gi·o·sper′ma·tous** (-spûr′mə·təs), **an′gi·o·sper′mous** *adj.*

an·gle¹ (ang′gəl) *v.i.* **gled, ·gling** **1.** To fish with a hook and line. **2.** To try to get something slyly or artfully: with *for.* [< OE *angel* fishhook]

an·gle² (ang′gəl) *n.* **1.** *Geom.* **a** The figure formed by the divergence of two straight lines from a common point or of two or more planes from a common straight line. **b** The space between these lines or surfaces. **c** The amount of divergence of these lines or surfaces, measured in degrees. **2.** A projecting corner, as of a building. **3.** The point of view or aspect from which something is regarded. **4.** *U.S. Slang* Special selfish motive or interest. — *v.* **an·gled, an·gling** *v.t.* **1.** To move or turn at an angle or by angles. **2.** *Informal* To impart a particular bias or interpretation to, as a story or report. — *v.i.* **3.** To proceed or turn itself at an angle or by angles. [< F < L *angulus* a corner, angle]

ANGLES
1. Acute: *aeb, bec*; Right: *aec, ced*;
Obtuse: *bed.* 2. Dihedral.

An·gle (ang′gel) *n.* A member of a Germanic tribe that migrated to Britain in the fifth century. [< L *Anglus,* sing. of *Angli* < Gmc.] — **An′gli·an** *adj. & n.*

angle iron A piece of iron in the form of an angle, for joining or strengthening beams, girders, etc.

angle of incidence *Physics* The angle relative to the perpendicular drawn from the point of impact at which an object, beam of light, etc., strikes a surface.

an·gler (ang′glər) *n.* **1.** One who fishes with rod, hook, and line. **2.** A fish having antennalike filaments on its head.

an·gle·worm (ang′gəl·wûrm′) *n.* An earthworm, commonly used as bait on fishhooks.

An·gli·can (ang′glə·kən) *adj.* Pertaining to or characteristic of the Church of England, or of the churches that agree with it in faith and order. — *n.* **1.** A member of an Anglican Church. [< Med.L *Anglicanus* < L *Angli* the Angles]

Anglican Church 1. The Church of England. **2.** A body of churches, including the Protestant Episcopal Church, mostly derived from the Church of England and in communion with it. — **An·gli·can·ism** (ang′glə·kən·iz′əm) *n.*

An·gli·cism (ang′glə·siz′əm) *n.* **1.** An idiom or turn of phrase peculiar to the English language. **2.** A Briticism. **3.** The state or quality of being English.

An·gli·cize (ang′glə·sīz) *v.* **·cized, ·ciz·ing** *v.t.* **1.** To give an English form, style, or idiom to. — *v.i.* **2.** To acquire some English trait or peculiarity; become like the English. Also *Brit.* **An′gli·cise.** — **An′gli·ci·za′tion** *n.*

An·gli·fy (ang′glə·fī) *v.t. & v.i.* **·fied, ·fy·ing** To Anglicize.

an·gling (ang′gling) *n.* The act or art of fishing with a hook, line, and rod.

Anglo- *combining form* English; English and: *Anglophile, Anglo-Norman.*

An·glo·ma·ni·a (ang′glō·mā′nē·ə) *n.* Overfondness for or imitation of English manners, speech, institutions, etc.

An·glo-Nor·man (ang′glō·nôr′mən) *adj.* Pertaining to the Normans who settled in England after the Norman Conquest, their descendants, or their language. — *n.* **1.** One of the Norman settlers in England after the Norman Conquest. **2.** The dialect of Old French of these settlers.

An·glo·phile (ang′glə·fīl, -fil) *n.* A lover of England or its people, customs, institutions, or manners. — *adj.* Of or like Anglophiles. Also **An′glo·phil** (fil).

An·glo·pho·bi·a (ang′glə·fō′bē·ə) *n.* Hatred or dread of England, its customs, people, or institutions. — **An′glo·phobe** *n. & adj.* — **An′glo·pho′bic** (-fō′bik, -fob′ik) *adj.*

An·glo-Sax·on (ang′glō·sak′sən) *n.* **1.** A member of one of the Germanic tribes (Angles, Saxons, and Jutes) that dominated England until the Norman Conquest. **2.** Their West Germanic language; Old English. **3.** A person of English nationality or descent. — *adj.* Of or pertaining to the Anglo-Saxons, their language or descendants.

An·go·ra (ang·gôr′ə, -gō′rə) *n.* **1.** A goat, originally from Ankara, having long, silky hair. **2.** A shawl, cloth, etc., made of Angora wool or its imitations. **3.** An Angora cat. **Angora cat** A variety of cat with long, silky hair.

an·gos·tu·ra bark (ang′gəs·tŏŏr′ə, -tyŏŏr′ə) A bark from a South American tree, used in the preparation of a tonic and flavoring. Also **an′gos·tu′ra.** [after *Angostura*, former name of Ciudad Bolívar, Venezuela]

an·gry (ang′grē) *adj.* **ang·ri·er, an·gri·est 1.** Feeling, showing, or excited by anger; indignant. **2.** Showing signs of anger; wrathful. **3.** Seeming to be in anger. **4.** Badly inflamed. — **an·gri·ly** (ang′grə·lē) *adv.* — **an′gri·ness** *n.*

ang·strom (ang′strəm) *n.* A linear unit equal to 10^{-8} centimeter or 3.937×10^{-9} inch, used for minute measurements, as of wavelengths of light. Also **angstrom unit.** [after A. J. *Ångström*, 1814–75, Swedish physicist]

an·guish (ang′gwish) *n.* Excruciating mental or bodily pain; agony; torture. — *v.t. & v.i.* To affect or suffer with anguish. [< OF *anguisse* < L *angustia* tightness, difficulty]

an·gu·lar (ang′gyə·lər) *adj.* **1.** Having, forming, or constituting an angle or angles; sharp-cornered. **2.** Measured by an angle. **3.** Pertaining to angles. **4.** Bony; gaunt. **5.** Awkward or ungraceful. [< L < *angulus* corner, angle] — **an′gu·lar·ly** *adv.*

an·gu·lar·i·ty (ang′gyə·lar′ə·tē) *n. pl.* **·ties 1.** The state of being angular: also **an′gu·lar·ness. 2.** *pl.* Angular outlines or parts.

an·hy·dride (an·hī′drīd, -drid) *n. Chem.* **1.** Any organic or inorganic compound that has been dehydrated. **2.** A compound formed from another compound, especially an acid or base, by the removal of one or more molecules of water, the process being generally reversible. [See ANHYDROUS]

an·hy·drous (an·hī′drəs) *adj. Chem.* Pertaining to or designating a compound that has no water of crystallization in its composition. [< Gk. < *an-* without + *hydōr* water]

an·il (an′il) *n.* **1.** A West Indian indigo plant. **2.** The indigo dye made from this plant. [< F < Pg. < Arabic *al-nīl* the blue < Skt.]

an·i·line (an′ə·lin, -līn) *n. Chem.* A colorless oily, poisonous compound, $C_6H_5NH_2$, the base of many coal-tar dyes, chiefly made from nitrobenzene. Also called *phenylamine.* — *adj.* Made of, derived from, or pertaining to aniline. Also **an·i·lin** (an′ə·lin). [< ANIL + -INE²]

an·i·ma (an′ə·mə) *n.* The vital principle; soul. [< L]

an·i·mad·ver·sion (an′ə·mad·vûr′zhən, -shən) *n.* A censorious comment or reflection: with *on* or *upon.*

an·i·mad·vert (an′ə·mad·vûrt′) *v.i.* To comment critically, usu. in an adverse sense: with *on* or *upon.* [< L < *animus* mind + *advertere* to turn to]

an·i·mal (an′ə·məl) *n.* **1.** A sentient living organism typically capable of voluntary motion and sensation: distinguished from *plant.* **2.** Any such creature as distinguished from man. **3.** A bestial human being. — *adj.* **1.** Of, characteristic of, derived from, or resembling animals. **2.** Carnal; sensual: *animal appetites.* [< L, < *anima* breath, soul, life]

an·i·mal·cule (an′ə·mal′kyōōl) *n.* An animal of microscopic smallness, as an ameba. Also **an′i′mal′cu·lum** (-kyə·ləm). [< L *animalculum,* dim. of *animal* animal] — **an′i·mal′cu·lar** (-kyə·lər) *adj.*

animal husbandry The branch of agriculture specializing in the breeding, raising, and care of farm animals.

an·i·mal·ism (an′ə·məl·iz′əm) *n.* **1.** The state or condition of a mere animal. **2.** Animal activity. **3.** The doctrine that man is entirely animal, having no soul. — **an′i·mal·ist** *n.* — **an′i·mal·is′tic** *adj.*

an·i·mal·i·ty (an′ə·mal′ə·tē) *n.* **1.** The nature or qualities of an animal. **2.** Animal life; the animal kingdom.

an·i·mal·ize (an′ə·məl·īz′) *v.t.* **ized, ·iz·ing** To render brutal; sensualize. — **an·i·mal·i·za·tion** (an′ə·mel·ə·zā′shən, -ī·zā′-) *n.*

animal kingdom Animal organisms collectively, as distinguished from plants.

an·i·mal·ly (an′ə·məl·ē) *adv.* Physically, as distinguished from spiritually or mentally.

animal magnetism Mesmerism.

an·i·mate (*v.* an′ə·māt; *adj.* an′ə·mit) *v.t.* **·mat·ed, ·mat·ing 1.** To impart life to; make alive. **2.** To move to action; incite; inspire. **3.** To produce activity or energy in. — *adj.* **1.** Possessing animal life; living. **2.** Full of life; vivacious; lively: also **an′i·mat′ed** (-mā′tid). [< L *anima* breath, soul] — **an′i·mat′ed·ly** *adv.* — **an′i·ma′tor, an′i·ma′ter** *n.*

animated cartoon See CARTOON.

an·i·ma·tion (an′ə·mā′shən) *n.* **1.** The act of imparting life, or the state of possessing life. **2.** The quality of being lively or quick; vivacity. **3.** The process and technique of preparing animated cartoons.

a·ni·ma·to (ä′nē·mä′tō) *adj. & adv. Music* With animation. [< Ital.]

an·i·mism (an′ə·miz′əm) *n.* **1.** The belief in the existence of spirit or soul, as distinct from matter. **2.** The doctrine that natural objects and phenomena possess a soul. [< L *anima* soul] — **an′i·mist** *n.* — **an′i·mis′tic** *adj.*

an·i·mos·i·ty (an′ə·mos′ə·tē) *n. pl.* **·ties** Active and vehement enmity; hatred. [< L *animositas, -talis* high spirit]

an·i·mus (an′ə·məs) *n.* **1.** Hostile feeling; animosity. **2.** The animating thought or purpose; intention. [< L]

an·i·on (an′ī′ən) *n. Chem.* A negative ion: opposed to *cation.* [< Gk. *anienai* to go up] — **an′i·on′ic** (-on′ik) *adj.*

an·ise (an′is) *n.* **1.** A small South European and North African plant that furnishes aniseed. **2.** Aniseed. [< OF < L < Gk. *anison*]

an·i·seed (an′i·sēd′) *n.* The fragrant seed of the anise plant.

an·i·sette (an′ə·zet′, -set′) *n.* A cordial made from or flavored with aniseed. [< F,

an·kle (ang′kəl) *n.* **1.** The joint connecting the foot and the leg. **2.** The part of the leg between the foot and the calf near the ankle joint. [ME *ankel* < OE *anclēow*]

an·kle·bone (ang′kəl·bōn′) *n.* The talus. Also **ankle bone.**

an·klet (ang′klit) *n.* **1.** An ornament or fetter for the ankle. **2.** A short sock reaching just above the ankle.

ankylo- *combining form* Bent; crooked: in anatomy, referring to adhesion of bones. [< Gk. *ankylos* crooked]

an·ky·lose (ang′kə·lōs) *v.t. & v.i.* **losed, ·los·ing** To unite or join by ankylosis: also spelled *anchylose.*

an·ky·lo·sis (ang′kə·lō′sis) *n.* **1.** *Anat.* The fusing of bones or parts of bones. **2.** *Pathol.* The abnormal adhesion of bones, especially those forming a joint; stiffening of a joint. Also spelled *anchylosis.* [< NL < Gk. *ankylōsis* < *ankyloein* to bend < *ankylos* crooked] — **an′ky·lot′ic** (-lo t′ik) *adj.*

an·nal·ist (an′əl·ist) *n.* A writer of annals; a historian. — **an′nal·is′tic** *adj.*

an·nals (an′əlz) *n.pl.* **1.** A record of events in their chronological order, year by year. **2.** History or records. **3.** A periodical publication of discoveries, transactions, etc. [< L *annus* year]

An·na·mese (an′ə·mēz′, -mēs′) *n. pl.* **An·na·mese 1.** A native or inhabitant of Annam. **2.** Formerly, the Vietnamese language. — *adj.* Of Annam or the Annamese.

Anne, Saint Traditionally, the mother of the Virgin Mary.

an·neal (ə·nēl′) *v.t.* **1.** To reduce the brittleness of, as glass and various metals, by heating and then slowly cooling. **2.** To toughen, as the will. [OE *onælan* to burn]

an·ne·lid (an′ə·lid) *Zool. adj.* Belonging to a phylum of segmented worms, including the earthworm and leeches. — *n.* An annelid worm. [< NL < F < L *annellus* a ring]

---

an·nex (*v.* ə·neks′; *n.* an′eks) *v.t.* **1.** To add or append, as an additional or minor part, to existing possessions; affix. **2.** To attach, as an attribute, condition, or consequence. — **Syn.** See ADD. — *n.* **1.** An addition to a building. **2.** An addition to a document; addendum. [< F < L < *ad-* to + *nectere* to tie] — **an·nex′a·ble** *adj.*

an·nex·a·tion (an′ek·sā′shən) *n.* **1.** The act of annexing. **2.** That which is added or attached. Also **an·nex′ment**.

an·ni·hi·late (ə·nī′ə·lāt) *v.t.* **·lat·ed**, **·lat·ing** To destroy utterly. [< L *ad-* to + *nihil* nothing] — **an·ni′hi·la·ble** *adj.* — **an·ni′hi·la′tive** *adj.* — **an·ni·hi·la·tion** (ə·nī′ə·lā′shən) *n.* — **an·ni′hi·la′tor** *n.*

an·ni·ver·sa·ry (an′ə·vûr′sər·ē) *n. pl.* **·ries 1.** A day in the year on the date of which an event occurred in some preceding year. **2.** A celebration on such occasion. — *adj.* **1.** Recurring annually or at the same date every year. **2.** Pertaining to or occurring on an anniversary. [< L *annus* year + *versus*, pp. of *vertere* to turn]

an·no Dom·i·ni (an′ō dom′ə·nī) *Latin* In the year of our Lord or of the Christian era. Abbr. *A.D.*

an·no·tate (an′ō·tāt) *v.t. & v.i.* **·tat·ed**, **·tat·ing** To provide (a text, etc.) with explanatory or critical notes. [< L < *ad-* to + *notare* to note, mark] — **an′no·ta′tion** *n.* — **an′no·ta′tive** *adj.* — **an′no·ta′tor** *n.*

an·nounce (ə·nouns′) *v.t.* **·nounced**, **·nounc·ing 1.** To make known publicly or officially; proclaim. **2.** To give notice of the approach or appearance of: to *announce* guests. **3.** To make known to the senses. **4.** To serve as the announcer for, as a radio program. [< OF < L < *ad-* to + *nuntiare* to report] — **an·nounce′ment** *n.*

an·nounc·er (ə·noun′sər) *n.* **1.** One who announces. **2.** A person who identifies the station from which a radio or television program is broadcast, introduces the performers, etc.

an·noy (ə·noi′) *v.t.* **1.** To be troublesome to; bother; irritate. **2.** To do harm to or injure. [< OF *anuier*, *anoier*, ult. < L *in odio* in hatred] — **an·noy′er** *n.*

an·noy·ance (ə·noi′əns) *n.* **1.** One who or that which annoys. **2.** The act of annoying or of being annoyed.

an·noy·ing (ə·noi′ing) *adj.* Vexatious; troublesome. — **an·noy′ing·ly** *adv.* — **an·noy′ing·ness** *n.*

an·nu·al (an′yōō·əl) *adj.* **1.** Returning, performed, or occurring every year. **2.** Reckoned by the year. — *n.* **1.** A book or pamphlet issued once a year. **2.** *Bot.* A plant living for a single year or season. Abbr. *ann.* [< L *annualis* yearly] — **an′nu·al·ly** *adv.*

an·nu·i·tant (ə·nōō′ə·tənt, ə·nyōō′-) *n.* One receiving, or entitled to receive, an annuity.

an·nu·i·ty (ə·nōō′ə·tē, ə·nyōō′-) *n. pl.* **·ties 1.** An income paid yearly. **2.** The right to receive such an allowance, or the duty of paying it. **3.** Interest from an investment in yearly payments. [< OF < Med.L *annuitas*, *-tatis*]

an·nul (ə·nul′) *v.t.* **·nulled**, **·nul·ling** To put an end to; nullify, esp. a marriage. [< OF < LL < L *ad-* to + *nullus* none] — **an·nul′ment** *n.* — **an·nul′la·ble** *adj.*

— **Syn. 1.** *Annul* and *nullify* are general terms; *nullify* may also be used in an extralegal sense. A marriage is *annulled*; a law may be *nullified* by a new law, or by the effects of popular defiance. *Cancel*, *abate*, *void*, *vacate*, *quash*, *abrogate*, *repeal*, *rescind*, and *revoke* differ chiefly in technical usage. Typically, we *cancel* a lease, *abate* or *void* a writ, *vacate* an injunction, *quash* an indictment, *abrogate* a treaty, *repeal* a law, *rescind* a ruling, and *revoke* a will.

an·nu·lar (an′yə·lər) *adj.* Formed like a ring; ring-shaped. [< L *annularis* < *annulus*, *anulus* ring] — **an′nu·lar·ly** *adv.*

annular eclipse *Astron.* A solar eclipse in which a narrow ring of the sun is visible beyond the dark mass of the moon.

an·nu·late (an′yə·lit, -lāt) *adj.* Furnished with rings; ringed. [< L *annulatus* < *annulus* a ring] — **an′nu·la′tion** *n.*

an·nu·lus (an′yə·ləs) *n. pl.* **·li** (-lī) or **·lus·es** A ringlike part, body, or space. [< L, a ring]

an·nun·ci·ate (ə·nun′shē·āt, -sē-) *v.t.* **·at·ed**, **·at·ing** To announce. [< L *annuntiare* to report]

an·nun·ci·a·tion (ə·nun′sē·ā′shən, -shē-) *n.* The act of announcing, or that which is announced; proclamation.

An·nun·ci·a·tion (ə·nun′sē·ā′shən, -shē-) *n. Eccl.* **1.** The announcement of the Incarnation to the Virgin Mary by an angel. *Luke* i 28–38. **2.** The festival (March 25) commemorating this event.

an·nun·ci·a·tor (ə·nun′shē·ā′tər, -sē-) *n.* **1.** An announcer. **2.** An electrical indicator used in hotels, etc., that shows a number or name when a bell is rung.

an·ode (an′ōd) *n. Electr.* **1.** The positive electrode toward which anions migrate in an electrolytic cell. **2.** The plate of an electron tube toward which electrons are attracted. [< Gk. *anodos* a way up] — **an·od·ic** (an·od′ik) *adj.*

an·o·dyne (an′ə·dīn) *adj.* Having power to allay pain; soothing. — *n. Med.* Anything that relieves pain or soothes. [< L < Gk. < *an-* without + *odynē* pain]

a·noint (ə·noint′) *v.t.* **1.** To smear with oil or ointment. **2.** To put oil on in a religious ceremony. [< OF < L < *in-* on + *ungere* to smear] — **a·noint′er** *n.* — **a·noint′ment** *n.*

a·nom·a·lous (ə·nom′ə·ləs) *adj.* Deviating from the common rule; exceptional; abnormal. [< L < Gk. < *an-* not + *homalos* even] — **a·nom′a·lous·ly** *adv.* — **a·nom′a·lous·ness** *n.*

a·nom·a·ly (ə·nom′ə·lē) *n. pl.* **·lies 1.** Deviation from rule, type, or form; irregularity. **2.** Anything anomalous. — **a·nom′a·lism** *n.* — **a·nom·a·lis·tic** (ə·nom′ə·lis′tik) or **·ti·cal** *adj.*

a·non (ə·non′) *adv.* **1.** In a little while; soon. **2.** At another time; again. [OE *on ān* in one]

an·o·nym (an′ə·nim) *n.* **1.** An anonymous person or writer. **2.** A pseudonym.

a·non·y·mous (ə·non′ə·məs) *adj.* **1.** Having or bearing no name. **2.** Of unknown authorship or agency. [< Gk. < *an-* without + *onoma* name] — **an·o·nym·i·ty** (an′ə·nim′ə·tē), **a·non′y·mous·ness** *n.* — **a·non′y·mous·ly** *adv.*

a·noph·e·les (ə·nof′ə·lēz) *n.* A mosquito carrying the malaria parasite. [< NL < Gk. *anōphelēs* harmful] — **a·noph·e·line** (ə·nof′ə·līn, -lin) *adj.*

an·o·rex·i·a (an′ə·rek′sē·ə) *n. Med.* Loss of appetite. Also **an′o·rex′y.** [< NL < Gk. < *an-* without + *orexis* appetite] — **an·o·rec·tic** (an′ə·rek′tik), **an/o·rec′tous** *adj.*

an·oth·er (ə·nuth′ər) *adj.* **1.** An additional; one more. **2.** Not the same; different: *another* man. — *pron.* **1.** An additional one; one more. **2.** A different one. **3.** A similar or identical one. [< *an other*]

an·ox·i·a (an·ok′sē·ə) *n. Pathol.* An insufficient oxygen supply to the body tissues.

An·schluss (än′shlŏŏs) *n. German* Political union.

an·swer (an′sər, än′-) *v.i.* **1.** To reply or respond, as by words or actions. **2.** To be responsible or accountable: with *for*. **3.** To serve the purpose. **4.** To correspond or match, as in appearance: with *to*. — *v.t.* **5.** To speak, write, or act in response or reply to. **6.** To be sufficient for; fulfill. **7.** To pay for: to *answer* damages. **8.** To conform or correspond to; match. **9.** *Law* To reply favorably to, as a petition or petitioner. — **to answer back** To talk back, as in contradiction. — *n.* **1.** A reply. **2.** Any action in return or in kind; retaliation. **3.** The result of a calculation or solution. **4.** *Law* The defense of a defendant. **5.** *Music* The restatement of a musical theme or phrase. [OE *andswarian*] — **an′swer·er** *n.*

an·swer·a·ble (an′sər·ə·bəl, än′-) *adj.* **1.** Accountable; responsible. **2.** That may be answered. — **an·swer·a·ble·ness** *n.* — **an′swer·a·bly** *adv.*

ant (ant) *n.* A small insect, usu. wingless, and living in colonies. [OE *æmete*]

ant- Var. of ANTI-.

-ant *suffix* **1.** Forming adjectives that mean in the act or process of doing (what is denoted by the stem): *militant*, *litigant*, etc. **2.** One who or that which does (what is indicated by the stem): *servant*, one who serves. [< F < L *-ans*, *-ens*, present participial suffixes]

ant·ac·id (ant·as′id) *adj.* Correcting acidity. — *n.* An alkaline remedy for stomach acidity.

an·tag·o·nism (an·tag′ə·niz′əm) *n.* **1.** Mutual opposition or resistance; hostility. **2.** An opposing principle or force.

an·tag·o·nist (an·tag′ə·nist) *n.* **1.** An adversary; opponent. **2.** *Anat.* A muscle that acts counter to another muscle. — **Syn.** See ENEMY.

an·tag·o·nis·tic (an·tag′ə·nis′tik) *adj.* Opposed; hostile. — **an·tag′o·nis′ti·cal·ly** *adv.*

an·tag·o·nize (an·tag′ə·nīz) *v.* **·nized**, **·niz·ing** *v.t.* **1.** To make unfriendly; make an enemy of. **2.** To struggle against; oppose. — *v.i.* **3.** To act antagonistically. [< Gk. < *anti-* against + *agōnizesthai* to struggle, strive]

ant·al·ka·li (ant·al′kə·lī) *n. pl.* **·lis** or **·lies** Any substance able to neutralize alkalis.

Ant·arc·tic (ant·ärk′tik, -är′tik) *adj.* Of or relating to the South Pole, or the regions within the Antarctic Crcle. [< Gk. < *anti-* opposite + *arktos* the Bear (a northern constellation), the north]

An·tar·es (an·târ′ēz) *n.* A giant red star, one of the 20 brightest; Alpha in the constellation Scorpio. [< Gk.]

ant bear A mammal of tropical America feeding on ants.

an·te (an′te) *v.t. & v.i.* **·ted** or **·teed**, **·te·ing 1.** In poker, to put up (one's stake). **2.** *Slang* To pay (one's share). — *n.* **1.** In poker, the stake put up before receiving the hand. **2.** *Slang* One's share. [< L, before]

ante- *prefix* **1.** Before in time or order: *antemeridiem*. **2.** Before in position; in front of: *antechamber*. [< L *ante* before]

ANT BEAR
(8 feet long;
2 feet high)

ant·eat·er (ant′ē′tər) *n.* **1.** The ant bear. **2.** One of several other mammals that feed partly on ants, as the aardvark.

an·te·bel·lum (an′tē bel′əm) *adj.* Before the war; esp., before the Civil War in the United States. [< L]

an·te·cede (an′tə·sēd′) *v.t. & v.i.* **·ced·ed**, **·ced·ing** To go or come before. [< L < *ante-* before + *cedere* to go]

an·te·ce·dence (an′tə·sēd′ns) *n.* **1.** A going before; prece-

dence; priority. **2.** *Astron.* The apparent retrograde motion of a planet. Also **an·te·ce′den·cy.**
an·te·ce·dent (an′tə·sēd′nt) *adj.* **1.** Prior; preceding. — *n.* **1.** One who or that which precedes. **2.** *Gram.* The word, phrase, or clause to which a pronoun refers. **3.** *pl.* The past events, circumstances, etc., of a person's life; also, ancestry. **4.** *Math.* The first term of a ratio; in a proportion, the first and third terms. **5.** *Logic* The condition on which a hypothetical proposition depends. [< L < *ante-* before + *cedere* to go] — **an′te·ce′dent·ly** *adv.*
an·te·cham·ber (an′ti·chām′bər) *n.* A room serving as an entranceway to another room
an·te·date (an′ti·dāt′) *v.t.* **·dat·ed, ·dat·ing 1.** To precede in time. **2.** To assign to a date earlier than the actual one. **3.** To cause to happen at an earlier date.
an·te·di·lu·vi·an (an′ti·di·lōō′vē·ən) *adj.* **1.** Before the Flood. **2.** Antiquated; primitive. — *n.* **1.** A person, animal, or plant that lived before the Flood. **2.** An old or old-fashioned person. [< ANTE- + L *diluvium* deluge]
an·te·lope (an′tə·lōp) *n. pl.* **·lope** or **·lopes 1.** Any of various swift, hollow-horned animals, as the gazelle, chamois, gnu, etc. **2.** Leather made from its hide. **3.** *U.S.* The pronghorn. [< OF < Med.L < LGk. *antholops*]
an·te me·rid·i·em (an′tē mə·rid′ē·em) *Latin* Before noon. Abbr. *a.m.*, *A.M.* — **an′te·me·rid′i·an** *adj.*
an·ten·na (an·ten′ə) *n. pl.* **·ten·nae** (-ten′ē) *for def. 1* **·ten·nas** *for def. 2* **1.** *Entomol.* One of the paired, movable sense organs on the head of an insect or other arthropod. **2.** *Telecom.* A system of wires, etc., for transmitting or receiving electromagnetic waves. [< NL < L, a yard for a sail]
an·te·pe·nult (an′ti·pē′nult, -pi·nult′) *n.* The last syllable but two in a word, as *te* in *antepenult.* [< L]
an·te·pe·nul·ti·mate (an′ti·pi·nul′tə·mit) *adj.* Pertaining to the last but two of any series. — *n.* The antepenult.
an·te·ri·or (an·tir′ē·ər) *adj.* **1.** Antecedent in time; prior. **2.** Farther front or forward in space. [< L, compar. of *ante* before] — **an·te′ri·or·ly** *adv.*
antero- *combining form* Anterior; placed in front. [< L *anterus* (assumed form)]
an·te·room (an′ti·rōōm′, -rŏŏm′) *n.* A waiting room.
anth- Var. of ANTI-.
an·them (an′thəm) *n.* **1.** A hymn of gladness or praise: a national *anthem.* **2.** A musical composition, usually set to words from the Bible. — *v.t.* To celebrate with an anthem. [OE < L < Gk., < *anti-* against + *phōnē* voice]
an·ther (an′thər) *n. Bot.* The pollen-bearing part of a stamen. For illustration see FLOWER. [< F < L < Gk. *anthos* flower]
an·ther·id·i·um (an′thə·rid′ē·əm) *n. pl.* **·ther·id·i·a** (-thə·rid′ē·ə) *Bot.* The male sexual organ in cryptogams. [< NL, dim. of Gk. *anthēros* flowery] — **an′ther·id′i·al** *adj.*
antho- *combining form* Flower. [< Gk. *anthos* a flower]
an·thol·o·gize (an·thol′ə·jīz) *v.* **·gized, ·giz·ing** *v.i.* **1.** To make an anthology or anthologies. — *v.t.* **2.** To put into an anthology or make an anthology of.
an·thol·o·gy (an·thol′ə·jē) *n. pl.* **·gies** A collection of choice or representative literary extracts. [< L < Gk. < *anthos* flower + *legein* to gather] — **an·tho·log′i·cal** (an′thə·loj′i·kəl) *adj.* — **an·thol′o·gist** *n.*
an·tho·zo·an (an′thə·zō′ən) *Zool. adj.* Of or belonging to a class of marine animals including the sea anemones and corals. — *n.* An anthozoan animal. [< NL < ANTHO- + Gk. *zōion* animal] — **an′tho·zo′ic** *adj.*
an·thra·cene (an′thrə·sēn) *n. Chem.* A crystalline compound, $C_{14}H_{11}$, obtained from coal tar and used in manufacturing dyes. [< Gk. *anthrax, -akos* coal + -ENE]
an·thra·cite (an′thrə·sīt) *n.* Coal that burns slowly and with great heat: also called *hard coal.* [< L < Gk. *anthrax* coal] — **an·thra·cit·ic** (an′thr·sit′ik) *adj.*
an·thrax (an′thraks) *n. pl.* **·thra·ces** (-thrə·sēz) *Pathol.* An infectious, malignant disease of man and some animals, often with carbuncles; also, the carbuncle. [< Gk., coal]
anthropo- *combining form* Man; human: *anthropology.* Also, before vowels, **anthrop-.** [< Gk. *anthrōpos* man]
an·thro·po·cen·tric (an′thrə·pō·sen′trik) *adj.* Regarding man as the central fact or final aim of the universe.
an·thro·pog·e·ny (an′thrə·poj′ə·nē) *n.* The branch of anthropology that treats of the origin and development of man. Also **an·thro·po·gen·e·sis** (an′thrə·pō·jen′ə·sis).
an·thro·poid (an′thrə·poid) *adj.* Like a human being in form or other characteristics, as the gorilla, chimpanzee, and orang-utan. Also **an′thro·poi′dal.** — *n.* An ape.
an·thro·pol·o·gy (an′thrə·pol′ə·jē) *n.* **1.** The science treating of the physical, social, material, and cultural development of man, including his origin, evolution, distribution, customs, beliefs, folkways, etc. — **an·thro·po·log·i·cal** (an′thrə·pə·loj′i·kəl) or **·log′ic** *adj.* — **an′thro·po·log′i·cal·ly** *adv.* — **an′thro·pol′o·gist** *n.*

an·thro·pom·e·try (an′thrə·pom′ə·trē) *n.* The science and technique of human anatomical measurements. — **an·thro·po·met′ric** (an′thrə·pō·met′rik) or **·ri·cal** *adj.*
an·thro·po·mor·phic (an′thrə·pō·môr′fik) *adj.* Of or characterized by anthropomorphism.
an·thro·po·mor·phism (an′thrə·pō·môr′fiz·əm) *n.* The ascription of human form or characteristics to a deity, or to any being or thing not human. — **an′thro·po·mor′phist** *n.*
an·thro·po·mor·phize (an′thrə·pō·môr′fīz) *v.t. & v.i.* **·phized, ·phiz·ing** To ascribe human characteristics (to).
an·thro·po·mor·phous (an′thrə·pō·môr′fəs) *adj.* Having or resembling human form. [< Gk. < *anthrōpos* man + *morphē* form, shape]
an·ti (an′tī, an′tē) *n. pl.* **·tis** *Informal* One opposed to some policy, group, etc.
anti- A prefix having the following meanings: **1.** Against; opposed to, as in: **antitobacco, anti-Fascist. 2.** Opposite to; reverse, as in: **anticyclic, antilogic. 3.** *Med.* Counteracting; curative, as in: **antianemic, antivirus.** *Anti-* usu. changes to *ant-* before words beginning with a vowel, as in *antacid.* [< Gk. *anti* against]
an·ti·air·craft (an′tē·âr′kraft′, -âr′kräft′, an′tī-) *adj.* Used for defense against enemy aircraft. Abbr. *AA*, *A.A.*
an·ti·bi·o·sis (an′ti·bī·ō′sis) *n. Biol.* The condition of associated organisms in which one is detrimental to the other.
an·ti·bi·ot·ic (an′ti·bī·ot′ik, an′ti-, an′ti·bē·ot′ik) *n. Biochem.* Any of a large class of substances, as penicillin, streptomycin, etc., having the power of destroying or arresting the growth of microorganisms. [< ANTI- + Gk. *bios* life]
an·ti·bod·y (an′ti·bod′ē) *n. pl.* **·bod·ies** *Biochem.* Any of a class of proteins serving to immunize the body against specific antigens.
an·tic (an′tik) *n.* **1.** *Usually pl.* A prank; caper. **2.** A clown; buffoon. — *adj.* Odd; fantastic; ludicrous. — *v.i.* **an·ticked, an·tick·ing** To play the clown; perform antics. [< Ital. *antico* old, grotesque] — **an′tic·ly** *adv.*
an·ti·christ (an′ti·krīst′) *n. Often cap.* A denier or opponent of Christ or Christianity. — **an′ti·chris′tian** *adj. & n.*
An·ti·christ (an′ti·krīst′) *n.* The blasphemous antagonist of Christ. *I John* ii 18.
an·tic·i·pant (an·tis′ə·pənt) *adj.* Coming or acting in advance; anticipating; expectant. — *n.* One who anticipates.
an·tic·i·pate (an·tis′ə·pāt) *v.t.* **·pat·ed, ·pat·ing 1.** To experience or realize beforehand. **2.** To look forward to. **3.** To act or arrive sooner than, especially so as to forestall. **4.** To foresee and fulfill beforehand, as desires. **5.** To make use of beforehand. **6.** To discharge, as a debt, before it is due. **7.** To cause to happen earlier. [< L < *ante-* before + *capere* to take] — **an·tic′i·pa′tor** *n.*
an·tic·i·pa·tion (an·tis′ə·pā′shən) *n.* **1.** The act of anticipating; also, that which is anticipated. **2.** An expectation. **3.** An intuitive prevision.
an·tic·i·pa·tive (an·tis′ə·pā′tiv) *adj.* Anticipating, or characterized by anticipation. — **an·tic′i·pa·tive·ly** *adv.*
an·tic·i·pa·to·ry (an·tis′ə·pə·tôr′ē, -tō′rē) *adj.* Of, showing, or embodying anticipation. — **an·tic′i·pa·to′ri·ly** *adv.*
an·ti·cler·i·cal (an′ti·kler′i·kəl) *adj.* Opposed to clerical influence in political and civic affairs. — **an′ti cler′i·cal ism** *n.*
an·ti·cli·max (an′ti·klī′maks) *n.* **1.** In rhetoric, a ludicrous decrease in the importance or impressiveness of what is said. **2.** Any sudden descent or fall contrasted with a previous rise. — **an′ti·cli·mac′tic** (-klī·mak′tik) *adj.*
an·ti·cline (an′ti·klīn) *n. Geol.* A system of roughly parallel folds in stratified rock in which the folds slope downward from the crest in opposite directions. Compare SYNCLINE. [< ANTI- + Gk. *klinein* to slope] — **an′ti·cli′nal** *adj.*

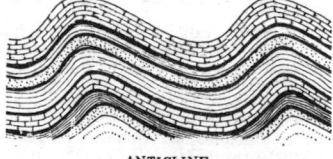

ANTICLINE

an·ti·cy·clone (an′ti·sī′klōn) *n. Meteorol.* An atmospheric condition in which winds spiral outward from a central point of high pressure. — **an′ti·cy·clon′ic** (-klon′ik) *adj.*
an·ti·dote (an′ti·dōt) *n.* Anything that will counteract or remove the effects of poison, disease, or any evil. [< L < Gk. < *anti-* against + *didonai* to give] — **an′ti·do′tal** *adj.* — **an′ti·do′tal·ly** *adv.*
An·ti·fed·er·al·ist (an′ti·fed′ər·əl·ist, -fed′rəl-) *n.* A member of the political party that opposed the ratification of the U.S. Constitution. — **An′ti·fed′er·al** *adj.*
an·ti·freeze (an′ti·frēz′) *n.* A liquid of low freezing point, added to or substituted for the cooling agent in combustion-engine radiators, to prevent freezing.
an·ti·gen (an′tə·jən) *n. Biochem.* Any of several substances

that cause the development of antibodies. Also **an'ti·gene** (-jēn). — **an·ti·gen·ic** (an'tə·jen'ik) *adj.*

An·tig·o·ne (an·tig'ə·nē) In Greek legend, a daughter of Oedipus and Jocasta, who was sentenced to death for illegally burying her brother.

an·ti·his·ta·mine (an'ti·his'tə·mēn, -min) *n. Med.* Any of certain drugs that neutralize the action of histamine in the treatment of hay fever, asthma, etc. — **an'ti·his'ta·min'ic** (-min'ik) *adj.*

an·ti·knock (an'ti·nok') *n.* An agent that prevents premature combustion when added to the fuel of an internal-combustion engine.

an·ti·log·a·rithm (an'ti·lôg'ə·rith'əm, -log'-) *n. Math.* The number corresponding to a given logarithm. Also, in shortened form, **an·ti·log** (an'ti·lôg, -log).

an·ti·ma·cas·sar (an'ti·mə·kas'ər) *n.* A covering for the backs and arms of chairs and sofas to prevent soiling; a tidy.

an·ti·mat·ter (an'ti·mat'ər) *n. Physics* A form of matter composed of antiparticles.

an·ti·mo·ni·al (an'tə·mō'nē·əl) *adj.* Of or containing antimony. — *n.* A medicine containing antimony.

an·ti·mo·ny (an'tə·mō'nē) *n.* A silver-white, crystalline, metallic element (symbol Sb) used in chemistry, medicine, in alloys, etc.: also called *stibium.* See ELEMENT. ◆ Collateral adjective: *stibial.* [< Med.L *antimonium*]

an·ti·par·ti·cle (an'ti·pär'ti·kəl) *n. Physics* Any of a group of atomic particles having masses equal to the electron, proton, neutron, etc., but with opposite charges and magnetic characteristics.

an·ti·pas·to (än'tē·päs'tō) *n.* A course of smoked or salted meat, fish, vegetables, etc., served as an appetizer. [< Ital.]

an·tip·a·thet·ic (an·tip'ə·thet'ik, an'ti·pə-) *adj.* Having a natural aversion; constitutionally opposed: often with *to.* Also **an·tip'a·thet'i·cal.** — **an·tip'a·thet'i·cal·ly** *adv.*

an·tip·a·thy (an·tip'ə·thē) *n. pl.* **·thies** 1. An instinctive feeling of aversion or dislike. 2. The object of such a feeling. [< L < Gk. < *anti-* against + *pathein* to feel, suffer]

an·ti·per·son·nel (an'ti·pûr'sə·nel', an'tī-) *adj. Mil.* Designating weapons that are employed against troops rather than against defenses or mechanized equipment.

an·ti·per·spi·rant (an'ti·pûr'spə·rənt, an'tī-) *n.* A skin astringent that prevents or diminishes perspiration.

an·ti·phlo·gis·tic (an'ti·flō·jis'tik) *Med. adj.* Capable of reducing inflammation. — *n.* A remedy for inflammation. [< ANTI- + Gk. *phlogizein* to burn]

an·ti·phon (an'tə·fon) *n.* A verse of a psalm or hymn said or chanted in response to another. [< LL < Gk. < *anti-* against + *phōnē* voice]

an·tiph·o·nal (an·tif'ə·nəl) *adj.* Of or like an antiphon; sung responsively. Also **an·tiph·on·ic** (an'tə·fon'ik). — *n.* An antiphonary. — **an·tiph'o·nal·ly** *adv.*

an·tiph·o·nar·y (an·tif'ə·ner'ē) *n. pl.* **·nar·ies** A book of antiphons. — *adj.* Of or pertaining to a book of antiphons.

an·tip·o·dal (an·tip'ə·dəl) *adj.* 1. Pertaining to or situated on the opposite side of the earth. 2. Diametrically opposed. Also **an·tip·o·de·an** (an·tip'ə·dē'ən).

an·ti·pode (an'ti·pōd) *n.* An exact opposite.

an·tip·o·des (an·tip'ə·dēz) *n.* (*construed as sing. or pl.*) A place or region on the opposite side of the earth, or its inhabitants. [< L < Gk. < *anti-* opposite + *pous* foot]

an·ti·py·ret·ic (an'ti·pī·ret'ik) *Med. adj.* Reducing fever. — *n.* A medicine to reduce fever. [< ANTI- + Gk. *pyretos* fever]

an·ti·quar·i·an (an'ti·kwâr'ē·ən) *adj.* Pertaining to antiques or antiquaries. — *n.* An antiquary. — **an'ti·quar'i·an·ism** *n.*

an·ti·quar·y (an'ti·kwer'ē) *n. pl.* **·quar·ies** One who collects, deals in, or studies antiques or antiquities.

an·ti·quate (an'ti·kwāt) *v.t.* **·quat·ed, ·quat·ing** 1. To make old or out-of-date. 2. To cause to look antique. [< L *antiquare* to make old] — **an'ti·qua'tion** *n.*

an·ti·quat·ed (an'ti·kwā'tid) *adj.* 1. Out-of-date; old-fashioned; obsolete. 2. Ancient; very old.

an·tique (an·tēk') *adj.* 1. Of or pertaining to ancient times. 2. Of an earlier period: an *antique* chair. 3. Old-fashioned; out-of-date. — *n.* 1. The style of ancient art, or a specimen of it. 2. Any old object, usually prized for its rarity, style or craft, etc. 3. *Printing* A style of type with all the lines of nearly equal thickness. — *v.t.* **an·tiqued, an·ti·quing** To give the appearance of antiquity to. [< F < L *antiquus* ancient] — **an·tique'ly** *adv.* — **an·tique'ness** *n.*

an·tiq·ui·ty (an·tik'wə·tē) *n. pl.* **·ties** 1. The quality of being ancient. 2. Ancient times, esp. before the Middle Ages. 3. The people of ancient times collectively; the ancients. 4. *Usually pl.* Ancient relics.

an·ti·Sem·i·tism (an'ti·sem'ə·tiz'əm, an'tī-) *n.* Opposition to, discrimination against, or intolerance of Jews, Jewish culture, etc. — **an·ti–Sem·ite** (an'ti·sem'īt) *n.* — **an'ti Se·mit'ic** (-sə·mit'ik) *adj.* — **an'ti Se·mit'i·cal·ly** *adv.*

an·ti·sep·sis (an'tə·sep'sis) *n.* The condition of being free of pathogenic bacteria; also, the method of obtaining this.

an·ti·sep·tic (an'tə·sep'tik) *adj.* 1. Of, pertaining to, or used in antisepsis. 2. Preventing or counteracting infection. Also **an'ti·sep'ti·cal.** — *n.* Any antiseptic substance. [< ANTI- + Gk. *sēpsis* putrefaction] — **an'ti·sep'ti·cal·ly** *adv.*

an·ti·se·rum (an'ti·sir'əm) *n.* A serum that provides immunity from specific diseases.

an·ti·slav·er·y (an'ti·slā'vər·ē, -slāv'rē, an'tī-) *adj.* Opposed to human slavery.

an·ti·so·cial (an'ti·sō'shəl, an'tī-) *adj.* 1. Unsociable. 2. Opposed to or disruptive of society or the general good.

an·ti·spas·mod·ic (an'ti·spaz·mod'ik) *Med. adj.* Relieving or checking spasms. — *n.* An antispasmodic agent.

an·tis·tro·phe (an·tis'trə·fē) *n.* In ancient Greek drama, the verses sung by the chorus while returning from left to right, in answer to the previous strophe. [< L < Gk. < *anti-* against, opposite + *strephein* to turn] — **an·ti·stroph·ic** (an'ti·strof'ik) *adj.*

an·ti·tank (an'ti·tangk') *adj. Mil.* Designed to combat tanks and other armored vehicles: *antitank* guns. Abbr. *AT*

an·tith·e·sis (an·tith'ə·sis) *n. pl.* **·ses** (-sēz) 1. The balancing of two contrasted words, ideas, or phrases against each other. Example: *My prayers go up; my thoughts remain below.* 2. Opposition; contrast: the *antithesis* of peace and war. 3. The direct opposite. 4. One of the three categories found in the dialectic systems of Hegel, Marx, etc. [< L < Gk. < *anti-* against + *tithenai* to place] — **an·ti·thet·i·cal** (an'tə·thet'i·kəl) — **an'ti·thet'i·cal·ly** *adv.*

an·ti·tox·in (an'ti·tok'sin) *n. Biochem.* A substance formed in the living tissues of an animal, that neutralizes a specific bacterial poison; also, serum containing this. Also **an'ti·tox'ine** (-tok'sin, -sēn). — **an'ti·tox'ic** *adj.*

an·ti·trade (an'ti·trād') *n.* One of the upper air currents in the tropics, moving contrary to the trade winds.

an·ti·trust (an'ti·trust') *adj.* Pertaining to the regulation of or opposition to trusts, cartels, monopolies, etc.

ant·ler (ant'lər) *n. Usu. pl.* Either of the branched horns on the head of members of the deer family. [< OF < L *ante-* before + *oculus* eye] — **ant'lered** *adj.*

ant lion An insect resembling a dragonfly, whose larva preys on ants and other insects.

an·to·nym (an'tə·nim) *n.* A word that is the opposite of another in meaning: opposed to *synonym.* Abbr. *ant.* [< Gk. < *anti-* opposite + *onoma, onyma* name]

an·trum (an'trəm) *n. pl.* **·tra** (-trə) *Anat.* A cavity, usually in a bone; esp., the cavity in the upper jaw opening into the nose. [< L < Gk. *antron* cave]

a·nus (ā'nəs) *n. Anat.* The excretory opening at the lower extremity of the alimentary canal. [< L, orig., a ring]

an·vil (an'vil, -vəl) *n.* 1. A heavy block of iron or steel on which metal may be forged. 2. *Anat.* The incus. — *v.t. & v.i.* **an·viled** or **·villed, an·vil·ing** or **·vil·ling** To work at or shape on an anvil. [OE *anfilt*]

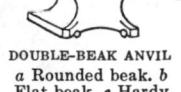

DOUBLE-BEAK ANVIL
a Rounded beak. *b* Flat beak. *c* Hardy hole, cutter, or chisel hole.

anx·i·e·ty (ang·zī'ə·tē) *n. pl.* **·ties** 1. Disturbance of mind regarding some uncertain event; misgiving; worry. 2. Strained or solicitous desire; eagerness. 3. *Psychiatry* A tense emotional state characterized by and apprehension without apparent cause.

anx·ious (angk'shəs, ang'-) *adj.* 1. Troubled in mind respecting some uncertain matter. 2. Causing anxiety; distressing: an *anxious* matter. 3. Intent; eagerly desirous: with *for* or the infinitive. [< L *angere* to choke, distress] — **anx'ious·ly** *adv.* — **anx'ious·ness** *n.*

an·y (en'ē) *adj.* 1. One, no matter which; a or an, or (plural) some: Have we *any* choice? 2. Some, however much or little: Did he eat *any* supper? 3. Every: *Any* fool knows that. — *pron.* One or more persons or things of a number: Have *any* of the guests arrived? — *adv.* At all; to any extent: Are they *any* nearer? [OE *ǣnig* < *ān* one]

an·y·bod·y (en'i·bod'ē, -bud'ē) *pron.* Any person whatever; anyone. — *n. pl.* **·bod·ies** A person of importance.

an·y·how (en'i·hou') *adv.* 1. In any way whatever; by any means. 2. Notwithstanding; in any case. 3. Carelessly.

an·y·one (en'i·wun', -wən) *pron.* Any person. ◆ **any one, anyone** *Any one* is used to distinguish one person from others in the same group or class: *Any one* of these men may be guilty. *Anyone* (indefinite pronoun) means any person at all.

an·y·thing (en'i·thing') *pron.* Any thing, event, or matter whatever. — *n.* A thing of any kind. — *adv.* To any degree; in any way: now only in the expression **anything like. anything but** By no means; far from: *anything but* safe.

an·y·way (en'i·wā') *adv.* 1. In any manner. 2. Nevertheless; anyhow. 3. Carelessly; haphazardly.

an·y·where (en'i·hwâr') *adv.* In, at, or to any place.

an·y·wise (en'i·wīz') *adv.* In any manner.

An·zac (an'zak) *adj.* Pertaining to the Australian and New Zealand Army Corps during World War I. — *n.* Any soldier from Australia or New Zealand.

A-one (ā'wun') *adj.* *Informal* Excellent. Also **A-1.**

a·or·ta (ā-ôr'tə) *n.* *pl.* **·tas** or **·tae** (-tē) *Anat.* The great artery springing from the left ventricle of the heart and forming the main arterial trunk that distributes blood to all of the body except the lungs. [< NL < Gk. < *aeirein* to raise, heave] — **a·or'tal, a·or'tic** *adj.*

ap-¹ Assimilated var. of AD-.

ap-² Var. of APO-.

a·pace (ə-pās') *adv.* Rapidly; quickly. [< A-¹ on + PACE]

a·pache (ə-päsh', ə-pash'; *Fr.* ä-päsh') *n.* A ruffian or gangster of Paris. [< F < APACHE]

A·pach·e (ə-pach'ē) *n.* *pl.* **A·pach·es** or **A·pach·e** One of a group of Indians, inhabiting the southern and SW U.S.

Apache State Nickname of ARIZONA.

a·part (ə·pärt') *adv.* **1.** Separated; not together. **2.** One from another. **3.** Separately for some use or purpose. **4.** Independently in logic or thought: Let us view this matter *apart.* **5.** Aside; to one side. **6.** In pieces or to pieces: The ship broke *apart.* — *adj.* Separate; distinct. [< MF < L *ad* to + *pars, partis* part]

a·part·heid (ə-pärt'hīt) *n.* In the Republic of South Africa, the official policy of political, social, and economic discrimination and segregation enforced against nonwhites. [< Afrikaans, *apartness, separation*]

a·part·ment (ə-pärt'mənt) *n.* **1.** Any of several suites of rooms in a building, each equipped for housekeeping; a flat. **2.** A room. Abbr. *apt.* (pl. *apts.*). [< F < Ital., ult. < L *ad* to + *pars, partis* part]

apartment house *U.S.* A multiple-dwelling building divided into a number of apartments.

ap·a·thet·ic (ap'ə-thet'ĭk) *adj.* **1.** Lacking emotion. **2.** Indifferent; unconcerned. Also **ap'a·thet'i·cal.** [< APATHY, on analogy with *sympathetic*] — **ap'a·thet'i·cal·ly** *adv.*

ap·a·thy (ap'ə-thē) *n.* *pl.* **·thies** **1.** Lack of emotion. **2.** Indifference. [< L < Gk. < *a-* without + *pathos* feeling]
— **Syn.** 1, 2. *Apathy* may refer to a habitual lack of feeling, or it may be used in the sense of *indifference* to describe a temporary lack of interest caused by depression, sorrow, ignorance, despair, etc. *Insensibility* is a lack of feeling for other persons.

ape (āp) *n.* **1.** A large, tailless, Old World primate, as a gorilla or chimpanzee. **2.** Loosely, any monkey. **3.** A mimic. — *v.t.* **aped, ap·ing** To imitate; mimic. [OE *apa*]

a·pe·ri·ent (ə-pir'ē·ənt) *Med. adj.* Laxative. — *n.* A gentle purgative. Also **a·per·i·tive** (ə-per'ə·tiv). [< L *aperire* to open]

a·pé·ri·tif (ä·pā·rē·tēf') *n.* *French* A drink of alcoholic liquor or wine taken as an appetizer.

ap·er·ture (ap'ər-chŏŏr, -chər) *n.* **1.** An opening; orifice. **2.** *Optics* An opening, often adjustable in diameter, through which light enters the lens of a camera, etc. [< L *aperire* to open] — **ap'er·tur·al** *adj.* — **ap'er·tured** *adj.*

a·pet·al·ous (ā-pet'l-əs) *adj.* *Bot.* Without petals.

a·pex (ā'peks) *n.* *pl.* **a·pex·es** or **ap·i·ces** (ap'ə-sēz, ā'pə-) **1.** The highest point; tip; top. **2.** *Geom.* The vertex of an angle. **3.** Climax. [< L]

aph- Var. of APO-.

a·pha·sia (ə-fā'zhə, -zhē-ə) *n.* *Pathol.* Any partial or total loss of the power of articulate speech, usu. due to a brain lesion. [< NL < Gk. < *a-* not + *phanai* to speak] — **a·pha·sic** (ə-fā'zik, -sik), **a·pha·si·ac** (ə-fā'zē-ak) *adj. & n.*

a·phe·li·on (ə-fē'lē-ən) *n.* *pl.* **·li·a** (-lē-ə) *Astron.* The point in an orbit, as of a planet, farthest from the sun: opposed to *perihelion.* [< APH (APO-) away from + Gk. *hēlios* sun] — **a·phe'li·an** (-ən) *adj.*

a·phid (ā'fid, af'id) *n.* A small, juice-sucking insect, injurious to plants: also called *plant louse.* Also **a'phis.** [Origin uncertain] — **a·phid·i·an** (ə-fid'ē-ən) *adj.*

APHELION
P Perihelion.
S Sun. *A* Aphelion.

aph·o·rism (af'ə-riz'əm) *n.* **1.** A brief statement of a truth or principle. **2.** A proverb; maxim. [< MF < Med.L < Gk. < *apo-* from + *horizein* to divide] — **aph'o·rist** *n.* — **aph'o·ris'tic** (af'ə-ris'tik) or **·i·cal** *adj.* — **aph'o·ris'ti·cal·ly** *adv.*

aph·ro·dis·i·ac (af'rə-diz'ē-ak) *adj.* Arousing or increasing sexual desire or potency. — *n.* An aphrodisiac drug, food, etc. [< Gk. *aphrodisiakos* < *Aphroditē*, goddess of love]

Aph·ro·di·te (af'rə-dī'tē) In Greek mythology, the goddess of love and beauty, the daughter of Zeus: identified with the Roman *Venus.* [< Gk. *Aphroditē* the foam-born]

a·pi·ar·i·an (ā'pē-âr'ē-ən) *adj.* Of or relating to bees or the keeping of bees. — *n.* An apiarist.

a·pi·a·rist (ā'pē-ə-rist) *n.* A beekeeper.

a·pi·a·ry (ā'pē-er'ē) *n.* *pl.* **·ar·ies** A place where bees are kept; a set of hives, bees, etc. [< L *apiarium* < *apis* bee]

ap·i·cal (ap'i-kəl, ā'pi-) *adj.* Situated at or belonging to the apex or top. [< L *apex, apicis* tip]

ap·i·ces (ap'ə-sēz, ā'pə-) Alternative plural of APEX.

a·pi·cul·ture (ā'pi-kul'chər) *n.* The raising and care of bees. [< L *apis* bee + CULTURE] — **a'pi·cul'tur·ist** *n.*

a·piece (ə-pēs') *adv.* For or to each one; each.

ap·ish (ā'pish) *adj.* Like an ape; servilely imitative; foolish and tricky. — **ap'ish·ly** *adv.* — **ap'ish·ness** *n.*

a·plomb (ə·plom', *Fr.* ä·plôn') *n.* Assurance; self-confidence. [< F < *à* according to + *plomb* plumb bob]

apo- *prefix* Off; from; away: *apostasy.* Also **ap-** before vowels; *aph-* before an aspirate. [< Gk. < *apo* from, off]

ap·o·ca·lypse (ə-pok'ə-lips) *n.* A prophecy or revelation. [< L < Gk. < *apo-* from + *kalyptein* to cover]

A·poc·a·lypse (ə-pok'ə-lips) The book of Revelaton, the last book of the New Testament. Abbr. *Apoc.*

a·poc·a·lyp·tic (ə-pok'ə-lip'tik) *adj.* **1.** Of or of the nature of a revelation. **2.** Pertaining to the Apocalypse. Also **a·poc'·a·lyp'ti·cal.** — **a·poc'a·lyp'ti·cal·ly** *adv.*

a·poc·o·pe (ə-pok'ə-pē) *n.* A cutting off or elision of the last sound or syllable of a word. [< Gk. *apokopē* < *apokoptein* to cut off < *apo-* off + *koptein* to cut]

A·poc·ry·pha (ə-pok'rə-fə) *n.pl.* (*often construed as sing.*) Those books of the Septuagint included in the Vulgate but rejected by Protestants as uncanonical because not in the Hebrew Scriptures. [< LL < Gk. *apokryphos* hidden]

a·poc·ry·phal (ə-pok'rə-fəl) *adj.* Having little or no authenticity. — **a·poc'ry·phal·ly** *adv.* — **a·poc'ry·phal·ness** *n.*

ap·o·gee (ap'ə-jē) *n.* **1.** *Astron.* That point in the orbit of a celestial body which is farthest from the earth: opposed to *perigee.* **2.** The highest point; climax. [< MF < L < Gk. < *apo-* away from + *gē, gaia* earth] — **ap·o·ge·al** (ap'ə-jē'əl), **ap'o·ge'an** *adj.*

A·pol·lo (ə-pol'ō) In Greek and Roman mythology, the god of music, poetry, prophecy, and medicine, and later of the sun. — *n.* Any handsome young man.

APOGEE
P Moon at perigee. *E* Earth.
A Moon at apogee.

a·pol·o·get·ic (ə-pol'ə-jet'ik) *adj.* **1.** Of the nature of an apology; excusing. **2.** Defending or explaining. Also **a·pol'o·get'i·cal.** — *n.* An apology or defense. [< F < L < Gk. < *apologia* a speech in defense] — **a·pol'o·get'i·cal·ly** *adv.*

a·pol·o·get·ics (ə-pol'ə-jet'iks) *n.pl.* (*construed as sing.*) The branch of theology that defends Christianity.

a·pol·o·gist (ə-pol'ə-jist) *n.* One who argues in defense of any person or cause.

a·pol·o·gize (ə-pol'ə-jīz) *v.i.* **·gized, ·giz·ing** **1.** To offer an excuse; acknowledge, with regret, any offense. **2.** To make a formal defense in speech or writing. — **a·pol'o·giz'er** *n.*

ap·o·logue (ap'ə-lôg, -log) *n.* A fable or tale having a moral. Also **ap'o·log.** [< L < Gk. < *apo-* from + *logos* speech]

a·pol·o·gy (ə-pol'ə-jē) *n.* *pl.* **·gies** **1.** A statement or explanation expressing regret for some error or offense. **2.** A poor substitute. [< L < Gk. *apologia* a speech in defense]

ap·o·phthegm (ap'ə-them) See APOTHEGM.

ap·o·plec·tic (ap'ə-plek'tik) *adj.* Pertaining to, affected with, or tending toward apoplexy. Also **ap'o·plec'ti·cal.** — *n.* A person subject to apoplexy.

ap·o·plex·y (ap'ə-plek'sē) *n.* *Pathol.* Sudden paralysis and loss of sensation caused by a bloodclot or hemorrhage in the brain. [< Gk. < *apo-* from, off + *plēssein* to strike]

a·port (ə-pôrt', ə-pōrt') *adj. Naut.* On or toward the port side.

a·pos·ta·sy (ə-pos'tə-sē) *n.* *pl.* **·sies** Desertion of one's faith, religion, party, or principles. Also **a·pos'ta·cy.** [< L < Gk. < *apo-* away + *stasis* a standing] — **a·pos·tate** (ə-pos'-tāt, -tit) *adj. & n.*

a·pos·ta·tize (ə-pos'tə-tīz) *v.i.* **·tized, ·tiz·ing** To forsake one's faith or principles; become an apostate.

a pos·te·ri·o·ri (ā' pos-tir'ē-ôr'ī, -ô'rī) **1.** *Logic* Reasoning from facts to principles or from effect to cause. **2.** Inductive; empirical. [< L, from the later]

a·pos·tle (ə-pos'əl) *n.* **1.** One of the twelve disciples originally commissioned by Christ to preach the gospel (*Matt.* x 2–4). **2.** One of a class of missionaries in the early church (*I Cor.* xii 28). **3.** A Christian missionary who first evangelizes a nation or place. **4.** The earliest or foremost advocate of a cause. [OE *apostol* < L < Gk. a messenger]

Apostles' Creed A traditional and still widely accepted Christian confession of faith.

a·pos·to·late (ə-pos'tə-lit, -lāt) *n.* The dignity or office of an apostle. Also **a·pos'tle·ship.**

ap·os·tol·ic (ap'ə-stol'ik) *adj.* **1.** Of or pertaining to an apostle, the apostles, or their times. **2.** According to the doctrine or practice of the apostles. **3.** *Often cap.* Papal. Also **ap/os·tol'i·cal.** — **ap'os·tol'i cism** *n.* — **a·pos·to·lic·i·ty** (ə-pos'tə·lis'ə·tē) *n.*

Apostolic See 1. The Church of Rome, regarded as having been founded by St. Peter. **2.** The papacy.

a·pos·tro·phe¹ (ə·pos′trə·fē) *n.* A symbol (') written above the line to mark the omission of a letter or letters from a word, to indicate the possessive case, and to denote certain plurals, as 5's, cross your *t*'s. [< F < L < Gk. < *apo-* away + *strephein* to turn] — **ap·os·troph·ic** (ap′ə·strof′ik) *adj.*

a·pos·tro·phe² (ə·pos′trə·fē) *n.* A digression from a discourse; esp., a turning aside to speak to an absent person. — **ap·os·troph·ic** (ap′ə·strof′ik) *adj.*

a·pos·tro·phize¹ (ə·pos′trə·fīz) *v.t. & v.i.* **·phized, ·phiz·ing** To shorten (a word) by the omission of a letter or letters.

a·pos·tro·phize² (ə·pos′trə·fīz) *v.t. & v.i.* **·phized, ·phiz·ing** To speak or write an apostrophe (to).

apothecaries' measure A system of liquid measure used in pharmacy. See table front of book. Abbr. *ap.*

apothecaries' weight A system of weights used in pharmacy. See table front of book. Abbr. *ap.*

a·poth·e·car·y (ə·poth′ə·ker′ē) *n. pl.* **·car·ies** A druggist. [< OF < L < Gk. < *apo-* away + *tithenai* to put]

ap·o·thegm (ap′ə·them) *n.* A terse, instructive, practical saying; maxim: also spelled *apophthegm.* [< Gk. < *apo-* from + *pthengesthai* to utter] — **ap·o·theg·mat·ic** (ap′ə·theg·mat′ik) or **·i·cal** *adj.*

a·poth·e·o·sis (ə·poth′ē·ō′sis, ap′ə·thē′ə·sis) *n. pl.* **·ses** (-sēz) **1.** Exaltation to divine rank; deification. **2.** Supreme exaltation of any person, principle, etc. [< L < Gk. < *apo-* from + *theos* a god]

a·poth·e·o·size (ə·poth′ē·ə·sīz′, ap′ə·thē′ə·sīz) *v.t.* **·sized, ·siz·ing 1.** To deify. **2.** To glorify; exalt.

ap·pal (ə·pôl′) *v.t.* **·palled, ·pal·ling** *Brit.* Appall.

ap·pall (ə·pôl′) *v.t.* To fill with dismay or horror; shock: also, *Brit., appal.* [< OF *apallir* to pale < L *pallidus*]

ap·pal·ling (ə·pô′ling) *adj.* Causing dismay or terror; frightful. — **ap·pal′ling·ly** *adv.*

ap·pa·ra·tus (ap′ə·rā′təs, -rat′əs) *n. pl.* **·tus** or (rarely) **·tus·es 1.** A device, machine, or assembly of tools, instruments, etc., for a particular purpose. **2.** *Physiol.* Those organs and parts of the body by means of which natural processes are carried on. [< L < *ad-* to + *parare* to prepare]

ap·par·el (ə·par′əl) *n.* **1.** Clothing; attire. **2.** Equipment or furnishings, especially for a ship. — *v.t.* **·eled** or **·elled, ·el·ing** or **·el·ling.** To clothe; dress. [< OF *apareiller* to prepare, ult. < L *ad-* to + *par* equal]

ap·par·ent (ə·par′ənt, ə·pâr′-) *adj.* **1.** Readily perceived by the mind; evident; obvious. **2.** Easily seen; visible. **3.** Seeming, in distinction from real or actual. [< OF < L *apparere*] — **ap·par′ent·ness** *n.*

ap·par·ent·ly (ə·par′ənt·lē, ə·pâr′-) *adv.* **1.** Obviously; plainly. **2.** Seemingly.

ap·pa·ri·tion (ap′ə·rish′ən) *n.* **1.** A visual appearance of a disembodied spirit; phantom; ghost. **2.** Anything that appears, esp. if remarkable or startling. [< MF < L *apparitio, -onis* < *apparere* to appear] — **ap′pa·ri′tion·al** *adj.*

ap·peal (ə·pēl′) *n.* **1.** An earnest entreaty for aid, sympathy, or the like; prayer; supplication. **2.** The quality of being attractive. **3.** A resort to some higher power or final means, for sanction, proof, or aid. **4.** *Law* **a** The carrying of a case from a lower to a higher tribunal for a rehearing. **b** A case so carried. — *v.t.* **1.** *Law* To refer or remove, as a case, to a higher court. — *v.i.* **2.** To make an earnest supplication or request, as for sympathy, corroboration, or aid. **3.** To awaken a favorable response; be interesting. **4.** *Law* To remove a case, or request that a case be moved, to a higher court. **5.** To resort to or have recourse: with *to.* [< OF < L *appellare* to accost, call upon] — **ap·peal′a·ble** *adj.* — **ap·peal′er** *n.* — **ap·peal′ing·ly** *adv.*

ap·pear (ə·pir′) *v.i.* **1.** To come into view; become visible. **2.** To seem, or seem likely. **3.** To be clear to the mind; be obvious. **4.** To come before the public; also, to be published, as a book. **5.** *Law* To come formally into court. [< OF < L *ad-* to + *parere* to come forth, appear]

ap·pear·ance (ə·pir′əns) *n.* **1.** The act of appearing or coming into view. **2.** External or physical aspect; presence: a commanding *appearance.* **3.** *pl.* Circumstances or indications: *Appearances* are against him. **4.** Outward show; pretense. **5.** An apparition; phenomenon.

ap·pease (ə·pēz′) *v.t.* **·peased, ·peas·ing 1.** To placate by making concessions or yielding to demands. **2.** To satisfy or allay. [< OF *apaisier* < L *pax*] — **ap·peas′a·ble** *adj.* — **ap·peas′a·bly** *adv.* — **ap·peas′er** *n.* — **ap·peas′ing·ly** *adv.*

ap·pease·ment (ə·pēz′mənt) *n.* **1.** The act of appeasing or being appeased. **2.** The policy of making concessions to potential aggressors in order to maintain peace.

ap·pel·lant (ə·pel′ənt) *adj. Law* Of or pertaining to an appeal; appellate. — *n.* One who appeals, in any sense.

ap·pel·late (ə·pel′it) *adj. Law* Pertaining to or having jurisdiction of appeals: an *appellate* court.

ap·pel·la·tion (ap′ə·lā′shən) *n.* **1.** A name or title. **2.** The act of calling or naming.

ap·pel·la·tive (ə·pel′ə·tiv) *adj.* **1.** Serving to designate or name. **2.** *Gram.* Denoting a class: said of common nouns.

— *n.* **1.** A title; appellation. **2.** A common noun. — **ap·pel′la·tive·ly** *adv.* — **ap·pel′la·tive·ness** *n.*

ap·pend (ə·pend′) *v.t.* **1.** To add, as something subordinate or supplemental. **2.** To hang or attach: to *append* a seal. — **Syn.** See ADD. [< L < *ad-* to + *pendere* to hang]

ap·pend·age (ə·pen′dij) *n.* **1.** Anything appended. **2.** *Zool.* Any part joined to or diverging from the axial trunk, as a limb.

ap·pen·dant (ə·pen′dənt) *adj.* **1.** Attached; adjunct. **2.** Hanging attached. **3.** Attendant; consequent. — *n.* Something appended or attached. Also **ap·pen′dent.**

ap·pen·dec·to·my (ap′ən·dek′tə·mē) *n. pl.* **·mies** *Surg.* The removal of the vermiform appendix.

ap·pen·di·ces (ə·pen′də·sēz) Alternative plural of APPENDIX.

ap·pen·di·ci·tis (ə·pen′də·sī′tis) *n. Pathol.* Inflammation of the vermiform appendix.

ap·pen·dix (ə·pen′diks) *n. pl.* **·dix·es** or **·di·ces** (-də·sēz) **1.** An addition or appendage, as of supplementary matter at the end of a book. **2.** *Anat.* **a** The vermiform appendix. **b** An outgrowth of an organ. [< L, an appendage]

ap·per·cep·tion (ap′ər·sep′shən) *n. Psychol.* Conscious perception. [< F *apercevoir* to see, recognize] — **ap′per·cep′tive** *adj.*

ap·per·tain (ap′ər·tān′) *v.i.* To pertain or belong as by custom, function, nature, right, or fitness; relate: with *to.* [< OF < LL < L *ad-* to + *pertinere* to reach to]

ap·pe·tence (ap′ə·təns) *n.* **1.** Strong craving or propensity. **2.** Instinct or tendency. Also **ap′pe·ten·cy.** [< L < *appetere* to seek] — **ap′pe·tent** *adj.*

ap·pe·tite (ap′ə·tīt) *n.* **1.** A desire for food or drink. **2.** Any physical craving or natural desire. **3.** A strong liking. [< OF < L < *ad-* to + *petere* to seek] — **ap′pe·ti′tive** *adj.*

ap·pe·tiz·er (ap′ə·tī′zər) *n.* Anything that excites appetite or gives relish before a meal. Also *Brit.* **ap′pe·tis·er.**

ap·pe·tiz·ing (ap′ə·tī′zing) *adj.* Stimulating or tempting to the appetite. Also *Brit.* **ap′pe·tis′ing.** [Orig. ppr. of rare *appetize*] — **ap′pe·tiz′ing·ly** *adv.*

ap·plaud (ə·plôd′) *v.t. & v.i.* **1.** To express approval (of) by clapping the hands. **2.** To commend; praise. — **Syn.** See PRAISE. [< L < *ad-* to + *plaudere* to clap hands, strike] — **ap·plaud′er** *n.* — **ap·plaud′ing·ly** *adv.*

ap·plause (ə·plôz′) *n.* Approval or commendation, esp. as shown by clapping the hands, shouting, etc. — **ap·plau·sive** (ə·plô′siv) *adj.* — **ap·plau′sive·ly** *adv.*

ap·ple (ap′əl) *n.* **1.** The fleshy, edible fruit of a widely distributed tree of the rose family, usually of a roundish or conical shape. **2.** The similar fruit of several allied species, as the crab apple. **3.** One of several fruits or plants with little or no resemblance to the apple. [OE *æppel*]

apple cart A handcart used for peddling apples, etc. — **to upset the apple cart** To ruin someone's plans.

ap·ple·jack (ap′əl·jak′) *n.* Brandy made from cider.

ap·ple·sauce (ap′əl·sôs′) *n.* **1.** Apples stewed to a pulp. **2.** *U.S. Slang* Nonsense; bunk.

Ap·ple·ton layer (ap′əl·tən) A region of the ionosphere about 150 miles above sea level that acts as a reflector of certain frequencies of radio waves: also called *F layer.* [after Sir E. V. *Appleton,* born 1892, English physicist.]

ap·pli·ance (ə·plī′əns) *n.* A device or instrument; esp., an electrically powered device for household work.

ap·pli·ca·ble (ap′li·kə·bəl, ə·plik′ə-) *adj.* Capable of or suitable for application; relevant; fitting. [< L *applicare* to apply + -ABLE] — **ap′pli·ca·bil′i·ty, ap′pli·ca·ble·ness** *n.* **ap′pli·ca·bly** *adv.*

ap·pli·cant (ap′li·kənt) *n.* One who applies, as for a job.

ap·pli·ca·tion (ap′li·kā′shən) *n.* **1.** The act of applying. **2.** That which is applied, especially as a remedial agent. **3.** Employment for a special purpose or use. **4.** Capacity of being used; relevance. **5.** Close attention. **6.** A formal, written request, esp. for employment.

ap·pli·ca·tive (ap′li·kā′tiv) *adj.* Applicatory.

ap·pli·ca·tor (ap′li·kā′tər) *n.* An instrument or utensil for applying medication, etc.

ap·pli·ca·to·ry (ap′li·kə·tôr′ē, -tō′rē) *adj.* Fit for application; practical; applicative.

ap·plied (ə·plīd′) *adj.* Put in practice; utilized: opposed to *abstract, theoretical,* or *pure: applied* science.

ap·pli·qué (ap′li·kā′) *adj.* Applied: said of ornaments, as in needlework, sewn to the surface of another. — *n.* Decoration or ornaments so applied. — *v.t.* **·quéd** (-kād′), **·qué·ing** (-kā′ing) To decorate with appliqué work. [< F]

ap·ply (ə·plī′) *v.* **·plied, ·ply·ing** *v.t.* **1.** To bring into contact with something; put on or to. **2.** To devote or put to a particular use: to *apply* steam to navigation. **3.** To connect, as an epithet, with a particular person or thing. **4.** To give (oneself) wholly to; devote. — *v.i.* **5.** To make a request or petition; ask: with *for.* **6.** To be relevant: This order *applies* to all. [< OF < L < *ad-* to + *plicare* to fold]

ap·point (ə·point′) *v.t.* **1.** To name or select, as a person, a time and place, etc. **2.** To ordain, as by decree; command; prescribe. **3.** To fit out; equip: used chiefly in combination in the past participle: a *well-appointed* yacht. [< OF < LL < L *ad-* to + *punctum* a point]

ap·point·ee (ə·poin'tē′) *n.* One appointed to an office.

ap·point·ive (ə·poin′tiv) *adj.* Filled by appointment.

ap·point·ment (ə·point′mənt) *n.* **1.** The act of appointing or placing in office. **2.** A position held by someone appointed. **3.** An agreement to meet someone or to be somewhere at a specified time; engagement. **4.** *Usually pl.* Furniture.

Ap·po·mat·tox (ap′ə·mat′əks) A village in central Virginia. At **Appomattox Court House** Lee surrendered to Grant, April 9, 1865, virtually ending the Civil War.

ap·por·tion (ə·pôr′shən, ə·pōr′-) *v.t.* To divide and assign proportionally; allot. [< OF < a- to + *portionner* to divide] — **ap·por'tion·ment** *n.*

ap·pose (ə·pōz′) *v.t.* **·posed, ·pos·ing** **1.** To apply or put, as one thing to another: with *to*: to *appose* a seal to a document. **2.** To arrange side by side. [< OF < a- to + *poser* to put]

ap·po·site (ap′ə·zit) *adj.* Fit for or appropriate. [< L *apponere* to put near to] — **ap'po·site·ly** *adv.* — **ap'po·site·ness** *n.*

ap·po·si·tion (ap′ə·zish′ən) *n.* **1.** *Gram.* **a** The placing of one word beside another so that the second adds to or explains the first, and both have the same grammatical form, as *John, president* of the class. **b** The syntactical relationship between such words. **2.** An apposing or being apposed. — **ap'po·si'tion·al** *adj.* — **ap'po·si'tion·al·ly** *adv.*

ap·pos·i·tive (ə·poz′ə·tiv) *adj.* Of or in apposition. — *n.* A word or phrase in apposition. — **ap·pos'i·tive·ly** *adv.*

ap·prais·al (ə·prā′zəl) *n.* **1.** An appraising. **2.** An official valuation, as for sale, taxation, etc. Also **ap·praise'ment.**

ap·praise (ə·prāz′) *v.t.* **praised, ·prais·ing** **1.** To make an official valuation of; set a price or value on. **2.** To estimate the amount, quality, or worth of; judge. — **ap·prais'a·ble** *adj.* — **ap·prais'er** *n.*

— **Syn.** 1. evaluate, value, assess, assay.

ap·pre·ci·a·ble (ə·prē′shē·ə·bəl) *adj.* Capable of being valued or estimated. — **ap·pre'ci·a·bly** *adv.*

ap·pre·ci·ate (ə·prē′shē·āt) *v.* **·at·ed, ·at·ing** *v.t.* **1.** To be fully aware of the value, importance, magnitude, etc., of. **2.** To esteem adequately or highly. **3.** To be keenly sensible of or sensitive to. **4.** To show gratitude for. **5.** To increase the price or value of. **6.** To estimate the worth of. — *v.i.* **7.** To rise in value. [< LL < ad- to + *pretium* price] — **ap·pre'ci·a'tor** *n.*

ap·pre·ci·a·tion (ə·prē′shē·ā′shən) *n.* **1.** The act of placing an estimate on persons or things; judgment. **2.** Perception or awareness, as of qualities, values, etc. **3.** Gratitude. **4.** Increase in value.

ap·pre·ci·a·tive (ə·prē′shē·ā′tiv, -shə·tiv) *adj.* Capable of showing appreciation; manifesting appreciation. — **ap·pre'ci·a·tive·ly** *adv.* — **ap·pre'ci·a·tive·ness** *n.*

ap·pre·ci·a·to·ry (ə·prē′shē·ə·tôr′ē, -tō′rē, -shə-) *adj.* Appreciative. — **ap·pre'ci·a·to'ri·ly** *adv.*

ap·pre·hend (ap′rə·hend′) *v.t.* **1.** To lay hold of or grasp mentally; understand; perceive. **2.** To expect with anxious foreboding; dread. **3.** To arrest; take into custody. **4.** *Obs.* To take hold of. — *v.i.* **5.** To understand. [< L < ad- to + *prehendere* to seize] — **ap'pre·hend'er** *n.*

— **Syn.** 1. To *apprehend* is merely to perceive, while to *comprehend* something is to grasp its meaning in its entirety. *Understand* is close in meaning to *comprehend*, but can also mean to have insight into or sympathy with.

ap·pre·hen·si·ble (ap′rə·hen′sə·bəl) *adj.* Capable of being apprehended. — **ap'pre·hen'si·bil'i·ty** *n.*

ap·pre·hen·sion (ap′rə·hen′shən) *n.* **1.** Foreboding; misgiving. **2.** The power of apprehending; understanding. **3.** An estimate; opinion. **4.** Arrest; capture. — **Syn.** See KNOWLEDGE.

ap·pre·hen·sive (ap′rə·hen′siv) *adj.* **1.** Fearful; anxious. **2.** Quick to apprehend or perceive. — **ap'pre·hen'sive·ly** *adv.* — **ap'pre·hen'sive·ness** *n.*

ap·pren·tice (ə·pren′tis) *n.* **1.** One who is bound by a legal agreement to serve another for a fixed period of time in order to learn a trade or business. **2.** Any learner or beginner. — *v.t.* **·ticed, ·tic·ing** To bind or take on as an apprentice. [< OF < L *apprehendere* to comprehend] — **ap·pren'tice·ship** *n.*

ap·prise (ə·prīz′) *v.t.* **·prised, ·pris·ing** To notify, as of an event; inform. Also **ap·prize'.** [< F < L *apprehendere* to comprehend] — **ap·prise'ment** *n.* — **ap·pris'er** *n.*

ap·prize (ə·prīz′) *v.t.* **·prized, ·priz·ing** To appraise. Also **ap·prise'.** [Prob. < OF < a- on, to + *prisier* to value]

ap·proach (ə·prōch′) *v.i.* **1.** To come near or nearer in time or space. — *v.t.* **2.** To come near or nearer to. **3.** To come close to; approximate. **4.** To make advances to; offer a proposal, or bribe to. **5.** To cause to move nearer. **6.** To start to deal with: to *approach* a problem. — *n.* **1.** The act of approaching; a coming near. **2.** An approxi-

mation; nearness. **3.** A way or means of approaching; access. **4.** A method of beginning or accomplishing something. **5.** *Often pl.* An overture of friendship, etc.; advance. **6.** In golf, a stroke made after the tee shot, intended to land the ball on the putting green. [< OF < LL < L *ad-* to + *prope* near] — **ap·proach'a·ble** *adj.* — **ap·proach'a·bil'i·ty, ap·proach'a·ble·ness** *n.*

ap·pro·ba·tion (ap′rə·bā′shən) *n.* **1.** The act of approving; approval. **2.** Sanction. — **ap·pro·ba'tive, ap·pro·ba·to·ry** (ə·prō′bə·tôr′ē, -tō′rē) *adj.*

ap·pro·pri·ate (*adj.* ə·prō′prē·it; *v.* ə·prō′prē·āt) *adj.* Suitable; fit; proper; relevant. — *v.t.* **·at·ed, ·at·ing** **1.** To set apart for a particular use. **2.** To take for one's own use. [< L < ad- to + *proprius* one's own] — **ap·pro'pri·ate·ly** *adv.* — **ap·pro'pri·ate·ness** *n.* — **ap·pro'pri·a'tor** *n.*

ap·pro·pri·a·tion (ə·prō′prē·ā′shən) *n.* **1.** The act of appropriating or setting apart. **2.** Anything, esp. money, set apart for a special use. — **ap·pro'pri·a'tive** *adj.*

ap·prov·al (ə·prōō′vəl) *n.* **1.** The act of approving; approbation. **2.** Official consent; sanction. **3.** Favorable opinion; praise, commendation. — **on approval** For (a customer's) examination without obligation to purchase.

ap·prove (ə·prōōv′) *v.* **·proved, ·prov·ing** *v.t.* **1.** To regard as worthy, proper, or right. **2.** To confirm formally or authoritatively; sanction; ratify. — *v.i.* **3.** To show or state approval: often with *of*. [< OF < L < ad- to + *probare* to approve, prove] — **ap·prov'a·ble** *adj.* — **ap·prov'er** *n.* — **ap·prov'ing·ly** *adv.*

ap·prox·i·mate (*adj.* ə·prok′sə·mit; *v.* ə·prok′sə·māt) *adj.* **1.** Nearly exact, accurate, or complete. **2.** Like; resembling. **3.** Near; close together. — *v.* **·mat·ed, ·mat·ing** *v.t.* **1.** To come close to, as in quality, degree, or quantity. **2.** To cause to come near. — *v.i.* **3.** To come near in quality, degree, etc. [< L < ad- to + *proximus*, superl. of *prope* near] — **ap·prox'i·mate·ly** *adv.*

ap·prox·i·ma·tion (ə·prok′sə·mā′shən) *n.* **1.** The act or result of approximating. **2.** *Math.* A result sufficiently exact for a specified purpose.

ap·pur·te·nance (ə·pûr′tə·nəns) *n.* **1.** Something attached to another, more important thing. **2.** *pl.* Apparatus. **3.** *Law* Something passing as an incident to a principal thing. [< AF, OF < LL < L *ad-* to + *pertinere* to reach to]

ap·pur·te·nant (ə·pûr′tə·nənt) *adj.* Appertaining or belonging, as by right; accessory. — *n.* An appurtenance.

a·pri·cot (ā′pri·kot, ap′ri·kot) *n.* **1.** A yellow fruit of a tree, similar to a small peach. **2.** The tree bearing this fruit. **3.** A pinkish yellow color. [Earlier *apricock* (prob. directly < Pg.) < F < Pg. or Sp. < L *praecoquus* early ripe]

A·pril (ā′prəl) *n.* The fourth month of the year, containing 30 days. [< L *Aprilis*]

April fool The victim of a practical joke on April 1, known as **April** (or **All**) **Fools' Day.**

a pri·o·ri (ā′ prī·ô′rī, ā′ prē·ôr′ē) **1.** *Logic* Proceeding from cause to effect, or from an assumption to its logical conclusion. **2.** Based on theory rather than on experience or examination. [< L, from what is before] — **a·pri·or'i·ty** (ā′prī·ôr′ə·tē, -or′-) *n.*

a·pron (ā′prən, ā′pərn) *n.* **1.** A garment of cloth, leather, etc., worn to protect or adorn the front of a person's clothes. **2.** *Mech.* Any of various overlapping pieces protecting parts of machines. **3.** *Engin.* **a** The platform or sill at the entrance to a dock. **b** The platform below a dam or in a sluiceway. **4.** *Aeron.* A hard-surfaced area in front of and around a hangar or aircraft shelter. **5.** The part of a theater stage in front of the curtain. — *v.t.* To cover or furnish with an apron. [< OF < L *mappa* cloth, napkin]

ap·ro·pos (ap′rə·pō′) *adj.* Suited to the occasion; opportune: an *apropos* remark. — *adv.* **1.** With reference or regard; in respect: with *of*: *apropos* of spring. **2.** To the purpose; pertinently. **3.** By the way; incidentally: used to introduce a remark. [< F < à to + *propos* purpose]

apse (aps) *n.* *Archit.* An extending portion of an edifice, usually semicircular with a half dome; especially, the eastern or altar end of a church. [< L *apsis* arch]

apt (apt) *adj.* **1.** Inclined; liable; likely. **2.** Quick to learn; intelligent. **3.** Pertinent; relevant. [< L *aptus* fitted, suited] — **apt'ly** *adv.* — **apt'ness** *n.*

ap·ter·ous (ap′tər·əs) *adj.* *Biol.* Without wings; wingless.

ap·ter·yx (ap′tər·iks) *n.* A New Zealand bird with undeveloped wings, now nearly extinct: also called *kiwi*. [< NL < Gk. a- without + *pteryx* wing]

ap·ti·tude (ap′tə·tōōd, -tyōōd) *n.* **1.** Natural or acquired ability or bent. **2.** Quickness of understanding; intelligence. **3.** The state or quality of being apt or fitting. [< F < LL < L *aptus* fitted, suited]

aq·ua (ak′wə, ä′kwə) *n.* *pl.* **aq·uae** (ak′wē, ä′kwē) or **aq·uas** Water: used in Latin phrases applied to different kinds of water. — *adj. & n.* Bluish green. [< L]

aqua for·tis (fôr′tis)   Commercial nitric acid.

Aq·ua-Lung (ak′wə-lung′)   n.   A scuba: a trade name. Also **aq′ua·lung′.**

aq·ua·ma·rine (ak′wə-mə-rēn′)   n.   **1.** A sea-green variety of precious beryl. **2.** A bluish green color.   — adj.   Bluish green.   [< L aqua marina sea water]

aq·ua·naut (ak′wə-nôt)   n.   One who is trained to live and work underwater over a period of time.   [< L aqua water + -naut < Gk. nautēs sailor), after aeronaut, astronaut]

aq·ua·plane (ak′wə-plān)   n.   A board on which one stands while being towed by a motorboat.   — v.i. -planed, -plan·ing   To ride an aquaplane.   [< L aqua water + PLANE⁴]

aqua re·gi·a (rē′jē-ə)   A mixture of nitric and hydrochloric acid, a solvent for gold and platinum.   [< L, royal water]

a·quar·i·um (ə-kwâr′ē-əm)   n.   pl. **a·quar·i·ums** or **a·quar·i·a** (ə-kwâr′ē-ə)   **1.** A tank, pond, or the like for the exhibition or study of aquatic animals or plants. **2.** A public building containing such an exhibition.   [< L aqua water]

A·quar·i·us (ə-kwâr′ē-əs)   n.   A constellation, the Water Bearer; also, a sign of the zodiac. See ZODIAC.   [< L]

a·quat·ic (ə-kwat′ik, ə-kwot′-)   adj.   **1.** Living or growing in or near water. **2.** Performed on or in water.   — n.   An aquatic animal or plant.   [< L aqua water]

aq·ua·tint (ak′wə-tint′)   n.   **1.** A technique of engraving by treating the surface of a copper plate with an acid to give the effect of a water color. **2.** Such an engraving.   — v.t. To etch by aquatint.   [< F < Ital. < L aqua tincta]

aqua vi·tae (vī′tē)   **1.** Alcohol. **2.** Whisky; brandy.   [< L]

aq·ue·duct (ak′wə-dukt)   n.   **1.** A water conduit, esp. one for supplying water to a community from a distance. **2.** A structure supporting a canal carried across a river or over low ground.   [< L < aqua water + ducere to lead]

a·que·ous (ā′kwē-əs, ak′wē-)   adj.   **1.** Of or like water; watery. **2.** Composed of matter deposited by water.

aqueous humor   Physiol.   A clear fluid filling the space in the eye between the cornea and the lens.

aqui-   combining form   Water.   [< L aqua]

aq·ui·line (ak′wə-līn, -lin)   adj.   **1.** Of or like an eagle. **2.** Curving or hooked: an aquiline nose.   [< L aquila eagle]

ar-   Assimilated var. of AD-.

-ar¹   suffix   **1.** Pertaining to; like: regular, singular. **2.** The person or thing pertaining to: scholar.   [< OF -er, -ier < L -aris (in nouns -are), var. of -alis, suffix of adjectives; or directly < L]

-ar²   suffix   A form of -ARY, -ER², refashioned in imitation of -AR¹: vicar, in ME vicary, viker.

-ar³   suffix   A form of -ER¹, refashioned in imitation of -AR²: pedlar.

Ar·ab (ar′əb)   n.   **1.** A native or inhabitant of Arabia. **2.** Any of a Semitic-speaking people inhabiting Arabia. **3.** A horse of a graceful, intelligent breed originally native to Arabia.   — adj. Arabian.

ar·a·besque (ar′ə-besk′)   n.   **1.** An ornament or design, as used in Moorish architecture, of intertwined scrollwork, leaves or flowers, etc. **2.** In ballet, a position in which the dancer extends one leg straight backward, one arm forward, and the other arm backward.   — adj.   Relating to, executed in, or resembling arabesque; fanciful; ornamental.   [< F < Ital. Arabo Arab]

A·ra·bi·an (ə-rā′bē-ən)   adj.   Of or pertaining to Arabia or the Arabs.   — n.   An Arab (defs. 1 and 3).

Arabian Nights   A collection of stories from Arabia, India, Persia, etc., from the tenth century.

Ar·a·bic (ar′ə-bik)   adj.   Of or pertaining to Arabia, the Arabs, their language, culture, etc.   — n.   The Southwest Semitic language of the Arabs.

Arabic numerals   The symbols 1, 2, 3, 4, 5, 6, 7, 8, 9, and 0, in general use in Europe since about the tenth century.

ar·a·ble (ar′ə-bəl)   adj.   Capable of being plowed.   — n.   Arable land.   [< L arare to plow]   — **ar′a·bil′i·ty** n.

Arab League   A confederation, established 1945, of the states of Iraq, Jordan (then Trans-Jordan), Lebanon, Saudi Arabia, the United Arab Republic (Egypt), Syria, and Yemen, joined by 1959 by Libya, Morocco, Sudan, and Tunisia, and in 1961 by Kuwait.

a·rach·nid (ə-rak′nid)   n.   Any of a class of arthropods, including the spiders, scorpions, mites, etc.   [< NL < Gk. arachnē spider]   — **a·rach·ni·dan** (ə-rak′nə-dən) adj. & n.

Ar·a·gon (ar′ə-gon)   A former kingdom in Spain.   — **Ar·a·go·nese** (ar′ə-gə-nēz′, -nēs′) adj. & n.

Ar·am (âr′əm)   The Biblical name of ancient Syria. Also **Ar·a·me·a** (ar′ə-mē′ə).

Ar·a·ma·ic (ar′ə-mā′ik)   n.   Any of a group of Semitic languages including Syriac and the language spoken by Christ. **Ar·a·me·an** (ar′ə-mē′ən)   adj.   Of or pertaining to ancient Aram or Arameans, or its peoples, languages, etc.   — n.   **1.** An inhabitant of Aram. **2.** Aramaic. Also **Ar′a·mae′an.**

A·rap·a·ho (ə-rap′ə-hō)   n.   pl. **-ho** or **-hoes**   A member of a nomadic Algonquian tribe, now dwelling primarily in Oklahoma and Wyoming. Also **A·rap′a·hoe.**

ar·ba·lest (är′bə-list)   n.   A medieval crossbow requiring a mechanical appliance to bend it. Also **ar′ba·list.**   [< OF < L arcus a bow + ballista to throw]   — **ar′ba·lest′er** n.

ar·bi·ter (är′bə-tər)   n.   **1.** A chosen or appointed judge or umpire, as between parties in a dispute. **2.** One who has matters under his sole control; an absolute and final judge.   — Syn. See JUDGE.   [< L < ad- to + bitere, betere to go]   — **ar′bi·tress** n.fem.   — **ar′bi·tral** (-trəl) adj.

ar·bi·tra·ble (är′bə-trə-bəl)   adj.   Subject to, capable of, or suitable for arbitration.

ar·bit·ra·ment (är-bit′rə-mənt)   n.   **1.** Arbitration. **2.** The decision of an arbitrator; an award. **3.** The power or right to make such decision. Also **ar·bit′re·ment.**

ar·bi·trar·y (är′bə-trer′ē)   adj.   **1.** Based on or subject to one's opinion, judgment, prejudice, etc. **2.** Absolute; despotic. **3.** Law Not determined by statute. [See ARBITER.]   — **ar′bi·trar′i·ly** adv.   — **ar′bi·trar′i·ness** n.

ar·bi·trate (är′bə-trāt)   v.   -trat·ed, -trat·ing   v.t.   **1.** To decide as arbitrator. **2.** To submit to or settle by arbitration.   — v.i.   **3.** To act as arbitrator. **4.** To submit a dispute to arbitration.   — **ar′bi·tra′tive** adj.

ar·bi·tra·tion (är′bə-trā′shən)   n.   The settlement of a dispute by the decision of a third party or court.

ar·bi·tra·tor (är′bə-trā′tər)   n.   A person chosen to decide a dispute.   — Syn. See JUDGE.   [< L]

ar·bor¹ (är′bər)   n.   A bower, as of latticework, supporting vines or trees. Also Brit. **ar′bour.**   [Earlier erber, herber < AF < L < herba grass, herb]

ar·bor² (är′bər)   n.   pl. **ar·bo·res** (är′bər-ēz) for def. 1; **ar·bors** for def. 2.   **1.** A tree: used chiefly in botanical names. **2.** Mech. **a** A shaft, mandrel, spindle, or axle. **b** A principal support of a machine.   [< L, tree]

ar·bo·re·al (är-bôr′ē-əl, -bō′rē-)   adj.   **1.** Of or like a tree. **2.** Inhabiting trees, or adapted to life in trees.

ar·bo·res·cent (är′bə-res′ənt)   adj.   Treelike; branching.

ar·bo·re·tum (är′bə-rē′təm)   n.   pl. **-tums** or **-ta** (-tə)   A botanical garden exhibiting trees for display or study.

arbori-   combining form   Tree.   [< L arbor tree]

ar·bor·vi·tae (är′bər-vī′tē)   n.   An evergreen shrub or tree of the pine family.   [< L arbor vitae tree of life]

ar·bu·tus (är-byōō′təs)   n.   **1.** An evergreen tree or shrub of the heath family. **2.** The trailing arbutus.   [< L, strawberry tree]

arc (ärk)   n.   **1.** Anything in the shape of an arch, a curve, or a part of a circle; a bow; arch. **2.** Geom. A part of any curve. **3.** Electr. The bow of flame formed by the passage of an electric current across the gap between two conductors. **4.** Astron. A part of the apparent path of a heavenly body.   — v.i. **arced** (ärkt) or **arcked, arc·ing** (är′king) or **arck·ing** Electr. To form an arc.   [< L arcus bow, arch]

ar·cade (är-kād′)   n.   **1.** Archit. A series of arches with supporting columns or piers, standing against the face of a wall or free. **2.** A roofed passageway or street, esp. one having shops, etc., opening from it.   — v.t. -cad·ed, -cad·ing   To furnish with or form into an arcade or arcades.   [< F < Med.L < L arcus bow, arch]

Ar·ca·di·a (är-kā′dē-ə)   Any region of ideal rustic simplicity and contentment. Also **Ar·ca·dy** (är′kə-dē).

Ar·ca·di·an (är-kā′dē-ən)   adj.   **1.** Of or pertaining to Arcadia. **2.** Rural or simple; pastoral.   — n.   **1.** A native of or dweller in Arcadia. **2.** One with simple, pastoral tastes.

ar·cane (är-kān′)   adj.   Secret; hidden.   [< L arcanus hidden]

ar·ca·num (är-kā′nəm)   n.   pl. **-na** (-nə)   An inner secret.

arch¹ (ärch)   n.   **1.** A curved structure spanning an opening, formed of wedge-shaped parts resting on supports at the two extremities. **2.** Any similar structure or object. **3.** A bowlike curve. **4.** Anat. A curved or archlike part, as of the foot.   — v.t.   **1.** To cause to form an arch or arches. **2.** To furnish with an arch or arches. **3.** To span; extend over, as an arch.   — v.i. **4.** To form an arch or arches.   [< OF < Med.L < L arcus bow, arch]

arch² (ärch)   adj.   **1.** Cunning; roguish; sly. **2.** Most eminent; chief.   [< ARCH-]   — **arch′ly** adv.   — **arch′ness** n.

arch-   prefix   **1.** Chief; principal. **2.** Very great; extreme. Also archi-.   [OE < L < Gk. archos ruler]

archaeo-   See ARCHEO-.

ar·chae·ol·o·gy (är′kē-ol′ə-jē), etc.   See ARCHEOLOGY, etc.

ar·cha·ic (är-kā′ik)   adj.   **1.** Old-fashioned; antiquated. **2.** Characterizing a word, an inflectional form, or a phrase no longer in current use. Also **ar·cha′i·cal.**   — Syn. See OBSOLETE.   [< Gk. archaios ancient]

ar·cha·ism (är′kē-iz′əm, -kā-)   n.   An archaic word, idiom, or style.   — **ar′cha·ist** n.   — **ar·cha·is′tic** adj.

arch·an·gel (ärk′ān′jəl)   n.   **1.** An angel of highest rank. **2.** The angelica.   — **the Archangel** In Christian theology, usually Michael.   [< LL < Gk. < arch- chief + angelos angel]   — **arch·an·gel·ic** (ärk′an-jel′ik) or **-i·cal** adj.

arch·bish·op (ärch′bish′əp)   n.   Eccl.   The chief bishop of a province.   — **arch′bish′op·ric** n.

arch·dea·con (ärch′dē′kən) *n. Eccl.* A chief deacon, ranking just below a bishop.

arch·dea·con·ry (ärch′dē′kən·rē) *n. pl.* **·ries 1.** The jurisdiction or office of an archdeacon. Also **arch′dea′con·ate** (-it), **arch′dea′con·ship. 2.** An archdeacon's residence.

arch·di·o·cese (ärch′dī′ə·sēs, -sis) *n.* The diocese or jurisdiction of an archbishop.

arch·du·cal (ärch′dōō′kəl, -dyōō′-) *adj.* Of or pertaining to an archduke or an archduchy.

arch·duch·ess (ärch′duch′is) *n.* **1.** The wife or widow of an archduke. **2.** A princess of the former royal family of Austria.

arch·duch·y (ärch′duch′ē) *n. pl.* **·duch·ies** The territory ruled by an archduke. Also **arch′duke/dom.**

arch·duke (ärch′dōōk′, -dyōōk′) *n.* A chief duke, especially a prince of the former royal family of Austria. Abbr. *Archd.*

arched (ärcht) *adj.* **1.** Having the form of an arch. **2.** Covered or furnished with arches.

ar·che·go·ni·um (är′kə·gō′nē·əm) *n. pl.* **·ni·a** (-nē·ə) *Bot.* The female sexual organ of the higher cryptogams. Also **ar·che·gone** (är′kə·gōn). [< NL < Gk. < *archos* chief, first + *gonos* race, offspring] — **ar′che·go′ni·al** *adj.* — **ar′che·go′ni·ate** *adj.*

archeo- *combining form* Ancient: *Archeozoic.* Also **archaeo-.** [< Gk. *archaios* ancient]

ar·che·ol·o·gy (är′kē·ol′ə·jē) *n.* The science or study of history from the remains of early human cultures as discovered chiefly by systematic excavations: also, *esp. Brit.,* archaeology. — **ar·che·o·log·i·cal** (är′kē·ə·loj′i·kəl) or **·log′ic** *adj.* — **ar′che·ol′o·gist** *n.*

Ar·che·o·zo·ic (är′kē·ə·zō′ik) *adj. Geol.* Of or pertaining to the oldest of the eras making up the geological record. See chart for GEOLOGY. Also spelled *Archaeozoic.* [< ARCHEO- + Gk. *zōion* animal]

arch·er (är′chər) *n.* One who shoots with a bow and arrow. [< AF < L *arcus* bow]

Arch·er (är′chər) *n.* The constellation and sign of the zodiac Sagittarius.

arch·er·y (är′chər·ē) *n.* **1.** The art or sport of shooting with bow and arrows. **2.** The weapons and outfit of an archer.

ar·che·type (är′kə·tīp) *n.* An original or standard pattern or model; a prototype. [< L < Gk. < *arche-* first + *typos* stamp, pattern] — **ar′che·typ′al** (-tī′pəl), **ar′che·typ′ic** (-tip′ik) or **·i·cal** *adj.*

archi- *prefix* **1.** Var. of ARCH-. **2.** *Biol.* Original; primitive: *archicarp.* [See ARCH-.]

ar·chi·e·pis·co·pate (är′kē·i·pis′kə·pit, -pāt) *n.* The office or tenure of an archbishop. — **ar′chi·e·pis′co·pal** *adj.*

Ar·chi·me·de·an (är′kə·mē′dē·ən, mə·dē′ən) *adj.* Of, discovered by, or pertaining to Archimedes.

ar·chi·pel·a·go (är′kə·pel′ə·gō) *n. pl.* **·goes** or **·gos 1.** A sea with many islands. **2.** The islands in such a sea. [< Ital. < Gk. *archi-* chief + *pelagos* sea] — **ar·chi·pe·lag·ic** (är′kə·pə·laj′ik) *adj.*

ar·chi·tect (är′kə·tekt) *n.* **1.** One whose profession is to design and draw up the plans for buildings, etc., and supervise their construction. **2.** One who devises or creates anything. [< F < L < Gk. < *archi-* chief + *tektōn* worker]

ar·chi·tec·ton·ic (är′kə·tek·ton′ik) *adj.* **1.** Pertaining to an architect or architecture; constructive. **2.** Having architectural qualities of design and structure.

ar·chi·tec·ton·ics (är′kə·tek·ton′iks) *n.pl. (construed as sing.)* **1.** The science of architecture. **2.** Structural design, as in works of music or art.

ar·chi·tec·ture (är′kə·tek′chər) *n.* **1.** The science, art, or profession of designing and constructing buildings or other structures. **2.** A style or system of building: Gothic *architecture.* **3.** Construction or structure generally. **4.** A building, or buildings collectively. Abbr. *arch., archit.* — **ar′chi·tec′tur·al** *adj.* — **ar′chi·tec′tur·al·ly** *adv.*

ar·chi·trave (är′kə·trāv) *n. Archit.* **1.** The part of an entablature that rests upon the column heads and supports the frieze. For illus. see COLUMN. **2.** A molded ornament skirting the head and sides of a door or window. [< F < Ital. < Gk. < *archi-* chief + Ital. *trave* beam]

ar·chives (är′kīvz) *n.pl.* **1.** A place where public records and historical documents are kept. **2.** Public records, documents, etc., as kept in such a depository. [< F < LL < Gk. *archeion* a public office] — **ar·chi·val** (är·kī′vəl) *adj.*

ar·chi·vist (är′kə·vist) *n.* A keeper of archives.

arch·priest (ärch′prēst′) *n.* **1.** Formerly, the senior priest of a cathedral chapter, serving as assistant to a bishop: later called *dean.* **2.** A chief priest. — **arch′priest′hood.**

arch·way (ärch′wā′) *n.* A passage under an arch.

-archy *combining form* Rule; government: *monarchy.* [< Gk. *-archia < archos* ruler]

arc light A lamp in which light of high intensity is produced between two adjacent electrodes. Also **arc lamp.**

arc·tic (ärk′tik, är′tik) *adj.* Characteristic of the Arctic; extremely cold; frigid. [Earlier *artik* < OF < L < Gk. < *arktos* a bear]

Arctic Circle The parallel at 66°33′ north latitude; the boundary of the North Frigid Zone.

Arc·tu·rus (ärk·tŏŏr′əs, -tyōōr′-) *n.* An orange-red star, one of the 20 brightest, 0.24 magnitude; Alpha in the constellation Boötes. [< L < Gk. *arktos* a bear + *ouros* a guard]

-ard *suffix of nouns* One who does something to excess or who is to be disparaged: *drunkard, coward;* sometimes changed to *-art: braggart.* [< OF *-ard, -art* < G *-hard, -hart* hardy]

ar·den·cy (är′dən·sē) *n.* Intensity of emotion; ardor.

ar·dent (är′dənt) *adj.* **1.** Passionate; zealous; intense. **2.** Glowing; flashing. **3.** Hot; burning. [< L *ardere* to burn] — **ar′dent·ly** *adv.* — **ar′dent·ness** *n.*

ar·dor (är′dər) *n.* **1.** Warmth or intensity of passion or affection; eagerness; vehemence; zeal. **2.** Great heat, as of fire. Also *Brit.* **ar′dour.** [< L *ardere* to burn]

ar·du·ous (är′jōō·əs) *adj.* **1.** Involving great labor or hardship; difficult. **2.** Toiling strenuously; energetic. **3.** Steep; hard to climb or surmount. [< L *arduus* steep] — **ar′du·ous·ly** *adv.* — **ar′du·ous·ness** *n.*

are¹ (är, *unstressed* ər, r, ə) *v.* First, second, and third person plural, present indicative, of BE: also used as second person singular. [OE (Northumbrian) *aron*]

are² (âr, är) *n.* In the metric system, a surface measure equal to one hundred square meters; also spelled *ar.* See table inside back cover. [< F < L *area* area]

ar·e·a (âr′ē·ə) *n. pl.* **ar·e·as 1.** A particular portion of the earth's surface; region. **2.** The surface included within a bounding line. **3.** The extent or scope of anything. **4.** The yard of a building. **5.** Any flat, open space. [< L, an open space] — **ar′e·al** *adj.*

ar·e·a·way (âr′ē·ə·wā′) *n.* **1.** A small sunken court before a basement door. **2.** A passageway.

a·re·na (ə·rē′nə) *n.* **1.** The oval space in a Roman amphitheater, where contests and shows were held. **2.** Any place of this nature: a football *arena.* **3.** A scene or sphere of action or contest: the political *arena.* [< L, sand, sandy place]

arena theater A stage in the center of an auditorium, surrounded by seats: also called *theater-in-the-round.*

aren't (ärnt) Are not.

aren't I ♦ See note under AIN'T.

areo- *combining form* Mars. [< Gk. *Arēs*]

a·re·o·la (ə·rē′ə·lə) *n. pl.* **·lae** (-lē) or **·las 1.** *Bot.* An interstice in a network of leaf veins. **2.** *Anat.* The colored circle about a nipple or about a vesicle. Also **ar·e·ole** (âr′ē·ōl). [< L, dim. of *area* open space] — **a·re′o·lar, a·re·o·late** (ə·rē′ə·lit, -lāt) *adj.* — **ar·e·o·la·tion** (âr′ē·ə·lā′shən) *n.*

Ar·e·op·a·gus (ar′ē·op′ə·gəs) **1.** A hill NW of the Acropolis on which the highest court of ancient Athens held its sessions; also, the court itself. **2.** Any high law court. [< L < Gk. *Areios* of Ares + *pagos* hill]

Ar·es (âr′ēz) In Greek mythology, the god of war: identified with the Roman *Mars.*

ar·ga·li (är′gə·lē) *n. pl.* **·lis** or **·li 1.** An Asian wild sheep with large horns curved spirally outward. **2.** Any of several other wild sheep. Also **ar·gal** (är′gəl). [< Mongolian]

ar·gent (är′jənt) *n. Archaic & Poetic* Silver. — *adj.* Like or made of silver; white; silvery: also **ar·gen·tal** (är·jen′təl). [< F < L *argentum* silver]

ar·gen·tine (är′jən·tin, -tīn) *adj.* Silvery. [< F < L *argentum* silver]

Ar·gen·tine (är′jən·tēn, -tīn) *adj.* Of or pertaining to Argentina. — *n.* A native or citizen of Argentina: also **Ar·gen·tin·e·an** (är′jən·tin′ē·ən).

ar·gen·tum (är·jen′təm) *n. Chem.* Silver. [< L]

ar·gil (är′jil) *n.* Potters' clay; white clay. [< MF < L < Gk. < *argos* white]

ar·gi·nine (är′jə·nēn, -nin, -nīn) *n. Biochem.* One of the amino acids essential to nutrition, $C_6H_{14}O_2N_4$. [< NL *argin-* + -INE²]

Ar·give (är′jīv, -gīv) *adj. & n.* Greek.

Ar·go (är′gō) *n.* In Greek legend, the ship in which Jason and the Argonauts sailed for the Golden Fleece.

ar·gol (är′gəl) *n.* Crude potassium bitartrate, the base of tartaric acid. [ME < AF *argoil*]

ar·gon (är′gon) *n.* A colorless, gaseous element (symbol Ar) present in the atmosphere, used in electric display signs and as a filter for incandescent electric lamps. [< NL < Gk. neut. of *argos* idle, inert + -ON]

Ar·go·naut (är′gə·nôt) *n.* **1.** In Greek legend, one who sailed with Jason in the ship Argo to find the Golden Fleece. **2.** One who went to California in 1849 to hunt gold. [< L

ARGALI (4 feet high at shoulder)

< Gk. < *Argō*, the ship + *nautēs* sailor] **—ar′go·nau′tic** *adj.*

ar·go·sy (är′gə·sē) *n. pl.* **·sies 1.** A large merchant ship. **2.** A fleet of merchant vessels. [Earlier *ragusy*, after *Ragusa*, Italian name of Dubrovnik, Yugoslav port]

ar·got (är′gō, -gət) *n.* The specialized vocabulary or jargon of any class or group, as that of the underworld. [< F] **—ar·got·ic** (är·got′ik) *adj.*

ar·gue (är′gyōō) *v.* **·gued, ·gu·ing** *v.i.* **1.** To present reasons to support or contest a measure or opinion. **2.** To contend in argument; quarrel. **—** *v.t.* **3.** To present reasons for or against; discuss, as a proposal. **4.** To contend or maintain, by reasoning. **5.** To prove or indicate, as from evidence. **6.** To influence or convince, as by argument. [< OF < L *arguere* to prove] **—ar′gu·a·ble** *adj.* **—ar′gu·er** *n.*

ar·gu·ment (är′gyə·mənt) *n.* **1.** An angry discussion or quarrel. **2.** A reason or reasons offered for or against something. **3.** Discourse intended to persuade or to convince. **4.** A short summary of a piece of subject matter.

ar·gu·men·ta·tion (är′gyə·men·tā′shən) *n.* **1.** The methodical setting forth of premises and the drawing of conclusions therefrom. **2.** Discussion; debate.

ar·gu·men·ta·tive (är′gyə·men′tə·tiv) *adj.* **1.** Controversial. **2.** Given to argumentation; disputatious. **—ar′gu·men′ta·tive·ly** *adv.* **—ar′gu·men′ta·tive·ness** *n.*

Ar·gus (är′gəs) *n.* **1.** In Greek mythology, a giant with a hundred eyes, killed by Hermes. **2.** Any vigilant watchman.

Ar·gus-eyed (är′gəs·īd′) *adj.* Sharp-sighted; vigilant.

a·ri·a (ä′rē·ə, âr′ē·ə) *n.* **1.** An air; melody. **2.** An elaborate melody for single voice, as in an opera or oratorio, often with instrumental accompaniment. [< Ital. < L *aer* air]

-aria *suffix* Used in forming new Latin names, esp. in zoological and botanical classifications. [< NL < L *-arius*]

Ar·i·ad·ne (ar′ē·ad′nē) In Greek mythology, the daughter of Minos, who gave Theseus the thread by which he found his way out of the Labyrinth.

-arian *suffix* Used in forming adjectives and adjectival nouns denoting occupation, age, sect, beliefs, etc.: *nonagenarian, predestinarian.* [< L *-arius* -ary + -AN]

Ar·i·an (âr′ē·ən, ar′-, är′yən) See ARYAN.

Ar·i·an·ism (âr′ē·ən·iz′əm) *n. Theol.* The doctrine denying that Christ is of one substance with God the Father. [after *Arius*, 250?–336, Greek theologian] **—Ar′i·an** *adj. & n.*

ar·id (ar′id) *adj.* **1.** Parched with heat; dry. **2.** Without interest or feeling; dull. [< L *arere* to be dry] **—a·rid·i·ty** (ə·rid′ə·tē), **ar′id·ness** *n.* **—ar′id·ly** *adv.*

Ar·ies (âr′ēz, âr′i·ēz) *n.* A constellation, the Ram; also, the first sign of the zodiac. See ZODIAC. [< L]

a·right (ə·rīt′) *adv.* In a right way; correctly; rightly.

a·ri·o·so (ä·ryō′sō) *adj. Music* Characteristic of an aria. **—** *adv.* In the manner of an aria. **—** *n.* A passage, composition, etc., resembling an aria. [< Ital.]

-arious *suffix of adjectives* Connected with; pertaining to: *gregarious.* [< L *-arius* -ary + -OUS]

a·rise (ə·rīz′) *v.i.* **a·rose** (ə·rōz′), **a·ris·en** (ə·riz′ən), **a·ris·ing 1.** To get up, as from a prone position. **2.** To rise; ascend. **3.** To come into being; originate; issue. **4.** To result; proceed. [OE < ā- up + *rīsan* to rise]

aristo- *combining form* Best; finest. [< Gk. *aristos*]

ar·is·toc·ra·cy (ar′is·tok′rə·sē) *n. pl.* **·cies 1.** A hereditary nobility or privileged class. **2.** A state ruled by a privileged upper class, or by the nobility. **3.** Government by an upper class or the nobility. **4.** Originally, government by its best citizens or a state governed by its best citizens. **5.** Any preeminent group: the *aristocracy* of talent. [< L < Gk. < *aristos* best + *krateein* to rule]

a·ris·to·crat (ə·ris′tə·krat, ar′is·tə·krat′) *n.* **1.** A member of an aristocracy. **2.** A proud and exclusive person. **3.** One who prefers an aristocratic form of government. **—a·ris′to·crat′ic** or **·i·cal** *adj.* **—a·ris′o·crat′i·cal·ly** *adv.*

Ar·is·to·te·li·an (ar′is·tə·tē′lē·ən, -tēl′yən, ə·ris′tə-) *adj.* Pertaining to or characteristic of Aristotle or his philosophy. **—** *n.* An adherent of Aristotle's teachings; one who tends to be empirical or scientific in his method, rather than speculative. Also **Ar′is·to·te′le·an. —Ar′is·to·te′li·an·ism** *n.*

Aristotelian logic The deductive method of logic of Aristotle, characterized by the syllogism.

a·rith·me·tic (*n.* ə·rith′mə·tik; *adj.* ar′ith·met′ik) *n.* The science of computing with numbers by the operations of addition, subtraction, multiplication, and division. **—** *adj.* Of or pertaining to arithmetic: also **ar′ith·met′i·cal.** [< L < Gr. *arithmos* number] **—ar′ith·met′i·cal·ly** *adv.*

a·rith·me·ti·cian (ə·rith′mə·tish′ən, ar′ith-) *n.* One who uses or is skilled in arithmetic.

arithmetic mean (ar′ith·met′ik) *Math.* The sum of a set of numbers, divided by the number of terms in the set.

arithmetic progression (ar′ith·met′ik) *Math.* A sequence of terms in which each, except the first, differs from the preceding one by a constant quantity, as 2, 4, 6, 8.

-arium *suffix of nouns* **1.** A place for: *herbarium.* **2.** Connected with: *honorarium.* [< L < -arius. See -ARY[1].]

ark (ärk) *n.* **1.** In the Bible: **a** The ship of Noah. *Gen.* vi-viii. **b** The chest containing the stone tablets bearing the Ten Commandments: also called **ark of the covenant.** *Ex.* xxv 10. **2.** A large, flat-bottomed or awkward boat; scow. [OE *arc* < L *arca* chest]

arm[1] (ärm) *n.* **1.** *Anat.* An upper limb of the human body, from the shoulder to the hand or wrist. ◆ Collateral adjective: *brachial.* **2.** The forelimb of certain other vertebrates. **3.** An armlike part or appendage. **4.** Something intended to support or cover the human arm. **5.** Anything branching out like an arm from a main body, as the end of a spar. **— at arm's length** At a distance. **— with open arms** Cordially; warmly. [OE *earm, arm*]

arm[2] (ärm) *n.* **1.** A weapon. **2.** A distinct branch of the military service: the air *arm.* **—** *v.t.* **1.** To supply with weapons. **2.** To make secure, as with a protective covering. **—** *v.i.* **3.** To supply or equip oneself with weapons. [< OF < L *arma* weapons] **—arm′er** *n.*

ar·ma·da (är·mä′də, -mä′-) *n.* A fleet of war vessels. **— the Armada** The fleet sent against England by Spain in 1588, defeated by the English navy: also **Invincible Armada, Spanish Armada.** [< Sp. < L *armare* to arm]

ar·ma·dil·lo (är′mə·dil′ō) *n. pl.* **·los** An American burrowing nocturnal mammal having an armorlike covering of jointed plates. [< Sp. < L *armare* to arm]

Ar·ma·ged·don (är′mə·ged′n) *n.* **1.** In Biblical prophecy, the scene of a great battle between the forces of good and evil, to occur at the end of the world. *Rev.* xvi 16. **2.** Any great or decisive conflict.

ARMADILLO
(30 inches long; tail 12 inches)

ar·ma·ment (är′mə·mənt) *n.* **1.** *Often pl.* The guns and other military equipment of a fortification, military unit, warship, etc. **2.** The act of arming or equipping for war. [< L *armare* to arm]

ar·ma·ture (är mə·chŏŏr) *n.* **1.** A piece of soft iron joining the poles of a magnet to prevent the loss of magnetic power. **2.** *Electr.* **a** In a dynamo or motor, the cylindrical, laminated iron core carrying the coils of insulated wire to be revolved through the magnetic field. **b** The part of a relay, as a buzzer or bell, that vibrates when activated. **3.** *Biol.* Protective covering, as the shells of animals. **4.** In sculpture, a framework to support the clay or other substance in modeling. **5.** Arms; armor. [< MF < L *armare* to arm]

arm·chair (ärm′châr′) *n.* A chair with supports for the arms.

armed (ärmd) *adj.* **1.** Provided with weapons. **2.** Having upper limbs: used in combination: *strong-armed.*

armed forces The military and naval forces of a nation.

Ar·me·ni·an (är·mē′nē·ən, -mēn′yən) *adj.* Of or pertaining to the country, people, or language of Armenia. **—** *n.* **1.** A native of Armenia. **2.** The language of the Armenians.

arm·ful (ärm′fŏŏl′) *n. pl.* **·fuls** That which is held, or as much as can be held, in the arm or arms.

Ar·min·i·an·ism (är·min′ē·ən·iz′əm) *n. Theol.* The doctrines holding a less rigorous view of predestination than Calvinism. [after Jacobus *Arminius*, 1560–1609, Dutch Protestant theologian] **—Ar·min′i·an** *adj. & n.*

ar·mi·stice (är′mə·stis) *n.* A temporary cessation of hostilities by mutual agreement; a truce. [< F < L < *arma* arms + *sistere* to stop, stand still]

Armistice Day See VETERANS DAY.

arm·let (ärm′lit) *n.* **1.** A little arm, as of the sea. **2.** A band worn around the arm. **3.** A small, short sleeve.

ar·moire (är·mwär′) *n.* A large, movable, often ornate cabinet or cupboard. [< F < OF < L *armarium* a chest]

ar·mor (är′mər) *n.* **1.** A defensive covering, as of metallic plates for a war vessel, a tank, etc. **2.** The armored vehicles of an army. **3.** Any protective covering, as the shell of a turtle. **—** *v.t. & v.i.* To furnish with or put on armor. Also *Brit.* **ar′mour.** [< OF *armeür* < L *armare* to arm]

ar·mored (är′mərd) *adj.* **1.** Protected by armor. **2.** Equipped with armored vehicles, as a military unit.

ar·mor·er (är′mər·ər) *n.* **1.** A maker or repairer, of arms or armor. **2.** A manufacturer of arms. **3.** *Mil.* An enlisted man in charge of small arms. Also *Brit.* **ar′mour·er.**

ar·mo·ri·al (är·môr′ē·əl, -mō′rē-) *adj.* Pertaining to heraldry.

armor plate A covering of very hard steel plating, used on warships, tanks, etc. **— ar·mor-plat·ed** (är′mər·plā′tid) *adj.*

ar·mo·ry (är′mər·ē) *n. pl.* **·mor·ies 1.** A place where arms are kept; arsenal. **2.** *U.S.* A building for the use of a body of militia, including storage for arms and equipment, drill rooms, etc. **3.** *U.S.* A factory for making firearms. Also *Brit.* **ar′mour·y.** [Prob. < ARMOR]

arm·pit (ärm′pit′) *n.* The cavity under the arm at the shoulder; axilla.

arms (ärmz) *n.pl.* **1.** Weapons collectively. **2.** Warfare. **3.** The official insignia of a state, etc. **4.** Heraldic symbols. **— to arms!** Make ready for battle! **— to bear arms 1.** To carry weapons. **2.** To serve in the armed forces. **— under arms** Provided with weapons; ready for war. **— up in arms** Aroused and ready to fight. [< F < L *arma* weapons]

ar·my (är′mē) *n. pl.* **·mies** **1.** A large organized body of men armed for military service on land. **2.** The total military land forces of a country. **3.** Any large body of people, animals, etc.; host; multitude. [< OF < L *armare* to arm]

ar·ni·ca (är′ni·kə) *n.* **1.** A widely distributed herbaceous perennial of the composite family. **2.** A tincture prepared from this herb, used for sprains and bruises. [< NL]

a·ro·ma (ə·rō′mə) *n.* **1.** Fragrance, as from appetizing food, spices, etc.; agreeable odor. **2.** Characteristic quality or style. — **Syn.** See SMELL. [< L < Gk. *arōma, -atos* spice] — **a·ro·ma·tous** (ə·rō′mə·təs) *adj.*

ar·o·mat·ic (ar′ə·mat′ik) *adj.* Having an aroma; fragrant; spicy. Also **ar′o·mat′i·cal.** — *n.* Any vegetable or drug of agreeable odor. — **ar′o·mat′i·cal·ly** *adv.*

a·ro·ma·tize (ə·rō′mə·tīz) *v.t.* **·tized, ·tiz·ing** To make fragrant or aromatic.

a·rose (ə·rōz′) Past tense of ARISE.

a·round (ə·round′) *adv.* **1.** On all sides; in various directions: It is raining all *around.* **2.** In the opposite direction: to turn *around.* **3.** *U.S.* From place to place; here and there: to walk *around.* **4.** *U.S. Informal* Nearby; in the vicinity: Wait *around* until I call. **5.** In or to a particular place: Come *around* to see us again. — **to get around** *U.S. Informal* **1.** To be experienced and up to date. **2.** To overcome or cope with (someone or something). — **to get around to** *U.S. Informal* To give attention to or accomplish. — **to have been around** *U.S. Informal* To be experienced in the ways of the world. — *prep.* **1.** About the circumference or circuit of. **2.** On all sides of; surrounding or enveloping. **3.** *U.S. Informal* Here and there in: He wandered *around* the city. **4.** *U.S. Informal* Somewhere near or within. **5.** *U.S. Informal* Somewhere near in time, amount, etc.; about.

a·rouse (ə·rouz′) *v.* **a·roused, a·rous·ing** *v.t.* **1.** To awaken. **2.** To excite, as to a state of high emotion. — *v.i.* **3.** To arouse oneself. [< A-² + ROUSE] — **a·rous′al** (-zəl) *n.*

ar·peg·gi·o (är·pej′ē·ō, -pej′ō) *n. pl.* **·gi·os** *Music* **1.** The sounding or playing of the notes of a chord in rapid succession. **2.** A chord so played. [< Ital. *arpa* a harp]

ar·que·bus (är′kwə·bəs) *n.* A harquebus.

ar·raign (ə·rān′) *v.t.* **1.** *Law* To call into court and cause to answer to an indictment. **2.** To call upon for an answer; accuse. — **Syn.** See ACCUSE. [< AF < LL *arrationare* to call to account] — **ar·raign′er** *n.* — **ar·raign′ment** *n.*

ar·range (ə·rānj′) *v.* **·ranged, ·rang·ing** *v.t.* **1.** To put in definite or proper order. **2.** To plan the details of; prepare for. **3.** To adjust, as a conflict or dispute; settle. **4.** *Music* To change or adapt for other instruments or voices. — *v.i.* **5.** To come to an agreement or understanding. **6.** To see about the details; make plans. [< OF *arangier* < *a-* to + *rangier* to put in order] — **ar·rang′er** *n.*

ar·range·ment (ə·rānj′mənt) *n.* **1.** The act of arranging, or the state of being arranged; disposition. **2.** That which is arranged. **3.** The style in which something is arranged; order. **4.** A settlement, as of a dispute; adjustment. **5.** *Usually pl.* The plans or preparations made, or measures taken, for a particular purpose. **6.** *Music* The adaptation of a composition to other voices or instruments.

ar·rant (ar′ənt) *adj.* Notoriously bad; unmitigated. [Var. of ERRANT] — **ar′rant·ly** *adv.*

ar·ras (ar′əs) *n.* **1.** A tapestry. **2.** A wall hanging, esp. of tapestry. [after *Arras*, France]

ar·ray (ə·rā′) *n.* **1.** Regular or proper order, esp. of troops. **2.** The persons or things arrayed. **3.** Clothing; fine dress. — *v.t.* **1.** To draw up in order of battle; set in order. **2.** To adorn; dress, as for display. [< AF < OF *arei* < *a-* to + *rei* order]

ar·ray·al (ə·rā′əl) *n.* **1.** The act or process of arraying. **2.** Anything arrayed; an array.

ar·rear·age (ə·rir′ij) *n.* **1.** The state of being in arrears. **2.** The amount in arrears. **3.** A thing kept in reserve.

ar·rears (ə·rirz′) *n.pl.* That which is behindhand; a part, as of a debt, overdue and unpaid. — **in arrears** (or **arrear**) Behind in meeting payment, completing work, etc. [< OF < L *ad-* to + *retro* backward]

ar·rest (ə·rest′) *v.t.* **1.** To stop suddenly; check. **2.** To take into legal custody. **3.** To attract and fix, as the attention. — *n.* **1.** The act of arresting, or the state of being arrested. **2.** Seizure by legal authority. **3.** A device for arresting motion. — **under arrest** In custody; arrested. [< OF < LL < L *ad-* to + *restare* to stop, remain] — **ar·rest′er, ar·rest′or** *n.*

ar·ri·val (ə·rī′vəl) *n.* **1.** The act of arriving. **2.** One who or that which arrives or has arrived.

ar·rive (ə·rīv′) *v.i.* **·rived, ·riv·ing** **1.** To reach a destination or place. **2.** To come to a desired object, state, etc.: often with *at.* **3.** To attain success or fame. **4.** To come at length: The hour has *arrived.* [< OF < LL < L *ad-* to + *ripa* shore]

ar·ro·gance (ar′ə·gəns) *n.* The quality or state of being arrogant or haughty. Also **ar′ro·gan·cy, ar′ro·gant·ness.**

ar·ro·gant (ar′ə·gənt) *adj.* **1.** Overbearing; haughty. **2.** Characterized by or due to arrogance. [< OF < L < *ad-* to + *rogare* to ask] — **ar′ro·gant·ly** *adv.*

ar·ro·gate (ar′ə·gāt) *v.t.* **·gat·ed, ·gat·ing** **1.** To claim or take without right. **2.** To ascribe to another without reason. [< L < *ad-* to + *rogare* to ask] — **ar′ro·ga′tive** *adj.* — **ar′ro·ga′tion** *n.*

ar·row (ar′ō, -ə) *n.* **1.** A slender shaft, generally feathered at one end and with a pointed head at the other, to be shot from a bow. **2.** Anything resembling an arrow in shape, speed, etc. **3.** A sign or figure in the shape of an arrow, used to indicate directions. [OE *earh, arwe*] — **ar·row·y** (ar′ō·ē) *adj.*

ar·row·head (ar′ō·hed′, -ə-) *n.* **1.** The sharp-pointed head of an arrow. **2.** Something resembling an arrowhead, as a mark used to point direction, etc. **3.** *Bot.* An aquatic plant with arrow-shaped leaves.

ar·row·root (ar′ō·rōōt′, -ə-, -rŏŏt′) *n.* **1.** A nutritious starch obtained from a tropical American plant. **2.** The plant itself. [Plant so called because used to treat arrow wounds]

ar·roy·o (ə·roi′ō) *n. pl.* **·os** (-ōz) *SW U.S.* **1.** A deep, dry gully. **2.** A brook. [< Sp., ult. < L *arrugia* pit, shaft]

ar·se·nal (är′sə·nəl) *n.* **1.** A government facility for manufacturing and storing arms and munitions. **2.** A store of arms. [< Ital. < Arabic *dār aṣ-ṣin′ah* workshop]

ar·se·nic (är′sə·nik) *n.* A grayish white, brittle metallic element (symbol As), forming many poisonous compounds and used in medicine, industry, and the arts. [< OF < L < Gk. *arsenikon* yellow orpiment]

ar·sen·i·cal (är·sen′i·kəl) *adj.* Of or containing arsenic. Also **ar·sen′ic.** — *n.* Any arsenical insecticide or drug.

ar·son (är′sən) *n. Law* The crime of setting fire to a building or other property. [< OF < LL < L *ardere* to burn]

ars po·et·i·ca (ärz pō·et′i·kə) *Latin* The art of poetry.

art¹ (ärt) *n.* **1.** An esthetically pleasing and meaningful arrangement of elements, as words, sounds, colors, shapes, etc. **2.** Literature, music, and esp. painting, sculpture, drawing, etc. **3.** Any system of rules and principles that facilitates skilled human accomplishment. **4.** A pursuit or occupation that depends upon the skilled application of such a system of rules and principles. **5.** Practical skill; dexterity: the *art* of a craftsman. **6.** *pl.* The liberal arts. **7.** *Usu. pl.* Cunning. [< OF < L *ars, artis* skill]

art² (ärt) *Archaic* or *Poetic* Second person singular present tense of BE: used with *thou.* [OE *eart*]

-art *suffix* Var. of -ARD.

Ar·te·mis (är′tə·mis) In Greek mythology, the goddess identified with the Roman *Diana.*

ar·te·ri·al (är·tir′ē·əl) *adj.* **1.** Of or pertaining to the arteries or an artery. **2.** *Physiol.* Pertaining to the bright red blood that has undergone aeration in the lungs. **3.** Resembling an artery: an *arterial* highway.

ar·te·ri·al·ize (är·tir′ē·əl·īz′) *v.t.* **·ized, ·iz·ing** *Physiol.* To convert (venous blood) into arterial blood by oxygenation. Also *Brit.* **ar·te′ri·al·ise′.** — **ar·te′ri·al·i·za′tion** *n.*

arterio- *combining form* Artery. Also, before vowels, **arter-.** [< Gk. *artēria*]

ar·te·ri·o·scle·ro·sis (är·tir′ē·ō·sklə·rō′sis) *n. Pathol.* The thickening and hardening of the walls of an artery. — **ar·te′ri·o·scle·rot′ic** (-rot′ik) *adj.*

ar·ter·y (är′tər·ē) *n. pl.* **·ter·ies** **1.** *Anat.* Any of a large number of muscular vessels conveying blood away from the heart to every part of the body. **2.** Any main channel or route. [< L *arteria* artery, windpipe]

ar·te·sian well (är·tē′zhən) A well that penetrates to a water-bearing stratum from a surface lower than the source of the water supply, so that the water pressure forces a flow of water out at the surface. [< F, after *Artois*, town in France]

art·ful (ärt′fəl) *adj.* **1.** Crafty; cunning. **2.** Skillful; ingenious. **3.** Artificial. — **art′ful·ly** *adv.* — **art′ful·ness** *n.*

ar·thri·tis (är·thrī′tis) *n. Pathol.* Inflammation of a joint or joints. [< L < Gk. *arthron* joint] — **ar·thrit·ic** (är·thrit′ik) *adj. & n.*

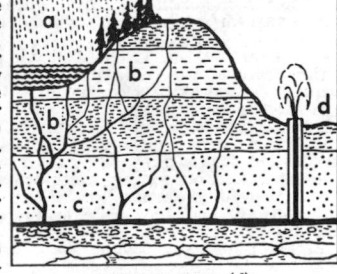

ARTESIAN WELL (*d*)
a Precipitation. *b* Seepage.
c Water table.

arthro- *combining form* Joint. Also, before vowels, **arthr-**. [< Gk. *arthron*]

ar·thro·pod (är′thrə-pod) *Zool. n.* Any of a large phylum of invertebrate animals having jointed legs and segmented body parts, including insects, spiders, and crabs. [< AR-THRO- + Gk. *pous, podos* foot] — **ar·throp·o·dous** (är-throp′ə-dəs), **ar·throp′o·dal** *adj.*

Ar·thur (är′thər) Legendary sixth-century British king; hero of the Round Table. [? < Celtic, high, admirable] — **Ar·thu′ri·an** (-thōōr′ē-en) *adj.*

ar·ti·choke (är′tə-chōk) *n.* 1. A thistlelike garden plant. 2. Its flower head, used as a vegetable. 3. The Jerusalem artichoke. [< Ital. ult. < Arabic *al-kharshūf*]

ar·ti·cle (är′ti-kəl) *n.* 1. A particular object or substance; a thing. 2. An individual item in a class: an *article* of food. 3. A literary composition forming an independent part of a newspaper, magazine, etc. 4. A separate section in a document, as in a treaty, contract, statute, etc. 5. *Gram.* One of a class of auxiliary words inserted before a noun to limit or modify it in some way, as English *a, an* (**indefinite article**) and *the* (**definite article**). — *v.* **·cled, ·cling** *v.t.* 1. To bind to service by a written contract. 2. To accuse by formal articles. — *v.i.* 3. To make accusations: with *against.* [< F < L *artus* a joint]

ar·tic·u·lar (är-tik′yə-lər) *adj.* Pertaining to a joint or the joints. [< L *articularis*]

ar·tic·u·late (*adj.* är-tik′yə-lit; *v.* är-tik′yə-lāt) *adj.* 1. Able to speak, esp. well or expressively. 2. Clearly enunciated. 3. Coherent; well presented: an *articulate* thesis. 4. Jointed; segmented, as limbs. Also **ar·tic′u·lat′ed.** — **·lat·ed, ·lat·ing** *v.t.* 1. To utter distinctly; enunciate. 2. To give utterance to; express in words. 3. To joint together; unite by joints. — *v.i.* 4. To speak distinctly. 5. *Phonet.* To produce a speech sound. [< L *articulare* to divide into joints, utter distinctly] — **ar·tic′u·late·ly** *adv.* — **ar·tic′u·late·ness** *n.*

ar·tic·u·la·tion (är-tik′yə-lā′shən) *n.* 1. A jointing or being jointed together. 2. The manner or method of jointing. 3. *Anat.* The union forming a joint, as of bones. 4. The utterance of speech sounds; enunciation. 5. *Phonet.* **a** A speech sound. **b** The movements of the organs of speech in producing a speech sound. 6. *Bot.* A node or the space between two nodes. — **ar·tic·u·la·tive** (är-tik′yə-lā′tiv, -lə-tiv), **ar·tic·u·la·to·ry** (är-tik′yə-lə-tôr′ē, -tō′rē) *adj.*

ar·tic·u·la·tor (är-tik′yə-lā′tər) *n.* One who or that which articulates.

ar·ti·fact (är′tə-fakt) *n.* Anything made by human work or art. Also **ar′te·fact.** [< L *ars, artis* art, skill + *facere* to make]

ar·ti·fice (är′tə-fis) *n.* 1. An ingenious expedient; stratagem; maneuver. 2. Subtle or deceptive craft; trickery. 3. Skill; ingenuity. [< F < L *ars, artis* art + *facere* to make]

ar·tif·i·cer (är-tif′ə-sər) *n.* 1. One who constructs with skill. 2. *Mil.* A skilled mechanic. 3. An inventor.

ar·ti·fi·cial (är′tə-fish′əl) *adj.* 1. Produced by human art. 2. Made in imitation of something natural. 3. Feigned; fictitious. 4. Not genuine or natural; affected. [See ARTIFICE.] — **ar′ti·fi′cial·ly** *adv.* — **ar′ti·fi′cial·ness** *n.*

artificial horizon *Aeron.* An instrument that shows the deviations of an aircraft from level flight.

artificial insemination Impregnation of the female without direct sexual contact.

ar·ti·fi·ci·al·i·ty (är′tə-fish′ē-al′ə-tē) *n. pl.* **·ties** 1. The quality or state of being artificial. 2. Something artificial.

ar·til·ler·y (är-til′ə-rē) *n.* 1. Guns of larger caliber than machine guns. 2. Military units armed with such guns. 3. A branch of the U.S. Army. 4. The science of gunnery. 5. *U.S. Slang* A firearm. [< OF *artiller* to fortify]

ar·til·ler·y·man (är-til′ə-rē-mən) *n. pl.* **·men** (-mən) A soldier in the artillery. Also **ar·til′ler·ist.**

ar·ti·san (är′tə-zən) *n.* A trained or skilled workman. [< F < Ital. < L *ars, artis* art]

ar·tist (är′tist) *n.* 1. One skilled in any of the fine arts, esp. the graphic arts. 2. One whose work exhibits artistic qualities and skill; a craftsman. 3. An artiste. [< F < Ital. < L *ars, artis* art]

ar·tiste (är-tēst′) *n.* 1. An entertainer, as a dancer or singer. 2. An artist: often used ironically.

ar·tis·tic (är-tis′tik) *adj.* 1. Of or pertaining to art or artists. 2. Conforming or conformable to the principles of art; tastefully executed. 3. Fond of or sensitive to art. Also **ar·tis′ti·cal.** — **ar·tis′ti·cal·ly** *adv.*

art·ist·ry (är′tis-trē) *n.* 1. Artistic workmanship or ability. 2. The pursuits or occupation of an artist.

art·less (ärt′lis) *adj.* 1. Lacking craft or deceit; guileless; naive. 2. Natural; simple. 3. Devoid of art or skill; clumsy. 4. Uncultured; ignorant. — **Syn.** See INGENUOUS. — **art′less·ly** *adv.* — **art′less·ness** *n.*

art·y (är′tē) *adj.* Ostentatiously claiming artistic worth or interest. — **art′i·ness** *n.*

ar·um (âr′əm) *n.* Any of a genus of Old World herbs, including the philodendron. [< L < Gk. *aron*]

-ary¹ *suffix of adjectives and nouns* 1. Connected with or pertaining to what is expressed in the root word: *elementary.* 2. A person employed as or engaged in: *apothecary.* 3. A thing connected with or a place dedicated to: *dictionary.* [< L *-arius, -arium*]

-ary² *suffix of adjectives* Of or pertaining to; belonging to: *military, salutary.* See -AR¹. [< L *-aris*]

Ar·y·an (âr′ē-ən, ar′-, är′yən) *n.* 1. A member or descendant of a prehistoric people who spoke Indo-European. 2. In Nazi ideology, a Caucasian gentile, esp. one of Nordic stock. — *adj.* 1. Of or pertaining to the Aryans or their languages. 2. In Nazi ideology, of or pertaining to Caucasian gentiles. Also spelled *Arian.* [< Skt. *ārya* noble]

Ar·y·an·ize (âr′ē-ən-īz′, ar′-, är′yən-) *v.t.* **·ized, ·iz·ing** In Nazi ideology, to make characteristically Aryan or to free from (so-called) non-Aryan influences, control, etc.

as¹ (az, *unstressed* əz) *adv.* To the same degree; equally. — *conj.* 1. To the same degree or extent that: often used in correlative constructions with *as* or *so* to denote equality or identity: *as* fair *as* the sun. 2. In the way that; in the same manner that: Do *as* I do. 3. In proportion that; to the degree in which: He became gentler *as* he grew older. 4. At the same time that; while. 5. Because; since. ◆ This sense, though standard, often involves an ambiguity in meaning, and should be used with care. In the sentence *As it was raining, we stayed at home,* as may mean *while, when,* or *because.* 6. With the result or purpose that: Speak louder, so *as* to make yourself heard. 7. For instance: used to introduce examples or illustrations: Some animals are cunning, *as* the fox. 8. Though; however: Bad *as* it was, it might have been worse. — **as for** (or **as to**) In the matter of; concerning. — **as if** (or **as though**) The same, or in the same manner, that it would be if. — **as is** *Informal* Just as it is; in its present condition. — *pron.* 1. That; who; which: after *same* and *such:* He lived in the same city *as* I did. 2. A fact which: He is dead, *as* everyone knows. — *prep.* 1. In the role or character of: to act *as* umpire. 2. In the manner of; like: to use a board *as* a hammer. [ME *as, als, alse,* OE *ealswā* entirely so, just as]

as- Assimilated var. of AD-.

As (äs) Singular of ÆSIR.

as·a·fet·i·da (as′ə-fet′ə-də) *n.* A fetid substance prepared from certain plants of the parsley family, formerly used in medicine as an antispasmodic. Also **as′a·foet′i·da.** [< Med.L *asa* gum + L *foetida,* fem., ill-smelling]

as·bes·tos (as-bes′təs, az-) *n.* 1. A white or light gray silicate mineral, occurring in long slender needles or fibrous masses that may be woven or shaped into acid-resisting, nonconducting, and fireproof articles. 2. A fireproof curtain, as in a theater. — *adj.* Of or made of asbestos. Also **as·bes′tus.** [< L < Gk., *a-* not + *sbennynai* to quench] — **as·bes·tine** (as-bes′tin, az-), **as·bes′tic** *adj.*

as·ca·rid (as′kə-rid) *n. Zool.* A nematode worm parasitic in the intestines. [< Gk. *askaris, -idos*]

as·cend (ə-send′) *v.i.* 1. To go or move upward; rise. 2. To lie along an ascending slope. — *v.t.* 3. To mount; climb. [< L < *ad-* to + *scandere* to climb] — **as·cend′a·ble** or **as·cend′i·ble** *adj.* — **as·cen′sive** *adj.* — **as·cen′der** *n.*

as·cen·dan·cy (ə-sen′dən-sē) *n.* The quality, fact, or state of being in the ascendant; domination; sway. Also **as·cen′dance, as·cen′dence, as·cen′den·cy.**

as·cen·dant (ə-sen′dənt) *adj.* 1. Ascending; rising. 2. Superior; dominant. 3. *Astron.* Coming to or above the horizon. — *n.* A position of preeminence; domination. Also **as·cen′dent.** — **to be in the ascendant** To approach or occupy a predominating position.

as·cen·sion (ə-sen′shən) *n.* The act of ascending. — **the Ascension** *Theol.* The bodily assent of Christ into heaven after the Resurrection, commemorated on **Ascension Day,** the fortieth day after Easter. — **as·cen′sion·al** *adj.*

as·cent (ə-sent′) *n.* 1. The act of ascending in space; a rising, soaring, or climbing. 2. A rise in state, rank, or station; advancement. 3. A way or means of ascending; upward slope. 4. The degree of acclivity: an *ascent* of 30°.

as·cer·tain (as′ər-tān′) *v.t.* To learn with certainty; find out by experiment or investigation. [< OF < *a-* to (< L *ad-*) + *certain*] — **as′cer·tain′a·ble** *adj.* — **as′cer′tain′a·ble·ness** *n.* — **as′cer·tain′a·bly** *adv.* — **as′cer·tain′ment** *n.*

as·cet·ic (ə-set′ik) *n.* One who leads a very austere and self-denying life, esp. for religious purposes. — *adj.* 1. Pertaining to ascetics or asceticism. 2. Rigidly abstinent; austere. Also **as·cet′i·cal.** [< Gk. *askētēs* one who practices (self-denial), a monk] — **as·cet′i·cal·ly** *adv.*

as·cet·i·cism (ə-set′ə-siz′əm) *n.* Ascetic belief or conduct.

as·cid·i·an (ə-sid′ē-ən) *Zool. n.* One of a class of marine animals having a leathery sac; a tunicate. — *adj.* Of or pertaining to this class of animals. [< NL < ASCIDIUM]

as·cid·i·um (ə-sid′ē-əm) *n. pl.* **·cid·i·a** (-sid′ē-ə) *Bot.* A flask-shaped plant appendage. [< NL < Gk. *askos* bag]

As·cle·pi·us (as-klē′pē-əs) In Greek mythology, the god of medicine: identified with the Roman *Aesculapius.*

as·co·my·ce·tous (as′kə·mī·sē′təs) *adj. Bot.* Belonging to a large class of fungi, including mildews and yeasts. [< NL *Ascomycetes*]

a·scor·bic (ə·skôr′bik) *adj.* Antiscorbutic.

ascorbic acid *Biochem.* The scurvy-preventing vitamin C, a white, odorless, crystalline compound, $C_6H_8O_6$, present in citrus and other fresh fruits, tomatoes, potatoes, and green leafy vegetables, and also made synthetically.

as·cot (as′kət, -kot) *n.* A kind of necktie knotted so that the broad ends are laid one across the other. [after *Ascot*, a village in England.]

as·cribe (ə·skrīb′) *v.t.* **·cribed, ·crib·ing 1.** To attribute or impute, as to a cause or source: I *ascribe* his conduct to insanity. **2.** To consider or declare as belonging (to); assign as a quality or attribute. — **Syn.** See ATTRIBUTE. [< L < *ad-* to + *scribere* to write] — **as·crib′a·ble** *adj.*

as·crip·tion (ə·skrip′shən) *n.* **1.** The act of ascribing. **2.** That which ascribes; esp., a text or sentence of praise to God.

-ase *suffix Chem.* Used in naming enzymes: *amylase, casease.*

a·sea (ə·sē′) *adv.* To or toward the sea; at sea.

a·sep·sis (ə·sep′sis, ā-) *n. Med.* **1.** Absence of pathogenic organisms. **2.** The prevention of infection by the use of sterilized instruments, dressings, etc. [< A-⁴ + SEPSIS]

a·sep·tic (ə·sep′tik, ā-) *adj.* Free of pathogenic microorganisms. — **a·sep′ti·cal·ly** *adv.*

a·sex·u·al (ā·sek′shoō·əl) *adj. Biol.* **1.** Having no distinct sexual organs; without sex. **2.** Occurring or performed without union of male and female gametes. — **a·sex·u·al·i·ty** (ā·sek′shoō·al′ə·tē) *n.* — **a·sex′u·al·ly** *adv.*

As·gard (as′gärd, äs′-) In Norse mythology, the home of the gods and of heroes slain in battle. Also **As·garth** (äs′gärth). [< ON < *āss* god + *gardhr* yard, dwelling]

ash¹ (ash) *n.* The powdery, whitish gray residue of a substance that has been burned. [OE *æsce, asce*]

ash² (ash) *n.* **1.** A tree of the olive family. **2.** The light, tough, elastic wood of this tree. — *adj.* Made of ash wood. [OE *æsc*]

a·shamed (ə·shāmd′) *adj.* **1.** Feeling shame. **2.** Deterred by fear of shame. [OE *āscamod,* pp. of *āscamian*] — **a·sham·ed·ly** (ə·shā′mid·lē) *adv.* — **a·sham′ed·ness** *n.*

ash·en¹ (ash′ən) *adj.* **1.** Of, pertaining to, or like ashes. **2.** Pale in color; gray.

ash·en² (ash′ən) *adj.* Pertaining to or made of ash wood.

ash·es (ash′iz) *n.pl.* **1.** The grayish white, powdery particles remaining after something has been burned. **2.** The remains of the human body after cremation. **3.** Mortal remains. **4.** Volcanic lava. [pl. of ASH¹]

ash·lar (ash′lər) *n.* **1.** In masonry, a roughhewn block of stone. **2.** A thin, dressed, squared stone, used for facing a wall. **3.** Masonry made of such blocks. Also **ash′ler.** [< OF < L *axis* board, plank]

a·shore (ə·shôr′, ə·shōr′) *adv. & adj.* **1.** To or on the shore. **2.** On land; aground.

Ash Wednesday The first day of Lent: from the sprinkling of ashes on the heads of penitents.

ash·y (ash′ē) *adj.* **ash·i·er, ash·i·est 1.** Of, pertaining to, or like ashes; ash-covered. **2.** Ash-colored; ashen.

A·sian (ā′zhən, ā′shən) *adj.* Of or characteristic of Asia or its peoples. — *n.* A native or inhabitant of Asia.

A·si·at·ic (ā′zhē·at′ik, ā′shē-) *adj. & n.* Asian. ◆ In most cases, esp. in the ethnic sense, *Asian* is now preferred.

a·side (ə·sīd′) *adv.* **1.** On or to one side; apart. **2.** Out of thought or use: to put grief *aside.* **3.** Away from the general company; in seclusion: He drew me *aside.* **4.** Away from one's person; down. **5.** In reserve. — **aside from** *U.S.* **1.** Apart from. **2.** Excepting. — *n.* Lines spoken privately by an actor and supposed to be heard by the audience but not by the other actors.

as·i·nine (as′ə·nīn) *adj.* Pertaining to or like an ass, considered a stupid, obstinate animal. [< L *asinus* ass] — **as′i·nine·ly** *adv.* — **as·i·nin·i·ty** (as′ə·nin′ə·tē) *n.*

ask (ask, äsk) *v.t.* **1.** To put a question to: Don't *ask* me. **2.** To put a question about: to *ask* the time. **3.** To make a request of or for; solicit. **4.** To need or require: This job *asks* too much time. **5.** To state the price of; demand. **6.** To invite. — *v.i.* **7.** To make inquiries: with *for, after,* or *about.* **8.** To make a request: often with *for:* He *asked* for aid. [OE *āscian*] — **ask′er** *n.*

— **Syn. 1.** *Ask* is the most direct and inclusive term of putting a question to a person. *Query* suggests the effort to settle a doubt. To *question* is to put a series of questions; to *interrogate* is to question formally or by right of authority. We *quiz* as a test of knowledge. *Inquire* suggests the effort to ascertain facts or the truth. **3.** *Ask* and *request* mean to urge that something desired be granted or handed over. *Ask* suggests the expectation of compliance; *request* is more formal, and allows for refusal.

a·skance (ə·skans′) *adv.* **1.** With a side glance; sidewise. **2.** Disdainfully; distrustfully. Also **a·skant′.** [Origin unknown]

a·skew (ə·skyoō′) *adj.* Oblique. — *adv.* In an oblique position or manner; to one side; awry.

a·slant (ə·slant′, ə·slänt′) *adj.* Slanting; oblique. — *adv.* At a slant; obliquely. — *prep.* Slantingly across or over.

a·sleep (ə·slēp′) *adj.* **1.** In a state of sleep; sleeping. **2.** Dormant; inactive. **3.** Benumbed, as an arm or leg. **4.** Dead. — *adv.* Into a sleeping condition: to fall *asleep.*

a·slope (ə·slōp′) *adj.* Sloping. — *adv.* At a slope.

a·so·cial (ā·sō′shəl) *adj.* **1.** Avoiding society; not gregarious. **2.** Heedless of one's fellow beings; self-centered.

asp (asp) *n.* The common European viper. [< L < Gk.]

as·par·a·gus (ə·spar′ə·gəs) *n.* **1.** The succulent, edible shoots of a cultivated variety of a perennial herb of the lily family. **2.** Any related plant. [< L < Gk. *aspharagos*]

as·pect (as′pekt) *n.* **1.** The look of a person; facial expression. **2.** Appearance to the eye; look: the pleasant *aspect* of a lake. **3.** Appearance presented to the mind by circumstances, etc.; interpretation: all *aspects* of a problem. **4.** A looking or facing in a given direction: the southern *aspect* of a house. **5.** The side or surface facing in a certain direction: ventral *aspect.* **6.** In astrology: **a** Any configuration of the planets. **b** The supposed influence of this for good or evil. — **Syn.** See PHASE. [< L < *ad-* at + *specere* to look]

asp·en (as′pən) *n.* Any of several species of poplar of North America or Europe with leaves that tremble in the slightest breeze. — *adj.* **1.** Of the aspen. **2.** Shaking, like aspen leaves. [OE *æspe*]

as·per·i·ty (as·per′ə·tē) *n. pl.* **·ties 1.** Roughness or harshness, as of surface, sound, etc. **2.** Sharpness of temper; acrimony. [< OF < L *asper* rough]

as·perse (ə·spûrs′) *v.t.* **as·persed** (ə·spûrst′), **as·pers·ing** To spread false charges against; slander. [< L < *ad-* to + *spargere* to sprinkle] — **as·pers′er** or **as·per′sor** *n.* — **as·per′sive** (-siv) *adj.*

as·per·sion (ə·spûr′zhən, -shən) *n.* **1.** A slandering; defamation. **2.** A slanderous or damaging report; calumny.

as·phalt (as′fôlt, -falt) *n.* **1.** A solid, brownish black, combustible mixture of bituminous hydrocarbons, found native in various parts of the world and also obtained as a residue in the refining of petroleum. **2.** A mixture of this with sand or gravel, used for paving, etc. Also **as·phal·tum** (as·fal′təm), **as·phal′tus.** — *v.t.* To pave with asphalt. [< LL < Gk. *asphalton*] — **as·phal·tic** (as·fôl′tik, -fal′-) *adj.*

as·pho·del (as′fə·del) *n.* A plant of the lily family, bearing white, pink, or yellow flowers. [< L < Gk. *asphodelos*]

as·phyx·i·a (as·fik′sē·ə) *n. Pathol.* Unconsciousness caused by too little oxygen and too much carbon dioxide in the blood. [< NL < Gk. < *a-* not + *sphyzein* to beat] — **as·phyx′i·al** *adj.* — **as·phyx′i·ant** *adj. & n.*

as·phyx·i·ate (as·fik′sē·āt) *v.t.* **·at·ed, ·at·ing** *v.t.* **1.** To cause asphyxia in; suffocate. — *v.i.* **2.** To undergo asphyxia. — **as·phyx′i·a′tion** *n.* — **as·phyx′i·a′tor** *n.*

as·pic (as′pik) *n.* A jelly of meat or vegetable juices, served as a relish or as a mold for meat, vegetables, etc. [< F]

as·pi·dis·tra (as′pə·dis′trə) *n.* A stemless, Asian herb of the lily family, with large, glossy, evergreen leaves. [< NL < Gk. *aspis, aspidos* shield + *astron* star]

as·pir·ant (ə·spīr′ənt, as′pər·ənt) *n.* One who aspires, as after honors or place; a candidate. — *adj.* Aspiring.

as·pi·rate (*v.* as′pə·rāt; *n. & adj.* as′pər·it) *v.t.* **·rat·ed, ·rat·ing 1.** To utter with a puff of breath or as if preceded by an *h* sound. **2.** To follow with a puff of breath, as (p), (t), and (k) when before a vowel. **3.** *Med.* To draw out with an aspirator. — *n.* An aspirated sound. — *adj. Phonet.* Uttered with an aspirate: also **as′pi·rat′ed** (-rā′tid). [See ASPIRE.]

as·pi·ra·tion (as′pə·rā′shən) *n.* **1.** Exalted desire; high ambition. **2.** The act of breathing; breath. **3.** *Med.* The use of an aspirator. **4.** *Phonet.* An aspirate.

as·pi·ra·tor (as′pə·rā′tər) *n. Med.* A device for drawing off fluid matter or gases from the body by suction.

as·pi·ra·to·ry (ə·spīr′ə·tôr′ē, -tō′rē) *adj.* Of, pertaining to, or adapted for breathing or suction.

as·pire (ə·spīr′) *v.i.* **·spired, ·spir·ing** To have an earnest desire or ambition. [< L < *ad-* to + *spirare* to breathe] — **as·pir′er** *n.* — **as·pir′ing** *adj.* — **as·pir′ing·ly** *adv.*

as·pi·rin (as′pər·in, -prin) *n.* A white crystalline compound, the acetyl derivative of salicylic acid, $C_9H_8O_4$, used for the relief of fever, pain, etc. [< A(CETYL) + SPIR(AEIC ACID), former name of salicylic acid, + -IN]

a·squint (ə·skwint′) *adj. & adv.* With sidelong glance.

ass (as, äs) *n. pl.* **ass·es 1.** A long-eared quadruped smaller than the ordinary horse, used as a beast of burden; the donkey. **2.** A stupid person; fool. [OE *assa* ? < OIrish < L *asinus*]

as·sail (ə·sāl′) *v.t.* To attack violently, as by force, argument, etc. — **Syn.** See ATTACK. [< OF < LL < L *ad-* to + *salire* to leap] — **as·sail′a·ble** *adj.* — **as·sail′a·ble·ness** *n.*

as·sail·ant (ə-sā′lənt) *n.* One who assails. Also **as·sail′er.** — *adj.* Attacking; hostile.

as·sas·sin (ə-sas′in) *n.* One who kills; esp., one who murders a political figure from fanaticism or for a price.

as·sas·si·nate (ə-sas′ə-nāt) *v.t.* **·nat·ed, ·nat·ing** **1.** To kill by secret or surprise assault. **2.** To destroy or injure by treachery, as a reputation. — **Syn.** See KILL. — **as·sas′si·na′tion** *n.* — **as·sas′si·na′tor** *n.*

as·sault (ə-sôlt′) *n.* **1.** Any violent attack, as an act, speech, or writing. **2.** *Law* An unlawful attempt or offer to do bodily injury to another. **3.** A rape. **4.** *Mil.* **a** An attack upon a fortified place. **b** A closing with the enemy. — *v.t. & v.i.* To attack with violence. — **Syn.** See ATTACK. [< OF < L *ad-* to + *salire* to leap]

assault and battery *Law* The carrying out of an assault with force and violence; a beating.

as·say (n. ə-sā′, as′ā; v. ə-sā′) *n.* **1.** The analysis or testing of an alloy or ore to ascertain the ingredients and their proportions. **2.** The substance to be so examined. **3.** The result of such a test. **4.** Any examination or testing. — *v.t.* **1.** To subject to chemical analysis; make an assay of. **2.** To prove; test. — *v.i.* **3.** *U.S.* To show by analysis a certain value or proportion, as of a precious metal. [< OF *assai*, var. of *essai* trial] — **as·say′er** *n.*

as·sem·blage (ə-sem′blij, *for def. 4, also Fr.* à-sän-bläzh′) *n.* **1.** The act of assembling, or the state of being assembled. **2.** Any gathering of persons or things; collection; assembly. **3.** A fitting together, as of the parts of a machine. **4.** A work of art created by assembling materials and objects; also, the technique of making such works: compare COLLAGE. — **Syn.** See COMPANY. [< F]

as·sem·ble (ə-sem′bəl) *v.t. & v.i.* **bled, ·bling** **1.** To come or bring together; collect or congregate. **2.** To fit or join together, as the parts of a mechanism. [< OF < L *ad-* to + *simul* together] — **as·sem′bler** *n.*

as·sem·bly (ə-sem′blē) *n. pl.* **·blies** **1.** The act of assembling, or the state of being assembled. **2.** A number of persons met together for a common purpose. **3.** The act or process of fitting together the parts of a machine, etc.; also, the parts themselves. **4.** *Mil.* The signal calling troops to form ranks.

assembly line An arrangement of industrial equipment and workers in which the product passes from one specialized operation to another until completed.

as·sem·bly·man (ə-sem′blē-mən) *n. pl.* **·men** (-men′, -mən) *U.S. & Canadian* A member of a legislative assembly, esp. of a State or Provincial legislature.

as·sent (ə-sent′) *v.i.* To express agreement; acquiesce; concur: usually with *to.* — *n.* **1.** Mental concurrence or agreement. **2.** Consent; sanction. [< OF < L *ad-* to + *sentire* to feel] — **as′sen·ta′tion** *n.* — **as·sent′er** *n.*

as·sert (ə-sûrt′) *v.t.* **1.** To state positively; affirm; declare. **2.** To maintain as a right or claim, as by words or force. — **to assert oneself** To put forward and defend one's own rights or claims. [< L < *ad-* to + *serere* to bind] — **as·sert′a·ble** or **as·sert′i·ble** *adj.* — **as·sert′er** or **as·ser′tor** *n.*

as·ser·tion (ə-sûr′shən) *n.* **1.** The act of asserting. **2.** A positive declaration without attempt at proof.

as·ser·tive (ə-sûr′tiv) *adj.* Confident; aggressive. — **as·ser′tive·ly** *adv.* — **as·ser′tive·ness** *n.*

as·sess (ə-ses′) *v.t.* **1.** To charge with a tax, fine, or other payment, as a person or property. **2.** To determine the amount of, as a tax or other fine on a person or property. **3.** To evaluate, as property, for taxation. [< OF < LL < L *assidere* to sit by (as a judge in court)] — **as·sess′a·ble** *adj.*

as·sess·ment (ə-ses′mənt) *n.* **1.** The act of assessing. **2.** An amount assessed.

as·ses·sor (ə-ses′ər) *n.* One who makes assessments, as for taxation. — **as·ses·so·ri·al** (as′ə-sôr′ē-əl, -sō′rē-) *adj.*

as·set (as′et) *n.* **1.** An item of property. **2.** A useful or valuable thing or quality.

as·sets (as′ets) *n.pl.* **1.** In accounting, a balance sheet showing all the property or resources of a person or business, and money owed: opposed to *liabilities.* **2.** *Law* All the property, real and personal, of a person, corporation, or partnership, that is or may be chargeable with their debts or legacies. [< OF < LL *ad-* to + *satis* enough]

as·sev·er·ate (ə-sev′ə-rāt) *v.t.* **·at·ed, ·at·ing** To affirm or declare emphatically or solemnly. [< L < *ad-* to + *severus* serious] — **as·sev′er·a′tion** *n.*

as·si·du·i·ty (as′ə-doo̅′ə-tē, -dyoo̅′-) *n. pl.* **·ties** Close and continuous application or effort; diligence.

as·sid·u·ous (ə-sij′oo̅-əs) *adj.* **1.** Devoted; attentive. **2.** Unremitting; persistent: *assiduous* study. [< L < *ad-* to + *sedere* to sit] — **as·sid′u·ous·ly** *adv.* — **as·sid′u·ous·ness** *n.*

as·sign (ə-sīn′) *v.t.* **1.** To set apart, as for a particular function; designate: to *assign* a day for trial. **2.** To appoint, as to or for a post or duty. **3.** To allot as a task: to *assign* a lesson. **4.** To ascribe or attribute; refer: to *assign* a monument to Roman times. **5.** *Law* To transfer, as personal property, rights, or interests. — *v.i.* **6.** To transfer property, especially for the benefit of creditors. — **Syn.** See ATTRIBUTE. — *n. Law Usually pl.* Assignee. [< OF < L < *ad-* to + *signare* make a sign] — **as·sign′a·bil′i·ty** *n.* — **as·sign′a·ble** *adj.* — **as·sign′a·bly** *adv.* — **as·sign′er,** *Law* **as·sign·or** (ə-sī′nôr′, as′ə-nôr′) *n.*

as·sig·na·tion (as′ig-nā′shən) *n.* **1.** An appointment for meeting, esp. a secret or illicit one as made by lovers. **2.** An assignment. [See ASSIGN.]

as·sign·ee (ə-sī′nē′, as′ə-nē′) *n. Law* A person to whom property, rights, or powers are transferred.

as·sign·ment (ə-sīn′mənt) *n.* **1.** The act of assigning. **2.** Anything assigned, as a lesson or task. **3.** *Law* **a** The transfer of a claim, right, or property, or the instrument or writing of transfer. **b** The claim, right, or property transferred.

as·sim·i·la·ble (ə-sim′ə-lə-bəl) *adj.* Capable of being assimilated. — **as·sim′i·la·bil′i·ty** *n.*

as·sim·i·late (ə-sim′ə-lāt) *v.t.* **·lat·ed, ·lat·ing** *v.t.* **1.** *Biol.* To take up and incorporate into living organisms, as food. **2.** To make into a homogeneous part, as of a substance or system. **3.** To make alike or similar; cause to resemble. **4.** To become alike or similar. **5.** To become absorbed or assimilated. [< L < *ad-* to + *similare* to make like] — **as·sim′i·la·tive, as·sim·i·la·to·ry** (ə-sim′ə-lə-tôr′ē, -tō′rē) *adj.*

as·sim·i·la·tion (ə-sim′ə-lā′shən) *n.* **1.** The act or process of assimilating. **2.** *Biol.* The transformation of nutriment into an integral part of a plant or animal. **3.** *Phonet.* The process whereby a sound is influenced by a neighboring sound, as when *horseshoe* is pronounced (hôrsh′shoo̅′).

as·sist (ə-sist′) *v.t.* **1.** To give or render help to; relieve; succor. **2.** To act as subordinate or deputy to. — *v.i.* **3.** To give help or support. **4.** In baseball, to aid a teammate in a put-out. — **to assist at** To be present at (a ceremony, etc.). — *n.* **1.** An act of helping. **2.** In baseball, a play that helps to put out a runner. [< MF < L < *ad-* to + *sistere* to cause to stand] — **as·sist′er,** *Law* **as·sis′tor** *n.*

as·sis·tance (ə-sis′təns) *n.* The act of helping, or the help given; aid; support.

as·sis·tant (ə-sis′tənt) *n.* One who assists; a subordinate or helper. — *adj.* **1.** Holding a subordinate or auxiliary place, office, or rank. **2.** Affording aid; assisting.

as·size (ə-sīz′) *n.* **1.** Originally, a session of a legislative or judicial body. **2.** *pl.* In England, one of the regular court sessions held in each county for the trial of civil and criminal cases by jury; also, the time and place of such sessions. [< OF < L *assidere* to sit by (as a judge at court)]

as·so·ci·ate (*n. & adj.* ə-sō′shē-it, -āt, -sē-; *v.* ə-sō′shē-āt, -sē-) *n.* **1.** A companion. **2.** A partner, colleague, or fellow employee. **3.** Anything that habitually accompanies something else; a concomitant. **4.** One admitted to partial membership in an association, society, or institution. — *adj.* **1.** Joined with another or others in a common pursuit or office. **2.** Having subordinate or secondary status: an *associate* professor. **3.** Existing or occurring together; concomitant. — *v.* **·at·ed, ·at·ing** *v.t.* **1.** To ally; unite. **2.** To combine. **3.** To connect mentally. — *v.i.* **4.** To unite for a common purpose. **5.** To keep or be in company: with *with.* [< L < *ad-* to + *sociare* to join]

Associated Press An organization for collecting news and distributing it to member newspapers.

as·so·ci·a·tion (ə-sō′sē-ā′shən, -shē-) *n.* **1.** The act of associating. **2.** The state of being associated; fellowship; companionship. **3.** A body of persons associated for some common purpose; society; league. Abbr. *ass., assn., assoc.* **4.** *Ecol.* A group of plants or animals sharing a common habitat and similar geographic conditions. **5.** The connection or relation of ideas, feelings, etc. — **as·so′ci·a′tion·al** *adj.*

association football Soccer.

as·so·ci·a·tive (ə-sō′shē-ā′tiv, -shē-ə-) *adj.* **1.** Of or characterized by association. **2.** Causing association. — **as·so′ci·a′tive·ly** *adv.*

as·so·nance (as′ə-nəns) *n.* **1.** Resemblance in sound; especially, in prosody, correspondence of accented vowels, but not of consonants, as in *main, came.* **2.** Rough likeness; approximation. [< F, ult. < L < *ad-* to + *sonare* to sound] — **as′so·nant** *adj. & n.*

as·sort (ə-sôrt′) *v.t.* **1.** To distribute into groups according to kinds; classify. **2.** To furnish, as a warehouse, with a variety of goods, etc. — *v.i.* **3.** To fall into groups or classes of the same kind. **4.** To associate: with *with.* [< OF < *a-* to + *sorte* sort] — **as·sort′er** *n.*

as·sort·ed (ə-sôr′tid) *adj.* **1.** Containing or arranged in various sorts or kinds; miscellaneous. **2.** Classified. **3.** Matched.

as·sort·ment (ə-sôrt′mənt) *n.* **1.** The act of assorting; classification. **2.** A varied collection; miscellany.

as·suage (ə-swāj′) *v.t.* **·suaged, ·suag·ing** **1.** To make less harsh or severe; alleviate. **2.** To satisfy, as thirst. **3.** To calm; pacify. [< OF < L *ad-* to + *suavis* sweet] — **as·suage′ment** *n.*

as·sume (ə-soo̅m′) *v.t.* **·sumed, ·sum·ing** **1.** To take on or adopt, as a style of dress, aspect, or character. **2.** To undertake, as an office or duty. **3.** To usurp, as powers of state. **4.** To take for granted. **5.** To affect; feign. [< L < *ad-* to + *sumere* to take] **—as·sum·a·ble** (ə-sŏŏ′mə-bəl) *adj.*

as·sump·tion (ə-sump′shən) *n.* **1.** The act of assuming, or that which is assumed. **2.** That which is taken for granted; a supposition. **3.** Presumption; arrogance. **4.** *Logic* A minor premise. **— Syn.** See HYPOTHESIS. **— the Assumption** A church feast, observed on August 15, commemorating the bodily ascent of the Virgin Mary into heaven. **—as·sump′tive** *adj.* **—as·sump′tive·ly** *adv.*

as·sur·ance (ə-shŏŏr′əns) *n.* **1.** The act of assuring, or the state of being assured. **2.** A positive statement, intended to give confidence, encouragement, etc. **3.** Self-confidence. **4.** Boldness; effrontery. **5.** *Chiefly Brit.* Insurance.

as·sure (ə-shŏŏr′) *v.t.* **·sured, ·sur·ing** **1.** To make sure or secure; establish firmly. **2.** To make (something) certain; guarantee. **3.** To cause to feel certain; convince. **4.** To promise; make positive declaration to. **5.** To encourage; reassure. **6.** To insure, as against loss. [< OF < LL < L *ad-* to + *securus* safe] **—as·sur′a·ble** *adj.* **—as·sur′er** *n.*

as·sured (ə-shŏŏrd′) *adj.* **1.** Made certain; undoubted; sure: His defeat is *assured.* **2.** Self-possessed; confident. **3.** Insured. **—** *n.* An insured person. **—as·sur·ed·ly** (ə-shŏŏr′id-lē) *adv.* **—as·sur′ed·ness** *n.*

As·syr·i·a (ə-sir′ē-ə) An ancient empire of western Asia; capital, Nineveh. **—As·syr′i·an** *adj. & n.*

as·ta·tine (as′tə-tēn, -tin) *n.* An unstable chemical element (symbol At) of atomic number 85, related to the halogens and occupying the place formerly assigned to alabamine. [< Gk. *astatos* unstable + -INE²]

as·ter (as′tər) *n.* A plant of the composite family, having flowers with white, purple, or blue rays and yellow disc. [< L < Gk. *astēr* star]

-aster *suffix* Little; inferior: *poetaster.* [< L *-aster,* dim. suffix]

as·ter·isk (as′tər-isk) *n.* *Printing* A starlike figure (*) used to indicate omissions, footnotes, references, etc. **—** *v.t.* To mark with an asterisk. [< L < Gk. *astēr* star]

a·stern (ə-stûrn′) *adv. & adj. Naut.* **1.** In the rear; at any point behind a vessel. **2.** To the rear; backward.

astero- *combining form* Of or related to a star. Also *aster-* (before vowels): also **asteri-.** [< Gk. *astēr* a star]

as·ter·oid (as′tə-roid) *adj.* Star-shaped. **—** *n.* **1.** *Astron.* Any of several hundred small planets between Mars and Jupiter: also called *planetoid.* **2.** A starfish. [< Gk. *astēr* a star] **—as′ter·oi′dal** *adj.*

asth·ma (az′mə, as′-) *n. Pathol.* A chronic respiratory disorder characterized by recurrent paroxysmal coughing and constriction of the chest. [< Gk. *azein* to breathe hard]

asth·mat·ic (az-mat′ik, as-) *adj.* Of, pertaining to, or affected with asthma. Also **asth·mat′i·cal.** **—** *n.* A person suffering from asthma. **—asth·mat′i·cal·ly** *adv.*

as·tig·mat·ic (as′tig-mat′ik) *adj.* Of, having, or correcting astigmatism.

a·stig·ma·tism (ə-stig′mə-tiz′əm) *n.* A defect of the eye or of a lens such that the rays of light from an object do not converge to a focus, thus causing imperfect vision or images. [< A-⁴ without + Gk. *stigma,* -*atos* mark, spot + -ISM]

a·stir (ə-stûr′) *adv. & adj.* Stirring; moving about.

a·ston·ish (ə-ston′ish) *v.t.* To affect with wonder and surprise; amaze; confound. [OF *estoner* < L *ex-* out + *tonare* to thunder] **—a·ston′ish·er** *n.* **—a·ston′ish·ing** *adj.* **—a·ston′ish·ing·ly** *adv.*

a·ston·ish·ment (ə-ston′ish-mənt) *n.* **1.** The state of being astonished. **2.** A cause of such emotion.

a·stound (ə-stound′) *v.t.* To overwhelm with wonder; confound. [ME < OF *estoner* < L *ex-* out + *tonare* to thunder] **—a·stound′ing** *adj.* **—a·stound′ing·ly** *adv.*

as·trag·a·lus (as-trag′ə-ləs) *n. pl.* **·li** (-lī) *Anat.* The talus. [< L < Gk. *astragalos*] **—as·trag′a·lar** (-lər) *adj.*

as·tra·khan (as′trə-kan, -kən) *n.* **1.** The black or gray, loosely curled fur made from the pelt of lambs raised near Astrakhan. **2.** A fabric with a curled pile imitative of this. Also **as′tra·chan.**

as·tral (as′trəl) *adj.* **1.** Of, pertaining to, coming from, or like the stars; starry. **2.** Of or designating a supposedly supernatural substance. **—** *n.* An astral body. [< LL < L < Gk. *astron* star] **—as′tral·ly** *adv.*

a·stray (ə-strā′) *adv. & adj.* Away from the right path; wandering. [< OF < L *extra-* beyond + *vagare* to wander]

a·stride (ə-strīd′) *adv. & adj.* **1.** With one leg on each side. **2.** With the legs far apart. **—** *prep.* With one leg on each side of: *astride* a horse.

as·trin·gent (ə-strin′jənt) *adj.* **1.** *Med.* Tending to contract or draw together organic tissues; binding; styptic. **2.** Harsh; stern; austere. **—** *n.* An astringent substance. [< L < *ad-* to + *stringere* to bind fast] **—as·trin′gen·cy** *n.* **—as·trin′gent·ly** *adv.*

astro- *combining form* **1.** Star. **2.** Of, pertaining to, occurring in, or characteristic of outer space: *astronautics.* [< Gk. *astron* star]

as·tro·dy·nam·ics (as′trō-dī-nam′iks) *n.pl.* (*construed as sing.*) The branch of dynamics concerned with the motions of celestial bodies.

as·tro·labe (as′trə-lāb) *n.* An instrument formerly used for obtaining the altitudes of planets and stars. [< OF < Med.L < Gk. *astron* star + *lambanein* to take]

as·trol·o·gy (ə-strol′ə-jē) *n.* The study professing to foretell the future and interpret the influence of the heavenly bodies upon the destinies of men. [< L < Gk. < *astron* star + *logos* discourse] **—as·trol′o·ger** *n.* **—as·tro·log·ic** (as′trə-loj′ik) or **·i·cal, as·trol′o·gous** (-gəs) *adj.* **—as′tro·log′i·cal·ly** *adv.*

as·tro·naut (as′trə-nôt) *n.* One who travels in space. [< ASTRO- + *-naut* (< Gk. *nautēs* sailor), after *aeronaut*]

as·tro·nau·tics (as′trə-nô′tiks) *n.pl.* (*construed as sing.*) The science and art of space travel. **—as′tro·nau′tic** or **·ti·cal** *adj.* **—as′tro·nau′ti·cal·ly** *adv.*

as·tron·o·mer (ə-stron′ə-mər) *n.* One learned or expert in astronomy. *Abbr. astr., astron.*

as·tro·nom·i·cal (as′trə-nom′i-kəl) *adj.* **1.** Of or pertaining to astronomy. **2.** Enormously or inconceivably large. Also **as′tro·nom′ic.** **—as′tro·nom′i·cal·ly** *adv.*

astronomical unit A space unit for expressing the distances of the stars, equal to the mean distance of the earth from the sun.

astronomical year The period between two passages of the sun through the same equinox, equal to about 365 days, 5 hours, 48 minutes, and 46 seconds.

as·tron·o·my (ə-stron′ə-mē) *n.* The science that treats of the heavenly bodies, their motions, magnitudes, distances, and constitution. [< OF < L < Gk. *astron* star + *nomos* law]

as·tro·phys·ics (as′trō-fiz′iks) *n.pl.* (*construed as sing.*) The branch of astronomy that treats of the physical constitution and properties of the heavenly bodies. **—as′tro·phys′i·cal** *adj.* **—as·tro·phys·i·cist** (as′trō-fiz′ə-sist) *n.*

as·tute (ə-stŏŏt′, ə-styŏŏt′) *adj.* Keen in discernment; acute; shrewd; cunning. [< L *astus* cunning] **—as·tute′ly** *adv.* **—as·tute′ness** *n.*

a·sun·der (ə-sun′dər) *adv.* **1.** Apart; into pieces. **2.** In or into a different place or direction. **—** *adj.* Separated; apart. [OE *on sundran*]

a·sy·lum (ə-sī′ləm) *n. pl.* **·lums** or **·la** (-lə) **1.** An institution for the care of the mentally ill, the aged, the destitute, etc. **2.** A place of refuge. **3.** An inviolable shelter from arrest or punishment, as a temple or church in ancient times. [< L < Gk. < *a-* without + *sylon* right of seizure]

a·sym·met·ric (ā′si-met′rik, as′i-) *adj.* **1.** Not symmetrical. **2.** *Chem.* Designating an unbalanced spatial arrangement of atoms and radicals within a molecule. Also **a′sym·met′ri·cal.** **—a′sym·met′ri·cal·ly** *adv.*

a·sym·me·try (ā-sim′ə-trē) *n.* Lack of symmetry.

as·ymp·tote (as′im-tōt) *n. Math.* A straight line that an indefinitely extended curve continually approaches as a tangent. [< Gk. < *a-* not + *syn-* together + *piptein* to fall] **—as′ymp·tot′ic** or **·i·cal** *adj.* **—as′ymp·tot′i·cal·ly** *adv.*

at (at, *unstressed* ət) *prep.* **1.** In or on the position of: *at* the center of the circle. **2.** Of time, on or upon the point or stroke of: *at* noon. **3.** During the course or lapse of: *at* night. **4.** In contact with; on; upon: *at* sea. **5.** To or toward: Look *at* that sunset! **6.** Through; by way of: Smoke came out *at* the windows. **7.** Within the limits of; present in: *at* home. **8.** Engaged or occupied in: *at* work. **9.** Attending: *at* a party. **10.** In the state or condition of: *at* war. **11.** In the region or vicinity of: *at* the door. **12.** With an interval of: *at* sixty paces. **13.** Having reference to; in connection with: He winced *at* the thought. **14.** In the manner of: *at* a trot. **15.** In pursuit or quest of; in the direction of; against: to catch *at* straws. **16.** Dependent upon: *at* an enemy's mercy. **17.** According to: Proceed *at* your discretion. **18.** Amounting to: interest *at* two percent. **19.** From; out of: to draw water *at* a well. **20.** On the occasion of. [OE *æt*]

— Syn. 2. *At, in,* and *on* may be used with reference to time. An event occurs *at* an hour of the day, *in* a month or year, *on* a day of the week, a date, or a precise division of time: to arrive *on* the hour. **7.** *At, in,* and *on* may be used of spatial location. Something is *at* a place regarded as a point: *at* a city, displayed *at* the museum. It is *in* a place regarded as embracing it: *in* a country, *in* a suburb. A building is said to be *on* a street.

At·a·brine (at′ə·brin, -brēn) *n.* Proprietary name for a brand of quinacrine. Also **at′a·brine.**

at·a·rac·tic (at′ə-rak′tik) *n. Med.* A drug having the power to tranquilize and to lessen nervous tension. Also **at′a·rax′ic** (-rak′sik). [< NL < Gk. *ata+akteein* to be calm]

at·a·vism (at′ə-viz′əm) *n.* **1.** Reversion to an earlier or primitive type. **2.** *Biol.* Reversion. [< F < L < *at-* be-

---

PRONUNCIATION KEY: add, āce, câre, pälm; end, ēven; it, īce; odd, ōpen, ôrder; tŏŏk, pōōl; up, bûrn; ə = a in *above*, e in *sicken*, i in *flexible*, o in *melon*, u in *focus*; yōō = u in *fuse*; oil; pout; check; go; ring; thin; this; zh, vision.

yond + *avus* grandfather] — **at′a·vist** *n.* — **at′a·vis′tic** *adj.*

a·tax·i·a (ə·tak′sē-ə) *n. Pathol.* Loss or failure of muscular coordination. Also **a·tax·y** (ə·tak′sē). [< NL < Gk. < *a-* not + *tattein* to arrange] — **a·tax′ic** *adj. & n.*

ate (āt, *chiefly Brit.* et) Past tense of EAT.

-ate[1] *suffix* Forming: **1.** Participial adjectives equivalent to those in *-ated.* **2.** Adjectives from nouns with the meaning "possessing or characterized by": *caudate.* **3.** Verbs, originally from stems of Latin verbs of the first conjugation, and, by analogy, extended to other stems: *fascinate.* **4.** *Chem.* Verbs with the meaning "combine or treat with": *chlorinate.* [< L *-atus,* pp. ending of 1st conjugation verbs]

-ate[2] *suffix* Forming: **1.** Nouns denoting office, function, or agent: *magistrate.* **2.** Nouns denoting the object or result of an action: *mandate.* [< L *-atus,* suffix of nouns]

at·el·ier (at′əl·yā, *Fr.* ȧ·tə·lyā′) *n.* A workshop, esp. of an artist; studio. [< F]

a·the·ism (ā′thē·iz′əm) *n.* The belief that there is no God. [< MF < Gk. < *a-* without + *theos* god]

a·the·ist (ā′thē·ist) *n.* One who denies or disbelieves in the existence of God. — **a′the·is′tic** or **-tic·al** *adj.* — **a′the·is′ti·cal·ly** *adv.*

A·the·na (ə·thē′nə) In Greek mythology, the goddess identified with the Roman *Minerva.* Also **Athena Parthenos,** **A·the·ne** (ə·thē′nē). [< Gk. *Athēnē*]

ath·e·ne·um (ath′ə·nē′əm) *n.* **1.** A literary club, academy, or other institution for the promotion of learning. **2.** A reading room, library, etc. Also **ath′e·nae′um.**

A·the·ni·an (ə·thē′nē-ən) *adj.* Of or pertaining to Athens, or to its art or culture. — *n.* A native or citizen of Athens.

ath·er·o·scle·ro·sis (ath′ər·ō·sklə·rō′sis) *n. Pathol.* Hardening of the arteries, accompanied by the deposit of fat in the inner arterial walls. [< NL < Gk. *athērē* gruel + *sklēros* hard]

a·thirst (ə·thûrst′) *adj.* Keenly desirous; longing; eager: with *for.* [OE < *of-,* intensive + *thyrstan* to thirst]

ath·lete (ath′lēt) *n.* One trained in acts or feats of physical strength and agility, as in sports. [< L < Gk. *athleein* to contend for a prize]

athlete's foot Ringworm of the foot, caused by a fungus.

ath·let·ic (ath·let′ik) *adj.* **1.** Of, pertaining to, or befitting an athlete or athletics. **2.** Strong; vigorous; muscular. — **ath·let′i·cal·ly** *adv.* — **ath·let·i·cism** (ath·let′ə·siz′əm) *n.*

ath·let·ics (ath·let′iks) *n.pl.* Athletic games and exercises, as rowing, wrestling, etc.

ath·o·dyd (ath′ō·did) *n.* A jet engine consisting of a pipe to which air is admitted, heated, and expelled from the rear at high velocity.

at-home (ət·hōm′) *n.* An informal party or reception given at one's home.

a·thwart (ə·thwôrt′) *adv.* **1.** From side to side; across. **2.** So as to thwart; perversely. — *prep.* **1.** From side to side of. **2.** Contrary to. **3.** *Naut.* Across the course of.

-atic *suffix* Of; of the kind of: *erratic.* [< F < L < Gk. *-atikos*]

a·tilt (ə·tilt′) *adv. & adj.* In a tilted manner; tilted up.

-ation *suffix of nouns* **1.** Action or process of: *creation.* **2.** Condition or quality of: *affectation.* **3.** Result of: *reformation.* Also *-ion, -tion.* [< F *-ation* or L *-atio, -ationis*]

-ative *suffix* Denoting relation, tendency, or characteristic: *remunerative.* [< F *-atif,* masc., *-ative,* fem. or < L *-ativus*]

At·lan·tic (at·lan′tik) *adj.* Of, near, in, or pertaining to the Atlantic Ocean. [< L < Gk. *Atlantikos* pertaining to Atlas]

Atlantic Charter A statement issued in August, 1941, by Churchill and Roosevelt, setting forth the basic aims of the Allied Nations for the peace after World War II.

At·lan·tis (at·lan′tis) A mythical island west of Gibraltar, said by Plato to have been engulfed by the sea.

at·las (at′ləs) *n.* **1.** A volume of maps usu. bound together. **2.** Any book of tables or charts on a given subject.

At·las (at′ləs) *n.* **1.** In Greek mythology, a Titan who supported the heavens on his shoulders. **2.** An intercontinental ballistic missile of the U.S. Air Force.

at·man (ät′mən) *n.* In Hinduism, the soul; the divine life principle in man. — **Atman** The supreme soul, the source and goal of all individual souls. [< Skt.]

atmo- *combining form* Vapor. [< Gk. *atmos*]

at·mos·phere (at′məs·fir) *n.* **1.** The body of gases surrounding the earth or a celestial body. **2.** The particular climatic condition of any place or region. **3.** Any surrounding or pervasive element or influence. **4.** *Informal* A quality regarded as especially characteristic or interesting: This café has *atmosphere.* **5.** *Physics* A unit of pressure, equal to 14.69 pounds per square inch. [< NL < Gk. *atmos* vapor + *sphaira* sphere]

at·mos·pher·ic (at′məs·fer′ik) *adj.* **1.** Of or in the atmosphere. **2.** Dependent on or resulting from the atmosphere. Also **at′mos·pher′i·cal.** — **at′mos·pher′i·cal·ly** *adv.*

at·mos·pher·ics (at′məs·fer′iks) *n.pl.* (*construed as sing.*) In radio transmission, static.

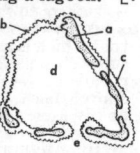

ATOLL
a Islets. *b* Barrier reef. *c* Fringing reef. *d* Lagoon. *e* Passage.

at·oll (at′ôl, -ol, ə·tol′) *n.* A ring-shaped coral island and its associated reef, nearly or completely enclosing a lagoon. [? < Malayalam *adal* closing, uniting]

a·tom (at′əm) *n.* **1.** *Chem.* The smallest part of an element capable of existing alone or in combination, and that cannot be changed or destroyed in any chemical reaction. **2.** *Physics* One of the particles of which all matter is formed, regarded as an aggregate of nucleons and electrons variously organized within and around a central nucleus, and exhibiting complex mass-energy characteristics. **3.** A hypothetical entity admitting of no division into smaller parts. **4.** The smallest quantity or particle; iota. [< L < Gk. < *a-* not + *temnein* to cut]

a·tom·ic (ə·tom′ik) *adj.* **1.** Of or pertaining to an atom or atoms. **2.** Very minute; infinitesimal. — **a·tom′i·cal·ly** *adv.*

atomic age The era characterized by the use and growing importance of atomic energy.

atomic bomb A bomb of formidable destructive power using the energy released by the fission of atomic nuclei, esp. those of radioactive elements, as uranium: also called *A-bomb.* Also **atom bomb.**

atomic clock A high-precision instrument for the measurement of time by the vibration rate of suitable molecules.

atomic energy The energy contained within the nucleus of the atom, esp. when made available for human use by controlled nuclear fission or thermonuclear reactions.

atomic number *Physics* A number that represents the unit positive charges (protons) in the atomic nucleus of each element and corresponds to the number of extranuclear electrons. Hydrogen is assigned an atomic number of 1.

atomic power Atomic energy as a source of power.

atomic reactor Reactor (def. 4).

at·om·ics (ə·tom′iks) *n.pl.* (*construed as sing.*) Nuclear physics, esp. in its practical applications.

atomic structure *Physics* The conception of the atom as a system of particles consisting of a central positive nucleus and a cluster of negatively charged electrons, the number and arrangement of the particles determining the energy relations within and between atoms.

atomic theory **1.** *Chem.* The doctrine that elements unite with one another, atom by atom, and in definite simple proportions by weight. **2.** *Physics* The modern concept of atomic structure as a complex of mass-energy relationships.

atomic weight *Chem.* **a** Since 1961, the weight of an atom of an element relative to that of an atom of carbon, taken as 12. **b** Formerly, the weight of an atom of an element relative to that of an atom of oxygen, taken as 16.

at·om·ize (at′əm·īz) *v.t.* **·ized, ·iz·ing 1.** To reduce to atoms. **2.** To spray or reduce to a spray, as by an atomizer. Also *Brit.* **at′om·ise.** — **at′om·i·za′tion** *n.*

at·om·iz·er (at′əm·ī′zər) *n.* An apparatus for reducing a liquid, esp. medicine or perfume, to a spray.

atom smasher *Physics* An accelerator.

a·to·nal (ā·tō′nəl) *adj. Music* Without tonality; lacking key or tonal center. — **a·to′nal·ly** *adv.*

a·to·nal·i·ty (ā′tō·nal′ə·tē) *n. Music* The use of a system of tones, especially the chromatic scale, so that each tone is equal in its relation to the others and no one tone holds a central or primary position; absence of key or tonal center.

a·tone (ə·tōn′) *v.i.* **a·toned, a·ton·ing** To make expiation, as for sin or wrongdoing. [< earlier adverbial phrase *at one* in accord, short for *to set at one,* i.e., reconcile] — **a·ton′a·ble** or **a·tone′a·ble** *adj.* — **a·ton′er** *n.*

a·tone·ment (ə·tōn′mənt) *n.* **1.** Satisfaction, reparation, or expiation made for wrong or injury. **2.** *Usually cap. Theol.* The reconciliation between God and man effected by Christ.

a·ton·ic (ə·ton′ik, ā-) *adj.* **1.** Not accented, as a word or syllable. **2.** Lacking tone or vigor. [< Med.L < Gk. < *a-* not + *teinein* to stretch]

a·top (ə·top′) *adv. & adj.* On or at the top. — *prep. Chiefly U.S.* On the top of.

-ator *suffix of nouns* An agent; doer; actor; one who or that which: *arbitrator, mediator.* [< L]

-atory *suffix of adjectives* Characterized by; producing or produced by: *conciliatory.* [< L *-atorius,* adj. suffix]

at·ra·bil·ious (at′rə·bil′yəs) *adj.* Disposed to hypochondria; melancholy; splenetic. Also **at′ra·bil′i·ar** (-bil′ē·ər). [< L *atra bilis* black bile] — **at′ra·bil′ious·ness** *n.*

a·tri·um (ā′trē·əm) *n. pl.* **a·tri·a** (ā′trē·ə) **1.** The entrance hall or central open court of an ancient Roman house. **2.** A court or hall. **3.** *Anat.* One of the upper chambers of the heart: also called *auricle.* [< L, a hall] — **a′tri·al** *adj.*

a·tro·cious (ə·trō′shəs) *adj.* **1.** Very wicked, cruel, etc. **2.** *Informal* Very bad; of in bad taste. [< L *atrox, atrocis* harsh, cruel] — **a·tro′cious·ly** *adv.* — **a·tro′cious·ness** *n.*

a·troc·i·ty (ə·tros′ə·tē) *n. pl.* **·ties 1.** The state or quality of being atrocious. **2.** An atrocious deed or act. **3.** *Informal.* Something in very bad taste.

at·ro·phy (at′rə-fē) *n. pl.* **·phies** *Pathol.* A wasting or failure in development of the body or any of its parts. — *v.* **·phied, ·phy·ing** *v.t.* **1.** To cause to waste away or wither. — *v.i.* **2.** To waste away; wither. [< F < L < Gk. < a- not + *trephein* to nourish] — **a·troph·ic** (ə-trof′ik) *adj.* — **at′ro·phied** *adj.*

at·ro·pine (at′rə-pēn, -pin) *n.* A crystalline, poisonous alkaloid, C₁₇H₂₃O₃N, found in the deadly nightshade and in certain other plants, used as an antispasmodic and to enlarge the pupil of the eye. Also **at′ro·pin** (-pin). [See ATROPOS.]

At·ro·pos (at′rə-pos) One of the three Fates. [< Gk., inflexible < a- not + *trepein* to turn]

at·tach (ə-tach′) *v.t.* **1.** To make fast to something; fasten on; affix. **2.** To join on as a part or adjunct. **3.** To add or append, as a signature. **4.** To connect by personal ties, as of affection. **5.** To ascribe: with *to*. **6.** To appoint officially; assign. **7.** *Law* To secure for legal jurisdiction; seize by legal process: to *attach* an employee's salary. — *v.i.* **8.** To be attached; connect. [< OF < a- to + *tache* nail] — **at·tach′a·ble** *adj.*

at·ta·ché (at′ə-shā′, *esp. Brit.* ə-tash′ā) *n.* A person officially attached to a diplomatic mission or staff in a specified capacity: military *attaché*. [< F, pp. of *attacher* to attach]

attaché case A boxlike hinged briefcase.

at·tach·ment (ə-tach′mənt) *n.* **1.** The act of attaching, or the state of being attached. **2.** A bond; band; tie. **3.** Affection; devoted regard. **4.** An appendage or adjunct. **5.** *Law* Seizure of a person or property.

at·tack (ə-tak′) *v.t.* **1.** To set upon violently; begin battle or conflict with. **2.** To assail with hostile words; criticize. **3.** To begin work on; set about, as an undertaking. **4.** To begin to affect injuriously. — *v.i.* **5.** To make an attack; begin battle. — *n.* **1.** The act of attacking; assault; onset. **2.** The first movement toward any undertaking. **3.** A seizure, as by disease. [< F, ult. < same source as ATTACH] — **Syn.** (verb) **1.** *Attack* is applied loosely to any offensive action, but strictly means to begin hostilities. *Assault* always suggests close physical contact and extreme violence. To *assail* is to belabor with repeated words or blows. — (noun) **1.** assault, onslaught, onset, invasion, incursion, raid.

at·tain (ə-tān′) *v.t.* **1.** To gain by exertion of body or mind; achieve. **2.** To come to, as in time; arrive at: He *attained* old age. — **to attain to** To arrive at with effort; succeed in reaching. [< OF < L < ad- to + *tangere* to touch] — **at·tain′a·ble** *adj.* That can be attained. — **at·tain′a·bil′i·ty, at·tain′a·ble·ness** *n.*

at·tain·der (ə-tān′dər) *n.* The loss of all civil rights consequent to a sentence of death or of outlawry for a capital offense. — **bill of attainder** Formerly, a legislative act inflicting attainder upon a person guilty of a capital offense. [< OF *ataindre* to attain, strike]

at·tain·ment (ə-tān′mənt) *n.* **1.** The act of attaining. **2.** That which is attained; an acquisition, as of skill.

at·taint (ə-tānt′) *v.t.* **1.** To inflict attainder upon; condemn. **2.** To touch or affect injuriously; disgrace; taint. — *n.* **1.** Imputation; stigma. **2.** Attainder. [See ATTAIN.]

at·tar (at′ər) *n.* The fragrant essential oil extracted from the petals of flowers, esp. roses. [< Arabic *itr* perfume]

at·tempt (ə-tempt′) *v.t.* **1.** To make an effort to do or accomplish; try. **2.** To try to take by force; attack: to *attempt* the life of someone. — *n.* **1.** A putting forth of effort; a trial; endeavor. **2.** An attack; assault. [< OF < L < ad- toward + *tendere* to stretch] — **at·tempt′a·bil′i·ty** *n.* — **at·tempt′a·ble** *adj.* — **at·tempt′er** *n.*

at·tend (ə-tend′) *v.t.* **1.** To be present at, as a meeting. **2.** To wait upon or go with as an attendant; escort. **3.** To visit or minister to (a sick person). **4.** To accompany as a result. **5.** To give heed to; listen to. — *v.i.* **6.** To be present. **7.** To give heed; listen. — **to attend to 1.** To apply oneself to. **2.** To take care of; tend to. [< OF < L < ad- toward + *tendere* to stretch]

at·ten·dance (ə-ten′dəns) *n.* **1.** The act of attending. **2.** Those who attend; an audience or retinue.

at·ten·dant (ə-ten′dənt) *n.* **1.** One who attends, esp. as a servant. **2.** One who is present. **3.** A concomitant; consequence. — *adj.* Following or accompanying.

at·ten·tion (ə-ten′shən) *n.* **1.** Close or earnest attending. **2.** The power or faculty of mental concentration. **3.** Practical consideration; care: *attention* to one's appearance. **4.** *Usu. pl.* Acts of courtesy, esp. on the part of a lover. **5.** *Mil.* The prescribed position of readiness: to stand at *attention*; also, the order to take this position.

at·ten·tive (ə-ten′tiv) *adj.* **1.** Observant. **2.** Courteous or gallant. — **at·ten′tive·ly** *adv.* — **at·ten′tive·ness** *n.*

at·ten·u·ate (*v.* ə-ten′yōō-āt; *adj.* ə-ten′yōō-it) *v.* **·at·ed, ·at·ing** *v.t.* **1.** To make thin, small, or fine; draw out, as a wire.

2. To weaken; lessen. **3.** To reduce in density; rarefy, as a liquid or gas. **4.** *Bacteriol.* To weaken the virulence of (a microorganism). — *v.i.* **5.** To become thin, weak, rarefied, etc. — *adj.* Attenuated. [< L < ad- (intensive) + *tenuare* to make thin] — **at·ten′u·a·ble** *adj.*

at·ten·u·a·tion (ə-ten′yōō-ā′shən) *n.* The act or process of attenuating, or the state of being attenuated.

at·test (ə-test′) *v.t.* **1.** To confirm as accurate, true, or genuine; vouch for. **2.** To certify, as by signature or oath. **3.** To be proof of. **4.** To put upon oath. — *v.i.* **5.** To bear witness; testify: with *to*. — *n.* Attestation. [< MF < L < ad- to + *testari* to bear witness]

at·tes·ta·tion (at′es-tā′shən) *n.* **1.** The act of attesting. **2.** Testimony.

at·tic (at′ik) *n.* **1.** A low story beneath the roof of a building; a garret. **2.** *Archit.* A low structure, above a cornice or entablature. [< F < L *Atticus*, architectural term]

At·tic (at′ik) *adj.* **1.** Of Attica. **2.** Of or characteristic of Athens or the Athenians. **3.** Simple and graceful; delicate; refined: also **at′tic.** — *n.* The dialect of Attica. [< L < Gk. *Attikē* Attica]

At·ti·ca (at′i-kə) In ancient times, the region of Greece surrounding Athens.

Attic salt Delicate, refined, graceful wit. Also **Attic wit.**

at·tire (ə-tīr′) *v.t.* **·tired, ·tir·ing** To dress; array; adorn. — *n.* Dress or clothing. [< OF *atirer* to arrange, adorn]

at·ti·tude (at′ə-tōōd, -tyōōd) *n.* **1.** Position of the body, as suggesting some thought or feeling. **2.** State of mind, behavior, or conduct regarding some matter, as indicating opinion or purpose. [< F < Ital. < LL < L *aptus* fitted, suited] — **at·ti·tu·di·nal** (at′ə-tōō′də-nəl, -tyōō′-) *adj.*

at·ti·tu·di·nize (at′ə-tōō′də-nīz, -tyōō′-) *v.i.* **·nized, ·niz·ing** To take a pose for effect. Also *Brit.* **at·ti·tu′di·nise.**

atto- *combining form* One quintillionth (10⁻¹⁸) of a specific quantity or dimension.

at·tor·ney (ə-tûr′nē) *n.* A person empowered by another to act in his stead; esp., a lawyer. — **by attorney** By proxy. [< OF *atorner* to turn to, appoint] — **at·tor′ney·ship** *n.*

attorney at law A lawyer.

attorney general *pl.* **attorneys general, attorney generals** The chief law officer of a government. *Abbr. A.G., Atty. Gen.*

at·tract (ə-trakt′) *v.t.* **1.** To draw to or cause to come near by some physical force, as magnetism. **2.** To draw, as the admiration or attention of. — *v.i.* **3.** To exert attractive influence. [< L < ad- toward + *trahere* to draw, drag] — **at·tract′a·ble** *adj.* — **at·tract′a·ble·ness, at·tract′a·bil′i·ty** *n.* — **at·trac′tile** *adj.* — **at·trac′tor** or **at·tract′er** *n.*

at·trac·tion (ə-trak′shən) *n.* **1.** The act or power of attracting. **2.** Attractive quality or characteristic; enticement; charm. **3.** Something that attracts. **4.** *Physics* A force that, exerted between or among bodies, tends to make them approach each other or prevents their separating.

at·trac·tive (ə-trak′tiv) *adj.* **1.** Pleasing; winning; charming. **2.** Having the power to attract. — **at·trac′tive·ly** *adv.* — **at·trac′tive·ness** *n.*

at·trib·ute (ə-trib′yōōt) *v.t.* **·ut·ed, ·ut·ing** To ascribe as belonging to or resulting from: to *attribute* wisdom to old age. — **at·tri·bute** (at′rə-byōōt) *n.* **1.** A quality or characteristic of a person or thing. **2.** *Gram.* An adjective or its equivalent. **3.** In art and mythology, a distinctive mark or symbol. [< L < ad- to + *tribuere* to allot, give over] — **at·trib′ut·a·ble** *adj.* — **at·trib′u·ter** or **at·trib′u·tor** *n.* — **Syn.** (verb) *Attribute, impute,* and *ascribe* are largely interchangeable, but usually we *attribute* good things, *impute* bad, and *ascribe* either. We usually *assign* or *refer* a thing to a category, as time, place, cause, etc., rather than to a person.

at·tri·bu·tion (at′rə-byōō′shən) *n.* **1.** The act of attributing. **2.** An ascribed characteristic or quality; attribute.

at·trib·u·tive (ə-trib′yə-tiv) *adj.* **1.** Pertaining to or of the nature of an attribute. **2.** Ascribed, as a work of art: an *attributive* Vermeer. **3.** *Gram.* Designating an adjective or its equivalent that stands before the noun it modifies. — *n. Gram.* An attributive word or phrase. — **at·trib′u·tive·ly** *adv.* — **at·trib′u·tive·ness** *n.*

at·tri·tion (ə-trish′ən) *n.* **1.** A rubbing out or grinding down, as by friction. **2.** A gradual wearing down or weakening. [< L < ad- to, against + *terere* to rub]

at·tune (ə-tōōn′, ə-tyōōn′) *v.t.* **·tuned, ·tun·ing 1.** To bring into accord; harmonize. **2.** To tune.

a·typ·i·cal (ā-tip′i-kəl) *adj.* Not typical; differing from the type; irregular. Also **a·typ′ic.** — **a·typ′i·cal·ly** *adv.*

au·burn (ô′bûrn) *adj. & n.* Reddish brown. [< OF < LL < L *albus* white; infl. in meaning by ME *brun* brown]

au cou·rant (ō kōō-räṅ′) *French* Up to date; well informed.

auc·tion (ôk′shən) *n.* **1.** A public sale in which the price is increased by bids until the highest bidder becomes the purchaser. **2.** The bidding in bridge. — *v.t.* To sell by or at auction: usually with *off*. [< L *augere* to increase]

auction bridge A variety of the game of bridge in which tricks made by the declarer in excess of the contract count toward game. Compare CONTRACT BRIDGE.

auc·tion·eer (ôk′shən·ir′) *n.* One who conducts an auction, usu. as a business. — *v.t.* To sell at aucton.

au·da·cious (ô·dā′shəs) *adj.* 1. Showing no fear; daring; bold. 2. Shameless; impudent. [< L *audere* to dare + -OUS] — **au·da′cious·ly** *adv.* — **au·da′cious·ness** *n.*

au·dac·i·ty (ô·das′ə·tē) *n.* 1. Boldness; daring. 2. Impudence; shamelessness. — **Syn.** See TEMERITY.

au·di·ble (ô′də·bəl) *adj.* Perceptible by the ear; loud enough to be heard. [< Med.L < L *audire* to hear] — **au·di·bil′i·ty, au′di·ble·ness** *n.* — **au′di·bly** *adv.*

au·di·ence (ô′dē·əns) *n.* 1. An assembly of listeners or spectators, as at a concert. 2. Those who are reached by a book, television program, etc. 3. A formal hearing, interview, or conference. 4. Opportunity to be heard. [<OF < L *audire* to hear]

au·di·o (ô′dē·ō) *adj.* 1. Of or pertaining to characteristics associated with sound waves. 2. *Electronics* Designating devices used in transmission or reception of sound waves: in television, distinguished from *video*. [< L *audire* to hear]

audio- *combining form* Pertaining to hearing: Also **audi-**. [< L *audire* to hear]

audio frequency *Physics* A frequency of electrical, sound, or other wave vibrations within the range of normal human hearing, or from about 20 to 20,000 cycles a second.

au·di·o·vis·u·al aids (ô′dē·ō·vizh′ōō·əl) Motion pictures, photographs, recordings, etc., used as teaching devices.

au·dit (ô′dit) *v.t.* 1. To examine, adjust, and certify, as accounts. 2. *U.S.* To attend (a college course) as a listener and without earning credit. — *v.i.* 2. To make an audit. — *n.* 1. An examination of an accounting document and of the evidence in support of its correctness. 2. A final statement of such an account. 3. An adjustment and settling of accounts. [< L *audire* to hear]

au·di·tion (ô·dish′ən) *n.* 1. The act or sense of hearing. 2. A test or hearing, as of an actor or singer. — *v.t. & v.i.* To give an audition. [< L *audire* to hear]

au·di·tor (ô′də·tər) *n.* 1. One who audits accounts. 2. A listener. 3. *U.S.* One who audits classes [< L]

au·di·to·ri·um (ô′də·tôr′ē·əm, -tō′rē·əm) *n. pl.* **·to·ri·ums** or **·to·ri·a** (-tôr′ē·ə, -tō′rē·ə) 1. The room or part of a school, church, theater, etc., occupied by the audience. 2. A building for concerts, public meetings, etc. [< L, lecture room]

au·di·to·ry (ô′də·tôr′ē, -tō′rē) *adj.* Of or pertaining to hearing or the organs or sense of hearing. — *n. pl.* **·ries** 1. An audience. 2. The nave of a church. [< L *audire* to hear]

auditory canal *Anat.* The passage leading from the auricle to the tympanic membrane. For illustration see EAR.

auf Wie·der·seh·en (ouf vē′dər·zā′ən) *German* Till we meet again; good-by for now.

Au·ge·an stables (ô·jē′ən) In Greek mythology, the stables that were cleaned in a day by Hercules.

au·gend (ô′jend) *n. Math.* A number to which another is to be added. See ADDEND. [< L *augere* to increase]

au·ger (ô′gər) *n.* Any of various tools for boring wood. [OE *nafugār,* < *nafu* nave of a wheel + *gār* borer, spear]

aught¹ (ôt) *n.* Anything; any part or item. — *adv.* By any chance; at all. [OE *āwiht, ōwiht* < *ā* ever + *wiht* thing]

aught² (ôt) *n.* The figure 0; cipher; a naught; nothing. [*a naught* taken as *an aught*]

aug·ment (*v.* ôg·ment′; *n.* ôg′ment) *v.t.* 1. To make greater, as in size, number, or amount; enlarge; intensify. — *v.i.* 2. To become greater, as in size. — **Syn.** see INCREASE. — *n.* Increase; enlargement. [< F < L *augere* to increase] — **aug·ment′a·ble** *adj.*

aug·men·ta·tion (ôg′men·tā′shən) *n.* 1. The act of augmenting, or the state of being augmented. 2. An addition.

aug·men·ta·tive (ôg·men′tə·tiv) *adj.* 1. Having the quality or power of augmenting. 2. *Gram.* Denoting greater size or intensity, as a suffix. — *n. Gram.* An augmentative form. Also **aug·men′tive.** Abbr. *aug.*

aug·ment·er (ôg·men′tər) *n.* One who or that which augments. 2. *Aeron.* Afterburner.

au gra·tin (ō grät′n, grat′n; *Fr.* ō grà·taṅ′) Sprinkled with bread crumbs or grated cheese and baked until brown. [< F]

au·gur (ô′gər, -gyər) *n.* A prophet; soothsayer. — *v.t. & v.i.* 1. To prophesy. 2. To betoken; be an omen of. [< L *augere* to increase] — **au′gu·ral** *adj.*

au·gu·ry (ô′gyə·rē) *n. pl.* **·ries** 1. The art or practice of divination. 2. A portent or omen.

au·gust (ô·gust′) *adj.* Inspiring awe, admiration, or reverence; majestic; imposing. [< L *augere* to increase, exalt] — **au·gust′ly** *adv.* — **au·gust′ness** *n.*

Au·gust (ô′gəst) *n.* The eighth month of the year, containing 31 days. Abbr. *Ag., Aug, Aug.* [< L *Augustus Caesar*]

Au·gus·tan (ô·gus′tən) *adj.* 1. Of or pertaining to Augustus Caesar or to his times. 2. Pertaining to any similar era — *n.* A writer or artist of an Augustan age.

Augustan age 1. The period of the reign of Augustus Cae-

sar, the golden age of Roman literature. 2. A similar period in English literature during the reign of Queen Anne.

auk (ôk) *n.* A short-winged, web-footed diving bird of northern seas; the **razor-billed** auk of the North Atlantic. [< ON *ālka*]

auld lang syne (ôld′ lang sīn′, zīn′) *Scot.* Literally, old long since; long ago.

au na·tu·rel (ō nȧ·tü·rel′) *French* 1. Plainly cooked; ungarnished. 2. In the natural condition; nude.

aunt (ant, änt) *n.* A sister of one's father or mother, or the wife of one's uncle. [< OF *aunte, ante*]

au pair (ō pâr) *Chiefly Brit.* 1. An arrangement whereby one receives room and board in a foreign household in exchange for doing certain chores, as caring for children: often used attributively: *au pair* girls. 2. *Informal* An au pair girl. [< F, lit., at par, even (with)]

RAZOR–BILLED AUK
(About 16 inches high)

au·ra (ôr′ə) *n. pl.* **au·ras** or **au·rae** (ôr′ē) 1. An invisible emanation or exhalation. 2. A distinctive air or quality enveloping or characterizing a person or thing. 3. *Pathol.* The sensory, motor, or psychic manifestations preceding an epileptic attack or other paroxysm. [< L, breeze < Gk. *aurē* breath] — **au′ral** *adj.*

au·ral (ôr′əl) *adj.* Pertaining to the ear or the sense of hearing; auricular. [< L *auris* ear + -AL]

au·re·ate (ôr′ē·it) *adj.* 1. Of the color of gold; golden. 2. Splendid. [< L *aureus* < *aurum* gold]

au·re·ole (ôr′ē·ōl) *n.* 1. In art, a halo. 2. Any radiance or halo around a body. Also **au·re·o·la** (ô·rē′ə·lə). [< L *aureola (corona)* golden (crown) < *aurum* gold]

Au·re·o·my·cin (ôr′ē·ō·mī′sin) *n.* Proprietary name for a type of antibiotic. Also **au′re·o·my′cin.** [< L *aureus* golden + Gk. *mykes* fungus]

au re·voir (ō rə·vwàr′) *French* Good-by; till we meet again.

au·ri·cle (ôr′i·kəl) *n.* 1. *Anat.* **a** An atrium of the heart. **b** The external ear; pinna. 2. An ear-shaped part. [< L *auricula,* dim. of *auris* ear] — **au′ri·cled** *adj.*

au·ric·u·lar (ô·rik′yə·lər) *adj.* 1. Of or pertaining to the ear or the sense of hearing. 2. Intended for the ear. 3. Ear-shaped. 4. Of or pertaining to an auricle.

au·rif·er·ous (ô·rif′ər·əs) *adj.* Containing gold. [< L *aurum* gold + *ferre* to bear]

au·ri·form (ôr′ə·fôrm) *adj.* Ear-shaped.

Au·ri·ga (ô·rī′gə) *n.* A constellation, the Charioteer or Wagoner, containing the bright star Capella. [< L]

au·ro·ra (ô·rôr′ə, ô·rō′rə) *n.* 1. *Meteorol.* A display of arcs, bands, streamers, etc., of light occasionally seen in the skies of polar latitudes. 2. The dawn. [< L, dawn]

Au·ro·ra (ô·rôr′ə, ô·rō′rə) In Roman mythology, the goddess of the dawn: identified with the Greek *Eos.*

aurora aus·tra·lis (ôs·trā′lis) *Meteorol.* The aurora seen in far southern latitudes; also called *southern lights.* [< NL, southern aurora < L *auster* south wind]

aurora bo·re·al·is (bôr′ē·al′is, -ā′lis, bō′rē-) *Meteorol.* The aurora seen in high northern latitudes: also called *northern lights.* [< NL, northern aurora < Gk. *boreas* north wind]

au·ro·ral (ô·rôr′əl, ô·rō′rəl) *adj.* 1. Pertaining to or like the dawn; roseate. 2. *Meteorol.* Of, like, or caused by an aurora.

au·rum (ôr′əm) *n.* Gold. [< L]

aus·cul·tate (ôs′kəl·tāt) *v.t. & v.i.* **·tat·ed, ·tat·ing** *Med.* To examine by auscultation. [< L *auscultare* to listen, give ear to] — **aus′cul·ta′tor** *n.*

aus·cul·ta·tion (ôs′kəl·tā′shən) *n.* 1. *Med.* The act of listening, as with a stethoscope. 2. A listening.

aus·pice (ôs′pis) *n. pl.* **aus·pi·ces** (ôs′pə·sēz) 1. *Usu. pl.* Patronage. 2. An omen, or sign. [< F < L *auspex*]

aus·pi·cious (ôs·pish′əs) *adj.* 1. Of good omen; propitious. 2. Prosperous; fortunate. — **Syn.** See PROPITIOUS. — **aus·pi′cious·ly** *adv.* — **aus·pi′cious·ness** *n.*

aus·tere (ô·stir′) *adj.* 1. Severe, grave, or stern, as in aspect or conduct. 2. Morally strict; abstemious; ascetic. 3. Sour and astringent. 4. Severely simple; unadorned. [< OF < L < Gk. *austēros* harsh, bitter] — **aus·tere′ly** *adv.*

aus·ter·i·ty (ô·ster′ə·tē) *n. pl.* **·ties** 1. The quality of being austere; severity of demeanor, way of life, etc.: also **aus·tere′ness.** 2. *Usually pl.* Severe or ascetic acts.

aus·tral (ôs′trəl) *adj.* Southern; torrid. [< L *southern < auster* south wind]

Aus·tral·a·sian (ôs′tral·ā′zhən, -ā′shən) *n.* A native or inhabitant of Australasia. — *adj.* Of Australasia.

Aus·tral·ian (ôs·strāl′yən) *n.* A native or naturalized inhabitant of Australia. — *adj.* Of or pertaining to Australia or to its people.

Australian English The English language as spoken and written in Australia.

Aus·tri·an (ôs′trē·ən) *n.* An inhabitant or citizen of Austria. — *adj.* Of Austria or its people.

Austro- *combining form* 1. Austrian. 2. Australian.

Aus·tro·ne·sian (ôs′trō-nē′zhən, -shən) *adj.* Of or pertaining to Austronesia, its inhabitants, or their languages. — *n.* A family of languages of the Pacific comprising the Indonesian, Oceanic (including Melanesian and Micronesian), and Polynesian subfamilies. Also *Malayo-Polynesian.*

aut- Var. of AUTO-¹.

au·tar·chy (ô′tär-kē) *n. pl.* ·chies 1. Absolute rule or sovereignty, or a country under such rule. 2. Self-government. 3. Autarky. [< Gk. < *autos* self + *archein* to rule] — **au·tar·chic** (ô-tär′kik) or **·chi·cal** *adj.*

au·tar·ky (ô′tär-kē) *n.* National economic self-sufficiency. [< Gk. *autarkeia* self-sufficiency] — **au·tar·kik** (ô-tär′kik) or **·ki·kal** *adj.*

au·then·tic (ô-then′tik) *adj.* 1. Authoritative; reliable. 2. Of undisputed origin; genuine. 3. *Law* Duly executed before the proper officer. Also **au·then′ti·cal.** [< OF < L < Gk. < *authentēs* the doer of a deed] — **au·then′ti·cal·ly** *adv.* — **Syn.** 1. true, veritable. 2. real, legitimate, authorized, accredited. — **Ant.** spurious, counterfeit, fictitious, false.

au·then·ti·cate (ô-then′ti-kāt) *v.t.* ·cat·ed, ·cat·ing 1. To make authentic or authoritative. 2. To give legal validity to. 3. To establish the authenticity of. — **au·then·ti·ca′tion** *n.* — **au·then′ti·ca′tor** *n.*

au·then·tic·i·ty (ô·then·tis′ə·tē) *n.* The state or quality of being authentic, authoritative, or genuine.

au·thor (ô′thər) *n.* 1. The writer of a book, treatise, etc.; also, one who makes literary composition his profession. 2. One who begins or originates; creator. 3. An author's writings collectively. — *v.t. Informal* To be the author of; write. [< AF < L *auctor* originator, producer] — **au′thor·ess** *n.fem.* — **au·tho·ri·al** (ô-thôr′ē-əl, ô-thō′rē-) *adj.*

au·thor·i·tar·i·an (ə-thôr′ə-târ′ē-ən, ə-thor′-) *adj.* Favoring subjection to authority as opposed to individual freedom. — *n.* One who favors the principle of authority. — **au·thor′i·tar′i·an·ism** *n.*

au·thor·i·ta·tive (ə-thôr′ə-tā′tiv, ə-thor′-) *adj.* 1. Possessing or proceeding from proper authority; duly sanctioned. 2. Exercising authority; commanding; dictatorial. — **au·thor′i·ta′tive·ly** *adv.* — **au·thor′i·ta′tive·ness** *n.*

au·thor·i·ty (ə-thôr′ə-tē, ə-thor′-) *n. pl.* ·ties 1. The right to command and to enforce obedience; the right to act, decide, etc. 2. Delegated right or power; authorization. 3. *pl.* Those having the power to govern or command. 4. Title to respect, confidence, etc.; personal influence. 5. A person, volume, etc., appealed to in support of action or belief. 6. One who has special knowledge; an expert. 7. An official or group having administrative control in a specified area. 8. An authoritative opinion, decision, or precedent. Abbr. *auth.* [< OF < L < *augere* to increase]

au·thor·ize (ô′thə-rīz) *v.t.* ·ized, ·iz·ing 1. To confer authority upon; empower; commission. 2. To warrant; justify. 3. To sanction. [< OF < Med.L < L *auctor* originator] — **au·thor·i·za′tion** *n.* — **au′thor·iz′er** *n.*

au·thor·ized (ô′thə-rīzd) *adj.* 1. Endowed with authority; accepted as authoritative. 2. Formally or legally sanctioned.

au·thor·ship (ô′thər-ship) *n.* 1. The profession or occupation of an author. 2. Origin or source.

au·to (ô′tō) *U.S. Informal n.* An automobile. — *v.i.* **au·toed, au·to·ing** To ride in or travel by an automobile.

au·to-¹ *combining form* 1. Arising from some process or action within the object; not induced by any stimulus from without; as in:

autoagglutination	autodiffusion	autoinduction

2. Acting, acted, or directed upon the self; as in:

autoanalysis	autodiagnosis	autolavage

Also, before vowels, *aut-.* [< Gk. *autos* self]

au·to-² *combining form* Self-propelled. [< Gk. *autos* self]

au·to·bi·og·ra·phy (ô′tə-bī·og′rə-fē, -bē·og′-) *n. pl.* ·phies The story of a person's life written by that person. — **au′to·bi·og′ra·pher** *n.* — **au·to·bi·o·graph·ic** (ô′tə-bī′ə-graf′ik) or **·i·cal** *adj.* — **au′to·bi·o·graph′i·cal·ly** *adv.*

au·to·clave (ô′tə-klāv) *n.* 1. An enclosed chamber for the sterilization of drugs, vaccines, instruments, etc. 2. A pressure cooker. [< F < *auto-* self + L *clavis* a key]

au·toc·ra·cy (ô-tok′rə-sē) *n. pl.* ·cies 1. Absolute government by an individual; rule or authority of an autocrat. 2. A state ruled by an autocrat.

au·to·crat (ô′tə-krat) *n.* 1. A supreme ruler of unrestricted power. 2. An arrogant, dictatorial person. [< F < Gk. < *autos* self + *kratos* power] — **au′to·crat′ic** or **·i·cal** *adj.* — **au′to·crat′i·cal·ly** *adv.*

au·to·da·fé (ô′tə-dä-fā′, ou′-) *n. pl.* **au·tos-da-fé** (ô′tōz-, ou′tōz-) The public announcement and execution of a sentence of the Inquisition; esp., the burning of heretics at the stake. [< Pg., lit., act of the faith]

au·tog·e·nous (ô-toj′ə-nəs) *adj.* Self-produced or self-generated. Also **au·to·gen·ic** (ô′tō-jen′ik). [< Gk. *autogenēs* self-produced]

au·to·gi·ro (ô′tō-jī′rō) *n. pl.* ·ros An airplane that is supported in the air chiefly by freely-turning rotors but is drawn forward by a conventional propeller. Also **au′to·gy′ro.** [< AUTO-¹ + Gk. *gyros* a circle]

au·to·graph (ô′tə-graf, -gräf) *n.* 1. One's own signature or handwriting. 2. A manuscript in the author's handwriting. — *v.t.* 1. To write one's name in or affix one's signature to. 2. To write in one's own handwriting. — *adj.* Written by one's own hand, as a will. [< L < Gk. < *autos* self + *graphein* to write] — **au′to·graph′ic** or **·i·cal** *adj.* — **au′to·graph′i·cal·ly** *adv.*

au·to·in·tox·i·ca·tion (ô′tō-in-tok′sə-kā′shən) *n.* Poisoning from noxious secretions of one's own body.

au·to·mat (ô′tə-mat) *n. U.S.* A restaurant in which food is automatically made available from a receptacle when coins are deposited in a slot alongside.

au·to·mate (ô′tə-māt) ·mat·ed, ·mat·ing *v.t.* To adapt, as a machine, factory, or process, for automation. [Back formation < AUTOMATION]

au·to·mat·ic (ô′tə-mat′ik) *adj.* 1. Acting from forces inherent in itself; self-moving. 2. Self-acting and self-regulating, as machinery; mechanical. 3. *Psychol.* Done from force of habit or without volition. 4. Of firearms, extracting and ejecting the empty case and chambering the next round, using the force of recoil or of part of the exploding gas, and firing continuously until the trigger is released. Also (*except for def. 4*) **au′to·mat′i·cal, au·tom·a·tous** (ô-tom′ə-təs) — *n.* An automatic device, pistol, etc. [< Gk. *automatos* acting of oneself] — **au′to·mat′i·cal·ly** *adv.*

automatic pilot *Aeron.* An automatic-control mechanism designed to keep an aircraft level and on an even course.

automatic pistol A pistol using the force of recoil to extract and eject used shells and chamber the next round.

automatic rifle A rifle capable of automatic fire.

au·to·ma·tion (ô′tə-mā′shən) *n.* The automatic transfer of one unit of a complex industrial assembly to a succession of machines, each of which completes another stage in manufacture. — **au·to·ma·tive** (ô′tə-mā′tiv) *adj.*

au·tom·a·tism (ô-tom′ə-tiz′əm) *n.* 1. The state or quality of being automatic or of having no voluntary action. 2. *Physiol.* The functioning or power of functioning of muscular or other processes in response to external stimuli but independent of conscious control. — **au·tom′a·tist** *n.*

au·tom·a·ton (ô-tom′ə-ton, -tən) *n. pl.* ·tons or ·ta (-tə) 1. An apparatus that appears to function of itself by the action of a concealed mechanism. 2. Any living being whose actions are or appear to be involuntary or mechanical. 3. Anything capable of spontaneous movement or action. [< Gk. *automaton*, neut. of *automatos* acting of oneself, independent]

au·to·mo·bile (*n. & v.* ô′tə-mə-bēl′, ô′tə-mə-bēl′, ô′tə-mō′-bēl; *adj.* ô′tə-mō′bil) *n.* A four-wheeled passenger vehicle that carries its own source of power and travels on roads or streets; motorcar. — *v.i.* ·biled, ·bil·ing To ride in or drive an automobile. — *adj.* Automotive. [< F < Gk. *auto-* + *mobile* moving] — **au·to·mo·bil·ist** (ô′tə-mə-bēl′ist, -mō′-bil·ist) *n.*

au·to·mo·tive (ô′tə-mō′tiv) *adj.* 1. Self-propelling. 2. Of or for automobiles.

au·to·nom·ic (ô′tə-nom′ik) *adj.* 1. Autonomous. 2. *Physiol.* Pertaining to the autonomic nervous system. Also **au′to·nom′i·cal.** — **au′to·nom′i·cal·ly** *adv.*

autonomic nervous system A plexus of nerve ganglia and fibers originating in the spinal column and acting to innervate and control the efferent functions of all body tissues and organs not subject to voluntary control, as the heart, blood vessels, smooth muscle, glands, stomach, and intestines.

au·ton·o·mous (ô-ton′ə-məs) *adj.* 1. Independent; self-governing. 2. *Biol.* Independent. [< Gk. < *autos* self + *nomos* law, rule] — **au·ton′o·mous·ly** *adv.*

au·ton·o·my (ô-ton′ə-mē) *n. pl.* ·mies 1. The condition or quality of being autonomous; esp., the power or right of self-government. 2. A self-governing community or group. 3. Self-determination. — **au·ton′o·mist** *n.*

au·top·sy (ô′top-sē, ô′təp-) *n. pl.* ·sies Post-mortem examination of a human body, esp. when ordered by a coroner. [< NL < Gk. < *autos* self + *opsis* a seeing]

au·to·sug·ges·tion (ô′tō-səg-jes′chən) *n. Psychol.* Suggestion emanating from one's self only. — **au′to·sug·gest′i·bil′i·ty** *n.* — **au′to·sug·gest′i·ble** *adj.*

au·tumn (ô′təm) *n.* 1. The season of the year occurring between summer and winter. Often called *fall.* 2. A time of maturity and incipient decline. [< OF < L *autumnus*]

au·tum·nal (ô-tum′nəl) *adj.* 1. Of, pertaining to, or like autumn. 2. Ripening or harvested in autumn. 3. Past maturity; declining. — **au·tum′nal·ly** *adv.*

autumnal equinox See under EQUINOX.

aux·il·ia·ry (ôg-zil′yər-ē, -zil′ər-) *adj.* 1. Giving or furnishing aid. 2. Subsidiary; accessory. 3. Supplementary; reserve. — *n. pl.* ·ries 1. One who or that which aids or helps; assistant; associate. 2. *Gram.* A verb that helps to express tense, mood, etc., as have in *We have gone:* also **auxiliary verb.** 3. *pl.* Foreign troops associated with those of a nation at war. [< L < *auxilium* help]

a·vail (ə·vāl′) *v.t.* 1. To assist or aid; profit. — *v.i.* 2. To be of value or advantage; suffice. — **to avail oneself of** To take advantage of; utilize. — *n.* 1. Utility for a purpose; benefit; good: His efforts were of no *avail.* 2. *pl.* Proceeds. [< OF < L *ad-* to + *valere* to be strong]

a·vail·a·ble (ə·vā′lə·bəl) *adj.* 1. Capable of being used; at hand; usable. 2. *Law* Valid. — **a·vail′a·bil′i·ty, a·vail′a·ble·ness.** — **a·vail′a·bly** *adv.*

av·a·lanche (av′ə·lanch, -länch) *n.* A large mass of snow or ice falling down a slope. 2. Something like an avalanche, as in power, destructiveness, etc. — *v.* **·lanched, ·lanch·ing** *v.i.* 1. To fall or slide like an avalanche. — *v.t.* 2. To fall or come down upon like an avalanche. [< F < dial. F (Swiss) *lavenche* < L *ad vallem*]

a·vant-garde (ə·vänt′gärd′, *Fr.* á·vän·gárd′) *n.* The vanguard; esp., in art, the group regarded as most advanced or daring in technique and ideas. — *adj.* Of or pertaining to this group. [< F, lit., advance guard]

av·a·rice (av′ə·ris) *n.* Passion for acquiring and hoarding riches; greed. [< OF < L < *avere* to desire, crave]

av·a·ri·cious (av′ə·rish′əs) *adj.* Greedy of gain; grasping; miserly. — **av′a·ri′cious·ly** *adv.* — **av′a·ri′cious·ness** *n.*

a·vast (ə·vast′, ə·väst′) *interj. Naut.* Stop! hold! cease! [< Du. *hou' vast, houd vast* hold fast]

av·a·tar (av′ə·tär′) *n.* 1. In Hindu mythology, the incarnation of a god. 2. Any incarnation. [< Skt. *avatāra* descent]

a·ve (ä′vē, ä′vā) *interj.* 1. Hail! 2. Farewell! — *n.* The salutation *ave.* [< L, hail, farewell]

A·ve Ma·ri·a (ä′vā mə·rē′ə, ä′vē) A Roman Catholic prayer to the Virgin Mary: also called *Hail Mary.* Also **A′ve, Mar·y** (ä′vē mâr′ē). [< L, Hail, Mary]

a·venge (ə·venj′) *v.* **a·venged, a·veng·ing** *v.t.* 1. To take vengeance or exact exemplary punishment for or in behalf of. — *v.i.* 2. To take vengeance. [< OF < L < *ad-* to + *vindicare* to avenge] — **a·veng′er** *n.* — **a·veng′ing·ly** *adv.*

av·e·nue (av′ə·nōō, -nyōō) *n.* 1. A broad street. 2. A way of approach, as to a building, often bordered with trees. 3. A mode of access or attainment. [< F *avenue* < L < *ad-* toward + *venire* to come]

a·ver (ə·vûr′) *v.t.* **a·verred, a·ver·ring** 1. To declare confidently as fact; affirm. 2. *Law* To assert formally; prove or justify (a plea). [< OF < L *ad-* to + *verus* true] — **a·ver′ment** *n.* — **a·ver′ra·ble** *adj.*

av·er·age (av′rij, av′ər·ij) *n.* 1. *Math.* An arithmetic mean. 2. A mean, ratio, etc., showing a specific standing or accomplishment: batting *average;* B *average.* 3. The ordinary rank, degree, or amount; general type. 4. In marine law: **a** The loss arising by damage to a ship or cargo. **b** The proportion of such loss falling to a single person in an equitable distribution among those interested. — *adj.* 1. Obtained by calculating the mean of several. 2. Medium; ordinary. — *v.* **·aged, ·ag·ing** *v.t.* 1. To fix or calculate as the mean. 2. To amount to or obtain an average of: He *averages* three dollars an hour. 3. To apportion on the average. — *v.i.* 4. To be or amount to an average. 5. To buy or sell more goods, shares, etc., in order to get a better average price. [< F *avarie* damage to a ship] — **av′er·age·ly** *adv.*

A·ver·nus (ä·ver′nəs) In Roman mythology, hell; Hades. — **A·ver′nal** *adj.*

a·verse (ə·vûrs′) *adj.* Opposed; unfavorable; reluctant: with *to.* [< L *aversus,* pp. of *avertere* to turn aside] — **a·verse′ly** *adv.* — **a·verse′ness** *n.*

a·ver·sion (ə·vûr′zhən, -shən) *n.* 1. Extreme dislike; opposition; antipathy. 2. A cause of repugnance or dislike.

a·vert (ə·vûrt′) *v.t.* 1. To turn or direct away or aside, as one's regard. 2. To prevent or ward off, as a danger. — **Syn.** See PREVENT. [< OF *avertir* < L *avertere* to turn aside < *ab-* away + *vertere* to turn] — **a·vert′ed·ly** *adv.* — **a·vert′i·ble** or **a·vert′a·ble** *adj.*

A·ves·ta (ə·ves′tə) The sacred writings of Zoroastrianism, written in **A·ves·tan,** (ə·ves′tən), an ancient Iranian language. See ZEND-AVESTA. — **A·ves′tan** *adj.*

avi- *combining form* Bird; of or related to birds. [< L *avis* bird]

a·vi·ar·y (ā′vē·er′ē) *n. pl.* ·ar·ies An enclosure or large cage for live birds. [< L < *avis* bird] — **a·vi·a·rist** (ā′vē·er′ist, -ə·rist) *n.*

a·vi·a·tion (ā′vē·ā′shən, av′ē-) *n.* The act, science, or art of flying heavier-than-air aircraft. [< F < L *avis* bird]

a·vi·a·tor (ā′vē·ā′tər, av′ē-) *n.* An airplane pilot. — **a′vi·a′tress** (-tris) or **a·vi·a·trix** (ā′vē·ā′triks, av′ē-) *n.fem.*

av·id (av′id) *adj.* Very desirous; eager; greedy. [< L < *avere* to crave] — **a·vid·i·ty** (ə·vid′ə·tē) *n.* — **av′id·ly** *adv.*

a·vi·on·ics (ā′vē·on′iks, av′ē-) *n pl.* (*construed as sing.*) The applications of electronics to aviation, astronautics, etc.

av·o·ca·do (av′ə·kä′dō, ä′və-) *n. pl.* **·dos** 1. The pear-

shaped fruit of a West Indian tree: also called *alligator pear.* 2. The tree bearing this fruit. [< Sp. < Nahuatl *ahuacatl*]

av·o·ca·tion (av′ə·kā′shən) *n.* A casual or occasional occupation; diversion; hobby. — **Syn.** See OCCUPATION. [< L < *ab-* away + *vocare* to call]

av·o·cet (av′ə·set) *n.* A long-legged shore bird having webbed feet and an upcurved bill. Also **av′o·set.** [< F < Ital. *avocetta*]

a·void (ə·void′) *v.t.* 1. To keep away or at a distance from; shun; evade. 2. *Law* To make void. [< OF < L *ex-* out + *viduare* to empty, deprive] — **a·void′a·ble** *adj.* — **a·void′a·bly** *adv.* — **a·void′ance** *n.*

av·oir·du·pois (av′ər·də·poiz′) *n.* 1. The ordinary system of weights of the U.S. and Great Britain in which 16 ounces avoirdupois make a pound. Abbr. *av., avdp., avoir.* See table front of book. 2. *Informal* Weight; corpulence. [< OF *avoir de pois* goods of (i.e., sold by) weight]

a·vouch (ə·vouch′) *v.t.* 1. To vouch for; guarantee. 2. To affirm positively; proclaim. 3. To acknowledge; avow. [< OF < L < *ad-* to + *vocare* to call]

a·vow (ə·vou′) *v.t.* To declare openly, as facts; own; acknowledge. [< OF < L *advocare* to summon] — **a·vow′a·ble** *adj.* — **a·vow′a·bly** *adv.* — **a·vow′er** *n.*

a·vow·al (ə·vou′əl) *n.* Frank admission or acknowledgment.

a·vowed (ə·voud′) *adj.* Openly acknowledged; plainly declared. — **a·vow·ed·ly** (ə·vou′id·lē) *adv.* — **a·vow′ed·ness** *n.*

a·vun·cu·lar (ə·vung′kyə·lər) *adj.* Of or pertaining to an uncle. [< L *avunculus* maternal uncle]

a·wait (ə·wāt′) *v.t.* 1. To wait for; expect. 2. To be ready or in store for. [< OF *awaitier* to watch for < *a-* to (< L *ad-*) + *waitier* to watch < OHG *wahtēn* to watch]

a·wake (ə·wāk′) *adj.* Not asleep; alert; vigilant. [< v.] — *v.* **a·woke** (*Rare* **a·waked**), **a·waked** (*Rare* **a·woke**), **a·wak·ing** *v.t.* 1. To arouse from sleep. 2. To stir up; excite. — *v.i.* 3. To cease to sleep; become awake. 4. To become alert or aroused. [OE *onwæcnan* rise from sleep]

a·wak·en (ə·wā′kən) *v.t. & v.i.* To awake. — **a·wak′en·er** *n.*

a·wak·en·ing (ə·wā′kən·ing) *adj.* Stirring; exciting. — *n.* 1. The act of waking. 2. A reviving, as of interest.

a·ward (ə·wôrd′) *v.t.* 1. To adjudge as due, as by legal decision. 2. To bestow as the result of a contest or examination, as a prize. — *n.* 1. A decision, as by a judge or arbitrator. 2. The document containing it. 3. That which is awarded, as a medal. [< AF, OF < *es-* out (< L *ex-*) + *guarder* to watch] — **a·ward′a·ble** *adj.* — **a·ward′er** *n.*

a·ware (ə·wâr′) *adj.* Conscious; cognizant: often with *of.* [OE *gewær* watchful] — **a·ware′ness** *n.*

a·wash (ə·wosh′, ə·wôsh′) *adv. & adj.* 1. Level with or just above the surface of the water. 2. Tossed or washed about by waves. 3. Covered or overflowed by water.

a·way (ə·wā′) *adv.* 1. From a given place; off. 2. Far; at or to a distance. 3. In another direction; aside. 4. Out of existence; at or to an end: to waste *away.* 5. On and on; continuously: to peg *away* at a task. 6. From one's keeping, attention, or possession: to give food *away.* 7. At once, without hesitation: Fire *away!* — **to do away with** 1. To get rid of. 2. To kill. — *adj.* 1. Absent. 2. At a distance. — *interj.* Begone! [OE *on weg* on (one's) way]

awe (ô) *n.* Reverential fear; dread mingled with veneration. — *v.t.* **awed, aw·ing** or **awe·ing** To impress with reverential fear. [< ON *agi* fear]

a·weigh (ə·wā′) *adv. Naut.* Hanging with the flukes just clear of the bottom: said of an anchor.

awe·some (ô′səm) *adj.* 1. Inspiring awe. 2. Characterized by or expressing awe; reverential. — **awe′some·ly** *adv.* — **awe′some·ness** *n.*

aw·ful (ô′fəl) *adj.* 1. *Informal* Exceedingly bad or unpleasant; ugly. 2. Inspiring awe; majestically or solemnly impressive. 3. Causing fear or dread. 4. *Informal* Very great. — **aw′ful·ness** *n.*

aw·ful·ly (ô′fəl·ē for def. 1; ô′flē for def. 2) *adv.* 1. In an awful manner. 2. *Informal* Excessively; very: *awfully* rich.

a·while (ə·hwīl′) *adv.* For a brief time. [OE *āne hwīle* a while]

awk·ward (ôk′wərd) *adj.* 1. Ungraceful in bearing. 2. Unskillful in action; bungling. 3. Embarrassing or perplexing. 4. Difficult or dangerous to deal with. 5. Inconvenient for use; uncomfortable. [< ON *öfugr* turned the wrong way + -WARD] — **awk′ward·ly** *adv.* — **awk′ward·ness** *n.*

awl (ôl) *n.* A pointed instrument for making small holes, as in wood or leather. [ME *awel* < OE *æl*]

awn (ôn) *n. Bot.* A bristlelike appendage of certain grasses; beard, as of wheat or rye. [ME < ON *ögn* chaff] — **awned** (ônd) *adj.* — **awn′less** *adj.* — **awn′y** *adj.*

awn·ing (ô′ning) *n.* A rooflike cover, as of canvas, for protection from sun or rain. [Origin unknown]

a·woke (ə·wōk′) Past tense of AWAKE.

AWOL (*as an acronym pronounced* ā′wôl) *Mil.* Absent or absent without leave. Also **awol, A.W.O.L., a.w.o.l.**

a·wry (ə·rī′) *adj. & adv.* 1. Toward one side; askew. 2. Out of the right course; amiss; wrong.

ax (aks) *n. pl.* **ax·es** A tool with a bladed head mounted on a handle, used for chopping, hewing, etc. — **to have an ax to grind** *Informal* To have a private purpose or interest to pursue. — *v.t.* 1. To cut or trim with an ax. 2. To behead with an ax. Also *Brit.* **axe.** [OE *æx*] — **ax/like/** *adj.*

ax·es¹ (ak/sēz) Plural of AXIS¹.

ax·es² (ak/siz) Plural of AX.

ax·i·al (ak/sē-əl) *adj.* 1. Of, pertaining to, or forming an axis. 2. Situated on or along an axis. Also **ax·ile** (ak/sil, -sīl).

ax·il (ak/sil) *n. Bot.* The cavity or angle formed by the junction of the upper side of a leafstalk, branch, etc., with a stem or branch. [< L *axilla* armpit]

ax·il·la (ak-sil/ə) *n. pl.* **ax·il·lae** (-sil/ē) 1. *Anat.* The armpit. 2. An axil. [< L]

ax·il·lar (ak/sə-lər) *adj.* Axillary.

ax·il·lar·y (ak/sə-ler/ē) *adj.* 1. *Bot.* Of, pertaining to, or situated in an axil. 2. *Anat.* Pertaining to the axilla.

ax·i·om (ak/sē-əm) *n.* 1. A self-evident or universally recognized truth. 2. An established principle or rule. 3. *Logic & Math.* A self-evident proposition accepted as true without proof. [< L < Gk. < *axioein* to think worthy]

ax·i·o·mat·ic (ak/sē-ə-mat/ik) *adj.* 1. Of, pertaining to, or resembling an axiom; self-evident. 2. Aphoristic. Also **ax/·i·o·mat/i·cal.** — **ax/i·o·mat/i·cal·ly** *adv.*

ax·is¹ (ak/sis) *n. pl.* **ax·es** (ak/sēz) 1. A line around which a turning body rotates or may be supposed to rotate. 2. *Geom.* **a** A straight line through the center of a plane or solid figure, esp. the line in relation to which the figure is symmetrical. **b** A fixed line, as in a graph, along which distances are measured or to which positions are referred. 3. The central line about which the parts of a body or thing are regularly arranged. 4. An affiliation of two or more nations to promote and ensure mutual interest, cooperation, and solidarity in their foreign relations. [< axis, axle]

ax·le (ak/səl) *n.* 1. A crossbar on which a wheel or wheels turn. 2. An axletree. [< AXLETREE] — **ax/led** *adj.*

ax·le·tree (ak/səl·trē/) *n.* A bar or beam on the ends of which the opposite wheels of a carriage or wagon revolve. [< ON < öxull axle + trē tree, beam]

ax·man (aks/mən) *n. pl.* **·men** (-mən) One who wields an ax; a woodsman. Also **axe/man.**

Ax·min·ster (aks/min·stər) *n.* 1. A carpet with a long, soft pile. 2. A carpet made in imitation of this. [after *Axminster*, England, where first made]

ax·o·lotl (ak/sə·lot/l) *n.* A North American tailed amphibian that retains its external gills and breeds in a larval state. [< Sp. < Nahuatl, lit., servant of water]

ax·on (ak/son) *n. Physiol.* The central process of a neuron, usu. carrying impulses away from the cells. Also **ax·one** (ak/sōn). [< NL < Gk. *axōn* axis]

a·yah (ä/yə) *n. Anglo-Indian* A native nurse or lady's maid. [< Hind. *āyā* < Pg. *aia* nurse]

aye (ī) *n.* An affirmative vote or voter. — *adv.* Yes; yea. Also **ay.** [Origin unknown]

a·zal·ea (ə·zāl/yə) *n.* A flowering shrub of the heath family, esp. the **flame azalea,** with showy scarlet or orange flowers. [< NL < Gk. < *azein* to parch, dry up]

az·i·muth (az/ə·məth) *n.* 1. The angular distance in a horizontal plane measured clockwise from true north to a given course or celestial object. 2. In celestial navigation, the angle measured at the zenith, clockwise, from true north to a vertical plane passing through a heavenly body; in astronomy, measured clockwise from the south point. [< OF < Arabic *as-sumūt* the ways, pl. of *samt* way] — **az·i·muth·al** (az/ə·muth/əl) *adj.* — **az/i·muth/al·ly** *adv.*

az·o (az/ō, ā/zō) *adj. Chem.* Containing nitrogen. [< *azote*, former name for nitrogen]

a·zo·ic (ə·zō/ik) *adj. Geol.* Of or pertaining to those periods on earth before life appeared; without organic remains. [< Gk. < *a-* without + *zōē* life]

Az·tec (az/tek) *n.* 1. One of a tribe of Indians of Nahuatlan stock, founders of an empire that was at its height when Cortés invaded Mexico in 1519. 2. Nahuatl. — *adj.* Of or pertaining to the Aztec Indians, their language, culture, or empire: also **Az·tec·an** (az/tek·ən).

az·ure (azh/ər, ā/zhər) *adj.* Sky blue. — *n.* 1. A clear, sky-blue color or pigment. 2. *Poetic* The sky. [< OF < Arabic < Persian *lāzhward* lapis lazuli]

az·u·rite (azh/ə·rīt) *n.* A vitreous, monoclinic, azure-blue, basic copper carbonate, often used as a gemstone.

az·y·gous (az/i·gəs) *adj. Biol.* Occurring singly; not paired. [< Gk. < *a-* without + *zygon* a yoke]

B

b, B (bē) *n. pl.* **b's** or **bs, B's** or **Bs, bees** (bēz) 1. The second letter of the English alphabet. 2. The sound represented by the letter b. — *symbol* 1. *Music* **a** One of a series of tones, the seventh in the natural diatonic scale of C. **b** A written note representing it. **c** A scale built upon B. 2. *Chem.* Boron (symbol B). 3. The second in sequence, etc.

baa (bä, ba) *v.i.* **baaed, baa·ing** To bleat, as a sheep. — *n.* A bleat, as of a sheep. [Imit.]

Ba·al (bā/əl, bäl) *n. pl.* **Ba·al·im** (bā/əl·im) 1. Any of several ancient Semitic gods of fertility and flocks; esp., the sun god of the Phoenicians. 2. An idol or false god. [< Hebrew *ba'al* lord] — **Ba/al·ish** *adj.* — **Ba/al·ist, Ba/al·ite** *n.* — **Ba/al·ism** *n.*

bab·bitt (bab/it) *v.t.* To line, fill, etc., with Babbitt metal.

Bab·bitt (bab/it) *n.* A type of conventional American businessman who is mediocre and smug; philistine. [after Sinclair Lewis's novel *Babbitt* (1922)] — **Bab/bitt·ry** *n.*

Babbitt metal 1. A soft, white, antifriction alloy of tin, copper, and antimony. 2. Any of a group of similar alloys. [after Isaac *Babbitt*, 1799–1862, U.S. metallurgist]

bab·ble (bab/əl) *v.* **·bled, ·bling** *v.i.* 1. To utter inarticulate or meaningless sounds. 2. To make a murmuring or rippling sound, as a stream. 3. To talk unwisely or foolishly. — *v.t.* 4. To utter unintelligibly. 5. To blurt out thoughtlessly. — *n.* 1. Inarticulate or confused speech. 2. Prattle, as of an infant. 3. A murmuring or rippling sound. [ME *babelen;* ult. origin unknown] — **bab/bler** *n.*

babe (bāb) *n.* 1. An infant; baby. 2. *U.S. Informal* An artless or inexperienced person. 3. *U.S. Slang* A girl. [ME]

ba·bel (bā/bəl, bab/əl) *n.* A confusion of many voices or languages; tumult. Also **Ba/bel.** [after (*Tower of*) *Babel*]

Ba·bel (bā/bəl, bab/əl) In the Bible, an ancient city in Shinar, now identified with Babylon. — **Tower of Babel** 1. A tower begun in Babel by the descendants of Noah and intended to reach heaven, but abandoned. *Gen.* xi 9. 2. Any impractical scheme or structure.

ba·bies'-breath (bā/bēz·breth/) See BABY'S-BREATH.

ba·boon (ba·bōon/) *n.* 1. A large, terrestrial monkey of Africa and Asia, having a doglike muzzle and usu. a short tail. 2. *Slang* A coarse or stupid person. [< OF *babuin*]

ba·bush·ka (bə·bŏosh/kə) *n.* A woman's scarf, worn over the head. [< Russian, grandmother]

ba·by (bā/bē) *n. pl.* **·bies** 1. A very young child of either sex; an infant. 2. The youngest or smallest member of a family or group. 3. One who looks or acts like a child. 4. Any young animal. 5. *Slang* A girl. — *adj.* 1. For a baby. 2. Childish; infantile. 3. Small; diminutive; miniature. — *v.t.* **·bied, ·by·ing** To treat as a baby; pamper. [ME *baby*, dim. of *babe*] — **ba/by·hood** *n.* — **ba/by·like/** *adj.*

ba·by-blue-eyes (bā/bē·blōo/īz/) *n.* An annual plant with showy, sky-blue flowers. Also **baby blue-eyes.**

ba·by·ish (bā/bē·ish) *adj.* Childish; infantile. — **ba/by·ish·ly** *adv.* — **ba/by·ish·ness** *n.*

Bab·y·lon (bab/ə·lən, -lon) 1. An ancient city of Mesopotamia on the Euphrates, capital of Babylonia from about 2100 B.C.; celebrated as a seat of wealth, luxury, and vice. 2. Any city or place of great wealth, luxury, or vice.

Bab·y·lo·ni·a (bab/ə·lō/nē·ə) An ancient empire of Mesopotamia; capital, Babylon; conquered by Persia, 538 B.C. — **Bab·y·lo/ni·an** *adj. & n.*

ba·by's-breath (bā/bēz·breth/) *n.* 1. An Old World perennial with numerous clusters of small, white or pink, fragrant flowers. 2. Any of certain other fragrant herbs, as the wild madder. Also spelled *babies'-breath.*

baby-sit (bā/bē·sit/) *v.i.* **-sat, -sit·ting** To act as a baby sitter.

baby sitter A person employed to take care of young children while the parents are absent: also called *sitter*.

bac·ca·lau·re·ate (bak/ə·lôr/ē·it) *n.* **1.** The degree of bachelor of arts, bachelor of science, etc. **2.** An address to a graduating class at commencement: also **baccalaureate sermon.** [< Med.L < *baccalaureus*, var. of *baccalaris*, a young farmer; infl. in form by L *bacca lauri* laurel berry]

bac·ca·rat (bak/ə·rä/, bak/ə·rä) *n.* A gambling game in which winnings are decided by comparing cards held by the banker with those held by the players. Also **bac·ca·ra** (bak/. ə·rä/, bak/ə·rä). [< F *baccara*, a game of cards]

bac·cha·nal (bak/ə·nəl) *n.* **1.** A votary of Bacchus. **2.** A drunken reveler. **3.** *pl.* Bacchanalia. — *adj.* Bacchanalian. [< L *bacchanalis* of Bacchus]

bac·cha·na·li·a (bak/ə·nā/lē·ə, -nāl/yə) *n.pl.* Drunken revelries; orgies. [< L, neut. pl. of *bacchanalis* of Bacchus] — **bac/cha·na/li·an** *adj.* — **bac/cha·na/li·an·ism** *n.*

bac·chant (bak/ənt) *n.* *pl.* **bac·chants** or **bac·chan·tes** (bə·kan/tēz) **1.** A votary of Bacchus. **2.** A carouser; reveler. — *adj.* Given to drunkenness. — **bac·chan·te** (bə· kan/tē, bə·kant/, bak/ənt) *n. fem.*

bac·chic (bak/ik) *adj.* Riotous; orgiastic; drunken.

Bac·chus (bak/əs) In classical mythology, the god of wine and revelry: identified with *Dionysus.* — **Bac·chic** *adj.*

bacci- *combining form* Berry or berries. [< L *bacca* berry]

bach·e·lor (bach/ə·lər, bach/lər) *n.* **1.** An unmarried man. **2.** One who has taken his first university or college degree. **3.** A young knight serving under another's banner: also **bach/e·lor-at-arms/.** [< OF < Med.L *baccalaris*, a young farmer] — **bach/e·lor·hood/, bach/e·lor·ship/** *n.*

Bachelor of Arts **1.** A degree usu. given by a college or university to a person who has completed a four-year course in the humanities. **2.** One who has received this degree.

Bachelor of Science **1.** A degree given by a college or university to a person who has completed a four-year course in the sciences. **2.** One who has received this degree.

bach·e·lor's-but·ton (bach/ə·lərz·but/n, bach/lərz-) *n.* **1.** Any of several plants with button-shaped flowers or flower heads. **2.** The cornflower.

bac·il·lar·y (bas/ə·ler/ē) *adj.* **1.** Rod-shaped. **2.** Pertaining to or caused by bacilli. Also **ba·cil·lar** (bə·sil/ər).

ba·cil·lus (bə·sil/əs) *n.* *pl.* **·cil·li** (-sil/ī) **1.** *Bacteriol.* Any of a large class of straight, rod-shaped bacteria including both beneficial and pathogenic species. **2.** A bacterium. — **Syn.** See MICROBE. [< NL < L *baculus* stick]

back¹ (bak) *n.* **1.** The part of the body nearest the spine; in man the hinder, in quadrupeds the upper part, extending from the neck to the base of the spine. ◆ Collateral adjective: *dorsal.* **2.** The backbone. **3.** The rear or posterior part of anything. **4.** The farther or other side; the reverse. **5.** The part behind or opposite to the part used: the *back* of a knife. **6.** Anything to cover or support the back. **7.** The part of a garment covering the back. **8.** Physical strength: Put your *back* into it. **9.** In football, a player in a position behind the line of scrimmage. **10.** *Phonet.* The part of the tongue directly behind the front and below the velum. — **at one's back** Following closely. — **behind one's back 1.** Secretly. **2.** Treacherously. — **in back of** Behind; at or to the rear of. — **to be (flat) on one's back** To be helplessly ill. — **to turn one's back on 1.** To show contempt or ill feeling toward by ignoring. **2.** To renounce. — *v.t.* **1.** To cause to move backward; reverse the action of. **2.** To furnish with a back. **3.** To support, as by financing or by endorsing: to *back* a candidate; to *back* a business. **4.** To bet on. **5.** To form a background for. **6.** To mount, as a horse. **7.** To write on the back of. — *v.i.* **8.** To move backward. **9.** To shift counterclockwise: said of the wind. — **to back down** To withdraw from a position, abandon a claim, etc. — **to back off** To retreat, as from contact. — **to back out (of)** To withdraw from or refuse to carry out a promise, contest, etc. — *adj.* **1.** In the rear; behind. **2.** Distant; remote: the *back* country. **3.** Of or for a date earlier than the present: a *back* issue. **4.** In arrears; overdue: *back* taxes. **5.** In a backward direction. [OE *bæc*]

back² (bak) *adv.* **1.** At, to, or toward the rear. **2.** In, to, or toward a former place or condition. **3.** Into time past. **4.** In return or retort. **5.** In reserve or concealment. **6.** In check or hindrance. **7.** In withdrawal or repudiation. — **back and forth** First in one direction and then in the opposite. — **back of** *U.S.* Behind. — **to go back on** *Informal* **1.** To fail to keep (an engagement, promise, etc.). **2.** To desert or betray. [< ABACK]

back·bite (bak/bīt/) *v.t. & v.i.* **·bit, ·bit·ten** (*Informal* ·bit), **·bit·ing** To revile behind one's back; slander. — **back/bit/-er** *n.*

back·board (bak/bôrd/, -bōrd/) *n.* **1.** A board forming or supporting the back of something. **2.** In basketball, the vertical board behind the basket.

back·bone (bak/bōn/) *n.* **1.** The spine or vertebral column. **2.** Something likened to a backbone in function or appearance. **3.** Strength of character. — **back/boned/** *adj.*

back·break·ing (bak/brā/king) *adj.* Physically exhausting.

back·door (bak/dôr/, -dōr/) *adj.* Clandestine; underhand.

back·drop (bak/drop/) *n.* The curtain hung at the rear of a stage, often representing a scene. Also **back cloth.**

backed (bakt) *adj.* Having a (specified kind of) back or backing: used in combination: *low-backed; cardboard-backed.*

back·er (bak/ər) *n.* **1.** One who supports with money; a patron. **2.** One who bets on a contestant.

back·field (bak/fēld/) *n.* In football, the players behind the line of scrimmage, usu. the fullback, two halfbacks, and the quarterback.

back·fire (bak/fīr/) *n.* **1.** A fire built to check an advancing forest or prairie fire by creating a barren area in its path. **2.** Premature explosion in the cylinder of an internal-combustion engine. **3.** An explosion of unburned fuel in the muffler of an internal combustion engine. **4.** An explosion in the back part of a gun. — *v.i.* **·fired, ·fir·ing 1.** To set or use a backfire. **2.** To explode in a backfire. **3.** To react in an unexpected and unwelcome manner: His scheme *backfired.*

back formation *Ling.* **1.** The creation by analogy of a new word from an existing word. **2.** A word so formed, as *enthuse* from *enthusiasm.*

back·gam·mon (bak/gam/ən, bak/gam/ən) *n.* **1.** A game played by two persons, on a special board, the moves of the pieces being determined by dice throws. **2.** A victory in this game. — *v.t.* To win a backgammon from. [ME *back gammen* back game]

back·ground (bak/ground/) *n.* **1.** That part in a picture against which the principal elements, motifs, or subjects are represented. **2.** Ground in the rear or distance. **3.** A subordinate position; obscurity; retirement. **4.** The aggregate of one's experiences, education, etc. **5.** The events leading up to or causing a situation, event, etc. **6.** Music or sound effects employed in a motion picture, radio program, etc.

back·hand (bak/hand/) *n.* **1.** Handwriting that slopes toward the left. **2.** The hand turned backward in making a stroke, as with a racket. **3.** A stroke made with the hand turned backward, as in tennis. — *adj.* Backhanded. — *adv.* With a backhand stroke.

back·hand·ed (bak/han/did) *adj.* **1.** Delivered or made with the back of the hand turned forward, as a stroke in tennis. **2.** Insincere; equivocal: a *backhanded* compliment. **3.** Sloping to the left, as handwriting. — **back/hand/ed·ly** *adv.* — **back/hand/ed·ness** *n.*

back·ing (bak/ing) *n.* **1.** Support or assistance. **2.** Supporters or promoters collectively. **3.** Endorsement. **4.** Motion backward. **5.** The back of anything, as for support.

back·lash (bak/lash/) *n.* **1.** *Mech.* **a** A jarring recoil, as of the parts of a machine when poorly fitted. **b** The amount of loose play in such parts. **2.** In angling, a snarl or tangle of line on a reel, caused by a faulty cast.

back·log (bak/lôg/, -log/) *n.* *U.S.* **1.** A large log at the back of an open fireplace to maintain and concentrate the heat. **2.** Any reserve supply, as of funds, business orders, etc.

back·most (bak/mōst) *adj.* Farthest to the rear; hindmost.

back number 1. An old issue of a magazine or newspaper. **2.** *U.S. Informal* An old-fashioned person or thing.

back·rest (bak/rest/) *n.* A support for or at the back.

back seat 1. A seat in the rear, as of a vehicle, hall, etc. **2.** An inconspicuous or subordinate position.

back-seat driver (bak/sēt/) A passenger in an automobile who persists in directing and advising the driver.

back·side (bak/sīd/) *n.* **1.** The hind part. **2.** The rump.

back·slide (bak/slīd/) *v.i.* **·slid, ·slid** or **·slid·den, ·slid·ing** To return to wrong or sinful ways. — **back·slid/er** *n.*

back·spin (bak/spin/) *n.* Reverse rotation of a round object that is moving forward, as a golf ball, baseball, etc.

back·stage (*n., adv.* bak/stāj/; *adj.* bak/stāj/) *adv.* **1.** In or toward the portion of a theater behind the stage, including the wings, dressing rooms, etc. **2.** To or toward the back portion of the stage. — *n.* The back portion of the stage. — *adj.* Situated or occurring backstage.

back·stairs (bak/stârz/) *adj.* Indirect; underhand. Also **back/stair/.**

back·stay (bak/stā/) *n.* *Naut.* A stay supporting a mast on the aft side.

back·stitch (bak/stich/) *n.* A stitch made by carrying the thread back half the length of the preceding stitch. — *v.t. & v.i.* To sew with backstitches.

back·stop (bak/stop/) *n.* *U.S.* A fence, wire screen, or net to stop the ball from going too far, as in baseball, tennis, etc.

back·stretch (bak/strech/) *n.* That part of a racecourse farthest from the spectators, usually a straightaway.

back·stroke (bak/strōk/) *n.* **1.** A backhanded stroke. **2.** In swimming, a stroke executed while on one's back. — *v.* **·stroked, ·strok·ing** *v.t.* **1.** To strike, as a ball, with a backstroke. — *v.i.* **2.** To swim with a backstroke.

back talk Impudent retort; insolent answering back.

back·track (bak/trak/) *v.i.* *U.S.* **1.** To retrace one's steps. **2.** To withdraw from a position, undertaking, etc.

back·ward (bak/wərd) *adv.* **1.** Toward the back; to the rear. **2.** With the back foremost. **3.** In reverse order. **4.** From better to worse. **5.** To or into time past. Also **back'·wards. — adj. 1.** Turned to the back or rear; reversed. **2.** Done the reverse or wrong way. **3.** Behind in growth or development; retarded; slow. **4.** Hesitating; reluctant; bashful. **— back'ward·ly** adv. **— back'ward·ness** n.

back·wash (bak'wosh', -wôsh') n. **1.** Water moved backward, as by a boat. **2.** A backward current or flow.

back·wa·ter (bak'wô'tər, -wot'ər) n. **1.** Water turned or held back, as by a dam, a current, etc. **2.** Any place or condition regarded as stagnant, backward, etc.

back·woods (bak'wŏŏdz') U.S. n.pl. Wild, heavily wooded, or sparsely settled districts. **— adj.** In, from, or like the backwoods: also **back'wood'. — back'woods'man** (-mən) n.

ba·con (bā'kən) n. The salted and dried or smoked back and sides of the hog. **— to bring home the bacon** U.S. Informal **1.** To provide food, etc. **2.** To succeed. [< OF < OHG bacho, bahho ham, side of bacon]

Ba·co·ni·an (bā-kō'nē-ən) adj. Of or pertaining to Francis Bacon, his philosophy, or his literary style. **— n.** A believer in the Baconian theory.

Baconian theory The theory that Francis Bacon wrote the plays attributed to Shakespeare.

bac·te·ri·a (bak-tir'ē-ə) Plural of BACTERIUM.

bac·te·ri·cide (bak-tir'ə-sīd) n. An agent destructive of bacteria. **— bac'te'ri·ci'dal** adj.

bacterio- combining form Of or pertaining to bacteria. Also, before vowels, **bacter-.** Also **bacteri-, bactero-.** [< Gk. baktron rod, staff]

bac·te·ri·ol·o·gy (bak-tir'ē-ol'ə-jē) n. The branch of biology and medicine that deals with bacteria. **— bac'te·ri·o·log'·i·cal** (bak-tir'ē-ə-loj'i-kəl) adj. **— bac'te'ri·o·log'i·cal·ly** adv. **— bac'te·ri·ol'o·gist** n.

bac·te·ri·o·phage (bak-tir'ē-ə-fāj') n. Bacteriol. An ultramicroscopic filter-passing agent that has the power of destroying bacteria in a living organism.

bac·te·ri·um (bak-tir'ē-əm) n. pl. **·te·ri·a** (-tir'ē-ə) Any of numerous widely distributed unicellular microorganisms exhibiting both plant and animal characteristics, and ranging from the harmless and beneficial to those that cause disease. **— Syn.** See MICROBE. [< NL < Gk. baktron staff, stick] **— bac'te'ri·al** adj. **— bac'te'ri·al·ly** adv.

bad (bad) adj. **worse, worst 1.** Not good in any manner or degree. **2.** Evil; wicked; immoral. **3.** Defective; worthless: bad wiring. **4.** Faulty or incorrect: bad grammar. **5.** Not valid or sound. **6.** Not sufficient; inadequate. **7.** Lacking skill or proficiency: a bad poet. **8.** Distressing; unfavorable: bad news. **9.** Offensive; disagreeable: a bad taste. **10.** Harmful; noxious: bad for the eyes. **11.** Rotted; spoiled. **12.** Severe: a bad storm. **13.** Sick; in ill health. **14.** Sorry; regretful: He felt bad about it. **— in bad** Informal **1.** In difficulty. **2.** In disfavor. **— not bad** Rather good: also **not half bad, not so bad. — n. 1.** That which is bad. **2.** Those who are bad: with the. **3.** A bad state or condition; wickedness. **— adv.** Informal Badly. [ME bad, baddle, ? < OE bæddel effeminate man] **— bad'ness** n.

bade (bad) Past tense of BID.

badge (baj) n. **1.** Any device worn to indicate rank, office, membership in an organization, an award or prize, etc. **2.** Any distinguishing mark, token, or insignia. **— v.t. badged, badg·ing** To decorate or provide with a badge. [ME bage]

badg·er (baj'ər) n. **1.** A small, burrowing, nocturnal, carnivorous mammal, with a broad body, short legs, and long-clawed toes. **2.** The fur of a badger, or a brush made of its hair. **— v.t.** To harass; nag at. [Origin unknown]

Badger State Nickname of WISCONSIN.

AMERICAN
BADGER
(About 30
inches long;
tail 6 inches)

bad·i·nage (bad'ə-näzh', bad'ə-nij) n. Playful raillery; banter. **— v.t. ·naged, ·nag·ing** To subject or to tease with badinage. [< F badin silly, jesting]

bad·lands (bad'landz') n.pl. A barren area characterized by numerous ridges, peaks, and mesas cut by erosion.

Bad Lands An arid, eroded plateau in South Dakota and Nebraska. Also **Bad'lands.**

bad·ly (bad'lē) adv. **1.** In a bad manner; improperly, imperfectly, or grievously. **2.** Informal Very much; greatly.

bad·min·ton (bad'min·tən) n. A game played by batting a shuttlecock back and forth over a high, narrow net with a light racket. [after Badminton, an estate in England]

bad-tem·pered (bad'tem'pərd) adj. Cross; irritable.

Bae·de·ker (bā'di·kər) n. **1.** Any of a series of travelers' guidebooks. **2.** Loosely, any guidebook. [after Karl Baedeker, 1801–59, German publisher who issued them]

baf·fle (baf'əl) v. **·fled, ·fling** v.t. **1.** To confuse mentally; perplex: The problem baffled him. **2.** To foil or frustrate;

hinder. **— v.i. 3.** To struggle to no avail. **— n. 1.** A partition or wall used to control and direct sound effects in radio or motion pictures. **2.** A partition or grating used to alter the flow of gases or liquids: also **baf·fle·plate** (baf'əl·plāt'). [Origin uncertain] **— baf'fle·ment** n. **— baf'fler** n. **— baf'fling** adj. **— baf'fling·ly** adv.

bag (bag) n. **1.** A sack or pouch, usu. of paper, cloth, or leather, used as a receptacle. **2.** The amount a bag will hold. **3.** A woman's purse. **4.** A suitcase or satchel. **5.** The quantity of game caught or killed in hunting. **6.** A bulging or baggy part, as of a sail. **7.** A sac or similar part in various animals, as the udder of a cow. **8.** In baseball slang, a base. **9.** U.S. Slang A slovenly woman. **— in the bag** U.S. Slang Assured; certain. **— to be left holding the bag** U.S. Informal To be left to assume full responsibility or blame. **— v. bagged, bag·ging** v.t. **1.** To put into a bag. **2.** To cause to fill out or bulge like a bag. **3.** To capture or kill, as game. **— v.i. 4.** To bulge or swell like a bag. **5.** To hang loosely. [? < ON baggi pack, bundle]

bag and baggage Informal **1.** With all one's possessions: He cleared out bag and baggage. **2.** Entirely; completely.

ba·gasse (bə-gas') n. The dry refuse of sugar cane after the juice has been expressed, used in making paper and fiberboard. Also **ba·gass'.** [< F < Sp. bagazo refuse of grapes, olives, etc., after pressing]

bag·a·telle (bag'ə·tel') n. **1.** A trifle. **2.** A game similar to billiards. [< F < Ital. bagatella, dim of baga sack]

ba·gel (bā'gəl) n. A doughnut-shaped roll of yeast dough simmered in water and baked. [< Yiddish < beigen to twist]

bag·gage (bag'ij) n. **1.** Chiefly U.S. The trunks, packages, etc., of a traveler. **2.** An army's movable equipment. **3.** A lively or impudent woman. [< MF < Med.L baga sack]

bag·ging (bag'ing) n. A coarse cloth for making bags.

bag·gy (bag'ē) adj. **bag·gi·er, bag·gi·est** Like a bag; loose; bulging. **— bag'gi·ly** adv. **— bag'gi·ness** n.

bagn·io (ban'yō, bän'-) n. **1.** A brothel. **2.** In the Orient, a prison. [< Ital. < L < Gk. balaneion bath]

bag·pipe (bag'pīp') n. Often pl. A reed musical instrument having several pipes, the air being forced through them from an inflated leather bag. **— bag'pip'er** n.

ba·guette (ba·get') n. A gem or crystal cut in long, narrow, rectangular form. Also **ba·guet'.** [< F < Ital. < L baculum staff, stick]

bah (bä, ba) interj. An exclamation of contempt or dismissal.

bail[1] (bāl) n. A scoop or bucket for dipping out fluids, as from a boat. **— v.t. & v.i. 1.** To dip (water) from a boat with a bail. **2.** To clear (a boat) of water by dipping out. **— to bail out** To jump with parachute from an aircraft. [< OF < LL baca, bacca tub] **— bail'er** n.

bail[2] (bāl) n. In cricket, one of the crosspieces of the wicket. [< OF bailler to enclose]

bail[3] (bāl) Law n. **1.** One who becomes surety for the debt or default of another, esp. of a person under arrest. **2.** The security or guaranty given or agreed upon. **3.** Release, or the privilege of release, on bail. **— to go bail for** U.S. Slang To provide bail for. **— v.t.** To obtain the release of (an arrested person) by giving bail: often with out. [< OF < L bajulare to carry] **— bail'a·ble** adj. **— bail'ment** n.

bail[4] (bāl) n. **1.** The semicircular handle of a pail, kettle, etc. **2.** An arch-shaped support, as for a canopy. **— v.t.** To provide with a bail or handle. [< ON beygla hook, ring]

bai·liff (bā'lif) n. **1.** A court officer having custody of prisoners under arraignment. **2.** A sheriff's deputy for serving processes and warrants of arrest. **3.** One who oversees an estate for the owner; a steward. **4.** Brit. A subordinate magistrate with jurisdiction limited to a certain district or to certain functions. [< OF < L bajulus porter, manager]

bai·li·wick (bā'lə·wik) n. **1.** The office, jurisdiction, or district of a bailiff. **2.** U.S. A person's own area of authority or competence. [ME bailie bailiff + wick village]

bails·man (bālz'mən) n. pl. **·men** (-mən) One who provides bail for another.

bairn (bârn) n. Scot. A young child; a son or daughter.

bait (bāt) n. **1.** Food or other enticement placed as a lure in a trap, on a hook, etc. **2.** Any allurement or enticement. **3.** A halt for food or refreshment during a journey. **— v.t. 1.** To put food or some other lure on or in: to bait a trap. **2.** To set dogs upon for sport: to bait a bear. **3.** To harass; torment. **4.** To lure; entice. [< ON beita food] **— bait'er** n.

baize (bāz) n. A plain woolen fabric, usu. dyed green and napped to imitate felt, used for pool table covers, etc. [< OF baies, fem. pl. of bai chestnut brown]

bake (bāk) v. **baked, bak·ing** v.t. **1.** To cook (bread, pastry, etc.) by dry heat, as in an oven. **2.** To harden or vitrify by heat, as bricks or pottery. **— v.i. 3.** To bake bread, pastry, etc. **4.** To become baked or hardened by heat, as soil. **— n.** A baking, or the amount baked. [OE bacan]

bake·house (bāk′hous′) *n.* A bakery.

Ba·ke·lite (bā′kə·līt) *n.* Any of a group of thermosetting plastics having many uses: a trade name. Also **ba/ke·lite.** [after Leo Hendrik *Baekeland*, 1863–1944, U.S. chemist]

bak·er (bā′kər) *n.* **1.** One who bakes and sells bread, cake, etc. **2.** A portable oven.

baker's dozen Thirteen.

bak·er·y (bā′kər·ē, bāk′rē) *n. pl.* **·er·ies 1.** A place for baking bread, cake, etc. **2.** A shop where bread, cake, etc., are sold: also **bake/shop/.**

bak·ing (bā′king) *n.* **1.** The act of one who or that which bakes. **2.** The quantity baked.

baking powder A finely powdered mixture of baking soda and an acid salt, giving off carbon dioxide when moist, used as a leavening agent in baking.

baking soda Sodium bicarbonate.

bak·sheesh (bak′shēsh) *n.* In India, Turkey, etc., a gratuity or a gift of alms. — *v.t. & v.i.* To give a tip or alms (to). Also **bak/shish.** [< Persian *bakhshīdan* to give]

Ba·laam (bā′ləm) In the Bible, a prophet hired to curse the Israelites but who blessed them by God's command after his donkey spoke to him. *Num.* xxii.

bal·a·lai·ka (bal′ə·lī′kə) *n.* A Russian stringed instrument of the guitar family. [< Russian]

bal·ance (bal′əns) *n.* **1.** *Sometimes pl.* An instrument for weighing; esp., a bar that pivots on a central point as weights are placed in the pans suspended from each end. **2.** Figuratively, the scale by which deeds and principles are weighed and destinies determined. **3.** The power or authority to decide and determine. **4.** A state of equilibrium or equal relationship; equipoise. **5.** Bodily poise. **6.** Mental or emotional stability. **7.** Harmonious proportion, as in the design or arrangement of parts in a whole. **8.** Something used to produce an equilibrium; counterpoise. **9.** The act of balancing or weighing. **10.** In book-keeping: **a** Equality between the debit and credit totals of an account. **b** A difference between such totals; the excess on either side. **11.** *U.S.* Whatever is left over; remainder. **12.** A balance wheel. **13.** A movement in dancing. — **to strike a balance** To find or take an intermediate position; compromise. — *v.* **·anced, ·anc·ing** *v.t.* **1.** To bring into or keep in equilibrium; poise. **2.** To weigh in a balance. **3.** To compare or weigh in the mind, as alternative courses of action. **4.** To offset or counteract. **5.** To place or keep in proportion. **6.** To be equal or in proportion to. **7.** In bookkeeping: **a** To compute the difference between the debit and credit sides of (an account). **b** To reconcile, as by making certain entries, the debit and credit sides of (an account). **c** To adjust (an account) by paying what is owed. — *v.i.* **8.** To be or come into equilibrium. **9.** To be equal. **10.** To hesitate; tilt. [< F < L *bis* two + *lanx, lancis* dish, plate] — **bal/ance·a·ble** *adj.* — **bal/an·cer** *n.*

Bal·ance (bal′əns) *n.* The constellation and sign of the zodiac Libra.

balance of power A distribution of forces among nations such that none may acquire a degree of power dangerous to the others.

balance of trade The difference in value between exports and imports of a country.

balance sheet A statement in tabular form to show assets and liabilities, profit and loss, etc., of a business.

balance wheel The oscillating wheel of a watch or chronometer, that determines its rate of motion.

bal·a·ta (bal′ə·tə) *n.* The juice of one of several tropical American trees, used as an elastic gum for making golf balls, insulating wires, etc. [< Sp. < Tupi]

bal·bo·a (bal·bō′ə) *n.* A silver monetary unit of Panama, in 1960 worth $1.00. [after Vasco de *Balboa*]

bal·brig·gan (bal·brig′ən) *n.* **1.** A fine, unbleached, knitted cotton fabric. **2.** *pl.* Underwear and hose made of this fabric. [after *Balbriggan*, a town in Ireland]

bal·co·ny (bal′kə·nē) *n. pl.* **·nies 1.** A balustraded platform projecting from a wall of a building. **2.** A projecting gallery in a theater or public building. [< Ital. < OHG *balcho* beam] — **bal/co·nied** *adj.*

bald (bôld) *adj.* **1.** Without hair on the head. **2.** Without natural covering or growth. **3.** Unadorned. **4.** Without disguise; forthright. **5.** *Zool.* Having white feathers or fur on the head. [? < Welsh *bāl* white] — **bald/ly** *adv.* — **bald/ness** *n.*

BALCONY
(With balusters and balustrade)

Bal·der (bôl′dər) In Norse mythology, god of sunlight, spring, and joy; son of Odin. Also **Bal/dr.**

bal·der·dash (bôl′dər·dash) *n.* A meaningless flow of words; nonsense. [Origin uncertain]

bald·head (bôld′hed′) *n.* One whose head is bald. — **bald/head/ed** *adj.*

bald·pate (bôld′pāt′) *n.* **1.** A baldheaded person. **2.** See under WIDGEON. — **bald/pat/ed** *adj.*

bal·dric (bôl′drik) *n.* A belt worn over one shoulder and across the breast, to support a sword, bugle, etc. Also **bal/drick.** [Cf. OF *baldrei,* ult. < L *balteus* belt]

bale (bāl) *n.* A large package of bulky goods corded or otherwise prepared for transportation. — *v.t.* **baled, bal·ing** To make into a bale or bales. [< OF *bale* round package] — **bal/er** *n.*

ba·leen (bə·lēn′) *n.* Whalebone. [< F < L < Gk. *phalaina* whale]

bale·ful (bāl′fəl) *adj.* **1.** Hurtful; malignant. **2.** Ominous: *baleful* predictions of his political future. [OE *bealu* evil + -FUL] — **bale/ful·ly** *adv.* — **bale/ful·ness** *n.*

Ba·li·nese (bä′lə·nēz′, -nēs′) *adj.* Of or pertaining to Bali, its people, or their language. — *n. pl.* **·nese 1.** A native or inhabitant of Bali. **2.** The Indonesian language of Bali.

balk (bôk) *v.i.* **1.** To stop short and refuse to proceed or take action. — *v.t.* **2.** To render unsuccessful; thwart; frustrate. — *n.* **1.** A hindrance or check; defeat; disappointment. **2.** An error or slip; blunder. **3.** In baseball, an illegal motion made by the pitcher when one or more runners are on base. **4.** A ridge between furrows. **5.** A squared beam. Also spelled *baulk.* [OE *balca* bank, ridge]

Bal·kan (bôl′kən) *adj.* **1.** Of or pertaining to the Balkan Peninsula, its people, or their customs. **2.** Of or pertaining to the Balkan Mountains.

balk·y (bô′kē) *adj.* **balk·i·er, balk·i·est** Given to balking.

ball¹ (bôl) *n.* **1.** A spherical or nearly spherical body. **2.** Such a body, of any size and made of various substances, used in a number of games. **3.** A game played with a ball, esp. baseball. **4.** In sports, a ball moving, thrown, or struck in a specified manner. **5.** In baseball, a pitch in which the ball fails to pass over the home plate between the batter's armpits and knees and is not struck at by him. **6.** A roundish protuberance or part of something. **7.** *Usu. pl. Slang* A testicle. — **to be on the ball** *U.S. Slang* To be alert or competent. — **to have something on the ball** *U.S. Slang* To have ability. — **to play ball 1.** To begin or resume playing a ball game or some other activity. **2.** *U.S. Informal* To cooperate. — *v.t. & v.i.* To form, gather, or wind into a ball. — **to ball up** *Slang* To confuse. [< ON *böllr*]

ball² (bôl) *n.* A formal social dance. [< F *bal*]

bal·lad (bal′əd) *n.* **1.** A narrative poem or song of popular origin in short stanzas, often with a refrain. **2.** A sentimental song of several stanzas, in which the melody is usually repeated for each stanza. [Var. of BALLADE]

bal·lade (bə·läd′, ba-) *n.* **1.** A verse form having three stanzas of eight or ten lines each and an envoy of four or five lines. The last line of each stanza and of the envoy is the same. **2.** A musical composition of romantic or dramatic nature, usually for piano or orchestra. [< OF *balade* dancing song]

bal·lad·ry (bal′əd·rē) *n.* **1.** Ballad poetry. **2.** The art of making or singing ballads.

ball-and-sock·et joint (bôl′ən·sok′it) **1.** *Mech.* A joint composed of a sphere in a bearing, permitting a degree of free turning in any direction. **2.** *Anat.* An enarthrosis.

bal·last (bal′əst) *n.* **1.** Any heavy substance, as sand, stone, etc., laid in the hold of a vessel or in the car of a balloon to steady it. **2.** Gravel or broken stone laid down as a stabilizer for a rail bed. **3.** That which gives stability to character, morality, etc. — *v.t.* **1.** To provide or fill with ballast. **2.** To steady with ballast; stabilize. [< ODan. *bar* bare, mere + *last* load]

ball bearing *Mech.* **1.** A bearing in which a shaft bears on small metal balls that turn freely as it revolves. **2.** A metal ball in such a bearing.

bal·le·ri·na (bal′ə·rē′nə) *n.* A female ballet dancer. [< Ital., fem. of *ballerino* dancer]

bal·let (bal′ā, ba·lā′) *n.* **1.** An elaborate dramatic group dance using conventionalized movements, often for narrative effects. **2.** The performers or troupe of such dancing. [< F, dim. of *bal* dance]

bal·lis·tic (bə·lis′tik) *adj.* Of or pertaining to projectiles or to ballistics.

ballistic missile A missile controlled to the apex of its trajectory, falling free thereafter.

bal·lis·tics (bə·lis′tiks) *n.pl.* (construed as sing.) **1.** The science that deals with the motion of projectiles, either while they are still in the bore (**interior ballistics**) or after they leave the muzzle (**exterior ballistics**). **2.** The study of the flight of all missiles. — **bal·lis·ti·cian** (bal′ə·stish′ən) *n.*

bal·loon (bə·lōōn′) *n.* **1.** A large, impermeable bag, inflated with gas lighter than air, and designed to rise and float in the atmosphere; esp., such a bag having a car or basket attached, for carrying passengers, instruments, etc. **2.** A small, inflatable rubber bag, used as a toy. — *v.i.* **1.** To increase quickly in scope or magnitude; expand: The rumor threatened to *balloon* into a full-fledged scandal. **2.** To swell out like a balloon, as a sail. **3.** To ascend or travel in a balloon. — *v.t.* **4.** To inflate or distend with air. — *adj.* Like a balloon. [< Ital. *balla* ball, sphere < Gmc.] — **bal·loon/ist** *n.*

bal·lot (bal′ət) *n.* **1.** A written or printed slip or ticket used in casting a secret vote. **2.** The total number of votes cast in an election. **3.** The act or system of voting secretly by ballots or by voting machines. **4.** A list of candidates for office; ticket. —*v.* **·lot·ed, ·lot·ing** *v.i.* **1.** To cast a ballot in voting. —*v.t.* **2.** To vote for or decide on by ballot. [< Ital. *ballotta*, dim. of *balla* ball]

ball·play·er (bôl′plā′ər) *n.* *U.S.* A baseball player.

ball-point pen (bôl′point′) A fountain pen having for a point a ball bearing that rolls to ink itself from a cartridge.

ball·room (bôl′rōōm′, -rōōm′) *n.* A large room for dancing.

ballroom dancing Social dancing for two people.

ball valve *Mech.* A valve controlled by a ball that is free to rise when the upward pressure exceeds gravity.

bal·ly·hoo (bal′ē·hōō′) *n.* *U.S. Informal* **1.** Blatant or sensational advertising; noisy propaganda. **2.** Clamor; uproar. —*v.t. & v.i.* **·hooed, ·hoo·ing** To advocate or promote by ballyhoo. [Origin unknown]

balm (bäm) *n.* **1.** An aromatic, resinous exudation from various trees or shrubs, used as medicine; balsam. **2.** Any oily, fragrant, resinous substance. **3.** A tree or shrub yielding such a substance. **4.** Any of various aromatic plants resembling mint. **5.** A pleasing fragrance. **6.** Anything that soothes. [< OF < L < Gk. *balsamon* balsam tree]

balm of Gilead **1.** The resinous, fragrant juice obtained from a small evergreen tree growing on the shores of the Red Sea. **2.** The balsam fir.

balm·y (bä′mē) *adj.* **balm·i·er, balm·i·est** **1.** Mild and soothing; soft. **2.** Having the fragrance of balm; aromatic. **3.** *Brit. Slang* Crazy. —**balm′i·ly** *adv.* —**balm′i·ness** *n.*

ba·lo·ney (bə·lō′nē) *n.* **1.** *Slang* Nonsense. **2.** Bologna sausage. Also spelled *boloney*. [def. 1 < BOLOGNA SAUSAGE]

bal·sa (bôl′sə, bäl′-) *n.* **1.** A tree of tropical America and the West Indies. **2.** The very light wood of this tree. **3.** A raft made of light logs. [< Sp. *balza*]

bal·sam (bôl′səm) *n.* **1.** Any of a group of fragrant oleoresins obtained chiefly from the exudations of various trees. **2.** Any tree yielding such a resinous substance, as the balsam fir. **3.** Any fragrant ointment, esp. one used medicinally. —*v.t.* To anoint with balsam. [< L < Gk. *balsamon* balsam] —**bal·sam·ic** (bôl·sam′ik) *adj.*

balsam fir A tree of the pine family, growing in the U.S. and Canada and yielding Canada balsam: also *balm of Gilead*.

Bal·tic (bôl′tik) *adj.* Of or pertaining to the Baltic Sea or the Baltic States.

Baltimore oriole An American oriole of which the male has orange and black plumage. [after the colors of the coat of arms of Lord *Baltimore*]

bal·us·ter (bal′əs·tər) *n.* One of a set of small pillars supporting a handrail. For illus. see BALCONY. [< MF < Ital. *balaustra* pomegranate flower]

bal·us·trade (bal′ə·strād′, bal′ə·strād) *n.* A handrail supported by balusters. For illus. see BALCONY. See BALUSTER.

bam·bi·no (bam·bē′nō) *n.* *pl.* **·ni** (-nē) or **·nos** **1.** A little child; a baby. **2.** A figure of the child Jesus. [< Ital., dim. of *bumbo* simple, childish]

bam·boo (bam·bōō′) *n.* **1.** A tall, treelike or shrubby grass of tropical and semitropical regions. **2.** Its tough, hollow, jointed stem, used for furniture, etc. [< Malay *bambu*]

bam·boo·zle (bam·bōō′zəl) *v.* **·zled, ·zling** *Informal v.t.* **1.** To mislead; cheat. **2.** To perplex. —*v.i.* **3.** To practice trickery or deception. [Origin unknown] —**bam·boo′zle·ment** *n.* —**bam·boo′zler** *n.*

ban (ban) *v.t.* **banned, ban·ning** **1.** To proscribe or prohibit; forbid. **2.** To place under a ban; anathematize; interdict. —*n.* **1.** An official proclamation, especially of prohibition. **2.** *Eccl.* An edict of excommunication or interdiction. **3.** A sentence of outlawry. [< OE *bannan* to proclaim and ON *banna* to curse, prohibit]

ba·nal (bā′nəl, bə·nal′, ban′əl) *adj.* Hackneyed; trite. [< F < OF *ban* feudal summons hence, ordinary, common] —**ba·nal·i·ty** (bə·nal′ə·tē) *n.* —**ba′nal·ly** *adv.*

ba·nan·a (bə·nan′ə) *n.* **1.** The elongated, edible, pulpy fruit of a herbaceous plant of tropical regions, having an easily removed rind and growing in drooping clusters. **2.** The plant bearing this fruit. [< Sp. < native African name]

band¹ (band) *n.* **1.** A flat flexible strip of any material, often used for binding or securing. **2.** A strip of fabric used to finish, strengthen, or trim an article of dress: often in combination: *hatband*. **3.** Any broad stripe of contrasting color, material, or surface. **4.** *pl.* Geneva bands (which see). **5.** A high collar worn in the 16th and 17th centuries. **6.** *Telecom.* A range of frequencies or wavelengths between two stated limits. —*v.t.* **1.** To unite or tie with a band; encircle. **2.** To mark by attaching a band to. [< F *bande*.]

band² (band) *n.* **1.** A company of persons associated for a common purpose; a group, troop, or gang. **2.** A company of persons organized to play musical instruments. **3.** *Cana-*

dian A group of reservation Indians having elective chiefs. —*v.t. & v.i.* To unite in a band. [< MF *bande*]

band·age (ban′dij) *n.* A strip of soft cloth or other material used in dressing wounds, etc. —*v.t.* **·aged, ag·ing** To bind or cover with a bandage. [< F < *bande* band]

Band-Aid (band′ād′) *n.* An adhesive strip with a gauze patch for covering minor wounds: a trade name. Also **band′-aid′.**

ban·dan·na (ban·dan′ə) *n.* A large, brightly colored handkerchief decorated with spots or figures. Also **ban·dan′a.** [< Hind. *bāndhnū*, a method of dyeing]

band·box (band′boks′) *n.* A light round or oval box, originally used to hold collars, and now used for carrying hats.

ban·deau (ban·dō′, band′dō) *n.* *pl.* **·deaux** (-dōz′, -dōz) **1.** A narrow band, esp. one worn about the hair. **2.** A narrow brassiere. [< F < OF *bande* band]

ban·di·coot (ban′di·kōōt) *n.* **1.** A large rat of India and Ceylon. **2.** A small marsupial of Australia, Tasmania, etc. [Alter. of Telugu *pandikokku* pig-rat]

ban·dit (ban′dit) *n.* *pl.* **ban·dits** or **ban·dit·ti** (ban·dit′ē) **1.** A robber. **2.** An outlaw; brigand. [< Ital. *bandire* to proscribe, outlaw] —**ban′dit·ry** *n.*

band·mas·ter (band′mas′tər, -mäs′tər) *n.* The conductor of a musical band.

ban·do·leer (ban′də·lir′) *n.* A broad belt fitted with loops or cases for holding cartridges, and worn over the shoulder. Also **ban′do·lier′.** [< MF < Ital. *banda* band]

band saw *Mech.* A saw consisting of a toothed endless belt mounted on pulleys.

band shell A bandstand having a concave hemispherical rear wall.

band·stand (band′stand′) *n.* A platform for a band of musicians, often roofed when outdoors.

band·wag·on (band′wag′ən) *n.* A high, decorated wagon used to carry a band in a parade. —**to climb (hop, get, etc.) on the bandwagon** *U.S. Informal* To give one's support to a principle or candidate apparently assured of success.

ban·dy (ban′dē) *v.t.* **·died, ·dy·ing** **1.** To give and take; exchange, as blows or words. **2.** To pass along; circulate: to *bandy* stories. **3.** To pass, throw, or knock back and forth, as a ball. —*n.pl.* **·dies** A game resembling hockey; also, a crooked stick used in this game. [Origin uncertain]

ban·dy-leg·ged (ban′dē-leg′id, -legd′) *adj.* Bowlegged.

bane (bān) *n.* **1.** Anything destructive or ruinous. **2.** Poison: now only in combination: *henbane.* [OE *bana* killer]

bane·ful (bān′fəl) *adj.* Poisonous; destructive. —**Syn.** See PERNICIOUS. —**bane′ful·ly** *adv.* —**bane′ful·ness** *n.*

bang¹ (bang) *n.* **1.** A heavy, noisy blow or thump. **2.** A sudden, loud noise or explosion. **3.** *Informal* A sudden spurt of activity: To start with a *bang.* **4.** *U.S. Slang* Thrill; enjoyment. —*v.t.* **1.** To beat or strike heavily and noisily. —*v.i.* **2.** To make a loud sound. **3.** To strike noisily; crash. —*adv.* Abruptly and loudly. [< ON *banga* to hammer]

bang² (bang) *n.* *Usu. pl.* A fringe of hair cut straight across the forehead. —*v.t.* To cut short and straight across. [< BANG¹, *adv.*; from the hair being cut off abruptly]

bang³ (bang) See BHANG.

ban·gle (bang′gəl) *n.* A decorative bracelet or anklet. [< Hind. *bangrī* glass bracelet]

bang-up (bang′up′) *adj.* *Slang* Excellent.

ban·ish (ban′ish) *v.t.* **1.** To compel to leave a country by political decree; exile. **2.** To expel, as from any customary or desired place; drive away; dismiss. [< OF < LL *bannire* to banish] —**ban′ish·er** *n.* —**ban′ish·ment** *n.*

ban·is·ter (ban′is·tər) *n.* **1.** Often *pl.* A balustrade. **2.** Loosely, a baluster. Also *bannister*. [BALUSTER]

ban·jo (ban′jō) *n.* *pl.* **·jos** or **·joes** A long-necked, four- or five-stringed musical instrument having a hoop-shaped body covered on top with stretched skin and played by plucking the strings with the fingers or a plectrum. [< a West African language; cf. Mandingo *bania*] —**ban′jo·ist** *n.*

bank¹ (bangk) *n.* **1.** Any moundlike formation or mass; ridge. **2.** A steep slope; rising ground. **3.** *Often pl.* The slope of land at the edge of a watercourse or of any cut or channel. —**Syn.** See SHORE. **4.** A raised portion of the ocean floor, a river bed, etc.; a shoal; shallow: the Newfoundland *banks.* **5.** *Aeron.* The controlled sidewise tilt of an airplane in a turn, used to prevent skidding. —*v.t.* **1.** To enclose, cover, or protect by a bank, dike, or border; embank. **2.** To heap up into a bank or mound. **3.** To give an upward slant to, as the curve of a road. **4.** To tilt (an airplane) laterally in flight. **5.** In billiards and pool: To cause (a ball) to rebound at an angle from a cushion. —*v.i.* **6.** To form or lie in banks. **7.** To tilt an airplane laterally in flight. [ME *banke*]

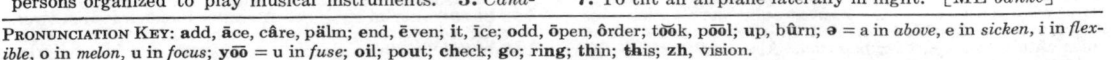

BANJO

bank² (bangk) *n.* **1.** An institution for lending, borrowing, exchanging, issuing, or safeguarding money. **2.** An office or building used for such purposes. **3.** The funds of a gambling house or the fund held by the dealer or banker in some gambling games. **4.** A store or reserve supply of anything needed for future use: a blood *bank.* — *v.t.* **1.** To deposit in a bank. — *v.i.* **2.** To do business as or with a bank or banker. **3.** In gambling, to keep the bank in a game. — **to bank on** *Informal* To rely on; be sure about. [< F < Ital. *banca* money-changer's table, ult. < Gmc.]

bank³ (bangk) *n.* **1.** A set of like articles arranged in a row. **2.** *Naut.* A rowers' bench or tier of oars in a galley. **3.** A rank of keys in a piano or organ. **4.** In journalism, lines under a headline; deck. — *v.t.* To arrange in a bank. [< OF < LL *bancus* bench, ult. < Gmc.]

bank account Money deposited in a bank to the credit of, and subject to withdrawal by, the depositor.

bank bill **1.** A bank note. **2.** A draft drawn on one bank by another: also **banker's bill.**

bank-book (bangk/bŏŏk/) *n.* A book kept by a depositor in which his accounts are entered: also called *passbook.*

bank-er¹ (bangk/ər) *n.* **1.** An employee or officer of a bank. **2.** One who keeps the bank in certain gambling games.

bank-er² (bangk/ər) *n. U.S. & Canadian* A vessel or person engaged in cod fishing on the Newfoundland banks.

bank-ing (bangk/ing) *n.* The business of a bank or banker.

bank note A promissory note issued by a bank, payable on demand and serving as currency. Abbr. *B.N.*

bank-rupt (bangk/rupt) *n.* **1.** *Law* One who is judicially declared insolvent, his property being administered for and distributed among his creditors, under a bankruptcy law. **2.** Any person unable to pay his debts, or without resources. **3.** One ruined and unproductive in some way: a spiritual *bankrupt.* — *adj.* **1.** Subject to the conditions of a bankruptcy law; insolvent. **2.** Destitute; lacking: with *in.* — *v.t.* To make bankrupt. [< F < Ital. < L *rumpere* to break]

bank-rupt-cy (bangk/rupt-sē, -rəp-sē) *n. pl.* **-cies** The state of being bankrupt.

ban-ner (ban/ər) *n.* **1.** A flag or standard bearing a motto or device. **2.** In journalism, a headline extending across a newspaper page. — *adj.* Leading; foremost; outstanding. [< OF < LL *bandum* banner]

ban-nis-ter (ban/is-tər) See BANISTER.

banns (banz) *n.pl. Eccl.* A public announcement in church of a proposed marriage, usu. made on three successive Sundays. Also **bans.** [< BAN]

ban-quet (bang/kwit) *n.* **1.** A sumptuous feast. **2.** A formal or ceremonial dinner, often followed by speeches. — *v.t. & v.i.* To entertain at a banquet; feast sumptuously or formally. [< MF, dim. of *banc* table] — **ban/quet-er** *n.*

ban-quette (bang-ket/) *n.* **1.** *Mil.* A platform or bank behind a parapet, on which soldiers may stand and fire. **2.** An upholstered bench, as along a wall. **3.** A sidewalk. [< F < Ital. *banchetta,* dim. of *banca* bench]

ban-shee (ban/shē, ban-shē/) *n.* In Gaelic folklore, a spirit whose wailing was supposed to foretell a death. Also **ban/shie.** [< Irish *bean* woman + *sidhe* fairy]

ban-tam (ban/təm) *n.* **1.** *Often cap.* Any of various breeds of very small domestic fowl, characterized by combativeness. **2.** A small, pugnacious person. — *adj.* Like a bantam; small and combative. [after *Bantam,* Java]

ban-tam-weight (ban/təm-wāt/) *n.* A boxer or wrestler who weighs between 113 and 118 pounds.

ban-ter (ban/tər) *n.* Good-humored ridicule; raillery. — *v.t.* **1.** To tease good-naturedly. — *v.i.* **2.** To exchange good-natured repartee. [Origin unknown] — **ban/ter-er** *n.* — **ban/ter-ing-ly** *adv.*

Ban-tu (ban/tōō) *n. pl.* **-tu** or **-tus** (-tōōz) **1.** A member of any of numerous Negro tribes of central and southern Africa, including the Kaffirs, Zulus, Bechuanas, and Damaras. **2.** A family of languages spoken by these tribes. — *adj.* Of or pertaining to the Bantu tribes or their languages.

ban-yan (ban/yən) *n.* An East Indian fig-bearing tree whose branches send down roots that develop into new trunks. [< *banian,* Hindu merchant, from the use of the ground under the tree as a market place]

ban-zai (bän-zī) *Japanese* (May you live) ten thousand years: used as a cheer, battle cry, etc.

ba-o-bab (bā/ō-bab, bä/ō-) *n.* An African tree with a thick trunk, bearing edible fruit. [< native African name]

bap-tism (bap/tiz-əm) *n.* **1.** The act of baptizing or of being baptized; esp., the Christian sacrament of initiation into the Church. **2.** Any initiatory or purifying experience. [< OF < LL < Gk. *baptismos* immersion] — **bap-tis-mal** (bap-tiz/məl) *adj.* — **bap-tis/mal-ly** *adv.*

Bap-tist (bap/tist) *n.* **1.** A member of any of various Protestant denominations holding that baptism (generally by immersion) should be given only to professed believers. **2.** One who baptizes. — **the Baptist** John the Baptist.

bap-tis-ter-y (bap/tis-tər-ē, -tis trē) *n. pl.* **-ter-ies** A part of a church set apart for baptism. Also **bap/tis-try** (-trē).

bap-tize (bap-tīz/, bap/tīz) *v.* **-tized, -tiz-ing** *v.t.* **1.** To immerse in water or sprinkle water on in Christian baptism. **2.** To christen. **3.** To cleanse or initiate. — *v.i.* **4.** To administer baptism. Also *Brit.* **bap-tise/.** [< OF < LL < Gk. *baptizein* to immerse, wash] — **bap-tiz/er** *n.*

bar (bär) *n.* **1.** A piece of wood, metal, etc., evenly shaped and long in proportion to its width and thickness, used as a fastening, lever, etc. **2.** An oblong block of solid material, as of soap or a precious metal. **3.** Any barrier or obstacle. **4.** A bank, as of sand, at the entrance to a harbor or river. **5.** The railing about the place in a court occupied by the judge and lawyers, or where prisoners are brought to trial. **6.** A court of law. **7.** Lawyers collectively; also, the legal profession. **8.** Any tribunal or place of judgment. **9.** *Music* **a** The vertical line that divides a staff into measures. **b** A measure. **10** A counter or establishment serving drinks and food, esp. alcoholic drinks. **11.** A stripe, as of color. **12.** The metal mouthpiece of a horse's bridle. — *v.t.* **barred, bar-ring 1.** To fasten or secure with a bar. **2.** To prevent or prohibit. **3.** To obstruct or hinder. **4.** To exclude. **5.** To mark with stripes. — *prep.* Excepting: *bar* none. [< OF < LL *barra* bar]

Ba-rab-bas (bə-rab/əs) A thief released in place of Jesus at the demand of the multitude. *Matt.* xxvii 16–21.

barb¹ (bärb) *n.* **1.** A point projecting backward on a sharp weapon, as on an arrow, fishhook, or spear, intended to prevent easy extraction. **2.** Any similar sharp point, as on barbed wire. **3.** Pointedness; sting, as of wit; also, a stinging remark. **4.** *Ornithol.* One of the lateral processes of a bird's feather. — *v.t.* To provide with a barb or barbs: to *barb* an arrow. [< F < L *barba* beard]

barb² (bärb) *n.* A horse of the breed introduced by the Moors from Barbary into Spain. [< F < Arabic *Barbar* native of North Africa]

bar-bar-i-an (bär-bâr/ē-ən) *n.* **1.** One who belongs to a people, group, or tribe characterized by a primitive civilization. **2.** A rude, coarse, or brutal person. **3.** Formerly, a foreigner; esp., in ancient Greece, one who was non-Hellenic. — *adj.* **1.** Of or resembling a barbarian; uncivilized. **2.** Foreign. — **bar-bar/i-an-ism** *n.*

bar-bar-ic (bär-bar/ik) *adj.* **1.** Of or befitting barbarians; uncivilized. **2.** Coarse; unrestrained.

bar-ba-rism (bär/bə-riz/əm) *n.* **1.** The use of words or forms not approved or standard in a language. **2.** Such a word or form. **3.** A primitive stage of civilization. **4.** A trait, condition, act, etc., characteristic of such a stage.

bar-bar-i-ty (bär-bar/ə-tē) *n. pl.* **-ties 1.** Barbaric conduct. **2.** A barbaric act. **3.** Crudity in style or taste.

bar-ba-rize (bär/bə-rīz) *v.t. & v.i.* **-rized, -riz-ing** To make or become barbarous or corrupt, as a language.

bar-ba-rous (bär/bər-əs) *adj.* **1.** Uncivilized; primitive. **2.** Lacking in refinement; coarse. **3.** Cruel; brutal. **4.** Rude or harsh in sound: *barbarous* music. **5.** Of language, abounding in barbarisms; also, non classical. **6.** Formerly, foreign; esp. in ancient Greece, non-Hellenic. [< L < Gk. *barbaros* non-Hellenic, foreign, rude] — **bar/ba-rous-ly** *adv.* — **bar/ba-rous-ness** *n.*

Bar-ba-ry (bär/bər-ē) North Africa west of Egypt, including the former Barbary States.

Barbary ape An easily trained, tailless ape of North Africa and southern Spain.

bar-bate (bär/bāt) *adj.* **1.** Bearded. **2.** *Bot.* Tufted with long hairs. [< L *barba* beard]

bar-be-cue (bär/bə-kyōō) *n.* **1.** *U.S.* A social gathering, usu. outdoors, at which animals are roasted whole over an open fire. **2.** A whole animal carcass or other meat roasted over an open fire. **3.** A grill, framework, or pit for roasting meat in this fashion. — *v.t.* **-cued, -cu-ing** To roast (usu. beef or pork) in large pieces or whole over an open fire or in a trench, often using a highly seasoned sauce. [< Sp. *barbacoa* < Taino *barbacoa* framework of sticks]

barbed (bärbd) *adj.* **1.** Having a barb or barbs. **2.** Pointed, piercing, or wounding: a *barbed* remark.

barbed wire Fence wire having barbs at short intervals.

bar-bel (bär/bəl) *n.* **1.** One of the soft threadlike appendages to the jaws, chin, or nostrils of certain fishes, functioning as an organ of touch. **2.** A carplike, Old World fish. [< OF < LL < L *barba* beard]

bar-ber (bär/bər) *n.* One who cuts hair, shaves beards, etc., as a business. ◆ Collateral adjective: *tonsorial.* — *v.t.* To cut or dress the hair of; shave or trim the beard of. [< AF, ult. < L *barba* beard]

bar-ber-ry (bär/ber/ē, -bər-ē) *n.* **-ries 1.** A shrub bearing yellow flowers and bright red, oblong berries. **2.** Its acid berry. [< Med.L *berberis, barbaris*]

bar-ber-shop (bär/bər-shop/) *n.* The place of business of a barber. — *adj. Informal* Characterized by close harmony and sentimentality of theme: said of a singing group.

bar-bi-can (bär/bi-kən) *n.* An outer fortification; outwork. [< OF *barbacane;* ult. origin uncertain]

bar-bi-tal (bär/bə-tôl, -tal) *n. Chem.* A white, odorless, crystalline powder, $C_8H_{12}O_3N_2$, with a bitter taste, used as a sedative and hypnotic. Also *Brit.* **bar/bi·tone** (-tōn).

bar·bit·u·rate (bär-bich/ər·it, bär/bə·tŏŏr/it, -tyŏŏr/it) *n. Chem.* A salt or ester of barbituric acid, esp. one used as a sedative or sleeping pill.

bar·bi·tu·ric acid (bär/bə·tŏŏr/ik, -tyŏŏr/-) *Chem.* A crystalline powder, $C_4H_4O_3N_2$, from which several sedative and hypnotic drugs are derived. [< NL (*Usnea*) *barbata* bearded (lichen) + -URIC]

bar·bule (bär/byŏŏl) *n.* **1.** A small barb or beard. **2.** *Ornithol.* A process fringing the barb of a feather. [< L *barbula*, dim. of *barba* beard]

bar·ca·role (bär/kə·rōl) *n.* **1.** A Venetian gondolier's song. **2.** A melody in imitation of this. Also **bar/ca·rolle.** [< F < Ital. *barcaruola* boatman's song]

bard (bärd) *n.* **1.** A Celtic poet and minstrel. **2.** A poet. [< Celtic] — **bard/ic** *adj.*

bare[1] (bâr) *adj.* **1.** Without clothing or covering; naked. **2.** Open to view; exposed. **3.** Without the usual furnishings or equipment; empty. **4.** Unadorned; plain; bald. **5.** Just sufficient; mere. **6.** Threadbare. — *v.t.* **bared, bar·ing** To make or lay bare; reveal; expose. [OE *bær*]

bare[2] (bâr) *Archaic* past tense of BEAR[1].

bare·back (bâr/bak/) *adj.* Riding a horse without a saddle. — *adv.* Without a saddle. — **bare/backed/** *adj.*

bare·faced (bâr/fāst/) *adj.* **1.** Having the face bare. **2.** Unconcealed; open. **3.** Impudent; audacious. — **bare·fac·ed·ly** (bâr/fā/sid·lē, -fāst/lē) *adv.* — **bare/fac·ed·ness** *n.*

bare·foot (bâr/fŏŏt/) *adj. & adv.* With the feet bare.

bare·foot·ed (bâr/fŏŏt/id) *adj.* Having the feet bare.

bare·hand·ed (bâr/han/did) *adj. & adv.* **1.** With the hands uncovered. **2.** Without a weapon, tool, etc.

bare·head·ed (bâr/hed/id) *adj. & adv.* With the head bare. Also **bare/head/.**

bare·leg·ged (bâr/leg/id, -legd/) *adj. & adv.* With the legs bare.

bare·ly (bâr/lē) *adv.* **1.** Only just; scarcely. **2.** Openly; boldly; plainly. **3.** Nakedly.

bar·gain (bär/gən) *n.* **1.** A mutual agreement between persons, especially an agreement to buy or sell goods. **2.** That which is agreed upon or the terms of the agreement. **3.** The agreement as it affects one of the parties: He made a bad *bargain.* **4.** An article bought or offered at a low price. — **into the bargain** In addition to what was agreed; besides. — **to strike a bargain** To come to an agreement on terms. — *v.i.* **1.** To discuss terms for selling or buying. **2.** To make a bargain; reach an agreement. **3.** To negotiate. — *v.t.* **4.** To trade or arrange by bargaining. — **to bargain for** To expect; count on: more than I *bargained for.* [< OF *bargaine*] — **bar/gain·er, *Law* bar/gain·or** *n.*

barge (bärj) *n.* **1.** A flat-bottomed freight boat or lighter for harbors and inland waters. **2.** A large boat, for pleasure, pageants, or for state occasions. **3.** *Naval* A ship's boat for the use of a flag officer. — *v.* **barged, barg·ing** *v.i.* **1.** To transport by barge. — *v.i.* **2.** To move clumsily and slowly. **3.** *Informal* To collide: with *into.* **4.** *Informal* To enter or intrude rudely or awkwardly. [< OF < LL *barga*]

barge·man (bärj/mən) *n. pl.* **·men** (-mən) One in charge of or employed on a barge. Also *Brit.* **bar·gee** (bär·jē/).

bar·ite (bâr/īt) *n.* A heavy, vitreous, usu. white, orthorhombic barium sulfate, $BaSO_4$: also called *heavy spar.*

bar·i·tone (bar/ə·tōn) *n.* **1.** A male voice of a register higher than bass and lower than tenor. **2.** One having such a voice. **3.** A brass instrument having a similar range. — *adj.* **1.** Of or pertaining to a baritone. **2.** Having the range of a baritone. [< Ital. < Gk. < *barys* deep + *tonos* tone]

bar·i·um (bâr/ē·əm) *n.* A silver white to yellow, malleable, metallic element (symbol Ba) occurring in combination and forming salts, of which the soluble ones and the carbonate are poisonous. See ELEMENT. [< NL < Gk. *barys* heavy] — **bar·ic** (bâr/ik) *adj.*

barium sulfate An insoluble compound, $BaSO_4$, used to facilitate X-ray pictures of the stomach and intestines.

bark[1] (bärk) *n.* **1.** The short, abrupt, explosive cry of a dog. **2.** Any sound like this. — *v.i.* **1.** To utter a bark, as a dog, or to make a sound like a bark. **2.** *Informal* To cough. **3.** To speak loudly and sharply. **4.** *U.S. Slang* To solicit customers at the entrance to a show by proclaiming its attractions. — *v.t.* **5.** To say roughly and curtly: He *barked* an order. — **to bark up the wrong tree** *U.S. Informal* To be mistaken as to one's object or as to the means of attaining it. [OE *beorcan*]

bark[2] (bärk) *n.* The rind or covering of the stems, branches, and roots of a tree or other plant. — *v.t* **1.** To remove the bark from; scrape; girdle. **2.** To rub off the skin of. **3.** To tan or treat with an infusion of bark. [< Scand.]

bark[3] (bärk) *n.* A sailing vessel of three or more masts, square-rigged on all but the mizzenmast, which is fore-and-aft-rigged. [< MF < LL *barca* bark]

bar·keep·er (bär/kē·pər) *n.* **1.** One who owns or manages a bar where alcoholic liquors are served. **2.** A bartender. Also **bar/keep/.**

bar·ken·tine (bär/kən·tēn) *n.* A sailing vessel of three or more masts, square-rigged on the foremast and fore-and-aft-rigged on the other masts: also spelled *barquentine.* [< BARK[3], on analogy with *brigantine*]

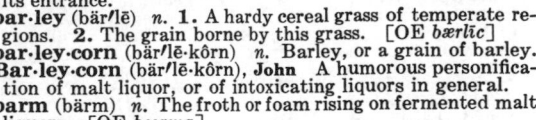

BARK

bark·er (bär/kər) *n. U.S. Informal* One who advertises a show, etc., at its entrance.

bar·ley (bär/lē) *n.* **1.** A hardy cereal grass of temperate regions. **2.** The grain borne by this grass. [OE *bærlic*]

bar·ley·corn (bär/lē·kôrn) *n.* Barley, or a grain of barley.

Bar·ley·corn (bär/lē·kôrn), **John** A humorous personification of malt liquor, or of intoxicating liquors in general.

barm (bärm) *n.* The froth or foam rising on fermented malt liquors. [OE *beorma*]

bar·maid (bär/mād) *n.* A female bartender.

bar·man (bär/mən) *n. pl.* **·men** (mən) A bartender.

bar mitz·vah (bär mits/və) In Judaism, a boy commencing his thirteenth year, the age of religious duty; also, the ceremony celebrating this. [< Hebrew, son of the commandment]

barm·y (bär/mē) *adj.* **barm·i·er, barm·i·est 1.** Full of barm; frothy. **2.** *Brit. Slang* Silly; flighty. Also *Scot.* **barm/ie.**

barn (bärn) *n.* **1.** A building for storing hay, stabling livestock, etc. **2.** *Brit.* A building for storing grain. [OE *bern*]

bar·na·cle (bär/nə·kəl) *n.* **1.** A marine shellfish that attaches itself to rocks, ship bottoms, etc. **2.** A European wild goose of northern seas: also **barnacle goose. 3.** One who or that which clings tenaciously. [< ME *bernacle*; origin uncertain] — **bar/na·cled** *adj.*

barn dance A social dance held in a barn and usu. consisting of square dances with appropriate music and calls.

barn owl An owl of nearly world-wide distribution, often found in barns, where it preys on mice.

barn·storm (bärn/stôrm/) *v.i. U.S Informal* To tour rural districts, giving shows, political speeches, exhibitions of stunt flying, etc. — **barn/storm/er** *n.* — **barn/storm/ing** *adj. & n.*

barn·yard (bärn/yärd/) *n.* A yard adjoining a barn. — *adj.* Of or fit for a barnyard; broad; smutty.

baro- *combining form* Weight; atmospheric pressure: *barometer.* [< Gk. *baros* weight]

bar·o·gram (bar/ə·gram) *n.* The record of a barograph.

bar·o·graph (bar/ə·graf, -gräf) *n.* An automatically recording barometer. — **bar/o·graph/ic** *adj.*

ba·rom·e·ter (bə·rom/ə·tər) *n.* **1.** An instrument for measuring atmospheric pressure, used in forecasting weather, measuring elevations, etc. **2.** Anything that indicates changes. — **bar·o·met·ric** (bar/ə·met/rik) or **·ri·cal** *adj.* — **bar/o·met/ri·cal·ly** *adv.* — **ba·rom/e·try** *n.*

bar·on (bar/ən) *n.* **1.** A member of the lowest order of hereditary nobility in several European countries. **2.** *U.S.* One who has great power in a commercial field. [< OF < LL *baro, -onis* man < Gmc.] — **ba·ro·ni·al** (bə·rō/nē·əl) *adj.*

bar·on·age (bar/ən·ij) *n.* **1.** Barons collectively. **2.** The dignity or rank of a baron.

bar·on·ess (bar/ən·is) *n.* **1.** The wife or widow of a baron. **2.** A woman holding a barony in her own right.

bar·on·et (bar/ən·it, -ə·net) *n.* **1.** An inheritable English title, below that of baron and not part of the nobility. **2.** The bearer of the title. — **bar/on·et·age, bar/on·et·cy** *n.*

bar·o·ny (bar/ə·nē) *n. pl.* **·nies** The rank, dignity, or domain of a baron.

ba·roque (bə·rōk/) *adj.* **1.** Of or characteristic of a style of art and architecture developed in Europe in the late 16th and 17th centuries, characterized by extravagantly contorted classical forms and curvilinear ornament. **2.** Fantastic in style; elaborately ornamented. **3.** Loosely, rococo. **4.** Irregular in shape: said of pearls. — *n.* **1.** The baroque style in art. **2.** An object, ornament, design, or composition in this style. [< F < Pg. *barroco* rough or imperfect pearl]

ba·rouche (bə·rōōsh/) *n.* A four-wheeled carriage with folding top, four inside seats, and an outside seat for the driver. [< G < Ital. < L *bis* twice + *rota* wheel]

barque (bärk), **bar·quen·tine** (bär/kən·tēn) See BARK[3], BARKENTINE.

bar·racks (bar/əks) *n.pl. (construed as sing. or pl.)* **1.** A building or group

BAROQUE ARCHITECTURE (Church of Santa Maria della Salute, Venice, 1631–56)

of buildings for the housing of soldiers. **2.** Any large, plain building used for temporary housing. Also **bar′rack.** [< F *baraque* < Ital. *baracca* soldier's tent; ult. origin uncertain]

barracks bag A soldier's cloth bag with a draw cord, for holding clothing and equipment. Also **barrack bag.**

bar·ra·cu·da (bar′ə·kōō′də) *n. pl.* **·da** or **·das** A voracious pikelike fish of tropical seas. [< Sp.]

bar·rage (bə·räzh′) *n.* **1.** *Mil.* A curtain of fire designed to protect troops by impeding enemy movements across defensive lines or areas. **2.** Any overwhelming attack, as of words or blows. — *v.t. & v.i.* **·raged, ·rag·ing** To lay down or subject to a barrage. [< F (*tir de*) *barrage* barrage (fire)]

bar·ran·ca (bə·rang′kə) *n. SW U.S.* A deep ravine. [< Sp.]

bar·ra·try (bar′ə·trē) *n. pl.* **·tries** *Law* **1.** Any willful and unlawful act by the master or crew of a ship, whereby the owners sustain injury. **2.** The offense of exciting lawsuits, stirring up quarrels, etc. Also **bar′re·try.** [< OF < *barat* fraud] — **bar′ra·tor** *n.* — **bar′ra·trous** *adj.*

barred (bärd) *adj.* **1.** Having or secured with bars. **2.** Prohibited. **3.** Marked with bars or stripes.

bar·rel (bar′əl) *n.* **1.** A large, approximately cylindrical vessel usu. of wood, flat at the base and top and bulging slightly in the middle. **2.** As much as a barrel will hold, as the standard U.S. barrel containing 3.28 bushels dry measure, or 31.5 liquid measure. **3.** Something resembling or having the form of a barrel, as the tube of a gun, the drum of a windlass, the cylindrical box containing the mainspring of a watch, etc. — *v.* **bar·reled** or **·relled, ·rel·ing** or **·rel·ling** *v.t.* **1.** To put or pack in a barrel. — *v.i.* **2.** *U.S Slang* To move fast. [< OF *baril*]

bar·rel·house (bar′əl·hous′) *n. U.S. Slang* **1.** A cheap drinking house. **2.** *Music* An early style of jazz.

barrel organ A hand organ.

barrel roll *Aeron.* A maneuver in which an airplane rolls on its own axis as it spirals about its original path.

bar·ren (bar′ən) *adj.* **1.** Not producing or incapable of producing offspring; sterile. **2.** Not productive; unfruitful. **3.** Unprofitable, as an enterprise. **4.** Lacking in interest or attractiveness; dull. **5.** Empty; devoid. — *n. Usu. pl.* A tract of level, scrubby land. [< OF *baraigne*] — **bar′ren·ly** *adv.* — **bar′ren·ness** *n.*

bar·rette (bə·ret′) *n.* A small bar with a clasp used for keeping a woman's hair in place. [< F, dim. of *barre* bar]

bar·ri·cade (bar′ə·kād′, bar′ə·kād) *n.* **1.** A barrier hastily built for obstruction or defense. **2.** Any barrier or obstruction blocking passage. — *v.t.* **·cad·ed, ·cad·ing** To enclose, obstruct, or defend with a barricade or barricades. [< F < Sp. *barricada* barrier < *barrica* barrel; the first barricades were barrels filled with earth, stones, etc.] — **bar′ri·cad′er** *n.*

bar·ri·er (bar′ē·ər) *n.* **1.** A fence, wall, gate, etc., erected to bar passage. **2.** Any obstacle or obstruction, natural or otherwise. **3.** Something that separates or keeps apart: a *barrier* of suspicion. [< OF < *barre* bar]

barrier reef A long, narrow ridge of rock or coral parallel to the coast and close to or above the surface of the sea.

bar·ring (bär′ing) *prep.* Excepting; apart from.

bar·ris·ter (bar′is·tər) *n.* In England, a member of the legal profession who argues cases in the courts.

bar·room (bär′rōōm′, -rŏŏm′) *n.* A room where alcoholic liquors are served across a counter or bar.

bar·row[1] (bar′ō) *n.* **1.** A frame or tray with handles at either end by which it is carried, used for transporting loads. **2.** A wheelbarrow. **3.** The load carried on a barrow. **4.** *Brit.* A pushcart. [OE *bearwe* < *beran* to bear]

bar·row[2] (bar′ō) *n.* **1.** *Anthropol.* A mound of earth or stones built over a grave. **2.** A hill. [OE *beorg*]

bar sinister Erroneously, a bend sinister.

bar·tend·er (bär′ten′dər) *n.* A man who mixes and serves alcoholic drinks over a bar.

bar·ter (bär′tər) *v.i.* **1.** To trade by exchange of goods or services without use of money. — *v.t.* **2.** To trade (goods or services) for something of equal value. — *n.* **1.** The act of bartering; exchange of goods. **2.** Anything bartered. [< OF *barater* to exchange] — **bar′ter·er** *n.*

Bart·lett (bärt′lit) *n.* A variety of pear introduced by Enoch Bartlett of Massachusetts. Also **Bartlett pear.**

Bar·uch (bâr′ək) A book in the Old Testament Apocrypha.

bar·y·tes (bə·rī′tēz) *n.* Barite.

ba·sal (bā′səl) *adj.* **1.** Of, at, or forming the base. **2.** Basic; fundamental. — **ba′sal·ly** *adv.*

basal metabolism *Physiol.* The minimum energy required by the body at rest in maintaining essential vital activities, measured by the rate (**basal metabolic rate**) of oxygen intake and heat discharge.

ba·salt (bə·sôlt′, bas′ôlt) *n.* A dense, dark volcanic rock, having a columnar structure. [< L *basaltes* dark marble] — **ba·sal′tic** *adj.*

bas·cule (bas′kyōōl) *n.* A mechanical apparatus of which each end counterbalances the other, used in a kind of drawbridge (**bascule bridge**) operated by a counterpoise. [< F, seesaw]

base[1] (bās) *n.* **1.** The lowest or supporting part of anything; bottom. **2.** An underlying principle or foundation. **3.** The essential or preponderant element; chief or fundamental ingredient. **4.** Any point, line, or quantity from which an inference, measurement, or reckoning is made. **5.** *Archit.* The lowest member of a structure, as the basement of a building. **6.** *Geom.* The side of a polygon or solid figure on which it appears to rest. **7.** *Math.* A number on which a numerical system depends: The *base* of the decimal system is 10. **8.** *Mil.* A locality or installation from which operations are projected or supported. **9.** *Chem.* A compound that is capable of so uniting with an acid as to neutralize it and form a salt. **10.** *Biol.* The point of attachment of an organ. **11.** In baseball, any of the four points of the diamond, or the bag or plate marking one of these. **12.** A base line. **13.** *Ling.* A form to which prefixes, suffixes, or infixes are added; root or stem. — **off base 1.** In baseball, not in contact with the base occupied: said of base runners. **2.** *U.S. Slang* Thinking, speaking, etc., erroneously. — *v.t.* **based, bas·ing 1.** To place on a foundation or basis; ground; establish: with *on* or *upon.* **2.** To form a base for. — *adj.* **1.** Serving as a base: a *base* line. **2.** Situated at or near the base: a *base* angle. [< OF < L < Gk. < *bainein* to go]

BASCULE BRIDGE
(Tower Bridge, London)

base[2] (bās) *adj.* **1.** Morally low; mean; vile; contemptible. **2.** Like or befitting an inferior person or thing; menial; degrading: *base* flattery. **3.** Comparatively low in value: said of metals. **4.** Debased, as money; counterfeit: *base* coin. **5.** Not classical; corrupted: said of languages. [< OF < LL *bassus* low] — **base′ly** *adv.* — **base′ness** *n.*

base·ball (bās′bôl′) *n.* **1.** A game played with a wooden bat and a hard ball by two teams of nine players each, one team being at bat and the other in the field, alternately, the object of the game being to make as many runs as possible within nine innings of play. **2.** The ball used in this game.

base·board (bās′bôrd′, -bōrd′) *n.* **1.** A board skirting the interior wall of a room, next to the floor. **2.** Any board forming a base.

base·born (bās′bôrn′) *adj.* **1.** Of humble birth; plebeian. **2.** Born out of wedlock. **3.** Mean; vile.

base burn·er (bās′bûr′nər) *n.* A coal stove or furnace in which the fuel is fed from above into a central fuel chamber.

base hit In baseball, a batted ball that enables the batter to reach a base unaided by a defensive error, an attempt to put out a preceding base runner, or a force play: also called *hit.*

base·less (bās′lis) *adj.* Without foundation in fact; unfounded; groundless. — **base′less·ness** *n.*

base line 1. In baseball, a path of definite width connecting successive bases. **2.** A line, value, etc., taken as a base for measurement or comparison.

base·ment (bās′mənt) *n.* **1.** The lowest story of a building, usu. wholly or partly underground and just beneath the main floor. **2.** The basal portion of any building.

base runner In baseball, a member of the team at bat who has reached a base.

bas·es[1] (bā′siz) Plural of BASE[1].

bas·es[2] (bā′sēz) Plural of BASIS.

bash (bash) *Informal v.t.* To strike heavily; smash in. — *n.* A smashing blow. [? Akin to Dan. *baske* thwack]

bash·ful (bash′fəl) *adj.* **1.** Shrinking from notice; shy; timid; diffident. **2.** Characterized by or indicating sensitiveness and timid modesty: a *bashful* glance. [< *bash*, var. of ABASH + -FUL] — **bash′ful·ly** *adv.* — **bash′ful·ness** *n.*

ba·sic (bā′sik) *adj.* **1.** Pertaining to, forming, or like a base or basis; essential; fundamental. **2.** *Chem.* Of, pertaining to, or producing a base. — **ba′si·cal·ly** *adv.*

Basic English A simplified form of English, devised for use as an international language and in the teaching of English. It contains 850 words of general vocabulary, supplemented by an additional 150 for scientific purposes. Also **Basic.**

bas·il (baz′əl) *n.* An aromatic plant of the mint family, sometimes used in cooking. [< OF < L < Gk. *basilikon* (*phyton*) royal (plant), basil]

bas·i·lar (bas′ə·lər) *adj.* Pertaining to or situated at the base, esp. of the skull; basal. Also **bas·i·lar·y** (bas′ə·ler′ē).

ba·sil·i·ca (bə·sil′i·kə) *n.* **1.** In ancient Rome, a rectangular building divided by columns into a nave and two side aisles, used as a place of assembly. **2.** A building of this type used as a Christian church. [< L < Gk. *basilikē* (*stoa*) royal (hall), fem. of *basilikos*] — **ba·sil′i·can** *adj.*

bas·i·lisk (bas′ə·lisk) *n.* **1.** A fabled reptile whose breath and look were said to be fatal. **2.** A tropical American lizard having an erectile crest on the head. [< L < Gk. *basiliskos*, dim. of *basileus* king]

ba·sin (bā′sən) *n.* **1.** A round, wide, shallow vessel, often with sloping sides, used for holding liquids. **2.** A vessel resembling this, as the scale or pan of a balance. **3.** The amount that a basin will hold. **4.** A sink or washbowl. **5.** *Geog.* **a** Any large depression in the earth's surface, as the bed of a lake or ocean. **b** The region drained by a river. **6.** An enclosed place or hollow containing water, as a cistern, pond, etc. [< OF < LL < *bacca* bowl] — **ba′sined** *adj.*

ba·sis (bā′sis) *n.* *pl.* **ba·ses** (bā′sēz) **1.** That on which anything rests; support; foundation; base. **2.** Fundamental principle; groundwork. **3.** The chief component or ingredient of a thing. [< L < Gk., base, pedestal]

bask (bask, bäsk) *v.i.* **1.** To lie in and enjoy a pleasant warmth, as of the sun or a fire. **2.** To enjoy or benefit from a similar warmth, as of regard: to *bask* in royal favor. — *v.t.* **3.** To expose to warmth. [< ON *badhask* to bathe oneself]

bas·ket (bas′kit, bäs′-) *n.* **1.** A container made of interwoven splints, rushes, strips of wood, etc. **2.** Something like a basket in form or use. **3.** The amount a basket will hold. **4.** In basketball: **a** One of the goals, consisting of a metal ring with a cord net suspended from it. **b** The point or points made by throwing the ball through the basket. [ME]

bas·ket·ball (bas′kit·bôl′, bäs′-) *n.* **1.** A game played by two teams of five men each, in which the object is to throw the ball through an elevated goal (basket) at the opponent's end of an oblong court. **2.** The ball used in this game.

bas·ket·ry (bas′kit·rē, bäs′-) *n.* **1.** Baskets collectively; basketwork. **2.** The art or craft of making baskets.

basket weave A weave with two or more warp and filling threads woven side by side to resemble a plaited basket.

bas·ket·work (bas′kit·wûrk′, bäs′-) *n.* Work made of or resembling interlaced osiers, twigs, etc.; wickerwork.

ba·so·phile (bā′sə·fil, -fil) *Biol.* A tissue or cell having a special affinity for basic staining dyes. Also **ba′si·phile.** — **ba·so·phil·ic** (bā′sə·fil′ik), **ba·soph·i·lous** (bā·sof′ə·ləs) *adj.*

basque (bask) *n.* A woman's closely fitting bodice, separate from the dress skirt.

Basque (bask) *n.* **1.** One of a people of unknown origin living in the western Pyrenees in Spain and France. **2.** The language of the Basque people. — *adj.* Of the Basques.

bas-re·lief (bä′ri·lēf′, bas′-) *n.* That type of sculpture in which the figures project only slightly from the background: also called *low relief.* [< F < Ital. *basso* low + *rilievo* relief]

bass¹ (bas) *n.* *pl.* **bass** or **bass·es** Any of various spiny-finned, marine and fresh-water food fishes. [OE *bærs*]

bass² (bās) *n.* *Music* **1.** The lowest-pitched male singing voice. **2.** The notes in the lowest register of the piano, pipe organ, etc. **3.** The lowest part in vocal or instrumental music; also, these parts collectively. **4.** One who sings or an instrument that plays such a part, esp., a bass viol. — *adj.* **1.** Low in pitch; having a low musical range. **2.** Of or for a bass or basses. [< OF *bas* low]

bass³ (bas) *n.* **1.** The basswood or linden. **2.** Bast. [Alter. of BAST]

bass drum (bās) The largest of the drums, beaten on both heads and having a deep sound.

bas·set (bas′it) *n.* A hound characterized by a long, low body, long head and nose, and short, heavy, crooked forelegs. Also **basset hound.** [< OF *basset*, dim. of *bas* low]

bas·si·net (bas′ə·net′) *n.* A basket used as a baby's cradle, usu. with a hood over one end. [< F]

bas·so (bas′ō, bäs′ō; *Ital.* bäs′sō) *n.* *pl.* **bas·sos** (bas′ōz, bäs′ōz), *Ital.* **bas·si** (bäs′sē) **1.** A bass singer. **2.** The bass part. [< Ital., low]

bas·soon (ba·sōōn′, bə-) *n.* *Music* A large, low-pitched, double-reed woodwind instrument. [< F < It. *basso* low]

bass viol (bās) *Music* The double bass.

bass·wood (bas′wŏŏd′) *n.* The American linden. See under LINDEN. Also called *bass.*

bast (bast) *n.* *Bot.* The fibrous inner bark of trees, originally of the linden, used in making cordage: also called *bass.* [OE *bæst*]

bas·tard (bas′tərd) *n.* **1.** An illegitimate child. **2.** Any irregular, inferior, or counterfeit thing. **3.** *U.S. Slang* A worthless or cruel man. **4.** *Brit. Informal* A fellow; chap: a somewhat disparaging term. — *adj.* **1.** Born out of wedlock. **2.** False; spurious. **3.** Resembling but not typical of the genuine thing. **4.** Abnormal or irregular in size, shape, or proportion. [< OF < *fils de bast* packsaddle child] — **bas′tard·ly** *adj.* — **bas′tard·y** *n.*

bas·tard·ize (bas′tər·dīz) *v.* **·ized, ·iz·ing** *v.t.* **1.** To prove to be or proclaim to be a bastard. **2.** To make degenerate; debase. — *v.i.* **3.** To become debased. — **bas·tard·i·za′tion** *n.*

baste¹ (bāst) *v.t.* **bast·ed, bast·ing** To sew loosely together, as with long, temporary stitches. [< OF < OHG *bestan* to sew with bast]

baste² (bāst) *v.t.* **bast·ed, bast·ing** To moisten (meat or fish) with drippings, butter, etc., while cooking. [? < OF *basser* to soak, moisten]

baste³ (bāst) *v.t.* **bast·ed, bast·ing** *Informal* **1.** To beat; thrash. **2.** To attack verbally; abuse. [Prob. < Scand.]

bas·tille (bas·tēl′) *n.* A prison, esp. one operated tyrannically. Also **bas·tile′.** [< OF < LL < *bastire* to build]

Bas·tille (bas·tēl′, *Fr.* bȧs·tē′y′) A fortress in Paris, stormed and destroyed in the French Revolution on July 14, 1789.

bas·ti·na·do (bas′tə·nā′dō) *n.* *pl.* **·does** **1.** A beating with a stick, usu. on the soles of the feet. **2.** A stick or cudgel. Also **bas′ti·nade′** (-nād′). [< Sp. < *baston* cudgel]

bast·ing (bās′ting) *n.* **1.** The act of sewing loosely together. **2.** The thread used for this purpose. **3.** *pl.* Long, loose, temporary stitches.

bas·tion (bas′chən, -tē·ən) *n.* **1.** In fortifications, a projecting part of a rampart. **2.** Any fortified position. [< MF < Ital. < *bastire* to build] — **bas′tioned** *adj.*

bat¹ (bat) *n.* **1.** In baseball, cricket, and similar games: **a** A stick or club for striking the ball. **b** The act of batting. **c** A turn at bat. **2.** In cricket, the batsman. **3.** In tennis, badminton, etc., a racket. **4.** Any heavy cudgel or club. **5.** *Informal* A blow, as with a stick. **6.** *Slang* A drunken spree. — **to go to bat for** *Informal* To defend or advocate the cause of. — *v.* **bat·ted, bat·ting** *v.i.* **1.** In baseball, cricket, and other games, to use a bat or take a turn at bat. — *v.t.* **2.** To strike with or as with a bat. **3.** To have a batting average of: to *bat* .400. — **to bat around** *Slang* **1.** To travel about. **2.** To discuss. [OE *batt* cudgel]

bat² (bat) *n.* A nocturnal flying mammal having elongated forelimbs and digits that support a thin wing membrane. — **blind as a bat** Altogether blind. — **to have bats in the belfry** *U.S. Slang* To be crazy. [ME *bakke*, ? < Scand.]

bat³ (bat) *v.t.* **bat·ted, bat·ting** *Informal* To wink. — **not bat an eye** or **eyelash** *Informal* Not show surprise.

batch (bach) *n.* **1.** A quantity or number taken together. **2.** The amount of bread produced at one time. **3.** The quantity of material used for one operation. **4.** Any set of things made, done, etc., at one time. [ME *bacche*]

bate (bāt) *v.t. & v.i.* **bat·ed, bat·ing** To restrain; decrease. — **with bated breath** In a state of fear, suspense, expectation, etc. [Var. of ABATE]

ba·teau (ba·tō′) *n.* *pl.* **·teaux** (-tōz′) **1.** *U.S. & Canadian* A light, flat-bottomed boat. **2.** A pontoon for a floating bridge. [< F < OF *batel*, ult. < Gmc.]

bat·fish (bat′fish′) *n.* **1.** A North American marine fish having a batlike appearance. **2.** A sting ray.

bath (bath, bäth) *n.* *pl.* **baths** (bathz, bäthz; baths, bäths) **1.** A washing or immersing of something, esp. the body, in water or other liquid. **2.** The liquid used for this. **3.** The container for such a liquid; a bathtub. **4.** A bathroom. **5.** *Often pl.* A set of rooms or a building equipped for bathing. **6.** *Often pl.* An establishment or resort where bathing is part of a medical treatment. — *v.t. Brit.* To place or wash in a bath; immerse. [OE *bæth*]

bathe (bāth) *v.* **bathed, bath·ing** *v.t.* **1.** To place in liquid; immerse. **2.** To wash; wet. **3.** To apply liquid to for comfort or healing. **4.** To cover or suffuse as with liquid. — *v.i.* **5.** To wash oneself; take a bath. **6.** To be covered or suffused as if with liquid: to *bathe* in sunshine. — *n. Brit.* A swim. [OE *bathian*] — **bath′a·ble** *adj.* — **bath′er** *n.*

bath·house (bath′hous′, bäth′-) *n.* **1.** A building with facilities for bathing. **2.** A small structure at a bathing resort used as a dressing room.

bathing suit (bāth′ing) A garment, sometimes consisting of two pieces, worn for swimming.

batho- *combining form* Depth. [< Gk. *bathos* depth]

bath·o·lith (bath′ə·lith) *n.* *Geol.* A large, irregular mass of igneous rock, often forming the core of mountain ranges. Also **bath′o·lite** (-līt). [< BATHO- + -LITH] — **bath′o·lith′ic** or **bath·o·lit′ic** (-lit′ik) *adj.*

ba·thos (bā′thos) *n.* **1.** A descent from the lofty to the commonplace in discourse; anticlimax. **2.** Insincere pathos; sentimentality. [< Gk. < *bathys* deep]

bath·robe (bath′rōb′, bäth′-) *n.* A long, loose garment for wear before and after bathing.

bath·room (bath′rōōm′, -rŏŏm′, bäth′-) *n.* **1.** A room in which to bathe. **2.** A toilet.

Bath·she·ba (bath·shē′bə, bath′shi·bə) In the Bible, the wife of Uriah and later of David; mother of Solomon. II *Sam.*

bath·tub (bath′tub′, bäth′-) *n.* A vessel in which to bathe, esp. one installed as a permanent fixture in a bathroom.

bathy- *combining form* Deep; of the sea or ocean depths: *bathysphere.* [< Gk. *bathys* deep]

bath·y·scaph (bath′ə·skaf) *n.* A free bathysphere with ballast and a gasoline-filled float to control depth, capable of ocean depths over 35,000 feet. Also **bath′y·scaphe** (-skāf). [< BATHY- + Gk. *skaphē* bowl]

---

bath·y·sphere (bath'ə·sfir) *n.* A spherical diving bell equipped with windows for deep-sea observations.

ba·tik (bə·tēk', bat'ik) *n.* **1.** A process for coloring fabrics, in which the parts not to be dyed are covered with wax. **2.** The fabric so colored. Also spelled **battik**. [< Malay]

ba·tiste (bə·tēst') *n.* A fine cotton fabric in plain weave. [< F; after Jean *Baptiste*, 13th c. French linen weaver]

ba·ton (ba·ton', bat'n; *Fr.* bà·tôn') *n.* **1.** A short staff or truncheon borne as an emblem of authority or privilege. **2.** *Music* A slender stick or rod used by a conductor. [< F < OF *baston* < LL *bastum* stick]

ba·tra·chi·an (bə·trā'kē·ən) *adj.* Of or pertaining to a former class of amphibians, esp. to frogs and toads; amphibian. — *n.* A frog or toad. [< NL < Gk. *batrachos* frog]

bats (bats) *adj. Slang* Batty.

bats·man (bats'mən) *n. pl.* **·men** (-mən) In baseball or cricket, the batter.

bat·tal·ion (bə·tal'yən) *n.* **1.** *Mil.* **a** A unit consisting of a headquarters and two or more companies, batteries, or comparable units. **b** A body of troops. **2.** *Usu. pl.* A large group or number. [< MF < Ital. < *battaglia* battle]

bat·ten[1] (bat'n) *v.i.* **1.** To grow fat; thrive. — *v.t.* **2.** To make fat, as cattle. [< ON *batna* to grow better, improve]

bat·ten[2] (bat'n) *n.* **1.** A light strip of wood, as for covering a joint between boards. **2.** A strip of sawed timber, used for flooring, scantling, etc. **3.** *Naut.* A thin strip of wood placed in a sail to keep it flat or for fastening a tarpaulin over a hatch. — *v.t.* To fasten with battens: with *up* or *down*.

bat·ter[1] (bat'ər) *v.t.* **1.** To strike with repeated, violent blows. **2.** To damage or injure with such blows or with hard usage. — *v.i.* **3.** To pound or beat with blow after blow; hammer. [Partly < OF < L *battuere* to beat]

bat·ter[2] (bat'ər) *n.* In baseball and cricket, the player whose turn it is to bat.

bat·ter[3] (bat'ər) *n.* A mixture, as of eggs, flour, and milk, beaten for use in cookery. [? < OF < *battre* to beat]

bat·ter·ing-ram (bat'ər·ing·ram') *n.* A long, stout beam, used in ancient warfare for battering down walls.

bat·ter·y (bat'ər·ē, ba'trē) *n. pl.* **·ter·ies** **1.** Any unit, apparatus, or grouping in which a series or set of parts or components is assembled to serve a common end. **2.** *Electr.* One or more cells operating together as a single source of direct current. **3.** *Mil.* **a** An artillery unit equivalent to an infantry company. **b** A group of guns, rockets, or related equipment forming an artillery unit. **4.** *Naval* The guns of a warship, or a specific group of them. **5.** *Law* The illegal beating or touching of another person. [< OF < *battre* to beat]

bat·tik (bə·tēk', bat'ik) See BATIK.

bat·ting (bat'ing) *n.* Wadded cotton or wool prepared in sheets or rolls, used for interlining, stuffing mattresses, etc.

bat·tle (bat'l) *n.* **1.** A combat between hostile armies or fleets. **2.** Any fighting, conflict, or struggle. — *v.* **·tled**, **·tling** *v.i.* **1.** To contend in or as in battle; struggle; strive. — *v.t.* **2.** *U.S.* To fight. [< OF < LL < L *battuere* to beat] — **bat'tler** *n.*

— **Syn.** (noun) **1.** A *battle* is a more or less continuous fight and may last for many days, while a *skirmish* is brief and involves small groups of combatants. An *action* is one of the events in a *battle*, as by a part of the forces engaged. *Engagement* refers to a period of active combat, but may also be a complete *battle* or war.

bat·tle-ax (bat'l·aks') *n.* **1.** A large ax formerly used in battle; a broadax. **2.** *U.S. Slang* A formidable, disagreeable woman. Also **bat'tle-axe'**.

battle cruiser *Naval* A war vessel having cruiser speed, but less heavily armored than a battleship.

battle cry **1.** A shout uttered by troops in battle. **2.** A slogan or distinctive phrase used in any conflict or contest.

bat·tle·dore (bat'l·dôr, -dōr) *n.* **1.** A flat paddle or bat used to strike a shuttlecock. **2.** A game in which a shuttlecock is battered back and forth: also **battledore and shuttlecock**. — *v.t. & v.i.* **·dored**, **·dor·ing** To volley or hurl back and forth. [? < Provençal *batedor*, an implement for beating laundry]

battle fatigue *Psychiatry* Combat fatigue.

bat·tle·field (bat'l·fēld') *n.* The terrain on which a battle is fought. Also **bat'tle·ground'**.

bat·tle·ment (bat'l·mənt) *n.* A parapet indented along its upper line. [< OF < *ba(s)tillier* to fortify]

battle royal **1.** A fight involving numerous combatants. **2.** A protracted, vehement altercation.

bat·tle·ship (bat'l·ship') *n. Naval* A warship of great size, belonging to the class with heaviest armor and armament.

bat·ty (bat'ē) *adj.* **·ti·er**, **·ti·est** *Slang* Crazy; odd.

bau·ble (bô'bəl) *n.* A worthless, showy trinket; gewgaw; toy. [< OF *baubel* toy, ? < L *bellus* pretty]

baulk (bôk), **baulk·y** (bô'kē) See BALK, BALKY.

baux·ite (bôk'sīt, bō'zīt) *n.* A white to red claylike substance containing aluminum oxide or hydroxide, the principal ore of aluminum. [after Les *Baux*, France]

Ba·var·i·an (bə·vâr'ē·ən) *adj.* Of or pertaining to Bavaria, its people, or their dialect. — *n.* **1.** A native or inhabitant of Bavaria. **2.** The High German dialect spoken in Bavaria.

bawd (bôd) *n.* The keeper of a brothel. [ME *bawde*]

bawd·y (bô'dē) *adj.* **bawd·i·er**, **bawd·i·est** Obscene; indecent. — **bawd'i·ly** *adv.* — **bawd'i·ness** *n.*

bawd·y·house (bô'dē·hous') *n.* A brothel.

bawl (bôl) *v.t.* **1.** To call out noisily; bellow. **2.** To cry for sale. — *v.i.* **3.** To cry or sob noisily. — **to bawl out** *U.S. Slang* To berate; scold. — *n.* A loud outcry. [Cf. Med.L *baulare* to bark and ON *baula* to low, moo] — **bawl'er** *n.*

bay[1] (bā) *n.* A body of water partly enclosed by land; an inlet of the sea. [< OF *baie* < LL *baia*]

bay[2] (bā) *n.* **1.** *Archit.* **a** A bay window. **b** A principal part or division of a structure. **c** An extension or wing of a building. **2.** Any opening or recess in a wall. **3.** *Aeron.* A compartment in an aircraft. [< OF < L *badare* to gape]

bay[3] (bā) *adj.* Reddish brown: said esp. of horses. — *n.* **1.** A reddish brown color. **2.** A horse (or other animal) of this color. [< F *bai* < L *badius*]

bay[4] (bā) *n.* **1.** A deep bark or cry, as of dogs in hunting. **2.** The position of or as of a hunted animal forced to turn and fight. **3.** The condition of being kept off by or as by one's quarry. — **at bay** **1.** Unable to escape; cornered. **2.** Kept off, as by one's quarry. — *v.i.* **1.** To utter a deep-throated, prolonged bark, as a hound. — *v.t.* **2.** To utter with or as with such a bark. **3.** To pursue or beset with barking. **4.** To bring to bay. [< OF < L *badare* to gape]

bay[5] (bā) *n.* **1.** A laurel wreath, bestowed as a garland of honor, esp. on a poet. **2.** *pl.* Fame; renown. **3.** The bayberry. **4.** Any of several plants resembling the laurels. [< F *baie* < L *bacca* berry]

bay·ber·ry (bā'ber'ē, -bər·ē) *n. pl.* **·ries** **1.** A tree or shrub having aromatic berries, as the wax myrtle or laurel; also, its fruit. **2.** A tropical tree yielding an oil used in bay rum.

bay leaf The leaf of the laurel, used as a cooking herb.

bay·o·net (bā'ə·nit, -net, bā'ə·net') *n.* A daggerlike weapon attachable to the muzzle of a firearm, used in close fighting. — *v.t.* **·net·ed**, **·net·ing** To stab or pierce with a bayonet. [< F after *Bayonne*, France, where first made]

bay·ou (bī'ōō) *n. U.S.* A marshy inlet or outlet of a lake, river, etc. [< dial. F < Choctaw *bayuk* small stream]

Bayou State Nickname of Mississippi.

bay rum An aromatic liquid used in medicines and cosmetics, originally distilled from the leaves of the bayberry, but now also made from alcohol, water, and essential oils.

Bay State Nickname of Massachusetts.

bay window **1.** A window structure projecting from the wall of a building and forming a recess within. **2.** *Slang* A protruding belly, as of a fat person.

ba·zaar (bə·zär') *n.* **1.** An Oriental market or street of shops. **2.** A shop or store for the sale of miscellaneous wares. **3.** A sale of miscellaneous articles, as for charity. Also **ba·zar'**. [Ult. < Persian *bāzār* market]

ba·zoo·ka (bə·zōō'kə) *n. Mil.* A tubular, portable weapon that fires an explosive rocket, used against tanks and fortifications. [from *bazooka*, a comical musical instrument]

be (bē, *unstressed* bi) *v.i.* **been**, **be·ing** Present indicative: I **am**, he, she, it **is**, we, you, they **are**; past indicative: I, he, she, it **was**, we, you, they **were**; present subjunctive: **be**; past subjunctive: **were**; archaic forms: thou **art** (present), thou **wast** or **wert** (past) **1.** As the substantive verb, *be* is used to mean: **a** To have existence, truth, or actuality: God *is*; There *are* bears in the zoo. **b** To take place; happen: The party *is* today. **c** To stay or continue: She *was* here for one week. **d** To belong; befall: a subjunctive use, often with *to* or *unto*: Joy *be* unto you. **2.** As a copulative verb *be* forms a link between the subject and predicate nominative or qualifying word or phrase in sentences, and also forms infinitive and participial phrases: George *is* my friend; He *is* sick; the pleasure of *being* here. **3.** As an auxiliary verb *be* is used: **a** With the present participle of other verbs to express continuous or progressive action: I *am* working. **b** With the past participle of transitive verbs to form the passive voice: He *was* injured. **c** With the past participle of intransitive verbs to form the perfect tense: Christ *is* come; I *am* finished. **d** With the infinitive or present participle to express purpose, duty, possibility, futurity, etc.: We *are* to start on Monday.

be- *prefix* Used to form words from nouns, adjectives, and verbs with the following meanings: **1.** (*from verbs*) Around; all over; throughout; as in: **bedrape; befinger**. **2.** (*from verbs*) Completely; thoroughly; as in: **bedrench; bemuddle**. **3.** (*from verbs*) Off; away from; as in: **behead**. **4.** (*from intransitive verbs*) About; at; on; over; against; for; as in: **becrawl; bethunder**. **5.** (*from adjectives and nouns*) To make; cause to be; as in: **becripple; bedirty**. **6.** (*from nouns*) To provide with; affect by; cover with; as in: **becarpet; bejewel**. **7.** (*from nouns*, in the form of participial adjectives) Furnished with; as in: **bechained; beflowered**. [OE *be-*, *bi-*, var. of *bī* near, by]

beach (bēch) *n.* The sloping shore of a body of water; strand; esp., a sandy shore used for swimming. — **Syn.** See SHORE[1]. — *v.t. & v.i.* To drive or haul up (a boat or ship) on a beach; strand. [Origin unknown]

beach·comb·er (bēch′kō′mər) *n.* **1.** A vagrant living on what he can find or beg around the wharves and beaches of ports. **2.** A long wave rolling upon the beach.
beach·head (bēch′hed′) *n. Mil.* An area on a hostile shore established by an advance force for the landing of troops and supplies and the launching of subsequent operations.
bea·con (bē′kən) *n.* **1.** A signal; esp., a signal fire or light on a hill, building, etc., intended as a warning or guide. **2.** A light, buoy, etc., set on a shore, shoal, or similar place to guide or warn mariners. **3.** A lighthouse. **4.** Anything that warns or signals. **5.** *Aeron.* A mark, light, or radio transmitter used to plot flight courses. — *v.t.* **1.** To furnish with or guide by a beacon. — *v.i.* **2.** To shine as a beacon. [OE *bēacn* sign, signal. Akin to BECKON.]
bead (bēd) *n.* **1.** A small, usually round, piece of glass, wood, stone, etc., pierced for stringing on thread or attaching to fabric as decoration. **2.** *pl.* A string of beads; necklace. **3.** *pl.* A rosary. **4.** Any small body resembling a bead, as a bubble or a drop of liquid. **5.** Froth; foam. **6.** A small knob used as the front sight of a gun. **7.** *Archit.* A molding composed of a row of half-oval ornaments resembling a string of beads. — **to draw a bead on** To take careful aim at. — **to tell** (**count,** or **say**) **one's beads** To recite prayers with a rosary. — *v.t.* **1.** To decorate with beads or beading. — *v.i.* **2.** To collect in beads or drops. [OE *gebed* prayer]
bead·ing (bē′ding) *n.* **1.** Ornamentation with beads. **2.** Material consisting of or ornamented with beads. **3.** *Archit.* A bead, or beads collectively.
bea·dle (bēd′l) *n.* In the Church of England, a lay officer who ushers or keeps order. [< OF *bedel* messenger]
beads·man (bēdz′mən) *n. pl.* **·men** (-mən) One who prays for another. — **heads/wom/an** *n.fem.*
bead·work (bēd′wûrk′) *n.* **1.** Decorative work made with or of beads. **2.** *Archit.* A bead.
bead·y (bē′dē) *adj.* **bead·i·er, bead·i·est 1.** Small and glittering: *beady* eyes. **2.** Covered with beads. **3.** Foamy.
bea·gle (bē′gəl) *n.* A small, short-coated hound with short legs and drooping ears. [ME *begle*]
beak (bēk) *n.* **1.** The horny, projecting mouth parts of birds. **2.** A beaklike part or organ, as the horny jaws of turtles. **3.** Something resembling a bird's beak, as the spout of a pitcher. **4.** *Slang* A person's nose. [< F *bec* < LL *beccus*] — **beaked** *adj.* — **beak/less** *adj.* — **beak/like** *adj.*

BEAGLE
(About 15 inches high at shoulder)

beak·er (bē′kər) *n.* **1.** A large, wide-mouthed drinking cup or goblet. **2.** A cylindrical, flat-bottomed vessel of glass, aluminum, etc., with a lip for pouring, used in chemical analysis, etc. **3.** The contents or capacity of a beaker. [< ON *bikarr*; spelling infl. by *beak*]
beam (bēm) *n.* **1.** A long, heavy piece of wood, metal, or stone, shaped for use. **2.** A horizontal piece forming part of the frame of a building or other structure. **3.** *Naut.* **a** One of the heavy pieces of timber or iron set across a vessel to support the decks and stay the sides. **b** The greatest width of a vessel. **c** The shank of an anchor. **4.** The bar of a balance; also, the balance. **5.** A ray of light, or a group of nearly parallel rays. **6.** *Aeron.* A radio beam. **7.** The area of maximum sound clarity in front of a microphone. **8.** The horizontal piece in a plow to which the share and handles are attached. **9.** The widest part of anything. **10.** *Slang* The hips: broad in the *beam*. — **off the beam 1.** *Aeron.* Not following the radio beam. **2.** *Informal* On the wrong track; wrong. — **on the beam 1.** *Naut.* In a direction at right angles with the keel; abeam. **2.** *Aeron.* Following the radio beam. **3.** *Informal* In the right direction; just right; correct. — *v.t.* **1.** To send out in beams or rays. **2.** *Telecom.* To aim or transmit (a signal) in a specific direction. **3.** *Aeron.* To guide (an airplane) by radio beams. — *v.i.* **4.** To emit light. **5.** To smile or grin radiantly. [OE *bēam* tree] — **beam/less** *adj.* — **beam/like** *adj.*
beam-ends (bēm′endz′) *n.pl. Naut.* The ends of a ship's beams. — **on her beam-ends** Of a ship, tipped over so far as to be in danger of capsizing.
beam·ing (bē′ming) *adj.* Radiant; bright; smiling; cheerful. — **beam/ing·ly** *adv.*
beam·y (bē′mē) *adj.* **beam·i·er, beam·i·est 1.** Sending out beams of light; radiant. **2.** Like a beam; massive.
bean (bēn) *n.* **1.** The oval, edible seed of any of various leguminous plants. **2.** A plant that bears beans. **3.** Any of several beanlike seeds or plants. **4.** *Slang* The head. **5.** *Brit. Slang* Person; chap. — *v.t. U.S. Slang* To hit on the head. [OE *bēan*]
bean·ie (bē′nē) *n.* A small, brimless cap.
bean·pole (bēn′pōl′) *n.* **1.** A tall pole for a bean plant to climb on. **2.** *Slang* A tall, thin person.

bear[1] (bâr) *v.* **bore′** (*Archaic* **bare**), **borne, bear·ing** *v.t.* **1.** To support; hold up. **2.** To carry; convey. **3.** To show visibly; carry. **4.** To conduct or guide. **5.** To spread; disseminate. **6.** To hold in the mind; maintain or entertain. **7.** To suffer or endure; undergo. **8.** To accept or acknowledge; assume, as responsibility or expense. **9.** To produce; give birth to. ◆ In this sense, the participial form in the passive is **born,** except when followed by *by*. **10.** To conduct or comport (oneself). **11.** To manage or carry (oneself or a part of oneself). **12.** To move by pressing against; drive. **13.** To render; give: to *bear* witness. **14.** To be able to withstand; allow. **15.** To have or stand in (comparison or relation) with *to*: What relation does his story *bear* to yours? **16.** To possess as a right or power: to *bear* title. — *v.i.* **17.** To rest heavily; lean; press. **18.** To endure patiently; suffer. **19.** To produce fruit or young. **20.** To carry burdens. **21.** To move or lie in a certain direction; be pointed or aimed. **22.** To be relevant; have reference. — **to bear down 1.** To force down; overpower or overcome. **2.** To exert oneself; make an effort. — **to bear down on** (or **upon**) **1.** To put pressure on; press hard on. **2.** To make a great effort. **3.** To approach, especially another vessel from windward. — **to bear out** To support; confirm; justify. — **to bear up** To keep up strength and spirits. [OE *beran* to carry, wear]
bear[2] (bâr) *n.* **1.** A large mammal having a massive, thickly furred body and a very short tail, as the grizzly bear, polar bear, etc. ◆ Collateral adjective: *ursine.* **2.** Any of various other animals resembling or likened to the bear: ant *bear.* **3.** A gruff, ill-mannered, or clumsy person. **4.** A speculator, esp. one in the stock exchange, who seeks to depress prices or who sells in the belief that a decline in prices is likely: opposed to *bull.* — **the Bear** Russia. — *adj.* Of, pertaining to, or caused by stock-market bears, or a decline in prices. — *v.t.* To endeavor to depress the price of (stocks etc.) by selling or offering to sell. [OE *bera*]
bear·a·ble (bâr′ə·bəl) *adj.* Capable of being borne; endurable. — **bear/a·ble·ness** *n.* — **bear/a·bly** *adv.*
bear·cat (bâr′kat′) *n.* The panda (def. 1).
beard (bird) *n.* **1.** The hair on a man's face, esp. on the chin, usu. excluding the mustache. **2.** Any similar growth or appendage, as the long hair on the chin of some animals. **3.** *Bot.* An awn. For illus. see WHEAT. — *v.t.* **1.** To take by the beard; pull the beard of. **2.** To defy courageously. **3.** To furnish with a beard. [OE] — **beard/ed** *adj.* — **beard/less** *adj.* — **beard/less·ness** *n.* — **beard/like** *adj.*
bear·er (bâr′ər) *n.* **1.** One who or that which bears, carries, or upholds. **2.** A person who bears or presents for payment a check, money order, etc. **3.** A tree or vine producing fruit. **4.** A carrier or porter. **5.** A pallbearer.
bear·ing (bâr′ing) *n.* **1.** Manner of conducting or carrying oneself; deportment. **2.** The act, capacity, or period of producing. **3.** That which is produced; crops; yield. **4.** Endurance. **5.** *Mech.* A part on which something rests, or in which a pin, journal, etc., turns. **6.** The position or direction of an object or point. **7.** *Often pl.* The situation of an object relative to that of another, or of other points or places: to lose one's *bearings.* **8.** Reference or relation.
bear·ish (bâr′ish) *adj.* **1.** Like a bear; rough; surly. **2.** Tending toward, counting on, or causing a depression in the price of stocks. — **bear/ish·ly** *adv.* — **bear/ish·ness** *n.*
bear·skin (bâr′skin′) *n.* The skin of a bear, or a coat or robe made of it.
beast (bēst) *n.* **1.** Any creature except man; esp., any large, quadruped. **2.** Animal characteristics or animal nature. **3.** A cruel, rude, or filthy person. [< OF < LL < L *bestia* beast] — **beast/like** *adj.*
beast·ly (bēst′lē) *adj.* **·li·er, ·li·est 1.** Resembling a beast; bestial. **2.** *Informal* Disagreeable or unpleasant; nasty. — *adv. Brit. Slang* Very. — **beast/li·ness** *n.*
beat (bēt) *v.* **beat, beat·en** or **beat, beat·ing** *v.t.* **1.** To strike repeatedly; pound. **2.** To punish by repeated blows; thrash; whip. **3.** To dash or strike against. **4.** To shape or break by blows. **5.** To make flat by tramping or treading. **6.** To make, as one's way, by or as by blows. **7.** To flap; flutter, as wings. **8.** To stir or mix rapidly so as to make lighter or frothier: to *beat* eggs. **9.** To mark or measure as with a baton: to *beat* time. **10.** To sound (a signal), as on a drum. **11.** To hunt over; search. **12.** To subdue or defeat; master. **13.** To surpass; be superior to. **14.** *Informal* To baffle; perplex: it *beats* me. **15.** *U.S. Slang* To defraud; swindle. — *v.i.* **16.** To strike repeated blows. **17.** To strike or smite as if with blows: The sound *beat* on my ears. **18.** To throb; pulsate. **19.** To give forth sound, as when tapped or struck. **20.** To sound a signal, as on a drum. **21.** *Physics* To alternate in intensity so as to pulsate. **22.** To be adaptable to beating. **23.** To hunt through underbrush, etc., as for game. **24.** To win a victory or contest. — **to beat about** To search by one means and then another. — **to beat**

about the bush To approach a subject in a roundabout way. **— to beat a retreat** 1. To give a signal for retreat, as by the beat of drums. 2. To turn back; flee. **— to beat down** To force or persuade (a seller) to accept a lower price. **— to beat it** *Slang* To depart hastily. **— to beat off** To repel; drive away. **— to beat up** *Informal* To thrash thoroughly. **—** *n.* 1. A stroke or blow. 2. A regular stroke, or its sound; pulsation; throb. 3. *Physics* A regularly recurring pulsation or throb heard when two tones not quite in unison are sounded together, and caused by the interference of sound waves. 4. *Music* a A regular pulsation; the basic unit of musical time. b The gesture or symbol designating this. 5. The measured sound of verse; rhythm. 6. A round, line, or district regularly traversed, as by a sentry, policeman, or reporter. 7. *U.S.* A subdivision of a county, esp. in the South. 8. In newspaper slang, a scoop. 9. *U.S. Slang* A deadbeat. 10. A beatnik. **— on the beat** *Music* In tempo. **—** *adj.* 1. *U.S. Informal* Fatigued; worn out. 2. *Informal* Of or pertaining to beatniks. [OE *bēatan*] **— beat′er** *n.*

beat·en (bēt′n) Past participle of BEAT. **—** *adj.* 1. Shaped or made thin by beating. 2. Mixed by beating. 3. Worn by use; customary. 4. Defeated; baffled. 5. Exhausted.

be·a·tif·ic (bē′ə-tif′ik) *adj.* Imparting or expressing bliss or blessedness. **— be′a·tif′i·cal·ly** *adv.*

be·at·i·fi·ca·tion (bē-at′ə-fi-kā′shən) *n.* 1. The act of beatifying, or the state of being beatified. 2. In the Roman Catholic Church, an act of the pope declaring a deceased person beatified, usually the last step toward canonization.

be·at·i·fy (bē-at′ə-fī) *v.t.* **·fied, ·fy·ing** 1. To make supremely happy. 2. In the Roman Catholic Church, to declare as blessed and worthy of public honor, by an act of the pope. 3. To exalt above others. [< F < LL < L *beatus* happy + *facere* to make]

beat·ing (bē′ting) *n.* 1. The act of one who or that which beats. 2. Punishment by blows; flogging. 3. Pulsation; throbbing, as of the heart. 4. A defeat.

be·at·i·tude (bē-at′ə-tood, -tyood) *n.* Supreme blessedness or felicity. **— the Beatitudes** Eight declarations made by Jesus in the Sermon on the Mount. *Matt.* v 3–11. [< MF < L *beatitudo* blessedness]

beat·nik (bēt′nik) *n. Informal* One who acts and dresses in a manner calculated to be unconventional.

beau (bō) *n. pl.* **beaus** or **beaux** (bōz) 1. A sweetheart or lover of a girl or woman. 2. A dandy. [< OF, var. of *bel* < L *bellus* fine, pretty] **— beau′ish** *adj.*

Beau Brum·mell (brum′əl) A dandy or fop. [after George "*Beau*" *Brummell*, 1778–1840, English dandy]

Beau·fort scale (bō′fərt) *Meteorol.* A scale of wind velocities, ranging from 0 (calm) to 12 (hurricane). [after Sir Francis *Beaufort*, 1774–1857, British admiral]

beau monde (bō mônd′) *French* The fashionable world.

beau·te·ous (byoo′tē-əs) *adj.* Beautiful. **— beau′te·ous·ly** *adv.* **— beau′te·ous·ness** *n.*

beau·ti·cian (byoo-tish′ən) *n.* One who works in or operates a beauty parlor.

beau·ti·ful (byoo′tə-fəl) *adj.* Possessing the qualities or presenting an appearance of beauty, as in form or grace. **— beau′ti·ful·ly** *adv.* **— beau′ti·ful·ness** *n.*

beau·ti·fy (byoo′tə-fī) *v.t. & v.i.* **·fied, ·fy·ing** To make or grow beautiful. **— beau′ti·fi·ca′tion** *n.* **— beau′ti·fied** *adj.* **— beau′ti·fi′er** *n.*

beau·ty (byoo′tē) *n. pl.* **·ties** 1. The quality of objects, sounds, ideas, etc., that pleases and gratifies, as by their harmony, pattern, excellence, or truth. 2. One who or that which is beautiful, esp. a woman. 3. A special grace or charm. [< OF *beaute*, ult. < L *bellus* handsome, fine]

beauty parlor An establishment where women may go for hairdressing, complexion care, or other cosmetic treatment. Also **beauty salon, beauty shop.**

beauty spot 1. A small patch or mark put on the face to set off the whiteness of the skin. 2. A mole or other natural mark resembling this. Also **beauty mark.**

beaux (bōz) Plural of BEAU.

beaux-arts (bō-zär′) *n.pl. French* The fine arts.

bea·ver[1] (bē′vər) *n.* 1. An amphibious rodent with a scaly, flat, oval tail and webbed hind feet, valued for its fur, and noted for its skill in damming shallow streams. 2. The fur of the beaver. 3. A high silk hat. [OE *beofor*]

bea·ver[2] (bē′vər) *n.* 1. A movable piece of medieval armor covering the lower face. 2. The visor of a helmet. 3. *Slang* A beard. [< OF *bavé* saliva]

bea·ver·board (bē′vər-bôrd′, -bōrd′) *n.* A light, stiff building material made of compressed or laminated wood pulp, used chiefly for walls and partitions.

Beaver State Nickname of Oregon.

be·calm (bi-käm′) *v.t.* 1. *Naut.* To make (a sailing vessel) motionless for lack of wind. 2. To make calm; quiet.

be·came (bi-kām′) Past tense of BECOME.

be·cause (bi-kôz′) *conj.* For the reason that; on account of the fact that; since. **— because of** By reason of; on account of. [ME *bi cause* by cause]

be·chance (bi-chans′, -chäns′) *v.t. & v.i.* **·chanced, ·chanc·ing** To befall; happen by chance.

beck (bek) *n.* A nod or other gesture of summons. **— at one's beck and call** Subject to one's slightest wish. **—** *v.t. & v.i.* To beckon. [Short for BECKON]

beck·on (bek′ən) *v.t. & v.i.* 1. To signal, direct, or summon by sign or gesture. 2. To entice or lure. **—** *n.* A summoning gesture; beck. [OE *bīecnan, bēacnian* to make signs to]

be·cloud (bē-kloud′) *v.t.* 1. To obscure with clouds; darken. 2. To confuse, as an issue: to *becloud* his senses.

be·come (bi-kum′) *v.* **·came, ·come, ·com·ing** *v.i.* 1. To come to be; grow to be. **—** *v.t.* 2. To be appropriate to; befit. 3. To be suitable to; show to advantage. **— become of** To be the condition or fate of: What *became of* him? [OE *becuman* to happen, come about]

be·com·ing (bi-kum′ing) *adj.* 1. Appropriate; suitable. 2. Pleasing; attractive. **—** *n.* A coming to be. **— be·com′ing·ly** *adv.* **— be·com′ing·ness** *n.*

bed (bed) *n.* 1. An article of furniture to rest or sleep on, consisting of a bedstead, mattress, spring, and bedclothes. 2. Any place or thing used for resting or sleeping. 3. A lodging, esp. for the night. 4. A heap or mass resembling a bed. 5. A plot of ground prepared for planting; also the plants themselves. 6. The ground at the bottom of a body of water. 7. A part or surface that serves as a foundation or support. 8. *Geol.* Any layer in a mass of stratified rock; a seam. **— to get up on the wrong side of the bed** To be irritable, grouchy, or cross. **— to put (or go) to bed** *U.S. Slang* To go to press; be printed. **—** *v.* **bed·ded, bed·ding** *v.t.* 1. To furnish with a bed. 2. To put to bed. 3. To make a bed for; provide with litter: often with *down*: to bed down cattle. 4. To set out or plant in a bed of earth. 5. To lay flat or arrange in layers: to *bed* oysters. 6. To place firmly; embed. **—** *v.i.* 7. To go to bed. 8. To form a closely packed layer; stratify. [OE] **— bed′der** *n.*

bed and board Lodging and meals.

be·daub (bi-dôb′) *v.t.* 1. To smear or daub; besmirch; soil. 2. To ornament vulgarly or excessively.

be·daz·zle (bi-daz′əl) *v.t.* **·zled, ·zling** To confuse or blind by dazzling.

bed·bug (bed′bug) *n.* A bloodsucking insect of reddish brown color, infesting houses and esp. beds.

bed·cham·ber (bed′chām′bər) *n.* A bedroom.

bed·clothes (bed′klōz′, -klōthz′) *n.pl.* Covering for a bed, as sheets, blankets, quilts, etc.

bed·ding (bed′ing) *n.* 1. Mattress and bedclothes. 2. Straw or other litter for animals to sleep on. 3. That which forms a bed or foundation. 4. *Geol.* Stratification of rocks.

be·deck (bi-dek′) *v.t.* To adorn.

be·dev·il (bi-dev′əl) *v.t.* **·iled** or **·illed, ·il·ing** or **·il·ling** 1. To treat diabolically; harass or torment. 2. To worry or confuse; bewilder. 3. To possess with or as with a devil; bewitch. 4. To spoil; corrupt. **— be·dev′il·ment** *n.*

be·dew (bi-doo′, -dyoo′) *v.t.* To moisten with dew.

bed·fel·low (bed′fel′ō) *n.* 1. One who shares a bed with another. 2. A companion; associate.

be·dim (bi-dim′) *v.t.* **·dimmed, ·dim·ming** To make dim.

bed·lam (bed′ləm) *n.* 1. A place or scene of noisy confusion. 2. An incoherent uproar. 3. A lunatic asylum. [after *Bedlam*, an old London hospital for the insane]

bed linen Sheets, pillowcases, etc., for beds.

Bed·ou·in (bed′oo-in) *n.* 1. One of the nomadic Arabs of Syria, Arabia, etc. 2. Any nomad or vagabond. **—** *adj.* 1. Of or pertaining to the Bedouins. 2. Roving; nomadic. Also spelled *Beduin*. [< F < Arabic *badāwin* desert dweller]

bed·pan (bed′pan′) *n.* 1. A shallow vessel to be used as a toilet by one confined to bed. 2. A warming pan.

be·drag·gle (bi-drag′əl) *v.t.* **·gled, ·gling** To make wet, soiled, or untidy, as by dragging through mire.

bed·rid·den (bed′rid′n) *adj.* Confined to bed. Also **bed′rid′.** [Earlier *bedrid* < OE *bedrida* < *bed* bed + *rida* rider]

bed·rock (bed′rok′) *n.* 1. *Geol.* The solid rock underlying the looser materials of the earth's surface. 2. The lowest level; bottom. 3. Fundamental principles; foundation.

bed·roll (bed′rōl′) *n.* Bedding rolled to facilitate carrying.

bed·room (bed′room′, -room′) *n.* A room for sleeping.

bed·side (bed′sīd′) *n.* The space beside a bed, especially of a sick person; the side of a bed. **—** *adj.* Placed beside a bed.

bed·sore (bed′sôr′, -sōr′) *n.* A sore caused by prolonged pressure against a bed, occurring among bedridden persons.

bed·spread (bed′spred′) *n.* A cloth covering for a bed, usually for ornament.

bed·spring (bed′spring′) *n.* The framework of springs supporting the mattress of a bed; also, any of such springs.

bed·stead (bed′sted′) *n.* A framework for supporting the springs and mattress of a bed.

bed·time (bed′tīm′) *n.* The time for retiring to bed.

Bed·u·in (bed′oo-in) See BEDOUIN.

bed-wet·ting (bed′wet′ing) *n.* Urination in bed.

bee (bē) *n.* 1. A four-winged insect feeding largely upon nectar and pollen, esp. the honey bee. 2. *U.S.* A social gathering for work, competition, entertainment, etc.: a quilting *bee*. **— to have a bee in one's bonnet** To be excessively concerned about or obsessed with one idea. [OE *bēo*]

bee·bread (bē′bred′) *n.* A mixture of pollen and certain proteins stored by bees for food.

beech (bēch) *n.* **1.** A tree of temperate regions with smooth, ash-gray bark, and bearing an edible nut. **2.** The wood of the beech. **3.** A tree similar to the beech, as the hornbeam. [OE *bēce*] **— beech′en** *adj.*

beech mast Beechnuts.

beech·nut (bēch′nut′) *n.* The edible nut of the beech.

beef (bēf) *n.* *pl.* **beeves** (bēvz) or **beefs** *for def. 2*; **beefs** *for def. 4* **1.** The flesh of a slaughtered adult bovine animal. **2.** Any adult bovine animal, as an ox, cow, steer, bull, etc., fattened for the table. **3.** *Informal* Muscle; brawn. **4.** *U.S. Slang* A complaint. — *v.i. U.S. Slang* To complain. [< OF < L *bos, bovis* ox]

beef·eat·er (bēf′ē′tər) *n* **1.** A yeoman of the guard, or one of the similarly uniformed warders of the Tower of London. **2.** *Slang* An Englishman.

beef·steak (bēf′stāk′) *n.* A slice of beef suitable for broiling.

beef tea A beverage made by boiling lean beef or made from a beef extract.

beef·y (bē′fē) *adj.* **beef·i·er, beef·i·est 1.** Muscular and heavy. **2.** Beeflike. **3.** Stolid. **— beef′i·ness** *n.*

bee·hive (bē′hīv′) *n.* **1.** A hive for a colony of honeybees. **2.** A place full of activity.

Beehive State Nickname of UTAH.

bee·keep·er (bē′kē′pər) *n.* One who keeps bees; an apiarist.

bee·line (bē′līn′) *n.* The shortest course from one place to another: chiefly in the phrase **to make a beeline for.**

Be·el·ze·bub (bē·el′zə·bub) **1.** The prince of the demons; the devil. **2.** Any devil. [< Hebrew *ba'alzebūb* lord of flies]

been (bin, *Brit.* bēn) Past participle of BE.

beep (bēp) *n.* A short, piercing sound used as a signal or warning. — *v.i.* **1.** To make such a sound. — *v.t.* **2.** To sound (a horn). **3.** To transmit (a message) by beeps. [Imit.]

beer (bir) *n.* **1.** An alcoholic fermented beverage made from malt and hops. **2.** A beverage made from the roots, etc., of various plants: ginger *beer* [OE *bēor*]

Beer·she·ba (bir·shē′bə, bir′shi·ba) An ancient city in southwest Palestine.

beer·y (bir′ē) *adj.* **beer·i·er, beer·i·est 1.** Of or like beer. **2.** Influenced by beer; tipsy. **— beer′i·ness** *n.*

beest·ings (bēs′tingz) *n.pl. & sing.* The first milk from a cow after calving; the colostrum: also *biestings*. [OE *bēost*]

bees·wax (bēz′waks′) *n.* A yellow fatty solid secreted by honeybees for honeycombs, used in medicine and the arts.

beet (bēt) *n.* **1.** The fleshy succulent root of a biennial herb of the goosefoot family, esp. the common or red beet, and the sugar beet. **2.** The plant itself. [OE < L *beta*]

bee·tle[1] (bēt′l) *n.* **1.** An insect having biting mouth parts and hard, horny front wings that serve as a cover for the posterior wings when at rest. **2.** Loosely, any insect resembling a beetle. — *adj.* Jutting; overhanging: a *beetle* brow: also **beet′ling.** — *v.i.* **tled, ·tling** To jut out; overhang. [OE *bittan* to bite]

bee·tle[2] (bēt′l) *n.* **1.** A heavy instrument, usu. with a wooden head, for ramming paving stones, driving wedges, etc. **2.** A pestle or mallet for pounding, etc. — *v.t.* **·tled, ·tling** To beat or stamp with a beetle. [OE *bīetel* mallet]

bee·tle-browed (bēt′l·broud′) *adj.* **1.** Having prominent, overhanging eyebrows. **2.** Scowling; frowning.

beet sugar Sucrose obtained from the sugar beet.

beeves (bēvz) Alternative plural of BEEF.

be·fall (bi·fôl′) *v.* **·fell, ·fall·en, ·fall·ing** *v.i.* **1.** To come about; happen; occur. — *v.t* **2.** To happen to. [OE *be-f(e)allan* to fall]

be·fit (bi·fit′) *v.t.* **·fit·ted, ·fit·ting** To be suited to; be appropriate for. **— be·fit′ting** *adj.* **— be·fit′ting·ly** *adv.*

be·fit·ting (bi·fit′ing) *adj.* Becoming; proper; suitable. **— be·fit·ting·ly** *adv.*

be·fog (bi·fôg′, -fog′) *v.t* **·fogged, ·fog·ging 1.** To envelop in fog. **2.** To confuse; obscure.

be·fore (bi·fôr′, -fōr′) *adv.* **1.** In front; ahead. **2.** Preceding in time; previously. **3.** Earlier; sooner. — *prep.* **1.** In front of; ahead of. **2.** Earlier or sooner than. **3.** In advance of in development, rank, etc. **4.** In preference to; rather than. **5.** In the presence of; face to face with. **6.** Under the consideration or cognizance of: the issue *before* you. **7.** Ahead of; awaiting. — *conj.* **1.** Previous to the time when. **2.** Rather than. [OE *beforan* in front of]

be·fore·hand (bi·fôr′hand′, -fōr′-) *adv. & adj.* In anticipation or advance; ahead of time.

be·foul (bi·foul′) *v.t* To make foul or dirty; sully.

be·friend (bi·frend′) *v.t.* To act as a friend to; help.

be·fud·dle (bi·fud′l) *v.t.* **·dled, ·dling** To confuse, as with liquor or glib arguments.

beg (beg) *v.* **begged, beg·ging** *v.t.* **1.** To ask for in charity: to *beg* alms. **2.** To ask for or of earnestly; beseech: to *beg* forgiveness. — *v.i.* **3.** To ask alms or charity; be a beggar. **4.** To ask humbly or earnestly. **— to beg off** To ask to be excused or released (from an engagement, obligation, etc.). **— to beg the question 1.** To take for granted the very matter in dispute. **2.** Loosely, to avoid answering directly. **— to go begging** To fail of acceptance, adoption, or use. [? < AF < OF *begard* mendicant friar]

be·gan (bi·gan′) Past tense of BEGIN.

be·get (bi·get′) *v.t.* **·got** (*Archaic* ·gat), **·got·ten** or **·got, ·get·ting 1.** To procreate; be the father of. **2.** To cause to be; occasion. [OE *begitan*] **— be·get′ter** *n.*

beg·gar (beg′ər) *n.* **1.** One who asks alms, or lives by begging. **2.** A poor person; pauper. **3.** A rogue; rascal. — *v.t.* **1.** To reduce to want; impoverish. **2.** To exhaust the resources of: It *beggars* analysis. [< OF *begard* mendicant friar] **— beg′gar·dom, beg′gar·hood** *n.*

beg·gar·ly (beg′ər·lē) *adj.* Appropriate for a beggar; miserably poor; mean; sordid. **— beg′gar·li·ness** *n.*

be·gin (bi·gin′) *v.* **·gan, ·gun, gin·ning** *v.i.* **1.** To start to do something; take the first step; commence. **2.** To come into being; arise. — *v.t.* **3.** To do the first act or part of; start to do. **4.** To give origin to; start; originate. [OE *beginnan*]

be·gin·ner (bi·gin′ər) *n.* **1.** One beginning to learn a trade, study a subject, etc.; a novice; tyro. **— Syn.** See NOVICE. **2.** One who begins or originates; a founder.

be·gin·ning (bi·gin′ing) *n.* **1.** The act of starting; commencement. **2.** The point in time at which a thing begins. **3.** Source or first cause; origin. **4.** The first part. **5.** *Usually pl.* The first or rudimentary stage. — *adj.* **1.** First; opening: the *beginning* chapter. **2.** Elementary; introductory: a *beginning* course in physics.

be·gird (bi·gûrd′) *v.t.* **·girt** or **·gird·ed, ·gird·ing** To gird; encircle. [OE *begyrdan*]

be·gon·ia (bi·gōn′yə) *n.* A plant having brilliantly colored leaves and showy flowers. [after Michel *Bégon*, 1638–1710, French colonial administrator]

be·got (bi·got′) Past tense and past participle of BEGET.

be·got·ten (bi·got′n) Alternative past participle of BEGET.

be·grime (bi·grīm′) *v.t.* **·grimed, ·grim·ing** To soil.

be·grudge (bi·gruj′) *v.t.* **·grudged, ·grudg·ing 1.** To envy one the possession or enjoyment of (something). **2.** To give or grant reluctantly. **— be·grudg′ing·ly** *adv.*

be·guile (bi·gīl′) *v.t.* **·guiled, ·guil·ing 1.** To deceive; mislead by guile. **2.** To cheat; defraud: with *of* or *out of*. **3.** To while away pleasantly, as time. **4.** To charm; divert. **— be·guile′ment** *n.* **— be·guil′er** *n*

be·gum (bē′gəm) *n.* A Moslem princess, or woman of rank in India. [< Hind. < Turkish *bigim* princess]

be·gun (bi·gun′) Past participle of BEGIN.

be·half (bi·haf′, -häf′) *n.* The interest, part, or defense: usu. preceded by *in* or *on* and followed by *of*. **— Syn.** See SAKE. [OE *be healfe* by the side (of)]

be·have (bi·hāv′) *v.* **·haved, ·hav·ing** *v.i* **1.** To act; conduct oneself or itself. **2.** To comport oneself properly. **3.** To react to stimuli or environment. — *v.t.* **4.** To conduct (oneself), esp. in a proper or suitable manner. [ME *behaven = be- + haven* to hold oneself, act]

be·hav·ior (bi·hāv′yər) *n.* **1.** Manner of conducting oneself; demeanor; deportment. **2.** The way a person, substance, machine, etc., acts under given circumstances. Also *Brit.* **be·hav′iour.**

be·hav·ior·ism (bi·hāv′yər·iz′əm) *n.* *Psychol.* The theory that the behavior of animals and man is determined by measurable external and internal stimuli acting independently. **— be·hav′ior·ist** *n.* **— be·hav′ior·is′tic** *adj.*

be·head (bi·hed′) *v.t.* To decapitate. [OE *behēafdian*]

be·held (bi·held′) Past tense and past participle of BEHOLD.

be·he·moth (bi·hē′məth, bē′ə-) *n.* **1.** In the Bible, a huge beast. **2.** Anything large. [< Hebrew *bĕhēmāh* beast]

be·hest (bi·hest′) *n.* An authoritative request; command. [OE *behǣs* promise, vow]

be·hind (bi·hīnd′) *adv.* **1.** In, at, or toward the rear. **2.** In a place, condition, or time previously passed or departed from. **3.** In arrears; late. **4.** Slow, as a watch. — *prep.* **1.** At the back or rear of. **2.** Toward the rear of; backward from. **3.** In a place, condition, or time left by (one): Leave your problems *behind* you. **4.** After (a set time). **5.** Not so well advanced as; inferior to. **6.** Hidden by: What is *behind* your actions? **7.** Backing up; supporting: to be *behind* a venture. **8.** Following: the man *behind* me. **2.** In arrears. — *n. Informal* The buttocks. [OE *behindan*]

be·hind·hand (bi·hīnd′hand′) *adv. & adj.* **1.** Behind time; late. **2.** In arrears. **3.** Behind in development; backward.

be·hold (bi·hōld′) *v.t.* **·held, ·hold·ing** To look at or upon; observe. — *interj.* Look! See! [OE *beh(e)aldan* to hold] **— be·hold′er** *n.*

be·hold·en (bi-hōl/dən) *adj.* Indebted; obligated.
be·hoof (bi-hōōf/) *n.* That which benefits; advantage; use. [OE *behōf* advantage]
be·hoove (bi-hōōv/) *v.* **·hooved, ·hoov·ing** *v.t.* To be incumbent upon; be needful or right for: It *behooves* me to leave. Also *Brit.* **be·hove** (bi-hōv/). [OE *behōfian*]
beige (bāzh, bāj) *n.* The color of natural, undyed, unbleached wool; grayish tan. — *adj.* Of the color beige. [< F]
be·ing (bē/ing) Present participle of BE. — *n.* **1.** Existence, as opposed to nonexistence. **2.** Essential nature; substance: His whole *being* is musical. **3.** A living thing. **4.** A human individual; person. **5.** *Philos.* **a** Perfect or unqualified subsistence; essence. **b** That which has reality in time, space, or idea; anything that exists actually or potentially.
Be·ing (bē/ing) *n.* The Supreme Being; God.
bel (bel) *n. Physics* A unit expressing the logarithmic ratio of the values of two amounts of power: a measure of sound intensity. Compare DECIBEL. [after A. G. *Bell*]
be·la·bor (bi-lā/bər) *v.t.* **1.** To beat soundly; assail with blows; drub. **2.** To assail verbally. Also *Brit.* **be·la/bour.**
be·lat·ed (bi-lā/tid) *adj.* Late or too late. — **be·lat/ed·ly** *adv.* — **be·lat/ed·ness** *n.*
be·lay (bi-lā/) *v.t. & v.i.* **·layed, ·lay·ing 1.** *Naut.* To make fast (a rope) by winding on a cleat or pin (**belaying pin**). **2.** *Informal* To stop or hold: *Belay* there! [OE *belecgan*]
belch (belch) *v.i.* **1.** To eject wind noisily from the stomach through the mouth; eructate. **2.** To issue spasmodically from within; gush. **3.** To expel its contents violently, as a volcano. — *v.t.* **4.** To eject or throw forth violently; give vent to. — *n.* A belching. [OE *bealcian*] — **belch/er** *n.*
be·lea·guer (bi-lē/gər) *v.t.* **1.** To surround or shut in with an armed force. **2.** To surround; beset. [< Du. < *be·* about + *leger* camp] — **be·lea/guered** *adj.*
bel·fry (bel/frē) *n. pl.* **·fries 1.** A tower in which a bell is hung. **2.** The part of a tower or steeple containing the bell. [< OF *berfrei* tower, infl. by BELL[1]] — **bel/fried** *adj.*
Bel·gian (bel/jən, -jē·ən) *adj.* Of or pertaining to Belgium. — *n.* A native or citizen of Belgium.
Be·li·al (bē/lē·əl, bēl/yəl) In the Bible, the devil.
be·lie (bi-lī/) *v.t.* **·lied, ·ly·ing 1.** To misrepresent; disguise: His clothes *belie* his station. **2.** To prove false; contradict: Her actions *belied* her words. **3.** To fail to fulfill: to *belie* hopes. **4.** To slander. [OE *belēogan*] — **be·li/er** *n.*
be·lief (bi-lēf/) *n.* **1.** Acceptance of the truth or actuality of anything without certain proof. **2.** Something held to be true or actual. **3.** Trust in another person; confidence. **4.** A doctrine; creed. [ME < *bi·* complete + *leafe* belief]
— **Syn. 1.** *Belief* denotes acceptance with or without proof or strong emotional feelings. *Faith* is always the acceptance of something not susceptible of proof, while *conviction* is strong *belief* arising from a deep feeling of certainty.
be·lieve (bi-lēv/) *v.* **·lieved, ·liev·ing** *v.t.* **1.** To accept as true or real. **2.** To credit (a person) with veracity. **3.** To think; assume: with a clause as object. — *v.i.* **4.** To accept the truth, existence, worth, etc., of something: with *in*: to *believe* in freedom. **5.** To have confidence; place one's trust: with *in.* **6.** To have religious faith. **7.** To think: I cannot *believe* badly of you. [ME *beleven* < OE *gelēfan* to believe] — **be·liev/a·ble** *adj.* — **be·liev/er** *n.*
be·lit·tle (bi-lit/l) *v.t.* **·tled, ·tling** To cause to seem small or less; disparage; minimize.
bell[1] (bel) *n.* **1.** A hollow metallic instrument, usu. cup-shaped, which gives forth a ringing sound when struck. **2.** Anything in the shape of or suggesting a bell. **3.** The lower termination of a tubular musical instrument. **4.** A bell-shaped flower or corolla. **5.** *Naut.* A stroke on a bell every half hour to mark the periods of the watch; also, each of these periods. — *v.t.* **1.** To put a bell on. **2.** To shape like a bell. — *v.i.* **3.** To take the shape of a bell. [OE *belle*]
bell[2] (bel) *v.i.* To cry, as a hound, rutting stag, etc. — *n.* The cry of a deer, bittern, etc. [OE *bellan* to bellow]
bel·la·don·na (bel/ə·don/ə) *n.* **1.** A perennial herb with purple-red flowers and black berries: also called *deadly nightshade.* **2.** A poisonous alkaloid, as atropine, used in medicine. [< Ital. *bella donna,* lit., beautiful lady]
bell·boy (bel/boi/) *n. U.S.* A boy or man employed by a hotel to answer calls for service, carry suitcases, etc.
belle (bel) *n.* A beautiful and attractive woman or girl; a reigning social beauty. [< F, fem. of *beau* beautiful]
belles-let·tres (bel/let/rə) *n.pl.* Literature having esthetic appeal, rather than didactic or informational value; poetry, drama, fiction, etc. [< F, fine letters] — **bel·let·rist** (bel/let/rist) *n.* — **bel·le·tris·tic** (bel/lə·tris/tik) *adj.*
bell·flow·er (bel/flou/ər) *n.* The campanula.
bell·hop (bel/hop/) *n. U.S. Informal* A bellboy.
bel·li·cose (bel/ə·kōs) *adj.* Pugnacious. [< L *bellum* war] — **bel/li·cose/ly** *adv.* — **bel·li·cos/i·ty** (-kos/ə·tē) *n.*
bel·lig·er·ence (bə·lij/ər·əns) *n.* **1.** The state or quality of being warlike. **2.** Belligerency.
bel·lig·er·en·cy (bə·lij/ər·ən·sē) *n.* The status of a belligerent; condition of being at war.

bel·lig·er·ent (bə·lij/ər·ənt) *adj.* **1.** Warlike; bellicose. **2.** Engaged in or pertaining to warfare. — *n.* A person or nation engaged in warfare or fighting. [< F < L *belligerare* to wage war] — **bel·lig/er·ent·ly** *adv.*
bell·man (bel/mən) *n. pl.* **·men** (-mən) A town crier.
bel·low (bel/ō) *v.i.* **1.** To utter a loud, hollow cry, as a bull. **2.** To roar; shout: to *bellow* with anger. — *v.t.* **3.** To utter with a loud, roaring voice. — *n.* A loud, hollow cry or roar. [ME *belwen,* ? < OE *bylgian*] — **bel/low·er** *n.*
bel·lows (bel/ōz, *earlier* bel/əs) *n.pl. (construed as sing. or pl.)* **1.** An instrument with an air chamber and flexible sides, for drawing in air and expelling it under strong pressure through a nozzle or tube, used for blowing fires, filling the pipes of an organ, etc. **2.** The expansible portion of a camera. **3.** The lungs. [OE *belg, belig* bag]
bell·weth·er (bel/weth/ər) *n.* **1.** A ram with a bell about its neck, that leads a flock of sheep. **2.** One who leads a group, esp. a thoughtless, sheeplike group.
bel·ly (bel/ē) *n. pl.* **·lies 1.** The abdomen in vertebrates, or the underpart of other animals. **2.** The stomach. **3.** The protuberance of a bulging muscle. **4.** Any curved or protrusive line or surface: the *belly* of a sail. **5.** The front or underpart of anything. **6.** A deep, interior cavity: the *belly* of a ship. **7.** The curved front piece, containing the sound holes, of a violin, viola, etc. — *v.t. & v.i.* **·lied, ·ly·ing** To swell out or fill, as a sail. [OE *belg, belig* bag]
bel·ly·ache (bel/ē·āk/) *n.* A pain in the stomach or bowels. — *v.i.* **·ached, ·ach·ing** *Slang* To complain sullenly.
bel·ly·band (bel/ē·band/) *n.* A strap passing around the belly, as of a draft animal, to hold the shafts.
bel·ly·but·ton (bel/ē·but/n) *n. Informal* The navel.
bel·ly·ful (bel/ē·fŏŏl/) *n.* **1.** All that the stomach will hold. **2.** *Slang* All that one wants, or can endure.
be·long (bi-lông/, -long/) *v.i.* **1.** To be the property of someone: with *to.* **2.** To be a part of or an appurtenance to something: with *to.* **3.** To have a proper place; be suitable. **4.** To have relation or be a member. [ME < *be·* completely + *longen* to go along with]
be·long·ing (bi-lông/ing, -long/-) *n.* **1.** That which belongs to a person or thing. **2.** *pl.* Possessions; effects.
be·lov·ed (bi-luv/id, -luvd/) *adj.* Greatly loved. — *n.* One greatly loved. [Orig. pp. of obs. *belove* love dearly]
be·low (bi-lō/) *adv.* **1.** In or to a lower place. **2.** On or to a lower floor or deck. **3.** Farther down on a page or farther on in a list, book, etc. **4.** On earth, as distinguished from heaven. **5.** In or to hell or Hades. **6.** In a lower rank or authority. — *prep.* **1.** Lower than in place, grade, degree, etc. **2.** Unworthy of. [ME < *bi·* near + *loogh* low]
Bel·shaz·zar (bel-shaz/ər) In the Old Testament, the last ruler of Babylon.
belt (belt) *n.* **1.** A strap or band of leather or other flexible material worn about the waist to support clothing, tools, weapons, etc. **2.** Any band or strip resembling a belt. **3.** *Mech.* An endless band of flexible material for transmitting power from one wheel or shaft to another. **4.** A region or zone exhibiting some specific quality or condition: a storm *belt.* **5.** *Slang* A blow, as with the fist. — **below the belt** In violation of the rules; unfair. — **to tighten one's belt** To practice thrift. — *v.t.* **1.** To gird with or as with a belt. **2.** To fasten with a belt. **3.** To mark with belts or bands. **4.** To strike with a belt. **5.** *Informal* To give a blow to; strike. [OE < L *balteus* girdle]
be·lu·ga (bə·lōō/gə) *n.* A dolphin of Arctic and sub-Arctic seas: also called *white whale.* [< Russian *byelukha*]
bel·ve·dere (bel/və·dir/) *n. Archit.* A building, or an upper story of a building, that commands a view.
be·mire (bi-mīr/) *v.t.* **·mired, ·mir·ing 1.** To soil with mud or mire. **2.** To sink or stall in mud.
be·moan (bi-mōn/) *v.t.* **1.** To lament, as a loss. **2.** To express sympathy or pity for. — *v.i.* **3.** To mourn or lament. [OE *bemænan*] — **be·moan/a·ble** *adj.*
be·muse (bi-myōōz/) *v.t.* **·mused, ·mus·ing** To stupefy or preoccupy. — **be·mused/** *adj.*
bench (bench) *n.* **1.** A long seat of wood, marble, etc., with or without a back. **2.** A table for mechanical work. **3.** A seat or thwart in a boat. **4.** The seat for judges in a court. **5.** The judge, or the judges collectively. **6.** The office or dignity of a judge. **7.** A seat for persons sitting in an official capacity. **8.** Level, elevated ground along a shore or coast, or on a slope. — **on the bench** In sports, not participating. — *v.t.* **1.** To furnish with benches. **2.** To seat on a bench. **3.** In sports, to remove (a player) from a game. [OE *benc*]
bench mark A permanent mark, of known position and elevation, for use as a reference point in surveys, etc.
bench warrant *Law* A warrant issued by a judge, directing that an offender be brought into court.
bend[1] (bend) *v.* **bent** (*Archaic* **bend·ed**), **bend·ing** *v.t.* **1.** To cause to take the form of a curve; crook; bow. **2.** To direct or turn, as one's course, in a certain direction; deflect. **3.** To subdue or cause to yield. **4.** To apply closely; concentrate. **5.** *Naut.* To make fast, as a rope or sail. — *v.i.* **6.** To as-

sume the form of a curve. **7.** To take a certain direction. **8.** To bow in submission or respect. **9.** To apply one's energies: with *to.* — *n.* **1.** An act of bending, or the state of being bent. **2.** Something curved or bent; a curve or crook. **3.** *Naut.* A knot by which a rope is fastened to something else. [OE *bendan*]

bend[2] (bend) *n. Heraldry* A diagonal band across a shield from the upper left to the lower right. [OE *bend* strap]

bend·er (ben'dər) *n.* **1.** One who or that which bends. **2.** *U.S. Slang* A drinking spree. **3.** *Brit. Slang* A sixpence.

bends (bendz) *n.pl. Informal* Caisson disease.

bend sinister *Heraldry* A band drawn diagonally from the upper right to the lower left, used to indicate bastardy.

be·neath (bi-nēth') *adv.* **1.** In a lower place; below. **2.** underneath; directly below. — *prep.* **1.** Under; underneath; below. **2.** On the underside of; covered by. **3.** Under the power or sway of; subdued by. **4.** Lower in rank or station. **5.** Unworthy of; unbefitting. [OE *beneothan*]

ben·e·dic·i·te (ben'ə-dis'ə-tē) *n.* A blessing; grace or thanksgiving, esp. at table. — *interj.* Bless you!

Ben·e·dic·tine (ben'ə-dik'tin, -tēn; *for n. def. 3,* -tēn) *adj.* Pertaining to St. Benedict or his order. — *n.* **1.** A monk of the order established by St. Benedict at Subiaco, in Italy, about 530. **2.** A nun following the Benedictine rule. **3.** A brandy liqueur formerly made by French Benedictines.

ben·e·dic·tion (ben'ə-dik'shən) *n.* **1.** The act of blessing. **2.** The invocation of divine favor upon a person. [< LL *benedicere* to bless] — **ben·e·dic'tive, ben·e·dic·to·ry** (ben'ə-dik'tər·ē) *adj.*

Ben·e·dic·tus (ben'ə-dik'təs) *n.* **1.** Either of two canticles *Luke* i 68–71, and *Matt.* xxi 9: so called from their first word in Latin. **2.** A musical setting of either canticle.

ben·e·fac·tion (ben'ə-fak'shən) *n.* **1.** The act of giving help or conferring a benefit. **2.** A charitable deed; generous act. [< LL < *benefacere* to do well]

ben·e·fac·tor (ben'ə-fak'tər, ben'ə-fak'-) *n.* One who gives help or confers a benefit. — **ben'e·fac'tress** *n. fem.*

ben·e·fice (ben'ə-fis) *n. Brit. Eccl.* **1.** A church office endowed with funds or property; a living. **2.** The revenue of such an office. — *v.t.* **·ficed, ·fic·ing** To invest with a benefice. [OE < L *beneficium* favor] — **ben'e·ficed** *adj.*

be·nef·i·cence (bə-nef'ə-səns) *n.* **1.** The quality of being beneficent. **2.** A beneficent act or gift.

be·nef·i·cent (bə-nef'ə-sənt) *adj.* **1.** Bringing about or doing good. **2.** Resulting in benefit. — **be·nef'i·cent·ly** *adv.*

ben·e·fi·cial (ben'ə-fish'əl) *adj.* Producing benefit; advantageous; helpful. [< F *bénéficial* < LL < L *beneficium* favor] — **ben'e·fi'cial·ly** *adv.* — **ben'e·fi'cial·ness** *n.*

ben·e·fi·ci·ar·y (ben'ə-fish'ē-er'ē, -fish'ər-ē) *n. pl.* **·ar·ies** **1.** One who receives benefits or advantages. **2.** *Eccl.* The holder of a benefice. **3.** *Law* One entitled to the proceeds of property held in trust, or to whom an insurance policy or annuity is payable. [< L < *beneficium* favor]

ben·e·fit (ben'ə-fit) *n.* **1.** That which is helpful; advantage; profit. **2.** An act of kindness; charitable deed. **3.** A theatrical or musical performance given to raise funds for a worthy cause. *Often pl.* Payments made by an insurance company, etc — *v.* **·fit·ed, ·fit·ing** *v.t.* **1.** To be helpful or useful to. — *v.i.* **2.** To profit; gain advantage. [<OF < L *bene·facere* to do well]

benefit of clergy. 1. Churchly approval or sanction. **2.** Formerly, the privilege accorded to the clergy of demanding trial by an ecclesiastical rather than a secular court.

Ben·e·lux (ben'ə-luks) *n.* The economic union of Belgium, the Netherlands, and Luxembourg. [< BE(LGIUM) + NE(THERLANDS) + LUX(EMBOURG)]

be·nev·o·lence (bə-nev'ə-ləns) *n.* **1.** Disposition to do good; kindliness. **2.** Any act of kindness.

be·nev·o·lent (bə-nev'ə-lənt) *adj.* Disposed to do good; kindly. [< OF < L < *bene* well + *volens,* ppr. of *velle* to wish] — **be·nev'o·lent·ly** *adv.*

Ben·ga·li (ben-gô'lē, beng-) *adj.* Of or pertaining to Bengal. — *n.* **1.** A native of Bengal. **2.** The modern vernacular Indic language of Bengal.

ben·ga·line (beng'gə-lēn, beng'gə-lēn') *n.* A corded silk, wool, or rayon fabric of fine weave. [< BENGAL]

be·night·ed (bi-nī'tid) *adj.* **1.** Ignorant; unenlightened. **2.** Overtaken by night. — **be·night'ed·ness** *n.*

be·nign (bi-nīn') *adj.* **1.** Of a kind disposition; kindly. **2.** Gentle; mild. **3.** Favorable. **4.** *Med.* Favorable for recovery. [< OF < L *benignus* kindly] — **be·nign'ly** *adv.*

be·nig·nant (bi-nig'nənt) *adj.* **1.** Kind; gracious, esp.to inferiors. **2.** Favorable; benign. — **be·nig'nant·ly** *adv.*

be·nig·ni·ty (bi-nig'nə-tē) *n. pl.* **·ties 1.** The quality of being benign. Also **be·nig·nan·cy** (bi-nig'nən-sē). **2.** A gracious action or influence.

ben·i·son (ben'ə-zən, -sən) *n.* A benediction; blessing. [< OF < LL *benedictio, -onis* benediction]

Ben·ja·min (ben'jə-mən) In the Old Testament, the youngest son of Jacob and Rachel. *Gen* xxxv 18. — *n.* The tribe of Israel descended from him.

ben·ne (ben'ē) *n.* The sesame. [< Malay *bijen* seed]

bent[1] (bent) Past tense and past participle of BEND[1]. — *adj.* **1.** Not straight; crooked. **2.** Set in a course; resolved. — *n.* **1.** State of being bent or turned. **2.** A personal inclination or penchant. **3.** Limit of endurance or capacity: usually in the phrase **to the top of (one's) bent.**

bent[2] (bent) *n.* **1.** A stiff, wiry grass. Also **bent grass. 2.** The stiff flower stalk of various grasses. [OE *beonet*]

Ben·tham·ism (ben'thəm·iz'əm, -təm-) *n.* The philosophy of Jeremy Bentham, maintaining that the happiness of the greatest number is the supreme goal of society. — **Ben'tham·ite** (-īt) *n.*

be·numb (bi-num') *v.t.* **1.** To make numb; deaden. **2.** To stupefy. [OE *benumen* pp. of *beniman* to deprive.] — **be·numbed** (bi-numd') *adj.* — **be·numb'ment** *n.*

Ben·ze·drine (ben'zə-drēn, -drin) *n.* Proprietary name of a brand of amphetamine. Also **ben'ze·drine.**

ben·zene (ben'zēn, ben-zēn') *n. Chem.* A colorless, volatile, flammable, liquid hydrocarbon, C_6H_6, obtained chiefly from coal tar, used as a solvent and in organic synthesis.

ben·zine (ben'zēn, ben-zēn') *n.* A colorless, flammable liquid derived from crude petroleum and consisting of various hydrocarbons, used as a solvent, cleaner, and motor fuel. Also **ben'zin** (-zin), **ben·zo·line** (ben'zə-lēn).

ben·zo·ate (ben'zō·it, -āt) *n. Chem.* A salt of benzoic acid.

ben·zo·ic (ben·zō'ik) *adj.* **1.** Pertaining to or derived from benzoin. **2.** Pertaining to benzoic acid.

benzoic acid *Chem.* An aromatic compound, $C_7H_6O_2$, used as a food preservative and in medicine.

ben·zo·in (ben'zō·in, -zoin) *n.* **1.** A gum resin from various East Indian plants, used in medicine and as a perfume. [< F < Pg. or Ital. < Arabic *lubān jāwī* incense of Java]

ben·zol (ben'zōl, -zol) *n.* A grade of crude benzene.

Be·o·wulf (bā'ə·wŏŏlf) The princely hero of an Anglo-Saxon epic poem of the eighth century; also, the poem.

be·queath (bi·kwēth', -kwēth') *v.t.* **1.** *Law* To give (property) by will. **2.** To hand down. [OE *becwethan*]

be·quest (bi·kwest') *n.* The act of bequeathing, or that which is bequeathed. [ME *biqueste*]

be·rate (bi·rāt') *v.t.* **·rat·ed, ·rat·ing** To scold severely.

Ber·ber (bûr'bər) *n.* **1.** One who belongs to a group of Moslem tribes, esp. the Kabyles, inhabiting northern Africa. **2.** The Hamitic language of the Berbers. — *adj.* Of or pertaining to the Berbers or their language.

ber·ceuse (ber·sœz') *n. pl.* **·ceuses** (-sœz') A lullaby. [< F]

be·reave (bi·rēv') *v.t.* **·reaved** or **·reft** (-reft'), **·reav·ing 1.** To deprive, as of hope or happiness. **2.** To leave saddened through death. [OE *berēafian*] — **be·reave'ment** *n.*

be·reft (bi·reft') Alternative past tense and past participle of BEREAVE. — *adj.* Deprived: *bereft of all hope.*

be·ret (bə·rā', ber'ā) *n.* A soft, flat cap, usu. of wool, originating in the Basque regions of France and Spain. [< F]

berg (bûrg) *n.* An iceberg.

ber·ga·mot[1] (bûr'gə·mot) *n.* **1.** A small tree whose fruit furnishes a fragrant essential oil. **2.** The oil itself. **3.** Any of several plants of the mint family. [? after *Bergamo,* Italy]

ber·ga·mot[2] (bûr'gə·mot) *n.* A minor variety of pear. [< F < Ital. < Turkish *beg-armŭdi* prince's pear]

Berg·son·ism (berg'sən·iz'əm) *n.* The philosophy of Henri Bergson. — **Berg·so·ni·an** (berg·sō'nē·ən) *adv. & n.*

be·rhyme (bi·rīm') *v.t.* **·rhymed, ·rhym·ing 1.** To celebrate in rhyme. **2.** To compose in rhyme. Also **be·rime'.**

ber·i·ber·i (ber'ē·ber'ē) *n. Pathol.* A disease of the peripheral nerves resulting from the absence of B vitamins in the diet. [< Singhalese *beri* weakness] — **ber'i·ber'ic** *adj.*

berke·li·um (bûrk'lē·əm) *n.* The unstable radioactive element of atomic number 97 (symbol Bk), obtained by bombarding americium with alpha particles. [after *Berkeley,* California, location of the University of California]

Berk·shire (bûrk'shir, -shər) *n.* One of a breed of black and white swine originating in Berkshire, England.

berm (bûrm) *n.* A narrow ledge, shelf, or shoulder, as on a slope or at the side of a road: also **berme.** [< F *berme*]

Ber·mu·da shorts (bər·myōō'də) Knee-length shorts.

ber·ret·ta (bə·ret'ə) *n.* A biretta.

ber·ry (ber'ē) *n. pl.* **·ries 1.** Any small, succulent fruit: often used in combination: *strawberry.* **2.** *Bot.* A simple fruit with the seeds in a juicy pulp, as the grape. **3.** The dry kernel of various grains, or the fruit of certain plants, as a coffee bean, etc. — *v.i.* **·ried, ·ry·ing 1.** To form or bear berries. **2.** To gather berries. [OE *berie*]

ber·serk (bər·sûrk', bûr'sûrk) *adj.* Violently or frenetically destructive. — **to go (or run) berserk** To have a fit of destructive rage. — *n.* A berserker. [< ON *berserkr*]

ber·serk·er (bûr′sûr′kər) *n.* In Norse legend, a warrior who fought with frenzied fury.

berth (bûrth) *n.* **1.** A bunk or bed in a vessel, sleeping car, etc. **2.** *Naut.* Any place in which a vessel may lie at anchor or at a dock. **3.** Situation or employment on a vessel. **4.** Office or employment in general. **— to give a wide berth to** To avoid; keep out of the way of. *— v.t.* **1.** *Naut.* To bring to a berth. **2.** To provide with a berth. *— v.i.* **3.** *Naut.* To come to a berth. [Origin uncertain.]

ber·tha (bûr′thə) *n.* A deep collar worn by women, falling over the shoulders from a low neckline. [< F *berthe*]

Ber·til·lon system (bûr′tə·lon, *Fr.* ber·tē·yôn′) A system of coded physical measurements, used as a means of identification, esp. of criminals. [after Alphonse Bertillon, 1853–1914, French anthropologist]

ber·yl (ber′əl) *n.* A vitreous, green, light blue, yellow, pink, or white silicate of aluminum and beryllium, of which the aquamarine and emerald are varieties used as gems. [< OF < L < Gk. *bēryllos* beryl] **— ber·yl·line** (ber′ə·lin, -līn) *adj.*

be·ryl·li·um (bə·ril′ē·əm) *n.* A hard, grayish black, noncorrosive metallic element (symbol Be), used in copper and aluminum alloys and for windows of X-ray tubes. See ELEMENT. [< NL < L *beryllus* beryl]

be·seech (bi·sēch′) *v.t.* **·sought, ·seech·ing 1.** To entreat earnestly; implore. **2.** To beg for earnestly; crave. [ME < *bi-* greatly + *sēcan* to seek] **— be·seech′er** *n.*

be·seem (bi·sēm′) *v.i.* To be fitting or appropriate: It ill *beseems* you to speak thus. **— be·seem′ing** *adj.*

be·set (bi·set′) *v.t.* **·set, ·set·ting 1.** To attack on all sides; harass. **2.** To hem in; encircle. **3.** To set or stud, as with gems. [OE *besettan*] **— be·set′ment** *n.*

be·set·ting (bi·set′ing) *adj.* Constantly attacking or troubling.

be·side (bi·sīd′) *prep.* **1.** At the side of; in proximity to. **2.** In comparison with. **3.** Away or apart from: This discussion is *beside* the point. **4.** Other than; over and above. **— beside oneself** Out of one's senses, as from anger, fear, etc. *— adv.* In addition; besides. [OE *be sīdan* by the side (of)]

be·sides (bi·sīdz′) *adv.* **1.** In addition; as well. **2.** Moreover; furthermore. **3.** Apart from that mentioned; otherwise; else. *— prep.* **1.** In addition to; other than. **2.** Beyond; apart from: I care for nothing *besides* this.

be·siege (bi·sēj′) *v.t.* **·sieged, ·sieg·ing 1.** To lay siege to, as a castle. **2.** To crowd around. **3.** To overwhelm, as with gifts. **— be·siege′ment** *n.* **— be·sieg′er** *n.*

be·smear (bi·smir′) *v.t.* To smear over; sully.

be·smirch (bi·smûrch′) *v.t.* **1.** To soil; stain. **2.** To sully; dim the luster of. **— be·smirch′er** *n.* **— be·smirch′ment** *n.*

be·som (bē′zəm) *n.* **1.** A bundle of twigs used as a broom. **2.** Broom (def. 2). [OE *besma* broom]

be·sot (bi·sot′) *v.t.* **·sot·ted, ·sot·ting 1.** To stupefy, as with drink. **2.** To make foolish or stupid. **3.** To infatuate.

be·sought (bi·sôt′) Past tense and past participle of BESEECH.

be·span·gle (bi·spang′gəl) *v.t.* **·gled, ·gling** To decorate with or as with spangles.

be·spat·ter (bi·spat′ər) *v.t.* **1.** To cover or soil by spattering, as with mud. **2.** To sully; slander.

be·speak (bi·spēk′) *v.t.* **spoke** (Archaic ·spake), ·spo·ken or ·spoke, ·speak·ing 1. To ask or arrange for in advance. **2.** To give evidence of. **3.** To foretell. [OE *bisprecan*]

be·spec·ta·cled (bi·spek′tə·kəld) *adj.* Wearing spectacles.

be·spoke (bi·spōk′) Past tense and alternative past participle of BESPEAK.

be·spread (bi·spred′) *v.t.* **·spread, ·spread·ing** To cover or spread over thickly.

Bes·se·mer converter (bes′ə·mər) *Metall.* A large, pear-shaped vessel for containing the molten iron to be converted into steel by the Bessemer process.

Bessemer process *Metall.* A process for eliminating impurities from pig iron by forcing a blast of air through the molten metal before its conversion into steel or ingot iron.

best (best) Superlative of GOOD, WELL[2]. *— adj.* **1.** Excelling all others; of the highest quality. **2.** Most advantageous, desirable, or serviceable. **3.** Most; largest: the *best* part of an hour. *— adv.* **1.** In the most excellent way; most advantageously. **2.** To the utmost degree; most thoroughly. *— n.* **1.** The best thing, part, etc. **2.** Best condition or quality; utmost: Be at your *best*; Do your *best*. **3.** One's best clothes. **— at best** Under the most favorable circumstances. **— to get (or have) the best of** To defeat or outwit **— to make the best of** To adapt oneself to the disadvantages of. *— v.t.* To defeat, surpass. [OE *betst*]

be·stead (bi·sted′) *v.t.* To be of service to; help; avail.

BESSEMER CONVERTER
a, b Exhaust gases. *c* Silica refractory lining. *d* Flames. *e* Steel shell. *f* Compressed air. *g* Molten iron.

bes·tial (bes′chəl, best′yəl) *adj.* **1.** Of or pertaining to beasts. **2.** Brutish; depraved. [< OF < L < *bestia* beast] **— bes·ti·al·i·ty** (bes′chē·al′ə·tē, -tē·al′-) *n.* **— bes′tial·ly** *adv.*

bes·tial·ize (bes′chəl·īz, best′yəl-) *v.t.* **·ized, ·iz·ing** To brutalize.

be·stir (bi·stûr′) *v.t.* **·stirred, ·stir·ring** To rouse to activity.

best man The chief attendant of a bridegroom at a wedding.

be·stow (bi·stō′) *v.t.* **1.** To present as a gift; with *on* or *upon.* **2.** To apply; expend, as time. **3.** To give in marriage. **— be·stow′a·ble** *adj.* **— be·stow′al, be·stow′ment** *n.*

be·strad·dle (bi·strad′l) *v.t.* **·dled, ·dling** To bestride.

be·strew (bi·strō̄′) *v.t.* **·strewed, ·strewed** or **·strewn, ·strew·ing 1.** To cover or strew (a surface). **2.** To scatter about. **3.** To lie scattered over. Also **be·strow** (bi·strō′).

be·stride (bi·strīd′) *v.t.* **·strode, ·strid·den, ·strid·ing 1.** To mount; sit or stand astride of; straddle. **2.** To stride across.

best seller A book, phonograph record, etc., that sells or has sold in large numbers.

bet (bet) *n.* **1.** An agreement to risk something of one's own in return for the chance of winning something belonging to another or others. **2.** That which is risked in a bet, as a sum of money; a stake. **3.** The subject or event about which a bet is made. Also called *wager.* *— v.* **bet** or (less commonly) **bet·ted, bet·ting** *v.t.* **1.** To stake or pledge (money, etc.) in a bet. **2.** To declare as in a bet: I *bet* he doesn't come. *— v.i.* **3.** To place a bet. Also *wager.* **— you bet** *U.S. Slang* Certainly. [Origin uncertain]

be·ta (bā′tə, bē′-) *n.* **1.** The second letter of the Greek alphabet (B, β), corresponding to English b. See ALPHABET. **2.** The second object in any series, etc. [< Gk.]

beta particle A electron.

beta rays *Physics* A stream of electrons projected by radioactive substances.

be·ta·tron (bā′tə·tron) *n. Physics* An accelerator that uses a magnetic field to increase the velocity of electrons.

be·tel (bēt′l) *n.* A climbing plant of Asia, the leaves of which are chewed by the natives of Malaya and other Asian countries. [< Pg. < Malay *vettila*]

Be·tel·geuse (bēt′l·jōoz, bet′l·jœz) *n.* A giant red star, one of the 20 brightest, 1.2 magnitude; Alpha in the constellation Orion. Also **Be′tel·geux.** [< F *Bételgeuse* < Arabic *bat al-jauza,* ? shoulder of the giant]

be·tel·nut (bēt′l·nut′) *n.* The astringent seed of an East Indian palm, the **betel palm** (*Areca catechu*), used for chewing with betel leaves and lime.

bête noire (bāt′nwär′, *Fr.* bet nwâr′) Anything that is an object of hate or dread; a bugaboo. [< F, black beast]

Beth·a·ny (beth′ə·nē) In the New Testament, a village near Jerusalem: the home of Lazarus, Martha, and Mary.

beth·el (beth′əl) *n.* **1.** A hallowed place. *Gen.* xxviii 19. **2.** A seamen's church. [< Hebrew *bēth-el* house of God]

be·think (bi·thingk′) *v.* **·thought, ·think·ing** *v.t.* To bear in mind; consider: generally used reflexively.

be·thought (bi·thôt′) Past tense and past participle of BETHINK.

be·tide (be·tīd′) *v.t. & v.i.* **·tid·ed, ·tid·ing** To happen (to) or befall. [ME *bitiden*]

be·times (bi·tīmz′) *adv.* In good time; early; also, soon. [ME *betymes* in time, seasonably]

be·to·ken (bi·tō′kən) *v.t.* **1.** To be a sign of; presage. **2.** To give evidence of. [ME *bitacnien*] **— be·to′ken·er** *n.*

be·took (bi·tŏŏk′) Past tense of BETAKE.

be·tray (bi·trā′) *v.t.* **1.** To aid an enemy of; be a traitor to. **2.** To prove faithless to. **3.** To disclose, as secret information. **4.** To reveal unwittingly. **5.** To seduce and desert. **6.** To indicate; show: The smoke *betrays* a fire. [ME *bitraien*] **— be·tray′al, be·tray′ment** *n.* **— be·tray′er** *n.*

be·troth (bi·trōth′, -trôth′) *v.t.* To engage to marry; affiance. [ME < *bi-* to + *treuthe* truth]

be·troth·al (bi·trō′thəl, -trôth′əl) *n.* The act of betrothing; engagement or contract to marry. Also **be·troth′ment.**

be·trothed (bi·trōthd′, -trôtht′) *adj.* Engaged to be married; affianced. *— n.* A person engaged to be married.

bet·ter[1] (bet′ər) Comparative of GOOD, WELL[2]. *— adj.* **1.** Superior in quality. **2.** More advantageous, desirable, or serviceable. **3.** Larger; greater: the *better* part of the cake. **4.** Improved in health; convalescent. *— adv.* **1.** More advantageously. **2.** To a larger degree; more thoroughly. **3.** More: *better* than a week. **— better off** In a better condition or improved circumstances. *— v.t.* **1.** To make better; improve. **2.** To surpass; excel. *— v.i.* **3.** To become better. *— n.* **1.** That which is better. **2.** *Usu. pl.* One's superiors, as in ability, rank, etc. **3.** Advantage. [OE *betera*]

bet·ter[2] (bet′ər) *n.* One who lays bets. Also **bet′tor.**

bet·ter·ment (bet′ər·mənt) *n.* **1.** Improvement. **2.** *Law* An improvement adding to the value of real property.

be·tween (bi·twēn′) *prep.* **1.** In the space that separates (two places or objects). **2.** Intermediate in relation to, as times, qualities, etc. **3.** From one to another of; connecting. **4.** Involving reciprocal action among. **5.** By the joint action of: *Between* them, they killed three deer. **6.** In the joint possession of: not a cent *between* them. **7.** Being one alternative over another: to judge *between* right and wrong. **— between you and me** Confidentially. **— adv.** In intervening time, space, position, or relation: few and far *between.* **— in between** In an intermediate position or state; undecided. [Fusion of OE *bitwēonum* and *bitwēon* < *bi-* by + *-tweonum* and *-tweon,* both < *twā* two]

be·twixt (bi·twikst′) *adv. & prep. Archaic* Between. **— betwixt and between** In an intermediate or indecisive state. [OE *betweons* twofold < *be-* by + *-tweons* < *twā* two]

bev·el (bev′əl) *n.* **1.** Any inclination of two surfaces other than 90°, as at the edge of a timber, etc. **2.** An adjustable instrument for measuring angles: also **bevel square. — adj.** Oblique; slanting. **— v.** **bev·eled** or **·elled, bev·el·ing** or **·el·ling** *v.t.* **1.** To cut or bring to a bevel. **— v.i.** **2.** To slant. [? < OF. Cf. F *beveau* bevel (n. def. 2).]

bevel gear *Mech.* A gear having beveled teeth, as for transmitting rotary motion at an angle. For illus. see GEAR.

bev·er·age (bev′rij, bev′ər·ij) *n.* That which is drunk; any drink. [< OF < L *bibere* to drink]

bev·y (bev′ē) *n.* *pl.* **bev·ies** **1.** A group, esp. of girls or women. **2.** A flock, esp. of quail, grouse, or larks. **— Syn.** See FLOCK. [ME *bevey;* origin uncertain]

be·wail (bi·wāl′) *v.t. & v.i.* To lament. **— Syn.** See MOURN.

be·ware (bi·wâr′) *v.t. & v.i.* **·wared, ·war·ing** To look out (for); be cautious or wary (of). [OE *wær* cautious]

be·wil·der (bi·wil′dər) *v.t.* To confuse utterly; perplex. **— be·wil′dered** *adj.* **— be·wil′dered·ly** *adv.* **— be·wil′der·ment** *n.*

be·witch (bi·wich′) *v.t.* **1.** To gain power over by charms or incantations. **2.** To attract irresistibly; charm; fascinate. [ME < *bi-* completely + *wicchen* to enchant] **— be·witch′er** *n.* **— be·witch′ment, be·witch′er·y** *n.*

be·witch·ing (bi·wich′ing) *adj.* Charming; captivating. **— be·witch′ing·ly** *adv.*

bey (bā) *n.* **1.** The governor of a minor Turkish province or district. **2.** A Turkish title of respect. [< Turkish *beg* lord]

be·yond (bi·yond′) *prep.* **1.** On or to the far side of; farther on than. **2.** Later than. **3.** Outside the reach or scope of: *beyond* help. **4.** Surpassing; superior to: lovely *beyond* description. **5.** More than; over and above. **— adv.** Farther on or away; at a distance. **— the (great) beyond** Whatever comes after death. [OE < *be-* near + *geondan* yonder]

bez·el (bez′əl) *n.* **1.** A bevel on the edge of a cutting tool. **2.** The upper part of a cut gem, including the table and surrounding facets. [? < OF. Cf. F *biseau* bias.]

be·zique (bə·zēk′) *n.* A game of cards resembling pinochle, played with a deck of 64 cards. [Alter. of F *bésique*]

bhang (bang) *n.* **1.** Hemp (def. 1). **2.** Hashish. Also spelled *bang.* [< Hind. < Skt. *bhangā* hemp]

Bhu·tan·ese (bōō′tan·ēz′, -ēs′) *n.* *pl.* **·ese** **1.** A native of Bhutan. **2.** The Sino-Tibetan language of Bhutan. **— adj.** Of or pertaining to Bhutan, its people, or their language.

bi- *prefix* **1.** Twice; doubly; two; especially, occurring twice or having two: *biangular.* **2.** *Chem.* **a** Indicating the doubling of a radical, etc., in an organic compound. **b** Having double the proportion of the substance named: *bicarbonate.* Also: *bin-* before a vowel, as in *binaural; bis-* before *c, s,* as in *bissextile.* [< L *bi-* < *bis* twice]

bi·an·gu·lar (bī·ang′gyə·lər) *adj.* Having two angles.

bi·an·nu·al (bī·an′yōō·əl) *adj.* Occurring twice a year; semiannual. Compare BIENNIAL. **— bi·an′nu·al·ly** *adv.*

bi·as (bī′əs) *n.* *pl.* **bi·as·es** **1.** A line running obliquely across a fabric: to cut on the *bias.* **2.** A mental tendency, preference, or prejudice. **— Syn.** See PREJUDICE. **— adj.** Cut, running, set, or folded diagonally; slanting. **— adv.** Slantingly; diagonally. **— v.t.** **bi·ased** or **·assed, bi·as·ing** or **·as·sing** To influence or affect unduly or unfairly. [< MF *biais* oblique]

bi·ax·i·al (bī·ak′sē·əl) *adj.* Having two axes, as a crystal. Also **bi·ax·al** (bī·ak′səl). **— bi·ax′i·al·ly** *adv.*

bib (bib) *n.* **1.** A cloth worn under a child's chin at meals to protect the clothing. **2.** The upper front part of an apron or of overalls. [? < L *bibere* to drink]

bib and tucker *Informal* Clothes.

bib·ber (bib′ər) *n.* A habitual drinker; tippler.

bib·cock (bib′kok′) *n.* A faucet having the nozzle bent downward.

bibe·lot (bib′lō, *Fr.* bēb·lō′) *n.* A small, decorative and often rare object or trinket. [< F]

Bi·ble (bī′bəl) *n.* **1.** In Christianity, the Old Testament and the New Testament. **2.** In Judaism, the Old Testament. **3.** The sacred book or writings of any religion. [< OF < L < Gk., pl. of *biblion* book]

Bib·li·cal (bib′li·kəl) *adj.* **1.** Of or in the Bible. **2.** In harmony with the Bible. Also **bib′li·cal. — Bib′li·cal·ly** *adv.*

Bib·li·cist (bib′lə·sist) *n.* **1.** One versed in the Bible. **2.** One who adheres to the letter of the Bible.

biblio- *combining form* Pertaining to books, or to the Bible: *bibliophile.* [< Gk. *biblion* book]

bib·li·og·ra·phy (bib′lē·og′rə·fē) *n.* *pl.* **·phies** **1.** A list of the works of an author, or of the literature bearing on a subject. **2.** A list of books or other sources mentioned or consulted by an author, usu. appended to the end of his text. **3.** The description and history of books, including details of authorship, editions, dates, etc. **— bib′li·og′ra·pher** *n.* **— bib·li·o·graph·ic** (bib′lē·ə·graf′ik) or **·i·cal** *adj.*

bib·li·o·ma·ni·a (bib′lē·ō·mā′nē·ə) *n.* A passion for collecting books. **— bib′li·o·ma′ni·ac** (-ak) *n. & adj.*

bib·li·o·phile (bib′lē·ə·fīl′, -fil′) *n.* One who loves books. Also **bib′li·o·phil′** (-fil′), **bib·li·oph′i·list** (bib′lē·of′ə·list). **— bib′li·oph′i·lism** *n.* **— bib′li·oph′i·lis′tic** *adj.*

bib·u·lous (bib′yə·ləs) *adj.* **1.** Given to drink; fond of drinking. **2.** Absorbent. [< L *bibere* to drink]

bi·cam·er·al (bī·kam′ər·əl) *adj.* Consisting of two chambers, houses, or branches. [< BI- + L *camera* chamber]

bi·car·bo·nate (bī·kär′bə·nit, -nāt) *n. Chem.* A salt of carbonic acid in which one of the hydrogen atoms of the acid is replaced by a metal: sodium *bicarbonate.*

bicarbonate of soda Sodium bicarbonate.

bi·cen·ten·ni·al (bī′sen·ten′ē·əl) *adj.* **1.** Occurring once in 200 years. **2.** Lasting or consisting of 200 years. **— n.** A 200th anniversary. Also **bi·cen·te·nar·y** (bī·sen′tə·ner′ē, bī′-sen·ten′ər·ē).

bi·ceps (bī′seps) *n.* *pl.* **bi·ceps** *Anat.* **1.** The large front muscle of the upper arm. **2.** The large flexor muscle at the back of the thigh. [< L < *bis* twofold + *caput* head]

bi·chlo·ride (bī·klôr′īd, -id, -klō′rīd, -rid) *n. Chem.* **1.** A salt having two atoms of chlorine. **2.** Bichloride of mercury.

bi·chro·mate (bī·krō′māt, -mit) *n. Chem.* Dichromate.

bick·er (bik′ər) *v.i.* **1.** To dispute petulantly; wrangle. **2.** To flicker, as a flame; twinkle. **— n.** A petty altercation. **— Syn.** See QUARREL[1]. [ME *bikeren*] **— bick′er·er** *n.*

bi·col·or (bī′kul′ər) *adj.* Two-colored. Also **bi′col′ored.**

bi·con·cave (bī·kon′kāv, -kong′-, bī′kon·kāv′) *adj.* Concave on both sides, as a lens.

bi·con·vex (bī·kon′veks, bī′kon·veks′) *adj.* Convex on both sides, as a lens.

bi·cus·pid (bī·kus′pid) *adj.* Having two cusps or points. Also **bi·cus′pi·dal** (-dəl), **bi·cus′pi·date** (-dāt). **— n.** A premolar tooth. For illus. see TOOTH. [< BI- + L *cuspis,* point]

bi·cy·cle (bī′sik·əl) *n.* A vehicle consisting of a metal frame mounted on two wheels, one in back of the other, having a saddle, handlebars, and pedals. **— v.i.** **·cled, ·cling** To ride a bicycle. [< F < *bi-* two + Gk. *kyklos* wheel] **— bi′cy·cler, bi′cy·clist** *n.*

bid (bid) *n.* **1.** An offer to pay a price; also, the amount offered. **2.** In card games, the number of tricks or points that a player engages to make; also, a player's turn to bid. **3.** An effort to acquire, win, or attain: a *bid* for the governorship. **4.** *Informal* An invitation. **— v. bade** for *defs. 3, 4, 6,* or **bid** for *defs. 1, 2, 5, 7,* **bid·den** or **bid, bid·ding** *v.t.* **1.** To make an offer of (a price). **2.** In card games, to declare (the number of tricks or points one will engage to make). **3.** To command; order. **4.** To say to, as a greeting or farewell. **— v.i.** **5.** To make a bid. **— to bid fair** To seem probable. **— to bid in** At an auction, to outbid a prospective purchaser on behalf of the owner, when the price offered is too low. **— to bid up** To increase the price by offering higher bids. [Fusion of OE *biddan* to ask, demand and *bēodan* to proclaim] **— bid′da·ble** *adj.* **— bid′der** *n.*

bid·ding (bid′ing) *n.* **1.** A command. **2.** An invitation or summons. **3.** Bids, or the making of a bid or bids.

bid·dy (bid′ē) *n.* *pl.* **·dies** A hen. [Origin uncertain]

bide (bīd) *v.* **bid·ed** (*Archaic* **bode**), **bid·ing** *v.t.* **1.** To endure; withstand. **2.** *Archaic* To tolerate; submit to. **— v.i.** **3.** To dwell; abide; stay. **— to bide one's time** To await the best opportunity. [OE *bīdan*]

bi·en·ni·al (bī·en′ē·əl) *adj.* **1.** Occurring every second year. **2.** Lasting or living for two years. **— n.** **1.** *Bot.* A plant that produces flowers and fruit in its second year, then dies. **2.** An event occurring once in two years. [< L < *bis* twofold + *annus* year] **— bi·en′ni·al·ly** *adv.*

bien·ve·nue (byań·və·nü′) *n. French* A welcome.

bier (bir) *n.* A framework for carrying a corpse to the grave; also, a coffin. [OE *bær*]

biest·ings (bēs′tingz) See BEESTINGS.

biff (bif) *U.S. Slang v.t.* To strike; hit. **— n.** A blow. [Imit.]

bi·fid (bī′fid) *adj.* Cleft; forked. [< L < *bis* twofold + *findere* to split] **— bi·fid′i·ty** *n.* **— bi′fid·ly** *adv.*

bi·fo·cal (bī′fō′kəl) *adj. Optics* Having two foci: said of a lens ground for both near and far vision.

---

bi·fo·cals (bī·fō′kəlz, bĭ′fō·kəlz) *n.pl.* Eyeglasses with bifocal lenses.

bi·fur·cate (bī′fər·kāt, bī·fûr′kāt; *adj. also* bī·fûr′kit) *v.t. & v.i.* **·cat·ed, ·cat·ing** To divide into two branches or stems; fork. — *adj.* Forked: also **bi′fur·cat′ed** (-kā′tid), **bi·fur·cous** (-kəs). [< L *bi-* two + *furca* fork] — **bi·fur·cate·ly** (bī′fər·kit·lē, bī·fûr′kit·lē) *adv.* — **bi·fur·ca′tion** *n.*

big (big) *adj.* **big·ger, big·gest** **1.** Of great size, extent, etc. **2.** Pregnant: usu. with *with.* **3.** Grown. **4.** Pompous; pretentious. **5.** Important; prominent. **6.** Loud. **7.** Generous; magnanimous. — *adv. Informal* Pompously; extravagantly: to talk *big.* [ME; origin uncertain] — **big′gish** *adj.* — **big′ly** *adv.* — **big′ness** *n.*

big·a·my (big′ə·mē) *n. Law* The criminal offense of marrying any other person while having a legal spouse living. [< OF < LL < L *bis* twice + Gk. *gamos* wedding] — **big′a·mist** *n.* — **big′a·mous** *adj.* — **big′a·mous·ly** *adv.*

Big Ben **1.** A bell in the Westminster clock in the tower of the House of Parliament, London. **2.** The clock itself.

Big Dipper The constellation Ursa Major.

big-heart·ed (big′här′tid) *adj.* Generous; charitable.

big·horn (big′hôrn) *n. pl.* **·horns** *or* **·horn** The Rocky Mountain sheep, remarkable for its large curved horns.

big house *U.S. Slang* A penitentiary.

bight (bīt) *n.* **1.** The loop, or middle part, of a rope. **2.** A bend or curve in a shoreline, a river, etc. **3.** A bay bounded by such a bend. — *v.t.* To secure with a bight. [OE *byht*]

big·no·ni·a (big·nō′nē·ə) *n.* A climbing plant having clusters of large, trumpet-shaped flowers. [after Abbé *Bignon,* 1711–1772, librarian to Louis XV]

big·ot (big′ət) *n.* One whose attitude or behavior expresses intolerance, as because of race, religion, politics, etc. [< F; ult. origin unknown] — **big′ot·ed** *adj.* — **big′ot·ed·ly** *adv.*

big·ot·ry (big′ə·trē) *n. pl.* **·ries** Attitudes, beliefs, or actions characteristic of a bigot; intolerance.

big shot *Slang* Someone of importance. Also **big wheel.**

big top *U.S. Informal* The main tent of a circus.

big·wig (big′wig′) *n. Informal* Someone of importance.

bi·jou (bē′zhōō, bē·zhōō′) *n. pl.* **bi·joux** (bē′zhōōz, bē·zhōōz′) A jewel, or a finely wrought trinket. [< MF]

bi·ju·gate (bī′jōō·gāt, bĭ·jōō′git) *adj. Bot.* Two-paired, as leaves. Also **bi·ju·gous** (bī′jōō·gəs).

bike (bīk) *n. Informal* A bicycle. [Alter. of BICYCLE]

bi·ki·ni (bi·kē′nē) *n.* A type of very scanty bathing suit.

bi·la·bi·al (bī·lā′bē·əl) *adj.* **1.** *Phonet.* Articulated with both lips, as certain consonants. **2.** Having two lips. — *n. Phonet.* A bilabial speech sound, as (b), (p), (m), and (w).

bi·la·bi·ate (bī·lā′bē·āt, -it) *adj. Bot.* Two-lipped: said of a corolla.

bi·lat·er·al (bī·lat′ər·əl) *adj.* **1.** Pertaining to or having two sides; two-sided. **2.** On two sides. **3.** Mutually binding. — **bi·lat′er·al·ly** *adv.* — **bi·lat′er·al·ness** *n.*

bil·ber·ry (bil′ber′ē, -bər·ē) *n. pl.* **·ries** The whortleberry.

bil·bo (bil′bō) *n. pl.* **·boes** *pl.* A fetter consisting of two sliding shackles attached to an iron bar. [after *Bilbao*]

bile (bīl) *n.* **1.** *Physiol.* A bitter yellow or greenish liquid secreted by the liver and serving to promote digestion. **2.** Anger; peevishness. [< F < L *bilis* bile, anger]

bile ducts *Physiol.* The excretory ducts of the gall bladder.

bilge (bilj) *n.* **1.** *Naut.* The rounded part of a ship's bottom. **2.** The bulge of a barrel. **3.** Bilge water. **4.** *Slang* Stupid or trivial talk or writing. — *v.t. & v.i.* **bilged, bilg·ing** **1.** To break open in the bilge: said of a ship. **2.** To bulge. [Var. of BULGE] — **bilg′y** *adj.*

bilge water Foul water that collects in the bilge of a ship.

bil·i·ar·y (bil′ē·er′ē) *adj.* Pertaining to or conveying bile. [< F *biliare*]

bi·lin·gual (bī·ling′gwəl) *adj.* **1.** Written or expressed in or using two languages. **2.** Able to speak two languages, often with equal skill. — *n.* A bilingual person. [< L *bilinguis*] — **bi·lin′gual·ism** *n.* — **bi·lin′gual·ly** *adv.*

bil·ious (bil′yəs) *adj.* **1.** Affected or caused by an excess of bile. **2.** Of or containing bile. **3.** Ill-tempered. **4.** Of a sickly color. [< F < L *biliosus*] — **bil′ious·ly** *adv.* — **bil′ious·ness** *n.*

-bility *suffix* Forming nouns from adjectives ending in *-ble: probability* from *probable.* [< F < L *-bilitas, -tatis*]

bilk (bilk) *v.t.* **1.** To cheat; deceive. **2.** To evade payment of. **3.** To balk. — *n.* **1.** A swindler; cheat. **2.** A hoax. [Origin unknown] — **bilk′er** *n.*

bill¹ (bil) *n.* **1.** A statement listing charges for goods delivered or services rendered. **2.** A statement of particulars; itemized list. **3.** *U.S.* A piece of paper money; a bank note. **4.** A bill of exchange; also, loosely, a promissory note. **5.** A draft of a proposed law. **6.** A handbill or advertising poster. **7.** The program of a theatrical performance. **8.** *Law* A formal statement of a case, a complaint, a petition for relief, etc. — *v.t.* **1.** To enter in a bill or list. **2.** To present a bill to. **3.** To advertise by bills or placards. [< LL *billa, var* of L *bulla* edict, document] — **bill′a·ble** *adj.*

bill² (bil) *n.* A beak, as of a bird. — *v.i.* To join bills, as

doves; caress. — **to bill and coo** To caress lovingly and speak in soft, murmuring tones. [OE *bile*]

bill³ (bil) *n.* **1.** A hook-shaped instrument used in pruning, etc.: also **bill′hook′.** **2.** An ancient weapon with a hook-shaped blade; a halberd. [OE]

bil·la·bong (bil′ə·bong) *n. Austral.* A stagnant backwater. [< native Australian < *billa* water + *bong* dead]

bill·board (bil′bôrd′, -bōrd′) *n.* A panel, usu. outdoors, for notices or advertisements.

bil·let¹ (bil′it) *n.* **1.** Lodging for troops in private or non-military buildings. **2.** An order for such lodging. **3.** A place assigned, as for a sailor to sling his hammock; quarters. **4.** A job; berth. — *v.t.* To lodge (soldiers, etc.) in a private house by billet. [< OF < L *bulla* seal, document]

bil·let² (bil′it) *n.* **1.** A short, thick stick, as of firewood. **2.** *Metall.* A mass of iron or steel drawn into a small bar. [< OF *billete,* dim. of *bille* log]

bil·let-doux (bil′ā·dōō′, *Fr.* bē·yä·dōō′) *n. pl.* **bil·lets-doux** (bil′ā·dōōz′, *Fr.* bē·yä·dōō′) A love letter. [<F]

bill·fold (bil′fōld′) *n.* A wallet.

bill·head (bil′hed′) *n.* A heading on paper used for making out bills; also, a blank with such a heading.

bil·liard (bil′yərd) *n. U.S. Informal* A carom. — *adj.* Of or pertaining to billiards: *billiard* player.

bil·liards (bil′yərdz) *n.pl.* (construed as sing.) Any of various games played with hard balls (**billiard balls**) hit by cues on an oblong, cloth-covered table (**billiard table**) having cushioned edges. [< F < OF *billart* cue] — **bil′liard·ist** *n.*

bill·ing (bil′ing) *n.* The relative eminence given to an actor or an act on a theater marquee, playbill, etc.

bil·lings·gate (bil′ingz·gāt) *n.* Vulgar or abusive language. [after *Billingsgate* fish market, London]

bil·lion (bil′yən) *n.* **1.** *U.S.* A thousand millions, written as 1,000,000,000: called a *milliard* in Great Britain. **2.** *Brit.* A million millions, written as 1,000,000,000,000: called a *trillion* in the U.S. [< F < *bi-* two + (*mi*)*llion* million] — **bil′lionth** *n. & adj.*

bil·lion·aire (bil′yən·âr′) *n.* One who owns a billion of money. [< BILLION, on analogy with *millionaire*]

bill of exchange A written order for the payment of a given sum to a designated person.

bill of fare A list of the dishes provided at a meal; menu.

bill of health An official certificate of the crew's health issued to a ship's master on departure from a port. — **a clean bill of health** *Informal* A good record; favorable report.

bill of lading A written acknowledgment of goods received for transportation.

bill of rights **1.** A formal summary and declaration of the fundamental principles and rights of individuals. **2.** *Often cap.* The first ten amendments to the U.S. Constitution.

bill of sale An instrument attesting the transfer of property.

bil·low (bil′ō) *n.* **1.** A great wave or swell of the sea. **2.** Any wave or surge, as of sound. — **Syn.** See WAVE. — *v.t.* To rise or roll in billows; surge; swell. [< ON *bylgja*]

bil·low·y (bil′ō·ē) *adj.* **·low·i·er, ·low·i·est** Of, full of, or resembling billows; surging; swelling. — **bil′low·i·ness** *n.*

bill·post·er (bil′pōs′tər) *n.* A person who posts bills, notices, or advertisements on walls, fences, etc. Also **bill′·stick′er.** — **bill′post′ing** *n.*

bil·ly (bil′ē) *n. pl.* **·lies** A short bludgeon, as a policeman's club. [< *Billy,* a nickname for William]

billy goat *Informal* A male goat.

bi·lo·bate (bī·lō′bāt) *adj* Divided into or having two lobes. Also **bi·lo′bat·ed.**

Bi·lox·i (bi·lok′sē) *n.* One of a tribe of North American Indians of Siouan stock.

bi·man·u·al (bī·man′yōō·əl) *adj.* Employing or involving both hands. — **bi·man′u·al·ly** *adv.*

bi·met·al·ism (bī·met′l·iz′əm) *n.* The concurrent use of both gold and silver as the standard of currency and value. Also **bi·met′al·lism.** — **bi·met′al·ist** *or* **bi·met′al·list** *n.*

bi·me·tal·lic (bī′mə·tal′ik) *adj.* **1.** Consisting of or relating to two metals. **2.** Of or using bimetalism.

bi·month·ly (bī·munth′lē) *adj.* **1.** Occurring once every two months. **2.** Occurring twice a month; semimonthly. — *n.* A bimonthly publication. — *adv.* **1.** Once in two months. **2.** Twice a month.

bin (bin) *n.* An enclosed place or large receptacle for holding meal, coal, etc. — *v.t.* **binned, bin·ning** To store or deposit in a bin. [OE *binn* basket, crib < Celtic]

bin- Var. of BI-.

bi·na·ry (bī′nər·ē) *adj.* Pertaining to, characterized by, or made up of two; double; paired. — *n. pl.* **·ries** **1.** A combination of two things. **2.** *Astron.* A binary star. [< L *binarius* < *bini* two, double]

binary star *Astron.* A pair of stars revolving about a common center of gravity.

bi·nate (bī′nāt) *adj. Bot.* Being or growing in pairs, as leaves. [< NL < L *bīnī* double, two] — **bi′nate·ly** *adv.*

bin·au·ral (bin·ôr′əl) *adj.* **1.** Hearing with both ears. **2.** *Electronics* Stereophonic.

bind (bīnd) *v.* **bound, bind·ing** *v.t.* **1.** To tie or fasten with a band, cord, etc. **2.** To fasten around; encircle; gird. **3.** To bandage; swathe: often with *up*. **4.** To constrain or obligate, as by moral authority. **5.** *Law* To subject to a definite legal obligation. **6.** To enclose between covers, as a book. **7.** To provide with a border for reinforcement or decoration. **8.** To cause to cohere; cement. **9.** To constipate. **10.** To make irrevocable; seal, as a bargain. **11.** To apprentice or indenture: often with *out* or *over*. — *v.i.* **12.** To tie up anything. **13.** To cohere; stick together. **14.** To have binding force; be obligatory. **15.** To become stiff or hard, as cement; jam, as gears. — **to bind over** *Law* To hold on bail or under bond for future appearance in court. — *n.* That which binds. [OE *bindan*]

bind·er (bīn′dər) *n.* **1.** One who binds; esp., a bookbinder. **2.** Anything used to bind or tie, as a cord or band, or to cause cohesion, as tar, glue, etc. **3.** A cover in which sheets of paper may be fastened. **4.** *Law* A written statement binding parties to an agreement pending preparation of a contract. **5.** *Agric.* A machine that cuts and ties grain.

bind·er·y (bīn′dər·ē) *n. pl.* **·er·ies** A place where books are bound.

bind·ing (bīn′ding) *n.* **1.** The act of one who binds. **2.** Anything that binds; binder. **3.** The cover holding together and enclosing the leaves of a book. **4.** A strip sewed over an edge for protection. — *adj.* **1.** Tying; restraining. **2.** Obligatory. — **bind′ing·ly** *adv.* — **bind′ing·ness** *n.*

bind·weed (bīnd′wēd′) *n.* Any strongly twining plant.

bine (bīn) *n.* **1.** A flexible shoot or climbing stem, as of the hop. **2.** The bindweed. **3.** The woodbine. [Var. of BIND]

binge (binj) *n.* *Slang* A drunken carousal; spree. [? < dial. F *binge* to soak]

bin·go (bing′gō) *n.* A gambling game resembling lotto, usu. played in large groups. [Origin unknown]

bin·na·cle (bin′ə·kəl) *n. Naut.* A stand or case for a ship's compass, usu. placed before the steering wheel. [Earlier *bittacle* < Pg. < L *habitaculum* little house]

bin·oc·u·lar (bə·nok′yə·lər, bī-) *adj.* Pertaining to, using, or intended for both eyes at once. — *n. Often pl.* A telescope, opera glass, etc., adapted for use by both eyes. [< L *bini* two, double + *ocularis* of the eyes < *oculus* eye]

bi·no·mi·al (bī·nō′mē·əl) *adj.* Consisting of two names or terms. — *n. Math.* An algebraic expression consisting of two terms joined by a plus or minus sign. [< LL *binominus* having two names] — **bi·no′mi·al·ly** *adv.*

bio- *combining form* Life: *biology*. [< Gk. *bios* life]

bi·o·chem·is·try (bī′ō·kem′is·trē) *n.* The branch of chemistry relating to the processes and physical properties of living organisms. — **bi′o·chem′i·cal** or **bi′o·chem′ic** *adj.* — **bi′·o·chem′i·cal·ly** *adv.* — **bi′o·chem′ist** *n.*

bi·o·gen·e·sis (bī′ō·jen′ə·sis) *n.* The doctrine that life is generated from living organisms only. Also **bi·og·e·ny** (bī·oj′ə·nē). — **bi·o·ge·net·ic** (bī′ō·jə·net′ik) or **·i·cal** *adj.* — **bi′o·ge·net′i·cal·ly** *adv.*

bi·og·ra·pher (bī·og′rə·fər, bē-) *n.* A writer of biography.

bi·o·graph·i·cal (bī·ə·graf′i·kəl) *adj.* **1.** Of or concerning a person's life. **2.** Pertaining to biography. Also **bi′o·graph′ic.** — **bi′o·graph′i·cal·ly** *adv.*

bi·og·ra·phy (bī·og′rə·fē, bē-) *n. pl.* **·phies** An account of a person's life; also, such accounts as a form of literature. [< LGk. < Gk. *bios* life + *graphein* to write]

bi·o·log·i·cal (bī′ə·loj′i·kəl) *adj.* **1.** Of or pertaining to biology. **2.** Used for or produced by biological research or practice. Also **bi′o·log′ic.** — **bi′o·log′i·cal·ly** *adv.*

biological warfare Warfare that employs bacteria, viruses, and other biological agents noxious to or destructive of life.

bi·ol·o·gy (bī·ol′ə·jē) *n.* The science of life in all its manifestations, and of the origin, structure, reproduction, growth, and development of living organisms collectively. Its two main divisions are botany and zoology. — **bi·ol′o·gist** *n.*

bi·om·e·try (bī·om′ə·trē) *n.* **1.** A measuring or calculating of the probable duration of human life. **2.** Biology from a statistical point of view, esp. with reference to problems of variation: also **bi·o·met·rics** (bī′ə·met′riks). — **bi·o·met′ric** or **·ri·cal** *adj.* — **bi′o·met′ri·cal·ly** *adv.*

bi·o·phys·ics (bī′ō·fiz′iks) *n.pl.* (*construed as sing.*) The study of biological function, structure, and organization in relation to and using the methods of physics. — **bi′o·phys′i·cal** *adj.* — **bi′o·phys′i·cist** *n.*

bi·op·sy (bī′op·sē) *n. pl.* **·sies** *Med.* The examination of tissue from a living subject. — **bi·op·sic** (bī·op′sik) *adj.*

bi·os·co·py (bī·os′kə·pē) *n. Med.* An examination to ascertain whether life exists. — **bi·o·scop·ic** (bī′ə·skop′ik) *adj.*

-biosis *combining form* Manner of living: *symbiosis*. [< Gk. *biōsis* < *bios* life]

bi·o·tin (bī′ə·tin) *n. Biochem.* A crystalline acid, $C_{10}H_{16}O_3\cdot N_2S$, forming part of the vitamin B complex. [< Gk. *biotos* life + -IN]

bi·par·ti·san (bī·pär′tə·zən) *adj.* Advocated by or consisting of members of two parties, esp. the Democratic and Republican parties. — **bi·par′ti·san·ship′** *n.*

bi·par·tite (bī·pär′tīt) *adj.* **1.** Consisting of two parts, esp. two corresponding parts. **2.** *Bot.* Divided into two parts almost to the base, as certain leaves. Also **bi·part′ed.** [< L *bipartire* to divide] — **bi·par′tite·ly** *adv.* — **bi·par·ti·tion** (bī′pär·tish′ən) *n.*

bi·ped (bī′ped) *n.* An animal having two feet. — *adj.* Two-footed: also **bi·pe·dal** (bī′pə·dəl, bip′ə-). [< L *bipes, bipedis*]

bi·pin·nate (bī·pin′āt) *adj. Bot.* Twice or doubly pinnate, as a leaf. Also **bi·pin′nat·ed.** — **bi·pin′nate·ly** *adv.*

bi·plane (bī′plān′) *n.* A type of airplane having two wings, one above the other.

bi·po·lar (bī·pō′lər) *adj.* **1.** Relating to or possessing two poles. **2.** Denoting or belonging to both polar regions. **3.** Containing two contradictory qualities, opinions, etc. — **bi·po·lar·i·ty** (bī′pō·lar′ə·tē) *n.*

birch (bûrch) *n.* **1.** A tree or shrub having the outer bark separable in thin layers; esp. the **canoe** or **paper birch** of North America: also called *white birch*. **2.** A rod from this tree, used as a whip. **3.** The tough, close-grained hardwood of the birch. — *v.t.* To whip with a birch rod. [OE *birce*] — **birch·en** (bûr′chən) *adj.*

bird (bûrd) *n.* **1.** A warm-blooded, feathered, egg-laying vertebrate having the forelimbs modified as wings. ◆ Collateral adjective: *avian*. **2.** A game bird. **3.** A shuttlecock. **4.** A clay pigeon. **5.** *Slang* A person, esp. one who is peculiar or remarkable. **6.** *Slang* A hiss or jeer. [OE *bridd*]

bird·call (bûrd′kôl′) *n.* **1.** A bird's note in calling. **2.** A sound imitating this, or an instrument for producing it.

bird dog A dog used in hunting game birds.

bird·ie (bûr′dē) *n.* **1.** *Informal* A small bird. **2.** In golf, one stroke less than par on a given hole.

bird·lime (bûrd′līm′) *n.* A sticky substance made from holly or mistletoe and smeared on twigs to catch small birds.

bird·man (bûrd′man′, -mən) *n. pl.* **·men** (-men′, -mən) **1.** *Informal* An aviator. **2.** A fowler. **3.** An ornithologist.

bird of paradise A tropical bird noted for the beauty of the plumage in the male.

bird of passage A migratory bird.

bird of prey A predatory bird, as an eagle, hawk, etc.

bird's-eye (bûrdz′ī′) *adj.* **1.** Marked with spots resembling birds' eyes: *bird's-eye* maple. **2.** Seen from above or from afar: a *bird's-eye* view. — *n.* **1.** A pattern woven with small, eyelike indentations. **2.** Any of various fabrics having such a pattern. Also **birds′eye′.**

bird watcher One who observes or identifies wild birds in their natural habitats as a pastime. — **bird watching**

bi·ret·ta (bi·ret′ə) *n.* A stiff, square cap with three or four upright projections on the crown, worn by clerics of the Roman Catholic church: also called *berretta*. [< Ital.]

birl (bûrl) *v.t. & v.i.* **1.** To rotate (a floating log). **2.** To whirl. — *n.* A droning noise.

birl·ing (bûr′ling) *n.* A sport in which two contestants balance on a floating log and try to dislodge one another.

birth (bûrth) *n.* **1.** The fact or act of being born. **2.** The bringing forth of offspring. **3.** Beginning; origin. **4.** Ancestry or descent. **5.** Noble lineage; good family. **6.** Natural or inherited tendency.

birth control The regulation of conception by preventive methods or devices.

birth·day (bûrth′dā) *n.* The day of one's birth or its anniversary.

birth·mark (bûrth′märk′) *n.* A mark or stain existing on the body from birth; nevus.

birth·place (bûrth′plās′) *n.* **1.** Place of birth. Abbr. *bp.* **2.** Place where something originates.

birth rate The number of births per a given number of individuals (usually 1,000), in a specified district and in a specified period of time.

birth·right (bûrth′rīt′) *n.* A privilege or possession into which one is born.

birth·stone (bûrth′stōn′) *n.* A jewel identified with the month of one's birth.

bis (bis) *adv.* Twice: used to denote repetition. [< L]

bis- Var. of BI-.

bis·cuit (bis′kit) *n.* **1.** *U.S.* A kind of shortened bread baked in small cakes, raised with baking powder or soda. **2.** *Brit.* A thin, crisp wafer. **3.** A light brown color. **4.** In ceramics, pottery baked once but not glazed. [< OF < L < *bis* twice + *coctus*, pp. of *coquere* to cook]

bi·sect (bī·sekt′) *v.t.* **1.** To cut into two parts; halve. **2.** *Geom.* To divide into two parts of equal size. — *v.i.* **3.** To fork, as a road. [< BI- + L *sectus*, pp. of *secare* to cut] — **bi·sec′tion** *n.* — **bi·sec′tion·al** *adj.* — **bi·sec′tion·al·ly** *adv.*

bi·sec·tor (bī·sek′tər) *n.* **1.** That which bisects. **2.** *Geom.* A line or plane that bisects an angle or another line.

bi·sex·u·al (bī-sek′shŏŏ-əl) *adj.* **1.** Of both sexes. **2.** Having the organs of both sexes; hermaphrodite. **3.** Sexually attracted to both sexes. — *n.* **1.** A hermaphrodite. **2.** A bisexual person. — **bi·sex′u·al·ism, bi·sex·u·al·i·ty** (bī-sek′-shŏŏ·al′ə·tē) *n.* — **bi·sex′u·al·ly** *adv.*

bish·op (bish′əp) *n.* **1.** A prelate in the Christian church; esp., the head of a diocese. **2.** A miter-shaped chess piece that may be moved only diagonally. [OE *biscop*]

bish·op·ric (bish′əp·rik) *n.* The office or the diocese of a bishop.

bis·muth (biz′məth) *n.* A lustrous, reddish white metallic element (symbol Bi) occurring native as well as in combination, used in medicine, in the manufacture of cosmetics, etc. See ELEMENT. [< G] — **bis·muth·al** (biz′məth·əl) *adj.*

bi·son (bī′sən, -zən) *n. pl.* **bi·son** A bovine ruminant, closely related to the true ox; esp., the North American buffalo. [< L *bison* wild ox, ult. < Gmc.]

bisque (bisk) *n.* **1.** A thick, rich soup made from meat or fish, esp. shellfish. **2.** Any thickened, creamy soup. **3.** A kind of ice cream containing crushed macaroons or nuts. [< F]

bis·ter (bis′tər) *n.* **1.** A yellowish brown pigment made from soot, used chiefly as a watercolor wash. **2.** A dark brown color. Also **bis′tre.** [< F *bistre* dark brown] — **bis′tered** *adj.*

NORTH AMERICAN BISON (5 to 6 feet high at shoulder)

bis·tro (bis′tro, *Fr.* bē-strō′) *n. Informal* A small bar, tavern or night club. [< F]

bi·sul·fate (bī-sul′fāt) *n. Chem.* An acid sulfate containing the radical HSO₄; also called *disulfate*. Also **bi·sul′phate.**

bi·sul·fide (bī-sul′fīd) *n. Chem.* A disulfide. Also **bi·sul′phide.**

bit¹ (bit) *n.* **1.** A small piece, portion, or quantity. **2.** A short time. **3.** A small part, as in a play or movie. **4.** *U.S.* The Spanish real, worth 12½ cents: now used chiefly in the expression *two bits.* — **to do one's bit** To make one's contribution; do one's share. — *adj.* Small; insignificant; minor. [OE *bita* < *bītan* to bite]

bit² (bit) *n.* **1.** A sharp-edged tool for boring or drilling, having a shank for attachment to a brace, drill press, etc. **2.** The sharp or cutting part of a tool. **3.** The metallic mouthpiece of a bridle. **4.** Anything that controls or restrains. **5.** The part of a key that turns a lock. — *v.t.* **bit·ted, bit·ting** **1.** To put a bit in the mouth of (a horse). **2.** To curb; restrain. [OE *bite* a biting < *bītan* to bite]

bit³ (bit) Past tense and alternative past participle of BITE.

bit⁴ (bit) *n.* A unit of information, expressed as a choice between two equally probable alternative messages or symbols, as a "yes" and a "no" or a dot and a dash. [< *b(inary)* + *(dig)it*]

BITS AND BRACE
a Brace (or bitstock). Bits: *b* Screwdriver, *c* Drill, *d* Ship auger, *e* Auger, *f* Expanding, *g* Chuck (cross-section).

bitch (bich) *n.* **1.** The female of the dog or other canine animal **2.** *Slang* A malicious or promiscuous woman: an abusive term. — *v.i. Slang* To complain. — **to bitch up** *Slang* To botch. [< OE *bicce*] — **bitch′y** *adj.*

bite (bīt) *v.* **bit, bit·ten** or **bit, bit·ing** *v.t.* **1.** To seize, tear, or wound with the teeth. **2.** To cut or tear off with or as with the teeth: usually with *off.* **3.** To puncture the skin of with a sting or fangs. **4.** To cut or pierce. **5.** To cause to sting or smart. **6.** To eat into; corrode. **7.** To grip; take hold of. **8.** To cheat; deceive: usually passive. — *v.i.* **9.** To seize or cut into something with the teeth. **10.** To have the effect of biting, as mustard; sting. **11.** To take firm hold; grip. **12.** To take as bait, as fish. **13.** To be tricked. — **to bite off more than one can chew** To attempt something beyond one's capabilities. — *n.* **1.** The act of biting. **2.** A wound inflicted by biting. **3.** A painful sensation; smart; sting. **4.** A morsel of food; mouthful. **5.** *Informal* A light meal; snack. **6.** The grip or hold taken by a tool, etc. [OE *bītan*] — **bit′a·ble** or **bite′a·ble** *adj.* — **bit′er** *n.*

bit·ing (bī′ting) *adj.* **1.** Sharp; stinging. **2.** Sarcastic; caustic. — **bit′ing·ly** *adv.* — **bit′ing·ness** *n.*

bit·stock (bit′stok′) *n.* A brace for a bit. For illus. see BIT².

bitt (bit) *Naut. n.* A post or vertical timber on a ship's deck, to which cables, etc., are made fast, usually in pairs. — *v t.* To wind (a cable) around a bitt. [? < ON *biti* beam]

bit·ten (bit′n) Past participle of BITE.

bit·ter (bit′ər) *adj.* **1.** Having an acrid, disagreeable taste. **2.** Unpleasant to accept; distasteful. **3.** Painful to body or mind; harsh. **4.** Feeling or showing intense animosity. **5.** Stinging; sharp. — **Syn.** See SOUR. — *n.* That which is bitter. — *v.t. & v.i.* To make or become bitter. [OE *biter* < *bītan* to bite] — **bit′ter·ly** *adv.* — **bit′ter·ness** *n.*

bit·tern (bit′ərn) *n.* Any of various wading birds related to the heron. [< OF *butor*, ? < L *butio, -onis* bittern]

bit·ter·root (bit′ər·rŏŏt′, -rōōt′) *n.* An herb with nutritious roots and pink or white flowers.

bit·ters (bit′ərz) *n.pl.* A liquor, usu. spirituous, prepared with an infusion of bitter herbs, etc.

bit·ter·sweet (bit′ər·swēt′) *n.* A shrubby or climbing plant having green flowers succeeded by orange pods. — *adj.* **1.** Bitter and sweet. **2.** Pleasant and unpleasant.

bi·tu·men (bi-tōō′mən, -tyōō′-, bich′ōō·mən) *n.* **1.** Any natural mixture of solid and semisolid hydrocarbons, as asphalt. **2.** A brown paint made by mixing asphalt with a drying oil. [< L] — **bi·tu·mi·noid** (bi-tōō′mə·noid) *adj.*

bi·tu·mi·nize (bi-tōō′mə·nīz, -tyōō′-) *v.t.* **-nized, -niz·ing** To render bituminous. — **bi·tu·mi·ni·za′tion** *n.*

bi·tu·mi·nous (bi-tōō′mə·nəs, -tyōō′-, bī-) *adj.* **1.** Of, pertaining to, or containing bitumen. **2.** Containing many volatile hydrocarbons, as shale. [< F *bitumineux*]

bituminous coal A mineral coal low in carbon and burning with a yellow, smoky flame: also called *soft coal.*

bi·va·lent (bī-vā′lənt, biv′ə-) *adj. Chem.* **a** Having a valence of two. **b** Having two valences. Also *divalent.* — **bi·va·lence** (bī-vā′ləns, biv′ə-), **bi·va·len·cy** (-vā′ən·sē) *n.*

bi·valve (bī′valv′) *n. Zool.* A mollusk having a shell of two lateral valves hinged together, as the oyster or clam. — *adj.* Having two valves or parts: also **bi′valved′, bi·val′vous** (bī-val′vəs), **bi·val·vu·lar** (bī-val′vyə·lər).

biv·ou·ac (biv′ōō·ak, biv′wak) *n.* A temporary encampment, esp. for soldiers in the field. — *v.i.* **·acked, ·ack·ing** To encamp in a bivouac. [< F < G *beiwacht* guard]

bi·week·ly (bī-wēk′lē) *adj.* **1.** Occuring once every two weeks. **2.** Occurring twice a week; semiweekly. — *n.* A biweekly publication. — *adv.* **1.** Once in two weeks. **2.** Twice a week.

bi·year·ly (bī-yir′lē) *adj. & adv.* **1.** Occurring twice yearly. **2.** Biennial. — *adv.* Twice a year.

bi·zarre (bi-zär′) *adj.* Singular or eccentric in style, manner, etc.; odd; fantastic; grotesque. [< F, ? ult. < Basque] — **bi·zarre′ly** *adv.* — **bi·zarre′ness** *n.*

blab (blab) *v.t. & v.i.* **blabbed, blab·bing** **1.** To disclose indiscreetly. **2.** To prattle. — *n.* **1.** One who blabs. **2.** Idle chatter. Also **blab′ber.** [ME *blabbe* idle talker]

blab·ber·mouth (blab′ər·mouth′) *n.* One who talks too much and can't be trusted to keep secrets.

black (blak) *adj.* **1.** Having no brightness or color; reflecting no light. **2.** Destitute of light. **3.** Gloomy; dismal; forbidding. **4.** Belonging to a racial group characterized by dark skin; esp., Negroid. **5.** Of, pertaining to, or controlled by black men: *black* power. **6.** Soiled; stained. **7.** Indicating disgrace or censure. **8.** Angry; threatening. **9.** Evil; wicked; malignant. **10.** Wearing black garments. **11.** Of coffee, without cream. — *n.* **1.** The absence of light; the darkest of all colors. **2.** Something black, as soot. **3.** A Negro. — *v.t.* **1.** To make black; blacken. **2.** To put blacking on and polish (shoes). — *v.i.* **3.** To become black. — **to black out** **1.** To delete by scoring through. **2.** To suffer a temporary loss of vision or consciousness. **3.** To extinguish or screen all lights. [OE *blæc* dark] — **black′ness** *n.*

black Africa Those states or parts of Africa whose inhabitants are mainly dark-skinned and belong to the Negroid ethnic division of mankind. — **black African**

black-and-blue (blak′ən-blŏŏ′) *adj.* Discolored: said of skin that has been bruised.

black and white **1.** Writing or print. **2.** A sketch or picture in various shades of black and white.

black art Necromancy; magic.

black·ball (blak′bôl′) *n.* A negative vote. — *v.t.* **1.** To vote against. **2.** To ostracize; exclude. — **black′ball′er** *n.*

black bass A fresh-water game fish of the eastern U.S. and Canada.

black bear The common North American bear, having fur that varies from glossy black to cinnamon brown.

black·ber·ry (blak′ber′ē, -bər·ē) *n. pl.* **·ries.** **1.** The black, edible fruit of certain shrubs of the rose family. **2.** Any of the plants producing it.

black·bird (blak′bûrd′) *n.* A common European thrush, the male of which is black with a yellow bill.

black·board (blak′bôrd′, -bōrd′) *n.* A blackened surface, often of slate, for drawing and writing upon with chalk.

Black Death An exceptionally virulent plague, epidemic in Asia and Europe during the 14th century: also called *plague.*

black·en (blak′ən) *v.* **·ened, ·en·ing** **1.** To make black or dark. **2.** To slander; defame. — *v.i.* **3.** To become black; darken. [ME *blaknen* < *blak* black] — **black′en·er** *n.*

black eye **1.** An eye with a black iris. **2.** An eye having the adjacent surface discolored by a blow or bruise. **3.** *Informal* A cause of discredit; blot. — **black′ eyed′** *adj.*

black-eyed Susan One of the coneflowers, with black-centered yellow flowers: also called *yellow daisy.*

black·face (blak′fās′) n. 1. An entertainer with exaggerated Negro make-up, esp. a minstrel comedian. 2. The make-up worn by such an entertainer.
black flag The Jolly Roger.
Black·foot (blak′foŏt′) n. pl. ·feet (-fēt′) A member of any of the tribes of Algonquian North American Indians living in Alberta and Montana. — adj. Of the Blackfeet.
black·guard (blag′ərd, -ärd) n. An unprincipled scoundrel; a rogue. — v.t. 1. To revile; vilify. — v.i. 2. To act like a blackguard. — adj. Of or like a blackguard; base; vile: also **black′guard·ly**. [< black guard] — **black′guard·ism** n.
black·head (blak′hed′) n. 1. A bird having a black head, as the American scaup duck. 2. Vet. A disease of turkeys. 3. A plug of dried, fatty matter in a pore of the skin.
black-heart·ed (blak′här′tid) adj. Evil; wicked.
black·ing (blak′ing) n. A preparation used to give blackness or luster to shoes, stoves, etc.
black·jack (blak′jak′) n. 1. A small bludgeon with a flexible handle. 2. A pirate's flag. 3. A small oak of the SE U.S. having black bark. 4. Twenty-one, a card game. 5. A large drinking cup. — v.t. 1. To strike with a blackjack. 2. To coerce by threat.
black lead Graphite.
black letter Printing A type face characterized by heavy black letters resembling those of early 𝕿𝖍𝖎𝖘 𝖑𝖎𝖓𝖊 𝖎𝖘 𝖎𝖓 𝖇𝖑𝖆𝖈𝖐 𝖑𝖊𝖙𝖙𝖊𝖗. printed works: also called gothic, Old English. — **black·let·ter** (blak′let′ər) adj.
black·list (blak′list′) n. A list of persons or organizations under suspicion or censure, or refused approval or employment for any cause. — v.t. To place on a blacklist.
black·ly (blak′lē) adv. Darkly, gloomily, or threateningly.
black magic Witchcraft.
black·mail (blak′māl′) n. Extortion by threats of public accusation or of exposure; also, that which is so extorted, as money. — v.t. 1. To levy blackmail upon. 2. To force (to do something), as by threats: with into. [< BLACK + MAIL³] — **black′mail·er** n.
black man 1. A person belonging to a racial group characterized by dark skin; esp., in the U.S., an Afro-American. 2. A male member of the so-called black race.
Black Ma·ri·a (mə-rī′ə) Informal A patrol wagon.
black mark A mark of censure, failure, etc.
black market A market where goods are sold in violation of official prices, quotas, etc.
Black Muslim A member of a sect (the **Nation of Islam**) of Negroes in the U.S., which follows the practices of Islam and rejects integration with the white race.
black·out (blak′out′) n. 1. The extinguishing or screening of all lights, esp. as a precaution against air raids. 2. Physiol. Partial or complete loss of vision and sometimes of consciousness, as experienced by airplane pilots during rapid changes in velocity. 3. In the theater, the extinguishing of the lights on a stage. 4. A ban, as on news.
black race The Negroid ethnic division of mankind.
black sheep One regarded as a disgrace by his family.
black·smith (blak′smith′) n. 1. One who shoes horses. 2. One who works iron on an anvil and uses a forge.
black·snake (blak′snāk′) n. 1. Any of various agile, nonvenomous snakes of the eastern U.S., having smooth, black scales. 2. U.S. A heavy, pliant whip of braided leather.
black·thorn (blak′thôrn′) n. 1. A thorny European shrub of the rose family. 2. Its small, plumlike, astringent fruit. Also called sloe. 3. A cane made from its wood.
black tie 1. A black bow tie. 2. A tuxedo and its correct accessories.
black widow The venomous female of a North American spider: so called from its color and its eating of its mate.
blad·der (blad′ər) n. 1. Anat. A distensible membranous sac in the anterior part of the pelvic cavity, for the temporary retention of urine. ◆ Collateral adjective: vesical. 2. An inflatable object resembling a bladder: the bladder of a basketball. [OE blǽdre] — **blad′der·y** adj.
blad·der·wort (blad′ər-wûrt′) n. An aquatic herb having little bladders on the leaves in which minute organisms are trapped for nutriment.
blade (blād) n. 1. The flat, cutting part of any edged tool or weapon. 2. The thin, flat part of an oar, plow, etc. 3. The leaf of grasses of other plants. 4. A sword. 5. A dashing or reckless young man. 6. Phonet. The upper surface of the tongue behind the tip. 7. Bot. The broad, flat part of a leaf, petal, etc. [OE blǽd] — **blad′ed** adj.
blah (blä) n. U.S. Slang Nonsense.
blain (blān) n. Pathol. A pustule; blister. [OE blegen]
blam·a·ble (blā′mə-bəl) adj. Derserving blame; culpable. Also **blame′a·ble**. — **blam′a·ble·ness** n. — **blam′a·bly** adv.
blame (blām) v.t. blamed, blam·ing 1. To hold responsible; accuse. 2. To find fault with; reproach. 3. To place

the responsibility for (an action or error). — **to be to blame** To be at fault. — n. 1. Expression of censure; reproof. 2. Responsibility for something wrong; culpability. [< OF < LL blasphemare to revile, reproach] — **blame′ful** adj. — **blame′ful·ly** adv. — **blame′ful·ness** n. — **blame′·less** adj. — **blame′less·ly** adv. — **blame′less·ness** n.
blame·wor·thy (blām′wûr′thē) adj. Deserving of blame. — **blame′wor′thi·ness** n.
blanch (blanch, blänch) v.t. 1. To remove the color from; bleach. 2. To cause to turn pale. 3. To remove the skin of or whiten. — v.i. 4. To turn or become white or pale. — Syn. See WHITEN. [< F blanc white] — **blanch′er** n.
blanc·mange (blə-mänzh′) n. A whitish, jellylike preparation of milk, eggs, sugar, cornstarch, flavoring, etc., used chiefly for desserts. [< OF blanc-manger, lit., white food]
bland (bland) adj. 1. Gentle and soothing; suave. 2. Not stimulating or irritating; mild. [< L blandus mild] — **bland′ly** adv. — **bland′ness** n.
blan·dish (blan′dish) v.t. To wheedle; flatter. [< OF < L blandus mild] — **blan′dish·er** n. — **blan′dish·ment** n.
blank (blangk) adj. 1. Free from writing or print. 2. Not completed or filled out, as a check. 3. Showing no expression or interest; vacant. 4. Lacking variety or interest. 5. Disconcerted; bewildered. 6. Utter; complete: blank dismay. 7. Empty or void; also, fruitless. — n. 1. An empty space; void. 2. A blank space in a printed document, to be filled in. 3. A paper or document with such spaces. 4. A lottery ticket that has drawn no prize. 5. A partially prepared piece, as of metal, ready for forming into a finished object, as a key. 6. A cartridge filled with powder but having no bullets: also **blank cartridge**. — v.t. 1. To delete; invalidate: often with out. 2. In games, to prevent (an opponent) from scoring. [< OF blanc white] — **blank′·ly** adv. — **blank′ness** n.
blank check Informal 1. A check bearing a signature but no specified amount. 2. Unlimited authority or freedom.
blan·ket (blang′kit) n. 1. A large piece of woolen or other soft, warm fabric, used as a covering in bed, as a robe, etc. 2. Anything that covers, conceals, or protects: a blanket of fog. — adj. Covering a wide range of conditions, items, or the like: a blanket indictment. — v.t. 1. To cover with or as with a blanket. 2. To cover or apply to uniformly. 3. To obscure or suppress; interfere with. [< OF blankete, dim. of blanc white; orig. a white or undyed woolen cloth]
blank verse Verse without rhyme; esp., iambic pentameter verse, used in English epic and dramatic poetry.
blare (blâr) v.t. & v.i. blared, blar·ing 1. To sound loudly, as a trumpet. 2. To exclaim noisily. — n. 1. A loud brazen sound. 2. Brightness or glare, as of color. [Prob. imit.]
blar·ney (blär′nē) n. Wheedling flattery; cajolery. — v.t. & v.i. To flatter, cajole, or wheedle. [< BLARNEY STONE]
Blarney Stone A stone in a castle in Blarney, Ireland, that reputedly endows one who kisses it with skill in flattery.
bla·sé (blä-zā′, blä′zä) adj. Wearied or bored, as from over-indulgence in pleasure. [< F blaser to satiate]
blas·pheme (blas-fēm′) v. ·phemed, ·phem·ing v.t. 1. To speak in an impious manner of (God or sacred things). 2. To speak ill of; malign. — v.i. 3. To utter blasphemy. [< OF < LL < Gk. blasphēmos evil-speaking]
blas·phe·mous (blas′fə-məs) adj. Expressing blasphemy. — **blas′phe·mous·ly** adv. — **blas′phe·mous·ness** n.
blas·phe·my (blas′fə-mē) n. pl. ·mies Impious or profane speaking of God, or of sacred persons or things. — **Syn.** See PROFANITY. [< OF < LL < Gk. blasphēmia]
blast (blast, bläst) v.t. 1. To rend in pieces by or as by explosion. 2. To cause to wither or shrivel; destroy. — **to blast off** Aerospace To begin an ascent by means of rocket or jet propulsion. — n. 1. A strong wind; gust. 2. A loud, sudden sound, as of a trumpet. 3. A rush of air, as from the mouth. 4. A strong, artificial current of air, steam, etc. 5. An explosion of dynamite, etc.; also, the charge set off. 6. A blight. — **at full blast** At capacity operation or maximum speed. [OE blǽst] — **blast′er** n.
blast·ed (blas′tid, bläs′-) adj. 1. Withered or destroyed; blighted. 2. Damned: a euphemism.
blast furnace Metall. A smelting furnace in which the fire is intensified by an air blast.
blasto- combining form Biol. Growth; sprout. Also, before vowels, **blast-**. [< Gk. blastos sprout]
blast·off (blast′ôf′, -of′, bläst′-) n. Aerospace The series of events immediately before and after a rocket leaves its launching pad; also the moment of leaving.
blas·tu·la (blas′choŏ-lə) n. pl. ·lae (-lē) Biol. The stage of the embryo just preceding the formation of the gastrula; a hollow sphere of one layer of cells. [< NL < Gk. blastos sprout] — **blas′tu·lar** adj.
blat (blat) v. blat·ted, blat·ting v.t. 1. Informal To blurt out. — v.i. 2. To bleat, as a sheep. [Var. of BLEAT]

bla·tant (blā'tənt) *adj.* **1.** Offensively loud or noisy; clamorous. **2.** Obvious; obtrusive: *blatant* stupidity. [Coined by Edmund Spenser] **— bla'tan·cy** *n.* **— bla'tant·ly** *adv.*

blath·er (blath'ər) *v.t. & v.i.* To speak or utter foolishly; babble. **—** *n.* Foolish talk. [< ON *blathr* nonsense]

blath·er·skite (blath'ər·skīt) *n.* **1.** A blustering, talkative person. **2.** Foolish talk.

blaze¹ (blāz) *v.* blazed, blaz·ing *v.i.* **1.** To burn brightly. **2.** To burn as with emotion. **3.** To shine; be resplendent. **—** *n.* **1.** A vivid glowing flame; fire. **2.** Brilliance; glow. **3.** Sudden activity; outburst, as of anger. [OE *blæse*]

blaze² (blāz) *v.t.* blazed, blaz·ing **1.** To mark (a tree) by chipping off a piece of bark. **2.** To indicate (a trail) by marking trees in this way. **—** *n.* **1.** A white spot on the face of a horse, etc. **2.** A mark chipped on a tree to indicate a trail. [Akin to ON *blesi* white spot on a horse's face]

blaz·er (blā'zər) *n.* A lightweight, often striped, jacket for informal wear. [< BLAZE¹]

bla·zon (blā'zən) *v.t.* **1.** To inscribe or adorn, as with names or symbols. **2.** To describe or depict (coats of arms) in technical detail. **3.** To proclaim; publish. **—** *n.* **1.** A coat of arms. **2.** A technical description of armorial bearings. **3.** Ostentatious display. [< OF *blason* coat of arms, shield] **— bla'zon·er** *n.* **— bla'zon·ment** *n.* **— bla'zon·ry** *n.*

-ble See -ABLE.

bleach (blēch) *v.t. & v.i.* To make or become colorless or white; whiten. **— Syn.** See WHITEN. **—** *n.* **1.** The act of bleaching. **2.** The degree of bleaching obtained. **3.** A fluid or powder used as a bleaching agent. [OE *blǣcean*]

bleach·er (blē'chər) *n.* **1.** One who or that which bleaches. **2.** *pl. U.S.* Unroofed outdoor seats for spectators.

bleak (blēk) *adj.* **1.** Exposed to wind and weather; bare; barren. **2.** Cold; cutting. **3.** Cheerless; dreary. [? < ON *bleikr* pale] **— bleak'ly** *adv.* **— bleak'ness** *n.*

blear (blir) *v.t.* **1.** To dim (the eyes) with or as with tears. **2.** To blur or make dim. **—** *adj.* Bleary. [ME *blere*]

blear-eyed (blir'īd') *adj.* **1.** Having eyes bleared by tears, old age, etc. **2.** Dull of perception.

blear·y (blir'ē) *adj.* ·i·er, ·i·est **1.** Made dim, as by tears. **2.** Blurred; dim. **— blear'i·ly** *adv.* **— blear'i·ness** *n.*

bleat (blēt) *v.i.* **1.** To utter the cry of a sheep, goat, or calf. **2.** To speak or complain with a similar sound. **—** *v.t.* **3.** To utter with a bleat. **4.** To babble; prate. **—** *n.* The act or sound of bleating. [OE *blǣtan*] **— bleat'er** *n.*

bleed (blēd) *v.* bled, bleed·ing *v.i.* **1.** To lose or shed blood. **2.** To suffer wounds or die. **3.** To feel grief, sympathy, or anguish. **4.** To exude sap or other fluid. **5.** *Printing* To extend to or beyond the edge of a page, as an illustration. **—** *v.t.* **6.** To draw blood from; leech. **7.** To exude, as sap, blood, etc. **8.** *Printing* To print (an illustration, etc.) so that it will bleed. [OE *blēdan*]

bleed·er (blē'dər) *n.* **1.** One who bleeds profusely, even from a slight wound. **2.** A hemophiliac.

bleeding heart A plant having racemes of pink, drooping flowers.

blem·ish (blem'ish) *v.t.* To mar the perfection of; sully. **—** *n.* **1.** A disfiguring defect, esp. of the skin. **2.** A moral fault or stain. [< OF *blemir* to make livid] **— blem'ish·er** *n.*

blench¹ (blench) *v.i.* To shrink back; flinch. [OE *blencan* to deceive] **— blench'er** *n.*

blench² (blench) *v.t. & v.i.* To make or become pale; blanch. [Var. of BLANCH¹]

BLEEDING
HEART
(1 to 3
feet high)

blend (blend) *v.* blend·ed or (less commonly) blent, blend·ing *v.t.* **1.** To mingle and combine so as to obscure or harmonize the varying components. **2.** To mix so as to obtain a uniform product: to *blend* paints. **—** *v.i.* **3.** To mix; intermingle. **4.** To pass or shade imperceptibly into each other, as colors. **5.** To harmonize. **—** *n.* The act or result of mixing. [Prob. < ON *blanda* to mix] **— blend'er** *n.*

blende (blend) *n. Mineral.* One of a number of rather bright minerals combining sulfur with a metallic element. [< G *blendendes erz* deceptive ore]

blended whisky *U.S.* Whisky that has been blended with other whisky or neutral spirits.

blen·ny (blen'ē) *n. pl.* ·nies A small marine fish having an elongated body. [< L < Gk. *blennos* slime]

bless (bles) *v.t.* blessed or blest, bless·ing **1.** To consecrate; make holy by religious rite. **2.** To honor and exalt; glorify. **3.** To make the sign of the cross over, as for sanctification or protection. **4.** To invoke God's favor upon (a person or thing). **5.** To bestow prosperity upon; make happy. **6.** To endow, as with a gift: She was *blessed* with a beautiful face. **7.** To guard; protect: *Bless* me! [OE *blēdsian* to consecrate (with blood) < *blōd* blood] **— bless'er** *n.*

bless·ed (bles'id, blest) *adj.* **1.** Made holy by a religious rite; consecrated. **2.** Enjoying the happiness of heaven; beatified. **3.** Blissful; happy. **4.** Causing happiness. Also spelled *blest.* **— bless'ed·ly** *adv.* **— bless'ed·ness** *n.*

bless·ed event (bles'id) *Informal* The birth of a baby.

Blessed Virgin The Virgin Mary.

bless·ing (bles'ing) *n.* **1.** An invocation or benediction of grace. **2.** The bestowal of divine favor. **3.** That which makes happy or prosperous. **4.** Grateful adoration.

blest (blest) Alternative past participle of BLESS. **—** *adj.* Blessed.

blew (bloo) Past tense of BLOW.

blight (blīt) *n.* **1.** Any of a number of destructive plant diseases, as mildew, rust, smut, etc. **2.** Anything causing such a disease. **3.** Anything that withers hopes, destroys prospects, or impairs growth. **4.** The state of being blighted. **—** *v.t.* **1.** To cause to decay; blast. **2.** To ruin; frustrate. **—** *v.i.* **3.** To suffer blight. [Origin unknown]

blimp (blimp) *n. Informal* A nonrigid dirigible. [< Type *B-Limp*, a kind of British dirigible]

blind (blīnd) *adj.* **1.** Unable to see. **2.** Lacking in perception or judgment. **3.** Acting or done without intelligent control; random. **4.** Unreasoning; heedless: *blind* prejudice. **5.** Concealed: a *blind* ditch. **6.** Closed at one end: a *blind* alley. **7.** Having no opening or outlet: a *blind* wall. **8.** Insensible. **9.** Done without the aid of visual reference: *blind* flying. **10.** Of or for blind persons. **—** *n.* **1.** Something that obstructs vision or shuts off light; esp., a window shade. **2.** A hiding place, as for a hunter; ambush. **3.** Something intended to deceive. **—** *adv.* **1.** Blindly. **2.** Without the aid of visual reference: to fly *blind*. **—** *v.t.* **1.** To make blind. **2.** To dazzle. **3.** To deprive of judgment or discernment. **4.** To darken; obscure. **5.** To eclipse. [OE] **— blind'ing** *adj.* **— blind'ing·ly** *adv.* **— blind'ly** *adv.* **— blind'ness** *n.*

blind alley **1.** An alley, road, etc., open at one end only. **2.** Any search, pursuit, etc., in which progress is blocked.

blind date *Informal* A date with a person of the opposite sex whom one has not previously met.

blind·er (blīn'dər) *n.* **1.** One who or that which blinds. **2.** *U.S.* A flap on the side of a horse's bridle, serving to obstruct sideways vision, also called *blinker*.

blind·fold (blīnd'fōld') *v.t.* **1.** To cover or bandage the eyes of. **2.** To hoodwink; mislead. **—** *n.* A bandage over the eyes. **—** *adj.* **1.** Having the eyes bandaged. **2.** Reckless; rash. [ME < *blind* blind + *fellen* to strike]

blind·man's buff (blīnd'manz') A game in which one player is blindfolded and must catch and identify another player.

blind spot **1.** *Anat.* A small area on the retina of the eye that is insensible to light because of the entrance of the optic nerve. **2.** A subject about which one is ignorant, or incapable of objective thought.

blink (blingk) *v.i.* **1.** To wink rapidly. **2.** To squint, as in sunlight. **3.** To twinkle; also, to flash on and off. **4.** To look indifferently or evasively: with *at*. **—** *v.t.* **5.** To cause to wink. **6.** To shut the eyes to; evade. **—** *n.* **1.** A blinking; wink. **2.** A gleam. **3.** A glance or glimpse. [< Du. *blinken*; ult. origin uncertain]

blink·er (blingk'ər) *n.* **1.** A light that blinks, as in warning or for sending messages. **2.** *pl.* Goggles. **3.** Blinder (def. 2).

blint·ze (blint'sə) *n.* A thin pancake folded about a filling of cottage cheese, potato, fruit, etc., and usu. eaten with sour cream or jam. Also **blintz.** [< Yiddish]

blip (blip) *n. Telecom.* One of the luminous signals recorded on a radarscope. [? Var. of *flip*]

bliss (blis) *n.* **1.** Gladness; joy. **2.** A cause of delight or happiness. [OE *blithe* joyous] **— bliss'ful** *adj.* **— bliss'ful·ly** *adv.* **— bliss'ful·ness** *n.*

blis·ter (blis'tər) *n.* **1.** A thin vesicle, esp. on the skin, containing watery matter, as from rubbing, a burn, etc. **2.** A similar swelling on various other surfaces. **—** *v.t.* **1.** To produce a blister or blisters upon. **2.** To rebuke severely. **—** *v.i.* **3.** To become blistered. [< OF < ON *blāstr* swelling] **— blis'ter·y** *adj.*

blister beetle The Spanish fly.

blithe (blīth, blith) *adj.* **1.** Cheerful; gay. **2.** Casual or airy in manner. [OE] **— blithe'ly** *adv.* **— blithe'ness** *n.*

blithe·some (blīth'səm, blith'-) *adj.* Showing or imparting gladness. **— blithe'some·ly** *adv.* **— blithe'some·ness** *n.*

blitz (blits) *Informal n.* A sudden attack; blitzkrieg. **—** *v.t.* To subject to a blitzkrieg.

blitz·krieg (blits'krēg) *n.* **1.** *Mil.* A swift, sudden attack by tanks, aircraft, etc.; also, warfare so waged. **2.** Any sudden attack or assault. [< G < *blitz* lightning + *krieg* war]

bliz·zard (bliz'ərd) *n.* A severe snowstorm, often with high, cold winds. [< dial. E *blizzer* sudden blow]

bloat (blōt) *v.t.* **1.** To cause to swell, as with fluid. **2.** To puff up; make proud or vain. **—** *v.i.* **3.** To swell; become puffed up. [ME, ? < ON *blautr* soft, soaked]

bloat·er (blō'tər) *n.* **1.** A smoked herring. **2.** A whitefish of the Great Lakes of North America.

blob (blob) *n.* **1.** A soft, globular mass; a drop, as of viscous liquid. **2.** A daub or spot, as of color. **—** *v.t.* blobbed, blobbing To mark with ink or color; blot. [Origin unknown]

bloc (blok) *n.* A group, as of politicians, nations, etc., combined to foster special interests. **— Syn.** See FACTION. [< F]

block¹ (blok) *n.* **1.** A solid piece of wood, metal, etc., usu. with one or more flat surfaces. **2.** Such a piece on which cutting or chopping is done. **3.** A support or form on which something is shaped or displayed: a hat *block.* **4.** A stand from which articles are sold at auction. **5.** A small cube used by children for building. **6.** A set or section, as of tickets, etc., handled as a unit. **7.** A section of railroad controlled by signals. **8.** *U.S.* An area bounded, usu. on four sides, by streets; also, one side of such an area. **9.** *U.S. & Canadian* An office building. **10.** *Canadian* A group of townships in the midst of unsurveyed land. **11.** A pulley, or set of pulleys, in a frame with a hook or the like at one end. **12.** A piece of wood prepared for engraving. — *v.t.* **1.** To shape into blocks. **2.** To shape, with a block, as a hat. **3.** To secure or strengthen with blocks. — **to block out** To plan broadly without details. [< F *bloc,* ult. < Gmc.] — **block′er** *n.*

BLOCKS¹ (*def.* 13)

a Tackle. *b* Dock, with attaching screw. *c* Snatch. *d* Triple-sheave steel. *e* Gin. *f* Square-cheeked.

block² (blok) *n.* **1.** An obstacle or hindrance. **2.** The act of obstructing, or the state of being obstructed. **3.** In sports, interference with an opponent's actions. **4.** *Med. & Pathol.* **a** An obstruction, as of a nerve or blood vessel. **b** Anesthesia of a specific region: saddle *block.* **5.** *Psychol.* The inability to think or act in certain situations. — *v.t.* **1.** To obstruct. **2.** In sports, to hinder the movements of (an opposing player); also, to stop (a ball), as with the body. **3.** *Med. & Pathol.* To stop (a nerve) from functioning, as with an anesthetic. — *v.i.* **4.** To obstruct an opponent's actions. — **to block out** To obscure from view. — **to block up** To fill (an area or space) so as to prevent movement into or through. [< MF *bloquer* to obstruct] — **block′age** *n.* — **block′er** *n.*

block·ade (blo·kād′) *n.* **1.** The closing by hostile ships or forces of a coast, city, etc., to traffic or communication. **2.** The ships or forces used for this. **3.** An obstruction to action or passage. — **to run the blockade** To elude a blockade. — *v.t.* **·ad·ed, ·ad·ing** To subject to a blockade; obstruct. — **block·ad′er** *n.*

block and tackle A set of pulley blocks and ropes for pulling or hoisting.

block·bust·er (blok′bus′tər) *n. Informal* An aerial bomb, capable of demolishing a large area.

block·head (blok′hed′) *n.* A stupid person; dolt.

block·house (blok′hous′) *n.* **1.** A fortification, formerly of logs and heavy timbers, having loopholes from which to fire. **2.** *U.S.* A house made of hewn logs set square.

block·ish (blok′ish) *adj.* Like a block; stupid; dull. Also **block′like′.** — **block′ish·ly** *adv.* — **block′ish·ness** *n.*

block letter **1.** Printing type cut from wood. **2.** A style of letters without serifs. — **block-let·ter** (blok′let′ər) *adj.*

block·y (blok′ē) *adj.* **block·i·er, block·i·est** **1.** Unequally shaded, as if printed in blocks. **2.** Short and stout; stocky.

bloke (blōk) *n. Brit. Slang* A fellow; guy.

blond (blond) *adj.* **1.** Having fair hair with light eyes and skin. **2.** Flaxen or golden, as hair. — *n.* A blond person. [< F < Med.L *blondus,* prob. < Gmc.]

blonde (blond) *adj.* Blond: feminine form. — *n.* A blonde woman or girl.

blood (blud) *n.* **1.** *Physiol.* The typically red fluid that circulates through the heart, arteries, and veins of animals and delivers oxygen and nutrients to the cells and tissues of the body. ◆ Collateral adjective: *hemal.* **2.** A liquid or juice resembling this in some way, as the sap of plants. **3.** The shedding of blood; slaughter; murder. **4.** Disposition of mind; temperament: hot *blood.* **5.** The principle of life; vitality; lifeblood. **6.** Descent from a common ancestor; kinship. **7.** Noble descent. **8.** Racial or national extraction. **9.** A dashing young man; also, a rake. — **in cold blood** **1.** Deliberately; without passion. **2.** Cruelly; without mercy. — **to make one's blood boil** (or **run cold**) To make one angry (or frightened). [OE *blōd*]

blood bank A place where blood is stored, either in liquid form or as dried plasma, for use in transfusion.

blood bath Wanton killing; a massacre.

blood count *Med.* A measure of the number and proportion of red and white cells in a given sample of blood.

blood·cur·dling (blud′kûrd′ling) *adj.* Terrifying.

blood·ed (blud′id) *adj.* **1.** Having blood or temper of a specified character: *cold-blooded.* **2.** Thoroughbred.

blood group *Physiol.* One of the classes into which blood may be divided on the basis of specific differences in its composition: also called *blood type.*

blood·hound (blud′hound′) *n.* **1.** A large, smooth-coated hound remarkable for its keen sense of smell, and often used to track fugitives. **2.** *Informal* Any persistent pursuer.

blood·less (blud′lis) *adj.* **1.** Devoid of blood; pale. **2.** Without bloodshed. **3.** Lacking vigor; listless. **4.** Cold-hearted. — **blood′less·ly** *adv.* — **blood′less·ness** *n.*

blood·let·ting (blud′let′ing) *n.* **1.** Bleeding for a therapeutic purpose. **2.** Bloodshed.

blood money **1.** *Informal* Money obtained at the cost of another's life, welfare, etc. **2.** Money paid to a hired murderer. **3.** Compensation paid to the kin of a murdered man.

blood plasma *Physiol.* The liquid part of the blood, without its cellular components.

blood platelet *Physiol.* One of the minute bodies found in the blood of higher vertebrates, essential to coagulation.

blood poisoning *Pathol.* Deterioration of the blood caused by bacterial substances: also called *toxemia.*

blood pressure *Physiol.* The pressure of the blood on the walls of the arteries, varying with the force of the heart action, with age, general condition, etc.

blood relation One who is related by birth; kinsman.

blood·root (blud′root′, -root′) *n.* A perennial North American herb having a fleshy rootstalk with deep red sap.

blood·shed (blud′shed′) *n.* The shedding of blood; slaughter; carnage. Also **blood′shed·ding.** — **blood′shed·der** *n.*

blood·shot (blud′shot′) *adj.* Suffused or shot with blood; red and inflamed or irritated: said of the eye.

blood·stain (blud′stān′) *n.* A spot produced by blood. — *v.t.* To stain with blood. — **blood′stained′** *adj.*

blood·stone (blud′stōn′) *n.* A stone of green chalcedony flecked with particles of red jasper: also called *heliotrope.*

blood stream The blood coursing through a living body.

blood·suck·er (blud′suk′ər) *n.* **1.** An animal that sucks blood, as a leech. **2.** *Informal* One who extorts or sponges.

blood·thirst·y (blud′thûrs′tē) *adj.* Thirsting for blood; cruel. — **blood′thirst·i·ly** *adv.* — **blood′thirst·i·ness** *n.*

blood transfusion *Med.* The transfer of blood from one person or animal into another.

blood type Blood group.

blood vessel Any tubular canal, as an artery, vein, or capillary, through which the blood circulates.

blood·y (blud′ē) *adj.* **blood·i·er, blood·i·est** **1.** Stained with blood. **2.** Of, like, or containing blood. **3.** Involving bloodshed. **4.** Bloodthirsty. **5.** Deep red. **6.** *Brit. Slang* Damned: a vulgarism. — *v.t.* **blood·ied, blood·y·ing** To stain with blood. — *adv. Brit. Slang* Very: a vulgarism. [OE *blōdig*] — **blood′i·ly** *adv.* — **blood′i·ness** *n.*

bloom (bloom) *n.* **1.** The flower of a plant; blossom. **2.** The state of being in flower. **3.** A growing or flourishing condition; freshness. **4.** The rosy tint of the cheeks or skin; glow. **5.** *Bot.* The powdery, waxy substance on certain fruits and leaves. **6.** Any of various earthy minerals found as a powdery incrustation on certain ores. — *v.i.* **1.** To bear flowers; blossom. **2.** To glow with health; flourish. **3.** To glow with a warm color. — *v.t.* **4.** To bring into bloom; cause to flourish. **5.** To give a bloom to. [< ON *blōm* blossom] — **bloom′y** *adj.*

bloom·ers (bloo′mərz) *n.pl.* **1.** Loose, wide trousers gathered at the knee, worn by women as a gymnasium costume. **2.** A woman's undergarment resembling these.

bloom·ing (bloo′ming) *adj.* **1.** In flower; blossoming. **2.** Flourishing. — **bloom′ing·ly** *adv.* — **bloom′ing·ness** *n.*

blos·som (blos′əm) *n.* **1.** A flower, esp. one of a plant yielding edible fruit. **2.** The state or period of flowering; bloom. — *v.i.* **1.** To come into blossom. **2.** To prosper; thrive. [OE *blōstm*] — **blos′som·less** *adj.* — **blos′som·y** *adj.*

blot (blot) *n.* **1.** A spot or stain, as of ink. **2.** A stain on reputation or character; blemish. **3.** A detraction from beauty, excellence, etc. **4.** An erasure. — *v.* **blot·ted, blot·ting** *v.t.* **1.** To spot, as with ink; stain. **2.** To disgrace; sully. **3.** To mark over or obliterate, as writing: often with *out.* **4.** To obscure: usually with *out.* **5.** To dry, as with blotting paper. **6.** To paint roughly; daub. — *v.i.* **7.** To spread in a blot or blots, as ink. **8.** To become blotted; stain. **9.** To absorb. [ME *blotte*]

blotch (bloch) *n.* **1.** A spot or blot. **2.** An eruption on the skin. — *v.t.* **1.** To mark or cover with blotches. **2.** To become blotched. [Blend of BLOT and BOTCH.] — **blotch′i·ness** *n.* — **blotch′y** *adj.*

blot·ter (blot′ər) *n.* **1.** A sheet or pad of blotting paper. **2.** The daily record of arrests in a police station.

blotting paper Unsized paper for absorbing excess ink.

blouse (blous, blouz) *n.* **1.** A woman's garment extending from the neck to the waist or just below. **2.** A loose, knee-length smock, usu. belted at the waist, worn chiefly by European workmen. **3.** The service coat of the U.S. Army uniform. — *v.t. & v.i.* **bloused** (bloust, blouzd), **blous·ing** To drape loosely or fully. [< F] — **blouse′like′** *adj.*

blow¹ (blō) *v.* **blew, blown, blow·ing** *v.i.* **1.** To be in motion: said of wind or air. **2.** To move in a current of air. **3.** To emit a current or jet of air, steam, etc., as from the mouth. **4.** To produce sound by blowing or being blown, as a trumpet. **5.** To pant; gasp for breath. **6.** To spout air and water before breathing, as a whale. **7.** To fail or become useless, as a fuse, tire, etc.: often with *out*. **8.** *Informal* To brag. **9.** *U.S. Slang* To depart; go. — *v.t.* **10.** To drive or impel by a current of air. **11.** To direct a current of air upon, as from the mouth. **12.** To sound by blowing into, as a bugle. **13.** To sound (a signal): to *blow* taps. **14.** To emit, as air or smoke, from the mouth. **15.** To clear by forcing air into or through. **16.** To put out of breath, as a horse. **17.** To form by inflating a material: to *blow* bubbles. **18.** To break, shatter, or destroy by explosion: usu. with *up, down*, etc. **19.** *Informal* To melt (a fuse). **20.** *U.S. Slang* To spend (money) lavishly; also, to treat or entertain. **21.** *U.S. Slang* To depart from; leave. **— to blow hot and cold** *Informal* To vacillate; be uncertain. **— to blow off** **1.** To let off, as steam from a boiler. **2.** *Slang* To speak in anger. **— to blow out** **1.** To extinguish by blowing. **2.** To burst, as a tire. **3.** To melt, as a fuse. **— to blow over** **1.** To pass, as a storm; subside. **2.** To pass without bad result. **— to blow up** **1.** To inflate. **2.** To make an enlargement of (a photograph). **3.** To explode. **4.** *Informal* To lose one's temper. **5.** To arise; become intense, as a storm. — *n.* **1.** A blowing, as of wind. **2.** A storm or gale. [OE *blāwan*]

blow² (blō) *n.* **1.** A sudden stroke dealt with the fist, a weapon, etc. **2.** A sudden disaster. **3.** A hostile act; assault. **— Syn.** See MISFORTUNE. **— to come to blows** To start fighting. [ME *blaw*]

blow³ (blō) *Archaic & Poetic v.* **blew, blown, blow·ing** *v.i.* **1.** To bloom; blossom. — *v.t.* **2.** To cause to bloom. — *n.* A display, as of blossoms. [OE *blōwan* to blossom]

blow·er (blō′ər) *n.* **1.** One who or that which blows. **2.** A device for forcing air through a building, furnace, etc.

blow·fly (blō′flī′) *n.* *pl.* **·flies** A blue or green fly whose larvae live in carrion or in living flesh: also called *bluebottle*.

blow·gun (blō′gun′) *n.* A long tube through which a missile, as a dart, may be blown by the breath.

blow·hole (blō′hōl′) *n.* **1.** *Zool.* The nasal openings in the heads of certain whales or other cetaceans. **2.** A vent for gas and bad air, as in mines. **3.** A hole in the ice to which seals, etc., come to breathe.

blown (blōn) Past participle of BLOW¹. — *adj.* **1.** Out of breath, as from overexertion. **2.** Inflated; swollen, esp. with gas. **3.** Made with a blowtube, blowpipe, etc.

blow·out (blō′out′) *n.* **1.** A bursting, as of a tire, or the hole so made. **2.** The melting of a fuse. **3.** *Slang* An elaborate meal or party. **4.** A flameout.

blow·pipe (blō′pīp′) *n.* **1.** A tube for blowing air or gas through a flame to direct and intensify its heat. **2.** A blowgun.

blow·torch (blō′tôrch′) *n.* An apparatus for vaporizing a combustible fluid under pressure and expelling it from a nozzle as a long, intensely hot flame, used for soldering, etc.

blow·up (blō′up′) *n.* **1.** An explosion. **2.** *Informal* A loss of self-control; outburst; also, a fight; quarrel. **3.** An enlargement, as of a photograph.

blow·y (blō′ē) *adj.* **blow·i·er, blow·i·est** Windy.

blowz·y (blou′zē) *adj.* **blowz·i·er, blowz·i·est** **1.** Disheveled; slovenly. **2.** Fat and red-faced. Also **blowzed** (blouzd). [< earlier *blowse* a fat, ruddy woman; origin uncertain]

blub·ber (blub′ər) *v.i.* **1.** To weep and sob noisily. — *v.t.* **2.** To utter with sobs. — *n.* **1.** *Zool.* The layer of fat beneath the skin of a whale or other cetacean, used as a source of oil. **2.** The act of blubbering; weeping. — *adj.* Swollen; protruding. [ME *blubren*; imit.] **— blub′ber·er** *n.* **— blub′ber·ing·ly** *adv.* **— blub′ber·y** *adj.*

blu·cher (bloo′chər, -kər) *n.* A shoe in which there is no front seam, the upper meeting above in two projecting flaps. [after G. L. *Blücher*, 1742–1819, Prussian field marshal]

bludg·eon (bluj′ən) *n.* A short club, commonly loaded at one end, used as a weapon. — *v.t.* **1.** To strike with or as with a bludgeon. **2.** To coerce; bully. [Origin unknown]

blue (bloo) *adj.* **blu·er, blu·est** **1.** Having the color of the clear sky seen in daylight. **2.** Livid, as the skin from bruising or cold. **3.** Depressed in spirits; melancholy. **4.** Dismal; dreary. **5.** Puritanical; strict. **— once in a blue moon** Very seldom. — *n.* **1.** The color of the clear sky; azure. **2.** Any pigment or dye used to impart a blue color. **3.** Bluing. **4.** *Sometimes cap.* One who wears a blue uniform. **— out of the blue** From an unsuspected source. **— the blue** **1.** The sky. **2.** The sea. — *v.t.* **blued, blu·ing** **1.** To make blue. **2.** To treat with bluing. [< OF *bleu*, ult. < Gmc.] **— blue′ly** *adv.* **— blue′ness** *n.*

blue baby An infant born with cyanosis resulting from a congenital heart lesion or from defective lungs.

Blue·beard (bloo′bird′) In folklore, a man who married and then murdered six women in succession.

blue·bell (bloo′bel′) *n.* Any one of various plants that bear blue, bell-shaped flowers.

blue·ber·ry (bloo′ber′ē, -bər·ē) *n.* *pl.* **·ries** **1.** An edible, blue or black American berry. **2.** The plant that bears it.

blue·bird (bloo′bûrd′) *n.* A small American passerine bird with predominantly blue plumage.

blue blood **1.** Aristocratic blood or descent. **2.** One of aristocratic family: also **blue-blood** (bloo′blud′). **— blue′-blood′ed** *adj.* **— blue′blood′ed·ness** *n.*

blue·bon·net (bloo′bon′it) *n.* **1.** The cornflower. **2.** An annual leguminous herb with blue flowers.

blue book **1.** A register of persons employed by the U.S. government. **2.** A register of socially prominent people. Also **blue·book** (bloo′book′).

blue·bot·tle (bloo′bot′l) *n.* **1.** A blowfly. **2.** Any of various flowers with tubular, usu. blue florets.

blue cheese A type of cheese resembling Roquefort.

blue chip **1.** In finance, the stock of a well-known company with a good sustained record of dividends, earnings, etc. **2.** A gambling chip of the highest value.

blue·coat (bloo′kōt′) *n.* A policeman.

blue devils **1.** Despondency. **2.** Delirium tremens.

blue·fish (bloo′fish′) *n.* *pl.* **·fish** or **·fish·es** A voracious food fish common along the Atlantic coast of the U.S.

blue fox A small fox of arctic regions whose pelt acquires a bluish color in summer; also, its fur.

blue·grass (bloo′gras′, -gräs′) *n.* One of various grasses; esp., the **Kentucky bluegrass.**

Bluegrass State Nickname of Kentucky.

blue·gum (bloo′gum′) *n.* Any of several eucalyptus trees.

blue·ing (bloo′ing), **blue·ish** (bloo′ish) See BLUING, etc.

blue·jack·et (bloo′jak′it) *n.* An enlisted man in the United States or British navy.

blue jay A crested, corvine bird of North America. Also **blue·jay** (bloo′jā′).

blue law *Often pl. U.S.* A puritanical law, esp. one prohibiting entertainment on Sunday.

blue·nose (bloo′nōz′) *n.* *Informal* A puritanical person.

blue-pen·cil (bloo′pen′səl) *v.t.* **·ciled** or **·cilled, ·cil·ing** or **·cil·ing** To edit or cancel with or as with a blue pencil.

blue point An oyster found off the shore of Long Island.

blue·print (bloo′print′) *n.* **1.** A plan or drawing made by printing on sensitized paper, the drawing showing in white lines on a blue ground. **2.** Any detailed plan. — *v.t.* To make a blueprint of.

blue ribbon The highest award or distinction; first prize.

blues (blooz) *n.pl.* **1.** Depression of spirits; melancholy. **2.** *Music* A style using deliberately mistuned scale degrees (**blue notes**), often in 4/4 meter with 12-measure phrases; also, the often mournful songs sung to this music.

blue·stock·ing (bloo′stok′ing) *n.* A learned, pedantic, or literary woman. [from the informal blue stockings worn by a leading literary figure in 18th-century London]

blu·et (bloo′it) *n.* **1.** One of various plants having blue flowers. **2.** A delicate meadow flower of the madder family.

bluff¹ (bluf) *v.t. & v.i.* **1.** To deceive by putting on a bold front. **2.** To frighten with empty threats. **— to bluff one's way** To obtain an object by bluffing. — *n.* **1.** The act of bluffing. **2.** One who bluffs. [? < Du. *bluffen* to deceive, mislead] **— bluff′er** *n.*

bluff² (bluf) *n.* **1.** A steep headland or bank. **2.** *Canadian* A clump of trees on a prairie. — *adj.* **1.** Rough and hearty in manner. **2.** Having a broad, steep appearance. [? < Du. *blaf* flat] **— bluff′ly** *adv.* **— bluff′ness** *n.*

blu·ing (bloo′ing) *n.* A blue coloring matter used in laundry work to counteract yellowing in linen: also spelled *blueing.*

blu·ish (bloo′ish) *adj.* Somewhat blue: also spelled *blueish.* **— blu′ish·ness** *n.*

blun·der (blun′dər) *n.* A stupid mistake; error. — *v.i.* **1.** To act or move awkwardly; stumble. **2.** To make a stupid mistake. — *v.t.* **3.** To utter stupidly or confusedly: often with *out*. **4.** To bungle. [ME *blondren* to mix up, confuse] **— blun′der·er** *n.* **— blun′der·ing·ly** *adv.*

blun·der·buss (blun′dər·bus) *n.* **1.** An old-fashioned, short gun with large bore and flaring mouth, used for scattering shot at close range. **2.** A stupid, blustering person. [Blend of BLUNDER and Du. *donderbus* thunder box]

BLUNDERBUSS (def. 1)

blunt (blunt) *adj.* **1.** Having a dull end or edge. **2.** Abrupt in manner; brusque. **3.** Slow of wit; dull. — *v.t. & v.i.* To make or become dull or less hurtful. [ME; origin unknown] **— blunt′ly** *adv.* **— blunt′ness** *n.*

— Syn. (adj.) **1.** dull, round, smooth. **2.** *Blunt* suggests an unpleasant frankness and *abrupt* a disconcerting directness: a *blunt* opinion, an *abrupt* departure. *Brusque* implies ungraciousness, while *curt* connotes undue brevity, and often intentional rudeness: a *brusque* handshake, a *curt* rejoinder.

blur (blûr) *v.t. & v.i.* **blurred, blur·ring** **1.** To make or become vague and indistinct in outline. **2.** To dim. **3.** To smear; smudge. — *n.* **1.** A smear; smudge. **2.** Something indistinct. — **blur′ry** *adj.*

blurb (blûrb) *n.* A brief and highly commendatory description or advertisement, esp. one on a book jacket. [Coined by Gelett Burgess, 1866–1951, U.S. humorist]

blurt (blûrt) *v.t.* To utter abruptly or impulsively: often with *out.* [? Blend of BLOW and SPURT]

blush (blush) *v.i.* **1.** To become red in the face from modesty or confusion; flush. **2.** To become red or rosy, as flowers. **3.** To feel shame or regret: usually with *at* or *for.* — *v.t.* **4.** To make red. — *n.* **1.** A reddening of the face from modesty, etc. **2.** A red or rosy tint. **3.** A glance; glimpse: now only in the phrase **at** or **on first blush** — *adj.* Reddish. [OE *blyscan* to redden] — **blush′er** *n.* — **blush′ful** *adj.* — **blush′ing·ly** *adv.*

blus·ter (blus′tər) *v.i.* **1.** To blow gustily and with violence and noise, as the wind. **2.** To utter threats. — *v.t.* **3.** To utter noisily and boisterously. **4.** To force or bully by blustering. — *n.* **1.** Boisterous talk or swagger. **2.** Fitful and noisy blowing of the wind; blast. — **blus′ter·er** *n.* — **blus′ter·ing·ly** *adv.* — **blus′ter·y, blus′ter·ous** *adj.*

bo·a (bō′ə) *n. pl.* **bo·as** **1.** Any of several nonvenomous serpents notable for the crushing power of their coils, as the anaconda and python; esp. the **boa constrictor** of South America. **2.** A long feather or fur scarf for women. [< L]

boar (bôr, bōr) *n. pl.* **boars** or **boar.** **1.** An uncastrated male swine. **2.** The wild boar. [OE *bār*]

board (bôrd, bōrd) *n.* **1.** A flat, thin slab of sawed wood much longer than it is wide. **2.** A thin slab of wood or the like for a specific purpose: an ironing *board.* **2.** One of the pasteboard covers of a book. **4.** A table set for serving food. **5.** Food or meals; esp., meals furnished for pay, and sometimes including lodging. **6.** An organized official body. **7.** A table at which meetings are held. — **across the board** *Informal* **1.** Designating a racing bet whereby equal sums are wagered on a single horse, etc., to win, place, and show. **2.** Affecting all members or categories in the same degree: said of changes in salary, taxes, etc. — **by the board** Overboard. — **on board** On or in a vessel or other conveyance. — **the boards** The stage. — **to go by the board** To fall into ruin, disuse, etc. — *v.t.* **1.** To cover or enclose with boards: often with *up.* **2.** To furnish with meals, or meals and lodging, for pay. **3.** To place (someone) where meals are provided, as in a boarding school. **4.** To enter, as a ship or train. **5.** *Naut.* To come alongside or go on board of (a ship), as to attack. — *v.i.* **6.** To take meals, or meals and lodging. [OE *bord* board, side of a ship, table]

board·er (bôr′dər, bōr′-) *n.* **1.** One who receives regular meals, or meals and lodging, for pay. **2.** One who is detailed to board an enemy's ship.

board foot *pl.* **board feet** The contents of a board 1 foot square and 1 inch thick; the common unit of measure for logs and lumber in the U.S., equal to 144 cubic inches or 2359.8 cubic centimeters. Abbr. *bd. ft.*

boarding house A house where meals, or meals and lodging, can be had regularly for pay. Also **board·ing·house** (bôr′ding·hous′, bōr′-).

boarding school A school in which pupils are boarded.

board measure A cubic measure applied to boards, the unit of which is the board foot. Abbr. *b.m.*

board·walk (bôrd′wôk′, bōrd′-) *n.* **1.** A promenade along a beach, usually of boards. **2.** A walk made of planks.

boast (bōst) *v.i.* **1.** To talk in a vain or bragging manner. **2.** To speak or possess with pride: used with *of.* — *v.t.* **3.** To brag about; extol. **4.** To be proud to possess; take pride in. — *n.* **1.** A boastful speech. **2.** That which is boasted about. [ME *bosten*] — **boast′er** *n.* — **boast′ing·ly** *adv.*

boast·ful (bōst′fəl) *adj.* Characterized by or addicted to boasting. — **boast′ful·ly** *adv.* — **boast′ful·ness** *n.*

boat (bōt) *n.* **1.** A small, open watercraft propelled by oars, sails, or an engine. **2.** *Informal* Any watercraft of any size, from a rowboat to an ocean liner. **3.** A boat-shaped object, as a dish. — **in the same boat** In the same situation or condition; equally involved. — *v.i.* **1.** To travel by boat. **2.** To go boating for pleasure. — *v.t.* **3.** To transport or place in a boat: to *boat* oars. [OE *bāt*]

boat·house (bōt′hous′) *n.* A building for storing boats.

boat·ing (bō′ting) *n.* The act or sport of one who boats.

boat·load (bōt′lōd′) *n.* **1.** The amount that a boat can hold. **2.** The load carried by a boat.

boat·man (bōt′mən) *n. pl.* **·men** (-mən) **1.** A man who deals in or works on boats. **2.** An aquatic insect.

boat·swain (bō′sən, *rarely* bōt′swān′) *n.* A warrant officer of a naval ship, or a subordinate officer of a merchantman who is in charge of the rigging, anchors, etc. Also spelled **bosun, bo's'n.** [OE *bātswegen*]

bob¹ (bob) *v.* **bobbed, bob·bing** *v.i.* **1.** To move up and down with an irregular motion. **2.** To curtsy. — *v.t.* **3.** To move up and down. — **to bob up** To appear or emerge suddenly. — *n.* **1.** A short, jerky movement: a *bob* of the head. **2.** A quick bow or curtsy. **3.** In fishing, a float or cork. [ME; origin uncertain] — **bob′ber** *n.*

bob² (bob) *n.* **1.** A short haircut for a woman or child. **2.** The docked tail of a horse. **3.** A small, pendant object, as the weight on a plumb line. For illus. see PLUMB BOB. **4.** In fishing, a large, ball-shaped bait made of worms, rags, etc. — *v.* **bobbed, bob·bing** *v.t.* **1.** To cut short, as hair. — *v.i.* **2.** To fish with a bob. [ME *bobbe*] — **bob′ber** *n.*

bob³ (bob) *n. pl.* **bob** *Brit. Informal* A shilling. [< *Bob,* a nickname for *Robert,* a personal name]

bob·bin (bob′in) *n.* A spool or reel holding thread for spinning, weaving, or machine sewing. [< F *bobine*]

bob·by (bob′ē) *n. pl.* **·bies** *Brit. Informal* A policeman. [after Sir Robert Peel, 1788–1850, who introduced police reforms]

bobby pin A metal hairpin shaped so as to clasp and hold the hair tightly. Also **bob′bie pin.**

bobby socks *Informal* Short socks worn by girls.

bob·by·sox·er (bob′ē·sok′sər) *U.S. Informal* A young girl who follows fads and fashions current among adolescents.

bob·cat (bob′kat′) *n.* The American lynx.

bob·o·link (bob′ə·lingk) *n.* A thrushlike singing bird of North America. [Imit.; from its call]

bob·sled (bob′sled′) *n.* **1.** A racing sled steered by a steering wheel controlling the front runners. **2.** Either of two short sleds connected in tandem; also, the vehicle so formed. — *v.i.* **·sled·ded, ·sled·ding** To go coasting on a bobsled. Also **bob′sleigh′** (-slā′). [Origin unknown]

bob·tail (bob′tāl′) *n.* **1.** A short tail or a tail cut short. **2.** An animal with such a tail. — *adj.* **1.** Having the tail docked. **2.** Cut short; incomplete. — *v.t.* **1.** To cut the tail of; dock. **2.** To cut short. — **bob′tailed′** *adj.*

bob·white (bob′hwīt′) *n.* A quail of North America having brownish, mottled plumage. [Imit.; from its call]

bock beer (bok) A dark, strong beer brewed in the winter and served in early spring. Also **bock.** [< G *bockbier*]

bode¹ (bōd) Archaic past tense and past participle of BIDE.

bode² (bōd) *v.* **bod·ed, bod·ing** *v.t.* **1.** To be a foretoken of; presage. — *v.i.* **2.** To presage good or ill. [OE *bodian* to announce] — **bode′ment** *n.*

bod·ice (bod′is) *n.* **1.** The upper portion of a woman's dress. **2.** A woman's ornamental vest. [Var. of *bodies*]

bod·ied (bod′ēd) *adj.* **1.** Having a body. **2.** Having a (specified kind of) body: used in combination: *full-bodied.*

bod·i·less (bod′i·lis) *adj.* Having no body; incorporeal.

bod·i·ly (bod′ə·lē) *adj.* **1.** Of or pertaining to the body. **2.** Physical, as opposed to mental: *bodily* illness. — *adv.* **1.** In the flesh; in person. **2.** All together; completely.

bod·kin (bod′kin) *n.* **1.** A pointed instrument for piercing holes in cloth, etc. **2.** A blunt needle for drawing tape through a hem. **3.** A long pin for fastening the hair. [ME *boydekin* dagger; origin unknown]

bod·y (bod′ē) *n. pl.* **bod·ies 1.** The entire physical part of a human being, animal, or plant. **2.** A corpse; carcass. **3.** The torso of a human being or animal; the trunk. **4.** The principal part or mass of anything. **5.** A collection of persons or things taken as a whole. **6.** A distinct mass or portion of matter: a *body* of clear water. **7.** Density or consistency; substance: a wine with *body.* **8.** That part of a garment that covers the body or the upper body. **9.** *Informal* A person. — *v.t.* **bod·ied, bod·y·ing 1.** To furnish with or as with a body. **2.** To exhibit in bodily form; represent: usually with *forth.* [OE *bodig*]

bod·y·guard (bod′ē·gärd′) *n.* **1.** A guard responsible for the physical safety of an individual. **2.** A retinue; escort.

body politic The state or nation as an organized political entity; the people collectively.

body snatcher One who steals bodies from graves.

Boe·o·tia (bē·ō′shə, -shē·o) A state of ancient Greece; capital Thebes.

Boe·o·tian (bē·ō′shən) *adj.* **1.** Of or pertaining to Boeotia. **2.** Dull; clownish. — *n.* **1.** A native of Boeotia. **2.** A stupid, doltish person.

Boer (bôr, bōr, boor) *n.* A Dutch colonist, or person of Dutch descent, in South Africa. — *adj.* Of or pertaining to the Boers. [< Du., farmer]

bog (bog, bôg) *n.* Wet and spongy ground; marsh; morass. — *v.t. & v.i.* **bogged, bog·ging** To sink or be impeded in or as in a bog: often with *down.* [< Irish < *bog* soft] — **bog′gish** *adj.* — **bog′gish·ness** *n.*

bo·gey¹ (bō′gē) *n. pl.* **·geys** In golf: **a** An estimated standard score. **b** One stroke over par on a hole. Also **bo′gie.** [after Col *Bogey,* an imaginary faultless golfer]

bo·gey² (bō′gē) See BOGY.

bog·gle (bog'əl) *v.* **·gled, ·gling** *v.i.* **1.** To hesitate, as from doubt or scruples; shrink back: often with *at.* **2.** To start with fright, as a horse. **3.** To equivocate; dissemble. **4.** To work clumsily; fumble. — *v.t.* **5.** To make a botch of; bungle. — *n.* **1.** The act of boggling. **2.** A scruple; objection. **3.** *Informal* A botch. [< Scot. *bogle* a hobgoblin]

bog·gy (bog'ē, bôg'ē) *adj.* **·gi·er, ·gi·est** Swampy; miry.

bo·gie (bō'gē) See BOGY.

bo·gus (bō'gəs) *adj. U.S.* Counterfeit; spurious; fake.

bo·gy (bō'gē) *n. pl.* **·gies** A goblin; bugbear: also spelled *bogey, bogie.* [? Akin to BUG²] — **bo'gy·ism** *n.*

Bo·he·mi·an (bō·hē'mē·ən) *adj.* **1.** Of or pertaining to Bohemia. **2.** Leading the life of a Bohemian; unconventional. — *n.* **1.** An inhabitant of Bohemia. **2.** A gypsy. **3.** A person, usu. of artistic or literary tastes, who lives in an unconventional manner. Also (for *adj.* def. 2, *n.* def. 3) **bo·he'mi·an. 4.** A former name for the Czech dialect of Czechoslovakian. — **Bo·he'mi·an·ism** *n.*

boil¹ (boil) *v.i.* **1.** To be agitated by escaping gaseous bubbles, usu. from the effect of heat: said of liquids. **2.** To reach the boiling point. **3.** To undergo the action of a boiling liquid. **4.** To be agitated like boiling water; seethe. **5.** To be stirred by rage or passion. — *v.t.* **6.** To bring to the boiling point. **7.** To cook or cleanse by boiling. **8.** To separate by means of evaporation caused by boiling. — **to boil away** To evaporate in boiling. — **to boil down 1.** To reduce in bulk by boiling. **2.** To condense; summarize. — **to boil over 1.** To overflow while boiling. **2.** To give vent to one's rage or passion. — *n.* The act or state of boiling. [< OF < L *bullire* to boil]

boil² (boil) *n. Pathol.* A painful purulent nodule of bacterial origin beneath the skin: also called *furuncle.* [OE *byl*]

boil·er (boi'lər) *n.* **1.** A closed vessel containing a system of tubes, used for generating steam, as for heating or power. **2.** A container in which something is boiled. **3.** A tank for hot water.

boiling point The temperature at which a liquid boils; at normal atmospheric pressure the boiling point of water is 212° F. or 100° C.

bois·ter·ous (bois'tər·əs, -trəs) *adj.* **1.** Noisy and unrestrained; uproarious. **2.** Stormy; violent, as the weather. [ME *boistous*] — **bois'ter·ous·ly** *adv.* — **bois'ter·ous·ness** *n.*

bo·la (bō'lə) *n.* A throwing weapon, consisting of balls fastened to cords. Also **bo·las** (bō'ləs) [< Sp., a ball]

bold (bōld) *adj.* **1.** Having courage; fearless. **2.** Showing or requiring courage; daring. **3.** Presuming unduly; brazen; forward. **4.** Vigorous in conception or expression; unconventional. **5.** Abrupt; steep, as a cliff. — **to make bold** To venture. [OE *bald*] — **bold'ly** *adv.* — **bold'ness** *n.*

bold·face (bōld'fās') *n. Printing* A type in which the lines have been thickened to give a very black impression.

bole (bōl) *n.* The trunk of a tree. [< ON *bolr*]

bo·le·ro (bō·lâr'ō) *n. pl.* **·ros 1.** A short jacket open at the front. **2.** A Spanish dance, usu. accompanied by castanets. **3.** The music for this dance. [< Sp.]

bol·i·var (bol'ə·vər, -vär; Sp. bō·lē'vär) *n. pl.* **bol·i·vars,** *Sp.* **bo·li·va·res** (bō'lē·vä'rās) The monetary unit of Venezuela. [after Simón *Bolívar*]

bo·li·via·no (bō·lē'vyä'nō) *n. pl.* **·nos** (-nōs) The monetary unit of Bolivia.

boll (bōl) *n.* A round pod or seed capsule, as of flax or cotton. — *v.i.* To form pods.

bol·lix (bol'iks) *v.t.* **·lixed, ·lix·ing** *Slang* To bungle; botch: often with *up.* [Alter. of *ballocks* testicles]

boll weevil A beetle that destroys cotton bolls.

boll·worm (bōl'wûrm') *n.* The very destructive larva of a pale brown moth that feeds on cotton bolls.

bo·lo (bō'lō) *n. pl.* **·los** (-lōz) A large, single-edged knife used by natives of the Philippines. [< Sp. < Visayan]

Bo·lo·gna sausage (bə·lō'nə, -lōn'yə, -lō'nē) A highly seasoned sausage of mixed meats: also *baloney, boloney.*

bo·lo·ney (bə·lō'nē) See BALONEY.

Bol·she·vik (bōl'shə·vik, bol'-) *n. pl.* **Bol·she·viks** or **Bol·she·vi·ki** (bōl'shə·vē'kē, bol'-) **1.** A member of the dominant branch of the Russian Social Democratic Party or, since 1918, of the Russian Communist Party. **2.** A member of any Communist party. **3.** Loosely, any radical. Also **bol'she·vik.** [< Russian *bolshe* the majority]

Bol·she·vism (bōl'shə·viz'əm, bol'-) *n.* The Marxian doctrines and policies of the Bolsheviks; also, any practice, government, etc., based on them. Also **bol'she·vism.**

Bol·she·vist (bōl'shə·vist, bol'-) *n.* A Bolshevik. Also **bol'she·vist.** — **Bol·she·vis'tic** *adj.*

bol·ster (bōl'stər) *n.* **1.** A narrow pillow as long as a bed's width. **2.** A pad used as a support or for protection. **3.** Anything shaped like a bolster or used as a support. — *v.t.* To prop or reinforce, as something ready to fall: with *up.* [OE] — **bol'ster·er** *n.*

bolt¹ (bōlt) *n.* **1.** A sliding bar or piece for fastening a door, etc. **2.** A pin or rod for holding something in place, usu. having a head at one end, and threaded at the other. **3.** The part of a lock that is shot or withdrawn by turning the key. **4.** A sliding mechanism that closes the breech of some small firearms. **5.** An arrow, esp. for a crossbow. **6.** A stroke of lightning; thunderbolt. **7.** Anything that comes suddenly or unexpectedly: a bolt of bad luck. **8.** A sudden start or spring: He made a *bolt* for the door. **9.** *U.S.* A desertion of one's party, its candidate, etc. **10.** A roll of cloth, wallpaper, etc. — **a bolt from the blue 1.** A thunderbolt on a clear day. **2.** A sudden and wholly unexpected event. — **to shoot one's bolt** To do one's utmost. — *v.i.* **1.** To move, go, or spring suddenly: He *bolted* from the room. **2.** *U.S.* To break away, as from a political party; refuse to support party policy. — *v.t.* **3.** To fasten or lock with or as with a bolt or bolts. **4.** *U.S.* To break away from, as a political party. **5.** To gulp, as food. **6.** To arrange into bolts, as cloth. **7.** To blurt out. — *adv.* Like an arrow; suddenly. — **bolt upright** Stiffly erect. [OE, arrow for a crossbow]

bolt² (bōlt) *v.t.* **1.** To sift. **2.** To examine as by sifting. [< OF *bulter* to sift] — **bolt'er** *n.*

bo·lus (bō'ləs) *n. pl.* **·lus·es 1.** A large pill. **2.** Any rounded lump or mass. [< Med.L < Gk. *bōlos* a lump]

bomb (bom) *n.* **1.** *Mil.* A hollow projectile containing explosive, incendiary, or chemical material to be discharged by concussion or by a time fuse. **2.** Any sudden or unexpected event. — *v.t. & v.i.* To attack or destroy with or as with bombs. [< F < Sp. < L < Gk. *bombos* hollow noise]

bom·bard (*v.* bom·bärd'; *n.* bom'bärd) *v.t.* **1.** To attack with bombs or shells. **2.** To attack as with bombs. — *n.* The earliest form of cannon, originally hurling stones. [< MF < OF < L < Gk. *bombos* hollow noise] — **bom·bard'er** *n.* — **bom·bard'ment** *n.*

bom·bar·dier (bom'bər·dir') *n.* **1.** *Mil.* The member of the crew of a bomber who operates the bombsight and releases bombs. **2.** *Brit. & Canadian* An artillery corporal. [< F]

bom·bast (bom'bast) *n.* Grandiloquent or pompous language. [< OF < LL *bombax, -acis* cotton]

bom·bas·tic (bom·bas'tik) *adj.* High-flown; grandiloquent. Also **bom·bas'ti·cal.** — **bom·bas'ti·cal·ly** *adv.*

bom·ba·zine (bom'bə·zēn', bom'bə·zēn) *n.* A twilled fabric usu. with silk warp and worsted filling. Also **bom'ba·sine'.** [< F < LL *bombax* cotton]

bomb bay A compartment in military aircraft in which bombs are carried and from which they are dropped.

bomb·er (bom'ər) *n.* **1.** An airplane designed to carry and drop bombs. **2.** One who bombs.

bomb·shell (bom'shel') *n.* **1.** A bomb. **2.** A complete surprise.

bomb·sight (bom'sīt') *n. Mil.* An instrument on an aircraft that enables the bombardier to aim accurately.

bo·na fide (bō'nə·fīd', -fī'dē) *adj.* Being, acting, or carried out in good faith; authentic; genuine. [< L]

bo·nan·za (bə·nan'zə) *n. U.S.* **1.** A rich mine or find of ore. **2.** A source of great wealth. [< Sp. < L *bonus* good]

bon-bon (bon'bon', *Fr.* bôn·bôn') *n.* A sugared candy. [< F < *bon* good]

bond (bond) *n.* **1.** That which binds or holds together; a band; tie. **2.** A uniting force or influence. **3.** A voluntary obligation. **4.** A substance that cements or unites; also, the union itself. **5.** *Law* An obligation in writing under seal. **6.** In finance, an interest-bearing certificate of debt, usu. issued by a government or corporation, obligating the issuer to pay the principal at a specified time. **7.** In insurance, a policy covering losses suffered through the acts of an employee. **8.** In commerce, the condition of goods stored in a bonded warehouse until duties are paid. **9.** A bondsman; also, bail; surety. **10.** *Chem.* A unit of combining power between the atoms of a molecule. — **Syn.** See SECURITY. — **bottled in bond** *U.S.* Bottled under government supervision and stored in a warehouse for a stated period, as certain whiskies. — *v.t.* **1.** To put a certified debt upon; mortgage. **2.** To furnish bond for; be surety for (someone). **3.** To place, as goods or an employee, under bond. **4.** To unite, as with glue, etc. **5.** To lay (bricks, etc.) in interlocking patterns for strength. — *v.i.* **6.** To interlock or cohere. — *adj.* In bondage; enslaved. [Var. of BAND¹] — **bond'er** *n.*

bond·age (bon'dij) *n.* **1.** Involuntary servitude; slavery; serfdom. **2.** Subjection to any influence or domination. [< Med.L < OE < ON *bōnde* peasant]

bond·ed (bon'did) *adj.* **1.** Secured or pledged by a bond or bonds. **2.** Stored in a warehouse; placed in bond.

bond·hold·er (bond'hōl'dər) *n.* One owning or holding bonds. — **bond'hold'ing** *adj. & n.*

bond·man (bond'mən) *n. pl.* **·men** (-mən) **1.** A slave or serf. **2.** A man bound to serve without wages. — **bond'·maid, bond'wom·an, bonds'wom·an** *n. fem.*

bond paper A strong grade of paper, used for documents.

bond·ser·vant (bond'sûr'vənt) *n.* **1.** A person bound to serve without wages. **2.** A slave; serf; also **bond'slave'.**

bonds·man (bondz'mən) *n. pl.* **·men** (-mən) **1.** One who provides bond for another. **2.** A bondman.

bone (bōn) *n.* **1.** *Anat.* **a** A hard, dense porous material

forming the skeleton of vertebrate animals. **b** A piece of this material. ◆ Collateral adjectives: *osseous, osteal.* **2.** *pl.* The skeleton as a whole. **3.** A substance resembling bone. **4.** Something made of bone or similar material. **5.** *pl. Informal* Dice. **6.** A strip of whalebone. **— to feel in (one's) bones** To be sure of; have an intuition of. **— to have a bone to pick** To have grounds for complaint or dispute. **— to make no bones about** To be direct or straightforward about or with. **—** *v.* **boned, bon·ing** *v.t.* **1.** To remove the bones from. **2.** To stiffen with whalebone. **—** *v.i.* **3.** *Slang* To study intensely and quickly: often with *up*. [OE *bān*]
bone·black (bōn′blak′) *n.* A black pigment made by calcining bones in airtight containers. Also **bone black.**
bone·head (bōn′hed′) *n. Informal* A stupid person.
bone meal Pulverized bone, used as feed and fertilizer.
bone of contention A cause or subject of disagreement.
bon·er (bō′nər) *n. Slang* An error; blunder.
bone·set (bōn′set′) *n.* A composite herb, formerly used in medicine as a tonic.
bon·fire (bon′fīr′) *n.* **1.** A large fire built in the open air. **2.** Formerly, a fire for burning corpses. [< BONE + FIRE]
bon·go drums (bong′gō) A pair of connected drums played with the hands, originally from Africa. Also **bon′gos.**
bon·ho·mie (bon′ə·mē′, Fr. bô·nô·mē′) *n.* Good nature; genial disposition. Also **bon/hom·mie′.** [< F]
bo·ni·to (bə·nē′tō) *n. pl.* **·to** or **·toes** A large mackerellike marine food fish: also called *skipjack.* [< Sp.]
bon jour (bôn zhōōr′) *French* Good day; good morning.
bon mot (bôn mō′) *pl.* **bons mots** (bôn mōz′, Fr. mō′) A clever saying; terse witticism. [< F]
bon·net (bon′it) *n.* **1.** An outdoor headdress for women or children, typically held in place by ribbons tied under the chin. **2.** *Chiefly Scot.* A cap for men and boys. **3.** An American Indian headdress of feathers. **—** *v.t.* To cover with a bonnet. [< OF < Med.L *bonetus*]
bon·ny (bon′ē) *adj.* **·ni·er, ·ni·est 1.** Having beauty; comely. **2.** Fine; good. **3.** Robust; healthy. Also **bon′nie.** [< F *bon* good] **— bon′ni·ly** *adv.* **— bon′ni·ness** *n.*
bon·sai (bon′sī′, bōn′) *n. pl.* **·sai 1.** A dwarfed tree or shrub trained, as by pruning, into a pleasing design. **2.** The art of creating such trees or shrubs. [< Japanese]
bon soir (bôn swär′) *French* Good evening; good night.
bo·nus (bō′nəs) *n. pl.* **·nus·es** Something paid or given in addition to a usual or stipulated amount. [< L, good]
bon vi·vant (bôn vē·väň′) *pl.* **bons vi·vants** (bôn vē·väň′) *French* One who enjoys luxurious living; an epicure.
bon vo·yage (bôn vwä·yäzh′) *French* Pleasant trip.
bon·y (bō′nē) *adj.* **bon·i·er, bon·i·est 1.** Of, like, pertaining to, or consisting of bone or bones. **2.** Having prominent bones; thin; gaunt. **— bon′i·ness** *n.*
boo (bōō) *n. & interj.* A vocal sound made to indicate contempt or to frighten. **—** *v.* **booed, boo·ing** *v.i.* **1.** To utter "boo." **—** *v.t.* **2.** To shout "boo" at. [Imit.]
boob (bōōb) *n. Slang* A simpleton; booby.
boo·boo (bōō′bōō′) *n. pl.* **·boos** *Slang* An embarrassing error; blunder. Also **boo′-boo′.** [Origin uncertain]
boo·by (bōō′bē) *n. pl.* **·bies 1.** A stupid person; dunce. **2.** In some games, the person who makes the poorest score. **3.** Any of several gannets of tropical America. [< Sp. *bobo* fool]
booby hatch 1. *Naut.* A raised hood over a small hatchway. **2.** *U.S. Slang* A hospital for the mentally ill.
booby prize A mock award for a worst score or performance.
booby trap A concealed bomb, mine, etc., placed so as to be detonated by casual or careless movements of the victim. **2.** Any device for taking someone unawares.
boo·dle (bōōd′l) *U.S. Slang n.* **1.** Bribery money; graft. **2.** Loot; plunder. **3.** A mob. **—** *v.i.* **·dled, ·dling** To receive money corruptly. [Cf. Du. *boedel* property]
boog·ie-woog·ie (bōōg′ē·wōōg′ē) *n.* A style of jazz piano playing marked by repetition of bass rhythms and melodic variations in the treble. [Origin uncertain]
boo·hoo (bōō′hōō′) *v.i.* **·hooed, ·hoo·ing** To weep loudly. **—** *n. pl.* **·hoos** Noisy sobbing. [Imit.]
book (bōōk) *n.* **1.** A bound set of printed sheets of paper, usually between covers. **2.** A literary composition of some length, written or printed. **3.** A ledger, register, etc. **4.** A main division of a literary composition: a *book* of the Bible. **5.** A libretto. **6.** The script of a play. **7.** A booklike packet, as of matches. **8.** Something regarded as a source of instruction: the *book* of experience. **9.** A record of bets, especially on a horse race. **10.** A specific number of tricks or cards won. **— by the book** According to rule. **— like a book** Thoroughly. **— on the books 1.** Recorded. **2.** Enrolled. **— to make book** *U.S. Slang* To bet or accept bets. **—** *v.t.* **1.** To enter or list in a book. **2.** To arrange for beforehand, as accommodations or seats. **3.** To engage, as actors or a play, for performance. **4.** To make a record of charges against (someone) on a police blotter. [OE]

book·bind·er (bōōk′bīn′dər) *n.* One whose trade is the binding of books. **— book′bind′er·y** *n.* **— book′bind′ing** *n.*
book·case (bōōk′kās′) *n.* A case with shelves for books.
book club 1. An organization that sells books at reduced rates to members who agree to buy a certain number. **2.** A club given over to the reading and discussion of books.
book end A support or prop used to hold books upright.
book·ie (bōōk′ē) *n. Informal* A bookmaker (def. 2).
book·ing (bōōk′ing) *n.* An engagement to perform, etc.
book·ish (bōōk′ish) *adj.* **1.** Fond of books; studious. **2.** Knowing only what has been read in books; pedantic. **3.** Of books. **— book′ish·ly** *adv.* **— book′ish·ness** *n.*
book jacket A dust jacket.
book·keep·ing (bōōk′kē′ping) *n.* The practice of recording business transactions systematically. **— book′keep′er** *n.*
book learning Knowledge obtained from books rather than from experience. **— book·learn·ed** (bōōk′lûr′nid) *adj.*
book·let (bōōk′lit) *n.* A small book or pamphlet.
book·mak·er (bōōk′mā′kər) *n.* **1.** One who compiles, prints, or binds books. **2.** One who makes a business of accepting bets, as in horse racing.
book·mark (bōōk′märk′) *n.* **1.** Any object, as a ribbon, inserted in a book to mark a place. **2.** A bookplate.
book·mo·bile (bōōk′mə·bēl) *n.* A motor truck equipped to serve as a traveling library.
Book of Common Prayer The book of ritual used in the Anglican church.
book·rack (bōōk′rak′) *n.* **1.** A frame to hold an open book. Also **book′rest′. 2.** A rack to hold books.
book review An article or essay discussing or critically examining a book, esp. a recently published book.
book·sell·er (bōōk′sel′ər) *n.* One who sells books.
book·stack (bōōk′stak′) *n.* A tall rack containing shelves for books, as in a library.
book·stall (bōōk′stôl′) *n.* **1.** A stall or stand where books are sold. **2.** *Brit.* A newsstand.
book·store (bōōk′stôr′, -stōr′) *n.* A store where books are sold. Also **book/shop′.**
book·worm (bōōk′wûrm′) *n.* **1.** One excessively devoted to books and study. **2.** Any insect destructive to books.
boom¹ (bōōm) *v.i.* **1.** To emit a deep, resonant sound. **2.** *U.S.* To grow rapidly; flourish. **—** *v.t.* **3.** To utter or sound in a deep resonant tone: often with *out.* **4.** *U.S.* To praise or advertise vigorously. **5.** *U.S.* To cause to flourish. **—** *n.* **1.** A deep, reverberating sound, as of a supersonic aircraft, of waves, etc. **2.** *U.S.* A sudden increase, as in growth; spurt. **—** *adj. U.S.* Caused or maintained by a boom: *boom* prices. [Imit.]
boom² (bōōm) *n.* **1.** *Naut.* A long spar or pole used to hold or extend the bottom of certain sails. **2.** A long pole or beam extending upward at an angle from the foot of the mast of a derrick, and from which are suspended the objects to be lifted. **3.** *U.S.* A floating chain of connected logs used to enclose other floating logs, to retard the advance of a vessel, etc. **—** *v.t.* **1.** To extend (a sail) by means of a boom: with *out.* **2.** To shove off or away, as a vessel from a wharf: with *off.* [< Du. *boom* tree, beam]

BOOM²
(def. 2)

boom·e·rang (bōō′mə·rang) *n.* **1.** A curved, wooden missile originated in Australia, one form of which will return to the thrower. **2.** A plan, statement, etc., that recoils upon the originator. **—** *v.i.* To react harmfully on the originator. [< native Australian name]
boom town A town showing sudden development or prosperity, as from a discovery of gold.
boon¹ (bōōn) *n.* **1.** A good thing bestowed; blessing. **2.** *Archaic* A request. [< ON *bōn* petition]
boon² (bōōn) *adj.* Convivial; merry: now only in the phrase **boon companion.** [< F < L *bonus* good]
boon·docks (bōōn′doks′) *n.pl. U.S. Slang* An uncivilized or backwoods area: with *the.* [< Tagalog *bundok* mountain]
boon·dog·gle (bōōn′dôg′əl, -dog′əl) *U.S. Informal v.i.* **·gled, ·gling** To work on wasteful or unnecessary projects. **—** *n.* Unnecessary work. [Origin uncertain] **— boon′dog′gler** *n.*
boor (bōōr) *n.* An awkward, rude, or ill-mannered person. [< Du. *boer* farmer, rustic] **— boor′ish** *adj.* **— boor′ish·ly** *adv.* **— boor′ish·ness** *n.*
boost (bōōst) *U.S. v.t.* **1.** To raise by pushing from beneath or behind. **2.** To increase: to *boost* prices. **3.** To advance by speaking well of; promote or extol vigorously. **—** *n.* **1.** A lift; help. **2.** An increase. [Origin uncertain]
boost·er (bōōs′tər) *U.S. n.* **1.** Any device or substance for increasing power. **2.** *Informal* One who gives enthusiastic support to a person, cause, etc.
boot¹ (bōōt) *n.* **1.** A covering, usu. of leather, for the foot and part or most of the leg. **2.** A flap on an open vehicle for shielding the driver against rain or mud. **3.** A thick patch

for the inside of a tire casing. **4.** A kick. **5.** In U.S. Navy and Marine Corps slang, a recent recruit. **— too big for one's boots** *U.S.* Proud; conceited. **— the boot** *Slang* Dismissal; discharge. **— to die with one's boots on** To die fighting or working. — *v.t.* **1.** To put boots on. **2.** To kick or to punt. **3.** *Slang* To dismiss; fire. [< OF *bote*]

boot[2] (boot) *Obs. n.* Advantage. **— to boot** In addition; over and above. [ME < OE *bōt* profit]

boot·black (boot/blak') *n.* One whose business is shining boots and shoes.

boo·tee (boo·tē', boo/tē) *n.* **1.** A baby's knitted woolen boot. **2.** A light half boot for women. Also **boo·tie** (boo/tē).

Bo·ö·tes (bō·ō/tēz) *n.* A constellation, the Bear Keeper: also called *Herdsman.* [< L < Gk. *boōtēs* plowman]

booth (booth, booth) *n.* **1.** A small compartment or cubicle for privacy or for keeping out sound, etc. **2.** A seating compartment, as in a restaurant. **3.** A small stall for the display or sale of goods. [ME *bothe* < Scand.]

boot·jack (boot/jak') *n.* A forked device for holding a boot while the foot is withdrawn.

boot·leg (boot/leg') *U.S. v.t. & v.i.* **·legged, ·leg·ging** To make, sell, or carry for sale (liquor, etc.) illegally; smuggle. — *adj.* Unlawful: *bootleg* whisky. — *n.* **1.** The part of a boot above the instep. **2.** Bootleg liquor or other merchandise. [With ref. to the smuggling of liquor in bootlegs] — **boot/leg'ger** *n.* — **boot/leg'ging** *n.*

boot·less (boot/lis) *adj.* Profitless; useless; unavailing. — **boot/less·ly** *adv.* — **boot/less·ness** *n.*

boot·lick (boot/lik') *U.S. Slang v.t. & v.i.* To flatter servilely; toady. — **boot/lick'er** *n.* — **boot/lick'ing** *n. & adj.*

boo·ty (boo/tē) *n. pl.* **·ties** **1.** The spoil of war; plunder. **2.** Goods taken by violence. **3.** Any prize or gain. [< F *butin* < MLG; infl. by obs. *boot* advantage]

booze (booz) *Informal n.* **1.** Alcoholic drink. **2.** A drunken spree. — *v.i.* **boozed, booz·ing** To drink to excess; tipple. [< MDu. *busen* to drink, tipple] — **booz/er** *n.*

booz·y (boo/zē) *adj. Informal* Drunken; alcoholic. — **booz/i·ly** *adv.* — **booz/i·ness** *n.*

bop[1] (bop) *v.t.* **bopped, bop·ping** *Slang* To hit. [Imit.]

bop[2] (bop) *n.* A variety of jazz.

bo·rac·ic (bə·ras/ik) *adj. Chem.* Boric.

bor·age (bûr/ij, bor/-, bor/-) *n.* A European herb having blue flowers and hairy leaves, used medicinally and in salads. [< Med.L *borra, burra* rough hair]

bo·rate (bôr/āt, bō/rāt) *n. Chem.* A salt of boric acid. — **bo/rat·ed** *adj.*

bo·rax (bôr/aks, bō/raks) *n.* A white crystalline compound, $Na_2B_4O_7·10H_2O$, found native and used in medicine, industry, etc. [< OF < Med.L < Arabic < Persian *būrah*]

bo·ra·zon (bôr/ə·zon, bō/rə-) *n. Chem.* A crystalline compound of boron and nitrogen, BN, equaling the diamond in hardness but with a much higher melting point.

Bor·deaux (bôr·dō/) *n.* A white or red wine produced in the vicinity of Bordeaux, France. Red Bordeaux is called *claret.*

bor·der (bôr/dər) *n.* **1.** A margin or edge. **2.** The frontier line or district of a country or state; boundary. **3.** A design or stripe in the margins of a page of a book, etc. **4.** A decorative edging or margin. — *adj.* Of, on, or forming the border. — *v.t.* **1.** To put a border or edging on. **2.** To lie along the border of; bound. **— to border on** (or **upon**) **1.** To lie adjacent to. **2.** To approach; verge on: That act *borders on* piracy. [< OF < *bord* edge] — **bor/der·er** *n.*

bor·der·land (bôr/dər·land') *n.* **1.** Land on or near the border of two adjoining countries. **2.** Debatable or indeterminate ground: the *borderland* between love and hate.

bor·der·line (bôr/dər·līn') *n.* A line of demarcation. Also **border line.** — *adj.* Difficult to classify; doubtful.

bore[1] (bôr, bōr) *v.* **bored, bor·ing** *v.t.* **1.** To make a hole in or through, as with a drill. **2.** To make (a tunnel, etc.) by or as by drilling. **3.** To force (one's way). **4.** To weary by being dull, long-winded, etc.; tire. — *v.i.* **5.** To make a hole, etc., by or as by drilling. **6.** To force one's way. — *n.* **1.** A hole made by or as if by boring. **2.** The interior diameter of a firearm or cylinder; caliber. **3.** One who or that which is tiresome. [OE *bor* auger]

bore[2] (bôr, bōr) *n.* A high, crested wave caused by the rush of a flood tide, as in the Amazon. [< ON *bāra* billow]

bore[3] (bôr, bōr) *Past tense of* BEAR[1].

bo·re·al (bôr/ē·əl, bō/rē-) *adj.* Of the north or the north wind. [< LL < L *Boreas,* the north wind]

Bo·re·as (bôr/ē·as, bō/rē-) In Greek mythology, the god of the north wind. [< L < Gk.]

bore·dom (bôr/dəm, bōr/-) *n.* The condition of being bored.

bor·er (bôr/ər, bō/rər) *n.* **1.** A tool used for boring. **2.** A beetle, moth, or worm that burrows in plants, wood, etc.

bo·ric (bôr/ik, bō/rik) *adj. Chem.* Of, pertaining to, or derived from boron: also *boracic.*

boric acid *Chem.* A white crystalline compound, H_3BO_3, used as a preservative and as a mild antiseptic.

born (bôrn) *adj.* **1.** Brought forth, as offspring. **2.** Natural; by birth: a *born* musician. [OE *beran* to bear]

borne (bôrn, bōrn) Past participle of BEAR[1].

bo·ron (bôr/on, bō/ron) *n.* A nonmetallic element (symbol B) found only in combination. See ELEMENT.

bor·ough (bûr/ō, -ə) *n.* **1.** An incorporated village or town. **2.** One of the five administrative divisions of New York, N.Y. **3.** *Brit.* **a** A town with a municipal corporation and certain privileges granted by royal charter: also **municipal borough. b** A town entitled to representation in Parliament: also **parliamentary borough.** [OE *burg, burh* fort, town]

bor·row (bôr/ō, bor/ō) *v.t.* **1.** To take or obtain (something) with the promise or understanding that one will return it. **2.** To adopt for one's own use, as ideas. **3.** In arithmetical subtraction, to withdraw (a unit of ten) from any figure of the minuend in order to add it to the next lower denomination. — *v.i.* **4.** To borrow something. [OE *borg* pledge] — **bor/row·er** *n.*

borscht (bôrsht) *n.* A Russian beet soup, eaten hot or cold. Also **borsch** (bôrsh). [< Russian *borshch*]

bort (bôrt) *n.* An impure diamond, used only for cutting and polishing. Also **bortz** (bôrts). [? < OF *bort* bastard]

bor·zoi (bôr/zoi) *n.* A breed of Russian hounds, resembling the greyhound but larger, and having a long, silky coat: also called *Russian wolfhound.* [< Russian, swift]

bosh (bosh) *n. Informal* Empty words; nonsense. [< Turkish, empty, worthless]

bo's'n (bō/sən) See BOATSWAIN.

Bos·ni·an (boz/nē·ən) *adj.* Of or pertaining to Bosnia. Also **Bos·ni·ac** (boz/nē·ak). — *n.* **1.** A native or inhabitant of Bosnia. **2.** The Serbo-Croatian language of the Bosnians.

bos·om (booz/əm, boo/zəm) *n.* **1.** The breast of a human being, esp. of a woman. **2.** The breast as the seat of thought and emotion. **3.** Something suggesting the human breast. **4.** Inner circle; midst: in the *bosom* of the church. — *adj.* **1.** Close; intimate: a *bosom* friend. **2.** Of or pertaining to the bosom. — *v.t.* **1.** To have or cherish in the bosom; embrace. **2.** To hide; conceal. [OE *bōsm*]

boss[1] (bôs, bos) *U.S. Informal n.* **1.** A superintendent or employer of workmen. **2.** A professional politician who controls a political organization. — *v.t.* **1.** To supervise; direct. **2.** To order in a highhanded manner. — *v.i.* **3.** To act as boss. — *adj.* Head; chief. [< Du. *baas* master]

boss[2] (bôs, bos) *n.* **1.** A circular prominence; a knob or projecting ornament. **2.** *Mech.* An enlarged part of a shaft, coupling with a wheel or another shaft. — *v.t.* **1.** To ornament with bosses. **2.** To emboss. [< OF *boce* bump, knob]

boss·ism (bôs/iz·əm, bos/-) *n. U.S.* Control by political bosses.

boss·y[1] (bôs/ē, bos/ē) *adj.* **boss·i·er, boss·i·est** *U.S. Informal* Tending to boss; domineering.

boss·y[2] (bos/ē, bôs/ē) *n. U.S. Informal* A cow or a calf.

Boston terrier A small terrier having a short, smooth, brindled coat with white markings. Also **Boston bull.**

bo·sun (bō/sən) See BOATSWAIN.

bot (bot) *n.* The larva of a botfly: also spelled **bott.** [Origin unknown]

bo·tan·i·cal (bə·tan/i·kəl) *adj.* Of or pertaining to botany or to plants. Also **bo·tan/ic.** — *n.* A drug derived from the leaves, roots, stems, etc., of a plant. [< F < Gk. *botanē* plant, pasture] — **bo·tan/i·cal·ly** *adv.* — **bot/a·nist** *n.*

bot·a·nize (bot/ə·nīz) *v.* **·nized, ·niz·ing** *v.i.* **1.** To study botanical specimens. **2.** To gather plants for study. — *v.t.* **3.** To search for botanical specimens. — **bot/a·niz/er** *n.*

bot·a·ny (bot/ə·nē) *n.* **1.** The division of biology that treats of plants, their structure, functions, classification, etc. **2.** The total plant life of a region, country, etc. **3.** The characteristics of a group of plants treated collectively.

botch (boch) *v.t.* **1.** To bungle. **2.** To patch or mend clumsily. — *n.* **1.** A bungled piece of work. **2.** A clumsy patch. [ME *bocchen*; origin unknown] — **botch/er** *n.* — **botch/er·y** *n.* — **botch/i·ly** *adv.* — **botch/y** *adj.*

bot·fly (bot/flī') *n.* A fly of which the larvae are parasitic in vertebrates; esp., the **horse botfly.**

both (bōth) *adj. & pron.* The two together: *Both* girls laughed. — *conj. & adv.* Equally; alike; as well: with *and.* [< ON *bādhar*]

both·er (both/ər) *v.t.* **1.** To pester; give trouble to. **2.** To confuse; fluster. — *v.i.* **3.** To trouble or concern oneself. — *n.* **1.** A source or state of annoyance; vexation; trouble. **2.** One who or that which bothers. [? dial. E (Irish)]

both·er·some (both/ər·səm) *adj.* Causing bother.

bott (bot) See BOT.

bot·tle (bot/l) *n.* **1.** A vessel, usu. of glass, for holding liquids, having a neck and a narrow mouth that can be stopped. **2.** As much as a bottle will hold: also **bot/tle·ful'.** **— to hit the bottle** *U.S. Slang* To drink liquor to excess. — *v.t.* **·tled, ·tling** **1.** To put into a bottle or bottles. **2.** To restrain: often with *up* or *in.* [< LL *buticula* flask] — **bot/tler** *n.*

bottle green A dark, dull green.

bot·tle·neck (bot/l·nek') *n.* **1.** A narrow or congested passageway. **2.** Anything that retards progress; hindrance.

bot·tle·nose (bot/l·nōz') *n.* A variety of dolphin.

bot·tom (bot'əm) _n._ **1.** The lowest part of anything. **2.** The underside or undersurface. **3.** The ground beneath a body of water. **4.** Source or foundation. **5.** _Often pl._ Bottom land. **6.** _Naut._ The part of a vessel below the water line. **7.** _Informal_ The buttocks. **8.** The seat of a chair. **9.** Staying power; stamina. **— at bottom** Fundamentally. **— bottoms up!** _Informal_ Empty your glass! — _adj._ Lowest; fundamental; basal. — _v.t._ **1.** To provide with a bottom. **2.** To base or found: with _on_ or _upon_. **3.** To fathom; comprehend. — _v.i._ **4.** To be founded; rest. **5.** To touch or rest on the bottom. [OE]

bottom land Lowland along a river.

bot·tom·less (bot'əm·lis) _adj._ **1.** Having no bottom. **2.** Unfathomable; limitless; endless. **— the bottomless pit** Hell.

bot·tom·ry (bot'əm·rē) _n._ A contract whereby the owner of a vessel borrows money, pledging the vessel as security.

bot·u·lism (boch'ŏŏ·liz'əm) _n._ Poisoning caused by a toxin produced by a bacillus sometimes present in improperly preserved food. [< G < L _botulus_ sausage]

bou·clé (bōō·klā') _n._ A woven or knitted fabric with a looped or knotted surface; also, the yarn from which this is made. [< F, pp. of _boucler_ to buckle, curl]

bou·doir (bōō'dwär, bōō·dwär') _n._ A lady's private sitting room or bedroom. [< F, lit., pouting room]

bouf·fant (bōō·fänt') _adj._ Puffed-out; flaring, as a skirt. [< F, ppr. of _bouffer_ to swell]

bough (bou) _n._ A large branch of a tree. [OE _bōg_ shoulder.]

bought (bôt) Past tense and past participle of BUY.

bouil·la·baisse (bōōl'yə·bās', _Fr._ bōō·yà·bes') _n._ A chowder made of several varieties of fish. [< F < Provençal < _boui_ boil + _abaisso_ to settle, go down]

bouil·lon (bōōl'yon, -yən; _Fr._ bōō·yôn') _n._ Clear soup from beef or other meats. [< F < _bouillir_ to boil]

boul·der (bōl'dər) _n._ A large, rounded rock that has been detached: also spelled _bowlder_. [ME _bulderston_]

boul·e·vard (bōōl'ə·värd, bōō'lə-) _n._ **1.** A broad avenue, often lined with trees. **2.** _Chiefly Canadian_ The grass between sidewalk and street; also, the center strip of a divided highway. _Abbr._ _blvd._ [< F < G _bollwerk_ fortification]

bounce (bouns) _v._ **bounced**, **bounc·ing** _v.i._ **1.** To move with a bound or bounds, as a ball; rebound. **2.** To move suddenly and violently; spring. **3.** _U.S. Slang_ To be returned by a bank as worthless: said of a check. — _v.t._ **4.** To cause to bounce. **5.** _Slang_ To eject (a person) forcibly; also, to discharge from employment. — _n._ **1.** A bound or rebound. **2.** A sudden spring or leap. **3.** Ability or capacity to bounce or spring. **1.** _Informal_ Vivacity; verve; spirit. [ME _bunsen_ to thump < MLG] **— bounc'y** _adj._

bounc·er (boun'sər) _n._ _U.S. Slang_ One employed in a bar, night club, etc., to eject disorderly persons.

bounc·ing (boun'sing) _adj._ Strong and active; strapping.

bound¹ (bound) _v.i._ **1.** To strike and spring back from a surface, as a ball. **2.** To leap; move by a series of leaps. — _v.t._ **3.** To cause to bound. — _n._ A leap or spring; also, a rebound. [< MF _bondir_ to resound, rebound]

bound² (bound) _n._ **1.** _Usu. pl._ A boundary; limit: out of _bounds_. **2.** _pl._ The area near or within a boundary. — _v.t._ **1.** To set limits to; restrict. **2.** To form the boundary of. **3.** To name the boundaries of. — _v.i._ **4.** To adjoin; abut. [< OF < LL _bodina_ limit.]

bound³ (bound) Past tense and past participle of BIND. — _adj._ **1.** Made fast; tied with bonds. **2.** Having a cover or binding. **3.** Morally or legally obligated. **4.** Certain; sure: It's _bound_ to rain. **5.** _U.S. Informal_ Determined; resolved. **— bound up in** (or **with**) **1.** Inseparably connected with. **2.** Devotedly attached to.

bound⁴ (bound) _adj._ Having one's course directed; on the way: _bound_ for home. [< ON < _būa_ to prepare]

bound·a·ry (boun'də·rē, -drē) _n._ _pl._ **·ries** Anything indicating a limit or confine.

bound·en (boun'dən) _adj._ **1.** Obligatory: our _bounden_ duty. **2.** Under obligations; obliged.

bound·er (boun'dər) _n._ _Chiefly Brit. Informal_ An offensive, ill-mannered person; a cad.

bound·less (bound'lis) _adj._ Having no limit; vast. — **bound'less·ly** _adv._ — **bound'less·ness** _n._

boun·te·ous (boun'tē·əs) _adj._ **1.** Generous; beneficent. **2.** Marked by abundance; plentiful. [ME < OF < _bonté_ goodness] — **boun'te·ous·ly** _adv._ — **boun'te·ous·ness** _n._

boun·ti·ful (boun'tə·fəl) _adj._ **1.** Free and generous in bestowing gifts. **2.** Showing abundance; plentiful. — **boun'ti·ful·ly** _adv._ — **boun'ti·ful·ness** _n._

boun·ty (boun'tē) _n._ _pl._ **·ties** **1.** Liberality in giving. **2.** Gifts or favors generously bestowed. **3.** A reward from a government, as for the killing of predatory animals, etc. [< OF < L _bonitas, -tatis_ goodness]

bou·quet (bōō·kā', bōō·kā' _for def._ 1; bōō·kā' _for def._ 2) _n._ **1.** A bunch of flowers. **2.** Delicate odor; esp. the distinctive aroma of a wine. [< F < OF _boschet_]

bour·bon (bûr'bən) _n._ A whiskey distilled from a fermented mash containing at least 51 per cent corn. Also **bourbon whiskey.** [after _Bourbon_ County, Ky., where first made]

Bour·bon (bōōr'bən) _n._ **1.** A dynasty that reigned over France, 1589–1792, 1815–48, or a related branch that ruled Spain, 1700–1931. **2.** One who is stubbornly conservative in politics. — **Bour'bon·ism** _n._ — **Bour'bon·ist** _n._

bour·geois¹ (bŏŏr'zhwä, bŏŏr·zhwä') _n._ _pl._ **·geois** **1.** A member of the middle class; a tradesman. **2.** _pl._ The middle class. **3.** In Marxism, a member of the class in conflict with the working class. — _adj._ Of or characteristic of the middle class: often used disparagingly. [< F < OF < LL < _burgus_ town] — **bour·geoise** (bŏŏr·zhwäz') _n. & adj. fem._

bour·geois² (bər·jois') _n._ A size of type, about 9-point. [? after a French printer]

bour·geoi·sie (bŏŏr'zhwä·zē') _n._ **1.** The middle class of society, esp. in France. **2.** In Marxism, that social class opposed in the class struggle to the proletariat or working class.

bour·geon (bûr'jən) See BURGEON.

Bourse (bŏŏrs) _n._ An exchange or money market; esp., the Paris stock exchange. [< F, purse < LL _bursa_ bag]

bout (bout) _n._ **1.** A contest; trial. **2.** A fit or spell, as of drinking or illness. [Var. of ME _bought_ bending, turn]

bou·tique (bōō·tēk') _n._ _French_ A small retail shop.

bou·ton·niere (bōō'tən·yâr') _n._ A bouquet or flower worn in the buttonhole. Also **bou'ton·nière'.** [< F]

bo·vine (bō'vīn, -vin) _adj._ **1.** Of or pertaining to oxen, cows, etc. **2.** Stolid; null. — _n._ A bovine animal. [< LL < L _bos, bovis_ ox]

bow¹ (bou) _n._ **1.** _Naut._ The forward part of a ship, boat, etc. **2.** The forward oarsman of a boat. — _adj._ Of or at the bow. [< LG or Scand.]

bow² (bou) _v._ **bowed**, **bow·ing** _v.i._ **1.** To bend the body or head, as in salutation, worship, or assent. **2.** To bend or incline downward. **3.** To submit; yield. — _v.t._ **4.** To bend (the body, head, etc.) in reverence, courtesy, or submission. **5.** To express by bowing. **6.** To escort with bows. **7.** To cause to yield; subdue. **8.** To cause to bend or stoop. **— to bow out** To withdraw; resign. — _n._ An inclination of the body or head. [OE _būgan_ to bend]

bow³ (bō) _n._ **1.** A weapon made from a strip of elastic wood or other pliable material, bent by a string and used to project an arrow. **2.** An archer. **3.** Something bent or curved; a bend. **4.** A knot with a loop or loops, as of ribbon, etc. **5.** _Music_ **a** A rod with hairs stretched between raised ends, used for playing a violin or related stringed instrument. **b** A stroke with a bow. — _adj._ Bent; curved; bowed. — _v.t. & v.i._ **bowed**, **bow·ing** **1.** To bend into the shape of a bow. **2.** _Music_ To play (a stringed instrument) with a bow. — **Syn.** See BEND¹. [OE _boga_]

bowd·ler·ize (boud'lər·īz) _v.t._ **·ized**, **·iz·ing** To expurgate or edit prudishly. [after Dr. Thomas _Bowdler's_ "family" edition of Shakespeare (1818)] — **bowd'ler·ism** _n._ — **bowd'ler·i·za'tion** _n._

bow·el (bou'əl, boul) _n._ **1.** An intestine. **2.** _pl._ The inner part of anything: the _bowels_ of the earth. — _v.t._ **bow·eled** or **·elled**, **bow·el·ing** or **·el·ling** To disembowel. [< OF < L _botellus_, dim. of _botulus_ sausage]

bow·er (bou'ər) _n._ A shaded recess. — _v.t._ To enclose in or as in a bower. [OE _būr_ chamber] — **bow'er·y** _adj._

Bow·er·y (bou'ər·ē) A street in New York City noted for its saloons, shabby hotels, etc.: often preceded by _the._

bow·ie knife (bō'ē, bōō'ē) A strong, single-edged hunting knife. [after James _Bowie_, 1799–1836, its reputed inventor]

bow·knot (bō'not') _n._ An ornamental slipknot made with one or more loops. For illus. see KNOT.

BOWIE KNIFE

bowl¹ (bōl) _n._ **1.** A deep, round dish. **2.** The amount a bowl will hold. **3.** A large goblet. **4.** Convivial drinking. **5.** An amphitheater. **6.** Something shaped like a bowl: the _bowl_ of a pipe. [OE _bolla_]

bowl² (bōl) _n._ **1.** A large ball for bowls or tenpins. **2.** A throw of the ball in bowling. — _v.i._ **1.** To play at bowls, tenpins, etc. **2.** To roll a ball or rounded object. **3.** To move smoothly and swiftly: usually with _along._ — _v.t._ **4.** To roll or throw, as a ball. **5.** To carry or transport on or as on wheels. **— to bowl over 1.** To cause to be confused or helpless. **2.** To knock down. [< F _boule_ ball] — **bowl'er** _n._

bowl·der (bōl'dər) See BOULDER.

bow·leg (bō'leg') _n._ A leg with an outward curvature at or below the knee. — **bow·leg·ged** (bō'leg'id, -legd') _adj._

bowl·er (bō'lər) _n._ _Brit._ A derby. [< BOWL²]

bow·line (bō'lin, -līn') _n._ **1.** A knot tied so as to form a loop. Also **bowline knot.** **2.** _Naut._ A rope to keep a sail taut when sailing close-hauled.

---

bowl·ing (bō′ling) *n.* The game of bowls or of tenpins.
bowling alley A long, narrow space for playing tenpins, or the building containing it.
bowling green A smooth lawn for playing at bowls.
bowls (bōlz) *n.pl.* **1.** *Brit.* An outdoor game played by rolling slightly flattened or weighted balls at a stationary ball. **2.** Tenpins, ninepins, or skittles.
bow·man (bō′mən) *n. pl.* **·men** (-mən) An archer.
bow·shot (bō′shot′) *n.* The distance to which an arrow may be sent from the bow.
bow·sprit (bou′sprit′, bō′-) *n.* *Naut.* A spar projecting forward from the bow of a vessel. [? < M.Du. < *boeg* bow of a ship + *spriet* spear]
bow·string (bō′string′) *n.* The string of a bow, which projects the arrow.
bow tie A necktie worn in a bowknot.
bow window (bō) A projecting, usually curved window built up from the ground level.
box[1] (boks) *n.* **1.** A receptacle or case of wood, metal, etc., in many sizes and shapes and usu. having a lid. **2.** The quantity contained in a box. **3.** Something resembling a box in form or use. **4.** A small booth for a sentry, watchman, etc. **5.** The raised driver's seat of a coach. **6.** A space partitioned off for seating, as in a theater, courtroom, stadium, etc. **7.** In baseball, any of several designated spaces, as for the pitcher, batter, coach, etc. **8.** *Mech.* An axle bearing, casing, or other enclosed cavity. **9.** An enclosed space on a page of a newspaper, magazine, etc. — *v.t.* **1.** To place in a box. **2.** To furnish with a bushing or box. — **to box in 1.** In racing, to block (another contestant) so that he is unable to get ahead. **2.** To box up. — **to box the compass 1.** To recite in order the 32 points of the compass. **2.** To make a complete revolution or turn. — **to box up** To confine in, or as in, a small space. [OE < Med.L < Gk. *pyxos* boxwood] — **box′er** *n.*
box[2] (boks) *v.t.* **1.** To strike or buffet with the hand; cuff. **2.** To fight (another) in a boxing match. — *v.i.* **3.** To fight with one's fists; be a boxer. — *n.* A blow on the ear or cheek; cuff. [ME]
box[3] (boks) *n.* **1.** Any of a small family of evergreen herbs, shrubs, and trees, used as borders and hedges. **2.** The hard wood of these plants. [OE < L < Gk. *pyxos* boxwood]
box·car (boks′kär′) *n.* A roofed, enclosed freight car.
box elder A North American tree of the maple family, having compound leaflets: also called *Manitoba maple.*
box·er[1] (bok′sər) *n.* One who fights with his fists; pugilist.
box·er[2] (bok′sər) *n.* A breed of dog, related to the bulldog, having a sturdy body, smooth fawn coat, and a black mask.
Box·er (bok′sər) *n.* A member of a Chinese secret society, active in 1900, that aimed to rid China of foreigners by force.
box·ing (bok′sing) *n.* The art or practice of fighting with the fists, esp. when gloved; pugilism.
boxing glove A padded mitten used for prizefighting.
box office 1. The ticket office of a theater, etc. **2.** *Informal* Receipts at the box office, as a measure of success.
box seat A seat in a box of a theater, stadium, etc.
box spring A mattress foundation consisting of an upholstered frame set with coil springs to provide resiliency.
box·wood (boks′wŏŏd′) *n.* **1.** The hard, close-grained, durable wood of box. **2.** The shrub.
boy (boi) *n.* **1.** A male child; lad; youth. **2.** A man; fellow; a familiar use. **3.** A male servant. [ME *boi*] — **boy′ish** *adj.* — **boy′ish·ly** *adv.* — **boy′ish·ness** *n.*
boy·cott (boi′kot) *v.t.* **1.** To combine together in refusing to deal or associate with, so as to punish or coerce. **2.** To refuse to use or buy. — *n.* The act or practice of boycotting. [after Capt. C. *Boycott*, 1832–97, Irish landlord's agent, who was the first victim] — **boy′cot·ter** *n.*
boy friend 1. *Informal* A preferred male companion or intimate friend of a girl or woman. **2.** A male friend.
boy·hood (boi′hŏŏd) *n.* **1.** The state or period of being a boy. **2.** Boys collectively.
boy scout A member of the **Boy Scouts**, an organization for boys, stressing self-reliance and good citizenship.
boy·sen·ber·ry (boi′zən·ber′ē) *n. pl.* **·ries** The edible fruit obtained by crossing the blackberry, raspberry, and loganberry. [after Rudolph *Boysen*, 20th c. U.S. horticulturist]
bra (brä) *n.* *U.S. Informal* A brassiere.
brace (brās) *v.* **braced, brac·ing** *v.t.* **1.** To make firm or steady; strengthen by or as by braces. **2.** To make ready to withstand pressure, impact, assault, etc. **3.** To increase the tension or strain. **4.** To tie or fasten firmly, as with straps. **5.** To stimulate; enliven. — *v.i.* **6.** To strain against pressure. — **to brace up** *Informal* To rouse one's courage or resolution. — *n.* **1.** A support, as of wood or metal, used to strengthen something or hold it in place. **2.** A clasp or clamp for fastening, connecting, etc. **3.** A cranklike handle for holding and turning a bit or other boring tool. **4.** A pair; couple. **5.** *Printing* A doubly curved line, [or] used to connect words, lines, staves of music, etc. **6.** *pl. Brit.* Suspenders. **7.** *Often pl. Dent.* A wire or wires fastened on ir-

regular teeth and gradually tightened to align them. **8.** *Med.* Any of various devices for supporting a joint, limb, or other part. [< OF < L *brachia*, pl. of *brachium* arm]
brace·let (brās′lit) *n.* **1.** An ornamental band worn around the wrist or arm. **2.** *Informal* A handcuff. [< OF, dim. of *bracel* < L *brachiale* bracelet]
brac·er (brā′sər) *n.* **1.** One who or that which braces or steadies. **2.** *U.S. Informal* A stimulating drink.
bra·chi·al (brā′kē·əl, brak′ē-) *adj.* Of or pertaining to the arm or to armlike appendages. [< L < *brachium* arm]
brachio- *combining form* Arm; of the arm: *brachiopod.* Also, before vowels, **brachi-**. [< Gk. *brachiōn* arm]
bra·chi·o·pod (brā′kē·ə·pod′, brak′ē-) *n. Zool.* One of a phylum or class of marine animals having a bivalve shell and a pair of armlike parts on the sides of the mouth. [< NL]
bra·chi·um (brā′kē·əm, brak′ē-) *n. pl.* **bra·chi·a** (brā′kē·ə, brak′ē-) **1.** *Anat.* The arm, esp. that part above the elbow. **2.** Any armlike process or appendage. [< L]
brachy- *combining form* Short. [< Gk. *brachys* short]
brach·y·ce·phal·ic (brak′i·sə·fal′ik) *adj.* Having a short, broad skull; short-headed. Also **brach·y·ceph·a·lous** (brak′i·sef′ə·ləs). [< NL < Gk. < *brachys* short + *kephalē* head] — **brach′y·ceph′a·lism, brach′y·ceph′a·ly** *n.*
brac·ing (brā′sing) *adj.* Strengthening; invigorating. — *n.* A brace or system of braces, as in bridge building.
brack·en (brak′en) *n.* **1.** A coarse, hardy fern with very large fronds: also called *brake.* **2.** A clump of such ferns. [ME *braken* < Scand.]
brack·et (brak′it) *n.* **1.** A piece of wood, metal, stone, etc., projecting from a wall, used to support a shelf or other weight. **2.** A brace used to strengthen an angle. **3.** A projecting wall fixture for a gaslight, electric lamp, etc. **4.** A classification according to income for tax purposes: the high-income *bracket.* **5.** *Printing* One of two marks [] used to enclose any part of a text. — *v.t.* **1.** To provide or support with a bracket or brackets. **2.** To enclose within brackets. **3.** To group or categorize together. [< Sp. < L *bracae*, pl., breeches]
brack·ish (brak′ish) *adj.* **1.** Somewhat saline; briny. **2.** Distasteful. [< Du. *brak* salty] — **brack′ish·ness** *n.*
bract (brakt) *n. Bot.* A modified leaf situated at the base of a flower. [< L *bractea* thin metal plate] — **brac·te·al** (brak′tē·əl) *adj.* — **brac·te·ate** (brak′tē·it, -āt) *adj.*
brad (brad) *n.* A small, slender nail with a small head. [< ON *broddr* spike]
brad·awl (brad′ôl′) *n.* A short awl for making holes in wood, as for brads or screws.
brady- *combining form* Slow. [< Gk. *bradys* slow]
brae (brā) *n. Scot.* A bank; hillside; slope.
brag (brag) *v.* **bragged, brag·ging** *v.i.* **1.** To boast about oneself or one's deeds or abilities. — *v.t.* **2.** To declare or assert boastfully; boast of. — *n.* **1.** Boastful language; boasting. **2.** A boast. **3.** One who brags. [Origin uncertain] — **brag′ger** *n.*
brag·ga·do·ci·o (brag′ə·dō′shē·ō) *n. pl.* **·ci·os 1.** Pretentious boasting. **2.** One who boasts; a swaggerer. [after *Braggadochio*, a boastful character in Spenser's *Faerie Queene*]
brag·gart (brag′ərt) *n.* A bragger. — *adj.* Boastful. [< MF < *braguer* to brag] — **brag′gart·ism** *n.*
brah·ma (brä′mə, brä′-) *n. Often cap.* A large breed of domestic fowl developed in Asia. [after *Brahmaputra*]
Brah·ma (brä′mə) *n.* **1.** In Hindu religion, the supreme soul of the universe. **2.** God, comprising the Hindu trinity Brahma, Vishnu, and Siva; esp. the first of the trinity as supreme creator. [< Skt. *Brahmā*]
Brah·man (brä′mən) *n. pl.* **·mans 1.** A member of the highest Hindu caste, the sacerdotal caste: also spelled *Brahmin.* **2.** A breed of cattle originating in India. [< Skt. *brāhmana* < *brahman* praise, worship] — **Brah·man·i** (brä′mən·ē) *n.fem.* — **Brah·man·ic** (brä·man′ik) *adj.*
Brah·man·ism (brä′mən·iz′əm) *n.* The religious and social system of the Brahmans: also **Brah′min·ism** (brä′min-).
Brah·min (brä′min) *n.* **1.** A Brahman. **2.** A highly cultured or aristocratic person, esp. an ultraconservative or snobbish one.
braid (brād) *v.t.* **1.** To weave or intertwine several strands of hair, etc. **2.** To bind or ornament (the hair) with ribbons, etc. **3.** To form by braiding. **4.** To ornament (garments) with braid. — *n.* **1.** A narrow, flat tape or strip for binding or ornamenting fabrics. **2.** Anything braided or plaited. **3.** A string or band used in arranging the hair. [OE *bregdan* to brandish, weave, braid] — **braid′er** *n.* — **braid′ing** *n.*
Braille (brāl) *n.* A system of printing or writing for the blind in which the characters consist of raised dots to be read by the fingers; also, the characters themselves. Also **braille**. [after Louis *Braille*, 1809–52, French educator, the inventor]
brain (brān) *n.* **1.** *Anat.* The enlarged and greatly modified part of the central nervous system contained in the cranium of vertebrates. **2.** *Often pl.* Mind; intellect. — **to have on**

BRACTS
(Around a composite flower)

the brain To be obsessed by. — *v.t.* **1.** To dash out the brains of. **2.** *Slang* To hit on the head. [OE *brægen*]

brain child *Informal* That which one has created or originated, as an idea, technique, device, etc.

brain·less (brān/lis) *adj.* Lacking intelligence; senseless; stupid. — **brain/less·ly** *adv.* — **brain/less·ness** *n.*

brain·pan (brān/pan/) *n.* The cranium; skull.

brain·sick (brān/sik) *adj.* Affected with mental disorder.

brain·storm (brān/stôrm/) *n. Informal* A sudden inspiration. Also **brain storm.**

brain trust A group of experts who act as consultants on matters of policy, etc. — **brain truster**

brain·wash (brān/wosh , -wôsh/) *v.t.* To alter the convictions, beliefs, etc., of by means of intensive, coercive indoctrination. — **brain/wash/ing** *n.*

brain wave *Physiol.* A rhythmical fluctuation of electrical potential in the brain.

brain·y (brā/nē) *adj.* **brain·i·er, brain·i·est** *Informal* Intelligent; smart. — **brain/i·ly** *adv.* — **brain/i·ness** *n.*

braise (brāz) *v.t.* **braised, brais·ing** To cook (meat) by searing till brown and then simmering in a covered pan. [< F < *braise* charcoal]

brake¹ (brāk) *n.* **1.** A device for slowing or stopping a vehicle or wheel, esp. by friction. **2.** An instrument for separating the fiber of flax, hemp, etc., by bruising or crushing. — *v.* **braked, brak·ing** *v.t.* **1.** To apply a brake to. **2.** To bruise and crush, as flax. — *v.i.* **3.** To operate a brake or brakes. [< MDu. *braeke* brake for flax] — **brake/age** *n.*

brake² (brāk) *n.* Bracken, a kind of fern. [ME]

brake³ (brāk) *n.* An area covered with brushwood, briers, cane, etc.; thicket.

brake·man (brāk/mən) *n. pl.* **·men** (-mən) One who tends brakes on a railroad car or assists in operating a train.

brake shoe A rigid metal casting shaped to press against a wheel or brake when braking action is applied.

bram·ble (bram/bəl) *n.* **1.** A plant of the rose family, esp. the blackberry of Europe. **2.** Any prickly plant. Also **bram/ble·bush/** (-bŏŏsh/). [OE *bræmble*] — **bram/bly** *adj.*

bran (bran) *n.* **1.** The coarse, outer coat of cereals, as separated from the flour by sifting or bolting. **2.** Grain by-products used as feed. [< OF *bran, bren*] — **bran/ny** *adj.*

branch (branch, bränch) *n.* **1.** A woody outgrowth from the trunk of a tree or other large plant; limb. **2.** A part analogous to a branch; an offshoot, as of a deer's antlers. **3.** Any separate part or division of a system, subject, etc.; department. **4.** A subordinate or local store, office, etc. **5.** A division of a family, tribe, nation, etc., having or thought to have a common ancestor. **6.** A tributary stream of a river. **7.** Any small stream or brook. — *v.i.* **1.** To put forth branches. **2.** To separate into branches or subdivisions. — *v.t.* **3.** To divide into branches. — **to branch off 1.** To separate into branches; fork, as a road. **2.** To diverge; go off on a tangent. — **to branch out** To extend or expand, as one's business. [< OF < LL *branca* paw]

bran·chi·ae (brang/ki·ē) *n. pl.* of **bran·chi·a** (brang/kē-ə) *Zool.* Gills, the respiratory organs of fish. [< L < Gk. *branchia,* pl., gills] — **bran/chi·al** *adj.*

bran·chi·ate (brang/kē·it, -āt) *adj.* Having gills.

brand (brand) *n.* **1.** A distinctive name or trademark identifying the product of a manufacturer. **2.** The kind or make of a product: a good *brand* of coffee. **3.** A mark made with a hot iron, as on cattle, to indicate ownership. **4.** Formerly, a mark burned on criminals. **5.** Any mark of disgrace; stigma. **6.** A branding iron. **7.** A burning piece of wood; also, a torch. — *v.t.* **1.** To mark with a brand. **2.** To stigmatize. [OE, torch, sword.] — **brand/er** *n.*

bran·died (bran/dēd) *adj.* Mixed, flavored with, or preserved in brandy: *brandied* cherries.

branding iron An iron for burning in a brand.

bran·dish (bran/dish) *v.t.* To wave or flourish triumphantly, menacingly, or defiantly. — *n.* A flourish, as with a weapon. [< OF *brandir*] — **bran/dish·er** *n.*

brand-new (brand/nōō/, -nyōō/, bran/-) *adj.* Very new; fresh and bright. Also **bran/-new/** (bran/-).

bran·dy (bran/dē) *n. pl.* **·dies** An alcoholic liquor distilled from wine or other fermented fruit juices. — *v.t.* **·died, ·dy·ing** To mix, flavor, strengthen, or preserve with brandy. [< Du. *brandewijn,* lit., distilled (burned) wine]

brant (brant) *n. pl.* **brants** or **brant** A small, black-necked wild goose of Europe and North America. Also **brant goose.**

brash¹ (brash) *adj. U.S.* **1.** Acting hastily; rash; impetuous. **2.** Impudent; saucy; pert. [Cf. G *barsch* harsh and Sw. *barsk* impetuous] — **brash/ly** *adv.* — **brash/ness** *n.*

brash² (brash) *n. Brit.* A shower of rain. [? Blend of *break* and *crash, dash,* etc.] — **brash/i·ness** *n.* — **brash/y** *adj.*

bra·sier (brā/zhər) See BRAZIER.

brass (bras, bräs) *n.* **1.** An alloy essentially of copper and zinc, harder than copper, and both ductile and malleable.

2. Formerly, any alloy of copper, esp. one with tin. **3.** *Usu. pl.* Ornaments or utensils of brass. **4.** *Sometimes pl. Music* The brass instruments of an orchestra or band collectively: also *Rare* **brass winds. 5.** *Informal* Effrontery. **6.** *U.S. Informal* High-ranking military officers; any high officials. — *adj.* Made of brass; brazen. [OE *bræs*]

bras·sard (bras/ärd, brə·särd/) *n.* **1.** A band worn on the upper arm as a badge or insignia. **2.** A piece of armor for the arm. Also **bras·sart** (bras/ärt). [< F < *bras* arm]

brass band *Music* A band using mostly brass instruments.

brass hat *Informal* A high-ranking military officer.

brass·ie (bras/ē, bräs/ē) *n.* A wooden golf club with a brass plate on the sole. Also **brass/y.**

bras·siere (brə·zir/) *n.* A woman's undergarment to support or shape the breasts. Also **bras·sière/.** [< F]

brass knuckles A metal device that fits over the knuckles of a closed fist, used in rough fighting: also called *knuckledusters.* Also **brass knucks** (nuks).

brass tacks *Informal* Basic facts; essentials: usu. in the phrase **to get** (or **come**) **down to brass tacks.**

brass·y (bras/ē, bräs/ē) *adj.* **brass·i·er, brass·i·est 1.** Of or ornamented with brass. **2.** Like brass, as in sound or color. **3.** Cheap and showy. **4.** *Informal* Insolent; brazen. — **brass/i·ly** *adv.* — **brass/i·ness** *n.*

brat (brat) *n.* A nasty child.

bra·va·do (brə·vä/dō) *n. pl.* **·does** or **·dos** Boastful defiance; affectation of bravery. [< Sp. < *bravo* brave]

brave (brāv) *adj.* **brav·er, brav·est 1.** Having or showing courage; intrepid. **2.** Making a fine display; elegant. — *v.* **braved, brav·ing** *v.t.* **1.** To meet with courage and fortitude. **2.** To defy; challenge. — *n.* **1.** A man of courage. **2.** A North American Indian warrior. [< F < Ital. *bravo*] — **brave/ly** *adv.* — **brave/ness** *n.*

brav·er·y (brā/vər·ē) *n. pl.* **·er·ies 1.** The quality of being brave; valor; heroism. **2.** Elegance of attire; show; splendor.

bra·vo (brä/vō) *interj.* Good! well done! — *n. pl.* **·vos** A shout of "bravo!" [< Ital.]

bra·vu·ra (brə·vyŏŏr/ə, *Ital.* brä·vōō/rä) *n.* **1.** *Music* A passage requiring dashing and brilliant execution; also, a brilliant style of execution. **2.** Any brilliant or daring performance. [< Ital., dash, daring < *bravo.*]

brawl (brôl) *n.* **1.** A noisy quarrel; fight. **2.** *U.S. Slang* An uproarious party. — *v.i.* **1.** To quarrel noisily; fight. **2.** To move noisily, as water. [ME *braulen,* ? < LG] — **brawl/er** *n.* — **brawl/ing·ly** *adv.*

brawn (brôn) *n.* **1.** Firm or well-developed muscles. **2.** Muscular power. [< OF *braun* slice of flesh, ult. < Gmc.]

brawn·y (brô/nē) *adj.* **brawn·i·er, brawn·i·est** Muscular; strong. — **brawn/i·ness** *n.*

bray (brā) *v.i.* **1.** To utter a loud, harsh cry, as an ass. **2.** To sound harshly, as a trumpet. — *v.t.* **3.** To utter loudly and harshly. — *n.* **1.** The cry of an ass, mule, etc. **2.** Any loud, harsh sound. [< OF *braire* to cry out] — **bray/er** *n.*

braze¹ (brāz) *v.t.* **brazed, braz·ing 1.** To make of brass. **2.** To make like brass in hardness or appearance. **3.** To ornament with or as with brass. [OE < *bræs* brass]

braze² (brāz) *v.t.* **brazed, braz·ing** *Metall.* To join the surfaces of (similar or dissimilar metals) with a layer of a soldering alloy applied under very high temperature. [< F *braser* solder < OF, burn, ult. < Gmc.] — **braz/er** *n.*

bra·zen (brā/zən) *adj.* **1.** Made of brass. **2.** Resembling brass in hardness, color, etc. **3.** Impudent; shameless. — *v.t.* **1.** To face with effrontery or impudence: with *out.* **2.** To make bold or reckless. [OE < *bræs* brass] — **bra/zen·ly** *adv.* — **bra/zen·ness** *n.*

bra·zen·face (brā/zən·fās/) *n.* An impudent, shameless person. — **bra/zen·faced/** *adj.*

bra·zier¹ (brā/zhər) *n.* A worker in brass. [ME *brasiere*]

bra·zier² (brā/zhər) *n.* An open pan for holding live coals: also spelled *brasier.* [< F < *braise* hot coals]

Bra·zil·ian (brə·zil/yən) *adj.* Of or pertaining to Brazil or its people. — *n.* A citizen or native of Brazil.

Brazil nut The edible seed of a South American tree.

breach (brēch) *n.* **1.** The act of breaking, or the state of being broken; infraction. **2.** Violation of a legal obligation, promise, etc. **3.** A gap or break in a dike, wall, etc. **4.** A breaking up of friendly relations; estrangement. — *v.t.* To break through. [OE *bryce*]

bread (bred) *n.* **1.** A food made with flour or meal, commonly leavened with yeast and baked. **2.** Food in general. **3.** The necessities of life. — *v.t.* To roll in bread crumbs before cooking. [OE *brēad* bit, crumb] — **bread/ed** *adj.*

bread-and-but·ter (bred/n-but/ər) *adj.* Expressing gratitude for hospitality: a *bread-and-butter* letter.

bread and butter *Informal* Subsistence; livelihood.

bread·bas·ket (bred/bas/kit, -bäs/-) *n. Slang* The stomach.

bread·fruit (bred/frōōt/) *n.* **1.** The fruit of a tree native to the South Sea Islands. **2.** The tree.

PRONUNCIATION KEY: add, āce, câre, pälm; end, ēven; it, īce; odd, ōpen, ôrder; tŏŏk, pōōl; up, bûrn; ə = a in *above,* e in *sicken,* i in *flexible,* o in *melon,* u in *focus;* yōō = u in *fuse;* oil; pout; check; go; ring; thin; this; zh, vision.

bread line A line of persons waiting to be given bread or other food as charity.

bread·stuff (bred/stuff/) *n.* **1.** Material for bread; grain, meal, or flour. **2.** Bread.

breadth (bredth, bretth) *n.* **1.** Measure or distance from side to side, as distinguished from length and thickness; width. **2.** Freedom from narrowness; liberality. **3.** That which is measured by its width, or which has a definite width: a *breadth* of cloth. [OE < *brād* broad]

breadth·wise (bredth/wiz/, bretth/-) *adv.* In the direction of the breadth. Also **breadth/ways/** (-wāz/).

bread·win·ner (bred/win/ər) *n.* One who supports himself and others by his earnings.

break (brāk) *v.* **broke** (*Archaic* **brake**), **bro·ken** (*Archaic* **broke**), **break·ing** *v.t.* **1.** To separate into pieces or fragments, as by a blow; shatter. **2.** To crack. **3.** To part the surface of; pierce: to *break* ground. **4.** To burst or cause to discharge, as an abscess. **5.** To disable; render useless. **6.** To destroy the order, continuity, or completeness of: to *break* ranks. **7.** To diminish the force or effect of: to *break* a fall. **8.** To overcome by opposing; end: to *break* a strike. **9.** To interrupt the course of, as a journey. **10.** To violate: to *break* one's promise. **11.** To reduce in spirit or health, as by toil. **12.** To tame, as a horse. **13.** To demote. **14.** To give or obtain smaller units for: to *break* a dollar. **15.** To make bankrupt or short of money. **16.** To force (a way), as through a barrier. **17.** To escape from. **18.** To surpass; excel: to *break* a record. **19.** To make known; tell, as news. **20.** To cause to discontinue a habit. **21.** *Law* To invalidate (a will) by court action. — *v.i.* **22.** To become separated into pieces or fragments. **23.** To give way; become unusable: His pencil *broke*. **24.** To dissolve and disperse: The clouds *broke*. **25.** To come into being or evidence: The storm *broke* suddenly. **26.** To appear above the surface. **27.** To start or move suddenly: He *broke* from the crowd. **28.** To become overwhelmed with grief: His heart *broke*. **29.** To fall off abruptly: The fever *broke*. **30.** To change tone, as a boy's voice. **31.** In baseball, to curve at or near the plate: said of a pitch. — **to break bread** To take or share a meal. — **to break down** **1.** To undergo mechanical failure. **2.** To suffer physical or mental collapse. **3.** To yield, especially to grief or strong feelings. **4.** To cause to yield. **5.** To analyze or be analyzed. **6.** To decompose. — **to break in** To cause to obey; train; adapt. — **to break into** (or **in**) **1.** To interrupt or intervene. **2.** To enter by force. — **to break in on** (or **upon**) To interrupt. — **to break off** **1.** To stop or cease, as from speaking. **2.** To sever (relations); discontinue. **3.** To become separate or detached. — **to break out** **1.** To start unexpectedly or suddenly, as a fire or plague. **2.** To have an eruption or rash, as the skin. **3.** To escape, as from prison. — **to break out into** (or **forth in, into,** etc.) To begin to do or perform: The birds *broke out into song.* — **to break up** **1.** To disperse; scatter: The meeting *broke up.* **2.** To dismantle. **3.** To put an end to. **4.** *Informal* To distress: The loss *broke up* the old man. **5.** *Informal* To sever relations. — **to break with** To sever relations with. — *n.* **1.** The act or result of breaking; fracture; rupture. **2.** A starting or opening: the *break* of day. **3.** *U.S.* A dash or run; especially, an attempt to escape: to make a *break* for the door. **4.** A breach of continuity, as a pause from work or an interruption in a discourse. **5.** *U.S. Informal* A chance or opportunity. **6.** *Electr.* The opening of a circuit; interruption of current. **7.** A rupture in friendship; quarrel. **8.** In prosody, a caesura. **9.** A sudden decline, as in prices, temperature, etc. **10.** *Music* **a** The point where one register or quality of a voice changes to another in singing. **b** In jazz, a syncopated cadenza bridging two phrases or choruses. **11.** In baseball or cricket, the swerving of a ball from a straight course when thrown. — **break/a·ble** *adj.* — **break/a·ble·ness** *n.*

break·age (brā/kij) *n.* **1.** A breaking, or being broken. **2.** Articles broken. **3.** Compensation for articles broken.

break·down (brāk/doun/) *n.* **1.** A collapse or failure, as of a machine, one's health, etc. **2.** An analysis or summary.

break·er (brā/kər) *n.* **1.** One who or that which breaks. **2.** A wave of the sea that breaks on rocks, a reef, etc.

break·fast (brek/fəst) *n.* The morning meal. — *v.t.* **1.** To furnish with a breakfast. — *v.i.* **2.** To eat breakfast.

break·neck (brāk/nek/) *adj.* Likely to break the neck; dangrous: *breakneck* speed.

break·through (brāk/thrōō/) *n.* **1.** *Mil.* An attack that penetrates through an enemy's defenses into the rear area. **2.** Any sudden, important success, as in scientific research.

break·up (brāk/up/) *n.* **1.** A breaking up or separation; dissolution; disruption. **2.** An ending.

break·wa·ter (brāk/wô/tər, -wot/ər) *n.* A barrier for protecting a harbor or beach from the force of waves.

bream (brēm) *n.* *pl.* **breams** or **bream** **1.** Any of several fresh-water fishes with deep, compressed bodies. **2.** Any of various fresh-water sunfishes. [OF *bresme*]

breast (brest) *n.* **1.** *Anat.* The front of the chest from the neck to the abdomen. **2.** One of the mammary glands. **3.** That part of a garment that covers the breast. **4.** The breast as the seat of the emotions. **5.** Anything likened to the human or animal breast. — **to make a clean breast of** To confess. — *v.t.* To meet boldly. [OE *brēost*]

breast·bone (brest/bōn/) *n.* *Anat.* The sternum.

breast-feed (brest/fēd/) *v.t. & v.i.* **-fed, -feed·ing** To suckle.

breast·pin (brest/pin/) *n.* A pin worn at the breast.

breast·plate (brest/plāt/) *n.* Plate armor for the breast.

breast stroke In swimming, a stroke made by thrusting the arms forward simultaneously from the breast.

breast·work (brest/wûrk/) *n.* A low, temporary defensive work, usu. breast-high.

breath (breth) *n.* **1.** Air inhaled and exhaled in respiration. **2.** Power or ability to breathe. **3.** The act of breathing; also, life; existence: while *breath* remains. **4.** A single respiration. **5.** The time of a single respiration; instant. **6.** A slight delay. **7.** A slight movement of air. **8.** Anything slight; trifle. **9.** A murmur; whisper. **10.** Moisture from exhaled air, when visible in cold air. **11.** *Phonet.* An exhalation of air without vibration of the vocal cords, as in the production of (p) and (f). — **in the same breath** At the same moment; without a pause or break. — **out of breath** Breathless; gasping. — **to take one's breath away** To awe or produce sudden emotion in. — **under one's breath** In a whisper or mutter. [OE *bræth* vapor, odor]

breathe (brēth) *v.* **breathed** (brēthd), **breath·ing** *v.i.* **1.** To inhale and exhale air. **2.** To be alive; live. **3.** To pause for breath; rest. **4.** To murmur; whisper. **5.** To move gently, as breezes. **6.** To be exhaled, as fragrance. — *v.t.* **7.** To inhale and expel from the lungs, as air; respire. **8.** To inject or infuse: to *breathe* life into a statue. **9.** To express; manifest: to *breathe* confidence. **10.** To exhale. **11.** To allow a rest to, as for breath. **12.** *Phonet.* To utter with the breath only. [ME *breth* breath] — **breath/a·ble** *adj.*

breath·er (brē/thər) *n.* *Informal* A brief rest period.

breath·ing (brē/thing) *adj.* Respiring; living. — *n.* **1.** The act of respiration; also, a single breath. **2.** A gentle breeze. **3.** Words spoken; utterance. **4.** Aspiration; longing. **5.** Time to breathe. **6.** *Phonet.* An aspiration; aspirate.

breath·less (breth/lis) *adj.* **1.** Out of breath. **2.** Holding the breath from fear, excitement, etc. **3.** That takes the breath away: *breathless* speed. **4.** Devoid of breath; dead. **5.** Motionless. — **breath/less·ly** *adv.* — **breath/less·ness** *n.*

breath·tak·ing (breth/tā/king) *adj.* Thrilling; overawing.

breath·y (breth/ē) *adj.* Characterized by audible breathing.

brec·ci·a (brech/ē·ə, bresh/-) *n.* *Geol.* A rock made up of angular fragments. [< Ital., grave] — **brec·ci·at·ed** (brech/ē·ā/tid, bresh/-) *adj.*

bred (bred) Past tense and past participle of BREED.

breech (brēch; *for v. def. 1, also* brich) *n.* **1.** The posterior and lower part of the body; the buttocks. **2.** The part of a gun, cannon, etc., that is behind the bore or barrel. **3.** The lower part of something, as of a pulley. — *v.t.* **1.** To clothe with breeches. **2.** To provide with a breech. [OE *brēc*]

breech·cloth (brēch/klôth/, -kloth/) *n.* A loincloth. Also **breech/clout/** (-klout/).

breech·es (brich/iz) *n.pl.* **1.** A man's garment covering the hips and thighs. **2.** Trousers. [OE *brēc*]

breeches buoy *Naut.* A lifesaving apparatus consisting of canvas breeches attached to a life buoy and run on a rope from one vessel to another or to the shore.

breech·ing (brich/ing, brē/ching) *n.* A harness strap passing behind a horse's haunches.

breech·load·er (brēch/lō/dər) *n.* A firearm loaded at the breech. — **breech/load/ing** *adj.*

breed (brēd) *v.* **bred, breed·ing** *v.t.* **1.** To produce (offspring). **2.** To cause: Familiarity *breeds* contempt. **3.** To raise: to *breed* horses. **4.** To bring up; train. — *v.i.* **5.** To procreate. **6.** To originate or be caused: Militarism *breeds* in armies. — *n.* **1.** A race or strain of animals. **2.** A sort or kind. [OE *brōd* brood] — **breed/er** *n.*

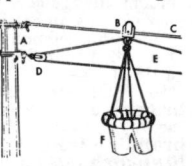

BREECHES BUOY *A* Mast. *B* Traveling block. *C* Hawser. *D* Fixed block. *E* Hauling line. *F* Breeches buoy.

breed·ing (brē/ding) *n.* **1.** The act of bearing young. **2.** The rearing of the young. **3.** Good manners. **4.** The scientific production of improved varieties of plants, animals, etc.

breeze (brēz) *n.* **1.** *Meteorol.* A moderate current of air; a gentle wind. **2.** *Brit. Informal* A flutter of excitement. — **in a breeze** *Slang* Without difficulty; easily. — *v.i.* **breezed, breez·ing** *Slang* To go quickly and blithely. [< Sp. and Pg. *brisa, briza* northeast wind]

breeze·way (brēz/wā/) *n.* A roofed, open passageway between two structures, as a house and garage.

breez·y (brē/nō) *adj.* **breez·i·er, breez·i·est** **1.** Having breezes; windy. **2.** Brisk or carefree; sprightly. — **breeze/i·ly** *adv.* — **breez/i·ness** *n.*

breth·ren (breth'rən) *n.pl.* **1.** Brothers. **2.** Members of a brotherhood. [ME]

Bret·on (bret'n) *adj.* Of or pertaining to Brittany, its inhabitants, or their language. — *n.* **1.** A native of Brittany. **2.** The Celtic language of the Bretons.

breve (brev, brēv) *n.* **1.** A mark (˘) placed over a vowel to indicate that it has a short sound, as *a* in *hat*. **2.** In prosody, a similar mark (◡) indicating a short or unstressed syllable. **3.** *Music* A note equivalent to two whole notes, or the symbol for it. [< Ital. < L *brevis* short]

bre·vet (brə·vet', *esp. Brit.* brev'it) *n. Mil.* A commission advancing an officer in honorary rank without advance in pay or in command. — *v.t.* **bre·vet·ted** (brə·vet'id) or **brev·et·ed** (brev'it·id), **bre·vet·ting** (brə·vet'ing) or **brev·et·ing** (brev'it·ing) To raise in rank by brevet. — *adj.* Held or conferred by brevet. [< OF *bref* letter, document] — **bre·vet·cy** (brə·vet'sē) *n.*

brevi- *combining form* Short. [< L *brevis* short]

bre·vi·ar·y (brē'vē·er'ē, brev'ē-) *n. pl.* **·ar·ies** *Eccl.* In the Roman Catholic and Eastern Orthodox churches, a book of daily prayers for the canonical hours. [< L *brevis* short]

bre·vier (brə·vir') *n. Printing* A size of type, about 8-point. [? < L, breviary; because once used in breviaries]

brev·i·ty (brev'ə·tē) *n.* **1.** Shortness of time. **2.** Condensation of language; conciseness. [< L *brevis* short]

brew (brōō) *v.t.* **1.** To make, as beer or ale, by steeping, boiling, and fermenting malt, hops, etc. **2.** To prepare (any beverage) as by boiling or mixing. **3.** To plot; devise. — *v.i.* **4.** To make ale, beer, or the like. **5.** To commence to form, as a storm. — *n.* **1.** Something brewed. **2.** The amount brewed. [OE *brēowan*] — **brew'er** *n.*

brew·er·y (brōō'ər·ē) *n. pl.* **·er·ies** An establishment for brewing; also, the apparatus used in brewing.

brew·ing (brōō'ing) *n.* **1.** The process of making a brew. **2.** The amount brewed at one time.

bri·ar (brī'ər) See BRIER.

bri·ar·root (brī'ər·rōōt', -rŏŏt') See BRIERROOT.

bri·ar·wood (brī'ər·wŏŏd') *n.* Brierroot.

bribe (brīb) *n.* **1.** A reward or emolument used corruptly to influence a person. **2.** Anything that seduces or allures. — *v.* **bribed, brib·ing** *v.t.* **1.** To offer or give a bribe to. **2.** To gain or influence by means of bribery. — *v.i.* **3.** To give bribes. [< OF, piece of bread given a beggar] — **brib'a·ble** *adj.* — **brib'er** *n.*

brib·er·y (brī'bər·ē) *n. pl.* **·er·ies** The giving, offering, or accepting of a bribe.

bric-a-brac (brik'ə·brak) *n.* Small objects of curiosity or decoration; antiques; knickknacks. [< F]

brick (brik) *n.* **1.** A molded block of clay, baked in various shapes and sizes, used for building, etc. **2.** Bricks collectively. **3.** Any object shaped like a brick. **4.** *Informal* An admirable fellow. — *v.t.* **1.** To build or line with bricks. **2.** To cover with bricks: with *up* or *in.* — *adj.* **1.** Of brick. **2.** Brick-red. [< MF *brique* fragment]

brick·bat (brik'bat') *n.* **1.** A piece of a brick, esp. when used as a missile. **2.** *Informal* An insulting remark.

brick·kiln (brik'kil', -kiln') *n.* A structure in which bricks are burned or baked.

brick·lay·er (brik'lā'ər) *n.* One who builds with bricks. — **brick'lay'ing** *n.*

brick red Dull yellowish or brownish red.

brick·work (brik'wûrk') *n.* Construction of or with bricks.

brick·yard (brik'yärd') *n.* A place where bricks are made.

bri·dal (brīd'l) *adj.* Pertaining to a bride or a wedding; nuptial. — *n.* A wedding. [OE *brȳdealo* wedding feast]

bridal wreath A flowering shrub of the rose family, with small white flowers.

bride (brīd) *n.* A newly married woman, or a woman about to be married. [OE *brȳd*]

bride·groom (brīd'grōōm', -grŏŏm') *n.* A man newly married or about to be married. [OE < *brȳd* bride + *guma* man]

brides·maid (brīdz'mād') *n.* A young, usu. unmarried woman who attends a bride at her wedding.

bridge¹ (brij) *n.* **1.** A structure erected across a waterway, ravine, road, etc., to afford passage. **2.** An observation platform built athwart the forward part of a ship for the officers, pilot, etc. **3.** The upper bony ridge of the nose. **4.** The central part of a pair of spectacles that rests on the nose. **5.** In some string instruments, a thin piece of wood that raises the strings above the soundboard. For illus. see VIOLIN. **6.** *Music* A transitional passage connecting two sections of a composition. **7.** *Dent.* A mounting for false teeth, attached on each side to a natural tooth. — **to burn one's bridges** (**behind one**) To cut off all means of retreat. — *v.t.* **bridged, bridg·ing** **1.** To construct a bridge or bridges over. **2.** To make a passage over. [OE *brycg*] — **bridge'a·ble** *adj.*

bridge² (brij) *n.* A card game, derived from whist, in which the trump suit (or the fact that there will be no trumps) is

determined by the side proposing to take the higher number of tricks. See AUCTION BRIDGE, CONTRACT BRIDGE.

bridge·head (brij'hed') *n. Mil.* A position on the hostile side of a river or defile, established by advance troops.

bridge·work (brij'wûrk') *n.* **1.** *Dent.* A dental bridge. **2.** The construction of bridges.

bri·dle (brīd'l) *n.* **1.** The head harness, including bit and reins, used to guide or restrain a horse. **2.** Anything that restrains or limits. — *v.* **·dled, ·dling** *v.t.* **1.** To put a bridle on. **2.** To check or control with or as with a bridle. — *v.i.* **3.** To raise the head and draw in the chin through resentment, pride, etc. [OE *brīdel*] — **bri'dler** *n.*

bridle path A path for saddle horses or pack animals only.

brief (brēf) *adj.* **1.** Short in time or extent; quickly ending. **2.** Of few words; concise. **3.** Curt or abrupt. — *n.* **1.** A short or abridged statement; summary. **2.** *Law* A memorandum of the material facts, points of law, precedents, etc., of a case. **3.** *pl.* Short underpants. — **in brief** In short; briefly. — **to hold a brief for** To be on the side of. — *v.t.* **1.** To make a summary of; epitomize. **2.** To give a briefing to. **3.** *Brit.* To inform by a legal brief. **4.** *Brit.* To retain as counsel. [< OF < L *brevis* short] — **brief'ly** *adv.* — **brief'ness** *n.*

brief·case (brēf'kās') *n.* A flexible, rectangular case, usually of leather, for carrying documents, papers, books, etc.

brief·ing (brē'fing) *n.* A short lecture setting forth the details of an operation or procedure.

bri·er¹ (brī'ər) *n.* **1.** A prickly bush or shrub, esp. one of the rose family, as the sweetbrier. **2.** A growth of such prickly bushes. **3.** A thorny or prickly twig. Also spelled *briar.* [OE *brær, brēr*] — **bri'er·y** *adj.*

bri·er² (brī'ər) *n.* **1.** The tree heath of southern Europe. **2.** A pipe made of brierroot. [< F *bruyère* heath]

bri·er·root (brī'ər·rōōt', -rŏŏt') *n.* **1.** The root of the brier or tree heath, used in making tobacco pipes. **2.** A pipe made from this wood. Also **bri·er·wood** (brī'ər·wŏŏd').

brig¹ (brig) *n. Naut.* A two-masted ship, square-rigged on both masts. [Short for BRIGANTINE]

brig² (brig) *n.* A place of confinement on shipboard. [Origin unknown]

bri·gade (bri·gād') *n.* **1.** *Mil.* A unit of two or more groups or regiments. **2.** Any considerable body of persons more or less organized: a fire *brigade.* — *v.t.* **·gad·ed, ·gad·ing** **1.** To form into a brigade. **2.** To classify or combine. [< MF < Ital. *brigare* to brawl, fight]

BRIG

brig·a·dier (brig'ə·dir') *n.* **1.** *Mil.* A brigadier general. **2.** In the British, Canadian, and other Commonwealth armies, an office ranking next below a major general. See table at GRADE.

brigadier general *Mil.* An officer ranking next above a colonel and next below a major general. See table at GRADE.

brig·and (brig'ənd) *n.* A robber, esp. in a band of outlaws. [< MF < Ital. *brigare* to brawl, fight] — **brig'and·ish** *adj.*

brig·an·tine (brig'ən·tēn, -tin) *n. Naut.* A two-masted vessel, square-rigged on the foremast, and fore-and-aft rigged on the mainmast: also called *hermaphrodite brig.* [< MF < Ital. *brigare* to fight]

bright (brīt) *adj.* **1.** Emitting or reflecting much light; full of light; shining. **2.** Of brilliant color; vivid. **3.** Glorious; illustrious. **4.** Having or showing high intelligence; quick-witted. **5.** Lively; vivacious. **6.** Hopeful; auspicious. — *adv.* In a bright manner; brightly. [OE *beorht, bryht*] — **bright·ly** *adv.* — **bright'ness** *n.*

bright·en (brīt'n) *v.t. & v.i.* To make or become bright or brighter. — **bright'en·er** *n.*

Bright's disease (brīts) A disease marked by degeneration of the kidneys and imperfect elimination of uric acid. [after Richard *Bright,* 1789–1858, English physician]

bril·liance (bril'yəns) *n.* **1.** Intense brightness or luster. **2.** Great talent or intellect. **3.** Excellence; preeminence. **4.** *Music* Clarity of sound; vivid tone. Also **bril'lian·cy.**

bril·liant (bril'yənt) *adj.* **1.** Sparkling or glowing with light; very bright. **2.** Splendid; illustrious. **3.** Having great intellect or talent. **4.** *Music* Clear; vivid; intense. — *n.* **1.** A diamond of the finest cut, having as many as 58 facets above and below the girdle. **2.** *Printing* A very small size of type, about 3½-point. [< F *briller* to sparkle] — **bril'liant·ly** *adv.* — **bril'liant·ness** *n.*

bril·lian·tine (bril'yən·tēn) *n.* An oily hairdressing. [< F]

brim (brim) *n.* **1.** The rim or upper edge of a cup, bowl, etc. **2.** A projecting rim, as of a hat. **3.** An edge or margin. — *v.t. & v.i.* **brimmed, brim·ming** To fill or be full to the brim. — **to brim over** To overflow. [OE *brim* seashore]

brim·ful (brim'fŏŏl', brim'fŏŏl') *adj.* Full to the brim.

brim·stone (brim'stōn') *n.* Sulfur. [OE *bryn*- burning + *stān* stone] — **brim'ston'y** *adj.*

brin·dle (brin'dəl) *adj.* Brindled. — *n.* A brindled color, or a brindled animal.

brin·dled (brin'dəld) *adj.* Tawny or grayish with irregular streaks or spots; barred; streaked.

brine (brīn) *n.* 1. Water saturated with salt. 2. The water of the sea; the ocean. — *v.t.* **brined, brin·ing** To treat with or steep in brine. [OE *brȳne*] — **brin'ish** *adj.*

bring (bring) *v.t.* **brought, bring·ing** 1. To convey or cause (a person or thing) to come with oneself to or toward a place. 2. To cause to come about; involve as a consequence: War *brings* destruction. 3. To introduce into the mind. 4. To cause (a person or oneself) to adopt or admit, as a course of action. 5. To sell for: The house *brought* a good price. 6. *Law* **a** To prefer, as a charge. **b** To institute: to *bring* suit. **c** To set forth, as evidence or an argument. — **to bring about** 1. To accomplish; cause to happen. 2. *Naut.* To reverse; turn, as a ship. — **to bring around** (or **round**) 1. To cause to adopt or admit, as an opinion. 2. To revive; restore to consciousness. — **to bring down the house** To evoke wild applause. — **to bring forth** 1. To give birth or produce. 2. To give rise to. — **to bring forward** 1. To adduce, as an argument. 2. In bookkeeping, to carry, as a sum, from one page or column to another. — **to bring in** 1. To import. 2. To render or submit (a verdict). 3. To yield or produce, as profits. — **to bring off** To do successfully. — **to bring on** 1. To cause; lead to. 2. To produce; cause to appear: *Bring on* the actors. — **to bring out** 1. To reveal; cause to be evident. 2. To publish or produce. 3. To introduce, as a young girl to society. — **to bring to** 1. To revive; restore to consciousness. 2. *Naut.* To cause (a ship) to come up into the wind and lie to. — **to bring up** 1. To rear; educate. 2. To suggest or call attention to, as a subject. 3. To cough or vomit up. [OE *bringan*]

bring·ing-up (bring'ing-up') *n.* Care, training, and education of a person in childhood; upbringing.

brink (bringk) *n.* 1. The edge or verge, as of a steep place. 2. The shore of a river, etc. [ME < Scand.]

brink·man·ship (bringk'mən-ship') *n.* The willingness to take major risks in order to achieve some end. [< BRINK + *manship*, on analogy with *showmanship*, etc.]

brin·y (brī'nē) *adj.* **brin·i·er, brin·i·est** Of the nature of or like brine. — **the briny** *Slang* The sea. — **brin'i·ness** *n.*

bri·oche (brē'ōsh, -osh; *Fr.* brē-ôsh') *n.* A soft roll. [< F]

bri·quette (bri·ket') *n.* A block of compressed coal dust, used for fuel. Also **bri·quet'.** [< F *brique* brick]

brisk (brisk) *adj.* 1. Moving, acting, or taking place quickly; lively; energetic. 2. Sharp or stimulating. [Cf. F *brusque* abrupt, sudden] — **brisk'ly** *adv.* — **brisk'ness** *n.*

bris·ket (bris'kit) *n.* The breast of an animal, esp. of one used as food. [< OF *bruschet*]

bris·tle (bris'əl) *n.* 1. One of the coarse, stiff hairs of swine, used in making brushes. 2. Any similar hair. — *v.* ·**tled, ·tling** *v.i.* 1. To erect the bristles in anger or excitement. 2. To show anger or irritation. 3. To stand or become erect, like bristles. 4. To be thickly set as if with bristles. — *v.t.* 5. To erect as or like bristles. 6. To ruffle or agitate. [ME < OE *byrst*] — **bris'tly** *adj.*

Bri·tan·ni·a (bri·tan'ē-ə, -tan'yə) 1. The ancient Roman name for Great Britain. 2. The British Empire.

Bri·tan·nic (bri·tan'ik) *adj.* British. [< L *Britannicus*]

Brit·i·cism (brit'ə·siz'əm) *n.* An idiom or turn of phrase peculiar to the British.

Brit·ish (brit'ish) *adj.* Pertaining to Great Britain or the United Kingdom. — *n.* 1. The people of Great Britain or of the British Empire: preceded by *the.* 2. British English. [OE *Bretisc* < *Bret* a Briton]

British America 1. Canada. 2. British possessions in or adjacent to North America. Also **British North America.**

British Commonwealth of Nations A political association comprising the United Kingdom, Canada, Australia, New Zealand, Ghana, India, Pakistan, Ceylon, Malaysia, Nigeria, Nyasaland, Cyprus, Sierra Leone, Tanganyika, Trinidad, and Tobago, Jamaica, Uganda, Western Samoa, Kenya, and Zanzibar, and including the dependencies of member nations: officially *The Commonwealth.* Also *Commonwealth of Nations.*

British Empire The sovereign states under the British Crown, comprising those in the British Commonwealth of Nations with their dependencies.

Brit·ish·er (brit'ish·ər) *n.* A native or subject of Great Britain, esp. an Englishman.

British Isles Great Britain, Ireland, the Isle of Man, and the Channel Islands.

British thermal unit *Physics* The quantity of heat required to raise the temperature of one pound of water one degree Fahrenheit.

Brit·on (brit'n) *n.* 1. A member of a Celtic people inhabiting ancient Britain, conquered by the Romans. 2. A Britisher. [< OF < L *Britto* < Celtic]

brit·tle (brit'l) *adj.* Liable to break or snap; fragile. — Syn. See FRAGILE. [ME *britil*] **brit'tle·ness** *n.*

broach (brōch) *v.t.* 1. To mention or suggest for the first time; introduce. 2. To pierce so as to withdraw a liquid. — *n.* 1. *Mech.* A pointed, tapering tool for boring; a reamer. 2. A spit for roasting. [< OF < Med.L *brocca* spike, spit] — **broach'er** *n.*

broad (brôd) *adj.* 1. Extended from side to side; wide. 2. Of great extent; vast or spacious. 3. Fully diffused; open and clear: *broad* daylight. 4. Of wide scope or application; extensive. 5. Liberal in spirit; tolerant. 6. Not detailed; general. 7. Obvious; clear: a *broad* hint. 8. Vulgar and indelicate; unrefined. 9. Outspoken or unrestrained. 10. Strongly dialectal: a *broad* pronunciation. 11. *Phonet.* Formed with the oral passage open wide and the tongue low and flat, as the *a* in *calm.* — *n.* 1. The broad part of anything. 2. *Slang* A woman or girl. — *adv.* Completely; fully. [OE *brād*] — **broad'ly** *adv.* — **broad'ness** *n.*

broad·ax (brôd'aks') *n.* An ax with a broad edge and a short handle. Also **broad'axe'.**

broad·cast (brôd'kast', -käst') *v.* ·**cast** or (*esp. for defs.* 1, 4) ·**cast·ed, ·cast·ing** *v.t.* 1. To send or transmit (music, newscasts, etc.) by radio or television. 2. To scatter, as seed, over a wide area. 3. To disseminate; make public. — *v.i.* 4. To make a radio or television broadcast. — *n.* 1. The act of broadcasting. 2. A radio or television program. — *adj.* 1. By or for radio or television transmission. 2. Scattered far and wide. — *adv.* So as to be scattered over a wide area. — **broad'cast'er** *n.*

broad·cloth (brôd'kloth', -klôth') *n.* 1. A fine woolen cloth used for suits, skirts, etc. 2. A closely woven fabric of silk, cotton, etc., used for shirts, dresses, etc.

broad·en (brôd'n) *v.t. & v.i.* To make or become broad.

broad-gauge (brôd'gāj') *adj.* Having a width of railroad track greater than the standard gauge of 56½ inches. Also **broad'gage', broad'-gaged', broad-gauged'.**

broad jump A jump or jumping contest for distance.

broad·loom (brôd'lōom') *n.* Carpet woven in widths of from 6 to 18 feet. Also **broadloom carpet.**

broad-mind·ed (brôd'mīn'did) *adj.* Liberal and tolerant; free from bigotry and prejudice. — **broad'-mind'ed·ly** *adv.* — **broad'-mind'ed·ness** *n.*

broad·side (brôd'sīd') *n.* 1. All the guns on one side of a man-of-war, or their simultaneous discharge. 2. A volley of abuse or denunciation. 3. *Naut.* A vessel's side above the water line. 4. A large sheet of paper, printed on one side: also **broad'sheet'.** — *adv.* With the broadside exposed.

broad·sword (brôd'sôrd', -sōrd') *n.* A sword with a broad cutting blade.

broad·tail (brôd'tāl') *n.* The lustrous black fur obtained from lambs of the karakul sheep.

Broad·way (brôd'wā) A street in New York City, noted for its theatres and entertainment district.

bro·cade (brō·kād') *n.* A rich fabric interwoven with a raised design, as in silken or gold or silver threads. — *v.t.* ·**cad·ed, ·cad·ing** To weave (a cloth) with a raised design or figure. [< Sp. < Med.L *broccare* to embroider]

broc·co·li (brok'ə·lē) *n.* A variety of cauliflower. [< Ital., pl. of *broccolo* cabbage sprout]

bro·chure (brō·shōor') *n.* A pamphlet or similar publication. [< F, lit., a stitched book < *brocher* to stitch]

bro·gan (brō'gən) *n.* A coarse, heavy shoe. [< Irish *brōgan*, dim. of *brōg* shoe]

brogue[1] (brōg) *n.* An Irish accent in the pronunciation of English. [< Irish *barrōg* defect of speech]

brogue[2] (brōg) *n.* 1. A heavy oxford shoe, decorated with perforations. 2. A shoe of untanned hide worn formerly in Ireland and the Scottish Highlands. [< Irish *brōg* a shoe]

broil[1] (broil) *v.t.* 1. To cook, as meat, by subjecting to direct heat. 2. To expose to great heat; scorch. — *v.i.* 3. To be exposed to great heat; cook. — *n.* 1. Something broiled. 2. A broiling heat. [< OF *bruller, bruillir* to burn]

broil[2] (broil) *n.* A turmoil; noisy quarrel; brawl. — *v.i.* To engage in a broil; brawl. [< F *brouiller* to confuse]

broil·er (broi'lər) *n.* 1. A device for broiling. 2. A young, tender chicken suitable for broiling.

broke (brōk) Past tense and archaic past participle of BREAK. — *adj. Informal* Having no money; bankrupt.

bro·ken (brō'kən) Past participle of BREAK. — *adj.* 1. Forcibly separated into pieces; fractured. 2. Violated; transgressed: *broken* vows. 3. Interrupted; disturbed. 4. Incomplete; fragmentary. 5. Rough; uneven, as terrain. 6. In disorder; scattered, as troops. 7. Humbled; crushed. 8. Weakened or infirm. 9. Bankrupt. 10. Trained in procedure; adapted: often with *in.* 11. Imperfectly spoken; disjointed. — **bro'ken·ly** *adv.* — **bro'ken·ness** *n.*

bro·ken-down (brō'kən·doun') *adj.* 1. Incapable of functioning; out of repair. 2. Ruined; decayed.

bro·ken-heart·ed (brō'kən·här'tid) *adj.* Overwhelmed or crushed in spirit, as by grief.

bro·ker (brō'kər) *n.* One who buys and sells for another, arranges contracts, etc; esp., a stockbroker. [< AF < OF *brochier* to tap, broach (a wine cask)]

bro·ker·age (brō′kər·ij) *n.* The business or commission of a broker. Also **bro′kage.**

bro·mide[1] (brō′mīd,- mid) *n. Chem.* A compound of bromine with an element or an organic radical. Also **bro′mid** (-mid).

bro·mide[2] (brō′mīd, -mid) *n. Informal* A platitude.

bro·mid·ic (brō·mid′ik) *adj. Informal* Commonplace; trite.

bro·mine (brō′mēn, -min) *n.* A dark reddish brown, non-metallic, fuming liquid element (symbol Br) with a suffocating odor. Also **bro′min** (-min). See ELEMENT. [< F *brome* (< Gk. *brōmos* stench) + -INE[2]]

bromo- *combining form* Used to indicate bromine in chemical compounds. Also, before vowels, **brom-.**

bron·chi (brong′kī) Plural of BRONCHUS.

bron·chi·a (brong′kē·ə) *n.pl. Anat.* The bronchial tubes. [< LL < Gk. *bronchia*]

bron·chi·al (brong′kē·əl) *adj. Anat.* Of or pertaining to the chief air passages of the lungs.

bronchial tube *Anat.* Any of the subdivisions of the trachea conveying air into the lungs.

bron·chi·tis (brong·kī′tis) *n. Pathol.* Inflammation of the bronchial tubes. — **bron·chit·ic** (brong·kit′ik) *adj.*

broncho- *combining form* Windpipe. Also, before vowels, **bronch-.** [< Gk. *bronchos*]

bron·cho·scope (brong′kə·skōp) *n. Med.* An instrument for inspecting or treating the interior of the bronchi.

bron·chus (brong′kəs) *n.* pl. **·chi** (-kī) *Anat.* One of the two forked branches of the trachea. For illus. see LUNG. [< NL < Gk. *bronchos* windpipe]

bron·co (brong′kō) *n.* pl. **·cos** 1. *U.S.* A small, wild or partly broken horse of the West. 2. *Canadian* An Englishman. Also **bronc, bron′cho.** [< Sp. *bronco* rough]

bron·co·bust·er (brong′kō·bus′tər) *n. U.S. Informal* One who breaks a bronco to the saddle. Also **bron′cho·bust′er.**

bron·to·sau·rus (bron′tə·sôr′əs) *n.* pl. **·rus·es** *Paleontol.* A huge, herbivorous dinosaur of the Jurassic period. Also **bron′to·saur.** [< Gk. *brontē* thunder + *sauros* lizard]

Bronx cheer *U.S. Slang* A noisy fluttering of the lips to show contempt or derision: also called *raspberry, razzberry.*

BRONTOSAURUS
(To 70 feet long; about 20 tons)

bronze (bronz) *n.* 1. *Metall.* **a** A reddish brown alloy essentially of copper and tin. **b** A similar alloy of copper and some other metal, as aluminum. 2. A pigment of the color of bronze. 3. A reddish brown color similar to bronze. 4. A statue, bust, etc., done in bronze. — *v.* **bronzed, bronz·ing** *v.t.* 1. To color like bronze. — *v.i.* 2. To become bronze or tan. [< MF < Ital. *bronzo, bronzino*] — **bronz′y** *adj.*

Bronze Age *Archeol.* A stage of prehistory following the Stone Age and preceding the Iron Age, during which weapons and implements were made of bronze.

Bronze Star A U.S. military decoration, awarded for heroism or exemplary conduct in ground combat.

brooch (brōch, brōōch) *n.* An ornamental pin with a clasp for wearing on the breast or shoulder. [Var. of BROACH]

brood (brōōd) *n.* 1. The young of animals, esp. of birds, produced at one time. 2. All the young of the same mother. 3. Kind or species. — *v.i.* 1. To meditate moodily and deeply: usu. with *on* or *over.* 2. To sit on eggs. — *v.t.* 3. To sit upon or incubate (eggs). 4. To protect (young) by covering with the wings. [OE *brōd*]

brood·er (brōō′dər) *n.* 1. A warmed structure for artificially rearing young fowl. 2. One who or that which broods.

brood·y (brōō′dē) *adj.* **brood·i·er, brood·i·est** 1. Meditative; moody. 2. Inclined to sit on eggs: said of hens.

brook[1] (brōōk) *n.* A natural stream, smaller than a river or creek; a rivulet. [OE *brōc*]

brook[2] (brōōk) *v.t.* To put up with; tolerate: usu. with the negative: I cannot brook such conduct. [OE *brūcan* to use]

brook·let (brōōk′lit) *n.* A little brook.

brook trout The speckled trout of eastern North America.

broom (brōōm, brōōm) *n.* 1. A brush attached to a long handle for sweeping, formerly made from twigs of broom. 2. Any of various shrubs with yellow flowers and stiff green branches: also called *besom.* — *v.t.* To sweep. [OE *brōm*]

broom·corn (brōōm′kôrn′, brōōm′-) *n.* A canelike grass of which brooms are made.

broom·stick (brōōm′stik′, brōōm′-) *n.* The handle of a broom.

broth (brôth, broth) *n.* A soup made by boiling meat, vegetables, etc., in water; a thin or strained soup. [OE]

broth·el (broth′əl, broth′-, brôth′əl, brôth′-) *n.* A house of prostitution. [ME, a worthless person]

broth·er (bruth′ər) *n. pl.* **broth·ers** (*Archaic* **breth·ren**) 1. A male individual having the same parents as another or others of either sex. 2. A kinsman, or one of the same tribe, etc. 3. A fellow member, as of an organization. 4. A comrade. 5. One of a male religious order who is not a priest. — *v.t.* To treat or address as a brother. [OE *brōthor*]

broth·er·hood (bruth′ər·hŏŏd) *n.* 1. The relationship of or state of being brothers, esp. by blood. 2. A society, fraternity, guild, etc. 3. All the persons engaged in an enterprise, profession, etc.

broth·er-in-law (bruth′ər·in·lô′) *n. pl.* **broth·ers-in-law** 1. A brother of one's husband or wife. 2. The husband of one's sister. 3. The husband of one's spouse's sister.

broth·er·ly (bruth′ər·lē) *adj.* Pertaining to or characteristic of a brother; fraternal; affectionate. — *adv.* As a brother; kindly. — **broth′er·li·ness** *n.*

brougham (brōōm, brōō′əm, brō′əm) *n.* 1. A closed, four-wheeled carriage having a high, uncovered driver's seat. 2. A limousine with the driver's seat outside. [after Lord Henry *Brougham,* 1778–1868, British statesman]

brought (brôt) Past tense and past participle of BRING.

brow (brou) *n.* 1. The front upper part of the head; forehead. 2. The eyebrow. 3. The countenance in general. 4. The upper edge of a steep place: the *brow* of a hill. [OE *brū*]

brow·beat (brou′bēt′) *v.t.* **·beat, ·beat·en, ·beat·ing** To intimidate; bully.

brown (broun) *adj.* 1. Of a dark color combining red, yellow, and black. 2. Dark-complexioned; tanned. — **to do up brown** *Informal* To do thoroughly. — *n.* 1. A brown color. 2. A brown pigment or dye. — *v.t. & v.i.* To make or become brown. [OE *brūn*] — **brown′ness** *n.*

brown bear 1. The black bear. 2. One of several very large bears of North America and Europe, with fur varying from yellowish to dark brown.

brown Bet·ty (bet′ē) Baked pudding made of bread crumbs, apples, sugar, and spices. Also **brown bet′ty.**

brown bread Any bread made of a dark-colored flour.

Brown·i·an movement (brou′nē·ən) *Physics* The rapid oscillatory movement of small particles when suspended in fluids. Also **Brownian motion.** [after Robert *Brown,* 1773–1858, Scottish botanist, who discovered it]

brown·ie (brou′nē) *n.* 1. In folklore, a goblin or sprite, supposed to do useful work at night. 2. *U.S.* A small, flat chocolate cake with nuts. [< BROWN; from its color]

Brown·ie (brou′nē) *n.* A junior girl scout of the age group seven through nine.

brown·out (broun′out′) *n.* A partial diminishing of lights either as a defensive measure or to save fuel.

brown rice Unpolished rice grains.

Brown Shirt 1. A storm trooper. 2. A Nazi.

brown·stone (broun′stōn′) *n.* A brownish red sandstone used for building; also, a house with a front of brownstone.

brown study A state of absent-mindedness; reverie.

brown sugar Sugar that is unrefined or partly refined.

browse (brouz) *v.* **browsed, brows·ing** *v.i.* 1. To feed on leaves, shoots, etc. 2. To glance through a book or books or look over merchandise casually. — *v.t.* 3. To nibble at; crop; also, to graze on. — *n.* Growing shoots or twigs used as fodder. [< MF *broust* bud, sprout] — **brows′er** *n.*

bru·cel·lo·sis (brōō′sə·lō′sis) *n. Pathol.* Undulant fever. [after Sir David *Bruce,* 1855–1931, English physician]

bru·in (brōō′in) *n.* A bear; esp., a brown bear. [< MDu.]

bruise (brōōz) *v.* **bruised, bruis·ing** *v.t.* 1. To injure, as by a blow, without breaking the surface of the skin; contuse. 2. To dent or mar the surface of. 3. To hurt or offend slightly, as feelings. 4. To crush; pound small, as in a mortar. — *v.i.* 5. To become discolored as from a blow. — *n.* An injury caused by bruising; contusion. [Fusion of OE *brȳsan* to crush and OF *bruisier* to break, shatter]

bruis·er (brōō′zər) *n.* 1. A professional boxer. 2. *Informal* A bully.

bruit (brōōt) *v.t.* To noise abroad; talk about: usu. in the passive. [< F < *bruire* to roar, ? < L *rugire*] — **bruit′er** *n.*

brunch (brunch) *n. U.S. Informal* A late morning meal combining breakfast and lunch. [< BR(EAKFAST) + (L)UNCH]

bru·net (brōō·net′) *adj.* Dark-hued; having dark complexion, hair, and eyes. — *n.* A brunet man or boy. [< F]

bru·nette (brōō·net′) *adj.* Brunet: feminine form. — *n.* A brunette woman or girl. [< F]

Brun·hild (brōōn′hild, *Ger.* brōōn′hilt) In the *Nibelungenlied,* a queen of Iceland. Compare BRÜNNHILDE.

Brünn·hil·de (brün·hil′də) In Wagner's *Ring of the Nibelung,* a Valkyrie put in a trance and encircled by flames, but eventually released by Siegfried.

brunt (brunt) *n.* The main force or strain of a blow, attack, etc. [? < ON *bruna* to advance quickly, as a fire]

brush[1] (brush) *n.* **1.** An implement having bristles, wires, or other flexible fibrous material, fixed in a handle or a back, and used for sweeping, painting, smoothing the hair, etc. **2.** The act of brushing. **3.** A light, grazing touch. **4.** A brief encounter, esp. a skirmish. **5.** Brushwork. **6.** *Electr.* A conductor, resting on the commutator cylinder of a dynamo, for carrying off the current or for an external current through a motor. —*v.t.* **1.** To use a brush on; sweep, paint, etc., with a brush. **2.** To remove with or as with a brush. **3.** To touch lightly in passing. —*v.i.* **4.** To move lightly and quickly. —**to brush aside** To deny consideration to. —**to brush off** *U.S. Slang* To dismiss or refuse abruptly. —**to brush up** **1.** To refresh one's knowledge of. **2.** To renovate. [< OF *brosse,* ? < Gmc.]

brush[2] (brush) *n.* **1.** A growth of small trees and shrubs. **2.** Wooded country sparsely settled; backwoods. **3.** Brushwood. [< OF *broche, brosse,* ? < Gmc.] —**brush'y** *adj.*

brush-off (brush'ôf', -of') *n. U.S. Slang* An abrupt refusal or dismissal.

brush-wood (brush'wŏŏd') *n.* **1.** Bushes or branches cut or broken off. **2.** A thicket of small trees or shrubs.

brusque (brusk, *esp. Brit.* brŏŏsk) *adj.* Rude or curt; blunt. Also **brusk.** — **Syn.** See BLUNT. [< MF < Ital. *brusco* rude, rough] —**brusque'ly** *adv.* —**brusque'ness** *n.*

Brussels sprouts **1.** A variety of cabbage having stems covered with heads like little cabbages. **2.** The small, edible heads of this plant.

brut (brüt, brŏŏt) *adj.* Dry: said of wines, esp. champagne. [< F, lit., rough < L *brutus*]

bru·tal (brŏŏt'l) *adj.* **1.** Characteristic of or like a brute; cruel; savage. **2.** Unfeeling; rude; coarse. [< L *brutus* stupid, rough] —**bru'tal·ly** *adv.*

bru·tal·i·ty (brŏŏ·tal'ə·tē) *n. pl.* **·ties** **1.** The state or quality of being brutal; cruelty. **2.** A brutal act.

bru·tal·ize (brŏŏt'l·īz) *v.t. & v.i.* **·ized, ·iz·ing** To make or become brutal. —**bru'tal·i·za'tion** *n.*

brute (brŏŏt) *n.* **1.** Any animal other than man. **2.** A brutal person. —*adj.* **1.** Incapable of reasoning; merely animal. **2.** Like a brute or animal; unintelligent. **3.** Dominated by appetite; gross; sensual. [< F < L *brutus* stupid]

bru·ti·fy (brŏŏt'tə·fī) *v.t. & v.i.* **·fied, ·fy·ing** To brutalize.

brut·ish (brŏŏt'tish) *adj.* Of, relating to, or characteristic of a brute or brutes; stupid; gross; sensual. —**brut'ish·ly** *adv.* —**brut'ish·ness, brut'ism** *n.*

Bryn·hild (brün'hilt) In the *Volsunga Saga,* a Valkyrie awakened by Sigurd from an enchanted sleep. Compare BRUNHILD, BRÜNNHILDE.

bry·ol·o·gy (brī·ol'ə·jē) *n.* The branch of botany that treats of mosses. [< Gk. *bryon* moss + -LOGY] —**bry·o·log·i·cal** (brī'ə·loj'i·kəl) *adj.* —**bry·ol'o·gist** *n.*

bry·o·ny (brī'ə·nē) *n.* A common English herb of the gourd family, with white or yellowish flowers. [< L < Gk. *bryōnia*]

bry·o·phyte (brī'ə·fīt) *n. Bot.* Any moss or liverwort. [< Gk. *bryon* moss + -PHYTE] —**bry'o·phyt'ic** (-fit'ik) *adj.*

Bry·thon·ic (bri·thon'ik) *n.* The branch of the Celtic languages that includes Welsh, Breton, and the extinct Cornish; Cymric: distinguished from *Goidelic.*

bub·ble (bub'əl) *n.* **1.** A liquid globule filled with air or other gas. **2.** A globule of air or other gas confined in a liquid or solid substance. **3.** Anything unsubstantial; a delusion; fraud. **4.** The process or sound of bubbling. **5.** A glass or plastic dome. —*v.* **·bled, ·bling** *v.i.* **1.** To form or emit bubbles; rise in bubbles. **2.** To move or flow with a gurgling sound. **3.** To express joy, delight, exultation, etc., in an irrepressible manner. —*v.t.* **4.** To cause to bubble. [ME *buble*] —**bub'bly** *adj.*

bu·bo (byŏŏ'bō) *n. pl.* **bu·boes** *Pathol.* An inflammatory swelling of a lymph gland in the groin or armpit. [< LL < Gk. *boubōn* groin] —**bu·bon·ic** (byŏŏ·bon'ik) *adj.*

bubonic plague *Pathol.* A contagious, epidemic disease, usually fatal, characterized by fever and buboes and transmitted to man by fleas from infected rats.

buc·cal (buk'əl) *adj. Anat.* **1.** Of or pertaining to the cheek. **2.** Pertaining to the mouth. [< L *bucca* cheek]

buc·ca·neer (buk'ə·nir') *n.* A pirate or freebooter, esp. one who preyed along the Spanish coasts of America. [< F < Tupi *boucan* a frame for smoking and curing meat]

buck[1] (buk) *n.* **1.** The male of certain animals, as of antelopes, deer, goats, rabbits, and rats. **2.** A dandy; fop. **3.** *Informal* A young man. —*v.i.* **1.** To leap upward suddenly, as a horse or pack animal, in an attempt to dislodge rider or burden. **2.** *U.S. Informal* To resist stubbornly; object. **3.** *U.S. Informal* To move with jerks and jolts. —*v.t.* **4.** To throw by bucking. **5.** *U.S. Dial.* To butt with the head. **6.** *U.S. Informal* To resist stubbornly; oppose. **7.** In football, to charge into (the opponent's line) with the ball. —**to buck for** *U.S. Slang* To try hard to obtain (a promotion, raise, etc.). —**to buck up** *Informal* To encourage or take courage. [OE *bucca* he-goat]

buck[2] (buk) *n.* **1.** A sawhorse. **2.** A padded frame like a sawhorse, used for vaulting, etc. [< Du. *zaagbok* sawbuck]

buck[3] (buk) *n.* In poker, a marker put into a jackpot, indicating that he who receives it must order another jackpot when it is his deal. —**to pass the buck** *U.S. Informal* To shift responsibility, blame, etc., to someone else.

buck and wing An intricate, fast tap dance.

buck·a·roo (buk'ə·rŏŏ, buk'ə·rŏŏ') *n. U.S.* A cowboy. Also **buck·ay·ro** (buk·ā'rō). [Alter. of Sp. *vaquero* cowboy]

buck·board (buk'bôrd', -bōrd') *n.* A light, four-wheeled, open carriage having a long, flexible board in place of body and springs.

buck·et (buk'it) *n.* **1.** A deep cylindrical vessel, with a rounded handle, used for carrying water, coal, etc.; a pail. **2.** As much as a bucket will hold: also **buck'et·ful'.** —*v.t. & v.i.* **1.** To draw or carry in a bucket. [? < OF *buket* tub]

buck·eye (buk'ī') *n. Chiefly U.S.* **1.** The horse chestnut. **2.** The glossy brown seed or nut of this tree.

Buck·eye (buk'ī') *n.* A native or inhabitant of Ohio.

Buckeye State Nickname of Ohio.

Buck·ing·ham Palace (buk'ing·əm) The official London residence of the British sovereign.

buck·le[1] (buk'əl) *n.* **1.** A device for fastening together two loose ends, as of a strap. **2.** An ornament for shoes, etc., resembling a buckle. —*v.* **led, ·ling** *v.t.* **1.** To fasten or attach with or as with a buckle. —*v.i.* **2.** To be fastened or joined by a buckle. —**to buckle down** To apply oneself vigorously. [< F *boucle* cheekstrap, boss of a shield]

buck·le[2] (buk'əl) *v.t. & v.i.* **led, ·ling** To bend under pressure; warp, curl, or crumple. —*n.* A bend, bulge, kink, or twist. [< F *boucler* to bulge]

buck·ler (buk'lər) *n.* **1.** A small, round shield. **2.** A means of defense. [< OF *boucler* having a boss]

buck·o (buk'ō) *n. pl.* **buck·oes** A bully.

buck private *U.S. Slang* A private in the U.S. Army.

buck·ram (buk'rəm) *n.* A coarse cotton fabric sized with glue, used for stiffening garments, in bookbinding, etc. —*v.t.* To stiffen with or as with buckram. [OF *boquerant* coarse cloth < *Bokhara,* Persia, where first made]

buck·saw (buk'sô') *n.* A wood-cutting saw set in an adjustable H-shaped frame.

buck·shot (buk'shot') *n.* Shot of a large size, used in hunting deer and other large game.

buck·skin (buk'skin') *n.* **1.** The skin of a buck. **2.** A soft, strong, grayish yellow leather, formerly made from deerskins, now chiefly from sheepskins. **3.** *pl.* Breeches or clothing made of such skin.

buck·thorn (buk'thôrn') *n.* A shrub or small tree having veined leaves and axillary flowers.

buck·tooth (buk'tŏŏth') *n. pl.* **·teeth** A projecting tooth. —**buck'toothed'** *adj.*

buck·wheat (buk'hwēt') *n.* **1.** A plant yielding triangular seeds used as fodder and for flour. **2.** Its seeds. **3.** The flour. [OE *bōc* beech + WHEAT]

bu·col·ic (byŏŏ·kol'ik) *adj.* Pertaining to or characteristic of shepherds or herdsmen; pastoral; rustic. — **Syn.** See RURAL. —*n.* **1.** A pastoral poem. **2.** A rustic; farmer. [< L < Gk. < *boukolos* herdsmen] —**bu·col'i·cal·ly** *adv.*

bud (bud) *n.* **1.** *Bot.* **a** An undeveloped stem, branch, or shoot of a plant, with rudimentary leaves or unexpanded flowers. **b** The act or stage of budding. **2.** *Zool.* A budlike projection or part, as in some lower animals. **3.** Any immature person or thing. —**to nip in the bud** To stop in the initial stage. —*v.* **bud·ded, bud·ding** *v.i.* **1.** To put forth buds. **2.** To begin to grow or develop. —*v.t.* **3.** To cause to bud. **4.** To graft to another type of tree or plant. [ME *budde;* origin uncertain] —**bud'der** *n.*

Bud·dhism (bŏŏd'iz·əm, bŏŏ'diz-) *n.* A mystical and ascetic religious faith of eastern Asia, founded in northern India by Buddha in the sixth century B.C., and teaching that the ideal state of nirvana is reached by right living and believing, and peace of mind through meditation. — **Bud'dhist** *adj. & n.* — **Bud·dhis'tic** or **·ti·cal** *adj.*

bud·ding (bud'ing) *adj.* Just beginning; incipient.

bud·dy (bud'ē) *n. pl.* **·dies** *U.S. Informal* Pal; chum.

budge (buj) *v.t. & v.i.* **budged, budg·ing** To move or stir slightly. [< F *bouger* to stir, move]

budg·et (buj'it) *n.* **1.** A plan for adjusting expenditures to income. **2.** A collection or stock. —*v.t.* **1.** To determine in advance the expenditure of (time, money, etc.). **2.** To provide for or plan according to a budget. [< F < L *bulga* leather bag] —**budg·et·ar·y** (buj'ə·ter'ē) *adj.*

buff[1] (buf) *n.* **1.** A thick, soft, flexible leather made from the skins of buffalo, elk, oxen, etc. **2.** Its color, a light brownish yellow. **3.** A military coat made of buff leather. **4.** *Informal* The bare skin; the nude. **5.** A stick or wheel covered with leather, velvet, etc., and used for polishing. —*adj.* **1.** Made of buff. **2.** Light, brownish yellow. —*v.t.* To clean or polish with or as with a buff. [< F *buffle* buffalo] —**buff'y** *adj.*

buff[2] (buf) *v.t.* To deaden the shock of. —*n.* A blow; buffet: now only in *blindman's buff.* [< OF *buffe* blow]

buff[3] (buf) *n.* An enthusiast or devotee. [Origin uncertain]

buf·fa·lo (buf′ə·lō) *n. pl.* **·loes** or **·los** **1.** Any of various large Old World oxen, as the **Cape buffalo** of Africa, and the water buffalo. **2.** The North American bison. — *v.t.* **·loed**, **·lo·ing** *U.S. Slang* To overawe; intimidate; hoodwink. [< Ital. < LL < Gk. *boubalos* buffalo]

buffalo grass A low, creeping grass covering prairies east of the Rocky Mountains.

buff·er[1] (buf′ər) *n.* One who or that which buffs or polishes. [< BUFF[1], v.]

buff·er[2] (buf′ər) *n.* **1.** A shock absorber. **2.** One who or that which diminishes shock of any kind.

buffer state A small country situated between two larger rival powers and regarded as lessening the danger of conflict between them.

buf·fet[1] (bŏŏ·fā′, *Brit.* buf′it) *n.* **1.** A sideboard for china, glassware, etc. **2.** A counter for serving meals or refreshments, or a restaurant with such a counter. **3.** A light meal at which the guests serve themselves. [< F]

buf·fet[2] (buf′it) *v.t.* **1.** To strike or cuff, as with the hand. **2.** To strike repeatedly; knock about. — *v.i.* **3.** To fight; struggle. — *n.* A blow or cuff, as with the hand. [< OF *buffet*, dim. of *buffe* a blow, slap] — **buf′fet·er** *n.*

buf·foon (bu·fōōn′) *n.* **1.** A clown. **2.** One given to jokes, coarse pranks, etc. [< F < Ital. clown < *buffa* jest] — **buf·foon′er·y** *n.* — **buf·foon′ish** *adj.*

bug (bug) *n.* **1.** Any crawling insect with sucking mouth parts, wingless or with two pairs of wings. **2.** Loosely, any insect or small arthropod. **3.** *Brit.* A bedbug. **4.** *Informal* A microorganism; germ. **5.** *Slang* An enthusiast; monomaniac. **6.** *U.S. Slang* A minor defect, as in a machine. **7.** *U.S. Slang* A miniature electronic microphone, used in wiretapping, etc. — *v.* **bugged**, **bug·ging** *v.i.* **1.** To stare; stick out: said of eyes. — *v.t. U.S. Slang* **2.** To annoy; pester. **3.** To fit (a room, telephone circuit, etc.) with a concealed listening device.

bug·bear (bug′bâr′) *n.* **1.** A real or imaginary object of dread. **2.** A hobgoblin. Also **bug·a·boo** (bug′ə·bōō).

bug-eyed (bug′īd′) *adj. Slang* With the eyes bulging.

bug·gy[1] (bug′ē) *n. pl.* **·gies** **1.** A light, four-wheeled carriage. **2.** A baby carriage. [Origin uncertain]

bug·gy[2] (bug′ē) *adj.* **·gi·er**, **·gi·est** **1.** Infested with bugs. **2.** *U.S. Slang* Crazy. — **bug′gi·ness** *n.*

bu·gle[1] (hyōō′gəl) *n.* **1.** A brass wind instrument resembling a trumpet, usu. without keys or valves. **2.** A huntsman's horn. — *v.* **·gled**, **·gling** *v.t.* **1.** To summon with a bugle. — *v.i.* **2.** To sound a bugle. [< OF < L *buculus*, dim. of *bos* ox] — **bu′gler** *n.*

bu·gle[2] (byōō′gəl) *n.* A tube-shaped glass bead used for ornamenting garments. — **bu′gled** *adj.*

buhl (bōōl) *n.* Decoration of furniture with inlaid tortoise shell, ivory, etc.; also a piece so decorated. Also **buhl′work′**. [after A. C. *Boulle*, 1642–1732, French cabinetmaker]

build (bild) *v.* **built** (*Archaic* **build·ed**), **build·ing** *v.t.* **1.** To construct, erect, or make by assembling separate parts or materials. **2.** To establish and increase. **3.** To found; make a basis for. — *v.i.* **4.** To construct or erect a house, etc. **5.** To base or develop an idea, theory, etc.: with *on* or *upon.* — **to build up 1.** To create or build by degrees. **2.** To renew or strengthen; also, to increase. — *n.* The manner or style in which anything is constructed; form; figure. [OE *byldan* < *bold* house] — **build′er** *n.*

build·ing (bil′ding) *n.* **1.** That which is built; a structure; edifice, as a house or barn. **2.** The occupation, act, or art of constructing.

build-up (bild′up′) *n.* **1.** The act of increasing or strengthening. **2.** *Informal* Extravagant publicity or praise.

built-in (bilt′in′) *adj.* Built as a part of the structure.

bulb (bulb) *n.* **1.** *Bot.* A leaf bud comprising a cluster of thickened, scalelike leaves growing usu. underground and sending forth roots, as the onion or lily. **2.** Any plant growing from a bulb. **3.** A rounded protuberance, as at the end of a tube. **4.** An incandescent lamp. [< L < Gk. *bolbos* bulbous root] — **bul·bar** (bul′bər) *adj.*

bul·bous (bul′bəs) *adj.* **1.** Of, producing, or growing from bulbs. Also **bul·ba·ceous** (bul·bā′shəs). **2.** Shaped like a bulb; swollen.

Bul·gar·i·an (bul·gâr′ē·ən, bŏŏl-) *adj.* Of Bulgaria, the Bulgarians, or their language. — *n.* **1.** A native or citizen of Bulgaria. **2.** The Slavic language of the Bulgarians.

bulge (bulj) *n.* A protuberant, rounded part. — *v.t. & v.i.* **bulged**, **bulg·ing** To swell out. [< OF < L *bulga*] — **bulg′i·ness** *n.* — **bulg′y** *adj.*

bulk (bulk, bŏŏlk) *n.* **1.** Magnitude, volume, or size. **2.** The greater or principal part; main body. **3.** A large body or mass. — **in bulk 1.** Not packaged; loose. **2.** In large quantities. — *v.i.* **1.** To appear large or important; loom. **2.** To increase in magnitude; grow: with *up.* — *v.t.* **3.** To cause to expand or grow large: with *out.* [Cf. ON *bulki* heap, cargo, and Dan. *bulk* rump]

bulk·head (bulk′hed′) *n.* **1.** *Naut.* An upright partition in a vessel, separating compartments. **2.** A partition or wall to keep back earth, gas, etc. **3.** A small structure built on a roof to cover an elevator shaft.

bulk·y (bul′kē, bŏŏl′kē) *adj.* **bulk·i·er**, **bulk·i·est** Of great size; massive; also, large and unwieldy. — **bulk′i·ly** *adv.* — **bulk′i·ness** *n.*

bull[1] (bŏŏl) *n.* **1.** The uncastrated male of a bovine animal, esp. of the domesticated types. ◆ Collateral adjective: *taurine.* **2.** The male of some other animals, as of the elephant, whale, etc. **3.** One likened to a bull, as in strength or manner. **4.** A speculator who buys so as to profit from a rise in prices he anticipates or hopes to cause: opposed to *bear*[2]. **5.** *U.S. Slang* A policeman or detective. **6.** *U.S. Slang* Empty talk; nonsense. — *v.t.* **1.** To speculate for a rise in price of or in. **2.** To push or force (a way). — *v.i.* **3.** To go up in price. **4.** To go or push ahead. — *adj.* **1.** Male; masculine. **2.** Like a bull; large. **3.** Marked by rising prices: a *bull* market. [ME *bule*]

bull[2] (bŏŏl) *n.* An official and authoritative document issued by the Pope. [< L *bulla* edict, seal]

bull·dog (bŏŏl′dôg′, -dog′) *n.* A medium-sized, short-haired, powerful dog, with strong jaws. — *adj.* Resembling a bulldog; courageous; tenacious. — *v.t.* **·dogged**, **·dog·ging** *U.S. Informal* To throw (a steer) by gripping its horns and twisting its neck.

bull·doze (bŏŏl′dōz′) *v.t.* **·dozed**, **·doz·ing** **1.** *U.S. Slang* To intimidate; bully. **2.** To clear, dig, scrape, etc., with a bulldozer. [? < BULL[1], adj. + DOSE, with ref. to the violent or excessive treatment given to the victim]

bull·doz·er (bŏŏl′dō′zər) *n.* **1.** A tractor equipped with a heavy steel blade, used for moving earth, clearing wooded areas, etc. **2.** *U.S. Slang* One who intimidates.

bul·let (bŏŏl′it) *n.* **1.** A small projectile for a firearm. **2.** Any small ball. [< F *boulette*, dim. of *boule* ball]

bul·le·tin (bŏŏl′ə·tən, -tin) *n.* **1.** A brief account of news, in a newspaper or on radio. **2.** A periodical publication, as of the proceedings of a society. — *v.t.* To make public by bulletin. [< F < Ital. *bulletino* < L]

bulletin board A board on which bulletins, etc., are posted.

bul·let-proof (bŏŏl′it·prōōf′) *adj.* Not penetrable by bullets.

bull·fight (bŏŏl′fīt′) *n.* A combat in an arena between men and a bull or bulls, popular among the Spanish and Spanish Americans. — **bull′fight′er** *n.* — **bull′fight′ing** *n.*

bull·finch (bŏŏl′finch′) *n.* A European songbird having a short bill and red breast.

bull·frog (bŏŏl′frog′, -frôg′) *n.* A large frog with a deep bass croak. [< BULL[1], adj. + FROG]

bull·head (bŏŏl′hed′) *n.* A fresh-water catfish.

bull·head·ed (bŏŏl′hed′id) *adj.* Stubborn; headstrong.

bull·horn (bŏŏl′hôrn′) *n.* An electrical, hand-held voice amplifier resembling a megaphone.

bul·lion (bŏŏl′yən) *n.* Gold or silver uncoined or in mass, as in bars, plates, etc. [< AF, OF < *bouillir* to boil]

bull·ish (bŏŏl′ish) *adj.* **1.** Bull-like. **2.** Tending to cause prices to rise; also, marked by rising prices. **3.** Bullheaded. — **bull′ish·ly** *adv.* — **bull′ish·ness** *n.*

bul·lock (bŏŏl′ək) *n.* A gelded bull; a steer or ox. [OE *bulluc*]

bull·pen (bŏŏl′pen′) *n. U.S.* **1.** An enclosure for bulls. **2.** *Informal* A place for temporary detention of prisoners. **3.** In baseball, a place where pitchers practice during a game.

bull·ring (bŏŏl′ring′) *n.* A circular enclosure for bullfights.

bull session *U.S. Informal* An informal discussion.

bull's-eye (bŏŏlz′ī′) *n.* **1.** The central colored disk on a target; also, a shot that hits this disk. **2.** A thick disk of glass set in a pavement, deck, etc., to admit light. **3.** A convex lens. **4.** A lantern with such a lens.

bull terrier A white terrier having a long head and stiff coat, originally bred from a bulldog and a white terrier.

bull·whip (bŏŏl′hwip′) *n.* A long, heavy whip. — *v.t.* **·whipped**, **·whip·ping** To strike with a bullwhip.

bul·ly[1] (bŏŏl′ē) *n. pl.* **·lies** A swaggering, quarrelsome, usu. cowardly person who terrorizes weaker people. — *v.* **·lied**, **·ly·ing** *v.t.* **1.** To intimidate or coerce by threats. — *v.i.* **2.** To act the bully. — *adj.* **1.** *U.S. Informal* Excellent; admirable. **2.** Jolly; dashing; gallant. — *interj. U.S. Informal* Well done! [Cf. Du. *boel* friend, lover]

bul·ly[2] (bŏŏl′ē) *n.* Canned or pickled beef. Also **bully beef**. [Prob. < F *bouillir* to boil]

bul·ly·rag (bŏŏl′ē·rag′) *v.t.* **·ragged**, **·rag·ging** To bully; intimidate. [? < BULLY, v. + RAG[1]]

bul·rush (bŏŏl′rush′) *n.* **1.** A tall, rushlike plant growing in water or damp ground. **2.** In the Bible, papyrus. *Ex.* ii 3. [< BULL¹, adj. + RUSH²]

bul·wark (bŏŏl'wərk) *n.* **1.** A defensive wall or rampart; fortification. **2.** Any safeguard or defense. **3.** *Usu. pl. Naut.* The raised side of a ship, above the upper deck. — *v.t.* To surround and fortify with a bulwark. [< MHG *bolwerc*]

bum (bum) *U.S. Slang n.* A worthless or dissolute loafer; tramp. — **on the bum.** **1.** Out of order; broken. **2.** Living as a vagrant. — **the bum's rush** Forcible ejection. — *adj.* Bad; inferior. — *v.* **bummed, bum·ming** *v.i.* **1.** To live by sponging on others. **2.** To live idly and in dissipation. — *v.t.* **3.** To get by begging: to *bum* a ride. [Short for *bummer*, alter. of G *bummler* loafer, dawdler] — **bum'mer** *n.*

bum·ble (bum'bəl) *v.t. & v.i.* **·bled, ·bling** To bungle, esp. in an officious manner. [? Imit.] — **bum'bling** *adj. & n.*

bum·ble·bee (bum'bəl-bē') *n.* Any of various large, hairy bees. [< dial. E *bumble* to hum + BEE¹]

bump (bump) *v.t.* **1.** To come into contact with; knock into. **2.** To cause to knock into or against. **3.** *U.S. Slang* To displace, as from a position or seat. — *v.i.* **4.** To strike heavily or with force: often with *into* or *against*. **5.** To move with jerks and jolts. — **to bump off** *Slang* To kill, esp. with a gun. — *n.* **1.** An impact or collision; a blow; jolt. **2.** A protuberance or uneven place. [Imit.]

bump·er¹ (bum'pər) *n.* The horizontal bar at the front or rear of an automobile to absorb the shock of collision.

bump·er² (bum'pər) *n.* A cup or glass filled to the brim. — *adj.* Unusually full or large: a *bumper* crop. [? Alter. of F *bombarde* large cup; infl. in form by *bump*]

bump·kin (bump'kin) *n.* An awkward rustic; a lout. [? < Du. *boomkin* little tree, block]

bump·tious (bump'shəs) *adj.* Aggressively self-assertive. [Appar. < BUMP] — **bump'tious·ly** *adv.* — **bump'tious·ness** *n.*

bump·y (bum'pē) *adj.* **bump·i·er, bump·i·est** **1.** Having bumps. **2.** Jolting. — **bump'i·ly** *adv.* — **bump'i·ness** *n.*

bun (bun) *n.* **1.** A small bread roll, sometimes sweetened or spiced. **2.** A roll of hair shaped like a bun. [ME *bunne*]

bu·na (bōō'nə, byōō'-) *n. Chem.* A synthetic rubber made by the polymerization of butadiene with certain other substances. [< BU(TADIENE) + NA(TRIUM)]

bunch (bunch) *n.* **1.** A number of things of the same kind growing, occurring, or fastened together; a cluster. **2.** *Informal* A group: a *bunch* of boys. **3.** *Rare* A hump; protuberance. — *v.t. & v.i.* **1.** To form bunches or groups. **2.** To gather, as in folds. [ME *bunche*] — **bunch'y** *adj.*

bun·co (bung'kō) *U.S. Informal n.* A swindle; confidence game. — *v.t.* **·coed, ·co·ing** To swindle or rob. Also spelled *bunko.* [Prob. < Sp. *banco*, a card game]

bun·combe (bung'kəm) *n.* *U.S. Informal* **1.** Empty speechmaking for political effect or to please constituents. **2.** Empty talk; humbug. Also spelled *bunkum.* [from *Buncombe* County, N.C., whose congressman (1919–21) insisted on making unimportant speeches "for Buncombe"]

bund (bŏŏnd, *Ger.* bŏŏnt) *n.* A league; society. [< G]

bun·dle (bun'dəl) *n.* **1.** A number of things or a quantity of anything bound together. **2.** Anything folded or wrapped and tied up; a package. **3.** A group; collection. ♦ Collateral adjective: *fascicular.* — *v.* **·dled, ·dling** *v.t.* **1.** To tie, roll, or otherwise secure in a bundle. **2.** To send or put hastily and unceremoniously: with *away, off, out,* or *into.* — *v.i.* **3.** To go hastily; hustle. **4.** To lie or sleep in the same bed without undressing, formerly a courting custom in Wales and New England. — **to bundle up** To dress warmly. [< MDu. *bond* group] — **bun'dler** *n.*

bung (bung) *n.* **1.** A stopper for the hole through which a cask is filled. **2.** Bunghole. — *v.t.* **1.** To close with or as with a bung: often with *up* or *down.* **2.** *Slang* To damage; maul: usually with *up.* [< MDu. *bonghe*]

bun·ga·low (bung'gə-lō) *n.* A small house or cottage, usually with one or one and a half stories. [< Hind. *banglā,* lit., Bengalese (house) < *Banga* Bengal]

bung·hole (bung'hōl') *n.* A hole in a keg or barrel from which liquid is tapped. [< BUNG + HOLE]

bun·gle (bung'gəl) *v.t. & v.i.* **·gled, ·gling** To work, make, or do (something) clumsily. — *n.* A clumsy job or performance; botch. — **bun'gler** *n.* — **bun'gling·ly** *adv.*

bun·ion (bun'yən) *n.* A painful swelling of the foot, usually at the base of the great toe. [< OF *bugne* swelling]

bunk¹ (bungk) *n.* **1.** A narrow, built-in bed or shelf for sleeping; a berth. **2.** *Informal* A bed. — *v.i. Informal* **1.** To sleep in a bunk. **2.** To go to bed. [Cf. MDu. *banc* bench]

bunk² (bungk) *n. U.S. Slang* Empty talk; buncombe.

bun·ker (bung'kər) *n.* **1.** A large bin, as for coal on a ship. **2.** In golf, a mound of earth serving as an obstacle. **3.** *Mil.* A steel and concrete fortification. [Cf. OSw. *bunke* hold of a ship and BANK³ rowers' bench]

bun·ko (bung'kō) See BUNCO.

bun·kum (bung'kəm) See BUNCOMBE.

bun·ny (bun'ē) *n. pl.* **·nies** A rabbit: a pet name. [Dim. of dial. E *bun* a rabbit; ult. origin unknown]

Bun·sen burner (bun'sən) A type of gas burner in which a mixture of gas and air is burned at the top of a short metal tube, producing a very hot flame. [after R. W. *Bunsen,* 1811–1899, German chemist]

bunt (bunt) *v.t. & v.i.* **1.** To strike or push as with horns; butt. **2.** In baseball, to bat (the ball) lightly into the infield, without swinging the bat. — *n.* **1.** A push or shove; a butt. **2.** In baseball: **a** The act of bunting. **b** A ball that has been bunted. [Nasalized var. of BUTT¹]

bunt·ing¹ (bun'ting) *n.* **1.** A light woolen stuff or cotton fabric used for flags, etc. **2.** Flags, banners, etc., collectively. **3.** A type of sleeping bag for infants. [? ME *bonten* to sift]

bunt·ing² (bun'ting) *n.* One of various birds related to the finches and sparrows. [ME *bountyng*; origin unknown]

bunt·line (bunt'lin, -lĭn') *n. Naut.* A rope used in hauling a square sail up to the yard for furling.

Bun·yan (bun'yən), Paul See PAUL BUNYAN.

buoy (boi, bōō'ē) *n.* **1.** *Naut.* A warning float moored on a dangerous rock or shoal or at the ends of a channel. **2.** A device for keeping a person afloat; a life buoy. — *v.t.* **1.** To keep from sinking in a liquid; keep afloat. **2.** To sustain the courage or heart of; encourage: usu. with *up.* **3.** *Naut.* To mark with buoys. [< MDu. or OF < L *boia* fetter; because it is chained to one spot]

buoy·an·cy (boi'ən-sē, bōō'yən-sē) *n.* **1.** The tendency or ability to keep afloat. **2.** The power of a fluid to keep an object afloat. **3.** Cheerfulness. Also **buoy'ance.**

buoy·ant (boi'ənt, bōō'yənt) *adj.* Having buoyancy. [Prob. < Sp. < *boyar* to float] — **buoy'ant·ly** *adv.*

bur¹ (bûr) *n.* **1.** *Bot.* A rough or prickly flower head or seedcase. **2.** A plant that bears burs. **3.** A person or thing that clings like a bur. — *v.t.* **burred, bur·ring** To remove burs from. Also spelled *burr.* [< Scand.]

bur² (bûr) See BURR².

bur·ble (bûr'bəl) *v.i.* **·bled, ·bling** **1.** To bubble; gurgle. **2.** To talk excitedly and confusedly. [ME; imit.]

bur·bot (bûr'bət) *n. pl.* **·bot** A fresh-water fish with barbels on the chin. [< F, ult., < L *barbata* bearded]

bur·den¹ (bûr'dən) *n.* **1.** Something carried; a load. **2.** Something that weighs heavily, as responsibility or anxiety. **3.** *Naut.* **a** The carrying capacity of a vessel. **b** The weight of the cargo. **4.** The carrying of loads: beasts of *burden.* — *v.t.* To load or overload. [OE *byrthen* load]

bur·den² (bûr'dən) *n.* **1.** Something often repeated or dwelt upon; the prevailing idea. **2.** A refrain of a song. [< LL *burdo* drone]

burden of proof The obligation to prove a point.

bur·den·some (bûr'dən-səm) *adj.* Hard or heavy to bear; oppressive. — **bur'den·some·ly** *adv.* — **bur'den·some·ness** *n.*

bur·dock (bûr'dok) *n.* A coarse weed of the composite family having prickly burs. [< BUR¹ + DOCK⁴]

bu·reau (byŏŏr'ō) *n. pl.* **bu·reaus** or **bu·reaux** (byŏŏr'ōz) **1.** *U.S.* A chest of drawers for clothing, etc., usu. with a mirror. **2.** A government department, or a division thereof. **3.** An office for transacting business. **4.** *Brit.* A writing desk or table with drawers. [< F, a desk]

bu·reauc·ra·cy (byŏŏ-rok'rə-sē) *n. pl.* **·cies** **1.** Government by bureaus; also, the group of officials so governing. **2.** The undue extension of bureaus in the departments of a government. **3.** Rigid adherence to administrative routine. [< F < *bureau* office, bureau + Gk. *kratia* power, rule]

bu·reau·crat (byŏŏr'ə-krat) *n.* **1.** A member of a bureaucracy. **2.** An official who narrowly adheres to a rigid routine. — **bu'reau·crat'ic** or **·i·cal** *adj.* — **bu'reau·crat'i·cal·ly** *adv.*

bu·rette (byŏŏ-ret') *n. Chem.* A finely graduated glass tube with a stopcock at the bottom. Also **bu·ret'.** [< F, dim. of *buire* a vase, vial]

burg (bûrg) *n. U.S. Informal* A town; esp., a rural town. [OE *burg*]

bur·geon (bûr'jən) *v.i.* **1.** To flourish; grow. **2.** To bud; sprout. — *v.t.* **3.** To put forth (buds, etc.). — *n.* A bud; sprout. Also spelled *bourgeon.* [< OF *burjon*]

bur·gess (bûr'jis) *n.* **1.** A citizen or officer of a borough. **2.** In colonial times, a member of the lower house (**House of Burgesses**) of the legislature of Virginia. [< OF *burgeis*]

burgh (bûrg, *Scot.* bûr'ō, -ə) *n.* In Scottish law, a chartered town. [Var. of BOROUGH] — **burgh·al** (bûr'gəl) *adj.*

burgh·er (bûr'gər) *n.* A citizen of a burgh, town, or city.

bur·glar (bûr'glər) *n.* One who commits burglary. [< Med.L < OF < *bourg* dwelling + *laire* robbery]

bur·glar·ize (bûr'glə-rīz') *v.t.* **·ized, ·iz·ing** To commit burglary upon.

bur·gla·ry (bûr'glər-ē) *n. pl.* **·ries** *Law* The breaking and entering of a dwelling at night, with intent to commit a crime. — **Syn.** See THEFT.

bur·gle (bûr'gəl) *v.t. & v.i.* **·gled, ·gling** *Informal* To commit burglary (upon).

bur·go·mas·ter (bûr'gə-mas'tər, -mäs'-) *n.* A Dutch, Flemish, or German mayor. [< Du. *burgemeester*]

Bur·gun·dy (bûr'gən-dē) *n. pl.* **·dies** A kind of red or white wine originally made in Burgundy.

bur·i·al (ber'ē-əl) *n.* The burying of a dead body; interment. — *adj.* Of or pertaining to burial. [ME *buryel*, *biriels* < *biriels* (mistaken as plural) < OE *brygels* tomb]

bu·rin (byoor'in) *n.* A steel tool with a lozenge-shaped point for engraving or carving.

burl (bûrl) *n.* 1. A knot or lump in wool, cloth, or thread. 2. A large wartlike excrescence formed on the trunks of trees. — *v.t.* To dress (cloth) by removing burls. [< OF < LL *burra* shaggy hair] — **burled** *adj.* — **burl'er** *n.*

bur·lap (bûr'lap) *n.* A coarse fabric made of jute or hemp, used for wrapping, bagging, etc. [Origin uncertain]

bur·lesque (bər-lesk') *n.* 1. A satire or ludicrous imitation, usually of a serious, dignified subject; parody. 2. *U.S.* A theatrical entertainment marked by low comedy, striptease, etc. — *adj.* 1. Marked by ridiculous incongruity or broad caricature. 2. *U.S.* Of or pertaining to theatrical burlesque. — *v.* **·lesqued, ·les·quing** *v.t.* 1. To represent laughably; satirize. — *v.i.* 2. To use broad caricature. [< F < Ital. < *burla* joke]

bur·ley (bûr'lē) *n.* A fine, light tobacco grown principally in Kentucky. Also **Bur'ley.** [? after *Burley*, a grower]

bur·ly (bûr'lē) *adj.* **·li·er, ·li·est** Large of body; bulky; stout; lusty. [ME *borlich*] — **bur'li·ly** *adv.* — **bur'li·ness** *n.*

Bur·mese (bər-mēz', -mēs') *adj.* Of or pertaining to Burma, its inhabitants, or their language. Also **Bur'man** (-mən). — *n.* *pl.* **·mese** 1. A native or inhabitant of Burma. 2. The Sino-Tibetan language of Burma.

burn (bûrn) *v.* **burned** or **burnt, burn·ing** *v.t.* 1. To destroy or consume by fire. 2. To set afire; ignite. 3. To injure or kill by fire; execute by fire. 4. To injure or damage by friction, heat, steam, etc.; scale; wither. 5. To produce by fire. 6. To brand; also, to cauterize. 7. To finish or harden by intense heat; fire. 8. To use or employ, so as to give off light, heat, etc. 9. To cause a feeling of heat in. 10. To sunburn. 11. *Chem.* To cause to undergo combustion. 12. *U.S. Slang* To electrocute. — *v.i.* 13. To be on fire; blaze. 14. To be destroyed or scorched by fire. 15. To give off light, heat, etc.; shine. 16. To die by fire. 17. To appear or feel hot: He *burns* with fever. 18. To be eager, excited, or inflamed. 19. *Chem.* To oxidize; undergo combustion. 20. *U.S. Slang* To be electrocuted. — **to burn down** To raze or be razed by fire. — **to burn out** 1. To become extinguished through lack of fuel. 2. To destroy or wear out by heat, friction, etc. 3. To burn up the house, store, or property of. 4. To drive out by heat. — **to burn up** 1. To consume by fire. 2. *Slang* To make or become irritated or enraged. — *n.* 1. A burned place. 2. *Pathol.* A lesion caused by heat, extreme cold, corrosive chemicals, gases, electricity, radiation, etc. [Fusion of OE *beornan* to be on fire, and OE *bærnan* to set afire]

burn·er (bûr'nər) *n.* 1. One who or that which burns. 2. That part of a stove, lamp, etc., from which the flame comes.

burn·ing (bûr'ning) *adj.* 1. Consuming or being consumed by or as if by fire. 2. Causing intense feeling; urgent.

burning glass A convex lens for concentrating the sun's rays upon an object so as to heat or ignite it.

bur·nish (bûr'nish) *v.t. & v.i.* To polish by friction; make or become shiny. — *n.* Polish; luster. [< OF *burnir* to polish] — **bur'nish·er** *n.* — **bur'nish·ment** *n.*

bur·noose (bər-nōōs', bûr'nōōs) *n.* An Arab hooded cloak. Also **bur·nous'.** [< F < Arabic *burnus*]

burn·out (bûrn'out') *n.* 1. A destruction or failure due to burning or to excessive heat. 2. *Aerospace* The cessation of burning in a jet or rocket engine, esp. when caused by stoppage or exhaustion of fuel.

burn·sides (bûrn'sīdz) *n.pl.* Side whiskers and mustache: also called *sideburns.* [after A. E. *Burnside*, 1824–81, Union general in the Civil War]

burnt (bûrnt) Alternative past tense and past participle of BURN.

burnt ocher A permanent, brick red pigment.

burnt offering An animal, food, etc., burned upon an altar as a sacrifice or offering to a god.

burnt sienna A dark brown pigment.

burnt umber A reddish brown pigment.

burp (bûrp) *U.S. Informal n.* A belch. — *v.i.* To belch. — *v.t.* To cause to belch: to *burp* a baby. [Imit.]

burr¹ (bûr) *n.* 1. A roughness or rough edge, esp. one left on metal in casting or cutting. 2. Any of several tools for cutting, reaming, etc. 3. A dentist's drill with a rough head. 4. A protuberant knot on a tree. — *v.t.* 1. To form a rough edge on. 2. To remove a rough edge from. Also spelled *bur.* [Var. of BUR¹] — **bur'ry** *adj.*

burr² (bûr) *n.* 1. A rough guttural sound of *r* produced by vibration of the uvula against the back of the tongue. 2. Any rough, dialectal pronunciation: the Scottish *burr.* 3. A buzz. — *v.t.* 1. To pronounce with a rough or guttural articulation. — *v.i.* 2. To speak with a burr. [Imit.]

bur·ro (bûr'ō, bŏŏr'ō) *n. pl.* **·ros** A small donkey. [< Sp.]

bur·row (bûr'ō) *n.* 1. A hole made in the ground, as by a rabbit. 2. Any similar place of refuge. — *v.i.* 1. To live or hide in a burrow. 2. To dig a burrow or burrows. 3. To dig into, under, or through something. — *v.t.* 4. To dig a burrow or burrows in. 5. To make by burrowing. 6. To hide (oneself) in a burrow. [ME *borow*] — **bur'row·er** *n.*

bur·sa (bûr'sə) *n. pl.* **·sae** (-sē) or **·sas** *Anat.* A pouch or saclike cavity; esp. one containing synovia and located at points of friction in the bodies of vertebrates. [< Med.L, sac, pouch] — **bur'sal** *adj.*

bur·sar (bûr'sər, -sär) *n.* A treasurer, as of a college. [< Med.L *bursa* bag, purse] — **bur·sar·i·al** (bər-sâr'ē-əl) *adj.*

bur·sa·ry (bûr'sər-ē) *n. pl.* **·ries** The treasury of a public institution or a religious order.

bur·si·tis (bər-sī'tis) *n. Pathol.* Inflammation of a bursa.

burst (bûrst) *n.* **burst, burst·ing** *v.i.* 1. To break open or apart suddenly and violently. 2. To be full to the point of breaking open; bulge. 3. To appear or enter suddenly or violently. 4. To become audible or evident. 5. To give sudden expression to passion, grief, etc. — *v.t.* 6. To cause to break open suddenly or violently; force open; puncture. 7. To cause to swell to the point of breaking open. — *n.* 1. A sudden exploding or breaking forth. 2. A sudden effort or spurt; rush. 3. A crack or break. [OE *berstan*] — **burst'er** *n.*

bur·y (ber'ē) *v.t.* **bur·ied, bur·y·ing** 1. To put (a dead body) in a grave, tomb, or the sea; perform burial rites for; inter. 2. To put underground; to conceal, as by covering. 3. To embed; sink: to *bury* a nail in a wall. 4. To end; put out of mind: to *bury* a friendship. 5. To occupy deeply; engross: He *buried* himself in study. [OE *byrgan*]

burying ground A cemetery.

bus (bus) *n. pl.* **bus·es** or **bus·ses** 1. A large passenger vehicle usu. following a prescribed route. 2. *Informal* An automobile. — *v.t.* **bused** or **bussed, bus·ing** or **bus·sing** 1. To transport by bus. — *v.i.* 2. To go by bus. 3. *Informal* To work as a bus boy. [Short form of OMNIBUS]

bus boy An employee in a restaurant who clears tables of soiled dishes, assists the waiters, etc.

bus·by (buz'bē) *n. pl.* **·bies** A tall fur cap worn by British hussars, artillerymen, and engineers. [Origin uncertain]

bush¹ (bŏŏsh) *n.* 1. A low, treelike or thickly branching shrub. 2. A clump of shrubs; thicket; undergrowth. 3. Wild, uncleared land covered with scrub; also, any rural or unsettled area. 4. A fox's tail. 5. *Canadian* Wood lot. — *v.i.* 1. To grow or branch like a bush. 2. To be or become bushy. — *v.t.* 3. To decorate or support with bushes. [< ON *buskr*]

bush² (bŏŏsh) *v.t.* To put a bushing in, as a bearing. — *n.* A bushing. [< MDu. *busse* box]

BUSBY

bushed (bŏŏsht) *adj. Informal* 1. *U.S. & Canadian* Exhausted. 2. Odd from living in isolation. [< BUSH¹]

bush·el¹ (bŏŏsh'əl) *n.* 1. A unit of dry capacity. 2. A container holding this amount. See table front of book. [< OF *boissiel*, dim. of *boisse* box]

bush·el² (bŏŏsh'əl) *v.t. & v.i.* **bush·eled** or **·elled, bush·el·ing** or **·el·ling** *U.S.* To repair and restore (a garment). [Cf. G *bosseln* to do small jobs] — **bush'el·er** or **bush'el·ler** *n.*

bu·shi·do (bōō'shē-dō) *n.* The chivalric code of the feudal Samurai. Also **Bu'shi·do.** [< Japanese, way of the warrior]

bush·ing (bŏŏsh'ing) *n.* 1. *Mech.* A metallic lining for a hole, as in the hub of a wheel, designed to insulate or to prevent abrasion between parts. 2. *Electr.* A lining inserted in a socket to insulate an electric current. [< BUSH²]

bush league In baseball slang, an obscure minor league.

bush leaguer 1. In baseball slang, a player in a bush league. 2. *U.S. Slang* A mediocre person.

bush·man (bŏŏsh'mən) *n. pl.* **·men** (-mən) *Austral.* A dweller or farmer in the bush.

Bush·man (bŏŏsh'mən) *n. pl.* **·men** (-mən) 1. One of a nomadic people of South Africa. 2. The language of the Bushmen. [Trans. of Du. *boschjesman*]

bush·mas·ter (bŏŏsh'mas'tər, -mäs') *n.* A venomous pit viper of Central and South America.

bush·whack (bŏŏsh'hwak') *U.S. v.t.* 1. To attack or fire upon from hiding; ambush. — *v.i.* 2. To fight as a guerrilla. [< Du. *boschwachter* forest keeper; infl. by *whack*] — **bush'whack·er** *n.* — **bush'whack·ing** *n.*

bush·y (bŏŏsh'ē) *adj.* **bush·i·er, bush·i·est** 1. Covered with bushes. 2. Shaggy. — **bush'i·ly** *adv.* — **bush'i·ness** *n.*

bus·ied (biz'ēd) Past tense and past participle of BUSY.

bus·i·ly (biz'ə-lē) *adv.* In a busy manner; industriously.

busi·ness (biz'nis) *n.* 1. An occupation, trade, or profession. 2. Any of the various operations or details of trade or industry. 3. A commercial enterprise or establishment.

---

a firm, factory, store, etc. **4.** The amount or volume of trade. **5.** A proper interest or concern; responsibility; duty. **6.** A matter or affair. **7.** In the theater, the movements, facial expressions, etc., apart from dialogue, by which actors interpret a part. — **Syn.** See OCCUPATION. — **to give (someone) the business** *Slang* **1.** To deal with harshly or summarily. **2.** To beat severely or kill. **3.** To cheat or defraud. — **to have no business** To have no right (to do something). — **to mean business** *Informal* To have a serious intention. [OE *bysignis*]

business college A school that gives training in clerical and secretarial skills for positions in commerce and industry.

busi·ness·like (biz′nis-līk′) *adj.* Methodical; systematic.

busi·ness·man (biz′nis-man′) *n.* *pl.* **-men** (-men′) One engaged in commercial or industrial activity. — **busi′ness·wom′an** (-wŏŏm′an) *n.fem.*

bus·kin (bus′kin) *n.* **1.** A boot reaching halfway to the knee, and strapped or laced to the ankle. **2.** A laced half boot, worn by Greek and Roman tragic actors. **3.** Tragedy. [Origin uncertain] — **bus′kined** *adj.*

bus·man (bus′mən) *n.* *pl.* **men** (-mən) A bus driver.

busman's holiday A holiday spent by choice in activity similar to one's regular work.

buss (bus) *Archaic & Dial.* *n.* A kiss; smack. — *v.t. & v.i.* To kiss heartily. [Imit.]

bus·ses (bus′iz) Alternative plural of BUS.

bust[1] (bust) *n.* **1.** The human breast, esp. the bosom of a woman. **2.** A piece of statuary representing the human head, shoulders, and breast. [< F < Ital. *busto*]

bust[2] (bust) *Slang* *v.t.* **1.** To burst. **2.** To tame; train, as a horse. **3.** To make bankrupt or short of funds. **4.** To reduce in rank; demote. **5.** To hit; strike. — *v.i.* **6.** To burst. **7.** To become bankrupt or short of funds. — *n.* **1.** Failure; bankruptcy. **2.** A spree. **3.** A blow. [Alter. of BURST]

bus·tard (bus′tərd) *n.* A large Old World game bird related to the plovers and cranes. [< OF *bistarde, oustarde* < L *avis tarda*, lit., slow bird]

bust·er (bus′tər) *n.* *U.S. Slang* One who breaks or breaks up: trust *buster.*

bus·tle[1] (bus′əl) *n.* Excited activity; noisy stir; fuss. — *v.* **·tled, ·tling** *v.i.* **1.** To move noisily or energetically; hurry. — *v.t.* **2.** To cause to hurry. [? Akin to BUSK²]

bus·tle[2] (bus′əl) *n.* A frame or pad formerly worn by women on the back of the body below the waist to distend the skirt. [? < BUSTLE¹]

bus·tling (bus′ling) *adj.* Active; busy. — **bus′tling·ly** *adv.*

bus·y (biz′ē) *adj.* **bus·i·er, bus·i·est** **1.** Actively engaged in something; occupied. **2.** Filled with activity; never still. **3.** Officiously active; meddling; prying. **4.** Temporarily engaged, as a telephone line. — *v.t.* **bus·ied, bus·y·ing** To make busy. [OE *bysig* active] — **bus′y·ness** *n.*

bus·y·bod·y (biz′ē-bod′ē) *n.* *pl.* **·bodies** One who officiously meddles in the affairs of others.

busy signal In a dial telephone, a recurrent buzzing tone indicating that the number called is already connected.

but (but, *unstressed* bət) *conj.* **1.** On the other hand; yet. **2.** Without the result that: It never rains *but* it pours. **3.** Other than; otherwise than. **4.** Except: anything *but* that. **5.** With the exception that: often with *that*: Nothing will do *but* I must leave. **6.** That: We don't doubt *but* he is there. **7.** That . . . not: He is not so ill *but* exercise will benefit him. **8.** Who . . . not; which . . . not: Few sought his advice *but* were helped by it. — *prep.* With the exception of; save: owning nothing *but* his clothes. — *adv.* Only; just: She is *but* a child. — **all but** Almost; nearly. — **but for** Were it not for. — *n.* An objection or condition; exception: no ifs or *buts.* [OE < *be* by + *ūtan* outside]
— **Syn.** (conj.) **1.** *But* ranges in meaning from faintest contrast to absolute negation. *However* suggests a moderate concession or a second point to be considered. *Nevertheless* emphasizes direct opposition, and *yet* serves to introduce a mildly inconsequential outcome.

bu·ta·di·ene (byŏŏ′tə·dī′ēn, -dī·ēn′) *n.* *Chem.* A hydrocarbon, C₄H₆, similar to isoprene, used in the manufacture of synthetic rubber. [< BUTA(NE) + DI-² (def. 2) + -ENE]

bu·tane (byŏŏ′tān, byŏŏ·tān′) *n.* *Chem.* A colorless, flammable, gaseous hydrocarbon, C₄H₁₀, of the methane series. [< L *but(yrum)* butter + -ANE²]

butch·er (bŏŏch′ər) *n.* **1.** One who slaughters or dresses animals for market; also, a dealer in meats. **2.** One guilty of needless bloodshed. **3.** *U.S.* A vendor of candy, etc., on trains. **4.** A botcher. — *v.t.* **1.** To slaughter or dress for market. **2.** To kill cruelly or indiscriminately. **3.** To botch. [< OF *bouchier* slaughterer of bucks] — **butch′er·er** *n.*

butch·er·bird (bŏŏch′ər·bûrd′) *n.* The shrike, a bird.

butch·er's-broom (bŏŏch′ərz·brŏŏm′, -brŏŏm′) *n.* A low, evergreen shrub with leathery, leaflike branches bearing scarlet berries. Also **butch′er·broom′.**

butch·er·y (bŏŏch′ər·ē) *n.* *pl.* **·er·ies** **1.** Wanton slaughter. **2.** A slaughterhouse. **3.** The butcher's trade.

but·ler (but′lər) *n.* A manservant in charge of the dining

room, wine, etc., usu. the head servant in a household. [< AF, OF < Med.L < *buticula* bottle] — **but′ler·ship** *n.*

butler's pantry A room between the kitchen and the dining room, suitable for storage, serving, etc.

butt[1] (but) *v.t.* **1.** To strike with the head or horns; ram. **2.** To drive, push, or bump as with the head. — *v.i.* **3.** To strike or attempt to strike something with the head or horns. **4.** To move or drive head foremost. **5.** To project; jut. — **to butt in** *Informal* To interrupt; intrude. — *n.* **1.** A blow or push with the head. **2.** A thrust in fencing. [< OF *buter* to strike, push, project] — **but′ter** *n.*

butt[2] (but) *n.* **1.** A person or thing subjected to jokes, ridicule, criticism, etc. **2.** A target, as on a rifle range. **3.** *pl.* A target range. **4.** An embankment or wall behind a target to stop the shot. [< OF *but* end, goal]

butt[3] (but) *n.* **1.** The larger or thicker end of anything. **2.** An end or extremity. **3.** An unused end, as of a cigar or cigarette; stub; stump. **4.** The thick part of a tanned hide. **5.** *U.S. Informal* The buttocks. [Akin to Dan. *but* blunt]

butt[4] (but) *n.* **1.** A large cask. **2.** A measure of wine, 126 U.S. gallons. [< OF *boute*]

butte (byŏŏt) *n.* *U.S. & Canadian* A conspicuous hill, esp. one with steep sides and a flattened top. [< F]

but·ter (but′ər) *n.* **1.** The fatty constituent of milk churned and prepared for cooking and table use. **2.** A substance having the consistency or some of the qualities of butter. **3.** Any of several food preparations of semisolid consistency: apple *butter*. **4.** *Informal* Flattery. — *v.t.* **1.** To put butter on. **2.** *Informal* To flatter: usu. with *up.* — **to know which side one's bread is buttered on** To be aware of the true sources of one's fortune or security. [OE < L < Gk. < *bous* cow + *tyros* cheese]

butter bean **1.** The wax bean. **2.** In the southern U.S., the lima bean.

but·ter·cup (but′ər·kup′) *n.* A plant of the crowfoot family, with yellow, cup-shaped flowers.

but·ter·fat (but′ər·fat′) *n.* The fatty substance of milk, from which butter is made.

but·ter·fin·gers (but′ər·fing′gərz) *n.* *Informal* One who drops things easily or often. — **but′ter·fin′gered** *adj.*

but·ter·fish (but′ər·fish′) *n.* *pl.* **·fish** or **·fishes** A silvery, laterally compressed fish common along the Atlantic coast.

but·ter·fly (but′ər·flī′) *n.* *pl.* **·flies** **1.** An insect with large, often brightly colored wings, club-shaped antennae, and slender body. **2.** A frivolous person. [OE *buttorfléoge*]

butter knife A small, blunt-edged knife for cutting or spreading butter.

but·ter·milk (but′ər·milk′) *n.* The sour liquid left after the butterfat has been separated from milk or cream.

but·ter·nut (but′ər·nut′) *n.* **1.** The oily, edible nut of a walnut of North America. **2.** The tree or its cathartic inner bark. **3.** A yellowish brown.

but·ter·scotch (but′ər·skoch′) *n.* **1.** Hard, sticky candy made with brown sugar, butter, and flavoring. **2.** A syrup or flavoring consisting of similar ingredients. — *adj.* Made of or flavored with butterscotch.

but·ter·y[1] (but′ər·ē) *adj.* **1.** Containing, like, or smeared with butter. **2.** *Informal* Grossly flattering; adulatory.

but·ter·y[2] (but′ər·ē, but′rē) *n.* *pl.* **·ter·ies** *Chiefly Brit.* A pantry or wine cellar. [< OF < LL *butta* bottle]

but·tock (but′ək) *n.* **1.** *Anat.* Either of the two fleshy prominences that form the rump. **2.** *pl.* The rump. [Dim. of BUTT³]

but·ton (but′n) *n.* **1.** A knob or disk sewn to a garment, etc., serving as a fastening or for ornamentation. **2.** Anything resembling a button, as the knob for operating an electric bell or an electric lamp. **3.** *Slang* The point of the chin. — **on the button** *Informal* Exactly; precisely. — *v.t.* **1.** To fasten or provide with a button or buttons. — *v.i.* **2.** To be capable of being fastened with or as with buttons. [< OF *boton* button, bud] — **but′ton·er** *n.*

but·ton·hole (but′n·hōl′) *n.* A slit or loop to receive and hold a button. — *v.t.* **·holed, ·hol·ing** **1.** To work buttonholes in. **2.** To seize as by the buttonhole so as to detain.

but·tons (but′nz) *n.pl.* (*construed as sing.*) *Brit. Informal* A bellboy; page.

but·ton·wood (but′n·wŏŏd′) *n.* **1.** A plane tree of North America, yielding a wood used for furniture, etc. Also **but·ton·ball** (-bôl′). **2.** The wood of this tree.

but·ton·y (but′n·ē) *adj.* Of, having, or like a button.

but·tress (but′tris) *n.* **1.** *Archit.* A structure built against a wall to strengthen it. **2.** Any support or prop. **3.** Something suggesting a buttress, as a projecting rock or hillside. — *v.t.* **1.** To support with a buttress. **2.** To prop up; sustain. [< OF *bouter, buter* to push, thrust]

bu·tyl (byŏŏ′til) *n.* *Chem.* A univalent hydrocarbon radical, C₄H₉, from butane. [< BUT(YRIC) + -YL]

butyl alcohols *Chem.* A group of three isomeric alcohols having the formula C₄H₉OH.

bu·ty·lene (byŏŏ′tə·lēn) *n.* *Chem.* A gaseous hydrocarbon, C₄H₈, an ingredient of synthetic rubber.

bu·tyr·ic (byoo·tir′ik) *adj.* Of or derived from butter.
bux·om (buk′səm) *adj.* Characterized by health and vigor; plump; comely: said of women. [ME *buhsum* pliant] — **bux′om·ly** *adv.* — **bux′om·ness** *n.*
buy (bī) *v.* **bought, buying** *v.t.* **1.** To acquire with money; purchase. **2.** To obtain by some exchange or sacrifice: to *buy* wisdom with experience. **3.** To bribe; corrupt: He was *bought* cheap. — *v.i.* **4.** To make purchases; be a purchaser. — **to buy in 1.** To buy back for the owner, as at an auction when the bids are too low. **2.** To buy stock in a company. **3.** *Slang* To pay money as a price for joining. — **to buy off** To bribe. — **to buy out** To purchase the stock, interests, etc., of. — **to buy over** To win over to one's interest by a bribe. — **to buy up** To purchase the entire supply of. — *n. Informal* **1.** Anything bought or about to be bought. **2.** A bargain. [OE *bycgan*] — **buy′a·ble** *adj.*
buy·er (bī′ər) *n.* **1.** One who makes purchases. **2.** A purchasing agent, as for a department store.
buzz (buz) *v.i.* **1.** To make the humming, vibrating sound of the bee. **2.** To talk or gossip excitedly. **3.** To go busily or hastily. — *v.t.* **4.** To cause to buzz. **5.** To spread by buzzing. **6.** To signal with a buzz. **7.** *Informal* To fly an airplane low over. **8.** *Informal* To call by telephone. — *n.* **1.** A vibrating hum. **2.** A low murmur, as of many voices. **3.** *Informal* A phone call. [Imit.]
buz·zard (buz′ərd) *n.* **1.** One of several large, slow-flying hawks. **2.** A turkey buzzard. [< OF *busart*]
buzz bomb A robot bomb.
buzz·er (buz′ər) *n.* An electric signal making a buzzing sound, as on a telephone switchboard.
buzz saw A circular saw, so called from the sound it emits.
by (bī) *prep.* **1.** Next to; near: the house *by* the river. **2.** Past and beyond: The train roared *by* us. **3.** Through the agency or by means of: to hang *by* a rope; to travel *by* plane. **4.** By way of: Come *by* the nearest road. **5.** On the part of: a loss felt *by* all. **6.** According to: *by* law. **7.** In the course of; during: to travel *by* night. **8.** Not later than: Be here by noon. **9.** After: day *by* day. **10.** According to as a standard: to work *by* the day. **11.** To the extent or amount of: insects *by* the thousands. **12.** In multiplication or measurement with: Multiply 6 *by* 8. **13.** With reference to: to do well *by* one's friends. **14.** In the name of: *by* all that's holy. — **by the way** (or **by the by, bye the bye**) Incidentally. — *adv.* **1.** At hand; near. **2.** Up to and beyond something; past: The years go *by*. **3.** Apart; aside: to lay something *by*. — **by and by** After a time; before long. — **by and large** On the whole; generally. — *adj.* & *n.* See BYE. [OE *bī* near, about]
by- *combining form* **1.** Secondary; incidental: *by-product*. **2.** Near; close: *bystander*. **3.** Aside; out of the way: *byway*.
by-and-by (bī′ən·bī′) *n.* Future time; hereafter.
bye (bī) *n.* **1.** Something of minor or secondary importance. **2.** The position of one who, assigned no opponent, automatically advances to the next round, as in a tennis tournament. **3.** In golf, any hole remaining unplayed when the match ends. — *adj.* Secondary. Also spelled *by*. [< BY]

bye-bye (bī′bī′) *interj.* Good-by.
by-e·lec·tion (bī′i·lek′shən) *n. Brit.* A parliamentary election between general elections, held to fill a vacancy.
Bye·lo·rus·sian (bye′lə·rush′ən) *adj.* Of or pertaining to the Byelorussian S.S.R., its people, or their language. — *n.* **1.** A native or inhabitant of the Byelorussian S.S.R. **2.** The language of the Byelorussians. Also *White Russian.*
by·gone (bī′gôn′, -gon′) *adj.* Gone by; past. — *n. Often pl.* Something past. — **to let bygones be bygones** To let disagreements and difficulties in the past be overlooked.
by·law (bī′lô′) *n.* **1.** A law adopted by a corporation, etc., and subordinate to a constitution or charter. **2.** A secondary law. [ME < *by*, *bi* village + *lawe* law]
by-line (bī′līn′) *n.* The line at the head of an article in a newspaper, etc., giving the name of the writer.
by-pass (bī′pas′, -päs′) *n.* **1.** Any road, path, or route connecting two points in a course other than that normally used; a detour. **2.** *Electr.* A shunt. — *v.t.* **1.** To go around or avoid (an obstacle). **2.** To provide with a by-pass.
by-path (bī′path′, -päth′) *n.* A secluded or indirect path.
by-play (bī′plā′) *n.* Action or speech apart from the main action, especially in a play.
by-prod·uct (bī′prod′əkt) *n.* A secondary product or result.
by·road (bī′rōd′) *n.* A back or side road.
By·ron·ic (bī·ron′ik) *adj.* **1.** Of or pertaining to Lord Byron. **2.** Like Byron; melancholy, romantic, passionate, etc.
by·stand·er (bī′stan′dər) *n.* One present but not taking part; an onlooker.
by·way (bī′wā′) *n.* A branch or side road.
by·word (bī′wûrd′) *n.* **1.** A proverbial saying; also, a pet phrase. **2.** A person, institution, etc., that proverbially represents a type, usually an object of scorn.
Byz·an·tine (biz′ən·tēn, -tīn, bi·zan′tin) *adj.* **1.** Of or pertaining to Byzantium or its civilization. **2.** Pertaining to the style of architecture developed in Byzantium during the fifth and sixth centuries, using rounded arches, centralized plans surmounted by large domes, and lavishness of mosaic and other decoration. — *n.* A native or inhabitant of Byzantium. Also **By·zan·ti·an** (bi·zan′shē·ən, -shən). [< L *Byzantinus* < *Byzantium*]

BYZANTINE ARCHITECTURE
(Santa Sophia, Constantinople, A.D. 538)

Byzantine Empire The eastern part of the later Roman Empire (395–1453); capital, Constantinople: also, *Byzantium, Eastern Roman Empire.*
By·zan·ti·um (bi·zan′shē·əm, -tē·əm) **1.** An ancient city on the Bosporus, later Constantinople. **2.** The Byzantine Empire.

C

c, C (sē) *n. pl.* **c's** or **cs, C's** or **Cs, cees** (sēz) **1.** The third letter of the English alphabet. **2.** Any sound represented by the letter *c*. — *symbol* **1.** The Roman numeral for 100. **2.** *Chem.* Carbon (symbol C). **3.** *Music* **a** The tonic note of the natural scale; do. **b** A written note representing it. **c** The scale built upon C. **4.** The third in sequence or class.
Caa·ba (kä′bə, kä′ə·bə) See KAABA.
cab (kab) *n.* **1.** A taxicab. **2.** A one-horse carriage for hire. **3.** A covered compartment of a locomotive, motor truck, etc., for the operator. [Short form of CABRIOLET]
ca·bal (kə·bal′) *n.* **1.** A number of persons secretly united for some private purpose. **2.** An intrigue; plot. — *v.i.* **·balled, ·bal·ling** To form a cabal; plot. [< MF *cabale*]
cab·a·la (kab′ə·lə, kə·bä′lə) *n.* **1.** *Often cap.* An occult system originating in a mystical interpretation of the Scriptures among certain Jewish rabbis. **2.** Any secret, occult, or mystic system. Also spelled *kabala, kabbala.* [< Hebrew *qābal* to receive] — **cab′a·lism** *n.* — **cab′a·list** *n. & adj.*

cab·a·lis·tic (kab′ə·lis′tik) *adj.* **1.** Pertaining to the cabala. **2.** Having a mystic meaning; mysterious. Also **ca·bal·ic** (kə·bal′ik), **cab·a·lis′ti·cal.** — **cab′a·lis′ti·cal·ly** *adv.*
cab·al·le·ro (kab′əl·yâr′ō) *n. pl.* **·ros. 1.** A Spanish cavalier. **2.** *SW U.S.* A horseman. [< Sp. < L *caballus* horse]
ca·ban·a (kə·ban′ə, -bä′nə) *n.* **1.** A small cabin. **2.** A beach bathhouse. Also **ca·ba·ña** (kə·bän′yə, -ban′-). [< Sp.]
cab·a·ret (kab′ə·rā′) *n.* **1.** A restaurant that provides singing, dancing, etc. **2.** Entertainment of this type. [< F]
cab·bage (kab′ij) *n.* The close-leaved edible head of a plant of the mustard family. — *v.i.* **·baged, ·bag·ing** To form a head, as cabbage. [< OF, ult. < L *caput* head]
cabbage palm A palm with a terminal leaf bud used as a vegetable.
cab·by (kab′ē) *n. pl.* **·bies** *Informal* The driver of a cab.
cab·in (kab′in) *n.* **1.** A small, rude house; a hut. **2.** In the U.S. Navy, the quarters of the captain. **3.** *Naut.* On passenger vessels, the living quarters for passengers and officers.

4. *Aeron.* The enclosed space in an aircraft for the crew, passengers, or cargo. — *v.t. & v.i.* To confine or dwell in or as in a cabin. [< F < LL *capanna* cabin]

cabin boy A boy who waits on the officers and passengers of a ship.

cabin class A class of accommodations for steamship passengers, higher than tourist class, lower than first class.

cabin cruiser A cruiser (def. 3).

cab·i·net (kab′ə·nit) *n.* **1.** A piece of furniture fitted with shelves and drawers; a cupboard. **2.** A council, or the chamber in which it meets. **3.** *Often cap.* The body of official advisers and executive chiefs serving a head of state. — *adj.* **1.** Of or suitable for a cabinet. **2.** Secret; confidential. [< F < Ital. *gabinetto* closet, chest of drawers]

cab·i·net·mak·er (kab′ə·nit·mā′kər) *n.* One who does fine woodworking, as for cabinets, furniture, etc.

cab·i·net·work (kab′ə·nit·wûrk′) *n.* Expert woodwork.

ca·ble (kā′bəl) *n.* **1.** A heavy rope, now usu. of steel wire. **2.** A cable's length. **3.** *Electr.* **a** An insulated electrical conductor or group of conductors. **b** An underwater telegraph line. **4.** A cablegram. — *v.* **·bled, ·bling** *v.t.* **1.** To make fast by a cable. **2.** To signal by underwater telegraph. — *v.i.* **3.** To send a message by underwater telegraph. [< LL < L *capere* to take, grasp]

cable car A car pulled by a moving cable.

ca·ble·gram (kā′bəl·gram) *n.* A telegraphic message sent by underwater cable.

cable's length A unit of nautical measure, in the United States 720 feet, in England 608 feet.

cab·man (kab′mən) *n. pl.* **·men** (-mən) A cab driver.

ca·boo·dle (kə·bōōd′l) *n. Informal* Collection; lot: usu. in the phrase **the whole (kit and) caboodle.**

ca·boose (kə·bōōs′) *n.* **1.** *U.S.* A car, usu. at the rear of a freight or work train, for use by the train crew. **2.** *Brit.* The galley of a ship. [< MDu. *cabuse* galley]

cab·ri·o·let (kab′rē·ə·lā′, -let′) *n.* **1.** A light, one-horse carriage with two seats and a folding top. **2.** An automobile of the coupé type. [< MF *cabriole* leap, caper]

ca·ca·o (kə·kā′ō, -kā′ō) *n. pl.* **·ca·os 1.** A small, evergreen tree of tropical America. **2.** The large, nutritive seeds of this tree, used in making cocoa and chocolate. [< Sp. < Nahuatl *cacauatl* cacao seed]

cacao butter Cocoa butter.

cach·a·lot (kash′ə·lot, -lō) *n.* The sperm whale. [< F]

cache (kash) *v.t.* **cached, cach·ing** To conceal or store, as in the earth. — *n.* A place for hiding or storing things; also, the things stored or hidden. [< F *cacher* to hide]

ca·chet (ka·shā′, kash′ā) *n.* **1.** A seal, as for a letter. **2.** A distinctive mark; stamp of individuality. **3.** A mark, slogan, etc., printed on mail. [< F *cacher* to hide]

cach·in·nate (kak′ə·nāt) *v.i.* **·nat·ed, ·nat·ing** To laugh immoderately or noisily. [< L *cachinnare* to laugh loudly]

ca·cique (kə·sēk′) *n.* A chief among the Indians of the West Indies, Mexico, etc. [< Sp. < native Haitian word]

cack·le (kak′əl) *v.* **·led, ·ling** *v.i.* **1.** To make a shrill, broken cry, as a hen that has laid an egg. **2.** To laugh or talk with a similar sound. — *v.t.* **3.** To utter in a cackling manner. — *n.* **1.** The shrill, broken cry of a hen or goose. **2.** Idle talk; chatter. **3.** A short, shrill laugh. [Imit.] — **cack′ler** *n.*

caco- *combining form* Bad; vile. [< Gk. *kakos* bad, evil]

ca·cog·ra·phy (kə·kog′rə·fē) *n.* Bad handwriting or spelling. — **ca·cog′ra·pher** *n.* — **cac·o·graph·ic** (kak′ə·graf′ik) or **·i·cal** *adj.*

ca·coph·o·nous (kə·kof′ə·nəs) *adj.* Having a harsh, disagreeable sound; discordant. Also **cac·o·phon·ic** (kak′ə·fon′ik) or **·i·cal.** — **ca·coph′o·nous·ly, cac′o·phon′i·cal·ly** *adv.*

ca·coph·o·ny (kə·kof′ə·nē) *n.* Disagreeable or discordant sound. [< F < Gk. < *kakos* bad + *phōnein* to sound]

cac·tus (kak′təs) *n. pl.* **·tus·es** or **·ti** (-tī) Any of various green, fleshy, mostly leafless and spiny plants, often having showy flowers, and native in arid regions of America. [< L < Gk. *kaktos,* prickly plant]

cad (kad) *n.* An ungentlemanly or despicable fellow. — **cad′dish** *adj.* — **cad′dish·ly** *adv.* — **cad′dish·ness** *n.*

ca·dav·er (kə·dav′ər, -dā′vər) *n.* A dead body; esp., a human body for dissection; a corpse. [< L]

ca·dav·er·ous (kə·dav′ər·əs) *adj.* Resembling or characteristic of a corpse; pale; ghastly; gaunt. Also **ca·dav′er·ic.** — **ca·dav′er·ous·ly** *adv.* — **ca·dav′er·ous·ness** *n.*

cad·die (kad′ē) *n.* One paid to carry clubs for golf players. — *v.i.* **·died, ·dy·ing** To act as a caddie. Also spelled **caddy.**

cad·dis fly (kad′is) Any of certain four-winged insects whose aquatic larvae (**caddis worms**) construct cylindrical cases covered with sand, gravel, etc. [Origin uncertain]

cad·dy¹ (kad′ē) *n. pl.* **·dies** A small box or case, as for tea. [< Malay *kāti,* a measure of weight]

cad·dy² (kad′ē) *n. pl.* **·dies** A caddie.

ca·dence (kād′ns) *n.* **1.** Rhythmic or measured flow, as of poetry. **2.** The measure or beat of music, marching, etc. **3.** Modulation, as of the voice; intonation. **4.** *Music* A melodic, harmonic, or rhythmic formula ending a phrase, movement, etc. Also **ca′den·cy.** [< F < Ital. < LL < L *cadere* to fall] — **ca′denced** *adj.*

ca·dent (kād′nt) *adj.* Having cadence or rhythm.

ca·den·za (kə·den′zə, *Ital.* kä·dent′sä) *n. Music* A flourish or thematic ornamentation, often improvised, for displaying the virtuosity of a solo performer, usu. introduced just before the end of a composition or movement. [< Ital.]

ca·det (kə·det′) *n.* **1.** A student at a military or naval school, esp. one in training for commissioning as an officer. **2.** A younger son or brother. [< F, ult. < L *caput* head, chief] — **ca·det′ship** *n.*

cadge (kaj) *v.* **cadged, cadg·ing** *v.t.* **1.** *Informal* To get by begging. — *v.i.* **2.** *Dial.* To go begging. — **cadg′er** *n.*

cad·mi·um (kad′mē·əm) *n.* A bluish white metallic element (symbol Cd), occurring in small quantities in zinc ores, and used in the manufacture of fusible alloys, in electroplating, and in the control of atomic fission. See ELEMENT. [< NL < L < Gk. *kadmeia* (*gē*) calamine]

Cad·mus (kad′məs) In Greek mythology, a Phoenician prince who killed a dragon and sowed its teeth, from which sprang armed men who fought one another.

cad·re (kad′rē, *Fr.* kä′dr′) *n.* **1.** *Mil.* The nucleus of officers and men needed to train a new military unit. **2.** A framework; nucleus; core. [< F, frame of a picture]

ca·du·ce·us (kə·dōō′sē·əs, -dyōō′-) *n. pl.* **·ce·i** (-sē·ī) **1.** In ancient Greece and Rome, a herald's wand or staff; esp., the staff of Mercury. **2.** A similar staff used as the emblem of a medical corps or of the medical profession. [< L < Gk. (Doric) *karykion* herald's staff] — **ca·du′ce·an** *adj.*

cae- For those words not entered below, see under CE-.

cae·cum (sē′kəm) See CECUM.

Cae·sar (sē′zər) *n.* **1.** The title of the Roman emperors from Augustus to Hadrian. **2.** Any despot.

CADUCEUS

cae·sar·e·an (si·zâr′ē·ən), **cae·sar·i·an,** See CESAREAN, etc.

Cae·sar·e·an (si·zâr′ē·ən) *adj.* Pertaining to Caesar. — *n.* Loosely, a cesarean section. Also **Cae·sar′i·an.**

cae·si·um (sē′zē·əm) See CESIUM.

caes·tus (ses′təs) See CESTUS.

cae·su·ra (si·zhōōr′ə, -zyōōr′ə) *n. pl.* **·su·ras** or **·su·rae** (-zhōōr′ē, -zyōōr′ē) **1.** In Greek and Latin prosody, a break occurring when a word ends within a foot. **2.** In modern prosody, a pause usu. near the middle of a line. Caesura is indicated by two vertical lines (‖). **3.** *Music* A pause indicating a rhythmic division point. Also spelled *cesura.* [< L *caedere* to cut] — **cae·su′ral** *adj.*

ca·fé (ka·fā′, kə-) *n.* **1.** A coffee house; restaurant. **2.** A barroom. **3.** Coffee. Also *esp. U.S.* **ca·fe′.** [< F]

ca·fé au lait (kà·fā′ ō lā′) *French* **1.** Coffee with scalded milk. **2.** A light brown.

ca·fé noir (kà·fā′ nwàr′) *French* Black coffee.

caf·e·te·ri·a (kaf′ə·tir′ē·ə) *n.* A restaurant where the patrons wait upon themselves. [< Am. Sp., coffee store].

caf·feine (kaf′ēn, *in technical usage* kaf′ē·in) *n. Chem.* A slightly bitter alkaloid, $C_8H_{10}O_2N_4$, obtained from the leaves and berries of coffee, used as a stimulant and diuretic. Also **caf′fein.** [< F *café* coffee]

caf·tan (kaf′tan, kaf·tän′) *n.* An undercoat having long sleeves and a sash, worn in eastern Mediterranean countries: also spelled *kaftan.* [< F < Turkish *qaftān*]

cage (kāj) *n.* **1.** A boxlike structure with openwork of wires or bars, for confining birds or beasts. **2.** Any cagelike structure or framework. **3.** In baseball, a movable backstop for batting practice. **4.** In hockey, the frame and net used as the goal. **5.** In basketball, the basket. — *v.t.* **caged, cag·ing** To shut up in a cage; confine; imprison. [< OF, ult. < L *cavus* empty, hollow]

cage·ling (kāj′ling) *n.* A caged bird.

cage·y (kā′jē) *adj.* **cag·i·er, cag·i·est** *Informal* Wary of being duped; shrewd and careful. Also **cag′y.** [Origin uncertain] — **cag′i·ly** *adv.* — **cag′i·ness** *n.*

ca·hier (kä·yā′) *n.* **1.** A number of sheets, as of printed matter, loosely bound together. **2.** A report, as of proceedings, etc. [< F < OF, ult. < L *quaterni* a set of four]

ca·hoots (kə·hōōts′) *n.pl. U.S. Slang* Affiliation; partnership, as in the phrase **in cahoots.** [? < F *cahute* cabin]

cai·man (kā′mən) See CAYMAN.

Cain (kān) The eldest son of Adam, who slew his brother Abel. *Gen.* iv. — *n.* A murderer. — **to raise Cain** *U.S. Slang* To cause a disturbance.

ca·ique (kä·ēk′) *n.* A long, narrow skiff used on the Bosporus. [< F < Ital. < Turkish *kāyik*]

cairn (kârn) *n.* A mound or heap of stones set up as a memorial or a marker. [< Scottish Gaelic *carn* heap of stones]

cais·son (kā′sən, -son) *n.* **1.** A large watertight chamber within which work is done under water, as on a bridge pier. **2.** *Naut.* A watertight device used to raise sunken ships. **3.** A two-wheeled vehicle carrying a chest of ammunition to serve a gun. [< F, aug. of *caisse* box, chest]

caisson disease *Pathol.* A painful, paralyzing, sometimes fatal disease caused by too rapid a transition from the compressed air of caissons, diving bells, etc., while the system still contains an excess of nitrogen.

ca·jole (kə·jōl′) *v.t. & v.i.* **·joled, ·jol·ing** To coax with flattery or false promises; wheedle. [< F *cajoler*] **— ca·jole′·ment** *n.* **— ca·jol′er** *n.* **— ca·jol′ing·ly** *adv.*

ca·jol·er·y (kə·jō′lər·ē) *n. pl.* **·er·ies** The act or practice of cajoling or wheedling; artful persuasion; coaxing.

Ca·jun (kā′jən) *n.* A reputed descendant of the Acadian French in Louisiana. [Alter. of ACADIAN]

cake (kāk) *n.* **1.** A mixture of flour, milk, sugar, etc., baked in various forms and generally sweeter and richer than bread. **2.** A small, usu. thin mass of dough, or other food, baked or fried: fish *cake*. **3.** A mass of matter compressed or hardened into a compact form: a *cake* of soap. **— to take the cake** *Informal* To take or deserve a prize; excel: often used sarcastically. **— v.t. & v.i.** **caked, cak·ing** To form into a hardened mass. [< ON *kaka*]

cakes and ale Pleasures of life; easy living.

cake·walk (kāk′wôk′) *n.* Formerly, a dance which American Negroes performed, a cake being awarded for the most original steps. **— v.i.** To do a cakewalk strut.

cal·a·bash (kal′ə·bash) *n.* **1.** The calabash tree. **2.** A gourd from this tree, used for making pipes, bowls, etc. [< F < Sp. *calabaza* pumpkin]

calabash tree 1. A tropical American tree of the gourd family, bearing a hard-shelled fruit. **2.** A tropical American tree of the bignonia family, with a gourdlike fruit.

cal·a·boose (kal′ə·bōōs) *n.* *U.S. Informal* A jail; lockup. [< Sp. *calabozo*]

ca·la·di·um (kə·lā′dē·əm) *n.* A tuberous tropical American herb of the arum family. [< NL < Malay *kelady*]

cal·a·mine (kal′ə·mīn, -min) *n.* A vitreous zinc carbonate, ZnCO₃, used in the form of a lotion or ointment for the treatment of skin ailments. **— v.t.** **·mined, ·min·ing** To apply calamine to. [< F < LL < L < Gk. *kadmeia* calamine]

ca·lam·i·tous (kə·lam′ə·təs) *adj.* Causing or resulting in a calamity; disastrous. **— ca·lam′i·tous·ly** *adv.*

ca·lam·i·ty (kə·lam′ə·tē) *n. pl.* **·ties 1.** A disaster. **2.** A state of great distress. [< F < L *calamitas, -tatis*]

cal·a·mus (kal′ə·məs) *n. pl.* **·mi** (-mī) **1.** The sweet flag, a plant. **2.** The quill of a feather. [< Gk. *kalamos* reed]

ca·lash (kə·lash′) *n.* **1.** A low-wheeled light carriage with folding top. **2.** A folding carriage top; also **calash top. 3.** A folding bonnet of the 18th century. [< F *calèche*]

cal·ca·ne·us (kal·kā′nē·əs) *n. pl.* **·ne·i** (-nē·ī) *Anat.* The large bone at the back of the foot: also called *heel bone.* Also **cal·ca′ne·um.** [< L (*os*) *calcaneum* heel bone < *calx* heel]

cal·car·e·ous (kal·kâr′ē·əs) *adj.* **1.** Composed of, containing, or like limestone or calcium carbonate. **2.** Containing calcium. [< L *calcarius* of lime < *calx, calcis* lime]

cal·ced·o·ny (kal·sed′ə·nē) See CHALCEDONY.

cal·ces (kal′sēz) Alternative plural of CALX.

calci- *combining form* Lime. [< L *calx, calcis* lime]

cal·cif·er·ol (kal·sif′ər·ōl, -ol) *n. Biochem.* The antirachitic vitamin D₂, a white, crystalline compound, C₂₈H₄₄O. [< CALCIFER(OUS) + (ERGOSTER)OL]

cal·cif·er·ous (kal·sif′ər·əs) *adj.* Yielding or containing calcium carbonate, as rocks.

cal·ci·fy (kal′sə·fī) *v.t. & v.i.* **·fied, ·fy·ing** To make or become stony by the deposit of lime salts. **— cal·ci·fi·ca·tion** (kal′sə·fi·kā′shən) *n.*

cal·ci·mine (kal′sə·mīn, -min) *n.* A white or tinted wash for ceilings, walls, etc. **— v.t.** **·mined, ·min·ing** To apply calcimine to. Also, *Brit.*, *distemper*: also spelled *kalsomine.* [< L *calx, calcis* lime; orig. a trade name]

cal·cin·a·to·ry (kal·sin′ə·tôr′ē, -tō′rē) *adj.* For calcining. **— n. pl. ·ries** An apparatus for calcining, as a furnace.

cal·cine (kal′sīn, -sin) *v.* **·cined, ·cin·ing** *v.t.* **1.** To render (a substance) friable by the expulsion of its volatile content through heat. **2.** To reduce to a calx by subjecting to heat. **— v.i. 3.** To become changed by dry heat into a friable powder. Also **cal′cin·ize.** [< F < Med.L *calcinare* < L *calx* lime] **— cal·ci·na·tion** (kal′sə·nā′shən) *n.*

cal·cite (kal′sīt) *n.* A widely distributed calcium carbonate mineral, white or variously tinted, including chalk, limestone, marble, etc. **— cal·cit·ic** (kal·sit′ik) *adj.*

cal·ci·um (kal′sē·əm) *n.* A silver-white, malleable, metallic element (symbol Ca), widely distributed in combination, as in chalk, gypsum, and limestone. See ELEMENT. [< NL < L *calx, calcis* lime]

calcium carbide *Chem.* A compound, CaC₂, made from quicklime and carbon and used to make acetylene.

calcium carbonate *Chem.* A compound, CaCO₃, forming the principal constituent of certain rocks and minerals, as limestone, aragonite, and calcite, and used in the preparation of lime and as the basis of dentifrices.

calcium chloride *Chem.* A white salt, CaCl₂, used as a drying agent, preservative, refrigerant, and dust preventer.

calcium hydroxide *Chem.* Slaked lime, Ca(OH)₂: when used in solution called *limewater.*

calc·spar (kalk′spär′) *n.* Crystallized carbonate of lime.

cal·cu·la·ble (kal′kyə·lə·bəl) *adj.* **1.** Capable of being calculated. **2.** Reliable; dependable. **— cal′cu·la·bly** *adv.*

cal·cu·late (kal′kyə·lāt) *v.* **·lat·ed, ·lat·ing** *v.t.* **1.** To determine by computation; arrive at by arithmetical means. **2.** To ascertain beforehand; form an estimate of. **3.** To plan or design: used chiefly in the passive: *calculated* to carry two tons. **4.** *U.S. Dial.* To think; expect. **— v.i. 5.** To compute. **— to calculate on** To depend or rely on. [< L < *calculus* pebble; with ref. to the use of pebbles in counting]

cal·cu·lat·ing (kal′kyə·lā′ting) *adj.* Inclined to reckon or estimate, esp. for one's own interests; scheming.

cal·cu·la·tion (kal′kyə·lā′shən) *n.* **1.** The act, process, or result of computing. **2.** An estimate; forecast. **3.** Forethought; prudence. **— cal·cu·la′tive** *adj.*

cal·cu·la·tor (kal′kyə·lā′tər) *n.* **1.** One who calculates. **2.** A keyboard machine that adds, subtracts, multiplies, and divides: also **calculating machine.**

cal·cu·lous (kal′kyə·ləs) *adj. Pathol.* Pertaining to or affected with a calculus or calculi. [< L *calculosus* pebbly]

cal·cu·lus (kal′kyə·ləs) | *n. pl.* **·li** (-lī) or **·lus·es 1.** *Pathol.* A stonelike mass, as in the bladder. **2.** *Math.* A method of calculating by the use of a highly specialized system of algebraic symbols. **— differential calculus** The branch of analysis that investigates the infinitesimal changes of constantly varying quantities when the relations between the quantities are given. **— integral calculus** The branch of analysis that, from the relations among the infinitesimal changes or variations of quantities, deduces relations among the quantities themselves. [< L, a pebble (used in counting)]

cal·dron (kôl′drən) See CAULDRON.

ca·lèche (kà·lesh′) *n.* A calash.

Cal·e·do·ni·a (kal′ə·dō′nē·ə, -dōn′yə) *Poetic* Scotland. [< L] **— Cal′e·do′ni·an** *adj. & n.*

cal·e·fa·cient (kal′ə·fā′shənt) *adj.* Causing heat or warmth. **— n.** *Med.* A remedy that produces heat. [< L < *calere* to be warm + *facere* to make, cause]

cal·en·dar (kal′ən·dər) *n.* **1.** Any of various systems of fixing the order, length, and subdivisions of the years and months. **2.** A table showing the days, weeks, and months of a year. **3.** A schedule or list, esp. one arranged in chronological order: a court *calendar.* **— v.t.** To place in a calendar; schedule. [< L < *calendae* calends]

— Gregorian calendar The calendar now in general use in most parts of the world; first prescribed in 1582 by Pope Gregory XIII to correct the Julian year to the astronomical year, the first being the **Old Style** (*O.S.*) date and the second being the **New Style** (*N.S.*).

— Hebrew (or **Jewish**) **calendar** A calendar used by the Jews, based on the lunar month and reckoning the year of creation as 3761 B.C. Since the Hebrew months are mostly shorter, they do not coincide in any systematic manner with those of the Gregorian calendar except by approximation.

Months	Number of days	Approximate month in Gregorian calendar
1 Tishri	30	October
2 Heshwan	29 or 30	November
3 Kislew	29 or 30	December
4 Tebet	29	January
5 Shebat	30	February
6 Adar	29 or 30	March
– Veadar¹	29	
7 Nisan	30	April
8 Iyyar	29	May
9 Sivan	30	June
10 Tammuz	29	July
11 Ab	30	August
12 Elul	29	September

¹The additional intercalary month.

— Julian calendar The calendar prescribed by Julius Caesar, in which the ordinary year had 365 days and every fourth year 366 (leap year). It is now replaced by the Gregorian calendar.

— Moslem (or **Mohammedan**) **calendar** The calendar generally used in all Moslem countries, reckoning time from July 16 A.D. 622, the day following Mohammed's flight from Mecca to Medina, and consisting of 12 lunar months.

— Republican (or **Revolutionary**) **calendar** The calendar instituted on Oct. 5, 1793, by the first French republic, and abolished Dec. 31, 1805. It divided the year into 12 months of 30 days each, with five (in leap years six) supplementary days (*sansculottides*) at the end of the last month.

— Roman calendar A lunar calendar, attributed to Numa.

The day of the new moon was the *calends*, and the day of the full moon the *ides* (the 13th or 15th of the month).

calendar year The 365, or, in leap year, 366 days from midnight of December 31 to the same hour twelve months thereafter.

cal·en·der (kalʹən·dər) *n.* A machine for giving a gloss to cloth, paper, etc., by pressing between rollers. — *v.t.* To press in a calender. [< F < L < Gk. *kylindros* roller]

cal·ends (kalʹəndz) *n.pl.* The first day of the Roman month: also spelled *kalends.* [< L *calendae*]

ca·len·du·la (kə·lenʹjoo·lə) *n.* An annual or perennial herb of the composite family, having bright orange or yellow flowers. [< NL, dim. of L *calendae* calends]

ca·les·cence (kə·lesʹəns) *n.* The condition of growing warm. [< L *calescere* to grow warm] — **ca·les·cent** *adj.*

calf¹ (kaf, käf) *n.* *pl.* **calves** (kavz, kävz) **1.** The young of the cow or various other bovine animals. **2.** The young of various mammals, as the elephant, whale, etc. **3.** Calfskin. **4.** *Informal* A gawky, witless young man. [OE *cealf*]

calf² (kaf, käf) *n.* *pl.* **calves** (kavz, kävz) The muscular rear part of the human leg below the knee. [< ON *kālfi*]

calf love *Informal* Adolescent infatuation; puppy love.

calf·skin (kafʹskin′, käfʹ-) *n.* **1.** The skin or hide of a calf. **2.** Leather made from this.

Cal·i·ban (kalʹə·ban) In Shakespeare's *Tempest*, a deformed, savage slave of Prospero.

cal·i·ber (kalʹə·bər) *n.* **1.** The internal diameter of a tube. **2.** *Mil.* **a** The internal diameter of the barrel of a gun, cannon, etc. **b** The diameter of a bullet, shell, etc. **3.** Degree of personal excellence. Also *Brit.* **cal′i·bre.** [< F *calibre*]

cal·i·brate (kalʹə·brāt) *v.t.* **·brat·ed, ·brat·ing 1.** To graduate, correct, or adjust the scale of (a measuring instrument) into appropriate units. **2.** To determine the reading of (such an instrument). **3.** To ascertain the caliber of. [Cf. F *calibrer*] — **cal′i·bra′tion** *n.* — **cal′i·bra′tor** *n.*

cal·i·ces (kalʹə·sēz) Plural of CALIX.

cal·i·co (kalʹi·kō) *n.* *pl.* **·coes** or **·cos** Cheap cotton cloth printed in a figured pattern of bright colors. — *adj.* **1.** Made of calico. **2.** Resembling printed calico; dappled or streaked: a *calico* cat. [after *Calicut*, where first obtained]

California poppy A plant of the poppy family having showy yellow flowers: the State flower of California.

cal·i·for·ni·um (kalʹə·fôrʹnē·əm) *n.* An unstable radioactive element (symbol Cf), artificially produced by bombardment of curium with alpha particles. See ELEMENT. [after the University of *California* where first produced]

ca·lig·ra·phy (kə·ligʹrə·fē) See CALLIGRAPHY.

cal·i·per (kalʹə·pər) *n.* *Usu. pl.* An instrument resembling a pair of compasses, usu. with curved legs, used for measuring diameters. Also **caliper compass.** — *v.t. & v.i.* To measure by using calipers. Also **calliper.** [< CALIBER]

ca·liph (kāʹlif, kalʹif) *n.* The spiritual and civil head of a Moslem state: also spelled *calif, kalif, kaliph, khalif.* [< F < Arabic *khalīfah* successor (to Mohammed)]

cal·i·phate (kalʹə·fāt, -fit) *n.* The office, dominion, or reign of a caliph.

cal·is·then·ics (kalʹis·thenʹiks) *n.pl.* (*construed as sing. def. 2*) **1.** Light gymnastics to promote grace and health. **2.** The science of such exercises. [<Gk. *kalli-* beautiful + *sthenos* strength] — **cal′is·then′ic** or **·i·cal** *adj.*

calk¹ (kôk) See CAULK.

calk² (kôk) *n.* **1.** A spur on a horse's shoe to prevent slipping. **2.** *U.S.* A plate with sharp points worn on the sole of a boot or shoe to prevent slipping. Also **calk′er.** — *v.t.* To furnish with calks. [Prob. < L *calx* heel]

call (kôl) *v.t.* **1.** To say in a loud voice; shout; proclaim. **2.** To summon. **3.** To convoke; convene: to *call* a meeting. **4.** To invoke solemnly. **5.** To summon to a specific work: to *call* someone to the ministry. **6.** To arouse, as from sleep. **7.** To telephone to. **8.** To summon or lure (birds or animals) by imitating their cry, whistling, etc. **9.** To name. **10.** To designate or characterize in any way. **11.** To estimate loosely; consider: I *call* it 10 pounds. **12.** To bring to action or consideration: to *call* a case to court. **13.** To insist upon payment of, as by written notice. **14.** In baseball: **a** To stop or suspend (a game). **b** To designate a point as (a ball or strike). **c** To declare (a player) out, safe, etc. **15.** In poker, to demand a show of hands by a bet equal to that of (another). **16.** In pool, etc., to predict (a shot) before making the play. — *v.i.* **17.** To raise one's voice; speak loudly. **18.** To make a brief visit, stop, or stay: with *at, on,* or *upon.* **19.** To communicate by telephone. **20.** In poker, to demand a show of hands. **21.** In some card games, to make a demand or signal, as for trumps. — **to call back 1.** To summon back; recall. **2.** To call in return, as by telephone. — **to call down 1.** To invoke from heaven. **2.** *Informal* To rebuke; reprimand. — **to call for 1.** To stop so as to obtain. **2.** To require; need. — **to call forth** To summon into action; draw out. — **to call in 1.** To collect, as debts. **2.** To retire, as currency, from circulation. **3.** To summon, as for consultation. — **to call off 1.** To summon away. **2.** To say or read aloud. **3.** To cancel. — **to call out** To shout. — **to call up 1.** To recollect. **2.** To summon. **3.** To telephone. — *n.* **1.** A shout or cry. **2.** A summons or invitation. **3.** A signal, as on a bell or horn. **4.** A demand; claim: the *call* of duty. **5.** A communication by telephone. **6.** A roll call. **7.** An inward urge to a religious vocation. **8.** A brief, often formal, visit. **9.** The cry of an animal, esp. of a bird. **10.** A whistle, etc., with which to imitate such a cry. **11.** A need; occasion: You've no *call* to do that. **12.** A request for payment. — **on call 1.** Payable on demand. **2.** Available when sent for. [< ON *kalla*]

cal·la (kalʹə) *n.* **1.** A plant of the arum family having a large white leaf that resembles a flower. Also **calla lily. 2.** A marsh plant bearing red berries in dense clusters. [< L]

call·board (kôlʹbôrd′, -bōrd′) *n.* A theater bulletin board for posting notices of rehearsals, instructions, etc.

call·boy (kôlʹboi′) *n.* **1.** A boy who calls actors to go on stage. **2.** A bellboy.

call·er (kôʹlər) *n.* **1.** One who or that which calls. **2.** One making a brief visit.

calli- For words not found here, see under CALI-.

cal·lig·ra·phy (kə·ligʹrə·fē) *n.* **1.** Beautiful penmanship. **2.** Handwriting in general. Also spelled *caligraphy.* [< Gk. < *kalos* beautiful + *graphein* to write] — **cal·lig′ra·pher, cal·lig′ra·phist** *n.* — **cal·li·graph′ic** *adj.*

call·ing (kôʹling) *n.* **1.** A speaking or crying aloud. **2.** A convocation or summons. **3.** A vocation or profession.

calling card A small card, printed or engraved with one's name, used to announce a visit or call: also *visiting card.*

cal·li·o·pe (kə·līʹə·pē, kalʹē·ōp) *n.* A musical instrument consisting of a series of steam whistles played by means of a keyboard: also called *steam organ.* [after *Calliope*]

Cal·li·o·pe (kə·līʹə·pē) The Muse of eloquence and epic poetry. [< L < Gk. < *kalos* beautiful + *ops* voice]

cal·lis·then·ics (kalʹis·thenʹiks) See CALISTHENICS.

call letters The code letters identifying a radio or television transmitting station. Also **call sign.**

call loan A loan of money to be repaid on demand.

call money Money borrowed as a call loan.

call number A classifying number employed by libraries to indicate the subject of a book and its place on the shelves.

cal·los·i·ty (kə·losʹə·tē) *n.* *pl.* **·ties 1.** *Physiol.* A callus. **2.** Callousness of feelings; insensibility.

cal·lous (kalʹəs) *adj.* **1.** Thickened and hardened, as a callus. **2.** Hardened in feelings; insensible. — *v.t. & v.i.* To make or become callous. [< L < *callus* hard skin] — **cal′lous·ly** *adv.* — **cal′lous·ness** *n.*

cal·low (kalʹō) *adj.* **1.** Inexperienced; immature. **2.** Unfledged, as a bird. [OE *calu* bare, bald]

cal·lus (kalʹəs) *n.* *pl.* **·lus·es 1.** *Physiol.* A thickened, hardened part of the skin: also called *callosity.* **2.** *Anat.* The new bony tissue between and around the fractured ends of a broken bone in the process of reuniting. **3.** *Bot.* The tissue that forms over a cut on a stem and protects the exposed wood. — *v.i.* To form a callus. [< L, hard skin]

calm (käm) *adj.* **1.** Free from agitation; still or nearly still. **2.** Not excited by passion or emotion; peaceful. — *n.* **1.** Lack of wind or motion; stillness. **2.** Serenity. — *v.t. & v.i.* To make or become quiet or calm: often with *down.* [< MF < Ital. < LL < Gk. *kauma* heat; with ref. to the midday siesta] — **calm′ly** *adv.* — **calm′ness** *n.*

— **Syn.** (*adj.*) *Calm* describes a state that may be transient; *tranquil* suggests a more enduring condition: a *calm* sea, a *tranquil* life. A *placid* person is regarded as temperamentally stolid; a *placid* lake is always peaceful. Things elevated above earthly turmoil are *serene*: a *serene* sky, a *serene* smile. *Quiet* and *still* imply absence of noise as well as of bustle.

cal·o·mel (kalʹə·mel, -məl) *n.* *Med.* Mercurous chloride, $HgCl$, a heavy, white, tasteless compound, used as a purgative, etc. [< F < Gk. *kalos* beautiful + *melas* black]

ca·lor·ic (kə·lôrʹik, -lorʹ-) *adj.* Of or pertaining to heat. — *n.* Heat. [< F < L *calor* heat] — **cal·o·ric·i·ty** (kalʹə·risʹə·tē) *n.*

cal·o·rie (kalʹə·rē) *n.* **1.** One of two recognized units of heat. The **large** or **great calorie** is the amount of heat required to raise the temperature of one kilogram of water 1° C. The **small calorie** is the amount of heat required to raise one gram of water 1° C. **2.** *Physiol.* The large calorie, a measure of the energy value of foods or the heat output of organisms. Also **cal′o·ry.** [< F < L *calor* heat]

cal·o·rif·ic (kalʹə·rifʹik) *adj.* Pertaining to or producing heat. [< F < L *calorificus*]

cal·o·rim·e·ter (kalʹə·rimʹə·tər) *n.* Any apparatus for measuring the quantity of heat generated by friction, combustion, or chemical change.

cal·o·rim·e·try (kalʹə·rimʹə·trē) *n.* The measurement of heat. — **ca·lor·i·met·ric** (kə·lôrʹə·metʹrik, -lorʹ-) or **·met·ri·cal** *adj.*

ca·lotte (kə·lotʹ) *n.* A skullcap. [< F]

cal·u·met (kalʹyə·met, kalʹyə·metʹ) *n.* A tobacco pipe with a long, ornamented stem, used by American Indians in ceremonies, to ratify treaties, etc.: also called *peace pipe*. [< dial. F, pipe stem < L *calamus* reed]

ca·lum·ni·ate (kə·lum'nē·āt) *v.t.* & *v.i.* **·at·ed, ·at·ing** To accuse falsely; defame; slander. [< L *calumnia* slander] — **ca·lum'ni·a'tion** *n.* — **ca·lum'ni·a'tor** *n.*

ca·lum·ni·ous (kə·lum'nē·əs) *adj.* Slanderous. Also **ca·lum·ni·a·to·ry** (-tôr'ē, -tōr'ē). — **ca·lum'ni·ous·ly** *adv.*

cal·um·ny (kal'əm·nē) *n. pl.* **·nies** 1. A false and malicious accusation or report, made to injure another. 2. Defamation; slander. [< MF < L *calumnia* slander]

Cal·va·ry (kal'və·rē) The place, near the site of ancient Jerusalem, where Christ was crucified; Golgotha. *Luke* xxiii 33. [< L *calvaria* skull, trans. of Aramaic *golgothā*]

calve (kav, käv) *v.t.* & *v.i.* **calved, calv·ing** To bring forth (a calf). [OE *cealfian* < *cealf* calf]

calves (kavz, kävz) Plural of CALF.

Cal·vin·ism (kal'vin·iz'əm) *n. Theol.* The system or doctrines of John Calvin, emphasizing the depravity and helplessness of man, the sovereignty of God, and predestination, and characterized by an austere moral code. — **Cal'vin·ist** *n.* — **Cal'vin·is'tic** or **·ti·cal** *adj.* — **Cal'vin·is'ti·cal·ly** *adv.*

calx (kalks) *n. pl.* **calx·es** or **cal·ces** (kal'sēz) The residue from the calcination of minerals. [< L]

cal·y·ces (kal'ə·sēz, kā'lə-) Alternative plural of CALYX.

ca·lyp·so (kə·lip'sō) *n.* An improvised song, originally Trinidadian, dealing with news, love, etc. [Origin uncertain]

Ca·lyp·so (kə·lip'sō) In the *Odyssey*, a nymph who kept Odysseus for seven years on her island.

ca·lyx (kā'liks, kal'iks) *n. pl.* **ca·lyx·es** or **cal·y·ces** (kal'ə·sēz, kā'lə-) *Bot.* The outermost series of leaflike parts of a flower; the sepals. [< L < Gk. *kalyx*, husk, pod]

cam (kam) *n. Mech.* An irregularly shaped piece or projection, as on a wheel or rotating shaft, that imparts reciprocating or variable motion to another piece bearing on it. [< Du., tooth, cog of a wheel.]

ca·ma·ra·de·rie (kä'mə·rä'dər·ē) *n.* Comradeship. [< F]

cam·a·ril·la (kam'ə·ril'ə, *Sp.* kä·mä·rē'lyä) *n.* A clique; cabal. [< Sp., dim. of *camara* chamber]

cam·ass (kam'əs) *n.* An herb of the lily family having an edible bulb. Also **cam'as.** [< Chinook jargon]

cam·ber (kam'bər) *v.t.* 1. To cut or bend to a slight upward convex form. — *v.i.* 2. To have or assume a slight upward curve, as a ship's deck. — *n.* A slight upward bend, as of a timber. [< ME < L *camera* curved roof, vault]

cam·bi·um (kam'bē·əm) *n. Bot.* A layer of tissue in exogenous plants, from which new wood and bark are formed. [< LL, exchange]

Cam·bri·a (kam'brē·ə) Medieval Latin name for WALES.

Cam·bri·an (kam'brē·ən) *adj.* 1. Of or pertaining to Cambria; Welsh. 2. *Geol.* Denoting or of the earliest of the periods of the Paleozoic era. See chart under GEOLOGY. — *n.* 1. The Cambrian strata or period. 2. A Welshman.

cam·bric (kām'brik) *n.* A fine white linen, or a similar fabric of cotton. [< Flemish *Kameryk* Cambrai]

cambric tea A drink made of sweetened hot water and milk, sometimes flavored with a little sugar.

came (kām) Past tense of COME.

cam·el (kam'əl) *n.* A large Asian or African ruminant with a humped back, used in the desert as a beast of burden. The **Arabian camel**, or dromedary, has one hump, and the **Bactrian camel** has two. [OE < L < Gk. *kamēlos* < Semitic]

cam·el·hair (kam'əl·hâr') *n.* Camel's hair.

ca·mel·lia (kə·mēl'yə, -mel'ē·ə) *n.* A tropical Asian tree or shrub with glossy leaves and white, pink, red, or variegated flowers: also called *japonica*. [< NL, after G. J. *Kamel*, 1661–1706, Jesuit traveler]

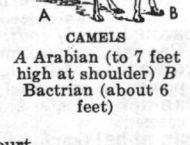
CAMELS
A Arabian (to 7 feet high at shoulder) *B* Bactrian (about 6 feet)

Cam·e·lot (kam'ə·lot) In Arthurian legend, the seat of King Arthur's court.

camel's hair 1. The hair of the camel. 2. A soft, warm, usually tan cloth made of camel's hair, sometimes mixed with wool or other fibers. — **cam·el's-hair** (kam'əlz·hâr') *adj.*

Cam·em·bert (kam'əm·bâr, *Fr.* kâ·män·bâr') *n.* A rich, creamy, soft cheese. [after *Camembert*, town in NW France]

cam·e·o (kam'ē·ō) *n. pl.* **·os** 1. A gem of differently colored layers, having a design carved in relief on one with the other layer or layers serving as background. 2. Carving done in this manner. [< Ital. *cammeo*; ult. origin unknown]

cam·er·a (kam'ər·ə, kam'rə) *n. pl.* **·er·as** for defs. 1 and 2, **·er·ae** (-ə·rē) for def. 3 1. A lightproof chamber or box for taking photographs and consisting of a sensitized plate or film on which light rays are projected through a lens. 2. *Telecom.* An enclosed unit containing the light-sensitive elec-

tron tube that converts optical images into electrical impulses for television transmission. 3. A chamber; esp. a judge's private room. — **in camera** *Law* Not in public court; privately. [< L, vaulted room < Gk. *kamara*]

cam·er·a·man (kam'ər·ə·man', kam'rə-) *n. pl.* **·men** (-men') The operator of a camera, esp. a motion-picture camera.

cam·i·sole (kam'ə·sōl) *n.* 1. A woman's fancy underwaist, worn with a sheer bodice. 2. A brief negligée. 3. A type of straitjacket. [< F < Sp. *camisola*, dim. of *camisa* shirt]

cam·o·mile (kam'ə·mīl) *n.* A strongly scented, bitter herb whose aromatic flowers and leaves are used in medicine. [< F < L < Gk. < *chamai* on the ground + *mēlon* apple]

cam·ou·flage (kam'ə·fläzh, -fläj) *n.* 1. *Mil.* Measures or material used to conceal or misrepresent the identity of installations, ships, etc. 2. Any disguise or pretense. — *v.t.* & *v.i.* **·flaged, ·flag·ing** To hide or obscure, as with disguises. [< F < *camoufler* to disguise] — **cam'ou·flag'er** *n.*

camp¹ (kamp) *n.* 1. A group of tents or other temporary shelters, as for soldiers, hunters, or vacationers. Also, the ground or area so employed. 2. The persons occupying a group of tents, etc. 3. *U.S.* A town hastily constructed near a mine. 4. Military life. 5. A body of persons supporting a policy, theory, or doctrine; also, the position so upheld. — *v.i.* 1. To set up or live in a camp; encamp. 2. To hold stubbornly to a position. — *v.t.* 3. To shelter or station in a camp. — **to camp out** To sleep in a tent; live in the open. [< MF < Ital. < L *campus* level plain]

camp² (kamp) *n.* A comical style or quality perceived in theatrical or flamboyant gestures, literary works, etc. [? < dial. E *camp* or *kemp* bold, impetuous fellow]

cam·paign (kam·pān') *n.* 1. A series of connected military operations conducted for a common objective, in a particular area, etc. 2. An organized series of activities designed to obtain a definite result. — *v.i.* To serve in, conduct, or go on a campaign. [< F < Ital. *campagna*] — **cam·paign'er** *n.*

cam·pa·ni·le (kam'pə·nē'lē, *Ital.* käm'pä·nē'lā) *n. pl.* **·les** or **·li** (-lē) A bell tower. [< Ital. < LL *campana* bell]

cam·pan·u·la (kam·pan'yə·lə) *n.* A plant having bell-shaped flowers. [< NL, dim. of LL *campana* bell]

camp chair A light, folding chair.

camp·er (kamp'ər) *n.* 1. One who camps out or is a member of a camp, as a children's summer camp. 2. A vehicle affording shelter and usu. sleeping facilities: also **camper wagon.**

cam·pes·tral (kam·pes'trəl) *adj.* Growing in or pertaining to fields or open country. [< L *campus* field]

camp·fire (kamp'fīr') *n.* 1. A fire in an outdoor camp, for cooking, warmth, etc. 2. A gathering around a campfire.

campfire girl A girl between seven and eighteen years of age, belonging to the **Camp Fire Girls of America.**

camp·ground (kamp'ground') *n.* An area used for a camp or a camp meeting.

cam·phor (kam'fər) *n.* A white, volatile, translucent crystalline compound, $C_{10}H_{16}O$, with a penetrating odor, obtained from the camphor tree, used in medicine, etc. [< Malay *kāpūr*] — **cam·phor·ic** (kam·fôr'ik, -for'-) *adj.*

cam·phor·ate (kam'fə·rāt) *v.t.* **·at·ed, ·at·ing** To treat or saturate with camphor.

camphor ball A moth ball.

camphor ice A mixture of camphor, white wax, spermaceti, and castor oil, used for chapped skin, etc.

camphor tree A large evergreen tree of eastern Asia yielding the camphor of commerce.

camp·ing (kamp'ing) *n.* The act or practice of living outdoors, as in tents or without shelter, esp. for recreation.

cam·pi·on (kam'pē·ən) *n.* One of various herbs of the pink family, as the rose campion.

camp meeting A series of religious meetings held in a grove or field, usu. in a tent; also, one such meeting.

camp·stool (kamp'stool') *n.* A light, folding stool.

cam·pus (kam'pəs) *n. U.S.* The grounds of a school or college, or the court enclosed by the buildings. [< L, field]

cam·shaft (kam'shaft', -shäft') *n.* A shaft having one or more cams on it.

can¹ (kan, *unstressed* kən) *v.* Present *3rd person sing.* **can**; past **could** A defective verb now used only in the present and past tenses as an auxiliary and having the following senses: 1. To be able to. 2. To know how to. 3. To have the right to. 4. *Informal* To be permitted to; may. [OE *cunnan*]

◆ **can, may** In informal speech and writing, *can* is now acceptable in the sense of *may*, to express permission, esp. in questions or negative statements: *Can* I leave now? You *cannot*. At the formal level, the distinction between *can* and *may* is still observed: *can*, to express ability to perform, either mentally or physically; *may*, to denote permission.

can² (kan) *n.* 1. A vessel, usu. of tinned iron, for holding or carrying liquids, garbage, etc. 2. *U.S.* A container in which fruits, tobacco, etc., are hermetically sealed. 3. *U.S.* The contents of a sealed tin container. 4. *U.S. Slang* **a** Jail. **b** A toilet. **c** The buttocks. — *v.t.* **canned, can·ning** 1. To put up in cans, jars, etc.; preserve. 2. *Slang* To record for sound or film reproduction. 3. *U.S. Slang* **a** To dismiss. **b** To cease: *Can* it! [OE *canne* cup] — **can′ner** *n.*

Ca·naan (kā′nən) The Promised Land of the Israelites.

Ca·naan·ite (kā′nən·īt) *n.* A dweller in Canaan prior to the Israelite conquest.

Canada balsam A yellowish turpentine derived from the balsam fir, used as a mounting cement in microscopy.

Canada goose The common wild goose of North America, brownish gray with black neck and head.

Canada jay A sooty gray bird of the crow family, native in Canada and the NE United States.

Canada sparrow A tree sparrow.

Ca·na·di·an (kə·nā′dē·ən) *adj.* Of or pertaining to Canada or its people. — *n.* A native or inhabitant of Canada.

Canadian English The English language as spoken and written in Canada.

Canadian French The French language as spoken and written in Canada.

CANADA GOOSE
(To 43 inches long)

Ca·na·di·an·ism (kə·nā′dē·ən·iz′əm) *n.* 1. A trait, custom, or tradition characteristic of the people of Canada or some of them. 2. A word, phrase, etc. characteristic of Canadian English or French.

ca·naille (kə·nāl′, *Fr.* kà·nä′y′) *n.* The rabble; mob. [< F < Ital. *canaglia* pack of dogs < L *canis* dog]

ca·nal (kə·nal′) *n.* 1. An artificial waterway for inland navigation, irrigation, etc. 2. *Anat.* A passage or duct; tube: the auditory *canal.* 3. *Astron.* One of the faint, linear markings visible on Mars. — *v.t.* **ca·nalled** or **·naled, ca·nal·ling** or **·nal·ing** To dig a canal through, or provide with canals. [< MF < L *canalis* groove]

canal boat A long barge, used on canals.

can·a·lic·u·late (kan′ə·lik′yə·lit, -lāt) *adj.* Channeled or grooved. Also **can′a·lic′u·lar** (-lər), **can′a·lic′u·lat′ed.**

can·a·lic·u·lus (kan′ə·lik′yə·ləs) *n.* *pl.* **·li** (-lī) *Anat.* A small tube or canal, as in a bone. [< L *canalis* groove]

ca·nal·i·za·tion (kə·nal′ə·zā′shən, kan′əl·ə-) *n.* 1. The act of making canals. 2. A system of canals.

ca·nal·ize (kə·nal′īz, kan′əl·īz) *v.t.* **·ized, ·iz·ing** 1. To convert into a canal. 2. To furnish with a canal, or a system of canals. 3. To furnish with an outlet.

can·a·pé (kan′ə·pē, -pā, *Fr.* kà·nà·pā′) *n.* A thin piece of toast or a cracker spread with cheese, caviar, etc. [< F]

ca·nard (kə·närd′, *Fr.* kà·när′) *n.* A false or absurd story or rumor; a hoax. [< F, duck]

ca·nar·y (kə·nâr′ē) *n.* *pl.* **·nar·ies** 1. A small finch having generally yellow plumage, popular as a cage bird. 2. A bright yellow color. Also **canary yellow.** 3. A sweet, white wine from the Canary Islands. [< F < Sp. < L *Canaria* (*Insula*) Dog (Island)]

ca·nas·ta (kə·nas′tə) *n.* A card game for two to six players, based on rummy. [< Sp., basket]

can·can (kan′kan′, *Fr.* kän·kän′) *n.* A fast dance with much high kicking and wild movements. [< MF, noise]

can·cel (kan′səl) *v.* **can·celed** or **·celled, can·cel·ing** or **·cel·ling** *v.t.* 1. To mark out or off, as by drawing lines through. 2. To render null and void; annul. 3. To delete or withdraw; call off. 4. To mark or otherwise deface, as a postage stamp. 5. To make up for; neutralize. 6. *Math.* To eliminate (a common factor) from the numerator and denominator of a fraction, or from both sides of an equation. — *v.i.* 7. To cancel one another: with *out.* — **Syn.** See ANNUL. — *n.* A cancellation. [< MF < L *cancellare* to cross out] — **can′cel·a·ble** or **can′cel·la·ble** *adj.* — **can′cel·er** or **can′·cel·ler** *n.*

can·cel·la·tion (kan′sə·lā′shən) *n.* 1. The act of canceling or rendering void. 2. The marks used in canceling. 3. That which is canceled. Also **can′ce·la′tion.**

can·cer (kan′sər) *n.* 1. Any of a group of often fatal diseases characterized by abnormal cellular growth and by malignancy. 2. A malignant tumor. 3. Any dangerous and spreading evil. [< L, crab] — **can′cer·ous** *adj.*

Can·cer (kan′sər) *n.* A constellation, the Crab; also, the fourth sign of the zodiac. See ZODIAC.

can·de·la·brum (kan′də·lä′brəm, -lā′/-) *n.* *pl.* **·bra** (-brə) or **·brums** A large, branched candlestick. Also **can′de·la′bra** (-brə) *pl.* **·bras.** [< L < *candela* candle]

can·des·cence (kan·des′əns) *n.* Incandescence. [< L *candere* to gleam] — **can·des′cent** *adj.* — **can·des′cent·ly** *adv.*

can·did (kan′did) *adj.* 1. Honest and open; sincere; frank. 2. Impartial; fair. [< MF < L *candere* to gleam] — **can′·did·ly** *adv.* — **can′did·ness** *n.*

can·di·da·cy (kan′də·də·sē) *n.* *pl.* **·cies** The state or position of being a candidate. Also **can·di·da·ture** (kan′də·də·chŏŏr, -dā′chər), **can′di·date·ship′** (-dit·ship′).

can·di·date (kan′də·dāt, -dit) *n.* One who seeks, or is nominated for, an office, honor, or privilege. [< L *candidus* white; because office seekers in Rome wore white togas]

candid camera A small camera with a fast lens, used for taking informal, unposed pictures.

can·died (kan′dēd) *adj.* 1. Cooked with or in sugar. 2. Crystallized or granulated. 3. Flattering; honeyed.

can·dle (kan′dəl) *n.* 1. A cylinder of tallow, wax, or other solid fat, containing a wick, that gives light when burning. 2. Anything like a candle in shape or purpose. 3. *Physics* A unit of luminous intensity now equal to that of ⅟₆₀ square centimeter of a black body operating at the temperature of solidification of platinum: also called *standard candle.* — **to hold a candle to** To compare with favorably: usually used in the negative. — *v.t.* **·dled, ·dling** To test, as eggs, by holding between the eye and a light. [OE < L *candere* to gleam]

can·dle·ber·ry (kan′dəl·ber′ē) *n.* *pl.* **·ries** 1. The wax myrtle. 2. Its fruit.

can·dle·light (kan′dəl·līt′) *n.* Light given by a candle; artificial light. 2. Twilight.

Can·dle·mas (kan′dəl·məs) *n.* February 2, the feast of the Purification, or of the Presentation of Christ in the temple.

can·dle·pow·er (kan′dəl·pou′ər) *n.* The illuminating power of a standard candle, used as a measure.

can·dle·stick (kan′dəl·stik′) *n.* A holder with sockets or spikes for a candle or candles.

can·dle·wick (kan′dəl·wik′) *n.* The wick of a candle.

can·dor (kan′dər) *n.* 1. Openness; frankness. 2. Impartiality; fairness. Also *Brit.* **can′dour.** [< L, sincerity]

can·dy (kan′dē) *n.* *pl.* **·dies** Any of numerous confections consisting chiefly of sugar or syrup, usu. with chocolate, nuts, fruits, etc., added; also, such confections collectively: usu. called *sweets* in Great Britain. — *v.* **·died, ·dy·ing** *v.t.* 1. To cause to form into crystals of sugar. 2. To preserve by boiling or coating with sugar. 3. To render pleasant; sweeten. — *v.i.* 4. To become covered with sugar. [< Arabic *qandī* made of sugar < *qand* sugar, ult. < Skt.]

cane (kān) *n.* 1. A walking stick. 2. The jointed, woody stem of the bamboo, rattan, and certain palm trees, used as a weaving material in chairs, etc. 3. Sugar cane. 4. The stem of a raspberry or allied plant. 5. Any rod, especially one used for flogging. — *v.t.* **caned, can·ing** 1. To strike or beat with a cane. 2. To make or repair with cane, as a chair. [< OF < L < Gk. *kanna* reed] — **can′er** *n.*

cane·brake (kān′brāk′) *n.* A thick growth of cane.

cane sugar Sucrose obtained from the sugar cane.

ca·nine (kā′nīn) *adj.* 1. Of or like a dog. 2. *Zool.* Of the dog family. 3. Of or pertaining to a canine tooth. — *n.* 1. A dog or other canine animal. 2. *Anat.* One of the four pointed teeth situated one on either side of the upper and lower incisors. For illus. see TOOTH. [< L *canis* dog]

Ca·nis Ma·jor (kā′nis mā′jər) A constellation containing the bright star Sirius. [< L, greater dog]

Canis Mi·nor (mī′nər) A constellation containing the bright star Procyon. [< L, lesser dog]

can·is·ter (kan′is·ter) *n.* 1. A container, usu. metal, for tea, spices, etc. 2. Formerly, fragments in a metallic cylinder, to be fired from a cannon: also **canister shot.** [< L *canistrum* basket]

can·ker (kang′kər) *n.* 1. *Pathol.* An ulceration, chiefly of the mouth and lips. 2. Anything that causes corruption, evil, decay, etc. 3. A disease of trees, causing decay of the bark and wood. — *v.t.* 1. To affect with canker. 2. To eat away like a canker. — *v.i.* 3. To become infected with canker. [< AF < L *cancer* crab] — **can′ker·ous** *adj.*

can·ker·worm (kang′kər·wûrm′) *n.* Any of several insect larvae that destroy fruit and shade trees.

can·na (kan′ə) *n.* An erect, mostly tropical American plant with red or yellow irregular flowers. [< L < Gk. *kanna* reed] — **can·na·ceous** (kə·nā′shəs) *adj.*

canned (kand) *adj.* 1. Preserved in a can or jar. 2. *Slang* Recorded: *canned* music.

can·nel (kan′əl) *n.* A bituminous coal with low heating power. Also **cannel coal.**

can·ner·y (kan′ər·ē) *n.* *pl.* **·ner·ies** A place where foods are canned.

can·ni·bal (kan′ə·bəl) *n.* 1. One who eats human flesh. 2. An animal that devours its own species. — *adj.* Of or like cannibals. [< Sp. *Canibales,* var. of *Caribes* Caribs]

can·ni·bal·ism (kan′ə·bəl·iz′əm) *n.* 1. The act or practice of eating the flesh of one's own kind. 2. Inhuman cruelty. — **can′ni·bal·is′tic** *adj.* — **can′ni·bal·is′ti·cal·ly** *adv.*

can·ni·bal·ize (kan′ə·bəl·īz′) *v.t.* **·ized, ·iz·ing** *Mil.* To take parts from (damaged tanks, etc.) in order to repair others.

can·ni·kin (kan′ə·kin) *n.* 1. A small can. 2. A wooden pail.

can·ning (kan′ing) *n.* The act, process, or business of preserving foods in hermetically sealed tin cans, glass jars, etc.

can·non (kan′ən) *n.* *pl.* **·nons** or **·non** 1. *Mil.* A large tubular weapon, usu. mounted on a fixed or mobile carriage, that discharges a projectile by the use of an explosive. 2. The large bone between the fetlock and knee or hock of the horse and allied animals. Also **cannon bone.** 3. *Brit.* A carom. — *v.i.* 1. To fire cannon. 2. *Brit.* To carom. — *v.t.* 3. To attack with cannon shot. **4.** *Brit.* To cause to carom. [< OF < Ital. *canna* tube, pipe]

can·non·ade (kan/ən-ād/) *v.* **·ad·ed, ·ad·ing** *v.t.* **1.** To attack with cannon shot. —*v.i.* **2.** To fire cannon repeatedly. —*n.* A continued discharge of or attack with cannon.

cannon ball A spherical solid shot fired from a cannon.

can·non·eer (kan/ən-ir/) *n.* An artillery gunner.

cannon fodder Soldiers considered as that which is consumed by war.

can·not (kan/ot, ka·not/) The negative of the auxiliary verb CAN: written *can not* for emphasis. —**cannot but** Have no alternative except to.

can·ny (kan/ē) *adj.* *Originally Scot.* **·ni·er, ·ni·est 1.** Cautiously shrewd. **2.** Frugal; thrifty. **3.** Skillful. —*adv.* In a canny manner. —**can/ni·ly** *adv.* —**can/ni·ness** *n.*

ca·noe (kə·nōō/) *n.* A small, long, narrow boat, pointed at both ends, and propelled by paddles. —*v.* **·noed, ·noe·ing** *v.t.* **1.** To convey by canoe. —*v.i.* **2.** To paddle, sail, or travel in a canoe. [< Sp. *canoa*] —**ca·noe/ist** *n.*

can·on¹ (kan/ən) *n.* **1.** A rule or law; esp., a rule or body of rules of faith and practice enacted by a church council. **2.** An established rule; principle. **3.** A standard for judgment; criterion. **4.** The books of the Bible. **5.** The sacred books of any sect or religion. **6.** A list, as of the recognized works of an author. **7.** The list of canonized saints. **8.** *Often cap. Eccl.* The portion of the Mass between the Sanctus and the Lord's Prayer. **9.** *Music* A composition or passage in which one or more voices follow and imitate the melody of the first voice. [OE < L < Gk. *kanōn* rule, straight rod]

can·on² (kan/ən) *n.* A member of the chapter of a cathedral or collegiate church. [See CANON¹.]

ca·ñon (kan/yən, *Sp.* kän·yōn/) See CANYON.

can·on·ess (kan/ən·is) *n.* A member of a religious community of women living under a rule but not under vows.

ca·non·i·cal (kə·non/i·kəl) *adj.* **1.** Relating or conforming to or prescribed by, a canon or canons. **2.** Of or contained in the canon of Scripture. **3.** Authoritative; recognized. Also **ca·non/ic.** —**ca·non/i·cal·ly** *adv.*

canonical hours *Eccl.* The seven daily periods, fixed by canon, for prayer and devotion: also called *Divine Office.*

ca·non·i·cals (kə·non/i·kəlz) *n.pl.* The habits or robes prescribed by canon to be worn by the clergy when officiating.

can·on·ist (kan/ən·ist) *n.* One skilled in canon law. —**can/on·is/tic** or **·ti·cal** *adj.*

can·on·ize (kan/ən·īz) *v.t.* **·ized, ·iz·ing 1.** To declare (a deceased person) to be a saint. **2.** To recognize as part of the canon of Scripture. **3.** To sanction as being conformable to church canons. **4.** To glorify. —**can/on·i·za/tion** *n.*

canon law The ecclesiastical laws of a Christian church.

can·on·ry (kan/ən·rē) *n.* *pl.* **·ries 1.** The office, dignity, or benefice of a canon. **2.** Canons collectively. Also **can/on·ship.**

Ca·no·pus (kə·nō/pəs) *n.* One of the 20 brightest stars, 0.86 magnitude; Alpha in the constellation Carina. [< L]

can·o·py (kan/ə·pē) *n.* *pl.* **·pies 1.** A covering suspended over a throne, bed, shrine, etc., or held over a person. **2.** Any covering overhead, as the sky. **3.** *Archit.* An ornamental covering over a niche, altar, or tomb. **4.** *Aeron.* The main lifting surface of a parachute. —*v.t.* **·pied, ·py·ing** To cover with or as with a canopy. [< MF < L < Gk. *kōnōpeion* bed with mosquito net]

canst (kanst) Archaic second person singular, present tense of CAN¹: used with *thou.*

cant¹ (kant) *n.* **1.** An inclination from the vertical or horizontal; a slope or tilt. **2.** A sudden motion that tilts or overturns. **3.** An outer corner or angle. **4.** A slant surface, as one produced by cutting off a corner or edge. —*v.t.* **1.** To set slantingly; tilt. **2.** To give a bevel to. **3.** To throw out or off; jerk; toss. —*v.i.* **4.** To tilt; slant. —*adj.* **1.** Oblique; slanting. **2.** Having canted sides or corners. [Prob. < OF < Med.L *cantus* corner, side]

cant² (kant) *n.* **1.** Insincere religious or moralistic talk. **2.** Phraseology used merely for effect; stock phrases. **3.** Words or phraseology peculiar to a sect, class, or calling: *legal cant.* **4.** The secret jargon of thieves, gypsies, etc.; argot. **5.** Whining speech, esp. of beggars. —*v.i.* To use cant. —*adj.* Having the character of cant; hypocritical. [< AF < L < *canere* to sing] —**cant/er** *n.*

can't (kant, känt) Cannot.

can·ta·bi·le (kän·tä/bē·lā) *Music adj.* Melodious; flowing. —*n.* Music characterized by flowing melody. [< Ital.]

Can·ta·brig·i·an (kan/tə·brij/ē·ən) *adj.* Of or pertaining to Cambridge, England, or Cambridge University. —*n.* A resident of Cambridge, England; also, a student or graduate of Cambridge University. [< LL *Cantabrigia* Cambridge]

can·ta·loupe (kan/tə·lōp) *n.* A muskmelon having a ribbed, warty rind and sweet, orange flesh. Also **can/ta·loup.** [< F, after *Cantalupo,* Italian castle where first grown]

can·tank·er·ous (kan·tang/kər·əs) *adj.* Quarrelsome; ill

natured; perverse. [Prob. akin to ME *contak* strife] —**can·tank/er·ous·ly** *adv.* —**can·tank/er·ous·ness** *n.*

can·ta·ta (kən·tä/tə) *n.* *Music* A vocal composition in the style of a drama, to be sung but not acted. [< Ital.]

can·teen (kan·tēn/) *n.* **1.** A small, usu. metal flask for carrying water or other liquids. **2.** A shop at a military camp where soldiers can buy provisions, refreshments, etc. **3.** A place for refreshments. [< F < Ital. *cantina* cellar]

can·ter (kan/tər) *n.* A moderate, easy gallop. —*v.t. & v.i.* To ride or go at a canter. [Short for *Canterbury gallop;* with ref. to the pace of pilgrims riding to Canterbury]

Canterbury bell One of various cultivated bellflowers.

Canterbury Tales An uncompleted work (1387–1400) by Chaucer, consisting of a series of tales, largely in verse, told by a group of pilgrims on their way to Canterbury.

cant hook A lever equipped with an adjustable hook for handling logs. Also **cant·dog** (kant/dôg/, -dog/).

can·thus (kan/thəs) *n.* *pl.* **·thi** (-thī) *Anat.* The angle at the junction of the eyelids. [< Gk. *kanthos*]

can·ti·cle (kan/ti·kəl) *n.* A nonmetrical hymn, said or chanted in church. [< L *canticum* song]

Canticle of Can·ti·cles (kan/ti·kəlz) In the Bible, the Song of Solomon.

can·ti·lev·er (kan/tə·lev/ər, -lē/vər) *n.* **1.** *Engin.* A long structural member, as a truss, beam, or slab, lying across a support with the projecting arms in balance. **2.** *Archit.* Any structural part projecting horizontally and anchored at one end only. —*v.t. & v.i.* To project (a building member) outward and in balance beyond the base. [Origin uncertain]

CANTILEVER BRIDGE
(Section of Queensboro Bridge, New York City)

cantilever bridge A bridge formed by the meeting of two freely projecting beams, trusses, etc.

can·tle (kan/təl) *n.* The hind part of a saddle, projecting upward. [< AF < Med.L *cantus* corner]

can·to (kan/tō) *n.* *pl.* **·tos** A division of an extended poem. [< Ital. < L *cantus* song]

can·ton (kan/tən, -ton, kan·ton/; *for v. def. 2* kan·ton/, -tōn/, -tōōn/) *n.* A district; esp., one of the states of Switzerland, or a subdivision of an arrondissement in France. —*v.t.* **1.** To divide into cantons or districts. **2.** To assign quarters to, as troops. [< OF] —**can·ton·al** (kan/tən·ol) *adj.*

Can·ton·ese (kan/tən·ēz/, -ēs/) *n.* *pl.* **·ese 1.** A native of Canton, China. **2.** The Chinese language spoken in parts of southern China.

Canton flannel (kan/tən) A heavy cotton flannel.

can·ton·ment (kan·ton/mənt, -tōn/-, -tōōn/-, kan/tən·mənt) *n.* The assignment of troops to temporary quarters; also, such quarters. [< F *cantonner* to quarter]

can·tor (kan/tər, -tôr) *n.* **1.** The chief liturgical singer in a synagogue. **2.** A precentor, or chief singer. [< L]

can·vas (kan/vəs) *n.* **1.** A heavy, closely woven cloth of hemp, flax, or cotton, used for sails, tents, etc. **2.** A piece of such material on which to paint, esp. in oils. **3.** A painting on canvas. **4.** Sailcloth. **5.** Sails collectively. **6.** A tent, esp. a circus tent. —**under canvas 1.** With sails set. **2.** In tents. [< AF, ult. < L *cannabis* hemp]

can·vas·back (kan/vəs·bak/) *n.* A sea duck of North America, having a grayish white back.

can·vass (kan/vəs) *v.t.* **1.** To go about (a region) or among (persons) to solicit votes, opinions, etc. **2.** To scrutinize. —*v.i.* **3.** To go about seeking votes, opinions, etc. —*n.* **1.** A solicitation of votes, orders, etc., often to determine the public's attitude toward a candidate, a product, etc. **2.** A detailed examination or discussion. [< CANVAS; with ref. to its early use for sifting] —**can/vass·er** *n.*

can·yon (kan/yən) *n.* A deep gorge or ravine, with steep sides: also spelled *cañon.* [< Sp. *cañón*]

caout·chouc (kōō/chōōk, kou·chōōk/) *n.* Rubber; esp., crude rubber. [< F < Tupi *cahuchu*]

cap (kap) *n.* **1.** A covering for the head, usu. snug, brimless, and of soft material. **2.** Any headgear designed to denote rank, function, membership, etc. **3.** Something suggesting a cap in form, function, or position. **4.** A primer, as of a cartridge. —**to set one's cap for** To try to win as a suitor or husband. —*v.t.* **capped, cap·ping 1.** To put a cap on; cover. **2.** To serve as a cap or cover to; lie on top of. **3.** To add the final touch to. **4.** To excel. —**to cap the climax** To surpass the climax. [OE < LL, prob. < L *caput* head]

ca·pa·bil·i·ty (kā/pə·bil/ə·tē) *n.* *pl.* **·ties 1.** The quality of being capable; capacity or ability. **2.** *Usu. pl.* Qualities that may be used or developed; potentialities.

ca·pa·ble (kā/pə·bəl) _adj._ Having ability; competent. — **capable of 1.** Having the capacity or qualities needed for. **2.** Susceptible to. [< F < LL < L _capere_ to take] — **ca/pa·ble·ness** _n._ — **ca/pa·bly** _adv._

ca·pa·cious (kə·pā/shəs) _adj._ Able to contain much; roomy. [< L < _capere_ to take] — **ca·pa/cious·ly** _adv._ — **ca·pa/cious·ness** _n._

ca·pac·i·tance (kə·pas/ə·təns) _n. Electr._ The property of a circuit or body that permits it to store an electrical charge. — **ca·pac/i·tive** (-tiv) _adj._

ca·pac·i·tate (kə·pas/ə·tāt) _v.t._ **·tat·ed, ·tat·ing 1.** To render capable. **2.** To qualify according to law.

ca·pac·i·tor (kə·pas/ə·tər) _n. Electr._ A device consisting of conductors isolated in a dielectric medium, with each of them attached to only one side of a circuit, used to increase the capacitance to a desired value: also called _condenser._

ca·pac·i·ty (kə·pas/ə·tē) _n. pl._ **·ties 1.** Ability to receive, contain, or absorb. **2.** Maximum ability to hold, contain, etc. **3.** Adequate mental power to understand, act. **4.** The ability or aptitude to do something: with _for, of,_ or the infinitive. **5.** Specific position or office. **6.** Legal qualification. **7.** Maximum output or production. **8.** _Electr._ Capacitance. [< MF < L < _capax_ able to hold]

cap and bells A jester's cap ornamented with little bells.

cap and gown Ceremonial academic garb consisting of a cap or mortarboard and a characteristic robe or gown.

cap-a-pie (kap/ə·pē/) _adv._ From head to foot. Also **cap/à·pie/.** [< OF]

ca·par·i·son (kə·par/ə·sən) _n._ **1.** An ornamental covering for a horse. **2.** Rich apparel or trappings. — _v.t._ To clothe richly. [< OF < Sp., ult. < LL _cappa_ cape]

cape¹ (kāp) _n._ A point of land extending into the sea or a lake. [< F _cap,_ ult. < L _caput_ head]

cape² (kāp) _n._ A sleeveless garment fastened at the neck and hanging loosely from the shoulders. [< F < LL _cappa_]

cap·e·lin (kap/ə·lin) _n. pl._ **·lin** or **·lins** _U.S. & Canadian_ A small, edible fish of northern seas, much used as bait. Also **cap/e·lan.** [< dial. F (Canadian) _capelan_ < F]

Ca·pel·la (kə·pel/ə) _n._ One of the 20 brightest stars, 0.21 magnitude, in the constellation Auriga. [< L, she-goat]

ca·per¹ (kā/pər) _n._ **1.** A playful leap; a skip. **2.** A wild prank; antic. — **to cut a caper** (or **capers**) To caper; frolic. — _v.i._ To leap playfully. [Short for CAPRIOLE] — **ca/per·er** _n._

ca·per² (kā/pər) _n._ **1.** The flower bud of a low shrub of Mediterranean countries, pickled and used as a condiment. **2.** The shrub itself. [< L < Gk. _kapparis_]

cap·er·cail·lie (kap/ər·kāl/yē) _n._ A large, black European grouse. Also **cap/er·cail/zie** (-yē, -zē) [Alter. of Gaelic _capullcoille,_ lit., horse of the wood]

Ca·pe·tian (kə·pē/shən) _adj._ Of or belonging to the dynasty (987–1328) founded in France by Hugh Capet.

ca·pi·as (kā/pē·əs, kap/ē·əs) _n. pl._ **·as·es** _Law_ A judicial writ commanding an officer to take and hold in custody the person named therein. [< L, you may take]

cap·il·lar·i·ty (kap/ə·lar/ə·tē) _n. pl._ **·ties 1.** The state of being capillary. **2.** _Physics_ A form of surface tension between the molecules of a liquid and those of a solid. When the adhesive force is stronger (**capillary attraction**) the liquid will tend to rise in a capillary tube; when cohesion dominates (**capillary repulsion**), the liquid tends to fall. [< F]

cap·il·lar·y (kap/ə·ler/ē) _adj._ **1.** Of, pertaining to, or like hair; fine. **2.** Having a hairlike bore, as a tube or vessel. — _n. pl._ **·lar·ies 1.** _Anat._ A minute vessel, as those connecting the arteries and veins. **2.** Any tube with a fine bore. [< L _capillus_ hair]

cap·i·ta (kap/ə·tə) Plural of CAPUT.

cap·i·tal¹ (kap/ə·təl) _n._ **1.** The city or town that is the seat of government of a country, state, etc. **2.** A capital letter. **3.** The total amount of money or property owned or used by an individual or corporation. **4.** Wealth in any form employed in or available for the production of more wealth. **5.** In accounting, the net worth of a business after the deduction of all liabilities. **6.** Possessors of wealth as a class. — **to make capital of** To turn to advantage. — _adj._ **1.** Chief, as comprising the seat of government. **2.** Standing at the head; principal. **3.** Of or pertaining to funds or capital. **4.** Of the first quality. **5.** Punishable by or involving the death penalty. **6.** Very injurious; grave. [< OF < L < _caput_ head]

cap·i·tal² (kap/ə·təl) _n. Archit._ The upper member of a column or pillar. [< L _caput_ head]

capital expenditure Expenditure for permanent additions or improvements to property.

capital gain Profit from the sale of capital investments, such as stocks, real estate, etc.

cap·i·tal·ism (kap/ə·təl·iz/əm) _n._ **1.** An economic system in which the means of production and distribution are mostly privately owned and operated for private profit. **2.** The possession of private capital and its resulting power.

cap·i·tal·ist (kap/ə·təl·ist) _n._ **1.** An owner of capital; esp.

one who has large means employed in productive enterprise. **2.** Loosely, any person of wealth. **3.** A supporter of capitalism. — **cap/i·tal·is/tic** _adj._ — **cap/i·tal·is/ti·cal·ly** _adv._

cap·i·tal·i·za·tion (kap/ə·təl·ə·zā/shən, -ī·zā/-) _n._ **1.** The act or process of capitalizing. **2.** A sum arrived at by capitalizing. **3.** The total capital employed in a business.

cap·i·tal·ize (kap/ə·təl·īz/) _v._ **·ized, ·iz·ing** _v.t._ **1.** To begin with capital letters, or print or write in capital letters. **2.** To convert into capital. **3.** To provide capital for; organize on a basis of capital. **4.** To estimate the worth of (a business or stock) from earnings or potential earnings. **5.** In accounting, to record (expenses) as assets. — _v.i._ **6.** To acquire an advantage; profit: with _on_ or _by._ **7.** To accumulate capital.

capital letter The form of a letter used at the beginning of a sentence, with proper names, etc., as the A in Africa.

cap·i·tal·ly (kap/ə·təl·ē) _adv._ In a capital or excellent way.

capital punishment The death penalty for a crime.

capital ship A warship of large size, as a battleship or aircraft carrier, carrying guns of over 8-inch caliber.

capital stock 1. The amount of stock a corporation is authorized to issue. **2.** The total face value of such stock.

cap·i·ta·tion (kap/ə·tā/shən) _n._ An assessment on each person (or head); poll tax. [< LL < L _caput_ head]

cap·i·tol (kap/ə·təl) _n._ The building in which a State legislature convenes; a statehouse.

Cap·i·tol (kap/ə·təl) **1.** The official building of the U.S. Congress in Washington, D.C. **2.** The temple of Jupiter Capitolinus in ancient Rome. [< L _Capitolium_ the Capitoline]

ca·pit·u·lar (kə·pich/ŏo·lər) _adj._ Of or pertaining to an ecclesiastical chapter. [< Med.L _capitulum_ chapter]

ca·pit·u·late (kə·pich/ŏo·lāt) _v.i._ **·lat·ed, ·lat·ing 1.** To surrender on stipulated terms. **2.** To surrender. [< L _capitulare_ to draw up in chapters] — **ca·pit/u·la/tor** _n._

ca·pit·u·la·tion (kə·pich/ŏo·lā/shən) _n._ **1.** The act of surrendering conditionally; also, the instrument containing the terms of surrender. **2.** A surrender or giving up; yielding. **3.** A summary of a subject. — **ca·pit·u·la·to·ry** (kə·pich/ŏo·lə·tôr/ē, -tō/rē) _adj._

cap·lin (kap/lin) See CAPELIN.

ca·pon (kā/pon, -pən) _n._ A rooster gelded to improve the flesh for eating. [OE < L _capo, -onis_]

ca·pote (kə·pōt/) _n._ **1.** A hooded cloak or overcoat. **2.** A bonnet worn by women. [< F, dim. of _cape_ hood]

ca·pric·ci·o (kə·prē/chē·ō, _Ital._ kä·prēt/chō) _n. pl._ **·ci·os** or _Ital._ **ca·pric·ci** (kä·prēt/chē) **1.** _Music_ A composition of lively and spirited mood, fancifully irregular in form. **2.** A prank; also, a caprice. [< Ital., whim < _capro_ goat < L _caper_]

ca·price (kə·prēs/) _n._ **1.** A sudden change of mind or action without adequate motive; a whim. **2.** A tendency to make such changes; capriciousness. **3.** _Music_ A capriccio. [< F < Ital. _capriccio_ whim]

ca·pri·cious (kə·prish/əs) _adj._ Characterized by or resulting from caprice; fickle; whimsical. — **ca·pri/cious·ly** _adv._ — **ca·pri/cious·ness** _n._

Cap·ri·corn (kap/rə·kôrn) _n._ A constellation, the Goat; also, the tenth sign of the zodiac. See ZODIAC. Also **Cap/ri·cor/nus** (-kôr/nəs). [< L < _caper_ goat + _cornu_ horn]

cap·ri·ole (kap/rē·ōl) _n._ **1.** A leap made by a trained horse, with all feet off the ground and no forward motion. **2.** A leap. — _v.i._ **·oled, ·ol·ing** To perform a capriole. [< F, leap]

caps or **caps.** _Printing_ Capital letters.

cap·si·cum (kap/si·kəm) _n._ **1.** An herb or shrub of the nightshade family, producing pods prepared as condiments or gastric stimulants. **2.** The fruit of these plants; red pepper. [< L _capsa_ box (from the shape of the fruit)]

cap·size (kap·sīz/, kap/sīz) _v.t. & v.i._ **·sized, ·siz·ing** To upset or overturn. [? < Sp. _capuzar_ to sink a ship by the head]

cap·stan (kap/stən) _n. Naut._ A drumlike apparatus, turned by bars or levers, for hoisting anchors by exerting traction upon a cable. [< F _cabestan,_ ult. < L _capere_ to hold]

capstan bar A lever used in turning a capstan.

cap·stone (kap/stōn/) _n._ Copestone.

cap·su·late (kap/sə·lāt, -syŏō-) _adj._ In or formed into a capsule. Also **cap/su·lat/ed.** — **cap/su·la/tion** _n._

cap·sule (kap/səl, -syŏol) _n._ **1.** A small container, usu. made of gelatin, for a dose of medicine. **2.** A detachable part of an airplane, rocket, etc., containing the pilot, instruments, etc. **3.** A thin covering or seal, as over the cork of a bottle. **4.** _Bot._ **a** A dry seed vessel made up of more than one carpel. **b** The spore case of a cryptogam. **5.** _Anat._ A fibrous or membranous structure that envelops some part of the body. — _adj._ In concise form; condensed. [< F < L _capsula,_ dim. of _capsa_ box] — **cap/su·lar** _adj._

cap·tain (kap/tən, -tin) _n._ **1.** One at the head or in command; a chief; leader. **2.** The master or commander of a vessel. **3.** _Mil._ A commissioned officer ranking below a major. See tables at GRADE. **4.** _Naval_ A commissioned officer ranking below a commodore or rear admiral. See tables at GRADE. **5.** A member of a team designated as its leader. — _v.t._ To act as captain to; command; lead. [< OF < LL < L _caput_ head] — **cap/tain·cy, cap/tain·ship** _n._

captain's walk A widow's walk.
cap·tion (kap/shən) *n.* **1.** A heading, as of a chapter, document, or newspaper article. **2.** The title and descriptive matter for an illustration. **3.** A subtitle in a motion picture. — *v.t.* To provide a caption for. [< L *capere* to take]
cap·tious (kap/shəs) *adj.* **1.** Apt to find fault; disposed to criticize. **2.** Designed to ensnare or perplex: a *captious* question. [< L *captiosus* fallacious] — **cap/tious·ly** *adv.* — **cap/tious·ness** *n.*
cap·ti·vate (kap/tə·vāt) *v.t.* **·vat·ed, ·vat·ing** To enthrall; fascinate; charm. [< LL *captivare* to capture] — **cap/ti·va/tion** *n.* — **cap/ti·va/tor** *n.*
cap·tive (kap/tiv) *n.* **1.** One who or that which is captured and held in confinement; a prisoner. **2.** One enthralled by beauty, passion, etc. — *adj.* **1.** Taken or held prisoner, as in war. **2.** Held in restraint; confined: a *captive* balloon. **3.** Captivated. **4.** Of or pertaining to a captive or captivity. [< F < L *capere* to take]
captive audience *U.S.* A group of people forced by circumstances to listen to something.
cap·tiv·i·ty (kap·tiv/ə·tē) *n. pl.* **·ties** The state of being held captive; thralldom.
cap·tor (kap/tər) *n.* One who takes or holds captive.
cap·ture (kap/chər) *v.t.* **·tured, ·tur·ing 1.** To take by force, stratagem, etc., as in war. **2.** To gain or win, as in competition. — *n.* **1.** The act of capturing; seizure. **2.** The person or thing captured. [< MF < L *capere* to take]
cap·u·chin (kap/yŏŏ·chin, -shin) *n.* **1.** A woman's hooded cloak. **2.** A long-tailed South American monkey whose head is covered with a cowl-like growth of hair. [< MF <I tal. *cappa* head]
Cap·u·chin (kap/yŏŏ·chin, -shin) *n.* A member of a branch of the Franciscan order.
ca·put (kā/pət, kap/ət) *n. pl.* **cap·i·ta** (kap/ə·tə) A head or headline part. [< L]
car (kär) *n.* **1.** An automobile. **2.** A vehicle for use on rails. **3.** *Brit.* Any of various wheeled vehicles. **4.** *Poetic* A chariot. **5.** *U.S.* The enclosed platform of an elevator. [< AF < LL < L *carrus* wagon]
ca·ra·ba·o (kä/rə·bä/ō) *n. pl.* **·ba·os** or **·ba·o** In the Philippines, the water buffalo. [< Sp. < Malay *karbau*]
car·a·bin (kar/ə·bin), **car·a·bine** (-bīn) See CARBINE.
car·a·bin·eer (kar/ə·bin·ir/), **car·a·bin·ier** See CARBINEER.
ca·ra·ca·ra (kä/rə·kä/rə) A large, vulturelike hawk found in South America and southern U.S. [< Sp. *caracará*]
car·ack (kar/ək) See CARRACK.
car·a·cole (kar/ə·kōl) *n.* A half turn to the right or left made by a horseman's mount in riding. — *v.i.* **·coled, ·col·ing** To perform caracoles; wheel. Also **car/a·col** (-kol). [< F < Ital. < Sp. *caracol* snail shell]
car·a·cul (kar/ə·kəl) See KARAKUL.
ca·rafe (kə·raf/, -räf/) *n.* A glass water bottle. [< F]
car·a·mel (kar/ə·məl, -mel, kär/məl) *n.* **1.** A chewy confection composed of sugar, butter, milk, etc. **2.** Burnt sugar, used to flavor foods. [< OF < Med.L *canna mellis* sugar cane]
car·a·mel·ize (kar/ə·məl·īz/, kär/məl-) *v.t. & v.i.* **·ized, ·iz·ing** To convert into caramel. — **car/a·mel·i·za/tion** *n.*
car·a·pace (kar/ə·pās) *n. Zool.* A hard, bony, or chitinous outer case or covering, as of a turtle or lobster. Also **car/a·pax** (-paks). [< F < Sp. *carapacho*]
car·at (kar/ət) *n.* **1.** A unit of weight for gems, one metric carat being 200 milligrams, or 3.086 grains. **2.** Loosely, a karat. [< F < Ital. < Arabic < Gk. *keration* seed]
car·a·van (kar/ə·van) *n.* **1.** A company of traders, pilgrims, or the like, traveling together, esp. across deserts. **2.** A number of vehicles traveling together. **3.** A large, covered vehicle; a van. [< F < Persian *kārwān* caravan]
car·a·van·sa·ry (kar/ə·van/sə·rē) *n. pl.* **·ries 1.** In Oriental countries, an inn enclosing a court for sheltering caravans. **2.** Any hostelry or inn. Also **car/a·van/se·rai** (-rī, -rā). [< F < Persian *kārwān* caravan + *sarāī* inn]
car·a·vel (kar/ə·vel) *n.* A small ship of the 15th and 16th centuries, used esp. by the Portuguese and Spanish. Also **car/a·velle**. [< MF < Sp. *caraba* boat]
car·a·way (kar/ə·wā) *n.* An herb of the parsley family having small, spicy seeds (**caraway seeds**), used for flavoring. [< Sp. < Arabic *karwiyā* caraway]
car·bide (kär/bīd, -bid) *n. Chem.* A compound of carbon with a more electropositive element.
car·bine (kär/bīn, -bēn) *n.* **1.** A light, short-barreled rifle originally devised for mounted troops: also *carabin, carabine.* **2.** *U.S. Mil.* A semi-automatic and now automatic, gas-operated, .30-caliber rifle. [Earlier *carabine* < F]
car·bi·neer (kär/bə·nir/) *n.* A soldier armed with a carbine: also *carabineer, carabinier.*
carbo- *combining form* Carbon: *carbohydrate.* Also, before vowels, **carb-**. [< L *carbo* coal]
car·bo·hy·drate (kär/bō·hī/drāt) *n. Biochem.* Any of

a group of compounds containing carbon combined with hydrogen and oxygen, and including sugars, starches, and cellulose.
car·bo·lat·ed (kär/bə·lā/tid) *adj.* Containing carbolic acid.
carbolic acid (kär·bol/ik) *Chem.* Phenol.
car·bo·lize (kär/bə·līz) *v.t.* **·lized, ·liz·ing** *Chem.* To treat or impregnate with carbolic acid.
car·bon (kär/bən) *n.* **1.** A nonmetallic element (symbol C) found in all organic substances and in some inorganic substances, as diamonds, graphite, coal, charcoal, lampblack, etc. See ELEMENT. **2.** *Electr.* **a** A rod of carbon, used as an electrode in an arc light. **b** The negative electrode of a primary cell. **3.** A piece of carbon paper. **4.** A carbon copy. — *adj.* **1.** Of, pertaining to, or like carbon. **2.** Treated with carbon. [< F < L *carbo, -onis* coal]
carbon 14 *Physics* Radiocarbon.
car·bo·na·ceous (kär/bə·nā/shəs) *adj.* Of, pertaining to, or yielding carbon.
car·bon·ate (kär/bə·nāt; *for n., also* kär/bə·nit) *Chem. v.t.* **·at·ed, ·at·ing 1.** To impregnate or charge with carbon dioxide. **2.** To carbonize. — *n.* A salt or ester of carbonic acid. [< F] — **car/bon·a/tion** *n.*
carbon copy 1. A copy of a letter, etc., made by means of carbon paper. **2.** An exact or close replica; duplicate.
carbon dioxide *Chem.* A heavy, odorless, incombustible gas, CO_2, taken from the atmosphere in the photosynthesis of plants and returned to it by the respiration of both plants and animals.
carboni- *combining form* Carbon; coal. [< L *carbo, -onis* coal]
car·bon·ic (kär·bon/ik) *adj.* Of, pertaining to, or obtained from carbon.
carbonic acid *Chem.* A weak, unstable acid, H_2CO_3, existing only in solution.
car·bon·if·er·ous (kär/bə·nif/ər·əs) *adj.* Of, pertaining to, containing, or yielding carbon or coal.
Car·bon·if·er·ous (kär/bə·nif/ər·əs) *adj. Geol.* Of or pertaining to a period of the Paleozoic era characterized by the formation of extensive coal beds. — *n.* The Carboniferous period or system of rocks. See chart under GEOLOGY.
car·bon·ize (kär/bən·īz) *v.t.* **·ized, ·iz·ing 1.** To reduce to carbon. **2.** To coat with carbon, as paper. **3.** To charge with carbon. — **car/bon·i·za/tion** *n.* — **car/bon·iz/er** *n.*
carbon monoxide *Chem.* A colorless, odorless gas, CO, formed by the incomplete oxidation of carbon, burning with a blue flame and highly poisonous when inhaled.
carbon paper Thin paper coated with carbon or the like, placed between two sheets of paper to reproduce on the bottom sheet what is written or typed on the upper sheet.
carbon tetrachloride *Chem.* A colorless, nonflammable liquid, CCl_4, used as a solvent, cleaning fluid, etc.
Car·bo·run·dum (kär/bə·run/dəm) *n.* An abrasive of silicon carbide: a trade name. Also **car/bo·run/dum.**
car·box·yl (kär·bok/sil) *n. Chem.* A univalent acid radical, COOH, the characteristic group of most organic acids.
car·boy (kär/boi) *n.* A large glass bottle enclosed in a box or in wickerwork, used as a container for corrosive acids, etc. [Alter. of Persian *qarābah* demijohn]
car·bun·cle (kär/bung·kəl) *n.* **1.** *Pathol.* An inflammation of the subcutaneous tissue, resembling a boil but larger. **2.** A red garnet cut without facets. [< AF < L *carbo, -onis* coal] — **car·bun·cu·lar** (kär·bung/kyə·lər) *adj.*
car·bu·ret (kär/bə·rāt, -byə·ret) *v.t.* **·ret·ed** or **·ret·ted, ·ret·ing** or **·ret·ting** To combine chemically with carbon; esp. to charge (air or gas) with carbon compounds. — **car·bu·re·tion** (kär/bə·rā/shən, -byə·resh/ən) *n.*
car·bu·re·tor (kär/bə·rā/tər, -byə·ret/ər) *n.* An apparatus used to charge air or gas with volatile hydrocarbons to give it illuminative or explosive power. Also *Brit.* **car·bu·ret·tor** (kär/byə·ret/ər) or **car/bu·ret/ter.**
car·bu·rize (kär/bə·rīz, -byə-) *v.t.* **·rized, ·riz·ing 1.** To carburet. **2.** *Metall.* To impregnate the surface layer of (low-carbon steel) with carbon, a stage in casehardening.
car·ca·jou (kär/kə·jōō, -zhōō) *n. Canadian* The wolverine. [< dial. F (Canadian) < native Algonquian name]
car·cass (kär/kəs) *n.* **1.** The dead body of an animal. **2.** The human body, living or dead: a contemptuous or humorous use. **3.** Something from which the life or essence is gone; shell. **4.** A framework or skeleton. Also **car/case.** [< AF < Med.L *carcasium*]
car·cin·o·gen (kär·sin/ə·jən) *n. Pathol.* A substance that causes cancer. — **car·ci·no·gen·ic** (kär·sə·nō·jen/ik) *adj.*
car·ci·no·ma (kär/sə·nō/mə) *n. pl.* **·mas** or **·ma·ta** (-mə·tə) *Pathol.* A malignant epithelial tumor; cancer. Also **car·ci·nus** (kär/sə·nəs). [< L < Gk. *karkīnos* cancer] — **car·ci·nom·a·tous** (kär/sə·nom/ə·təs, -nō/mə-) *adj.*
card[1] (kärd) *n.* **1.** A small, usu. rectangular piece of thin pasteboard or stiff paper, used for a variety of purposes. **2.**

One of a pack of such pieces with figures, numbers, or other symbols, used for various games. **3.** *pl.* Games played with playing cards. **4.** A greeting card. **5.** A card certifying the identity of its owner or bearer: library *card*. **6.** A program or form of events, as at the races. **7.** *Naut.* The dial of a compass. **8.** An advertisement or public announcement printed on a card. **9.** *Informal* A person manifesting some peculiarity: a queer *card*. **10.** *Informal* A witty person. **— in the cards** Likely to happen; possible. **— to put one's cards on the table** To reveal one's intentions with complete frankness. **—** *v.t.* **1.** To fasten or write upon a card or cards. **2.** To provide with a card. [< MF < Ital. < L < Gk. *chartēs* leaf of paper]

card² (kärd) *n.* **1.** A wire-toothed brush for combing and cleansing wool, etc. **2.** A similar instrument for raising a nap. **—** *v.t. & v.i.* To comb, dress, or cleanse with a card. [< MF < Ital. < Med.L < L *carduus* thistle] **— card′er** *n.*

car·da·mom (kär′də-məm) *n.* **1.** The aromatic seeds of either of two Asian plants of the ginger family. **2.** One of the plants yielding these seeds. Also **car′da·mon** (-mən), **car′da·mum.** [< L < Gk. *kardamon* cress + *amōmon* spice]

card·board (kärd′bôrd′, -bōrd′) *n.* A thin, stiff pasteboard used for making cards, boxes, etc.

card catalogue A catalogue made out on cards, esp. one showing the books in a library.

cardi- Var. of CARDIO-.

car·di·ac (kär′dē-ak) *Med. adj.* **1.** Pertaining to, situated near, or affecting the heart. **2.** Of or pertaining to the upper orifice of the stomach. Also **car·di·a·cal** (kär-dī′ə-kəl). **—** *n.* **1.** One suffering from a heart disease. **2.** A cardiac remedy or stimulant. [< F < L < Gk. *kardia* heart]

car·di·gan (kär′də-gən) *n.* A jacket or sweater opening down the front. Also **cardigan jacket, cardigan sweater.** [after the seventh Earl of *Cardigan*, 1797–1868]

car·di·nal (kär′də-nəl, kärd′nəl) *adj.* **1.** Of prime importance; chief; principal. **2.** Of a deep scarlet color. **3.** Of or relating to a cardinal or cardinals. **—** *n.* **1.** In the Roman Catholic Church, a member of the College of Cardinals, or Sacred College. **2.** A bright red, crested finch of the eastern United States: also called *redbird*: also **cardinal bird, cardinal grosbeak. 3.** A deep scarlet. **4.** A cardinal number. [< F < L *cardo, cardinis* hinge, that on which something turns or depends] **— car′di·nal·ly** *adv.*

car·di·nal·ate (kär′də-nəl-āt, kärd′nəl-āt) *n.* The rank, dignity, or term of office of a cardinal. Also **car′di·nal·ship.**

cardinal flower An herb of North America having large red flowers.

cardinal number *Math.* Any number that expresses the number of objects or units under consideration, as 1, 2, 3, etc.: distinguished from *ordinal number.*

cardinal point Any of the four main points of the compass.

cardinal sins The seven deadly sins.

cardinal virtues Justice, prudence, temperance, and fortitude, classified by Plato as the four types of moral excellence.

card·ing (kär′ding) *n.* **1.** The cleansing and combing of wool, flax, etc., before spinning. **2.** Carded fibers.

cardio- *combining form* Heart: *cardiogram.* Also, before vowels, **cardi-.** [< Gk. *kardia* heart]

car·di·o·gram (kär′dē-ə-gram′) *n.* The graphic record of heart movements produced by the cardiograph.

car·di·o·graph (kär′dē-ə-graf′, -gräf′) *n.* An instrument for tracing and recording the force and character of the heart movements. **— car′di·o·graph′ic** *adj.* **— car·di·og·ra·phy** (kär′dē-og′rə-fē) *n.*

car·di·tis (kär-dī′tis) *n. Pathol.* Inflammation of the heart.

cards (kärdz) *n.pl.* (*construed as sing.*) **1.** Any game played with playing cards. **2.** The playing of card games.

card·sharp (kärd′shärp′) *n.* One who cheats at cards, esp. as a livelihood. Also **card′sharp′er.**

care (kâr) *n.* **1.** A feeling of anxiety or concern; worry. **2.** A cause of worry or anxiety. **3.** Watchful regard or attention; heed. **4.** Charge or guardianship; custody; supervision. **5.** An object of solicitude or attention. **—** *v.i.* **cared, car·ing 1.** To have or show regard, interest, or concern. **2.** To be inclined; desire: with *to.* **3.** To mind or be concerned: I don't *care* if it rains. **— to care for 1.** To look after or provide for. **2.** To feel interest concerning; also, to have a fondness for; like. **3.** To want; desire. [OE *caru, cearu*]

ca·reen (kə-rēn′) *v.i.* **1.** *U.S.* To lurch or twist from side to side while moving. **2.** To lean sideways. **3.** To clean a ship when it is on one side. **—** *v.t.* **4.** To turn (a ship, etc.) on one side; tip. **5.** To clean, repair, or caulk (a careened ship). **—** *n.* **1.** The act of careening a vessel. **2.** The position of a ship careened or heeled over. [< F < L *carina* keel of a ship] **— ca·reen′er** *n.*

ca·reer (kə-rir′) *n.* **1.** The course or progress of a person's life: a remarkable *career.* **2.** One's lifework; profession. **3.** Successful pursuit of an occupation. **4.** Speed; full speed. **—** *adj. U.S.* Making one's profession a lifework: *career* diplomat. **—** *v.i.* To move with a swift, free motion. [< F < LL < L *carrus* wagon] **— ca·reer′er** *n.*

ca·reer·ist (kə-rir′ist) *n.* A person chiefly concerned with advancing himself professionally. **— ca·reer′ism** *n.*

care·free (kâr′frē′) *adj.* Free of troubles or anxiety.

care·ful (kâr′fəl) *adj.* **1.** Exercising care in one's work; painstaking. **2.** Done with care: a *careful* job. **3.** Watchful; cautious. **— care′ful·ly** *adv.* **— care′ful·ness** *n.*

care·less (kâr′lis) *adj.* **1.** Not attentive; reckless: a *careless* worker. **2.** Not done with care; neglectful. **3.** Without care or concern; indifferent: with *about, in,* or *of.* **4.** Artless; unstudied: *careless* elegance. **5.** Carefree: a *careless* life. **— care′less·ly** *adv.* **— care′less·ness** *n.*

ca·ress (kə-res′) *n.* An affectionate touch or gesture, as an embrace, pat, etc. **—** *v.t.* To touch or treat lovingly; fondle. [< MF < Ital. < L *carus* dear] **— ca·ress′er** *n.* **— ca·ress′ing·ly** *adv.* **— ca·res′sive** *adj.* **— ca·res′sive·ly** *adv.*

car·et (kar′ət) *n.* A sign (∧) placed below a line to indicate where something should be inserted. [< L, it is missing]

care·tak·er (kâr′tā′kər) *n.* One who takes care of a place, thing, or person; a custodian.

care·worn (kâr′wôrn′, -wōrn′) *adj.* Showing the effects of care and anxiety; haggard; weary.

car·fare (kär′fâr′) *n.* The fare for a ride on a bus, etc.

car·go (kär′gō) *n. pl.* **·goes** or **·gos** Goods and merchandise carried by a vessel, aircraft, etc.; freight; load. [< Sp. < LL < L *carrus* wagon]

car·hop (kär′hop′) *n. U.S. Informal* A waiter or waitress at a drive-in restaurant.

Car·ib (kar′ib) *n.* **1.** One of a tribe of Indians now surviving on the coasts of Guiana, Venezuela, Dominica, Honduras, Guatemala, and Nicaragua. **2.** The family of languages spoken by these Indians. [< Sp. < Cariban *caribe* brave] **— Car′ib·an** *adj. & n.*

Car·ib·be·an (kar′ə-bē′ən, kə-rib′ē-ən) *n.* **1.** The Caribbean Sea. **2.** A Carib. **— adj. 1.** Of or pertaining to the Caribbean Sea. **2.** Of or pertaining to the Caribs, their language, or their culture.

car·i·bou (kar′ə-bōō) *n. pl.* **·bou** or **·bous** A North American reindeer found from Maine to the Arctic. [< dial. F (Canadian) < Alonquian *khalibu* pawer]

car·i·ca·ture (kar′i·kə-chŏŏr, -chər) *n.* **1.** A picture or description in which features are exaggerated or distorted so as to produce an absurd effect. **2.** The act or art of caricaturing. **3.** A poor imitation. **—** *v.t.* **·tured, ·tur·ing** To represent so as to make ridiculous; burlesque. [< F < Ital. *caricare* to load, exaggerate] **— car′i·ca·tur′al** *adj.* **— car′i·ca·tur′ist** *n.*

CARIBOU
(4 feet high at shoulder; 6 feet long; tail 4 inches)

car·ies (kâr′ēz, -i·ēz) *n. Pathol.* Decay of a bone or of a tooth. [< L]

car·il·lon (kar′ə·lon, kə·ril′yən) *n.* **1.** A set of stationary bells rung by hammers operated from a keyboard or by a mechanism. **2.** A melody rung on a carillon. **3.** An organ stop imitating bells. **—** *v.i.* **·lonned, ·lon·ning** To play a carillon. [< F < Med.L *quadrilio, -onis* set of four bells]

car·il·lon·neur (kar′ə·lə·nûr′) *n.* One who plays a carillon.

car·i·o·ca (kar′ē·ō′kə) *n.* A type of South American dance, or the music for it. [after Sierra de *Carioca*, a mountain range near Rio de Janeiro]

car·i·ole (kar′ē·ōl) *n.* **1.** A small, open carriage. **2.** A light cart. **3.** *Canadian* A dog sled for one person lying down. Also spelled **carriole.** [< F < Ital. *carra* cart, wagon]

car·i·ous (kâr′ē·əs) *adj.* Affected with caries; decayed. Also **car·ied** (kâr′ēd) **— car′i·os′i·ty** (-os′ə·tē), **car′i·ous·ness** *n.*

carl (kärl) *n.* **1.** *Archaic* A countryman; peasant. **2.** *Scot.* A churl. Also **carle.** [< ON *karl* man, freeman]

car·load (kär′lōd′) *n.* **1.** The load carried in a car. **2.** The minimum load required to ship at the **carload rate,** a rate lower than that for smaller loads.

carload lot A freight shipment meeting the official minimum weight for a carload rate.

car·ma·gnole (kär′mən·yōl′, *Fr.* kår·må·nyôl′) *n.* **1.** A wild dance and song of the French revolutionists of 1789. **2.** The costume of the French revolutionists. [< F, after *Carmagnola,* a town in Piedmont]

car·man (kär′mən) *n. pl.* **·men** (-mən) **1.** The driver, or one of the crew, of a streetcar, etc. **2.** One who drives a cart.

Car·mel·ite (kär′məl·īt) *n.* A monk or nun of the order of Our Lady of Mt. Carmel. **—** *adj.* Of or relating to the Carmelites.

car·min·a·tive (kär·min′ə·tiv, kär′mə·nā′tiv) *Med. adj.* Tending to, or used to, relieve flatulence. **—** *n.* A remedy for flatulence. [< L *carminare* to cleanse]

car·mine (kär′min, -mīn) *n.* **1.** A deep red or purplish red color. **2.** A crimson pigment obtained from cochineal; rouge. **—** *adj.* Deep red or purplish red. [< F < Med.L < O Sp. *carmesin* crimson]

car·nage (kär′nij) *n.* Extensive and bloody slaughter, as in war; massacre. **— Syn.** See MASSACRE. [< MF < Ital. < LL < L *caro, carnis* flesh, meat]

car·nal (kär′nəl) *adj.* **1.** Relating to bodily appetites; sensual. **2.** Sexual. **3.** Not spiritual; worldly. [< LL < L *caro, carnis* flesh] — **car′nal·ist** *n.* — **car·nal·i·ty** (kär·nal′ə·tē) *n.* — **car′nal·ly** *adv.*

car·na·tion (kär·nā′shən) *n.* **1.** The perennial, herbaceous, fragrant flower of any of the many varieties of the pink family. **2.** A light pink, bright rose, or scarlet color. [< F < L *caro, carnis* flesh]

car·nel·ian (kär·nēl′yən) *n.* A clear red chalcedony, used as a gem: also *cornelian*. [< L *carnis* flesh]

car·ni·fy (kär′nə·fī) *v.t. & v.i.* **·fied, ·fy·ing** To form into flesh or a fleshlike consistency. [< L < *carnis* flesh + *facere* to make] — **car′ni·fi·ca′tion** *n.*

car·ni·val (kär′nə·vəl) *n.* **1.** An amusement show with merry-go-round, Ferris wheel, side shows, etc. **2.** Any gay festival, wild revel, or merrymaking. **3.** A period of festivity immediately preceding Lent. [< Ital. < Med.L < L < *carnis* flesh + *levare* to remove]

car·ni·vore (kär′nə·vôr, -vōr) *n.* A flesh-eating mammal, as a cat, dog, etc.

car·niv·o·rous (kär·niv′ə·rəs) *adj.* **1.** Eating or living on flesh. **2.** Of or pertaining to carnivores. [< L < *carnis* flesh + *vorare* to eat, devour] — **car·niv′o·rous·ly** *adv.* — **car·niv′o·rous·ness** *n.*

car·ol (kar′əl) *n.* A song of joy or praise; esp., a Christmas song. — *v.* **car·oled** or **·olled, car·ol·ing** or **·ol·ling** *v.i.* **1.** To sing, esp. in a joyous strain. — *v.t.* **2.** To utter or praise in song. [< OF < L < Gk. < *choros* a dance + *auleein* to play the flute] — **car′ol·er** or **car′ol·ler** *n.*

Car·o·li·nas (kar′ə·lī′nəz), **the** North and South Carolina.

Car·o·lin·gi·an (kar′ə·lin′jē·ən) *adj.* Of or pertaining to the dynasty of Charlemagne.

Car·o·lin·i·an (kar′ə·lin′ē·ən) *adj.* **1.** Of or pertaining to North or South Carolina. **2.** Carolingian. — *n.* A native or inhabitant of North or South Carolina.

car·om (kar′əm) *n.* **1.** In billiards, a shot in which the cue ball strikes against two other balls in succession: in England, called a *cannon*. Also called *billiard*. **2.** Any impact followed by a rebound. — *v.i.* **1.** To hit and rebound. — *v.t.* **2.** To cause to make a carom. [Earlier *carambole* < F]

car·o·tene (kar′ə·tēn) *n. Biochem.* A deep yellow or red crystalline hydrocarbon, $C_{40}H_{56}$, found in carrots, etc., and changed in the body to vitamin A. Also **car′o·tin** (-tin). [< L *carota* carrot + -ENE]

ca·rot·e·noid (kə·rot′ə·noid) *n. Biochem.* One of a large variety of pigments found in plant and animal tissues. — *adj.* Of carotene or carotenoids. Also **ca·rot′i·noid.**

ca·rot·id (kə·rot′id) *adj. Anat.* Of, pertaining to, or near one of the two major arteries on each side of the neck. Also **ca·rot′i·dal.** [< Gk. *karos* stupor]

ca·rou·sal (kə·rou′zəl) *n.* A feast or banquet.

ca·rouse (kə·rouz′) *v.i.* **·roused, ·rous·ing** To drink freely and boisterously. — *n.* A carousal. [< G *gar aus (trinken)* (to drink) all out] — **ca·rous′er** *n.*

car·ou·sel (kar′ə·sel′, -zel′) *n.* **1.** A merry-go-round (def. 1). **2.** A tournament in which horsemen perform. Also spelled *carrousel*. [< F < Ital. *carosello* tournament]

carp¹ (kärp) *v.i.* To find fault unreasonably; complain; cavil. [< ON *karpa* to boast] — **carp′er** *n.*

carp² (kärp) *n. pl.* **carp** or **carps 1.** A fresh-water food fish widely distributed in Europe and America. **2.** Any of various related fishes, as goldfish. [< OF < LL *carpa*]

-carp *combining form* Fruit; fruit (or seed) vessel: *pericarp.* [< Gk. *karpos* fruit]

car·pal (kär′pəl) *Anat. adj.* Of, pertaining to, or near the wrist. — *n.* A carpale. [< NL < L < Gk. *karpos* wrist]

car·pa·le (kär·pā′lē) *n. pl.* **·li·a** (-lē·ə) *Anat.* A bone of the carpus or wrist. [See CARPAL.]

car·pe di·em (kär′pē dī′em) *Latin* Enjoy the present; seize today's opportunities; literally, seize the day.

car·pel (kär′pəl) *n. Bot.* A simple pistil or seed vessel. [< NL < Gk. *karpos* fruit] — **car·pel·lar·y** (kär′pə·ler′ē) *adj.*

car·pen·ter (kär′pən·tər) *n.* A workman who builds and repairs wooden structures, as houses, ships, etc. — *v.i.* **1.** To work as a carpenter. — *v.t.* **2.** To make or build as a carpenter. [< AF < LL < L *carpentum* two-wheeled carriage] — **car′pen·ter·ing** *n.* — **car′pen·try** *n.*

car·pet (kär′pit) *n.* **1.** A heavy covering for floors; also, the fabric used for it. **2.** A surface or covering suggesting this. — **on the carpet 1.** Subjected to reproof or reprimand. **2.** Under consideration or discussion. — *v.t.* To cover with or as with a carpet. [< OF < LL < L *carpere* to pluck, card wool]

car·pet·bag (kär′pit·bag′) *n.* An old type of traveling bag, made of carpeting.

car·pet·bag·ger (kär′pit·bag′ər) *n. U.S.* One of the Northern adventurers who sought to gain advantages in the South from the unsettled conditions after the Civil War.

carpet beetle A beetle whose larvae feed on carpets, fur, etc. Also **carpet bug.**

car·pet·ing (kär′pit·ing) *n.* Carpets or carpet fabric.

carpet sweeper A hand-operated apparatus for sweeping carpets, combining a revolving brush and closed dustpan.

carp·ing (kär′ping) *adj. & n.* Faultfinding. — **carp′ing·ly** *adv.*

carpo- *combining form* Fruit. [< Gk. *karpos* fruit]

car·port (kär′pôrt′, -pōrt′) *n. U.S.* A shelter for an automobile, usu. a roof projecting from the side of a building.

-carpous *combining form* Having a certain kind or number of fruits. Also **-carpic.** [< Gk. *karpos* fruit]

car·pus (kär′pəs) *n. pl.* **·pi** (-pī) *Anat.* The wrist, or the wrist bones collectively. [< NL < Gk. *karpos* wrist]

car·rack (kar′ək) *n.* A galleon: also spelled *carack.* [< OF < Med.L, ? < Arabic *qorqûr* merchant ship]

car·ra·geen (kar′ə·gēn) *n.* An edible seaweed known commercially as Irish moss and used in medicine. Also **car′ra·gheen.** [after *Carragheen*, Ireland, where it grows]

car·rel (kar′əl) *n.* A small space, as among the stacks in a library, for solitary study. Also **car′rell.** [Var. of CAROL]

car·riage (kar′ij; *for def. 7, also* kar′ē·ij) *n.* **1.** A wheeled, usu. horse-drawn vehicle for carrying persons. **2.** *Brit.* A railroad passenger car. **3.** Manner of carrying the head and limbs; bearing. **4.** A moving portion of a machine carrying another part: the *carriage* of a lathe. **5.** A wheeled frame for carrying something heavy. **6.** The act of carrying; transportation. **7.** The cost of transportation.

carriage trade The wealthy patrons of a restaurant, theater, etc., so called because they came in private carriages.

car·ried (kar′ēd) Past tense and past participle of CARRY.

car·ri·er (kar′ē·ər) *n.* **1.** One who or that which carries. **2.** A person or company that carries persons or goods for hire. **3.** *Med.* A person who is immune to a disease but transmits it to others.

carrier pigeon A homing pigeon.

carrier wave *Telecom.* The radio-frequency wave that is varied in some respect in order to transmit intelligence.

car·ri·ole (kar′ē·ōl) *n.* See CARIOLE.

car·ri·on (kar′ē·ən) *n.* Dead and putrefying flesh. — *adj.* **1.** Feeding on carrion. **2.** Like or pertaining to carrion; putrefying. [< AF < L *caro, carnis* flesh]

carrion crow The common crow of Europe.

car·rom (kar′əm) *n.* See CAROM.

car·rot (kar′ət) *n.* **1.** The long, reddish yellow, edible root of an umbelliferous plant. **2.** The plant itself. [< F < L < Gk. *karôton* carrot]

car·rot·y (kar′ət·ē) *adj.* **1.** Like a carrot, esp. in color. **2.** Having red hair.

car·rou·sel (kar′ə·sel′, -zel′) *n.* See CAROUSEL.

car·ry (kar′ē) *v.* **·ried, ·ry·ing** *v.t.* **1.** To bear from one place to another; transport; convey. **2.** To serve as a medium of conveyance for; transmit. **3.** To have or bear upon or about one's person. **4.** To bear the weight, burden, or responsibility of. **5.** To give support to; confirm. **6.** To bear as a mark or attribute: Her words *carried* conviction. **7.** To be pregnant with. **8.** To bear (the body, or a part of it) in a specified manner. **9.** To conduct or comport (oneself). **10.** To take by force or effort; capture; win. **11.** To win the support or interest of. **12.** To gain victory or acceptance for; also, to achieve success in. **13.** To cause to go or come; urge. **14.** To extend; continue. **15.** To have or keep for sale. **16.** To transfer, as a number or figure, to another column. **17.** To maintain on one's account books for a future settlement. **18.** *U.S.* To sing or play (a part or melody). **19.** *Southern U.S.* To escort. — *v.i.* **20.** To act as bearer or carrier. **21.** To have or exert propelling or projecting power: The rifle *carries* well. **22.** To hold the neck and head in a particular manner. **23.** To gain victory or acceptance: The motion *carried.* — **to carry all before one** To meet with uniform success. — **to carry arms 1.** To belong to the army. **2.** To bear weapons. **3.** To hold a weapon in a prescribed position against the shoulder. — **to carry away** To move the feelings greatly; enchant. — **to carry forward 1.** To progress or proceed with. **2.** In bookkeeping, to transfer (an item, etc.) to the next column or page. — **to carry off 1.** To cause to die. **2.** To win, as a prize or honor. **3.** To face consequences boldly; brazen out. **4.** To abduct. — **to carry on 1.** To keep up; keep going; continue. **2.** To behave in a wild, excited, or foolish manner. **3.** To engage in. — **to carry out** To accomplish; bring to completion. — **to carry over 1.** In bookkeeping, to repeat (an item, etc.) on another page or in another column. **2.** To postpone; put off. — **to carry through 1.** To carry to completion or success. **2.** To sustain or support to the end. — *n. pl.* **·ries 1.** Range, as of a gun; also, the distance covered by a projectile, golf ball, etc. **2.** *U.S.* A portage, as between streams. **3.** The act of carrying. [< L *carrus* cart]

---

car·ry·all[1] (kar'ē·ôl')   n.   A light, four-wheeled covered vehicle having room for several people.

car·ry·all[2] (kar'ē·ôl')   n.   A large basket or bag.

carrying charge In installment buying, the interest charged on the unpaid balance.

carrying place *Canadian* A portage (def. 2).

car·ry·o·ver (kar'ē·ō'vər)   n.   1. Something left over or kept until later.   2. In bookkeeping, a sum carried forward.

car·sick (kär'sik')   adj.   Nauseated from riding in a car.

cart (kärt)   n.   1. A two-wheeled vehicle, for carrying loads.   2. A light, two-wheeled vehicle with springs, used for business or pleasure.   — *v.t.*   1. To carry in or as in a cart. — *v.i.*   2. To drive or use a cart.   [ON *kartr*]   — **cart'er** *n.*

cart·age (kär'tij)   n.   The act of or charge for carting.

carte blanche (kärt' blänsh', *Fr.* kärt blänsh')   *pl.* **cartes blanches** (kärts' blänsh', *Fr.* kärt blänsh')   1. A signed paper granting its possessor the freedom to write his own conditions.   2. Unrestricted authority.   [< F, white card]

car·tel (kär·tel', kär'təl)   n.   1. An international trust that aims at monopolistic control of a particular market.   2. An official agreement between governments, esp. for the exchange of prisoners.   3. A challenge to single combat.   [< F < Ital. *carta* paper]

Car·te·sian·ism (kär·tē'zhən·iz'əm)   n.   The philosophy of Descartes who defended complete dualism between thought (or mind) and extension (the subject matter of physical science).   [< NL *Cartesius*, Latinized form of *Descartes*]   — **Car·te'sian** *n. & adj.*

Car·thage (kär'thij)   An ancient city state in North Africa; destroyed by the Romans in 146 B.C. Ancient **Car·tha·go** (kär·thā'gō).   — **Car·tha·gin·i·an** (kär'thə·jin'ē·ən) *adj. & n.*

Car·thu·sian (kär·thōō'zhən)   n.   A monk or nun of a contemplative order founded at Chartreuse in the French Alps by St. Bruno in 1084.   — *adj.*   Of or pertaining to the Carthusians.   [< Med.L *Carturissium* Chartreuse]

car·ti·lage (kär'tə·lij)   n.   *Zool.*   1. A tough, elastic form of connective tissue in man and animals; gristle.   2. A part consisting of cartilage.   [< MF < L *cartilago* gristle]

car·ti·lag·i·nous (kär'tə·laj'ə·nəs)   adj.   1. Of or like cartilage; gristly.   2. Having a gristly skeleton, as sharks.

cart·load (kärt'lōd')   n.   As much as a cart can hold.

car·tog·ra·phy (kär·tog'rə·fē)   n.   The art of making maps or charts.   [< L *carta* map + -GRAPHY]   — **car·tog'ra·pher** *n.* — **car·to·graph·ic** (kär'tə·graf'ik) or **·i·cal** *adj.*

car·ton (kär'tən)   n.   1. A cardboard box.   2. A paper or plastic container for liquids.   [< F, pasteboard]

car·toon (kär·tōōn')   n.   1. A drawing or caricature depicting a humorous or satirical person or situation.   2. A comic strip.   3. A motion-picture film (**animated cartoon**) produced by photographing a series of action drawings.   4. A full-size sketch for a fresco, mosaic, etc.   — *v.t.*   1. To make a caricature or cartoon of.   — *v.i.*   2. To make cartoons.   [< F < Ital. *charta* paper]   — **car·toon'ist** *n.*

car·tridge (kär'trij)   n.   1. A casing of metal, pasteboard, or the like, containing a charge of powder for a firearm and, usu., the projectile or shot and the primer.   2. Any small similar container, as the removable case in a tone arm of a record player.   3. *Photog.*   A roll of protected sensitized film.   [< F < Ital. *cartoccio* < L *charta* paper]

cartridge clip   A metal container holding cartridges for a rapid-fire gun, as an automatic rifle.

cart·wheel (kärt'hwēl')   n.   1. A sideways handspring.   2. *U.S. Informal* A large coin, esp. a silver dollar.

carve (kärv)   v.   **carved**, **carv·ing**   *v.t.*   1. To make by cutting, or as if by cutting.   2. To create, design, or fashion by cutting.   3. To cut up, as cooked meat; divide.   — *v.i.*   4. To make carved work.   5. To cut up meat.   — n.   A cut or stroke in carving.   [OE *ceorfan*]   — **carv'er** *n.*

carv·en (kär'vən)   adj.   *Poetic* or *Archaic* Carved.

carv·ing (kär'ving)   n.   1. The act of one who carves.   2. Carved work; a carved figure or design.

car·y·at·id (kar'ē·at'id)   n.   *pl.* **·at·ids** or **·at·i·des** (-at'ə·dēz)   *Archit.*   A supporting column in the form of a sculptured female figure.   [< L < Gk. *Karyatis* a Greek priestess]

caryo-   See KARYO-.

car·y·o·tin (kar'ē·ō'tin)   See KARYOTIN.

ca·sa·ba (kə·sä'bə)   n.   A winter variety of muskmelon with sweet white flesh and yellow rind: also spelled *cassaba*. Also **casaba melon.**   [after *Kasaba*, a town in western Turkey]

ca·sa·va (kə·sä'və)   See CASSAVA.

Cas·bah (käz'bä)   The native quarter of Algiers or of other cities with a large Arab population: also *Kasbah.*

cas·cade (kas·kād')   n.   1. A fall of water over steep rocks, or one of a series of such falls.   2. Anything resembling a waterfall.   — *v.i.*   **·cad·ed**, **·cad·ing** To fall in the form of a waterfall.   [< F < Ital. < L *cadere* to fall]

cas·car·a (kas·kâr'ə)   n.   A buckthorn of the NW United States, yielding cascara sagrada. Also **cascara buckthorn.**   [< Sp. *cáscara* bark]

cascara sa·gra·da (sə·grä'də)   A laxative obtained from the bark of the cascara.

case[1] (kās)   n.   1. A particular instance or occurrence: a *case* of mistaken identity.   2. The actual circumstance or state of affairs: Such is not the *case*.   3. An instance of disease or injury; also, a patient.   4. A set of arguments, reasons, etc.: the *case* for capital punishment.   5. A question or problem: a *case* of conscience.   6. *Law* A An action or suit at law. **b** The set of facts offered in support of a claim.   7. Condition or situation; plight.   8. *Informal* A peculiar or exceptional person.   9. *Gram.*   The syntactical relationship of a noun, pronoun, or adjective to other words in a sentence.   — **in any case** No matter what; regardless.   — **in case** In the event that; if.   — **in case of** In the event of: *in case of* fire.   — *v.t.*   **cased**, **cas·ing** *U.S. Slang* To look over carefully, especially with intent to rob.   [< OF < L *casus* event]

case[2] (kās)   n.   1. A box, sheath, bag, etc., for containing something.   2. A box and its contents.   3. A set or pair.   4. *Printing* A tray with compartments for holding type, called *upper case* for capital letters, and *lower case* for small letters.   5. The covers and spine in which a book, when sewed, is bound.   6. An outer or protective part, as of a watch.   7. A frame or casing, as for a door.   — *v.t.*   **cased**, **cas·ing** To put into or cover with a case; incase.   [< AF < L *capsa* box]

ca·se·fy (kā'sə·fī)   *v.t. & v.i.*   **·fied**, **·fy·ing** To make or become like cheese.   [< L *caseus* cheese + -FY]

case·hard·en (kās'här'dən)   *v.t.*   1. *Metall.*   To harden the surface of (low-carbon steel).   2. To make callous, esp. in feelings.

case history   A record of an individual or a family unit, in which salient facts are collected for use in medical, psychiatric, sociological, or similar studies. Also **case study.**

ca·se·in (kā'sē·in, -sēn)   n.   *Biochem.*   A protein found esp. in milk and constituting the principal ingredient in cheese.   [< L *caseus* cheese]   — **ca·se·ic** (kā'sē·ik) *adj.*

case knife   1. A knife kept in a sheath.   2. A table knife.

case law   Law based on judicial decisions, as distinguished from that based on statute or other sources of law.

case·mate (kās'māt)   n.   A bombproof shelter in a fortification, or an armored compartment on a warship, for a gun and crew.   [< MF < Ital. *casamatta*]   — **case'mat·ed** *adj.*

case·ment (kās'mənt)   n.   1. The sash of a window that opens on hinges at the side, or a window having such sashes.   2. A case; covering.   — **case'ment·ed** *adj.*

ca·se·ous (kā'sē·əs)   adj.   Of or like cheese; cheesy.

ca·sern (kə·zûrn')   n.   A barrack for soldiers. Also **ca·serne'.**   [< F < Sp. *caserna* small hut < L *quaterna* four each]

case·work (kās'wûrk')   n.   The investigation and guidance by a social worker of maladjusted individuals and families.   — **case'work·er** *n.*

cash[1] (kash)   n.   1. Current money in hand or readily available.   2. Money paid down; immediate payment.   — *v.t.*   To convert into ready money, as a check.   — **to cash in** 1. In gambling, to turn in one's chips and receive cash.   2. *U.S. Slang* To die.   — **to cash in on** *U.S. Informal* 1. To make a profit from.   2. To turn to advantage.   [< F < Ital. < L *capsa* box]   — **cash'a·ble** *adj.*

cash[2] (kash)   n.   *pl.* **cash** Coins of low value of the East Indies and China.   [< Pg. < Tamil *kāsu* small coin]

cash-and-car·ry (kash'ən·kar'ē)   adj.   Operated on a system of cash purchase and no delivery.

cash·book (kash'book')   n.   A book in which a record is kept of money taken in and paid out.

cash discount   A discount from the purchase price allowed the buyer if he pays within a stipulated period.

cash·ew (kash'ōō, kə·shōō')   n.   1. A tropical American tree of the sumac family that yields a gum.   2. Its small, edible fruit: also **cashew nut.**   [< F < Pg. < Tupi *acajoba*]

cash·ier[1] (ka·shir')   n.   1. One employed to collect cash payments, as in a restaurant.   2. A bank officer responsible for the bank's assets.   [< F < Ital. < L *capsa* box]

cash·ier[2] (ka·shir')   *v.t.*   1. To dismiss in disgrace, as a military officer.   2. To discard.   [< Du. < F < LL *cassare* to annul and L *quassare* to destroy]

cash·mere (kash'mir, kazh'-)   n.   1. A fine wool obtained from Kashmir goats.   2. A soft fabric made from this.   3. Something made of cashmere.   [after *Kashmir*, India]

cash register   A device usu. with a money drawer, that records, adds, and displays the amount of cash received.

cas·ing (kā'sing)   n.   1. A protective case or covering.   2. A framework, as about a door.   3. *U.S.* The shoe of a tire.

ca·si·no (kə·sē'nō)   n.   *pl.* **·nos**   1. A place for dancing, gambling, etc.   2. Cassino.   [< Ital., dim. of *casa* house]

cask (kask, käsk)   n.   1. A barrel-shaped wooden vessel, made of staves, hoops, and flat heads.   2. The quantity a cask will hold.   [< Sp. *casco* skull, potsherd, cask]

cas·ket (kas'kit, käs'-)   n.   1. *U.S.* A coffin.   2. A small box or chest.   — *v.t.*   To enclose in a casket.   [Orig. uncertain]

casque (kask)   n.   A helmet.   [< F, ult. < L *quassare*. Related to CASK.]   — **casqued** (kaskt) *adj.*

cas·sa·ba (kə·sä'bə)   See CASABA.

Cas·san·dra (kə·san'drə)   In Greek mythology, a daughter of Priam whose prophecies were fated by Apollo to be true but never believed. — *n.* Anyone who utters unheeded prophecies of disaster.

cas·sa·va (kə-sä′və) *n.* **1.** A tropical American shrub or herb, cultivated for the edible roots. **2.** A starch made from these roots, the source of tapioca. [< F < Taino *casavi*]

cas·se·role (kas′ə-rōl) *n.* **1.** An earthenware or glass dish in which food is baked and served. **2.** Any food so prepared and served. **3.** *Brit.* A saucepan. [< F]

cas·sette (kə-set′) *n.* **1.** *Photog.* A lightproof magazine for film. **2.** *Electronics* A cartridge containing magnetic tape, used in tape recorders. [< F, lit., small box]

cas·sia (kash′ə, kas′ē-ə) *n.* **1.** A variety of cinnamon obtained from the bark (**cassia bark**) of a tree native to China. **2.** The tree itself. **3.** Any shrub, herb, or tree of tropical regions whose dried pods (**cassia pods**) yield a mild laxative. [< L < Gk. < Hebrew *qātsa′* to strip off bark]

cas·si·no (kə-sē′nō) *n.* A card game for two to four players.

cas·si·o·ber·ry (kas′ē-ō-ber′ē) *n. pl.* **·ries** The shining black edible drupe of a North American shrub. [< N. Am. Ind.]

Cas·si·o·pe·ia (kas′ē-ə-pē′ə) In Greek mythology, the mother of Andromeda. — *n.* A constellation: also **Cassiopeia's Chair.**

cas·sock (kas′ək) *n. Eccl.* A close-fitting vestment, usu. black, reaching to the feet, and worn by clergymen, choir singers, etc. [< set′) < Ital. *casacca* greatcoat]

cas·so·war·y (kas′ə-wer′ē) *n. pl.* **·war·ies** A large, three-toed, flightless bird of Australia and New Guinea, related to the emu. [< Malay *kasuārī*]

cast (kast, käst) *v.* **cast, cast·ing** *v.t.* **1.** To throw or hurl with force; fling. **2.** To put with violence or force. **3.** To throw down. **4.** To cause to fall upon or over or in a particular direction: to *cast* a shadow. **5.** To direct, as a glance of the eyes. **6.** To let down; drop: to *cast* anchor. **7.** To throw forth or out. **8.** To throw off; lose; also, to shed; molt. **9.** To throw aside; reject or dismiss. **10.** To give birth to, esp. prematurely. **11.** To deposit; give: He *cast* his vote. **12.** To throw, as dice. **13.** In the theater, movies, etc., to assign the parts of (a play) or a part in a play to (an actor). **14.** To throw up, as with a shovel: to *cast* a mound of earth. **15.** To calculate; add. **16.** To compute astrologically: to *cast* a horoscope. **17.** To arrange by some system. **18.** To contrive; devise. **19.** *Metall.* To shape in a mold. **20.** *Printing* To stereotype or electroplate. **21.** To twist; warp. *Naut.* To turn (a ship); tack. — *v.i.* **23.** To make a throw, as with dice, a fishing line, etc. **24.** To deliberate mentally; also, to scheme. **25.** To conjecture; forecast. **26.** To make arithmetical calculations; add. **27.** *Metall.* To take shape in a mold. **28.** To warp, as timber. **29.** *Naut.* To veer; fall off; also, to tack. — **to cast about** To consider ways and means; scheme. — **to cast away 1.** To discard. **2.** To shipwreck or maroon. — **to cast down 1.** To overthrow; destroy. **2.** To discourage; depress. — **to cast off 1.** To reject or discard. **2.** To let go, as a ship from a dock. **3.** *Printing* To estimate the number of pages, columns, etc., a manuscript will yield. — **to cast up 1.** To eject; vomit. **2.** To compute; add. **3.** To drive ashore. **4.** To direct upward. — *n.* **1.** The act of casting or throwing. **2.** The distance to which a thing may be thrown. **3.** The throwing of a line or fishing net into the water. **4.** A throw of dice; also, the number thrown. **5.** Anything thrown out, off, or away. **6.** *Pathol.* A plastic substance formed in and often taking the shape of diseased cavities and organs: a renal *cast*. **7.** *Surg.* A rigid dressing or bandage, usu. made of plaster of Paris, for preventing movement of fractured bones. **8.** The actors who portray the characters in a play, movie, etc. **9.** The act of casting or founding. **10.** An impression made of anything; a mold. **11.** Something shaped or formed in a mold; a casting. **12.** The material poured into molds at one operation. **13.** Kind; sort; type. **14.** The appearance or form of something. **15.** A tinge; shade. **16.** A twist to one side; squint. **17.** A glance; look. **18.** A warp. **19.** A stroke of fortune. [< ON *kasta* to throw]

cas·ta·net (kas′tə-net′) *n.* One of a pair of small concave disks of wood or ivory, clapped together with the fingers, as a rhythmical accompaniment to song or dance. [< Sp. < L *castanea* chestnut]

cast·a·way (kast′ə-wā′, käst′-) *adj.* **1.** Adrift; shipwrecked. **2.** Thrown away. — *n.* **1.** One who is shipwrecked. **2.** An outcast.

caste (kast, käst) *n.* **1.** In India, one of the hereditary social classes into which Hindus are divided. **2.** Any rigid social class. **3.** The system or principles of such class divisions. **4.** The position conferred by such a system. [< Pg. < L *castus* pure]

cas·tel·lat·ed (kas′tə-lā′tid) *adj.* Having battlements and turrets. [< Med.L < L *castellum* castle] — **cas/tel·la′tion** *n.*

CASTANETS
a Outer and inner sides.
b Position in use.

cast·er (kas′tər, käs′-) *n.* **1.** One who or that which casts. **2.** One of a set of small, swiveling wheels or rollers, fastened under articles of furniture, or the like, to allow them to be moved about. **3.** A cruet for condiments; also, a stand for such cruets. Also (for defs. 2 and 3) *castor*.

cas·ti·gate (kas′tə-gāt) *v.t.* **·gat·ed, ·gat·ing** To rebuke or chastise severely; criticize. — **Syn.** See CHASTEN. [< L *castigare* to chasten] — **cas/ti·ga/tion** *n.* — **cas/ti·ga/tor** *n.*

Cas·tile soap (kas′tēl, kas·tēl′) A hard, white, odorless soap made with olive oil and soda. Also **castile soap.** [after *Castile*, where first made]

Cas·til·ian (kas-til′yən) *n.* **1.** A native or citizen of Castile. **2.** The standard form of Spanish as spoken in Spain, originally the dialect of Castile. — *adj.* Of or pertaining to Castile, its people, language, or culture.

cast·ing (kas′ting, käs′-) *n.* **1.** The act of one who or that which casts. **2.** That which is cast or formed in a mold.

casting vote A deciding vote, given by the chairman of an assembly in cases where the votes of the members tie.

cast-i·ron (kast′ī′ərn, käst′-) *adj.* **1.** Made of cast iron. **2.** Like cast iron; rigid or strong; unyielding.

cast iron Iron having a high carbon content, and usu. hard, brittle, and not malleable.

cas·tle (kas′əl, käs′-) *n.* **1.** In feudal times, the fortified dwelling of a prince or noble. **2.** Any large, imposing house. **3.** A place of refuge; stronghold. **4.** In chess, a rook. — *v.* **·tled, ·tling** *v.t. & v.i.* In chess, to move (the king) two squares to the right or left and place the rook from that side on the square over which the king has passed. [Ult. < L *castrum* camp, fort]

castle in the air A fanciful, impractical scheme; daydream.

cast-off (kast′ôf′, -of′, käst′-) *adj.* Thrown or laid aside. — *n.* One who or that which is no longer wanted or used.

cas·tor¹ (kas′tər, käs′-) *n.* **1.** An oily, odorous secretion of beavers, used in medicine and perfumery: also **cas·to·re·um** (kas-tôr′ē·əm, -tō′rē·əm) **2.** A hat of beaver or other fur. [< L < Gk. *kastōr* beaver]

cas·tor² (kas′tər, käs′-) See CASTER (defs. 2 and 3).

Cas·tor and Pol·lux (kas′tər, käs′-; pol′əks) **1.** In Greek mythology, twin brothers set by Zeus among the stars. **2.** *Astron.* The two brightest stars in the constellation Gemini.

castor bean The seed of the castor-oil plant.

castor oil A viscid oil extracted from castor beans and used as a cathartic and lubricant.

cas·tor-oil plant (kas′tər-oil′, käs′-) A plant native in India, yielding the castor bean.

cas·trate (kas′trāt) *v.t.* **·trat·ed, ·trat·ing 1.** To remove the testicles from; emasculate; geld. **2.** To remove the ovaries from; spay. [< L *castrare*] — **cas·tra/tion** *n.*

cas·u·al (kazh′ōō-əl) *adj.* **1.** Occurring by chance; accidental. **2.** Irregular; occasional: *casual* visits. **3.** Without intention or plan; offhand: a *casual* question. **4.** Negligent; nonchalant: a *casual* manner. **5.** Designed for informal wear: *casual* clothes. **6.** *Med.* Pertaining to accidental injuries. — *n.* **1.** One who is employed at irregular intervals. **2.** An occasional visitor. **3.** *Mil.* A soldier temporarily attached to a unit. [< MF < L *casus* accident < *cadere* to fall] — **cas/u·al·ly** *adv.* — **cas/u·al·ness** *n.*

cas·u·al·ty (kazh′ōō-əl-tē) *n. pl.* **·ties 1.** One who or that which is destroyed, injured, or otherwise made ineffective by an accident. **2.** *Mil.* A soldier who is killed, wounded, captured, or otherwise lost to his command through combat action. **3.** An accident, esp. a fatal or serious one.

cas·u·ist (kazh′ōō-ist) *n.* One who studies or resolves ethical problems: often used for one who rationalizes about such matters. [< F < L *casus* event, case] — **cas/u·is/tic** or **·ti·cal** *adj.* — **cas/u·is/ti·cal·ly** *adv.*

cas·u·ist·ry (kazh′ōō-is-trē) *n. pl.* **·ries 1.** The science that treats of or solves ambiguous cases of conscience or questions of right and wrong. **2.** Sophistical or equivocal reasoning, esp. in cases of conscience.

ca·sus bel·li (kā′səs bel′ī) *Latin* A cause justifying war.

cat (kat) *n.* **1.** A domesticated carnivorous mammal having retractile claws, and valued because it kills mice and rats. **2.** Any other animal of the cat family, as a lion, tiger, lynx, ocelot, etc. ◆ Collateral adjective: *feline.* **3.** A gossiping or backbiting woman. **4.** *Naut.* A tackle for hoisting an anchor to the cathead. **5.** A catboat. **6.** A cat-o'-nine-tails. **7.** A catfish. **8.** *U.S. Slang* A man; guy. **9.** *U.S. & Canadian* A catepillar tractor. — **to let the cat out of the bag** To divulge a secret. — *v.t.* **cat·ted, cat·ting 1.** To hoist and fasten at the cathead. **2.** To flog. [OE *cat, catte*]

cata- *prefix* **1.** Down; against; upon. **2.** Back; over. Also, before vowels, **cat-**: also **cath-**. Also spelled **kata-**. [< Gk. *kata* down, against, back]

ca·tab·o·lism (kə-tab′ə-liz′əm) *n. Biol.* The process by which living tissue breaks down into simpler and more stable substances; destructive metabolism: opposed to *anab-*

olism. [< Gk. < *kata*- down + *ballein* to throw] **—cat·a·bol·ic** (kat/ə·bol/ik) *adj.* **—cat/a·bol/i·cal·ly** *adv.*

cat·a·clysm (kat/ə·kliz/əm) *n.* **1.** Any violent upheaval or change, as a war, revolution, etc. **2.** Any violent disturbance. **3.** A deluge. [< MF < Gk. < *kata*- down + *klyzein* to wash] **—cat/a·clys/mic, cat/a·clys/mal** (-məl) *adj.*

cat·a·comb (kat/ə·kōm) *n. Usu. pl.* An underground place of burial, consisting of passages and small rooms with excavations in their sides for tombs. [< F < LL *catacumbas*]

cat·a·falque (kat/ə·falk) *n.* A structure supporting a coffin during a funeral. Also **cat/a·fal/co.** [< F < Ital. *catafalco*]

Cat·a·lan (kat/ə·lan, -lən) *adj.* Of or pertaining to Catalonia, its people, or their language. **—n.** **1.** A native or citizen of Catalonia. **2.** The Romance language of Catalonia and Valencia, closely related to Provençal.

cat·a·lep·sy (kat/ə·lep/sē) *n. Psychiatry* An abnormal maintenance of physical postures, accompanied by intense muscular rigidity. [< Med.L < Gk. < *kata*- upon + *lēpsis* seizure] **—cat/a·lep/tic** (-lep/tik) *adj. & n.*

cat·a·log (kat/ə·lôg, -log) *n., v.t., & v.i.* **·loged, ·log·ing** Catalogue. **—cat/a·log/er, cat/a·log/ist** *n.*

cat·a·logue (kat/ə·lôg, -log) *n.* **1.** A list or enumeration of names, objects, etc., usu. in alphabetical order. **2.** A publication containing such a list, as of articles for sale. **3.** A card catalogue (which see). Abbr. *cat.* **—v.t. & v.i. ·logued, ·logu·ing** To make a catalogue (of); enter (items) in a catalogue. [< F < LL < Gk. < *kata*- down + *legein* to select, choose] **—cat/a·logu/er, cat/a·logu/ist** *n.*

ca·tal·pa (kə·tal/pə) *n.* A tree of China, Japan, and North America, having large, ovate leaves, fragrant flowers, and long, slender pods. [< N. Am. Ind.]

ca·tal·y·sis (kə·tal/ə·sis) *n. pl.* **·ses** (-sēz) *Chem.* An increase in the rate of a chemical reaction, caused by the addition of a substance that is not permanently altered by the reaction: also spelled *katalysis.* [< Gk. < *kata*- wholly, completely + *lyein* to loosen] **—cat·a·lyt·ic** (kat/ə·lit/ik) *adj. & n.* **—cat/a·lyt/i·cal·ly** *adv.*

cat·a·lyst (kat/ə·list) *n. Chem.* Any substance that causes catalysis. Also **cat/a·lyz/er.**

cat·a·lyze (kat/ə·līz) *v.t.* **·lyzed, ·lyz·ing** To submit to or decompose by catalysis.

cat·a·ma·ran (kat/ə·mə·ran/) *n. Naut.* **1.** A long, narrow raft of logs, often with an outrigger. **2.** A boat having twin hulls. **3.** *Canadian* In Newfoundland, a heavy-duty wooden sled. [< Tamil *katta-maran* tied wood]

cat·a·mount (kat/ə·mount) *n. U.S.* The puma; also, the lynx. [Short form of *cat of the mountain*]

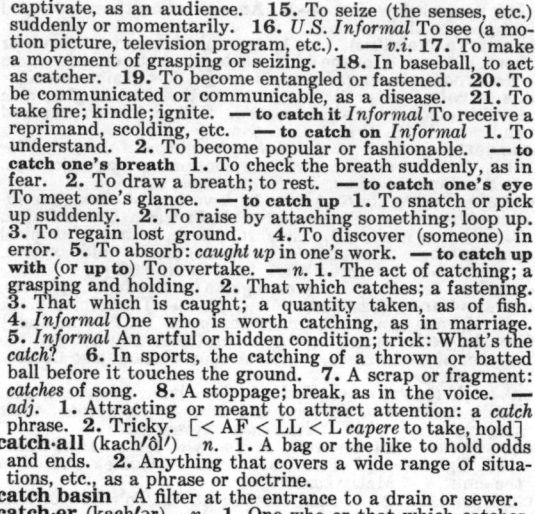

CATAMARAN (def. 2)
(Tahitian war canoe)

cat·a·pult (kat/ə·pult) *n.* **1.** An ancient military device for throwing stones, arrows, etc. **2.** *Aeron.* A device for launching an airplane at flight speed, as from the deck of a ship. **3.** A slingshot. **—v.t.** **1.** To hurl from or as from a catapult. **—v.i.** **2.** To hurtle through the air. [< L < Gk. < *kata*- down + *pallein* to brandish, hurl]

cat·a·ract (kat/ə·rakt) *n.* **1.** A waterfall. **2.** A downpour. **3.** *Pathol.* **a** Opacity of the lens of the eye, causing partial or total blindness. **b** The opaque area. [< MF *cataracte* < L < Gk. < *kata*- down + *arassein* to fall headlong]

ca·tarrh (kə·tär/) *n. Pathol.* Inflammation of the mucous membrane of the air passages in the throat and head, with excessive secretion of mucus. [< MF < L < Gk. < *kata*- down + *rhein* to flow] **—ca·tarrh/al, ca·tarrh/ous** *adj.*

ca·tas·tro·phe (kə·tas/trə·fē) *n.* **1.** A great and sudden disaster; calamity. **2.** A sudden, violent change or upheaval. **3.** In a drama, the conclusion of the plot; dénouement. [< Gk. < *kata*- over, down + *strephein* to turn] **—cat/a·stroph/ic** *adj.* **—cat/a·stroph/i·cal·ly** *adv.*

Ca·taw·ba (kə·tô/bə) *n.* An American red grape; also, a dry white wine made from it.

cat·bird (kat/bûrd/) *n.* A small, slate-colored North American songbird, having a catlike cry.

cat·boat (kat/bōt/) *n. Naut.* A small sailboat, having its mast well forward and carrying a single fore-and-aft sail.

cat·call (kat/kôl/) *n.* A shrill, discordant call or whistle expressing impatience or derision. **—v.t.** **1.** To deride or show contempt for with catcalls. **—v.i.** **2.** To utter catcalls.

catch (kach) *v.* **caught, catch·ing** *v.t.* **1.** To take, seize, or come upon. **2.** To take by trapping; ensnare. **3.** To surprise in the act. **4.** To take hold of suddenly so as to detain. **5.** To grip; entangle. **6.** To grasp and retain: to *catch* rain water in a barrel. **7.** To overtake: We were *caught* by the storm. **8.** To reach in time: to *catch* a train. **9.** To strike. **10.** To check (oneself) in speaking. **11.** To become affected with, as by contagion: to *catch* cold. **12.** To take; get: to *catch* fire. **13.** To apprehend or perceive; also, to reproduce accurately: The artist has not *caught* her expression. **14.** To captivate, as an audience. **15.** To seize (the senses, etc.) suddenly or momentarily. **16.** *U.S. Informal* To see (a motion picture, television program, etc.). **—v.i. 17.** To make a movement of grasping or seizing. **18.** In baseball, to act as catcher. **19.** To become entangled or fastened. **20.** To be communicated or communicable, as a disease. **21.** To take fire; kindle; ignite. **—to catch it** *Informal* To receive a reprimand, scolding, etc. **—to catch on** *Informal* **1.** To understand. **2.** To become popular or fashionable. **—to catch one's breath 1.** To check the breath suddenly, as in fear. **2.** To draw a breath; to rest. **—to catch one's eye** To meet one's glance. **—to catch up 1.** To snatch or pick up suddenly. **2.** To raise by attaching something; loop up. **3.** To regain lost ground. **4.** To discover (someone) in error. **5.** To absorb: *caught up* in one's work. **—to catch up with** (or **up to**) To overtake. **—n. 1.** The act of catching; a grasping and holding. **2.** That which catches; a fastening. **3.** That which is caught; a quantity taken, as of fish. **4.** *Informal* One who is worth catching, as in marriage. **5.** *Informal* An artful or hidden condition; trick: What's the *catch?* **6.** In sports, the catching of a thrown or batted ball before it touches the ground. **7.** A scrap or fragment: *catches* of song. **8.** A stoppage; break, as in the voice. **—adj. 1.** Attracting or meant to attract attention: a *catch* phrase. **2.** Tricky. [< AF < LL < L *capere* to take, hold]

catch·all (kach/ôl/) *n.* **1.** A bag or the like to hold odds and ends. **2.** Anything that covers a wide range of situations, etc., as a phrase or doctrine.

catch basin A filter at the entrance to a drain or sewer.

catch·er (kach/ər) *n.* **1.** One who or that which catches. **2.** In baseball, the player stationed behind home plate to catch balls that pass the batter.

catch·ing (kach/ing) *adj.* **1.** Infectious. **2.** Attractive.

catch·pen·ny (kach/pen/ē) *adj.* Designed merely to sell; cheap and showy. **—n. pl. ·nies** A catchpenny article.

catch·up (kach/əp, kech/-) See KETCHUP.

catch·word (kach/wûrd/) *n.* **1.** A word or phrase taken up and often repeated, esp. as a political slogan. Also **catch phrase. 2.** A word at the head of a page or column, identifying the first or last item on the page.

catch·y (kach/ē) *adj.* **catch·i·er, catch·i·est 1.** Attractive; catching the fancy; also, easily remembered: *catchy* tunes. **2.** Deceptive; tricky. **3.** Fitful: *catchy* winds.

cat·e·chet·ic (kat/ə·ket/ik) *adj.* Pertaining to oral instruction by question and answer. Also **cat/e·chet/i·cal.**

cat·e·chism (kat/ə·kiz/əm) *n.* **1.** A short manual giving, in the form of questions and answers, an outline of the principles of a religious creed. **2.** Any similar manual giving instructions. **3.** Examination by questions and answers. [< Med.L < Gk. *katēchizein* to instruct]

cat·e·chist (kat/ə·kist) *n.* One who catechizes; esp., an instructor of catechumens. Also **cat/e·chiz/er, cat/e·chis/er.** **—cat/e·chis/tic** or **·ti·cal** *adj.*

cat·e·chize (kat/ə·kīz) *v.t.* **·chized, ·chiz·ing 1.** To instruct, esp. in the principles of Christianity, by asking questions and discussing the answers. **2.** To question searchingly and at length. [< L < Gk. *katēchizein* to instruct] **—cat/e·chi·za/tion** *n.*

cat·e·chu·men (kat/ə·kyoo/mən) *n.* **1.** One who is under instruction in the elements of Christianity. **2.** One undergoing elementary instruction in any subject. **—cat/e·chu/me·nal, cat·e·chu·men·i·cal** (kat/ə·kyoo·men/i·kəl) *adj.*

cat·e·gor·i·cal (kat/ə·gôr/i·kəl, -gor/-) *adj.* **1.** Without qualification; absolute; unequivocal. **2.** Of, pertaining to, or included in a category. **—cat/e·gor/i·cal·ly** *adv.*

cat·e·go·rize (kat/ə·gə·rīz/) *v.t.* **·rized, ·riz·ing** To put into a category; classify.

cat·e·go·ry (kat/ə·gôr/ē, -gō/rē) *n. pl.* **·ries 1.** A division in any system of classification; a class: Drama is a *category* of literature. **2.** *Logic* Any of the fundamental concepts or classifications into which all knowledge can be placed. [< L < Gk. *katēgoreein* to allege, predicate]

cat·e·nate (kat/ə·nāt) *v.t.* **·nat·ed, ·nat·ing** To connect like the links of a chain. [< L *catena* chain] **—cat/e·na/tion** *n.*

ca·ter (kā/tər) *v.i.* **1.** To furnish food or entertainment. **2.** To provide for the gratification of any need or taste. **—v.t. 3.** To furnish food for: to *cater* a party. [< AF < LL < L *ad-* toward + *captare* to grasp, seize]

cat·er-cor·nered (kat/ər-kôr/nərd) *adj.* Diagonal. **—adv.** Diagonally. Also **catty-cornered, kitty-cornered.** Also **cat/er-cor/ner.** [< dial. F < F < L *quattuor* four + CORNERED]

ca·ter·er (kā/tər·ər) *n.* One who caters; esp., one who provides food and services for social functions.

cat·er·pil·lar (kat/ər·pil/ər) *n.* The larva of a butterfly or moth, or of certain other insects, as the sawfly. **—adj.** Moving or fitted with treads mounted on endless belts. [< AF < L < *catta* cat + *pilosus* < *pilum* hair]

Cat·er·pil·lar (kat/ər·pil/ər) *n.* A tractor that moves by means of two endless metal tracks running along each side: a trade name. Also **cat/er·pil/lar, caterpillar tractor.**

cat·er·waul (kat/ər·wôl) *v.i.* **1.** To utter the discordant cry of cats at mating time. **2.** To make any discordant screeching. — *n.* Such a sound. [ME < *cater* cat + *wawen* to wail, howl]

cat·fish (kat′fish′) *n.* *pl.* **·fish** or **·fish·es** Any of numerous scaleless fishes having sensitive barbels around the mouth.

cat·gut (kat′gut′) *n.* A very tough cord made from the intestines of certain animals, as sheep, and used for stringing musical instruments, making surgical ligatures, etc.

cath- Var. of CATA-.

ca·thar·sis (kə·thär′sis) *n.* **1.** *Med.* Purgation, esp. of the alimentary canal. **2.** A purifying or purging of the emotions through the effect of art. **3.** *Psychoanal.* A method of psychotherapy that induces the discharge of repressed emotions. Also spelled *katharsis.* [< Gk. *katharos* pure]

ca·thar·tic (kə·thär′tik) *adj.* Purgative; purifying. Also **ca·thar′ti·cal.** — *n.* A laxative. [< Gk. *katharos* pure]

Ca·thay (ka·thā′) *Poetic* or *Archaic* China.

cat·head (kat′hed′) *n.* *Naut.* A beam projecting over the bow, by which the anchor is supported clear of the ship.

ca·the·dra (kə·thē′drə, kath′ə-) *n.* **1.** A bishop's seat or throne in the cathedral of his diocese. **2.** The see or office of a bishop. [< L < Gk. < *kata-* down + *hedra* seat]

ca·the·dral (kə·thē′drəl) *n.* **1.** The church containing the official chair of a bishop. **2.** Loosely, any large or important church. — *adj.* **1.** Pertaining to or containing a bishop's chair or see. **2.** Authoritative; dogmatic. **3.** Of, pertaining to, or resembling a cathedral.

cath·e·ter (kath′ə·tər) *n.* *Med.* A slender, flexible tube introduced into body cavities for drainage, esp. one to draw urine from the bladder. [< L < Gk. *kata-* down + *hienai* to send, let go]

cath·e·ter·ize (kath′ə·tə·rīz′) *v.t.* **·ized,** **·iz·ing** To introduce a catheter into.

cath·ode (kath′ōd) *n.* *Electr.* The negatively charged electrode that receives cations during electrolysis. Also spelled *kathode.* [< Gk. < *kata-* down + *hodos* road, way] — **ca·thod·ic** (kə·thod′ik) or **·i·cal** *adj.*

cathode rays *Physics* A stream of electrons that pass from a cathode to the opposite wall of an evacuated electron tube when it is excited by a current of electricity.

cathode-ray tube *Electronics* A special type of electron tube in which a beam of electrons is focused by an electric or magnetic field and deflected so as to impinge upon a sensitized screen, forming an image, as on a television receiver.

cath·o·lic (kath′ə·lik, kath′lik) *adj.* **1.** Broad-minded, as in belief or tastes; liberal; comprehensive; large. **2.** Universal in reach; general. [< L < Gk. < *kata* thoroughly | *holos* whole] — **ca·thol·i·cal·ly** (kə·thol′ik·lē) *adv.*

Cath·o·lic (kath′ə·lik, kath′lik) *adj.* **1.** Since the Reformation: **a** Of or pertaining to the Roman Catholic Church. **b** Designating those churches that claim to have the apostolic doctrine and sacraments of the ancient, undivided church, and including the Anglican, Old Catholic, Orthodox, and Roman Catholic churches. **2.** Of the ancient, undivided Christian church. — *n.* A member of any Catholic church.

Catholic Church The Roman Catholic Church.

Ca·thol·i·cism (kə·thol′ə·siz′əm) *n.* The doctrine, system, and practice of a Catholic church, esp. the Roman Catholic Church. Also **Cath·o·lic·i·ty** (kath′ə·lis′ə·tē).

cath·o·lic·i·ty (kath′ə·lis′ə·tē) *n.* **1.** Freedom from narrowness; liberality. **2.** Universality.

ca·thol·i·cize (kə·thol′ə·sīz) *v.t.* & *v.i.* **·cized,** **·ciz·ing** To make or become catholic or Catholic.

cat·i·on (kat′ī·ən) *n.* *Chem.* The electropositive ion of an electrolyte, that moves toward the cathode in electrolysis: opposed to *anion:* also spelled *kation.* [< Gk. < *kata-* down + *ienai* to go] — **cat′i·on′ic** (-ī·on′ik) *adj.*

cat·kin (kat′kin) *n.* *Bot.* A deciduous, scaly spike of flowers, as in the willow. [MDu. *katteken,* dim. of *katte* cat]

cat nap A short, light nap; doze.

cat·nip (kat′nip′) *n.* An aromatic herb of the mint family, of which cats are fond. Also *Brit.* **cat′mint′.** [< CAT + dial. E *nep* catnip]

cat-o'-nine-tails (kat′ə·nīn′tālz′) *n.* A whip with nine knotted lines fastened to a handle.

cat rig The rig of a catboat, consisting of one sail on a mast far forward. — **cat-rigged** (kat′rigd′) *adj.*

cat's cradle A game played with a loop of string stretched in an intricate arrangement over the fingers.

cat's-eye (kats′ī′) *n.* **1.** A gemstone, usually chrysoberyl or quartz, that shows a line of light across the dome when cut. **2.** A small metal or glass reflector.

cat's-paw (kats′pô′) *n.* **1.** A person used as a tool or dupe. **2.** A light wind that ruffles the water. Also **cats′paw′.**

cat·sup (kat′səp, kech′əp) *See* KETCHUP.

cat·tail (kat′tāl′) *n.* A marsh plant having flowers in cylindrical terminal spikes and long leaves used for making mats, chair seats, etc.

cat·tle (kat′l) *n.* **1.** Domesticated bovine animals, as cows, bulls, and steers. **2.** Formerly, all livestock, as horses, sheep, etc. **3.** Human beings: a contemptuous term. [< AF < LL < L *capitale* capital, wealth]

cat·tle·man (kat′l·mən) *n.* *pl.* **·men** (-mən) One who raises or tends cattle.

cat·ty (kat′ē) *adj.* **·ti·er,** **·ti·est** **1.** Like or pertaining to cats. **2.** Slyly malicious; spiteful. — **cat′ti·ly** *adv.* — **cat′ti·ness** *n.*

cat·ty-cor·nered (kat′ē·kôr′nərd) *adj.* Cater-cornered.

cat·walk (kat′wôk′) *n.* Any narrow walking space, as at the side of a bridge.

Cau·ca·sian (kô·kā′zhən, -shən, -kash′ən) *adj.* **1.** Of or pertaining to the Caucasus region, its people, and their languages. **2.** Of or belonging to a major ethnic division of the human species loosely called the white race. Also **Cau·cas·ic** (kô·kas′ik). — *n.* **1.** A native of the Caucasus region. **2.** A member of the Caucasian division of the human race.

cau·cus (kô′kəs) *n.* A meeting of members of a political party to select candidates, plan a campaign, etc. — *v.i.* **cau·cused** or **·cussed, cau·cus·ing** or **·cus·sing** To meet in or hold a caucus. [after the 18th c. *Caucus* Club, Boston, Mass.]

cau·dal (kôd′l) *adj.* *Zool.* **1.** Of, pertaining to, or near the tail or posterior part of the body. **2.** Taillike. [< NL < L *cauda* tail] — **cau′dal·ly** *adv.*

cau·date (kô′dāt) *adj.* *Zool.* Having a tail or taillike appendage. Also **cau′dat·ed.** [< L *caudatus* < *cauda* tail]

cau·dle (kôd′l) *n.* A warm drink of gruel with wine, eggs, sugar, etc., for invalids. [< AF < Med.L < L *caldus* warm]

caught (kôt, kot) Past tense and past participle of CATCH.

caul (kôl) *n.* The part of the prenatal sac that sometimes envelops the head of a child at birth. [< OF *cale* cap]

caul·dron (kôl′drən) *n.* A large kettle or boiler: also spelled *caldron.* [< AF < L *calidus* hot]

cau·li·flow·er (kô′lə·flou′ər, kol′i-) *n.* **1.** The fleshy, edible head of a variety of cabbage. **2.** The plant bearing this. [Alter. of NL *cauliflora* a flowering cabbage]

cauliflower ear An ear that has been deformed by blows.

cau·lis (kô′lis) *n.* *pl.* **·les** (-lēz) *Bot.* The stem of a plant. [< L < Gk. *kaulos*] — **cau·line** (kô′lin, -līn) *adj.*

caulk (kôk) *v.t.* **1.** To make tight, as a boat's seams, window frame, etc., by plugging with soft material, such as oakum or tar. Also spelled *calk.* [< OF < L *calcare* to tread] — **caulk′er** *n.* — **caulk′ing** *n.*

cau·sal (kô′zəl) *adj.* Pertaining to, constituting, involving, or expressing a cause. — *n. Gram.* A form expressing cause or reason, as *therefore.* [< L *causa* cause] — **caus′al·ly** *adv.*

cau·sal·i·ty (kô·zal′ə·tē) *n.* *pl.* **·ties** **1.** The relation of cause and effect. **2.** Causal character or agency.

cau·sa·tion (kô·zā′shən) *n.* **1.** The act of causing. **2.** That which produces an effect; cause. **3.** The relation of cause and effect. [< Med.L < L *causa* cause]

caus·a·tive (kô′zə·tiv) *adj.* **1.** Effective as a cause. **2.** *Gram.* Expressing cause or agency: *to lay* (to cause to lie) is a *causative* verb. — *n. Gram.* A form that expresses or suggests causation. [< MF < L *causa* cause] — **caus′a·tive·ly** *adv.* — **caus′a·tive·ness** *n.*

cause (kôz) *n.* **1.** The agent or force producing an effect or a result. **2.** A ground for choice or action: *cause* for complaint. **3.** Sufficient ground; good reason: no *cause* to strike. **4.** An aim, object, or principle advocated and supported by an individual or group. **5.** *Law* A matter to be decided in court. **6.** A matter under discussion or in dispute. — *v.t.* **caused, caus·ing** To be the cause of; produce; effect. [< MF < L *causa* cause, legal case] — **caus′a·ble** *adj.* — **cause′less** *adj.* — **caus′er** *n.*

cause cé·lè·bre (kōz sā·leb′r′) *French* **1.** A famous legal case. **2.** Any well-known controversial issue.

cau·se·rie (kō′zə·rē′, *Fr.* kōz·rē′) *n.* **1.** An informal conversation; a chat. **2.** A short, chatty piece of writing. [< F]

cause·way (kôz′wā′) *n.* **1.** A raised road or way, as over marshy ground. **2.** A paved way; a highway. — *v.t.* To make a causeway for or through, as a marshy tract. [Earlier *causeyway* < AF < LL < L *calx, calcis* heel + WAY]

caus·tic (kôs′tik) *adj.* **1.** Capable of corroding or eating away tissues; burning; corrosive. **2.** Sarcastic; biting: *caustic* wit. — *n.* A caustic substance. [< L < Gk. *kaiein* to burn] — **caus′ti·cal·ly** *adv.* — **caus·tic·i·ty** (kôs·tis′ə·tē) *n.*

caustic potash Potassium hydroxide.

caustic soda Sodium hydroxide.

cau·ter·ize (kô′tə·rīz) *v.t.* **·ized,** **·iz·ing** To sear with a caustic agent or heated iron. — **cau′ter·i·za′tion** *n.*

cau·ter·y (kô′tər·ē) *n.* *pl.* **·ter·ies** *Med.* **1.** The destruction of tissue by the application of a caustic substance or a searing iron. **2.** A cauterizing agent. [< L < Gk. *kauterion* < *kaiein* to burn]

cau·tion (kô′shən) *n.* **1.** Care to avoid injury or misfortune; prudence; wariness; discretion. **2.** An admonition or warning. **3.** *Informal* One who or that which alarms, astonishes, etc. — *v.t.* To advise to be prudent; warn. [< OF < L *cautio, -onis* < *cavere* to beware]

cau·tion·ar·y (kô′shən·er′ē) *adj.* Urging caution.

cau·tious (kô′shəs) *adj.* Using great care or prudence; wary. — **cau′tious·ly** *adv.* — **cau′tious·ness** *n.*

cav·al·cade (kav′əl·kād′, kav′əl·kād) *n.* **1.** A company of horsemen on the march or in procession. **2.** A procession; parade. [< MF < Ital. < LL < L *caballus* horse]

cav·a·lier (kav′ə·lir′) *n.* **1.** A horseman; knight. **2.** A courtly or dashing gentleman; a gallant; also, a lady's escort. — *adj.* **1.** Haughty; supercilious. **2.** Free and easy; offhand. — *v.i.* To behave in a cavalier fashion; show arrogance. [< MF < Ital. < LL < L *caballus* horse, nag] — **cav′a·lier′ly** *adj. & adv.*

Cav·a·lier (kav′ə·lir′) *n.* A supporter of Charles I of England; a Royalist. — *adj.* Pertaining to the Cavaliers.

cav·al·ry (kav′əl·rē) *n. pl.* **·ries** Troops trained to maneuver and fight on horseback or, more recently, in armored motor vehicles. Abbr. *cav.* [< MF < Ital. < LL < L *caballus* horse] — **cav′al·ry·man** (-mən) *n.*

cave (kāv) *n.* A chamber beneath the earth, in a mountain or mountainside, etc. ◆ Collateral adjective: *spelean.* — *v.* **caved, cav·ing** *v.t.* **1.** To hollow out. — *v.i.* **2.** *Informal* To fall in or down; give way. — **to cave in 1.** To fall in or down, as when undermined; cause to fall in. **2.** *Informal* To yield utterly; give in. [< OF < L *cavus* hollow]

ca·ve·at (kā′vē·at) *n.* **1.** *Law* A formal notification given by an interested party to a court or officer not to do a certain act. **2.** A caution or warning, esp. to avoid misinterpretation. [< L, let him beware]

ca·ve·at emp·tor (kā′vē·at emp′tôr) *Latin* Let the buyer beware, implying that the purchase is made at his own risk.

ca·ve·a·tor (kā′vē·ā′tər) *n.* One who enters a caveat.

cave-in (kāv′in′) *n.* A collapse or falling in, as of a mine.

cave man 1. A Paleolithic man; prehistoric cave dweller; troglodyte (def. 1). **2.** *Informal* A man who is rough and brutal, esp. in his approach to women.

cav·ern (kav′ərn) *n.* A cave, esp. one that is large or extensive. — *v.t.* **1.** To shut in or as in a cavern. **2.** To hollow out. [< MF < L < *cavus* hollow]

cav·ern·ous (kav′ər·nəs) *adj.* **1.** Full of caverns. **2.** Characteristic of a cavern. **3.** Hollow. — **cav′ern·ous·ly** *adv.*

cav·i·ar (kav′ē·är, kä′vē-) *n.* The salted roe of sturgeon or other fish, used as a relish. Also **cav′i·are.** [< F < Turkish *khāvyār*]

cav·il (kav′əl) *v.* **cav·iled** or **·illed, cav·il·ing** or **·il·ling** *v.i.* **1.** To raise trivial objections; argue captiously; carp: with *at* or *about.* — *v.t.* **2.** To find fault with. — *n.* A captious objection. [< MF < L *cavilla* a jeering, a scoffing] — **cav′il·er** or **cav′il·ler** *n.* — **cav′il·ing·ness** or **cav′il·ling·ness** *n.* — **cav′il·ing·ly** or **cav′il·ling·ly** *adv.*

cav·i·ty (kav′ə·tē) *n. pl.* **·ties 1.** A hollow or sunken space; hole. **2.** A natural hollow in the body. **3.** A decayed place in a tooth. [< MF < LL < L *cavus* hollow]

ca·vort (kə·vôrt′) *v.i. U.S.* To prance about; caper; frisk.

ca·vy (kā′vē) *n. pl.* **·vies** A small South American rodent with the tail absent or rudimentary, as the guinea pig. [< NL *Cavia* < Carib]

caw (kô) *v.i.* To make the high harsh sound of a crow, rook, etc. — *n.* The cry of a crow, raven, etc. [Imit.]

cay (kā, kē) *n.* A coastal reef or sandy islet, as in the Gulf of Mexico. See KEY². [< Sp. *cayo* shoal]

cay·enne pepper (kī·en′, kā-) Red pepper. Also **cay·enne′.**

cay·man (kā′mən) *n. pl.* **·mans** A tropical American crocodilian related to the alligator. [< Sp. *caiman* < Carib]

Ca·yu·ga (kā·yōō′gə, kī-) *n. pl.* **·ga** or **·gas** One of a tribe of Iroquois Indians formerly living near Cayuga Lake, N.Y.

cay·use (kī·yōōs′) *n. U.S.* An Indian pony.

Cay·use (kī·yōōs′) *n.* A member of a tribe of North American Indians formerly inhabiting Oregon.

cease (sēs) *v.* **ceased, ceas·ing** *v.t.* **1.** To leave off or discontinue, as one's own actions. — *v.i.* **2.** To come to an end; stop; desist. — *n.* End; stopping: now only in the phrase **without cease.** [< MF < L *cedere* to withdraw, yield] — **cease′less** *adj.* — **cease′less·ly** *adv.*

cease-fire (sēs′fīr′) *n.* An armistice; truce.

ce·cro·pi·a moth (si·krō′pē·ə) A large, strikingly marked moth common in the eastern U.S.

ce·cum (sē′kəm) *n. pl.* **ce·ca** (sē′kə) *Anat.* A pouch, or cavity, open at one end, esp. that situated between the large and small intestine: also spelled *caecum.* For illus. see IN-TESTINE. [< L < *caecus* blind] — **ce′cal** *adj.*

ce·dar (sē′dər) *n.* **1.** A large tree of the pine family, having evergreen leaves and fragrant wood. **2.** The red cedar (def. 1). **3.** The wood of these and related trees. — *adj.* Pertaining to or made of cedar. [< OF < L < Gk. *kedros*]

ce·dar·bird (sē′dər·bûrd′) *n.* The cedar waxwing. See under WAXWING.

cede (sēd) *v.t.* **ced·ed, ced·ing 1.** To yield or give up. **2.** To surrender title to; transfer: to *cede* land. [< MF *céder* < L *cedere* to withdraw, yield]

ce·dil·la (si·dil′ə) *n.* A mark put under the letter *c* (ç) before *a, o,* or *u* in some French words, as in *français,* to indicate that it is to be sounded as (s). [< Sp. < Gk. *zēta* letter *z*]

ceil (sēl) *v.t.* To furnish with a ceiling. [< F < L *caelum* heaven, sky]

ceil·ing (sē′ling) *n.* **1.** The overhead covering or lining of a room. **2.** An upper limit; maximum, as one set on prices or wages. **3.** *Aeron.* The maximum height to which a given aircraft can be flown under specified conditions.

cel·an·dine (sel′ən·dīn) *n.* **1.** A plant of the poppy family, with yellow flowers. **2.** A crowfoot having tuberous roots and yellow flowers. [< OF < L < Gk. *chelidōn* a swallow]

-cele¹ *combining form* Tumor or hernia. [< Gk. *kēlē* tumor]

-cele² *combining form* Cavity; hollow space: *blastocele:* also spelled *-coele.* [< Gk. *koilos* hollow]

cel·e·brant (sel′ə·brənt) *n.* **1.** One who participates in a celebration. **2.** The officiating priest at the Eucharist.

cel·e·brate (sel′ə·brāt) *v.* **·brat·ed, ·brat·ing** *v.t.* **1.** To observe, as a festival, with rejoicing. **2.** To make known or famous; extol. **3.** To perform (a ceremony) publicly and as ordained. — *v.i.* **4.** To observe or commemorate a day or event. **5.** To perform a religious ceremony. [< L *celeber* famous] — **cel′e·bra′tor** *n.*

— **Syn. 1.** *Celebrate* is used for joyous occasions: to *celebrate* a holiday or birthday. *Commemorate* refers to the solemnity of an event, as does *solemnize,* but *commemorate* looks to the past, often with sorrow, while *solemnize* refers to a present occasion: to *commemorate* a great man's death, to *solemnize* a marriage.

cel·e·brat·ed (sel′ə·brā′tid) *adj.* Well-known; much publicized: a *celebrated* murder trial.

cel·e·bra·tion (sel′ə·brā′shən) *n.* **1.** The act of celebrating. **2.** That which is done in commemoration of any event.

ce·leb·ri·ty (sə·leb′rə·tē) *n. pl.* **·ties 1.** A famous or celebrated person. **2.** Fame or renown. [< L *celeber* famous]

ce·ler·i·ty (sə·ler′ə·tē) *n.* Quickness of motion; speed; rapidity. [< L *celer* swift]

cel·er·y (sel′ər·ē, sel′rē) *n.* A biennial herb whose stems are used as a vegetable or salad. [< F < dial. Ital. < *selinon* parsley < Gk.]

ce·les·ta (sə·les′tə) *n.* A musical instrument having a keyboard and steel plates struck by hammers. [< F *célesta*]

ce·les·tial (sə·les′chəl) *adj.* **1.** Of or pertaining to the sky or heavens. **2.** Of heaven; divine. **3.** *Often cap.* Chinese. — *n.* **1.** A heavenly being. **2.** *Often cap.* A Chinese. [< OF < L < *caelum* sky, heaven] — **ce·les′tial·ly** *adv.*

Celestial Empire The former Chinese Empire.

celestial equator *Astron.* The great circle in which the plane of the earth's equator cuts the celestial sphere.

celestial sphere *Astron.* The imaginary spherical surface on which the heavenly bodies seem to lie, commonly conceived as of infinite diameter and enclosing the universe.

ce·li·ac (sē′lē·ak) *adj.* Of or pertaining to the abdomen. Also spelled *coeliac.* [< L *coeliacus* < Gk. *koilos* hollow]

cel·i·ba·cy (sel′ə·bə·sē) *n.* The state of being unmarried, esp. in accordance with religious vows. [< L *caelebs* unmarried]

cel·i·bate (sel′ə·bit, -bāt) *n.* One who remains unmarried, esp. by vow. — *adj.* Unmarried, esp. by vow.

cell (sel) *n.* **1.** A small room, as for a prisoner or monk. **2.** A small compartment, receptacle, or cavity. **3.** A body of persons forming a single unit in an organization of similar groups. **4.** *Biol.* The fundamental structural unit of plant and animal life, consisting of a small mass of cytoplasm and usu. enclosing a central nucleus and surrounded by a membrane (animal) or a rigid cell wall (plant). **5.** A single

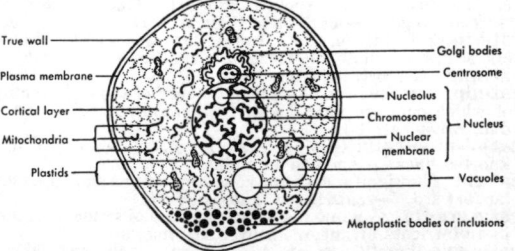

True wall — Golgi bodies
Plasma membrane — Centrosome
— Nucleolus
Cortical layer — Chromosomes — Nucleus
Mitochondria — Nuclear membrane
Plastids — Vacuoles
— Metaplastic bodies or inclusions

GENERALIZED CELL

compartment of a honeycomb. **6.** *Bot.* The seed-bearing cavity of an ovary or pericarp. **7.** *Electr.* The unit composing all or part of a battery, consisting of electrodes in contact with an electrolyte and in which a current is generated by means of chemical action. — **dry cell** *Electr.* A primary cell with its electrolyte distributed in some porous substance. [< OF < L *cella* cell, small room]

cel·lar (sel′ər) *n.* **1.** A space wholly or partly underground and usu. beneath a building, used for storage, etc. **2.** A wine cellar; also, a stock of wines. — *v.t.* To put or keep in a cellar. [< AF, OF < L *cella* cell, small room]

cel·lar·age (sel′ər·ij) *n.* **1.** Space in or for a cellar. **2.** The charge for storing goods in a cellar.

cel·lar·er (sel′ər·ər) *n.* The keeper of a cellar, as the steward in a monastery.

cel·lar·et (sel′ə·ret′) *n.* A case or small cabinet for wine and liquor bottles, decanters, glasses, etc. Also **cel′lar·ette′**.

cell-block (sel′blok′) *n.* In prisons, a unit of cells.

cel·lo (chel′ō) *n. pl.* **·los** A bass instrument of the violin family, tuned an octave lower than the viola, and held between the performer's knees: also called *violoncello.* Also **'cel′lo.** [Short for VIOLONCELLO] — **cel′list** or **'cel′list** *n.*

cel·lo·phane (sel′ə·fān) *n.* A treated cellulose that has been processed in thin, transparent strips or sheets.

cel·lu·lar (sel′yə·lər) *adj.* **1.** Of or like a cell or cells. **2.** Consisting of cells. [See CELLULE.]

cel·lule (sel′yōōl) *n.* A small cell. [< L *cellula,* dim. of *cella* cell, small room]

Cel·lu·loid (sel′yə·loid) *n.* A hard, elastic, flammable plastic, made from guncotton mixed with camphor and other substances: a trade name. Also **cel′lu·loid.**

cel·lu·lose (sel′yə·lōs) *n. Biochem.* An amorphous white carbohydrate, insoluble in all ordinary solvents, and forming the fundamental material of the structure of plants. [< L *cellula.* See CELLULE.]

cellulose acetate *Chem.* **1.** A derivative of cellulose, used in making synthetic yarns and fabrics. **2.** Acetate rayon.

ce·lom (sē′ləm) See COELOM.

Cel·o·tex (sel′ə·teks) *n.* A composition board used for insulation: a trade name. Also **cel′o·tex.**

Cel·si·us scale (sel′sē·əs) A temperature scale in which the freezing point of water at normal atmospheric pressure is 0° and the boiling point is 100°; the centigrade scale. [after Anders *Celsius,* 1701–44, Swedish astronomer]

Celt (selt, kelt) *n.* A person of Celtic linguistic stock, now represented by the Irish, Welsh, Highland Scots, and Bretons, formerly by the Gauls and Britons. Also spelled *Kelt.*

Celt·ic (sel′tik, kel′-) *n.* A subfamily of the Indo-European family of languages, including ancient Gaulish, the Brythonic or Cymric branch (Cornish, Welsh, Breton), and the Goidelic or Gaelic branch (Irish, Scottish Gaelic, Manx). — *adj.* Of or pertaining to the Celtic peoples, their languages, or culture. Also spelled *Keltic.*

Celtic cross An upright cross having a circle behind the crossbeam.

ce·ment (si·ment′) *n.* **1.** A mixture, usu. of burned limestone and clay, that is applied as a mortar or used for pavements and other smooth surfaces. **Portland cement** is made by calcining limestone with chalk, mud, etc. **2.** Any material, as glue, that, when hardened, will bind objects together. **3.** Something that unites. **4.** An adhesive material used in filling teeth and in other dental work. **5.** *Anat.* Cementum. — *v.t.* **1.** To unite or join with or as with cement. **2.** To cover or coat with cement. — *v.i.* **3.** To become united by means of cement; cohere. [< OF *ciment* < L *caedere* to cut] — **ce·men·ta·tion** (sē′mən·tā′shən, sem′ən-) *n.* — **ce·ment′er** *n.*

ce·men·tum (si·men′təm) *n. Anat.* The layer of bony tissue developed over the roots of the teeth: also called *cement.* For illus. see TOOTH. [< L]

cem·e·ter·y (sem′ə·ter′ē) *n. pl.* **·ter·ies** A place for burying the dead; graveyard. [< L *coemeterium* < Gk. *koimaein* to put to sleep]

-cene *combining form Geol.* Recent; new: used in the names of geological periods: *Pliocene.* [< Gk. *kainos* new]

ceno- *combining form* Common. Also spelled *coeno-*: also, before vowels, **cen-.** [< Gk. *koinos* common]

cen·o·bite (sen′ə·bīt, sē′nə-) *n.* A member of a religious community: also spelled *coenobite.* [< LL *coenobita* < Gk. < *koinos* common + *bios* life] — **cen′o·bit′ic** (-bit′ik) or **·i·cal** *adj.* — **cen′o·bit·izm,** **sē′nə-)** *n.*

cen·o·taph (sen′ə·taf, -täf) *n.* A monument erected to the dead but not containing the remains. [< MF < L < Gk. < *kenos* empty + *taphos* tomb] — **cen′o·taph′ic** *adj.*

Ce·no·zo·ic (sē′nə·zō′ik, sen′ə-) *Geol. adj.* Of or pertaining to the fourth and latest of the eras of geologic time, following the Mesozoic, and extending to and including the present. See chart for GEOLOGY. — *n.* The Cenozoic period. [< Gk. *kainos* new + *zoē* life]

cen·ser (sen′sər) *n.* A vessel for burning incense: also called *thurible.* [< OF *censier* < Med.L *incensum* incense]

cen·sor (sen′sər) *n.* **1.** An official examiner of manuscripts, plays, etc., empowered to suppress them, wholly or in part, if objectionable. **2.** An official who examines dispatches, letters, etc., in time of war. **3.** Anyone who censures or arraigns. **4.** In ancient Rome, one of two magistrates who drew up the census and supervised public morals. — *v.t.*

To act as censor of. [< L < *censere* to judge] — **cen·so·ri·al** (sen·sôr′ē·əl, -sō′rē-) *adj.*

cen·so·ri·ous (sen·sôr′ē·əs, -sō′rē-) *adj.* Given to censure; judging severely; faultfinding. — **cen·so′ri·ous·ly** *adv.* — **cen·so′ri·ous·ness** *n.*

cen·sor·ship (sen′sər·ship) *n.* **1.** The action of censoring. **2.** The office or power of a censor. **3.** A system of censoring.

cen·sur·a·ble (sen′shər·ə·bəl) *adj.* Deserving censure. — **cen·sur·a·ble·ness** *n.* — **cen·sur·a·bly** *adv.*

cen·sure (sen′shər) *n.* The expression of disapproval or blame; adverse or hostile criticism; reprimand. — **Syn.** See REPROOF. — *v.* **·sured, ·sur·ing** *v.t.* **1.** To express disapproval of; condemn; blame. — *v.i.* **2.** To express disapproval. [< F < L < *censere* to judge] — **cen′sur·er** *n.*

cen·sus (sen′səs) *n. pl.* **·sus·es 1.** An official count of the people of a country or district, with statistics as to age, sex, employment, etc. **2.** In ancient Rome, a similar enumeration to determine taxation. [< L *censere* to assess] — **cen·su·al** (sen′shōō·əl) *adj.*

cent (sent) *n.* **1.** The hundredth part of a dollar; also, a coin of this value: symbol ¢. **2.** A hundred: used only in *percent, per cent.* [< F < L *centum* hundred]

cen·tare (sen′târ, *Fr.* sän·tår′) *n.* A measure of land area, equal to one square meter: also *centiare.* See table front of book. [< F *centi-* hundredth (< L *centum* hundred) + *are.* See ARE².]

cen·taur (sen′tôr) *n.* In Greek mythology, one of a race of monsters, having the head, arms, and torso of a man united to the body and legs of a horse. [< L < Gk. *Kentauros*]

CENTAUR

cen·ta·vo (sen·tä′vō) *n. pl.* **·vos** (-vōz, *Sp.* -vōs) **1.** A small coin of the Philippines and various Spanish-American countries, equal to one hundredth of the peso. **2.** A similar coin of Portugal and of Brazil. [< Sp.]

cen·te·nar·i·an (sen′tə·nâr′ē·ən) *n.* One who is 100 years old. — *adj.* **1.** Of the age of 100 years. **2.** Pertaining to a period of 100 years.

cen·te·nar·y (sen′tə·ner′ē, sen·ten′ə·rē) *adj.* **1.** Of or pertaining to 100 or 100 years. **2.** Occurring every 100 years. — *n. pl.* **·nar·ies 1.** A period of 100 years. **2.** A centennial. [< L *centum* hundred]

cen·ten·ni·al (sen·ten′ē·əl) *adj.* **1.** Of an age or duration of 100 years. **2.** Of or marking a period of 100 years or its completion. **3.** Occurring every 100 years. — *n.* A 100th anniversary or its celebration. [< L < *centum* hundred + *annus* year] — **cen·ten′ni·al·ly** *adv.*

Centennial State Nickname of Colorado.

cen·ter (sen′tər) *n.* **1.** The point or place equally distant from the extremities or sides of anything. **2.** *Geom.* The point within a circle or sphere equidistant from every point on the circumference or surface. **3.** A point about which a thing revolves. **4.** A place or point at which activity is concentrated or toward which people seem to converge. **5.** A point from which effects, influences, etc., proceed; source. **6.** *Mil.* The part of an army occupying the front between the wings. **7.** *Often cap.* A group, party, etc., having moderate views or tendencies. **8.** In football, basketball, etc., a player who occupies a middle position, as in the forward line. — *v.t.* **1.** To place in or at the center. **2.** To direct toward one place; concentrate. **3.** To determine or mark the center of. — *v.i.* **4.** To be at the center of. — *adj.* Central; middle. Also, *Brit.,* centre. [< L *centrum* < Gk. *kentron* point]

cen·ter·board (sen′tər·bôrd′, -bōrd′) *n.* A board so hung that it can be lowered below the bottom of a sailboat through a slot to prevent leeway. Also **cen′tre·board′.**

center of gravity *Physics* The point about which a body acted upon by gravity is in equilibrium in all positions.

cen·ter·piece (sen′tər·pēs′) *n.* A piece at the center of anything; esp., an ornament in the center of a table.

cen·tes·i·mal (sen·tes′ə·məl) *adj.* **1.** Hundredth. **2.** Pertaining to or divided into hundredths. [< L *centesimus* hundredth] — **cen·tes′i·mal·ly** *adv.*

centi- *combining form* **1.** Hundred: *centipede.* **2.** In the metric system and in technical usage, one hundredth of (a specified unit): *centiliter.* [< L *centum* hundred]

cen·ti·are (sen′tē·âr) See CENTARE.

cen·ti·grade (sen′tə·grād) *adj.* Graduated to a scale of a hundred. [< F < L *centum* hundred + *gradus* step, degree]

centigrade scale A temperature scale in which the freezing point of water at normal atmospheric pressure is 0° and the boiling point is 100°: also called *Celsius scale.*

cen·ti·gram (sen′tə·gram) *n.* In the metric system, the hundredth part of a gram. Also **cen′ti·gramme.** See table inside back cover.

cen·ti·li·ter (sen′tə·lē′tər) *n.* In the metric system, the hundredth part of a liter. Also *esp. Brit.* **cen′ti·li′tre.** See table inside back cover.

cen·time (sän′tēm, *Fr.* sän·têm′) *n.* A small coin, the hundredth part of a franc. [< F < OF < L *centesimus* hundredth]

cen·ti·me·ter (sen′tə·mē′tər) *n.* In the metric system, the hundredth part of a meter. Also *esp. Brit.* **cen′ti·me′tre.** See table inside back cover.

cen·ti·me·ter-gram-sec·ond (sen′tə·mē′tər·gram′sek′ənd) *adj.* See CGS.

cen·ti·pede (sen′tə·pēd) *n.* A wormlike animal having many pairs of legs. [< F < L < *centum* hundred + *pes, pedis* foot]

cen·ti·stere (sen′tə·stir) *n.* A hundredth of a stere. See table inside back cover. [< F *centistère*]

cen·tral (sen′trəl) *adj.* 1. At, in, or near the center. 2. Of or constituting the center. 3. That exercises a controlling influence; dominant. 4. Most important; principal; chief. [< L < *centrum* center] — **cen′tral·ly** *adv.*

cen·tral·ism (sen′trəl·iz′əm) *n.* A centralizing tendency or system; concentration of control in a central authority. — **cen′tral·ist** *n. & adj.* — **cen′tral·is′tic** *adj.*

cen·tral·i·ty (sen·tral′ə·tē) *n.* 1. The state of being central. 2. Tendency toward or situation at a center.

cen·tral·ize (sen′trəl·īz) *v.* ·ized, ·iz·ing *v.t.* 1. To bring to a center; make central; especially, to bring under a central authority. — *v.i.* 2. To come to a center; concentrate. — **cen′tral·i·za′tion** *n.* — **cen′tral·iz′er** *n.*

central nervous system *Anat.* That part of the nervous system consisting of the brain and spinal cord.

cen·tre (sen′tər) *n., adj., v.t. & v.i.* ·tred, ·tring *Brit.* Center.

centri- *combining form* Center: used in words of Latin origin. Compare CENTRO-. [< L *centrum* center]

cen·tric (sen′trik) *adj.* At, relating to, or having a center. Also **cen′tri·cal.** [< Gk. *kentrikos* < *kentron* center] — **cen′tri·cal·ly** *adv.* — **cen·tric·i·ty** (sen·tris′ə·tē) *n.*

cen·trif·u·gal (sen·trif′yə·gəl, -trif′ə·gəl) *adj.* 1. Directed or tending away from a center; radiating: opposed to *centripetal.* 2. Employing centrifugal force: a *centrifugal* pump. — *n.* A centrifuge. [< NL < L *centrum* center + *fugere* to flee] — **cen·trif′u·gal·ly** *adv.*

centrifugal force *Physics* The inertial reaction by which a body tends to move away from the center of rotation.

cen·tri·fuge (sen′trə·fyōoj) *n.* A rotary machine for the separation of substances having different densities. — *v.t.* **·fuged, ·fug·ing** To subject to the action of a centrifuge. [< F] — **cen·trif·u·ga·tion** (sen·trif′yə·gā′shən, -ə·gā′-) *n.*

cen·trip·e·tal (sen·trip′ə·təl) *adj.* 1. Directed, tending, or drawing toward a center: opposed to *centrifugal.* 2. Acting by drawing toward a center. [< NL < L *centrum* center + *petere* to seek] — **cen·trip′e·tal·ly** *adv.*

centripetal force *Physics* A force attracting a body toward a center around which it revolves.

cen·trist (sen′trist) *n.* One who takes a moderate position in politics.

centro- *combining form* Center: used in words of Greek origin, as in *centrosphere.* Also, before vowels, **centr-.** [< Gk. *kentron* center]

cen·tro·some (sen′trə·sōm) *n. Biol.* The small area of protoplasm external to the nucleus of the cell. — **cen′tro·som′ic** (-som′ik) *adj.* For illus. see CELL.

cen·tro·sphere (sen′trə·sfir′) *n. Biol.* In living cells, the sphere that surrounds the centrosome. For illus. see CELL.

cen·tu·ple (sen′tə·pəl, sen·tōo′pəl, -tyōō′-) *v.t.* **·pled, ·pling** To increase a hundredfold. — *adj.* Increased a hundredfold. [< F < LL *centuplus* hundredfold]

cen·tu·pli·cate (*v.* sen·tōo′plə·kāt, -tyōo′-; *adj. & n.* sen·tōo′plə·kit, -tyōo′-) *v.t.* **·cat·ed, ·cat·ing** To multiply by a hundred; centuple. — *adj. & n.* Hundredfold. [< LL < L *centuplex* hundredfold] — **cen·tu′pli·ca′tion** *n.*

cen·tu·ri·on (sen·tŏŏr′ē·ən, -tyŏŏr′-) *n.* In the ancient Roman army, a captain of a century. [< L *centurio, -onis*]

cen·tu·ry (sen′chə·rē) *n. pl.* **·ries** 1. A period of 100 years in any system of chronology, esp. in reckoning from the first year of the Christian era. 2. In ancient Rome: **a** A body of foot soldiers, originally of 100 men. **b** One of 193 electoral divisions. 3. A group or series of a hundred. [< L *centuria* < *centum* hundred] — **cen·tu·ri·al** (sen·tŏŏr′ē·əl) *adj.*

century plant A succulent plant of the amaryllis family, flowering in twenty to thirty years and then dying, popularly supposed to bloom once in a century.

ce·phal·ic (sə·fal′ik) *adj.* 1. Of or pertaining to the head. 2. At, on, in, or near the head. [< F < Gk. *kephalē* head]

-cephalic *combining form* Head; skull: *brachycephalic.*

cephalic index *Anat.* The ratio of the greatest breadth of the human head from side to side, multiplied by 100, to the greatest length.

cephalo- *combining form* Head. Also, before vowels, **cephal-.** [< Gk. *kephalē* head]

ceph·a·lo·pod (sef′ə·lə·pod′) *Zool. n.* Any of a class of marine mollusks having a clearly defined head and eyes, ink sac, and tentacles or arms around the mouth, as squids and octopuses. — *adj.* Of or pertaining to cephalopods: also **ceph′-**

a·lo·pod′ic, ceph·a·lop·o·dous (sef′ə·lop′ə·dəs). — **ceph·a·lop·o·dan** (sef′ə·lop′ə·dən) *n. & adj.*

ceph·a·lo·tho·rax (sef′ə·lō·thôr′aks, -thō′raks) *n. Zool.* The anterior portion of certain crustaceans and arachnids, consisting of the united head and thorax. For illus. see SHRIMP. — **ceph′a·lo·tho·rac′ic** (-thə·ras′ik) *adj.*

ceph·a·lous (sef′ə·ləs) *adj.* Having a head.

-cephalous *combining form* Headed: *hydrocephalous.* [< Gk. *kephalē* head]

cer- Var. of CERO-.

ce·ram·ic (sə·ram′ik) *adj.* Pertaining to articles made of fired and baked clay. [< Gk. *keramos* potter's clay]

ce·ram·ics (sə·ram′iks) *n.pl.* (*construed as sing in def.* 1.) 1. The art of modeling and baking in clay. 2. Objects made of fired and baked clay. — **ce·ram′ist** *n.*

Cer·ber·us (sûr′bər·əs) In classical mythology, the three-headed dog guarding the portals of Hades. — **Cer·be·re·an** (sər·bir′ē·ən) *adj.*

cere[1] (sir) *v.t.* **cered, cer·ing** To wrap in cerecloth. [< MF < L *cera* wax]

cere[2] (sir) *n. Ornithol.* In parrots and birds of prey, a waxlike area about the bill. [< F < L *cera* wax]

ce·re·al (sir′ē·əl) *n.* 1. An edible, starchy grain yielded by certain plants of the grass family, as rice, wheat, rye, oats, etc. 2. Any of such plants. 3. A breakfast food made from a cereal grain. [< L *Ceres,* goddess of grain]

cer·e·bel·lum (ser′ə·bel′əm) *n. pl.* **·bel·lums** or **·bel·la** (-bel′ə) *Anat.* The part of the brain below and behind the cerebrum serving as the coordination center of voluntary movements, posture, and equilibrium. [< L, dim. of *cerebrum* brain] — **cer′e·bel′lar** *adj.*

cer·e·bral (ser′ə·brəl, sə·rē′-) *adj.* 1. Of or pertaining to the cerebrum or the brain. 2. Appealing to or involving the intellect; intellectual. [< F < L *cerebrum* brain]

cerebral palsy *Pathol.* Any paralysis affecting the ability to control movement and caused by brain lesions resulting from prenatal defect or birth injury.

cer·e·brate (ser′ə·brāt) **·brat·ed, ·brat·ing** *v.i.* 1. To have or manifest brain action. 2. To think. [< L *cerebrum* brain] — **cer′e·bra′tion** *n.*

cerebro- *combining form* Brain: *cerebrospinal.* Also, before vowels, **cerebr-.** [< L *cerebrum* brain]

cer·e·bro·spi·nal (ser′ə·brō·spī′nəl) *adj. Anat.* Of or affecting the brain and the spinal cord.

cer·e·brum (ser′ə·brəm, sə·rē′brəm) *n. pl.* **·bra** (-brə) *Anat.* The upper anterior part of the brain, consisting of two hemispherical masses enclosed within the cortex and constituting the seat of conscious processes. [< L] — **cer·e·bric** (ser′ə·brik, sə·rē′-) *adj.*

cere·cloth (sir′klôth′, -kloth′) *n.* Cloth treated with wax, used to wrap the dead. [Orig. *cered cloth* < L *cera* wax]

cere·ment (sir′mənt) *n. Usu. pl.* 1. A cerecloth. 2. A shroud. [< F < MF < L *cera* wax]

cer·e·mo·ni·al (ser′ə·mō′nē·əl) *adj.* Of, pertaining to, or characterized by ceremony; ritual; formal. — *n.* 1. A prescribed set of ceremonies for some particular occasion; ritual. 2. A rite; ceremony. — **cer′e·mo′ni·al·ism** *n.* — **cer′e·mo′ni·al·ist** *n.* — **cer′e·mo′ni·al·ly** *adv.*

cer·e·mo·ni·ous (ser′ə·mō′nē·əs) *adj.* 1. Studiously or overly polite. 2. Characterized by ceremony; formal. — **cer′e·mo′ni·ous·ly** *adv.* — **cer′e·mo′ni·ous·ness** *n.*

cer·e·mo·ny (ser′ə·mō′nē) *n. pl.* **·nies** 1. A formal act or ritual, or a series of them, performed in a prescribed manner. 2. Formal observances collectively; ritual. 3. An empty ritual. 4. Adherence to ritual forms; formality. 5. An act of formal courtesy. — **to stand on** (or **upon**) **ceremony** To insist upon formalities. [< OF < L *caerimonia* awe]

Ce·res (sir′ēz) In Roman mythology, the goddess of grain and harvests: identified with the Greek *Demeter.*

cer·iph (ser′if) See SERIF.

ce·rise (sə·rēz′, -rēs′) *n. & adj.* Vivid red. [< F, cherry]

ce·ri·um (sir′ē·əm) *n.* A silver-white, ductile, highly reactive and electropositive element (symbol Ce) of the lanthanide series. See ELEMENT. [after the asteroid *Ceres*]

cero- *combining form* Wax: *cerotype.* Also, before vowels, **cer-.** [< L *cera* or Gk. *kēros* wax]

ce·ro·plas·tic (sir′ə·plas′tik) *adj.* 1. Pertaining to wax modeling. 2. Modeled in wax. [< Gk. < *kēros* wax + *plassein* to mold]

cer·tain (sûr′tən) *adj.* 1. Absolutely confident; convinced. 2. Sure; destined. 3. Beyond doubt; indisputable. 4. Sure in its workings or results; dependable; also, unerring. 5. Fixed; determined. 6. Not explicitly stated or identified: *certain* persons. 7. Some, or some at least: a *certain* improvement. — *n.* An indefinite number or quantity: *certain* of the students were absent. — **for certain** Without doubt; surely. [< OF, ult. < L *cernere* to determine]

cer·tain·ly (sûr′tən·lē) *adv.* Without doubt; surely.

cer·tain·ty (sûr′tən·tē) *n. pl.* **·ties** 1. The state, quality, or fact of being certain. 2. A known fact.

cer·tif·i·cate (*n.* sər·tif′ə·kit; *v.* sər·tif′ə·kāt) *n.* An official or sworn document stating something to be a fact. — *v.t.* **·cat·ed, ·cat·ing** To furnish with or attest by a certificate. [< Med.L < L < *certus* certain + *facere* to make] — **cer·tif'i·ca·tor** (-kā'tər) *n.* — **cer·tif'i·ca·to'ry** *adj.*

cer·ti·fi·ca·tion (sûr'tə·fi·kā'shən) *n.* **1.** The act of certifying or guaranteeing. **2.** The state of being certified. **3.** That which guarantees or vouches for. **4.** A certificate.

cer·ti·fied (sûr'tə·fīd) *adj.* **1.** Vouched for in writing; endorsed. **2.** Affirmed or guaranteed by a certificate. **3.** Legally committed to a mental institution.

certified check A check issued by a bank that guarantees that it is drawn on an account having sufficient funds.

cer·ti·fy (sûr'tə·fī) *v.* **·fied, ·fy·ing** *v.t.* **1.** To give certain information of; attest. **2.** To testify to in writing; vouch for. **3.** To endorse as meeting set standards or requirements. **4.** To guarantee in writing on the face of (a check) that the account drawn on has sufficient funds for payment: said of banks. **5.** To make certain; assure. **6.** To commit to a mental institution. — *v.i.* **7.** To make attestation; vouch (*for*) or testify (*to*). [< OF < Med.L < L < *certus* certain + *facere* to make] — **cer'ti·fi'a·ble** *adj.* — **cer'ti·fi'er** *n.*

cer·ti·o·ra·ri (sûr'shē·ə·râr'ē, -râr'ī) *n. Law* A writ from a superior to an inferior court, directing that a record of a designated case be sent up for review. [< L, to be certified]

cer·ti·tude (sûr'tə·tood, -tyood) *n.* Complete confidence. [< MF < LL < L < *certus* certain + *facere* to make]

ce·ru·le·an (sə·roo'lē·ən, -lyən) *adj. & n.* Sky blue; vivid blue. [< L *caeruleus* dark blue]

ce·ru·men (sə·roo'mən) *n.* Earwax. [< NL < L *cera* wax]

cer·vi·cal (sûr'vi·kəl) *adj. Anat.* Of, pertaining to, in, or near the neck of the cervix uteri. [< L *cervix* neck]

cer·vine (sûr'vīn, -vin) *adj.* **1.** Deerlike. **2.** Of or pertaining to deer. [< L *cervinus* < *cervus* deer]

cer·vix (sûr'viks) *n. pl.* **cer·vix·es** or **cer·vi·ces** (sər·vī'sēz, sûs'və·sēz) *Anat.* **1.** The neck. **2.** The cervix uteri. **3.** A necklike part. [< L] — **cer·vi·cal** (sûr'vi·kəl) *adj.*

cervix u·ter·i (yoo'tə·rī) *Anat.* The constricted neck of the uterus that distends during parturition. [< L]

ce·sar·e·an (si·zâr'ē·ən) *Surg. n.* A cesarean section. — *adj.* Of or pertaining to a cesarean section. Also **ce·sar'i·an.**

Ce·sar·e·an (si·zâr'ē·ən), **Ce·sar·i·an** See CAESAREAN.

cesarean section *Surg.* The birth of a child by section of the abdominal walls and the uterus. Also **cesarean operation.** [< L *sectio caesarea* < *caedere* to cut]

ce·si·um (sē'zē·əm) *n.* A ductile metallic element (symbol Cs) of the alkali group: also spelled *caesium.* See ELEMENT. [< NL < L *caesius* bluish gray]

ces·sa·tion (se·sā'shən) *n.* A ceasing; stop; pause. [< L *cessatio, -onis* < *cessare* to stop]

ces·sion (sesh'ən) *n.* The act of ceding; a giving up, as of territory or rights, to another. [< L pp. of *cedere* to yield]

cess·pool (ses'pool') *n.* **1.** A covered well or pit for the drainage from sinks, toilets, etc. **2.** Any repository of filth. Also **cess'pit'.** [Origin uncertain]

c'est la guerre (se là gâr') *French* That's war.

c'est la vie (se là vē') *French* That's life.

ces·tus (ses'təs) *n. pl.* **·tus** A wrapping of thongs, often weighted, worn about the hands by boxers in ancient Rome: also spelled *caestus.* [< L *caedere* to kill]

ce·su·ra (si·zhoor'ə, -zyoor'ə) See CAESURA.

ce·ta·cean (si·tā'shən) *adj.* Of or belonging to the aquatic mammals, including the whales, dolphins, and porpoises. Also **ce·ta'ceous.** — *n.* A cetacean animal. [< NL < L Gk. *kētos* whale]

CESTUS[1]

ce·tane (sē'tān) *n. Chem.* A saturated hydrocarbon of the methane series, $C_{16}H_{34}$, used as fuel for diesel engines. [< L *cetus* whale + -ANE[2]]

Cey·lon·ese (sēl'ən·ēz, -ēs) *adj.* Of or pertaining to Ceylon or to its people. — *n.* A native or resident of Ceylon.

cgs The centimeter-gram-second system of measurement in which the unit of length is the centimeter, the unit of mass is the gram, and the unit of time is one second. Also **c.g.s., CGS, C.G.S.**

Cha·blis (shà·blē') *n.* A dry, white, Burgundy wine made in the region of Chablis, a town in north central France.

cha·conne (shà·kôn') *n.* A musical form, important in the Baroque period, usu. in slow triple meter, probably derived from a 16th century Spanish colonial dance: often called *passacaglia.* [< F < Sp. *chacona*]

chaeto- *combining form* Hair. Also, before vowels, **chaet-.** [< Gk. *chaitē* hair, bristle]

chafe (chāf) *v.* **chafed, chaf·ing** *v.t.* **1.** To abrade or make sore by rubbing. **2.** To make warm by rubbing. **3.** To irritate; annoy. — *v.i.* **4.** To rub. **5.** To be irritated; fret; fume: to *chafe* under the abuse. — **to chafe at the bit** To be

impatient and irritable because of delay. — *n.* **1.** Soreness or wear from rubbing; friction. **2.** Irritation or vexation. [< OF < L < *calere* to be warm + *facere* to make]

chaf·er (chā'fər) *n.* The cockchafer or other scarabaeid beetle. Also **chaf·fer** (chaf'ər). [OE *ceafor*]

chaff[1] (chaf, chäf) *n.* **1.** The husks of grain. **2.** Any trivial or worthless matter. [OE *ceaf*] — **chaff'y** *adj.*

chaff[2] (chaf, chäf) *v.t. & v.i.* To poke fun (at). — *n.* Good-natured raillery. [Origin uncertain] — **chaff'er** *n.*

chaf·fer (chaf'ər) *v.i.* To haggle about price; bargain. — *n.* A haggling about terms; bargaining. [ME < OE *cēap* bargain + *faru* going] — **chaf'fer·er** *n.*

chaf·finch (chaf'inch) *n.* A song finch of Europe.

chafing dish A vessel with a heating apparatus beneath it, to cook or keep food warm at the table.

cha·grin (shə·grin') *n.* Distress or vexation caused by disappointment, failure, etc.; mortification. — *v.t.* To humiliate; mortify: used in the passive. [< F]

chain (chān) *n.* **1.** A series of connected rings or links, usu. of metal, serving to bind, drag, hold, or ornament. **2.** *pl.* Anything that confines or restrains; shackles; bonds. **3.** *pl.* Bondage. **4.** Any connected series; a succession. **5.** A series of chain stores. **6.** *Chem.* A series of atoms or radicals of the same or different kinds, linked together and acting as a unit. — *v.t.* **1.** To fasten or connect with a chain. **2.** To fetter; bind. [< OF < L *catena*] — **chain'less** *adj.*

chain gang A gang of convicts chained together while doing hard labor.

chain letter A letter intended to be sent on from one to another in a series of recipients.

chain mail Flexible armor consisting of interlinked metal chains, rings, or scales.

chain reaction **1.** *Physics* The self-sustaining fission of atomic nuclei, in which neutrons released by one fission induce fission in neighboring nuclei, as in a nuclear reactor. **2.** Any series of reactions or events, each of which develops from the preceding one.

chain stitch An ornamental stitch resembling a chain, used in sewing, crocheting, etc.

chain store *U.S.* One of a number of retail stores under the same ownership and selling similar merchandise.

chair (châr) *n.* **1.** A seat, usu. having four legs and a back, for one person. **2.** A seat of office, authority, etc., as that of a professor or bishop. **3.** The office or dignity of one who presides or is in authority. **4.** A presiding officer; chairman. **5.** The electric chair; also, execution in the electric chair. — **to take the chair** To preside at or open a meeting. — *v.t.* **1.** To seat in a chair. **2.** To install in office. **3.** To preside over (a meeting). [< OF *chaiere* < L *cathedra*.]

chair car A parlor car.

chair·man (châr'mən) *n. pl.* **·men** (-mən) One who presides over an assembly, committee, etc. — **chair·wom·an** (châr'woom'ən) *n.fem.*

chaise (shāz) *n.* **1.** A two-wheeled, one-horse vehicle for two persons, having a calash top. **2.** A similar carriage with four wheels. Also, *Dial., shay.* [< F, var. of *chaire* chair]

chaise longue (shāz' lông', *Fr.* shez lông') A couchlike chair having the seat prolonged to support the sitter's outstretched legs. [< F, lit., long chair]

cha·la·za (kə·lā'zə) *n. pl.* **·zas** or **·zae** (-zē) *Biol.* One of the two threads attached to each end of the lining membrane of an egg. [< NL < Gk., hailstone, small lump]

chal·ced·o·ny (kal·sed'ə·nē, kal'sə·dō'nē) *n. pl.* **·nies** A waxy, translucent variety of quartz, often of a pale blue or grayish color: also spelled *calcedony.* [after *Chalcedon,* an ancient Greek port]

Chal·de·a (kal·dē'ə) In Biblical times, the southernmost Tigris and Euphrates valley, sometimes including Babylonia. Also **Chal·dae'a.** — **Chal·de'an** *adj. & n.*

cha·let (sha·lā', shal'ā) *n.* **1.** A Swiss cottage with a gently sloping, projecting roof; also, any cottage built in this style. **2.** A herdsman's hut of the Alpine regions of Europe. [< F]

chal·ice (chal'is) *n.* **1.** A drinking cup or goblet. **2.** *Eccl.* In the Eucharist, a cup in which the wine is consecrated. **3.** A cup-shaped flower. [< OF < L *calix, calicis* cup]

chalk (chôk) *n.* **1.** A soft, grayish white or yellowish compact limestone, largely composed of the shells of marine animals. **2.** A piece of limestone or similar material, frequently colored, used for marking, etc. **3.** A score, tally, or notation of credit given. — *v.t.* **1.** To mark, write, or draw with chalk. **2.** To treat or dress with chalk. **3.** To make pale. — **to chalk up** To score; credit. — *adj.* Made with chalk. [OE < L *calx* limestone] — **chalk'i·ness** *n.* — **chalk'y** *adj.*

chal·lenge (chal'ənj) *v.* **·lenged, ·leng·ing** *v.t.* **1.** To demand a contest with. **2.** To demand defiantly. **3.** To call in question; dispute. **4.** *Law* To object to. **5.** To claim as due; demand. **6.** *Mil.* To stop and demand the countersign from. **7.** *U.S.* To claim that (a person) is not qualified to vote, or that (a vote) is invalid. —*v.i.* **8.** To make a challenge. —*n.* **1.** An invitation or dare to participate in a contest. **2.** *Mil.* A sentry's call, requiring one to halt and give the countersign. **3.** A calling in question; dispute. **4.** *U.S.* A claim that a voter is not qualified, or that a vote is not valid. **5.** *Law* A formal objection, as to a juror. **6.** *Telecom.* An electromagnetic signal requesting identification, as in radar communication. [< OF < L *calumnia* slander] — **chal′lenge·a·ble** *adj.* — **chal′leng·er** *n.*

chal·lis (shal′ē) *n.* A light fabric, usu. of printed wool, rayon, etc. Also **chal′lie**. [Origin uncertain]

cha·ly·be·ate (kə·lib′ē·āt, -it) *adj.* **1.** Impregnated with compounds of iron, as mineral waters. **2.** Tasting of iron. —*n.* A medicine or water containing iron in solution. [< NL < L, ult. < Gk. *chalyps, chalybos* steel]

cham·ber (chām′bər) *n.* **1.** A room in a house; esp., a bedroom. **2.** *pl.* An office or suite of rooms, as of a judge. **3.** *pl. Brit.* A set of rooms for one living alone. **4.** A hall where an assembly meets; also, the assembly itself. **5.** A council; board. **6.** An enclosed space or cavity, as in a gun. —*v.t.* **1.** To provide with a chamber. **2.** To fit into or as into a chamber. [< F < L *camera* vaulted room]

chamber concert A concert of chamber music.

cham·ber·lain (chām′bər·lin) *n.* **1.** An official charged with the domestic affairs of a monarch or lord. **2.** A high officer of a royal court. **3.** A treasurer. [< OF < OHG < L *camera* vaulted room] — **cham′ber·lain·ship′** *n.*

cham·ber·maid (chām′bər·mād′) *n.* A female servant who cleans and tends bedrooms in a house, hotel, etc.

chamber music Music composed for a small group of instruments, as for a quartet.

chamber of commerce An association of merchants and businessmen for the regulation and promotion of business in a city or locality.

chamber pot A portable vessel used as a toilet.

cham·bray (sham′brā) *n.* A cotton fabric woven with colored warp and white filling. [after *Cambrai,* France]

cha·me·le·on (kə·mē′lē·ən, -mēl′yən) *n.* **1.** A lizard capable of changing color. **2.** A person of changeable disposition or habits. [< L < Gk. *chamai* on the ground + *leōn* lion]

cham·fer (cham′fər) *v.t.* **1.** To cut away the corner of. **2.** To cut a furrow in; flute. —*n.* A surface produced by chamfering. [< F < OF *chanfraindre* to cut off an edge]

cham·ois (sham′ē, *Fr.* shä·mwä′) *n. pl.* **·ois 1.** A mountain antelope of Europe and western Asia. **2.** A soft leather prepared from the skin of the chamois, sheep, goats, deer, etc.: also spelled *shammy, shamois:* also **cham′my. 3.** The color of this leather, a yellowish beige. —*v.t.* To dress (leather or skin) like chamois. [< MF]

cham·o·mile (kam′ə·mīl) See CAMOMILE.

champ[1] (champ) *v.t.* **1.** To crush and chew noisily; munch. **2.** To bite upon restlessly. —*v.i.* **3.** To make a biting or chewing movement with the jaws. —*n.* The action of chewing or biting. [Prob. imit.]

champ[2] (champ) *n. Slang* Champion.

cham·pagne (sham·pān′) *n.* **1.** A sparkling white wine made in the area of Champagne, France; also, any wine made in imitation of this. **2.** A pale or greenish yellow. —*adj.* Pertaining to champagne.

cham·paign (sham·pān′) *n.* Flat and open country. —*adj.* Flat and open. [< OF < LL < L *campus* field]

cham·pi·on (cham′pē·ən) *n.* **1.** One who has defeated all opponents and is ranked first, esp. in a sport. **2.** Anything awarded first place. **3.** One who fights for another or defends a principle or cause. —*adj.* Having won first prize or rank; superior to all others. —*v.t.* To fight in behalf of; defend; support. [< OF < LL *campio, -onis* fighter]

cham·pi·on·ship (cham′pē·ən·ship′) *n.* **1.** The state of being a champion. **2.** The position or honor of a champion. **3.** The act of championing; advocacy; defense.

Champs É·ly·sées (shän zā·lē·zā′) A fashionable avenue in Paris. [< F, lit., Elysian fields]

chance (chans, chäns) *n.* **1.** The unknown or undefined cause of events; fortune; luck. **2.** An unusual and unexplained event. **3.** The probability of anything happening; possibility. **4.** An opportunity: Now is your *chance.* **5.** A risk or gamble; hazard. **6.** A ticket in a lottery. —*v.* **chanced, chanc·ing** *v.i.* **1.** To occur accidentally; happen. —*v.t.* **2.** To take the chance of; risk: I'll *chance* it. — **to chance upon** (or **on**) To find or meet unexpectedly. —*adj.* Occurring by chance. [< OF < LL *cadentia* a falling]

chan·cel (chan′səl, chän′-) *n.* The space near the altar of a church for the clergy and choir, often set apart by a screen or railing. [< OF < LL < L *cancelli,* pl., lattice, railing]

chan·cel·ler·y (chan′sə·lər·ē, -slər·ē, chän′-) *n. pl.* **·ler·ies 1.** The office or dignity of a chancellor. **2.** The building or

room in which a chancellor has his office. **3.** The office of an embassy or legation. Also **chan·cel·ry** (chan′səl·rē, chän′-).

chan·cel·lor (chan′sə·lər, -slər, chän′-) *n.* **1.** In some European countries, a chief minister of state. **2.** The chief secretary of an embassy. **3.** A secretary, as of a nobleman or ruler. **4.** The head of some universities. **5.** *U.S.* A judge of a court of chancery or equity. Also **chan′cel·or.** — **Lord High Chancellor** *Brit.* The highest judicial officer of the crown: also **Lord Chancellor.** [< OF < LL *cancellarius* one who stands at the bar in a court] — **chan′cel·lor·ship′** *n.*

Chancellor of the Exchequer The minister of finance in the British cabinet.

chance-med·ley (chans′med′lē, chäns′-) *n.* **1.** *Law* Unpremeditated homicide in self-defense. **2.** Inadvertent or random action. [< OF < *chance* chance + *medlee* mixed]

chan·cer·y (chan′sər·ē, chän′-) *n. pl.* **·cer·ies 1.** In the United States: **a** A court of equity. Also **court of chancery. b** Equity, or proceedings in equity. **2.** *Brit.* One of the five divisions of the High Court of Justice. **3.** A chancellery. **4.** A court of records; archives. — **in chancery 1.** *Law* Pending in a court of chancery; in litigation. **2.** In wrestling, with the head caught and held under an opponent's arm. **3.** In a hopeless predicament. [See CHANCELLOR.]

chan·cre (shang′kər) *n. Pathol.* A primary syphilitic lesion resembling a sore with a hard base. [< F < L *cancer* crab, ulcer] — **chan·crous** (shang′krəs) *adj.*

chan·croid (shang′kroid) *n. Pathol.* A nonsyphilitic, localized venereal lesion.

chanc·y (chan′sē, chän′-) *adj.* **chanc·i·er, chanc·i·est** *Informal* Subject to chance; risky. — **chan′ci·ly** *adv.*

chan·de·lier (shan′də·lir′) *n.* A branched support for a number of lights, suspended from a ceiling. [< F < Med.L < L *candela* candle]

chan·dler (chan′dlər, chän′-) *n.* **1.** A trader; dealer: ship *chandler.* **2.** One who makes or sells candles. **3.** *Brit.* A shopkeeper. [< OF *chandelier* chandler, candlestick]

change (chānj) *v.* **changed, chang·ing** *v.t.* **1.** To make different; alter. **2.** To exchange: to *change* places. **3.** To give or obtain the equivalent of. **4.** To put other garments, coverings, etc., on: to *change* the bed. —*v.i.* **5.** To become different. **6.** To make a change or exchange. **7.** To transfer from one train, etc., to another. **8.** To put on other garments. — **to change color 1.** To blush. **2.** To turn pale. — **to change hands** To pass from one possessor to another. —*n.* **1.** The act or fact of changing. **2.** A substitution of one thing for another. **3.** Something new or different; variety. **4.** A clean or different set of clothes. **5.** The amount returned when a coin or bill of greater value than the sum due has been tendered. **6.** Money of lower denomination given in exchange for higher. **7.** Small coins. **8.** *Usu. pl.* Any order in which a peal of bells may be struck. **9.** A place for transacting business; an exchange: also **'change.** — **to ring the changes 1.** To operate a chime of bells in every possible order. **2.** To repeat something with every possible variation. [< OF < LL *cambiare* to exchange] — **chang′er** *n.*

change·a·ble (chān′jə·bəl) *adj.* **1.** Likely to change or vary; inconstant; fickle. **2.** Capable of being changed. **3.** Reflecting light so as to appear of different color from different points of view. — **change·a·bil·i·ty** (chān′jə·bil′ə·tē,) **change′a·ble·ness** *n.* — **change′a·bly** *adv.*

change·ful (chānj′fəl) *adj.* Full of or given to change; variable. — **change′ful·ly** *adv.* — **change′ful·ness** *n.*

change·less (chānj′lis) *adj.* Free from change; enduring; unchanging. — **change′less·ly** *adv.* — **change′less·ness** *n.*

change·ling (chānj′ling) *n.* A child secretly left in place of another.

change of life The menopause.

change ringing The production of every possible variation in the ringing of a set of bells.

chan·nel (chan′əl) *n.* **1.** The bed of a stream. **2.** A wide strait: the English *Channel.* **3.** *Naut.* The deep part of a river, harbor, etc. **4.** A tubular passage, as for liquids. **5.** The course through which anything moves or passes. **6.** *pl.* The official or proper routes of communication: to put a request through *channels.* **7.** *Telecom.* **a** A path for the transmission of telegraph, telephone, or radio communications. **b** A range of frequencies assigned for television transmission. **8.** A groove or furrow. —*v.t.* **chan·neled** or **·nelled, chan·nel·ing** or **·nel·ling 1.** To cut or wear channels in. **2.** To direct or convey through or as through a channel. [< OF < L *canalis* groove]

chan·son (shan′sən, *Fr.* shän·sôn′) *n.* A song. [< F < L *canere* to sing]

chant (chant, chänt) *n.* **1.** A simple melody in which a varying number of syllables are sung or intoned on each note. **2.** A psalm or canticle so sung or intoned. **3.** A song; melody. **4.** Any monotonous singing or shouting of words, as from a mob. **5.** A singing intonation in speech. —*v.t.* **1.** To sing to a chant. **2.** To celebrate in song. **3.** To recite or say in the manner of a chant. —*v.t.* **4.** To sing

CHAMOIS
(2 feet high at shoulder; 45 inches long)

chants. **5.** To make melody; sing. **6.** To talk monotonously. [< OF < L *canere* to sing] — **chant'er** *n.*

chan·teuse (shän·tœz') *n. French* A woman singer.

chant·ey (shan'tē, chan'-) *n. pl.* **·eys** A rhythmical working song of sailors: also spelled *shantey, shanty.* Also **chan'ty.** [Alter. of F *chantez*, imperative of *chanter* to sing]

chan·ti·cleer (chan'tə·klir) *n.* A cock. [< OF < *chanter* to sing, crow + *cler* aloud]

chan·try (chan'trē, chän'-) *n, pl.* **·tries** An endowment for the daily masses or special prayers; also, a chapel or altar so endowed. [< OF < L *canere* to sing]

Cha·nu·kah (khä'nŏŏ·kə) See HANUKKAH.

cha·os (kā'os) *n.* **1.** Utter disorder and confusion. **2.** The supposed unformed original state of the universe. [< L < Gk., abyss]

cha·ot·ic (kā·ot'ik) *adj.* Utterly disordered and confused. Also **cha·ot'i·cal.** — **cha·ot'i·cal·ly** *adv.*

chap¹ (chap) *n. Informal* A fellow; lad.

chap² (chap) *v.* **chapped** or **chapt, chap·ping** *v.t.* **1.** To cause to split, crack, or become rough: The cold has *chapped* my hands. — *v.i.* **2.** To split, crack, or redden. — *n.* A crack or roughened place in the skin. [ME *chappen*]

chap³ (chap, chop) *n.* **1.** A jaw. **2.** *pl.* The mouth and cheeks. Also spelled *chop.* [Cf. ME *chaft* jaw]

chap·ar·ral (chap'ə·ral') *n.* A thicket of dwarf oak, low thorny shrubs, etc. [< Sp. < *chaparra* evergreen oak]

chap·book (chap'bŏŏk') *n.* A small book containing tales, ballads, etc.

cha·peau (sha·pō', *Fr.* shà·pō') *n. pl.* **·peaux** (-pōz', *Fr.* -pō') or **·peaus** (-pōz') A hat. [< F]

chap·el (chap'əl) *n.* **1.** A place of worship smaller than a church. **2.** A recess or enclosed part of a church, for small or special services. **3.** *Brit.* A place of worship not connected with the established church. **4.** A building or room in a college, school, etc., for religious services; also, the services. [< OF < Med.L < *cappa* cloak; orig., a sanctuary where the cloak of St. Martin was kept as a relic]

chap·er·on (shap'ə·rōn) *n.* An older person who accompanies and supervises a group of young people. — *v.t.* To act as chaperon to. Also **chap'er·one.** [< F, hood < *chape* cape] — **chap·er·on·age** (shap'ə·rōn'nij) *n.*

chap·fall·en (chap'fô'lən, chop'-) *adj.* Dejected; crestfallen. Also *chopfallen.*

chap·lain (chap'lin) *n.* A clergyman who conducts religious services in a legislative assembly, for a military unit, etc. [< OF < Med.L *cappa* cloak] — **chap'lain·cy, chap'·lain·ship** *n.*

chap·let (chap'lit) *n.* **1.** A wreath or garland for the head. **2.** A rosary, or, more strictly, one third of a rosary. **3.** A string of beads, or anything resembling it. [< OF < LL *cappa* hooded cape]

chap·man (chap'mən) *n. pl.* **·men** (-mən) *Brit.* A peddler; hawker. [OE < *cēap* business + *man* man]

chaps (chaps, shaps) *n.pl. U.S.* Leather overalls without a seat, worn over trousers by cowboys to protect the legs.

chap·ter (chap'tər) *n.* **1.** A main division of a book or treatise, usually numbered. **2.** A branch of a society or fraternity. **3.** *Eccl.* An assembly of the canons of a cathedral or collegiate church; also, the canons collectively. **4.** A meeting of any order or society. **5.** A period of time: an important *chapter* in history. — *v.t.* To divide into chapters, as a book. [< F < OF < L *caput* head, capital]

chapter house **1.** A place of assembly for a cathedral or monastery chapter. **2.** The house of a fraternity or sorority.

char¹ (chär) *v.* **charred, char·ring** *v.t.* **1.** To burn or scorch the surface of, as timber. **2.** To convert into charcoal by incomplete combustion. — *v.i.* **3.** To become charred. — *n.* Charcoal. [? < CHARCOAL]

char² (chär) *n. pl.* **chars** or **char** Any of various fishes allied to the lake trout. [< Scottish Gaelic *ceara* blood red]

char³ (chär) *Brit. n.* **1.** A chore; esp., a household task: also called *chare.* **2.** A charwoman. — *v.i.* **charred, char·ring** To work as a charwoman. [OE *cerr* turn of work]

char·a·banc (shar'ə·bangk, -bang) *n. pl.* **·bancs** *Brit.* A long, open vehicle with rows of seats facing forward. Also **char'-a-banc.** [< F *char à bancs* car with benches]

char·ac·ter (kar'ik·tər) *n.* **1.** The combination of qualities or traits that distinguishes an individual or group; personality. **2.** Any distinguishing attribute; characteristic; property. **3.** Moral force; integrity. **4.** A good reputation. **5.** Status; capacity: in his *character* as president. **6.** A personage. **7.** A person in a play, novel, etc. **8.** *Informal* An eccentric or humorous person. **9.** A figure engraved, written, or printed; mark; sign; letter. **10.** *Genetics* Any structural or functional trait in a plant or animal resulting from the interaction of genes and regarded as hereditary as to origin. — **in** (or **out of**) **character** In keeping (or not in keeping) with the general character or role. — *v.t.* To

write, print, or engrave. [< MF < L < Gk. < *charassein* to sharpen, engrave, carve, scratch] — **char'ac·ter·less** *adj.*

character actor An actor who portrays characters markedly different from himself in age, temperament, etc.

char·ac·ter·is·tic (kar'ik·tə·ris'tik) *adj.* Indicating or constituting the distinctive quality, character, or disposition; typical: a *characteristic* gesture. — *n.* **1.** A distinctive feature or trait. **2.** *Math.* The integral part of a logarithm; index. — **char'ac·ter·is'ti·cal·ly** *adv.*

— **Syn.** (noun) A *characteristic* is that by which we recognize something for what it is; a hump is one of a camel's *characteristics.* A *peculiarity* is a *characteristic* that distinguishes one individual or kind from another. We speak of the qualities of persons as *traits*, and of the qualities of objects or substances as *properties.*

char·ac·ter·ize (kar'ik·tə·rīz') *v.t.* **·ized, ·iz·ing** **1.** To describe by qualities or peculiarities; designate. **2.** To be a mark or peculiarity of; distinguish. **3.** To give character to, as in writing or acting. — **char·ac·ter·i·za·tion** (kar'ik·tər·ə·zā'shən) *n.* — **char'ac·ter·iz'er** *n.*

cha·rades (shə·rādz', *Brit.* shə·rädz') *n.pl.* (construed as sing.) A game in which words and phrases are to be guessed, sometimes syllable by syllable, from their representation in pantomime. [< F < Provençal < *charra* to chatter, prattle]

char·coal (chär'kōl') *n.* **1.** A black, porous substance obtained by the imperfect combustion of organic matter, as wood, used as a fuel, adsorbent, filter, etc. **2.** A drawing pencil made of charcoal dust. **3.** A drawing made with such a pencil. — *v.t.* To write, draw, mark, or blacken with charcoal. [ME *charcole*; origin unknown]

chard (chärd) *n.* A variety of edible white beet cultivated for its large leaves and leafstalks. [< F < L *carduus* thistle]

charge (chärj) *v.* **charged, charg·ing** *v.t.* **1.** To place a load upon. **2.** To place in or on (a thing) what it is intended or able to receive: to *charge* a furnace with ore. **3.** To load (a firearm). **4.** To diffuse something throughout, as water with carbon dioxide. **5.** To fill as if with electricity; make vibrant. **6.** To supply (a storage battery) with a quantity of electricity. **7.** To accuse; impute something to. **8.** To command; enjoin. **9.** To instruct, exhort: to *charge* a jury. **10.** To entrust with a duty, responsibility, etc.; burden, as with care. **11.** To set or state as a price: to *charge* a dollar. **12.** To make financially liable. **13.** To set down or record as a debt to be paid: to *charge* a purchase. **14.** To attack forcefully: to *charge* a fort. **15.** To place (a weapon) in position for use. — *v.i.* **16.** To make an onset; rush violently. **17.** To demand or fix a price. — **Syn.** See ACCUSE. — **to charge off** To regard as a loss. — *n.* **1.** A load or burden. **2.** The quantity of anything that an apparatus or receptacle can hold at one time. **3.** The amount of explosive to be detonated at one time. **4.** The quantity of static electricity present in or on an apparatus, as a storage battery. **5.** Care and custody; superintendence. **6.** A person or thing entrusted to one's care. **7.** A responsibility or duty. **8.** An accusation; allegation. **9.** An address of instruction or admonition given by a judge to a jury at the close of a trial. **10.** An order or injunction; command. **11.** The expense or cost of something; price. **12.** Any pecuniary burden; tax; lien; expense. **13.** A debt or charged purchase, or an entry recording it. **14.** An onslaught or attack; also, the signal for this. **15.** *Physics* The energy present in an atomic particle. — **in charge of** Having responsibility for or control of. [< OF < LL < L *carrus* cart]

charge·a·ble (chär'jə·bəl) *adj.* **1.** That may be or is liable to be charged. **2.** Liable to become a public charge.

charge account A retail credit account to which purchases or services may be charged for future payment.

char·gé d'af·faires (shär·zhā' də·fâr', *Fr.* shàr·zhā' dà·fâr') *pl.* **char·gés d'af·faires** (shär·zhāz' də·fâr', *Fr.* shàr·zhā' dà·fâr') **1.** One who temporarily heads a diplomatic mission in the absence of the ambassador or minister. **2.** A diplomatic of lower rank than an ambassador. Also **char·gé'.**

charg·er (chär'jər) *n.* **1.** One who or that which charges. **2.** A horse trained for use in battle; a war horse. **3.** An apparatus for charging storage batteries.

char·i·ly (châr'ə·lē) *adv.* In a chary manner; carefully.

char·i·ness (châr'ē·nis) *n.* The quality of being chary.

char·i·ot (char'ē·ət) *n.* An ancient two-wheeled vehicle used in war, racing, etc. — *v.t. & v.i.* To convey, ride, or drive in a chariot. [< OF < L *carrus* cart, wagon]

char·i·o·teer (char'ē·ə·tir') *n.* One who drives a chariot.

cha·ris·ma (kə·riz'mə) *n.* **1.** *Theol.* An extraordinary spiritual grace that benefits others. **2.** Extraordinary personal power or charm. [< Gk., grace, favor]

char·is·mat·ic (kar'iz·mat'ik) *adj.* Possessing charisma.

char·i·ta·ble (char'ə·tə·bəl) *adj.* **1.** Generous in giving gifts to the poor; beneficent. **2.** Inclined to judge others leniently. **3.** Of or concerned with charity: a *charitable* enterprise. — **char'i·ta·ble·ness** *n.* — **char'i·ta·bly** *adv.*

PRONUNCIATION KEY: add, āce, câre, pälm; end, ēven; it, īce; odd, ōpen, ôrder; tŏŏk, pōōl; up, bûrn; ə = a in *above*, e in *sicken*, i in *flex-ible*, o in *melon*, u in *focus*; yōō = u in *fuse*; oil; pout; check; go; ring; thin; this; zh, vision.

char·i·ty (char'ə·tē) *n. pl.* **·ties** **1.** The providing of help to the poor. **2.** That which is given to help the needy; alms. **3.** An institution, organization, or fund to aid those in need. **4.** Tolerance; leniency. **5.** An act of good will. **6.** Brotherly love. [< OF < L *carus* dear]

cha·riv·a·ri (shə·riv'ə·rē', shiv'ə·rē', shä'rē·vä'rē) *n. pl.* **·ris** A mock serenade, as to a newly married couple, performed with tin pans, horns, etc.: also *chivaree, shivaree.* [< MF]

char·la·tan (shär'lə·tən) *n.* One who makes claim to skill and knowledge he does not possess; an impostor; quack. [< F < Ital. *ciarla* chat, idle talk] — **char'la·tan'ic** (-tan'ik) *adj.* — **char'la·tan·ism, char'la·tan·ry** *n.*

Charles's Wain The constellation Ursa Major.

Charles·ton (chärl'stən) *n.* A fast dance in ¼ time, popular in the 1920's. [after *Charleston, S.C.*]

char·ley horse (chär'lē) *U.S. Informal* A muscular cramp in the arm or leg, caused by strain. [Origin unknown]

char·lock (chär'lək) *n.* Any of several herbs of the mustard family having yellow flowers. [OE *cerlic*]

char·lotte russe (shär'lət rōōs) A small sponge cake with a filling of whipped cream or custard. [< F, Russian charlotte]

charm (chärm) *n.* **1.** The power to allure or delight; fascination. **2.** Any fascinating quality or feature. **3.** A small ornament worn on a necklace, bracelet, etc. **4.** Something worn to ward off evil or ensure good luck; an amulet. **5.** Any formula or action supposed to have magic power. — *v.t.* **1.** To attract irresistibly; delight; fascinate. **2.** To cast a spell upon or influence as if by a spell; bewitch. **3.** To protect by or as by magic power. — *v.i.* **4.** To be pleasing or fascinating. [< F < L *carmen* song] — **charm'er** *n.*

charm·ing (chär'ming) *adj.* **1.** Delightful; very attractive. **2.** Magically powerful. — **charm'ing·ly** *adv.*

char·nel (chär'nəl) *n.* A charnel house. — *adj.* Suggesting or fit for receiving the dead; sepulchral; ghastly. [< OF < LL < L *caro, carnis* flesh]

charnel house A room or vault where bones or bodies of the dead are placed.

Char·on (kâr'ən, kar'-) In Greek mythology, the ferryman who carried the dead over the river Styx to Hades. — *n.* A ferryman: a humorous use.

char·ry (chär'ē) *adj.* **·ri·er, ·ri·est** Like charcoal.

chart (chärt) *n.* **1.** A map, esp. one for the use of mariners. **2.** An outline map on which climatic data, military operations, etc., can be shown. **3.** A sheet showing facts graphically or in tabular form. **4.** A graph showing changes and variation of temperature, population, prices, wages, etc. — *v.t.* To lay out on a chart; map out. [< OF < L < Gk. *chartēs* leaf of paper] — **chart'less** *adj.*

char·ter (chär'tər) *n.* **1.** A document of incorporation of a municipality, institution, or the like, specifying its privileges and purposes. **2.** A formal document by which a sovereign or government grants special rights or privileges to a person, company, or the people. **3.** An authorization to establish a branch or chapter of some larger organization. **4.** A contract for the lease of a vessel, bus, airplane, etc. — *v.t.* **1.** To hire (an airplane, train, etc.). **2.** To give a charter to. [< OF < L *chartula,* dim. of *charta* paper] — **char'ter·age** *n.* — **char'ter·er** *n.*

charter member An original member of a corporation, order, or society.

char·treuse (shar·trœz'; *for def. 2,* also shär·trōōz') *n.* **1.** A yellow, pale green, or white liqueur made by the Carthusian monks. **2.** A pale, yellowish green color. — *adj.* Of the color chartreuse. [< F < *La Grande Chartreuse,* chief Carthusian monastery in France]

char·wom·an (chär'wŏŏm'ən) *n. pl.* **·wom·en** (-wim'ən) *Brit.* A woman employed to do housework, or cleaning and scrubbing, as in office buildings.

char·y (châr'ē) *adj.* **char·i·er, char·i·est** **1.** Cautious; wary. **2.** Fastidious; particular. **3.** Sparing; frugal; stingy. [OE *cearig* sorrowful, sad < *cearu* care]

Cha·ryb·dis (kə·rib'dis) In Greek mythology, a monster dwelling in a whirlpool on the Sicilian coast opposite the cave of Scylla; also, the whirlpool. See SCYLLA.

chase¹ (chās) *v.* **chased, chas·ing** *v.t.* **1.** To pursue with intent to catch or harm. **2.** To follow persistently; run after. **3.** To put to flight; drive. — *v.i.* **4.** To follow in pursuit. **5.** *Informal* To rush; go hurriedly. — *n.* **1.** The act of chasing or pursuing. **2.** The sport of hunting: preceded by *the.* **3.** That which is pursued; prey; quarry. — **to give chase** To pursue. [< OF < LL < L *capere* to take]

chase² (chās) *n.* **1.** *Printing* A rectangular metal frame into which pages of type are fastened for printing or platemaking. **2.** A groove or slot; hollow; trench. — *v.t.* **chased, chas·ing** **1.** To indent or groove. **2.** To ornament by embossing; engrave. [Fusion of F *chasse* and *chas,* both ult. < L *capsa* box; in def. 2 < ENCHASE] — **chas'er** *n.*

chas·er (chā'sər) *n.* **1.** One who chases or pursues. **2.** *U.S. Informal* Water, etc. taken after strong liquor.

chasm (kaz'əm) *n.* **1.** A yawning crack in the earth's sur-

face; a gorge. **2.** An abrupt interruption; a gap or void. **3.** Any great difference of opinion, sentiment, loyalty, etc. [< Gk. *chainein* to gape] — **chas·mal** (kaz'məl) *adj.*

chas·seur (sha·sûr') *n.* **1.** One of a body of light cavalry or infantry trained for rapid maneuvers, as in the French army. **2.** A liveried servant. **3.** A huntsman. [< F, hunter]

Chas·si·dim (khä·sē'dim) *n. pl. of* **Chas·sid** (khä'sid) A sect of Jewish mystics: also spelled *Hasidim.* [< Hebrew, pious] — **Chas·si·dic** (khä·sē'dik) *adj.*

chas·sis (shas'ē, chas'ē) *n. pl.* **chas·sis** (shas'ēz, chas'ēz) **1.** The flat, rectangular frame that supports the body of a motor vehicle and includes the wheels, springs, motor, etc. **2.** *Aeron.* The landing gear of an aircraft. **3.** *Telecom.* The metal framework to which the tubes and other components of a radio receiver, amplifier, etc., are attached. **4.** A movable frame on which the top carriage of a gun moves backward and forward. [< F *chassis* < *chas.* See CHASE².]

chaste (chāst) *adj.* **1.** Not guilty of unlawful sexual intercourse; virtuous. **2.** Pure in character or conduct; not indecent. **3.** Pure in artistic or literary style; simple. [< OF < L *castus* pure] — **chaste'ly** *adv.* — **chaste'ness** *n.*

chas·ten (chā'sən) *v.t.* **1.** To discipline by punishment or affliction; chastise. **2.** To moderate; soften; temper. [< OF < L *castigare* to correct] — **chast'en·er** *n.*
— **Syn. 1.** *Chasten* is a general term to cover mild or severe punishment, whether physical or moral. *Correct* suggests mild punishment or sometimes mere verbal reproof. *Discipline,* like *correct,* looks to future conduct, and stresses training rather than punishment. *Chastise* and *castigate* refer to corporal punishment for past misconduct rather than as a corrective measure.

chas·tise (chas·tīz') *v.t.* **·tised, ·tis·ing** To punish, esp. by beating. — **Syn.** See CHASTEN. [ME *chastisen*] — **chas·tis'a·ble** *adj.* — **chas·tise·ment** (chas'tiz·mənt, chas·tīz'-) *n.* — **chas·tis'er** *n.*

chas·ti·ty (chas'tə·tē) *n.* **1.** The state or quality of being chaste. **2.** Virginity or celibacy. [< OF < L < *castus* pure]

chas·u·ble (chaz'yə·bəl, chas'-) *n.* A long, sleeveless vestment worn over the alb by a priest when celebrating the Eucharist. [< F < Med.L < L, dim. of *casa* house]

chat (chat) *v.i.* **chat·ted, chat·ting** To converse in an easy or gossipy manner; talk familiarly. — *n.* **1.** Easy, informal conversation. **2.** Any of several singing birds: so called from their notes. [Short for CHATTER]

cha·teau (sha·tō', *Fr.* shä·tō') *n. pl.* **·teaux** (-tōz', *Fr.* -tō') **1.** A French castle. **2.** A house on a country estate. Also *French* **châ·teau'.** [< F < OF < L *castrum* camp, fort]

chat·e·laine (shat'ə·lān) *n.* **1.** A chain hanging from a woman's belt to hold small articles, as keys; also, a clasp to hold a watch or purse. **2.** The mistress of a chateau, castle, or any fashionable household. [< F *châtelaine*]

chat·tel (chat'l) *n. Law* An article of personal property; a movable, as distinguished from real property. [< OF *chatel* < L *caput* head]

chattel mortgage A mortgage on personal property.

chat·ter (chat'ər) *v.i.* **1.** To click together rapidly, as the teeth in shivering. **2.** To talk rapidly and trivially. **3.** To utter a rapid series of short, inarticulate sounds, as a squirrel. — *v.t.* **4.** To utter in a trivial or chattering manner. — *n.* **1.** Idle or foolish talk; prattle. **2.** Jabbering, as of a monkey. **3.** A rattling of the teeth. [Imit.] — **chat'ter·er** *n.*

chat·ter·box (chat'ər·boks') *n.* An incessant talker.

chat·ty (chat'ē) *adj.* **·ti·er, ·ti·est** **1.** Given to chat; loquacious. **2.** Easy and familiar; informal: a *chatty* style of writing. — **chat'ti·ly** *adv.* — **chat'ti·ness** *n.*

Chau·ce·ri·an (chô·sir'ē·ən) *adj.* Of or like the writings of Chaucer. — *n.* A specialist in Chaucer's works.

chauf·feur (shō'fər, shō·fûr') *n.* One who is employed as the driver of an automobile. — *v.t.* To serve as driver for. [< F, stoker < *chauffer* to warm]

chaul·moo·gra (chôl·mōō'grə) *n.* An East Indian and Malayan tree whose seeds yield **chaulmoogra oil,** formerly used in treating leprosy. [< Bengali *câulmugrā*]

chau·vin·ism (shō'vən·iz'əm) *n.* **1.** Militant and vainglorious patriotism. **2.** Unreasoning attachment to one's race, group, etc. [after Nicholas *Chauvin,* a soldier and overzealous supporter of Napoleon Bonaparte] — **chau'vin·ist** *n.* — **chau'vin·is'tic** *adj.* — **chau'vin·is'ti·cal·ly** *adv.*

cheap (chēp) *adj.* **1.** Bringing a low price; inexpensive. **2.** Charging low prices, as a store. **3.** Obtainable at a low price in proportion to its value. **4.** Easily obtained; costing little trouble. **5.** Being of little value; poor; inferior. **6.** Not esteemed. **7.** Vulgar; mean: a *cheap* person. — *adv.* At a low price; cheaply. [Earlier *good cheap* a bargain < OE *cēap* business, trade] — **cheap'ly** *adv.* — **cheap'ness** *n.*

cheap·en (chē'pən) *v.t. & v.i.* To make or become cheap or cheaper. — **cheap'en·er** *n.*

cheap·skate (chēp'skāt') *n. U.S. Slang* A miserly person.

cheat (chēt) *v.t.* **1.** To swindle or defraud. **2.** To mislead or delude; trick. **3.** To elude or escape; foil. — *v.i.* **4.** To practice fraud or act dishonestly. **5.** *U.S. Slang* To be sexually unfaithful. — *n.* **1.** A fraud; swindle. **2.** One who cheats or defrauds. [ME *chete*, short for *achete* to confiscate, deprive] **— cheat′er** *n.* **— cheat′ing·ly** *adv.*

check (chek) *n.* **1.** A break in progress or advance; a stopping; rebuff; delay. **2.** One who or that which stops or controls. **3.** Control maintained to secure accuracy, honesty etc.; supervision. **4.** A test, examination, or comparison. **5.** A mark to show that something has been verified or investigated. **6.** An order, in writing, upon a bank or banker to pay a designated sum: also, *Brit*. *cheque*. **7.** *U.S.* A tag, slip, or the like, issued for identification: a baggage *check*. **8.** *U.S.* A slip listing the amount one owes, as in a restaurant. **9.** A counter used in various games; a chip. **10.** A square in a checkered surface, as on a chessboard. **11.** A fabric having a checkered pattern. **12.** In chess, the condition of a king that is subject to capture on the next opposing move. **13.** A crack, as in timber or steel. **— in check** Under control or restraint. **—** *v.t.* **1.** To bring to a stop suddenly or sharply; halt. **2.** To hold back; curb; restrain. **3.** To test or verify as to accuracy, completeness, etc.; also, to investigate. **4.** To mark with a check, as to indicate correctness. **5.** To mark with squares or crossed lines. checker. **6.** To deposit or accept for temporary safekeeping: to *check* luggage. **7.** In chess, to put (an opponent's king) in check. **8.** To cause to crack. **—** *v.i.* **9.** To come to a stop; pause. **10.** *U.S.* To agree item for item; correspond accurately. **11.** In chess, to put an opponent's king in check. **12.** *U.S.* To draw on a checking account. **13.** To crack, as paint. **— to check in** *U.S.* To register as a guest at a hotel, etc. **— to check on** (or **up on**) *U.S.* To inquire into; investigate. **— to check out 1.** *U.S.* To pay one's bill and leave, as from a hotel. **2.** To investigate or confirm. **3.** To be true or as expected, upon investigation. **4.** *Slang* To die. **—** *interj.* In chess, an exclamation proclaiming that an opponent's king is in check. **—** *adj.* **1.** *Chiefly Brit.* Formed or marked in a pattern of checks. **2.** Serving to verify or check. [< OF *eschec* defeat, check] **— check′a·ble** *adj.*

check·book (chek′bŏŏk′) *n.* A book of blank bank checks.

checked (chekt) *adj.* **1.** Marked with squares: *checked* gingham. **2.** Kept in check; restrained. **3.** Stopped.

check·er (chek′ər) *n.* **1.** A piece used in the game of checkers, usually a small disk. **2.** One of the squares in a checkered surface; also, a pattern of such squares. **3.** One who checks; esp., one who inspects, counts, or supervises the disposal of merchandise. **—** *v.t.* **1.** To mark with squares or crossed lines. **2.** To fill with variations or vicissitudes. Also, *Brit.*, *chequer*. [< ME < OF *eschec* defeat, check]

check·er·board (chek′ər·bôrd′, -bôrd′) *n.* A board divided into 64 squares, used in playing checkers or chess.

check·ered (chek′ərd) *adj.* **1.** Divided into squares. **2.** Marked by light and dark patches. **3.** Marked by alternations; eventful: a *checkered* career.

check·ers (chek′ərz) *n.pl.* (*construed as sing.*) A game played by two persons on a checkerboard, each player starting with twelve pieces: in England usu. called *draughts*.

check·ing account (chek′ing) A bank account against which a depositor may draw checks.

check list A list of items to be checked.

check·mate (chek′māt) *v.t.* **·mat·ed**, **·mat·ing 1.** In chess, to put (an opponent's king) in check from which no escape is possible, thus winning the game. **2.** To defeat by a skillful maneuver. **—** *n.* **1.** In chess: **a** The move that checkmates a king. **b** The condition of a king when checkmated. **2.** Utter defeat. Also *mate*. [< OF < Arabic *shāh māt* the king is dead < Persian]

check·off (chek′ôf′, -of′) *n.* The collection of trade-union dues by deduction from the pay of each employee.

check·out (chek′out′) *n.* **1.** The procedure or time of checking out of a hotel. **2.** The itemization of goods and payment for purchases, as at a supermarket: often used attributively: a *check-out* counter. Also **check′out′**.

check·rein (chek′rān′) *n.* A rein from the bit to the saddle of a harness to keep a horse's head up.

check·room (chek′rŏŏm′, -rŏŏm′) *n.* A room in which packages, coats, etc., may be left temporarily.

check·up (chek′up′) *n.* An examining or searching.

Ched·dar (ched′ər) *n.* Any of several kinds of white to yellow, hard, smooth cheese. Also **ched′dar, Cheddar cheese**. [after *Cheddar*, Somerset, England, where originally made]

cheek (chēk) *n.* **1.** Either side of the face below the eye and above the mouth. ◆ Collateral adjective: *buccal*. **2.** A side or part analogous to the side of the face. **3.** *Informal* Impudent self-assurance. [OE *cēce, cēace*]

cheek·bone (bhēk′bŏn′) *n.* Either of two bony prominences of the cheek below the eye socket.

cheek by jowl Side by side; in close intimacy.

cheek·y (chē′kē) *adj.* **cheek·i·er, cheek·i·est** *Informal* Impudent; brazen. **— cheek′i·ly** *adv.* **— cheek′i·ness** *n.*

cheep (chēp) *v.t. & v.i.* To make, or utter with, a faint, shrill sound, as a young bird. **—** *n.* A weak chirp or squeak. [Imit.] **— cheep′er** *n.*

cheer (chir) *n.* **1.** A shout of acclamation or encouragement. **2.** Gladness or gaiety. **3.** State of mind; mood. **4.** That which promotes happiness or joy; encouragement. **—** *v.t.* **1.** To make cheerful; gladden: often with *up*. **2.** To acclaim with cheers. **3.** To urge; incite: often with *on*. **—** *v.i.* **4.** To become cheerful or glad: often with *up*. **5.** To utter cries of encouragement, approval, etc. [< OF *chiere, chere* face] **— cheer′er** *n.* **— cheer′ing·ly** *adv.*

cheer·ful (chir′fəl) *adj.* **1.** In good spirits; joyous; lively. **2.** Pleasant: a *cheerful* color. **3.** Willing; ungrudging: a *cheerful* giver. **— cheer′ful·ly** *adv.* **— cheer′ful·ness** *n.*

cheer·i·o (chir′ē·ō) *interj. & n. pl.* **cheer·i·os** *Brit. Informal* **1.** Hello. **2.** Good-by. Also **cheer′o**.

cheer·lead·er (chir′lē′dər) *n.* A person who leads organized cheering at an athletic event. Also **cheer leader**.

cheer·less (chir′lis) *adj.* Destitute of cheer; gloomy. **— cheer′less·ly** *adv.* **— cheer′less·ness** *n.*

cheer·y (chir′ē) *adj.* **cheer·i·er, cheer·i·est** Abounding in cheerfulness; gay. **— cheer′i·ly** *adv.* **— cheer′i·ness** *n.*

cheese[1] (chēz) *n.* **1.** The pressed curd of milk, variously prepared and flavored. **2.** Any of various substances like cheese in consistency or shape. [OE *cēse* < L *caseus* cheese]

cheese[2] (chēz) *v.t.* **cheesed, chees·ing** *Slang* To stop: esp. in the phrase **cheese it!** Look out! Run! [< CEASE]

cheese[3] (chēz) *n. Slang* Personage: a big *cheese*. [? < Urdu *chīz* thing]

cheese·cake (chēz′kāk′) *n.* **1.** A cake containing sweetened curds, eggs, milk, etc.: also **cheese cake**. **2.** *Slang* A photograph featuring a pretty girl's legs and figure.

cheese·cloth (chēz′klôth′, -kloth′) *n.* A thin, loosely woven cotton fabric, originally used for wrapping cheese.

chees·y (chē′zē) *adj.* **chees·i·er, chees·i·est 1.** Of or like cheese. **2.** *U.S. Slang* Inferior. **— chees′i·ness** *n.*

chee·tah (chē′tə) *n.* An animal of the cat family, resembling the leopard, native to SW Asia and northern Africa. [< Hind. *chītā* leopard < Skt. *chitraka* speckled]

chef (shef) *n.* A head cook; also, any cook. [< F *chef* (de *cuisine*) head (of the kitchen) < OF]

cheg·oe (cheg′ō) *n.* The chigoe (def. 1).

cheilo- See CHILO-.

cheiro- See CHIRO-.

che·la (kē′lə) *n. pl.* **·lae** (-lē) *Zool.* A pincerlike claw in crustaceans and arachnids. [< NL < Gk. *chēlē* claw] **— che·late** (kē′lāt) *adj.*

chem·i·cal (kem′i·kəl) *adj.* Of or pertaining to chemistry or its phenomena, laws, operations, or results. **—** *n.* A substance obtained by or used in a chemical process. [< F < Med.L *alchimicus* of alchemy] **— chem′i·cal·ly** *adv.*

chemical warfare The technique of using smoke screens, gases, incendiary materials, etc., in warfare.

che·mise (shə·mēz′) *n.* **1.** A woman's loose undergarment resembling a short slip. **2.** A dress hanging straight from the shoulders. [< OF < LL *camisia* shirt]

chem·ist (kem′ist) *n.* **1.** One versed in chemistry. **2.** *Brit.* A druggist. [< ALCHEMIST]

chem·is·try (kem′is·trē) *n. pl.* **·tries 1.** The science that treats of the structure, composition, and properties of substances and of their transformations. **2.** Chemical composition or processes.

chemo- *combining form* Chemical; of or with chemicals or chemical reactions. Also **chemi-**. Also, before vowels, **chem-**.

chem·o·ther·a·py (kem′ō·ther′ə·pē, kē′mō-) *n. Med.* The treatment of infections by the use of chemically synthesized drugs. Also **chem′o·ther′a·peu′tics**. **— chem′o·ther′a·peu′tic** *adj.* **— chem′o·ther′a·pist** *n.*

chem·ur·gy (kem′ər·jē) *n.* The chemical exploitation of organic raw materials, esp. agricultural products, in the industrial development of new products. **— chem·ur·gic** (kem·ûr′jik) or **·gi·cal** *adj.*

che·nille (shə·nēl′) *n.* **1.** A soft, fuzzy cord, used for embroidery, fringes, etc. **2.** A fabric made with filling of this cord, used for rugs, bedspreads, or the like. [< F < L *canicula*, dim. of *canis* dog]

cheque (chek) *n. Brit.* A check (def. 6).

chequer (chek′ər) *n. Brit.* A checker.

cher·ish (cher′ish) *v.t.* **1.** To hold dear; treat with tenderness; foster. **2.** To entertain fondly, as a hope or an idea to. [< OF *cheriss-*, stem of *cherir* to hold dear < L *carus*] **— cher′ish·er** *n.* **— cher′ish·ing·ly** *adv.*

Cher·o·kee (cher′ə·kē, cher′ə·kē′) *n. pl.* **·kee** or **·kees 1.** One of a great tribe of Iroquoian Indians formerly occupying northern Georgia and North Carolina, now dwelling in Oklahoma. **2.** The Iroquoian language of this tribe.

Cherokee rose A trailing rose having large, solitary white flowers: the State flower of Georgia.

che·root (shə·rōōt′) *n.* A cigar cut square at both ends: also spelled *sheroot*. [< F < Tamil *shuruttu* roll, cigar]

cher·ry (cher′ē) *n. pl.* **·ries 1.** Any of various trees of the rose family, related to the plum and the peach and bearing small, round or heart-shaped drupes enclosing a smooth pit. **2.** The wood or fruit of a cherry tree. **3.** A bright red color resembling that of certain cherries: also **cherry red.** — *adj.* **1.** Bright red. **2.** Made of or with cherries. **3.** Made of cherry wood. [ME *chery* < L *cerasus* cherry tree]

cher·ub (cher′əb) *n. pl.* **cher·ubs** or **cher·u·bim** (cher′ə·bim, -yə·bim) *for def. 1,* **cherubs** *for def. 2,* **cherubim** *for def. 3* **1.** A representation of a beautiful winged child, the accepted type of the angelic cherub. **2.** A beautiful child; also, a chubby, innocent-looking adult. **3.** In Scripture, a celestial being. [< LL < Hebrew *kerūb*, an angelic being] — **che·ru·bic** (chə·rōō′bik) *adj.* — **che·ru′bi·cal·ly** *adv.*

cher·vil (chûr′vəl) *n.* A garden herb of the parsley family, the young leaves of which are used for soups, salads, etc. [OE < L < Gk. *chairephyllon*]

cher·vo·nets (cher·vô′nets) *n. pl.* **·vont·si** (-vônt′sē) A former gold monetary unit of the U.S.S.R. [< Russian]

Chesh·ire cat (chesh′ər, -ir) In Lewis Carroll's *Alice's Adventures in Wonderland,* a grinning cat that gradually faded away until only its grin remained.

chess (ches) *n.* A game of skill played on a chessboard by two persons, with 16 pieces on each side. The aim of each player is to checkmate his opponent's king. [< OF *esches,* pl. of *eschec* < Arabic *shāh* king < Persian]

chess·board (ches′bôrd′, -bōrd′) *n.* A board divided into 64 alternately colored squares, used in playing chess.

chess·man (ches′man′, -mən) *n. pl.* **·men** (men′, -mən) Any of the pieces used in playing chess.

chest (chest) *n.* **1.** The part of the body enclosed by the ribs; thorax. ◆ Collateral adjective: *pectoral.* **2.** A box, usu. with a hinged lid, for storing or protecting articles, as tools, jewelry, etc. **3.** The treasury of a public institution; also, the funds contained there. **4.** A chest of drawers. [< OE < L < Gk. *kistē* basket, box]

ches·ter·field (ches′tər·fēld) *n.* **1.** A single-breasted topcoat, generally with concealed buttons. **2.** *Chiefly Canadian* A sofa. [after a 19th c. Earl of *Chesterfield*]

Ches·ter·field·i·an (ches′tər·fēl′dē·ən) *adj.* **1.** Of or pertaining to Lord Chesterfield. **2.** Suave; polished; elegant.

chest·nut (ches′nut′, -nət) *n.* **1.** The edible nut of various trees of the beech family, growing in a prickly bur; also, a tree that bears this nut. **2.** One of certain similar trees, or their fruit, as the horse chestnut. **3.** A reddish brown color. **4.** A horse of this color. **5.** *Informal* A stale joke. **b** Anything trite, as a story, song, etc. — *adj.* Reddish brown. [ME < OF < L < Gk. *kastanea* + NUT]

chest of drawers A piece of furniture containing a set of drawers for storing linens, clothing, etc.

chest·y (ches′tē) *adj.* **chest·i·er, chest·i·est** *Informal* **1.** Self-assertive; proud. **2.** Large in the chest.

che·val-de-frise (shə·val′də·frēz′) *n. pl.* **che·vaux-de-frise** (shə-vō′-) A protecting line, as of broken glass or spikes, on top of a wall. [< F, lit., horse of Friesland]

che·val glass (shə·val′) A long mirror mounted on horizontal pivots in a frame.

chev·a·lier (shev′ə·lir′) *n.* **1.** A member of certain orders of knighthood or honor, as of the French Legion of Honor. **2.** A knight or cavalier. **3.** A chivalrous man; a gallant. [< OF *chevalier* < LL < L *caballus* horse]

chev·i·ot (shev′ē·ət) *n.* A rough cloth of twill weave, used for suits, overcoats, etc., originally made from Cheviot wool.

Chev·i·ot (chev′ē·ət, chē′vē-) *n.* One of a breed of large sheep, originating in the Cheviot Hills, esteemed for their wool (**Cheviot wool**).

chev·ron (shev′rən) *n.* An emblem or insignia usu. consisting of stripes meeting at an angle, worn on a uniform sleeve to indicate rank, length of service, etc., used by military, naval, and police forces. [< OF, chevron, rafter]

chev·y (chev′ē) *n. pl.* **chev·ies** *Brit.* A hunt, or a shout in hunting. — *v.* **chev·ied, chev·y·ing** *v.t.* **1.** To chase about; hunt. **2.** To harass; worry. — *v.i.* **3.** To race; scamper. Also *chivy, chivvy.* [Prob. < *Chevy* Chase]

chew (chōō) *v.t. & v.i.* **1.** To crush or grind with the teeth; masticate. **2.** To meditate upon; consider carefully. — **to chew out** *U.S. Slang* To reprimand severely; berate. — *n.* **1.** The act of chewing. **2.** That which is chewed; a quid; cut. [OE *cēowan*] — **chew′er** *n.*

chew·ing gum (chōō′ing) A preparation of some natural gum, usu. chicle, flavored for chewing.

che·wink (chi·wingk′) *n.* The towhee, a bird. [Imit.]

chew·y (chōō′ē) *adj.* **chew·i·er, chew·i·est** Relatively soft and requiring chewing: Caramels are chewy.

Chey·enne (chī·en′) *n. pl.* **·enne** or **·ennes** One of a tribe of North American Indians now inhabiting Montana and Oklahoma.

chi (kī) *n.* The twenty-second letter in the Greek alphabet (X, χ), transliterated as *ch.* See ALPHABET. [< Gk.]

chi·an·ti (kē·an′tē, *Ital.* kyän′tē) *n.* A dry, red, Italian wine; also, any similar wine. [after Monti *Chianti,* a region in Italy]

chi·a·ro·scu·ro (kē·är′ə·skyōōr′ō) *n. pl.* **·ros 1.** The distribution and treatment of light and shade in a picture. **2.** A kind of painting or drawing using only light and shade. **3.** An artist's treatment of light and shade. Also **chi·a·ro·o·scu·ro** (kē·är′ə·ō·skyōōr′ō). [< Ital. < L < *clarus* clear + *obscurus* dark] — **chi·a′ro·scu′rist** *n.*

chic (shēk. shik) *adj.* Smart; stylish; elegant. — *n.* Originality, elegance, and taste, esp. in dress. [< F]

chi·cane (shi·kān′) *v.* **·caned, ·can·ing** *v.t.* **1.** To deceive by chicanery; trick. **2.** To quibble about. — *v.i.* **3.** To resort to chicanery; use tricks. — *n.* **1.** Chicanery. **2.** A bridge or whist hand containing no trumps. [< F *chicaner*]

chi·can·er·y (shi·kā′nər·ē) *n. pl.* **·er·ies 1.** Trickery and subterfuge; sophistry; quibbling. **2.** A trick; quibble.

chic·co·ry (chik′ər·ē) See CHICORY.

chi·chi (shē′shē) *adj. Informal* Ostentatiously stylish or elegant. [< F, frill]

chick (chik) *n.* **1.** A young chicken. **2.** Any young bird. **3.** A child. **4.** *U.S. Slang* A girl. [Short for CHICKEN]

chick·a·dee (chik′ə·dē) *n.* An American titmouse with the top of the head and the throat black or dark colored. [Imit. of its cry]

chick·a·ree (chik′ə·rē) *n.* The red squirrel. See under SQUIRREL. [Imit. of its cry]

Chick·a·saw (chik′ə·sô) *n. pl.* **·saw** or **·saws** One of a tribe of Muskhogean North American Indians now living in Oklahoma.

chick·en (chik′ən) *n.* **1.** The young of domestic fowl. **2.** A cock or hen of any age. **3.** The flesh of the chicken, used as food. **4.** *Informal* A child or a young person: now chiefly in the phrase **no chicken,** one no longer young. — *adj.* *U.S. Slang* Afraid, cowardly. — *v.i.* *U.S. Slang* To lose one's nerve: often with *out.* [OE *cicen*]

CHICKADEE (5¾ inches long; tail 2¾ inches; wingspread 8½ inches)

chicken feed *Slang* **1.** Small change, as pennies, nickels, dimes, etc. **2.** Food for chickens.

chicken hawk Any of various hawks that prey on poultry.

chick·en-heart·ed (chik′ən·här′tid) *adj.* Cowardly.

chicken pox *Pathol.* A contagious disease, principally of children, characterized by skin eruptions and a slight fever.

chick·pea (chik′pē′) *n.* **1.** A plant of Mediterranean regions and central Asia. **2.** Its seed, widely used as a food. [ME *chichpease*]

chick·weed (chik′wēd) *n.* Any of various weeds having seeds and leaves that birds eat.

chic·le (chik′əl) *n.* The milky juice or latex of the sapodilla, used as the basic principle of chewing gum. Also **chicle gum.** [< Sp. < Nahuatl *chictli*]

chic·o·ry (chik′ər·ē) *n. pl.* **·ries 1.** A perennial herb, having usu. blue flowers and used as a salad plant. **2.** Its dried, roasted, and ground roots, used for mixing with coffee or as a coffee substitute. [< MF < L < Gk. *kichora*]

chide (chīd) *v.t. & v.i.* **chid·ed** or **chid** (chid), **chid·ed** or **chid** or **chid·den** (chid′n), **chid·ing** To speak reprovingly (to); scold. [OE *cīdan*] — **chid′er** *n.* — **chid′ing·ly** *adv.*

chief (chēf) *n.* **1.** *Often cap.* The person highest in rank or authority, as the leader or head of a tribe, band, police force, government bureau, etc. **2.** *Usu. cap.* A ship's chief engineer; also, a chief petty officer. **3.** *Slang* A boss. — **in chief** Having the highest authority: commander in chief. — *adj.* **1.** Highest in rank or authority. **2.** Most important or eminent; leading. [< OF *chef,* chief < L *caput* head]

chief justice The presiding judge of a court composed of several justices.

chief·ly (chēf′lē) *adv.* **1.** Most of all; above all; especially. **2.** Principally; mainly. — *adj.* Of or like a chief.

chief of staff *U.S.* The principal staff officer of a division or a higher level.

Chief of Staff *U.S.* The ranking officer in the Army or Air Force, responsible to the Secretary of his department.

chief·tain (chēf′tən) *n.* **1.** The head of a clan or tribe. **2.** Any chief; leader. [< OF < LL < L *caput* head] — **chief′tain·cy, chief′tain·ship** *n.*

chif·fon (shi·fon′, shif′on) *n.* **1.** A sheer silk or rayon fabric. **2.** *pl.* Ornamental adjuncts of feminine attire, as ribbons or lace. — *adj.* **1.** Of or pertaining to chiffon. **2.** In cooking, having a fluffy texture. [< F, dim. of *chiffe* rag]

chif·fo·nier (shif′ə·nir′) *n.* A high chest of drawers, often with a mirror at the top. Also **chif′fon·nier′.** [< F < *chiffon*]

chig·ger (chig′ər) *n.* **1.** The larva of various mites of the southern U.S., that attaches itself to the skin, causing intense itching. **2.** The chigoe (def. 1). [Alter. of CHIGOE]

chi·gnon (shēn′yon, *Fr.* shēnyôN′) *n.* A knot or roll of hair worn at the back of the head by women. [< F]

chig·oe (chig′ō) *n.* **1.** A flea of the West Indies and South America. **2.** A chigger (def. 1) [< Carib]

Chi·hua·hua (chi·wä′wä) *n.* One of an ancient breed of very small, smooth-coated dogs with large, pointed ears, originally native to Mexico. [after *Chihuahua,* Mexico]

chil- Var. of CHILO-.

chil·blain (chil′blān) *n. Pathol.* An inflammation of the hands or feet caused by exposure to cold.

child (chīld) *n. pl.* **chil·dren** 1. An offspring of human parents. 2. A boy or girl, most commonly one between infancy and youth. 3. A descendant. 4. A childish person. 5. A product of a specified condition, quality, etc.: a *child* of joy. — **with child** Pregnant. [OE *cild*] — **child′less** *adj.*

child·bear·ing (chīld′bâr′ing) *n.* The bringing forth of children.

child·bed (chīld′bed′) *n.* The state of a woman giving birth to a child.

child·birth (chīld′bûrth′) *n.* Parturition.

child·hood (chīld′hŏod) *n.* The state or time of being a child. [OE *cildhād*]

child·ish (chīl′dish) *adj.* 1. Of, like, or proper to a child. 2. Unduly like a child; immature; puerile; weak. [OE *cildisc*] — **child′ish·ly** *adv.* — **child′ish·ness** *n.*

child·like (chīld′līk′) *adj.* Like, characteristic of, or appropriate to a child; artless, docile, etc. — **child′like′ness** *n.*

chil·dren (chil′dran) Plural of CHILD.

child's play Something easy to do.

chil·i (chil′ē) *n. pl.* **chil·ies** 1. The acrid pod or fruit of the red pepper, used as a seasoning. 2. Chile con carne. Also **chil′e, chil′li.** [< Sp. < Nahuatl *chilli*]

chile con car·ne (kon kär′nē) A highly seasoned dish made with meat, chili, and often beans. [< Sp., chili with meat]

chili sauce A spiced tomato sauce made with chili.

chill (chil) *n.* 1. A sensation of cold, often with shivering. 2. A moderate degree of coldness. 3. A check to enthusiasm, joy, etc. 4. A numbing sensation of dread or anxiety. — *v.t.* 1. To reduce to a low temperature. 2. To affect with cold; seize with a chill. 3. To check, as ardor; dispirit. 4. To harden the surface of (metal) by sudden cooling. — *v.i.* 5. To become cold. 6. To be stricken with a chill. 7. To become hard by sudden cooling, as metal. — *adj.* 1. Moderately or unpleasantly cold. 2. Affected by or shivering with cold. 3. Cold in manner; distant. 4. Discouraging. [OE *ciele*] — **chill′ing·ly** *adv.* — **chill′ness** *n.*

chill·er (chil′ar) *n.* 1. That which chills. 2. A horror story or movie.

chill·y (chil′ē) *adj.* **chill·i·er, chill·i·est** 1. Causing chill; cold or chilling. 2. Feeling cold; affected by chill. 3. Disheartening, unfriendly. — **chill′i·ly** *adv.* — **chill′i·ness** *n.*

chilo- *combining form* Lip. Also spelled *cheilo-*: also, before vowels, *chil-*. [< Gk. *cheilos* lip]

chime¹ (chīm) *n.* 1. *Often pl.* A set of bells, as in a bell tower, tuned to a scale. 2. A single bell: the *chime* of a clock. 3. *Often pl.* The sounds or music produced by a chime. 4. Agreement; accord. — *v.* **chimed, chim·ing** 1. To cause to sound musically by striking; ring. 2. To announce (the hour) by the sound of bells. 3. To summon, welcome, or send by chimes. 4. To say rhythmically; prate. — *v.i.* 5. To sound musically. 6. To ring chimes. 7. To harmonize; agree: with *with.* — **to chime in** 1. To join in harmoniously. 2. To join, and so interrupt, a conversation. [ME < L *cymbalum* cymbal] — **chim′er** *n.*

chime² (chīm) *n.* The rim of a cask, barrel, etc. Also **chimb** (chīm). [OE *cimb-* edge, as in *cimbing* joint]

chi·me·ra (ka·mir′a, kī-) *n.* 1. An absurd creation of the imagination. 2. In painting, sculpture, etc., an imaginary, grotesque monster. [< L < Gk. *chimaira* she-goat]

chi·mer·i·cal (ka·mer′i·kal, kī-) *adj.* 1. Of the nature of a chimera; fantastic; imaginary. 2. Given to fanciful dreams; visionary. Also **chi·mer′ic.** — **chi·mer′i·cal·ly** *adv.*

chim·ney (chim′nē) *n.* 1. A flue to conduct gases and smoke from a fire to the outer air. 2. A structure containing such a flue, usually vertical and rising above the roof of a building. 3. A smokestack; funnel. 4. A tube, usually of glass, for enclosing the flame of a lamp. 5. A vent of a volcano. [< OF *cheminee* < LL < L < Gk. *kaminos*]

chimney corner 1. The space between the jamb or side of a large fireplace and the fire. 2. The fireside.

chimney piece A mantel.

chimney pot A pipe placed on the top of a chimney to improve the draft and prevent smoking.

chimney sweep One whose occupation is the cleaning of soot from inside chimneys. Also **chimney sweeper.**

chim·pan·zee (chim′pan·zē′, chim·pan′zē) *n.* An arboreal anthropoid ape of equatorial Africa, having large ears and dark brown hair, and smaller and more intelligent than the gorilla. [< native West African name]

chin (chin) *n.* 1. The lower part of the face, between the mouth and the neck. 2. *Anat.* The central and anterior part of the lower jaw. — *v.* **chinned, chin·ning** *v.t.* 1. To

lift (oneself) while grasping an overhead bar until the chin is level with the hands. — *v.i.* 2. *U.S. Informal* To talk idly. 3. To chin oneself. [OE *cin*]

chi·na (chī′na) *n.* 1. Fine porcelain or ceramic ware, originally made in China. 2. Any crockery. Also **chi′na·ware′.**

chi·na·ber·ry (chī′na·ber′ē) *n. pl.* **·ries** 1. Either of two trees of the soapberry family, found in Mexico and the SW U.S. Also **China tree.** 2. Its berrylike fruit.

Chi·na·man (chī′na·man) *n. pl.* **·men** (man) A Chinese: an offensive term.

Chi·na·town (chī′na·toun′) The Chinese quarter of any city outside China.

chin·ca·pin (ching′ka·pin) See CHINQUAPIN.

chinch (chinch) *n.* 1. A small, brown and black hemipterous insect destructive to grain. Also **chinch bug.** 2. The bedbug. [< Sp. *chinche* < L *cimex* bug]

chin·chil·la (chin·chil′a) *n.* 1. A small rodent native in the Andes. 2. The soft, valuable, pearl gray fur of the chinchilla. 3. A closely woven, twilled fabric having a tufted surface. [< Sp., ? alter. of Quechua *sinchi* strong]

chine¹ (chīn) *n.* 1. The spine, backbone, or back. 2. A piece of meat including all or part of the backbone. [< OF *eschine* backbone < Gmc.]

chine² (chīn) *n.* Chime².

Chi·nese (chī·nēz′, -nēs) *adj.* Of or pertaining to China, its people, or their languages. — *n. pl.* **·nese** 1. A native of China, or a person of Chinese ancestry. 2. The standard language of China.

Chinese lantern A collapsible lantern made of thin paper.

Chinese puzzle 1. An intricate puzzle originally made by the Chinese. 2. Any problem difficult to solve.

chink¹ (chingk) *n.* A small, narrow cleft; crevice. — *v.t.* 1. To make cracks or fissures in. 2. To fill the cracks of, as a wall; plug up. [ME *chynke*] — **chink′y** *adj.*

chink² (chingk) *n.* 1. A short, sharp, metallic sound. 2. *Slang* Coin; cash. — *v.t. & v.i.* To make or cause to make a sharp, clinking sound. [Imit.]

chi·no (chē′nō) *n.* 1. A strong cotton fabric with a twilled weave. 2. *pl.* Boys' or men's trousers of this material. [< Sp., toasted; with ref. to the original tan color]

Chino- *combining form* Connected with China.

chi·nook (chi·nŏok′, -nŏok′) *n. U.S. & Canadian* 1. A warm wind of the Oregon and Washington coasts. 2. A warm, dry wind that blows off the eastern slopes of the Rocky Mountains in the NW U.S. and western Canada. [after *Chinook*]

Chi·nook (chi·nŏok′, -nŏok′) *n. pl.* **·nook** or **·nooks** 1. One of a tribe of North American Indians formerly occupying the region of the Columbia River, Oregon. 2. The language of this tribe. — **Chi·nook′an** *adj. & n.*

Chinook jargon A pidgin language comprising words from Chinook, mixed with English, French, etc.

Chinook salmon A salmon of North Pacific coastal waters.

chin·qua·pin (ching′ka·pin) *n.* 1. Any of several trees of North America. 2. A related tree of the Pacific coast. 3. The edible nut of these trees. Also **chin′ka·pin.** [< N. Am. Ind.]

chintz (chints) *n.* A cotton fabric usu. glazed and printed in bright colors. Also **chints.** [< Skt. *chitra* variegated]

chip (chip) *n.* 1. A small piece cut or broken off. 2. A small disk or counter used in certain games, as in poker. 3. A crack or imperfection caused by chipping. 4. A thinly sliced morsel: potato *chips.* 5. *pl. Brit.* French fried potatoes. 6. *Usu. pl.* Dried animal droppings used as fuel. 7. Anything of little or no value. 8. Wood, palm leaves, etc., cut into strips for weaving. — **a chip off** (or **of**) **the old block** One who resembles either of his parents in behavior, appearance, etc. — **a chip on one's shoulder** A willingness to take offense; belligerent manner. — **in the chips** *Slang* Possessing money; affluent. — *v.* **chipped, chip·ping** *v.t.* 1. To break off small pieces of, as china. — *v.i.* 2. To become chipped. — **to chip in** *Informal* To contribute, as to a fund. [ME *chippe*] — **chip′per** *n.*

Chip·e·wy·an (chip·a·wī′an) *n.* 1. One of a tribe of Indians living in NW Canada. 2. The language of this tribe.

chip·munk (chip′mungk) *n.* Any of various striped North American rodents of the squirrel family: also called *ground squirrel.* Also **chip·muck** (chip′muk). [< N. Am. Ind.]

chipped beef (chipt) Beef smoked and sliced thin.

Chip·pen·dale (chip′an·dāl) *adj.* Designating or in the style of a graceful, rococo type of furniture made in 18th-century England. [after Thomas *Chippendale,* 1718–79, English cabinetmaker.]

chip·per (chip′ar) *adj. U.S. Informal* 1. Brisk; cheerful. 2. Smartly dressed; spruce. [< Brit. Dial. *kipper* frisky]

CHIPMUNK

(About 6½ inches long; tail 4½ inches)

Chip·pe·wa (chip/ə·wä, -wā, -wə) *n. pl.* **·wa** or **·was** Ojibwa. Also **Chip·pe·way** (chip/ə·wā).

chip·py (chip/ē) *n. pl.* **·pies** 1. A chipmunk. 2. *Slang* A young woman of easy morals; also, a prostitute.

chip shot In golf, a short, lofted shot made in approaching the green.

chiro- *combining form* Hand; of or with the hand: *chirography.* Also spelled *cheiro-.* Also, before vowels, **chir-.** [< Gk. *cheir, cheiros* hand]

chi·rog·ra·phy (kī·rog/rə·fē) *n.* The art, style, or character of handwriting. — **chi·rog/ra·pher** *n.* — **chi·ro·graph·ic** (kī/rə·graf/ik) or **·i·cal** *adj.*

chi·ro·man·cy (kī/rə·man/sē) *n.* Palmistry. [< F < Gk. < *cheir* hand + *manteia* divination] — **chi/ro·man/cer** *n.*

chi·rop·o·dy (kə·rop/ə·dē, kī-) *n.* The branch of medicine that deals with ailments of the foot: also called *pedicure, podiatry.* [< CHIRO- + Gk. *podos* foot] — **chi·rop/o·dist** *n.*

chi·ro·prac·tic (kī/rə·prak/tik) *n.* A medical therapy based on the manipulation of bodily structures, esp. the spinal column. [< CHIRO- + Gk. *praktikos* effective] — **chi·ro·prac/tor** (kī/rə·prak/tər) *n.*

chirp (chûrp) *v.i.* 1. To give a short, acute cry, as a sparrow or locust; cheep, as a young bird. 2. To talk in a quick and shrill manner. — *v.t.* 3. To utter with a quick, sharp sound. — *n.* The sound of chirping. [Var. of CHIRK] — **chirp/er** *n.*

chirr (chûr) *v.i.* To make a sharp trilling sound, as that of the grasshopper, cicada, and some birds. — *n.* The trilling sound of crickets, locusts, etc. Also **chirre.** [Imit.]

chir·rup (chir/əp) *v.i.* 1. To chirp continuously or repeatedly, as a bird. 2. To chirp with the lips, as in urging a horse. — *v.t.* 3. To utter with chirps. — *n.* A sound of chirruping. [< CHIRP] — **chir/rup·y** *adj.*

chis·el (chiz/əl) *n.* A cutting tool with a beveled edge, used for cutting, engraving, or mortising metal, stone, or wood. — *v.t. & v.i.* **chis·eled** or **·elled, chis·el·ing** or **·el·ling** 1. To cut, engrave, or carve with or as with a chisel. 2. *Slang* To cheat; swindle; also, to obtain by dishonest methods. [< AF < L *caedere* to cut] — **chis/el·er** or **chis/el·ler** *n.*

chit¹ (chit) *n.* 1. A voucher of a sum owed, as for food. 2. *Brit.* A memorandum: also **chit/ty.** [< Hind. *chitthī* note]

chit² (chit) *n.* A pert girl. [ME *chit*]

chit·chat (chit/chat/) *n.* 1. Small talk. 2. Gossip.

chi·tin (kī/tin) *n. Biochem.* A horny substance forming the hard outer covering of insects and crustaceans. [< F < Gk. *chitōn* tunic] — **chi/tin·ous** *adj.*

chit·ter·lings (chit/ər·lingz) *n.pl.* The small intestines of pigs, esp. as used for food; also **chit/lin** (chit/lin), **chit/ling.** [Cf. G. *kutteln* entrails]

chiv·al·ric (shiv/əl·rik, shi·val/rik) *adj.* Chivalrous.

chiv·al·rous (shiv/əl·rəs) *adj.* 1. Having the qualities of the ideal knight; gallant, courteous, generous, etc. 2. Pertaining to chivalry. [< OF < *chevalier* knight] — **chiv/al·rous·ly** *adv.* — **chiv/al·rous·ness** *n.*

chiv·al·ry (shiv/əl·rē) *n.* 1. The feudal system of knighthood. 2. The spirit or principles of this system; knight-errantry. 3. The ideal qualities of knighthood, as courtesy, valor, skill in arms, etc. 4. A body of knights, gallant gentlemen, etc. [< OF < LL *caballarius* cavalier]

chiv·a·ree (shiv/ə·rē/) See CHARIVARI.

chive (chīv) *n.* A perennial herb allied to the leek and onion, used as a flavoring in cooking. [< AF < L *cepa* onion]

chiv·y (chiv/ē), **chiv·vy** See CHEVY (def. 1).

chlor- Var. of CHLORO-.

chlo·ral (klôr/əl, klō/rəl) *n. Chem.* 1. A colorless, oily, liquid compound, $CCl_3 \cdot CHO$, with a penetrating odor. 2. A white, crystalline, pungent compound, $CCl_3CHO \cdot H_2O$, used medicinally as a hypnotic: also **chloral hydrate.** [< CHLOR(INE) + AL(COHOL)]

chlo·ram·phen·i·col (klôr/am·fen/i·kōl, -kol, klō/ram-) *n. Chem.* A crystalline nitrogenous compound, $C_{11}H_{12}Cl_2O_5N_2$, used as an antibiotic.

chlo·rate (klôr/āt, klō/rāt) *n. Chem.* A salt of chloric acid.

chlor·dane (klôr/dān, klōr/-) *n. Chem.* A toxic compound of chlorine, $C_{10}H_6Cl_8$ used as a fumigant and insecticide.

chlo·ric (klôr/ik, klō/rik) *adj. Chem.* Of, pertaining to, or combined with chlorine in its higher valence.

chlo·ride (klôr/īd, klō/rīd, -rid) *n. Chem.* A compound of chlorine with a more positive element or radical. Also **chlo·rid** (klôr/id, klō/rid). — **chlo·rid·ic** (klə·rid/ik) *adj.*

chloride of lime *Chem.* A disinfecting and bleaching agent made by the action of chlorine on slaked lime.

chlo·rin·ate (klôr/ə·nāt, klō/rə-) *v.t.* **·at·ed, ·at·ing** *Chem.* To treat or cause to combine with chlorine, as in purifying water, whitening fabrics, etc. — **chlo/rin·a/tion** *n.*

chlo·rine (klôr/ēn, -in, klō/rēn, -rin) *n.* A greenish yellow, poisonous, gaseous element (symbol Cl), with a suffocating odor, widely used as a bleach and disinfectant. Also **chlo·rin** (klôr/in, klō/rin). See ELEMENT. [< Gk. *chlōros* green]

chloro- *combining form* 1. Light green: *chlorophyll.* 2. Chlorine. Also, before vowels, *chlor-.* [< Gk. *chlōros* green]

chlo·ro·form (klôr/ə·fôrm, klō/rə-) *n. Chem.* A colorless, volatile, sweetish liquid compound, $CHCl_3$, used as an anesthetic and solvent. — *v.t.* 1. To administer chloroform to. 2. To anesthetize or kill with chloroform.

Chlo·ro·my·ce·tin (klôr/ə·mī·sē/tən, klō/rə-) *n.* Proprietary name for a brand of chloramphenicol, used as an antibiotic: also **chlo/ro·my·ce/tin.**

chlo·ro·phyll (klôr/ə·fil, klō/rə-) *n. Biochem.* The green nitrogenous coloring matter contained in the chloroplasts of plants, essential to the production of carbohydrates by photosynthesis. Also **chlo/ro·phyl.** [< CHLORO- + Gk. *phyllon* leaf] — **chlo·ro·phyl·la·ceous** (klôr/ə·fi·lā/shəs, klō/rə-), **chlo/ro·phyl/lose** (-fil/ōs), **chlo/ro·phyl/lous** (-fil/əs) *adj.*

chlo·ro·plast (klôr/ə·plast, klō/rə-) *n. Bot.* One of the flattened bodies containing chlorophyll. Also **chlo/ro·plas/tid.**

chlor·pro·ma·zine (klôr·prō/mə·zēn, -zin, klōr-) *n.* A synthetic tranquilizing drug used to control severe excitement in certain mental disorders.

chock (chok) *n.* 1. A block or wedge, so placed as to prevent or limit motion. 2. *Naut.* **a** A heavy piece of metal or wood fastened to a deck, etc., and having jaws through which a rope or cable may pass. **b** A block or support on which to rest a boat, etc. — *v.t.* 1. To make fast or fit with a chock or chocks. 2. To place on chocks, as a boat. — *adv.* As far or as close as possible. [< AF *choque* log]

chock-a-block (chok/ə·blok/) *adj.* 1. Drawn to the limit, with blocks touching: said of a tackle. 2. Close together; jammed. — *adv.* Close; very near.

chock-full (chok/fool/) *adj.* Completely full; stuffed: also *choke-full, chuck-full.* [ME *chokke-fulle*]

choc·o·late (chôk/lit, chôk/ə·lit, chok/-) *n.* 1. A preparation of cacao nuts roasted and ground and usu. sweetened. 2. A beverage or confection made from this. 3. A dark brown color. — *adj.* Flavored with or made with chocolate. [< Sp. < Nahuatl *chocolatl*] — **choc/o·lat·y** *adj.*

Choc·taw (chok/tô) *n. pl.* **·taw** or **·taws** 1. A member of a tribe of North American Indians of Muskhogean stock, now living in Oklahoma. 2. The language of this tribe.

choice (chois) *n.* 1. The act of choosing; selection. 2. The right or privilege of choosing; option. 3. The person or thing chosen. 4. A number or variety from which to choose: a great *choice* of dishes. 5. A well-selected supply. 6. An alternative: He had no *choice.* 7. The best or preferred part of anything. 8. Excellence: wine of *choice.* — *adj.* **choic·er, choic·est** 1. Select; excellent. 2. Chosen with care. [< OF < *choisir* to choose] — **choice/ly** *adv.* — **choice/ness** *n.*

choir (kwīr) *n.* 1. An organized body of singers, esp. in a church. 2. The part of a church occupied by such singers; chancel. — *v.i.* 1. To sing, as in a choir. — *v.t.* 2. To sing or utter in chorus. [< OF *cuer* < L *chorus*]

choke (chōk) *v.* **choked, chok·ing** *v.t.* 1. To stop the breathing of by obstructing the windpipe; strangle. 2. To keep back; suppress. 3. To obstruct or close up by filling; clog. 4. To retard the progress, growth, or action of. 5. To lessen the air intake of the carburetor in order to enrich the fuel mixture of (a gasoline engine). — *v.i.* 6. To become suffocated or stifled. 7. To become clogged, fouled, or obstructed. — **to choke up** 1. To be overcome by emotion, tears, etc. 2. To perform poorly because of tension, agitation, etc. — *n.* 1. The act or sound of choking. 2. *Mech.* A device to control the flow of air, as to a gasoline engine. [OE *acēocian*]

choke·bore (chōk/bôr/, -bōr/) *n.* In shotguns, a bore narrowed at the muzzle to concentrate the shot; also, a shotgun with such a bore.

choke·cher·ry (chōk/cher/ē) *n. pl.* **·ries** A wild cherry of North America, or its sour fruit.

choke·damp (chōk/damp/) *n.* Any condition of the atmosphere resulting in choking or suffocation.

choke-full (chōk/fool/) See CHOCK-FULL.

chok·er (chō/kər) *n.* 1. One who or that which chokes. 2. *Informal* A neckcloth or necklace worn high around the throat; also, a high, tight collar. 3. A small fur neckpiece.

chok·y (chō/kē) *adj.* **chok·i·er, chok·i·est** 1. Causing one to choke. 2. Somewhat choked. Also **chok/ey.**

chole- *combining form* Bile; gall: *cholesterol.* Also **cholo-:** also, before vowels, **chol-.** [< Gk. *cholē* bile]

chol·er (kol/ər) *n.* Anger; hastiness of temper, formerly thought to be caused by an excess of bile. [< OF < L < Gk. *cholē* bile] — **chol/er·ic** *adj.*

chol·er·a (kol/ər·ə) *n. Pathol.* An acute, infectious, epidemic disease characterized principally by serious intestinal disorders. In its more malignant forms, as **Asiatic cholera,** it is usu. fatal. [< L < Gk. *cholē* bile]

cho·les·ter·ol (kə·les/tə·rōl, -rol) *n. Biochem.* A fatty, crystalline alcohol, $C_{27}H_{45}OH$, derived principally from bile, present in most gallstones, and very widely distributed in animal fats and tissues. Also **cho·les/ter·in** (-in). [< CHOLE- + Gk. *stereos* solid + -OL²]

chondro- *combining form* Cartilage. Also, before vowels, **chondr-.** [< Gk. *chondros* cartilage]

choose (chōōz) *v.* **chose, cho·sen, choos·ing** *v.t.* **1.** To select as most desirable; take by preference. **2.** To desire or have a preference for. **3.** To prefer (to do something): He has *chosen* to remain. — *v.i.* **4.** To make a choice. — **cannot choose but** Must. [OE *cēosan*] — **choos'er** *n.*

choos·y (chōō'zē) *adj.* **choos·i·er, choos·i·est** *Informal* Particular or fussy in one's choices. Also **choos'ey.**

chop¹ (chop) *v.* **chopped, chop·ping** *v.t.* **1.** To cut or make by strokes of a sharp tool: to *chop* a hole. **2.** To cut up in small pieces. **3.** To utter jerkily. **4.** To make a cutting, downward stroke at (the ball), as in tennis. — *v.i.* **5.** To make cutting strokes. **6.** To go, come, or move with sudden or violent motion. — *n.* **1.** The act of chopping. **2.** A piece chopped off; *esp.* a cut of meat, *usu.* lamb, pork, or veal. **3.** A sharp, downward blow or stroke, as in boxing, tennis, etc. **4.** A quick, broken motion of waves. **5.** A cleft or fissure. [ME *choppen*] — **chop'per** *n.*

chop² (chop) *v.* **chopped, chop·ping** *v.i.* To veer suddenly; shift, as the wind.

chop³ (chop) *n.* **1.** *Usually pl.* A jaw; also the part of the face about the mouth or jaws. **2.** A sudden bite or snap. — *v.t.* **chopped, chop·ping** **1.** To utter in a quick, abrupt manner. **2.** To seize with the jaws; snap.

chop⁴ (chop) *n.* **1.** In India, China, etc., an official stamp or seal; also, a clearance, passport, or permit. **2.** *Anglo-Indian* Quality: first *chop*. [< Hind. *chhāp* stamp]

chop chop (chop'chop') In Pidgin English, quickly!

chop·fal·len (chop'fô'lən) *adj.* Chapfallen.

chop·house (chop'hous') *n.* An eating house specializing in chops and steaks.

chop·py¹ (chop'ē) *adj.* **·pi·er, ·pi·est** **1.** Full of short, rough waves. **2.** Full of cracks or fissures. [< CHOP¹, n.]

chop·py² (chop'ē) *adj.* **·pi·er, ·pi·est** Variable, shifting, as wind. [< CHOP²]

chop·sticks (chop'stiks') *n.pl.* Slender rods of ivory or wood, used in pairs by the Chinese, Japanese, etc., to convey food to the mouth. [< Pidgin English *chop* quick + STICK]

chop su·ey (sōō'ē) A Chinese-American dish consisting of bits of meat or chicken, bean sprouts, onions, etc., served with rice. [< Chinese *tsa-sui*, lit., mixed pieces]

cho·ral (kôr'əl, kō'rəl) *adj.* Pertaining to, written for, or sung by a chorus or choir. — **cho'ral·ly** *adv.*

cho·rale (kô·ral', kə-) *n.* A hymn marked by a simple melody, often sung in unison. Also **cho·ral'.** [< G *choral*]

chord¹ (kôrd) *n.* *Music* A combination of three or more tones sounded together. [Earlier *cord*, short for ACCORD]

chord² (kôrd) *n.* **1.** A string of a musical instrument. **2.** An emotional response or reaction. **3.** *Geom.* **a** A straight line connecting the extremities of an arc. **b** The portion of a straight line contained by its intersections with a curve. **4.** *Engin.* One of the principal members of a bridge truss. [< L < Gk. *chordē* string of a musical instrument] — **chord'al** *adj.*

CHORD
(def. 3)
Lines *cb* and *ab* are chords respectively of arcs *cab* and *ab*.

chor·date (kôr'dāt) *Zool.* *n.* Any of a large phylum of the animal kingdom that includes the vertebrates and whose members are characterized by an internal skeleton (in primitive forms a notochord) and a dorsally located central nervous system. — *adj.* Of, pertaining to, or belonging to this phylum or to a chordate. [< NL < L < Gk. *chordē.*]

chore (chôr, chōr) *n.* *U.S.* **1.** A small or minor job. **2.** An unpleasant or hard task. Also, *Brit., char, chare.*

cho·re·a (kô·rē'ə, kō-) *n.* *Pathol.* An acute nervous disease characterized by involuntary and uncontrollable muscular twitching: also called *St. Vitus' dance.* [< NL < Gk. *choreia* dance] — **cho·re'al, cho·re'ic** *adj.*

choreo- *combining form* Dance. Also **choro-.** [< Gk. *choreia* dance]

cho·re·og·ra·pher (kôr'ē·og'rə·fər, kō'rē-) *n.* One who devises ballet and other dance compositions.

cho·re·og·ra·phy (kôr'ē·og'rə·fē, kō'rē-) *n.* **1.** The devising of ballets and incidental dances, esp. for the stage. **2.** The written representation of figures and steps of dancing. **3.** The art of dancing; ballet. Also **cho·reg'ra·phy** (kə·reg'rə·fē). — **cho·re·o·graph·ic** (kôr'ē·ə·graf'ik, kō'rē-) *adj.*

cho·ric (kôr'ik, kō'rik) *adj.* Of or like a chorus (defs. 7–9).

chor·is·ter (kôr'is·tər, kor'-) *n.* **1.** A member of a choir; esp., a choirboy. **2.** A leader of a choir. [< AF < L *chorus*]

cho·roid (kôr'oid, kō'roid) *Anat. adj.* Pertaining to or designating a highly vascular membrane. — *n.* The vascular tunic of the eyeball, between the sclera and the retina. For illus. see EYE. Also **cho·ri·oid** (kôr'ē·oid, kō'rē-).

chor·tle (chôr'təl) *v.t. & v.i.* **·tled, ·tling** To utter or utter with chuckles of glee. — *n.* A chuckle; joyful vocal sound. [Blend of CHUCKLE and SNORT; coined by Lewis Carroll]

cho·rus (kôr'əs, kō'rəs) *n.* **1.** A musical composition, *usu.* in parts, to be sung by a large group. **2.** A group of singers who perform such works. **3.** A body of singers and dancers who perform together in opera, musical comedy, etc. **4.** A group of persons singing or speaking something simultaneously. **5.** A simultaneous utterance of words, cries, etc., by many individuals. **6.** A refrain, as of a song. **7.** In ancient Greece, a ceremonial dance, *usu.* religious, accompanied by the singing of odes. **8.** In Greek drama, a body of actors who comment upon and sometimes take part in the main action of a play. **9.** The part of a drama performed by a chorus. — *v.t. & v.i.* **cho·rused** or **·russed, cho·rus·ing** or **·rus·sing** To sing or speak all together in unison. [< L < Gk. *choros* dance]

chorus girl A woman in the chorus of a musical comedy, etc. — **chorus boy** *masc.*

chose (chōz) Past tense of CHOOSE.

cho·sen (chō'zən) Past participle of CHOOSE. — *adj.* **1.** Made an object of choice; selected. **2.** *Theol.* Elect.

chow (chou) *n.* **1.** A medium-sized dog having a thick, brown or black coat: also *chow-chow.* **2.** *Slang* Food.

chow-chow (chou'chou') *n.* **1.** A relish of chopped mixed vegetables pickled in mustard. **2.** Chow¹ (def. 1). [< Pidgin English]

chow·der (chou'dər) *n.* A dish *usu.* made of clams or fish stewed with vegetables, often in milk. [< F *chaudière* kettle < *calidus* hot]

chow·mein (chou'mān') A Chinese-American dish made of shredded meat, onions, celery, etc., stewed and served with fried noodles. [< Chinese *ch'ao* to fry + *mein* flour]

chrism (kriz'əm) *n.* *Eccl.* **1.** Consecrated oil used for anointing at baptism, confirmation, unction, etc. **2.** Any sacramental anointing. [OE < LL < Gk. *chriein* to anoint]

Christ (krīst) *n.* **1.** The Anointed; the Messiah: the deliverer of Israel foretold by the Hebrew prophets. **2.** Jesus of Nazareth, regarded as fulfilling this prophecy: at first a title (*Jesus the Christ*), later a proper name (*Jesus Christ*). [OE < L < Gk. *Christos* (< *chriein* to anoint); trans. of Hebrew *māshīah* anointed] — **Christ'li·ness** *n.* — **Christ'ly** *adv.*

chris·ten (kris'ən) *v.t.* **1.** To name in baptism. **2.** To administer Christian baptism to. **3.** To give a name to. **4.** *Informal* To use for the first time. [See CHRIST.]

Chris·ten·dom (kris'ən·dəm) *n.* **1.** Christian lands. **2.** Christians collectively.

chris·ten·ing (kris'ən·ing) *n.* A Christian baptismal ceremony, esp. the baptizing of an infant.

Chris·tian (kris'chən) *adj.* **1.** Professing or following the religion of Christ; esp., affirming the divinity of Christ. **2.** Relating to or derived from Christ or his doctrine. **3.** Characteristic of Christianity or Christendom. **4.** *Informal* Human; civilized; decent. — *n.* **1.** One who believes in or professes belief in Jesus as the Christ; a member of any of the Christian churches. **2.** *Informal* A civilized, decent, or respectable person. — **Chris'tian·ly** *adv.*

Christian era The era beginning at the approximate date of Christ's birth, but now considered four to six years too late. Dates in this era are denoted A.D., those before it, B.C.

Chris·ti·an·i·ty (kris'chē·an'ə·tē) *n.* **1.** The Christian religion. **2.** Christians collectively. **3.** The state of being a Christian.

Chris·tian·ize (kris'chən·īz) *v.* **·ized, ·iz·ing** *v.t.* **1.** To convert to Christianity. **2.** To imbue with Christian principles, etc. — **Chris'tian·i·za'tion** *n.* — **Chris'tian·iz'er** *n.*

Christian name A baptismal name.

Christian Science A religion and system of healing, founded in 1866 by Mary Baker Eddy: officially called the **Church of Christ, Scientist.** — **Christian Scientist**

Christ·like (krīst'līk') *adj.* Resembling Christ; having the spirit of Christ. — **Christ'like·ness** *n.*

Christ·mas (kris'məs) *n.* December 25, held as the anniversary of the birth of Jesus Christ and widely observed as a holy day or a holiday. Also **Christmas Day.**

Christmas Eve The evening before Christmas Day.

Christ·mas·tide (kris'mas·tīd') *n.* The season of Christmas extending from Christmas Eve to Epiphany (Jan. 6).

Christmas tree An evergreen tree decorated with ornaments and lights at Christmas.

chrom- Var. of CHROMO-.

chro·mate (krō'māt) *n.* *Chem.* A salt of chromic acid.

chro·mat·ic (krō·mat'ik) *adj.* **1.** Pertaining to color or colors. **2.** *Music* Of or pertaining to a chromatic scale, or to an instrument that can play such a scale. — **chro·mat'i·cal·ly** *adv.*

chro·mat·ics (krō·mat'iks) *n.pl.* (*construed as sing.*) The science of colors.

chromatic scale *Music* A scale proceeding by semitones.

chro·ma·tin (krō'mə·tin) *n.* *Biol.* The readily stainable substance in the protoplasm of the cell nucleus, developing into chromosomes during mitosis. For illus. see CELL.

chromato- *combining form* Color; coloring or pigmentation. Also, before vowels, **chromat-**. [< Gk. *chrōma, -atos* color]

chro·ma·tog·ra·phy (krō/mə·tog/rə·fē) *n. Chem.* A method for the analysis of mixtures, in which a solution is passed through a column of powder that selectively adsorbs the constituents in one or more sharply defined, often colored bands. — **chro·mat·o·graph·ic** (krō·mat/ə·graf/ik) *adj.*

chrome (krōm) *n.* 1. Chrome yellow. 2. Chromium. — *v.t.* **chromed, chrom·ing** To plate with chromium. [< F < Gk. *chrōma* color]

-chrome *combining form* 1. Color; colored. 2. *Chem.* Chromium. [< Gk. *chrōma* color]

chrome steel *Metall.* A very hard steel alloyed with chromium. Also **chromium steel.**

chro·mic (krō/mik) *adj. Chem.* 1. Of, from, or pertaining to chromium. 2. Pertaining to compounds of chromium in its higher valence.

chromic acid *Chem.* An acid, H_2CrO_4, existing only in solution and forming chromates.

chro·mi·um (krō/mē·əm) *n.* A grayish white, very hard metallic element (symbol Cr), used in making alloys and pigments. See ELEMENT. [< NL < F < Gk. *chrōma* color; so called from its many brightly colored, poisonous compounds]

chro·mo (krō/mō) *n. pl.* **·mos** A chromolithograph.

chromo- *combining form* 1. Color; in or with color. 2. *Chem.* Chromium. Also, before vowels, **chrom-**. [< G *chrōma* color]

chro·mo·li·thog·ra·phy (krō/mō·li·thog/rə·fē) *n.* The process of reproducing a color print by lithography. — **chro/mo·lith/o·graph** *n.* — **chro/mo·li·thog/ra·pher** *n.* — **chro/mo·lith·o·graph·ic** (krō/mō·lith/ə·graf/ik) *adj.*

chro·mo·some (krō/mə·sōm) *n. Biol.* One of the deeply staining, rod- or loop-shaped bodies into which the chromatin of the cell nucleus divides during cell division, and in which the genes are located.

chro·mo·sphere (krō/mə·sfir/) *n. Astron.* 1. An incandescent, gaseous envelope, consisting mostly of hydrogen and helium, that surrounds the sun beyond the photosphere. 2. A similar envelope surrounding a star. — **chro/mo·spher/ic** (-sfir/ik, -sfer/-) *adj.*

chro·mous (krō/məs) *adj. Chem.* Of or pertaining to chromium in its lower valence.

chron·ic (kron/ik) *adj.* 1. Continuing for a long period; constant. 2. Prolonged; lingering; also, recurrent: said of a disease: opposed to *acute.* 3. Long affected by a disease, or given to a habit; confirmed. [< F < L < Gk. *chronos* time] — **chron/i·cal·ly** *adv.*

chron·i·cle (kron/i·kəl) *n.* A register of events in the order in which they occurred. — *v.t.* **·cled, ·cling** To record in, or in the manner of, a chronicle. [< AF < L < Gk. *chronos* time] — **chron/i·cler** *n.*

Chron·i·cles (kron/i·kəlz) *n.pl.* Either of two historical books, I and II Chronicles, of the Old Testament: also, in the Douai Bible, called *I* and *II Paralipomenon.*

chrono- *combining form* Time: *chronometer.* Also, before vowels, **chron-**. [< Gk. *chronos* time]

chron·o·log·i·cal (kron/ə·loj/i·kəl) *adj.* 1. Arranged according to sequence in time. 2. Pertaining to chronology. Also **chron/o·log/ic.** — **chron/o·log/i·cal·ly** *adv.*

chro·nol·o·gy (krə·nol/ə·jē) *n. pl.* **·gies** 1. The science of determining the proper sequence of historical events. 2. Arrangement or relationship according to order of occurrence. 3. A chronological list or table. [< NL < Gk. *chronos* time + *-logia* study] — **chro·nol/o·ger, chro·nol/o·gist** *n.*

chro·nom·e·ter (krə·nom/ə·tər) *n.* A timekeeping instrument of high precision. — **chron·o·met·ric** (kron/ə·met/rik) or **·ri·cal** *adj.* — **chron/o·met/ri·cal·ly** *adv.*

chro·nom·e·try (krə·nom/ə·trē) *n.* The science or method of measuring time or periods of time.

-chroous *combining form* Having (a certain) color. [< Gk. *chrōs, chroos* color]

chrys·a·lid (kris/ə·lid) *Entomol. n.* A chrysalis. — *adj.* Of or like a chrysalis: also **chrys·al·i·dal** (kri·sal/ə·dəl).

chrys·a·lis (kris/ə·lis) *n. pl.* **chrys·a·lis·es** or **chry·sal·i·des** (kri·sal/ə·dēz) 1. *Entomol.* The capsule-enclosed pupa from which the butterfly or moth develops. 2. Anything in an undeveloped state. [< L < Gk. *chrysos* gold]

chrys·an·the·mum (kri·san/thə·məm) *n.* 1. Any of a number of cultivated varieties of plants of the genus *Chrysanthemum,* with large heads of showy flowers. 2. The flower. [< L < Gk. *chrysanthemon* golden flower]

chryso- *combining form* Gold; of a golden color. Also, before vowels, **chrys-**. [< Gk. *chrysos* gold]

chrys·o·lite (kris/ə·līt) *n.* A variety of olivine. [< OF < Med.L < L < Gk. < *chrysos* gold + *lithos* stone]

chrys·o·prase (kris/ə·prāz) *n.* A semiprecious, apple-green variety of chalcedony, used as a gem. [< OF < L < Gk. < *chrysos* gold + *prason* leek]

chub (chub) *n. pl.* **chubs** or **chub** 1. A carplike fish common in European rivers. 2. Any of various other unrelated fishes. [ME *chubbe*]

chub·by (chub/ē) *adj.* **·bi·er, ·bi·est** Plump; rounded. — **chub/bi·ness** *n.*

chuck¹ (chuk) *v.t.* 1. To pat or tap affectionately, esp. under the chin. 2. To throw or pitch. 3. *Informal* To throw away; discard. 4. *Informal* To eject forcibly: with *out.* 5. *Slang* To quit. — *n.* 1. A playful pat under the chin. 2. A throw; toss. [Cf. F *choquer* shake, jolt]

chuck² (chuk) *n.* 1. The cut of beef extending from the neck to the shoulder blade. 2. *Mech.* A clamp, chock, or wedge used to hold a tool or work in a machine, as in a lathe.

chuck-full (chuk/fŏŏl/) *adj.* Chockfull.

chuck·le (chuk/əl) *v.i.* **·led, ·ling** 1. To laugh quietly and with satisfaction. 2. To cluck, as a hen. — *n.* A low, mildly amused laugh. [Freq. of CLUCK] — **chuck/ler** *n.*

chuck·le·head (chuk/əl·hed/) *n. Informal* A stupid fellow; blockhead. — **chuck/le·head/ed** *adj.*

chuck wagon *U.S.* A wagon fitted with cooking equipment and provisions for cowboys, harvest hands, etc.

chug (chug) *n.* A dull, explosive sound, as of the exhaust of an engine. — *v.i.* **chugged, chug·ging** To move or operate with a series of such sounds. [Imit.]

chuk·ker (chuk/ər) *n.* In polo, one of the eight periods of continuous play, lasting 7½ minutes. Also **chuk/kar.** [< Hind. < Skt. *chakra* wheel]

chum (chum) *n.* 1. An intimate companion. 2. Originally, a roommate. — *v.i.* **chummed, chum·ming** 1. To associate very closely with another. 2. To share the same room. [? Short for *chamber fellow*]

chum·my (chum/ē) *adj.* **·mi·er, ·mi·est** *Informal* Friendly; intimate. — **chum/mi·ly** *adv.*

chump¹ (chump) *n.* 1. *Informal* A stupid or foolish person. 2. A chunk of wood. 3. The thick end of anything, as of a loin of mutton. 4. *Slang* The head. [? Var. of CHUNK]

chump² (chump) *v.t. & v.i.* To chew; munch. [< CHAMP¹]

chunk (chungk) *n.* 1. A thick mass or piece of anything, as of wood. 2. A considerable quantity of something. 3. *U.S. Informal* A strong, stocky person or animal. [Var. of CHUCK²]

chunk·y (chung/kē) *adj.* **chunk·i·er, chunk·i·est** 1. Short and thickset; stocky. 2. In chunks. — **chunk/i·ness** *n.*

church (chûrch) *n.* 1. A building for Christian worship. 2. Regular religious services; public worship. 3. A congregation of Christians. 4. *Usu. cap.* A distinct body of Christians having a common faith and discipline; a denomination. Abbr. *c., C., ch., Ch.* 5. All Christian believers collectively. 6. Ecclesiastical organization and authority: the separation of *church* and state. 7. The clerical profession. — *v.t.* 1. To subject to church discipline. 2. To conduct a religious service for (a person, esp. a woman after childbirth). [OE *circe,* ult. < Gk. *kyrios* Lord]

church·go·er (chûrch/gō/ər) *n.* One who goes regularly to church. — **church/go/ing** *adj. & n.*

church·ly (chûrch/lē) *adj.* Of, pertaining to, or suitable to a church. — **church/li·ness** *n.*

church·man (chûrch/mən) *n. pl.* **·men** (-mən) 1. A member of a church. 2. A clergyman. — **church/man·ly** *adj.* — **church/man·ship** *n.* — **church/wom/an** *n.fem.*

church mouse A mouse that lives in a church: usually in the phrase **poor as a church mouse,** very poor.

Church of Christ, Scientist See CHRISTIAN SCIENCE.

Church of England The national church of England, established by law in the 16th century, claiming to be an independent branch of the ancient Catholic church, and repudiating papal authority: also called *Anglican Church.*

Church of Jesus Christ of Latter-day Saints The Mormon Church: its official name.

church·war·den (chûrch/wôr/dən) *n.* 1. In the Church of England, an elected lay officer who assists in the administration of a parish. 2. In the Protestant Episcopal Church, one of two elected lay officers of a vestry. 3. A long-stemmed clay pipe. Also **church warden.**

church·yard (chûrch/yärd/) *n.* The ground surrounding or adjoining a church, often used as a cemetery.

churl (chûrl) *n.* 1. A rude or surly person. 2. A stingy person. 3. A rustic; countryman. [OE *ceorl*] — **churl/ish** *adj.* — **churl/ish·ly** *adv.* — **churl/ish·ness** *n.*

churn (chûrn) *n.* 1. A vessel in which milk or cream is agitated to separate the oily globules and gather them as butter. 2. A state of unrest or agitation. — *v.t.* 1. To stir or agitate (cream or milk), as in a churn. 2. To make in a churn, as butter. 3. To agitate violently: The oars *churned* the water. — *v.i.* 4. To work a churn. 5. To move with violent agitation; seethe. [OE *cyrin*] — **churn/er** *n.*

chute (shoot) *n.* 1. An inclined trough or vertical passage down which water, coal, etc., may pass. 2. A steep, narrow watercourse; a rapid; shoot. 3. A narrow pen for branding or controlling cattle. 4. A slide, as for toboggans. 5. *Informal* A parachute. [Fusion of F *chute* a fall and SHOOT, n.]

chut·ney (chut/nē) *n.* A piquant relish of fruit, spices, etc. Also **chut/nee.** [< Hind. *chatni*]

chutz·pah (hŏŏts/pə, khŏŏts/-) *n. U.S. Slang* Brazen effrontery; gall. [< Yiddish < Hebrew]

chyle (kīl) *n. Physiol.* The milky emulsion of lymph and fat taken up from the small intestine during digestion and passed from the thoracic duct into the veins. [< F < L < Gk. *chylos* juice] — **chy·la·ceous** (kī·lā′shəs), **chy·lous** (kī′ləs) *adj.*

chyme (kīm) *n. Physiol.* The partly digested food in semiliquid form as it passes from the stomach into the small intestine. [< L < Gk. *chymos* juice] — **chy·mous** (kī′məs) *adj.*

ci·bo·ri·um (si·bôr′ē·əm, -bō′rē-) *n. pl.* **·bo·ri·a** (-bôr′ē·ə, -bō′rē·ə) **1.** An arched canopy over an altar, esp. a permanent one. **2.** A covered receptacle for the consecrated bread of the Eucharist. [< Med.L < Gk. *kibōrion* cup]

ci·ca·da (si·kā′də, -kä′-) *n. pl.* **·das** or **·dae** (-dē) A large winged insect, the male of which is equipped with vibrating membranes that produce a loud, shrill sound: often called *locust.* [< L]

CICADA

cic·a·trix (sik′ə·triks) *n. pl.* **cic·a·tri·ces** (sik′ə·trī′sēz) **1.** *Med.* A scar or seam of new tissue remaining after the healing of wounded or ulcerous parts. **2.** *Biol.* A scar left by the healing of a wound, the fall of a leaf, etc. Also **cic·a·trice** (sik′ə·tris). [< L] — **cic·a·tri·cial** (sik′ə·trish′əl), **ci·cat·ri·cose** (si·kat′ri·kōs) *adj.*

(1 to 1½ inches long)

cic·a·trize (sik′ə·trīz) *v.t. & v.i.* **·trized, ·triz·ing** To heal by the formation of a scar. — **cic′a·tri·za′tion** *n.*

cic·e·ro·ne (sis′ə·rō′nē, *Ital.* chē′chä·rō′nä) *n. pl.* **·nes**, *Ital.* **·ni** (-nē) A guide for tourists. [< Ital., Cicero]

Cic·e·ro·ni·an (sis′ə·rō′nē·ən) *adj.* Of or pertaining to Cicero, or to his rhetorical style; eloquent.

-cidal *combining form* Killing; able to kill: *homicidal.* [< L *caedere* to kill]

-cide *combining form* **1.** Killer or destroyer of: *regicide.* **2.** Murder or killing of: *parricide.* [def. 1 < L -*cida* killer < *caedere* to kill; def. 2 < L -*cidium* slaughter < *caedere*]

ci·der (sī′dər) *n.* The expressed juice of apples used to make vinegar, and as a beverage before fermentation (**sweet cider**), or after fermentation (**hard cider**). [< OF < LL < Hebrew *shēkār* strong drink]

ci·gar (si·gär′) *n.* A small roll of tobacco leaves prepared and shaped for smoking. [< Sp. *cigarro*]

cig·a·rette (sig′ə·ret′, sig′ə·ret) *n.* A small roll of finely cut tobacco for smoking, usu. enclosed in thin paper. Also *U.S.* **cig′a·ret′.** [< F, dim. of *cigare* cigar]

cil·i·a (sil′ē·ə) Plural of CILIUM.

cil·i·ar·y (sil′ē·er′ē) *adj. Biol.* Of, pertaining to, or like cilia. [< L *cilium* eyelid]

cil·i·ate (sil′ō·it, -āt) *adj. Biol.* Having cilia. Also **cil′i·at′ed.**

cil·i·um (sil′ē·əm) *n. pl.* **cil·i·a** (sil′ē·ə) **1.** *Biol.* A vibratile, microscopic, hairlike process on the surface of a cell, organ, plant, etc. **2.** An eyelash. [< L, eyelid]

Cim·me·ri·an (si·mir′ē·ən) *adj.* **1.** Of or pertaining to the Cimmerians, a mythical people mentioned by Homer as living in perpetual darkness. **2.** Densely dark; gloomy.

cinch (sinch) *n. U.S.* **1.** A pack or saddle girth. **2.** *Informal* A tight grip. **3.** *Slang* Something easy or sure. — *v.t.* **1.** To fasten a saddle girth around. **2.** *Slang* To get a tight hold upon. **3.** *Slang* To make sure of. — *v.i.* **4.** To tighten a saddle girth. [< Sp. < L *cingere* to bind]

cin·cho·na (sin·kō′nə) *n.* **1.** A tropical tree or shrub of the madder family, widely cultivated as a source of quinine and related alkaloids. **2.** The bark of any of these trees: also called *Peruvian bark.* [after the Countess of *Chinchón*, 1576–1639] — **cin·chon·ic** (sin·kon′ik) *adj.*

cin·cho·nize (sin′kə·nīz) *v.t.* **·nized, ·niz·ing** To treat with cinchona or quinine. — **cin′cho·ni·za′tion** *n.*

cinc·ture (singk′chər) *n.* **1.** A belt, cord, etc., put around the waist. **2.** The act of girding or surrounding. — *v.t.* **·tured, ·tur·ing** To encircle with or as with a cincture. [< L *cingere* to bind, gird]

cin·der (sin′dər) *n.* **1.** Any partly burned substance, not reduced to ashes; esp. a tiny particle of such a substance. **2.** A bit of wood, coal, etc., that can burn but without flame. **3.** *pl.* Ashes. — *v.t.* To burn or reduce to a cinder. [OE *sinder*] — **cin′der·y** *adj.*

Cin·der·el·la (sin′də·rel′ə) *n.* **1.** The heroine of a popular fairy tale, who is treated as a drudge, but eventually marries a prince. **2.** Any girl who achieves happiness or success after a period of neglect.

cine- *combining form* Cinema. [< CINEMA]

cin·e·ma (sin′ə·mə) *n.* **1.** A motion picture (def. 2). **2.** A motion-picture theater. — **the cinema** Motion pictures collectively; also, the art or business of making motion pictures. [Short for CINEMATOGRAPH] — **cin·e·mat·ic** (sin′ə·mat′ik) *adj.* — **cin′e·mat′i·cal·ly** *adv.*

cin·e·mat·o·graph (sin′ə·mat′ə·graf, -gräf) *n.* A motion-picture camera or projector. — *v.t. & v.i.* To take photographs (of) with a motion-picture camera: also **cin·e·ma·tize**

(sin′ə·mə·tīz′). Also *kinematograph.* [< Gk. *kinēma*, *-atos* movement + -GRAPH]

cin·e·ma·tog·ra·phy (sin′ə·mə·tog′rə·fē) *n.* The art and process of making motion pictures. — **cin′e·ma·tog′ra·pher** *n.* — **cin·e·mat·o·graph·ic** (sin′ə·mat′ə·graf′ik) *adj.* — **cin′·e·mat/o·graph′i·cal·ly** *adv.*

cin·e·rar·i·a (sin′ə·râr′ē·ə) *n.* A cultivated plant having heart-shaped leaves and white, red, or purple flowers. [< NL < L, fem. of *cinerarius* ashy]

cin·e·rar·i·um (sin′ə·râr′ē·əm) *n. pl.* **·rar·i·a** (-râr′ē·ə) A place for keeping the ashes of a cremated body. [< L] — **cin·e·rar·y** (sin′ə·rer′ē) *adj.*

cin·er·a·tor (sin′ə·rā′tər) *n.* A furnace for cremating dead bodies; crematory. [Short for INCINERATOR]

cin·na·bar (sin′ə·bär) *n.* **1.** A heavy, crystallized red mercuric sulfide, HgS, the chief ore of mercury. **2.** Vermilion. [< L < Gk. < Persian *zanjifrah*]

cin·na·mon (sin′ə·mən) *n.* **1.** The aromatic inner bark of any of several tropical trees of the laurel family, used as a spice. **2.** Any tree that yields this bark. **3.** A shade of light reddish brown. [< L < Gk. < Hebrew *quinnāmōn*]

cinque·foil (singk′foil) *n.* **1.** *Archit.* A five-cusped ornament or window. **2.** Any of several plants of the rose family, with five-lobed leaves: also called *five-fingers.* [< F < L < *quinque* five + *folium* leaf]

ci·on (sī′ən) *n.* A twig or shoot cut from a plant or tree, esp. for grafting: also spelled *scion.* [Var. of SCION]

-cion Var. of -TION.

Ci·pan·go (si·pang′gō) *Poetic* Japan.

CINQUE-FOIL (def. 1)

ci·pher (sī′fər) *n.* **1.** The figure 0, the symbol of the absence of quantity; zero. **2.** A person or thing of no value or importance. **3.** Any system of secret writing that uses a prearranged scheme or key. **4.** A message in cipher; also, its key. **5.** A monogram. **6.** Any Arabic number. — *v.t.* **1.** To calculate arithmetically. **2.** To write in characters of hidden meaning. — *v.i.* **3.** To work out arithmetical examples. **4.** To sound continuously, as an organ pipe. Also spelled *cypher.* [< OF < Arabic *sifr* nothing]

cir·ca (sûr′kə) *prep. Latin* About; around; used before approximate date or figures.

Cir·cas·sian (sər·kash′ən, -kash′ē·ən) *n.* **1.** A member of a group of tribes of the Caucasus region. **2.** The language of these tribes. — *adj.* Of or pertaining to Circassia, its people, or their language: also **Cir·cas·sic** (sər·kas′ik).

Cir·ce (sûr′sē) In the *Odyssey,* an enchantress who changed Odysseus's companions into swine by a magic drink.

Cir·ce·an (sər·sē′ən) *adj.* **1.** Of, pertaining to, or characteristic of Circe. **2.** Bewitching and degrading.

cir·cle (sûr′kəl) *n.* **1.** A plane figure bounded by a curved line every point of which is equally distant from the center. **2.** The circumference of such a figure. **3.** Something like a circle, as a crown, halo, or ring. **4.** A round or spherical body; an orb. **5.** A group of persons united by some common interest or pursuit; a set; coterie. **6.** The domain or scope of a special influence or action. **7.** A gallery or tier of seats in a theater: the family *circle.* **8.** A series or process that finishes at its starting point or that repeats itself without end: the *circle* of the seasons. **9.** *Astron.* The orbit of a heavenly body. — *v.* **·cled, ·cling** *v.t.* **1.** To enclose in a circle; encompass. **2.** To move around, as in a circle. — *v.i.* **3.** To move in a circle. [< L *circus* ring] — **cir′cler** *n.*

cir·clet (sûr′klit) *n.* A small ring or ring-shaped object, especially one worn as an ornament. [< F *cercle* ring]

cir·cuit (sûr′kit) *n.* **1.** A moving or traveling round; a circular route or course. **2.** A periodic journey from place to place, as by a judge or minister. **3.** The route traversed, or the district visited, in such a journey. **4.** A group of associated theaters presenting plays, films, etc., in turn. **5.** The line or distance around an area; circumference; also, the area enclosed. **6.** *Electr.* The entire course traversed by an electric current. **7.** *Telecom.* A transmission and reception system. — *v.t. & v.i.* To go or move (about) in a circuit. [< F < L < *circum-* around + *ire* to go]

circuit breaker *Electr.* A switch or relay for breaking a circuit under specified or abnormal conditions of current flow.

circuit court A court of law that sits in various counties or districts over which its jurisdiction extends.

circuit judge A judge of a circuit court.

cir·cu·i·tous (sər·kyōō′ə·təs) *adj.* Roundabout; indirect. — **cir·cu′i·tous·ly** *adv.* — **cir·cu′i·tous·ness** *n.*

circuit rider A minister who preaches at churches on a circuit or district route.

cir·cuit·ry (sûr′kit·rē) *n. Electr.* The design and arrangement of circuits in any device, instrument, or system.

cir·cu·i·ty (sər·kyōō′ə·tē) *n. pl.* **·ties** Roundabout procedure or speech; indirectness.

cir·cu·lar (sûr′kyə·lər) *adj.* **1.** Shaped like a circle; round. **2.** Moving in a circle. **3.** Of or referring to a circle. **4.** Roundabout; indirect; devious. **5.** Addressed to several persons, or intended for general circulation. — *n.* A statement, notice, or advertisement printed for general distribution. [See CIRCLE.] — **cir·cu·lar·i·ty** (sûr′kyə·lar′ə·tē), **cir′·cu·lar·ness** *n.* — **cir′cu·lar·ly** *adv.*

cir·cu·lar·ize (sûr′kyə·lə·rīz′) *v.t.* **·ized, ·iz·ing 1.** To make circular. **2.** To make into a circular. **3.** To distribute circulars to. — **cir′cu·lar·i·za′tion** *n.* — **cir′cu·lar·iz′er** *n.*

circular saw A disk-shaped saw having a toothed edge, rotated at high speed by a motor.

cir·cu·late (sûr′kyə·lāt) *v.* **·lat·ed, ·lat·ing** *v.i.* **1.** To move by a circuitous course back to the starting point, as the blood. **2.** To pass from place to place or person to person: Rumors *circulate* quickly. **3.** To be in free motion, as air. — *v.t.* **4.** To cause to circulate. [See CIRCLE.] — **cir·cu·la·tive** (sûr′·kyə·lā′tiv) *adj.* — **cir′cu·la′tor** *n.*

circulating library A library from which books may be borrowed or rented: also called *lending library*.

cir·cu·la·tion (sûr′kyə·lā′shən) *n.* **1.** A moving around or through something back to the starting point. **2.** The motion of the blood from and to the heart through the arteries and veins. **3.** A transmission or spreading from one person or place to another; dissemination. **4.** The extent or amount of distribution of a periodical; also, the number of copies distributed. **5.** A current medium of exchange, as coin.

cir·cu·la·to·ry (sûr′kyə·lə·tôr′ē, -tō′rē) *adj.* Of, pertaining to or affecting circulation: a *circulatory* disorder.

circum- *prefix* **1.** About; around; on all sides; surrounding. **2.** Revolving around. [< L *circum-* around, about]

cir·cum·am·bi·ent (sûr′kəm·am′bē·ənt) *adj.* Encompassing; surrounding. — **cir′cum·am′bi·ence, cir′cum·am′bi·en·cy** *n.*

cir·cum·cise (sûr′kəm·sīz) *v.t.* **·cised, ·cis·ing** To cut off all or part of the prepuce (of a male) or the clitoris (of a female). [< OF < L < *circum-* around + *caedere* to cut] — **cir′cum·cis′er** *n.* — **cir·cum·ci·sion** (sûr′kəm·sizh′ən) *n.*

cir·cum·fer·ence (sər·kum′fər·əns) *n.* **1.** The boundary line of any area; esp., the boundary of a circle. **2.** The length of such a line. [< L < *circum-* around + *ferre* to bear] — **cir·cum·fer·en·tial** (sər·kum′fə·ren′shəl) *adj.* — **cir′cum·fer·en′tial·ly** *adv.*

cir·cum·flex (sûr′kəm·fleks) *n.* A mark (^, ˆ, ˘) written over certain letters in ancient Greek, and later, in other languages, to mark a long vowel, contraction, etc., or used as a diacritical mark in phonetic transcription. — *adj.* **1.** Pronounced or marked with the circumflex accent. **2.** *Physiol.* Bent or curving around, as certain nerves. — *v.t.* **1.** To pronounce or mark with a circumflex. **2.** To wind around. [< L < *circum-* around + *flectere* to bend] — **cir·cum·flex·ion** (sûr′kəm·flek′shən) *n.*

cir·cum·flu·ous (sər·kum′floo·əs) *adj.* Flowing around; surrounding. Also **cir·cum·flu·ent** (sər·kum′floo·ənt). [< L < *circum-* around + *fluere* to flow]

cir·cum·fuse (sûr′kəm·fyooz′) *v.t.* **·fused, ·fus·ing 1.** To pour, scatter, or spread about. **2.** To surround, as with a liquid. [< L < *circum-* around + *fundere* to pour] — **cir·cum·fu·sion** (sûr′kəm·fyoo′zhən) *n.*

cir·cum·lo·cu·tion (sûr′kəm·lō·kyoo′shən) *n.* An indirect lengthy way of expressing something; also, an example of this. [< L < *circum-* around + *loqui* to speak] — **cir·cum·loc·u·to·ry** (sûr′kəm·lok′yə·tôr′ē, -tō′rē) *adj.*

cir·cum·nav·i·gate (sûr′kəm·nav′ə·gāt) *v.t.* **·gat·ed, ·gat·ing** To sail around. [< L < *circum-* around + *navigare* to sail] — **cir·cum·nav·i·ga·ble** (sûr′kəm·nav′ə·gə·bəl) *adj.* — **cir′cum·nav′i·ga′tion** *n.* — **cir′cum·nav′i·ga′tor** *n.*

cir·cum·scribe (sûr′kəm·skrīb′) *v.t.* **·scribed, ·scrib·ing 1.** To mark out the limits of; define. **2.** To draw a line or figure around. **3.** *Geom.* **a** To draw (a figure) about another figure so that it touches at every possible point without intersecting. **b** To surround (another figure) in this way. [< L < *circum-* around + *scribere* to write] — **cir·cum·scrib·a·ble** *adj.* — **cir′cum·scrib′er** *n.*

cir·cum·scrip·tion (sûr′kəm·skrip′shən) *n.* **1.** The act of circumscribing, or the state of being circumscribed. **2.** Anything that limits or encloses. **3.** The periphery of an object. **4.** A space marked out or bounded. **5.** An inscription around a coin, medallion, etc. — **cir′cum·scrip′tive** *adj.*

cir·cum·spect (sûr′kəm·spekt) *adj.* Attentive to everything; watchful; cautious; wary. Also **cir′cum·spec′tive** *adj.* [< L < *circum-* around + *specere* to look] — **cir′cum·spec′tion, cir′cum·spect′ness** *n.* — **cir′cum·spect′ly** *adv.*

cir·cum·stance (sûr′kəm·stans) *n.* **1.** A factor connected with an act, event, or condition, either as an accessory or as a determining element. **2.** *Often pl.* The conditions, influences, etc., affecting persons or actions. **3.** *pl.* Financial condition in life: in poor *circumstances*. **4.** An occurrence: a happy *circumstance*. **5.** Detail, especially superfluous detail, as in narrative. **6.** Formal display: pomp and *circumstance*. — **under no circumstances** Never; under no conditions. —

under the circumstances Since such is (or was) the case. — *v.t.* **·stanced, ·stanc·ing** To place in or under limiting circumstances or conditions. [< OF < L < *circum-* around + *stare* to stand] — **cir′cum·stanced** *adj.*

cir·cum·stan·tial (sûr′kəm·stan′shəl) *adj.* **1.** Pertaining to or dependent on circumstances. **2.** Incidental; not essential. **3.** Full of details. — **cir′cum·stan′tial·ly** *adv.*

circumstantial evidence *Law* Evidence that furnishes reasonable ground for inferring the existence of a fact.

cir·cum·stan·ti·al·i·ty (sûr′kəm·stan′shē·al′ə·tē) *n. pl.* **·ties 1.** The quality of being particular, detailed, or minute. **2.** A particular matter; detail.

cir·cum·stan·ti·ate (sûr′kəm·stan′shē·āt) *v.t.* **·at·ed, ·at·ing** To set forth or establish by circumstances or in detail. — **cir′cum·stan′ti·a′tion** *n.*

cir·cum·val·late (sûr′kəm·val′āt) *v.t.* **·lat·ed, ·lat·ing** To surround with a rampart or a trench. — *adj.* Enclosed by or as by a wall. [< L < *circum-* around + *vallare* to fortify] — **cir′cum·val·la′tion** *n.*

cir·cum·vent (sûr′kəm·vent′) *v.t.* **1.** To surround or entrap, as an enemy, by stratagem. **2.** To gain an advantage over; outwit. **3.** To go around or avoid. [< L < *circum-* around + *venire* to come] — **cir′cum·vent′er** or **cir′cum·vent′or** *n.* — **cir′cum·ven′tive** *adj.* — **cir′cum·ven′tion** *n.*

cir·cus (sûr′kəs) *n.* **1.** A traveling show of acrobats, clowns, etc.; also, a performance of such a show. **2.** A circular, usu. tented area used for such shows. **3.** In ancient Rome, an oblong enclosure with tiers of seats around three sides, used for races, games, etc. **4.** *Brit.* An open, usu. circular junction of several streets. **5.** *U.S. Informal* Something or someone uproariously entertaining. [< L, a ring, racecourse]

cir·rho·sis (si·rō′sis) *n. Pathol.* A disease of the liver, characterized by an abnormal formation of connective tissue with progressive cellular breakdown. [< NL < Gk. *kirrhos* tawny; with ref. to the color of the cirrhotic liver] — **cir·rhot·ic** (si·rot′ik) *adj.*

cir·ri (sir′ī) Plural of CIRRUS.

cirro- *combining form* Cirrus. Also **cirri-.** [< L *cirrus* curl]

cir·ro·cu·mu·lus (sir′ō·kyoom′yə·ləs) *n. Meteorol.* A mass of fleecy, globular cloudlets (Symbol Cc) in contact with one another; mackerel sky.

cir·ro·stra·tus (sir′ō·strā′təs) *n. Meteorol.* A fine, whitish veil of cloud (Symbol Cs).

cir·rous (sir′əs) *adj.* **1.** Having or like cirri. **2.** Of or pertaining to a cirrus cloud. Also **cir·rose** (sir′ōs).

cir·rus (sir′əs) *n. pl.* **cir·ri** (sir′ī) **1.** *Meteorol.* A type of white, wispy cloud (Symbol Ci), usually consisting of ice crystals and seen in tufts or feathery bands across the sky. **2.** *Bot.* A tendril. **3.** *Zool.* A threadlike appendage serving as an organ of touch. [< L, ringlet, curl]

cis- *prefix* **1.** On this side of. **2.** Since; following: *cis-Elizabethan.* [< L *cis* on this side]

cis·al·pine (sis·al′pīn, -pin) *adj.* On the Roman side of the Alps. [< L < *cis* on this side + *Alpes* the Alps]

cis·co (sis′kō) *n. pl.* **·coes** or **·cos** *U.S. & Canadian* A whitefish of North America. [? < N. Am. Ind.]

Cis·ter·cian (sis·tûr′shən) *n.* A monk of a very strict contemplative order founded in 1098 at Cistercium (modern *Cîteaux*), France, as an offshoot of the Benedictines. — *adj.* Of or pertaining to this order.

cis·tern (sis′tərn) *n.* **1.** An artificial reservoir, as a tank, for holding water or other liquids. **2.** *Anat.* A large lymph space; a sac. [< OF < L *cista* chest]

cit·a·del (sit′ə·dəl, -del) *n.* **1.** A fortress commanding a city. **2.** Any fortress or stronghold. **3.** The heavily plated casemate in a war vessel. [< MF < Ital. *città* city]

ci·ta·tion (sī·tā′shən) *n.* **1.** A citing or quoting; also, a passage or authority so cited. **2.** A public commendation for outstanding achievement. **3.** A summons, as to appear in court. [See CITE.] — **ci·ta·to·ry** (sī′tə·tôr′ē, -tō′rē) *adj.*

cite (sīt) *v.t.* **cit·ed, cit·ing 1.** To quote as authority or illustration. **2.** To bring forward or refer to as proof or support. **3.** *Mil.* To mention in a report, esp. for bravery. **4.** To mention or enumerate. **5.** To summon to appear in court. **6.** To summon to action; rouse. [< F < L *citare* < *ciere* to set in motion] — **cit′a·ble** or **cite′a·ble** *adj.*

cith·a·ra (sith′ə·rə) *n.* An ancient Greek stringed instrument resembling a lyre. [< L < Gk. *kithara*]

cith·er (sith′ər) *n.* **1.** A zither. **2.** A cittern. Also **cith′ern** (sith′ərn). **3.** A cithara.

cit·i·fied (sit′i·fīd) *adj.* Having the ways, habits, fashions, etc., of city life.

cit·i·zen (sit′ə·zən) *n.* **1.** A native or naturalized person owing allegiance to, and entitled to protection from, a government. **2.** A resident of a city or town. **3.** A civilian, as distinguished from a military official, police officer, soldier, etc. [< AF < L *civis* citizen] — **cit′i·zen·ess** *n.fem.*

cit·i·zen·ry (sit′ə·zən·rē) *n. pl.* **·ries** Citizens collectively.

cit·i·zen·ship (sit′ə·zən·ship′) *n.* The status of a citizen, with its rights, privileges, and duties.

citra- *prefix* On this side; cis-. [< L]

cit·rate (sit'rāt, -rit, sī'trāt) *n. Chem.* A salt of citric acid.

cit·ric (sit'rik) *adj.* Of or derived from citrus fruits.

citric acid *Chem.* A white, crystalline, sharply sour compound, $C_6H_8O_7$, contained in various fruits, and also made synthetically.

cit·rine (sit'rin) *adj.* Lemon yellow. — *n.* 1. Citrine color. 2. A light yellow variety of quartz. [< F *citrin*]

cit·ron (sit'rən) *n.* 1. A fruit like a lemon, but larger and less acid. 2. The tree producing this fruit. 3. A watermelon with a small, hard-fleshed fruit. Also **citron melon.** 4. The rind of either of these fruits, preserved and used in confections. [< MF < Ital. < L *citrus* citrus tree]

cit·ron·el·la (sit'rə·nel'ə) *n.* A grass cultivated in Ceylon, yielding **citronella oil,** used in perfumery, in cooking, and as protection against mosquitoes. Also **citronella grass.** [< NL < CITRON; so called from its odor]

cit·rus (sit'rəs) *adj.* Of or pertaining to trees bearing oranges, lemons, etc. Also **cit'rous.** [< L, citron tree]

cit·tern (sit'ərn) *n.* Any of a group of old stringed instruments resembling a lute or guitar. [< L < Gk. *kithara*]

cit·y (sit'ē) *n. pl.* **cit·ies** 1. A place inhabited by a large, permanent community. 2. In the United States, a municipality of the first class with definite boundaries and various legal powers. 3. In Canada, a municipality of high rank. 4. In Great Britain, a large incorporated town. 5. The people of a city, collectively. [< OF < L *civis* citizen]

cit·y-bred (sit'ē·bred') *adj.* Brought up in a city.

city desk A department in a newspaper office where local news is received, rewritten, and edited.

city father One who directs the public affairs of a city.

city manager An administrator not publicly elected but appointed by a city council to manage the city.

city planning Public control of the physical development of a city, as by regulation of the size and use of buildings, etc.

cit·y-state (sit'ē·stāt') *n.* A state consisting of a city and its contiguous territories, as ancient Athens.

civ·et (siv'it) *n.* 1. A substance of musklike odor, secreted by the genital glands of the civet cat, used in perfumery. 2. The civet cat or its fur. [< MF *civette*]

civet cat A feline carnivore of Africa.

civ·ic (siv'ik) *adj.* Of or pertaining to a city, a citizen, or citizenship; civil. [< L < *civis* citizen]

civ·ics (siv'iks) *n.pl.* (*construed as sing.*) The division of political science dealing with citizenship and civic affairs.

civ·il (siv'əl) *adj.* 1. Of or pertaining to community life rather than military or ecclesiastical affairs. 2. Of or pertaining to citizens and their government: *civil* affairs. 3. Occurring within the state; domestic: *civil* war. 4. Of, proper to, or befitting a citizen. 5. Civilized. 6. Proper; polite. 7. *Law* Related to the rights of citizens and to legal proceedings involving such rights. — **Syn.** See POLITE. [< MF < L *civis* citizen] — **civ'il·ly** *adv.*

civil defense A civilian program for the maintenance of essential services in wartime.

civil disobedience A refusal to comply with certain civil laws, usually done by means of passive resistance.

civil engineer A professional engineer trained to design, build, and maintain public works, as roads, bridges, etc.

ci·vil·ian (sə·vil'yən) *n.* One who is not in the military or naval service. — *adj.* Of or pertaining to a civilian.

ci·vil·i·ty (sə·vil'ə·tē) *n. pl.* **·ties** 1. The quality of being civil; courtesy; politeness. 2. A polite act or speech.

civ·i·li·za·tion (siv'ə·lə·zā'shən, -lī·zā'-) *n.* 1. A state of human society characterized by a high level of intellectual, social, and cultural development. 2. The countries and peoples considered to have reached this stage. 3. The cultural development of a specific people, country, or region. 4. The act of civilizing, or the process of becoming civilized.

civ·i·lize (siv'ə·līz) *v.t.* **·lized, ·liz·ing** To bring into a state of civilization; bring out of savagery; refine; enlighten. Also *Brit.* **civ'i·lise.** [< MF < Med.L < L *civis* citizen] — **civ'i·liz·a·ble** *adj.* — **civ'i·liz·er** *n.*

civil law The body of laws having to do with the rights and privileges of private citizens.

civil liberty A liberty guaranteed to the individual by the laws of a government.

civil marriage A marriage solemnized by a civil or government official rather than by a clergyman.

civil rights Private, nonpolitical privileges; esp., exemption from involuntary servitude, as established by the 13th and 14th amendments to the U.S. Constitution.

civil service 1. The branches of governmental service that are not military, naval, legislative, or judicial. 2. The persons employed in these branches. — **civil servant**

civil war War between parties or sections of the same country.

Civil War See table for WAR.

civ·vies (siv'ēz) *n.pl. Informal* Civilian clothes, as distinguished from military dress; mufti.

clab·ber (klab'ər) *n.* Milk curdled by souring. — *v.t. & v.i.* To curdle, as milk. [< Irish *bainne clabair*]

clack (klak) *v.i.* 1. To make a sharp, dry sound. 2. To chatter heedlessly. 3. To cluck, as a hen. — *v.t.* 4. To cause to clack. 5. To babble. — *n.* 1. A short, sharp sound. 2. Something that makes a clack. 3. Chatter. [Imit.] — **clack'er** *n.*

clad (klad) Alternative past tense and past participle of CLOTHE.

claim (klām) *v.t.* 1. To demand as one's right or due; assert ownership or title to. 2. To hold to be true; assert. 3. To require or deserve: The problem *claims* our attention. — *n.* 1. A demand or an assertion of a right. 2. An assertion of something as true. 3. A ground for claiming something. 4. That which is claimed, as a piece of land. [< OF < L *clamere* to declare] — **claim'a·ble** *adj.* — **claim'er** *n.*

claim·ant (klā'mənt) *n.* One who makes a claim.

clair·voy·ance (klâr·voi'əns) *n.* 1. The alleged ability to perceive distant or hidden objects. 2. Knowledge of things beyond the area of normal perception. [< MF]

clair·voy·ant (klâr·voi'ənt) *adj.* Having clairvoyance or second sight. — *n.* A clairvoyant person.

clam[1] (klam) *n.* 1. Any of various bivalve mollusks, as the quahog. 2. *Informal* A close-mouthed person. — *v.i.* **clammed, clam·ming** To hunt for or dig clams. — **to clam up** *U.S. Slang* To become or keep silent. [< obs. *clam* a clamp]

clam·bake (klam'bāk') *n. U.S.* 1. A picnic where clams and other foods are baked. 2. Any noisy gathering.

clam·ber (klam'bər, -ər) *v.t. & v.i.* To climb by using the hands and feet; mount or descend with difficulty. — *n.* The act of clambering. [Akin to CLIMB] — **clam'ber·er** *n.*

clam·my (klam'ē) *adj.* **·mi·er, ·mi·est** Stickily soft and damp, and usually cold. [< Du. *klam* sticky] — **clam'mi·ly** *adv.* — **clam'mi·ness** *n.*

clam·or (klam'ər) *n.* 1. A loud, repeated outcry. 2. A vehement protest or demand. 3. Any loud and continuous noise; din. — *v.i.* 1. To make loud outcries, demands, or complaints. — *v.t.* 2. To utter with clamor. 3. To move or drive by clamor. Also *Brit.* **clam'our.** [< OF < L *clamare* to cry out] — **clam'or·er** *n.*

clam·or·ous (klam'ər·əs) *adj.* Making, or made with, a clamor; noisy. — **clam'or·ous·ly** *adv.* — **clam'or·ous·ness** *n.*

clamp (klamp) *n.* Any of a number of devices for holding objects together, securing a piece in position, etc.; esp. one having two opposite parts that can be brought together by a screw or spring action. — *v.t.* To hold or bind with or as with a clamp. — **to clamp down** *U.S. Informal* To become more strict. [Cf. OE *clamm,* M.Du *klampe*]

clan (klan) *n.* 1. A united group of relatives, or families, claiming a common ancestor and having the same surname. 2. A clique; fraternity; club. [< Scottish Gaelic *clann*]

clan·des·tine (klan·des'tin) *adj.* Kept secret for a purpose, usually for something evil or illicit; surreptitious; furtive; — **Syn.** See STEALTHY. [< F < L *clandestinus* < *clam* in secret] — **clan·des'tine·ly** *adv.* — **clan·des'tine·ness** *n.*

clang (klang) *v.t. & v.i.* To make or cause to make a loud, ringing, metallic sound; ring loudly. — *n.* A ringing sound.

clan·gor (klang'gər, klang'ər) *n.* Repeated clanging; clamor; din. — *v.i.* To ring noisily; clang. Also *Brit.* **clan'gour.** [< L < *clangere* to clang] — **clan'gor·ous** *adj.* — **clan'gor·ous·ly** *adv.*

clank (klangk) *n.* A short, harsh, metallic sound. — *v.t. & v.i.* To emit, or cause to emit, a clank. [Imit.]

clan·nish (klan'ish) *adj.* 1. Of or characteristic of a clan. 2. Disposed to cling together, or bound by family prejudices, traditions, etc. — **clan'nish·ly** *adv.* — **clan'nish·ness** *n.*

clans·man (klanz'mən) *n. pl.* **·men** (-mən) A member of a clan. — **clans'wom'an** *n.fem.*

clap (klap) *v.* **clapped, clap·ping** *v.i.* 1. To strike the hands together, as in applauding. 2. To make a sound, as of two boards striking together. — *v.t.* 3. To bring (the hands) together sharply and with an explosive sound. 4. To strike with the open hand, as in greeting. 5. To applaud (someone or something) by clapping. 6. To put, place, or fling quickly or suddenly: They *clapped* him into jail. 7. To flap, as the wings. — *n.* 1. The act or sound of clapping the hands. 2. A loud, explosive sound, esp. of thunder. 3. A blow with the open hand. [OE *clæppan*]

clap·board (klab'ərd, klap'bôrd', -bōrd') *n.* A narrow board having one edge thinner than the other, nailed overlapping as siding on frame buildings: sometimes called *weatherboard.* — *v.t.* To cover with clapboards. [Partial trans. of M.Du. *klapholt* barrel stave]

clap·per (klap'ər) *n.* 1. The tongue of a bell. 2. One who or that which claps.

---

clap·trap (klap'trap) *n.* Pretentious language; cheap, sensational artifice. [< CLAP[1], n. + TRAP[1], n.]

claque (klak) *n.* **1.** A group of hired applauders in a theater. **2.** Any set of persons who praise or applaud from interested motives. [< F < *claquer* to clap]

clar·et (klar'ət) *n.* **1.** Any dry red wine, esp. red Bordeaux. **2.** Ruby to deep purplish red. [< OF < L *clarus* bright]

clar·i·fy (klar'ə-fī) *v.t. & v.i.* ·fied, ·fy·ing **1.** To make or become clear or free from impurities. **2.** To make or become understandable; explain. [< OF < LL < L *clarus* clear + *facere* to make] — **clar/i·fi·ca/tion** — **clar/i·fi/er** *n.*

clar·i·net (klar'ə-net') *n.* A cylindrical woodwind instrument having a single-reed mouthpiece, finger holes, and keys. Also *Rare* **clar·i·o·net** (klar'ē·ə-net'). [< F < Ital. *clarinetto*] — **clar/i·net/ist** or **clar/i·net/tist** *n.*

clar·i·on (klar'ē-ən) *n.* **1.** An obsolete kind of trumpet having a shrill tone. **2.** The sound of a clarion. — *v.t. & v.i.* To proclaim as with a clarion. — *adj.* Clear and resounding. [< OF < L *clarus* clear]

clar·i·ty (klar'ə-tē) *n.* Clearness; lucidity.

clash (klash) *v.t.* **1.** To strike or dash together with a harsh, metallic sound. — *v.i.* **2.** To collide with loud and confused noise. **3.** To conflict; be in opposition. — *n.* **1.** A resounding, metallic noise. **2.** A conflict or opposition. [Imit.]

clasp (klasp, kläsp) *n.* **1.** A fastening, as a hook, by which things or parts are held together. **2.** A firm grasp of the hand or embrace. — *v.t.* **1.** To embrace. **2.** To fasten with or as with a clasp. **3.** To grasp firmly in or with the hand. [ME *claspe*] — **clasp/er** *n.*

class (klas, kläs) *n.* **1.** A body of persons considered to have certain social or other characteristics in common. **2.** The division of society by relative standing; social rank, caste. **3.** A category of objects, persons, etc., based on quality or rank: of the first *class*. **4.** A number of things grouped together as having common properties; a category. **5.** A group of students under one teacher, or pursuing a study together; also, a meeting of such a group. **6.** *U.S.* A group of students in a school or college graduating together. **7.** *Biol.* A group of plants or animals standing below a phylum and above an order. **8.** *Slang* Superiority; elegance. — *v.t.* **1.** To assign to a class; classify. — *v.i.* **2.** *Rare* To be placed or ranked, as in a class. [< MF < L *classis* class]

class consciousness Awareness of the nature, interest, and unity of one's social group. — **class/-con/scious** *adj.*

clas·sic (klas/ik) *adj.* **1.** Belonging to the first class or highest rank; approved as a model. **2.** Of or characteristic of ancient Greece and Rome, their literature or art. **3.** In the style of ancient Greek and Roman authors and artists; balanced; formal; austere. — *n.* **1.** An author, artist, or work generally recognized as a standard of excellence. **2.** *Informal* Any well-known event thought of as being typical or traditional. — **the classics** Ancient Greek and Roman literature. [< L *classis* order, class]

clas·si·cal (klas/i·kəl) *adj.* **1.** Classic. **2.** Generally accepted as being standard and authoritative; not new or experimental: *classical* economic theory. **3.** Of ancient Greece and Rome: *classical* civilization. **4.** Versed in the Greek and Roman classics: a *classical* scholar. **5.** Consisting of or pertaining to studies based on Greek and Roman language, literature, and thought: a *classical* curriculum. **6.** *Music* Loosely, of a serious nature, as distinguished from jazz or popular music. — **clas/si·cal·ly** *adv.* — **clas/si·cal/i·ty** *n.*

clas·si·cal·ism (klas/i·kəl·iz/əm) *n.* Classicism. — **clas/·si·cal·ist** *n.*

clas·si·cism (klas/ə·siz/əm) *n.* **1.** A group of esthetic principles (simplicity, restraint, balance, dignity, etc.) as manifested in ancient Greek and Roman art and literature: distinguished from *romanticism*. **2.** Adherence to these principles. **3.** The style of ancient Greek and Roman literature, architecture, etc. **4.** Classical scholarship. **5.** A Greek or Latin idiom or form.

clas·si·cist (klas/ə·sist) *n.* **1.** One versed in the classics. **2.** An adherent or imitator of classic style. **3.** One who actively supports the study of the classics.

clas·si·fi·ca·tion (klas/ə·fə·kā/shən) *n.* The act, process, or result of classifying. — **clas·si·fi·ca·to·ry** (klas/ə·fə·kā/tər·ē, klə·sif/ə·kə·tôr/ē, -tō/rē) *adj.*

classified advertisement An advertisement under any of various subject headings. Also **classified ad.**

clas·si·fy (klas/ə·fī) *v.t.* ·fied, ·fy·ing **1.** To arrange or put in a class or classes on the basis of resemblances or differences. **2.** To designate as of aid to an enemy and restrict as to circulation or use, as a government document. [< L *classis* class + -FY] — **clas/si·fi/a·ble** *adj.* — **clas/si·fi/er** *n.*

class·mate (klas/māt, kläs/-) *n.* A member of the same class in school or college.

class·room (klas/room', -rŏŏm', kläs/-) *n.* A room in a school or college in which classes are held.

class struggle **1.** The conflict between classes in society. **2.** In Marxist theory, the economic and political struggle for power between the dominant class and the rising class.

class·y (klas/ē) *adj.* **class·i·er, class·i·est** *Slang* Elegant.

clat·ter (klat/ər) *v.i.* **1.** To make a rattling noise; give out short, sharp noises rapidly or repeatedly. **2.** To move with a rattling noise. **3.** To talk noisily; chatter. — *v.t.* **4.** To cause to clatter. — *n.* **1.** A rattling or clattering sound. **2.** A disturbance or commotion. **3.** Noisy talk; chatter. [OE *clatrunge* a clattering noise] — **clat/ter·er** *n.*

clause (klôz) *n.* **1.** A distinct part of a composition, as an article in a statute, will, treaty, etc. **2.** *Gram.* A group of words containing a subject and a predicate: distinguished from *phrase*. Abbr. *cl.* — **dependent clause** A clause that functions as a subject or complement (noun clause) or as a modifier (adjective or adverb clause) within a sentence: also called *subordinate clause*. — **independent clause** A clause that can stand alone as a simple sentence, or combine with other clauses to form compound or complex sentences: also called *main clause, principal clause.* [< OF < Med.L < L *clausus*, pp. of *claudere* to close] — **claus/al** *adj.*

claus·tro·pho·bi·a (klôs/trə-fō/bē·ə) *n.* *Psychiatry* Morbid fear of enclosed or confined places. [< L *claustrum* a closed place + -PHOBIA] — **claus/tro·pho/bic** *adj.*

cla·vate (klā/vāt) *adj.* Club-shaped. [< L *clava* a club]

clave (klāv) Archaic past tense of CLEAVE[1] and CLEAVE[2].

clav·i·chord (klav/ə-kôrd) *n.* A keyboard musical instrument that is a forerunner of the piano. [< Med.L < L < *clavis* key + *chorda* string]

clav·i·cle (klav/ə-kəl) *n.* *Anat.* The bone connecting the shoulder blade and breastbone: also called *collarbone.* For illus. see SKELETON. [< L *clavis* key] — **cla·vic·u·lar** (klə-vik/yə-lər) *adj.*

clav·i·er (klə-vir/; for defs. 1 and 3, also klav/ē-ər) *n.* **1.** A keyboard. **2.** Any keyboard stringed instrument, as a harpsichord, piano, etc. **3.** A dummy keyboard for silent practicing. [< F, keyboard < L *clavis* key]

claw (klô) *n.* **1.** A sharp, usu. curved, horny nail on the toe of a bird, mammal, or reptile. **2.** A chela or pincer of certain insects and crustaceans. **3.** Anything sharp and hooked, as the cleft part of a hammerhead. — *v.t. & v.i.* To tear, scratch, dig, pull, etc., with or as with claws. [OE *clawu*]

claw hammer A hammer with one end of its head forked and curved like a claw for drawing nails.

clay (klā) *n.* **1.** A fine-grained, variously colored earth, plastic when wet, used in the making of bricks, tiles, pottery, etc. **2.** Earth. **3.** The human body. — *v.t.* To mix or treat with clay. [OE *clæg*] — **clay/ey** *adj.* — **clay/ish** *adj.*

clay·more (klā/môr, -mōr) *n.* A double-edged broadsword formerly used by the Scottish Highlanders. [< Scottish Gaelic *claidheamh* sword + *mor* great]

clay pigeon In trapshooting, a saucer-shaped disk, as of baked clay, projected from a trap as a flying target.

-cle *suffix of nouns* Small; minute; *particle, corpuscle.* [< F < L *-culus*, dim. suffix]

clean (klēn) *adj.* **1.** Free from dirt or stain; unsoiled. **2.** Morally pure; wholesome. **3.** Without obstructions, encumbrances, or restrictions: a *clean* title to land. **4.** Thorough; complete: a *clean* getaway. **5.** Clever; dexterous: a *clean* jump. **6.** Well-proportioned; trim; shapely. **7.** Neat in habits. **8.** Producing an explosion relatively free of radioactive fallout: said of an atomic or thermonuclear bomb. — *v.t.* **1.** To render free of dirt or other impurities. **2.** To prepare (fowl, game, etc.) for cooking. — *v.i.* **3.** To undergo or perform the act of cleaning. — **to clean out 1.** To clear of trash or rubbish. **2.** To empty (a place) of contents or occupants. **3.** *Informal* To leave without money: The depression *cleaned* him *out*. — **to clean up 1.** To clean completely and thoroughly. **2.** *Slang* To make a large profit. **3.** *Informal* To finish: to *clean up* one's work. — *adv.* **1.** In a clean manner; cleanly. **2.** Wholly; completely. [OE *clæne* clear, pure] — **clean/a·ble** *adj.* — **clean/ness** *n.*

clean-cut (klēn/kut') *adj.* **1.** Cut with smooth edge or surface; well-made. **2.** Sharply defined; clear. **3.** Pleasing in appearance; wholesome; neat: a *clean-cut* young man.

clean·er (klē/nər) *n.* **1.** A person whose work is cleaning, esp. clothing. **2.** Any substance or device that cleans.

clean·ly *adj.* (klen/lē; *adv.* klēn/lē) *adj.* Habitually and carefully clean; neat; tidy. — *adv.* In a clean manner. — **clean·li·ly** (klen/lə-lē) *adv.* — **clean·li·ness** (klen/lē·nis) *n.*

cleanse (klenz) *v.t.* **cleansed, cleans·ing** To free from dirt or defilement; clean; purge. [OE *clænsian* < *clæne* clean]

cleans·er (klenz/ər) *n.* One who or that which cleanses; esp., a soap, detergent, etc., used for cleansing.

clean·up (klēn/up') *n.* **1.** A complete cleaning. **2.** *Slang* A large profit; gain.

clear (klir) *adj.* **1.** Bright; unclouded. **2.** Without impurity or blemish. **3.** Of great transparency. **4.** Free from obstructions: a *clear* road. **5.** Understandable; plain to the mind. **6.** Plain to the eye, ear, etc. **7.** Able to discern; keen: a *clear* mind. **8.** Free from uncertainty; sure: Are you *clear* on that point? **9.** Free from guilt or blame. **10.** Not in contact: usu. with *of*: to stand *clear* of a fire. **11.** Emptied of cargo. **12.** Without deductions; net: a *clear* $5,000.

— adv. **1.** In a clear manner. **2.** *Informal* All the way: *clear* through the day. *— v.t.* **1.** To make clear; brighten. **2.** To free from foreign matter, impurities, or obstructions. **3.** To remove (obstacles, etc.) in making something clear. **4.** To free from blame or guilt. **5.** To make plain. **6.** To pass or get under or over without touching: to *clear* a fence. **7.** To free from debt by payment. **8.** To settle (a debt). **9.** To obtain or give clearance for. **10.** To gain over and above expenses. **11.** To pass (a check) through a clearing-house. *— v.i.* **12.** To become free from fog, rain, etc.: become fair. **13.** To pass away, as mist or clouds. **14.** To settle accounts by exchange of bills and checks, as in a clearing-house. **15.** To obtain clearance. **— to clear away** (or **off**) **1.** To remove out of the way. **2.** To go away; disappear. **— to clear out 1.** *Informal* To go away. **2.** To empty of contents. **— to clear the air** To dispel tensions; settle differences. **— to clear up 1.** To make clear. **2.** To grow fair, as the weather. **3.** To free from confusion or mystery. **4.** To put in order; tidy. *— n.* **1.** An unobstructed space. **2.** Clearance. **— in the clear 1.** Free from limitations or obstructions. **2.** *Informal* Free from guilt or blame. [< OF < L *clarus* clear, bright] **— clear′a·ble** *adj.* **— clear′ly** *adv.* **— clear′ness** *n.*
— Syn. (adj.) 1, 3. A thing is *clear* when it presents no obstructions to the sight. We see objects clearly through something *transparent*; that which is *translucent* allows the passage of light, but may obscure form and color.

clear·ance (klir′əns) *n.* **1.** The act or instance of clearing. **2.** A space cleared. **3.** The space by which a moving object clears something. **4.** Permission for a ship, airplane, truck, etc., to proceed, as after a check of its load. **5.** The passage of checks, bank drafts, etc. through a clearing-house.

clear-cut (klir′kut′) *adj.* **1.** Distinctly and sharply outlined. **2.** Plain; evident; obvious.

clear-head·ed (klir′hed′id) *adj.* Not mentally confused; clear in thought; sensible. **— clear′-head′ed·ness** *n.*

clear·ing (klir′ing) *n.* **1.** A making or becoming clear. **2.** That which is clear or cleared, as a tract of land. **3.** In banking, clearance.

clear·ing-house (klir′ing·hous′) *n.* An office where bankers exchange drafts and checks and adjust balances. Also **clear′ing·house′.**

clear-sight·ed (klir′sī′tid) *adj.* **1.** Having accurate perception and good judgment; discerning. **2.** Having keen vision. **— clear′-sight′ed·ly** *adv.* **— clear′-sight′ed·ness** *n.*

clear-sto·ry (klir′stôr′ē, -stō′rē) See CLERESTORY.

cleat (klēt) *n.* **1.** A strip of wood or iron fastened across a surface to strengthen or support. **2.** A piece of metal or wood with arms on which to wind or secure a rope. *— v.t.* **1.** To furnish or strengthen with a cleat or cleats. **2.** *Naut.* To fasten (rope, etc.) to or with a cleat. [ME *clete*]

cleav·age (klē′vij) *n.* **1.** A cleaving or being cleft. **2.** A split or cleft. **3.** *Mineral.* A tendency in certain rocks or crystals to split in certain directions.

cleave[1] (klēv) *v.* **cleft** or **cleaved** or **clove** (*Archaic* **clave**), **cleft** or **cleaved** or **clo·ven, cleav·ing** *v.t.* **1.** To split or sunder, as with an ax or wedge. **2.** To make or achieve by cutting: to *cleave* a path. **3.** To pass through; penetrate: to *cleave* the air. *— v.i.* **4.** To part or divide along natural lines of separation. **5.** To make one's way; pass: with *through.* [OE *cleofan*] **— cleav′a·ble** *adj.*

cleave[2] (klēv) *v.i.* **cleaved** (*Archaic* **clave, clove**), **cleaved, cleav·ing 1.** To stick fast; adhere: with *to.* **2.** To be faithful: with *to.* [Fusion of OE *clifan* and *clifian*]

cleav·er (klē′vər) *n.* **1.** One who or that which cleaves. **2.** A butcher's heavy, axlike knife. [< CLEAVE[1]]

clef (klef) *n. Music* A symbol placed on the staff to show the pitch of the notes. [< MF < L *clavis* key]

cleft (kleft) Past tense and past participle of CLEAVE[1]. *— adj.* Divided partially or completely. *— n.* A fissure; crevice; rift. [ME *clift*]

cleft palate A congenital longitudinal fissure in the roof of the mouth.

clem·a·tis (klem′ə·tis) *n.* A perennial shrub or vine of the crowfoot family. [< Gk. *klēmatis*]

clem·en·cy (klem′ən·sē) *n., pl.* **·cies 1.** Leniency; mercy. **2.** An act of mercy or leniency. **3.** Mildness of weather, etc. **— Syn.** See MERCY. [< L *clemens* mild]

clem·ent (klem′ənt) *adj.* **1.** Lenient or merciful in temperament; compassionate. **2.** Mild: said of weather. [< L *clemens, -entis* mild, merciful] **— clem′ent·ly** *adv.*

clench (klench) *v.t.* **1.** To grasp or grip firmly. **2.** To close tightly or lock, as the fist or teeth. **3.** To clinch, as a nail. *— n.* **1.** A tight grip. **2.** A device that clenches or grips. [OE *-clenc(e)an* in *beclencan* to hold fast]

clere·sto·ry (klir′stôr′ē, -stō′rē) *n., pl.* **·ries 1.** *Archit.* The highest story of the nave and choir of a church, with windows opening above the aisle roofs, etc. **2.** A similar part in other structures. Also spelled *clearstory.* Also **clere′sto′rey.** [< earlier *clere* clear + STORY]

cler·gy (klûr′jē) *n., pl.* **·gies** The whole body of men set apart by ordination for religious service. [< OF < LL < Gk. *klēros* lot, portion]

cler·gy·man (klûr′jē·mən) *n., pl.* **·men** (-mən) One of the clergy; an ordained minister. Abbr. *cl.*

cler·ic (kler′ik) *adj.* Clerical. *— n.* A member of the clergy.

cler·i·cal (kler′i·kəl) *adj.* **1.** Of or related to clerks or office workers or their work. **2.** Belonging to or characteristic of the clergy. **3.** Advocating great political influence for the clergy. *— n.* **1.** A clergyman. **2.** *pl.* The distinctive dress of a clergyman. **— cler′i·cal·ly** *adv.*

cler·i·cal·ism (kler′i·kəl·iz′əm) *n.* Excessive clerical influence in politics. **— cler′i·cal·ist** *n.*

clerk (klûrk, *Brit.* klärk) *n.* **1.** A worker in an office who keeps records or accounts, attends to correspondence, etc. **2.** An official or employee of a court, legislative body, or the like, charged with the care of records, etc. **3.** *U.S.* A salesperson in a store. *— v.i.* To work or act as clerk. [OE < LL < Gk. *klēros* lot, portion] **— clerk′ship** *n.*

clerk·ly (klûrk′lē, *Brit.* klärk′-) *adj.* **clerk·li·er, clerk·li·est** Of a clerk: *clerkly* duties. *— adv.* In the manner of a clerk. **— clerk′li·ness** *n.*

clev·er (klev′ər) *adj.* **1.** Mentally keen; intelligent; quick-witted. **2.** Physically adroit, esp. with the hands; dexterous. **3.** Ingeniously made, said, done, etc. [Cf. ME *cliver* adroit] **— clev′er·ly** *adv.* **— clev′er·ness** *n.*

clev·is (klev′is) *n.* A U-shaped metal fastening pierced for a bolt, used to attach chains, cables, etc. [Akin to CLEAVE[1]]

clew (kloō) *n.* **1.** In legends, a ball of thread that guides through a maze. **2.** Something that serves as a guide in solving a problem or mystery: usu. spelled *clue.* **3.** *Naut.* A lower corner of a square sail or the lower aft corner of a fore-and-aft sail; also, a loop at the corner. *— v.t.* **1.** To coil into a ball. **2.** To guide or track by or as by a clew. **3.** *Naut.* To raise the clews of (a square sail): with *up.* [OE *cliwen*]

cli·ché (klē·shā′) *n.* A trite or hackneyed expression, action, etc. [< F, pp. of *clicher* to stereotype]

click (klik) *n.* **1.** A short, sharp, nonresonant metallic sound, as that made by a latch. **2.** *Phonet.* A speech sound made by clicking the tongue, characteristic of certain African languages: also called *suction stop.* *— v.t.* **1.** To cause to make a click or clicks. *— v.i.* **2.** To produce a click or clicks. **3.** *Slang* To succeed. [Imit.] **— click′er** *n.*

cli·ent (klī′ənt) *n.* **1.** One in whose interest a lawyer acts. **2.** One who engages the services of any professional adviser. **3.** A customer. [< L *cliens, -entis* follower] **— cli·en·tal** (klī·en′təl, klī′ən·təl) *adj.*

cli·en·tele (klī′ən·tel′) *n.* A body of clients, patients, customers, etc. Also **cli·ent·age** (klī′ən·tij). [< F]

cliff (klif) *n.* A high steep face of rock; a precipice. [OE]

cliff swallow A North American swallow that builds mud nests under eaves or against cliffs.

cliff·y (klif′ē) *adj.* Abounding in or resembling cliffs.

cli·mac·ter·ic (klī·mak′tər·ik, klī′mak·ter′ik) *n.* **1.** An age or period of life characterized by marked physiological change, as the menopause. **2.** Any critical year or period. *— adj.* Pertaining to a critical year or period: also **cli·mac·ter·i·cal** (klī·mak·ter′i·kəl). [< L < Gk. *klimaktēr* rung of a ladder]

cli·mac·tic (klī·mak′tik) *adj.* Pertaining to or constituting a climax. Also **cli·mac′ti·cal.**

cli·mate (klī′mit) *n.* **1.** The temperature, precipitation, winds, etc., characteristic of a region. **2.** A region in reference to its characteristic weather. **3.** A prevailing trend or condition in human affairs: the *climate* of opinion. [< OF < LL < Gk. *klima, -atos* region, zone] **— cli·mat·ic** (klī·mat′ik) or **·i·cal** *adj.* **— cli·mat′i·cal·ly** *adv.*

climato- *combining form* Climate; pertaining to climate or climatic conditions: *climatology.* Also, before vowels, **climat-.** [< Gk. *klima, -atos* region]

cli·ma·tol·o·gy (klī′mə·tol′ə·jē) *n.* The branch of science dealing with the phenomena of climate. **— cli·ma·to·log·ic** (klī′mə·tə·loj′ik) or **·i·cal** *adj.* **— cli′ma·tol′o·gist** *n.*

cli·max (klī′maks) *n.* **1.** The point of greatest intensity or fullest development; culmination; acme. **2.** In drama, fiction, etc., the scene or moment of action that determines the dénouement. *— v.t. & v.i.* To reach or bring to a climax. [< L < Gk. *klimax* ladder]

climb (klīm) *v.* **climbed, climb·ing** *v.t.* **1.** To ascend or mount (something), by means of the hands and feet. *— v.i.* **2.** To rise or advance in status, rank, etc. **3.** To incline or slope upward. **4.** To rise during growth, as certain vines, by entwining a support. **— to climb down** To descend, esp. by using the hands and feet. *— n.* **1.** The act or process of climbing; ascent. **2.** A place ascended by climbing. [OE *climban*] **— climb′a·ble** *adj.* **— climb′er** *n.*

clinch (klinch) *v.t.* **1.** To secure, as a driven nail or staple, by bending down the protruding point. **2.** To fasten together by this means. **3.** To make sure; settle. — *v.i.* **4.** To grapple, as combatants. **5.** *Slang* To embrace, as lovers. — *n.* **1.** The act of clinching. **2.** That which clinches; a clamp. **3.** A grip or struggle at close quarters, as in boxing. **4.** *Slang* A close embrace. [Var. of CLENCH]

clinch·er (klin′chər) *n.* **1.** One who or that which clinches. **2.** A nail made for clinching. **3.** *Informal* A deciding statement, point, etc.

cling (kling) *v.i.* **clung, cling·ing 1.** To hold fast, as by grasping, sticking, or winding round. **2.** To resist separation: with *together*. [OE *clingan*] — **cling′er** *n.* — **cling′ing·ly** *adv.* — **cling′y** *adj.*

clinging vine *Informal* A woman who displays extreme dependence on a man.

cling·stone (kling′stōn′) *n.* A variety of peach in which the pulp adheres to the stone.

clin·ic (klin′ik) *n.* **1.** An infirmary, usu. connected with a hospital or medical school, for the treatment of nonresident patients. **2.** The teaching of medicine by treating patients in the presence of a class; also, a class receiving such instruction. **3.** A place where patients are studied and treated by specialists. **4.** An organization that offers advice on specific problems. [< F < Gk. *klinein* to recline]

clin·i·cal (klin′i·kəl) *adj.* **1.** Of or pertaining to a clinic. **2.** Concerned with the observation and treatment of patients in clinics, as distinguished from laboratory experimentation. **3.** Coldly scientific or detached. — **clin′i·cal·ly** *adv.*

clinical thermometer An accurately calibrated thermometer used for determining body temperature.

cli·ni·cian (kli·nish′ən) *n.* A physician trained in clinical methods, or one who gives instruction in clinics.

clink¹ (klingk) *v.t. & v.i.* To make or cause to make a short, slight, ringing sound. — *n.* A slight tinkling sound. [Imit.]

clink² (klingk) *n. Slang* A prison. [? after *Clink* prison in London]

clink·er (kling′kər) *n.* **1.** The fused residue left by coal, etc., in burning. **2.** A very hard brick. — *v.i.* To form clinkers, as coal in burning. [< Du. *klinckaerd* brick]

clino- *combining form* Bend; slope; incline: *clinometer*. [< Gk. *klinein* to bend]

cli·nom·e·ter (kli·nom′ə·tər, kli-) *n.* An instrument for determining angular inclination, as of guns, slopes, etc. — **cli·no·met·ric** (kli′nə·met′rik) or **·ri·cal** *adj.*

Cli·o (klī′ō) The Muse of history.

clip¹ (klip) *n.* A device that clasps, grips, or holds articles together, as letters or papers. — *v.t.* **clipped, clip·ping** To fasten with or as with a clip. [OE *clyppan* to clasp]

clip² (klip) *v.* **clipped, clip·ping** *v.t.* **1.** To cut with shears or scissors, as hair or fleece; trim. **2.** To cut short; curtail: to *clip* the ends of words. **3.** *Informal* To strike with a sharp blow. **4.** *U.S. Slang* To cheat or defraud. — *v.i.* **5.** To cut or trim. **6.** *Informal* To run or move swiftly. — **to clip the wings of** To check the aspirations or ambitions of. — *n.* **1.** The act of clipping, or that which is clipped off. **2.** The wool yielded at one shearing or during one season. **3.** A sharp blow; punch. **4.** *Informal* A quick pace. [< ON *klippa*]

clip·board (klip′bôrd′, -bōrd′) *n.* A board providing a writing surface, with a spring clip for holding paper.

clipped form A shortened form of a polysyllabic word, as *bus* for *omnibus.* Also **clipped word.**

clip·per (klip′ər) *n.* **1.** *pl.* An instrument or tool for clipping or cutting. **2.** A sailing vessel of the mid-19th century, built for speed: also **clipper ship. 3.** One who clips.

clip·ping (klip′ing) *n.* **1.** The act of one who or that which clips. **2.** *Chiefly U.S.* That which is cut off or out by clipping: a newspaper *clipping.* — *adj.* That cuts or clips.

clique (klēk, klik) *n.* An exclusive or clannish group of people. — *v.i.* **cliqued, cli·quing** To unite in a clique; act clannishly. [< MF < *cliquer* to click, clap]

cli·quish (klē′kish, klik′ish) *adj.* Inclined to form cliques; exclusive. Also **cli·quey, cli·quy.** — **cli′quish·ly** *adv.* — **cli′quish·ness** *n.*

cli·to·ris (klī′tə·ris, klit′ə-) *n. Anat.* A small erectile organ at the upper part of the vulva, homologous to the penis. [< NL < Gk. *kleitoris*] — **clit′o·ral** (-rəl) *adj.*

clo·a·ca (klō·ā′kə) *n. pl.* **·cae** (-sē) **1.** *Zool.* The common cavity into which the various ducts of the body open in certain fishes, reptiles, birds, and some mammals. **2.** A sewer or a privy. [< L, a drain] — **clo·a′cal** *adj.*

cloak (klōk) *n.* **1.** A loose outer garment, usu. without sleeves. **2.** Something that covers or hides. — *v.t.* **1.** To cover with a cloak. **2.** To conceal; disguise. [< OF < Med.L *cloca* bell, cape; so called from its bell-like shape]

cloak·room (klōk′rōōm′, -rŏŏm′) *n.* A room where hats, coats, luggage, etc., are left temporarily, as in a theater.

clob·ber (klob′ər) *v.t. U.S. Slang* **1.** To beat severely; trounce; maul. **2.** To defeat utterly. [? Freq. of CLUB¹, v.]

cloche (klōsh, *Fr.* klôsh) *n.* A woman's close-fitting, bell-shaped hat. [< F, bell]

clock¹ (klok) *n.* An instrument for measuring time; esp., a sizable mechanism having pointers that move over a dial marked off in hours. — *v.t.* To ascertain the speed or the time of with a stopwatch. [< MDu. < OF < Med.L *cloca*]

clock² (klok) *n.* An embroidered or woven ornament on the side of a stocking or sock at the ankle. [Origin uncertain]

clock·wise (klok′wīz′) *adj. & adv.* Going in the direction traveled by the hands of a clock.

clock·work (klok′wûrk′) *n.* The machinery of a clock, or any similar mechanism, usu. driven by a spring. — **like clockwork** With regularity and precision.

clod (klod) *n.* **1.** A lump of earth, clay, etc. **2.** Earth. **3.** A dull, stupid person. [Var. of CLOT] — **clod′dish** *adj.* — **clod′dish·ness** *n.* — **clod′dy** *adj.*

clod·hop·per (klod′hop′ər) *n.* **1.** *Informal* A rustic; hick; lout. **2.** *pl.* Large, heavy shoes.

clog (klog) *n.* **1.** Anything that impedes motion; an obstruction; hindrance. **2.** A block or weight attached, as to a horse, to hinder movement. **3.** A wooden-soled shoe. **4.** A clog dance. — *v.* **clogged, clog·ging** *v.t.* **1.** To choke up or obstruct. **2.** To impede; hinder. **3.** To fasten a clog to; hobble. — *v.i.* **4.** To become clogged or choked. **5.** To adhere in a mass; coagulate. **6.** To perform a clog dance. [ME *clogge* block of wood] — **clog′gi·ness** *n.* — **clog′gy** *adj.*

cloi·son·né (kloi′zə·nā′) *n.* **1.** Enamel work made by laying out the pattern with metal strips and filling the interstices with enamel. **2.** The ware so produced. — *adj.* Of, pertaining to, or made by this method. [< F, partitioned]

clois·ter (klois′tər) *n.* **1.** A covered walk along the inside walls of buildings in a quadrangle, as in a monastery or college. **2.** A monastery; convent. **3.** Any place of quiet seclusion. **4.** Monastic life. — *v.t.* To seclude; confine, as in a cloister. [OF < L *claustrum* enclosed place] — **clois′tered** *adj.* — **clois′tral** *adj.*

— **Syn.** (noun) **2.** *Cloister* refers to a retreat for either sex, and stresses loneliness. *Convent* was originally a general term, but is now usually restricted to a retreat for women, replacing the former *nunnery.* *Monasteries* are *cloisters* for men.

clo·nus (klō′nəs) *n. Pathol.* A succession of muscle spasms. [< NL < Gk. *klonos* motion, turmoil] — **clon·ic** (klon′ik) *adj.* — **clo·nic·i·ty** (klō·nis′ə·tē) *n.* — **clo′nism** *n.*

close (*adj., adv., n. defs. 4 and 5* klōs; *v., n. def. 2* klōz) *adj.* **clos·er, clos·est 1.** Near or near together in space, time, etc. **2.** Dense; compact: a *close* weave. **3.** Near to the surface; short: a *close* haircut. **4.** Near to the mark: a *close* shot. **5.** Nearly even or equal: said of contests. **6.** Fitting tightly. **7.** Conforming to an original: a *close* resemblance. **8.** Logically exact: *close* reasoning. **9.** Thorough; rigorous: *close* attention. **10.** Bound by strong affection, loyalty, etc.: a *close* friend. **11.** Shut in or about; not open. **12.** Confined in space; cramped: *close* quarters. **13.** Open only to a few; restricted. **14.** Strictly guarded: a *close* secret. **15.** Concealing one's thoughts or feelings; reticent. **16.** Hidden; secluded. **17.** Close-fisted; stingy. **18.** Difficult to obtain: said of money or credit. **19.** Stifling and humid; stuffy. **20.** *Phonet.* Of vowels, pronounced with a part of the tongue relatively close to the palate, as (ē): opposed to *open.* — *v.* **closed, clos·ing** *v.t.* **1.** To shut. **2.** To obstruct, as an opening or passage. **3.** To bring to an end; terminate. — *v.i.* **4.** To become shut or closed. **5.** To come to an end. **6.** To grapple; come to close quarters. **7.** To come to an agreement. **8.** To be worth at the end of a business day: stocks *closed* three points higher. — **to close down** To cease operations, as a factory. — **to close in** To advance from all sides so as to prevent escape. — **to close out** *U.S.* To sell all of, usu. at reduced prices. — **to close up 1.** To close completely. **2.** To come nearer together, as troops. — *n.* **1.** The end; conclusion. **2.** An enclosed place, esp. about a cathedral or building. — *adv.* In a close manner; nearly; closely. [< OF < L *claudere* to close] — **close·ly** (klōs′lē) *adv.* — **close·ness** (klōs′nis) *n.* — **clos·er** (klō′zər) *n.*

close call (klōs) *U.S. Informal* A narrow escape.

closed circuit (klōzd) *Telecom.* A form of television in which broadcasts are transmitted by cable to a restricted number of receivers.

closed shop An establishment where only union members are hired, by agreement with the union.

close-fist·ed (klōs′fis′tid) *adj.* Stingy; miserly. — **close′-fist′ed·ness** *n.*

close-fit·ting (klōs′fit′ing) *adj.* Fitting snugly.

close-hauled (klōs′hôld′) *adj. & adv. Naut.* With sails set for sailing as close to the wind as possible.

close-mouthed (klōs′mouthd′, -moutht′) *adj.* Not given to speaking; taciturn; uncommunicative.

close quarters (klōs) **1.** In fighting, an encounter at close range or hand-to-hand. **2.** A small, confined space.

close shave (klōs) *U.S. Informal* A narrow escape.

clos·et (klok′it) *n. Chiefly U.S.* A small room or recess for storing clothes, linen, etc. **2.** A small, private room. **3.** A ruler's council chamber. — *v.t.* To shut up or conceal in or as in a closet: usu. reflexive. — *adj.* **1.** Private; confidential. **2.** Based on theory rather than practice: *closet* strategy. [< OF, dim. of *clos* < L *claudere* to close]

close-up (klōs/up/) *n.* **1.** A picture taken at close range, or with a telescopic lens. **2.** A close look or view.

clo·sure (klō/zhər) *n.* **1.** A closing or shutting up. **2.** That which closes or shuts. **3.** An end; conclusion. **4.** Cloture. — *v.t. & v.i.* **·sured, ·sur·ing** To cloture. [< OF < L *claudere* to close]

clot (klot) *n.* A thick, viscid, or coagulated mass, as of blood. — *v.t. & v.i.* **·ted, ·ting** To form into clots; coagulate. [OE *clott* lump, mass] — **clot/ty** *adj.*

cloth (klôth, kloth) *n. pl.* **cloths** (klôthz, klothz, klôths, kloths) **1.** A woven, knitted, or felted fabric of wool, cotton, rayon, etc.; also, a piece of such fabric. **2.** A piece of cloth for a special use, as a tablecloth. **3.** Professional attire, esp. of the clergy. — **the cloth** The clergy. [OE *clāth*]

clothe (klōth) *v.t.* **clothed** or **clad, cloth·ing 1.** To cover or provide with clothes; dress. **2.** To cover as if with clothing; invest. [Fusion of OE *clāthian* and *clǣthan*]

clothes (klōz, klōthz) *n.pl.* **1.** Garments; clothing. **2.** Bedclothes. [OE *clāthas,* pl. of *clāth* cloth]

clothes·horse (klōz/hôrs/, klōthz/-) *n.* **1.** A frame on which to hang or dry clothes. **2.** *U.S. Slang* A person regarded as excessively concerned with dress.

clothes·line (klōz/līn, klōthz/-) *n.* A cord, rope, or wire on which to hang clothes to dry.

clothes·pin (klōz/pin/, klōthz/-) *n.* A forked peg or clamp with which to fasten clothes on a line.

clothes·press (klōz/pres/, klōthz/-) *n.* A closet; wardrobe.

cloth·ier (klōth/yər) *n.* One who makes or sells cloth or clothing.

cloth·ing (klō/thing) *n.* **1.** Dress collectively; apparel. **2.** A covering.

Clo·tho (klō/thō) One of the three Fates.

clot·ty (klot/ē) *adj.* **1.** Full of clots. **2.** Tending to clot.

clo·ture (klō/chər) *n.* A parliamentary device to stop debate in a legislative body in order to secure a vote. — *v.t.* To stop (debate) by cloture. Also *closure.* [< F *clôture*]

cloud (kloud) *n.* **1.** A mass of visible vapor or an aggregation of watery or icy particles floating in the atmosphere. **2.** Any visible collection of particles in the air, as steam, smoke, or dust. **3.** A cloudlike mass of things in motion, esp. in flight: a *cloud* of gnats. **4.** Something that darkens, obscures, or threatens. **5.** A dimness or milkiness, as in glass or liquids. — **in the clouds 1.** In the realm of the unreal or fanciful. **2.** Impractical. — **under a cloud 1.** Overshadowed by reproach or distrust. **2.** Troubled or depressed. — *v.t.* **1.** To cover with or as with clouds; dim; obscure. **2.** To render gloomy or troubled. **3.** To disgrace; sully, as a reputation. **4.** To mark with different colors; variegate. — *v.i.* **5.** To become overcast: often with *up* or *over.* [OE *clūd* rocky mass, hill] — **cloud/less** *adj.*

cloud·burst (kloud/bûrst/) *n.* A sudden, heavy downpour.

cloud chamber *Physics* An enclosed receptacle containing air or gas saturated with water vapor whose sudden cooling indicates the presence of ions by the tracks of water droplets they produce: also called *fog chamber, Wilson Cloud Chamber.*

cloud·y (klou/dē) *adj.* **cloud·i·er, cloud·i·est 1.** Overspread with clouds. **2.** Of or like a cloud or clouds. **3.** Marked with cloudlike spots. **4.** Not limpid or clear. **5.** Obscure; vague; confused: *cloudy* thinking. **6.** Full of foreboding; gloomy. [OE *clūdig*] — **cloud/i·ly** *adv.* — **cloud/i·ness** *n.*

clout (klout) *n.* **1.** *Informal* A heavy blow or cuff with the hand. **2.** In baseball slang, a long hit. **3.** In archery, the center of a target, or a shot that strikes it. **4.** A type of flatheaded nail: also **clout nail.** — *v.t. Informal* To hit or strike, as with the hand. [OE *clūt*]

clove (klōv) *n.* A dried flower bud of a tree of the myrtle family, used as a spice. [< OF < L *clavus* nail]

clove hitch *Naut.* A knot consisting of two half hitches, with the ends of the rope going in opposite directions, used for fastening a rope around a spar. For illustration see HITCH.

clo·ven (klō/vən) Alternative past participle of CLEAVE[1]. — *adj.* Parted; split.

cloven-hoofed (klō/vən-hōōft/, -hōōft/) *adj.* **1.** Having the foot cleft, as cattle. **2.** Satanic. Also **clo/ven-foot/ed.**

clo·ver (klō/vər) *n.* Any of several plants having dense flower heads and trifoliolate leaves; esp., the **red clover,** used for forage and adopted as the State flower of Vermont. — **in clover** In a prosperous condition. [OE *clāfre* trefoil]

clo·ver·leaf (klō/vər·lēf/) *n. pl.* **·leafs** A type of intersection resembling a four-leaf clover, in which two highways crossing at different levels are connected by curving ramps.

clown (kloun) *n.* **1.** A professional buffoon in a play or circus, who entertains by jokes, tricks, etc.; a zany; jester. **2.** A coarse or vulgar person; boor. — *v.i.* To behave like a clown. [Earlier *cloune* < MLG] — **clown/er·y** *n.* — **clown/ish** *adj.* — **clown/ish·ly** *adv.* — **clown/ish·ness** *n.*

cloy (kloi) *v.t.* **1.** To gratify beyond desire; surfeit. — *v.i.* **2.** To cause a feeling of surfeit. [< OF < LL < L *clavus* a nail] — **cloy/ing·ly** *adv.* — **cloy/ing·ness** *n.*

club[1] (klub) *n.* **1.** A stout stick or staff; a cudgel. **2.** A stick or bat used in games to strike a ball; esp., a stick with a curved head used in golf. **3.** In card games: **a** A black marking on a playing card, shaped like a three-leaf clover. **b** A card so marked. **c** *pl.* The suit so marked. — *v.t.* **clubbed, club·bing** *v.t.* To beat, as with a club. [< ON *klubba*]

club[2] (klub) *n.* **1.** A group of persons organized for some mutual aim or pursuit, esp. a group that meets regularly. **2.** A house or room reserved for the meetings of such an organization. — *v.* **clubbed, club·bing** *v.t.* **1.** To contribute for a common purpose: to *club* resources. — *v.i.* **2.** To combine or unite: often with *together.* [Special use of CLUB[1]]

club car A railroad passenger car furnished with easy chairs, tables, a buffet or bar, etc.

club·foot (klub/fŏŏt/) *n. pl.* **·feet** *Pathol.* **1.** Congenital distortion of the foot: also called *talipes.* **2.** A foot so affected. — **club/foot/ed** *adj.*

club·house (klub/hous/) *n.* **1.** The building occupied by a club. **2.** Dressing rooms for an athletic team.

club moss A perennial evergreen herb allied to the ferns.

club sandwich A sandwich consisting of three slices of toast and layers of various meats, lettuce, tomatoes, etc.

club steak A small beefsteak cut from the loin.

club topsail *Naut.* A gaff topsail, extended at its foot by a small spar. For illus. see SCHOONER.

cluck (kluk) *v.i.* **1.** To give the low, guttural cry of a hen calling her chicks. **2.** To utter any similar sound, as in urging a horse. — *v.t.* **3.** To call by clucking. **4.** To express with a like sound: to *cluck* disapproval. — *n.* The sound of clucking. [OE *cloccian;* imit.]

clue (klōō) *n.* Something that leads to the solution of a problem or mystery. — *v.t.* **clued, clu·ing 1.** To clew. **2.** *U.S. Informal* To give (someone) information. [Var. of CLEW]

clump (klump) *n.* **1.** A thick cluster: a *clump* of bushes. **2.** A heavy, dull sound, as of tramping. **3.** An irregular mass; a lump. — *v.i.* **1.** To walk clumsily and noisily. **2.** To form clumps. — *v.t.* **3.** To place or plant in a clump. [Var. of CLUB[1]] — **clump/y, clump/ish** *adj.*

clum·sy (klum/zē) *adj.* **·si·er, ·si·est 1.** Lacking dexterity, ease, or grace. **2.** Ungainly or unwieldy. **3.** Ill-contrived: a *clumsy* excuse. [< obs. *clumse* to be numb with cold] — **clum/si·ly** *adv.* — **clum/si·ness** *n.*

clung (klung) Past tense and past participle of CLING.

clus·ter (klus/tər) *n.* **1.** A collection of objects of the same kind growing or fastened together. **2.** A number of persons or things close together; group. — *v.t. & v.i.* To grow or form into a cluster or clusters. [OE *clyster*] — **clus/tered** *adj.* — **clus/ter·y** *adj.*

clutch[1] (kluch) *v.t.* **1.** To snatch, as with hands or talons. **2.** To grasp and hold firmly. — *v.i.* **3.** To attempt to seize, snatch, or reach: with *at:* He *clutched* at her hand. — *n.* **1.** A tight grip; grasp. **2.** *pl.* Power or control: in the *clutches* of the police. **3.** *Mech.* **a** Any of a number of devices for coupling two working parts, as the engine and driveshaft of an automobile. **b** A lever or pedal for operating such a device. **4.** A contrivance for gripping and holding. [ME *clucchen*]

clutch[2] (kluch) *n.* **1.** The number of eggs laid at one time. **2.** A brood of chickens. — *v.t.* To hatch. [< ON *klekja* hatch]

clut·ter (klut/ər) *n.* **1.** A disordered state or collection; litter. **2.** A clatter. — *v.t.* **1.** To litter, heap, or pile in a confused manner. — *v.i.* **2.** To make a clatter. [Var. of earlier *clotter*]

Clydes·dale (klīdz/dāl) *n.* A breed of draft horses originating in the valley of the Clyde, Scotland.

clyp·e·ate (klip/ē-āt) *adj.* Shield-shaped. Also **clyp·e·i·form** (klip/ē-ə-fôrm/). Also **clyp/e·at/ed.**

clys·ter (klis/tər) *n. Med.* An enema. [< OF < Gk. *klyster* < *klyzein* to wash out, rinse]

Cly·tem·nes·tra (klī/təm·nes/trə) The wife of Agamemnon, daughter of Leda. See ORESTES. Also **Cly/taem·nes/tra.**

co-[1] *prefix* With; together; joint or jointly; equally: used with verbs, nouns, adjectives, and adverbs. [< L *co-* var. of *com-* before *gn, h,* and vowels < *cum* with]

Following is a list of self-explanatory words containing the prefix *co-*:

coadminister	codefendant	co-owner
coadministrator	coeditor	copartner
coambassador	coheir	copassionate
coarrange	coinvolve	copatron
coauthor	co-oblige	coreign

co-² *prefix* **1.** *Math.* Of the complement: *cosine.* **2.** *Astron.* Complement of. [< L *complementum* complement]

coach (kōch) *n.* **1.** A large, four-wheeled closed carriage. **2.** A passenger bus. **3.** Air coach (which see). **4.** A railroad passenger car; esp., one having only seats and offering the cheapest travel. **5.** A private tutor. **6.** A trainer or director in athletics, dramatics, etc. — *v.t.* **1.** To tutor or train; act as coach to. — *v.i.* **2.** To study with or be trained by a coach. **3.** To act as coach. **4.** To ride or drive in a coach. [< MF < Hung. *kocsi* (*szeker*) (wagon) of Kocs, the village where first used]

coach-and-four (kōch′ən·fôr′, -fōr′) *n.* A coach drawn by four horses.

coach dog A Dalmatian.

coach·man (kōch′mən) *n. pl.* **·men** (-mən) One who drives a coach.

co·ad·ju·tant (kō·aj′ŏŏ·tənt) *adj.* Cooperating. — *n.* An assistant or co-worker. [< CO-¹ + L *adjutare* to help]

co·ad·ju·tor (kō·aj′ŏŏ·tər, kō′ə·jōō′tər) *n.* **1.** An assistant or co-worker. **2.** A bishop who assists a diocesan bishop.

co·ae·val (kō·ē′vəl) See COEVAL.

co·ag·u·la·ble (kō·ag′yə·lə·bəl) *adj.* Capable of being coagulated. — **co·ag′u·la·bil′i·ty** *n.*

co·ag·u·lant (kō·ag′yə·lənt) *n.* A coagulating agent, as rennet. [< L *coagulare* to curdle]

co·ag·u·late (kō·ag′yə·lāt) *v.t. & v.i.* **·lat·ed, ·lat·ing** To change from a liquid into a clot or jelly, as blood. [< L *coagulare* to curdle] — **co·ag′u·la′tion** *n.* — **co·ag′u·la′tive** *adj.* — **co·ag′u·la′tor** *n.*

coal (kōl) *n.* **1.** A dark brown to black, combustible mineral produced by the carbonization of prehistoric vegetation, found in beds or veins in the earth and used as fuel and a source of hydrocarbons. **2.** A piece of coal. **3.** A glowing or charred fragment of wood or other fuel; an ember. — **to carry coals to Newcastle** To provide something already in abundant supply. — **to haul** (**rake**, etc.) **over the coals** To criticize severely; reprimand. — *v.t.* **1.** To supply with coal. — *v.i.* **2.** To take on coal. [OE *col*]

Coal may appear as a combining form or as the first element in two-word phrases as in: **coalbin, coal-burning, coal dust, coal mine, coal-producing.**

co·a·lesce (kō′ə·les′) *v.i.* **·lesced, ·lesc·ing** To grow or come together into one; blend. [< L *co-* together + *alescere* to grow up] — **co′a·les′cence** *n.* — **co′a·les′cent** *adj.*

coal gas 1. The poisonous gas produced by the combustion of coal. **2.** A gas used for illuminating and heating, produced by the distillation of bituminous coal.

co·a·li·tion (kō′ə·lish′ən) *n.* **1.** An alliance of persons, parties, or states. **2.** A fusion into one mass. [< L < *co-* together + *alescere* to grow up] — **co′a·li′tion·ist** *n.*

coal oil 1. Kerosene. **2.** Crude petroleum.

coal·scut·tle (kōl′skut′l) *n.* A bucketlike container in which coal may be kept or carried. Also **coal hod.**

coal tar A black, viscid liquid produced in the distillation of bituminous coal, yielding a variety of compounds used in making dyestuffs, drugs, plastics, etc. — **coal′-tar′** *adj.*

coam·ing (kō′ming) *n.* A curb about a hatchway or skylight, to keep water from entering. [Origin unknown]

coarse (kôrs, kōrs) *adj.* **1.** Lacking refinement; vulgar; low. **2.** Inferior; base; common. **3.** Composed of large parts or particles; not fine in texture. [Adjectival use of COURSE, meaning usual, ordinary] — **coarse′ly** *adv.* — **coarse′ness** *n.*

coarse-grained (kôrs′grānd′, kōrs′-) *adj.* **1.** Having a coarse grain or texture. **2.** Not delicate or refined; crude.

coars·en (kôr′sən, kōr′-) *v.t. & v.i.* To make or become coarse.

coast (kōst) *n.* **1.** The land next to the sea; the seashore. **2.** A slope suitable for sliding, as on a sled; also, a slide down it. — **Syn.** See SHORE¹. — **the Coast** *U.S.* That part of the United States bordering on the Pacific Ocean. — **the coast is clear** There is no danger or difficulty now. — *v.i.* **1.** To slide down a slope by force of gravity alone, as on a sled. **2.** To continue moving on acquired momentum alone. **3.** To sail along a coast. — *v.t.* **4.** To sail along, as a coast; skirt. [< OF < L *costa* rib, flank] — **coast′al** *adj.*

coast·er (kōs′tər) *n.* **1.** One who or that which coasts, as a person or vessel engaged in the coasting trade. **2.** A sled or toboggan. **3.** A small disk of glass, metal, etc., set under a drinking glass to protect the surface beneath.

coaster brake A clutchlike brake on a bicycle, operated by reversing the pressure on the pedals.

coast guard Naval or military coastal patrol and police. — **United States Coast Guard** A force set up to protect life and property at sea and to enforce customs, immigration, and navigation laws, operating under the Department of the Treasury.

coast·line (kōst′līn′) *n.* The contour or boundary of a coast.

coast·ward (kōst′wərd) *adj.* Directed or facing toward the coast. — *adv.* Toward the coast: also **coast′wards.**

coast·wise (kōst′wīz′) *adj.* Following, or along the coast. — *adv.* Along the coast: also **coast′ways′** (-wāz′).

coat (kōt) *n.* **1.** A sleeved outer garment, as the jacket of a suit, or an overcoat or topcoat. **2.** A natural covering or integument, as the fur of an animal, the rind of a melon, etc. **3.** Any layer covering a surface, as paint, ice, etc. — *v.t.* **1.** To cover with a surface layer, as of paint. **2.** To provide with a coat. [< OF *cote*] — **coat′ed** *adj.* — **coat′less** *adj.*

co·a·ti (kō·ä′tē) *n. pl.* **·tis** (-tēz) A small, carnivorous, raccoonlike mammal of tropical America, with a mobile snout and plantigrade feet. Also **co·a′ti·mon′di** (-mun′dē), **co·a′ti·mun′di** (-mun′dē). [< Tupi]

coat·ing (kō′ting) *n.* **1.** A covering layer; coat. **2.** Cloth for coats.

coat of arms 1. A shield marked with the insignia of a person or family. **2.** A representation of such insignia.

coat of mail *pl.* **coats of mail** A defensive garment made of chain mail; a hauberk.

coat·tail (kōt′tāl′) *n.* The loose, back part of a coat below the waist; also, either half of this in a coat split at the back.

coax (kōks) *v.t.* **1.** To persuade or seek to persuade by gentleness, tact, flattery, etc.; wheedle. **2.** To obtain by coaxing: to *coax* a promise from someone. — *v.i.* **3.** To use persuasion or cajolery. — *n.* One who coaxes. [< earlier *cokes* a fool, dupe] — **coax′er** *n.* — **coax′ing·ly** *adv.*

co·ax·i·al (kō·ak′sē·əl) *adj.* **1.** Having a common axis or coincident axes. Also **co·ax·al** (kō·ak′səl). **2.** Describing a cable consisting of two or more insulated conductors capable of transmitting radio or television signals or multiple telegraph or telephone messages.

cob (kob) *n.* **1.** A corncob. **2.** A male swan. **3.** A thickset horse with short legs. **4.** A lump. [ME *cobbe*]

co·balt (kō′bôlt) *n.* A tough, lustrous, pinkish gray, metallic element (symbol Co), used as an alloy and in pigments. See ELEMENT. [< G *kobalt*, var. of *kobold* goblin] — **co·bal′tic** *adj.* — **co·bal′tous** *adj.*

cobalt blue 1. A permanent, deep blue pigment, made from oxides of cobalt and aluminum. **2.** An intense blue.

cob·ble¹ (kob′əl) *n.* A cobblestone. — *v.t.* **·bled, ·bling** To pave with cobblestones. [Akin to COB¹]

cob·ble² (kob′əl) *v.t.* **·bled, ·bling 1.** To repair, as shoes. **2.** To put together roughly. [Origin uncertain]

cob·bler¹ (kob′lər) *n.* One who patches boots and shoes.

cob·bler² (kob′lər) *n.* **1.** An iced drink made of wine, sugar, fruit juices, etc. **2.** *U.S.* A deep-dish fruit pie with no bottom crust. [Origin unknown]

cob·ble·stone (kob′əl·stōn′) *n.* A naturally rounded stone, formerly used for paving.

cob coal Coal in large, round lumps.

co·bel·lig·er·ent (kō′bə·lij′ər·ənt) *n.* A country waging war in cooperation with another or others.

co·bra (kō′brə) *n.* A venomous snake of Asia and Africa that when excited can dilate its neck into a broad hood; esp., the **spectacled cobra** of India, and the **king cobra.** [< Pg. < L *colubra* snake]

cob·web (kob′web′) *n.* **1.** The network of fine thread spun by a spider; also, a single thread of this. **2.** Something like a cobweb in flimsiness, or in its ability to ensnare. — *v.t.* **·webbed, ·web·bing** To cover with or as with cobwebs. [ME *coppeweb* < *coppe* spider + WEB] — **cob′web′by** *adj.*

co·ca (kō′kə) *n.* **1.** The dried leaves of a South American shrub, yielding cocaine and other alkaloids. **2.** The shrub itself. [< Sp. < Quechua]

co·caine (kō·kān′, kō′kān; *in technical usage* kō′kə·ēn) *n.* A bitter, crystalline alkaloid, $C_{17}H_{21}NO_4$, contained in coca leaves, used as a local anesthetic and as a narcotic. Also **co·cain′, co·cain′.** [< COCA + -INE²]

cocci- *combining form* Berry; berry-shaped. [< Gk. *kokkos* berry, seed]

coc·coid (kok′oid) *adj. Bacteriol.* Like a coccus, as certain forms of bacteria.

coc·cus (kok′əs) *n. pl.* **coc·ci** (kok′sī) *Bacteriol.* One of the principal forms of bacteria, characterized by an ovoid or spherical shape. [< NL < Gk. *kokkos* berry]

-coccus *combining form* Berry-shaped. [< Gk. *kokkos* berry, seed]

coc·cyx (kok′siks) *n. pl.* **coc·cy·ges** (kok·sī′jēz) *Anat.* The small triangular bone consisting of four or five rudimentary vertebrae at the caudal end of the spine. For illus. see PELVIS. [< L < Gk. *kokkyx* cuckoo; from a fancied resemblance to a cuckoo's bill] — **coc·cyg·e·al** (kok·sij′ē·əl) *adj.*

coch·i·neal (koch′ə·nēl′, koch′ə·nēl′) *n.* A brilliant scarlet dye prepared from the dried bodies of the female of a scale insect of tropical America and Java. [< F < Sp. < L < Gk. *kokkos*]

COBRA

a Indian or spectacled cobra.
b Markings or "spectacles" on back of head. (To 6 feet long)

coch·le·a (kok′lē·ə)   *n.*   *pl.* **·le·ae** (-li·ē)   *Anat.* A spirally wound tube in the internal ear, forming an essential part of the mechanism of hearing. For illus. see EAR. [< L, snail] — **coch′le·ar** *adj.*

coch·le·ate (kok′lē·āt)   *adj.* Spirally twisted like a snail shell. Also **coch′le·at′ed.**

cock[1] (kok)   *n.* **1.** A full-grown male of the domestic fowl; a rooster. **2.** Any male bird. **3.** A leader; champion. **4.** A faucet, often with the nozzle bent downward. **5.** In a firearm, the hammer; also, the condition of readiness for firing. **6.** A significant jaunty tip or upward turn, as of a hat brim. — *v.t.* **1.** To set the mechanism of (a firearm) so as to be ready for firing. **2.** To turn up or to one side alertly, jauntily, or inquiringly, as the head, eye, ears, etc. **3.** To bring to a position of readiness. — *v.i.* **4.** To cock a firearm. **5.** To stick up prominently. — *adj.* Male. [OE *cocc*]

cock[2] (kok)   *n.* A conical pile of straw or hay. — *v.t.* To arrange in piles or cocks, as hay. [< ON *kökkr* lump, heap]

cock·ade (kok·ād′)   *n.* A knot of ribbon, or the like, worn on the hat as a badge. [< MF *coq* cock] — **cock·ad′ed** *adj.*

Cockade State Nickname of Maryland.

cock·a·too (kok′ə·too′, kok′ə·too)   *n.*   *pl.* **·toos** Any of various brightly colored, crested parrots of the East Indies or Australia. [< Du. < Malay *kakatūa*]

cock·a·trice (kok′ə·tris)   *n.* A fabulous serpent, said to be hatched from a cock's egg, deadly to those who felt its breath or met its glance. [< OF *cocatris* (infl. by *coq* cock)]

cock·boat (kok′bōt)   *n.* A ship's small rowboat: also called **cockle boat.** [< obs. *cock* (< MF *coque* small boat) + BOAT]

cock·chaf·er (kok′chā′fər)   *n.* A large European beetle destructive to vegetation. [< COCK[1] (def. 3) + CHAFER]

cock·crow (kok′krō′)   *n.* Early morning. Also **cock′crow′·ing.**

cocked hat (kokt) A hat with the brim turned up, esp. in three places; a tricorn. — **to knock into a cocked hat** To demolish; ruin.

cock·er·el (kok′ər·əl)   *n.* A cock less than a year old.

cock·er spaniel (kok′ər) A small, sturdy spaniel of solid or variegated coloring, used for hunting and as a house pet. Also **cocker.** [? Because used in hunting woodcock]

cock·eye (kok′ī)   *n.* A squinting eye.

cock·eyed (kok′īd′)   *adj.* **1.** Cross-eyed. **2.** *Slang* Off center; askew. **3.** *Slang* Absurd; ridiculous. **4.** *Slang* Drunk.

cock·fight (kok′fīt′)   *n.* A fight between gamecocks that are usually fitted with steel spurs. — **cock′fight′ing** *adj. & n.*

cock·horse (kok′hôrs′)   *n.* A rocking horse or hobbyhorse.

cock·le[1] (kok′əl)   *n.* **1.** A European bivalve mollusk, esp. an edible species, with ridged, somewhat heart-shaped shells. **2.** Any of various similar mollusks. **3.** A cockleshell. **4.** A wrinkle; pucker. — **the cockles of one's heart** The depths of one's heart or feelings. — *v.t. & v.i.* **·led, ·ling** To wrinkle; pucker. [< F < L < Gk. *konchē* a shell, mussel]

cock·le[2] (kok′əl)   *n.* A weed that grows among grain, as the darnel. [OE *coccel*]

cock·le·bur (kok′əl·bûr′)   *n.* **1.** A coarse, branching weed having burs about an inch long. **2.** The burdock.

cock·le·shell (kok′əl·shel′)   *n.* **1.** The shell of a cockle. **2.** A scallop shell. **3.** A frail, light boat. [< COCKLE[1] + SHELL]

cock·ney (kok′nē)   *n.* **1.** *Often cap.* A resident of the East End of London. **2.** The dialect or accent of East End Londoners: also **cock′ney·ese′** (-ēz′, -ēs′). — *adj.* Of or like cockneys or their speech. [ME *cokeney*, lit., a pampered child, a soft person, a city man] — **cock′ney·ish** *adj.*

cock·ney·ism (kok′nē·iz′əm)   *n.* A mannerism, idiom, or way of speaking peculiar to cockneys.

cock·pit (kok′pit′)   *n.* **1.** A compartment in the fuselage of some small airplanes, where the pilot and copilot sit. **2.** A pit or ring for cockfighting. **3.** *Naut.* In small vessels, a space toward the stern lower than the rest of the deck.

cock·roach (kok′rōch′)   *n.* Any of a large group of swift-running, chiefly nocturnal insects, many of which are household pests. [< Sp. *cucaracha*]

cocks·comb (koks′kōm′)   *n.* **1.** The comb of a cock. **2.** A plant with showy red or yellowish flowers. **3.** A coxcomb.

cock·spur (kok′spûr′)   *n.* **1.** A spur on the leg of a cock. **2.** A kind of hawthorn with long thorns.

cock·sure (kok′shoor′)   *adj.* **1.** Absolutely sure. **2.** Overly self-confident; presumptuously sure. — **cock′sure′ness** *n.*

cock·swain (kok′sən, -swān′)   See COXSWAIN.

cock·tail (kok′tāl′)   *n.* **1.** Any of various chilled alcoholic drinks, consisting usu. of brandy, whisky, gin, etc., mixed with other liquors, fruit juice, etc. **2.** An appetizer, as chilled diced fruits, fruit juices, or seafood seasoned with sauce. [? Alter. of F *coquetel*]

cock·y (kok′ē)   *adj.* **cock·i·er, cock·i·est** *Informal* Pertly or swaggeringly self-confident; conceited. — **cock′i·ly** *adv.* — **cock′i·ness** *n.*

co·co (kō′kō)   *n.*   *pl.* **·cos 1.** The coconut palm. **2.** The fruit of the coconut palm. — *adj.* Made of the fiber of the coconut. [< Pg., grinning face]

co·coa (kō′kō)   *n.* **1.** A powder made from the roasted, husked seed kernels of the cacao; chocolate. **2.** A beverage made from this. **3.** A reddish brown color. [Alter. of CACAO]

cocoa butter A fatty substance obtained from cacoa seeds, used for making soap, cosmetics, etc.: also called *cacao butter.*

co·co·nut (kō′kə·nut′, -nət)   *n.* The fruit of the coconut palm, having white meat enclosed in a hard shell, and containing a milky liquid. Also **co′coa·nut′.**

coconut milk The milky fluid within the fresh coconut.

coconut oil The oil derived from the dried meat of the coconut, used in soaps, foodstuffs, etc.

coconut palm A tropical palm tree bearing coconuts. Also **coco palm, coconut tree.**

co·coon (kə·koon′)   *n.* The envelope spun by the larvae of certain insects, in which they are enclosed in the pupal or chrysalis state. [< F *coque* shell]

cod (kod)   *n.*   *pl.* **cod** or **cods** An important food fish of the North Atlantic. [Origin unknown]

co·da (kō′də)   *n.*   *Music* A passage at the end of a composition or movement that brings it to a formal, complete close. [< Ital. < L *cauda* tail]

cod·dle (kod′l)   *v.t.* **·dled, ·dling 1.** To boil gently; simmer in water. **2.** To treat as a baby or an invalid; pamper. [? Akin to CAUDLE] — **cod′dler** *n.*

code (kōd)   *n.* **1.** A systematized body of law. **2.** Any system of principles or regulations. **3.** A set of signals, characters, or symbols used in communication. **4.** A set of words, letters, or numerals, used for secrecy or brevity in transmitting messages. — *v.t.* **cod·ed, cod·ing 1.** To systematize, as laws; make a digest of. **2.** To put into the symbols of a code. [< F < L *codex* writing tablet]

co·deine (kō′dēn, kō′di·ēn)   *n.*   *Chem.* A white crystalline alkaloid, $C_{18}H_{21}NO_3$, derived from morphine and used in medicine as a mild narcotic. Also **co·de·in** (kō′dē·in, kō′dēn), **co·de·ia** (kō·dē′ə). [< Gk. *kōdeia* head of a poppy + -INE[2]]

co·dex (kō′deks)   *n.*   *pl.* **co·di·ces** (kō′də·sēz, kod′ə-) An ancient manuscript volume, as of Scripture. [< L, tablet]

codg·er (koj′ər)   *n. Informal* An eccentric or testy man, esp. an old one. [Prob. var. of *cadger*]

cod·i·cil (kod′ə·səl)   *n.* **1.** *Law* A supplement to a will, changing or explaining something in it. **2.** An appendix; addition. [< L *codex* writing tablet] — **cod·i·cil·la·ry** (kod′ə·sil′ər·ē) *adj.*

cod·i·fy (kod′ə·fī, kō′də-)   *v.t.* **·fied, ·fy·ing** To systematize, as laws. [< F *code* system, code] — **cod′i·fi·ca′tion** *n.* — **cod′i·fi′er** *n.*

cod·ling[1] (kod′ling)   *n.*   *pl.* **·lings** (*Rare* **·ling**) **1.** A young cod. **2.** Any of certain related fishes. [Dim. of COD[1]]

cod·ling[2] (kod′ling)   *n.* **1.** One of a variety of elongated tapering cooking apples. **2.** Any hard, unripe apple for stewing. Also **cod·lin** (kod′lin). [ME *querdling*]

codling moth A moth whose larvae feed on apples, pears, quinces, etc. Also **codlin moth.**

cod-liver oil (kod′liv′ər, kod′liv′ər) Oil from the livers of cod, used in medicine as a source of vitamins A and D.

co·ed (kō′ed′)   *Informal n.* A woman student at a coeducational institution. — *adj.* Coeducational. Also **co′-ed′.**

co·ed·u·ca·tion (kō′ej·oo·kā′shən)   *n.* The education of both sexes in the same school. — **co′ed·u·ca′tion·al** *adj.*

co·ef·fi·cient (kō′ə·fish′ənt)   *n.* **1.** *Math.* A number or letter put before an algebraic expression and multiplying it. **2.** *Physics* A number indicating the kind and amount of change in a substance, body, or process under given conditions. — *adj.* Acting together.

coe·la·canth (sē′lə·kanth)   *n. Zool.* A large-bodied, hollow-spined fish, extinct except for one species. [< COEL(O)- + Gk. *akantha* spine]

-coele Var. of -CELE[2].

coe·len·ter·ate (si·len′tə·rāt)   *Zool. n.* Any of a phylum of invertebrate animals having a large body cavity that functions as a vascular as well as a digestive system, including sea anemones, corals, jellyfish, and hydras. — *adj.* Belonging or pertaining to this phylum. [< COEL(O)- + Gk. *enteron* intestine] — **coe·len·ter·ic** (sē′len·ter′ik) *adj.*

COELACANTH (4 to 5½ feet long)

coe·li·ac (sē′lē·ak)   See CELIAC.

coelo- *combining form* Cavity; cavity of the body, or of an organ. Also, before vowels, **coel-.** [< Gk. *koilos* hollow]

coe·lom (sē′ləm)   *n. Zool.* The body cavity of a metazoan, between the viscera and the body wall: also spelled *celom.* Also **coe·lome** (sē′lōm). [< Gk. *koilōma* cavity]

coeno- See CENO-.

coe·no·bite (sen′ə·bīt, sē′nə-)   See CENOBITE.

co·e·qual (kō·ē′kwəl)   *adj.* Of the same value, age, size, etc. — *n.* The equal of another or others.

co·erce (kō-ûrs′) *v.t.* **·erced, ·erc·ing** **1.** To compel by force, law, authority, or fear. **2.** To restrain or repress by superior force. **3.** To bring about by forcible measures: to *coerce* compliance. [< L < co- together + *arcere* to shut up, restrain] **— co·er′cer** *n.* **— co·er′ci·ble** *adj.*

co·er·cion (kō-ûr′shən) *n.* **1.** Forcible constraint or restraint, moral or physical. **2.** Government by force. **— co·er·cion·ar·y** (kō-ûr′shən-er′ē) *adj.* **— co·er′cion·ist** *n.*

co·er·cive (kō-ûr′siv) *adj.* Serving or tending to coerce. **— co·er′cive·ly** *adv.* **— co·er′cive·ness** *n.*

co·e·val (kō-ē′vəl) *adj.* **1.** Of or belonging to the same age, time, or duration. **2.** Contemporary. **—** *n.* **1.** One of the same age. **2.** A contemporary. Also spelled *coaeval*. [< L < co- together + *aevum* age] **— co·e′val·ly** *adv.*

co·ex·ist (kō′ig-zist′) *v.i.* To exist together, in or at the same place or time. **— co′ex·ist′ence** *n.* **— co′ex·ist′ent** *adj.*

co·ex·tend (kō′ik-stend′) *v.t. & v.i.* To extend through the same space or time. [< CO-1 + EXTEND] **— co′ex·ten′sion** *n.* **— co′ex·ten′sive** *adj.* **— co′ex·ten′sive·ly** *adv.*

cof·fee (kôf′ē, kof′ē) *n.* **1.** A beverage made from the roasted and ground beans of a tropical evergreen shrub. **2.** The seeds or beans of this shrub: also **coffee beans**. **3.** The shrub itself, native to Asia and Africa and widely grown in Brazil. **4.** The brown color of coffee with cream. [< Ital. < Turkish < Arabic *qahwah*]

coffee break *U.S.* A short recess from work during which coffee or other refreshments are taken.

coffee cake A kind of cake to be eaten with coffee, often containing raisins or nuts and topped with sugar or icing.

coffee house A public room where coffee is the main beverage. Also **cof·fee·house** (kôf′ē·hous′, kof′ē-).

coffee shop A restaurant or public room where coffee and food are served. Also **coffee room**.

coffee table A low table, generally placed in front of a sofa, for serving refreshments, etc.

cof·fer (kôf′ər, kof′-) *n.* **1.** A chest or box, esp. one for valuables. **2.** *pl.* Financial resources; a treasury. **3.** A decorative, sunken panel in a ceiling, dome, etc. **4.** A lock in a canal. **5.** A cofferdam. **—** *v.t.* **1.** To place in a coffer. **2.** To adorn with coffers. [< F < L < Gk. *kophinos* basket]

cof·fer·dam (kôf′ər-dam, kof′-) *n.* **1.** A temporary enclosure built in the water and pumped dry to permit work on bridge piers and the like. **2.** A watertight structure attached to a ship's side for repairs made below the water line.

cof·fin (kôf′in, kof′-) *n.* A box or case in which a corpse is buried. **—** *v.t.* To put into or as into a coffin. [< OF < L < Gk. *kophinos* basket]

cog (kog) *n.* **1.** *Mech.* A tooth or one of a series of teeth projecting from the surface of a wheel or gear to impart or receive motion. **2.** One who plays a minor but necessary part in a large or complex process. **3.** A projecting part on the end of a timber, used for forming a joint; tenon. [ME *cogge* < Scand.] **— cogged** *adj.*

co·gent (kō′jənt) *adj.* Compelling belief, assent, or action; forcible; convincing. [< L < *cogere* to compel] **— co′gen·cy** *n.* **— co′gent·ly** *adv.*

cog·i·tate (koj′ə-tāt) *v.t. & v.i.* **·tat·ed, ·tat·ing** To give careful thought (to); ponder; meditate. [< L < co- together + *agitare* to consider] **— cog·i·ta·ble** (koj′ə-tə-bəl) *adj.* **— cog′i·ta·tor** *n.*

— Syn. think, deliberate, reflect, reason, cerebrate.

cog·i·ta·tion (koj′ə-tā′shən) *n.* Careful consideration; reflection; thought.

cog·i·ta·tive (koj′ə-tā′tiv) *adj.* Capable of or given to cogitation. **— cog′i·ta′tive·ly** *adv.* **— cog′i·ta′tive·ness** *n.*

co·gnac (kōn′yak, kon′-) *n.* **1.** Brandy produced in the Cognac region of western France. **2.** Any brandy. [< F]

cog·nate (kog′nāt) *adj.* **1.** Allied by blood; kindred. **2.** Allied by derivation from the same source; belonging to the same stock or root: English "cold" and Latin "gelidus" are *cognate* words. **3.** Allied in characteristics; similar. **—** *n.* A cognate person or thing. [< L < co- together + pp. of (*g*)*nasci* to be born] **— cog·na′tion** *n.*

cog·ni·tion (kog-nish′ən) *n.* **1.** The act or faculty of knowing or perceiving. **2.** A thing known; a perception. **— Syn.** See KNOWLEDGE. [< L < co- together + (*g*)*noscere* to know] **— cog·ni′tion·al** *adj.* **— cog′ni·tive** *adj.*

cog·ni·za·ble (kog′nə-zə-bəl, kon′ə-, kog-nī′zə-bəl) *adj.* **1.** Capable of being known. **2.** Capable of being tried or examined by a court. **— cog′ni·za·bly** *adv.*

cog·ni·zance (kog′nə-zəns, kon′ə-) *n.* **1.** Apprehension or perception of fact; knowledge; notice. **2.** *Law* **a** The hearing of a case by a court. **b** The right of a court to hear a case. **3.** Range or sphere of what can be known. **— to take cognizance of** To acknowledge; recognize; notice. [< OF < L < co- together + pp. of (*g*)*nasci* to be born]

cog·ni·zant (kog′nə-zənt, kon′ə-) *adj.* Having knowledge; aware; with *of*.

cog·nize (kog′nīz) *v.t.* **·nized, ·niz·ing** To know, perceive, or recognize. Also *Brit.* **cog′nise**.

cog·no·men (kog-nō′mən) *n.* *pl.* **·no·mens** or **·nom·i·na** (-nom′ə-nə) **1.** A surname. **2.** In ancient Rome, the last of a citizen's three names. **3.** Loosely, any name, nickname, or appellation. [< L < co- together + (*g*)*nomen* name] **— cog·nom·i·nal** (kog-nom′ə-nəl) *adj.*

cog·wheel (kog′hwēl′) *n.* A wheel with cogs, used to transmit or receive motion: also called *gearwheel*.

co·hab·it (kō-hab′it) *v.i.* To live together as husband and wife, esp. illegally. [< LL < L < co- together + *habitare* to live] **— co·hab′i·tant, co·hab′it·er** *n.* **— co·hab′i·ta′tion** *n.*

co·here (kō-hir′) *v.i.* **·hered, ·her·ing** **1.** To stick or hold firmly together. **2.** To be logically connected, as the parts of a story. [< L < co- together + *haerere* to stick]

co·her·ence (kō-hir′əns) *n.* **1.** A sticking together; conjunction; cohesion. **2.** Logical connection or consistency; congruity: the *coherence* of his thoughts. Also **co·her′en·cy**.

co·her·ent (kō-hir′ənt) *adj.* **1.** Sticking together, as particles of the same substance. **2.** Observing logical order and connection; consistent. **3.** Intelligible or articulate, as speech. **— co·her′ent·ly** *adv.*

co·he·sion (kō-hē′zhən) *n.* **1.** The act or state of cohering. **2.** *Physics* That force by which molecules of the same kind or the same body are held together.

co·he·sive (kō-hē′siv) *adj.* Having or exhibiting cohesion. **— co·he′sive·ly** *adv.* **— co·he′sive·ness** *n.*

co·hort (kō′hôrt) *n.* **1.** The tenth of an ancient Roman legion, 300 to 600 men. **2.** A band or group, esp. of warriors. **3.** A companion or follower. [< L *cohors, cohortis*]

coif (koif) *n.* A close-fitting cap or hood, as that worn by nuns under the veil. **—** *v.t.* To cover with or as with a coif. [< OF < LL *cofea* < Gmc.]

coif·feur (kwä-fœr′) *n.* *French* A hairdresser.

coif·fure (kwä-fyŏŏr′, *Fr.* kwä-für′) *n.* **1.** A style of arranging or dressing the hair. **2.** A headdress. **—** *v.t.* To dress (the hair). Also **coif** (kwäf). [< F < OF *coife*. See COIF.]

coign (koin) *n.* A projecting angle or stone; a corner. Also **coigne**. [Var. of QUOIN]

coil (koil) *n.* **1.** A series of concentric rings or spirals, as that formed by winding a rope. **2.** A single ring or spiral of such a series. **3.** A spiral pipe, or series of pipes, forming a continuous conduit, as in a radiator. **4.** *Electr.* **a** A conductor consisting of a number of turns of wire wound on an insulating coil. **b** An induction coil. **5.** *Canadian* A small stack of hay. **—** *v.t.* **1.** To wind spirally or in rings. **—** *v.i.* **2.** To form rings or coils. [< OF < L < com- together + *legere* to choose] **— coil′er** *n.*

coin (koin) *n.* **1.** A piece of metal stamped by government authority for use as money. **2.** Metal currency collectively. **3.** *Archit.* A corner or angle of a building; quoin. **—** *v.t.* **1.** To stamp (coins) from metal. **2.** To make into coins. **3.** To originate or invent, as a word or phrase. **— to coin money** *Informal* To make money rapidly. [< F, wedge, die < L *cuneus* wedge] **— coin′a·ble** *adj.* **— coin′er** *n.*

coin·age (koi′nij) *n.* **1.** The act or right of making coins. **2.** The coins made; metal money. **3.** The system of coins of a country; currency. **4.** The act of fabricating or inventing anything, esp. a word or phrase. **5.** Something fabricated, as an artificially created word.

co·in·cide (kō′in-sīd′) *v.i.* **·cid·ed, ·cid·ing** **1.** To have the same dimensions and position in space. **2.** To occur at the same time. **3.** To agree exactly; accord. [< MF < Med.L < L co- together + *incidere* to happen]

co·in·ci·dence (kō-in′sə-dəns) *n.* **1.** The fact or condition of coinciding; correspondence. **2.** A remarkable concurrence of events, ideas, etc., apparently by mere chance.

co·in·ci·dent (kō-in′sə-dənt) *adj.* **1.** Having the same position and extent. **2.** Occurring at the same time. **3.** In exact agreement; consonant: with *with*. **— co·in′ci·dent·ly** *adv.*

co·in·ci·den·tal (kō-in′sə-den′təl) *adj.* Characterized by or involving coincidence. **— co·in′ci·den′tal·ly** *adv.*

coir (koir) *n.* Coconut-husk fiber, used in making ropes, matting, etc.: also called *kyar*. [< Malay *kāyar* rope]

co·i·tion (kō-ish′ən) *n.* Sexual intercourse. Also **co·i·tus** (kō′i·təs). [< L < co- together + *ire* to go]

coke (kōk) *n.* A solid, carbonaceous fuel obtained by heating coal in ovens or retorts to remove its gases. **—** *v.t. & v.i.* **coked, cok·ing** To change into coke. [? ME *colke*.]

col-¹ Var. of COM-.

col-² Var. of COLO-.

co·la (kō′lə) A small tropical tree bearing cola nuts: also spelled *kolo*. [< *kola* native African name]

cola nut The seed of the cola, yielding an extract used in the manufacture of soft drinks: also spelled *kola nut*.

col·an·der (kul′ən·dər, kol′-) *n.* A perforated vessel for draining off liquids: also *cullender*. [< L *colare* to strain]

cold (kōld) *adj.* **1.** Having a relatively low temperature; having little or no perceptible heat: a *cold* night. **2.** Having a relatively low temperature as compared with a normal body temperature: *cold* hands. **3.** Feeling no or insufficient warmth; chilled. **4.** Without vital heat; dead. **5.** Detached; objective: *cold* reason. **6.** Lacking in affection. **7.**

Lacking in sexual desire; frigid. **8.** Unfriendly. **9.** Chilling to the spirit; depressing. **10.** *U.S. Informal* Unconscious, as from a blow. **11.** Lacking freshness; stale; old: a *cold* trail. **12.** *Informal* Distant from the object sought: said of a seeker in a game, etc. **13.** In art, bluish in tone. **— cold feet** *Informal* Loss of courage; timidity. **— to throw cold water on** To discourage by being unenthusiastic or indifferent (about something). *— adv. U.S. Slang* Thoroughly; with certainty: to know it *cold*. *— n.* **1.** The comparative lack of heat. **2.** The sensation caused by loss or lack of heat. **3.** An acute infection of the mucous membranes of the upper respiratory tract, caused by a virus, and characterized by sneezing, coughing, etc. **— out in the cold** Ignored; neglected. **— to catch** (or **take**) **cold** To become affected with a cold. [OE *cald*] **—cold/ly** *adv.* **—cold/ness** *n.*
cold-blood·ed (kōld/blud/id) *adj.* **1.** Unsympathetic; heartless. **2.** Sensitive to cold. **3.** *Zool.* Having a blood temperature that varies with the environments, as in reptiles. **—cold/-blood/ed·ly** *adv.* **—cold/-blood/ed·ness** *n.*
cold chisel A chisel of tempered steel for cutting cold metal.
cold cream A cleansing and soothing ointment for the skin.
cold front *Meteorol.* The irregular, forward edge of a cold air mass advancing beneath and against a warmer mass.
cold-heart·ed (kōld/här/tid) *adj.* Without sympathy; unkind. **—cold/heart/ed·ly** *adv.* **—cold/heart/ed·ness** *n.*
cold shoulder *Informal* A deliberate slight.
cold sore An eruption about the mouth or nostrils, often accompanying a cold or fever.
cold turkey *U.S. Slang* **1.** The abrupt and total deprivation of a substance, as a narcotic drug, from one addicted to its use. **2.** Blunt talk, often unwelcome to the listener.
cold war An intense rivalry between nations, as in diplomatic strategy, falling just short of armed conflict.
cold wave *Meteorol.* An unusual drop in temperature; a spell of cold weather, usu. moving along a specified course.
cole (kōl) *n.* A plant related to the cabbage, esp. rape. Also **cole/wort/** (-wûrt). [OE *cāl, cāwl* < L *caulis* cabbage]
co·le·op·ter·ous (kō/lē·op/tər·əs, kol/ē-) *adj.* Belonging to a large order of insects, including the beetles and weevils, having horny front wings that fit as cases over the hind wings. [< NL < Gk. *koleos* sheath + *pteron* wing]
cole·slaw (kōl/slô/) *n.* A salad of shredded raw cabbage. Also **cole slaw.** [< Du *kool sla* cabbage salad]
col·ic (kol/ik) *n.* Acute abdominal pain resulting from muscular spasms. *— adj.* Pertaining to, near, or affecting the colon. [< F < L < Gk. *kolon* colon] **—col/ick·y** *adj.*
-coline Var. of -COLOUS.
col·i·se·um (kol/ə·sē/əm) *n.* A large building or stadium for exhibitions, sports events, etc.: also spelled *colosseum.*
Col·i·se·um (kol/ə·sē/əm) See COLOSSEUM.
co·li·tis (kō·lī/tis) *n. Pathol.* Inflammation of the colon.
col·lab·o·rate (kə·lab/ə·rāt) *v.i.* **·rat·ed, ·rat·ing** **1.** To work or cooperate with another, esp. in literary or scientific pursuits. **2.** To be a collaborationist. [< LL < L *com-* with + *laborare* to work] **—col·la/bo·ra/tion** *n.* **—col·lab/o·ra/tive** *adj.* **—col·lab/o·ra/tor** *n.*
col·lab·o·ra·tion·ist (kə·lab/ə·rā/shən·ist) *n.* A citizen of an occupied country who cooperates with the enemy.
col·lage (kə·läzh/) *n.* An artistic composition consisting of or including flat materials pasted on a picture surface; also, the technique of making such compositions. Compare ASSEMBLAGE (def. 4). [< F, pasting < *colle* glue]
col·lapse (kə·laps/) *v.* **·lapsed, ·laps·ing** *v.i.* **1.** To give way; cave in. **2.** To fail utterly; come to naught. **3.** To assume a more compact form by being folded. **4.** To lose health, strength, etc., suddenly. **5.** To lose all or part of its air content, as a lung. *— v.t.* **6.** To cause to collapse. *— n.* **1.** The act or process of collapsing. **2.** Extreme prostration. **3.** Utter failure; ruin. [< L < *com-* together + *labi* to fall] **—col·laps/i·ble** or **col·laps/a·ble** *adj.* **—col·laps/i·bil/i·ty** *n.*
col·lar (kol/ər) *n.* **1.** The part of a garment at the neck, often folded over. **2.** A band of leather or metal for the neck of an animal. **3.** A cushion placed around the neck of a draft animal to bear most of the strain of the pull. **4.** *Mech.* Any of various devices encircling a rod or shaft, to form a connection, etc. *— v.t.* **1.** To provide with a collar. **2.** To grasp by the collar; capture. [< OF, AF < L *collum* neck]
col·lar·bone (kol/ər·bōn/) *n.* The clavicle.
col·lard (kol/ərd) *n. Usu. pl.* A variety of cabbage that does not form a head. [Alter. of *colewort.* See COLE.]
col·late (kə·lāt/, kol/āt) *v.t.* **·lat·ed, ·lat·ing** **1.** To compare critically, as writings or facts. **2.** In bookbinding, to examine (the gathered sheets to be bound) in order to verify and correct their arrangement. [< L < *com-* together + *ferre* to bear, carry] **—col·la·tor** (kə·lā/tər, kol/ā·tər) *n.*
col·lat·er·al (kə·lat/ər·əl) *adj.* **1.** Lying or running side by side; parallel. **2.** Concomitant. **3.** Tending to the same conclusion; corroborative. **4.** Subordinate; secondary. **5.**

Guaranteed by stocks, bonds, property, etc.: a *collateral* loan. **6.** Descended from a common ancestor, but in a different line. *— n.* **1.** *U.S.* Security pledge for a loan or obligation. **2.** A collateral kinsman. [< Med.L < L *com-* together + *lateralis* lateral] **—col·lat/er·al·ly** *adv.*
collateral adjective An adjective closely related to a given noun in meaning, but not in immediate origin, as *brachial* is to *arm.*
col·la·tion (kə·lā/shən) *n.* **1.** The act or process of collating. **2.** Any light, informal meal. [See COLLATE.]
col·league (kol/ēg) *n.* A fellow member of a profession, official body, etc.; an associate. [< F < L < *com-* together + *legere* to choose] **—col/league·ship** *n.*
col·lect[1] (kə·lekt/) *v.t.* **1.** To gather together; assemble. **2.** To bring together as a hobby: to *collect* stamps. **3.** To request and obtain (payments of money). **4.** To regain control: to *collect* one's wits. *— v.i.* **5.** To assemble or congregate, as people. **6.** To accumulate, as sand or dust. **7.** To gather payments or donations. *— adj. & adv.* To be paid for by the receiver: Send it *collect*; a *collect* call. [< L *collectus*, pp. of *colligere* < *com-* together + *legere* to choose] **—col·lect/a·ble** or **col·lect/i·ble** *adj.*
col·lect[2] (kol/ekt) *n. Eccl.* A short, formal prayer used in several Western liturgies. [See COLLECT[1].]
col·lect·ed (kə·lek/tid) *adj.* Composed; self-possessed. **col·lect/ed·ly** *adv.* **—col·lect/ed·ness** *n.*
col·lec·tion (kə·lek/shən) *n.* **1.** The act or process of collecting. **2.** That which is collected. **3.** That which has accumulated: a *collection* of dirt. **4.** A soliciting of money, as for church expenses; also, the money.
col·lec·tive (kə·lek/tiv) *adj.* **1.** Formed or gathered together by collecting. **2.** Of, relating to, or proceeding from a number of persons or things together. **3.** *Gram.* Denoting in the singular number a collection or aggregate of individuals: a *collective* noun. *— n.* **1.** A collective enterprise or body, as a farm. **2.** The individuals comprising such a body or enterprise. **—col·lec/tive·ly** *adv.* **—col·lec/tive·ness, col·lec·tiv·i·ty** (kol/ek·tiv/ə·tē) *n.*
collective bargaining Negotiation between organized workers and employers on wages, hours, etc.
collective noun *Gram.* A singular noun naming a collection or group. It takes either a singular or a plural verb, depending upon whether it refers to the objects composing it as one aggregate or as separate individuals: The *audience was* large; The *audience were* divided in opinion.
col·lec·tiv·ism (kə·lek/tiv·iz/əm) *n.* A system in which the people as a whole, or the state, own and control the material and means of production and distribution. **—col·lec/tiv·ist** *adj. & n.* **—col·lec/tiv·is/tic** *adj.*
col·lec·tiv·ize (kə·lek/tiv·īz) *v.t.* **·ized, ·iz·ing** To organize (an agricultural settlement, industry, economy, etc.) on a collectivist basis. **—col·lec/tiv·i·za/tion** *n.*
col·lec·tor (kə·lek/tər) *n.* **1.** One who or that which collects. **2.** One who collects taxes, duties, debts, etc.
col·leen (kol/ēn, kə·lēn/) *n. Irish* A girl. [< Irish *cailín*]
col·lege (kol/ij) *n.* **1.** A school of higher learning that grants a bachelor's degree at the completion of a course of study. **2.** Any of the undergraduate divisions or schools of a university. **3.** A school for instruction in a special field or a profession. **4.** A building or buildings used by a college or university. **5.** A body of associates engaged in a common task and having certain rights: the electoral *college.* [< OF < L *collegium* body of associates]
College of Cardinals In the Roman Catholic Church, the body of cardinals who elect and advise the Pope, and, in his absence, administer the Holy See: also called *Sacred College.*
col·le·gian (kə·lē/jən, -jē·ən) *n.* A college student.
col·le·giate (kə·lē/jit, -jē·it) *adj.* Of, like, or intended for a college or for college students.
col·lide (kə·līd/) *v.i.* **·lid·ed, ·lid·ing** **1.** To come together with violent impact; crash. **2.** To come into conflict; clash. [< L < *com-* together + *laedere* to strike]
col·lie (kol/ē) *n.* A large sheep dog of Scottish breed, characterized by a long, narrow head and full, long-haired coat. [Prob. < Scottish Gaelic *cuilean* puppy]
col·lier (kol/yər) *n.* **1.** *Chiefly Brit.* A coal miner. **2.** A vessel for carrying coal. [OE *col* coal + -IER]
col·lier·y (kol/yər·ē) *n. pl.* **·lier·ies** A coal mine.
col·li·mate (kol/ə·māt) *v.t.* **·mat·ed, ·mat·ing** **1.** To bring into line or make parallel, as refracted rays of light. **2.** To adjust the line of sight of (a telescope, etc.). [< L < *com-* together + *lineare* to align] **—col/li·ma/tion** *n.*
col·li·ma·tor (kol/ə·mā/tər) *n. Optics.* A device used to obtain parallel rays of light, as a fixed telescope or the convex lens in a spectroscope. For illus. see SPECTROSCOPE.
col·li·sion (kə·lizh/ən) *n.* **1.** The act of colliding; a violent striking together. **2.** A clash of views or interests; conflict.
col·lo·cate (kol/ō·kāt) *v.t.* **·cat·ed, ·cat·ing** To place to-

gether or in relation; arrange. [< L < *com-* together + *locare* to place] — **col'lo·ca'tion** *n.*

col·lo·di·on (kə·lō′dē·ən) *n.* A flammable solution used as a coating for wounds and formerly for photographic plates. Also **col·lo·di·um** (kə·lō′dē·əm). [< Gk. < *kolla* glue]

col·loid (kol′oid) *n.* **1.** Any gluelike or jellylike substance, as gelatin, starch, raw egg white, etc., that diffuses not at all or very slowly through vegetable and animal membranes. **2.** *Chem.* A state of matter in which finely divided particles of one substance are suspended in another in such manner that the electrical and surface properties acquire special importance. — *adj.* Of or pertaining to a colloid or the colloid state: also **col·loi·dal** (kə·loid′l). [< Gk. *kolla* glue + -OID] — **col·loi·dal·i·ty** (kol′oi·dal′ə·tē) *n.*

col·lo·qui·al (kə·lō′kwē·əl) *adj.* **1.** Denoting a manner of speaking or writing that is characteristic of familiar conversation; informal. **2.** Conversational. — **col·lo′qui·al·ly** *adv.* — **col·lo′qui·al·ness** *n.*

col·lo·qui·al·ism (kə·lō′kwē·əl·iz′əm) *n.* **1.** An expression or form of speech of the type used in informal conversation. **2.** Informal, conversational style.

col·lo·quy (kol′ə·kwē) *n.* *pl.* **·quies** A conversation or conference, esp. a formal one. [< L < *com-* together + *loqui* to speak] — **col′lo·quist** *n.*

col·lude (kə·lood′) *v.i.* **·lud·ed, ·lud·ing** To cooperate secretly; conspire; connive. [< L < *com-* together + *ludere* to play, trick] — **col·lud′er** *n.*

col·lu·sion (kə·lōō′zhən) *n.* A secret agreement for a wrongful purpose; conspiracy. [See COLLUDE.]

col·lu·sive (kə·lōō′siv) *adj.* Secretly arranged to defraud another or to circumvent the law. — **col·lu′sive·ly** *adv.* — **col·lu′sive·ness** *n.*

colo- *combining form Anat.* Colon. Also, before vowels, **col-**. [< Gk. *kolon* colon]

co·logne (kə·lōn′) *n.* A toilet water consisting of alcohol scented with aromatic oils: also called *eau de Cologne.* Also **Cologne water.** [after *Cologne*]

co·lon¹ (kō′lən) *n.* *pl.* **co·lons** A punctuation mark (:), used as a sign of apposition or equality to connect one clause with another that explains it, after a word introducing a quotation, citation, etc., after the salutation in a formal letter, in expressing clock time, and in mathematical proportions. [< L < Gk. *kōlon* member, limb, clause]

co·lon² (kō′lən) *n.* *pl.* **co·lons** or **co·la** (kō′lə) *Anat.* The portion of the large intestine between the cecum and the rectum. For illus. see INTESTINE. [< L < Gk. *kolon*] — **co·lon·ic** (kə·lon′ik) *adj.*

co·lón (kō·lōn′) *n.* *pl.* **co·lons** (kō·lōnz′), *Sp.* **co·lo·nes** (kō·lō′nās) The monetary unit of Costa Rica and El Salvador.

colo·nel (kûr′nəl) *n.* *Mil.* A commissioned officer ranking next above a lieutenant colonel and next below a brigadier or brigadier general. See tables at GRADE. Abbr. *Col.* [< MF < Ital. *colonna* column of soldiers] — **colo′nel·cy, colo′nel·ship** *n.*

co·lo·ni·al (kə·lō′nē·əl) *adj.* **1.** Of, pertaining to, or living in a colony or colonies. **2.** Of or referring to the thirteen original colonies of the U.S. **3.** Describing a style of architecture that originated in the American colonies. — *n.* A citizen or inhabitant of a colony. — **co·lo′ni·al·ly** *adv.*

co·lo·ni·al·ism (kə·lō′nē·əl·iz′əm) *n.* The policy of a nation seeking to acquire, extend, or retain overseas dependencies.

col·o·nist (kol′ə·nist) *n.* **1.** A member or inhabitant of a colony. **2.** A settler or founder of a colony.

col·o·nize (kol′ə·nīz) *v.* **·nized, ·niz·ing** *v.t.* **1.** To set up a colony in; settle. **2.** To establish as colonists. — *v.i.* **3.** To establish or unite in a colony or colonies. Also *Brit.* **col′o·nise.** — **col′o·ni·za′tion** *n.* — **col′o·niz′er** *n.*

col·on·nade (kol′ə·nād′) *n.* *Archit.* A series of regularly spaced columns, usually supporting an entablature. [< F < *colonne* column] — **col′on·nad′ed** *adj.*

col·o·ny (kol′ə·nē) *n.* *pl.* **·nies** **1.** A body of emigrants living in a land apart from, but under the control of, the parent country. **2.** The region thus settled. **3.** Any territory politically controlled by a distant state. **4.** A group of individuals from the same country, of the same occupation, etc., living in a particular part of a city, state, or country: a Chinese *colony.* **5.** The region or quarter occupied by such a group. **6.** *Biol.* A group of organisms of the same species functioning in close association as certain bacteria. **7.** *Ecol.* A group of similar plants or animals living in a particular locality. — **the Colonies** The British colonies that became the original thirteen States of the United States: New Hampshire, Massachusetts, Rhode Island, Connecticut, New York, New Jersey, Pennsylvania, Delaware, Maryland, Virginia, North Carolina, South Carolina, and Georgia. [< L *colonus* farmer]

col·o·phon (kol′ə·fon, -fən) *n.* An emblematic device adopted by a publisher, usu. printed on the title page of his books. [< LL < Gk. *koluphon* summit, finishing touch]

col·or (kul′ər) *n.* **1.** A visual attribute of bodies or substances that depends upon the spectral composition of the wavelengths stimulating the retina and its associated neural structures. Colors are classified as *achromatic* (black and white and the grays), and *chromatic* (green, blue, red, etc.). **2.** A paint, dyestuff, or pigment. **3.** Complexion; hue of the skin. **4.** Ruddy complexion; also, a blush. **5.** The complexion of those peoples not classed as Caucasians, esp. of Negroes. **6.** *pl.* The ensign or flag of a nation, military or naval unit, etc. **7.** A color, ribbon, badge, etc., used for identification: college *colors.* **8.** *pl.* The side, or the opinions, arguments, etc., one upholds: Stick to your *colors.* **9.** Outward appearance; semblance; aspect: a *color* of reason. **10.** A false appearance; pretext; disguise: under *color* of religion. **11.** General character; sort; kind. **12.** Liveliness or vividness, esp. in literary work. **13.** In art and literature, the use of characteristic details to produce a realistic effect: local *color.* **14.** In art, the total effect of the colors in a painting. **15.** *Music* Timbre. **16.** *pl.* In the U.S. Navy, the salute made when the national flag is hoisted in the morning or lowered in the evening. — **to change color** **1.** To turn pale. **2.** To blush. — **to lose color** To turn pale. — **to show one's (true) colors** To show one's real nature, beliefs, etc. — *v.t.* **1.** To apply or give color to, as by painting, staining, or dyeing. **2.** To misrepresent by distortion or exaggeration. **3.** To modify, influence, or change in nature or character. — *v.t.* **4.** To take on or change color, as ripening fruit. **5.** To blush. Also *Brit.* **col′our.** [< OF < L *color*] — **col′or·er** *n.*

col·or·a·ble (kul′ər·ə·bəl) *adj.* **1.** That may be colored. **2.** Capable of appearing true or right. **3.** Specious but apparently plausible; deceptive. Also *Brit.* **col′our·a·ble.** — **col′or·a·bil′i·ty, col′or·a·ble·ness** *n.* — **col′or·a·bly** *adv.*

co·lo·ra·do (kol′ə·rä′dō) *adj.* Having medium strength and color: said of cigars. [< Sp., colored, red]

col·or·a·tion (kul′ə·rā′shən) *n.* Arrangement of colors, as in an animal or plant; coloring.

col·or·a·tu·ra (kul′ər·ə·toor′ə, -tyoor′ə) *n.* **1.** In vocal music, runs, trills, or other florid decoration. **2.** Music characterized by this. **3.** A coloratura soprano. — *adj.* Characterized by or suitable for coloratura. [< Ital., coloration]

coloratura soprano A soprano voice or a singer able to sing coloratura.

color blindness The inability to perceive chromatic color, or, more commonly, to distinguish one of the three primary colors. — **col·or·blind** (kul′ər·blīnd′) *adj.*

col·or·cast (kul′ər·kast′, -käst′) *n.* A television broadcast in color. — *v.t. & v.i.* In television, to broadcast in color.

col·ored (kul′ərd) *adj.* **1.** Having color. **2.** Of a race other than the Caucasoid; especially, wholly or partially Negro. **3.** Of or relating to Negroes. **4.** Influenced or distorted; biased; tainted. **5.** False or misleading; specious.

Col·ored (kul′ərd) *n.* **pl. Col·ored** In South Africa, a person of mixed African and European or Asian parentage.

col·or·fast (kul′ər·fast′, -fäst′) *adj.* Resistant to fading or running: *colorfast* fabrics.

col·or·ful (kul′ər·fəl) *adj.* **1.** Full of colors, especially contrasting colors. **2.** Full of variety; vivid; picturesque: a *colorful* story. — **col′or·ful·ly** *adv.* — **col′or·ful·ness** *n.*

color guard Those who conduct the colors in a ceremony.

col·or·im·e·ter (kul′ə·rim′ə·tər) *n.* An apparatus for determining the hue, purity, and brightness of a color.

col·or·ing (kul′ər·ing) *n.* **1.** The act or manner of applying colors. **2.** A substance used to impart color. **3.** Appearance of anything as to color. **4.** False appearance.

col·or·ist (kul′ər·ist) *n.* **1.** One who uses color. **2.** An artist who uses colors skillfully. — **col′or·is′tic** *adj.*

col·or·less (kul′ər·lis) *adj.* **1.** Without color. **2.** Weak in color; pallid. **3.** Lacking vividness or variety; dull.

color line A social, political, and economic distinction drawn between the white and other races.

co·los·sal (kə·los′əl) *adj.* **1.** Of immense size or extent; enormous; huge. **2.** *Informal* Beyond belief or understanding: *colossal* pride. [< COLOSSUS] — **co·los′sal·ly** *adv.*

col·os·se·um (kol′ə·sē′əm) See COLISEUM.

Col·os·se·um (kol′ə·sē′əm) An amphitheater in Rome built by Vespasian and Titus in A.D. 75–80: also *Coliseum.*

Co·los·sian (kə·losh′ən) *n.* **1.** A native or inhabitant of Colossae. **2.** *pl.* (construed as sing.) A book of the New Testament, Saint Paul's epistle to the Colossians.

co·los·sus (kə·los′əs) *n.* *pl.* **co·los·si** (kə·los′ī) or **co·los·sus·es** **1.** A gigantic statue. **2.** Something of great size or stature. [< L < Gk. *kolossos* gigantic statue]

Colossus of Rhodes A gigantic bronze statue of Apollo at the entrance to the harbor of ancient Rhodes about 285 B.C.

col·our (kul′ər) See COLOR.

-colous *combining form* Dwelling in or inhabiting. Also *-coline.* [< L *colere* to dwell, inhabit]

colt (kōlt) *n.* **1.** A young horse, donkey, etc.; esp., a young male horse. **2.** A young or inexperienced person. [OE] — **colt′ish** *adj.*

col·ter (kōl′tər) *n.* A blade or disk on a plow that cuts the sod: also spelled *coulter.* [OE < L *culter* knife]

col·u·brine (kol'yə·brīn, -brin) *adj.* **1.** Of or like a snake. **2.** Of or pertaining to a family of snakes that includes the garter snake, blacksnake, etc. [< L *coluber* snake]

col·um·bar·i·um (kol'əm·bâr'ē·əm) *n. pl.* **·bar·i·a** (-bâr'ē·ə) A dovecote; also, a pigeonhole in a dovecote. Also **col·um·bar·y** (kol'əm·ber'ē). [< L < *columba* dove]

Co·lum·bi·a (kə·lum'bē·ə) *n. Poetic* The personification of the United States of America. [after Christopher *Columbus*] **— Co·lum'bi·an** *adj.*

col·um·bine (kol'əm·bīn) *n.* A herbaceous plant with variously colored flowers of five petals; esp., the **Colorado columbine**, State flower of Colorado. **—** *adj.* Dovelike. [< F < L *columba* dove]

Col·um·bine (kol'əm·bīn) A stock character in pantomimes, the daughter of Pantaloon and sweetheart of Harlequin.

co·lum·bi·um (kə·lum'bē·əm) *n.* Former name for the element niobium. [< NL < *Columbia*, the United States]

Columbus Day October 12, a holiday in most of the U.S. commemorating the discovery of America by Columbus.

col·umn (kol'əm) *n.* **1.** *Archit.* A post or pillar; esp., such a member consisting of base, shaft, and capital, serving as support or ornament. **2.** Something suggesting a column: the spinal *column*. **3.** *Printing* A section of printed matter on a page, usu. narrow and enclosed by a rule or blank space. **4.** An entertaining or instructive feature article that appears regularly in a newspaper or periodical. **5.** *Mil. & Naval* A formation in which elements of troops, vehicles, ships, or aircraft are placed one behind another. [< L *columna*] **— co·lum·nar** (kə·lum'nər), **col·umned** (kol'əmd) *adj.*

co·lum·ni·a·tion (kə·lum'nē·ā'shən) *n. Arch.* The use or grouping of columns.

col·um·nist (kol'əm·nist, -əm·ist) *n.* One who writes or conducts a special column in a newspaper or periodical.

col·za (kol'zə) *n.* The summer rape whose seeds produce rape oil. [< F < Du. *kool* cabbage + *zaad* seed]

colza oil Rape oil.

com- *prefix* With; together: *combine, compare.* Also: **co-** before *gn, h* and vowels; **col-** before *l*, as in *collide*; **con-** before *c, d, f, g, j, n, q, s, t, v*, as in *concur, confluence, connect, conspire*; **cor-** before *r*, as in *correspond.* [< L *com- < cum* with]

co·ma¹ (kō'mə) *n. pl.* **·mas** **1.** *Pathol.* A condition of profound unconsciousness caused by disease, poison, or severe physical or nervous injury. **2.** Stupor. [< NL < Gk. *kōma* deep sleep]

co·ma² (kō'mə) *n. pl.* **·mae** (-mē) **1.** *Astron.* A luminous, gaseous envelope around the nucleus of a comet. **2.** *Bot.* A tuft of silky hairs, as at the end of certain seeds. [< L, hair < Gk. *komē*] **— co'mal** *adj.*

Co·man·che (kō·man'chē, kə-) *n. pl.* **·ches** **1.** An Indian of Shoshonean stock, ranging between Kansas and northern Mexico, now in Oklahoma. **2.** The language of this tribe.

co·ma·tose (kō'mə·tōs, kom'ə-) *adj.* **1.** Relating to or affected with coma or unconsciousness. **2.** Lethargic; torpid. [< COMA¹] **— co'ma·tose·ly** *adv.*

comb (kōm) *n.* **1.** A toothed strip of hard, often flexible material, used for smoothing, dressing, or fastening the hair. **2.** A thing resembling this, as a card for dressing wool or flax. **3.** The fleshy crest on the head of a fowl. **4.** Honeycomb. **—** *v.t.* **1.** To dress or smooth with or as with a comb. **2.** To card, as wool or flax. **3.** To search carefully. **—** *v.i.* **4.** To crest and break: said of waves. [OE *camb*]

com·bat (*n.* kom'bat, kum'-; *v.* kəm·bat') *n.* A battle or fight; struggle. **— close combat** Hand-to-hand fighting. **— single combat** A fight between two persons. **—** *v.* **·bat·ed** or **·bat·ted, ·bat·ing** or **·bat·ting** *v.t.* **1.** To fight or contend with; oppose in battle. **2.** To resist. **—** *v.i.* **3.** To do battle; struggle: with *with* or *against.* [< F < L *com-* with + *batuere* to fight, beat] **— com·bat·a·ble** (kəm·bat'ə·bəl, kom'bat·ə·bəl, kum'-) *adj.* **— com·bat·er** (kom'bat·ər, kum'-, kəm·bat'ər) *n.*

com·bat·ant (kəm·bat'nt, kom'bə·tənt, kum'-) *n.* One engaged in or prepared for combat or hostilities. **—** *adj.* **1.** Fighting; battling. **2.** Ready or disposed to fight.

combat fatigue *Psychiatry* A psychoneurotic disorder characterized by anxiety, depression, loss of control, etc., associated with the stresses of modern warfare: formerly called *shell shock*: also called *battle fatigue.*

com·bat·ive (kəm·bat'iv, kom'bə·tiv, kum'-) *adj.* Apt or eager to fight. **— com·bat'ive·ly** *adv.* **— com·bat'ive·ness** *n.*

comb·er (kō'mər) *n.* **1.** One who or that which combs wool, flax, etc. **2.** A long, crested wave.

com·bi·na·tion (kom'bə·nā'shən) *n.* **1.** The act of joining together or the state of being joined; union. **2.** That which is formed by combining. **3.** An alliance, as of persons, to further a common interest, activity, etc. **4.** The series of numbers or letters forming the key to a combination lock; also, the mechanism of such a lock. **5.** Underwear consisting of an undershirt and underpants made in one piece. **6.** *Math.* Any selection of a group of units such that the order of selection is immaterial, as 123, 321, and 213. **— com·bi·na'tion·al, com'bi·na'tive** *adj.*

combination lock A lock that can be opened only by moving a dial in a set sequence of turns.

com·bine (*v.* kəm·bīn'; *n.* kom'bīn) *v.* **·bined, ·bin·ing** *v.t.* **1.** To bring together into close union; blend; merge; unite. **2.** To possess in union. **—** *v.i.* **3.** To become one, or parts of a whole. **4.** To associate for a purpose. **5.** *Chem.* To enter into combination. **—** *n.* **1.** A combination. **2.** *U.S. Informal* A group of persons united in pursuit of selfish commercial or political ends; a trust; ring. **3.** *Agric.* A machine that reaps, threshes, and cleans grain while harvesting it. [< LL < L *com-* together + *bini* two by two] **— com·bin'a·ble** *adj.* **— com·bin'er** *n.*

combining form The stem of a word, usu. of Greek or Latin origin, as *tele-* and *-phone* in *telephone*, or an English word unchanged, as *over* in *overeat*, used in combination with other forms to create compounds.

com·bo (kom'bō) *n. Informal* **1.** Combination. **2.** A small jazz or dance band, usually three or four musicians.

com·bus·ti·ble (kəm·bus'tə·bəl) *adj.* **1.** Capable of burning easily. **2.** Easily excited; fiery. **—** *n.* Any substance that will readily burn, as paper or wood. **— com·bus'ti·ble·ness, com·bus'ti·bil'i·ty** *n.* **— com·bus'ti·bly** *adv.*

com·bus·tion (kəm·bus'chən) *n.* **1.** The action or operation of burning. **2.** *Chem.* **a** Oxidation of a substance, accompanied by the generation of heat and sometimes light. **b** Slow oxidation, as of food in the body. **3.** Violent disturbance; tumult. [< LL < L *comburere* to burn up] **— com·bus'tive** *adj.*

come (kum) *v.i.* **came, come, com·ing** **1.** To move to or toward the speaker; approach. **2.** To arrive as the result of motion or progress. **3.** To advance or move into view. **4.** To arrive in due course or in orderly progression: when your turn *comes.* **5.** To occur in time: Labor Day *came* late that year. **6.** To reach or extend. **7.** To arrive at some state or condition: to *come* to harm. **8.** To happen; occur: *come* what may. **9.** To exist as an effect or result: This *comes* of trifling. **10.** To emanate or proceed; be derived. **11.** To become: The wheel *came* loose. **12.** To turn out or prove to be: His prediction *came* true. **13.** To be offered, obtainable, or produced: The car *comes* in many colors. **14.** To act as the speaker wishes: used in the imperative and expressing impatience, anger, protest, etc. **— to come about 1.** To take place; happen. **2.** *Naut.* To turn to the opposite tack. **— to come across 1.** To meet with or find by chance. **2.** *Slang* To give or do what is requested. **— to come around** (or **round**) **1.** To recover or revive. **2.** To change or turn, as in direction or opinion. **3.** *Informal* To pay a visit. **— to come at 1.** To reach. **2.** To attain. **3.** To attack. **— to come back 1.** To return. **2.** *Informal* To regain former status; make a comeback. **3.** *Slang* To reply sharply. **— to come by 1.** To pass near. **2.** To acquire; get. **— to come down 1.** To lose status, wealth, etc. **2.** To descend as by inheritance. **— to come in 1.** To enter. **2.** To arrive. **3.** To be brought into use. **— to come in for** *Informal* **1.** To be eligible to receive. **2.** To acquire; get. **— to come into 1.** To inherit. **2.** To enter into; join. **— to come of 1.** To be descended from. **2.** To result from. **— to come off 1.** To become detached. **2.** To happen; occur. **3.** To emerge from action or trial; acquit oneself. **— to come on 1.** To meet by chance. **2.** To make progress; develop. **3.** To enter, as on stage. **— to come out 1.** To be made public; be published. **2.** To make one's debut. **3.** To speak frankly; declare oneself. **4.** To result; end. **— to come out with 1.** To declare openly. **2.** To offer; publish. **— to come through 1.** To be successful (in). **2.** To survive. **3.** To wear through. **4.** *Informal* To give or do what is required. **— to come to 1.** To recover; revive. **2.** To amount to. **3.** To result in. **4.** *Naut.* **a** To turn close to the wind. **b** To anchor. **— to come up 1.** To arise; appear. **2.** *Naut.* **a** To come closer to the wind. **b** To slacken. **— to come upon 1.** To chance upon. **2.** To attack. **— to come up to 1.** To equal; rival. **2.** To reach. **— to come up with** *U.S. Informal* **1.** To propose or produce: to *come up* with an idea. **2.** To overtake. [OE *cuman*]

come·back (kum'bak') *n.* **1.** *Informal* A return, as to health or lost position. **2.** *Slang* A smart retort.

co·me·di·an (kə·mē′dē·ən) *n.* **1.** An actor in comedies. **2.** An entertainer specializing in jokes, comic skits, and the like. **3.** One who continually tries to be funny. **4.** A person who writes comedy. [< F *comédien*]

co·me·di·enne (kə·mē′dē·en′) *n.* A female comedian. [< F]

come·down (kum′doun′) *n.* A descent to a lower condition or position; a humiliating or disappointing setback.

com·e·dy (kom′ə·dē) *n. pl.* **·dies 1.** A play, motion picture, etc., dealing with human folly in a light and humorous manner, and having a happy ending. **2.** The branch of drama treating of such themes. **3.** The art or theory of composing comedy. **4.** An incident, situation, etc., resembling comedy. [< MF < L < Gk. < *kōmos* revel + *aeidein* to sing] — **co·me·dic** (kə·mē′dik, -med′ik) *adj.* — **co·me′di·cal·ly** *adv.*

comedy of manners A satiric comedy portraying the manners, customs, and foibles of the fashionable world.

come·ly (kum′lē) *adj.* **·li·er, ·li·est 1.** Pleasing in person; handsome; graceful. **2.** Suitable; becoming. [OE *cýmlic* > *cýme* fine] — **come′li·ly** *adv.* — **come′li·ness** *n.*

come-on (kum′on′, -ôn′) *n. U.S. Slang* **1.** Someone or something that lures. **2.** A beckoning look or gesture.

com·er (kum′ər) *n.* **1.** One who comes or arrives. **2.** *Informal* One who or that which shows great promise.

co·mes·ti·ble (kə·mes′tə·bəl) *Rare adj.* Edible. — *n. Usu. pl.* Food. [< MF < LL < L *comedere* to eat up]

com·et (kom′it) *n. Astron.* A celestial body moving in an orbit about the sun and consisting of a nucleus of more or less condensed material, accompanied by a tenuous coma pointing away from the sun. [OE < L < Gk. *kométēs* longhaired] — **com·et·ar·y, co·met·ic** (kə·met′ik) *adj.*

come·up·pance (kum′up′əns) *n. U.S. Informal* The punishment one deserves; just deserts. Also **come′up′ance.**

com·fit (kum′fit, kom′-) *n.* A sweetmeat; confection. [< OF < L *confectus.* Related to CONFECT.]

com·fort (kum′fərt) *n.* **1.** A state of mental or physical ease. **2.** Relief from sorrow, distress, etc. **3.** One who or that which brings ease or consolation. **4.** Help or support: aid and *comfort.* **5.** *U.S.* A bed comforter. — *v.t.* **1.** To cheer in time of grief or trouble; solace; console. **2.** *Law* To aid; help. [< OF < LL < L *com-* with + *fortis* strong] — **com′fort·ing** *adj.* — **com′fort·ing·ly** *adv.*

com·fort·a·ble (kum′fər·tə·bəl, kumf′tə·bəl, -tər-) *adj.* **1.** Imparting comfort and satisfaction. **2.** Free from physical or mental distress; content; at ease. **3.** *Informal* Moderate; adequate: a *comfortable* income. — **com′fort·a·ble·ness** *n.* — **com′fort·a·bly** *adv.*

com·fort·er (kum′fər·tər) *n.* **1.** One who comforts. **2.** *U.S.* A thick, quilted bedcover: also called *comfort.*

comfort station A public toilet or rest room.

com·ic (kom′ik) *adj.* **1.** Of or pertaining to comedy. **2.** Provoking mirth; funny; ludicrous. — *n.* **1.** A comic actor or entertainer. **2.** The humorous element in art, life, etc. **3.** *pl. Informal* Comic strips or a book of comic strips. [< L < Gk. *kōmos* revelry]

com·i·cal (kom′i·kəl) *adj.* Causing merriment; funny; ludicrous. — **Syn.** See HUMOROUS. — **com·i·cal·i·ty** (kom′·ə·kal′ə·tē), **com′i·cal·ness** *n.* — **com′i·cal·ly** *adv.*

comic opera An opera or operetta having a humorous plot and spoken dialogue.

comic strip A strip of cartoons printed in a newspaper, etc.

Com·in·form (kom′in·fôrm) *n.* The Communist Information Bureau, established in 1947 and dissolved in 1956. [< COM(MUNIST) INFORM(ATION)]

com·ing (kum′ing) *adj.* **1.** Approaching, esp. in time: the *coming* year. **2.** On the way to fame or distinction. — *n.* The act of approaching; arrival; advent.

com·ing-out (kum′ing·out′) *n. Informal* Debut into society.

Com·in·tern (kom′in·tûrn) *n.* An international organization formed in 1919 for extending the scope of Marxist socialism, and dissolved in 1943: also called *Third International.* [< COM(MUNIST) INTERN(ATIONAL)]

com·i·ty (kom′ə·tē) *n. pl.* **·ties** Courtesy; civility. [< L *comitas, -tatis* courtesy]

comity of nations The courteous recognition that one nation accords to the laws and usages of another.

com·ma (kom′ə) *n.* **1.** A punctuation mark (,) indicating a slight separation in ideas or in grammatical construction within a sentence. **2.** Any pause or separation. [< L < Gk. *komma* short phrase]

comma bacillus *Bacteriol.* A bacillus shaped like a comma and causing Asiatic cholera.

com·mand (kə·mand′, -mänd′) *v.t.* **1.** To order, require, or enjoin with authority. **2.** To control or direct authoritatively; rule; have at one's disposal or use. **3.** To overlook, as from a height. **4.** To exact as being due or proper: to *command* respect. — *v.i.* **5.** To be in authority; rule. **6.** To overlook something from a superior position. — *n.* **1.** The act of commanding; bidding. **2.** The authority to command. **3.** That which is commanded; an order. **4.** Dominating power as achieved through superior position.

5. Ability to control; mastery: *command* of one's emotions. **6.** *Mil. & Naval* The unit or units under the command of one person; also, the base of operations of such a unit. [< OF < LL < L *com-* thoroughly + *mandare* to order]

com·man·dant (kom′ən·dant′, -dänt′) *n.* A commanding officer, as of a service school, military district, etc.

com·man·deer (kom′ən·dir′) *v.t.* **1.** To force into military service. **2.** To seize for public use, especially under military necessity. **3.** *Informal* To take by force or constraint.

com·mand·er (kə·man′dər, -män′-) *n.* **1.** One who commands or is in command. **2.** *Mil.* The commissioned officer in command of a force or post. **3.** *Naval* A commissioned officer ranking next above a lieutenant commander and next below a captain. See table at GRADE. — **com·mand′·er·ship** *n.*

commander in chief *pl.* **commanders in chief 1.** *Often cap.* One holding supreme command of the armed forces of a nation: in the U.S., the President. **2.** The officer commanding a fleet, major force, etc.

com·mand·ing (kə·man′ding, -män′-) *adj.* **1.** Exercising command. **2.** Impressive; imperious. **3.** Dominating, as from a height. — **com·mand′ing·ly** *adv.*

commanding officer In the Royal, Royal Canadian, and other Commonwealth navies, a commissioned officer. See table at GRADE.

com·mand·ment (kə·mand′mənt, -mänd′-) *n.* **1.** An authoritative mandate; edict; order; law. **2.** *Sometimes cap.* One of the Ten Commandments.

com·man·do (kə·man′dō, -män′-) *n. pl.* **·dos** or **·does 1.** A special fighting force trained for quick, destructive raids into enemy territory. **2.** A member of such a unit. **3.** In South Africa, especially in the Boer War, a force of militia; also, a raid. [< Afrikaans < Pg., a group commanded]

command post The field headquarters of a military unit.

com·mem·o·rate (kə·mem′ə·rāt) *v.t.* **·rat·ed, ·rat·ing** To celebrate the memory of. Also **com·mem′o·rize** (-ə·rīz). — **Syn.** See CELEBRATE. [< L *com-* together + *memorare* to remember] — **com·mem′o·ra′tor** *n.*

com·mem·o·ra·tion (kə·mem′ə·rā′shən) *n.* **1.** The act of commemorating, or that which commemorates. **2.** A commemorative observance. — **com·mem′o·ra′tion·al** *adj.*

com·mem·o·ra·tive (kə·mem′ə·rā′tiv, -rə·tiv) *adj.* Serving to commemorate. Also **com·mem·o·ra·to·ry** (kə·mem′ər·ə·tôr′ē, -tō′rē). — *n.* Anything that commemorates.

com·mence (kə·mens′) *v.t. & v.i.* **·menced, ·menc·ing** To start; begin; originate. [< OF < L *com-* thoroughly + *initiare* to begin] — **com·menc′er** *n.*

com·mence·ment (kə·mens′mənt) *n.* **1.** A beginning; origin. **2.** The ceremony at a college or school during which degrees are conferred; also, the day such a ceremony is held.

com·mend (kə·mend′) *v.t.* **1.** To express a favorable opinion of; praise. **2.** To recommend. **3.** To present the regards of. **4.** To commit with confidence. [< L *com-* thoroughly + *mandare* to order] — **com·mend′a·ble** *adj.* — **com·mend′a·ble·ness** *n.* — **com·mend′a·bly** *adv.*

com·men·da·tion (kom′ən·dā′shən) *n.* **1.** The act of commending; approbation. **2.** Something that commends.

Commendation Ribbon A U.S. military decoration consisting of a ribbon and medallion. See DECORATION.

com·mend·a·to·ry (kə·men′də·tôr′ē, -tō′rē) *adj.* Serving to commend; expressing commendation.

com·men·sal (kə·men′səl) *adj.* **1.** Eating together. **2.** *Zool.* Associated with another in close but nonparasitic relationship. [< OF < L *com-* together + *mensa* table]

com·men·su·ra·ble (kə·men′shər·ə·bəl, -sər·ə-) *adj.* **1.** Capable of being measured by a common standard or unit. **2.** Fitting as to proportion; proportionate. [< LL < L *com-* together + *mensurabilis* measurable] — **com·men′su·ra·bil′i·ty** *n.* — **com·men′su·ra·bly** *adv.*

com·men·su·rate (kə·men′shə·rit, -sə·rit) *adj.* **1.** Having the same measure or extent. **2.** In proper proportion; adequate. **3.** Commensurable. [< LL < L *com-* together + *mensurare* to measure] — **com·men′su·rate·ly** *adv.* — **com·men′su·rate·ness** *n.* — **com·men′su·ra′tion** *n.*

com·ment (kom′ent) *n.* **1.** A written note of explanation, illustration, or criticism, as of a literary passage. **2.** A remark made in observation or criticism. **3.** Talk; conversation. — *v.i.* **1.** To make a comment or comments. — *v.t.* **2.** To make comments on. [< OF < L *comminisci* to contrive] — **com′ment·er** *n.*

com·men·tar·y (kom′ən·ter′ē) *n. pl.* **·ries 1.** A series of illustrative or explanatory notes. **2.** A comment. **3.** A series of remarks. **4.** *Usu. pl.* A historical narrative or memoir. [< L *comminisci* to contrive, devise] — **com·men·tar·i·al** (kom′ən·târ′ē·əl) *adj.*

com·men·ta·tor (kom′ən·tā′tər) *n.* **1.** One who writes commentaries. **2.** One who discusses or analyzes news events.

com·merce (kom′ərs) *n.* **1.** The exchange of materials, products, etc., esp. on a large scale between states or nations; extended trade. **2.** Social intercourse. **3.** Sexual intercourse. — **Department of Commerce** An executive department of the U.S. government headed by the Secretary of Commerce, that supervises transportation and shipping, the census, and food and drug laws. [< F < L < com- together + merx, mercis wares]

com·mer·cial (kə·mûr′shəl) *adj.* 1. Of, relating to, or engaged in commerce; mercantile. 2. Produced in large quantities. 3. Having financial gain as an object. — *n.* In radio and television, an advertisement. — **com·mer·ci·al·i·ty** (kə·mûr′shē·al′ə·tē) *n.* — **com·mer′cial·ly** *adv.*

com·mer·cial·ism (kə·mûr′shəl·iz′əm) *n.* 1. The spirit or methods of commerce. 2. Commercial practices or customs. — **com·mer′cial·ist** *n.* — **com·mer′cial·is′tic** *adj.*

com·mer·cial·ize (kə·mûr′shəl·īz) *v.t.* **·ized**, **·iz·ing** To put on a commercial basis; make a matter of business or profit. — **com·mer′cial·i·za′tion** *n.*

commercial paper Any of various short-term negotiable papers, as drafts, bills of exchange, promissory notes, etc.

com·mie (kom′ē) *n. Often cap. Informal* A Communist.

com·min·gle (kə·ming′gəl) *v.t. & v.i.* **·gled**, **·gling** To mix together; mingle. [< COM- + MINGLE]

com·mi·nute (kom′ə·nōot, -nyōot) *v.t.* **·nut·ed**, **·nut·ing** To reduce to minute particles; pulverize. [< L < com- thoroughly + minuere to lessen] — **com/mi·nu′tion** *n.*

com·mis·er·ate (kə·miz′ə·rāt) *v.* **·at·ed**, **·at·ing** *v.t.* 1. To feel or express sympathy for; pity. — *v.i.* 2. To express sympathy; condole: used with *with*. [< L < com- with + miserari to feel pity] — **com·mis′er·a′tive** *adj.* — **com·mis′er·a′tive·ly** *adv.* — **com·mis′er·a′tor** *n.*

com·mis·er·a·tion (kə·miz′ə·rā′shən) *n.* A feeling or expression of sympathy; compassion.

com·mis·sar (kom′ə·sär, kom′ə·sär′) *n.* Formerly, an official in charge of a commissariat of the Soviet government. [< Russ. *komissar*]

com·mis·sar·i·at (kom′ə·sâr′ē·ət) *n.* 1. The department of an army charged with providing food and daily necessities; also, the officers or supplies of such a department. 2. Formerly, any major department of the Soviet government.

com·mis·sar·y (kom′ə·ser′ē) *n. pl.* **·sar·ies** 1. A store selling food, equipment, etc., as at a camp or military post. 2. An authority delegated for a special duty. 3. In the Soviet Union, a commissar. [See COMMISSAR.] — **com·mis·sar·i·al** (kom′ə·sâr′ē·əl) *adj.* — **com′mis·sar′y·ship** *n.*

com·mis·sion (kə·mish′ən) *n.* 1. The act of committing to the charge of another; an entrusting. 2. The matter or trust so committed; a charge. 3. Authorization or command to act as specified. 4. A written warrant conferring a particular authority or power. 5. *Mil.* **a** An official document conferring rank and authority. **b** The rank or authority conferred. 6. A body of persons acting under lawful authority to perform certain duties. 7. The fee or percentage given an agent or salesman for his services. 8. The condition of being authorized or delegated. 9. The act of committing; also, the act itself. — **in commission** In active service or use; usable. — **out of commission** Not in active service or use; laid up for repairs, etc. — *v.t.* 1. To give rank or authority to. 2. *Naval* To put into active service under a commander, as a ship. 3. To appoint; delegate. [< OF < L committere. See COMMIT.]

com·mis·sion·er (kə·mish′ən·ər) *n.* 1. One who holds a commission. 2. A member of a commission. 3. A public official in charge of a department: fire *commissioner*. 4. In baseball, etc., an official selected as supreme authority.

com·mit (kə·mit′) *v.t.* **·mit·ted**, **·mit·ting** 1. To do; perpetrate. 2. To place in trust or charge; consign. 3. To consign for preservation: to *commit* a speech to memory. 4. To devote (oneself) unreservedly. 5. To refer, as to a committee for consideration. [< L committere to join, entrust < com- together + mittere to send] — **com·mit′ta·ble** *adj.*

com·mit·ment (kə·mit′mənt) *n.* 1. The act or process of entrusting or consigning. 2. The state of being committed. 3. An engagement or pledge to do something. 4. A consignment to a prison, mental institution, etc.

com·mit·tal (kə·mit′l) *n.* Commitment (defs. 1 and 3).

com·mit·tee (kə·mit′ē) *n.* 1. A group of people chosen to investigate, report, or act on a matter. 2. *Law* One appointed by a court to care for the person or property of another. — **in committee** Under consideration by a committee. [< AF *committere* to entrust]

com·mit·tee·man (kə·mit′ē·mən) *n. pl.* **·men** (-mən) A member of a committee. — **com·mit′tee·wom′an** *n.fem.*

com·mode (kə·mōd′) *n.* 1. A low chest of drawers. 2. A covered washstand. 3. A woman's high headdress, worn about 1700. 4. A toilet. [< MF < L commodus convenient]

com·mo·di·ous (kə·mō′dē·əs) *adj.* Containing ample room; spacious. [See COMMODE.] — **com·mo′di·ous·ly** *adv.* — **com·mo′di·ous·ness** *n.*

com·mod·i·ty (kə·mod′ə·tē) *n. pl.* **·ties** 1. Something

bought and sold. 2. Anything of use or profit. [< MF < L commoditas, -tatis convenience]

com·mo·dore (kom′ə·dôr, -dōr) *n.* 1. In the U.S. Navy, an officer next above a captain and next below a rear admiral: a rank last used during World War II. 2. In the Royal, Royal Canadian, and other Commonwealth navies, an officer ranking next below a rear-admiral. See table at GRADE. 3. A title given to the presiding officer of a yacht club. [Earlier commandore, ? < Du. kommandeur]

com·mon (kom′ən) *adj.* 1. Frequent or usual; unexceptional. 2. Widespread; general. 3. Shared equally by two or more, or by all. 4. Pertaining to the entire community; public. 5. Habitual; notorious: a *common* thief. 6. Of low rank; ordinary. 7. Vulgar; low; coarse. 8. *Gram.* **a** Of gender, applied to either sex, as *parent*, *spouse*, *cat*. **b** Of a noun, applicable to any individual of a class of similar objects; not proper or personal, as *dog*. 9. *Math.* Referring to a number or quantity belonging equally to two or more quantities: a *common* denominator. — *n.* 1. A tract of land considered as the property of the community, open to the use of all. 2. *Sometimes cap. Eccl.* An office or service used for any of certain classes of feast. — **in common** Equally with another or others; jointly. [< OF < L communis common] — **com′mon·ly** *adv.* — **com′mon·ness** *n.*

com·mon·al·ty (kom′ən·əl·tē) *n. pl.* **·ties** 1. The common people, as opposed to the nobility. 2. A body corporate, or its members. 3. The entire mass; whole.

common carrier An individual or company that, for a fee, provides public transportation for goods or persons.

com·mon·er (kom′ən·ər) *n.* One of the common people.

common fraction *Math.* A fraction expressed by two numbers, a denominator and a numerator.

common law A system of jurisprudence based on custom, traditional usage, and precedent, as that of England.

com·mon-law marriage (kom′ən-lô′) A marriage in which both members consent to live as man and wife without undergoing a religious or civil ceremony.

Common Market Any of several customs unions, esp. the European Economic Community.

common noun *Gram.* A noun that names any member of a class of things, as *man*, *boat*: distinguished from *proper noun*.

com·mon·place (kom′ən·plās′) *adj.* Not remarkable or interesting; ordinary. — *n.* 1. A trite or obvious remark. 2. Something common. — **com′mon·place′ness** *n.*

Common Prayer The public worship of the Anglican Church, as contained in the Book of Common Prayer.

com·mons (kom′ənz) *n.pl. Chiefly Brit.* 1. The common people. 2. (construed as sing.) Food provided for a common table, as in a college. 3. Rations; fare. 4. (construed as sing.) The dining hall of a college.

Com·mons (kom′ənz) *n.pl.* The House of Commons.

common sense Practical understanding; sound judgment. — **com′mon-sense′** *adj.*

common stock Corporation stock the ownership of which entitles the holder to dividends or a share in the profits only after other obligations have been met.

common time *Music* Meter in which there are four quarter notes to a measure: also **common measure**.

com·mon·weal (kom′ən·wēl′) *n.* The general welfare; common good. Also **common weal**.

com·mon·wealth (kom′ən·welth′) *n.* 1. The whole people of a state or nation. 2. A state or republic in which the sovereignty is vested in the people; loosely, any of the United States. — **The Commonwealth** The official name of the British Commonwealth of Nations.

Commonwealth of England The English government from 1649 to 1660.

Commonwealth of Nations See BRITISH COMMONWEALTH OF NATIONS.

com·mo·tion (kə·mō′shən) *n.* 1. A violent agitation; excitement. 2. Popular tumult; social disorder; insurrection. [< L < com- thoroughly + movere to move]

com·mu·nal (kom′yə·nəl, kə·myōo′nəl) *adj.* 1. Of or pertaining to a commune. 2. Of or belonging to a community; common; public. — **com′mu·nal·ly** *adv.*

com·mu·nal·ism (kom′yə·nəl·iz′əm, kə·myōo′nəl-) *n.* A theory or system of government in which the state exists merely as a federation of virtually self-governing communes. — **com′mu·nal·ist** *n.* — **com′mu·nal·is′tic** *adj.*

com·mu·nal·ize (kom′yə·nəl·īz′, kə·myōo′nəl·īz) *v.t.* **·ized**, **·iz·ing** To render communal. — **com′mu·nal·i·za′tion** *n.*

com·mune[1] (*v.* kə·myōon′; *n.* kom′yōon) *v.i.* **·muned**, **·mun·ing** 1. To converse intimately. 2. To partake of the Eucharist. — *n.* Intimate conversation. [< OF *comuner* to share]

com·mune[2] (kom′yōon) *n.* 1. The smallest political division of France, Belgium, Italy, etc.; also, the people of such a district. 2. Any community. — **the Commune** or the

Commune of Paris   1. The revolutionary government of Paris between 1789 and 1794.   2. The revolutionary government of Paris in 1871.   [< L *communa* community]

com·mu·ni·ca·ble (kə-myōō′ni·kə-bəl)   *adj.*   Capable of being communicated, as a disease.   — **com·mun′i·ca·bil′i·ty, com·mu′ni·ca·ble·ness** *n.*   — **com·mu′ni·ca·bly** *adv.*

com·mu·ni·cant (kə-myōō′nə·kənt)   *n.*   1. One who communicates.   2. One who partakes or has a right to partake of the Eucharist.   — *adj.* Communicating.

com·mu·ni·cate (kə-myōō′nə·kāt)   *v.*   **·cat·ed, ·cat·ing** *v.t.*   1. To cause another or others to partake of or share in; impart.   2. To transmit, as a disease.   — *v.i.*   3. To transmit or exchange thought or knowledge.   4. To be connected.   5. To partake of the Eucharist.   [< L *communicare* to share < *communis* common]   — **com·mu′ni·ca′tor** *n.*

com·mu·ni·ca·tion (kə-myōō′nə·kā′shən)   *n.*   1. The act of imparting or transmitting.   2. The transmission of ideas, information, etc., as by speech or writing.   3. A message.   4. A means of passage or of transmitting messages between places or persons.   5. *pl.* The science of communicating.

com·mu·ni·ca·tive (kə-myōō′nə·kā′tiv, -kə·tiv)   *adj.*   1. Talkative.   2. Of or pertaining to communication.   — **com·mu′ni·ca′tive·ly** *adv.*   — **com·mu′ni·ca′tive·ness** *n.*

com·mun·ion (kə-myōōn′yən)   *n.*   1. A having or sharing in common; mutual participation.   2. A mutual sharing of thoughts, feelings, etc.   3. Religious fellowship, as between members of a church; also, a religious denomination.   4. *Usu. cap.* The Eucharist.   [< OF < L *communis* common]

com·mu·ni·qué (kə-myōō′nə·kā′, kə·myōō′nə·kā)   *n.*   An official announcement or bulletin.   [< F]

com·mu·nism (kom′yə·niz′əm)   *n.*   1. A social system characterized by the communal sharing of goods and services.   2. A theory of social change advocating a classless society, public ownership of almost all productive property, and the sharing of the products of labor.   3. *Often cap.* The system in force in any state based on this theory.   [< F *commun* common, shared equally + -ISM]

com·mu·nist (kom′yə·nist)   *n.*   1. *Often cap.* A member of a Communist party.   2. One who advocates communism.   — *adj.* Pertaining to communism and communists.

com·mu·nis·tic (kom′yə·nis′tik)   *adj.*   1. Of, or of the nature of, communism.   2. Tending to or in accordance with communism.   — **com′mu·nis′ti·cal·ly** *adv.*

Communist Party   1. The dominant party in Russia since 1917, previously called the Bolshevik Party.   2. Any political party advocating communism.

com·mu·ni·ty (kə-myōō′nə·tē)   *n. pl.* **·ties**   1. A group of people living together or in one locality and subject to the same laws, having common interests, etc.   2. The district or area in which they live.   3. The public; society in general.   4. Common ownership or participation.   5. Identity or likeness: *community* of interests.   6. *Ecol.* A group of plants or animals living under relatively similar conditions in a definite area.   [< L *communitas, -tatis* fellowship]

community center   A building or grounds used by a community for social and recreational activities.

community chest   A welfare fund of contributions drawn upon by various charitable organizations.

com·mu·nize (kom′yə·nīz)   *v.t.*   **·nized, ·niz·ing**   To make public property or cause to become communistic.   — **com′·mu·ni·za′tion** *n.*

com·mu·tate (kom′yə·tāt)   *v.t.*   **·tat·ed, ·tat·ing** *Electr.*   To alter or reverse the direction of (a current).

com·mu·ta·tion (kom′yə·tā′shən)   *n.*   1. A substitution or interchange, as of one kind of payment for another.   2. A payment or service substituted.   3. *U.S.* Regular travel to and from work.   4. *Electr.* The reversing of the direction of current.   5. *Law* A reduction of a judicial penalty or sentence.   [< L *com-* thoroughly + *mutare* change]

commutation ticket   *U.S.*   A railroad or other ticket issued at a reduced rate and good for a specified number of trips, or for a specified period, over a given route.

com·mu·ta·tor (kom′yə·tā′tər)   *n. Electr.*   1. Any contrivance for reversing the direction of current.   2. A part within a dynamo or generator, serving to collect and transmit the induced current.

com·mute (kə-myōōt′)   *v.* **·mut·ed, ·mut·ing** *v.t.*   1. To exchange reciprocally; interchange.   2. To exchange for something less severe.   3. To pay in gross at a reduced rate.   — *v.i.*   4. To serve as a substitute.   5. *U.S.* To make regular trips of some distance to and from work.   — **com·mut′a·ble** *adj.*   — **com·mut′a·ble·ness, com·mut′a·bil′i·ty** *n.*   — **com·mut′er** *n.*

com·pact¹ (*adj.* kəm-pakt′, kom′pakt; *v.* kəm-pakt′; *n.* kom′·pakt)   *adj.*   1. Closely and firmly united; pressed together.   2. Brief and to the point; terse.   3. Packed into a small space.   4. Composed; made up: with *of*.   — *v.t.* To pack or press closely; compress.   — *n.* A small, hinged box with a mirror, in which a woman carries face powder.   [< L *com-* together + *pangere* to fasten]   — **com·pact′ly** *adv.*   — **com·pact′ness** *n.*

com·pact² (kom′pakt)   *n.*   A covenant, agreement, or contract.   [< L < *com-* together + *pacisci* to agree]

com·pan·ion¹ (kəm-pan′yən)   *n.*   1. A comrade; associate.   2. A person employed to live with, accompany, or assist another.   3. One of a pair; a mate.   — *v.t.* To be a companion to.   [< OF < LL < L *com-* together + *panis* bread]

com·pan·ion² (kəm-pan′yən)   *n. Naut.*   A companionway; also, the hood or covering over a companionway.   [< Du. *kampanje* quarter-deck, storeroom]

com·pan·ion·a·ble (kəm-pan′yən-ə-bəl)   *adj.*   Fitted for companionship; friendly; sociable.   — **com·pan′ion·a·bil′i·ty** *n.*   — **com·pan′ion·a·bly** *adv.*

com·pan·ion·ate (kəm-pan′yən-it)   *adj.*   1. Of or characteristic of companions.   2. Agreed upon; shared.

com·pan·ion·ship (kəm-pan′yən-ship)   *n.*   Fellowship.

com·pan·ion·way (kəm-pan′yən-wā′)   *n. Naut.*   A staircase leading below from a ship's deck; also, the space it occupies.

com·pa·ny (kum′pə·nē)   *n. pl.* **·nies**   1. A group of people.   2. A gathering of persons for social purposes; society.   3. A guest or guests; visitors.   4. Companionship; society.   5. A number of persons associated for some common purpose, as in business.   6. A partner or partners not named in the title of a firm.   7. A body of actors and actresses; troupe.   8. *Mil.* A body of men commanded by a captain, larger than a platoon and smaller than a battalion.   9. *Naut.* The entire crew of a ship, including the officers.   — **to keep company (with)**   1. To associate (with).   2. To court, as lovers; go together.   — **to part company (with)**   To end friendship or association (with).   — *v.t. & v.i.* **·nied, ·ny·ing** *Archaic* To keep or go in company (with).   [See COMPANION¹.]

com·pa·ra·ble (kom′pər·ə·bəl)   *adj.*   1. Capable of comparison.   2. Worthy of comparison.   — **com′pa·ra·ble·ness, com′pa·ra·bil′i·ty** *n.*   — **com′pa·ra·bly** *adv.*

com·par·a·tive (kəm-par′ə·tiv)   *adj.*   1. Pertaining to, resulting from, or making use of comparison: *comparative* anatomy.   2. Not positive or absolute; relative.   3. *Gram.* Expressing a degree of an adjective or adverb higher than the positive and lower than the superlative.   — *n. Gram.* The comparative degree, or a word or form by which it is expressed: "Better" is the *comparative* of "good."   — **com·par′a·tive·ly** *adv.*

com·pare (kəm-pâr′)   *v.* **·pared, ·par·ing** *v.t.*   1. To represent or speak of as similar or equal: with *to*.   2. To examine so as to perceive similarity or dissimilarity: with *with*.   3. *Gram.* To form or state the degrees of comparison of (an adjective or adverb).   — *v.i.*   4. To be worthy of comparison: with *with*.   5. To vie or compete.   — *n.* Comparison: usually in the phrase **beyond compare**.   [< MF < L < *com-* together + *par* equal]

com·par·i·son (kəm-par′ə·sən)   *n.*   1. A comparing or being compared; a statement of relative likeness or unlikeness.   2. Similarity.   3. *Gram.* That inflection of adjectives or adverbs that indicates the three differences of degree, the positive, comparative, and superlative, as *short, shorter, shortest.*

com·part·ment (kəm-pärt′mənt)   *n.*   1. One of the parts into which an enclosed space is subdivided.   2. Any separate section.   [< F < L < *com-* together + *partiri* to share]

com·pass (kum′pəs, kom′-)   *n.*   1. An instrument for determining direction, consisting essentially of a freely suspended magnetic needle that points toward the magnetic north.   2. The reach or extent of something; area or range; scope.   3. An enclosing line or boundary; circumference.   4. *Sometimes pl.* An instrument having two usually pointed legs hinged at one end, used for taking measurements, describing circles, etc.: also **pair of compasses**.   — *v.t.*   1. To go round.   2. To surround; encompass.   3. To comprehend.   4. To attain or accomplish.   5. To plot; devise.   [< OF < L *com-* together + *passus* step]   — **com′pass·a·ble** *adj.*

compass card   The circular card or dial resting on the pivot of a mariner's compass, on which the 32 points and 360 degrees of the circle are marked.

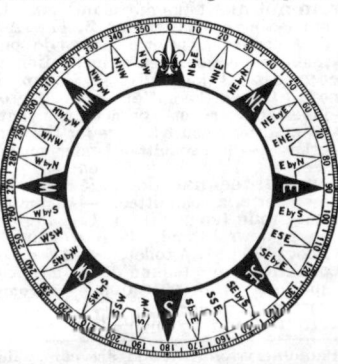

com·pas·sion (kəm·pash′ən)   *n.*   Pity for the suffering or distress of another, with the desire to help or spare.   — **Syn.** See PITY.   [< MF < LL < *com-* together + *pati* to feel, suffer]

com·pas·sion·ate (*adj.* kəm·pash′ən·it; *v.* kəm·pash′ən·āt)   *adj.*   Feeling compassion or pity; merciful; sympathetic.   — *v.t.* **·at·ed, ·at·ing**   To have compassion for; pity; sympathize. **— com·pas'sion·ate·ly** adv. **— com·pas'sion·ate·ness** n.

com·pat·i·ble (kəm·pat'ə·bəl) adj. **1.** Capable of existing together; congruous; congenial: usu. with with. **2.** In television capable of being received in black and white on sets not adapted for color reception. [< MF < Med.L < L com- together + pati to feel, suffer] **— com·pat'i·bil'i·ty, com·pat'i·ble·ness** n. **— com·pat'i·bly** adv.

com·pa·tri·ot (kəm·pā'trē·ət, -pat'rē·ət) n. A fellow countryman. **—** adj. Of the same country. [< F < LL < L com- together + patriota countryman]

com·peer (kəm·pir', kom'pir) n. **1.** One of equal rank; a peer. **2.** A comrade. [< OF < L < com- with + par equal]

com·pel (kəm·pel') v.t. ·pelled, ·pel·ling **1.** To urge irresistibly; constrain. **2.** To obtain by force; exact. **3.** To force to yield; overpower. [OF < L < com- together + pellere to drive] **— com·pel'la·ble** adj. **— com·pel'la·bly** adv. **— com·pel'ler** n.

com·pen·di·ous (kəm·pen'dē·əs) adj. Stating briefly and succinctly the substance of something; concise. **— com·pend'i·ous·ly** adv. **— com·pen'di·ous·ness** n.

com·pen·di·um (kəm·pen'dē·əm) n. pl. ·di·ums or ·di·a (-dē·ə) A brief, comprehensive summary; an abridgment. [< L < com- together + pendere to weigh]

com·pen·sa·ble (kəm·pen'sə·bəl) adj. That may be compensated. **— com·pen'sa·bil'i·ty** n.

com·pen·sate (kom'pən·sāt) v. ·sat·ed, ·sat·ing v.t. **1.** To make suitable amends to or for; requite; remunerate; pay; reimburse. **2.** To counterbalance or make up for; offset. **—** v.i. **3.** To make returns or amends: often with for. [< L < com- together + pendere to weigh] **— com'pen·sa'tor** n. **— com·pen·sa·tive** (kom'pən·sā'tiv, kəm·pen'sə·tiv) adj. **— com·pen·sa·to·ry** (kəm·pen'sə·tôr'ē) adj.

com·pen·sa·tion (kom'pən·sā'shən) n. **1.** The act of compensating, or that which compensates; payment; amends. **2.** Biol. The offsetting of defects of an organ or part by the development of another organ. **— com'pen·sa'tion·al** adj.

com·pete (kəm·pēt') v.i. ·pet·ed, ·pet·ing To contend with another or others; engage in a contest or competition; vie. [< L < com- together + petere to seek]

com·pe·tence (kom'pə·təns) n. **1.** The state of being competent; ability. **2.** Sufficient means for comfortable living. **3.** Law Legal authority, qualification, or jurisdiction. Also **com'pe·ten·cy.**

com·pe·tent (kom'pə·tənt) adj. **1.** Having sufficient ability; capable. **2.** Sufficient; adequate. **3.** Law Having legal qualification. [< MF < L < com- together + petere to go, seek] **— com'pe·tent·ly** adv. **— com'pe·tent·ness** n.

com·pe·ti·tion (kom'pə·tish'ən) n. **1.** A striving against another or others for some object, as a prize, or for superiority. **2.** A trial of skill or ability; a contest. **3.** Business rivalry between persons or firms striving for the same market.

com·pet·i·tive (kəm·pet'ə·tiv) adj. Of, pertaining to, or characterized by competition. Also **com·pet·i·to·ry** (kəm·pet'ə·tôr'ē, -tō'rē) **— com·pet'i·tive·ly** adv. **— com·pet'i·tive·ness** n.

com·pet·i·tor (kəm·pet'ə·tər) n. One who competes, as in games or in business.

com·pile (kəm·pīl') v.t. ·piled, ·pil·ing **1.** To put together from materials collected from other sources. **2.** To gather (various materials) into a volume. **3.** To amass; collect. [< L < com- thoroughly + pilare to strip, plunder] **— com·pi·la·tion** (kom'pə·lā'shən) n. **— com·pil'er** n.

com·pla·cen·cy (kəm·plā'sən·sē) n. pl. ·cies Self-satisfaction; smugness. Also **com·pla'cence.**

com·pla·cent (kəm·plā'sənt) adj. **1.** Smug; self-satisfied. **2.** Complaisant. [< L < com- thoroughly + placere to please] **— com·pla'cent·ly** adv.

com·plain (kəm·plān') v.i. **1.** To express feelings of dissatisfaction, resentment, pain, etc.; grumble. **2.** To describe one's pains or ills. **3.** To make a formal accusation; present a complaint. [< OF < LL < L com- thoroughly + plangere to beat (the breast in grief)] **— com·plain'er** n.

com·plain·ant (kəm·plā'nənt) n. One who enters a complaint, as before a magistrate.

com·plaint (kəm·plānt') n. **1.** An expression of pain, grief, or dissatisfaction. **2.** A cause for complaining; grievance. **3.** An ailment; disorder. **4.** Law A formal charge.

com·plai·sant (kəm·plā'zənt, kom'plə·zant) adj. Showing a desire to please; yielding; compliant. [< MF < L com- placere] **— com·plai'sance** n. **— com·plai'sant·ly** adv.

com·ple·ment (n. kom'plə·mənt; v. kom'plə·ment) n. **1.** That which fills up or completes a thing. **2.** Full or complete number, allowance, or amount: The vessel has her complement of men. **3.** One of two parts that mutually complete each other. **4.** Geom. An angle that when added to another angle equals 90°. **5.** Gram. A word or phrase used after a verb to complete predication. A **subjective comple-**

ment describes the subject, as happy in She is happy. An **objective complement** describes or identifies the direct object, as happy in It made her happy. **—** v.t. To make complete. [< L < com- thoroughly + plere to fill]

com·ple·men·tal (kom'plə·men'təl) adj. Complementary.

com·ple·men·ta·ry (kom'plə·men'tər·ē, -trē) adj. **1.** Serving as a complement; completing. **2.** Mutually providing each other's needs.

complementary color Either of a pair of spectrum colors that when combined give a white or nearly white light.

com·plete (kəm·plēt') adj. **1.** Having all needed or normal parts; lacking nothing; entire; full. **2.** Wholly finished; ended; concluded. **3.** Perfect in quality or nature. **—** v.t. ·plet·ed, ·plet·ing **1.** To make entire or perfect. **2.** To finish; end. [< L < com- thoroughly + plere to fill] **— com·plete'ly** adv. **— com·plete'ness** n.

com·ple·tion (kəm·plē'shən) n. The act of completing, or the state of being completed.

com·plex (adj. kəm·pleks', kom'pleks; n. kom'pleks) adj. **1.** Consisting of various connected or interwoven parts; composite. **2.** Complicated, as in structure; involved; intricate. **—** n. **1.** A whole made up of interwoven or connected parts. **2.** Psychoanal. A group of interrelated feelings, desires, memories, and ideas, that function as a unit to dominate the personality, and which, when repressed, often lead to abnormal patterns of behavior. **3.** Loosely, an excessive concern or fear; an obsession. [< L < com- together + plectere to twist] **— com·plex'ly** adv. **— com·plex'ness** n.

complex fraction Math. A fraction in which either the numerator or the denominator is a fraction.

com·plex·ion (kəm·plek'shən) n. **1.** The color and appearance of the skin, esp. of the face. **2.** General aspect or appearance; quality; character. [< F < L < complecti to put together] **— com·plex'ion·al** adj.

com·plex·ioned (kəm·plek'shənd) adj. Of a certain complexion: used in compounds: light-complexioned.

com·plex·i·ty (kəm·plek'sə·tē) n. pl. ·ties **1.** The state of being complex. **2.** Something complex.

complex sentence. See under SENTENCE.

com·pli·a·ble (kəm·plī'ə·bəl) adj. Compliant. **— com·pli'a·ble·ness** n. **— com·pli'a·bly** adv.

com·pli·ance (kəm·plī'əns) n. **1.** The act of complying or yielding. **2.** A disposition to comply; complaisance. Also **com·pli'an·cy.** **— in compliance with** In agreement with.

com·pli·ant (kəm·plī'ənt) adj. Complying; yielding. **— com·pli'ant·ly** adv.

com·pli·cate (v. kom'plə·kāt; adj. kom'plə·kit) v. ·cat·ed, ·cat·ing v.t. **1.** To make complex, difficult, or perplexing. **2.** To twist or wind around; intertwine. **—** v.i. **3.** To become complex or difficult. **—** adj. Complicated; complex. [< L < com- together + plicare to fold]

com·pli·cat·ed (kom'plə·kā'tid) adj. Difficult to separate, analyze, or understand; intricate; involved. **— com'pli·cat'ed·ly** adv. **— com'pli·cat'ed·ness** n.

com·pli·ca·tion (kom'plə·kā'shən) n. **1.** The act of complicating. **2.** An intricate or perplexing structure, condition, or relationship. **3.** Anything that complicates.

com·plic·i·ty (kəm·plis'ə·tē) n. pl. ·ties **1.** The state of being an accomplice, as in a wrong act. **2.** Complexity.

com·pli·ment (n. kom'plə·mənt; v. kom'plə·ment) n. **1.** An expression of admiration, praise, or congratulation. **2.** Usu. pl. A formal greeting or remembrance. **—** v.t. **1.** To pay a compliment to. **2.** To show regard for, as by a gift. [< MF < Ital. < L complementum]

com·pli·men·ta·ry (kom'plə·men'tər·ē, -trē) adj. **1.** Conveying, using, or like a compliment. **2.** Given free: a complimentary copy of a book. **— com'pli·men'ta·ri·ly** adv.

com·plin (kom'plin) n. Often cap. Eccl. Prescribed prayers constituting the last of the seven canonical hours. Also **com·pline** (kom'plin, -plīn) [< OF < L L com- thoroughly + plere to fill]

com·ply (kəm·plī') v.i. ·plied, ·ply·ing **1.** To act in conformity; consent; obey: with with. [< Ital. complire < Sp. < L < com- thoroughly + plere to fill] **— com·pli'er** n.

com·po·nent (kəm·pō'nənt) n. A constituent element or part. **—** adj. Forming a part or ingredient; constituent. [< L < com- together + ponere to put]

com·port (kəm·pôrt', -pōrt') v.t. **1.** To conduct or behave (oneself). **—** v.i. **2.** To be compatible; agree: with with. [< F < L < com- together + portare to carry] **— com·port'ment** n.

com·pose (kəm·pōz') v. ·posed, ·pos·ing v.t. **1.** To constitute; form. **2.** To make of elements or parts; fashion. **3.** To create (a literary or musical work). **4.** To make calm or tranquil; quiet. **5.** To reconcile or settle, as differences. **6.** Printing To arrange (type) in lines; set. **—** v.i. **7.** To engage in composition, as of musical works. **8.** Printing To set type. [< MF < com- together + poser to place]

com·posed (kəm-pōzd′) *adj.* Free from agitation; calm. — **com·pos·ed·ly** (kəm-pō′zid-lē) *adv.* — **com·pos′ed·ness** *n.*

com·pos·er (kəm-pō′zər) *n.* One who composes; esp., one who writes music.

com·pos·ite (kəm-poz′it) *adj.* **1.** Made up of separate parts or elements; combined or compounded. **2.** *Bot.* Characteristic of or pertaining to a family of plants, as the dandelion, chrysanthemum, etc., the flowers usu. occurring in dense clusters. — *n.* **1.** That which is composed or made up of parts. **2.** *Bot.* A composite plant. [< L < *com-* together + *ponere* to put] — **com·pos′ite·ly** *adv.* — **com·pos′ite·ness** *n.*

com·po·si·tion (kom′pə-zish′ən) *n.* **1.** A putting together of parts, ingredients, etc., to form a whole. **2.** That which is so formed. **3.** Constitution; make-up. **4.** The act or art of creating a literary, musical, or artistic work. **5.** The work so created, or its general structure. **6.** A short essay written as an exercise for school. **7.** An agreement or settlement, esp. by compromise. **8.** *Printing* The setting of type.

com·pos·i·tor (kəm-poz′ə-tər) *n.* One who sets type.

com·pos men·tis (kom′pəs men′tis) *Latin* Of sound mind.

com·post (kom′pōst) *n.* **1.** A fertilizing mixture of decomposed vegetable matter. **2.** A compound. [< OF, mixture]

com·po·sure (kəm-pō′zhər) *n.* Tranquillity, as of mind; calmness; serenity.

com·pote (kom′pōt, *Fr.* kôṅ-pôt′) *n.* **1.** Fruit stewed or preserved in syrup **2.** A dish for holding fruits, etc. [< F < OF *composte*]

com·pound¹ (*n.* kom′pound; *v.* kom-pound′, kəm-; *adj.* kom′pound, kom-pound′) *n.* **1.** A combination of two or more elements or parts. **2.** *Gram.* A word composed of two or more words joined with a hyphen or written in solid form, as *fly-by-night, shoestring*. **3.** *Chem.* A definite substance resulting from the combination of specific elements or radicals in fixed proportions: distinguished from *mixture*. — *v.t.* **1.** To make by combining various elements or ingredients. **2.** To mix (elements or parts). **3.** To compute (interest) on both the principal and whatever interest has accrued. **4.** To settle for less than the sum due, as a debt; compromise. — *adj.* Composed of two or more elements or parts. [< OF < L < *com-* together + *ponere* to put] — **com·pound′a·ble** *adj.* — **com·pound′er** *n.*

com·pound² (kom′pound) *n.* **1.** In the Orient, an enclosure containing a building, esp. one occupied by Europeans. **2.** Any similar enclosed place. [< Malay *kampong*]

compound fraction *Math.* A complex fraction.

compound interest Interest computed on the original principal together with its accrued interest.

compound leaf *Bot.* A leaf having several distinct blades on a common leafstalk.

compound number *Math.* A quantity containing more than one unit or denomination, as 6 feet 3 inches.

compound sentence See under SENTENCE.

com·pre·hend (kom′pri-hend′) *v.t.* **1.** To grasp mentally; understand fully. **2.** To take in or embrace; include. — *v.i.* **3.** To understand. — **Syn.** See APPREHEND. [< L < *com-* together + *prehendere* to grasp, seize]

com·pre·hen·si·ble (kom′pri-hen′sə-bəl) *adj.* Capable of being comprehended; understandable; intelligible. Also **com′·pre·hend′i·ble.** — **com′pre·hen·si·bil′i·ty, com′pre·hen′si·ble·ness** *n.* — **com′pre·hen′si·bly** *adv.*

com·pre·hen·sion (kom′pri-hen′shən) *n.* **1.** The mental grasping of ideas, facts, etc., or the power of so doing; understanding. **2.** An including or taking in; comprehensiveness. — **Syn.** See KNOWLEDGE.

com·pre·hen·sive (kom′pri-hen′siv) *adj.* **1.** Large in scope or content; broad. **2.** Understanding or comprehending. — **com′pre·hen′sive·ly** *adv.* — **com′pre·hen′sive·ness** *n.*

com·press (*v.* kəm-pres′; *n.* kom′pres) *v.t.* To press together or into smaller space; condense; compact. — *n.* **1.** *Med.* A cloth or pad, sometimes medicated, for applying moisture, cold, heat, or pressure to a part of the body. **2.** An apparatus for compressing bales of cotton, etc. [< OF < LL < L < *com-* together + *premere* to press] — **com·pressed′** *adj.* — **com·press′i·bil·i·ty, com·press′i·ble·ness** *n.* — **com·press′i·ble** *adj.* — **com·pres′sive** *adj.*

com·pres·sion (kəm-presh′ən) *n.* **1.** The act of compressing or the state of being compressed. Also **com·pres·sure** (kəm-presh′ər). **2.** The process by which a confined gas is reduced in volume through the application of pressure, as in the cylinder of an internal-combustion engine.

com·pres·sor (kəm-pres′ər) *n.* **1.** One who or that which compresses. **2.** *Anat.* A muscle that compresses a part. **3.** *Mech.* A power-driven machine for compressing a gas in order to utilize its expansion, as for refrigeration.

com·prise (kəm-prīz′) *v.t.* **·prised, ·pris·ing** To consist of or contain; include. [< F < OF < L < *com-* together + *premere* to press] — **com·pris′a·ble** *adj.* — **com·pri′sal** *n.*

com·pro·mise (kom′prə-mīz) *n.* **1.** An adjustment or settlement by which each side makes concessions. **2.** The result of such concessions. **3.** Something lying midway be-

tween, or combining the qualities of, two different things. **4.** An imperiling, as of character or reputation. — *v.* **·mised, ·mis·ing** *v.t.* **1.** To adjust by concessions. **2.** To expose to risk, suspicion, or disrepute; imperil. — *v.i.* **3.** To make a compromise. [< MF < L < *com-* together + *promittere* to promise] — **com′pro·mis′er** *n.*

compte ren·du (kôṅt räṅ-dü′) *French* An official report; literally, account rendered.

Comp·tom·e·ter (komp-tom′ə-tər) *n.* A high-speed calculating machine: a trade name. Also **comp·tom′e·ter.**

comp·trol·ler (kən-trō′lər) See CONTROLLER (def. 2).

com·pul·sion (kəm-pul′shən) *n.* **1.** The act of compelling; coercion. **2.** The state of being compelled. **3.** *Psychol.* An irresistible impulse or tendency to perform an act. [< MF < L < *com-* together + *pellere* to drive]

com·pul·sive (kəm-pul′siv) *adj.* Compelling; compulsory. — **com·pul′sive·ly** *adv.* — **com·pul′sive·ness** *n.*

com·pul·so·ry (kəm-pul′sər-ē) *adj.* **1.** Employing compulsion; coercive. **2.** Required; obligatory: *compulsory* education. — **com·pul′so·ri·ly** *adv.* — **com·pul′so·ri·ness** *n.*

com·punc·tion (kəm-pungk′shən) *n.* **1.** An uneasiness of mind arising from wrongdoing; a sense of guilt or remorse. **2.** A feeling of slight regret or pity. [< OF < LL < L *com-* greatly + *pungere* to prick, sting] — **com·punc′tious** *adj.* — **com·punc′tious·ly** *adv.*

com·pu·ta·tion (kom′pyə-tā′shən) *n.* **1.** The act or method of computing. **2.** A computed amount or number.

com·pute (kəm-pyōōt′) *v.t. & v.i.* **·put·ed, ·put·ing** To ascertain (an amount or number) by calculation; reckon. — *n.* Computation. [< MF < L < *com-* together + *putare* to reckon.] — **com·put′a·bil′i·ty** *n.* — **com·put′a·ble** *adj.*

com·put·er (kəm-pyōō′tər) *n.* **1.** One who or that which computes. **2.** An electronic machine for the high-speed performance of mathematical and logical operations, or for the processing of large masses of coded information.

com·rade (kom′rad, -rid, kum′-) *n.* **1.** An intimate companion or friend. **2.** A person who shares one's own occupation, interests, etc. [< MF *camarade* < Sp. < L *camera* room] — **com′rade·ship** *n.*

Com·tism (kom′tiz-əm, kôṅ′-) *n.* The philosophy of Comte; positivism. — **Com·ti·an** (kom′tē·ən, kôṅ′-) *adj.*

con¹ (kon) *v.t.* **conned, con·ning** To study; peruse carefully; commit to memory. [Var. of CAN¹] — **con′ner** *n.*

con² (kon) *Naut. v.t.* **conned, con·ning** To direct the steering of (a vessel). — *n.* The act of conning. Also **conn.** [Earlier *cond* < F < L < *com-* together + *ducere* to lead]

con³ (kon) *U.S. Slang adj.* Confidence: *con* man; *con* game. — *v.t.* **conned, con·ning** To defraud; dupe; swindle. [< CONFIDENCE]

con- Var. of COM-.

con·cat·e·nate (kon-kat′ə-nāt) *v.t.* **·nat·ed, ·nat·ing** To join or link together; connect in a series. — *adj.* Connected in a series. [< L < *com-* together + *catena* chain]

con·cat·e·na·tion (kon-kat′ə-nā′shən) *n.* **1.** The act of linking together. **2.** A chainlike series, as of events, etc.

con·cave (*adj.* kon-kāv′, kon′kāv, kong′-; *n.* kon′kāv, kong′-; *v.* kon-kāv′) *adj.* Hollow and curving inward, as the interior of a sphere or bowl: opposed to *convex*. — *n.* A concave surface; vault. — *v.t.* **·caved, ·cav·ing** To make concave. [< MF < L < *com-* thoroughly + *cavus* hollow] — **con·cave′ly** *adv.* — **con·cave′ness** *n.*

con·cav·i·ty (kon-kav′ə-tē) *n., pl.* **·ties 1.** The state of being concave. **2.** A concave surface; a hollow.

con·ca·vo-con·cave (kon-kā′vō-kon-kāv′) *adj.* Biconcave.

con·ca·vo-con·vex (kon-kā′vō-kon-veks′) *adj.* Concave on one side and convex on the other, as a lens.

con·ceal (kən-sēl′) *v.t.* To keep from sight, discovery, or knowledge; hide; secrete. — **Syn.** See HIDE. [< OF < L < *com-* thoroughly + *celare* to hide] — **con·ceal′a·ble** *adj.* — **con·ceal′er** *n.* — **con·ceal′ment** *n.*

con·cede (kən-sēd′) *v.* **·ced·ed, ·ced·ing** *v.t.* **1.** To acknowledge as true, correct, or proper; admit. **2.** To grant; yield, as a right or privilege. — *v.i.* **3.** To make a concession; yield. — **Syn.** See CONFESS. [< L < *com-* thoroughly + *cedere* to yield, go away] — **con·ced′er** *n.*

con·ceit (kən-sēt′) *n.* **1.** Overweening self-esteem. **2.** An ingenious, fanciful thought or expression. **3.** In poetry, an elaborate, extended metaphor. **4.** Imagination; fancy. — **Syn.** See PRIDE. [< CONCEIVE]

con·ceit·ed (kən-sē′tid) *adj.* Having an excessively high opinion of oneself; vain. — **con·ceit′ed·ly** *adv.* — **con·ceit′ed·ness** *n.*

con·ceive (kən-sēv′) *v.* **·ceived, ·ceiv·ing** *v.t.* **1.** To become pregnant with. **2.** To form a concept or notion of; imagine: to *conceive* the perfect man. **3.** To understand; grasp. **4.** To express in a particular way. — *v.i.* **5.** To form a mental image; think: with *of*. **6.** To become pregnant. [< OF < L < *com-* thoroughly + *capere* to grasp, take] — **con·ceiv′·a·ble** *adj.* — **con·ceiv′a·bil′i·ty, con·ceiv′a·ble·ness** *n.* — **con·ceiv′a·bly** *adv.* — **con·ceiv′er** *n.*

con·cen·ter (kon-sen′tər) *v.t. & v.i.* To direct or come to a common point or center; focus. Also *Brit.* **con·cen′tre.** [< F < L < *com-* together + *centrum* center]

con·cen·trate (kon′sən-trāt) *v.* **·trat·ed, ·trat·ing** *v.t.* **1.** To draw or direct to a common point; focus: to *concentrate* troops. **2.** To intensify or purify by removing certain constituents; condense. — *v.i.* **3.** To converge toward a center. **4.** To become compacted, intensified, or more pure. **5.** To direct one's entire attention: often with *on* or *upon.* — *n.* A product of concentration, as in chemistry or metallurgy. — *adj.* Concentrated. — **con′cen·tra′tor** *n.*

con·cen·tra·tion (kon′sən-trā′shən) *n.* **1.** The act of concentrating, or the state of being concentrated. **2.** That which is concentrated, as a solution. **3.** Complete attention to some single problem, task, etc.

concentration camp An enclosed camp for the confinement of prisoners of war, political prisoners, aliens, etc.

con·cen·tra·tive (kon′sən-trā′tiv, kən-sen′trə-tiv) *adj.* Tending to concentrate, or characterized by concentration. — **con′cen·tra′tive·ly** *adv.* — **con′cen·tra′tive·ness** *n.*

con·cen·tric (kən-sen′trik) *adj.* Having a common center, as circles: opposed to *eccentric.* Also **con·cen′tri·cal.** — **con·cen′tri·cal·ly** *adv.* — **con·cen·tric·i·ty** (kon′sen-tris′ə-tē) *n.*

con·cept (kon′sept) *n.* A mental image; esp., a generalized idea formed by combining the elements of a class into the notion of one object; also, a thought or opinion. — **Syn.** See IDEA. [< L *conceptus* a conceiving]

con·cep·tion (kən-sep′shən) *n.* **1.** A conceiving, or a being conceived, in the womb. **2.** An embryo or fetus. **3.** A beginning; commencement. **4.** The act of forming concepts or ideas. **5.** A concept, idea, plan, or design. — **con·cep′tion·al** *adj.* — **con·cep′tive** *adj.*

con·cep·tu·al (kən-sep′chōō-əl) *adj.* Of or pertaining to conception or concepts. — **con·cep′tu·al·ly** *adv.*

con·cern (kən-sûrn′) *v.t.* **1.** To be of interest or importance to. **2.** To occupy the attention or mind of; engage; involve: used as a reflexive or in the passive. **3.** To affect with anxiety; trouble: often in the passive. — *n.* **1.** That which concerns or affects one; affair; business. **2.** Anxiety or interest; solicitous regard; care. **3.** Relation or bearing. **4.** A business enterprise; a firm. [< MF < Med.L < L *com-* thoroughly + *cernere* to see, discern] — **con·cerned′** *adj.*

con·cern·ing (kən-sûr′ning) *prep.* In relation to; regarding; about.

con·cern·ment (kən-sûrn′mənt) *n.* **1.** Importance. **2.** Concern; anxiety. **3.** Anything that relates to one; affair.

con·cert (*n.* kon′ûrt; *v.* kən-sûrt′) *n.* **1.** A musical performance by singers or instrumentalists. **2.** Agreement; harmony. — **in concert** In unison; all together. — *adj.* Of or for concerts. [< MF < Ital. < *concertare* to agree]

con·cert·ed (kən-sûr′tid) *adj.* **1.** Arranged, agreed upon, or done together; combined. **2.** *Music* Arranged in parts for voices or instruments. — **con·cert′ed·ly** *adv.*

con·cer·ti·na (kon′sər-tē′nə) *n.* A small bellowslike musical instrument with buttons for keys and handles on each of the two hexagonal ends. [< CONCERT + -INA]

con·cert·mas·ter (kon′sərt·mas′tər, -mäs′-) *n.* The leader of the first violin section of an orchestra, who acts as assistant to the conductor. Also **con′cert·meis′ter** (mīs′-)

con·cer·to (kən-cher′tō) *n.* *pl.* **·tos,** *Ital.* **·ti** (-tē) *Music* A composition, usu. of three movements, for performance by a solo instrument or instruments accompanied by an orchestra. Abbr. *con.* [< Ital. See CONCERT.]

concerto gros·so (grô′sō) *pl.* **concerti gros·si** (grô′sē) A concerto for a group of solo instruments and an orchestra. [< Ital., lit., big concerto]

con·ces·sion (kən-sesh′ən) *n.* **1.** The act of conceding. **2.** Anything so yielded. **3.** A right or privilege granted by a government. **4.** *U.S.* The right to operate a subsidiary business on certain premises. **5.** *Canadian* In Ontario and Quebec, a subdivision of land in township surveys. — **con·ces′sive** *adj.*

con·ces·sion·aire (kən-sesh′ən-âr′) *n.* One who holds or operates a concession. Also **con·ces′sion·er** [< F]

con·ces·sion·ar·y (kən-sesh′ən-er′ē) *adj.* Of or pertaining to a concession. — *n. pl.* **·ar·ies** A concessionaire.

concession road *Canadian* A road following a survey line.

conch (kongk, konch) *n. pl.* **conchs** (kongks) or **conch·es** (kon′chiz) **1.** Any of various marine mollusks having large, spiral, univalve shells. **2.** Such a shell. [< L < Gk. *konchē* shell]

con·chol·o·gy (kong·kol′ə-jē) *n.* The study of shells and mollusks. [< L *concha* shell + -LOGY] — **con·cho·log·i·cal** (kong′kə-loj′i-kəl) *adj.* — **con·chol′o·gist** *n.*

con·ci·erge (kon′sē-ûrzh′, *Fr.* kôɴ-syârzh′) *n.* An attendant or doorkeeper of a building, esp. in France, who performs custodial services. [< F]

CONCH
SHELL

con·cil·i·ate (kən-sil′ē-āt) *v.t.* **·at·ed, ·at·ing** **1.** To win over; placate; appease. **2.** To secure or attract by favorable measures; win. **3.** To make consistent. [< L < *concilium* council] — **con·cil·i·a·ble** (kən-sil′ē-ə-bəl) *adj.* — **con·cil′i·a′tion** *n.* — **con·cil′i·a′tor** *n.*

con·cil·i·a·to·ry (kən-sil′ē-ə-tôr′ē, -tō′rē) *adj.* Tending to reconcile or conciliate. Also **con·cil′i·a′tive.** — **con·cil′i·a·to′ri·ly** *adv.* — **con·cil′i·a·to′ri·ness** *n.*

con·cise (kən-sīs′) *adj.* Expressing much in brief form; compact. — **Syn.** See TERSE. [< L < *com-* thoroughly + *caedere* to cut] — **con·cise′ly** *adv.* — **con·cise′ness** *n.*

con·clave (kon′klāv, kong′-) *n.* **1.** A private or secret meeting. **2.** The private chambers in which the College of Cardinals meets to elect a pope; also, the meeting. [< F < L < *com-* together + *clavis* key] — **con′clav·ist** *n.*

con·clude (kən-klōōd′) *v.* **·clud·ed, ·clud·ing** *v.t.* **1.** To bring to an end; terminate. **2.** To arrange or settle finally; effect. **3.** To form an opinion or judgment about; decide. **4.** To resolve (to do); determine. — *v.i.* **5.** To come to an end. **6.** To come to a decision or agreement. [< L < *com-* thoroughly + *claudere* to close, shut off] — **con·clud′er** *n.*

con·clu·sion (kən-klōō′zhən) *n.* **1.** The end or termination of something. **2.** A closing part, as of a speech. **3.** The result of an act or process; outcome. **4.** A judgment or opinion obtained by reasoning. **5.** A final decision; resolve. **6.** A final arranging; settlement, as of a treaty. — **in conclusion** As a final statement or summing up.

con·clu·sive (kən-klōō′siv) *adj.* Putting an end to a question; decisive. — **con·clu′sive·ly** *adv.* — **con·clu′sive·ness** *n.*

con·coct (kon-kokt′, kən-) *v.t.* **1.** To make by mixing ingredients, as food, a drink, etc. **2.** To make up; devise: to *concoct* a plan. [< L < *com-* together + *coquere* to cook, boil] — **con·coct′er** or **con·coc′tor** *n.* — **con·coc′tive** *adj.*

con·coc·tion (kon-kok′shən, kən-) *n.* **1.** The act of concocting. **2.** Something concocted.

con·com·i·tance (kon-kom′ə-təns, kən-) *n.* Existence or occurrence together; accompaniment. Also **con·com′i·tan·cy.**

con·com·i·tant (kon-kom′ə-tənt, kən-) *adj.* Existing or occurring together; attendant. — *n.* An attendant circumstance, state, or thing. [< L < *com-* with + *comitari* to accompany] — **con·com′i·tant·ly** *adv.*

con·cord (kon′kôrd, kong′-) *n.* **1.** Unity of feeling or interest; agreement; accord. **2.** Peace; friendly relations. **3.** A treaty establishing this. **4.** *Music* Consonance. — **Syn.** See HARMONY. [< MF < L < *com-* together + *cor, cordis* heart]

con·cor·dance (kon·kôr′dəns, kən-) *n.* **1.** Agreement; concord. **2.** An alphabetical index of the important words in a book as they occur in context: a *concordance* of the Bible.

con·cor·dant (kon-kôr′dənt, kən-) *adj.* Existing in concord; agreeing; harmonious. — **con·cor′dant·ly** *adv.*

con·cor·dat (kon-kôr′dat) *n.* **1.** An agreement between the papacy and a government on church affairs. **2.** Any official agreement or pact.

con·course (kon′kôrs, -kōrs, kong′-) *n.* **1.** A coming together; confluence. **2.** A crowd; throng. **3.** A large place for the assembling or passage of crowds. [< MF < L < *com-* together + *currere* to run]

con·crete (kon′krēt; *for adj., n., & v. def. 3,* also kon·krēt′) *adj.* **1.** Specific, as opposed to general: a *concrete* example. **2.** Physically perceptible; objectively real. **3.** *Gram.* Naming a specific thing or class of things, rather than an abstract quality or state. **4.** Constituting a composite mass or substance; solid. **5.** Made of concrete. — *n.* **1.** A building material of sand and gravel or broken rock united by cement, used for roadways, bridges, walls, etc. **2.** That which is concrete: often preceded by *the.* — *v.* **·cret·ed, ·cret·ing** *v.t.* **1.** To bring together in one mass or body; cause to coalesce. **2.** To cover with concrete. — *v.i.* **3.** To coalesce; solidify. [< L < *com-* together + *crescere* to grow] — **con·crete′ly** *adv.* — **con·crete′ness** *n.*

con·cre·tion (kon-krē′shən) *n.* **1.** The act or process of growing or coming together; a solidifying. **2.** A concrete mass. — **con·cre′tive** *adj.* — **con·cre′tive·ly** *adv.*

con·cre·tize (kon′kri·tīz) *v.t.* **·tized, ·tiz·ing** To render concrete; make specific.

con·cu·bine (kong′kyə·bīn, kon′-) *n.* **1.** A woman who cohabits with a man without being married to him. **2.** In certain polygamous societies, a secondary wife. [< F < L < *com-* with + *cumbere* to lie] — **con·cu·bi·nage** (kon-kyōō′bə·nij) *n.* — **con·cu′bi·nar·y** *adj.*

con·cu·pis·cence (kon-kyōō′pə-səns) *n.* **1.** Sexual desire; lust. **2.** Any immoderate desire. [< L < *com-* thoroughly + *cupere* to desire] — **con·cu′pis·cent** *adj.*

con·cur (kən-kûr′) *v.i.* **·curred, ·cur·ring** **1.** To agree or approve, as in opinion or action. **2.** To cooperate or combine. **3.** To happen at the same time. **4.** To converge to a point, as lines. [< L < *com-* together + *currere* to run]

con·cur·rence (kən·kûr'əns) n. 1. The act of concurring. 2. Cooperation or combination to effect some purpose or end. 3. Agreement in mind or opinion; assent; consent. 4. Simultaneous occurrence; coincidence. 5. Geom. The point where three or more lines meet. Also **con·cur'ren·cy.**

con·cur·rent (kən·kûr'ənt) adj. 1. Occurring together at the same time. 2. United in action or application; cooperating; coordinate. 3. Law Having the same authority or jurisdiction. 4. Meeting at or going toward the same point. 5. In agreement or accordance. — **con·cur'rent·ly** adv.

con·cus·sion (kən·kush'ən) n. 1. A violent shaking; jar. 2. Pathol. A violent shock to some organ, esp. to the brain, by a fall, sudden blow, or blast. [< L < com- together + quatere to strike, beat] — **con·cus·sive** (kən·kus'iv) adj.

con·demn (kən·dem') v.t. 1. To hold to be wrong; censure. 2. To pronounce judicial sentence against. 3. To show the guilt of; convict. 4. To pronounce or declare to be unfit for use, usually by official order. 5. U.S. To appropriate for public use by judicial decree; declare forfeited. [< L < com- thoroughly + damnare to condemn] — **con·dem·na·ble** (kən·dem'nə·bəl) adj. — **con·demn·er** (kən·dem'ər) n.

con·dem·na·tion (kon'dem·nā'shən) n. 1. The act of condemning, or the state of being condemned. 2. A cause or occasion for condemning. — **con·dem·na·to·ry** (kən·dem'nə·tô'rē, -tō'rē) adj.

con·den·sa·tion (kon'den·sā'shən) n. 1. The act of condensing, or the state of being condensed. 2. Any product of condensing.

con·dense (kən·dens') v. ·densed, ·dens·ing v.t. 1. To compress or make dense; consolidate. 2. To abridge or make concise, as an essay. 3. To change from the gaseous to the liquid state, or from the liquid to the solid state, as by cooling or compression. — v.i. 4. To become condensed. [< L < com- together + densus crowded, close] — **con·den'sa·bil'i·ty** or **con·den'si·bil'i·ty** n. — **con·den'sa·ble** or **con·den'si·ble** adj.

condensed milk Cow's milk, sweetened with sugar, and thickened by evaporation of its water content.

con·dens·er (kən·den'sər) n. 1. One who or that which condenses. 2. Any device for reducing a vapor to liquid or solid form. 3. Electr. A capacitor. 4. Optics A combination of lenses for effectively focusing light rays.

con·de·scend (kon'di·send') v.i. 1. To lower oneself (to do something); deign. 2. To behave in a patronizing manner. [< MF < LL < com- together + descendere to stoop] — **con'de·scen'sion, con'de·scen'dence** n.

con·de·scend·ing (kon'di·sen'ding) adj. Showing conscious courtesy toward inferiors; esp., making a display of such courtesy; patronizing. — **con'de·scend'ing·ly** adv.

con·di·ment (kon'də·mənt) n. A sauce, relish, spice, etc., used to season food. [< L condire to pickle]

con·di·tion (kən·dish'ən) n. 1. The state or mode of existence of a person or thing. 2. State of health; esp., a healthful state. 3. Informal An ailment: a heart condition. 4. An event, fact, or circumstance necessary to the occurrence of some other; a prerequisite: Hard work is the condition of success. 5. Usu. pl. The circumstances affecting an activity or a mode of existence: poor living conditions. 6. Social status. 7. In a will, contract, etc., a provision allowing for modification upon the occurrence of some uncertain future event. — **in** (or **out of**) **condition** Fit (or unfit) for proper performance, esp. of some physical activity. — **on condition that** Provided that; if. — v.t. 1. To be a condition or prerequisite of. 2. To specify as a condition; stipulate. 3. To render fit or in good condition. 4. Psychol. To train to a behavior pattern or conditioned response. 5. To accustom (someone) to. — v.i. 6. To bargain; stipulate. [< OF < L < com- together + dicere to say] — **con·di'tion·er** n.

con·di·tion·al (kən·dish'ən·əl) adj. 1. Not absolute; tentative. 2. Gram. Expressing or implying a condition. — n. Gram. A conditional word, tense, clause, or mood. — **con·di'·tion·al'i·ty** (-al'ə·tē) n. — **con·di'tion·al·ly** adv.

con·di·tioned response (kən·dish'ənd) Psychol. A learned response to a previously neutral stimulus, made directly effective by its repeated association with a stimulus normally evoking the response. Also **conditioned reflex.**

con·dole (kən·dōl') v. ·doled, ·dol·ing v.i. To grieve or express sympathy with one in affliction: with with. [< LL < L com- together + dolere to grieve] — **con·do·la·to·ry** (kən·dō'lə·tôr'ē, -tō'rē) adj. — **con·dol'er** n.

con·do·lence (kən·dō'ləns, occasionally kon'də·ləns) n. Expression of sympathy with a person in pain or sorrow. Also **con·dole·ment** (kən·dōl'mənt).

con·dom (kon'dəm, kun'-) n. A sheath for the penis, usu. made of rubber and having an antivenereal or contraceptive function. [? Alter. of Conton, 18th c. English physician]

con·do·min·i·um (kon'də·min'ē·əm) n. 1. Joint sovereignty or ownership ? U.S. An apartment house in which the units are owned separately; also, an apartment in such a house. [< NL < L com- together + dominium rule]

con·done (kən·dōn') v.t. ·doned, ·don·ing To treat (an of-

fense) as overlooked or as if it had not been committed. [< L < com- thoroughly + donare to give] — **con'do·na'tion** n. — **con·don'er** n.

con·dor (kon'dôr, -dər) n. A vulture of the high Andes, one of the largest flying birds, having a bare head and a white, downy neck. [< Sp. < Quechua cuntur]

con·duce (kən·dōōs', -dyōōs') v.i. ·duced, ·duc·ing To help or tend toward a result; contribute: with to. [< L conducere to bring together]

con·du·cive (kən·dōō'siv, -dyōō'-) adj. Contributive or promotive; leading; helping: with to. Also **con·du·cent** (kən·dōō'sənt, -dyōō'-). — **con·du'cive·ness** n.

con·duct (v. kən·dukt'; n. kon'dukt) v.t. 1. To accompany and show the way; guide; escort. 2. To manage or control. 3. To direct and lead the performance of, as an orchestra, opera, etc. 4. To serve as a medium of transmission for; convey; transmit. 5. To act or behave: use reflexively. — v.i. 6. To serve as a conductor. 7. To direct or lead. — n. 1. The way a person acts; behavior. 2. Management; control. 3. The act of guiding or leading. [< L < com- together + ducere to lead] — **con·duct'i·bil'i·ty** n. — **con·duct'i·ble** adj. — **con·duc·tive** (kən·duk'tiv) adj.

con·duc·tance (kən·duk'təns) n. Electr. The ability of a body to pass a current: the reciprocal of resistance.

con·duc·tion (kən·duk'shən) n. 1. Physics The transmission of heat, sound, or electricity through matter without motion of the conducting body as a whole. 2. Physiol. The transference of a stimulus along nerve fibers.

con·duc·tiv·i·ty (kon'duk·tiv'ə·tē) n. Physics The capacity to transmit sound, heat, or electricity.

con·duc·tor (kən·duk'tər) n. 1. One who conducts or leads. 2. Chiefly U.S. One who has charge of a railroad car, bus, etc. 3. The director of an orchestra or chorus. 4. Any substance, material, or medium that conducts electricity, heat, etc. — **con·duc'tor·ship** n. — **con·duc'tress** n.fem.

con·duit (kon'dit, -dōō·it) n. 1. A channel or pipe for conveying water or other liquid; a canal; aqueduct. 2. A covered passage or tube for electric wires. [< MF < L < com- together + ducere to lead]

cone (kōn) n. 1. Geom. a A surface generated by a straight line passing through all the points of a fixed closed curve and a fixed point (the vertex) outside the plane of the curve. b A solid bounded by such a surface. 2. A thing that tapers uniformly from a circular part to a point, as a machine part or the pastry shell used to hold ice cream. 3. Bot. A dry multiple fruit, as of the pine, composed of scales arranged symmetrically around an axis and enclosing seeds. — v.t. coned, con·ing To shape conically. [< L < Gk. kōnos]

con·el·rad (kon'əl·rad) n. A technique for controlling radio signals from stations so as to prevent enemy aircraft from using the signals for navigation or information. [< CON(TROL OF) EL(ECTROMAGNETIC) RAD(IATION)]

Con·es·to·ga wagon (kon'is·tō'gə) U.S. A type of covered wagon with broad wheels, used by American pioneers for westward travel over the prairies. [after Conestoga, Pa., where first made]

CONESTOGA WAGON

co·ney (kō'nē, kun'ē) See CONY.

con·fab (kon'fab) Informal v.i. ·fabbed, ·fab·bing To converse. — n. A conversation. [Short for CONFABULATION]

con·fab·u·late (kən·fab'yə·lāt) v.i. ·lat·ed, ·lat·ing To chat; gossip; converse. [< L < com- together + fabulari to chat] — **con·fab'u·la'tion** n. — **con·fab·u·la·to·ry** (kən·fab'yə·lə·tôr'ē, -tō'rē) adj.

con·fec·tion (kən·fek'shən) n. 1. The act or process of mixing or compounding. 2. Any of various sweet preparations, as candy or preserves. — **con·fec'tion·ar·y** adj. & n.

con·fec·tion·er (kən·fek'shən·ər) n. One who makes or deals in confectionery.

confectioner's sugar A finely ground powdered sugar, used in icings, confections, etc.

con·fec·tion·er·y (kən·fek'shən·er'ē) n. pl. ·er·ies 1. Sweetmeats collectively. 2. A confectioner's shop, or the business of a confectioner.

con·fed·er·a·cy (kən·fed'ər·ə·sē) n. pl. ·cies 1. A union of states or persons for mutual support or action; a league; alliance. 2. An unlawful combination; conspiracy. — **the Confederacy** The Confederate States of America: also Southern Confederacy.

con·fed·er·ate (n., adj. kən·fed'ər·it; v. kən·fed'ə·rāt) n. One who takes part in a league or plot; an associate; accomplice. — adj. Associated in a confederacy. — v.t. & v.i. ·at·ed, ·at·ing To form or join in a confederacy. [< LL < L com- together + fœdus league] — **con·fed'er·a'tive** adj.

Con·fed·er·ate (kən·fed'ər·it) adj. Pertaining to the Confederate States of America. — n. An adherent of the Confederate States of America. Abbr. Confed.

Confederate States of America A league of eleven southern States that seceded from the United States during the period from December, 1860 to May, 1861.

con·fed·er·a·tion (kən·fed′ə·rā′shən) *n.* **1.** The act of confederating, or the state of being confederated. **2.** An association of states usu. less permanent than a federation.

Con·fed·er·a·tion (kən·fed′ə·rā′shən) *n.* **1.** The federation formed by Ontario, Quebec, Nova Scotia, and New Brunswick in 1867, now including ten provinces. **2.** The union of the American colonies, 1781–89, under the Articles of Confederation.

con·fer (kən·fûr′) *v.* **·ferred, ·fer·ring** *v.t.* **1.** To grant as a gift or benefit; bestow. Abbr. *cf.* — *v.i.* **2.** To hold a conference; consult together; take counsel. [< L < *com*- together + *ferre* to bring, carry] — **con·fer′ment** *n.* — **con·fer′ra·ble** *adj.* — **con·fer′rer** *n.*

con·fer·ee (kon′fə·rē′) *n.* One who takes part in conference or a conference. Also **con·fer·ree′**.

con·fer·ence (kon′fər·əns, -frəns) *n.* **1.** A discussion or consultation on some important matter; also, a formal meeting for this. **2.** A league or association, as of athletic teams, schools, churches, etc. — **con′fer·en′tial** (-fə·ren′shəl) *adj.*

con·fess (kən·fes′) *v.t.* **1.** To acknowledge or admit, as a fault, guilt, or sin. **2.** To concede or admit to be true. **3.** To acknowledge belief or faith in. **4.** *Eccl.* **a** To admit or make known (one's sins), esp. to a priest, in order to obtain absolution. **b** To hear the confession of: said of a priest. — *v.i.* **5.** To make acknowledgment, as of fault or crime: with *to.* **6.** To make confession to a priest. [< MF < L < *com*- thoroughly + *fateri* to own, declare] — **con·fess′ed·ly** *adv.*

— **Syn. 1.** *Confess* is now generally restricted to the sense of making known to others one's own error or wrongdoing: to *confess* a robbery. We *acknowledge* that for which we are responsible, often with no bad implication: to *acknowledge* one's signature. *Admit* and *concede* indicate a yielding to the assertion or wish of another; we *admit* the truth of an allegation; we *concede* a demand, claim, opposing view, etc. — **Ant.** deny, disavow, repudiate.

con·fes·sion (kən·fesh′ən) *n.* **1.** The act of confessing; acknowledgment; admission, esp. of guilt. **2.** That which is confessed. **3.** A statement, esp. a formal document, in which something is confessed. **4.** *Eccl.* The contrite acknowledgment of one's sins to a priest in order to obtain absolution. **5.** A body of doctrine put forth as the belief of a church: also **confession of faith. 6.** A church holding a particular confession of faith.

con·fes·sion·al (kən·fesh′ən·əl) *adj.* Of, pertaining to, or like confession. — *n.* A small enclosure or stall where a priest hears confessions. Also *Rare* **con·fes′sion·ar′y** (-er′ē).

con·fes·sor (kən·fes′ər) *n.* **1.** A priest who hears confessions. **2.** One who confesses. Also **con·fess′er.** Abbr. *conf.*

con·fet·ti (kən·fet′ē) *n.pl.* **1.** (construed as *sing.*) Small pieces of colored paper thrown at carnivals, weddings, etc. **2.** Bonbons. [< Ital., pl. of *confetto* confection]

con·fi·dant (kon′fə·dant′, -dänt′, kon′fə·dant, -dänt) *n.* A person to whom secrets are confided. — **con′fi·dante′** *n.fem.*

con·fide (kən·fīd′) *v.* **·fid·ed, ·fid·ing** *v.t.* **1.** To reveal in trust or confidence. **2.** To put into another's trust or keeping. — *v.i.* **3.** To have trust; impart secrets trustingly: with *in.* [< L < *com*- thoroughly + *fidere* to trust] — **con·fid′er** *n.*

con·fi·dence (kon′fə·dəns) *n.* **1.** A feeling of trust in a person or thing; reliance; faith. **2.** A relationship of trustful intimacy. **3.** Self-assurance; also, fearlessness. **4.** Excessive self-assurance. **5.** A feeling of certainty. **6.** A secret. — **to take into one's confidence** To trust with one's secrets.

confidence game A swindle in which the victim is defrauded after his confidence has been won: also, *U.S. Slang,* **con game.** Also **confidence trick.**

confidence man A swindler in a confidence game.

con·fi·dent (kon′fə·dənt) *adj.* **1.** Having confidence; assured: *confident* of success. **2.** Self-assured; also, bold; presumptuous. — *n.* A confidant. — **con′fi·dent·ly** *adv.*

con·fi·den·tial (kon′fə·den′shəl) *adj.* **1.** Secret: *confidential* information. **2.** Enjoying another's confidence; trusted. **3.** Denoting the confiding of secrets: a *confidential* manner. — **con·fi·den·ti·al·i·ty** (kon′fə·den′shē·al′ə·tē), **con′fi·den′tial·ness** *n.* — **con′fi·den′tial·ly** *adv.*

con·fid·ing (kən·fī′ding) *adj.* That trusts or confides; unsuspicious. — **con·fid′ing·ly** *adv.* — **con·fid′ing·ness** *n.*

con·fig·u·ra·tion (kən·fig′yə·rā′shən) *n.* **1.** The arrangement of the parts of a thing, or the form resulting therefrom; conformation; contour. **2.** *Psychol.* A gestalt. [< LL < L *com*- together + *figurare* to shape, fashion] — **con·fig′u·ra′tion·al, con·fig·u·ra·tive** (kən·fig′yər·ə·tiv, -yə·rā′tiv) *adj.*

con·fine (*v.* kən·fīn′; *n.* kon′fīn) *v.* **·fined, ·fin·ing** *v.t.* **1.** To shut within an enclosure; imprison. **2.** To restrain or oblige to stay within doors. **3.** To hold within limits; restrict: to *confine* remarks. — *n.* Usu. *pl.* A boundary or border. [< MF < L < *com*- together + *finis* border] — **con·fin′a·ble** or **con·fine′a·ble** *adj.* — **con·fin′er** *n.*

con·fine·ment (kən·fīn′mənt) *n.* **1.** The act of confining, or the state of being confined. **2.** Childbirth.

con·firm (kən·fûrm′) *v.t.* **1.** To assure the validity of; verify. **2.** To add firmness to; strengthen. **3.** To render valid and binding by formal approval. **4.** To receive into the church by confirmation. [< OF < L < *com*- thoroughly + *firmus* strong] — **con·firm′a·ble** *adj.* — **con·firm′er,** *Law* **con·firm·or** (kon′fər·môr′, kən·fûr′mər) *n.*

con·fir·ma·tion (kon′fər·mā′shən) *n.* **1.** The act of confirming. **2.** That which confirms; proof. **3.** A religious rite in which a person is admitted to all the privileges of a church.

con·firm·a·to·ry (kən·fûr′mə·tôr′ē, -tō′rē) *adj.* Confirming.

con·firmed (kən·fûrmd′) *adj.* **1.** Firmly established; ratified. **2.** Inveterate; chronic; habitual: a *confirmed* skeptic. **3.** Having received the rites of religious confirmation.

con·fis·cate (kon′fis·kāt) *v.t.* **·cat·ed, ·cat·ing 1.** To seize or appropriate for the public use or treasury, usu. as a penalty. **2.** To appropriate by or as by authority. — *adj.* **1.** Appropriated or forfeited. **2.** Deprived of property through confiscation. [< L < *com*- together + *fiscus* chest, treasury] — **con′fis·ca′tion** *n.* — **con′fis·ca′tor** *n.* — **con·fis·ca·to·ry** (kən·fis′kə·tôr′ē, -tō′rē) *adj.*

con·fla·gra·tion (kon′flə·grā′shən) *n.* A great or extensive fire. [< L < *com*- thoroughly + *flagrare* to burn]

con·flict (*n.* kon′flikt; *v.* kən·flikt′) *n.* **1.** A struggle; battle. **2.** Mutual antagonism, as of ideas, interests, etc. **3.** A clash between contradictory impulses within an individual. — *v.i.* **1.** To come into collision; be in mutual opposition; clash. **2.** To engage in battle; struggle. [< L < *com*- together + *fligere* to strike] — **con·flic′tive** *adj.*

con·flu·ence (kon′floo·əns) *n.* **1.** A flowing together of streams; also, the place where they meet. **2.** The body or stream of water so formed. **3.** A flocking together; crowd. Also **con·flux** (kon′fluks). [< L < *com*- together + *fluere* to flow] — **con′flu·ent** *adj.* — **con′flu·ent·ly** *adv.*

con·form (kən·fôrm′) *v.i.* **1.** To show identity or resemblance; correspond: with *to*: to *conform* to specification. **2.** To adhere to conventional behavior. — *v.t.* **3.** To make the same or similar: with *to.* **4.** To bring (oneself) into harmony or agreement: with *to.* [< F < L < *com*- together + *formare* to shape] — **con·form′er** *n.*

con·form·a·ble (kən·fôr′mə·bəl) *adj.* **1.** In agreement; harmonious. **2.** Corresponding in form, character, or use; similar. **3.** Compliant or obedient; submissive. — **con·form′a·bil′i·ty, con·form′a·ble·ness** *n.* — **con·form′a·bly** *adv.*

con·form·ance (kən·fôr′məns) *n.* Conformity.

con·for·ma·tion (kon′fôr·mā′shən) *n.* **1.** The manner in which a thing is formed; structure or outline. **2.** The symmetrical arrangement and shaping of parts. **3.** The act of conforming, or the state of being conformed.

con·form·ist (kən·fôr′mist) *n.* One who conforms.

con·form·i·ty (kən·fôr′mə·tē) *n.* *pl.* **·ties 1.** Correspondence in form, manner, or use; agreement; harmony; congruity. **2.** The act or habit of conforming; acquiescence.

con·found (kon·found′, kən-; *for def. 4* kon′found′) *v.t.* **1.** To confuse, amaze, or bewilder. **2.** To confuse with something else; fail to distinguish. **3.** To confuse or mingle indistinguishably. **4.** To damn: used as an oath. [< AF, OF < L < *com*- together + *fundere* to pour] — **con·found′er** *n.*

— **Syn. 1.** puzzle, perplex, dumfound, mystify.

con·found·ed (kon·foun′did, kən-) *adj.* **1.** Confused or abashed. **2.** *Informal* Damned; detestable: a *confounded* cheat. — **con·found′ed·ly** *adv.*

con·frere (kon′frâr) *n.* A fellow member; a colleague. [< MF < L *com*- with + *frater* brother]

con·front (kən·frunt′) *v.t.* **1.** To stand face to face with; face defiantly. **2.** To put face to face: to *confront* a liar with the truth. [< F < L *com*- together + *frons, frontis* face, forehead] — **con·front′ment** *n.* — **con·front′er** *n.*

con·fron·ta·tion (kon′frən·tā′shən) *n.* **1.** The act of confronting, or the state of being confronted. **2.** The provocation of conflict as a means of effecting political change; also, a crisis or conflict so caused.

Con·fu·cian·ism (kən·fyōō′shən·iz′əm) *n.* The ethical system taught by Confucius, emphasizing ancestor worship, devotion to family and friends, and the maintenance of justice and peace. — **Con·fu′cian·ist** *n.* — **Con·fu′cian** *n.* & *adj.*

con·fuse (kən·fyōōz′) *v.t.* **·fused, ·fus·ing 1.** To perplex or perturb; confound; bewilder. **2.** To mix indiscriminately; jumble. **3.** To mistake one for the other. [< L < *com*- together + *fundere* to pour] — **con·fus′ed·ly** (kən·fyōō′zid·lē) *adv.* — **con·fus′ed·ness** *n.* — **con·fus′ing·ly** *adv.*

con·fu·sion (kən·fyōō′zhən) *n.* **1.** The act of confusing, or the state of being confused. **2.** Disarray; disorder. **3.** Perplexity of mind. **4.** Embarrassment. — **con·fu′sion·al** *adj.*

con·fute (kən·fyōōt′) *v.t.* **·fut·ed, ·fut·ing 1.** To prove to be wrong, false, or invalid; refute successfully. **2.** To overwhelm with proofs or disproofs; prove (a person) to be in the wrong. **3.** To bring to naught; confound. **— Syn.** See REFUTE. [< L *confutare* to check, restrain] **— con·fu·ta·tion** (kon′fyoō-tā′shən) *n.* **— con·fut′er** *n.*

con·ga (kong′gə) *n.* **1.** A dance of Latin American origin in which the dancers form a winding line. **2.** The music for this dance, in fast 4/4 time. [< Am. Sp.]

con game *U.S. Slang* A confidence game.

con·gé (kon′zhā, *Fr.* kôṅ-zhā′) *n.* **1.** A formal leave-taking. **2.** Dismissal. [< F < L < *com-* thoroughly + *ire* to go]

con·geal (kən-jēl′) *v.t. & v.i.* **1.** To change from a fluid to a solid condition, as by freezing or curdling. **2.** To clot or co-agulate, as blood. [< MF < L < *com-* together + *gelare* to freeze] **— con·geal′a·ble** *adj.* **— con·geal′er** *n.* **— con·geal′ment** *n.*

con·gen·ial (kən-jēn′yəl) *adj.* **1.** Having similar character or tastes; sympathetic. **2.** Suited to one's disposition; agree-able: a *congenial* job. **— con·ge·ni·al·i·ty** (kən-jē′nē-al′ə-tē) *n.* **— con·gen′ial·ly** *adv.*

con·gen·i·tal (kən-jen′ə-təl) *adj.* **1.** Existing prior to or at birth: a *congenital* defect. **2.** Loosely, disposed as if by birth: a *congenital* liar. [< L < *com-* together + *genitus*, pp. of *gignere* to bear] **— con·gen′i·tal·ly** *adv.*

con·ger (kong′gər) *n.* A marine eel, used as a food fish. Also **conger eel.** [< OF < L < Gk. *gongros*]

con·ge·ries (kon′jə-rēz, kon-jir′ēz) *n.pl.* (*usu.* construed as *sing.*) A collection of things; a mass; heap. [< L < *con-gerere* to bring together]

con·gest (kən-jest′) *v.t.* **1.** To collect or crowd together; overcrowd. **2.** *Pathol.* To surcharge (an organ or part) with an excess of blood. **— v.i. 3.** To become congested. [< L < *com-* together + *gerere* to bear, carry] **— con·ges′tion** *n.* **— con·ges′tive** *adj.*

con·glom·er·ate (*adj., n.* kən-glom′ər-it; *v.* kən-glom′ə-rāt) *adj.* **1.** Massed or clustered. **2.** *Geol.* Consisting of loosely cemented heterogeneous material: *conglomerate* clay: also **con·glom·er·at·ic** (kən-glom′ə-rat′ik), **con·glom′er·it′ic** (-ə-rit′ik). **— n. 1.** A heterogeneous collection; cluster. **2.** *Geol.* A rock composed of pebbles, etc., loosely cemented to-gether. **— v.t. & v.i. ·at·ed, ·at·ing** To gather into a cohering mass. [< L < *com-* together + *glomus, glomeris* ball] **— con·glom′er·a′tion** *n.*

con·glu·ti·nate (kən-gloō′tə-nāt) *v.t. & v.i.* **·nat·ed, ·nat·ing** To glue or stick together; adhere. **— adj.** Glued together; united by adhesion. [< L < *com-* together + *glutinare* to stick] **— con·glu′ti·na′tion** *n.* **— con·glu′ti·na′tive** *adj.*

congo snake A tailed aquatic salamander of the SE U.S. Also **congo eel.**

con·grat·u·late (kən-grach′oō-lāt) *v.t.* **·lat·ed, ·lat·ing** To express pleasure in or otherwise acknowledge the achieve-ment or good fortune of (another); felicitate. [< L < *com-* together + *gratulari* to rejoice] **— con·grat′u·lant** *adj. & n.* **— con·grat′u·la′tor** *n.* **— con·grat′u·la·to·ry** *adj.*

con·grat·u·la·tion (kən-grach′oō-lā′shən) *n.* **1.** The act of congratulating. **2.** *pl.* Expressions of pleasure and good wishes on another's fortune or success.

con·gre·gate (*v.* kong′grə-gāt; *adj.* kong′grə-git) *v.t. & v.i.* **·gat·ed, ·gat·ing** To bring or come together into a crowd; as-semble. **— adj. 1.** Relating to a congregation. **2.** Gath-ered together; collected. [< L < *com-* together + *gregare* to collect] **— con′gre·ga′tive** *adj.* **— con′gre·ga′tor** *n.*

con·gre·ga·tion (kong′grə-gā′shən) *n.* **1.** The act of con-gregating; a collecting into one mass, body, or assembly. **2.** An assemblage of people or things. **3.** A group of people met together for worship; also, the body of persons who worship in a local church; a parish. **— con′gre·ga′tion·al** *adj.*

con·gre·ga·tion·al·ism (kong′grə-gā′shən-əl-iz′əm) *n.* A form of church government in which each local congregation is autonomous in all church matters.

Con·gre·ga·tion·al·ism (kong′grə-gā′shən-əl-iz′əm) *n.* The type of organization and system of beliefs of an evan-gelical Protestant denomination (**Congregational Christian Churches**) practicing congregationalism. **— Con′gre·ga′·tion·al** *adj.* **— Con′gre·ga′tion·al·ist** *n.*

con·gress (kong′gris) *n.* **1.** An assembly or conference. **2.** A coming together; meeting. **3.** The legislature of various nations, esp. of a republic. **— v.i.** To meet at a congress. [< L < *com-* together + *gradi* to walk]

Con·gress (kong′gris) *n.* The legislative body of the U.S., consisting of the Senate and the House of Representatives; also, this body during one of the two-year periods between elections to the House of Representatives.

con·gres·sion·al (kən-gresh′ən-əl) *adj. Often cap. U.S.* Pertaining to a congress, esp. to the U.S. Congress.

Congressional district *U.S.* A division of a State, en-titled to one representative in Congress.

Congressional Medal of Honor See MEDAL OF HONOR.

Congressional Record *U.S.* An official publication con-taining the debates and proceedings of Congress.

con·gress·man (kong′gris-mən) *n. pl.* **·men** (-mən) *Often cap.* A member of the U.S. Congress, esp. of the House of Representatives. **— con′gress·wom′an** *n.fem.*

con·gru·ence (kong′groō-əns) *n.* Conformity; agreement.

con·gru·ent (kong′groō-ənt) *adj.* **1.** Agreeing or conform-ing; congruous. **2.** *Geom.* Exactly coinciding when super-imposed. [< L *congruere* to agree] **— con′gru·en·cy** *n.* **— con′gru·ent·ly** *adv.*

con·gru·i·ty (kən-groō′ə-tē) *n. pl.* **·ties** **1.** The state or quality of being congruous; agreement or fitness. **2.** An example of agreement. **3.** *Geom.* Exact correspondence when superimposed. **— Syn.** See HARMONY.

con·gru·ous (kong′groō-əs) *adj.* **1.** Agreeing in nature or qualities; harmonious. **2.** Appropriate; fit. **3.** *Geom.* Con-gruent. **— con′gru·ous·ly** *adv.* **— con′gru·ous·ness** *n.*

con·ic (kon′ik) *adj.* **1.** Cone-shaped. **2.** Of or formed by or upon a cone. Also **con′i·cal. — n.** *Math.* A conic section. [< Gk. *kōnos* cone] **— con′i·cal·ly** *adv.*

conic section *Math.* A curve formed by the intersection of a plane with a cone having a circular base, being an ellipse, parabola, or hyperbola, according to the inclination of the cutting plane to the axis.

co·nid·i·um (kō-nid′ē-əm) *n. pl.* **·nid·i·a** (-nid′ē-ə) *Bot.* An asexual propagative spore of many species of fungi. Also **co·nid·i·o·spore** (kō-nid′ē-ə-spôr′, -spōr′). [< NL < Gk. *konis* dust] **— co·nid′i·al** *adj.*

CONIC SECTIONS

a Circle. *b* Pa-rabola. *c* Hyper-bola. *d* Ellipse. *e* Right-line.

con·i·fer (kon′ə-fər, kō′nə-) *n.* Any of a large and widely distributed family of evergreen shrubs and trees, as the pines, spruces, firs, and junipers. [< L < *conus* cone + *ferre* to bear] **— co·nif·er·ous** (kō-nif′ər-əs) *adj.*

con·jec·tur·al (kən-jek′chər-əl) *adj.* **1.** Involving or de-pendent upon conjecture. **2.** Given to conjecture. **— con·jec′tur·al·ly** *adv.*

con·jec·ture (kən-jek′chər) *v.* **·tured, ·tur·ing** *v.t.* **1.** To conclude from incomplete evidence; guess; infer. **— v.i. 2.** To make a conjecture. **— Syn.** See SUPPOSE. **— n. 1.** In-ference from incomplete evidence. **2.** A conclusion based on this; a guess; surmise. **— Syn.** See HYPOTHESIS. [< L < *com-* together + *jacere* to throw] **— con·jec′tur·a·ble** *adj.* **— con·jec′tur·a·bly** *adv.* **— con·jec′tur·er** *n.*

con·join (kən-join′) *v.t. & v.i.* To join together; associate; connect; unite. [< MF < L < *com-* together + *jungere* to join] **— con·join′er** *n.*

con·joint (kən-joint′) *adj.* **1.** Associated; conjoined. **2.** Joint. **— con·joint′ly** *adv.*

con·ju·gal (kon′joō-gəl, -jə-) *adj.* Pertaining to marriage or to the relation of husband and wife; connubial. [< F < L *conjungere* to join in marriage] **— con·ju·gal·i·ty** (kon′joō-gal′ə-tē) *n.* **— con′ju·gal·ly** *adv.*

con·ju·gate (kon′joō-gāt, -jə-; *for adj., n., also* kon′joō-git, -jə-) *v.* **·gat·ed, ·gat·ing** *v.t.* **1.** *Gram.* To give the inflec-tions of (a verb) for person, number, tense, mood, and voice. **— v.i. 2.** *Biol.* To unite in conjugation. **— adj. 1.** Joined in pairs; coupled. **2.** Kindred in origin and, usually, mean-ing: said of words. **— n. 1.** A conjugate word. **2.** A mem-ber of any conjugate pair. [< L < *com-* together + *jugare* to join] **— con′ju·ga′tive** *adj.* **— con′ju·ga′tor** *n.*

con·ju·ga·tion (kon′joō-gā′shən, -jə-) *n.* **1.** A joining or being joined together. **2.** *Gram.* **a** The inflection of verbs. **b** A schematic presentation of the entire inflection of a verb. **c** A class of verbs that are inflected in the same manner. **— con′ju·ga′tion·al** *adj.* **— con′ju·ga′tion·al·ly** *adv.*

con·junct (kən-jungkt′, kon′jungkt) *adj.* Joined together; conjoined. [See CONJOIN.] **— con·junct′ly** *adv.*

con·junc·tion (kən-jungk′shən) *n.* **1.** The act of joining to-gether, or the state of being so joined. **2.** A coincidence. **3.** *Astron.* **a** The position of two celestial bodies when they are in the same celestial longitude. **b** The position of a planet when it is on a direct line with the earth and the sun. **4.** *Gram.* A word used to connect words, phrases, clauses, or sentences; one of the eight traditional parts of speech. **— coordinate conjunction** A conjunction, as *and, but, or,* that joins words or groups of words of equal rank. **— subordi-nate conjunction** A conjunction, as *as, because, if, that, though,* that joins clauses of minor rank to principal clauses. **— con·junc′tion·al** *adj.* **— con·junc′tion·al·ly** *adv.*

con·junc·ti·va (kon′jungk-tī′və, kən-jungk′tə-və) *n. pl.* **·vas** or **·vae** (-vē) *Anat.* The mucous membrane lining the eyelids and covering the front part of the eyeball. For illus. see EYE. [< NL (*membrana*) *conjunctiva* connective (mem-brane)] **— con′junc·ti′val** *adj.*

con·junc·tive (kən-jungk′tiv) *adj.* **1.** Joining; connective. **2.** Joined together. **3.** *Gram.* **a** Serving as a conjunction. **b** Of an adverb, serving to unite sentences in larger units, as *furthermore, nevertheless,* etc. **— n.** *Gram.* A conjunctive word. [See CONJOIN.] **— con·junc′tive·ly** *adv.*

con·junc·ti·vi·tis (kən-jungk′tə-vī′tis) *n. Pathol.* Inflam-mation of the conjunctiva.

con·junc·ture (kən-jungk′chər) *n.* **1.** A combination of cir-cumstances or events; juncture. **2.** A critical situation; cri-sis. **3.** Conjunction; union.

con·ju·ra·tion (kon'jŏŏ·rā'shən) n. 1. The doing of something by magic. 2. A magic spell or expression.
con·jure (v. def. 1 kən·jŏŏr'; v. defs. 2-5, adj. kon'jər, kun'-) v. ·jured, ·jur·ing v.t. 1. To call on or appeal to solemnly; adjure. 2. To summon by incantation or spell, as a devil. 3. To accomplish by or as by magic. — v.i. 4. To practice magic, especially legerdemain. 5. To summon a devil or spirit by incantation. — adj. U.S. Dial. Practicing magic. [< OF < L < com- together + jurare to swear]
con·jur·er (kon'jər·ər, kun'- for def. 1; kən·jŏŏr'ər for def. 2) n. 1. One who practices magic; a sorcerer or magician. 2. One who appeals solemnly. Also con·jur·or.
conk (kongk) n. Slang 1. U.S. The head. 2. The nose. — v.t. U.S. Slang To hit on the head. — to conk out 1. Informal To stall or fail: said of engines. 2. U.S. Slang To become suddenly weak and tired. [? < CONCH]
con man (kon) U.S. Slang A confidence man.
conn (kon) See CON².
con·nect (kə·nekt') v.t. 1. To join or fasten together; link. 2. To associate by some relation, as in thought or action. — v.i. 3. To join or fit. 4. To meet so that passengers can transfer from one route to another: said of trains, buses, etc. [< L < com- together + nectere to bind] — con·nec'tor or con·nect'er n.
connecting rod Mech. A rod joining a piston with the crankshaft in an engine, pump, etc.: also called piston rod.
con·nec·tion (kə·nek'shən) n. 1. The act of connecting, or the state of being connected. 2. That which joins or relates; a bond; link. 3. Logical sequence of words or ideas; coherence. 4. Context. 5. Family relationship. 6. A religious sect. 7. Usually pl. A group of friends or associates, often considered as influential in some way. 8. Often pl. A transfer or continuation from one route or vehicle to another. Also Brit. con·nex'ion. — con·nec'tion·al adj.
con·nec·tive (kə·nek'tiv) adj. Capable of connecting, or serving to connect. — n. 1. That which connects. 2. Gram. A connecting word or particle, as a conjunction. — con·nec'tive·ly adv. — con·nec·tiv·i·ty (kon'ek·tiv'ə·tē) n.
connective tissue Anat. The fibrous tissue that serves to unite and support the various organs and tissues of the body.
conning tower 1. The armored pilothouse of a warship. 2. In submarines, an observation tower.
con·nip·tion (kə·nip'shən) n. U.S. Informal A fit of hysteria, rage, etc. [Cf. dial. E canaphus ill-tempered]
con·niv·ance (kə·nī'vəns) n. The act or fact of conniving; silent assent, esp. to wrongdoing. Also con·niv'ence.
con·nive (kə·nīv') n.i. ·nived, ·niv·ing 1. To encourage or assent to a wrong by silence or feigned ignorance: with at. 2. To be in collusion: with with. [< L conivere to wink, shut the eyes] — con·niv'er n.
con·nois·seur (kon'ə·sûr') n. One competent to judge critically because of thorough knowledge, esp. in matters of art and taste. — Syn. See AMATEUR. [< F, ult. < L cognoscere to know, understand] — con·nois·seur'ship n.
con·no·ta·tion (kon'ə·tā'shən) n. 1. The suggestive or associative significance of an expression, additional to the literal meaning. Compare DENOTATION. 2. The act of connoting.
con·no·ta·tive (kon'ə·tā'tiv, kə·nō'tə·tiv) adj. Having or of the nature of connotation. — con'no·ta'tive·ly adv.
con·note (kə·nōt') v.t. ·not·ed, ·not·ing To suggest or imply along with the literal meaning. [< Med.L < L com- together + notare to mark]
con·nu·bi·al (kə·nōō'bē·əl, -nyōō'-) adj. Pertaining to marriage or to the married state. [< L < com- together + nubere to marry] — con·nu'bi·al'i·ty n. — con·nu'bi·al·ly adv.
co·noid (kō'noid) adj. Cone-shaped. Also co·noi'dal. — n. Something cone-shaped. [< Gk. kōnoeidēs conical]
con·quer (kong'kər) v.t. 1. To overcome or subdue by force, as in war; vanquish. 2. To overcome by mental or moral force; surmount. — v.i. 3. To be victorious. [< OF < com- thoroughly + quaerere to search for, procure] — con'quer·or n. — con'quer·a·ble adj.
con·quest (kon'kwest, kong'-) n. 1. The act of conquering. 2. The thing conquered. 3. A winning of another's favor or love. 4. One whose favor or love has been won.
con·quis·ta·dor (kon·kwis'tə·dôr, -kis'-; Sp. kōng·kēs'tä·thōr') n. pl. ·dors, Sp. ·do·res (-thō'rās) A conqueror; esp., any of the Spanish conquerors of Mexico and Peru in the 16th century. [< Sp. < conquistar to conquer]
con·san·guin·e·ous (kon'sang·gwin'ē·əs) adj. Of the same blood or ancestry; akin. Also con·san·guine (kon·sang'gwin). [< L < com- together + sanguis blood] — con'san·guin'e·ous·ly adv.
con·san·guin·i·ty (kon'sang·gwin'ə·tē) n. 1. Relationship resulting from common ancestry; blood relationship. 2. Any close affinity or connection. — Syn. See RELATIONSHIP.
con·science (kon'shəns) n. 1. The faculty by which distinctions are made between moral right and wrong. 2. Con-

formity in conduct to the prescribed moral standard. — in (all) conscience 1. In truth; in reason and honesty. 2. Certainly; assuredly. [< OF < L conscire to know inwardly] — con'science·less adj.
con·sci·en·tious (kon'shē·en'shəs, kon'sē-) adj. 1. Governed by or done in accordance with conscience; scrupulous. 2. Careful and thorough; painstaking. — con'sci·en'tious·ly adv. — con'sci·en'tious·ness n.
conscientious objector One who, on grounds of religious or moral convictions, refuses to perform military service.
con·scion·a·ble (kon'shən·ə·bəl) adj. Rare Conformable to conscience or right; just. — con'scion·a·bly adv.
con·scious (kon'shəs) adj. 1. Aware of one's own existence or of external objects and conditions. 2. Aware of some object or fact; conscious of one's shortcomings. 3. Felt by oneself; internally known: conscious superiority. 4. Overly aware of oneself; self-conscious. 5. Deliberate; intentional. — n. That part of mental life of which an individual is aware. [< L conscius knowing inwardly < com- together + scire to know] — con'scious·ly adv.
con·scious·ness (kon'shəs·nis) n. 1. The state of being conscious; awareness of oneself and one's surroundings. 2. Awareness of some object, influence, etc. 3. The mental and emotional awareness of an individual, or of a group.
con·script (n., adj. kon'skript; v. kən·skript') n. One who is compulsorily enrolled for some service or job. — adj. Enlisted by compulsion; conscripted. — v.t. To force into military, naval, or other service. [< L < com- together + scribere to write] — con·scrip'tion n.
conscript fathers (kon'skript) 1. The senators of ancient Rome. 2. The members of any legislative body.
con·se·crate (kon'sə·krāt) v.t. ·crat·ed, ·crat·ing 1. To set apart as sacred; dedicate to sacred uses. 2. To dedicate; devote: He consecrated his life to the cause. 3. To make revered; hallow: consecrated by time. [< L < com- thoroughly + sacer holy] — con'se·cra'tion n. — con'se·cra'tor n. — con·se·cra·to·ry (kon'sə·krə·tôr'ē, -tō'rē) adj.
con·sec·u·tive (kən·sek'yə·tiv) adj. 1. Following in uninterrupted succession; successive. 2. Characterized by logical sequence. — con·sec'u·tive·ly adv. — con·sec'u·tive·ness n.
con·sen·sus (kən·sen'səs) n. A collective opinion; general agreement. ◆ The phrase consensus of opinion, although redundant, is now widely used. [< L < com- together + sentire to feel, think]
con·sent (kən·sent') v.i. To give assent; agree or acquiesce. — n. 1. A voluntary yielding; compliance. 2. Agreement; harmony; concord. [See CONSENSUS.] — con·sent'er n.
con·se·quence (kon'sə·kwens, -kwəns) n. 1. That which naturally follows from a preceding action or condition; result. 2. A logical conclusion. 3. Distinction: a man of consequence. 4. Importance: an event of no consequence.
con·se·quent (kon'sə·kwent, -kwənt) adj. 1. Following as a natural result, or as a logical conclusion. 2. Characterized by correctness of reasoning; logical. — n. 1. That which follows something else, as in time. 2. An outcome; result. [< L < com- together + sequi to follow]
con·se·quen·tial (kon'sə·kwen'shəl) adj. 1. Following as an effect or conclusion. 2. Of consequence; important. 3. Having or showing self-importance. — con'se·quen'ti·al'i·ty n. — con'se·quen'tial·ness n. — con'se·quen'tial·ly adv.
con·se·quent·ly (kon'sə·kwent'lē, -kwənt·lē) adv. As a result; therefore.
con·ser·va·tion (kon'sər·vā'shən) n. 1. The act of keeping or protecting from loss or injury. 2. The preservation of natural resources, as forests, fisheries, etc., for economic or recreational use; also, an area so preserved. [See CONSERVE] — con'ser·va'tion·al adj. — con'ser·va'tion·ist n.
conservation of energy Physics The principle that in any closed material system the total amount of energy remains constant, though it may assume different forms successively.
con·ser·va·tism (kən·sûr'və·tiz'əm) n. 1. Devotion to the existing order of things; opposition to change. 2. The principles of people or groups so devoted.
Con·ser·va·tism (kən·sûr'və·tiz'əm) n. The doctrines and policies of the Conservative Party.
con·ser·va·tive (kən·sûr'və·tiv) adj. 1. Inclined to preserve the existing order of things; opposed to change. 2. Moderate; cautious: a conservative estimate. 3. Conserving; preservative. — n. 1. A conservative person. 2. A preservative. — con·ser'va·tive·ly adv. — con·ser'va·tive·ness n.
Con·ser·va·tive (kən·sûr'və·tiv) adj. Of or pertaining to the Conservative Party. — n. 1. A member of this party. 2. A member of the Progressive-Conservative Party in Canada. Abbr. C.
Conservative Judaism That branch of Judaism that accepts as binding the Mosaic Laws, but allows some adjustments to the changed conditions of today.

Conservative Party In Great Britain, the principal right-wing party. See TORY.

con·ser·va·to·ry (kən·sûr'və·tôr'ē, -tō'rē) *n. pl.* **·ries 1.** A small greenhouse or glass-enclosed room in which plants are grown and displayed. **2.** A school of music. Also **con·ser·va·toire** (kən·sûr'və·twär'). — *adj.* Adapted to preserve.

con·serve (kən·sûrv'; *for n., also* kon'sûrv) *v.t.* **·served, ·serv·ing 1.** To keep from loss, decay, or depletion; maintain. **2.** To preserve with sugar. — *n. Often pl.* A kind of jam made of several fruits stewed together in sugar, often with nuts, raisins, etc. [< MF < L < *com-* thoroughly + *servare* to keep] — **con·serv'a·ble** *adj.* — **con·serv'er** *n.*

con·sid·er (kən·sid'ər) *v.t.* **1.** To think about or deliberate upon; examine mentally; weigh. **2.** To look upon or regard (as); think (to be). **3.** To hold as an opinion; believe. **4.** To take into account; have regard for: to *consider* the feelings of others. — *v.i.* **5.** To think carefully; deliberate. [< MF < L *considerare* to observe]

con·sid·er·a·ble (kən·sid'ər·ə·bəl) *adj.* **1.** Somewhat large in amount, extent, etc.; much; *considerable* trouble. **2.** Worthy of consideration. — **con·sid'er·a·bly** *adv.*

con·sid·er·ate (kən·sid'ər·it) *adj.* **1.** Thoughtful of others; kind. **2.** Deliberate; considered. — **con·sid'er·ate·ly** *adv.* — **con·sid'er·ate·ness** *n.*

con·sid·er·a·tion (kən·sid'ə·rā'shən) *n.* **1.** The act of considering; deliberation. **2.** A circumstance to be taken into account, as in forming an opinion. **3.** Thoughtful or kindly feeling or treatment; solicitude. **4.** A thought or reflection; opinion. **5.** Something given for a service; fee; recompense. **6.** Claim to be considered; importance. **7.** High regard; esteem. — **in consideration of** In view of, or in return for. — **under consideration** Being thought about or discussed.

con·sid·er·ing (kən·sid'ər·ing) *prep.* In view of; taking into account. — *adv. Informal* Taking all the facts into account.

con·sign (kən·sīn') *v.t.* **1.** To entrust or commit to the care of another. **2.** To give up or turn over. **3.** To forward or deliver, as merchandise. **4.** To set apart or devote, as for a specific use. [< MF < L < *com-* with + *signum* a seal] — **con·sign'a·ble** *adj.* — **con·sig·na·tion** (kon'sig·nā'shən) *n.*

con·sign·ee (kon'sī·nē') *n.* One to whom goods are consigned.

con·sign·ment (kən·sīn'mənt) *n.* **1.** A consigning of something, esp. of goods, for sale or disposal. **2.** That which is consigned. — **on consignment** Of goods, paid for by the retailer only after they have been sold.

con·sign·or (kən·sī'nər, kon'sī·nôr') *n.* One who consigns, esp. goods for sale. Also **con·sign'er.**

con·sist (kən·sist') *v.i.* **1.** To be made up or constituted: with *of.* **2.** To have as source or basis; exist; inhere: with *in.* **3.** To be compatible; harmonize: with *with.* [< L < *com-* together + *sistere* to stand]

con·sis·ten·cy (kən·sis'tən·sē) *n. pl.* **·cies 1.** Agreement between things, acts, or statements; logical connection. **2.** Agreement with previous acts, statements, or decisions. **3.** Firmness, nearness, or density. **4.** Degree of firmness, thickness, or density. Also **con·sis'tence.**

con·sis·tent (kən·sis'tənt) *adj.* **1.** Not contradictory or self-contradictory; compatible; harmonious. **2.** Conforming to a single set of principles, or to previous action or belief. [See CONSIST.] — **con·sis'tent·ly** *adv.*

con·sis·to·ry (kən·sis'tər·ē) *n. pl.* **·ries 1.** *Eccl.* The highest council of the Roman Catholic Church, composed of all the cardinals, and usually presided over by the Pope. **2.** The place where any such body meets, or the meeting itself. [< AF < Med.L *consistere* to stand still, wait] — **con·sis·to·ri·al** (kon'sis·tôr'ē·əl, -tō'rē-), **con'sis·to'ri·an** *adj.*

con·so·la·tion (kon'sə·lā'shən) *n.* **1.** A consoling or being consoled. **2.** One who or that which consoles.

con·sol·a·to·ry (kən·sol'ə·tôr'ē, -tō'rē) *adj.* Consoling.

con·sole¹ (kən·sōl') *v.t.* **·soled, ·sol·ing** To comfort (a person) in grief or sorrow; cheer. [< MF < L < *com-* together + *solari* to solace] — **con·sol'a·ble** *adj.*

— **Syn.** We *console* a person by soothing or sustaining his fallen spirits, or *comfort* him by any act that brings relief to his mind or body. *Solace* stresses the feeling of relief that results from our actions. — **Ant.** distress, grieve, sadden.

con·sole² (kon'sōl) *n.* **1.** A bracket, especially one used to support a cornice or ornamental fixture. **2.** A console table. **3.** The portion of an organ containing the manuals and stops. **4.** A cabinet for a radio, phonograph, or television set, designed to rest on the floor. [< MF, a bracket]

console table A table supported by consoles.

con·sol·i·date (kən·sol'ə·dāt) *v.* **·dat·ed, ·dat·ing** *v.t.* **1.** To make solid, firm, or coherent; strengthen. **2.** To combine in one; form a union of. — *v.i.* **3.** To become united, solid, or firm. — *adj.* Consolidated. [< L < *com-* together + *solidus* solid] — **con·sol'i·da'tion** *n.* — **con·sol'i·da'tor** *n.*

— **Syn.** (verb) **1.** solidify. **2.** merge, unite. **3.** unify.

consolidated school *U.S. & Canadian* A school, usu. rural, for pupils from more than one district.

con·som·mé (kon'sə·mā', *Fr.* kôǹ·sô·mā') *n.* A clear soup

made of meat and sometimes vegetables boiled in water. [< F, *consommer* to complete, finish]

con·so·nance (kon'sə·nəns) *n.* **1.** Agreement; accord. **2.** Correspondence of sounds; esp. resemblance of consonants but not of vowels. **3.** *Music* A combination of tones regarded as stable and not requiring resolution: also *concord.* Also **con'so·nan·cy.** — **Syn.** See HARMONY.

con·so·nant (kon'sə·nənt) *adj.* **1.** Being in agreement; consistent. **2.** Corresponding in sound; having consonance. **3.** Consonantal. — *n.* **1.** *Phonet.* A sound produced by contact or constriction of the speech organs resulting in complete or partial blockage of the breath stream, as the sounds of *b, f, k, s, t,* etc. **2.** A letter or written symbol representing such a sound. [< MF < L < *com-* together + *sonare* to sound] — **con'so·nant·ly** *adv.*

con·so·nan·tal (kon'sə·nan'təl) *adj.* **1.** Of the nature of a consonant. **2.** Having a consonant or consonants.

con·sort (*n.* kon'sôrt; *v.* kən·sôrt') *n.* **1.** A husband or wife; spouse. **2.** A companion or partner; mate. **3.** *Naut.* A vessel sailing with another. — *v.i.* **1.** To keep company; associate. **2.** To be in agreement; harmonize. — *v.t.* **3.** To join; associate. [< MF < L < *com-* together + *sors* share, lot]

con·sor·ti·um (kən·sôr'shē·əm) *n. pl.* **·ti·a** (-shē-ə) A coalition, as of banks or corporations for a venture requiring vast resources. [< L, fellowship]

con·spec·tus (kən·spek'təs) *n. pl.* **·tus·es 1.** A general view of a subject. **2.** A summary. [See CONSPICUOUS.]

con·spic·u·ous (kən·spik'yoo·əs) *adj.* **1.** Clearly visible; easy to be seen. **2.** Readily attracting attention; striking. [< L < *com-* together + *specere* to look at] — **con·spic'u·ous·ly** *adv.* — **con·spic'u·ous·ness** *n.*

con·spir·a·cy (kən·spir'ə·sē) *n. pl.* **·cies 1.** The planning of two or more persons to do an evil act; also, the plan so made. **2.** An acting together: a *conspiracy* of the elements.

con·spir·a·tor (kən·spir'ə·tər) *n.* One who is involved in a conspiracy. [See CONSPIRE.]

con·spir·a·to·ri·al (kən·spir'ə·tôr'ē·əl, -tō'rē-) *adj.* Of, pertaining to, or like conspiracy or conspirators.

con·spire (kən·spīr') *v.* **·spired, ·spir·ing** *v.i.* **1.** To combine secretly in an evil or unlawful enterprise. **2.** To act together: The winds *conspire* against us. — *v.t.* **3.** To plan secretly; plot. [< MF < L < *com-* together + *spirare* to breathe] — **con·spir'er** *n.*

con·sta·ble (kon'stə·bəl, kun'-) *n.* A peace officer who arrests offenders, serves writs, executes warrants, etc. [< OF < LL *comes stabuli* chief groom] — **con'sta·ble·ship'** *n.*

con·stab·u·lar·y (kən·stab'yə·ler'ē) *n. pl.* **·lar·ies 1.** The body of constables of a city, etc. **2.** The district of a constable. **3.** A police force organized in a military fashion. — *adj.* Pertaining to constables or their functions.

con·stan·cy (kon'stən·sē) *n.* **1.** Steadiness or faithfulness in purpose, action, affections, etc. **2.** Unchanging quality.

con·stant (kon'stənt) *adj.* **1.** Long-continuing, or continually recurring; persistent. **2.** Unchanging; invariable. **3.** Steady in purpose, action, affection, etc.; persevering; faithful. — *n.* **1.** That which is permanent or invariable. **2.** *Math.* A quantity that retains a fixed value throughout a given discussion. **3.** In the sciences, any characteristic of a substance, event, etc., numerically determined, that remains the same under specified conditions. [< MF < L < *com-* thoroughly + *stare* to stand] — **con'stant·ly** *adv.*

con·stel·late (kon'stə·lāt) *v.t. & v.i.* **·lat·ed, ·lat·ing** To group in constellations.

con·stel·la·tion (kon'stə·lā'shən) *n.* **1.** *Astron.* Any of various groups of stars imagined to represent the outline of a being or thing, usu. mythological, and named accordingly. **2.** Any brilliant group of persons or things. **3.** In astrology, the aspect of the planets at the time of one's birth. **4.** *Psychol.* A group of associated emotions, ideas, etc., centering upon a dominant element. [< LL < L *com-* together + *stella* star] — **con·stel·la·to·ry** (kən·stel'ə·tôr'ē, -tō'rē) *adj.*

con·ster·nate (kon'stər·nāt) *v.t.* **·nat·ed, ·nat·ing** To overwhelm with terror and confusion; dismay. [< L < *com-* thoroughly + *sternere* to cast down, prostrate]

con·ster·na·tion (kon'stər·nā'shən) *n.* Sudden, paralyzing fear or amazement; panic. — **Syn.** See ALARM.

con·sti·pate (kon'stə·pāt) *v.t.* **·pat·ed, ·pat·ing** To cause constipation in. [< L < *com-* together + *stipare* to press, crowd] — **con'sti·pat'ed** *adj.*

con·sti·pa·tion (kon'stə·pā'shən) *n.* A condition of the bowels characterized by suppressed or difficult evacuation.

con·stit·u·en·cy (kən·stich'oo·ən·sē) *n. pl.* **·cies 1.** A body of voters who elect a representative to a legislative body; also, the district represented. **2.** Any body of supporters.

con·stit·u·ent (kən·stich'oo·ənt) *adj.* **1.** Serving to form or compose; constituting. **2.** Entitled to elect a representative. **3.** Having the power to frame or modify a constitution. — *n.* **1.** One represented politically or in business, a voter or client. **2.** A necessary part or element.

con·sti·tute (kon'stə·toot, -tyoot) *v.t.* **·tut·ed, ·tut·ing 1.**

To be the substance or elements of; make up; compose. **2.** To enact (a law, etc.). **3.** To found, as a school; establish, as an assembly, in legal form. **4.** To empower; appoint: I *constitute* you my spokesman. **5.** To make by combining elements or parts; frame. [< L < *com-* together + *statuere* to place, station] — **con′sti·tut′er** or **con′sti·tu′tor** *n.*

con·sti·tu·tion (kon′stə·tōō′shən, -tyōō′-) *n.* **1.** The act of constituting; a setting up or appointing. **2.** The composition or make-up of a thing; esp., physical make-up: a weak *constitution.* **3.** The fundamental laws and principles that normally govern the operation of a state or association; also, a document recording such laws and principles. — **the Constitution** The Constitution of the U.S., framed and adopted in 1787 and put into effect March 4, 1789.

con·sti·tu·tion·al (kon′stə·tōō′shən·əl, -tyōō′-) *adj.* **1.** Of or inherent in the constitution of a person or thing; essential: a *constitutional* weakness. **2.** Consistent with or pertaining to the constitution of a state; lawful. **3.** Acting under and controlled by a constitution: a *constitutional* monarchy. **4.** Loyal to the constitution. **5.** Benefiting one's health. — *n.* Exercise taken for one's health. — **con·sti·tu·tion·al·i·ty** (kon′sti·tōō′shən·al′ə·tē) *n.* — **con′sti·tu′tion·al·ly** *adv.*

Constitutional amendment A legal alteration of the U.S. Constitution, ratified by three fourths of the States.

Constitution State Nickname of CONNECTICUT.

con·sti·tu·tive (kon′stə·tōō′tiv, -tyōō′-) *adj.* **1.** Forming an essential element of something; basic. **2.** Having power to enact, institute, or establish. — **con′sti·tu′tive·ly** *adv.*

con·strain (kən·strān′) *v.t.* **1.** To compel by physical or moral means; coerce. **2.** To confine, as by bonds. **3.** To restrain; compel to inaction. [< OF < L < *com-* together + *stringere* to bind] — **con·strain′a·ble** *adj.* — **con·strain′er** *n.*

con·strained (kən·strānd′) *adj.* Forced; unnatural: a *constrained* smile. — **con·strain·ed·ly** (kən·strā′nid·lē) *adv.*

con·straint (kən·strānt′) *n.* **1.** The use of force; coercion. **2.** Confinement; restriction. **3.** Unnaturalness of manner; awkwardness. **4.** A constraining or being constrained.

con·strict (kən·strikt′) *v.t.* To draw together by force; cause to shrink or contract; bind; cramp. [< L < *com-* together + *stringere* to bind]

con·stric·tion (kən·strik′shən) *n.* **1.** The act of constricting, or the state of being constricted. **2.** A feeling of tightness. **3.** That which constricts or is constricted. — **con·stric′tive** *adj.*

con·stric·tor (kən·strik′tər) *n.* **1.** That which constricts. **2.** *Anat.* A muscle that contracts an organ of the body. **3.** A serpent that coils about and crushes its prey.

con·struct (*v.* kən·strukt′; *n.* kon′strukt) *v.t.* **1.** To form by combining materials or parts; build; erect. **2.** To form mentally; devise. **3.** To form (anything) systematically. — *n.* Something constructed. [< L < *com-* together + *struere* to build] — **con·struct′er** or **con·struc′tor** *n.*

con·struc·tion (kən·struk′shən) *n.* **1.** The act of constructing; also, the business of building. **2.** Something constructed; a structure or building. **3.** The way in which a thing is put together. **4.** Interpretation given a statement, law, etc.; explanation. **5.** *Gram.* The arrangement of forms syntactically, as in sentences. — **con·struc′tion·al** *adj.*

con·struc·tive (kən·struk′tiv) *adj.* **1.** Tending to build, improve, or advance; resulting in positive conclusions. **2.** Pertaining to construction; structural. **3.** Assumed by interpretation; inferred though not expressly stated. — **con·struc′tive·ly** *adv.* — **con·struc′tive·ness** *n.*

con·strue (*v.* kən·strōō′; *n.* kon′strōō) *v.* **-strued, -stru·ing** *v.t.* **1.** To analyze the grammatical structure of (a clause or sentence); parse. **2.** To interpret; explain; also, to deduce by inference. **3.** To translate orally. **4.** *Gram.* To use syntactically: The noun "aerodynamics" is *construed* as a singular. — *v.i.* **5.** To determine grammatical structure. **6.** To infer; deduce. **7.** To admit of grammatical analysis. — *n.* An act of construing. [< L < *com-* together + *struere* to build up] — **con·stru′a·ble** *adj.* — **con·stru′er** *n.*

con·sul (kon′səl) *n.* **1.** An officer residing in a foreign city to protect his country's commercial interests and the welfare of its citizens. **2.** Either of the two chief magistrates ruling conjointly in the Roman republic. **3.** Any of the three chief magistrates of the French republic, 1799–1804. [< L] — **con′su·lar** (-sə·lər, -syə·lər) *adj.*

con·su·late (kon′sə·lit, -syə-) *n.* **1.** The office or term of office of a consul. Also **con′sul·ship. 2.** The official place of business of a consul. **3.** Government by consuls. — **the Consulate** The government of France from 1799 to 1804. [< L *consulatus* < *consul* consul]

consul general A consular officer of the highest rank stationed in an important foreign commercial city, who supervises the other consuls in his district.

con·sult (kən·sult′) *v.t.* **1.** To ask the advice of; go to for counsel; refer to. **2.** To have regard to in deciding or acting;

consider: to *consult* one's best interests. — *v.i.* **3.** To ask advice. **4.** To compare views; take counsel: with *with.* **5.** To give professional advice. [< L *consultare,* freq. of *consulere* to seek advice] — **con·sult′er** or **con·sul′tor** *n.*

con·sult·ant (kən·sul′tənt) *n.* **1.** A person referred to for expert or professional advice. **2.** One who consults.

con·sul·ta·tion (kon′səl·tā′shən) *n.* **1.** The act or practice of consulting. **2.** A meeting of consulters. — **con·sult·a·tive** (kən·sul′tə·tiv), **con·sult′a·to′ry** (-tôr′ē, -tō′rē) *adj.*

con·sume (kən·sōōm′) *v.* **·sumed, ·sum·ing** *v.t.* **1.** To destroy, as by burning. **2.** To eat, drink, or use up. **3.** To squander, as money or time. **4.** To engross or absorb. — *v.i.* **5.** To be wasted or destroyed. [< L < *com-* thoroughly + *sumere* to take up, use] — **con·sum′a·ble** *adj.*

con·sum·ed·ly (kən·sōō′mid·lē) *adv.* Excessively.

con·sum·er (kən·sōō′mər) *n.* **1.** One who or that which consumes. **2.** One who uses an article or service, as distinguished from a producer; one of the buying public.

con·sum·mate (*v.* kon′sə·māt; *adj.* kən·sum′it) *v.t.* **·mat·ed, ·mat·ing 1.** To bring to completion or perfection; achieve. **2.** To fulfill (a marriage) by sexual intercourse. — *adj.* Of the highest degree; perfect; complete. [< L < *com-* together + *summa* sum, total] — **con·sum′mate·ly** *adv.* — **con·sum′ma·tive** *adj.* — **con′sum·ma′tor** *n.*

con·sum·ma·tion (kon′sə·mā′shən) *n.* The act of consummating, or the state of being consummated; fulfillment.

con·sump·tion (kən·sump′shən) *n.* **1.** The act or process of consuming; destruction, as by burning, use, etc. **2.** The amount consumed. **3.** *Econ.* The using up of goods and services. **4.** *Pathol.* Pulmonary tuberculosis.

con·sump·tive (kən·sump′tiv) *adj. Pathol.* Pertaining to, affected with, or disposed to pulmonary tuberculosis. — *n.* A person affected with pulmonary tuberculosis. — **con·sump′tive·ly** *adv.* — **con·sump′tive·ness** *n.*

con·tact (kon′takt) *n.* **1.** A coming together or touching. **2.** A potentially helpful acquaintance: He has many *contacts.* **3.** *Electr.* The touching or joining of conductors, permitting the flow of a current; also, a conducting part for completing or breaking a circuit. **4.** *Med.* One who has been exposed to a contagious disease. — *v.t.* **1.** To bring or place in contact; touch. **2.** *Informal* To get in touch with (someone). — *v.i.* **3.** To be or come in contact; touch: with *with.* [< L < *com-* together + *tangere* to touch]

contact lens *Optics* A thin lens of glass or plastic ground to optical prescription and worn directly on the eyeball.

con·ta·gion (kən·tā′jən) *n.* **1.** The communication of disease by contact. **2.** A disease that is or may be communicated. **3.** The medium of transmission of disease. **4.** The communication of mental states, of ideas, etc., as by association. [< MF < L < *con-* together + *tangere* to touch]

con·ta·gious (kən·tā′jəs) *adj.* **1.** Transmissible by contact, as a disease. **2.** Spreading contagion. **3.** Exciting or tending to excite similar feelings, etc., in others; spreading; catching. — **con·ta′gious·ly** *adv.* — **con·ta′gious·ness** *n.*

con·tain (kən·tān′) *v.t.* **1.** To hold or enclose. **2.** To include or comprise. **3.** To be capable of containing; be able to hold. **4.** To keep within bounds; restrain, as oneself or one's feelings. **5.** *Math.* To be exactly divisible by. [< OF < L < *com-* together + *tenere* to hold] — **con·tain′a·ble** *adj.*

con·tain·er (kən·tā′nər) *n.* Something that contains, as a box, can, etc.

con·tain·ment (kən·tān′mənt) *n.* The prevention of territorial or ideological expansion on the part of another power.

con·tam·i·nate (kən·tam′ə·nāt) *v.t.* **·nat·ed, ·nat·ing** To make impure by contact or admixture; taint; defile; pollute. [< L < *contamen* pollution] — **con·tam′i·na·tion** *n.* — **con·tam′i·na·tive** *adj.* — **con·tam′i·na′tor** *n.*

con·temn (kən·tem′) *v.t.* To despise; scorn. [< OF < L < *com-* thoroughly + *temnere* to slight, scorn] — **con·temn′er** (kən·tem′ər, -tem′nər) or **con·tem·nor** (kən·tem′nər) *n.*

con·tem·plate (kon′təm·plāt) *v.* **·plat·ed, ·plat·ing** *v.t.* **1.** To look at attentively; gaze at. **2.** To consider thoughtfully; meditate upon. **3.** To intend or plan: to *contemplate* marriage. — *v.i.* **4.** To meditate; muse. [< L < *com-* together + *templum* temple; with ref. to divination] — **con·tem·pla·tion** (kon′təm·plā′shən) *n.* — **con′tem·pla′tor** *n.*

con·tem·pla·tive (kən·tem′plə·tiv, kon′təm·plā′tiv) *adj.* Of or given to contemplation; meditative. — *n.* A member of a religious order devoted to prayer and penance. — **con·tem′pla·tive·ly** *adv.* — **con·tem′pla·tive·ness** *n.*

con·tem·po·ra·ne·ous (kən·tem′pə·rā′nē·əs) *adj.* Living or occurring at the same time: also *cotemporaneous.* [< L < *com-* together + *tempus, -oris* time] — **con·tem·po·ra·ne·i·ty** (kən·tem′pə·rə·nē′ə·tē), **con·tem′po·ra′ne·ous·ness** *n.* — **con·tem′po·ra·ne·ous·ly** *adv.*

con·tem·po·rar·y (kən·tem′pə·rer′ē) *adj.* **1.** Belonging to the same age; living or occurring at the same time. **2.** Of the same age. **3.** Current; modern. — *n. pl.* **·rar·ies** A contemporary person or thing. Also *cotemporary*. [< L *com-* together + *tempus, -oris* time]

con·tempt (kən·tempt′) *n.* **1.** The feeling of one who views something as mean, vile, and worthless; disdain; scorn. **2.** The state of being despised. **3.** *Law* Willful disregard or disrespect of authority, as of a court. [< L < *com-* thoroughly + *temnere* to scorn]

con·tempt·i·ble (kən·temp′tə·bəl) *adj.* Deserving of contempt; despicable. — **con·tempt′i·bil′i·ty, con·tempt′i·ble·ness** *n.* — **con·tempt′i·bly** *adv.*

con·temp·tu·ous (kən·temp′chŏŏ·əs) *adj.* Showing or feeling contempt; disdainful; scornful. — **con·temp′tu·ous·ly** *adv.* — **con·temp′tu·ous·ness** *n.*

con·tend (kən·tend′) *v.i.* **1.** To strive in competition or rivalry; vie: to *contend* for a prize. **2.** To argue; debate. **3.** To struggle; fight. — *v.t.* **4.** To assert; affirm. [< L < *com-* together + *tendere* to strive, strain] — **con·tend′er** *n.*

con·tent[1] (kon′tent) *n.* **1.** *Usu. pl.* That which a thing contains: the *contents* of a box. **2.** Subject matter, as of a document. **3.** Ability to contain; capacity. **4.** Extent or size. **5.** The quantity of a specified part. [See CONTAIN.]

con·tent[2] (kən·tent′) *adj.* **1.** Satisfied with what one has. **2.** Resigned; accepting. — *n.* Ease of mind; satisfaction. — *v.t.* To satisfy. [See CONTAIN.] — **con·tent′ment** *n.*

con·tent·ed (kən·ten′tid) *adj.* Satisfied with things as they are; content. — **con·tent′ed·ly** *adv.* — **con·tent′ed·ness** *n.*

con·ten·tion (kən·ten′shən) *n.* **1.** Controversy; argument. **2.** Competition; rivalry. **3.** A point asserted in argument. — **in contention** Being contended over. [See CONTEND.]

con·ten·tious (kən·ten′shəs) *adj.* **1.** Given to contention; quarrelsome. **2.** Involving or characterized by contention. — **con·ten′tious·ly** *adv.* — **con·ten′tious·ness** *n.*

con·ter·mi·nous (kən·tûr′mə·nəs) *adj.* **1.** Having a common boundary line. **2.** Contained within the same limits. Also **coterminous**: also **con·ter′mi·nal.** [< L < *com-* together + *terminus* limit] — **con·ter′mi·nous·ly** *adv.*

con·test (*n.* kon′test; *v.* kən·test′) *n.* **1.** A struggling against one another; conflict; strife. **2.** Verbal controversy; dispute. **3.** A competition, game, match, etc. — *v.t.* **1.** To fight for; strive to keep or win. **2.** To call in question; challenge: to *contest* a decision. — *v.i.* **3.** To struggle or dispute; contend: with *with* or *against*. [< F < L < *com-* together + *testari* to bear witness] — **con·test′a·ble** *adj.* — **con·tes·ta·tion** (kon′tes·tā′shən) *n.* — **con·test′er** *n.*

con·test·ant (kən·tes′tənt) *n.* **1.** One who enters a contest; a competitor. **2.** One who contests; a litigant.

con·text (kon′tekst) *n.* **1.** Any phrase, sentence, or passage so closely connected to a word or words as to affect their meaning. **2.** Something that surrounds and influences, as environment or circumstances. [< L < *com-* together + *texere* to weave] — **con·tex·tu·al** (kən·teks′chŏŏ·əl) *adj.* — **con·tex′tu·al·ly** *adv.*

con·ti·gu·i·ty (kon′tə·gyŏŏ′ə·tē) *n.* *pl.* **·ties** The state of being contiguous or in actual contact; nearness.

con·tig·u·ous (kən·tig′yŏŏ·əs) *adj.* **1.** Touching at the edge or boundary. **2.** Close, but not touching; adjacent. [See CONTACT.] — **con·tig′u·ous·ly** *adv.* — **con·tig′u·ous·ness** *n.*

con·ti·nence (kon′tə·nəns) *n.* Self-restraint, esp. abstinence from sexual intercourse. Also **con′ti·nen·cy.**

con·ti·nent (kon′tə·nənt) *n.* One of the large land masses of the earth: Africa, Australia, Europe and Asia (the conventional divisions of the Eurasian land mass), North America, South America, and, usually, Antarctica. — **the Continent** Europe, as distinct from the British Isles. — *adj.* **1.** Self-restrained; moderate. **2.** Abstinent, esp. sexually; chaste. [See CONTAIN.] — **con′ti·nent·ly** *adv.*

con·ti·nen·tal (kon′tə·nen′təl) *adj.* **1.** Of, or of the proportions of, a continent. **2.** *Often cap.* Pertaining to the European continent; European. — *n.* **1.** *Usu. cap.* An inhabitant of the European continent; a European. **2.** A note of the money issued by the Continental Congress.

Con·ti·nen·tal (kon′tə·nen′təl) *adj.* Pertaining to the thirteen American colonies during and just after the Revolution. — *n.* A regular soldier in the Continental army.

Continental Congress The legislative and governing body of the Revolutionary American colonies, that convened in 1774, 1775–76, and 1776–81. It was de facto until 1781 when it became de jure the **Congress of the Confederation.**

con·tin·gen·cy (kən·tin′jən·sē) *n.* *pl.* **·cies** **1.** Uncertainty of occurrence; the condition of being subject to chance or accident. **2.** An unforeseen but possible occurrence. **3.** Something incidental; an adjunct. Also **con·tin′gence.**

con·tin·gent (kən·tin′jənt) *adj.* **1.** Liable, but not certain, to happen; possible. **2.** Occurring by chance; accidental. **3.** Dependent upon an uncertain event or condition: with *on* or *upon*. — *n.* **1.** An accidental or possible occurrence: contingency. **2.** A proportionate share or quota of something to be furnished, as of troops. **3.** A representative group in an assemblage. [< L < *com-* together + *tangere* to touch] — **con·tin′gent·ly** *adv.*

con·tin·u·al (kən·tin′yŏŏ·əl) *adj.* **1.** Renewed frequently;

often repeated. **2.** Continuous (in time). [< OF < L *continuus* hanging together] — **con·tin′u·al·ly** *adv.*

con·tin·u·ance (kən·tin′yŏŏ·əns) *n.* **1.** A continuing of something, as an action or condition, or a remaining in something, as in a place or state. **2.** Continuation, as of a novel. **3.** Duration: a disease of long *continuance*. **4.** *Law* Adjournment to a future time.

con·tin·u·a·tion (kən·tin′yŏŏ·ā′shən) *n.* **1.** The act of continuing or the state of being continued. **2.** The extension or a carrying to a further point: the *continuation* of a history. **3.** Addition; sequel.

con·tin·ue (kən·tin′yŏŏ) *v.* **·tin·ued, ·tin·u·ing** *v.i.* **1.** To go on in some action or condition; persist. **2.** To resume after an interruption. **3.** To remain in the same place, condition, or capacity. **4.** To last; endure. — *v.t.* **5.** To persevere or persist in; carry forward. **6.** To take up again after interruption. **7.** To extend or prolong in space, time, or development. **8.** To cause to last or endure; also, to keep on; retain, as in office. **9.** *Law* To postpone; grant a continuance of. [< OF < L < *com-* together + *tenere* to hold] — **con·tin′u·a·ble** *adj.* — **con·tin′u·er** *n.*

con·ti·nu·i·ty (kon′tə·nŏŏ′ə·tē, -nyŏŏ′-) *n.* *pl.* **·ties** **1.** The state or quality of being continuous. **2.** An unbroken series; succession. **3.** In motion pictures, television, etc., a scenario outlining the sequence of scenes; also, the script.

con·tin·u·ous (kən·tin′yŏŏ·əs) *adj.* Extended or prolonged without break; uninterrupted. — **con·tin′u·ous·ly** *adv.* — **con·tin′u·ous·ness** *n.*

con·tin·u·um (kən·tin′yŏŏ·əm) *n.* *pl.* **·tin·u·a** (-tin′yŏŏ·ə) Something that is continuous, of which no separate parts are discernible. [< L, neut. of *continuus* continuous]

con·tort (kən·tôrt′) *v.t.* & *v.i.* To twist violently; wrench out of shape or place. [< L < *com-* together + *torquere* to twist] — **con·tor′tion** *n.* — **con·tor′tive** *adj.*

con·tor·tion·ist (kən·tôr′shən·ist) *n.* A performer trained to twist his limbs and body into unnatural positions.

con·tour (kon′tŏŏr) *n.* The outline of a figure or body, or a line representing it. — *v.t.* To draw the contour lines of. — *adj.* **1.** *Agric.* Following the contours of land in such a way in plowing as to minimize erosion. **2.** Shaped to fit the outline or contour of something: *contour* sheets. [< F < LL *com-* together + *tornare* to make round]

contour map A map showing topographic configuration by lines (**contour lines**) that connect the points of a surface having similar elevation.

contra- *prefix* Against; opposite. [< L < *contra* against]

con·tra·band (kon′trə·band) *n.* **1.** Goods that, by law or treaty, may not be imported or exported. **2.** Smuggled goods. **3.** Goods that, by international law, a neutral may not furnish to a belligerent, and which are subject to seizure: in full **contraband of war.** — *adj.* Prohibited by law from being imported or exported. [< Sp. < Ital. < *contra* against + *bando* < LL *bannum* law] — **con′tra·ban′dist** *n.*

con·tra·bass (kon′trə·bās) *Music n.* The member of a family of instruments whose range is below the bass; esp., the double bass. Also **con′tra·bas′so** (-bä′sō). — *adj.* Pitched lower than the normal bass: the *contrabass* clarinet. [< Ital. *contrabasso*] — **con·tra·bass·ist** (kon′trə·bā′sist) *n.*

con·tra·bas·soon (kon′trə·bə·sŏŏn′) *n.* The double bassoon.

con·tra·cep·tion (kon′trə·sep′shən) *n.* The deliberate prevention of fertilization of the human ovum. [< CONTRA- + (CON)CEPTION] — **con′tra·cep′tive** *n.* & *adj.*

con·tra·clock·wise (kon′trə·klok′wīz′) *adj.* & *adv.* Counterclockwise.

con·tract (*v.* kən·trakt′; *for v. def. 2, also* kon′trakt; *n.* kon′trakt) *v.t.* **1.** To cause to draw together; reduce in size. **2.** To enter upon or settle by contract. **3.** To acquire or become affected with, as a disease or habit. **4.** *Gram.* To shorten, as a word, by omitting or combining medial letters or sounds. — *v.i.* **5.** To become smaller, shrink. **6.** To make a contract. — *n.* **1.** A formal agreement between two or more parties, esp. one that is legally binding. **2.** The paper or writing containing such an agreement. **3.** The department of law dealing with contracts. **4.** A betrothal or marriage. **5.** In bridge: **a** The highest and final bid of a hand, stating a denomination and the number of tricks to be made. **b** Contract bridge. Abbr. *cont., contr.* [< L < *com-* together + *trahere* to pull, draw] — **con·tract′i·bil′i·ty, con·tract′i·ble·ness** *n.* — **con·tract′i·ble** *adj.*

contract bridge A variety of the game of bridge in which tricks made by the declarer in excess of the contract do not count toward game.

con·trac·tile (kən·trak′təl) *adj.* Able to contract or to induce contraction. — **con·trac·til·i·ty** (kon′trak·til′ə·tē) *n.*

con·trac·tion (kən·trak′shən) *n.* **1.** The act of contracting, or the state of being contracted. **2.** *Gram.* The shortening of a word or phrase by the omission of medial letters or sounds, as it is not for *do not*; also, the new word formed. — **Syn.** See ABBREVIATION. — **con·trac′tive** *adj.*

con·trac·tor (kən·trak′tər; *for def. 1, also* kon′trak·tər) *n.* **1.**

One who agrees to supply materals or perform services for a sum, esp. for the construction of buildings. **2.** That which contracts, as a muscle.

con·trac·tu·al (kən·trak′chŏo·əl) *adj.* Connected with or implying a contract.

con·tra·dance (kon′trə·dans′, -däns′), **con·tra·danse** See CONTREDANSE.

con·tra·dict (kon′trə·dikt′) *v.t.* **1.** To maintain or assert the opposite of (a statement). **2.** To deny a statement of (a person). **3.** To be contrary to or inconsistent with. — *v.i.* **4.** To utter a contradiction. [< L < *contra* against + *dicere* to say, speak] — **con′tra·dict′a·ble** *adj.* — **con′tra·dict′er** or **con′tra·dic′tor** *n.*

con·tra·dic·tion (kon′trə·dik′shən) *n.* **1.** Assertion of the opposite of a statement; denial. **2.** A statement that denies the validity of another. **3.** Obvious inconsistency, as between two statements; discrepancy.

con·tra·dic·to·ry (kon′trə·dik′tər·ē) *adj.* **1.** Involving or of the nature of a contradiction; inconsistent; contrary. **2.** Given to contradicting. — *n. pl.* **·ries** *Logic* Either of two statements so related that if one is true the other must be false. — **con′tra·dic′to·ri·ly** *adv.* — **con′tra·dic′to·ri·ness** *n.*

con·tra·dis·tinc·tion (kon′trə·dis·tingk′shən) *n.* Distinction by contrast or by contrasting qualities. — **con′tra·dis·tinct′,** **con′tra·dis·tinc′tive** *adj.*

con·trail (kon′trāl) *n. Aeron.* A trail of condensed water vapor created by an airplane or rocket flying through super-cooled air. [< (*con*)*densation trail*]

con·tra·in·di·cate (kon′trə·in′də·kāt) *v.t. Med.* To indicate the danger or undesirability of (a given drug or treatment). — **con′tra·in′di·cant** *n.* — **con′tra·in′di·ca′tion** *n.*

con·tral·to (kən·tral′tō) *n. pl.* **·tos** or **·ti** (-tē) **1.** The lowest female voice, intermediate between soprano and tenor. **2.** One having such a voice. — *adj.* Of or pertaining to the contralto or its range. *Abbr. contr.* [< Ital.]

con·trap·tion (kən·trap′shən) *n. Informal* A contrivance or gadget. [? < CONTRIVE]

con·tra·pun·tal (kon′trə·pun′təl) *adj. Music* **1.** Of or pertaining to counterpoint. **2.** According with the principles of counterpoint. [< Ital. *contrapunto* counterpoint] — **con′tra·pun′tal·ly** *adv.* — **con′tra·pun′tist, con′tra·pun′tal·ist** *n.*

con·tra·ri·e·ty (kon′trə·rī′ə·tē) *n. pl.* **·ties 1.** The quality or state of being contrary. **2.** An inconsistency. [< OF < LL < L *contrarius* opposite]

con·trar·i·wise (kon′trer·ē·wīz′; *for def. 3, also* kən·trâr′ē·wīz′) *adv.* **1.** On the contrary; on the other hand. **2.** In the reverse order; conversely. **3.** Contrarily; perversely.

con·trar·y (kon′trer·ō; *for adj. def. 4, also* kən·trâr′ē) *adj.* **1.** Opposed in essence, purpose, aim, etc. **2.** Opposite as to position or direction. **3.** Adverse; unfavorable: *contrary winds.* **4.** Inclined to oppose and contradict; perverse. — *n. pl.* **·trar·ies 1.** One of two contrary things. **2.** The opposite: the *contrary* is true. **3.** *Logic* A statement the truth of which is undetermined by the falsity of another, but which cannot be true if the latter is true. — **on the contrary** On the other hand; conversely. — **to the contrary** To the opposite effect. — *adv.* In a contrary manner. [< OF < L < *contra* against] — **con′trar·i·ly** *adv.* — **con′trar·i·ness** *n.* — **Syn.** (adj.) **1.** contradictory, opposed, opposite, antithetical.

con·trast (*v.* kən·trast′; *n.* kon′trast) *v.t.* **1.** To place in opposition so as to set off differences or discrepancies. **2.** To set (one another) off by opposition, difference, etc. — *v.i.* **3.** To reveal differences when set in opposition. — *n.* **1.** The act of contrasting, or the state of being contrasted. **2.** A dissimilarity revealed by contrasting. **3.** One who or that which shows unlikeness to another. [< OF to oppose < LL < L *contra-* against + *stare* to stand] — **con·trast′a·ble** *adj.*

con·tra·vene (kon′trə·vēn′) *v.t.* **·vened, ·ven·ing 1.** To come into conflict with; run counter to; infringe; transgress: to *contravene* a law. **2.** To oppose or contradict. [< F < L *contra-* against + *venire* to come] — **con′tra·ven′er** *n.* — **con·tra·ven·tion** (kon′trə·ven′shən) *n.*

contre- *prefix* Counter; against; in opposition to. [< F < L *contra.* See CONTRA-.]

con·tre·danse (kôṅ′trə·däns′) *n.* A country-dance: also **contradance, contradanse.** Also **con·tre·dance** (kôṅ′trə·dans′, -däns′). [< F, alter. of COUNTRY-DANCE]

con·tre·temps (kôṅ′trə·täṅ′) *n. pl.* **·temps** (-täṅz′, *Fr.* -täṅ′) An embarrassing or awkward occurrence. [< F]

con·trib·ute (kən·trib′yŏot) *v.* **·ut·ed, ·ut·ing** *v.t.* **1.** To give with others for a common purpose. **2.** To furnish (an article, story, etc.) to a publication. — *v.i.* **3.** To share in effecting a result: These causes *contributed* to the king's downfall. **4.** To make a contribution. [< L < *com-* together + *tribuere* to grant, allot] — **con·trib′ut·a·ble** *adj.* — **con·trib′u·tive** *adj.* — **con·trib′u·tive·ly** *adv.* — **con·trib′u·tive·ness** *n.* — **con·trib′u·tor** *n.*

con·tri·bu·tion (kon′trə·byŏo′shən) *n.* **1.** The act of con-tributing. **2.** Something contributed. **3.** An article, story, etc., furnished to a periodical. **4.** A tax or levy.

con·trib·u·to·ry (kən·trib′yə·tôr′ē, -tō′rē) *adj.* **1.** Contributing, as money or aid. **2.** That forms a contribution. — *n. pl.* **·ries** One who or that which contributes.

con·trite (kən·trīt′, kon′trīt) *adj.* **1.** Deeply and humbly sorry for one's sins; penitent. **2.** Resulting from remorse. [< OF < L < *com-* together + *terere* to rub] — **con·trite′ly** *adv.* — **con·trite′ness, con·tri′tion** (-trish′ən) *n.*

con·triv·ance (kən·trī′vəns) *n.* **1.** The act or manner of contriving; also, the ability to do this. **2.** A device or mechanical apparatus. **3.** An ingenious plan.

con·trive (kən·trīv′) *v.* **·trived, ·triv·ing** *v.t.* **1.** To plan, scheme, or plot. **2.** To improvise; invent. **3.** To manage, as by some scheme. — *v.i.* **4.** To plan, scheme, or plot. [OF < L *com-* together + *turbare* to stir up, disclose, find] — **con·triv′a·ble** *adj.* — **con·triv′er** *n.*

con·trol (kən·trōl′) *v.t.* **·trolled, ·trol·ling 1.** To exercise authority over. **2.** To restrain; curb. **3.** To regulate or verify, as an experiment. **4.** To check, as an account, by means of a duplicate register; verify or rectify. — *n.* **1.** Power to regulate and direct. **2.** A restraining influence; check. **3.** A standard of comparison against which to check the results of a scientific experiment. **4.** *Often pl. Mech.* A device used for operating a machine, airplane, automobile, etc. [< MF < OF < Med.L < L *contra-* against + *rotulus* list] — **con·trol′la·bil′i·ty, con·trol′la·ble·ness** *n.* — **con·trol′la·ble** *adj.*

con·trol·ler (kən·trō′lər) *n.* **1.** One who controls, regulates, or directs. **2.** An officer appointed to examine and verify accounts: also spelled *comptroller.* **3.** A mechanism that regulates the speed of a machine, etc. — **con·trol′ler·ship** *n.*

control tower A specially equipped structure at an airfield, from which aircraft traffic is directed.

con·tro·ver·sial (kon′trə·vûr′shəl) *adj.* **1.** Subject to or characterized by controversy. **2.** Given to controversy; disputatious. — **con′tro·ver′sial·ist** *n.* — **con′tro·ver′sial·ly** *adv.*

con·tro·ver·sy (kon′trə·vûr′sē) *n. pl.* **·sies 1.** Dispute regarding a matter on which opinions differ. **2.** A dispute. [< L < *contra-* against + *versus,* pp. of *vertere* to turn]

con·tro·vert (kon′trə·vûrt, kon′trə·vûrt′) *v.t.* **1.** To argue against; contradict; oppose. **2.** To argue about. — **con′tro·vert′er** *n.* — **con′tro·vert′i·ble** *adj.* — **con′tro·vert′i·bly** *adv.*

con·tu·ma·cious (kon′tŏo·mā′shəs, -tyŏo-) *adj.* Stubbornly disobedient. — **con′tu·ma′cious·ly** *adv.* — **con′tu·ma′cious·ness** *n.*

con·tu·ma·cy (kon′tŏo·mə·sē, -tyŏo-) *n. pl.* **·cies** Contemptuous disobedience of authority; insolent defiance; insubordination. [< L < *contumax, -acis* stubborn]

con·tu·me·ly (kon′tŏo·mə·lē, -tyŏo-, -mē′lē; kən·tŏo′mə·lē, -tyŏo′-) *n. pl.* **·lies 1.** Insulting rudeness in speech or manner; insolence. **2.** An insult. [< OF < L *contumelia* reproach] — **con·tu·me·li·ous** (kon′tŏo·mē′lē·əs, -tyŏo-) *adj.* — **con′tu·me′li·ous·ly** *adv.* — **con′tu·me′li·ous·ness** *n.*

con·tuse (kən·tŏoz′, -tyŏoz′) *v.t.* **·tused, ·tus·ing** To bruise by a blow. [< L < *com-* together + *tundere* to beat]

con·tu·sion (kən·tŏo′zhən, -tyŏo′-) *n.* A bruise.

co·nun·drum (kə·nun′drəm) *n.* **1.** A riddle of which the answer depends on a pun. **2.** Any problem or puzzle. — **Syn.** See PUZZLE. [Origin unknown]

con·va·lesce (kon′və·les′) *v.i.* **·lesced, ·lesc·ing** To recover after illness; regain good health. [< L < *com-* thoroughly + *valescere,* inceptive of *valere* to be strong]

con·va·les·cence (kon′və·les′əns) *n.* **1.** Gradual recovery from illness. **2.** The period of such recovery. — **con′va·les′cent** *adj. & n.*

con·vec·tion (kən·vek′shən) *n.* **1.** *Physics* The transference of heat in a gas or liquid by currents resulting from unequal temperature and the consequent unequal densities. **2.** The act of conveying. [< L < *com-* together + *vehere* to carry] — **con·vec′tion·al** *adj.* — **con·vec′tive** *adj.* — **con·vec′tive·ly** *adv.*

con·vene (kən·vēn′) *v.* **·vened, ·ven·ing** *v.t.* **1.** To cause to assemble; convoke. **2.** To summon to appear, as by judicial authority. — *v.i.* **3.** To come together; assemble. [< MF < *com-* together + *venire* to come] — **con·ven′a·ble** *adj.* — **con·ven′er** *n.*

con·ven·ience (kən·vēn′yəns) *n.* **1.** The quality of being convenient; suitability. **2.** Personal comfort; ease. **3.** Anything that increases comfort or saves work. Also *Rare* **con·ven′ien·cy.** — **at one's convenience** At a time or occasion suiting one's needs or preference.

con·ven·ient (kən·vēn′yənt) *adj.* **1.** Well suited to one's purpose or needs; conducive to ease or comfort. **2.** Within easy reach; handy. [See CONVENE.] — **con·ven′ient·ly** *adv.*

con·vent (kon′vent, -vənt) *n.* **1.** A religious community, esp. of nuns, living according to an established rule. **2.** The building or buildings of such a community. — **Syn.** See CLOISTER. [< AF, OF < L *conventus* meeting, assembly]

con·ven·ti·cle (kən·ven'ti·kəl) *n.* **1.** A meeting for religious worship, esp. a secret one. **2.** The meeting place of such an assembly. [See CONVENE.] — **con·ven'ti·cler** *n.*

con·ven·tion (kən·ven'shən) *n.* **1.** A formal meeting of delegates or members, as for political or professional purposes. **2.** The persons attending such a meeting. **3.** A rule or approved technique in conduct or art; a custom or usage. **4.** Conventionality. **5.** An agreement or contract.

con·ven·tion·al (kən·ven'shən·əl) *adj.* **1.** Growing out of or established by convention or custom. **2.** Following or conforming to approved or established practice. **3.** Formal; stylized. **4.** In art, simplified or abstracted. **5.** Established by general agreement or acceptance: a *conventional* symbol. **6.** Of or pertaining to a convention. — **con·ven'tion·al·ist** *n.* — **con·ven'tion·al·ly** *adv.*

con·ven·tion·al·ism (kən·ven'shən·əl·iz'əm) *n.* **1.** Regard for or adherence to custom. **2.** Anything conventional.

con·ven·tion·al·i·ty (kən·ven'shən·al'ə·tē) *n.* *pl.* **·ties 1.** The state or quality of being in accord with convention; adherence to established forms, customs, or usages. **2.** A conventional act, principle, custom, etc.

con·ven·tion·al·ize (kən·ven'shən·əl·īz') *v.t.* **·ized, ·iz·ing 1.** To make conventional. **2.** To represent in a conventional manner. — **con·ven'tion·al·i·za'tion** *n.*

con·ven·tu·al (kən·ven'chōō·əl) *adj.* Belonging or pertaining to a convent. — *n.* One who belongs to a convent.

con·verge (kən·vûrj') *v.* **·verged, ·verg·ing** *v.i.* **1.** To move toward one point; come together gradually. — *v.t.* **2.** To cause to tend toward one point. [< LL < L *com-* together + *vergere* to bend]

con·ver·gence (kən·vûr'jəns) *n.* **1.** The act, fact, or state of converging. **2.** The degree or point of converging. Also **con·ver'gen·cy.**

con·vers·a·ble (kən·vûr'sə·bəl) *adj.* **1.** Approachable in conversation; affable. **2.** Fond of talking. — **con·vers'a·ble·ness** *n.* — **con·vers'a·bly** *adv.*

con·ver·sant (kon'vər·sənt, kən·vûr'sənt) *adj.* Well acquainted or familiar, as by study. [See CONVERSE¹.] — **con·ver·sance** (kon'vər·səns, kən·vûr'səns), **con'ver·san·cy** *n.* — **con'ver·sant·ly** *adv.*

con·ver·sa·tion (kon'vər·sā'shən) *n.* **1.** An informal talk with another or others. **2.** Intimate association or social intercourse. **3.** Sexual intercourse. [See CONVERSE¹.]

con·ver·sa·tion·al (kon'vər·sā'shən·əl) *adj.* **1.** Of or characteristic of conversation. **2.** Disposed to or adept at conversation. — **con'ver·sa'tion·al·ly** *adv.*

con·ver·sa·tion·al·ist (kon'vər·sā'shən·əl·ist) *n.* One who enjoys or excels in conversation. Also **con'ver·sa'tion·ist.**

conversation piece Something, as a piece of furniture, that arouses comment.

con·verse¹ (*v.* kən·vûrs'; *n.* kon'vûrs) *v.i.* **·versed, ·vers·ing** To speak together informally; engage in conversation. — *n.* **1.** Conversation. **2.** Social fellowship. [< OF *converser* to live with < L < *com-* together + *vertere* to turn] — **con·vers'er** *n.*

con·verse² (kon'vûrs; *for adj., also* kon·vûrs') *adj.* Turned about so that two parts are interchanged; reversed; contrary. — *n.* That which exists in a converse relation; opposite. [< L < *com-* thoroughly + *vertere* to turn] — **con·verse·ly** (kən·vûrs'lē, kon'vûrs·lē) *adv.*

con·ver·sion (kən·vûr'zhən, -shən) *n.* **1.** The act of converting, or the state of being converted. **2.** A change in which one comes to adopt new opinions, esp. a spiritual turning to righteousness and faith. — **con·ver'sion·al, con·ver·sion·ar·y** (kən·vûr'zhən·er'ē, -shən-) *adj.*

con·vert (*v.* kən·vûrt'; *n.* kon'vûrt) *v.t.* **1.** To change into another state, form, or substance; transform. **2.** To apply or adapt to a new or different purpose or use. **3.** To change from one belief, religion, or course of action to another. **4.** To exchange for an equivalent value, as goods for money. **5.** To exchange for value of another form, as preferred for common stock. **6.** To change chemically. **7.** *Law* To assume possession of illegally. — *v.i.* **8.** To become changed in character. **9.** In football, to score an extra point after the touchdown. — *n.* A person who has been converted, as from one religion to another. [See CONVERSE²]

con·vert·er (kən·vûr'tər) *n.* **1.** One who or that which converts. **2.** A Bessemer converter. **3.** *Electr.* An apparatus for converting direct into alternating current, or vice versa. Also **con·ver'tor.**

con·vert·i·ble (kən·vûr'tə·bəl) *adj.* Capable of being converted. — *n.* **1.** A convertible thing. **2.** An automobile with a top that folds back. — **con·vert'i·bil'i·ty, con·vert'i·ble·ness** *n.* — **con·vert'i·bly** *adv.*

con·vex (kon'veks; *for adj., also* kon·veks') *adj.* Curving outward, as the exterior of a globe: opposed to *concave.* — *n.* A convex surface or body, convexity. [< L *convexus* vaulted, curved] — **con·vex'i·ty** *n.* — **con·vex'ly** *adv.*

con·vex·o·con·cave (kon·vek'sō·kon·kāv') *adj.* Convex on one side and concave on the other, as a lens.

con·vey (kən·vā') *v.t.* **1.** To carry from one place to another; transport. **2.** To serve as a medium or path for; transmit. **3.** To make known; impart; communicate. **4.** To transfer ownership of, as real estate. [< AF < L *com-* together + *via* road, way] — **con·vey'a·ble** *adj.*

con·vey·ance (kən·vā'əns) *n.* **1.** The act of conveying; communication; transportation. **2.** Something used for conveying, as a truck or bus. **3.** *Law* The transfer of title to property; also, the document whereby title is transferred.

con·vey·anc·ing (kən·vā'ən·sing) *n. Law* The business of preparing conveyances of property. — **con·vey'anc·er** *n.*

con·vey·er (kən·vā'ər) *n.* **1.** One who or that which conveys, transports, or transfers. **2.** Any mechanical contrivance for conveying articles or materials, as an endless belt, a series of rollers, etc. Also (*for def. 2*) **con·vey'or.**

con·vict (*v. adj.* kən·vikt'; *n.* kon'vikt) *v.t.* To prove guilty; find guilty after a judicial trial. — *n.* **1.** One serving a sentence in prison. **2.** One found guilty of a crime. [See CONVINCE.]

con·vic·tion (kən·vik'shən) *n.* **1.** The state of being convinced; firm belief. **2.** A firm belief. **3.** A convincing, as of a truth. **4.** A pronouncing or being guilty. — **Syn.** See BELIEF. — **con·vic'tion·al, con·vic'tive** *adj.*

con·vince (kən·vins') *v.t.* **·vinced, ·vinc·ing** To cause to believe something, as by proof; bring to belief: often with *of.* [< L < *com-* thoroughly + *vincere* to conquer] — **con·vince'ment** *n.* — **con·vinc'er** *n.* — **con·vin'ci·ble** *adj.* — **Syn. 1.** *Convince* and *persuade* agree in the sense of making one's view or will prevail over another's. A man is *convinced* by argument or evidence; he is *persuaded* by appeals to his affections. We *convince* a man of a truth, but *persuade* him to act.

con·vinc·ing (kən·vin'sing) *adj.* **1.** Satisfying by evidence: *convincing* testimony. **2.** Credible or believable: a *convincing* act. — **con·vinc'ing·ly** *adv.* — **con·vinc'ing·ness** *n.*

con·viv·i·al (kən·viv'ē·əl) *adj.* **1.** Fond of feasting and good fellowship; jovial. **2.** Of or befitting a feast; festive. [< L *convivium* a feast, banquet < *com-* together + *vivere* to live] — **con·viv'i·al·ist** *n.* — **con·viv·i·al·i·ty** (kən·viv'ē·al'ə·tē) *n.* — **con·viv'i·al·ly** *adv.*

con·vo·ca·tion (kon'vō·kā'shən) *n.* **1.** A calling together; a summoning to assemble. **2.** A meeting, esp. an ecclesiastical one. — **con'vo·ca'tion·al** *adj.* — **con'vo·ca'tor** *n.*

con·voke (kən·vōk') *v.t.* **·voked, ·vok·ing** To call together; summon to meet. [< F < L < *com-* together + *vocare* to call, summon] — **con·vok'er** *n.*

con·vo·lute (kon'və·lōōt) *adj.* Rolled one part over another or inward from one side. — *v.t. & v.i.* **·lut·ed, ·lut·ing** To coil up. [See CONVOLVE.] — **con'vo·lute'ly** *adv.*

con·vo·lu·tion (kon'və·lōō'shən) *n.* **1.** A coiled or convoluted state. **2.** A fold or twist in something convoluted. **3.** *Anat.* One of the folds of the cortex of the brain.

con·volve (kən·volv') *v.t. & v.i.* **·volved, ·volv·ing** To coil up, wind, or twist together. [< L < *com-* together + *volvere* to spin, twist]

con·vol·vu·lus (kən·vol'vyə·ləs) *n.* A twining herb with large flowers, esp. the morning-glory. [< L, bindweed]

con·voy (kon'voi; *for v., also* kən·voi') *n.* **1.** A protecting escort, as for ships at sea. **2.** A formation of ships, military vehicles, etc., traveling together. **3.** The act of convoying, or the state of being convoyed. — *v.t.* To act as convoy to; escort. [< MF < L *com-* together + *via* road]

con·vulse (kən·vuls') *v.t.* **·vulsed, ·vuls·ing 1.** To effect with violent movements; agitate or shake. **2.** To throw into convulsions. **3.** To cause to laugh violently. [< L < *com-* together + *vellere* to pull]

con·vul·sion (kən·vul'shən) *n.* **1.** *Often pl. Pathol.* A violent and involuntary contraction or series of contractions of the voluntary muscles. **2.** Any violent commotion or disturbance, as an earthquake. **3.** A violent fit of laughter. — **con·vul'sion·ar·y** *adj. & n.*

con·vul·sive (kən·vul'siv) *adj.* Producing, characterized by, or of the nature of convulsions: *convulsive* anger. — **con·vul'sive·ly** *adv.* — **con·vul'sive·ness** *n.*

co·ny (kō'nē, kun'ē) *n. pl.* **·nies 1.** A rabbit. **2.** Rabbit fur. Also spelled **coney.** [< OF < L *cuniculus* rabbit]

coo (kōō) *v.* **cooed, coo·ing** *v.i.* **1.** To utter the murmuring note of a dove. **2.** To talk amorously in murmurs: to bill and coo. — *v.t.* **3.** To utter with a coo. — *n.* A murmuring sound, as of a dove. [Imit.] — **coo'er** *n.* — **coo'ing·ly** *adv.*

cook (kŏŏk) *v.t.* **1.** To prepare (food) for eating by the action of heat. **2.** *Informal* To tamper with. **3.** *Slang* To ruin. — *v.i.* **4.** To act as a cook. **5.** To undergo cooking. — **to cook up** *Informal* To invent; concoct: to *cook up* a scandal. — *n.* One who prepares food for eating. [OE < LL < L *coquus* a cook] — **cook'er** *n.*

cook·book (kŏŏk'bŏŏk') *n.* A book containing recipes and other information about cooking.

cook·er·y (kŏŏk'ər·ē) *n. pl.* **·er·ies 1.** The art or practice of cooking. **2.** A place for cooking.

cook·out (kŏŏk′out′) *n. U.S. Informal* A meal cooked outdoors.

cook·y (kŏŏk′ē) *n. pl.* **cook·ies** *U.S.* A small, thin, dry cake, usu. sweetened. Also **cook′ey, cook′ie.** [< Du. *koekje,* dim. of *koek* cake]

cool (kōōl) *adj.* **1.** Moderately cold; lacking warmth. **2.** Producing a feeling of coolness: a *cool* suit. **3.** Calm in action or thought; composed. **4.** Not cordial; chilling: a *cool* reception. **5.** Suggesting coolness: said of colors. **6.** *U.S. Informal* Not exaggerated; actual: a *cool* million. **7.** *U.S. Slang* Excellent. — *adv. U.S. Informal* Coolly. — *v.t. & v.i.* **1.** To make or become less warm. **2.** To make or become less angry, ardent, or zealous. — *n.* A cool time, thing, place, etc. [OE *cōl*] — **cool′ly** *adv.* — **cool′ness** *n.*

cool·er (kōō′lər) *n.* **1.** A vessel or apparatus that serves to cool something or to keep it cool. **2.** *Slang* A jail.

cool-head·ed (kōōl′hed′id) *adj.* Not readily excited; calm.

coo·lie (kōō′lē) *n.* An unskilled Oriental laborer. Also **coo′· ly.** [Prob. < *Kuli,* an aboriginal Indian tribe]

coon (kōōn) *n.* **1.** A raccoon. **2.** *Slang* A Negro: an offensive term. [Short for RACCOON]

coop (kōōp, kŏŏp) *n.* **1.** An enclosure or box, as for fowls. **2.** *Slang* A jail. — **to fly the coop** *Slang* To escape from prison, etc. — *v.t.* To put into a coop.

co-op (kō′op, kō·op′) *n. Informal* A cooperative.

coop·er (kōō′pər, kŏŏp′ər) *n.* One who makes and repairs casks, barrels, etc. — *v.t. & v.i.* To make or mend (casks, barrels, etc.). [ME < LG. Cf. MDu. *kupe* cask.]

coop·er·age (kōō′pər·ij, kŏŏp′ər·) *n.* **1.** The work or workshop of a cooper. Also **coop′er·y. 2.** A cooper's fee.

co·op·er·ate (kō·op′ə·rāt) *v.i.* **·at·ed, ·at·ing** To work together for a common objective; act in combination. Also **co·öp′er·ate, co·ŏp′er·ate.** [< L < *co-* together + *operari* to work] — **co·op′er·a′tor** *n.*

co·op·er·a·tion (kō·op′ə·rā′shən) *n.* **1.** A working together toward a common end. **2.** The association of laborers, farmers, small capitalists, etc., for mutual economic benefit. Also **co·op′er·a′tion, co·öp′er·a′tion.** — **co·op′er·a′tion·ist** *n.*

co·op·er·a·tive (kō·op′rə·tiv, -ə·rā′tiv) *adj.* **1.** Cooperating or willing to cooperate. **2.** Of or organized for economic cooperation. — *n.* A business enterprise, association, or property organized or owned by a group for its common economic benefit. Also **co·op′er·a·tive, co·öp′er·a·tive.** — **co·op′er·a·tive·ly** *adv.* — **co·op′er·a·tive·ness** *n.*

Cooperative Commonwealth Federation *Canadian* Former name of the NEW DEMOCRATIC PARTY.

co-opt (kō·opt′) *v.t.* **1.** To elect as a fellow member of a committee, etc. **2.** To appoint. **3.** To make ineffectual as an instrument for radical change by incorporating within the established order. [< L < *co-* together + *optare* to choose] — **co′-op·ta′tion, co-op′tion** *n.* — **co-op′ta·tive** (kō′op′tə·tiv) *adj.*

co·or·di·nate (kō·ôr′də·nāt; *for adj., n.,* also kō·ôr′də·nit) *adj.* **1.** Of equal importance or rank; not subordinate. **2.** Of or pertaining to coordinates or coordination. — *n.* **1.** One who or that which is of the same order, rank, power, etc. **2.** *Math.* Any of a set of magnitudes by means of which the position of a point, line, or angle is determined with reference to fixed elements. — *v.* **·nat·ed, ·nat·ing** *v.t.* **1.** To put in the same rank, class, or order. **2.** To bring into harmonious relation or action; adjust. — *v.i.* **3.** To become coordinate. **4.** To act in harmonious or reciprocal relation. Also **co·or′di·nate.** [< Med.L < L *co-* together + *ordinare* to set in order] — **co·or′di·nate·ly** *adv.* — **co·or′di·nate·ness** *n.* — **co·or′· di·na′tive** *adj.* — **co·or′di·na′tor** *n.*

co·or·di·na·tion (kō·ôr′də·nā′shən) *n.* **1.** The act of coordinating, or the state of being coordinated. **2.** Harmonious, integrated action or interaction. Also **co·or′di·na′tion.**

coot (kōōt) *n.* **1.** A short-winged aquatic bird resembling the rail. **2.** *Informal* A simpleton. [ME *cote* < LG]

coot·ie (kōō′tē) *n. Slang* A louse. [? < Indonesian *kutu,* a parasitic insect; orig. nautical slang]

cop (kop) *n. Informal* A policeman. — *v.t.* **copped, cop·ping** *Slang* **1.** To steal. **2.** To catch. — **to cop out** *U.S. Slang* To back down; renege. [? Var. of *cap* to catch, take]

co·pa·cet·ic (kō′pə·set′ik) See COPESETIC.

co·pal (kō′pəl) *n.* A hard resin of various tropical trees, used in varnishes. [< Sp. < Nahuatl *copalli* incense]

cope¹ (kōp) *v. coped, cop·ing* *v.i.* To contend or strive, esp. successfully: often with *with.* [< OF *coup* blow]

cope² (kōp) *n.* **1.** A semicircular mantle worn by priests on ceremonial occasions. **2.** Something that arches overhead; a vault: the *cope* of heaven. — *v.t.* **coped, cop·ing** To dress or cover in or as in a cope. [See CAP¹.]

co·peck (kō′pek) See KOPECK.

Co·per·ni·can system (kō·pûr′nə·kən) *Astron.* The theory of the solar system of Copernicus that the earth and other planets revolve about the sun.

co·pe·set·ic (kō′pə·set′ik) *adj. U.S. Slang* Fine; excellent: also spelled *copacetic.* Also **co′pa·set·ic, co′pe·set·ic.** [< Creole *coupesètique* able to be coped with]

cope·stone (kōp′stōn) *n.* **1.** One of the stones of a coping. **2.** The final stroke. Also called *capstone.*

cop·i·er (kop′ē·ər) *n.* **1.** An imitator. **2.** A copyist.

co·pi·lot (kō′pī′lət) *n.* The assistant pilot of an aircraft.

cop·ing (kō′ping) *n.* The top course of a wall, roof, etc., usually sloping to shed water. [< COPE², v.]

coping saw A narrow-bladed saw set in a recessed frame and used for cutting curved pieces from wood.

co·pi·ous (kō′pē·əs) *adj.* **1.** Abundant; plentiful. **2.** Diffuse; wordy. [< L *copia* abundance] — **co′pi·ous·ly** *adv.* — **co′pi·ous·ness** *n.*

cop-out (kop′out′) *n. U.S. Slang* **1.** A way of avoiding responsibility; evasion. **2.** One who cops out.

cop·per¹ (kop′ər) *n.* **1.** A reddish, ductile, metallic element (symbol Cu) that is one of the best conductors of heat and electricity. See ELEMENT. **2.** A large pot. **3.** A coin of copper, or of bronze. **4.** A lustrous, reddish brown. — *v.t.* **1.** To cover or coat with copper. **2.** *U.S. Slang* To bet against (another bet). — *adj.* Of, or of the color of, copper. [OE < LL < L < Gk. *Kypros* Cyprus where copper abounded] — **cop′per·y** *adj.*

cop·per² (kop′ər) *n. Slang* A policeman. [< COP¹]

cop·per·as (kop′ər·əs) *n.* A green, crystalline, astringent ferrous sulfate, FeSO₄·7H₂O, used in dyeing, inkmaking, etc. [< MF < Med.L < (*aqua*) *cuprosa* copper (water)]

cop·per·head (kop′ər·hed′) *n.* A venomous North American snake having reddish brown markings.

Cop·per·head (kop′ər·hed′) *n. U.S.* During the Civil War, a Northerner who sympathized with the South.

cop·per·plate (kop′ər·plāt′) *n.* **1.** An engraved or etched plate of copper. **2.** A print or engraving from such a plate.

cop·per·smith (kop′ər·smith′) *n.* One who works in copper.

copper sulfate A deep blue, crystalline substance, CuSO₄· 5 H₂O, used in electric batteries, etc.

cop·pice (kop′is) *n.* A copse. [Alter. of COPSE]

cop·ra (kop′rə, kō′prə) *n.* The dried kernel of the coconut, yielding coconut oil. Also **cop·per·ah** (kop′ər·ə), **cop′rah, cop′pra.** [< Pg. < Malayalam *koppara*]

copse (kops) *n.* A thicket of bushes or small trees: also called *coppice.* [Earlier *coppice* < OF *copeiz* < *coper* to cut]

Copt (kopt) *n.* **1.** A native Egyptian of ancient Egyptian stock. **2.** A member of the Coptic Church. [< Med.L < Arabic < Coptic < Gk. *Aigyptios* Egyptian]

Cop·tic (kop′tik) *adj.* Of or pertaining to the Copts, or to their language. — *n.* The Hamitic language of the Copts.

Coptic Church The principal Christian sect of Egypt.

cop·u·la (kop′yə·lə) *n. pl.* **·las** or **·lae** (-lē) *Gram.* A linking verb. [< L, a link, band] — **cop′u·lar** *adj.*

cop·u·late (kop′yə·lāt) *v.i.* **·lat·ed, ·lat·ing** To unite in sexual intercourse. [< L *copula* a link] — **cop′u·la′tion** *n.*

cop·u·la·tive (kop′yə·lā′tiv, -lə·tiv) *adj.* **1.** Serving to join. **2.** *Gram.* **a** Serving as a copula. **b** Connecting words or clauses in a coordinate relationship. **3.** Copulatory. — *n. Gram.* A copulative word. — **cop′u·la′tive·ly** *adv.*

cop·y (kop′ē) *n. pl.* **cop·ies** **1.** A reproduction or imitation of an original; duplicate. **2.** A single specimen of a book, print, etc. **3.** Written matter as distinct from graphic matter, as in advertising, etc. **4.** Something to be reproduced or imitated. **5.** *Printing* Manuscript or other matter to be reproduced in type. **6.** In journalism, subject matter for an article, etc.: The president is good *copy.* Abbr. *c., C.* — *v.* **cop·ied, cop·y·ing** *v.t.* **1.** To make a copy of; reproduce or transcribe. **2.** To follow as a model; imitate. — *v.i.* **3.** To make a copy. [< MF < Med.L *copia* transcript]

cop·y·book (kop′ē·bŏŏk′) *n.* A book containing copies to be imitated in penmanship. — *adj.* Ordinary; trite.

copy boy An errand boy in a newspaper office.

cop·y·cat (kop′ē·kat′) *n.* An imitator: a child's term.

copy desk A desk in a newspaper office where copy is edited and prepared for the typesetters.

cop·y·ist (kop′ē·ist) *n.* **1.** One who makes copies, esp. of documents. **2.** One who imitates or copies.

cop·y·read·er (kop′ē·rē′dər) *n.* A person who edits work intended for publication.

cop·y·right (kop′ē·rīt) *n.* The exclusive statutory right of authors, composers, playwrights, artists, publishers, and distributors to publish and dispose of their works for a specified period of time. In the U.S. this period is 28 years, with the privilege of one renewal. — *v.t.* To secure copyright for. — *adj.* Of or protected by copyright. — **cop′y· right′a·ble** *adj.* — **cop′y·right′er** *n.*

cop·y·writ·er (kop′ē·rī′tər) *n.* One who writes copy for advertisements.

co·quet (kō·ket′) *v.* **·quet·ted, ·quet·ting** *v.i.* To flirt. [< F *coq* a cock; with ref. to its strutting] — **co·quet′ry** *n.*

---

co·quette (kō·ket′) *n.* A woman who tries to attract men merely to gratify her vanity; a flirt. — *v.t.* & *v.i.* **·quet·ted, ·quet·ting** To coquet. — **co·quet′tish** *adj.* — **co·quet′tish·ly** *adv.* — **co·quet′tish·ness** *n.*

co·qui·na (kō·kē′nə) *n.* A soft, highly porous limestone used as building material. [< Sp., shell, ult. < L *concha*]

cor- Var. of COM-.

cor·a·cle (kôr′ə·kəl, kor′-) *n.* A small, rounded boat of hide or oilcloth on a wicker frame. [< Welsh *corwg* boat]

cor·al (kôr′əl, kor′-) *n.* 1. The calcareous skeleton secreted in or by the tissues of various marine coelenterates, deposited in many forms and colors. 2. A mass of these skeletons forming an island, reef, etc. 3. An animal of this type. 4. A pinkish or yellowish red. 5. An object, as a jewel, made of coral. — *adj.* Of, relating to, or of the color of coral. [< OF < L < Gk. *korallion* red coral]

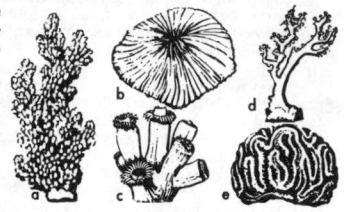

CORAL

a Reef. *b* Mushroom. *c* Bud. *d* Red. *e* Brain.

coral reef A reef, often of great extent, formed by the gradual deposit of coral skeletons.

coral snake A venomous snake of tropical America and the southern U.S., noted for its red, black, and yellow rings.

cor·bel (kôr′bəl, -bel) *n. Archit.* 1. A projection from the face of a wall to support an overhanging weight. 2. A short timber placed under a girder to increase its bearing. — *v.t.* **cor·beled** or **·belled, cor·bel·ing** or **·bel·ling** To support by or furnish with corbels. [< OF < L *corvus* crow]

cor·bel·ing (kôr′bəl·ing) *n. Archit.* An arrangement of stones or bricks in which each successive course projects beyond the one below it. Also **cor′bel·ling.**

cor·bie (kôr′bē) *n. Scot.* A crow or raven. Also **cor′by.**

cord (kôrd) *n.* 1. A string or small rope; twine. 2. A flexible, insulated electric wire, usu. with a plug at one end. 3. A measure for wood, usu. for firewood, equaling a pile 4 × 4 × 8 feet, or 128 cubic feet. See table front of book. 4. An influence that draws or restrains. 5. A raised rib in fabric; also, fabric with such ribs. 6. *pl.* Corduroy trousers. 7. *Anat.* A cordlike structure: spinal *cord.* — *v.t.* 1. To bind with cord. 2. To furnish or ornament with cords. 3. To pile (firewood) by the cord. [< MF < L < Gk. *chordē* string of a musical instrument] — **cord′er** *n.*

cord·age (kôr′dij) *n.* 1. Ropes and cords collectively, especially in a ship's rigging. 2. The amount of wood, in cords.

cor·date (kôr′dāt) *adj. Bot.* Heart-shaped, as a leaf. [< L *cordis* heart] — **cor′date·ly** *adv.*

cord·ed (kôr′did) *adj.* 1. Bound or fastened with cord. 2. Ribbed with cords: a *corded* fabric. 3. Piled in cords.

cor·dial (kôr′jəl, *esp. Brit.* -dyəl) *adj.* 1. Warm and hearty; sincere. 2. Giving heart; invigorating. — *n.* 1. A liqueur. 2. Something that invigorates, as a medical stimulant. [< L *cor, cordis* heart] — **cor′dial·ly** *adv.* — **cor′dial·ness** *n.*

cor·dial·i·ty (kôr·jal′ə·tē, -jē·al′-, *esp. Brit.* -dē·al′-) *n. pl.* **·ties** Cordial quality; sincerity of feeling; warmth.

cor·dil·le·ra (kôr·dil·yâr′ə, kôr·dil′ər·ə) *n. Geog.* An entire system of mountain ranges continuous within a great land mass. [< Sp. < OSp. *cordilla,* dim. of *cuerda* rope] — **cor·dil·ler·an** (kôr·dil·yâr′ən, kôr·dil′ər·ən) *adj.*

cord·ite (kôr′dīt) *n.* A smokeless explosive consisting of cellulose nitrate or guncotton, nitroglycerin, and a mineral jelly. [< CORD; with ref. to its appearance]

cor·don (kôr′dən) *n.* 1. A line, as of men or ships, stationed so as to guard or enclose an area. 2. A ribbon or cord worn as an insignia of honor. [< F < *corde* cord]

cor·do·van (kôr′də·vən) *n.* A fine leather first made at Córdoba, Spain, originally of goatskin, but now usu. of split horsehide. Also **cordovan leather.** — *adj.* Made of cordovan. [< OSp. *cordovan* of Córdoba]

cor·du·roy (kôr′də·roi, kôr′də·roi′) *n.* 1. A durable fabric, usu. of cotton, having a ribbed pile. 2. *pl.* Trousers made of corduroy. — *adj.* Made of corduroy. [? < *cord* (ribbed fabric) + obs. *duroy* coarse woolen cloth; prob. < F *corde du roi* king's cord]

corduroy road A road formed from logs laid transversely.

cord·wood (kôrd′wŏŏd′) *n.* Firewood or pulpwood cut for stacking in a cord or sold by the cord.

core (kôr, kōr) *n.* 1. The central or innermost part of a thing. 2. The fibrous central part of a fruit, containing the seeds. 3. A cylindrical mass of rock. 4. *Electr.* The central iron mass of an induction coil, armature, or electromagnet. — *v.t.* **cored, cor·ing** To remove the core of. [ME; origin uncertain] — **core′less** *adj.* — **cor′er** *n.*

co·re·la·tion (kō′ri·lā′shən) See CORRELATION.

co·re·lig·ion·ist (kō′ri·lij′ən·ist) *n.* An adherent of the same religion, church, or sect as another.

co·re·op·sis (kôr′ē·op′sis, kō′rē-) *n.* A plant of the composite family, with yellow or reddish flowers. [< NL < Gk. *koris* bug + -OPSIS; with ref. to the shape of the seed]

co·re·spon·dent (kō′ri·spon′dənt) *n. Law* In a suit for divorce, one charged with having committed adultery with the husband or wife. — **co′re·spon′den·cy** *n.*

co·ri·an·der (kôr′ē·an′dər, kō′rē-) *n.* 1. A plant of the parsley family, bearing aromatic seeds used for seasoning and in medicine. 2. The seeds of this plant. [< MF < L < Gk. *koriannon*]

Cor·inth (kôr′inth, kor′-) An ancient city in Argolis, Greece.

Co·rin·thi·an (kə·rin′thē·ən) *adj.* 1. Of or pertaining to ancient Corinth, noted for its luxury, licentiousness, and ornate art. 2. Given to luxury and dissipation. 3. *Archit.* Of or pertaining to an order of Greek architecture characterized by ornate, bell-shaped capitals decorated with simulated acanthus leaves. — *n.* A native or inhabitant of Corinth. — **Epistle to the Corinthians** Either of two letters addressed by Saint Paul to the Christians at Corinth, each forming a book of the New Testament. Also **Corinthians.**

co·ri·um (kôr′ē·əm, kō′rē-) *n. Anat.* The dermis. [< L]

cork (kôrk) *n.* 1. The light, porous, elastic outer bark of the cork oak, widely used in industry and the arts. 2. Something made of cork, esp. when used as a bottle stopper; also, a stopper made of other material. — *v.t.* 1. To stop with a cork. 2. To restrain; check. 3. *U.S.* To blacken with burnt cork. [Appar. < OSp. < Arabic ? < L *quercus* oak]

cork·er (kôr′kər) *n.* 1. One who or that which corks. 2. *Slang* Something outstanding or astonishing. 3. An argument, remark, etc., that puts an end to discussion.

cork·ing (kôr′king) *Slang adj.* Excellent; splendid.

cork oak An evergreen oak of southern Europe and North Africa, from whose bark cork is produced.

cork·screw (kôrk′skrōō′) *n.* An instrument for drawing corks from bottles. — *v.t.* & *v.i.* To move or twist spirally. — *adj.* Shaped like a corkscrew; twisted; spiral.

cork·y (kôr′kē) *adj.* **cork·i·er, cork·i·est** 1. Of or resembling cork. 2. Tasting of cork, as wine. — **cork′i·ness** *n.*

corm (kôrm) *n. Bot.* A bulblike enlargement of the underground stem in certain plants, as the gladiolus. [< NL *cormus* < Gk. *kormos* tree trunk]

cor·mo·rant (kôr′mər·ənt) *n.* 1. A large, web-footed aquatic bird having a hooked bill and a pouch under the beak. 2. A greedy or voracious person. — *adj.* Greedy; rapacious. [< MF < L *corvus marinus* sea crow]

corn[1] (kôrn) *n.* 1. *U.S.* A tall, extensively cultivated cereal plant bearing seeds on a large ear or cob; also, the seeds of this plant: also called *Indian corn, maize.* 2. *Brit.* In England, wheat. 3. In Scotland and Ireland, oats. 4. A single seed of a cereal plant; kernel; grain. 5. *U.S. Informal* Corn whisky. 6. *U.S. Slang* Anything trite or sentimental. — *v.t.* To preserve in coarse salt or in brine. [OE]

corn[2] (kôrn) *n.* A horny thickening of the skin, commonly on a toe. [< OF < L *cornu*]

Corn Belt *U.S.* The chief corn-growing States, Illinois, Indiana, Iowa, Kansas, Missouri, Nebraska, and Ohio.

corn borer The larva of a moth that feeds on the ears and stalks of corn.

corn·bread (kôrn′bred′) *n.* Bread made from cornmeal.

corn·cob (kôrn′kob′) *n. U.S.* The woody spike of corn around which the kernels grow.

corncob pipe A pipe whose bowl is cut from a corncob.

corn·cock·le (kôrn′kok′əl) *n.* A tall weed of the pink family, with purple flowers.

cor·ne·a (kôr′nē·ə) *n. Anat.* The transparent part of the coat of the eyeball, continuous with the sclera. For illus. see EYE. [< Med.L < L *cornu* horn] — **cor′ne·al** *adj.*

corned (kôrnd) *adj.* Preserved in salt or brine, as beef.

cor·nel (kôr′nəl) *n.* A shrub or small tree with hard wood, as the dogwood. [< MF < L *cornus* cornel]

cor·nel·ian (kôr·nēl′yən) *n.* Carnelian.

cor·ne·ous (kôr′nē·əs) *adj.* Consisting of horn; of a hornlike texture; horny. [< L < *cornu* horn]

cor·ner (kôr′nər) *n.* 1. The point formed by the meeting of two lines or surfaces. 2. The place where two streets meet. 3. A threatening or embarrassing position. 4. A region or place: in every *corner* of the land. 5. A piece for forming, ornamenting, or guarding a corner, as of a book. 6. *Econ.* An operation in which a commodity or security is bought up by an individual or group of individuals with a view to forcing higher prices. — **to cut corners** To economize; reduce expenditures. — *v.t.* 1. To force into a corner; place in a dangerous or embarrassing position. 2. To form a corner in (a stock or commodity). 3. To furnish with corners. 4. To place in a corner. — *v.i.* 5. To form a corner in a stock or commodity. 6. *U.S.* To come together or be located on or at a corner. — *adj.* 1. Located on a corner. 2. Designed for a corner. [< OF < L *cornu* horn] — **cor′nered** *adj.*

cor·ner·stone (kôr′nər·stōn′) *n.* 1. A stone uniting two walls at the corner of a building. **2.** Such a stone ceremoniously laid into the foundation of a building under construction. **3.** Something of primary importance.

cor·ner·wise (kôr′nər·wīz′) *adv.* **1.** With the corner in front. **2.** Diagonally. Also **cor′ner·ways′.**

cor·net (kôr·net′) *n.* **1.** A small wind instrument of the trumpet class, with a somewhat wider bore. **2.** A cone-shaped paper wrapper, as for candy, nuts, etc. [< OF < L *cornu* horn] — **cor·net′tist, cor·net′ist** *n.*

corn·flow·er (kôrn′flou′ər) *n.* A hardy annual plant of the composite family, with heads of blue, purple, pink, or white flowers: also called *bachelor's-button, bluebonnet, bluebottle.*

corn·husk (kôrn′husk′) *n. U.S.* The leaves or husk enclosing an ear of corn: also called *corn shuck.*

Corn·husk·er State (kôrn′husk′ər) Nickname of Nebraska.

corn·husk·ing (kôrn′hus′king) *n. U.S.* A social gathering for husking corn, usu. followed by refreshments, dancing, etc.: also called *husking bee.* — **corn′husk′er** *n.*

cor·nice (kôr′nis) *n.* **1.** *Archit.* **a** The horizontal molded projection at the top of a building. **b** The uppermost member of an entablature. **2.** A molding around the walls of a room, close to the ceiling. — *v.t.* **·niced, ·nic·ing** To adorn with a cornice. [< Ital., ? < L < Gk. *korōnis* wreath]

Cor·nish (kôr′nish) *adj.* Pertaining to Cornwall, England, or its people. — *n.* The former language of Cornwall, belonging to the Brythonic branch of the Celtic languages. — **Cor′nish·man** (-mən) *n.*

corn·meal (kôrn′mēl′) *n.* **1.** Meal made from corn: also called *Indian meal.* **2.** *Scot.* Oatmeal. Also **corn meal.**

corn pone *Southern U.S.* Bread made of cornmeal, water, and salt, usu. without milk or eggs.

corn silk The soft, silky styles on an ear of corn.

corn·stalk (kôrn′stôk′) *n.* A stalk of corn. Also **corn stalk.**

corn·starch (kôrn′stärch′) *n.* **1.** Starch made from corn. **2.** A purified starchy cornmeal used in making puddings.

corn syrup Syrup extracted from corn grains, containing glucose mixed with dextrine and maltose.

cor·nu·co·pi·a (kôr′nə·kō′pē·ə) *n.* **1.** A symbol of prosperity, represented as a curved horn overflowing with fruit, vegetables, grains, etc. **2.** A great abundance. Also called *horn of plenty.* [< LL < L *cornu copiae* horn of plenty] — **cor′nu·co′pi·an** *adj.*

corn whisky Whisky distilled from corn.

corn·y (kôr′nē) *adj.* **corn·i·er, corn·i·est** **1.** *Slang* Trite, banal, or sentimental. **2.** Of or producing corn.

co·rol·la (kə·rol′ə) *n. Bot.* The circle of flower leaves, usu. colored, forming the inner floral envelope; the petals of a flower. [< L, dim. of *corona* crown] — **cor·ol·la·ceous** (kôr′ə·lā′shəs, kor′-) *adj.* — **cor·ol·late** (kôr′ə·lāt, kor′-) *adj.*

cor·ol·lar·y (kôr′ə·ler′ē, kor′-; *Brit.* kə·rol′ər·ē) *n. pl.* **·lar·ies** **1.** A proposition following so obviously from another that it requires little or no proof. **2.** An inference or deduction. **3.** A natural consequence; result. — *adj.* Like a corollary; consequent. [< L *corolla* garland]

co·ro·na (kə·rō′nə) *n. pl.* **·nas** or **·nae** (-nē) **1.** A crownlike structure or part, as the top of the head, the upper part of a tooth, etc. **2.** *Astron.* **a** A luminous circle around one of the heavenly bodies, as when seen through cloud or mist. **b** The luminous envelope of ionized gases visible during a total eclipse of the sun. **3.** Anything resembling a corona or halo. **4.** *Bot.* A crownlike process at the top of the tube of a corolla, as in jonquils. **5.** *Electr.* The luminous discharge appearing at the surface or between the terminals of an electrical conductor under high voltage. [< L, crown] — **co·ro′nal** *adj.*

cor·o·nar·y (kôr′ə·ner′ē, kor′-) *adj.* **1.** Pertaining to or like a crown. **2.** *Anat.* Designating either of two arteries rising from the aorta and supplying blood to the heart muscle. For illus. see HEART. — *n.* Coronary thrombosis. [< L *corona* crown]

coronary thrombosis *Pathol.* The formation of a thrombus, or blood clot, in one of the coronary arteries, resulting in interruption of blood supply to the heart muscle.

cor·o·na·tion (kôr′ə·nā′shən, kor′-) *n.* The act or ceremony of crowning a monarch. [< MF, ult. < L *corona* crown]

cor·o·ner (kôr′ə·nər, kor′-) *n.* A public officer whose principal duty is the investigation, with the aid of a jury (**coroner's jury**), of the cause of deaths not clearly due to natural causes. [< AF < L *corona*] **cor′o·ner·ship′** *n.*

cor·o·net (kôr′ə·net, -nit, kor′-) *n.* **1.** A small crown, denoting noble rank less than sovereign. **2.** A headband ornamented with jewels, etc. [< OF < L *corona*] — **cor′o·net′ed** *adj.*

cor·po·ra (kôr′pər·ə) Plural of CORPUS.

cor·po·ral[1] (kôr′pər·əl) *adj.* **1.** Belonging or related to the body: *corporal* punishment. **2.** Personal: *corporal* possession. [< L *corpus, -oris* body] — **cor·po·ral·i·ty** (kôr′pə·ral′ə·tē) *n.* — **cor′po·ral·ly** *adv.*

cor·po·ral[2] (kôr′pər·əl, -prəl) *n. Mil.* A noncommissioned

officer of the lowest rank. See tables at GRADE. [< MF < Ital. < L *caput*]

corporal punishment Physical punishment given an offender, as flogging.

cor·po·rate (kôr′pər·it) *adj.* **1.** Of or related to a corporation; incorporated. **2.** Combined as a whole; collective. [< L *corpus, -oris* body] — **cor′po·rate·ly** *adv.*

cor·po·ra·tion (kôr′pə·rā′shən) *n.* **1.** A body of persons recognized by law as an individual person or entity having its own name and identity, and with rights, privileges, and liabilities distinct from those of its members. **2.** Any group of persons acting as one body. **3.** *Informal* A bulging abdomen; paunch. — **cor′po·ra′tive** *adj.* — **cor′po·ra′tor** *n.*

cor·po·re·al (kôr·pôr′ē·əl, -pō′rē·əl) *adj.* **1.** Of, or of the nature of, the body; bodily; mortal. **2.** Of a material nature; physical. — **cor·po·re·al·i·ty** (kôr·pôr′ē·al′ə·tē, -pō′rē-) *n.* — **cor·po′re·al·ly** *adv.* — **cor·po′re·al·ness** *n.*

cor·po·re·i·ty (kôr′pə·rē′ə·tē) *n.* Bodily or material existence. [< Med.L < L *corpus, -oris* body]

corps (kôr, kōr) *n. pl.* **corps** (kôrz, kōrz) **1.** *Mil.* **a** A tactical unit, intermediate between a division and an army, consisting of two or more divisions and auxiliary arms and services. **b** A special department: the Transportation *Corps.* **2.** A number of persons acting together. [See CORPSE.]

corps de bal·let (kôr′ de ba·lā′, *Fr.* bà·le′) The ballet dancers who perform as a group and have no solo parts. [< F]

corpse (kôrps) *n.* A dead body, usu. of a human being. [ME < OF < L *corpus* body]

corps·man (kôr′mən, kōr′-) *n. pl.* **·men** (-mən) **1.** In the U.S. Navy, an enlisted man trained as a pharmacist or hospital assistant. **2.** In the U.S. Army, an enlisted man in the Medical Corps assigned to a combat area.

cor·pu·lence (kôr′pyə·ləns) *n.* An excess accumulation of fat in the body; obesity. Also **cor′pu·len·cy.** [< F < L < *corpus* body] — **cor′pu·lent** *adj.* — **cor′pu·lent·ly** *adv.*

cor·pus (kôr′pəs) *n. pl.* **·po·ra** (-pər·ə) **1.** A human or animal body. **2.** A collection of writings, generally on one subject or by one author. **3.** The main part or mass of anything. [< L]

Cor·pus Chris·ti (kôr′pəs kris′tē, -tī) In the Roman Catholic Church, a festival honoring the Eucharist on the first Thursday after Trinity Sunday. [< L, body of Christ]

cor·pus·cle (kôr′pəs·əl, -pus·əl) *n.* **1.** *Biol.* Any protoplasmic granule of distinct shape or characteristic function, esp. one of the particles forming part of the blood of vertebrates. **2.** A minute particle of matter, as a molecule, atom, or electron. Also **cor·pus·cule** (kôr·pus′kyōōl). [< L *corpus, -oris* body] — **cor·pus·cu·lar** (kôr·pus′kyə·lər) *adj.*

cor·pus de·lic·ti (kôr′pəs di·lik′tī) **1.** *Law* The essential fact of the commission of a crime, as, in a case of murder, the finding of the body of the victim. **2.** Loosely, the victim's body in a murder case. [< L, the body of the offense]

corpus ju·ris (jŏŏr′is) *Latin* The body of law.

cor·ral (kə·ral′) *n.* An enclosed space or pen for livestock. — *v.t.* **·ralled, ·ral·ling** **1.** To drive into and enclose in a corral. **2.** *U.S. Informal* To seize or capture; secure. [< Sp.]

cor·rect (kə·rekt′) *v.t.* **1.** To make free from error or mistake; set right: to *correct* false notions. **2.** To remedy or counteract; rectify. **3.** To mark the errors of: to *correct* proofs. **4.** To punish or rebuke so as to improve. **5.** To adjust, as to a standard: to *correct* a lens. — *adj.* **1.** Free from fault or mistake; true or exact; accurate. **2.** Conforming to custom or other standard; proper: *correct* behavior. [< L < *com-* together + *regere* to make straight] — **cor·rect′a·ble** or **cor·rect′i·ble** *adj.* — **cor·rect′ly** *adv.* — **cor·rect′ness** *n.* — **cor·rec′tor** *n.*

cor·rec·tion (kə·rek′shən) *n.* **1.** The act of correcting. **2.** That which is offered or used as an improvement; an emendation. **3.** The act or process of disciplining or chastening; punishment. **4.** A quantity added or subtracted for correcting: chronometer *corrections.* — **cor·rec′tion·al** *adj.*

cor·rec·tive (kə·rek′tiv) *adj.* Tending or intended to set right. — *n.* That which corrects. — **cor·rec′tive·ly** *adv.*

cor·re·late (kôr′ə·lāt, kor′-) *v.* **·lat·ed, ·lat·ing** *v.t.* **1.** To place or put in reciprocal relation: to *correlate* literature and philosophy. — *v.i.* **2.** To be mutually or reciprocally related. — *adj.* Having a mutual or reciprocal relation. — *n.* Either of two things mutually related.

cor·re·la·tion (kôr′ə·lā′shən, kor′-) *n.* **1.** Mutual or reciprocal relation. **2.** The act of correlating. — **cor′re·la′tion·al** *adj.*

cor·rel·a·tive (kə·rel′ə·tiv) *adj.* **1.** Having correlation or mutual relation. **2.** Mutually related in grammatical or logical significance: *Either . . . or* are *correlative* conjunctions. — *n.* **1.** A correlate. **2.** A correlative term. — **cor·rel′a·tively** *adv.* — **cor·rel′a·tive·ness, cor·rel′a·tiv′i·ty** *n.*

cor·re·spond (kôr′ə·spond′, kor′-) *v.i.* **1.** To conform in fitness or appropriateness; be in agreement; suit: often with

with or *to.* **2.** To be similar in character or function: with *to.* **3.** To hold communication by means of letters. [< Med.L < L *com-* together + *respondere* to answer]

cor·re·spon·dence (kôr′ə·spon′dəns, kor′-) *n.* **1.** The act or state of corresponding; agreement; congruity; also, analogy; similarity. Also **cor′re·spon′den·cy. 2.** Communication by letters; also, the letters written.

correspondence school A school that offers courses of study by mail.

cor·re·spon·dent (kôr′ə·spon′dənt, kor′-) *n.* **1.** One who communicates by means of letters. **2.** A person employed to report news, etc., from a distant place. **3.** A thing that corresponds; a correlative. — *adj.* Corresponding.

cor·re·spond·ing (kôr′ə·spon′ding, kor′-) *adj.* **1.** That corresponds in character or place; similar or equivalent. **2.** Handling correspondence. — **cor′re·spond′ing·ly** *adv.*

cor·ri·dor (kôr′ə·dər, -dôr, kor′-) *n.* **1.** A gallery or passageway, usu. having rooms opening upon it. **2.** A strip of land across a foreign country, as one affording a landlocked nation access to the sea. **3.** A relatively long, narrow, densely-populated region joining two or more major cities. [< MF < Ital. < L *currere* to run]

cor·ri·gen·dum (kôr′ə·jen′dəm, kor′-) *n. pl.* **·da** (-də) Something to be corrected, as a printer's error. [< L, gerundive of *corrigere* < *com-* together + *regere* to make straight]

cor·ri·gi·ble (kôr′ə·jə·bəl, kor′-) *adj.* **1.** Capable of being corrected or reformed **2.** Submissive to correction. [See CORRECT.] — **cor′ri·gi·bil′i·ty** *n.* — **cor′ri·gi·bly** *adv.*

cor·rob·o·rate (kə·rob′ə·rāt) *v.t.* **·rat·ed, ·rat·ing** To strengthen or support, as conviction; confirm. [< L < *com-* together + *robur, -oris* strength] — **cor·rob′o·ra′tion** *n.* — **cor·rob′o·ra′tor** *n.*

cor·rob·o·ra·tive (kə·rob′ə·rā′tiv, -ər·ə·tiv) *adj.* Tending to strengthen or confirm. Also **cor·rob·o·ra·to·ry** (kə·rob′·ər·ə·tôr′ē, -tō′rē). — **cor·rob′o·ra·tive·ly** *adv.*

cor·rode (kə·rōd′) *v.* **·rod·ed, ·rod·ing** *v.t.* **1.** To eat away or destroy gradually, as by chemical action. **2.** To destroy, consume, or impair (character, strength, etc.). — *v.i.* **3.** To be eaten away. [< L < *com-* thoroughly + *rodere* to gnaw] — **cor·rod′i·ble** or **cor·ro·si·ble** (kə·rō′sə·bəl) *adj.*

cor·ro·sion (kə·rō′zhən) *n.* **1.** An eating or wearing away. **2.** A product of corrosive action, as rust.

cor·ro·sive (kə·rō′siv) *adj.* Having the power of corroding or eating away. — *n.* A corroding substance. — **cor·ro′sive·ly** *adv.* — **cor·ro′sive·ness** *n.*

corrosive sublimate *Chem.* Mercuric chloride.

cor·ru·gate (kôr′ə·gāt, -gə-, kor′-) *v.t. & v.i.* **·gat·ed, ·gat·ing** To contract into alternate ridges and furrows; wrinkle. — *adj.* Contracted into ridges or folds; wrinkled, furrowed: also **cor′ru·gat′ed.** [< L *com-* thoroughly + *rugare* to wrinkle] — **cor′ru·ga′tion** *n.*

cor·rupt (kə·rupt′) *adj.* **1.** Open to bribery; dishonest. **2.** Immoral or perverted. **3.** Rotting; putrid. **4.** Debased by changes or errors; altered, as a text. — *v.t. & v.i.* To make or become corrupt. [< OF < L < *com-* thoroughly + *rumpere* to break] — **cor·rupt′er** or **cor·rup′tor** *n.* — **cor·rupt′ly** *adv.* — **cor·rupt′ness** *n.*

cor·rupt·i·ble (kə·rup′tə·bəl) *adj.* Capable of being corrupted. — **cor·rupt′i·bil′i·ty, cor·rupt′i·ble·ness** *n.* — **cor·rupt′i·bly** *adv.*

cor·rup·tion (kə·rup′shən) *n.* **1.** The act of corrupting, or the state of being corrupt. **2.** Dishonesty and lack of integrity; also, bribery. **3.** Moral deterioration. **4.** Physical decay; rot. **5.** Any corrupting influence.

cor·sage (kôr·säzh′) *n.* **1.** A small bouquet of flowers for a woman to wear, as at the waist or shoulder. **2.** The bodice or waist of a woman's dress. [< OF < *cors* body]

cor·sair (kôr′sâr) *n.* **1.** A privateer. **2.** A pirate. **3.** A corsair's vessel. [< MF < Med.L < L *currere* to run]

corse·let (kôrs′lit) **1.** Body armor; also, a breastplate. Also **cors′let. 2.** A light corset, usu. without stays. [< MF, double dim. of OF *cors* body]

cor·set (kôr′sit) *n.* **1.** A close-fitting undergarment, usu. tightened with laces and reinforced by stays, worn chiefly by women to give support or desired shape to the body. **2.** A close-fitting medieval garment. — *v.t.* To enclose or dress in a corset. [< OF, dim. of *cors* body]

cor·tege (kôr·tezh′, -tāzh′) *n.* **1.** A train of attendants. **2.** A ceremonial procession. Also *Chiefly Brit.* **cor·tège** (-tezh′). [< F < Ital. *corteggio* < *corte* court]

cor·tex (kôr′teks) *n. pl.* **·ti·ces** (-tə·sēz) **1.** *Bot.* The bark of trees or the rind of fruits. **2.** *Anat.* The external layer of various organs, esp. the gray matter covering the brain. [< L, bark] — **cor′ti·cal** *adj.* — **cor′ti·cal·ly** *adv.*

cor·ti·cate (kôr′ti·kit, -kāt) *adj.* Sheathed in bark or in a cortex. Also **cor′ti·cat′ed.** [< L *cortex* bark]

cor·ti·sone (kôr′tə·sōn, -zōn) *n.* A powerful hormone extracted from the cortex of the adrenal gland and also made synthetically, used in the treatment of rheumatoid arthritis and certain other diseases. [Short for *corticosterone*]

co·run·dum (kə·run′dəm) *n.* An aluminum oxide, Al_2O_3,

used as an abrasive, varieties of which include the ruby and sapphire. [< Tamil *kurundam*]

cor·us·cate (kôr′ə·skāt, kor′-) *v.i.* **·cat·ed, ·cat·ing** To sparkle. [< L *coruscare* to glitter] — **cor′us·ca′tion** *n.*

cor·vette (kôr·vet′) *n.* **1.** A small, swift warship, used chiefly as an antisubmarine escort vessel. **2.** Formerly, a warship equipped with sails and a single tier of guns, smaller than a frigate. Also **cor·vet** (kôr·vet′, kôr′vet). [< F < Pg. < L *corbita* (*navis*) cargo (ship)]

cor·vine (kôr′vīn, -vin) *adj.* Of or pertaining to a crow; crowlike. [< L *corvinus* < *corvus* crow]

cor·ymb (kôr′imb, -im, kor′-) *n. Bot.* A flat-topped or convex open flower cluster. [< F < L < Gk. *korymbos* flower cluster] — **co·rym·bose** (kə·rim′bōs) *adj.* — **co·rym′bose·ly** *adv.* — **co·rym·bous** (kə·rim′bəs) *adj.*

co·ry·za (kə·rī′zə) *n. Pathol.* A cold in the head. [< L < Gk. *koryza* catarrh]

co·se·cant (kō·sē′kant) *n. Trig.* The secant of the complement of an acute angle. [< CO-² + SECANT]

co·sig·na·to·ry (kō·sig′nə·tôr′ē, -tō′rē) *adj.* Signing together or jointly. — *n. pl.* **·ries** One of the joint signers of a document: also called *cosigner.*

co·sign·er (kō′sī′nər) *n.* **1.** One who endorses the signature of another, as for a loan. **2.** A cosignatory.

co·sine (kō′sīn) *n. Trig.* The sine of the complement of an acute angle.

cos·met·ic (koz·met′ik) *adj.* Used to beautify, esp. the complexion. Also **cos·met′i·cal.** — *n.* A cosmetic preparation. [< Gk. < *kosmos* order] — **cos·met′i·cal·ly** *adv.*

cos·mic (koz′mik) *adj.* **1.** Of or relating to the universe or cosmos. **2.** Limitless; vast. Also **cos′mi·cal.** [< Gk. < *kosmos* order, the universe] — **cos′mi·cal·ly** *adv.*

cosmic dust Fine particles of matter collected by the earth from outer space.

cosmic rays *Physics* Radiation of intense penetrating power and high frequency, emanating from outer space and consisting principally of high-energy rays formed from many types of atomic particles, positive and negative in charge.

cosmo- *combining form* The universe. Also, before vowels, **cosm-.** [< Gk. *kosmos* the universe]

cos·mog·o·ny (koz·mog′ə·nē) *n. pl.* **·nies 1.** A theory concerning the origin of the material universe. **2.** The creation of the universe. [< Gk. < *kosmos* the universe + *-gonia* < *-gon*, stem of *gignesthai* to be born] — **cos·mo·gon·ic** (koz′mə·gon′ik) or **·i·cal, cos·mog′o·nal** *adj.* — **cos·mog′o·nist** *n.*

cos·mog·ra·phy (koz·mog′rə·fē) *n. pl.* **·phies** The science that describes the universe, including astronomy, geology, and geography. [< Gk. < *kosmos* the universe + *graphein* to write] — **cos·mog′ra·pher, cos·mog′ra·phist** *n.* — **cos·mo·graph·ic** (koz′mə·graf′ik) or **·i·cal** *adj.*

cos·mol·o·gy (koz·mol′ə·jē) *n. pl.* **·gies** The general philosophy of the universe considered as a totality of parts and phenomena subject to laws. [< NL < Gk. *kosmos* the universe + *-logia* study] — **cos·mo·log·i·cal** (koz′mə·loj′i·kəl) or **cos·mo·log′ic** *adj.* — **cos·mol′o·gist** *n.*

cos·mo·naut (koz′mə·nôt) *n.* An astronaut.

cos·mo·pol·i·tan (koz′mə·pol′ə·tən) *adj.* **1.** Common to all the world; not local or limited. **2.** At home in all parts of the world; free from local attachments or prejudices. — *n.* A cosmopolitan person. — **cos′mo·pol′i·tan·ism, cos·mop·o·lit·ism** (koz·mop′ə·lit·iz′əm) *n.*

cos·mop·o·lite (koz·mop′ə·līt) *n.* **1.** A cosmopolitan person. **2.** A plant or animal widely distributed over the world. [< Gk. < *kosmos* world + *politēs* citizen < *polis* city]

cos·mos (koz′məs, -mos) *n.* **1.** The world or universe considered as an orderly system. **2.** Any complete system. **3.** *Bot.* A plant related to the dahlia. [< Gk. *kosmos* order]

Cos·sack (kos′ak, -ək) *n.* One of a people of the southern U.S.S.R., famous as cavalrymen. [< Russ. *kazak* < Turkic *quzzāq* guerrilla, freebooter]

cos·set (kos′it) *v.t.* To pamper; pet. — *n.* **1.** A pet lamb. **2.** Any pet. [? OE *cot-sǣta* dweller in a cottage]

cost (kôst) *v.* **cost** (*for def. 3, also* **cost·ed**), **cost·ing** *v.i.* **1.** To be acquirable for or have the value of a price, sum, consideration, etc. **2.** To be gained by the expenditure of a specified thing, as health, pain, effort, etc. — *v.t.* **3.** To estimate the amount spent for the production of. — *n.* **1.** The price paid for anything. **2.** Loss; suffering; detriment. **3.** *pl. Law* The expenses of a lawsuit in court. — **at all costs** (or **at any cost**) Regardless of cost; by all means. [< OF < *com-* together + *stare* to stand]

cost accountant One who keeps track of the costs incurred in production and distribution. — **cost accounting**

cos·tal (kos′təl) *adj.* Of, on, or near a rib or the ribs.

cos·ter·mon·ger (kos′tər·mung′gər, -mong′-, kôs′-) *n. Brit.* A street hawker of vegetables, fruits, etc. Also **cos′ter.** [< *costard* a variety of apple + MONGER]

cos·tive (kos′tiv, kôs′-) *adj.* Constipated. [< OF *costivé*] — **cos′tive·ly** *adv.* — **cos′tive·ness** *n.*

cost·ly (kôst′lē, kost′-) *adj.* **·li·er, ·li·est 1.** Costing very much; expensive. **2.** Sumptuous. — **cost′li·ness** *n.*

costo- *combining form* Rib: used in anatomical and surgical terms. Also, before vowels, **cost-**. [< L *costa* rib]

cost of living The average cost, as to an individual or family, of food, clothing, shelter, etc.

cos·tume (n. kos′tōōm, -tyōōm; v. kos·tōōm′, -tyōōm′) n. **1.** The mode of dress, including ornaments and hair style, of a given region, time, or class. **2.** Such dress as worn by actors, dancers, etc. **3.** A set of garments for some occasion or activity: summer *costume*. **4.** Garb; apparel, esp. that of a woman. — v.t. **·tumed**, **·tum·ing** To furnish with costumes. [< F < Ital. < L *consuetudo* custom]

cos·tum·er (kos·tōō′mər, -tyōō′-) n. One who makes or furnishes costumes. Also **cos·tum·ier** (kos·tōōm′yər, -tyōōm′-; *Fr.* kôs·tü·myā′).

cot¹ (kot) n. A light, narrow bed, commonly of canvas stretched on a folding frame. [< Hind. *khāt* < Skt. *khaṭvā*]

cot² (kot) n. **1.** A small house; cottage. **2.** A cote. **3.** A protective covering for an injured finger. [OE]

co·tan·gent (kō·tan′jənt) n. *Trig.* The tangent of the complement of an acute angle. — **co·tan·gen·tial** (kō′tan·jen′shəl) *adj.*

cote (kōt) n. **1.** A small shelter for sheep or birds. **2.** *Dial.* A little house; hut. [OE. Akin to COT².]

co·tem·po·ra·ne·ous (kō·tem′pə·rā′nē·əs), **co·tem·po·rar·y** (kō·tem′pə·rer′ē), etc. See CONTEMPORANEOUS, etc.

co·ten·ant (kō·ten′ənt) n. One of several tenants holding the same property. — **co·ten′an·cy** n.

co·te·rie (kō′tə·rē) n. A small, exclusive group of persons who share certain interests or pursuits. [< F]

co·ter·mi·nous (kō·tûr′mə·nəs) See CONTERMINOUS.

co·til·lion (kō·til′yən, kə-) n. **1.** *U.S.* An elaborate dance marked by frequent change of partners: also called *german*. **2.** *U.S.* A formal ball at which young ladies are presented to society. **3.** A lively, quick dance. **4.** The music for this dance. Also **co·til·lon** (kō·til′yən, kə-; *Fr.* kô·tē·yôṅ′). [< F *cotillon* petticoat]

cot·tage (kot′ij) n. **1.** A small house in the suburbs or the country. **2.** *U.S.* A temporary home at a resort. [< COT²]

cottage cheese A soft, white cheese made of milk curds.

cottage pudding Plain cake covered with a sweet sauce.

cot·tag·er (kot′ij·ər) n. **1.** One who lives in a cottage. **2.** *Brit.* A rural laborer. **3.** *Canadian* A summer resident.

cotter pin A key, wedge, pin, etc., that is split lengthwise so that the ends may be spread apart to hold parts of machinery together.

cot·ton (kot′n) n. **1.** The soft, fibrous, white or yellowish material, of high cellulose content, attached to the seeds of the cotton plant and widely used as a textile. **2.** The plant itself. **3.** Cotton plants collectively. **4.** Cotton cloth or thread. — *adj.* Woven or composed of cotton cloth or thread. — **to cotton to** *Informal* **1.** To become friendly with. **2.** To take a liking to. — **to cotton up to** *Informal* To attempt to please by friendly overtures or flattery. [< F *coton* < OSp. < Arabic *qutun*] — **cot′ton·y** *adj.*

cotton belt *U.S.* The region of the southern U.S. in which cotton is the chief crop.

cotton flannel A soft, warm cotton fabric, napped on one or both sides.

cotton gin A machine used to separate the seeds from the fiber of cotton.

cot·ton·mouth (kot′n·mouth′) n. The water moccasin, a snake.

COTTON
a Boll ready for picking.

cotton picker A machine designed to remove the ripe cotton from standing cotton plants.

cot·ton·seed (kot′n·sēd′) n. The seed of the cotton plant.

cottonseed oil A pale yellow, viscid oil pressed from cottonseeds, used in cooking, paints, and as a lubricant.

cot·ton·tail (kot′n·tāl′) n. The American gray rabbit.

cot·ton·wood (kot′n·wŏŏd′) n. An American poplar tree whose seeds discharge a cottony substance.

cotton wool 1. Raw cotton. **2.** *Brit.* Absorbent cotton.

cot·y·le·don (kot′ə·lēd′n) n. *Bot.* A seed leaf, or one of a pair of the first leaves from a sprouting seed. [< L < Gk. < *kotylē* a cavity] — **cot′y·le′do·nous, cot′y·le′do·nal** *adj.*

couch (kouch) n. A piece of furniture, usu. upholstered and having a back, on which several may sit or one may recline; also, a bed, or any place of repose. — v.t. **1.** To phrase; put into words. **2.** To cause to recline, as on a bed. **3.** To bend or bring down; lower, as a spear for attack. — v.i. **4.** To lie down; recline. **5.** To lie in ambush. [< OF < *coucher* to put to bed] — **couch′er** n.

couch·ant (kou′chənt) *adj.* Lying down. [See COUCH.]

couch grass A perennial grass multiplying injuriously in cultivated grounds by its long rootstocks: also called *quitch grass*. [Var. of QUITCH (GRASS)]

cou·gar (kōō′gər) n. The puma. [< F < Tupi]

cough (kôf, kof) v.i. **1.** To expel air from the lungs in a noisy or spasmodic manner. — v.t. **2.** To expel by a cough. — **to cough up 1.** To expel by coughing. **2.** *Slang* To surrender; hand over, as money. — n. **1.** A sudden, harsh expulsion of breath. **2.** An illness in which there is frequent coughing. [ME *cozen*, *couzen*] — **cough′er** n.

cough drop A medicated lozenge to relieve coughing, etc.

could (kŏŏd) Past tense of CAN¹. [ME *coude*, OE *cuthe* knew how; *l* inserted on analogy with *should* and *would*]

could·n't (kŏŏd′nt) Could not.

cou·lee (kōō′lē) n. **1.** *U.S.* A deep gulch cut by rainstorms or melting snow. **2.** *Geol.* A sheet of solidified lava. Also *French* **cou·lée** (kōō·lā′). [< F *couler* to flow]

cou·lomb (kōō·lom′) n. The practical unit of quantity in measuring electricity; the amount conveyed by one ampere in one second. [after C. A. de *Coulomb*, 1736–1806, French physicist]

coul·ter (kōl′tər) See COLTER.

coun·cil (koun′səl) n. **1.** An assembly of persons convened for consultation or deliberation. **2.** A body of men elected or appointed to act in an administrative, legislative, or advisory capacity in a government. **3.** The deliberation that takes place in a council chamber. [< AF, OF < L < *com-* together + *calare* to call]

coun·cil·man (koun′səl·mən) n. *pl.* **·men** (-mən) A member of a council, esp. the governing council of a city.

coun·cil·or (koun′səl·ər, -slər) n. A member of a council. Also *Brit.* **coun′cil·lor.** — **coun′cil·or·ship′** n.

coun·sel (koun′səl) n. **1.** Mutual exchange of advice, opinions, etc.; consultation. **2.** Advice; guidance. **3.** A deliberate purpose; plan. **4.** A secret intent or opinion: obsolete except in **to keep one's own counsel. 5.** A lawyer or lawyers. — v. **coun·seled** or **·selled, coun·sel·ing** or **·sel·ling** v.t. **1.** To give advice to; advise. **2.** To advise in favor of; recommend. — v.i. **3.** To give or take counsel. [< AF, OF < L *consulere* to deliberate]

coun·sel·or (koun′səl·ər, -slər) n. **1.** One who gives counsel; an adviser. **2.** An attorney at law. **3.** A supervisor at a children's camp. Also **coun′sel·lor.**

count¹ (kount) v.t. **1.** To list or call off one by one to ascertain the total. **2.** To list numerals in a progressive sequence up to: to *count* ten. **3.** To consider to be; judge. **4.** To take note of; include in a reckoning. — v.i. **5.** To list numbers in sequence. **6.** To have worth; be of importance. **7.** To be accounted or included. — **to count in** To include. — **to count on** (or **upon**) To rely on. — **to count out 1.** In boxing, to reach a count of ten over (a downed boxer), thus declaring him defeated. **2.** To omit or exclude; disregard. — n. **1.** The act of counting. **2.** The number arrived at by counting; total. **3.** An accounting or reckoning. **4.** *Law* A separate and distinct charge, as in an indictment. **5.** In boxing, the ten seconds given a contestant to get up or lose the fight. [< OF < L < *com-* together + *putare* to reckon] — **count′a·ble** *adj.*

count² (kount) n. In some European countries, a nobleman having a rank corresponding to that of an earl in England. [< AF *counte*, OF *coute* < L *comes* an associate]

count·down (kount′doun′) n. A reverse counting of time units, reaching zero at the instant when an operation, as a rocket launching, nuclear blast, etc., is to be executed.

coun·te·nance (koun′tə·nəns) n. **1.** The face or features. **2.** Facial expression. **3.** An encouraging look; also, approval; support. **4.** Self-control; composure. — **out of countenance** Disconcerted; embarrassed; abashed. — v.t. **·nanced, ·nanc·ing** To approve; encourage. [< OF < L *continere* to hang together] — **coun′te·nanc·er** n.

coun·ter¹ (koun′tər) n. **1.** An opposite or contrary. **2.** In boxing, a blow given while receiving or parrying another. **3.** In fencing, a parry in which one foil follows another. **4.** A piece encircling the heel of a shoe. **5.** *Naut.* The curved part of a vessel's stern extending from the water line to the point of fullest outward swell. — v.t. **1.** To return, as a blow, by another blow. **2.** To oppose; contradict; controvert. **3.** To put a new counter on (a shoe, etc.). — v.i. **4.** To give a blow while receiving or parrying one. **5.** To make a countermove. — *adj.* Opposing; opposite; contrary. — *adv.* Contrary. [< F < L *contra* against]

coun·ter² (koun′tər) n. **1.** A board, table, or the like, on which to expose goods for sale, transact business, or serve refreshments or meals. **2.** A piece of wood, ivory, etc., used in counting, as in billiards. **3.** A piece in chess, checkers, etc. **4.** An imitation coin. [< AF < Med.L < L *computare* to compute]

counter- *combining form* **1.** Opposing; contrary; acting in opposition or response to the action of the main element; as in:

counteraccusation   counterblow   countercharge

counterdemand   counterpropaganda   counterstatement
counterforce   counterproposal   countertheory
counterinfluence   counterreform   counterthreat
countermeasure   counterresolution   counterthrust

2. Done or acting in reciprocation or exchange; as in:
counteroffer   counterquestion

3. Complementing or corresponding; denoting the duplicate or parallel; as in:
countercheck   counterfugue   countersecurity

4. Opposite in direction or position; as in:
countercurrent   counterflow   counterpressure
counterflight   counterposition   counterturn
[< F *contra-* against]

coun·ter·act (koun/tər·akt/) *v.t.* To act in opposition to; check. — **coun/ter·ac/tion** *n.* — **coun·ter·ac/tive** *adj.*

coun·ter·at·tack (*n.* koun/tər·ə·tak/; *v.* koun/tər·ə·tak/) *n.* An attack designed to counter another attack. — *v.t. & v.i.* To make a counterattack (against).

coun·ter·bal·ance (*v.* koun/tər·bal/əns; *n.* koun/tər·bal/əns) *v.t.* ·anced, ·anc·ing To oppose with an equal weight or force; offset. — *n.* **1.** Any power equally opposing another. **2.** A weight that balances another; counterpoise.

coun·ter·claim (*n.* koun/tər·klām/; *v.* koun/tər·klām/) *n.* A claim that opposes another claim. — *v.t. & v.i.* To make or plead (as) a counterclaim. — **coun/ter·claim/ant** *n.*

coun·ter·clock·wise (koun/tər·klok/wīz/) *adj. & adv.* Opposite to the direction taken by the hands of a clock.

coun·ter·es·pi·o·nage (koun/tər·es/pē·ə·näzh/, -nij) *n.* Measures intended to counteract enemy spying.

coun·ter·feit (koun/tər·fit) *v.t.* **1.** To make an imitation of, as money or stamps, with the intent to defraud. **2.** To copy; imitate; also, to feign; dissemble: to *counterfeit* sorrow. — *v.i.* **3.** To practice deception; feign. **4.** To make counterfeits. — *adj.* **1.** Made to resemble some genuine thing with the intent to defraud. **2.** Pretended; feigned; deceitful. — *n.* **1.** Something made fraudulently to resemble the genuine. **2.** Any imitation of copy. [< OF < L *contra-* against + *facere* to make] — **coun/ter·feit/er** *n.*

coun·ter·foil (koun/tər·foil/) *n.* The part of a check, money order, etc., kept by the issuer as a record; a stub.

coun·ter·in·tel·li·gence (koun/tər·in·tel/ə·jəns) *n.* Activities to oppose espionage, subversion, and sabotage.

coun·ter·ir·ri·tant (koun/tər·ir/ə·tənt) *n.* Anything used to excite irritation in one place so as to counteract more serious irritation elsewhere.

coun·ter·man (koun/tər·mən) *n.* A man who serves at a lunch counter.

coun·ter·mand (*v.* koun/tər·mand/, -mänd/; *n.* koun/tər·mand, -mänd) *v.t.* **1.** To revoke or reverse (a command, order, etc.). **2.** To recall or order back by a contrary command. — *n.* An order contrary to or revoking one previously issued. [< OF < L *contra-* against + *mandare* to order]

coun·ter·march (*n.* koun/tər·märch/; *v.* koun/tər·märch/) *n.* **1.** A return march. **2.** *Mil.* A reversal of direction while marching, keeping the same order. — *v.t. & v.i.* To execute or cause to execute a countermarch.

coun·ter·move (*n.* koun/tər·mōōv/; *v.* koun/tər·mōōv/) *n.* A move designed to counter another move. — *v.t. & v.i.* ·moved, ·mov·ing To move in opposition (to).

coun·ter·of·fen·sive (koun/tər·ə·fen/siv, koun/tər·ə·fen/siv) *n.* A large-scale attack designed to stop the offensive of an enemy and to seize the initiative along an extended front.

coun·ter·pane (koun/tər·pān/) *n.* A coverlet for a bed. [< F *pan* quilt]

coun·ter·part (koun/tər·pärt/) *n.* **1.** Someone or something resembling another. **2.** One who or that which supplements or completes another.

coun·ter·plot (*n.* koun/tər·plot/; *v.* koun/tər·plot/) *n.* A plot designed to foil another plot. — *v.t. & v.i.* ·plot·ted, ·plot·ting To oppose (a plot) by another plot.

coun·ter·point (koun/tər·point/) *n.* *Music* **1.** The technique or practice of composing two or more melodic parts to be heard simultaneously; also, the arrangement of parts so composed. **2.** Any of such parts in relation to the principal part. [< MF < Med.L < L *contra-* against + *punctus* point, note]

coun·ter·poise (*v.* koun/tər·poiz/; *n.* koun/tər·poiz/) *v.t.* ·poised, ·pois·ing To bring to a balance by opposing with an equal weight, power, or force; counterbalance. — *n.* **1.** A counterbalancing weight, force, power, or influence. **2.** A state of equilibrium. [< OF < L *contra-* against + *pensare* to weigh]

Counter Reformation The reform movement within the Roman Catholic Church in the 16th century in reaction to the Protestant Reformation.

coun·ter·rev·o·lu·tion (koun/tər·rev/ə·lōō/shən) *n.* A revolution designed to counteract a previous revolution and to reverse its effects. — **coun/ter·rev/o·lu/tion·ar/y** *adj. & n.* — **coun/ter·rev/o·lu/tion·ist** *n.*

coun·ter·shaft (koun/tər·shaft/, -shäft/) *n.* *Mech.* An intermediate shaft driven by a main shaft.

coun·ter·sign (*v.* koun/tər·sīn/, koun/tər·sīn/; *n.* koun/tər·sīn/) *v.t.* To sign (a document already signed by another), as in authenticating. — *n.* *Mil.* A password. [< OF *contresigner*] — **coun/ter·sig/na·ture** *n.*

coun·ter·sink (*v.* koun/tər·singk/, koun/tər·singk/; *n.* koun/·tər·singk/) *v.t.* ·sank or ·sunk, ·sunk (*Obs.* ·sunk·en), ·sink·ing **1.** To cut the edges of (a hole) so that a screw, bolthead, etc., will lie flush with or below the surface. **2.** To sink, as a bolt or screw, into such a depression. — *n.* **1.** A tool for countersinking. **2.** A countersunk hole.

coun·ter·ten·or (koun/tər·ten/ər) *n.* An adult male singing voice higher than the tenor. [< MF *contreteneur*]

coun·ter·vail (koun/tər·vāl/, koun/tər·vāl) *v.t.* **1.** To oppose with equal force or effect; counteract. **2.** To compensate or make up for; offset. — *v.i.* **3.** To be of avail: with *against*. [< AF < L *contra valere* to avail against]

coun·ter·weigh (koun/tər·wā/) *v.t. & v.i.* To counterbalance.

coun·ter·weight (koun/tər·wāt/) *n.* Any counterbalancing weight, force, or influence. — **coun/ter·weight/ed** *adj.*

counter word A word widely used without regard to its exact meaning, as *nice, awful, fix.*

count·ess (koun/tis) *n.* **1.** The wife or widow of a count, or, in Great Britain, of an earl. **2.** A woman equal in rank to a count or earl. [See COUNT².]

count·ing house (koun/ting) A building or office in which a mercantile or other firm carries on bookkeeping, correspondence, etc. Also **count/ing·house/, counting room.**

count·less (kount/lis) *adj.* That cannot be counted; innumerable. — **Syn.** See INFINITE.

coun·tri·fied (kun/tri·fīd) *adj.* Having the appearance, manner, etc., associated with the country or with country people; rural; rustic. Also **coun/try·fied.**

coun·try (kun/trē) *n. pl.* ·tries **1.** A land under a particular government, inhabited by a certain people, or within definite geographical limits. **2.** The land of one's birth or allegiance. **3.** The district outside cities and towns; rural areas. **4.** A region of a specified character: sheep *country.* **5.** The people of a nation. — **Syn.** See NATION. — *adj.* Rustic. [< OF < LL < L *contra* on the opposite side]

country club A club in the outskirts of a town or city, with a clubhouse, grounds, and facilities for outdoor sports.

coun·try-dance (kun/trē·dans/, -däns/) *n.* A folk dance of English origin, in which the partners are in opposite lines.

country gentleman A landed proprietor who lives on his country estate.

coun·try·man (kun/trē·mən) *n. pl.* ·men (-mən) **1.** A man of the same country as another. **2.** A native of a particular country. **3.** A rustic. — **coun/try·wom·an** *n.fem.*

coun·try·seat (kun/trē·sēt/) *n.* A country estate.

coun·try·side (kun/trē·sīd/) *n.* A rural district, or its inhabitants.

coun·ty (koun/tē) *n. pl.* ·ties **1.** An administrative division of a state or kingdom. In the United States, it is the division next below a State. In England a county is sometimes called a *shire.* **2.** The people of a county. [< AF, OF < L *comes* count, companion]

county seat The seat of government of a county.

coup (kōō) *n. pl.* **coups** (kōōz, *Fr.* kōō) A sudden, telling blow; a masterstroke; brilliant stratagem. [< F < L < Gk. *kolaphos* a blow with the fist]

coup de grâce (kōō/ də gräs/) *French* **1.** The mortal stroke, as delivered to a wounded enemy. **2.** Any finishing stroke.

coup d'é·tat (kōō/dā·tä/) *French* An unexpected stroke of policy; esp., a sudden seizure of government.

coupe (kōōp, kōō·pā/) *n.* A closed automobile with two doors, seating two to six persons: also *coupé.* [< COUPÉ]

cou·pé (kōō·pā/) *n.* **1.** A low, four-wheeled, closed carriage with a seat for two and an outside seat for the driver. **2.** A coupe. [< F, pp. of *couper* to cut]

coup·le (kup/əl) *n.* **1.** Two of a kind; a pair. **2.** Two persons of opposite sex, wedded or otherwise paired, as in dances, games, etc. **3.** *Informal* A few: a *couple* of hours. **4.** Something joining two things together. — *v.* ·led, ·ling *v.t.* **1.** To join, as one thing to another; link. **2.** To join in wedlock; marry. — *v.i.* **3.** To pair. [< OF < L *copula* bond]

coup·ler (kup/lər) *n.* **1.** One who or that which couples. **2.** A device that connects objects; esp.: **a** A contrivance for linking railroad cars. **b** A device enabling two or more organ keys or keyboards to play together.

coup·let (kup/lit) *n.* **1.** Two successive lines of verse, usu. rhymed and in the same meter. **2.** A pair.

coup·ling (kup/ling) *n.* **1.** The act of one who or that which couples. **2.** A linking device, as for joining railroad cars.

cou·pon (kōō/pon, kyōō/-) *n.* **1.** One of a number of dated certificates attached to a bond, representing interest accrued. **2.** A section of a ticket, advertisement, etc., entitling the holder to something in exchange. [< F *couper* to cut]

cour·age (kur/ij) *n.* That quality of mind or spirit enabling one to meet danger or opposition with fearlessness. [< OF *corage*, ult. < L *cor* heart]

cou·ra·geous (kə-rā′jəs) *adj.* Possessing or characterized by courage; brave; daring: *courageous* words. — **cou·ra′·geous·ly** *adv.* — **cou·ra′geous·ness** *n.*

cou·ri·er (koŏr′ē-ər, kûr′-) *n.* **1.** A messenger, esp. one traveling in haste or on official diplomatic business. **2.** One who arranges a journey. [< OF < L *currere* to run]

course (kôrs, kōrs) *n.* **1.** Onward movement in a certain direction; progress. **2.** The path or ground passed over. **3.** Direction: to take an eastward *course*. **4.** Passage or duration in time. **5.** Advance; progression: the *course* of evolution. **6.** Natural or usual development: to run its *course*. **7.** A series of actions, events, etc., constituting a unit. **8.** Line of conduct: a wise *course*. **9.** A prescribed curriculum of studies leading to a degree: a liberal arts *course*; also, any unit of study in a school curriculum: a history *course*. **10.** A portion of a meal served at one time. **11.** A horizontal row or layer, as of stones in a wall. — **in due course** In the proper sequence; at the right time. — **of course 1.** As might be expected; naturally. **2.** Certainly. — *v.* **coursed, cours·ing** *v.t.* **1.** To run through or over. **2.** To pursue. **3.** To cause (hounds) to chase game. — *v.i.* **4.** To race. **5.** To hunt game with hounds. [< L *currere* to run]

cours·er (kôr′sər, kōr′-) *n. Poetic* A fleet, spirited horse. [< F < OF < L *currere* to run]

court (kôrt, kōrt) *n.* **1.** A courtyard. **2.** A short street enclosed by buildings on three sides. **3.** The residence of a sovereign; palace. **4.** A sovereign together with his council and retinue. **5.** A formal assembly held by a sovereign. **6.** A place where justice is judicially administered; also, those judges who administer justice. **7.** The regular session of a judicial tribunal. **8.** A level space laid out for tennis, basketball, squash, or similar games; also, a subdivision of such a space. **9.** Flattering attention paid another to win favor; homage. **10.** Wooing; courtship. — **out of court 1.** Without a trial. **2.** Without claim to a hearing. — *v.t.* **1.** To try to gain the favor of. **2.** To seek the love of; woo. **3.** To attempt to gain: to *court* applause. **4.** To invite: to *cour* disaster. — *v.i.* **5.** To engage in courtship. — *adj.* Of ot pertaining to a court. [< OF < L *cohors, cohortis* yard] r

Court of Common Pleas A common-law court having original jurisdiction over civil and criminal matters.

cour·te·ous (kûr′tē·əs) *adj.* Showing courtesy; polite. — **Syn.** See POLITE. [< OF *corteis* befitting a court] — **cour′te·ous·ly** *adv.* — **cour′te·ous·ness** *n.*

cour·te·san (kôr′tə·zən, kōr′-, kûr′-) *n.* A prostitute. Also **cour′te·zan.** [< MF < Ital. *cortigiana* court lady]

cour·te·sy (kûr′tə·sē) *n. pl.* **·sies 1.** Habitual politeness; good manners. **2.** A courteous favor or act. **3.** Common consent or allowance, as opposed to right: an aunt by *courtesy*. **4.** A curtsy. [< OF *corteis* courteous]

court·house (kôrt′hous′, kōrt′-) *n.* A public building occupied by judicial courts and other administrative offices.

court·i·er (kôr′tē·ər, -tyər, kōr′-) *n.* **1.** A member of a sovereign's court. **2.** One who seeks favor by flattery.

court·ly (kôrt′lē, kōrt′-) *adj.* **·li·er, ·li·est 1.** Pertaining to or befitting a court. **2.** Elegant in manners. — *adv.* In a courtly manner. — **court′li·ness** *n.*

court-mar·tial (kôrt′mär′shəl, kōrt′-) *n. pl.* **courts-mar·tial 1.** A military court to try persons subject to military law. **2.** A trial by such a court. — *v.t.* **-mar·tialed** or **·tialled, -mar·tial·ing** or **·tial·ling** To try by court-martial.

court plaster Adhesive tape.

court·room (kôrt′rōōm′, -rŏŏm′, kōrt′-) *n.* A room in which judicial proceedings are held.

court·ship (kôrt′ship, kōrt′-) *n.* The act or period of courting and wooing.

court·yard (kôrt′yärd′, kōrt′-) *n.* An enclosed yard adjoining a building or surrounded by buildings or walls; a court.

cous·in (kuz′ən) *n.* **1.** One collaterally related by descent from a common ancestor, but not a brother or sister. Children of brothers and sisters are **first** or **full cousins** to each other; children of first cousins are **second cousins** to each other. **2.** One of a kindred group or nation: our English *cousins*. **3.** A title of address used by a sovereign to a noble or a fellow sovereign. [< OF < L *consobrinus* child of a maternal aunt] — **cous′in·hood, cous′in·ship** *n.* — **cous′in·ly** *adj. & adv.*

cous·in-ger·man (kuz′ən·jûr′mən) *n. pl.* **cous·ins-ger·man** A first or full cousin. [< OF *cousin germain*]

cous·in·ry (kuz′ən·rē) *n. pl.* **·ries** Cousins collectively.

cou·tu·rier (koo·tü·ryā′) *n.* A male dress designer. [< F] — **cou·tu·rière** (koo·tü·ryâr′) *n. fem.*

co·va·lence (kō′vā′ləns) *n. Chem.* A bond formed by the sharing of electrons between the atoms of a compound. — **co′va·lent** *adj.*

cove¹ (kōv) *n.* **1.** A small bay or baylike recess in a shoreline. **2.** A recess among hills, in a wood, etc. **3.** *Archit.* a A concave vault. For illus. see VAULT. b A concave molding. c A concave curved portion where a ceiling meets a wall. — *v.t.* **coved, cov·ing** To curve over or inward. [OE *cofa* cave]

cove² (kōv) *n. Brit. Slang* A boy or man; fellow. [< Romany *covo* that man]

cov·e·nant (kuv′ə·nənt) *n.* **1.** An agreement entered into by two or more persons or parties; a compact. **2.** *Theol.* The promise of God to bless those who obey him or fulfill some other condition. **3.** *Law* A written agreement, as a contract, under seal. — **Covenant of the League of Nations** The first twenty-six articles of the Treaty of Versailles. — *v.t. & v.i.* To promise by or in a covenant. [< OF, < L *convenire* to meet together, agree] — **cov·e·nant·al** (kuv′ə·nan′təl) *adj.* — **cov′e·nant·al·ly** *adv.* — **cov′e·nant·er** *n.*

cov·er (kuv′ər) *v.t.* **1.** To place something over or upon, as to protect or conceal. **2.** To provide with a cover or covering; clothe. **3.** To invest as if with a covering: *covered* with confusion. **4.** To hide; conceal: often with *up*. **5.** To provide shelter or protection for. **6.** To occupy the surface of: Snow *covered* the house. **7.** To treat of; include: His speech *covered* the tax problem. **8.** To be sufficient to pay, defray, or offset. **9.** To protect or guarantee (life, property, etc.) with insurance. **10.** To incubate or sit on, as eggs. **11.** To travel over: to *cover* 200 miles. **12.** To aim directly at, as with a firearm. **13.** *Mil.* To provide protective fire for (another person, unit, etc.). **14.** In journalism, to report the details of. **15.** In sports, to guard the activity of (an opponent); also, to protect (an area or position). **16.** To match; equal, as the wager of an opponent. **17.** In card games, to play a higher card than (the one previously played). — *v.i.* **18.** To spread over so as to overlay something. **19.** To put on a hat, cap, or the like. — *n.* **1.** That which covers or is laid over something else. **2.** Shelter; protection; concealment, as from enemy fire. **3.** Shrubbery, underbrush, etc. **4.** A pretense or pretext. **5.** In stamp collecting, an envelope or wrapper that bears a postmark. **6.** The table articles, as plate, silverware, napkin, etc., for one person. — **to break cover** To come from hiding. — **under cover 1.** Protected. **2.** Secret or secretly. [< OF < L *co-* thoroughly + *operire* to hide] — **cov′er·er** *n.*

cov·er·age (kuv′ər·ij) *n.* **1.** The extent to which anything is covered, included, or reported. **2.** The protection afforded by an insurance policy.

cov·er·alls (kuv′ər·ôlz) *n.pl.* A one-piece work garment with sleeves, worn to protect the clothes. Also **cov′er·all.**

cover charge A fixed charge added to the bill at cabarets, hotels, etc., for entertainment or service.

cover crop *Agric.* A crop sown to protect the ground through winter and to enrich it when plowed under in the spring.

covered wagon *U.S.* A large wagon covered with canvas stretched over hoops, used esp. by American pioneers.

cover girl A female model who poses for magazine covers.

cov·er·ing (kuv′ər·ing) *n.* That which covers, protects, etc.

cov·er·let (kuv′ər·lit) *n.* A bedspread. Also **cov′er·lid.**

cov·ert (kuv′ərt, kō′vərt) *adj.* Concealed; secret; sheltered. — *n.* **1.** A covering. **2.** A shelter or hiding place, esp. for game. **3.** *pl. Ornithol.* Small feathers overlying the bases of tail and wing quills. [See COVER.] — **cov′ert·ly** *adv.*

covert cloth (kō′vərt, kuv′ərt) A twilled, chiefly woolen cloth of speckled appearance, used for suits, overcoats, etc.

cov·er·ture (kuv′ər·chər) *n.* **1.** *Law* The legal status of a married woman. **2.** A covering; esp., a shelter.

cov·et (kuv′it) *v.t.* **1.** To long for, esp. for something belonging to another. — *v.i.* **2.** To feel desire. [< OF < L *cupere* to desire] — **cov′et·a·ble** *adj.* — **cov′et·er** *n.*

cov·et·ous (kuv′ə·təs) *adj.* Excessively desirous (of something); avaricious; greedy. [< OF *coveitus*] — **cov′et·ous·ly** *adv.* — **cov′et·ous·ness** *n.*

cov·ey (kuv′ē) *n. pl.* **·eys 1.** A flock of quails or partridges. **2.** A company; set. — **Syn.** See FLOCK¹. [< OF < L *cubare* to lie down]

cow¹ (kou) *n. pl.* **cows** (*Archaic* **kine**) **1.** The mature female of a bovine animal, esp. of the domesticated species. **2.** The mature female of some other animals, as of the whale, elephant, moose, etc. [OE *cū*]

cow² (kou) *v.t.* To overawe; intimidate; daunt. [< ON *kūga* to tyrannize over]

cow·ard (kou′ərd) *n.* One who yields unworthily to fear of pain or harm. — *adj.* Cowardly. [< OF < L *cauda* tail]

cow·ard·ice (kou′ər·dis) *n.* Lack of courage in the face of danger, pain, opposition, etc.; unworthy timidity.

cow·ard·ly (kou′ərd·lē) *adj.* **1.** Lacking courage; ignobly fearful. **2.** Befitting a coward: a *cowardly* lie. — *adv.* Like a coward; meanly. — **cow′ard·li·ness** *n.* — **Syn.** (adj.) **1.** craven, pusillanimous, spineless, yellow.

cow·bell (kou′bel) *n.* A bell hung around a cow's neck to indicate her whereabouts.

cow·ber·ry (kou′ber′ē, -bər·ē) *n. pl.* **·ries** A trailing evergreen shrub of the heath family, bearing red berries.

cow·bird (kou′bûrd′) *n.* An American blackbird, often found with cattle. Also **cow blackbird**.

cow·boy (kou′boi′) *n. U.S.* A man, usu. working on horseback, who herds and tends cattle on a ranch.

cow·catch·er (kou′kach′ər) *n.* An iron frame on the front of a locomotive or streetcar for clearing the track.

cow·er (kou′ər) *v.i.* To crouch, as in fear; tremble; quail. [ME *couren*, prob. < Scand.]

cow·fish (kou′fish) *n. pl.* **·fish** or **·fish·es** 1. Any of various small cetaceans, as the grampus, dolphin, etc. 2. A sirenian.

cow·girl (kou′gûrl′) *n.* A girl who helps to herd and tend cattle or who dresses like a cowboy.

cow·hand (kou′hand′) *n.* A cowboy.

cow·herd (kou′hûrd′) *n.* One who herds cattle.

cow·hide (kou′hīd′) *n.* 1. The skin of a cow, either before or after tanning. 2. A heavy, flexible leather whip. — *v.t.* **·hid·ed, ·hid·ing** To whip as with a cowhide.

cow killer A large, antlike wasp of the SW U.S.

cowl (koul) *n.* 1. A monk's hood; also, a hooded cloak. 2. A hood-shaped top for a chimney, to increase the draft. 3. *Aeron.* A cowling. 4. The part of an automobile body to which the windshield, instrument board, and the rear end of the hood are attached. — *v.t.* To cover with or as with a cowl. [OE < LL < L *cucullus* hood]

cowled (kould) *adj.* 1. Wearing a cowl. 2. Like a cowl.

cow·lick (kou′lik′) *n.* A tuft of hair turned up.

cowl·ing (kou′ling) *n. Aeron.* The covering over or around the engine or any component of an aircraft. [< COWL]

cow·man (kou′mən) *n. pl.* **·men** (-mən) A rancher.

co-work·er (kō′wûr′kər) *n.* A fellow worker.

cow·pea (kou′pē′) *n.* 1. A twining herb of the bean family, cultivated in the southern U.S. 2. The edible pea of this herb: also called *black-eyed pea.*

cow pony *U.S.* A small horse used in herding cattle.

cow·pox (kou′poks′) *n. Vet.* An acute contagious disease of cows, forming pustules containing a virus that is used in making smallpox vaccine: also called *vaccinia.*

cow·punch·er (kou′pun′chər) *n. U.S. Informal* A cowboy. Also **cow′poke′.**

cow·ry (kou′rē) *n. pl.* **·ries** A glossy seashell of warm seas; esp. one used as money in Africa and southern Asia. Also **cow′rie.** [< Hind. *kaurī*]

cow·slip (kou′slip′) *n.* 1. An English wildflower of the primrose family. 2. The marsh marigold of the U.S. [OE < *cū* cow + *slyppe* dung]

cox (koks) *n. Informal* Coxswain. — *v.t. & v.i.* To act as coxswain to (a boat).

cox·a (kok′sə) *n. pl.* **cox·ae** (kok′sē) *Anat.* The hip or hip joint. [< L, hip] — **cox′al** *adj.*

cox·comb (koks′kōm′) *n.* 1. A pretentious and conceited young man. 2. A cockscomb. [Var. of *cockscomb*] — **cox·comb·i·cal** (koks·kom′i·kəl, -kō′mi-) *adj.*

cox·comb·ry (koks′kōm′rē) *n. pl.* **·ries** Vain, foppish behavior; silly conceit; also, an instance of this.

cox·swain (kok′sən, kok′swān′) *n.* One who steers or has charge of a small boat or a racing shell: also spelled *cockswain.* [< *cock* (see COCKBOAT) + SWAIN]

coy (koi) *adj.* 1. Shy and retiring. 2. Feigning shyness to attract attention. [< MF < OF < L *quietus* rest] — **coy′ish** *adj.* — **coy′ly** *adv.* — **coy′ness** *n.*

coy·o·te (kī·ō′tē, kī′ōt) *n.* A small wolf of western North America: also called *prairie wolf.* [< Am. Sp. < Nahuatl]

Coyote State Nickname of South Dakota.

coy·pu (koi′pōō) *n. pl.* **·pus** or **·pu** A South American rodent that yields a beaverlike fur known as nutria. Also **coy′pou.** [< native name]

coz (kuz) *n. Informal* A cousin.

coz·en (kuz′ən) *v.t. & v.i.* To cheat, esp. in a petty way; deceive. [< F *cousiner* to deceive by claiming kinship < *cousin.* See COUSIN.] — **coz′en·age** *n.* — **coz′en·er** *n.*

co·zy (kō′zē) *adj.* **·zi·er, ·zi·est** Snugly comfortable. — *n.* A padded cover for a teapot to keep it hot: also called *tea cozy.* [< dial. E *cosie*] — **co′zi·ly** *adv.* — **co′zi·ness** *n.*

crab¹ (krab) *n.* 1. A ten-footed crustacean having four pairs of legs, a pair of pincers, and a flattened carapace. 2. The hermit crab. 3. The horseshoe crab. — *v.* **crabbed, crab·bing** *v.t.* 1. To take or hunt crabs. 2. *U.S. Informal* To back out. [OE *crabba*]

crab² (krab) *n.* 1. The crab apple or crab tree. 2. An ill-tempered person. — *v.* **crabbed, crab·bing** *v.i.* 1. *Informal* To find fault; complain. — *v.t.* 2. *Informal* To spoil or ruin. 3. *Informal* To criticize; disparage. [? < Scand.]

crab apple 1. A kind of small, sour apple: also called *crab.* 2. A tree bearing crab apples.

crab·bed (krab′id) *adj.* 1. Sour-tempered; surly. 2. Hard to understand; abstruse. 3. Irregular in form; cramped. [< CRAB²] — **crab′bed·ly** *adv.* — **crab′bed·ness** *n.*

crab·ber (krab′ər) *n.* 1. One who fishes for crabs. 2. A boat used for crab fishing.

crab·by (krab′ē) *adj.* **·bi·er, ·bi·est** Ill-tempered; peevish.

crab grass A low-growing grass, a lawn pest.

crack (krak) *v.i.* 1. To break without separation of parts; also, to break apart or to pieces. 2. To make a sharp snapping sound, as in breaking. 3. To change tone abruptly to a higher register: said of the voice. 4. *Informal* To break down; fail. 5. *Slang* To speak flippantly; make remarks. — *v.t.* 6. To break partially or completely. 7. To cause to give forth a short, sharp sound: to *crack* a whip. 8. *Informal* To break into; open: to *crack* a safe. 9. *Informal* To find the solution of. 10. To cause (the voice) to crack. 11. *Informal* To strike sharply or with a sharp sound. 12. *Slang* To tell (a joke). 13. To break mentally; derange. 14. To reduce by distillation, as petroleum. — **to crack a book** *U.S. Slang* To open, as a textbook, and read or study. — **crack a smile** *Slang* To smile. — **to crack down** *U.S. Informal* To take severe repressive measures: with *on.* — **to crack up** *Informal* 1. To crash or be in a crash. 2. To have a breakdown, nervous or physical. 3. *U.S. Slang* To become convulsed with laughter. — **to crack wise** *U.S. Slang* To wisecrack. — *n.* 1. A partial break, in which parts are not completely separated; a fissure. 2. A narrow space: Open the door a *crack.* 3. A sudden sharp sound, as of a rifle discharging. 4. *Informal* A resounding blow. 5. A defect; flaw. 6. A cracked tone of the voice. 7. *Informal* A try. 8. *Informal* A witty or sarcastic remark. — *adj. Informal* Of superior excellence: a *crack* shot. [OE *cracian*]

crack·brain (krak′brān′) *n.* A weak-minded person.

crack·brained (krak′brānd′) *adj.* Foolish; crazy.

cracked (krakt) *adj.* 1. Having a crack or cracks. 2. Broken to pieces. 3. Damaged or blemished. 4. *Informal* Mentally deranged. 5. Uneven in tone: said of the voice.

crack·er (krak′ər) *n.* 1. *U.S.* A thin, crisp biscuit. 2. *U.S.* A firecracker. 3. *U.S.* A cylindrical paper roll containing candy, etc., and a weak explosive set off by pulling strips of paper at either end: also **cracker bonbon.** 4. An impoverished white person of parts of the SE United States: a contemptuous term.

crack·er-bar·rel (krak′ər-bar′əl) *adj.* Characteristic of the informal, rambling discussions of those habitually gathered in a country store: *cracker-barrel* philosophy.

crack·er·jack (krak′ər-jak′) *Slang adj.* Of exceptional quality; excellent. — *n.* A person or thing of exceptional merit or skill. Also **crack′a·jack′.**

Cracker State Nickname of Georgia.

crack·ing (krak′ing) *n. Chem.* A process by which the molecular structure of petroleum is changed under pressure by heat, etc., so that nonvolatile fractions are broken down to volatile fractions to produce high-octane gasoline.

crack·le (krak′əl) *v.* **·led, ·ling** *v.i.* 1. To make a succession of light, sharp sounds. — *v.t.* 2. To crush with such sounds. 3. To cover, as china, with a delicate network of cracks. — *n.* 1. A sound of crackling. 2. A network of fine cracks produced in the glaze of china, porcelain, etc. 3. Ware having such an appearance: also **crack′le·ware′** (-wâr′).

crack·ling (krak′ling) *n.* 1. The giving forth of small sharp sounds. 2. The crisp browned skin of roasted pork. 3. *pl.* The crisp remains of fat after rendering.

crack·ly (krak′lē) *adj.* Likely to crackle; brittle.

crack·pot (krak′pot′) *Slang n.* A weak-minded or eccentric person; a crank. — *adj.* Eccentric; foolish; insane.

crack-up (krak′up′) *n.* 1. A crash, as of an airplane or automobile. 2. *Informal* A physical or mental breakdown.

-cracy *combining form* Government or authority: *democracy.* [< Gk. *-krateia* power < *krateein* to rule]

cra·dle (krād′l) *n.* 1. A small bed for an infant, usu. on rockers. 2. A place of origin. 3. A framework for supporting something under construction or repair. 4. A frame to protect an injured limb. 5. The holder for the receiver or handset of a telephone. 6. A frame attached to a scythe to catch the cut grain; also, such a scythe. 7. A low frame on casters for a mechanic to lie on while working under an automobile. — **to rob the cradle** *Informal* To marry or take as a sweetheart one much younger than oneself. — *v.* **·dled, ·dling** *v.t.* 1. To put into or rock in or as in a cradle; soothe. 2. To nurse in infancy; nurture. 3. To cut (grain) with a cradle. 4. To place or support in a cradle, as a ship. 5. *Mining* To wash, as gold-bearing gravel, in a cradle. — *v.i.* 6. To lie in or as in a cradle. 7. To cut or reap. [OE *cradol*]

cra·dle-song (krād′l-sông′, -song′) *n.* A lullaby (def. 1).

craft (kraft, kräft) *n.* 1. Skill or proficiency, esp. in hand work; loosely, art. 2. Skill in deception. 3. An occupation or trade, usually one calling for manual skill. 4. The membership of a particular trade. 5. A vessel or an aircraft: also used collectively. — *Syn.* See OCCUPATION. [OE *cræft* skill, art, strength, courage]

-craft *combining form* Skill; trade; art of: *woodcraft.*

crafts·man (krafts′mən, kräfts′-) *n. pl.* **·men** (-mən) One skilled in a craft or art. — **crafts′man·ship** *n.*

craft union A labor union limited to workers who perform the same type of work: also called *horizontal union.*

craft·y (kraf′tē, kräf′-) *adj.* **craft·i·er, craft·i·est** Skillful in deceiving; cunning. — **craft′i·ly** *adv.* — **craft′i·ness** *n.*

crag (krag) *n.* A rough, steep, or prominently projecting rock. [ME *cragg* < Celtic]

crag·gy (krag′ē) *adj.* **·gi·er**, **·gi·est** Having numerous crags. Also **crag·ged** (krag′id). — **crag′gi·ness** *n.*

crake (krāk) *n.* Any of various small, harsh-voiced birds of the rail family. [< ON *kraka* crow]

cram (kram) *v.* **crammed**, **cram·ming** *v.t.* **1.** To force into an inadequate space; stuff. **2.** To fill or pack tightly. **3.** To feed to excess. **4.** To force (information) into the mind, or to fill (a person or his mind) with information, as in intensive study. — *v.i.* **5.** To eat greedily; stuff oneself with food. **6.** To engage in intensive, hurried study. — *n.* **1.** The act or process of cramming. **2.** A crowded condition; a crush. [OE *crammian* to stuff] — **cram′mer** *n.*

cramp[1] (kramp) *n.* **1.** An involuntary, sudden, painful muscular contraction. **2.** A paralysis of local muscles caused by overexertion. **3.** *pl.* Acute abdominal pains. — *v.t.* To affect with a cramp. [< OF *crampe*]

cramp[2] (kramp) *n.* **1.** An iron bar bent at both ends, used to bind two stones, timbers, etc., together. **2.** An adjustable frame in which pieces may be held together; a clamp. **3.** Anything that presses or confines. — *v.t.* **1.** To fasten with a cramp. **2.** To restrain or confine; hamper. **3.** To steer; also, to jam (a wheel) by turning too short. — **to cramp one's style** *Slang* To hamper one's customary skill or self-confidence. — *adj.* **1.** Narrowed; contracted. **2.** Difficult to read or make out. [ME < MDu. *krampe* hook.]

cramp·fish (kramp′fish′) *n. pl.* **·fish** or **·fish·es** The electric ray.

cram·pon (kram′pən) *n.* **1.** A pair of hooked pieces of iron for raising heavy stones, etc. **2.** *Usu. pl.* An iron attachment for the shoe to aid in walking on ice or in climbing. Also **cram·poon** (kram·pōōn′). [< MF *crampe* hook]

CRAMPON
(def. 2)

cran·ber·ry (kran′ber′ē, -bər·ē) *n. pl.* **·ries 1.** The edible, scarlet, acid berry of a plant growing in marshy land. **2.** The plant itself.

crane (krān) *n.* **1.** One of a family of large, long-necked, long-legged birds, as the rare **whooping crane** of North America. **2.** Loosely, any of various herons or cormorants. **3.** A hoisting machine, usually having a projecting movable arm, by which a heavy object can be raised and moved. **4.** Any arm swinging horizontally, by which something is suspended. — *v.* **craned**, **cran·ing** *v.t.* & *v.i.* **1.** To stretch out one's neck, as a crane does. **2.** To lift or move by or as if by a crane. [OE *cran*]

crane·bill (krān′bil′) *n.* Any species of geranium. Also **cranes·bill** (krānz′bil′), **crane's′-bill′**.

crane fly A fly with very long, slender legs.

cranio- *combining form* Cranium; cranial. Also, before vowels, **crani-**. [< Med.L *cranium* skull]

cra·ni·ol·o·gy (krā′nē·ol′ə·jē) *n.* The branch of anatomy that treats of skulls. — **cra·ni·o·log·i·cal** (krā′nē·ə·loj′i·kəl) *adj.* — **cra′ni·ol′o·gist** *n.*

cra·ni·om·e·ter (krā′nē·om′ə·ter) *n.* An instrument for measuring skulls. — **cra·ni·o·met·ric** (-ə·met′rik) or **·ri·cal** *adj.* — **cra·ni·o·met′ri·cal·ly** *adv.* — **cra·ni·om′e·try** *n.*

cra·ni·um (krā′nē·əm) *n. pl.* **·ni·ums** or **·ni·a** (-nē·ə) The skull, esp. the part enclosing the brain. [< Med.L < Gk. *kranion* skull] — **cra′ni·al** *adj.*

crank (krangk) *n.* **1.** A device for transmitting motion, usu. a handle attached at right angles to a shaft. **2.** *Informal* One given to eccentric or hostile behavior. **3.** *Informal* A grouchy person. **4.** A fantastic turn of speech; conceit. **5.** A perverse notion or action; whim. — *v.t.* **1.** To bend into the shape of a crank. **2.** To furnish with a crank. **3.** To start or operate by means of a crank. — *v.i.* **4.** To turn a crank. [OE *cranc*]

crank·case (krangk′kās′) *n. Mech.* The case enclosing an engine crankshaft, as of an automobile.

cran·kle (krang′kəl) *n.* A bend; crinkle. — *v.t.* & *v.i.* **·kled**, **·kling** To bend; crinkle. [Dim. of CRANK]

crank·shaft (krangk′shaft′, -shäft′) *n. Mech.* A shaft driven by or driving a crank.

crank·y (krang′kē) *adj.* **crank·i·er**, **crank·i·est 1.** Irritable; peevish. **2.** Eccentric; queer. **3.** Loose and rickety; shaky. **4.** *Naut.* Liable to heel; top-heavy: also **crank**. [< CRANK] — **crank′i·ly** *adv.* — **crank′i·ness** *n.*

cran·ny (kran′ē) *n. pl.* **·nies** A narrow crevice or chink, as in a wall. [? < OF *cran*, *cren* notch] — **cran′nied** *adj.*

crap (krap) *U.S. n.* **1.** The game of craps. **2.** A losing throw in craps. **3.** *Slang* Statements that lie, mislead, or exaggerate. **4.** *Slang* Anything worthless. [See CRAPS]

crape (krāp) *n.* See CREPE.

crap·pie (krap′ē) *n. pl.* **·pies** or **·pie** An edible fresh-water fish of the central U.S.

craps (kraps) *n.pl.* (*construed as sing.*) *U.S.* A game of chance, played with two dice. [< F < E *crabs*, the lowest throw (two aces) in hazard]

crap·shoot·er (krap′shōō′tər) *n. U.S.* One who plays the game of craps.

crap·u·lent (krap′yŏŏ·lənt) *adj.* **1.** Grossly intemperate in eating or drinking. **2.** Sick from eating or drinking too much. Also **crap′u·lous**. [< LL < L < Gk. *kraipalē* drunken headache] — **crap′u·lence** *n.*

crash[1] (krash) *v.i.* **1.** To break to pieces with a loud noise. **2.** To suffer damage or destruction, as by falling or striking something. **3.** To make a loud, sharp noise of breaking. **4.** To move with such a noise. **5.** To fail or come to ruin. — *v.t.* **6.** To dash violently to pieces; smash. **7.** To force or drive with a sound of crashing. **8.** To cause (an airplane, automobile, etc.) to crash. **9.** *Informal* To enter without invitation or without paying admission. — *n.* **1.** A loud noise, as of things being violently broken. **2.** A sudden collapse, as of a business enterprise. **3.** The act of crashing, as of an airplane, automobile, etc. — *adj. U.S. Informal* Of, pertaining to, or resembling a crash program. [Imit.]

crash[2] (krash) *n.* A coarse fabric woven of thick, uneven yarns, used for towels, etc. [? < Russian *krashenina*]

crash dive *Naval* The quick submergence of a submarine.

crash helmet A heavy, padded helmet.

crash landing An emergency landing of an airplane.

crash program *U.S. Informal* An intensive emergency undertaking in government, science, etc., having priority over all others. Also **crash project**.

crass (kras) *adj.* **1.** Grossly vulgar or stupid. **2.** Coarse or thick. [< L *crassus* thick] — **crass′ly** *adv.* — **crass′ness** *n.*

-crat *combining form* A supporter or member of a social class or of a type of government: *democrat*, *aristocrat*. [< F *-crate* < Gk. *-kratēs* < *krateein* to rule, govern]

crate (krāt) *n.* **1.** A protective case or framework of slats in which to pack something for shipment. **2.** *Slang* A decrepit vehicle or airplane. — *v.t.* **crat·ed**, **crat·ing** To pack in a crate. [Prob. < L *cratis* wickerwork] — **crat′er** *n.*

cra·ter (krā′tər) *n.* **1.** A bowl-shaped depression at the outlet of a volcano. **2.** Any similar cavity, as one resulting from the explosion of a bomb. [< L < Gk. *kratēr* bowl]

cra·vat (krə·vat′) *n.* **1.** A necktie. **2.** A scarf. [< F *Cravate* a Croatian; with ref. to the neckcloths worn by Croatian soldiers]

crave (krāv) *v.* **craved**, **crav·ing** *v.t.* **1.** To long for; desire greatly. **2.** To be in need of; require. **3.** To ask for earnestly, beg. — *v.i.* **4.** To desire or long: with *for* or *after*. [OE *crafian*] — **crav′er** *n.*

cra·ven (krā′vən) *adj.* Conspicuously lacking in courage; cowardly. — *n.* A base coward. [? < OF < L *crepare* to creak, break] — **cra′ven·ly** *adv.* — **cra′ven·ness** *n.*

craw (krô) *n.* **1.** The crop of a bird. **2.** The stomach of any animal. — **to stick in one's craw** To be displeasing or unacceptable. [ME *crawe*. Akin to Du. *kraag* neck.]

craw·fish (krô′fish′) *n. pl.* **·fish** or **·fish·es** A crayfish.

crawl[1] (krôl) *v.i.* **1.** To move along slowly with the body on or close to the ground. **2.** To move slowly, feebly, or cautiously. **3.** To be covered with things that crawl. **4.** To feel as if covered with crawling things. **5.** To behave with servility. — *n.* **1.** The act of crawling. **2.** An overarm swimming stroke performed face down, combined with a flutter kick. [Prob. < ON *krafla* to paw] — **crawl′er** *n.* — **crawl′ing·ly** *adv.*

crawl[2] (krôl) *n.* A pen in shallow water for confining fish, turtles, etc. [See KRAAL.]

crawl·y (krô′lē) *adj.* **crawl·i·er**, **crawl·i·est** *Informal* Creepy.

cray·fish (krā′fish′) *n. pl.* **·fish** or **·fish·es 1.** A fresh-water crustacean resembling the lobster. **2.** Loosely, the spiny lobster. Also **crawfish**. [Earlier *crevice* < OF < OHG *krebiz*]

cray·on (krā′ən, -on) *n.* **1.** A stick of colored wax, chalk, etc., for use in drawing. **2.** A drawing made with crayons. — *v.t.* & *v.i.* To sketch or draw with crayons. [< F, pencil]

craze (krāz) *v.* **crazed**, **craz·ing** *v.t.* **1.** To render insane or demented. **2.** To make full of minute cracks, as the glaze of pottery. — *v.i.* **3.** To become insane. **4.** To become full of minute cracks. — *n.* **1.** A brief fashion or fad; rage. **2.** An extravagant liking or enthusiasm. **3.** Mental disorder; insanity. **4.** A minute flaw in the glaze of pottery, etc. [ME *crasen* to crack] — **crazed** *adj.*

cra·zy (krā′zē) *adj* **·zi·er**, **·zi·est 1.** Disordered in mind; insane; demented; mad; maniacal. **2.** *Informal* Very enthusiastic or excited. **3.** *Informal* Unpredictable or inexplicable: *a crazy driver*. **4.** Dilapidated; rickety; unsound. — **cra′zi·ly** *adv.* — **cra′zi·ness** *n.*

crazy bone The funny bone.

crazy quilt A patchwork quilt made of pieces of various sizes, shapes, and colors.

creak (krēk) *n.* A sharp, squeaking sound, as from friction. — *v.t.* & *v.i.* To produce or cause to make a creak. [Imit.]

creak·y (krē'kē) *adj.* ·i·er, ·i·est 1. Creaking. 2. Likely to creak: a *creaky* step. — **creak'i·ly** *adv.* — **creak'i·ness** *n.*

cream (krēm) *n.* 1. An oily, yellowish substance contained in milk. 2. The best part. 3. The yellowish white color of cream. 4. A food or delicacy made with or resembling cream. 5. Something resembling cream. 6. A soft, oily cosmetic for cleansing or protecting the skin. — *v.t.* 1. To skim cream from. 2. To take the best part from. 3. To add cream to, as coffee. 4. To permit (milk) to form cream. 5. To beat, as butter and sugar, to a creamy consistency. 6. To cook or prepare (food) with cream or cream sauce. 7. *U.S. Slang* To defeat decisively. — *v.i.* 8. To froth or foam. 9. To form cream. [< OF < LL *chriȝma* chrism]

cream cheese Soft, white cheese made of cream or a mixture of cream and milk.

cream·er (krē'mər) *n.* 1. A small pitcher used for serving cream. 2. Any device in which cream is separated.

cream·er·y (krē'mər·ē) *n.* *pl.* ·er·ies 1. A place where milk and cream are prepared for market. 2. An establishment at which dairy products are sold.

cream of tartar Potassium bitartrate.

cream puff 1. A shell of pastry filled with whipped cream or custard. 2. *Slang* A sissy; weakling.

cream·y (krē'mē) *adj.* cream·i·er, cream·i·est 1. Containing cream. 2. Resembling cream. — **cream'i·ness** *n.*

crease¹ (krēs) *n.* A mark or line made by folding or wrinkling. — *v.* **creased, creas·ing** *v.t.* 1. To make a crease, line, or fold in; wrinkle. 2. To graze with a bullet. — *v.i.* 3. To become wrinkled. [ME *creaste*, ? var. of *creste* crest, ridge] — **creas'er** *n.*

crease² (krēs) See KRIS.

creas·y (krē'sē) *adj.* creas·i·er, creas·i·est Creased.

cre·ate (krē·āt') *v.t.* ·at·ed, ·at·ing 1. To cause to come into existence; originate. 2. To be the cause of; occasion: To *create* interest. 3. To produce (a work of art, etc.). 4. To be the first to portray, as a character or part. 5. To invest with new office, rank, etc.; appoint. [< L *creare* to produce, create]

cre·a·tion (krē·ā'shən) *n.* 1. The act of creating, or the fact of being created. 2. Anything created. 3. *Usu. cap.* God's bringing of the universe into existence. 4. The universe; also, all living creatures. — **cre·a'tion·al** *adj.*

cre·a·tive (krē·ā'tiv) *adj.* 1. Having the power or ability to create. 2. Characterized by originality of thought and execution. 3. Productive: with *of.* — **cre·a'tive·ly** *adv.* — **cre·a'tive·ness, cre·a·tiv·i·ty** (krē'ā·tiv'ə·tē, -ə·tiv'-) *n.*

cre·a·tor (krē·ā'tər) *n.* One who or that which creates. — **the Creator** God. — **cre·a'tor·ship** *n.*

crea·ture (krē'chər) *n.* 1. A living being; especially, an animal. 2. A person. 3. That which has been created. 4. One who is dependent upon, influenced by, or subordinate to something or someone; puppet; tool. 5. *U.S.* A domestic animal. [< OF < LL < *creare* to produce]

crèche (kresh, krāsh) *n.* 1. A group of figures representing the scene in the stable at the Nativity. 2. A foundling asylum. 3. *Brit.* A public day nursery. [< F, crib, cradle]

cre·dence (krēd'ns) *n.* Belief, esp. as based upon the evidence of others. [< MF < L *credere* to believe]

cre·den·tial (kri·den'shəl) *n.* 1. That which entitles one to authority or confidence. 2. *Usually pl.* A certificate or letter giving evidence of one's authority or identity. [< Med.L *credentia* belief + -AL¹]

cre·den·za (kri·den'zə) *n.* A sideboard or buffet. [< Ital. < Med.L < L *credere* to believe.]

cred·i·ble (kred'ə·bəl) *adj.* 1. Capable of being believed. 2. Worthy of confidence; reliable. [< L < *credere* to believe] — **cred'i·bil'i·ty, cred'i·ble·ness** *n.* — **cred'i·bly** *adv.*

cred·it (kred'it) *n.* 1. Belief in the genuineness or truth of something; trust; faith. 2. The quality of being trustworthy. 3. A good reputation. 4. A source of honor or good repute: a *credit* to one's family. 5. Approval for some action or quality. 6. Influence derived from the good opinion of others. 7. *Usu. pl.* Acknowledgment of a book, motion picture, play, etc. 8. Confidence in the ability of an individual, firm, etc., to fulfill financial obligations: to buy on *credit.* 9. Reputation for commercial integrity. 10. The time extended for payment of a liability. 11. In bookkeeping: **a** The entry of any amount paid by a debtor, or the amount entered. **b** The right-hand side of an account, where values received are entered. 12. In an account, the balance in one's favor. 13. *U.S.* Official certification that a student has passed a course of study; also, a unit of academic study. — *v.t.* 1. To accept as true. 2. To ascribe, as intelligence or honor, to: with *with.* 3. In bookkeeping, to give credit for or enter as credit to. 4. *U.S.* to give educational credits to (a student). [< MF < L < *credere* to believe, trust]

cred·it·a·ble (kred'it·ə·bəl) *adj.* Deserving credit or esteem; praiseworthy. — **cred'it·a·bil'i·ty, cred'it·a·ble·ness** *n.* — **cred'it·a·bly** *adv.*

cred·i·tor (kred'i·tər) *n.* One to whom money is owed. [< AF < L < *credere* to believe, trust]

credit union A cooperative group for making loans to its members at low rates of interest.

cre·do (krē'dō, krā'-) *n.* *pl.* ·dos 1. A set of beliefs; a creed. 2. *Often cap.* The Apostles' Creed or the Nicene Creed; also, a musical setting for this. [< L, I believe]

cre·du·li·ty (krə·dōō'lə·tē, -dyōō'-) *n.* Readiness to believe on slight evidence; gullibility.

cred·u·lous (krej'ōō·ləs) *adj.* 1. Disposed to believe on slight evidence. 2. Arising from credulity. [< L < *credere* to believe] — **cred'u·lous·ly** *adv.* — **cred'u·lous·ness** *n.*

Cree (krē) *n.* *pl.* **Cree** or **Crees** 1. One of an Algonquian tribe of North American Indians formerly dwelling in Manitoba and Saskatchewan. 2. The language of this tribe.

creed (krēd) *n.* 1. A formal statement of religious belief or doctrine. 2. Any organized system or statement of beliefs, principles, etc. — **Syn.** See DOCTRINE. — **the Creed** The Apostles' Creed. [OE < L *credo* I believe.]

creek (krēk, krik) *n.* 1. *U.S.* A stream intermediate in size between a brook and a river. 2. *Chiefly Brit.* A narrow inlet or cove in a shoreline. [ME *creke, crike* < Scand.]

Creek (krēk) *n.* 1. A member of one of various tribes of North American Indians, once occupying parts of Georgia, Alabama, and Florida. 2. Their Muskhogean language.

creel (krēl) *n.* An angler's wicker basket for carrying fish. [Appar. related to OF *greille* grating]

creep (krēp) *v.i.* **crept, creep·ing** 1. To move with the body close to or touching the ground; crawl. 2. To move imperceptibly, stealthily, or timidly. 3. To act servilely; cringe. 4. To grow along a surface or support, as a vine. 5. To have a sensation of being covered with creeping things. 6. To slip out of position. — *n.* 1. The act of creeping. 2. *pl. Informal* A feeling of apprehension. [OE *crēopan*]

creep·er (krē'pər) *n.* 1. One who or that which creeps. 2. *Bot.* A plant growing along or across a surface by sending out short, flowering stems. 3. *pl.* A baby's garment resembling overalls.

creep·y (krē'pē) *adj.* creep·i·er, creep·i·est 1. Having or producing a feeling of fear or repugnance. 2. Characterized by a creeping motion. — **creep'i·ly** *adv.* — **creep'i·ness** *n.*

creese (krēs) See KRIS.

cre·mate (krē'māt, kri·māt') *v.t.* ·mat·ed, ·mat·ing To burn (a dead body) to ashes. [< L *cremare* to burn to ashes] — **cre·ma·tion** (kri·mā'shən) *n.* — **cre'ma·tor** *n.*

cre·ma·to·ry (krē'mə·tôr'ē, -tō'rē, krem'ə-) *adj.* Related to cremation. — *n.* *pl.* ·ries A furnace or establishment for cremating dead bodies: also **cre'ma·to'ri·um.**

crème (krem) *n.* *French* Cream: used in names of sauces and liqueurs.

crème de ca·ca·o (də kə·kā'ō, -kä'ō) *French* A sweet, chocolate-flavored liqueur.

crème de menthe (də mänt) *French* A sweet, green or white cordial with a strong flavor of mint.

Cre·mo·na (kri·mō'nə, *Ital.* krā·mô'nä) *n.* Any violin made at Cremona, Italy, from the 16th to the 18th century, by the Amati family, by Antonio Stradivari, and others.

cre·nate (krē'nāt) *adj. Bot.* Scalloped or toothed with even, rounded notches, as a leaf or margin. Also **cre'nat·ed.** [< NL < *crena* notch] — **cre'nate·ly** *adv.* — **cre·na'tion** *n.*

cren·el (kren'əl) *n.* 1. One of the embrasures, or indentations of a battlement. 2. A crenature. — *v.t.* **cren·eled** or **·elled, cren·el·ing** or **·el·ling** To crenelate. Also **cre·nelle** (kri·nel'). [< OF, dim. of *cren* notch]

cren·el·ate (kren'ə·lāt) *v.t.* ·lat·ed, ·lat·ing To provide with battlements or crenels. Also *Brit.* **cren'el·late.** — **cren'·el·a'tion, cren'el·la'tion** *n.*

Cre·ole (krē'ōl) *n.* 1. A native of Spanish America or the West Indies but of European descent. 2. A descendant of the original French settlers of the southern U.S., esp. of Louisiana. 3. The French patois spoken by the Louisiana Creoles. — *adj.* Of, relating to, or peculiar to the Creoles. [< F *créole* < Sp. < L *creare* to create]

Creole State Nickname of Louisiana.

cre·o·sol (krē'ə·sōl, -sol) *n. Chem.* A colorless, aromatic, oily liquid compound, $C_8H_{10}O_2$, derived from beechwood tar by distillation. [< CREOS(OTE) + -OL²]

cre·o·sote (krē'ə·sōt) *n. Chem.* An oily liquid obtained by the distillation of wood tar and coal tar, used as an antiseptic and preservative. — *v.t.* ·sot·ed, ·sot·ing To treat or impregnate with creosote, as shingles, etc. [< Gk. *kreas* flesh + *sōtēr* preserver < *sōzein* to save]

crepe (krāp) *n.* 1. A thin fabric of silk, cotton, wool, or synthetic fiber, having a crinkled surface. 2. Black crepe used as a sign of mourning, as in an armband: in this sense usu. *crape.* 3. Tissue paper resembling crepe: also **crepe paper.** Also spelled *crape:* also **crêpe.** [< F (*tissu*) *crêpe* crinkled (cloth) < L *crispus* curled]

crêpes su·zette (krep' sōō·zet') Thin egg pancakes usu. served aflame in cognac or curaçao.

crep·i·tate (krep'ə·tāt) *v.i.* ·tat·ed, ·tat·ing To crackle; rattle. [< L *crepitare*, freq. of *crepare* to creak] — **crep'i·tant** *adj.* — **crep'i·ta'tion** *n.*

crept (krept) Past tense of CREEP.
cre·pus·cu·lar (kri·pus′kyə·lər) *adj.* **1.** Dim; obscure. **2.** *Zool.* Appearing or flying in the twilight.
cres·cen·do (krə·shen′dŏ, -sen′-) *Music* *n.* *pl.* **-dos** A gradual increase in volume: expressed by the sign ⦦: opposed to *diminuendo.* — *v.i.* **-doed, -do·ing** To produce a crescendo. [< Ital., ppr. of *crescere* to increase < L]
cres·cent (kres′ənt) *n.* **1.** The visible part of the moon in its first or last quarter, having one concave edge and one convex edge. **2.** Something crescent-shaped. **3.** The device on the Turkish standard. — **the Crescent** Turkish or Moslem power. — *adj.* **1.** Increasing: said of the moon in its first quarter. **2.** Shaped like the moon in its first quarter. [< L *crescens, -entis,* ppr. of *crescere* to increase]
cre·sol (krē′sŏl, -sol) *n. Chem.* A liquid or crystalline compound, C₇H₈O, obtained by the destructive distillation of coal tar, used as an antiseptic. [Var. of CREOSOL]
cress (kres) *n.* One of various plants of the mustard family, as watercress, pungent to taste, used in salads. [OE *cresse*]
cres·set (kres′it) *n.* A metal holder for burning oil, wood, etc., for illumination. [< OF *craicet, craisset*]
crest (krest) *n.* **1.** A comb, tuft, or projection on the head of an animal, esp. of birds. **2.** The top of a wave. **3.** The highest point or stage: the *crest* of a flood. **4.** The projection on the top of a helmet; a plume. — *v.t.* **1.** To furnish with a crest. **2.** To reach the crest of. — *v.i.* **3.** To come to a crest, as a wave. [< OF < L *crista* tuft] — **crest′ed** *adj.* — **crest′less** *adj.*
crest·fall·en (krest′fô′lən) *adj.* **1.** Depressed; dispirited; dejected. **2.** Having a fallen or drooping crest.
cre·ta·ceous (kri·tā′shəs) *adj.* Consisting of, containing, or resembling chalk. [< L *creta* chalk]
Cre·ta·ceous (kri·tā′shəs) *Geol. adj.* Of or pertaining to the third geologic period of the Mesozoic era. — *n.* The system of rocks deposited during this period. See chart under GEOLOGY.
cre·tin (krē′tin, krēt′n) *n.* A person afflicted with cretinism. [< F *crétin,* var. of *chrétien* Christian, human being, i.e., not an animal] — **cre′tin·ous** *adj.*
cre·tin·ism (krē′tən·iz′əm) *n. Pathol.* A congenital condition associated with thyroid deficiency, marked by arrested physical development, goiter, and mental retardation.
cre·tonne (kri·ton′, krē′ton) *n.* A heavy, unglazed cotton, linen, or rayon fabric printed in colored patterns, used esp. for draperies. [after *Creton,* a village in Normandy]
cre·vasse (krə·vas′) *n.* **1.** A deep fissure or chasm, as in a glacier. **2.** *U.S.* A breach in a levee. — *v.t.* **-vassed, -vass·ing** To split with crevasses. [See CREVICE]
crev·ice (krev′is) *n.* A fissure or crack on or through the surface of something; cleft; chink. [< OF *crevace* < LL < L *crepare* to crack, creak] — **crev′iced** *adj.*
crew¹ (krōō) *n.* **1.** The company of men belonging to one ship, aircraft, etc. **2.** A body of men organized or detailed for a particular job: a repair *crew.* **3.** A group trained to handle a racing shell. **4.** A company of people; crowd; gang. [< OF < L *crescere* to increase]
crew² (krōō) Past tense of CROW.
crew cut *U.S.* A closely cropped haircut.
crew·el (krōō′əl) *n.* A slackly twisted worsted yarn, used in fancywork. [Origin uncertain] — **crew′el·work′** *n.*
crib (krib) *n.* **1.** A child's bed, with side railings. **2.** A box, bin, or small building for grain, having slat or openwork sides. **3.** A rack or manger for fodder. **4.** A stall for cattle. **5.** A small house, cottage, or room. **6.** A framework of wood or metal, used to retain or support something, as in mines. **7.** *Informal* A plagiarism. **8.** *Informal* A translation or other unauthorized aid employed by students. — *v.* **cribbed, crib·bing** *v.t.* **1.** To enclose in or as in a crib. **2.** To line or bolster, as the walls of a pit, with timbers or planking. **3.** *Informal* To plagiarize. — *v.i.* **4.** *Informal* To use a crib in translating. [OE *cribb*] — **crib′ber** *n.*
crib·bage (krib′ij) *n.* A game of cards for two, three, or four players, the score being kept on a pegboard.
crick (krik) *n.* A painful spasm of the muscles, as of the neck; a cramp. — *v.t.* To turn or twist so as to produce a crick. [Origin uncertain]
crick·et¹ (krik′it) *n.* A leaping insect having long antennae, the male of which makes a chirping sound by friction of the forewings. [< OF < LG; orig. imit.]
crick·et² (krik′it) *n.* **1.** An outdoor game played with bats, a ball, and wickets, between two sides of eleven each, popular in England. **2.** *Informal* Fair play; sportsmanship. — *v.i.* To play cricket. [< F] — **crick′et·er** *n.*
crick·et³ (krik′it) *n.* A footstool. [Origin unknown]
cried (krīd) Past tense and past participle of CRY.
cri·er (krī′ər) *n.* **1.** One who cries. **2.** One who makes public announcements, as of sales, news, etc. **3.** A hawker.
crime (krīm) *n.* **1.** *Law* An act or omission in violation of

public law, esp. a felony. **2.** Any grave offense against morality or social order. **3.** *Informal* Any apparent injustice; a shame. [< OF < L *crimen* accusation]
Crimean War See table for WAR.
crim·i·nal (krim′ə·nəl) *adj.* **1.** Implying or involving crime. **2.** *Law* Pertaining to the administration of penal as opposed to civil law: a *criminal* court. **3.** Guilty of crime. — *n.* One who has committed a crime. [< OF < L < *crimen* charge] — **crim′i·nal·ly** *adv.* — **crim′i·nal′i·ty** *n.*
crim·i·nol·o·gy (krim′ə·nol′ə·jē) *n.* The scientific study and investigation of crime and the behavior of criminals. [< L *crimen, criminis* crime + -LOGY] — **crim·i·no·log·i·cal** (krim′ə·nə·loj′i·kəl) *adj.* — **crim′i·nol′o·gist** *n.*
crimp¹ (krimp) *v.t.* **1.** To bend or press into ridges or folds; corrugate; flute. **2.** To curl or wave: to *crimp* the hair. — *n.* **1.** Something that has been crimped. **2.** *pl.* Waved or curled hair. — **to put a crimp in** *Informal* To hinder or obstruct. [< MDu. *crimpen* to wrinkle] — **crimp′er** *n.*
crimp² (krimp) *n.* One who gets sailors, soldiers, etc., to serve by decoying or entrapping them. — *v.t.* To decoy or entrap into forced military service. [Origin uncertain]
crimp·y (krim′pē) *adj.* **crimp·i·er, crimp·i·est** Having a crimped appearance; wavy; curly.
crim·son (krim′zən) *n.* A deep red color. — *adj.* **1.** Of a deep red color. **2.** Bloody. — *v.t. & v.i.* To make or become crimson. [ME < Sp. < Arabic < *qirmiz* insect]
cringe (krinj) *v.i.* **cringed, cring·ing** **1.** To shrink or crouch in fear or cowardice. **2.** To fawn. — *n.* A servile crouching. [ME *cringen, crengen*] — **cring′er** *n.*
crin·gle (kring′gəl) *n. Naut.* A small loop or grommet of rope or metal, attached to the edge of a sail. [Appar. < LG]
crin·kle (kring′kəl) *v.t. & v.i.* **-kled, -kling** **1.** To form or cause to form wrinkles, turns, etc. **2.** To rustle or crackle. — *n.* A wrinkle or fold. [ME *crenklen* to curl up] — **crin′kly** *adj.*
cri·noid (krī′noid, krin′oid) *adj.* **1.** *Zool.* Of or pertaining to animals having jointed stems attached by stalks to the sea bottom, and radial arms. **2.** Lilylike. — *n.* A crinoid animal. [< NL < Gk. < *krinon* lily + *eidos* form]
crin·o·line (krin′ə·lin, -lēn) *n.* **1.** A stiff fabric, used in puffed sleeves, hems, interlinings, etc., originally made of horsehair and linen. **2.** A petticoat of this fabric. **3.** A hoop skirt. [< F < L *crinis* hair + *linum* linen]
crip·ple (krip′əl) *n.* A lame or disabled person or animal; one lacking the natural use of a limb or the body. — *v.t.* **-pled, -pling** **1.** To make lame. **2.** To impair or disable. [OE *crypel*] — **crip′pler** *n.*
cri·sis (krī′sis) *n.* *pl.* **-ses** (-sēz) **1.** A crucial turning point in an affair or of a series of events. **2.** A critical moment. **3.** *Pathol.* Any decisive change in the course of a disease, favorable or unfavorable. [< L < Gk. < *krinein* to decide]
crisp (krisp) *adj.* **1.** Brittle; easily crumbled. **2.** Fresh and firm: *crisp* vegetables. **3.** Brisk; invigorating: a *crisp* breeze. **4.** Stimulating; lively: a *crisp* conversation. **5.** Terse or pithy; curt: a *crisp* retort. **6.** Having tight curls or waves, as hair. — *v.t. & v.i.* To make or become crisp. [OE < L *crispus* curled] — **crisp′ly** *adv.* — **crisp′ness** *n.*
crisp·y (kris′pē) *adj.* **crisp·i·er, crisp·i·est** Crisp.
criss·cross (kris′krôs′, -kros′) *v.t.* **1.** To cross with interlacing lines. — *v.i.* **2.** To move in crisscrosses. — *adj.* Marked by crossings. — *n.* **1.** The cross of one who cannot write. **2.** A group of intersecting lines. — *adv.* Crosswise. [Alter. of *Christcross*]
cri·te·ri·on (krī·tir′ē·ən) *n.* *pl.* **·te·ri·a** (-tir′ē·ə) or **·te·ri·ons** A standard or rule by which a judgment can be made; a model, test, or measure. [< Gk. < *krinein* to decide]
crit·ic (krit′ik) *n.* **1.** One who judges the merits of anything by some standard or criterion. **2.** A skilled judge of literary, theatrical, or other artistic creations. **3.** One who judges severely. [< L < Gk. < *kritēs* judge]
crit·i·cal (krit′i·kəl) *adj.* **1.** Given to faultfinding or severe judgments; carping. **2.** Exhibiting careful, precise judgments; analytical: a *critical* report. **3.** Of or characteristic of a critic or criticism. **4.** Of the nature of a crisis or turning point; crucial; decisive. **5.** Attended with danger; risky; perilous. **6.** Necessary for the prosecution of a war: *critical* materiel. **7.** *Physics* Indicating a decisive change in a specified condition. — **crit′i·cal·ly** *adv.* — **crit′i·cal·ness** *n.*
crit·i·cism (krit′ə·siz′əm) *n.* **1.** The act of criticizing, esp. disapprovingly. **2.** A severe or unfavorable judgment. **3.** The art of making informed and discriminating judgments. **4.** The occupation or profession of a critic. **5.** A review, article, or commentary expressing a critical judgment.
crit·i·cize (krit′ə·sīz) *v.t. & v.i.* **1.** To judge severely; censure. **2.** To pass judgment on the merits or faults of. Also *Brit.* **crit′i·cise.** — **crit′i·ciz′a·ble** *adj.* — **crit′i·ciz′er** *n.*
cri·tique (kri·tēk′) *n.* **1.** A critical review, esp. of a work of art or literature. **2.** The art of criticism. [< F]

crit·ter (krit′ər) *n. U.S. Dial.* A creature.

croak (krōk) *v.i.* **1.** To utter a hoarse, low-pitched cry, as a frog or crow. **2.** To speak in a low, hoarse voice. **3.** To talk in a doleful tone; grumble. **4.** *Slang* To die. —*v.t.* **5.** To utter with a croak. **6.** *Slang* To kill. —*n.* A hoarse vocal sound, as of a frog. [Imit.] —**croak′y** *adj.*

croak·er (krō′kər) *n.* **1.** Any of various animals that croak, as the grunt, a fish. **2.** One who speaks dolefully.

Cro·at (krō′at, -ət) *n.* **1.** A Slavic native of Croatia. **2.** The Croatian language.

Cro·a·tian (krō-ā′shən) *adj.* Pertaining to Croatia or the Croats. —*n.* **1.** A Croat. **2.** The South Slavic language of the Croats; Serbo-Croatian.

cro·chet (krō-shā′) *v.t. & v.i.* **·cheted** (-shād′), **·chet·ing** (-shā′ing) To form or ornament (a fabric) by interlacing thread with a hooked needle. —*n.* A kind of fancywork produced by crocheting. [< F, dim., of *croche* hook]

crock (krok) *n.* An earthenware pot or jar. [OE *croc*]

crocked (krokt) *adj. U.S. Slang* Drunk.

crock·er·y (krok′ər·ē) *n.* Earthen vessels collectively.

croc·o·dile (krok′ə-dīl) *n.* **1.** A large lizardlike, amphibious reptile of tropical regions, with long jaws and armored skin. **2.** A gavial. [< OF < Med.L Gk. *krokodilos* lizard, crocodile]

crocodile tears False weeping; hypocritical grief.

croc·o·dil·i·an (krok′-ə-dil′ē-ən) *adj.* **1.** Of or like a crocodile. **2.** Belonging to an order of reptiles that includes crocodiles, alligators, and caymans. —*n.* A crocodilian reptile. Also **croc′o·dil′e·an.**

CROCODILE
(To 18 feet long)

cro·cus (krō′kəs) *n. pl.* **cro·cus·es** or **cro·ci** (krō′sī) **1.** A plant of the iris family, with long grasslike leaves and large flowers. **2.** A deep orange yellow. [< L < Gk. *krokos*]

Croe·sus (krē′səs) Sixth-century B.C. Lydian king, noted for his wealth. —*n.* Any very wealthy man.

croft (krôft, kroft) *n. Brit.* **1.** A small field near a house. **2.** A small tenant farm. [OE, field] —**croft′er** *n.*

Croix de Guerre (krwä də gâr′) A French military decoration for bravery; literally, cross of war.

Cro-Mag·non (krō-mag′non, *Fr.* krō-mà-nyôǹ′) *Anthropol. n.* A member of a prehistoric European race considered to be a forerunner of modern man. —*adj.* Pertaining to or belonging to the Cro-Magnon race. [after the cave in France where their remains have been found]

crom·lech (krom′lek) *n.* **1.** An ancient monument of large standing stones arranged roughly in a circle. **2.** A dolmen. [< Welsh < *crom* bent + *llech* flat stone]

crone (krōn) *n.* A withered old woman. [Prob. < OF *carogne* carcass]

Cro·nus (krō′nəs) In Greek mythology, the youngest of the Titans, who deposed his father Uranus and was himself overcome by his son Zeus: identified with the Roman *Saturn:* also spelled *Kronos.*

cro·ny (krō′nē) *n. pl.* **·nies** A friend. [Orig. university slang < Gk. *chronios* contemporary]

crook (krŏŏk) *n.* **1.** A bend or curve. **2.** The curved or bent part of a thing. **3.** Something with a crook in it, as a shepherd's staff. **4.** *Informal* A thief. —*v.t.* **1.** To bend; make crooked. —*v.i.* **2.** To grow crooked. [< ON *krōkr*]

crook·ed (krŏŏk′id) *adj.* **1.** Bent; not straight. **2.** Tricky; dishonest. —**crook′ed·ly** *adv.* —**crook′ed·ness** *n.*

crook·neck (krŏŏk′nek′) *n.* Any of several varieties of squash with a long, curved neck.

croon (krōōn) *v.t. & v.i.* **1.** To sing or hum in a low tone. **2.** To sing (popular songs) in a soft and sentimental manner. —*n.* A low, mournful humming or singing. [< MDu. *kronen* to sing softly, lament] —**croon′er** *n.*

crop (krop) *n.* **1.** The cultivated produce of the land, as grain or vegetables. **2.** The product of a particular kind, place, or season. **3.** A collection or quantity of anything. **4.** A cropping, esp. of the hair. **5.** An earmark, as on cattle. **6.** An enlargement of the gullet, as in birds; the craw. **7.** The handle of a whip. **8.** A whip having a leather loop for a lash. —*v.* cropped, crop·ping *v.t.* **1.** To cut or eat off the stems of, as grass. **2.** To reap. **3.** To trim or clip (the hair, ears, tail, etc.) of. **4.** To raise a crop or crops on. —*v.i.* **5.** To bear or yield a crop or crops. —**to crop up** (or **out**) **1.** To appear above the surface; sprout. **2.** To develop or happen unexpectedly. [OE]

crop·per¹ (krop′ər) *n.* **1.** One who or that which crops. **2.** *U.S.* One who cultivates another's land for part of the crop.

crop·per² (krop′ər) *n.* A bad fall, as when one is thrown over a horse's head. —**to come a cropper 1.** To fall headlong. **2.** To fail. [? < dial. *neck and crop* completely]

cro·quet (krō-kā′) *n.* An outdoor game played by driving wooden balls through a series of wire arches by means of long-handled mallets. [Var. of *crochet.* See CROCHET.]

cro·quette (krō-ket′) *n.* A ball or cake of minced food fried brown in deep fat. [< F < *croquer* to crunch]

cro·sier (krō′zhər) *n.* A staff surmounted by a crook or cross, borne by or before a bishop or archbishop on occasions of ceremony. [< OF < Med.L < *crocia* bishop's crook]

cross (krôs, kros) *n.* **1.** An ancient instrument of execution, an upright with a horizontal piece near the top, upon which the condemned persons were fastened. **2.** The emblem of Christianity, a representation of the cross upon which Christ died. **3.** Any severe trial, affliction, or suffering: to bear one's *cross.* **4.** The sign of the cross, made with the right hand as a devotional act. **5.** A monument, staff, or other structure in the form of a cross. **6.** The mark of one who cannot write. **7.** Anything that resembles or is intermediate between two other things: a *cross* between poetry and prose. **8.** A mixture of varieties or breeds of plants or animals; a hybrid. —**the Cross 1.** The cross on which Christ was crucified. **2.** Christianity. —*v.t.* **1.** To move or pass from one side to the other side of; go across; traverse. **2.** To extend from side to side of; span: An overpass *crosses* a highway. **3.** To pass across or intersect, as streets or lines. **4.** To transport or convey across. **5.** To make the sign of the cross upon or over. **6.** To draw or put a line across: to *cross* a t. **7.** To lay or place across or over: to *cross* the legs, fingers, etc. **8.** To meet and pass: Your ship *crossed* mine. **9.** To obstruct or hinder; thwart. **10.** *Biol.* To crossbreed (plants or animals). —*v.i.* **11.** To pass, move, or extend from side to side. **12.** To intersect; lie athwart. **13.** To meet and pass: Our paths *crossed.* **14.** *Biol.* To crossbreed. —**to cross one's mind** To occur to one. —**to cross up** *Informal* To betray. —*adj.* **1.** Peevish; ill-humored. **2.** Lying across each other: *cross* streets. **3.** Embodying interchange; reciprocal. **4.** Contrary; adverse: at *cross* purposes. **5.** Hybrid. —*adv.* **1.** Across; crosswise; transversely. **2.** Adversely; contrarily. [< OE < ON < L *crux*] —**cross′ly** *adv.* —**cross′ness** *n.*

cross·bar (krôs′bär′, kros′-) *n.* A transverse bar or line. —*v.t.* **·barred**, **·bar·ring** To secure or mark with crossbars.

cross·beam (krôs′bēm′, kros′-) *n.* **1.** A large beam or girder going from wall to wall. **2.** Any beam that crosses another.

cross·bill (krôs′bil′, kros′-) *n.* A finchlike bird having points on its mandibles that cross each other.

cross·bones (krôs′bōnz′, kros′-) *n.* A representation of two bones crossing each other, usu. surmounted by a skull, and used as a symbol of death.

cross·bow (krôs′bō′, kros′-) *n.* A medieval weapon consisting of a bow fixed transversely on a grooved stock along which arrows or stones are released. —**cross′bow′man** *n.*

cross·breed (krôs′brēd′, kros′-) *v.t. & v.i.* **bred**, **breed·ing** *Biol.* To produce (a strain or animal) by interbreeding or blending two varieties. —*n.* A strain or animal produced by crossbreeding; a hybrid.

cross·check (krôs′chek′) *v.t. & v.i.* To confirm or make certain by using parallel or additional data.

cross-coun·try (krôs′kun′trē, kros′-) *adj. & adv.* Across open country and disregarding roads, lanes, etc.

cross·cur·rent (krôs′kûr′ənt, kros′-) *n.* **1.** A current flowing across another. **2.** A contradictory tendency.

cross·cut (krôs′kut′, kros′-) *v.t. & v.i.* **·cut**, **·cut·ting** To cut crosswise or through. —*adj.* **1.** Used or made for the purpose of crosscutting. **2.** Cut across or on the bias: *crosscut* silk. —*n.* **1.** A cut across or a shortcut. **2.** *Mining* A cutting that intersects the lode or the main workings.

cross-ex·am·ine (krôs′ig-zam′in, kros′-) *v.t. & v.i.* **·ined**, **·in·ing 1.** To question anew (a witness called by the opposing party) for the purpose of testing the reliability of his previous testimony. **2.** To question carefully. —**cross′-ex·am′i·na′tion** *n.* —**cross′-ex·am′in·er** *n.*

cross-eye (krôs′ī′, kros′-) *n.* Strabismus in which one or both eyes are turned inward. —**cross′-eyed** *adj.*

cross-fer·ti·li·za·tion (krôs′fûr′tə-lə-zā′shən, kros′-) *n.* **1.** *Biol.* The fertilization of an organism by sexually differentiated reproductive cells. **2.** *Bot.* The fertilization of one plant or flower by the pollen from another.

cross-fer·ti·lize (krôs′fûr′tə-līz, kros′-) *v.t.* **·lized**, **·liz·ing** To fertilize (a plant or animal) by cross-fertilization.

cross-grained (krôs′grānd′, kros′-) *adj.* **1.** Having the grain running transversely: a *cross-grained* board. **2.** Stubborn; perverse: a *cross-grained* man.

cross·hatch (krôs′hach′, kros′-) *v.t.* To shade, as a picture, by crossed lines. —**cross′hatch′ing** *n.*

cross-in·dex (krôs′in′deks, kros′-) *v.t. & v.i.* To insert cross-references in (an index, etc.).

cross·ing (krôs′ing, kros′-) *n.* **1.** The act of going across, hindering, etc. **2.** The place where something, as a road, may be crossed. **3.** Intersection, as of roads.

cross·patch (krôs′pach′, kros′-) *n. Informal* A cranky, ill-tempered person.

cross·piece (krôs'pēs', kros'-)   n. Any piece of material that crosses another.

cross·pol·li·nate (krôs'pol'ə·nāt, kros'-) v.t. **·nat·ed, ·nat·ing** To cross-fertilize (a plant). **— cross'·pol'li·na'tion** n.

cross·pur·pose (krôs'pûr'pəs, kros'-)   n. A purpose or aim in conflict with another. **— to be at cross-purposes** To misunderstand or act counter to each other's purposes.

cross·ques·tion (krôs'kwes'chən, kros'-)   v.t. To cross-examine. **—** n. A question asked in a cross-examination.

cross·re·fer (krôs'ri·fûr', kros'-) v. **·ferred, ·fer·ring** v.t. **1.** To refer to another passage or part. **—** v.i. **2.** To make a cross-reference.

cross·ref·er·ence (krôs'ref'rəns, kros'-)   n. A note or statement directing a reader from one part of a book, index, etc., to another part.

cross·road (krôs'rōd', kros'-)   n. **1.** A road that intersects another. **2.** A road connecting one road to another.

cross·roads (krôs'rōdz', kros'-) n.pl. (construed as sing.) **1.** The place where roads meet: in rural areas, often a settlement. **2.** The meeting place of different cultures. **— at the crossroads** At any critical point or moment.

cross·ruff (krôs'ruf', kros'-)   n. In cards, a play in which each of two partners alternately trumps the other's lead.

cross section 1. A plane section of any object cut at right angles to its length. **2.** A sampling meant to be characteristic or typical of the whole: a cross section of opinion. **3.** A cutting through anything at right angles.

cross·stitch (krôs'stich', kros'-)   n. **1.** A double stitch in the form of an x. **2.** Needlework made with this stitch. **—** v.t. To make or mark with a cross-stitch.

cross·tie (krôs'tī', kros'-)   n. Chiefly U.S. A beam or tie laid crosswise under railroad tracks to support them.

cross·town (krôs'toun', kros'-)   adj. Going across a town or city: a cross-town bus. **—** adv. Across a town or city.

cross·tree (krôs'trē', kros'-)   n. Usu. pl. Naut. Pieces of wood or metal set crosswise at the head of a mast to sustain the top or to extend the topgallant shrouds.

cross·walk (krôs'wôk', kros'-)   n. A lane marked off for use by pedestrians in crossing a street.

cross·way (krôs'wā', kros'-)   n. A crossroad.

cross·wise (krôs'wīz', kros'-)   adv. **1.** Across. **2.** In the form of a cross. **3.** Contrarily. Also **cross'ways'** (-wāz').

cross·word puzzle (krôs'wûrd', kros'-) A puzzle worked on a pattern of white and black space, of which the white spaces are to be filled with letters that form words to agree with numbered definitions or similar clues.

crotch (kroch)   n. **1.** The fork or angle formed by two diverging parts, as by the branches of a tree. **2.** The region of the human body where the legs separate from the pelvis. **3.** A forked pole, support, etc. [? < AF croche crook]

crotched (krocht)   adj. Having a crotch; forked.

crotch·et (kroch'it)   n. **1.** A whimsical or perverse notion or whim; an eccentricity. **2.** A small hook or hooklike instrument. **3.** Entomol. A hooklike process. **4.** Music Chiefly Brit. A quarter note. [< F croche hook]

crotch·et·y (kroch'ə·tē)   adj. **1.** Full of eccentric or stubborn notions; perverse; contrary. **2.** Like a crotchet. **— crotch'et·i·ness** n.

cro·ton (krōt'n)   n. **1.** A tree or shrub of the spurge family, often used medicinally. **2.** An ornamental tropical shrub. [< NL < Gk. krotōn a tick]

Cro·ton bug (krōt'n)   A small, light-colored cockroach. [after Croton Aqueduct; the first infestation in New York City occurred after this aqueduct was opened in 1842]

crouch (krouch)   v.i. **1.** To stoop or bend low, as an animal ready to spring. **2.** To cringe; abase oneself; cower. **—** v.t. **3.** To bend low. **—** n. A crouching or crouching position. [? < OF crochir to be bent]

croup[1] (krōōp)   n. Pathol. **1.** A disease of the throat characterized by hoarse coughing, laryngeal spasm, and difficult breathing. **2.** Loosely, inflammation of the larynx. [Imit.]

croup[2] (krōōp)   n. The rump of certain animals, esp. of a horse. Also **croupe.** [< OF crope]

crou·pi·er (krōō'pē·ər, Fr. krōō·pyā')   n. One who collects the stakes lost and pays out those won at a gaming table. [< F, lit., one who rides on the croup]

croup·y (krōō'pē)   adj. **1.** Of or indicating croup. **2.** Having croup. Also **croup'ous. — crou'pi·ness** n.

crou·ton (krōō'ton, krōō·ton', Fr. krōō·tôn')   n. A small piece of toasted bread used in soups. [< F]

crow[1] (krō)   n. **1.** An omnivorous, raucous bird having glossy black plumage. **2.** Loosely, the rook or raven. **—** Collateral adjective: corvine. **3.** A crowbar. **— as the crow flies** In a straight line. **— to eat crow** Informal To recant a statement; back down; humiliate oneself. [OE crāwe]

crow[2] (krō)   v.i. **crowed** or (for def. 1) **crew, crowed, crow·ing 1.** To utter the shrill cry of a cock. **2.** To exult; boast. **3.** To utter sounds expressive of delight, as an infant. **—** n.

1. The cry of a cock. **2.** Any shrill, inarticulate sound resembling this, as an infant's cry of pleasure. [OE crāwan]

Crow (krō)   n. **1.** A North American Indian of a Siouan tribe formerly inhabiting the region between the Platte and Yellowstone rivers. **2.** The language of this tribe.

crow·bar (krō'bär')   n. A straight iron or steel bar with a flattened point often set at an angle, used as a lever.

crowd (kroud)   n. **1.** A large number of persons gathered closely together. **2.** The populace in general; mob. **3.** Informal A particular set of people; a clique. **—** v.t. **1.** To shove or push. **2.** To fill to overflowing. **3.** To cram together; force into a confined space. **4.** Informal To put pressure on, esp. for payment. **—** v.i. **5.** To gather in large numbers. **6.** To force one's way. **7.** To shove or push. [OE crūdan] **— crowd'ed** adj. **— crowd'er** n.

crow·foot (krō'fŏŏt')   n. pl. **·foots 1.** Any of a genus of plants that includes the buttercup, columbine, etc. **2.** A plant having leaves, etc., suggestive of a bird's foot.

crown (kroun)   n. **1.** A circlet, often of precious metal set with jewels, worn on the head as a mark of sovereign power. **2.** A decorative covering for the head. **3.** Anything shaped like a crown. **4.** A coin stamped with a crown or a crowned head, esp. the English crown, worth five shillings. **5.** The top part of the head. **6.** The head itself. **7.** The upper part of a hat. **8.** The top or summit of something. **9.** The most perfect or complete state or type. **10.** A reward or prize for achievement. **11.** Dent. The part of a tooth that is covered with enamel or an artificial substitute for it. **12.** Naut. The lowest point of junction of the two arms of an anchor. **— the Crown 1.** The sovereign ruler; monarch. **2.** The power or the empire of a monarch. **—** v.t. **1.** To place a crown or garland on the head of. **2.** To make a monarch of. **3.** To endow with honor or dignity. **4.** To form the crown, ornament, or top to. **5.** To finish or make complete. **6.** Informal To strike on the head. **7.** In checkers, to make (a piece) into a king by placing another piece upon it. [< AF, OF < L corona] **— crown'er** n.

crown colony A colony of Great Britain in which the Crown retains control of legislation.

crown glass Hard optical glass of low refraction.

crown prince The male heir apparent to a throne.

crown princess 1. The wife of a crown prince. **2.** The female heir apparent to a throne.

crow's-foot (krōz'fŏŏt')   n. pl. **-feet** One of the wrinkles diverging from the outer corner of the eye.

crow's-nest (krōz'nest')   n. **1.** Naut. An observation platform near the top of a ship's mast. **2.** Any similar platform.

cro·zier (krō'zhər) See CROSIER.

cru·ces (krōō'sēz) Alternative plural of CRUX.

cruci- combining form Cross. [< L crux, crucis cross]

cru·cial (krōō'shəl)   adj. **1.** Of a critical or decisive nature. **2.** Involving difficulties; severe. [< MF < L crux, crucis cross, torture] **— cru'cial·ly** adv.

cru·ci·ble (krōō'sə·bəl)   n. **1.** A heat-resistant vessel for melting metals or minerals. **2.** A severely trying test or experience. [< Med.L crucibulum earthen pot, lamp]

cru·ci·fix (krōō'sə·fiks)   n. **1.** A cross bearing an effigy of Christ crucified. **2.** The cross as a Christian emblem. [< OF < L cruci fixus one hanged on a cross]

cru·ci·fix·ion (krōō'sə·fik'shən)   n. **1.** The act of crucifying, or the state of being crucified. **2.** A painting, etc., that represents Christ's death on the cross. **— the Crucifixion** The execution of Jesus Christ on the cross.

cru·ci·form (krōō'sə·fôrm)   adj. Cross-shaped.

cru·ci·fy (krōō'sə·fī)   v.t. **·fied, ·fy·ing 1.** To put to death by nailing or fastening the hands and feet to a cross. **2.** To torture; torment. [< OF < L cruci figere to fasten to a cross] **— cru'ci·fi'er** n.

crude (krōōd)   adj. **crud·er, crud·est 1.** In an unrefined or unprepared state; raw: crude oil. **2.** Immature; unripe. **3.** Showing a lack of skill or knowledge. **4.** Roughly made; unfinished. **5.** Lacking tact, refinement, or taste. [< L crudus rough] **— crude'ly** adv. **— crude'ness** n.

cru·di·ty (krōō'də·tē)   n. pl. **·ties 1.** The state or quality of being crude. **2.** A crude act, remark, etc.

cru·el (krōō'əl)   adj. **cru·el·er** or **·el·ler, cru·el·est** or **·el·lest 1.** Indifferent to or enjoying the suffering of others. **2.** Causing or inflicting mental or physical suffering. [< OF < L crudelis severe] **— cru'el·ly** adv. **— cru'el·ness** n.

cru·el·ty (krōō'əl·tē)   n. pl. **·ties 1.** The quality or condition of being cruel; merciless; inhumanity. **2.** That which causes suffering; an inhuman act; brutal treatment.

cru·et (krōō'it)   n. A small glass bottle for vinegar, oil, etc. [< AF, dim. of OF crue pot]

cruise (krōōz)   v. **cruised, cruis·ing** v.i. **1.** To sail about with no fixed destination, as for pleasure. **2.** To travel about at a moderate speed, as a police squad car. **3.** To move at the optimum speed for sustained travel: said of aircraft, etc. —*v.t.* 4. To cruise over. —*n.* A cruising trip, esp. a voyage at sea. [< Du. *kruisen* to cross, traverse]

cruis·er (krōō′zər) *n.* 1. One who or that which cruises. 2. A fast, maneuverable warship, having medium tonnage and armament. 3. A small power vessel equipped with living facilities: also called *cabin cruiser.*

crul·ler (krul′ər) *n.* A small cake of sweetened dough, fried in deep fat. [< Du. < *krullen* to curl]

crumb (krum) *n.* 1. A tiny fragment of bread, cake, or the like. 2. A bit or scrap of anything: *crumbs* of information. 3. The soft inner part of bread, as distinguished from the crust. 4. *U.S. Slang* A contemptible person. —*v.t.* 1. To break into small pieces; crumble. 2. In cooking, to dress or cover with bread crumbs. [OE *cruma*]

crum·ble (krum′bəl) *v.* **·bled, ·bling** *v.t.* 1. To cause to break into tiny parts. —*v.i.* 2. To fall to small pieces; disintegrate. [ME < OE *cruma* crumb]

crum·bly (krum′blē) *adj.* **·bli·er, ·bli·est** Apt to crumble; friable. — **crum′bli·ness** *n.*

crumb·y (krum′ē) *adj.* **crumb·i·er, crumb·i·est** 1. Full of crumbs. 2. Soft, like the inner part of bread.

crum·my (krum′ē) *adj.* **crum·mi·er, crum·mi·est** *U.S. Slang* Inferior; cheap; shabby.

crum·pet (krum′pit) *n.* A thin, leavened batter cake baked on a gridiron, then usu. toasted. [< ME *crompen* to curl up]

crum·ple (krum′pəl) *v.* **·pled, ·pling** *v.t.* 1. To press into wrinkles; rumple. —*v.i.* 2. To become wrinkled; shrivel. 3. *Informal* To collapse. —*n.* Anything crumpled; a wrinkle. [Freq. of obs. *crump,* var. of CRIMP]

crunch (krunch) *v.t. & v.i.* 1. To chew with a crushing or crackling sound. 2. To move, press, or advance with a crushing sound. —*n.* A crunching, or its sound. [Imit.]

crup·per (krup′ər) *n.* 1. The strap that goes under a horse's tail. 2. The rump of a horse. [< OF *crope* croup?]

cru·sade (krōō·sād′) *n.* *Usu. cap.* Any of the military expeditions undertaken by Christians to recover the Holy Land from the Moslems. 2. Any expedition under papal sanction against heathens or heretics. 3. Any vigorous concerted movement or cause, esp. a reform movement. —*v.i.* **·sad·ed, ·sad·ing** To engage in a crusade. [< Sp. < Med.L *cruciare* to mark with a cross] — **cru·sad′er** *n.*

cruse (krōōz, krōōs) *n.* A small bottle, flask, or jug; cruet. [? < MDu. *cruyse* jar, pot]

crush (krush) *v.t.* 1. To press or squeeze out of shape; mash. 2. To smash or grind into fine particles. 3. To obtain or extract by pressure. 4. To crowd. 5. To subdue; conquer. —*v.i.* 6. To become broken or misshapen by pressure. 7. To move ahead by crushing or pressing. —*n.* 1. The act of crushing. 2. The state of being crushed. 3. A crowd or throng; jam. 4. A substance obtained by crushing: orange *crush.* 5. *Informal* An infatuation. [< OF < MHG *krosen* to crush] — **crush′a·ble** *adj.* — **crush′er** *n.*

crust (krust) *n.* 1. The hard outer part of bread. 2. A piece of bread consisting mostly of crust (def. 1); also, any dry, hard piece of bread. 3. The pastry shell of a pie, tart, etc. 4. Any hard, crisp surface, as of snow. 5. *Slang* Insolence; impertinence. 6. *Geol.* The exterior shell of the earth. —*v.t. & v.i.* 1. To cover with or acquire a crust. 2. To form into a crust. [< OF < L *crusta*] — **crus′tal** *adj.*

crus·ta·cean (krus·tā′shən) *n.* One of a class of arthropods having crustlike shells, and generally aquatic, including lobsters, crabs, shrimps, etc. — *adj.* Of or pertaining to this class of arthropods. [< NL *Crustacea* < L *crusta* crust] — **crus·ta′ceous** *adj.*

crust·y (krus′tē) *adj.* **crust·i·er, crust·i·est** 1. Like or having a crust. 2. Harshly curt in manner or speech; surly. — **crust′i·ly** *adv.* — **crust′i·ness** *n.*

crutch (kruch) *n.* 1. A staff used by the lame as a support in walking, esp. one having a crosspiece to fit under the armpit and a grip for the hand. 2. Anything that gives support. 3. Any of various devices resembling a crutch. — *v.t.* To prop up or support, as on crutches. [OE *crycc*]

crux (kruks) *n. pl.* **crux·es** or **cru·ces** (krōō′sēz) 1. A pivotal, fundamental, or vital point. 2. A cross. 3. A tormenting or baffling problem. [< L, cross]

Crux (kruks) *n.* A constellation, the Southern Cross, containing the bright star Acrux.

cry (krī) *v.* **cried, cry·ing** *v.i.* 1. To utter sobbing sounds of grief, pain, fear, etc., usu. accompanied by tears. 2. To call out or appeal loudly; shout: often with *out.* 3. To make characteristic calls: said of animals. —*v.t.* 4. To utter loudly or shout out; exclaim. 5. To affect (oneself) by weeping: to *cry* oneself to sleep. 6. To beg for. — **to cry down** 1. To belittle; disparage. 2. To silence or put down by cries. — **to cry up** To praise highly. —*n. pl.* **cries** 1. A loud or emotional utterance; shout; call. 2. A fit of weeping. 3. An appeal; entreaty. 4. Advertisement by outcry. 5. General report or rumor. 6. A rallying call; battle cry. 7. A catchword. 8. A demand; clamor. 9. The characteristic call of a bird or animal. 10. A pack of hounds. — **a far cry** 1. A long distance away. 2. Some-

thing very unlike. — **in full cry** In full pursuit, as a pack of hounds. [< OF < L *quiritare* to call out]

cry·ba·by (krī′bā′bē) *n. pl.* **·bies** A person, esp. a child, given to crying or complaining.

cry·ing (krī′ing) *adj.* 1. That cries: a *crying* child. 2. Calling for immediate action or remedy: a *crying* shame.

cryo- *combining form* Cold; frost. [< Gk. *kryos* frost]

cry·o·gen·ics (krī′ə·jen′iks) *n.pl. (construed as sing.)* The branch of physics dealing with very low temperatures.

cry·o·lite (krī′ə·līt) *n.* A fluoride of sodium and aluminum, used in the production of aluminum, soda, and glass.

crypt (kript) *n.* A chamber or vault, esp. one beneath a church, used as a place of burial. [< L < Gk. *kryptos* hidden]

cryp·ta·nal·y·sis (krip′tə·nal′ə·sis) *n. pl.* **·ses** (-sēz) The scientific study of cryptograms, ciphers, codes, etc., to which the key is not known. — **cryp·tan·a·lyst** (krip·tan′ə·list) *n.* — **cryp′tan·a·lyt′ic** *adj.*

cryp·tic (krip′tik) *adj.* 1. Secret or hidden; occult. 2. Puzzling; mystifying. Also **cryp′ti·cal.** [< LL < Gk. *kryptos* hidden]

crypto- *combining form* Hidden; secret. Also, before vowels, **crypt-.** [< Gk. *kryptos* hidden]

cryp·to·gam (krip′tə·gam) *n. Bot.* Any of a former division of plants that have no seeds or flowers, but propagate by spores, as algae, fungi, ferns, and mosses. [< F < Gk. *kryptos* hidden + *gamos* marriage] — **cryp′to·gam′ic, cryp·tog·a·mous** (krip·tog′ə·məs) *adj.*

cryp·to·gram (krip′tə·gram) *n.* A message written in code or cipher. — **cryp′to·gram′mic** *adj.*

cryp·tog·ra·phy (krip·tog′rə·fē) *n.* 1. The art or process of writing in or reconverting cipher. 2. Any system of writing in secret characters. — **cryp·tog′ra·pher, cryp·tog′ra·phist** *n.* — **cryp·to·graph·ic** (krip′tə·graf′ik) *adj.*

crys·tal (kris′təl) *n.* 1. Colorless transparent quartz, or rock crystal. 2. *Physics* A homogeneous solid body, exhibiting a symmetrical structure, with geometrically arranged planes and faces that assume any of various patterns associated with peculiarities of atomic structure. 3. Flint glass, or any fine clear glass; also, articles made of such glass, as bowls, etc. 4. Anything transparent and colorless. 5. A glass or plastic covering over the face of a watch. 6. A crystal detector. — *adj.* 1. Composed of crystal. 2. Like crystal; extremely clear; limpid. [< OF < L < Gk. *krystallos* ice, crystal]

crystal ball A ball of crystal or glass used in crystal gazing.

crystal detector *Telecom.* A device consisting of metal electrodes in contact with suitable crystal materials, used to rectify incoming radio signals.

crystal gazing The act of looking into a crystal ball in order to induce a vision of distant objects or future events; also, the alleged ability to do this. — **crys·tal-gaz·er** (kris′təl·gā′zər) *n.*

a   b

c   d

CRYSTALS
a Tetragonal pyramid.
b Tetragonal prism.
c Dodecahedron.
d Deltahedron.

crys·tal·line (kris′tə·lin, -lēn) *adj.* 1. Of, pertaining to, like, or made of crystal or crystals. 2. Transparent; clear.

crys·tal·lize (kris′tə·līz) *v.* **·lized, ·liz·ing** *v.t.* 1. To cause to form crystals or become crystalline. 2. To bring to definite and permanent form. 3. To coat with sugar. —*v.i.* 4. To assume the form of crystals. 5. To assume definite and permanent form. Also **crys′tal·ize.** — **crys′tal·liz′a·ble** *adj.* — **crys′tal·li·za′tion** *n.*

crystallo- *combining form* Crystal. Also, before vowels, **crystall-.** [< Gk. *krystallos* crystal]

crys·tal·log·ra·phy (kris′tə·log′rə·fē) *n.* The science and study of crystals. — **crys′tal·log′ra·pher** *n.*

crys·tal·loid (kris′tə·loid) *adj.* Like or having the nature of a crystal or a crystalloid. Also **crys′tal·loi′dal.** — *n. Chem.* One of a class of substances, usu. crystallizable, whose solutions pass easily through membranes. [< Gk. *krystalloeidēs* like crystal]

crystal pickup A pickup that utilizes a piezoelectric crystal to transform mechanical motion into sound, etc., often used in electric record players.

crystal set A radio receiving set operating with a crystal detector but without electron tubes.

cub (kub) *n.* 1. The young of the bear, fox, wolf, and certain other carnivores; a whelp. 2. An awkward youth. 3. A beginner or learner. [Origin uncertain]

cub·by·hole (kub′ē·hōl′) *n.* A small, enclosed space. Also **cub′by.** [< *cubby,* dim. of dial. E *cub* shed + HOLE]

cube (kyōōb) *n.* 1. A solid bounded by six equal squares and having all its angles right angles. 2. *Math.* The third power of a quantity: the *cube* of 3 is 27, or $3^3 = 3 \times 3 \times 3 = 27.$ —*v.t.* **cubed, cub·ing** 1. To raise (a number or quantity) to the third power. 2. To find the cubic capacity of. **3.** To form or cut into cubes or cubelike shapes; dice: to *cube* potatoes. [< OF < L < Gk. *kybos* cube]

cu·beb (kyōō′beb) *n.* A berry of an East Indian shrub of the pepper family, often smoked in the form of cigarettes to treat catarrh. [< OF < Arabic *kabābah*]

cube root The number that, taken three times as a factor, produces a number called its cube: 4 is the *cube root* of 64.

cu·bic (kyōō′bik) *adj.* **1.** Shaped like a cube. **2.** Having three dimensions, or pertaining to three-dimensional content: a *cubic* foot. **3.** *Math.* Of the third power or degree.

cu·bi·cal (kyōō′bi·kəl) *adj.* Shaped like a cube. — **cu′bi·cal·ly** *adv.* — **cu′bi·cal·ness** *n.*

cu·bi·cle (kyōō′bi·kəl) *n.* **1.** A bedroom, esp. a partially enclosed section in a dormitory. **2.** Any small partitioned area, as a carrell. [< L *cubiculum* bedroom]

cubic measure A unit or system of units for measuring volume, or the amount of space occupied in three dimensions. See table front of book.

cu·bism (kyōō′biz·əm) *n.* A movement in modern art concerned with the abstract and geometric interpretation of form, rather than with a realistic representation of nature. — **cu′bist** *adj. & n.* — **cu·bis′tic** *adj.*

cu·bit (kyōō′bit) *n.* An ancient measure of length, usu. about 18 to 20 inches. [< L *cubitum* elbow]

cu·boid (kyōō′boid) *adj.* Shaped like a cube. Also **cu·boi′·dal.** — *n. Geom.* A rectangular parallelepiped.

cub reporter A young, inexperienced newspaper reporter.

cub scout A member of a subdivision of the Boy Scouts, comprising boys eight to ten years of age.

cuck·old (kuk′əld) *n.* The husband of an unfaithful wife. — *v.t.* To make a cuckold of. [< OF *cucu* cuckoo]

cuck·old·ry (kuk′əl·drē) *n.* The cuckolding of a husband.

cuck·oo (kōōk′ōō; *for adj., also* kōō′kōō) *n.* **1.** A bird, as the common European cuckoo, that deposits its eggs in the nests of other birds. **2.** A simpleton; fool. **3.** A cuckoo's cry. — *v.* **·ooed, ·oo·ing** *v.t.* **1.** To repeat without cessation. — *v.i.* **2.** To utter or imitate the cry of the cuckoo. — *adj. Slang* Crazy; silly. [< OF *cucu, coucou;* imit.]

cuckoo clock A clock in which a mechanical cuckoo announces the hours.

cuckoo spit **1.** A frothy secretion exuded upon plants by certain insect larvae. **2.** An insect that secretes such froth.

cu·cul·late (kyōō′kə·lāt, kyōō·kul′āt) *adj. Bot.* Shaped like a hood as certain leaves. [< LL < L *cucullus* hood]

cu·cum·ber (kyōō′kum·bər) *n.* **1.** The cylindrical, hard-rinded fruit of a plant of the gourd family, cultivated as a vegetable. **2.** The plant. [< OF < L *cucumis, -eris*]

cud (kud) *n.* Food forced up into the mouth from the first stomach of a ruminant and chewed over again. [OE *cwidu*]

cud·dle (kud′l) *v.* **·dled, ·dling** *v.t.* **1.** To caress fondly within a close embrace; fondle. — *v.i.* **2.** To lie close; nestle together. — *n.* An embrace or caress; a hug. [? < dial. E *couth* snug] — **cud′dle·some** (-səm) *adj.* — **cud′dly** *adj.*

cud·dy (kud′ē) *n. pl.* **·dies** *Naut.* A small cabin or galley.

cudg·el (kuj′əl) *n.* A short, thick club. — **to take up the cudgels** To enter into a contest or controversy. — *v.t.* **cudg·eled** or **·elled, cudg·el·ing** or **·el·ling** To beat with a cudgel. — **to cudgel one's brains** To think hard; puzzle. [OE *cycgel*] — **cudg′el·er** or **cudg′el·ler** *n.*

cue¹ (kyōō) *n.* **1.** A long, tapering rod, used to strike the cue ball. **2.** A queue of hair. **3.** A queue of persons. — *v.t.* **cued, cu·ing** **1.** To braid, or tie into a cue. **2.** In billiards, etc., to hit with a cue. [< F *queue* tail]

cue² (kyōō) *n.* **1.** In plays, movies, etc., any action or sound that signals the start of another action, speech, etc. **2.** Anything that serves as a signal to begin. **3.** A hint or suggestion. **4.** State of mind; mood. — *v.t.* **cued, cu·ing** To call a cue to (an actor); prompt. [Earlier *Q, qu,* supposedly an abbreviation of L *quando* when]

cue ball The ball struck by the cue in billiards or pool.

cuff¹ (kuf) *n.* **1.** A band or fold at the lower end of a sleeve. **2.** *U.S.* The turned-up fold on the bottom of a trouser leg. **3.** A detachable band of fabric worn about the wrist. **4.** A handcuff. — **off the cuff** *U.S. Slang* Spontaneously. — **on the cuff** *U.S. Slang* On credit. [ME *cuffe, coffe*]

cuff² (kuf) *v.t.* **1.** To strike, as with the open hand; buffet. — *v.i.* **2.** To scuffle or fight; box. — *n.* A blow, esp. with the open hand. [? < Scand.]

cuff links Linked buttons or the like, used to fasten shirt cuffs.

cui bo·no (kwē′ bō′nō, kī′) *Latin* For whose benefit? Also, inaccurately, for what purpose?

cui·rass (kwi·ras′) *n.* A piece of armor consisting of a breastplate and backplate; also, the breastplate alone. — *v.t.* To equip with a cuirass. [< MF, ult. < L < *corium* leather]

cui·ras·sier (kwi′rə·sir′) *n.* A mounted soldier wearing a cuirass.

cui·sine (kwi·zēn′) *n.* **1.** The style or quality of cooking. **2.** The food prepared. [< F < L < *coquere* to cook]

cuisse (kwis) *n.* A piece of plate armor for the thigh. Also **cuish** (kwish). [< OF < *cuisse* thigh < L *coxa* hip]

cul-de-sac (kul′də·sak′, kōōl′-; *Fr.* kü′də·säk′) *n. pl.* **cul-de-sacs,** *Fr.* **culs-de-sac** (kü-) A passage open only at one end; blind alley; trap. [< F, bottom of the bag]

-cule *suffix of nouns* Small; little; *animalcule.* [< F < L *-culus,* dim. suffix]

cu·li·nar·y (kyōō′lə·ner′ē, kul′-) *adj.* Of or pertaining to cookery or the kitchen. [< L < *culina* kitchen]

cull (kul) *v.t.* **1.** To pick or sort out; select. **2.** To gather. **3.** To pick over and divide as to quality. — *n.* Something picked or sorted out, esp. something rejected as inferior. [< OF < L *colligere* to collect] — **cull′er** *n.*

culm¹ (kulm) *n. Bot.* The jointed, usu. hollow, stem or straw of grasses. — *v.i.* To form a culm. [< L *culmus* stalk] — **culm·if·er·ous** (kul·mif′ər·əs) *adj.*

culm² (kulm) *n.* **1.** Coal refuse or dust. **2.** An inferior anthracite coal. [Var. of dial. *coom* soot]

cul·mi·nate (kul′min·āt) *v.i.* **·nat·ed, ·nat·ing** **1.** To reach the highest point or degree; come to a final result: with *in.* **2.** *Astron.* To reach the meridian. [< LL < L *culmen,* highest point] — **cul′mi·nant** *adj.*

cul·mi·na·tion (kul′mə·nā′shən) *n.* **1.** The act of culminating. **2.** The highest point, condition, or degree.

cu·lottes (kyōō·lots′, kōō-; *Fr.* kü·lôt′) *n.pl.* A woman's trouserlike garment cut to resemble a skirt. [< F]

cul·pa·ble (kul′pə·bəl) *adj.* Deserving of blame or censure. [< OF < L < *culpa* fault] — **cul′pa·bil′i·ty, cul′pa·ble·ness** *n.* — **cul′pa·bly** *adv.*

cul·prit (kul′prit) *n.* **1.** One guilty of some offense or crime. **2.** One charged with or arraigned for a crime. [AF *cul prit,* short for *culpable* guilty + *prit* ready for trial]

cult (kult) *n.* **1.** A system of religious rites and observances. **2.** Zealous devotion to a person, ideal, or thing. **3.** The object of this devotion. **4.** The followers of a cult. [< F < L < *colere* to cultivate, worship]

cul·ti·va·ble (kul′tə·və·bəl) *adj.* Capable of cultivation. Also **cul′ti·vat·a·ble** (-vā′tə·bəl). — **cul′ti·va·bil′i·ty** *n.*

cul·ti·vate (kul′tə·vāt) *v.t.* **·vat·ed, ·vat·ing** **1.** To make fit for raising crops, as by plowing, fertilizing, etc.; till. **2.** To care for (plants, etc.) so as to promote growth and abundance. **3.** To raise from seeds, bulbs, etc., for later planting. **4.** To produce or improve (plants, etc.) by selective breeding or other techniques. **5.** To improve or develop by study, or training; refine: to *cultivate* one's mind. **6.** To give one's attention to in order to acquire: to *cultivate* a habit, good manners, etc. **7.** To promote the development or advancement of. **8.** To court the friendship of. [< Med.L < L *cultus,* pp. of *colere* to care for, cherish] — **cul′ti·vat·ed** *adj.*

cul·ti·va·tion (kul′tə·vā′shən) *n.* **1.** The act of cultivating the ground, plants, etc. **2.** The improvement or development of anything through study and effort. **3.** Culture; refinement. — **Syn.** See REFINEMENT.

cul·ti·va·tor (kul′tə·vā′tər) *n.* **1.** One who cultivates. **2.** *Agric.* A machine for cultivating, commonly having several blades that loosen the ground and destroy weeds

cul·tur·al (kul′chər·əl) *adj.* **1.** Of, pertaining to, or developing culture: *cultural* studies. **2.** Produced by breeding, as certain varieties of fruits or plants. — **cul′tur·al·ly** *adv.*

cul·ture (kul′chər) *n.* **1.** The cultivation of plants or animals, esp. to improve the breed. **2.** The development, and refinement of mind, morals, or taste. **3.** The condition thus produced; refinement. **4.** A specific stage in the development of a civilization. **5.** Cultivation of the soil. **6.** *Anthropol.* The sum total of the attainments and learned behavior patterns of any specific period, race, or people. **7.** *Biol.* **a** The development of microorganisms in artificial media. **b** The organisms so developed. — **Syn.** See REFINEMENT. — *v.t.* **·tured, ·tur·ing** **1.** To cultivate (plants or animals). **2.** *Biol.* **a** To develop or grow (microorganisms) in an artificial medium. **b** To inoculate with a prepared culture. [< F < L < *colere* to care for] — **cul′tur·ist** *n.*

cul·tured (kul′chərd) *adj.* **1.** Possessing or manifesting culture. **2.** Created or grown by cultivation.

cul·tus (kul′təs) *n. pl.* **·tuses** or **·ti** (-tī) A cult.

cul·ver·in (kul′vər·in) *n.* **1.** A long cannon used in the 16th and 17th centuries. **2.** An early form of musket. [< F < *couleuvre* serpent]

cul·vert (kul′vərt) *n.* An artificial, covered channel for water, as under a road. [Origin uncertain]

cum·ber (kum′bər) *v.t.* **1.** To hinder; obstruct; hamper. **2.** To weigh down; burden. — *n.* A hindrance or encumbrance. [Cf. OF *encombrer* to hinder]

cum·ber·some (kum′bər·səm) *adj.* **1.** Unwieldy; clumsy. **2.** Vexatious; burdensome. — **cum′ber·some·ly** *adv.* — **cum′ber·some·ness** *n.*

cum·brance (kum′brəns) *n.* An encumbrance.
cum·brous (kum′brəs) *adj.* Cumbersome. **—cum′brous·ly** *adv.* **—cum′brous·ness** *n.*
cum·in (kum′in) *n.* **1.** An annual of the parsley family. **2.** Its seeds, used as a condiment. Also **cum′min.** [OE < L < Gk. *kyminon* < Semitic]
cum lau·de (kum lô′dē, kŏŏm lou′de) *Latin* With praise: used on diplomas to denote the special merit of the recipient's work. **—magna cum laude** With high praise. **—summa cum laude** With highest praise.
cum·mer·bund (kum′ər·bund) *n.* A broad sash worn as a waistband. [< Persian < *kamar* loin + *band* band]
cu·mu·late (kyōōm′yə·lāt; *for adj., also* kyōōm′yə·lit) *v.t. & v.i.* **·lat·ed, ·lat·ing** To collect into a heap; accumulate. **—** *adj.* Massed; accumulated. [< L < *cumulus* a heap] **—cu·mu·la′tion** *n.*
cu·mu·la·tive (kyōōm′yə·lā′tiv, -lə·tiv) *adj.* **1.** Gathering volume, strength, or value. **2.** Gained by accumulation: *cumulative* knowledge. **3.** Increasing or accruing, as unpaid interest or dividends. **—cu′mu·la′tive·ly** *adv.*
cu·mu·lo·cir·rus (kyōōm′yə·lō·sir′əs) *n. Meteorol.* Altocumulus.
cu·mu·lo·nim·bus (kyōōm′yə·lō·nim′bəs) *n. Meteorol.* A massive cloud formation (Symbol Cb) in the shape of mountains, and producing thunder and showers.
cu·mu·lo·stra·tus (kyōōm′yə·lō·strā′təs) *n. Meteorol.* Stratocumulus.
cu·mu·lus (kyōōm′yə·ləs) *n. pl.* **·li** (-lī) **1.** A mass; pile. **2.** *Meteorol.* A dense, usu. white cloud formation (Symbol Cu) with dome-shaped upper surfaces and horizontal bases, seen in fair weather. [< L] **—cu′mu·lous** *adj.*
cu·ne·ate (kyōō′nē·it, -āt) *adj.* Wedge-shaped: said esp. of leaves. Also **cu′ne·at′ed, cu·ne·at·ic** (kyōō′nē·at′ik). [< L < *cuneus* wedge] **—cu′ne·ate·ly** *adv.*
cu·ne·i·form (kyōō·nē′ə·fôrm, kyōō′nē·ə·fôrm′) *adj.* **1.** Wedge-shaped, as the characters in some ancient Sumerian, Assyrian, Babylonian, and Persian inscriptions. **2.** *Anat.* Designating a wedge-shaped bone in the wrist, or one of three in the human foot. **—** *n.* Cuneiform writing. Also **cu·ni·form** (kyōō′nə·fôrm). [< L *cuneus* wedge + -FORM]

CUNEIFORM
a Earth. *b* Woman. *c* Man. *d* Food.

cun·ning (kun′ing) *n.* **1.** Skill in deception; craftiness. **2.** Knowledge combined with manual skill; dexterity. **—** *adj.* **1.** Crafty or shrewd. **2.** Executed with skill; ingenious. **3.** *U.S.* Innocently amusing; cute. [OE < *cunnan* to know, be able] **—cun′ning·ly** *adv.* **—cun′ning·ness** *n.*
cup (kup) *n.* **1.** A small, open vessel, often with a handle, used chiefly for drinking from. **2.** The contents of a cup; a cupful: as a measure, equal to 8 ounces or half a pint. **3.** The bowl of a drinking vessel that has a stem and base. **4.** In the Eucharist, the chalice, or its contents. **5.** One's lot in life: the bitter *cup* of exile. **6.** Intoxicating drink, or the habit of drinking. **7.** An alcoholic beverage, usu. chilled and served with herbs, fruits, etc. **8.** A cup-shaped object or part, as of a flower. **9.** A cup-shaped vessel given as a prize, esp. in sports. **10.** In golf, a hole, or the metal receptacle within it. **—in one's cups** Drunk. **—** *v.t.* **cupped, cup·ping 1.** To shape like a cup. **2.** To place in or as in a cup. **3.** *Med.* To perform cupping on. [OE < L *cupa* tub]
cup·bear·er (kup′bâr′ər) *n.* One who serves drinks.
cup·board (kub′ərd) *n.* **1.** A closet or cabinet with shelves, as for dishes. **2.** Any small cabinet or closet.
cup·cake (kup′kāk′) *n.* A small individual cake.
cup·ful (kup′fŏŏl′) *n. pl.* **·fuls** The quantity held by a cup.
Cu·pid (kyōō′pid) In Roman mythology, the god of love: identified with the Greek *Eros.* **—** *n.* **1.** A representation of the god of love as a naked, winged boy with a bow and arrow. **2.** One who helps to arrange meetings between lovers; chiefly in the phrase **to play Cupid.** [< L < *cupido* desire]
cu·pid·i·ty (kyōō·pid′ə·tē) *n.* Eager desire for possession, esp. of wealth; avarice; greed. [< L *cupiditas, -tatis*]
cup of tea *Informal* A favorite object, activity, etc.
cu·po·la (kyōō′pə·lə) *n.* **1.** *Archit.* **a** A rounded roof; dome. **b** A small, vaulted structure, usu. hemispherical, rising above a roof. **2.** Any of various dome-shaped structures, organs, etc. **—** *v.t.* **·laed, ·la·ing** To provide with or shape like a cupola. [< Ital. < LL < L *cupa* tub]
cup·ping (kup′ing) *n. Med.* The process of drawing blood to the surface of the skin by creating a vacuum at that point.
cupping glass *Med.* A cup used for cupping.
cu·pre·ous (kyōō′prē·əs) *adj.* Of, pertaining to, containing, or resembling copper. [< LL < L *cuprum* copper]
cu·pric (kyōō′prik) *adj. Chem.* Of or pertaining to copper, esp. in its highest valence: *cupric* oxide, CuO.
cupro- *combining form* Copper. Also, *before vowels,* **cupri-.**
cu·prous (kyōō′prəs) *adj. Chem.* Of or pertaining to copper, esp. in its lowest valence: *cuprous* oxide, Cu_2O.
cu·prum (kyōō′prəm) *n.* Copper. [< L]

cur (kûr) *n.* **1.** A mongrel dog. **2.** A mean or despicable person. [Short for earlier *kur-dogge*]
cur·a·ble (kyōōr′ə·bəl) *adj.* Capable of being cured. **—cur′a·bil′i·ty, cur′a·ble·ness** *n.* **—cur′a·bly** *adv.*
cu·ra·çao (kyōōr′ə·sō′, kōō′rä·sou′) *n.* A liqueur made by distilling spirits with the peel of the sour orange. Also **cu′·ra·çoa′** (-sō′). [after *Curaçao*]
cu·ra·cy (kyōōr′ə·sē) *n. pl.* **·cies** The position, duties, or term of office of a curate.
cu·ra·re (kyōō·rä′rē) *n.* **1.** A blackish, resinous extract of certain South American trees, that, when introduced into the blood stream, paralyzes the motor nerves; used as an arrow poison and in general anesthesia. **2.** A plant from which this is extracted. Also called *oorali, urare, urari, woorali:* also **cu·ra·ra** (kyōō·rä′rə), **cu·ra·ri.** [< Sp. < Tupi]
cu·rate (kyōōr′it) *n.* A clergyman assisting a parish priest, rector, or vicar. [< Med.L < L *cura* care, cure]
cur·a·tive (kyōōr′ə·tiv) *adj.* Having the power to cure. **—** *n.* A remedy. **—cur′a·tive·ly** *adv.* **—cur′a·tive·ness** *n.*
cu·ra·tor (kyōō·rā′tər) *n.* A person in charge of a museum or similar institution. [< L < *cura* care] **—cu·ra·to·ri·al** (kyōōr′ə·tôr′ē·əl, -tō′rē-) *adj.* **—cu·ra′tor·ship** *n.*
curb (kûrb) *n.* **1.** Anything that restrains or controls: a *curb* on inflation. **2.** A border of concrete or stone along the edge of a street: also, *Brit.,* **kerb. 3.** A chain or strap bracing a bit against the lower jaw of a horse, used to check the horse. **4.** An enclosing or confining framework, margin, etc. **—** *v.t.* **1.** To control, as with reins and curb. **2.** To provide with a curb. **3.** To lead (a dog) off a curb for defecation in the street. [< F *courbe,* orig. adj., curved < L *curvus*]
curb·ing (kûr′bing) *n.* Material forming a curb.
curb roof *Archit.* A roof consisting of two slopes of varying pitch; a mansard or gambrel roof.
curb·stone (kûrb′stōn′) *n.* A stone, row of stones, etc., on the outer edge of a sidewalk. Also, *Brit.,* **kerbstone.**
cur·cu·li·o (kûr·kyōō′lē·ō) *n. pl.* **·os** Any of various long-snouted weevils, injurious to fruits and nuts. [< L, weevil]
curd (kûrd) *n. Often pl.* The coagulated portion of milk, of which cheese is made, as distinct from the watery whey. **—** *v.t. & v.i.* To form into or become curd. [Metathetic var. of CRUD] **—curd′y** *adj.*
cur·dle (kûr′dəl) *v.t. & v.i.* **·dled, ·dling** To change or turn to curd; coagulate; congeal; thicken. [Freq. of CURD]
cure (kyōōr) *n.* **1.** A restoration to a sound or healthy condition. **2.** That which restores health or removes an evil. **3.** A special method or course of remedial or medicinal treatment. **4.** Spiritual care, esp. of a clergyman for his congregation: also **cure of souls. 5.** A process of preserving food or other products. **—** *v.* **cured, cur·ing** *v.t.* **1.** To restore to a healthy or sound condition. **2.** To remedy or eradicate: to *cure* a bad habit. **3.** To preserve, as by salting, smoking, or aging. **—** *v.i.* **4.** To bring about recovery. **5.** To be or become cured by a preserving process. [< OF < L *cura* care] **—cure′less** *adj.* **—cur′er** *n.*
cu·ré (kyōō·rā′) *n.* A parish priest, esp. in France. [< F]
cure-all (kyōōr′ôl′) *n.* A cure for all ills; panacea.
cur·few (kûr′fyōō) *n.* **1.** A police or military regulation requiring persons to keep off the streets after a designated hour; also, a similar order applying to children. **2.** A medieval regulation requiring fires to be put out at the tolling of a bell. **3.** The bell itself. **4.** The hour of ringing such a bell, or the ringing itself. [< OF *couvrir* to cover + *feu* fire]
cu·ri·a (kyōōr′ē·ə) *n. pl.* **cu·ri·ae** (kyōōr′ē·ē) **1.** A court of justice. **2.** *Often cap.* The collective body of officials of the papal government: also **Cu′ri·a Ro·ma·na** (rō·mä′nə). [< L] **—cu′ri·al** *adj.*
cu·rie (kyōōr′ē, kyōō·rē′) *n. Physics* The unit of radioactivity, equal to 3.70×10^{10} nuclear disintegrations per second. [after Marie *Curie*]
cu·ri·o (kyōōr′ē·ō) *n. pl.* **·os** A rare or curious art object, piece of bric-a-brac, etc. [Short for CURIOSITY]
cu·ri·os·i·ty (kyōōr′ē·os′ə·tē) *n. pl.* **·ties 1.** Eager desire for knowledge of something, esp. of something novel or unusual. **2.** Interest in the private affairs of others. **3.** That which excites interest by its strangeness or rarity.
cu·ri·ous (kyōōr′ē·əs) *adj.* **1.** Eager for information or knowledge. **2.** Given to prying or meddling. **3.** Attracting interest because of novelty or unusualness; odd; strange. **4.** Executed with ingenuity or skill. [< OF < L *curiosus* < *cura* care] **—cu′ri·ous·ly** *adv.* **—cu′ri·ous·ness** *n.*
cu·ri·um (kyōōr′ē·əm) *n.* An unstable radioactive element (symbol Cm), produced originally by the bombardment of uranium and plutonium with alpha particles. See ELEMENT. [after Marie and Pierre *Curie*]
curl (kûrl) *v.t.* **1.** To twist into ringlets or curves, as the hair. **2.** To form into a curved or spiral shape. **—** *v.i.* **3.** To form ringlets, as the hair. **4.** To become curved; take a spiral shape. **5.** To play at the game of curling. **—to curl up 1.** To assume a position with the back curved and the legs drawn close to the body. **2.** To form into a curved or spiral shape. **—** *n.* **1.** Something coiled or spiral, as a ring-

let of hair.   **2.** A curled or circular shape or mark.   **3.** The act of curling, or the state of being curled. [Metathetic var. of ME *crollid, crulled* curled < *crull* curly < MLG]

curl·er (kûr′lər)   *n.*   **1.** One who or that which curls.   **2.** One who plays the game of curling.

cur·lew (kûr′lōō)   *n.* A shore bird with a long bill and long legs. [< OF *corlieu, courlieus*; orig. imit.]

curl·i·cue (kûr′li·kyōō)   *n.* Any fancy curl or twist, as a flourish with a pen. Also **curl′y·cue.**

curl·ing (kûr′ling)   *n.* A game played on ice in which the opposing players slide heavy, smooth, circular stones (**curling stones**) toward a goal or tee at either end.

curling iron An implement of metal, used when heated for curling or waving the hair. Also **curling irons.**

curl·y (kûr′lē)   *adj.* **1.** Having curls.   **2.** Tending to curl.   **3.** Containing curllike marks: *curly* maple.   — **curl′i·ness** *n.*

cur·mudg·eon (kər·muj′ən)   *n.* A gruff or irritable person, esp. an elderly man. [Origin unknown]

cur·rant (kûr′ənt)   *n.*   **1.** A small, round, acid berry, used for making jelly.   **2.** The bush producing this berry.   **3.** A small seedless raisin of the Levant. [Back formation < AF (*raisins de*) *Corauntz* (raisins from) Corinth]

cur·ren·cy (kûr′ən·sē)   *n.*   *pl.* **·cies 1.** The current medium of exchange; money.   **2.** General acceptance or circulation.   **3.** The time during which something is current.

cur·rent (kûr′ənt)   *adj.* **1.** Belonging to the immediate present: the *current* year.   **2.** Passing from person to person; circulating, as money or news.   **3.** Generally accepted; prevalent.   — *n.* **1.** A continuous onward movement, as of water.   **2.** The part of any body of water or air that has a more or less steady flow in a definite direction: an ocean *current.*   **3.** Any perceptible course or trend.   **4.** *Electr.* **a** A movement or flow of electricity passing through a conductor. **b** The rate at which it flows.   — **alternating current** *Electr.* A current that periodically reverses its direction of flow, each complete cycle having the same value. Abbr. *AC, a.c., A.C.*   — **direct current** *Electr.* A current flowing in one direction. Abbr. *DC, d.c., D.C.*   [< OF < L *currere* to run]   — **cur′rent·ly** *adv.*   — **cur′rent·ness** *n.*

cur·ric·u·lum (kə·rik′yə·ləm)   *n.*   *pl.* **·lums** or **·la** (-lə) **1.** All the courses of study offered at a university or school.   **2.** A regular or particular course of study. [< L, a race < *currere* to run]   — **cur·ric′u·lar** *adj.*

cur·ry¹ (kûr′ē)   *v.t.* **·ried, ·ry·ing 1.** To rub down and clean with a currycomb.   **2.** To dress (tanned hides) by soaking, smoothing, etc.   — **to curry favor** To seek favor by flattery, etc.   [< OF *correier, conreder* to prepare]

cur·ry² (kûr′ē)   *n.*   *pl.* **·ries 1.** A pungent sauce of East Indian origin.   **2.** A dish of meat, fish, etc., cooked with this sauce.   **3.** Curry powder.   — *v.t.* **·ried, ·ry·ing** To flavor with curry.   [< Tamil *kari* sauce]

cur·ry·comb (kûr′ē·kōm′)   *n.* A comb consisting of a series of teeth or upright serrated ridges, for grooming horses, etc.   — *v.t.* To comb with a currycomb.

curry powder A condiment prepared from pungent spices, turmeric, etc., used in making curry and curried dishes.

curse (kûrs)   *n.*   **1.** An appeal for evil or injury to befall another, as through the intercession of God or gods.   **2.** The evil or injury so invoked.   **3.** Any profane oath; imprecation.   **4.** A source of calamity or evil.   **5.** Something cursed.   — *v.* **cursed** (kûrst) or **curst, curs·ing** *v.t.* **1.** To invoke evil or injury upon; damn.   **2.** To swear at.   **3.** To cause evil or injury to; afflict.   — *v.i.* **4.** To utter curses; swear.   [OE < OIrish *cursagim* to blame]

curs·ed (kûrst; *for adj., also* kûr′sid) A past tense and past participle of CURSE.   — *adj.* **1.** Under a curse.   **2.** Deserving a curse; wicked.   Also **curst.**   — **curs′ed·ly** *adv.*   — **curs′ed·ness** *n.*

cur·sive (kûr′siv)   *adj.* Running; flowing: said of writing in which the letters are joined.   — *n.* **1.** A cursive character.   **2.** *Printing* A typeface resembling handwriting. [< Med.L < L *currere* to run]   — **cur′sive·ly** *adv.*

cur·so·ry (kûr′sər·ē)   *adj.* Rapid and superficial. [< LL < L *currere* to run]   — **cur′so·ri·ly** *adv.*   — **cur′so·ri·ness** *n.*

curt (kûrt)   *adj.* **1.** Brief and abrupt; esp., rudely brief: a *curt* nod.   **2.** Short or shortened.   — **Syn.** See BLUNT.   [< L *curtus* shortened]   — **curt′ly** *adv.*   — **curt′ness** *n.*

cur·tail (kər·tāl′)   *v.t.* To cut off or cut short; reduce. [< obs. *curtal* cut short]   — **cur·tail′er** *n.*   — **cur·tail′ment** *n.*

cur·tain (kûr′tən)   *n.* **1.** A piece or pieces of cloth, etc. hanging in a window or opening, usu. capable of being drawn to the sides or raised.   **2.** Something that conceals or separates like a curtain: the *curtain* of darkness.   **3.** *pl. Slang* Ruin; death.   — *v.t.* To provide, shut off, or conceal with or as with a curtain.   [< OF < LL *cortina*]

curtain call Prolonged applause of an audience at the end of a play, scene, etc., as a call for the performers to reappear and acknowledge it; also, their reappearance.

curtain raiser   **1.** A short play or sketch presented before a longer or more important play.   **2.** Any introductory event.

curtain wall *Archit.* An outside wall providing enclosure but giving no structural support.

curt·sy (kûrt′sē)   *n.*   *pl.* **·sies** A bending of the knees and lowering of the body as a gesture of civility or respect, performed by women: sometimes spelled *courtesy.*   — *v.i.* **·sied, ·sy·ing** To make a curtsy. Also **curt′sey.** [Var. of COURTESY]

cur·va·ceous (kûr·vā′shəs)   *adj. U.S. Informal* Having voluptuous curves; shapely: said of a woman.

cur·va·ture (kûr′və·chər)   *n.* **1.** The act of curving, or the state of being curved.   **2.** *Physiol.* A curving, esp. when abnormal: *curvature* of the spine.   [< L *curvare* to bend]

curve (kûrv)   *n.* **1.** A line continuously bent, as the arc of a circle.   **2.** A curving, or something curved.   **3.** An instrument for drawing curves.   **4.** *Math.* The locus of a point moving in such a way that its course can be defined by an equation.   **5.** In baseball, a ball pitched with a spin that causes it to veer to one side.   **6.** A grading system based upon a theoretical frequency distribution.   — *v.* **curved, curv·ing** *v.t.* **1.** To cause to assume the form of or move in the path of a curve.   — *v.i.* **2.** To assume the form of a curve.   **3.** To move in a curve.   — *adj.* Curved.   [< L *curvus* bent]   — **curv′ed·ly** *adv.*   — **curv′ed·ness** *n.*

cur·vet (*n.* kûr′vit; *v.* kər·vet′, kûr′vit)   *n.* A light, low leap of a horse, made so that all four legs are off the ground at one time.   — *v.* **cur·vet·ted** or **·vet·ed, cur·vet·ting** or **·vet·ing** *v.i.* **1.** To make a curvet.   **2.** To prance; frisk.   — *v.t.* **3.** To cause to curvet.   [< Ital. < L *curvus* bent]

curvi- *combining form* Curved.   [< L *curvus* curved]

cur·vi·lin·e·ar (kûr′və·lin′ē·ər)   *adj.* Formed or enclosed by curved lines. Also **cur′vi·lin′e·al.**

cush·ion (kŏŏsh′ən)   *n.* **1.** A flexible bag or casing filled with some soft or elastic material, as feathers, air, etc., used for lying or resting on.   **2.** Anything resembling a cushion in appearance or use; esp., any device to deaden the jar or impact of parts, as padding, etc.   **3.** The elastic rim of a billiard table.   **4.** *Canadian* The ice of a hockey rink.   — *v.t.* **1.** To seat or arrange on or as on a cushion.   **2.** To provide with a cushion.   **3.** To absorb the shock or effect of.   [< F *coussin,* ult. < L *coxa* hip, thigh]   — **cush′ion·y** *adj.*

Cush·it·ic (kŏŏsh·it′ik)   *n.* A group of Hamitic languages spoken in Ethiopia and Somaliland.   — *adj.* Pertaining to this group of languages.   Also spelled *Kushitic.*

cush·y (kŏŏsh′ē)   *adj. Slang* **cush·i·er, cush·i·est** Comfortable; agreeable; easy.   [< CUSHION; orig. Brit. slang]

cusp (kusp)   *n.* **1.** A point or pointed end.   **2.** Either point of a crescent moon.   **3.** *Geom.* A point at which two branches of a curve meet and end, with a common tangent.   [< L *cuspis, -idis* a point]   — **cus·pate** (kus′pāt), **cus′pated, cusped** (kuspt) *adj.*

cus·pid (kus′pid)   *n.* A canine tooth.

cus·pi·date (kus′pə·dāt)   *adj.* Having a cusp or cusps. Also **cus·pi·dal** (kus′pə·dəl), **cus′pi·dat′ed.**

cus·pi·dor (kus′pə·dôr)   *n.* A spittoon.   [< Pg. < L < com- thoroughly + *spuere* to spit]

cuss (kus)   *U.S. Informal v.t. & v.i.* To curse.   — *n.* **1.** A curse.   **2.** A perverse person or animal.   [Var. of CURSE]   — **cuss·ed** (kus′id) *adj.*   — **cuss′ed·ly** *adv.*   — **cuss′ed·ness** *n.*

cus·tard (kus′tərd)   *n.* A mixture of milk, eggs, sugar, and flavoring, either boiled or baked.   [< F < L *crusta* crust]

cus·to·di·an (kus·tō′dē·ən)   *n.* A guardian; caretaker.   — **cus·to′di·an·ship′** *n.*

cus·to·dy (kus′tə·dē)   *n.*   *pl.* **·dies 1.** A keeping; guardianship.   **2.** The state of being held in keeping or under guard.   [< L < *custos* guardian]   — **cus·to·di·al** (kus·tō′dē·əl) *adj.*

cus·tom (kus′təm)   *n.* **1.** The habitual practice of a community or a people.   **2.** An ordinary or usual manner of doing or acting; habit.   **3.** *Law* An old and general usage that has obtained the force of law.   **4.** Habitual patronage, as of a hotel, store, etc.   **5.** *pl.* A tariff or duty upon imported or, rarely, exported goods; also, the agency of the government that collects such duties.   — *adj.* **1.** Made to order.   **2.** Specializing in made-to-order goods.   [< OF < L < com- thoroughly + *suescere* to become used to]

cus·tom·ar·y (kus′tə·mer′ē)   *adj.* **1.** Conforming to or established by custom; usual; habitual.   **2.** *Law* Holding or held by custom, as a feudal estate.   — *n.*   *pl.* **·ar·ies** A written statement of laws and customs. [See CUSTOM.]   — **cus·tom·ar·i·ly** (kus′tə·mer′ə·lē, kus′tə·mer′ə·lē) *adv.*

cus·tom-built (kus′təm·bilt′)   *adj.* Built to order or to individual specifications: a *custom-built* boat.

cus·tom·er (kus′təm·ər)   *n.* **1.** One who buys something; esp., one who deals regularly at a given establishment.   **2.** *Informal* One to be dealt with: a queer *customer.*

cus·tom·house (kus′təm·hous′)   *n.* The government office where duties are collected and vessels cleared for entering or leaving. Also **custom house.**

---

cus·tom-made (kus'təm-mād') *adj.* Made to order.
cus·toms union (kus'təmz) An association of nations that remove tariff restrictions among themselves and have a common tariff policy toward other nations: also *common market.*
cut (kut) *v.* **cut, cut·ting** *v.t.* **1.** To open or penetrate with a sharp edge; gash; pierce. **2.** To divide with a sharp edge into parts or segments. **3.** To make or shape by cutting, as gems. **4.** To fell or hew: often with *down.* **5.** To strike sharply, as with a whip. **6.** To hurt the feelings of. **7.** *Informal* To pretend not to know; snub. **8.** *Informal* To absent oneself from: to *cut* a class. **9.** To cross or intersect. **10.** To shorten or trim, as hair, grass, etc. **11.** To shorten or edit by removing parts. **12.** To mow or reap (wheat, etc.) **13.** To reduce or lessen: to *cut* prices. **14.** To dilute or weaken, as whisky. **15.** To dissolve or break down: to *cut* grease. **16.** To have (a new tooth) grow through the gum. **17.** In certain games, to strike the ball so as to deflect it to one side. **18.** To divide (a pack of cards), as before dealing. — *v.i.* **19.** To make an incision. **20.** To act as a sharp edge. **21.** To penetrate like a knife. **22.** To veer sharply in one's course. **23.** To go by the shortest and most direct route: with *across, through,* etc. **24.** In certain sports and games, to deflect the ball. **25.** To grow through the gum: said of teeth. **26.** To divide a pack of cards, as before dealing. **— to cut back 1.** To shorten by removing the end. **2.** To reduce or curtail. **3.** To reverse one's direction. **— to cut down 1.** To reduce; curtail. **2.** To kill, as with a sword. **— to cut in 1.** To move into a line or queue abruptly or out of turn. **2.** To interrupt a dancing couple so as to take the place of one partner. **3.** To break in, as on a conversation; interrupt. **— to cut off 1.** To remove or detach by cutting. **2.** To put an end to; stop. **3.** To interrupt. **4.** To intercept. **5.** To disinherit. **— to cut out 1.** To remove by cutting; excise. **2.** To shape by cutting. **3.** To be suited for: He's not *cut out* for the work. **4.** To move sharply from one's course, as in traffic. **5.** To oust and supplant, as a rival. **6.** *Slang* To stop doing; cease. **— to cut up 1.** To cut in pieces. **2.** To affect deeply; distress. **3.** *Informal* To behave in an unruly manner. — *n.* **1.** A severing, slashing, or piercing stroke: a clean *cut.* **2.** The opening or sound made by such a stroke; gash; cleft. **3.** A part cut off; esp. the part of a meat animal. **4.** A deletion or excision of a part. **5.** A passage or channel that has been cut or dug out. **6.** A direct route: a short *cut.* **7.** Something that hurts the feelings, as an insult. **8.** *Informal* A refusal to recognize an acquaintance. **9.** The manner in which a thing is cut; fashion; style: the *cut* of a suit. **10.** A reduction in prices, wages, etc. **11.** *U.S. Slang* A share or commission. **12.** *Informal* An absence from a class at school. **13.** *Printing* An engraved block or plate; also, an impression made from this. **14.** A stroke imparting spin to a ball, as in tennis, billiards, etc. **15.** A cutting of a deck of cards. **16.** *Chem.* A fraction, as of petroleum, obtained in distillation. **— a cut above** A degree better than. — *adj.* **1.** That has been cut off, into, or through: a *cut* finger. **2.** Dressed or finished by a tool, as stone or glass. **3.** Reduced, as rates or prices. **4.** Diluted, as whisky. **— cut and dried 1.** Prepared or arranged beforehand. **2.** Lacking interest or suspense. [ME < Scand.]
cu·ta·ne·ous (kyōō·tā'nē·əs) *adj.* Of, pertaining to, affecting, or like skin. [< Med.L < L *cutis* skin]
cut·a·way (kut'ə·wā') *n.* A man's formal daytime coat, having the front corners cut slopingly away from the waist down to the tails at the back: also **cutaway coat.**
cut·back (kut'bak') *n.* **1.** A sharp reduction, as in personnel or scheduled production. **2.** A reduction.
cute (kyōōt) *adj.* **cut·er, cut·est** *U.S. Informal* Pretty, dainty, or attractive. [Var. of ACUTE] **— cute'ly** *adv.* **— cute'ness** *n.*
cut glass Glass that has been shaped or ornamented by cutting on a wheel of stone, iron, copper, etc.
cu·ti·cle (kyōō'ti·kəl) *n.* **1.** *Anat.* The epidermis. **2.** Any superficial covering. **3.** The crescent of toughened skin around the base of a fingernail or toenail. [< L *cuticula,* dim. of *cutis* skin] **— cu·tic'u·lar** *adj.*
cu·tin (kyōō'tin) *n.* *Bot.* A fatty or waxy protective cuticle of leaves, stems, etc., of plants. [< L *cutis* skin + -IN]
cu·tin·i·za·tion (kyōō'tən·ə·za'shən, -ī·zā'-) *n.* *Bot.* The modification of cell walls by the presence of cutin, making them waterproof.
cu·tin·ize (kyōō'tən·īz) *v.t. & v.i.* **·ized, ·iz·ing** To undergo or cause to undergo cutinization.
cut·lass (kut'ləs) *n.* A short, swordlike weapon, often curved. Also **cut'las.** [< F < L *culter* knife]
cut·ler (kut'lər) *n.* One who makes repairs, or deals in cutlery. [< OF < Med.L < L *cultellus,* dim. of *culter* knife]
cut·ler·y (kut'lər·ē) *n.* **1.** Cutting instruments collectively, esp. those for use at the dinner table. **2.** The occupation of a cutler.
cut·let (kut'lit) *n.* **1.** A thin piece of meat for frying or broiling, usu. veal or mutton. **2.** A flat croquette of chopped meat, fish, etc. [< F < L *costa* rib]

cut·off (kut'ôf', -of') *n.* **1.** The prescribed termination or limit of a process or series. **2.** *U.S.* A shorter route; short cut. **3.** *Mech.* **a** A cutting off of the flow of something, as fluid or steam. **b** The mechanism that does this.
cut·out (kut'out') *n.* **1.** Something cut out or intended to be cut out. **2.** *Electr.* A device that cuts off the current when the flow reaches an unsafe level. **3.** A device to let the exhaust gases from an internal-combustion engine pass directly to the air without going through the muffler.
cut·o·ver (kut'ō'vər) *adj.* Cleared of timber, as land.
cut·purse (kut'pûrs') *n.* A pickpocket; formerly, one who cut away purses that were attached to a girdle or belt.
cut-rate (kut'rāt') *adj.* Sold or selling at reduced prices.
cut·ter (kut'ər) *n.* **1.** One who cuts, esp. one who shapes, fits, decorates, or edits by cutting. **2.** A device that cuts. **3.** *Naut.* **a** A single-masted, fast-sailing vessel of narrow beam and deep draft, and normally spreading no more than four sails. **b** A small, swift, armed, and engined vessel, as used by the Coast Guard for coastal patrol, etc. **c** A small to medium-sized boat either employed by or carried on a larger vessel (such as a warship) and used to discharge passengers, transport stores, etc. **4.** A small sleigh.
cut·throat (kut'thrōt') *adj.* **1.** Bloodthirsty; murderous. **2.** Ruinous; merciless. — *n.* A murderer.
cut·ting (kut'ing) *adj.* **1.** Adapted to cut; edged. **2.** Sharp; chilling. **3.** Unkind; sarcastic. — *n.* **1.** The act of one who or that which cuts. **2.** Something obtained or made by cutting. **3.** *Brit.* A newspaper clipping.
cut·tle·bone (kut'l·bōn') *n.* The internal calcareous plate of a cuttlefish, used as a dietary supplement for birds and, when powdered, as a polishing agent.
cut·tle·fish (kut'l·fish') *n. pl.* **·fish** or **·fish·es** A sea mollusk having lateral fins, ten sucker-bearing arms, a hard inner shell, and concealing itself by ejecting an inky fluid.
cut·up (kut'up') *n. Informal* A person who tries to seem funny, as a practical joker.
cut·wa·ter (kut'wô'tər, -wot'ər) *n.* The forward part of the prow of a vessel.
cut·work (kut'wûrk') *n.* Openwork embroidery with cut-out edges.
cut·worm (kut'wûrm') *n.* Any of several nocturnal caterpillars that cut off plants at the surface of the ground.
-cy *suffix* Forming nouns: **1.** (*from adjectives*) Quality, state, or condition of: *secrecy, bankruptcy.* **2.** (*from nouns*) Rank or condition of: *chaplaincy.* [< F *-cie* < L *-cia* < Gk. *-kia*]
cyan- Var. of CYANO-.
cy·an·ic (sī·an'ik) *adj.* **1.** Of, pertaining to, or containing cyanogen. **2.** Blue.
cy·a·nide (sī'ə·nīd) *n. Chem.* A compound of cyanogen with a metallic element or radical. Also **cy'a·nid** (-nid). — *v.t.* **·nid·ed, ·nid·ing** *Metall.* To subject to the action of cyanide: to extract gold by *cyaniding* the ore. **— cy'a·ni·da'tion** *n.*
cyano- *combining form* **1.** Characterized by bluish coloring: *cyanosis.* **2.** *Chem.* Cyanide. Also, before vowels, **cyan-.** [< Gk. *kyanos* dark blue]
cy·an·o·gen (sī·an'ə·jən) *n. Chem.* **1.** A colorless, flammable, poisonous, liquefiable gas, C_2N_2, having an almondlike odor. **2.** The univalent radical CN. [< F *cyanogène*]
cy·a·no·sis (sī'ə·nō'sis) *n. Pathol.* A disordered condition due to inadequate oxygenation of the bood, causing the skin to look blue. **— cy·a·not·ic** (sī'ə·not'ik) *adj.*
cy·ber·net·ics (sī'bər·net'iks) *n.pl.* (*construed as sing.*) The science that treats of the principles of control and communication as they apply both to the operation of complex machines and the functions of organisms. [< Gk. *kybernetēs* steersman + -ICS] **— cy'ber·net'ic** *adj.*
cy·cad (sī'kad) *n.* Any of a family of primitive, seed-bearing, mostly tropical plants of fernlike or palmlike appearance. [< Gk. *kykas,* erroneous pl. of *koix* a palm tree] —
cyc·a·da·ceous (sik'ə·dā'shəs) *adj.*
cyc·la·men (sik'lə·mən, -men) *n.* An Old World bulbous flowering herb of the primrose family, with white, pink, or crimson flowers. [< NL < L < Gk. *kyklaminos, kyklamis*]
cy·cle (sī'kəl) *n.* **1.** A recurring period within which certain events or phenomena occur in a definite sequence. **2.** A completed round of events or phenomena in which there is a final return to the original state. **3.** A pattern of regularly recurring events. **4.** A vast period of time; an eon. **5.** A body of poems or stories relating to the same character or subject. **6.** A bicycle, tricycle, etc. — *v.i.* **·cled, ·cling 1.** To pass through cycles. **2.** To ride a bicycle, tricycle, etc. [< OF < LL < Gk. *kyklos* circle]
cy·clic (sī'klik, sik'lik) *adj.* **1.** Pertaining to or characterized by cycles; recurring in cycles. **2.** *Chem.* Arranged in a closed chain or ring formation, as the atoms of benzene, naphthalene, etc. Also **cy'cli·cal.**
cy·clist (sī'klist) *n.* One who rides a bicycle, tricycle, etc.
cyclo- *combining form* **1.** Circular. **2.** *Chem.* A cyclic compound. Also, before vowels, **cycl-.** [< Gk *kyklos* circle]
cy·cloid (sī'kloid) *adj.* Resembling a circle or somewhat circular. — *n. Geom.* The curve described by a point on the

circumference of a circle rolling along a straight line in a single plane. [< Gk. *kykloeidēs* circular] — **cy·cloi′dal** *adj.*

cy·clom·e·ter (sī-klom′ə-tər) *n.* An instrument for recording the rotations of a wheel to show speed and distance.

cy·clone (sī′klōn) *n.* **1.** *Meteorol.* A system of winds circulating about a center of relatively low barometric pressure, and advancing at the earth's surface with clockwise rotation in the Southern Hemisphere, counterclockwise in the Northern. **2.** Loosely, any violent storm. [< Gk. < *kyklos* circle] — **cy·clon·ic** (sī-klon′ik) or **-i·cal** *adj.* — **cy·clon′i·cal·ly** *adv.*

cy·clo·pe·an (sī′klə-pē′ən) *adj.* **1.** *Usu. cap.* Of or pertaining to the Cyclopes. **2.** Gigantic: a *cyclopean* task.

cy·clo·pe·di·a (sī′klə-pē′dē·ə) *n.* An encyclopedia (which see). Also **cy′clo·pae′di·a.** — **cy′clo·pe′dic** *adj.* — **cy′clo·pe′di·cal·ly** *adv.* — **cy′clo·pe′dist,** or **cy′clo·pae′dist** *n.*

cy·clo·pro·pane (sī′klə-prō′pān) *n. Chem.* A colorless, pungent, inflammable gas, C_3H_6, used as an anesthetic.

Cy·clops (sī′klops) *n. pl.* **Cy·clo·pes** (sī-klō′pēz) In Homeric legend, any of a race of one-eyed giants of Sicily.

cy·clo·ram·a (sī′klə-ram′ə, -rä′mə) *n.* **1.** A series of pictures on the interior of a cylindrical surface, appearing in natural perspective to a spectator standing in the center. **2.** A backdrop curtain, often concave, used on theater stages. [< CYCLO- + Gk. *horama* a view] — **cy′clo·ram′ic** *adj.*

cy·clo·tron (sī′klə-tron) *n. Physics* An accelerator that obtains high-energy electrified particles by whirling them at very high speeds in a strong magnetic field.

cyg·net (sig′nit) *n.* A young swan. [< MF *cygne* a swan]

Cyg·nus (cig′nəs) *n.* A constellation, the Swan, containing the bright star Deneb: also called *Northern Cross.* [< L]

cyl·in·der (sil′in·dər) *n* **1.** *Geom.* A solid figure generated by one side of a rectangle rotated about the opposite fixed side, the ends of the figure being equal, parallel circles. **2.** Any object or container resembling a cylinder in form. **3.** *Mech.* In a reciprocating engine, the chamber in which the pistons move. **4.** In a revolver, the rotating part that holds the cartridges. — *v.t.* To press or fit with a cylinder. [< L < Gk. < *kylindein* to roll]

cy·lin·dri·cal (si·lin/dri·kəl) *adj.* **1.** Of a cylinder. **2.** Shaped like a cylinder. Also **cy·lin′dric.** Abbr. *cyl.* — **cy·lin·dri·cal·i·ty** (si·lin/dri·kal/ə·tē) *n.* — **cy·lin′dri·cal·ly** *adv.*

cym·bal (sim′bəl) *n.* One of a pair of concave metal plates clashed to produce a musical ringing sound. [OE and OF < L < Gk. *kymbē* cup, hollow of a vessel] — **cym′bal·ist** *n.*

cyme (sīm) *n. Bot* A flat-topped flower cluster in which the central flowers bloom first. [< F < L < Gk *kyma*] — **cy·mose** (sī′mōs, sī mōs′) *adj.*

cymo- *combining form* Wave. [< Gk. *kymo-* < *kyma* wave]

Cym·ric (kim′rik, sim′-) *adj.* Of or pertaining to the Cymry; Brythonic. — *n.* **1.** The Welsh language. **2.** The Brythonic branch of the Celtic languages.

Cym·ry (kim′rē, sim′-) *n.* A collective name for the Welsh and their Cornish and Breton kin: also *Kymry.* Also **Cym′ri.**

cyn·ic (sin′ik) *n.* A sneering, faultfinding person; esp., one who believes that all men are motivated by selfishness. — *adj.* Cynical. [< L < Gk < *kyōn, kynos* dog]

Cyn·ic (sin′ik) *n.* One of a sect of Greek philosophers of the fifth and fourth centuries B.C., who held that virtue was the goal of life. Their doctrine eventually came to represent insolent self-righteousness. — *adj.* Pertaining to or characteristic of the Cynics: also **Cyn′i·cal.**

cyn·i·cal (sin′i·kəl, -ə-) *adj.* Distrusting or contemptuous of virtue in others; sneering; sarcastic. — **cyn′i·cal·ly** *adv.*

cyn·i·cism (sin′ə·siz′əm, -i-) *n.* **1.** Cynical character or attitude; contempt for or disbelief in the virtues of others. **2.** A cynical remark, action, etc. Also **cyn′i·cal·ness.**

cy·no·sure (sī′nə·shŏŏr, sin′ə-) *n.* **1.** A person or object that attracts notice and admiration. **2.** Something that guides. [< MF < L < Gk. < *kyōn, kynos* dog + *oura* tail]

Cy·no·sure (sī′nə·shŏŏr, sin′ə-) *n.* **1.** The constellation Ursa Minor, containing the polestar. **2.** Polaris.

Cyn·thi·a (sin′thē·ə) Artemis. — *n. Poetic* The moon.

cy·pher (sī′fər) See CIPHER.

cy·press [1] (sī′prəs) *n.* **1.** An evergreen tree of the pine family, having flat, scalelike foliage. **2.** A related tree. **3.** The wood of these trees. [< OF < LL < Gk. *kyparissos*]

Cyp·ri·an (sip′rē·ən) *adj.* Of or pertaining to Cyprus. — *n.* A Cypriote.

cyp·ri·noid (sip′rə·noid, si·prī′-) *adj.* Of or pertaining to the carp family of fishes. Also **cy·pri·nid** (si·prī′nid, sip′rə·nid). [< Gk. *kyprinos* carp + -OID]

Cyp·ri·ote (sip′rē·ōt) *n.* **1.** A native or inhabitant of Cyprus. **2.** The ancient or modern Greek dialect of Cyprus. — *adj.* Of or pertaining to Cyprus. Also **Cyp·ri·ot** (sip′rē·ət). [< F *cypriote*]

Cy·ril·lic alphabet (si·ril′ik) A Slavic alphabet based mainly on that of the Greeks, ascribed traditionally to Saint Cyril, used for Russian, Bulgarian, Serbo-Croatian, Ukrainian, Byelorussian, and Macedonian. See ALPHABET.

cyst (sist) *n.* **1.** *Pathol.* Any abnormal sac or vesicle in which matter may collect and be retained. **2.** *Biol.* Any saclike organ in plants or animals. [< Med.L < Gk. *kyein* to contain] — **cys′tic, cys′toid** *adj.*

cys·ti·tis (sis·tī′tis) *n. Pathol.* Inflammation of the bladder.

cysto- *combining form* Bladder; cyst. Also, before vowels, **cyst-:** also **cysti-.** [< Gk. *kystis* bladder]

cys·to·scope (sis′tə·skōp) *n. Med.* A device for examining the interior of the urinary bladder. — **cys·to·scop·ic** (sis′tə·skop′ik) *adj.*

-cyte *combining form* Cell: *phagocyte.* [< Gk. *kytos* hollow vessel]

Cyth·e·re·a (sith′ə·rē′ə) Aphrodite. — **Cyth′e·re′an** *adj.*

cyto- *combining form* Cell. Also, before vowels, **cyt-.** [< Gk. *kytos* hollow vessel < *kyein* to contain, be pregnant with]

cy·to·ge·net·ics (sī′tō·jə·net′iks) *n.pl.* (*construed as sing.*) The study of the role of cells in heredity.

cy·tol·o·gy (sī·tol′ə·jē) *n.* The study of the structure, organization, and function of cells. — **cy·to·log·ic** (sī′tə·loj′ik) or **-i·cal** *adj.* — **cy′to·log′i·cal·ly** *adv.* — **cy·tol′o·gist** *n.*

cy·to·plasm (sī′tə·plaz′əm) *n. Biol.* All the protoplasm of a cell except that in the nucleus. Also **cy′to·plast.**

czar (zär) *n.* **1.** An emperor or king; esp., one of the former emperors of Russia. **2.** An absolute ruler; despot. Also *tsar, tzar.* [< Russ. *tsar′,* ult. < L *Caesar* Caesar] — **czar′dom** *n.* — **czar′ism** *n.* — **czar′ist** *adj. & n.*

czar·e·vitch (zär′ə·vich) *n.* The eldest son of a czar: also *tsarevitch, tzarevitch.* [< Russ. *tsarevich*]

cza·rev·na (zä·rev′nə) *n.* **1.** The wife of the czarevitch. **2.** Formerly, the title of any daughter of the czar. Also *tsarevna, tzarevna.* [< Russ. *tsarevna*]

cza·ri·na (zä·rē′nə) *n.* The wife of a czar; an empress of Russia: also *tsarina, tzarina.* Also **cza·rit·za** (zä·rit′sə) [< G *czarin,* for Russ. *tzaritsa*]

Czech (chek) *n.* **1.** A member of the western branch of Slavs, including the peoples of Bohemia and Moravia. **2.** The West Slavic language of the Czechs, formerly called Bohemian. — *adj.* Relating to Czechoslovakia, the Czechs, or their language: also **Czech′ic, Czech′ish.**

Czech·o·slo·vak (chek′ə·slō′vak, -väk) *n.* A Czech or Slovak inhabiting Czechoslovakia. — *adj.* Of or pertaining to the Czechoslovaks. Also **Czech·o·slo·va·ki·an** (chek′ə·slō·väk′ē·ən, -vak′ē·ən).

D

d, D (dē) *n. pl.* **d's** or **ds, D's** or **Ds, dees** (dēz) **1.** The fourth letter of the English alphabet. **2.** The sound represented by the letter *d.* **3.** Anything shaped like the letter D. — *symbol* **1.** The Roman numeral for 500. **2.** *Music* **a** The second tone in the natural scale of C; re. **b** A written note representing it. **c** The scale built upon D. **3.** *Math.* Differential. **4.** The fourth in a series or group. **5.** Pence **6.** *Chem.* Deuterium (symbol D). **7.** *Physics* Density.

dab [1] (dab) *n.* **1.** Any of various flounders. **2.** Any flatfish.

dab [2] (dab) *n.* **1.** A gentle pat. **2.** A soft, moist patch: a *dab* of paint. **3.** A little bit. — *v.t. & v.i.* **dabbed, dab·bing 1.** To strike softly; tap. **2.** To peck. **3.** To pat with something soft and damp. **4.** To apply (paint, etc.) with light strokes. [ME *dabben*] — **dab′ber** *n.*

dab·chick (dab′chik) *n.* A small grebe of Europe, or the pied-billed grebe of North America.

dab·ble (dab′əl) v. ·bled, ·bling v.i. 1. To play in a liquid, as with the hands; splash gently. 2. To engage oneself slightly or superficially: to *dabble* in art. — v.t. 3. To wet slightly; bespatter. [Freq. of DAB², v.] — **dab′bler** n.

da ca·po (dä kä′pō) *Music* From the beginning: a direction to repeat the opening section of a piece.

dace (dās) n. pl. **dac·es** or **dace** A small fresh-water fish of the carp family. [< L of *dars*, a small fish, lit., dart]

dachs·hund (däks′hŏont/, daks′hŏond/, dash′-) n. A breed of dog native to Germany, having a long, compact body, short legs, and a short coat, usu. of red, tan, or black and tan. [< G < *dachs* badger + *hund* dog]

Da·cron (dā′kron, dak′ron) n. A synthetic polyester textile fiber of high tensile strength, having great resistance to stretching and wrinkling: a trade name. Also **da′cron**.

DACHSHUND
(7 to 9 inches high at shoulder)

dac·tyl (dak′təl) n. In prosody, a metrical foot consisting of one long or accented syllable followed by two short or unaccented ones (—◡◡). [< L < Gk. *daktylos* finger, dactyl] — **dac·tyl·ic** (dak·til′ik) adj. & n.

dactylo- *combining form* Finger; toe. Also, before vowels, **dactyl-**. [< L < Gk. *daktylos* finger]

dad (dad) n. *Informal* Father. Also **dad·dy** (dad′ē). [Origin unknown]

da·da (dä′dä, -də) n. *Often cap.* A movement in art and literature, occurring esp. in France, Germany, and Switzerland about 1916–20, that protested against civilization and violently satirized all previous art. Also **da′da·ism**. [< F *dada*, a nonsense word] — **da′da·ist** n. — **da·da·ist′ic** adj.

dad·dle (dad′l) v.t. & v.i. ·dled, ·dling Diddle¹.

dad·dy-long·legs (dad′ē·lông′legz′, -long′-) n. pl. ·legs A longlegged insect resembling a spider: also called *harvestman*.

da·do (dā′dō) n. pl. ·does 1. *Archit.* The part of a pedestal between the base and the cornice; the die. 2. The lower part of an interior wall, often ornamented. [< Ital., a cube]

Daed·a·lus (ded′ə·ləs, *Brit.* dē′də-) In Greek mythology, an Athenian architect who devised the Cretan Labyrinth in which he was later imprisoned with his son Icarus, and from which they escaped by artificial wings.

daf·fo·dil (daf′ə·dil) n. A plant of the amaryllis family, with solitary yellow flowers. Also *Dial.* or *Poetic* **daf·fa·dil·ly** (daf′ə·dil′ē), **daf·fa·down·dil·ly** (daf′ə·doun-dil′ē), **daf·fy·down·dil·ly** (daf′ē-). [Var. of ME *affodile*]

daf·fy (daf′ē) adj. **daf·fi·er, daf·fi·est** *Informal* Crazy; silly; zany. [< DAFF²]

daft (daft, däft) adj. 1. *Chiefly Brit.* Of weak mind; insane. 2. *Chiefly Brit.* Foolish; silly. [OE *gedæfte* mild, meek] — **daft′ly** adv. — **daft′ness** n.

dag·ger (dag′ər) n. 1. A short, pointed and edged weapon for stabbing. 2. *Printing* A reference mark (†). — **double dagger** *Printing* A reference mark (‡); a diesis. — **to look daggers (at)** To glare or scowl (at). — v.t. 1. To stab. 2. *Printing* To mark with a dagger. [? ME *dag* to stab]

da·go (dā′gō) n. pl. ·gos or ·goes *U.S. Slang* An Italian, or less commonly, a Spaniard or Portuguese: an offensive term. [Alter. of Sp. *Diego*, a personal name]

da·guerre·o·type (də·ger′ə·tīp′, -ē·ə·tīp′) n. 1. An early photographic process using silver-coated metallic plates that were sensitive to light. 2. A picture made by this process. [after Louis Jacques Mandé *Daguerre*, 1789–1851, French inventor] — **da·guerre′o·typ′er, da·guerre′o·typ′ist** n. — **da·guerre′o·typ′y** n.

dahl·ia (dal′yə, däl′-, dāl′-) n. A tender perennial plant of the composite family, having tuberous roots and showy red, purple, yellow, or white flowers; also, the flowers. [after Anders *Dahl*, 18th c. botanist]

Dail Ei·reann (dô·əl âr′ən) The lower house of the legislature of Ireland.

dai·ly (dā′lē) adj. Of, occurring, or appearing every day or every weekday. — n. pl. ·lies A daily publication. — adv. Day after day; on every day. [OE *dæg* day]

dain·ty (dān′tē) adj. ·ti·er, ·ti·est 1. Delicately pretty or graceful. 2. Of pleasing taste; delicious. 3. Of fine sensibilities; fastidious; also, too fastidious; overnice. — n. pl. ·ties Something tasty or delicious; a delicacy. [< OF < L *dignitas* worth, dignity] — **dain′ti·ly** adv. — **dain′ti·ness** n.

dai·qui·ri (dī′kər·ē, dak′ər-ē) n. A cocktail made of rum, lime or lemon juice, and sugar. [after *Daiquiri*, Cuba]

dair·y (dâr′ē) n. pl. ·ies 1. A commercial establishment that sells milk products. 2. A room or building on a farm where milk and cream are kept and processed. 3. A dairy farm or dairy cattle. 4. Dairying. [ME *deie* dairymaid]

dairy cattle Cows of a breed adapted for milk production.

dairy farm A farm for producing dairy products.

dair·y·ing (dâr′ē·ing) n. The business of a dairy.

dair·y·maid (dâr′ē mād′) n. A female worker in a dairy.

dair·y·man (dâr′ē·mən) n. pl. ·men (-mən) A man who works in or owns a dairy.

da·is (dā′is, dās) n. A raised platform in a room or hall on which a speaker, eminent guests, etc., may sit or stand. [< OF *deis* < LL *discus* table]

dai·sy (dā′zē) n. pl. ·sies 1. Any of various plants of the composite family; esp., the **oxeye daisy**, of the U.S., having a yellow disk and white rays, and the **English daisy**, having a small yellow disk and numerous white or rose rays. 2. *Slang* Something excellent or exceptional. [OE *dægas ēage* day's eye] — **dai′sied** adj.

Da·ko·ta (də·kō′tə) n. 1. A member of the largest division of the Siouan stock of North American Plains Indians, now on reservations in North and South Dakota, Minnesota, and Montana. 2. The Siouan language of the Dakotas. 3. A Sioux Indian. — **Da·ko′tan** adj. & n.

Da·lai La·ma (dä·lī′ lä′mə) The pontiff of the principal Buddhist faith in Tibet, and traditional chief of state.

dale (dāl) n. A small valley. [OE *dæl*]

dal·li·ance (dal′ē·əns) n. 1. Amorous play, flirting, or fondling. 2. Idle wasting of time; trifling.

dal·ly (dal′ē) v. ·lied, ·ly·ing v.i. 1. To make love sportively; frolic. 2. To play; trifle. 3. To waste time. — v.t. 4. To waste (time): with *away*. [< OF *dalier* to converse, chat] — **dal′li·er** n.

Dal·ma·tian (dal·mā′shən) n. 1. A large, short-haired dog, white with black spots: also called *coach dog*. 2. One of the Slavic people of Dalmatia. — adj. Of or pertaining to Dalmatia or its people.

dal·mat·ic (dal·mat′ik) n. *Eccl.* A wide-sleeved vestment worn by a deacon over the alb, as at High Mass. [< OF < L *dalmatica* (*vestis*) Dalmatian (robe)]

dal se·gno (däl sā′nyō) *Music* From the sign: a direction to repeat from the sign :S: to the end. [< Ital.]

dam¹ (dam) n. 1. A barrier to obstruct or control the flow of water. 2. The water held back by such a barrier. 3. Any obstruction. — v.t. **dammed, dam·ming** 1. To erect a dam in; obstruct or confine by a dam. 2. To keep back; restrain: with *up* or *in*. [ME. Akin to OE *demman* to block.]

dam² (dam) n. A female parent: said of animals. [< DAME]

dam·age (dam′ij) n. 1. Injury to person or property. 2. pl. *Law* Money to compensate for an injury or wrong. 3. *Sometimes pl. Informal* Price or expense. — v. ·aged, ·ag·ing v.t. 1. To cause damage to. — v.i. 2. To be susceptible to damage. [< OF < L *damnum* loss] — **dam′age·a·ble** adj.

dam·as·cene (dam′ə·sēn, dam′ə·sēn′) v.t. ·cened, ·cen·ing To ornament (iron, steel, etc.) with wavy patterns or by inlaying or etching. Also **dam·as·keen** (dam′ə·skēn, dam′ə·skēn′). — adj. Relating to damascening or to damask. — n. Work ornamented by damascening.

Damascus steel A steel with wavy markings, formerly used in swords made at Damascus. Also **damask steel**.

dam·ask (dam′əsk) n. 1. A rich, reversible, elaborately patterned fabric, originally made of silk. 2. A fine, twilled table linen. 3. Damascus steel, or the wavy pattern on such steel. 4. A deep pink or rose color. — adj. 1. Of or from Damascus. 2. Made of Damascus steel or of damask. 3. Deep pink or rose-colored. — v.t. 1. To damascene. 2. To weave or ornament with rich patterns. [after *Damascus*]

damask rose A large, fragrant, pink rose of the Near East.

dame (dām) n. 1. A mature woman; matron. 2. *U.S. Slang* A woman. 3. In Great Britain: a A title of the Order of the British Empire conferred on women, equivalent to that of knight. b The legal title of the wife of a knight or baronet. [< OF < L *domina* lady]

damn (dam) v.t. 1. To pronounce worthless, bad, a failure, etc. 2. To curse or swear at. 3. *Theol.* To condemn to eternal punishment. 4. To pronounce guilty; bring ruin upon. — v.i. 5. To swear; curse. — **to damn with faint praise** To praise so reluctantly as to imply adverse criticism. — n. 1. The saying of "damn" as an oath. 2. The smallest, most contemptible bit. — *interj.* An oath expressive of irritation, disappointment, etc. — adj. & adv. *Informal* Damned. [< OF < L *damnare* to condemn to punishment]

dam·na·ble (dam′nə·bəl) adj. Meriting damnation; detestable; outrageous. [< OF < L *damnare* to condemn] — **dam′na·ble·ness** n. — **dam′na·bly** adv.

dam·na·tion (dam·nā′shən) n. 1. The act of damning, or the state of being damned. 2. *Theol.* Condemnation to eternal punishment; also, eternal punishment. — *interj.* Damn. — **dam·na·to·ry** (dam′nə·tôr′ē, -tō′rē) adj.

damn·dest (dam′dist) *Informal* adj. 1. Most detestable or outrageous: the *damndest* lie. 2. Most extraordinary. — n. The utmost: Do your *damndest*. Also **damned′est**.

damned (damd, *poetic or rhetorical* dam′nid) adj. 1. Doomed; condemned, esp. to eternal punishment. 2. Deserving damnation. — adv. *Informal* Very: *damned* funny.

damn·ing (dam′ing, dam′ning) adj. That damns or condemns; inculpating: *damning* evidence. — **damn′ing·ly** adv.

Dam·o·cles (dam′ə·klēz) In Greek legend, a courtier who was forced to sit at a banquet under a sword suspended by a hair that he might learn the perilous nature of a ruler's life. — **sword of Damocles** Any impending calamity.

Da·mon and Pyth·i·as (dā′mən; pith′ē-əs) In Roman legend, two devoted friends.

damp (damp) *adj.* Somewhat wet; moist. — *n.* **1.** Moisture or moistness; vapor; mist. **2.** Foul air or poisonous gas, especially in a mine. **3.** Depression of spirits. — *v.t.* **1.** To make damp; moisten. **2.** To discourage or dull (energy, ardor, etc.). **3.** To stifle, check, reduce, etc. **4.** *Physics* To reduce the amplitude of (a series of waves). [< MDu., vapor, steam] — **damp′ly** *adv.* — **damp′ness** *n.*

damp·en (dam′pən) *v.t.* **1.** To make damp; moisten. **2.** To check; depress, as ardor or spirits. — *v.i.* **3.** To become damp. — **damp′en·er** *n.*

damp·er (dam′pər) *n.* **1.** One who or that which damps, depresses, or checks. **2.** A flat plate in the flue of a stove, furnace, etc., for controlling the draft. **3.** *Music* **a** A mechanism for stopping the vibrations of the strings in a piano. **b** In brass instruments, a mute.

damp·ish (dam′pish) *adj.* Slightly damp.

dam·sel (dam′zəl) *n.* A young unmarried woman; maiden. Also, *Archaic*, **dam′o·sel.** [< OF *dameisele* gentlewoman]

dam·son (dam′zən, -sən) *n.* **1.** An oval purple plum. **2.** The tree producing it. Also **damson plum.** [ME < L *Damascenum* from Damascus]

Dan (dan) In the Old Testament, a son of Jacob and Bilhah. *Gen.* xxx 6. — *n.* The tribe of Israel descended from him.

Dan (dan) In the Bible, a city at the north end of Palestine.

Dan·a·id (dan′ē-id) *n.* One of the Danaides.

Da·na·i·des (də-nā′ə-dēz) *n.pl.* In Greek mythology, the forty-nine daughters of a King of Argos who murdered their husbands on their bridal night and who were punished by having to draw water in a sieve forever.

dance (dans, däns) *v.* **danced, danc·ing** *v.i.* **1.** To move the body and feet rhythmically, esp. to music. **2.** To move about lightly or excitedly; leap about. **3.** To move up and down jerkily; bob. — *v.t.* **4.** To perform the steps of (a waltz, tango, etc.). **5.** To cause to dance. — **to dance at-tendance** To wait upon another constantly. — *n.* **1.** A series of regular rhythmic steps or movements, usually performed to music. **2.** An act or instance of dancing. **3.** A musical composition for dancing. **4.** A gathering of people for dancing; a ball. [< OF *danser*] — **danc′er** *n.*

dan·de·li·on (dan′də-lī′ən, -dē-) *n.* A widespread plant having yellow flowers and toothed, edible leaves. [< F *dent de lion* lion's tooth; with ref. to the shape of the leaves]

dan·der (dan′dər) *n.* *U.S. Informal* Ruffled temper; anger. — **to get one's dander up** To become angry. [? Var. of Scottish *dunder* to ferment]

dan·di·fy (dan′də-fī) *v.t.* **·fied, ·fy·ing** To cause to resemble a dandy or fop. — **dan′di·fi·ca′tion** *n.*

dan·dle (dan′dəl) *v.t.* **·dled, ·dling** **1.** To move up and down lightly on the knees or in the arms, as an infant or child. **2.** To fondle; caress. [< Ital. *dandolare*] — **dan′dler** *n.*

dan·druff (dan′drəf) *n.* A fine scurf that forms on the scalp and comes off in small scales. [Origin unknown]

dan·dy (dan′dē) *n.* *pl.* **·dies** **1.** A man who is excessively interested in fine clothes and elegant appearance; a fop. **2.** *Informal* A particularly fine specimen of its kind. — *adj.* **1.** Like a dandy; foppish. **2.** *U.S. Informal* Excellent; very fine. [Alter. of *Andy*, a personal name] — **dan′dy·ish** *adj.*

Dane (dān) *n.* A native or inhabitant of Denmark, or a person of Danish descent. [< ON *Danir* the Danes]

Dane·law (dān′lô′) *n.* A ninth-century code of laws established by Danish settlers in NE England; also, the region of England under these laws. Also **Dane′lagh** (-lô′). [OE]

dan·ger (dān′jər) *n.* **1.** Exposure to evil, injury, or loss; peril; risk. **2.** A cause or instance of peril or risk. [< OF, power to harm]

dan·ger·ous (dān′jər-əs) *adj.* Attended with danger; perilous; unsafe. — **dan′ger·ous·ly** *adv.* — **dan′ger·ous·ness** *n.*

dan·gle (dang′gəl) *v.* **·gled, ·gling** *v.i.* **1.** To hang loosely; swing to and fro. **2.** To follow or hover near someone as a suitor or hanger-on. — *v.t.* **3.** To hold so as to swing loosely. — *n.* **1.** Manner or act of dangling. **2.** Something that dangles. Cf. Scand. Cf. Dan. *dangle*.] — **dan′gler** *n.*

Dan·iel (dan′y l) In the Bible, a young Hebrew prophet, captive in Babylon. *Dan.* i 3–6. — *n.* A book of the Old Testament, containing the story and prophecies of Daniel.

Dan·ish (dā′nish) *adj.* Of or pertaining to Denmark, the Danes, or their language. — *n.* The North Germanic language of the Danes. Abbr. *Dan.* [OE *Denisc*]

dank (dangk) *adj.* Unpleasantly damp; cold and wet. [ME *danke*] — **dank′ly** *adv.* — **dank′ness** *n.*

dan·seuse (dän-sœz′) *n.* *pl.* **·seus·es** (-sœ′ziz, *Fr.* -sœz′) A female ballet dancer. [< F, fem. of *danseur*]

Dan·tesque (dan-tesk′) *adj.* Pertaining to or in the style of Dante Alighieri. Also **Dan·te·an** (dan′tē-ən, dan·tē′ən).

Daph·ne (daf′nē) In Greek mythology, a nymph changed into a laurel tree to escape the pursuit of Apollo.

dap·per (dap′ər) *adj.* **1.** Smartly dressed; trim; natty. **2.** Small and active. [< MDu., strong]

dap·ple (dap′əl) *v.t.* **·pled, ·pling** To make spotted or variegated in color. — *adj.* Spotted; variegated: also **dap′pled.** — *n.* **1.** A spot or dot, as on the skin of a horse. **2.** An animal marked with spots. [Origin uncertain]

dap·ple-gray (dap′əl-grā′) *adj.* Gray with a pattern of variegated rounded markings: usu. said of horses.

dare (dâr) *v.* **dared, dar·ing** *v.t.* **1.** To have the courage or boldness to undertake; venture on. **2.** To challenge (someone) to attempt something as proof of courage, etc. **3.** To oppose and challenge; defy. — *v.i.* **4.** To have the courage or boldness to do or attempt something; venture. — **I dare say** I believe (it): also **I dare·say** (dâr′sā). — *n.* A challenge; taunt. [OE *durran*] — **dar′er** *n.*

dare·dev·il (dâr′dev′əl) *n.* One who is recklessly bold. — *adj.* Rash; reckless. — **dare·dev′il·ry, dare·dev′il·try** *n.*

dar·ing (dâr′ing) *adj.* **1.** Brave and adventurous; bold; fearless. **2.** Audacious; presuming. — *n.* Adventurous courage; bravery. — **dar′ing·ly** *adv.* — **dar′ing·ness** *n.*

dark (därk) *adj.* **1.** Having little or no light; dim: a *dark* cave. **2.** Giving off or reflecting little light; gloomy: a *dark* day. **3.** Of a deep shade; black, or almost black: a *dark* color. **4.** Brunet in complexion. **5.** Cheerless or disheartening. **6.** Sullen in disposition or appearance; frowning; dour. **7.** Unenlightened in mind or spirit; ignorant. **8.** Evil or sinister; wicked; atrocious: a *dark* deed. **9.** Not understandable; mysterious: a *dark* saying. **10.** Not known; secret. — *n.* **1.** Lack of light. **2.** A place or condition of little or no light. **3.** Night. **4.** Obscurity; secrecy. **5.** Ignorance. **6.** A dark shadow or color. — **in the dark** **1.** In secret. **2.** Ignorant; uninformed. [OE *deorc*] — **dark′ness** *n.*

Dark Ages The period in European history between the fall of the Western Roman Empire (A.D. 476) and the Italian Renaissance; the Middle Ages, esp. the early part.

Dark Continent Africa: so called because little was known about it until the 19th century.

dark·en (där′kən) *v.t.* **1.** To make dark or darker; deprive of light. **2.** To make dark in color; make black. **3.** To fill with gloom; sadden. **4.** To obscure; confuse. **5.** To blind. — *v.i.* **6.** To grow dark or darker; become obscure. **7.** To grow clouded or flushed. **8.** To become blind. — **dark′-en·er** *n.*

dark horse One who unexpectedly wins a race, contest, nomination, etc.

dark lantern A lantern having a case with one transparent side that can be covered by a shield to hide the light.

dark·ling (därk′ling) *Poetic adj.* Occurring or being in the dark; dim. — *adv.* In the dark. [< DARK + -LING²]

dark·ly (därk′lē) *adv.* **1.** Obscurely. **2.** Mysteriously.

dark·room (därk′rōōm′, -rŏŏm′) *n. Photog.* A room equipped to exclude actinic rays, for treating plates, films, etc.

dark star *Astron.* An invisible or dimly shining star, known only through spectrum analysis, gravitational effect, etc.

dar·ling (där′ling) *n.* **1.** A person tenderly loved: often a term of address. **2.** A person in great favor. — *adj.* Beloved; very dear. [OE *dēorling*, dim. of *dēor* dear]

darn¹ (därn) *v.t. & v.i.* To repair (a garment or a hole) by filling the gap with interlacing stitches. — *n.* **1.** A place mended by darning. **2.** The act of darning. [? OE *dernan* to conceal < *derne* hidden] — **darn′er** *n.*

darn² (därn) *v.t., adj., n., & interj. U.S. Informal* Damn: a euphemism. [Alter. of DAMN]

dar·nel (där′nəl) *n.* An annual grass often found in grain fields: also called *cockle, ryegrass.* [< dial. F *darnelle*]

darn·ing needle (därn′ing) **1.** A large-eyed needle used in darning. **2.** A dragonfly.

dart (därt) *n.* **1.** A thin, pointed weapon to be thrown or shot. **2.** Anything like a dart in appearance. **3.** A sudden, rapid motion. **4.** The stinger of an insect. **5.** A tapering tuck made in a garment to make it fit. — *v.i.* **1.** To move suddenly like a dart; rush. — *v.t.* **2.** To throw or emit suddenly or swiftly. [< OF < Gmc.]

dart·er (där′tər) *n.* **1.** One who or that which darts. **2.** A small American percoid fish.

dar·tle (där′təl) *v.t. & v.i.* **·tled, ·tling** To dart or shoot out repeatedly.

darts (därts) *n.pl.* (*construed as sing.*) A game of skill in which small darts are thrown at a bull's-eye target.

Dar·win·i·an (där-win′ē-ən) *adj.* Pertaining to Charles Darwin, or to Darwinism. — *n.* An advocate of Darwinism: also **Dar′win·ite** (-īt).

Dar·win·ism (där′win-iz′əm) *n.* The biological doctrine of the origin of species through descent by natural selection with variation, advocated by Charles Darwin. — **Dar′win·ist** *n. & adj.* — **Dar′win·is′tic** *adj.*

dash (dash) *v.t.* **1.** To strike with violence, esp. so as to break or shatter. **2.** To throw, thrust, or knock suddenly and violently: usually with *away, out, down*, etc. **3.** To be-spatter. **4.** To do, write, etc., hastily: with *off* or *down*. **5.** To frustrate; confound: to *dash* hopes. **6.** To daunt or dis-courage. **7.** To put to shame; abash. **8.** To adulterate; mix: with *with*: to *dash* with salt. —*v.i.* **9.** To strike; hit: The waves *dashed* against the shore. **10.** To rush or move im-petuously. —*n.* **1.** A collision; impact. **2.** The splashing of water or other liquid against an object. **3.** A small addi-tion of some other ingredient: a *dash* of bitters. **4.** A hasty stroke, as with a pen or brush. **5.** A check or hindrance. **6.** A sudden advance or onset; a short rush. **7.** A short race run at full speed: the 100-yard *dash*. **8.** Spirited action. **9.** Vigor of style; verve. **10.** A horizontal line (—) used as a mark of punctuation to set off words or phrases in a sen-tence, to indicate an abrupt breaking off, to mark omissions of words or letters, etc. **11.** *Telecom.* The long sound in the Morse or similar code, used in combination with the dot to represent letters or numbers. [ME *daschen* < Scand.]

dash·board (dash′bôrd′, -bōrd′) *n.* **1.** The instrument panel of an automobile. **2.** An upright screen on the front of a vehicle to intercept mud, spray, etc.

dash·er (dash′ər) *n.* **1.** One who or that which dashes. **2.** A lively or showy person. **3.** The plunger of a churn.

dash·ing (dash′ing) *adj.* **1.** Spirited; bold; impetuous. **2.** Ostentatiously showy or gay. —**dash′ing·ly** *adv.*

dash·y (dash′ē) *adj.* **dash·i·er, dash·i·est** Stylish; showy.

das·tard (das′tərd) *n.* A base coward; a sneak. —*adj.* **Dastardly.** [? ME *dased, dast*, pp. of *dasen* to daze + -ARD]

das·tard·ly (das′tərd-lē) *adj.* Base; cowardly. —**das′-tard·li·ness** *n.*

da·ta (dā′tə, dat′ə, dä′tə) *n.orig. pl.* of **datum** Facts or fig-ures from which conclusions may be drawn. ◆ Those who continue to regard *data* as a Latin plural use it with a plural verb (These data *are* new), but its use with a singular verb (This data *is* new) is widespread. [< L, neut. pl. of *datus*, pp. of *dare* to give]

data processing The operations involved in handling and storing information, using computers and other machines.

date¹ (dāt) *n.* **1.** A particular point of time; esp., the time of the occurrence of an event. **2.** The part of a writing, coin, statue, etc., that tells when, or where and when, it was writ-ten or made. **3.** The age or period to which a thing belongs: a town of ancient *date*. **4.** The term or duration of a thing. **5.** The day of the month. **6.** *Informal* A social appointment or engagement for a specified time. **7.** *Informal* A person of the opposite sex with whom such an appointment is made. —**to date** Up to and including the present day; till now. —*v. dat·ed, dat·ing* *v.t.* **1.** To furnish or mark with a date. **2.** To ascertain the time or era of; assign a date to. **3.** *U.S. Informal* To make an appointment with (a member of the opposite sex). —*v.i.* **4.** To have origin in an era or time: usually with *from*: This coin *dates* from the Renaissance. **5.** To reckon time. **6.** *Informal* To have appointments with members of the opposite sex. [< F < L *data*, fem. pp. of *dare* to give] —**dat′a·ble** *adj.* —**dat′er** *n.*

date² (dāt) *n.* **1.** The sweet fruit of a palm, enclosing a sin-gle hard seed. **2.** A palm bearing this fruit: also **date palm**. [< OF < L < Gk. *daktylos* finger]

dat·ed (dā′tid) *adj.* **1.** Marked with a date. **2.** Antiquat-ed; old-fashioned.

date·less (dāt′lis) *adj.* **1.** Bearing no date. **2.** Without end or limit. **3.** Immemorial. **4.** Of permanent interest.

date line **1.** The line containing the date of publication of a periodical or of any contribution printed in it. **2.** An imagi-nary line roughly corresponding to 180° longitude from Greenwich, internationally agreed upon as determining those points on the earth's surface where a day is dropped on cross-ing it from west to east and added crossing east to west.

da·tive (dā′tiv) *n. Gram.* **1.** In inflected Indo-European languages, the case of a noun, pronoun, or adjective denoting the indirect object. It is expressed in English by *to* or *for* with the objective or by word order, as in *I told the story to him, I told him the story*. **2.** A word in this case. —*adj. Gram.* Pertaining to or designating the dative case or a word in this case: also **da·ti·val** (dā-tī′vəl). [< L *dativus*, trans. of Gk. (*ptōsis*) *dotikē* (the case of) giving] —**da′tive·ly** *adv.*

da·tum (dā′təm, dat′əm, dä′təm) Singular of DATA.

daub (dôb) *v.t. & v.i.* **1.** To smear or coat (something), as with plaster, grease, etc. **2.** To paint without skill. —*n.* **1.** Any sticky application, as of mud, plaster, clay, etc. **2.** A smear or spot. **3.** A poor painting. **4.** An instance or act of daubing. [< OF < L *dealbare* to whitewash] —**daub′er** *n.* —**daub′y** *adj.*

daugh·ter (dô′tər) *n.* **1.** A female child, considered in re-lationship to either or both of her parents. **2.** A female descendant. **3.** A woman or girl considered to be in a rela-tionship like that of a daughter: a *daughter* of nobility. **4.** Anything regarded as a female descendant. [OE *dohtor*] —**daugh′ter·ly** *adj.* —**daugh′ter·li·ness** *n.*

daugh·ter-in-law (dô′tər·in·lô′) *n. pl.* **daugh·ters-in-law** The wife of one's son.

daunt (dônt, dänt) *v.t.* To dishearten or intimidate; cow. [< OF < L *domare* to tame]

daunt·less (dônt′lis, dänt′-) *adj.* Fearless; intrepid. —**daunt′less·ly** *adv.* —**daunt′less·ness** *n.*

dau·phin (dô′fin, *Fr.* dô-faṅ′) *n.* The eldest son of a king of France, a title used from 1349 to 1830. [< F, a dolphin]

dav·en·port (dav′ən-pôrt, -pōrt) *n. U.S.* A large, uphol-stered sofa, often usable as a bed. [Prob. from the name of the first manufacturer]

Da·vid (dā′vid), 1040?–970? B.C., second king of Judah and Israel 1010?–970? B.C., succeeded Solomon. —**Da·vid·ic** (də-vid′ik) *adj.*

dav·it (dav′it, dā′vit) *n. Naut.* One of a pair of small cranes on a ship's side for hoisting its boats, stores, etc. [Appar. from *David*, proper name]

da·vy (dā′vē) *n. pl.* **·vies** A safety lamp (def. 1). [after Sir Humphry *Davy*, who invented it] Also **Davy lamp.**

Da·vy Jones (dā′vē jōnz′) The spir-it of the sea.

Davy Jones's locker The bottom of the ocean, esp. as the grave of the drowned.

DAVIT
a Position on deck.
b Position when low-ering lifeboat.

daw·dle (dôd′l) *v.t. & v.i.* **·dled, ·dling** To waste (time) in slow tri-fling; loiter: often with *away*. [? Var. of DADDLE] —**daw′dler** *n.*

dawn (dôn) *n.* **1.** Daybreak. ◆ Collateral adjective: *au-roral*. **2.** A beginning or unfolding. —*v.i.* **1.** To begin to grow light in the morning. **2.** To begin to be understood: with *on* or *upon*. **3.** To begin to expand or develop. [ME *dawenyng* daybreak < Scand.]

day (dā) *n.* **1.** The period of light from dawn to dark; day-light. **2.** The interval represented by one rotation of the earth upon its axis; twenty-four hours. ◆ Collateral adjec-tive: *diurnal*. **3.** A portion of a day spent in a particular way or place: a shopping *day*; a *day* outdoors. **4.** The hours of a day devoted to work: a seven-hour *day*. **5.** A time or period; age; epoch: in Caesar's *day*. **6.** *Usu. cap.* A particu-lar day: Labor *Day*. **7.** *Often pl.* A lifetime: in my *day*. **8.** A period of success, influence, accomplishment, etc.: Your *day* will come. **9.** The contest or battle of the day: to win the *day*. —**day after day** Every day. —**day by day** Each day. —**day in, day out** Every day. —**(from) day to day** From one day to the next. [OE *dæg*]

day bed A lounge or couch that can be converted into a bed.

day·book (dā′book′) *n.* **1.** In bookkeeping, the book in which transactions are recorded in the order of their occur-rence. **2.** A diary or journal.

day·break (dā′brāk′) *n.* The time each morning when day-light replaces darkness.

day camp A camp where children spend the day in super-vised activities, returning home each evening.

day coach A railroad car without special accommodations, as distinguished from a sleeping car, dining car, etc.

day·dream (dā′drēm′) *n.* A dreamlike thought, as of a fu-ture or desired event, situation, etc.; reverie. —*v.i.* To have daydreams. —**day′dream′er** *n.*

day·fly (dā′flī′) *n.* A May fly.

day laborer One who works for pay by the day, esp. at unskilled manual tasks.

day letter A long telegram, slower and cheaper than a regu-lar telegram, sent during the day.

day·light (dā′līt′) *n.* **1.** The light received from the sun; the light of day. **2.** Insight into or understanding of some-thing formerly puzzling. **3.** Exposure to view; publicity. **4.** The period of light during the day.

day·light-sav·ing time (dā′līt′sā′ving) Time in which more daylight is obtained at the end of each working day by setting clocks one or more hours ahead of standard time, esp. during the summer months.

day·long (dā′lông′, -long′) *adj.* Lasting all day. —*adv.* Through the entire day.

day nursery A place for the care of small children, esp. those of working mothers, during the day.

Day of Atonement Yom Kippur.

Day of Judgment *Theol.* Judgment Day.

day school **1.** A school that holds classes only during the daytime. **2.** A private school for pupils who live at home.

day·time (dā′tīm′) *n.* The time of daylight.

daze (dāz) *v.t.* **dazed, daz·ing** To stupefy or bewilder; stun. —*n.* The state of being dazed. [ME *dasen*] —**daz·ed·ly** (dā′zid·lē) *adv.*

daz·zle (daz′əl) *v.* **·zled, ·zling** *v.t.* **1.** To blind or dim the vision of by excess of light. **2.** To bewilder or charm, as with brilliant display. —*v.i.* **3.** To be blinded by lights or glare. **4.** To excite admiration. —*n.* **1.** The act of dazzling; daz-zled condition. **2.** Something that dazzles; brightness. [Freq. of DAZE] —**daz′zling·ly** *adv.*

D-day (dē′dā′) *n.* In military operations, the unspecified date of the launching of an attack; especially, June 6, 1944, the day on which the Allies invaded France in World War II.

DDT A powerful insecticide effective on contact. [< D(I-CHLORO)D(IPHENYL)T(RICHLOROETHANE)]

de- *prefix* **1.** Away; off: *deflect, decapitate.* **2.** Down: *decline, descend.* **3.** Completely; utterly: *derelict, denude.* **4.** The undoing, reversing, or ridding of (the action, condition or substance expressed by the main element: *decode, decentralization, decarbonization.* [< L *de* from, away, down; also < F *dé-* < L *de-*, or < OF *des-* < L *dis-* (see DIS-¹)]

dea·con (dē′kən) *n.* **1.** A lay church officer or subordinate minister. **2.** In the Anglican, Eastern Orthodox, and Roman Catholic churches, a clergyman ranking next below a priest. [OE < L < Gk. *diakonos* servant, minister] — **dea·con·ry** (dē′kən-rē), **dea′con·ship** *n.*

dea·con·ess (dē′kən-is) *n.* A woman appointed or chosen as a lay church worker or officer.

de·ac·ti·vate (dē-ak′tə-vāt) *v.t.* **·vat·ed, ·vat·ing 1.** To render inactive or ineffective, as an explosive, chemical, etc. **2.** *Mil.* To release (a military unit, ship, etc.) from active duty; demobilize. — **de·ac′ti·va′tion** *n.*

dead (ded) *adj.* **1.** Having ceased to live; lifeless. **2.** Deathlike: a *dead* faint. **3.** Inanimate. **4.** Insensible: with *to*: *dead* to pity. **5.** Lacking sensation; numb. **6.** Extinct: a *dead* language. **7.** No longer in force: a *dead* law. **8.** Not productively used: *dead* capital. **9.** *Informal* Very tired. **10.** Lacking activity, excitement, etc.: a *dead* town. **11.** Extinguished: a *dead* fire. **12.** Dull: said of colors. **13.** Muffled: said of sounds. **14.** Without elasticity. **15.** Complete; utter: *dead* silence. **16.** Having no outlet or opening: a *dead* end. **17.** Perfect; exact: a *dead* center. **18.** Unerring; sure: a *dead* shot. **19.** In certain games, out of play: said of the ball. — *n.* **1.** A dead person, or dead persons collectively: preceded by *the*. **2.** The coldest, darkest, or most intense part: the *dead* of winter. — *adv.* **1.** Completely: to stop *dead*. **2.** Directly: *dead* ahead. [OE *dēad*] — **dead′ness** *n.*

dead·beat (ded′bēt′) *n. U.S. Slang* **1.** One who avoids paying his bills. **2.** A sponger.

dead center *Mech.* One of two points in the motion of a crank and connecting rod when they are in alignment and the connecting rod has no power to turn the crank.

dead·en (ded′n) *v.t.* **1.** To diminish the sensitivity, force, or intensity of. **2.** To impede the velocity of; retard. **3.** To render soundproof. **4.** To make dull or less brilliant in color. — *v.i.* **5.** To become dead. — **dead′en·er** *n.*

dead end **1.** A passage, street, etc., having no outlet. **2.** A point from which no progress can be made.

dead·eye (ded′ī′) *n. Naut.* A wooden disk pierced by holes through which lanyards are passed, and having a grooved circumference, used to set up shrouds, stays, etc.

dead·fall (ded′fôl′) *n.* A trap operated by a weight that falls upon and kills or holds an animal.

dead·head (ded′hed′) *Informal n.* **1.** One who is admitted, entertained, or accommodated free of charge. **2.** A dull, stupid person. — *v.t. & v.i.* To treat or go as a deadhead. — *adj.* Traveling without passengers or freight.

dead heat A race in which two or more competitors tie.

dead letter **1.** A letter that is unclaimed, or cannot be delivered because of a faulty address. **2.** A law, issue, etc., no longer valid or enforced, though still formally in effect.

dead·line (ded′līn′) *n.* **1.** A time limit, as for the completion of newspaper copy, payment of debts, etc. **2.** Originally, a boundary line that prisoners might not cross.

dead·lock (ded′lok′) *n.* A standstill or stoppage of activity resulting from the unrelenting opposition of equally powerful forces. — *v.t. & v.i.* To bring or come to a deadlock.

dead·ly (ded′lē) *adj.* **·li·er, ·li·est 1.** Likely or certain to cause death. **2.** Implacable; mortal: a *deadly* enemy. **3.** Resembling death: *deadly* pallor. **4.** *Theol.* Causing spiritual death: a *deadly* sin. **5.** Excessive. — *adv.* **1.** As in death; deathly. **2.** *Informal* Very. — **dead′li·ness** *n.*

deadly nightshade Belladonna.

dead pan *U.S. Slang* A completely expressionless face. — **dead·pan** (ded′pan′) *adj. & adv.*

dead reckoning *Naut.* The computation of a vessel's position by log and compass without astronomical observations.

Dead Sea Scrolls A number of scrolls of parchment, leather, or copper, dating from about 100 B.C. to A.D. 100, containing Hebrew and Aramaic texts of Biblical works, found in 1947 and after in caves near the Dead Sea.

dead weight **1.** A heavy weight or load, as of something inert. **2.** In transportation, the weight of a vehicle as distinguished from its load.

dead·wood (ded′wŏŏd′) *n.* **1.** Wood dead on the tree. **2.** *U.S.* Worthless material; a useless person or thing.

deaf (def) *adj.* **1.** Partly or completely lacking the power to hear. **2.** Determined not to hear; unwilling to listen. [OE *dēaf*] — **deaf′ly** *adv.* — **deaf′ness** *n.*

deaf-and-dumb alphabet (def′ən-dum′) Manual alphabet (which see).

deaf·en (def′ən) *v.t.* **1.** To make deaf. **2.** To confuse, stupefy, or overwhelm, as with noise. **3.** To drown (a sound) by a louder sound. **4.** To make soundproof.

deaf-mute (def′myōōt′) *n.* A deaf person who cannot speak, usu. because of deafness from early life. Also **deaf mute.**

deal¹ (dēl) *v.* **dealt** (delt), **deal·ing** *v.t.* **1.** To distribute or portion out, as playing cards. **2.** To apportion to (one person) as his or her share. **3.** To deliver or inflict, as a blow. — *v.i.* **4.** To conduct oneself; behave toward: with *with*. **5.** To be concerned or occupied: with *in* or *with*: to *deal* in facts. **6.** To consider, discuss, or take action: with *with*. **7.** To do business: with *in, with*, or *at*. **8.** In card games, to act as dealer. — *n.* **1.** The act of dealing. **2.** In card games: **a** The distribution of the cards to the players. **b** The right or turn to distribute the cards. **c** The cards distributed to a player; a hand. **d** A single round of play. **3.** An indefinite amount, degree, extent, etc.: a great *deal* of time. **4.** *Informal* A business transaction. **5.** *Informal* A secret arrangement, as in politics. **6.** *Informal* A plan, agreement, or treatment: a rough *deal*. [OE *dǣlan*.]

deal² (dēl) *n.* **1.** A fir or pine plank. **2.** Such planks collectively. — *adj.* Made of deal. [< MDu. *dele* plank]

deal·er (dē′lər) *n.* **1.** One engaged in a specified business; a trader. **2.** In card games, one who distributes the cards.

deal·ing (dē′ling) *n.* **1.** The act of distributing. **2.** *Usu. pl.* Transactions or relations with others. **3.** Method or manner of treatment: honest *dealing*.

dealt (delt) Past tense and past participle of DEAL.

dean (dēn) *n.* **1.** An officer of a college or university, having jurisdiction over a particular group of students, area of study, or acting as head of a faculty. **2.** The senior member, in length of service, of a group of men. **3.** The chief ecclesiastical officer of a cathedral or of a collegiate church. [< OF < LL < L *decem* ten] — **dean′ship** *n.*

dean·er·y (dē′nər-ē) *n. pl.* **·er·ies** The office, revenue, jurisdiction, or place of residence of a dean.

dear (dir) *adj.* **1.** Beloved; precious. **2.** Highly esteemed: used in letter salutations. **3.** Expensive; costly. **4.** Characterized by high prices. **5.** Intense; earnest: our *dearest* wish. — *n.* One who is much beloved; a darling. — *adv.* Dearly. — *interj.* An exclamation of regret, surprise, etc. [OE *dēore*] — **dear′ly** *adv.* — **dear′ness** *n.*

dearth (dûrth) *n.* Scarcity; lack; famine. [ME *derthe*]

dear·y (dir′ē) *n. pl.* **dear·ies** *Informal* Darling; dear. Also **dear′ie.**

death (deth) *n.* **1.** The permanent cessation of all vital functions in an animal or plant. **2.** The condition of being dead. **3.** *Usu. cap.* A personification of death, usu. a skeleton holding a scythe. **4.** The extinction of anything; destruction. **5.** The cause of dying. **6.** The time or manner of dying: to meet a tyrant's *death*. **7.** Something considered as terrible as death. ◆ Collateral adjectives: *lethal, mortal.* — **to death** Very much: He frightened me *to death*. — **to put to death** To kill; execute. [OE *dēath*]

death·bed (deth′bed′) *n.* **1.** The bed on which a person dies or died. **2.** The last hours of life.

death·blow (deth′blō′) *n.* That which causes the death or the end of a person or thing.

death-cup (deth′kup′) *n.* A poisonous mushroom having a usu. white, olive, or umber cap.

death house That part of a prison, as a block of cells, in which prisoners condemned to death are confined.

death·less (deth′lis) *adj.* Not liable to die; perpetual; immortal. — **death′less·ly** *adv.* — **death′less·ness** *n.*

death·ly (deth′lē) *adj.* **1.** Resembling or suggesting death. Also **death′like.** **2.** Causing death; fatal. — *adv.* **1.** In a deathlike manner. **2.** Extremely: *deathly* ill.

death mask A cast of the face taken just after death.

death rate The number of persons per thousand of population who die within a given time.

death rattle The rattling sound caused by the breath passing through mucus in the throat of one dying.

death's-head (deths′hed′) *n.* A human skull, or a representation of it, as a symbol of death.

death trap (deth′trap′) *n.* **1.** An unsafe building or structure. **2.** Any very dangerous situation.

death warrant **1.** *Law* An official order for the execution of a person. **2.** Anything that destroys hope, happiness, etc.

death·watch (deth′woch′, -wôch′) *n.* **1.** A vigil kept at the side of one who is dying or has recently died. **2.** A guard set over a condemned man before his execution.

de·ba·cle (dā-bäk′əl, -bak′əl, di-) *n.* **1.** A sudden and disastrous breakdown or collapse. **2.** The breaking up of ice in a river. **3.** A violent flood. [< F < débâcler to unbar]

de·bar (di·bär′) *v.t.* ·barred, ·bar·ring 1. To bar or shut out: usu. with *from*. 2. To hinder. [< F < dé- away + *barrer* to bar] — **de·bar′ment** *n.*

de·bark (di·bärk′) *v.t. & v.i.* To put or go ashore from a ship. [< F < dé- away + *barque* ship] — **de·bar·ka·tion** (dē′bär·kā′shən) *n.*

de·base (di·bās′) *v.t.* ·based, ·bas·ing To lower in character or worth; degrade. [< DE- + obs. *base*] — **de·base′ment** *n.* — **de·bas′er** *n.*

de·bate (di·bāt′) *n.* 1. A discussion of any question; argument; dispute. 2. A formal contest in argumentation conducted between persons taking opposite sides of a question. — *v.* ·bat·ed, ·bat·ing *v.t.* 1. To argue about; discuss, as in a public meeting. 2. To deliberate upon; consider, as alternatives. 3. To discuss in formal debate. — *v.i.* 4. To engage in argument; discuss a question. 5. To take part in a formal debate. 6. To deliberate; ponder. [< OF < *de-* down + *batre* to strike] — **de·bat′a·ble** *adj.* — **de·bat′er** *n.*

de·bauch (di·bôch′) *v.t.* 1. To corrupt in morals; seduce; deprave. — *v.i.* 2. To indulge in debauchery; dissipate. — *n.* 1. An act or period of debauchery. 2. Debauchery. [< F < OF *desbaucher* to lure from work] — **de·bauch·ed·ly** (di·bô′chid·lē) *adv.* — **de·bauch′er** *n.* — **de·bauch′ment** *n.*

deb·au·chee (deb′ô·chē′, -shē′) *n.* One habitually profligate, drunken, or lewd; a libertine.

de·bauch·er·y (di·bô′chər·ē) *n.* *pl.* ·er·ies Gross indulgence of one's sensual appetites.

de·ben·ture (di·ben′chər) *n.* 1. A certificate given as acknowledgment of debt. 2. A bond, usu. without security, issued by a corporation and often convertible into common stock. Also **debenture bond**. [< L *debere* to owe]

de·bil·i·tate (di·bil′ə·tāt) *v.t.* ·tat·ed, ·tat·ing To make feeble or languid; weaken. [< L *debilitare* < *debilis* weak] — **de·bil′i·ta′tion** *n.* — **de·bil′i·ta′tive** *adj.*

de·bil·i·ty (di·bil′ə·tē) *n.* *pl.* ·ties Abnormal weakness; languor; feebleness. [< F < L < *debilis* weak]

deb·it (deb′it) *n.* 1. An item of debt recorded in an account. 2. An entry of debit in an account, or the sum of such entries. 3. The left-hand side of an account, where debts are recorded. — *v.t.* 1. To enter (a debt) in an account. 2. To charge (someone) with a debt. [< L *debere* to owe]

deb·o·nair (deb′ə·nâr′) *adj.* 1. Urbane; nonchalant. 2. Pleasantly gracious. 3. Cheerful; lively; gay. Also **deb′o·naire′, deb′on·naire′**. [< OF *de bon aire* of good mien] — **deb′o·nair′ly** *adv.* — **deb′o·nair′ness** *n.*

de·bouch (di·bōōsh′) *v.i.* 1. *Mil.* To march from a narrow passage, wood, etc., into the open. 2. To come forth; emerge; issue. — *v.t.* 3. To cause to emerge. [< F < dé- from + *bouche* a mouth] — **de·bouch′ment** *n.*

de·bris (də·brē′, dā′brē; *Brit.* deb′rē) *n.* 1. Fragments, or scattered remains, as of something destroyed; ruins; rubble. 2. *Geol.* An accumulation of detached fragments of rocks. Also **dé·bris′**. [< F < OF *debrisier* to break away]

debt (det) *n.* 1. That which one owes, as money, goods, or services. 2. The obligation to pay or render something to another. 3. The condition of owing something. 4. *Theol.* A sin. [< OF < L *debere* to owe]

debt of honor A gambling debt.

debt·or (det′ər) *n.* One who owes a debt.

de·bunk (di·bungk′) *v.t. Informal* To expose or deride the sham, false pretensions, etc., of. [< BUNK²]

de·but (di·byōō′, dā-, dā′byōō) *n.* 1. A first public appearance. 2. A formal introduction to society. 3. The beginning, as of a career. — *v.i.* To make a debut. Also **dé·but′**. [< F < *débuter* to begin]

deb·u·tante (deb′yōō·tänt, -yə-, *Fr.* deb′yōō·tänt′) *n.fem.* A young woman making a debut in society. Also **dé′bu·tante′**.

deca- *combining form* 1. Ten. 2. In the metric system, deka-. Also, before vowels, **dec-**.

dec·ade (dek′ād, de·kād′) *n.* 1. A period of ten years. 2. A group or set of ten. [< MF < L < Gk. < *deka* ten]

de·ca·dence (di·kād′ns, dek′ə·dəns) *n.* 1. A process of deterioration; decay. 2. A condition or period of decline, as in morals. [< F < Med.L < L < *de-* down + *cadere* to fall]

de·ca·dent (dek′ə·dənt, di·kād′nt) *adj.* Falling into, or characteristic of, decay and decline. — *n.* A decadent person, esp. an artist or writer. — **de·ca′dent·ly** *adv.*

dec·a·gon (dek′ə·gon) *n.* *Geom.* A polygon with ten sides and ten angles. [< Gk. < *deka* ten + *gōnia* angle] — **de·cag·o·nal** (di·kag′ə·nəl) *adj.* — **de·cag′o·nal·ly** *adv.*

dec·a·gram (dek′ə·gram) See DEKAGRAM.

dec·a·he·dron (dek′ə·hē′drən) *n.* *pl.* ·drons or ·dra (-drə) *Geom.* A polyhedron bounded by ten plane faces. [< DECA- + Gk. *hedra* seat] — **dec′a·he′dral** *adj.*

de·cal (dē′kal, di·kal′) *n.* A decalcomania.

de·cal·ci·fy (dē·kal′sə·fī) *v.t.* ·fied, ·fy·ing To remove lime or calcareous matter from (bones, teeth, etc.). — **de·cal′ci·fi·ca′tion** *n.*

de·cal·co·ma·ni·a (di·kal′kə·mā′nē·ə, -mān′yə) *n.* 1. A process of transferring prints, designs, etc., from specially prepared paper to glass, porcelain, or other material. 2. The design or print to be transferred. [< F < *décalquer* to transfer a tracing + -manie -mania]

dec·a·li·ter (dek′ə·lē′tər) See DEKALITER.

Dec·a·logue (dek′ə·lôg, -log) *n.* The Ten Commandments. Also **Dec′a·log**. [< Gk. < *deka* ten + *logos* word]

dec·a·me·ter (dek′ə·mē′tər) See DEKAMETER.

de·camp (di·kamp′) *v.i.* 1. To break camp. 2. To leave suddenly or secretly; run away. — **de·camp′ment** *n.*

de·cant (di·kant′) *v.t.* 1. To pour off (a liquid) without disturbing its sediment. 2. To pour from one container into another. [< F < Med.L < *de-* from + *canthus* lip of a jug] — **de·can·ta·tion** (dē′kan·tā′shən) *n.*

de·cant·er (di·kan′tər) *n.* A vessel for decanting; esp. a decorative, stoppered bottle for serving wine, etc.

de·cap·i·tate (di·kap′ə·tāt) *v.t.* ·tat·ed, ·tat·ing To cut off the head of; behead. [< Med.L < L *de-* off + *caput* head] — **de·cap′i·ta′tion** *n.* — **de·cap′i·ta′tor** *n.*

dec·a·pod (dek′ə·pod) *adj.* Ten-footed or ten-armed. — *n. Zool.* 1. A crustacean having five pairs of legs, including the crabs, lobsters, shrimps, etc. 2. Any ten-armed cephalopod, as a cuttlefish or squid. [< Gk. < *deka* ten + *pous* foot] — **de·cap·o·dal** (di·kap′ə·dəl), **de·cap′o·dous** *adj.*

de·car·bon·ate (dē·kär′bə·nāt) *v.t.* ·at·ed, ·at·ing To free from carbon dioxide. — **de·car·bon·a′tor** *n.*

de·car·bon·ize (dē·kär′bən·īz) *v.t.* ·ized, ·iz·ing To decarburize. — **de·car′bon·i·za′tion** *n.* — **de·car′bon·iz′er** *n.*

de·car·bu·rize (dē·kär′byə·rīz) *v.t.* ·rized, ·riz·ing To remove carbon from (molten steel or the cylinders of an internal-combustion engine). — **de·car′bu·ri·za′tion** *n.*

dec·are (dek′âr, dek·âr′) See DEKARE.

dec·a·stere (dek′ə·stir) See DEKASTERE.

dec·a·syl·la·ble (dek′ə·sil′ə·bəl) *n.* A line of verse having ten syllables. — **dec·a·syl·lab·ic** (dek′ə·si·lab′ik) *adj.*

de·cath·lon (di·kath′lon) *n.* An athletic contest consisting of ten different track and field events in all of which each contestant participates. [< DEC(A)- + Gk. *athlon* a contest]

de·cay (di·kā′) *v.i.* 1. To fail slowly in health, beauty, quality, or any form of excellence. 2. To decompose; rot. — *v.t.* 3. To cause to decay. — *n.* 1. A falling into a ruined or reduced condition. 2. Decomposition, as of a dead organism. 3. Rottenness. [< OF < L < *de-* down + *cadere* to fall]
— **Syn.** (verb) 2. Dead organic matter *decays* by the action of bacteria; also, a great mind may *decay* with age. *Putrefy* is used only of animal matter, as is also the strong, direct *rot*. *Spoil* suggests mild decay or taint; food *spoils* if not refrigerated.

de·cease (di·sēs′) *v.i.* ·ceased, ·ceas·ing To die. — *n.* Death. [< OF < L < *de-* away + *cedere* to go]

de·ceased (di·sēst′) *adj.* Dead. — **the deceased** The dead person or persons.

de·ce·dent (di·sēd′nt) *n. Law* A person deceased.

de·ceit (di·sēt′) *n.* 1. The act of deceiving. 2. An instance of deception or a device that deceives; a trick. 3. The quality of being deceptive; falseness. [See DECEIVE.]

de·ceit·ful (di·sēt′fəl) *adj.* 1. Given to deceiving; lying or treacherous. 2. Tending to deceive; false. — **Syn.** See DECEPTIVE. — **de·ceit′ful·ly** *adv.* — **de·ceit′ful·ness** *n.*

de·ceive (di·sēv′) *v.* ·ceived, ·ceiv·ing *v.t.* 1. To mislead by falsehood; lead into error; delude. — *v.i.* 2. To practice deceit. [< OF < L < *de-* away, down + *capere* to take] — **de·ceiv′er** *n.* — **de·ceiv′ing·ly** *adv.*

de·cel·er·ate (dē·sel′ə·rāt) *v.t. & v.i.* ·at·ed, ·at·ing To diminish in velocity. [< DE- + L *celerare* to hasten] — **de·cel′er·a′tion** *n.* — **de·cel′er·a′tor** *n.*

De·cem·ber (di·sem′bər) *n.* The twelfth month of the year, having 31 days. [< L < *decem* ten; December was the tenth month in the old Roman calendar]

de·cem·vir (di·sem′vər) *n.* *pl.* ·virs or ·vi·ri (-və·rī) A member of any body of ten magistrates; esp. one in ancient Rome. [< L < *decem* ten + *vir* man] — **de·cem′vi·ral** *adj.*

de·cem·vi·rate (di·sem′və·rit, -rāt) *n.* 1. A body of ten men in authority. 2. The government of such a body.

de·cen·cy (dē′sən·sē) *n.* *pl.* ·cies 1. The quality or state of being decent; propriety in conduct, speech, or dress. 2. *Usu. pl.* Those things that are proper or decent. 3. *pl.* The requirements for a proper manner of life.

de·cen·ni·al (di·sen′ē·əl) *adj.* 1. Of or continuing for ten years. 2. Occurring every ten years. — *n.* An anniversary observed every ten years. — **de·cen′ni·al·ly** *adv.*

de·cent (dē′sənt) *adj.* 1. Characterized by propriety of conduct, speech, or dress; proper; respectable. 2. Free of coarseness or indelicacy; modest; chaste. 3. Adequate; satisfactory. 4. Generous; kind. 5. *Informal* Adequately or properly clothed. [< L *decere* to be fitting, proper] — **de′cent·ly** *adv.* — **de′cent·ness** *n.*

de·cen·tral·ize (dē·sen′trəl·īz) *v.t.* ·ized, ·iz·ing To undo the centralization of; reorganize from smaller and more dispersed parts. — **de·cen′tral·i·za′tion** *n.*

de·cep·tion (di·sep′shən) *n.* 1. The act of deceiving. 2. The state of being deceived. 3. Anything that deceives or is meant to deceive; a delusion. [See DECEIVE.]

DECA-
HEDRON

de·cep·tive (di-sep′tiv) *adj.* Having power or tendency to deceive. **— de·cep′tive·ly** *adv.* **— de·cep′tive·ness** *n.*

deci- *combining form* In the metric system, one tenth of (a specified unit): *decimeter*. [< L *decimus* tenth < *decem* ten]

dec·i·are (des′ē-âr) *n.* In the metric system, one tenth of an are. Abbr. *da.* [< F *déciare*]

dec·i·bel (des′ə-bəl) *n. Physics* One tenth of a bel: a measure of sound intensity.

de·cide (di-sīd′) *v.* **·cid·ed, cid·ing** *v.t.* **1.** To determine; settle, as a controversy, contest, etc. **2.** To determine the issue or conclusion of: The charge *decided* the battle. **3.** To bring (someone) to a decision. *— v.i.* **4.** To give a decision or verdict. **5.** To make a decision. [< MF < L < *de-* down, away + *caedere* to cut] **— de·cid′a·ble** *adj.*

de·cid·ed (di-sī′did) *adj.* **1.** Free from uncertainty; definite. **2.** Exhibiting determination; resolute; emphatic. **— de·cid′ed·ly** *adv.* **— de·cid′ed·ness** *n.*

de·cid·u·ous (di-sij′o͞o-əs) *adj.* **1.** *Biol.* Falling off or shed at maturity or at specific seasons, as petals, fruit, leaves, antlers, etc. **2.** Characterized by such a falling off: distinguished from *evergreen.* [< L < *de-* down, away + *cadere* to fall] **— de·cid′u·ous·ly** *adv.* **— de·cid′u·ous·ness** *n.*

dec·i·gram (des′ə-gram) *n.* In the metric system, the tenth part of a gram. Also **dec′i·gramme.** See table front of book.

dec·i·li·ter (des′ə-lē′tər) *n.* In the metric system, the tenth part of a liter. Also *esp. Brit.* **dec′i·li′tre.** Abbr. *dl, dl.* See table front of book.

de·cil·lion (di-sil′yən) *n.* **1.** *U.S.* A thousand nonillions, written as 1 followed by thirty-three zeros: a cardinal number. **2.** *Brit.* A million nonillions (def. 2), written as 1 followed by sixty zeros: a cardinal number. *— adj.* Being a decillion. [< DEC(A)- + (M)ILLION] **— de·cil′lionth** *adj.*

dec·i·mal (des′ə-məl) *adj.* **1.** Pertaining to or founded on the number 10. **2.** Proceeding by tens. *— n.* A decimal fraction or one of its digits. [< Med.L < L *decem* ten]

decimal fraction *Math.* A fraction whose denominator is any power of 10 and which may be expressed in decimal form, as 7/10 (0.7), 3/100 (0.03), etc.

decimal point A dot used before a decimal fraction.

decimal system A system of reckoning by tens or tenths.

dec·i·mate (des′ə-māt) *v.t.* **·mat·ed, ·mat·ing 1.** To destroy or kill a large proportion of. **2.** To select by lot and kill one out of every ten of. [< L *decimare* to take a tenth part from] **— dec′i·ma′tion** *n.* **— dec′i·ma′tor** *n.*

dec·i·me·ter (des′ə-mē′tər) *n.* In the metric system, the tenth part of a meter. Also *esp. Brit.* **dec′i·me′tre.** Abbr. *dec., decim., dm, dm.* See table front of book.

de·ci·pher (di-sī′fər) *v.t.* **1.** To determine the meaning of (something obscure, illegible, etc.). **2.** To translate from cipher or code into plain text; decode. **— de·ci′pher·a·ble** *adj.* **— de·ci′pher·er** *n.* **— de·ci′pher·ment** *n.*

de·ci·sion (di-sizh′ən) *n.* **1.** The act of deciding (an issue, question, etc.). **2.** A conclusion or judgment reached by deciding. **3.** The making up of one's mind. **4.** Firmness in judgment, action, or character. **5.** In boxing, a victory decided when there has not been a knockout. [See DECIDE.]

de·ci·sive (di-sī′siv) *adj.* **1.** Ending uncertainty or dispute; conclusive. **2.** Characterized by decision and firmness; determined. **3.** Unquestionable; unmistakable. **— deci′-sive·ly** *adv.* **— de·ci′sive·ness** *n.*

dec·i·stere (des′ə-stir) *n.* In the metric system, a cubic decimeter, or the tenth part of a stere. Abbr. *ds.*

deck (dek) *n.* **1.** *Naut.* **a** A platform covering or extending horizontally across a vessel, and serving as both floor and roof. **b** The space between two such platforms. **2.** Any similar flat surface. **3.** *U.S.* A pack of playing cards. *— to hit the deck Slang* **1.** To rise from bed; get up. **2.** To prepare for action. *— on deck Slang* Present and ready for action. *— v.t.* **1.** To dress or decorate elegantly; adorn. **2.** *Naut.* To furnish with a deck. [< MDu. *dek* roof, covering]

deck·er (dek′ər) *n.* Something with one or more decks, layers, levels, etc.: usu. in combination: a *double-decker.*

deck hand A common sailor employed on deck.

deck·le (dek′əl) *n.* **1.** In making paper by hand, a frame that limits the size of the sheet. **2.** The ragged edge of handmade paper: also **deckle edge.** Also **deck′el.** [< G *decke* cover] **— deck′le-edged′** *adj.*

de·claim (di-klām′) *v.i.* **1.** To speak loudly and rhetorically. **2.** To give a formal, set speech. **3.** To attack verbally and vehemently: with *against. — v.t.* **4.** To utter rhetorically. [< L < *de-* completely + *clamare* to shout] **— de·claim′er** *n.* **— dec·la·ma·tion** (dek′lə-mā′shən) *n.*

de·clam·a·to·ry (di-klam′ə-tôr′ē, -tō′rē) *adj.* Of, like, or pertaining to declamation. **— de·clam′a·to′ri·ly** *adv.*

dec·la·ra·tion (dek′lə-rā′shən) *n.* **1.** The act of declaring or proclaiming. **2.** That which is declared. **3.** A statement of goods liable to taxation. **4.** In bridge, a contract.

Declaration of Independence The manifesto that formally declared the political independence of the American colonies from Britain. It was written by Thomas Jefferson and adopted July 4, 1776.

de·clar·a·tive (di-klar′ə-tiv) *adj.* Making a declaration or statement. Also **de·clar·a·to·ry** (di-klar′ə-tôr′ē, -tō′rē).

de·clare (di-klâr′) *v.* **·clared, ·clar·ing** *v.t.* **1.** To make known or clear; esp. to announce formally; proclaim. **2.** To say emphatically; assert; avow. **3.** To reveal; prove. **4.** To make full statement of, as goods liable to duty. **5.** In bridge, to make a final bid designating (a trump suit or no-trump). *— v.i.* **6.** To make a declaration. **7.** To proclaim a choice or opinion: with *for* or *against.* [< L < *de-* completely + *clarare* to make clear] **— de·clar′er** *n.*

dé·clas·sé (dā-klä-sā′) *adj. French* Fallen or lowered in social status, class, rank, etc.

de·clen·sion (di-klen′shən) *n.* **1.** *Gram.* **a** The inflection of nouns, pronouns, and adjectives according to case, number, and gender. **b** A class of words similarly inflected. **2.** A sloping downward; descent. **3.** A decline. **4.** Deviation, as from a belief. [See DECLINE.] **— de·clen′sion·al** *adj.*

dec·li·na·tion (dek′lə-nā′shən) *n.* **1.** The act of inclining or bending downward. **2.** Deviation, as in direction or conduct. **3.** The angle formed between the direction of a compass needle and true north. **4.** *Astron.* The angular distance of a heavenly body north or south from the celestial equator. **5.** A polite refusal.

de·cline (di-klīn′) *v.* **·clined, ·clin·ing** *v.i.* **1.** To refuse politely to accept, comply with, or do something. **2.** To lessen or fail gradually, as in health. **3.** To draw to an end. **4.** To lower oneself, as to a mean action. **5.** To bend or incline downward or aside. *— v.t.* **6.** To refuse politely to accept, comply with, or do. **7.** To cause to bend or incline downward or aside. **8.** *Gram.* To give the inflected forms of (a noun, pronoun, or adjective). *— n.* **1.** The act or result of declining; deterioration. **2.** A period of declining. **3.** A condition in which one's mental or physical faculties weaken or deteriorate. **4.** A downward slope. [< OF < L *declinare* to lean down] **— de·clin′a·ble** *adj.* **— de·clin′er** *n.*

de·cliv·i·ty (di-kliv′ə-tē) *n. pl.* **·ties** A downward slope or surface: opposed to *acclivity.* [< L < *de-* down + *clivus* hill, slope] **— de·cliv′i·tous, de·cli′vous** (-klī′vəs) *adj.*

de·coct (di-kokt′) *v.t.* To extract by boiling; condense. [< L < *de-* down + *coquere* to cook] **— de·coc′tion** *n.*

de·code (dē-kōd′) *v.t.* **·cod·ed, ·cod·ing** To convert from code into plain language. **— de·cod′er** *n.*

dé·col·le·té (dā′kol-tā′, *Fr.* dā·kôl·tā′) *adj.* **1.** Cut low in the neck, as a gown. **2.** Wearing a low-necked gown. [< F]

de·com·mis·sion (dē′kə-mish′ən) *v.t.* To take out of active service, as a ship; retire from use.

de·com·pose (dē′kəm-pōz′) *v.t. & v.i.* **·posed, ·pos·ing 1.** To separate into constituent parts. **2.** To decay. **— de′·com·pos′a·ble** *adj.* **— de′com·pos′er** *n.*

de·com·po·si·tion (dē′kom-pə-zish′ən) *n.* The act, process, or result of decomposing.

de·com·press (dē′kəm-pres′) *v.t.* **1.** To free of pressure. **2.** To remove the pressure on (divers, caisson workers, etc.). **— de′com·pres′sion** *n.*

decompression sickness Caisson disease.

de·con·tam·i·nate (dē′kən-tam′ə-nāt) *v.t.* **·nat·ed, ·nat·ing** To make (a contaminated object or area) safe by destroying or neutralizing poisonous chemicals, radioactivity, etc.

de·con·trol (dē′kən-trōl′) *v.t.* **·trolled, ·trol·ling** To remove from control. *— n.* The removal of controls.

dé·cor (dā′kôr, dā-kôr′) *n.* **1.** The scheme or style of decoration in a room, home, club, etc. **2.** In the theater, the scenery. Also **de′cor.** [< F < *décorer* to decorate]

dec·o·rate (dek′ə-rāt) *v.t.* **·rat·ed, ·rat·ing 1.** To embellish or furnish with things beautiful; adorn. **2.** To confer a decoration or medal upon. [< L *decus, decoris* grace, embellishment] **— dec′o·ra′tor** *n.*

dec·o·ra·tion (dek′ə-rā′shən) *n.* **1.** The act, process, or art of decorating. **2.** A thing or group of things that decorate; ornamentation. **3.** A badge or emblem; medal. ◆ The U.S. military decorations in order of precedence are: Medal of Honor, Distinguished Service Cross or Navy Cross (Navy and Marine Corps), Distinguished Service Medal, Silver Star, Legion of Merit, Distinguished Flying Cross, Soldier's Medal, Bronze Star, Air Medal, Commendation Ribbon, and Purple Heart.

Decoration Day Memorial Day.

dec·o·ra·tive (dek′ər-ə-tiv, dek′rə-tiv, dek′ə-rā′tiv) *adj.* Of, pertaining to, or suitable for decoration; ornamental. **— dec′o·ra·tive·ly** *adv.* **— dec′o·ra·tive·ness** *n.*

dec·o·rous (dek′ər-əs, di-kôr′əs, -kō′rəs) *adj.* Marked by decorum; seemly; proper. [< L *decus, decoris* grace] **— dec′o·rous·ly** *adv.* **— dec′o·rous·ness** *n.*

de·co·rum (di-kôr′əm, -kō′rəm) *n.* **1.** Conformity to the requirements of good taste or social convention; propriety in behavior, dress, etc.; seemliness. **2.** *Usu. pl.* The proprieties. [See DECOROUS.]

de·coy (n. di·koi′, dē′koi; v. di·koi′) *n.* **1.** A person or thing that lures into danger, deception, etc. **2.** A bird or animal, or the likeness of one, used to lure game. **3.** An enclosed place into which game may be lured. — *v.t. & v.i.* To lure or be lured into danger or a trap. [Earlier *coy* < Du. *kooi* a cage] — **de·coy′er** *n.*

de·crease (*v.* di·krēs′; *n.* dē′krēs, di·krēs′) *v.t. & v.i.* **·creased, ·creas·ing** To grow, or cause to grow, gradually less or smaller; diminish. — *n.* **1.** The act, process, or state of decreasing. **2.** The amount or degree of decreasing. [< OF < L < *de-* down + *crescere* to grow] — **de·creas′ing·ly** *adv.*
— **Syn.** *Decrease* is applied to amount, *lessen* to number, *dwindle* to size, and *abate* to force. To *diminish* is to grow smaller by the removal of a part. *Reduce* is used in all the foregoing senses, but is usually transitive: to *reduce* the temperature of a room.

de·cree (di·krē′) *n.* **1.** A formal and authoritative order or decision. **2.** A foreordained and eternal purpose. — *v.* **·creed, ·cree·ing** *v.t.* **1.** To order, adjudge, ordain, or appoint by law or edict. — *v.i.* **2.** To issue an edict or decree. [< Of < L < *de-* down + *cernere* to decide]

dec·re·ment (dek′rə·mənt) *n.* **1.** The act or process of decreasing. **2.** The amount lost by decrease.

de·crep·it (di·krep′it) *adj.* Enfeebled or worn out by old age or excessive use. [< L < *de-* completely + *crepare* to creak] — **de·crep′it·ly** *adv.*

de·crep·i·tude (di·krep′ə·tood, -tyood) *n.* A decrepit or enfeebled condition, as from infirmity or old age.

de·cre·tal (di·krēt′l) *n.* A decree; esp. a papal decree.

de·cry (di·krī′) *v.t.* **·cried, ·cry·ing** **1.** To condemn or disparage openly. **2.** To depreciate, as foreign coins. [< F < *dé-* down + *crier* to cry] — **de·cri′al** *n.* — **de·cri′er** *n.*

de·cum·bent (di·kum′bənt) *adj.* **1.** Lying down. **2.** *Bot.* Prostrate: said of stems, shoots, etc., growing along the ground. [< L < *de-* down + *cumbere* to lie, recline] — **de·cum′bence, de·cum′ben·cy** *n.*

de·cus·sate (di·kus′āt, -it) *adj.* *Bot.* Having each pair of leaves at right angles with the pair below or above. [< L *decussare* to mark with an X] — **de·cus′sate·ly** *adv.* — **de·cus·sa·tion** (dē′ku·sā′shən, dek′ə-) *n.*

ded·i·cate (ded′ə·kāt, -i-) *v.t.* **·cat·ed, ·cat·ing** **1.** To set apart for sacred uses. **2.** To set apart for any special use, duty, or purpose. **3.** To inscribe (a work of literature, etc.) to someone. **4.** To commit (oneself) to a certain course of action or thought. **5.** To open or unveil (a bridge, statue, etc.) to the public. [< L < *de-* down + *dicare* to proclaim]

ded·i·ca·tion (ded′ə·kā′shən, -i-) *n.* **1.** The act of dedicating or the state of being dedicated. **2.** An inscription dedicating a literary work, etc. to someone or something.

ded·i·ca·tive (ded′ə·kā′tiv, -i-) *adj.* That dedicates.

ded·i·ca·to·ry (ded′ə·kə·tôr′ē, -tō′rē, -i-) *adj.* Constituting, containing, or serving as a dedication: a *dedicatory* preface.

de·duce (di·dōōs′, -dyōōs′) *v.t.* **·duced, ·duc·ing** **1.** To derive as a conclusion by reasoning. **2.** To trace, as origin. [< L < *de-* down + *ducere* to lead] — **de·duc′i·ble** *adj.*

de·duct (di·dukt′) *v.t.* To take away or subtract. [See DEDUCE.] — **de·duct′i·ble** *adj.*

de·duc·tion (di·duk′shən) *n.* **1.** The act of deducing. **2.** *Logic* Reasoning from the general to the particular; also, reasoning from stated premises to logical conclusions. **3.** The act of deducting; also, the amount deducted. — **de·duc′tive** *adj.* — **de·duc′tive·ly** *adv.*

deed (dēd) *n.* **1.** Anything done; an act. **2.** A notable achievement; feat. **3.** Action in general, as opposed to words. **4.** *Law* Any written, sealed instrument of bond, contract, transfer, etc., especially of real estate conveyance. — **Syn.** See ACT. — **in deed** In fact; in truth; actually. — *v.t.* To transfer by deed. [OE *dǣd*] — **deed′less** *adj.*

deem (dēm) *v.t. & v.i.* To judge; think; believe. [OE *dēman* to judge]

deep (dēp) *adj.* **1.** Extending or situated far below a surface. **2.** Extending far inward or backward, or to either side. **3.** Having a (specified) depth or dimension: six feet *deep.* **4.** Rising to the level of: used in combination: *knee-deep.* **5.** Coming from or penetrating to a depth: a *deep* sigh. **6.** Difficult to understand. **7.** Learned and penetrating; wise. **8.** Of great intensity; extreme: *deep* sorrow. **9.** Of intense or dark hue. **10.** Of low, sonorous tone. **11.** Absorbed: *deep* in thought. **12.** Artful; cunning. — **to go off the deep end** *Informal* To become excited or hysterical. — *n.* **1.** A place or thing of great depth; an abyss. **2.** The most intense or profound part. **3.** *Naut.* The interval between two successive marked fathoms. — **the deep** *Poetic* The sea or ocean. — *adv.* **1.** Deeply. **2.** Far along in time. [OE *dēop*] — **deep′ly** *adv.* — **deep′ness** *n.*

deep-dyed (dēp′dīd′) *adj.* Thoroughgoing; absolute.

deep·en (dē′pən) *v.t. & v.i.* To make or become deep or deeper.

deep-freeze (dēp′frēz′) *n.* **1.** A refrigerator for freezing and storing foods for long periods of time at temperatures approximating 0° F. **2.** Storage, esp. of long duration. — *v.t.* **·froze** or **·freezed, ·fro·zen** or **·freezed, ·freez·ing** To place or store in or as in a deepfreeze.

deep-fry (dēp′frī) *v.t.* **·fried, -fry·ing** To fry in deep fat.

deep-root·ed (dēp′rōō′tid, -rōōt′id) *adj.* **1.** Having roots far below the surface. **2.** Firmly held: said of beliefs, etc.

deep-seat·ed (dēp′sē′tid) *adj.* Established far within; difficult to remove, as a fear or disease.

deep-set (dēp′set′) *adj.* Deeply placed, as eyes.

deer (dir) *n. pl.* **deer** A ruminant animal having deciduous antlers, usu. in the male only, as the moose, elk, and reindeer. ◆ Collateral adjective: *cervine.* [OE *dēor* beast]

deer·hound (dir′hound′) *n.* A breed of hunting dog, having a shaggy, dark gray or brindle coat: also called *staghound.*

deer·skin (dir′skin′) *n.* A deer's hide, or leather made from it.

de·es·ca·late (dē·es′kə·lāt) *v.t. & v.i.* **·lat·ed, ·lat·ing** To decrease or be decreased gradually, as in scope, effect, or intensity: to *de-escalate* a war. — **de·es′ca·la′tion** *n.*

de·face (di·fās′) *v.t.* **·faced, ·fac·ing** To mar the surface or appearance of; disfigure. [< F < OF < *de-* down, away + *face* face] — **de·fac′a·ble** *adj.* — **de·face′ment** *n.*

de fac·to (dē fak′tō) Actually or really existing. [< L]

de·fal·cate (di·fal′kāt) *v.t.* **·cat·ed, ·cat·ing** To embezzle. [< Med.L < L *de-* down, away + *falx* scythe] — **de·fal·ca·tion** (dē′fal·kā′shən) *n.* — **de·fal′ca·tor** *n.*

de·fam·a·to·ry (di·fam′ə·tôr′ē, -tō′rē) *adj.* Slanderous.

de·fame (di·fām′) *v.t.* **·famed, ·fam·ing** To attack the good name or reputation of; slander; libel. [< L < *dis-* away, from + *fama* a report, reputation] — **def·a·ma·tion** (def′·ə·mā′shən) *n.* — **de·fam′er** *n.*

de·fault (di·fôlt′) *n.* A failure or neglect to fulfill an obligation or requirement, as to pay money due, to appear in court, or to appear for or finish a contest. — **in default of** Owing to lack or failure of. — *v.i.* **1.** To fail to do or fulfill something required. **2.** To fail to meet financial obligations. **3.** *Law* To fail to appear in court. **4.** In sports, to fail to compete or to complete a game, etc. — *v.t.* **5.** To fail to perform or pay. **6.** In sports, to fail to compete in, as a game; also, to forfeit by default. [< OF < L *de-* down + *fallere* to deceive] — **de·fault′er** *n.*

de·feat (di·fēt′) *v.t.* **1.** To overcome in any conflict or competition; vanquish. **2.** To prevent the successful outcome of; baffle; frustrate. **3.** *Law* To make void; annul. — *n.* **1.** The act or result of defeating; an overthrow; failure. **2.** Frustration; bafflement. **3.** *Law* An annulment. [< OF < *des-* not + *faire* to do]

de·feat·ism (di·fē′tiz·əm) *n.* The practice of those who accept defeat as inevitable. — **de·feat′ist** *n. & adj.*

def·e·cate (def′ə·kāt) *v.* **·cat·ed, ·cat·ing** *v.i.* **1.** To discharge excrement. **2.** To become free of dregs. — *v.t.* **3.** To refine; purify. [< L < *de-* down, away + *faex* dregs] — **def′e·ca′tion** *n.* — **def′e·ca′tor** *n.*

de·fect (*n.* di·fekt′, dē′fekt; *v.* di·fekt′) *n.* **1.** Lack of something necessary for perfection or completeness. **2.** A blemish; failing; fault. — *v.i.* To desert. [< L < *de-* not + *facere* to do] — **de·fec′tion** *n.*

de·fec·tive (di·fek′tiv) *adj.* **1.** Having a defect; imperfect; faulty. **2.** *Gram.* Lacking one or more of the inflected forms normal for its class: *Can* is a *defective* verb. **3.** *Psychol.* Having less than normal intelligence. — *n.* One who or that which is imperfect; esp., a mentally defective person. — **de·fec′tive·ly** *adv.* — **de·fec′tive·ness** *n.*

de·fec·tor (di·fek′tər) *n.* One who deserts.

de·fend (di·fend′) *v.t.* **1.** To shield from danger, attack, or injury; protect. **2.** To justify or vindicate; support. **3.** *Law* **a** To act in behalf of (an accused). **b** To contest (a claim, charge, or suit). — *v.i.* **4.** To make a defense. [< L < *de-* down, away + *fendere* to strike] — **de·fend′a·ble** *adj.* — **de·fend′er** *n.*

de·fen·dant (di·fen′dənt) *n.* *Law* One against whom an action is brought: opposed to *plaintiff.* — *adj.* Defending.

de·fense (di·fens′) *n.* **1.** The act of defending against danger or attack. **2.** Anything that defends or serves to defend. **3.** A plea or argument in justification or support of something. **4.** *Law* **a** The defendant's denial of the truth of a complaint; also, whatever is alleged in such denial. **b** A defendant and his legal counsel, collectively. **5.** The act or science of protecting oneself or a goal, as in sports. Also, *Brit.,* **defence.** — **Department of Defense** An executive department of the U.S. government (established 1949), headed by the Secretary of Defense, that supervises military and civil defense operations. [See DEFEND.] — **de·fense′less** *adj.* — **de·fense′less·ly** *adv.* — **de·fense′less·ness** *n.*

defense mechanism *Psychoanal.* An unconscious adjustment of behavior or mental attitude directed toward shutting out painful emotions and unacceptable impulses.

de·fen·si·ble (di·fen′sə·bəl) *adj.* Capable of being defended, maintained, or justified. **—de·fen′si·bil′i·ty, de·fen′si·ble·ness** *n.* **—de·fen′si·bly** *adv.*

de·fen·sive (di·fen′siv) *adj.* **1.** Intended or suitable for defense. **2.** Carried on for the purpose of defense: distinguished from *offensive.* **3.** Having an attitude of defense. **—** *n.* **1.** An attitude or position of defense. **2.** A means of defense. **—de·fen′sive·ly** *adv.* **—de·fen′sive·ness** *n.*

de·fer[1] (di·fûr′) *v.t. & v.i.* **·ferred, ·fer·ring** To delay or put off to some other time; postpone. [See DIFFER.] **—de·fer′·ra·ble** *adj.* **—de·fer′ment, de·fer′ral** *n.*

de·fer[2] (di·fûr′) *v.i.* **·ferred, ·fer·ring** To yield to the opinions or decisions of another: with *to.* [< MF < L < *de-* down + *ferre* to bear, carry] **—de·fer′rer** *n.*

def·er·ence (def′ər·əns) *n.* **1.** Submission or yielding to the will, opinions, etc., of another. **2.** Respectful regard.

def·er·ent (def′ər·ənt) *adj.* Deferential; respectful.

def·er·en·tial (def′ə·ren′shəl) *adj.* Marked by deference; respectful; courteous. **—def′er·en′tial·ly** *adv.*

de·ferred (di·fûrd′) *adj.* **1.** Postponed. **2.** With benefits or payments held back for a specific time: *deferred* stock. **3.** Temporarily exempted from military draft.

de·fi·ance (di·fī′əns) *n.* **1.** Bold opposition; disposition to oppose or resist. **2.** A challenge to meet in combat. **—de·fi′ant** *adj.* **—de·fi′ant·ly** *adv.*

de·fi·cien·cy (di·fish′ən·sē) *n. pl.* **·cies 1.** The state of being deficient. **2.** A lack; insufficiency.

de·fi·cient (di·fish′ənt) *adj.* **1.** Lacking an adequate or proper supply. **2.** Lacking some essential; incomplete. [See DEFECT.] **—de·fi′cient·ly** *adv.*

def·i·cit (def′ə·sit) *n.* The amount by which an expected or required sum of money falls short. [< L, it is lacking]

de·fi·er (di·fī′ər) *n.* One who defies.

de·file[1] (di·fīl′) *v.t.* **·filed, ·fil·ing 1.** To make foul or dirty. **2.** To tarnish the brightness of; corrupt the purity of. **3.** To sully or profane (a name, reputation, etc.). **4.** To violate the chastity of. [< OF < *de-* down + *fouler* to trample] **—de·file′ment** *n.* **—de·fil′er** *n.*

de·file[2] (di·fīl′, dē′fīl) *v.i.* **·filed, ·fil·ing** To march in a line. **—** *n.* **1.** A long, narrow pass, as between mountains. **2.** A marching in file. [< MF < *de* down + *file* row]

de·fine (di·fīn′) *v.t.* **·fined, ·fin·ing 1.** To state precisely the meaning of (a word, etc.). **2.** To describe the nature or properties of; explain. **3.** To determine the boundary or extent of. **4.** To bring out the outline of; show clearly. **5.** To fix with precision; specify, as the limits of power. **—** *v.i.* **6.** To make definitions. [< OF < L *de-* down + *finire* to finish] **—de·fin′a·ble** *adj.* **—de·fin′er** *n.*

def·i·nite (def′ə·nit) *adj.* **1.** Having precise limits, quantity, etc.: a *definite* sum. **2.** Known for certain; positive: It is *definite* that he won. **3.** Clearly defined; explicit; precise. **4.** *Gram.* Limiting; particularizing. [< L. See DEFINE.] **—def′i·nite·ly** *adv.* **—def′i·nite·ness** *n.*

definite article *Gram.* In English, the article *the*, which limits or particularizes the noun before which it stands.

def·i·ni·tion (def′ə·nish′ən) *n.* **1.** The act of stating what a word, phrase, set of terms, etc., means or signifies. **2.** A statement of the meaning of a word, phrase, etc. **3.** The determining of the outline or limits of anything. **4.** The state of being clearly outlined or determined. **5.** *Optics* The power of a lens to give a distinct image. **6.** *Telecom.* clarity of detail in a televised image, or of sounds received in a radio set. **— Syn.** See EXPLANATION.

de·fin·i·tive (di·fin′ə·tiv) *adj.* **1.** Sharply defining or limiting; explicit. **2.** Conclusive and unalterable; final. **3.** Most nearly accurate and complete: a *definitive* edition of Chaucer. **—** *n. Gram.* A word that defines or limits, as the definite article. **—de·fin′i·tive·ly** *adv.* **—de·fin′i·tive·ness** *n.*

de·flate (di·flāt′) *v.* **·flat·ed, ·flat·ing** *v.t.* **1.** To cause to collapse by removing air or gas. **2.** To take the conceit or self-esteem out of. **3.** *Econ.* To reduce or restrict (money or spending) so that prices decline. **—** *v.i.* **4.** To become deflated. [< L < *de-* down + *flare* to blow] **—de·fla′tor** *n.*

de·fla·tion (di·flā′shən) *n.* **1.** The act of deflating, or the state of being deflated. **2.** *Econ.* A decline in prices caused by a decrease in money supply or spending. **—de·fla′tion·ar′y** (-er′ē) *adj.* **—de·fla′tion·ist** *n. & adj.*

de·flect (di·flekt′) *v.t. & v.i.* To turn aside; swerve or cause to swerve from a course. [< L *de-* down + *flectere* to bend] **—de·flec′tive** *adj.* **—de·flec′tor** *n.*

de·flec·tion (di·flek′shən) *n.* **1.** The act of deflecting, or the state of being deflected. **2.** The amount of deviation. Also *Brit.* **de·flex′ion.**

de·flow·er (di·flou′ər) *v.t.* **1.** To despoil of flowers. **2.** To deprive (a woman) of virginity. **3.** To violate; rob of beauty, charm, etc. Also **de·flo·rate** (di·flôr′āte, -flō′rāte). [< OF < LL < L *de-* down, away + *flos, floris* flower; infl. in form by *flower*] **—def·lo·ra·tion** (def′lə·rā′shən) *n.*

de·for·est (dē·fôr′ist, -for′-) *v.t.* To clear of forests or trees. **—de·for′es·ta′tion** *n.* **—de·for′est·er** *n.*

de·form (di·fôrm′) *v.t.* **1.** To distort the form of; render misshapen. **2.** To mar the beauty or excellence of. **—** *v.i.* **3.** To become deformed. [< L < *de-* away, down + *forma* form] **—de·form′a·bil′i·ty** *n.* **—de·form′a·ble** *adj.* **—de·form′er** *n.*

de·form·a·tion (dē′fôr·mā′shən, def′ər-) *n.* **1.** The act of deforming, or the state of being deformed. **2.** A change in form or condition for the worse. **3.** An altered form.

de·formed (di·fôrmd′) *adj.* **1.** Marred in form; misshapen. **2.** Morally distorted; perverted; warped. **—de·form·ed·ly** (di·fôr′mid·lē) *adv.* **—de·form′ed·ness** *n.*

de·form·i·ty (di·fôr′mə·tē) *n. pl.* **·ties 1.** A deformed condition. **2.** An abnormally shaped part, as of the body. **3.** A deformed person or thing. **4.** Moral defect; also, depravity. [< OF < L < *de-* away, down + *forma* figure, form]

de·fraud (di·frôd′) *v.t.* To take or withhold from by fraud; cheat; swindle. [< OF < L < *de-* completely + *fraus, fraudis* cheat] **—de·fraud·a·tion** (dē′frô·dā′shən), **de·fraud′·ment** *n.* **—de·fraud′er** *n.*

de·fray (di·frā′) *v.t.* To pay (the costs, expenses, etc.). [< F < OF < *de-* away + *fraier* to spend] **—de·fray′a·ble** *adj.* **—de·fray′al, de·fray′ment** *n.* **—de·fray′er** *n.*

de·frock (dē·frok′) *v.t.* To unfrock.

de·frost (dē·frôst′, -frost′) *v.t.* To remove ice or frost from.

de·frost·er (dē·frôs′tər, -fros′-) *n.* A device for removing ice or frost, or for preventing their formation.

deft (deft) *adj.* Neat and skillful in action; adroit. [OE *gedæfte* meek, gentle] **—deft′ly** *adv.* **—deft′ness** *n.*

de·funct (di·fungkt′) *adj.* Dead; deceased. **— the defunct** The dead person. [< L < *de-* not + *fungi* to perform]

de·fy (*v.* di·fī′; *n.* dē′fī) *v.t.* **·fied, ·fy·ing 1.** To resist or confront openly and boldly. **2.** To resist or withstand successfully. **3.** To challenge (someone) to do something; dare. **—** *n. pl.* **·fies** *U.S.* A challenge; defiance. [< OF < Med.L < L *di-* not + *fidare* to be faithful]

de·gen·er·a·cy (di·jen′ər·ə·sē) *n.* **1.** The process of degenerating; deterioration. **2.** The state of being degenerate.

de·gen·er·ate (*v.* di·jen′ə·rāt; *adj., n.* di·jen′ər·it) *v.i.* **·at·ed, ·at·ing 1.** To become worse, or more debased. **2.** *Biol.* To revert to a lower type; deteriorate. **— Syn.** See RETROGRESS. **—** *adj.* Having become worse; degraded. **—** *n.* **1.** A deteriorated or degraded animal or human. **2.** A morally degraded person. [< L < *de-* down + *generare* to create] **—de·gen′er·ate·ly** *adv.* **—de·gen′er·ate·ness** *n.* **—de·gen·er·a·tive** (di·jen′o·rā′tiv, or o·tiv) *adj.*

de·gen·er·a·tion (di·jen′ə·rā′shən) *n.* **1.** The process of degenerating. **2.** A degenerate condition. **3.** *Biol.* The reversion of a group of organisms into a less complex type. **4.** *Pathol.* Progressive deterioration of an organ or part.

deg·ra·da·tion (deg′rə·dā′shən) *n.* **1.** The act of degrading. **2.** The state of being reduced in rank, honor, quality, etc.

de·grade (di·grād′) *v.t.* **·grad·ed, ·grad·ing 1.** To debase or lower in character, morals, etc. **2.** To bring into contempt; dishonor. **3.** To reduce in rank; remove from office, dignity, etc. **4.** To reduce in quality, intensity, etc. **5.** *Geol.* To reduce the height of by erosion. [< OF < LL < L *de-* down + *gradi* to step] **—de·grad′ed** *adj.* **—de·grad′ed·ly** *adv.* **—de·grad′ed·ness** *n.*

de·grad·ing (di·grā′ding) *adj.* Debasing; humiliating. **—de·grad′ing·ly** *adv.* **—de·grad′ing·ness** *n.*

de·gree (di·grē′) *n.* **1.** One of a succession of steps or stages. **2.** Relative extent, amount, or intensity. **3.** Relative dignity or rank, or position. **4.** Relative condition, manner, or respect. **5.** An academic title conferred by an institution of learning upon the completion of a course of study, or as an honorary distinction. **6.** A division or unit of a scale, as of a thermometer. **7.** A step in a line of genealogical descent. **8.** *Law* Measure of culpability: murder in the first *degree.* **9.** *Geom.* One 360th of the circumference of a circle. **10.** *Math* **a** The sum of the exponents of the unknowns of an algebraic term: x^3 and xy^2 are both of the third *degree.* **b** The exponent of the highest degree term in a polynomial or equation: $x^4 + 2x^2$ is of the fourth *degree.* **11.** *Geog.* A line or point of the earth's surface defined by its angular distance east or west of a standard meridian, or north or south of the equator. **12.** *Gram.* One of the forms of comparison (positive, comparative, or superlative) of an adjective or adverb. **13.** *Music* **a** The interval between consecutive tones of a scale. **b** A line or space in a staff. **— by degrees** Little by little; gradually. **— to a degree 1.** Somewhat. **2.** Greatly. [< OF < *de-* down + *gre* < L *gradus* a step]

de·hisce (di·his′) *v.i.* **·hisced, ·hisc·ing** To split open, as the capsule of a plant. [< L < *de-* down + *hiscere*, inceptive of *hiare* to gape] **—de·his′cence** *n.* **—de·his′cent** *adj.*

de·horn (dē·hôrn′) *v.t.* To remove the horns of (cattle).

de·hu·man·ize (dē·hyōō′mən·īz) *v.t.* **·ized, ·iz·ing 1.** To deprive of human qualities or attributes. **2.** To make mechanical, abstract, or artificial. **— de·hu′man·i·za′tion** n.

de·hu·mid·i·fi·er (dē/hyōō·mid/ə·fī/ər) n. An apparatus by which moisture is removed from the air.

de·hu·mid·i·fy (dē/hyōō·mid/ə·fī) v.t. **·fied, ·fy·ing** To render less humid. **— de/hu·mid/i·fi·ca/tion** n.

de·hy·drate (dē/hī/drāt) v. **·drat·ed, ·drat·ing** v.t. **1.** To deprive of water, as a chemical compound, vegetables, etc. **— v.i. 2.** To suffer loss of water. **— de/hy·dra/tion** n.

de·ice (dē/īs′) v.t. **·iced, ·ic·ing** To free from ice.

de·ic·er (dē/ī/sər) n. A mechanical or thermal device that breaks up formations of ice, as on an airplane wing.

de·if·ic (dē·if/ik) adj. **1.** Making, or tending to make, divine. **2.** Divine. Also **de·if/i·cal.**

de·i·fy (dē/ə·fī) v.t. **·fied, ·fy·ing 1.** To make a god of. **2.** To regard or worship as a god. **3.** To glorify or idealize. [< F < LL < L deus god + facere to make] **— de/i·fi·ca/tion** n. **— de/i·fi/er** n.

deign (dān) v.i. **1.** To think it befitting oneself (to do something); condescend. **— v.t. 2.** To condescend to grant or allow: He deigned no reply. [< OF < L dignus worthy]

De·i gra·ti·a (dē/ī grā/shē·ə, dā/ē grä/tē·ä) Latin By the grace of God. Abbr. D.G.

de·ism (dē/iz·əm) n. **1.** Belief in the existence of a personal God, based solely on the testimony of reason. **2.** Belief that God created the world subject to natural laws, but takes no interest in it. [< L deus a god + -ISM] **— de/ist** n. **— de·is/tic** or **·ti·cal** adj. **— de·is/ti·cal·ly** adv.

de·i·ty (dē/ə·tē) n. pl. **·ties 1.** A god, goddess, or divine person. **2.** Divine nature or status; godhead; divinity. **— the Deity** God. [< F < LL < L deus a god]

de·ject (di·jekt′) v.t. To depress in spirit; dishearten. [< L < de- down + jacere to throw]

de·ject·ed (di·jek/tid) adj. Depressed in spirits; disheartened. **— de·ject/ed·ly** adv. **— de·ject/ed·ness** n.

de·jec·tion (di·jek/shən) n. A state or condition of being dejected; lowness of spirits; depression; melancholy.

dé·jeu·ner (dā·zhœ·nā′) n. **1.** A late breakfast. **2.** Luncheon. [< F < dé- away + jeun fasting < L jejunus empty]

de ju·re (dē jōōr/ē) Latin By right; rightfully or legally; distinguished from de facto.

deka- combining form In the metric system, ten times (a specified unit). Also, before vowels, **dek-.** [< Gk. deka ten]

dek·a·gram (dek/ə·gram) n. In the metric system, a measure of weight equal to 10 grams: also spelled decagram. Also **dek/a·gramme.** See table front of book.

dek·a·li·ter (dek/ə·lē/tər) n. In the metric system, a measure of capacity equal to 10 liters: also spelled decaliter. Also esp. Brit. **dek/a·li/tre.** See table front of book.

dek·a·me·ter (dek/ə·mē/tər) n. In the metric system, a measure of length equal to 10 meters: also spelled decameter. Also esp. Brit. **dek/a·me/tre.** See table front of book.

dek·are (dek/âr) n. In the metric system, a thousand square meters or 10 ares: also spelled decare.

dek·a·stere (dek/ə·stir) n. In the metric system, a measure of volume equal to 10 steres: also spelled decastere.

Del·a·ware (del/ə·wâr) n. **1.** A confederacy of Algonquian tribes of North America, formerly occupying the whole Delaware River valley. **2.** The language of these people. Also called Lenape, Leni-Lenape, Lenni-Lenape.

de·lay (di·lā′) v.t. **1.** To put off to a future time; postpone; defer. **2.** To cause to be late; detain. **— v.i. 3.** To linger; procrastinate. **— n. 1.** The act of delaying. **2.** The fact or condition of being delayed. [< OF delaier] **— de·lay/er** n.

de·le (dē/lē) v.t. **·led, ·le·ing** Printing To take out; delete: usu. an imperative represented by a sign (ϑ). Compare STET. [< L, imperative of delere to erase]

de·lec·ta·ble (di·lek/tə·bəl) adj. Giving great pleasure; delightful. [< OF < L delectare. See DELIGHT.] **— de·lec/ta·ble·ness, de·lec/ta·bil/i·ty** n. **— de·lec/ta·bly** adv.

de·lec·ta·tion (dē/lek·tā/shən) n. Delight, enjoyment.

del·e·ga·cy (del/ə·gə·sē) n. pl. **·cies 1.** The act of delegating, or the state of being delegated. **2.** The office or authority given a delegate. **3.** A body of delegates.

del·e·gate (n. del/ə·gāt, -git; v. del/ə·gāt) n. **1.** A person sent with authority to represent or act for another or others. **2.** U.S. **a** A person elected or appointed to represent a Territory in the House of Representatives, where he may speak but not vote. **b** A member of the lower house (**House of Delegates**) of the legislature in Maryland, Virginia, and West Virginia. **— v.t. ·gat·ed, ·gat·ing 1.** To send as a representative, with authority to act. **2.** To commit or entrust (powers, authority, etc.) to another as an agent. **3.** To assign (a debtor of one's own) to one's creditor to satisfy a claim. [< L < de- down + legare to send]

del·e·ga·tion (del/ə·gā/shən) n. **1.** The act of delegating, or the state of being delegated; deputation. **2.** A person or persons appointed to represent others; delegates collectively.

de·lete (di·lēt′) v.t. **·let·ed, ·let·ing** To take out (written or printed matter); cancel. [< L deletus, pp. of delere to erase, destroy] **— de·le/tion** n.

del·e·te·ri·ous (del/ə·tir/ē·əs) adj. Causing moral or physical injury. **— Syn.** See PERNICIOUS. [< NL < Gk. dēlētērios harmful] **— del/e·te/ri·ous·ly** adv. **— del/e·te/ri·ous·ness** n.

Del·fi (del/fī) See DELPHI.

delft (delft) n. **1.** A glazed earthenware, usu. white or blue, first made at Delft, Holland, about 1310. **2.** Any tableware resembling this. Also **delf** (delf), **delft/ware/.**

de·lib·er·ate (v. di·lib/ə·rāt; adj. di·lib/ər·it) v. **·at·ed, ·at·ing** v.i. **1.** To consider carefully and at length. **2.** To take counsel together so as to reach a decision. **— v.t. 3.** To think about or consider carefully; weigh. **— adj. 1.** Carefully thought out; intentional. **2.** Slow and cautious in determining or deciding. **3.** Leisurely in movement or manner. [< L de- completely + librare to weigh] **— de·lib/er·ate·ly** adv. **— de·lib/er·ate·ness** n.

de·lib·er·a·tion (di·lib/ə·rā/shən) n. **1.** Careful and prolonged consideration. **1.** Often pl. Examination and discussion of the arguments for and against a measure. **3.** Slowness and care in decision or action.

de·lib·er·a·tive (di·lib/ə·rā/tiv, -rə·tiv) adj. Involved in or characterized by deliberation: a deliberative body.

del·i·ca·cy (del/ə·kə·sē) n. pl. **·cies 1.** The quality of being delicate. **2.** Frailty or weakness of body or health. **3.** Refinement of feeling, appreciation, etc. **4.** Consideration for the feelings of others. **5.** Nicety of touch or execution. **6.** Sensitivity in reaction, as of instruments. **7.** Need of cautious, tactful treatment: a subject of great delicacy. **8.** Something choice and dainty, as an item of food.

del·i·cate (del/ə·kit) adj. **1.** Exquisite and fine in workmanship, texture, etc. **2.** Daintily pleasing, as in taste, aroma, or color. **3.** Easily injured or destroyed; frail. **4.** Requiring tactful treatment. **5.** Gentle and skilled: a delicate touch. **6.** Sensitive and subtle in feeling, perception, or expression: a delicate eye for color. **7.** Showing a fine appreciation for what is proper and becoming. **8.** Considerate of the feelings of others. **9.** Sensitively accurate: a delicate thermometer. **10.** Subtle: a delicate distinction. [< L delicatus pleasing] **— del/i·cate·ly** adv. **— del/i·cate·ness** n.

del·i·ca·tes·sen (del/ə·kə·tes/ən) n.pl. **1.** (often construed as sing.) Cooked or preserved foods, as cooked meats, cheeses, pickles, etc. **2.** (construed as sing.) A store that sells such foods. [< G, pl. of delicatesse delicacy]

de·li·cious (di·lish/əs) adj. Extremely pleasant or enjoyable, esp. to the taste. [< OF < LL < L delicia delight] **— de·li/cious·ly** adv. **— de·li/cious·ness** n.

De·li·cious (di·lish/əs) n. A variety of sweet, red apple.

de·light (di·līt′) n. **1.** Great pleasure; gratification; joy. **2.** That which gives extreme pleasure. **3.** Poetic The quality of delighting; charm. **— v.i. 1.** To take great pleasure; rejoice: with in or the infinitive. **2.** To give great enjoyment. **— v.t. 3.** To please or gratify highly. [< OF < L delectare, freq. of delicere < de- away + lacere to entice] **— de·light/ed** adj. **— de·light/ed·ly** adv.

de·light·ful (di·līt/fəl) adj. Affording delight; extremely pleasing. **— de·light/ful·ly** adv. **— de·light/ful·ness** n.

De·li·lah (di·lī/lə) A Philistine woman, the mistress of Samson, who betrayed him to the Philistines by cutting off his hair, thus depriving him of his strength. Judg. xvi 4–20. **— n.** A voluptuous but treacherous woman.

de·lim·it (di·lim/it) v.t. To prescribe the limits of. Also **de·lim/i·tate.** [< F < L < de- completely + limitare to bound] **— de·lim/i·ta/tion** n. **— de·lim/i·ta·tive** adj.

de·lin·e·ate (di·lin/ē·āt) v.t. **·at·ed, ·at·ing 1.** To draw in outline. **2.** To represent by a drawing. **3.** To portray verbally; describe. [< L < de- completely + lineare to draw a line] **— de·lin/e·a/tion** n. **— de·lin/e·a/tive** adj. **— de·lin/e·a/tor** n.

de·lin·quen·cy (di·ling/kwən·sē) n. pl. **·cies 1.** Neglect of duty. **2.** A fault; offense. **3.** Juvenile delinquency.

de·lin·quent (di·ling/kwənt) adj. **1.** Neglectful of or failing in duty or obligation; guilty of an offense. **2.** Due and unpaid, as taxes. **— n. 1.** One who fails to perform a duty or commits a fault. **2.** A juvenile delinquent. [< L < de- down, away + linquere to leave] **— de·lin/quent·ly** adv.

del·i·quesce (del/ə·kwes′) v.i. **·quesced, ·quesc·ing 1.** To melt or pass away gradually. **2.** To become liquid by absorption of moisture from the air, as certain salts. [< L < de- completely + liquescere to melt] **— del/i·ques/cence** n. **— del/i·ques/cent** adj.

de·lir·i·ous (di·lir/ē·əs) adj. **1.** Suffering from delirium. **2.** Characteristic of delirium: delirious dreams. **3.** Wildly excited. **— de·lir/i·ous·ly** adv. **— de·lir/i·ous·ness** n.

de·lir·i·um (di·lir/ē·əm) n. **1.** A sporadic or temporary mental disturbance associated with fever, intoxication, etc., and marked by excitement, hallucinations, and general incoherence. **2.** Wild emotion or excitement. [< L < de- down, away < lira turrow, track]

delirium tre·mens (trē/mənz) A violent delirium caused esp. by excessive use of alcoholic liquors.

de·liv·er (di·liv/ər) v.t. **1.** To hand over; surrender. **2.** To carry and distribute: to *deliver* newspapers. **3.** To give forth; send forth: to *deliver* a blow. **4.** To give forth in words; utter. **5.** To throw or pitch, as a ball. **6.** To free from restraint, evil, danger, etc. **7.** To assist in the birth of (offspring). **— to be delivered of** To give birth. **— to deliver oneself of** To put into words; express. [< OF < LL < L *de-* down, away + *liberare* to set free] **— de·liv′er·a·ble** *adj.* **— de·liv′er·er** *n.*

de·liv·er·ance (di-liv′ər-əns) *n.* **1.** The act of delivering, or the state of being delivered. **2.** An expression of opinion.

de·liv·er·y (di-liv′ər-ē) *n. pl.* **·er·ies 1.** The act of delivering or distributing something. **2.** That which is distributed, as mail. **3.** The act of liberating; release. **4.** A transferring or handing over. **5.** The bringing forth of offspring. **6.** Manner of utterance, as in public speaking. **7.** The act or manner of giving forth or discharging a ball, a blow, etc.

dell (del) *n.* A small, secluded, usu. wooded valley. [ME]

de·louse (dē-lous′) *v.t.* **·loused, ·lous·ing** To remove lice or other insect vermin from.

Del·phi (del′fī) An ancient city in Phocis, Greece; famous for its oracle: also *Delfi.* **— Del·phi·an** (del′fē-ən) *adj. & n.*

Del·phic (del′fik) *adj.* **1.** Relating to Delphi or to Apollo's oracle there. **2.** Oracular.

del·phin·i·um (del-fin′ē-əm) *n.* Any of a genus of perennial plants of the crowfoot family, having large, spurred flowers, usu. blue; the larkspur. [< NL < Gk. *delphis* dolphin; so called from the shape of the nectary]

del·ta (del′tə) *n.* **1.** The fourth letter in the Greek alphabet (Δ, δ), corresponding to English *d*. See ALPHABET. **2.** *Geog.* An alluvial, typically triangular-shaped, silt deposit at or in the mouth of a river. **3.** Anything triangular. [< Gk.]

del·ta·he·dron (del′tə-hē′drən) *n. pl.* **·dra** (-drə) *Crystall.* A crystal form having twelve equal, trapezoidal faces. Also **del′to·he′dron.** For illus. see CRYSTAL.

del·toid (del′toid) *n. Anat.* A triangular muscle covering the shoulder joint. **—** *adj.* Shaped like a delta; triangular. [< Gk. < *delta* the letter Δ + *eidos* form]

de·lude (di-lood′) *v.t.* **·lud·ed, ·lud·ing** To mislead the mind or judgment of; deceive. [< L < *de-* from, away + *ludere* to play] **— de·lud′er** *n.* **— de·lud′ing·ly** *adv.*

del·uge (del′yooj) *v.t.* **·uged, ·ug·ing 1.** To flood with water. **2.** To overwhelm; destroy. **—** *n.* **1.** A great flood or inundation. **2.** Something that overwhelms or engulfs: a *deluge* of tears. **— the Deluge** The flood in the time of Noah. *Gen.* vii. [< OF < L < *dis-* away + *luere* to wash]

de·lu·sion (di-loo′zhən) *n.* **1.** The act of deluding. **2.** The state of being deluded. **3.** A false, fixed belief, held in spite of evidence to the contrary. **— de·lu′sion·al** *adj.*

de·lu·sive (di-loo′siv) *adj.* Tending to delude; misleading. Also **de·lu·so·ry** (di-loo′sər-ē). **— de·lu′sive·ly** *adv.* **— de·lu′sive·ness** *n.*

de luxe (di looks′, di luks′; *Fr.* də lüks′) Elegant and expensive; of superfine quality. [< F, lit., of luxury]

delve (delv) *v.* **delved, delv·ing** *v.i.* To make careful investigation; search for information. [OE *delfan*] **— delv′er** *n.*

de·mag·net·ize (dē-mag′nə-tīz) *v.t.* **·ized, ·iz·ing** To deprive (a substance) of magnetism. **— de·mag′net·i·za′tion** *n.* **— de·mag′net·iz′er** *n.*

dem·a·gog·ic (dem′ə-goj′ik, -gog′ik) *adj.* Of or like a demagogue. Also **dem′a·gog′i·cal.** **— dem′a·gog′i·cal·ly** *adv.*

dem·a·gogue (dem′ə-gôg, -gog) *n.* One who leads the populace by appealing to prejudices and emotions. Also **dem′a·gog.** [< Gk. < *dēmos* people + *agein* to lead]

dem·a·gogu·er·y (dem′ə-gôg′ər-ē, -gog′ər-ē) *n.* The spirit, method, or conduct of a demagogue. Also **dem′a·gog′ism.**

dem·a·go·gy (dem′ə-gō′jē, -gôg′ē, -gog′ē) *n.* **1.** Demagoguery. **2.** The rule of a demagogue. **3.** Demagogues collectively.

de·mand (di-mand′, -mänd′) *v.t.* **1.** To ask for boldly or preemptorily. **2.** To claim as due. **3.** To inquire formally. **4.** To have need for; require. **5.** *Law* **a** To summon to court. **b** To make formal claim to (property). **—** *v.i.* **6.** To make a demand. **—** *n.* **1.** The act of demanding. **2.** That which is demanded. **3.** A claim or requirement: the *demands* on one's time. **4.** An inquiry. **5.** *Law* A request or claim. **6.** *Econ.* **a** The desire to possess combined with the ability to purchase. **b** The potential amount of certain goods that will be purchased at a given time for a given price. **— in demand** Desired; sought after. **— on demand** On presentation: a note payable *on demand.* [< F < L < *de-* down, away + *mandare* to command, order] **— de·mand′a·ble** *adj.* **— de·mand′er** *n.*

de·mar·cate (di-mär′kāt, dē′mär-kāt) *v.t.* **·cat·ed, ·cat·ing 1.** To mark the limits of. **2.** To differentiate; separate.

de·mar·ca·tion (dē′mär-kā′shən) *n.* **1.** The fixing or marking of boundaries or limits. **2.** The limits or boundaries fixed. **3.** A limiting or separating. [< Sp. < *de-* down (< L *de-*) + *marcar* to mark a boundary]

dé·marche (dā-mȧrsh′) *n. French* **1.** A mode of procedure. **2.** In diplomacy, a change in policy.

de·mean¹ (di-mēn′) *v.t.* To behave or conduct (oneself) in a particular way. [< OF < *de-* down (< L *de-*) + *mener* to lead < LL *minare* to threaten, drive]

de·mean² (di-mēn′) *v.t.* To lower in dignity or reputation; debase; degrade. **— Syn.** See ABASE.

de·mean·or (di-mē′nər) *n.* The manner in which one behaves or bears oneself. Also, *Brit.,* **de·mean′our.**

de·ment (di-ment′) *v.t.* To make insane.

de·ment·ed (di-men′tid) *adj.* Mentally ill; insane. **— de·ment′ed·ly** *adv.* **— de·ment′ed·ness** *n.*

de·men·tia (di-men′shə, -shē-ə) *n.* Loss or serious impairment of mental powers. [< L, madness]

dementia pre·cox (prē′koks) *Psychiatry* Schizophrenia: a former name. Also **de·men′tia prae′cox.**

de·mer·it (di-mer′it) *n.* **1.** A defect; fault. **2.** In schools, etc., a mark for failure or misconduct. [< Med.L < L < *de-* down, away + *merere* to deserve]

de·mesne (di-mān′, -mēn′) *n.* **1.** In law, lands held in one's own power. **2.** A manor house and the adjoining lands. **3.** A region; domain. [< OF *demeine, demaine*]

De·me·ter (di-mē′tər) The Greek goddess of agriculture, marriage, and fertility: identified with *Ceres.*

demi- *prefix* **1.** Half; intermediate. **2.** Inferior or less in size, quality, etc.; partial. [< F < L < *dis-* from, apart + *medius* middle]

dem·i·god (dem′ē-god′) *n.* **1.** An inferior diety. **2.** A man with the attributes of a god. **— dem′i·god′dess** *n.fem.*

dem·i·john (dem′ē·jon′) *n.* A narrow-necked jug, often enclosed in wickerwork. [< F *dame-jeanne,* lit., Lady Jane]

de·mil·i·ta·rize (dē-mil′ə-tə-rīz′) *v.t.* **·rized, ·riz·ing** To remove military characteristics from; free from militarism.

dem·i·mon·daine (dem′ē-mon-dān′) *n.* A woman of the demimonde. Also **dem·i·rep** (dem′ē-rep′). [< F]

dem·i·monde (dem′ē-mond, dem′ē-mond′) *n.* The class of women who have lost social position because of their scandalous behavior. [< F < *demi-* half, partial + *monde* world]

de·mise (di-mīz′) *n.* **1.** Death. **2.** *Law* A transfer of rights or an estate. **—** *v.* **·mised, ·mis·ing** *v.t.* **1.** To bestow (royal power) by death or abdication. **2.** *Law* To lease or transfer (an estate). **—** *v.i.* **3.** To pass by will or inheritance. [< OF < L < *de-* down, away + *mittere* to send]

dem·i·sem·i·qua·ver (dem′ē-sem′ē-kwā′vər) *n. Music Chiefly Brit.* A thirty-second note.

dem·i·tasse (dem′ē-tas′, -täs′) *n.* **1.** A small cup in which after-dinner coffee is served. **2.** Coffee served in such a cup. [< F, a half cup]

demo- *combining form* People. [< Gk. *dēmos* people]

de·mo·bi·lize (dē-mō′bə-līz) *v.t.* **·lized, ·liz·ing** To disband (an army or troops). **— de·mo′bi·li·za′tion** *n.*

de·moc·ra·cy (di-mok′rə-sē) *n. pl.* **·cies 1.** A form of government in which political power resides in all the people and is exercised by them directly or is given to elected representatives. **2.** A state so governed. **3.** The spirit or practice of political, legal, or social equality. [< F < Med.L < Gk. < *dēmos* people + *kratein* to rule]

De·moc·ra·cy (di-mok′rə-sē) *n.* The principles of the Democratic Party; also, the party, or its members collectively.

dem·o·crat (dem′ə-krat) *n.* **1.** One who favors a democracy. **2.** One who believes in political and social equality.

Dem·o·crat (dem′ə-krat) *n.* A member of the Democratic Party in the United States. *Abbr. D., Dem.*

dem·o·crat·ic (dem′ə-krat′ik) *adj.* **1.** Of, pertaining to, or characterized by the principles of democracy. **2.** Existing or provided for the benefit or enjoyment of all. **3.** Practicing social equality. **— dem′o·crat′i·cal·ly** *adv.*

Dem·o·crat·ic (dem′ə-krat′ik) *adj.* Of, pertaining to, or characteristic of the Democratic Party.

Democratic Party One of the two major political parties in the United States, dating from 1828.

de·moc·ra·tize (di-mok′rə-tīz) *v.* **& *v.i.* ·tized, ·tiz·ing** To make or become democratic. **— de·moc′ra·ti·za′tion** *n.*

de·mol·ish (di-mol′ish) *v.t.* **1.** To tear down, as a building. **2.** To destroy utterly; ruin. [< F < L < *de-* down + *moliri* to build] **— de·mol′ish·er** *n.* **— de·mol′ish·ment** *n.* **— Syn.** A building is *demolished* if smashed to fragments, and *razed* if leveled to the ground. It is *ruined* if made unfit for habitation or use, though much of its structure may remain. *Destroy* is a very general term, covering all these senses.

dem·o·li·tion (dem′ə-lish′ən) *n.* The act or result of demolishing; destruction. **— dem′o·li′tion·ist** *n.*

de·mon (dē′mən) *n.* **1.** An evil spirit; devil. **2.** A very wicked or cruel person. **3.** *Informal* A person of great skill or zeal: a *demon* with a gun. [< L < Gk. *daimōn*]

de·mon·e·tize (dē-mon′ə-tīz) *v.t.* **·tized, ·tiz·ing 1.** To deprive (currency) of standard value. **2.** To withdraw from use, as currency. **— de·mon′e·ti·za′tion** *n.*

---

de·mo·ni·ac (di·mō′nē·ak) *adj.* 1. Of, like, or befitting a demon. 2. Influenced or possessed by or as by demons; frenzied. Also **de·mo·ni·a·cal** (dē′mə·nī′ə·kəl). — *n.* One supposedly possessed of a demon. — **de′mo·ni′a·cal·ly** *adv.*

de·mon·ic (di·mon′ik) *adj.* 1. Of or like a demon. Also **de·mo·ni·an** (di·mō′nē·ən). 2. Inspired, as by a demon.

de·mon·ism (dē′mən·iz′əm) *n.* 1. Belief in demons. 2. Demonolatry. 3. Demonology. — **de′mon·ist** *n.*

demono- *combining form* Demon. Also, before vowels, **demon-**. [< Gk. *daimōn* spirit, god]

de·mon·ol·a·try (dē′mən·ol′ə·trē) *n.* The worship of demons. [< DEMONO- + Gk. *latreia* worship] — **de′mon·ol′·a·ter** *n.*

de·mon·ol·o·gy (dē′mən·ol′ə·jē) *n.* The study of demons or of belief in demons. — **de′mon·ol′o·gist** *n.*

de·mon·stra·ble (di·mon′strə·bəl, dem′ən-) *adj.* Capable of being demonstrated or proved. — **de·mon′stra·bil′i·ty**, **de·mon′stra·ble·ness** *n.* — **de·mon′stra·bly** *adv.*

dem·on·strate (dem′ən·strāt) *v.* **·strat·ed**, **·strat·ing** *v.t.* 1. To explain or describe by use of experiments, examples, etc. 2. To prove or show by reasoning; make evident. 3. To show feelings clearly. — *v.i.* 4. To take part in a public demonstration. 5. To make a show of military force. [< L < *de-* completely + *monstrare* to show, point out]

dem·on·stra·tion (dem′ən·strā′shən) *n.* 1. The act of making known or evident. 2. Undeniable proof or evidence. 3. An explanation or showing of how something works, as a product. 4. A show or expression: a *demonstration* of love. 5. A display of public feeling, as a mass meeting or parade. 6. A show of military force or readiness.

de·mon·stra·tive (di·mon′strə·tiv) *adj.* 1. Serving to demonstrate or point out. 2. Able to prove beyond doubt; convincing and conclusive. 3. Inclined to strong expression. 4. *Gram.* Indicating the person or object referred to. — *n. Gram.* A demonstrative pronoun. — **de·mon′stra·tive·ly** *adv.* — **de·mon′stra·tive·ness** *n.*

demonstrative pronoun *Gram.* A pronoun that directly points out its antecedents, as *this*, *those.*

dem·on·stra·tor (dem′ən·strā′tər) *n.* One who or that which demonstrates.

de·mor·al·ize (di·môr′əl·īz, -mor′-) *v.t.* **·ized**, **·iz·ing** 1. To corrupt or deprave. 2. To lower the morale of. 3. To throw into disorder. — **de·mor′al·i·za′tion** *n.* — **de·mor′·al·iz′er** *n.*

de·mote (di·mōt′) *v.t.* **·mot·ed**, **·mot·ing** To reduce to a lower grade or rank. — **de·mo′tion** *n.*

de·mul·cent (di·mul′sənt) *adj.* Soothing. — *n. Med.* A soothing substance. [< L < *de-* down + *mulcere* to soothe]

de·mur (di·mûr′) *v.i.* **·murred**, **·mur·ring** 1. To offer objections; take exception. 2. To delay; hesitate. 3. *Law* To interpose a demurrer. — *n.* 1. The act of demurring. 2. An objection, as to proposed action. 3. A delay. [< OF < L < *de-* completely + *morari* to delay]

de·mure (di·myŏŏr′) *adj.* **·mur·er**, **·mur·est** 1. Grave; reserved. 2. Prim; coy. [ME < OF < L *maturus* mature, discreet] — **de·mure′ly** *adv.* — **de·mure′ness** *n.*

de·mur·rage (di·mûr′ij) *n.* 1. The detention of a vessel, railway freight car, or other commercial conveyance, beyond the specified time for departure, as a result of loading, unloading, etc. 2. Compensation for such delay.

de·mur·rer (di·mûr′ər) *n.* 1. *Law* A pleading that allows the truth of the facts stated by the opposite party, but denies that they are sufficient to constitute a good cause of action or defense in law. 2. Any objection or exception taken. 3. One who demurs. [< AF]

den (den) *n.* 1. The cave or retreat of a wild animal; a lair. 2. A site or dwelling: used pejoratively: a *den* of thieves. 3. A small, private room for relaxation or study. — *v.i.* **denned**, **den·ning** To dwell in or as in a den. [OE *denn*]

de·nar·i·us (di·nâr′ē·əs) *n.* *pl.* **·nar·i·i** (-nâr′ē·ī) 1. A silver coin of ancient Rome; the penny of the New Testament. 2. A gold coin of ancient Rome. [< L < *decem* ten]

de·na·tion·al·ize (dē·nash′ən·əl·īz′) *v.t.* **·ized**, **·iz·ing** To deprive of national character, status, or rights. Also *Brit.* **de·na′tion·al·ise′.** — **de·na′tion·al·i·za′tion** *n.*

de·nat·u·ral·ize (dē·nach′ər·əl·īz′) *v.t.* **·ized**, **·iz·ing** 1. To render unnatural. 2. To deprive of citizenship. Also *Brit.* **de·nat′u·ral·ise′.** — **de·nat′u·ral·i·za′tion** *n.*

de·na·ture (dē·nā′chər) *v.t.* **·tured**, **·tur·ing** 1. To change the nature of. 2. To adulterate (alcohol, fat, etc.) so as to make unfit for drinking or eating without destroying other useful properties. Also **de·na′tur·ize.** — **de·na′tur·ant** *n.*

den·drite (den′drīt) *n. Physiol.* A threadlike, branching process of a nerve cell that conducts impulses toward the cell body. [< Gk. < *dendron* tree] — **den·drit′ic** (-drit′ik) or **·i·cal** *adj.* — **den·drit′i·cal·ly** *adv.*

dendro- *combining form* Tree. Also **dendr-** (before vowels), **dendri-**. [< Gk. *dendron* tree]

-dendron *combining form* Tree. [< Gk. *dendron* tree]

Den·eb (den′eb) *n.* One of the 20 brightest stars, 1.33 magnitude; Alpha in the constellation Cygnus.

den·gue (deng′gē, -gā) *n. Pathol.* An acute, tropical, virus disease transmitted by the bite of a mosquito and characterized by fever, eruptions, and severe pains in the joints. [< Sp., ult. < Swahili]

de·ni·a·ble (di·nī′ə·bəl) *adj.* That can be denied. — **de·ni′a·bly** *adv.*

de·ni·al (di·nī′əl) *n.* 1. A contradiction, as of a statement. 2. Refusal to believe a doctrine, etc. 3. A disowning or disavowal. 4. Refusal to grant, give, or allow.

de·nic·o·tin·ize (dē·nik′ə·tin·īz′) *v.t.* **·ized**, **·iz·ing** To remove nicotine from (tobacco). Also **de·nic′o·tine.**

de·ni·er¹ (di·nī′ər) *n.* One who makes denial.

den·ier² (den′yər, də·nir′) *n.* A unit of weight for denoting the coarseness or fineness of rayon, nylon, or silk yarns. [See DENARIUS.]

den·im (den′əm) *n.* 1. A strong, twilled cotton used for overalls, uniforms, etc.; also, a finer grade of this fabric used for hangings, upholstery, etc. 2. *pl.* Garments made of this material. [< F (*serge*) *de Nîmes* (serge) of Nîmes]

den·i·zen (den′ə·zən) *n.* 1. An inhabitant. 2. A person, animal, or thing at home or naturalized in a region or condition not native to it. — *v.t.* To make (someone or something) a denizen. [< AF < *deinz* inside < *de intus* from within] — **den′i·zen·a′tion** *n.*

de·nom·i·nate (*v.* di·nom′ə·nāt; *adj.* di·nom′ə·nit) *v.t.* **·nat·ed**, **·nat·ing** To give a name to; call. — *adj.* Having a specific name. [< L < *de-* down + *nomen* name]

de·nom·i·na·tion (di·nom′ə·nā′shən) *n.* 1. The act of naming or calling by name. 2. A name. 3. Any specifically named class or group of things or people: There were many *denominations* of criminals. 4. A religious group; a sect.

de·nom·i·na·tion·al (di·nom′ə·nā′shən·əl) *adj.* Of, pertaining to, or supported by a religious denomination or sect; sectarian. — **de·nom′i·na′tion·al·ly** *adv.*

de·nom·i·na·tion·al·ism (di·nom′ə·nā′shən·əl·iz′əm) *n.* 1. A disposition to divide into or form denominations. 2. Rigid adherence or devotion to a denomination or sect; sectarianism. — **de·nom′i·na′tion·al·ist** *n. & adj.*

de·nom·i·na·tive (di·nom′ə·nā′tiv, -nə·tiv) *adj.* 1. That gives or constitutes a name; appellative. 2. *Gram.* Derived from a noun or adjective, as the verb *to garden*. — *n. Gram.* A denominative word. — **de·nom′i·na′tive·ly** *adv.*

de·nom·i·na·tor (di·nom′ə·nā′tər) *n. Math.* The term of a fraction below the line indicating the number of equal parts into which the unit is divided.

de·no·ta·tion (dē′nō·tā′shən) *n.* 1. The specific meaning of, or the object or objects designated by, a word. 2. The act of denoting. 3. That which indicates, as a sign.

de·note (di·nōt′) *v.t.* **·not·ed**, **·not·ing** 1. To point out or make known; mark. 2. To signify; indicate. 3. To designate; mean: said of words, symbols, etc. [< L < *de-* down + *notare* to mark] — **de·not′a·ble** *adj.* — **de·no·ta·tive** (di·nō′tə·tiv, dē′nō·tā′tiv) *adj.*

dé·noue·ment (dā·nōō·män′) *n.* 1. The final solution of the plot of a play, novel, etc. 2. Any final outcome. [< OF < *des-* away (< L *dis-*) + *nouer* to knot]

de·nounce (di·nouns′) *v.t.* **·nounced**, **·nounc·ing** 1. To attack or condemn openly and vehemently; inveigh against. 2. To inform against; accuse. 3. To announce as a threat. 4. To give formal notice of the termination of (a treaty, etc.). [< OF < L < *de-* down + *nuntiare* to announce] — **de·nounce′ment** *n.* — **de·nounc′er** *n.*

dense (dens) *adj.* **dens·er**, **dens·est** 1. Compact; thick; close. 2. Hard to penetrate. 3. Stupid. [< L *densus*] — **dense′ly** *adv.* — **dense′ness** *n.*

den·si·ty (den′sə·tē) *n.* *pl.* **·ties** 1. The state or quality of being dense; closeness of parts; compactness. 2. Stupidity. 3. *Physics* The mass of a substance per unit of its volume. 4. *Sociol.* The number of specified units, as persons, families, or dwellings, per unit of area. [< MF < L < *densus* thick]

dent (dent) *n.* A small depression made by striking or pressing. — *v.t.* 1. To make a dent in. — *v.i.* 2. To become dented. [Var. of DINT]

den·tal (den′təl) *adj.* 1. Of or pertaining to the teeth. 2. Of or pertaining to dentistry. 3. *Phonet.* Produced with the tip of the tongue against or near the upper front teeth. — *n. Phonet.* A dental consonant. [< NL < L *dens*, tooth]

dental plate A denture.

den·tate (den′tāt) *adj.* Having teeth or toothlike processes; toothed; notched. [< L *dentatus* having teeth] — **den′tate·ly** *adv.* — **den·ta′tion** *n.*

denti- *combining form* Tooth. Also, before vowels, **dent-**.

den·ti·frice (den′tə·fris) *n.* A preparation, as a powder or paste, for cleaning the teeth. [< MF < L < *dens*, *dentis* tooth + *fricare* to rub]

den·tine (den′tēn, -tin) *n. Anat.* The hard, calcified substance forming the body of a tooth, situated just beneath the enamel and cementum. Also **den′tin** (-tin). For illus. see TOOTH. — **den′ti·nal** *adj.*

den·tist (den′tist) *n.* One who practices dentistry. [< F *dentiste* < *dent* a tooth]

den·tist·ry (den′tis·trē) *n.* **1.** The branch of medicine concerned with the diagnosis, prevention, and treatment of diseases affecting the teeth. **2.** The work of a dentist.

den·ti·tion (den·tish′ən) *n.* **1.** The process or period of cutting teeth; teething. **2.** The kind, number, and arrangement of teeth in man and other animals.

den·ture (den′chər) *n.* **1.** A set of teeth. **2.** A set of artificial teeth, either partial or full: also called *dental plate.* [< F < *dent* tooth] — **den′tur·al** *adj.*

de·nu·date (di·nōō′dāt, -nyōō′-, den′yōō·dāt) *adj.* Stripped of foliage or other covering; naked. — *v.t.* **·dat·ed, ·dat·ing** To denude. [< L *denudatus,* pp. of *denudare.* See DENUDE.]

de·nude (di·nōōd′, -nyōōd′) *v.t.* **·nud·ed, ·nud·ing** **1.** To strip the covering from; make naked. **2.** *Geol.* To expose to view by erosion. [< L < *de-* down, completely + *nudare* to strip] — **den·u·da·tion** (den′yōō·dā′shən, dē′nōō-, -nyōō-) *n.*

de·nun·ci·ate (di·nun′sē·āt, -shē-) *v.t. & v.i.* **·at·ed, ·at·ing** To denounce. [< L < *de-* down + *nuntiare* to announce]

de·nun·ci·a·tion (di·nun′sē·ā′shən, -shē-) *n.* **1.** Open disapproval or condemnation of a person or action. **2.** An accusation. **3.** A threat or warning. **4.** Formal notice that a treaty is to be terminated.

de·nun·ci·a·to·ry (di·nun′sē·ə·tôr′ē, -tō′rē, -shē-) *adj.* Of the nature of or containing denunciation; accusing.

de·ny (di·nī′) *v.t.* **·nied, ·ny·ing** **1.** To declare to be untrue; contradict. **2.** To refuse to believe; declare to be false or invalid, as a doctrine. **3.** To refuse to give; withhold. **4.** To refuse (someone) a request. **5.** To refuse to acknowledge; disown; repudiate. **6.** To refuse access to. — **to deny oneself** To refuse oneself something desired; practice self-denial. [< OF < L < *de-* completely + *negare* to say no, refuse]

de·o·dar (dē′ə·där) *n.* The East Indian cedar, prized for its durable, light red wood. [< Skt. < *deva* god + *dāru* wood]

de·o·dor·ant (dē·ō′dər·ənt) *adj.* Destroying, absorbing, or disguising bad odors. — *n.* A deodorant substance.

de·o·dor·ize (dē·ō′dər·īz) *v.t.* **·ized, ·iz·ing** To modify, destroy, or disguise the odor of. — **de·o′dor·i·za′tion** *n.* — **de·o′dor·iz′er** *n.*

de·ox·i·dize (dē·ok′sə·dīz) *v.t.* **·dized, ·diz·ing** **1.** To remove oxygen from. **2.** To reduce from the state of an oxide. — **de·ox′i·di·za′tion** *n.* — **de·ox′i·diz′er** *n.*

de·ox·y- *combining form* Containing less oxygen than. Also *desoxy-.*

de·ox·y·ri·bo·nu·cle·ic acid (dē·ok′sē·rī′bō·nōō·klē′ik, -nyōō-) *Biochem.* A nucleic acid forming a principal constituent of the genes and known to play an important role in the genetic action of the chromosomes. Abbr. *DNA.*

de·part (di·pärt′) *v.i.* **1.** To go away; leave. **2.** To deviate; differ; vary: with *from:* to *depart* from tradition. **3.** To die. — *v.t.* **4.** To leave: now archaic except in the phrase **to depart this life.** [< OF < *de-* away + *partir* to divide]

de·part·ed (di·pär′tid) *adj.* **1.** Gone; past. **2.** Dead. — **the departed** The dead person, or the dead collectively.

de·part·ment (di·pärt′mənt) *n.* **1.** A distinct part or division of something, as of a business or college: the English *department.* **2.** *Usu. cap. U.S.* An executive division of the government, headed by a cabinet officer. **3.** In France, an administrative district. [See DEPART.] — **de·part·men·tal** (dē′pärt·men′təl) *adj.* — **de′part·men′tal·ly** *adv.*

de·part·men·tal·ize (dē′pärt·men′təl·īz) *v.t. & v.i.* **·ized, ·iz·ing** To divide into departments.

department store A large retail establishment selling various types of merchandise and service.

de·par·ture (di·pär′chər) *n.* **1.** The act of going away or taking leave. **2.** Deviation from an accepted or ordinary method, course, etc. **3.** *Archaic* Death.

de·pend (di·pend′) *v.i.* **1.** To rely; trust: with *on* or *upon.* **2.** To be conditioned or determined; be contingent: with *on* or *upon.* **3.** To rely for maintenance, etc.: with *on* or *upon.* **4.** To hang down: with *from.* [< OF < L < *de-* down + *pendere* to hang]

de·pend·a·ble (di·pen′də·bəl) *adj.* That can be depended upon; trustworthy. — **de·pend′a·bil′i·ty, de·pend′a·ble·ness** *n.* — **de·pend′a·bly** *adv.*

de·pen·dence (di·pen′dəns) *n.* **1.** The state of relying on something or someone. **2.** Reliance or trust. **3.** The state of being contingent on or determined by something else. **4.** Subjection to the control or guidance of another. **5.** The object of one's reliance. Also **de·pen′dance.**

de·pen·den·cy (di·pen′dən·sē) *n. pl.* **·cies** **1.** The state of being dependent; dependence. **2.** That which is dependent or subordinate. **3.** A territory or state separate from but subject to another state or country. Also **de·pen′dan·cy.**

de·pen·dent (di·pen′dənt) *adj.* **1.** Conditioned by or contingent upon something else. **2.** Subordinate. **3.** Relying on someone or something for support. **4.** Hanging down. — *n.* One who depends on another. Also **de·pen′dant.**

dependent clause *Gram.* See under CLAUSE.

de·pict (di·pikt′) *v.t.* **1.** To portray or represent by or as by drawing, etc. **2.** To portray in words. [< L < *de-* down + *pingere* to paint] — **de·pic′tion** *n.*

dep·i·late (dep′ə·lāt) *v.t.* **·lat·ed, ·lat·ing** To remove hair from. [< L < *de-* away + *pilus* hair] — **dep′i·la′tion** *n.* **dep′i·la′tor** *n.*

de·pil·a·to·ry (di·pil′ə·tôr′ē, -tō′rē) *adj.* Having the power to remove hair. — *n. pl.* **·ries** A depilatory agent.

de·plane (dē·plān′) *v.i.* **·planed, ·plan·ing** To alight from an airplane: to *deplane* in Boston.

de·plete (di·plēt′) *v.t.* **·plet·ed, ·plet·ing** **1.** To reduce or lessen, as by use, exhaustion, or waste. **2.** To empty completely or partially. [< L < *de-* not + *plere* to fill] — **de·ple′tion** *n.* — **de·ple′tive** *adj. & n.*

de·plor·a·ble (di·plôr′ə·bəl, -plō′rə-) *adj.* **1.** To be deplored; lamentable. **2.** Wretched; sad. — **de·plor′a·ble·ness, de·plor′a·bil′i·ty** *n.* — **de·plor′a·bly** *adv.*

de·plore (di·plôr′, -plōr′) *v.t.* **·plored, ·plor·ing** To have or show regret or sadness over; lament. — **Syn.** See MOURN. [< L < *de-* completely + *plorare* to bewail]

de·ploy (di·ploi′) *v.t. & v.i.* To place or position (forces, people, etc.) according to a plan. [< F < OF < LL < L *dis-* from + *plicare* to fold] — **de·ploy′ment** *n.*

de·po·nent (di·pō′nənt) *adj.* In Latin and Greek grammar, denoting a verb that has the form of the passive but is active in meaning. — *n.* **1.** A deponent verb. **2.** *Law* One who gives sworn testimony, especially in writing.

de·pop·u·late (dē·pop′yə·lāt) *v.t.* **·lat·ed, ·lat·ing** To remove the inhabitants from, as by massacre, famine, eviction, etc. [< L < *de-* down + *populari* to lay waste] — **de·pop′·u·la′tion** *n.* — **de·pop′u·la′tor** *n.*

de·port (di·pôrt′, -pōrt′) *v.t.* **1.** To expel from a country. **2.** To behave or conduct (oneself). [< OF < L < *de-* away + *portare* to carry] — **de′por·ta′tion** *n.*

de·port·ment (di·pôrt′mənt, -pōrt′-) *n.* Conduct or behavior; demeanor; bearing.

de·pose (di·pōz′) *v.* **·posed, ·pos·ing** *v.t.* **1.** To deprive of rank or office; oust. **2.** *Law* To declare under oath. — *v.i.* **3.** *Law* To give testimony under oath. [< OF < *de-* down + *poser* to put down] — **de·pos′a·ble** *adj.* — **de·pos′al** *n.*

de·pos·it (di·poz′it) *v.t.* **1.** To set down; place; put. **2.** To put down in the form of a layer, as silt. **3.** To entrust (money, valuables, etc.) for safekeeping, as in a bank. **4.** To give as partial payment or security. — *v.i.* **5.** To be collected or precipitated: Sediments *deposit* in layers. — *n.* **1.** Something entrusted for safekeeping, especially money placed in a bank. **2.** The state of being placed for safekeeping: chiefly in the phrase **on deposit.** **3.** Anything given as partial payment or security. **4.** That which is or has been deposited, as sediment. **5.** *Geol.* A mass of iron, coal, oil, etc. [< L < *de-* down + *ponere* to place]

de·pos·i·tar·y (di·poz′ə·ter′ē) *n. pl.* **·tar·ies** **1.** One entrusted with anything for safekeeping. **2.** A depository.

dep·o·si·tion (dep′ə·zish′ən, dē′pə-) *n.* **1.** The act of deposing, as from an office. **2.** The act of depositing; also, that which is deposited. **3.** *Law* The written testimony of a witness who is under oath. — **Syn.** See TESTIMONY.

de·pos·i·tor (di·poz′ə·tər) *n.* One who makes a deposit.

de·pos·i·to·ry (di·poz′ə·tôr′ē, -tō′rē) *n. pl.* **·ries** **1.** A place where anything is deposited. **2.** A depositary.

de·pot (dē′pō, *Mil. & Brit.* dep′ō) *n.* **1.** A warehouse or storehouse. **2.** *U.S.* A railroad station. **3.** *Mil.* **a** An installation that manufactures, procures, stores, or repairs military materiel. **b** An installation for assembling and processing personnel. — **Syn.** See STATION. [See DEPOSIT.]

de·prave (di·prāv′) *v.t.* **·praved, ·prav·ing** To render bad or worse, especially in morals; corrupt; pervert. [< L < *de-* completely + *pravus* corrupt, wicked] — **dep·ra·va·tion** (dep′rə·vā′shən) *n.* — **de·prav′er** *n.*

de·prav·i·ty (di·prav′ə·tē) *n. pl.* **·ties** **1.** The state of being depraved; wickedness. **2.** A depraved act or habit.

dep·re·cate (dep′rə·kāt) *v.t.* **·cat·ed, ·cat·ing** **1.** To express disapproval of or regret for. **2.** To disparage or belittle. [< L < *de-* away + *precari* to pray] — **dep′re·cat′ing·ly** *adv.* — **dep′re·ca′tion** *n.* — **dep′re·ca′tor** *n.*

dep·re·ca·to·ry (dep′rə·kə·tôr′ē, -tō′rē) *adj.* Expressing deprecation. Also **dep′re·ca′tive.**

de·pre·ci·ate (di·prē′shē·āt) *v.* **·at·ed, ·at·ing** *v.t.* **1.** To lessen the value of; lower the price or rate of. **2.** To disparage; belittle. — *v.i.* **3.** To become less in value, etc. [< L < *de-* down + *pretium* price] — **de·pre′ci·a′tor** *n.* — **de·pre′ci·a·tive, de·pre′ci·a·to·ry** *adj.*

de·pre·ci·a·tion (di·prē′shē·ā′shən) *n.* **1.** A loss in value or efficiency resulting from usage, age, etc. **2.** A decline in the purchasing value of money. **3.** A disparagement.

dep·re·date (dep′rə·dāt) *v.t. & v.i.* **·dat·ed, ·dat·ing** To prey upon; pillage; plunder. [< LL < L *de-* completely +

praeda booty, prey] **—dep·re·da·tion** (dep/rə-dā/shən) *n.* **—dep/re·da/tor** *n.* **—dep·re·da·to·ry** (dep/rə-dā/tər-ē, di-pred/ə-tôr/ē, -tō/rē) *adj.*

de·press (di-pres/) *v.t.* **1.** To lower the spirits of; make gloomy; sadden. **2.** To lessen in vigor, force, or energy. **3.** To lower in price or value. **4.** To press or push down. [< OF < L < *de*- down + *primere* to press]

de·pres·sant (di-pres/ənt) *Med. adj.* Tending to lessen nervous or functional activity. **—** *n.* A sedative.

de·pressed (di-prest/) *adj.* **1.** Sad; dejected. **2.** Pressed down; flattened. **3.** Lowered or sunk even with or below the surface. **4.** Reduced in power, amount, value, etc.

depressed area A region characterized by unemployment.

de·pres·sion (di-presh/ən) *n.* **1.** The act of depressing, or the state of being depressed. **2.** Low spirits or vitality. **3.** A low or depressed place or surface. **4.** A severe decline in business, accompanied by increasing unemployment, falling prices, etc. **5.** *Psychiatry* Deep dejection characterized by withdrawal, lack of response to stimulation, etc. **—de·pres/sive** *adj.* **—de·pres/sive·ly** *adv.*

de·pres·sor (di-pres/ər) *n.* **1.** One who or that which depresses. **2.** *Physiol.* An afferent nerve connected with the heart, controlling heart rate and blood pressure.

dep·ri·va·tion (dep/rə-vā/shən) *n.* The act of depriving, or the state of being deprived. Also **de·priv·al** (di-prī/vəl).

de·prive (di-prīv/) *v.t.* **·prived, ·priv·ing** **1.** To take something away from; divest. **2.** To keep from acquiring, using, or enjoying something. [< OF < L *de*- completely + *privare* to strip, remove] **—de·priv/a·ble** *adj.*

depth (depth) *n.* **1.** The state or degree of being deep; deepness. **2.** Extent or distance downward, inward, or backward. **3.** Profundity of thought or feeling. **4.** *Usu. pl.* An extremely remote, deep, or distant part. **5.** *Usu. pl.* An intense state of being or feeling. **6.** The most intense part or stage: the *depth* of night. **7.** Richness or intensity of color, sound, etc. **8.** Lowness of pitch. [ME *depthe*]

depth charge A drum-shaped bomb that explodes under water at a desired depth. Also **depth bomb.**

dep·u·ta·tion (dep/yə-tā/shən) *n.* **1.** A person or persons acting for another or others; a delegation. **2.** The act of deputing, or the state of being deputed.

de·pute (di-pyoot/) *v.t.* **·put·ed, ·put·ing** **1.** To appoint as an agent, deputy, etc. **2.** To transfer (authority, etc.) to another. [< OF < LL < L *de*- away + *putare* to think]

dep·u·tize (dep/yə-tīz) *v.* **·tized, ·tiz·ing** *v.t.* **1.** To appoint as a deputy. **—** *v.i.* **2.** To act as a deputy.

dep·u·ty (dep/yə-tē) *n. pl.* **·ties** **1.** One appointed to act for another: a sheriff's *deputy.* **2.** A member of a legislative assembly in certain countries. **—** *adj.* Acting as deputy.

de·rail (dē-rāl/) *v.t.* **1.** To cause (a train, etc.) to run off the rails. **—** *v.i.* **2.** To run off the rails. [< F < *dé*- from + *rail* rail] **—de·rail/ment** *n.*

de·range (di-rānj/) *v.t.* **·ranged, ·rang·ing** **1.** To disturb the arrangement, working, or order of. **2.** To unbalance the reason of; render insane. [< F < *dé*- away + *ranger* to set in line] **—de·ranged/** *adj.* **—de·range/ment** *n.*

der·by (dûr/bē) *n. pl.* **·bies** A stiff felt hat with a curved, narrow brim and round crown: also, *Brit., bowler.* [< DERBY]

Der·by (dûr/bē, *Brit.* där/bē) *n.* **1.** An annual horse race for three-year-olds run at Epsom Downs in Surrey, England, since 1780. **2.** Any similar horse race, as the Kentucky Derby. [after the 12th Earl of *Derby,* the founder]

der·e·lict (der/ə-likt) *adj.* **1.** Neglectful of obligation; remiss. **2.** Deserted or abandoned. **—** *n.* **1.** That which is deserted or abandoned, as a ship at sea. **2.** A social outcast, etc. [< L < *de*- completely + *relinquere* to abandon]

der·e·lic·tion (der/ə-lik/shən) *n.* **1.** Neglect of or failure in duty. **2.** Voluntary abandonment of something. **3.** The state or fact of being abandoned.

de·ride (di-rīd/) *v.t.* **·rid·ed, ·rid·ing** To treat with scornful mirth; ridicule. [< L < *de*- completely + *ridere* to laugh, mock] **—de·rid/er** *n.* **—de·rid/ing·ly** *adv.*

de ri·gueur (də rē-gœr/) *French* Necessary according to etiquette; required by good form.

de·ri·sion (di-rizh/ən) *n.* **1.** The act of deriding; ridicule; mockery. **2.** An object of ridicule or scorn.

de·ri·sive (di-rī/siv) *adj.* Expressive of or characterized by derision; mocking. Also **de·ri·so·ry** (di-rī/sər-ē). **—de·ri/sive·ly** *adv.* **—de·ri/sive·ness** *n.*

der·i·va·tion (der/ə-vā/shən) *n.* **1.** The act of deriving, or the condition of being derived. **2.** That which is derived; a derivative. **3.** Origin or descent. **4.** The tracing of a word from its original form and meaning; also, a statement of this; an etymology. **—der/i·va/tion·al** *adj.*

de·riv·a·tive (di-riv/ə-tiv) *adj.* **1.** Resulting from or characterized by derivation. **2.** Not original or primary; based on other sources. **—** *n.* **1.** That which is derived. **2.** *Gram.* A word developed from another, as by the addition of affixes. **3.** *Chem.* A compound formed or regarded as being formed from a specified substance, usu. by partial substitution: a benzene *derivative.* **—de·riv/a·tive·ly** *adv.*

de·rive (di-rīv/) *v.* **·rived, ·riv·ing** *v.t.* **1.** To draw or receive, as from a source or principle. **2.** To deduce, as from a premise. **3.** To trace the source of (a word, etc.). **4.** *Chem.* To obtain (a compound) from another, as by partial substitution. **—** *v.i.* **5.** To originate; proceed. [< L < *de*- from + *rivus* stream] **—de·riv/a·ble** *adj.* **—de·riv/er** *n.*

derm- Var. of DERMO-.

-derm *suffix* Skin. [< Gk. *derma* skin]

der·ma (dûr/mə) *n. Anat.* The dermis. [< Gk., skin] **—der/mal** *adj.*

dermato- *combining form* Skin. Also, before vowels, **dermat-.** [< Gk. *derma, dermatos* skin]

der·ma·tol·o·gy (dûr/mə-tol/ə-jē) *n.* The branch of medical science that relates to the skin and its diseases. **—der·ma·to·log·i·cal** (dûr/mə-tə-loj/i-kəl) *adj.* **—der/ma·tol/o·gist** *n.*

der·mis (dûr/mis) *n. Anat.* **1.** The sensitive, vascular portion of the skin below the epidermis: also called *corium, derma.* **2.** The skin. [< LL < Gk. *derma* skin]

dermo- *combining form* Skin. Also, before vowels, **derm-.**

der·o·gate (der/ə-gāt) **·gat·ed, ·gat·ing** *v.t. & v.i.* **1.** To take or cause to take away; detract: with *from.* **2.** To become or cause to become inferior: with *from.* **2.** To be away + *rogare* to ask] **—der/o·ga/tion** *n.*

de·rog·a·tive (di-rog/ə-tiv) *adj.* Tending to derogate or detract; derogatory. **—de·rog/a·tive·ly** *adv.*

de·rog·a·to·ry (di-rog/ə-tôr/ē, -tō/rē) *adj.* Having the effect of lessening or detracting; belittling; disparaging. **—de·rog/a·to/ri·ly** *adv.* **—de·rog/a·to/ri·ness** *n.*

der·rick (der/ik) *n.* **1.** An apparatus for hoisting and swinging heavy weights, usu. consisting of a tackle at the end of a boom or mast. **2.** The framework over the mouth of an oil well. [after *Derrick,* 17th c. London hangman]

DERRICKS

a Hoisting. *b* Oil-well.

der·ring-do (der/ing-doo/) *n.* Courageous or daring action. [ME *dorrying don* daring to do]

der·rin·ger (der/in-jər) *n.* A pistol having a short barrel and a large bore. [after Henry *Deringer,* 19th c. U.S. gunsmith]

der·vish (dûr/vish) *n.* A member of any of various Moslem orders, some of whom express their devotion in whirling, howling, etc. [< Turkish < Persian *darvēsh*]

de·salt (dē-sôlt/) *v.t.* To remove the salt from, as sea water, to make potable. **—de·salt/er** *n.* **—de·salt/ing** *n.*

des·cant (*n.* des/kant; *v.* des·kant/, dis-) *n.* **1.** A discussion or a series of remarks. **2.** *Music* **a** A varied melody or song. **b** A counterpoint above the basic melody. **c** The upper part in part music. **—** *v.i.* **1.** To discourse at length: with *on* or *upon.* **2.** *Music* **a** To make or perform a descant. **b** To sing. [< AF < Med.L < L *dis*- away + *cantus* a song]

de·scend (di-send/) *v.i.* **1.** To move from a higher to a lower point. **2.** To slope downward, as a path. **3.** To lower oneself; stoop: to *descend* to begging. **4.** To come by inheritance; be inherited. **5.** *Biol.* To be derived by heredity. **6.** To pass from the general to the specific. **7.** To arrive or come in great numbers. **8.** *Astron.* To move toward the horizon. **—** *v.t.* **9.** To move from an upper to a lower part of; go down, as stairs. [< OF < L < *de*- down + *scandere* to climb] **—de·scend/er** *n.*

de·scend·ant (di-sen/dənt) *n.* One who is descended lineally from another; offspring.

de·scend·ent (di-sen/dənt) *adj.* Proceeding downward.

de·scent (di-sent/) *n.* **1.** The act of descending. **2.** A decline or deterioration. **3.** A declivity; slope. **4.** Ancestral derivation; lineage. **5.** In genealogy, a generation. **6.** *Law* The succession of property or title by inheritance.

de·scribe (di-skrīb/) *v.t.* **·scribed, ·scrib·ing** **1.** To present in spoken or written words. **2.** To give a picture or idea of by means of words; depict. **3.** To draw the figure of; trace; outline. [< L < *de*- down + *scribere* to write] **—de·scrib/a·ble** *adj.* **—de·scrib/er** *n.*

de·scrip·tion (di-skrip/shən) *n.* **1.** The act or technique of describing. **2.** An account that describes. **3.** A drawing or tracing, as of an arc. **4.** Sort, kind, or variety: birds of every *description.* **—Syn.** See EXPLANATION.

de·scrip·tive (di-skrip/tiv) *adj.* Characterized by or containing description; serving to describe. **—de·scrip/tive·ly** *adv.* **—de·scrip/tive·ness** *n.*

de·scry (di-skrī/) *v.t.* **·scried, ·scry·ing** **1.** To discover with the eye, as something distant. **2.** To discover by observation. [< OF < *des*- away + *crier* to cry]

des·e·crate (des/ə-krāt) *v.t.* **·crat·ed, ·crat·ing** To divert from a sacred to a common use; treat sacrilegiously; profane. [< DE- + L *sacrare* to make holy] **—des/e·crat/er** or **des/e·cra/tor** *n.* **—des/e·cra/tion** *n.*

de·seg·re·gate (dē-seg/rə-gāt) *v.t.* **·gat·ed, ·gat·ing** To eliminate racial segregation in. **—de/seg·re·ga/tion** *n.*

de·sen·si·tize (dē-sen′sə-tīz) *v.t.* **-tized, -tiz·ing** To make less sensitive, esp. in medicine, to lessen or eliminate the sensitiveness of (an individual, organ, tissue, etc.), as to an allergen. — **de·sen′si·ti·za′tion** *n.* — **de·sen′si·tiz′er** *n.*

des·ert[1] (dez′ərt) *n.* **1.** A region greatly lacking in rainfall, moisture, and vegetation. **2.** Any region that is uncultivated and desolate. — *adj.* Of or like a desert; uninhabited. [< OF < LL < L *deserere* < *de-* away + *serere* to join]

de·sert[2] (di-zûrt′) *v.t.* **1.** To forsake or abandon. **2.** To forsake in violation of one's oath or orders, as a service, post, etc. — *v.i.* **3.** To abandon one's post, duty, etc. **4.** *Mil.* To be absent without leave with the intention of not returning.

de·sert[3] (di-zûrt′) *n.* **1.** *Often pl.* That which is deserved or merited: to get one's just *deserts*. **2.** The state of deserving reward or punishment. [See DESERVE.]

de·sert·er (di-zûr′tər) *n.* One who forsakes a duty, friends, etc.; esp., one who deserts from a military service.

de·ser·tion (di-zûr′shən) *n.* **1.** The act of deserting. **2.** The state of being deserted; desolation. **3.** *Law* The willful abandonment of one's spouse or children, or both.

de·serve (di-zûrv′) *v.* **-served, -serv·ing** *v.t.* **1.** To be entitled to or worthy of. — *v.i.* **2.** To be worthy. [< OF < L < *de-* completely + *servire* to serve] — **de·serv′er** *n.*

de·served (di-zûrvd′) *adj.* Earned or merited. — **de·serv′·ed·ly** (di-zûr′vid-lē) *adv.* — **de·serv′ed·ness** *n.*

de·serv·ing (di-zûr′ving) *adj.* Worthy; meritorious: *deserving* of praise. — **de·serv′ing·ly** *adv.* — **de·serv′ing·ness** *n.*

des·ha·bille (dez′ə-bēl′) *n.* Dishabille.

des·ic·cant (des′ə-kənt) *adj.* Producing dryness; desiccating, as a medicine. — *n.* A drying agent or substance.

des·ic·cate (des′ə-kāt) *v.* **-cat·ed, -cat·ing** *v.t* **1.** To dry thoroughly. **2.** To preserve (foods) by drying. — *v.i.* **3.** To become dry. [< L < *de-* completely + *siccare* to dry out] — **des′ic·ca′tion** *n.* — **des′ic·ca′tive** *adj. & n.*

de·sid·er·a·tum (di-sid′ə-rā′təm) *n. pl.* **·ta** (-tə) Something needed or regarded as desirable. [< L]

de·sign (di-zīn′) *v.t* **1.** To draw or prepare preliminary plans or sketches of. **2.** To plan and make with skill, as a work of art. **3.** To form or make (plans, schemes, etc.) in the mind; conceive; invent. **4.** To intend; purpose. — *v.i.* **5.** To be a designer. **6.** To plan; conceive. — *n.* **1.** A preliminary sketch or outline; pattern. **2.** The arrangement and coordination of the parts or details of any object: the *design* of a jet airplane. **3.** A piece of artistic or decorative work. **4.** The art of making designs. **5.** A visual pattern or composition. **6.** A plan or project. **7.** An object or purpose. **8.** *Often pl.* A sinister scheme or plot. **9.** Intelligent, purposeful, or discoverable pattern, as opposed to chaos. [See DESIGNATE.] — **de·sig′na·ble** *adj.*

des·ig·nate (*v.* dez′ig-nāt; *for adj., also* dez′ig-nit) *v.t.* **-nat·ed, -nat·ing 1.** To indicate or specify. **2.** To name or entitle; characterize. **3.** To select or appoint for a specific purpose, duty, etc. — *adj.* Designated; selected. [< L *de-* completely + *signare* to mark] — **des′ig·na′tive** (-nā′tiv) *adj.* — **des′ig·na′tor** *n.*

des·ig·na·tion (dez′ig-nā′shən) *n.* **1.** A distinctive mark or title. **2.** The act of pointing out something. **3.** Appointment or nomination.

de·sign·ed·ly (di-zī′nid-lē) *adv.* By design; intentionally.

des·ig·nee (dez′ig-nē′) *n.* A person designated.

de·sign·er (di-zī′nər) *n.* **1.** One who creates designs, as for dresses, machinery, etc. **2.** A schemer; contriver.

de·sign·ing (di-zī′ning) *n.* **1.** The act or art of making designs. **2.** The act of plotting or scheming. — *adj.* **1.** Scheming. **2.** Exercising foresight. — **de·sign′ing·ly** *adv.*

de·sir·a·ble (di-zīr′ə-bəl) *adj.* Worthy of or exciting desire. — **de·sir′a·bil′i·ty, de·sir′a·ble·ness** *n.* — **de·sir′a·bly** *adv.*

de·sire (di-zīr′) *v.t.* **-sired, -sir·ing 1.** To wish or long for; crave. **2.** To ask for; request. — *n.* **1.** A longing or craving. **2.** A request or wish. **3.** An object desired. **4.** Sexual appetite; passion; lust. [< OF < L *de-* from + *sidus, sideris* star; with ref. to astrology] — **de·sir′er** *n.*

de·sir·ous (di-zīr′əs) *adj.* Having a desire or craving.

de·sist (di-zist′) *v.i.* To cease, as from an action. [< L < *de-* from + *sistere* to stop] — **de·sis′tance,** or **de·sis′tence** *n.*

desk (desk) *n.* **1.** A table or case adapted for writing or studying, usu. having compartments or drawers. **2.** A table or stand to hold reading matter; also, a pulpit. **3.** A division or post in an organization: the service *desk.* **4.** *U.S.* A department in a newspaper office: the copy *desk.* **5.** *Music* An orchestral music stand. [< Med.L < LL *discus* table]

des·o·late (*adj.* des′ə-lit; *v.* des′ə-lāt) *adj.* **1.** Destitute of inhabitants or dwellings; deserted. **2.** Made unfit for habitation. **3.** Gloomy; dreary. **4.** Without friends; forlorn. — *v.t.* **-lat·ed, -lat·ing 1.** To deprive of inhabitants. **2.** To lay waste; devastate. **3.** To make sorrowful or forlorn. **4.** To forsake; abandon. [< L < *de-* completely + *solus* alone] — **des′o·late·ly** *adv.* — **des′o·late·ness** *n.*

des·o·la·tion (des′ə-lā′shən) *n.* **1.** The act of making desolate; a laying waste. **2.** The condition of being ruined or deserted. **3.** Loneliness. **4.** A desolate region; waste.

des·ox·y- Var. of DEOXY-.

de·spair (di-spâr′) *v.i.* To lose or abandon hope; be or become hopeless: with *of.* — *n.* **1.** Utter hopelessness and discouragement. **2.** That which causes despair. [< OF < L < *de-* away + *sperare* to hope] — **de·spair′ing** *adj.* — **de·spair′ing·ly** *adv.*

— **Syn.** (noun) *Despair* is the utter abandonment of hope that leaves the mind apathetic or numb. *Desperation* is energized *despair,* vigorous in action and reckless of consequences. *Despondency* is paralyzing *despair* coupled with deep sorrow. The mere absence of hope is *hopelessness* and is often used to characterize circumstances. — **Ant.** hope, expectation, confidence.

des·per·a·do (des′pə-rā′dō, -rä′dō) *n. pl.* **·does** or **·dos** A desperate or violent criminal. [< OSp. See DESPAIR.]

des·per·ate (des′pər-it) *adj.* **1.** Without care for danger; reckless, as from despair. **2.** Resorted to in desperation. **3.** Regarded as almost hopeless; critical. **4.** Extreme; very great. — **des′per·ate·ly** *adv.* — **des′per·ate·ness** *n.*

des·per·a·tion (des′pə-rā′shən) *n.* The state of being desperate; also, the recklessness growing out of despair.

des·pi·ca·ble (des′pi·kə-bəl, di-spik′ə-bəl) *adj.* That is to be despised; contemptible; vile. [See DESPISE.] — **des′pi·ca·bil′i·ty, des′pi·ca·ble·ness** *n.* — **des′pi·ca·bly** *adv.*

de·spise (di-spīz′) *v.t.* **-spised, -spis·ing** To regard as contemptible or worthless; disdain; scorn. [< OF < L < *de-* down + *specere* to look at] — **de·spis′er** *n.*

de·spite (di-spīt′) *prep.* In spite of; notwithstanding. — *n.* **1.** Contemptuous defiance. **2.** An act of defiance, malice, or injury. — **in despite of** In spite of. [See DESPISE.]

de·spoil (di-spoil′) *v.t.* To deprive of possessions; rob. [< OF < L < *de-* completely + *spoliare* to rob] — **de·spoil′er** *n.* — **de·spoil′ment, de·spo·li·a·tion** (di-spō′lē·ā′shən) *n.*

de·spond (di-spond′) *v.i.* To lose spirit, courage, or hope. — *n. Archaic* Despondency. [< L < *de-* away + *spondere* to promise] — **de·spond′ing·ly** *adv.*

de·spon·den·cy (di-spon′dən-sē) *n.* Dejection of spirits from loss of hope or courage. Also **de·spon′dence.**

de·spon·dent (di-spon′dənt) *adj.* Dejected in spirit; disheartened. — **de·spond′ent·ly** *adv.*

des·pot (des′pət, -pot) *n.* **1.** An absolute monarch; autocrat. **2.** A tyrant. [< OF < Gk. *despotēs* master]

des·pot·ic (di-spot′ik) *adj.* Of or like a despot; tyrannical; autocratic. — **des·pot′i·cal·ly** *adv.*

des·pot·ism (des′pə-tiz′əm) *n.* **1.** Unlimited authority; absolute power. **2.** A state ruled by a despot.

des·sert (di-zûrt′) *n.* **1.** *U.S.* A serving of pastry, ice cream, etc., as the last course of a meal. **2.** *Brit.* Fruits, nuts, etc., served after a dinner. [< F < *desservir* to clear a table]

des·ti·na·tion (des′tə-nā′shən) *n.* **1.** The point or place set for a journey's end, or to which something is directed. **2.** The purpose or end for which anything is created or intended. **3.** The act of designating or appointing.

des·tine (des′tin) *v.t.* **-tined, -tin·ing 1.** To design for or appoint to a distinct purpose. **2.** To determine the future of, as by destiny. [< OF < L *destinare* to make fast, ult. < *de-* completely + *stare* to stand] — **des′tined** *adj.*

des·ti·ny (des′tə-nē) *n. pl.* **·nies 1.** The fate to which a person or thing is destined. **2.** The preordained or predetermined ordering of events. **3.** The power that is thought to predetermine the course of events. [See DESTINE.]

des·ti·tute (des′tə-tōōt, -tyōōt) *adj.* **1.** Not having; entirely lacking: with *of.* **2.** Extremely poor. [< L < *de-* down + *statuere* to set]

des·ti·tu·tion (des′tə-tōō′shən, -tyōō′-) *n.* **1.** Extreme poverty. **2.** Deficiency; lack.

de·stroy (di-stroi′) *v.t.* **1.** To ruin utterly; consume. **2.** To tear down; demolish. **3.** To put an end to. **4.** To kill. **5.** To make ineffective or useless. — **Syn.** See DEMOLISH. [< OF, ult. < L < *de-* down + *struere* to construct]

de·stroy·er (di-stroi′ər) *n.* **1.** One who or that which destroys. **2.** A speedy war vessel, smaller than a cruiser.

de·struct (di-strukt′) *n. Aerospace* The act of destroying a defective or dangerous missile or rocket after launch.

de·struc·ti·ble (di-struk′tə-bəl) *adj.* Capable of being destroyed. — **de·struc′ti·bil′i·ty, de·struc′ti·ble·ness** *n.*

de·struc·tion (di-struk′shən) *n.* **1.** The act of destroying, or the state of being destroyed; demolition; ruin. **2.** That which destroys, or is a means of destroying.

de·struc·tive (di-struk′tiv) *adj.* **1.** Causing destruction; tending to destroy; ruinous: with *of* or *to.* **2.** Tending to tear down or discredit. — **de·struc′tive·ly** *adv.* — **de·struc′tive·ness, de·struc·tiv·i·ty** (dē′struk′tiv′ə-tē) *n.*

destructive distillation *Chem.* The distillation of organic substances, as wood and coal, in such a way as to decompose them chemically: also called *dry distillation.*

des·ue·tude (des′wə-tood, -tyood) *n.* A condition of disuse. [< MF < L < *de-* away + *suescere* to be used to]

de·sul·fur·ize (dē-sul′fə-rīz) *v.t.* ·ized, ·iz·ing To remove sulfur from. Also **de·sul′fur, de·sul′fur·ate, de·sul′phur·ize.** — **de·sul′fur·i·za′tion** *n.* — **de·sul′fur·iz′er** *n.*

des·ul·to·ry (des′əl-tôr′ē, -tō′rē) *adj.* 1. Passing abruptly from one thing to another; unmethodical. 2. Occurring by chance. [< L < *de-* down + *sultus*, pp. of *salire* to leap] — **des′ul·to′ri·ly** *adv.* — **des′ul·to′ri·ness** *n.*

de·tach (di-tach′) *v.t.* 1. To unfasten and separate; disconnect. 2. To send off for special duty, as a regiment or a ship. [< F < *de-* away + OF *tache* nail] — **de·tach′a·bil′i·ty** *n.* — **de·tach′a·ble** *adj.* — **de·tach′er** *n.*

de·tached (di-tacht′) *adj.* 1. Separated from others; disconnected. 2. Unconcerned; impartial.

detached retina *Pathol.* A disconnection of the inner layers of the retina from the pigment layer.

de·tach·ment (di-tach′mənt) *n.* 1. The act of detaching or separating. 2. The state of being detached. 3. Dissociation from surroundings or worldly affairs. 4. Absence of prejudice or partiality. 5. *Mil.* **a** A part of a unit separated from its parent organization for duty. **b** A permanent unit organized for a specific purpose.

de·tail (*n.* di·tāl′, dē′tāl; *v.* di-tāl′; *Mil.* dē′tāl) *n.* 1. A separately considered part or item; particular. 2. A dealing with particulars: to go into *detail*. 3. A narrative account giving particulars. 4. In art, architecture, etc., a minor or secondary part. 5. *Mil.* A small detachment designated for a particular task. — **in detail** Item by item. — *v.t.* 1. To report or narrate minutely. 2. *Mil.* To select and send off for a special service, duty, etc. [< F < *dé-* completely + *tailler* to cut up]

de·tain (di-tān′) *v.t.* 1. To keep from proceeding; stop; delay. 2. To withhold (what belongs to another). 3. To hold in custody; confine. [< OF < L < *de-* away + *tenere* to hold] — **de·tain′ment** *n.*

de·tect (di-tekt′) *v.t.* 1. To perceive or find, as something obscure: to *detect* an error in spelling. 2. To expose or uncover, as a crime. 3. *Telecom.* To recover the (signal, audio component, etc.) from a modulated carrier wave. [< L < *de-* away, off + *tegere* to cover] — **de·tect′a·ble** or **de·tect′i·ble** *adj.* — **de·tect′er** *n.*

de·tec·tion (di-tek′shən) *n.* 1. The act of detecting, or the fact of being detected. 2. *Telecom.* Any method of operating on a modulated signal wave so as to obtain the signal imparted to it; demodulation of incoming electrical signals.

de·tec·tive (di-tek′tiv) *n.* A person, often a policeman, whose work is to investigate crimes, discover evidence, capture criminals, etc. — *adj.* 1. Belonging or pertaining to detectives or their work. 2. Fitted for or used in detection.

de·tec·tor (di-tek′tər) *n.* 1. One who or that which detects. 2. *Telecom.* A device for obtaining the signal from a modulated carrier.

dé·tente (dā-tänt′) *n.* An easing, as of discord between nations. [< F]

de·ten·tion (di-ten′shən) *n.* 1. The act of detaining; a restraining. 2. The state of being detained. [See DETAIN.]

de·ter (di-tûr′) *v.t.* ·terred, ·ter·ring To prevent or discourage (someone) from acting by arousing fear, uncertainty, etc. [< L < *de-* away + *terrere* to frighten] — **de·ter′ment** *n.*

de·terge (di-tûrj′) *v.t.* ·terged, ·terg·ing 1. To cleanse, as a wound. 2. To wipe off. [< L < *de-* away + *tergere* to wipe]

de·ter·gent (di-tûr′jənt) *adj.* Having cleansing or purging qualities. — *n.* A cleansing agent. — **de·ter′gen·cy, de·ter′gence** *n.*

de·te·ri·o·rate (di-tir′ē·ə-rāt′) *v.t. & v.i.* ·rat·ed, ·rat·ing To make or become worse; depreciate. [< L < *deterior* worse] — **de·te′ri·o·ra′tion** *n.* — **de·te′ri·o·ra′tive** *adj.*

de·ter·mi·na·ble (di-tûr′mi·nə-bəl) *adj.* 1. That may be found out, settled, or decided. 2. *Law* Liable to be ended.

de·ter·mi·nant (di-tûr′mə-nənt) *adj.* Determinative. — *n.* That which influences or determines.

de·ter·mi·nate (di-tûr′mə-nit) *adj.* 1. Definitely limited or fixed; specific; distinct. 2. Settled and conclusive; decided; final. 3. Fixed in purpose; resolute. 4. *Bot.* Terminating in a flower or bud, as each axis of an inflorescence. — **de·ter′mi·nate·ly** *adv.* — **de·ter′mi·nate·ness** *n.*

de·ter·mi·na·tion (di-tûr′mə-nā′shən) *n.* 1. The act of reaching a decision; also, the decision reached. 2. The quality of being firm in purpose or action; resoluteness. 3. The determining or fixing of the quality, degree, etc., of anything; also, the result of this. 4. A decisive tendency or movement toward some object or end.

de·ter·mi·na·tive (di-tûr′mə-nā′tiv, -mə-nə-tiv) *adj.* Tending or having power to determine. — *n.* That which determines. — **de·ter′mi·na′tive·ly** *adv.*

de·ter·mine (di-tûr′min) *v.* ·mined, ·min·ing *v.t.* 1. To settle or decide, as an argument, question, or debate. 2. To ascertain or fix. 3. To cause to reach a decision. 4. To fix or give definite form to; influence. 5. To give purpose or

direction to. 6. To set bounds to; limit. 7. *Law* To limit; terminate: to *determine* a contract. — *v.i.* 8. To come to a decision; resolve. 9. *Law* To come to an end. [< OF < L < *de-* completely + *terminare* to end] — **de·ter′min·er** *n.*

de·ter·mined (di-tûr′mind) *adj.* Having or showing fixed purpose; resolute; firm. — **de·ter·mined·ly** (di-tûr′mind·lē, -min·id·lē) *adv.* — **de·ter′mined·ness** *n.*

de·ter·min·ism (di-tûr′mə-niz′əm) *n.* *Philos.* The doctrine that every event is the inevitable result of antecedent conditions, and that human beings do not have free will.

de·ter·rent (di-tûr′ənt) *adj.* Tending or serving to deter. — *n.* Something that deters. — **de·ter′rence** *n.*

de·test (di-test′) *v.t.* To dislike with intensity; hate; abhor. [< MF < L *detestari* to denounce < *de-* away + *testis* a witness] — **de·test′er** *n.*

de·test·a·ble (di-tes′tə-bəl) *adj.* Deserving to be detested; extremely hateful; abominable. — **de·test′a·bil′i·ty, de·test′a·ble·ness** *n.* — **de·test′a·bly** *adv.*

de·tes·ta·tion (dē′tes-tā′shən) *n.* 1. Extreme dislike; hatred; abhorrence. 2. One who or that which is detested.

de·throne (dē-thrōn′) *v.t.* ·throned, ·thron·ing To remove from the throne. — **de·throne′ment** *n.* — **de·thron′er** *n.*

det·o·nate (det′ə-nāt, dē′tə-) *v.* ·nat·ed, ·nat·ing *v.t.* 1. To cause to explode suddenly and with violence. — *v.i.* 2. To explode suddenly with a loud report. [< L < *de-* down + *tonare* to thunder] — **det′o·na′tion** *n.* — **det′o·na′tor** *n.*

de·tour (dē′tŏŏr, di-tŏŏr′) *n.* A deviation from a direct route or course of action; esp., a byroad used when a main road is impassable. — *v.t. & v.i.* To go or cause to go by a roundabout way. [< F < *dé-* away + *tourner* to turn]

de·tract (di-trakt′) *v.i.* 1. To take away a part; diminish: with *from.* — *v.t.* 2. To take away (a part). 3. To distract; divert. [< L < *de-* away + *trahere* to pull] — **de·trac′tion** *n.* — **de·trac′tive** *adj.* — **de·trac′tor** *n.*

de·train (dē-trān′) *v.t. & v.i.* *Chiefly Brit.* To leave or cause to leave a railroad train. — **de·train′ment** *n.*

det·ri·ment (det′rə-mənt) *n.* 1. Damage or loss. 2. Something that impairs, injures, or causes loss. [< L < *de-* away + *terere* to rub]

det·ri·men·tal (det′rə-men′təl) *adj.* Causing damage or loss. — **Syn.** See PERNICIOUS. — **det′ri·men′tal·ly** *adv.*

de·tri·tus (di-trī′təs) *n.* 1. Loose fragments or particles separated from masses of rock by erosion, glacial action, or other forces. 2. Debris. [See DETRIMENT.]

de trop (də trō′) *French* Too much; superfluous.

deuce[1] (doos, dyoos) *n.* 1. Two; esp., a card or side of a die having two spots. 2. In tennis, a score tied at 40 or at five or more games each, requiring either side to win two successive points for the game or two successive games for the set. [< F < OF < L *duos*, accusative of *duo* two]

deuce[2] (doos, dyoos) *n.* *Informal* The devil; bad luck: a mild oath. [< LG *de duus* the deuce (throw at dice)]

deu·ced (doo′sid, dyoo′-, doost, dyoost) *Informal adj.* Confounded; excessive. — *adv.* Devilishly. — **deu′ced·ly** *adv.*

De·us (dē′əs, dā′ŏŏs) *n.* *Latin* God.

deu·te·ri·um (doo-tir′ē·əm, dyoo-) *n.* The isotope of hydrogen having the atomic weight 2.01 (symbol, D or H^2): also called *heavy hydrogen.* [< NL < Gk. *deuteros* second]

deuterium oxide Heavy water.

deutero- *combining form* Second; secondary. Also, **deuter-** (before vowels), **deuto-.** [< Gk. *deuteros* second]

deu·ter·on (doo′tə-ron, dyoo′-) *n.* *Physics* The nucleus of a deuterium atom. [< NL < Gk. *deuteros* second]

Deu·ter·on·o·my (doo′tə-ron′ə-mē, dyoo′-) The fifth book of the Old Testament, containing a second statement of the Mosaic law. [< Gk. < *deuteros* second + *nomos* law]

deut·sche mark (doi′chə-märk′) *n.* 1. The standard monetary unit of West Germany, equivalent to 100 pfennigs; in 1960 worth about 24 U.S. cents. 2. The standard monetary unit of East Germany. Also **deutsche mark.**

de·val·u·ate (dē-val′yŏŏ-āt) *v.t.* ·at·ed, ·at·ing To reduce the value or worth of. Also **de·val′ue.** — **de·val′u·a′tion** *n.*

dev·as·tate (dev′ə-stāt) *v.t.* ·tat·ed, ·tat·ing 1. To lay waste, as by war, fire, etc. 2. *Informal* To confound; crush. [< L < *de-* completely + *vastare* to lay waste] — **dev′as·tat′ing·ly** *adv.* — **dev′as·ta′tion** *n.* — **dev′as·ta′tor** *n.*

de·vel·op (di-vel′əp) *v.t.* 1. To expand or bring out the potentialities, capabilities, etc., of. 2. To work out in detail; enlarge upon: to *develop* an idea. 3. To reveal or unfold gradually: to *develop* a plot. 4. To bring into active existence: to *develop* patience. 5. *Photog.* **a** To make visible (the hidden image) upon a sensitized plate that has been exposed to the action of light. **b** To subject (a plate or film) to a developer. 6. *Music* To elaborate on (a theme). — *v.i.* 7. To increase in capabilities, maturity, etc. 8. To advance from a lower to a higher stage; evolve. 9. To be disclosed; as events, a plot, etc. 10. To come into existence: Some tastes *develop* slowly. [< F < *dé-* away | OF *voluper* to fold, wrap up] — **de·vel′op·a·ble** *adj.*

de·vel·op·er (di-vel′əp·ər) *n.* 1. One who or that which develops. 2. *Photog.* A solution for developing photographs.

de·vel·op·ment (di-vel′əp-mənt) *n.* **1.** The act of developing. **2.** The state or condition of that which has been developed. **3.** A result or product of developing. **4.** An event or occurrence: a political *development*.

de·vel·op·men·tal (di-vel′əp-men′təl) *adj.* Of or pertaining to development; evolutionary. — **de·vel′op·men′tal·ly** *adv.*

de·vi·ate (*n.* dē′vē-it; *v.* dē′vē-āt) — *n.* One whose actions and beliefs differ considerably from the standards of his society. Also **de·vi·ant** (dē′vē-ənt). — *v.* **·at·ed, ·at·ing** *v.i.* **1.** To turn aside from a straight or appointed way or course. **2.** To differ, as in belief. — *v.t.* **3.** To cause to turn aside. [< LL < L *de-* from + *via* road] — **de′vi·a′tor** *n.*

de·vi·a·tion (dē′vē-ā′shən) *n.* **1.** The act of deviating, or its result. **2.** *Stat.* The difference between one value in a series of observations and the arithmetic mean of the series.

de·vice (di-vīs′) *n.* **1.** Something devised or constructed for a specific purpose. **2.** A scheme or plan, esp. a crafty or evil one. **3.** An ornamental design, as in embroidery. **4.** An emblem in a coat of arms; also, any emblem or motto. — **to leave (someone) to his own devices** To allow (someone) to do as he wishes. [< OF < L *dividere* to divide]

dev·il (dev′əl) *n.* **1.** *Sometimes cap.* In Jewish and Christian theology, the prince and ruler of the kingdom of evil; Satan. **2.** Any subordinate evil spirit; a demon. **3.** A wicked or malicious person. **4.** A wretched fellow: poor *devil*. **5.** A person of great energy or daring. **6.** A machine for any of various purposes, as for cutting or tearing up rags. **7.** A printer's apprentice: also called *printer's devil*. — **between the devil and the deep blue sea** Between equally bad alternatives. — **the devil** An exclamation of anger, surprise, etc. — **the devil to pay** Trouble to be expected as a consequence. — **to give the devil his due** To acknowledge the ability or success of even a disliked person, antagonist, etc. — *v.t.* **dev·iled** or **·illed, dev·il·ing** or **·il·ling 1.** To prepare for eating by seasoning highly. **2.** To cut up (cloth, etc.) in a devil. **3.** To annoy or harass. [OE < LL < Gk. *diabolos* slanderer]

dev·il·fish (dev′əl-fish′) *n. pl.* **·fish** or **·fish·es 1.** The manta. **2.** Any of various large cephalopods, as the octopus.

dev·il·ish (dev′əl-ish, dev′lish) *adj.* **1.** Having the qualities of the devil; diabolical. **2.** *Informal* Excessive. — *adv. Informal* Excessively. — **dev′il·ish·ly** *adv.* — **dev′il·ish·ness** *n.*

dev·il-may-care (dev′əl-mā-kâr′) *adj.* Careless; reckless.

dev·il·ment (dev′əl-mənt) *n.* Impish conduct; mischief.

devil's advocate (dev′əlz) **1.** In the Roman Catholic Church, an official appointed to argue against a candidate for canonization. **2.** One who argues perversely.

devil's-food cake (dev′əlz-fōōd′) A chocolate cake.

dev·il·try (dev′əl-trē) *n. pl.* **·tries 1.** Wanton or malicious mischief. **2.** Wickedness or cruelty. Also *Brit.* **dev′il·ry.**

de·vi·ous (dē′vē-əs) *adj.* **1.** Winding or leading away from the regular, straight, or direct course; rambling; swerving. **2.** Straying from the proper way; erring. [< L *de-* from + *via* way] — **de′vi·ous·ly** *adv.* — **de′vi·ous·ness** *n.*

de·vis·al (di-vī′zəl) *n.* A contriving or bequeathing.

de·vise (di-vīz′) *v.* **·vised, ·vis·ing** *v.t.* **1.** To form in the mind; invent; contrive; plan. **2.** *Law* To transmit (real estate) by will. — *v.i.* **3.** To form a plan. — *n. Law* **1.** The act of bequeathing lands. **2.** A gift of lands by will. **3.** A will, or clause in a will, conveying real estate. [< OF < L *dividere* to separate] — **de·vis′a·ble** *adj.* — **de·vis′er** *n.*

dev·i·see (di-vī′zē′, dev′ə-zē′) *n. Law* The person to whom a devise is made.

de·vi·sor (di-vī′zər, -zôr) *n. Law* One who devises property.

de·vi·tal·ize (dē-vīt′l-īz) *v.t.* **·ized, ·iz·ing** To destroy the vitality of; make weak. — **de·vi′tal·i·za′tion** *n.*

de·void (di-void′) *adj.* Not possessing; destitute; empty: with *of*. [ME *devoided*, pp. of obs. *devoid* to empty out]

de·voir (də-vwär′, dev′wär) *n.* **1.** *Usu. pl.* Courteous attentions; respects. **2.** Duty. [< OF < L *debere* to owe]

dev·o·lu·tion (dev′ə-lōō′shən) *n.* **1.** A passing down from one stage to another. **2.** The passing of authority, property, etc., to a successor. [See DEVOLVE.]

de·volve (di-volv′) *v.* **·volved, ·volv·ing** *v.t.* **1.** To cause (authority, duty, etc.) to pass to a successor. — *v.i.* **2.** To pass to a successor or substitute: with *on, upon,* or *to*. [< L *de-* down + *volvere* to roll] — **de·volve′ment** *n.*

De·vo·ni·an (di-vō′nē-ən) *adj.* **1.** Of or pertaining to Devon in England. **2.** *Geol.* Of or pertaining to the period in the Paleozoic era following the Silurian. See chart for GEOLOGY. — *n. Geol.* The Devonian period or its rock system. [after *Devon*, England; with ref. to rocks found there]

de·vote (di-vōt′) *v.t.* **·vot·ed, ·vot·ing 1.** To apply (attention, time, or oneself) completely to some activity, purpose, etc. **2.** To dedicate. [< OF < L *de-* completely + *vovere* to vow] — **de·vote′ment** *n.*

de·vot·ed (di-vō′tid) *adj.* **1.** Feeling or showing devotion; devout. **2.** Set apart, as by a vow; consecrated. — **de·vot′ed·ly** *adv.* — **de·vot′ed·ness** *n.*

dev·o·tee (dev′ə-tē′) *n.* **1.** One who is deeply devoted to anything. **2.** One who is marked by religious ardor.

de·vo·tion (di-vō′shən) *n.* **1.** Strong attachment or affection, as to a person or cause. **2.** Ardor or zeal in the performance of religious acts or duties. **3.** *Usu. pl.* An act of worship or prayer. **4.** The act of devoting, or the state of being devoted. — **de·vo′tion·al** *adj.* — **de·vo′tion·al·ly** *adv.*

de·vour (di-vour′) *v.t.* **1.** To eat up greedily. **2.** To destroy; waste. **3.** To take in greedily with the senses or the intellect. **4.** To engross the attention of. **5.** To engulf; absorb. [< OF < L *de-* down + *vorare* to gulp, swallow] — **de·vour′er** *n.* — **de·vour′ing·ly** *adv.*

de·vout (di-vout′) *adj.* **1.** Earnestly religious; pious. **2.** Heartfelt; sincere. **3.** Containing or expressing devotion. [See DEVOTE.] — **de·vout′ly** *adv.* — **de·vout′ness** *n.*

dew (dōō, dyōō) *n.* **1.** Moisture condensed from the atmosphere in small drops upon cool surfaces. **2.** Anything moist, pure, or refreshing as dew. **3.** Moisture generally, esp. that which appears in minute drops, as perspiration, tears, etc. — *v.t.* To wet with or as with dew. [OE *dēaw*]

dew·ber·ry (dōō′ber′ē, -bər-ē, dyōō′-) *n. pl.* **·ries** The fruit of several species of trailing blackberry; also, the plant.

dew·claw (dōō′klô′, dyōō′-) *n.* **1.** A rudimentary toe in some dogs and other mammals. **2.** The false hoof above the true hoof of hogs, deer, etc. — **dew′clawed′** *adj.*

dew·drop (dōō′drop′, dyōō′-) *n.* A drop of dew.

dew·lap (dōō′lap′, dyōō′-) *n.* The pendulous skin under the throat of cattle, certain dogs, etc. [ME < *dew*, origin uncertain + *lappe* pendulous piece, lobe] — **dew′lapped′** *adj.*

DEW line A chain of radar stations in North America, maintained by the United States in cooperation with Canada. [< D(istant) E(arly) W(arning)]

dew point The temperature at which dew forms or condensation of vapor occurs.

dew·y (dōō′ē, dyōō′ē) *adj.* **dew·i·er, dew·i·est 1.** Moist. **2.** Of, resembling, or forming dew. — **dew′i·ness** *n.*

dex·ter (dek′stər) *adj.* **1.** Of or situated on the right side. **2.** *Heraldry* Being on the wearer's right, and thus on the observer's left: opposed to *sinister*. [< L, right]

dex·ter·i·ty (dek-ster′ə-tē) *n.* **1.** Skill in using the hands or body. **2.** Mental adroitness. [< L *dexter* on the right] — **Syn.** Both *dexterity* and *adroitness* are, literally, "right-handedness," or proficiency in manual tasks. In extended use, *dexterity* is applied to technical proficiency in the use of tools, methods, etc.: the *dexterity* of a magician. *Adroitness* has become cleverness in dealing with people or in handling situations. *Handiness* applies chiefly to manual work; *skill* is acquired, at least in part and sometimes wholly, by mental training.

dex·ter·ous (dek′strəs, -stər-əs) *adj.* **1.** Possessing dexterity; adroit. **2.** Done with dexterity. Also **dex·trous** (dek′strəs) — **dex′ter·ous·ly** *adv.* — **dex′ter·ous·ness** *n.*

dex·tral (dek′strəl) *adj.* **1.** Of or pertaining to, or turned toward the right side; right-hand. **2.** Right-handed. — **dex·tral·i·ty** (dek-stral′ə-tē) *n.* — **dex′tral·ly** *adv.*

dex·trin (dek′strin) *n. Biochem.* A gummy, water-soluble substance formed from starch, and used as a substitute for gum arabic. Also **dex·trine** (dek′strin, -strēn).

dextro- *combining form* Turned or turning to the right, or clockwise; used esp. in chemistry and physics. Also, before vowels, **dextr-.** [< L *dexter* right]

dex·trorse (dek′strôrs, dek-strôrs′) *adj. Bot.* Twining spirally toward the right, as certain climbing plants: opposed to *sinistrorse*. Also **dex·tror′sal.** [< L < *dexter* right + *vertere* to turn] — **dex′trorse·ly** *adv.*

dex·trose (dek′strōs) *n. Biochem.* A sugar occurring in plants. Also **dex·tro·glu·cose** (dek′strō-glōō′kōs).

di-¹ Var. of DIS-¹.

di-² *prefix* **1.** Twice; double. **2.** *Chem.* Containing two atoms, molecules, radicals, etc. Also, before *s*, **dis-.** [< Gk. *di-* < *dis* twice]

di-³ Var. of DIA-.

dia- *prefix* **1.** Through; across; between; apart. **2.** Thoroughly. Also, before vowels, **di-.** [< Gk. *dia-* through]

di·a·be·tes (dī′ə-bē′tis, -tēz) *n. Pathol.* A disease, **diabetes mel·li·tus** (mə-lī′təs), associated with deficient insulin secretion, leading to excess sugar in the blood and urine, extreme hunger and thirst, and metabolic failure. [< NL < Gk. < *dia-* through + *bainein* to go]

di·a·bet·ic (dī′ə-bet′ik, -bē′tik) *Med. adj.* Of, pertaining to, or affected with diabetes. — *n.* One who has diabetes.

di·a·bol·ic (dī′ə-bol′ik) *adj.* **1.** Of, belonging to, or proceeding from the devil; satanic; infernal. **2.** Atrociously wicked or inhuman. Also **di′a·bol′i·cal.** [< OF < LL < Gk. *diabolos*] — **di′a·bol′i·cal·ly** *adv.* — **di′a·bol′i·cal·ness** *n.*

di·ac·o·nal (dī-ak′ə-nəl) *adj.* Of, pertaining to, or befitting a deacon or the diaconate. [< LL *diaconus* deacon]

di·ac·o·nate (dī-ak′ə-nit, -nāt) *n.* **1.** The office or rank of a deacon. **2.** Deacons collectively.

di·a·crit·ic (dī'ə·krit'ik) *n.* A diacritical mark. — *adj.* Diacritical. [< Gk. < *dia-* between + *krinein* to distinguish]
di·a·crit·i·cal (dī'ə·krit'i·kəl) *adj.* Serving to mark a distinction, as between phonetic values assigned to a letter; distinguishing. — **di·a·crit'i·cal·ly** *adv.*
diacritical mark A mark, point, or sign attached to a letter to indicate its phonetic value, or to distinguish it from another letter: also called *diacritic.*
di·a·dem (dī'ə·dem) *n.* **1.** A crown or headband worn as a symbol of royalty or honor. **2.** Regal power. — *v.t.* To crown. [< OF < L < Gk. < *dia-* across + *deein* to bind]
di·aer·e·sis (dī·er'ə·sis) See DIERESIS.
di·ag·nose (dī'əg·nōs', -nōz') *v.t. & v.i.* **·nosed, ·nos·ing** To make a diagnosis.
di·ag·no·sis (dī'əg·nō'sis) *n. pl.* **·ses** (-sēz) **1.** *Med.* **a** The act or process of recognizing diseases by their characteristic symptoms. **b** The conclusion arrived at. **2.** Any similar examination, summary, and conclusion. [< NL < Gk. < *dia-* between + *gignōskein* to know] — **di·ag·nos·tic** (dī'əg·nos'tik) *adj.* — **di·ag·nos'ti·cal·ly** *adv.*
di·ag·nos·ti·cian (dī'əg·nos·tish'ən) *n.* One who is versed in diagnosis.
di·ag·o·nal (dī·ag'ə·nəl) *adj.* **1.** Having an oblique direction from corner to corner or from side to side. **2.** Marked by oblique lines, ridges, etc. — *n.* **1.** *Geom.* A diagonal line or plane. **2.** Anything running diagonally. [< L < Gk. < *dia-* across + *gōnia* angle] — **di·ag'o·nal·ly** *adv.*
di·a·gram (dī'ə·gram) *n.* **1.** An outline figure or scheme of lines, spaces, points, etc., intended to demonstrate a geometrical proposition, represent an object or area, show the relation between parts or places, etc. **2.** A graph or chart. — *v.t.* **di·a·gramed** or **·grammed, di·a·gram·ing** or **·gram·ming** To represent or illustrate by a diagram. [< Gk. < *dia-* across + *graphein* to write] — **di·a·gram·mat·ic** (dī'ə·grə·mat'ik) or **·i·cal** *adj.* — **di·a·gram·mat'i·cal·ly** *adv.*
di·al (dī'əl, dīl) *n.* **1.** Any graduated circular plate or face upon which pressure, temperature, etc., is indicated by means of a pointer or needle. **2.** The face of a watch or clock; also, a sundial. **3.** A knob or disk on a radio or television set, used to tune in stations. **4.** A rotating disk, used to make connections in an automatic telephone system. — *v.* **di·aled** or **·alled, di·al·ing** or **·al·ling** *v.t.* **1.** To measure with a dial. **2.** To turn to or indicate by means of a dial. **3.** To call by means of a dial telephone. **4.** To adjust a radio or television set to (a station, program, etc.). — *v.i.* **5.** To use a dial, as in telephoning. [< Med.L *dialis* daily < L *dies* day] — **di'al·er** or **di'al·ler** *n.*
di·a·lect (dī'ə·lekt) *n.* **1.** A variety of speech distinguished from the standard language by variations of idiom, vocabulary, pronunciation, etc.: the Yorkshire *dialect* of England. **2.** Any of the regional forms of the standard language: the Southern *dialect* of American English. **3.** A manner of speech characteristic of the members of a particular class, trade, or profession. **4.** A language developed from an earlier language; a linguistic branch. [< MF < L < Gk. < *dia-* across + *legein* to speak]
di·a·lec·tal (dī'ə·lek'təl) *adj.* Of or characteristic of a dialect. — **di'a·lec'tal·ly** *adv.*
di·a·lec·tic (dī'ə·lek'tik) *n.* **1.** *Often pl.* The art or practice of examining statements logically, as by question and answer, to establish validity. **2.** A specific logical mode of argument: Hegel's *dialectic.* **3.** Formerly, logic. — *adj.* **1.** Pertaining to or using dialectic. **2.** Dialectal. [< OF < L < Gk. < *dia-* across + *legein* to speak]
di·a·lec·ti·cal (dī'ə·lek'ti·kəl) *adj.* Dialectic. — **di'a·lec'ti·cal·ly** *adv.*
dialectical materialism *Philos.* The doctrine of Karl Marx and Friedrich Engels.
di·a·lec·ti·cian (dī'ə·lek·tish'ən) *n.* **1.** A logician. **2.** One who specializes in the study of dialects.
di·a·logue (dī'ə·lôg, -log) *n.* **1.** A conversation in which two or more take part. **2.** The conversation in a play, novel, etc. **3.** A literary work in which two or more characters are represented as conversing: a Platonic *dialogue.* **4.** An exchange of opinions or ideas; discussion. — *v.* **·logued, ·logu·ing** *v.t.* **1.** To express in dialogue form. — *v.i.* **2.** To carry on a dialogue. Also **di'a·log.** [< F < L < Gk. < *dialegesthai* to converse] — **di'a·log'uer** or **di'a·log'er** *n.*
di·al·y·sis (dī·al'ə·sis) *n. pl.* **·ses** (-sēz) **1.** Separation of parts previously or normally joined together. **2.** *Chem.* The separating of solutions of unequal diffusibility by means of moist membranes; esp., the separation of a colloid from a crystalloid. [< Gk. < *dia-* completely + *lyein* to loosen] — **di·a·lyt·ic** (dī'ə·lit'ik) *adj.* — **di'a·lyt'i·cal·ly** *adv.*
di·a·mag·net·ic (dī'ə·mag·net'ik) *Physics adj.* Pertaining to or designating the property of substances that tend to lie at right angles to the poles of a magnet. — **di'a·mag·net'i·cal·ly** *adv.* — **di'a·mag'net·ism** *n.*
di·am·e·ter (dī·am'ə·tər) *n. Math.* **1.** A straight line passing through the center of a circle or sphere and terminating at the circumference or surface. **2.** The length of such a line.

3. *Optics* A unit used to measure the magnifying power of binoculars, microscopes, etc. [< OF < L < Gk. < *dia-* through + *metron* measure]
di·a·met·ri·cal (dī'ə·met'ri·kəl) *adj.* **1.** Of, pertaining to, or coinciding with a diameter. Also **di·am·e·tral** (dī·am'ə·trəl). **2.** Directly opposite; as far removed as possible: *diametrical* motives. Also **di'a·met'ric.** — **di'a·met'ri·cal·ly** *adv.*
di·am·ine (dī·am'ēn, -in, dī'ə·mēn, -min) *n. Chem.* Any of a group of compounds containing two amino (NH₂) radicals; a double amine. Also **di·am·in** (dī·am'in, dī'ə·min).
di·a·mond (dī'mənd, dī'ə-) *n.* **1.** A mineral of great hardness and refractive power, consisting of carbon crystallized under great pressure and temperature; also, this mineral when used as a gem. **2.** The uncut face of this stone, used in cutting glass, etc. **3.** A figure bounded by four equal straight lines, having two of the angles acute and two obtuse; a lozenge. **4.** In card games: **a** A red, lozenge-shaped spot on a playing card. **b** A card with such a mark. **c** *pl.* A suit of cards so marked. **5.** In baseball, the infield of a baseball field; also, the entire field. **6.** *Printing* A size of type next above brilliant, 4- or 4½-point. — *adj.* Made of or like diamonds. — *v.t.* To adorn with or as with diamonds. [< OF < LL < L < Gk. *adamas* adamantine] — **dia'mond·ed** *adj.*
diamond anniversary A 60th or 75th anniversary.
di·a·mond·back (dī'mənd·bak', dī'ə-) *n.* **1.** An edible turtle of the southern U.S., having diamond-shaped markings on the shell. Also **diamondback terrapin.** **2.** A large rattlesnake of the SE U.S., having diamond-shaped markings on the back: also **dia'mond-rat'tler** (-rat'lər).

DIAMONDBACK
TERRAPIN
(Upper shell 5 to
7½ inches long)

Diamond State Nickname of Delaware.
Di·an·a (dī·an'ə) In Roman mythology, goddess of the hunt, virginity, and the moon.
di·a·pa·son (dī'ə·pā'sən, -zən) *n.* **1.** In a pipe organ, either of two principal stops (the **open diapason** and the **stopped diapason**) that extend throughout the entire compass of the instrument and produce its fundamental tone. **2.** The entire compass of an instrument or voice. [< L < Gk. dia pa-sōn (*chordōn*) through all (the notes)]
di·a·per (dī'ə·pər; *for n. def. 1, v. def. 1, also* dī'pər) *n.* **1.** A folded piece of soft fabric used as a baby's breechcloth. **2.** A decorative pattern consisting of a system of repeated figures or designs. — *v.t.* **1.** To put a diaper on (a baby). **2.** To decorate with a repeated figure or similar figures. [< OF < Med.Gk. < *dia-* completely + *aspros* white]
di·aph·a·nous (dī·af'ə·nəs) *adj.* Showing light through its substance; transparent; translucent. [< Med.L < Gk. < *dia-* through + *phainein* to show] — **di·aph'a·nous·ly** *adv.* — **di·aph'a·nous·ness** *n.*
di·a·pho·re·sis (dī'ə·fə·rē'sis) *n. Med.* Copious perspiration, esp. when produced artificially. [< L < Gk. < *dia-* across + *phorein* to carry] — **di'a·pho·ret'ic** *adj. & n.*
di·a·phragm (dī'ə·fram) *n.* **1.** *Anat.* A muscular wall separating the thoracic and abdominal cavities in mammals. **2.** Any membrane or partition that separates. **3.** Any device resembling a diaphragm in appearance or elasticity, as the thin vibrating disk of a telephone. **4.** *Optics* A disk with an adjustable aperture that can control the amount of light passing through the lens of a camera, telescope, etc. — *v.t.* To act upon or furnish with a diaphragm. [< LL < Gk. < *dia-* across + *phragma* fence]
di·a·phrag·mat·ic (dī'ə·frag·mat'ik) *adj.* Of, pertaining to, or like a diaphragm. — **di'a·phrag·mat'i·cal·ly** *adv.*
di·ar·rhe·a (dī'ə·rē'ə) *n. Pathol.* A disorder of the intestine marked by abnormally frequent and fluid evacuation of the bowels. Also **di'ar·rhoe'a.** [< L < Gk. < *dia-* through + *rheein* to flow] — **di'ar·rhe'al** or **·rhoe'al, di'ar·rhe'ic** or **·rhoe'ic, di'ar·rhet'ic** or **·rhoet'ic** (-ret'ik) *adj.*
di·a·ry (dī'ə·rē, dī'rē) *n. pl.* **·ries. 1.** A record of daily events; esp., a personal record of one's activities, experiences, or observations; journal. **2.** A book for keeping such a record. [< L < *dies* day] — **di'a·rist** *n.*
Di·as·po·ra (dī·as'pər·ə) *n.* The dispersion of the Jews among the Gentiles after the Babylonian captivity. [< Gk. dispersion < *dia-* completely + *speirein* to sow, scatter]
di·a·stase (dī'ə·stās) *n. Biochem.* An enzyme that converts starch and glycogen into dextrin and maltose. [< F < Gk. < *dia-* apart + *histanai* to set, cause to stand] — **di'a·sta'·sic, di'a·stat'ic** (-stat') *adj.*
di·as·to·le (dī·as'tə·lē) *n.* **1.** *Physiol.* The usual rhythmic dilatation of the heart, esp. of the ventricles, after each contraction. Compare SYSTOLE. **2.** In classical prosody, the lengthening of a syllable. [< LL < Gk. < *dia-* apart + *stellein* to send, put] — **di·a·stol·ic** (dī'ə·stol'ik) *adj.*
di·as·tro·phism (dī·as'trə·fiz'əm) *n. Geol.* **1.** Any of the processes through which the earth's crust is deformed, producing continents, mountains, etc. **2.** Any deformation resulting from this. [< Gk. < *dia-* apart + *strephein* to turn] — **di·a·stroph·ic** (dī'ə·strof'ik) *adj.*

di·a·ther·my (dī′ə·thûr′mē) *n. pl. ·mies Med.* **1.** The generation of heat in the body tissues through their resistance to the passage of high-frequency electric currents. **2.** The apparatus used. Also **di·a·ther·mi·a** (dī′ə·thûr′mē·ə). [< NL < Gk. *dia-* through + *thermē* heat]

di·a·tom (dī′ə·tom, -təm) *n.* Any of various marine and fresh-water plankton, unicellular or colonial whose walls contain silica. [< NL < Gk. *dia-* through + *temnein* to cut]

di·a·ton·ic (dī′ə·ton′ik) *adj. Music* Pertaining to the order of intervals in a major or minor scale of eight tones without the chromatic intervals. [< MF < LL < Gk. < *dia-* through, at the interval of + *tenein* to stretch] — **di′a·ton′·i·cal·ly** *adv.* — **di·a·ton·i·cism** (dī′ə·ton′i·siz′əm) *n.*

di·a·tribe (dī′ə·trīb) *n.* A bitter or malicious denunciation. [< MF < L < Gk. < *dia-* thoroughly + *tribein* to rub]

di·ba·sic (dī-bā′sik) *adj. Chem.* **1.** Of an acid, containing two atoms of hydrogen replaceable by a base or basic radical, as sulfuric acid. **2.** Of or derived from such an acid: said of salts. Also **bibasic.** — **di·ba·sic·i·ty** (dī′bā·sis′ə·tē) *n.*

dib·ble (dib′əl) *n.* A gardener's pointed tool for planting seeds, setting slips, etc. Also **dib·ber** (dib′ər). — *v.t.* ·**bled,** ·**bling** To make holes for seeds or plants in (soil) with a dibble. [ME, ? < *dib,* var. of DAB³] — **dib′bler** *n.*

dice (dīs) *n. pl.* of **die** **1.** Small cubes of bone, ivory, etc., having the sides marked with spots from one to six. **2.** A game of chance played with such cubes. — *v.* **diced, dic·ing** *v.t.* **1.** To cut into small cubes. **2.** To gamble away or win with dice. — *v.i.* **3.** To play at dice. [See DIE²] — **dic′er** *n.*

di·chlo·ro·di·phen·yl·tri·chlor·o·eth·ane (dī-klôr′ō-dī-fen′əl-trī-klôr′ō-eth′ān, -klō′rō-) *n.* DDT.

dicho- *combining form* In two; in pairs. Also, before vowels, **dich-.** [< Gk. *dicha* in two < *dis* twice]

di·chot·o·my (dī-kot′ə·mē) *n. pl. ·mies* **1.** Division into two parts or by pairs; a cutting in two. **2.** *Logic* The division of a class into two mutually exclusive subclasses, as minerals into gold and not-gold. **3.** *Bot.* A system of branching in which each successive axis forks into two equally developed branches. [< Gk. < *dicho-* in two + *temnein* to cut] — **di·chot′o·mous** *adj.* — **di·chot′o·mous·ly** *adv.*

di·chro·mat·ic (dī′krō·mat′ik) *adj.* **1.** Having two colors. **2.** *Zool.* Having two color phases within the species apart from changes due to age or sex. **3.** *Pathol.* Able to see only two of the three primary colors. Also *dichromic.*

di·chro·ma·tism (dī-krō′mə·tiz′əm) *n.* The state of being dichromatic, esp. with reference to color blindness.

di·chro·mic (dī-krō′mik) *adj.* **1.** Containing two atoms of chromium or their equivalents. **2.** Dichromatic.

dick·er (dik′ər) *U.S. v.i.* **1.** To make a petty trade; haggle. **2.** In politics, to work toward a deal; bargain. — *v.t.* **3.** To barter; exchange. — *n.* The act of dickering; also, a petty trade; a bargain. [ME *dyker* lot of ten, esp. skins or hides]

dick·ey (dik′ē) *n. pl. ·eys* **1.** A blouse front worn by women under a jacket or low-necked dress. **2.** A detachable shirt front for a man. **3.** Any small bird. Also **dick′ey·bird′, dick′y·bird′** (-bûrd′) **4.** A driver's outside seat on a carriage; also, a seat for servants in the rear. Also **dick′y.** [< *Dicky,* double dim. of *Richard,* a personal name]

di·cot·y·le·don (dī′kot·ə·lēd′n, dī·kot′-) *n. Bot.* A plant having two seed leaves. — **di′cot·y·le′do·nous** *adj.*

dic·ta (dik′tə) Plural of DICTUM.

Dic·ta·phone (dik′tə·fōn) *n.* A type of phonographic instrument that records and reproduces speech, as for dictation to a stenographer: a trade name. Also **dic′ta·phone.**

dic·tate (dik′tāt; *for v.,* also dik·tāt′) *v.* ·**tat·ed, ·tat·ing** *v.t.* **1.** To utter or read aloud (something) to be recorded by another. **2.** To prescribe authoritatively, as commands, terms, rules, etc. — *v.i.* **3.** To utter aloud something to be recorded by another. **4.** To give orders. — *n.* An authoritative suggestion, rule, or command: the *dictates* of reason. [< L, pp. of *dictare,* freq. of *dicere* to say, speak]

dic·ta·tion (dik·tā′shən) *n.* **1.** The act of dictating material to a copyist. **2.** That which is dictated. **3.** Authoritative direction. — **dic·ta′tion·al** *adj.*

dic·ta·tor (dik′tā·tər, dik·tā′tər) *n.* **1.** A person having absolute powers of government, esp. one considered to be an oppressor. **2.** A person who rules, prescribes, or suggests authoritatively: a *dictator* of fashion. **3.** One who dictates words to be written down.

dic·ta·to·ri·al (dik′tə·tôr′ē·əl, -tō′rē-) *adj.* **1.** Given to dictating; overbearing. **2.** Of or pertaining to a dictator; autocratic. — **dic′ta·to′ri·al·ly** *adv.* — **dic′ta·to′ri·al·ness** *n.*

dic·ta·tor·ship (dik′tā·tər·ship′, dik·tā′tər·ship′) *n.* **1.** The office or term of office of a dictator. **2.** A state under the rule of a dictator. **3.** Supreme or despotic control.

dic·tion (dik′shən) *n.* **1.** The use, choice, and arrangement of words in writing and speaking. **2.** The manner of uttering speech sounds; enunciation. [< L < *dicere* to say, speak]

dic·tion·ar·y (dik′shən·er′ē) *n. pl. ·ar·ies* **1.** A reference work containing alphabetically arranged words together with their definitions, pronunciations, etymologies, etc.; a lexicon. **2.** A lexicon whose words are given in one language together with their equivalents in another. **3.** A reference work containing information relating to a special branch of knowledge and arranged alphabetically. [< Med.L *dictionarium* a collection of words and phrases < L *dicere* to speak.]

Dic·to·graph (dik′tə·graf, -gräf) *n.* A telephonic device capable of reproducing or recording sounds made at a considerable distance from the transmitter, used to transmit or overhear conversations: a trade name. Also **dic′to·graph.**

dic·tum (dik′təm) *n. pl. ·ta* (-tə) **1.** An authoritative, dogmatic, or positive utterance; pronouncement. **2.** A popular saying; maxim. [< L < *dicere* to say]

did (did) Past tense of DO¹.

di·dac·tic (dī-dak′tik, di-) *adj.* **1.** Intended to instruct. **2.** Morally instructive; preceptive. **3.** Overly inclined to teach or moralize; pedantic. Also **di·dac′ti·cal.** [< Gk. < *didaskein* to teach] — **di·dac′ti·cal·ly** *adv.* — **di·dac′ti·cism** (-siz·əm) *n.*

di·dac·tics (dī-dak′tiks, di-) *n.pl. (construed as sing.)* The science or art of instruction or education.

did·dle (did′l) *v.* ·**dled, ·dling** *Informal v.t.* **1.** To cheat. — *v.i.* **2.** To dawdle; pass time idly. Also *daddle.* [? < DIDDLE²] — **did′dler** *n.*

did·dle² (did′l) *v.t. & v.i.* ·**dled, ·dling** To jerk up and down or back and forth; jiggle. [? Var. of dial. *didder,* ME *didderen* to quiver, shake, tremble]

did·n't (did′nt) Did not.

di·do (dī′dō) *n. pl. ·dos* or **·does** *Informal* A caper; antic. [Origin unknown]

Di·do (dī′dō) In the *Aeneid,* the queen of Carthage in love with Aeneas.

didst (didst) *Archaic* second person singular past tense of DO¹: used with *thou.*

di·dym·i·um (dī-dim′ē-əm, di-) *n.* A mixture of the elements neodymium and praseodymium, formerly regarded as one of the elements. [< NL < Gk. *didymos* double]

die¹ (dī) *v.i.* **died, dy·ing** **1.** To suffer death; expire. **2.** To suffer the pains of death: The coward *dies* many times. **3.** To pass gradually: with *away, down,* or *out.* **4.** To cease to exist; fade away: The smile *died* on his lips. **5.** To become extinct: often with *out* or *of.* **6.** *Informal* To desire exceedingly. **7.** To stop functioning, as an engine. **8.** To faint. **9.** *Theol.* To suffer spiritual death. — **to die hard** To resist death or defeat to the end. — **to die off** To be removed one after another by death. [< ON *deyja*]

die² (dī) *n. pl.* **dies** *for def. 2 and 3.* **1.** *Mech.* Any of various hard metal devices for stamping, shaping, or cutting out some object. **2.** A small marked cube. See DICE. **3.** A cast, as in playing dice; stake; hazard. — **the die is cast** The choice or course of action is irrevocable. — *v.t.* **died, die·ing** To cut, stamp, or shape with or as with a die. [< OF *de* < L *datum* something given]

die casting *Metall.* **1.** The process of giving a metal or alloy a desired shape by forcing the molten material into a mold under pressure. **2.** A metal object so made.

di·e·cious (dī-ē′shəs), etc. See DIOECIOUS, etc.

die-hard (dī′härd′) *n.* One who obstinately refuses to abandon or modify his views; esp., a political conservative. — *adj.* Characterized by obstinate resistance. Also **die′hard′.**

di·e·lec·tric (dī′ə·lek′trik) *Electr. adj.* **1.** Nonconducting. **2.** Capable of sustaining an electric field, as by induction. Also **di′e·lec′tri·cal.** — *n.* A dielectric substance, medium, or material. — **di′e·lec′tri·cal·ly** *adv.*

di·en·ceph·a·lon (dī′en·sef′ə·lon) *n. Anat.* That part of the brain forming the posterior part of the forebrain. [< NL < Gk. *di(a)-* between + *enkephalos* brain]

-diene *suffix Chem.* Denoting an open-chain unsaturated hydrocarbon compound having two double bonds: *butadiene.*

di·er·e·sis (dī·er′ə·sis) *n. pl. ·ses* (-sēz) Two dots (¨) placed over the second of two adjacent letters to indicate that two separate vowel sounds are to be pronounced, as in *Noël.* Also spelled *diaeresis.* [< LL < Gk. < *dia-* apart + *hairein* to take, seize] — **di·e·ret·ic** (dī′ə·ret′ik) *adj.*

die·sel engine (dē′zəl) An internal-combustion engine in which fuel oil is sprayed directly into the cylinder, where it is ignited by the high temperature of the air held within the cylinder at a constant pressure. Also **Diesel engine.** [after Rudolf *Diesel,* 1858–1913, German inventor]

die·sink·er (dī′singk′ər) *n.* One who engraves metal dies.

Di·es I·rae (dī′ēz ī′rē) The name of a medieval Latin hymn on the Day of Judgment, used in masses for the dead: so called from its opening words. [< L, day of wrath]

di·e·sis (dī′ə·sis) *n. pl. ·ses* (-sēz) *Printing* The double dagger (‡). [< L < Gk. < *dia-* through + *hienai* to send]

die·stock (dī′stok′) *n. Mech.* A device for holding dies that are used to cut threads on screws, bolts, etc.

di·et[1] (dī'ət) *n.* **1.** A regulated course of eating and drink-ing, esp. one followed for medical or hygienic reasons. **2.** The daily fare. **3.** Food, as regards its nutritive value. — *v.t.* **1.** To regulate the food and drink of. — *v.i.* **2.** To take food and drink according to a regimen. [< OF < L < Gk. *diaita* way of living] — **di'et·er** *n.*

di·et[2] (dī'ət) *n.* A legislative assembly. [< Med.L < L *dies* a day]

Di·et (dī'ət) *n.* **1.** The legislature of certain countries, as Japan. **2.** The semiannual meeting of the estates of the Holy Roman Empire.

di·e·tar·y (dī'ə·ter'ē) *adj.* Pertaining to diet. — *n. pl.* **·tar·ies** **1.** A system or regimen of dieting. **2.** A standard or regulated allowance of food.

di·e·tet·ic (dī'ə·tet'ik) *adj.* Relating to diet or the regula-tion of diet. Also **di·e·tet'i·cal.** — **di·e·tet'i·cal·ly** *adv.*

di·e·tet·ics (dī'ə·tet'iks) *n.pl.* (*construed as sing.*) The branch of hygiene that treats of diet and dieting.

di·e·ti·tian (dī'ə·tish'ən) *n.* One skilled in the principles of dietetics. Also **di·e·tet·ist** (dī'ə·tet'ist), **di'e·ti'cian.**

dif- Assimilated var. of DIS-.

dif·fer (dif'ər) *v.i.* **1.** To be unlike in quality, degree, etc.: often with *from.* **2.** To disagree: often with *with.* **3.** To quarrel. [< OF < L < *dis-* apart + *ferre* to carry]

dif·fer·ence (dif'ər·əns, dif'rəns) *n.* **1.** The state, quality, or degree of being unlike or different. **2.** A specific instance of such unlikeness. **3.** A distinguishing characteristic or peculiarity. **4.** A disagreement or controversy; dispute. **5.** A discrimination: She makes no *difference* between truth and falsehood. **6.** *Math.* The amount by which one quantity differs from another. — **to make a difference** **1.** To affect or change the case or situation. **2.** To distinguish between. — *v.t.* **·enced, ·enc·ing** To make or mark as different.

dif·fer·ent (dif'ər·ənt, dif'rənt) *adj.* **1.** Marked by a differ-ence; unlike. **2.** Not the same; separate; other: There is a *different* clerk there now. **3.** Differing from the ordinary; unusual. — **dif'fer·ent·ly** *adv.* — **dif'fer·ent·ness** *n.*

◆ **different from, than** In American usage, *from* is estab-lished as the idiomatic preposition to follow *different*; when, however, a clause follows the connective, *than* is gaining in-creasing acceptance.

dif·fer·en·ti·a (dif'ə·ren'shē·ə) *n. pl.* **·ti·ae** (shi·ē) *Logic* A specific difference; a characteristic attribute distinguishing a species from others of the same genus. [< L]

dif·fer·en·tial (dif'ə·ren'shəl) *adj.* **1.** Relating to, indicat-ing, or exhibiting a difference or differences. **2.** Constituting or creating a difference. **3.** Based on a difference or distinc-tion. **4.** *Math.* Pertaining to or involving differentials or differentiation. **5.** *Mech.* Of or having a construction in which a movement is obtained by the difference in two mo-tions in the same direction. — *n.* **1.** *Math.* An infinitesimal increment of a quantity: symbol *d.* **2.** *Mech.* A differential gear. **3.** *Electr.* One of two resistance coils, the current of which flows in a direc-tion opposite to that of the other. **4.** In commerce, a difference in rates charged. — **dif'fer·en'tial·ly** *adv.*

differential gear or **gearing** *Mech.* A coupling consisting of a train of gears used to connect two or more shafts so that the wheels can move at different speeds on curves.

differential windlass *Mech.* A windlass having two drums of differ-ent diameters on the same axis, the power being increased in inverse pro-portion to the difference between the diameters.

DIFFERENTIAL GEAR
a Drive shaft. *b* Drive-shaft gear.   *c* Axles.
d Ring gear. *e* Epicyclic train of gears.

dif·fer·en·ti·ate (dif'ə·ren'shē·āt) *v.* **·at·ed, ·at·ing** *v.t.* **1.** To constitute the difference between. **2.** To perceive and indicate the differences in or between. **3.** *Biol.* To develop differences in, as a species. **4.** *Math.* To find the derivative of (a function): opposed to *integrate.* — *v.i.* **5.** To acquire a distinct character; become specialized. **6.** To discriminate. **7.** *Biol.* Of cells during embryological growth, to diversify and develop into specialized organs and tissues. — **dif'fer·en'ti·a'tion** *n.*

dif·fi·cult (dif'ə·kult, -kəlt) *adj.* **1.** Hard to do, accomplish, or deal with; demanding effort or great care. **2.** Not easy to understand; perplexing. **3.** Hard to please: a *difficult* cus-tomer. **4.** Hard to persuade; stubborn. — **dif'fi·cult·ly** *adv.*

dif·fi·cul·ty (dif'ə·kul'tē, -kəl-) *n. pl.* **·ties** **1.** The state, fact, or quality of being difficult. **2.** That which is difficult to do, overcome, or understand. **3.** *Usu. pl.* A troublesome state of affairs, especially financial embarrassment. **4.** A dispute. **5.** Reluctance or objection. **6.** A trouble; worry. [< L < *dis* away, not | *facilis* easy < *facere* to do, make]

dif·fi·dent (dif'ə·dənt) *adj.* Lacking confidence in one-self; timid. [< L *diffidens, -entis*, ppr. of *diffidere* < *dis-* away + *fidere* to trust] — **dif'fi·dence** *n.* — **dif'fi·dent·ly** *adv.*

dif·fract (di·frakt') *v.t.* **1.** To separate into parts. **2.** To subject to diffraction. [< L < *dis-* away + *frangere* to break] — **dif·frac'tive** *adj.* — **dif·frac'tive·ly** *adv.* — **dif·frac'tive·ness** *n.*

dif·frac·tion (di·frak'shən) *n.* *Physics* **1.** A modification of light rays when partially cut off by any obstacle or passing near the edges of an opening, or through a minute hole, gen-erally accompanied by light and dark, or colored, bands due to interference. **2.** An analogous modification of other kinds of wave motion, as of sound, electricity, X-rays, etc.

dif·fuse (*v.* di·fyooz'; *adj.* di·fyoos') *v.t. & v.i.* **·fused, ·fus·ing** **1.** To pour or send out so as to spread in all directions; permeate. **2.** To subject to or spread by diffusion. — *adj.* **1.** Characterized by the excessive use of words. **2.** Widely spread out; dispersed. [< L < *dis-* from + *fundere* to pour] — **dif·fuse'ly** (di·fyoos'lē) *adv.* — **dif·fuse·ness** (di·fyoos'nis) *n.* — **dif·fus'er** or **dif·fus'or** *n.*

dif·fus·i·ble (di·fyoo'zə·bəl) *adj.* Capable of being diffused. — **dif·fus'i·bil'i·ty, dif·fus'i·ble·ness** *n.*

dif·fu·sion (di·fyoo'zhən) *n.* **1.** The act or process of diffus-ing, or the state of being diffused. **2.** Imprecision of verbal expression; verbosity. **3.** *Physics* **a** The intermingling by thermal agitation of the molecules of two fluids, as of gases. **b** The scattering and crisscrossing of light rays, producing general illumination rather than direct radiation.

dif·fu·sive (di·fyoo'siv) *adj.* Tending to diffuse; marked by diffusion. — **dif·fu'sive·ly** *adv.* — **dif·fu'sive·ness** *n.*

dig (dig) *v.* **dug, dig·ging** *v.t.* **1.** To break up, turn up, or re-move (earth, etc.), as with a spade, claws, or the hands. **2.** To make or form by or as by digging. **3.** To take out or ob-tain by digging: to *dig* clams. **4.** To thrust or force into or against, as a heel. **5.** To discover or bring out by careful effort or study: often with *up* or *out.* **6.** *U.S. Slang* To understand or like. — *v.i.* **7.** To break or turn up earth, etc. **8.** To force or make a way by or as by digging. **9.** *U.S. Informal* To study hard; plod. — **to dig in** **1.** To dig trench-es. **2.** *U.S. Informal* To entrench (oneself). **3.** *U.S. In-formal* To begin to work intensively. — *n. Informal* **1.** A thrust; poke. **2.** A sarcastic remark; slur. [< MF *diguer*]

di·gest (*v.* di·jest', dī-; *n.* dī'jest) *v.t.* **1.** *Physiol.* To change (food) chemically in the alimentary canal into material suit-able for assimilation by the body. **2.** To take in or assimi-late mentally. **3.** To arrange in systematic form, usu. by condensing. **4.** To tolerate patiently; endure. **5.** *Chem.* **a** To soften or decompose with heat or moisture. **b** To treat, as wood, with chemical agents under pressure so as to obtain a desired result. — *v.i.* **6.** To be assimilated, as food. **7.** To assimilate food. **8.** To be subjected to heat, moisture, chem-ical agents, or pressure. — *n.* A systematically arranged collection or summary of literary, scientific, legal, or other material; a synopsis. — *Syn.* See ABRIDGEMENT. [< L < *dis-* away + *gerere* to carry] — **di·gest'er** *n.*

di·ges·tant (di·jes'tənt, dī-) *n. Med.* Any agent that assists digestion. — *adj.* Digestive.

di·gest·i·ble (di·jes'tə·bəl, dī-) *adj.* Capable of being di-gested. — **di·gest'i·bil'i·ty, di·gest'i·ble·ness** *n.* — **di·gest'·i·bly** *adv.*

di·ges·tion (di·jes'chən, dī-) *n.* **1.** *Physiol.* The act, process, or function of digesting; also, the resulting condition or state of this process. **2.** Mental reception and assimilation.

di·ges·tive (di·jes'tiv, dī-) *adj.* Pertaining to or promoting digestion: *digestive* tract. — *n.* A medicine to aid digestion.

dig·ger (dig'ər) *n.* **1.** One who digs. **2.** Any implement or part of a machine for digging.

dig·gings (dig'ingz) *n.pl.* **1.** A place of excavation; esp., a mining region. **2.** The materials dug out of such a region. **3.** *Informal* One's lodgings.

dig·it (dij'it) *n.* **1.** A finger or toe. **2.** Any one of the ten Arabic numeral symbols, 0 to 9. **3.** *Electronics* One of a set of characters by which, a digital computer provides required information. [< L *digitus* finger]

dig·i·tal (dij'ə·təl) *adj.* **1.** Of, pertaining to, or like the fin-gers or digits. **2.** Having digits. **3.** Digitate. — *n.* A key on a piano, organ, etc. — **dig'i·tal·ly** *adv.*

digital computer A computing machine that receives problems and processes the answers in digital form. Compare ANALOG COMPUTER.

dig·i·tal·is (dij'ə·tal'is, -tā'lis) *n.* **1.** Any of a genus of herbs of the figwort family, as the foxglove. **2.** The dried leaves of foxglove, containing several substances, that are used as a heart stimulant. [< NL < L *digitus* finger]

dig·i·tate (dij'ə·tāt) *adj. Bot.* Having parts, as leaflets, ar-ranged like the fingers of a hand. Also **dig'i·tat'ed.** [< L < *digitus* finger] — **dig'i·tate·ly** *adv.*

digiti- *combining form* Finger; toe. [< L *digitus* finger, toe]

dig·i·ti·grade (dij'ə·tə·grād') *Zool. adj.* Walking on the toes, without resting on the whole sole of the foot. See PLANTIGRADE. [< DIGITI- + L *gradus* a step, going]

dig·ni·fied (dig'nə·fīd) *adj.* Characterized by or invested with dignity; stately. — **dig'ni·fied·ly** *adv.*

dig·ni·fy (dig'nə·fī) *v.t.* **·fied, ·fy·ing** **1.** To impart or add dignity to. **2.** To give a high-sounding name to. [< OF < Med.L < L *dignus* worthy + *facere* to make]

dig·ni·tar·y (dig′nə·ter′ē) *n.* *pl.* **·tar·ies** One having high official position, as in the government or church.

dig·ni·ty (dig′nə·tē) *n.* *pl.* **·ties 1.** Stateliness and nobility of manner; gravity. **2.** The state or quality of being excellent, worthy, or honorable. **3.** Relative importance or position. **4.** A high rank, title, or office, esp. in the church. **5.** A dignitary. **6.** Persons of high rank or position collectively: preceded by *the.* [< OF < L *dignus* worthy]

di·graph (dī′graf, -gräf) *n.* A combination of two characters representing a single sound, as *oa* in *boat*, *sh* in *she*.

di·gress (di·gres′, dī-) *v.i.* **1.** To turn aside from the main subject. **2.** To ramble; wander. [< L < *di-* away, apart + *gradi* to go, step] — **di·gres′sion** *n.* — **di·gres′sion·al** *adj.*

di·gres·sive (di·gres′iv, dī-) *adj.* Given to or marked by digression. — **di·gres′sive·ly** *adv.* — **di·gres′sive·ness** *n.*

di·he·dral (dī·hē′drəl) *adj.* **1.** Two-sided; formed by or having two plane faces. **2.** Pertaining to or having a dihedral angle. — *n. Aeron.* The upward or downward inclination of an airplane's supporting surfaces. [< DI-² + Gk. *hedra* base, face of a regular solid]

dihedral angle *Geom.* The angle formed by two intersecting planes.

dik·dik (dik′dik′) *n.* A NE African antelope about a foot tall. [< native East African name]

dike (dīk) *n.* **1.** An embankment to protect low land from being flooded. **2.** A bank formed by earth thrown up during the excavation of a ditch. **3.** A ditch. **4.** A causeway. **5.** A barrier or obstruction. **6.** *Geol.* A mass of igneous rock intruded into a fissure in other rocks. — *v.t.* **diked**, **dik·ing 1.** To surround or furnish with a dike. **2.** To drain by ditching. Also, *Chiefly Brit.*, **dyke.** [OE *dīc*] — **dik′er** *n.*

di·lap·i·date (di·lap′ə·dāt) *v.t. & v.i.* **·dat·ed**, **·dat·ing** To fall or cause to fall into partial ruin or decay. [< L < *dis-* away + *lapidare* to throw stones] — **di·lap′i·da′tion** *n.*

di·la·tate (dī·lā′tāt, dil′ə·tāt) *adj.* Dilated.

dil·a·ta·tion (dil′ə·tā′shən, dī′lə-) *n.* **1.** The process of dilating, or the state of being dilated. **2.** That which is dilated. **3.** *Pathol.* An excessive enlargement of an organ, etc.

di·late (di·lāt′, dī-) *v.* **·lat·ed**, **·lat·ing** *v.t.* **1.** To make wider or larger; cause to expand. — *v.i.* **2.** To become larger or wider. **3.** To speak or write diffusely; enlarge; expatiate: with *on* or *upon*. [< F < L < *dis-* apart + *latus* wide] — **di·lat′a·ble** *adj.* — **di·lat′a·bil′i·ty**, **di·lat′a·ble·ness** *n.* — **di·lat′a·bly** *adv.* — **di·la′tive** *adj.*

di·la·tion (di·lā′shən, dī-) *n.* **1.** Dilatation. **2.** *Med.* The expanding of an abnormally small canal or orifice.

di·la·tor (di·lā′tər, dī-) *n.* **1.** One who or that which dilates. **2.** *Med.* An instrument for expanding a wound, aperture, or cavity. Also **di·la·ta·tor** (dil′ə·tā′tər, dīl′ə-), **di·lat′er.**

dil·a·to·ry (dil′ə·tôr′ē, -tō′rē) *adj.* **1.** Given to or characterized by delay; tardy; slow. **2.** Tending to cause delay. [< LL < L *dilatus*, pp. of *differe* to delay] — **dil′a·to′ri·ly** *adv.* — **dil′a·to′ri·ness** *n.*

di·lem·ma (di·lem′ə) *n.* **1.** A situation requiring a choice between equally undesirable alternatives. **2.** *Logic* An argument that presents an antagonist with alternatives that are equally conclusive against him. — **the horns of a dilemma** The equal and usu. undesirable alternatives between which a choice must be made. [< LL < Gk. < *di-* two + *lēmma* a premise] — **dil·em·mat·ic** (dil′ə·mat′ik) *adj.*

dil·et·tan·te (dil′ə·tan′tē, dil′ə·tänt′) *n.* *pl.* **·ti** (-tē) or **·tes 1.** One who interests himself in a subject superficially or merely for amusement; a dabbler. **2.** One who loves the fine arts. — **Syn.** See AMATEUR. — *adj.* Pertaining to or like a dilettante. [< Ital., ppr. of *dilettare* to delight < L < *de-* away + *lacio* to allure] — **dil′et·tan′tish** or **dil′et·tan′te·ish** *adj.* — **dil′et·tan′tism** or **dil′et·tan′te·ism** *n.*

dil·i·gence¹ (dil′ə·jəns) *n.* **1.** Persistent application to one's work or duty; persevering effort. **2.** Proper heed; care.

dil·i·gence² (dil′ə·jəns, *Fr.* dē·lē·zhäns′) *n.* A public stagecoach used in the 18th century in Europe, esp. France. Also **dil·ly** (dil′ē). [< F (*carrosse de*) *diligence* fast coach]

dil·i·gent (dil′ə·jənt) *adj.* **1.** Showing perseverance and application in whatever is undertaken; industrious. **2.** Pursued with painstaking effort: a *diligent* search. [< OF < L *diligere* to care for] — **dil′i·gent·ly** *adv.*

dill (dil) *n.* **1.** An Old World annual of the parsley family, with aromatic seeds, used medicinally and for flavoring. **2.** The seeds or leaves of this plant. [OE *dile*]

dill pickle A pickle flavored with dill.

dil·ly·dal·ly (dil′ē·dal′ē) *v.i.* **·dal·lied**, **·dal·ly·ing** To waste time, esp. in indecision. [Varied reduplication of DALLY]

dil·u·ent (dil′yōō·ənt) *adj.* Serving to dilute. — *n.* A diluent.

di·lute (di·lōōt′, dī-; *for adj., also* dī′lōōt) *v.t.* **·lut·ed**, **·lut·ing 1.** To make weaker or more fluid by adding a liquid, as

water. **2.** To weaken or reduce the intensity, strength, or purity of. — *adj.* Weak; diluted. [< L *dilutus*, pp. of *diluere* < *dis-* away + *luere* to wash] — **di·lu′tion** *n.*

di·lu·vi·al (di·lōō′vē·əl) *adj.* **1.** Of or pertaining to a flood, esp. the Deluge. **2.** *Geol.* **a** Produced by a deluge or by floods. **b** Made of or related to diluvium. Also **di·lu′vi·an.**

di·lu·vi·um (di·lōō′vē·əm) *n. Geol.* Coarse rock deposited by glaciers; glacial drift. [< NL < L, a flood]

dim (dim) *adj.* **dim·mer**, **dim·mest 1.** Obscured or darkened from faintness of light. **2.** Not clearly seen or recognized; indistinct: a *dim* figure. **3.** Not clear to the understanding or memory; vague. **4.** Not perceiving clearly; obtuse. **5.** Not seeing clearly: said of the eye. **6.** Lacking luster or brilliance. **7.** Faint: a *dim* sound. **8.** Discouraging; pessimistic. — *v.t. & v.i.* **dimmed**, **dim·ming** To render or grow dim. [OE *dimm, dim*] — **dim′·ly** *adv.* — **dim′ness** *n.*

dime (dīm) *n.* A silver coin of the United States and Canada, equal to ten cents or one tenth of a dollar. [< OF < L *decima*, fem. of *decimus* a tenth part]

dime novel *Chiefly U.S.* **1.** A cheap, sensational novel, originally costing a dime. **2.** Any trashy novel.

di·men·sion (di·men′shən) *n.* **1.** Any measurable extent, as length, breadth, or thickness. **2.** *Usu. pl.* Extent or magnitude: the *dimensions* of the case. [< MF < L *-onis* < *dis-* apart + *metiri* to measure] — **di·men′sion·al** *adj.*

dime store A five-and-ten-cent store.

di·min·ish (di·min′ish) *v.t.* **1.** To make smaller or less; decrease, as in size, amount, or degree. **2.** To reduce in rank, power, or authority. — *v.i.* **3.** To dwindle; decrease. — **Syn.** See DECREASE. [Fusion of ME *diminuen* to lessen and OF *menusier* to make small] — **di·min′ish·a·ble** *adj.*

di·min·ished (di·min′isht) *adj. Music* **1.** One semitone smaller than the corresponding minor or perfect interval. **2.** Denoting a theme that has been subjected to diminution.

di·min·u·en·do (di·min′yōō·en′dō) *Music n.* *pl.* **·dos** A gradual lessening in volume: expressed by the sign ——— : opposed to *crescendo*. — *v.i.* **·doed**, **·do·ing** To produce a diminuendo. [< Ital., ppr. of *diminuire* to lessen]

dim·i·nu·tion (dim′ə·nōō′shən, -nyōō′-) *n.* The act of diminishing or the condition of being diminished; decrease.

di·min·u·tive (di·min′yə·tiv) *adj.* **1.** Of relatively small size. **2.** Diminishing or tending to diminish. **3.** *Gram.* Expressing diminished size: said of certain suffixes. — *n.* **1.** *Gram.* A word formed from another to express diminished size, familiarity, affection, etc. **2.** Anything very small. — **dim·in′u·tive·ly** *adv.*

dim·i·ty (dim′ə·tē) *n.* *pl.* **·ties** A sheer cotton fabric woven with stripes, cords, or checks, used for dresses, curtains, etc. [< Ital. < ML < Gk. < *di-* two + *mitos* thread]

dim·mer (dim′ər) *n.* A rheostat used for varying the intensity of illumination, as in a theater lighting system.

di·mor·phism (dī·môr′fiz·əm) *n.* The existence of two distinct forms of the same organ or substance. [< Gk. < *di-* two + *morphē* form] — **di·mor′phic**, **di·mor′phous** *adj.*

dim-out (dim′out′) *n.* A form of modified lighting in a city, etc., used as a precautionary measure against aerial attack.

dim·ple (dim′pəl) *n.* **1.** A slight depression in the surface of the human body, esp. one made visible in the cheek by smiling. **2.** A similar depression in any smooth surface. — *v.t. & v.i.* **pled**, **pling** To mark with or form dimples. [ME *dympull*] — **dim′ply** *adj.*

dim·wit (dim′wit′) *n. Slang* A stupid or simple-minded person. — **dim′wit′ted** *adj.* — **dim′wit′ted·ly** *adv.*

din (din) *n.* A loud, continuous noise or clamor; a rattling or clattering sound. — *v.* **dinned**, **din·ning** *v.t.* **1.** To assail with confusing noise. **2.** To urge or press with repetition or insistence. — *v.i.* **3.** To make a din. [OE *dyne*]

dine (dīn) *v.* **dined**, **din·ing** *v.i.* **1.** To eat dinner. **2.** To eat; feed: with *on* or *upon*. — *v.t.* **3.** To entertain at dinner. [< F < OF, prob. < L *dis-* away + *jejunus* fast]

din·er (dī′nər) *n.* **1.** One who dines. **2.** A dining car. **3.** A restaurant resembling a railroad car.

di·nette (dī·net′) *n.* An alcove or small room used as a dining room.

ding (ding) *v.t.* **1.** To sound, as a bell; ring. **2.** *Informal* To instill by constant repetition; din. — *v.i.* **3.** To ring or sound. **4.** *Informal* To speak with constant repetition. — *n.* The sound of a bell, or a sound resembling this. [Imit.]

ding-dong (ding′dông′, -dong′) *n.* **1.** The peal of a bell. **2.** Any monotonous repetition. — *adj. Informal* Energetically and closely contested, as a fight. [Imit.]

din·ghy (ding′gē, ding′ē) *n.* *pl.* **·ghies** Any of various kinds of small rowing boats. Also **din′gey**, **din′gy**, **din′gy.** [< Hind. *dingī*]

din·go (ding′gō) *n.* *pl.* **·goes** The native wild dog of Australia. [< native name]

ding·us (ding′əs) *n. Informal* A thing or device of which the name is unknown or forgotten; a gadget or thingamabob. [< Afrikaans < Du. *ding* thing]

---

din·gy (din'jē) *adj.* **·gi·er, ·gi·est** Darkened or discolored, as if soiled; dull; grimy; shabby. [Origin unknown] — **din'gi·ly** *adv.* — **din'gi·ness** *n.*

dining car A railway car in which meals are served en route.

dining room A room in which meals are served, esp. dinner.

dink·y (ding'kē) *adj.* **dink·i·er, dink·i·est** *Informal* **1.** *U.S.* Small; insignificant. **2.** *Brit.* Little; cute; neat. — *n. pl.* **din·kies** A dinkey. [< Scot. *dink* neat, tidy]

din·ner (din'ər) *n.* **1.** The principal meal of the day, taken usu. at some hour between noon and nine P.M. **2.** A banquet in honor of a person or event. [< F *dîner* to dine]

dinner coat or **jacket** A tuxedo jacket.

din·ner·ware (din'ər-wâr') *n.* Dishes, etc., used for meals.

di·no·saur (dī'nə-sôr) *n. Paleontol.* One of a group of extinct reptiles, widely distributed during the Mesozoic period and including the largest known land animals. [< DINO- + Gk. *sauros* lizard] — **di'no·sau'ri·an** *adj. & n.*

dint (dint) *n.* **1.** Active agency; means; force: to win by *dint* of effort. **2.** A dent. — *v.t.* **1.** To make a dent in. **2.** To drive in forcibly. [OE *dynt* a blow]

di·oc·e·san (dī-os'ə-sən, dī'ə-sē'sən) *adj.* Of or pertaining to a diocese. — *n.* A bishop in charge of a diocese.

di·o·cese (dī'ə-sēs, -sis) *n.* The territory or the churches under a bishop's jurisdiction. [< OF < Med.L < L < Gk. < *dia-* completely + *oikeein* to dwell, manage]

di·ode (dī'ōd) *n. Electronics* An electron tube that permits electrons to pass in one direction only, used as a rectifier.

di·oe·cious (dī-ē'shəs) *adj. Bot.* Having the male and female organs borne by different plants; unisexual: also spelled *diecious.* [< DI-² + Gk. *oikia* house, dwelling]

Di·o·nys·ian (dī'ə-nish'ən, -nis'ē-ən) *adj.* Of or characteristic of Dionysius. Also **Di·o·nys·i·ac** (dī'ə-nis'ē-ak).

Di·o·ny·sus (dī'ə-nī'səs) In Greek mythology, the god of wine, fertility, etc., worshiped with orgiastic rites: identified with the Roman *Bacchus.* Also **Di'o·ny'sos.**

di·op·ter (dī-op'tər) *n. Optics* The unit for measuring the refractive power of a lens, expressed as the reciprocal of its focal length in meters. Also **di·op'tre.** [< MF < L < Gk., optical instrument]

di·op·tric (dī-op'trik) *adj. Optics* **1.** Aiding the vision by refraction, as a lens. **2.** Of or pertaining to dioptrics. **3.** Of or pertaining to a diopter. Also **di·op'tri·cal.**

di·op·trics (dī-op'triks) *n.pl.* (construed as sing.) The branch of optics treating of light refraction by transparent media.

di·o·ra·ma (dī'ə-rä'mə, -ram'ə) *n.* **1.** An exhibit consisting of modeled figures, etc., set in a naturalistic foreground. **2.** A picture that changes by means of cloth transparencies, etc. [< Gk. *dia-* through + *horama* a sight] — **di·o·ram·ic** (dī'ə-ram'ik) *adj.*

di·ox·ide (dī-ok'sīd, -sid) *n. Chem.* An oxide containing two atoms of oxygen to the molecule. Also **di·ox·id** (dī-ok'sid).

dip (dip) *v.* **dipped, dip·ping** *v.t.* **1.** To put or let down into a liquid momentarily. **2.** To obtain or lift up and out by scooping, bailing, etc. **3.** To lower and then raise, as a flag in salute. **4.** To baptize by immersion. **5.** To plunge (animals) into a disinfectant. **6.** To dye by immersion. **7.** To make (candles) by repeatedly immersing wicks in wax or tallow. — *v.i.* **8.** To plunge into and quickly come out of water or other liquid. **9.** To plunge one's hand or a receptacle into water, etc., or into a container, especially so as to take something out. **10.** To sink or go down suddenly. **11.** To incline downward; go down; decline. **12.** *Geol.* To lie at an angle to the horizon, as rock strata. **13.** *Aeron.* To drop rapidly and then climb. **14.** To engage in or read something slightly or superficially. — *n.* **1.** An act of dipping; a brief immersion or plunge. **2.** A liquid sauce, etc., into which something is to be dipped. **3.** The quantity of something taken up at a dipping; also, the object used for dipping. **4.** A candle made by dipping. **5.** A sloping downward; also, the degree of such a sloping. **6.** A hollow or depression. **7.** The angle that a magnetic needle makes with the horizon. **8.** *Aeron.* A rapid drop of an airplane followed by a climb. **9.** *Slang* A pickpocket. [OE *dyppan*]

diph·the·ri·a (dif-thir'ē-ə, dip-) *n. Pathol.* An acute contagious disease, caused by a bacillus and characterized by the formation of a false membrane in the air passages, fever, and weakness. [< F < Gk. *diphthera* leather, membrane]

diph·the·ri·al (dif-thir'ē-əl, dip-) *adj.* Of, pertaining to, or having diphtheria. Also **diph·the'ri·an, diph·the·ric** (dif-thir'ik, dip-), **diph·the·rit·ic** (dif'thə-rit'ik, dip'-).

diph·thong (dif'thông, -thong, dip'-) *n. Phonet.* A blend of two vowel sounds in one syllable, as *oi* in *coil*, or as *i* in *fine*. [< F < LL < Gk. < *di-* two + *phthongos* sound] — **diph·thon'gal** *adj.*

diph·thong·ize (dif'thông-īz, -thong-, dip'-) *v.* **·ized, ·iz·ing** *v.t.* **1.** To make a diphthong of; pronounce as a diphthong. — *v.i.* **2.** To become a diphthong. — **diph'thong·i·za·tion** *n.* [< Gk. *diploos* double]

dip·lo· *combining form* Double. Also, before vowels, **dipl-.**

dip·loid (dip'loid) *adj. Biol.* Having two sets of chromosomes.

di·plo·ma (di-plō'mə) *n.* **1.** A certificate given by a school, college, or university testifying that a student has earned a degree or completed a course of study. **2.** A certificate conferring some honor or privilege. [< L < Gk. *diplōma* paper folded double, a letter]

di·plo·ma·cy (di-plō'mə-sē) *n. pl.* **·cies** **1.** The art, science, or practice of conducting negotiations between nations. **2.** Skill or tact in dealing with others, etc.

dip·lo·mat (dip'lə-mat) *n.* **1.** One engaged in diplomacy. **2.** Any individual possessing skill or tact in dealing with others. [See DIPLOMA.]

dip·lo·mat·ic (dip'lə-mat'ik) *adj.* **1.** Of or pertaining to diplomacy. **2.** Tactful and skillful in dealing with people. Also **dip'lo·mat'i·cal.** — **dip'lo·mat'i·cal·ly** *adv.*

diplomatic corps The corps of officials, as ambassadors and envoys, who are assigned to represent their country in another country. Also **diplomatic body.**

diplomatic immunity Exemption of the members of a diplomatic corps from the ordinary processes of local law.

di·plo·ma·tist (di-plō'mə-tist) *n. Brit.* A diplomat.

dip·per (dip'ər) *n.* **1.** One who dips. **2.** A long-handled cup used to dip liquids. **3.** Any of several American birds that are quick divers; esp. the water ouzel.

Dip·per (dip'ər) *n.* Either of two northern constellations, the Big Dipper or the Little Dipper.

dip·so·ma·ni·a (dip'sə-mā'nē-ə) *n.* Uncontrollable craving for alcoholic drink. [< Gk. *dipsa* thirst + -MANIA]

dip·so·ma·ni·ac (dip'sə-mā'nē·ak) *n.* A person affected with dipsomania. — *adj.* Pertaining to or affected with dipsomania: also **dip·so·ma·ni·a·cal** (dip'sə-mə-nī'ə-kəl).

dip·ter·ous (dip'tər-əs) *adj.* **1.** *Entomol.* Of or pertaining to insects having a single pair of wings, including the flies, gnats, mosquitoes, etc. **2.** Two-winged, as a seed or fruit. [< Gk. < *di-* twice + *pteron* wing]

dip·tych (dip'tik) *n.* **1.** An ancient Greek or Roman hinged double writing tablet. **2.** A double picture or carving, often of a religious subject. [< Gk., pair of tablets]

dire (dīr) *adj.* **dir·er, dir·est** Calamitous; dreadful; terrible. [< L *dirus* awful] — **dire'ly** *adv.* — **dire'ness** *n.*

di·rect (di-rekt', dī-) *v.t.* **1.** To control or conduct the affairs of; manage. **2.** To order or instruct with authority; command. **3.** *Music* To lead as a conductor. **4.** To tell (someone) the way. **5.** To cause to move or face in a desired direction: to *direct* one's gaze. **6.** To indicate the destination of, as a letter. **7.** To intend, as remarks or insults, to be heard by a person; address. **8.** To guide or supervise (the performance of a play, film, etc.). — *v.i.* **9.** To give commands or guidance. **10.** To guide the production or interpretation of a play, film, etc. — *adj.* **1.** Having or being the straightest course; shortest; nearest. **2.** Free from intervening agencies or conditions. **3.** Straightforward; candid; plain. **4.** Complete; absolute: the *direct* antithesis. **5.** In a continuous line of descent; lineal. **6.** In the exact words of the speaker or writer: a *direct* quote. **7.** *Govt.* By the efforts of the people through referendum, etc., without the intervention of delegates or representatives. **8.** *Electr.* Continuous as opposed to alternating, as a current. — *adv.* In a direct line or manner; directly. [< L < *dis-* apart + *regere* to guide, conduct] — **di·rect'ness** *n.*

di·rec·tion (di-rek'shən, dī-) *n.* **1.** The act of directing. **2.** The course or position of an object or point in relation to another object or point: in the *direction* of Chicago. **3.** *Usu. pl.* Instructions about how to do or use something. **4.** An order, command, or regulation. **5.** Management, control, or administration. **6.** Supervision and organization of a play, film, etc. **7.** Tendency or movement. **8.** The address on a letter, parcel, etc., that indicates the intended recipient.

di·rec·tion·al (di-rek'shən-əl, dī-) *adj.* **1.** Pertaining to direction in space. **2.** *Telecom.* **a** Adapted for indicating from which of several directions signals are received. **b** Describing an antenna that radiates or receives radio waves more effectively in or from some directions than from others.

direction finder *Telecom.* A receiving device with which the direction of incoming radio signals may be determined.

di·rec·tive (di-rek'tiv, dī-) *n.* An order or regulation; esp., a governmental or military pronouncement. — *adj.* That directs or points out, rules, or governs.

di·rect·ly (di-rekt'lē, dī-) *adv.* **1.** In a direct line or manner. **2.** Without medium, agent, or go-between. **3.** As soon as possible; immediately. **4.** Exactly; precisely. — *conj. Brit.* As soon as.

di·rec·tor (di-rek'tər, dī-) *n.* **1.** One who directs, as the head member of a corporation, the conductor of an orchestra, etc. **2.** *Mil.* An apparatus that computes firing data for use against moving targets. — **di·rec'tress** *n.fem.*

di·rec·to·rate (di-rek'tər-it, dī-) *n.* **1.** A body of directors. **2.** The office or power of a director; also **di·rec'tor·ship.**

di·rec·to·ri·al (di-rek'tôr'ē-əl, -tō'rē, dī-) *adj.* **1.** That directs; directive. **2.** Pertaining to a director or directorate.

di·rec·to·ry (di-rek'tər-ē, dī-) *n. pl.* **·ries** **1.** An alphabetical or classified list, as of the names and addresses of the inhabitants or businesses of a city. **2.** A collection of rules. **3.** A directorate. — *adj.* Serving to direct.

direct primary *Govt.* A preliminary election in which a party chooses its candidates for public office by direct vote.

direct tax A tax charged directly to the taxpayer.

dire·ful (dīr′fŏŏl, -fəl) *adj.* Dreadful; terrible; dire. — **dire′ful·ly** *adv.* — **dire′ful·ness** *n.*

dirge (dûrj) *n.* **1.** A song or melody expressing mourning. **2.** A funeral hymn. [< L *dirige* (imperative of *dirigere* to direct), the first word of the antiphon (*Ps.* v 8) of matins]

dir·i·gi·ble (dĭr′ə·jə·bəl) *n.* A lighter-than-air aircraft that may be steered by means of its own motive power. — *adj.* That can be steered. [< L *dirigere* to direct]

dirk (dûrk) *n.* A dagger. [Origin uncertain]

dirn·dl (dûrn′dəl) *n.* **1.** A woman's dress with a full skirt gathered to a tight bodice. **2.** The skirt of such a dress: also **dirndl skirt.** [< G *dirndl,* dim. of *dirne* girl]

dirt (dûrt) *n.* **1.** Any foul or filthy substance, as mud, dust, excrement, etc. **2.** Loose earth or soil; loam. **3.** Something contemptible, mean, or of small worth. **4.** Obscene speech, pictures, or writing. **5.** Rude language. **6.** Gossip. **7.** *Mining* Washed-down earth, broken ore or rock, etc., containing precious metal. — *adj.* Made of earth: a *dirt* road. [ME *drit* < ON, dirt, bird droppings]

dirt-cheap (dûrt′chēp′) *adj.* Very inexpensive. — *adv.* At a very low price.

dirt farmer *U.S. Informal* A farmer who does his own work.

dirt·y (dûr′tē) *adj.* **dirt·i·er, dirt·i·est** **1.** Soiled with or as with dirt; unclean; filthy. **2.** Imparting dirt; making filthy. **3.** Indecent; obscene. **4.** Despicable; mean. **5.** Lacking brightness or clarity: said of colors. **6.** Stormy: *dirty* weather. **7.** Having excessive radioactive fallout: a *dirty* atomic bomb. — *v.t. & v.i.* **dirt·ied, dirt·y·ing** To make or become dirty. — **dirt′i·ly** *adv.* — **dirt′i·ness** *n.*

dis-¹ *prefix* **1.** Away from; apart: *disembody.* **2.** The reverse of or the undoing of (what is expressed in the rest of the word): *disconnect.* **3.** Deprivation of some quality, power, rank, etc.: *disable.* **4.** Not: *disloyal.* **5.** Completely; thoroughly (with an already negative word): *disannul.* Also: *di-* before *b, d, l, m, n, r, s, v,* and usu. before *g,* as in *digress, direct, diverge; dif-* before *f,* as in *differ.* The living English prefix is always in the form *dis-.* [< L *dis-,* sometimes replacing OF *des-* (see DE-), ult. < *duo* two]

dis-² *prefix* Var. of DI-². [< MF, ult. < Gk. *dis* twice]

Dis (dĭs) In Roman mythology: **a** God of the lower world: identified with *Pluto.* **b** The kingdom of the dead.

dis·a·bil·i·ty (dĭs′ə·bĭl′ə·tē) *n. pl.* **·ties** **1.** That which disables. **2.** Lack of ability. **3.** Legal incapacity to act.

dis·a·ble (dĭs·ā′bəl) *v.t.* **·bled, ·bling 1.** To render incapable; cripple. **2.** To render legally incapable. — **dis·a′ble·ment** *n.*

dis·a·buse (dĭs′ə·byōōz′) *v.t.* **·bused, ·bus·ing** To free from false or mistaken ideas; undeceive.

dis·ad·van·tage (dĭs′əd·van′tij, -vän′-) *n.* **1.** An unfavorable condition or situation. **2.** That which produces an unfavorable condition or situation; drawback; handicap. **3.** Loss, injury, or detriment. — **at a disadvantage** In an unfavorable condition or situation. — *v.t.* **·taged, ·tag·ing** To subject to a disadvantage.

dis·ad·van·taged (dĭs′əd·van′tijd, -vän′-) *adj.* Having less money, social status, etc., than is needed for decent living.

dis·ad·van·ta·geous (dĭs·ad′vən·tā′jəs) *adj.* Attended with disadvantage; detrimental; inconvenient. — **dis·ad′van·ta′geous·ly** *adv.* — **dis·ad′van·ta′geous·ness** *n.*

dis·af·fect (dĭs′ə·fekt′) *v.t.* To destroy or weaken the affection or loyalty of; alienate; estrange. — **dis′af·fec′tion** *n.*

dis·af·fect·ed (dĭs′ə·fek′tid) *adj.* Alienated in feeling or loyalty; estranged; unfriendly. — **dis′af·fect′ed·ly** *adv.*

dis·a·gree (dĭs′ə·grē′) *v.i.* **·greed, ·gree·ing** **1.** To vary in opinion; differ; dissent. **2.** To quarrel; argue. **3.** To fail to agree or harmonize, as facts. **4.** To be unacceptable or unfavorable: with *with:* Heat *disagreed* with him.

dis·a·gree·a·ble (dĭs′ə·grē′ə·bəl) *adj.* **1.** Repugnant or offensive; not agreeable; unpleasant. **2.** Of unpleasant disposition; quarrelsome; bad-tempered. — **dis′a·gree′a·bil′i·ty, dis′a·gree′a·ble·ness** *n.* — **dis′a·gree′a·bly** *adv.*

dis·a·gree·ment (dĭs′ə·grē′mənt) *n.* **1.** Failure to agree. **2.** Dissimilarity; inconsistency; discrepancy. **3.** Difference in views; dissent. **4.** A quarrel; dispute.

dis·al·low (dĭs′ə·lou′) *v.t.* **1.** To refuse to allow. **2.** To reject as untrue or invalid. — **dis′al·low′ance** *n.*

dis·ap·pear (dĭs′ə·pir′) *v.i.* **1.** To pass from sight; fade away; vanish. **2.** To cease to exist. — **dis′ap·pear′ance** *n.*

dis·ap·point (dĭs′ə·point′) *v.t.* **1.** To fail to fulfill the expectation, hope, or desire of (a person). **2.** To prevent the fulfillment of (a hope or plan). — **dis′ap·point′ing·ly** *adv.*

dis·ap·point·ed (dĭs′ə·poin′tid) *adj.* Frustrated in one's expectations or hopes.

dis·ap·point·ment (dĭs′ə·point′mənt) *n.* **1.** The act of disappointing. **2.** The feeling of being disappointed. **3.** One who or that which disappoints.

dis·ap·pro·ba·tion (dĭs′ap·rə·bā′shən) *n.* Disapproval.

dis·ap·prov·al (dĭs′ə·prōō′vəl) *n.* The act of disapproving; the withholding of approval; censure.

dis·ap·prove (dĭs′ə·prōōv′) *v.* **·proved, ·prov·ing** *v.t.* **1.** To regard with disfavor or censure; condemn. **2.** To refuse to approve. — *v.i.* **3.** To have or express an unfavorable opinion: often with *of.* — **dis′ap·rov′ing·ly** *adv.*

dis·arm (dis·ärm′) *v.t.* **1.** To deprive of weapons or of any means of attack or defense. **2.** To overcome the suspicion, antagonism, etc., of. **3.** To allay or reduce (suspicion, antagonism, etc.). — *v.i.* **4.** To lay down arms. **5.** To reduce or eliminate one's military forces, equipment, etc.

dis·ar·ma·ment (dis·är′mə·mənt) *n.* The act of disarming; esp., the elimination, reduction, or limitation of armed forces, military equipment, or weapons of war.

dis·arm·ing (dis·är′ming) *adj.* Tending to overcome suspicion, etc.: a *disarming* smile. — **dis·arm′ing·ly** *adv.*

dis·ar·range (dĭs′ə·rānj′) *v.t.* **·ranged, ·rang·ing** To disturb the arrangement of; disorder. — **dis′ar·range′ment** *n.*

dis·ar·ray (dĭs′ə·rā′) *n.* **1.** Disorder; confusion. **2.** Disorder of clothing. — *v.t.* To throw into disarray.

dis·as·sem·ble (dĭs′ə·sem′bəl) *v.t.* **·bled, ·bling** To take apart. — **dis′as·sem′bly** *n.*

dis·as·so·ci·ate (dĭs′ə·sō′shē·āt) *v.t.* **·at·ed, ·at·ing** To dissociate. — **dis′as·so′ci·a′tion** *n.*

dis·as·ter (di·zas′tər, -zäs′-) *n.* An event causing great distress or ruin; sudden and crushing misfortune. [< MF < *des-* away + *astre* a star]

dis·as·trous (di·zas′trəs, -zäs′-) *adj.* Causing or accompanied by disaster; calamitous. — **dis·as′trous·ly** *adv.* — **dis·as′trous·ness** *n.*

dis·a·vow (dĭs′ə·vou′) *v.t.* To disclaim responsibility for or approval of; refuse to acknowledge. — **dis′a·vow′al** *n.*

dis·band (dis·band′) *v.t.* **1.** To break up the organization of; dissolve; especially, to break up (an army or similar unit) by dismissing the members. — *v.i.* **2.** To become disbanded. — **dis·band′ment** *n.*

dis·bar (dis·bär′) *v.t.* **·barred, ·bar·ring** To expel officially from the legal profession. — **dis·bar′ment** *n.*

dis·be·lief (dĭs′bi·lēf′) *n.* Lack of belief.

dis·be·lieve (dĭs′bi·lēv′) *v.t. & v.i.* **·lieved, ·liev·ing** To withhold belief (from); reject. — **dis′be·liev′er** *n.*

dis·bur·den (dis·bûr′dən) *v.t.* **1.** To relieve of a burden. **2.** To get rid of (a burden). — *v.i.* **3.** To put off a burden.

dis·burse (dis·bûrs′) *v.t.* **·bursed, ·burs·ing** To pay out; expend. [< OF < *des-* away + *bourse* a purse] — **dis·burs′a·ble** *adj.* — **dis·burse′ment** *n.* — **dis·burs′er** *n.*

disc (disk) *n.* **1.** See DISK. **2.** *Anat.* Any approximately flat, circular outgowth, organ, or structure, as of cartilage between the joints of certain bones. [Var. of DISK]

dis·calced (dis·kalst′) *adj.* Barefooted, as certain orders of monks [< L < *dis-* not + *calceatus* a shoe]

dis·cant (dis′kant, dis·kant′) *n. & v.i.* Descant.

dis·card (*v.* dis·kärd′; *n.* dis′kärd) *v.t.* **1.** To cast aside as useless or undesirable; reject; dismiss. **2.** In card games, to throw out (a card or cards) from one's hand; also, to play (a card, other than a trump, not of the suit led). — *v.i.* **3.** In card games, to throw out a card or cards. — *n.* **1.** The act of discarding, or the state of being discarded. **2.** A card or cards discarded. **3.** One who or that which is discarded.

dis·cern (di·sûrn′, di·zûrn′) *v.t.* **1.** To perceive, as with sight or mind. **2.** To recognize as separate and different. — *v.i.* **3.** To distinguish or discriminate something. [< OF < L < *dis-* apart + *cernere* to separate] — **dis·cern′er** *n.* — **dis·cern′i·ble** *adj.* — **dis·cern′i·bly** *adv.*

dis·cern·ing (di·sûr′ning, -zûr′-) *adj.* Quick to discern; discriminating; penetrating. — **dis·cern′ing·ly** *adv.*

dis·cern·ment (di·sûrn′mənt, -zûrn′-) *n.* **1.** The act or process of discerning. **2.** Keenness of judgment; insight.

dis·charge (dis·chärj′; *n. also* dis′chärj) *v.* **charged, charg·ing** *v.t.* **1.** To remove the contents of; unload. **2.** To remove by unloading. **3.** To emit (fluid). **4.** To shoot or fire, as a gun. **5.** To dismiss from office or employment. **6.** To set at liberty, as a prisoner. **7.** To relieve of duty or obligation. **8.** To perform the duties of (a trust, office, etc.). **9.** To pay (a debt) or meet and satisfy (an obligation or duty). **10.** To set aside legally; annul. **11.** *Electr.* To free of an electrical charge. — *v.i.* **12.** To get rid of a load, burden, etc. **13.** To go off, as a cannon. **14.** To give or send forth contents. **15.** *Electr.* To lose a charge of electricity. — *n.* **1.** The act of discharging or the state of being discharged. **2.** The firing of a weapon or missile. **3.** An issuing forth; emission. **4.** That which is discharged, as pus. **5.** Release or dismissal from service, employment, or custody. **6.** Something that discharges, as a certificate separating one from military service. **7.** *Electr.* The flow of electricity between the terminals of a condenser when placed in very near contact. [< OF *deschargier* < *des-* away (< L *dis-*) + *chargier* to carry] **— dis·charge′a·ble** *adj.* **— dis·charg′er** *n.*

dis·ci·ple (di·sī′pəl) *n.* **1.** One who accepts and follows a teacher or a doctrine. **2.** One of the twelve chosen companions and apostles of Jesus Christ. **— Syn.** See ADHERENT. [OE < L *discere* to learn] **— dis·ci′ple·ship** *n.*

dis·ci·pli·nar·i·an (dis′ə·plə·nâr′ē·ən) *n.* One who administers or advocates discipline. **—** *adj.* Disciplinary.

dis·ci·pli·nar·y (dis′ə·plə·ner′ē) *adj.* Of, relating to, or of the nature of discipline; used for discipline.

dis·ci·pline (dis′ə·plin) *n.* **1.** Training of the mental, moral, and physical powers by instruction, control, and exercise. **2.** The state or condition resulting from such training. **3.** Subjection to rule and authority. **4.** Punishment or disciplinary action for the sake of training. **5.** A system of rules, or method of practice, as of a church. **6.** A branch of knowledge or instruction. **7.** A penitential instrument; a scourge. **—** *v.t.* **·plined, ·plin·ing 1.** To train to obedience or subjection. **2.** To drill; educate. **3.** To punish. **— Syn.** CHASTEN, TEACH. [< OF < L *disciplina* instruction] **— dis′ci·plin′a·ble** *adj.* **— dis′ci·plin·er** *n.*

disc jockey See DISK JOCKEY.

dis·claim (dis·klām′) *v.t.* **1.** To disavow any claim to, or responsibility for. **2.** To reject or deny the authority of. **—** *v.i.* **3.** *Law* To renounce a legal claim. **— dis·cla·ma·tion** (dis′klə·mā′shən) *n.*

dis·claim·er (dis·klā′mər) *n.* **1.** One who disclaims. **2.** A disclaiming act, notice, or instrument.

dis·close (dis·klōz′) *v.t.* **·closed, ·clos·ing 1.** To expose to view; uncover. **2.** To make known. **— dis·clos′er** *n.*

dis·clo·sure (dis·klō′zhər) *n.* **1.** The act or process of disclosing. **2.** That which is disclosed.

dis·coid (dis′koid) *adj.* Having the form of a disk. Also **dis·coi′dal.** **—** *n.* A disk or disklike object. [< L < Gk. *diskos discus* < *eidos* form]

dis·col·or (dis·kul′ər) *v.t.* **1.** To change or destroy the color of; stain. **—** *v.i.* **2.** To become discolored. Also *Brit.* **dis·col′our. — dis·col′or·a′tion, dis·col′or·ment** *n.*

dis·com·bob·u·late (dis′kəm·bob′yə·lāt) *v.t.* **·lat·ed, ·lat·ing** *U.S. Slang* To throw into confusion. [Origin uncertain]

dis·com·fit (dis·kum′fit) *v.t.* **1.** To defeat the plans or purposes of; frustrate. **2.** To throw into confusion. **3.** To vanquish. [< OF < *des-* away + *confire* to prepare]

dis·com·fi·ture (dis·kum′fi·chər) *n.* The act of discomfiting, or the state of being discomfited; defeat; frustration.

dis·com·fort (dis·kum′fərt) *n.* **1.** Lack of ease or comfort; disquietude. **2.** That which interferes with comfort. **—** *v.t.* To make uneasy; distress.

dis·com·mode (dis′kə·mōd′) *v.t.* **·mod·ed, ·mod·ing** To cause inconvenience to; trouble; disturb. [< DIS-¹ + L *commodus* fit, suitable, convenient]

dis·com·pose (dis′kəm·pōz′) *v.t.* **·posed, ·pos·ing 1.** To disturb the calm of; make uneasy. **2.** To disorder or disarrange. **— dis′com·pos′ed·ly** *adv.* **— dis′com·pos′ing·ly** *adv.*

dis·com·po·sure (dis′kəm·pō′zhər) *n.* The state of being discomposed; agitation; perturbation.

dis·con·cert (dis′kən·sûrt′) *v.t.* **1.** To disturb the composure of; confuse; upset. **2.** To frustrate, as a plan. [< MF < *dis-* apart + *concerter* to agree] **— dis′con·cert′ed** *adj.* **— dis′con·cert′ed·ly** *adv.* **— dis′con·cert′ed·ness** *n.* **— dis′con·cert′ing·ly** *adv.*

dis·con·form·i·ty (dis′kən·fôr′mə·tē) *n. pl.* **·ties** Lack of conformity; nonconformity.

dis·con·nect (dis′kə·nekt′) *v.t.* To break the connection of or between. **— dis′con·nec′tion** *n.*

dis·con·nect·ed (dis′kə·nek′tid) *adj.* **1.** Not connected; disjointed. **2.** Incoherent; rambling. **— dis′con·nect′ed·ly** *adv.* **— dis′con·nect′ed·ness** *n.*

dis·con·so·late (dis·kon′sə·lit) *adj.* **1.** Not to be consoled; inconsolable; dejected. **2.** Producing or marked by gloominess; cheerless. [< Med.L < L *dis-* not + *consolari* to cheer, console] **— dis·con′so·late·ly** *adv.* **— dis·con′so·late·ness, dis·con·so·la′tion** *n.*

dis·con·tent (dis′kən·tent′) *adj.* Discontented. **—** *n.* Lack of contentment; dissatisfaction; uneasiness: also **dis′con·tent′ment.** **—** *v.t.* To make discontent.

dis·con·tent·ed (dis′kən·ten′tid) *adj.* Restless; uneasy in mind, as through frustration; dissatisfied. **— dis′con·tent′ed·ly** *adv.* **— dis′con·tent′ed·ness** *n.*

dis·con·tin·ue (dis′kən·tin′yōō) *v.* **·tin·ued, ·tin·u·ing** *v.t.* **1.** To break off or cease from; stop. **2.** To cease using, receiving, etc. **—** *v.i.* **3.** To come to an end; cease. **— dis·con·tin′u·ance, dis·con·tin′u·a′tion** *n.*

dis·con·ti·nu·i·ty (dis′kon·tə·nōō′ə·tē, ·nyōō′-) *n. pl.* **·ties 1.** Lack of continuity. **2.** A gap or break.

dis·con·tin·u·ous (dis′kən·tin′yōō·əs) *adj.* Not continuous; characterized by interruptions or breaks. **— dis′con·tin′u·ous·ly** *adv.* **— dis′con·tin′u·ous·ness** *n.*

dis·cord (*n.* dis′kôrd; *v.* dis·kôrd′) *n.* **1.** Lack of agreement

or concord; contention; conflict; strife. **2.** A harsh or disagreeable mingling of noises; din. **3.** *Music* Dissonance. **—** *v.i.* To be out of accord or harmony; clash. [< OF < L *dis-* apart + *cor, cordis* heart]

dis·cor·dant (dis·kôr′dənt) *adj.* **1.** Characterized by lack of agreement or concord; differing; clashing. **2.** Dissonant, harsh, or disagreeable in sound. [See DISCORD.] **— dis·cor′dance, dis·cor′dan·cy** *n.* **— dis·cor′dant·ly** *adv.*

dis·co·thèque (dis·kə·tek′) *n.* A night club offering recorded music for dancing instead of music played by a band of live musicians. [< F, lit., record library]

dis·count (*v.* dis′kount, dis·kount′; *n.* dis′kount) *v.t.* **1.** To deduct (an indicated sum or percent) from the full amount that would otherwise be charged or owed. **2.** To buy or sell (a bill, note, or other negotiable paper), less the amount of interest to be accumulated before maturity. **3.** To lend money on (negotiable notes, etc., not immediately payable), deducting the interest. **4.** To reduce the cost or value of: to *discount* merchandise. **5.** To take little or no account of; disregard: *Discount* what she says. **6.** To allow for exaggeration, prejudice, etc., in; accept with reservation: to *discount* stories of great heroism. **7.** To take into account in advance and so lessen the full intensity or effect of. **—** *v.i.* **8.** To lend money, deducting the interest beforehand. **—** *n.* **1.** A deduction of a particular sum or percent, as one made for immediate cash payment. **2.** The interest deducted beforehand in buying, selling, or lending money on negotiable notes, etc. **3.** The rate of interest so deducted: also **discount rate. 4.** The act of discounting. **— at a discount 1.** Below the amount regularly charged; at less than face value. **2.** In little demand and of little value. [< MF < OF < Med.L < L *dis-* away + *computare.* See COMPUTE.] **— dis′count·a·ble** *adj.* **— dis′count·er** *n.*

dis·coun·te·nance (dis·koun′tə·nəns) *v.t.* **·nanced, ·nanc·ing 1.** To disapprove of. **2.** To abash; disconcert.

dis·cour·age (dis·kûr′ij) *v.t.* **·aged, ·ag·ing 1.** To weaken the courage or lessen the confidence of; dishearten. **2.** To deter or dissuade: with *from.* **3.** To obstruct; hinder. **4.** To attempt to repress or prevent by disapproval. [< OF < *des-* away + *corage* courage] **— dis·cour′ag·er** *n.* **— dis·cour′ag·ing·ly** *adv.* **— dis·cour′age·ment** *n.*

dis·course (*n.* dis′kôrs, -kōrs, dis·kôrs′, -kōrs′; *v.* dis·kôrs′, -kōrs′) *n.* **1.** Communication, as in conversation or writing. **2.** A formal, extensive, oral or written treatment of a subject. **—** *v.* **·coursed, ·cours·ing** *v.i.* **1.** To set forth one's ideas concerning a subject: with *on* or *upon.* **2.** To converse; confer. [< F < L < *dis-* apart + *cursus* a running, pp. of *currere* to run] **— dis·cours′er** *n.*

dis·cour·te·ous (dis·kûr′tē·əs) *adj.* Not courteous; impolite. **— dis·cour′te·ous·ly** *adv.* **— dis·cour′te·ous·ness** *n.*

dis·cour·te·sy (dis·kûr′tə·sē) *n. pl.* **·sies 1.** Lack of courtesy; rudeness. **2.** A discourteous act.

dis·cov·er (dis·kuv′ər) *v.t.* To find out, get knowledge of, or come upon, esp. for the first time. [< OF < *des-* away + *covrir* to cover] **— dis·cov′er·a·ble** *adj.* **— dis·cov′er·er** *n.*

dis·cov·er·y (dis·kuv′ər·ē) *n. pl.* **·er·ies 1.** The act of discovering. **2.** Something discovered.

dis·cred·it (dis·kred′it) *v.t.* **1.** To harm the credit or reputation of; bring into disrepute. **2.** To cause to be doubted, disbelieved, or distrusted. **3.** To refuse to believe (something asserted). **—** *n.* **1.** The state of being discredited; as: **a** Lack or loss of credit, reputation, or general esteem. **b** Doubt; disbelief; distrust. **2.** Something that discredits. **— dis·cred′it·a·ble** *adj.* **— dis·cred′it·a·bly** *adv.*

dis·creet (dis·krēt′) *adj.* Tactful and judicious, esp. in dealing with others. [< OF < LL *discretus,* orig. pp. of L *discernere* to discern] **— dis·creet′ly** *adv.* **— dis·creet′ness** *n.*

dis·crep·an·cy (dis·krep′ən·sē) *n. pl.* **·cies 1.** Lack of agreement or consistency; contradiction. **2.** An instance of this. Also **dis·crep′ance.** [< OF < L *dis-* apart + *crepare* to creak] **— dis·crep′ant** *adj.* **— dis·crep′ant·ly** *adv.*

dis·crete (dis·krēt′) *adj.* **1.** Distinct or separate. **2.** Made up of distinct parts. [Var. of DISCREET] **— dis·crete′ly** *adv.* **— dis·crete′ness** *n.*

dis·cre·tion (dis·kresh′ən) *n.* **1.** The quality of being discreet; tactfulness; prudence. **2.** Freedom or power to make one's own judgments. **— at one's discretion** According to one's own judgment. [< OF < L < *discernere* to discern] **— dis·cre′tion·ar·y** (dis·kresh′ən·er′ē) *adj.* Left to or determined by one's discretion. Also **dis·cre′tion·al.**

dis·crim·i·nate (*v.* dis·krim′ə·nāt; *adj.* dis·krim′ə·nit) *v.* **·nat·ed, ·nat·ing** *v.i.* **1.** To act toward someone or something with partiality or prejudice: to *discriminate* against a minority. **2.** To draw a clear distinction; distinguish: to *discriminate* between good and evil. **—** *v.t.* **3.** To draw or constitute a clear distinction between: differentiate: to *discriminate* good and evil. **4.** To recognize as being different. **—** *adj.* Discriminating. [< L < *dis-* apart + *crimen* judgment] **— dis·crim′i·nate·ly** *adv.* **— dis·crim′i·nat·ing** *adj.* **— dis·crim′i·nat·ing·ly** *adv.* **— dis·crim′i·na′tion** *n.* **— dis·crim′i·na′tor** *n.*

dis·crim·i·na·to·ry (dis-krim′ə-nə-tôr′ē, -tō′rē) *adj.* Showing prejudice or bias: *discriminatory* practices.

dis·cur·sive (dis-kûr′siv) *adj.* Passing quickly or disjointedly from one subject to another digressive. [See DISCOURSE.] — **dis·cur′sive·ly** *adv.* — **dis·cur′sive·ness** *n.*

dis·cus (dis′kəs) *n. pl.* **dis·cus·es** or **dis·ci** (dis′ī) 1. A flat, heavy disk, as of metal or stone, hurled for distance in athletic contests. 2. Such a contest. [< L < Gk. *diskos*]

dis·cuss (dis-kus′) *v.t.* To have as the subject of conversation or writing; treat or consider formally. [< L, pp. of *discutere* to discuss < *dis-* apart + *quatere* to shake] — **dis·cuss′er** *n.* — **dis·cuss′i·ble** *adj.*

dis·cus·sion (dis-kush′ən) *n.* The act of discussing; examination or consideration of a subject in speech or writing.

dis·dain (dis-dān′) *v.t.* 1. To consider unworthy of one's regard or notice: to *disdain* a coward. 2. To refuse scornfully: to *disdain* to beg for food. — *n.* A feeling or attitude of superiority and dislike. [< OF < L < *dis-* away + *dignare* to deign] — **dis·dain′ful** *adj.* — **dis·dain′ful·ly** *adv.* — **dis·dain′ful·ness** *n.*

dis·ease (di-zēz′) *n.* 1. A condition of ill health or malfunctioning in a living organism, esp. one having particular symptoms. 2. Any disordered or unwholesome condition. — *v.t.* **·eased, ·eas·ing** To cause disease in; make unhealthy; corrupt. [< AF *desaise*. See EASE.] — **dis·eased′** *adj.*

dis·em·bark (dis′em-bärk′) *v.t. & v.i.* To put or go ashore from a ship; land; unload. — **dis·em′bar·ka′tion** *n.*

dis·em·bar·rass (dis′em-bar′əs) *v.t.* To free from embarrassment, entanglement, etc. — **dis′em·bar′rass·ment** *n.*

dis·em·bod·y (dis′em-bod′ē) *v.t.* **·bod·ied, ·bod·y·ing** To free from the body or from physical existence: a *disembodied* spirit. — **dis′em·bod′i·ment** *n.*

dis·em·bow·el (dis′em-bou′əl, -boul′) *v.t.* **·bow·eled** or **·elled, ·bow·el·ing** or **·el·ling** To take out the bowels or entrails of; eviscerate. — **dis′em·bow′el·ment** *n.*

dis·en·chant (dis′en-chant′, -chänt′) *v.t.* To free from enchantment; disillusion. — **dis′en·chant′er** *n.* — **dis′en·chant′ment** *n.*

dis·en·cum·ber (dis′en-kum′bər) *v.t.* To free from encumbrance.

dis·en·fran·chise (dis′en-fran′chīz) *v.t.* **·chised, ·chis·ing** To disfranchise. — **dis′en·fran′chise·ment** (-chiz-mənt, -chīz-) *n.*

dis·en·gage (dis′en-gāj′) *v.* **·gaged, ·gag·ing** *v.t.* 1. To free from entanglement, obligation, occupation, etc.; set free. — *v.i.* 2. To free oneself; get loose. — **dis′en·gage′ment** *n.*

dis·en·tan·gle (dis′en-tang′gəl) *v.t.* **·gled, ·gling** *v.t.* 1. To free or relieve of entanglement, confusion, etc. — *v.i.* 2. To become disentangled. — **dis′en·tan′gle·ment** *n.*

dis·en·twine (dis′en-twīn′) *v.t. & v.i.* **·twined, ·twin·ing** To untwine; disentangle.

dis·es·tab·lish (dis′es-tab′lish) *v.t.* 1. To deprive of fixed or established status or character. 2. To take away government support from (a state church). — **dis′es·tab′lish·ment** *n.*

dis·es·teem (dis′es-tēm′) *v.t.* To regard with little esteem; have a low opinion of. — *n.* Lack of esteem.

di·seuse (dē-zœz′) *n. French* A woman entertainer who performs dramatic impersonations, monologues, etc.

dis·fa·vor (dis-fā′vər) *n.* 1. Lack of favor; disapproval; dislike. 2. The state of being frowned upon or disliked. — *v.t.* To treat or regard disapprovingly. Also *Brit.* **dis·fa′vour.**

dis·fig·ure (dis-fig′yər) *v.t.* **·ured, ·ur·ing** To mar or destroy the appearance or form of; make unsightly; deform. — **dis·fig′ur·er** *n.* — **dis·fig′ure·ment** *n.*

dis·fran·chise (dis-fran′chīz) *v.t.* **·chised, ·chis·ing** 1. To deprive (a citizen) of a right or privilege, esp. of the ballot. 2. To deprive of a franchise, privilege, or right, as a corporation. Also *disenfranchise.* — **dis·fran′chise·ment** (-chiz-mənt, -chīz-) *n.* — **dis·fran′chis·er** *n.*

dis·gorge (dis-gôrj′) *v.t.* **gorged, ·gorg·ing** 1. To throw out, as from the throat or stomach; eject; vomit. 2. To give up unwillingly. — *v.i.* 3. To disgorge something. [< OF < *des-* from + *gorge* throat]

dis·grace (dis-grās′) *n.* 1. A condition of shame, dishonor, or infamy; ignominy. 2. Anything that brings about dishonor or shame. 3. A state of being out of favor: in *disgrace* at court. — *v.t.* **graced, grac·ing** 1. To bring reproach or shame upon. 2. To treat with dishonor. [< MF < Ital. < *dis-* away + *grazia* favor] — **dis·grac′er** *n.*

dis·grace·ful (dis-grās′fəl) *adj.* Characterized by or causing disgrace; shameful; disreputable. — **dis·grace′ful·ly** *adv.* — **dis·grace′ful·ness** *n.*

dis·grun·tle (dis-grun′təl) *v.t.* **·tled, ·tling** To make dissatisfied or sulky; put out of humor.

dis·guise (dis-gīz′) *v.t.* **·guised, ·guis·ing** 1. To alter the appearance of so as to make unrecognizable. 2. To conceal the actual nature of: to *disguise* the facts. — *n.* 1. The act of disguising or the state of being disguised. 2. Something

that disguises, as a mask or costume. [< OF < *des-* down + *guise*. See GUISE.] — **dis·guis′er** *n.*

dis·gust (dis-gust′) *v.t.* 1. To affect with nausea or loathing. 2. To offend the sensibilities, moral values, or good taste of; sicken. — *n.* Strong aversion aroused by something offensive. [< MF < *des-* not + *gouster* to taste] — **dis·gust′ed** *adj.* — **dis·gust′ed·ly** *adv.*

dis·gust·ing (dis-gus′ting) *adj.* Provoking disgust; repugnant; revolting; offensive. — **dis·gust′ing·ly** *adv.*

dish (dish) *n.* 1. An open, concave, usu. shallow container, as of china or glass, typically used for holding or serving food. 2. A particular kind or preparation of food: a delicious *dish.* 3. A dishful. 4. A hollow or depression like that in a dish. — *v.t.* 1. To put (food, etc.) into a dish; serve: usu. with *up* or *out.* 2. To hollow out (a surface). — **to dish it out** *Slang* 1. To administer severe punishment or reproof. 2. To talk glibly. [OE < L *discus* disk] — **dish′like′** *adj.*

dis·ha·bille (dis′ə-bēl′) *n.* 1. A state of being partially or negligently dressed. 2. The garments worn in this state. Also *deshabille.* [< F < *des-* away + *habiller* to dress]

dis·har·mo·ny (dis-här′mə-nē) *n. pl.* **·nies** Lack of harmony or agreement; discord. — **dis′har·mo′ni·ous** *adj.* — **dis′har·mo′ni·ous·ly** *adv.*

dish·cloth (dish′klôth′, -kloth′) *n.* A cloth used in washing dishes: also called *dishrag.*

dis·heart·en (dis-här′tən) *v.t.* To discourage. — **dis·heart′en·ing·ly** *adv.* — **dis·heart′en·ment** *n.*

di·shev·el (di-shev′əl) *v.t.* **di·shev·eled** or **·elled, di·shev·el·ing** or **·el·ling** 1. To muss up, disarrange, or rumple (the hair or clothing). 2. To disorder the hair or clothing of. [< MF < *des-* away + *chevel* hair] — **di·shev′el·ment** *n.*

di·shev·eled (di-shev′əld) *adj.* 1. Tousled or rumpled. 2. Untidy; unkempt. Also **di·shev′elled.**

dish·ful (dish′fool′) *n.* As much as a dish holds.

dis·hon·est (dis-on′ist) *adj.* 1. Not honest; not trustworthy. 2. Marked by a lack of honesty. [< OF < LL *dis-* away + *honestus* honest] — **dis·hon′est·ly** *adv.*

dis·hon·es·ty (dis-on′is-tē) *n. pl.* **·ties** 1. Lack of honesty or integrity. 2. A dishonest act or statement.

dis·hon·or (dis-on′ər) *v.t.* 1. To deprive of honor; disgrace; insult. 2. To decline or fail to pay, as a note. — *n.* 1. Lack or loss of honor or of honorable character. 2. An insult, indignity, taint, etc. 3. Refusal or failure to pay a note, etc., when due. Also *Brit.* **dis·hon′our.** — **dis·hon′or·er** *n.*

dis·hon·or·a·ble (dis-on′ər·ə-bəl) *adj.* 1. Characterized by or bringing dishonor; discreditable: a *dishonorable* act. 2. Lacking honor or honorableness: a *dishonorable* lawyer. — **dis·hon′or·a·ble·ness** *n.* — **dis·hon′or·a·bly** *adv.*

dish·rag (dish′rag′) *n.* A dishcloth.

dis·il·lu·sion (dis′i-lōō′zhən) *v.t.* To free from illusion; disenchant. — *n.* The state or process of being disillusioned; also **dis·il′lu′sion·ment.**

dis·in·cli·na·tion (dis-in′klə-nā′shən) *n.* Distaste; aversion; unwillingness.

dis·in·cline (dis′in-klīn′) *v.t. & v.i.* **·clined, ·clin·ing** To make or be unwilling or averse.

dis·in·fect (dis′in-fekt′) *v.t.* To cleanse of disease germs; sterilize. — **dis′in·fec′tion** *n.* — **dis′in·fec′tor** *n.*

dis·in·fec·tant (dis′in-fek′tənt) *n.* A substance or agent used to disinfect. — *adj.* Capable of disinfecting.

dis·in·gen·u·ous (dis′in-jen′yōō-əs) *adj.* Lacking simplicity, frankness, or sincerity; not straightforward; crafty. — **dis′in·gen′u·ous·ly** *adv.* — **dis′in·gen′u·ous·ness** *n.*

dis·in·her·it (dis′in-her′it) *v.t.* To deprive of an inheritance. — **dis′in·her′i·tance** *n.*

dis·in·te·grate (dis-in′tə-grāt) *v.* **·grat·ed, ·grat·ing** *v.t.* 1. To break or reduce into component parts or particles; destroy the wholeness of. — *v.i.* 2. To become reduced to fragments or particles; crumble. — **dis·in′te·gra·ble** (-grə-bəl) *adj.* — **dis·in′te·gra′tion** *n.* — **dis·in′te·gra′tor** *n.*

dis·in·ter (dis′in-tûr′) *v.t.* **·terred, ·ter·ring** 1. To dig up, as from a grave; exhume. 2. To bring to light or life as if from a grave. — **dis′in·ter′ment** *n.*

dis·in·ter·est (dis-in′tər-ist, -trist) *n.* 1. Freedom from self-seeking and personal bias; impartiality. 2. Loosely, lack of interest; indifference. — **dis·in′ter·est·ed** *adj.* — **dis·in′ter·est·ed·ly** *adv.* — **dis·in′ter·est·ed·ness** *n.*

dis·join (dis-join′) *v.t.* 1. To undo or prevent the joining of; separate. — *v.i.* 2. To become divided or separated.

dis·joint (dis-joint′) *v.t.* 1. To take apart at the joints; dismember. 2. To put out of joint; dislocate. 3. To separate forcibly; disunite. 4. To upset or destroy the coherence, connection, or sequence of. — *v.i.* 5. To come apart at the joints; fall apart. 6. To get out of joint. — **dis·joint′ed** *adj.* — **dis·joint′ed·ly** *adv.* — **dis·joint′ed·ness** *n.*

dis·junct (dis-jungkt′) *adj.* Not connected; detached. [< L < *dis-* not + *jungere* to join] — **dis·junc′tion** *n.*

dis·junc·tive (dis-jungk′tiv) *adj.* 1. Serving to disconnect or separate; dividing. **2.** *Gram.* Indicating alternation or opposition, as *either* or *or* in *either you or I.* **3.** *Logic* Involving choice between two or more predicates in a proposition. — *n.* **1.** *Gram.* A disjunctive conjunction. **2.** *Logic* A disjunctive proposition. — **dis·junc′tive·ly** *adv.*

disk (disk) *n.* **1.** A fairly flat, circular plate. **2.** *Biol.* A disc. **3.** A phonograph record. **4.** A discus. — *v.t. & v.i.* To break up or plow (land) with a disk harrow. Also, *esp. Brit., disc.* [< L *discus* < Gk. *diskos* disk, platter]

disk harrow A harrow consisting of a series of rolling saucer-shaped disks set on edge and at an angle along one or more axles, used for pulverizing the soil, covering seeds, etc.

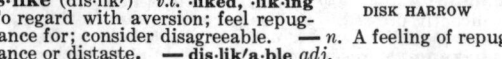

DISK HARROW

disk jockey *U.S. Informal* An announcer and commentator on a radio program presenting recorded music.

dis·like (dis·līk′) *v.t.* **·liked, ·lik·ing** To regard with aversion; feel repugnance for; consider disagreeable. — *n.* A feeling of repugnance or distaste. — **dis·lik′a·ble** *adj.*

dis·lo·cate (dis′lō·kāt, dis·lō′kāt) *v.t.* **·cat·ed, ·cat·ing** **1.** To put out of proper place or order. **2.** *Med.* To displace an organ or part, esp. a bone from a joint. — **dis′lo·ca′tion** *n.*

dis·lodge (dis·loj′) *v.* **·lodged, ·lodg·ing** *v.t.* **1.** To remove or drive out, as from an abode, hiding place, or firm position. — *v.i.* **2.** To leave a place of abode; move. — **dis·lodg′·ment,** or **dis·lodge′ment** *n.*

dis·loy·al (dis·loi′əl) *adj.* Not loyal; false to one's allegiance or obligations; faithless. — **dis·loy′al·ly** *adv.*

dis·loy·al·ty (dis·loi′əl·tē) *n. pl.* **·ties** **1.** The quality of being disloyal; unfaithfulness. **2.** A disloyal action.

dis·mal (diz′məl) *adj.* **1.** Cheerless and depressing; dark and gloomy: a *dismal* day. **2.** Devoid of joy; bleak: to feel *dismal.* [uit. < L *dies mali* evil or unpropitious days] — **dis′mal·ly** *adv.* — **dis′mal·ness** *n.*

dis·man·tle (dis·man′təl) *v.t.* **·tled, ·tling** **1.** To strip of furniture or equipment. **2.** To raze. **3.** To take apart. [< MF < *des-* away + *manteller* to cover with a cloak] — **dis·man′tle·ment** *n.*

dis·may (dis·mā′) *v.t.* To fill with consternation or apprehension; dishearten and depress. — *n.* An onrush of consternation or downheartedness. [ME *dismayen*]

dis·mem·ber (dis·mem′bər) *v.t.* **1.** To cut off or pull off the limbs or members of; tear asunder. **2.** To divide forcibly into pieces; mangle. [< OF < L *dis-* apart + *membrum* limb, member] — **dis·mem′ber·ment** *n.*

dis·miss (dis·mis′) *v.t.* **1.** To discharge, as from a job. **2.** To tell or allow to go or disperse. **3.** To get rid of: to *dismiss* all fear. **4.** To have done with quickly: He *dismissed* the matter in a few words. **5.** *Law* To put out of court without further hearing. [< LL < L *dimissus,* pp. of *dimittere* to send away] — **dis·miss′al** *n.* — **dis·miss′i·ble** *adj.*

dis·mount (dis·mount′) *v.i.* **1.** To get off, as from a horse; alight. — *v.t.* **2.** To remove from a setting, support, etc. **3.** To disassemble. **4.** To knock off or throw down, as from a horse; unseat. — **dis·mount′a·ble** *adj.*

dis·o·be·di·ence (dis′ə·bē′dē·əns) *n.* Refusal or failure to obey; lack of obedience; insubordination. — **dis′o·be′di·ent** *adj.* — **dis′o·be′di·ent·ly** *adv.*

dis·o·bey (dis′ə·bā′) *v.t. & v.i.* To refuse or fail to obey. — **dis′o·bey′er** *n.*

dis·o·blige (dis′ə·blīj′) *v.t.* **·bliged, ·blig·ing** **1.** To act contrary to the wishes of. **2.** To slight; affront. — **dis′o·blig′·ing** *adj.* — **dis′o·blig′ing·ly** *adv.*

dis·or·der (dis·ôr′dər) *n.* **1.** Lack of good order; disarrangement or confusion. **2.** Disturbance of proper civic order; tumult; riot. **3.** A sickness; ailment. **4.** An act, occurrence, or condition marked by disorder. — *v.t.* **1.** To put out of order; throw into disorder; disarrange. **2.** To disturb or upset the normal health or functions of. — **dis·or′dered** *adj.*

dis·or·der·ly (dis·ôr′dər·lē) *adj.* **1.** Devoid of good order or arrangement; full of disorder. **2.** Devoid of method; unsystematic. **3.** Undisciplined and unruly; tumultuous: a *disorderly* mob. **4.** Violating public order or decency. — *adv.* In a disorderly manner. — **dis·or′der·li·ness** *n.*

dis·or·gan·ize (dis·ôr′gən·īz) *v.t.* **·ized, ·iz·ing** **1.** To destroy the organization of; break up the systematic arrangement or unity of. **2.** To throw into confusion; disorder. — **dis·or′gan·i·za′tion** *n.* — **dis·or′gan·i′zer** *n.*

dis·o·ri·ent (dis·ôr′ē·ent′, -ō′rē-) *v.t.* To mix up; confuse; esp., to cause to lose one's sense of direction, perspective, or time. — **dis·o′ri·en·ta′tion** *n.*

dis·own (dis·ōn′) *v.t.* To refuse to acknowledge or to admit responsibility for or connection with; deny; repudiate.

dis·par·age (dis·par′ij) *v.t.* **·aged, ·ag·ing** **1.** To treat or speak of with disrespect or contempt; belittle. **2.** To bring discredit upon; cause to have less esteem. [< OF < *des-* down, away + *parage* equality of rank] — **dis·par′age·ment** *n.* — **dis·par′ag·er** *n.* — **dis·par′ag·ing·ly** *adv.*

dis·pa·rate (dis′pər·it) *adj.* Essentially different; altogether

dissimilar. [< L < *dis-* apart + *parare* to make ready] — **dis′pa·rate·ly** *adv.* — **dis′pa·rate·ness** *n.*

dis·par·i·ty (dis·par′ə·tē) *n. pl.* **·ties** **1.** Lack of equality, as in age or rank. **2.** Dissimilarity. **3.** An instance of inequality. [< MF < L *dis-* apart + *paritas* equality]

dis·pas·sion (dis·pash′ən) *n.* Freedom from passion or bias.

dis·pas·sion·ate (dis·pash′ən·it) *adj.* Free from passion or bias. — **dis·pas′sion·ate·ly** *adv.* — **dis·pas′sion·ate·ness** *n.*

dis·patch (dis·pach′) *v.t.* **1.** To send off, as a messenger, telegram, or vehicle, to a particular destination. **2.** To dispose of quickly, as a business matter. **3.** To kill summarily. — *n.* **1.** The act of dispatching. **2.** Efficient quickness; promptness: to finish a job with *dispatch.* **3.** A message, usu. in writing, sent with speed; esp., an official communication, as a military report. **4.** A news story sent to a newspaper. [< Ital. *dispacciare* or Sp. *despachar*]

dis·patch·er (dis·pach′ər) *n.* **1.** One who dispatches. **2.** One who sends out trains, buses, etc., on schedule.

dis·pel (dis·pel′) *v.t.* **·pelled, ·pel·ling** To drive away by or as by scattering; disperse: to *dispel* fear, rumors, etc. [< L < *dis-* away, apart + *pellere* to drive]

dis·pen·sa·ble (dis·pen′sə·bəl) *adj.* **1.** That can be relinquished or dispensed with. **2.** That can be removed by dispensation. — **dis·pen′sa·bil′i·ty, dis·pen′sa·ble·ness** *n.*

dis·pen·sa·ry (dis·pen′sər·ē) *n. pl.* **·ries** A place where medicines and medical advice are given out.

dis·pen·sa·tion (dis′pən·sā′shən) *n.* **1.** The act of dispensing; a dealing out; distribution. **2.** That which is dispensed or distributed. **3.** A specific plan, order, or system of dispensing or administering. **4.** A special exemption from something, as from a law or obligation; esp., an exemption by ecclesiastical authority from an obligation or from church law. **5.** *Theol.* **a** The arrangement or ordering of events, as by a divine Providence. **b** A religious or moral system: the Mosaic *dispensation.* — **dis′pen·sa′tion·al** *adj.*

dis·pen·sa·to·ry (dis·pen′sə·tôr′ē, -tō′rē) *adj.* Of or pertaining to dispensation. — *n. pl.* **·ries** A book in which medicinal substances are described; a pharmacopoeia.

dis·pense (dis·pens′) *v.* **·pensed, ·pens·ing** *v.t.* **1.** To give or deal out in portions: to *dispense* patronage. **2.** To compound and give out (medicines). **3.** To administer, as laws. **4.** To excuse or exempt, as from an obligation, esp., a religious obligation. — *v.i.* **5.** To grant dispensation. — **to dispense with 1.** To get along without. **2.** To dispose of. [< OF < L < *dis-* away + *pendere* to weigh]

dis·pens·er (dis·pen′sər) *n.* One who or that which dispenses, manages, or administers: a soap *dispenser.*

dis·perse (dis·pûrs′) *v.* **·persed, ·pers·ing** *v.t.* **1.** To cause to scatter in various directions. **2.** To drive away; dispel: The sun *dispersed* the mists. **3.** To spread abroad; diffuse. **4.** To separate (light) into a spectrum. — *v.i.* **5.** To scatter in various directions. [< MF < L < *dis-* away + *spargere* to scatter] — **dis·per′sal** *n.* — **dis·pers′ed·ly** *adv.* — **dis·pers′er** *n.* — **dis·pers′i·ble** *adj.*

dis·per·sion (dis·pûr′zhən, -shən) *n.* **1.** The act of dispersing, or the state of being dispersed. **2.** *Mil.* The pattern of hits made, as by bombs. **3.** *Physics* The separation of white or complex light into different colors by passing it through a prism. **4.** *Stat.* The arrangement of a series of values around the median or mean of a distribution.

dis·per·sive (dis·pûr′siv) *adj.* Tending to disperse.

dis·pir·it (dis·pir′it) *v.t.* To make downhearted or depressed. — **dis·pir′it·ed** *adj.* — **dis·pir′it·ed·ly** *adv.*

dis·place (dis·plās′) *v.t.* **·placed, ·plac·ing** **1.** To remove or shift from the usual or proper place. **2.** To take the place of; supplant. **3.** To remove from a position or office; discharge. [< OF < *des-* away (< L *dis-*) + *placer* to place]

displaced person A person made homeless by war and forced to live in a foreign country.

dis·place·ment (dis·plās′mənt) *n.* **1.** The act of displacing, or the state of being displaced. **2.** *Astron.* An apparent change of position, as of a star. **3.** *Physics* The weight of a fluid displaced by a floating body, being equal to the weight of the body.

dis·play (dis·plā′) *v.t.* **1.** To make evident or noticeable; reveal: to *display* ignorance. **2.** To expose to the sight; exhibit. **3.** To make a prominent or ostentatious show of. **4.** *Printing* To make (printed matter) stand out prominently, as by the use of large type or wide spacing. — *n.* **1.** The act of displaying; exhibition. **2.** That which is displayed. **3.** Ostentatious show. **4.** *Printing* A style or arrangement of type designed to make printed matter stand out prominently. [< OF < LL < *dis-* apart + *plicare* to fold, add]

dis·please (dis·plēz′) *v.* **·pleased, ·pleas·ing** *v.t.* **1.** To cause displeasure in or annoyance to; vex; offend. — *v.i.* **2.** To cause displeasure or annoyance. [< OF, ult. < L < *dis-* not + *placere* to please] — **dis·pleas′ing·ly** *adv.*

dis·pleas·ure (dis·plezh′ər) *n.* The state of being displeased.

dis·port (dis·pôrt′, -pōrt′) *v.t.* **1.** To divert or amuse (oneself). — *v.i.* **2.** To frisk about playfully. — *n.* Diversion; sport. [< OF < L *dis-* away + *portare* to carry]

dis·pos·a·ble (dis·pō′zə·bəl) *adj.* **1.** Capable of being disposed of; esp., designed to be discarded after use. **2.** Free to be used as occasion may require: *disposable* funds.

dis·po·sal (dis·pō′zəl) *n.* **1.** A particular ordering or arrangement; disposition. **2.** A particular way of attending to or settling something, as business affairs. **3.** Transfer, as by gift or sale. **4.** A getting rid of something. **5.** Liberty to deal with or dispose of in any way.

dis·pose (dis·pōz′) *v.* **·posed**, **·pos·ing** *v.t.* **1.** To put into a receptive frame of mind for. **2.** To condition toward something; esp., to make susceptible. **3.** To put or set in a particular arrangement or position. **4.** To put into proper, definitive, or final shape; settle. — *v.i.* **5.** To control the course of events. — **to dispose of 1.** To attend to; deal with. **2.** To finish up with; settle. **3.** To transfer to another, as by gift or sale. **4.** To throw away. [< OF < *dis-* apart + *poser* to place] — **dis·pos′er** *n.*

dis·posed (dis·pōzd′) *adj.* Having a particular inclination, frame of mind, or mood: *disposed* to take offense.

dis·po·si·tion (dis′pə·zish′ən) *n.* **1.** One's usual frame of mind; temperament. **2.** Acquired tendency or inclination, esp. when habitual: a *disposition* to drink. **3.** Natural organic tendency or inclination. **4.** A particular ordering, arrangement, or distribution, as of troops. **5.** Management, as of business affairs. **6.** Transfer, as by gift or sale. **7.** A getting rid of something, as by throwing away. **8.** Liberty to deal with or dispose of in any way.

dis·pos·sess (dis′pə·zes′) *v.t.* To deprive of possession of something, as a house or land; oust. — **dis′pos·ses′sion** (-zesh′ən) *n.* — **dis′pos·ses′sor** *n.*

dis·praise (dis·prāz′) *v.t.* **·praised**, **·prais·ing** To express disapproval of; disparage. — *n.* Disparagement; censure. — **dis·prais′er** *n.* — **dis·prais′ing·ly** *adv.*

dis·proof (dis·prōōf′) *n.* **1.** The act of disproving. **2.** Something that disproves, as evidence.

dis·pro·por·tion (dis′prə·pôr′shən, -pōr′-) *n.* **1.** Lack of proportion or symmetry; disparity. **2.** An instance of this. — *v.t.* To make disproportionate. — **dis′pro·por′tion·al** *adj.* — **dis′pro·por′tion·al·ly** *adv.*

dis·pro·por·tion·ate (dis′prə·pôr′shən·it, -pōr′-) *adj.* Out of proportion, as in size, form, or value. — **dis′pro·por′tion·ate·ly** *adv.* — **dis′pro·por′tion·ate·ness** *n.*

dis·prove (dis·prōōv′) *v.t.* **·proved**, **·proved** or **·prov·en**, **·prov·ing** To prove to be false, invalid, or erroneous. — **Syn.** See REFUTE. [< OF < *des-* not + *prouver* to prove] — **dis·prov′a·ble** *adj.* — **dis·prov′al** *n.*

dis·put·a·ble (dis·pyōō′tə·bəl, dis′pyōō·tə·bəl) *adj.* Open to being disputed or called into question; arguable; debatable. — **dis·put′a·bil′i·ty** *n.* — **dis·put′a·bly** *adv.*

dis·pu·tant (dis′pyōō·tənt, dis·pyōō′tənt) *adj.* Engaged in controversy; disputing. — *n.* One who disputes; a debater.

dis·pu·ta·tion (dis′pyōō·tā′shən) *n.* **1.** The act of disputing; argumentation; controversy. **2.** A formal debate; esp., formal argumentation in philosophy or theology.

dis·pu·ta·tious (dis′pyōō·tā′shəs) *adj.* Given to disputing; argumentative. Also **dis·pu·ta·tive** (dis·pyōō′tə·tiv). — **dis′pu·ta′tious·ly** *adv.* — **dis′pu·ta′tious·ness** *n.*

dis·pute (dis·pyōōt′) *v.* **·put·ed**, **·put·ing** *v.t.* **1.** To argue about. **2.** To question the validity, genuineness, etc., of. **3.** To strive or contest for, as a prize. **4.** To resist; oppose. — *v.i.* **5.** To argue. **6.** To quarrel. — *n.* **1.** A discussion; debate. **2.** A quarrel. [< OF < L < *dis-* away + *putare* to think] — **dis·put′er** *n.*

dis·qual·i·fy (dis·kwol′ə·fī) *v.t.* **·fied**, **·fy·ing** **1.** To make unqualified or unfit; incapacitate. **2.** To pronounce unqualified or ineligible. **3.** In sports, to bar from competition because of rule infractions, etc. — **dis·qual′i·fi·ca′tion** *n.*

dis·qui·et (dis·kwī′ət) *n.* An unsettled or disturbed condition. — *v.t.* To make anxious or uneasy. — **dis·qui′et·ly** *adv.*

dis·qui·e·tude (dis·kwī′ə·tōōd, -tyōōd) *n.* Uneasiness.

dis·qui·si·tion (dis′kwi·zish′ən) *n.* A formal treatise or discourse. [< L < *dis-* thoroughly + *quaerere* to seek]

dis·re·gard (dis′ri·gärd′) *v.t.* **1.** To pay no attention to; ignore. **2.** To treat as undeserving of consideration. — *n.* Lack of notice or due regard, esp. when deliberate. — **dis′re·gard′er** *n.* — **dis′re·gard′ful** *adj.*

dis·re·pair (dis′ri·pâr′) *n.* The state of being out of repair.

dis·rep·u·ta·ble (dis·rep′yə·tə·bəl) *adj.* **1.** Not in good repute; not esteemed. **2.** Not respectable: a *disreputable* tavern. — **dis·rep′u·ta·ble·ness** *n.* — **dis·rep′u·ta·bly** *adv.*

dis·re·spect (dis′ri·spekt′) *n.* Lack of courtesy or respect. — *v.t.* To treat without respect. — **dis′re·spect′ful** *adj.* — **dis′re·spect′ful·ly** *adv.* — **dis′re·spect′ful·ness** *n.*

dis·robe (dis·rōb′) *v.t. & v.i.* **·robed**, **·rob·ing** To undress.

dis·rupt (dis·rupt′) *v.t.* **1.** To throw into disorder; upset. **2.** To halt or impede the movement of, procedure of, etc. **3.** To break or burst apart. — *v.i.* **4.** To break; burst. [< L < *dis-* apart + *rumpere* to burst] — **dis·rupt′er** or **dis·rup′**

tor *n.* — **dis·rup′tion** *n.* — **dis·rup′tive** *adj.* — **dis·rup′tive·ly** *adv.*

dis·sat·is·fac·tion (dis′sat·is·fak′shən) *n.* **1.** A dissatisfied state or feeling; discontent. **2.** That which dissatisfies.

dis·sat·is·fac·to·ry (dis′sat·is·fak′tər·ē) *adj.* Causing dissatisfaction; unsatisfactory.

dis·sat·is·fy (dis·sat′is·fī) *v.t.* **·fied**, **·fy·ing** To fail to satisfy; disappoint; displease. — **dis·sat′is·fied** *adj.*

dis·sect (di·sekt′, dī-) *v.t.* **1.** To cut apart or divide, as an animal body or a plant, in order to examine the structure; anatomize. **2.** To analyze in detail. [< L < *dis-* apart + *secare* to cut] — **dis·sec′tion** *n.* — **dis·sec′tor** *n.*

dis·sect·ed (di·sek′tid, dī-) *adj.* **1.** Cut in pieces; separated at the joints. **2.** *Geol.* Cut into ridges, as a plateau. **3.** *Bot.* Deeply cut into lobes or segments, as a leaf.

dis·sem·blance (di·sem′bləns) *n.* **1.** The act of dissembling; dissimulation. **2.** Lack of resemblance; dissimilarity.

dis·sem·ble (di·sem′bəl) *v.* **·bled**, **·bling** *v.t.* **1.** To conceal or disguise the actual nature of (intentions, feelings, etc.). **2.** To make a false show of; feign. — *v.i.* **3.** To conceal one's true nature, intentions, etc.; act hypocritically. [Var. of earlier *dissimule* < OF < L < *dis-* not, away + *similis* alike] — **dis·sem′bler** *n.* — **dis·sem′bling·ly** *adv.*

dis·sem·i·nate (di·sem′ə·nāt) *v.t.* **·nat·ed**, **·nat·ing** To scatter, as if sowing: to *disseminate* knowledge. [< L < *dis-* away + *seminare* to sow] — **dis·sem′i·na′tion** *n.* — **dis·sem′i·na′tive** *adj.* — **dis·sem′i·na′tor** *n.*

dis·sen·sion (di·sen′shən) *n.* **1.** Difference of opinion, esp. arising from dissatisfaction or anger; discord; strife. **2.** A heated quarrel or disagreement.

dis·sent (di·sent′) *v.i.* **1.** To differ in thought or opinion: with *from*. **2.** To withhold approval or consent. **3.** To refuse adherence to an established church. — *n.* **1.** Difference of opinion. **2.** Refusal to conform to an established church. [< L < *dis-* apart + *sentire* to think, feel]

dis·sent·er (di·sen′tər) *n.* One who dissents or disagrees.

dis·sen·tient (di·sen′shənt) *adj.* Dissenting. — *n.* A dissenter. — **dis·sen′tience** *n.*

dis·sent·ing (di·sen′ting) *adj.* Expressing disagreement: a *dissenting* opinion. — **dis·sent′ing·ly** *adv.*

dis·sen·tious (di·sen′shəs) *adj.* Quarrelsome; disputatious.

dis·ser·ta·tion (dis′ər·tā′shən) *n.* An extended formal treatise or discourse; esp., a written treatise required of a doctoral candidate. [< L < *dis-* apart + *serere* to join]

dis·serve (dis·sûrv′) *v.t.* **·served**, **·serv·ing** To serve poorly or treat badly; do an ill turn to.

dis·ser·vice (dis·sûr′vis) *n.* Ill service; an ill turn; injury.

dis·sev·er (di·sev′ər) *v.t.* **1.** To divide; separate. **2.** To separate into parts. — *v.i.* **3.** To become separated. — **dis·sev′er·ance, dis·sev′er·ment** *n.*

dis·si·dent (dis′ə·dənt) *adj.* Dissenting; differing. — *n.* A dissenter. [< L < *dis-* apart + *sedere* to sit] — **dis′si·dence** *n.*

dis·sim·i·lar (di·sim′ə·lər) *adj.* Not similar; unlike; different: sometimes with *to*. — **dis·sim′i·lar·ly** *adv.*

dis·sim·i·lar·i·ty (di·sim′ə·lar′ə·tē) *n.* *pl.* **·ties** **1.** Lack of similarity; unlikeness; difference. **2.** An example of this.

dis·sim·i·late (di·sim′ə·lāt) *v.t. & v.i.* **·lat·ed**, **·lat·ing** **1.** To make or become unlike. **2.** *Phonet.* To undergo or cause to undergo dissimilation. [< DIS-¹ + L *similis* alike]

dis·sim·i·la·tion (di·sim′ə·lā′shən) *n.* **1.** The act or process of making or becoming dissimilar. **2.** *Phonet.* The process whereby one of two or more similar sounds in a word is omitted, as in the pronunciation (li′ber′ē) for *library*, or replaced by another sound, as *turtle* from Latin *turtur*.

dis·si·mil·i·tude (dis′si·mil′ə·tōōd, tyōōd) *n.* **1.** Lack of resemblance; unlikeness. **2.** An instance of this.

dis·sim·u·late (di·sim′yə·lāt) *v.t. & v.i.* **·lat·ed**, **·lat·ing** To conceal (intentions, feelings, etc.) by pretense. — **dis·sim′u·la′tion** *n.* — **dis·sim′u·la′tive** *adj.* — **dis·sim′u·la′tor** *n.*

dis·si·pate (dis′ə·pāt) *v.* **·pat·ed**, **·pat·ing** *v.t.* **1.** To disperse or drive away; dispel. **2.** To squander. — *v.i.* **3.** To become dispersed. **4.** To engage in excessive or dissolute pleasures. [< L < *dis-* away + *supare* to scatter] — **dis′si·pat′er** or **dis′si·pa′tor** *n.* — **dis′si·pa′tive** *adj.*

dis·si·pat·ed (dis′ə·pā′tid) *adj.* **1.** Wasted; scattered. **2.** Pursuing pleasure to excess; dissolute. — **dis′si·pat′ed·ly** *adv.* — **dis′si·pat′ed·ness** *n.*

dis·si·pa·tion (dis′ə·pā′shən) *n.* **1.** The act of dissipating, or the state of being dissipated; dispersion; scattering. **2.** Excessive indulgence, esp. in dissolute pleasures. **3.** Distraction or diversion, as of the mind.

dis·so·ci·ate (di·sō′shē·āt, -sē-) *v.* **·at·ed**, **·at·ing** *v.t.* **1.** To break the association of; disconnect; separate. **2.** To regard as separate in concept or nature. **3.** To subject to dissociation. — *v.i.* **4.** To break an association. **5.** To undergo dissociation. Also *disassociate*. [< L < *dis-* apart + *sociare* to join together] — **dis·so′ci·a′tive** *adj.*

dis·so·ci·a·tion (di-sō′sē-ā′shən, -shē-ā′-) *n.* **1.** The act of dissociating, or the state of being dissociated. **2.** *Chem.* **a** The resolution of a compound into simpler constituents by a change in physical state, as by heat or pressure.

dis·sol·u·ble (di-sol′yə-bəl) *adj.* Capable of being dissolved or decomposed. **— dis′sol·u·bil′i·ty, dis·sol′u·ble·ness** *n.*

dis·so·lute (dis′ə-lōōt) *adj.* Not governed by moral restraints. **— dis′so·lute·ly** *adv.* **— dis′so·lute·ness** *n.*

dis·so·lu·tion (dis′ə-lōō′shən) *n.* **1.** Separation into parts; disintegration. **2.** Change from a solid to a fluid form; liquefaction. **3.** The breaking up or liquidation of a formal or legal union, bond, or tie. **4.** Dismissal of a meeting or assembly. **5.** Termination or destruction. **6.** Separation of soul and body; death. **— dis′so·lu′tive** *adj.*

dis·solve (di-zolv′) *v.* **·solved, ·solv·ing** *v.t.* **1.** To cause to pass into solution. **2.** To overcome, as by emotion. **3.** To disintegrate. **4.** To put an end to: to *dissolve* a partnership. **5.** To dismiss (a meeting or assembly). **—** *v.i.* **6.** To pass into solution. **7.** To be overcome: to *dissolve* in tears. **8.** To come to an end; break up. **9.** To dwindle or fade away. **10.** In motion pictures and television, to change gradually from one scene to another by overlapping two shots. **—** *n.* A lap dissolve. [< L < *dis-* apart + *solvere* to loosen] **— dis·solv′a·ble** *adj.* **— dis·solv′er** *n.*

dis·so·nance (dis′ə-nəns) *n.* **1.** A discordant mingling of sounds; discord. **2.** Harsh disagreement; incongruity. **3.** *Music* A simultaneous combination of tones that seem to clash and require resolution. Also **dis′so·nan·cy.**

dis·so·nant (dis′ə-nənt) *adj.* **1.** Harsh in sound; inharmonious. **2.** Naturally hostile; incongruous. **3.** *Music* Consisting of or containing a dissonance. [< L < *dis-* away + *sonare* to sound] **— dis′so·nant·ly** *adv.*

dis·suade (di-swād′) *v.t.* **·suad·ed, ·suad·ing** To alter the plans or intentions of (someone) by persuasion or advice: with *from.* [< L < *dis-* away + *suadere* to persuade] **— dis·suad′er** *n.* **— dis·sua′sive** *n.* **— dis·sua′sive** *adj.*

dis·syl·la·ble (di-sil′ə-bəl, dis′sil′ə-bəl) *n.* A word of two syllables: also spelled *disyllable.* [< F < L < Gk. < *di-* two + *syllabē* syllable] **— dis′syl·lab′ic** *adj.*

dis·taff (dis′taf, -täf) *n.* *pl.* **·taffs** or *Rare* **·taves** (-tāvz) **1.** A rotating vertical staff that holds a bunch of flax or wool for spinning by hand. **2.** Women in general. **3.** Woman's work or domain. [OE < *dis* bundle of flax + *stæf* staff]

distaff side The maternal branch or female line of a family.

dis·tal (dis′təl) *adj.* *Anat.* Relatively remote from the center of the body or point of attachment. **— dis′tal·ly** *adv.*

dis·tance (dis′təns) *n.* **1.** The extent of spatial separation between things, places, or locations. **2.** The extent of separation between points of time; interval. **3.** The state or fact of being separated from something else, esp. to a notable extent, in space, time, or condition. **4.** A gap, as in relationship or rank, between persons or things. **5.** Remoteness; esp., reserve or aloofness: to keep one's *distance.* **6.** A point or location removed from another, esp. to a notable extent. **7.** *Music* The interval between two tones. **—** *v.t.* **·tanced, ·tanc·ing 1.** To leave behind; outdo. **2.** To cause to appear distant. **3.** To hold off or place at some distance.

dis·tant (dis′tənt) *adj.* **1.** Separated or apart by a specified amount of space or time; away: often with *from.* **2.** Remote in time or space. **3.** At, from, or to a distance: a *distant* journey. **4.** Not closely related; remote, as to similarity, kinship, etc. **5.** Reserved or unapproachable. [< F < L < *dis-* apart + *stare* to stand] **— dis′tant·ly** *adv.*

dis·taste (dis·tāst′) *n.* Dislike; aversion: a *distaste* for work.

dis·taste·ful (dis·tāst′fəl) *adj.* Causing dislike; offensive; disagreeable. **— dis·taste′ful·ly** *adv.* **— dis·taste′ful·ness** *n.*

dis·tem·per¹ (dis·tem′pər) *n.* **1.** *Vet.* Any of several infectious diseases of animals; esp., a catarrhal disease of puppies. **2.** A disorder of the mind or body; illness. **3.** Political or civil disturbance. **—** *v.t.* **1.** To derange the faculties or functions of. **2.** To ruffle; disturb. [< Med.L < L *dis-* away + *temperare* to regulate, mix]

dis·tem·per² (dis·tem′pər) *n.* **1.** Tempera. **2.** A painting medium in which size is the only agent used to bind the pigments. **3.** The art or method of using this medium. **4.** A painting done in distemper. **5.** *Brit.* Calcimine. **—** *v.t.* **1.** To mix (colors or pigments) with a binding medium, such as casein. **2.** To paint in distemper. [< OF < Med.L < L *dis-* apart + *temperare* to mix, soak]

dis·tend (dis·tend′) *v.t. & v.i.* **1.** To expand by or as by pressure from within. **2.** To stretch out; swell. [< L < *dis-* apart + *tendere* to stretch] **— dis·ten′si·ble** *adj.* **— dis·ten′tion, dis·ten′sion** *n.*

dis·tich (dis′tik) *n.* In prosody, a couplet. [< L < Gk. < *di-* two + *stichos* a row, line]

dis·till (dis·til′) *v.* **·tilled, ·till·ing** *v.t.* **1.** To subject to distillation so as to purify or produce, concentrate, or refine. **2.** To extract by distillation. **3.** To give forth or send down in drops. **—** *v.i.* **4.** To undergo distillation. **5.** To exude in drops. Also *Brit.* **dis·til′.** [< L < *de-* down + *stillare* to drop, trickle] **— dis·till′a·ble** *adj.*

dis·til·late (dis′tə-lit, -lāt) *n.* The condensed product separated by distillation: also called *distillation.*

dis·til·la·tion (dis′tə-lā′shən) *n.* **1.** The act or process of separating the more volatile parts of a substance from those less volatile by heating in a retort or still and then condensing the vapor thus produced by cooling. **2.** The purification or rectification of a substance by this process. **3.** A distillate. **4.** The essential or abstract quality of anything. Also **dis·till·ment** (dis·til′mənt), *Brit.* **dis·til′ment.**

dis·til·ler (dis·til′ər) *n.* **1.** One who distills; esp., a maker of distilled liquors. **2.** A condenser for distilling.

dis·til·ler·y (dis·til′ər-ē) *n.* *pl.* **·ler·ies** An establishment for distilling, esp. alcoholic liquors.

dis·tinct (dis·tingkt′) *adj.* **1.** Recognizably not the same; clearly different. **2.** Differentiated by individualizing features. **3.** Sharp and clear to the senses or mind; definite. **4.** Undeniably such: a *distinct* step forward. [< L *distinguere* to separate] **— dis·tinct′ly** *adv.* **— dis·tinct′ness** *n.*

dis·tinc·tion (dis·tingk′shən) *n.* **1.** The act of distinguishing; discrimination. **2.** A difference that may be distinguished: the *distinction* between thrift and avarice. **3.** The state of being different or distinguishable. **4.** A characteristic difference or distinctive quality. **5.** A mark of honor. **6.** A distinguishing superiority or preeminence.

dis·tinc·tive (dis·tingk′tiv) *adj.* Serving to distinguish; characteristic. **— dis·tinc′tive·ly** *adv.* **— dis·tinc′tive·ness** *n.*

dis·tin·gué (dis′tang-gā′, *Fr.* dēs·tañ·gā′) *adj.* Eminently well-bred and dignified. [< F] **— dis·tin·guée′** *adj.fem.*

dis·tin·guish (dis·ting′gwish) *v.t.* **1.** To indicate the differences of or between. **2.** To be an outstanding or individualizing characteristic of: Honesty *distinguished* his career. **3.** To classify. **4.** To bring fame or credit upon. **5.** To perceive with the senses. **—** *v.i.* **6.** To make or discern differences; discriminate: often with *among* or *between.* [< MF < L *distinguere* to separate] **— dis·tin′guish·a·ble** *adj.* **— dis·tin′guish·a·bly** *adv.* **— dis·tin′guish·er** *n.*

dis·tin·guished (dis·ting′gwisht) *adj.* **1.** Conspicuous for qualities of excellence; celebrated; eminent; famous. **2.** Having an air of distinction; distingué.

Distinguished Flying Cross A U.S. military decoration awarded for heroism or exceptional achievement in aerial flight. See DECORATION.

Distinguished Service Cross A U.S. military decoration awarded for heroism in combat. See DECORATION.

Distinguished Service Medal A U.S. military decoration awarded for meritorious service in a duty of great responsibility. See DECORATION.

dis·tort (dis·tôrt′) *v.t.* **1.** To twist or bend out of shape; make misshapen. **2.** To twist the meaning of; misrepresent; pervert. [< L < *dis-* apart + *torquere* to twist] **— dis·tort′ed** *adj.* **— dis·tort′ed·ly** *adv.* **— dis·tort′ed·ness** *n.* **— dis·tort′er** *n.*

dis·tor·tion (dis·tôr′shən) *n.* **1.** The act of distorting. **2.** The condition of being distorted; deformity. **3.** That which is distorted, as a misleading statement. **4.** *Telecom.* A change in the wave form of a signal caused by nonuniform transmission at different frequencies. **— dis·tor′tion·al** *adj.*

dis·tract (dis·trakt′) *v.t.* **1.** To draw or divert (the mind, etc.) from something claiming attention. **2.** To bewilder; confuse. **3.** To make frantic; craze. [< L < *dis-* away + *trahere* to draw] **— dis·tract′er** *n.* **— dis·trac′tion** *n.*

dis·tract·ed (dis·trak′tid) *adj.* **1.** Bewildered or harassed. **2.** Mentally deranged; mad. **— dis·tract′ed·ly** *adv.*

dis·sract·ing (dis·trak′ting) *adj.* Serving or tending to distract. Also **dis·trac′tive.** **— dis·tract′ing·ly** *adv.*

dis·train (dis·trān′) *Law v.t. & v.i.* To seize and detain (personal property) as security for a debt, claim, etc. [< OF < L *distringere* to detain, hinder] **— dis·train′a·ble** *adj.* **— dis·train′or or dis·train′er** *n.* **— dis·traint′** *n.*

dis·trait (dis·trā′, *Fr.* dēs·tre′) *adj.* Absent-minded. [< F. See DISTRACT.]

dis·traught (dis·trôt′) *adj.* **1.** Deeply agitated in mind; worried, tense, and bewildered. **2.** Driven insane; crazed. [Var. of earlier *distract,* pp. of DISTRACT]

dis·tress (dis·tres′) *v.t.* To inflict suffering upon; cause agony or worry to; afflict; harass. **—** *n.* **1.** Acute or extreme suffering or its cause; pain; trouble. **2.** A state of extreme need: a ship in *distress.* **3.** *Law* **a** The act of distraining. **b** The goods distrained. **— Syn.** See SUFFERING. [< OF < LL < L *distringere* to detain, hinder] **— dis·tress′ful** *adj.* **— dis·tress′ful·ly** *adv.* **— dis·tress′ful·ness** *n.* **— dis·tress′ing** *adj.* **— dis·tress′ing·ly** *adv.*

dis·trib·u·tar·y (dis′trib′yōō·ter′ē) *n.* *pl.* **·tar·ies** A river branch flowing away from the main branch.

dis·trib·ute (dis·trib′yōōt) *v.t.* **·ut·ed, ·ut·ing 1.** To divide and deal out in shares; apportion; allot. **2.** To divide and classify; arrange. **3.** To scatter or spread out, as over a surface. [< L < *dis-* away, apart + *tribuere* to give, allot] **— dis·trib′ut·a·ble** *adj.*

dis·tri·bu·tion (dis′trə·byōō′shən) *n.* **1.** The act of distributing or the state of being distributed. **2.** The manner in which something is distributed: random *distribution*. **3.** That which is distributed. **4.** In commerce, the system of distributing goods among consumers. **5.** *Stat.* Frequency: symbolized by *t*. — **dis·tri·bu·tion·al** *adj.*

dis·trib·u·tive (dis-trib′yə-tiv) *adj.* **1.** Pertaining to or caused by distribution. **2.** Serving or tending to distribute. **3.** *Gram.* Singling out the separate individuals of a group: *Each* and *every* are *distributive* adjectives. — *n. Gram.* A distributive word or expression. — **dis·trib′u·tive·ly** *adv.* — **dis·trib′u·tive·ness** *n.*

dis·trib·u·tor (dis-trib′yə-tər, -tôr) *n.* **1.** One who or that which distributes or sells merchandise. **2.** In a gasoline engine, a device that directs the electrical current to the spark plugs. Also **dis·trib′ut·er** (-yə-tər).

dis·trict (dis′trikt) *n.* A particular region or locality; esp., an area, as within a city or state, set off for adminstrative or judicial purposes. — *v.t.* To divide into districts. [< MF < Med.L *districtus* jurisdiction]

district attorney The prosecuting officer of a Federal or State judicial district.

dis·trust (dis-trust′) *v.t.* To doubt; suspect. — *n.* Doubt; suspicion. — **dis·trust′ful** *adj.* — **dis·trust′ful·ly** *adv.*

dis·turb (dis-tûrb′) *v.t.* **1.** To destroy the repose, tranquility, or peace of. **2.** To agitate the mind of; trouble. **3.** To upset the order, system, or progression of. **4.** To interrupt; break in on. **5.** To inconvenience. [< OF < *dis-* completely + *turbare* to disorder] — **dis·turb′er** *n.*

dis·tur·bance (dis-tûr′bəns) *n.* **1.** The act of disturbing, or the state of being disturbed. **2.** Something that disturbs. **3.** A tumult or commotion; especially, a public disorder.

dis·turbed (dis-tûrbd′) *adj.* **1.** Characterized by disturbance. **2.** Troubled emotionally or mentally; neurotic.

di·sul·fate (dī-sul′fāt) *n. Chem.* A bisulfate. Also **di·sul′-phate.**

di·sul·fide (dī-sul′fīd) *n. Chem.* A sulfide containing two atoms of sulfur to the molecule: also called *bisulfide*. Also **di·sul′fid** (-fid), **di·sul′phide.**

dis·un·ion (dis-yōōn′yən) *n.* **1.** The state of being disunited; severance; rupture. **2.** A condition of disagreement.

dis·u·nite (dis′yōō-nīt′) *v.* **·nit·ed, ·nit·ing** *v.t.* To break the union of; separate; part. **2.** To alienate; estrange. — *v.i.* **3.** To come apart. — **dis·u′ni·ty** *n.*

dis·use (*n.* dis-yōōs′; *v.* dis-yōōz′) *n.* The state of not being used; out of use. — *v.t.* **·used, ·us·ing** To stop using.

ditch (dich) *n.* A long, narrow trench or channel dug in the ground, typically used for irrigation or drainage. — *v.t.* **1.** To make a ditch in. **2.** To surround with a ditch. **3.** To throw into or as into a ditch. **4.** *U.S. Slang* To get rid of. — *v.i.* **5.** To make a ditch. [OE *dīc*] — **ditch′er** *n.*

dith·er (dith′ər) *n.* A state of nervous excitement or anxiety, or of trembling agitation. — *v.i.* To be in a dither. [Var. of earlier *didder* to tremble, shake; origin uncertain]

dith·y·ramb (dith′ə-ram, -ramb) *n.* **1.** In ancient Greece, a wild, passionate choric hymn in honor of Dionysus. **2.** A highly emotional speech or piece of writing. [< L < Gk. *dithyrambos*] — **dith′y·ram′bic** *adj. & n.*

dit·to (dit′ō) *n. pl.* **·tos 1.** The same thing (as something written above or mentioned or done before), usually symbolized by ditto marks. **2.** A duplicate or copy of something. **3.** Ditto marks. — *adv.* As written above or as mentioned before. — *interj. Informal* I agree. — *v.t.* **·toed, ·to·ing 1.** To repeat. **2.** To duplicate. [< Ital. < L *dicere* to say]

ditto marks Two small marks (″) placed beneath an item to indicate that it is to be repeated. Also **ditto mark.**

dit·ty (dit′ē) *n. pl.* **·ties** A short, simple song. [< OF *dittie, ditie* < L *distatum* a thing said]

ditty bag A sailor's bag for needles, thread, personal belongings, etc. Also **ditty box.** [Origin uncertain]

di·u·ret·ic (dī′yōō-ret′ik) *adj.* Increasing the secretion of urine. — *n.* A diuretic medicine.

di·ur·nal (dī-ûr′nəl) *adj.* **1.** Of, belonging to, or occurring each day; daily. **2.** Of or occurring during the daytime; not nocturnal. [< L *diurnus* daily] — **di·ur′nal·ly** *adv.*

di·va (dē′və) *n. pl.* **·vas** or **·ve** (-vā) A celebrated female operatic singer; a prima donna. [< Ital., fem of *divo* divine]

di·va·gate (dī′və-gāt) *v.i.* **·gat·ed, ·gat·ing 1.** To wander or stray aimlessly. **2.** To digress. [< L < *dis-* about + *vagari* to wander] — **di′va·ga′tion** *n.*

di·va·lent (dī-vā′lənt, div′ə-) *adj. Chem.* Bivalent.

di·van (di-van′, dī′van) *n.* **1.** A sofa or couch, usu. without arm rests or back. **2.** A room for smoking or drinking. [< Turkish *divan* < Persian *dēvān* council, chamber]

dive (dīv) *v.* **dived** or **dove, dived, div·ing** *v.i.* **1.** To plunge, esp. headfirst, as into water. **2.** To go underwater or to the bottom; submerge. **3.** To plunge downward at a sharp angle. **4.** To dart away or leap into something. **5.** To rush into and become deeply engrossed in something. **6.** To reach into something eagerly. — *v.t.* **7.** To cause to plunge;

especially, to cause (an airplane) to move swiftly downward at a sharp angle. — *n.* **1.** A plunge, as into water. **2.** A sharp, swift descent, as of an airplane. **3.** *Informal* A cheap, disreputable place, as a saloon, etc. — **to take a dive** *U.S. Slang* In boxing, to allow an opponent to win by prearrangement. [Blend of OE *dūfan* to dive and *dȳfan* to immerse]

dive bomber An airplane designed to bomb a target while in a steep dive.

div·er (dī′vər) *n.* **1.** One who dives, esp. one who dives to salvage sunken cargo, etc. **2.** A bird that dives, as a loon.

di·verge (di-vûrj′, dī-) *v.* **·verged, ·verg·ing** *v.i.* **1.** To move or extend in different directions from a common point or from each other. **2.** To deviate. **3.** To differ. — *v.t.* **4.** To cause to diverge. [< NL < L *dis-* apart + *vergere* to incline]

di·ver·gence (di-vûr′jəns, dī-) *n.* **1.** The act of diverging, or the state of being divergent. **2.** Deviation or difference, as of opinion. Also **di·ver′gen·cy.** — **di·ver′gent** *adj.* — **di·ver′gent·ly** *adv.*

di·vers (dī′vərz) *adj.* **1.** Several. **2.** Various. [< OF < L *diversus* different]

di·verse (di-vûrs′, dī-, dī′vûrs) *adj.* **1.** Marked by distinct differences; not alike. **2.** Varied in kind or form; diversified. [See DIVERS.] — **di·verse′ly** *adv.* — **di·verse′ness** *n.*

di·ver·si·fy (di-vûr′sə-fī, dī-) *v.t.* **·fied, ·fy·ing 1.** To make diverse; give variety to; vary. **2.** To make or distribute (investments) among different types of securities so as to minimize risk. — **di·ver·si·fi·ca·tion** (di-vûr′sə-fə-kā′shən, dī-) *n.*

di·ver·sion (di-vûr′zhən, -shən, dī-) *n.* **1.** The act of diverting or turning aside, as from a course. **2.** A drawing away of the attention from something. **3.** An amusement.

di·ver·sion·ar·y (di-vûr′zhən-er′ē, -shən, dī-) *adj.* Designed to distract the enemy from the point of operation.

di·ver·si·ty (di-vûr′sə-tē, dī-) *n. pl.* **·ties 1.** Unlikeness; difference. **2.** Variety; multiplicity.

di·vert (di-vûrt′, dī-) *v.t.* **1.** To turn aside, as from a set course; deflect. **2.** To distract the attention of. **3.** To amuse; entertain. [< L < *dis-* apart + *vertere* to turn] — **di·vert′ing** *adj.* — **di·vert′ing·ly** *adv.*

di·ver·ti·men·to (di-vûr′ti-men′tō) *n. pl.* **·ti** (-tē) *Music* A light instrumental composition in several movements. [< Ital., diversion]

di·ver·tisse·ment (də-vûr′təs-mənt, dē-ver-tēs-män′) *n.* **1.** A diversion; amusement. **2.** *Music* A divertimento. **3.** A short ballet, etc. performed during or between the parts of an opera or play. [< MF]

di·vest (di-vest′, dī-) *v.t.* **1.** To strip, as of clothes. **2.** To deprive, as of rights or possessions. [See DEVEST.]

di·vest·i·ture (di-ves′tə-chər, dī-) *n.* The act of divesting, or the state of being divested. Also **di·vest′ment, di·ves′ture.**

di·vide (di-vīd′) *v.* **·vid·ed, ·vid·ing** *v.t.* **1.** To separate into pieces or portions, as by cutting. **2.** To distribute the pieces or portions of. **3.** To separate into sections. **4.** To separate into groups; classify. **5.** To split up into opposed sides; cause dissent in. **6.** To cause to be apart. **7.** *Math.* **a** To subject to the process of division. **b** To be an exact divisor of. **8.** *Mech.* To graduate; calibrate. — *v.i.* **9.** To become separated into parts; diverge. **10.** To be at variance. **11.** *Brit.* In Parliament and other legislative bodies, to separate into two groups in order to vote. **12.** To share. **13.** To perform mathematical division. — *n.* A mountain range separating one drainage system from another; watershed. [< L *dividere* to separate, divide] — **di·vid′a·ble** *adj.*

di·vid·ed (di-vī′did) *adj.* **1.** Separated into parts; parted. **2.** Disunited. **3.** *Bot.* Having incisions or indentations.

div·i·dend (div′ə-dend) *n.* **1.** *Math.* A quantity divided into equal parts. **2.** A sum of money to be distributed to stockholders, etc. **3.** The portion of such a sum given to each individual. [< L *dividendum* thing to be divided]

di·vid·er (di-vī′dər) *n.* **1.** One who or that which divides, separates, or apportions. **2.** *pl.* A pair of compasses typically used for measuring or marking off short intervals.

div·i·na·tion (div′ə-nā′shən) *n.* **1.** The act or art of knowing the future or that which is hidden or unknown. **2.** A prophecy. **3.** A clever guess. — **di·vin·a·to·ry** (div·in′ə-tôr′ē, -tō′rē) *adj.*

di·vine (di-vīn′) *adj.* **1.** Of or pertaining to God or a god. **2.** Given by or derived from God or a god. **3.** Directed or devoted to God or a god; sacred. **4.** Like a god. **5.** Extraordinarily perfect. **6.** *Informal* Altogether delightful. — *n.* **1.** A clergyman. **2.** A theologian. — *v.* **vined, ·vin·ing** *v.t.* **1.** To foretell or find out by occult means. **2.** To locate (water, etc.) by means of a divining rod. **3.** To conjecture or surmise by instinct. — *v.i.* **4.** To practice divination. **5.** To guess. [< L *deus* god] — **di·vine′ly** *adv.* — **di·vine′ness** *n.* — **di·vin′er** *n.*

Divine Comedy A narrative poem by Dante Alighieri.

Divine Office The canonical hours.

diving bell A large, hollow, inverted vessel supplied with air under pressure, in which men may work under water.

diving board A flexible board upon which divers jump to gain impetus for the dive: also called *springboard*.

diving suit A waterproof garment with detachable helmet that is supplied with air through a hose, worn by divers.

divining rod A forked branch popularly asserted to indicate underground water or metal: also called *dowsing rod*.

di·vin·i·ty (di·vin′ə·tē) *n.* *pl.* **·ties** 1. The state or quality of being divine. 2. A godlike character or attribute. 3. A deity. 4. Theology. 5. A soft, creamy candy. **— the Divinity** God. [< OF < L *divinitas* godhead, deity]

di·vis·i·ble (di·viz′ə·bəl) *adj.* 1. Capable of being divided. 2. *Math.* That can be divided and leave no remainder. **— di·vis′i·bil′i·ty, di·vis′i·ble·ness** *n.* **— di·vis′i·bly** *adv.*

di·vi·sion (di·vizh′ən) *n.* 1. The act of dividing; separation. 2. The state of being divided. 3. One of the parts into which a thing is divided. 4. A part or section of a country, government, etc., that has been divided for administrative, political, or other reasons. 5. Something that divides or separates. 6. Disagreement; discord. 7. *Math.* The operation of finding how many times a number or quantity (the *divisor*) is contained in another number or quantity (the *dividend*), the number or quantity found being called the *quotient*. 8. A voting of a legislative body. 9. *Mil.* A major administrative and tactical unit that is larger than a regiment and smaller than a corps. 10. In the U.S. Navy, a number of ships grouped for operational command. 11. In the U.S. Air Force, an air combat organization with appropriate service units. [< OF < L *dividere* to divide] **— di·vi′sion·al** *adj.*

division sign *Math.* The symbol (÷) that denotes a first number is to be divided by a second, as 6 ÷ 2 = 3.

di·vi·sive (di·vī′siv) *adj.* 1. Causing or expressing division or distribution. 2. Creating division, dissension, or strife.

di·vi·sor (di·vī′zər) *n. Math.* 1. A number by which another number is divided. 2. A common divisor.

di·vorce (di·vôrs′, -vōrs′) *n.* 1. Dissolution of a marriage bond by legal process or by accepted custom. 2. Any radical or complete separation. Also **di·vorce′ment.** **—** *v.* **·vorced, ·vorc·ing** *v.t.* 1. To dissolve the marriage of. 2. To free oneself from (one's husband or wife) by divorce. 3. To separate; cut off; disunite. **—** *v.i.* 4. To get a divorce. [< MF < L *divertere* to divert]

di·vor·cé (di·vôr′sā′, -vōr′-, di·vôr′sā, -vōr′-) *n.* A divorced man. [< F, pp. of *divorcer* to divorce] **— di·vor·cée′** *n.fem.*

di·vor·cee (di·vôr′sē′, -vōr′-) *n.* A divorced person.

div·ot (div′ət) *n.* A piece of turf torn by a golf club.

di·vulge (di·vulj′) *v.t.* **·vulged, ·vulg·ing** To tell, as a secret; disclose; reveal. [< L < *dis-* away + *vulgare* to make public] **— di·vulge′ment, di·vul′gence** *n.* **— di·vulg′er** *n.*

div·vy (div′ē) *Slang* *n.* *pl.* **·vies** A share; portion. **—** *v.t.* **·vied, ·vy·ing** To divide: often with *up.* [Short for DIVIDE]

Dix·ie (dik′sē) 1. Traditionally, those States that comprised the Confederacy during the Civil War. Also **Dixie Land.** 2. A Confederate marching song.

Dix·ie·land (dik′sē·land′) *n.* A style of jazz in two-beat or four-beat rhythm, originally played in New Orleans.

diz·en (diz′ən, dī′zən) *v.t.* To dress in finery; deck out. [< M.Du. *disen* to put flax on a distaff] **— diz′en·ment** *n.*

diz·zy (diz′ē) *adj.* **·zi·er, ·zi·est** 1. Having a feeling of whirling or unsteadiness. 2. Causing giddiness. 3. *Informal* Silly; stupid. **—** *v.t.* **·zied, ·zy·ing** To make giddy; confuse. [OE *dysig* foolish, stupid] **— diz′zi·ly** *adv.* **— diz′zi·ness** *n.*

djin·ni (ji·nē′) See JINNI.

DNA *Biochem.* Deoxyribonucleic acid.

do[1] (dōo) *v.* **did, done, do·ing** Present: *sing.* **do, do** (*Archaic* **thou do·est** or **dost**), **does** (*Archaic* **do·eth** or **doth**), *pl.* **do**; past: **did** (*Archaic* **thou didst**); pp. **done**; ppr. **do·ing** *v.t.* 1. To perform, as an action; produce, as a piece of work. 2. To fulfill; complete; accomplish. 3. To cause; bring about: to do no wrong. 4. To put forth: He *did* his best. 5. To render: to *do* homage. 6. To work at. 7. To work out; solve. 8. To translate. 9. To present (a play, reading, etc.). 10. To enact the part of. 11. To cover (a distance); travel. 12. *Informal* To make a tour of; visit. 13. To be sufficient for. 14. *Informal* To serve, as a term in prison. 15. *Informal* To cheat; swindle. **—** *v.i.* 16. To exert oneself; be active: to *do* or die. 17. To conduct oneself. 18. To fare; get along. 19. To serve the purpose; suffice. **— to do away with** 1. To throw away. 2. To kill; destroy. **— to do by** To act toward. **— to do for** 1. To provide for; care for. 2. *Informal* To ruin; kill. **— to do in** *Slang* To kill. **— to do over** *Informal* To redecorate. **— to do up** 1. To wrap or tie up. 2. To roll up or arrange. 3. To clean; repair. 4. To tire out. **— to do without** To get along without. **— to have to do with** To be involved with. **— to make do** To get along with (whatever is available). **—** *auxiliary* As an auxiliary, *do* is used: 1. Without specific meaning in negative, interrogative, and inverted constructions: I *do* not want it; *Do* you want to leave? 2. To add force to impera-

tives: *Do* hurry. 3. To express emphasis: I *do* believe you. 4. As a substitute for another verb to avoid repetition: I will not affirm, as some *do.* **—** *n.* *pl.* **do's** or **dos** 1. *Informal* A trick; cheat. 2. Deed; duty: chiefly in the phrase **to do one's do.** 3. *Informal* Festivity; celebration. 4. *pl.* That which ought to be done: used chiefly in the expression **do's and don'ts.** [OE *dōn*]

do[2] (dō) *n.* *Music* The keynote syllable of a major scale; also, the tone C. [< Ital.]

do·a·ble (dōō′ə·bəl) *adj.* Capable of being done.

do·all (dōō′ôl′) *n.* A general helper; factotum.

dob·bin (dob′in) *n.* A horse, esp. a plodding one. [after *Dobbin*, var. of *Robin* < *Robert*, a personal name]

Do·ber·man pinscher (dō′bər·mən) A breed of large, short-haired dogs originally developed in Germany. [after Ludwig *Dobermann*, its first breeder]

doc·ile (dos′əl, *Brit.* dō′sīl) *adj.* 1. Amenable to training; easy to manage; tractable. 2. Easily worked or handled. [< MF < L *docilis* able to be taught] **— doc′ile·ly** *adv.* **— do·cil·i·ty** (do·sil′ə·tē, dō-) *n.*

dock[1] (dok) *n.* 1. The water space between two adjoining piers or wharves where ships can remain for loading, unloading, or repair. 2. A wharf or pier. 3. *Often pl.* A group of wharves or piers. 4. A shipping or loading platform, as for trucks, trains, etc. **— Syn.** See WHARF. **—** *v.t.* 1. To bring (a vessel, truck, etc.) into or next to a dock. **—** *v.i.* 2. To come into a dock. [< MDu. *docke*]

dock[2] (dok) *n.* 1. The fleshy part of an animal's tail. 2. The stump of a tail that remains after clipping. **—** *v.t.* 1. To cut off the end of (a tail, etc.), or clip short the tail of. 2. To take a part from (wages, etc.). 3. To take from the wages, etc. of. [Cf. ME *docken* to cut short] **— dock′er** *n.*

dock[3] (dok) *n.* An enclosed space for the defendant in a criminal court. [< Flemish *dok* cage]

dock[4] (dok) *n.* Any of various plants of the buckwheat family, as the **sour dock.** [OE *docce*]

dock·age[1] (dok′ij) *n.* 1. A charge for docking (a ship, etc.). 2. Facilities for docking a vessel. 3. The act of docking.

dock·age[2] (dok′ij) *n.* 1. Curtailment, as of wages; deduction. 2. Waste matter in grain, easily separated by cleaning.

dock·et (dok′it) *n.* 1. A written summary or abstract. 2. *Law* a A record of court judgments. b The book in which such a record is kept. c A court calendar of the cases still pending. 3. Any calendar of things to be done. 4. A tag or label attached to a parcel, listing contents, directions, etc. **—** *v.t.* 1. To enter in a docket. 2. To put a tag or label on (a parcel, etc.). [ME; origin uncertain]

dock·yard (dok′yärd′) *n.* 1. An area of docks, etc., where ships are built, repaired, etc. 2. *Brit.* A navy yard.

doc·tor (dok′tər) *n.* 1. A licensed practitioner of medicine, surgery, or any of certain other healing arts, as a dentist, veterinarian, etc. 2. A person who has received a diploma of the highest degree, as in law, literature, etc. 3. A medicine man. 4. *Informal* One who or that which removes defects, mends broken parts, etc. **—** *v.t. Informal* 1. To prescribe for or treat medically. 2. To repair. 3. To falsify or alter, as evidence. **—** *v.i. Informal* 4. To practice medicine. 5. To undergo medical treatment. [< L *docere* to teach] **— doc′tor·al** *adj.*

doc·tor·ate (dok′tər·it) *n.* The degree or status of a doctor.

doc·tri·naire (dok′trə·nâr′) *adj.* Theoretical; visionary. **—** *n.* One whose views are derived from theories rather than from facts; an impractical theorist. **— doc′tri·nair′ism** *n.*

doc·trine (dok′trin) *n.* 1. That which is presented for acceptance or belief; teachings, as of a religious group. 2. A particular principle or tenet that is taught. [< OF < L *docere* to teach] **— doc′tri·nal** *adj.* **— doc′tri·nal·ly** *adv.*
— Syn. *Doctrine* primarily signifies a principle that is taught. A *theory* is a proposition regarded as susceptible of verification, and thus is usually scientific. A *dogma* rests on authority, such as the decision of a church council. Any *doctrine* is a *belief* on the part of those who accept it, but *belief* more often suggests matters of faith rather than of reason. A *creed* is the list of *doctrines* or *dogmas* of a religion or church; any single item of such a list is a *tenet.*

doc·u·ment (*n.* dok′yə·mənt; *v.* dok′yə·ment) *n.* Something written or printed that furnishes conclusive information or evidence, as an official paper or record. **—** *v.t.* 1. To furnish with documents. 2. To support by conclusive information or evidence. 3. To supply (a book, etc.) with citations that prove what is stated. [< OF < L *docere* to teach] **— doc′u·men·ta′tion** *n.*

doc·u·men·ta·ry (dok′yə·men′tər·ē) *adj.* 1. Pertaining to, consisting of, or based upon documents. 2. That presents factual material objectively without fictionalizing. Also **doc′u·men′tal.** **—** *n.* *pl.* **·ries** A motion picture dealing with events, circumstances, etc., in a factual way.

dod·der (dod′ər) *v.i.* To tremble or totter, as from age. [Cf. ME *dildder* to tremble] **— dod′der·ing** *adj.*

do·dec·a- *combining form* Twelve; of or having twelve. Also before vowels, **dodec-.** [< Gk. *dōdeka* twelve]

do·dec·a·gon (dō·dek′ə·gon) *n. Geom.* A polygon having

twelve sides and twelve angles. [< Gk. *dōdekagōnon*] —
do·dec·a·ge·o·nal (dō′dek·a·kag′ə·nəl) *adj.*
do·dec·a·he·dron (dō′dek·a·hē′drən) *n. pl.* **·drons** or **·dra**
(-drə) *Geom.* A polyhedron bounded by twelve plane faces.
For illus. see CRYSTAL. — **do′dec·a·he′dral** *adj.*
dodge (doj) *v.* **dodged, dodg·ing** *v.t.* **1.** To avoid, as a blow,
by a sudden turn or twist. **2.** To evade, as a duty or issue.
— *v.i.* **3.** To move suddenly, as to avoid a blow. **4.** To
practice trickery. — *n.* **1.** An act of dodging. **2.** A trick
to deceive or cheat. [Origin unknown]
dodg·er (doj′ər) *n.* **1.** One who dodges; a tricky fellow. **2.**
U.S. A small handbill. **3.** *U.S.* A cake of Indian meal.
do·do (dō′dō) *n. pl.* **·does** or **·dos 1.** An extinct bird about
the size of a turkey, with rudimentary, functionless wings.
2. *Informal* One who is slow or dull. [< Pg. *doudo*]
doe (dō) *n.* **1.** The female of the deer, antelope, rabbit, kangaroo, and certain other animals. **2.** Loosely, the female of
the moose or elk (properly called *cow*). [OE *dā*]
do·er (dōō′ər) *n.* One who acts, does, or performs; an agent.
does (duz) Present tense, third person singular, of DO¹.
doe·skin (dō′skin′) *n.* **1.** The skin of the female deer. **2.**
Leather made from this, used especially for gloves. **3.** A
heavy, short-napped, woolen or cotton fabric.
does·n't (duz′ənt) Does not. ◆ See note at DON'T.
doff (dof, dôf) *v.t.* **1.** To take off, as a hat or clothing. **2.**
To discard. [Contraction of *do off*] — **doff′er** *n.*
dog (dôg, dog) *n.* **1.** A domesticated, carnivorous mammal
of many varieties. ◆ Collateral adjective: *canine.* **2.** Any
of various other species of this family, as wolves, foxes, etc.
3. The male of any of these species. **4.** One of various animals having an appearance suggestive of a dog, as a prairie
dog. **5.** A despicable person. **6.** *Informal* A man or boy;
fellow. **7.** An andiron. **8.** *Mech.* One of several devices for
gripping or holding logs, etc. **9.** *pl. U.S. Slang* The feet.
— **to go to the dogs** *Informal* To go to ruin. — **to put on
the dog.** *U.S. Informal* To make a pretentious display. —
adv. Very; utterly: used in combination: *dog-tired.* — *v.t.*
dogged, dog·ging 1. To pursue persistently; hound. **2.**
Mech. To grip or fasten (a log, etc.) with a dog. [OE *docga*]
Dog (dôg, dog) *n.* Either of two constellations, Canis Major
(the Greater Dog) or Canis Minor (the Little Dog).
dog·bane (dôg′bān′, dog′-) *n.* A smooth, reddish-stemmed
herb having a milky juice.
dog biscuit A hard biscuit made with meat scraps, ground
bones, etc., for feeding dogs.
dog cart (dôg′kärt′, dog′-) *n.* **1.** A one-horse vehicle, usu.
two-wheeled, with two seats set back to back. **2.** A cart
hauled by one or more dogs.
dog·catch·er (dôg′kach′ər, dog′-) *n. U.S.* A person employed or elected to pick up and impound stray dogs.
dog days The hot, sultry days of July and early August.
doge (dōj) *n.* The elective chief magistrate in the former republics of Venice and Genoa. [< Ital. < L *dux-, ducis* chief]
dog-ear (dôg′ir′, dog′-) *n.* A turned-down corner of a book
page. — *v.t.* To turn down the corner of (a page). Also
dog's-ear. — **dog′-eared′** *adj.*
dog·face (dôg′fās′, dog′-) *n. U.S. Slang* A soldier in the
U.S. Army; esp., an infantryman.
dog·fight (dôg′fit′, dog′-) *n.* **1.** A fight between or as between dogs. **2.** *Mil.* An aerial battle between planes.
dog·fish (dôg′fish′, dog′-) *n. pl.* **·fish** or **·fish·es** One of various small, littoral sharks of North American waters.
dog·ged (dôg′id, dog′-) *adj.* Stubborn; obdurate. — **dog′-
ged·ly** *adv.* — **dog′ged·ness** *n.*
dog·ger·el (dôg′ər·əl, dog′-) *n.* Trivial, awkwardly written
verse, usu. comic or burlesque. — *adj.* Of or composed of
such verse. Also **dog′grel.** [ME; origin unknown]
dog·gish (dôg′ish, dog′-) *adj.* **1.** Relating to or suggestive
of a dog. **2.** Bad-tempered; snappish. **3.** *U.S. Informal*
Pretentiously stylish. — **dog′gish·ly** *adv.* — **dog′gish·ness** *n.*
dog·gone (dôg′gôn′, dog′gon′) *Informal interj.* Damn!;
darn! — *v.t.* **·goned, ·gon·ing** To damn.
dog·gy (dôg′ē, dog′ē) *n. pl.* **·gies** A dog; esp., a small dog.
Also **dog′gie.** — *adj.* **dog·gi·er, dog·gi·est 1.** Of or like a
dog: *doggy* odor. **2.** *U.S. Informal* Showily fashionable.
dog·house (dôg′hous′, dog′-) *n.* A small house for a dog.
— **in the doghouse** *U.S. Informal* In disfavor with someone.
do·gie (dō′gē) *n.* In the western U.S., a stray or motherless
calf: also spelled *dogy.* [Origin unknown]
dog·ma (dôg′mə, dog′-) *n. pl.* **·mas** or **·ma·ta** (-mə·tə) *n.*
Theol. A doctrine or system of doctrine maintained by a religious body as true and necessary of belief. **2.** A belief,
principle, or tenet. **3.** A system of such beliefs or principles.
— **Syn.** See DOCTRINE. [< L < Gk. *dogma* opinion]
dog·mat·ic (dôg·mat′ik, dog-) *adj.* **1.** Of, like, or pertaining to dogma. **2.** Marked by authoritative, often arrogant,
assertion of opinions or beliefs. — **dog·
mat′i·cal.** — **dog·
mat′i·cal·ly** *adv.*

dog·ma·tism (dôg′mə·tiz′əm, dog′-) *n.* Positive or arrogant assertion, as of opinions or beliefs. — **dog′ma·tist** *n.*
dog·ma·tize (dôg′mə·tiz, dog′-) *v.* **·tized, ·tiz·ing** *v.i.* **1.** To
express oneself dogmatically. — *v.t.* **2.** To declare or assert
as a dogma. — **dog′ma·ti·za′tion** *n.* — **dog′ma·tiz′er** *n.*
do-good·er (dōō′good′ər) *n. Informal* An idealistic philanthropist or reformer: a derisive term.
dog rose The wild brier of European hedges and thickets,
bearing single pink flowers.
dog's-ear (dôgz′ir′, dogz′-) *n.* Dog-ear.
dog sled A sled drawn by one or more dogs. Also **dog sledge.**
Dog Star 1. The star Sirius. **2.** Procyon.
dog tag 1. A small metal plate on the collar of a dog, usu.
indicating ownership. **2.** *U.S. Informal* A soldier's identification tag, worn on a chain around the neck.
dog·tooth (dôg′tōōth′, dog′-) *n.* A canine tooth.
dogtooth violet 1. A European herb of the lily family: also
called *adder's tongue.* **2.** One of various American plants,
bearing yellow or pinkish flowers. Also **dog's-tooth violet.**
dog·trot (dôg′trot′, dog′-) *n.* A regular and easy trot.
dog·watch (dôg′woch′, dog′-) *n. Naut.* Either of two short
watches aboard ship, from 4 to 6 or 6 to 8 P.M.
dog·wood (dôg′wood′, dog′-) *n.* Any of certain trees or
shrubs, esp. the **flowering dogwood** or **Virginia dogwood** of
the U.S., with white or pink flowers. Also called *cornel.*
do·gy (dō′gē) See DOGIE.
doi·ly (doi′lē) *n. pl.* **·lies** A small, ornamental piece of
lace, etc., used to protect surfaces. Also spelled *doyley,
doily.* [after *Doily* or *Doyley,* 17th c. English draper]
do·ings (dōō′ingz) *n.pl.* **1.** Activities or proceedings. **2.**
Behavior; conduct.
do-it-your·self (dōō′it-yŏŏr-self′) *adj. U.S. Informal* Designed to be used or done without special or hired help.
dol (dol) *n. Psychol.* A unit of pain intensity based on the
sensation of heat rays on the skin. [< L *dolor* pain]
dol·drums (dol′drəmz, dōl′-) *n.pl.* **1.** Those parts of the
ocean near the equator where calms or baffling winds prevail. **2.** A becalmed state. **3.** A dull, depressed, or bored
condition of mind; the dumps. [Cf. OE *dol* dull, stupid]
dole (dōl) *n.* **1.** That which, as food or money, is distributed,
esp. in charity. **2.** A giving out of something. **3.** A sum
of money paid to an unemployed person. — **on the dole**
Receiving relief payments from the government. — *v.t.*
doled, dol·ing To dispense in small quantities; distribute:
usually with *out.* [OE *dāl*]
dole·ful (dōl′fəl) *adj.* Melancholy. [< OF < LL < *dolere*
to feel pain] — **dole′ful·ly** *adv.* — **dole′ful·ness** *n.*
dol·i·cho·ce·phal·ic (dol′i·kō·sə·fal′ik) *adj.* Having a long
skull; longheaded. Also **dol′i·cho·ceph′a·lous** (-sef′ə·ləs).
[< Gk. *dolichos* long + *kephalē* head] — **dol′i·cho·ceph′a·
lism, dol′i·cho·ceph′a·ly** *n.*
doll (dol) *n.* **1.** A child's toy made to resemble the human
figure. **2.** A pretty but superficial woman. **3.** A pretty or
lovable child. **4.** *Slang* An attractive or charming person of
either sex. — *v.t. & v.i. Informal* To adorn or dress smartly: with *up.* [from *Doll,* nickname for *Dorothy*]
dol·lar (dol′ər) *n.* **1.** The standard monetary unit of the
United States, equivalent to 100 cents. **2.** The standard
monetary unit of Canada, China, various British colonies,
etc. **3.** A coin or a piece of paper currently worth one dollar.
4. Loosely, a Mexican peso. **5.** Any of various coins or
currency originally issued for trade. Symbol $ or $. [<
earlier *daler* < LG < G *taler, thaler,* short for *Joachimstaler,*
a coin of *Joachimstal,* a village in Bohemia]
dol·lar-a-year (dol′ər·ə·yir′) *adj. U.S.* Designating a
government employee, job, etc., having only token pay.
dollar diplomacy A practice or policy whereby a government uses public or private funds to advance its own interests abroad.
dol·lop (dol′əp) *n. Informal* A portion, serving, etc., of indefinite form or amount, as of a soft substance or liquid.
dol·ly (dol′ē) *n. pl.* **·lies 1.** A doll: a child's term. **2.** A
low, flat frame set on small wheels or rollers, used for moving
heavy loads, cameras, etc. **3.** A wooden instrument for beating or stirring clothes, etc. — *v.i.* **·lied, ·ly·ing** To move a
motion-picture or television camera toward or away from
the action.
dol·man (dol′mən) *n.* A woman's coat with dolman sleeves
or capelike arm pieces. [< F < Turkish *dōlāmān* long robe]
dolman sleeve A sleeve tapering from a wide opening at
the armhole to a narrow one at the wrist.
dol·men (dol′mən) *n.* A prehistoric monument made of a
huge stone set on upright stones. [< F]
dol·o·mite (dol′ə·mit) *n.* A marblelike rock consisting
principally of a brittle calcium and magnesium carbonate.
[after D. de Dolomieu, 1750–1801, French geologist]
do·lor (dō′lər) *n. Poetic* Sorrow; anguish. Also *Brit.* **do′-
lour.** [< OF < L, pain]

do·lor·ous (dō'lər-əs, dol'ər-) *adj.* **1.** Sad; mournful. **2.** Painful. **—do'lor·ous·ly** *adv.* **—do'lor·ous·ness** *n.*

dol·phin (dol'fin) *n.* **1.** Any of various cetaceans with beaklike snouts; esp. the **common dolphin** of the Mediterranean and Atlantic. **2.** *Naut.* A buoy or post to which a boat can be moored. [< OF *daulphin* < L *delphinus* < Gk. *delphis, -inos*]

DOLPHIN (def. 1)
(To 8 feet long)

dolt (dōlt) *n.* A stupid person. [ME *dold* stupid] **—dolt'·ish** *adj.* **—dolt'ish·ly** *adv.* **—dolt'ish·ness** *n.*

-dom *suffix of nouns* **1.** State or condition of being: *freedom.* **2.** Domain of: *kingdom.* **3.** Rank of: *earldom.* **4.** The totality of those having a certain rank, state, or condition: *Christendom.* [OE *-dōm* < *dōm* state, condition]

do·main (dō-mān') *n.* **1.** A territory under a sovereign or one government. **2.** A sphere or field of action, knowledge, etc. **3.** A landed estate. [< MF < OF < L *dominus* lord]

dome (dōm) *n.* **1.** A roof resembling an inverted cup or hemisphere. **2.** Something shaped like this. **3.** *Slang* The head. **—** *v.* **domed, dom·ing** *v.t.* **1.** To furnish or cover with a dome. **2.** To shape like a dome. **—** *v.i.* **3.** To rise or swell upward like a dome. [< MF < Ital. < L *domus* house]

domes·day (dōōmz'dā') *n.* See DOOMSDAY.

do·mes·tic (də·mes'tik) *adj.* **1.** Of or pertaining to the home or family. **2.** Given to or fond of things concerning the home or family. **3.** Tame; domesticated: *domestic animals.* **4.** Of, produced, or pertaining to one's own country. **—** *n.* **1.** A household servant. **2.** *pl.* Native products. [< MF < L *domus* house] **—do·mes'ti·cal·ly** *adv.*

do·mes·ti·cate (də·mes'tə·kāt) *v.* **·cat·ed, ·cat·ing** *v.t.* **1.** To tame. **2.** To civilize. **3.** To cause to feel at ease or at home. **—** *v.i.* **4.** To become domestic. Also **do·mes'ti·cize.** [< Med.L < L *domus* house] **—do·mes'ti·ca'tion** *n.*

do·mes·tic·i·ty (dō'mes·tis'ə·tē) *n. pl.* **·ties** **1.** Life at home or with one's family. **2.** Devotion to home and family. **3.** *pl.* Domestic matters.

domestic science Home economics.

dom·i·cile (dom'ə·səl, -sīl) *n.* **1.** A home, house, or dwelling. **2.** The place of one's legal abode. **—** *v.* **·ciled, ·cil·ing** *v.t.* **1.** To establish in a place of abode. **—** *v.i.* To dwell. [< MF < L *domus* house] **—dom·i·cil·i·ar·y** (dom'ə·sil'ē·er'ē) *adj.*

dom·i·nance (dom'ə·nəns) *n.* The state or fact of being dominant; control; ascendancy. Also **dom'i·nan·cy.**

dom·i·nant (dom'ə·nənt) *adj.* **1.** Dominating; ruling; governing. **2.** Conspicuously prominent, as in position. **3.** *Genetics* Designating one of a pair of hereditary characters that, appearing in hybrid offspring, masks a contrasting character: opposed to *recessive.* **4.** *Music* Of or based upon the dominant. **—** *n.* **1.** *Genetics* A dominant character. **2.** *Music* The fifth tone of a diatonic scale, a perfect fifth above the tonic. [See DOMINATE.] **—dom'i·nant·ly** *adv.*

dom·i·nate (dom'ə·nāt) *v.* **·nat·ed, ·nat·ing** *v.t.* **1.** To exercise control over; govern. **2.** To tower above; loom over. **—** *v.i.* **3.** To be dominant, as in power. [< L *dominari* to rule, dominate] **—dom'i·na'tor** *n.*

dom·i·na·tion (dom'ə·nā'shən) *n.* **1.** The act of dominating, or the state of being dominated. **2.** Control; authority.

dom·i·neer (dom'ə·nir') *v.t. & v.i.* To rule arrogantly or insolently. [< Du. < F < L *dominus* lord] **—dom'i·neer'ing** *adj.* **—dom'i·neer'ing·ly** *adv.*

Do·min·i·can (də·min'i·kən) *adj.* **1.** Of or pertaining to St. Dominic or to his monastic order. **2.** Of the Dominican Republic. **—** *n.* **1.** A member of the monastic order founded by St. Dominic. **2.** A native of the Dominican Republic.

do·min·ion (də·min'yən) *n.* **1.** Sovereign or supreme authority. **2.** A country under a particular government. **3.** A self-governing member of the British Commonwealth of Nations. [< F < L < *dominus* lord]

Dominion Day In Canada, July 1, the anniversary of Canada's federation into a dominion, 1867: a legal holiday.

dom·i·no¹ (dom'ə·nō) *n. pl.* **·noes** or **·nos** **1.** A small mask for the eyes. For illus. see MASK¹. **2.** A loose robe, hood, and mask worn at masquerades. **3.** A person wearing this. [< MF, hood worn by clerics]

dom·i·no² (dom'ə·nō) *n. pl.* **·noes** or **·nos** **1.** A small, oblong piece of wood, plastic, etc., with the upper side marked with dots. **2.** *pl.* (construed *as sing.*) A game: usu. played with a set of 28 of these pieces. [? < DOMINO¹]

don¹ (don) *n.* **1.** A Spanish gentleman or nobleman. **2.** An important personage. **3.** *Brit. Informal* A head, fellow, or tutor of a college. [< Sp. < L *dominus* lord]

don² (don) *v.t.* **donned, don·ning** To put on, as a garment. [Contraction of *do on*]

Don (don) *n.* Sir: a title of respect or address, used with the given name in Spanish-speaking countries.

Do·ña (dō'nyä) *n.* Lady; Madam: a title of respect or address used with the given name in Spanish-speaking countries.

do·nate (dō'nāt, dō-nāt') *v.t.* **·nat·ed, ·nat·ing** *Chiefly U.S.* To give, as to a charitable organization; contribute. [Back formation < DONATION] **—do'na·tor** *n.*

do·na·tion (dō-nā'shən) *n.* **1.** The act of giving. **2.** A gift. [< F < L *donare* to give]

done (dun) Past participle of DO¹. **—** *adj.* **1.** Completed; finished; ended; agreed. **2.** Cooked sufficiently.

do·nee (dō-nē') *n.* One who receives a gift.

done for *U.S. Informal* **1.** Ruined; finished; exhausted. **2.** Dead or about to die.

done in *U.S. Informal* **1.** Utterly exhausted; worn out with fatigue. Also **done up.** **2.** Killed; destroyed.

don·jon (dun'jən, don'-) *n.* The main tower or keep of a castle. [< OF, the lord's tower]

Don Juan (don wän') **1.** A legendary Spanish nobleman and seducer of women. **2.** Any rake or seducer.

don·key (dong'kē, dung'-) *n. pl.* **·keys** **1.** The ass. **2.** A stupid or stubborn person. [? after *Duncan,* a personal name]

Don·na (don'ə, *Ital.* dôn'nä) *n.* Lady; Madam, a title of respect or address in Italian-speaking countries.

don·nish (don'ish) *adj.* **1.** Of or suggestive of a university don. **2.** Formal; pedantic. **—don'nish·ness** *n.*

don·ny·brook (don'ē·brook') *n.* A brawl marked by roughness and abusive lamguage; free-for-all. [after *Donnybrook Fair,* an event known for its brawls, held in Ireland]

do·nor (dō'nər) *n.* **1.** One who gives. **2.** *Med.* One who furnishes blood, skin, etc. [< AF < L *donare* to give]

Don Quix·ote (don kwik'sət, kē-hō'tē; *Sp.* dôn kē-hō'tä) **1.** A satirical novel by Cervantes. **2.** The hero of this novel, a naive, dreamy, befuddled idealist.

don't (dōnt) **1.** Do not. **2.** Does not: now nonstandard in general American speech.

doo·dad (dōō'dad) *n. Informal* **1.** A small ornament; bauble. **2.** A doohickey. [Humorous coinage; extension of DO]

doo·dle (dōōd'l) *Informal* *v.t. & v.i.* **·dled, ·dling** To draw or scribble in an aimless, preoccupied way. **—** *n.* A design so made. [Cf. dial. E *doodle* to be idle, trifle]

doo·dle·bug (dōōd'l·bug') *n.* **1.** *U.S. Dial.* The larva of several insects. **2.** Loosely, the tumblebug. [? < dial. E *doodle* idler, fool + BUG]

doo·hick·ey (dōō'hik'ē) *n. pl.* **·eys** *U.S. Informal* A small object whose exact name is not known or remembered. [Humorous coinage; extension of DO]

doom (dōōm) *v.t.* **1.** To pronounce judgment or sentence upon; condemn. **2.** To destine to an unhappy fate. **—** *n.* **1.** An unhappy fate. **2.** An adverse judicial sentence. **3.** Death or ruin. **4.** The Last Judgment. [OE *dōm*]

dooms·day (dōōmz'dā') *n.* **1.** The day of the Last Judgment; the end of the world. **2.** Any day of final judgment. Also spelled *domesday.* [OE *dōm* doom + *dæg* day]

door (dôr, dōr) *n.* **1.** A hinged, sliding, folding, or rotating structure, as of wood, used for closing or opening an entrance to a house, vehicle, etc. **2.** A doorway, often representing an entire building or room: to live six *doors* away. **3.** Any means of entrance or exit. **— Syn.** See ENTRANCE¹. [Fusion of OE *duru* pair of doors and *dor* gate]

door·bell (dôr'bel', dōr'-) *n.* A bell at a doorway.

door·jamb (dôr'jam', dōr'-) *n.* A vertical piece at the side of a doorway supporting the lintel.

door·keep·er (dôr'kē'pər, dōr'-) *n.* A guardian or keeper of a doorway.

door·knob (dôr'nob', dōr'-) *n.* A handle to open a door.

door·man (dôr'man', -mən, dōr'-) *n. pl.* **·men** (-men', -mən) An attendant at the door of a hotel, apartment house, etc., who assists persons entering and leaving the building.

door mat A mat placed at an entrance for wiping the shoes.

door·nail (dôr'nāl', dōr'-) *n.* A large-headed nail, formerly used in the construction and ornamentation of doors. **— dead as a doornail** Unquestionably dead.

door·plate (dôr'plāt', dōr'-) *n.* A metal plate on a door, with the occupant's name, street number, etc.

door·post (dôr'pōst', dōr'-) *n.* A doorjamb.

door·sill (dôr'sil', dōr'-) *n.* The sill or threshold of a door.

door·step (dôr'step', dōr'-) *n.* A step or one of a series of steps leading to a door.

door·stop (dôr'stop', dōr'-) *n.* A device to keep a door open.

door·way (dôr'wā', dōr'-) *n.* The passage for entrance and exit into and out of a building, room, etc. **— Syn.** See ENTRANCE¹.

door·yard (dôr'yärd', dōr'-) *n.* A yard around, or esp. in front of, a house.

dope (dōp) *n.* **1.** A viscid substance or unusually thick liquid used as a lubricant. **2.** A filler, varnish, or similar preparation used for protecting and making taut the fabric of airplane wings, etc. **3.** *Photog.* A developer. **4.** *Slang* A drug or narcotic. **5.** *Slang* A dull witted or inapable individual. **6.** *Slang* Inside information. **—** *v.t.* **doped, dop·ing** **1.** To apply dope to. **2.** To adulterate or treat (a substance) with another. **3.** *Slang* To give drugs to; drug.

often with *up*. **4.** *Slang* To plan or solve: usu. with *out*. [Orig. U.S., prob. < Du. *doop* a dipping, sauce]

do·pey (dō′pē) *adj.* **·pi·er**, **·pi·est** *Slang* **1.** Lethargic from or as from narcotics. **2.** Stupid. Also **do′py**.

Doppler effect *Physics* The change in the frequency of a sound, light, or other wave caused by movement of its source relative to the observer. Also **Doppler shift**. [after C. J. *Doppler*, 1803–53, German physicist and mathematician]

Dor·ic (dôr′ik, dor′-) *adj. Archit.* Of or pertaining to the simplest of the three orders of Greek architecture characterized by heavy, fluted columns and unadorned capitals.

dorm (dôrm) *n. Informal* A dormitory.

dor·mant (dôr′mənt) *adj.* **1.** Asleep or as if asleep; motionless through sleep or torpidity. **2.** Not active; inoperative. **3.** *Biol.* Marked by partial suspension of vital processes, as many animals and plants in winter. [< OF < L *dormire* to sleep] **— dor′man·cy** *n.*

dor·mer (dôr′mər) *n.* **1.** A vertical window set in a small gable that projects from a sloping roof. Also **dormer window**. **2.** The roofed projection or gable itself. [< OF *dormeor* < L < *dormire* to sleep]

dor·mi·to·ry (dôr′mə·tôr′ē, -tō′rē) *n. pl.* **·ries** **1.** A large room with sleeping accommodations for many persons. **2.** A building providing sleeping and living accommodations, esp. at a school, college, or resort. [< L < *dormire* to sleep]

DORMER WINDOW

dor·mouse (dôr′mous′) *n. pl.* **·mice** A small, arboreal European rodent. [ME ? dial. E *dorm* to doze + MOUSE]

dor·sal (dôr′səl) *adj. Anat.* Of, pertaining to, on or near the back. [< L *dorsum* back] **— dor′sal·ly** *adv.*

dorsi- *combining form* **1.** On, to, or of the back. **2.** Dorso-. [< L *dorsum* back]

dorso- *combining form* Dorsal. [< L *dorsum* back]

do·ry (dôr′ē, dō′rē) *n. pl.* **·ries** A deep, flat-bottomed rowboat with a sharp prow, used esp. by North Atlantic fishermen. [< native Honduran name]

dos·age (dō′sij) *n.* **1.** The administering of medicine in prescribed quantity. **2.** The amount of medicine to be given.

dose (dōs) *n.* **1.** A particular quantity of medicine given or prescribed to be given at one time. **2.** *Informal* A particular amount of something usually disagreeable or painful. **— v.** **dosed**, **dos·ing** *v.t.* **1.** To give medicine, etc., to in doses. **2.** To give, as medicine or drugs, in doses. **— v.i. 3.** To take medicines. [< MF < Med.L < Gk. *dosis* gift]

do·sim·e·ter (dō·sim′ə·tər) *n. Med.* An instrument for measuring the total amount of radiation absorbed in a given time. [< Gk. *dosis* dose + -METER]

dos·si·er (dos′ē·ā, dos′ē·ər; *Fr.* dô·syā′) *n.* A collection of papers, documents, etc., relating to a particular matter or person. [< F, bundle of papers]

dost (dust) Do: archaic or poetic second person singular, present tense of DO¹: used with *thou*.

dot¹ (dot) *n.* **1.** A tiny, usu. round, mark; a speck, spot, or point. **2.** A small amount. **3.** In writing and printing, a point used as a part of a letter, in punctuation, etc. **4.** *Music* **a** A point written after a note or rest that increases its time value by half. **b** A point placed over a note to indicate staccato treatment. **5.** A signal in Morse code that is of shorter duration than the dash. **— on the dot** At exactly the specified time. **— v. dot·ted**, **dot·ting** *v.t.* **1.** To mark with a dot or dots. **2.** To make by means of dots; stud. **3.** To be scattered thickly over or about. **— v.i. 4.** To make a dot or dots. **— to dot one's i's and cross one's t's** To be exact or correct. [OE *dott* head of a boil] **— dot′ter** *n.*

dot² (dot, *Fr.* dô) *n.* A woman's marriage portion; dowry. [< F < L *dos, dotis*] **— do·tal** (dōt′l) *adj.*

do·tage (dō′tij) *n.* **1.** Feebleness of mind as a result of old age; senility. **2.** Foolish and excessive affection.

do·tard (dō′tərd) *n.* A foolish old person.

dote (dōt) *v.i.* **dot·ed**, **dot·ing** **1.** To lavish extreme fondness: with *on* or *upon*. **2.** To be feeble-minded as a result of old age. [ME *doten*] **— dot′er** *n.*

doth (duth) Does: archaic or poetic third person singular, present tense of DO¹.

dot·ing (dō′ting) *adj.* **1.** Extravagantly or foolishly fond. **2.** Feeble-minded; senile. **— dot′ing·ly** *adv.*

dot·ter·el (dot′ər·əl) *n.* A migratory plover of northern Europe and Asia. Also **dot′trel** (-rəl). [ME *dotrelle*]

dot·tle (dot′l) *n.* The plug of tobacco ash left in a pipe after smoking. Also **dot′tel**. [? Dim. of DOT¹]

dot·ty (dot′ē) *adj.* **·ti·er**, **·ti·est 1.** Consisting of or marked with dots. **2.** *Informal* Of unsteady or feeble gait. **3.** *Informal* Slightly demented; mentally weak.

Douai Bible An English translation of the Vulgate Bible made by Roman Catholic scholars at Reims and Douai and completed in 1610. A revision of the New Testament was published in 1941. Also **Douay Bible** or **Version**.

doub·le (dub′əl) *adj.* **1.** Combined with another usu. identical one: a *double* consonant. **2.** Two together: *double* lines. **3.** Twofold; duple. **4.** More than one; not single; dual: a *double* role. **5.** Consisting of two layers. **6.** Made for two: a *double* bed. **7.** Twice as great, as large, as many, etc.: *double* fare. **8.** Extra heavy, large, wide, etc.: a *double* blanket. **9.** Marked by duplicity; two-faced: a *double* life. **10.** *Music* Producing tones one octave lower than the notes indicated on a score: said of an instrument. **11.** *Bot.* Having the petals increased in number. **— n. 1.** Something that is twice as much. **2.** A duplicate. **3.** A player or singer who can substitute for another; understudy. **4.** A sharp or backward turn, as of a hunted fox. **5.** A trick or stratagem. **6.** A fold or pleat. **7.** *pl.* In tennis, etc., a game having two players on each side. **8.** In baseball, a fair hit that enables the batter to reach second base. **9.** In bridge, the act of challenging an opponent's bid by increasing its value and thus the penalty if the contract is not fulfilled; also, a hand warranting such an act. **— on** (or **at**) **the double 1.** In double time. **2.** *Informal* Quickly. **— v. ·led**, **·ling** *v.t.* **1.** To make twice as great in number, size, value, force, etc. **2.** To be twice the quantity or number of. **3.** To fold or bend one part of upon another: usu. with *over*, *up*, *back*. **4.** To clench (the fist): often with *up*. **5.** *Naut.* To sail around: to *double* a cape. **6.** *Music* To duplicate a voice or part in unison or in another octave. **7.** In baseball, to advance (a base runner) by making a two-base hit: He *doubled* him home. **8.** In bridge, to challenge (an opponent) by announcing a double. **— v.i. 9.** To become double; increase by an equal amount. **10.** To turn and go back on a course: often with *back*. **11.** To act or perform in two capacities. **12.** To serve as a double: to *double* for an actress. **13.** In baseball, to make a two-base hit. **14.** In bridge, to announce a double. **— to double in brass** *U.S. Slang* **1.** To be useful or adept in another capacity apart from one's (or its) specialty. **2.** Originally, of musicians, to play a second instrument in addition to the regular one. **— to double back 1.** To fold back. **2.** To turn and go back on the same or a parallel course. **— to double up 1.** To bend over or cause to bend over, as from pain or laughter. **2.** *U.S. Informal* To share one's quarters, bed, etc., with another. **— adv.** In pairs; twofold; doubly. [< OF < L *duplus* double]

doub·le-bar·reled (dub′əl·bar′əld) *adj.* **1.** Having two barrels, as a shotgun. **2.** Ambiguous, as a remark.

double bass 1. The largest and deepest-toned of the stringed instruments played with a bow: also called *bass viol*. **2.** The contrabass.

double bassoon A double-reed instrument pitched an octave below the ordinary bassoon: also called *contrabassoon*.

double bed A bed wide enough for two people.

double boiler A cooking utensil consisting of two pots, one fitting into the other. Food in the upper pot is cooked by the heat from water boiling in the lower pot.

dou·ble-breast·ed (dub′əl·bres′tid) *adj.* Having two rows of buttons and fastening so as to provide a double thickness of cloth across the breast: said of a coat or vest.

double chin A fat, fleshy fold under the chin.

doub·le-cross (*v.* dub′əl·krôs′, -kros′; *n.* dub′əl·krôs′, -kros′) *Slang v.t.* To betray by failing to act as promised. **— n.** A betrayal; a treacherous act. **— doub′le-cross′er** *n.*

doub·le-date (dub′əl·dāt′) *v.i.* **-dat·ed**, **-dat·ing** *U.S. Informal* To make or go out on a social engagement of two couples. **— double date**

doub·le-deal·ing (dub′əl·dē′ling) *adj.* Treacherous; deceitful. **— n.** Treachery; duplicity. **— doub′le-deal′er** *n.*

doub·le-deck·er (dub′əl·dek′ər) *n.* **1.** A ship, vehicle, etc., having two levels. **2.** *U.S. Informal* A sandwich made with three slices of bread and two layers of filling.

doub·le-edged (dub′əl·ejd′) *adj.* **1.** Having two cutting edges. **2.** Applicable both ways, as an argument.

dou·ble-en·ten·dre (dōō·blän·tän′dr) *n.* A word or phrase of double meaning. [Alter. of F *double entente*]

double entry A method of bookkeeping in which every transaction is made to appear as both a debit and a credit.

double exposure *Photog.* The act of exposing the same film or plate twice, as in making a composite photograph; also, a print developed from a film or plate so exposed.

doub·le-faced (dub′əl·fāst′) *adj.* **1.** Having two faces. **2.** Deceitful; hypocritical; two-faced.

double feature A program of two motion pictures.

doub·le-head·er (dub′əl·hed′ər) *n.* **1.** In baseball, two games played in succession on the same day by the same two teams. **2.** A train pulled by two locomotives.

double indemnity A clause in a life insurance policy by which a payment of double the face value of the policy is made in the event of accidental death.

double jeopardy The peril under which a defendant is placed when he is tried more than once for the same offense.

doub·le-joint·ed (dub′əl·join′tid) *adj.* Having very flexible joints that allow limbs, fingers, etc., to be bent at unusual angles.

doub·le·ness (dub′əl·nis) *n.* **1.** The state or quality of being double. **2.** Duplicity; deceitfulness.

doub·le-park (dub′əl·pärk′) *v.t. & v.i.* To park (a motor vehicle) alongside another already parked at the curb.

double play In baseball, a play in which two base runners are put out during one continuous play of the ball.

double pneumonia Pneumonia affecting both lungs.

dou·ble-reed (dub′əl·rēd′) *adj. Music* Designating a group of wind instruments having two reeds united at the lower end and separated at the upper, as the oboe and bassoon.

double standard A moral standard that permits men greater freedom than women, esp. in sexual behavior.

doub·let (dub′lit) *n.* **1.** A short, close-fitting outer garment, with or without sleeves, worn by men during the Renaissance. **2.** A pair of like things; a couple. **3.** *Ling.* One of a pair of words derived from the same original but entering a language through different routes, as *regal* and *royal.* [< OF, something folded, orig. dim. of *double*]

double take Delayed reaction to a joke or unusual situation, characterized by blank acceptance initially and then sudden, startled realization of the actual significance.

double talk **1.** A rapid flow of actual words mixed with meaningless syllables, made to sound like talk. **2.** Ambiguous talk meant to deceive.

double time **1.** In the U.S. Army, a fast marching step at the rate of 180 three-foot steps per minute. **2.** A wage rate that is twice one's normal pay.

doub·le·tree (dub′əl·trē′) *n. U.S.* A crossbar on a wagon, carriage or plow.

doub·loon (du·blōōn′) *n.* A former Spanish gold coin, originally worth about 16 dollars. [< Sp. *doble* double]

doub·ly (dub′lē) *adv.* **1.** In twofold degree; twice. **2.** In pairs. **3.** In twice the quantity.

doubt (dout) *v.t.* **1.** To hold the truth, validity, or reliability of as uncertain; hesitate to believe or accept. —*v.i.* **2.** To be unconvinced or mistrustful. —*n.* **1.** Lack of certainty about the truth or fact of something. **2.** A condition or state of affairs giving rise to uncertainty: Their fate was in *doubt.* **3.** An unresolved point or matter. —**beyond doubt** Unquestionably; certainly. —**no doubt 1.** Certainly. **2.** Most likely; probably. —**without doubt** Certainly. [< OF < L *dubitare*] —**doubt′er** *n.*

doubt·ful (dout′fəl) *adj.* **1.** Subject to or causing doubt; uncertain; unsettled. **2.** Having or experiencing doubt; undecided. **3.** Indistinct or obscure in appearance, meaning, etc.; vague; ambiguous. **4.** Of questionable character: a *doubtful* reputation. —**doubt′ful·ly** *adv.* —**doubt′ful·ness** *n.*

doubt·less (dout′lis) *adv.* **1.** Unquestionably. **2.** Probably. Also **doubt′less·ly.** —*adj.* Free from uncertainty.

douche (dōōsh) *n.* **1.** A jet of water, etc., directed into or onto some part of the body. **2.** A cleansing or medicinal treatment of this kind. **3.** A syringe or other device for administering a douche. —*v.* **douched, douch·ing** *v.t.* **1.** To cleanse or treat medicinally with a douche. —*v.i.* **2.** To administer a douche. [< F < Ital. < L *ducere* to lead]

dough (dō) *n.* **1.** A soft mass of moistened flour or meal and other ingredients, mixed for making bread, pastry, etc. **2.** Any soft, pasty mass. **3.** *Slang* Money. [OE *dāh*]

dough·nut (dō′nut′) *n.* A small cake of usu. leavened and sweetened dough, cooked by frying in deep fat.

dough·ty (dou′tē) *adj.* **·ti·er, ·ti·est** Valiant; brave: chiefly humorous. [OE *dyhtig, dohtig*] —**dough′ti·ly** *adv.* —**dough′ti·ness** *n.*

dough·y (dō′ē) *adj.* **dough·i·er, dough·i·est** Resembling dough in consistency or appearance; soft, pasty, pale, etc.

Douglas fir A large timber tree of the pine family, growing on the Pacific coast of the U.S.: often called *red fir, Nootka fir.* Also **Douglas hemlock, Douglas pine, Douglas spruce.** [after David *Douglas,* 1798–1834, Scottish botanist]

dour (dōōr, dour) *adj.* Forbidding and surly; morosely stern; ill-tempered. [< OF < L *durus* hard] —**dour′ly** *adv.* —**dour′ness** *n.*

dou·ra (dōōr′ə) See DURRA.

douse¹ (dous) *v.* **doused, dous·ing** *v.t.* **1.** To plunge into water or other liquid; dip suddenly; duck. **2.** To drench with liquid. —*v.i.* **3.** To become drenched or immersed. —*n.* A ducking or drenching. [Origin unknown]

douse² (dous) *v.t.* **doused, dous·ing 1.** *Informal* To put out; extinguish. **2.** *Informal* To take off, as clothes. **3.** *Naut.* To take in or haul down quickly, esp. a sail. [Cf. MDu. *dossen* to beat, strike]

dove¹ (duv) *n.* **1.** Any bird of the pigeon family, esp. the mourning dove, turtle dove, etc. **2.** *Usu. cap.* A symbol of the Holy Ghost. **3.** A symbol of peace. **4.** A gentle, innocent, tender person. [ME *duve*]

dove² (dōv) *Informal* Alternative past tense of DIVE.

dove·cote (duv′kōt′, -kot′) *n.* A box set on a pole or on a building, used for breeding pigeons. Also **dove′cot′** (-kot′).

dove·tail (duv′tāl′) *n.* **1.** A tenon shaped like a wedge and designed to interlock with a mortise of similar shape. **2.** A joint thus formed. —*v.t. & v.i.* **1.** To join by dovetails. **2.** To fit together closely or harmoniously.

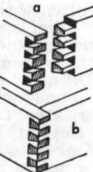

DOVETAIL JOINT
a Before joining.
b Joined.

dow·a·ger (dou′ə·jər) *n.* **1.** In English law, a widow holding property or title derived from her deceased husband. **2.** *Informal* An elderly woman of dignified bearing. [< OF *douagiere,* ult. < L *dotare* to give]

dow·dy (dou′dē) *adj.* **·di·er, ·di·est** Notably devoid of smartness in dress; frumpish. —*n. pl.* **·dies** A dowdy woman. [ME *doude* slut] —**dow′di·ly** *adv.* —**dow′di·ness** *n.*

dow·el (dou′əl) *n.* A pin or peg fitted tightly into adjacent holes of two pieces so as to hold them together. Also **dowel pin.** —*v.t.* **dow·eled** or **·elled, dow·el·ing** or **·el·ling** To furnish or fasten with dowels. [ME, ? < MLG *dovel* plug]

dow·er (dou′ər) *n.* **1.** The part of a deceased man's estate that is assigned by law to his widow for life. **2.** A natural talent or endowment. **3.** A dowry. —*v.t.* **1.** To provide with a dower. **2.** To endow, as with a talent or quality. [< OF < LL < L *dos, dotis* dowry]

dow·er·y (dou′ər·ē) See DOWRY.

down¹ (doun) *adv.* **1.** From a higher to a lower place. **2.** In or on a lower place, level, etc. **3.** On or to the ground. **4.** To or toward the south. **5.** To or in a place regarded as distant or outlying: *down* on the farm. **6.** Below the surface or horizon. **7.** From an upright to a prone or prostrate position: to knock a man *down.* **8.** To lesser bulk, heavier consistency, etc.: The mixture boiled *down.* **9.** To less activity, intensity, etc.: Things quieted *down.* **10.** To a lower amount, rate, etc.: Prices have gone *down.* **11.** In or into subjection or control: to put the rebels *down.* **12.** In or into a depressed or prostrate physical or mental state. **13.** Completely; fully: loaded *down* with honors. **14.** From an earlier time or individual. **15.** In cash as partial payment: five dollars *down.* **16.** In writing: Take *down* his name. —**down with** (Let us) do away with or overthrow. —*adj.* **1.** Directed downward: a *down* curve. **2.** *Informal* Downcast; depressed. **3.** Given in cash as a partial amount: a *down* payment. **4.** In games, behind an opponent by a specified number of points, strokes, etc. **5.** In football, not in play: said of the ball. —**down and out** In a completely miserable state, as of poverty or desolation. —**down on** *Informal* Annoyed with or hostile to. —*prep.* **1.** In a descending direction along, upon, or in. **2.** During the course of: *down* the years. —*v.t.* **1.** To knock, throw, or put down. **2.** *Informal* To swallow quickly; gulp. —*n.* **1.** A downward movement; descent. **2.** A reverse of fortune: chiefly in the phrase **ups and downs. 3.** In football, any of the four consecutive plays during which a team must advance the ball at least ten yards to keep possession of it; also, the declaring of the ball as out of play, or the play immediately preceding this declaration. [OE *dūne < of dūne* from the hill]

down² (doun) *n.* **1.** The fine, soft plumage of birds under the feathers, esp. that on the breast of water birds. **2.** Any feathery, fluffy substance. [< ON *dūnn*]

down³ (doun) *n.* **1.** *pl.* Turf-covered, undulating tracts of upland, esp. in southern and SE England. **2.** A hill, esp. of sand; dune. [OE *dūn.* Akin to DUNE.]

down·cast (doun′kast′, -käst′) *adj.* **1.** Directed downward: *downcast* eyes. **2.** Low in spirits; dejected; depressed. —*n.* **1.** The act of casting down. **2.** An air shaft, as in a mine.

Down East *Informal* New England, esp. Maine. —**down·east** (doun′ēst′) *adj.* —**down′east′er** *n.*

down·fall (doun′fôl′) *n.* **1.** A sudden descent, as in reputation or fortune; collapse; ruin. **2.** A sudden, heavy fall of rain, etc. **3.** A deadfall (def. 1). —**down′fall·en** *adj.*

down·grade (doun′grād′) *n.* A descending slope, as of a hill or road. —**on the downgrade** Declining in health, reputation, status, etc. —*adj.* Downhill. —*v.t.* **·grad·ed, ·grad·ing** To reduce in status, salary, etc.

down·heart·ed (doun′här′tid) *adj.* Dejected; discouraged. —**down′heart′ed·ly** *adv.* —**down′heart′ed·ness** *n.*

down·hill (*adv.* doun′hil′; *adj.* doun′hil′) *adv.* In a downward direction; toward the bottom of a hill. —**to go downhill** To decline, as in success or health. —*adj.* Descending.

Downing Street (dou′ning) **1.** A street in London; site of many British government offices. **2.** *Informal* The British government.

down payment An initial payment on a purchase.

down·pour (doun′pôr′, -pōr′) *n.* A heavy fall of rain.

down·right (doun′rīt′) *adj.* **1.** Thorough; utter: *downright* nonsense. **2.** Straightforward. —*adv.* Thoroughly; utterly.

down·stairs (*adv.* doun′stârz′) *adj. & n.* doun′stârz′) *adv.* **1.** Down the stairs. **2.** On or to a lower floor. —*adj.* Situated on a lower floor: also **down′stair′.** —*n.* The downstairs part of a house or other building.

down·stream (*adv.* doun′strēm′; *adj.* doun′strēm′) *adv.* Down the stream. — *adj.* In the direction of the current.
down·town (*adv.* doun′toun′; *adj.* doun′toun′) *adv.* To, toward, or in the geographically lower section of a town or city. — *adj.* Located in the geographically lower section of a town or city, usu. the chief business section.
down·trod·den (doun′trod′n) *adj.* 1. Trampled under foot. 2. Subjugated; oppressed. Also **down′trod′**.
down·ward (doun′wərd) *adv.* 1. From a higher to a lower level, position, etc. 2. From an earlier or more remote time, place, etc. Also **down′wards**, occasionally **down′ward·ly**. — *adj.* 1. Descending from a higher to a lower level. 2. Descending in course from that which is more remote.
down·y (dou′nē) *adj.* **down·i·er, down·i·est** 1. Of, like, or covered with down. 2. Soft; quiet. — **down′i·ness** *n.*
dow·ry (dou′rē) *n. pl.* **·ries** 1. The money or property a wife brings to her husband at marriage: also called *portion*. 2. A natural talent or endowment. [See DOWER]
dowse[1] (dous) See DOUSE[1].
dowse[2] (douz) *v.i.* **dowsed, dows·ing** To search for with a divining rod. [Origin uncertain] — **dows′er** *n.*
dows·ing rod (douz′ing) A divining rod.
dox·ol·o·gy (dok·sol′ə·jē) *n. pl.* **·gies** A hymn or verse of praise to God. — **greater doxology** The Gloria in excelsis Deo. — **lesser doxology** The Gloria Patri. [< Med.L < Gk. < *doxa* praise + *legein* to speak] — **dox·o·log·i·cal** (dok′sə·loj′i·kal) *adj.* — **dows′o·log′i·cal·ly** *adv.*
doy·ley, doy·ly (doi′lē) See DOILY.
doze (dōz) *v.* **dozed, doz·ing** *v.i.* 1. To sleep lightly or be drowsy for brief periods of time; nap. — *v.t.* 2. To spend (time) in napping or in being half asleep. — **to doze off** To fall into a light, brief sleep. — *n.* A light, brief sleep; nap. [< Scand., ? ult. < ON *dūsa* to doze]
doz·en (duz′ən) *n. pl.* **doz·ens**; *when preceded by a number,* **doz·en** A group or set of twelve things. Abbr. *doz., doz., dz.* [< OF < L < *duo* two + *decem* ten]
do·zy (dō′zē) *adj.* **·zi·er, ·zi·est** Drowsy. — **do′zi·ly** *adv.* — **do′zi·ness** *n.*
drab[1] (drab) *adj.* **drab·ber, drab·best** 1. Lacking brightness; dull and monotonous. 2. Having a dull, yellowish brown color. 3. Made of a thick, woolen, yellowish brown cloth. — *n.* 1. A dull, yellowish brown color. 2. A thick, woolen, yellowish brown cloth. [< F *drap* cloth < LL *drappus,* ? < Celtic] — **drab′ly** *adv.* — **drab′ness** *n.*
drab[2] (drab) *n.* 1. A slipshod, untidy woman. 2. A prostitute; slut. — *v.i.* **drabbed, drab·bing** 1. To associate with prostitutes. 2. To be a prostitute. [? < Celtic]
drachm (dram) *n.* 1. A dram. 2. A drachma.
drach·ma (drak′mə) *n. pl.* **·mas** or **·mae** (-mē) 1. An ancient Greek silver coin. 2. The standard monetary unit of Greece: in 1960 worth about 3 U.S. cents. 3. An ancient Greek unit of weight. 4. Any of several modern weights, as the dram. [< L < Gk. *drachmē* a handful]
draft (draft, dräft) *n.* 1. The act or process of selecting an individual or individuals for some special duty or purpose; esp., the selection of men for compulsory military service; conscription. 2. The condition of being selected for some special duty or purpose; also, those selected. 3. A current of air. 4. A device for controlling the airflow, as in a furnace. 5. A written order, as of an individual or bank, directing the payment of money. 6. A sketch, plan, or design of something to be made. 7. A preliminary or rough version of a writing. 8. A quantity of liquid for drinking: a *draft* of ale. 9. The act of drinking; also, the liquid taken at one drink. 10. The drawing of liquid from its container. 11. The act of drawing in a fishnet; also, the amount of fish taken with one drawing of a net. 12. The act of drawing air, smoke, etc., into the lungs; also, the air, etc., taken in. 13. The pulling of something, as a loaded wagon; also, the load pulled. 14. A heavy demand or drain on something. 15. *pl.* Draughts. 16. *Naut.* The depth of water required for a ship to float, esp. when loaded. — **on draft** Ready to be drawn, as beer, from a cask, etc. — *v.t.* 1. To draw up in preliminary form, esp. in writing. 2. To select and draw off, as for military service. 3. To draw off or away. 4. To cut a draft on (a stone). — *adj.* 1. Suitable to be used for pulling heavy loads: a *draft* animal. 2. Not bottled, as beer. Also *Brit.* **draught.** [ME < OE *dragan* to draw]
draft board An official board of civilians that selects men for compulsory service in the U.S. armed forces.
draft dodger One who avoids or attempts to avoid conscription into military service.
draft·ee (draf·tē′, dräf-) *n.* A person drafted for service in the armed forces.
drafts·man (drafts′mən, dräfts′-) *n. pl.* **·men** (-mən) 1. One who draws or prepares designs or plans of buildings, machinery, etc. 2. One who draws up documents, as deeds. 3. An artist esp. skilled in drawing.

draft·y (draf′tē, dräf′-) *adj.* **draft·i·er, draft·i·est** Having or exposed to drafts of air: a *drafty* room. Also spelled *draughty.* — **draft′i·ly** *adv.* — **draft′i·ness** *n.*
drag (drag) *v.* **dragged, drag·ging** *v.t.* 1. To pull along by main force; haul. 2. To sweep or search the bottom of, as with a net or grapnel; dredge. 3. To catch or recover, as with a grapnel or net. 4. To draw along heavily and wearily. 5. To harrow (land). 6. To continue tediously: often with *on* or *out.* 7. To introduce (an irrelevant subject or matter) into a discussion, argument, etc.: usu. with *in.* — *v.i.* 8. To be pulled or hauled along. 9. To move heavily or slowly. 10. To lag behind. 11. To pass slowly. 12. To use a grapnel, drag, or dredge. — **to drag one's feet** *U.S. Informal* To act with deliberate slowness. — *n.* 1. The act of dragging. 2. The resistance encountered in dragging: a heavy *drag* on the left wheel. 3. A slow, heavy, usu. impeded motion or movement. 4. Something that slows down movement, as a clog on a wheel. 5. Something heavy that is dragged. 6. A contrivance for dragging through water to find or bring up something. 7. Anything that hinders. 8. A stagecoach, with seats inside and on the top. 9. *U.S. Slang* Influence that brings special favors; pull. 10. *Slang* A puff on a cigarette, etc. 11. *U.S. Slang* One who or that which is tedious or colorless. [ME, prob. < OE *dragan*]
drag·gle (drag′əl) *v.* **·gled, ·gling** *v.t.* 1. To make soiled or wet by dragging in mud or water. — *v.i.* 2. To become wet or soiled. 3. To follow slowly; lag. [Freq. of DRAG]
drag·net (drag′net′) *n.* 1. A net to be drawn along the bottom of the water or along the ground, to find or capture something. 2. Any device or plan for catching a criminal.
drag·o·man (drag′ə·mən) *n. pl.* **·mans** (-mənz) or **·men** (-mən) An interpreter or guide for travelers in the Near East. [< F < LGk. < Arabic *tarjumān* translator]
drag·on (drag′ən) *n.* 1. A mythical, serpentlike, winged monster. 2. A fierce, violent person. 3. An overbearing, watchful woman. [< OF < L < Gk. *drakōn* serpent]
drag·on·fly (drag′ən·flī′) *n. pl.* **·flies** A predatory insect having a slender body, four wings, and strong jaws.
dra·goon (drə·gōōn′) *n.* In some European armies, a cavalryman. — *v.t.* 1. To harass by dragoons. 2. To coerce; browbeat. [< F *dragon,* a type of 17th c. firearm]
drain (drān) *v.t.* 1. To draw off (water, etc.) gradually. 2. To draw water, etc., from: to *drain* a swamp. 3. To empty (a glass, cup, etc.) by drinking. 4. To use up gradually; exhaust. 5. To filter. — *v.i.* 6. To flow off gradually. 7. To become dry by the flowing off or away of liquid. 8. To discharge waters contained: said of an area: The region *drains* into the lake. — *n.* 1. A trench, or similar device for draining. 2. *Surg.* A substance, or appliance inserted into a wound or cavity to afford a channel for discharge. 3. A continuous outflow, expenditure, or depletion. 4. The act of draining. [OE *drēahnian*] — **drain′er** *n.*
drain·age (drā′nij) *n.* 1. The act or method of draining. 2. A system of drains. 3. That which is drained off. 4. A drainage basin.
drainage basin A large surface area whose waters are drained off into a principal river system.
drain·pipe (drān′pīp′) *n.* A pipe used for draining.
drake (drāk) *n.* A male duck. [ME]
dram (dram) *n.* 1. An apothecaries' weight equal to 60 grains, 3.89 grams, or one eighth of an ounce. Abbr. *dr.* 2. An avoirdupois measure equal to 27.34 grains, 1.77 grams, or one sixteenth of an ounce. See table front of book. 3. A fluid dram. 4. A drink of alcoholic liquor. 5. A drachma. 6. A small portion. Also spelled *drachm.* — *v.* **drammed, dram·ming** *v.t.* 1. To ply with liquor. — *v.i.* 2. To use intoxicants freely. [< OF < L < Gk. *drachmē* a handful]
dra·ma (drä′mə. dram′ə) *n.* 1. A literary composition written to be performed upon a stage, telling a story, usu. of human conflicts and emotions; a play. 2. Stage plays as a branch of literature: the classical *drama.* 3. The art or profession of writing, acting, or producing plays. 4. A series of dramatic events. [< LL < Gk., action < *draein* to act, do]
Dram·a·mine (dram′ə·mēn) *n.* Proprietary name of a drug for relieving motion sickness. Also **dram′a·mine.**
dra·mat·ic (drə·mat′ik) *adj.* 1. Of, connected with, or like the drama. 2. Characterized by the action or spirit of the drama; theatrical. — **dra·mat′i·cal·ly** *adv.*
dra·mat·ics (drə·mat′iks) *n.pl.* (*usu. construed as sing. in def. 2*) 1. Dramatic performance, esp. by amateurs. 2. The art of staging or acting plays.
dram·a·tis per·so·nae (dram′ə·tis pər·sō′nē) *Latin* The characters of a play; also, a list of these.
dram·a·tist (dram′ə·tist) *n.* One who writes plays.
dram·a·tize (dram′ə·tīz) *v.* **·tized, ·tiz·ing** *v.t.* 1. To present in dramatic form; adapt for performance, as a play. 2. To represent or interpret (events, oneself, etc.) in a the-

atrical manner. —*v.i.* **3.** To be suitable for dramatizing. Also *Brit.* **dram′a·tise.** — **dram′a·ti·za′tion** *n.*

dram·a·turge (dram′ə·tûrj′) *n.* A dramatist. Also **dram′a·tur′gist.** [< F < Gk. < *drama* play + *ergein* to work]

dram·a·tur·gy (dram′ə·tûr′jē) *n.* The art of writing or producing plays, or of acting in them; dramatics. — **dram·a·tur′gic** (dram′ə·tûr′jik) or **·gi·cal** *adj.*

drank (drangk) Past tense of DRINK.

drape (drāp) *v.* **draped, drap·ing** *v.t.* **1.** To cover or adorn in a graceful fashion, as with drapery or clothing. **2.** To arrange in graceful folds. **3.** *Informal* To dispose in a leisurely or sloppy manner. — *v.i.* **4.** To hang in folds. — *n.* **1.** *U.S. & Canadian Usu. pl.* Drapery. **2.** The way in which cloth hangs, as in clothing. [< F *draper* to weave]

drap·er (drā′pər) *n. Brit.* A dealer in cloth or dry goods.

dra·per·y (drā′pər·ē) *n. pl.* **·er·ies 1.** Loosely hanging attire, esp. on figures in painting, sculpture, etc. **2.** *Often pl.* Hangings or curtains arranged in loose folds. **3.** Cloth.

dras·tic (dras′tik) *adj.* Acting vigorously; extreme. [< Gk. *drastikos* effective < *draein* to act] — **dras′ti·cal·ly** *adv.*

draught (draft, dräft) See DRAFT.

draughts (drafts, dräfts) *n.pl.* (construed as sing.) *Brit.* The game of checkers: also spelled *drafts.* [See DRAFT.]

draughts·man (drafts′mən, dräfts′-) *n. pl.* **·men** (-mən) See DRAFTSMAN.

draught·y (draf′tē, dräf′-) See DRAFTY.

Dra·vid·i·an (drə·vid′ē·ən) *n.* **1.** A member of an ancient people of southern India. **2.** A family of languages spoken in southern India and northern Ceylon. — *adj.* Of the Dravidians or their languages: also **Dra·vid′ic.**

draw (drô) *v.* **drew, drawn, draw·ing** *v.t.* **1.** To cause to move toward or to follow behind an agent exerting physical force; pull. **2.** To obtain, as from a receptacle: to *draw* water. **3.** To extract, as a tooth, cork, etc. **4.** To cause to flow forth, as blood. **5.** To bring forth; elicit: to *draw* praise. **6.** To take or pull off, on, or out, as a sword, gloves, etc. **7.** To portray with lines or words; sketch; delineate: to *draw* a portrait. **8.** To deduce or extract by a mental process: to *draw* a conclusion. **9.** To attract; entice: Honey *draws* flies. **10.** To pull tight, as a rope. **11.** To make or manufacture by stretching or hammering, as wire or dies. **12.** To take in, as air or a liquid, by inhaling or sucking. **13.** To close or shut as curtains. **14.** To disembowel. **15.** To cause (an abscess, etc.) to soften and drain by applying a poultice. **16.** To shrink or wrinkle. **17.** To extract (essence) by infusion, distillation, etc.: to *draw* tea. **18.** To select or obtain, as by chance; also, to win (a prize) in a lottery. **19.** To receive; earn, as a salary or interest. **20.** To withdraw, as money from a bank. **21.** To write out; draft (a check). **22.** *Naut.* Of a vessel, to sink to (a specified depth) in floating. **23.** To leave undecided, as a game or contest. — *v.i.* **24.** To practice the art of drawing; sketch. **25.** To exert a pulling or drawing force. **26.** To approach or retreat: to *draw* near or away. **27.** To exert an attracting influence. **28.** To pull out or unsheathe a weapon for action: usu. with *on.* **29.** To shrink or become contracted, as a wound. **30.** To cause redness or irritation of the skin, as a poultice or blister. **31.** To obtain by making an application to some source; with *on* or *upon*: to *draw* on one's credit; to *draw* on one's experience. **32.** To produce a current of air: This chimney *draws* well. **33.** To end a contest without a decision; tie. — **to draw a blank** To be unsuccessful. — **to draw on** To approach: Evening is *drawing on.* — **to draw oneself up** To straighten up or stiffen, as in anger or indignation. — **to draw out 1.** To prolong. **2.** To cause (someone) to talk freely. — **to draw the line** To fix a limit and refuse to go further. — **to draw up 1.** To write out in proper form: to *draw up* a deed. **2.** To bring or come to a standstill, as horses. **3.** To come alongside. — *n.* **1.** The act of drawing. **2.** The act of drawing out a weapon for action. **3.** Something drawn, as a ticket in a lottery. **4.** Something that attracts a large audience. **5.** A stalemate; tie. **6.** *U.S.* A gully or ravine into which water drains. [OE *dragan*]

draw·back (drô′bak′) *n.* **1.** Anything that hinders progress, success, etc. **2.** A refund on money paid, esp. on duties for reexported goods or on excess payment for freight.

draw·bridge (drô′brij′) *n.* A bridge of which the whole or a part may be raised, let down, or drawn aside.

draw·ee (drô′ē′) *n.* One on whom an order for the payment of money is drawn.

draw·er (drô′ər for *def. 1;* drôr for *def. 2*) *n.* **1.** One who draws; as. **a** A draftsman. **b** One who draws a check or money order. **c** One who draws beer, etc. **2.** A sliding receptacle, as in a desk, that can be drawn out.

DRAWBRIDGE

draw·ers (drôrz) *n.pl.* An undergarment covering the lower part of the body, including all or part of each leg.

draw·ing (drô′ing) *n.* **1.** The act of one who or that which draws. **2.** That which is drawn. **3.** The art of representing something, usu. by pen, pencil, or crayon. **4.** The picture, sketch, or design produced by this art. **5.** A lottery.

drawing board A smooth, flat board to which paper, etc., is attached for making drawings.

drawing card Something that attracts a large audience.

drawing room 1. A room in which visitors are received and entertained. **2.** *Chiefly Brit.* A formal reception in a drawing room. **3.** *U.S.* A private compartment in a sleeping car on a train. [Short for WITHDRAWING ROOM]

draw·knife (drô′nīf′) *n. pl.* **·knives** (-nīvz′) A knife with a handle at each end, used for shaving over a surface with a drawing motion. Also **drawing knife.**

drawl (drôl) *v.t. & v.i.* To speak or pronounce slowly, esp. with a drawing out of the vowels. — *n.* The act of drawling. [? Freq. of DRAW] — **drawl′er** *n.* — **drawl′ing·ly** *adv.* — **drawl·y** *adj.*

drawn (drôn) Past participle of DRAW.

drawn butter *U.S.* A sauce of melted butter.

drawn work Ornamental openwork made by pulling out threads of fabric and forming various patterns.

dray (drā) *n.* A low, strong cart with removable sides, for carrying heavy articles. — *v.t.* To transport by dray. [OE < *dragan* to draw] — **dray′man** *n.*

dray·age (drā′ij) *n.* **1.** The act of conveying in a dray. **2.** The charge for draying.

dread (dred) *v.t.* To anticipate with great fear or anxiety. — *adj.* **1.** Causing great fear; terrible. **2.** Exciting awe. — *n.* **1.** A terrifying anticipation, as of evil or danger. **2.** Fear mixed with deep respect; awe. **3.** A person or thing inspiring fear or awe. [ME < OE *ondrǣdan*]

dread·ful (dred′fəl) *adj.* **1.** Inspiring dread; terrible. **2.** *Informal* Disgusting; shocking; very bad; awful. — **dread′ful·ly** *adv.* — **dread′ful·ness** *n.*

dread·nought (dred′nôt′) *n.* Any battleship of great size carrying large-caliber guns. Also **dread′naught′.**

dream (drēm) *n.* **1.** A series of thoughts or images passing through the mind in sleep; also, the mental state in which this occurs. **2.** A daydream; reverie. **3.** A cherished or vain hope or ambition. **4.** Anything of dreamlike quality, esp. of unreal beauty or charm. — *v.* **dreamed** or **dreamt** (dremt), **dream·ing** *v.t.* **1.** To see or imagine in a dream. **2.** To imagine, as in a dream. **3.** To spend (time) in idle reverie: with *away.* — *v.i.* **4.** To have a dream or dreams. **5.** To indulge in daydreams. **6.** To consider something as possible: with *of*: I would not *dream* of staying. — **to dream up** *Informal* To concoct or create, as by ingenuity or cleverness. [ME < OE *drēam* joy] — **dream′er** *n.* — **dream′ful** *adj.* — **dream′ful·ly** *adv.* — **dream′ing·ly** *adv.* — **dream′less** *adj.* — **dream′less·ly** *adv.* — **dream′like′** *adj.*

dream·y (drē′mē) *adj.* **dream·i·er, dream·i·est 1.** Of, pertaining to, or causing dreams. **2.** Appropriate to dreams. **3.** Given to dreams; visionary. **4.** Soothing. **5.** *Informal* Wonderful. — **dream′i·ly** *adv.* — **dream′i·ness** *n.*

drear (drir) *adj. Poetic* Dreary.

drear·y (drir′ē) *adj.* **drear·i·er, drear·i·est 1.** Causing or manifesting sadness or gloom. **2.** Dull or monotonous. [OE < *drēor* gore] — **drear′i·ly** *adv.* — **drear′i·ness** *n.*

dredge¹ (drej) *n.* **1.** A large, powerful scoop or suction apparatus for removing mud or gravel from the bottoms of channels, harbors, etc. Also **dredging machine.** **2.** Any smaller device for bringing up something from under water. — *v.* **dredged, dredg·ing** *v.t.* **1.** To clear or widen by means of a dredge. **2.** To remove, catch, or gather with a dredge. — *v.i.* **3.** To use a dredge. [ME *dreg*] — **dredg′er** *n.*

dredge² (drej) *v.t.* **dredged, dredg·ing** To sprinkle or dust with a powdered substance, esp. flour. [ME < OF < L *tragemata* spices < Gk.]

dregs (dregz) *n.pl.* **1.** The sediment of liquids, esp. of beverages; lees. **2.** Coarse, worthless residue: the *dregs* of society. **3.** (construed as sing.) A small amount left over. [ME < ON *dregg*] — **dreg′gy** *adj.* — **dreg′gi·ness** *n.*

drench (drench) *v.t.* **1.** To wet thoroughly; soak. **2.** *Vet.* To administer a potion to by force. — *n.* **1.** *Vet.* A liquid medicine administered by force. **2.** A large quantity of fluid. **3.** A water solution for drenching. **4.** The act of drenching. [OE *drencan* to cause to drink] — **drench′er** *n.*

Dres·den (drez′dən) *n.* A china made in Dresden, Germany.

dress (dres) *v.* **dressed** or **drest, dress·ing** *v.t.* **1.** To put clothes on; clothe. **2.** To supply with clothing. **3.** To trim or decorate, as a store window. **4.** To treat medicinally, as a wound. **5.** To comb and arrange (hair). **6.** To curry (a horse). **7.** To prepare (stone, timber, etc.) for use or sale. **8.** To clean (fowl, game, etc.) for cooking. **9.** To till, trim, or prune. **10.** To put in proper alignment, as troops. — *v.i.* **11.** To put on or wear clothing, esp. formal clothing. **12.** To come into proper alignment. — **to dress down** *Informal* To rebuke severely; scold. — **to dress up** To put on or wear formal attire. — *n.* **1.** An outer garment for a woman or child, consisting of a skirt and waist, usu. in one piece. **2.** Clothing collectively. **3.** Formal or fashionable clothing. **4.** External adornment or appearance. — *adj.* **1.** Of, pertaining to, or suitable for a dress. **2.** To be worn on formal occasions: a *dress* suit. [< OF *dresser* to arrange, ult. < L < *dis-* apart + *regere* to guide]

dress circle A section of seats in a theater or concert hall, usu. the first gallery behind and above the orchestra.

dress·er¹ (dres'ər) *n.* **1.** One who dresses something. **2.** One who assists another in dressing. **3.** One who dresses well or in a particular way: a fancy *dresser*. **4.** A tool used in dressing stone, leather, etc. **5.** *Brit.* A surgical assistant.

dress·er² (dres'ər) *n.* **1.** A chest of drawers for articles of clothing, usu. with a mirror. **2.** A piece of furniture for holding dishes, silverware, etc. [< OF *dresser* to dress]

dress·ing (dres'ing) *n.* **1.** The act of one who or that which dresses. **2.** That with which something is dressed, as medicated bandages for a wound, manure for the soil, etc. **3.** A stuffing for poultry or roasts. **4.** A sauce for salads, etc.

dress·ing-down (dres'ing-doun') *n.* *U.S. Informal* **1.** A severe scolding. **2.** A beating.

dressing gown A loose gown worn while lounging at home.

dressing room A room for dressing, as in a theater.

dressing table A small table or stand with a mirror, used while putting on make-up, grooming the hair, etc.

dress·mak·er (dres'mā'kər) *n.* One who makes women's dresses or other articles of clothing. — *adj.* Not severely tailored; having soft, feminine lines. — **dress'mak'ing** *n.*

dress parade A formal military parade in dress uniform.

dress rehearsal A final rehearsal of a play, done with the costumes, lighting, etc., to be used in the public performance.

dress suit A man's suit for formal evening wear.

dress·y (dres'ē) *adj.* **dress·i·er, dress·i·est** *Informal* **1.** Having or giving an appearance of smart elegance; stylish; chic. **2.** Fond of dressing up. — **dress'i·ness** *n.*

drew (drōō) Past tense of DRAW.

drib (drib) *n.* *Dial.* Driblet. — **dribs and drabs** Small quantities. [Var. of DRIP]

drib·ble (drib'əl) *v.t. & v.i.* **·bled, ·bling** **1.** To fall or let fall in drops. **2.** To drool. **3.** In basketball, to propel (the ball) by bouncing. **4.** In soccer, to propel (the ball) by successive kicks. — *n.* **1.** A small quantity of a liquid falling in drops. **2.** The act of dribbling. — **drib'bler** *n.*

drib·let (drib'lit) *n.* **1.** A small drop of water or other liquid. **2.** A tiny quantity of something. Also **drib'blet.**

dried (drīd) Past tense and past participle of DRY.

dri·er (drī'ər) Comparative of DRY. — *n.* **1.** One who or that which dries. **2.** A substance added to paint, etc., to make it dry more quickly. **3.** A mechanical device for drying, as for drying clothes. Also spelled *dryer*.

dri·est (drī'ist) Superlative of DRY: also spelled *dryest*.

drift (drift) *n.* **1.** The act of moving along, or the fact of being carried along, in or as in a current of water, air, etc. **2.** A force or influence that drives something along. **3.** The course along which something is directed; tendency or intent: the *drift* of a conversation. **4.** A usu. slow, broad current of water, as in some parts of an ocean. **5.** The rate at which a current of water moves. **6.** The direction of a current of water. **7.** Something driven along or heaped up by air or water currents: a snow *drift*. **8.** Material carried along from one place to another. **9.** The act of driving something along. **10.** The distance a ship, aircraft, missile, etc., is driven from its direct or intended course by wind, sea, etc. **11.** *Mining* A horizontal passage in a mine. — *v.i.* **1.** To move along in or as in a current. **2.** To become heaped up by air currents or water currents. **3.** To move along aimlessly. — *v.t.* **4.** To cause to drift. [ME < OE *drīfan* to drive] — **drift'er** *n.* — **drift'y** *adj.*

drift·age (drif'tij) *n.* **1.** The act or process of drifting. **2.** Deviation caused by drifting. **3.** Something carried along or deposited by air currents or water currents.

drift·wood (drift'wŏŏd') *n.* Wood floated or drifted by water; esp., wood washed up on a seashore.

drill¹ (dril) *n.* **1.** A tool used for boring holes in metal, stone, wood, or other hard substances. **2.** A mollusk that kills oysters by drilling holes in their shells. **3.** A process of training marked by fixed procedures and much repetition, as in gymnastics, in arithmetic, etc. **4.** The act of teaching through such training; also, a particular exercise. — *Syn.* See PRACTICE. — *v.t.* **1.** To pierce with or as with a drill. **2.** To make (a hole) with a drill. **3.** To train in military procedures, etc. **4.** To teach by drill. — *v.i.* **5.** To make a hole with or as with a drill. **6.** To take part in a drill. **7.** To train someone by drill. [< Du. *drillen* to bore] — **drill'er** *n.*

drill² (dril) *Agric.* *n.* **1.** A machine for planting seeds in rows. **2.** A furrow in which seeds are sown. **3.** A row of seeds so planted. — *v.t. & v.i.* To sow or plant in rows.

drill³ (dril) *n.* Heavy, twilled linen or cotton cloth. Also **drill'ing.** [< G *drillich* cloth with three threads]

drill⁴ (dril) *n.* A baboon of West Africa, similar to the mandrill. [? < native name]

drill·mas·ter (dril'mas'tər, -mäs'-) *n.* One who teaches or trains by drilling; esp., a trainer in military exercises.

drill press A machine tool used in drilling holes.

dri·ly (drī'lē) See DRYLY.

drink (dringk) *v.* **drank** (*Archaic* **drunk**), **drunk** (*Archaic* **drunk·en** or **drank**), **drink·ing** *v.t.* **1.** To take into the mouth and swallow (a liquid). **2.** To soak up or absorb (liquid or moisture). **3.** To receive eagerly through the senses or the mind. **4.** To swallow the contents of (a glass, etc.). — *v.i.* **5.** To swallow a liquid. **6.** To drink alcoholic liquors, especially to excess. **7.** To drink a toast: with *to*. — **to drink the health of** To offer homage or good wishes to by a toast. — *n.* **1.** A drinkable liquid; beverage. **2.** A portion of liquid swallowed. **3.** Alcoholic liquor. **4.** The practice of drinking alcoholic liquor to excess. **5.** *Slang* A body of water. [OE *drincan*] — **drink'a·ble** *adj.* — **drink'er** *n.*

drip (drip) *n.* **1.** The falling of liquids in drops. **2.** Liquid falling in drops; also, the sound so made. **3.** Melted fat exuded from meat being roasted or fried. Also **drip'pings.** **4.** *Archit.* A projecting molding for shedding rain. **5.** *U.S. Slang* A disagreeable, insipid, or inept individual. — *v.t. & v.i.* **dripped** or **dript, drip·ping** To fall or cause to fall in drops. [OE *dryppan*] — **drip'py** *adj.*

drip-dry (drip'drī') *adj.* Designating or pertaining to a garment or fabric treated to dry quickly and retain its proper shape after being hung while dripping wet. — *v.i.* **-dried, -dry·ing** To dry in such a manner.

drive (drīv) *v.* **drove, driv·en, driv·ing** *v.t.* **1.** To push or propel onward with force. **2.** To force to work or activity. **3.** To goad by force or compulsion: Failure *drove* him to despair. **4.** To cause to penetrate by force. **5.** To produce by penetration: to *drive* a well. **6.** To cause to go rapidly by striking or throwing. **7.** To control the operation of (a vehicle). **8.** To transport in a vehicle. **9.** To provide the motive power for. **10.** To carry through without letup: to *drive* a hard bargain. — *v.i.* **11.** To move along rapidly. **12.** To strike, throw, or impel a ball, etc., with force. **13.** To drive a vehicle. **14.** To be transported in a vehicle. **15.** To work toward a particular objective or meaning: with *at.* — **to drive home** **1.** To force in all the way, as a nail. **2.** To make evident with force or emphasis: to *drive home* one's meaning. — **to let drive** To aim or release (a blow, shot, etc.). — *n.* **1.** The act of driving. **2.** A road for driving. **3.** A journey in a vehicle. **4.** Urgent pressure, as of business. **5.** The gathering together of cattle, logs, etc.; also, the cattle, logs, etc., being driven. **6.** An organized campaign: a *drive* for money. **7.** *U.S. Informal* Energy; aggressiveness. **8.** *Psychol.* A strong, motivating power or stimulus: the sex *drive*. **9.** *Mil.* A large-scale, sustained attack. **10.** *Mech.* A means of transmitting power, as from the motor of an automobile to the wheels. **11.** In certain games, as golf, the act of driving the ball. [OE *drīfan*]

drive-in (drīv'in') *n.* **1.** An outdoor motion-picture theater designed for viewing from parked cars. **2.** A restaurant, shop, etc., serving patrons in their cars.

driv·el (driv'əl) *v.* **driv·eled** or **·elled, driv·el·ing** or **·el·ling** *v.i.* **1.** To let saliva flow from the mouth. **2.** To flow like saliva. **3.** To talk foolishly. — *v.t.* **4.** To let flow from the mouth. **5.** To say in a foolish manner. — *n.* **1.** A flow of saliva from the mouth. **2.** Senseless talk; twaddle. [OE *dreflian*] — **driv'el·er** or **driv'el·ler** *n.*

driv·en (driv'ən) Past participle of DRIVE.

driv·er (drī'vər) *n.* **1.** One who drives a vehicle, animals, logs, etc. **2.** Something used for driving. **3.** In golf, a wooden-headed club with full-length shaft, for driving from the tee. **4.** *Mech.* A part that transmits motion.

drive·way (drīv'wā') *n.* **1.** A private road providing access to a garage, house, or other building. **2.** A road for driving.

driz·zle (driz'əl) *v.t. & v.i.* **·zled, ·zling** To rain steadily in fine drops. — *n.* A light rain. [? Freq. of ME *dresen*, OE *drēosan* to fall] — **driz'zly** *adj.*

droll (drōl) *adj.* Humorously odd; comical; funny. — *Syn.* See HUMOROUS. — *n.* A prankster; clown. — *v.i.* To clown. [< MF < MDu. *drol* a jolly man] — **droll'ly** *adv.*

droll·er·y (drō'lər-ē) *n.* *pl.* **·er·ies** **1.** The quality of being droll; humor. **2.** An amusing way of acting or talking. **3.** Something droll, as a funny remark.

-drome *combining form* Place for running; racecourse. [< Gk. < *dramein* to run]

drom·e·dar·y (drom'ə·der'ē, drum'-) *n.* *pl.* **·dar·ies** The swift, one-humped Arabian camel trained for riding. [< OF < LL < L *dromas* a running]

drone¹ (drōn) *v.* **droned, dron·ing** *v.i.* **1.** To make a dull, humming sound. **2.** To speak monotonously. — *v.t.* **3.** To utter in a monotonous tone. — *n.* **1.** A dull humming sound, as of a bee. **2.** One of the single-note pipes of the bagpipe; also, a bagpipe. [ME *drone* male bee]

drone[2] (drōn) *n.* **1.** The male of the bee, esp. of the honeybee, having no sting and gathering no honey. **2.** A loafer who lives by the labor of others. **3.** *Aeron.* An unmanned airplane piloted by remote control. — *v.i.* **droned, dron·ing** To live in idleness. [OE *drān*]

drool (drōōl) *v.t. & v.i.* To drivel; slaver. — *n.* **1.** Spittle. **2.** *Informal* Foolish talk; twaddle. [Contraction of DRIVEL]

droop (drōōp) *v.i.* **1.** To sink down; hang downward. **2.** To lose vigor or spirit; languish. — *v.t.* **3.** To let hang or sink down. — *n.* A drooping. [< ON *drūpa*]

droop·y (drōō′pē) *adj.* **droop·i·er, droop·i·est** Tending to droop. — **droop′i·ly** *adv.* — **droop′i·ness** *n.*

drop (drop) *n.* **1.** A small quantity of liquid, shaped like a tiny ball. **2.** A very small amount of anything. **3.** *pl.* A liquid medicine given in drops. **4.** Something resembling a drop in shape, size, etc. **5.** Something designed to fall, slide, or hang down, as a curtain. **6.** A slot or other aperture, as in a mailbox. **7.** A sudden or quick downward movement. **8.** A sudden or quick decrease, as in prices. **9.** The vertical distance from a higher to a lower level. **10.** A falling off or away: a sheer *drop*. **11.** A parachuting of men or supplies. **— at the drop of a hat** With little or no hesitation or provocation; at once. **— to have** (or **get**) **the drop on** To have (or get) the advantage over. — *v.* **dropped** or **dropt, drop·ping** *v.i.* **1.** To fall in drops, as a liquid. **2.** To fall or descend rapidly. **3.** To fall down exhausted, injured, or dead. **4.** To decline or decrease, as in amount. **5.** To crouch, as a hunting dog at the sight of game. **6.** To fall into some state or condition. **7.** To come to an end: to let the matter *drop*. — *v.t.* **8.** To let fall by letting go of. **9.** To let fall in drops. **10.** To give birth to: said of animals. **11.** To utter (a hint, etc.) in a casual way. **12.** To write and send (a note, etc.). **13.** To cause to fall, as by striking, etc. **14.** To have no more to do with. **15.** To let out or deposit at a particular place. **16.** To parachute (soldiers, supplies, etc.). **17.** To omit, as a word, line, or stitch. **18.** *U.S.* To discharge (an employee). **19.** To move down; lower. **20.** *Slang* To lose (money, etc.), as in gambling. **21.** In football, to drop-kick (the ball); also, to score (a goal) by drop-kicking. **— to drop behind** (or **back**) To fall behind or lag behind purposely or by necessity. **— to drop in** To make a casual visit. **— to drop off 1.** To decline or decrease. **2.** To go to sleep. **— to drop out** To withdraw, as from membership. [OE *dropa*]

drop·forge (drop′fôrj′) *v.t.* **·forged, ·forg·ing** To forge (metal) between dies with a drop hammer.

drop hammer A machine for forging, stamping, etc., in which a heavy weight sliding between vertical guides hammers the metal beneath it. Also **drop press.**

drop-kick (drop′kik′) *v.t. & v.i.* To give a drop kick (to).

drop kick In football, a kick given the ball just as it is rebounding after being dropped by the kicker.

drop·let (drop′lit) *n.* A tiny drop.

drop·out (drop′out′) *n.* *U.S. & Canadian* A child who leaves school as soon as attendance is not compulsory.

drop·sy (drop′sē) *n.* *Pathol.* An abnormal accumulation of serous fluid in body cavities. [< OF < L < Gk. *hydrōps* dropsy] — **drop′si·cal** (-si-kəl), **drop′sied** (-sēd) *adj.*

drosh·ky (drosh′kē, drôsh′-) *n.* *pl.* **·kies** A light, open, four-wheeled Russian carriage or any similar carriage.

dro·soph·i·la (drō-sof′ə-lə, drə-) *n.* *pl.* **·lae** (-lē) The fruit fly (def. 2). [< NL < Gk. *drosos* dew + *phileein* to love]

dross (drôs, dros) *n.* **1.** *Metall.* Refuse or impurity in melted metal; slag; cinders. **2.** Waste matter; refuse. [OE *drōs*] — **dross′i·ness** *n.* — **dross′y** *adj.*

drought (drout) *n.* **1.** Long-continued dry weather; lack of rain. **2.** Scarcity; dearth. **3.** *Dial.* Thirst. Also **drouth** (drouth). [OE *drūgath*] — **drought′y** *adj.*

drove[1] (drōv) Past tense of DRIVE.

drove[2] (drōv) *n.* **1.** A number of animals driven or herded for driving. **2.** A moving crowd of human beings. **3.** A stonemason's broad-edged chisel. Also **drove chisel.** — *Syn.* See FLOCK. — *v.t.* **droved, drov·ing 1.** To drive (cows, etc.) for some distance. **2.** To dress (stone) with a drove. [OE *drāf.* Akin to DRIVE.] — **drov′er** *n.*

drown (droun) *v.i.* **1.** To die by suffocation with a liquid. — *v.t.* **2.** To kill by suffocation with a liquid. **3.** To cover with or as with a flood; inundate. **4.** To lessen the sound of; muffle. **5.** To lessen or extinguish. [ME *drounen*]

drowse (drouz) *v.* **drowsed, drows·ing** *v.i.* **1.** To be only half awake; doze. — *v.t.* **2.** To make sleepy, dull, or lethargic. **3.** To pass (time) in drowsing. — *n.* The state of being half asleep; doze. [OE *drūsian* to become sluggish]

drow·sy (drou′zē) *adj.* **·si·er, ·si·est 1.** Heavy with sleepiness; dull. **2.** Produced by sleepiness or lethargy. **3.** Making sleepy; soporific. — **drow′si·ly** *adv.* — **drow′si·ness** *n.*

drub (drub) *v.t.* **drubbed, drub·bing 1.** To beat, as with a stick. **2.** To vanquish; overcome. — *n.* A blow; thump. [? < Arabic *darb* a beating] — **drub′ber** *n.*

drudge (druj) *v.i.* **drudged, drudg·ing** To work hard at wearisome or menial tasks. — *n.* One who drudges. [OE *drēogan* work, labor] — **drudg′er** *n.* — **drudg′ing·ly** *adv.*

drudg·er·y (druj′ər·ē) *n.* *pl.* **·er·ies** Dull, wearisome, or menial work. — *Syn.* See TOIL[1].

drug (drug) *n.* **1.** Any chemical or biological substance, other than food, intended for use in the treatment, prevention, or diagnosis of disease. **2.** A narcotic. **3.** A commodity that is overabundant: a *drug* on the market. — *v.t.* **drugged, drug·ging 1.** To mix drugs with (food, drink, etc.). **2.** To administer drugs to. **3.** To stupefy or poison with or as with drugs. [ME *drogge*]

drug addict One who uses narcotics habitually.

drug·gist (drug′ist) *n.* **1.** One who compounds prescriptions and sells drugs; a pharmacist. **2.** A dealer in drugs.

drug·store (drug′stôr′, -stōr′) *n.* *U.S.* A place where prescriptions are compounded, and drugs and miscellaneous merchandise are sold; pharmacy. Also **drug store.**

dru·id (drōō′id) *n.* One of an order of priests or teachers of an ancient Celtic religion. [< MF < L *druides* < Celtic] — **dru·id·ic** (drōō-id′ik) or **·i·cal** *adj.* — **dru′id·ism** *n.*

drum (drum) *n.* **1.** A hollow percussion instrument, typically shaped like a cylinder or hemisphere, having a membrane stretched tightly over one or both ends, and played by beating the membrane with sticks, the hands, etc. **2.** A sound produced by or as by a drum. **3.** Something resembling a drum in shape; as: **a** A metal cylinder around which cable, wire, etc., is wound. **b** A cylindrical metal container, as for oil. **4.** *Anat.* The middle ear, or the tympanic membrane. — *v.* **drummed, drum·ming** *v.i.* **1.** To beat a drum. **2.** To tap or thump continuously, as with the fingers. — *v.t.* **3.** To perform on or as on a drum. **4.** To summon by beating a drum. **5.** To force upon by constant repetition. **6.** To work up (business or trade) by advertising, canvassing, etc.: usually with *up.* **7.** To expel in disgrace: usually with *out.* [Prob. < MDu. *tromme*] — **drum′mer** *n.*

drum·head (drum′hed′) *n.* **1.** The membrane stretched over the end of a drum. **2.** *Naut.* The circular top of a capstan. **3.** *Anat.* The tympanic membrane.

drum major One who instructs or leads a band or drum corps. — **drum ma·jor·ette** (mā′jə·ret′) *fem.*

drum·stick (drum′stik′) *n.* **1.** A stick for beating a drum. **2.** The lower joint of the leg of a cooked fowl.

drunk (drungk) Past participle and archaic past tense of DRINK. — *adj.* **1.** Affected with alcoholic drink; intoxicated; inebriated. **2.** Overwhelmed by some powerful emotion. — *n.* *Informal* **1.** One who is drunk. **2.** A drunkard. **3.** A bout of drinking; binge.

drunk·ard (drungk′ərd) *n.* One who habitually drinks alcoholic beverages to excess.

drunk·en (drungk′ən) Archaic past participle of DRINK. — *adj.* **1.** Habitually drunk. **2.** Relating to or caused by a drunken state. — **drunk′en·ness** *n.* — **drunk′en·ly** *adv.*

drupe (drōōp) *n.* *Bot.* A soft, fleshy fruit, as a peach or cherry, enclosing a hard-shelled stone or seed. [< NL < L *drupa* (oliva) an overripe (olive)] — **dru·pa′ceous** *adj.*

dry (drī) *adj.* **dri·er** or, occasionally, **dry·er, dri·est** or, occasionally, **dry·est. 1.** Devoid of moisture; not wet or damp. **2.** Marked by little or no rainfall. **3.** Not lying under water: *dry* land. **4.** Parched. **5.** Having all or nearly all the water drained away, exhausted or evaporated: a *dry* stream. **6.** No longer giving milk. **7.** Devoid of tears. **8.** Thirsty. **9.** Eaten or served without butter, jam, etc.: *dry* toast. **10.** Unaccompanied by the discharge of phlegm, etc. **11.** Consisting of or pertaining to commodities, etc., that are not liquids: *dry* provisions. **12.** Lacking sweetness: said of wines. **13.** Plain; unadorned; bare: the *dry* facts. **14.** Dull; boring: a *dry* lecture. **15.** Devoid of warmth, color, or emotion: a *dry* welcome. **16.** Crisp; quietly shrewd: *dry* humor. **17.** *U.S. Informal* Opposing or prohibiting the sale of or indulgence in alcoholic beverages: a *dry* State. — *v.* **dried, dry·ing** *v.t.* **1.** To make dry. **2.** To preserve (meat, fish, etc.) by removing moisture. — *v.i.* **3.** To become dry. — **to dry up 1.** To become thoroughly dry. **2.** To become unproductive. **3.** *Slang* To stop talking. [OE *drȳge*]

dry·ad (drī′əd, -ad) *n.* In classical mythology, a nymph dwelling in or presiding over woods and trees. [< L < Gk. < *drys, dryos* tree] — **dry·ad′ic** *adj.*

dry cell *Electr.* A primary cell containing an electrolyte of liquid and powder combined to form a paste.

dry-clean (drī′klēn′) *v.t.* To clean (clothing, etc.) with solvents other than water, such as carbon tetrachloride. Also **dry′-cleanse′.** — **dry cleaner** — **dry cleaning**

dry distillation *Chem.* Destructive distillation.

dry-dock (drī′dok′) *v.t.* **1.** To put into dry dock. — *v.i.* **2.** To go into dry dock.

dry dock A floating or stationary structure from which water can be removed, used for repairing and cleaning ships.

dry·er (drī′ər) Alternative comparative of DRY. — *n.* A drier.

dry·est (drī′ist) Alternative superlative of DRY.

dry-eyed (drī′īd′) *adj.* Not weeping; tearless.
dry farming In an arid country, the raising of crops without irrigation, mainly by saving the moisture of the soil and by raising drought-resisting crops. **— dry farmer**
dry goods Textile fabrics, as distinguished from groceries, hardware, etc.
dry ice Solid carbon dioxide, having a temperature of about −110° F., and passing directly to the gaseous state, widely used as a refrigerant: also called *carbon dioxide snow*.
dry law *U.S.* A law banning the sale of alcoholic beverages.
dry·ly (drī′lē) *adv.* In a dry manner: also spelled *drily*.
dry measure A unit or system of units for measuring the volume of dry commodities, as fruits or grains. See table front of book.
dry·ness (drī′nis) *n.* The state or quality of being dry.
dry nurse A nurse who rears a child without suckling it.
dry point 1. A fine, hard etching needle used to incise fine lines on copperplate without the use of acid. 2. An engraving made by this method.
dry rot 1. A fungous disease of timber, causing it to crumble. 2. A disease of potato tubers and other vegetables.
dry run 1. *Mil.* A practice exercise in combat skills without using live ammunition. 2. Any rehearsal or trial run.
du·al (dōō′əl, dyōō′-) *adj.* 1. Denoting or relating to two. 2. Composed of two; twofold; double; binary. 3. *Gram.* In some languages, as Sanskrit and Greek, of or designating a word form that denotes two: distinguished from *singular*, *plural*. **—** *n.* *Gram.* The dual number, or a word form having this number. [< L *duo* two]
du·al·ism (dōō′əl-iz′əm, dyōō′-) *n.* 1. The state of being twofold; duality. 2. *Philos.* The theory that the universe is composed of two principles, as mind and matter. **— du′al·ist** *n.* **— du′al·is′tic** *adj.* **— du′al·is′ti·cal·ly** *adv.*
du·al·i·ty (dōō-al′ə-tē, dyōō-) *n.* *pl.* **·ties** The state, character, or quality of being two or composed of two.
dub[1] (dub) *v.t.* **dubbed, dub·bing** 1. To confer knighthood upon by tapping on the shoulder with a sword. 2. To name or style. 3. To smooth or rub, as timber. [OE *dubbian*]
dub[2] (dub) *U.S. Informal n.* A clumsy, blundering person. **—** *v.t.* **dubbed, dub·bing** To bungle. [? < DUB[1]]
dub[3] (dub) *v.t.* **dubbed, dub·bing** 1. To rerecord (a record, tape, etc.) in order to edit or add portions or to change volume, frequency, or tonal quality. 2. To insert a new sound track into (a film) [Short for DOUBLE]
du·bi·e·ty (dōō-bī′ə-tē, dyōō-) *n.* *pl.* **·ties** 1. The state of being dubious. 2. Something doubtful. Also **du·bi·os·i·ty** (dōō′bē-os′ə-tē, dyōō′-). [< LL < L *dubius* doubtful]
du·bi·ous (dōō′bē-əs, dyōō′-) *adj.* 1. Unsettled in judgment or opinion; doubtful. 2. Causing doubt; equivocal. 3. Not predictable; uncertain. 4. Open to criticism, objection, or suspicion: a *dubious* reputation. [< L *dubium* doubt] **— du′bi·ous·ly** *adv.* **— du′bi·ous·ness** *n.*
Du·bon·net (dōō′bə-nā′, *Fr.* dü-bô-ne′) *n.* 1. A fortified French wine used as an apéritif: a trade name. 2. A reddish purple, the color of red Dubonnet. Also **du′bon·net′**.
du·cal (dōō′kəl, dyōō′-) *adj.* Pertaining to a duke or a duchy. [< MF < LL < L *dux* leader] **— du′cal·ly** *adv.*
duc·at (duk′ət) *n.* 1. Any of several gold or silver coins, formerly current in Europe. 2. *Slang* A ticket, as to a show. [< MF < Ital. *ducato* a coin with a picture of a duke]
duch·ess (duch′is) *n.* 1. The wife or widow of a duke. 2. The female sovereign of a duchy [< OF < L *dux* leader]
duch·y (duch′ē) *n.* *pl.* **duch·ies** The territory of a duke or duchess; dukedom.
duck[1] (duk) *n.* 1. Any of various aquatic birds, with webbed feet and broad bills. 2. The female of this bird. The male is called a *drake*. 3. *Chiefly Brit. Informal* A dear; darling. 4. *U.S. Slang* A person; fellow. [OE *dūce* diver]
duck[2] (duk) *v.t* 1. To thrust suddenly under water. 2. To lower quickly; bob, as the head. 3. *Informal* To dodge; evade (a blow or punishment). 4. *Informal* To avoid (a duty, person, etc.) **—** *v.i.* 5. To submerge suddenly under water. 6. *Informal* To move quickly and abruptly, as in dodging. **—** *n.* The act of ducking; esp., a quick plunge under water. [ME *douken, duken* to dive, ult. < Gmc.]
duck[3] (duk) *n.* 1. A strong linen or cotton fabric similar to canvas. 2. *pl.* Trousers made of duck. [< Du. *doek* cloth]
duck·bill (duk′bil′) *n.* A platypus.
duck·ling (duk′ling) *n.* A young duck.
duck·pin (duk′pin′) *n.* 1. A small pin used in a variation of the game of tenpins. 2. *pl.* (*construed as sing.*) The game played with such pins.
duck·y (duk′ē) *adj.* **duck·i·er, duck·i·est** *Slang* Delightful.
duct (dukt) *n.* 1. Any tube, canal, or passage by which a liquid, gas, etc., is conveyed. 2. *Anat.* A tubular passage by which a secretion is carried away. 3. *Electr.* A tubular channel for carrying telegraph or telephone cables. [< L < *ducere* to lead]

duc·tile (duk′təl, -til) *adj.* 1. Capable of being hammered into thin layers, drawn out into wire, or otherwise subjected to stress without breaking, as certain metals. 2. Easily molded or shaped; plastic. 3. Ready to obey; easily led. [< F < L < *ducere* to lead] **— duc·til·i·ty** (duk-til′ə-tē) *n.*
duct·less gland (dukt′lis) *Physiol.* A gland that has no excretory duct but releases its secretions directly into the blood or lymph, as the thyroid gland, etc.
dud (dud) *n.* 1. *Mil.* A bomb or shell that fails to explode. 2. *Informal* One who or that which proves a failure. [< Du. *dood* dead]
dude (dōōd, dyōōd) *n.* *U.S.* 1. A man who dresses in a flashy or extremely fastidious manner; dandy; fop. 2. *U.S. Informal* A city person; esp., an Easterner vacationing on a ranch. [Origin unknown] **— dud′ish** *adj.*
dude ranch *U.S.* A ranch operated as a resort for tourists.
dudg·eon (duj′ən) *n.* Sullen displeasure; resentment: to leave in high *dudgeon*. [Origin unknown]
duds (dudz) *n.pl. Informal* 1. Clothing. 2. Belongings in general. [ME *dudde* cloak]
due (dōō, dyōō) *adj.* 1. Subject to demand for payment; esp., payable because of the arrival of a stipulated date. 2. That should be rendered or given; proper: the honor *due*. 3. Adequate; sufficient: *due* cause for alarm. 4. Appointed or expected to arrive, be present, or be ready: The bus is *due*. 5. That may be charged or attributed; ascribable: with *to*: The mistake was *due* to carelessness. **— due to** *Informal* Because of; on account of: widely used but still questioned by some. **—** *n.* 1. That which is owed or rightfully required; a debt. 2. *pl.* Charge or fee: club *dues*. **—** *adv.* Directly: *due* east. [< OF *deü*, pp. of *devoir* to owe < L *debere*]
du·el (dōō′əl, dyōō′-) *n.* 1. A prearranged combat between two persons, usu. fought with deadly weapons. 2. A struggle between two contending parties. **—** *v.t. & v.i.* **du·eled** or **·elled, du·el·ing** or **·el·ling** To fight, or fight with, in a duel. [< F < Ital. < L *duellum*, earliest form of *bellum* war] **— du′el·er** or **du′el·ler, du′el·ist** or **du′el·list** *n.*
du·en·na (dōō-en′ə, dyōō-) *n.* 1. In Spain and Portugal, an elderly woman who serves as a companion and protector to a young girl. 2. A chaperon. [< Sp. < L *domina* lady]
du·et (dōō-et′, dyōō-) *n.* A musical composition for two performers. [< Ital. < L *duo* two]
duff (duf) *n.* A thick flour pudding boiled in a cloth bag. [Var. of DOUGH]
duf·fel (duf′əl) *n.* 1. A coarse woolen fabric napped on both sides. 2. Equipment or supplies, esp. for camping. Also **duf′fle**. [after *Duffel*, a town near Antwerp]
duffel bag A sack, usu. of canvas or duck, used to carry clothing and personal possessions. Also **duffle bag**.
dug[1] (dug) Past tense and past participle of DIG.
dug[2] (dug) *n.* A teat or udder. [Cf. Dan. *dægge* to suckle]
du·gong (dōō′gong) *n.* A herbivorous marine mammal of warm seas, having flippers and a paddlelike tail: also called *sea cow*. [< Malay *duyong*]
dug·out (dug′out′) *n.* 1. A canoe made by hollowing out a log. 2. An excavated shelter or dwelling for protection against storms, bombs, etc. 3. In baseball, a structure set back from the diamond, in which team members sit when not at bat or in the field.
duke (dōōk, dyōōk) *n.* 1. In Great Britain and certain other European countries, a nobleman ranking immediately below a prince and above a marquis. 2. A European prince ruling over a duchy. [< F < L *dux* leader] **— duke′dom** *n.*
dul·cet (dul′sit) *adj.* Pleasing to the ear; melodious; also, soothing; pleasant. [< OF dim. of *douz*, sweet < L *dulcis*]
dul·ci·mer (dul′sə-mər) *n.* A stringed instrument played with two padded hammers or plucked with the fingers. [< OF, ? < LL < *dulcis* sweet + *melos* a song < Gk.]
dull (dul) *adj.* 1. Lacking in intelligence or understanding; stupid. 2. Wanting in perception or responsiveness: a *dull* audience. 3. Not brisk or active: Trade is *dull*. 4. Without spirit; listless. 5. Having a blunt edge or point. 6. Exciting little or no interest: a *dull* book. 7. Not acute or intense: a *dull* pain. 8. Cloudy; gloomy. 9. Not bright, clear, or vivid: a *dull* color. 10. Unclear in sound. **—** *v.t. & v.i.* To make or become dull. [ME *dul*] **— dull′ish** *adj.* **— dull′ness** or **dul′ness** *n.* **— dul′ly** *adv.*
dull·ard (dul′ərd) *n.* A stupid person; dolt.
dulse (duls) *n.* A reddish brown seaweed sometimes eaten as a vegetable. [< Irish *duileasg*]
du·ly (dōō′lē, dyōō′-) *adv.* 1. In due or proper manner; fitly. 2. At the proper time. 3. To an adequate degree.
dumb (dum) *adj.* 1. Having no power of speech; mute. 2. Temporarily speechless: *dumb* with grief. 3. Not inclined to speak; silent. 4. *U.S. Informal* Stupid; dull-witted. 5. Made or done without speech, as a pantomime. [OE] **— dumb′ly** *adv.* **— dumb′ness** *n.*
dumb·bell (dum′bel′) *n.* 1. A gymnastic hand instrument

used for exercising, consisting of a wood or metal handle with a weighted ball at each end. **2.** *U.S. Slang* A stupid person.

dumb·wait·er (dum′wā′tər) *n.* **1.** *U.S.* A small elevator for conveying food, dishes, garbage, etc., between floors. **2.** *Brit.* A movable serving stand placed near a dining table.

dum·dum bullet (dum′dum′) A small-arms bullet having a soft point or a jacket cut across at the point so that it will expand on impact and tear a gaping wound. [after *Dum-dum*, a town near Calcutta, India, where first made]

dum·found (dum′found′) *v.t.* To strike dumb; confuse; amaze. Also **dumb′found′.** [Blend of DUMB and CONFOUND]

dum·my (dum′ē) *n. pl.* **·mies 1.** A figure representing the human form, used for displaying clothing, for tackling in football practice, etc. **2.** An imitation object, as a false drawer. **3.** One who is dumb; a mute. **4.** *Slang* A stupid person. **5.** One who seems to be acting for his own interests while secretly representing another. **6.** *Printing* **a** A sample book or magazine, usually blank, used as a model of the final product. **b** A model page form for the printer, made up of proofs pasted into position. **7.** In certain card games, esp. bridge: **a** An exposed hand played in addition to his own by the person sitting opposite it. **b** The inactive player who has exposed such a hand. — *adj.* **1.** Sham; counterfeit. **2.** Silent; mute. **3.** Ostensibly acting for oneself, but actually for another. **4.** Played with a dummy, as in card games.

dump (dump) *v.t.* **1.** To drop or throw down heavily or abruptly. **2.** To empty out, as from a container. **3.** To empty (a container), as by overturning. **4.** To throw away, as rubbish. **5.** To put up (goods) for sale cheaply and in large quantities, esp. in a foreign market. — *v.i.* **6.** To fall or drop suddenly. **7.** To unload. **8.** To offer large quantities of goods for sale at low prices. — *n.* **1.** A dumping area, as for rubbish. **2.** That which is dumped. **3.** *Mil.* A temporary storage place for ammunition and supplies. **4.** *U.S. Slang* A shabby, poorly kept place. [ME < Scand.]

dump·ling (dump′ling) *n.* **1.** A ball of biscuit dough filled with fruit and baked or steamed. **2.** A small mass of dough dropped into boiling soup or stew.

dumps (dumps) *n.pl.* A gloomy state of mind: now only in the phrase **in the dumps.** [Cf. MDu. *domp* haze]

dump truck A truck for hauling gravel, coal, etc., that unloads by tilting back the cargo bin and opening the tailboard.

dump·y¹ (dump′ē) *adj.* **dump·i·er, dump·i·est** Sullen or discontented; sulky. [See DUMPS]

dump·y² (dump′ē) *adj.* **dump·i·er, dump·i·est** Short and thick; squat. — **dump′i·ly** *adv.* — **dump′i·ness** *n.*

dun¹ (dun) *v.t. & v.i.* **dunned, dun·ning** To press (a debtor) for payment; importune; pester. — *n.* **1.** One who duns. **2.** A repeated demand for payment. [Prob. var. of DIN.]

dun² (dun) *adj.* Of a grayish brown or reddish brown color. — *n.* **1.** Dun color. **2.** A dun-colored horse. — *v.t.* **dunned, dun·ning** To make dun-colored. [OE *dunn*]

dunce (duns) *n.* A stupid or ignorant person. [Earlier *Dunsman*, a follower of John *Duns* Scotus]

dunce cap A conical cap, formerly placed on the head of a dull student. Also **dunce's cap.**

dun·der·head (dun′dər·hed′) *n.* A blockhead; dunce. Also **dun′der·pate′** (-pāt′). [? < dial. E (Scottish) *dunder* thunder, noise + HEAD] — **dun′der·head′ed** *adj.*

dune (dōōn, dyōōn) *n.* A hill of loose sand heaped up by the wind. [< F < MDu.]

dung (dung) *n.* **1.** Animal excrement; manure. **2.** Anything foul. — *v.t.* To cover with or as with dung. [OE]

dun·ga·ree (dung′gə·rē′) *n.* **1.** A coarse cotton cloth used for work clothes, tents, sails, etc. **2.** *pl.* Trousers or overalls made of this fabric. [< Hind. *dungrī*]

dung beetle Any of various beetles that breed in dung.

dun·geon (dun′jən) *n.* **1.** A dark confining prison or cell, esp. one underground. **2.** A donjon. [< DONJON]

dung·hill (dung′hil′) *n.* **1.** A heap of manure. **2.** A vile thing, abode, or condition.

dunk (dungk) *v.t. & v.i.* To dip (bread, doughnuts, etc.) into tea, coffee, soup, etc. [< G *tunken* to dip] — **dunk′er** *n.*

dun·lin (dun′lin) *n.* A sandpiper having in summer plumage a black belly and a reddish back. [< DUN² + -LING¹]

dun·nage (dun′ij) *n.* **1.** *Naut.* Mats and battens used to protect cargo. **2.** Baggage.

du·o (dōō′ō, dyōō′ō) *n. pl.* **du·os** or **du·i** (-ē) *Music* An instrumental duet. [< Ital. < L *duo* two]

duo- *combining form* Two. [< L *duo* two]

du·o·dec·i·mal (dōō′ō·des′ə·məl, dyōō′-) *adj.* **1.** Pertaining to twelfth or twelfths. **2.** Reckoning by twelves. — *n.* **1.** One of the numbers used in duodecimal arithmetic; a twelfth. **2.** *pl.* A method of computing by twelves instead of by tens. [< L *duodecim* twelve]

du·o·dec·i·mo (dōō′ō·des′ə·mō, dyōō′-) *adj.* **1.** Having twelve pages to one sheet of printing paper. **2.** Measuring about 5 x 7¾ inches in size: said of a page or book. — *n. pl.* **·mos** The size of a page folded twelve to a sheet; also, a page or book of this size. Also **twelvemo.** Also written **12 mo., 12°.**

du·o·de·num (dōō′ō·dē′nəm, dyōō′-; dōō·od′ə·nəm) *n. pl.*

·na (-nə) *Anat.* The part of the small intestine extending from the stomach to the jejunum. For illus. see INTESTINE. [< Med.L *duodenum* (*digitorum*) of twelve (fingers); with ref. to its length] — **du/o·de′nal** *adj.*

du·o·logue (dōō′ə·lôg, -log, dyōō′-) *n.* **1.** A dramatic piece for two performers. **2.** A dialogue. Also **du′o·log.**

dupe (dōōp, dyōōp) *n.* One who is easily deceived or misled. — *v.t.* **duped, dup·ing** To make a dupe of; deceive. [< OF *huppe* hoopoe < L *upupa*] — **dup′er** *n.* — **dup′er·y** *n.*

du·ple (dōō′pəl, dyōō′-) *adj.* Double. [< L *duplus* double]

du·plex (dōō′pleks, dyōō′-) *adj.* **1.** Having two parts; twofold. **2.** *Mech.* Having two similar parts operating independently or in conjunction within one framework. **3.** *Telecom.* Pertaining to or allowing the transmission of two messages simultaneously over a single wire and in opposite directions. — *n.* A duplex apartment or house. [< L < *duo* two + stem of *plicare* to fold] — **du·plex′i·ty** *n.*

duplex apartment 1. *U.S.* An apartment having rooms on two floors. **2.** *Canadian* A two-story building having an apartment on each floor.

duplex house *U.S. & Canadian* A house having two one-family units.

du·pli·cate (*adj., n.* dōō′plə·kit, dyōō′-; *v.* dōō′plə·kāt, dyōō′-) *adj.* **1.** Made like or corresponding exactly to an original: a *duplicate* key. **2.** Growing or existing in pairs. **3.** In card-playing, replayed by other players with the same hands as originally dealt. — *n.* **1.** An exact copy. **2.** A double or counterpart. **3.** A duplicate game of cards. — *v.t.* **·cat·ed, ·cat·ing 1.** To copy exactly; reproduce. **2.** To double. **3.** To do a second time. [< L < *duplex* twofold] — **du′pli·cate·ly** *adv.* — **du/pli·ca′tion** *n.* — **du/pli·ca′tive** *adj.*

du·pli·ca·tor (dōō′plə·kā′tər, dyōō′-) *n.* A mechanical device for making duplicates.

du·plic·i·ty (dōō·plis′ə·tē, dyōō-) *n. pl.* **·ties** Tricky deceitfulness; double-dealing. [< OF < LL < L *duplex* twofold]

du·ra (dōōr′ə) See DURRA.

du·ra·ble (dōōr′ə·bəl, dyōōr′-) *adj.* **1.** Able to withstand decay or wear. **2.** Not easily changed or upset. [< OF < L *durus* hard] — **du/ra·bil′i·ty, du′ra·ble·ness** *n.*

Du·ral·u·min (dōō·ral′yə·min, dyōō-) *n.* A light, strong alloy of aluminum and copper, with addition of magnesium and manganese: a trade name. Also **du/ra·l′u·min.**

du·ra ma·ter (dōōr′ə mā′tər, dyōōr′ə) *Anat.* The tough fibrous membrane forming the outermost of the three coverings of the brain and spinal cord. Also **du′ra.** [< Med.L < L *dura* hard + *mater* mother] — **du/ral** *adj.*

du·ra·men (dōō·rā′min, dyōō-) *n. Bot.* The heartwood, or darker central portion, of an exogenous stem or tree trunk. [< L, a ligneous vine branch]

dur·ance (dōōr′əns, dyōōr′-) *n.* Forced confinement or imprisonment. [< OF < L *durare* to endure]

du·ra·tion (dōō·rā′shən, dyōō-) *n.* **1.** The period of time during which anything lasts. **2.** Continuance in time. [< LL < L *durare* to endure, last]

du·ress (dōō·res′, dyōō-; dōōr′is, dyōōr′-) *n.* **1.** Constraint by force or fear; compulsion. **2.** *Law* **a** Coercion to do or say something against one's will or judgment. **b** Imprisonment without full legal sanction. [< OF < L *durus* hard]

dur·ing (dōōr′ing, dyōōr′-) *prep.* **1.** Throughout the time, existence, or action of. **2.** In the course of; at some period in. [ME. Orig. ppr. of *duren* to endure]

dur·ra (dōōr′ə) *n.* A variety of sorghum of southern Asia and northern Africa: also spelled *doura, dura.* Also **durr** (dōōr). [< Arabic *dhura*]

du·rum (dōōr′əm, dyōōr′-) *n.* A species of wheat widely grown for macaroni products. [< L *durus* hard]

dusk (dusk) *n.* **1.** The partial darkness between day and night, usu. considered darker than twilight. **2.** Any degree of light or dark resembling this. — *adj.* Somewhat dark or dim; shadowy. — *v.t. & v.i.* To make grow, or appear shadowy or dim; darken. [OE *dox*] — **dusk′ish** *adj.*

dusk·y (dus′kē) *adj.* **dusk·i·er, dusk·i·est 1.** Somewhat dark; dim; obscure. **2.** Rather dark in shade or coloring; swarthy. **3.** Gloomy. — **dusk′i·ly** *adv.* — **dusk′i·ness** *n.*

dust (dust) **1.** Earthy matter reduced to particles so fine as to be easily borne in the air. **2.** Any substance reduced to fine powder. **3.** A cloud of powdered earth or other fine particles. **4.** Confusion; turmoil. **5.** Earth, esp. as the receptacle of the dead. **6.** The disintegrated remains of a human body. **7.** A low or despised condition. **8.** Something worthless. **9.** *Brit.* Sweepings, ashes, or other refuse. **10.** Pollen. **11.** Gold dust. **12.** *Slang* Money. — **to bite the dust** To be killed or injured. — **to lick the dust 1.** To be defeated; grovel. **2.** To be killed or wounded. — **to throw dust in someone's eyes** To deceive. — *v.t.* **1.** To wipe or brush dust from. **2.** To sprinkle with powder, insecticide, etc. **3.** To sprinkle (powder, etc.) over something. **4.** To soil with dust. — *v.i.* **5.** To wipe or brush dust from furniture, etc. **6.** To cover oneself with dust, as a bird. **7.** To become dusty. [OE *dūst*] — **dust′less** *adj.*

dust bowl An area subject to dust storms and drought. —

the Dust Bowl A region in the south central U.S. where the topsoil was blown away by dust storms during 1934–37.
dust·er (dus/tər) *n.* **1.** One who or that which dusts. **2.** A cloth or brush for removing dust. **3.** A device for sprinkling a powder, insecticide, etc., over something. **4.** An outer garment worn to protect clothing from dust.
dust jacket A removable paper cover that protects the binding of a book: also called *book jacket*. Also **dust cover.**
dust·pan (dust/pan/) *n.* An implement resembling a short-handled shovel into which dust from a floor is swept.
dust storm A windstorm of arid regions that carries clouds of dust with it.
dust·y (dus/tē) *adj.* **dust·i·er, dust·i·est** **1.** Covered with or as with dust. **2.** Like dust; powdery. **3.** Of the color of dust. **4.** Having a grayish or dull cast: *dusty* pink. — **dust/·i·ly** *adv.* — **dust/i·ness** *n.*
Dutch (duch) *adj.* **1.** Of or relating to the Netherlands, its people, culture, or language. **2.** Loosely, German. — *n.* **1.** The people of the Netherlands: preceded by *the.* **2.** Loosely, the German people: preceded by *the.* **3.** The language of the Netherlands. **4.** Pennsylvania Dutch. — **in Dutch** *U.S. Informal* In trouble or disgrace. — **to beat the Dutch** *U.S. Informal* To be most unusual or surprising. — **to go Dutch** *U.S. Informal* To have each participant in a meal or entertainment pay his own expenses. [< MDu. *dutsch* Germanic]
Dutch door A door divided horizontally in the middle, allowing either half to open individually.
Dutch·man (duch/mən) *n. pl.* **·men** (-mən) **1.** A native of the Netherlands. **2.** Loosely, a German. **3.** A Dutch ship.
dutch·man's-breech·es (duch/mənz·brich/iz) *n. sing. & pl.* A low herb with widely spreading spurs. Also **dutch/mans·breech/es.**
Dutch oven **1.** A cast-iron kettle with a tight-fitting cover, used for meats, stews, etc. **2.** A metal box with an open side, set before a fire for cooking.
Dutch treat *U.S. Informal* An entertainment or meal at which each person pays his own bill.
Dutch uncle A very frank and severe critic or adviser.
du·te·ous (dōō/tē·əs, dyōō/-) *adj.* Obedient; dutiful. — **du/te·ous·ly** *adv.* — **du/te·ous·ness** *n.*
du·ti·ful (dōō/ti·fəl, dyōō/-) *adj.* **1.** Performing one's duties; obedient. **2.** Expressive of a sense of duty; respectful: *dutiful* attentions. — **du/ti·ful·ly** *adv.* — **du/ti·ful·ness** *n.*
du·ty (dōō/tē, dyōō/-) *n. pl.* **·ties** **1.** That which one is morally or legally bound to do; obligation. **2.** The impelling or controlling force of such obligations: *Duty* calls. **3.** Action or conduct required by one's profession or position. **4.** Specific obligatory service, esp. of military personnel. **5.** A tax on imported or exported goods. — **off duty** Temporarily not at work. [< AF *dû.* See DUE.]
du·ve·tyn (dōō/və·tēn, dyōō/və·tēn/) *n.* Twill-weave fabric with a napped surface, made of wool, rayon, cotton, or silk. Also **du/ve·tine, du/ve·tyne.** [< F *duvet* down]
dwarf (dwôrf) *n.* A human being, animal, or plant that is stunted in its growth and often has abnormal physical proportions. — *v.t.* **1.** To prevent the natural development of; stunt. **2.** To cause to appear small or less by comparison. — *v.i.* **3.** To become stunted; grow smaller. — *adj.* Diminutive; stunted. [OE *dweorh*] — **dwarf/ish** *adj.* — **dwarf/ish·ly** *adv.* — **dwarf/ish·ness** *n.*
dwarf chestnut The chinquapin.
dwell (dwel) *v.i.* **dwelt** or **dwelled, dwell·ing** **1.** To have a fixed abode; reside. **2.** To linger, as on a subject: with *on* or *upon.* **3.** To continue in a state or place. — **Syn.** See LIVE. [OE *dwellan* to go astray] — **dwell/er** *n.*
dwell·ing (dwel/ing) *n.* A place of residence; abode; house.
dwin·dle (dwin/dəl) *v.t. & v.i.* **·dled, ·dling** To diminish or become less; make or become smaller. — **Syn.** See DECREASE. [OE *dwīnan* to waste away]

dye (dī) *v.* **dyed, dye·ing** *v.t.* **1.** To fix a color in (cloth, hair, etc.), esp. by soaking in liquid coloring matter. — *v.i.* **2.** To take or give color: This cloth *dyes* badly. — *n.* A coloring matter used for dyeing; also, the color so produced. [OE *dēagian* to dye < *dēag* dye] — **dy/er** *n.*
dyed-in-the-wool (dīd/in·tha·wōōl/) *adj.* **1.** Dyed before being woven. **2.** Thoroughgoing; complete.
dye·ing (dī/ing) *n.* The act of fixing colors in cloth, etc.
dye-stuff (dī/stuff/) *n.* Any material used for dyeing.
dy·ing (dī/ing) *adj.* **1.** Near death; expiring. **2.** Coming to a close; destined to end: a *dying* civilization. **3.** Given, uttered, or manifested just before death. — *n.* Death.
dyke (dīk) See DIKE.
dyna- *combining form* Power. Also, before vowels, **dyn-.** [< Gk. *dynamis* power]
dy·nam·ic (dī·nam/ik) *adj.* **1.** Of or pertaining to forces not in equilibrium, or to motion as the result of force: opposed to *static.* **2.** Pertaining to dynamics. **3.** Characterized by energy or forcefulness: a *dynamic* personality. [< Gk. *dynamis* power] — **dy·nam/i·cal·ly** *adv.*
dy·nam·ics (dī·nam/iks) *n.pl.* (*construed as sing. in defs. 1 and 2*) **1.** The branch of physics that treats of the motion of bodies and the effects of forces in producing motion, including kinetics. **2.** *Music* **a** The group of words, and symbols, etc., used to indicate degrees of loudness; also **dynamic marks. b** The act of producing varying degrees of loudness.
dy·na·mite (dī/nə·mīt) *n.* **1.** An explosive composed of nitroglycerin held in some absorbent substance. **2.** *Slang* Anything wonderful or spectacular: The news was *dynamite!* — *v.t.* **·mit·ed, ·mit·ing** To blow up or shatter with or as with dynamite. [< Gk. *dynamis* power] — **dy/na·mit/er** *n.*
dy·na·mo (dī/nə·mō) *n. pl.* **·mos** A generator for the conversion of mechanical energy into electrical energy.
dynamo- *combining form* Force; power. [< Gk. *dynamis* power]
dy·na·mo·e·lec·tric (dī/nə·mō·i·lek/trik) *adj.* Pertaining to the conversion of mechanical energy into electrical energy, or the reverse. Also **dy/na·mo·e·lec/tri·cal.**
dy·na·mom·e·ter (dī/nə·mom/ə·tər) *n.* An instrument for measuring force or power. — **dy·na·mo·met·ric** (dī/nə·mō·met/rik) or **·ri·cal** *adj.* — **dy/na·mom/e·try** *n.*
dy·na·mo·tor (dī/nə·mō/tər) *n.* A dynamoelectric machine having one field magnet, one armature core, and two armature windings, each being insulated from the other.
dy·nast (dī/nast, -nəst; *Brit.* din/əst) *n.* A ruler, esp. a hereditary one. [< L < Gk. < *dynasthai* to be powerful]
dy·nas·ty (dī/nəs·tē, *Brit.* din/əs·tē) *n. pl.* **·ties** A succession of sovereigns in one line of descent; also, the length of time during which one family is in power. — **dy·nas·tic** (dī·nas/tik, di-) or **·ti·cal** *adj.* — **dy·nas/ti·cal·ly** *adv.*
dyne (dīn) *n. Physics* The fundamental unit of force in the cgs system that, if applied to a mass of one gram, would give it an acceleration of one centimeter per second per second. Abbr. *d., D.* [< F < Gk. *dynamis* power]
dys·en·ter·y (dis/ən·ter/ē) *n. Pathol.* A painful inflammation of the large intestine, attended with bloody evacuations and some fever. [< OF < L < Gk. < *dys-* bad + *enteron* intestine] — **dys/en·ter/ic** or **·i·cal** *adj.*
dys·pep·sia (dis·pep/shə, -sē·ə) *n.* Difficult or painful digestion. [< L < Gk. < *dys-* hard + *peptein* to cook, digest]
dys·pep·tic (dis·pep/tik) *adj.* **1.** Relating to or suffering from dyspepsia. **2.** Gloomy; peevish. Also **dys·pep/ti·cal.** — *n.* A dyspeptic person. — **dys·pep/ti·cal·ly** *adv.*
dysp·ne·a (disp·nē/ə) *n. Pathol.* Labored breathing. Also **dysp·noe/a.** [< NL < L < Gk. < *dys-* hard + *pneein* to breathe] — **dysp·ne/al** or **dysp·ne/ic** *adj.*
dys·pro·si·um (dis·prō/sē·əm, -shē-) *n.* A highly magnetic element (symbol Dy) of the lanthanide series. See ELEMENT. [< NL < Gk. < *dys-* hard + *prosienai* to approach]

E

e, E (ē) *n. pl.* **e's, E's** or **es, Es, ees** (ēz) **1.** The fifth letter of the English alphabet. **2.** Any sound represented by the letter *e.* — *symbol* **1.** *Music* **a** The third tone in the natural scale of C, *mi.* **b** A written note representing it. **c** The scale built upon E. **2.** *Math.* The limit of the expression $(1 + 1/n)^n$, as *n* increases without limit: 2.7182818284+: the base to which Napierian logarithms are calculated: written *e.*
e- Reduced var. of EX-.

each (ēch) *adj.* Being one of two or more individuals that together form an aggregate; every. — *pron.* Every one of any number or group considered individually; each one. ◆ The pronoun *each* is usu. treated as a singular, as *Each* did *his* own work. — *adv.* For or to each person, article, etc.; apiece: one dollar *each.* [OE *ǣlc* < *ā* ever + *gelīc* alike]

each other A compound reciprocal pronoun used in oblique cases: They saw *each other.* The possessive is *each other's.*

ea·ger (ē'gər) *adj.* Impatiently desirous of something. [< OF < L *acer* sharp] — **ea'ger·ly** *adv.* — **ea'ger·ness** *n.*

ea·gle (ē'gəl) *n.* **1.** A large bird of prey related to the falcon, esp. the **bald** (or **American**) **eagle,** dark brown, with the head, neck, and tail white, the national emblem of the United States; and the **imperial eagle** of Europe. ◆ Collateral adjective: *aquiline.* **2.** Any national seal or standard that bears an eagle as symbol. **3.** A former gold coin of the U.S. having a value of $10. **4.** In golf, a score of two under par on any hole. [< OF *egle, aigle,* < L *aquila*]

ea·gle-eyed (ē'gəl-īd') *adj.* Having keen sight.

ea·glet (ē'glit) *n.* A young eagle.

ear[1] (ir) *n.* **1.** The organ of hearing in its entirety. ◆ Collateral adjective: *aural.* **2.** The fleshy or cartilaginous external part of the organ of hearing. **3.** The sense of hearing. **4.** The ability to perceive the refinements of music, poetry, or the like. **5.** Attentive consideration; heed. **6.** Something resembling the external ear in shape or position, as a projecting piece on a vase. — **to be all ears** To be eagerly attentive. — **to be up to the ears** To be submerged in work, problems, etc. — **to have an ear to the ground** To listen to or heed current public opinion. — **to lend an ear** To pay attention. [OE *ēare*] — **ear'less** *adj.*

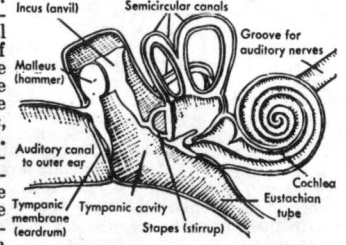

HUMAN EAR, FRONTAL SECTION
(Anatomical nomenclature)

(labels: Incus (anvil); Semicircular canals; Groove for auditory nerves; Malleus (hammer); Auditory canal to outer ear; Cochlea; Eustachian tube; Tympanic membrane (eardrum); Tympanic cavity; Stapes (stirrup))

ear[2] (ir) *n.* The fruit-bearing part of a cereal plant; the head. — **in** (or **on**) **the ear** On the cob, as corn; unhusked, as grain. — *v.i.* To form ears, as grain. [OE *ēar*]

ear·ache (ir'āk') *n.* Pain in the middle or internal ear.

ear·drum (ir'drum') *n.* The tympanic membrane.

eared (ird) *adj.* Having ears or earlike appendages.

earl (ûrl) *n.* A member of the British nobility next in rank above a viscount and below a marquis. [OE *eorl* nobleman] — **earl'dom** *n.*

ear·lap (ir'lap') *n.* **1.** One of two flaps attached to a cap for protecting the ears from the cold. **2.** The ear lobes.

ear lobe The fleshy lower part of the external ear.

car·ly (ûr'lē) *adj.* ·li·er, ·li·est **1.** Coming near the beginning of any specified period of time or of any series of related things: an *early* Shaw play. **2.** Belonging to a distant time or stage of development. **3.** Occurring ahead of the usual or arranged time: an *early* dinner. **4.** Occurring in the near future: An *early* truce is expected. — *adv.* **1.** Near the beginning of any specified period or series of things. **2.** Far back in time. **3.** Before the usual or arranged time. [OE *lice* < *ǣr* before + *-līce* -ly] — **ear'li·ness** *n.*

ear·mark (ir'märk') *n.* **1.** A distinctive mark made on an animal's ear to denote ownership. **2.** Any mark of identification. — *v.t.* **1.** To put an earmark on. **2.** To set aside, as money, for a particular purpose.

earn (ûrn) *v.t.* **1.** To receive or deserve as recompense for labor, service, or performance. **2.** To acquire as a consequence. **3.** To produce as profit. [OE *earnian*]

ear·nest[1] (ûr'nist) *adj.* **1.** Intent and direct in purpose; zealous: an *earnest* student. **2.** Of a serious or important nature. — **in earnest** With serious intent or determination. [OE *eornoste*] — **ear'nest·ly** *adv.* — **ear'nest·ness** *n.*

ear·nest[2] (ûr'nist) *n.* **1.** *Law* Money paid in advance to bind a contract. Also **earnest money.** **2.** An assurance or token of something to come. [Prob. < OF *erres* < L *arra, arrhabo* < Gk. *arrhabōn* < Hebrew *'ērābōn* pledge]

earn·ings (ûr'ningz) *n.pl.* Wages or profits.

ear·phone (ir'fōn') *n.* A radio or telephone device held at or inserted into the ear; also, a similar part of a hearing aid.

ear·ring (ir'ring') *n.* An ornament worn at the ear lobe.

ear·shot (ir'shot') *n.* The distance at which sounds may be heard.

earth (ûrth) *n.* **1.** The dry land surface of the globe, as distinguished from the oceans and sky; ground. **2.** Soil; dirt. **3.** The planet on which man dwells; also, the people who inhabit it. **4.** The abode of mortal man, as opposed to heaven and hell. **5.** Worldly or temporal affairs. **6.** The mortal body. **7.** The hole or lair of a burrowing animal. — **down to earth** Realistic; practical; unaffected. — **to run to earth**

To hunt down and find, as a fox. — *v.t.* **1.** To heap up (plants, etc.) with soil for protection. **2.** To chase into hiding. — *v.i.* **3.** To burrow in the earth. [OE *eorthe*]

Earth (ûrth) *n.* The planet fifth in order of size, having an area of about 196 million square miles and a mass of 6.57 sextillion tons (6.57 × 10²¹). See PLANET. Abbr. *E.*

earth·bound (ûrth'bound') *adj.* **1.** Having only material interests. **2.** Confined to the earth. Also **earth'bound'.**

earth·en (ûr'thən) *adj.* Made of earth or baked clay.

earth·en·ware (ûr'thən-wâr') *n.* Dishes, pots, and the like, made of a coarse grade of baked clay.

earth·ly (ûrth'lē) *adj.* **1.** Of or relating to the earth and its material qualities; worldly; secular. **2.** Possible; imaginable: of no *earthly* use. — **earth'li·ness** *n.*

earth·quake (ûrth'kwāk') *n.* A shaking of the earth's crust, caused by the splitting of a mass of rock or by volcanic disturbances. ◆ Collateral adjective: *seismic.*

earth·ward (ûrth'wərd) *adv.* Toward the earth. Also **earth'wards.** — *adj.* Moving toward the earth.

earth·work (ûrth'wûrk') *n.* *Mil.* A fortification made largely or wholly of earth.

earth·worm (ûrth'wûrm') *n.* Any burrowing worm.

earth·y (ûr'thē) *adj.* **earth·i·er, earth·i·est** **1.** Of or like earth. **2.** Unrefined; coarse. **3.** Natural; robust; lusty. — **earth'i·ness** *n.*

ear·wax (ir'waks') *n.* A substance secreted by glands lining the passages of the external ear: also called *cerumen.*

ear·wig (ir'wig') *n.* **1.** An insect with horny forewings and a tail pair of forceps, erroneously believed to enter the human ear. **2.** *U.S.* A small centipede. — *v.t.* ·**wigged,** ·**wigging** To insinuate against in secret. [OE *ēarwicga*]

ease (ēz) *n.* **1.** Freedom from physical discomfort or mental agitation. **2.** Freedom from great effort or difficulty. **3.** Naturalness; poise. — *v.* **eased, eas·ing** *v.t.* **1.** To relieve the mental or physical pain or oppression of; comfort. **2.** To make less painful or oppressive; alleviate. **3.** To lessen the pressure, weight, tension, etc., of: to *ease* an axle. **4.** To make easier; facilitate. **5.** To move, lower, or put in place slowly and carefully. — *v.i.* **6.** To lessen in severity, tension, speed, etc.: often with *up* or *off.* [< OF < L *adjacens, -entis* close at hand] — **ease'ful** *adj.* — **eas'er** *n.*

ea·sel (ē'zəl) *n.* A folding frame or tripod used to support an artist's canvas, etc. [< Du. *ezel* easel, orig. an ass]

ease·ment (ēz'mənt) *n.* **1.** Anything that gives ease or comfort. **2.** *Law* The right to use another's property.

eas·i·ly (ē'zə·lē) *adv.* **1.** In an easy manner. **2.** Beyond question. **3.** Very possibly.

eas·i·ness (ē'zi·nis) *n.* The state of being at ease, or of being easy to do.

east (ēst) *n.* **1.** The direction of the sun in relation to an observer on earth at sunrise. **2.** One of the four cardinal points of the compass, directly opposite *west* and 90° clockwise from *north.* See COMPASS CARD. **3.** Any direction near this point. **4.** *Sometimes cap.* Any region east of a specified point. — **the East** Asia and its adjacent islands; the Orient. — *adj.* **1.** To, toward, facing, or in the east. **2.** Coming from the east. — *adv.* In or toward the east. [OE *ēast*]

east·bound (ēst'bound') *adj.* Going eastward. Also **east'bound'.**

East·er (ēs'tər) *n.* **1.** A Christian festival commemorating the resurrection of Christ. **2.** The day on which this festival is celebrated, the Sunday immediately after the first full moon that occurs on or after March 21: also **Easter Sunday.** [OE *Eastre* goddess of spring]

east·er·ly (ēs'tər·lē) *adj.* **1.** In, of, toward, or pertaining to the east. **2.** From the east, as a wind. — *adv.* Toward or from the east. — *n., pl.* ·**lies** A wind or storm from the east.

east·ern (ēs'tərn) *adj.* **1.** To, toward, or in the east. **2.** Native to or inhabiting the east: an *eastern* species. **3.** *Sometimes cap.* Of, or like the east or the East.

Eastern Church The church of the Byzantine Empire, including the patriarchates of Constantinople, Alexandria, Antioch, and Jerusalem, that separated from the Western Church in 1054: also called *Greek Church.* **2.** The Eastern Orthodox Church. **3.** The Uniat Church.

east·ern·er (ēs'tərn·ər) *n. Often cap.* One who is native to or lives in the east, esp. the eastern U.S.

Eastern Orthodox Church The modern churches derived from the medieval Eastern Church, including the Greek and Russian Orthodox churches, that agree in faith and order with the patriarch of Constantinople: also called *Eastern Church, Orthodox Church,* or loosely *Greek Church.*

Eastern Roman Empire The Byzantine Empire.

East·er·tide (ēs'tər·tīd') *n.* The season of Easter, a period extending in various churches from Easter to Ascension Day, Whitsunday, or Trinity Sunday.

east·ward (ēst'wərd) *adv.* Toward the east. Also **east'wards.** — *adj.* To, toward, facing, or in the east. — *n.* An eastward direction or point; also, an eastern part or region.

east·ward·ly (ēst'wərd·lē) *adj. & adv.* **1.** Toward the east. **2.** Coming from the east, as a wind.

eas·y (ē′zē) *adj.* **eas·i·er, eas·i·est** **1.** Requiring little work or effort; offering few difficulties: an *easy* task. **2.** Free from discomfort, trouble, or anxiety: an *easy* mind. **3.** Characterized by rest or comfort: an *easy* life. **4.** Not stiff or formal; relaxed: an *easy* manner. **5.** Not strict; lenient; indulgent. **6.** Yielding; credulous: an *easy* victim. **7.** Complacent; easygoing. **8.** Unhurried; gentle: an *easy* trot. **9.** Not burdensome; moderate: to buy on *easy* terms. **10.** Well-to-do; affluent: in *easy* circumstances. **11.** *Econ.* In little demand: said of a commodity. **— to be on easy street** *Informal* To be well-to-do; live in comfort. **—** *adv. Informal* In an easy manner; easily. **— to go easy on** *Slang* **1.** To use with moderation, as liquor. **2.** To be lenient with. **3.** To be tactful about. **— to take it easy** *Informal* **1.** To relax. **2.** To remain calm. [< OF *aiser* to put at ease]

eas·y-go·ing (ē′zē-gō′ing) *adj.* **1.** Not inclined to effort or worry. **2.** Moving at an easy pace, as a horse.

eat (ēt) *v.* **ate** (āt, *Brit.* et) or *Archaic* **eat** (et, ēt), **eat·en, eat·ing** *v.t.* **1.** To take in through the mouth as nourishment; esp., to chew and swallow. **2.** To consume or destroy by or as by eating: usu. with *away* or *up*. **3.** To wear away; waste. **4.** To make (a hole, etc.) by gnawing or corroding. **—** *v.i.* **5.** To take food; have a meal. **— to eat one's words** To retract what one has said. [OE *etan*] **— eat′·a·ble** *adj. & n.* **— eat′er** *n.*

eau de Co·logne (ō′ də kə·lōn′) Cologne, a toilet water.

eaves (ēvz) *n.* (*orig. sing., now construed as pl.*) The lower projecting edge of a sloping roof. [OE *efes* edge]

eaves·drop (ēvz′drop′) *v.i.* **·dropped, ·drop·ping** To listen secretly, as to a private conversation. **—** *n.* Water that drops from the eaves. **— eaves′drop′per** *n.*

ebb (eb) *v.i.* **1.** To recede, as the tide: opposed to *flow.* **2.** To decline or weaken; fail. **—** *n.* **1.** The flowing back of tidewater to the ocean: opposed to *flood.* Also **ebb tide.** **2.** A condition or period of decline or decay. [OE *ebbian*]

eb·on·ite (eb′ən·īt) *n.* Vulcanite, a rubber product.

eb·on·y (eb′ən·ē) *n. pl.* **·ies** **1.** A hard, heavy wood, usu. black, used for cabinetwork, etc., furnished by various species of tropical hardwood trees. **2.** Any tree yielding this wood. **—** *adj.* **1.** Made of ebony. **2.** Like ebony; black. [< L < Gk. < Egyptian *hebni*]

e·bul·lient (i·bul′yənt) *adj.* **1.** Full of enthusiasm; exuberant. **2.** Boiling or bubbling up. [< L < *e-* out + *bullire* to boil] **— e·bul′lient·ly** *adv.* **— e·bul′lience, e·bul′lien·cy** *n.*

eb·ul·li·tion (eb′ə·lish′ən) *n.* **1.** The bubbling of a liquid; boiling. **2.** Any sudden or violent agitation, as of emotions.

ec- Var. or **EX-**[2].

ec·cen·tric (ek·sen′trik) *adj.* **1.** Differing conspicuously in behavior, appearance, or opinions. **2.** Not situated in the center, as an axis. **3.** Deviating from a perfect circle: said chiefly of an elliptical orbit. **4.** *Math.* Not having the same center: opposed to *concentric.* **—** *n.* An odd or erratic individual. [< LL < Gk. < *ek-* out, away + *kentron* center] **— ec·cen′tri·cal·ly** *adv.*

ec·cen·tric·i·ty (ek′sen·tris′ə·tē) *n. pl.* **·ties** **1.** Deviation from what is regular or expected; irregularity. **2.** A peculiarity. **3.** The quality or degree of being eccentric.

Ec·cle·si·as·tes (i·klē′zē·as′tēz) *n.* A book of the Old Testament: also, *Hebrew, Koheleth.* [< Gk. *ekklēsiastēs,* trans. of Hebrew *qōheleth* preacher]

ec·cle·si·as·tic (i·klē′zē·as′tik) *adj.* Ecclesiastical. **—** *n.* One officially in the service of the church; a cleric; churchman. [< Gk. < *ek-* out + *kaleein* to call]

ec·cle·si·as·ti·cal (i·klē′zē·as′ti·kəl) *adj.* Of or pertaining to the church, especially as an organized and governing power. **— ec·cle′si·as′ti·cal·ly** *adv.*

Ec·cle·si·as·ti·cus (i·klē′zē·as′ti·kəs) *n.* One of the didactic books of the Old Testament Apocrypha.

ech·e·lon (esh′ə·lon) *n.* **1.** A troop, fleet, or airplane formation resembling a series of steps, in which each rank, ship, or airplane extends behind and slightly to the right or left of the preceding one. **2.** *Mil.* **a** One of the different fractions of a command arranged from front to rear, to which a particular combat mission is assigned: assault *echelon;* support *echelon.* **b** One of the various subdivisions from front to rear of a military headquarters: forward *echelon;* rear *echelon.* **c** Level of command: command *echelon.* **—** *v.t. & v.i.* To form in echelon. [< F *échelon* < *échelle* ladder < L *scala*]

e·chid·na (i·kid′nə) *n. pl.* **·nae** (-nē) An egg-laying mammal of Australia, Tasmania, and New Guinea, having strong spines intermixed with fur. [< NL < Gk., viper]

e·chi·no·derm (i·kī′nə·dûrm) *n.* A marine animal having a radial body and a hard, spiny shell, as the starfish.

ech·o (ek′ō) *n. pl.* **ech·oes** **1.** The repetition of a sound by the reflection of sound waves from an opposing surface; also, the sound so produced. **2.** The repetition or reproduction of the views, style, etc., of another. **3.** One who imitates another or repeats his words. **4.** Prompt, sympathetic response. **—** *v.t.* **1.** To repeat or send back (sound) by echo: The walls *echoed* the shot. **2.** To repeat the words, opinions, etc., of. **3.** To repeat (words, opinions, etc.) in imitation. **—** *v.i.* **4.** To give back sound. **5.** To be repeated or given back. [< L < Gk. *ēche* sound, noise] **— ech′o·er** *n.* **— e·cho′ic** *adj.*

Ech·o (ek′ō) In Greek mythology, a nymph who, because of love for Narcissus, pined away until only her voice was left.

é·clair (ā·klâr′, i·klâr′) *n.* A small oblong pastry shell filled with custard or whipped cream. [< F, lit., flash of lightning]

é·clat (ā·klä′, i·klä′) *n.* **1.** Brilliance of action or effect; conspicuous success. **2.** Splendor of reputation; renown; also, notoriety. **3.** Acclaim. [< F < *éclater* to burst out]

ec·lec·tic (ek·lek′tik, ik-) *adj.* **1.** Selecting what is considered best from different systems or sources. **2.** Composed of elements selected from diverse sources. **—** *n.* One favoring no particular belief or practice, as in philosophy or art, but selecting from all schools or methods. [< Gk. < *ek-* out + *legein* to select] **— ec·lec′ti·cal·ly** *adv.* **— ec·lec′ti·cism** *n.*

e·clipse (i·klips′) *n.* **1.** *Astron.* The apparent dimming or elimination of light from one heavenly body by another. A **lunar eclipse** is caused by the passage of the moon through the earth's shadow; a **solar eclipse** by the passage of the moon between the sun and the observer. **2.** Any overshadowing or dimming, as of power or reputation. **—** *v.t.* **e·clipsed, e·clips·ing** **1.** To cause an eclipse of; darken. **2.** To obscure the beauty, fame, worth, etc., of; overshadow; surpass. [< OF < L < Gk. < *ek-* out + *leipein* to leave]

e·clip·tic (i·klip′tik, ē-) *n. Astron.* **1.** The plane, passing through the center of the sun, that contains the orbit of the earth: also **plane of the ecliptic.** **2.** The great circle in which this plane intersects the celestial sphere. **—** *adj.* Pertaining to eclipses or to the ecliptic: also **e·clip′ti·cal.** **— e·clip′ti·cal·ly** *adv.*

ec·logue (ek′lôg, -log) *n.* A short pastoral poem. [< F < L < Gk. < *ek-* out + *legein* to select]

e·col·o·gy (i·kol′ə·jē, ē-) *n.* The division of biology that treats of the relations between organisms and their environment. [< Gk. *oikos* home + -LOGY] **— ec·o·log·ic** (ek′ə·loj′ik) or **·i·cal** *adj.* **— ec′o·log′i·cal·ly** *adv.* **— e·col′o·gist** *n.*

ec·o·nom·ic (ek′ə·nom′ik, ē′kə-) *adj.* **1.** Of or pertaining to the development and management of the material wealth of a government or community: the French *economic* policy. **2.** Relating to the science of economics: *economic* theory. **3.** Of or pertaining to financial matters. **4.** Of practical use.

ec·o·nom·i·cal (ek′ə·nom′i·kəl, ē′kə-) *adj.* **1.** Frugal. **2.** Economic. **— ec·o·nom′i·cal·ly** *adv.*

economic determinism The theory that all human activities and institutions have economic origins.

ec·o·nom·ics (ek′ə·nom′iks, ē′kə-) *n.pl.* **1.** (*construed as sing.*) The science that treats of the production, distribution, and consumption of wealth. **2.** Economic matters.

e·con·o·mist (i·kon′ə·mist) *n.* **1.** One who is proficient in economics. **2.** One who is careful and thrifty.

e·con·o·mize (i·kon′ə·mīz) *v.* **·mized, ·miz·ing** *v.i.* **1.** To be sparing in expenditure; manage thriftily. **—** *v.t.* **2.** To use sparingly or to best advantage. Also *Brit.* **e·con′o·mise.**

e·con·o·my (i·kon′ə·mē) *n. pl.* **·mies** **1.** Frugal management of money, materials, resources, and the like; also, an example of this. **2.** The practical administration of the material resources of a country, community, or establishment: the national *economy.* **3.** The orderly distribution and interplay of parts in a structure or system: the *economy* of nature. [< L < Gk. < *oikos* house + *nemein* to manage]

ec·ru (ek′rōō, ā′krōō) *adj.* Of the color of unbleached linen. **—** *n.* A light, yellowish brown. Also **é·cru.** [< F < OF < L *ex-* thoroughly + *crudus* raw]

ec·sta·sy (ek′stə·sē) *n. pl.* **·sies** **1.** The state of being beside oneself through some overpowering emotion: in an *ecstasy* of anticipation. **2.** Intense delight; rapture. **3.** A trance. [< OF < LL < Gk. < *ek-* out + *histanai* to place]

ec·stat·ic (ek·stat′ik) *adj.* **1.** Pertaining to, of the nature of, or exciting to ecstasy; rapturous. **2.** In a state of ecstasy; transported. Also **ec·stat′i·cal.** **—** *n.* A person subject to ecstasies or trances. **— ec·stat′i·cal·ly** *adv.*

ecto- *combining form* Without; outside; external: *ectoderm.* Also, before vowels, **ect-.** [< Gk. *ekto-* < *ektos* outside]

ec·to·derm (ek′tə·dûrm) *n. Biol.* The outermost of the three primary germ layers in the embryo, developing into the skin, sense organs, and nervous system. **— ec′to·der′mal, ec′to·der′mic** *adj.*

ec·to·mor·phic (ek′tō·môr′fik) *adj.* Of human body types, characterized by a lean body structure. **— ec′to·morph** *n.*

-ectomy *combining form* Removal of a part by cutting out: used in surgical terms to indicate certain kinds of operations: *appendectomy.* [< Gk. < *ek-* out + *temnein* to cut]

ec·to·plasm (ek′tə·plaz′əm) *n.* **1.** *Biol.* The firm outer layer of the cytoplasm of a unicellular organism or of a plant cell.

2. The substance alleged to emanate from the body of a spiritualist medium during a trance. — **ec/to·plas/mic** *adj.*

ec·u·men·i·cal (ek/yŏŏ·men/i·kəl) *adj.* World-wide in scope, esp. of the Christian church: an *ecumenical* council. Also **ec/u·men/ic.** [< LL < Gk. *oikeein* to inhabit]

ec·u·men·ism (ek/yŏŏ·men/iz·əm) *n.* The movement for world-wide unity and cooperation among all Christian churches. Also **ec/u·men/i·cal·ism, ec/u·men/i·cism.**

ec·ze·ma (ek/sə·mə, eg/zə·mə, eg·zē/mə) *n. Pathol.* An inflammatory disease of the skin attended by itching, watery discharge, and the appearance of lesions. [< Gk. < *ek-* out + *zeein* to boil] — **ec·zem·a·tous** (eg·zem/ə·təs) *adj.*

-ed[1] *suffix* Forming the past tense of regular verbs: *walked, killed, played.* [OE *-ede, -ode, -ade*]

-ed[2] *suffix* **1.** Forming the past participle of regular verbs: *washed.* **2.** Forming adjectives from adjectives in *-ate*, with the same general meaning: *bipinnated.* [OE *-ed, -ad, -od*]

-ed[3] *suffix* Forming adjectives from nouns with the senses: **1.** Having; possessing; characterized by: *toothed, green-eyed.* **2.** Like; resembling: *bigoted.* [OE *-ede*]

ed·dy (ed/ē) *n. pl.* **·dies** A backward-circling current of water or air; whirlpool. — *v.t.* **·died, ·dy·ing** To move, or cause to move, in or as in an eddy. [Prob. < ON *idha*]

e·del·weiss (ā/dəl·vīs) *n.* A small, perennial herb growing chiefly in the Alps, with white, woolly leaves suggesting a flower. [< G *edel* noble + *weiss* white]

e·de·ma (i·dē/mə) *n. pl.* **·ma·ta** (-mə·tə) *Pathol.* An abnormal accumulation of serous fluid in various organs, cavities, or tissues of the body; swelling: also spelled *oedema.* [< NL < Gk. *oidein* to swell] — **e·dem·a·tous** (i·dem/ə·təs), **e·dem/a·tose** (-tōs) *adj.*

E·den (ēd/n) *n.* **1.** In the Bible, the garden that was the first home of Adam and Eve: often called *Paradise.* **2.** Any delightful place or condition. [< Hebrew *ēden* delight]

EDELWEISS
(To 4 inches high)

e·den·tate (ē·den/tāt, i·den/-) *adj.* **1.** Of or pertaining to an order of mammals, some of which lack teeth, including sloths, anteaters, and armadillos. **2.** Toothless. — *n.* An edentate mammal. [< L < *e-* without + *dens, dentis* tooth]

edge (ej) *n.* **1.** A bounding or dividing line; also, the part along a boundary; border; margin: the *edge* of a lawn. **2.** A verge or brink; rim: the *edge* of a cliff. **3.** The line where two surfaces of a solid meet: the *edge* of a cube. **4.** The thin, sharp, cutting side of a blade. **5.** Sharpness; keenness. **6.** *U.S. Informal* Advantage; superiority. — **on edge** **1.** Keenly sensitive; tense; irritable. **2.** Eager; impatient. — *v.* **edged, edg·ing** *v.t.* **1.** To sharpen. **2.** To furnish with an edge or border. **3.** To push sideways or by degrees. — *v.i.* **4.** To move sideways or by degrees. [OE *ecg*]

edge·wise (ej/wīz/) *adv.* **1.** With the edge forward. **2.** On, by, with, or toward the edge. Also **edge/ways/** (-wāz/).

edg·ing (ej/ing) *n.* A trimming; border.

edg·y (ej/ē) *adj.* **edg·i·er, edg·i·est** **1.** Tense, nervous, or irritable. **2.** Having an edge or edges. — **edg/i·ness** *n.*

ed·i·ble (ed/ə·bəl) *adj.* Fit to eat. — *n. Usu. pl.* Something fit to eat. [< LL < L *edere* to eat]

e·dict (ē/dikt) *n.* An official decree publicly proclaimed. [< L < *e-* out + *dicere* to say] — **e·dic·tal** (ē·dik/təl) *adj.*

ed·i·fi·ca·tion (ed/ə·fə·kā/shən) *n.* Intellectual or moral enlightenment and improvement.

ed·i·fice (ed/ə·fis) *n.* A building or other structure, esp. one that is large and imposing. [< F < L < *aedes* building + *facere* to make] — **ed·i·fi·cial** (ed/ə·fish/əl) *adj.*

ed·i·fy (ed/ə·fī) *v.t.* **·fied, ·fy·ing** To enlighten and benefit, esp. morally or spiritually. [< OF < L < *aedes* building + *facere* to make] — **ed/i·fi/er** *n.*

ed·it (ed/it) *v.t.* **1.** To correct and prepare for publication: to *edit* a manuscript. **2.** To compile, arrange, and emend for publication: to *edit* a collection of poems. **3.** To direct the preparation, publication, and editorial policies of (a newspaper, magazine, etc.). [Back formation < EDITOR]

e·di·tion (i·dish/ən) *n.* **1.** The form in which a book is published: a three-volume *edition.* **2.** The total number of copies of a publication issued at any one time; also, such a copy. [< F < L < *e-* out + *dare* to give]

ed·i·tor (ed/i·tər) *n.* **1.** One who edits. **2.** A writer of editorials. [< L] — **ed/i·tor·ship/** *n.*

ed·i·to·ri·al (ed/i·tôr/ē·əl, -tō/rē-) *n.* An article in a newspaper, magazine, or the like, published as the periodical's official expression of opinion on some issue. — *adj.* Of, pertaining to, or written by an editor. — **ed/i·to/ri·al·ly** *adv.*

ed·i·to·ri·al·ize (ed/i·tôr/ē·əl·īz/, -tō/rē-) *v.t. & v.i.* **·ized, ·iz·ing** **1.** To express opinions (on a subject) editorially. **2.** To insert editorial opinions (into a news item, etc.).

editor in chief *pl.* **editors in chief** The chief editor of a publication, who establishes its policy and supervises operations.

ed·u·cate (ej/ŏŏ·kāt) *v.t.* **·cat·ed, ·cat·ing** **1.** To develop or train the mind, capabilities, or character of by instruction or study; teach. **2.** To train for some special purpose. **3.** To

develop or train (taste, special ability, etc.). **4.** To provide schooling for. [< L < *e-* out + *ducere* to lead] — **ed/u·ca·ble** *adj.* — **ed/u·ca/tor** *n.*

ed·u·cat·ed (ej/ŏŏ·kā/tid) *adj.* **1.** Developed and informed by education; instructed; trained. **2.** Having a cultivated mind, speech, manner, etc.

ed·u·ca·tion (ej/ŏŏ·kā/shən) *n.* **1.** The act of educating; systematic development or training of the mind, capabilities, or character through instruction or study. **2.** Acquisition of knowledge or skills; esp., formal schooling in an institution of learning. **3.** Knowledge, skills, or cultivation acquired through instruction or study. **4.** The study of teaching methods and problems, the learning process, and other matters related to the classroom; pedagogy.

ed·u·ca·tion·al (ej/ŏŏ·kā/shən·əl) *adj.* Of, pertaining to, or imparting education: an *educational* trip. — **ed/u·ca/tion·al·ly** *adv.*

ed·u·ca·tive (ej/ŏŏ·kā/tiv) *adj.* **1.** That educates or tends to educate; educational. **2.** Of or relating to education.

e·duce (i·dōōs/, i·dyōōs/) *v.t.* **e·duced, e·duc·ing** **1.** To call forth; bring out; elicit. **2.** To infer or develop from data; deduce. [< L < *e-* out + *ducere* to lead] — **e·duc/i·ble** *adj.* — **e·duc·tion** (i·duk/shən) *n.* — **e·duc/tive** *adj.*

-ee *suffix of nouns* **1.** One who undergoes, or benefits from, some action: used esp. in legal terms, and opposed to *-er, -or,* as in *grantor, grantee.* **2.** One who is described by the main element: *absentee.* [< AF *-é,* suffix of pp. < L *-atus*]

eel (ēl) *n. pl.* **eels** or **eel** A fish having a snakelike body, usu. without scales or pelvic fins, and of both marine and fresh-water habitat. [OE *æl*] — **eel/y** *adj.*

e'en[1] (ēn) *adv. Poetic* Even.

e'en[2] (ēn) *n. Poetic & Dial.* Evening.

e'er (âr) *adv. Poetic* Ever.

-eer *suffix of nouns and verbs* **1.** One who is concerned with, works with, or makes something indicated: *engineer.* **2.** Be concerned with; work at: *electioneer.* [< F *-ier* < L *-arius*]

ee·rie (ir/ē, ē/rē) *adj.* **1.** Inspiring fear; weird; ghostly. **2.** Affected by superstitious fear. Also **ee/ry.** [ME *eri* timid, var. of *erg* < OE *earg*] — **ee/ri·ly** *adv.* — **ee/ri·ness** *n.*

ef·face (i·fās/) *v.t.* **·faced, ·fac·ing** **1.** To rub out, as written characters; erase. **2.** To obliterate, as a memory. **3.** To make (oneself) insignificant. [< F < L *ex-* out + *facies* face] — **ef·face/ment** *n.* — **ef·fac/er** *n.*

ef·fect (i·fekt/) *n.* **1.** Something brought about by some cause or agency; result; consequence. **2.** Capacity to produce some result; efficacy. **3.** The condition or fact of being in active force: to put a law into *effect.* **4.** The state of being actually accomplished or realized: to carry plans into *effect.* **5.** The particular way in which something affects or influences something else. **6.** The overall reaction or impression produced by something seen, heard, or done. **7.** A technique used in art, literature, music, etc., to achieve a certain result or produce a distinctive impression. **8.** The actual or basic meaning intended or conveyed; purport: usu. with *to:* She said something to that *effect.* **9.** *pl.* Movable goods; belongings. — **in effect** **1.** In actual fact. **2.** For all practical purposes; virtually. **3.** In active force or operation. — **to take effect** To begin to act upon something; be or become operative. — *v.t.* To bring about; cause; esp., to accomplish; achieve: to *effect* an escape. [< L < *ex-* out + *facere* to do, make] — **ef·fect/er** *n.* — **ef·fect/i·ble** *adj.*

ef·fec·tive (i·fek/tiv) *adj.* **1.** Producing or adapted to produce the proper result. **2.** Being in force, as a law. **3.** Producing a striking impression, as a speaker. **4.** Ready for action, as an army. — *n.* **1.** One who is fit for duty. **2.** The number of men available for military service. — **ef·fec/tive·ly** *adv.* — **ef·fec/tive·ness** *n.*

ef·fec·tu·al (i·fek/chōō·əl) *adj.* **1.** Producing or having adequate power to produce an intended effect. **2.** Legally valid or binding. — **ef·fec/tu·al·ly** *adv.* — **ef·fec/tu·al·ness, ef·fec/tu·al/i·ty** (-al/ə·tē) *n.*

ef·fec·tu·ate (i·fek/chōō·āt) *v.t.* **·at·ed, ·at·ing** To bring about; accomplish; effect. — **ef·fec/tu·a/tion** *n.*

ef·fem·i·nate (i·fem/ə·nit) *adj.* **1.** Having womanlike traits or qualities to a degree unbefitting a man; womanish; unmanly. **2.** Characterized by weakness or self-indulgence. [< L < *ex-* out + *femina* a woman] — **ef·fem/i·na·cy** (-nə·sē) *n.* — **ef·fem/i·nate·ly** *adv.* — **ef·fem/i·nate·ness** *n.*

ef·fer·ent (ef/ər·ənt) *adj. Physiol.* Carrying or carried outward: said esp. of impulses transmitted from the central nervous system to muscles, etc.; opposed to *afferent.* — *n. Physiol.* An efferent duct, vessel, or nerve. [< L < *ex-* out + *ferre* to carry]

ef·fer·vesce (ef/ər·ves/) *v.i.* **·vesced, ·vesc·ing** **1.** To give off bubbles of gas, as water charged with carbon dioxide. **2.** To issue out in bubbles, as a gas. **3.** To show exhilaration or lively spirits. [< L < *ex-* out + *fervescere* to boil] — **ef/fer·ves/cence** *n.* — **ef/fer·ves/cent** *adj.*

ef·fete (i·fēt/) *adj.* **1.** Having lost strength or virility. **2.** Incapable of further production; barren. [< L < *ex-* out + *fetus* a breeding] — **ef·fete/ly** *adv.* — **ef·fete/ness** *n.*

ef·fi·ca·cious (ef/ə·kā/shəs) *adj.* Producing or capable of producing an intended effect. [See EFFECT.] — **ef/fi·ca/·cious·ly** *adv.* — **ef/fi·ca/cious·ness** *n.*

ef·fi·ca·cy (ef/ə·kə·sē) *n. pl.* **·cies** Power to produce a desired or intended result.

ef·fi·cien·cy (i·fish/ən·sē) *n. pl.* **·cies 1.** The quality of being efficient. **2.** The ratio of work done or energy expended to the energy supplied in the form of food or fuel.

ef·fi·cient (i·fish/ənt) *adj.* **1.** Productive of results with a minimum of wasted effort. **2.** Producing an effect. [See EFFECT.] — **ef/fi·cient·ly** *adv.*

ef·fi·gy (ef/ə·jē) *n. pl.* **·gies 1.** A likeness or representation; esp., a sculptured portrait. **2.** A crude image of a disliked person. [< F < L < *ex-* out + *fingere* to fashion]

ef·flo·resce (ef/lôr·es/, -lō·res/) *v.i.* **·resced**, **·resc·ing 1.** To blossom, bloom, or flower. **2.** *Chem.* **a** To become powdery, wholly or in part, and lose crystalline structure through evaporation of water. **b** To become covered with a crust of saline particles left by evaporation or by chemical change. [< L < *ex-* thoroughly + *florescere* to bloom]

ef·flo·res·cence (ef/lôr·es/əns, -lō·res/-) *n.* **1.** The act or season of flowering. **2.** *Chem.* The act or process of efflorescing. **3.** *Pathol.* A rash. — **ef/flo·res/cent** *adj.*

ef·flu·ent (ef/lōō·ənt) *adj.* Flowing out. — *n.* An outflow, as of water from a lake, industrial sewage, etc. [< L < *ex-* out + *fluere* to flow] — **ef/flu·ence** *n.*

ef·flu·vi·um (i·flōō/vē·əm) *n. pl.* **·vi·a** (-vē·ə) or **·vi·ums 1.** An invisible emanation; esp., a foul-smelling exhalation, as from decaying matter. **2.** A supposed imponderable agent formerly regarded as the source of electric and magnetic forces. [< L, a flowing out] — **ef·flu/vi·al** *adj.*

ef·flux (ef/luks) *n.* **1.** A flowing out. **2.** That which flows forth; emanation. [< L < *ex-* out + *fluere* to flow]

ef·fort (ef/ərt) *n.* **1.** Expenditure of physical, mechanical, or mental energy to get something done; exertion. **2.** Something produced by exertion: a new theatrical *effort.* [< F < OF < L *ex-* thoroughly + *fortis* strong] — **ef/fort·less** *adj.* — **ef/fort·less·ly** *adv.*

ef·front·er·y (i·frun/tər·ē) *n. pl.* **·ies** Shameless or insolent boldness; audacity. [< F < L < *ex-* out + *frontis* face]

ef·fulge (i·fulj/) *v.t. & v.i.* **·fulged**, **·fulg·ing** To shine forth; radiate. [< L < *ex-* out + *fulgere* to shine]

ef·ful·gent (i·ful/jənt) *adj.* Shining brilliantly; radiant; splendid. — **ef·ful/gence** *n.* — **ef·ful/gent·ly** *adv.*

ef·fuse (*adj.* i·fyōōs/; *v.* i·fyōoz/) *adj.* **1.** *Bot.* Spreading out loosely or flat. **2.** *Zool.* Having the lips separated by a groove, as certain shells. — *v.* **·fused**, **·fus·ing** *v.t.* **1.** To pour forth; shed. — *v.t.* **2.** To emanate; exude. [< L < *ex-* out + *fundere* to pour] — **ef·fu/sion** *n.*

ef·fu·sive (i·fyōō/siv) *adj.* **1.** Overflowing with sentiment; demonstrative; gushing. **2.** Pouring forth; overflowing. — **ef·fu/sive·ly** *adv.* — **ef·fu/sive·ness** *n.*

e·gad (i·gad/, ē·gad/) *interj.* By God!: a mild oath.

e·gal·i·tar·i·an (i·gal/ə·târ/ē·ən) *adj.* Of, relating to, or believing in political and social equality. — *n.* One who believes in, or advocated political and social equality. Also **equalitarian.** [< F *égalitaire*] — **e·gal/i·tar/i·an·ism** *n.*

egg¹ (eg) *n.* **1.** The round or oval reproductive body produced by female birds, insects, and most reptiles and fishes, consisting of the germ and a nutritive yolk enclosed in a shell or membrane. **2.** *Biol.* The reproductive cell of female animals; ovum: also **egg cell. 3.** The hen's egg as a food. **4.** Something oval like a hen's egg. **5.** *U.S. Slang* Person: He's a good *egg.* — **to lay an egg** *U.S. Slang* To fail completely. — **to put all one's eggs in one basket** To risk all in a single venture. — *v.t.* **1.** To cover with beaten egg before cooking. **2.** *U.S. Informal* To pelt with eggs. [< ON]

egg² (eg) *v.t.* To incite; urge: usu. with *on.* [< ON *eggja*]

egg·head (eg/hed/) *n. U.S. Slang* An intellectual; highbrow: often derisive.

egg·nog (eg/nog/) *n.* A drink made of beaten eggs and milk with sugar and nutmeg and sometimes with liquor.

egg·plant (eg/plant/, -plänt/) *n.* **1.** A widely cultivated herb with large, egg-shaped, usu. purple-skinned fruit. **2.** The fruit of this plant, used as a vegetable.

egg·shell (eg/shel/) *n.* The hard, brittle covering of a bird's egg. — *adj.* **1.** Thin and fragile. **2.** Pale yellow or ivory.

egg white The uncooked albumen of an egg.

e·gis (ē/jis) See AEGIS.

eg·lan·tine (eg/lən·tīn, -tēn) *n.* Any of various fragrant wild roses. [< F < OF, ult. < L *acus* needle]

e·go (ē/gō, eg/ō) *n. pl.* **e·gos 1.** The thinking, feeling, and acting self that is conscious of itself and aware of its distinction from the objects of its thought and perceptions. **2.** *Psychoanal.* The conscious aspect of the psyche that develops through contact with the external world and resolves conflicts between the id and the superego. **3.** *Informal* Self-centeredness; conceit. [< L, I]

e·go·cen·tric (ē/gō·sen/trik, eg/ō-) *adj.* Regarding oneself as the object of all experience and acts. — *n.* An egocentric person. — **e/go·cen·tric/i·ty** (-sen·tris/ə·tē) *n.*

e·go·ism (ē/gō·iz/əm, eg/ō-) *n.* **1.** Inordinate concern for one's own welfare and interests. **2.** Self-conceit; egotism.

e·go·ist (ē/gō·ist, eg/ō-) *n.* **1.** One who is completely devoted to his own interests. **2.** A conceited person; egotist. — **e/go·is/tic** or **·ti·cal** *adj.* — **e/go·is/ti·cal·ly** *adv.*

e·go·ma·ni·a (ē/gō·mā/nē·ə, -mān/yə, eg/ō-) *n.* Abnormal or excessive egotism. — **e/go·ma/ni·ac** (-ak) *n.*

e·go·tism (ē/gə·tiz/əm, eg/ə-) *n.* **1.** Excessive reference to oneself in speech or writing; self-conceit. **2.** Selfishness; egoism. — **e/go·tist** *n.* — **e/go·tis/tic** or **·ti·cal** *adj.* — **e/go·tis/ti·cal·ly** *adv.*

e·gre·gious (i·grē/jəs, -jē·əs) *adj.* Conspicuously bad; glaring; flagrant. [< L < *e-* out + *grex, gregis* herd] — **e·gre/gious·ly** *adv.* — **e·gre/gious·ness** *n.*

e·gress (ē/gres) *n.* **1.** A going out, as from a building; emergence; also, the right of going out. Also **e·gres/sion. 2.** A place of exit. [< L < *e-* out + *gradi* to walk]

e·gret (ē/grit, eg/rit) *n.* **1.** One of various herons characterized in the breeding season by long and loose plumes drooping over the tail. **2.** Aigrette (def. 1). [Var. of AIGRETTE]

E·gyp·tian (i·jip/shən) *adj.* Of or pertaining to Egypt, its people, or their culture. — *n.* **1.** One of the people of Egypt. **2.** The ancient Hamitic language of Egypt.

E·gyp·tol·o·gy (ē/jip·tol/ə·jē) *n.* The study of the antiquities of Egypt. — **E/gyp·tol/o·gist** *n.*

eh (ā, e) *interj.* What: used to express uncertainty: surprise, etc.

ei·der (ī/dər) *n.* A large sea duck of northern regions. [< ON *æðhr-* in *æðhar-dūn* eiderdown]

ei·der·down (ī/dər·doun/) *n.* The down of the eider used for stuffing pillows and quilts; such also, a quilt.

eight (āt) *n.* **1.** The sum of seven and one: a cardinal number. **2.** Any symbol of this number, as 8, viii, VIII. **3.** Anything consisting of eight units. — *adj.* Being one more than seven. [OE *eahta*] — **eighth** (ātth, āth) *adj. & n.*

eight·een (ā/tēn/) *n.* **1.** The sum of seventeen and one: a cardinal number. **2.** Any symbol of this number, as 18, xviii, XVIII. **3.** Anything consisting of or representing eighteen units. — *adj.* Being one more than seventeen. [OE *eahtatiene*] — **eight·eenth/** *adj. & n.*

eight·een·mo (ā/tēn/mō/) *adj. & n.* Octodecimo.

eighth note *Music* A note having one eighth the time value of a whole note: also, *Chiefly Brit.,* quaver.

eight·vo (āt/vō) *adj. & n.* Octavo.

eight·y (ā/tē) *n. pl.* **·ies 1.** The sum of seventy and ten: a cardinal number. **2.** Any symbol of this number, as 80, lxxx, LXXX. **3.** Anything consisting of or representing eighty units. — *adj.* Being ten more than seventy. [OE *eahtatig*] — **eight/i·eth** *adj. & n.*

-ein Var. of -IN.

ein·stein·i·um (īn·stī/nē·əm) *n.* A radioactive element (symbol Es), originally detected in the debris of a thermonuclear explosion and artificially produced by the irradiation of plutonium. See ELEMENT. [after Albert *Einstein*]

ei·ther (ē/thər, ī/thər) *adj.* **1.** One or the other of two: Use *either* foot. **2.** Each of two; one and the other: They sat on *either* side of him. — *pron.* One or the other: Choose *either.* — *conj.* In one of two or more cases, indeterminately or indifferently: a disjunctive correlative used with *or:* *Either* I shall go or he will come. — *adv.* Any more so: used after the denial of an alternative, or to emphasize a preceding negative: He could not speak, and I could not *either*; I shall leave, and you can't stop me *either.* [OE *ægther*]

♦ **either, neither** *Either,* like *neither,* is singular and in formal writing takes a singular verb: *Either* of them *is* suitable. In informal speech and writing, however, a plural verb is commonly used: *Are either* of you going to the party? When there are two subjects of differing number, the verb agrees with the nearer: *Neither he nor they are* ever there.

e·jac·u·late (i·jak/yə·lāt) *v.* **·lat·ed**, **·lat·ing** *v.t.* **1.** To utter suddenly, as a brief exclamation. **2.** To discharge suddenly and quickly, as seminal fluid. — *v.i.* **3.** To ejaculate something. — *n.* That which is ejaculated. — **Syn.** See EXCLAIM. [< L < *e-* out + *jaculari* to throw] — **e·jac/u·la/tion** *n.* — **e·jac/u·la/tive** (-lā/tiv, -lə·tiv) *adj.* — **e·jac/·u·la·tor** *n.* — **e·jac/u·la·to/ry** *adj.*

e·ject (i·jekt/) *v.t.* **1.** To throw out with sudden force. **2.** To put forcibly outside; expel: to *eject* an intruder. **3.** *Law* To dispossess; evict. [< L < *e-* out + *jacere* to throw] — **e·jec/tion** *n.* — **e·jec/tive** *adj.* — **e·ject/ment** *n.* — **e·jec/·tor** *n.*

eke (ēk) *v.t.* **eked**, **ek·ing 1.** To piece out; supplement: usually with *out.* **2.** To make a (living) with difficulty: usually with *out.* [Var. of obs. *eche* to increase]

el- Assimilated var. of EN-².

e·lab·o·rate (*adj.* i·lab/ər·it; *v.* i·lab/ə·rāt) *adj.* Worked out with great thoroughness or exactness; developed in minute detail: *elaborate* precautions. — *v.* **·rat·ed**, **·rat·ing** *v.t.* **1.** To work out in detail; develop carefully and thoroughly. **2.** To produce by labor. — *v.i.* **3.** To add details or embellishments: with *on* or *upon*: to *elaborate* on a subject. [< L < *e-* out + *laborare* to work] — **e·lab/o·rate·ly** *adv.* — **e·lab/o·rate·ness** *n.* — **e·lab/o·ra/tion** *n.* — **e·lab/o·ra·tive** *adj.* — **e·lab/o·ra/tor** *n.*

E·lam (ē/ləm) An ancient country of SW Asia between the Persian Gulf and the Caspian Sea. *Gen.* xiv 1. — **E/lam·ite** (-īt) *adj.* & *n.* — **E/lam·it/ic** (-lə·mit/ik) *adj.* & *n.*

é·lan (ā·län/) *n.* Enthusiasm; dash; vivacity. [< F]

e·land (ē/lənd) *n.* A large, oxlike African antelope with twisted horns. [< Du., elk]

e·lapse (i·laps/) *v.i.* **e·lapsed**, **e·laps·ing** To slip by; pass away: said of time. [< L < *e-* out, away + *labi* to glide]

e·las·mo·branch (i·las/mō·brangk, i·laz/-) *n. Zool.* One of a class or subclass of sharks, rays, etc., having cartilaginous skeletons, and lacking air bladders. [< NL < Gk. *elasmos* metal plate + *branchia* gills]

e·las·tic (i·las/tik) *adj.* **1.** Spontaneously regaining former size, shape, or bulk after compression, extension, or other distortion. **2.** Adjusting readily to fit the circumstances; flexible. **3.** Recovering quickly, as from emotional or physical distress; resilient. **4.** Marked by a springy motion. — *n.* **1.** Fabric made stretchable by interwoven threads of rubber. **2.** An article manufactured of this fabric, as a garter. **3.** A rubber band. [< NL < Gk. < *elaunein* to drive] — **e·las/ti·cal·ly** *adv.*

e·las·tic·i·ty (i·las/tis/ə·tē, ē/las-) *n. pl.* **·ties** The property or quality of being elastic; flexibility; resilience.

e·late (i·lāt/) *v.t.* **e·lat·ed**, **e·lat·ing** To raise the spirits of; stimulate; excite. [< L < *ex-* out + *ferre* to bear]

e·lat·ed (i·lā/tid) *adj.* Filled with joy or triumph, as over good fortune. — **e·lat/ed·ly** *adv.* — **e·lat/ed·ness** *n.*

e·la·tion (i·lā/shən) *n.* Exalted feeling, as from success.

E layer The Heaviside layer.

el·bow (el/bō) *n.* **1.** The joint at the bend of the arm between the forearm and the upper arm; esp., the projecting outer side of this joint. **2.** The joint corresponding to an elbow in the shoulder or hock of a quadruped. **3.** Something having an angle or bend like an elbow. — **at one's elbow** Within easy reach. — **out at the elbows** Shabby; impoverished. — **to rub elbows with** To associate closely with (celebrities, etc.). — **up to the elbows** (in) Deeply immersed (in). — *v.t.* **1.** To push or jostle with or as with the elbows. **2.** To make (one's way) by such pushing. — *v.i.* **3.** To push one's way along. [OE *elnboga*]

eld·er[1] (el/dər) *adj.* **1.** Of earlier birth; older; senior. **2.** Superior or prior in rank, office, etc. **3.** Pertaining to a previous time; earlier; former. — *n.* **1.** *Often pl.* An older person; also, a forefather or predecessor. **2.** An influential senior member of a family, community, etc. **3.** *Eccl.* A governing or counseling officer in certain Christian churches. **4.** An aged person. [OE *eldra*] — **eld/er·ship** *n.*

el·der[2] (el/dər) *n.* **1.** A shrub of the honeysuckle family, with white flowers and purple-black or red berries. **2.** Any trees or plants resembling this shrub. [OE *ellæn*]

el·der·ber·ry (el/dər·ber/ē, -bər·ē) *n. pl.* **·ber·ries 1.** The berry of the elder, used to make wine. **2.** The elder.

eld·er·ly (el/dər·lē) *adj.* Rather advanced in age; approaching old age; quite old. — **Syn.** See OLD.

eld·est (el/dist) *adj.* Alternative superlative of OLD.

e·lect (i·lekt/) *v.t.* **1.** To choose (a person or persons) for an office by vote. **2.** To pick out; select. **3.** *Theol.* To set aside by divine will for salvation: used in the passive voice. — *v.i.* **4.** To make a choice. — *adj.* **1.** Chosen; selected. **2.** Elected to office, but not yet inducted: used in compounds: president-*elect.* — *n.* An elect person or group. [< L < *e-* out + *legere* to choose]

e·lec·tion (i·lek/shən) *n.* **1.** The formal choice of a person or persons for any position or dignity, usu. by ballot. **2.** A popular vote upon any question officially proposed. **3.** In Calvinism, the predestination of individuals to salvation.

e·lec·tion·eer (i·lek/shən·ir/) *v.i.* To work for votes for a particular candidate or political party.

e·lec·tive (i·lek/tiv) *adj.* **1.** Of or pertaining to a choice by vote. **2.** Obtained or settled by election. **3.** Having the power to elect. **4.** Subject to choice; optional. — *n. U.S.* An optional subject in a school or college curriculum.

e·lec·tor (i·lek/tər) *n.* **1.** One who elects; a person qualified to vote. **2.** *U.S.* A member of the electoral college. **3.** *Usu. cap.* One of the German princes who formerly elected the Holy Roman emperor. — **e·lec/tor·al** *adj.*

electoral college A body of electors, chosen by the voters in the States and the District of Columbia, which formally elects the president and vice president of the United States.

e·lec·tor·ate (i·lek/tər·it) *n.* **1.** The whole body of voters. **2.** A district of voters. **3.** The rank or territory of an elector.

E·lec·tra (i·lek/trə) In Greek legend, the sister of Orestes.

She persuaded him to kill their mother and their mother's lover to avenge their father's murder. Also *Elektra.*

e·lec·tric (i·lek/trik) *adj.* **1.** Relating to, produced by, or operated by electricity. **2.** Producing or carrying electricity: an *electric* cable. **3.** Thrillingly exciting or magnetic: an *electric* personality. — *n.* A vehicle run by electricity. [< NL < L < Gk. *ēlektron* amber]

e·lec·tri·cal (i·lek/tri·kəl) *adj.* **1.** Electric. **2.** Concerned with the use of electricity. — **e·lec/tri·cal·ly** *adv.*

electrical transcription *Telecom.* A transcription.

electric eel An eellike, fresh-water fish of tropical America, that is capable of delivering powerful electric shocks.

electric eye A photoelectric cell.

electric field A field of force surrounding a charged object or a moving magnet.

e·lec·tri·cian (i·lek/trish/ən, ē/lek-) *n.* A technician who designs, installs, operates, or repairs electrical apparatus.

e·lec·tric·i·ty (i·lek/tris/ə·tē, ē/lek-) *n.* **1.** A fundamental property of matter, associated with atomic particles whose movements develop fields of force and generate kinetic or potential energy. **2.** A current or charge of energy so generated. **3.** The science that deals with the laws, theory, and application of electric energy. **4.** The property of many substances to attract or repel each other when subjected to friction. **5.** A state of great tension or excitement.

electric motor A machine for transforming electric energy into mechanical power: distinguished from *generator.*

electric needle A high-frequency, needle-shaped electrode used in surgery for simultaneous cutting and cautery.

electric ray A fish having muscles that store and discharge electricity: also called *crampfish, torpedo.*

e·lec·tri·fy (i·lek/trə·fī) *v.t.* **·fied**, **·fy·ing 1.** To charge with or subject to electricity. **2.** To equip or adapt for operation by electric power, as a railroad, house, etc. **3.** To arouse; startle. — **e·lec/tri·fi/a·ble** *adj.* — **e·lec/tri·fi·ca/tion** *n.*

electro- *combining form* **1.** Electric; by, with, or of electricity. **2.** Electrolytic. Also, before vowels, sometimes **electr-.** [< Gk. *ēlektron* amber]

e·lec·tro·car·di·o·gram (i·lek/trō·kär/dē·ə·gram/) *n. Med.* The record made by an electrocardiograph.

e·lec·tro·car·di·o·graph (i·lek/trō·kär/dē·ə·graf/, -gräf/) *n. Med.* An instrument for recording the electric current produced by the action of the heart muscle, used in the diagnosis of diseases affecting the heart.

e·lec·tro·chem·is·try (i·lek/trō·kem/is·trē) *n.* The study of electricity as active in effecting chemical change. — **e·lec/tro·chem/i·cal** *adj.* — **e·lec/tro·chem/i·cal·ly** *adv.*

e·lec·tro·cute (i·lek/trə·kyōōt) *v.t.* **·cut·ed**, **·cut·ing 1.** To execute in the electric chair. **2.** To kill by electricity. — **e·lec/tro·cu/tion** *n.*

e·lec·trode (i·lek/trōd) *n. Electr.* **1.** Any terminal connecting a conductor, as copper wire, with an electrolyte. **2.** Any of the elements in an electron tube, transistor, etc., that emit, collect, or control the movement of electrons.

e·lec·tro·de·pos·it (i·lek/trō·di·poz/it) *v.i.* To precipitate metal from an electrolyte containing it in ionic form. — *n.* That which is precipitated by electrolysis. — **e·lec/tro·dep/o·si/tion** (-dep/ə·zish/ən, -dē/pə-) *n.*

e·lec·tro·dy·nam·ics (i·lek/trō·dī·nam/iks) *n.pl.* (*construed as sing.*) The branch of physics that deals with the forces of electrical attraction and repulsion and with the energy transformations of magnetic fields and electric currents. — **e·lec/tro·dy·nam/ic** or **·i·cal** *adj.*

e·lec·tro·en·ceph·a·lo·gram (i·lek/trō·en·sef/ə·lə·gram/) *n. Med.* The record made by an electroencephalograph.

e·lec·tro·en·ceph·a·lo·graph (i·lek/trō·en·sef/ə·lə·graf/, -gräf/) *n. Med.* An instrument for recording the strength and character of electrical impulses in the brain used in the diagnosis of brain disorders. — **e·lec/tro·en·ceph/a·lo·graph/ic** *adj.*

e·lec·tro·lu·mi·nes·cence (i·lek/trō·lōō/mə·nes/əns) *n.* The emission of light from a specially coated surface subjected to the action of an alternating current.

e·lec·trol·y·sis (i·lek/trol/ə·sis) *n.* **1.** The application of a direct current to an electrolyte so as to attract its positive ions to the cathode and its negative ions to the anode. **2.** The removal of hair by treating the follicle with an electrically charged needle.

e·lec·tro·lyte (i·lek/trə·līt) *n. Chem.* A compound that when in solution or a fluid state conducts electricity by the dissociation of its constituents into free ions. **2.** A solution that conducts electricity; esp., the solution used in a cell or battery. — **e·lec·tro·lyt·ic** (i·lek/trə·lit/ik) or **·i·cal** *adj.* — **e·lec/tro·lyt/i·cal·ly** *adv.*

e·lec·tro·lyze (i·lek/trə·līz) *v.t.* **·lyzed**, **·lyz·ing** To decompose by electric current. — **e·lec/tro·ly·za/tion** *n.*

e·lec·tro·mag·net (i·lek/trō·mag/nit) *n.* A core of soft iron that temporarily becomes a magnet when an electric current passes through a coil of wire surrounding it.

e·lec·tro·mag·net·ism (i·lek/trō·mag/nə·tiz/əm) *n.* **1.** Magnetism developed by electricity. **2.** The science that treats of the relations between electricity and magnetism and the resulting phenomena. — **e·lec′tro·mag·net′ic** (-mag·net′ik) *adj.* — **e·lec′tro·mag·net′i·cal·ly** *adv.*

electromagnetic wave *Physics* Any of a class of waves propagated by a system of electric and magnetic fields and including all forms of radiant energy from radio and light waves to gamma and cosmic rays.

e·lec·trom·e·ter (i·lek′trom′ə·tər, ē′lek-) *n.* An instrument for measuring the voltage of an electric current.

e·lec·trom·e·try (i·lek′trom′ə·trē, ē′lek-) *n.* The science of making electrical measurements. — **e·lec·tro·met·ric** (i·lek′trō·met′rik) or **·ri·cal** *adj.*

e·lec·tro·mo·tive (i·lek′trə·mō′tiv) *adj.* Producing, or tending to produce, a flow of electric current.

electromotive force 1. That which tends to produce a flow of electricity from one point to another. 2. Difference of electrical potential between two points in a circuit, a battery, etc.; voltage. Abbr. *emf., e.m.f., E.M.F.*

e·lec·tron (i·lek′tron) *n.* An atomic particle carrying a unit charge of negative electricity, and having a mass approximately one eighteen-hundredth of that of the proton. [< Gk. *ēlektron* amber]

e·lec·tro·neg·a·tive (i·lek′trō·neg′ə·tiv) *adj.* 1. Appearing at the positive electrode in electrolysis. 2. Having the property of becoming negatively electrified by contact or chemical action. 3. Nonmetallic.

e·lec·tron·ic (i·lek′tron′ik, ē′lek-) *adj.* 1. Of or pertaining to electrons. 2. Operating or produced by the movement of free electrons, as in radio and radar. 3. Pertaining to electronics. — **e·lec′tron′i·cal·ly** *adv.*

e·lec·tron·ics (i·lek′tron′iks, ē′lek-) *n.pl.* (*construed as sing.*) The study of the properties and behavior of electrons under all conditions, esp. with reference to technical and industrial applications.

electron microscope A powerful microscope that projects a greatly enlarged image of an object held in the path of a sharply focused electron beam.

electron tube A device in which a stream of electrons is conducted through a vacuum or a rarefied gas and usu. controlled by a grid: also called *vacuum tube.*

electron volt The energy acquired by an electron that passes through a potential difference of one volt.

e·lec·tro·pho·re·sis (i·lek′trō·fə·rē′sis) *n. Chem.* The movement of the electrically charged colloidal particles in a fluid, when under the influence of an electric field.

e·lec·troph·o·rus (i·lek′trof′ər·əs, ē′lek-) *n. pl.* **·ri** (-rī) An instrument for generating static electricity by induction. Also **e·lec·tro·phore** (i·lek′trə·fôr, -fōr).

e·lec·tro·plate (i·lek′trə·plāt′) *v.t.* **·plat·ed, ·plat·ing** To coat (an object) with metal by electrodeposition. — *n.* An electroplated article. — **e·lec′tro·plat′er** *n.*

e·lec·tro·pos·i·tive (i·lek′trō·poz′ə·tiv) *adj.* 1. Appearing at the negative electrode in electrolysis. 2. Having the property of becoming positively electrified by contact or chemical action. 3. Basic; not acid.

e·lec·tro·scope (i·lek′trə·skōp) *n.* An instrument for detecting the presence of an electric charge upon a conductor by the attraction or repulsion of pith balls or strips of gold leaf. — **e·lec′tro·scop′ic** (-skop′ik) *adj.*

e·lec·tro·stat·ics (i·lek′trō·stat′iks) *n.pl.* (*construed as sing.*) A branch of physics that deals primarily with electric charges, fields, induction in conductors, and polarization in dielectrics. — **e·lec′tro·stat′ic** or **·i·cal** *adj.* — **e·lec′tro·stat′i·cal·ly** *adv.*

e·lec·tro·ther·a·peu·tics (i·lek′trō·ther′ə·pyōō′tiks) *n.pl.* (*construed as sing.*) 1. The treatment of disease by electricity. 2. The principles of such treatment. Also **e·lec′tro·ther′a·py.** — **e·lec′tro·ther′a·peu′tic** or **·ti·cal** *adj.*

e·lec·tro·type (i·lek′trə·tīp′) *n.* 1. A metallic copy, made by electrodeposition, of any surface, esp. of a page of type for printing. 2. An impression from an electrotype. — *v.t.* **·typed, ·typ·ing** To make an electrotype of. — **e·lec′tro·typ′er, e·lec′tro·typ′ist** *n.* — **e·lec′tro·typ′ic** *adj.* — **e·lec′tro·typ′ing** *n.*

e·lec·trum (i·lek′trəm) *n.* An alloy of native gold and silver. [< L < Gk. *ēlektron* amber]

el·ee·mos·y·nar·y (el′ə·mos′ə·ner′ē, el′ē·ə-) *adj.* 1. Of or pertaining to charity or alms. 2. Aided by or dependent upon charity. 3. Done as a charitable act. [See ALMS.]

el·e·gance (el′ə·gəns) *n.* 1. The state or quality of being elegant or refined; tasteful opulence. 2. Something elegant, as a fastidiously chosen word or phrase. Also **el′e·gan·cy.**

el·e·gant (el′ə·gənt) *adj.* 1. Tastefully ornate in dress, furnishings, etc. 2. Marked by grace and refinement, as in style, manners, etc. 3. Marked by ingenuity and simplicity. 4. *Informal* Excellent; first-rate. [< F < L < *e-* out + *legare* to choose] — **el′e·gant·ly** *adv.*

el·e·gi·ac (el′ə·jī′ək, i·lē′jē·ak) *adj.* 1. Pertaining to ele-

gies. 2. Like an elegy; sad; lamenting. — *n. Usu. pl.* Verse composed in elegiac form.

el·e·gize (el′ə·jīz) *v.* **·gized, ·giz·ing** *v.i.* 1. To write elegiac verse. — *v.t.* 2. To lament or commemorate in elegy.

el·e·gy (el′ə·jē) *n. pl.* **·gies** 1. In classical prosody, a poem written in elegiac verse. 2. Any meditative poem of lamentation. 3. *Music* A work of lamentation or mourning. [< F < L < Gk. *elegos* a song of lament] — **el′e·gist** *n.*

E·lek·tra (i·lek′trə) See ELECTRA.

el·e·ment (el′ə·mənt) *n.* 1. A relatively simple constituent that is a basic part of a whole; an essential, principle, fact, etc.: the *elements* of poetry. 2. A group or class of people belonging to a larger group but distinguished from it by belief, behavior, etc.: a rowdy *element* in a crowd; the conservative *element.* 3. One of four substances (earth, air, fire, water) anciently viewed as composing the physical universe. 4. The surrounding conditions best suited to some person or thing. 5. *pl.* Atmospheric powers or forces: the fury of the *elements.* 6. *Physics & Chem.* One of a limited number of substances, as gold or carbon, each of which is composed entirely of atoms having the same atomic number, and none of which may be decomposed by ordinary chemical means. See table below. 7. *Mil.* A subdivision of an organization or formation: a command *element.* 8. *Eccl.* The bread or wine of the Eucharist. [< L *elementum* first principle]

TABLE OF ELEMENTS

Name	Symbol	Atomic No.	Atomic Wt.
Actinium	Ac	89	227
Aluminum	Al	13	26.9815
Americium	Am	95	243
Antimony (*stibium*)	Sb	51	121.75
Argon	Ar	18	39.948
Arsenic	As	33	74.9216
Astatine	At	85	210
Barium	Ba	56	137.34
Berkelium	Bk	97	249
Beryllium	Be	4	9.0122
Bismuth	Bi	83	208.98
Boron	B	5	10.811
Bromine	Br	35	79.909
Cadmium	Cd	48	112.40
Calcium	Ca	20	40.08
Californium	Cf	98	251
Carbon	C	6	12.01115
Cerium	Ce	58	140.12
Cesium	Cs	55	132.905
Chlorine	Cl	17	35.453
Chromium	Cr	24	51.996
Cobalt	Co	27	58.9332
Columbium	(Cb)		
See NIOBIUM			
Copper (*cuprum*)	Cu	29	63.54
Curium	Cm	96	247
Dysprosium	Dy	66	162.50
Einsteinium	Es	99	254
Erbium	Er	68	167.26
Europium	Eu	63	151.96
Fermium	Fm	100	253
Fluorine	F	9	18.9984
Francium	Fr	87	223
Gadolinium	Gd	64	157.25
Gallium	Ga	31	69.72
Germanium	Ge	32	72.59
Glucinum			
See BERYLLIUM			
Gold (*aurum*)	Au	79	196.967
Hafnium	Hf	72	178.44
Helium	He	2	4.0026
Holmium	Ho	67	164.93
Hydrogen	H	1	1.00797
Indium	In	49	114.82
Iodine	I	53	126.9044
Iridium	Ir	77	192.2
Iron (*ferrum*)	Fe	26	55.847
Krypton	Kr	36	83.80
Lanthanum	La	57	138.91
Lawrencium	Lw	103	257?
Lead (*plumbum*)	Pb	82	207.19
Lithium	Li	3	6.939
Lutetium	Lu	71	174.97
Magnesium	Mg	12	24.312
Manganese	Mn	25	54.938
Mendelevium	Md	101	256
Mercury (*hydrargyrum*)	Hg	80	200.59
Molybdenum	Mo	42	95.94
Neodymium	Nd	60	144.24
Neon	Ne	10	20.183
Neoytterbium			
See YTTERBIUM			
Neptunium	Np	93	237
Nickel	Ni	28	58.71
Niobium	Nb	41	92.906

(*continued*)

NAME	Symbol	Atomic No.	Atomic Wt.
Niton	See RADON		
Nitrogen	N	7	14.0067
Nobelium	No	102	253
Osmium	Os	76	190.2
Oxygen	O	8	15.9994
Palladium	Pd	46	106.4
Phosphorus	P	15	30.9738
Platinum	Pt	78	195.09
Plutonium	Pu	94	242
Polonium	Po	84	210
Potassium (*kalium*)	K	19	39.102
Praseodymium	Pr	59	140.90
Promethium	Pm	61	147
Proctactinium	Pa	91	231
Radium	Ra	88	226.05
Radon	Rn	86	222
Rhenium	Re	75	186.20
Rhodium	Rh	45	102.905
Rubidium	Rb	37	85.47
Ruthenium	Ru	44	101.07
Samarium	Sm	62	150.35
Scandium	Sc	21	44.956
Selenium	Se	34	78.96
Silicon	Si	14	28.086
Silver (*argentum*)	Ag	47	107.87
Sodium (*natrium*)	Na	11	22.9898
Strontium	Sr	38	87.62
Sulfur	S	16	32.064
Tantalum	Ta	73	180.948
Technetium	Tc	43	99
Tellurium	Te	52	127.60
Terbium	Tb	65	158.924
Thallium	Tl	81	204.37
Thorium	Th	90	232.038
Thulium	Tm	69	168.934
Tin (*stannum*)	Sn	50	118.69
Titanium	Ti	22	47.90
Tungsten	W	74	183.85
Uranium	U	92	238.03
Vanadium	V	23	50.942
Wolfram	See TUNGSTEN		
Xenon	Xe	54	131.30
Ytterbium	Yb	70	173.04
Yttrium	Y	39	88.90
Zinc	Zn	30	65.37
Zirconium	Zr	40	91.22

el·e·men·tal (el'ə·men'təl) *adj.* **1.** Of or relating to an element or elements. **2.** Fundamental and relatively simple; basic. **3.** Relating to first principles; rudimentary. **4.** Of or suggestive of the powerful forces at work in nature or in man. **5.** Chemically uncombined. — **el'e·men'tal·ly** *adv.*

el·e·men·ta·ry (el'ə·men'tər·ē, -men'trē) *adj.* **1.** Elemental. **2.** Fundamental; basic. **3.** Simple and rudimentary. — **el·e·men'ta·ri·ly** *adv.* — **el'e·men'ta·ri·ness** *n.*

elementary school A school giving a course of education of from six to eight years, pupils usu. entering at about six years of age: also called *grade school, grammar school*.

el·e·phant (el'ə·fənt) *n.* A massively built, almost hairless mammal of Asia and Africa, having a flexible trunk, and the upper incisors developed as tusks, which are the chief source of ivory. The **Asian elephant** has relatively small ears, and the **African elephant** has large, flapping ears. [< OF < L < Gk. *elephas*, *-antos* ivory]

el·e·phan·ti·a·sis (el'ə·fən·tī'ə·sis) *n. Pathol.* A disease caused by a parasitic worm, characterized by a hardening of the skin, and an enormous enlargement of the part affected. [< L < Gk. < *elephas* elephant]

el·e·phan·tine (el'ə·fən'tin, -tēn, -tīn) *adj.* **1.** Of or pertaining to an elephant. **2.** Enormous; unwieldy; ponderous.

El·eu·sin·i·an (el'yōō·sin'ē·ən) **mysteries** The secret religious rites originated in ancient Greece at Eleusis.

el·e·vate (el'ə·vāt) *v.t.* **·vat·ed, ·vat·ing** **1.** To lift up; raise. **2.** To raise in rank, status, etc. **3.** To raise the spirits of; cheer; elate. **4.** To raise the pitch or loudness of (the voice). **5.** To raise the moral character or intellectual level of. [< L *e-* out + *levare* to lighten, raise]

el·e·vat·ed (el'ə·vā'tid) *adj.* **1.** Raised up; high. **2.** Lofty in character; sublime. **3.** In high spirits; elated. — *n. U.S. Informal* An overhead railroad.

el·e·va·tion (el'ə·vā'shən) *n.* **1.** The act of elevating, or the state of being elevated. **2.** An elevated place. **3.** Height above sea level. **4.** Loftiness of thought, feeling, station, etc. **5.** In dancing, the ability to leap. **6.** *Often cap. Eccl.* The raising of the eucharistic elements for adoration during the Mass. **7.** *Astron.* The angular distance of a celestial body above the horizon. **8.** In drafting, a side, front, or rear view of a machine or other structure.

el·e·va·tor (el'ə·vā'tər) *n.* **1.** One who or that which elevates. **2.** A mechanism for hoisting grain. **3.** *U.S.* A granary. **4.** *U.S.* A movable platform or car that carries passengers or freight up and down.

e·lev·en (i·lev'ən) *n.* **1.** The sum of ten and one: a cardinal number. **2.** Any symbol of this number, as 11, xi, XI. **3.** Anything consisting of or representing eleven units. — *adj.* Being one more than ten. [OE *endleofan* one left over (after ten)] — **e·lev'enth** *adj. & n.*

elf (elf) *n. pl.* **elves** (elvz) **1.** In folklore, a dwarfish sprite with magical powers, usu. intent upon playful mischief. **2.** Any mischievous creature. **3.** A tiny person. [OE *æľf*] — **elf'ish** *adj.* — **elf'ish·ly** *adv.* — **elf'ish·ness** *n.*

elf·in (el'fin) *adj.* Elfish. — *n.* An elf.

elf·lock (elf'lok') *n.* A lock of hair tangled as if by elves.

e·lic·it (i·lis'it) *v.t.* **1.** To draw out or forth; evoke: to *elicit* a reply. **2.** To bring to light: to *elicit* the truth. [< L < *e-* out + *lacere* to entice] — **e·lic'i·ta'tion** *n.* — **e·lic'i·tor** *n.*

e·lide (i·līd') *v.t.* **e·lid·ed, e·lid·ing** **1.** To omit (a vowel or syllable) in pronunciation. **2.** To suppress; omit; ignore. [< L < *e-* out + *laedere* to strike] — **e·lid/i·ble** *adj.*

el·i·gi·bil·i·ty (el'ə·jə·bil'ə·tē) *n. pl.* **·ties** **1.** The quality of being eligible; suitableness. **2.** *pl.* Qualities that make a person or thing eligible.

el·i·gi·ble (el'ə·jə·bəl) *adj.* **1.** Capable of and qualified for an office, position, function, etc. **2.** Fit for or worthy of choice or adoption. **3.** Agreeable to have; suitable. — *n.* An eligible person. [See ELECT.] — **el'i·gi·bly** *adv.*

E·li·jah (i·lī'jə) Ninth-century B.C. Hebrew prophet: also **E·li·as** (i·lī'əs). [< Hebrew, Jehovah is my God]

e·lim·i·nate (i·lim'ə·nāt) *v.t.* **·nat·ed, ·nat·ing** **1.** To get rid of. **2.** To ignore. **3.** To remove (a contestant, team, etc.) from further competition by defeating. **4.** *Physiol.* To void; excrete. **5.** *Math.* To remove (a quantity) from a system of algebraic equations. [< L < *e-* out + *limen* threshold] — **e·lim/i·na'tion** *n.* — **e·lim/i·na'tor** *n.* — **e·lim/i·na'tive, e·lim/i·na·to/ry** (-nə·tôr'ē, -tō'rē) *adj.*

E·li·sha (i·lī'shə) Ninth-century B.C. Hebrew prophet, successor of Elijah. [< Hebrew, God is Salvation]

e·li·sion (i·lizh'ən) *n.* Omission of a vowel or syllable, as in "th' imperial towers." [See ELIDE.]

e·lite (ā·lēt') *n.* **1.** The choicest part, as of a social group. **2.** A size of typewriter type, equivalent to 10-point, with 12 characters to the inch. *Also U.S.* **e·lite'**. [See ELECT.]

e·lix·ir (i·lik'sər) *n.* **1.** A sweetened alcoholic medicinal preparation. **2.** In ancient philosophy, a substance sought by alchemists for changing base metals into gold, or for prolonging life: also **elixir vi·tae** (vī'tē). **3.** The essential principle of anything. **4.** A cure-all. [< Med.L < Arabic *al-iksīr* < Gk. *zērion* medicated powder]

E·liz·a·be·than (i·liz'ə·bē'thən, -beth'ən) *adj.* Of or pertaining to Elizabeth I of England, or to her era. — *n.* An Englishman living during the reign of Elizabeth I.

Elizabethan sonnet A Shakespearean sonnet.

elk (elk) *n. pl.* **elks** or **elk** **1.** A large deer of northern Europe and Asia. **2.** The wapiti. **3.** A pliant, tanned leather of calfskin, horsehide, etc. [ME < OE *elh*]

ell¹ (el) *n.* A measure of length now rarely used: in England, 45 inches or 1.114 meters. [OE *eln* an arm's length]

ell² (el) *n.* Anything shaped like the letter L.

el·lipse (i·lips') *n. Geom.* A plane curve such that the sum of the distances from any point of the curve to two fixed points, called *foci*, is a constant; a conic section. [< L *ellipsis*.] See ELLIPSIS.

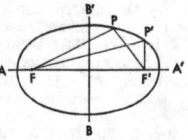

ELLIPSE

AA' Major axis. *BB'* Minor axis. *F, F'* Foci. *P, P'* Points on curve.
$(FP + F'P = FP' + F'P')$

el·lip·sis (i·lip'sis) *n. pl.* **·ses** (-sēz) **1.** *Gram.* The omission of a word or words necessary for the complete grammatical construction of a sentence, but not required for the understanding of it. **2.** Marks (... or ***) indicating omission. [< L < Gk. < *en-* in + *leipsis* a leaving < *leipein* to leave]

el·lip·tic (i·lip'tik) *adj.* **1.** Of, pertaining to, or shaped like an ellipse. **2.** *Gram.* Characterized by ellipsis; shortened. *Also* **el·lip'ti·cal**. — **el·lip'ti·cal·ly** *adv.*

elm (elm) *n.* **1.** A shade tree of America, Europe, and Asia, having a broad, spreading, or overarching top. **2.** The wood of this tree. [OE] — **elm'y** *adj.*

el·o·cu·tion (el'ə·kyōō'shən) *n.* **1.** The art of public speaking, including vocal delivery and gesture. **2.** Manner of speaking. [< L < *e-* out + *loqui* to speak] — **el/o·cu'·tion·ar'y** *adj.* — **el'o·cu'tion·ist** *n.*

E·lo·him (e·lō·him', e·lō'him) God: Hebrew name used in the Old Testament. [< Hebrew *'Elōhim*, pl. of *'Elōah* God]

e·lon·gate (i·lông'gāt, i·long'-) *v.t. & v.i.* **·gat·ed, ·gat·ing** To increase in length; stretch. — *adj.* Drawn out; lengthened. [< LL < L *e-* out + *longe* far off] — **e·lon·ga'tion** *n.*

e·lope (i·lōp') *v.i.* **e·loped, e·lop·ing** **1.** To run away with a lover, usu. to get married. **2.** To abscond. [< AF *aloper*.] — **e·lope'ment** *n.* — **e·lop'er** *n.*

el·o·quence (el'ə·kwəns) *n.* **1.** Fluent, polished, and effective use of language, esp. in public speaking. **2.** The quality of being moving, forceful, or persuasive.

el·o·quent (el'ə·kwənt) *adj.* **1.** Possessed of or manifesting eloquence. **2.** Visibly expressive of emotion: *eloquent* tears. [< L < e- out + *loqui* to speak] — **el'o·quent·ly** *adv.*

else (els) *adv.* **1.** In a different place, time, or way; instead: Where *else*? How *else*? **2.** If the case or facts were different; otherwise: Hurry, or *else* you will be caught. — *adj.* Additional; different: somebody *else*. [OE *elles*. Akin to L *alius*.]

else·where (els'hwâr') *adv.* In or to another place or places; somewhere or anywhere else.

e·lu·ci·date (i·lōō'sə·dāt) *v.* **·dat·ed, ·dat·ing** *v.t.* **1.** To make clear; explain. — *v.i.* **2.** To clarify something. [< LL < L e- out + *lucidus* clear] — **e·lu'ci·da'tion** *n.* — **e·lu'ci·da'tive** *adj.* — **e·lu'ci·da'tor** *n.*

e·lude (i·lōōd') *v.t.* **e·lud·ed, e·lud·ing** **1.** To avoid or escape from by dexterity or artifice; evade. **2.** To escape the notice or understanding of: The meaning *eludes* me. [< L < e- out + *ludere* to play]

E·lul (e·lōōl', el'ōōl) *n.* The twelfth month of the Hebrew year. See (Hebrew) CALENDAR.

e·lu·sive (i·lōō'siv) *adj.* Tending to slip away; hard to grasp or perceive: an *elusive* fragrance. Also **e·lu'so·ry** (-sər·ē). — **e·lu'sive·ly** *adv.* — **e·lu'sive·ness** *n.*

elves (elvz) Plural of ELF.

elv·ish (el'vish) *adj.* Elfish. — **elv'ish·ly** *adv.*

E·ly·si·um (i·lizh'ē·əm, i·liz'-) **1.** In Greek mythology, the land of the blessed dead. Also **Elysian Fields. 2.** A place or condition of supreme delight; paradise. [< L < Gk. *Elysion* (*pedion*) the Elysian (field)] — **E·ly·sian** (i·lizh'ən, -ē·ən) *adj.*

em (em) *n. Printing* The square of the body size of a type; esp., a pica em, about ⅙ of an inch, used as a standard unit of measurement: originally, the size of the letter M.

em-[1] Var. of EN-[1].

em-[2] Var. of EN-[2].

'em (əm, m) *pron. Informal* Them.

e·ma·ci·ate (i·mā'shē·āt) *v.t.* **·at·ed, ·at·ing** To make abnormally lean; cause to lose flesh. [< L *macies* leanness] — **e·ma'ci·at'ed** *adj.* — **e·ma'ci·a'tion** *n.*

em·a·nate (em'ə·nāt) *v.i.* **nat·ed, nat·ing** To flow forth from a source; issue. [< L < e- out + *manare* to flow]

em·a·na·tion (em'ə·nā'shən) *n.* **1.** The act of emanating. **2.** Something that emanates; efflux; effluence. **3.** *Physics* A gaseous product of disintegration in certain radioactive substances, as radon and thoron. — **em'a·na'tive** *adj.*

e·man·ci·pate (i·man'sə·pāt) *v.t.* **·pat·ed, ·pat·ing** **1.** To release from bondage, oppression, or authority; set free. **2.** *Law* To free (a child) from paternal control. [< L < e- out + *manus* hand + *capere* to take] — **e·man'ci·pa'tive** *adj.* — **e·man'ci·pa'tion** *n.* — **e·man'ci·pa'tor** *n.*

Emancipation Proclamation A proclamation issued by President Abraham Lincoln on January 1, 1863, declaring free all Negro slaves in all States.

e·mas·cu·late (*v.* i·mas'kyə·lāt; *adj.* i·mas'kyə·lit) *v.t.* **·lat·ed, ·lat·ing 1.** To deprive of procreative power; castrate; geld. **2.** To deprive of strength and vigor; weaken. — *adj.* Emasculated; effeminate; weakened. [< L *emasculare* < e- away + *masculus* male] — **e·mas'cu·la'tion** *n.* — **e·mas'cu·la·tor** *n.* — **e·mas·cu·la·to·ry** (i·mas'kyə·lə·tôr'ē, -tō'rē), **e·mas'cu·la·tive** *adj.*

em·balm (im·bäm') *v.t.* **1.** To preserve (a dead body) from decay by treatment with chemicals, etc. **2.** To perfume or keep in memory. [< F *embaumer*] — **em·balm'er** *n.*

em·bank·ment (im·bangk'mənt) *n.* A mound or bank raised to hold back water, support a roadway, etc.

em·bar·go (im·bär'gō) *n. pl.* **·goes 1.** An order by a government restraining merchant vessels from leaving or entering its ports. **2.** Authoritative stoppage of foreign commerce or of any special trade. **3.** A restraint or prohibition. — *v.t.* **·goes, ·go·ing** To lay an embargo upon. [< Sp. < *embargar*, ult. < LL *barra* bar]

em·bark (im·bärk') *v.t.* **1.** To put or take aboard a vessel. **2.** To invest (money) or involve (a person) in a venture. — *v.i.* **3.** To go aboard a vessel for a voyage. **4.** To engage in a venture. [< F < LL < *in-* in + *barca* boat] — **em·bar·ka·tion, em·bar·ca·tion** (em'bär·kā'shən) *n.* — **em·bark'ment** *n.*

em·bar·rass (im·bar'əs) *v.t.* **1.** To make self-conscious and uncomfortable; abash; disconcert. **2.** To involve in financial difficulties. **3.** To hamper; impede. **4.** To render difficult; complicate. [< F < em- in + *barre* < OF] — **em·bar'rass·ing** *adj.* — **em·bar'rass·ing·ly** *adv.* — **em·bar'rass·ment** *n.*

em·bas·sy (em'bə·sē) *n. pl.* **·sies 1.** An ambassador together with his staff. **2.** The mission, function, or position of an ambassador. **3.** The official residence or headquarters of an ambassador. [< OF < Med.L < L *ambactus* servant]

em·bat·tle (em·bat'l) *v.t.* **·tled, ·tling** To form in line of battle; prepare or equip for battle. [< OF < *em*[1]- in + *bataille* < L *battuere* to beat]

em·bed (im·bed') *v.t.* **·bed·ded, ·bed·ding 1.** To set firmly in surrounding matter. **2.** To place in or as in a bed. — **em·bed'ment** *n.*

em·bel·lish (im·bel'ish) *v.t.* **1.** To beautify by adding ornamental features; decorate. **2.** To heighten the interest of (a narrative) by adding fictitious details. [< OF < em- in + *bel* beautiful] — **em·bel'lish·er** *n.* — **em·bel'lish·ment** *n.*

em·ber (em'bər) *n.* **1.** A live coal or unextinguished brand. **2.** *pl.* A dying fire. [OE *æmerge*]

em·bez·zle (im·bez'əl) *v.t.* **·zled, ·zling** To appropriate fraudulently to one's own use, as money or securities entrusted to one's care. [< AF < em- in + *besiler* to destroy] — **em·bez'zle·ment** *n.* — **em·bez'zler** *n.*

em·bit·ter (im·bit'ər) *v.t.* To make bitter, unhappy, or resentful. — **em·bit'ter·ment** *n.*

em·bla·zon (em·blā'zən) *v.t.* **1.** To adorn magnificently, esp. with heraldic devices. **2.** To extol; celebrate. — **em·bla'zon·er** *n.* — **em·bla'zon·ment** *n.* — **em·bla'zon·ry** *n.*

em·blem (em'bləm) *n.* **1.** An object or pictorial device that serves to represent something more or less abstract; symbol. **2.** A distinctive badge or figured object. [< L < Gk. < *em-* in + *ballein* to throw]

em·blem·at·ic (em'blə·mat'ik) *adj.* Of, pertaining to, or serving as an emblem; symbolic. Also **em'blem·at'i·cal.** — **em'blem·at'i·cal·ly** *adv.*

em·bod·i·ment (im·bod'i·mənt) *n.* **1.** The act of embodying, or the state of being embodied. **2.** That which embodies, or in which something is embodied.

em·bod·y (im·bod'ē) *v.t.* **·bod·ied, ·bod·y·ing 1.** To invest with or as with a body; put into visible or concrete form: to *embody* ideals in action. **2.** To collect into, or make part of, an organized whole; incorporate.

em·bold·en (im·bōl'dən) *v.t.* To give courage to.

em·bo·lism (em'bə·liz'əm) *n. Pathol.* The stopping up of a vein or artery by an embolus.

em·bo·lus (em'bə·ləs) *n. pl.* **·li** (-lī) *Pathol.* A foreign body that forms an obstruction in a blood vessel, as a piece of fibrin, a blood clot, or an air bubble. [< L < Gk. < en- in + *ballein* to throw] — **em·bol·ic** (em·bol'ik) *adj.*

em·bos·om (em·bōoz'əm, -bōo'zəm) *v.t.* **1.** To embrace. **2.** To cherish. **3.** To enclose protectively; shelter.

em·boss (im·bôs', -bos') *v.t.* **1.** To cover or adorn (a surface) with raised figures, designs, etc. **2.** To raise or represent (designs, figures, etc.) from or upon a surface. **3.** To decorate sumptuously. [Origin unknown] — **em·boss'er** *n.* — **em·boss'ment** *n.*

em·bou·chure (äm·bōo·shōor', Fr. än·bōo·shür') *n.* **1.** The mouth of a river. **2.** The opening out of a river valley into flat land. **3.** *Music* a The mouthpiece of a wind instrument. b The position or application of the lips and tongue in playing a wind instrument. [< F < em- in + *bouche* mouth]

em·bow·er (em·bou'ər) *v.t. & v.i.* To cover or shelter in or as in a bower.

em·brace (im·brās') *v.* **·braced, ·brac·ing** *v.t.* **1.** To clasp or infold in the arms; hug. **2.** To accept willingly; adopt, as a religion or doctrine. **3.** To avail oneself of: to *embrace* an offer. **4.** To surround; encircle. **5.** To include; contain. **6.** To take in visually or mentally. **7.** To have sexual intercourse with. — *v.i.* **8.** To hug each other. — *n.* The act of embracing. [< OF *embracer*, ult. < L in- in + *bracchium* arm] — **em·brace'ment** *n.* — **em·brac'er** *n.*

em·bra·sure (em·brā'zhər) *n.* **1.** *Archit.* An opening in a wall, as for a window or door, sloped or beveled so as to enlarge its interior outline. **2.** An opening that enlarges inwardly or outwardly in a parapet, battlement, or wall. [< F < *embraser* (*ébraser*) to widen (an opening)]

em·broi·der (im·broi'dər) *v.t.* **1.** To ornament (cloth) with designs in needlework. **2.** To execute (a design) in needlework. **3.** To exaggerate. — *v.i.* **4.** To make embroidery. [< MF *broder* to stitch] — **em·broi'der·er** *n.*

em·broi·der·y (im·broi'dər·ē) *n. pl.* **·der·ies 1.** Ornamental needlework. **2.** Any elaborate ornamentation.

em·broil (em·broil') *v.t.* **1.** To involve in dissension or strife. **2.** To complicate or confuse. [< F < em- + *brouiller* to confuse] — **em·broil'ment** *n.*

em·bry·o (em'brē·ō) *n. pl.* **·os 1.** *Biol.* The earliest stages in the development of an organism, before it has assumed its distinctive form, in the human species, the first eight weeks. **2.** *Bot.* The rudimentary plant within the seed. **3.** The rudimentary stage of anything. Also **em'bry·on.** — *adj.* Rudimentary. [< Gk < en- in + *bryein* to swell]

embryo- *combining form* Embryo; embryonic. Also, before vowels, **embry-.** [< Gk. *embryon* embryo]

em·bry·ol·o·gy (em'brē·ol'ə·jē) *n.* The science that deals with the origin, structure, and development of the embryo.

—em·bry·o·log·i·cal (em'brē·ə·loj'i·kəl) or em'bry·o·log'ic adj. — em'bry·o·log'i·cal·ly adv. — em'bry·ol'o·gist n.

em·bry·on·ic (em'brē·on'ik) adj. Of, pertaining to, or in the state of an embryo; rudimentary; immature; undeveloped.

em·cee (em'sē') Informal n. Master of ceremonies. — v.t. & v.i. ·ceed, ·cee·ing To act as master of ceremonies.

e·meer (ə·mir') See EMIR.

e·mend (i·mend') v.t. 1. To make corrections or changes in (a literary work, etc.), esp. after scholarly study. 2. To free from faults. [< L < e- out + menda fault] — e·mend'a·ble adj. — e·mend'er n.

e·men·date (ē'men·dāt) v.t. ·dat·ed, ·dat·ing To emend (a text). — e·men·da·tion (ē'men·dā'shən, em'en-) n. — e'men·da'tor n. — e·mend·a·to·ry (i·men'də·tôr'ē) adj.

em·er·ald (em'ər·əld, em'rəld) n. 1. A bright green variety of beryl, valued as a jewel. 2. A rich green. — adj. 1. Of, pertaining to, or like the emerald. 2. Of a rich green color. [< OF emeraude, esmeralde < L < Gk. smaragdos]

Emerald Isle Ireland: so called from its green landscape.

e·merge (i·mûrj') v.i. e·merged, e·merg·ing 1. To come forth as from water, a hiding place, etc. 2. To come to light; become apparent. [< L < e- out + mergere to dip] — e·mer'gence n. — e·mer'gent adj.

e·mer·gen·cy (i·mûr'jən·sē) n. pl. ·cies A sudden and unexpected turn of events calling for immediate action.

e·mer·i·tus (i·mer'ə·təs) adj. Retired from active service, usu. because of age, but retained in an honorary position: professor emeritus. — n. pl. ·ti (-tī) One who is emeritus. [< L, pp. of emerere < e- out + merere to earn]

e·mer·sion (ē·mûr'shən, -zhən) n. An emerging.

em·er·y (em'ər·ē, em'rē) n. A very hard, black or grayish black variety of corundum mixed with magnesite and other minerals, used as an abrasive. [F < OF < LL < Gk. smēris emery powder]

e·met·ic (i·met'ik) adj. Tending to produce vomiting. — n. An emetic agent. [< Gk. < emeein to vomit]

-emia combining form Med. Blood; condition of the blood: used in names of diseases: leukemia. Also spelled -aemia, -haemia, -hemia. [< Gk. haima blood]

em·i·grant (em'ə·grənt) adj. Moving from one place or country to settle in another. — n. A person who emigrates.

em·i·grate (em'ə·grāt) v.i. ·grat·ed, ·grat·ing To move away from one country, or section of a country, to settle in another. — Syn. see MIGRATE. [< L < e- out + migrare to move] — em'i·gra'tion n.

é·mi·gré (em'ə·grā, Fr. ā·mē·grā') An emigrant; esp. one who fled to escape the French or Russian revolution.

em·i·nence (em'ə·nəns) n. 1. Superiority in rank, power, achievement, etc. 2. A high place or elevation, as a hill. Also em'i·nen·cy. [< L < e- out + minere to jut out]

Em·i·nence (em'ə·nəns) n. A title for cardinals.

em·i·nent (em'ə·nənt) adj. 1. High in station, merit, or esteem; distinguished: an eminent scholar. 2. Noteworthy; conspicuous: eminent valor. 3. High; lofty: an eminent tower. [< L eminere to stand out] — em'i·nent·ly adv.

eminent domain Law The right or power of the state to take or control private property for public use.

e·mir (ə·mir') n. 1. A Moslem prince or commander. 2. A descendant of Mohammed. 3. A high Turkish official. Also spelled emeer. [< Arabic amīr ruler] — e·mir'ate n.

em·is·sar·y (em'ə·ser'ē) n. pl. ·sar·ies 1. A person sent on a mission as an agent or representative of a government. 2. A secret agent; spy. — adj. Of, pertaining to, or serving as an emissary. [< L emissarius < emittere to send out]

e·mis·sion (i·mish'ən) n. 1. The act of emitting. 2. That which is emitted. 3. The issuance of currency, notes, shares, etc. [< L emissio, -onis < -e out + mittere to send]

e·mis·sive (i·mis'iv) adj. Sending or sent forth; emitting.

e·mit (i·mit') v.t. e·mit·ted, e·mit·ting 1. To send forth or give off (light, heat, sound, etc.); discharge. 2. To give expression to; utter, as an opinion. 3. To issue authoritatively, as an edict. 4. To put into circulation, as money. [< L < e- out + mittere to send] — e·mit'ter n.

Em·man·u·el (i·man'yōō·əl) See IMMANUEL.

e·mol·lient (i·mol'yənt, -ē·ənt) adj. Softening or relaxing; soothing, esp. to the skin. — n. Med. A softening or soothing medicament. [< L < e- thoroughly + mollire to soften]

e·mol·u·ment (i·mol'yə·mənt) n. A salary or fee as for a service. [< L < e- out + molere to grind]

e·mote (i·mōt') v.i. e·mot·ed, e·mot·ing Informal To exhibit an exaggerated emotion, as in acting. [< EMOTION]

e·mo·tion (i·mō'shən) n. 1. A strong surge of feeling marked by an impulse to outward expression and often accompanied by complex bodily reactions; any strong feeling, as love, hate, or joy. 2. The power of feeling; sensibility. [< L emotio, -onis < e- out + movere to move]

e·mo·tion·al (i·mō'shən·əl) adj. 1. Of, pertaining to, or expressive of emotion. 2. Easily or excessively affected by emotion. 3. Arousing the emotions. — e·mo·tion·al·ist n. — e·mo·tion·al'i·ty n. — e·mo·tion·al·ly adv.

e·mo·tion·al·ism (i·mō'shən·əl·iz'əm) n. 1. The tendency to overindulge the emotions or to be too much affected by them. 2. A display of emotion. 3. Appeal to the emotions.

e·mo·tion·al·ize (i·mō'shən·əl·īz') v.t. ·ized, ·iz·ing To treat in an emotional manner. — e·mo'tion·al·i·za'tion n.

e·mo·tive (i·mō'tiv) adj. Characterized by, expressing, or tending to excite emotion: emotive eloquence. — e·mo'tive·ly adv. — e·mo'tive·ness, e·mo·tiv·i·ty (ē'mō·tiv'ə·tē) n.

em·pan·el (im·pan'əl) See IMPANEL.

em·pa·thize (em'pə·thīz) v.t. & v.i. ·thized, ·thiz·ing To regard with or feel empathy.

em·pa·thy (em'pə·thē) n. Psychol. Intellectual or imaginative apprehension of another's condition or state of mind. — em·path·ic (em·path'ik) adj. — em·path'i·cal·ly adv.

em·per·or (em'pər·ər) n. The sovereign of an empire. [< OF < L imperator commander] — em'per·or·ship' n.

em·pha·sis (em'fə·sis) n. pl. ·ses (-sēz) 1. Special significance or importance assigned to something. 2. Stress given by voice or rhetorical contrivance to a particular syllable, word, or phrase. 3. Force or intensity of meaning, action, etc. [< L < Gk. < en- in + phainein to show]

em·pha·size (em'fə·sīz) v.t. ·sized, ·siz·ing To give emphasis to; make specially prominent or important; stress.

em·phat·ic (em·fat'ik) adj. 1. Spoken or done with emphasis; forcibly expressive. 2. Characterized by forcefulness or intensity. 3. Striking; decisive. — em·phat'i·cal·ly adv.

em·phy·se·ma (em'fə·sē'mə) n. Pathol. A lung condition marked by loss of elasticity of the air sacs, causing difficulty in breathing. [< NL < Gk. emphysēma inflation]

em·pire (em'pīr) n. 1. A state, or union of states, governed by an emperor; also, the historical period of such government. 2. A union of dispersed states and unrelated peoples under one rule. 3. Wide and supreme dominion. [< F < L imperium rule, authority]

Empire State Nickname of New York.

em·pir·i·cal (em·pir'i·kəl) adj. 1. Relating to or based upon direct experience or observation alone: empirical knowledge. 2. Relying on practical experience without benefit of scientific knowledge or theory. Also em·pir'ic. [< L < Gk. < en- in + peira trial] — em·pir'i·cal·ly adv.

em·pir·i·cism (em·pir'ə·siz'əm) n. 1. Empirical method or practice. 2. Philos. The doctrine that all knowledge is derived from sensory experience. 3. Reliance on sensory observation and experiment as the bases of knowledge. 4. Quackery. — em·pir'i·cist n.

em·place·ment (im·plās'mənt) n. 1. The position assigned to guns or to a battery within a fortification; also, a gun platform, the parapet, or the like. 2. A setting in place; location. [< F < emplacer to put into position]

em·ploy (im·ploi') v.t. 1. To engage the services of; hire. 2. To provide work and livelihood for. 3. To make use of as a means or instrument: to employ cunning. 4. To devote or apply: to employ one's energies in research. — n. The state of being employed; service. [< F employer < L in- in + plicare to fold] — em·ploy'a·ble adj. — em·ploy'ment n.

em·ploy·ee (im·ploi'ē, em'ploi·ē') n. One who works for another in return for salary. Also em·ploy'e, em·ploy'é.

em·ploy·er (im·ploi'ər) n. 1. One who employs. 2. A person or business firm that employs persons for wages or salary.

em·po·ri·um (em·pôr'ē·əm, -pō'rē-) n. pl. ·po·ri·ums or ·po·ri·a (-pôr'ē·ə, -pō'rē·ə) 1. A store carrying general merchandise. 2. A trading or market center. [< L < Gk. emporion market < en- in + poros way]

em·pow·er (im·pou'ər) v.t. 1. To authorize; delegate authority to. 2. To enable; permit.

em·press (em'pris) n. 1. A woman who rules an empire. 2. The wife or widow of an emperor.

emp·ty (emp'tē) adj. ·ti·er, ·ti·est 1. Containing nothing; void; vacant: an empty pitcher; an empty room. 2. Without significance; unsubstantial; hollow: empty promises. 3. Carrying nothing: empty hands. 4. Destitute or devoid: with of: empty of compassion. 5. Informal Hungry. — v. ·tied, ·ty·ing v.t. 1. To remove the contents of. 2. To transfer the contents of (a container): to empty a bucket onto a fire. 3. To pour out or draw off (the contents of something). 4. To unburden; clear: with of. — v.i. 5. To become empty. 6. To discharge itself or its contents. — n. pl. ·ties An empty container, vehicle, etc. [OE æmetig < æmetta leisure] — emp'ti·ly adv. — emp'ti·ness n.

emp·ty-hand·ed (emp'tē·han'did) adj. Carrying nothing.

em·pyr·e·al (em·pir'ē·əl, em'pə·rē'əl, -pī-) adj. 1. Of or pertaining to the highest region of heaven. 2. Of pure fire; fiery. [< Med.L < Gk. < en- in + pyr fire]

em·py·re·an (em'pə·rē'ən, -pī-) n. 1. The highest heaven; the abode of God and the angels, anciently conceived as a region of pure fire. 2. The firmament. — adj. Empyreal.

e·mu (ē'myōō) n. A flightless, three-toed Australian bird related to the ostrich. [Prob. < Pg. ema ostrich]

em·u·late (em'yə·lāt) v.t. ·lat·ed, ·lat·ing 1. To try to equal or surpass. 2. To rival or vie with successfully. [< L < aemulus jealous] — em'u·la'tive adj. — em'u·la'tion n. — em'u·la'tive·ly adv. — em'u·la'tor n.

em·u·lous (em′yə-ləs) *adj.* **1.** Eager to equal or excel another; competitive. **2.** Pertaining to or arising from emulation. — **em′u·lous·ly** *adv.* — **em′u·lous·ness** *n.*

e·mul·si·fy (i·mul′sə-fī) *v.t.* **·fied, ·fy·ing** To make into an emulsion. — **e·mul′si·fi·ca′tion** *n.* — **e·mul′si·fi′er** *n.*

e·mul·sion (i·mul′shən) *n.* **1.** A liquid mixture in which a fatty or resinous substance is suspended in minute globules, as butter in milk. **2.** Any milky liquid. **3.** *Photog.* A light-sensitive coating for film, plates, papers, etc. [< LL < L < *e-* out + *mulgere* to milk] — **e·mul′sive** *adj.*

en (en) *n. Printing* A space half the width of an em.

en-¹ *prefix* Forming transitive verbs: **1.** (from nouns) To cover or surround with; place into or upon: *encircle.* **2.** (from adjectives and nouns) To make; cause to be or to resemble: *enable, enfeeble.* **3.** (from verbs) Often with simple intensive force, or used to form transitive verbs from intransitives: *enact.* Also *em-* before *b, p,* and sometimes *m,* as in *embark.* Many words in *en-* or *em-* have variant forms in *in-* or *im-* respectively. [< OF < L *in-* < *in* in, into]

en-² *prefix* In; into; on: *endemic.* Also *el-* before *l,* as in *ellipse; em-* before *b, m, p, ph,* as in *embolism, empathy; er-* before *r,* as in *errhine.* [< Gk. *en-* < *en* in, into]

-en¹ *suffix* Forming verbs: **1.** (from adjectives) Cause to be; become: *deepen, harden.* **2.** (from nouns) Cause to have; gain: *hearten, strengthen.* [OE *-nian*]

-en² *suffix of adjectives* Made of; resembling: *woolen.* [OE]

-en³ *suffix* Used in the past participles of many strong verbs: *broken, beaten.* [OE]

-en⁴ *suffix* Used in the plurals of certain nouns: *oxen, children.* [OE *-an,* plural ending of the weak declension]

-en⁵ *suffix* Small; little: *chicken, kitten.* [OE]

en·a·ble (in·ā′bəl) *v.t.* **·bled, ·bling** **1.** To supply with adequate power or opportunity; make able. **2.** To make possible or practicable.

en·act (in·akt′) *v.t.* **1.** To make into a law; decree. **2.** To carry out in action; perform. **3.** To represent in or as in a play; act the part of. — **en·act′a·ble** *adj.* — **en·ac′tor** *n.*

en·act·ment (in·akt′mənt) *n.* **1.** The act of enacting, or the state of being enacted. **2.** That which is enacted; a law.

en·am·el (in·am′əl) *n.* **1.** A vitreous, usu. opaque material applied by fusion to surfaces of metal, glass, or porcelain as a decoration or a protective surface. **2.** A piece executed in enamel. **3.** A paint, varnish, or lacquer that dries to form a hard, glossy surface. **4.** Any coating resembling enamel. **5.** *Anat.* The hard, glossy, calcareous outer layer of the teeth. For illus. see TOOTH. — *v.t.* **en·am·eled** or **·elled, en·am·el·ing** or **·el·ling** **1.** To cover or inlay with enamel. **2.** To surface with or as with enamel. **3.** To adorn with different colors. [< AF < *en-* on + *amayl,* OF *esmail* enamel] — **en·am′el·er** or **en·am′el·ler, en·am′el·ist** or **en·am′el·list** *n.*

en·am·el·ware (in·am′əl-wâr′) *n.* Enameled kitchenware.

en·am·or (in·am′ər) *v.t.* To inflame with love; also, to charm; fascinate: chiefly in the passive, followed by *of:* He is *enamored* of his cousin. Also *Brit.* **en·am′our.** [< OF < *en-* in + *amour* love] — **en·am′ored** *adj.*

en·camp (in·kamp′) *v.i.* **1.** To go into camp; live in a camp. — *v.t.* **2.** To place in a camp. — **en·camp′ment** *n.*

en·case (in·kās′) See INCASE.

en·caus·tic (en·kôs′tik) *adj.* Having the pigments burned in: *encaustic* tile. [< L < Gk. < *en-* in + *kaiein* to burn]

-ence *suffix of nouns* Forming nouns of action, quality, or condition from adjectives in *-ent,* as *prominence.* Compare -ENCY. See note under -ANCE. [< F < L *-entia,* suffix used to form nouns from present participles]

en·ce·phal·ic (en′sə·fal′ik) *adj.* **1.** Of or pertaining to the brain. **2.** Situated within the cranial cavity.

en·ceph·a·li·tis (en·sef′ə·lī′tis, en·sef′-) *n. Pathol.* Inflammation of the brain. — **en′ceph·a·lit′ic** (-lit′ik) *adj.*

encephalitis le·thar·gi·ca (li·thär′ji·kə) *Pathol.* An acute virus form of encephalitis, affecting the central nervous system and accompanied by fever, lethargy, and sensory disturbances: also called *sleeping sickness.*

encephalo- *combining form* The brain. Also, before vowels, **encephal-.** [< Gk. < *en-* in + *kephalē* head]

en·ceph·a·lon (en·sef′ə·lon) *n. pl.* **·la** (-lə) *Anat.* The brain. [< NL < Gk. *enkephalos*] — **en·ceph′a·lous** *adj.*

en·chain (in·chān′) *v.t.* **1.** To bind with or as with a chain. **2.** To hold fast or captive, as attention. — **en·chain′ment** *n.*

en·chant (in·chant′, -chänt′) *v.t.* **1.** To put a spell upon; bewitch. **2.** To charm completely; delight. [< F < L < *in-* in + *cantare* to sing] — **en·chant′er** *n.* — **en·chant′ment** *n.* — **en·chant′ress** *n. fem.*

en·chant·ing (in·chan′ting, -chän′-) *adj.* Having power to enchant; charming; fascinating. — **en·chant′ing·ly** *adv.*

en·ci·pher (en·sī′fər) *v.t.* To convert (a message, report, etc.) from plain text into cipher.

en·cir·cle (en·sûr′kəl) *v.t.* **·cled, ·cling** **1.** To form a circle around. **2.** To go around. — **en·cir′cle·ment** *n.*

en·clave (en′klāv) *n.* **1.** A territory completely or partially enclosed by the territory of a power to which it is not politically subject, as San Marino and Vatican City in Italy. **2.** A district, as in a city, inhabited by a minority group. [< F < LL < L *in-* in + *clavis* key]

en·clit·ic (en·klit′ik) *adj.* Having no independent accent, but pronounced as part of a preceding word, as English *is* in *Tom's going,* French *je* in *ai-je.* — *n. Gram.* An enclitic form. [< LL < Gk. < *en-* on + *klinein* to lean]

en·close (in·klōz′) *v.t.* **·closed, ·clos·ing** **1.** To close in on all sides; surround. **2.** To transmit within the cover of a letter. **3.** To contain. Also spelled *inclose.*

en·clo·sure (in·klō′zhər) *n.* **1.** The act of enclosing, or the state of being enclosed. **2.** An enclosed object or area. **3.** That which encloses, as a wall. Also spelled *inclosure.*

en·code (en·kōd′) *v.t.* **·cod·ed, ·cod·ing** To convert (a message, document, etc.) from plain text into code.

en·co·mi·um (en·kō′mē·əm) *n. pl.* **·mi·ums** or **·mi·a** (-me·ə) A formal expression of praise; eulogy. [< L < Gk. *enkōmion* eulogy]

en·com·pass (in·kum′pəs) *v.t.* **1.** To form a circle around; surround. **2.** To enclose; contain. — **en·com′pass·ment** *n.*

en·core (äng′kôr, -kōr, än′-) *interj.* Again! once more! — *n.* The call by an audience, as by prolonged applause, for repetition of a performance or for an additional performance; also, that which is performed in response to this call. — *v.t.* **·cored, ·cor·ing** To call for a repetition of (a performance) or by (a performer). [< F]

en·coun·ter (in·koun′tər) *n.* **1.** A meeting with a person or thing, esp. when casual or unexpected. **2.** A hostile meeting; contest. — *v.t.* **1.** To meet, esp. casually or unexpectedly. **2.** To meet in battle. **3.** To be faced with or contend against (opposition, difficulties, etc.). — *v.i.* **4.** To meet each other unexpectedly or in conflict. [< OF < LL < L *in-* in + *contra* against]

en·cour·age (in·kûr′ij) *v.t.* **·aged, ·ag·ing** **1.** To inspire with courage, hope, or resolution. **2.** To help or foster. [< OF < *en-* in + *corage* courage] — **en·cour′age·ment** *n.*

en·cour·ag·ing (in·kûr′ij·ing) *adj.* Giving, or tending to give, courage or confidence. — **en·cour′ag·ing·ly** *adv.*

en·croach (in·krōch′) *v.i.* **1.** To intrude stealthily or gradually upon the possessions or rights of another: with *on* or *upon.* **2.** To advance beyond the proper or usual limits. [< OF < *en-* in + *croc* hook] — **en·croach′ment** *n.*

en·crust (in·krust′), etc. See INCRUST, etc.

en·cum·ber (in·kum′bər) *v.t.* **1.** To hinder in action or motion, as with a burden; impede. **2.** To block up; crowd, as with obstacles or useless additions. **3.** To weigh down, as with debts. Also spelled *incumber.* [< OF < LL < *in-* in + *combrus* obstacle]

en·cum·brance (in·kum′brəns) *n.* **1.** That which encumbers; a hindrance. **2.** A dependent, esp. a child. **3.** *Law* A lien attached to real property. Also spelled *incumbrance.*

-ency *suffix of nouns* A variant of -ENCE, as in *decency,* used to form words expressing quality or condition, the earlier form being used largely for nouns of action. [< L *-entia*]

en·cyc·li·cal (en·sik′li·kəl, -sī′kli-) *adj.* Intended for general circulation; circular: said of letters. Also **en·cyc′lic.** — *n.* A circular letter addressed by the Pope to the bishops of the world. [< LL < Gk. < *en-* in + *kyklos* circle]

en·cy·clo·pe·di·a (en·sī′klə·pē′dē·ə) *n.* **1.** A comprehensive work made up of systematically arranged articles broadly covering the whole range of knowledge or treating of one particular field. **2.** The entire circle of knowledge. Also **en·cy′clo·pae′di·a.** [< NL < Gk. < *enkyklios paideia* a general education] — **en·cy′clo·pe′dic** or **·di·cal, en·cy′clo·pae′dic** *adj.* — **en·cy′clo·pe′di·cal·ly** *adv.*

en·cy·clo·pe·dist (en·sī′klə·pē′dist) *n.* A writer for or compiler of an encyclopedia. Also **en·cy′clo·pae′dist.**

en·cyst (en·sist′) *v.t. & v.i. Biol.* To enclose or become enclosed in a cyst or sac. — **en·cyst′ment, en′cys·ta′tion** *n.*

end (end) *n.* **1.** The terminal point or part of anything that has length: the *end* of a street. **2.** The extreme limit of the space occupied by any extended object; boundary: the *ends* of the earth. **3.** The point in time at which something ceases. **4.** The purpose of an action. **5.** An inevitable or natural consequence. **6.** Ultimate state. **7.** The termination of existence; death. **8.** Fragment; remnant: odds and *ends.* **9.** In football, the outermost player at each side of the line of scrimmage; also, the position of this player. — **to make (both) ends meet** To live within one's income. — *v.t.* **1.** To bring to a finish or termination. **2.** To be the end of. **3.** To cause the death of. — *v.i.* **4.** To come to an end. **5.** To die. [OE *ende*]

en·da·me·ba (en′də·mē′bə) *n.* A parasitic ameba; esp. one causing dysentery and liver abscess. Also **en′da·moe′ba.**

en·dan·ger (in·dān′jər) *v.t.* To expose to danger; imperil.

en·dear (in·dir′) *v.t.* To make dear or beloved.

en·dear·ing (in-dîr'ing) *adj.* **1.** Making dear or beloved. **2.** Manifesting affection; caressing. **— en·dear'ing·ly** *adv.*

en·dear·ment (in-dîr'mənt) *n.* **1.** The act of endearing, or the state of being endeared. **2.** A loving word, act, etc.

en·deav·or (in-dev'ər) *n.* An attempt or effort to do or attain something. **—** *v.t.* **1.** To make an effort to do or effect; try: usu. with an infinitive as object. **—** *v.i.* **2.** To strive. Also *Brit.* **en·deav'our.** [ME < EN-¹ + DEVOIR]

en·dem·ic (en-dem'ik) *adj.* **1.** Peculiar to a particular country or people. **2.** *Med.* Confined to or characteristic of a given locality: said of a disease. Also **en·dem'i·cal.** **— Syn.** See NATIVE. [< Gk. < *en-* in + *dēmos* people]

end·ing (en'ding) *n.* **1.** The act of bringing or coming to an end. **2.** The concluding or final part; end; extremity. **3.** One or more concluding letters or syllables added to the base of a word, esp. to indicate an inflection.

en·dive (en'dīv, än'dēv) *n.* An herb whose blanched leaves are used as a salad. [< F < L *intibus* endive]

end·less (end'lis) *adj.* **1.** Enduring forever; eternal. **2.** Having no end in space; infinite. **3.** Continually recurring; incessant. **4.** Forming a closed loop or circle. **— end'less·ly** *adv.* **— end'less·ness** *n.*

end·most (end'mōst') *adj.* Most remote; farthest.

endo- *combining form* Within; inside. Also, before vowels, **end-.** [< Gk. < *endon* within]

en·do·blast (en'dō-blast) *n. Biol.* The endoderm. **— en'do·blas'tic** *adj.*

en·do·carp (en'dō-kärp) *n. Bot.* The inner layer of a ripened fruit, as of a cherry stone.

en·do·crine (en'dō-krin, -krēn, -krīn) *Physiol. adj.* **1.** Secreting internally. **2.** Of or pertaining to an endocrine gland or its secretion. Also **en'do·cri'nal** (-krī'nəl), **en'do·crin'ic** (-krin'ik), **en·doc·ri·nous** (en-dok'rə-nəs) *adj.* [< ENDO- + Gk. *krinein* to separate]

endocrine gland One of several ductless glands, as the thyroid, pituitary, and suprarenal glands, whose secretions, released directly into the blood or lymph, have a critical importance in many phases of physiological activity.

en·do·cri·nol·o·gy (en'dō·kri·nol'ə·jē, -krī-) *n.* The branch of medicine dealing with the endocrine glands and the various internal secretions. **— en'do·cri·nol'o·gist** *n.*

en·do·derm (en'dō-dûrm) *n. Biol.* The innermost of the three germ layers of the embryo, developing into the digestive and respiratory systems: also called *endoblast, entoblast, entoderm.* **— en'do·der'mal, en'do·der'mic** *adj.*

en·dog·a·my (en·dog'ə·mē) *n. Anthropol.* Marriage within the group, class, caste, or tribe. **— en·dog'a·mous** *adj.*

en·dog·e·nous (en·doj'ə·nəs) *adj. Biol.* Originating or growing from within, as cells within the wall of the parent cell. **— en·dog'e·nous·ly** *adv.* **— en·dog'e·ny** *n.*

en·do·mor·phic (en'dō-môr'fik) *adj.* Of human body types, characterized by a heavy body structure. **— en'do·morph** *n.* **— en'do·mor'phy** *n.*

en·do·plasm (en'dō-plaz'əm) *n. Biol.* The inner granular portion of the cytoplasm of the cell, enclosing the nucleus. Also **en·do·sarc** (en'dō-särk). **— en'do·plas'mic** *adj.*

end organ *Physiol.* Any organ adapted for the reception or delivery of nervous stimuli.

en·dorse (in-dôrs') *v.t.* **·dorsed, ·dors·ing** **1.** To write on the back of (a paper); esp., to transfer ownership or assign payment of (a check, note, etc.) by signing on the reverse side. **2.** To give sanction or support to. Also spelled *indorse.* [< OF < Med.L < L *in-* on + *dorsum* back] **— en·dors'a·ble** *adj.* **— en·dors'er** or **en·dor'sor** *n.*

en·dor·see (in'dôr-sē', in·dôr'sē) *n.* One to whom transference by endorsement is made.

en·dorse·ment (in-dôrs'mənt) *n.* **1.** The act of endorsing. **2.** That which endorses, as a signature. **3.** Confirmation; approval. Also spelled *indorsement.*

en·do·skel·e·ton (en'dō-skel'ə-tən) *n. Anat.* The internal supporting structure of an animal, as in all vertebrates. **— en'do·skel'e·tal** *adj.*

en·do·sperm (en'dō-spûrm) *n. Bot.* The nutritive substance with the embryo sac of an ovule.

en·do·ther·mic (en'dō-thûr'mik) *adj. Chem.* Pertaining to, attended by, or produced from the absorption of heat. Also **en'do·ther'mal.** [< ENDO- + Gk. *thermē* heat]

en·dow (in-dou') *v.t.* **1.** To bestow a permanent fund or income upon. **2.** To furnish or equip, as with talents or natural gifts: usu. with *with.* [< OF < *en-* in + L *dotare* to give]

en·dow·ment (in-dou'mənt) *n.* **1.** Money or property given for the permanent use of an institution, person, etc. **2.** Any natural gift, as talent or beauty. **3.** The act of endowing.

end table *U.S.* A small table beside a chair, sofa, etc.

en·due (in-dōo', -dyōo') *v.t.* **·dued, ·du·ing** **1.** To endow with some quality, power, etc. **2.** To put on. **3.** To clothe. [Fusion of OF *enduire* to introduce and *enduire* to clothe]

en·dur·ance (in-dōor'əns, -dyōor'-) *n.* **1.** The act or capacity of bearing up, as under hardship or prolonged stress. **2.** Duration. **3.** That which is endured.

en·dure (in-dōor', -dyōor') *v.* **·dured, ·dur·ing** *v.t.* **1.** To bear up under: to *endure* hardships. **2.** To put up with; tolerate. **—** *v.i.* **3.** To continue to be; last. **4.** To suffer without yielding. [< OF < L < *in-* in + *durare* to harden] **— en·dur'a·ble** *adj.* **— en·dur'a·bly** *adv.*

en·dur·ing (in-dōor'ing, -dyōor'-) *adj.* **1.** Lasting; permanent. **2.** Long-suffering. **— en·dur'ing·ly** *adv.* **— en·dur'ing·ness** *n.*

end·wise (end'wīz') *adv.* **1.** With the end foremost or uppermost. **2.** On end. **3.** Lengthwise. **4.** End to end. Also **end'ways'** (-wāz').

En·dym·i·on (en-dim'ē-ən) In Greek mythology, a beautiful youth loved by Selene and granted eternal youth.

-ene *suffix Chem.* **1.** Denoting a hydrocarbon compound having one double bond: *ethylene.* **2.** Denoting a compound of the benzene series.

en·e·ma (en'ə·mə) *n.* *pl.* **en·e·mas** or **en·em·a·ta** (e·nem'ə·tə) *Med.* **1.** A liquid injected into the rectum for cleansing, diagnostic, or nutritive purposes. **2.** The injection of such a liquid. [< Gk. < *en-* in + *hienai* to send]

en·e·my (en'ə·mē) *n.* *pl.* **·mies** **1.** One who harbors hatred or malicious intent toward another; also, one who or that which opposes a person, cause, etc. **2.** A hostile power or military force; also, a member of a hostile force. **— adj.** Of or pertaining to a hostile army or power. [< OF < L < *in-* not + *amicus* friend]
— Syn. (noun) An *enemy* is one who manifests ill will, or broadly anyone on the opposite side in a struggle. An *opponent* may vie with one in a friendly contest, while an *antagonist* is always hostile and unfriendly. *Adversary* is a general word and may be applied to a friendly *opponent* or to the most implacable *enemy.*

en·er·get·ic (en'ər·jet'ik) *adj.* Having or displaying energy; forceful and efficient. **— en'er·get'i·cal·ly** *adv.*

en·er·gize (en'ər·jīz) *v.* **·gized, ·giz·ing** *v.t.* **1.** To give energy, force, or strength to; activate. **—** *v.i.* **2.** To be in operation; be active. **— en'er·giz'er** *n.*

en·er·gy (en'ər·jē) *n.* *pl.* **·gies** **1.** Vigor or intensity of action, expression, or utterance. **2.** Capacity or tendency for vigorous action. **3.** Inherent power to produce an effect. **4.** *Often pl.* Power forcefully and effectively exercised. **5.** *Physics* The capacity for doing work and for overcoming inertia. **Potential energy** is due to the position of one body relative to another, and **kinetic energy** is manifested by bodies in motion. [< LL < Gk. < *en-* + *ergon* work]

en·er·vate (*v.* en'ər·vāt; *adj.* i·nûr'vit) *v.t.* **·vat·ed, ·vat·ing** To sap the strength or vitality of; weaken in body or will. **— adj.** Weakened; devitalized. [< L < *e-* out + *nervus* sinew] **— en'er·va'tion** *n.* **— en'er·va'tor** *n.*

en·fee·ble (en-fē'bəl) *v.t.* **·bled, ·bling** To make feeble. **— en·fee'ble·ment** *n.* **— en·fee'bler** *n.*

en·fi·lade (en'fə·lād') *Mil. v.t.* **·lad·ed, ·lad·ing** To fire or be in a position to fire down the length of, as a column of troops. **—** *n.* **1.** Gunfire that can rake lengthwise a line of troops, etc. **2.** A position exposed to such fire. [< F < *en-* in + *fil* thread]

en·fold (in-fōld') See INFOLD.

en·force (in-fôrs', -fōrs') *v.t.* **·forced, ·forc·ing** **1.** To compel observance of (a law, etc.). **2.** To impose (obedience, etc.) by force. **3.** To lay stress upon; emphasize. [< OF < LL < L *in-* in + *fortis* strong] **— en·force'a·ble** *adj.* **— en·force'ment** *n.* **— en·forc'er** *n.*

en·fran·chise (in-fran'chīz) *v.t.* **·chised, ·chis·ing** **1.** To endow with a franchise, as with the right to vote. **2.** To set free, as from bondage or legal liabilities. [< OF < *en-* in + *franc* free] **— en·fran'chise·ment** (-chiz·mənt) *n.*

en·gage (in-gāj') *v.* **·gaged, ·gag·ing** *v.t.* **1.** To hire or employ (a person); also, to secure or contract for (professional services, assistance, etc.). **2.** To reserve the use of, as lodgings. **3.** To hold the interest or attention of; engross. **4.** To occupy; keep busy: to *engage* one's time in revelry. **5.** To bind by a pledge, contract, etc. **6.** To betroth: usu. in the passive. **7.** To enter into conflict with: to *engage* the enemy. **8.** *Mech.* To mesh or interlock with. **—** *v.i.* **9.** To occupy oneself in an undertaking. **10.** To pledge oneself; warrant. **11.** To enter into combat. **12.** *Mech.* To mesh. [< F < *en-* in + *gager* to pledge]

en·gaged (in-gājd') *adj.* **1.** Occupied or busy. **2.** Betrothed. **3.** Involved in conflict. **4.** *Mech.* Geared together. **5.** *Archit.* Partially sunk into another part of a structure.

en·gage·ment (in-gāj'mənt) *n.* **1.** The act of engaging, or the state of being engaged. **2.** Something that engages or binds, as an obligation. **3.** Betrothal. **4.** A business appointment. **5.** A salaried position, esp. for a limited period. **6.** A hostile encounter. **7.** *Mech.* The state of being in gear. **8.** *pl.* Financial obligations. **— Syn.** See BATTLE.

en·gag·ing (in-gā'jing) *adj.* Attracting interest or affection; winning; pleasing. **— en·gag'ing·ly** *adv.*

en·garde (än gärd') *French* On guard: a fencing position.

en·gen·der (in-jen'dər) *v.t.* **1.** To cause to exist; produce. **2.** *Rare* To beget. **—** *v.i.* **3.** To come into being. [< OF < L *ingenerare* to create < *in-* in + *genus, generis* race]

en·gine (en'jən) *n.* **1.** A machine that converts heat energy into mechanical work. **2.** A locomotive. **3.** An apparatus or mechanical contrivance for producing some effect. **4.** Any agency, means, or instrument. [< OF < L *in-* in + *gen-*, root of *gignere* to beget]

en·gi·neer (en′jə·nir′) *n.* **1.** One versed in or practicing any branch of engineering. **2.** One who operates an engine. **3.** *Mil.* A member of a corps of men engaged in constructing forts and bridges, clearing and building roads, etc. — *v.t.* **1.** To put through or manage by contrivance: to *engineer* a scheme. **2.** To plan and superintend as engineer.

en·gi·neer·ing (en′jə·nir′ing) *n.* **1.** The art and science of designing, constructing, and operating roads, bridges, buildings, etc. **2.** Clever planning or maneuvering.

Eng·lish (ing′glish) *adj.* **1.** Of, pertaining to, or derived from England or its people. **2.** Expressed in or belonging to the English language. — *n.* **1.** The people of England collectively: with *the.* **2.** The language spoken by the people of the British Isles and most of the British Commonwealth, and of the United States, its territories, and possessions. — **Old English** or **Anglo-Saxon** The English language from about A.D. 450 to 1050, consisting of a basically Germanic vocabulary. — **Middle English** The language of England after the Norman Conquest, from about 1050 to 1475, represented by the works of Chaucer and having extensive borrowings from Latin, French, and the Low German languages. — **Modern English** The English language since 1475. **3.** *U.S.* In billiards, a horizontal twist or spin given to the cue ball by striking it on one side. — *v.t.* **1.** To translate into English. **2.** To Anglicize, as a foreign word. **3.** *U.S.* In billiards, to apply English to. [OE *Engle* the Angles]

English horn A double-reed instrument having a pitch a fifth lower than an oboe.

Eng·lish·man (ing′glish·mən) *n.* *pl.* **·men** (-mən) **1.** A native or citizen of England. **2.** An English ship.

English muffin A round, flat muffin made with little shortening, and usu. eaten toasted.

English sonnet The Shakespearean sonnet.

Eng·lish·wom·an (ing′glish·wŏŏm′ən) *n.* *pl.* **·wom·en** (-wim′in) A woman who is a native or citizen of England.

en·gorge (en·gôrj′) *v.t.* **·gorged, ·gorg·ing 1.** To fill with blood, as an artery. **2.** To devour or swallow greedily. [< F < *en-* in + *gorge* throat] — **en·gorge′ment** *n.*

en·graft (en·graft′, -gräft′) *v.t.* **1.** *Bot.* To graft. **2.** To set firmly; implant.

en·gram (en′gram) *n.* A permanently altered state in the protoplasm of animal cells assumed to result from the temporary excitation of certain stimuli.

en·grave (en·grāv′) *v.t.* **·graved, ·grav·ing 1.** To carve or etch figures, letters, etc., into (a surface). **2.** To impress deeply on the mind. **3.** To cut (pictures, lettering, etc.) into metal, stone, or wood, for printing. **4.** To print from plates so made. [< EN-¹ + *grave* to carve] — **en·grav′er** *n.*

en·grav·ing (en·grā′ving) *n.* **1.** The act or art of cutting designs, etc., into a surface. **2.** An engraved design; plate. **3.** An impression printed from an engraved plate; print.

en·gross (en·grōs′) *v.t.* **1.** To occupy completely; absorb. **2.** To copy legibly in a large hand, as a document. **3.** In business, to monopolize (goods already on the market). [< AF < LL *ingrossare* to write large] — **en·gross′ment** *n.*

en·gross·ing (en·grō′sing) *adj.* Holding the attention or interest completely; absorbing. — **en·gross′ing·ly** *adv.*

en·gulf (en·gulf′) *v.t.* To swallow up in or as in a gulf; bury or overwhelm completely.

en·hance (in·hans′, -häns′) *v.t.* **·hanced, ·hanc·ing** To heighten or increase, as in reputation, cost, beauty, quality, etc. [< AF < *en-* in, on + *haucer* to lift] — **en·hanc′er** *n.* — **en·hance′ment** *n.*

en·har·mon·ic (en′här·mon′ik) *adj.* *Music* Of or relating to tones, as C♯ and D♭, having different notation but the same pitch. [< L < *en-* in + *harmonia* harmony]

e·nig·ma (i·nig′mə) *n.* **1.** An obscure or ambiguous saying. **2.** Anything that puzzles or baffles. — **Syn.** See PUZZLE. [< L < Gk. *ainissesthai* to speak in riddles]

en·ig·mat·ic (en′ig·mat′ik, ē′nig-) *adj.* Of or like an enigma; puzzling. Also **en′ig·mat′i·cal.** — **en′ig·mat′i·cal·ly** *adv.*

en·join (en·join′) *v.t.* **1.** To order or command (a person or group). **2.** To impose (a condition, course of action, etc.) on a person or group. **3.** To forbid or prohibit, especially by judicial order. [< OF < L < *in-* on + *jungere* to join] — **en·join′er** *n.* — **en·join′ment** *n.*

en·joy (en·joi′) *v.t.* **1.** To experience joy or pleasure in. **2.** To have the use or benefit of. [< OF < *en-* in + *joir* to rejoice] — **en·joy′a·ble** *adj.* — **en·joy′a·ble·ness** *n.* — **en·joy′a·bly** *adv.* — **en·joy′er** *n.* — **en·joy′ment** *n.*

en·kin·dle (en·kin′dəl) *v.t.* **·dled, ·dling 1.** To set on fire; kindle. **2.** To stir to action; excite. — **en·kin′dler** *n.*

en·large (in·lärj′) *v.* **·larged, ·larg·ing** *v.t.* **1.** To make larger. — *v.i.* **2.** To become larger. **3.** To express oneself

in greater detail or at greater length: with *on* or *upon.* — **Syn.** See INCREASE. — **en·large′ment** *n.* — **en·larg′er** *n.*

en·light·en (in·līt′n) *v.t.* To give revealing or broadening knowledge to; cause to know. — **en·light′en·er** *n.*

en·light·en·ment (in·līt′n·mənt) *n.* The act of enlightening, or the state of being enlightened. — **the Enlightenment** A philosophical movement of the 18th century, characterized by rationalistic methods.

en·list (in·list′) *v.t.* **1.** To engage (someone) for the armed forces. **2.** To secure the active aid or participation of (a person, etc.). — *v.i.* **3.** To enter military service without being drafted. **4.** To join some venture, cause, etc.: with *in.*

en·list·ed man (in·lis′tid) Any male member of the armed forces who is not a commissioned officer or warrant officer.

en·list·ment (in·list′mənt) *n.* **1.** An enlisting or being enlisted. **2.** The term for which one enlists.

en·li·ven (in·lī′vən) *v.t.* **1.** To make lively, cheerful, or sprightly. **2.** To make active or vigorous; stimulate. — **en·li′ven·er** *n.* — **en·li′ven·ment** *n.*

en masse (en mas′, *Fr.* än mås′) All together. [< F]

en·mesh (en·mesh′) *v.t.* To ensnare in or as in a net.

en·mi·ty (en′mə·tē) *n.* *pl.* **·ties** Deep-seated unfriendliness; hostility. [< OF < L *in-* not + *amicus* friend]

en·no·ble (i·nō′bəl, en-) *v.t.* **·bled, ·bling 1.** To make honorable or noble in nature, quality, etc.; dignify. **2.** To confer a title of nobility upon. — **en·no′ble·ment** *n.* — **en·no′bler** *n.*

en·nui (än·wē′, än′wē, *Fr.* än·nwē′) *n.* A feeling of listless weariness and boredom. [< F < L *in odio* in hatred]

e·nor·mi·ty (i·nôr′mə·tē) *n.* *pl.* **·ties 1.** The quality of being outrageous; heinousness. **2.** An outrageous offense; atrocity. [See ENORMOUS.]

e·nor·mous (i·nôr′məs) *adj.* Far exceeding the usual size, amount, degree, etc. [< L *enormis* < *e-* out + *norma* rule] — **e·nor′mous·ly** *adv.* — **e·nor′mous·ness** *n.*

e·nough (i·nuf′) *adj.* Adequate for any demand or need; sufficient. — *n.* An ample supply; a sufficiency. — *adv.* **1.** So as to be sufficient. **2.** Quite; very. **3.** Adequately; fairly; tolerably. — *interj.* That's enough! [OE *genōh, genōg*]

en·plane (en·plān′) *v.i.* **·planed, ·plan·ing** To board an airplane.

en·quire (in·kwīr′), **en·quir·y** (in·kwīr′ē, in′kwər·ē) See INQUIRE, INQUIRY.

en·rage (in·rāj′) *v.t.* **·raged, ·rag·ing** To throw into a rage.

en rap·port (än rå·pôr′) *French* In sympathy; in accord.

on rapt (in rapt′) *adj.* Rapt; enraptured.

en·rap·ture (in·rap′chər) *v.t.* **·tured, ·tur·ing** To bring into a state of rapture; delight extravagantly.

en·rich (in·rich′) *v.t.* **1.** To make rich or increase the wealth of. **2.** To make more productive, as soil. **3.** To add attractive or desirable elements to; make better, more interesting, etc., by adding. **4.** To increase the food value of. — **en·rich′er** *n.* — **en·rich′ment** *n.*

en·roll (in·rōl′) *v.t.* **1.** To write or record (a name) in a roll; register; list. **2.** To enlist. **3.** To place on record; record, as a document or decree. **4.** To roll up; wrap. — *v.i.* **5.** To place one's name on a list; register oneself. Also *Brit.* **en·rol′.**

en·roll·ment (in·rōl′mənt) *n.* **1.** An enrolling or being enrolled. **2.** A record of persons or things enrolled. **3.** The number of persons or things enrolled. Also **en·rol′ment.**

en route (än·rōōt′, en-, *Fr.* än·rōōt′) On the way.

en·sconce (en·skons′) *v.t.* **·sconced, ·sconc·ing 1.** To fix securely or comfortably in some place. **2.** To shelter; hide.

en·sem·ble (än·säm′bəl, *Fr.* än·sän′bl′) *n.* **1.** All the parts of a thing viewed as a whole. **2.** An individual's entire costume, including accessories. **3.** The over-all effect of something. **4.** The entire cast of a play, ballet, etc. **5.** *Music* **a** The degree of precision, balance, and unification achieved by a group of performers. **b** A group of players or singers performing together. [< F < L < *in-* in + *simul* at the same time]

en·shrine (in·shrīn′) *v.t.* **·shrined, ·shrin·ing 1.** To place in or as in a shrine. **2.** To cherish devoutly; hold sacred. Also spelled *inshrine.* — **en·shrine′ment** *n.*

en·shroud (in·shroud′) *v.t.* To shroud; conceal.

en·sign (en′sīn; *also, and always for def. 2,* en′sən) *n.* **1.** A flag or banner. **2.** In the U.S. Navy or Coast Guard, a commissioned officer of the lowest grade. See table at GRADE. **3.** A badge, symbol, or distinguishing mark. [< OF < L < *in-* in + *signum* mark] — **en′sign·ship, en′sign·cy** *n.*

en·si·lage (en′sə·lij) *n.* **1.** The process of preserving green fodder in closed pits or silos. **2.** Fodder preserved in silos: also called *silage.* — *v.t.* **·laged, ·lag·ing** To store in a silo for preservation: also **en·sile** (en·sīl′). [< F]

en·slave (in·slāv′) *v.t.* **·slaved, ·slav·ing 1.** To make a slave of. **2.** To dominate; control. — **en·slave′ment** *n.*

en·snare (en·snâr′) *v.t.* **·snared, ·snar·ing** To catch in a snare; trick: also *insnare.* — **en·snare′ment** *n.*

en·sue (en·sōō′) *v.i.* **·sued, ·su·ing 1.** To follow subsequently; occur afterward. **2.** To follow as a consequence; result. [< OF < L < *in-* on, in + *sequi* to follow]

en·sure (in·shŏŏr′) *v.t.* **·sured, ·sur·ing 1.** To make sure or certain: to *ensure* victory. **2.** To make safe or secure: with *from* or *against*: to *ensure* liberty against tyranny. **3.** To insure (life, etc.). [< OF < *en-* in + *seur* sure]

-ent *suffix of nouns and adjectives* **1.** Having the quality, or performing the action of (the main element); *dependent.* **2.** One who or that which performs the action of (the main element); *superintendent.* Compare -ANT. [< F *-ent* < L *-ens*, *-entis*, suffix of present participle]

ent- See ENTO-.

en·tab·la·ture (en·tab′lə·chər) *n. Archit.* **1.** The uppermost member of a classical order or columnar system, consisting of the architrave, frieze, and cornice. **2.** Any projecting frieze or cornice of several members. [< MF < Ital. < *in-* in + *tavola* base, table]

en·tail (in·tāl′) *v.t.* **1.** To impose, involve, or result in by necessity. **2.** *Law* To restrict or leave the inheritance of (real property) to an unalterable succession of heirs. — *n.* **1.** The act of entailing, or the state of being entailed. **2.** Something entailed, as an inherited estate. **3.** A restricted line of succession or inheritance. [< OF < *en-* + *taillier* to cut] — **en·tail′ment** *n.*

en·ta·me·ba (en′tə·mē′bə) *n.* Endameba.

en·tan·gle (in·tang′gəl) *v.t.* **·gled, ·gling 1.** To catch in or as in a snare; hamper. **2.** To make tangled; snarl. **3.** To involve in difficulties; perplex; embarrass. — **en·tan′gle·ment** *n.* — **en·tan′gler** *n.*

en·tente (än·tänt′, *Fr.* än·tänt′) *n.* A mutual agreement; also, the parties entering into a mutual agreement. [< F] **entente cor·diale** (kôr·dyäl′) Cordial understanding, as between governments; friendly agreement. [< F]

en·ter (en′tər) *v.t.* **1.** To come or go into. **2.** To penetrate; pierce. **3.** To set in; insert. **4.** To become a member of; join. **5.** To start out upon; embark on. **6.** To obtain admission to (a school, etc.). **7.** To cause to be admitted to; enroll in. **8.** To write down, as in a list. **9.** To file notice of (goods, a ship, etc.) at a custom house. **10.** *Law* **a** To place (a plea, evidence, etc.) on the records of a court. **b** To file a claim to (public lands). — *v.i.* **11.** To come or go into a particular place. **12.** To begin to sing, play an instrument, etc. — **to enter into 1.** To start out; embark on. **2.** To engage in. **3.** To form a part or constituent of. **4.** To consider or discuss. — **to enter on** (or **upon**) **1.** To start out on. **2.** To start to have or use. [< OF < L *intra* within]

en·ter·ic (en·ter′ik) *adj.* Intestinal. [< Gk. *enteron* intestine]

en·ter·i·tis (en′tə·rī′tis) *n. Pathol.* Inflammation of the intestines, chiefly the small intestine.

entero- *combining form* Intestine. Also, before vowels, **enter-.** [< Gk. *enteron* intestine]

en·ter·prise (en′tər·prīz) *n.* **1.** Any project, undertaking, or task, especially when difficult, demanding, or of major importance. **2.** Boldness, energy, and venturesomeness in practical affairs. **3.** Active engagement in projects. [< OF < *entre-* between + *prendre* to take]

en·ter·pris·ing (en′tər·prī′zing) *adj.* Energetic, bold, and full of initiative; venturesome. — **en′ter·pris′ing·ly** *adv.*

en·ter·tain (en′tər·tān′) *v.t.* **1.** To amuse; divert. **2.** To extend hospitality to; receive as a guest. **3.** To take into consideration, as a proposal. **4.** To keep or bear in mind: to *entertain* a grudge. — *v.i.* **5.** To receive and care for guests. [< F < *entre-* between + *tenir* to hold] — **en′ter·tain′er** *n.*

en·ter·tain·ing (en′tər·tā′ning) *adj.* That entertains; amusing; diverting. — **en′ter·tain′ing·ly** *adv.*

en·ter·tain·ment (en′tər·tān′mənt) *n.* **1.** The act of entertaining, or the state of being entertained. **2.** Something that entertains, as a play. **3.** The care of guests.

en·thrall (in·thrôl′) *v.t.* **1.** To keep spellbound; fascinate; charm. **2.** To enslave. Also **en·thral′.** — **en·thrall′ment** or **en·thral′ment** *n.*

en·throne (in·thrōn′) *v.t.* **·throned, ·thron·ing 1.** To put upon a throne. **2.** To invest with authority. **3.** To exalt; revere. — **en·throne′ment** *n.*

en·thuse (in·thōōz′) *v.* **·thused, ·thus·ing** *U.S. Informal v.t.* **1.** To make enthusiastic. — *v.i.* **2.** To become enthusiastic.

en·thu·si·asm (in·thōō′zē·az′əm) *n.* **1.** Keen, animated interest in and preoccupation with something; ardor; zeal. **2.** A cause or object of intense, lively interest. [< LL < Gk. < *entheos, enthous* inspired, possessed]

en·thu·si·ast (in·thōō′zē·ast, ·ist) *n.* **1.** One given to or moved by enthusiasm. **2.** A religious fanatic.

en·thu·si·as·tic (in·thōō′zē·as′tik) *adj.* Full of or marked by enthusiasm; ardent. — **en·thu′si·as′ti·cal·ly** *adv.*

en·tice (in·tīs′) *v.t.* **·ticed, ·tic·ing** To lead on or attract by arousing hope of pleasure, profit, etc., allure. [< OF *en* *ticier* to set afire] — **en·tice′ment** *n.* — **en·tic′ing·ly** *adv.*

en·tire (in·tīr′) *adj.* **1.** Having no part missing; whole; complete. **2.** Not broken; intact. **3.** Not lessened; full; total. **4.** Consisting wholly of one piece; not divided into

sections. — *n.* The whole of something; total. [< OF < L *integer* whole] — **en·tire′ly** *adv.* — **en·tire′ness** *n.*

en·tire·ty (in·tī′rə·tē) *n. pl.* **·ties 1.** The state or condition of being entire; completeness. **2.** That which is entire.

en·ti·tle (in·tīt′l) *v.t.* **·tled, ·tling 1.** To give (a person or thing) the right to receive, demand, or do something. **2.** To give a name or designation to. **3.** To give (a person) a title designating rank, honor, etc.

en·ti·ty (en′tə·tē) *n. pl.* **·ties 1.** Something existing objectively or in the mind; an actual or conceivable being. **2.** Existence as opposed to nonexistence. **3.** Essence; substance. [< L ppr. of *esse* to be]

ento- *combining form* Interior. Also, before vowels, **ent-.**

en·to·blast (en′tō·blast) *n. Biol.* The endoderm. — **en′to·blas′tic** *adj.*

en·to·derm (en′tō·dûrm) *n.* Endoderm.

en·tomb (in·tōōm′) *v.t.* **1.** To place in or as in a tomb; bury. **2.** To serve as a tomb for. Also spelled *intomb.* [< OF < *en-* in + *tombe* tomb] — **en·tomb′ment** *n.*

entomo- *combining form* Insect. Also, before vowels, **entom-.** [< Gk. *entoma* insects]

en·to·mol·o·gy (en′tə·mol′ə·jē) *n.* The branch of zoology that treats of insects. — **en′to·mo·log′i·cal** or **en′to·mo·log′ic** *adj.* — **en′to·mo·log′i·cal·ly** *adv.* — **en·to·mol′o·gist** *n.*

en·tou·rage (än′tōō·räzh′, *Fr.* än·tōō·räzh′) *n.* **1.** A group of followers, retainers, or attendants; retinue. **2.** Environment. [< F < *entourer* to surround]

en·tr'acte (än·trakt′, *Fr.* än·träkt′) *n.* **1.** The interval between the acts of a play, opera, etc. **2.** A musical interlude, dance, or the like, performed between acts. [< F]

en·trails (en′trālz, ·trəlz) *n.pl.* **1.** The internal parts of a man or animal; esp., the intestines; bowels; guts. **2.** The internal parts of anything. [< OF < LL *intralia* intestines]

en·train (en·trān′) *v.i.* **1.** To board a train. — *v.t.* **2.** To put aboard a train. — **en·train′ment** *n.*

en·trance¹ (en′trəns) *n.* **1.** The act of entering. **2.** A passage, opening, or the like, affording a means of entering. **3.** The right or power of entering; admittance. **4.** The point in a play, ballet, etc., at which a performer is cued to enter.

en·trance² (in·trans′, ·träns′) *v.t.* **·tranced, ·tranc·ing 1.** To fill with rapture or wonder; delight; charm. **2.** To put into a trance. — **en·trance′ment** *n.* — **en·tranc′ing·ly** *adv.*

en·trance·way (en′trəns·wā′) *n.* A means of entrance.

en·trant (en′trənt) *n.* **1.** One who enters; a beginner. **2.** One who competes in a contest.

en·trap (in·trap′) *v.t.* **·trapped, ·trap·ping 1.** To catch in or as in a trap. **2.** To trick into danger of difficulty; deceive; ensnare. — **en·trap′ment** *n.*

en·treat (in·trēt′) *v.t.* **1.** To beseech with great intensity; implore; beg. **2.** To make an earnest request of or for; petition. — *v.i.* **3.** To ask earnestly. [< OF < *en-* in + *traitier* to treat] — **en·treat′ing·ly** *adv.* — **en·treat′ment** *n.*

en·treat·y (in·trē′tē) *n. pl.* **·ies** An earnest request.

en·tre·chat (än′trə·shä′) *n. French* In ballet, a leap upward in which the dancer repeatedly crosses his feet.

en·trée (än′trā, *Fr.* än·trā′) *n.* **1.** The act or privilege of entering; entrance; admission. **2.** The principal course at a meal. **3.** In lavish or formal dinners, a dish served between the fish and meat courses or directly before the main course. Also *U.S.* **en′tree.** [< F, orig. pp. of *entrer.* See ENTER.]

en·trench (in·trench′) *v.t.* **1.** To fortify or protect with or as with a trench or trenches. **2.** To establish firmly: The idea was *entrenched* in his mind. — *v.i.* **3.** To encroach or trespass: with *on* or *upon.* — **en·trench′ment** *n.*

en·tre·pre·neur (än′trə·prə·nûr′, *Fr.* än·trə·prə·nœr′) *n.* One who undertakes to start and conduct an enterprise or business. [< F < *entreprendre.* See ENTERPRISE.]

en·tro·py (en′trə·pē) *n. Physics* **1.** A mathematical expression of the degree to which the energy of a thermodynamic system is unavailable for conversion into work. **2.** The irreversible tendency of a system, including the universe, toward increasing disorder; also, the final state predictable from this. [< Gk. < *en-* in + *trepein* to turn]

en·trust (in·trust′) *v.t.* **1.** To give over (something) for care, safekeeping, or performance. **2.** To place something in the care or trust of. Also spelled *intrust.*

en·try (en′trē) *n. pl.* **·tries 1.** The act of coming in; entrance. **2.** A place of entrance; a small hallway or vestibule. **3.** The act of entering anything in a register, list, etc.; also, the item entered. **4.** The act of reporting at a customhouse the arrival of a ship in port and the nature of her cargo. **5.** The act of assuming possession of lands or tenements by entering upon them. **6.** A contestant listed for a race, competition, etc. **7.** In bridge and whist, a card that will win a trick and place the lead in a specified hand: also *reentry.*

en·twine (in·twīn′) *v.t. & v.i.* **·twined, ·twin·ing** To twine around; twine or twist together: also spelled *intwine.*

e·nu·mer·ate (i·nōō′mə·rāt, ·nyōō′-) *v.t.* **·at·ed, ·at·ing 1.** To name one by one; list. **2.** To ascertain the number of. [< L < *e-* out + *numerare* to count] — **e·nu′mer·a′tion** *n.* — **e·nu′mer·a′tive** *adj.* — **e·nu′mer·a′tor** *n.*

e·nun·ci·ate (i·nun/sē·āt, -shē-) *v.* **·at·ed, ·at·ing** *v.t.* **1.** To articulate (speech sounds), esp. in a clear and distinct manner. **2.** To state with exactness, as a theory or dogma. **3.** To announce or proclaim. — *v.i.* **4.** To pronounce words, esp. with distinct articulation. [< L < *e-* out + *nuntiare* to announce] — **e·nun·ci·a·ble** (i·nun/sē·ə·bəl, -shē-) *adj.* — **e·nun/ci·a/tive, e·nun/ci·a·to/ry** (-sē·ə·tôr/ē, -tō/rē) *adj.* — **e·nun/ci·a/tive·ly** *adv.* — **e·nun/ci·a/tor** *n.*

e·nun·ci·a·tion (i·nun/sē·ā/shən, -shē-) *n.* **1.** The utterance or mode of utterance of speech sounds. **2.** A declaration.

en·u·re·sis (en/yə·rē/sis) *n. Pathol.* Involuntary urination. [< NL < Gk. < *en-* in + *oureein* to urinate]

en·vel·op (in·vel/əp) *v.t.* **·oped, ·op·ing 1.** To wrap; enclose. **2.** To hide; conceal. [< OF < *en-* in + *voluper* to wrap] — **en·vel/op·er** *n.*

en·ve·lope (en/və·lōp, än/-) *n.* **1.** A paper case or wrapper for enclosing a letter or the like, usu. having a gummed flap for sealing. **2.** Any enveloping cover or wrapper. **3.** *Aeron.* The outer fabric covering of a dirigible, balloon, etc.

en·vel·op·ment (in·vel/əp·mənt) *n.* **1.** The act of enveloping, or the state of being enveloped. **2.** A covering.

en·ven·om (en·ven/əm) *v.t.* **1.** To impregnate with venom; poison. **2.** To make vindictive; embitter.

en·vi·a·ble (en/vē·ə·bəl) *adj.* So admirable or desirable as to arouse envy. — **en/vi·a·bly** *adv.*

en·vi·ous (en/vē·əs) *adj.* Full of, characterized by, or expressing envy. — **en/vi·ous·ly** *adv.* — **en/vi·ous·ness** *n.*

en·vi·ron (en·vi/rən) *v.t.* To extend around; encircle; surround. [< F < *environ* around]

en·vi·ron·ment (in·vi/rən·mənt, -vi/ərn-) *n.* **1.** The external circumstances, conditions, and things that affect the existence and development of an individual, organism, or group. **2.** The act of surrounding or being surrounded. **3.** Surroundings. — **en·vi/ron·men/tal** *adj.*

en·vi·rons (in·vi/rənz) *n.pl.* A surrounding, outlying area, as about a city; outskirts; suburbs.

en·vis·age (en·viz/ij) *v.t.* **·aged, ·ag·ing 1.** To form a mental image of; visualize. **2.** To conceive of in advance; contemplate. [< EN- + VISAGE] — **en·vis/age·ment** *n.*

en·vi·sion (en·vizh/ən) *v.t.* To see or foresee in the mind.

en·voy¹ (en/voi, än/-) *n.* **1.** A diplomatic representative of the second class ranking next below an ambassador. **2.** A diplomat on a special mission. **3.** Anyone entrusted with a mission. [< F *envoyé* < OF < L *in-* in + *via* way, road]

en·voy² (en/voi, än/-) *n.* The closing lines of a poem or prose work, often in the form of a dedication: also *l'envoie, l'envoy.* Also **envoi.** [See ENVOY¹.]

en·vy (en/vē) *n. pl.* **·vies 1.** A feeling of resentment or discontent over another's superior attainments, endowments, or possessions. **2.** A desire to possess the goods of another. **3.** Any object of envy. — *v.* **·vied, ·vy·ing** *v.t.* **1.** To regard with envy; feel envy because of: *I envy you your calm.* — *v.i.* **2.** To feel or show envy. [< OF < L < *in-* on + *videre* to see, look] — **en/vi·er** *n.* — **en/vy·ing·ly** *adv.*

en·zyme (en/zim, -zim) *n. Biochem.* A protein able to initiate or accelerate specific chemical reactions in the metabolism of plants and animals; an organic catalyst. Also **en/zym** (-zim). [< L < Gk. < *en-* in + *zymē* leaven] — **en·zy·mat·ic** (en/zi·mat/ik, -zi-) *adj.*

eo- *combining form* Earliest; early part or early representative of. [< Gk. *ēos* dawn, daybreak]

E·o·cene (ē/ə·sēn) *Geol. adj.* Of, pertaining to, or existing in the Early Tertiary period of the Cenozoic era. — *n.* The second epoch of the Cenozoic era. See chart for GEOLOGY. [< EO- + Gk. *kainos* new]

e·o·lith (ē/ə·lith) *n.* A stone tool of the earliest form; celt. [< EO- + Gk. *lithos* stone]

E·o·lith·ic (ē/ə·lith/ik) *adj. Anthropol.* Of or pertaining to a period of early human culture, known only by the rudest implements of bone and chipped stone.

e·on (ē/on, ē/ən) *n.* **1.** An incalculable period of time; an age; eternity. **2.** *Geol.* A time interval including two or more eras. Also spelled **aeon.** [< L *aeon* < Gk. *aiōn* age]

E·os (ē/əs) In Greek mythology, the goddess of the dawn, daughter of Hyperion; identified with the Roman *Aurora.*

e·o·sin (ē/ə·sin) *n. Chem.* A reddish coloring matter, $C_{20}H_8Br_4O_5$, derived from coal tar, used for dyeing and as a stain in microscopy. Also **e/o·sine** (-sin, -sēn). [< Gk. *ēos* morning red, dawn + -IN] — **e/o·sin/ic** *adj.*

-eous *suffix* Of the nature of. [< L *-eus*]

E·o·zo·ic (ē/ə·zō/ik) *adj. Geol.* Of or pertaining to the portion of Pre-Cambrian time immediately before the Paleozoic era and showing the first signs of invertebrate life. [< EO- + Gk. *zōē* life]

ep- Var. of EPI-.

ep·au·let (ep/ə·let) *n. Mil.* A shoulder ornament, as on military and naval uniforms. Also **ep/au·lette.** [< F *épaulette* < OF < LL < L < Gk. *spathē* blade]

é·pée (ā·pā/) *n.* A dueling sword with a sharp point and no cutting edge. [< F < OF < L] — **é·pée·ist** *n.*

eph- Var. of EPI-.

e·phed·rine (i·fed/rin, ef/ə·drēn) *n. Chem.* An alkaloid, $C_{10}H_{15}ON$, used for relief of asthma, hay fever, nasal congestion, etc. Also **e·phed·rin** (i·fed/rin, ef/ə·drin). [< NL *Ephedra*, a genus of plants + -INE²]

e·phem·er·a (i·fem/ər·ə) *n. pl.* **·er·as** or **·er·ae** (-ə·rē) **1.** An ephemerid or May fly. **2.** Anything of very short life or duration. [< Gk. < *epi-* on + *hēmera* day]

e·phem·er·al (i·fem/ər·əl) *adj.* **1.** Lasting but a short time. **2.** Living one day only, as certain insects. — *n.* Anything lasting for a very short time. — **e·phem/er·al·ly** *adv.*

e·phem·er·id (i·fem/ər·id) *n.* A May fly.

E·phe·sian (i·fē/zhən) *adj.* Of or pertaining to Ephesus. — *n.* A citizen of Ephesus.

E·phe·sians (i·fē/zhəns) *n.pl.* (*construed as sing.*) A book of the New Testament, consisting of St. Paul's epistle to the church at Ephesus.

E·phra·im (ē/frē·əm, ē/frəm) In the Old Testament, Joseph's younger son, who obtained the birthright. *Gen.* xlvi 20. — *n.* **1.** The tribe of Israel descended from this son. *Josh.* xiv 4. **2.** The kingdom of Israel. — **E/phra·im·ite** *n.*

epi- *prefix* **1.** Upon; above; among; outside: *epidermis.* **2.** Besides; over; in addition to: *epilogue.* **3.** Near; close to; beside. Also: *ep-*, before vowels, as in *eponym*; *eph-*, before an aspirate, as in *ephemeral.* [< Gk. *epi* upon, on, besides]

ep·ic (ep/ik) *n.* **1.** A long, formal, narrative poem in elevated style, typically having as its subject heroic exploits and achievements or grandiose events. **2.** A novel, drama, etc., that in scale or subject resembles such a poem. — *adj.* **1.** Of, pertaining to, or suitable as a theme for an epic. **2.** Heroic; grandiose. Also **ep/i·cal** *adj.* [< L *epicus* < Gk. *epikos* < *epos* word, tale, song] — **ep/i·cal·ly** *adv.*

ep·i·ca·lyx (ep/ə·kā/liks, -kal/iks) *n. pl.* **·ca·lyx·es** or **·ca·ly·ces** (-kā/lə·sēz, -kal/ə-) *Bot.* An involucre resembling an accessory calyx and lying outside the true calyx of a flower.

ep·i·can·thus (ep/ə·kan/thəs) *n. pl.* **·thi** (-thi) A small fold of skin over the inner corner of the eye, typical of Mongoloid peoples. Also **epicanthic fold.** [< NL < Gk. *epi-* upon + *kanthos* corner of the eye] — **ep/i·can/thic** *adj.*

ep·i·car·di·um (ep/ə·kär/dē·əm) *n. pl.* **·di·a** (-dē·ə) *Anat.* The inner portion of the pericardium that is directly united with the substance of the heart. [< NL < Gk. *epi-* upon + *kardia* heart] — **ep/i·car/di·ac** (-ak), **ep/i·car/di·al** *adj.*

ep·i·carp (ep/ə·kärp) *n. Bot.* The outer layer of a pericarp.

ep·i·cene (ep/ə·sēn) *adj.* Belonging to or partaking of the characteristics of both sexes; hermaphrodite. — *n.* An epicene person. [< L < Gk. < *epi-* upon + *koinos* common]

ep·i·cen·ter (ep/ə·sen/tər) *n. Geol.* The point or area on the earth's surface directly above the focus of an earthquake.

ep·i·cure (ep/ə·kyŏŏr) *n.* One given to luxurious living and discriminating gratification of the senses; a sensualist; esp., a fastidious devotee of good food and drink; a gourmet. [after *Epicurus*, Greek philosopher] — **ep/i·cu·re/an** *adj. & n.*

Ep·i·cu·re·an·ism (ep/ə·kyŏŏ·rē/ən·iz/əm) *n.* The doctrines of Epicurus, Greek philosopher, who taught that the chief aims of life are pleasure regulated by temperance, peace of mind, and cultural pursuits. Also **Ep/i·cur·ism.** — **Ep/i·cu·re/an** *adj. & n.*

ep·i·cy·clic train (ep/ə·si/klik, -sik/lik) *Mech.* A train of gear wheels in which, in addition to the motions of the wheels about their respective axes, one has a fixed axis about which the other axes revolve.

ep·i·dem·ic (ep/ə·dem/ik) *adj.* Breaking out suddenly in a particular area so as to affect many individuals at the same time: used esp. of contagious diseases. Also **ep/i·dem/i·cal.** — *n.* **1.** An epidemic disease. **2.** Anything temporarily widespread, as a fad. [< F < LL < Gk. < *epi-* among + *dēmos* people] — **ep/i·dem/i·cal·ly** *adv.*

ep·i·der·mis (ep/ə·dûr/mis) *n.* **1.** *Anat.* The outer, nonvascular covering of the skin: also called *cuticle.* **2.** Any of various other outer coverings. **3.** *Bot.* The outermost layer of cells covering the surface of a plant when there are several layers of tissue. [< NL < Gk. < *epi-* upon + *derma* skin] — **ep/i·der/mal, ep/i·der/mic** *adj.*

ep·i·der·moid (ep/ə·dûr/moid) *adj.* Of the nature of epidermis. Also **ep/i·der·moi/dal.**

ep·i·glot·tis (ep/ə·glot/is) *n. Anat.* A leaf-shaped, cartilaginous lid at the base of the tongue that covers the windpipe during the act of swallowing. [< NL < Gk. < *epi-* upon + *glōtta* tongue] — **ep/i·glot/tal** *adj.*

ep·i·gram (ep/ə·gram) *n.* **1.** A brief, clever, pointed remark or observation typically marked by antithesis. **2.** A short, pithy piece of verse with a witty, often satirical point. **3.** Epigrammatic expression. [< L < Gk. < *epi-* upon + *graphein* to write] — **ep·i·gram·mat·ic** (ep/i·grə·mat/ik) *adj.* — **ep/i·gram·mat/i·cal·ly** *adv.* — **ep/i·gram/ma·tist** *n.*

ep·i·graph (ep′ə·graf, -gräf) n. 1. An inscription on a monument, tomb, etc. 2. A quotation or motto prefixed to a book, etc. [< Gk. < epi- upon + graphein to write]

ep·i·graph·ic (ep′ə·graf′ik) adj. Of epigraphs or epigraphy. Also **ep′i·graph′i·cal**. — **ep′i·graph′i·cal·ly** adv.

e·pig·ra·phy (i·pig′rə·fē) n. 1. The science that treats of the study, interpretation, etc., of inscriptions. 2. Epigraphs collectively. — **e·pig′ra·pher, e·pig′ra·phist** n.

ep·i·lep·sy (ep′ə·lep′sē) n. Pathol. A disorder of cerebral function marked by attacks of unconsciousness with or without convulsions. See GRAND MAL, PETIT MAL. [< OF < LL < Gk. < epi- upon + lambanein to seize]

ep·i·lep·tic (ep′ə·lep′tik) adj. 1. Of, relating to, or resembling epilepsy. 2. Affected with epilepsy. — n. One affected with epilepsy. — **ep′i·lep′ti·cal·ly** adv.

ep·i·logue (ep′ə·lôg, -log) n. 1. A short section appended to a novel, poem, etc., by way of commentary. 2. A short speech appended to a play. Also **ep′i·log**. [< F < L < Gk. < epi- in addition + legein to say]

ep·i·neph·rine (ep′ə·nef′rin, -rēn) n. Chem. The active principle of the medullary portion of the adrenal glands, $C_9H_{13}O_3N$, used as a heart stimulant: also called adrenalin. Also **ep′i·neph′rin** (-rin). [< EPI- + Gk. nephros kidney]

E·piph·a·ny (i·pif′ə·nē) n. Eccl. A festival, held on January 6, commemorating the manifestation of Christ to the Gentiles as represented by the Magi: also called Twelfth day.

ep·i·phyte (ep′ə·fīt) n. Bot. A plant growing upon, but not receiving its nourishment from, another plant, as an orchid, moss, or lichen. — **ep′i·phyt′ic** (-fit′ik) or **·i·cal** adj.

e·pis·co·pa·cy (i·pis′kə·pə·sē) n. pl. ·cies 1. Government of a church by bishops. 2. The rank, office, or incumbency of a bishop; episcopate. 3. Bishops, collectively. [< LL < Gk. < epi- over + scopein to look]

e·pis·co·pal (i·pis′kə·pəl) adj. 1. Of, pertaining to, or governed by bishops. 2. Advocating episcopacy. [< LL episcopalis < episcopus] — **e·pis′co·pal·ly** adv.

Episcopal Church The Protestant Episcopal Church.

E·pis·co·pa·li·an (i·pis′kə·pā′lē·ən, -pāl′yən) n. A member of the Protestant Episcopal Church. — adj. Belonging to the Protestant Episcopal Church, etc.; Episcopal.

e·pis·co·pate (i·pis′kə·pit, -pāt) n. 1. The office, dignity, or term of office of a bishop. 2. Bishops collectively.

ep·i·sode (ep′ə·sōd) n. 1. A section of a novel, poem, etc., complete in itself. 2. A part of a serialized story or play; installment. [< Gk. < epi- beside + eisodos entrance]

ep·i·sod·ic (ep′ə·sod′ik) adj. 1. Of, relating to, or resembling an episode. 2. Broken up into episodes; esp., disjointed. Also **ep′i·sod′i·cal**. — **ep′i·sod′i·cal·ly** adv.

e·pis·te·mol·o·gy (i·pis′tə·mol′ə·jē) n. pl. ·gies The branch of philosophy that investigates the nature, limits, criteria, or validity of human knowledge; also, a particular theory of cognition. [< Gk. epistēmē knowledge + -LOGY] — **e·pis·te·mo·log·i·cal** (i·pis′tə·mə·loj′i·kəl) adj. — **e·pis′te·mo·log′i·cal·ly** adv. — **e·pis′te·mol′o·gist** n.

e·pis·tle (i·pis′əl) n. 1. A letter, esp. when long or formal. 2. Usu. cap. Eccl. a One of the letters written by an apostle. b A selection taken from one of these letters and read as part of a service. [OE < L < Gk. < epi- to + stellein to send]

e·pis·to·lar·y (i·pis′tə·ler′ē) adj. 1. Of or relating to a letter or an Epistle. 2. Included in or maintained by a letter.

ep·i·taph (ep′ə·taf, -täf) n. An inscription on a tomb or monument in memory of the dead. [< L < Gk. < epi- upon, at + taphos a tomb] — **ep′i·taph′ic** (-taf′ik) adj.

ep·i·the·li·um (ep′ə·thē′lē·əm) n. pl. ·li·ums or ·li·a (-lē·ə) Biol. A membranous tissue consisting of one or more layers of cells, serving to line the cavities and ducts of the body. [< NL < Gk. epi- upon + thēlē nipple] — **ep′i·the′li·al** adj.

ep·i·thet (ep′ə·thet) n. 1. A descriptive word or phrase qualifying or used in place of the usual name of a person or thing. 2. Loosely, any disparaging name. [< L < Gk. < epi- upon + tithenai to place] — **ep′i·thet′ic** or **·i·cal** adj.

e·pit·o·me (i·pit′ə·mē) n. 1. A typical or extreme example; embodiment: the epitome of arrogance. 2. A concise summary; abridgement. [< L < Gk. < epi- upon + temnein to cut]

e·pit·o·mize (i·pit′ə·mīz) v.t. ·mized, ·miz·ing To make or be an epitome of. Also Brit. **e·pit′o·mise**. — **e·pit′o·miz′er** n.

ep·i·zo·ot·ic (ep′ə·zō·ot′ik) adj. Affecting many animals within a wide area: said esp. of diseases. — n. An epizootic disease: also **ep′i·zo′o·ty** (-zō′ə·tē).

e plu·ri·bus u·num (ē plŏŏr′ə·bəs yōō′nəm) Latin One out of many: motto of the U.S.

ep·och (ep′ək, Brit. ē′pok) n. 1. A point in time marked by the beginning of a new development or state of things. 2. An interval of time memorable for extraordinary events, important influences, unusual circumstances, etc. 3. Geol. A minor subdivision of time; a time interval less than a period. See chart for GEOLOGY. 4. Astron. A moment of time when a planet reaches a certain known position in relation to the sun, selected arbitrarily and thereafter used as a reference point. [< Gk. < epi- upon + echein to hold] — **ep′och·al** adj. — **ep′och·al·ly** adv.

ep·o·nym (ep′ə·nim) n. A real or legendary personage from whom a nation, city, epoch, theory, etc., is reputed to derive its name. [< Gk. < epi- upon + onyma name] — **e·pon′y·mous** adj. — **e·pon′y·my** n.

e·pox·y (e·pok′sē) n. Chem. The radical -O-, esp. as bonded to different atoms already joined in different ways, to form the durable, thermosetting epoxy resins much used for varnishes and adhesives. [< EP(I)- + OXY-[2]]

ep·si·lon (ep′sə·lon) n. The fifth letter and second vowel in the Greek alphabet (E, ϵ), corresponding to English short e. See ALPHABET. [< Gk. epsilon < e e + psilon simple]

Epsom salts A hydrous magnesium sulfate, used as a purge or to reduce inflammation. Also Epsom salt.

eq·ua·ble (ek′wə·bəl, ē′kwə-) adj. 1. Not changing or varying greatly; even. 2. Not easily upset; tranquil. 3. Evenly proportioned; uniform. [< L aequare to make equal] — **eq·ua·bil′i·ty, eq′ua·ble·ness** n. — **eq′ua·bly** adv.

e·qual (ē′kwəl) adj. 1. Identical in size, extent, etc. 2. Having the same rights, rank, etc. 3. Having the same abilities, degree of excellence, etc. 4. Evenly proportioned; balanced. 5. Affecting or shared by all alike: equal rights. 6. Having the requisite ability, power, etc.: with to: equal to the task. — v.t. e·qualed or e·qualled, e·qual·ing or e·qual·ling 1. To be equal to; match. 2. To do or produce something equal to. 3. To recompense in full. — n. A person or thing equal to another. [< L aequus even] — **e′qual·ly** adv.

e·qual·i·tar·i·an (i·kwol′ə·târ′ē·ən) adj. & n. Egalitarian. — **e·qual′i·tar′i·an·ism** n.

e·qual·i·ty (i·kwol′ə·tē) n. pl. ·ties The state or quality of being equal; also an instance of this.

e·qual·ize (ē′kwəl·īz) v.t. ·ized, ·iz·ing To make equal or uniform. — **e′qual·iz′er** n. — **e′qual·i·za′tion** n.

equal sign A sign (=) denoting numbers, quantities, etc., equal to one another.

e·qua·nim·i·ty (ē′kwə·nim′ə·tē, ek′wə-) n. Evenness of mind or temper. [< L < aequus even + animus mind]

e·quate (i·kwāt′) v.t. e·quat·ed, e·quat·ing 1. To make equal; treat or consider as equivalent. 2. To reduce to a common standard. 3. Math. To indicate the equality of; express as an equation. [< L aequus even]

e·qua·tion (i·kwā′zhən, -shən) n. 1. The process or act of making equal. 2. The state of being equal. 3. Math. A statement expressing (usu. by =) the equality of two quantities. 4. Chem. A symbolic representation of a chemical reaction, as $Na_2CO_3 + H_2SO_4 \rightarrow Na_2SO_4 + CO_2 + H_2O$.

e·qua·tor (i·kwā′tər) n. 1. The great circle of the earth, a line lying in a plane perpendicular to the earth's polar axis. 2. Any similar circle, as of the sun. 3. Astron. The celestial equator. [< LL (circulus) aequator equalizer (circle)]

e·qua·to·ri·al (ē′kwə·tôr′ē·əl, -tō′rē) adj. 1. Of, pertaining to, or like the equator. 2. Relating to conditions prevailing at the earth's equator.

eq·uer·ry (ek′wər·ē) n. pl. ·ries 1. An officer in charge of the horses of a prince or nobleman. 2. A personal attendant on a member of the royal household of England. [Confusion of F écurie stable (< OF escuerie) with OF escuier esquire]

e·ques·tri·an (i·kwes′trē·ən) adj. 1. Pertaining to horses or horsemanship. 2. Mounted on horseback; also, representing someone as being on horseback: an equestrian portrait. — n. A rider on horseback, esp. when skilled. [< L equus horse] — **e·ques′tri·enne** n.fem.

equi- combining form Equal; equally. [< L aequus equal]

e·qui·dis·tant (ē′kwə·dis′tənt) adj. Equally distant. — **e′qui·dis′tance** n. — **e′qui·dis′tant·ly** adv.

e·qui·lat·er·al (ē′kwə·lat′ər·əl) n. 1. A side of equal length with another. 2. A geometric figure with equal sides. — adj. Having all the sides equal. — **e′qui·lat′er·al·ly** adv.

e·qui·li·brate (ē′kwə·lī′brāt, i·kwil′ə·brāt) v.t. & v.i. ·brat·ed, ·brat·ing 1. To bring into or be in a state of equilibrium. 2. To counterpoise. — **e′qui·li·bra′tion** n.

e·qui·lib·ri·um (ē′kwə·lib′rē·əm) n. 1. Physics A state of balance between two or more forces acting within or upon a body such that there is no change in the state of rest or motion of the body. 2. Any state of balance, compromise, or adjustment. [< L < aequus equal + libra balance]

e·quine (ē′kwīn) adj. Of, pertaining to, or like a horse. — n. A horse. [< L equus horse]

e·qui·noc·tial (ē′kwə·nok′shəl) adj. 1. Occurring at or near the time of the equinox. 2. Of or pertaining to the equinox. — n. Meteorol. A severe storm occurring usu. at or near the time of the equinox.

equinoctial line Astron. The celestial equator.

e·qui·nox (ē′kwə·noks) n. One of two opposite points at which the sun crosses the celestial equator, when the days and nights are equal; also, the time of this crossing (about March 21, the vernal or spring equinox, and Sept. 21, the autumnal equinox). [< F < L < aequus equal + nox night]

e·quip (i·kwip′) v.t. e·quipped, e·quip·ping 1. To furnish or fit out with whatever is needed for any purpose or undertaking. 2. To dress or attire. [< F < OF, prob. < ON skipa to outfit a vessel]

eq·ui·page (ek'wə·pij) *n.* **1.** The equipment for a camp, army, etc. **2.** A carriage, esp. when outfitted with horses, attendants, etc.

e·quip·ment (i·kwip'mənt) *n.* **1.** The act of equipping, or the state of being equipped. **2.** Material with which a person or organization is provided for some special purpose.

e·qui·poise (ē'kwə·poiz, ek'wə-) *n.* **1.** Equality of weight; equal balance. **2.** A counterpoise.

eq·ui·ta·ble (ek'wə·tə·bəl) *adj.* **1.** Marked by equity; impartially just, fair, and reasonable. **2.** *Law* Of, relating to, or valid in equity as distinguished from statute law and common law. — **eq'ui·ta·ble·ness** *n.* — **eq'ui·ta·bly** *adv.*

eq·ui·ty (ek'wə·tē) *n. pl.* **·ties 1.** Fairness or impartiality. **2.** Something that is fair or equitable. **3.** *Law* **a** Justice based on the concepts of ethics and fairness. **b** A system of jurisprudence administered by courts of equity and designed primarily to mitigate the rigors of common law. **4.** In business or property, the value remaining in excess of any liability or mortgage. [< F < L *aequus* equal]

e·quiv·a·lent (i·kwiv'ə·lənt) *adj.* **1.** Equal in value, force, meaning, effect, etc. **2.** *Geom.* Equal in area, but not identical or congruent. **3.** *Chem.* Having the same valence or the same combining weight. — *n.* **1.** That which is equivalent. **2.** *Chem.* The weight of an element that combines with or displaces 1.008 grams of hydrogen. [< LL < L *aequus* equal + *valere* to be worth] — **e·quiv'a·lence, e·quiv'a·len·cy** *n.*

e·quiv·o·cal (i·kwiv'ə·kəl) *adj.* **1.** Having a doubtful meaning; ambiguous. **2.** Of uncertain origin, character, value, etc.; dubious. **3.** Questionable or suspicious: *equivocal* kindness. [< LL < L *aequus* equal + *vox, vocis* voice] — **e·quiv'o·cal·ly** *adv.* — **e·quiv'o·cal·ness** *n.*

e·quiv·o·cate (i·kwiv'ə·kāt) *v.i.* **·cat·ed, ·cat·ing** To use ambiguous language with intent to mislead or deceive. — **e·quiv'o·ca'tion** *n.* — **e·quiv'o·ca'tor** *n.* — **e·quiv'o·ca·to·ry** (-kə·tôr'ē, -tō'rē) *adj.*

er- Assimilated var. of EN-².

-er¹ *suffix of nouns* **1.** A person or thing that performs the action of the root verb: *maker, reaper.* See **-EE** (def. 1). **2.** A person concerned with or practicing a trade or profession: *geographer, hatter.* **3.** One who lives in or comes from: *New Yorker, southerner.* **4.** A person, thing, or action related to or characterized by: *three-decker.* ◆ Nouns of agency are generally formed in English by adding *-er* to a verb, as in *leader,* but some such nouns have the suffix *-or,* as in *creditor, elevator.* [OE < L *-arius, -arium*]

-er² *suffix of nouns* A person or thing connected with: *grocer, jailer.* [< AF, OF < L *-arius, -arium*]

-er³ *suffix* Forming the comparative degree of adjectives and adverbs: *harder, later.* [OE *-ra, -or*]

-er⁴ *suffix* Repeatedly: used in frequentative verbs: *stutter.* [OE *-rian*]

-er⁵ *suffix of nouns* Denoting the action expressed by the root word: *rejoinder, waiver.* [< F *-er,* infinitive ending]

e·ra (ir'ə, ē'rə) *n.* **1.** An extended period of time reckoned from some fixed point in the past and used as the basis of a chronology: the Christian *era.* **2.** A period of time characterized by certain events, conditions, influences, etc. **3.** The beginning of a particular period; an epoch. **4.** *Geol.* A division of geological history of highest rank. See chart for GEOLOGY. [< LL *aera* counters, orig. pl. of L *aes* brass, money]

e·ra·di·ate (i·rā'dē·āt) *v.t. & v.i.* **·at·ed, ·at·ing** To radiate. — **e·ra'di·a'tion** *n.*

e·rad·i·cate (i·rad'ə·kāt) *v.t.* **·cat·ed, ·cat·ing 1.** To pull up by the roots. **2.** To destroy utterly. [< L < *e-* out + *radix, -icis* a root] — **e·rad'i·ca·ble** (-kə·bəl) *adj.* — **e·rad'i·ca'tion** *n.* — **e·rad'i·ca'tive** *adj.*

e·rad·i·ca·tor (i·rad'ə·kā'tər) *n.* One who or that which eradicates; esp., a preparation for removing ink, etc.

e·rase (i·rās') *v.t.* **e·rased, e·ras·ing 1.** To obliterate, as by scraping or rubbing out; efface. **2.** *U.S. Slang* To kill. [< L < *e-* out + *radere* to scrape] — **e·ras'a·ble** *adj.*

e·ras·er (i·rā'sər) *n.* Something used for erasing, as a piece of rubber, felt, etc.

e·ra·sure (i·rā'shər, -zhər) *n.* **1.** The act of erasing, or the state of being erased. **2.** That which is erased. **3.** A mark left on a surface by erasing something.

Er·a·to (er'ə·tō) The Muse of lyric and love poetry.

er·bi·um (ûr'bē·əm) *n.* A metallic element (symbol Er) of the lanthanide series, found in gadolinite. See ELEMENT. [< NL < (*Ytt*)*erby,* town in Sweden where first found]

ere (âr) *Archaic & Poetic prep.* Prior to; before in time. — *conj.* **1.** Before. **2.** Sooner than; rather than. [OE *ǣr*]

Er·e·bus (er'ə·bəs) In Greek mythology, a dark region through which the dead pass on their way to Hades.

e·rect (i·rekt') *v.t.* **1.** To put up (a building, etc.). **2.** To assemble the parts of; set up. **3.** To set upright; raise. **4.** To establish or found, as an empire. **5.** To work out or formulate, as a theory or system. **6.** To make into; form: with

into. — *v.i.* **7.** *Physiol.* To become rigidly upright, as through an influx of blood. — *adj.* **1.** Marked by a vertical position or posture; upright. **2.** Directed or pointed upward. [< L < *e-* out + *regere* to direct] — **e·rect'ly** *adv.* — **e·rect'ness** *n.* — **e·rec'tion** *n.*

e·rec·tile (i·rek'təl, -til) *adj.* Capable of becoming erected.

e·rec·tor (i·rek'tər) *n.* **1.** One who or that which erects. **2.** *Anat.* Any of various muscles that stiffen or hold up a part of the body. Also **e·rect'er.**

erg (ûrg) *n. Physics* In the cgs system, the unit of work and of energy, being the work done in moving a body one centimeter against the force of one dyne. [< Gk. *ergon* work]

er·go (ûr'gō) *conj. & adv. Latin* Hence; therefore. [< L]

er·got (ûr'gət) *n.* **1.** A fungus sometimes replacing the grain in rye and other cereal grasses. **2.** The disease caused by this fungus growth. **3.** The dried sclerotia of rye ergot, used in medicine to contract involuntary muscle and to check hemorrhage. [< OF *argot* spur of a cock]

E·rid·a·nus (i·rid'ə·nəs) *n.* A constellation, the River. [< L, the Po river]

E·rie (ir'ē) *n. pl.* **E·rie** or **E·ries** One of a tribe of North American Indians of Iroquoian stock, formerly inhabiting the southern shores of Lake Erie.

Er·in (âr'in, ir'in) *Chiefly Poetic* Ireland.

erl·king (ûrl'king') *n.* In Germanic folklore, an evil spirit, malicious toward children. [< G *erlkönig,* wrong trans. of Dan. *ellerkonge, elverkonge* king of the elves]

er·mine (ûr'min) *n.* **1.** One of several weasels of the northern hemisphere, having brown fur that in winter turns white with a black tip on the tail. **2.** The white fur of the ermine, used in Europe for the facings of the official robes of judges, etc. **3.** The rank or functions of a judge. [< OF (*h*)*ermine,* ? < Gmc.] — **er'mined** *adj.*

ERMINE (def. 1)
(Body 9 to 12 inches long; tail 3 to 3½ inches)

erne (ûrn) *n.* A sea eagle. Also **ern.** [OE *earn*]

e·rode (i·rōd') *v.* **e·rod·ed, e·rod·ing** *v.t.* **1.** To wear away gradually by constant friction; wear down by scraping, rubbing, etc. **2.** To eat into; corrode. **3.** To make (a channel, gully, etc.) by wearing away or eating into. — *v.i.* **4.** To become eroded. [< L < *e-* off + *rodere* to gnaw]

Er·os (ir'os, er'os) In Greek mythology, the god of love, son of Aphrodite: identified with the Roman *Cupid.*

e·ro·sion (i·rō'zhən) *n.* **1.** The act of eroding, or the state of being eroded. **2.** *Geol.* The wearing away of the earth's surface by the action of wind, water, glaciers, etc.

e·ro·sive (i·rō'siv) *adj.* **1.** Eroding or tending to erode. **2.** Caustic or corrosive. Also **e·ro·dent** (i·rōd'nt).

e·rot·ic (i·rot'ik) *adj.* **1.** Of, pertaining to, or concerned with sexual love; amatory. **2.** Designed to arouse sexual desire. **3.** Strongly moved by sexual desire. — *n.* **1.** An erotic person. **2.** An erotic poem. [< Gk. < *erōs, -erōtos* love] — **e·rot'i·cal·ly** *adv.* — **e·rot'i·cism** *n.*

err (ûr, er) *v.i.* **erred, err·ing 1.** To make a mistake. **2.** To go astray morally. [< OF < L *errare* to wander] — **err'ing** *adj.* — **err'ing·ly** *adv.*

er·rand (er'ənd) *n.* **1.** A trip made to carry a message or perform some task, usu. for someone else. **2.** The business or purpose of such a trip. [OE *ǣrende* message, news]

er·rant (er'rənt) *adj.* **1.** Roving or wandering, esp. in search of adventure. **2.** Straying from the proper course or standard. [< OF < L *iter* journey] — **er'rant·ly** *adv.*

er·rat·ic (i·rat'ik) *adj.* **1.** Not conforming to usual standards; eccentric. **2.** Lacking a fixed or certain course; straying. **3.** *Geol.* Transported from the original site by glaciers, currents, etc. — *n.* An erratic person or thing. [< L < *errare* to wander] — **er·rat'i·cal·ly** *adv.*

er·ra·tum (i·rā'təm, i·rä'təm) *n. pl.* **·ra·ta** (-rä'tə, -rā'tə) An error, as in writing or printing. [< L]

er·ro·ne·ous (ə·rō'nē·əs, e·rō'-) *adj.* Marked by error; incorrect. — **er·ro'ne·ous·ly** *adv.* — **er·ro'ne·ous·ness** *n.*

er·ror (er'ər) *n.* **1.** Something done, said, or believed incorrectly; a mistake. **2.** The condition of deviating from what is correct or true in judgment, belief, or action. **3.** An offense against morals; sin. **4.** In baseball, a misplay by a member of the team not batting. **5.** *Math.* **a** The difference between the observed value of a magnitude and the true or mean value. **b** Any deviation from the true or mean value not due to gross blunders of observation or measurement.

er·satz (er·zäts', er'zäts) *adj.* Substitute, and usu. inferior. — *n.* A usu. inferior substitute. [< G]

Erse (ûrs) *n.* **1.** Scottish Gaelic. **2.** Irish Gaelic. — *adj.* Of or pertaining to the Celts of Ireland or Scotland or their language. [Var. of IRISH]

erst (ûrst) *Archaic adv.* **1.** Formerly; long ago. **2.** In the beginning. — *adj.* First. [OE *ǣrest,* superl. of *ǣr* before]

erst·while (ûrst′hwīl′) *adj.* Former: an *erstwhile* colleague.

e·ruct (i·rukt′) *v.t. & v.i.* To belch. Also **e·ruc′tate**. [< L < *e-* out + *ructare* to belch] **— e·ruc·ta′tion** *n.* **— e·ruc′-ta·tive** *adj.*

er·u·dite (er′yŏŏ·dīt, er′ŏŏ-)   *adj.* Very learned; scholarly. [< L < *e-* out + *rudis* untrained] **— er′u·dite·ly** *adv.* **— er′u·dite·ness** *n.*

er·u·di·tion (er′yŏŏ·dish′ən, er′ŏŏ-)   *n.* Great learning.

e·rupt (i·rupt′) *v.i.* **1.** To cast forth lava, steam, etc., as a volcano or geyser. **2.** To be cast forth from a volcano, geyser, etc. **3.** To burst forth suddenly and violently. **4.** To show a rash or become covered with pimples, etc. **5.** Of new teeth, to break through the gums. *— v.t.* **6.** To make erupt. **7.** To cast forth (lava, etc.). [< L < *e-* out + *rumpere* to burst] **— e·rup′tion** *n.* **— e·rup′tive** *adj.*

-ery *suffix of nouns* **1.** A business, place of business, or place where something is done: *brewery*. **2.** A place or residence for: *nunnery*. **3.** A collection of things: *finery*. **4.** The qualities, principles, or practices of: *snobbery*. **5.** An art, trade, or profession: *cookery*. **6.** A state, or condition of being: *slavery*. Also *-ry*, as in *jewelry*. [< OF < *-ier* (< L *-arius*) + *-ie* < L *-ia*]

erythro- *combining form* Red. Also, before vowels, **erythr-**. [< Gk. *erythros* red]

e·ryth·ro·cyte (i·rith′rō·sīt)   *n. Anat.* A disk-shaped red blood cell formed in bone marrow; it contains hemoglobin and transports oxygen to all tissues of the body. **— e·ryth′-ro·cyt′ic** (-sit′ik) *adj.*

es- *prefix* Out: used in words borrowed from Old French: *escape, escheat*. [< OF < L *ex* from, out of]

-es[1] An inflectional ending used to form the plural of nouns ending in a sibilant (*fuses, fishes*), an affricate (*witches*), or, in some cases, a vowel. Compare -s[1]. [OE *-as*]

-es[2] An inflectional ending used to form the third person singular present indicative of verbs ending in a sibilant, affricate, or vowel: *goes, poaches*. Compare -s[2]. [ME *-es*]

E·sau (ē′sô) The eldest son of Isaac, who sold his birthright to his brother Jacob. *Gen.* xxv 25. [< Hebrew ′ēsāw hairy]

es·ca·drille (es′kə·dril′, *Fr.* es·kà·drē′y′)   *n.* **1.** In France, a unit of military airplanes. **2.** A squadron of naval vessels. [< F, dim. of *escadre* squadron]

es·ca·late (es′kə·lāt)   *v.t. & v.i.* **·lat·ed, ·lat·ing** **1.** To increase or be increased gradually: to *escalate* a war. **2.** To ascend an escalator. [Back formation < ESCALATOR] **— es′ca·la′tion** *n.*

es·ca·la·tor (es′kə·lā′tər)   *n.* A moving stairway built on the conveyor-belt principle.

es·cal·lop (e·skol′əp, e·skal′-)   *n.* Scallop. *— v.t.* To scallop.

es·ca·pade (es′kə·pād)   *n.* **1.** A brief piece of reckless behavior or prankish disregard of convention; fling; spree. **2.** An act of getting away from rigid restraint or confinement. [< F < Sp. < *escapar* to escape]

es·cape (ə·skāp′, e·skāp′)   *v.* **·caped, ·cap·ing** *v.i.* **1.** To get free from confinement, restraint, or capture. **2.** To manage to avoid some danger or evil. **3.** To come out gradually from a container or enclosure, as by seeping, leaking, etc. **4.** To fade away and disappear; vanish. *— v.t.* **5.** To get away from (prison, captors, etc.). **6.** To succeed in avoiding (capture, harm, etc.). **7.** To get away from the notice or recollection of: No detail *escaped* him. **8.** To slip out from unintentionally: A cry *escaped* his lips. *— n.* **1.** The act of escaping, or the fact of having escaped. **2.** A means of escaping something: Drinking is an *escape* for him. **3.** A gradual leaking or seeping. *— adj.* **1.** That provides a means of getting away from reality, etc.; escapist: *escape* literature. **2.** That provides a means of lessening or avoiding liability, etc.: an *escape* clause in a contract. [< AF < L *ex-* out + *cappa* cloak] **— es·cap′a·ble** *adj.*

es·cap·ee (e·skā·pē′, ə·skā′pē, e·skā′pē)   *n.* One who has escaped, as from prison.

es·cape·ment (ə·skāp′mənt, e·skāp′-)   *n.* **1.** *Mech.* A device used in timepieces for securing a uniform movement, consisting of a notched escape wheel that is released one tooth at a time by a small lock. **2.** A typewriter mechanism controlling the horizontal movement of the carriage.

escape velocity *Physics* The minimum velocity a body must attain to escape a gravitational field: on the earth this velocity is approximately 7 miles per second.

escape wheel *Mech.* A notched wheel in an escapement.

es·cap·ism (ə·skā′piz·əm, e·skā′-)   *n.* A desire or tendency to escape unpleasant reality by resorting to diversions, or by indulging in daydreaming.

es·cap·ist (ə·skā′pist, e·skā′-)   *adj.* Catering to or providing a means of indulging in escapism: *escapist* literature. *— n.* One given to escapism.

es·ca·role (es′kə·rōl)   *n.* A variety of endive whose leaves are used for salads. [< F < ML *escarius* fit for eating]

es·carp·ment (es·kärp′mənt)   *n.* **1.** A precipitous artificial slope about a fortification or position. **2.** A steep slope or drop; esp., the precipitous face of a line of cliffs.

-esce *suffix of verbs* To become or grow; begin to be or do

(what is indicated by the main element): *phosphoresce*. [< L *-escere*, suffix of inceptive verbs]

-escence *suffix of nouns* Forming nouns of state or quality corresponding to adjectives in *-escent*. [< L *-escentia*]

-escent *suffix of adjectives* Beginning to be, have, or do (what is indicated by the main element): *effervescent*. [< L *-escens, -escentis*, suffix of ppr. of inceptive verbs]

es·cheat (es·chēt′)   *Law n.* **1.** Reversion of property to the state or to the crown in default of legal heirs or other qualified claimants. **2.** Property entering possession of the state, etc., by this process. *— v.i. & v.t.* To revert or cause to revert to the state, etc., by escheat. [< OF < *es-* out + *cheoir* to fall] **— es·cheat′a·ble** *adj.*

es·chew (es·chōō′)   *v.t.* To shun, as something unworthy or injurious. [< OF *eschiver*] **— es·chew′al** *n.*

es·cort (*n.* es′kôrt; *v.* es·kôrt′)   *n.* **1.** An individual or group of individuals accompanying another so as to give protection or guidance. **2.** A male who takes a girl or woman to a dance, party, etc. **3.** One or more planes, ships, cars, etc., moving along with another so as to give protection, guidance, etc. *— v.t.* To accompany in the capacity of an escort. [< F < Ital. *scorgere* to lead]

es·cri·toire (es′kri·twär′)   *n.* A writing desk; secretary. [< OF < LL *scriptorium* place for writing]

es·crow (es′krō, es·krō′)   *n. Law* **1.** A written deed, contract, etc., placed in the custody of a third party and effective upon fulfillment of a stipulated condition. **2.** The condition of being an escrow: a bond in *escrow*. [< OF *escrowe*, OF *escroe* scroll]

es·cu·do (es·kōō′dō; *Pg.* ish·kōō′thōō; *Sp.* es·kōō′thō)   *n. pl.* **·dos** (-dōz; *Pg.* -thōōs; *Sp.* -thōs) The monetary unit of Portugal, containing 100 centavos: in 1960 worth about 4 U.S. cents. [< Pg. < L *scutum* shield]

es·cu·lent (es′kyə·lənt)   *adj.* Edible. *— n.* Anything edible, esp. a plant. [< L *esca* food]

es·cutch·eon (i·skuch′ən)   *n. Heraldry* A usu. shield-shaped surface carrying armorial bearings. Also *scutcheon*. [< AF < L *scutum* shield]

Es·dras (ez′drəs) The Douai Bible name for EZRA. *— n.* In the Douai Bible, either of two books of the Old Testament. I Esdras corresponds to the book of Ezra, and II Esdras corresponds to the book of Nehemiah. [< Gk.]

-ese *suffix of nouns and adjectives* **1.** A native or inhabitant of: *Milanese*. **2.** The language or dialect of: *Chinese*. **3.** Originating in: *Tirolese*. **4.** In the manner or style of: *journalese*. [< OF *-eis, -ese* < L *-ensis*]

Es·ki·mo (es′kə·mō)   *n. pl.* **·mos** or **·mo** **1.** One of a Mongoloid people indigenous to the Arctic coasts of North America, Greenland, and NE Siberia. **2.** The language of the Eskimos. *— adj.* Of or relating to the Eskimos, their language, or their culture. Also spelled *Esquimau*. [< Dan. (< F *Esquimaux*) < N. Am. Ind., eaters of raw flesh]

Es·ki·mo·an (es′kə·mō′ən) *adj.* Eskimo. Also **Es′ki·mau′an**.

Eskimo dog One of a breed of large, sturdy, broad-chested dogs used by the Eskimos to draw sledges.

e·soph·a·gus (i·sof′ə·gəs)   *n. pl.* **·gi** (-jī) *Anat.* The tube through which food passes from the mouth to the stomach; gullet: also spelled *oesophagus*. For illus. see MOUTH, THROAT. [< NL < Gk. *oisophagos*] **— e·so·phag·e·al** (ē′sō·faj′ē·əl, i·sof′ə·jē′əl) or **e·soph′a·gal** (-ə·gəl) *adj.*

es·o·ter·ic (es′ə·ter′ik)   *adj.* **1.** Understood by or meant for only a few specially instructed or initiated individuals: *esoteric* doctrine. **2.** Confidential; kept secret: an *esoteric* motive. **— Syn.** See MYSTERIOUS. [< Gk. *esōterikos* inner] **— es′o·ter′i·cal·ly** *adv.*

ESP Extrasensory perception.

es·pal·ier (es·pal′yər)   *n.* **1.** A trellis or other flat framework on which small trees, shrubs, etc., are trained to grow. **2.** A tree or row of plants so trained. *— v.t.* To furnish with an espalier. [< F < Ital. < L *spatula* shoulder]

es·pe·cial (es·pesh′əl)   *adj.* Preeminent in place or degree; very special. [< OF < L *species* kind, type]

es·pe·cial·ly (es·pesh′əl·ē)   *adv.* To a very special extent or degree; particularly: *especially* frequent; *especially* good.

Es·pe·ran·to (es′pə·rän′tō, -rän′tō)   *n.* An artificial language having a vocabulary based on words in the major European languages. [after pseudonym of the inventor]

es·pi·al (es·pī′əl)   *n.* **1.** The act of noticing something, or the fact of being noticed. **2.** The act of spying upon. [< OF *espier* to look]

es·pi·o·nage (es′pē·ə·nij′, -näzh′; *Fr.* es·pyô·näzh′)   *n.* **1.** The practice of spying. **2.** The work of spies; esp., the securing of secret information. [< F *espier* to espy]

es·pla·nade (es′plə·nād′, -näd′)   *n.* **1.** A level, open stretch of land, as along a shore, used as a roadway or public walk. **2.** An open embankment or level area before a fortress. [< F < Sp. < L < *ex-* out + *planus* level]

es·pou·sal (es·pou′zəl)   *n.* **1.** Adoption or support, as of a cause. **2.** A betrothal. **3.** *Often pl.* A marriage ceremony.

es·pouse (es·pouz′)   *v.t.* **·poused, ·pous·ing** **1.** To make one's own; support, as a cause or doctrine. **2.** To take as a spouse; marry. **3.** To give in marriage. [< OF < L *spondere* to promise] **— es·pous/er** *n.*

es·pres·so (es·pres/ō) *n. pl.* **·sos** Coffee brewed from darkly roasted beans by steam pressure. [< Ital. *espresso*]

es·prit (es·prē/) *n.* Spirit; wit. [< F < L *spiritus*]

esprit de corps (də kôr) *French* A spirit of enthusiastic devotedness to and support of the common goals of a group.

es·py (es·pī/) *v.t.* **·pied**, **·py·ing** To catch sight of (something); see; descry. [< OF *espier* to look, spy]

-esque *suffix of adjectives* Having the manner or style of; resembling; like: *picturesque*. [< F < Ital. < L *-iscus*]

Es·qui·mau (es/kə·mō) *n. pl.* **·maux** (-mōz) See Eskimo.

es·quire (es·kwīr/; *for n.*, also es/kwīr) *n.* **1.** *Usu. cap.* A title of courtesy or respect sometimes written abbreviated after a man's surname: John Smith, *Esq.* **2.** In England, a man ranking just below a knight. **3.** A squire or young candidate for knighthood. [< OF < LL *scutarius* shield-bearer]

-ess *suffix* Used to form the feminine of many nouns: *goddess*, *lioness*. [< F *-esse* < LL *-issa* < Gk.]

es·say (*n. def. 1* es/ā; *n. defs. 2 and 3* es/ā, e·sā/; *v.* e·sā/) *n.* **1.** A short composition dealing with a single topic and typically personal in approach. **2.** An attempt; endeavor. **— v.t. 1.** To attempt to do or accomplish; try. **2.** To test the nature, etc., of. [< OF *essai* trial] **— es·say/er** *n.*

es·say·ist (es/ā·ist) *n.* A writer of essays.

es·sence (es/əns) *n.* **1.** That in which the real nature of a thing consists; intrinsic or fundamental nature. **2.** The distinctive quality of something. **3.** *Philos.* A real or true substance. **4.** An immaterial being; spirit. **5.** An extract, as of a plant or food, containing the distinctive properties of the plant; also, an alcoholic solution of such an extract. **6.** A perfume. [< F < L *esse* to be]

es·sen·tial (ə·sen/shəl) *adj.* **1.** Of, belonging to, or constituting the intrinsic nature of something. **2.** Extremely important; vital; indispensable. **3.** Derived from the extract of a plant, etc.: an *essential* oil. **4.** Complete, total, or absolute. **— n.** Something fundamental, indispensable, or extremely important. **— es·sen/tial·ly** *adv.*

es·sen·ti·al·i·ty (ə·sen/shē·al/ə·tē) *n. pl.* **·ties 1.** The state or quality of being essential. **2.** Something essential.

essential oil Any of a group of volatile oils that give to plants their characteristic odors, flavors, etc.

-est[1] *suffix* Forming the superlative degree of adjectives and adverbs: *hardest*, *latest*. [OE *-ast*, *-est*, *-ost*]

-est[2] An archaic inflectional ending used in the second person singular present and past indicative, with *thou*: *eatest*, *walkest*. Also, in contracted forms, *-st*, as in *hast*, *didst*. [OE *-est*, *-ast*]

es·tab·lish (ə·stab/lish) *v.t.* **1.** To make secure, stable, or permanent. **2.** To set up, found, or institute: to *establish* a government. **3.** To install: to *establish* oneself in a new home. **4.** To initiate and cause to last: to *establish* a precedent. **5.** To cause to be recognized and accepted: to *establish* oneself as a writer. **6.** To clear from doubt; demonstrate; prove. **8.** To cause to be the official church of a state. [< OF < L *stabilis* stable] **— es·tab/lish·er** *n.*

established church A church recognized by a government and supported in part by public funds.

es·tab·lish·ment (ə·stab/lish·mənt) *n.* **1.** The act of establishing, or the state or fact of being established. **2.** Something established, as a business, residence, etc. **— the Establishment** Those collectively who occupy positions of influence and status in a society.

es·tate (ə·stāt/) *n.* **1.** A usu. extensive piece of landed property or the residence built on it. **2.** One's entire property and possessions. **3.** A particular condition or state: to rise to high *estate*; man's *estate*. **4.** A particular class of persons with distinct political or social status, rights, and powers. **5.** *Law* The degree, nature, and extent of ownership or use of property. [< OF < L *status* a state]

es·teem (ə·stēm/) *v.t.* **1.** To have a high opinion of; value greatly. **2.** To think of as; rate. **— n. 1.** High regard or respect. **2.** Judgment. [< F < L *aestimare* to value]

es·ter (es/tər) *n.* *Chem.* Any of a class of organic compounds formed by the reaction of an acid with an alcohol. [Coined by Leopold Gmelin, 1788–1853, German chemist]

Es·ther (es/tər) In the Old Testament, the Jewish queen, wife of King Ahasuerus (Xerxes) of Persia, who saved her people from massacre. **— n.** A book of the Old Testament containing her story. [< Hebrew *ester*, ? < Babylonian]

es·thete (es/thēt) *n.* **1.** One who is very responsive to beauty in art, nature, etc. **2.** One who cultivates an extravagant, usu. artificial admiration for beauty and art. Also *Brit.*, *aesthete*. [< Gk. *aisthētēs* one who perceives]

es·thet·ic (es·thet/ik) *adj.* **1.** Of or relating to esthetics. **2.** Of or relating to the beauty in art, nature, etc. **3.** Keenly responsive to beauty in art, nature, etc. Also spelled *aesthetic*: also **es·thet/i·cal.** **— es·thet/i·cal·ly** *adv.*

es·thet·i·cism (es·thet/ə·siz/əm) *n.* **1.** A particular theory or outlook relating to the nature, forms, and importance of beauty. **2.** Keen responsiveness to and appreciation of beauty in art, etc. Also spelled *aestheticism*.

es·thet·ics (es·thet/iks) *n.pl.* (*construed as sing.*) **1.** A branch of philosophy relating to the nature and forms of beauty. **2.** Study of the mental and emotional responses to the beauty in art, etc. Also spelled *aesthetics*.

es·ti·ma·ble (es/tə·mə·bəl) *adj.* **1.** Worthy of respect or admiration. **2.** That may be estimated or calculated. **— es/ti·ma·ble·ness** *n.* **— es/ti·ma·bly** *adv.*

es·ti·mate (*v.* es/tə·māt; *n.* es/tə·mit) *v.* **·mat·ed**, **·mat·ing** *v.t.* **1.** To form an approximate opinion of (size, amount, number, etc.). **2.** To form an opinion about; judge. **— v.i. 3.** To make or submit an estimate. **— n. 1.** A rough calculation based on incomplete data. **2.** A preliminary statement of the approximate cost for certain work. **3.** A judgment or opinion. [< L *aestimare* to value] **— es/ti·ma/tive** *adj.* **— es/ti·ma/tor** *n.*

es·ti·ma·tion (es/tə·mā/shən) *n.* **1.** The act of estimating. **2.** A conclusion arrived at by estimating. **3.** Esteem; regard: I hold him in high *estimation*.

es·ti·val (es/tə·vəl, es·tī/-) *adj.* Of or pertaining to summer.

es·ti·vate (es/tə·vāt) *v.i.* **·vat·ed**, **·vat·ing** To pass the summer in a dormant state. [< L *aestivare* to spend the summer] **— es/ti·va/tion** *n.* **— es/ti·va/tor** *n.*

Es·to·ni·an (es·tō/nē·ən) *adj.* Of or pertaining to Estonia. **— n. 1.** One of a people inhabiting Estonia and part of Livonia. **2.** The Finno-Ugric language of this people.

es·trange (es·trānj/) *v.t.* **·tranged**, **·trang·ing 1.** To make (someone previously friendly or affectionate) indifferent or hostile; alienate. **2.** To remove or dissociate (oneself, etc.). [< OF < L *extraneus* foreign] **— es·trange/ment** *n.*

es·tro·gen (es/trə·jən) *n.* *Biochem.* Any of various substances that influence estrus or produce changes in the sexual characteristics of female mammals: also spelled *oestrogen*. **— es/tro·gen/ic** (-jen/ik) *adj.*

es·trus (es/trəs, ēs/-) *n.* **1.** *Biol.* **a** The entire cycle of physiological changes in female mammals, preparing the generative organs for their fertile period. **b** The peak of the sexual cycle, culminating in ovulation; heat. Also called *oestru m*: also spelled *oestrus*. Also **es/trum** (-trum). [< L *oestrus* frenzy, passion < Gk. *oistros* gadfly]

es·tu·ar·y (es/chōo·er/ē) *n. pl.* **·ar·ies 1.** A wide mouth of a river where its current meets the sea and is influenced by the tides. **2.** An inlet or arm of the sea. [< L < *aestus* tide] **— es/tu·ar/i·al** (-âr/ē·əl) *adj.*

-et *suffix* Small; little: *islet*: often without appreciable force, as in *sonnet*. [< F]

e·ta (ā/tə, ē/-) *n.* The seventh letter and third vowel in the Greek alphabet (H, η), corresponding to English long *e*. See alphabet. [< Gk. *ēta* < Phoenician *hēth*]

et cet·er·a (et set/ər·ə, set/rə) And other things; and the rest; and so forth. Also **et caet/er·a.** Abbr. *etc.*, *&c.* [< L]

etch (ech) *v.t.* **1.** To engrave by means of acid or other corrosive fluid, esp. in making a design on a plate for printing. **2.** To outline or sketch by scratching lines with a pointed instrument. **— v.i. 3.** To engage in etching. [< Du. *etsen* < G *ätzen* < OHG *ezjan* to corrode] **— etch/er** *n.*

etch·ing (ech/ing) *n.* **1.** A process of engraving in which lines are scratched with a needle on a plate covered with wax or other coating, and the parts exposed are subjected to the corrosive action of an acid. **2.** A figure or design formed by etching. **3.** An impression from an etched plate.

e·ter·nal (i·tûr/nəl) *adj.* **1.** Existing without beginning or end; forever existent. **2.** Unending: *eternal* happiness. **3.** Valid and true for and beyond all time. **4.** Seemingly endless. **— the Eternal** God. [< OF < LL < L *aevum* age] **— e·ter/nal·ly** *adv.* **— e·ter/nal·ness** *n.*

Eternal City Rome.

e·ter·ni·ty (i·tûr/nə·tē) *n. pl.* **·ties 1.** Existence without beginning or end; endless duration. **2.** An immeasurable extent of time. **3.** The endless time following death.

e·ter·nize (i·tûr/nīz) *v.t.* **·nized**, **·niz·ing 1.** To make eternal. **2.** To perpetuate the fame of; immortalize. Also **e·ter/nal·ize** (-nəl·īz). **— e·ter/ni·za/tion** *n.*

eth (eth) See EDH.

-eth[1] An archaic inflectional ending used in the third person singular present indicative of some verbs: *eateth*, *drinketh*. Also, in contracted forms, *-th*, as in *hath*, *doth*. [OE *-eth*, *-ath*]

-eth[2] *suffix* Var. of -TH[2].

eth·ane (eth/ān) *n.* *Chem.* A colorless, odorless, gaseous hydrocarbon, C_2H_6, of the methane series contained in crude petroleum and in illuminating gas. [< ETHER]

eth·a·nol (eth/ə·nōl, -nol) *n.* *Chem.* An alcohol, C_2H_5OH, obtained by the distillation of certain fermented sugars or starches, the intoxicant in liquors, wines, and beers: also called *ethyl alcohol*, *grain alcohol*. [< ETHANE + -OL[1]]

---

e·ther (ē'thər) *n.* **1.** Ethyl ether. **2.** *Chem.* Any of a group of organic compounds in which an oxygen atom is joined with two organic radicals. **3.** A solid or semisolid medium formerly assumed to pervade all of space: also spelled *aether.* **4.** The clear, upper regions of space: also spelled *aether.* [< L *aether* sky]

e·the·re·al (i·thir'ē·əl) *adj.* **1.** Resembling ether or air; airy. **2.** Delicate or exquisite in line, feature, etc.: an *ethereal* face. **3.** Spiritual; celestial. **4.** Of or existing in the upper regions. **5.** *Chem.* Of or pertaining to ether. — **e·the're·al·ly** *adv.* — **e·the're·al·i·ty** (-əl/ə·tē), **e·the're·al·ness** *n.*

e·the·re·al·ize (i·thir'ē·əl·īz') *v.t.* **·ized, ·iz·ing** To make ethereal; spiritualize. — **e·the're·al·i·za'tion** *n.*

e·ther·ize (ē'thə·rīz) *v.t.* **·ized, ·iz·ing** To subject to the fumes of ether; anesthetize. — **e'ther·i·za'tion** *n.*

eth·ic (eth'ik) *n.* A philosophy or system of morals; ethics. — *adj.* Ethical; moral. [< L < Gk. *ēthos* character]

eth·i·cal (eth'i·kəl) *adj.* **1.** Pertaining to or treating of ethics and morality. **2.** Conforming to right principles of conduct as accepted by a specific profession, etc. — **eth'i·cal·ly** *adv.* — **eth'i·cal·ness, eth'i·cal'i·ty** (-kal'ə·tē) *n.*

eth·ics (eth'iks) *n.pl.* (*construed as sing. in defs. 1 and 3*) **1.** The study and philosophy of human conduct, with emphasis on the determination of right and wrong. **2.** The principles of right conduct with reference to a specific profession, mode of life, etc. **3.** A treatise on morals.

E·thi·o·pi·an (ē'thē·ō'pē·ən) *adj.* Of or pertaining to Ethiopia, its people, or their language. — *n.* A native or inhabitant of Ethiopia.

E·thi·op·ic (ē'thē·op'ik, -ō'pik) *n.* A Semitic language of ancient Ethiopia. — *adj.* Ethiopian.

eth·nic (eth'nik) *adj.* **1.** Of, belonging to, or distinctive of a particular racial, cultural, or language division of mankind. **2.** Of or belonging to a people neither Jewish nor Christian; heathen. Also **eth'ni·cal.** [< Gk. < *ethnos* nation] — **eth'ni·cal·ly** *adv.*

ethno- *combining form* Race; nation; peoples. Also, before vowels, **ethn-.**

eth·nog·ra·phy (eth·nog'rə·fē) *n.* *pl.* **·phies** **1.** The branch of anthropology concerned with the classification and description of regional, chiefly primitive human cultures. **2.** Loosely, ethnology. — **eth·nog'ra·pher** *n.* — **eth·no·graph·ic** (eth'nə·graf'ik) or **·i·cal** *adj.* — **eth'no·graph'i·cal·ly** *adv.*

eth·nol·o·gy (eth·nol'ə·jē) *n.* *pl.* **·gies** **1.** The branch of anthropology concerned with the study of racial and ethnic groups in their origins, distribution, and cultures. **2.** Loosely, ethnography. — **eth·nol'o·gist** *n.* — **eth·no·log·ic** (eth'nə·loj'ik) or **·i·cal** *adj.* — **eth'no·log'i·cal·ly** *adv.*

eth·yl (eth'əl) *n.* *Chem.* **1.** A univalent hydrocarbon radical, C_2H_5. **2.** Any gasoline treated with tetraethyl lead to reduce knock. [< ETH(ER) + -YL] — **e·thyl·ic** (i·thil'ik) *adj.*

ethyl alcohol Ethanol.

eth·y·lene (eth'ə·lēn) *n.* *Chem.* A colorless, flammable, gaseous hydrocarbon, C_2H_4, contained in coal gas, used as an anesthetic and in organic syntheses.

ethylene glycol *Chem.* A colorless, sweetish alcohol, $C_2H_4(OH)_2$, formed by decomposing certain ethylene compounds and used as an antifreeze, solvent, and lubricant.

ethyl ether *Chem.* A colorless, volatile, flammable liquid compound, $(C_2H_5)_2O$, having a characteristic odor, used as an anesthetic and solvent: also called *ether.*

e·ti·ol·o·gy (ē'tē·ol'ə·jē) *n.* *pl.* **·gies** **1.** The science of causes or reasons. **2.** *Med.* A theory of the cause of a particular disease. **3.** The giving of a cause or reason for anything; also, the reason given. Also spelled *aetiology.* [< LL < Gk. < *aitia* cause + *logos* word, study] — **e·ti·o·log'i·cal** *adj.* — **e·ti·o·log'i·cal·ly** *adv.* — **e·ti·ol'o·gist** *n.*

et·i·quette (et'ə·ket) *n.* The rules conventionally established for behavior in polite society or in official or professional life. [< F < OF *estiquette*; orig., label]

Eton College A public school for boys in Eton, England.

E·to·ni·an (i·tō'nē·ən) *n.* One who is or has been a student at Eton College. — *adj.* Of or relating to Eton College.

Eton jacket A short jacket cut off square at the hips and generally worn with a wide, overlapping, stiff collar (the **Eton collar**), originally worn at Eton College.

E·trus·can (i·trus'kən) *adj.* Of or relating to Etruria, its people, or language. Also **E·tru'ri·an.** — *n.* **1.** One of the people of Etruria. **2.** The extinct Etruscan language.

-ette *suffix of nouns* **1.** Little; small: *kitchenette.* **2.** Resembling; imitating: *leatherette.* **3.** Feminine: *farmerette.* [< F *-ette,* fem. of *-et,* dim. suffix]

é·tude (ā'tood, -tyood; *Fr.* ā·tüd') *n.* *Music* An exercise for solo instrument or voice, designed to perfect some phase of technique. [< F. See STUDY.]

et·y·mol·o·gize (et'ə·mol'ə·jīz) *v.* **·gized, ·giz·ing** *v.t.* **1.** To give the etymology of. — *v.i.* **2.** To give an etymology.

et·y·mol·o·gy (et'ə·mol'ə·jē) *n.* *pl.* **·gies** **1.** The history of a word as shown by breaking it down into basic elements or by tracing it back to the earliest known form and indicating its changes in form and meaning; also, a statement of this. **2.** The study of the derivation of words. [< F < L < Gk. < *etymon* true meaning + *logos* word, study] — **et·y·mo·log·i·cal** (et'ə·mə·loj'i·kəl) or **et'y·mo·log'ic** *adj.* — **et'y·mo·log'i·cal·ly** *adv.* — **et'y·mol'o·gist** *n.*

eu- *prefix* Good; well; easy; agreeable: *euphony.* [< Gk. *eu*]

eu·ca·lyp·tus (yoo'kə·lip'təs) *n.* *pl.* **·tus·es** or **·ti** (-tī) Any of a genus of large, chiefly Australian evergreen trees, widely used as timber and yielding a volatile, pungent oil (**oil of eucalyptus**) used in medicine. [< NL < Gk. *eu-* well + *kalyptos* covered, from the covering of the buds]

Eu·cha·rist (yoo'kə·rist) *n.* **1.** A Christian sacrament in which bread and wine are consecrated and received in commemoration of the passion and death of Christ: also called *Communion, Holy Communion.* **2.** The consecrated bread and wine of this sacrament. [< OF < LL < Gk. *eu-* well + *charizesthai* to show favor] — **Eu'cha·ris'tic** or **·ti·cal** *adj.*

eu·chre (yoo'kər) *n.* **1.** A card game for two to four players, played with 32 cards. **2.** An instance of euchring an opponent. — *v.t.* **·chred** (-kərd), **·chring** **1.** In the game of euchre, to defeat (the trump-making side) by taking three tricks. **2.** *Informal* To outwit or defeat. [Origin uncertain]

Eu·clid·e·an (yoo·klid'ē·ən) *adj.* Of or relating to the geometric principles of Euclid. Also **Eu·clid'i·an.**

eu·gen·ic (yoo·jen'ik) *adj.* Of or pertaining to eugenics. Also **eu·gen'i·cal.** [< Gk. (< *eu-* well + *genēs* born) + -IC] — **eu·gen'i·cal·ly** *adv.*

eu·gen·i·cist (yoo·jen'ə·sist) *n.* A specialist in or a student of eugenics. Also **eu·ge·nist** (yoo'jə·nist, yoo·jen'ist).

eu·gen·ics (yoo·jen'iks) *n.pl.* (*construed as sing.*) The science of improving the physical and mental qualities of human beings through control of the factors influencing heredity.

eu·lo·gist (yoo'lə·jist) *n.* One who eulogizes.

eu·lo·gis·tic (yoo'lə·jis'tik) *adj.* Relating to or having the nature of eulogy; laudatory. Also **eu'lo·gis'ti·cal.** — **eu'lo·gis'ti·cal·ly** *adv.*

eu·lo·gize (yoo'lə·jīz) *v.t.* **·gized, ·giz·ing** To speak or write a eulogy about; praise highly; extol. — **eu'lo·giz'er** *n.*

eu·lo·gy (yoo'lə·jē) *n.* *pl.* **·gies** **1.** A spoken or written piece of high praise, esp. when delivered publicly. **2.** Great praise. [< Gk. < *eu-* well + *legein* to speak]

Eu·men·i·des (yoo·men'ə·dēz) *n.pl.* The Furies. [< Gk., the kind ones: a euphemistic name]

eu·nuch (yoo'nək) *n.* A castrated man, esp. one employed as a harem attendant or as an Oriental palace official. [< L < Gk. < *eunē* bed + *echein* to keep, guard]

eu·phe·mism (yoo'fə·miz'əm) *n.* **1.** Substitution of a mild or roundabout word or expression for another felt to be too blunt or painful. **2.** A word or expression so substituted, as "the departed" for "the dead." [< Gk. < *eu-* well + *phēmizein* < *phanai* to speak] — **eu'phe·mist** *n.* — **eu'phe·mis'tic** or **·ti·cal** *adj.* — **eu'phe·mis'ti·cal·ly** *adv.*

eu·phe·mize (yoo'fə·mīz) *v.* **·mized, ·miz·ing** *v.t. & v.i.* To speak or write of (something) by using a euphemism.

eu·phon·ic (yoo·fon'ik) *adj.* **1.** Of or relating to euphony. **2.** Agreeable in sound; euphonious. — **eu·phon'i·cal·ly** *adv.*

eu·pho·ni·ous (yoo·fō'nē·əs) *adj.* Marked by euphony; agreeable and pleasant in sound. — **eu·pho'ni·ous·ly** *adv.*

eu·pho·ni·um (yoo·fō'nē·əm) *n.* A brass instrument having a tone resembling that of a tuba but slightly higher in range.

eu·pho·ny (yoo'fə·nē) *n.* *pl.* **·nies** **1.** The quality of being pleasant and agreeable in sound, as in speech or music. **2.** Progressive change in speech sounds through assimilation, allowing greater ease of pronunciation. [< Gk. < *eu-* good + *phōnē* sound]

eu·phor·bi·a (yoo·fôr'bē·ə) *n.* An herb having a milky juice and various medicinal properties: also called *spurge.* [< NL < L < Gk. *euphorbion*] — **eu·phor'bi·al** *adj.*

eu·pho·ri·a (yoo·fôr'ē·ə, -fō'rē-) *n.* A feeling of wellbeing, relaxation, and happiness. [< NL < Gk. *eu-* well + *pherein* to bear] — **eu·phor'ic** *adj.*

eu·phu·ism (yoo'fyoo·iz'əm) *n.* **1.** An artificially elegant style of speech or writing, characterized by strained similes, excessive use of alliteration and antithesis, etc. **2.** An expression or rhetorical device typical of such a style. [after *Euphues,* character created by John Lyly, English writer, 1554?-1606 < Gk. < *eu-* well + *phyein* to grow, form] — **eu'phu·ist** *n.* — **eu'phu·is'tic** *adj.* — **eu'phu·is'ti·cal·ly** *adv.*

Eur·a·sian (yoo·rā'zhən, -shən) *adj.* **1.** Pertaining to Eurasia. **2.** Of European and Asian descent. — *n.* A person of mixed European and Asian parentage.

eu·re·ka (yoo·rē'kə) *interj.* I have found (it): an exclamation of triumph or achievement. [< Gk. *heurēka*]

Eu·ro·pa (yoo·rō'pə) In Greek mythology, a Phoenician princess abducted by Zeus, in the guise of a bull, to Crete.

Eu·ro·pe·an (yoor'ə·pē'ən) *adj.* Relating to or derived from Europe or its inhabitants. — *n.* **1.** A native or inhabitant of Europe. **2.** A person of European descent.

European Economic Community A customs union of

France, Italy, West Germany, and the Benelux nations: also called *Common Market*. Also **European Common Market**.

Eu·ro·pe·an·ize (yŏŏr'ə·pē'ən·īz) *v.t.* **·ized, ·iz·ing** To make European, as in culture. **— Eu'ro·pe'an·i·za'tion** *n.*

European plan At a hotel, the system of paying for room and service separately from the charge for meals.

eu·ro·pi·um (yŏŏ·rō'pē·əm) *n.* A steel-gray, malleable metallic element (symbol Eu) of the lanthanide series. See ELEMENT. [< NL < L *Europa* Europe]

eury- *combining form* Wide; broad. [< Gk. *eurys* wide]

Eu·ryd·i·ce (yŏŏ·rid'ə·sē) In Greek mythology, the wife of Orpheus. See ORPHEUS.

eu·ryth·mics (yŏŏ·riŧʰ'miks) *n.pl.* (*construed as sing.*) A system for developing grace and rhythm through bodily movements made in response to music: also **eu·rhyth'mics**. [< L < Gk. < *eu-* good + *rhythmos* symmetry] **— eu·ryth'mic** or **·mi·cal** *adj.*

Eu·sta·chi·an tube (yŏŏ·stā'kē·ən, -shē·ən, -shən) *Anat.* A passage between the pharynx and the middle ear, serving to equalize air pressure between the tympanic cavity and the atmosphere: also called *syrinx*. For illus. see EAR. [after Bartolomeo *Eustachio*, died 1574, Italian anatomist]

Eu·ter·pe (yŏŏ·tûr'pē) The Muse of lyric song and music.

eu·tha·na·si·a (yŏŏ'thə·nā'zhə, -zhē·ə) *n.* 1. Painless, peaceful death. 2. The deliberate putting to death painlessly of a person suffering from an incurable disease: also called *mercy killing*. [< Gk. < *eu-* easy + *thanatos* death]

eu·then·ics (yŏŏ·then'iks) *n.pl.* (*construed as sing.*) The science of improving the physical and mental qualities of human beings, through control of environmental factors. [< Gk. *euthēnein* to thrive]

e·vac·u·ant (i·vak'yŏŏ·ənt) *Med. adj.* Cathartic or emetic. **—** *n.* An evacuant medicine, drug, etc.

e·vac·u·ate (i·vak'yŏŏ·āt) *v.* **·at·ed, ·at·ing** *v.t.* 1. *Mil.* **a** To give up or abandon possession of, as a fortress or city. **b** To move out or withdraw (troops, inhabitants, etc.) from a threatened area or place. 2. To depart from and leave vacant; vacate. 3. To remove the contents of. 4. *Physiol.* To discharge or eject, as from the bowels. **—** *v.i.* 5. To withdraw, as from a threatened area [< L < *ex-* out + *vacuare* to make empty] **— e·vac'u·a'tion** *n.* **— e·vac'u·a'tor** *n.*

e·vac·u·ee (i·vak'yŏŏ·ē') *n.* A person moved out or withdrawn from a destroyed or threatened area. [See EVACUATE]

e·vade (i·vād') *v.* **e·vad·ed, e·vad·ing** *v.t.* 1. To get away from by tricks or cleverness: to *evade* pursuers. 2. To get out of or avoid: to *evade* a question. 3. To baffle; elude: The facts *evade* explanation. **—** *v.i.* 4. To dodge a question, responsibility, etc. [< L < *e-* out + *vadere* to go] **— e·vad'·a·ble** or **e·vad'i·ble** *adj.* **— e·vad'er** *n.*

e·val·u·ate (i·val'yŏŏ·āt) *v.t.* **·at·ed, ·at·ing** To find or determine the amount, worth, etc., of. [< F < OF *valoir* to be worth] **— e·val'u·a'tion** *n.*

ev·a·nesce (ev'ə·nes') *v.i.* **·nesced, ·nesc·ing** To disappear by degrees; vanish gradually. [< L < *e-* out + *vanescere* to vanish] **— ev'a·nes'cence** *n.*

ev·a·nes·cent (ev'ə·nes'ənt) *adj.* Passing away, or liable to pass away, gradually or imperceptibly; fleeting. **— ev'a·nes'cent·ly** *adv.*

e·van·gel (i·van'jəl) *n.* 1. The gospel. 2. *Usu. cap.* One of the four Gospels. 3. Any good news or glad tidings. [< OF < LL < Gk. < *eu-* good + *angellein* to announce]

e·van·gel·i·cal (ē'van·jel'i·kəl, ev'ən-) *adj.* 1. Of, relating to, or contained in the New Testament, esp. the Gospels. 2. Of, relating to, or maintaining the doctrine that the Bible is the only rule of faith. 3. Evangelistic. **—** *n.* A member of an evangelical church. Also **e'van·gel'ic**. **— e'van·gel'i·cal·ism** *n.* **— e'van·gel'i·cal·ly** *adv.*

e·van·gel·ism (i·van'jə·liz'əm) *n.* The zealous preaching or spreading of the gospel.

e·van·gel·ist (i·van'jə·list) *n.* 1. *Usu. cap.* One of the four writers of the New Testament Gospels: Matthew, Mark, Luke, or John. 2. An itinerant or missionary preacher. **— e·van'gel·is'tic** *adj.* **— e·van·gel·is'ti·cal·ly** *adv.*

e·van·gel·ize (i·van'jəl·īz) *v.* **·ized, ·iz·ing** *v.t.* 1. To preach the gospel to. 2. To convert to Christianity. **—** *v.i.* 3. To preach or act as an evangelist. **— e·van'gel·i·za'tion** *n.*

e·vap·o·rate (i·vap'ə·rāt) *v.* **·rat·ed, ·rat·ing** *v.t.* 1. To convert into vapor; vaporize. 2. To remove moisture or liquid from (milk, fruit, etc.) so as to dry or concentrate. **—** *v.i.* 3. To become vapor. 4. To yield vapor. 5. To vanish; disappear. [< L < *e-* out, away + *vaporare* to emit vapor] **— e·vap'o·ra·ble** *adj.* **— e·vap'o·ra'tive** *adj.* **— e·vap'o·ra'tion** *n.* **— e·vap'o·ra'tor** *n.*

evaporated milk Unsweetened canned milk slightly thickened by removal of some of the water.

e·va·sion (i·vā'zhən) *n.* 1. The act of evading; esp., the act of dodging something difficult or distasteful. 2. A piece of trickery or shrewdness used in dodging a question, etc.

e·va·sive (i·vā'siv) *adj.* 1. Given to or characterized by evasion; not direct and frank: an *evasive* person; *evasive* promises. 2. Elusive. **— e·va'sive·ly** *adv.* **— e·va'sive·ness** *n.*

eve (ēv) *n.* 1. The evening before a holiday: Christmas *Eve*. 2. The time immediately preceding some event. 3. *Poetic* Evening. [Var. of EVEN²]

Eve (ēv) The first woman; wife of Adam and mother of the human race. *Gen.* iii 20. [< Hebrew *hawwah* life]

e·ven¹ (ē'vən) *adj.* 1. Flat and smooth; level: an *even* surface. 2. Extending to the same height or depth: a tree *even* with the housetop. 3. Extending along; parallel to: a bookcase *even* with the wall. 4. Equally distributed; uniform: an *even* coat of paint. 5. Calm and controlled: an *even* disposition. 6. Equally matched: an *even* struggle. 7. Being about the same for any one of several alternatives: The chances for success or failure are *even*. 8. Being the same (score) for each side or competitor. 9. Having accomplished exact settlement of a debt. 10. Identical in quantity, number, measure, etc.: *even* portions. 11. Exactly divisible by 2: an *even* number: opposed to *odd*. **— to break even** *Informal* To end up with neither profit nor loss, as in a business deal. **— to get even** To exact one's full measure of revenge. **—** *adv.* 1. To all the greater extent or degree; still: an *even* better plan. 2. During the very same moment: with *as*: *Even* as they watched, the ship sank. 3. In exactly the same way; precisely; just: with *as*: Do *even* as I do. 4. In very fact; indeed; actually: to feel glad, *even* delighted. 5. Unlikely or inconceivable as it may seem: He was kind *even* to his enemies. 6. All the way; as far as: faithful *even* to death. 7. All the same; nevertheless; notwithstanding: *Even* with that handicap, he managed to win. 8. Not otherwise than; right: It is happening *even* now. 9. *Informal* In a smooth manner; evenly: to keep things running *even*. **— even if** Although; notwithstanding. **—** *v.t.* 1. To make even: often with *up* or *off*: to *even* up accounts. **—** *v.i.* 2. To become even: often with *up* or *off*. [OE *efen*] **— e'ven·ly** *adv.* **— e'ven·ness** *n.*

e·ven² (ē'vən) *n. Archaic* Evening. [OE *ǣfen*]

e·ven·fall (ē'vən·fôl') *n.* Early evening; twilight; dusk.

e·ven·hand·ed (ē'vən·han'did) *adj.* Treating all alike; impartial. **— e'ven·hand'ed·ly** *adv.* **— e'ven·hand'ed·ness** *n.*

eve·ning (ēv'ning) *n.* 1. The latter part of day and the first part of night. ♦ Collateral adjective: *vesperal*. 2. An evening's entertainment or activity. 3. The declining years of life, a career, etc. [OE *ǣfnian* to approach evening]

evening dress Formal evening wear. Also **evening clothes**.

evening gown A woman's formal dress for evening wear

evening primrose An erect American biennial herb with conspicuous yellow flowers that open in the evening.

evening star A bright planet visible in the west just after sunset, especially Venus. Also called *Hesperus, Vesper*.

e·vent (i·vent') *n.* 1. Something that takes place; a happening or an incident: the *events* of that period. 2. An actual or possible set of circumstances; a real or contingent situation: in the *event* of failure. 3. Final outcome: In the *event*, she decided not to go. 4. One of the items forming part of a variegated program of sports: the skating exhibition and other *events*. **— in any event** or **at all events** Regardless of what happens. [< OF < L < *e-* out + *venire* to come]

e·vent·ful (i·vent'fəl) *adj.* 1. Marked by important events: an *eventful* era. 2. Having important consequences: an *eventful* decision. **— e·vent'ful·ly** *adv.* **— e·vent'ful·ness** *n.*

e·ven·tide (ē'vən·tīd') *n. Poetic* Evening.

e·ven·tu·al (i·ven'chŏŏ·əl) *adj.* Occurring or resulting in due course of time. **— e·ven'tu·al·ly** *adv.*

e·ven·tu·al·i·ty (i·ven'chŏŏ·al'ə·tē) *n. pl.* **·ties** A likely or possible occurrence; a conceivable outcome.

e·ven·tu·ate (i·ven'chŏŏ·āt) *v.i.* **·at·ed, ·at·ing** To result ultimately: His efforts *eventuated* in success.

ev·er (ev'ər) *adv.* 1. At any time; on any occasion: Did you *ever* see it? 2. By any possible chance: If the sun *ever* comes out, the fog will disappear. 3. In any possible or conceivable way: Do it as fast as *ever* you can. 4. At all times; invariably: They remained *ever* on guard. 5. Throughout the entire course of time; always; forever: now usually followed by *since, after*, or *afterward*. ♦ In informal speech, *ever* is often used merely to add force: Was I *ever* glad! **— ever so** *Informal* To an extremely great extent or degree: It was *ever* so pleasant. **— ever so often** *Informal* 1. Extremely often; repeatedly. 2. Now and then; every so often. **— for ever and ever** Forever: an intensive form. [OE *ǣfre*]

ev·er·glade (ev'ər·glād) *n.* A tract of low swampy land.

Everglade State Nickname of Florida.

ev·er·green (ev'ər·grēn') *adj.* Having foliage that remains green until the formation of new foliage: distinguished from *deciduous*. **—** *n.* 1. An evergreen tree or plant. 2. *pl.* Evergreen branches or twigs, esp. as used for decorations.

Evergreen State Nickname of Washington.

ev·er·last·ing (ev'ər·las'ting, -läs'-) *adj.* 1. Existing or lasting forever; eternal: belief in an *everlasting* God. **2.** Continuing for an indefinitely long period; perpetual: *everlasting* happiness. **3.** Incessant; interminable: her *everlasting* chatter. — *n.* **1.** Endless duration; eternity: to love for *everlasting*. **2.** One of several plants, chiefly of the aster family, whose flowers keep their form and color when dried: also called *immortelle.* — **the Everlasting** God. [ME] — **ev′·er·last′ing·ly** *adv.* — **ev′er·last′ing·ness** *n.*

ev·er·more (ev′ər-môr′, -mōr′) *adv. Poetic* For and at all time to come; always. — **for evermore** Forever.

e·ver·sion (i-vûr′zhən) *n.* The act of everting, or the condition of being everted. — **e·ver′si·ble** (-sə-bəl) *adj.*

e·vert (i-vûrt′) *v.t.* To turn outward or inside out. [< L *e-* out + *vertere* to turn]

ev·er·y (ev′rē, ev′ər·ē) *adj.* **1.** Each without excepting any of all those that together form an aggregate. **2.** Each (member or unit singled out in some way) of a series: *every* tenth man. **3.** The utmost; all possible: Show him *every* consideration. — **every bit** *Informal* In all respects: He is *every bit* as good as you. — **every now and then** From time to time; occasionally. Also **every now and again, every once in a while.** — **every other** Each alternate (specified thing). — **every so often** *Informal* Every now and then. — **every which way** *Informal* In every way or direction and with little or no order. [ME < OE *ǣfre* ever + *ǣlc* each]

eve·ry·bod·y (ev′rē-bod′ē, -bud′ē) *pron.* Every person.

eve·ry·day (ev′rē-dā′, -dā′) *adj.* **1.** Happening every day; daily. **2.** Suitable for ordinary days: *everyday* clothes. **3.** Commonplace; ordinary: *everyday* folks.

eve·ry·one (ev′rē-wun′, -wən) *pron.* Everybody.

every one Each individual person or thing out of the whole number, excepting none: *Every one* of the men is ill.

eve·ry·thing (ev′rē-thing′) *pron.* **1.** Whatever exists; all things whatsoever. **2.** Whatever is relevant, needed, or important: I have *everything.* **3.** The only thing that really matters; the essential thing: Happiness is *everything.*

eve·ry·where (ev′rē-hwâr′) *adv.* At, in, or to every place.

e·vict (i-vikt′) *v.t.* **1.** To expel (a tenant) by legal process; dispossess; put out. **2.** To recover (property, etc.) by legal process or superior claim. — **Syn.** See EXPEL. [< L *e-* out + *vincere* to conquer] — **e·vic′tion** *n.* — **e·vic′tor** *n.*

ev·i·dence (ev′ə-dəns) *n.* **1.** That which serves to prove or disprove something; support; proof. **2.** That which serves as a ground for knowing something with certainty or for believing something with conviction; corroboration. **3.** An outward indication of the existence or fact of something: Her paleness was *evidence* of her distress. **4.** *Law* That which is properly presented before a court as a means of establishing or disproving something alleged or presumed, as the statements of witnesses. — **in evidence** In the condition of being readily seen or perceived; esp., conspicuously present. — **to turn state's evidence** To testify in court against one's accomplices. — *v.t.* **·denced, ·denc·ing 1.** To show unmistakably. **2.** To support by oral testimony.

ev·i·dent (ev′ə-dənt) *adj.* Easily perceived or recognized; clearly perceptible; plain. [< L < *e-* out + *videre* to see]

ev·i·den·tial (ev′ə-den′shəl) *adj.* Relating to, serving as, or based on evidence. — **ev′i·den′tial·ly** *adv.*

ev·i·dent·ly (ev′ə-dənt·lē, -dent′-, ev′ə-dent′lē) *adv.* **1.** To all appearances; apparently. **2.** Quite clearly; obviously.

e·vil (ē′vəl) *adj.* **1.** Morally bad; wicked. **2.** Causing injury or any other undesirable result. **3.** Marked by or threatening misfortune or distress: an *evil* omen. **4.** Low in public esteem: an *evil* reputation. — **the Evil One** Satan. — *n.* **1.** That which is evil; as: **a** That which is morally bad. **b** That which is injurious. **c** That which causes suffering or misfortune. **2.** Some particular act, characteristic, etc. that is evil: one of the *evils* of that political system. — *adv.* In an evil manner; badly: now chiefly in combinations: an *evil*-smelling plant. [OE *yfel*] — **e′vil·ly** *adv.* — **e′vil·ness** *n.*

e·vil·do·er (ē′vəl-dōō′ər) *n.* One who does evil. — **e′vil·do′ing** *n.*

evil eye A glance superstitiously supposed capable of inflicting misfortune or injury.

e·vil-mind·ed (ē′vəl-mīn′did) *adj.* Obsessed with vicious or depraved thoughts; esp., sexually indecent thoughts. — **e′vil-mind′ed·ly** *adv.* — **e′vil-mind′ed·ness** *n.*

e·vince (i-vins′) *v.t.* **e·vinced, e·vinc·ing 1.** To indicate clearly; demonstrate convincingly. **2.** To give an outward sign of having (a quality, feeling, etc.). [< L < *e-* out + *vincere* to conquer] — **e·vin′ci·ble** *adj.* — **e·vin′cive** *adj.*

e·vis·cer·ate (*v.* i·vis′ə·rāt; *adj.* i·vis′ər·it) *v.t.* **·at·ed, ·at·ing 1.** To disembowel. **2.** To remove the vital part of. — *adj. Surg.* Disemboweled: an *eviscerate* abdomen. [< L *e-* out + *viscera* entrails] — **e·vis′cer·a′tion** *n.*

ev·o·ca·tion (ev′ə-kā′shən) *n.* The act of evoking; a summoning, as of memories. — **ev′o·ca′tor** *n.*

o·vo·a·tive (i voḱ′tiv, -vō′kə?) *adj.* Tending to evoke.

e·voke (i-vōk′) *v.t.* **e·voked, e·vok·ing 1.** To call or summon forth, as memories. **2.** To draw forth or produce (a response, reaction, etc.). **3.** To summon up (spirits) by or as

by incantations. [< L < *e-* out + *vocare* to call] — **ev·o·ca·ble** (ev′ə·kə·bəl, i·vō′kə·bəl) *adj.*

ev·o·lu·tion (ev′ə-loō′shən) *n.* **1.** The process of unfolding, growing, or developing, usu. by slow stages. **2.** Anything developed by such a process. **3.** *Biol.* **a** The theory that all forms of life originated by descent from earlier forms. **b** The series of changes, as by natural selection, mutation, etc., through which a given type of organism has acquired its present characteristics. **4.** One of a series of complex movements. **5.** A movement or maneuver of troops, ships, etc. **6.** The process of giving off gas, heat, sound, etc. — **ev′o·lu′tion·al, ev′o·lu′tion·ar·y** *adj.* — **ev′o·lu′tion·al·ly** *adv.*

ev·o·lu·tion·ist (ev′ə-loō′shən·ist) *n.* **1.** A proponent of the theory of biological evolution. **2.** One who advocates progress through gradual stages, as in political structure. — *adj.* **1.** Evolutionary. **2.** Of or relating to evolutionists. — **ev′o·lu′tion·ism** *n.*

e·volve (i-volv′) *v.* **e·volved, e·volv·ing** *v.t.* **1.** To work out; develop gradually. **2.** *Biol.* To develop, as by a differentiation of parts or functions, to a more highly organized state: usu. in the passive. **3.** To give or throw off (vapor, heat, etc.). **4.** To unfold or expand. — *v.i.* **5.** To undergo the process of evolution. **6.** To develop. [< L < *e-* out + *volvere* to roll] — **e·volv′a·ble** *adj.* — **e·volve′ment** *n.*

ewe (yōō, *Dial.* yō) *n.* A female sheep. [OE *eowu*]

ew·er (yōō′ər) *n.* A large, wide-mouthed jug or pitcher for water. [ME < AF, OF < L *aqua* water]

ex (eks) *prep.* In finance, without the right to have or participate in: *ex* dividend. [< L *ex* out]

ex-[1] *prefix* **1.** Out of: *exit, exhale.* **2.** Thoroughly; *exasperate.* **3.** Not having; lacking. **4.** Being formerly: attached with a hyphen to the word it qualifies: *ex-president.* Also: *e-* before consonants except *c, f, p, q, s, t; ef-* before *f.* [< L *ex* from, out of]

ex-[2] *prefix* Out of; from; forth: *exodus.* Also, before consonants, *ec-,* as in *eclipse.* [< Gk. *ex* out]

ex-[3] Var. of EXO-.

ex·ac·er·bate (ig·zas′ər·bāt) *v.t.* **·bat·ed, ·bat·ing 1.** To make more sharp or severe; aggravate (feelings, a disease, pain, etc.). **2.** To embitter or irritate (someone). [< L < *ex-* very + *acerbus* bitter, harsh] — **ex·ac′er·ba′tion** *n.*

ex·act (ig·zakt′) *adj.* **1.** Perfectly clear and complete in every detail; precise. **2.** Altogether accurate: to ask for an *exact* answer. **3.** Being precisely (what is specified): the *exact* amount necessary. **4.** Corresponding in every detail with something taken as a model. **5.** Free from vagueness; clear: *exact* thinking. **6.** Extremely careful about detail and accuracy: an *exact* editor. **7.** Designed for use where the utmost precision is required: an *exact* scientific instrument. **8.** Rigorously demanding: an *exact* schoolmaster. — *v.t.* **1.** To demand rigorously the full payment of: to *exact* full compensation for an injury. **2.** To force unjustly the payment of. **3.** To obtain by or as if by forcing out: to *exact* a full reply. **4.** To insist upon the performance or yielding of as a strict right or obligation: to *exact* obedience. **5.** To require: The situation *exacted* quick thinking. [< L < *ex-* out + *agere* to drive] — **ex·act′ness, ex·act′i·tude** (-i·tōōd, -i·tyōōd) *n.* — **ex·ac′tor** or **ex·act′er** *n.* — **ex·ac′tion** *n.*

ex·act·ing (ig·zak′ting) *adj.* **1.** Making rigorous demands; severe. **2.** Involving constant hard work, attention, etc. — **ex·act′ing·ly** *adv.* — **ex·act′ing·ness** *n.*

ex·act·ly (ig·zakt′lē) *adv.* **1.** In an exact manner; with great precision or accuracy. **2.** Precisely right; just so.

ex·ag·ger·ate (ig·zaj′ə·rāt) *v.* **·at·ed, ·at·ing** *v.t.* **1.** To represent or look upon as greater than is actually the case: to *exaggerate* one's troubles. **2.** To make greater in size, intensity, etc., than what would be normal or expected. — *v.i.* **3.** To overstate or overemphasize something. [< L < *ex-* out + *agger* heap] — **ex·ag′ger·at′ed** *adj.* — **ex·ag′ger·a′tion** *n.* — **ex·ag′ger·a′tive** *adj.* — **ex·ag′ger·a′tor** *n.*

ex·alt (ig·zôlt′) *v.t.* **1.** To raise in rank, character, honor, etc. **2.** To glorify or praise. **3.** To fill with delight, pride, etc.; elate. **4.** To increase the intensity of, as colors; heighten. [< L < *ex-* out + *altus* high] — **ex·alt′ed** *adj.* — **ex·alt′ed·ly** *adv.* — **ex·alt′er** *n.*

ex·al·ta·tion (eg′zôl·tā′shən) *n.* **1.** The act of exalting, or the state of being exalted. **2.** A state or feeling of great, often extreme, exhilaration and well-being; ecstasy.

ex·am (ig·zam′) *n. Informal* An examination.

ex·am·i·na·tion (ig·zam′ə·nā′shən) *n.* **1.** The act of examining, or the state of being examined. **2.** Medical scrutiny and testing. **3.** A formal test of knowledge or skills; also, the questions or problems posed. — **ex·am′i·na′tion·al** *adj.*

ex·am·ine (ig·zam′in) *v.t.* **·ined, ·in·ing 1.** To inspect or scrutinize with care; inquire into. **2.** To subject (a person, organ, etc.) to medical scrutiny and testing. **3.** To test by questions or exercises as to qualifications, fitness, etc. **4.** To question formally in order to elicit facts, etc. [< OF < L < *ex-* out + *ag-,* root of *agere* to drive] — **ex·am′in·a·ble** *adj.* — **ex·am′in·er** *n.*

ex·am·ple (ig·zam′pəl, -zäm′-) *n.* **1.** A particular thing that belongs to and is typical of a group of things and that is singled out as a representative specimen. **2.** Something deserving imitation; model. **3.** An instance or object of punishment, reprimand, etc., designed to warn or deter others. **4.** A previous case or instance identical with or similar to something under consideration. **5.** A particular problem or exercise in arithmetic, algebra, etc. — **for example** By way of illustration. — **to set an example** To act in such a way as to arouse others to imitation. — *v.t.* **·pled, ·pling** To present an example of; exemplify: now only in the passive. [< OF < L < *ex-* out + *emere* to buy, take]

ex·as·per·ate (ig·zas′pə·rāt) *v.t.* **·at·ed, ·at·ing 1.** To make very annoyed or angry; infuriate. **2.** To make (a disagreeable condition, feeling, etc.) still worse; aggravate. — **Syn.** See OFFEND. [< L < *ex-* out + *asper* rough] — **ex·as′per·at′er** *n.* — **ex·as′per·at·ing** *adj.* — **ex·as′per·a′tion** *n.*

ex ca·the·dra (eks kə·thē′drə, kath′i-) *Latin* With authority; in one's official capacity; literally, from the chair.

ex·ca·vate (eks′kə·vāt) *v.t.* **·vat·ed, ·vat·ing 1.** To make a hole or cavity in. **2.** To form or make (a hole, tunnel, etc.) by hollowing, digging out, or scooping. **3.** To remove by digging or scooping out, as soil. **4.** To uncover by digging, as ruins; unearth. [< L < *ex-* out + *cavus* hollow] — **ex′ca·va′tion** *n.* — **ex′ca·va′tor** *n.*

ex·ceed (ik·sēd′) *v.t.* **1.** To surpass, as in quantity or quality. **2.** To go beyond the limit or extent of: to *exceed* one's income. — *v.i.* **3.** To be superior; surpass others. [< F < L < *ex-* out, beyond + *cedere* to go]

ex·ceed·ing (ik·sē′ding) *adj.* Greater than usual. — *adv. Archaic* Extremely. — **ex·ceed′ing·ly** *adv.*

ex·cel (ik·sel′) *v.* **·celled, ·cel·ling** *v.t.* **1.** To surpass, usu. in some good quality or action; be better than; outstrip: to *excel* all rivals. — *v.i.* **2.** To surpass others; be outstanding. [< OF < L *excellere* to rise]

ex·cel·lence (ek′sə·ləns) *n.* **1.** The state or quality of excelling; superiority. **2.** That in which someone or something excels; a superior trait or quality. Also **ex′cel·len·cy.**

Ex·cel·len·cy (ek′sə·lən·sē) *n. pl.* **·cies** An honorary title or form of address for certain dignitaries: often preceded by *His, Her, Your,* etc.

ex·cel·lent (ek′sə·lənt) *adj.* Being of the very best quality; exceptionally good. — **ex′cel·lent·ly** *adv.*

ex·cel·si·or (ik·sel′sē·ər) *n. U.S.* Long, fine wood shavings used as stuffing or as packing material.

ex·cept (ik·sept′) *prep.* With the exclusion or omission of; aside from. — *conj.* **1.** Aside from the fact that. Also **except that. 2.** Otherwise than. ◆ In this sense, *except* may also be construed as a preposition governing the following adverb, phrase, or clause. — **except for** If it were not for. — *v.t.* **1.** To exclude from consideration, enumeration, etc.; leave deliberately out of account. — *v.i.* **2.** To raise an objection, esp. a formal objection: now usu. with *to*: to *except* to an accusation. [< F < L < *ex-* out + *capere* to take]

ex·cept·ing (ik·sep′ting) *prep.* Barring; except.

ex·cep·tion (ik·sep′shən) *n.* **1.** The act of excepting, or the state of being excepted. **2.** Something excluded from or not conforming to a general class, principle, rule, etc. **3.** An objection or complaint; adverse criticism. **4.** *Law* A formal objection to the decision of a court during trial. — **to take exception 1.** To express disagreement. **2.** To feel resentful.

ex·cep·tion·a·ble (ik·sep′shən·ə·bəl) *adj.* Open to exception or objection. — **ex·cep′tion·a·bly** *adv.*

ex·cep·tion·al (ik·sep′shən·əl) *adj.* Being an exception; unusual or extraordinary. — **ex·cep′tion·al·ly** *adv.*

ex·cerpt (*n.* ek′sûrpt; *v.* ik·sûrpt′) *n.* An extract from a book, speech, etc. — *v.t.* To pick out and cite (a passage from a book, etc.). [< L < *ex-* out + *carpere* to pluck]

ex·cess (*n.* ik·ses′, ek′ses; *adj.* ek′ses, ik·ses′) *n.* **1.** The condition or fact of going beyond what is usual, necessary, proper, etc. **2.** An overabundance. **3.** The quantity, extent, or degree by which one thing is over and above another thing. **4.** Overindulgence, as in food or drink; intemperance. — *adj.* **1.** Being over and above what is expected or usual. **2.** Immoderate. [See EXCEED.]

ex·ces·sive (ik·ses′iv) *adj.* Going beyond what is usual, necessary, proper, etc.; extreme. — **ex·ces′sive·ly** *adv.*

excess profits Net profits exceeding the normal average for a specified period of years.

ex·change (iks·chānj′) *v.* **·changed, ·chang·ing** *v.t.* **1.** To give and receive reciprocally. **2.** To give up for something taken as a replacement. **3.** To return as unsatisfactory and get a replacement for. **4.** To transfer to another in return for the equivalent in goods or money; trade. — *v.i.* **5.** To exchange something. **6.** To be exchanged: money that *exchanges* at face value. — *n.* **1.** The act of giving or receiving one thing as equivalent for another. **2.** A giving and receiving in turn: an *exchange* of compliments. **3.** The substitution of one thing for another. **4.** That which is given or re-

ceived in trade or substitution. **5.** A place where brokers, etc., meet to buy, sell, or trade commodities or securities: stock *exchange*. **6.** A central telephone system in a part of a city or in a town. **7.** A bill of exchange; also, the system of using a bill of exchange, or the fee for it. **8.** Rate of exchange. **9.** The mutual giving and receiving of equal sums of money, as between two countries using different currencies, and allowing for differences in value. **10.** *pl.* Bills, drafts, etc., presented to a clearing-house for exchange or settlement. [< AF < LL < L *ex-* out + *cambiare* to exchange] — **ex·change′a·ble** *adj.* — **ex·change′a·bil′i·ty** *n.*

ex·cheq·uer (iks·chek′ər, eks′chek·ər) *n.* **1.** The treasury of a state, organization, etc. **2.** *Informal* One's total financial resources. [ME < OF *eschaquier* chessboard, then table marked in squares for keeping of accounts]

Ex·cheq·uer (iks·chek′ər, eks′chek·ər) *n.* The department of the British government managing the public revenue.

ex·cise¹ (*n.* ek′sīz, ik·sīz′; *v.* ik·sīz′) *n.* **1.** An indirect tax on such commodities as liquor, tobacco, etc., produced, sold, used, or transported within a country. Also **excise tax. 2.** A license fee charged for various sports, trades, etc. — *v.t.* **·cised, ·cis·ing** To levy an excise upon. [< MDu. < OF < L *ad-* to + *census* tax] — **ex·cis·a·ble** *adj.*

ex·cise² (ik·sīz′) *v.t.* **·cised, ·cis·ing 1.** To cut out, as a growth. **2.** To delete (a word, passage, etc.). [< L < *ex-* out + *caedere* to cut] — **ex·ci·sion** (ik·sizh′ən) *n.*

ex·cise·man (ik·sīz′mən) *n. pl.* **·men** (-mən) *Brit.* An officer who collects excise duties.

ex·cit·a·ble (ik·sī′tə·bəl) *adj.* **1.** Easily excited; highstrung. **2.** *Physiol.* Susceptible to stimuli. — **ex·cit′a·bil′i·ty** *n.* — **ex·cit′a·ble·ness** *n.* — **ex·cit′a·bly** *adv.*

ex·ci·tant (ik·sī′tənt, ek′sə·tənt) *n.* Something that excites or stimulates. — *adj.* Tending to excite or stimulate; stimulating: also **ex·ci·ta·tive, ex·ci·ta·to·ry** (-tôr′ē, -tō′rē).

ex·ci·ta·tion (ek′sī·tā′shən) *n.* The act of exciting, or the state of being excited; disturbance; agitation.

ex·cite (ik·sīt′) *v.t.* **·cit·ed, ·cit·ing 1.** To arouse (a feeling, reaction, etc.) into being or activity. **2.** To arouse strong feeling in; stimulate the emotions of. **3.** To provoke action in; rouse: to *excite* someone to greater endeavor. **4.** To bring about; stir up: to *excite* a riot. [< OF < L < *ex-* out + *ciere* to arouse] — **ex·cit′ed** *adj.* — **ex·cit′ed·ly** *adv.*

ex·cite·ment (ik·sīt′mənt) *n.* **1.** The state of being excited; agitation. **2.** That which excites.

ex·cit·ing (ik·sī′ting) *adj.* Causing excitement; stirring; rousing; thrilling. — **ex·cit′ing·ly** *adv.*

ex·claim (iks·klām′) *v.t. & v.i.* To cry out abruptly; speak vehemently, as in surprise or anger. [< F < L < *ex-* out + *clamare* to cry] — **ex·claim′er** *n.*

— **Syn.** *Exclaim* and *ejaculate* mean to say forcefully. *Exclaim* suggests merely vehement feeling; *ejaculate* adds a note of explosive utterance and incoherence.

ex·cla·ma·tion (eks′klə·mā′shən) *n.* **1.** The act of exclaiming. **2.** An abrupt or emphatic utterance, outcry, etc. — **ex·clam·a·to·ry** (iks·klam′ə·tôr′ē, -tō′rē) *adj.*

exclamation mark A mark (!) used in punctuation to indicate that the immediately preceding word, phrase, or sentence is an exclamation. Also **exclamation point.**

ex·clude (iks·klood′) *v.t.* **·clud·ed, ·clud·ing 1.** To keep from entering; bar. **2.** To refuse to notice, consider, or allow for; leave out. **3.** To put out; eject. [< L < *ex-* out + *claudere* to close] — **ex·clud′a·ble** *adj.* — **ex·clud′er** *n.*

ex·clu·sion (iks·kloo′zhən) *n.* **1.** The act of excluding, or the state of being excluded. **2.** That which is excluded.

ex·clu·sive (iks·kloo′siv) *adj.* **1.** Intended for or possessed by a single individual or group. **2.** Belonging to or found in a single source: an *exclusive* news story. **3.** Having no duplicate; altogether original: an *exclusive* design. **4.** Admitting or catering to only a very select group. **5.** Concentrated upon only one individual, thing, or group; complete and undivided: one's *exclusive* attention. **6.** Excluding the other or others by reason of being completely opposed or unrelated: mutually *exclusive* doctrines. **7.** Being the only one: the *exclusive* owner. **8.** Not including; not comprising: usu. with *of*: the expense *exclusive* of fees. **9.** Not including the items, dates, figures, etc., that are specified as the limits: from 1 to 10 *exclusive* (1 and 10 are not included). — **ex·clu′sive·ly** *adv.* — **ex·clu′sive·ness** *n.*

ex·cog·i·tate (eks·koj′ə·tāt) *v.t.* **·tat·ed, ·tat·ing** To think out carefully; think up; devise. [< L < *ex-* out + *cogitare* to think] — **ex·cog′i·ta′tion** *n.* — **ex·cog′i·ta′tive** *adj.*

ex·com·mu·ni·cate (*v.* eks′kə·myoo′nə·kāt; *adj. & n.* eks′kə·myoo′nə·kət) *v.t.* **·cat·ed, ·cat·ing** *Eccl.* To cut off by ecclesiastical authority from sharing in the sacraments, worship, privileges, or fellowship of a church. — *adj.* Excommunicated. — *n.* An excommunicated person. [< LL < *ex-* out + *communicare* to share] — **ex′com·mu′ni·ca·ble** *adj.* — **ex′com·mu′ni·ca′tion** *n.* — **ex′com·mu′ni·ca′tor** *n.*

ex·com·mu·ni·ca·tive (eks/kə·myōō/nə·kā/tiv, -kə·tiv) *adj.* Relating to, favoring, or effecting excommunication. Also **ex·com·mu·ni·ca·to·ry** (eks/kə·myōō/nə·kə·tôr/ē, -tō/rē).

ex·co·ri·ate (ik·skôr/ē·āt, -skō/rē-) *v.t.* **·at·ed, ·at·ing 1.** To tear, chafe, or burn away strips of (skin, bark, etc.). **2.** To upbraid or denounce scathingly. [< L ⌍ *ex*- out, off + *corium* skin] **— ex·co/ri·a/tion** *n.*

ex·cre·ment (eks/krə·mənt) *n.* Refuse matter expelled from the body; esp., feces. **— ex/cre·men/tal** *adj.*

ex·cres·cence (iks·kres/əns) *n.* **1.** An unnatural or disfiguring outgrowth, as a wart. **2.** Any unnatural addition or outgrowth. **3.** A natural outgrowth, as hair. [< L < *ex*- out + *crescere* to grow] **— ex·cres/cen·cy** *n.* **— ex·cres/cent** *adj.*

ex·cre·ta (iks·krē/tə) *n.pl.* Excretions, as sweat, urine, etc. **ex·crete** (iks·krēt/) *v.t.* **·cret·ed, ·cret·ing** To throw off or eliminate (waste matter) by normal discharge. [< L < *ex*- out + *cernere* to separate] **— ex·cre/tion** *n.*

ex·cre·to·ry (eks/krə·tôr/ē, -tō/rē, iks·krē/tər·ē) *adj.* Relating to or adapted for excretion. Also **ex·cre·tive** (iks·krē/tiv).

ex·cru·ci·ate (iks·krōō/shē·āt) *v.t.* **·at·ed, ·at·ing** To inflict extreme pain or agony upon; rack with pain. [< L < *ex*- completely + *cruciare* to torture] **— ex·cru/ci·at/ing** *adj.* **— ex·cru/ci·at/ing·ly** *adv.* **— ex·cru/ci·a/tion** *n.*

ex·cul·pate (eks/kul·pāt, ik·skul/-) *v.t.* **·pat·ed, ·pat·ing** To free from blame or prove innocent of guilt. [< EX-¹ + L *culpare* to blame] **— ex·culp·a·ble** (ik·skul/pə·bəl) *adj.* **— ex/cul·pa/tion** *n.* **— ex·cul/pa·to/ry** *adj.*

ex·cur·sion (ik·skûr/zhən, -shən) *n.* **1.** A short trip, as for relaxation, sightseeing, etc. **2.** A short trip on a train, etc., that is available at reduced rates. **3.** A group of people making such a trip. **4.** *Physics* An oscillating movement between two points; also, half of this total distance. [< L < *ex*- + *currere* to run] **— ex·cur/sion·ist** *n.*

ex·cur·sive (ik·skûr/siv) *adj.* Going in one direction and then another; rambling; discursive; digressive. **— ex·cur/sive·ly** *adv.* **— ex·cur/sive·ness** *n.*

ex·cuse (*v.* ik·skyōōz/; *n.* ik·skyōōs/) *v.t.* **·cused, ·cus·ing 1.** To ask pardon or forgiveness for (oneself). **2.** To grant pardon or forgiveness to. **3.** To accept or overlook: to *excuse* a child's mistakes. **4.** To free from censure or blame; extenuate. **5.** To release or exempt, as from a duty. **6.** To allow to leave. **— to excuse oneself 1.** To ask forgiveness for oneself. **2.** To ask that one be released from some duty, etc. **3.** To ask for permission to leave. **— n. 1.** A statement made or a reason given as a ground for being excused. **2.** A cause, factor, or circumstance that frees from blame, etc. [< OF < L < *ex*- out, away + *causa* charge, accusation] **— ex·cus/a·ble** *adj.* **— ex·cus/a·bly** *adv.*

ex·e·cra·ble (ek/sə·krə·bəl) *adj.* **1.** Detestable and revolting. **2.** Extremely bad. **— ex/e·cra·bly** *adv.*

ex·e·crate (ek/sə·krāt) *v.* **·crat·ed, ·crat·ing** *v.t.* **1.** To call down evil upon; curse. **2.** To detest; abhor. **— v.i. 3.** To utter curses. [< L < *ex*- out + *sacrare* to devote to good or evil] **— ex/e·cra/tion** *n.* **— ex/e·cra/tive, ex/e·cra·to/re** (-krə·tôr/ē, -krō/rē) *adj.* **— ex/e·cra/tor** *n.*

ex·e·cu·tant (ig·zek/yə·tənt) *n.* One who carries into effect something to be done; also, one who gives a performance.

ex·e·cute (ek/sə·kyōōt) *v.t.* **·cut·ed, ·cut·ing 1.** To follow or carry out fully. **2.** To put into force, as a law. **3.** To put to death legally. **4.** To make (a will, deed, etc.) legal or valid. **5.** To perform (something demanding skill). **6.** To produce or fashion. **— Syn.** See KILL. [< L < *ex*- throughout + *sequi* to follow] **— ex/e·cut/a·ble** *adj.* **— ex/e·cut/er** *n.*

ex·e·cu·tion (ek/sə·kyōō/shən) *n.* **1.** The act of executing, or the fact or condition of being executed. **2.** The particular way in which something is done or performed; style or technique. **3.** *Law* A judicial writ for carrying into effect a judgment or decree of a court.

ex·e·cu·tion·er (ek/sə·kyōō/shən·ər) *n.* One who executes a death sentence.

ex·e·cu·tive (ig·zek/yə·tiv) *adj.* **1.** Relating or adapted to the putting into effect of plans, projects, work programs, etc. **2.** Relating or adapted to the execution of laws and the administration of judgments, decrees, etc. **— n. 1.** An individual or a group managing the administrative affairs of a nation, state, or other political division. **2.** An individual responsible for the management of a business, etc.

executive officer *U.S.* The principal staff officer assisting a commanding officer in units smaller than a platoon.

ex·e·cu·tor (ek/sə·kyōō/tər *for def. 1,* ig·zek/yə·tər *for def. 2*) *n.* **1.** One who carries plans, etc., into effect. **2.** *Law* One who is appointed by a testator to carry out the terms of the will. **— ex·ec·u·to·ri·al** (ig·zek/yə·tôr/ē·əl, -tō/rē-) *adj.*

ex·ec·u·to·ry (ig·zek/yə·tôr/ē, -tō/rē) *adj.* **1.** Executive·

ex·ec·u·trix (ig·zek/yə·triks) *n.* *pl.* **·trix–es** or **·tri·ces** (-trī/sēz) *Law* A female executor.

ex·e·ge·sis (ek/sə·jē/sis) *n.* *pl.* **·ses** (-sēz) Critical explanation of the meaning of words and passages in a literary or Biblical work. [< Gk. *exēgeesthai* to explain] **— ex/e·get/·ic** (-jet/ik) *adj.* **— ex/e·get/i·cal·ly** *adv.*

ex·e·gete (ek/sə·jēt) *n.* One skilled in critical explanation, as of the Bible. Also **ex·e·ge·tist** (ek/sə·jē/tist).

ex·em·plar (ig·zem/plər, -plär) *n.* **1.** A model, pattern, or original. **2.** A typical example or specimen. [< OF < LL *exemplum* a pattern]

ex·em·pla·ry (ig·zem/plər·ē) *adj.* **1.** Serving as a worthy model or example. **2.** Serving as a warning: *exemplary* punishment. **— ex·em/pla·ri·ly** *adv.* **— ex·em/pla·ri·ness** *n.*

ex·em·pli·fy (ig·zem/plə·fī) *v.t.* **·fied, ·fy·ing 1.** To show by example; illustrate. **2.** *Law* To make an authenticated copy from. [< Med.L < L *exemplum* copy + *facere* to make] **— ex·em/pli·fi·ca/tion** *n.* **— ex·em/pli·fi·ca/tive** (-fə·kā/tiv) *adj.*

ex·empt (ig·zempt/) *v.t.* To free or excuse from some obligation to which others are subject. **— adj.** Free, clear, or excused, as from some duty, etc. **— n.** A person who is exempted. [< L < *ex*- out + *emere* to buy, take] **— ex·empt/i·ble** *adj.* **— ex·emp/tion** *n.*

ex·er·cise (ek/sər·sīz) *v.* **·cised, ·cis·ing** *v.t.* **1.** To subject to drills, etc., so as to train or develop. **2.** To make use of; employ. **3.** To perform, as duties. **4.** To exert, as influence or authority. **5.** To occupy the mind of; especially, to make anxious or fretful. **— v.i. 6.** To perform exercises. **— n. 1.** A putting into use: an *exercise* of patience. **2.** Activity performed for physical conditioning, etc. **3.** A lesson, problem, etc., designed to train some particular function or skill. **4.** *Usu. pl.* A ceremony, etc., as at a graduation. **— Syn.** See PRACTICE. [< OF < L *exercere* to practice] **— ex/er·cis/er** *n.* **— ex/er·cis/a·ble** *adj.*

ex·ert (ig·zûrt/) *v.t.* To put forth or into action, as force or influence. [< L *exserere* to thrust out] **— ex·er/tive** *adj.*

ex·er·tion (ig·zûr/shən) *n.* **1.** The act of exerting some power, faculty, etc. **2.** Strong action or effort; labor.

ex·e·unt (ek/sē·ənt, -sē·ŏŏnt) They go out: a stage direction. [< L]

ex·fo·li·ate (eks·fō/lē·āt) *v.t. & v.i.* **·at·ed, ·at·ing** To separate or peel off in scales, layers, flakes, etc., as skin, bark, rock, etc. [< LL < *ex*- off + *folium* leaf] **— ex·fo/li·a/tion** *n.* **— ex·fo/li·a/tive** *adj.*

ex·ha·la·tion (eks/hə·lā/shən, eg/zə-) *n.* **1.** The act of exhaling. **2.** That which is exhaled, as air.

ex·hale (eks·hāl/, ig·zāl/) *v.* **·haled, ·hal·ing** *v.i.* **1.** To expel air or vapor; breathe out. **2.** To pass off or rise as a vapor or emanation. **— v.t. 3.** To breathe forth or give off, as air, vapor, or an aroma. **4.** To draw off; cause to evaporate. [< F < L < *ex*- out + *halare* to breathe] **— ex·hal/a·ble** *adj.*

ex·haust (ig·zôst/) *v.t.* **1.** To make extremely tired. **2.** To drain of resources, strength, etc. **3.** To draw off, as gas, steam, etc., from or as from a container. **4.** To empty (a container) of contents; drain. **5.** To study, treat of, or develop thoroughly. **— v.i. 6.** To escape, as a waste gas, steam, etc. **— n. 1.** The escape or discharge of waste gases, working fluid, etc.; also, the waste gases, etc., that escape. **2.** A pipe or other engine part through which waste gases, etc., escape. **3.** Creation of a partial vacuum to suck out stale air, dust, etc., as from a room; also, a device to do this. [< L < *ex*- out + *haurire* to draw] **— ex·haust/i·ble** *adj.* **— ex·haust/i·bil/i·ty** *n.*

ex·haust·ed (ig·zôs/tid) *adj.* **1.** Entirely used up; drained; spent. **2.** Extremely tired. **— ex·haust/ed·ly** *adv.*

ex·haust·ing (ig·zôs/ting) *adj.* Extremely tiring; most fatiguing; wearying. **— ex·haust/ing·ly** *adv.*

ex·haus·tion (ig·zôs/chən) *n.* **1.** Extreme fatigue; utter weariness. **2.** The condition of being completely used up.

ex·haus·tive (ig·zôs/tiv) *adj.* **1.** That exhausts or tends to exhaust; exhausting. **2.** Thoroughly; comprehensive. **— ex·haus/tive·ly** *adv.* **— ex·haus/tive·ness** *n.*

ex·hib·it (ig·zib/it) *v.t.* **1.** To put on view, esp. publicly. **2.** To make evident; reveal. **3.** *Law* To submit (evidence, etc.) formally or officially to a court or officer. **— v.i. 4.** To put something on display. **— n. 1.** A putting on view; display. **2.** An object or objects displayed, as at a fair. **3.** *Law* An object submitted as a piece of evidence. [< L < *ex*- out + *habere* to hold, have] **— ex·hib/i·tive, ex·hib/i·to/ry** *adj.* **— ex·hib/i·tor, ex·hib/it·er** *n.*

ex·hi·bi·tion (ek/sə·bish/ən) *n.* **1.** The act of exhibiting. **2.** That which is exhibited. **3.** A public display of art works.

ex·hi·bi·tion·ism (ek/sə·bish/ən·iz/əm) *n.* **1.** A tendency to attract attention to oneself. **2.** *Psychiatry* The tendency to obtain sexual gratification by public exposure of one's body or genitalia. **— ex/hi·bi/tion·ist** *n.*

ex·hil·a·rant (ig·zil/ər·ənt) *adj.* Causing exhilaration. **—** *n.* Something that exhilarates.

ex·hil·a·rate (ig·zil/ə·rāt) *v.t.* **·rat·ed, ·rat·ing** To set aglow with happiness or elation; make cheerful. [< L < *ex*- completely + *hilarare* to gladden] **— ex·hil/a·ra/tion** *n.* **— ex·hil/a·ra/tor** *n.* **— ex·hil/a·ra/tive** *adj.*

ex·hort (ig·zôrt/) *v.t.* **1.** To urge by earnest appeal or argument, advise or recommend strongly. **— v.i.** To utter or give exhortation. [< L < *ex*- completely + *hortari* to urge] **— ex·hor·ta·tion** (eg/zôr·tā/shən, ek/sôr-) *n.* **— ex·hor/ta·tive** (-tə·tiv), **ex·hor/ta·to/ry** (-tôr/ē) *adj.* **— ex·hort/er** *n.*

ex·hume (ig·zyōōm′, iks·hyōōm′) *v.t.* **·humed, ·hum·ing 1.** To dig up; disinter. **2.** To bring to light; reveal. [< F < L *ex-* out + *humus* ground] — **ex·hu·ma·tion** (eks′hyōō·mā′·shən) *n.* — **ex·hum′er** *n.*

ex·i·gen·cy (ek′sə·jən·sē) *n. pl.* **·cies 1.** Urgency. **2.** A situation that requires immediate attention. **3.** *Usu. pl.* A pressing need or necessity. Also **ex′i·gence.**

ex·i·gent (ek′sə·jənt) *adj.* **1.** Urgent. **2.** Requiring or exacting a great deal; unreasonably demanding. [< L < *ex-* out + *agere* to drive] — **ex′i·gent·ly** *adv.*

ex·ig·u·ous (ig·zig′yōō·əs, ik·sig′-) *adj.* Small; scanty. [< L *exiguus* scanty] — **ex·i·gu·i·ty** (ek′sə·gyōō′ə·tē) *n.*

ex·ile (eg′zīl, ek′sīl) *n.* **1.** Separation by necessity or choice from one's native country, home, etc. **2.** One who is separated from his native country, home, etc. — *v.t.* **·iled, ·il·ing** To cause (a person) to leave and stay away from (the person's) native country, home, etc. [< OF < L *exsilium*]

ex·ist (ig·zist′) *v.i.* **1.** To have actual being or reality; be. **2.** To continue to live or be. **3.** To be present; occur. [< F < L < *ex-* out + *sistere* to be located] — **ex·is′tent** *adj.* & *n.*

ex·is·tence (ig·zis′təns) *n.* **1.** The state or fact of being or continuing to be. **2.** Possession or continuance of animate being; life. **3.** Way or mode of living. **4.** Presence; occurrence. **5.** Anything or all that exists. — **ex·is·ten′tial** (-ten′shəl) *adj.* — **ex·is·ten′tial·ly** *adv.*

ex·is·ten·tial·ism (eg′zis·ten′shəl·iz′əm) *n.* A philosophy that stresses the active role of the will rather than of reason in confronting problems posed by a hostile universe. — **ex′·is·ten′tial·ist** *adj.* & *n.*

ex·it (eg′zit, ek′sit) *n.* **1.** A way or passage out; egress. **2.** The departure of an actor from the stage. **3.** Any departure. — *v.i.* To go out; depart. [< L < *ex-* out + *ire* to go]

ex li·bris (eks lī′bris, lē′-) *Latin.* **1.** From the books (of): used as an inscription on a book. **2.** A bookplate.

exo- *combining form* Out; outside; external: *exocarp.* Also, before vowels, **ex-.** [< Gk. *exo-, ex-* < *exō* outside]

ex·o·carp (ek′sō·kärp) *n. Bot.* The epicarp.

ex·o·derm (ek′sō·dûrm) See ECTODERM.

ex·o·dus (ek′sə·dəs) *n.* A going forth. — **the Exodus** The departure of the Israelites from Egypt under the guidance of Moses, described in **Exodus,** the second book of the Old Testament. [< L < Gk. < *ex-* out + *hodos* way]

ex of·fi·ci·o (eks ə·fish′ē·ō) *Latin.* By virtue of or because of office or position.

ex·og·a·my (eks·og′ə·mē) *n.* The custom of marriage outside of the tribe, family, clan, etc. — **ex·og′a·mous** *adj.*

ex·o·gen (ek′sō·jen) *n. Bot.* A plant that increases in size by successive concentric additions beneath the bark. [< EXO- + -GEN] — **ex·og·e·nous** (eks·oj′ə·nəs) *adj.*

ex·on·er·ate (ig·zon′ə·rāt) *v.t.* **·at·ed, ·at·ing 1.** To free from accusation or blame. **2.** To relieve or free from a responsibility or the like. [< L < *ex-* out, away + *onus, oneris* burden] — **ex·on′er·a′tion** *n.* — **ex·on′er·a′tive** *adj.*

ex·oph·thal·mos (ek′sof·thal′məs) *n. Pathol.* Abnormal protrusion of the eyeball. Also **ex′oph·thal′mi·a** (-mē·ə), **ex′oph·thal′mus.** [< NL < Gk. < *ex-* out + *ophthalmos* eye] — **ex′oph·thal′mic** *adj.*

ex·or·bi·tant (ig·zôr′bə·tənt) *adj.* Going beyond usual and proper limits, as in price or demand; excessive; extravagant. [< LL *exorbitare* to go astray] — **ex·or′bi·tance, ex·or′bi·tan·cy** *n.* — **ex·or′bi·tant·ly** *adv.*

ex·or·cise (ek′sôr·sīz) *v.t.* **·cised, ·cis·ing 1.** To cast out (an evil spirit) by prayers or incantations. **2.** To free (a person, place, etc.) of an evil spirit. Also **ex′or·cize.** [< OF < LL < Gk. < *ex-* out + *horkos* oath] — **ex′or·cis′er, ex′or·cist** *n.* — **ex′or·cism** (ek′sôr·siz′əm) *n.*

ex·or·di·um (ig·zôr′dē·əm, ik·sôr′-) *n. pl.* **·di·ums** or **·di·a** (-dē·ə) The beginning or introductory part of anything, esp. of a discourse, treatise, etc. [< L < *ex-* out + *ordiri* to begin] — **ex·or′di·al** *adj.*

ex·o·sphere (ek′sō·sfir) *n. Meteorol.* The region of the earth's atmosphere beginning at about 400 miles up.

ex·ot·ic (ig·zot′ik) *adj.* **1.** Belonging by nature or origin to another part of the world; not native. **2.** Strangely different and fascinating. — *n.* Something exotic. [< L < Gk. *exōtikos* foreign] — **ex·ot′i·cal·ly** *adv.* — **ex·ot′i·cism** *n.*

ex·pand (ik·spand′) *v.t.* **1.** To increase the range, scope, volume, size, etc., of. **2.** To spread out by unfolding; open. **3.** To develop more fully the details or form of. — *v.i.* **4.** To grow larger, wider, etc. [< L < *ex-* out + *pandere* to spread] — **ex·pand′er** *n.*

ex·panse (ik·spans′) *n.* **1.** A wide, continuous area or stretch. **2.** Expansion. [See EXPAND.]

ex·pan·si·ble (ik·span′sə·bəl) *adj.* Capable of being expanded. — **ex·pan′si·bil′i·ty** *n.*

ex·pan·sion (ik·span′shən) *n.* **1.** The act of expanding, or the state of being expanded. **2.** The amount of increase in size, range, volume, etc. **3.** That which is expanded.

ex·pan·sive (ik·span′siv) *adj.* **1.** Capable of expanding or tending to expand. **2.** Characterized by expansion; broad; extensive. **3.** Open and effusive; outgoing. — **ex·pan′sive·ly** *adv.* — **ex·pan′sive·ness** *n.*

ex·pa·ti·ate (ik·spā′shē·āt) *v.i.* **·at·ed, ·at·ing** To speak or write at length; elaborate: with *on.* [< L < *ex-* out + *spatiari* to walk] — **ex·pa′ti·a′tion** *n.* — **ex·pa′ti·a′tor** *n.*

ex·pa·tri·ate (*v.* eks·pā′trē·āt; *n. & adj.* eks·pā′trē·it, -āt) *v.t.* **·at·ed, ·at·ing** To exile; banish. — *n.* An expatriated person. — *adj.* Banished; expatriated. [< Med.L < *ex-* out + *patria* native land] — **ex·pa′tri·a′tion** *n.*

ex·pect (ik·spekt′) *v.t.* **1.** To look forward to as certain or probable. **2.** To look for as right, proper, or necessary. **3.** *Informal* To presume; suppose. [< L < *ex-* out + *spectare* to look at] — **ex·pec′ta·ble** *adj.*

ex·pec·tan·cy (ik·spek′tən·sē) *n. pl.* **·cies 1.** The action or state of expecting. **2.** An object of expectation.

ex·pec·tant (ik·spek′tənt) *adj.* **1.** Having expectations. **2.** Awaiting the birth of a child. — **ex·pec′tant·ly** *adv.*

ex·pec·ta·tion (ek′spek·tā′shən) *n.* **1.** The action of expecting, or the state of mind of one who expects; anticipation. **2.** The state of being expected: preceded by *in.* **3.** Something expected or looked forward to.

ex·pect·ing (ik·spek′ting) *adj.* Pregnant; also, due to give birth: Is she *expecting*?; She is *expecting* in July.

ex·pec·to·rant (ik·spek′tər·ənt) *adj.* Promoting expectoration. — *n.* A medicine used to promote expectoration.

ex·pec·to·rate (ik·spek′tə·rāt) *v.t. & v.i.* **·rat·ed, ·rat·ing 1.** To discharge (phlegm, etc.) by spitting. **2.** To spit. [< L < *ex-* out + *pectus, -oris* breast] — **ex·pec′to·ra′tion** *n.*

ex·pe·di·en·cy (ik·spē′dē·ən·sē) *n. pl.* **·cies 1.** The state or quality of being expedient. **2.** That which is expedient. **3.** Adherence to what is opportune or politic, not for what is just or right. Also **ex·pe′di·ence.**

ex·pe·di·ent (ik·spē′dē·ənt) *adj.* **1.** Serving to promote a desired end; suitable, advisable, or proper. **2.** Pertaining to or prompted by utility, interest, or advantage rather than by what is right. — *n.* **1.** Something expedient. **2.** A device; shift. [< OF < L *expedire* to free the feet from fetters]

ex·pe·dite (ek′spə·dīt) *v.t.* **·dit·ed, ·dit·ing 1.** To speed up the process or progress of; facilitate. **2.** To do with quick efficiency. [< L *expedire* to free the feet from fetters]

ex·pe·dit·er (ek′spə·dī′tər) *n.* One who facilitates the delivery of needed material. Also **ex′pe·di′tor.**

ex·pe·di·tion (ek′spə·dish′ən) *n.* **1.** A journey or march for a definite purpose. **2.** The body of persons engaged in such a journey, together with their equipment. **3.** Speed.

ex·pe·di·tion·ar·y (ek′spə·dish′ən·er′ē) *adj.* Relating to, designed for, or constituting an expedition.

ex·pe·di·tious (ek′spə·dish′əs) *adj.* Quick; speedy. — **ex′·pe·di′tious·ly** *adv.* — **ex′pe·di′tious·ness** *n.*

ex·pel (ik·spel′) *v.t.* **·pelled, ·pel·ling 1.** To drive out by force. **2.** To force to end attendance at a school, terminate membership, etc.: oust. [< L < *ex-* out + *pellere* to drive, thrust] — **ex·pel′la·ble** *adj.*
— **Syn.** A school *expels* an unruly pupil; water in the lungs must be promptly *expelled.* A rifle *ejects* a shell automatically; a squid *ejects* an inky fluid. To *dislodge* is to move something heavy from its place; an avalanche may *dislodge* a large boulder. A man is *evicted* from his house; an official is *ousted* from office; an employee is *dismissed* from his job.

ex·pend (ik·spend′) *v.t.* To pay out or spend; use up. [< L < *ex-* out + *pendere* to weigh, pay]

ex·pend·a·ble (ik·spen′də·bəl) *adj.* **1.** Available for spending. **2.** *Mil.* Denoting supplies or equipment that can be sacrificed. — **ex·pend′a·bil′i·ty** *n.*

ex·pen·di·ture (ik·spen′də·chər) *n.* **1.** The act of expending; outlay. **2.** That which is expended; expense.

ex·pense (ik·spens′) *n.* **1.** Outlay or consumption of money. **2.** The amount of money required to buy or do something. **3.** Something that requires or involves the spending of money. **4.** *pl.* Funds allotted or spent to cover incidental costs. **5.** Loss or injury involved in doing something: preceded by *at.* [See EXPEND.]

ex·pen·sive (ik·spen′siv) *adj.* Involving much expense; costly. — **ex·pen′sive·ly** *adv.* — **ex·pen′sive·ness** *n.*

ex·pe·ri·ence (ik·spir′ē·əns) *n.* **1.** Actual participation in or direct contact with something. **2.** A particular activity or occurrence actually participated in. **3.** Knowledge or skill derived from actual participation or training. **4.** The period of such activity. **5.** The totality of one's judgments or reactions. **6.** The accumulated variety of whatever has been actually met with or engaged in: the entire *experience* of mankind. — *v.t.* **·enced, ·enc·ing** To be personally involved in; undergo. [< OF < L *experiri* to try out]

ex·pe·ri·enced (ik·spir′ē·ənst) *adj.* **1.** Having had considerable experience. **2.** Made skillful or proficient through actual practice, etc.

ex·pe·ri·en·tial (ik·spir′ē·en′shəl) *adj.* Pertaining to or acquired by experience; empirical. — **ex·pe′ri·en′tial·ly** *adv.*

ex·pe·ri·ment (ik·sper′ə·mənt, -ment) *n.* **1.** An act or operation designed to discover, test, or illustrate a truth, principle, or effect. **2.** The conducting of such operations. — *v.i.* To make experiments; make a test or trial. [< OF < L < *experiri* to try out] — **ex·per′i·ment′er** *n.*

ex·per·i·men·tal (ik·sper′ə·men′təl) *adj.* **1.** Pertaining to, resulting from, or known by experiment. **2.** Growing out of or based on experience; empirical. **3.** Having the nature of an experiment; provisional; tentative. — **ex·per′i·men·tal·ism** *n.* — **ex·per′i·men′tal·ist** *n.* — **ex·per′i·men′tal·ly** *adv.*

ex·per·i·men·ta·tion (ik·sper′ə·men·tā′shən) *n.* The act or practice of experimenting.

ex·pert (*n.* ek′spûrt; *for adj. also* ik·spûrt′) *n.* One who has special skill or knowledge; a specialist. — *adj.* **1.** Skillful as the result of training or experience. **2.** Characteristic of or produced by an expert. [< OF < L *expertus*, pp. of *experiri* to try out] — **ex·pert′ly** *adv.* — **ex·pert′ness** *n.*

ex·pi·ate (ek′spē·āt) *v.t.* **·at·ed, ·at·ing** To atone for; make amends for. [< L < *ex-* completely + *piare* to appease] — **ex′pi·a·ble** *adj.* — **ex′pi·a′tion** *n.* — **ex′pi·a′tor** *n.*

ex·pi·a·to·ry (eks′pē·ə·tôr′ē, -tō′rē) *adj.* Having the power or character of an expiation; offered in atonement.

ex·pi·ra·tion (ek′spə·rā′shən) *n.* **1.** The termination of anything; close. **2.** The act of breathing out air from the lungs.

ex·pire (ik·spīr′) *v.* **·pired, ·pir·ing** *v.i.* **1.** To come to an end, as a contract. **2.** To breathe out air from the lungs; exhale. **3.** To breathe one's last breath; die. **4.** To die out, as embers. — *v.t.* **5.** To breathe out from the lungs. [< F < L < *ex-* out + *spirare* to breathe] — **ex·pir′a·to′ry** *adj.*

ex·plain (ik·splān′) *v.t.* **1.** To make plain or understandable. **2.** To give the meaning of; interpret; expound. **3.** To give reasons for; account for. — *v.i.* **4.** To give an explanation. [< L < *ex-* out + *planare* to make level] — **ex·plain′a·ble** *adj.*

ex·pla·na·tion (ek′splə·nā′shən) *n.* **1.** The act or process of explaining. **2.** A statement that clarifies or accounts for something. **3.** The meaning assigned or adduced to explain something; sense; significance.

ex·plan·a·to·ry (ek·splan′ə·tôr′ē, -tō′rē) *adj.* Serving to explain. Also **ex·plan′a·tive.** — **ex·plan′a·to′ri·ly** *adv.*

ex·ple·tive (eks′plə·tiv) *n.* **1.** An exclamation, often profane. **2.** A word or syllable added solely for the completion of a syntactic pattern. — *adj.* Added merely to fill out a sentence, complete a rhythm, etc.: also **ex′ple·to′ry** (-tôr′ē, -tō′rē). [< LL < L < *ex-* completely + *plere* to fill]

ex·pli·ca·ble (eks′pli·kə·bəl, ik·splik′ə·bəl) *adj.* Capable of explanation.

ex·pli·cate (eks′plə·kāt) *v.t.* **·cat·ed, ·cat·ing** To clear from obscurity; explain. [< L < *ex-* out + *plicare* to fold] — **ex′pli·ca′tion** *n.* — **ex′pli·ca′tor** *n.*

ex·pli·ca·tive (eks′plə·kā′tiv, ik·splik′ə·tiv) *adj.* Serving to interpret or explain. Also **ex′pli·ca·to′ry** (-kə·tôr′ē).

ex·plic·it (ik·splis′it) *adj.* **1.** Plainly expressed; clear. **2.** Unreserved in expression; straightforward. [See EXPLICATE.] — **ex·plic′it·ly** *adv.* — **ex·plic′it·ness** *n.*

ex·plode (ik·splōd′) *v.* **·plod·ed, ·plod·ing** *v.t.* **1.** To cause to burst or blow up violently and with noise; detonate. **2.** To disprove utterly; refute. **3.** To cause to expand violently or pass suddenly from a solid to a gaseous state. — *v.i.* **4.** To burst into pieces or fragments; blow up. **5.** To make a noise as if bursting: to *explode* with laughter. **6.** To be exploded, as gunpowder. [< L < *ex-* out + *plaudere* to clap]

ex·ploit (*n.* eks′ploit, ik·sploit′; *v.* ik·sploit′) *n.* A deed or act, esp. one marked by heroism or daring; feat. — *v.t.* **1.** To use meanly for one's own gain or advantage: to *exploit* workers. **2.** To utilize for profitable ends: to *exploit* water power. [See EXPLICATE.] — **ex·ploit′a·ble** *adj.* — **ex′ploi·ta′tion** *n.* — **ex·ploit′a·tive** *n.* — **ex·ploit′er** *n.*

ex·plo·ra·tion (eks′plə·rā′shən) *n.* The act of exploring; esp., the exploring of unfamiliar or unknown regions.

ex·plor·a·to·ry (ik·splôr′ə·tôr′ē, ik·splō′rə·tō′rē) *adj.* Of, for, or relating to exploration. Also **ex·plor′a·tive.**

ex·plore (ik·splôr′, -splōr′) *v.* **·plored, ·plor·ing** *v.t.* **1.** To subject to a close search or examination; scrutinize carefully. **2.** To travel through (unfamiliar territory, etc.). — *v.i.* **3.** To make an exploration. [< L < *ex-* out + *plorare* to cry out] — **ex·plor′er** *n.*

ex·plo·sion (ik·splō′zhən) *n.* **1.** The act of exploding. **2.** The sudden, loud noise produced by exploding. **3.** A sudden, violent outbreak of feeling: an *explosion* of laughter.

ex·plo·sive (ik·splō′siv) *adj.* **1.** Pertaining to or marked by explosion. **2.** Liable to explode or to cause explosion. — *n.* Any substance or mixture of substances that, on impact or by ignition, reacts by a violent expansion of gases and the liberation of relatively large amounts of thermal energy. — **ex·plo′sive·ly** *adv.* — **ex·plo′sive·ness** *n.*

ex·po·nent (ik·spō′nənt; *for def. 3, also* ek′spō·nənt) *n.* **1.** One who or that which explains or expounds. **2.** One who or that which represents or symbolizes something: an *expo-*

nent of fair play. **3.** *Math.* A number or symbol placed as a superscript to the right of a quantity to indicate a power or the reciprocal or root of a power: 2 is an *exponent* in 3^2. [< L < *ex-* out + *ponere* to place]

ex·port (*v.* ik·spôrt′, -spōrt′, eks′pôrt, -pōrt; *n. & adj.* eks′·pôrt, -pōrt) *v.t.* To carry or send, as merchandise or raw materials, to other countries for sale or trade. — *n.* **1.** The act of exporting. **2.** That which is exported, as a commodity. — *adj.* Of or pertaining to exports or exportation. [< L < *ex-* out + *portare* to carry] — **ex·port′a·ble** *adj.* — **ex·port′a·bil′i·ty** *n.* — **ex′por·ta′tion** *n.* — **ex·port′er** *n.*

ex·pose (ik·spōz′) *v.t.* **·posed, ·pos·ing 1.** To lay open to criticism, ridicule, etc.: to *expose* oneself to scorn. **2.** To lay open to some force, influence, etc.: to *expose* a mixture to heat. **3.** To present to view by baring: to *expose* one's shoulders. **4.** To reveal (something evil, disgraceful, etc.): to *expose* a crime. **5.** To reveal the identity of (an evildoer, criminal, etc.); unmask. **6.** To place so as to cause the death of by cold, starvation, etc. **7.** *Photog.* To admit light to (a sensitized film or plate). [< MF < *ex-* out + *poser.* See POSE¹.] — **ex·pos′er** *n.*

ex·po·sé (ek′spō·zā′) *n.* A making known publicly of something evil or disgraceful. [< F, pp. of *exposer*]

ex·po·si·tion (eks′pə·zish′ən) *n.* **1.** The act of presenting, explaining, or expounding facts or ideas. **2.** A detailed presentation of subject matter; also, a commentary or interpretation. **3.** A large public display or show.

ex·pos·i·tor (ik·spoz′ə·tər) *n.* One who expounds.

ex·pos·i·to·ry (ik·spoz′ə·tôr′ē, -tō′rē) *adj.* Of or pertaining to exposition; explanatory. Also **ex·pos′i·tive.**

ex post fac·to (eks pōst fak′tō) *Latin* Arising or enacted after some act, occurrence, etc., and having retroactive effect: said esp. of a law.

ex·pos·tu·late (ik·spos′chŏo·lāt) *v.i.* **·lat·ed, ·lat·ing** To reason earnestly with a person concerning the inadvisability of his actions, etc.; remonstrate: usu. with *with.* [< L < *ex-* out + *postulare* to demand] — **ex·pos′tu·la′tion** *n.* — **ex·pos′tu·la′tor** *n.* — **ex·pos′tu·la·to′ry** (-lə·tôr′ē, -tō′rē), **ex·pos′tu·la′tive** *adj.*

ex·po·sure (ik·spō′zhər) *n.* **1.** The act of exposing, or the state of being exposed. **2.** Situation in relation to the sun, elements, or points of the compass: a room with southern *exposure.* **3.** *Photog.* **a** The act of subjecting a sensitized plate or film to the action of actinic rays. **b** The time required for this. **c** A single film or plate so acted upon.

ex·pound (ik·spound′) *v.t.* **1.** To set forth in detail; state; declare. **2.** To explain the meaning of; interpret. [< OF < L < *ex-* out + *ponere* to place] — **ex·pound′er** *n.*

ex·press (ik·spres′) *v.t.* **1.** To formulate in words; verbalize; state: to *express* an idea. **2.** To give an outward indication of; reveal: to *express* anger by frowning. **3.** To communicate through some medium other than words or signs. **4.** To indicate by means of a symbol, formula, etc., as in mathematics or chemistry. **5.** To squeeze out (a liquid, juice, etc.); press out. **6.** *U.S.* To send (goods, etc.) by special messenger or a system of rapid delivery. **— to express oneself 1.** To communicate one's thoughts. **2.** To give vent to one's feelings, desires, etc., through creative activity. — *adj.* **1.** Communicated or indicated in a clear and unmistakable way; explicit. **2.** Made or intended for a precise purpose. **3.** Designed for or operating at high speed: an *express* highway; an *express* train. **4.** Of or relating to a system of rapid delivery of goods, etc., as by railway: to send something by *express* delivery. **5.** Exact; precise. — *adv.* By rapid delivery: to send something *express.* — *n.* **1.** A system designed to convey goods, parcels, money, etc., rapidly from one point to another. **2.** Goods, parcels, etc., conveyed by this system. **3.** Any means of rapid conveyance. **4.** A company specializing in the rapid conveyance of goods, parcels, etc. **5.** A train or other conveyance operating at high speed and making few stops. **6.** A message sent with speed. [< OF < L < *ex-* out + *pressare* to press] — **ex·press′er** *n.* — **ex·press′i·ble** *adj.*

ex·press·age (ik·spres′ij) *n.* **1.** The transportation of goods by express. **2.** The charge for this.

ex·pres·sion (ik·spresh′ən) *n.* **1.** Communication of thought, opinion, etc. **2.** Outward indication or manifestation of some feeling, condition, quality, etc. **3.** A conventional sign or set of signs used to indicate something; symbolization. **4.** A particular cast of the features that expresses a feeling, meaning, etc. **5.** The particular way in which one expresses oneself. **6.** The quality of expressing oneself with understanding, insight, sensitivity, etc. **7.** A particular word, phrase, etc., used in communication. **8.** The kind of language used in communication: poetic *expression.* **9.** The action of pressing or squeezing out juice, etc.

ex·pres·sion·ism (ik·spresh′ən·iz′əm) *n.* An early 20th-century movement in the arts, originating in Europe, that had as its object the free expression of the inner experience of the artist rather than realistic representation. — **ex·pres′sion·ist** *n. & adj.* — **ex·pres′sion·is′tic** *adj.*

ex·pres·sive (ik-spres′iv) *adj.* **1.** Of or characterized by expression. **2.** Serving to express or indicate: a manner *expressive* of contempt. **3.** Significant: an *expressive* sigh. **— ex·pres′sive·ly** *adv.* **— ex·pres′sive·ness** *n.*

ex·press·ly (ik-spres′lē) *adv.* **1.** With definitely stated intent or application. **2.** Exactly and unmistakably; plainly.

ex·press·way (ik-spres′wā′) *n.* A road for rapid travel.

ex·pro·pri·ate (eks-prō′prē-āt) *v.t.* **·at·ed, ·at·ing** **1.** To take or transfer (property) from the owner, esp. for public use. **2.** To deprive (a person) of ownership or property. [< LL < L *ex-* out + *proprium* property < *proprius* one's own] **— ex·pro′pri·a′tion** *n.* **— ex·pro′pri·a′tor** *n.* **— ex·pro′pri·a·to′ry** (-ə-tôr′ē, -tō′rē) *adj.*

ex·pul·sion (ik-spul′shən) *n.* **1.** The act of expelling. **2.** The state or fact of being expelled. **— ex·pul′sive** *adj.*

ex·punge (ik-spunj′) *v.t.* **·punged, ·pung·ing** To erase or wipe out. [< L < *ex-* out + *pungere* to prick]

ex·pur·gate (eks′pər-gāt, ik-spûr′gāt) *v.t.* **·gat·ed, ·gat·ing** **1.** To take out obscene or otherwise objectionable material from: to *expurgate* a novel. **2.** To remove or omit (objectionable words, lines, etc.). [< L < *ex-* out + *purgare* to cleanse] **— ex′pur·ga′tion** *n.* **— ex′pur·ga′tor** *n.* **— ex·pur′ga·to′ry** *adj.*

ex·qui·site (eks′kwi·zit, ik·skwiz′it) *adj.* **1.** Marked by rare and delicate beauty, craftsmanship, etc. **2.** Being of a high degree of excellence; consummate; admirable: an *exquisite* skill. **3.** Highly sensitive to sounds, colors, forms, etc.; dscriminating: an *exquisite* eye for design. **4.** Extremely refined; very fastidious. **5.** Intensely keen or acute, as pleasure or pain. **— n.** A person, usu. a man, who is overelegant in dress, manners, etc. [< L < *ex-* out + *quaerere* to seek] **— ex′qui·site·ly** *adv.* **— ex′qui·site·ness** *n.*

ex·tant (ek′stənt, ik·stant′) *adj.* Still existing; not lost nor destroyed; surviving. [< L < *ex-* out + *stare* to stand]

ex·tem·po·ra·ne·ous (ik·stem′pə·rā′nē·əs) *adj.* **1.** Uttered, performed, or composed with little or no advance preparation: an *extemporaneous* talk. **2.** Prepared with regard to content but not read or memorized word for word: an *extemporaneous* political speech. **3.** Made with anything immediately available; improvised to meet circumstances. [< LL < L *ex-* out + *tempus, temporis* time] **— ex·tem′po·ra′ne·ous·ly** *adv.* **— ex·tem′po·ra′ne·ous·ness** *n.*

ex·tem·po·rar·y (ik·stem′pə·rer′ē) *adj.* Extemporaneous. **— ex·tem′po·rar′i·ly** *adv.* **— ex·tem′po·rar′i·ness** *n.*

ex·tem·po·re (ik·stem′pə·rē) *adj.* Extemporaneous. **—** *adv.* With little or no advance preparation; extemporaneously. [< L *ex tempore* out of the time]

ex·tem·po·rize (ik·stem′pə·rīz) *v.t. & v.i.* **·rized, ·riz·ing** To do, make or perform with little or no advance preparation. **— ex·tem′po·ri·za′tion** *n.* **— ex·tem′po·riz′er** *n.*

ex·tend (ik·stend′) *v.t.* **1.** To open or stretch to full length. **2.** To make longer. **3.** To prolong; continue. **4.** To spread out; expand. **5.** To hold out or put forth, as the hand. **6.** To give or offer to give: to *extend* hospitality. **—** *v.i.* **7.** To be extended; stretch. **— Syn.** See INCREASE. [< L < *ex-* out + *tendere* to stretch] **— ex·tend′ed** *adj.* **— ex·tend′i·bil′i·ty** *n.* **— ex·tend′i·ble** *adj.*

ex·ten·si·ble (ik·sten′sə·bəl) *adj.* Capable of being extended. **— ex·ten′si·bil′i·ty** *n.*

ex·ten·sion (ik·sten′shən) *n.* **1.** The act of extending, or the state of being extended. **2.** An extended part; addition. **3.** Range; extent. **4.** An agreement by which a creditor allows a debtor further time in which to pay a debt. **5.** *Physics* That property of matter by virtue of which it occupies space. **— ex·ten′sion·al** *adj.*

ex·ten·sive (ik·sten′siv) *adj.* **1.** Large in area: an *extensive* farm. **2.** Having a wide range; broad in scope: *extensive* experience. **3.** Widespread; far-reaching: *extensive* damage. **— ex·ten′sive·ly** *adv.* **— ex·ten′sive·ness** *n.*

ex·ten·sor (ik·sten′sər, -sôr) *n.* *Anat.* A muscle that straightens out a limb.

ex·tent (ik·stent′) *n.* **1.** The dimension, degree, or limit to which anything is extended; compass; reach; size. **2.** Size within given bounds; limits; scope: the *extent* of his powers. **3.** A vast area. [< L < *ex-* out + *tendere* to stretch]

ex·ten·u·ate (ik·sten′yōō·āt) *v.t.* **·at·ed, ·at·ing** **1.** To represent (a fault, crime, etc.) as less blameworthy; make excuses for. **2.** To belittle the importance of. [< L < *ex-* out + *tenuis* thin] **— ex·ten′u·a′tion** *n.* **— ex·ten′u·a′tor** *n.*

ex·ten·u·at·ing (ik·sten′yōō·ā′ting) *adj.* Serving to lessen the odiousness, as of a crime: *extenuating* circumstances.

ex·te·ri·or (ik·stir′ē·ər) *adj.* **1.** Of, pertaining to, or situated on the outside; external; outer. **2.** Coming or acting from without: *exterior* influences. **3.** Pertaining to foreign countries; foreign. **— n.** **1.** That which is outside, as an external surface. **2.** Outside appearance or demeanor. [< L *exterus* outside] **— ex·te′ri·or·ly** *adv.*

exterior angle *Geom.* **1.** Any of four angles formed on the

outside of two nonintersecting straight lines cut by a third line. **2.** The angle formed between any side of a polygon and the extension of an adjacent side.

ex·ter·mi·nate (ik·stûr′mə·nāt) *v.t.* **·nat·ed, ·nat·ing** To destroy (living things) entirely; annihilate. [< L < *ex-* out + *terminus* boundary] **— ex·ter′mi·na′tion** *n.* **— ex·ter′mi·na·to′ry** (-nə·tôr′ē, -tō′rē) *adj.*

ex·ter·mi·na·tor (ik·stûr′mə·nā′tər) *n.* One who or that which exterminates.

ex·ter·nal (ik·stûr′nəl) *adj.* **1.** Of, pertaining to, or situated on the outside; outer; exterior. **2.** Belonging to or derived from the outside; extrinsic: an *external* factor. **3.** Pertaining to the outer self; superficial. **4.** Pertaining to foreign countries: *external* affairs. **5.** Relating to, affecting, or meant for the outside of the body: *external* medication. **— n.** **1.** The outside; exterior. **2.** *Usu. pl.* Outward or superficial aspects, circumstances, etc. [< L *externus* outer] **— ex·ter·nal·i·ty** (ek′stər·nal′ə·tē) *n.* **— ex·ter′nal·ly** *adv.*

ex·ter·nal·ize (ik·stûr′nəl·īz) *v.t.* **·ized, ·iz·ing** **1.** To give external shape to; make external. **2.** To make outwardly real. **— ex·ter′nal·i·za′tion** *n.*

ex·tinct (ik·stingkt′) *adj.* **1.** Extinguished; inactive, as a volcano. **2.** No longer existing: an *extinct* animal. **3.** Void. [< L < *ex-* completely + *stinguere* to quench]

ex·tinc·tion (ik·stingk′shən) *n.* **1.** The act of extinguishing, or the state of being extinguished. **2.** The process or condition of becoming extinct; a dying out. **3.** Annihilation. **— ex·tinc′tive** *adj.*

ex·tin·guish (ik·sting′gwish, -wish) *v.t.* **1.** To put out or quench, as a fire. **2.** To make extinct; wipe out. **3.** To obscure; eclipse. [< L < *ex-* completely + *stinguere* to quench] **— ex·tin′guish·a·ble** *adj.* **— ex·tin′guish·er** *n.*

ex·tir·pate (ek′stər·pāt, ik·stûr′-) *v.t.* **·pat·ed, ·pat·ing** To root out or up; destroy wholly. [< L < *ex-* out + *stirps, stirpis* stem, root] **— ex′tir·pa′tion** *n.* **— ex′tir·pa′tive** *adj.* **— ex′tir·pa′tor** *n.*

ex·tol (ik·stōl′, -stol′) *v.t* **·tolled, ·tol·ling** To praise in the highest terms; exalt; laud. **— Syn.** See PRAISE. Also **ex·toll′.** [< L < *ex-* out, up + *tollere* to raise] **— ex·tol′ler** *n.* **— ex·tol′ment** or **ex·toll′ment** *n.*

ex·tort (ik·stôrt′) *v.t.* To obtain (money, etc.) from a person by threat, oppression, or abuse of authority. [< L < *ex-* out + *torquere* to twist] **— ex·tor′tive** *adj.*

ex·tor·tion (ik·stôr′shən) *n.* **1.** The act or practice of extorting. **2.** The act of exacting an exorbitant price for something. **3.** That which has been extorted. **— ex·tor′tion·ar·y, ex·tor′tion·ate** *adj.* **— ex·tor′tion·er** *n.*

ex·tor·tion·ist (ik·stôr′shən·ist) *n.* One guilty of extortion.

ex·tra (eks′trə) *adj.* **1.** Over and above what is normal, required, expected, etc.; additional. **2.** Larger or of better quality than usual. **— n.** **1.** Something beyond what is usual or required. **2.** A copy or an edition of a newspaper issued to cover news of special importance. **3.** Something for which a special charge is made: Meals are an *extra*. **4.** Something of special quality. **5.** In motion pictures, a person hired for a small part, as in a mob scene. **— adv.** Unusually: *extra* good. [< L, outside, beyond]

extra- *prefix* Beyond or outside the scope, area, or limits of: used chiefly in forming adjectives and usu. written without a hypen (*extracurricular, extragovernmental, extraterritorial*) except before words beginning with *a* (*extra-atmospheric*) or with a capital letter (*extra-Scriptural*).

ex·tract (*v.* ik·strakt′; *n.* eks′trakt) *v.t.* **1.** To draw or pull out by force. **2.** To derive (happiness, instruction, etc.) from some source. **3.** To draw out or formulate (a principle, doctrine, etc.); deduce. **4.** To obtain by force or contrivance: to *extract* money. **5.** To obtain from a substance as by pressure, distillation, etc.: to *extract* juice. **6.** To select or copy out (a passage, word, or the like), as for quotation. **7.** *Math.* To calculate (the root of a number). **— n.** Something extracted as: **a** A concentrated form of a food, drug, etc. **b** A passage selected from a book. [< L < *ex-* out + *trahere* to draw, pull] **— ex·trac′tive** *adj. & n.* **— ex·trac′tor** *n.* **— ex·tract′a·ble** or **ex·tract′i·ble** *adj.*

ex·trac·tion (ik·strak′shən) *n.* **1.** The act of extracting, or the state of being extracted. **2.** That which is extracted. **3.** Lineage; descent: of European *extraction*.

ex·tra·cur·ric·u·lar (eks′trə·kə·rik′yə·lər) *adj.* Of or pertaining to those activities not a direct part of the curriculum of school or college life, as athletics, fraternities, etc.

ex·tra·dite (eks′trə·dīt) *v.t.* **·dit·ed, ·dit·ing** **1.** To deliver up (an accused individual, prisoner, or fugitive) to the jurisdiction of some other state, country, etc. **2.** To obtain the extradition of. **— ex′tra·dit′a·ble** *adj.*

ex·tra·di·tion (eks′trə·dish′ən) *n.* The surrender of an accused individual, prisoner, or fugitive by one state, etc., to another. [< F < L < *ex-* out + *traditio* surrender]

ex·tra·mu·ral (eks′trə·myŏŏr′əl) *adj.* **1.** Situated without

or beyond the walls, as of a fortified city. **2.** Taking place outside of an educational institution: *extramural* games.
ex·tra·ne·ous (ik-strā′nē-əs) *adj.* **1.** Coming from without; foreign: *extraneous* rock. **2.** Unrelated to the matter at hand. [< L *extraneus* foreign, external < *extra*] **—ex·tra′ne·ous·ly** *adv.* **—ex·tra′ne·ous·ness** *n.*
ex·traor·di·nar·y (ik-strôr′də-ner′ē; *esp. for def. 3* eks′trə-ôr′də-ner′ē) *adj.* **1.** Being beyond or out of the common order, course, or method. **2.** Far exceeding the usual; exceptional; remarkable. **3.** Employed on an exceptional occasion; special: an envoy *extraordinary*. [< L < *extra* beyond + *ordo, ordinis* order] **—ex·traor′di·nar′i·ly** *adv.*
ex·trap·o·late (eks-trap′ə-lāt) *v.t. & v.i.* **·lat·ed, ·lat·ing 1.** *Math.* To project (those values of a magnitude or function that lie beyond the range of known values) on the basis of values that have already been determined: distinguished from *interpolate*. **2.** To infer (a possibility) beyond the strict evidence of a series of facts, events, observations, etc. [< EXTRA- + (INTER)POLATE] **—ex·trap′o·la·tion** *n.* **—ex·trap′o·la′tive** *adj.*
ex·tra·sen·so·ry (eks′trə-sen′sər-ē) *adj.* Beyond the range of normal sensory perception.
ex·trav·a·gance (ik-strav′ə-gəns) *n.* **1.** Wasteful expenditure of money. **2.** Extreme lack of moderation in behavior or speech. **3.** An instance of wastefulness or excess. [< F] Also **ex·trav′a·gan·cy.**
ex·trav·a·gant (ik-strav′ə-gənt) *adj.* **1.** Overly lavish in expenditure; wasteful. **2.** Exceeding reasonable limits; immoderate; unrestrained: *extravagant* praise. **3.** Flagrantly high; exorbitant: *extravagant* prices. [< MF < L *extra* outside + *vagari* to wander] **—ex·trav′a·gant·ly** *adv.*
ex·trav·a·gan·za (ik-strav′ə-gan′zə) *n.* A lavish, spectacular theatrical production. [< Ital. *estravaganza* extravagance.]
ex·treme (ik-strēm′) *adj.* **1.** Exceedingly great or severe: *extreme* danger; *extreme* weakness. **2.** Going far beyond the bounds of moderation; exceeding what is considered reasonable; immoderate; radical: an *extreme* fashion; an *extreme* reactionary; also, very strict or drastic: *extreme* measures. **3.** Outermost: the *extreme* border of a country. **4.** Last; final: *extreme* unction. **—n. 1.** The highest degree; utmost point or verge: the *extreme* of cruelty. **2.** One of the two ends or farthest limits of anything: the *extremes* of joy and sorrow. **3.** *pl.* A condition of great danger or distress: He is constantly in *extremes*. **4.** *Math.* The first or last term of a proportion or series. **—in the extreme** To the greatest or highest degree. **—to go to extremes** To carry something to excess. [< OF < L *extremus*, superl. of *exterus* outside]
ex·treme·ly (ik-strēm′lē) *adv.* Exceedingly; very.
extreme unction Unction (def. 2b).
ex·trem·ist (ik-strē′mist) *n.* **1.** One who advocates extreme measures or holds extreme views. **2.** One who carries something to excess. **—adj.** Of or pertaining to extreme measures or views. **—ex·trem′ism** *n.*
ex·trem·i·ty (ik-strem′ə-tē) *n., pl.* **·ties 1.** The utmost or farthest point; termination, end, or edge: the *extremity* of a line. **2.** The greatest degree: the *extremity* of grief. **3.** One's dying moments. **4.** *pl.* Extreme measures: to resort to *extremities*. **5.** A limb or appendage of the body; esp., the hands or feet.
ex·tri·ca·ble (eks′tri-kə-bəl) *adj.* That can be extricated.
ex·tri·cate (eks′trə-kāt) *v.t.* **·cat·ed, ·cat·ing 1.** To free from entanglement, hindrance, or difficulties; disentangle. **2.** To cause to be given off; emit, as gas or moisture. [< L < *ex-* out + *tricae* trifles, troubles] **—ex′tri·ca·tion** *n.*
ex·trin·sic (ek-strin′sik) *adj.* **1.** Being outside the nature of something; not inherent; opposed to *intrinsic*. **2.** Derived or acting from without; extraneous. Also **ex·trin′si·cal.** [< F < LL < *exter* outside + *secus* besides < *sequi* to follow] **—ex·trin′si·cal·ly** *adv.* **—ex·trin′si·cal·ness** *n.*
ex·tro·ver·sion (eks′trə-vûr′zhən, -shən) *n. Psychol.* The turning of one's interest toward objects and actions outside the self rather than toward one's own thoughts or feelings. [< *extro-* outwards + L *versio, -onis* a turning]
ex·tro·vert (eks′trə-vûrt) *n. Psychol.* **1.** A person characterized by extroversion. **2.** Loosely, one who is gregarious, exuberant, etc. **—adj.** Characterized by extroversion.
ex·trude (ik-strōōd′) *v.* **·trud·ed, ·trud·ing** *v.t.* **1.** To force, thrust, or push out. **2.** To shape (plastic, metal, etc.) by forcing through dies under pressure. **—v.i. 3.** To protrude. [< L < *ex-* out + *trudere* to thrust] **—ex·tru′sion** (ik-strōō′zhən) *n.* **—ex·tru′sive** *adj.*
ex·u·ber·ance (ig-zōō′bər-əns) *n.* **1.** The quality of being exuberant. **2.** An instance of this. Also **ex·u′ber·an·cy.**
ex·u·ber·ant (ig-zōō′bər-ənt) *adj.* **1.** Abounding in high spirits and vitality; full of joy and vigor. **2.** Overflowing; lavish; effusive: *exuberant* praise. **3.** Growing luxuriantly: *exuberant* foliage. [< L < *ex-* completely + *uberare* to be fruitful] **—ex·u′ber·ant·ly** *adv.*
ex·ude (ig-zōōd′, -zyōōd′, ik-sōōd′, -syōōd′) *v.* **·ud·ed, ·ud·ing** *v.i.* **1.** To ooze or trickle forth, as sweat, gum, etc. **—v.t.**

2. To discharge gradually in this manner. **3.** To manifest; display: to *exude* confidence. [< L < *ex-* out + *sudare* to sweat] **—ex·u·da·tion** (eks′yōō-dā′shən) *n.*
ex·ult (ig-zult′) *v.i.* To rejoice greatly, as in triumph; be jubilant. [< F < L < *ex-* out + *salire* to leap] **—ex·ul·ta·tion** (eg′zul-tā′shən, ek′sul-) **—ex·ult′ing·ly** *adv.*
ex·ul·tant (ig-zul′tənt) *adj.* Jubilant; triumphant; elated. **—ex·ul′tant·ly** *adv.*
ex·u·vi·ate (ig-zōō′vē-āt, ik-sōō′-) *v.t. & v.i.* **·at·ed, ·at·ing** To cast off or shed (a skin, shell, etc.). [< L *exuere* to cast off] **—ex·u′vi·a′tion** *n.*
-ey Var. of -Y[1].
eye (ī) *n.* **1.** The organ of vision in animals; in man, a nearly spherical mass set in the skull and consisting of the cornea, iris, pupil, retina, and lens, and protected by the eyelids, eyelashes, and eyebrows. **2.** The area around the eye. **3.** The iris, in regard to its color. **4.** A look; gaze. **5.** Attentive observation. **6.** Sight; view: in the public *eye*. **7.** Capacity to see or discern with discrimination. **8.** *Often pl.* Judgment; opinion. **9.** *Meteorol.* The calm central area of a hurricane or cyclone. **10.** Anything resembling the human eye: the *eye* of a needle. **—eye of the wind** *Naut.* The direction from which the wind blows. **—to catch one's eye** To get one's attention. **—to give (someone) the eye** *Slang* To look at (someone) admiringly or invitingly. **—to keep an eye out** (or **peeled**) To watch for something; keep alert. **—to lay** (or **set**) **eyes on** To catch sight of. **—to make eyes at** To look at amorously or covetously. **—with an eye to** With a view to; looking to. **—v. eyed, ey·ing** or **eye·ing** *v.t.* **1.** To look at carefully. **2.** To make a hole in (a needle, etc.). [OE *ēage*]

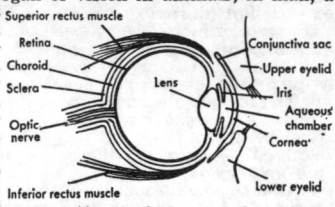
EYE (Anatomical nomenclature)

eye·ball (ī′bôl′) *n.* The globe or ball of the eye.
eye·brow (ī′brou′) *n.* **1.** The bony ridge over the eyes. **2.** The arch of small hairs growing on this ridge.
eye·cup (ī′kup′) *n.* A small cup with a rim curved to fit the eye, used in applying lotions.
eyed (īd) *adj.* Having an eye or eyes: *brown-eyed; one-eyed.*
eye·ful (ī′fŏŏl′) *n.* **1.** An amount of something in the eye. **2.** *Slang* A strikingly beautiful person.
eye·glass (ī′glas′, ī′gläs′) *n.* **1.** *pl.* A pair of corrective glass lenses mounted in a frame: also called *glasses, spectacles.* **2.** Any lens used to assist vision. **3.** An eyepiece.
eye·hole (ī′hōl′) *n.* **1.** An opening through which to pass a pin, hook, rope, etc. **2.** A peephole. **3.** The eye's socket.
eye·lash (ī′lash′) *n.* One of the stiff, curved hairs growing from the edge of the eyelids. ◆ Collateral adjective: *ciliary.*
eye·less (ī′lis) *adj.* Lacking eyes; blind.
eye·let (ī′lit) *n.* **1.** A small hole or opening. **2.** A hole made in leather, canvas, etc., and lined with metal. **3.** A metal ring for lining such a hole. **4.** In embroidery, a small hole edged with ornamental stitches. **—v.t. ·let·ted, ·let·ting** To make eyelets in. [< F *œillet*, dim. of *œil* eye]
eye·lid (ī′lid′) *n.* Either of the movable folds of skin by which the eyes are opened or closed.
eye opener *U.S.* **1.** That which opens the eyes or enlightens, as startling news, revelatory behavior, etc. **2.** *Informal* A drink of liquor, especially one taken early in the morning.
eye·piece (ī′pēs′) *n.* The lens or combination of lenses nearest the eye in a telescope, microscope, etc.
eye shadow A cosmetic preparation, tinted blue, green, gray, etc., applied to the eyelids.
eye·shot (ī′shot′) *n.* The range or scope of one's sight.
eye·sight (ī′sīt′) *n.* **1.** The power or faculty of sight. **2.** Extent or range of vision; view.
eye·sore (ī′sôr′, ī′sōr′) *n.* Something that offends the sight.
eye·strain (ī′strān′) *n.* Weariness or discomfort of the eyes caused by excessive or improper use.
eye·tooth (ī′tōōth′) *n. pl.* **·teeth** (-tēth′) One of the upper canine teeth.
eye·wash (ī′wosh′, ī′wôsh′) *n.* **1.** A medicinal wash for the eye. **2.** *U.S. Slang* Nonsense; bunk; flattery.
eye·wink (ī′wingk′) *n.* **1.** A wink or glance. **2.** An instant.
eye·wit·ness (ī′wit′nis) *n.* One who has seen something happen and can give testimony about it. **—adj.** Of or by an eyewitness: an *eyewitness* account.
ey·rie (âr′ē, ir′ē), **ey·ry** See AERIE.
E·ze·ki·el (i-zē′kē-əl, -kyəl) Sixth-century B.C. Hebrew prophet. **—n.** A book of the Old Testament written by him. Also, in the Douai Bible, **E·ze′chi·el.** [< Hebrew *yehez-qēl* God strengthens]
Ez·ra (ez′rə) Fifth-century B.C. Hebrew high priest. **—n.** A book of the Old Testament written in part by him. Also, in the Douai Bible, *Esdras*. [< Hebrew, help]

F

f, F (ef) *n. pl.* **f's** or **fs, F's** or **Fs, effs** (efs) **1.** The sixth letter of the English alphabet. **2.** The sound represented by the letter *f*. — *symbol* **1.** *Music* **a** The fourth tone in the musical scale of C. **b** A note representing it. **c** The scale built upon F. **d** The bass clef in musical notation. **e** Forte. **2.** *Chem.* Fluorine (symbol F). **3.** *Genetics* A filial generation, usu. followed by a subscript numeral, as F_1, F_2, for each successive filial generation offspring of a given mating.

fa (fä) *n. Music* The fourth syllable used in solmization; the fourth degree of a major scale; also, the tone F.

Fa·bi·an (fā′bē·ən) *adj.* Characterized by or practicing a policy of deliberate delay. — *n.* A member of the Fabian Society. [after *Fabius* Maximus, Roman general, died 203 B.C.] — **Fa′bi·an·ism** *n.* — **Fa′bi·an·ist** *n. & adj.*

Fabian Society An association formed in Great Britain in 1884, aiming at the gradual achievement of socialism.

fa·ble (fā′bəl) *n.* **1.** A brief tale embodying a moral and using persons, animals, or inanimate things as characters. **2.** A legend or myth. **3.** A foolish or improbable story. — *v.t. & v.i.* **·bled, ·bling** To invent or tell (fables or stories). [< OF < L *fari* to say, speak] — **fa′bled** *adj.* — **fa′bler** *n.* — **fab·u·list** (fab′yə·list) *n.*

fab·ric (fab′rik) *n.* **1.** A woven, felted, or knitted material, as cloth, felt, or lace. **2.** The texture or workmanship of such material. **3.** Structure or framework: the social *fabric*. [< F < L *faber* workman]

fab·ri·cate (fab′rə·kāt) *v.t.* **·cat·ed, ·cat·ing 1.** To make or manufacture; build. **2.** To make by combining parts. **3.** To make up or invent, as a lie or story. [< L *fabricare* to construct] — **fab′ri·ca′tion** *n.* — **fab′ri·ca′tor** *n.*

fab·u·lous (fab′yə·ləs) *adj.* **1.** Passing the limits of belief; incredible; astounding. **2.** Of, like, or recorded in fable; fictitious; mythical. — **fab′u·lous·ly** *adv.* — **fab′u·lous·ness** *n.*

fa·cade (fə·säd′) *n.* **1.** *Archit.* The front or principal face of a building. **2.** A front or a false appearance: a *façade* of respectability. Also **fa·cade.** [< F < Ital < LL < L *facies* face]

face (fās) *n.* **1.** The front portion of the head; countenance. **2.** The expression of the countenance. **3.** A grimacing expression. **4.** External aspect or appearance; look. **5.** *Informal* Effrontery; audacity. **6.** The value as written on the printed surface of a bond, note, etc. **7.** The front, principal, finished, or working surface of anything: the *face* of a clock, of a fabric, a golf club, etc. **8.** The surface of a coin. **9.** The side or surface of a solid. **10.** One of the sides of any military formation. **11.** The land surface or the geographical features of a region. **12.** *Printing* **a** The surface of a type body or printing plate that makes the impression. **b** The size or style of the letter or character on the type. **c** The letter or character itself: also *type face*. **13.** *Mining* The end of a drift or excavation. — **face to face 1.** In each other's immediate presence. **2.** Confronting; followed by *with*. — **in the face of 1.** Confronting. **2.** In spite of; notwithstanding. — **on the face of it** Judging by all appearances; apparently. — **to fly in the face of** To act in open defiance of. — **to lose face** To lose dignity or reputation. — **to one's face** Openly; frankly. — **to save face** To save oneself from embarrassment or disgrace; preserve one's dignity or reputation. — **to show one's face** To put in an appearance. — *v.* **faced, fac·ing** *v.t.* **1.** To bear or turn the face toward. **2.** To cause to turn in a given direction, as soldiers. **3.** To meet face to face; confront. **4.** To realize or be aware of. **5.** To cover with a layer or surface of another material. **6.** To make smooth the surface of. **7.** To turn face upward, as a playing card. — *v.i.* **8.** To turn or be turned with the face in a given direction. — **to face down** To disconcert or prevail over by a bold, fixed gaze or an audacious denial or assertion. — **to face out** To see to completion. — **to face the music** *U.S. Slang* To accept the consequences. — **to face up to** To meet with courage. [< F, ult. < L *facies* face] — **face′a·ble** *adj.*

face card In playing cards, a king, queen, or jack.

fac·et (fas′it) *n.* **1.** One of the small plane surfaces cut upon a gem. **2.** A phase, side, or aspect of a subject or person. — **Syn.** See PHASE. — *v.t.* **·fac·et·ed** or **·et·ted, fac·et·ing**

or **·et·ting** To cut or work facets upon. [< F *facette*, dim. of *face* face]

fa·ce·tious (fə·sē′shəs) *adj.* Given to or marked by levity or flippant humor. [< F < L *facetiae* jests] — **fa·ce′tious·ly** *adv.* — **fa·ce′tious·ness** *n.*

face value 1. The value stated on the face of a bond, coin, note, etc. **2.** Apparent value: at *face value*.

fa·cial (fā′shəl) *adj.* Of, near, or for the face. — *n. Informal* A massage or other treatment for the face.

facient *suffix* Causing; making: *sorbefacient*. [< L *faciens, -entis,* ppr. of *facere* to do]

fac·ile (fas′əl, -il) *adj.* **1.** Requiring little effort; easily achieved or performed; also, superficial: a *facile* prose style. **2.** Ready or quick in performance; also, smooth; glib. **3.** Easily moved or persuaded; affable; agreeable. [< F < L *facilis* easy to do] — **fac′ile·ly** *adv.* — **fac′ile·ness** *n.*

fa·cil·i·tate (fə·sil′ə·tāt) *v.t.* **·tat·ed, ·tat·ing** To make easier or more convenient. — **fa·cil′i·ta′tion** *n.*

fa·cil·i·ty (fə·sil′ə·tē) *n. pl.* **·ties 1.** Ease of performance or action. **2.** Ready skill or ability. **3.** *Usu. pl.* Something that makes an action or operation easier: *facilities* for research. **4.** Readiness to comply. [See FACILE.]

fac·ing (fā′sing) *n.* **1.** A lining or covering of a garment, often sewn on parts exposed by being turned back. **2.** A fabric used for this. **3.** Any covering, as on a building, that protects or is ornamental.

fac·sim·i·le (fak·sim′ə·lē) *n.* **1.** An exact copy. **2.** *Telecom.* A method of transmitting messages, drawings, or the like, by means of radio, telegraph, etc. — *adj.* Of or like a facsimile. [< L *fac simile* make like]

fact (fakt) *n.* **1.** Something that actually exists or has occurred. **2.** Something asserted to be true or to have happened. **3.** Reality or actuality. **4.** A criminal deed: now only in the legal phrases **before** (or **after) the fact, to deny the fact,** etc. — **as a matter of fact, in fact, in point of fact** In reality; actually. [< L *factum* < *facere* to do]

fac·tion (fak′shən) *n.* **1.** A group of people operating within, and often in opposition to, a larger group. **2.** Party strife; internal dissension. [< F < L *facere* to do] — **fac′tion·al** *adj.* — **fac′tion·al·ism** *n.* — **fac′tion·ist** *n.*
— **Syn. 1.** *Faction, wing,* and *bloc* refer to subgroups, especially within political parties. *Faction* is often applied to a disruptive subgroup: *wing* refers to either of two directly opposed groups: the liberal and conservative *wings* of the Republican party. A *bloc* is a coalition that cuts across party lines: the farm *bloc*.

fac·tious (fak′shəs) *adj.* Given to dissension.

fac·ti·tious (fak·tish′əs) *adj.* **1.** Not spontaneous; affected: *factitious* enthusiasm. **2.** Produced by artificial conditions or standards: a *factitious* demand. [< L *factitius* artificial] — **fac·ti′tious·ly** *adv.* — **fac·ti′tious·ness** *n.*

fac·tor (fak′tər) *n.* **1.** One of the elements or causes that contribute to produce a result. **2.** *Math.* One of two or more quantities that, when multiplied together, produce a given quantity. **3.** *Biol.* A gene. **4.** One who transacts business for another on a commission basis. — *v.t. Math.* To resolve into factors. [< L, maker] — **fac′tor·ship** *n.*

fac·tor·age (fak′tər·ij) *n.* **1.** A factor's commission. **2.** The business of a factor.

fac·to·ri·al (fak·tôr′ē·əl, -tō′rē-) *n. Math.* The product of a series of consecutive positive integers from 1 to a given number. The *factorial* of four (written 4!) $= 1 \times 2 \times 3 \times 4 = 24$. — *adj.* Pertaining to a factor or a factorial.

fac·tor·ize (fak′tə·rīz) *v.t.* **·ized, ·iz·ing** *Math.* To resolve into factors. — **fac′tor·i·za′tion** *n.*

fac·to·ry (fak′tər·ē) *n. pl.* **·ries** An establishment for the manufacture or assembly of goods. [< L *facere* to make]

fac·to·tum (fak·tō′təm) *n.* A man of all work. [< Med.L < L *fac,* sing. imperative of *facere* to do + *totum* everything]

fac·tu·al (fak′chōō·əl) *adj.* Pertaining to, containing, or consisting of facts; literal and exact. — **fac′tu·al·ly** *adv.*

fac·ul·ty (fak′əl·tē) *n. pl.* **·ties 1.** A natural or acquired power or ability. **2.** One of the inherent powers or capabilities of the body or mind. **3.** *U.S.* The entire teaching staff at an educational institution. **4.** A department of learning

---

at a university: the English *faculty*. **5.** The members of a learned profession collectively. **6.** Conferred power or privilege. **7.** *Eccl.* The right to perform certain ecclesiastical functions. [< OF < L < *facilis* easy to do]

fad (fad) *n.* A temporary style, amusement, fashion, etc. [Origin unknown] — **fad′dish** *adj.* — **fad′dist** *n.*

fade (fād) *v.* **·fad·ed, fad·ing** *v.i.* **1.** To lose brightness or clearness. **2.** To vanish slowly. **3.** To lose freshness, vigor, youth, etc, — *v.t.* **4.** To cause to fade. **5.** *U.S. Slang* In dice, to cover the bet of. — **to fade in** or **out** In television, motion pictures, and radio, to come into or depart from perception gradually. [< OF *fade* pale, insipid]

fae·ces (fē′sēz), **fae·cal** (fē′kəl) See FECES, FECAL.

fag[1] (fag) *v.* **fagged, fag·ging** *v.t.* **1.** To exhaust by hard work: usu. with *out*. **2.** *Brit.* To make a fag of. — *v.i.* **3.** To weary oneself by working. **4.** *Brit.* To serve as a fag. — *n.* **1.** *Brit.* In English public schools, a boy who does menial service for one in a higher class. **2.** *U.S. Slang* A homosexual: also **fag·got** (fag′ət). [Origin unknown]

fag[2] (fag) *n.* *Slang* A cigarette. [< FAG END]

fag end 1. The frayed end, as of a rope. **2.** A remnant or last part, usually of slight utility. [< FAG[1]]

fag·ot (fag′ət) *n.* **1.** A bundle of sticks, twigs, or branches, used for fuel, etc. **2.** A bundle of pieces of wrought iron or steel for working into bars, etc. — *v.t.* **1.** To make a fagot of. **2.** To ornament by fagoting. Also **fag′got**. [< OF]

fag·ot·ing (fag′ət·ing) *n.* **1.** A mode of ornamenting textile fabrics in which a number of threads of a material are drawn out and the cross threads tied together in the middle. **2.** A kind of criss-cross hemstitch. Also **fag′got·ing**.

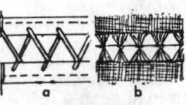

FAGOTING
a Hemstitch.
b Drawn work.

Fahr·en·heit scale (far′ən·hīt, *Ger.* fär′ən·hīt) A temperature scale in which the freezing point of water is 32° and the boiling point 212°, under standard atmospheric pressure. [after Gabriel Daniel *Fahrenheit*, 1686–1736, German physicist]

fail (fāl) *v.i.* **1.** To turn out to be deficient or wanting, as in ability, quality, etc. **2.** To miss doing or accomplishing something: He *failed* to make himself clear. **3.** To prove inadequate; fall short; give out. **4.** To decline in health or strength. **5.** To go bankrupt. **6.** In education, to receive a grade of failure. — *v.t.* **7.** To prove of no help to; desert: His friends *failed* him. **8.** In education: **a** To receive a grade of failure in (a course or examination). **b** To assign a grade of failure to (a student). — *n.* Failure: in the phrase **without fail**. [< OF < L *fallere* to deceive]

fail·ing (fā′ling) *n.* **1.** A minor fault; defect. **2.** The act of one who or that which fails. — **Syn.** See FOIBLE. — *prep.* In default of. — *adj.* That fails. — **fail′ing·ly** *adv.*

faille (fāl, fīl; *Fr.* fà′y′) *n.* An untwilled silk dress fabric having a light grain or cord. [< F]

fail-safe (fāl′sāf′) *adj.* Designating any of various systems designed to prevent equipment failure from causing operational failure, esp. such a system that makes the carrying out of a nuclear bombing automatically contingent upon a specific confirming order.

fail·ure (fāl′yər) *n.* **1.** A turning out to be unsuccessful, disappointing, or lacking. **2.** A breaking down in health, strength, action, efficiency, etc. **3.** Nonperformance; neglect: *failure* to obey the law. **4.** A becoming insolvent or bankrupt. **5.** One who or that which fails. **6.** In education, a failing to pass, or the grade indicating this.

fain (fān) *adv.* *Archaic & Poetic* Gladly; preferably: He would *fain* depart. — *adj.* **1.** *Archaic & Poetic* Glad; rejoiced. **2.** *Archaic & Poetic* Eager. [OE *fægen*]

faint (fānt) *v.i.* To lose consciousness; swoon. — *adj.* **1.** Feeble; weak. **2.** Lacking in distinctness, brightness. etc. **3.** Dizzy; weak. **4.** Lacking courage; timid. — *n.* A sudden, temporary loss of consciousness; swoon. [< OF, pp. of *faindre* to shape] — **faint′ly** *adv.* — **faint′ness** *n.*

faint·heart·ed (fānt′här′tid) *adj.* Cowardly; timorous; timid. — **faint′heart′ed·ly** *adv.* — **faint′heart′ed·ness** *n.*

fair[1] (fâr) *adj.* **1.** Light in coloring; not dark or sallow. **2.** Pleasing to the eye; beautiful. **3.** Free from blemish or imperfection: a *fair* name. **4.** Having no aspect of rain, snow, or hail. **5.** Just; upright. **6.** According to rules, principles, etc.; legitimate: a *fair* win. **7.** Properly open to attack: He is *fair* game. **8.** Moderately good or large: a *fair* crop. **9.** Likely; promising. **10.** Gracious or courteous; pleasant. **11.** In baseball, situated, falling or remaining in the area bounded by the foul lines; not foul. — *adv.* **1.** In a fair manner. **2.** Squarely; directly. — **to bid fair** To seem probable or favorable. — *n. Archaic* **1.** A fair woman. **2.** Beauty. — **for fair** For sure. [OE *fæger*]

fair[2] (fâr) *n.* **1.** A periodic and usually competitive exhibit of agricultural products, livestock, machinery, etc. **2.** A large exhibition or show of products, etc.: a world's *fair*.

3. An exhibit and sale of fancywork. **4.** A gathering of buyers and sellers. [< OF < L *feria* holiday]

fair-haired (fâr′hârd′) *adj.* **1.** Having blond hair. **2.** Favorite: the teacher's *fair-haired* boy.

fair·ing (fâr′ing) *n.* *Aeron.* In airplanes, an auxiliary structure or surface to reduce drag or resistance.

fair·ish (fâr′ish) *adj.* Moderately good, well, or large.

fair·ly (fâr′lē) *adv.* **1.** In a just manner; equitably. **2.** Moderately; somewhat. **3.** Positively; completely: The crowd *fairly* roared. **4.** Clearly; distinctly.

fair-mind·ed (fâr′mīn′did) *adj.* Free from bias or bigotry; open to reason; unprejudiced. — **fair′-mind′ed·ness** *n.*

fair-trade (fâr′trād′) *v.t.* **-trad·ed, -trad·ing** To set a price no less than the manufacturer's minimum retail price on (a branded or trademarked product). — *adj.* Of or pertaining to such a price.

fair·way (fâr′wā′) *n.* **1.** That part of a golf course, between the tees and putting greens, where the grass is kept short. **2.** *Naut.* The navigable or usual course through a channel or harbor.

fair-weath·er (fâr′weth′ər) *adj.* **1.** Suitable for fair weather, as a racetrack. **2.** Not helpful in adversity.

fair·y (fâr′ē) *n.* *pl.* **fair·ies 1.** An imaginary being, ordinarily small and capable of working good or ill. **2.** *Slang* A male homosexual. — *adj.* **1.** Of or pertaining to fairies. **2.** Resembling a fairy. [< OF *faerie* fairyland]

fair·y·land (fâr′ē·land′) *n.* **1.** The fancied abode of the fairies. **2.** Any delightful, enchanting place.

fairy tale 1. A tale about fairies. **2.** An incredible or highly imaginative story or statement.

fait ac·com·pli (fe·tà·kôṅ·plē′) *French* A thing done beyond recall or opposition; literally, an accomplished fact.

faith (fāth) *n.* **1.** Confidence in or dependence on a person, statement, or thing as trustworthy. **2.** Belief without need of certain proof. **3.** Belief in God or in the Scriptures or other religious writings. **4.** A system of religious belief. **5.** Anything given adherence or credence. **6.** Allegiance. — **Syn.** See BELIEF. — **bad faith** Deceit; dishonesty. — **in faith** Indeed; truly. — **in good faith** With honorable intentions. — **to break faith 1.** To betray one's principles or beliefs. **2.** To fail to keep a promise. — **to keep faith 1.** To adhere to one's principles or beliefs. **2.** To keep a promise. — *interj.* Indeed. [< OF < L *fidere* to trust]

faith·ful (fāth′fəl) *adj.* **1.** True or trustworthy in the performance of duty, the fulfillment of promises or obligations, etc.; loyal. **2.** Worthy of belief or confidence; truthful: a *faithful* saying. **3.** True in detail or accurate in description: a *faithful* copy. — **the faithful 1.** The followers of a religious faith. **2.** The loyal members of any group. — **faith′ful·ly** *adv.* — **faith′ful·ness** *n.*

faith·less (fāth′lis) *adj.* **1.** Untrue to promise or obligation; unfaithful. **2.** Not dependable or trustworthy. **3.** Devoid of faith. — **faith′less·ly** *adv.* — **faith′less·ness** *n.*

fake (fāk) *Informal n.* Any person or thing not genuine. — *adj.* Not genuine; spurious. — *v.* **faked, fak·ing** *v.t.* **1.** To make up and attempt to pass off as genuine: to *fake* a pedigree. **2.** To stimulate; feign. **3.** To improvise, as in music or a play. — *v.i.* **4.** To practice faking. [? Var. of obs. *feague, feak* < G *fegen* to sweep] — **fak′er** *n.*

fa·kir (fə·kir′, fā′kər) *n.* **1.** A Moslem ascetic or religious mendicant. **2.** Loosely, any Hindu yogi or religious devotee. Also **fa·keer** (fə·kir′). [< Arabic *faqīr* poor]

fal·chion (fôl′chən, -shən) *n.* **1.** A sword of the Middle Ages. **2.** *Poetic* Any sword. [< OF, ult. < L *falx* sickle]

fal·con (fal′kən, fôl-, fô′-) *n.* **1.** A bird of prey noted for its powerful wings, keen vision, and swiftness of attack upon its quarry. **2.** Any other birds of the same family, having long, pointed wings, a notched bill, and strong talons. [< OF < LL < L *falx, falcis* sickle, because of its curved beak]

fal·con·ry (fôl′kən·rē, fô′-, fal′-) *n.* **1.** The art of training falcons to hunt other birds and game. **2.** The sport of hunting with falcons: also called *hawking*. — **fal′con·er** *n.*

fal·de·ral (fal′də·ral) *n.* **1.** Any foolish nonsense or fancy. **2.** A trifling ornament. **3.** A meaningless refrain used in old songs. Also spelled *folderol*: also **fal·de·rol** (fal′də·rol).

fall (fôl) *v.* **fell, fall·en, fall·ing** *v.i.* **1.** To drop from a higher to a lower place or position because of removal of support or loss of hold or attachment. **2.** To drop suddenly from an erect position, striking the ground with some part of the body. **3.** To collapse. **4.** To become less in number, intensity, value, etc.: Prices *fell*. **5.** To become less in rank, importance, etc. **6.** To drop wounded or slain. **7.** To be overthrown, as a government. **8.** To be captured: The fort *fell*. **9.** To yield to temptation; sin. **10.** To hit; land: The bombs *fell* on target. **11.** To slope downward: The road *falls* into the valley. **12.** To hang down; droop. **13.** To come as though descending: Night *fell*. **14.** To pass into some specified condition: to *fall* asleep. **15.** To experience or show dejection: His face *fell*. **16.** To be cast down: His eyes *fell*. **17.** To come or happen by chance or lot: to *fall* among thieves. **18.** To happen; occur at a specified time or place. **19.** To pass by right or inheritance. **20.** To be uttered as if accidentally: An oath *fell* from his lips. **21.** To be classified or divided: with *into.* **22.** To be born: said of animals. — *v.t.* **23.** *U.S.* To fell or cut down, as a tree. — **to fall away 1.** To become lean or emaciated. **2.** To die; decline. — **to fall away from** To renounce allegiance to. — **to fall back** To recede; retreat. — **to fall back on** (or **upon**) **1.** To resort to; have recourse to. **2.** To retreat to. — **to fall behind 1.** To lose ground. **2.** To be in arrears. — **to fall down on** *U.S. Informal* To fail in. — **to fall flat** To fail to produce the intended effect or result. — **to fall for** *U.S. Informal* **1.** To be deceived by. **2.** To fall in love with. — **to fall in** *Mil.* To take proper place in a formation or group. — **to fall in with 1.** To meet and accompany. **2.** To agree with. — **to fall off 1.** To leave or withdraw. **2.** To become less. — **to fall on** (or **upon**) **1.** To attack. **2.** To discover. **3.** To light upon: said of the eyes, the glance, etc. — **to fall out 1.** To quarrel. **2.** To happen; result. **3.** *Mil.* To leave ranks. — **to fall short 1.** To fail to meet a standard, reach a particular place, etc.: with *of.* **2.** To be or prove deficient. — **to fall through** To come to nothing; fail. — **to fall to 1.** To set about; begin. **2.** To begin fighting. **3.** To begin eating. **4.** To come or drop into position. — **to fall under 1.** To be classified as or included in. **2.** To come under (a spell, power, etc.). — *n.* **1.** The act of falling; a descending. **2.** That which falls. **3.** The amount that falls. **4.** The distance through which anything falls. **5.** A more or less sudden descent from a vertical or erect position. **6.** A hanging down. **7.** A downward direction or slope. **8.** *Usu. pl.* A waterfall; cascade. **9.** A loss or reduction in value, price, reputation, etc. **10.** A moral lapse. **11.** A surrender, as of a city or fort. **12.** *Often cap. Chiefly U.S.* Autumn. **13.** In wrestling: **a** The throwing of an opponent to his back. **b** The method used. A wrestling match or part thereof. — **the fall of man** *Theol.* The disobedience of Adam and Eve that resulted in original sin. [OE *feallan*]

fal·la·cious (fə-lā′shəs) *adj.* **1.** Deceptive or misleading. **2.** Containing or involving a fallacy. **3.** Delusive: a *fallacious* hope. — **fal·la′cious·ly** *adv.* — **fal·la′cious·ness** *n.*

fal·la·cy (fal′ə-sē) *n. pl.* **·cies 1.** An erroneous or misleading notion. **2.** Unsoundness or incorrectness, as of belief, judgment, etc. **3.** Deceptive quality. **4.** Any reasoning contrary to the rules of logic. [< L *fallere* to deceive]

fall·en (fô′lən) Past participle of FALL. — *adj.* **1.** Having come down by falling. **2.** Brought down. **3.** Overthrown; vanquished. **4.** Disgraced; ruined. **5.** Slain.

fall guy *U.S. Slang* One who is left to receive the blame or penalties; a dupe; scapegoat.

fal·li·ble (fal′ə-bəl) *adj.* **1.** Liable to err. **2.** Liable to be misled or deceived. **3.** Liable to be erroneous or false. [< Med.L < L *fallere* to deceive] — **fal′li·bil′i·ty, fal′li·ble·ness** *n.* — **fal′li·bly** *adv.*

Fal·lo·pi·an tube (fə-lō′pē·ən) *Anat.* One of a pair of long, slender ducts serving as a passage for the ovum from the ovary to the uterus: also called *oviduct.* [after Gabriello *Fallopio*, 1523–62, Italian anatomist]

fall·out (fôl′out′) *n. Physics* **1.** The descent of minute particles of radioactive material resulting from the explosion of an atomic or thermonuclear bomb. **2.** The particles themselves. **3.** *Informal* A by-product. Also **fall′-out′.**

fal·low¹ (fal′ō) *adj.* Left unseeded after being plowed; uncultivated. — **to lie fallow** To remain unused, idle, dormant, etc. — *n.* **1.** Land left unseeded after plowing. **2.** The process of plowing or working land and leaving it unseeded for a time. — *v.t. & v.i.* To make, keep, or become fallow. [OE *fealging* fallow land] — **fal′low·ness** *n.*

fal·low² (fal′ō) *adj.* Light yellowish brown. [OE *fealu*]

fallow deer A European deer about 3 feet high at the shoulders and spotted white in the summer

FALLOW DEER

false (fôls) *adj.* **1.** Contrary to truth or fact. **2.** Incorrect: *false* reasoning. **3.** Not genuine; artificial. **4.** Deceptive or misleading: a *false* impression. **5.** Given to lying. **6.** Wanting in fidelity; faithless. **7.** Supplementary; substitutive. **8.** *Music* Not correct in pitch. — *adv.* In a false manner. [< OF < L *falsus*, orig. pp. of *fallere* to deceive] — **false′ly** *adv.* — **false′ness** *n.*

false face A mask.

false-heart·ed (fôls′här′tid) *adj.* Treacherous; deceitful.

false·hood (fôls′hŏŏd) *n.* **1.** Lack of accord to fact or truth. **2.** An intentional untruth; lie. — **Syn.** See LIE².

false ribs *Anat.* Ribs that do not unite directly with the sternum. In man there are five on each side.

fal·set·to (fôl·set′ō) *n. pl.* **·tos 1.** The higher, less colorful register of a voice, esp. of an adult male voice: also called *head voice.* **2.** A man who sings or speaks in this register: also **fal·set′tist.** — *adj.* Having the quality of falsetto; shrill. — *adv.* In falsetto. [< Ital., dim. of *falso* false]

fal·si·fy (fôl′sə-fī) *v.* **·fied, ·fy·ing** *v.t.* **1.** To tell lies about; misrepresent. **2.** To alter or tamper with, esp. in order to deceive. **3.** To prove to be false. — *v.i.* **4.** To tell lies. — **Syn.** See PERVERT. [< F < LL < L < *falsus* false + *facere* to make] — **fal′si·fi·ca′tion** *n.* — **fal′si·fi′er** *n.*

fal·si·ty (fôl′sə-tē) *n. pl.* **·ties 1.** The quality of being false. **2.** That which is false. — **Syn.** See ERROR.

Fal·staff (fôl′staf, -stäf), **Sir John** A fat, fun-loving old knight in Shakespeare's *Henry IV* and *The Merry Wives of Windsor.* — **Fal·staff′i·an** *adj.*

fal·ter (fôl′tər) *v.i.* **1.** To be hesitant or uncertain; waver. **2.** To move unsteadily. **3.** To speak haltingly. — *v.t.* **4.** To utter haltingly. — **Syn.** See VACILLATE. — *n.* **1.** An uncertainty or hesitation in voice or action. **2.** A quavering sound. [? < ON *faltrask* to be encumbered] — **fal′ter·er** *n.* — **fal′ter·ing** *adj.* — **fal′ter·ing·ly** *adv.*

fame (fām) *n.* **1.** Widespread and illustrious reputation; renown. **2.** Public reputation or estimation. — *v.t.* **famed,** **fam·ing** *Archaic* To speak of widely; celebrate. [< F < L *fama* report, reputation]

fa·mil·ial (fə-mil′yəl) *adj.* Of, pertaining to, associated with, or transmitted within the family.

fa·mil·iar (fə-mil′yər) *adj.* **1.** Having thorough knowledge of something; well-acquainted: followed by *with.* **2.** Well-known; customary. **3.** Intimate; close. **4.** Unduly intimate; forward. **5.** Informal or unconstrained. **6.** Domesticated: said of animals. — *n.* **1.** A friend or close associate. **2.** A spirit serving a witch, usu. in animal form. [< OF < L *familia* family] — **fa·mil′iar·ly** *adv.*

fa·mil·i·ar·i·ty (fə-mil′ē·ar′ə·tē, -mil′yar′-) *n. pl.* **·ties 1.** Thorough knowledge of or acquaintance with something. **2.** Friendly closeness; intimacy. **3.** Offensively familiar conduct; unwarranted intimacy. **4.** *Often pl.* An action warranted only by intimate acquaintance.

fa·mil·iar·ize (fə-mil′yə-rīz) *v.t.* **·ized, ·iz·ing 1.** To make (oneself or someone) familiar with something. **2.** To cause (something) to be familiar. — **fa·mil′iar·i·za′tion** *n.*

fam·i·ly (fam′ə-lē, fam′lē) *n. pl.* **·lies 1.** Parents and their children. **2.** The children as distinguished from the parents. **3.** A group of persons connected by blood or marriage. **4.** A succession of persons connected by blood, name, etc.; a house; clan. **5.** Distinguished or ancient lineage or descent. **6.** A household. **7.** Any class or group of like or related things. **8.** *Biol.* A taxonomic category higher than a genus and below an order. **9.** *Ling.* A grouping of languages assumed to be descended from a common parent, as the Indo-European family. — *adj.* Of, belonging to, or suitable for a family. [< L < *famulus* servant]

family name A surname.

family tree 1. A diagram showing family descent. **2.** The ancestors and descendants of a family, collectively.

fam·ine (fam′in) *n.* **1.** A widespread scarcity of food. **2.** A great scarcity of anything; dearth: a water *famine.* **3.** Starvation. [< OF < L *fames* hunger]

fam·ish (fam′ish) *v.t. & v.i.* To suffer or die, or to cause to suffer or die, from starvation. [Earlier *fame* < F *afamer* to starve] — **fam′ished** *adj.* — **fam′ish·ment** *n.*

fa·mous (fā′məs) *adj.* **1.** Celebrated in history or public report; well-known; renowned. **2.** *Informal* Excellent; admirable. — **fa′mous·ly** *adv.* — **fa′mous·ness** *n.*

fan¹ (fan) *n.* **1.** A device for putting the air into motion; esp., a light, flat implement, often collapsible and opening into a wedgelike shape, a circle, etc. **2.** Anything shaped like a fan. **3.** A machine fitted with blades that revolve rapidly about a central hub, for stirring air, etc. **4.** A machine for blowing away chaff. — *v.* **fanned, fan·ning** *v.t.* **1.** To move or stir (air) with or as with a fan. **2.** To direct air upon; cool or refresh with or as with a fan. **3.** To move or stir to action; excite: to *fan* someone's rage. **4.** To winnow (grain or chaff). **5.** To spread like a fan. **6.** In baseball, to cause (a batter) to strike out. — *v.i.* **7.** To spread out like a fan. **8.** In baseball, to strike out. [OE < L *vannus* winnowing basket] — **fan′ner** *n.*

fan² (fan) *n. Informal* An enthusiastic devotee or admirer of a sport, diversion, celebrity, etc. [? < FANATIC]

fa·nat·ic (fə-nat′ik) *n.* A person who is moved by a frenzy of enthusiasm or zeal; esp., a religious zealot. [< L *fanum* temple] — **fa·nat′i·cal** *adj.* — **fa·nat′i·cal·ly** *adv.* — **fa·nat′i·cism** (-siz′əm) *n.*

fan·cied (fan′sēd) *adj.* Imaginary: *fancied* insults.

fan·ci·er (fan′sē·ər) *n.* **1.** One having a special taste for or interest in something. **2.** A breeder of animals.

fan·ci·ful (fan′si·fəl) *adj.* **1.** Produced by or existing only in the fancy: *fanciful* schemes. **2.** Marked by fancy in design: a *fanciful* costume. **3.** Indulging in fancies: a *fanciful* mind. **— fan′ci·ful·ly** *adv.* **— fan′ci·ful·ness** *n.*

fan·cy (fan′sē) *n. pl.* **·cies 1.** Imagination of a capricious or whimsical sort. **2.** An extravagant, odd, or whimsical invention or image. **3.** An idea or notion not based on fact or evidence. **4.** A caprice or whim. **5.** A liking or inclination, as if resulting from caprice. **6.** Taste or judgment in art, style, etc. **— adj.** **·ci·er, ·ci·est 1.** Adapted to please the fancy; ornamental. **2.** Coming from the fancy; imaginary. **3.** Capricious; whimsical. **4.** Of higher grade than the average: *fancy* fruits. **5.** Exorbitant: *fancy* prices. **6.** Performed with exceptional grace and skill. **7.** Selectively bred for certain points, as an animal: also **fan′cy-bred′** **— v.t. ·cied, ·cy·ing 1.** To imagine; picture: *Fancy* that! **2.** To take a fancy to. **3.** To believe without proof or conviction; suppose. **4.** To breed, as animals, for conventional points of symmetry or beauty. **— interj.** An exclamation of surprise. [Contr. of FANTASY]

fan·cy-free (fan′sē-frē′) *adj.* **1.** Not in love. **2.** Carefree.

fan·cy·work (fan′sē-wûrk′) *n.* Ornamental needlework.

fan·dan·go (fan-dang′gō) *n. pl.* **·gos 1.** A Spanish dance in triple time. **2.** The music for this dance. [< Sp.]

fan·fare (fan′fâr′) *n.* **1.** A short, lively passage, as of trumpets. **2.** A noisy or showy parade. [< F]

fang (fang) *n.* **1.** A long, pointed tooth or tusk by which an animal seizes or tears at its prey. **2.** One of the long, hollow or grooved, usu. erectile teeth with which a venomous serpent injects its poison into its victim. [OE, a seizing] **— fanged** *adj.* **— fang′less** *adj.* **— fang′like′** *adj.*

fan·light (fan′līt′) *n. Archit.* **1.** A semicircular window containing a sash with bars radiating from the middle of its base: also called *fan window.* **2.** *Brit.* A transom.

fan·ny (fan′ē) *n. pl.* **·nies** *U.S. Slang* The buttocks.

fan·tail (fan′tāl′) *n.* **1.** A variety of domestic pigeon having fanlike tail feathers. **2.** Any fan-shaped end or tail.

fan·tan (fan′tan′) *n.* **1.** A Chinese gambling game. **2.** A game of cards played in sequence. [< Chinese *fan t′an*]

fan·ta·si·a (fan-tā′zhə, -zhē-ə, fan′tə-zē′ə) *n. Music* **1.** A fanciful composition observing no strict musical form. **2.** A medley of various themes, usu. with brilliant variations and embellishments. [< Ital., a fancy]

fan·ta·size (fan′tə-sīz) *v.i.* **·sized, ·siz·ing** To create mental fantasies.

fan·tas·tic (fan-tas′tik) *adj.* **1.** Odd, grotesque, or whimsical in appearance, construction, etc.: a *fantastic* room. **2.** Wildly fanciful or exaggerated. **3.** Capricious or impulsive, as moods, actions, etc. **4.** Coming from the imagination or fancy. **— n.** *Archaic* One who is fantastic. [< Med.L < L < Gk. < *phantastēs* a boaster]

fan·tas·ti·cal (fan-tas′ti-kəl) *adj.* **1.** Extremely capricious, odd, or eccentric. **2.** Extravagantly fanciful, imaginative or grotesque. **— fan·tas′ti·cal′i·ty** (-kal′ə-tē), **fan·tas′ti·cal·ness** *n.* **— fan·tas′ti·cal·ly** *adv.*

fan·ta·sy (fan′tə-sē, -zē) *n. pl.* **·sies 1.** Imagination unrestrained by reality; wild fancy. **2.** An odd, unreal, or grotesque mental image. **3.** An odd or whimsical notion. **4.** A capricious mood. **5.** An ingenious or highly imaginative creation. **6.** *Psychol.* A sequence of more or less pleasant mental images, usu. fulfilling a need not gratified in the real world. **7.** *Music* A fantasia. **— v.t.** **·sied, ·sy·ing** To envision; imagine. [< OF < L < Gk. *phainein* to show]

fan·tom (fan′təm) See PHANTOM.

fan window *Archit.* A fanlight.

far (fär) *adv.* **1.** At, to, or from a great distance. **2.** To or at a particular distance, point, or degree. **3.** To a great degree; very much: *far* wiser. **4.** Very remotely in time, degree, quality, etc.: *far* from pleasant. **— as far as** To the distance, extent, or degree that. **— by far** In a great degree; very much. **— far and away** Very much; decidedly. **— far and wide** Distantly and extensively; everywhere. Also **far and near. — far be it from me** I have not the audacity or desire. **— how far** To what extent, distance, or degree. **— in so far as** To the extent that. **— so far 1.** To that extent; up to that point. **2.** Up to now. **— so far as** To the extent that. **— so far so good** Up to now everything is all right. **— to go far 1.** To accomplish much; have success. **2.** To last a long time or cover a great extent. **3.** To tend strongly. **— adj. far·ther** or **fur·ther, far·thest** or **fur·thest** (See note under FARTHER.) **1.** Very remote in space or time. **2.** Extending widely or at length. **3.** More distant: the *far* end of the garden. [OE *feor*]

far·ad (far′əd, -ad) *n. Electr.* The unit of capacitance; the capacitance of a condenser that retains one coulomb of charge with one volt difference of potential. [after Michael Faraday]

far·a·way (fär′ə-wā′) *adj.* **1.** Distant: a *faraway* town. **2.** Absent-minded; abstracted: a *faraway* look.

farce (färs) *n.* **1.** A comedy employing ludicrous or exaggerated situations. **2.** A ridiculous action or situation. **— v.t. farced, farc·ing** To fill out with witticisms, jibes, etc., as a play. [< F < L *farcire* to stuff]

far·ci·cal (fär′si·kəl) *adj.* Of, belonging to, or resembling farce. **— far′ci·cal·ly** *adv.* **— far′ci·cal′i·ty, far′ci·cal·ness** *n.*

far cry A long way.

fare (fâr) *v.i.* **fared, far·ing 1.** To be in a specified state; get on: He *fares* poorly. **2.** To turn out: It *fared* well with him. **3.** To be supplied with food and drink. **— n. 1.** The fee for conveyance in a vehicle, etc. **2.** A passenger carried for hire. **3.** Food and drink; diet. [OE *faran* to go, travel]

Far East The countries of eastern Asia, including China, Japan, Korea, Manchuria, and adjacent islands.

fare·well (*n.* fâr′wel′; *interj.* fâr′wel′; *adj.* fâr′wel′) *n.* **1.** A parting salutation; a good-by. **2.** Leave-taking. **— interj.** Good-by. **— adj.** Parting; closing. [Earlier *fare well*]

far-fetched (fär′fecht′) *adj.* Neither natural nor obvious; forced; strained: a *far-fetched* joke.

far-flung (fär′flung′) *adj.* Extending over great distances.

fa·ri·na (fə-rē′nə) *n.* **1.** A meal or flour obtained chiefly from cereals, nuts, potatoes, or Indian corn, and used as a breakfast food. **2.** Starch. [< L < *far* spelt]

far·i·na·ceous (far′ə-nā′shəs) *adj.* **1.** Consisting or made of farina. **2.** Containing or yielding starch. **3.** Mealy.

far·kle·ber·ry (fär′kəl·ber′ē) *n. pl.* **·ries** A shrub or small tree with edible black berries. [Origin unknown]

farm (färm) *n.* **1.** A tract of land forming a single property and devoted to agriculture. **2.** A tract of water used for the cultivation of marine life. **3.** In baseball, a minor-league club used by a major-league club for training its recruits. **— v.t. 1.** To cultivate (land). **2.** To take a lease of, as the use of a business or the collection of taxes, for a fixed rental, retaining the profits. **3.** To let at a fixed rental, as the authority to collect taxes, etc.: usu. with *out.* **4.** To let out the services of (a person) for hire. **5.** To arrange for (work) to be performed by persons or a firm not in the main organization: with *out.* **6.** In baseball, to place (a player) with a minor-league team for training: often with *out.* **— v.i. 7.** To practice farming. [< F < Med.L < L *firmare* to fix]

farm·er (fär′mər) *n.* **1.** One who operates a farm. **2.** One who pays for the privilege of collecting taxes, etc.

farm hand One who works on a farm, esp. for hire.

farm·house (färm′hous′) *n.* The homestead on a farm.

farm·ing (fär′ming) *n.* **1.** The business of operating a farm; agriculture. **2.** The leasing of the authority to collect taxes, etc. **— adj.** Engaged in, suitable for, or used for agriculture.

farm·stead (färm′sted) *n.* A farm and the buildings on it.

farm·yard (färm′yärd′) *n.* A space surrounded by farm buildings, and enclosed for confining stock, etc.

far·o (fâr′ō) *n.* A game of cards in which the players bet against the dealer as to the order in which certain cards will appear. [Alter. of *Pharaoh*]

Far·o·ese (fâr′ō-ēz′) *n.* **1.** *pl.* **·ese** A native or inhabitant of the Faeroe Islands. **2.** The North Germanic language spoken in these islands, closely resembling Icelandic.

far-off (fär′ôf′, -of′) *adj.* Distant; remote.

far·ra·go (fə-rā′gō, -rä′-) *n. pl.* **·goes** A confused mixture; medley. [< L *far* spelt]

far-reach·ing (fär′rē′ching) *adj.* Having wide influence, range, or effect.

far·row (far′ō) *n.* A litter of pigs. **— v.t. & v.i.** To give birth to (young): said of swine. [OE *fearh* young pig]

far-see·ing (fär′sē′ing) *adj.* **1.** Having foresight; prudent; wise. **2.** Able to see distant objects clearly.

far·sight·ed (fär′sī′tid) *adj.* **1.** Able to see things at a distance more clearly than things at hand. **2.** Having foresight. **— far′sight′ed·ly** *adv.* **— far′sight′ed·ness** *n.*

far·ther (fär′thər) Comparative of FAR. **— adv.** To or at a more advanced point in space or, less often, time. **— adj. 1.** More distant or remote. **2.** Additional: in this sense usu. *further.* [ME *ferther*; var. of FURTHER]

far·ther·most (fär′thər-mōst′) *adj.* Most distant; farthest.

far·thest (fär′thist) Superlative of FAR. **— adv.** To or at the greatest distance. **— adj. 1.** Most distant or remote. **2.** Longest or most extended: the *farthest* way around.

far·thing (fär′thing) *n.* **1.** A small, bronze, English coin, formerly worth one fourth of a penny. **2.** Something of no value; a trifle. [OE < *fēortha* a fourth]

far·thin·gale (fär′thing-gāl′) *n.* A woman's hoop skirt of the 16th and 17th centuries. [< OF *verdugale*, alter. of Sp. *verdugado* < *verdugo* rod, hoop]

fas·ces (fas′ēz) *n.pl.* In ancient Rome, a bundle of rods enclosing an ax, used as a symbol of power. [< L, pl. of *fascis* bundle] **— fas·ci·al** (fash′ē-əl) *adj.*

fas·ci·a (fash′ē-ə) *n. pl.* **fas·ci·ae** (fash′i-ē) **1.** *Anat.* Fibrous connective tissue for enclosing or connecting muscles or internal organs. **2.** Something that binds together, as a fillet; a band. [< L, band] **— fas′ci·al** *adj.*

fas·ci·cle (fas′i-kəl) *n.* **1.** A small bundle or cluster, as of leaves, flowers, etc. **2.** One of the sections of a book that is published in installments. **— fas′ci·cled** (-kəld) *adj.* **— fas·cic·u·lar** (fə-sik′yə-lər) *adj.*

fas·ci·nate (fas′ə-nāt) *v.* **·nat·ed, ·nat·ing** *v.t.* **1.** To attract irresistibly, as by beauty or other qualities; captivate. **2.**

To hold spellbound, as by terror or awe. — *v.i.* **3.** To be fascinating. [< L *fascinum* spell] — **fas'ci·nat'ing** *adj.* — **fas'ci·nat'ing·ly** *adv.* — **fas'ci·na'tor** *n.*

fas·ci·na·tion (fas/ə·nā/shən) *n.* **1.** The act of fascinating, or the state of being fascinated. **2.** A fascinating attraction, influence, or quality; enchantment; charm.

fas·cism (fash/iz·əm) *n.* A one-party system of government in which the individual is subordinated to the state and control is maintained by military force, secret police, rigid censorship, and governmental regimentation of industry and finance. [See FASCISTI.]

fas·cist (fash/ist) *n.* **1.** An advocate of fascism. **2.** A member of a fascist party. — *adj.* Of, advocating, or practicing fascism: a *fascist* state: also **fa·scis·tic** (fə·shis/tik).

fash·ion (fash/ən) *n.* **1.** The mode of dress, manners, living, etc., prevailing in society, esp. in high society; also, good form or style. **2.** A current practice or usage. **3.** An object of enthusiasm among fashionable people. **4.** Fashionable people collectively; the élite. **5.** Manner: He walks in a peculiar *fashion*. **6.** Kind; sort. — **after a fashion** To a limited extent. — *v.t.* **1.** To give shape or form to; mold. **2.** To adapt, as to the occasion. [< AF, OF < L *factio*, *-onis* a (special) way of making] — **fash'ion·er** *n.*

fash·ion·a·ble (fash/ən·ə·bəl) *adj.* **1.** Conforming to the current fashion. **2.** Associated with, characteristic of, or patronized by persons of fashion. — *n.* A person of fashion. — **fash'ion·a·ble·ness** *n.* — **fash'ion·a·bly** *adv.*

fash·ioned (fash/ənd) *adj.* **1.** Made; shaped; formed· **2.** Of a certain style or fashion: *old-fashioned*.

fashion plate **1.** One who dresses in the latest fashion. **2.** A picture representing the prevailing fashions in dress.

fast¹ (fast, fäst) *adj.* **1.** Firm in place; not easily moved. **2.** Firmly secured. **3.** Constant; steadfast: *fast* friends. **4.** Not liable to fade: said of colors. **5.** Resistant: *acid-fast*. **6.** Sound or deep, as sleep. **7.** Acting or moving quickly. **8.** Performed quickly: *fast* work. **9.** Permitting or suitable for quick movement: a *fast* track. **10.** Requiring rapidity of action or motion: a *fast* schedule. **11.** In advance of the true time. **12.** Characterized by or given to dissipation or moral laxity. **13.** *Photog.* Intended for short exposure, as a high-velocity shutter or a highly sensitive film. — **to play fast and loose** To act in a tricky or untrustworthy fashion. — *adv.* **1.** Firmly; securely. **2.** Soundly: *fast* asleep. **3.** Quickly. **4.** Dissipatedly: to live *fast*. [OE *fæst*]

fast² (fast, fäst) *v.i.* To abstain from food; esp., to eat sparingly or abstain from certain foods, as in observance of a religious duty. — *n.* **1.** Abstinence from food or from prescribed kinds of food, particularly as a religious duty. **2.** A period prescribed for fasting. [OE *fæstan*]

fas·ten (fas/ən, fäs/-) *v.t.* **1.** To attach to something else; connect. **2.** To make fast; secure. **3.** To direct (the attention, eyes, etc.) steadily. **4.** To impute or attribute. — *v.i.* **5.** To take fast hold; cling: usu. with *on*. **6.** To become firm or attached. [OE *fæst* fixed] — **fas'ten·er** *n.*

fas·ten·ing (fas/ən·ing, fäs/-) *n.* **1.** The act of making fast. **2.** That which fastens, as a bolt.

fas·tid·i·ous (fas·tid/ē·əs, fəs-) *adj.* Hard to please in matters of taste; exceedingly delicate or refined; overnice; squeamish. — **Syn.** See METICULOUS. [< L *fastidium* disgust] — **fas·tid'i·ous·ly** *adv.* — **fas·tid'i·ous·ness** *n.*

fast·ness (fast/nis, fäst/-) *n.* **1.** A fortress; stronghold. **2.** The state of being firm or fixed. **3.** Swiftness.

fat (fat) *adj.* **fat·ter, fat·test** **1.** Having superfluous flesh or fat; obese; plump. **2.** Containing much fat, oil, etc. **3.** Rich or fertile, as land. **4.** Abundant; plentiful: a *fat* profit. **5.** Profitable: a *fat* job. **6.** Thick; broad. — **a fat chance** *Slang* Very little chance; no chance at all. — *n.* **1.** *Biochem.* Any of a large class of yellowish to white, greasy, solid or liquid substances widely distributed in plant and animal tissues. They are compounds of various fatty acids and glycerol, and are generally odorless, tasteless, and colorless. **2.** Animal tissue containing large quantities of such compounds. **3.** Any vegetable or animal fat or oil used in cooking. **4.** Plumpness; corpulence. **5.** The richest or most desirable part of anything. — **the fat is in the fire** The mischief is done. — **to chew the fat** *Slang* To talk. — *v.t.* & *v.i.* **fat·ted, fat·ting** To make or become fat. [OE *fæt*] — **fat'ly** *adv.* — **fat'ness** *n.* — **fat'tish** *adj.*

fa·tal (fāt/l) *adj.* **1.** Resulting in or capable of causing death. **2.** Bringing ruin or disaster; destructive. **3.** Highly significant or decisive; fateful: the *fatal* hour. **4.** Decreed or brought about by fate; destined; inevitable. [< L *fatum*. See FATE.] — **fa'tal·ly** *adv.*

fa·tal·ism (fāt/l·iz/əm) *n.* **1.** The doctrine that all events are predetermined and thus unalterable. **2.** A disposition to accept every event or condition as inevitable. — **fa'tal·ist** *n.* — **fa'tal·is'tic** *adj.* — **fa'tal·is'ti·cal·ly** *adv.*

fa·tal·i·ty (fā·tal/ə·tē, fə-) *n.* *pl.* **·ties** **1.** A death brought

about through some disaster or calamity. **2.** The capability of causing death or disaster. **3.** The state or quality of being subject to or determined by fate. **4.** A decree of fate.

fat·back (fat/bak/) *n.* Unsmoked salt pork.

fate (fāt) *n.* **1.** A force viewed as unalterably determining events in advance; destiny. **2.** That which inevitably happens as though determined by this force. **3.** Final result or outcome. **4.** An evil destiny; esp., death or destruction. — *v.t.* **fat·ed, fat·ing** To predestine: obsolete except in the passive. [< L *fatus*, pp. of *fari* to speak]

fat·ed (fā/tid) *adj.* **1.** Controlled by or subject to fate; destined. **2.** Condemned to ruin or destruction; doomed.

fate·ful (fāt/fəl) *adj.* **1.** Determining destiny; momentous. **2.** Brought about by or as if by fate. **3.** Bringing death or disaster; fatal. **4.** Ominously prophetic; portentous. — **fate'ful·ly** *adv.* — **fate'ful·ness** *n.*

Fates (fāts) In classical mythology, the three goddesses who control human destiny (Atropos, Clotho, and Lachesis).

fat·head (fat/hed/) *n.* A stupid person. — **fat'head'ed** *adj.*

fa·ther (fä/thər) *n.* **1.** A male parent. **2.** A male who adopts a child or who otherwise holds a paternal relationship toward another. **3.** Any male ancestor; forefather. **4.** A male who founds or establishes something. **5.** Any elderly man: a title of respect. **6.** One of the orthodox writers of the early Christian church. **7.** A leader or elder of a council, assembly, etc. **8.** A member of the ancient Roman senate. **9.** *Eccl.* a *Usu. cap.* A priest or other church dignitary, as in the Roman Catholic or Anglican church: often used as a title of respect. **b** A confessor. — *v.t.* **1.** To beget. **2.** To act as a father toward. **3.** To found or make. [OE *fæder*] — **fa'ther·less** *adj.*

fa·ther-in-law (fä/thər·in·lô/) *n.* *pl.* **fa·thers-in-law** **1.** The father of one's husband or wife. **2.** *Rare* A stepfather.

fa·ther·land (fä/thər·land/) *n.* **1.** The land of one's birth. **2.** The native country of one's forebears.

fa·ther·ly (fä/thər·lē) *adj.* **1.** Of or like a father. **2.** Showing the affection of a father. — **fa'ther·li·ness** *n.*

Father's Day The third Sunday in June.

fath·om (fath/əm) *n.* *pl.* **·oms** or **·om** A measure of length, 6 feet or 1.829 meters, used principally in marine and mining measurements. See table front of book. — *v.t.* **1.** To find the depth of; sound. **2.** To understand; interpret; puzzle out. [OE *fæthm* the span of two arms outstretched] — **fath'om·a·ble** *adj.* — **fath'om·less** *adj.*

fa·tigue (fə·tēg/) *n.* **1.** The condition of being very tired as a result of physical or mental exertion. **2.** *Mech.* Structural weakness or loss of resiliency in metals or other materials, produced by excessive subjection to strain. **3.** *Mil.* a A special work assignment done by soldiers in training: also **fatigue duty. b** *pl.* Strong, durable clothes worn on fatigue duty: also **fatigue clothes.** — *v.t.* & *v.i.* **·tigued, ·ti·guing** **1.** To tire out; weary. **2.** To weaken, as metal. [< F < L *fatigare* to tire] — **fat·i·ga·ble** (fat/ə·gə·bəl) *adj.*

fat·ling (fat/ling) *n.* A young animal fattened for slaughter.

fat·ten (fat/n) *v.t.* **1.** To cause to become fat. **2.** To make (land) rich by fertilizing. **3.** To add to (a sum of money, etc.) so as to make larger and more attractive. — *v.i.* **4.** To grow fatter, heavier, etc. — **fat'ten·er** *n.*

fat·ten·ing (fat/n·ing) *adj.* That fattens: a *fattening* food.

fat·ty (fat/ē) *adj.* **·ti·er, ·ti·est** **1.** Containing, possessing, or made of fat. **2.** Having the properties of fat; greasy; oily. — **fat'ti·ly** *adv.* — **fat'ti·ness** *n.*

fatty acid *Chem.* Any of a class of organic acids derived from hydrocarbons, and occurring in plant and animal fats.

fa·tu·i·ty (fə·tōō/ə·tē, -tyōō/-) *n.* *pl.* **·ties** **1.** Smug stupidity; asininity. **2.** An utterly stupid action, remark, etc.

fat·u·ous (fach/ōō·əs) *adj.* **1.** Foolish and silly in a self-satisfied way; inane. **2.** Stupid: a *fatuous* grin. [< L *fatuus* foolish] — **fat'u·ous·ly** *adv.* — **fat'u·ous·ness** *n.*

fau·ces (fô/sēz) *n.pl. Anat.* The passage from the back of the mouth onto the pharynx, formed by the membranous, muscular arches extending downward from each side of the soft palate. [< L] — **fau'cal** (-kəl), **fau'cial** (-shəl) *adj.*

fau·cet (fô/sit) *n.* A fixture with an adjustable valve that controls the flow of liquids from a pipe, vat, etc.; tap. [< OF, prob. < *fausser* to break into, create a fault]

faugh (fô) *interj.* An exclamation of disgust, contempt, etc.

fault (fôlt) *n.* **1.** Whatever impairs excellence; a flaw. **2.** A mistake or blunder. **3.** A slight offense; misdeed. **4.** Responsibility for some mishap, blunder, etc.; blame. **5.** *Geol.* A break in the continuity of rock strata or veins of ore. **6.** In tennis, squash, etc., failure to serve the ball into the prescribed area of the opponent's court; also, a ball that is improperly served according to rule. — **at fault 1.** Open to blame; in the wrong; culpable. **2.** At a loss; perplexed; astray.

FAULT (*def.* 5)

3. Off the scent. **— to a fault** Immoderately; excessively. **— to find fault** To seek out and complain about some imperfection, error, misdeed, etc.: often with *with*. **—** *v.t.* 1. *Geol.* To cause a fault in. 2. To find fault with; blame. **—** *v.i.* 3. *Geol.* To crack. [< OF, ult. < L *fallere* to deceive]
fault·find·ing (fôlt′fīn′ding) *n.* The act of one who finds fault. **—** *adj.* Inclined to find fault; critical; carping. **— fault′find′er** *n.*
fault·less (fôlt′lis) *adj.* Free from faults; flawless; perfect. **— fault′less·ly** *adv.* **— fault′less·ness** *n.*
fault·y (fôl′tē) *adj.* **fault·i·er, fault·i·est** Having faults; defective; imperfect. **— fault′i·ly** *adv.* **— fault′i·ness** *n.*
faun (fôn) *n.* In Roman mythology, a woodland deity typically represented as a man having the ears, horns, tail, and hind legs of a goat; satyr. [< L *Faunus*, a rural god]
fau·na (fô′nə) *n. pl.* **·nas** or **·nae** (-nē) The animals living within a given area or environment or during a stated period. [< NL, after L *Fauna*, a rural goddess] **— fau′nal** *adj.*
Faust (foust) In medieval legend, drama, etc., a philosopher who sells his soul to a devil, Mephistopheles, for wisdom.
faux pas (fō pä′) *pl.* **faux pas** (fō päz′, *Fr.* fō pä′) A false step; esp., a breach of etiquette. [< F, lit., false step]
fa·vor (fā′vər) *n.* 1. Helpful or considerate act. 2. An attitude of friendliness or approbation. 3. The condition of being looked upon with liking or approval. 4. Unfair discrimination; narrow partiality: to show *favor.* 5. The condition of leading one's opponent in the score of a game. 6. A small gift presented to each guest on some festive occasion, as at a birthday party. 7. *pl.* Consent to sexual intimacy. **— in favor** Having approval or support: a style much *in favor.* **— in favor of 1.** On the side of. 2. To the furtherance or advantage of. 3. Made out to the benefit of. **— in one's favor** Of such a kind as to help one or promote one's interests. **— out of favor** Lacking approval or support; not liked. **— to find favor** To come to be looked upon with approval or liking; gain acceptance. **—** *v.t.* 1. To do a favor for; oblige. 2. To look upon with approval or liking. 3. To show special consideration to, often in an unfair way. 4. To increase the chances of success of. 5. *Informal* To show a resemblance to in features. 6. To be careful of. Also *Brit.* **fa′vour.** [< OF < L < *favere* to favor] **— fa′vor·er** *n.*
fa·vor·a·ble (fā′vər·ə·bəl) *adj.* 1. Granting something requested or hoped for. 2. Building up hope or confidence. 3. Boding well; promising; approving. 4. Well-disposed or indulgent; friendly. Also *Brit.* **fa′vour·a·ble. — fa′vor·a·ble·ness** *n.* **— fa′vor·a·bly** *adv.*
fa·vored (fā′vərd) *adj.* 1. Treated with or looked upon with friendliness, liking, or approbation. 2. Endowed with esp. good qualities. 3. Having an (indicated) aspect or appearance: an *ill-favored* countenance. Also *Brit.* **fa′voured.**
fa·vor·ite (fā′vər·it) *adj.* Regarded with special favor; preferred. **—** *n.* 1. A person or thing greatly liked or preferred. 2. A person granted special privileges by a high official, etc. 3. In sports, the contestant considered to have the best chance of winning. Also *Brit.* **fa′vour·ite.**
fa·vor·it·ism (fā′vər·ə·tiz′əm) *n.* 1. Preferential treatment, esp. when unjust or narrowly discriminating. 2. The condition of being a favorite. Also *Brit.* **fa′vour·it·ism.**
fawn[1] (fôn) *v.i.* 1. To show cringing fondness, as a dog: often with *on* or *upon.* 2. To show affection or seek favor by or as by cringing. [OE *fahnian*, var. of *fægnian* to rejoice] **— fawn′er** *n.* **— fawn′ing·ly** *adv.*
fawn[2] (fôn) *n.* 1. A young deer, esp. in its first year. 2. The light yellowish brown color of a young deer. **—** *adj.* Light yellowish brown. [< OF < L *fetus* offspring]
fay (fā) *n.* A fairy. [< OF < L *fatum* fate]
faze (fāz) *v.t.* **fazed, faz·ing** *U.S. Informal* To worry; disconcert. [Var. of dial. E *fease*, OE *fēsian* to frighten]
fe·al·ty (fē′əl·tē) *n. pl.* **·ties** 1. The obligation of fidelity owed to a feudal lord by his vassal or tenant. 2. Faithfulness; loyalty. [< OF < L *fidelitas*]
fear (fir) *n.* 1. An agitated feeling aroused by awareness of actual or threatening danger, trouble, etc.; dread; terror. 2. An uneasy feeling that something may happen contrary to one's desires. 3. A feeling of deep, reverential awe and dread. 4. A continuing state or attitude of fright, dread, or alarmed concern: to live in *fear.* 5. The possibility that something dreaded or unwanted may occur: There is no *fear* that such a thing will happen. **— for fear of** So as to avoid or keep from happening. **— for fear that** (or **lest**) So that ... not: He held her hand *for fear that* she would fall. **—** *v.t.* 1. To be frightened of. 2. To be uneasy or apprehensive over (an unwanted or unpleasant possibility). 3. To have a deep, reverential awe of. **—** *v.i.* 4. To feel dread or terror. 5. To feel uneasy. [OE *fær* peril] **— fear′er** *n.*
fear·ful (fir′fəl) *adj.* 1. Filled with dread or terror. 2. Filled with uneasiness; apprehensive. 3. Filled with deep, reverential awe. 4. Causing dread or terror; terrifying; frightening. 5. Showing fear; moved by fear: a *fearful* look. 6. *Informal* Extremely bad. 6. Going to extremes: a *fearful* drinker. **— fear′ful·ly** *adv.* **— fear′ful·ness** *n.*

fear·less (fir′lis) *adj.* Devoid of fear; not at all afraid. **— fear′less·ly** *adv.* **— fear′less·ness** *n.*
fear·some (fir′səm) *adj.* 1. Causing fear; alarming. 2. Timid; frightened. **— fear′some·ly** *adv.* **— fear′some·ness** *n.*
fea·sance (fē′zəns) *n. Law* Fulfillment of a condition, obligation, etc. [< AF < F < L *facere* to do]
fea·si·ble (fē′zə·bəl) *adj.* 1. Capable of being put into effect or accomplished; practicable: a *feasible* project. 2. Capable of being successfully utilized; suitable. 3. Fairly probable; likely: a *feasible* explanation. [< OF < F < L *facere*] **— fea′si·bil′i·ty, fea′si·ble·ness** *n.* **— fea′si·bly** *adv.*
feast (fēst) *n.* 1. A sumptuous meal. 2. Something affording great pleasure to the senses or intellect. 3. An elaborate banquet for many persons. 4. A day or days of celebration regularly set aside for a religious purpose or in honor of some person, event, or thing; also **feast day.** **—** *v.t.* 1. To give a feast for; entertain lavishly. 2. To delight; gratify. **—** *v.i.* 3. To partake of a feast; eat heartily. 4. To dwell delightedly, as on a painting. [< OF < L *festa*, neut. pl. of *festus* joyful < *feriae* holidays] **— feast′er** *n.*
feat (fēt) *n.* A notable act, as one displaying skill or daring. **— Syn.** See ACT. [< OF *fait* < L *factum*. See FACT.]
feath·er (feth′ər) *n.* 1. Any of the horny, elongated structures that form the plumage of birds and much of the wing surface. 2. *pl.* Plumage. 3. *pl.* Dress; attire. 4. A lock or tuft of hair resembling a feather. 5. The hairy fringe on the legs and tails of some dogs. 6. A feather or feathers fastened to the shaft of an arrow to guide its flight. 7. Something resembling a bird's feather, as a key, wedge, etc. 8. Class or species; kind: birds of a *feather.* 9. The act of feathering (an oar blade or propeller). **— a feather in one's cap** An achievement to be proud of. **— in full feather** In full force; fully equipped. **— in high, fine,** or **good feather** In good spirits or health. **—** *v.t.* 1. To fit with a feather, as an arrow. 2. To cover, adorne, line, or fringe with feathers. 3. To join by a tongue-and-groove joint. 4. In rowing, to turn (the oar blade) following each stroke so that the blade is more or less horizontal as it is carried back to the position for reentering the water. 5. *Aeron.* To change the pitch of (a propeller) so that the blades are parallel with the line of flight. **—** *v.i.* 6. To grow feathers or become covered with feathers. 7. To move, spread, or expand like feathers. 8. To feather an oar or propeller blade. **— to feather one's nest** To grow prosperous. [OE *fether*] **— feath′ered** *adj.*
feather bed A mattress stuffed with feathers or down.
feath·er·bed·ding (feth′ər·bed′ing) *n.* The practice of requiring the employment of more workers than are needed so as to create more jobs and prevent unemployment.
feath·er·brain (feth′ər·brān′) *n.* A flighty, stupid, or mentally unbalanced individual. **— feath′er·brained** *adj.*
feath·er·edge (feth′ər·ej′) *n.* A very thin, tapering edge, as of a planed board. **— feath′er·edged** *adj.*
feath·er·stitch (feth′ər·stich′) *n.* An embroidery stitch resembling a feather, made by taking one or more short stitches alternately on either side of a straight line. **—** *v.t. & v.i.* To embroider with such a stitch.
feath·er·weight (feth′ər·wāt′) *n.* 1. A boxer or wrestler weighing between 118 pounds and 127 pounds. 2. Any person or thing relatively light in weight or size. **—** *adj.* 1. Of or like a featherweight. 2. Insignificant; trivial.
feath·er·y (feth′ər·ē) *adj.* 1. Provided with or as if with feathers; feathered. 2. Suggestive of feathers in lightness, etc. **— feath′er·i·ness** *n.*
fea·ture (fē′chər) *n.* 1. A distinctive part of the face, as the eyes, nose, or mouth. 2. *Usu. pl.* The overall appearance or structure of a face. 3. A distinguishing mark, part, or quality. 4. A full-length motion picture, esp. a principal attraction. 5. Anything given special prominence; as: **a** A special article, department, etc., in a magazine or newspaper. **b** An item publicized, as during a sale. **c** A special attraction, as on a program, etc. **—** *v.t.* **·tured, ·tur·ing** 1. To give special prominence to. 2. To be a distinctive characteristic of. 3. *Slang* To form an idea of; imagine. [< OF < L *facere* to do] **— fea′ture·less** *adj.*
fea·tured (fē′chərd) *adj.* 1. Having (specified) facial characteristics: *hard-featured.* 2. Presented as a special or central attraction.
febri- *combining form* Fever. Also, before vowels, **febr-.** [< L *febris* fever]
fe·brif·ic (fə·brif′ik) *adj.* 1. Causing fever. 2. Feverish.
feb·ri·fuge (feb′rə·fyōōj) *n.* A medicine efficacious in reducing or removing fever. **—** *adj.* Reducing or removing fever. [< F < L *febris* + *fugare* to drive away]
fe·brile (fē′brəl, feb′rəl) *adj.* Feverish.
Feb·ru·ar·y (feb′rōō·er′ē) *n. pl.* **·ar·ies** or **·ar·ys** The second month of the year, having twenty-eight, or, in leap years, twenty-nine days. Abbr. *F., Feb, Feb.* [< L *februa, a Roman purificatory festival celebrated on Feb. 15*]
fe·ces (fē′sēz) *n.pl.* 1. Animal excrement; ordure. 2. Any foul refuse matter or sediment. Also spelled *faeces.* [< L < *faex, faecis* sediment] **— fe′cal** (-kəl) *adj.*

feck·less (fek′lis) *adj.* **1.** Devoid of energy or effectiveness; feeble. **2.** Devoid of vitality; listless. **3.** Careless and irresponsible. **—feck′less·ly** *adv.* **—feck′less·ness** *n.*

fec·u·lent (fek′yə-lənt) *adj.* Turbid or foul with impurities; filthy. [< L *faex* dregs] **—fec′u·lence, fec′u·len·cy** *n.*

fe·cund (fē′kənd, fek′ənd) *adj.* Fruitful; prolific. [< OF < L *fecundus* fruitful] **—fe·cun·di·ty** (fi-kun′də-tē) *n.*

fe·cun·date (fē′kən-dāt, fek′ən-) *v.t.* **·dat·ed, ·dat·ing 1.** To make fruitful. **2.** To fertilize. **—fe′cun·da′tion** *n.*

fed (fed) Past tense and past participle of FEED. **—fed up** *Slang* Surfeited with something to an extreme degree.

fed·er·al (fed′ər-əl) *adj.* **1.** Of, relating to, or formed by an agreement among two or more states, groups, etc., to merge into a union in which control of common affairs is granted to a central authority, with each member retaining jurisdiction over its own internal affairs; also, of, relating to, or supporting such a union or central government. **2.** Of or pertaining to a confederacy (def. 1). **—** *n.* An advocate or supporter of a federal union or federal government. [< F < L *foedus, -eris* compact, league] **—fed′er·al·ly** *adv.*

Fed·er·al (fed′ər-əl) *adj.* **1.** Of, relating to, or supporting the central government of a specific country, as of the U.S. **2.** Of, relating to, or loyal to the Union cause in the American Civil War. **3.** Of, relating to, or supporting the Federalist Party. **—** *n.* **1.** One who favored the Union cause in the Civil War. **2.** A Federalist. **—Fed′er·al·ly** *adv.*

Federal Bureau of Investigation An agency of the U.S. government that investigates violations of Federal laws.

fed·er·al·ism (fed′ər-əl-iz′əm) *n.* The doctrine, system, or principle of federal union or federal government; also, advocacy or support of this doctrine, system, or principle.

fed·er·al·ist (fed′ər-əl-ist) *n.* An advocate or supporter of federalism. **—** *adj.* Of or relating to federalism or federalists: also **fed′er·al·is′tic.**

Fed·er·al·ist (fed′ər-əl-ist) *n.* **1.** One who supported the federal union of the American colonies and the adoption of the Constitution of the United States. **2.** A member of the Federalist Party. **—Fed′er·al·ism** *n.* **—** *adj.* Of or relating to the Federalist Party or Federalists: also **Fed′er·al·is′tic.**

Federalist Party A political party (1787–1830) that advocated the adoption of the U.S. Constitution and the formation of a strong national government. Also **Federal Party.**

fed·er·al·ize (fed′ər-əl-īz′) *v.t.* **·ized, ·iz·ing** To unite in a federal union; federate. **—fed′er·al·i·za′tion** *n.*

fed·er·ate (*v.* fed′ə-rāt; *adj.* fed′ər-it) *v.t. & v.i.* **·at·ed, ·at·ing** To unite in a federal union. [See FEDERAL.]

fed·er·a·tion (fed′ə-rā′shon) *n.* **1.** The joining together of two or more states, groups, etc., into a federal union or a confederacy. **2.** A league or confederacy.

fe·do·ra (fə-dôr′ə, -dō′rə) *n.* A soft hat, usu. of felt, with a curved brim and a crown creased lengthwise. [after *Fédora,* a play by V. Sardou, French dramatist]

fee (fē) *n.* **1.** A charge, compensation, or payment for something, as: **a** A sum charged for professional services: medical *fee.* **b** A sum charged for some privilege: membership *fee.* **c** A sum charged for admission: an entrance *fee.* **d** A gratuity or tip. **— to hold in fee** To have full and absolute possession of. **—** *v.t.* **feed, fee·ing** To pay a fee to. [< AF, var. of OF *fé, fief* < Med.L *feudum* fief, property, money]

fee·ble (fē′bəl) *adj.* **·bler, ·blest 1.** Lacking strength; very weak. **2.** Lacking energy, direction, or effectiveness: *feeble* efforts. **3.** Lacking point or substance: a *feeble* joke. **4.** Indistinct; faint: a *feeble* light. [< OF < L *flebilis* lamentable < *flere* to weep] **—fee′ble·ness** *n.* **—fee′bly** *adv.*

fee·ble-mind·ed (fē′bəl-mīn′did) *adj.* Mentally deficient. **—fee′ble-mind′ed·ly** *adv.* **—fee′ble-mind′ed·ness** *n.*

feed (fēd) *v.* **fed, feed·ing** *v.t.* **1.** To supply with food: to *feed* a hungry family. **2.** To give (something) as food or nourishment to: to *feed* carrots to rabbits. **3.** To serve as food or nourishment for; also, to produce food for: acreage that will *feed* many. **4.** To keep supplied, as with fuel: to *feed* a fire; also, to keep supplying: to *feed* data into a computing machine. **5.** To keep or make more intense or greater: to *feed* suspicions. **6.** To gratify; feast: to *feed* one's eyes on beauty. **—** *v.i.* **7.** To eat: said chiefly of animals. **— to feed on** (or **upon**) **1.** To consume (something) as food; use as food: said chiefly of animals. **2.** To draw support, encouragement, etc., from: to *feed on* hope. **—** *n.* **1.** Food given to animals. **2.** The amount of fodder, etc., given at one time. **3.** Material supplied, as to a machine. **4.** The supplying of such material. **5.** A mechanical part, as of a sewing machine, that keeps supplying material to be worked on, etc. **6.** *Informal* A meal. **— off one's feed** *Slang* Having little appetite. [OE *fēdan* < *fōda* food] **—feed′er** *n.*

feed·back (fēd′bak′) *n.* The return of part of the output of a system into the input for purposes of modification and control of the output, as in electronic amplifiers, automatic machines, certain biological and psychological processes, etc.

feel (fēl) *v.* **felt, feel·ing** *v.t.* **1.** To examine or explore with the hands, fingers, etc. **2.** To be aware of touch: to *feel* drops of sweat on one's forehead. **3.** To experience consciously (an emotion, pain, etc.): to *feel* joy. **4.** To be emotionally affected by: to *feel* disgrace deeply. **5.** To perceive or be aware of through thought: to *feel* the need for reform. **6.** To think; suppose; judge: I *feel* that you should do this. **7.** To have one's whole being respond to through understanding, etc. **8.** To experience the force or impact of: to *feel* the full weight of an attack. **—** *v.i.* **9.** To have physical sensation. **10.** To produce a sensory impression of being hard, soft, cold, hot, etc. **11.** To experience consciously the sensation or condition of being: He *feels* cold; to *feel* joyful. **12.** To produce an indicated overall condition, impression, or reaction: It *feels* good to be home. **13.** To experience compassion or pity: with *for*: I *feel* for you. **14.** To have convictions or opinions: to *feel* strongly about an issue. **15.** To search for by touching; grope: to *feel* around a darkened room. **— to feel like** *Informal* To have a desire or inclination for. **— to feel out 1.** To try to learn indirectly and cautiously the viewpoint, opinions, etc., of (a person); sound out. **2.** To explore the nature of (a situation, etc.) in a cautious way. **— to feel up to** To seem to oneself to be capable of or ready for. **—** *n.* **1.** Perception by touch or contact. **2.** The quality of something as perceived by touch. **3.** A sensation or impression. **4.** The act of feeling. [OE *fēlan*]

feel·er (fē′lər) *n.* **1.** One who or that which feels. **2.** Any action, hint, proposal, etc., intended to draw out the views or intentions of another. **3.** *Zool.* An organ of touch.

feel·ing (fē′ling) *n.* **1.** The faculty by which one perceives sensations of pain, pressure, heat, etc. **2.** Any particular sensation of this sort: a *feeling* of warmth. **3.** An emotion: a *feeling* of joy, sadness, etc. **4.** A sensation or awareness of something: a *feeling* of insecurity. **5.** A capacity to feel deeply: a woman of *feeling.* **6.** *pl.* Sensibilities; sensitivities: His *feelings* are easily hurt. **7.** A generous, sympathetic attitude; compassion. **8.** An impression produced upon a person by an object, place, etc. **9.** An opinion or sentiment; also, a foreboding. **—** *adj.* **1.** Having sensation; sentient. **2.** Having warm emotions; sympathetic: a *feeling* heart. **3.** Marked by or indicating emotion. **—feel′ing·ly** *adv.*

feet (fēt) Plural of FOOT. **— on one's** (or **its**) **feet 1.** In or into a condition of stability; well-established: to get a business *on its feet.* **2.** In or into a condition of restored health: to get a patient *on his feet.* **3.** Standing or walking.

feign (fān) *v.t.* **1.** To make a false show of; sham: to *feign* madness. **2.** To think up (a false story, a lying excuse, etc.) and give out as true; fabricate. **3.** To imitate so as to deceive. **—** *v.i.* **4.** To make pretense of something. [< OF < L *fingere* to shape] **—feigned** *adj.* **—feign′er** *n.*

feint (fānt) *n.* **1.** A deceptive appearance or movement; a ruse or pretense. **2.** An apparent or pretended blow or attack meant to divert attention. **—** *v.i.* To make a feint. [< F *feinte,* pp. of *feindre* < L *fingere* to shape]

feld·spar (feld′spär, fel′spär) *n.* Any one of a group of crystalline materials largely made up of silicates of aluminum: sometimes spelled *felspar.* Also **feld′spath** (-spath). [Partial trans. of G < *feld* field + *spat* spar] **—feld·spath′ic, feld·spath′ose** (-ōs) *adj.*

fe·lic·i·tate (fə-lis′ə-tāt) *v.t.* **·tat·ed, ·tat·ing** To congratulate. [< L < *felix, -icis* happy] **—fe·lic′i·ta′tion** *n.*

fe·lic·i·tous (fə-lis′ə-təs) *adj.* **1.** Most appropriate; apt. **2.** Using an agreeably pertinent or effective manner or style. **—fe·lic′i·tous·ly** *adv.* **—fe·lic′i·tous·ness** *n.*

fe·lic·i·ty (fə-lis′ə-tē) *n.* *pl.* **·ties 1.** Happiness; bliss. **2.** An instance of happiness. **3.** A source of happiness. **4.** An agreeably pertinent or effective manner or style. **5.** A pleasantly appropriate remark. [< OF < L *felix* happy]

fe·line (fē′līn) *adj.* **1.** Of or relating to a cat, as the domestic cat or lions, tigers, and leopards. **2.** Resembling a cat, as in stealthiness. **—** *n.* An animal of the cat family: also **fe·lid** (fē′lid). [< L *felis* cat] **—fe′line·ly** *adv.* **—fe′line·ness, fe·lin·i·ty** (fə-lin′ə-tē) *n.*

fell¹ (fel) Past tense of FALL.

fell² (fel) *v.t.* **felled, fell·ing 1.** To strike and cause to fall down. **2.** To cut down (timber). **3.** In sewing, to finish (a seam) with a flat, smooth strip made by joining edges, folding them under, and stitching flat. **—** *n.* **1.** The timber cut down during one season. **2.** In sewing, a felled seam. [OE *fellan,* causative of *feallan* to fall] **—fell′a·ble** *adj.*

fell³ (fel) *adj.* Cruel; vicious; inhuman. [< OF *fel* cruel]

fell⁴ (fel) *n.* The skin of an animal, esp. as covered with its natural hair, wool, etc. [OE *hide*]

fel·lah (fel′ə) *n.* *pl.* **fel·lahs** or *Arabic* **fel·la·hin, fel·la·heen** (fel′ə-hēn′) In Arabic-speaking countries, a peasant or laborer. [< Arabic *fellāh*]

fell·er (fel′ər) *n.* **1.** One who or that which fells. **2.** A sewing-machine attachment for the felling of seams.

fel·low (fel′ō) *n.* **1.** A man or boy: often in informal address. **2.** *U.S. Informal* The sweetheart of a woman or girl. **3.** A person in general; anybody; one. **4.** A comrade or companion. **5.** A person viewed as being of little importance or worth. **6.** A partner or accomplice: *fellows* in crime. **7.** An individual belonging to the same kind, class, or group as oneself. **8.** Either one of a pair; mate. **9.** A member of one of several learned societies. **10.** A graduate student of a university or college who, in recognition of merit, is granted financial assistance to pursue further study. — *adj.* Joined through some common occupation, interests, objectives, etc.: *fellow* citizens. [OE *fēolaga* business partner]

fel·low·ship (fel′ō-ship) *n.* **1.** Companionship; association. **2.** The condition or fact of having common interests, ideals, experiences, etc. **3.** A body of individuals joined together through similar interests, beliefs, etc.; brotherhood. **4.** The status of being a fellow at a university or college; also, the financial grant made to a fellow. — *v* ·shiped or ·shipped, ·ship·ing or ·ship·ping *Rare v.t.* **1.** To grant fellowship to. — *v.i.* **2.** To join in fellowship with others.

fellow traveler One who favors the ideology or program of a particular group without being a member.

fel·ly (fel′ē) *n. pl.* ·lies A segment of or the entire rim of a wooden wheel, in which the spokes are inserted. [OE *felg*]

fel·on[1] (fel′ən) *n. Law* One who has committed a felony. — *adj. Poetic* Wicked, or cruel. [< OF *felon* base]

fel·on[2] (fel′ən) *n. Pathol.* An inflammation of a finger or toe in the terminal joint or at the cuticle. [? < FELON[1]]

fe·lo·ni·ous (fə-lō′nē-əs) *adj.* **1.** *Law* **a** Of, relating to, or involving a felony: *felonious* intent. **b** Constituting, resembling, or having the nature of a felony: *felonious* assault. **2.** *Poetic* Wicked. — **fe·lo′ni·ous·ly** *adv.* — **fe·lo′ni·ous·ness** *n.*

fel·o·ny (fel′ə-nē) *n. pl.* ·nies *Law* Any of several grave crimes, as murder, rape, arson, or burglary, for which a punishment greater than that for a misdemeanor is provided.

fel·spar (fel′spär) See FELDSPAR.

felt[1] (felt) Past tense and past participle of FEEL.

felt[2] (felt) *n.* **1.** An unwoven fabric made by matting together fibers of wool, fur, or hair through pressure and the use of heat, chemicals, etc. **2.** Something made of felt, as a hat. — *adj.* Relating to, made of, or resembling felt. — *v.t.* **1.** To make into felt. **2.** To overlay with felt. — *v.i.* **3.** To become matted together like felt. [OE]

fe·luc·ca (fə-luk′ə, fe-) *n.* A small, swift vessel propelled by lateen sails and by oars. [< Ital. < Arabic *fulk* ship]

FELUCCA

fe·male (fē′māl) *adj.* **1.** Of or pertaining to the sex that brings forth young or produces ova. **2.** Typical of or suitable to this sex; feminine. **3.** Made up of women and girls: the *female* portion of the population. **4.** *Bot.* Designating a plant that has a pistil but no stamen and that is capable of being fertilized and of producing fruit. **5.** *Mech.* Denoting or having a bore or slot designed to receive a correlated inserted part, called *male*, as some electric plugs. — *n.* **1.** A human being of the female sex. **2.** A female animal or plant. [< OF < L *femina* woman]

fem·i·nine (fem′ə-nin) *adj.* **1.** Of or pertaining to the female sex; female. **2.** Of or pertaining to women and girls; typical of or appropriate to women and girls: *feminine* gentleness. **3.** Lacking manly qualities; effeminate. **4.** *Gram.* Applicable to females only or to persons or things classified, as in declension, as female. — *n. Gram.* **1.** The feminine gender. **2.** A word or form belonging to the feminine gender. — **fem′i·nine·ly** *adv.* — **fem′i·nine·ness** *n.*

feminine rhyme Rhyme in which the primary stress falls upon the next to the last syllable, as in *clever, never.*

fem·i·nin·i·ty (fem′ə-nin′ə-tē) *n. pl.* ·ties **1.** The quality or state of being feminine. **2.** A feminine trait.

fem·i·nism (fem′ə-niz′əm) *n.* **1.** A doctrine advocating the granting of the same social, political, and economic rights to women as the ones granted to men; also, a movement to win these. **2.** *Med.* The existence of female characteristics in the male. — **fem′i·nist** *n. & adj.* — **fem′i·nis′tic** *adj.*

fem·i·nize (fem′ə-nīz) *v.t. & v.i.* ·nized, ·niz·ing To make or become feminine or effeminate. — **fem′i·ni·za′tion** *n.*

femme (fàm) *n. French* Woman; wife.

femme fa·tale (fà·tàl′) *French* A seductive woman.

fe·mur (fē′mər) *n. pl.* fe·murs or fem·o·ra (fem′ər·ə) *Anat.* The long bone extending from the pelvis to the knee. Also called *thighbone.* For illustration see PELVIS. [< L, thigh] — **fem·o·ral** (fem′ər·əl) *adj.*

fen (fen) *n.* A marsh; bog. [OE *fenn*]

fence (fens) *n.* **1.** A structure of rails, stakes, strung wire, etc., erected as an enclosure, barrier, or boundary. **2.** Fencing. **3.** Skill at making quick, effective remarks or retorts, as in a discussion or debate. **4.** A dealer in stolen goods. — **on the fence** Unwilling or unable to commit oneself one way

or the other. — *v.* fenced, fenc·ing *v.t.* **1.** To enclose with or as with a fence. **2.** To cause to be separated by or as by a fence. — *v.i.* **3.** To practice the art of fencing. **4.** To avoid giving direct answers. **5.** To deal in stolen goods. [Aphetic var. of DEFENCE] — **fence′less** *adj.* — **fenc′er** *n.*

fenc·ing (fen′sing) *n.* **1.** The art or practice of using a foil, sword, or similar weapon. **2.** The art or practice of making quick, effective remarks or retorts, as in a debate. **3.** Material used in making fences; also, fences collectively.

fend (fend) *v.t.* **1.** To ward off; parry: usu. with *off.* — *v.i.* **2.** To offer resistance; parry. **3.** *Informal* To provide: shift: with *for:* to *fend* for oneself. [Aphetic var. of DEFEND]

fend·er (fen′dər) *n.* **1.** One who or that which fends or wards off. **2.** *U.S.* A part projecting over each wheel of a car or other vehicle, designed to keep water, mud, dirt, etc., from being thrown upwards. **3.** A metal guard set before an open fire. **4.** A part projecting from the front of a locomotive or streetcar, designed to push obstructions from the tracks.

Fe·ni·an (fē′nē·ən, fēn′yən) *n.* A member of an organization founded in New York about 1857 to seek independence for Ireland. — *adj.* Of Fenians. [< OIrish *fene* Irishman]

fen·nel (fen′əl) *n.* **1.** A tall herb of the parsley family that produces aromatic seeds used in cookery and pharmacy. **2.** The seeds of this plant. [OE < L *faeniculum* fennel]

feod (fyōōd) See FEUD[2].

feoff (*v.* fef; *n.* fēf) *Law v.t.* feoffed, feoff·ing To give or grant a fief to. — *n.* A fief. [See FIEF.] — **feof′fer** *n.* — **feoff′ment** *n.*

-fer *combining form* One who or that which bears: *conifer.* [< L < *ferre* to bear]

fe·ral (fir′əl) *adj.* **1.** Not tame nor domesticated; wild. **2.** Of, relating to, or typical of a wild beast; savage. [< LL *feralis* < L *fera* wild beast]

fer-de-lance (fâr′də-làns′) *n.* A large, venomous snake of tropical South America and Martinique. [< F, lance iron]

fer·ment (*n.* fûr′mənt; *v.* fər-ment′) *n.* **1.** Any substance or agent producing fermentation, as enzymes, yeast, certain bacteria, etc. **2.** Fermentation. **3.** Excitement or agitation. — *v.t.* **1.** To produce fermentation in. **2.** To excite with emotion or passion; agitate. — *v.i.* **3.** To undergo fermentation; work. **4.** To be agitated, as with emotion; seethe. [< F < L *fervere* to boil] — **fer·ment′a·ble** *adj.* — **fer·ment′a·bil′i·ty** *n.* — **fer·ment′a·tive** *adj.*

fer·men·ta·tion (fûr′mən·tā′shən) *n.* **1.** *Chem.* The gradual decomposition of organic compounds induced by the action of various ferments; specifically, the conversion of glucose into ethyl alcohol through the action of zymase. **2.** Commotion, agitation, or excitement.

fer·mi (fer′mē, fûr′-) *n. Physics* A unit for the measurement of the radii of nuclear atomic particles, equal to 10^{-13} centimeter. [after E. *Fermi*]

fer·mi·um (fer′mē·əm, fûr′-) *n.* A radioactive element (symbol Fm), artificially produced by the bombardment of einsteinium with alpha particles. See ELEMENT. [after E. *Fermi*]

fern (fûrn) *n.* A plant that bears no flowers or seeds, having roots, stems, and large, feathery fronds, and reproducing by means of asexual spores. [OE *fearn*] — **fern′y** *adj.*

fern·er·y (fûr′nər·ē) *n. pl.* ·er·ies **1.** A place in which ferns are grown. **2.** A standing growth or bed of ferns.

fe·ro·cious (fə-rō′shəs) *adj.* **1.** Extremely savage, fierce, bloodthirsty, or cruel. **2.** *Informal* Very intense: *ferocious* heat. [< L *ferox, ferocis* fierce + -OUS] — **fe·ro′cious·ly** *adv.* — **fe·ro′cious·ness** *n.*

fe·roc·i·ty (fə-ros′ə·tē) *n. pl.* ·ties The state or quality of being ferocious. [< F < L *ferox* fierce]

-ferous *combining form* Bearing or producing: *coniferous.* [< -FER + -OUS]

fer·rate (fer′āt) *n. Chem.* A salt of ferric acid. [< L *ferrum* iron + -ATE[3]]

fer·ret (fer′it) *n.* A small, red-eyed polecat of Europe, often domesticated and used in hunting rodents and other vermin. — *v.t.* **1.** To search out by careful investigation: with *out.* **2.** To drive out of hiding or hunt with a ferret. — *v.i.* **3.** To search. **4.** To hunt by means of ferrets. [< OF < LL < L *fur* thief] — **fer′ret·er** *n.* — **fer′ret·y** *adj.*

FERRET
(Body about 14 inches long; tail 5 inches)

ferri- *combining form Chem.* Containing iron in the ferric condition. [Var. of FERRO-]

fer·ric (fer′ik) *adj. Chem.* **1.** Pertaining to iron. **2.** Pertaining to or designating compounds of iron in its higher valence. [< L *ferrum* iron + -IC]

Fer·ris wheel (fer′is) *U.S.* A giant, vertical, power-driven wheel that revolves on a stationary axle and has hanging seats in which passengers ride for amusement. Also **ferris wheel.** [after G. W. G. Ferris, 1859–96, U.S. engineer]

fer·rite (fer′īt) *n.* **1.** *Geol.* A substance of uncertain composition that is found in igneous rocks and apparently contains iron. **2.** *Chem.* One of several compounds, often magnetic, containing ferric oxide. **3.** *Metall.* The pure metallic constituent in iron and steel. [< L *ferrum* iron + -ITE]

ferro- *combining form* **1.** Derived from, containing, or alloyed with iron. **2.** *Chem.* Containing iron in the ferrous condition. [< L *ferrum* iron]

fer·ro·con·crete (fer′ō·kon′krēt, -kon·krēt′) *n.* Reinforced concrete.

fer·ro·mag·net·ic (fer′ō·mag·net′ik) *adj. Physics* Highly magnetic, as is iron. — **fer′ro·mag′ne·tism** *n.*

fer·ro·man·ga·nese (fer′ō·mang′gə·nēs, -nēz) *n.* An alloy of iron rich in manganese, used in making tough steel.

fer·rous (fer′əs) *adj. Chem.* Of or pertaining to iron, esp. bivalent iron, where its combining value is lowest: *ferrous chloride*, FeCl₂. [< L *ferrum* iron + -OUS]

fer·ru·gi·nous (fə·rōō′jə·nəs) *adj.* **1.** Of or like iron. **2.** Rust-colored. [< L *ferrum* iron]

fer·rule (fer′əl, -ōōl) *n.* A metal ring or cap used on or near the end of a stick, as of a cane or a tool handle, to protect the end or reinforce the stick. — *v.t.* **·ruled, ·rul·ing** To equip with a ferrule. [< OF < L *viriae* bracelets]

fer·rum (fer′əm) *n.* Iron. [< L]

fer·ry (fer′ē) *n. pl.* **·ries 1.** A boat or other craft used in conveying people, cars, or merchandise across a river or other narrow extent of water. **2.** Delivery of a boat or other craft to a user under its own motive power. — *v.* **·ried, ·ry·ing** *v.t.* **1.** To convey across a river, etc., by a boat or other craft. **2.** To cross (a river, etc.) in a boat or other craft. **3.** To deliver by ferry (def. 2). — *v.i.* **4.** To cross a river, etc., by or as by a ferry. [OE *ferian* to carry, convey]

fer·ry·boat (fer′ē·bōt) *n.* A boat used as a ferry.

fer·tile (fûr′təl, *esp. Brit.* -tīl) *adj.* **1.** Yielding or capable of producing abundant crops or vegetation: *fertile* land. **2.** Reproducing or able to reproduce. **3.** Inventive or productive: a *fertile* talent. [< OF < L *fertilis* < *ferre* to bear] — **fer′·tile·ly** *adv.* — **fer′tile·ness** *n.*

fer·til·i·ty (fər·til′ə·tē) *n.* The state or quality of being fertile; productiveness.

fer·til·ize (fûr′təl·īz) *v.t.* **·ized, ·iz·ing 1.** To make fertile; cause to be productive or fruitful. **2.** To cause (a female reproductive cell to begin development of a new individual. **3.** To spread manure, nitrates, or other enriching material on (land). *adj.* — **fer′til·i·za′tion** (-tۈl·ə·zā′shən) *n.*

fer·til·iz·er (fûr′təl·ī′zər) *n.* That which fertilizes; esp., a material, as manure or nitrates, used to enrich land.

fer·ule (fer′əl, -ōōl) *n.* A flat stick or ruler sometimes used for punishing children. — *v.t.* **·uled, ·ul·ing** To punish with a ferule. [< L *ferula* whip, rod]

fer·vent (fûr′vənt) *adj.* **1.** Moved by or showing great warmth or intensity, as of emotion or enthusiasm; ardent. **2.** *Poetic* Very hot; burning. [< L *fervere* to boil] — **fer′·vent·ly** *adv.* — **fer′ven·cy, fer′vent·ness** *n.*

fer·vid (fûr′vid) *adj.* **1.** Fervent, esp. to an extreme degree; most impassioned. **2.** *Poetic* Very hot; burning. [< L *fervere* to boil] — **fer′vid·ly** *adv.* — **fer′vid·ness** *n.*

fer·vor (fûr′vər) *n.* **1.** Great warmth or intensity, as of emotion; fervency; ardor. **2.** Heat; warmth. Also *Brit.* **fer′·vour.** [< OF < L, violent heat, ardor]

fes·cue (fes′kyōō) *n.* Any of a genus of tough grasses, used for pasturage. [< OF < L *festuca* stalk, straw]

fess (fes) *n. Heraldry* A horizontal band across the middle of an escutcheon. Also **fesse.** [< OF < L *fascia* band]

-fest *combining form Slang* Bout; session: *gabfest.* [< G. *fest* festival]

fes·tal (fes′təl) *adj.* Pertaining to or typical of a festival, feast, or holiday. [< OF < L *festum* feast] — **fes′tal·ly** *adv.*

fes·ter (fes′tər) *v.i.* **1.** To develop pus; ulcerate. **2.** To or become rotten and foul. **3.** To be a constant source of vexation or irritation; rankle. — *v.i.* **4.** To cause to fester. — *n.* A small, ulcerous sore. [< OF < L *fistula* ulcer]

fes·ti·val (fes′tə·vəl) *n.* **1.** A particular feast, holiday, or celebration. **2.** Any occasion for rejoicing or feasting. **3.** A special series of performances, exhibitions, etc.: a Shakespeare *festival.* — *adj.* Festive. [See FESTIVE.]

fes·tive (fes′tiv) *adj.* Of, relating to, or suitable for a feast or other celebration. [< L < *festum* feast < *festus* joyful] — **fes′tive·ly** *adv.* — **fes′tive·ness** *n.*

fes·tiv·i·ty (fes·tiv′ə·tē) *n. pl.* **·ties 1.** A festival. **2.** Gladness and rejoicing. **3.** *pl.* Festive merrymaking.

fes·toon (fes·tōōn′) *n.* **1.** Flowers or leaves, or colored paper, ribbon, etc., hanging in loops between two points. **2.** An ornamental carving, sculpture, etc., representing this. — *v.t.* To decorate, fashion into, or link together by festoons. [< F < Ital. *festa* feast] — **fes·toon′er·y** *n.*

fe·tal (fēt′l) *adj.* Of or typical of a fetus: also spelled *foetal.*

fetch (fech) *v.t.* **1.** To go after and bring back. **2.** To draw forth; elicit. **3.** To draw in (breath); also, to give forth (a sigh, groan, etc.); heave. **4.** To infer. **5.** To cost or sell for.

6. *Informal* To attract or delight. **7.** *Informal* To give or deal (a blow, slap, etc.). **8.** *Naut.* To arrive at (a port, etc.). — *v.i.* **9.** To go after something and bring it back. **10.** *Naut.* To hold to a particular course; also, to swing around; veer. — *n.* **1.** The act of fetching. **2.** A trick; stratagem. [OE *feccan*] — **fetch′er** *n.*

fetch·ing (fech′ing) *adj. Informal* Very attractive or pleasing; charming. — **fetch′ing·ly** *adv.*

fete (fāt) *n.* **1.** A festival. **2.** An outdoor celebration: esp. a dinner, bazaar, etc. — *v.t.* **fet·ed, fet·ing** To honor with festivities. Also *Brit.* **fête.** [< F *fête*]

fet·id (fet′id) *adj.* Having a foul odor; stinking. [< L *fetere* to stink] — **fet′id·ly** *adv.* — **fet′id·ness** *n.*

fet·ish (fet′ish, fē′tish) *n.* **1.** An object regarded as having magical powers. **2.** Something to which one is devoted excessively or irrationally. **3.** *Psychiatry* Some object not in itself erotic but which is sexually stimulating to certain individuals. Also **fetich.** [< F < Pg. *feitiço* charm]

fet·ish·ism (fet′ish·iz′əm, fē′tish-) *n.* **1.** Superstitious belief in or worship of fetishes. **2.** Excessive or irrational devotion to something. **3.** *Psychiatry* Sexual stimulation produced by an object that is not in itself erotic. Also **fet′ich·ism.** — **fet′ish·ist** *n.* — **fet′ish·is′tic** *adj.*

fet·lock (fet′lok′) *n.* **1.** A tuft of hair growing at the back of the leg of a horse just above the hoof. **2.** The joint of the leg from which this tuft grows: also **fetlock joint.** [ME *fitlock, fetlak,* prob. < LG]

fet·ter (fet′ər) *n.* **1.** A chain or other bond put about the ankles to restrain movement or prevent escape. **2.** *Usu. pl.* Anything checking freedom of movement or expression. — *v.t.* **1.** To put fetters upon. **2.** To prevent the free movement or expression of. [OE *feter, fetor*]

fet·tle (fet′l) *v.t.* **·tled, ·tling** To put in proper order; attend to; arrange. — *n.* Proper condition of health or spirits: in fine *fettle.* [ME *fetlen* to prepare, lit., to gird up]

fe·tus (fē′təs) *n. pl.* **·tus·es** The individual unborn organism carried within the womb in the later stages of its development. Also spelled *foetus.* [< L, a bringing forth]

feud¹ (fyōōd) *n.* A state of bitter hostility existing between two or more individuals, families, etc., usu. lasting over a long period of time. — *v.i.* To take part in a feud. [ME < OF < OHG *fehida* hatred, revenge] — **feud′ist** *n.*

feud² (fyōōd) *n.* In feudal law, a fief: also spelled *feod.* [< Med.L *feudum* fief]

feu·dal (fyōōd′l) *adj.* **1.** Of, relating to, or typical of the feudal system. **2.** Of or relating to a fief. — **feu′dal·ly** *adv.*

feu·dal·ism (fyōōd′l·iz′əm) *n.* The mode of life produced by the feudal system. — **feu′dal·ist** *n.* — **feu′dal·is′tic** *adj.*

feudal system A social, political, and economic system in medieval Europe in which vassals were granted land holdings by their lords in return for military service or the performance of other duties.

feu·da·to·ry (fyōō′də·tôr′ē, -tō′rē) *n. pl.* **·ries** A vassal holding a fief; also, the fief held. — *adj.* **1.** Of or typical of a feudal relationship. **2.** Subject to a feudal lord.

fe·ver (fē′vər) *n.* **1.** A disorder marked by unduly high body temperature, rapid pulse, often delirium, etc. **2.** Any of several diseases that produce this symptom. **3.** Emotional excitement or restless eagerness. ◆ Collateral adjective: *febrile.* — *v.t.* To affect with fever. [OE *fēfer* < L *febris*] — **fe′vered** *adj.*

fever blister A cold sore. Also **fever sore.**

fe·ver·few (fē′vər·fyōō′) *n.* A plant bearing white flowers.

fe·ver·ish (fē′vər·ish) *adj.* **1.** Having a fever, esp. a low fever. **2.** Of or resembling a fever. **3.** Tending to produce fever. **4.** Agitated, uneasy, or restless. Also **fe′ver·ous.** — **fe′ver·ish·ly** *adv.* — **fe′ver·ish·ness** *n.*

fe·ver·wort (fē′vər·wûrt′) *n.* **1.** A perennial herb with brownish purple flowers and a root used medicinally. Also **fe′ver·root′** (-rōōt′, -rŏŏt′). **2.** Boneset, an herb.

few (fyōō) *adj.* Small in number; not very many. — *pron. & n.* A small number; not very many. — **quite a few** A considerable number. — **the few** The minority. [OE *fea* little]

fey (fā) *adj.* **1.** Acting as if enchanted or under a spell. **2.** Suggestive of a sprite. [< F < OF *fae* fairy]

fez (fez) *n. pl.* **fez·zes** A brimless, tapering, felt cap, usu. red and having a black tassel, often worn by Egyptian men. [after *Fez,* a city in Morocco]

fi·a·cre (fē·ä′kər, *Fr.* fyȧ′kr′) *n.* A small hackney coach. [after Hotel *St. Fiacre* in Paris, where they were first hired]

fi·an·cé (fē′än·sā′, fē·än′sā; *Fr.* fē·ȧn·sā′) *n.* A man to whom a woman is engaged to be married. [< F]

fi·an·cée (fē′än·sā′, fē·än′sā; *Fr.* fē·ȧn·sā′) *n.* A woman to whom a man is engaged to be married. [< F]

fi·as·co (fē·as′kō) *n. pl.* **·coes** or **·cos** A complete or humiliating failure. [< Ital., flask]

fi·at (fī′at, -ət) *n.* **1.** A positive and authoritative order or decree. **2.** Authorization. [< L, let it be done]

fiat money Paper money made legal tender by decree, as of a government, and not based on gold or silver reserves.

fib (fib) *n.* A lie about something unimportant. — *v.i.* **fibbed, fib·bing** To tell a fib. [? Alter. of FABLE] — **fib′ber** *n.*

fi·ber (fī′bər) *n.* 1. A fine, relatively long, continuous piece of something, suggestive of a thread, as a filament or asbestos, spun glass, textile or fabric. 2. *Biol.* One of similar filaments that together form animal or plant tissue or parts: a nerve *fiber*. 3. A material made up of fine filaments; also, collectively, the filaments themselves. 4. The particular composition or structure of something. 5. Character: to lack moral *fiber*. Also *Brit.* **fi′bre**. [< F < L *fibra*]

fi·ber·board (fī′bər-bôrd′, -bōrd′) *n.* 1. A tough, pliable building material made of wood fiber or other plant fiber.

Fi·ber·glas (fī′bər-glas′, -gläs′) *n.* A flexible, nonflammable material of glass spun into filaments, used for textiles, insulation, etc.: a trade name. Also **fi′ber·glas′, fi′ber·glass′**.

fibr- See FIBRO-

fi·bril (fī′brəl) *n.* 1. A minute fiber. 2. *Bot.* A root hair. [< NL < L *fibra* fiber] — **fi·bril·lar** (fī′brə-lər) *adj.*

fi·bril·la (fī-bril′ə) *n.* *pl.* **·bril·lae** (-bril′ē) A fibril. [< NL]

fi·bril·la·tion (fī′brə-lā′shən) *n.* 1. The formation of fibers. 2. *Pathol.* Rapid contraction of muscle fibers of the heart.

fi·brin (fī′brin) *n.* *Biochem.* An insoluble protein that promotes the clotting of blood. — **fi·bri·nous** (fī′brə-nəs) *adj.*

fi·brin·o·gen (fī-brin′ə-jən) *n.* *Biochem.* A complex protein occurring in the formation of fibrin.

fibro- *combining form* Pertaining to or composed of fibrous tissue. Also, before vowels, **fibr-**. [< L *fibra* fiber]

fi·broid (fī′broid) *adj.* Made up of or resembling fibrous tissue.

fi·brous (fī′brəs) *adj.* Made up of, having, or resembling fiber: *fibrous* tissue.

fib·u·la (fib′yŏŏ-lə) *n.* *pl.* **·lae** (-lē) or **·las** 1. *Anat.* The outer and smaller of the two bones forming the lower part of the human leg from the knee to the ankle. 2. *Zool.* In animals, a similar bone of the hind leg. 3. An ancient ornamental brooch. [< L, a clasp] — **fib′u·lar** *adj.*

-fic *suffix* Making, rendering, or causing: *beatific*. [< L *-ficus* < *facere* to make, render]

-fication *suffix* A causing to be (something indicated): *beatification*. [< L *facere* to make, render]

fi·chu (fish′ŏŏ, *Fr.* fē-shü′) *n.* A capelike piece of light material worn about the neck. [< F *ficher* to put on hastily]

fick·le (fik′əl) *adj.* Inconstant in feeling or purpose; changeful; capricious. [OE *ficol* crafty] — **fick′le·ness** *n.*

fic·tile (fik′til) *adj.* Produced by molding or able to be molded. [< L *fingere* to form]

fic·tion (fik′shən) *n.* 1. Prose works in narrative form, the characters and incidents of which are wholly or partly imaginary; also, such works collectively. 2. Something imagined or deliberately falsified. 3. The action of arbitrarily making up an explanation, etc. [< F < L *fictio* a making < *fingere* to form] — **fic′tion·al** *adj.* — **fic′tion·al·ly** *adv.*

fic·ti·tious (fik-tish′əs) *adj.* 1. Not corresponding to actual fact; artificially invented. 2. Not genuine; not real; false. 3. Fictional. — **fic·ti′tious·ly** *adv.* — **fic·ti′tious·ness** *n.*

fic·tive (fik′tiv) *adj.* 1. Fictitious. 2. Relating to the creation of fiction: *fictive* ability. — **fic′tive·ly** *adv.*

fid (fid) *n.* *Naut.* 1. A supporting bar or crosspiece to hold a topmast in place. 2. A large, tapering wooden pin used for opening ropes when splicing, etc. [Origin uncertain]

-fid *combining form* 1. Divided (into an indicated number of parts. 2. Separated into lobes (of an indicated kind). [< L *-fidus* < *findere* to split]

fid·dle (fid′l) *n.* 1. A violin; also, any other instrument of the violin or viol family. 2. *Naut.* A rack used at table to prevent things from sliding off. — **fit as a fiddle** Enjoying perfect health. — **to play second fiddle** To have a position subordinate to that of another. — *v.* **·dled** **·dling** *v.i.* 1. *Informal* To play a violin. 2. To make nervous or restless movements; fidget. — *v.t.* 3. To spend (time) in a careless way: usu. with *away*. [OE *fithele* < ML *fidula, fidella,* dim. of L *fides* lyre] — **fid′dler** *n.*

fid·dle-de-dee (fid′l-dē′dē′) *n. & interj.* Nonsense.

fid·dle-fad·dle (fid′l-fad′l) *n. & interj.* Nonsense. — *v.i.* **·dled, ·dling** To occupy oneself with unimportant things.

fiddler crab A small burrowing crab found chiefly off the Atlantic coast of the U.S., one of whose claws is, in the male, much larger than the other.

fid·dle·stick (fid′l-stik′) *n.* 1. A bow used on a violin, etc. 2. Something trifling.

fid·dle·sticks (fid′l-stiks′) *interj.* Nonsense!

FIDDLER CRAB
(Carapace ½ to 1 inch wide)

fi·del·i·ty (fī-del′ə-tē, fə-) *n.* *pl.* **·ties** 1. Faithfulness to duties, obligations, vows, truth, etc. 2. Exactness of reproductive detail. 3. *Electronics* The extent to which a phonograph, tape recorder, etc., receives and transmits input signals without distortion. [< L *fides* faith]

fidg·et (fij′it) *v.i.* 1. To make nervous or restless movements. — *v.i.* 2. To cause to fidget. — *n.* 1. *Usu. pl.* The condition of being restless or nervous. 2. One who fidgets. [ME *fiken* to fidget]

fi·du·cial (fi-dōō′shəl, -dyōō′-) *adj.* 1. Fiduciary. 2. Based on trust or faith. 3. *Physics* Fixed as a basis of measurement. [< L *fidere* to trust] — **fi·du′cial·ly** *adv.*

fi·du·ci·ar·y (fi-dōō′shē·er′ē, -shər·ē, -dyōō′-) *adj.* 1. Of, pertaining to, or acting as a trustee. 2. Held in trust. 3. Consisting of fiat money. — *n.* *pl.* **·ar·ies** One who holds something in trust. [< L *fidere* to trust]

fie (fī) *interj.* An expression of impatience or disapproval. [< OF *fi, fy* < L *fi,* an expression of disgust]

fief (fēf) *n.* A landed estate held under feudal tenure. [< OF < Med.L *feudum*]

field (fēld) *n.* 1. A piece of land with few or no trees, covered with grass, weeds, or similar vegetation. ◆ Collateral adjective: *campestral.* 2. A piece of land set aside for use as pasture or for crops. 3. A large expanse of open country; also, any wide expanse. 4. An area in which a natural resource is found: an oil *field*. 5. An airport. 6. The whole extent or a particular division of knowledge, research, study, etc.: the *field* of chemistry. 7. In sports and athletics: **a** The bounded area where a game is played or where athletic contests, exhibitions, etc., are held: a football *field*. **b** The members of a team, etc., actually engaged in active play. **c** The competitors in a race or other contest. 8. *Mil.* A region of active operations or maneuvers. 9. In business, the area away from the home office. 10. *Physics* An extent of space within which lines of magnetic or electric force are in operation: also called *field of force*. 11. *Optics* The area within which objects are seen in a telescope, etc. 12. The part of a painting canvas, flag, coin, etc., used for background. — **to leave the field** *U.S. Informal* To back out of a contest, struggle, dispute, etc — **to play the field** *U.S. Informal* To give one's energies, interest, or attention to the entire range of something. — **to take the field** To begin a game, military campaign, struggle, etc. — *v.t.* 1. In baseball, cricket, etc.: **a** To catch or pick up (a ball) and return to the inner field. **b** To send (a player) to a field position. — *v.i.* 2. In baseball, cricket, etc., to play in a field position. — *adj.* 1. Of, pertaining to, or growing in fields. 2. Used or designed for use in fields. 3. Played or held on an open field. [OE *feld*]

field artillery Artillery so mounted as to be freely movable, and suitable for use with troops in the field.

field day 1. A day of military maneuvers, athletic contests, etc. 2. A gala day full of pleasurable activities, etc.

field·er (fēl′dər) *n.* In baseball, etc., a player in the field.

field events The events at an athletic meet other than races.

field glass A compact, portable, binocular telescope. Also **field glasses**.

field goal 1. In football, a goal scored by a drop kick or a place kick, counting three points. 2. In basketball, a goal scored while the ball is in active play, counting two points.

field hospital A military hospital near a combat zone.

field magnet The magnet that produces the magnetic field in a generator or electric motor.

field marshal In the armies of several European nations, an officer just below the commander in chief.

Field-Mar·shal (fēld′mär′shəl) *n.* In the British and Canadian armies, an officer of the highest rank. See table at GRADE.

field officer *Mil.* A colonel, lieutenant colonel, or major.

field of force *Physics* Field (def. 10).

field sports Athletic events, as jumping and pole-vaulting, held on the field, as opposed to races held on the track.

field·stone (fēld′stōn′) *n.* Loose stone found near a construction site and used in building. — *adj.* Consisting of or having the appearance of fieldstone: a *fieldstone* house.

field·work (fēld′wûrk′) *n.* A temporary fortification.

field work Observations and investigations made in the field, as by a scientist. — **field worker**

fiend (fēnd) *n.* 1. An evil spirit; devil; demon. 2. An intensely wicked or cruel person. 3. *Informal* One who is highly skilled in a game, etc.: a bridge *fiend*. 4. *Informal* One addicted to an injurious habit. — **the Fiend** Satan; the devil. [OE *féond* enemy, devil] — **fiend′like** *adj.*

fiend·ish (fēn′dish) *adj.* Exceedingly cruel or malicious; diabolical. — **fiend′ish·ly** *adv.* — **fiend′ish·ness** *n.*

fierce (firs) *adj.* 1. Having a violent and cruel nature. 2. Violent in action or force. 3. Vehement; intense: *fierce* anger. 4. *Slang* Very disagreeable, bad, etc. [< OF < L *ferus* wild] — **fierce′ly** *adv.* — **fierce′ness** *n.*

fiery (fīr′ē, fī′ər·ē) *adj.* **fier·i·er, fier·i·est** 1. Like, containing, or composed of fire. 2. Brightly glowing; blazing. 3. Passionate; impetuous. 4. Inflamed, as a boil. — **fier′i·ly** *adv.* — **fier′i·ness** *n.*

fi·es·ta (fē·es′tə, *Sp.* fyes′tä) *n.* 1. A religious festival. 2. Any holiday or celebration. [< Sp. < L *festa*]

fife (fīf) *n.* A small, shrill-toned flute used chiefly for mili-

tary music. — *v.t.* & *v.i.* **fifed, fif·ing** To play on a fife. [<
G < LL < L *pipare* to peep, chirp] — **fif'er** *n.*
fif·teen (fif'tēn') *n.* **1.** The sum of fourteen and one: a cardinal number. **2.** Any symbol of this number, as 15, xv,
XV. **3.** Anything consisting of or representing fifteen units,
as an organization, game token, etc. — *adj.* Being one more
than fourteen. [OE *fīftēne*] — **fif'teenth** *n.* & *adj.*
fifth (fifth) *adj.* **1.** Next after the fourth: the ordinal of *five.*
2. Being one of five equal parts. — *n.* **1.** One of five equal
parts. **2.** That which follows the fourth. **3.** *Music* **a** The
interval between a tone and another tone five steps from it.
b One of these tones, esp. the one higher in pitch. **c** The fifth
above the tonic; the dominant. **4.** One fifth of a U.S. gallon,
used as a measure of liquors. — *adv.* In the fifth order, place,
or rank: also, in informal discourse, **fifth'ly.** [OE *fīfta*]
Fifth Amendment An amendment to the Constitution of
the U.S. guaranteeing due process of law and that no person
"shall be compelled to be a witness against himself".
fifth column In wartime, the civilians within defense lines
who secretly assist the enemy. — **fifth columnist**
fifth wheel A superfluous person or thing.
fif·ty (fif'tē) *n.* *pl.* **·ties 1.** The sum of forty and ten: a cardinal number. **2.** Any symbol of this number, as 50, l, L.
3. Anything consisting of or representing fifty units, as an
organization, bill, etc. — *adj.* Being ten more than forty.
[OE *fīftig*] — **fif'ti·eth** *n.* & *adj.*
fifty-fifty (fif'tē-fif'tē) *Informal adj.* Sharing equally, as in
benefits: *fifty-fifty* partners. — *adv.* Equally.
fig (fig) *n.* **1.** The small, edible, pear-shaped fruit of a tree,
cultivated in warm climates. **2.** The tree that bears this
fruit. [< OF < L *ficus*]
fight (fīt) *v.* **fought, fight·ing** *v.t.* **1.** To struggle against in
battle or physical combat. **2.** To struggle against in any
manner. **3.** To carry on or engage in (a duel, court action,
etc.) **4.** To make (one's way) by struggling. **5.** To manage
the fighting of, as boxers or gamecocks. — *v.i.* **6.** To take
part in combat. **7.** To struggle in any manner. — **to fight
it out** To fight until a final decision is reached. — **to fight
shy of** To avoid meeting (an opponent or an issue) squarely;
dodge. — *n.* **1.** Strife or struggle; battle; conflict; combat.
2. Power or disposition to fight; pugnacity. [OE *feohtan*]
fight·er (fī'tər) *n.* **1.** One who fights. **2.** *Mil.* A fast, highly maneuverable airplane for aerial fighting: formerly called
pursuit plane: also **fighter plane.**
fig·ment (fig'mənt) *n.* A capricious product of the mind; a
fiction; fabrication. [< L *figmentum* anything made]
fig·u·ra·tion (fig'yə-rā'shən) *n.* **1.** The act of shaping something. **2.** Form, shape, or outline. **3.** The act of representing figuratively. **4.** *Music* Ornamentation.
fig·ur·a·tive (fig'yər-ə-tiv) *adj.* **1.** Based on, like, or containing a figure or figures of speech; metaphorical. **2.** Representing by means of a form or figure. **3.** Pertaining to
pictorial or sculptural representation. — **fig'ur·a·tive·ly** *adv.*
fig·ure (fig'yər, *Brit.* fig'ər) *n.* **1.** A character or symbol
representing a number: the *figure* 5. **2.** *pl.* The use of such
characters in calculating. **3.** An amount stated in numbers,
as of price, etc. **4.** The visible form of anything; shape; outline. **5.** The human form or body. **6.** A personage or character, esp. a prominent one. **7.** The appearance or impression that a person makes. **8.** A representation or likeness,
as in painting or sculpture. **9.** A pattern or design, as in a
fabric. **10.** A printed illustration; a cut. **11.** One who or
that which represents or symbolizes something: a *figure* of
wisdom. **12.** A figure of speech. **13.** A movement or series
of movements, as in a dance. **14.** *Geom.* A surface enclosed
by lines, as a square or a space enclosed by planes, as a cube.
15. *Music* Any short succession of notes that produces a
single and distinct impression. — *v.* **·ured, ·ur·ing** *v.t.* **1.**
To compute numerically; calculate. **2.** To make an image
or other representation of; depict. **3.** To ornament with a
design. **4.** To picture mentally; imagine. **5.** To express by
a figure of speech; symbolize. **6.** *Informal* To believe; predict. **7.** *Music* To mark with figures above or below the
bass notes, indicating accompanying chords. — *v.i.* **8.** To
appear prominently; be conspicuous. **9.** To compute; reckon. — **to figure on** (or **upon**) *U.S. Informal* **1.** To count
on; rely on. **2.** To plan on. — **to figure out 1.** To solve;
compute. **2.** To make out; understand. [< F < L *fingere*
to form] — **fig'ur·er** *n.*
fig·ured (fig'yərd) *adj.* **1.** Adorned or marked with figures
or designs: *figured* cottons. **2.** Represented by figures.
figured bass *Music* A bass part with numerals, etc., indicating chords: also called *thorough bass.*
figure eight 1. A maneuver in ice skating that consists in
tracing the figure 8. **2.** A style of knot: for illus. see KNOT.
fig·ure·head (fig'yər-hed') *n.* **1.** A person having nominal
leadership but no real power. **2.** A carved or ornamental
figure on the prow of a vessel.

figure of speech An expression that intentionally deviates
from the literal meanings of words so as to create a more
vivid effect, as in simile, metaphor, etc.
figure skating The art or sport of skating in prescribed
dancelike patterns. — **figure skater**
fig·u·rine (fig'yə-rēn') *n.* A small, molded or carved figure;
statuette. [< F < Ital. *figurina*]
fig·wort (fig'wûrt') *n.* A plant with small, dark flowers,
formerly supposed to cure scrofula.
Fi·ji (fē'jē) *n.* **1.** One of the native people of the Fiji Islands.
2. The Melanesian language of the Fijis.
Fi·ji·an (fē'jē-ən, fi·jē'ən) *adj.* Of Fiji, its people, or their
language. — *n.* A Fiji.
fil·a·gree (fil'ə-grē) See FILIGREE.
fil·a·ment (fil'ə-mənt) *n.* **1.** A fine thread, fiber, or fibril;
also, any threadlike structure or appendage. **2.** *Bot.* The
stalk or support of an anther. For illus. see FLOWER. **3.**
Electr. The slender wire of tungsten, carbon, etc., which,
when heated by an electric current in a vacuum produces
light. **4.** A similar wire that forms or heats the cathode of
an electron tube. [< F < L *filum* thread] — **fil'a·men'tary** (-men'tər-ē), **fil·a·men'tous** (-men'təs) *adj.*
fi·lar·i·a (fi·lâr'ē-ə) *n.* *pl.* **·lar·i·ae** (-lâr'i-ē) A worm parasitic in the blood and intestines of vertebrates. [< NL < L
filum thread] — **fi·lar'i·al** (-əl), **fi·lar'i·an** (-ən) *adj.*
fil·bert (fil'bərt) *n.* The edible nut of the hazel or the tree it
grows on: also called *hazelnut.* [after St. *Philibert,* because
these nuts ripen about the time of his feast day (Aug. 22)]
filch (filch) *v.t.* To steal slyly and in small amounts; pilfer.
[Origin uncertain] — **filch'er** *n.*
file¹ (fīl) *n.* **1.** Any device in which papers are systematically arranged for quick reference, as a folder, drawer, or
cabinet. **2.** A collection of papers thus arranged. **3.** A line
of persons, animals, or things placed one behind another.
— **on file** Stored in systematic order for quick reference; in
a file. — **single file** An arrangement of persons or things
one behind another in a single line: also *Indian file.* — *v.*
filed, fil·ing *v.t.* **1.** To store (papers, etc.) in systematic
order. — *v.i.* **2.** To march in file, as soldiers. **3.** To make
an application, as for a job. [< L *filum* thread] — **fil'er** *n.*
file² (fīl) *n.* A hard steel instrument with ridged cutting
surfaces, used to abrade, smooth, or polish. — *v.t.* **filed,
fil·ing 1.** To cut, smooth, or sharpen with or as with a file.
2. To remove with a file. [OE *fīl*] — **fil'er** *n.*
fi·let (fi·lā', fil'ā; *Fr.* fē·le') *n.* **1.** Net lace having a square
mesh. **2.** Fillet (def. 2). — *v.t.* **fi·leted** (fi·lād', fil'ād);
fi·let·ing (fi·lā'ing, fil'ā·ing) To fillet (def. 2). [< F]
fi·let mi·gnon (fi·lā' min·yon', *Fr.* fē·le' mē·nyōn') A small,
choice, boneless cut of beef from the inside of the loin. [< F]
fil·i·al (fil'ē-əl, fil'yəl) *adj.* **1.** Of, pertaining to, or befitting
a son or daughter: *filial* devotion. **2.** *Genetics* Pertaining
to a generation following the parental. [< LL < L *filius*
son] — **fil'i·al·ly** *adv.*
fil·i·bus·ter (fil'ə·bus'tər) *n.* **1.** *U.S.* In a legislative body,
an instance of the use of delaying tactics, esp. the making of
time-consuming speeches; also, a legislator who makes such
speeches: also **fil'i·bus'ter·er.** **2.** An adventurer who takes
part in an unlawful military expedition. — *v.i.* **1.** *U.S.* To
obstruct legislation by long speeches and delay. **2.** To act
as an adventurer. — *v.t.* **3.** *U.S.* To block passage of (legislation) by dilatory tactics. [< Sp. *filibustero* < Du. *vrijbuit-
er* freebooter] — **fil'i·bus'trous** *adj.*
fil·i·form (fil'ə·fôrm) *adj.* Threadlike.
fil·i·gree (fil'ə·grē) *n.* **1.** Delicate ornamental work formed
of intertwisted gold or silver wire. **2.** Anything fanciful
and delicate. — *adj.* Resembling, made of, or adorned with
filigree; fanciful; ornate. — *v.t.* **·greed, ·gree·ing** To adorn
with or work in filigree. Sometimes spelled *filagree* or *filla-
gree.* [< F < Ital. < L *filum* thread + *granum* grain]
fil·ings (fī'lingz) *n.pl.* Particles removed by a file.
Fil·i·pi·no (fil'ə·pē'nō) *n.* *pl.* **·nos** A native or inhabitant
of the Philippine Islands. — *adj.* Of or pertaining to the
Philippine Islands or their inhabitants.
fill (fil) *v.t.* **1.** To supply (a container, space, etc.) with
as much of something as can be contained. **2.** To supply
fully, as with food. **3.** To occupy or pervade the whole of.
4. To stop up; plug: to *fill* a tooth. **5.** To put together or
make up what is indicated in (an order, prescription, etc.).
6. To satisfy or meet (a need, requirements, etc.). **7.** To
occupy (an office or position). **8.** To level out (an embankment, ravine, etc.) by adding fill. — *v.i.* **9.** To become full.
— **to fill away** *Naut.* To trim the yards so that the sails will
catch the wind. — **to fill in 1.** To fill completely, as an excavation. **2.** To insert (something): to *fill in* one's name.
3. To complete by inserting something; to *fill in* an application. **4.** To be a substitute. — **to fill (someone) in on** *Informal* To give (someone) additional facts or details about.
— **to fill out 1.** To make or become fuller or more rounded.

2. To make complete, as an application. **— to fill the bill** U.S. *Informal* To do or be what is wanted or needed. **— to fill up** To make or become full. **— n. 1.** That which fills or is sufficient to fill. **2.** An embankment built up by filling in with stone, gravel, etc. [OE *fyllan* fill]

fil·la·gree (fil′ə·grē) See FILIGREE.

fill·er (fil′ər) *n.* **1.** One who fills. **2.** That which fills; as: **a** A substance added to increase bulk, weight, etc. **b** A composition for filling pores or holes in wood. **c** Tobacco used for the inside of cigars. **d** A piece of writing used to fill space.

fil·let (fil′it; *for n. def. 2 and v.*, *also* fil′ā, fi·lā′) *n.* **1.** A narrow band or ribbon for binding the hair. **2.** A strip of boneless meat or fish. **3.** A narrow band of any material. **— v.t.** To slice into fillets. [< F < L *filum* thread]

fill-in (fil′in′) *n.* **1.** A person or thing included to fill a gap or omission. **2.** *Informal* A summary of facts.

fill·ing (fil′ing) *n.* **1.** That which is used to fill something; esp. the material put into a prepared cavity in a tooth. **2.** The act of becoming full. **3.** In weaving, the weft.

filling station *U.S.* A retail station for supplying gasoline, oil, etc., to motor vehicles: also called *gas station*.

fil·lip (fil′əp) *n.* **1.** The snap of a finger that has been pressed down by the thumb and suddenly released. **2.** Something that serves to excite or stimulate. **— v.t. 1.** To strike with a fillip. **2.** To project by or as by a fillip. **3.** To stimulate; arouse. **— v.i. 4.** To make a fillip. [Var. of FLIP]

fil·ly (fil′ē) *n.* *pl.* **·lies 1.** A young mare. **2.** *Informal* A spirited young girl. [< ON *fylja* < *foli* foal]

film (film) *n.* **1.** A thin covering, layer, or membrane. **2.** A thin haze or blur. **3.** *Photog.* A sheet, roll, or strip of transparent material coated with a light-sensitive emulsion and used for making photographs. **4.** In motion pictures: **a** The film containing the pictures projected on the screen. **b** The motion picture itself. **c** *pl.* Motion pictures collectively. **— v.t. 1.** To cover or obscure by or as by a film. **2.** To photograph on a film. **3.** To make a motion picture of: to *film* a play. **— v.i. 4.** To become covered or obscured by a film. **5.** To make a motion picture. **6.** To be adaptable for filming. [OE *filmen* membrane]

film·strip (film′strip′) *n.* A length of processed film containing frames of still pictures that are projected on a screen.

film·y (fil′mē) *adj.* **film·i·er, film·i·est 1.** Composed of or like film; gauzy. **2.** Covered with or as with a film; hazy; dim. **— film′i·ly** *adv.* **— film′i·ness** *n.*

fil·ter (fil′tər) *n.* **1.** Any device, as paper, cloth, or charcoal, used as a strainer for clearing or purifying liquids, air, etc. **2.** *Physics* A device that permits the passage of waves and currents of certain frequencies and limits the flow of certain others. **3.** *Photog.* A colored screen that controls the kind and intensity of light waves in an exposure. **— v.t. 1.** To pass (liquids, air, etc.) through a filter; strain. **2.** To separate or remove (impurities, etc.) by or as by a filter. **3.** To act as a filter for. **— v.i. 4.** To pass through a filter. **5.** To leak out, as news. [< OF < Med.L *feltrum* felt (used as a filter)] **— fil′ter·er** *n.*

fil·ter·a·ble (fil′tər·ə·bəl) *adj.* **1.** Capable of being filtered. **2.** Capable of passing through a filter. Also **fil·tra·ble** (fil′· trəb·əl) **— fil′ter·a·bil′i·ty** *n.*

filterable virus Virus (def. 1).

filth (filth) *n.* **1.** Anything that is foul or dirty. **2.** A foul condition. **3.** Moral defilement; obscenity. [OE *fylth*]

filth·y (fil′thē) *adj.* **filth·i·er, filth·i·est 1.** Of the nature of or containing filth. **2.** Morally foul; obscene. **3.** Highly unpleasant. **— filth′i·ly** *adv.* **— filth′i·ness** *n.*

fil·trate (fil′trāt) *v.t.* **·trat·ed, ·trat·ing** To filter. **— n.** The liquid that has been separated by filtration. [< NL < Med.L *filtrum* a filter] **— fil·tra′tion** *n.*

fin¹ (fin) *n.* **1.** A membranous extension from the body of a fish or other aquatic animal, serving to propel, balance, or steer it in the water. **2.** Any finlike or projecting part, appendage, or attachment. **3.** *Slang* The hand. **— v. finned, fin·ning** *v.t.* To cut up or trim off the fins of (a fish). **— v.i. 2.** To beat the water with the fins, as a whale when dying. [OE *finn*] **— fin′less** *adj.*

fin² (fin) *n.* *U.S. Slang* A five-dollar bill. [< Yiddish *finf* five]

fi·na·gle (fi·nā′gəl) *v.* **·gled, ·gling** *Informal v.t.* **1.** To get (something) by trickery or deceit. **2.** To cheat or trick (someone). **— v.i. 3.** To use trickery or deceit; be sly. [Origin uncertain] **— fi·na′gler** *n.*

fi·nal (fī′nəl) *adj.* **1.** Pertaining to, or coming at the end; ultimate; last. **2.** Precluding further action or controversy; conclusive. **3.** Relating to or consisting in the end or purpose aimed at: a *final* cause. **— n. 1.** Something that is terminal or last. **2.** *Often pl.* Something decisively final, as the last match in a tournament. [< F < L *finis* end]

fi·na·le (fi·nä′lē, ·nal′ē; *Ital.* fē·nä′lā) *n.* The last part, as the final scene in a play or the concluding section of a musical composition. [< Ital., *final*]

fi·nal·ist (fī′nəl·ist) *n.* In games, contests, etc., a contestant who takes part in the final matches.

fi·nal·i·ty (fī·nal′ə·tē) *n.* *pl.* **·ties 1.** The state or quality of being final or settled. **2.** A final act, offer, etc.

fi·nal·ize (fī′nəl·īz) *v.t.* **·ized, ·iz·ing** To put into final or complete form; bring to completion.

fi·nal·ly (fī′nəl·ē) *adv.* **1.** At or in the end; in conclusion; lastly. **2.** Completely; irrecoverably; decisively.

fi·nance (fi·nans′, fī′nans) *n.* **1.** The science of monetary affairs. **2.** *pl.* Monetary affairs; funds; revenue; income. **— v.t.** **·nanced, ·nanc·ing 1.** To supply the money for. **2.** To manage the finances of. [< OF, payment]

fi·nan·cial (fi·nan′shəl, fī-) *adj.* **1.** Of or pertaining to finance or finances. **2.** Of or pertaining to those dealing with money and credit. **— fi·nan′cial·ly** *adv.*

fin·an·cier (fin′ən·sir′) *n.* One engaged or skilled in financial operations. **— v.t.** To finance.

fin·back (fin′bak′) *n.* A rorqual. Also **finback whale.**

finch (finch) *n.* A small, seed-eating bird, as the bunting, sparrow, bullfinch, goldfinch, or canary. [OE *finc*]

find (find) *v.* **found, find·ing** *v.t.* **1.** To come upon unexpectedly. **2.** To discover after search, experience, or effort. **3.** To recover (something lost). **4.** To arrive at; reach. **5.** To gain or recover the use of: He *found* his tongue. **6.** To determine by legal inquiry and declare. **— v.i. 7.** To express a decision after legal inquiry: to *find* for the plaintiff. **— to find oneself** To discover one's special abilities or one's proper vocation. **— to find out 1.** To learn; discover. **2.** To detect the identity or the true nature of. **— n. 1.** The act of finding. **2.** Something found or discovered; esp., a valuable discovery. [OE *findan*]

find·er (fīn′dər) *n.* **1.** One who or that which finds. **2.** *Astron.* A small telescope by the side of a large one, used to locate a particular object. **3.** *Photog.* A camera attachment that shows the scene as it will appear in the photograph.

fin de siè·cle (fan də sye′kl′) *French* End of the century; esp. the close of the 19th century.

find·ing (fīn′ding) *n.* **1.** The act of one who finds. **2.** That which is found; a discovery or conclusion.

fine¹ (fīn) *adj.* **fin·er, fin·est 1.** Superior in quality; excellent. **2.** Highly satisfactory; very good. **3.** Light or delicate in texture, workmanship, structure, etc. **4.** Composed of very small particles: *fine* powder. **5.** Very thin: *fine* thread. **6.** Keen; sharp: a *fine* edge. **7.** Possessing superior ability or skill. **8.** Subtle; nice: a *fine* point. **9.** Discriminating: a *fine* ear for music. **10.** Elegant; polished; also, overelegant; showy; affected. **11.** Handsome; good-looking. **12.** Cloudless; clear: *fine* weather. **13.** Free from impurities. **14.** Containing a given proportion of pure metal: gold 18 karats *fine*. **— adv.** *Informal* Very well: It suits me *fine*. **— v.t. & v.i.** To make or become fine or finer. [< OF *fin* finished, perfected] **— fine′ly** *adv.* **— fine′ness** *n.*

fine² (fīn) *n.* A sum of money required as the penalty for an offense. **— in fine** Finally; in short. **— v.t. fined, fin·ing** To punish by fine. [< OF *fin* settlement]

fi·ne³ (fē′nä) *n.* *Music* The end; finis. [< Ital.]

fine arts The arts of painting, drawing, sculpture, and architecture, and sometimes including literature, music, drama, and the dance.

fine-drawn (fīn′drôn′) *adj.* Drawn out to extreme fineness or subtlety: a *fine-drawn* distinction.

fin·er·y (fī′nər·ē) *n.* *pl.* **·er·ies** Elaborate adornment; showy or fine clothes or decorations.

fine-spun (fīn′spun′) *adj.* **1.** Drawn or spun out to an extreme degree of fineness. **2.** Excessively subtle.

fi·nesse (fi·nes′) *n.* **1.** Highly refined skill; subtlety of style or performance. **2.** Smoothness and tact, as in handling a delicate situation; also, artful strategy; cunning. **3.** In bridge and other card games an attempt to take a trick with the lower of two nonsequential cards in the hope that the hand yet to play does not hold an intervening card. **— v. ·nessed, ·ness·ing** *v.t.* **1.** To change or bring about by finesse. **2.** In card games, to play as a finesse. **— v.i. 3.** To use finesse. **4.** In card games, to make a finesse. [< F < *fin*. See FINE¹.]

fine-toothed comb (fīn′tōōtht′) A comb with fine teeth set very close together. Also **fine′-tooth′ comb. — to go over with a fine-toothed comb** To examine minutely.

fin·ger (fing′gər) *n.* **1.** One of the terminating members of the hand, usu. excluding the thumb. **2.** That part of a glove made to fit the finger. **3.** Anything that resembles or serves as a finger. **4.** A unit of measure based on the width of a finger (from ¾ inch to one inch); or on the length of the middle finger (about 4 to 4½ inches). **— to burn one's fingers** To suffer the consequences of meddling or interfering. **— to have (or put) a finger in the pie 1.** To take part in some matter. **2.** To meddle. **— to put one's finger on** To identify or indicate correctly. **— to put the finger on** *U.S. Slang* **1.** To betray as, to the police, **2.** To point out (the victim of a planned crime). **— to twist around one's (little) finger** To influence or control with little or no effort. **— v.t. 1.** To touch or handle with the fingers; toy with. **2.** To steal; pilfer. **3.** *Music* **a** To play (an instrument) with the fingers. **b** To mark the fingering of (music). **4.** *U.S. Slang* To betray, as to the police. — *v.i.* **5.** To touch or feel anything with the fingers. [OE] — **fin′ger·er** *n.*

finger board In stringed instruments, as the violin, guitar, etc., the strip of wood upon which the strings are pressed by the fingers of the player. For illus. see VIOLIN.

finger bowl A bowl containing water for cleansing the fingers at the table after eating.

fin·gered (fing′gərd) *adj.* **1.** Having fingers. **2.** *Music* Having the fingering marked. **3.** Marked by fingers.

fin·ger·ing (fing′gər·ing) *n.* **1.** The act of touching or feeling with the fingers. **2.** *Music* **a** The action or technique of using the fingers in playing an instrument. **b** The notation indicating what fingers are to be used.

fin·ger·ling (fing′gər·ling) *n.* A young, small fish.

fin·ger·nail (fing′gər·nāl′) *n.* The horny substance along the upper surface of the end of a finger.

fin·ger·print (fing′gər·print′) *n.* An impression of the skin pattern on the inner surface of a finger tip, used for purposes of identification. — *v.t.* To take the fingerprints of.

finger tip The extreme end of a finger. — **to have at one's finger tips** To have ready and available knowledge of or access to.

fin·i·al (fin′ē·əl) *n. Archit.* An ornament at the apex of a spire, pinnacle, or the like. [< L *finis* end + -IAL]

fin·i·cal (fin′i·kəl) *adj.* Finicky. — **fin′i·cal·ly** *adv.* — **fin′i·cal·ness, fin·i·cal′i·ty** (-kal′ə·tē) *n.*

fin·ick·ing (fin′i·king) *adj.* Finicky.

fin·ick·y (fin′i·kē) *adj.* Excessively fastidious or precise; fussy; exacting. [< FINE¹ + -ICAL]

fin·is (fin′is, fī′nis) *n. pl.* **fin·is·es** The end. [< L]

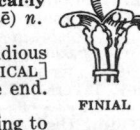

FINIAL

fin·ish (fin′ish) *v.t.* **1.** To complete or bring to an end. **2.** To use up completely. **3.** To perfect (a person) in social graces, education, etc. **4.** To give (fabric, wood, etc.) a particular surface quality. **5.** *Informal* To kill, destroy, or defeat. — *v.i.* **6.** To reach or come to an end; stop. — *n.* **1.** The conclusion or last stage of anything. **2.** Something that finishes, completes, or perfects. **3.** Completeness and perfection of detail. **4.** Perfection or polish in speech, manners, education, etc. **5.** The surface quality or appearance of textiles, paint, etc.: a glossy *finish.* [< OF < L *finis* end] — **fin′ish·er** *n.*

fin·ished (fin′isht) *adj.* **1.** Ended; completed. **2.** Perfected to a high degree; polished. **3.** Highly accomplished.

fin·ish·ing school (fin′ish·ing) A school that prepares girls for entrance into society.

fi·nite (fī′nīt) *adj.* **1.** Having bounds, ends, or limits. **2.** That may be determined, counted, or measured. **3.** Subject to human or natural limitations: our *finite* minds. — *n.* Finite things collectively, or that which is finite. [< L *finitus* limited] — **fi′nite·ly** *adv.* — **fi′nite·ness** *n.*

finite verb *Gram.* A verb form that is limited as to person, number, tense, and mood, and that can serve as a predicate.

fin·i·tude (fin′ə·tood, -tyood, fī′nə-) *n.* The state of being finite.

fink (fingk) *n. U.S. Slang* **1.** A strikebreaker. **2.** An unsavory person. [? < FINGER, v. (def. 4)]

Finn (fin) *n.* **1.** A native or inhabitant of Finland. **2.** One whose native language is Finnish. [OE *Finnas* Finns]

fin·nan had·die (fin′ən had′ē) Smoked haddock Also **fin′nan had·dock** (had′ək) [*Findhorn haddock,* after *Findhorn,* a Scottish fishing port where originally prepared]

finned (find) *adj.* Having fins or finlike extensions.

Finn·ish (fin′ish) *adj.* Of Finland, the Finns, or their language. — *n.* The Uralic language of the Finns.

Fin·no-U·gric (fin′ō-oo′grik, -yoo′grik) *n.* A subfamily of the Uralic languages, including Finnish, Estonian, Lapp, Magyar, etc. Also **Fin′no-U′gri·an.**

fin·ny (fin′ē) *adj.* **1.** Having fins. **2.** Resembling a fin. **3.** Of or pertaining to fish. **4.** Abounding in fish.

fiord (fyôrd, fyōrd) *n.* A long and narrow arm of the sea running between high, rocky cliffs or banks: also spelled *fjord.* [< Norw. *fjord*]

fip·ple (fip′əl) *n.* A plug of wood at the mouth of certain wind instruments, as recorders. [? < ON *flipi* lip of a horse]

fir (fûr) *n.* **1.** Any of several trees of the pine family. **2.** The wood of these trees. [OE *fyrh*] — **fir′ry** *adj.*

fire (fīr) *n.* **1.** The visible, active phase of combustion, manifested in light and heat. **2.** A burning mass of fuel, as in a fireplace **3.** A destructive burning, as of a building. **4.** A substance or device that produces fire or a firelike display: Greek *fire.* **5.** A flash or spark: to strike *fire.* **6.** A discharge of firearms: Cease *fire.* **7.** A rapid volley: a *fire* of questions. **8.** Flashing brightness; brilliance: the *fire* of a diamond. **9.** Intensity of spirit or feeling; ardor; passion. **10.** Vividness of imagination. **11.** Warmth or heat, as of

liquor. **12.** Fever or inflammation. **13.** An affliction or grievous trial. — **between two fires** Under attack or criticism from both sides. — **on fire 1.** Burning; ablaze. **2.** Ardent; zealous. — **to catch fire.** To start to burn. — **to go through fire and water** To experience great afflictions. — **to hang fire 1.** To fail to fire promptly, as a firearm. **2.** To be delayed or undecided. — **to lay a fire** To arrange fuel for igniting. — **to miss fire 1.** To fail to discharge: said of firearms. **2.** To be unsuccessful; fail. — **to open fire 1.** To begin to shoot. **2.** To commence. — **to play with fire** To do something rash or dangerous. — **to set fire to** or **to set on fire 1.** To make burn. **2.** To inflame or excite. — **to set the world on fire** To gain great success or fame. — **to strike fire 1.** To create a fire, as with flint. **2.** To get a reaction. — **to take fire 1.** To start to burn. **2.** To become excited, angry, or enthusiastic. — **under fire 1.** Exposed to gunshot or artillery fire. **2.** Subjected to severe criticism. — *v.* **fired, fir·ing** *v.t.* **1.** To set on fire. **2.** To tend the fire of. **3.** To subject to the heat of fire. **4.** To set off, as explosives. **5.** To set off explosives within or near: to *fire* an oil well. **6.** To discharge, as a gun or bullet. **7.** *Informal* To hurl: to *fire* questions. **8.** *Informal* To dismiss from employment. **9.** To bake, as pottery, in a kiln. **10.** To cure by heat. **11.** To cause to glow or shine. **12.** To inspire; excite. **13.** *Vet.* To cauterize. — *v.i.* **14.** To take fire; become ignited. **15.** To go off, as a gun. **16.** To set off firearms, a rocket, etc. **17.** *Informal* To hurl a missile. **18.** To tend a fire. — **to fire away** To start off and proceed energetically, esp. in asking questions. [OE *fȳr*]

fire·arm (fīr′ärm′) *n.* Any weapon, usu. small, from which a missile, as a bullet, is hurled by an explosive.

fire·ball (fīr′bôl′) *n.* **1.** A luminous meteor. **2.** Ball-shaped lightning. **3.** A hot, incandescent sphere of air and vaporized debris, formed around the center of a nuclear explosion. **4.** *U.S. Slang* A remarkably energetic person or thing.

fire·boat (fīr′bōt′) *n.* A boat equipped for fighting fires.

fire·box (fīr′boks′) *n.* The chamber in which the fuel of a locomotive, furnace, etc., is burned.

fire·brand (fīr′brand′) *n.* **1.** A piece of burning or glowing wood. **2.** One who stirs up trouble or dissension.

fire·break (fīr′brāk′) *n. U.S.* A strip of land that has been plowed or cleared to prevent the spread of fire.

fire·brick (fīr′brik′) *n.* A brick made of fire clay, used for lining furnaces.

fire·bug (fīr′bug′) *n. U.S. Informal* One who enjoys setting fire to buildings, etc.; a pyromaniac.

fire clay A refractory material, used to make crucibles, furnace linings, and the like.

fire control *Mil.* The control of the delivery of gunfire or of guided missiles by the use of special equipment.

fire·crack·er (fīr′krak′ər) *n.* A small paper cylinder charged with an explosive, used as a noisemaker.

fire·damp (fīr′damp′) *n.* **1.** A combustible gas, chiefly methane, that enters mines from coal seams. **2.** The explosive mixture formed by this gas and air.

fire·dog (fīr′dôg′, -dog′) *n.* An andiron.

fire·eat·er (fīr′ē′tər) *n.* **1.** A performer who pretends to eat fire. **2.** A hot-headed person eager to fight or quarrel.

fire engine A motor truck equipped to fight fires.

fire escape A metal stairway usu. attached to the outside of a building and furnishing a means of escape in case of fire.

fire extinguisher A portable apparatus containing fire-extinguishing chemicals ejected through a short hose.

fire·fly (fīr′flī′) *n. pl.* **·flies** A night-flying beetle emitting a phosphorescent light from an abdominal organ.

fire·house (fīr′hous′) *n. U.S.* A building housing fire-fighting equipment and personnel.

fire·light (fīr′līt′) *n.* Light from a fire, as from a campfire.

fire·man (fīr′mən) *n. pl.* **·men** (-mən) **1.** A man employed to prevent or extinguish fires. **2.** One who tends fires.

fire opal A variety of opal having translucent orange-yellow to red colors suggesting streaks of flame.

fire·place (fīr′plās′) *n.* A recess or structure in which a fire is built; esp., the part of a chimney opening into a room.

fire·plug (fīr′plug′) *n.* A hydrant for supplying water in case of fire.

fire·pow·er (fīr′pou′ər) *n. Mil.* **1.** Capacity for delivering fire, as from the guns of a ship, battery, etc. **2.** The amount or effectiveness of fire delivered by a given weapon or unit.

fire·proof (fīr′poof′) *adj.* Resistant to fire; relatively incombustible. — *v.t.* To make resistant to fire.

fire sale *U.S.* A sale of goods damaged by fire.

fire·side (fīr′sīd′) *n.* **1.** The hearth or space before the fireplace. **2.** Home or home life.

fire station A firehouse.

fire·trap (fīr′trap′) *n.* A building notoriously flammable.

fire·wa·ter (fīr′wô′tər, -wot′ər) *n.* Whiskey: term first used by the North American Indian.

fire·weed (fīr′wēd′) *n.* The willow herb.
fire·work (fīr′wûrk′) *n.* **1.** *Usu. pl.* A device containing combustibles or explosives that, when ignited, produce brilliant light or a loud noise. **2.** *pl.* A pyrotechnic display.
firing line 1. In combat, the front line from which gunfire is delivered. **2.** The foremost position in any activity.
firing pin The part of a firearm that strikes the primer or detonator, igniting the charge of the projectile.
firing squad 1. A military or naval detachment assigned to execute, by shooting, a person condemned to death. **2.** A similar squad to honor a deceased person with a salvo.
fir·kin (fûr′kən) *n.* **1.** A wooden vessel for butter, lard, etc. **2.** A measure of capacity, usu. equal to one fourth of a barrel. [ME < MDu. *vierde* fourth + -KIN]
firm¹ (fûrm) *adj.* **1.** Relatively solid, compact, or unyielding to touch or pressure. **2.** Difficult to move, loosen, etc. **3.** Fixedly settled and established. **4.** Constant and steadfast. **5.** Full of or indicating strength; vigorous; steady. **6.** Not fluctuating widely, as prices. —*v.t. & v.i.* To make or become firm. —*adv.* Solidly; resolutely; fixedly. [< L *firmus*] —**firm′ly** *adv.* —**firm′ness** *n.*
firm² (fûrm) *n.* A partnership of two or more persons for conducting business. [< Ital. < L < *firmus* firm]
fir·ma·ment (fûr′mə·mənt) *n.* The expanse of the heavens; sky. [< L *firmare* to make firm] —**fir′ma·men·tal** *adj.*
first (fûrst) *adj.* **1.** Preceding all others in the order of numbering: the ordinal of *one.* **2.** Prior to all others in time; earliest. **3.** Nearest or foremost in place. **4.** Highest or foremost in character, rank, etc.; chief. **5.** *Music* Designating one of two parts for like instruments or voices, usu. the one higher in pitch or the principal one. —**in the first place** To start with. —*n.* **1.** One who or that which is first in time, rank, order, or position. **2.** The beginning: from *first* to last. **3.** The winning position in a race or contest. **4.** *Music* One of two parts for like instruments or voices, usu. the one higher in pitch or the principal one. **5.** In English universities, the highest rank in examinations for honors; also, one winning this rank. **6.** *pl.* The best grade of certain merchandise, as of lumber, hosiery, etc. —**at first** At the beginning. —*adv.* **1.** Before all others in order, time, place, rank, etc.; also (more formally) *firstly.* **2.** For the first time. **3.** In preference to anything else: He would die *first.* [OE *fyrst,* superl. of *fore* before]
first aid Treatment given in an emergency before full medical care can be obtained. —**first-aid** (fûrst′ād′) *adj.*
First Amendment An amendment to the Constitution of the United States forbidding Congress to interfere with religion, free speech, a free press, the right to assemble peaceably, or the right to petition the government: ratified 1791.
first base In baseball, the base first reached by the runner, at the right-hand angle of the infield. —**first base′man**
first-born (fûrst′bôrn′) *adj.* First brought forth; eldest. —*n.* The first-born child.
first-class (fûrst′klas′, -kläs′) *adj.* **1.** Of highest rank or best quality. **2.** *U.S.* Of a class of sealed mail consisting wholly or partly of written matter. **3.** Of the most luxurious accommodations on a ship, plane, etc. —*adv.* By first-class mail or conveyance.
first-hand (fûrst′hand′) *adj.* Direct from the original source or producer. —*adv.* From the original source.
first lady The wife of the president of the U.S.
first lieutenant *Mil.* A commissioned officer ranking next above a second lieutenant and next below a captain.
first·ling (fûrst′ling) *n.* The first of a kind.
first·ly (fûrst′lē) *adv.* In the first place.
first mate A ship's officer ranking next below the captain.
first mortgage A mortgage having priority over all others.
first night The opening performance of a play, opera, etc. —**first-night** (fûrst′nīt′) *adj.* —**first′-night′er** *n.*
first papers Documents filed by an alien, declaring intention to be naturalized as a citizen of the U.S.
first-rate (fûrst′rāt′) *adj.* Of the finest class or quality; excellent. —*adv. Informal* Excellently.
firth (fûrth) *n. Scot.* An arm of the sea: also spelled *frith.*
fis·cal (fis′kəl) *adj.* Of or pertaining to the treasury or finances of a government; financial. [< F < L *fiscus* purse]
fiscal year Any twelve-month period at the end of which accounts are balanced.
fish (fish) *n. pl.* **fish** or (with reference to different species) **fish·es 1.** A vertebrate, cold-blooded aquatic animal with permanent gills, having a typically elongate, tapering body, usu. covered with scales and provided with fins for locomotion. ◆ Collateral adjective: *piscine.* **2.** Loosely, any animal habitually living in water. **3.** The flesh of fish used as food. —**like a fish out of water** Not comfortable or at ease. —*v.t.* **1.** To catch or try to catch fish in (a body of water). **2.** To catch or try to catch (fish, eels, etc.). **3.** To grope for and bring out: with *out* or *up*: to *fish* money out of one's pocket. —*v.i.* **1.** To catch or try to catch fish. **5.** To try to get something in an artful or indirect manner: with *for.* [OE *fisc*] —**fish′a·ble** *adj.* —**fish′like′** *adj.*

fish·bowl (fish′bōl′) *n.* A bowl, usu. of glass, serving as a small aquarium for fish.
fish cake A fried ball or cake of chopped fish, usu. salt codfish mixed with mashed potatoes. Also **fish ball.**
fish·er (fish′ər) *n.* **1.** A fisherman. **2.** A weasellike carnivore of eastern North America; also, its fur.
fish·er·man (fish′ər·mən) *n. pl.* **·men** (-mən) **1.** One who fishes as an occupation or for sport. **2.** A fishing boat.
fish·er·y (fish′ər·ē) *n. pl.* **·er·ies 1.** The operation or business of catching fish or other aquatic animals. **2.** The place for such an operation; a fishing ground. **3.** A fish hatchery.
fish hatchery A place designed for the artificial propagation, hatching, and nurture of fish.
fish hawk The osprey.
fish·hook (fish′hŏŏk′) *n.* A hook, usu. barbed, for fishing.
fishing rod A slender pole with a line and usu. a reel.
fishing tackle Equipment for fishing, as a rod, reel, etc.
fish·meal (fish′mēl′) *n.* Ground dried fish, used as fertilizer and feed for animals.
fish·mon·ger (fish′mung′gər, -mong′-) *n.* A dealer in fish.
fish stick *U.S. & Canadian* A frozen fish filet in bar form.
fish story *Informal* An extravagant or incredible narrative.
fish·tail (fish′tāl′) *adj.* Resembling the tail of a fish.
fish·wife (fish′wīf′) *n. pl.* **·wives** (-wīvz′) **1.** A woman who sells fish. **2.** A coarse, abusive woman.
fish·y (fish′ē) *adj.* **fish·i·er, fish·i·est 1.** Of or like fish. **2.** Abounding in fish. **3.** *Informal* Improbable. **4.** Vacant of expression. —**fish′i·ly** *adv.* —**fish′i·ness** *n.*
fissi- *combining form* Split; cleft. Also, before vowels, **fiss-.** [< L *fissus,* pp. of *findere* to split]
fis·sile (fis′əl) *adj.* **1.** Capable of being split or separated into layers. **2.** Tending to split. [< L *fissilis* < *findere* to split] —**fis·sil·i·ty** (fi·sil′ə·tē) *n.*
fis·sion (fish′ən) *n.* **1.** The act of splitting or breaking apart. **2.** *Biol.* Spontaneous division of a cell or organism into new cells or organisms, esp. as a mode of reproduction. **3.** *Physics* The disintegration of the nucleus of an atom, leading to the formation of more stable atoms and the release of energy. [< L *findere* to split] —**fis′sion·a·ble** *adj.*
fis·sure (fish′ər) *n.* **1.** A narrow opening, cleft or furrow. **2.** The act of cleaving, or the state of being cleft. **3.** *Anat.* Any cleft or furrow of the body, as on the surface of the brain. —*v.t. & v.i.* **·sured, ·sur·ing** To crack; split; cleave. [< L *fissura* < *findere* to split]
fist (fist) *n.* **1.** The hand closed tightly, as for striking; also, grip; clutch. **2.** *Informal* The hand. **3.** *Informal* Handwriting. **4.** *Printing* The index mark ☞. —*v.t.* To strike with the fist. [OE *fȳst*]
fist·ful (fist′fŏŏl) *n. pl.* **·fuls** *Informal* A handful.
fist·ic (fis′tik) *adj.* Of or pertaining to boxing; pugilistic.
fist·i·cuff (fis′ti·kuf′) *n.* **1.** *pl.* A fight with the fists. **2.** *pl.* The science of boxing. **3.** A blow with the fist. —*v.t. & v.i.* To fight with the fists. —**fist′i·cuff′er** *n.*
fis·tu·la (fis′chŏŏ·lə) *n. pl.* **·las** or **·lae** (-lē) *Pathol.* A duct or canal formed by the imperfect closing of a wound, abscess, or the like, and leading either to the body surface or from one cavity or hollow organ to another. [< L, a pipe]
fis·tu·lous (fis′chŏŏ·ləs) *adj.* **1.** Of, pertaining to, or like a fistula. **2.** Cylindrical and hollow like a reed. **3.** Having or consisting of cylindrical, hollow parts. Also **fis′tu·lar** (-lər).
fit¹ (fit) *adj.* **fit·ter, fit·test 1.** Adapted to an end, aim, or design; suited. **2.** Proper or appropriate; becoming **3.** Possessing the proper qualifications; competent. **4.** In a state of preparation; ready. **5.** In good physical condition; healthy. —*v.* **fit·ted** or **fit, fit·ting** *v.t.* **1.** To be suitable or proper for. **2.** To be of the right size and shape for. **3.** To prepare, make or alter to the proper size or purpose. **4.** To provide with what is suitable or necessary; equip. **5.** To put in place carefully or exactly. —*v.i.* **6.** To be suitable or proper. **7.** To be of the proper size, shape, etc. —**to fit out** (or **up**) To supply with what is necessary; outfit. —*n.* **1.** Condition or manner of fitting. **2.** Something that fits. **3.** The act of fitting. [ME *fyt*] —**fit′ness** *n.*
fit² (fit) *n.* **1.** A sudden onset of an organic or functional disorder, often attended by convulsions; spasm. **2.** A sudden overmastering emotion or feeling. **3.** Impulsive and irregular exertion or action. —**by fits** or **by fits and starts** Spasmodically; irregularly. [OE *fitt* struggle]
fitch (fich) *n.* The polecat of Europe or its fur. Also **fitch′et** (-it), **fitch′ew** (-ōō) [< MDu. *vitsche* polecat]
fit·ful (fit′fəl) *adj.* Characterized by irregular actions, moods; capricious. —**fit′ful·ly** *adv.* —**fit′ful·ness** *n.*
fit·ly (fit′lē) *adv.* In a fit manner, place, or time; properly.
fit·ter (fit′ər) *n.* One who or that which fits.
fit·ting (fit′ing) *adj.* Fit; suitable; proper; appropriate. —*n.* **1.** The act of one who fits. **2.** A piece of equipment or an appliance used in an adjustment. **3.** *pl.* Furnishings, fixtures, or decorations. —**fit′ting·ly** *adv.* —**fit′ting·ness** *n.*
Fitz- *prefix* Son of: formerly used in forming the surnames of illegitimate children of royalty. [< OF < L *filius* son]
five (fīv) *n.* **1.** The sum of four and one: a cardinal number.

2. Any symbol of this number, as 5, v, V.   **3.** Anything having five units, as a team, playing card, etc. — *adj.* Being one more than four. [OE fif]

five-and-ten-cent store (fīv′ən·ten′sent′)   **1.** Originally, a store selling miscellaneous articles priced at five and ten cents.   **2.** A store selling articles priced from a few cents to one dollar or more. Also called *dime store, ten-cent store.* Also **five′-and-ten′, five-and-dime** (fīv′ən·dīm′).

five iron In golf, an iron with a moderately sloping face, used in lofting the ball: also called *mashie.*

Five Nations A confederacy of five tribes of Iroquois Indians, the Mohawks, Oneidas, Onondagas, Cayugas, and Senecas, within New York State.

fiv·er (fī′vər)   *n.   Informal* A five-dollar bill or a five-pound note.   **2.** Anything counting as five.

Five-Year Plan (fīv′yir′)   A plan for national economic development: a term first used by the Soviet Union.

fix (fiks)   *v.t.*   **1.** To make firm or secure; fasten so as to be immovable.   **2.** To set or place permanently.   **3.** To render unchangeable: to *fix* color.   **4.** To hold or direct (the attention, gaze, etc.) steadily.   **5.** To look at steadily or piercingly.   **6.** To settle or decide definitely; to determine or establish.   **7.** To place (blame or responsibility) on a person.   **8.** *U.S.* To put in order; adjust.   **9.** To repair or mend.   **10.** *U.S.* To prepare (food or a meal).   **11.** *U.S. Informal* To prearrange or influence the outcome, etc., of (a race, game, jury, etc.) as by bribery.   **12.** *U.S. Informal* To chastise or discipline.   **13.** To prepare (specimens) for microscopic study.   **14.** *Chem.* To cause to form a nonvolatile or solid compound.   **15.** *Photog.* To bathe (a film or plate) in chemicals to remove light-sensitive substances and prevent fading.   **16.** *Informal* To castrate or spay (a dog, cat, etc.) — *v.i.*   **17.** To become firm or stable. — *n.*   **1.** *Informal* A difficult situation; predicament.   **2.** The position of a ship or aircraft as determined by fixed points on shore, astronomical observations, or bearings.   **3.** *U.S. Slang* A decision or outcome prearranged by bribery or other corrupt means.   **4.** *U.S. Slang* An injection of heroin or other narcotic. [< Med.L < L *fixus,* pp. of *figere* to fasten] — **fix′a·ble** *adj.* — **fix′er** *n.*

fix·a·tion (fik·sā′shən)   *n.*   **1.** The act of fixing, or the state of being fixed.   **2.** *Chem.* The conversion of free nitrogen from the air into useful compounds; also, any similar process applied to an oil or a gas.   **3.** *Psychoanal.* An arrested excessive attachment of the libido in a developmental stage.   **4.** Loosely, a preoccupation or obsession.

fix·a·tive (fik′sə·tiv)   *n.* That which serves to render permanent or fixed, as certain substances used on paintings.

fixed (fikst)   *adj.*   **1.** Placed or fastened securely; made firm in position.   **2.** Steadily or intently directed; set.   **3.** Stationary or unchanging in relative position.   **4.** Definite and unalterable.   **5.** Permanent.   **6.** *U.S. Informal* Prearranged as to outcome or decision.   **7.** *Chem.* **a** Formed into or forming part of a compound. **b** Not volatile.   **8.** *Biol.* Sessile. — **fix·ed·ly** (fik′sid·lē) *adv.* — **fix′ed·ness** *n.*

fixed charge   *Econ.* A charge that cannot be changed or avoided, esp. one payable at fixed intervals, as rent; taxes.

fixed idea   *Psychiatry* An obsessional, delusional idea that influences a person's attitude or thinking: also *idée fixe.*

fixed star   *Astron.* A star that seems to preserve the same position with respect to the stars around it.

fix·ings (fik′singz)   *n.pl.   U.S. Informal* Trimmings.

fix·i·ty (fik′sə·tē)   *n.   pl.* **·ties**   **1.** The state or quality of being fixed; stability; permanence.   **2.** That which is fixed.

fix·ture (fiks′chər)   *n.*   **1.** Anything securely fixed or fastened into position; esp., a permanent part or appendage of a house.   **2.** A person or thing regarded as fixed in a particular place or job.   **3.** *Law* **a** Any chattel or article of personal property affixed to reality to become a part thereof and thereafter governed by the law of real property. **b** Such chattel of a tenant, that can be removed without injury to the premises. [< FIXURE; infl. in form by *mixture*]

fizz (fiz)   *v.i.* To make a hissing or sputtering noise. — *n.*   **1.** A hissing sound.   **2.** An effervescent beverage made with soda water, liquor, flavoring, etc.: a gin *fizz.*

fiz·zle (fiz′əl)   *v.i.* **·zled, ·zling**   **1.** To make a hissing or sputtering sound.   **2.** *Informal* To fail, esp. after a good start. — *n.*   **1.** Hissing.   **2.** *Informal* A failure. [Freq. of obs. *fise* to fart]

fizz·y (fiz′ē)   *adj.* **fizz·i·er, fizz·i·est** Fizzing; effervescent.

fjord (fyôrd)   See FIORD.

flab·ber·gast (flab′ər·gast)   *v.t. Informal* To astound.

flab·by (flab′ē)   *adj.* **·bi·er, ·bi·est**   **1.** Lacking strength or firmness; soft.   **2.** Lacking vigor or force; weak, as language. — **flab′bi·ly** *adv.* — **flab′bi·ness** *n.*

flac·cid (flak′sid)   *adj.* Lacking firmness or elasticity; limp; flabby. [< F < L *flaccus* limp] — **flac′cid·ly** *adv.* — **flac·cid′i·ty, flac′cid·ness** *n.*

fla·con (flà·kôǹ′)   *n. French* A stoppered bottle or flask.

flag¹ (flag)   *n.*   **1.** A piece of cloth or bunting, usu. oblong, bearing devices and colors to designate a nation, state, organization, etc.   **2.** The bushy part of the tail of a dog.   **3.** The tail of a deer.   **4.** *pl. Ornithol.* The long leg- or wing-feathers of a hawk or bird of prey.   **5.** *Music* A hook. — *v.t.* **flagged, flag·ging**   **1.** To mark out or adorn with flags.   **2.** To signal as with a flag.   **3.** To send (information) by signals.   **4.** To decoy (deer, etc.), as by waving a flag. — **to flag down** To cause to stop, as a train, by signaling.

flag² (flag)   *n.*   **1.** Any of various irises having sword-shaped leaves and growing in moist places.   **2.** The leaf of a flag.

flag³ (flag)   *v.i.* **flagged, flag·ging**   **1.** To grow tired or weak.   **2.** To become limp. [? < obs. *flack* flutter]

flag⁴ (flag)   *n.* A flagstone. — *v.i.* **flagged, flag·ging** To pave with flags. [< ON *flaga* slab of stone]

Flag Day   June 14, the anniversary of the day in 1777 on which Congress proclaimed the Stars and Stripes the national standard of the United States.

flag·el·lant (flaj′ə·lənt, flə·jel′ənt)   *n.* One who whips; esp., one who whips himself or has himself whipped from religious motives or for sexual excitement. Also **flag·el·la·tor** (flaj′ə·lā′tər). [< L *flagellum* whip] — **flag′el·la′tion** (-shən) *n.*

flag·el·late (flaj′ə·lāt)   *v.t.* **·lat·ed, ·lat·ing** To whip; scourge. — *adj. Biol.*   **1.** Having or producing whiplike processes or branches.   **2.** Shaped like a flagellum. Also **flag′el·lat′ed.**

fla·gel·lum (flə·jel′əm)   *n.   pl.* **·la** (-ə)   **1.** *Biol.* A lashlike appendage, as of a protozoan.   **2.** A whip. [< L, whip]

flag·e·o·let (flaj′ə·let′)   *n.* A flutelike musical instrument blown at the end and having six finger holes. [< OF *flageol*]

flag·ging¹ (flag′ing)   *adj.* Growing weak; failing; drooping.

flag·ging² (flag′ing)   *n.*   **1.** A pavement of flagstones; also, flagstones collectively.   **2.** The act of paving with flagstones.

fla·gi·tious (flə·jish′əs)   *adj.* Flagrantly wicked. [< L *flagitium* disgraceful act] — **fla·gi′tious·ly** *adv.*

flag·man (flag′mən)   *n.   pl.* **·men** (-mən)   **1.** One who carries a flag.   **2.** One who signals with a flag, as on a railway.

flag officer   In the U.S. Navy, an officer above the rank of captain entitled to display a flag indicating his rank.

flag·on (flag′ən)   *n.* A vessel with a handle, spout, and often a hinged lid, used to serve liquids. [< OF < Med.L *flasco*]

flag·pole (flag′pōl′)   *n.* A pole on which a flag is displayed.

fla·grant (flā′grənt)   *adj.* Openly disgraceful; notorious; heinous. [< L *flagrare* to blaze, burn] — **fla′gran·cy, fla′grance** *n.* — **fla′grant·ly** *adv.*

fla·gran·te de·lic·to (flə·gran′tē di·lik′tō)   In the very act of committing a crime: literally, while the crime is blazing.

flag·ship (flag′ship′)   *n.* The ship in a naval formation that carries a flag officer and displays his flag.

flag·staff (flag′staf′, -stäf′)   *n.   pl.* **·staffs** or **·staves** (-stāvz′)   A staff on which a flag is hung or displayed.

flag·stone (flag′stōn′)   *n.* A broad, flat stone for pavements.

flail (flāl)   *n.* An implement for threshing grain by hand. — *v.t. & v.i.* To beat as with a flail. [OE *flygel,* prob. < L *flagellum* whip]

flair (flâr)   *n.*   **1.** A talent or aptitude.   **2.** Instinctive perceptiveness; discernment.   **3.** *Informal* A showy or dashing style. [< OF *flairer* to scent out]

flak (flak)   *n.* Antiaircraft fire. [< G *fl(ieger)* aircraft + *a(bwehr)* defense + *k(anone)* gun]

flake (flāk)   *n.*   **1.** A small, thin piece peeled or split off from a surface.   **2.** A small piece of light substance: a *flake* of snow.   **3.** A stratum, layer, or lamina. — *v.t. & v.i.* **flaked, flak·ing**   **1.** To peel off in flakes.   **2.** To form into flakes. [ME < Scand.] — **flak′er** *n.*

flak·y (flā′kē)   *adj.* **flak·i·er, flak·i·est**   **1.** Resembling or consisting of flakes.   **2.** Splitting off or easily separated into flakes. — **flak′i·ly** *adv.* — **flak′i·ness** *n.*

flam·beau (flam′bō)   *n.   pl.* **·beaux** (-bōz) or **·beaus**   **1.** A burning torch.   **2.** A large candlestick. [< F < OF *flamme*]

flam·boy·ant (flam′boi′ənt)   *adj.*   **1.** Extravagantly ornate; florid; showy.   **2.** Brilliant in color; resplendent.   **3.** *Archit.* Pertaining to a highly decorative style of architecture. [< F < OF *flambeïer*] — **flam·boy′ance, flam·boy′an·cy** *n.* — **flam·boy′ant·ly** *adv.*

flame (flām)   *n.*   **1.** A mass of burning vapor or gas rising from a fire in streams or darting tongues of light.   **2.** A single tongue of flame.   **3.** *Often pl.* A state of bright, intensely active combustion.   **4.** Something resembling a flame in brilliance, shape.   **5.** Intense passion or emotion; ardor.   **6.** *Informal* A sweetheart.   **7.** A bright, red-yellow color. — **Syn.** See FIRE. — *v.* **flamed, flam·ing** *v.i.*   **1.** To give out flame; blaze; burn.   **2.** To light up or glow as if on fire; flash.   **3.** To become enraged or excited. — *v.t.*   **4.** To subject to heat or fire. [< OF < L *flamma* flame]

fla·men·co (flə·meng′kō, -men′-, flä-)   *n.*   **1.** A fiery, percussive style of singing and dancing practiced esp. by the Gypsies of Andalusia.   **2.** A song or dance in this style. [< Sp.]

flame·out (flām′out′) *n.* Burnout, esp. of a jet engine.

flame thrower *Mil.* A weapon that throws a stream of burning napalm or other gasoline mixture.

flam·ing (flā′ming) *adj.* 1. In flames; blazing; fiery. 2. Brilliant. 3. Ardent. 4. Flagrant. — **flam′ing·ly** *adv.*

fla·min·go (flə-ming′gō) *n.* *pl.* **·gos** or **·goes** A long-necked wading bird of a pink or red color, having very long legs. [< Pg. or Sp. < L *flamma* flame + -ING³]

flam·ma·ble (flam′ə-bəl) *adj.* Capable of catching fire easily; combustible; inflammable. — **flam′ma·bil′i·ty** *n.*

flange (flanj) *n.* 1. A projecting rim or collar on a wheel, designed to keep it on a fixed track. 2. A similar projecting part of a beam, pipe, etc., designed to aid attachment or to increase stiffness. 3. A tool used to shape flanges. — *v.t.* & *v.i.* **flanged, flang·ing** To provide with or take the shape of a flange. [? < OF *flangir* to bend]

flank (flangk) *n.* 1. The part between the ribs and the hip at either side of the body of an animal or human being; also, a cut of meat from such a part. 2. Loosely, the outside part of the leg between the hip and the knee; thigh. 3. The extreme right or left part of something; side. 4. *Mil.* The right or left section of an army, fleet, fortification, etc. — *v.t.* 1. To be at the side of. 2. *Mil.* To defend, launch an attack against, or move around the flank of. — *v.i.* 3. To be located at the side of something. [< F *flanc* < Gmc.] — **flank′er** *n.*

flan·nel (flan′əl) *n.* 1. A woven fabric made of wool, or of wool and cotton. 2. A soft fabric made chiefly of cotton, with a nap on one or both sides: also **flan·nel·ette** (flan′əl·et′), **flan′nel·et′.** 3. *pl.* A garment or garments made of flannel. [Prob. < Welsh *gwlan* wool] — **flan′nel·ly** *adj.*

flap (flap) *v.* **flapped, flap·ping** *v.t.* 1. To move (wings, the arms, etc.) vigorously up and down, esp. with a muffled slapping sound. 2. To cause to move with an irregular waving or rippling motion, esp. with noise. 3. To strike with something flat or flexible; slap. 4. *Informal* To throw down or close up suddenly or noisily. — *v.i.* 5. To flap the wings, arms, etc. 6. To have an irregular waving motion, as a flag. — *n.* 1. The part of an envelope that is folded down in closing or sealing. 2. A loosely hanging covering over the entrance to a tent, etc. 3. A loose cover over the opening of a pocket; also, a lapel. 4. *Aeron.* A hinged section as on the wings of an airplane, used to increase the lift or decrease speed. 5. *Surg.* A partially detached piece of tissue. 6. The action or sound of flapping. 7. A blow given with something flat or flexible; slap.

flap·jack (flap′jak′) *n.* *U.S.* A griddlecake.

flap·per (flap′ər) *n.* 1. One who or that which flaps. 2. A broad flipper, as of a seal. 3. A young bird not yet able to fly. 4. *U.S. Informal* A young woman trying to appear sophisticated in dress and behavior: term current in the 1920's.

flare (flâr) *v.* **flared, flar·ing** *v.i.* 1. To blaze up or burn with a wavering light, esp. suddenly: often with *up.* 2. To break out in sudden or violent emotion or action: often with *up* or *out.* 3. To spread or gradually open outward, as the sides of a bell. — *v.t.* 4. To cause to flare. 5. To signal (information) with flares. — *n.* 1. A bright, flickering light. 2. An outburst, as of emotion. 3. A spreading outward; also, that which so flares. 4. *Photog.* Excess light striking a film. 5. *Mil.* A signal that gives off a bright white or colored light. — **Syn.** See FIRE. [Origin unknown]

flare-up (flâr′up′) *n.* 1. A sudden outburst of flame or light. 2. A sudden outbreak of emotion.

flar·ing (flâr′ing) *adj.* 1. Blazing with a bright, unsteady light. 2. Gaudy. 3. Spreading outward. — **flar′ing·ly** *adv.*

flash (flash) *v.i.* 1. To burst forth suddenly or repeatedly into brilliant light or fire. 2. To gleam brightly; glitter. 3. To move suddenly or with lightning speed. — *v.t.* 4. To cause to shine or glitter brightly. 5. To emit bursts of (light, fire, etc.). 6. To send or communicate with lightning speed. 7. *Informal* To show suddenly or abruptly; also, to make an ostentatious display of. 8. To provide (a roof, etc.) with sheet metal or flashing. 9. In glassmaking, to cover (glass) with a thin layer of differently colored glass. — *n.* 1. A quick blaze of light or fire, lasting an instant. 2. A sudden, brilliant manifestation, as of wit or talent. 3. Vulgar display. 4. An extremely brief space of time; instant. 5. *U.S.* A brief news dispatch sent by radio, etc. 6. A volatile mixture containing metal salts, used in applying a colored glaze to glass, etc. 7. A lock, dam, etc.; also, the sudden flow of water made available by such a device. — **flash in the pan** 1. Explosion of the powder in the pan of a flintlock musket without ignition of the charge. 2. A person, thing, or action that shows promise for a short time and then fails. — *adj.* Done or occurring very quickly. [ME *flaschen*; prob. imit.] — **flash′er** *n.*

flash·back (flash′bak′) *n.* A break in the continuity of a novel, drama, motion picture, etc., to give a scene occurring earlier; also, the scene itself.

flash bulb *Photog.* Any of various electrical devices that emit an intense light of brief duration for taking photographs.

flash flood A sudden, rushing flood caused by heavy rainfall.

flash gun *Photog.* A device that ignites a flash bulb.

flash·ing (flash′ing) *n.* Sheet metal or other protective material used to cover joints or angles, as of a roof.

flash·light (flash′līt′) *n.* *U.S.* A small, portable device that emits a beam of light, usu. powered by dry batteries.

flash point The lowest temperature at which the vapors of combustible liquids, esp. lubricating oils, will ignite.

flash·y (flash′ē) *adj.* **flash·i·er, flash·i·est** 1. Brilliant for a moment; sparkling; flashing. 2. Showy; cheap. — **flash′i·ly** *adv.* — **flash′i·ness** *n.*

flask (flask, fläsk) *n.* Any of various small containers made of glass, metal, etc., with a narrow neck; as: **a** A flat container, esp. for liquor, to be carried in the pocket. **b** A rounded receptacle with a long neck, for laboratory work. **c** A powder flask. [< F < Med.L *flasca*]

flat¹ (flat) *adj.* **flat·ter, flat·test** 1. Extended horizontally with little or no slope. 2. Smooth and regular with few or no hollows or projections. 3. Stretched out level or prostrate. 4. Having the front or back in full contact with an even surface. 5. Shallow: a *flat* dish. 6. Absolute and unqualified: a *flat* refusal. 7. Lacking interest or zestfulness; lifeless; dull. 8. Lacking variety or contrast. 9. Deflated: a *flat* tire. 10. *U.S. Informal* Having little or no money: broke. 11. Fixed; uniform: at a *flat* rate. 12. Marked by little or no commercial activity: Trade was *flat*. 13. Exact; precise: in a minute *flat*. 14. *Music* **a** Lowered in pitch by a semitone. **b** Lower than the right, true pitch. **c** Having flats in the key signature. 15. *Phonet.* Designating the vowel sound in *man*, as opposed to the sound in *calm*. — *adv.* 1. In a flat state, position, or manner. 2. Exactly. 3. In finance, without interest. 4. *Music* Below the right, true pitch. — **to fall flat** To fail to achieve a desired effect. — *n.* 1. The flat, plane surface or part of something. 2. Something that has a flat surface; as: **a** A piece of stage scenery. **b** A railroad flat car. **c** A level area of land. **d** *Usu. pl.* A partially submerged plain or shallow; shoal. 3. *Informal* A tire from which the air has escaped. 4. *pl. Informal* Women's shoes with flat heels. 5. *Music* A sign (♭) placed before a note to indicate it is at a lower semitone in pitch. — *v.t.* & *v.i.* **flat·ted, flat·ting** To make or become flat. [< ON *flatr*] — **flat′ly** *adv.*

flat² (flat) *n.* A suite of rooms on one floor, used as a residence; apartment. [Var. of obs. *flet* floor, OE *flet*]

flat·car (flat′kär′) *n.* *U.S.* A railroad car with no sides or roof, used for freight.

flat·fish (flat′fish′) *n.* *pl.* **·fish** or **·fish·es** One of several fishes, as the halibut, flounder, or sole, having a flat body.

flat·foot (flat′foot′) *n.* 1. *Pathol.* A condition caused by a flattened arch. 2. *Slang* A policeman.

flat-foot·ed (flat′foot′id) *adj.* 1. Having flat feet. 2. *U.S. Informal* Direct and uncompromising; plain and resolute. — **flat′-foot′ed·ly** *adv.* — **flat′-foot′ed·ness** *n.*

flat-i·ron (flat′ī′ərn) *n.* An iron (def. 4).

flat·ten (flat′n) *v.t.* & *v.i.* To make or become flat or flatter. — **flat′ten·er** *n.*

flat·ter (flat′ər) *v.t.* 1. To praise excessively, esp. without sincerity. 2. To try to gain favor by praising. 3. To play upon the hopes or vanity of; beguile. 4. To make pleased, as by compliments; to pamper. 5. To show as more attractive. — *v.i.* 6. To flatter someone or something. [< OF *flater* to fawn] — **flat′ter·er** *n.* — **flat′ter·ing·ly** *adv.*

flat·ter·y (flat′ər·ē) *n.* *pl.* **·ter·ies** 1. The act of flattering. 2. An overly complimentary remark.

flat·top (flat′top′) *n.* A *U.S.* naval aircraft carrier.

flat·u·lence (flach′oo·ləns, flat′yoo-) *n.* 1. Gas in the intestines. 2. Windy boastfulness. Also **flat′u·len·cy.** [< F < L *flatus* blowing] — **flat′u·lent** *adj.* — **flat′u·lent·ly** *adv.*

flat·ware (flat′wâr′) *n.* 1. Dishes that are flat, as plates and saucers. 2. Table utensils, as knives, forks, and spoons.

flat·work (flat′wûrk′) *n.* Sheets, tablecloths, etc., that can be ironed in a mangle and do not require hand ironing.

flaunt (flônt) *v.i.* 1. To make a brazen or gaudy display; parade impudently or boldly. 2. To wave freely. — *v.t.* 3. To display. — *n.* The act of flaunting. [ME *flant* < Scand.] — **flaunt′er** *n.* — **flaunt′ing·ly** *adv.*

flaunt·y (flôn′tē) *adj.* **flaunt·i·er, flaunt·i·est** Marked by or given to showy display. — **flaunt′i·ly** *adv.* — **flaunt′i·ness** *n.*

flau·tist (flô′tist) *n.* A flutist.

fla·vin (flā′vən) *n.* *Biochem.* One of a group of yellow pigments widely distributed in plant and animal tissues and including riboflavin. [< L *flavus* yellow + -IN]

fla·vor (flā′vər) *n.* 1. Taste; esp., a distinctive element in the overall taste of something. 2. Something added to increase or impart taste; flavoring. 3. A special, subtle quality pervading something. — *v.t.* To give flavor to. Also *Brit.* **fla′vour.** [< OF < L *flare* to blow] — **fla′vor·er** *n.*

fla·vor·ful (flā′vər·fəl) *adj.* Full of flavor; esp., pleasant to the taste. Also **fla′vor·ous, fla′vor·some, fla′vor·y.**

fla·vor·ing (flā′vər·ing) *n.* Something, as an essence or extract, added to heighten flavor or give a distinctive taste.

flaw¹ (flô) *n.* **1.** Something missing or faulty; defect. **2.** Something questionable. **3.** A crack or fissure. — *v.t.* **1.** To produce a flaw in. — *v.i.* **2.** To become cracked or torn. [? < ON *flaga* slab of stone] — **flaw′less** *adj.*

flaw² (flô) *n.* A gust; also, a brief windstorm, often accompanied by precipitation; squall. [Prob. < ON *flaga* gust]

flax (flaks) *n.* **1.** An annual plant that yields the fiber used in making linen. **2.** The fiber. [OE *fleax*]

flax·en (flak′sən) **1.** Pertaining to or made of flax. **2.** Having a light golden color like straw. Also **flax′y.**

flax·seed (flaks′sēd′, flak′sēd′) *n.* The mucilaginous seed of flax, yielding linseed oil: also called *linseed.*

flay (flā) *v.t.* **1.** To remove the skin, hide, bark, etc., of; esp., to rip off strips of skin from, as by lashing. **2.** To attack with scathing criticism. **3.** To get the money or goods of by extortion or swindling. [OE *flēan*] — **flay′er** *n.*

F′ layer Appleton layer.

flea (flē) *n.* A small, wingless, parasitic insect that sucks the blood of mammals and birds. [OE *flēa, flēah*]

flea-bit·ten (flē′bit′n) *adj.* **1.** Bitten by fleas; also, covered with fleas. **2.** *Informal* Broken-down; decrepit.

fleck (flek) *n.* **1.** A tiny streak or spot. **2.** A bit; speck. — *v.t.* To mark with flecks. [Cf. ON *flekkr* spot]

flec·tion (flek′shən) *n.* The act of bending, or the state of being bent. [< L *flectere* to bend] — **flec′tion·al** *adj.*

fled (fled) Past tense and past participle of FLEE.

fledge (flej) *v.* **fledged, fledg·ing** *v.t.* **1.** To furnish with feathers. **2.** To bring up (a young bird). — *v.i.* **3.** To grow enough feathers for flight. [< OE -*flycge* ready to fly]

fledg·ling (flej′ling) *n.* **1.** A fledged bird. **2.** A beginner. Also **fledge′ling.**

flee (flē) *v.* **fled, flee·ing** *v.i.* **1.** To run away, as from danger. **2.** To move swiftly; leave abruptly. — *v.t.* **3.** To run away from (a person, place, etc.). [OE *flēon*] — **fle′er** *n.*

fleece (flēs) *n.* **1.** The coat of wool covering a sheep or similar animal. **2.** The quantity of wool sheared from a sheep. **3.** Anything resembling fleece. **4.** A textile fabric with a soft, silky pile, used for linings, etc.; also, the pile. — *v.t.* **fleeced, fleec·ing 1.** To shear the fleece from. **2.** To swindle; defraud. [OE *flēos*] — **fleec′er** *n.*

fleec·y (flē′sē) *adj.* **fleec·i·er, fleec·i·est** Like, covered with, or made of fleece. — **fleec′i·ly** *adv.* — **fleec′i·ness** *n.*

fleet¹ (flēt) *n.* **1.** The entire number of ships belonging to one government; navy; also, a number of ships, esp. ships of war, operating together under one command. **2.** A group of aircraft, trucks, etc., organized into a unit. [OE *flēot* ship]

fleet² (flēt) *adj.* Swift; quick. — **Syn.** See SWIFT. — *v.i.* To move swiftly. [OE *flēotan* to float] — **fleet′ly** *adv.*

fleet·ing (flē′ting) *adj.* Passing quickly. — **fleet′ing·ly** *adv.* — **fleet′ing·ness** *n.*

Flem·ing (flem′ing) *n.* **1.** A native of Flanders, esp. of Belgian Flanders. **2.** A native speaker of Flemish.

Flem·ish (flem′ish) *adj.* Of or pertaining to Flanders, its people, or their language. — *n.* **1.** Flemings collectively. **2.** The language of the Flemings, closely related to Dutch.

flesh (flesh) *n.* **1.** The soft substance of the body of a human being or animal, esp. that consisting of muscle but usu. exclusive of fat. **2.** The edible substance of animals, excluding that of fish and sometimes of birds; meat. **3.** The soft, pulpy substance of fruits and vegetables. **4.** The surface of the body of a human being or animal. **5.** The color of the skin of a white person, usu. pink or pale orange-yellow. **6.** Plumpness; fatness; weight. **7.** The body of man as opposed to the soul or spirit; also, the physical, sensual nature. **8.** Mankind; also, living creatures. **9.** Kindred; kin. — *v.t.* **1.** To excite the hunting instinct of (dogs, etc.) by feeding with meat. **2.** To initiate into fighting, bloodshed, etc. — *v.i.* **3.** To become fat. [OE *flæsc*]

flesh-col·ored (flesh′kul′ərd) *adj.* Having moderate pink or pale orange-yellow color.

flesh·ly (flesh′lē) *adj.* **·li·er, ·li·est 1.** Pertaining to the body. **2.** Sensuous. **3.** Worldly. — **flesh′li·ness** *n.*

flesh·pot (flesh′pot′) *n. Usu. pl.* Material advantages or luxuries; also, places for indulgence, as night clubs, etc.

flesh·y (flesh′ē) *adj.* **flesh·i·er, flesh·i·est 1.** Of or resembling flesh. **2.** Plump; fat. **3.** Firm and pulpy. — **flesh′i·ness** *n.*

fleur-de-lis (flœr′də-lē′, -lēs′, flôôr′) *n. pl.* **fleurs-de-lis** (flœr′də-lēz′, flôôr′-) **1.** *Heraldry* A device of three leaves or petals bound near the base. **2.** The armorial bearings of the former royal family of France. **3.** The iris flower or plant. Also **fleur-de-lys′.** [< F, flower of lily]

flew (flôô) Past tense of FLY¹.

flex (fleks) *v.t. & v.i.* **1.** To bend, as the arm. **2.** To contract, as a muscle. [< L *flexus*, pp. of *flectere* to bend]

flexi- *combining form* Bent. [See FLEX.]

flex·i·ble (flek′sə-bəl) *adj.* **1.** Capable of being bent, twisted, etc.; pliant. **2.** Yielding; tractable. **3.** Able to adjust; adaptable. Also **flex·ile** (flek′sil). — **flex′i·bil′i·ty, flex′i·ble·ness** *n.* — **flex′i·bly** *adv.*

flex·or (flek′sər) *n. Anat.* A muscle that serves to bend a part of the body.

flex·ure (flek′shər) *n.* **1.** The act of bending, or the state of being bent. **2.** A turn; curve. [< L *flexura* a bending]

flib·ber·ti·gib·bet (flib′ər-tē-jib′it) *n.* An impulsive, flighty, or gossipy person. [Imit.]

flick (flik) *n.* **1.** A quick, light, snapping movement or blow. **2.** A slight, cracking sound made by such a blow. **3.** A slight trace of something. — *v.t.* **1.** To strike with a quick, light stroke, as with a whip. **2.** To cause to move or snap with a quick movement; also, to remove in such a way. — *v.i.* **3.** To move in a darting manner. **4.** To flutter.

flick·er¹ (flik′ər) *v.i.* **1.** To burn or shine with an unsteady or wavering light. **2.** To flash up and die away quickly, as lightning. **3.** To flutter or quiver. — *v.t.* **4.** To cause to flicker. — *n.* **1.** A wavering or unsteady light. **2.** A quivering or fluttering. **3.** A slight stirring, as of emotion. [OE *flicorian* to move the wings]

flick·er² (flik′ər) *n.* A woodpecker of eastern North America.

Flickertail State Nickname of North Dakota.

flied (flīd) Past tense and past participle of FLY¹ (def. 9).

fli·er (flī′ər) *n.* **1.** One who or that which flies, as an aviator. **2.** One who or that which moves very fast, as an express train. **3.** A big leap or jump. **4.** *U.S. Informal* A risky financial investment. **5.** *U.S.* A handbill. Also spelled *flyer.*

flight¹ (flīt) *n.* **1.** The act or manner of flying; also, the power of flying. **2.** Any swift movement through the air. **3.** The distance traveled or the course followed by an airplane, bird, projectile, etc. **4.** A journey by airplane; also, a scheduled trip by airplane. **5.** A group flying through the air together. **6.** In the U.S. Air Force, a tactical formation, usu. of four or more aircraft. **7.** A soaring or excursion: a *flight* of imagination. **8.** A continuous series of stairs. — *v.i.* To migrate, as wild fowl. [OE *flyht*]

flight² (flīt) *n.* The act of fleeing or escaping from danger.

flight engineer *Aeron.* The crew member of an airplane in charge of mechanical performance during flight.

flight lieutenant (lef-ten′ənt) In the Commonwealth air forces, a commissioned officer. See table at GRADE.

flight sergeant In the Commonwealth air forces, a non-commissioned officer. See table at GRADE.

flight·y (flī′tē) *adj.* **flight·i·er, flight·i·est 1.** Moving erratically from one idea or topic to another; unable to concentrate long or well; giddy. **2.** Moved by impulse or whim; frivolous; fickle. **3.** Not quite sane or clear-headed: a *flighty* old lady. — **flight′i·ly** *adv.* — **flight′i·ness** *n.*

flim·flam (flim′flam′) *Informal v.t.* **flammed, ·flam·ming** To swindle; hoax; trick. — *n.* **1.** Nonsense; silly talk. **2.** Petty trickery or deception. [Cf. Norw. *flim* lampoon]

flim·sy (flim′zē) *adj.* **·si·er, ·si·est 1.** Not strong or solid in structure. **2.** Light, thin, and delicate in texture. **3.** Lacking real validity or effectiveness: a *flimsy* excuse. — *n. pl.* **·sies 1.** Thin paper used for carbon copies or transfers. **2.** Copy written on this paper. [< FILM, by metathesis] — **flim′si·ly** *adv.* — **flim′si·ness** *n.*

flinch (flinch) *v.i.* To shrink back or wince, as from anything threatening or unpleasant. — *n.* **1.** Any act of shrinking back or wincing. **2.** A card game. [< OF *flechier* to bend] — **flinch′er** *n.* — **flinch′ing·ly** *adv.*

flin·der (flin′dər) *n. Usu. pl.* Small fragments; splinters; shreds. [Cf. Norw. *flindra* splinter]

fling (fling) *v.* **flung, fling·ing** *v.t.* **1.** To toss or hurl, esp. with violence. **2.** To put abruptly or violently: to *fling* someone into prison. **3.** To throw (oneself) into something completely or with energy. **4.** To send forth suddenly or rapidly: to *fling* reinforcements into battle. **5.** To move (a part of the body) with sudden vigor. **6.** To give off or diffuse. — *v.i.* **7.** To move, rush, or flounce, as in anger or contempt. **8.** To make abusive remarks; speak harshly: usu. with *out.* — *n.* **1.** The act of casting out, down, or away. **2.** A sneering or contemptuous comment. **3.** A brief period of self-indulgence, unrestraint, etc. **4.** *Informal* An attempt: to have a *fling* at painting. [ME *flingen* < Scand.]

flint (flint) *n.* **1.** A very hard, dull-colored variety of quartz that produces a spark when struck with steel. **2.** Anything very hard or cruel. — *v.t.* To provide with a flint. [OE]

flint glass A hard glass, used for lenses, cut glass, etc.

flint·lock (flint′lok′) *n.* **1.** A gunlock in which a flint is used to ignite the powder in the pan. **2.** An obsolete firearm that was equipped with such a gunlock.

flint·y (flin′tē) *adj.* **flint·i·er, flint·i·est 1.** Made of, containing, or resembling flint. **2.** Hard; cruel; obdurate. — **flint′i·ly** *adv.* — **flint′i·ness** *n.*

FLEUR-DE-LIS

flip (flip) *v.* **flipped, flip·ping** *v.t.* **1.** To throw or move with a jerk; flick. **2.** To propel, as a coin, by an outward snap of a finger pressed down by the thumb and suddenly released. — *v.i.* **3.** To move with a jerk. **4.** To strike lightly and quickly. **5.** *U.S. Slang* To become angry or upset. — *n.* **1.** A quick, light snapping movement, as of a lash. **2.** A drink made with liquor, as sherry, mixed with egg, sugar, and spices. — *adj. Informal* Pert; saucy; impertinent. [Imit.]

flip·pan·cy (flip′ən-sē) *n. pl.* **·cies 1.** Careless disrespect; impertinence; sauciness. **2.** An impertinent act or remark.

flip·pant (flip′ənt) *adj.* Lacking due respect or seriousness; impertinent; saucy. [< FLIP *v.* + -ANT] — **flip′pant·ly** *adv.* — **flip′pant·ness** *n.*

flip·per (flip′ər) *n.* **1.** A broad, flat limb adapted for swimming, as in seals, etc. **2.** A rubber, paddlelike shoe used by skin divers and other swimmers. **3.** *Slang* The hand.

flirt (flûrt) *v.i.* **1.** To act in a coquettish manner; play at love. **2.** To expose oneself to something carelessly or lightly: to *flirt* with danger. **3.** To dart; flit. — *v.t.* **4.** To move abruptly or briskly. **5.** To toss or snap quickly. — *n.* **1.** One who plays at love. **2.** A sudden movement. [Imit.]

flir·ta·tion (flûr·tā′shən) *n.* **1.** Coquettish behavior. **2.** A brief, casual love affair. — **flirt′y, flir·ta′tious** *adj.* — **flir·ta′tious·ly** *adv.*

flit (flit) *v.i.* **flit·ted, flit·ting** *v.i.* **1.** To move or fly rapidly and lightly; dart; skim. **2.** To pass away quickly. — *n.* A flitting movement. [< ON *flytja* to remove, move] — **flit′ter** *n.*

flitch (flich) *n.* **1.** A salted and smoked cut of meat from a pig. **2.** A piece of timber cut lengthwise. [OE *flicce*]

flit·ter (flit′ər) *v.t. & v.i. Dial.* To flutter. [Freq. of FLIT]

fliv·ver (fliv′ər) *n. U.S. Slang* **1.** An old, battered car. **2.** Formerly, the Model T Ford car. [Origin unknown]

float (flōt) *v.i.* **1.** To rest on or at the surface of a liquid. **2.** To remain suspended below the surface of a liquid. **3.** To remain suspended or be carried along in the air or some other gas. **4.** To move lightly and effortlessly. **5.** To go about from one person or thing to another in a random or unstable way. — *v.t.* **6.** To cause to float. **7.** To put (a stock, bond, etc.) on the market. **8.** To cause (a rumor, report, etc.) to circulate. **9.** To launch (a business venture, scheme, etc.). **10.** To irrigate by flooding. — *n.* **1.** An object that floats in a liquid or buoys up something in a liquid. **2.** A piece of cork or similar material attached to a fishing line. **3.** A hollow metal ball attached to a lever governing the supply of water in a tank. **4.** An anchored raft. **5.** A tableau or display carried atop a wheeled platform, truck, etc., in parades or pageants. **6.** A soda or milk shake with a ball of ice cream in it. [OE *flotian*] — **float′a·ble** *adj.*

float·age (flō′tij), **float·a·tion** (flō·tā′shən) See FLOTAGE, FLOTATION.

float·er (flō′tər) *n.* **1.** One who or that which floats. **2.** A person who drifts about from one thing to another.

float·ing (flō′ting) *adj.* **1.** That floats or is able to float. **2.** Moving about or inclined to move about from one place, job, etc., to another. **3.** *Pathol.* Abnormally movable or detached from the usual position: a *floating* kidney. **4.** *Econ.* **a** Due at various times and in various sums: said of a debt. **b** Not assigned to any particular investment: said of capital.

floating dock A type of dry dock that can be raised to leave the ship dry for repairs. Also **floating dry dock.**

floating rib A rib of either of the two lowest pairs of ribs in a human being, not attached to the other ribs or to the sternum.

floc·cu·late (flok′yə-lāt) *v.t. & v.i.* **·lat·ed, ·lat·ing** To form into small, lumpy masses, as clouds. — **floc′cu·la′tion** *n.*

floc·cu·lent (flok′yə-lənt) *adj.* **1.** Having soft, fluffy wool or hair. **2.** Marked by or producing woolly tufts. — **floc′cu·lence** *n.* — **floc′cu·lent·ly** *adv.*

flock¹ (flok) *n.* **1.** A group of animals of the same kind, esp. sheep, goats, or birds, feeding, living, or kept together. **2.** A group of members of the same church or congregation. **3.** Any group of persons under the care or supervision of someone. **4.** A large number or assemblage of persons or things. — *v.i.* To come or go in crowds. [OE *flocc*]
— **Syn.** (noun) **1.** *Flock* is applied to birds and to small mammals, now usually sheep or goats. Larger animals, as cattle and elephants, form a *herd*; when gathered together to be driven, they are a *drove.* Other terms are fairly restricted in application: a *bevy* of quail, a *covey* of partridges, a *gaggle* of geese, a *gam* of whales, a *pack* of dogs or wolves, a *pride* of lions, a *swarm* of bees.

flock² (flok) *n.* **1.** Refuse wool, rags, etc., used to stuff furniture. **2.** A tuft of wool, hair, etc. — *v.t.* To cover or fill with flock. [Prob. < OF < L *floccus* lock of wool]

floe (flō) *n.* A large, comparatively level field of floating ice; also, a detached section of such a field. [< ON *flō* a layer]

flog (flog, flôg) *v.t.* **flogged, flog·ging** To beat hard with a whip, rod, strap, etc. [? < L *flagellare* to whip] — **flog′ger** *n.*

flood (flud) *n.* **1.** An unusually large flow or rise of water, esp. over land not usu. covered with water; deluge. ◆ Collateral adjective: *diluvial.* **2.** The coming in of the tide; high tide: opposed to *ebb*: also **flood tide. 3.** Any copious flow or stream: a *flood* of words. **4.** *Poetic* Any great body of water, as the ocean, a lake, etc. — **the Flood** The Deluge. — *v.t.* **1.** To cover or inundate with a flood. **2.** To fill or overwhelm as with a flood. **3.** To supply excessively: to *flood* an engine with gasoline. — *v.i.* **4.** To rise to a flood; overflow. **5.** To flow in a flood. [OE *flōd*]

flood control The use of dikes, dams, etc., to regulate and control bodies of water that flood easily.

flood·gate (flud′gāt′) *n.* **1.** A gate or valve at the head of a water channel, designed to regulate the flow or depth of the water. **2.** Something restraining or checking an outburst.

flood·light (flud′līt′) *n.* **1.** A lamp that throws a bright, broad beam of light. **2.** The light of this lamp. — *v.t.* **·light·ed** or **·lit, ·light·ing** To illuminate with a floodlight.

floor (flôr, flōr) *n.* **1.** The surface in a room or building upon which one stands or walks. **2.** The area between two adjacent levels of a building; story. **3.** The bottom surface of any cavity: the ocean *floor.* **4.** A level structure or platform for some special purpose: a threshing *floor.* **5.** The part of a legislative house, stock exchange, etc., where the members gather to conduct business. **6.** In parliamentary procedure, the right to speak to the assembly: to be given the *floor.* **7.** The lowest or minimum price for anything. **8.** *Naut.* The more or less horizontal parts of a ship's bottom on each side of the keel. — *v.t.* **1.** To cover or provide with a floor. **2.** To knock down, as to the floor. **3.** *Informal* To puzzle or vanquish completely. [OE *flōr*]

floor·ing (flôr′ing, flō′ring) *n.* **1.** Material for the making of a floor. **2.** A floor; also, floors collectively.

floor leader A party leader in either house of the U.S. Congress, who directs his party's business on the floor.

floor plan An architectural plan of the rooms and other spaces on one floor of a building.

floor show Entertainment consisting of dancing, singing, etc., presented on the dance floor of a night club or cabaret.

floor·walk·er (flôr′wô′kər, flōr′-) *n.* In a department store, one who walks about so as to supervise the sales force, give information to customers, etc.: also, *Brit., shopwalker.*

flooz·y (floo′zē) *n. pl.* **flooz·ies** *U.S. Slang* A loose woman or a prostitute. Also **floos′y.** [Cf. FLOSSY]

flop (flop) *v.* **flopped, flop·ping** *v.i.* **1.** To move, flap, or beat about heavily or clumsily. **2.** To fall loosely and heavily. **3.** *Informal* To be completely unsuccessful. — *v.t.* **4.** To cause to drop or fall heavily. **5.** To flap in a loose, awkward, or noisy way, as wings. — *n.* **1.** The act of flopping. **2.** A flopping noise. **3.** *Informal* A total failure. [Var. of FLAP]

flop·house (flop′hous′) *n.* A cheap, shabby hotel.

flop·py (flop′ē) *adj.* **·pi·er, ·pi·est** *Informal* That flops or tends to flop. — **flop′pi·ly** *adv.* — **flop′pi·ness** *n.*

flo·ra (flôr′ə, flō′rə) *n. pl.* **flo·ras** or **flo·rae** (flôr′ē, flō′rē) The aggregate of plants growing in and usu. peculiar to a particular region or period: distinguished from *fauna.* [< NL, after L *Flora,* goddess of flowers]

flo·ral (flôr′əl, flō′rəl) *adj.* Of, like, or pertaining to flowers.

Flor·en·tine (flôr′ən·tēn, -tīn, flor′-) *adj.* Of or pertaining to Florence, Italy. — *n.* A native or inhabitant of Florence.

flo·res·cence (flō·res′əns, flō-) *n.* **1.** The state, period, or process of blossoming. **2.** A state or period of prosperity or success. [< NL < L *florere* to bloom] — **flo·res′cent** *adj.*

flo·ret (flôr′it, flō′rit) *n.* **1.** A little flower. **2.** *Bot.* One of the small individual flowers that make up the head of a composite flower. [< OF dim. of *flor* a flower < L *flos, floris*]

flo·ri·bun·da (flō′rə·bun′də, flôr′ə-) *n.* A long-flowering variety of rose with large blooms. [< NL, fem. of *floribundus* flowering freely < *flori-* + *-bundus* adj. suffix]

flo·ri·cul·ture (flôr′ə·kul′chər, flō′rə-) *n.* The cultivation of flowers. — **flo′ri·cul′tur·al** *adj.* — **flo′ri·cul′tur·ist** *n.*

flor·id (flôr′id, flor′-) *adj.* **1.** Having a ruddy color, esp. of the type typical of high blood pressure; flushed with redness. **2.** Ornate, esp. to an excessive degree; flowery: a *florid* style. [< L *floridus* flowery] — **flor′id·ly** *adv.*

flo·rid·i·ty (flō·rid′ə·tē) *n. pl.* **·ties 1.** Ruddiness. **2.** Floweriness. Also **flor′id·ness.**

flor·in (flôr′in, flor′-) *n.* **1.** A British silver coin, equal to two shillings. **2.** The guilder of the Netherlands. **3.** One of several former European coins. [< OF < Ital. < L *flos, floris* flower; from the figure of a lily stamped on it]

flo·rist (flôr′ist, flō′rist, flor′ist) *n.* A dealer in flowers.

-florous *combining form Bot.* Having a (specified number, kind, etc., of) flowers. [< L *flos, floris* a flower]

floss (flôs, flos) *n.* **1.** One of several light, silk or silklike substances or fibers. **2.** Soft fibers produced by some plants, as tassels of corn. **3.** The outside fibers on the cocoon of a silkworm. Also **floss silk.** [< OF *flosche*] — **floss′y** *adj.*

flo·ta·tion (flō·tā′shən) *n.* **1.** The act or state of floating. **2.** The act of financing a business undertaking, as by an issue of stocks or bonds. Also spelled *flotation.*

flo·til·la (flō·til′ə) *n.* A fleet of small vessels; also, a numerically small fleet. [< Sp. dim. of *flota* fleet]

flot·sam (flot′səm) *n.* Any goods from a wrecked or imperiled ship that are cast or swept into the sea and found floating there. [< AF < OE *flotian* to float]

flotsam and jetsam **1.** Parts of a wrecked ship or its cargo drifting on the water or cast ashore. **2.** Worthless or trifling things; oddments. **3.** Transients; drifters.

flounce[1] (flouns) *n.* A gathered or pleated strip of material used for trimming skirts, etc. — *v.t.* **flounced, flounc·ing** To furnish with flounces. [Earlier *frounce* < OF *fronce* fold]

flounce[2] (flouns) *v.i.* **flounced, flounc·ing** **1.** To move or go with exaggerated tosses of the body, as in anger or petulance. **2.** To plunge or flounder: said of animals. — *n.* The act of flouncing. [< Scand.]

floun·der[1] (floun′dər) *v.i.* **1.** To struggle clumsily; move awkwardly as if mired. **2.** To proceed, as in speech or action, in a stumbling or confused manner. — *n.* A stumbling or struggling motion. [? Blend of FLOUNCE[2] and FOUNDER[2]]

floun·der[2] (floun′dər) *n.* Any of certain flatfish, valued as food. [< AF *floundre*, prob. < Scand.]

flour (flour) *n.* **1.** A fine, soft, usu. white powder obtained by sifting and grinding the meal of a grain, esp. wheat. **2.** Any finely powdered substance. — *v.t.* **1.** To sprinkle or cover with flour. **2.** To make into flour by sifting and grinding. [Var. of FLOWER] — **flour′y** *adj.*

flour·ish (flûr′ish) *v.i.* **1.** To grow or fare well or prosperously; thrive. **2.** To be at the peak of success or development. **3.** To move with sweeping motions. **4.** To write with sweeping or ornamental strokes. **5.** To use elegant, flowery language. **6.** *Music* **a** To play or sing a showy passage or in a showy manner. **b** To sound a fanfare. — *v.t.* **7.** To wave about or brandish, as a weapon or flag. **8.** To display ostentatiously. **9.** To embellish, as with ornamental lines, notes, etc. — *n.* **1.** A brandishing, as of a sword. **2.** A curved or decorative stroke in penmanship. **3.** Something done primarily for display. **4.** Ornate language. **5.** *Music* **a** A fanfare, as of trumpets. **b** A florid passage. [< OF < L *florere* to bloom] — **flour′ish·er** *n.*

flout (flout) *v.t.* **1.** To scoff at; defy with open contempt: to *flout* convention. — *v.i.* **2.** To express one's contempt. — *n.* A contemptuous act or remark. [Prob. ME *flouten* to play the flute, to deride] — **flout′er** *n.* — **flout′ing·ly** *adv.*

flow (flō) *v.i.* **1.** Of fluids, to move steadily and smoothly along, as through a channel or over a surface; also, of electricity or other forms of energy, to pass along or be conveyed. **2.** To move along steadily and freely as a fluid. **3.** To well out or pour forth. **4.** To move steadily in an agreeably effortless or rhythmic way: Conversation *flowed.* **5.** To be marked by a satisfying, harmonious continuity: The lines of the statue *flow.* **6.** To hang or ripple down in rich profusion, as hair. **7.** To be abundant in something; also, to overflow. **8.** Of the tide, to rise: opposed to *ebb.* — *v.t.* **9.** To cover or flood with some fluid. **10.** To cause to flow. — *n.* **1.** The act of flowing. **2.** Something that flows, as a current or stream. **3.** A continuous stream or outpouring, as of words. **4.** The amount of that which flows. **5.** The manner of flowing. **6.** An overflowing. [OE *flōwan*] — **flow′ing** *adj.*

flow chart A schematic diagram showing a sequence of operations, stages, etc., as for an industrial process.

flow·er (flou′ər, flour) *n.* **1.** A simple or complex cluster of petals, usu. brightly colored, at or near the tip of a seed-bearing plant or sometimes along the stem, and enclosing the reproductive parts of the plant; blossom. **2.** *Bot.* The reproductive structure of any plant. **3.** The condition in which the reproductive parts of a plant are mature, esp. when marked by brightly colored, open petals. **4.** The condition of having arrived at fullest growth, development, or vigor;

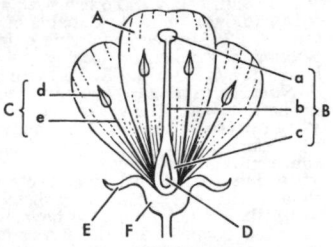

FLOWER
A Petal. *B* Pistil: *a* Stigma, *b* Style, *c* Ovary. *C* Stamen: *d* Anther, *e* Filament. *D* Ovule. *E* Sepal. *F* Receptacle.

prime: usu. preceded by *in.* **5.** The finest or choicest part or representative of something: the *flower* of youth. **6.** *Usu. pl.* A decorative feature; ornamentation. **7.** *pl. Chem.* A powdery substance usu. produced by heating a solid to a gaseous state and condensing the vapors: *flowers* of sulfur. — *v.i.* **1.** To produce flowers; bloom. **2.** To reach fullest development, or vigor. — *v.t.* **3.** To decorate with flowers or floral designs. [< OF < L *flos, floris* flower]

flower girl **1.** A girl or woman who sells flowers. **2.** A young girl who carries flowers in a procession.

flower head *Bot.* A dense cluster of tiny flowers all growing directly from the main stem of a plant.

flow·er·y (flou′ər·ē, flour′ē) *adj.* **·er·i·er, ·er·i·est** **1.** Full of or covered with flowers. **2.** Using or containing highly embellished language. **3.** Having a floral pattern. — **flow′er·i·ly** *adv.* — **flow′er·i·ness** *n.*

flown (flōn) Past participle of FLY[1].

flu (floo) *n. Informal* Influenza.

flub (flub) *U.S. Informal v.t. & v.i.* **flubbed, flub·bing** To make a mess of (an opportunity, performance, etc.). — *n.* A botch or blunder. [Origin unknown]

fluc·tu·ate (fluk′choo·āt) *v.* **·at·ed, ·at·ing** *v.i.* **1.** To change or vary often and in an irregular manner; waver. **2.** To undulate. — *v.t.* **3.** To cause to fluctuate. [< L *fluctus* wave] — **fluc′tu·ant** *adj.* — **fluc′tu·a′tion** *n.*

flue (floo) *n.* **1.** A pipe or tube through which smoke, hot air, etc., is drawn off, as from a furnace or stove. **2.** A pipe or tube, as of a boiler, through which steam or hot air is carried so as to heat water surrounding the pipe or tube. **3.** In an organ, a flue pipe. [Origin uncertain]

flu·ent (floo′ənt) *adj.* **1.** Capable of speaking or writing with effortless ease. **2.** Spoken or written with effortless ease. **3.** Marked by smoothness, grace, and expressiveness: *fluent* gestures. **4.** Running freely, as a stream of water; fluid; also, not stable; changeable. [< L *fluens, -entis,* ppr. of *fluere* to flow] — **flu′en·cy** *n.* — **flu′ent·ly** *adv.*

flue pipe An organ pipe in which the tone is produced by a stream of air passing over the lips of an opening in the side of the pipe rather than by the vibration of a reed.

fluff (fluf) *n.* **1.** A soft, light cluster, ball, or tuft of loosely gathered fibers of wool, cotton, etc. **2.** A mass of soft, fine feathers; down. **3.** *Informal* An error made in reading or speaking lines: said of actors, announcers, etc. — *v.t.* **1.** To make (pillows, blankets, etc.) soft and light by patting or shaking. **2.** *Informal* To make an error in reading or speaking (lines). — *v.i.* **3.** To become soft, light, or feathery. **4.** *Informal* To make an error in reading or speaking lines.

fluff·y (fluf′ē) *adj.* **fluff·i·er, fluff·i·est** Of, covered with, or resembling fluff. — **fluff′i·ly** *adv.* — **fluff′i·ness** *n.*

flu·id (floo′id) *adj.* **1.** Capable of flowing; not solid. **2.** Consisting of or pertaining to liquids. **3.** Readily changing; not fixed: a *fluid* policy. — *n.* A substance capable of flowing; esp., a liquid or gas. [< F < L < *fluere* to flow] — **flu·id′ic** *adj.* — **flu·id′i·ty** *n.* — **flu′id·ly** *adv.*

fluid dram A measure of capacity equal to one eighth of a fluid ounce. Also **fluid drachm.** See table front of book.

fluid ounce **1.** *U.S.* One sixteenth of a pint. **2.** *Brit.* One-twentieth of a pint. See table front of book.

fluke[1] (flook) *n.* **1.** One of several parasitic trematode worms. **2.** A flatfish or flounder. [OE *flōc*]

fluke[2] (flook) *n.* **1.** A sharp projection turned backward at an angle from the principal tip or point of an arrow, harpoon, etc.; also, the entire head of an arrow, etc. **2.** The triangular head at the end of either arm of an anchor. [? < FLUKE[1]]

fluke[3] (flook) *n.* **1.** A lucky stroke, as in the game of pool. **2.** Any piece of good luck. **3.** Anything that happens by chance. — *v.* **fluked, fluk·ing** *v.t.* **1.** To get, make, etc., by a fluke. — *v.i.* **2.** To make a fluke. [Origin unknown] — **fluk′ey, fluk′y** *adj.*

flume (floom) *n.* **1.** *U.S.* A narrow gap in a mountain through which a torrent passes. **2.** A chute or trough for carrying water, used as a source of water power, to convey logs, etc. — *v.t.* **flumed, flum·ing** **1.** To drain away or divert by means of a flume, as in mining. **2.** To transport, as logs, by means of a flume. [< OF < L *flumen* river]

flum·mer·y (flum′ər·ē) *n. pl.* **·mer·ies** **1.** One of several soft, light, easily digested foods, as a custard. **2.** Vapid flattery. **3.** Utter nonsense. [< Welsh *llymru*]

flung (flung) Past tense and past participle of FLING.

flunk (flungk) *U.S. Informal v.t.* **1.** To fail in (an examination, course, etc.). **2.** To give a failing grade to. — *v.i.* **3.** To fail, as in an examination. — **to flunk out** To leave or cause to leave a school or college because of failure in studies. — *n.* A failure, as in an examination. [Origin unknown]

flunk·y (flung′kē) *n. pl.* **flunk·ies** **1.** An obsequious, servile fellow; toady. **2.** A manservant in livery. Also **flunk′ey.** [? Alter. of *flanker* < FLANK, *v.*] — **flunk′y·ism** *n.*

fluo- See FLUORO-.

fluor- Var. of FLUORO-.

flu·o·resce (floo′ə·res′, floor·es′) *v.i.* **·resced, ·resc·ing** To become fluorescent. [Back formation < FLUORESCENCE]

flu·o·res·cence (floo′ə·res′əns, floor·es′-) *n.* **1.** The property possessed by certain substances of absorbing radiation of a particular wavelength and emitting it as light while the stimulus is active. **2.** The light so produced. [< FLUOR- (SPAR)] — **flu·o·res′cent** *adj.*

fluorescent lamp A tubular lamp in which ultraviolet light from a low-pressure mercury arc is reradiated as visible light after impact upon a coating of phosphors.

fluor·i·date (floor′ə·dāt, floo′ə·ri·dāt) *v.t.* **·dat·ed, ·dat·ing**

To add sodium fluoride to (drinking water), esp. as a means of preventing tooth decay. — **fluor′i·da′tion** *n.*

flu·o·ride (flōō′ə·rīd, -rĭd; flōōr′īd, -id) *n.* A compound of fluorine and another element. Also **flu′o·rid** (-rĭd).

flu·o·rine (flōō′ə·rēn, -rĭn; flōōr′ēn, -ĭn) *n.* A pale, greenish yellow, pungent, corrosive, and extremely reactive gaseous element (symbol F) belonging to the halogen group. See ELEMENT. Also **flu′o·rin** (-rĭn).

flu·o·rite (flōō′ə·rīt, flōōr′īt) *n.* A cleavable, isometric, variously colored calcium fluoride, CaF₂, used as a flux in making steel and glass.

fluoro- *combining form* 1. *Chem.* Indicating the presence of fluorine in a compound. 2. Fluorescence. Also, before vowels, **flour:**, also **fluo-**.

flu·o·ro·car·bon (flōō′ə·rō·kär′bən, flōōr′ō-) *n. Chem.* Any of a group of very stable compounds of carbon and fluorine used as solvents, lubricants, insulators, and refrigerants.

fluor·o·scope (flōōr′ə·skōp, flōō′ər·ə-) *n.* A device for observing the shadows projected upon a fluorescent screen by objects put between it and a direct beam of X-rays or other radiation. — **fluor′o·scop′ic** (-skŏp′ik) *adj.* — **fluor·os·co·py** (flōōr·os′kə·pē, flōō′ə·ros′-) *n.*

flur·ry (fûr′ē) *v.* **·ried, ·ry·ing** *v.t.* 1. To bewilder or confuse. — *v.i.* 2. To move in a flurry. — *n. pl.* **·ries** 1. A sudden commotion or excitement. 2. A sudden, light gust of wind. 3. A light, brief rain or snowfall, accompanied by small gusts. 4. In the stock exchange, a sudden, short-lived increase in trading. [Blend of FLUTTER and HURRY]

flush¹ (flush) *v.i.* 1. To become red in the face through a rush of blood; blush. 2. To glow or shine with a reddish brightness. 3. To flow or rush suddenly and copiously: Blood *flushed* into his face. 4. To become cleaned or purified through a quick gush of water, etc. — *v.t.* 5. To wash out, purify, etc., as a sewer, with a quick, sudden flow or gush of water. 6. To cause to glow red or blush. 7. To stir up or elate with the warmth of achievement, pride, etc.: usu. in the passive: to be *flushed* with success. — *n.* 1. A heightened, reddish color. 2. A pervasive feeling of being hot. 3. A pervasive, warm feeling of elation, excitement, etc. 4. Glowing bloom or freshness. 5. A sudden gush or flow of water, etc. [? < FLUSH⁴] — **flush′er** *n.*

flush² (flush) *adj.* 1. Even or level with another surface. 2. Of a line of print, even with the margin; not indented. 3. Of the deck of a ship, extending on one plane from stem to stern. 4. Having plenty of money on hand. 5. Of a period or epoch, marked by prosperity: *flush* times. 6. Having a heightened, reddish color: *flush* faces. 7. Of a blow, direct: a *flush* hit. — *adv.* 1. In an even position with another surface; also, in alignment with a margin. 2. In a direct manner; squarely: hit *flush* on the jaw. — *v.t.* To make even or level, as with another surface. [? < FLUSH¹]

flush³ (flush) *n.* In poker, etc., a hand of cards all of one suit. — **royal flush** In poker, a hand of cards made up of the ace, king, queen, jack, and ten of one suit. — **straight flush** In poker, a hand of cards made up entirely of cards of the same suit and in sequence.

flush⁴ (flush) *v.t.* 1. To drive (an animal) from cover; esp., to startle (birds) from cover. — *v.i.* 2. To rush out or fly from cover. [ME *flusschen*]

flus·ter (flus′tər) *v.t. & v.i.* To make or become confused, agitated, or befuddled. — *n.* Confusion or agitation of mind. [Cf. Icel. *flaustr* to hurry] — **flus·tra′tion** *n.*

flute (flōōt) *n.* 1. A tubular, reedless, woodwind instrument of small diameter, equipped with holes and keys and with a mouthpiece located either along the side or at the end, and producing tones of a high pitch and clear, silvery quality. 2. *Archit.* A groove, usu. of semicircular section, as in a column. 3. A small groove, as in pleated cloth. — *v.* **flut·ed, flut·ing** *v.i.* 1. To play on a flute. 2. To produce a flutelike sound. — *v.t.* 3. To sing, whistle, or utter with flutelike tones. 4. To make flutes in (a column, dress, etc.). [< OF *flaüte*]

flut·ing (flōō′tĭng) *n.* 1. The act of making flutes in a column, frill, etc. 2. Flutes or grooves collectively. 3. Ornamentation with flutes. 4. The act of playing on a flute.

flut·ist (flōō′tist) *n.* A flute player: also called *flautist*.

flut·ter (flut′ər) *v.i.* 1. To wave or flap rapidly and irregularly. 2. To flap the wings rapidly in or as in erratic flight. 3. To move or proceed with irregular motion. 4. To move about lightly and quickly; flit. 5. To be excited or nervous. 6. To beat rapidly and sometimes unevenly, as the heart. — *v.t.* 7. To cause to flutter; agitate. 8. To excite or confuse; fluster. — *n.* 1. A vibrating or quivering motion. 2. Nervous agitation; dither. 3. Excited interest; commotion. 4. *Aeron.* A periodic oscillation set up in any part of an airplane by mechanical disturbances and maintained by inertia, structural characteristics, etc. 5. *Telecom.* A distortion of sound caused by irregular variation in the frequency of a transmitter signal, message, or recording. 6. *Pathol.* An abnormally rapid contraction of the atria of the heart. [OE *floterian*] — **flut′ter·er** *n.* — **flut′ter·y** *adj.*

flut·y (flōō′tē) *adj.* Flutelike in tone; clear and mellow.

flu·vi·al (flōō′vē·əl) *adj.* Pertaining to, found in, or formed by a river. Also **flu·vi·a·tile** (flōō′vē·ə·til).

flux (fluks) *n.* 1. A flowing or discharge. 2. Constant movement or change. 3. The flowing in of the tide. 4. *Pathol.* An abnormal discharge of fluid matter from the body. 5. The act or process of melting. 6. *Metall.* A substance that promotes the fusing of metals, as borax, or that serves to purify metals or prevent undue oxidation of metal surfaces. 7. *Physics* The rate of flow of fluids, heat, electricity, light, etc. — **bloody flux** Dysentery. — *v.t.* 1. To make fluid; melt. 2. To treat, as metal, with a flux. [< F < L *fluere* to flow] — **flux·ion** (fluk′shən) *n.*

fly¹ (flī) *v.* **flew** or (*for def. 9*) **flied, flown** or (*for def. 9*) **flied, fly·ing** *v.i.* 1. To move through the air on wings, as a bird. 2. To move or travel through the air by aircraft. 3. To rush or be propelled through the air, as an arrow. 4. To wave or flutter in the air. 5. To move swiftly or with a rush. 6. To pass swiftly: Time *flies*. 7. To be used up quickly, as money. 8. To flee; escape. 9. In baseball, to bat the ball high over the field. — *v.t.* 10. To cause to fly or float in the air. 11. To operate (an aircraft). 12. To transport by aircraft. 13. To pass over in an aircraft. 14. To flee from. — **to fly at** To attack suddenly or violently. — **to fly in the face of** To defy openly. — **to fly into** To enter suddenly into (an outburst of rage, etc.). — **to fly off** To leave quickly. — **to fly off the handle** To lose one's temper. — **to fly out** In baseball, to be retired by batting a ball high over the field and having it caught by an opposing player. — **to fly the coop** *U.S. Slang* To sneak off; escape. — **to let fly** To utter, throw, or discharge violently, as an oath, a stone, etc. — *n. pl.* **flies** 1. A flap of material concealing the zipper or other fastening in a garment, esp. in a pair of trousers. 2. The flap at the entrance to a tent. 3. The flyleaf of a book. 4. The length of a flag from the staff to its farthest edge; also, the farthest edge. 5. In baseball, a ball batted high over the field. 6. A flywheel. 7. *pl.* In a theater, the space above the stage and behind the proscenium, containing drop curtains, overhead lights, etc. 8. *Brit.* A light hackney coach. — **on the fly** 1. While flying. 2. *U.S. Informal* While in great haste. [OE *flēogan*]

fly² (flī) *n. pl.* **flies** 1. Any of various small, two-winged insects; esp., the common housefly. 2. Any of various other flying insects, as the May fly. 3. A fishhook to which colored bits of material, feathers, etc., are attached to resemble an insect. — **fly in the ointment** Some small thing that detracts from the enjoyment of something. [OE *flyge*]

fly·blow (flī′blō′) *n.* The egg or young larva of a blowfly, deposited on food, etc. — *v.t. & v.i.* **blew, blown, blow·ing** 1. To taint (food) with flyblows. 2. To spoil.

fly·by (flī′bī′) *n. pl.* **-bys** *Aerospace* The passage of a spacecraft relatively near a heavenly body.

fly-by-night (flī′bī·nīt′) *adj.* Financially unsound. — *n.* One who cheats a creditor by departing secretly.

fly·catch·er (flī′kach′ər) *n.* Any of a large order of passerine birds of limited vocal powers and migratory habits.

fly·er (flī′ər) See FLIER.

fly-fish (flī′fish′) *v.i.* To fish with artificial flies as bait.

fly·ing (flī′ing) *adj.* 1. Capable of or adapted for flight in the air. 2. Moving or passing quickly, as if in flight. 3. Waving, streaming, or floating in or through the air. 4. Hurried: a *flying* trip. 5. Pertaining to or used in aviation. 6. *Naut.* Pertaining to sails not secured on all sides by stays or spars. — *n.* The act of one who or that which flies.

flying buttress *Archit.* A bracing structure, usu. a band of stone carried by a rampant arch from a wall to a supporting abutment and receiving the outward thrust of the wall.

flying fish A fish with large pectoral fins that enable it to glide through the air for short distances.

flying jib *Naut.* A jib set out beyond the standing jib, on an extended boom called the **flying-jib boom**. For illus. see SCHOONER.

flying officer In the Commonwealth air forces, a commissioned officer. See table at GRADE.

flying saucer Any of various objects of vaguely saucerlike shape, alleged to have been seen flying at high altitudes and great speeds; an unidentified flying object (UFO).

flying squirrel A squirrel having a fold of skin connecting its front and back limbs, enabling it to glide.

flying start 1. In racing, the passing of the starting post at full speed. 2. A speedy, efficient beginning.

fly·leaf (flī′lēf′) *n. pl.* **·leaves** (-lēvz′) A blank leaf at the beginning or end of a book, pamphlet, etc.

fly·pa·per (flī′pā′pər) *n.* A piece of paper coated with a sticky poisonous substance, placed so as to catch or kill flies.

fly·speck (flī′spek′) *n.* 1. The dot made by the excrement of a fly. 2. Any slight speck. — *v.t.* To mark with flyspecks.

fly·trap (flī′trap′) *n.* 1. A trap for catching flies. 2. A plant, as the Venus's-flytrap, that traps insects.

fly·weight (flī′wāt′) *n.* A boxer belonging to the lightest weight class, weighing 112 pounds or less.

fly·wheel (flī′hwēl′) *n.* A wheel heavy enough to resist sudden changes of speed, used to secure uniform motion in the working parts of a machine.

F number *Photog.* A number obtained by dividing the focal length of a lens by its effective diameter: the smaller the number, the shorter the exposure required.

foal (fōl) *n.* One of the young of an animal of the horse family. — *v.t. & v.i.* To give birth to (a foal). [OE *fola*]

foam (fōm) *n.* 1. A frothy mass of bubbles produced on the surface of a liquid by agitation, fermentation, etc. 2. A frothy mass of saliva, etc. 3. *Chem.* A colloid system of gas dispersed in a liquid. — *v.i.* 1. To become foam or become covered with foam. — *v.t.* 2. To cause to foam. [OE *fām*]

foam rubber A firm, spongy rubber produced by chemical treatment and used esp. in mattresses, cushions, etc.

foam·y (fō'mē) *adj.* **foam·i·er, foam·i·est** 1. Pertaining to, consisting of, or resembling foam. 2. Producing, covered with, or full of foam. — **foam'i·ly** *adv.* — **foam'i·ness** *n.*

fob¹ (fob) *n.* 1. A small pocket at the front waistline of trousers or at the front of a vest, designed to hold a watch, a small amount of change, etc. 2. *U.S.* A short chain or ribbon attached to a watch and worn dangling from such a pocket; also, a small ornament attached to the dangling end of such a chain or ribbon. [Cf. dial. G *fuppe* pocket]

fob² (fob) *v.t.* **fobbed, fob·bing** 1. To dispose of by fraud or trickery: with *off*. 2. To put off by lies, evasion, etc.; also, to try deceitfully to appease: with *off*. [? < FOB¹]

fo·cal (fō'kəl) *adj.* Of or placed at a focus. — **fo'cal·ly** *adv.*

focal distance *Optics* The distance from the center of a lens or curved mirror to the point where rays from a distant object converge. Also **focal length.**

fo·cal·ize (fō'kəl·īz) *v.t. & v.i.* **·ized, ·iz·ing** 1. To bring to a focus or become focused. 2. *Med.* To confine or be confined to a localized area of the body. — **fo'cal·i·za'tion** *n.*

fo'c's'le (fōk'səl) See FORECASTLE.

fo·cus (fō'kəs) *n.* *pl.* **·cus·es** or **·ci** (-sī) 1. *Optics* **a** The point (**real focus**) at which a system of light rays converges after passage through a lens or other optical arrangement or after reflection from a mirror. **b** The point (**virtual focus**) at which such rays appear to diverge and where they would meet if their direction were reversed. 2. The adjustment of the eye, a camera lens, etc., so that a clear image is produced; also, the position of the viewed object. 3. Focal distance. 4. Any central point, as of importance or interest. 5. *Physics* The meeting point of any system of rays, beams, or waves. 6. *Geom.* **a** One of two points, the sum or difference of whose distances to a conic section is a constant. **b** A similar point in some other curve. — *v.* **·cused** or **·cussed, ·cus·ing** or **·cus·sing** *v.t.* 1. To adjust the focus of (the eye, a lens, etc.) to receive a clear image. 2. To fix; concentrate. — *v.i.* 3. To become focused. [< L. hearth]

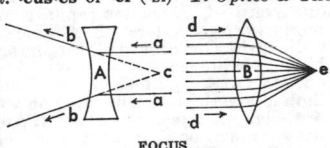

FOCUS

A Biconcave lens: light rays *a, a* refract as at *b, b* and form the virtual focus at *c.*
B Biconvex lens: light rays *d, d* converge to the real focus at *e.*

fod·der (fod'ər) *n.* Coarse feed for horses, cattle, etc., as the stalks and leaves of field corn. — *v.t.* To feed with fodder. [OE *fōdor*]

foe (fō) *n.* An enemy; adversary. [Fusion of OE *fāh* hostile and *gefā* enemy]

foe·man (fō'mən) *n.* *pl.* **·men** (-mən) A foe.

foe·tal (fēt'l), **foe·tus** (fē'təs), etc. See FETAL, FETUS, etc.

fog (fog, fôg) *n.* 1. A cloud of varying size formed at the surface of the earth by the condensation of atmospheric vapor and interfering to a greater or lesser extent with horizontal visibility. 2. Any hazy condition of the atmosphere caused by smoke, dust particles, etc. 3. A state of mental bewilderment or blurred perception. 4. *Photog.* A dark blur clouding part or all of a developed print or plate. — *v.* **fogged, fog·ging** *v.t.* 1. To surround with or as with fog. 2. To confuse or bewilder. 3. *Photog.* To cloud (a print or plate) with a dark blur. — *v.i.* 4. To become enveloped by or covered with or as with fog. 5. To become confused. 6. *Photog.* Of a print or plate, to become clouded with a dark blur. [Prob. back formation < *foggy*, in the sense "marshy"]

fog bank A mass of fog seen at a distance, esp. at sea.

fog·bound (fog'bound', fôg'-) *adj.* Prevented from traveling, sailing, flying, etc., because of fog.

fog chamber *Physics* A cloud chamber.

fog·gy (fog'ē, fôg'ē) *adj.* **·gi·er, ·gi·est** 1. Full of or marked by fog. 2. Resembling fog; cloudy. 3. Mentally confused; bewildered. — **fog'gi·ly** *adv.* — **fog'gi·ness** *n.*

fog·horn (fog'hôrn', fôg'-) *n.* 1. A horn or whistle for sounding a warning during a fog. 2. A loud, harsh voice.

fo·gy (fō'gē) *n.* *pl.* **·gies** A person of old-fashioned or ultra-conservative notions: usu. preceded by *old.* Also **fo'gey, fo'·gie.** [? < FOGGY] — **fo'gy·ish** *adj.* — **fo'gy·ism** *n.*

foi·ble (foi'bəl) *n.* A personal weakness or failing. [< F, obs. var. of *faible* weak]

foil¹ (foil) *v.t.* 1. To prevent the success of; thwart. 2. In hunting, to cross and recross (a scent or trail) to confuse pursuers. — *n.* An animal's trail. [< OF *fouler, fuler* to crush < LL *fullare* to full cloth]

foil² (foil) *n.* 1. A metal hammered or rolled into thin, pliant sheets. 2. A leaf of bright metal set beneath an artificial or inferior gem to add brilliance or color. 3. A person or thing serving by contrast to enhance the qualities of another. 4. *Archit.* A division, space, or piece of tracery suggestive of a leaf. — *v.t.* 1. To apply foil to; cover with foil. 2. To intensify or set off by contrast. 3. *Archit.* To adorn (windows, etc.) with foils. [< OF < L *folium* leaf]

foil³ (foil) *n.* 1. A blunted, rapierlike implement sometimes having a button on its end, used in fencing. 2. *pl.* The art of fencing with a foil. [Origin uncertain]

foist (foist) *v.t.* 1. To impose (someone or something) slyly or wrongfully; palm off. 2. To insert or introduce fraudulently. [Prob. < dial. Du. *vuisten* hold in the hand]

fold¹ (fōld) *v.t.* 1. To turn back or bend over so that one part covers or lies alongside another. 2. To close or collapse: often with *up.* 3. To wrap up; enclose. 4. To place together and interlock: to *fold* one's hands; also, to bring (wings) close to the body. 5. To embrace; enfold. 6. To wind; coil: with *about, around,* etc. 7. In cooking, to mix (beaten egg whites, etc.) into other ingredients by gently turning one part over the other: with *in.* — *v.i.* 8. To become folded. 9. *U.S. Slang* **a** To fail financially; close: The show *folded.* **b** To collapse, as from exhaustion. — *n.* 1. One part folded over another. 2. The space between two folded parts. 3. The crease made by folding. 4. The act of folding. 5. *Anat.* A thin edge or slip of tissue folded over an organ or part. 6. *Geol.* A bend in a layer of rock. [OE *fealdan*]

fold² (fōld) *n.* 1. A pen, as for sheep. 2. The sheep enclosed in a pen. 3. A flock of sheep. 4. A group of people, as the congregation of a church, having a leader, a common purpose, etc. — *v.t.* To shut up in a fold, as sheep. [OE *fald*]

-fold *suffix* 1. Having (a specified number of) parts: a *threefold* blessing. 2. (A specified number of) times as great or as much: to reward *tenfold.* 3. An amount multiplied by (a specified number): a *hundredfold.* [OE *fealdan* to fold]

fold·er (fōl'dər) *n.* 1. One who or that which folds. 2. A road map, timetable, etc., designed to be folded up into a small, compact form. 3. A large binder for loose papers.

fol·de·rol (fol'də·rol) See FALDERAL.

fo·li·a·ceous (fō'lē·ā'shəs) *adj.* 1. Of, pertaining to, or resembling the leaf of a plant: also **fo·li·ar** (fō'lē·ər). 2. Made up of thin, laminated sheets.

fo·li·age (fō'lē·ij) *n.* 1. The growth of leaves on a tree or other plant; also, leaves collectively. 2. An ornamental representation of leaves, flowers, and branches. [Earlier *foillage* < F < L *folium* leaf] — **fo'li·aged** *adj.*

fo·li·ate (fō'lē·āt; *for adj., also* fō'lē·it) *adj.* 1. Having leaves. 2. Foliaceous. — *v* **·at·ed, ·at·ing** *v.t.* 1. To roll or hammer (gold, etc.) into thin plates. — *v.i.* 2. To split into thin leaves or layers. 3. To produce leaves, as a tree.

fo·li·a·tion (fō'lē·ā'shən) *n.* 1. *Bot.* **a** The act of bursting into leaf, or the state of being in leaf. **b** The arrangement or formation of leaves in a bud. 2. *Geol.* In certain rocks, a crystalline formation into leaflike layers; also, the layers themselves. 3. The consecutive numbering of the leaves of a book. Also **fo·li·a·ture** (fō'lē·ə·chŏŏr').

fo·lic acid (fō'lik) *Biochem.* An orange-yellow crystalline compound, $C_{19}H_{19}N_7O_6$, included in the vitamin-B complex. It is found in green leaves, mushrooms, yeast, and some animal tissues: also *vitamin Bc.*

fo·li·o (fō'lē·ō) *n.* *pl.* **·li·os** 1. A sheet of paper folded once to form four pages (two leaves) of a book, the height of the pages usu. ranging from 13 to 19 inches. 2. A book, manuscript, etc., having the oversize pages made from such a sheet; also, the size of such a work. 3. A leaf of a book, manuscript, etc., only one side of which is numbered. 4. The page number of a book. — *adj.* Of, pertaining to, or being of the size of a folio. — *v.t. ·li·oed, ·li·o·ing* To number in order the pages of (a book, manuscript, etc.).

fo·li·o·late (fō'lē·ə·lāt') *adj. Bot.* Of, pertaining to, or composed of leaflets. [< L *foliolum,* dim. of *folium* leaf + -ATE¹]

-folious *suffix of adjectives* Leaflike or leafy. [< L *folium* leaf]

folk (fōk) *n.* *pl.* **folk** or **folks** 1. A people; nation. 2. *Usu. pl.* People of a particular group or class: old *folks.* 3. *pl. Informal* People in general. 4. *pl. Informal* One's family, esp. one's parents. — **Syn.** See PEOPLE. — *adj.* Originating among or characteristic of the common people. [OE *folc*]

folk dance 1. A dance originating among the common people of a district or country. 2. The music for such a dance.

folk etymology Popular modification of an unfamiliar word, thereby causing the word to correspond with better known forms, as *agnail* (in Middle English, a painful nail) becoming *hangnail*.

folk·lore (fōk′lôr′, -lōr′) *n.* 1. The traditions, beliefs, customs, sayings, stories, etc., preserved among the common people. 2. The study of folk cultures. **— folk′lor′ist** *n.*

folk music Music created and perpetuated by the common people.

folk singer One who sings folk songs.

folk song 1. A song, usu. of unknown authorship, originating among the common people and handed down orally. 2. A song copying the style of such a song.

folk·sy (fōk′sē) *adj.* **·si·er, ·si·est** *U.S. Informal* Friendly; sociable; unpretentious. **— folk′si·ness** *n.*

folk·ways (fōk′wāz′) *n.pl. Sociol.* The traditional habits, customs, and behavior of a group, tribe, or nation.

fol·li·cle (fol′i·kəl) *n.* 1. *Anat.* A small cavity or sac in certain parts of the body, having a protective or secretory function. 2. *Bot.* A dry seed vessel of one carpel. [< L, dim. of *follis* bag] **— fol·lic·u·lar** (fə·lik′yə·lər) *adj.*

fol·lic·u·lat·ed (fə·lik′yə·lā′tid) *adj.* 1. Having a follicle. 2. Encased in a cocoon. Also **fol·lic′u·late** (-lit).

fol·low (fol′ō) *v.t.* 1. To go or come after and in the same direction. 2. To succeed in time or order. 3. To pursue. 4. To hold to the course of: to *follow* a road. 5. To conform to: to *follow* the customs of a country. 6. To use or take as a model; imitate. 7. To watch or observe closely. 8. To have an active interest in: to *follow* sports. 9. To understand the course, sequence, or meaning of, as an explanation. 10. To come after as a consequence or result. 11. To work at as a profession or livelihood: men who *follow* the sea. 12. To be under the leadership or authority of. 13. To accompany; attend. **—** *v.i.* 14. To move or come after. 15. To pay attention. 16. To understand. 17. To come as a result or consequence. **— to follow out** 1. To follow to the end, as an argument. 2. To comply with, as orders or instructions. **— to follow suit** 1. In card games, to play a card of the suit led. 2. To follow another's example. **— to follow through** 1. To swing to the full extent of the stroke after having struck the ball, as in tennis or golf. 2. To perform fully. **— to follow up** 1. To pursue closely. 2. To bring to full completion. 3. To increase the effectiveness of by further action. **—** *n.* The act of following. [OE *folgian*]

fol·low·er (fol′ō·ər) *n.* One who or that which follows; as: **a** A pursuer. **b** A disciple or supporter. **c** A servant or attendant. **— Syn.** See ADHERENT. **— fol′low·er·ship**′ *n.*

fol·low·ing (fol′ō·ing) *adj.* That comes next in time or sequence: the *following* week. **—** *n.* A body of adherents, attendants, or disciples.

fol·low-through (fol′ō·thrō̄′) *n.* 1. In sports, the continuation and full completion of a motion; esp., in tennis and golf, the last part of the stroke after the ball has been hit. 2. Any continuing or completion.

fol·low-up (fol′ō-up′) *n.* 1. The act of following up. 2. Something, as an action, procedure, letter, etc., used in following up. **—** *adj.* Designed to follow up: a *follow-up* visit.

fol·ly (fol′ē) *n.* *pl.* **·lies** 1. The condition or state of being foolish; foolishness. 2. A foolish idea or action. 3. A foolish or ruinous undertaking. [< F < *fol* fool]

Fo·mal·haut (fō′mal·hôt) *n.* One of the 20 brightest stars, 1.29 magnitude; Alpha in the constellation Piscis Austrinus. [< F < Arabic *fom al-ḥūt* the whale's mouth]

fo·ment (fō·ment′) 1. To stir up or instigate (rebellion, discord, etc.). 2. To treat with warm water or medicated lotions, as in applying a poultice. [< F < LL < L *fomentum* poultice] **— fo′men·ta′tion** *n.* **— fo·ment′er** *n.*

fond (fond) *adj.* 1. Having affection (for someone or something specified): with *of*. 2. Loving or deeply affectionate. 3. Unwisely or indulgently affectionate; doting. 4. Affectionately nurtured; cherished. [ME *fonned*, pp. of *fonnen* to be foolish] **— fond′ly** *adv.*

fon·dant (fon′dənt, *Fr.* fôn·dän′) *n.* A soft, creamy confection. [< F, orig. ppr. of *fondre* to melt]

fon·dle (fon′dəl) *v.t.* **·dled, ·dling** To handle lovingly; caress. [Freq. of obs. *fond* to caress] **— fon′dler** *n.*

fond·ness (fond′nis) *n.* 1. Tender affection; liking. 2. Extravagant or foolish affection. 3. Strong preference.

fon·due (fon·dōō′, *Fr.* fôn·dü′) *n.* A dish made of grated cheese, cooked with eggs, butter, etc. [< F]

font¹ (font) *n.* 1. A basin, often of stone, for the water used in baptism. 2. A receptacle for holy water. 3. Source; origin. [OE < L *fons, fontis* fountain] **— font′al** *adj.*

font² (font) *n.* *Printing* A full assortment of type of a particular face and size: also, *Brit.*, **fount**. [< F *fondre* to melt]

fon·ta·nel (fon′tə·nel′) *n.* *Anat.* A soft, pulsating, unossified area in the fetal and infantile skull. [< F *fontanelle*]

food (fōōd) *n.* 1. That which is eaten, drunk, or absorbed by an organism for the maintenance of life and the growth

and repair of tissues. 2. Nourishment taken in more or less solid form as opposed to liquid form. 3. A particular kind of nourishment: breakfast *food*. 4. Anything that is used in a manner suggestive of food: intellectual *food*. [OE *fōda*]

food poi·son·ing (poi′zən·ing) A gastrointestinal disorder caused by certain bacterial toxins found in rancid or decomposed food: erroneously called *ptomaine poisoning*.

food·stuff (fōōd′stuf′) *n.* 1. Any substance suitable for food. 2. Any substance, as fat, protein, etc., that enters into the composition of food.

fool (fōōl) *n.* 1. A person lacking understanding, judgment, or common sense. 2. A clown formerly kept by noblemen for household entertainment; jester. 3. One who has been duped or imposed upon. **— to be nobody's fool** *Informal* To be shrewd. **.** **—** *v.i.* 1. To act like a fool. 2. To act, speak, etc., in a playful or teasing manner. **—** *v.t.* 1. To make a fool of; deceive. **— to fool around** or **about** *Informal* 1. To waste time on trifles; putter. 2. To loiter about idly. **— to fool with** *Informal* 1. To meddle with. 2. To play or toy aimlessly with. **—** *adj. Informal* Stupid or silly. [< F < L *follis* a bellows; later, simpleton]

fool·er·y (fōō′lə·rē) *n.* *pl.* **·er·ies** Foolish behavior, speech, etc.; also, an instance of this.

fool·har·dy (fōōl′här′dē) *adj.* **·di·er, ·di·est** Bold in a foolish or reckless way. **— fool′har′di·ly** *adv.* **— fool′har′di·ness** *n.*

fool·ish (fōō′lish) *adj.* 1. Marked by or showing a lack of good sense; silly. 2. Resulting from folly or stupidity: *foolish* consequences. 3. Utterly ridiculous; absurd. 4. *Archaic* Insignificant. **— fool′ish·ly** *adv.* **— fool′ish·ness** *n.*

fool·proof (fōōl′prōōf′) *adj.* 1. So simple and strong as to be incapable of damage or harm even through misuse. 2. Having no weak points; infallible: a *foolproof* plan.

fools·cap (fōōlz′kap) *n.* A writing paper measuring about 13 x 16 inches, usu. folded into a page measuring about 13 x 8 inches, so called from the watermark of a fool's cap.

fool's cap 1. A pointed cap, usu. with bells at its tip, formerly worn by jesters. 2. A dunce cap.

fool's gold One of several metallic sulfides, as pyrite, resembling gold in color.

foot (fōōt) *n.* *pl.* **feet** (fēt) 1. The terminal section of the limb of a vertebrate animal, upon which it stands or moves. ◆ Collateral adjective: *pedal*. 2. Any part, as of an invertebrate animal or of a plant, piece of furniture, etc., corresponding in form or position to the foot. 3. The part of a boot or stocking that covers the wearer's foot. 4. The lower part of anything; base; esp.: **a** The base of a hill or mountain. **b** The part of a bed, grave, etc., where the feet rest. **c** The bottom of a page, ladder, etc. **d** *Naut.* The lower edge of a sail. 5. The last part of a series; end. 6. The inferior part or section: the *foot* of the class. 7. A measure of length, equivalent to 12 inches: symbol (′). See table front of book. 8. In prosody, a group of syllables having a primary stress or accent on one of the syllables and forming a major unit of poetic rhythm. 9. Foot soldiers, collectively; infantry. 10. Step or manner of movement: a light *foot*. **— on foot** 1. Walking or standing. 2. In progress. **— to put one's best foot forward** 1. To do one's best. 2. To try to look one's best. **— to put one's foot down** To act firmly. **— to put one's foot in it** or **in one's mouth** To make an embarrassing mistake or blunder. **—** *v.i.* To walk or dance: often with indefinite *it*. **—** *v.t.* 3. To move on or through by foot. 4. To furnish with a foot, as a stocking. 5. *Informal* To pay, as a bill. 6. To add, as a column of figures: often with *up*. [OE *fōt*] **— foot′less** *adj.*

foot·age (fōōt′ij) *n.* The extent of something as measured in linear feet.

foot-and-mouth disease (fōōt′ən·mouth′) *Vet.* A contagious virus disease of cattle, swine, etc., marked by fever and blisters about the mouth and hoofs.

foot·ball (fōōt′bôl′) *n.* 1. *U.S.* A game played between two teams of eleven men on a field with goals at each end, in which points are made by carrying the ball across the opponent's goal line or by kicking the ball over the opponent's goal posts. 2. The ball used in this game, an inflated, leather-covered ball with an ellipsoidal shape. 3. *Canadian* A similar game played by teams of twelve men: also called *rugby, rugby football*. 4. In Great Britain: **a** Rugby football (def. 1); also, the ball. **b** Soccer; also, the inflated ball.

foot·board (fōōt′bôrd′, -bōrd′) *n.* 1. A board or small platform on which to prop or rest the feet. 2. An upright piece at the foot of a bedstead.

foot-can·dle (fōōt′kan′dəl) *n.* The illumination thrown on one square foot of surface, all points of which are at a distance of one foot from one international candle.

foot·ed (fōōt′id) *adj.* 1. Having a foot or feet: a *footed* goblet. 2. Having or characterized by a (specified kind of) foot or (a specified number of) feet: *light-footed; four-footed*.

foot·er (fōōt′ər) *n.* One who or that which has an indicated number of linear feet in height or length: a *six-footer*.

foot·fall (fōōt′fôl′) *n.* The sound of a footstep.

foot·hill (fōōt′hil′) *n.* A low hill at the base of a mountain.

foot·hold (fŏŏt′hōld′) *n.* **1.** A place on which the foot can rest securely, as in climbing. **2.** A good, firm position from which one can begin or carry forward some course of action.

foot·ing (fŏŏt′ĭng) *n.* **1.** A place on which to stand, walk, or climb securely. **2.** A secure support for the foot; foothold. **3.** An established or secure position or foundation. **4.** Social or professional status in relation to others; standing. **5.** The act of adding a foot to something, as a shoe; also, the material used for this. **6.** The adding up of a column of figures; also, the sum obtained. **7.** *Archit.* A base or foundation wider than the structure it supports, as for a pedestal.

foot·lights (fŏŏt′līts′) *n.pl.* **1.** Lights in a row near the front of the stage of a theater, nearly level with the performers' feet. **2.** The profession of acting on the stage.

foot·loose (fŏŏt′lōōs′) *adj.* Free to travel or do as one pleases; unattached.

foot·man (fŏŏt′mən) *n. pl.* **·men** (-mən) A male servant in livery who answers the door, waits at table, etc.

foot·note (fŏŏt′nōt′) *n.* An explanatory note, reference, or comment on the text, usu. appearing at the bottom of a page. — *v.t.* **·not·ed, ·not·ing** To furnish with footnotes.

foot·path (fŏŏt′păth′, -päth′) *n.* **1.** A path to be used only by persons on foot. **2.** *Brit.* A sidewalk.

foot·pound (fŏŏt′pound′) *n. Mech.* A unit of energy, equal to the amount of energy necessary to raise a one-pound mass through one linear foot.

foot·print (fŏŏt′print′) *n.* The outline or impression made by a foot treading on a surface.

foot·rest (fŏŏt′rest′) *n.* Something, as a small stool or platform, on which the feet can be propped or rested.

foot soldier A soldier trained and equipped to fight on foot.

foot·sore (fŏŏt′sôr, -sōr′) *adj.* Having sore or tired feet.

foot·step (fŏŏt′step′) *n.* **1.** The action of taking a step with the foot. **2.** The distance covered by a foot in stepping. **3.** The sound made by a foot in stepping. **4.** A footprint. **5.** A step of a stairway, etc. **— to follow in someone's foot·steps 1.** To repeat or duplicate the work or actions of another. **2.** To succeed to another's position.

foot·stool (fŏŏt′stōōl′) *n.* A low stool on which the feet can be rested while one is sitting.

foot·wear (fŏŏt′wâr′) *n.* Articles worn on the feet, as shoes.

foot·work (fŏŏt′wûrk′) *n.* Use or control of the feet, as in boxing or tennis.

foo·zle (fōō′zəl) *v.t. & v.i.* **·zled, ·zling** To do awkwardly; fumble. — *n.* A misstroke or misplay, esp. in golf. [Cf. dial. G *fuseln* to work badly] **— fooz′ler** *n.*

fop (fop) *n.* A man overly fastidious in dress or deportment; a dandy. [Cf. Du. *foppen* to cheat] **— fop′pish** *adj.* **— fop′pish·ly** *adv.* **— fop′pish·ness** *n.*

fop·per·y (fop′ər·ē) *n. pl.* **·per·ies 1.** The conduct or ways of a fop. **2.** Something worn by or typical of a fop.

for (fôr, *unstressed* fər) *prep.* **1.** To the extent of: The ground is flat *for* miles. **2.** Through the duration or period of: *for* a week. **3.** To the number or amount of: a check *for* six dollars. **4.** At the cost or payment of: a hat *for* ten dollars. **5.** On account of: He is respected *for* his ability. **6.** In honor of: He is named *for* his grandfather. **7.** Appropriate to: a time *for* work. **8.** In place of: using a book *for* a desk. **9.** In favor, support, or approval of. **10.** In the interest or behalf of. **11.** Directed toward: an eye *for* bargains. **12.** As affecting (in a particular way): good *for* your health. **13.** Sent, given, or assigned to. **14.** In proportion to: big *for* his age. **15.** As the equivalent to or requital of: blow *for* blow. **16.** In spite of. **17.** In order to reach or go toward: He left *for* his office. **18.** In order to find or obtain: looking *for* a hat. **19.** At (a particular time or occasion): to meet *for* the last time. **20.** As being or seeming: We took him *for* an honest man. **21.** In consideration of the usual characteristics of: She is strong *for* a woman. **22.** With the purpose of: walking *for* exercise. **— O for . . . !** Would that I had! — *conj.* Inasmuch as; because. [OE]

for-[1] *prefix* **1.** Away; off (in a privative sense): *forget, forgo.* **2.** Very; extremely; *forlorn.* [OE]

for-[2] See also words beginning FORE-.

for·age (fôr′ij, for′-) *n.* **1.** Food suitable for cattle or other domestic animals; fodder. **2.** A searching about for food or supplies; also, a raid to find or capture provisions. — *v.* **·aged, ·ag·ing** *v.i.* **1.** To search about or rummage around for something, esp. for food or supplies. **2.** To make a raid so as to find or capture supplies. — *v.t.* **3.** To search through for food, supplies, etc. **4.** To obtain by plundering or rummaging about. **5.** To provide with food or supplies. [< F < OF *feurre* fodder] **— for′ag·er** *n.*

fo·ra·men (fō-rā′mən) *n. pl.* **·ram·i·na** (-ram′ə·nə) *Biol.* A small opening or hole, usu. natural, as in a bone. [< L *forare* to bore]

for·a·min·i·fer (fôr′ə·min′ə·fər, for′-) *n.* One of a large order of extremely tiny unicellular marine animals, usu. hav-

ing bony shells perforated with many minute holes. [< L *foramen, -inis* hole + *-fer* having] **— fo·ram·i·nif·er·al** (fə-ram′ə·nif′ər·əl), **fo·ram·i·nif′er·ous** *adj.*

for·as·much as (fôr′əz·much′) Inasmuch as; since.

for·ay (fôr′ā, for′ā) *v.t. & v.i.* To plunder; raid. — *n.* An expedition or raid, as for plunder. [Prob. back formation < *forayer* raider < OF *feurre* fodder] **— for′ay·er** *n.*

for·bear[1] (fôr·bâr′) *v.* **·bore, ·borne, ·bear·ing** *v.t.* **1.** To refrain or abstain from (some action). **2.** To cease or desist from. — *v.i.* **3.** To abstain. **4.** To be patient. [OE] **— for·bear′er** *n.*

for·bear[2] (fôr′bâr′) See FOREBEAR.

for·bear·ance (fôr·bâr′əns) *n.* **1.** The act of forbearing. **2.** The quality of being forbearing; patience.

for·bear·ing (fôr·bâr′ing) *adj.* Disposed to forbear; patient.

for·bid (fər·bid′, fôr-) *v.t.* **·bade** (-bad′) or **·bad, ·bid·den** (*Archaic* **·bid**), **·bid·ding 1.** To command (a person) not to do something, etc.; prohibit from doing, having, etc. **2.** To prohibit the doing, use, etc., of. **3.** To have the effect of preventing; making impossible, impractical, etc. [OE *forbēodan*] **— for·bid′al, for·bid′dance** *n.*

for·bid·den (fər·bid′n, fôr-) *adj.* Not allowed; prohibited.

for·bid·ding (fər·bid′ing, fôr-) *adj.* **1.** Grim and unfriendly in appearance: a *forbidding* face. **2.** Having a threatening or ominous look: a *forbidding* swamp. **— for·bid′ding·ly** *adv.*

for·bore (fôr·bôr′, -bōr′) Past tense of FORBEAR[1].

for·borne (fôr·bôrn′, -bōrn′) Past participle of FORBEAR[1].

force (fôrs, fōrs) *n.* **1.** Power or energy; strength: the *force* of a gale. **2.** Power exerted on any resisting person or thing; also, the use of such power; coercion. **3.** The quality of anything that tends to produce an effect on the mind or will. **4.** Any moral, social, or political power or influence. **5.** A body of individuals belonging to one of a nation's military, naval, or air divisions: the armed *forces*. **6.** Any body of individuals organized for some specific work: police *force*. **7.** *Law* Binding effect; validity: the *force* of a contract. **8.** *Physics* Anything that changes or tends to change the state of rest or motion in a body. **— in (full) force 1.** Still operative or enforceable, as a law. **2.** With no one missing. — *v.t.* **forced, forc·ing 1.** To compel to do something; coerce. **2.** To get or obtain by or as by force. **3.** To bring forth or about by or as by effort: to *force* a smile. **4.** To drive or move despite resistance. **5.** To assault and capture, as a fortification. **6.** To break open, as a door or lock. **7.** To make, as a passage or way, by force. **8.** To press or impose upon someone as by force. **9.** To exert to the utmost; strain, as the voice. **10.** To rape. **11.** To stimulate the growth of artificially, as plants in a hothouse. **12.** In baseball: **a** To put out (a base runner compelled to leave one base for the next). **b** To cause (the base runner on third base) to score by walking the batter when the bases are full. **c** To allow (a run) in such a manner. **13.** In card games: **a** To compel (a player) to choose between losing a trick or playing a trump from his hand. **b** To play so as to compel (a player) to reveal the strength of a hand held. [< F < L *fortis* brave, strong] **— force′a·ble** *adj.* **— forc′er** *n.*

forced (fôrst, fōrst) *adj.* **1.** Done under force; compulsory: *forced* labor. **2.** Strained; affected: *forced* gaiety. **3.** Done in an emergency: a *forced* landing of an airplane.

force·ful (fôrs′fəl, fōrs′-) *adj.* Full of or done with force; vigorous; effective. **— force′ful·ly** *adv.* **— force′ful·ness** *n.*

force·meat (fôrs′mēt′, fōrs′-) *n.* Finely chopped, seasoned meat served separately or used as stuffing. [< *force*, alter. of FARCE, v. + MEAT]

for·ceps (fôr′saps) *n.* A pair of pincers for grasping and manipulating small or delicate objects, used by surgeons, dentists, etc. [< L < *formus* warm + *capere* to take]

for·ci·ble (fôr′sə·bəl) *adj.* **1.** Accomplished or brought about by force: a *forcible* exit. **2.** Characterized by or having force; vigorous. **— forc′i·ble·ness** *n.* **— for′ci·bly** *adv.*

ford (fôrd, fōrd) *n.* A shallow place in a stream, river, etc., that can be crossed by wading. — *v.t.* To cross (a river, stream, etc.) at a shallow place. [OE] **— ford′a·ble** *adj.*

fore (fôr, fōr) *adj.* Situated at or toward the front in relation to something else: the *fore* and hind legs of a horse. — *n.* **1.** The front part of something. **2.** *Naut.* A foremast; also, the bows of a ship. **— to the fore 1.** To or at the front part of something. **2.** In or into a prominent or conspicuous position. — *interj.* In golf, a cry made to warn anyone standing in the line of a ball. — *adv. Naut.* At or toward the bow of a ship. — *prep. & conj. Archaic* or *Dial.* Before: also *'fore.* [OE, adv. & prep.]

fore-[1] *prefix* **1.** Prior in time, place, or rank; as in:

foreacquaint	foreanswer	foreconclude

2. Situated at or near the front; as in:

forebody	forecabin	forecourt

[OE *fore-, for-* before]

fore-[2] See also words beginning FOR-.

fore-and-aft (fôr′ən·aft′, fôr′-, -äft′) *adj. Naut.* Lying or going in the direction of a ship's length: a *fore-and-aft* sail.

fore and aft *Naut.* **1.** Lengthwise of a boat. **2.** In, at, or toward both the stem and the stern of a boat.

fore-arm[1] (fôr′ärm′, fôr′-) *n.* The part of the arm between the elbow and the wrist. ◆ Collateral adjective: *cubital.*

fore-arm[2] (fôr·ärm′, fôr-) *v.t.* To arm beforehand.

fore-bear (fôr′bâr, fôr′-) *n.* An ancestor: also spelled *forbear.* [Earlier *for·be·er*]

fore-bode (fôr·bōd′, fôr′-) *v.t. & v.i.* **·bod·ed, ·bod·ing 1.** To indicate in advance; portend. **2.** To have a premonition of (something evil or harmful). [< FORE-[1] + BODE[2]]

fore-brain (fôr′brān′, fôr′-) *n. Anat.* The prosencephalon.

fore-cast (fôr′kast′, -käst′, fôr′-) *v.t.* **·cast** or **·cast·ed, ·cast·ing 1.** To calculate beforehand; especially, to predict (weather conditions). **2.** To foreshadow. **3.** To arrange or plan beforehand. **— n. 1.** A calculated prediction of weather conditions. **2.** A prediction or prophecy. **— fore′cast′er** *n.*

fore-cas-tle (fōk′səl) *n. Naut.* **1.** That part of the upper deck of a ship located forward of the mast nearest the bow. **2.** A section of a merchant ship near the bow, in which the sailors' living quarters are located. Also spelled *fo′c's′le.*

fore-close (fôr·klōz′, fôr-) *v.* **·closed, ·clos·ing** *v.t.* **1.** *Law* **a** To deprive (a mortgager in default) of the right to redeem mortgaged property. **b** To take away the power to redeem (a mortgage or pledge). **2.** To shut out; exclude. **— v.i. 3.** To foreclose a mortgage. [< OF *forclore* to exclude]

fore-clo-sure (fôr·klō′zhər, fôr-) *n.* The act of foreclosing.

fore-deck (fôr′dek′, fôr′-) *n. Naut.* The forward part of a deck, especially of an upper deck.

fore-doom (*v.* fôr·dōōm′, fôr-; *n.* fôr′dōōm′, fôr′-) *v.t.* To doom or condemn in advance. **— n.** Preordained doom.

fore-fa-ther (fôr′fä′thər, fôr′-) *n.* An ancestor.

fore-fin-ger (fôr′fing′gər, fôr′-) *n.* The finger next to the thumb; index finger.

fore-foot (fôr′fŏŏt′, fôr′-) *n. pl.* **·feet 1.** One of the front feet of an animal, insect, etc. **2.** *Naut.* The part of a boat where the prow and keel meet.

fore-front (fôr′frunt′, fôr′-) *n.* **1.** The very front of something. **2.** The position of most prominence, activity, etc.

fore-gath-er (fôr·gath′ər, fôr-) See FORGATHER.

fore-go[1] (fôr·gō′, fôr-) *v.t. & v.i.* **went, ·gone, ·go·ing** To go before or precede in time, place, etc. [OE *foregān*]

fore-go[2] (fôr·gō′, fôr-) See FORGO.

fore-go-ing (fôr·gō′ing, fôr-; fôr′gō′ing, fôr′-) *adj.* Said, written, or done previously; preceding; antecedent.

fore-gone (fôr·gôn′, fôr·gon′; fôr′gôn′, fôr′gon′) *adj.* Already gone or finished; also, previous or past: *foregone* eras.

foregone conclusion 1. A conclusion determined in advance of the evidence. **2.** A foreseen or inevitable result.

fore-ground (fôr′ground′, fôr′-) *n.* **1.** The part of a landscape, picture, etc., nearest or represented as nearest to the spectator. **2.** The position of most prominence or activity.

fore-hand (fôr′hand′, fôr′-) *adj.* **1.** Of or pertaining to a stroke in tennis, etc., in which the palm of the hand holding the racket faces the direction of the stroke. **2.** First or foremost; leading. **— n. 1.** A forehand stroke, as in tennis. **2.** A position of advantage.

fore-hand-ed (fôr′han′did, fôr′-) *adj.* **1.** *U.S.* Prudent; thrifty. **2.** Done in good time. **— fore′hand′ed·ness** *n.*

fore-head (fôr′id, fôr′-; *occasionally* fôr′hed′) *n.* **1.** The part of the face from the eyebrows to the hair. ◆ Collateral adjective: *frontal.* **2.** The front part of anything.

for-eign (fôr′in, for′-) *adj.* **1.** Belonging to, located in, characteristic of, or concerned with another country, region, society, etc. **2.** Unfamiliar; strange: Anything mechanical is *foreign* to him. **3.** Having little or no relation; not pertinent. **4.** Occurring in a place or body in which it is not normally found. [< F *forain,* ult. < L *foras* out of doors]

foreign affairs Matters of diplomacy, commerce, etc., in the dealings of one country or nation with another.

for-eign-born (fôr′in·bôrn′, for′-) *adj.* Born in a foreign country or state; not native to a country or region.

for-eign-er (fôr′in·ər, for′-) *n.* A native or citizen of a foreign country or region; alien. **— Syn.** See ALIEN.

foreign office The department of government in charge of foreign affairs.

fore-judge (fôr·juj′, fôr-) *v.t. & v.i.* **·judged, ·judg·ing** To judge in advance.

fore-know (fôr·nō′, fôr-) *v.t.* **·knew, ·known, ·know·ing** To know beforehand. **— fore′knowl′edge** *n.*

fore-land (fôr′land′, fôr′-) *n.* A projecting point of land.

fore-leg (fôr′leg′, fôr′-) *n.* One of the front legs of an animal, insect, etc. Also **fore′limb′** (-lim′).

fore-lock (fôr′lok′, fôr′-) *n.* A lock of hair growing over the forehead.

fore-man (fôr′man, fôr′-) *n. pl.* **·men** (-mən) **1.** The overseer of a body of workmen. **2.** The chairman and spokesman of a jury. **— fore′man·ship** *n.*

fore-mast (fôr′mast′, -mäst′, -məst, fôr′-) *n. Naut.* The mast that is closest to the bow of a ship.

fore-most (fôr′mōst, -məst, fôr′-) *adj.* First in place, time, rank, or order; chief. **— adv.** In the chief or principal place, rank, etc. [OE *formest*]

fore-named (fôr′nāmd′, fôr′-) *adj.* Previously named or mentioned; aforesaid.

fore-noon (fôr′nōōn′, fôr′-; fôr·nōōn′, fôr-) *n.* The period of daylight preceding midday, esp. the later business hours; morning. **— adj.** Of or occurring in the forenoon.

fo-ren-sic (fə·ren′sik) *adj.* Relating to, characteristic of, or used in courts of justice or public debate. [< L *forum* market place, forum] **— fo·ren′si·cal·ly** *adv.*

forensic medicine Medical jurisprudence.

fore-or-dain (fôr′ôr·dān′, fôr′-) *v.t.* **1.** To decree or appoint in advance. **2.** To fix the fate of in advance. **— fore′or·dain′ment, fore·or·di·na·tion** (fôr·ôr′də·nā′shən, fôr-) *n.*

fore-part (fôr′pärt′, fôr′-) *n.* The first part in time, place, or order. Also **fore part.**

fore-quar-ter (fôr′kwôr′tər, fôr′-) *n.* The front portion of a side of beef, etc., including the leg and adjacent parts.

fore-reach (fôr·rēch′, fôr-) *v.t.* **1.** To catch up with or get ahead of, as a ship. **— v.i. 2.** To catch up with or move ahead of a ship, etc.: usu. with *on, upon.*

fore-run (fôr·run′, fôr-) *v.t.* **·ran, ·run, ·run·ning 1.** To foreshadow; herald. **2.** To precede. **3.** To forestall.

fore-run-ner (fôr·run′ər, fôr-, fôr′run′ər, fôr′-) *n.* **1.** One who or that which precedes another; also, a forefather or ancestor. **2.** One who proclaims the coming of another. **3.** An advance indication of something; omen.

fore-sail (fôr′sāl′, -səl, fôr′-, fō′səl) *n. Naut.* **1.** The lowest sail on the foremast of a square-rigged vessel. **2.** The fore-and-aft sail on a schooner's foremast, set on a boom and gaff. For illus. see SCHOONER.

fore-see (fôr·sē′, fôr-) *v.t.* **·saw, ·seen, ·see·ing** To see or know in advance. **— fore·see′a·ble** *adj.* **— fore·se′er** *n.*

fore-shad-ow (fôr·shad′ō, fôr-) *v.t.* To give an advance indication or suggestion of; presage. **— fore·shad′ow·er** *n.*

fore-sheet (fôr′shēt′, fôr′-) *n. Naut.* **1.** A rope holding one of the clews of a foresail. **2.** *pl.* A boat's forward space.

fore-shore (fôr′shôr′, fôr′shōr′) *n.* That part of a shore uncovered at low tide.

fore-short-en (fôr·shôr′tən, fôr-) *v.t.* In drawing, to shorten parts of the representation of (an object) so as to create the illusion of depth and distance.

fore-sight (fôr′sīt′, fôr′-) *n.* **1.** The act or capacity of foreseeing; also, a look directed toward something distant. **2.** Prudent anticipation of the future. **— fore′sight′ed** *adj.* **— fore′sight′ed·ly** *adv.* **— fore′sight′ed·ness** *n.*

fore-skin (fôr′skin′, fôr′-) *n. Anat.* The prepuce.

for-est (fôr′ist, for′-) *n.* A large tract of land covered with a growth of trees and underbrush; also, the trees themselves. **— adj.** Of, pertaining to, or inhabiting forests; sylvan. **— v.t.** To plant with trees; make a forest of. [< OF < Med.L (*silva*) *foresta* an unenclosed (wood)]

fore-stall (fôr·stôl′, fôr-) *v.t.* **1.** To hinder, prevent, or guard against in advance. **2.** To deal with, think of, or realize beforehand; anticipate. **3.** To buy up (goods) for reselling. **— Syn.** See PREVENT. [OE *foresteall* ambush]

for-est-a-tion (fôr′is·tā′shən, for′-) *n.* **1.** The planting of trees so as to make a forest. **2.** The science of forestry.

fore-stay (fôr′stā′, fôr′-) *n. Naut.* A wire or rope running from the head of the foremast to the stem and used primarily to support the mast.

for-est-er (fôr′is·tər, for′-) *n.* **1.** One skilled in forestry or in charge of a forest. **2.** An animal dwelling in a forest.

for-est-ry (fôr′is·trē, for′-) *n.* **1.** The science of planting and managing forests. **2.** Forest land.

fore-taste (*n.* fôr′tāst′, fôr′-; *v.* fôr·tāst′, fôr-) *n.* An advance experiencing or sampling of something. **— v.t.** To have a foretaste of; taste in advance.

fore-tell (fôr·tel′, fôr-) *v.t. & v.i.* **·told, ·tell·ing** To tell of or about in advance; utter a prophecy of; predict. **— Syn.** See PROPHESY. **— fore·tell′er** *n.*

fore-thought (fôr′thôt′, fôr′-) *n.* **1.** Advance deliberation or consideration. **2.** Prudence; foresight.

fore-top (fôr′top′, fôr′-; *Naut.* fôr′təp, fôr′-) *n. Naut.* A platform at the top of the lower section of a foremast.

fore-top-gal-lant (fôr′tə·gal′ənt, for′-) *adj. Naut.* Of, pertaining to, or designating the mast, sail, yard, etc., immediately above the foretopmast.

fore-top-mast (fôr·top′mast, fôr-) *n. Naut.* The section of a mast above the foretop.

fore-top-sail (fôr·top′səl, fôr-) *n. Naut.* The sail set on the foretopmast.

for-ev-er (fôr·ev′ər, fər-) *adv.* **1.** Throughout eternity; to the end of time. **2.** Incessantly; constantly.

for-ev-er-more (fôr·ev′ər·môr′, -mōr′, fər-) *adv.* Forever: an intensive form. Also **for evermore.**

fore-warn (fôr·wôrn′, fôr-) *v.t.* To warn in advance.

fore-word (fôr′wûrd′, fôr′-) *n.* A prefatory statement preceding the text of a book.

for-feit (fôr′fit) *n.* **1.** Something taken away or given up

as a penalty for an offense, shortcoming, error, etc.; fine. **2.**
The giving up or loss of something as a penalty for an offense, etc. — *v.t.* To incur the deprivation of as a penalty
for an offense, mistake, etc. — *adj.* Taken away or lost as a
penalty for some offense, etc. [< OF *forfait* misdeed] —
for′feit·a·ble *adj.* — **for′feit·er** *n.*
for·fei·ture (fôr′fi·chər) *n.* **1.** The giving up or loss of
something by way of penalty. **2.** That which is forfeited.
for·gath·er (fôr·gath′ər) *v.i.* **1.** To meet or gather together; assemble. **2.** To meet by chance. **3.** To associate
or converse socially. Also spelled *foregather*.
for·gave (fər·gāv′, fôr-) Past tense of FORGIVE.
forge[1] (fôrj, fōrj) *n.* **1.** An apparatus in which intense heat
is maintained, used for heating and softening metal to be
worked into shape. **2.** A workshop or factory in which such
an apparatus is used. **3.** A furnace for melting or refining
metals, as in the production of wrought iron. — *v.* **forged,**
forg·ing *v.t.* **1.** To heat (metal) in a forge and work into
shape; also, to produce or form as if by hammering into
shape. **2.** To produce, change, or imitate so as to deceive;
especially, to counterfeit (a signature, etc.). — *v.i.* **3.** To
produce an imitation of something; esp. to counterfeit a
signature, etc. **4.** To work at a forge. [< OF, ult. < L
fabrica fabric] — **forg′er** *n.*
forge[2] (fôrj, fōrj) *v.i.* **forged, forg·ing** To move steadily
forward in spite of difficulties, etc. [? Alter. of FORCE]
for·ger·y (fôr′jər·ē, fōr′-) *n.* *pl.* **·ger·ies** **1.** The act of
making imitations of works of art, writings, signatures, etc.,
for fraudulent purposes. **2.** A fraudulent imitation.
for·get (fər·get′, fôr-) *v.* **·got, ·got·ten** or **·got, ·get·ting** *v.t.*
1. To be unable to recall (something previously known). **2.**
To neglect (to do or take something). **3.** To lose interest in
or regard for. — *v.i.* **4.** To lose remembrance of something.
— **to forget oneself 1.** To be unselfish. **2.** To lose self-
control and act in an unbecoming manner. **3.** To be lost in
thought. [OE *forgietan*] — **for·get′ta·ble** *adj.*
for·get·ful (fər·get′fəl, fôr-) *adj.* **1.** Inclined to forget. **2.**
Neglectful; inattentive. **3.** *Poetic* Producing forgetfulness.
— **for·get′ful·ly** *adv.* — **for·get′ful·ness** *n.*
for·get-me-not (fər·get′mē·not′) *n.* A small herb having
blue or white flowers growing in clusters.
for·give (fər·giv′, fôr-) *v.* **gave, ·giv·en, ·giv·ing** *v.t.* **1.** To
grant pardon for or remission of (something). **2.** To cease
to blame or feel resentment against. **3.** To remit, as a debt.
— *v.i.* **4.** To show forgiveness; grant pardon. [OE *forgie-
fan*] — **for·giv′a·ble** *adj.* — **for·giv′er** *n.*
for·give·ness (fər·giv′nis, fôr-) *n.* **1.** The act of forgiving,
or the state of being forgiven. **2.** A disposition to forgive.
for·giv·ing (fər·giv′ing, fôr-) *adj.* Disposed to forgive;
merciful. — **for·giv′ing·ly** *adv.* — **for·giv′ing·ness** *n.*
for·go (fôr·gō′) *v.t.* **·went, ·gone, ·go·ing** To give up or refrain from; go without. Also spelled *forego*. [OE *forgān* to
pass over] — **for·go′er** *n.*
for·got (fər·got′, fôr-) Past tense and alternative past
participle of FORGET.
for·got·ten (fər·got′n, fôr-) Past participle of FORGET.
fork (fôrk) *n.* **1.** An implement consisting of a handle at
the end of which are two or more prongs; as: **a** A utensil
used at table. **b** An agricultural tool used for digging, lifting,
tossing, etc. **2.** The division of something into two or more
separately continued parts; also, the point at which this division begins, or any one of the parts. — *v.t.* **1.** To convey,
lift, toss, etc., with or as with a fork. **2.** To give the shape
of a fork to. — *v.i.* **3.** To branch into two or more separately continued parts. [OE *forca* < L *furca*]
forked (fôrkt, *Poetic* fôr′kid) *adj.* Having a fork or forking
parts; also, sharply angled; zigzag.
for·lorn (fôr·lôrn′, fər-) *adj.* **1.** Left in distress; abandoned.
2. Wretched; cheerless; desolate. **3.** Hopeless. **4.** Bereft:
with *of*. [Orig. pp. of obs. *forlese* to lose, abandon] — **for·
lorn′ly** *adv.* — **for·lorn′ness** *n.*
form (fôrm) *n.* **1.** The shape or contour of something as
distinguished from its substance or color; external structure.
2. The body of a living being. **3.** A mold, frame, etc., that
gives shape to something. **4.** The particular state, character, etc., in which something presents itself: energy in the
form of light. **5.** A specific type or species: a *form* of government. **6.** The style or manner of a poem, play, picture, etc.:
traditional *forms*. **7.** Proper arrangement or order. **8.** The
manner in which something is done: diving *form*. **9.** Fitness
of mind or body for performance: He is in good *form*. **10.** A
document having spaces for the insertion of names, dates,
etc.: an application *form*. **11.** An established method of
doing something. **12.** Mere outward formality; convention.
13. A model formula or draft, as of a letter. **14.** A prescribed order of words, as in religious ceremonies, etc. **15.**
Philos. The intrinsic nature of something; essence. **16.**
Gram. Any of the various shapes assumed by a word in a

particular context, as *talk, talks, talked, talking.* **17.** *Printing* The body of type and cuts secured in a chase. **18.** *Brit.*
A grade or class in school. — *v.t.* **1.** To give shape or form
to; mold; fashion. **2.** To construct in the mind; devise: to
form a plan. **3.** To combine or organize into: to *form* a club.
4. To develop or acquire, as a habit. **5.** To be an element
of. — *v.i.* **6.** To take shape; assume a specific form or arrangement. **7.** To begin to exist. [< OF < L *forma*]
-form *combining form* Like; in the shape of: *cuneiform.*
[< L *-formis* -like < *forma* form]
for·mal[1] (fôr′məl) *adj.* **1.** Of, pertaining to, or based on
established methods, models, or forms: *formal* procedure.
2. Marked by and requiring more or less elaborate detail,
ceremony, dress, etc.: a *formal* dinner. **3.** Appropriate for
elaborate or state occasions: *formal* attire. **4.** Extremely
regular and well-proportioned as to form, design, etc.: a
formal garden. **5.** Adhering to rule, convention, or etiquette. **6.** Of or pertaining to external appearance, manner,
or form: the *formal* elements of a poem. **7.** Binding and
valid: a *formal* agreement. **8.** Pertaining to study in regular
academic institutions or classes: a *formal* education. **9.** Pertaining to or characterized by language of a more complex
and elaborate construction and vocabulary than that of informal speech or writing. — *n.* Something formal in character, as an evening gown. — **for′mal·ly** *adv.*
for·mal·de·hyde (fôr·mal′də·hīd) *n.* *Chem.* A colorless,
pungent gas, CH_2O, used in solution as an antiseptic, preservative, etc. [< FORM(IC) + ALDEHYDE]
for·mal·ism (fôr′məl·iz′əm) *n.* Scrupulous observance of
prescribed forms, as in religious worship, social life, art, etc.
— **for′mal·ist** *n.* — **for′mal·is′tic** *adj.*
for·mal·i·ty (fôr·mal′ə·tē) *n.* *pl.* **·ties** **1.** The state or
quality of being formal. **2.** Adherence to rules, conventions,
forms, etc. **3.** Excessive devotion to outward form. **4.** A
proper or customary act, method, practice, or observance.
for·mal·ize (fôr′məl·īz) *v.* **·ized, ·iz·ing** *v.t.* **1.** To make
formal. **2.** To give form to. — *v.i.* **3.** To be formal; act
formally. — **for′mal·i·za′tion** *n.* — **for′mal·iz′er** *n.*
for·mat (fôr′mat) *n.* **1.** The form, size, type face, margins,
and general style of a publication. **2.** The general form or
arrangement of anything. [< F < L *formare* to form]
for·ma·tion (fôr·mā′shən) *n.* **1.** The act or process of forming, or the state of being formed. **2.** That which is formed.
3. The manner in which a thing is shaped or formed. **4.**
Mil. The disposition of troops, as in a column, line, or square.
5. *Aeron.* A grouping of aircraft in flight. **6.** *Geol.* Mineral
deposits, or rock masses, having common characteristics.
form·a·tive (fôr′mə·tiv) *adj.* **1.** Having power to shape,
form, or mold: a *formative* influence. **2.** Of or pertaining to
formation or development: *formative* years. — *n. Gram.* **1.**
An element added to the base of a word to give it a new and
special grammatical form. **2.** A word so formed.
form·er[1] (fôr′mər) *n.* One who or that which forms.
form·er[2] (fôr′mər) *adj.* **1.** Being the first of two persons or
things referred to: often preceded by *the* and used absolutely:
opposed to *latter*. **2.** Previous: my *former* colleague. **3.**
Earlier: *former* times. [ME *formere*]
for·mer·ly (fôr′mər·lē) *adv.* Some time or a long time ago.
for·mic (fôr′mik) *adj.* **1.** Of or pertaining to ants. **2.** Designating or derived from formic acid. [< L *formica* ant]
formic acid *Chem.* A colorless, corrosive compound,
$HCOOH$, with a penetrating odor, occurring in ants and certain other insects and in some plants.
for·mi·da·ble (fôr′mi·də·bəl) *adj.* **1.** Exciting fear or dread
by reason of strength, size, etc. **2.** Extremely difficult. [<
MF < L *formidare* to fear] — **for′mi·da·bil′i·ty, for′mi·da·
ble·ness** *n.* — **for′mi·da·bly** *adv.*
form·less (fôrm′lis) *adj.* Lacking form or structure; shapeless. — **form′less·ly** *adv.* — **form′less·ness** *n.*
form letter One of many reproductions of a letter, etc.
For·mo·san (fôr·mō′sən) *n.* **1.** A native or inhabitant
of the island of Formosa (Taiwan). **2.** The Indonesian
language of the Malay aborigines of Formosa. — *adj.* Of or
pertaining to Formosa, its people, or their language.
for·mu·la (fôr′myə·lə) *n.* *pl.* **·las** or **·lae** (-lē) **1.** An exact
or prescribed method or form for doing something. **2.** A
fixed order or form of words. **3.** A prescription or recipe;
also, the mixture prepared. **4.** *Math.* A rule or combination
expressed in algebraic or symbolic form. **5.** *Chem.* A symbolic representation of the composition of a chemical compound, as H_2SO_4, acid. [< L, dim. of *forma* form]
for·mu·lar·ize (fôr′myə·lə·rīz′) *v.t.* **ized, ·iz·ing** To formulate. — **for′mu·lar·i·za′tion** *n.*
for·mu·lar·y (fôr′myə·ler′ē) *adj.* Pertaining to, stated in,
or resembling a formula. — *n. pl.* **·lar·ies** **1.** A compilation of formulas. **2.** A book listing pharmaceutical substances, their formulas, and preparation. **3.** A church ritual,
or a book containing such rituals. **4.** A formula.

for·mu·late (fôr′myə·lāt) *v.t.* **·lat·ed, ·lat·ing** 1. To express in or as a formula. 2. To put or state in exact and systematic form. — **for′mu·la′tion** *n.* — **for′mu·la′tor** *n.*

for·mu·lize (fôr′myə·līz) *v.t.* **·lized, ·liz·ing** To formulate.

for·ni·cate (fôr′nə·kāt) *v.i.* **·cat·ed, ·cat·ing** To commit fornication. [< L *fornix, -icis* brothel] — **for′ni·ca′tor** *n.*

for·ni·ca·tion (fôr′nə·kā′shən) *n.* Voluntary sexual intercourse between unmarried persons.

for·sake (fôr·sāk′, fər-) *v.t.* **·sook, ·sak·en, ·sak·ing** 1. To renounce or relinquish (an occupation, belief, etc.). 2. To abandon; desert. [OE *forsacan* to repudiate, deny]

for·sooth (fôr·sōōth′, fər-) *adv.* In truth; certainly. [OE]

for·swear (fôr·swâr′) *v.* **·swore, ·sworn, ·swear·ing** *v.t.* 1. To renounce or abandon emphatically or upon oath. 2. To deny absolutely or upon oath: to *forswear* a debt. — *v.i.* 3. To swear falsely; commit perjury. — **Syn.** See RENOUNCE. [OE *forswerian* to swear falsely]

for·sworn (fôr·swôrn′, -swōrn′) *adj.* Perjured.

for·syth·i·a (fôr·sith′ē·ə, -sī′thē·ə, fər-) *n.* A shrub of the olive family, cultivated for its bright yellow flowers. [after William *Forsyth,* 1737–1804, British botanist]

fort (fôrt, fōrt) *n.* 1. A fortified enclosure or structure capable of defense against an enemy. 2. A permanent U.S. army post. [< F, orig. adj. strong]

forte[1] (fôrt, fōrt, fôr′tā) *n.* That which one does with excellence; strong point. [See FORT.]

for·te[2] (fôr′tā, -tē) *Music adj.* Loud; forceful. — *adv.* Loudly; forcefully. [< Ital.]

forth (fôrth, fōrth) *adv.* 1. Forward in place, time, or order. 2. Out, as from seclusion, confinement, or inaction. 3. Away or out, as from a place of origin; abroad. — **and so forth** And the rest; and so on. [OE]

forth·com·ing (fôrth′kum′ing, fōrth′-) *adj.* 1. Drawing near in time; approaching. 2. Ready or about to appear, arrive, etc. 3. Available or produced when expected or due. — *n.* Arrival or appearance of something due or expected.

forth·right (fôrth′rīt′, fōrth′-) *adj.* 1. Coming straight to the point; candid; frank. 2. Going forward in a straight line; direct. — *adv.* 1. In a direct course or straightforward manner. 2. At once; straightway. — **forth′right′ness** *n.*

forth·with (fôrth′with′, -with′, fōrth′-) *adv.* Immediately.

for·ti·fi·ca·tion (fôr′tə·fə·kā′shən) *n.* 1. The act, art, or science of fortifying. 2. That which fortifies, as walls, ditches, etc. 3. A military place of defense.

for·ti·fy (fôr′tə·fī) *v.* **·fied, ·fy·ing** *v.t.* 1. To provide with defensive works; strengthen against attack. 2. To give physical or moral strength to. 3. To strengthen the structure of; reinforce. 4. To confirm. 5. To strengthen, as wine, by adding alcohol. 6. To enrich (food) by adding minerals, vitamins, etc. — *v.i.* 7. To raise defensive works. [< F < L *fortis* strong + *facere* to make] — **for′ti·fi′a·ble** *adj.* — **for′ti·fi′er** *n.*

for·tis·si·mo (fôr·tis′ə·mō, Ital. fôr·tēs′sē·mō) *adj. & adv. Music* Very loud. — *n. pl.* **·mos** A fortissimo note, chord, or passage. [< Ital., superl. of *forte* strong]

for·ti·tude (fôr′tə·tōōd, -tyōōd) *n.* Strength of mind in the face of pain, adversity, or peril; patient courage. — **for′ti·tu′di·nous** (-də·nəs) *adj.*

fort·night (fôrt′nīt′, -nit′) *n.* A period of two weeks; fourteen days. [OE *fēowertēne* fourteen + *niht* nights]

fort·night·ly (fôrt′nīt′lē) *adj.* Occurring, coming, or issued every fortnight. — *adv.* Once a fortnight.

for·tress (fôr′tris) *n.* 1. A large military stronghold; a fort, a series of forts, or a heavily fortified town. 2. Any place of security. — *v.t.* To furnish or strengthen with a fortress; fortify. [< OF < L *fortis* strong]

for·tu·i·tous (fôr·tōō′ə·təs, -tyōō′-) *adj.* Occurring by chance rather than by design; casual; accidental. — **Syn.** See ACCIDENTAL. [< L *fors* chance] — **for·tu′i·tous·ly** *adv.* — **for·tu′i·tous·ness** *n.*

for·tu·i·ty (fôr·tōō′ə·tē, -tyōō′-) *n. pl.* **·ties** Chance occurrence; also, chance.

for·tu·nate (fôr′chə·nit) *adj.* 1. Happening by a favorable chance; lucky. 2. Favored with good fortune. — **for′tu·nate·ly** *adv.* — **for′tu·nate·ness** *n.*

for·tune (fôr′chən) *n.* 1. That which happens or is to happen to one, whether good or bad. 2. A power supposed to control one's future; fate: often personified. 3. Luck or chance, esp. when favorable. 4. An amount of wealth or possessions. 5. Great wealth or riches. 6. A particular condition or state of life, usu. prosperous.

for·tune-tell·er (fôr′chən·tel′ər) *n.* One who claims to foretell events in a person's future. — **for′tune-tell′ing** *n. & adj.*

for·ty (fôr′tē) *n. pl.* **·ties** 1. The sum of thirty and ten: a cardinal number. 2. Any symbol of this number, as 40, xl, XL. 3. Anything consisting of or representing forty units. — *adj.* Being ten more than thirty. [OE *fēowertig*] — **for′ti·eth** *adj. & n.*

for·ty-nin·er (fôr′tē·nī′nər) *n.* U.S. A pioneer who went to California in 1849, the year of the gold rush.

forty winks *Informal* A short nap.

fo·rum (fôr′əm, fō′rəm) *n. pl.* **fo·rums** or **fo·ra** (fôr′ə, fō′rə) 1. The public market place of an ancient Roman city, where popular assemblies met, and most legal and political business was transacted. 2. A tribunal; court. 3. An assembly for discussion of public affairs. [< L]

for·ward (fôr′wərd) *adv.* 1. Toward what is ahead or what is in front; onward. Also **for′wards.** 2. At or in the front part, as of a ship. 3. Out into a conspicuous position; to the forefront. — **forward of** U.S. In front of. — *adj.* 1. Being at or near the front. 2. Moving or directed toward a point lying ahead. 3. Overstepping the usual bounds of propriety in an insolent or presumptuous way; bold. 4. Well-developed; not backward. 5. Developing or developed earlier than usual; also, precocious. 6. Extremely progressive or unconventional, as in political opinions. 7. Ready or prompt. 8. Made or done in advance: a *forward* contract for goods. — *n.* 1. In football, one of the players in the front lines of attack or defense. 2. In basketball, hockey, etc., a player who leads the offensive play. — *v.t.* 1. To help onward or ahead. 2. To send onward; esp., to send (mail) on to a new address. [OE *foreweard*] — **for′ward·er** *n.* — **for′ward·ly** *adv.* — **for′ward·ness** *n.*

forward pass In football, the throwing or passing of the ball toward the opponent's goal.

fos·sa (fos′ə) *n. pl.* **fos·sae** (fos′ē) *Anat.* A shallow depression or cavity in the body. [< L. See FOSSE.]

fos·sil (fos′əl) *n. Paleontol.* 1. The remains of plants or animals, preserved in the rocks of the earth's crust. 2. Some petrified trace of the existence of an early organism, as a petrified footprint. 3. *Informal* One who or that which is out of date. — *adj.* 1. Of or like a fossil. 2. Belonging to the past; out-of-date. [< F < L *fodire* to dig]

fos·sil·ize (fos′əl·īz) *v.* **·ized, ·iz·ing** *v.t.* 1. To change into a fossil; petrify. 2. To make antiquated or out of date. — *v.i.* 3. To become a fossil. — **fos′sil·i·za′tion** *n.*

fos·ter (fôs′tər, fos′-) *v.t.* 1. To bring up (a child); rear. 2. To promote the growth or development of: to *foster* genius. 3. To keep alive (feelings, hopes, etc.) within oneself; cherish. [OE *fōstrian* nourish] — **fos′ter·age** *n.*

foster child A child reared by a foster parent or parents.

foster parent A man or woman rearing a child not his or her own.

fought (fôt) Past tense and past participle of FIGHT.

foul (foul) *adj.* 1. Offensive or revolting to the senses; disgusting: a *foul* odor. 2. Full of dirt or impure matter; filthy. 3. Clogged or packed with dirt, etc. 4. Spoiled or rotten, as food. 5. Unfavorable; adverse: *foul* weather. 6. Obscene; vulgar. 7. Morally offensive; wicked. 8. Not according to rule or justice; unfair. 9. Impeded or entangled: a *foul* anchor. 10. In baseball, etc., of or pertaining to a foul ball or the foul lines. 11. *Informal* Very bad; unsatisfactory. — *n.* 1. An act of fouling, colliding, or becoming entangled. 2. Something foul, as: **a** A foul ball. **b** A breach of rule in various sports. **c** An entanglement or collision, as of ropes, boats, etc. — *v.t.* 1. To make foul or dirty. 2. To dishonor; disgrace. 3. To clog or choke, as a drain. 4. To entangle or snarl, as a rope. 5. To cover or encumber (a ship's bottom) with barnacles, seaweed, etc. 6. To collide with. 7. In sports, to commit a foul against. 8. In baseball, to bat (the ball) outside of the foul lines. — *v.i.* 9. To become foul or dirty. 10. To become clogged or encumbered. 11. To become entangled. 12. To collide. 13. In sports, to violate a rule. 14. In baseball, to bat a foul ball. — **to foul up** *Slang* 1. To throw into disorder or confusion. 2. To blunder. [OE *fūl*] — **foul′ly** *adv.* — **foul′ness** *n.*

fou·lard (fōō·lärd′) *n.* 1. A lightweight, satiny fabric of silk, rayon, cotton, etc., usu. with a printed design. 2. A scarf, necktie, or other article made of this fabric. [< F < Swiss F < OF < LL *fullare* to full cloth]

foul ball In baseball: **a** A batted ball that first hits the ground outside the foul lines. **b** A batted ball hitting the ground within the foul lines but passing outside the lines before reaching first or third base.

foul line 1. In baseball, either of the two lines extending from home plate past first and third base to the limits of the field. 2. In basketball, the free-throw line. 3. In bowling, etc., any line limiting the area of play or action.

foul-mouthed (foul′mouthd′, -moutht′) *adj.* Using abusive, profane, or obscene language.

foul play 1. Unfairness; in games and sports, a violation of rule. 2. Any unfair or treacherous action, often murder.

found[1] (found) *v.t.* 1. To give origin to; set up; establish. 2. To lay the foundation of; establish on a foundation or basis. — *v.i.* 3. To be established or based: with *on, upon.* [< OF < L *fundus* base, bottom]

found[2] (found) *v.t.* 1. To cast, as iron, by melting and pouring into a mold. 2. To make by casting molten metal. [< F < L *fundere* to pour]

found[3] (found) Past tense and past participle of FIND. — *adj.* Provided with food, lodging, equipment, etc.

foun·da·tion (foun·dā′shən) *n.* 1. The act of founding or establishing. **2.** The state of being founded or established. **3.** That on which anything is founded; basis: *Equality is the foundation of democracy.* **4.** A base on which something rests: *a machine's foundation.* **5.** That part of a building or wall, wholly or partly below the surface of the ground, that constitutes a base. **6.** A fund for the maintenance of an institution; an endowment. **7.** An endowed institution, esp. one that grants funds for research projects, charities, etc. **8.** A foundation garment. — **foun·da'tion·al** *adj.*

foundation garment *U.S.* A girdle or corset.

found·er[1] (foun'dər) *n.* One who establishes.

found·er[2] (foun'dər) *n.* One who makes metal castings.

foun·der[3] (foun'dər) *v.i.* **1.** To sink after filling with water, as a boat or ship. **2.** To fall or cave in, as land or buildings. **3.** To fail completely; collapse. **4.** To stumble and become lame, as a horse. — *v.t.* **5.** To cause to sink. — *n.* The act of foundering. [< OF < L *fundus* bottom]

found·ling (found'ling) *n.* A deserted infant of unknown parentage. [ME *funde*, pp. of *find* + -LING[1]]

foun·dry (foun'drē) *n. pl.* **·dries** **1.** An establishment in which metal, etc., is cast; also, an article made by casting. **2.** The act or operation of founding metal, etc.

fount[1] (fount) *n.* **1.** A fountain. **2.** Any source. [< F < L *fons, fontis* fountain]

fount[2] (fount) British spelling of FONT[2].

foun·tain (foun'tən) *n.* **1.** A spring or jet of water issuing from the earth; esp., the source of a stream. **2.** The origin or source of anything. **3.** A jet or spray of water forced upward artificially, as to provide water for drinking. **4.** A basinlike structure for such a jet to rise and fall in. [< OF < LL *fontana,* orig. fem. singular of L *fontanus* of a spring]

foun·tain·head (foun'tən·hed') *n.* **1.** A spring from which a stream takes its source. **2.** Any source or origin.

fountain pen A pen having a supply of ink automatically fed to the writing end from a reservoir or cartridge.

four (fôr, fōr) *n.* **1.** The sum of three and one: a cardinal number. **2.** Any symbol of this number, as 4, iv, IV. **3.** Anything consisting of or representing four units. — **on all fours** **1.** On hands and knees. **2.** On all four feet. — *adj.* Being one more than three; quaternary. [OE *fēower*] — **fourth** (fôrth, fōrth) *adj. & n.*

four-flush (fôr'flush', fōr'-) *v.i.* **1.** To bet on a poker hand lacking one card to a flush. **2.** *Slang* To bluff.

four-flush·er (fôr'flush'ər, fōr'-) *n. Slang* A fake or cheat.

four-foot·ed (fôr'fŏŏt'id, fōr'-) *adj.* Having four feet.

four hand·ed (fôr'han'did, fōr'-) *adj.* **1.** Designed for four players, as certain games. **2.** Designed for performance by two persons on a keyboard instrument, as a piano duet.

four hundred *U.S.* The most exclusive social group of a place.

four-in-hand (fôr'in·hand', fōr'-) *n.* **1.** A four-horse team driven by one person. **2.** A vehicle drawn by such a team. **3.** A necktie tied in a slip knot with the ends hanging.

four-leaf clover (fôr'lēf', fōr'-) A clover plant having four leaflets, supposed to bring good luck.

four-pence (fôr'pəns, fōr'-) *n.* The sum of four English pennies; also, a silver piece worth that sum.

four-post·er (fôr'pōs'tər, fōr'-) *n.* A bedstead with four tall posts at the corners and typically with a canopy or curtains.

four·some (fôr'səm, fōr'-) *n.* **1.** A game, esp. of golf, in which four players take part, two on each side; also, the players in such a game. **2.** Any group of four.

four·square (fôr'skwâr', fōr'-) *adj.* **1.** Having four equal sides; square. **2.** Firm; solid. **3.** Forthright; direct. — *n.* A square. — *adv.* Squarely; bluntly.

four·teen (fôr'tēn', fōr'-) *n.* **1.** The sum of thirteen and one: a cardinal number. **2.** Any symbol of this number, as 14, xiv, XIV. **3.** Anything consisting of or representing fourteen units. — *adj.* Being one more than thirteen. [OE *fēowertēne*] — **four'teenth** *adj. & n*

fourth dimension A hypothetical dimension in addition to height, width, and thickness; esp., in the theory of relativity. — **fourth'-di·men'sion·al** *adj.*

fourth estate The public press; journalism.

fourth·ly (fôrth'lē, fōrth'-) *adv.* In the fourth place.

Fourth of July Independence Day.

fowl (foul) *n. pl.* **fowl** or **fowls** **1.** The common domestic hen or cock; a chicken. **2.** Any related bird, as the duck, goose, etc. **3.** The flesh of fowl. **4.** Birds collectively. — *v.i.* To catch or hunt wild fowl. [OE *fugol*] — **fowl'er** *n.*

fowl·ing (fou'ling) *n.* The hunting of birds for sport.

fowling piece A light gun used for shooting birds.

fox (foks) *n.* **1.** Any of several small, wild mammals of the dog family, having long, pointed muzzles, bushy tails, and erect ears, esp. the **red fox** of North America, having a reddish brown fur. ♦ Collateral adjective: *vulpine.* **2.** The fur of the fox. **3.** A sly, crafty person. — *v.t.* **1.** To trick; outwit. **2.** To intoxicate. **3.** To stain, as paper

or timber, with a reddish color. **4.** To make sour, as beer, in fermenting. **5.** To repair (shoes) with new uppers. — *v.i.* **6.** To act slyly and cunningly. **7.** To become sour. **8.** To become stained with red. [OE]

fox·glove (foks'gluv') *n.* A plant of the figwort family, having flowers in long one-sided racemes.

NORTH AMERICAN RED FOX
(Body about 2 feet long; tail 16 inches)

fox·hole (foks'hōl') *n.* A shallow pit dug by a combatant as cover against enemy fire.

fox·hound (foks'hound') *n.* One of a breed of large, strong, very swift dogs trained for fox hunting.

fox·tail (foks'tāl') *n.* **1.** The tail of a fox. **2.** Any of various species of grass bearing a spike of flowers like a fox's tail.

fox terrier A small, white terrier with dark markings, formerly used to bring foxes out of their burrows.

fox-trot (foks'trot') *v.i.* **·trot·ted, ·trot·ting** To do a fox trot.

fox trot A ballroom dance in 2/4 or 4/4 time, consisting of a variety of rhythmic steps.

fox·y (fok'sē) *adj.* **fox·i·er, fox·i·est** **1.** Sly; crafty; sharp. **2.** Reddish brown. **3.** Discolored or stained, as from decay. **4.** Improperly fermented: said of beer, etc. **5.** Defective, esp. from age and damp. — **fox'i·ly** *adv.* — **fox'i·ness** *n.*

foy·er (foi'ər, foi'ā; *Fr.* fwá·yá') *n.* **1.** A public lobby in a hotel, theater, etc. **2.** An entrance room or hall in a house or apartment. [< F < LL < L *focus* hearth]

fra·cas (frā'kəs), *Brit.* frak'ä) *n.* A noisy disturbance, fight, or dispute; brawl; row. [< F < Ital. *fracassare* to shatter]

frac·tion (frak'shən) *n.* **1.** A disconnected part of anything; small portion; fragment. **2.** *Math.* A quantity less than a whole number, expressed as a decimal (0.3) or with numerator and denominator (3/10). **3.** *Chem.* One of the components separated from a substance by distilling, etc. — **Syn.** See PORTION. — *v.t.* To set or separate into fractions. [< OF < L *fractus,* pp. of *frangere* to break]

frac·tion·al (frak'shən·əl) *adj.* **1.** Pertaining to or constituting a fraction. **2.** Small in size or importance. Also **frac'tion·ar'y** (-er'ē). — **frac'tion·al·ly** *adv.*

frac·tious (frak'shəs) *adj.* **1.** Apt to be unruly or rebellious. **2.** Easily annoyed or angered. [< FRACTION, in obs. sense of discord] — **frac'tious·ly** *adv.* — **frac'tious·ness** *n.*

frac·ture (frak'chər) *n.* **1.** The act of breaking, or the state of being broken. **2.** A break; crack; rupture. **3.** *Med.* The breaking or cracking of a bone; also, sometimes, the tearing of a cartilage. **4.** *Mineral.* The characteristic appearance of the freshly broken surface of a mineral. — **compound** (or **open**) **fracture** *Med.* A fracture in which the broken ends of the bone protrude through the skin. — **simple** (or **closed**) **fracture** *Med.* A bone fracture in which the skin remains unbroken. — *v.t. & v.i.* **·tured, ·tur·ing** To break or be broken; crack. [< L *fractura* a breaking] — **frac'tur·al** *adj.*

frag·ile (fraj'əl) *adj.* Easily broken or damaged; frail; delicate. [< L *frangere* to break] — **frag'ile·ly** *adv.* — **fra·gil·i·ty** (frə·jil'ə·tē), **frag'ile·ness** *n.*
— **Syn.** That which cannot withstand even mild shocks or jars is *fragile* or, if constructed of parts poorly connected, *frail*: a *fragile* teacup, a *frail* scaffold. *Brittle* is used to describe things that are hard but so rigid or inelastic that they crack under stress.

frag·ment (n. frag'mənt; v. frag·ment') *n.* **1.** A part broken off; a small detached portion. **2.** A part or portion of something that has been left unfinished: *a fragment of a novel.* **3.** A separate or isolated bit: *He heard fragments of their conversation.* — *v.t. & v.i.* To break into fragments. [< F < L *fragmentum*] — **frag'ment·ed** *adj.*

frag·men·tar·y (frag'mən·ter'ē) *adj.* Composed of fragments; broken; incomplete. Also **frag·men'tal.** — **frag'men·tar'i·ly** *adv.* — **frag'men·tar'i·ness** *n.*

frag·men·ta·tion (frag'mən·tā'shən) *n.* **1.** A breaking up into fragments. **2.** *Mil.* The scattering in all directions of the fragments of an exploding grenade, shell, or bomb.

frag·ment·ize (frag'mən·tīz) *v.t. & v.i.* **·ized, ·iz·ing** To fragment.

fra·grance (frā'grəns) *n.* **1.** The state or quality of being fragrant. **2.** A pleasant scent; sweet odor. Also *Rare* **fra'gran·cy.** — **Syn.** See SMELL.

fra·grant (frā'grənt) *adj.* Having an agreeable or sweet smell. [< L *fragrare* to smell sweet] — **fra'grant·ly** *adv.*

frail (frāl) *adj.* **1.** Delicately constituted; weak. **2.** Fragile. **3.** Deficient in moral strength. — **Syn.** See FRAGILE. — *n. U.S. Slang* A young woman or girl. [< OF < L *fragilis*] — **frail'ly** *adv.* — **frail'ness** *n.*

frail·ty (frāl'tē) *n. pl.* **·ties** **1.** The state or quality of being frail; weakness. **2.** A fault or moral weakness.

frame (frām) *n.* **1.** A case or border made to enclose something, as a picture. **2.** A supporting structure surrounding something, as around a window or door. **3.** A framework; skeleton: the *frame* of a building, ship, etc. **4.** The general

arrangement, structure, or constitution of a thing. **5.** A system or order, as of a government. **6.** Bodily structure or build, esp. of the human body. **7.** A machine built in the form of or utilizing a framework: a silk *frame*. **8.** In pool or billiards: **a** The triangular form for grouping the balls. **b** The balls placed in this form. **c** The time required to pocket all the balls. **9.** In bowling, one of the ten divisions of the game. **10.** *Informal* In baseball, an inning. **11.** One of the individual exposures on a roll of motion-picture film. **12.** *Slang* A frame-up. **— frame of mind** Mental state; mood. — *v.* **framed, fram·ing** *v.t.* **1.** To surround with or put into a frame, as a picture. **2.** To put together: to *frame* a shelter. **3.** To put into words; utter. **4.** To conceive or create (a theory, idea, etc.). **5.** To draw up; devise: to *frame* a law. **6.** To shape or adapt to a purpose: Traffic rules are *framed* for safety. **7.** *Slang* To incriminate falsely. **8.** *Slang* To plan or set up dishonestly in advance, as a race, contest, etc. [OE *framian* to be of service to, provide for] **— fram′er** *n.*
frame house A house built on a wooden framework covered on the outside by shingles, boards, stucco, etc.
frame-up (frām′up′) *n. Slang* **1.** A prearranged plan to bring about a fraudulent outcome, as in a contest. **2.** A conspiracy to convict a person on a false charge.
frame·work (frām′wûrk′) *n.* **1.** A skeleton structure for supporting or enclosing something; also, frames, collectively. **2.** The arrangement of the basic or component parts of something: the *framework* of society.
fram·ing (frā′ming) *n.* **1.** A frame or framework. **2.** The act of erecting or fitting with frames or frameworks.
franc (frangk) *n.* **1.** The standard monetary unit of various countries, equivalent to 100 centimes; esp.: **a** The French franc, in 1960 worth about 20 U.S. cents. **b** The Belgian franc, in 1960 worth about 2 U.S. cents. **c** The Swiss franc, in 1960 worth about 23 U.S. cents. **d** A coin of this denomination. [< Med.L *Franc(orum rex)* (king of the) Franks, the motto on the earliest of these coins]
fran·chise (fran′chīz) *n.* **1.** The right to vote; suffrage. **2.** A right or privilege granted by a government or sovereign. **3.** A special privilege bestowed upon an individual or a corporate group of individuals by government grant: a *franchise* to operate a bus line. **4.** The territory over which any of the preceding special privileges or dispensations extend. [< OF < *franc, franche* free] **— fran′chised** *adj.*
Fran·cis·can (fran·sis′kən) *n.* A member of the mendicant order, the Gray Friars, founded in 1209 by St. Francis of Assisi. — *adj.* **1.** Of or pertaining to St. Francis. **2.** Belonging to a religious order following his rule.
fran·ci·um (fran′sē·əm) *n.* A radioactive element (symbol Fr), isolated from actinium, and replacing the hypothetical element known as *virginium*. See ELEMENT. [after *France*]
Franco- *combining form* French [< L *Francus* a Frank]
Fran·co·phile (frang′kə·fil) *n.* An admirer of France or of French customs, etc. — *adj.* Kindly disposed toward France.
Fran·co·phobe (frang′kə·fōb) *n.* A person who fears or dislikes France or French things. — *adj.* Fearful of France.
Fran·co-Prus·sian War (frang′kō-prush′ən) See table for WAR.
fran·gi·ble (fran′jə·bəl) *adj.* Easily broken; brittle. [< L *frangere* to break] **— fran′gi·bil′i·ty, fran′gi·ble·ness** *n.*
fran·gi·pan·i (fran′ji·pan′ē, -pä′nē) *n.* **1.** A perfume derived from or resembling that of the West Indian red jasmine. **2.** The West Indian plant. Also **fran′gi·pane** (-pān). [after Marquis *Frangipani*, the inventor]
frank[1] (frangk) *adj.* **1.** Completely honest and unreserved in speech; candid. **2.** Marked by no effort at concealment or disguise: *frank* hostility. — *v.t.* To mark (a letter, package, etc.) in indication that no charge is to be made for delivery; also, to send (a letter, etc.) without charge by marking in this way. — *n.* **1.** The right to send mail, etc., without charge; also, the mark used to indicate this right. **2.** Mail sent without charge. [< OF *franc* frank, free] **— frank′ly** *adv.* **— frank′ness** *n.*
frank[2] (frangk) *n. Informal* A frankfurter.
Frank (frangk) *n.* **1.** A member of one of the Germanic tribes living on the Rhine early in the Christian era who gave their name to France. **2.** In the Near East, any European. [< L *Francus* a Frank < Gmc., a spear]
Frank·en·stein (frangk′ən·stīn) The hero of Mary Shelley's *Frankenstein*, a medical student who fashions a manlike monster that slays its maker. — *n.* **1.** Loosely, Frankenstein's monster. **2.** Anything that destroys its own creator.
frank·furt·er (frangk′fər·tər) *n.* A smoked, often highly seasoned sausage made of beef or of beef and pork. Also **frank′fort·er** (-fər·tər), **frank′furt, frank′fort** (-fərt) [after *Frankfurt*, Germany]
frank·in·cense (frangk′in·sens) *n.* An aromatic gum or resin from various trees of East Africa, used as an incense and in medicine. [< OF *franc* pure + *encens* incense]
Frank·ish (frang′kish) *adj.* Of or pertaining to the Franks, or, in the Near East, to Europeans in general. — *n.* The West Germanic language of the Franks.

fran·tic (fran′tik) *adj.* **1.** Nearly driven out of one's mind, as with grief, fear, or rage. **2.** Madly excited. [< OF < LL < Gk. *phrenitis* delirium] **— fran′ti·cal·ly, fran′tic·ly** *adv.*
frap·pé (fra·pā′) *U.S. adj.* Iced; chilled. — *n.* **1.** A fruit juice or other beverage frozen to a soft, mushy consistency. **2.** A liqueur or other beverage poured over shaved ice. [< F, pp. of *frapper* to chill]
frat (frat) *n. U.S. Informal* A college fraternity.
fra·ter·nal (frə·tûr′nəl) *adj.* **1.** Pertaining to or befitting a brother; brotherly. **2.** Of or pertaining to a fraternal order or society. **3.** *Genetics* Designating either of a pair of twins that develop from separately fertilized ova: distinguished from *identical*. [< L *frater* brother] **— fra·ter′nal·ism** *n.* **— fra·ter′nal·ly** *adv.*
fraternal order A brotherhood of men organized to further their mutual benefit or to attain a common goal.
fra·ter·ni·ty (frə·tûr′nə·tē) *n.* *pl.* **·ties** **1.** The state of being brothers; also, the spirit of fraternal regard or affection. **2.** In U.S. schools, a society of male students, usu. having a Greek letter name, and represented by chapters in many institutions. **3.** A fraternal order. **4.** A body of people sharing the same interests, profession, etc.
frat·er·nize (frat′ər·nīz) *v.* **·nized, ·niz·ing** *v.i.* **1.** To associate closely with someone in a comradely way. **2.** To mingle intimately with the people of an enemy or conquered country. **— frat′er·ni·za′tion** *n.* **— frat′er·niz′er** *n.*
frat·ri·cide (frat′rə·sīd) *n.* **1.** The killing of one's brother. **2.** One who has killed his brother. [< L < *frater* brother + *caedere* to kill] **— frat′ri·ci′dal** *adj.*
Frau (frou) *n.* *pl.* **Frau·en** (-ən) *German* A married woman; wife: as a title, the equivalent of *Mrs.*
fraud (frôd) *n.* **1.** Willful deceit; trickery. **2.** An act or instance of this. **3.** *U.S. Informal* One who acts deceitfully; impostor. **4.** A deceptive or spurious thing. [< OF < L *fraus, fraudis* deceit]
fraud·u·lent (frô′jə·lent) *adj.* **1.** Practicing or given to fraud; dishonest or deceitful. **2.** Proceeding from, obtained by, or characterized by fraud. **— fraud′u·lence, fraud′u·len·cy** *n.* **— fraud′u·lent·ly** *adv.*
fraught (frôt) *adj.* Filled; laden: with *with*: a journey *fraught* with danger. [< MDu. *vrachten* freight]
Fräu·lein (froi′lin) *n. German* An unmarried woman: as a title, the equivalent of *Miss.*
fray[1] (frā) *n.* Conflict; fight; also a noisy, quarrelsome uproar or disturbance. [Aphetic var. of AFFRAY]
fray[2] (frā) *v.t.* **1.** To cause (cloth, rope, etc.) to become worn by friction. **2.** To wear holes in (cloth, etc.) by rubbing or chafing. — *v.i.* **3.** To become frayed. — *n.* A frayed place, as of a sleeve. [< F *frayer* < L *fricare* to rub]
fraz·zle (fraz′əl) *Informal* *v.t. & v.i.* **·zled, ·zling** **1.** To fray or become frayed; make or become tattered. **2.** To tire out; weary. — *n.* The state of being frazzled. **— worn to a frazzle** **1.** Worn to shreds. **2.** Tired out; exhausted. [? Blend of FRAY[2] + obs. *fasel* to ravel]
freak (frēk) *n.* **1.** A deformed human being, animal, or plant; monstrosity. **2.** Anything unusual or bizarre. **3.** A sudden whim; caprice. [Cf. OE *frician* to dance] **— freak′ish** *adj.* **— freak′ish·ly** *adv.* **— freak′ish·ness** *n.*
freck·le (frek′əl) *n.* A small brownish or dark-colored spot on the skin. — *v.t. & v.i.* **·led, ·ling** To mark or become marked with freckles. [< ON *freknur* freckles] **— freck′led, freck′ly** *adj.*
free (frē) *adj.* **fre·er, fre·est** **1.** Having personal liberty. **2.** Having civil, political, or religious liberty. **3.** Not controlled by a foreign power; autonomous. **4.** Not bound by restrictions or regulations: *free* trade. **5.** Released from legal charge of crime or misdeed; acquitted. **6.** Exempt from certain regulations or impositions, as some taxes. **7.** Cleared or devoid of something: with *from, of: free* from scandal. **8.** Allowed or permitted to do something: *free* to go. **9.** Not controlled, restricted, or hampered by external agents or influences. **10.** Released from or not hindered by burdens, debts, discomforts, etc.: with *from, of: free* from care. **11.** Not occupied; not busy. **12.** Available to all; open: a *free* port. **13.** Not attached, bound, fixed, or held; loose: the *free* end of a rope. **14.** Not obstructed; easy to pass through or over: The road is now *free*; also, unimpeded; profuse: a *free* flow of water. **15.** Given or provided without charge or cost: *free* seats. **16.** Easy and unconstrained: a *free* stride. **17.** Not adhering to strict form or rule: *free* verse. **18.** Not closely or literally following the original: a *free* translation. **19.** *Informal*; unconventional. **20.** Frank and honest; candid. **21.** Unrestrained by propriety, dignity, or decency. **22.** Generous in giving; liberal: *free* with advice. **23.** *Chem.* Uncombined: *free* hydrogen. **24.** *Physics* Available for work: *free* energy. **— free and clear** *Law* Pertaining to real property held without a mortgage or other encumbrance. **— to set free** To release, as from prison, slavery, or other restraint; disengage. — *adv.* **1.** In a free manner; easily. **2.** Without cost; gratuitously. **— to make free with** **1.** To use freely. **2.** To treat with undue famil-

iarity. —*v.t.* **freed, free·ing** 1. To release from confinement, worry, etc. 2. To clear or rid of obstruction or hindrance. [OE *frēo*] —**free'ly** *adv.* —**free'ness** *n.*

free association *Psychoanal.* A method of uncovering unconscious conflicts by encouraging spontaneous verbal association of memories, ideas, impressions, etc.

free·board (frē'bôrd', -bōrd') *n. Naut.* The side of a vessel between the water line and the main deck or gunwale.

free·boot·er (frē'boō'tər) *n.* A pirate or buccaneer. [< MDu. < *vrij* free + *buit* booty]

free·dom (frē'dəm) *n.* 1. The state or condition of being free; esp., the condition of enjoying civil liberty. 2. Political autonomy, as of a nation or people. 3. Liberty from bondage or slavery. 4. Liberation, as from prison or other confinement. 5. Liberty to move or act without outside interference, coercion, or restriction. 6. Liberty of personal choice, action, or thought. 7. Release or immunity from any stated thing or condition: with *from*: *freedom* from pain. 8. Exemption or release from obligations, ties, etc. 9. Facility or ease, as in moving or acting. 10. Boldness of concept or execution. 11. Openness or frankness. 12. Excessive familiarity or candor. [OE *frēodōm*]

freedom of the seas The doctrine that any waters not subject to the territorial jurisdiction of any one country or nation are open to unhampered navigation by any ships or, in war, by the ships of any neutral country or nation.

free enterprise An economic system based upon private ownership and operation of business with little or no governmental control: also called *private enterprise.*

free-for-all (frē'fər-ôl') *n.* A noisy, generalized fight.

free·hand (frē'hand') *adj.* Drawn or sketched by hand without the help of rulers, drafting instruments, etc.

free hand Full liberty to act as one sees fit.

free·hand·ed (frē'han'did) *adj.* 1. Having the hands free. 2. Openhanded; generous. —**free'hand'ed·ness** *n.*

free·hold (frē'hōld') *n. Law* 1. Tenure of an estate, or sometimes of an office or dignity, for life or as something capable of being transferred to another. 2. The estate, office, or dignity held by such tenure. —**free'hold'er** *n.*

free-lance (frē'lans', -läns') *v.i.* **-lanced, -lanc·ing** To work as a free lance. —*adj.* Working as a free lance.

free lance A writer, artist, etc., whose services are not sold exclusively to any one buyer.

free·man (frē'mən) *n. pl.* **·men,** (-mən) 1. A person not in bondage of any kind. 2. One having full political rights.

Free·ma·son (frē'mā'sən) *n.* A member of an extensive secret order or fraternity, the members denoting themselves *Free and Accepted Masons*: also called *Mason.* —**Free·ma·son·ic** (frē'mə·son'ik) *adj.* —**Free'ma'son·ry** *n.*

free on board Delivered, without charge to the buyer, for shipment by a common carrier. Abbr. *f.o.b., F.O.B.*

free·si·a (frē'zhē·ə, -sē·ə, -zhə) *n.* A South African plant having bell-shaped, variously colored, fragrant flowers. [< NL. after E. M. *Fries*, 1794–1878, Swedish botanist]

free silver The free and unlimited coinage of silver, particularly at a fixed ratio to gold.

free-spo·ken (frē'spō'kən) *adj.* Unreserved or frank in speech. —**free-spo'ken·ness** *n.*

Free State 1. Before the Civil War, any State where slavery was forbidden. 2. The Irish Free State.

free·stone (frē'stōn') *adj.* Having a pit from which the pulp easily separates, as a peach. —*n.* 1. Any stone, as sandstone or limestone, that can be cut in any direction without breaking. 2. A fruit easily freed from its pit.

free·style (frē'stīl') *adj.* In swimming, using or permitting any stroke the swimmer desires. —*n.* The use of freestyle swimming techniques.

free·think·er (frē'thing'kər) *n.* One who forms his own religious beliefs without regard to church authority. —**Syn.** See SKEPTIC. —**free'think'ing** *adj. & n.*

free-throw line (frē'thrō') In basketball, the line from which a free throw is made: also called *foul line.*

free trade 1. International commerce free from government regulations and from import and export duties. 2. A trade system where duties are levied only for revenue and not to protect home industries.

free verse Verse marked by an absence or irregularity of rhyme: also, *French, vers libre.*

free·way (frē'wā') *n.* A wide highway skirting populated areas and passing over or around intersections.

free will 1. The power of personal self-determination. 2. The doctrine that one's ability to choose between courses of action is not completely determined by circumstances.

free-will (frē'wil') *adj.* Of one's own free choice; voluntary.

freeze (frēz) *v.* **froze, fro·zen, freez·ing** *v.i.* 1. To become ice or a similar hard solid through loss of heat. 2. To become sheeted or filled with ice, as water pipes. 3. To become stiff or hard with cold, as wet clothes. 4. To adhere to

something by the formation of ice. 5. To be extremely cold. 6. To be damaged or killed by great cold. 7. To become suddenly motionless, inactive, or rigid, as through fear, shock, etc. 8. To become icily aloof: often with *up.* —*v.t.* 9. To cause to become ice or a similar hard solid through loss of heat. 10. To cause ice to form on or in. 11. To make stiff or hard by freezing the moisture of. 12. To make adhere by the formation of ice. 13. To make extremely cold. 14. To damage or kill by great cold. 15. To make motionless or rigid, as through fear; paralyze. 16. To make icily aloof, unfriendly, etc.; alienate. 17. To check abruptly the ardor, enthusiasm, etc., of. 18. To fix or stabilize (prices, wages, etc.) at a particular level. 19. To prohibit the continued making, use, or selling of (a raw material). 20. To make the liquidation, collection, or use of (funds or other assets) contrary to law or edict. —**to freeze one's blood** To fill one with terror. —**to freeze onto** (or **to**) To hold tightly to. —*n.* 1. The act of freezing, or the state of being frozen. 2. Freezing weather. [OE *frēosan*]

freez·er (frē'zər) *n.* 1. One who or that which freezes. 2. A refrigerator designed to freeze and preserve food.

freezing point *Physics* The temperature at which a liquid freezes under given pressure. For water at sea level it is 32° F. or 0° C.

freight (frāt) *n.* 1. In the United States and Canada: **a** The service of transporting commodities by land, air, or water; esp., ordinary transportation as opposed to express. **b** The commodities so transported. 2. The price paid for the transportation of commodities. 3. *U.S. & Canadian* A freight train. —*v.t.* 1. To load with commodities for transportation. 2. To load; burden. 3. To send or transport as or by freight. [< MDu. *vrecht*, var. of *vracht* a load]

freight·age (frā'tij) *n.* 1. A cargo; freight. 2. The price charged or paid for carrying goods. 3. The transportation of merchandise.

freight car A railway car for carrying freight.

freight·er (frā'tər) *n.* A ship used primarily for transporting cargo.

freight train *U.S.* A railroad train of freight cars.

French (french) *adj.* Of, pertaining to, or characteristic of France, its people, or their language; also, in Canada, pertaining to Canadian French persons, their speech, etc. —*n.* 1. The people of France collectively: preceded by *the*; also, in Canada, the French-speaking Canadians. 2. The Romance language of France. —**Old French** The French language from about 850 to 1400, descended from Vulgar Latin as it developed in Gaul. —**Middle French** The French language from about 1400 to 1600. —**Modern French** The language of France after 1600. [OE *Frencisc*]

French and Indian War See table for WAR.

French-Ca·na·di·an (french'kə·nā'dē·ən) *n.* A French settler in Canada or a descendant of French settlers. Also **French Canadian.** —*adj.* Of or pertaining to the language, culture, etc., of French-speaking people in Canada.

French cuff A cuff of a sleeve turned back and secured with a link.

French doors A pair of doors, usu. with glass panes, attached to opposite doorjambs and opening in the middle.

French dressing A salad dressing consisting of oil, vinegar, and spices.

French fried Cooked by frying crisp in deep fat.

French horn A valved, brass instrument with a long, coiled tube, flaring widely at the end and producing a mellow tone.

French·i·fy (fren'chə·fī) *v.t. & v.i.* **·fied, ·fy·ing** To make or become French in form or characteristics.

French leave An informal, secret, or hurried departure.

French·man (french'mən) *n. pl.* **·men** (-mən) A native or citizen of France. — FRENCH HORN **French·wom·an** (-wŏom'ən) *n.fem.*

French pastry A rich, fancy pastry often having a filling of whipped cream, custard, or preserved fruits.

French toast Bread dipped in a batter of beaten eggs and milk and fried in shallow fat.

French window A casement window with adjoining sashes attached to opposite jambs and opening in the middle.

fre·net·ic (frə·net'ik) *adj.* Feverishly excited; frenzied; frantic. Also **fre·net'i·cal.** —*n.* A frenetic person. —**fre·net'i·cal·ly** *adv.*

fren·zy (fren'zē) *n. pl.* **·zies** A state of extreme excitement or agitation suggestive of or bordering on delirium or insanity. —*v.t.* **·zied, ·zy·ing** To make frantic. [< OF < LL < Gk. *phrenitis* delirium] —**fren'zied** *adj.*

fre·quence (frē'kwəns) *n. Rare* Frequency (defs. 1, 2).

fre·quen·cy (frē'kwən·sē) *n. pl.* **·cies** 1. The state or fact of being frequent; repeated occurrence. 2. The number of times something occurs within a particular extent of time, a particular group, etc. **3.** *Stat.* The number of times a given case, value, or event occurs in relation to the total number of classified cases, values, or events; distribution. **4.** *Physics* The number of occurrences of a periodic phenomenon, as oscillation, per unit time, usu. expressed in cycles per second.

frequency modulation *Telecom.* A type of modulation in which the carrier wave of a transmitter is varied in frequency rather than in amplitude. Abbr. *FM, f-m, f.m., F.M.*

fre·quent (adj. frē′kwənt; v. fri·kwent′, frē′kwənt) *adj.* **1.** Happening time after time; occurring again and again: *frequent relapses.* **2.** Showing up often; appearing repeatedly: *frequent visitors.* —*v.t.* To go to repeatedly; be in or at often: to *frequent bars.* [< L *frequens, -entis* crowded] — **fre·quen·ta′tion** *n.* — **fre·quent′er** *n.* — **fre′quent·ly** *adv.*

fre·quen·ta·tive (fri·kwen′tə·tiv) *Gram. adj.* Denoting repeated or habitual action. — *n.* A frequentative verb.

frère (frâr) *n. pl.* **frères** (frâr) *French* **1.** Brother. **2.** Friar; monk.

fres·co (fres′kō) *n. pl.* **·coes** or **·cos** **1.** The art of painting on plaster that is still moist. **2.** A picture so painted. —*v.t.* **·coed, ·co·ing** To paint in fresco. [< Ital., fresh]

fresh[1] (fresh) *adj.* **1.** Newly made, obtained, received, etc.: *fresh* coffee; *fresh* footprints. **2.** New; novel: a *fresh* approach. **3.** Recent; latest: *fresh* news. **4.** Additional; further: *fresh* supplies. **5.** Not smoked, frozen, or otherwise preserved: *fresh* vegetables. **6.** Not spoiled, stale, musty, etc. **7.** Retaining original vividness; not faded or worn, as colors or memories. **8.** Not salt: *fresh* water. **9.** Pure and clear: *fresh* air. **10.** Appearing healthy or youthful. **11.** Not fatigued; energetic. **12.** Vivid; colorful; stimulating. **13.** Inexperienced; untrained: *fresh* recruits. **14.** *Meteorol.* Moderately rapid and strong: esp. designating a breeze or a gale on the Beaufort scale. **15.** Having a renewed supply of milk: said of a cow that has recently calved. [OE *fersc,* infl. by OF *freis,* both ult. < Gmc.] — **fresh′ly** *adv.* — **fresh′ness** *n.*

fresh[2] (fresh) *adj. U.S. Informal* Saucy; impudent; disrespectful. [< G *frech* impudent]

fresh·en (fresh′ən) *v.t. & v.i.* To make or become fresh. — **fresh′en·er** *n.*

fresh·et (fresh′it) *n.* **1.** A sudden rise or overflow of a stream. **2.** A fresh-water stream emptying into the sea.

fresh·man (fresh′mən) *n. pl.* **·men** (-mən) **1.** A student during the first year of studies in a high school, college, or university. **2.** A beginner; novice.

fresh-wa·ter (fresh′wô′tər, -wot/ər) *adj.* **1.** Pertaining to or living in fresh water: a *fresh-water* fish. **2.** Not situated on or near the seacoast; inland. **3.** Lacking skill or experience. **4.** *U.S.* Not well known; small: a *fresh-water* college.

fret[1] (fret) *v.* **fret·ted, fret·ting** *v.t.* **1.** To be vexed, annoyed, or troubled. **2.** To become worn, chafed, or corroded. **3.** To bite away bit after bit of something with or as with the teeth; gnaw: with *on, upon, into.* **4.** To eat through something by or as if by corrosion. **5.** To rankle; fester. **6.** To become rough or agitated, as water. —*v.t.* **7.** To vex, annoy, or trouble. **8.** To wear away or eat away by or as if by chafing, gnawing, or corrosion; also, to produce (a hole, frayed ends, etc.) in this way. **9.** To roughen or agitate (the surface of water). — *n.* **1.** Vexation. **2.** The act of chafing or gnawing. **3.** A worn spot. [OE *fretan* to devour]

fret[2] (fret) *n.* One of a series of ridges, as of metal, fixed across the fingerboard of a guitar, ukulele, etc., to guide the fingers in stopping the strings. —*v.t.* **fret·ted, fret·ting** To provide (a guitar, etc.) with frets. [Cf. OF *frete* ring]

FRETS[3]

fret[3] (fret) *n.* An ornamental band or border consisting of angular or sometimes curved lines symmetrically arranged. —*v.t.* **fret·ted, fret·ting** To adorn with a fret. [Prob. < OF *frette* lattice, trellis]

fret·ful (fret′fəl) *adj.* Inclined to fret; peevish or restless. — **fret′ful·ly** *adv.* — **fret′ful·ness** *n.* — **Syn.** complaining, impatient, pettish, petulant, restive.

fret·work (fret′wûrk′) *n.* **1.** Ornamental openwork, usu. composed of frets or interlaced parts. **2.** A pattern, as of light and shade, resembling such openwork.

Freu·di·an (froi′dē·ən) *adj.* Of, pertaining to, or conforming to the teachings of Sigmund Freud. — *n.* An adherent of the theories of Freud. — **Freu′di·an·ism** *n.*

fri·a·ble (frī′ə·bəl) *adj.* Easily crumbled or pulverized. [< F < L *friare* to crumble] — **fri·a·bil′i·ty, fri′a·ble·ness** *n.*

fri·ar (frī′ər) *n.* A man who is a member of one of several religious orders, esp. the mendicant orders, as the Dominicans or Franciscans. [< OF *frere* < L *frater* brother]

fri·ar·y (frī′ər·ē) *n. pl.* **·ar·ies** **1.** A monastery, especially of a mendicant order. **2.** A community of friars.

fric·as·see (frik′ə·sē′) *n.* A dish of meat cut small, stewed, and served with gravy. —*v.t.* **·seed, ·see·ing** To make into a fricassee. [< F *fricassé,* orig. pp. of *fricasser* to sauté]

fric·a·tive (frik′ə·tiv) *Phonet. adj.* Of consonants, produced by the passage of breath through a narrow aperture with resultant audible friction, as (f), (v), (th). — *n.* A consonant so produced. [< NL < L *fricare* to rub]

fric·tion (frik′shən) *n.* **1.** The rubbing of one object against another. **2.** Conflict of opinions, differences in temperament, etc. [< F < L *fricare* to rub] — **fric′tion·al** *adj.* — **fric′tion·al·ly** *adv.*

friction tape Cotton tape impregnated with an adhesive, moisture-resisting compound, used in electrical work.

Fri·day (frī′dē, -dā) *n.* The sixth day of the week. [OE *Frigedæg* Frigg's day]

Fri·day (frī′dē, -dā) In Defoe's *Robinson Crusoe,* Crusoe's native servant and companion. — *n.* Any devoted or faithful attendant or helper: man *Friday;* girl *Friday.*

fried (frīd) Past tense and past participle of FRY. — *adj. Slang* Intoxicated.

fried cake A small cake or doughnut fried in deep fat.

friend (frend) *n.* **1.** One who is personally well known by oneself and for whom one has warm regard or affection; intimate. **2.** One with whom one is on speaking terms; an associate or acquaintance. **3.** One who belongs to the same nation, party, etc., as oneself; also, one with whom one is united in some purpose, cause, etc. **4.** A patron or supporter. [OE *frēond*] — **friend′less** *adj.* — **friend′less·ness** *n.*

Friend (frend) *n.* A member of the Society of Friends; Quaker.

friend·ly (frend′lē) *adj.* **·li·er, ·li·est** **1.** Of, pertaining to, or typical of a friend. **2.** Well-disposed; not antagonistic. **3.** Acting as a friend; showing friendship. **4.** Helpful; favorable: a *friendly* wind. — *adv.* In a friendly manner: also **friend′li·ly.** — **friend′li·ness** *n.*

friend·ship (frend′ship) *n.* **1.** The state or fact of being friends. **2.** Mutual liking and esteem.

fri·er (frī′ər) See FRYER.

frieze[1] (frēz) *n.* **1.** The horizontal strip running between a cornice and architrave, either plain or decorated with sculpture, scrolls, etc. **2.** Any decorative horizontal strip, as along the top of a wall in a room. [< F < Med.L *frisium*]

frieze[2] (frēz) *n.* A coarse, woolen cloth with a shaggy nap. [< MF < *friser* to curl]

frig·ate (frig′it) *n.* A sailing war vessel of medium size, in use from about the 17th to the 19th centuries. [< F < Ital. *fregata*]

frigate bird Either of two large, rapacious, web-footed marine birds having hooked beaks and very long wings: also called *man-of-war bird.*

Frigg (frig) In Norse mythology, the wife of Odin and the goddess of marriage. Also **Frig·ga** (frig′ə).

fright (frīt) *n.* **1.** Sudden, violent alarm or fear. **2.** *Informal* One who or that which is ugly, etc. [OE *fryhto*]

fright·en (frīt′n) *v.t.* **1.** To make suddenly alarmed, fearful, or terrified; scare. **2.** To drive, force, etc., (away, out, into, etc.) by scaring. —*v.i.* **3.** To become afraid. — **fright′en·ing** *adj.* — **fright′en·ing·ly** *adv.*

fright·ful (frīt′fəl) *adj.* **1.** Repulsive, shocking, or contemptible. **2.** *Informal* Most distressing; very bad: a *frightful* headache. **3.** *Informal* Excessively great: a *frightful* number of losses. **4.** Such as fills with fright; alarming or terrifying. — **fright′ful·ly** *adv.* — **fright′ful·ness** *n.*

frig·id (frij′id) *adj.* **1.** Bitterly cold. **2.** Lacking warmth of feeling; formal. **3.** Habitually lacking sexual feeling or response: said of women. [< L *frigere* to be cold] — **frig′id·ly** *adv.* — **fri·gid·i·ty** (fri·jid′ə·tē), **frig′id·ness** *n.*

fri·jol (frē′hōl) *n. pl.* **fri·joles** (frē′hōlz, *Sp.* frē·hō′lās) A bean used as food, esp. by Latin-Americans. Also **fri·jole** (frē′hōl, *Sp.* frē·hō′lā). [< Sp.]

frill (fril) *n.* **1.** An ornamental strip of lace, etc., gathered together and attached along one edge and left free along the other; ruffle. **2.** *U.S. Informal* Any showy or superfluous detail of dress, manner, etc. **3.** *Zool.* A ruff of feathers about the neck of some birds or of hair about the neck of some animals. —*v.t.* **1.** To make into a frill. **2.** To put frills on. [Origin uncertain] — **frill′y** *adv.*

frill·ing (fril′ing) *n.* **1.** Frills collectively. **2.** A material or trimming suitable for use in a frill or frills.

fringe (frinj) *n.* **1.** An ornamental border of hanging cords, threads, etc. **2.** Something suggestive of such a border or trimming: a *fringe* of grass along a sidewalk. **3.** The area along the edge of something: the *fringes* of a city. —*v.t.* **fringed, fring·ing** **1.** To provide with or as with a fringe. **2.** To constitute a fringe on or along. — *adj.* Outer; marginal: a *fringe* area. [< OF < L *fimbria* fringe] — **fring′y** *adj.*

fringe benefit Anything of value given an employee in addition to his salary or wages, as insurance, pension, etc.

frin·gil·line (frin·jil′īn, -in) *adj.* Of, pertaining to, or resembling a family of small birds including the finches and sparrows. [< L *fringilla* small bird + -INE[1]]

frip·per·y (frip′ər·ē) *n. pl.* **·per·ies** **1.** Cheap, flashy dress or ornamentation. **2.** Showiness or affection in speech, manner, etc. [< F < OF *frepe* rag]

Fris·co (fris'kō) *Informal* San Francisco, California.
fri·sé (fri-zā') *n.* An upholstery or rug fabric faced with a thick pile of uncut loops or of cut and uncut loops in design. [< F, orig. pp. of *friser* to curl]
Fris·ian (frizh'ən, frizh'ē·ən) *adj.* Of or pertaining to the Dutch province of Friesland, its people, or their language. — *n.* **1.** A native or inhabitant of Friesland. **2.** The Germanic language of the Frisians. Also spelled *Friesian*.
frisk (frisk) *v.i.* **1.** To move or leap about playfully; frolic. — *v.t.* **2.** To move with quick jerks: a lamb *frisking* its tail. **3.** *U.S. Slang* To search (someone) for a concealed weapon, etc., by quickly feeling the pockets and clothing. **4.** *Slang* To rob of valuables in this way. — *n.* **1.** A playful skipping about. **2.** *U.S. Slang* A search of someone for a weapon, etc. [< obs. *frisk* lively < F *frisque*] — **frisk'er** *n.*
frisk·y (fris'kē) *adj.* **frisk·i·er, frisk·i·est** Lively or playful. — **frisk'i·ly** *adv.* — **frisk'i·ness** *n.*
frit (frit) *n.* The material formed by the partial fusion of sand and fluxes in the process of making glass. — *v.t.* To make (a mixture of sand, alkalis, etc.) into frit. Also **fritt.** [< F < Ital. *fritta*, pp. of *friggere* to fry]
frit·ter¹ (frit'ər) *v.t.* To waste or squander little by little, as money, time, etc.: usu. with *away*. [< L *frangere* to break]
frit·ter² (frit'ər) *n.* A small cake made of plain batter or of corn, meat, fruit, etc., covered with batter and fried in deep fat. [< F < L *frigere* to fry]
friv·o·lous (friv'ə·ləs) *adj.* **1.** Lacking importance or significance; petty. **2.** Inclined to levity; not serious; silly; fickle. [< L *frivolous* silly] — **fri·vol·i·ty** (fri·vol'ə·tē) *n.* — **friv'o·lous·ly** *adv.* — **friv'o·lous·ness** *n.*
frizz (friz) *v.t. & v.i.* **1.** To form into tight, crisp curls, as the hair. **2.** To make or form into small, tight tufts or knots, as the nap of cloth. — *n.* **1.** That which is frizzed, as hair. **2.** The condition of being frizzed. Also **friz.** [< F *friser* to curl] — **friz'zer** or **friz'er** *n.*
friz·zle¹ (friz'əl) *v.t. & v.i.* **·zled, ·zling 1.** To fry or cook with a sizzling noise. **2.** To make or become curled or crisp, as by frying. [Blend of FRY and SIZZLE; ? infl. by FRIZZLE²]
friz·zle² (friz'əl) *v.t. & v.i.* **·zled, ·zling** To form into tight curls, as the hair; frizz. — *n.* A crisp curl; frizz. [? Freq. of obs. *frieze* produce a nap on < MF *friser* to curl]
friz·zly (friz'lē) *adj.* Having tight, crisp curls.
frizz·y (friz'ē) *adj.* **frizz·i·er, frizz·i·est** Frizzly. — **friz'zi·ly** *adv.* — **friz'zi·ness** *n.*
fro (frō) *adv.* Away from; back: used in the phrase *to and fro.* — *prep. Scot.* From. [< ON *frā* from]
frock (frok) *n.* **1.** A long, loose-fitting robe with wide sleeves worn by monks; also, the clerical or priestly state. **2.** Any of several types of garments; as: **a** A dress. **b** A workers' smock. **c** A frock coat. — *v.t.* **1.** To furnish with or clothe in a frock. **2.** To invest with ecclesiastical office. [< OF *froc*]
frock coat A man's dress overcoat, worn esp. in the 19th century, having knee-length skirts and a tight-fitting, double-breasted upper part.
frog (frog, frôg) *n.* **1.** One of a genus of small, tailless, web-footed animals with short front legs and large, strong hind legs adapted to leaping. **2.** One of several similar amphibians, as a tree frog. **3.** A slight irritation, accumulation of phlegm, etc., producing difficulty or hoarseness in speaking: also **frog in the (or one's) throat. 4.** A triangular prominence in the sole of a horse's foot. **5.** A section of intersecting railroad tracks designed to permit wheels to pass over the junction without difficulty. **6.** An ornamental braid or cord, as on a jacket, often looped, so as to permit passage of a button. — *v.i.* **frogged, frog·ging** To hunt frogs. [OE *frogga*]

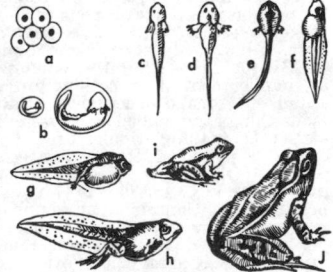

STAGES IN THE DEVELOPMENT OF THE FROG

a Eggs. *b* Embryo. *c–h* Development of the tadpole. *i* Young frog. *j* Adult frog.

frog·man (frog'mən, -man', frôg'-) *n.* *pl.* **·men** (-mən, -men') An underwater reconnaissance and demolition expert, able to swim and operate under water using a scuba.
frol·ic (frol'ik) *n.* **1.** Merriment. **2.** A gay occasion or diversion. **3.** A playful antic. — *v.i.* **·icked, ·ick·ing 1.** To move about or behave in a frisky way. **2.** To be prankish. [< Du. < MDu. *vro* glad] — **frol'ick·er** *n.*
frol·ic·some (frol'ik·səm) *adj.* Gay and lighthearted. Also **frol'ick·y.** — **frol'ic·some·ly** *adv.* — **frol'ic·some·ness** *n.*

from (frum, from; *unstressed* frəm) *prep.* **1.** Starting at (a particular place or time): the plane *from* New York. **2.** With (a particular person, place or thing) as the origin or instrument: a letter *from* your mother. **3.** Out of (a holder, container, etc.). **4.** Out of the control of: He escaped *from* his captors. **5.** Out of the totality of: to subtract 3 *from* 8. **6.** At a distance in relation to: far *from* the city. **7.** Beyond the possibility of: He kept her *from* falling. **8.** By reason of; because of. **9.** As being other or another than: He couldn't tell me *from* my brother. [OE *fram, from*]
frond (frond) *n. Bot.* **1.** A leaflike expansion in which the functions of stem and leaf are not fully differentiated, as in ferns and seaweeds. **2.** A large leaf of tropical plants and trees, as of the palm tree. [< L *frons, frondis* leaf]
front (frunt) *n.* **1.** The part or side of an object or body that faces forward or is viewed as facing forward. **2.** An area or position located directly ahead or before: He stood in *front* of her. **3.** An area or position of principal or most important activity. **4.** *Mil.* **a** The lateral space from flank to flank occupied by a unit. **b** The line of contact of two opposing forces. **5.** The outer side of a building, usu. the side where the main entrance is. **6.** An extent of land lying directly along a lake, road, etc. **7.** A group or movement uniting various individuals with a common aim. **8.** One chosen to head a group, movement, etc., to give it prestige, often lacking real authority. **9.** An apparently respectable person, business, etc., used for cloaking objectionable or illegal activities. **10.** One's bearing or attitude in facing a particular situation, problem, etc.: to put on a bold *front*. **11.** *Informal* An outward air of pretense of wealth, social importance, etc. **12.** A detachable, starched part of a man's formal dress shirt covering the chest. **13.** In hotels, the bellhop first in line. **14.** *Meteorol.* The fore part of a mass of warm or cold air; also, the line of separation between a mass of warm and cold air. **15.** *Phonet.* The part of the tongue immediately behind the blade and directly below the hard palate. — *adj.* **1.** Of, pertaining to, or directed toward the front. **2.** Located on, in, or at the front. — *v.t.* **1.** To face toward. **2.** To meet face to face. **3.** To provide with a front. **4.** To serve as a front for. — *v.i.* **5.** To face toward something. [< OF < L *frons, frontis* forehead]
front·age (frun'tij) *n.* **1.** The front part of a lot or building; also, the linear extent of this. **2.** The direction in which something faces; exposure. **3.** Land adjacent to a street, body of water, etc.
fron·tal (frun'təl) *adj.* **1.** Of or pertaining to the front. **2.** Of or pertaining to the forehead or to the bone forming the anterior part of the skull. — **fron'tal·ly** *adv.*
fron·tier (frun·tir') *n.* **1.** The part of a nation's territory lying along the border of another country. **2.** The part of a settled region lying along the border of an unsettled region. **3.** A new or unexplored area of thought or knowledge. — *adj.* Of or pertaining to a frontier. [< OF *front* front]
fron·tiers·man (frun·tirz'mən) *n.* *pl.* **·men** (-mən) One who lives on the frontier.
fron·tis·piece (frun'tis·pēs', fron'-) *n.* **1.** A picture or drawing on the page facing the title page of a book; also, formerly, the title page itself. **2.** *Archit.* **a** A façade; also, a highly decorated section of a façade. **b** A pediment. [< F < Med.L < Latin L *frons, frontis* forehead + *specere* to look at]
front matter *Printing* The pages preceding the actual text of a book or pamphlet.
front-page (frunt'pāj') *adj.* Appearing on or important enough to appear on the first page of a newspaper.
frosh (frosh) *n.* *pl.* **frosh** *U.S. Slang* A college freshman.
frost (frôst, frost) *n.* **1.** A feathery deposit of ice formed on the ground or on the surface of exposed objects by dew or water vapor that has frozen. **2.** Rime. **3.** Frozen moisture within a porous substance, as in the ground. **4.** Temperature cold enough to freeze. **5.** The act of freezing. **6.** Coldness of manner. **7.** *Slang* A cold reception by the public. — *v.t.* **1.** To cover with frost. **2.** To damage or kill by frost. **3.** To produce a frostlike surface or effect on (glass, etc.). **4.** To apply frosting to. [OE] — **frost'less** *adj.*
frost·bite (frôst'bīt', frost'-) *n.* The condition of having some part of the body partially frozen, often resulting in gangrene. — *v.t.* **·bit, ·bit·ten, ·bit·ing** To injure, as a part of the body, by partial freezing. — **frost'bit'ten** (-bit'n) *adj.*
frost·ed (frôs'tid, fros'-) *adj.* **1.** Covered with frost. **2.** Covered with frosting, as a cake. **3.** Presenting a surface resembling frost, as translucent glass. **4.** Frostbitten.
frost·ing (frôs'ting, fros'-) *n.* **1.** A mixture of sugar, egg white, butter, etc., cooked or beaten together, and used to cover cakes. **2.** The rough or lusterless surface produced on metal, glass, etc., in imitation of frost. **3.** Coarsely powdered glass, etc., used for decorative work.
frost·y (frôs'tē, fros'-) *adj.* **frost·i·er, frost·i·est 1.** Attended with frost; freezing: *frosty* weather. **2.** Composed of

or covered with frost. **3.** Lacking warmth of manner. **4.** Having white hair; hoary. — **frost′i·ly** *adv.* — **frost′i·ness** *n.*

froth (frôth, froth) *n.* **1.** A mass of bubbles resulting from fermentation or agitation. **2.** Any foamy excretion or exudation, as of saliva. **3.** Any unsubstantial or trivial thing, as a foolish conversation. — *v.t.* **1.** To cause to foam. **2.** To cover with froth. **3.** To give forth in the form of foam. — *v.i.* **4.** To form or give off froth. [< ON *frodha*]

froth·y (frô′thē, froth′ē) *adj.* **froth·i·er, froth·i·est 1.** Consisting of, covered with, or full of froth; foamy. **2.** Unsubstantial or trivial. — **froth′i·ly** *adv.* — **froth′i·ness** *n.*

frou-frou (frōō′frōō′) *n.* **1.** A rustling, as of silk; swish. **2.** *Informal* Affected elegance; fanciness. [< F]

fro·ward (frō′ərd, -wərd) *adj.* Disobedient; intractable. — **fro′ward·ly** *adv.* — **fro′ward·ness** *n.*

frown (froun) *v.i.* **1.** To contract the brow, as in displeasure or concentration; scowl. **2.** To look with distaste: with *on* or *upon.* — *v.t.* **3.** To make known (one's displeasure, disgust, etc.) by contracting one's brow. **4.** To silence, rebuke, etc., by or as by a frown. — *n.* **1.** A wrinkling of the brow, as in displeasure; scowl. **2.** Any showing of displeasure. [< OF *froignier*, prob. < Gmc.] — **frown′ing·ly** *adv.*

frow·zy (frou′zē) *adj.* **·zi·er, ·zi·est 1.** Slovenly in appearance; unkempt. **2.** Having a disagreeable smell; musty. Also **frou′zy, frow′sy.** [Origin uncertain]

froze (frōz) Past tense of FREEZE.

fro·zen (frō′zən) Past participle of FREEZE. — *adj.* **1.** Changed into or covered or clogged with ice, as a river. **2.** Killed or damaged by cold. **3.** Extremely cold, as a climate. **4.** Cold and unfeeling in manner. **5.** Made rigid or immobile: *frozen* with fear. **6.** *Econ.* **a** Arbitrarily maintained at a given level: said of prices, wages, etc. **b** Not readily convertible into cash: *frozen* assets. **7.** Made solid by cold.

fruc·ti·fy (fruk′tə·fī, frōōk′-) *v.* **·fied, ·fy·ing** *v.t.* **1.** To make fruitful; fertilize. — *v.i.* **2.** To bear fruit. [< F < L < *fructus* fruit + *facere* to do, make] — **fruc′ti·fi·ca′tion** *n.*

fruc·tose (fruk′tōs, frōōk′-) *n.* *Biochem.* A very sweet sugar, $C_6H_{12}O_6$, occurring in fruits: also called *fruit sugar, levulose.* [< L *fructus* + -OSE²]

fru·gal (frōō′gəl) *adj.* **1.** Exercising economy; saving. **2.** Costing little money: a *frugal* meal. [< F < *frugi* temperate, orig. dative singular of *frux* food] — **fru·gal′i·ty** (-gal′ə·tē) *n.* — **fru′gal·ly** *adv.* — **fru′gal·ness** *n.*

fru·giv·o·rous (frōō·jiv′ər·əs) *adj.* Fruit-eating. [< L *frux, frugis* fruit + -VOROUS]

fruit (frōōt) *n.* **1.** *Bot.* **a** The pulpy, usu. edible mass covering the seeds of various plants and trees. **b** In flowering plants, the mature seed vessel and its contents. **c** In spore plants, the spores with their enveloping or accessory organs. **2.** Any useful plant product, as cotton or flax. **3.** The outcome, consequence, or result of some action, effort, etc.: the *fruit* of labor. — *v.i.* & *v.t.* To produce or cause to produce fruit. [< OF < L *fructus* < *frui* to enjoy]

fruit·age (frōō′tij) *n.* **1.** Fruit collectively. **2.** The state, process, or time of producing fruit. **3.** Any result or effect.

fruit·cake (frōōt′kāk′) *n.* A rich, spiced cake containing nuts, raisins, citron, and other dried fruits.

fruit·er (frōō′tər) *n.* **1.** A ship that carries fruit; also, a fruit dealer or grower. **2.** A fruit-bearing tree or plant.

fruit fly 1. Any of various flies whose larvae attack fruit. **2.** A fly whose larvae feed on fruit and which is used in research in genetics: also called *drosophila.*

fruit·ful (frōōt′fəl) *adj.* **1.** Bearing fruit or offspring abundantly. **2.** Producing results: a *fruitful* discussion. — **fruit′ful·ly** *adv.* — **fruit′ful·ness** *n.*

fru·i·tion (frōō·ish′ən) *n.* **1.** The accomplishment or realization of things worked for or hoped for; fulfillment. **2.** The enjoyment of this. **3.** The bearing of fruit. [< OF < LL < L *frui* to enjoy]

fruit·less (frōōt′lis) *adj.* **1.** Yielding no fruit; barren. **2.** Ineffectual; useless; unproductive. — **Syn.** See FUTILE. — **fruit′less·ly** *adv.* — **fruit′less·ness** *n.*

fruit sugar Fructose.

frump (frump) *n.* A dowdy, sometimes ill-tempered woman. [? < MDu. *frompelen*, var. of *verrompelen* to wrinkle]

frump·ish (frum′pish) *adj.* **1.** Dowdy or old-fashioned in dress. **2.** Ill-tempered; peevish. Also **frump′y.** — **frump′ish·ly** *adv.* — **frump′ish·ness** *n.*

frus·trate (frus′trāt) *v.t.* **·trat·ed, ·trat·ing 1.** To keep (someone) from doing or achieving something; baffle the efforts, hopes, or desires of. **2.** To keep, as plans or schemes, from being fulfilled. [< L *frustrari* to disappoint]

frus·tra·tion (frus·trā′shən) *n.* **1.** The state of being frustrated or thwarted. **2.** Something that frustrates.

frus·tum (frus′təm) *n.* *pl.* **·tums** or **·ta** (-tə) *Geom.* **1.** That which is left of a cone or pyramid after cutting off the upper part along a plane parallel to the base. **2.** That part of a solid included between any two, usu. parallel planes. [< L, fragment]

FRUSTUM OF A PYRAMID

fry¹ (frī) *v.t.* & *v.i.* **fried, fry·ing** To cook in hot fat, usu. over direct heat. — *n.* *pl.* **fries 1.** A dish of anything fried. **2.** A social occasion, at which foods are fried and eaten. [< F *frier* < L *frigere*]

fry² (frī) *n.* *pl.* **fry 1.** Very young fish; also, small adult fish when together in large numbers. **2.** The young of certain animals, as of frogs, when produced in very large quantities. **3.** Young children, etc. See SMALL FRY. [< ON *friõ* seed]

fry·er (frī′ər) *n.* **1.** One who or that which fries. **2.** A young chicken suitable for frying. Also spelled *frier.*

fuch·sia (fyōō′shə, -shē·ə) *n.* **1.** Any of various plants of the evening-primrose family, with red, pink, white, or purple, drooping, four-petaled flowers. **2.** A bright bluish red, the typical color of the fuchsia. [after Leonhard *Fuchs*, 1501–66, German botanist]

fuch·sin (fōōk′sin) *n.* *Chem.* One of two deep red or violet dye compounds obtained from aniline, used as a bacterial stain, dye, etc.: also called *magenta.* Also **fuch·sine** (-sin, -sēn). [< FUCHSIA + -IN]

fud·dle (fud′l) *v.* **·dled, ·dling** *v.t.* **1.** To confuse or make stupid with or as with liquor. — *v.i.* **2.** To tipple. [Cf. dial. G *fuddeln* to swindle]

fud·dy-dud·dy (fud′ē-dud′ē) *n.* *pl.* **-dud·dies** *Informal* **1.** An old-fashioned person. **2.** A faultfinding, fussy person. [Varied reduplication, ? < dial. E *fud* the buttocks]

fudge (fuj) *n.* **1.** A soft, cooked confection made of butter, sugar, chocolate, etc. **2.** Humbug; nonsense. — *v.t.* **fudged, fudg·ing** To make, adjust, or fit together in a clumsy or dishonest manner. [Origin uncertain]

Fuehr·er (fyōō′rər, *Ger.* fü′rər) See FÜHRER.

fu·el (fyōō′əl) *n.* **1.** Combustible matter used as a source of heat energy or to feed a fire. **2.** Whatever sustains or heightens emotion, etc. — *v.t.* & *v.i.* **fu·eled** or **·elled, fu·el·ing** or **·el·ling** To supply with or take in fuel. [< OF *fouaille* < LL < L *focus* hearth] — **fu′el·er** or **fu′el·ler** *n.*

fu·gal (fyōō′gəl) *adj.* *Music* Of or pertaining to a fugue.

fu·gi·tive (fyōō′jə·tiv) *adj.* **1.** Fleeing or having fled, as from pursuit, arrest, etc. **2.** Not fixed or lasting; transient; fleeting. **3.** Treating of subjects of passing interest; occasional. **4.** Wandering about; shifting. — *n.* One who flees, as from pursuit, danger, etc.; runaway. [< F < L < *fugere* to flee] — **fu′gi·tive·ly** *adv.* — **fu′gi·tive·ness** *n.*

fugue (fyōōg) *n.* *Music* A contrapuntal composition in which a theme is introduced by one part, repeated by other parts, and subjected to complex development. [< F < Ital. *fuga* < L, flight]

Füh·rer (fyōōr′ər, *Ger.* fü′rər) *n.* *German* Leader: a title applied to Adolf Hitler by his adherents: also spelled *Fuehrer.*

-ful *suffix* **1.** Full of; characterized by: *joyful.* **2.** Able to; tending to: *helpful.* **3.** Having the character of: *manful.* **4.** The quantity or number that will fill: *cupful.* ◆ Nouns ending in *-ful* form the plural by adding *-s,* as in *cupfuls, spoonfuls.* [OE *-full, -ful* < *full* full]

ful·crum (fōōl′krəm) *n.* *pl.* **·crums** or **·cra** (-krə) **1.** The support on which a lever rests or about which it turns when raising a weight. For illus. see LEVER. **2.** Any prop or support. [< L, bedpost < *fulcire* to prop up]

ful·fill (fōōl·fil′) *v.t.* **·filled, ·fill·ing 1.** To bring about the accomplishment of (something promised, hoped for, anticipated, etc.); make an actuality of. **2.** To execute or perform (something commanded or requested). **3.** To come up to or satisfy (something stipulated). **4.** To get through to the end of (a period of time, a task, etc.); finish up. Also *Brit.* **ful·fil′.** [OE *fullfyllan*] — **ful·fill′ment** or **ful·fil′ment** *n.*

full¹ (fōōl) *adj.* **1.** Filled up with as much or as many as is possible. **2.** Containing an abundant or sufficient supply. **3.** Complete or sufficient in number, quantity, etc.; not deficient: a *full* dozen; also, whole or entire: to pay the *full* price. **4.** Maximum in size, extent, degree, etc.: a *full* load; *full* speed. **5.** Of the tide, risen to its highest level. **6.** Of the moon, having the face wholly illuminated. **7.** Having had ample food or drink. **8.** Of the face, figure, etc., well rounded out; plump. **9.** Engrossed or preoccupied: with *of: full* of plans for the future. **10.** Charged with emotion: a *full* heart. **11.** Having satisfying resonance and volume: *full* tones. **12.** Of garments, cut in ample folds; flowing: a long, *full* cape. — **in full cry** In close pursuit: said esp. of dogs. — **in full view** In a position allowing complete visibility. — *n.* The maximum size, extent, degree, etc. — **in full 1.** To the entire amount: paid *in full.* **2.** Without abridgement, condensation, or abbreviation: to reprint a text *in full.* — **to the full** To the most complete extent: to enjoy something *to the full.* — *adv.* **1.** To a complete degree or extent: now chiefly in compounds: *full-fledged.* **2.** Directly; straight; right: I looked him *full* in the face. — *v.t.* **1.** To gather or pleat (the fabric of a garment). — *v.i.* **2.** To become full: said of the moon. [OE *ful*]

full² (fōōl) *v.t.* **1.** To make (cloth, yarn, etc.) thicker and more compact, as by moistening and beating or pressing. — *v.i.* **2.** Of cloth, etc., to become thicker and more compact through special treatment. [Back formation < FULLER.]

full·back (fŏŏl′bak′) *n.* In football, a player stationed behind the line of scrimmage, usu. just behind the quarterback and the halfbacks; also, this position.

full-blood·ed (fŏŏl′blud′id) *adj.* Unmixed in race or breed; also, related to another through descent from the same parents: also **full-blood** (fŏŏl′blud′).

full-blown (fŏŏl′blōn′) *adj.* **1.** Blooming fully: a *full-blown* rose. **2.** Fully developed: a *full-blown* genius.

full-bod·ied (fŏŏl′bod′ēd) *adj.* Of beverages, having a satisfying richness and strength.

full-dress (fŏŏl′dres′) *adj.* **1.** Characterized by or requiring full dress; formal: a *full-dress* dinner. **2.** Undertaken or engaged in to the fullest possible extent: a *full-dress* debate.

full dress Formal or ceremonial attire.

full·er (fŏŏl′ər) *n.* One who fulls cloth, etc. [OE *fullere*]

full·er's earth (fŏŏl′ərz) A soft, absorbent material resembling clay, used in removing grease from material to be fulled, and also as a catalyst, and in talcs, poultices, etc.

full-fledged (fŏŏl′flejd′) *adj.* **1.** Having the feathers fully grown. **2.** Completely developed or trained.

full gainer A dive in which one springs forward off the board and makes a complete back somersault.

full-grown (fŏŏl′grōn′) *adj.* Having reached full growth.

full house In poker, a hand made up of three cards of one kind plus two cards of another kind. Also **full hand.**

full-length (fŏŏl′lengkth′) *adj.* **1.** Showing the entire length of an object or figure: a *full-length* portrait. **2.** Being of the original or usual length; not abridged.

full moon **1.** The moon when the whole of its face is illuminated. **2.** The time of month when this occurs.

full·ness (fŏŏl′nis) *n.* The state or quality of being full. Also **ful′ness.**

full-scale (fŏŏl′skāl′) *adj.* **1.** Scaled to actual size; not reduced: a *full-scale* drawing. **2.** Engaged in or undertaken to the fullest possible extent; all-out: a *full-scale* attack.

full swing **1.** The height of activity: a party in *full swing.* **2.** Freedom of activity: to be given *full swing.*

ful·ly (fŏŏl′ē) *adv.* **1.** To the fullest extent or degree; entirely: *fully* convinced. **2.** Adequately; sufficiently: *fully* fed. **3.** At the lowest estimate: *fully* three hundred.

ful·mi·nate (ful′mə-nāt) *v.* **·nat·ed, ·nat·ing** *v.i.* **1.** To make loud or violent denunciations; make scathing verbal attacks; inveigh: to *fulminate* against taxes. **2.** To explode suddenly and violently, as a chemical. — *v.t.* **3.** To issue (decrees, censures, etc.) in scathing rebuke or condemnation. **4.** To cause, as a chemical, to explode with sudden violence. — *n. Chem.* Any explosive compound. [< L *fulmen, fulminis* lightning] — **ful′mi·na′tion** *n.* — **ful·mi·na·to·ry** (ful′mə-nə-tôr′ē, -tō′rē) *adj.* — **ful′mi·na′tor** *n.*

ful·some (fŏŏl′səm, ful′-) *adj.* Distastefully excessive in an insincere way: a *fulsome* compliment. [< FULL, adj. + -SOME; infl. by FOUL] — **ful′some·ly** *adv.* — **ful′some·ness** *n.*

fum·ble (fum′bəl) *v.* **·bled, ·bling** *v.i.* **1.** To try to locate something by groping blindly or clumsily: with *for, after.* **2.** To try awkwardly to do something: with *at.* **3.** In football, etc., to get hold of the ball and then let it slip awkwardly from one's grasp. — *v.t.* **4.** To handle awkwardly or ineffectually; botch. **5.** To drop awkwardly (a ball in one's grasp). — *n.* The act of fumbling. [Prob. < Scand. *famla* to grope] — **fum′bler** *n.*

fume (fyōōm) *n.* **1.** A gaseous exhalation or smoke, esp. when acrid or otherwise disagreeable. **2.** A sharply penetrating odor. **3.** Something with no more substance than smoke. **4.** A state of rage: in a *fume.* — *v.* **fumed, fum·ing** *v.i.* **1.** To give off fumes. **2.** To pass off in a mist or vapor. **3.** To be filled with or show rage, irritation, etc. — *v.t.* **4.** To subject to fumes. [< OF < L *fumus* smoke]

fu·mi·gate (fyōō′mə-gāt) *v.t.* **·gat·ed, ·gat·ing** To subject to smoke or fumes, as for disinfection or to kill vermin. [< L < *fumus* smoke + *agere* to drive] — **fu′mi·ga′tion** *n.* — **fu′mi·ga′tor** *n.*

fun (fun) *n.* **1.** Pleasant diversion or amusement. **2.** Lighthearted playfulness: full of fun. — *adj. Informal* Full of fun: a *fun* game. — **for** (or in) **fun** In jest. — **like fun** *Informal* Absolutely not; by no means. — **to make fun of** To ridicule. — *v.i.* **funned, fun·ning** *Informal* To behave or speak in jest. [< obs. *fonnen* to befool]

func·tion (fungk′shən) *n.* **1.** The specific, natural, or proper action or activity of anything. **2.** The special duties or action required of anyone in an occupation, office, or role. **3.** Any more or less formal or elaborate social gathering or ceremony. **4.** Any fact, quality, or thing depending upon or varying with another. **5.** *Math.* A quantity whose value is dependent on the value of some other quantity. — *v.i.* **1.** To perform as expected or required. **2.** To perform the role of something else. [< OF < L *fungi* to perform]

func·tion·al (fungk′shən-əl) *adj.* **1.** Of or pertaining to a function or functions. **2.** Designed for or suited to a partic-

ular operation or use. **3.** Affecting the functions of an organ or part: *functional* disease: distinguished from *organic.* — **func′tion·al·ly** *adv.*

func·tion·al·ism (fungk′shən-əl-iz′əm) *n.* The doctrine that the function or use of an object should determine the form, structure, or material of the object.

func·tion·ar·y (fungk′shən-er′ē) *n. pl.* **·ar·ies** One who serves in a specific capacity; esp., an official.

fund (fund) *n.* **1.** A sum of money, or its equivalent, accumulated or reserved for a specific purpose. **2.** *pl.* Money readily available. **3.** A ready supply: a *fund* of humor. **4.** *pl. Brit.* The government debt; also, government securities: with *the.* — *v.t.* **1.** In finance: **a** To convert into a long-term debt. **b** To accumulate or furnish a fund for. **2.** To gather up a supply of.

fun·da·ment (fun′də-mənt) *n.* The buttocks; also, the anus. [< L *fundus* bottom]

fun·da·men·tal (fun′də-men′təl) *adj.* **1.** Pertaining to or constituting a foundation; basic. **2.** *Music* Of or pertaining to a root. **3.** *Physics* Designating the component of a wave form or other periodic oscillation on which all harmonic frequencies are based. — *n.* **1.** Anything that serves as the basis of a system, as a truth, law, etc. **2.** *Music* A root. **3.** *Physics* That frequency on which a harmonic or group of harmonics is based. — **fun′da·men′tal·ly** *adv.*

fun·da·men·tal·ism (fun′də-men′təl-iz′əm) *n.* **1.** The belief that all statements in the Bible are to be taken literally. **2.** In the U.S., a movement among Protestants holding such a belief. — **fun′da·men′tal·ist** *n. & adj.*

fu·ner·al (fyōō′nər-əl) *n.* **1.** The burial, cremation, or other final disposal of the body of a dead person, together with accompanying services. **2.** A procession held for the final disposal of the body of a dead person. — *adj.* Of, pertaining to, or suitable for a funeral. [< OF < Med.L < L *funus, funeri* burial rite] — **fu·ner·ar·y** (fyōō′nə·rer′ē) *adj.*

fu·ne·re·al (fyōō-nir′ē-əl) *adj.* **1.** Depressingly sad or gloomy; doleful: a *funereal* countenance. **2.** Pertaining to or suitable for a funeral. — **fu·ne′re·al·ly** *adv.*

fungi- *combining form* Fungus. Also, before vowels, **fung-.** [< L *fungus* mushroom]

fun·gi·cide (fun′jə-sīd, -gə-) *n.* Something, as a chemical compound, used in destroying fungi. — **fun′gi·ci′dal** *adj.*

fun·goid (fung′goid) *adj.* Resembling or typical of fungi. — *n. Pathol.* A fungus-like growth.

fun·gous (fung′gəs) *adj.* Of, pertaining to, or having the nature of a fungus.

fun·gus (fung′gəs) *n. pl.* **fun·gus·es** or **fun·gi** (fun′jī, -gī, -gē) **1.** Any nonflowering plants that have no chlorophyll, usu. reproduce asexually, and grow on dead organic matter or live parasitically, including mushrooms, molds, and mildews. **2.** Something that appears or spreads rapidly in a manner suggestive of a mushroom, etc. **3.** *Pathol.* A soft, spongy, granular growth of tissue. — *adj.* Fungous. [< L, mushroom.] — **fun′gal** *adj. & n.*

fu·nic·u·lar (fyōō-nik′yə-lər) *adj.* Moved by the pull of a cable, as a streetcar in a hilly section. — *n.* A railway along which cable cars are drawn: also **funicular railway.**

funk (fungk) *Chiefly Brit. Informal n.* **1.** A state of fear or panic: esp. in the phrase **to be in a blue funk. 2.** One who quails with fear. — *v.t.* **1.** To shrink back from (something difficult, etc.). **2.** To cause to quail. — *v.i.* **3.** To be in a funk. [Cf. Flemish *fonck* fear]

fun·nel (fun′əl) *n.* **1.** A utensil, usu. conical, with a wide mouth tapering to a small outlet or narrow tube, through which liquids, or other free-running substances are poured into bottles, etc., having narrow necks. **2.** One of the smokestacks of a large ship, locomotive, etc. **3.** Any chimney, flue, or similar shaft or tube. — *v.t. & v.i.* **fun·neled** or **·nelled, fun·nel·ing** or **·nel·ling** **1.** To pass through or as through a funnel. **2.** To converge to a particular point, area, etc. [Earlier *fonel,* ult. < L < *in-* into + *fundere* to pour]

fun·nies (fun′ēz) *n.pl. U.S. Informal* Comic strips, or the section of a newspaper containing them.

fun·ny (fun′ē) *adj.* **·ni·er, ·ni·est** **1.** Causing one to laugh or be amused; comical. **2.** *Informal* Peculiar; strange; odd. — **fun′ni·ly** *adv.* — **fun′ni·ness** *n.*

funny bone The part of the elbow where the ulnar nerve joins the humerus very close to the surface and which, when struck, produces an unpleasant, tingling sensation in the arm and hand: also called *crazy bone.*

fur (fûr) *n.* **1.** The soft, fine, hairy coat covering the skin of foxes, bears, squirrels, cats, and many other mammals. **2.** An animal skin or a part of an animal skin covered with such a coat, esp. when prepared for use in garments, rugs, etc.; also, such skins collectively. **3.** A layer of foul matter, as on the tongue when the digestive tract is upset. — **to make the fur fly** *U.S. Informal* To stir up a furor, as by making accusations, revealing faults, etc. — *adj.* Made of or lined or trimmed with fur. — *v.t.* **furred, fur·ring 1.** To cover, line, trim, or clothe with fur. **2.** To cover, as the tongue, with a layer of foul matter. **3.** To apply furring. [< OF *forrer* to line with fur < Gmc.]

fur·be·low (fûr′bə-lō) *n.* **1.** A ruffle, frill, or similar piece of ornamentation. **2.** Any showy bit of decoration. — *v.t.* To provide with furbelows. [Var. of obs. *falbala* < F]

fur·bish (fûr′bish) *v.t.* **1.** To make bright by rubbing; burnish. **2.** To restore to brightness or beauty; renovate: often with *up.* [< OF < OHG *furban* to clean] — **fur′bish·er** *n.*

fur·cate (fûr′kāt; *for adj., also* -kit) *v.i.* **·cat·ed, ·cat·ing** To divide into branches. — *adj.* Forked: also **fur′cat·ed** (-kāt-id). [< Med.L < L *furca* fork] — **fur·ca′tion** *n.*

Fu·ries (fyŏŏr′ēz) *n.pl.* In classical mythology, the three goddesses who avenge unpunished crimes: also called *Eumenides.*

fu·ri·ous (fyŏŏr′ē-əs) *adj.* **1.** Extremely angry; raging. **2.** Extremely violent or intense; fierce. **3.** Pushed to the limit; extremely great: a *furious* rate of speed. [< L *furere* to rage] — **fu′ri·ous·ly** *adv.* — **fu′ri·ous·ness** *n.*

furl (fûrl) *v.t.* **1.** To roll up (a sail, flag, etc.) and make secure, as to a mast or staff. — *v.i.* To become furled. — *n.* **1.** The act of furling, or the state of being furled. **2.** A rolled-up section of a sail, flag, etc. [< F *ferler* < OF < L *firmum* firm + *ligare* to tie]

fur·long (fûr′lông, -long) *n.* A measure of length, equal to ⅛ mile, 220 yards, or 201.168 meters. See table front of book. [OE *furlang* < *furh* furrow + *lang* long]

fur·lough (fûr′lō) *n.* Permission to be absent from duty, esp. in the armed services: now called *leave* or *leave of absence.* — *v.t.* To grant a furlough to. [< Du. *verlof*]

fur·nace (fûr′nis) *n.* **1.** A large apparatus with an enclosed chamber designed to produce intense heat for warming a building, melting metal, creating steam power, etc. **2.** Any intensely hot place. [< OF < L < *furnus* oven]

fur·nish (fûr′nish) *v.t.* **1.** To equip, or fit out, as with fittings or furniture. **2.** To supply; provide. [< OF *furnir* < OHG *frumjan* to provide]

fur·nish·ings (fûr′nish-ingz) *n.pl.* **1.** Articles of clothing, including accessories. **2.** Articles of furniture and other fixtures for a home, office, etc.

fur·ni·ture (fûr′nə-chər) *n.* **1.** The movable articles used in a home, office, etc., as sofas, chairs, tables, or mirrors. **2.** Any necessary equipment, as for a factory or ship. [< F *fourniture* < OF *furnir* < OHG *frumjan* to provide]

fu·ror (fyŏŏr′ôr) *n.* **1.** A great stir; commotion; rumpus. **2.** A state of intense excitement or enthusiasm. [< L *furor* < *furere* to rage]

furred (fûrd) *adj.* **1.** Having or clad in fur. **2.** Made of or trimmed with fur, as garments. **3.** Coated, as the tongue.

fur·ri·er (fûr′ē-ər, -yər) *n.* **1.** One who deals in, repairs, or stores furs. **2.** One who processes furs for garments, etc.

fur·ring (fûr′ing) *n.* **1.** A trimming or lining of fur. **2.** Furs collectively. **3.** An animal's coat of fur. **4.** A coating of foreign matter, as on the tongue. **5.** Strips of wood, metal, etc., fixed to a wall, floor, etc., so as to make a level surface or create air spaces.

fur·row (fûr′ō) *n.* **1.** A narrow channel made in the ground by or as if by a plow. **2.** Any long, narrow, deep depression, as a groove, rut, or deep wrinkle. — *v.t.* **1.** To make furrows or deep wrinkles in. **2.** To plow. — *v.i.* **3.** To become furrowed or wrinkled. [OE *furh*]

fur·ry (fûr′ē) *adj.* **fur·ri·er, fur·ri·est 1.** Of, pertaining to, or resembling fur. **2.** Covered or provided with fur. **3.** Coated, as the tongue. — **fur′ri·ness** *n.*

fur·ther (fûr′thər) Comparative of FAR. — *adv.* **1.** At or to a more distant or remote point in time or space. **2.** To a greater degree; more. **3.** In addition; besides; moreover. — *adj.* **1.** More distant or advanced in time or degree. **2.** More distant in space; farther. **3.** Additional. — *v.t.* To help forward; promote. [OE *furthra*] — **fur′ther·er** *n.*

fur·ther·ance (fûr′thər-əns) *n.* **1.** The act of furthering; advancement. **2.** That which furthers.

fur·ther·more (fûr′thər-môr′, -mōr′) *adv.* In addition; moreover.

fur·ther·most (fûr′thər-mōst′) *adj.* Furthest.

fur·thest (fûr′thist) Superlative of FAR. — *adv.* **1.** At or to the most remote or distant point in space of time. **2.** To the greatest degree. — *adj.* **1.** Most distant, remote, or advanced in time or degree. **2.** Most distant in space.

fur·tive (fûr′tiv) *adj.* **1.** Done in secret; surreptitious; stealthy. **2.** Evasive; shifty. — **Syn.** See STEALTHY. [< F < L < *fur* thief] — **fur′tive·ly** *adv.* — **fur′tive·ness** *n.*

fu·ry (fyŏŏr′ē) *n. pl.* **·ries 1.** Vehement and uncontrolled anger; ungovernable rage. **2.** A fit of such anger or rage. **3.** Violent action or agitation; fierceness: the storm's *fury.* **4.** A person of violent temper, esp. a woman. [< L *furia* < *furere* to rave]

furze (fûrz) *n.* A spiny evergreen shrub of the bean family, having many branches and yellow flowers: also called *gorse, whin.* [OE *fyrs*] — **furz′y** *adj.*

fuse¹ (fyŏŏz) *n.* **1.** A length of combustible material passing into the charge of an explosive, designed to be lit so as to ignite the charge. **2.** *Mil.* Any mechanical or electronic device designed to detonate a bomb, projectile, etc. **3.** *Electr.* A device consisting of a small strip of metal mounted in a casing and completing a circuit when put into position, the metal melting and breaking the circuit if the current becomes excessive. — *v.t.* To attach a fuse to (a rocket, bomb, etc.). Also spelled *fuze.* [< Ital. < L *fusus* spindle]

fuse² (fyŏŏz) *v.t. & v.i.* **fused, fus·ing 1.** To liquefy by heat; melt. **2.** To join by or as if by melting together. [< L *fusus,* pp. of *fundere* to pour]

fu·see (fyŏŏ-zē′) *n.* **1.** A friction match with a large head capable of burning in the wind. **2.** A flare used as a railroad signal. Also spelled *fuzee.* [< F < Med.L < L *fusus* spindle]

fu·se·lage (fyŏŏ′sə-läzh, -ləzh, -zə-) *n. Aeron.* The body of an airplane, containing the cockpit, cabin, etc. [< F]

fu·sel oil (fyŏŏ′zəl, -səl) A volatile, poisonous, oily liquid, obtained from rectified corn, potato, or grape spirits and used as a solvent in various chemical processes. Also **fu′sel.** [< G *fusel* inferior spirits]

fu·si·ble (fyŏŏ′zə-bəl) *adj.* Capable of being fused. — **fu′si·bil′i·ty** *n.* — **fu′si·ble·ness** *n.* — **fu′si·bly** *adv.*

fu·si·form (fyŏŏ′zə-fôrm) *adj.* Shaped like a spindle.

fu·sil (fyŏŏ′zəl) *n.* A flintlock musket. [< F < OF *foisil* a steel for striking sparks, ult. < L *focus* hearth]

fu·si·lier (fyŏŏ′zə-lir′) *n.* **1.** A soldier armed with a flintlock musket. **2.** *pl.* Soldiers of certain regiments of the British army: used in titles of the regiments. Also **fu′si·leer′.**

fu·si·lade (fyŏŏ′zə-lād′) *n.* **1.** A simultaneous or quickly repeated discharge of firearms. **2.** Anything resembling this: a *fusillade* of hail. — *v.t.* **·lad·ed, ·lad·ing** To attack or bring down with a fusillade. Also **fu′si·lade′.** [< F < *fusiller* to shoot < *fusil* musket]

fu·sion (fyŏŏ′zhən) *n.* **1.** A melting or blending together. **2.** Something formed by fusing. **3.** In politics, the union of two parties or two factions within a party. **4.** *Physics* A thermonuclear reaction in which the nuclei of a light element undergo transformation into those of a heavier element, with the release of great energy: also called *nuclear fusion.* [< L *fusio, -onis,* < *fundere* to pour]

fuss (fus) *n.* **1.** Nervous activity; bustle; commotion; ado. **2.** One excessively concerned with trifles: also **fuss′er.** — *v.i.* **1.** To be too much concerned with trifles. — *v.t.* **2.** To bother with trifles. [Origin unknown]

fuss·y (fus′ē) *adj.* **fuss·i·er, fuss·i·est 1.** Too much concerned with trifles; finicky. **2.** Fidgety; fretful. **3.** Requiring meticulous attention. **4.** Having elaborate and showy trimmings, as clothing. — **fuss′i·ly** *adv.* — **fuss′i·ness** *n.*

fus·tian (fus′chən) *n.* **1.** Formerly, a kind of stout cloth made of cotton and flax; now, a coarse, twilled cotton fabric, as corduroy. **2.** Pretentious verbiage; bombast. — *adj.* **1.** Made of fustian. **2.** Pompous; bombastic. [< OF < Med.L < L *fustis* cudgel]

fust·y (fus′tē) *adj.* **fust·i·er, fust·i·est 1.** Musty; moldy; rank. **2.** Old-fashioned; fogeyish. [< obs. *fust* moldy odor <OF, wine cask] — **fust′i·ly** *adv.* — **fust′i·ness** *n.*

fu·tile (fyŏŏ′təl, -til; *esp. Brit.* -tīl) *adj.* **1.** Being of no avail; done in vain; useless. **2.** Frivolous; trivial: *futile* chatter. [< F < L *futilis* pouring out easily, useless] — **fu′tile·ly** *adv.* — **fu′tile·ness** *n.* — **fu·til·i·ty** (fyŏŏ-til′ə-tē) *n.* — **Syn. 1.** vain, fruitless, abortive.

fu·ture (fyŏŏ′chər) *n.* **1.** The time yet to come. **2.** What will be in time to come. **3.** A condition, usu. of success or prosperity, in time to come: a man with a *future.* **4.** *Usu. pl.* Any commodity or security sold or bought upon agreement of future delivery. **5.** *Gram.* **a** A verb tense denoting action that will take place at some time to come. **b** A verb in this tense. — *adj.* **1.** Such as will be in time to come. **2.** Pertaining to or expressing time to come. [< OF < L *futurus,* future participle of *esse* to be] — **fu′ture·less** *adj.*

future perfect *Gram.* **1.** The verb tense expressing a future action or state completed before a specified future time: He *will have finished* by tomorrow. **2.** A verb in this tense.

fu·tur·ism (fyŏŏ′chə-riz′əm) *n.* A movement in art, music, and literature during World War I that rejected traditional forms in an effort to portray more vividly the intensity and speed of contemporary life. — **fu′tur·ist** *adj. & n.*

fu·tu·ri·ty (fyŏŏ-tŏŏr′ə-tē, -tyŏŏr′-) *n. pl.* **·ties 1.** Time to come; the future. **2.** The state or quality of being future. **3.** A future event or possibility.

fuze (fyŏŏz) See FUSE¹.

fu·zee (fyŏŏ-zē′) See FUSEE.

fuzz (fuz) *n.* **1.** Fine, loose particles, fibers, or hairs. **2.** A fluffy mass of these. — *v.t. & v.i.* To become or cause to become fuzzy. [Origin unknown]

fuzz·y (fuz′ē) *adj.* **fuzz·i·er, fuzz·i·est 1.** Having fuzz. **2.** Resembling fuzz. **3.** Lacking sharp distinctness or clarity; blurred. — **fuzz′i·ly** *adv.* — **fuzz′i·ness** *n.*

-fy *suffix of verbs* **1.** Cause to be or become: *deify.* **2.** Become: *liquefy.* [< OF < L *facere* to do, to make]

G

g, G (jē) *n. pl.* **g's** or **gs, G's** or **Gs, gees** (jēz) **1.** The seventh letter of the English alphabet. Also *gee.* **2.** Any sound represented by the letter *g.* **3.** *Usu. cap. U.S. Slang* One thousand dollars; a grand. — *symbol* **1.** *Music* **a** The fifth tone in the scale of C major or the seventh in the natural scale of A minor. **b** A written note representing this tone. **c** A scale built upon the tone of G. **d** The treble clef. **2.** *Physics* The acceleration of a body due to the earth's gravity, about 32 feet per second per second; also, a unit of acceleration equal to that due to the earth's gravity (symbol g).

gab (gab) *Informal v.i.* **gabbed, gab·bing** To talk, esp. glibly or excessively; chatter; prate. — *n.* Glib or excessive speech. [Prob. < ON *gabba* to mock] — **gab′ber** *n.*

gab·ar·dine (gab′ər-dēn, gab/ər-dēn′) *n.* **1.** A firm, twilled, worsted fabric, having a diagonal raised weave, used for coats, suits, etc. **2.** A similar, softer fabric of mercerized cotton. **3.** A gaberdine. [Var. of GABERDINE]

gab·ble (gab′əl) *v.* **·bled, ·bling** *v.i.* **1.** To talk quickly or incoherently. **2.** To utter rapid, cackling sounds, as geese. — *v.t.* **3.** To utter rapidly or incoherently. — *n.* **1.** Glib, incoherent, or foolish talk. **2.** Cackling sounds, as of geese. [Freq. of GAB] — **gab′bler** *n.*

gab·er·dine (gab′ər-dēn, gab/ər-dēn′) *n.* **1.** A loose, coarse coat or frock. **2.** A long, loose, coarse cloak worn by Jews in medieval times. **3.** Gabardine. [< Sp. *garbardina*]

ga·bi·on (gā′bē-ən) *n.* **1.** *Mil.* A cylindrical wicker basket filled with earth, stones, etc., used as a defense. **2.** An open cylinder, usu. of metal, filled with stones, etc., and used in the preliminary construction of dams, etc. [< F < Ital. *gabbione,* aug. of *gabbia* cage < L *cavea* cage]

ga·ble (gā′bəl) *n. Archit.* **1.** The outside, usu. triangular section of a wall extending upward from the level of the eaves of a sloped roof to the ridge pole. **2.** The end wall of a building whose upper part is a gable. **3.** Any gablelike feature, as above a door. — *v.t.* **1.** To cause to form a gable: a *gabled* roof. — *v.i.* **2.** To form a gable. [< OF, prob. < ON *gafl* gable]

gable roof A roof that forms a gable.

GABLES

Ga·bri·el (gā′brē-əl) In the Bible, one of the archangels, chosen as a special messenger of God.

gad¹ (gad) *v.i* **gad·ded, gad·ding** To roam about restlessly or capriciously; ramble. — *n.* The act of gadding. [? < obs. *gadling* vagabond] — **gad′der** *n.*

gad² (gad) *n.* **1.** In mining, a pointed tool. **2.** A goad. — *v.t.* **gad·ded, gad·ding** To break up (ore) with a gad. [< ON *gaddr* goad]

gad·a·bout (gad′ə·bout′) *Informal n.* One who goes about aimlessly, frivolously, etc. — *adj.* Fond of gadding.

gad·fly (gad′flī′) *n. pl.* **·flies 1.** One of various large flies, as a horsefly, that bite cattle, horses, etc. **2.** An irritating, bothersome individual. [< GAD² + FLY]

gadg·et (gaj′it) *n. Informal* **1.** Any small device or contrivance. **2.** Some little thing whose exact name is unknown.

gad·o·lin·i·um (gad′ə·lin′ē-əm) *n.* A metallic element (symbol Gd) of the lanthanide series. See ELEMENT. [after John *Gadolin,* 1760–1852, Finnish chemist]

gad·wall (gad′wôl) *n. pl.* **·walls** or **·wall** A large freshwater duck found in the northern hemisphere.

Gae·a (jē′ə) In Greek mythology, the goddess of earth and mother and wife of Uranus. [< Gk. *Gaia* Earth]

Gael (gāl) *n.* One of the Celts of Ireland or the Scottish Highlands. [< Scottish Gaelic *Gaidheal*]

Gael·ic (gā′lik) *adj.* Belonging or relating to the Gaels or their languages. — *n.* **1.** The languages of the Gaels. **2.** The Goidelic branch of the Celtic languages.

gaff (gaf) *n.* **1.** A sharp iron hook at the end of a pole, for landing a large fish; also, the pole. **2.** *Naut.* A spar for extending the upper edge of a fore-and-aft sail. **3.** *Slang* Loud or annoying talk. — *v.t.* To strike or land with a gaff. — **to stand the gaff** *U.S. Informal* To endure hardship, etc., patiently. [< OF *gaffe,* prob. < Celtic]

gaf·fer (gaf′ər) *n.* An old man. [Alter. of GODFATHER]

gag (gag) *n.* **1.** Something, as a wadded cloth, forced into or over the mouth to prevent a person from speaking or crying out. **2.** Any restraint or suppression of free speech, as by censorship. **3.** A device to keep the jaws open, as in dentistry. **4.** *Slang* A joke or hoax. **5.** *Slang* Something interpolated by an actor into a role, as a topical comment. — **to pull a gag** *U.S. Slang* To perform or perpetrate a practical joke, deception, etc. — *v.* **gagged, gag·ging** *v.t.* **1.** To keep from speaking out by means of a gag. **2.** To keep from speaking or discussing freely, as by force or authority. **3.** To cause nausea in; cause to retch. **4.** To keep (the mouth) open with a gag. — *v.i.* **5.** To heave with nausea; also, to choke on something. [ME *gaggen*] — **gag′ger** *n.*

ga·ga (gä′gä′) *adj. Slang* Foolish; crazy. [< F (slang), a foolish old man]

gage¹ (gāj) See GAUGE.

gage² (gāj) *n.* **1.** Something given as security for an action to be performed; pledge. **2.** Anything, as a glove, proffered as a challenge. **3.** Any challenge. [< OF *gage* pledge]

gag·gle (gag′əl) *v.i.* **·gled, ·gling** To cackle; gabble. — *n.* **1.** A flock of geese. **2.** A chattering group of women.

gai·e·ty (gā′ə·tē) *n. pl.* **·ties 1.** The state of being gay; cheerfulness. **2.** Bright colorfulness or showiness, as of dress. **3.** Fun; merrymaking. Also *gayety.* [< F *gai*]

gail·lar·di·a (gā-lär′dē-ə) *n.* A western American herb with showy yellow or reddish flowers.

gai·ly (gā′lē) *adv.* In a gay manner: also spelled *gayly.*

gain (gān) *v.t.* **1.** To obtain; acquire; get: to *gain* an advantage. **2.** To succeed in winning (a victory, etc.). **3.** To develop an increase of: to *gain* momentum. **4.** To put on (weight). **5.** To earn (a living, etc.). **6.** To arrive at; reach: to *gain* port. — *v.i.* **7.** To grow better: to *gain* in health. **8.** To draw nearer; also, to increase one's lead: usu. with *on* or *upon.* — *n.* **1.** *Often pl.* Something obtained by way of profit, winnings, etc.: small *gains.* **2.** An advantage or lead. **3.** An increase, as in size, amount, etc. **4.** The act of gaining. [< F < OF *gaaignier* < Gmc.] — **Syn.** (verb) **1.** See GET. **2.** attain, achieve. **7.** prosper, flourish.

gain·er (gā′nər) *n.* **1.** One who or that which gains. **2.** A full gainer. **3.** A half gainer.

gain·ful (gān′fəl) *adj.* Yielding profit; lucrative. — **gain′ful·ly** *adv.* — **gain′ful·ness** *n.*

gain·say (gān′sā′) *v.t.* **·said, ·say·ing 1.** To deny. **2.** To contradict. **3.** To act against; oppose. [OE *gegn-* against + SAY²] — **gain′say′er** *n.*

'gainst (genst, *esp. Brit.* gänst) *prep.* Against.

gait (gāt) *n.* **1.** One's manner of moving along on foot. **2.** One of the ways in which a horse steps or runs. — *v.t.* To train (a horse) to take a gait. [< ON *gata* way]

gai·ter (gā′tər) *n.* **1.** A covering, as of leather or canvas, worn over the leg, as a puttee. **2.** A similar covering for the ankle and instep; a spat. **3.** An old-fashioned shoe with a high top. [< F *guêtre*]

gal (gal) *n. Slang* **1.** A girl. **2.** A girl friend.

ga·la (gā′lə, gal′ə, gä′lə) *adj.* Appropriate to a festive occasion; festive. — *n.* An occasion marked by joyous festivity. [< F < Ital. holiday dress]

galacto- *combining form* Milk; milky. Also, before vowels, **galact-**. [< Gk. *galaktos* milk]

Gal·a·had (gal′ə·had) **1.** In Arthurian legend, the noblest knight of the Round Table, son of Lancelot, who accomplished the quest for the Holy Grail. **2.** Any pure man.

Gal·a·te·a (gal′ə·tē′ə) In Greek mythology, a statue of a maiden brought to life by Aphrodite after its sculptor, Pygmalion, had fallen in love with it.

Ga·la·tia (gə·lā′shə, -shē-ə) An ancient country of Asia Minor, so called from the Gauls who conquered it.

Ga·la·tian (gə·lā′shən) *adj.* Of ancient Galatia. — *n.* A native of Galatia. — **Epistle to the Galatians** A book of the New Testament, a letter written by the apostle Paul.

gal·ax·y (gal′ək·sē) *n. pl.* **·ax·ies 1.** *Astron.* Any very large system of stars, nebulae, or other celestial bodies. **2.** *Usu. cap.* The Milky Way. **3.** A brilliant group, as of persons. [< F < L < Gk. < *gala* milk]

gale (gāl) *n.* **1.** *Meteorol.* A wind stronger than a stiff breeze. **2.** An outburst, as of hilarity. [Origin uncertain]

ga·le·na (gə·lē′nə) *n.* A metallic, dull gray, cleavable, isometric lead sulfide, PbS, one of the principal ores of lead. Also **ga·le·nite** (gə·lē′nīt). [< L, lead ore]

Ga·li·cian (gə·lish′ən) *adj.* **1.** Of Spanish Galicia, its people, or their language. **2.** Of Polish Galicia or its people. —*n.* **1.** A native of Spanish Galicia. **2.** The Portuguese dialect spoken there. **3.** A native of Polish Galicia.

Gal·i·le·an (gal′ə·lē′ən) *adj.* Of Galilee, in ancient northern Palestine. —*n.* **1.** An inhabitant of Galilee. **2.** A Christian. —**the Galilean** Jesus Christ. Also **Gal′i·lae′an.**

Gal·i·le·an (gal′ə·lē′ən) *adj.* Of or pertaining to Galileo.

gall¹ (gôl) *n.* **1.** *Physiol.* The bitter fluid secreted by the liver; bile. **2.** Bitter feeling; rancor. **3.** Something bitter. **4.** *U.S. Slang* Impudence. [OE *gealla*]

gall² (gôl) *n.* **1.** An abrasion or sore produced by friction. **2.** Something that irritates or vexes. **3.** Exasperation. —*v.t.* **1.** To injure (the skin) by friction; chafe. **2.** To vex or irritate. —*v.i.* **3.** To become or be chafed. [Prob. < GALL¹]

gall³ (gôl) *n.* An abnormal plant growth that on certain oaks yields tannin. [< F < L *galla* gallnut]

gal·lant (gal′ənt *for adj. defs.* 1, 4, 5; gə·lant′, gal′ənt *for adj. defs.* 2 & 3; *n.* gal′ənt, gə·lant′; *v.* gə·lant′) *adj.* **1.** Possessing spirit and courage; brave: *gallant* soldiers. **2.** Chivalrously attentive to women; also, dashingly amorous. **3.** Stately; imposing. **4.** Showy: *gallant* attire. —*n.* **1.** A brave, spirited man. **2.** A man chivalrously attentive to women or amorous in a courtly way; a paramour. —*v.t.* **1.** To be chivalrously attentive to (a woman). **2.** To escort. —*v.i.* **3.** To be a suitor. [< OF *galer* to rejoice] —**gal′lant·ly** *adv.*

gal·lant·ry (gal′ən·trē) *n. pl.* **·ries** **1.** Nobility and bravery. **2.** Chivalrous or amorous behavior. **3.** An instance of gallant speech or behavior.

gall bladder *Anat.* A small, pear-shaped muscular pouch situated beneath the liver in man and serving as a reservoir for bile conducted through the **gall duct.**

gal·le·on (gal′ē·ən) *n.* A large sailing vessel of the 15th to 17th centuries. [< Sp. < Med.L]

gal·ler·y (gal′ər·ē) *n. pl.* **·ler·ies** **1.** A roofed promenade, esp. an open-sided one extending along an inner or outer wall of a building. **2.** Any similar long, usu. narrow enclosed area, as a hall. **3.** *Southern U.S.* A veranda. **4.** An elevated rear floor section for seating in a theater or other large building, over the back of the main floor. **5.** A group of spectators, as of those in a grandstand. **6.** A part of the general public viewed as shallow, undiscriminating, etc. **7.** A room or building in which statues, paintings, etc., are displayed. **8.** A room or building in which articles are sold to the highest bidder. **9.** An enclosed place, as at a fair, where one shoots at targets for amusement. **10.** A tunnel or underground passage, as in a mine. —**to play to the gallery** To play or cater to the common crowd. —*v.t.* **·ler·ied, ·ler·y·ing** To provide with a gallery. [< F < Med.L *galeria*]

gal·ley (gal′ē) *n. pl.* **·leys** **1.** A long, low vessel used in ancient times, propelled by oars and sails. **2.** A large rowboat. **3.** The kitchen of a ship. **4.** *Printing* **a** A long tray for holding composed type. **b** A galley proof. [< OF < Med.L < LGk. *galaia*]

galley proof *Printing* **1.** A proof taken from type composed in a galley and used for making corrections before page composition. **2.** Two or more such proofs collectively.

galley slave **1.** A slave or convict condemned to row a galley. **2.** One who does monotonous work; drudge.

gall·fly (gôl′flī′) *n. pl.* **·flies** A small insect that deposits eggs in plant tissue, with consequent production of galls.

gal·lic (gal′ik) *adj. Chem.* **1.** Of, pertaining to, or derived from gallium. **2.** Relating to or derived from gallnuts.

gallic acid *Chem.* A white, odorless, crystalline organic compound, $C_7H_6O_5·H_2O$, found in many plants and used in the making of inks, dyestuffs, paper, etc.

Gal·lic (gal′ik) *adj.* Of or pertaining to ancient Gaul or modern France; French. [< L *Gallus* inhabitant of Gaul]

Gal·li·cism (gal′ə·siz′əm) *n.* An idiom or turn of phrase peculiar to French.

Gal·li·cize (gal′ə·sīz) *v.t. & v.i.* **·cized, ·ciz·ing** To make French in character, language, etc.; Frenchify.

gal·li·na·ceous (gal′ə·nā′shəs) *adj.* Of or pertaining to an order of birds including the common hen, turkeys, partridges, etc. [< L < *gallina* hen] —**gal′li·na′cean** *n.*

gall·ing (gô′ling) *adj.* Very annoying or exasperating.

gal·li·nule (gal′ə·nyōōl, -nōōl) *n.* Any of several cootlike wading birds of the rail family. [< L *gallina* hen]

gal·li·pot (gal′i·pot) *n.* A small earthen jar, as for ointments, used esp. by druggists. [? < GALLEY + POT]

gal·li·um (gal′ē·əm) *n.* A rare, bluish white, metallic element in the aluminum group, having a low melting point (86° F.). See ELEMENT. [< NL < L *gallus* cock, trans. of Lecoq de Boisbaudran, 1838–1912, its discoverer]

gal·li·vant (gal′ə·vant, gal′ə·vant′) *v.i.* To roam about capriciously; gad. [? Alter. of GALLANT]

gall·nut (gôl′nut′) *n.* A gall produced on certain oaks or other plants.

Gallo- *combining form* Gaulish or French. [< L *Gallus*]

gal·lon (gal′ən) *n.* **1.** A liquid measure of capacity that by the U.S. standard contains 231 cubic inches or 4 quarts and by the British standard (**imperial gallon**) 277.3 cubic inches or 4 imperial quarts. **2.** A dry measure equivalent to ⅛ bushel. **3.** A container with a capacity of 1 gallon. See table front of book. [< OF < Celtic]

gal·lop (gal′əp) *n.* **1.** The fastest gait of a horse, etc., characterized by regular leaps during which all four feet are off the ground at once. **2.** A ride at a gallop. **3.** A rapid pace. —*v.i.* **1.** To ride at a gallop. **2.** To go very fast. —*v.t.* **3.** To cause to gallop. [< OF < *galoper* < Gmc.] —**gal′lop·er** *n.*

gal·lows (gal′ōz) *n. pl.* **·lows·es** or **·lows** **1.** A framework of two or more upright beams supporting a crossbeam, used for execution by hanging. Also **gallows tree.** **2.** Any similar structure, as a set of crossbars. [OE *galga*]

gallows bird *Informal* One who merits hanging.

gall·stone (gôl′stōn′) *n. Pathol.* A small, stony mass sometimes formed in the gall bladder or bile passages.

gal·op (gal′əp) *n.* **1.** A lively round dance. **2.** Music for this dance, written in duple meter. [< F, gallop]

ga·lore (gə·lôr′, -lōr′) *adv.* In great numbers or abundance: to offer bargains *galore*. [< Irish *go leōr* enough]

ga·losh (gə·losh′) *n. Usu. pl.* An overshoe reaching above the ankle and worn in bad weather. [< F *galoche*]

ga·lumph (gə·lumf′) *v.i.* To clump along pompously. [< GAL(LOP) + (TRI)UMPH; coined by Lewis Carroll]

gal·van·ic (gal·van′ik) *adj.* **1.** Of or caused by electricity as produced by chemical action. **2.** Pertaining to a reaction to an electric shock; convulsive. Also **gal·van′i·cal.**

gal·va·nism (gal′və·niz′əm) *n.* **1.** Electricity as produced by chemical action: also called *voltaism*. **2.** *Med.* The therapeutic application of a continuous electric current from voltaic cells. [after Luigi *Galvani* + -ISM]

gal·va·nize (gal′və·nīz) *v.t.* **·nized, ·niz·ing** **1.** To stimulate to muscular action by electricity. **2.** To rouse to action; excite. **3.** To provide with steel, etc. with a protective coating of zinc. —**gal′va·ni·za′tion** *n.* —**gal′va·niz′er** *n.*

galvanized iron Iron coated with zinc, as for protection against rust.

galvano- *combining form* Galvanic; galvanism.

gal·va·nom·e·ter (gal′və·nom′ə·tər) *n. Electr.* An apparatus for indicating the presence and determining the strength and direction of an electric current. —**gal·va·no·met·ric** (gal′və·nō·met′rik, gal·van′ō-) or **·ri·cal** *adj.*

gal·va·no·scope (gal′və·nō·skōp′, gal·van′ə-) *n.* An instrument for detecting an electric current and showing its direction. —**gal·va·no·scop·ic** (gal′və·nō·skop′ik, gal·van′ō-) *adj.* —**gal·va·nos′co·py** (-nos′kə·pē) *n.*

gam (gam) *n. Slang* A leg, esp. of a woman. Also **gamb.**

gam·bit (gam′bit) *n.* **1.** In chess, an opening in which a player risks or sacrifices a piece to gain a favorable position. **2.** Any opening move, as one to promote discussion. [< F < OF *gambet*, a tripping up, ult. < LL *gamba* leg]

gam·ble (gam′bəl) *v.* **·bled, ·bling** *v.i.* **1.** To risk or bet something of value on the outcome of a game of chance, etc. **2.** To take a risk to obtain a result. —*v.t.* **3.** To wager or bet (something of value). **4.** To lose by taking risks: usu. with *away*. —*n. Informal* **1.** Any risky venture. **2.** A gambling transaction. [Cf. OE *gamenian* to sport, play] —**gam·bler** (gam′blər) *n.*

gam·boge (gam·bōj′, -bōozh′) *n.* **1.** A gum resin obtained from a tropical tree, used as a pigment and cathartic. **2.** A bright yellow or orange-yellow color.

gam·bol (gam′bəl) *v.i.* **gam·boled** or **·bolled, gam·bol·ing** or **·bol·ling** To skip or leap about in play; frolic. —*n.* A skipping about in sport. [< F < Ital. *gamba* leg]

gam·brel (gam′brəl) *n.* **1.** The hock of a horse, etc. **2.** A gambrel roof. [< OF < LL *gamba*]

gambrel roof *Archit.* A ridged roof with the slope broken on each side.

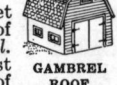

GAMBREL ROOF

game¹ (gām) *n.* **1.** A contest governed by set rules, entered into for amusement, as a test of prowess, or for money or other stakes. **2.** *pl.* Athletic competitions. **3.** A single contest forming part of a fixed series. **4.** The number of points for winning, as in tennis or cards. **5.** The score during a contest: The *game* was 6–6. **6.** The equipment used in playing games, as chess boards and pieces. **7.** The style or prowess in a contest: His *game* of golf is not good. **8.** A form of playful activity: Love is a *game*. **9.** *Informal* Any profession, business, etc.: the teaching *game*. **10.** A plan designed to attain an objective. **11.** Animals, fish, etc., that are hunted or taken; also, the flesh of such animals, etc. **12.** Anything hunted; quarry. **13.** A fit target for ridicule, criticism, etc.: They were fair *game*. —

to make game of To subject to ridicule, etc. **— to play the game 1.** To act with honor, consideration, etc. **2.** To act in accordance with what is expected. **— v. gamed, gam·ing v.i. 1.** To gamble at cards, etc., for money or other stakes. **— v.t. 2.** To lose by gambling: with *away.* **— adj. 1.** Of hunted animals, etc., or their flesh. **2.** Having a fighting spirit; plucky. **3.** *Informal* Ready; willing. [OE *gamen*]

game² (gām) *adj. Informal* Lame: a *game* leg.

game·cock (gām′kok′) *n.* A rooster bred and trained for cockfighting.

game·keep·er (gām′kē′pər) *n.* A person having the care of game, as on an estate.

game·ly (gām′lē) *adv.* In a game manner; pluckily.

game·ness (gām′nis) *n.* Pluck; bravery; endurance.

game·ster (gām′stər) *n.* One who gambles.

gam·ete (gam′ēt, gə-mēt′) *n. Biol.* Either of two mature reproductive cells, an ovum or sperm, that in uniting produce a zygote. [< NL < Gk. *gametē* wife, or *gametēs* husband] **— ga·met·ic** (gə-met′ik) *adj.*

gameto- *combining form* Gamete. [< Gk. < *gamos* marriage]

ga·me·to·phyte (gə-mē′tə-fīt) *n. Bot.* The phase or generation that produces the sexual organs of a plant.

gam·in (gam′in, *Fr.* gå·man′) *n.* A homeless youngster who wanders about the streets of a city or town. [< F]

gam·ma (gam′ə) *n.* The third letter in the Greek alphabet (Γ, γ), corresponding to *g* (as in *go*). See ALPHABET.

gamma globulin *Biochem.* A globulin present in blood plasma and containing antibodies effective against certain pathogenic microorganisms.

gamma rays *Physics* A type of electromagnetic radiation of great penetrating power.

gam·mer (gam′ər) *n.* An old woman: now humorous or contemptuous. Compare GAFFER. [Alter. of GODMOTHER]

gam·mon (gam′ən) *n.* In backgammon, a double victory, in which one player removes all his pieces before the other player removes any. **— v.t.** To obtain a gammon over. [? ME *gamen* game]

gamo- *combining form* **1.** *Biol.* Sexually joined. **2.** *Bot.* Fused; united. [< Gk. *gamos* marriage]

-gamous *combining form* Pertaining to marriage or union for reproduction: used in adjectives corresponding to nouns in *-gamy: polygamous.* [< Gk. *gamos* marriage + -OUS]

gam·ut (gam′ət) *n.* **1.** The whole range of anything: the *gamut* of emotions. **2.** *Music* **a** The entire range or compass of tones used in modern music. **b** The major diatonic scale. [< Med.L *gamma ut* < *gumma, the first note of the early* musical scale + *ut* (later, *do*). The names of the notes of the scale were taken from a medieval Latin hymn: *Ut* queant laxis *Resonare* fibris, *Mira* gestorum *Famuli* tuorum, *Solve* polluti *Labii* reatum, Sancte Iohannes.]

gam·y (gā′mē) *adj.* **gam·i·er, gam·i·est 1.** Having the flavor or odor of game, esp. game that has been kept raw until somewhat tainted. **2.** Full of pluck; disposed to fight.

-gamy *combining form* Marriage or union for reproduction: *polygamy.* [< Gk. *gamos* marriage]

gan·der (gan′dər) *n.* **1.** A male goose. **2.** *U.S. Slang* A look or glance: to take a *gander.* [OE *gandra*]

gang¹ (gang) *n.* **1.** A group of persons organized or associated together for disreputable or illegal purposes. **2.** A crew of persons who work together. **3.** *Informal* A group of persons associated together for some purpose. **4.** A set of similar tools or other devices designed to operate as a unit. **— v.t. 1.** To unite into or as into a gang. **2.** *Informal* To attack as a group. **— v.i. 3.** To form a gang. [OE *gangan* to go]

gang² (gang) *v.i. Scot.* To go or walk.

gan·gli·at·ed (gang′glē·ā′tid) *adj.* Possessing ganglia. Also **gan′gli·ate** (-it, -āt), **gan·gli·on·at·ed** (gang′glē·ən·ā′tid).

gan·gling (gang′gling) *adj.* Awkwardly tall and lanky. Also **gan′gly.** [Cf. dial. E *gangrel* a lanky person]

ganglio- *combining form* Ganglion. Also, before vowels, **gangli-** or **ganglion-.**

gan·gli·on (gang′glē·ən) *n. pl.* **·gli·ons** or **·gli·a** (glē·ə) **1.** *Physiol.* A collection of nerve cells, outside of the central nervous system. **2.** Any center of energy, activity, or strength. [< LL < Gk. *ganglion* tumor] **— gan·gli·on·ic** (gang′glē·on′ik) *adj.*

gang plank (gang′plangk′) *n.* A temporary bridge for passengers between a vessel and a wharf.

gan·grene (gang′grēn, gang-grēn′) *n. Pathol.* The rotting of tissue in the body, caused by a failure in the circulation of the blood, as from infection, etc. **— v.t. & v.i. ·grened ·gren·ing** To cause gangrene in or become affected by gangrene. [< L < Gk. *gangraina*] **— gan′gre·nous** (-grə-nəs) *adj.*

gang·ster (gang′stər) *n.* A member of a criminal gang.

gang·way (n. gang′wā, interj. gang′wā′) *n.* **1.** A passage-way through, into, or out of any enclosure. **2.** *Naut.* **a** A passage on a ship's upper deck. **b** An opening in a ship's side to give entrance to passengers or freight. **c** A gangplank. **— interj.** Get out of the way! [OE *gangweg*]

gan·net (gan′it) *n.* Any of several large sea birds related to the pelicans and herons. [OE *ganot*]

gan·oid (gan′oid) *adj.* **1.** Pertaining to a large division of fishes, including sturgeons, bowfins, etc. **2.** Having an enamellike appearance, as the scales of such fishes. **— n.** A ganoid fish. [< Gk. *ganos* brightness + -OID]

gant·let¹ (gônt′lit, gant′-) See GAUNTLET¹.

gant·let² (gônt′lit, gant′-) *n.* **1.** A former military punishment in which the offender ran between two lines of men armed with clubs, whips, etc., who struck him as he passed. **2.** An onslaught of difficulties or criticism from all sides. **— to run the gantlet 1.** To be punished by the gantlet. **2.** To be subjected to a fierce onslaught, as of criticism, difficulties, etc. Also spelled *gauntlet.* [Earlier *gantlope,* alter. of Sw. *gatlopp* a running down a lane]

gan·try (gan′trē) *n. pl.* **·tries 1.** A bridgelike framework for holding the rails of a traveling crane or for supporting railway signals. **2.** A gantry scaffold. **3.** A frame to support a barrel in a horizontal position. Also spelled *gauntry.* [< OF < L *canterius* beast of burden, framework]

gantry scaffold *Aerospace* A large mobile scaffolding used to assemble and service a large rocket on its launching pad.

gaol (jāl) *n. Brit.* Jail. [Var. of JAIL] **— gaol′er** *n.*

gap (gap) *n.* **1.** An opening or wide crack, as in a wall. **2.** A deep notch or ravine in a mountain ridge. **3.** A break in continuity; interruption. **4.** A difference, as in character, opinions, etc. **— v.t. gapped, gap·ping** To make or adjust a breach or opening in. [< ON *gap* gap, abyss]

gape (gāp, gap) *v.i.* **gaped, gap·ing 1.** To stare with or as with the mouth wide open. **2.** To open the mouth wide, as in yawning. **3.** To be or become open wide. **— n. 1.** The act of gaping. **2.** A wide opening; gap. **3.** *Zool.* The width of the fully opened mouth, as of birds, fishes, etc. [< ON *gapa*] **— gap′er** *n.*

gap·py (gap′ē) *adj.* **·pi·er, ·pi·est** Having gaps.

gar (gär) *n.* **1.** Any of several fresh-water fishes having a spearlike snout and elongate body. [Short for GARFISH]

ga·rage (gə-räzh′, -räj′; *Brit.* gar′ij) *n.* A building in which motor vehicles are stored, serviced, or repaired. **— v.t. ·raged, ·rag·ing** To put or keep in a garage. [< F < *garer* to protect]

Gar·and rifle (gar′ənd, gə-rand′) *U.S. Mil.* The M-1 rifle. [after J. C. *Garand,* born 1888, U.S. inventor]

garb (gärb) *n.* **1.** Clothes; esp., apparel characteristic of some office, rank, etc. **2.** External appearance, form, or expression. **— v.t.** To clothe; dress. [< MF *garbe* gracefulness]

gar·bage (gär′bij) *n.* **1.** Refuse from a kitchen, etc., consisting of unwanted or unusable pieces of meat, vegetable matter, eggshells, etc. **2.** Anything worthless or offensive. [Prob. < AF. Cf. OF *garbe* sheaf of grain, animal fodder.]

gar·ble (gär′bəl) *v.t.* **·bled, ·bling 1.** To mix up or confuse (a story, facts, etc.) unintentionally. **2.** To change or distort the meaning of (facts, texts, etc.) with intent to mislead or misrepresent. **— n. 1.** The act of garbling. **2.** That which is garbled. [< Ital. < Arabic *gharbala* to sift]

gar·çon (gàr·sôn′) *n. pl.* **·çons** (-sôn′) *French* **1.** A boy or youth. **2.** A waiter. **3.** A male servant.

gar·den (gär′dən) *n.* **1.** A place for the cultivation of flowers, vegetables, or small plants. **2.** Any territory remarkable for the beauty of its vegetation. **3.** *Often pl.* A piece of ground, commonly used as a place of public resort. **— adj. 1.** Grown or capable of being grown in a garden. **2.** Ordinary; common. **— v.t. 1.** To cultivate as a garden. **— v.i. 2.** To till or work in a garden. [< AF *gardin*] **— gar′den·er** *n.* **— gar′den·ing** *n.*

gar·de·ni·a (gär-dē′nē-ə, -dēn′yə) *n.* Any of mainly tropical shrubs or trees with large, fragrant, yellow or white flowers. [after Alexander *Garden,* 1730–91, U.S. botanist]

Garden State Nickname of New Jersey.

gar·fish (gär′fish′) *n. pl.* **·fish** or **·fish·es** A gar. Also **gar′·pike.** [OE *gar* spear + FISH]

Gar·gan·tu·a (gär-gan′chŏŏ-ə) The peace-loving giant of Rabelais' satirical romance *Gargantua* (1534), noted for his enormous appetite. **— Gar·gan′tu·an** *adj.*

gar·gle (gär′gəl) *v.* **·gled, ·gling v.i. 1.** To rinse the throat with a liquid kept agitated by slowly expelling air through the liquid. **— v.t. 2.** To rinse (the throat and mouth) by gargling. **3.** To utter throatily as if gargling. **— n.** A liquid used for gargling. [< OF *gargouille* throat]

gar·goyle (gär′goil) *n.* A waterspout, usu. made in the form of a grotesque human or animal figure, projecting from the gutter of a building. [< OF *gargouille* throat]

gar·ish (gâr′ish) *adj.* Vulgarly showy or gaudy: Her new dress is very *garish*. [Cf. obs. *gaure* to stare] — **gar′ish·ly** *adv.* — **gar′ish·ness** *n.*

gar·land (gär′lənd) *n.* **1.** A wreath or rope of flowers, leaves, vines, etc. **2.** Anything resembling a garland. **3.** A collection of poems, bits of prose, etc. **4.** *Naut.* A ring of rope, wire, etc., lashed to a spar to aid in hoisting it. — *v.t.* To decorate with or make into a garland. [< OF *garlande*]

gar·lic (gär′lik) *n.* **1.** A hardy bulbous perennial with a compound bulb. **2.** One of the cloves of this perennial, used in cooking and medicine. [OE *gār* spear + *lēac* leek] — **gar′lick·y** *adj.*

gar·ment (gär′mənt) *n.* **1.** An article of clothing, esp. of outer clothing. **2.** *pl.* Clothes. **3.** Outer covering. — *v.t.* To clothe. [< OF *garnir* to garnish]

gar·ner (gär′nər) *v.t.* To gather or store as in a granary; accumulate. — *n.* **1.** A granary. **2.** Any storage place. [< OF < L *granum* grain]

gar·net (gär′nit) *n.* **1.** Any of a group of vitreous silicate minerals varying in color; esp., any of the deep red varieties, used as gems. **2.** A deep red color. [< OF < Med.L *granatum* < L, pomegranate]

gar·nish (gär′nish) *v.t.* **1.** To add something to by way of decoration; embellish. **2.** In cookery, to decorate (a dish) with flavorsome or colorful trimmings. **3.** *Law* To garnishee. — *n.* **1.** Something that garnishes food. **2.** An added decoration; embellishment. [< OF *garnir* to prepare]

gar·nish·ee (gär′nish·ē′) *Law v.t.* **·nish·eed**, **·nish·ee·ing** **1.** To attach (any debt or property in the hands of a third person that is due or belongs to a defendant) with notice that no return or disposal is to be made until a court judgment is issued. **2.** To issue a garnishment to. — *n.* A person who has been garnisheed.

gar·nish·ment (gär′nish·mənt) *n.* **1.** The act of garnishing. **2.** That which garnishes; embellishment. **3.** *Law* **a** A summons to appear in court, issued to one who is not a litigant in the case. **b** A notice to a person holding money or effects belonging to a defendant not to return or dispose of the money or effects pending court judgment.

gar·ni·ture (gär′ni·chər) *n.* Anything used to garnish.

gar·ret (gar′it) *n.* A room or set of rooms in an attic. [< OF *garir* to watch, defend]

gar·ri·son (gar′ə·sən) *n.* **1.** The military force stationed in a fort, town, etc. **2.** The place where such a force is stationed. — *v.t.* **1.** To place troops in, as a fort or town, for defense. **2.** To station (troops) in a fort, town, etc. **3.** To occupy as a garrison. [< OF *garir* to defend]

gar·rote (gə·rot′, -rōt′) *n.* **1.** A former Spanish method of execution with a cord or metal collar tightened by a screw-like device; also, the cord or collar used. **2.** Any similar method of strangulation. — *v.t.* **·rot·ed**, **·rot·ing** **1.** To execute with a garrote. **2.** To throttle in order to rob, silence, etc. Also **ga·rote′, ga·rotte′.** [< Sp. *garrote*]

gar·ru·lous (gar′ə·ləs, -yə-) *adj.* **1.** Given to continual or glib talking. **2.** Rambling and wordy. [< L *garrulus* talkative] — **gar′ru·lous·ly** *adv.* — **gar·ru·li·ty** (ga·rōō′lə·tē), **gar′ru·lous·ness** *n.*

gar·ter (gär′tər) *n.* A band worn around the leg or a tab attached to an undergarment to hold a stocking in place. — *v.t.* To support or fasten with a garter. [< AF < OF *garet* bend of the knee < Celtic]

Gar·ter (gär′tər) *n.* **1.** The distinctive badge of the **Order of the Garter**, the highest order of knighthood in Great Britain. **2.** The order itself.

garter snake Any of various small, harmless, viviparous, brightly striped snakes.

gas (gas) *n.* *pl.* **gas·es** or **gas·ses** **1.** A form of matter having extreme molecular mobility and capable of diffusing and expanding rapidly in all directions. **2.** A combustible mixture used for lighting or heating. **3.** A mixture used to produce anesthesia; laughing *gas*. **4.** A chemical or mixture of chemicals designed to stupefy. **5.** An explosive mixture of air and methane, etc., sometimes accumulated in coal mines. **6.** A noxious exhalation given off by improperly digested food in the stomach or intestines. **7.** *U.S. Informal* Gasoline. **8.** *Slang* Long-winded talking. **9.** *Slang* Something very exciting, satisfying, etc. — *v.* **gassed**, **gas·sing**; he, she, it **gas·ses** or **gas·es** — *v.t.* **1.** To subject to or affect with gas. **2.** To fill or supply with gas. **3.** *U.S. Slang* To evoke a strong reaction, as of amusement or excitement, from: His remark *gassed* them. — *v.i.* **4.** To give off gas. **5.** *Slang* To talk excessively. [Coined by J. B. van Helmont, 1577–1644, Belgian chemist, either < Du. *geest* spirit or < L < Gk. *chaos* formless mass]

Gas·con (gas′kən) *adj.* Of or pertaining to Gascony or its assertedly boastful people. — *n.* A native of Gascony.

gas·e·ous (gas′ē·əs, -yəs) *adj.* **1.** Of, pertaining to, or resembling gas. **2.** Light and unsubstantial; superficial.

gas fitter One who fits and puts up gas fixtures.

gash (gash) *v.t.* To make a long, deep cut in. — *n.* A long, deep cut or flesh wound. [< OF *garser* to scratch]

gas·ket (gas′kit) *n.* **1.** *Mech.* A ring, disk or plate of packing to make a joint or closure watertight or gastight. **2.** *Naut.* A rope or cord used to confine furled sails to the yard or boom. [Cf. Ital. *gaschetta* end of rope]

gas·light (gas′līt′) *n.* Light produced by the burning of illuminating gas. Also **gas light.**

gas·man (gas′man′) *n.* *pl.* **·men** (-men′) A man employed to read gas meters and note the amount of gas used.

gas mantle A fabric tube that gives light when heated by gas.

gas mask A protective mask with an air filter worn to prevent poisoning or irritation by noxious gases.

gas meter An apparatus for measuring the quantity of gas that passes through it.

gas·o·line (gas′ə·lēn, gas′ə·lēn′) *n.* *U.S.* A colorless, volatile, flammable liquid hydrocarbon, made by the distillation of crude petroleum and used chiefly as a fuel and as a solvent for fats. Also **gas′o·lene.**

gas·om·e·ter (gas·om′ə·tər) *n.* **1.** An apparatus for measuring gases. **2.** A reservoir for gas. — **gas·om′e·try** *n.*

gasp (gasp, gäsp) *v.i.* **1.** To take in the breath suddenly and sharply, as from fear. **2.** To have great longing or desire: with *for* or *after*. — *v.t.* **3.** To say or utter while gasping. — *n.* **1.** An act of gasping. **2.** An utterance made while gasping. [< ON *geispa* yawn]

gas station *U.S.* A filling station.

gas·sy (gas′ē) *adj.* **·si·er**, **·si·est** **1.** Filled with, containing, or causing the formation of gas. **2.** Resembling or suggestive of gas. **3.** *Informal* Very talkative.

gas·tric (gas′trik) *adj.* Of or pertaining to the stomach.

gastric juice *Biochem.* A fluid secreted by stomach glands, essential to digestion and containing several enzymes.

gastric ulcer *Pathol.* An ulcer formed on the stomach lining, often by excess secretion of gastric juice.

gas·tri·tis (gas·trī′tis) *n.* *Pathol.* Inflammation of the lining of the stomach. — **gas·trit·ic** (gas·trit′ik) *adj.*

gastro- *combining form* **1.** Stomach. **2.** Stomach and. Also **gastero-** or, before vowels, **gastr-.** [< Gk. *gastēr* stomach]

gas·tro·in·tes·ti·nal (gas′trō·in·tes′tə·nəl) *adj.* *Anat.* Of or pertaining to the stomach and intestines.

gas·tro·nome (gas′trə·nōm) *n.* A gourmet. Also **gas·tron·o·mer** (gas·tron′ə·mər), **gas·tron′o·mist.**

gas·tro·nom·ic (gas′trə·nom′ik) *adj.* Of or pertaining to gastronomes or gastronomy. Also **gas′tro·nom′i·cal.**

gas·tron·o·my (gas·tron′ə·mē) *n.* The art of good eating; epicurism. [< F < Gk. < *gastēr* stomach + *nomos* law]

gas·tro·pod (gas′trə·pod) *n.* One of a large class of aquatic and terrestrial mollusks, including snails, slugs, limpets, etc., usu. having a univalve, spiral shell and a muscular creeping organ. — *adj.* Of or pertaining to this class. [< NL < Gk. *gastēr* stomach + *pous, podos* foot] — **gas·trop·o·dan** (gas·trop′ə·dən) *adj. & n.* — **gas·trop′o·dous** *adj.*

gas·tru·la (gas′trōō·lə) *n.* *pl.* **·lae** (-lē) *Biol.* An early embryonic form, consisting of a two-layered sac enclosing a central cavity opening to the outside at one end. [< NL, dim. of Gk. *gastēr* stomach] — **gas′tru·lar** *adj.*

gas turbine A turbine engine in which liquid or gaseous fuel is burned and the gases sent through a rotor unit.

gas·works (gas′wûrks′) *n.* *pl.* **·works** An establishment where illuminating gas or heating gas is made.

gat (gat) *n.* *Slang* A pistol. [Short for GATLING GUN]

gate (gāt) *n.* **1.** A movable barrier, commonly swinging on hinges, that closes or opens a passage through a wall, fence, etc. **2.** An opening for exit or entrance through a wall or fence. **3.** The structure on either side of such an opening. **4.** Anything that gives access: the *gate* to success. **5.** A mountain gap or other natural passageway. **6.** A protective barrier capable of being raised or lowered, as at a railroad crossing. **7.** A structure or valvelike device for controlling the supply of water, oil, gas, etc. **8.** The total paid attendance at a sports event, theatrical presentation, etc.; also, the money collected. — **to get the gate** *Slang* To be sent away or be rejected. — **to give the gate** *Slang* To dismiss, reject, or get rid of. [OE *gatu*, pl. of *geat* opening]

gate·crash·er (gāt′krash′ər) *n.* *Informal* One who gains admittance without paying or being invited.

gate-leg table (gāt′leg′) A table with swinging legs that support drop leaves and fold against the frame when the leaves are let down. Also **gate-legged table** (-legd′).

gate·way (gāt′wā′) *n.* **1.** An entrance that is or may be closed with a gate. **2.** That which is regarded as a means of entry or exit: the *gateway* to the Orient.

gath·er (gath′ər) *v.t.* **1.** To bring together into one place or group. **2.** To bring together from various places, sources, etc. **3.** To harvest or pick, as crops, fruit, etc. **4.** To accumulate or gain more and more of: The storm *gathered* force. **5.** To clasp or enfold. **6.** To wrinkle (the brow). **7.** To draw into folds, as cloth on a thread. **8.** To become aware of; infer. **9.** To summon up or muster, as one's energies. — *v.i.* **10.** To come together or assemble. **11.**

To increase by accumulation. **12.** To become wrinkled or creased, as the brow. **13.** To come to a head, as a boil. **— n.** *Usu. pl.* A pleat or fold in cloth, held by a thread passing through the folds. [OE *gadrian*] **— gath'er·er** *n.*

gath·er·ing (gath'ər·ing) *n.* **1.** The action of one who or that which gathers. **2.** That which is gathered. **3.** An assemblage of people; group. **4.** A series of gathers in cloth, etc. **5.** An abscess or boil. **6.** In bookbinding, a collection of printed sheets in proper order.

gauche (gōsh) *adj.* Awkward; clumsy; boorish. [< F, left-handed]

gauche·rie (gōsh·rē') *n.* **1.** An awkward or tactless action, statement, etc. **2.** Clumsiness; tactlessness. [< F]

Gau·cho (gou'chō) *n.* *pl.* **·chos** A cowboy of the South American pampas. [< Sp.]

gaud·y (gô'dē) *adj.* **gaud·i·er, gaud·i·est** Tastelessly brilliant or showy; garish. **— gaud'i·ly** *adv.* **— gaud'i·ness** *n.*

gauge (gāj) *v.t.* **gauged, gaug·ing 1.** To determine the dimensions, amount, force, etc., of. **2.** To determine the contents or capacity of, as a cask. **3.** To estimate, appraise, or judge. **4.** To make conform to a standard measurement. **— n. 1.** A standard measurement, dimension, or quantity. **2.** A means or standard of comparing, estimating, or judging; criterion. **3.** Any of various instruments or devices for measuring something. **4.** The distance between rails in a railway. **5.** The distance between wheel treads. **6.** The diameter of the bore of a gun. Also spelled *gage*. [< OF *gauger* to measure]

gaug·er (gā'jər) *n.* **1.** One who or that which gauges: a wind *gauger*. **2.** An officer of the revenue service who measures the contents of casks, etc. **3.** A tax collector.

Gaul (gôl) An ancient name for the territory south and west of the Rhine, west of the Alps, and north of the Pyrenees; roughly the area of modern France.

Gaul (gôl) *n.* **1.** A native of ancient Gaul. **2.** A Frenchman.

Gaul·ish (gô'lish) *adj.* Of ancient Gaul, its people, or their Celtic language. **— n.** The extinct Celtic language of Gaul.

gaunt (gônt) *adj.* **1.** Emaciated and hollow-eyed, as from hunger, illness, or age; haggard. **2.** Desolate or gloomy in appearance: a *gaunt* region. [? < OF *gent* elegant] **— gaunt'ly** *adv.* **— gaunt'ness** *n.*

gaunt·let¹ (gônt'lit, gänt'-) *n.* **1.** In medieval armor, a glove covered with metal plates to protect the hand. **2.** Any glove with a long, often flaring extension over the wrist. Sometimes spelled *gantlet*. **— to take up the gauntlet** To accept a challenge. **— to throw (or fling) down the gauntlet** To challenge to combat. [< OF *gant* mitten]

gaunt·let² (gônt'lit, gänt'-) See GANTLET².

gaun·try (gôn'trē) See GANTRY.

gauss (gous) *n.* *Physics* The electromagnetic unit of magnetic induction, equal to 1 maxwell per square centimeter. [after K. F. *Gauss*]

gauze (gôz) *n.* **1.** A lightweight, transparent fabric with an open weave, made of silk, cotton, etc. **2.** Any thin, open-mesh material: wire *gauze*. **3.** A mist or light fog. **— adj.** Resembling or made of gauze. [< MF *gaze*, appar. after *Gaza*, where originally made] **— gauz'y** *adj.* **— gauz'i·ness** *n.*

gave (gāv) Past tense of GIVE.

gav·el (gav'əl) *n.* A mallet used by a presiding officer to call for order or attention. [< OF (Norman) *keville* pin]

ga·vi·al (gā'vē·əl) *n.* A large crocodile of India, having long, slender jaws. [< F < Hind. *ghariyal*]

ga·votte (gə·vot') *n.* **1.** A dance of French origin, popular in the 17th and 18th centuries and resembling a quick-moving minuet. **2.** Music for this dance, written in duple meter. Also **ga·vot'.** [< F < Provençal *gavoto* Alpine dance]

gawk (gôk) *Informal v.i.* **1.** To stare stupidly; gape. **2.** To move about or behave awkwardly. **— n.** An ungainly, stupid individual. [Cf. dial. E *gawk* lefthanded]

gawk·y (gô'kē) *adj.* **gawk·i·er, gawk·i·est** Awkward or clumsy; ungainly. **— n.** *pl.* **gawk·ies** An awkward or ungainly person. **— gawk'i·ly** *adv.* **— gawk'i·ness** *n.*

gay (gā) *adj.* **1.** Happy and carefree; merry. **2.** Brightly colorful or ornamental. **3.** Jaunty; sporty. **4.** Full of or given to lighthearted pleasure. **5.** Rakish; libertine. [< OF < Gmc.] **— gay'ness** *n.*

gay·e·ty (gā'ə·tē) See GAIETY.

gay·ly (gā'lē) See GAILY.

gaze (gāz) *v.i.* **gazed, gaz·ing** To look steadily or fixedly at something, as in wonder or admiration; stare. **— n.** A steady or fixed look. [ME *gasen* < Scand.] **— gaz'er** *n.*

ga·zelle (gə·zel') *n.* A small, delicately formed antelope of northern Africa and Arabia, with curved horns and large eyes. [< OF < Arabic *ghazāl*]

ga·zette (gə·zet') *n.* **1.** A newspaper or similar periodical. **2.** An official publication, as of a government or society; esp.,

one of several publications issued by the British government listing government appointments, public bankruptcies, etc. **— v.t. ·zet·ted, ·zet·ting** To publish or announce in a gazette. [< F < Ital. < dial. Ital. (Venetian) *gazeta* coin]

gaz·et·teer (gaz'ə·tir') *n.* **1.** A work or section of a work listing countries, cities, rivers, etc., together with their location, size, etc. **2.** A writer for or publisher of a gazette.

gear (gir) *n.* **1.** *Mech.* **a** A mechanical assembly of interacting parts that serves to transmit motion or to change the rate or direction of motion. **b** A related group of parts that work together for a special purpose: steering *gear*. **2.** *Naut.* **a** The ropes, blocks, etc., used in working a spar or sail. **b** A ship's rigging or equipment. **c** The personal baggage or effects of a sailor. **3.** Any equipment, as clothing, tools, etc., used for a special task: a plumber's *gear*. **— v.t. 1.** *Mech.* **a** To put into gear. **b** To equip with gears. **c** To connect by means of gears. **2.** To regulate so as to match or suit something else: to *gear* production to demand. **3.** To put gear on; dress. **— v.i. 4.** To come into or be in gear; to mesh. **— out of gear 1.** Not engaged or connected, as one gear with another or with a motor. **2.** Not in working order or not in good condition. [< ON *gervi* equipment]

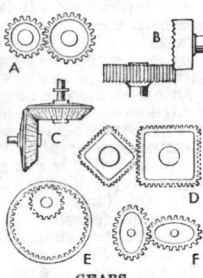

GEARS
A Spur. B Spur and crown. C Bevel. D Square. E Annular. F Elliptical.

gear·ing (gir'ing) *n.* **1.** *Mech.* Any system of gears or parts that transmit power or motion. **2.** *Naut.* Rope and tackle.

gear·shift (gir'shift') *n.* *Mech.* A device for engaging or disengaging the gears in a power-transmission system.

gear·wheel (gir'hwēl') *n.* *Mech.* A cogwheel. Also **gear wheel.**

geck·o (gek'ō) *n.* *pl.* **·os** or **·oes** Any of a family of small lizards having toes with adhesive disks. [< Malay *gēkoq*]

gee¹ (jē) *interj.* A cry used to guide horses, cattle, etc., to the right or (usu. with *up*) to urge them to move forward or faster. **— v.t. & v.i. geed, gee·ing 1.** To turn to the right. **2.** To move onward or faster: usu. with *up*. **3.** To evade. Opposed to *haw*: also spelled *jee*. [Origin uncertain]

gee² (jē) *interj.* An exclamation expressing mild surprise, sympathy, etc.: a euphemism for *Jesus*. Also **gee whiz.**

gee·zer (gē'zər) *n.* *Slang* A fellow, guy, esp., an old man. [Var. of *guiser* mummer < GUISE, v.]

Ge·hen·na (gi·hen'ə) *n.* **1.** A place of torment. **2.** In the New Testament, hell. [< LL < Gk. < Hebrew *ge hinnom* valley of Hinnom near Jerusalem where refuse was thrown]

Gei·ger counter (gī'gər) *Physics* An instrument for detecting ionizing radiation by means of a sealed tube containing a gas that when struck by ionizing particles conducts an electrical impulse between two electrodes connected to a suitable counting device. Also **Geiger-Müller counter** (mü'lər), **geiger counter.** [after Hans *Geiger* and W. *Müller*, 20th c. German physicists]

gei·sha (gā'shə) *n.* *pl.* **·sha** or **·shas** A Japanese girl furnishing entertainment by singing, dancing, etc. [< Japanese]

gel (jel) *n.* *Chem.* A colloidal dispersion of a solid in a liquid, typically having a jellylike consistency, as gelatin, mucilage, uncooked egg white, etc. **— v.t. & v.i. gelled, gel·ling** To change into a gel; jellify. [Short for GELATIN]

gel·a·tin (jel'ə·tin) *n.* **1.** An almost tasteless, odorless, dried protein soluble in water and extracted by boiling the bones, tendons, skins, etc., of animals, used in food and drug preparation and in the manufacture of photographic film, plastics, etc. **2.** A jelly made from gelatin. Also **gel'a·tine** (-tin, -tēn). [< F *gélatine*, orig. a soup made from fish]

ge·lat·i·nate (ji·lat'ə·nāt) *v.t. & v.i.* **·nat·ed, ·nat·ing** To change into gelatin or jelly. **— ge·lat'i·na'tion** *n.*

ge·lat·i·nize (ji·lat'ə·nīz) *v.* **·nized, ·niz·ing** *v.t.* **1.** To gelatinate. **2.** To treat or coat with gelatin. **— v.i. 3.** To be changed into gelatin or jelly. **— ge·lat'i·ni·za'tion** *n.*

ge·lat·i·nous (ji·lat'ə·nəs) *adj.* **1.** Having the nature of or resembling gelatin. **2.** Of or consisting of gelatin. **— ge·lat'i·nous·ly** *adv.* **— ge·lat'i·nous·ness** *n.*

geld (geld) *v.t.* **geld·ed** or **gelt, geld·ing 1.** To castrate or spay. **2.** To deprive of an essential part. [< ON *gelda*]

geld·ing (gel'ding) *n.* A castrated animal, esp. a horse.

gel·id (jel'id) *adj.* Very cold; icy; frozen. [< L *gelidus*] **— ge·lid·i·ty** (ji·lid'ə·tē) *n.* **— gel'id·ly** *adv.*

gem (jem) *n.* **1.** A cut and polished precious or semiprecious stone; jewel. **2.** One who or that which is treasured for having perfect or nearly perfect qualities. **3.** A kind of small, light cake. **— v.t. gemmed, gem·ming** To decorate or set with or as with gems. [OE < L *gemma* jewel]

gem·i·nate (jem′ə-nāt) *v.t.* & *v.i.* **·nat·ed, ·nat·ing** To double or become doubled; form into an identical pair. — *adj.* Formed into or appearing as a pair. [< L *geminus* twin]

Gem·i·ni (jem′ə-nī) *n.pl.* A constellation, the Twins; also, the third sign of the zodiac. See ZODIAC.

gem·ma (jem′ə) *n.* *pl.* **gem·mae** (jem′ē) *Biol.* **1.** A bud. **2.** A part of a plant or animal that grows outward, detaches, and forms a new individual. Also **gem′mule** (-yōōl). [< L]

gem·mate (jem′āt) *adj.* *Biol.* Bearing or reproducing by gemmae. — *v.i.* **·mat·ed, ·mat·ing** To form or reproduce by gemmae. — **gem·ma′tion** *n.*

gems·bok (gemz′bok) *n.* *pl.* **·bok** or **·boks** A South African antelope having long, sharp horns and a tufted tail. [< Afrikaans < G *gemse* chamois + *bock* a buck]

Gem State Nickname of Idaho.

gem·stone (jem′stōn′) *n.* A precious or semiprecious stone, esp. before it is cut and polished for use as a gem.

-gen *suffix of nouns* **1.** *Chem.* That which produces: *oxygen*. **2.** *Biol.* That which is produced: *antigen*. [< F < Gk. *gen-*, stem of *gignesthai* to be born, become]

gen·darme (zhän′därm, *Fr.* zhäṅ·därm′) *n.* *pl.* **·darmes** (-därmz, *Fr.* -därm′) **1.** One of a corps of armed police, esp. in France. **2.** Any policeman: a humorous use. [< F < *gens d'armes* men-at-arms]

gen·der (jen′dər) *n.* **1.** *Gram.* **a** One of two or more categories of words (esp. nouns and pronouns) or affixes based upon differences of sex or absence of sex or sometimes upon other distinctions (as of animateness or inanimateness), each category having distinctive forms for the words or affixes themselves or for the words modifying them. **b** Such categories collectively, or a system of such categories. **c** The distinctive form or forms used for such categories. **2.** *Informal* The quality of the male or female sex: a humorous use. [< OF < L *genus, -eris*]

gene (jēn) *n.* *Biol.* One of the complex protein molecules associated with the chromosomes of reproductive cells and acting, as a unit or in various biochemically determined combinations, in the transmission of specific hereditary characters from parents to offspring. [< Gk. *genea* breed, kind]

ge·ne·al·o·gist (jē′nē·al′ə·jist, jen′ē-, -nē·ol′-) *n.* One who traces genealogies or who is a student of genealogy.

ge·ne·al·o·gy (jē′nē·al′ə·jē, jen′ē-, -nē·ol′-) *n.* *pl.* **·gies** **1.** A record or table showing the descent of an individual or family from a certain ancestor. **2.** Descent in a direct line from a progenitor; pedigree. **3.** The study of pedigrees. [< Gk. *genea* race + -LOGY] — **ge·ne·a·log·i·cal** (jē′nē·ə·loj′i·kəl, jen′ē-) or **·log·ic** *adj.* — **ge·ne·a·log·i·cal·ly** *adv.*

gen·e·ra (jen′ər·ə) Plural of GENUS. [< L]

gen·er·al (jen′ər·əl) *adj.* **1.** Pertaining to, including, or affecting all or the whole; not particular. **2.** Common to or current among the majority: the *general* opinion. **3.** Not restricted in application: a *general* principle. **4.** Not limited to a special class; miscellaneous: a *general* cargo. **5.** Not detailed or precise: a *general* idea. **6.** Usual or customary. **7.** Dealing with all branches of a business or pursuit; not specialized: a *general* practitioner. **8.** Superior in rank: a second element in some titles: attorney *general*. **9.** *Med.* Relating to or affecting the entire body. — *n.* **1.** *Mil.* **a** In the U.S. Army, Air Force, or Marine Corps, a high-ranking officer. **b** In the Canadian Army, an officer ranking just below Field-Marshal. **c** An equivalent officer in other armies. *Abbr.* Gen. See tables at GRADE. **2.** A general officer: a shortened form. **3.** The head of a religious order. **4.** A general statement, fact, or principle. — **in general 1.** Without going into detail. **2.** All things considered. **3.** Usually; commonly. [< OF < L *generalis* of a race or king < *genus, generis* kind]

gen·er·al·cy (jen′ər·əl·sē) *n.* *pl.* **·cies 1.** The rank or office of a general. **2.** The time during which it is held.

general delivery *U.S.* **1.** A building or department of the post office in which an addressee's mail is kept until called for. **2.** Mail directed to this department.

general election 1. An election in which all the people vote. **2.** An election held to make a final choice for office among candidates selected in a preliminary election.

gen·er·al·is·si·mo (jen′ər·əl·is′i·mō) *n.* *pl.* **·mos 1.** In certain countries, one chosen as supreme commander of all the armed forces. **2.** The supreme commander of several armies in a particular campaign. [< Ital.]

gen·er·al·i·ty (jen′ə·ral′ə·tē) *n.* *pl.* **·ties 1.** The state or quality of being general. **2.** Something lacking detail or precision, as a statement or idea: a speech filled with *generalities*. **3.** The greater number of a group; mass.

gen·er·al·i·za·tion (jen′ər·əl·ə·zā′shən, -ī·zā′-) *n.* **1.** The act of generalizing. **2.** Something, as a broad, overall statement or conclusion, arrived at by generalizing.

gen·er·al·ize (jen′ər·əl·īz′) *v.* **·ized, ·iz·ing** *v.t.* **1.** To make general; as: **a** To make broad in application. **b** To avoid making detailed. **c** To cause to be widespread. **2.** To derive a broad conclusion, principle, etc., from (particular instances, facts, etc.). — *v.i.* **3.** To write or speak without going into details, etc. Also *Brit.* **gen′er·al·ise′**.

gen·er·al·ly (jen′ər·əl·ē) *adv.* **1.** For the most part; ordinarily. **2.** Without going into specific details or instances: *generally* speaking. **3.** Commonly: *generally* believed.

general officer *Mil.* Any officer ranking above a colonel, as a general, lieutenant general, major general, etc.

General of the Air Force The highest-ranking officer of the U.S. Air Force. See table at GRADE.

General of the Army The highest rank in the U.S. Army. See table at GRADE.

general paresis *Pathol.* Chronic paralysis of syphilitic origin, characterized by degeneration of body and brain tissue, and progressive dementia. Also **general paralysis**.

general practitioner A physician whose practice is not limited to a medical specialty.

gen·er·al·ship (jen′ər·əl·ship) *n.* **1.** A general's office or rank; generalcy. **2.** A general's military skill or management. **3.** Management or leadership of any sort.

general staff 1. A body of officers who direct the military policy and strategy of a national state. **2.** *Mil.* A group of officers who assist the commander in planning, coordination, and supervision of operations.

gen·er·ate (jen′ə·rāt) *v.t.* **·at·ed, ·at·ing 1.** To produce or cause to be; bring into being. **2.** To beget; procreate. **3.** *Geom.* To trace out by motion: A moving point *generates* a line. [< L *generatus*, pp. of *generare* to generate]

gen·er·a·tion (jen′ə·rā′shən) *n.* **1.** The process of begetting offspring. **2.** A successive step or degree in natural descent. **3.** The average period between any two such successive steps, about 30 years among human beings. **4.** Any group of individuals born at about the same time. **5.** The act or process of generating or being generated.

gen·er·a·tive (jen′ə·rā′tiv) *adj.* **1.** Of or pertaining to generation. **2.** Having the power to produce or originate.

gen·er·a·tor (jen′ə·rā′tər) *n.* **1.** One who or that which generates. **2.** *Chem.* An apparatus designed to generate a gas. **3.** Any of a class of machines for the conversion of mechanical energy into electrical energy.

gen·er·a·trix (jen′ə·rā′triks) *n.* *pl.* **gen·er·a·tri·ces** (jen′ər·ə·trī′sēz) **1.** *Geom.* A line, point, or figure that generates another figure by its motion. **2.** A female that generates.

ge·ner·ic (ji·ner′ik) *adj.* **1.** Pertaining to a genus or class of related things. **2.** Applicable to every member of a class or genus. **3.** Having a wide, general application. Also **ge·ner′i·cal.** [< L *genus, -eris* race, kind + -IC]

gen·er·os·i·ty (jen′ə·ros′ə·tē) *n.* *pl.* **·ties 1.** The quality of being generous. **2.** The quality of being free of pettiness; magnanimity. **3.** A generous act.

gen·er·ous (jen′ər·əs) *adj.* **1.** Marked by or showing great liberality; munificent. **2.** Having gracious or noble qualities: a *generous* nature. **3.** Abundant and overflowing: a *generous* serving. **4.** Stimulating or strong, as wine. **5.** Fertile: *generous* soil. [< F < L *generosus* of noble birth < *genus* race] — **gen′er·ous·ly** *adv.* — **gen′er·ous·ness** *n.*

gen·e·sis (jen′ə·sis) *n.* *pl.* **·ses** (-sēz) **1.** The act or mode of originating. **2.** Origin. [< L < Gk. *genesis* origin]

Gen·e·sis (jen′ə·sis) The first book of the Old Testament.

-genesis *combining form* Genesis; evolution: *biogenesis*.

gen·et[1] (jen′it, jə·net′) *n.* A small carnivore related to the civet. Also **ge·nette′.** [< F < Sp. < Arabic *jarnait* genet]

gen·et[2] (jen′it) *n.* A jennet.

ge·net·ic (jə·net′ik) *adj.* **1.** Of, pertaining to, or based on genetics. **2.** Of, or pertaining to the origin or development of something. Also **ge·net′i·cal.** [< GENESIS; formed on analogy with *synthetic*, etc.] — **ge·net′i·cal·ly** *adv.*

GENET[1]
(About 22 inches long; tail about 18 inches)

ge·net·ics (jə·net′iks) *n.pl.* **1.** (*construed as sing.*) The science dealing with the interaction of the genes in producing similarities and differences between individuals related by descent. **2.** The inherited characteristics of an organism. — **ge·net′i·cist** (-ə·sist) *n.*

Geneva Convention An international agreement signed at Geneva in 1864 governing the war-time treatment of prisoners of war and of the sick and the wounded.

gen·ial (jēn′yəl, jē′nē·əl) *adj.* **1.** Kindly, pleasant, or cordial in disposition or manner. **2.** Imparting warmth, comfort, or life. [< L *genius* tutelary spirit] — **ge·ni·al·i·ty** (jē′nē·al′ə·tē) *n.* — **gen′ial·ly** *adv.*

-genic *combining form* Related to generation or production: *biogenic*. [< -GEN + -IC]

ge·nie (jē′nē) See JINNI.

ge·ni·i (jē′nē·ī) Plural of GENIUS (def. 4).

gen·i·tal (jen′ə·təl) *adj.* Of or pertaining to the reproductive organs or the process of reproduction. [< L *genitus*, pp. of *gignere* to beget]

gen·i·tals (jen′ə·təlz) *n.pl.* The external sexual organs. Also **gen·i·ta·li·a** (jen′ə·tā′lē·ə, -tāl′yə).

gen·i·tive (jen′ə·tiv) *adj.* **1.** Indicating source, origin, possession, or the like. **2.** *Gram.* Pertaining to a case in Latin,

Greek, etc., corresponding in part to the English possessive. — *n. Gram.* **1.** The genitive case. **2.** A word in this case. [< L *gignere* to beget] — **gen′i·ti′val** (-tī′vəl) *adj.* — **gen′i·ti′val·ly** *adv.*

genito- *combining form* Genital. [< L *genitus*, pp. of *gignere* to beget]

gen·i·to·u·ri·nar·y (jen′ə·tō·yŏŏr′ə·ner′ē) *adj. Anat.* Of or pertaining to the genital and the urinary organs.

gen·ius (jēn′yəs) *n. pl.* **gen·ius·es** for *defs* 1, 2, 3, & 5; **ge·ni·i** (jē′nē·ī) *for def.* 4 **1.** Extraordinary intelligence surpassing that of most intellectually superior individuals; also, one who possesses such intelligence. **2.** An outstanding gift for some specialized activity; also, one who possesses such a gift. **3.** The essential spirit or distinguishing characteristics of a particular individual, people, era, etc. **4.** In ancient mythology, a supernatural being appointed to guide a person throughout life. **5.** A person who exerts a strong influence over another. [< L *gen-*, stem of *gignere* to beget]

gen·o·cide (jen′ə·sīd) *n.* The systematic extermination or destruction of an entire people or national group. [< Gk. *genos* race, tribe + -CIDE] — **gen′o·ci′dal** *adj.*

Gen·o·ese (jen′ō·ēz′, -ēs′) *adj.* Of or pertaining to Genoa. — *n. pl.* **·ese** A native or citizen of Genoa.

gen·o·type (jen′ə·tīp) *n. Biol.* **1.** The genetic constitution of an organism. **2.** A group of organisms with the same genetic constitution. **3.** A type species. — **gen·o·typ·ic** (jen′ə·tip′ik) or **·i·cal** *adj.* — **gen′o·typ′i·cal·ly** *adv.*

-genous *suffix of adjectives* **1.** Generating; yielding. **2.** Produced or generated by.

gen·re (zhän′rə, Fr. zhän′r′) *n.* **1.** A particular sort, kind, or category; esp., a category of art or literature characterized by a certain form, style, or subject matter. **2.** A class of painting or other art depicting everyday life. — *adj.* Of or pertaining to genre. [< F < L *genus*, *-eris* race, kind]

gens (jenz) *n. pl.* **gen·tes** (jen′tēz) **1.** *Anthropol.* In primitive society, a body of blood kindred having a common descent traced through the male line. **2.** In ancient Rome, a clan descended through the male line. [< L, race, kind]

gent (jent) *n. Slang* A gentleman. [Short for GENTLEMAN]

gen·teel (jen·tēl′) *adj.* **1.** Well-bred or refined; elegant; polite. **2.** Pertaining or appropriate to well-bred persons. **3.** Stylish or fashionable. ◆ This word is now used chiefly in a derogatory or humorous sense. [< MF *gentil*] — **gen·teel′ly** *adv.* — **gen·teel′ness** *n.*

gen·tian (jen′shən) *n.* An annual or perennial herb with showy blue, red, yellow, or white flowers. [< L *gentiana*, appar. after *Gentius*, an Illyrian king]

gen·tian·el·la (jen′shən·el′ə) *n.* **1.** A European alpine gentian having blue flowers. **2.** A bright blue color. [< NL, dim. of L *gentiana*. See GENTIAN.]

gentian violet *Chem.* A purple dye used as an antiseptic.

gen·tile (jen′tīl, -tĭl; *for adj. def.* 2 -tĭl) *adj.* **1.** Of or pertaining to a gens, tribe, or people. **2.** Of or pertaining to Gentiles. [< F < LL *gentilis* foreign]

Gen·tile (jen′tīl) *n.* **1.** Among Jews, one not a Jew. **2.** Among Christians, a heathen or pagan. **3.** Among Mormons, one not a Mormon. — *adj.* Of, pertaining to, or being a Gentile.

gen·til·i·ty (jen·til′ə·tē) *n. pl.* **·ties** **1.** The quality of being genteel; refinement: now often used ironically. **2.** Gentle birth; good extraction. **3.** Well-born or well-bred persons collectively. [< OF < L *gentilis* of good birth]

gen·tle (jen′təl) *adj.* **·tler** (-tlər), **·tlest** (-tlist) **1.** Mild and amiable in nature or disposition. **2.** Not harsh, rough, or loud; mild. **3.** Not steep or abrupt; gradual: a *gentle* ascent. **4.** Easily managed; docile. **5.** Of good family and breeding. **6.** Like or befitting one of good family; polite. **7.** *Meteorol.* Designating a moderate breeze. — *v.t.* **·tled, ·tling** To make easy to control; tame. — *n.* A bluebottle larva used as fish bait. [< OF < L *gentilis* of good birth < *gens, gentis* race, clan] — **gen′tly** (-tlē) *adv.* — **gen′tle·ness** *n.*

gen·tle·folk (jen′təl·fōk′) *n.pl.* Persons of good family and good breeding. Also **gen′tle·folks′.**

gen·tle·man (jen′təl·mən) *n. pl.* **·men** (-mən) **1.** A man of good birth and social position. **2.** A courteous, considerate man. **3.** Any man: in the plural, used as a form of address.

gen·tle·man-at-arms (jen′təl·mən-ət-ärmz′) *n. pl.* **·men** (-mən) *n. Brit.* One of forty gentlemen who attend the sovereign on various state and solemn occasions.

gen·tle·man-com·mon·er (jen′təl·mən·kom′ən·ər) *n. pl.* **gen·tle·men-com·mon·ers** (jen′təl·mən·kom′ən·ərz) *Brit.* Formerly, a commoner at Oxford and Cambridge Universities, enjoying special privileges.

gen·tle·man-farm·er (jen′təl·mən·fär′mər) *n.* One who owns a farm but hires others to work it.

gentleman in waiting A gentleman of a royal household staff, appointed to attend the sovereign or his son.

gen·tle·man·ly (jen′təl·mən·lē) *adj.* Pertaining to or be-

fitting a gentleman; courteous. Also **gen′tle·man·like′** (-līk′).

gentleman of fortune **1.** An adventurer or gambler. **2.** Formerly, a pirate.

gentleman of the road **1.** A highwayman. **2.** *U.S.* A hobo.

gen·tle·man's agreement (jen′təl·mənz) An understanding about something to be done, arrived at by informal mutual agreement and guaranteed solely by the pledged word of the parties involved. Also **gentlemen's agreement.**

gen·tle·man's gentleman (jen′təl·mənz) A valet.

gentle sex Women collectively. Also **gentler sex.**

gen·tle·wom·an (jen′təl·wŏŏm′ən) *n. pl.* **·wom·en** (-wim′in) **1.** A woman of good family or superior social position; lady. **2.** A gracious, well-mannered woman.

gen·try (jen′trē) *n.* **1.** People of good family or superior social background; in England, the upper ranks of the middle class. **2.** Individuals of a particular area, profession, etc.: the local *gentry*: now chiefly a patronizing or humorous term. [< OF *genterise* < *gentil* gentle]

ge·nu (jē′nōō, -nyōō) *n. pl.* **gen·u·a** (jen′yōō·ə) *Anat.* **1.** The knee. **2.** A kneelike structure or part. [< L].

gen·u·flect (jen′yə·flekt) *v.i.* To bend the knee, as in worship. [< Med.L < L *genu* knee + *flectere* to bend] — **gen′u·flec′tion** or **gen′u·flex′ion** *n.*

gen·u·ine (jen′yōō·in) *adj.* **1.** Being actually of the origin, authorship, or character claimed. **2.** Not spurious or counterfeit. **3.** Not affected or hypocritical; sincere. **4.** Being of the original or true stock: a *genuine* Indian. [< L *genuinus* innate] — **gen′u·ine·ly** *adv.* — **gen′u·ine·ness** *n.*

ge·nus (jē′nəs) *n. pl.* **gen·er·a** (jen′ər·ə) or, less commonly, **ge·nus·es** **1.** *Biol.* A grouping or category of plants and animals ranking next above the species and next below the family or subfamily. **2.** *Logic* A class of things divisible into two or more subordinate classes or species. **3.** A particular sort, kind, or class. [< L, race, kind]

-geny *combining form* Mode of production of; generation or development of: *anthropogeny*. [< F < L < Gk. *gen-*, stem of *gignesthai* to become]

geo- *combining form* Earth; ground; soil.

ge·o·cen·tric (jē′ō·sen′trik) *adj.* **1.** Calculated or viewed with relation to the earth's center. **2.** Formulated on the assumption that the earth is the center of the universe. Also **ge′o·cen′tri·cal** *adj.* — **ge′o·cen′tri·cal·ly** *adv.*

ge·o·chem·is·try (jē′ō·kem′is·trē) *n.* A specialized branch of chemistry dealing with the chemical composition of the earth's crust. — **ge′o·chem′i·cal** *adj.* — **ge′o·chem′ist** *n.*

ge·ode (jē′ōd) *n. Geol.* **1.** A rock, usually globular, having a cavity lined with crystals. **2.** The cavity in such a rock. [< F *géode* < L *geodes*, a precious stone < Gk. *geōdēs* earthy] — **ge·od·ic** (jē·od′ik) *adj.*

ge·o·des·ic (jē′ə·des′ik) *adj.* **1.** Of or pertaining to the geometry of geodesic lines or curved surfaces. **2.** Geodetic. Also **ge′o·des′i·cal.** — *n.* A geodesic line.

geodesic dome *Archit.* A light and strong hemispherical dome made of prefabricated polyhedral or triangular lattice nodules and covered with a thin, strong material.

geodesic line *Math.* The shortest line connecting two points on a given, esp. a curved, surface.

ge·od·e·sist (jē·od′ə·sist) *n.* One who specializes in geodesy.

ge·od·e·sy (jē·od′ə·sē) *n.* The science dealing with the determination of the shape, area, and curvature of the earth, with the precise mapping of continents or other large tracts, or location of specific points. Also **ge·o·det·ics** (jē′ə·det′iks). [< F < NL < Gk. < *gē* earth + *daiein* to divide]

ge·o·det·ic (jē′ə·det′ik) *adj.* **1.** Of or pertaining to geodesy. **2.** Geodesic. Also **ge′o·det′i·cal.** — **ge′o·det′i·cal·ly** *adv.*

ge·o·dy·nam·ics (jē′ō·dī·nam′iks, -di-) *n.pl.* (*construed as sing.*) The branch of geology concerned with the forces affecting the structure of the earth.

ge·o·graph·i·cal (jē′ə·graf′i·kəl) *adj.* **1.** Of or pertaining to geography. **2.** Relating to topographical facts and influences. Also **ge′o·graph′ic.** — **ge′o·graph′i·cal·ly** *adv.*

geographic determinism *Sociol.* The theory that attributes the forms and characteristics of a given society to geographic factors.

ge·og·ra·phy (jē·og′rə·fē) *n. pl.* **·phies** **1.** The science that describes the surface of the earth and its associated physical, biological, economic, political, and demographic characteristics. **2.** The natural aspect, features, etc., of a place or area: the *geography* of the Arctic. **3.** A particular work on or system of geography. [< L < Gk. < *gē* earth + *graphein* to write, describe] — **ge·og′ra·pher** *n.*

ge·oid (jē′oid) *n.* The earth considered hypothetically as an ellipsoidal solid whose surface coincides with the mean level of the ocean. [< Gk. *geoidēs* earthlike < *gē* earth + *eidos* form]

ge·o·log·ic (jē′ə·loj′ik) *adj.* Of or pertaining to geology. Also **ge′o·log′i·cal.** — **ge′o·log′i·cal·ly** *adv.*

ge·ol·o·gy (jē·ol′ə·jē) *n. pl.* **·gies 1.** The science that treats of the origin and structure of the earth, including the physical forces which have shaped it and its physical and organic history, esp. as shown by rocks and rock formations. **2.** The structure of the earth in a given region. — **ge·ol′o·gist** *n.*

ge·o·met·ric (jē′ə·met′rik) *adj.* **1.** Pertaining to or according to the rules and principles of geometry. **2.** Forming, consisting of, or characterized by straight lines, bars, crosses, zigzags, etc., as in painting or sculpture. Also **ge′o·met′ri·cal.** — **ge′o·met′ri·cal·ly** *adv.*

ge·o·pol·i·tics (jē′ō·pol′ə·tiks) *n.pl.* (*construed as sing.*) **1.** The study of political and economic geography. **2.** A doctrine, of Nazi Germany, advocating aggressive expansion: also German **Ge·o·pol·i·tik** (gā′ō·pōl·ē·tēk′). — **ge′o·po·lit′i·cal** (-pə·lit′i·kəl), **ge′o·po·lit′ic** *adj.* — **ge′o·po·lit′i·cal·ly** *adv.* — **ge′o·pol′i·ti′cian** (-pol′ə·tish′ən) *n.*

Geor·gian (jôr′jən) *adj.* **1.** Of or pertaining to the reigns or period of the first four Georges in England, 1714–1830, or of George V, 1910–36. **2.** Of or pertaining to Georgia or Georgians. **3.** Of or pertaining to the language of Georgia (def.

GEOLOGICAL TIME SCALE

Read from bottom to top.

ERAS	TIME PERIODS ROCK SYSTEMS	TIME EPOCHS ROCK SERIES	APPROX. DURATION MILLION YEARS	APPROX. PERCENT TOTAL AGE	LIFE FORMS
CENOZOIC	QUATERNARY	RECENT PLEISTOCENE	1		Rise and dominance of Man.
CENOZOIC	UPPER TERTIARY	PLIOCENE MIOCENE	65	2	Modern animals and plants.
CENOZOIC	LOWER TERTIARY	OLIGOCENE EOCENE PALEOCENE	65		Rapid development of modern mammals, insects, and plants.
MESOZOIC	UPPER CRETACEOUS		75	5	Primitive mammals; last dinosaurs; last ammonites.
MESOZOIC	LOWER CRETACEOUS		75	5	Rise of flowering plants.
MESOZOIC	JURASSIC		45	5	First birds, first mammals. Diversification of reptiles; climax of ammonites; coniferous trees.
MESOZOIC	TRIASSIC		45	5	Rise of dinosaurs; cycadlike plants; bony fishes.
PALEOZOIC	PERMIAN		45	9	Rise of reptiles. Modern insects. Last of many plant and animal groups.
PALEOZOIC	PENNSYLVANIAN (CARBONIFEROUS)		75	9	First reptiles. Amphibians; primitive insects; seed ferns; primitive conifers.
PALEOZOIC	MISSISSIPPIAN (CARBONIFEROUS)		75	9	Climax of shell-crushing sharks. Primitive ammonites.
PALEOZOIC	DEVONIAN		50	9	First amphibians, first land snails. Primitive land plants. Climax of brachiopods.
PALEOZOIC	SILURIAN		20	9	First traces of land life. Scorpions. First lungfishes. Widespread coral reefs.
PALEOZOIC	ORDOVICIAN		70	9	First fish. Climax of trilobites. First appearance of many marine invertebrates.
PALEOZOIC	CAMBRIAN		50	9	First marine invertebrates, including trilobites.
PROTEROZOIC (PRECAMBRIAN)			About 3000	84	First signs of life. Algae.
ARCHEOZOIC (PRECAMBRIAN)			About 3000	84	

Age of oldest dated rocks: about 3,500,000,000 years.

ge·om·e·tri·cian (jē·om′ə·trish′ən, jē′ə·mə-) *n.* A specialist in geometry. Also **ge·om′e·ter** (-ə·tər).

geometric progression *Math.* A sequence of terms of which each member is greater than its predecessor by a constant ratio, as 2, 4, 8, 16, 32, 64.

ge·om·e·try (jē·om′ə·trē) *n. pl.* **·tries** The branch of mathematics that treats of space and its relations, esp. as shown in the properties and measurement of points, lines, angles, surfaces, and solids. [< OF < L < Gk. < *gē* earth + *metreein* to measure]

ge·o·phys·ics (jē′ō·fiz′iks) *n.pl.* (*construed as sing.*) The study of the earth as the product of complex physico-chemical forces acting upon it internally and from outer space, esp. with reference to exploration of its less accessible regions. — **ge′o·phys′i·cal** *adj.* — **ge′o·phys′i·cist** *n.*

2.). — *n.* **1.** A native or inhabitant of Georgia. **2.** One of an ancient mountain people native to the Caucasus. **3.** The Caucasian language of the Georgians of the Soviet Union.

ge·o·stat·ics (jē′ə·stat′iks) *n.pl.* (*construed as sing.*) The statics of rigid bodies in relation to balanced forces on or beneath the earth's surface. — **ge′o·stat′ic** *adj.*

ge·ra·ni·um (ji·rā′nē·əm) *n.* **1.** A plant with showy pink or purple flowers: also called *cranebill.* **2.** A closely related plant, originally from South Africa. **3.** A very deep pink, almost red, color. [< L < Gk. *geranos* crane]

ger·fal·con (jûr′fal′kən, -fôl′-, -fô′-) *n.* A large falcon of the arctic regions, with feathered shanks: also spelled *gyrfalcon.* [< OF < OHG *gīr* vulture + OF *faucon* falcon]

ger·i·at·rics (jer′ē·at′riks) *n.pl.* (*construed as sing.*) **1.** The branch of medicine that deals with the structural changes, physiology, diseases, and hygiene of old age. **2.** Gerontology. [< Gk. *gēras* old age + -IATRICS] — **ger'i·at'ric** *adj.* — **ger'i·a·tri'cian** (-ə·trish'ən), **ger'i·at'rist** *n.*

germ (jûrm) *n.* **1.** A microorganism that causes disease; a microbe. **2.** Something in its essential though rudimentary form: the *germ* of an idea. **3.** That which gives rise to the production or development of something: to sow the *germs* of war. **4.** *Biol.* **a** A reproductive cell. **b** An organism in its embryonic form. [< F < L *germen* sprig]

ger·man¹ (jûr'mən) *n.* A cotillion (def. 1). [Short for *German cotillion*]

ger·man² (jûr'mən) *adj.* **1.** Having the same father and mother as oneself: *sister-german*. **2.** Related to oneself through being the child of one's uncle or aunt: *cousin-german*. **3.** Germane. [< OF < L *germanus* closely related]

Ger·man (jûr'mən) *adj.* Of, pertaining to, or characteristic of Germany, its people, or their language. — *n.* **1.** A native or inhabitant of Germany. **2.** The language of the Germans, belonging to the West Germanic branch. — **High German** The standard literary and spoken language used throughout Germany and Austria and in parts of Switzerland and Alsace: also called *New High German*. — **Low German** Collectively, the languages of the Low Countries, including Dutch, Flemish, and Frisian, and of the northern lowlands of Germany (*Plattdeutsch*). — **Old High German** The language of southern Germany from about 800 to 1100. — **Middle High German** The High German language from 1100 to 1450. — **Middle Low German** The Low German language from 1100 to 1450. [< L *Germanus*, prob. < Celtic]

ger·man·der (jər·man'dər) *n.* An herb of the mint family, with pale purple flowers. [< OF < Med.L < LGk. < Gk. < *chamai* on the ground + *drys* an oak]

ger·mane (jər·mān') *adj.* Related to what is being discussed or considered; pertinent; relevant. [See GERMAN²]

Ger·man·ic (jər·man'ik) *adj.* **1.** Of or pertaining to a group of early Indo-European tribes living in the region between the Rhine, Danube, and Vistula rivers: later including the Germans, English, Dutch, Flemings, Danes, Scandinavians, and German-Swiss. **2.** Relating to the language or customs of any of these people. — *n.* A sub-family of the Indo-European family of languages, divided into **East Germanic**, including Gothic (extinct); **North Germanic** or Scandinavian, including Norwegian, Swedish, Danish, Icelandic, and Faroese; and **West Germanic**, including all the High and Low German languages and dialects.

ger·ma·ni·um (jər·mā'nē·əm) *n.* A grayish white, metallic element (symbol Ge) of the silicon group, used in electronics and optics. See ELEMENT. [< NL < L *Germania* Germany]

German measles *Pathol.* A contagious virus disease accompanied by fever, sore throat, and a skin rash: also called *rubella, rubeola*.

Germano- *combining form* German.

German shepherd A breed of dog with a large, strong body and thick, smooth coat: also called *police dog*.

German silver A white alloy of copper, nickel, and zinc, used in the manufacture of cutlery and as a base for plated ware: also called *nickel silver*.

germ cell *Biol.* A cell specialized for reproduction.

ger·mi·cide (jûr'mə·sīd) *n.* An agent used to destroy disease germs or other microorganisms. — **ger·mi·ci·dal** (jûr'-mə·sī'dəl) *adj.*

ger·mi·nal (jûr'mə·nəl) *adj.* **1.** Of, relating to, or constituting a germ or germ cell. **2.** Pertaining to the earliest stage of development. [< NL < L *germen, -inis* sprig]

ger·mi·nate (jûr'mə·nāt) *v.* ·nat·ed, ·nat·ing *v.i.* **1.** To begin to grow or develop; sprout. — *v.t.* **2.** To cause to sprout. [< L *germinatus*, pp. of *germinare* to sprout] — **ger'mi·na·ble** (-nə·bəl) *adj.* — **ger'mi·na'tion** *n.* — **ger'mi·na'tive** *adj.* — **ger'mi·na'tor** *n.*

germ plasm *Biol.* The part of the protoplasm of a germ cell that contains the chromosomes and genes.

geronto- *combining form* Old age; pertaining to old people: *gerontology*. Also, before vowels, **geront-**. [< Gk. *gerōn, gerontos* old man]

ger·on·tol·o·gy (jer'on·tol'ə·jē) *n.* **1.** The scientific study of the processes and phenomena of aging. **2.** Geriatrics. — **ger'on·tol'o·gist** *n.*

-gerous *suffix* Bearing or producing. [< L *gerere* to bear + -OUS]

ger·ry·man·der (jer'i·man'dər, ger'-) *v.t.* **1.** To alter (a voting area) so as to advance unfairly the interests of a political party. **2.** To adapt to one's advantage; manipulate. — *n.* The act or result of gerrymandering. [after Elbridge *Gerry*, 1744–1814, + (SALA)MANDER; from the shape of a district formed in Massachusetts while he was governor]

ger·und (jer'ənd) *Gram. n.* **1.** A form of a verb used like a noun. **2.** In English, the *-ing* form of a verb, as *doing*, or a compound tense of a verb made with the *-ing* form of an

auxiliary, as *having done*, when used as the subject or object of a verb or as the object of a preposition. [< LL < L *gerere* to do] — **ge·run·di·al** (jə·run'dē·əl) *adj.*

ge·run·dive (jə·run'div) *Gram. n.* **1.** In Latin, a form of the verb constituting the future passive participle, having the stem of the gerund and expressing obligation, propriety, etc. **2.** In some other languages, a form similar to a gerundive in form or function. — *adj.* Of, pertaining to, or resembling a gerundive, or, sometimes, a gerund.

gest (jest) *n. Archaic* **1.** A noteworthy deed; exploit. **2.** A tale of adventure or romance; esp., a metrical romance. Also **geste.** [< OF < L *gesta* deeds < *gerere* to do]

ge·stalt (gə·shtält', -shtôlt') *n. pl.* ·**stalts** or ·**stalt·en** (-shtält'ən, -shtôlt'-) A synthesis of separate elements of emotion, experience, etc., that constitutes more than the mechanical sum of the parts. Also **Ge·stalt'.** [< G, form]

gestalt psychology Psychology based on the theory of the gestalt.

Ge·sta·po (gə·stä'pō, *Ger.* gə·shtä'pō) *n.* The German state secret police under the Nazi regime, noted for their brutality. [< G *Ge(heime) Sta(ats) Po(lizei)* Secret State Police]

ges·tate (jes'tāt) *v.t.* ·tat·ed, ·tat·ing To carry in the uterus during pregnancy. [< L *gestare* to carry] — **ges·ta'tion** *n.*

ges·tic·u·late (jes·tik'yə·lāt) *v.* ·lat·ed, ·lat·ing *v.i.* **1.** To make emphatic or expressive gestures, as in speaking. — *v.t.* **2.** To express by gestures. [< L *gesticulus*, dim. of *gestus* gesture] — **ges·tic'u·la'tive** *adj.* — **ges·tic'u·la'tor** *n.*

ges·tic·u·la·tion (jes·tik'yə·lā'shən) *n.* **1.** The act of gesticulating. **2.** An energetic or expressive gesture.

ges·ture (jes'chər) *n.* **1.** A bodily motion, as of the hands in speaking, used to emphasize or express some idea or emotion. **2.** Such motions collectively. **3.** Something said or done as a mere formality, or for effect. — *v.* ·tured, ·tur·ing *v.i.* **1.** To make gestures. — *v.t.* **2.** To express by gestures. [< Med.L < L *gerere* to carry on, do] — **ges'tur·er** *n.*

Ge·sund·heit (gə·zōont'hīt) *interj. German* (Your) health: said to someone who has just sneezed.

get (get) *v.* **got, got** or *U.S.* **got·ten, get·ting** *v.t.* **1.** To come into possession of; obtain. **2.** To go for and bring back. **3.** To capture; seize. **4.** To cause to come, go, etc.: to *get* baggage through customs. **5.** To carry away; take: *Get* this out of the house. **6.** To prepare: to *get* lunch. **7.** To bring to a state or condition: to *get* the work done. **8.** To persuade: *Get* her to sign the paper. **9.** To find out or obtain by calculation, experiment, etc.: to add the totals and *get* 100. **10.** To receive (reward or punishment). **11.** To learn or master, as by study or practice: Have you *got* your history lesson? **12.** To become sick with. **13.** To establish contact with: I'll *get* him on the phone. **14.** To catch, as a train; board. **15.** To beget: now said chiefly of animals. **16.** *Informal* To come to an understanding of. **17.** *Informal* To possess: with *have* or *has*: He has *got* quite a temper. **18.** *Informal* To obtain the advantage over: Drink will *get* him. **19.** *Informal* To square accounts with: I'll *get* you yet. **20.** *Informal* To be obliged or forced (to do something specified): with *have* or *has*. **21.** *Informal* To hit: The shrapnel *got* him in the arm. **22.** *Slang* To puzzle or baffle. **23.** *Slang* To please, irritate, etc.: That music *gets* me. **24.** *Slang* To take note of. **25.** To bring to or place in some specified location. — *v.i.* **26.** To arrive: When does the train *get* there? **27.** To come, go, or move: *Get* in here. **28.** To board; enter: with *on, in,* etc. **29.** To become. — **to get about 1.** To become known, as gossip. **2.** To move about. **3.** To be active socially. — **to get across 1.** To make or be convincing or clear, as to an audience. **2.** To be successful, as in projecting one's personality. — **to get ahead** To attain success. — **to get along 1.** To leave; go: *Get along* with you! **2.** To be successful, as in business. **3.** To be friendly or compatible. **4.** To proceed. **5.** To grow old or older. — **to get around 1.** To become known, as gossip. **2.** To move about. **3.** To attend social or public functions, etc. **4.** To flatter, cajole, etc., so as to obtain the favor of. **5.** To dodge; circumvent. — **to get around to** To give attention to after some delay. — **to get at 1.** To arrive at; reach. **2.** To intend; mean: I don't see what you're *getting at*. **3.** To apply oneself to: to *get at* a problem. **4.** *Informal* To prevail upon; influence. — **to get away 1.** To escape. **2.** To leave; go. **3.** To start, as a race horse. — **to get away with** *Slang* To do (something) without discovery, criticism, or punishment. — **to get back** To return to a previous position or state. — **to get back at** *Slang* To revenge oneself on. — **to get by 1.** To pass: This *got* by the censor. **2.** *Informal* To manage to survive. **3.** *Informal* To get away with. — **to get down** To descend, as from a horse or ladder. — **to get down to (business, facts,** etc.**)** To begin to act on, investigate, or consider. — **to get in 1.** To arrive or enter. **2.** To slip in (a remark, etc.). **3.** To become involved or familiar with. — **to get it** *Informal* **1.** To understand. **2.** To be

punished in some way. **— to get off** 1. To descend from; dismount. 2. To depart. 3. To be relieved or freed, as of a duty. 4. To be released with a lesser penalty, etc., or none at all. 5. To utter: to *get off* a joke. **— to get on** 1. To mount (a horse, vehicle, etc.). 2. To get along. **— to get out** 1. To depart or leave. 2. To escape. 3. To become known, as a secret. 4. To publish. 5. To express or utter with difficulty. 6. To take out. **— to get out of** 1. To obtain from. 2. To escape or evade. 3. To depart from. **— to get over** 1. To recover from (illness, surprise, anger, etc.). 2. To get across. **— to get there** *Informal* To succeed. **— to get through** 1. To complete. 2. To survive. **— to get through (to)** 1. To establish communication (with). 2. To make clear (to). **— to get to** 1. To begin. 2. To be able to (do something). 3. To get through to. **— to get together** 1. To assemble. 2. To come to an agreement. **— to get up** 1. To rise, as from sleep. 2. To climb. 3. To devise. 4. To acquire, develop, or work up. 5. *Informal* To dress up. [< ON *geta*] **— get′ta·ble** *adj.* **— get′ter** *n.*
— Syn. (verb) 1. obtain, procure, gain, acquire.
get·a·way (get′ə-wā′) *n.* 1. An escape, as of a criminal. 2. The start, as of an automobile, race horse, etc.
get-to·geth·er (get′tə-geth′ər) *n. Informal* A gathering.
get-up (get′up′) *n. Informal* 1. Overall arrangement and appearance, esp. of a book or magazine. 2. The combination of articles of dress worn on a particular occasion. 3. Vigorous initiative: also **get′-up′-and-go′** (-ən-gō′).
gew·gaw (gyōō′gô) *n.* Some little ornamental article of small value. *— adj.* Showy; gaudy. [ME *giue-goue*]
gey·ser (gī′zər, -sər) *n.* A natural hot spring from which intermittent jets of steam, hot water, or mud are ejected in a fountainlike column. [< Icel. *geysan* to gush]
ghast·ly (gast′lē, gäst′-) *adj.* **·li·er, ·li·est** 1. Horrible; terrifying. 2. Deathlike in appearance; pale; wan. 3. *Informal* Very bad or unpleasant. *— adv.* 1. Spectral in manner or appearance. 2. Fearfully; horribly. [ME < OE *gæstan* to terrify + *-lich* -ly¹] **— ghast′li·ness** *n.*
ghat (gôt) *n. Anglo-Indian* 1. A stairway leading down to the edge of a river. 2. A mountain pass. 3. A range or chain of mountains. Also **ghaut.** [< Hind. *ghāt*]
ghee (gē) *n. Anglo-Indian* A butterlike substance made with the butterfat of buffalo milk. [< Hind. < Skt. *ghrta*]
gher·kin (gûr′kin) *n.* 1. A very small, prickly cucumber pickled as a relish. 2. The plant producing it. 3. Any small, immature cucumber used for pickling. [< Du. *agurk* cucumber < G < Slavic, ult. < LGk. *angourion*]
ghet·to (get′ō) *n. pl.* **·tos** 1. An often run-down section of a city inhabited chiefly by a minority group that cannot live elsewhere, as because of racial or social prejudice. 2. A section of a city in certain European countries in which Jews were formerly required to live. [< Ital.]
ghost (gōst) *n.* 1. A disembodied spirit; a wraith, specter, or phantom. 2. The animating spirit or soul: now only in the phrase **to give up the ghost,** to die. 3. A haunting recollection of something: *ghosts* from the past. 4. A mere suggestion of something: the *ghost* of a smile. 5. *Informal* A ghostwriter. 6. *Optics & Telecom.* An unwanted false or secondary image. *— v.t. & v.i.* 1. To haunt as a ghost. 2. *Informal* To write as a ghostwriter. [OE *gāst* spirit]
ghost·ly (gōst′lē) *adj.* **·li·er, ·li·est** 1. Of or like an apparition; spectral. 2. Of religion; spiritual. **— ghost′li·ness** *n.*
ghost town A deserted town, esp. a former boom town.
ghost·write (gōst′rīt′) *v.t. & v.i.* **·wrote, ·writ·ten, ·writ·ing** To write or act as a ghostwriter.
ghost·writ·er (gōst′rī′tər) *n.* One who writes for someone else to whom the authorship is to be attributed.
ghoul (gōōl) *n.* 1. One who robs graves. 2. One who takes pleasure in revolting things. 3. In Moslem legend, an evil spirit who preys on corpses. [< Arabic *ghūl*] **— ghoul′ish** *adj.* **— ghoul′ish·ly** *adv.* **— ghoul′ish·ness** *n.*
GI (jē′ī′) *U.S. Informal n. pl.* **GIs** or **GI's** An enlisted man in the U.S. Army. **— the GIs** (or **GI's**) *Mil. Slang* Diarrhea. *— adj.* 1. Of or characteristic of GIs. 2. Furnished by the government for the use of the armed forces. *— v.t.* **GIed** or **GI'ed, GIing** or **GI'ing** To clean or scrub, as for military inspection. [< G(*overnment*) I(*ssue*)]
gi·ant (jī′ənt) *n.* 1. In legend, a manlike being of supernatural size and strength, as in Greek mythology, one of the race who warred against the gods of Olympus. 2. Any person or thing of great size, capability, etc. *— adj.* 1. Of or typical of a giant. 2. Huge; great. [< OF < L < Gk. *gigas, -antos*] **gi′ant·ess** *n. fem.*
gi·ant·ism (jī′ənt·iz′əm) *n.* Gigantism.
giant panda The panda (def. 2).
giaour (jour) *n.* Among Moslems, a nonbeliever; esp., a Christian. [< Turkish < Persian *gabr* infidel]
gib·ber (jib′ər, gib′-) *v.i. & v.t.* To talk rapidly and incoherently; jabber. **— n.** Gibberish.
gib·ber·ish (jib′ər·ish, gib′-) *n.* 1. Rapid or unintelligible talk; gabble. 2. Needlessly difficult or obscure language.
gib·bet (jib′it) *n.* Formerly a gallows. *— v.t.* **gib·bet·ed** or

·bet·ted, gib·bet·ing or **·bet·ting** 1. To execute by hanging. 2. To hold up to public contempt. [< OF *gibet* staff]
gib·bon (gib′ən) *n.* A slender, long-armed arboreal anthropoid ape of southern Asia and the East Indies. [< F]
gib·bos·i·ty (gi·bos′ə·tē) *n. pl.* **·ties** 1. The state of being gibbous or convex. 2. A rounded protuberance; hump.
gib·bous (gib′əs) *adj.* 1. Irregularly rounded or convex, as the moon when more than half full and less than full. 2. Hunchbacked. Also **gib·bose** (gib′ōs, gi·bōs′). [< L *gibbus* hump] **— gib′bous·ly** *adv.* **— gib′bous·ness** *n.*
gibe¹ (jīb) *v.* **gibed, gib·ing** *v.i.* 1. To utter jeers or derisive remarks. *— v.t.* 2. To taunt. *— n.* A jeer. [Cf. OF *giber* to treat roughly] **— gib′er** *n.* **— gib′ing·ly** *adv.*
gibe² (jīb) See JIBE¹.
gib·let (jib′lit) *n. Usu. pl.* The heart, liver, gizzard, etc., of a fowl. [< OF *gibelet* stew made from game]
gid·dy (gid′ē) *adj.* **·di·er, ·di·est** 1. Affected by a reeling or whirling sensation; dizzy. 2. Tending to cause such a sensation. 3. Rotating rapidly; whirling. 4. Frivolous; heedless. *— v.t. & v.i.* **·died, ·dy·ing** To make or become dizzy. [OE *gydig* insane] **— gid′di·ly** *adv.* **— gid′di·ness** *n.*
gift (gift) *n.* 1. Something that is given; present. 2. The action or right of giving. 3. A natural aptitude; talent. **— to look a gift horse in the mouth** To find fault with a gift or favor. [OE < *gifan* to give]
gift·ed (gif′tid) *adj.* Endowed with talent.
gig¹ (gig) *n.* 1. A light, two-wheeled vehicle drawn by one horse. 2. A machine for raising a nap on cloth. 3. *Naut.* A long ship's boat usu. for the captain; also, a speedy, light rowboat. *— v.* **gigged, gig·ging** *v.i.* 1. To ride in a gig. *— v.t.* 2. To raise the nap on (cloth).
gig² (gig) *n.* An arrangement of fishhooks. *— v.t. & v.i.* **gigged, gig·ging** To spear or catch (fish) with a gig. [< FISHGIG]
gig³ (gig) *Slang n.* A demerit, as in the army, school, etc. *— v.t.* **gigged, gig·ging** 1. To give a demerit to. 2. To punish.
gi·ga- *combining form* A billion (10⁹) times (a specified unit).
gi·gan·tic (jī·gan′tik) *adj.* 1. Of, like, or suited to a giant. 2. Tremendous; huge. Also **gi·gan·te·an** (jī′gan·tē′ən). [< L *gigas, -antis* giant + -IC] **— gi·gan′ti·cal·ly** *adv.*
gi·gan·tism (jī·gan′tiz·əm) *n.* Abnormal size, esp., excessive growth of the body due to disturbances in the pituitary gland: also called *giantism.*
gig·gle (gig′əl) *v.i.* **·gled, ·gling** To laugh in a high-pitched, silly, or nervous manner. *— n.* A titter. **— gig′gler** *n.*
gig·gly (gig′lē) *adj.* **·gli·er, ·gli·est** Tending to giggle.
gig·o·lo (jig′ə·lō, Fr. zhē·gô·lō′) *n. pl.* **·los** (-lōz, Fr. -lō′) 1. A professional male dancer who dances with women patrons; also, a woman's paid escort. 2. A man supported by a woman not his wife. [< F, prob. < *gigolette* prostitute]
gig·ot (jig′ət) *n.* 1. A leg-of-mutton sleeve. 2. A cooked haunch of lamb, veal, etc. [< F]
gigue (zhēg) *n.* 1. A jig (def. 1). 2. *Music* A lively dance form, often the final movement of a suite.
Gi·la monster (hē′lə) A large, venomous lizard of the N. American desert, having an orange and black body.
gild¹ (gild) *v.t.* **gild·ed** or **gilt, gild·ing** 1. To coat with a thin layer of gold. 2. To brighten or adorn. 3. To gloss over. [OE *gyldan*] **— gil′ding** *n.*
gild² (gild) *n.* A guild.
gild·er¹ (gil′dər) *n.* One who or that which gilds.
gild·er² (gil′dər) *n.* A guilder.
Gil·e·ad (gil′ē·əd) A mountainous region of ancient Palestine east of the Jordan. *Josh.* xii 2.
gill¹ (gil) *n.* 1. *Zool.* The organ for underwater breathing of fishes, amphibians, and other aquatic vertebrates. 2. *Usu. pl.* The wattles of a fowl. 3. *pl. Informal* The face and throat: usu. in the phrase **green around the gills,** Sickly in appearance. *— v.t.* 1. To catch by the gills. 2. To gut (fish). [ME *gile*]
gill² (jil) *n.* A liquid measure equal to ¼ pint. See table front of book. [< OF *gell* measure for wine]
gil·ly·flow·er (jil′ē·flou′ər) *n.* 1. A plant of the mustard family, as the wallflower. 2. A plant of the pink family, as the clove pink. Also **gil′li·flow′er.** [Alter. of ME *gilofre*]
gilt (gilt) Alternative past tense and past participle of GILD. *— adj.* Gold-colored; gilded. *— n.* A material for gilding.
gilt-edged (gilt′ejd′) *adj.* 1. Having the edges gilded. 2. Of the best quality: *gilt-edged* securities. Also **gilt′-edge′.**
gim·bals (jim′bəlz, gim′-) *n. pl.* A set of three metal rings so pivoted one within the other that it maintains an object supported by it, as a ship's compass, on a horizontal plane. [OF < L *geminus* twin]
gim·crack (jim′krak) *n.* A useless, gaudy object; knick-knack. *— adj.* Cheap and showy. **— gim′crack·er·y** *n.*
gim·let (gim′lit) *n.* A small, sharp tool with a bar handle and a pointed, spiral tip for boring holes. *— v.t.* To make a hole in with a gimlet. [< OF *guimbelet*]

GIMBALS

gim·let eyes Sharp eyes. — **gim′let-eyed′** adj.
gim·mick (gim′ik) n. *U.S. Slang* 1. A novel or tricky feature or detail. 2. A hidden or deceptive device, as one used by a magician. 3. Some little gadget of uncertain name. — **gim′mick·y** n. — **gim′mick·y** adj.
gimp¹ (gimp) n. A narrow piece of fabric, often stiffened with wire, used to trim curtains, etc. [Cf. OF *guimpre*, a kind of trimming]
gimp² (gimp) *U.S. Slang* n. One who limps; also, a limp.
gin¹ (jin) n. An aromatic alcoholic liquor distilled from various grains, esp. rye, and flavored with juniper berries or sometimes with other flavoring agents. [Short for GENEVA]
gin² (jin) n. 1. A cotton gin. 2. A tripodlike machine for hoisting. 3. A type of pulley and block. For illus. see BLOCK. 4. A snare or trap. — v.t. **ginned, gin·ning** 1. To remove the seeds from (cotton) in a gin. 2. To trap or snare. [Aphetic var. of OF *engin* ingenuity] — **gin′ner** n.
gin·ger (jin′jər) n. 1. The pungent, spicy rootstock of a tropical plant, used in medicine and cookery. 2. The plant itself. 3. A tawny, reddish brown color. 4. *Informal* Pep. — v.t. 1. To spice with ginger. 2. *Informal* To make lively: often with up. [< OF < LL < Gk. *zingiberis*, ult. < Skt.]
ginger ale An effervescent soft drink flavored with ginger.
ginger beer An effervescent, nonalcoholic ginger drink.
gin·ger·bread (jin′jər·bred′) n. 1. A dark, ginger-flavored cake or cooky. 2. Gaudy ornamentation, as ornate carvings on furniture, etc. — adj. Cheap and tawdry.
gin·ger·ly (jin′jər·lē) adv. In a cautious manner. — adj. Careful. [Cf. OF *gent* delicate] — **gin′ger·li·ness** n.
gin·ger·snap (jin′jər·snap′) n. A brittle, ginger cooky.
gin·ger·y (jin′jər·ē) adj. 1. Having the piquantly spicy flavor of ginger. 2. Having the reddish brown color of ginger. 3. Sharply pointed or peppery, as a remark.
ging·ham (ging′əm) n. A cotton fabric, yarn-dyed, woven in solid colors, checks, etc. [< F < Malay *ginggang* striped]
gin·gi·vi·tis (jin′jə·vī′tis) n. *Pathol.* Inflammation of the gums. [< L *gingiva* gum]
gink (gingk) n. *U.S. Slang* A man or boy; fellow; guy.
gink·go (ging′kō, jing′kō) n. pl. **·goes** A large tree native to China and cultivated in the U.S., with edible fruits and nuts. Also **ging′ko**. [< Japanese]
gin mill *Slang* A saloon.
gin rummy A variety of rummy.
gin·seng (jin′seng) n. 1. An herb native to China and North America, having a root of aromatic and stimulant properties. 2. The root of this herb as used in a medicinal preparation. [< Chinese *jen shen*]
gip·sy (jip′sē), **Gip·sy** See GYPSY, GYPSY.
gi·raffe (jə·raf′, -räf′) n. pl. **·raffes** or **·raffe** An African ruminant, the tallest of all mammals, having a very long neck and long slender legs. [< F, ult. < Arabic *zarāfah*]
gird¹ (gûrd) v.t. **gird·ed** or **girt, gird·ing** 1. To surround or make fast with a belt or girdle. 2. To encircle; surround. 3. To prepare (oneself) for action. 4. To clothe, equip, or endow, as with some quality or attribute. [OE *gyrdan*]
gird² (gûrd) v.t. & v.i. To attack with sarcasm; gibe. [ME *girden*; origin unknown]
gird·er (gûr′dər) n. A long heavy beam, as of steel or wood, that supports the joists of a floor, etc.
gir·dle (gûr′dəl) n. 1. A belt or cord worn around the waist; sash. 2. Anything that encircles like a belt. 3. A woman's flexible undergarment worn to give support and shape. 4. An encircling cut made through the bark of a tree trunk or branch. 5. The outer edge of a cut gem. — v.t. **·dled, ·dling** 1. To fasten a girdle or belt around. 2. To encircle; encompass. 3. To make an encircling cut through the bark of (a branch or tree). [OE *gyrdle*] — **gir′dler** n.
girl (gûrl) n. 1. A female infant or child. 2. A young, unmarried woman. 3. A female servant. 4. *Informal* A sweetheart. 5. *Informal* Any woman of any age. [ME *gurle*] — **girl′ish** adj. — **girl′ish·ly** adv. — **girl′ish·ness** n.
girl guide A member of a British and Canadian organization, the **Girl Guides**, resembling the Girl Scouts.
girl scout A member of an organization of girls between the ages of 7 and 17, founded in the U.S. in 1912 to develop health, character, etc.
girt¹ (gûrt) Past tense and past participle of GIRD¹.
girt² (gûrt) v.t. & v.i. 1. To gird. 2. To measure in girth. — n. Girth. [< GIRD¹]
girth (gûrth) n. 1. The circumference of anything. 2. A band passed under the belly of a horse or other animal to make fast a saddle, harness, pack, etc. 3. A girdle or band. — v.t. 1. To bind with a girth. 2. To encircle; girdle. — v.i. 3. To measure in girth. [< ON *gjorth*]
gis·mo (giz′mō) n. pl. **·mos** *U.S. Slang* A gadget. Also spelled *gizmo*.
gist (jist) n. The main idea or substance, as of an argument, question, etc. [< OF *giste* place of rest]

git·tern (git′ərn) n. A cittern. [< OF < L < Gk. *kithara*]
give (giv) v. **gave, giv·en, giv·ing** v.t. 1. To transfer freely (what is one's own) to the permanent possession of another without asking anything in return. 2. To put into the hands of another for temporary use; hand over; let have. 3. To put into the grasp of another: *Give* me your hand. 4. To make available; furnish. 5. To be a source of. 6. To grant or concede, as permission. 7. To impart: to *give* advice. 8. To administer (a dose of medicine, a treatment, etc.). 9. To assign or allot. 10. To deal, deliver, or inflict (a blow, beating, etc.). 11. To transmit or communicate (a disease, etc.). 12. To perform or do: to *give* a play. 13. To issue (an order, etc.). 14. To part with; relinquish or yield: to *give* one's life. 15. To devote, as oneself, to a cause, etc. — v.i. 16. To make donations; make free gifts. 17. To move down, back, etc., as under pressure: The door *gave*. 18. To be springy, flexible, etc.: The bed *gives* comfortably. 19. To furnish a view or passage; open: with *on* or *onto*. — **to give a good account of** To conduct (oneself) creditably. — **to give and take** To exchange on equal terms. — **to give away** 1. To bestow as a gift. 2. To hand over (the bride) to the bridegroom. 3. *Informal* To make known, as a secret; reveal. — **to give back** To restore or return. — **to give birth** To bear offspring. — **to give birth to** 1. To bear (offspring). 2. To create or originate, as an idea. 3. To result in. — **to give forth** To discharge; emit. — **to give in** 1. To yield, as to something demanded. 2. To cease opposition; acknowledge oneself vanquished. 3. To deliver or hand in (a report, resignation, etc.). — **to give it to** To administer a scolding, beating, etc., to. — **to give off** To send forth, as odors; emit. — **to give out** 1. To send forth; emit. 2. To hand out or distribute. 3. To make known; publish. 4. To become completely used up or exhausted. — **to give over** 1. To hand over, as to another's care. 2. To cease; desist. — **to give rise to** To cause or produce; result in. — **to give up** 1. To surrender. 2. To stop; cease. 3. To desist from as hopeless. 4. To lose all hope for, as a sick person. 5. To devote wholly: to *give* oneself up to art. — **to give way** 1. To collapse, bend, fail, etc., as under pressure or force. 2. To draw back. 3. To concede or yield. 4. To abandon oneself, as to despair. — n. 1. The quality of being resilient; elasticity. 2. The act or process of bending or yielding. [Fusion of OE *giefan* and ON *gefa*] — **giv′er** n.
give-and-take (giv′ən·tāk′) n. The making of mutual concessions, exchanges, etc.
give·a·way (giv′ə·wā′) *Informal* n. 1. A disclosure or betrayal, generally unintentional. 2. Something given free or at a greatly reduced price. — adj. Characterized by prizes.
giv·en (giv′ən) adj. 1. Presented; bestowed. 2. Habitually inclined; addicted: with *to*. 3. Specified; stated: a *given* date. 4. Issued on an indicated date: said of official documents, etc. 5. Admitted as a fact. — Syn. See ADDICTED.
given name The name bestowed on a person at birth, or shortly thereafter, as distinguished from his surname.
giz·mo (giz′mō) See GISMO.
giz·zard (giz′ərd) n. 1. A second stomach in birds, in which partly digested food is finely ground. 2. *Informal* The human stomach. [< OF < L *gigeria* cooked entrails of poultry]
gla·brous (glā′brəs) adj. *Biol.* 1. Devoid of hair or down. 2. Having a smooth surface. [< L *glaber* smooth]
gla·cé (gla·sā′) adj. 1. Sugared or candied, as preserved fruits. 2. Having a glossy surface, as certain leathers. 3. Iced; frozen. — v.t. **·céed, ·cé·ing** 1. To cover with icing. 2. To make smooth and glossy. [< F *glace* ice]
gla·cial (glā′shəl) adj. 1. Pertaining to, caused by, or marked by the presence of glaciers. 2. Freezingly cold. 3. Indifferent. [< L *glacies* ice] — **gla′cial·ly** adv.
glacial epoch *Geol.* Any portion of geological time characterized by ice sheets over much of the earth's surface.
gla·ci·ate (glā′shē·āt) v.t. **·at·ed, ·at·ing** To cover with or subject to the action of glaciers. — **gla′ci·a′tion** n.
gla·cier (glā′shər) n. A field of ice, formed in regions of perennial frost from compacted snow, that moves slowly until it either breaks off to form icebergs or melts in warmer regions. [< F < L *glacies* ice]
glad¹ (glad) adj. **glad·der, glad·dest** 1. Having a feeling of joy, pleasure, or content; gratified: often with *of* or *at*. 2. Showing joy; brightly cheerful: a *glad* face. 3. Giving reason to rejoice; bringing joy. 4. Very willing: He'd be *glad* to help. [OE *glæd* shining, glad]
glad² (glad) n. *Informal* A gladiolus.
glad·den (glad′n) v.t. To make glad. — **glad′den·er** n.
glade (glād) n. 1. A clearing in a wood. 2. *U.S.* An everglade. [Prob. akin to *glad* in obs. sense of "bright, sunny"]
glad eye *Slang* A flirtatious glance: esp. in the phrase **to get** (or **give**) **the glad eye.**
glad hand *Slang* A display, often insincere, of cordiality.
glad·i·a·tor (glad′ē·ā′tər) n. 1. In ancient Rome, a slave,

captive, or paid freeman who fought other men or animals as public entertainment. **2.** One who engages in any kind of struggle. [< L *gladius* sword] — **glad·i·a·to·ri·al** (glad/-ē·ə·tôr/ē·əl, -tō/rē-) *adj.*

glad·i·o·lus (glad/ē·ō/ləs, glə·dī/ə·ləs) *n. pl.* **·lus·es** or **·li** (-lī) A plant of the iris family with fleshy bulbs, sword-shaped leaves, and spikes of colored flowers. Also **glad/i·o/la.**

glad·ly (glad/lē) *adv.* In a glad manner; with joy; willingly.

glad·ness (glad/nis) *n.* The state of being glad; joy.

glad·some (glad/səm) *adj.* Glad. — **glad/some·ly** *adv.* — **glad/some·ness** *n.*

Glad·stone (glad/stōn, -stən) *n.* A suitcase hinged to open flat and form two equal compartments. Also **Gladstone bag.** [after W. E. *Gladstone*, 1809–98, English statesman]

glair (glâr) *n.* **1.** Raw egg white, used in making size or glaze; also, the glaze or size. **2.** Any sticky matter. — *v.t.* To coat with glair. [< F < L *clarus* clear] — **glair/y** *adj.*

glam·or·ize (glam/ər·īz) *v.t.* **·rized, ·riz·ing** To make glamorous.

glam·or·ous (glam/ər·əs) *adj.* Full of glamour; alluring. — **glam/or·ous·ly** *adv.* — **glam/or·ous·ness** *n.*

glam·our (glam/ər) *n.* Alluring charm or fascination. Also *U.S.* **glam/or.** [< Scot *gramarye* magic power]

glance (glans, gläns) *v.* **glanced, glanc·ing** *v.i.* **1.** To take a quick look. **2.** To touch briefly on some matter. **3.** To be deflected at an angle after obliquely striking. **4.** To flash intermittently; glint. — *v.t.* **5.** To cause to strike a surface obliquely. — *n.* **1.** A quick look. **2.** A flash; glint. **3.** Oblique impact and deflection. [< OF *glacier* to slip]

gland (gland) *n. Anat.* Any of various organs by means of which certain constituents are removed from the blood, either for use in the body or for elimination from it. [< F < L *glans, glandis* acorn]

glan·ders (glan/dərz) *n. Vet.* A contagious disease of horses and other equines, characterized by nasal discharges and ulcerative lesions of the lungs and other organs. [< OF *glandre* gland] — **glan/dered, glan/der·ous** *adj.*

glan·du·lar (glan/jə·lər) *adj.* **1.** Of, pertaining to, or resembling a gland. **2.** Having glands. Also **glan/du·lous.**

glan·dule (glan/jōōl) *n.* A small gland.

glare[1] (glâr) *v.* **glared, glar·ing** *v.i.* **1.** To shine with a steady and dazzling intensity. **2.** To gaze or stare fiercely or in hostility. **3.** To be conspicuous or showy. — *v.t.* **4.** To express or send forth with a glare. — *n.* **1.** A dazzling, steady light or reflection. **2.** An intense, piercing look or gaze, usually hostile. **3.** Gaudy or showy display; vulgar brilliance. [ME *glaren* < LG]

glare[2] (glâr) *U.S. n.* A glassy, smooth surface, as of ice. — *adj.* Having a glassy, smooth surface. [? < GLARE[1], n.]

glar·ing (glâr/ing) *adj.* **1.** Looking or staring fixedly or with hostility. **2.** Emitting an excessively brilliant light. **3.** Gaudy. **4.** Plainly conspicuous. — **glar/ing·ly** *adv.*

glar·y[1] (glâr/ē) *adj.* **glar·i·er, glar·i·est** Dazzling; glaring.

glar·y[2] (glâr/ē) *adj. U.S.* Slippery, as ice.

glass (glas, gläs) *n.* **1.** A hard, amorphous, brittle, usu. transparent substance made by fusing one or more of the oxides of silicon, boron, or phosphorus with certain basic oxides, followed by rapid cooling to prevent crystallization. ◆ Collateral adjective: *vitreous.* **2.** Any substance made of or resembling glass. **3.** An article made wholly or partly of glass; as: **a** A windowpane, lens, or mirror, tumbler, etc. **b** *pl.* A pair of eyeglasses; also, binoculars. **4.** Glassware. **5.** The contents of a drinking glass; glassful. — *v.t.* **1.** To put in a glass container. **2.** To enclose in or cover with glass. **3.** To equip with glass parts. **4.** To give a glassy surface or appearance to. — *adj.* **1.** Of, pertaining to, or consisting of glass. **2.** Fitted with glass: a *glass* frame. [OE *glæs*]

glass blowing The art or process of directing a controlled stream of air through a tube into a mass of molten glass at the end of the tube so as to form the glass into various shapes.

glass·ful (glas/fōōl, gläs/-) *n. pl.* **·fuls** The amount contained in a drinking glass.

glass snake A lizard of the southern U.S., having a very brittle tail.

glass·ware (glas/wâr/, gläs/-) *n.* Articles made of glass.

glass wool Fibers of spun glass of woollike appearance, used for insulation, filters, etc.

glass·work (glas/wûrk/, gläs/-) *n.* **1.** The manufacture of glass. **2.** Glass as a material used in glassware, decoration, etc. **3.** Glassware. **4.** The fitting of panes of glass.

glass·works (glas/wûrks/, gläs/-) *n.pl.* (*usu. construed as sing.*) A factory where glass is made.

glass·wort (glas/wûrt, gläs/-) *n.* Any of several seaside herbs: also called *saltwort.*

glass·y (glas/ē, gläs/ē) *adj.* **glass·i·er, glass·i·est** **1.** Resembling glass. **2.** Fixed, blank, and uncomprehending: a *glassy* stare. — **glass/i·ly** *adv.* — **glass/i·ness** *n.*

glau·co·ma (glô·kō/mə) *n. Pathol.* A disease of the eye characterized by pressure of fluids within the eyeball with gradual loss of vision. [< L < Gk. *glaukos* bluish gray] — **glau·co·ma·tous** (glô·kō/mə·təs, -kom/ə-) *adj.*

glau·cous (glô/kəs) *adj.* **1.** Yellowish green; also, sea-green. **2.** *Bot.* Covered with a whitish bloom, as grapes. [< L < Gk. *glaukos* bluish gray]

glaze (glāz) *v.* **glazed, glaz·ing** *v.t.* **1.** To fit, as a window, with glass panes; also, to provide (a building, etc.) with windows. **2.** To cover or coat with a thin film; as: **a** To coat (pottery) with a glasslike surface applied by fusing. **b** To cover (foods) with a thin coating of eggs, syrup, etc. **c** To cover (paintings) with a thin, transparent coating to modify the tone. — *v.i.* **3.** To become covered with a thin coating or film. — *n.* **1.** A thin, glossy coating; also, the substance used to make such a coating. **2.** A filmy haze. **3.** *U.S.* A thin coating of ice. [ME *glas* glass] — **glaz/er** *n.*

gla·zier (glā/zhər) *n.* **1.** One who fits windows, doors, etc., with panes of glass. **2.** One who applies glaze to pottery.

gla·zier·y (glā/zhər·ē) *n.* The work of a glazier.

glaz·ing (glā/zing) *n.* **1.** The act of setting glass, as in a window. **2.** The glass used. **3.** A glaze. **4.** The act or art of applying a glaze.

glaz·y (glā/zē) *adj.* **glaz·i·er, glaz·i·est** **1.** Covered with or as with a glaze. **2.** Resembling a glaze. — **glaz/i·ness** *n.*

gleam (glēm) *n.* **1.** An intermittent or momentary ray or beam of light. **2.** A soft radiance; glow; also, reflected light. **3.** A brief manifestation, as of humor; a faint trace, as of hope. — *v.i.* **1.** To shine softly; emit gleams. **2.** To appear briefly as in a small burst of light. — *v.t.* **3.** To emit in gleams. — **Syn.** See SHINE. [OE *glǣm*] — **gleam/y** *adj.*

glean (glēn) *v.t. & v.i.* **1.** To collect (facts, etc.) by patient effort. **2.** To gather (the leavings) from a field after the crop has been reaped. **3.** To gather the leavings from (a field, etc.). [< OF < LL *glenare* < Celtic] — **glean/er** *n.*

glean·ing (glē/ning) *n. Usu. pl.* That which is gleaned.

glebe (glēb) *n. Brit.* A portion of land attached to a church benefice as part of its endowment. [< OF < L *gleba* clod]

glee (glē) *n.* **1.** Lively, exuberant joy. **2.** A musical composition for male voices, without accompaniment. [OE *glēo*]

glee club A group of singers organized to sing part songs.

glee·ful (glē/fəl) *adj.* Feeling or exhibiting glee; mirthful. Also **glee/some** (-səm). — **glee/ful·ly** *adv.* — **glee/ful·ness** *n.*

glen (glen) *n.* A small, secluded valley. [< Scot. Gael. *glenn*]

Glen·gar·ry (glen·gar/ē) *n.* A Scottish cap having sloping sides and streamers in back. [after a valley in Scotland]

glib (glib) *adj.* **glib·ber, glib·best** **1.** Speaking fluently without much thought: a *glib* talker. **2.** More facile than sincere. **3.** Characterized by smoothness, as of manner. [< MLG *glibberich* slippery] — **glib/ly** *adv.* — **glib/ness** *n.*

glide (glīd) *v.* **glid·ed, glid·ing** *v.i.* **1.** To move, slip, or flow smoothly or effortlessly. **2.** To pass unnoticed or imperceptibly, as time: often with *by.* **3.** *Aeron.* To descend along an oblique line gradually without motor power; also, to fly a glider. **4.** *Music & Phonet.* To produce a glide. — *v.t.* **5.** To cause to glide. — *n.* **1.** The act of gliding. **2.** *Phonet.* A transitional sound made in passing from one speech sound to another. [OE *glīdan*] — **glid/ing·ly** *adv.*

glid·er (glī/dər) *n.* **1.** One who or that which glides. **2.** *Aeron.* An engineless airplane, constructed to soar on air currents. **3.** A swing gliding in a metal frame.

glim·mer (glim/ər) *v.i.* **1.** To gleam unsteadily; flicker. **2.** To appear fitfully or faintly. — *n.* **1.** A faint, unsteady light. **2.** A trace; inkling. [ME *glimeren* to shine] — **glim/mer·ing** *n. & adj.* — **glim/mer·ing·ly** *adv.*

glimpse (glimps) *n.* **1.** A momentary view or look. **2.** A faint intimation; inkling. — *v.* **glimpsed, glimps·ing** *v.t.* **1.** To see for an instant; catch a glimpse of. — *v.i.* **2.** To look for an instant: with *at.* [ME *glimsen* to shine faintly]

glint (glint) *v.i.* **1.** To gleam; glitter. **2.** To dart. — *v.t.* **3.** To reflect; shine. — *n.* **1.** A gleam. **2.** A luster, as of metal. [ME *glinten* to shine < Scand.]

glis·sade (gli·säd/, -sād/) *n.* **1.** The act of skillfully sliding down an icy slope. **2.** A gliding dance step. — *v.i.* **·sad·ed, ·sad·ing** To execute a glissade. [< F *glisser* to slip]

glis·san·do (gli·sän/dō) *Music n. pl.* **·di** (-dē) or **·dos** **1.** A passing from one tone to another by a continuous change of pitch; also, a rapid succession of tones. **2.** A passage so written or performed. — *adj.* Of a glissando. — *adv.* Like a glissando. [< F *glissant* slipping + Ital. *-ando*]

glis·ten (glis/ən) *v.i.* To shine, as reflected light. — *n.* Brightness; sparkle. [OE *glisnian* to shine]

glit·ter (glit/ər) *v.i.* **1.** To sparkle brightly or brilliantly, as a diamond. **2.** To display striking magnificence; be brilliantly showy. — *n.* Sparkling magnificence; brilliance. [< ON *glitra*] — **glit/ter·ing·ly** *adv.* — **glit/ter·y** *adj.*

gloam·ing (glō/ming) *n.* The dusk of early evening; twilight. [OE *glōmung*]

gloat (glōt) *v.i.* To take an intense, often malicious delight: usu. with *over.* [Cf. ON *glotta* to grin] — **gloat/ing** *adj.*

glob (glob) *n.* **1.** A small drop or ball of something. **2.** A rounded, often large mass of something.

glob·al (glō/bəl) *adj.* **1.** Involving the whole world: *global* war. **2.** Spherical. — **glob/al·ly** *adv.*

globe (glōb) *n.* **1.** A perfectly round body; ball; sphere;

also, anything like a sphere, as a fishbowl. **2.** The earth. **3.** A spherical model of the earth or heavens. **4.** A ball, usu. of gold, used as an emblem of authority. — *v.t. & v.i.* **globed, glob·ing** To form into a globe. [< F < L *globus* ball] — **glo·bate** (glō′bāt) *adj.*

globe·fish (glōb′fish) *n.* *pl.* **·fish** or **·fish·es** Any of various spiny-finned, tropical fishes that inflate their bodies into globular form.

globe·trot·ter (glōb′trot′ər) *n.* One who travels all over the world, esp. for sightseeing. — **globe′trot′ting** *n.*

glo·bin (glō′bin) *n.* *Biochem.* The protein constituent of hemoglobin. [< L *globus* ball + -IN]

glo·bose (glō′bōs, glō·bōs′) *adj.* Spherical. Also **glo′bous** (-bəs). [< L *globus* ball] — **glo·bos·i·ty** (glō·bos′ə·tē) *n.*

glob·u·lar (glob′yə·lər) *adj.* **1.** Spherical. **2.** Formed of globules.

glob·ule (glob′yōōl) *n.* A tiny sphere of matter or drop of liquid. [< F < L *globulus* ball]

glob·u·lin (glob′yə·lin) *n.* *Biochem.* Any of a group of simple plant and animal proteins, insoluble in water but soluble in dilute saline solutions.

glob·u·lous (glob′yə·ləs) *adj.* **1.** Containing or consisting of globules. **2.** Spherical; globular. Also **glob′u·lose** (-lōs).

glock·en·spiel (glok′ən·spēl) *n.* A portable musical instrument with a series of chromatically tuned metal bars played by hammers. [< G *glocken* bells + *spiel* play]

glom·er·ate (glom′ər·āt, -it) *adj.* Gathered or wound into a rounded mass. [< L *glomus* mass] — **glom′er·a′tion** *n.*

gloom (glōōm) *n.* **1.** Partial or total darkness; heavy shadow. **2.** Darkness or depression of the mind or spirits. **3.** A dark or gloomy place. — *v.i.* **1.** To look sullen or dejected. **2.** To be dark or threatening. — *v.t.* **3.** To make dark, sad, or sullen. [ME *glom(b)en* to look sad]

gloom·y (glōō′mē) *adj.* **gloom·i·er, gloom·i·est** **1.** Dark; dismal. **2.** Melancholy; morose. **3.** Producing gloom or melancholy. — **gloom′i·ly** *adv.* — **gloom′i·ness** *n.*

Glo·ri·a (glôr′ē·ə, glō′rē·ə) *n.* *Eccl.* **a** The section of the Mass consisting of the recitation or singing of *Gloria in excelsis Deo.* **b** Its musical setting. [< L, glory]

glo·ri·fi·ca·tion (glôr′ə·fə·kā′shən, glō′rə-) *n.* **1.** The act of glorifying or exalting. **2.** Invested with glory. **3.** *Informal* A glorified form of something.

glo·ri·fy (glôr′ə·fī, glō′rə-) *v.t.* **·fied, ·fy·ing** **1.** To make glorious. **2.** To honor; worship. **3.** To give great praise to; laud. **4.** To make seem more splendid than is so. [< OF < L *gloria* glory + *facere* to make] — **glo′ri·fi′er** *n.*

glo·ri·ous (glôr′ē·əs, glō′rē-) *adj.* **1.** Full of glory; illustrious. **2.** Bringing glory or honor. **3.** Resplendent. **4.** *Informal* Delightful. — **glo′ri·ous·ly** *adv.* — **glo′ri·ous·ness** *n.*

glo·ry (glôr′ē, glō′rē) *n.* *pl.* **·ries** **1.** Distinguished honor or praise; exalted reputation. **2.** Something bringing praise. **3.** Worshipful adoration: to give *glory* to God. **4.** Magnificence; splendor: the *glory* of Rome. **5.** The bliss of heaven. **6.** A state of extreme well-being: to be in one's *glory.* **7.** A nimbus; halo. — *v.i.* **·ried, ·ry·ing** **1.** To take pride with *in.* **2.** To boast; brag. [< OF < L *gloria*]

gloss¹ (glôs, glos) *n.* **1.** The luster or sheen of a polished surface. **2.** A deceptive or superficial appearance. — *v.t.* **1.** To make lustrous, as by polishing. **2.** To hide (errors, etc.) by falsehood: usu. with *over.* — *v.i.* **3.** To become shiny. [< Scand. Cf. ON *glossi* blaze.] — **gloss′er** *n.*

gloss² (glôs, glos) *n.* **1.** An explanatory note, esp. marginal or interlinear; a commentary; a translation; a glossary. **2.** An artful or deceptive explanation to cover up a fault, etc. — *v.t.* **1.** To write glosses for (a text, etc.); annotate. **2.** To excuse by false explanations. — *v.i.* **3.** To make glosses. [< OF < L < Gk. *glossa* foreign word] — **gloss′er** *n.*

glos·sa·ry (glos′ə·rē, glôs′-) *n.* *pl.* **·ries** A lexicon of the technical, obscure, or foreign words of a work or field. [< L < *glossa*] — **glos·sar·i·al** (glo·sâr′ē·əl, glô-) *adj.* — **glos·sar′i·al·ly** *adv.* — **glos·sa·rist** (glos′ə·rist, glôs′-) *n.*

glos·so- *combining form* The tongue; speech; language. Also, before vowels, **gloss-.** [< Gk. *glōssa* tongue]

gloss·y (glôs′ē, glos′ē) *adj.* **gloss·i·er, gloss·i·est** **1.** Having a bright sheen; lustrous. **2.** Made superficially attractive. **3.** Specious. — **gloss′i·ly** *adv.* — **gloss′i·ness** *n.*

-glot *combining form* Using or able to use (a number of) languages: *polyglot.* [< Gk. *glōssa* tongue, language]

glot·tal (glot′l) *adj.* Of or articulated in the glottis.

glot·tis (glot′is) *n.* *pl.* **glot·ti·des** (glot′ə·dēz) or **glot·tis·es** *Anat.* The cleft between the vocal cords at the upper opening of the larynx. [< NL < Gk. < *glōtta* tongue]

glot·to- *combining form* Language. [< Gk. *glōtta*]

glove (gluv) *n.* **1.** A covering for the hand, having a separate sheath for each finger. **2.** In baseball, a large leather mitt for catching the ball. **3.** A boxing glove. — **to be hand in glove** (with) To be in close relationship (with). — **to handle with kid gloves** To use great care and tact in dealing

with. — **to put on the gloves** *Informal* To box or spar. — *v.t.* **gloved, glov·ing** **1.** To put gloves on. **2.** To furnish with gloves. **3.** To be a glove for. [OE *glōf*]

glov·er (gluv′ər) *n.* A maker of or dealer in gloves.

glow (glō) *v.i.* **1.** To give off light and heat, esp. without flame; be incandescent. **2.** To shine but without heat. **3.** To be red, as from heat; flush. **4.** To be animated, as with emotion, etc. **5.** To be very hot; burn. — *n.* **1.** The incandescence given off by a heated substance. **2.** Vividness. **3.** Ruddiness, as from health. **4.** Strong emotion; ardor. [OE *glōwan*] — **glow′ing** *adj.* — **glow′ing·ly** *adv.*

glow·er (glou′ər) *v.i.* To stare with an angry frown; scowl sullenly. — *n.* The act of glowering; a fierce stare. [? Obs. *glow* to stare] — **glow′er·ing·ly** *adv.*

glow·worm (glō′wûrm′) *n.* **1.** A European beetle, the larva and wingless female of which display phosphorescent light. **2.** The firefly.

glox·in·i·a (glok·sin′ē·ə) *n.* A plant with large, bell-shaped flowers. [after *Gloxin*, 18th c. Ger. doctor]

gloze (glōz) *v.* **glozed, gloz·ing** *v.t.* To explain away.

glu·cose (glōō′kōs) *n.* **1.** *Chem.* A monosaccharide carbohydrate, $C_6H_{12}O_6$, less sweet than cane sugar, found as dextrose in plants and animals and obtained by hydrolysis. **2.** The thick yellowish syrup obtained by incomplete hydrolysis of starch and used in confectionery, baking, etc. [< F < Gk. *glykys* sweet] — **glu·cos′ic** (-kos′ik) *adj.*

glu·co·side (glōō′kə·sīd) *n.* *Chem.* Any of a class of carbohydrate compounds that yield glucose or other sugar.

glue (glōō) *n.* **1.** An adhesive in the form of a gelatine made from animal substances, as skin, bones, etc. **2.** An adhesive or cement made of casein or other synthetics. **3.** Any sticky adhesive. — *v.t.* **glued, glu·ing** To stick or fasten with or as with glue. [< OF *glu* birdlime]

glu·ey (glōō′ē) *adj.* **glu·i·er, glu·i·est** **1.** Having the nature of glue; sticky; viscous. **2.** Covered or spread with glue.

glum (glum) *adj.* **glum·mer, glum·mest** Moody and silent; sullen. — **glum′ly** *adv.* — **glum′ness** *n.*

glume (glōōm) *n.* *Bot.* One of the two lowest bracts on the spikelet of certain grassy plants. [< L *gluma* husk]

glut (glut) *v.* **glut·ted, glut·ting** *v.t.* **1.** To feed or supply to excess; satiate. **2.** To supply (the market) with an excess of goods so that the price falls. — *v.i.* **3.** To eat to excess. — *n.* **1.** An excessive supply. **2.** The act of glutting or being glutted. [< obs. *glut* glutton < OF *gloutir* to swallow]

glu·ten (glōōt′n) *n.* A tough, sticky mixture of proteins obtained by washing out the starch from wheat flour. [< L, glue] — **glu·te·nous** (glōōt′n·əs) *adj.*

glu·te·us (glōō·tē′əs) *n.* *pl.* **·te·i** (-tē′ī) *Anat.* Any of three muscles of the buttocks. [< NL < Gk. *gloutos* rump] — **glu·te′al** *adj.*

glu·ti·nous (glōōt′n·əs) *adj.* Resembling glue; sticky. — **glu′ti·nous·ly** *adv.* — **glu′ti·nous·ness** *n.*

glut·ton¹ (glut′n) *n.* **1.** One who eats to excess. **2.** One who has a great appetite or capacity for something. [< OF < L *gluto, -onis* glutton]

glut·ton² (glut′n) *n.* A wolverine, esp. of Asia or Europe. [Trans. of G *vielfrass* great eater]

glut·ton·ous (glut′n·əs) *adj.* **1.** Given to excess in eating; voracious. **2.** Desiring excessively. — **glut′ton·ous·ly** *adv.*

glut·ton·y (glut′n·ē) *n.* *pl.* **·ton·ies** The act or habit of eating to excess.

glyc·er·ide (glis′ər·īd, -id) *n.* *Chem.* An ether or ester of glycerol with a fatty acid.

glyc·er·in (glis′ər·in) *n.* Glycerol. Also **glyc′er·ine** (-in, -ēn).

glyc·er·ol (glis′ər·ōl, -ol) *n.* *Chem.* A sweet, oily, colorless alcohol, $C_3H_8O_3$, formed by decomposition of natural fats with alkalis or superheated steam, used in medicine, industry, and the arts. [< Gk. *glykeros* sweet + -OL²]

glyc·er·yl (glis′ər·il) *n.* *Chem.* The trivalent glycerol radical C_3H_5.

glyco- *combining form* Sweet. [< Gk. *glykys* sweet]

gly·co·gen (glī′kə·jən) *n.* *Biochem.* A white, mealy, amorphous polysaccharide, $(C_6H_{11}O_5)_x$, contained principally in the liver and hydrolized into glucose.

gly·co·gen·ic (glī′kə·jen′ik) *adj.* **1.** Relating to the formation of glycogen. **2.** Caused by glycogen.

gly·col (glī′kōl, -kol) *n.* *Chem.* **1.** One of several alcohols containing two hydroxyl radicals, having the general formula $C_nH_{2n}(OH)_2$. **2.** Ethylene glycol.

gly·co·side (glī′kə·sīd) *n.* *Chem.* Any of a group of carbohydrates that when decomposed yield glucose or other sugar.

G-man (jē′man′) *n.* *pl.* **-men** (-men′) An agent of the Federal Bureau of Investigation. [< G(OVERNMENT) MAN]

gnarl (närl) *n.* A protuberance on a tree; a tough knot. — *v.t.* To make knotty and twisted like an old tree.

gnarled (närld) *adj.* **1.** Having snarls. **2.** Weather-beaten and rugged. **3.** Of the hands, having prominent knuckles and twisted fingers as from hard work. Also **gnarl′y.**

gnash (nash) *v.t.* **1.** To grind or snap (the teeth) together, as in rage. **2.** To bite or chew by grinding the teeth. — *v.i.* **3.** To grind the teeth. — *n.* A bite of the teeth. [< Scand.]

gnat (nat) *n.* Any of various small stinging or biting flies. **— to strain at a gnat** To fuss. [OE *gnæt*]

-gnathous *combining form* Having a jaw of an indicated kind: *prognathous*. [< Gk. *gnathos* jaw + -OUS]

gnaw (nô) *v.t.* **gnawed, gnawed** or sometimes **gnawn, gnaw·ing 1.** To bite or eat away little by little as with the teeth; to make by gnawing; also, to bite on repeatedly. **2.** To torment or oppress with fear, pain, etc. — *v.i.* **3.** To bite, chew, or corrode persistently. **4.** To cause constant worry, etc. [OE *gnagan*] **— gnaw'er** *n.* **— gnaw'ing·ly** *adv.*

gnaw·ing (nô'ing) *n.* **1.** A dull, persistent sensation of discomfort or distress. **2.** *pl.* Pangs of hunger.

gneiss (nīs) *n.* A coarse-grained, banded rock like granite but having layered components. [< G] **— gneiss'ic** *adj.*

gnome (nōm) *n.* In folklore, one of a group of dwarfish, little old men, living in caves and guarding buried treasure, etc. [< F < NL *gnomus*] **— gnom'ish** *adj.*

gno·mic (nō'mik, nom'ik) *adj.* Consisting of or resembling maxims; aphoristic. Also **gno'mi·cal. — gno'mi·cal·ly** *adv.*

gno·mon (nō'mon) *n.* A pointer or similar device used to indicate time by the shadow it casts, as on a sundial. For illus. see SUNDIAL. [< Gk. < *gnō-* stem of *gignōskein* to know] **— gno·mon·ic** (nō·mon'ik) or **·i·cal** *adj.*

-gnomy *combining form* Knowledge or art of judging: *physiognomy*. [< Gk. *gnōmē* judgment]

-gnosis *combining form* *Med.* Knowledge; recognition: *prognosis*. [< Gk. *gnōsis* knowledge]

gnos·tic (nos'tik) *adj.* Of or possessing knowledge, esp. spiritual knowledge or insight. Also **gnos'ti·cal.**

Gnos·ti·cism (nos'tə·siz'əm) *n.* A system of ancient Greek and Oriental philosophy, an attempted synthesis with Christian doctrine, denounced as heretical by the Church. **— Gnos'tic** *adj. & n.*

gnu (nōō, nyōō) *n.* *pl.* **gnus** or **gnu** A South African antelope having an oxlike head with curved horns, a mane, and a long tail: also called *wildebeest*. [< Xhosa *nqu*]

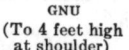

GNU
(To 4 feet high at shoulder)

go¹ (gō) *v.* **went, gone, go·ing;** *3rd person sing. present* **goes** *v.i.* **1.** To proceed or pass along; move. **2.** To move from a place; leave; depart: often used as a command or signal, as in a race: *Go!* **3.** To have a scheduled route destination: This train *goes* to Chicago daily. **4.** To be in operation; also, to work or function properly. **5.** To extend or reach: This pipe *goes* to the basement. **6.** To emit a specified sound or act in a certain way: The chain *goes* "clank." **7.** To fail, give away, or collapse; also, to disappear. **8.** To have a specific place: belong: The plates *go* on the shelf. **9.** To be awarded or given; also, to be allotted or applied: This *goes* for rent. **10.** To pass from one person to another. **11.** To pass into a condition; become: to *go* insane. **12.** To be, continue, or appear in a specified state: to *go* unpunished. **13.** To happen or end in a specific manner: The election *went* badly. **14.** To be considered or ranked: good as lunches *go*. **15.** To be suitable; harmonize; fit. **16.** To be phrased; have a certain form: How does the tune *go*? **17.** To have recourse; resort: to *go* to court. **18.** To die. **19.** To pass: said of time. **20.** To be abolished or given up; These expenses must *go*. **21.** To serve, contribute, or help; also, to make up a certain quantity: Two ounces *go* to each serving. **22.** To be sold or bid for: with *at* or *for*: These shoes will *go* at a high price. **23.** To subject oneself; put oneself: He *went* to great pains. **24.** To continue one's actions to or beyond certain limits: He *goes* too far in his criticism. **25.** To endure; last: Can he *go* two more rounds? **26.** To be about to: used in the progressive form and followed by the present infinitive: They are *going* to protest. — *v.t.* **27.** *Informal* To furnish or provide (bail). **28.** *Informal* To risk or bet; wager. **29.** *Informal* To put up with; tolerate: I cannot *go* that music. — *adj.* *Aerospace* Operating or proceeding as planned. **— to go** *Informal* **1.** Remaining: ten pages *to go*. **2.** Prepared for taking outside: a sandwich *to go*. **— to go about 1.** To be occupied or busy with. **2.** To circulate. **3.** *Naut.* To tack; turn. **— to go after 1.** To try to catch; chase. **2.** To follow in sequence. **— to go against 1.** To be opposed to; act contrary to. **— to go along 1.** To continue; carry on. **2.** To be in accord; agree: often with *with*. **3.** To escort; accompany: with *with*. **— to go around 1.** To move about or circulate. **2.** To enclose; encircle. **3.** To be enough for all to have some. **— to go at** To attack; work at. **— to go back on 1.** To be disloyal to; forsake. **2.** To fail to fulfill. **— to go behind** To inquire or investigate so as to test the validity of. **— to go beyond** To surpass; exceed. **— to go by 1.** To pass. **2.** To conform to or be guided by. **3.** To be known by. **— to go down 1.** To sink or descend. **2.** To experience defeat. **3.** To attain lasting remembrance, as

in history. **4.** To decrease, as prices. **— to go for 1.** To try to get. **2.** To advocate. **3.** *Informal* To attack. **4.** *Informal* To be attracted by. **— to go halves (or shares)** *Informal* To share equally. **— to go hard with** To bring trouble to. **— to go in for** *Informal* **1.** To strive for; advocate. **2.** To like or participate in. **— to go into 1.** To investigate. **2.** To take up, as a study. **3.** To be contained in. **— to go in with** To unite or join forces with. **— to go off 1.** To explode or be discharged, as a gun. **2.** To depart; leave. **3.** *Informal* To occur. **— to go on 1.** To act; behave. **2.** To happen: What's *going on* here? **3.** To persevere; endure. **4.** In the theater, to make an entrance. **— to go (someone) better** *Informal* To surpass (someone). **— to go out 1.** To go to social gatherings, etc. **2.** To be extinguished, as a light. **3.** To become outdated, as fashions. **4.** To go on strike. **5.** To sympathize. My heart *goes out* to him. **— to go over 1.** To repeat; also, to rehearse. **2.** To examine carefully. **3.** *Informal* To succeed. **4.** To change sides or allegiance. **— to go through 1.** To search thoroughly. **2.** To undergo; suffer; endure. **3.** To run over, as a role. **4.** To spend. **5.** To be accepted or approved. **— to go through with** To perform to the finish; complete. **— to go together 1.** To be suitable; harmonize. **2.** To be sweethearts. **— to go under 1.** To be overwhelmed. **2.** To fail, as a business. **— to go up** To increase, as prices. **— to go with 1.** To harmonize with. **2.** To accompany. **3.** *Informal* To be sweethearts. **— to go without** To do or be without. **— to go without saying** To be taken for granted. **— to let go 1.** To release one's hold; set free. **2.** To abandon. **— to let oneself go** To be uninhibited. **— n. 1.** The act of going. **2.** *Informal* The capacity for action; He has plenty of *go*. **3.** *Informal* A try: to have a *go* at something. **4.** *Informal* A success: He made a *go* of it. **5.** *Informal* An agreement; bargain: It's a *go*. **— no go** *Informal* Useless; hopeless. **— on the go** *Informal* In constant motion; very busy. [OE *gān*]

go² (gō) *n.* A Japanese game resembling chess or checkers.

goad (gōd) *n.* **1.** A stick for urging on oxen, etc. **2.** Something that drives. — *v.t.* To drive; incite. [OE *gād*]

go-a·head (gō'ə·hed') *n.* A signal or permission to move ahead or proceed.

goal (gōl) *n.* **1.** Something toward which effort or movement is directed; an end or objective. **2.** The terminal point of a journey or race. **3.** In some games, the point to which the players try to bring the ball, puck, etc., to score; also, the scoring; also, the score made. [ME *gol*]

goal·ie (gō'lē) *n.* *Informal* A goalkeeper.

goal·keep·er (gōl'kē'pər) *n.* In hockey, soccer, etc., a player whose function is to prevent the ball or puck from passing over the goal for a score. Also **goal'tend'er.**

goat (gōt) *n.* **1.** A cud-chewing mammal related to the sheep and having hollow horns. **2.** A lecherous man. **3.** *Slang* One who is the butt of a joke; scapegoat. **— to get one's goat** *Slang* To move one to anger or annoyance. [OE *gāt*] **— goat'ish** *adj.* **— goat'ish·ly** *adv.* **— goat'ish·ness** *n.*

Goat (gōt) *n.* The constellation and sign of the zodiac Capricorn.

goat·ee (gō·tē') *n.* A man's short, pointed beard.

goat·herd (gōt'hûrd') *n.* One who tends goats.

goat·skin (gōt'skin') *n.* **1.** The hide of a goat. **2.** Leather made from this hide. **3.** Something made from this leather.

goat·suck·er (gōt'suk'ər) *n.* Any of numerous nocturnal, insectivorous birds, as the whippoorwill.

gob¹ (gob) *n.* *Informal* **1.** A piece or lump, as of a soft substance. **2.** *pl.* Great quantities. [< OF *gobe* mouthful]

gob² (gob) *n.* *Slang* A sailor of the U.S. Navy.

gob·bet (gob'it) *n.* **1.** A piece or hunk of raw meat. **2.** *Archaic* A large lump of food. [See GOB¹.]

gob·ble¹ (gob'əl) *v.* **bled, ·bling** *v.t.* **1.** To swallow (food) greedily. **2.** *U.S. Slang* To seize in a grasping manner. — *v.i.* **3.** To eat greedily. [< F *gover* to bolt, devour]

gob·ble² (gob'əl) *v.i.* **bled, ·bling** To make the throaty sound of a male turkey. — *n.* This sound. [Var. of GABBLE.]

gob·ble·dy·gook (gob'əl·dē·gŏŏk') *n.* *Informal* Involved, pedantic, repetitious, and pompous jargon. [Coined by M. Maverick, U.S. Congressman, about 1940]

gob·bler (gob'lər) *n.* A male turkey.

Gob·e·lin (gob'ə·lin, gō'bə·; *Fr.* gō·blaṅ') *n.* A rich tapestry made in Paris or Beauvais, France. [after *Gobelin*, name of its first creator]

go-be·tween (gō'bə·twēn') *n.* One who acts as an agent or mediator between other persons.

gob·let (gob'lit) *n.* **1.** A drinking vessel, typically with a base and stem. **2.** A large, festive shallow drinking cup. [< OF *gobel* a drinking cup]

gob·lin (gob'lin) *n.* In folklore, an ugly elf regarded as evil or mischievous. [< OF *gobelin*]

go·bo (gō'bō) *n.* *pl.* **·bos 1.** A portable shield placed around a microphone to keep out extraneous sounds. **2.** A screen for shielding the lens of a television camera from the direct rays of light. [Origin uncertain]

go·by (gō'bē) *n.* *pl.* **·by** or **·bies** Any of a family of fishes having ventral fins and a funnel-shaped suction disk. [< L < Gk. *kōbios*, a small fish]

go-by (gō′bī′) *n. Informal* An intentional slight.

go-cart (gō′kärt′) *n.* **1.** A small wagon for young children. **2.** A framework with rollers, designed to support babies learning to walk. **3.** A handcart.

god (god) *n.* **1.** One of various beings, usu. male, in mythology, primitive religions, etc., conceived of as immortal, as embodying a particular quality or having special powers over some phase of life. **2.** A statue, image, or symbol of such a being. **3.** Any person or thing much loved. [OE]

God (god) *n.* In monotheism, the ruler of life and the universe.

god-child (god′chīld′) *n. pl.* **-chil-dren** One whom a person sponsors at baptism, circumcision, etc.

god-dam (god′dam′) *interj.* A strong oath used to express anger, annoyance, surprise, etc. Also **God damn.** — *adj. & adv.* Goddamned.

god-damned (god′damd′) *adj.* Utterly detestable or outrageous. — *adv. Informal* To an extreme degree; very.

god-daugh-ter (god′dô′tər) *n.* A female godchild.

god-dess (god′is) **1.** A female deity. **2.** A woman or girl of extraordinary beauty.

god-fa-ther (god′fä′thər) *n.* A man who sponsors a child at its baptism. — *v.t.* To act as a godfather to.

god-fear-ing (god′fir′ing) *adj.* **1.** *Often cap.* Having reverence for God. **2.** Pious; devout.

god-for-sak-en (god′fər-sā′kən) *adj.* **1.** *Often cap.* Abandoned by God. **2.** Totally wicked. **3.** Wretched; desolate.

god-head (god′hed′) *n.* Goodhood; divinity.

God-head (god′hed′) *n.* The essential nature of God.

god-hood (god′hŏŏd) *n.* The state or quality of being divine.

Go-di-va (gə-dī′və) A legendary lady who agreed to ride naked through Coventry if her husband would remove oppressive taxes.

god-less (god′lis) *adj.* **1.** Having or believing in no god. **2.** Wicked. — **god′less-ly** *adv.* — **god′less-ness** *n.*

god-like (god′līk) *adj.* **1.** Befitting or like God or a god. **2.** Being of supreme excellence, beauty, etc. — **god′like′ness** *n.*

god-ly (god′lē) *adj.* **-li-er, -li-est** Filled with love for God. — **god′li-ness** *n.*

god-moth-er (god′muth′ər) *n.* A woman who sponsors a child at its baptism. — *v.t.* To act as a godmother to.

god-par-ent (god′pâr′ənt) *n.* A godfather or godmother.

God's acre A burying ground.

god-send (god′send′) *n.* Something received or acquired unexpectedly that is just what one needed or wanted.

god-son (god′sun′) *n.* A male godchild.

God-speed (god′spēd′) *n.* Best wishes for someone's journey or venture. [Shortened form of *God speed you*]

god-wit (god′wit) *n.* A shore bird resembling a curlew, with long legs and bill. [Origin uncertain]

go-get-ter (gō′get′ər) *n. U.S. Informal* A hustling, energetic, aggressive person.

gog-gle (gog′əl) *n.* **1.** *pl.* Spectacles designed to protect the eyes against dust, sparks, wind, etc. **2.** An erratic movement or bulging of the eyes. — *v.* **-gled, -gling** *v.i.* **1.** To roll the eyes erratically. **2.** Of the eyes, to move erratically, bulge, or be fixed in a stare. — *v.t.* **3.** To cause (the eyes) to goggle. — *adj.* Of the eyes, rolling erratically, staring, or bulging. [ME *gogelen* to look aside]

gog-gle-eyed (gog′əl-īd′) *adj.* Having eyes that goggle.

Goi-del-ic (goi-del′ik) *n.* The branch of the Celtic languages including Irish, the Gaelic of the Scottish Highlands, and Manx; Gaelic: distinguished from *Brythonic.* — *adj.* Of or pertaining to the Gaels or their languages. Also **Goi-dhel′ic.** [< OIrish *Goídel* Gael]

go-ing (gō′ing) *n.* **1.** The act of departing or moving; leaving. **2.** The condition of ground or roads as affecting walking, riding, racing, etc. **3.** *Informal* A condition influencing progress or activity. — **goings on** *Informal* Actions or behavior: used chiefly to express disapproval. — *adj.* **1.** That goes, moves, or works. **2.** Continuing to function; moving ahead: a *going* concern. **3.** In existence; available.

goi-ter (goi′tər) *n. Pathol.* Any abnormal enlargement of the thyroid gland, visible as a swelling in the front of the neck. Also **goi′tre.** [< F, ult. < L *guttur* throat] — **goi-trous** (goi′trəs) *adj.*

gold (gōld) *n.* **1.** A precious, yellow, metallic element (symbol Au) that is highly ductile and resistant to oxidation: also called *aurum.* See ELEMENT. **2.** Coin made of this metal. **3.** Wealth; riches. **4.** A bright yellow color. **5.** Something valuable, etc.: a heart of *gold.* — *adj.* **1.** Pertaining to, made of, containing, or like gold. **2.** Based on or redeemable in gold. [OE]

gold-brick (gōld′brik′) *U.S. Slang n.* One who shirks work: said esp. of soldiers. Also **gold′brick′er.** — *v.t. & v.i.* **1.** To shirk (work or duty). **2.** To cheat or swindle.

gold brick *Informal* Anything deceitfully substituted for an object of value.

gold digger **1.** One who or that which digs for gold. **2.** *U.S. Slang* A woman who uses feminine wiles to get money.

gold-en (gōl′dən) *adj.* **1.** Made of or containing gold. **2.** Bright yellow. **3.** Resembling gold. **4.** Happy, prosperous, etc. — **gold′en-ly** *adv.* — **gold′en-ness** *n.*

golden age **1.** In Greek and Roman legend, an early period marked by perfect innocence, peace, and happiness. **2.** Any period of prosperity or excellence.

golden anniversary A 50th anniversary.

golden calf **1.** A molten image worshiped by the Israelites. *Ex.* xxxii. **2.** Riches, as unduly prized.

gold-en-eye (gōl′dən-ī′) *n.* A large diving duck of America and Europe with yellow eyes.

golden glow A tall garden plant having many-rayed yellow flowers.

golden mean Moderation; avoidance of extremes.

gold-en-rod (gōl′dən-rod′) *n.* A widely distributed North American herb of the composite family, having small, usu. yellow flowers: the State flower of Alabama, Kentucky, and Nebraska.

golden rule The rule or principle of treating others as one wants to be treated. *Matt.* vii 12.

golden section In esthetics, the division of a line or figure so that the smaller length is to the larger as the larger is to the whole, roughly a ratio of 3 to 5.

Golden State Nickname of California.

golden wedding The 50th anniversary of a marriage.

gold-filled (gōld′fild′) *adj.* Filled with a base metal over which a thick covering of gold is laid.

gold-finch (gōld′finch′) *n.* **1.** A European finch having a yellow patch on each wing. **2.** An American finch of which the male, in the summer, has a yellow body with black tail.

gold-fish (gōld′fish′) *n. pl.* **-fish** or **-fish-es** A small carp, usu. golden in color, cultivated as an aquarium fish.

gold foil Thin sheets of gold, thicker than gold leaf.

gold leaf Sheets of gold hammered to extreme thinness, used in gilding, etc.

gold mine **1.** A mine producing gold ore. **2.** *Informal* Any source of great profit, riches, etc.

gold plate Vessels and utensils of gold, collectively.

gold reserve **1.** Gold held in reserve by the U.S. Treasury to protect U.S. promissory notes. **2.** The quantity of gold bullion or coin owned by the central bank of a country.

gold rush A mass movement of people to an area where gold has been discovered, as that to California in 1849.

gold-smith (gōld′smith′) *n.* One who makes or deals in articles of gold.

gold standard A monetary system based on gold of a specified weight and fineness as the unit of value.

go-lem (gō′lem, -ləm) *n.* In medieval Jewish legend, an automaton made to resemble a human being and given life by a magic incantation. [< Hebrew, embryo, monster]

golf (gôlf, golf) *n.* An outdoor game played on a large course with a small resilient ball and a set of clubs, the object being to direct the ball into a series of variously distributed holes (usually nine or eighteen) in as few strokes as possible. — *v.i.* To play golf. [Cf. dial. E (Scot.) *gowf* strike] — **golf′er** *n.*

golf club **1.** One of several slender clubs with wooden or metal heads, used in playing golf. **2.** An organization of golfers; also, the building and grounds used by them.

golf course The course over which a game of golf is played. Also **golf links.**

Gol-gi body (gôl′jē) *Biol.* A netlike structure of rod-shaped elements found in the cytoplasm of animal cells. Also **Golgi apparatus.** For illus. see CELL. [after Camillo *Golgi,* 1844–1926, Italian pathologist]

Gol-go-tha (gol′gə-thə) A place near Jerusalem where Jesus was crucified; Calvary. *Matt.* xxvii 33. [< LL < Gk. < Aramaic *gogolthā* skull]

Go-li-ath (gə-lī′əth) In the Bible, a giant Philistine slain by David with a sling. I *Sam.* xvii 4.

gol-li-wog (gol′ē-wog) *n.* **1.** A grotesque black doll. **2.** A grotesque person. Also **gol′li-wogg.** [after illustrations by Florence Upton (1895) for a series of children's books]

gol-ly (gol′ē) *interj.* An exclamation of mild surprise, impatience, etc. [Euphemistic alter. of GOD]

Go-mor-rah (gə-môr′ə, -mor′ə), **Go-mor-rha** See SODOM.

gon- Var. of GONO-.

-gon *combining form* Having (an indicated number of) angles: *pentagon.* [< Gk. *gōnia* angle]

gon-ad (gon′ad, gōn′ad) *n. Anat.* A male or female sex gland, in which the reproductive cells develop; an ovary or testis. — **gon′a-dal, go-na-di-al** (gō-nā′dē-əl), **go-nad-ic** (gō-nad′ik) *adj.*

gon-do-la (gon′də-lə, gon-dō′lə) *n.* **1.** A long, narrow, flat-bottomed Venetian boat propelled by one man with an oar at the stern. **2.** *U.S.* A large, flat-bottomed, river boat; also, a gondola car. **3.** *Aeron.* The car attached below a dirigible. [< Ital. < *gondolar* to rock]

gondola car *U.S.* A long, shallow, open freight car.

gon·do·lier (gon'də·lir') *n.* The boatman of a gondola.

gone (gôn, gon) Past participle of GO. — *adj.* **1.** Moved away; left. **2.** Beyond hope; ruined; lost. **3.** Dead; departed. **4.** Ended; past. **5.** Marked by faintness or weakness. **6.** Consumed; spent. **— far gone 1.** Exhausted; wearied. **2.** Almost ended or dead.

gon·er (gôn'ər, gon'-) *n. Informal* A person or thing that is close to death, ruining, or beyond all hope of saving.

gon·fa·lon (gon'fə·lən) *n.* A banner or ensign, usu. cut so as to end in streamers. Also **gon·fa·non** (gon'fə·nən). [< Ital. < OHG *gundfano* war banner]

gong (gông, gong) *n.* **1.** A heavy metal disk giving a deep, resonant tone when struck. **2.** A flat, saucerlike bell struck with a small mechanical hammer. [< Malay]

gonio- *combining form* Angle; corner. [< Gk. *gōnia* angle]

-gonium *combining form* Reproductive cell; seed. [< Gk. *gonos* seed]

gono- *combining form* Procreative; sexual. Also, before vowels, **gon.-** [< Gk. *gonos* seed]

gon·o·coc·cus (gon'ə·kok'əs) *n. pl.* **·coc·ci** (-kok'sī) The bacterium that causes gonorrhea. [< NL]

gon·or·rhe·a (gon'ə·rē'ə) *n. Pathol.* A contagious venereal infection, caused by the gonococcus, in which there is a purulent inflammation of the mucous membranes of the genitourinary tract. Also **gon'or·rhoe'a.** [< LL < Gk. < *gonos* seed + *rheein* to flow] **— gon'or·rhe'al** *adj.*

-gony *combining form* Production of; generation: *cosmogony.* [< L *-gonia* < Gk. < *gonos* seed, reproduction. Cf. -GENY.]

goo (gōō) *n. U.S. Slang* Any sticky substance.

goo·ber (gōō'bər) *n. U.S.* A peanut. Also **goober pea.** [? < Bantu *nguba*]

good (gōōd) *adj.* **bet·ter, best 1.** Morally excellent; virtuous. **2.** Honorable; worthy: a *good* reputation. **3.** Generous; loving; kind. **4.** Well-behaved; tractable. **5.** Proper; desirable: *good* manners. **6.** Favorable: a *good* opinion. **7.** Pleasant; agreeable. **8.** Having beneficial effects; helpful: *good* advice. **9.** Reliable; safe: a *good* investment. **10.** Suitable; qualified: a *good* man for the job. **11.** Skillful; expert: He is *good* at sports. **12.** Genuine; valid: a *good* excuse. **13.** Backed by sufficient funds: a *good* check. **14.** Excellent in quality or degree: *good* literature. **15.** Orthodox; conforming. **16.** Sufficient; ample: a *good* rest. **17.** Unspoiled; fresh: *good* meat. **18.** Healthy: *good* lungs. **19.** Satisfactory or appropriate: *good* weather for flying. **20.** Attractive or striking: She looks *good* in that hat. **21.** Great in amount; also, maximum; full. **— as good as** Practically; virtually: *as good as* done. **— good and** *Informal* Completely; very: *good and* hot. **— good for 1.** Capable of lasting for. **2.** *Informal* Able to pay, give, or produce. **— no good** Worthless. **— n. 1.** That which is fitting, etc. **2.** Benefit: for the *good* of mankind. **3.** That which is morally or ethically desirable. **— for good (and all)** For the last time; forever. **— to make good 1.** To be successful. **2.** To compensate for. **3.** To fulfill. **4.** To prove; substantiate. **— interj.** An exclamation of satisfaction. **— adv.** *Informal* Well. ◆ *Good* is gaining acceptance in informal usage as a substitute for *well* when reference is made to the functioning of a machine or the like, as in *This watch runs good.* In other contexts it is usually nonstandard. [OE *gōd*]

good book The Bible. Also **Good Book.**

good-by (gōōd'bī') *adj., n. & interj. pl.* **-bys** (-bīz') Farewell. Also **good'-bye'.** [Contraction of *God be with you*]

good-for-noth·ing (gōōd'fər·nuth'ing) *n.* A worthless person. — *adj.* Having no use or worth.

Good Friday The Friday before Easter, a day observed by Christians as a commemoration of the crucifixion of Jesus.

good·heart·ed (gōōd'här'tid) *adj.* Kind; charitable; generous. **— good'heart'ed·ly** *adv.* **— good'heart'ed·ness** *n.*

good-hu·mored (gōōd'hyōō'mərd, -yōō'-) *adj.* Having a cheerful temper or mood. **— good'-hu'mored·ly** *adv.*

good·ish (gōōd'ish) *adj.* **1.** Somewhat good. **2.** Rather big.

good-look·ing (gōōd'lōōk'ing) *adj.* Handsome.

good·ly (gōōd'lē) *adj.* **·li·er, ·li·est 1.** Having a pleasing appearance. **2.** Of fine quality. **3.** Large. **— good'li·ness** *n.*

good-na·tured (gōōd'nā'chərd) *adj.* Having a pleasant disposition; not easily provoked. Also **good-tempered** (gōōd'tem'pərd). **— good'-na'tured·ly** *adv.* **— good'-na'tured·ness** *n.*

good·ness (gōōd'nis) *n.* **1.** The state or quality of being good; esp.: **a** Excellence of character, morals, etc.; virtue. **b.** Generous and kindly feelings; benevolence. **2.** The best part. **3.** God: *Goodness* knows. **— Syn.** See VIRTUE.

goods (gōōdz) *n.pl.* **1.** Merchandise; wares. **2.** Fabric; material. **3.** Property, esp. when personal and movable.

Good Samaritan 1. In a New Testament parable, the only passer-by to aid a man who had been injured and robbed. *Luke* x 30–37. **2.** A humane, compassionate person.

Good Shepherd A name for Jesus. *John* x 11, 12.

good will 1. A desire for the well-being of others; benevolence. **2.** Cheerful, ready consent or willingness. **3.** Intangible assets in terms of prestige and friendly relations. Also **good·will** (gōōd'wil').

good·y (gōōd'ē) *n. pl.* **good·ies** *Informal* **1.** *Usu. pl.* Something tasty. **2.** A prissy person: also **good'y-good'y.** — *adj.* Good or pious in a weak, sentimental way: also **good'y-good'y.** — *interj.* A childish exclamation.

goof (gōōf) *Slang n.* **1.** A dull-witted person; dope. **2.** A mistake; blunder. — *v.i.* **1.** To blunder. — *v.t.* **2.** To make a mess of. **— to goof off** *Slang* To loaf.

goon (gōōn) *n. U.S. Slang* **1.** A thug or hoodlum, esp. one hired to break strikes. **2.** A stupid person. [after a character created by E. C. Segar, 1894–1938, U.S. cartoonist]

goose (gōōs) *n. pl.* **geese** (gēs) **1.** A subfamily of web-footed birds larger than ducks. **2.** The female: distinguished from *gander.* **3.** The flesh as food. **4.** A fool. **— to cook one's goose** *Informal* To spoil one's chances. [OE *gos*]

goose·ber·ry (gōōs'ber'ē, -bər·ē, gōōz'-) *n. pl.* **·ries 1.** The tart berry of a spiny shrub of the saxifrage family, used for jams, pies, etc. **2.** The shrub itself.

goose flesh A taut, prickling sensation in the skin. Also **goose bumps, goose pimples, goose skin.**

goose·foot (gōōs'fōōt') *n. pl.* **·foots** A plant, having green flowers, as beets and spinach.

goose·neck (gōōs'nek') *n.* Any of various mechanical devices curved like a goose's neck.

goose-step (gōōs'step') *v.i.* **-stepped, -step·ping** To march along or mark time kicking stiffly and sharply.

goose step 1. The action of goose-stepping. **2.** The manner of moving the legs in goose-stepping.

go·pher (gō'fər) *n. U.S. & Canadian* **1.** A burrowing American rodent with large cheek pouches. **2.** A North American ground squirrel. [< F *gaufre* honeycomb]

Gor·di·an knot (gôr'dē·ən) **1.** A legendary knot tied by Gordius, king of Phrygia, which an oracle predicted would be undone by a ruler of Asia. Alexander the Great cut it. **2.** Any difficulty solved only by drastic measures.

gore[1] (gôr, gōr) *n.* Blood that has been shed; esp., a copious amount of thickened, clotted, or dried blood. [OE *gor* dirt]

gore[2] (gôr, gōr) *v.t.* **gored, gor·ing** To pierce with the horns or tusks. [ME *goren*]

gore[3] (gôr, gōr) *n.* A triangular or tapering section set into a garment, sail, etc., for greater fullness. — *v.t.* **gored, gor·ing 1.** To cut into gore-shaped pieces. **2.** To furnish with gores. [OE *gāra* triangular piece of land]

gorge (gôrj) *n.* **1.** A narrow, deep ravine, esp. with a stream flowing through. **2.** The act of gorging. **3.** That which is gorged, as a greedily swallowed meal. **4.** Deep or violent disgust. **5.** A mass obstructing a passage. — *v.* **gorged, gorg·ing** *v.t.* **1.** To stuff with food. **2.** To swallow gluttonously. — *v.i.* **3.** To stuff oneself with food. [< OF < L *gurges* whirlpool] **— gorg'er** *n.*

gor·geous (gôr'jəs) *adj.* **1.** Dazzlingly colorful; brilliant. **2.** *Informal* Extremely beautiful, etc. [< OF *gorgias* elegant] **— gor'geous·ly** *adv.* **— gor'geous·ness** *n.*

gor·gon (gôr'gən) *n.* A terrifyingly ugly woman.

Gor·gon (gôr'gən) In Greek mythology, one of three sisters with serpents for hair, so terrifying that the sight of them turned the beholder to stone. [< L < Gk. < *gorgos* terrible] **— Gor·go·ni·an** (gôr·gō'nē·ən) *adj.*

Gor·gon·zo·la (gôr'gən·zō'lə) *n.* A strongly flavored, white Italian cheese. [after *Gorgonzola,* a town]

go·ril·la (gə·ril'ə) *n.* An African jungle ape, the largest and most powerful of the anthropoids, having a massive body, long arms, and tusklike canine teeth. [< NL < Gk., appar. < native name]

gorse (gôrs) *n. Brit.* Furze, a plant. [OE *gors(t)*]

go·ry (gôr'ē, gō'rē) *adj.* **·ri·er, ·ri·est 1.** Covered, stained with, or resembling gore. **2.** Full of bloodshed: a *gory* battle. **— gor'i·ly** *adv.* **— go'ri·ness** *n.*

gosh (gosh) *interj.* An exclamation. [Euphemism for GOD]

gos·hawk (gos'hôk', gôs'-) *n.* Any of various large, short-winged hawks formerly used in falconry. [OE *gōshafoc*]

Go·shen (gō'shən) **1.** The region in Egypt inhabited by the Israelites. *Gen.* xlv 10. **2.** Any place of peace or plenty.

gos·ling (goz'ling) *n.* A young goose. [< ON *gæslingr*]

gos·pel (gos'pəl) *n.* **1.** The teachings of the Christian church as originally preached by Jesus Christ and the apostles. **2.** A narrative of Christ's life and teachings, as in the first four books of the New Testament. **3.** Any information accepted as unquestionably true. **4.** A doctrine considered of major importance. [OE *godspell* good news]

Gos·pel (gos'pəl) *n.* Any of the first four books of the New Testament, attributed to Matthew, Mark, Luke, and John.

gos·sa·mer (gos'ə·mər) *n.* **1.** Fine strands of spider's silk, esp. when floating in the air. **2.** Any filmsy, delicate substance, as filmy, gauzelike fabric. — *adj.* Resembling gossamer; flimsy; unsubstantial: also **gos'sa·mer·ry** (-mər·ē) [< ME *gossomer* Indian summer, lit., goose summer]

gos·sip (gos/əp) *n.* **1.** Idle, often malicious talk, esp. about others. **2.** Informal talk or writing, as of personages. **3.** A person, esp. a woman, who indulges in idle talk. — *v.* **·siped** or **·sipped**, **·sip·ing** or **·sip·ping** *v.t.* & *v.i.* To talk idly; repeat as gossip. [OE *god* + *sibb* a relative] — **gos/sip·er** *n.*
gos·sip·y (gos/əp·ē) *adj.* **1.** Indulging in gossip. **2.** Chatty.
got (got) Past tense and past participle of GET. ◆ See note under GOTTEN.
Goth (goth, gôth) *n.* **1.** A member of a Germanic people that invaded the Roman Empire in the third to fifth centuries: including the Ostrogoths (**East Goths**) and Visigoths (**West Goths**). **2.** A barbarian. [< LL < Gk. *Gothoi* < Gothic]
Goth·am (goth/əm, gō/thəm; *Brit.* got/əm) A nickname for New York City. — **Goth/am·ite** (-īt) *n.*
Goth·ic (goth/ik) *adj.* **1.** Of or pertaining to the Goths or to their language. **2.** Of a style of architecture used in Europe, from about 1200 to 1500, characterized by pointed arches, ribbed vaulting, flying buttresses, etc. **3.** Denoting a literature usu. medieval in setting, and emphasizing the grotesque and the supernatural. **4.** Of the Middle Ages. **5.** Barbarous. — *n.* **1.** The extinct East Germanic language of the Goths. **2.** Gothic architecture or art. Also (for *adj. defs. 3–5*) **goth/ic.** — **Goth/i·cal·ly** *adv.*
goth·ic (goth/ik) *n.* *Sometimes cap.* *Printing* **a** *U.S.* Sans serif. **b** *Brit.* Black letter.
got·ten (got/n) Past participle of GET. ◆ *Gotten*, obsolete in British, is current in American English along with *got*.

GOTHIC ARCHITECTURE
Westminster Abbey, London,
13th-15th century.

gouache (gwosh) *n.* **1.** A method of painting using opaque colors mixed with water and gum. **2.** The opaque pigment so used. **3.** A painting done in this medium. [< F < Ital. *guazzo* a spray < L *aqua* water]
Gou·da cheese (gou/də, gōō/-) A mild, yellow cheese similar to Edam cheese. [after *Gouda*, town in the Netherlands]
gouge (gouj) *n.* **1.** A chisel having a scoop-shaped blade, used for woodcarving. **2.** A groove made as by a gouge. **3.** *U.S. Informal* The action of cutting as with a gouge. **4.** *U.S. Informal* The act of cheating. — *v.t.* **gouged**, **goug·ing** **1.** To cut or carve as with a gouge. **2.** To scoop, force, or tear out. **3.** *U.S. Informal* To cheat; esp., to charge exorbitant prices. [< F < LL *gulbia*] — **goug/er** *n.*
gou·lash (gōō/läsh, -lash) *n.* A stew made with beef or veal and vegetables, seasoned with paprika, etc.: also called *Hungarian goulash.* [< Hung. *gulyas* (*hus*) shepherd's (meat)]
gou·ra·mi (gōō·rä/mē, gōō/rə·mē) *n.* **1.** A large, freshwater fish of SE Asia. **2.** Any of various related fishes frequently kept in home aquariums, as the **dwarf gourami** and the **three-spot gourami.** [< Malay *gurami*]
gourd (gôrd, gōōrd) *n.* **1.** The fruit of any of various plants, having hard, durable shells. **2.** The fruit of the calabash tree. **3.** A utensil, as a ladle, made from the dried shell. [< F *gourde* < L *cucurbita* gourd]
gour·mand (gōōr/mənd, Fr. gōōr·män/) *n.* One who takes hearty pleasure in eating. [< F, glutton]
gour·met (gōōr·mā/, Fr. gōōr·me/) *n.* A fastidious devotee of good food and drink. [< F < OF, winetaster]
gout (gout) *n.* *Pathol.* A disease arising from a defect in metabolism and characterized by attacks of painful inflammation of the joints. [< F *goutte* drop < L *guta*]
gout·y (gou/tē) *adj.* **gout·i·er**, **gout·i·est** **1.** Of, from or like gout. **2.** Affected with gout; swollen. — **gout/i·ly** *adv.* — **gout/i·ness** *n.*
gov·ern (guv/ərn) *v.t.* **1.** To rule or direct by right or authority: to *govern* a nation. **2.** To guide or control the action of; influence. **3.** To serve as a rule or deciding factor for. **4.** To keep in check. — *v.i.* **5.** To exercise authority; rule. [< OF < L *gubernare* to steer < Gk.] — **gov/ern·a·ble** *adj.*

gov·ern·ance (guv/ər·nəns) *n.* Exercise of authority.
gov·ern·ess (guv/ər·nis) *n.* A woman employed in a private household to train and instruct children.
gov·ern·ment (guv/ərn·mənt, -ər-) *n.* **1.** The authoritative administration of the affairs of a nation, state, city, etc.; the jurisdiction exercised over the people; rule. **2.** The official governing body of a nation, community, etc. **3.** The system or established form by which a nation, etc., is controlled: democratic *government.* **4.** Any governed territory, district, etc. **5.** Control. — **gov·ern·men·tal** (guv/ərn·men/təl, -ər-) *adj.* — **gov/ern·men/tal·ly** *adv.*
gov·er·nor (guv/ər·nər) *n.* **1.** One who governs; as: **a** The elected chief executive of any State in the U.S. **b** An official appointed to administer a province, territory, etc. **c** *Brit.* The manager of a society, etc. **2.** *Mech.* A device for controlling speed, as of a motor. — **gov/er·nor·ship** *n.*
governor general *pl.* **governors general** **1.** *Often cap. Brit.* The chief representative of the Crown in a dominion or colony. **2.** A governor or governors under his jurisdiction. Also *Brit.* **gov/er·nor-gen/er·al.**
gown (goun) *n.* **1.** A woman's dress, esp. one for formal occasions: evening *gown.* **2.** Any long, loose garment. **3.** A long, loose outer robe worn by certain officials, scholars, clergymen, etc. — *v.t.* & *v.i.* To dress in a gown. [< OF < Med.L *gunna* a loose robe]
Graaf·i·an follicle (gräf/ē·ən) *Anat.* One of the numerous, small, round sacs embedded in the cortex of a mammalian ovary, each of which contains a single ovum. Also **Graafian vesicle.** [after Regnier de *Graaf*, 1641–73, Dutch physician and anatomist]
grab (grab) *v.* **grabbed**, **grab·bing** *v.t.* **1.** To grasp or seize suddenly. **2.** To take possession of by force or by dishonest means. — *v.i.* **3.** To make a sudden grasp. — *n.* **1.** The act of grabbing. **2.** That which is grabbed. **3.** A dishonest acquisition. **4.** A mechanical apparatus used to grasp and lift. [Cf. M Du. *grabben* to grip] — **grab/ber** *n.*
grab bag *U.S.* A bag or other receptacle filled with miscellaneous unidentified articles, from which one draws an object at random.
grab·ble (grab/əl) *v.i.* **·bled**, **·bling** **1.** To feel about with the hands; grope. **2.** To flounder; sprawl. [Cf. Du. *grabbelen*, freq. of *grabben* to grab]
gra·ben (grä/bən) *n.* *Geol.* A generally elongate depression of the land caused by the downward faulting of a portion of the earth's crust. [< G, ditch]
grace (grās) *n.* **1.** Beauty or harmony of motion, form, or manner. **2.** Any attractive quality. **3.** Service freely rendered; good will. **4.** The act of showing favor. **5.** Clemency; mercy. **6.** The perception of what is appropriate: He had the *grace* to go. **7.** An extension of time granted after a set date, as for paying a debt. **8.** A short prayer at a meal. **9.** *Theol.* **a** The love of God toward man. **b** The divine influence operating in man. **c** The state of being pleasing to God. **d** Any divinely inspired spiritual virtue or excellence. **10.** *Music* A note or notes added as an ornament. — **to be in the good** (or **bad**) **graces of** To be regarded with favor (or disfavor) by. — **with good** (or **bad**) **grace** In a willing (or grudging) manner. — *v.t.* **graced**, **grac·ing** **1.** To add grace and beauty to; adorn. **2.** To dignify; honor. **3.** *Music* To ornament with grace notes. [< OF < L *gratia* favor]
Grace (grās) *n.* A title or form of address for a duke, duchess, archbishop, or bishop: preceded by *Your, His, Her,* etc.
grace·ful (grās/fəl) *adj.* Characterized by grace, elegance, or beauty. — **grace/ful·ly** *adv.* — **grace/ful·ness** *n.*
grace·less (grās/lis) *adj.* **1.** Lacking grace, charm, or elegance. **2.** Having no sense of what is right or decent. — **grace/less·ly** *adv.* — **grace/less·ness** *n.*
grace note *Music* A note written smaller than those of the main text, played or sung as an embellishment.
Grac·es (grā/siz) In Greek mythology, three sister goddesses who confer grace, beauty, and joy. Also **the three Graces.**
gra·cious (grā/shəs) *adj.* **1.** Having or showing kindness, affability, etc. **2.** Condescendingly polite or indulgent. **3.** Full of compassion; merciful. **4.** Refined. — *interj.* An exclamation of mild surprise. [< OF < L *gratia* favor] — **gra/cious·ly** *adv.* — **gra/cious·ness** *n.*
grack·le (grak/əl) *n.* Any of various New World blackbirds having long tails. [< NL < L *graculus* jackdaw]
grad (grad) *n.* *U.S. Informal* A graduate.
gra·date (grā/dāt) *v.t.* & *v.i.* **·dat·ed**, **·dat·ing** **1.** To pass or cause to pass imperceptibly from one shade or degree to another, as color. **2.** To arrange or be arranged in grades.
gra·da·tion (grā·dā/shən) *n.* **1.** An orderly and gradual progression or arrangement according to size, quality, rank, etc. **2.** *Usu. pl.* A step, degree, or relative position in such a progression. **3.** The act of arranging in grades. [< F < L *gradus* step] — **gra·da/tion·al** *adj.*

grade (grād) *n.* **1.** A degree or step in any scale, as of quality, merit, rank, etc. **2.** A stage or degree in an orderly progression, classification, or process. **3.** A group or category. **4.** *U.S.* In education: **a** A level of progress in school, generally constituting a year's work. **b** The pupils in such a division. **c** *pl.* Elementary school: preceded by *the.* **5.** *U.S.* A rating or mark indicating the quality of school work done. **6.** In the U.S. armed forces, rank or rating. See below. **7.** The degree of inclination of a road, track, or other surface as compared with the horizontal **8.** A rise or elevation in a road, track, etc. — **to make the grade** *Informal* To succeed in any undertaking. — **up to grade** In accordance with an established standard of quality, progress, etc. — *v.* **grad·ed,** **grad·ing** *v.t.* **1.** To arrange or classify by grades or degrees; sort according to size, quality, type, etc. **2.** In education, to assign a grade to. **3.** To level or reduce (a road, ground, etc.) to a desirable gradient. **4.** To gradate. — *v.i.* To be of a specific grade or rank. [< F < L *gradus* step] **-grade** *combining form* **1.** Progressing or moving: *retrograde.* **2.** *Zool.* Walking in a specified manner. [< L *gradi* to walk]

grade crossing An intersection of two railroads, or a road and a railroad, at the same level: also called *level crossing.* **gra·der** (grā'dər) *n.* **1.** One who or that which grades. **2.** *U.S.* A pupil in a specified school grade: a third *grader.* **grade school** An elementary school. **gra·di·ent** (grā'dē·ənt) *n.* **1.** Degree of inclination, as in a slope; grade. **2.** An incline; ramp. **3.** *Physics* A rate of change in certain variable factors, as pressure, temperature, etc. — *adj.* Rising or descending gradually or by uniform degrees. [< L *gradiens, -entis,* ppr. of *gradi* to walk] **grad·u·al** (graj'ōō·əl) *adj.* **1.** Moving, changing, etc., slowly and by degrees. **2.** Having a slight degree of inclination; not abrupt or steep, as a slope. [< Med.L < L *gradus* a step] — **grad'u·al·ly** *adv.* — **grad'u·al·ness** *n.* **grad·u·ate** (*v.* graj'ōō·āt; *n. & adj.* graj'ōō·it) *v.* **·at·ed, ·at·ing** *v.i.* **1.** To receive a diploma or degree upon completion of a course of study. **2.** To change gradually or by degrees. — *v.t.* **3.** To grant an academic diploma or degree to (someone). **4.** To arrange or sort according to size, degree, etc. **5.** To mark (a thermometer, scale, etc.) in units or degrees;

TABLE OF COMPARATIVE GRADES (UNITED STATES ARMED SERVICES)

Grade	Army	Air Force	Marine Corps	Navy	Coast Guard
O–11	General of the Army	General of the Air Force	(no equivalent)	Admiral of the Fleet	(no equivalent)
O–10	General	General	General	Admiral	Admiral
O–9	Lieutenant General	Lieutenant General	Lieutenant General	Vice Admiral	Vice Admiral
O–8	Major General	Major General	Major General	Rear Admiral (upper half)	Rear Admiral (upper half)
O–7	Brigadier General	Brigadier General	Brigadier General	Rear Admiral (lower half)	Rear Admiral (lower half)
O–6	Colonel	Colonel	Colonel	Captain	Captain
O–5	Lieutenant Colonel	Lieutenant Colonel	Lieutenant Colonel	Commander	Commander
O–4	Major	Major	Major	Lieutenant Commander	Lieutenant Commander
O–3	Captain	Captain	Captain	Lieutenant	Lieutenant
O–2	1st Lieutenant	1st Lieutenant	1st Lieutenant	Lieutenant (Junior Grade)	Lieutenant (Junior Grade)
O–1	2nd Lieutenant	2nd Lieutenant	2nd Lieutenant	Ensign	Ensign
W–4	Chief Warrant Officer	SAME	SAME	SAME	SAME
W–3	Chief Warrant Officer				
W–2	Chief Warrant Officer				
W–1	Warrant Officer				
E–9	Sergeant Major Specialist 9	Chief Master Sergeant	Master Gunnery Sergeant Sergeant Major	Master Chief Petty Officer	Master Chief Petty Officer
E–8	Master Sergeant First Sergeant Specialist 8	Senior Master Sergeant	Master Sergeant First Sergeant	Senior Chief Petty Officer	Senior Chief Petty Officer
E–7	Sergeant First Class Platoon Sergeant Specialist 7	Master Sergeant	Gunnery Sergeant	Chief Petty Officer	Chief Petty Officer
E–6	Staff Sergeant Specialist 6	Technical Sergeant	Staff Sergeant	Petty Officer First Class	Petty Officer First Class
E–5	Sergeant Specialist 5	Staff Sergeant	Sergeant	Petty Officer Second Class	Petty Officer Second Class
E–4	Corporal Specialist 4	Airman First Class	Corporal	Petty Officer Third Class	Petty Officer Third Class
E–3	Private First Class	Airman Second Class	Lance Corporal	Seaman	Seaman
E–2	Private	Airman Third Class	Private First Class	Seaman Apprentice	Seaman Apprentice
E–1	Recruit	Recruit	Private	Seaman Recruit	Seaman Recruit

TABLE OF COMPARATIVE GRADES

Royal Canadian Navy	Canadian Army	Royal Canadian Air Force
Admiral of the Fleet	Field-Marshal	Marshal of the Royal Canadian Air Force
Admiral	General	Air Chief Marshal
Vice-Admiral	Lieutenant-General	Air Marshal
Rear-Admiral	Major-General	Air Vice-Marshal
Commodore	Brigadier	Air Commodore
Captain	Colonel	Group Captain
Commander	Lieutenant-Colonel	Wing Commander
Lieutenant-Commander	Major	Squadron Leader
Lieutenant	Captain	Flight Lieutenant
Commanding Officer		
Sub-Lieutenant	Lieutenant	Flying Officer
Acting Sub-Lieutenant	Second Lieutenant	Pilot Officer
Midshipman		
Chief Petty Officer, First Class	Warrant Officer, First Class	Warrant Officer, First Class
Chief Petty Officer, Second Class	Warrant Officer, Second Class	Warrant Officer, Second Class
Petty Officer, First Class	Staff Sergeant	Flight Sergeant
Petty Officer, Second Class	Sergeant	Sergeant
Leading Seaman	Corporal	Corporal
Able Seaman	Private	Leading Aircraftman
Ordinary Seaman (trained)	Private (trained)	Aircraftman, First Class
Ordinary Seaman (entry)	Private (entry)	Aircraftman, Second Class
Ordinary Seaman (under 17 years)	Private (under 17 years)	Aircraftman, Second Class (under 17 years)

calibrate. — *n.* **1.** One who has been granted a diploma or degree by an educational institution. **2.** A beaker or similar vessel marked in units or degrees, used for measuring liquids, etc. — *adj.* **1.** Denoting a graduate student. **2.** Pertaining to or intended for such a student. [< Med.L < L *gradus* step, degree]

graduate student A student who has received a college degree and is working toward a more advanced degree.

grad·u·a·tion (graj′ōō·ā′shən) *n.* **1.** The act of graduating, or the state of being graduated. **2.** The ceremony of granting diplomas or degrees. **3.** A mark or division in a graduated scale; also, such divisions collectively.

Grae·cism (grē′siz·əm) *n.* A Grecism.

Grae·cize (grē′sīz) *v.t. & v.i.* **-cized, -ciz·ing** To Grecize.

Graeco- See GRECO-.

graft[1] (graft, gräft) *n.* **1.** A shoot (the cion) inserted into a prepared slit in a tree or plant (the stock) so as to become a living part of it. **2.** A plant, fruit, etc., obtained as a result of this operation. **3.** *Surg.* A piece of viable tissue transplanted to another part of the body or to the body of another individual. — *v.t.* **1.** To insert (a cion) into a tree or plant. **2.** To obtain (a plant, fruit, etc.) by grafting. **3.** *Surg.* To transplant (a piece of viable tissue) as a graft. **4.** To attach or incorporate, as by grafting: to *graft* new ideas on outworn concepts. — *v.i.* **5.** To insert or transplant grafts. **6.** To be or become grafted. [< OF < LL < Gk. *graphein* to write] — **graft′age** *n.* — **graft′er** *n.*

graft[2] (graft, gräft) *U.S. n.* **1.** The act of getting personal advantage or profit by dishonest or unfair means, esp. through one's political connections. **2.** Anything thus gained. — *v.t.* **1.** To acquire by graft. — *v.i.* **2.** To practice graft. [Cf. dial. E *graft* work, livelihood] — **graft′er** *n.*

gra·ham (grā′əm) *adj.* Made of unsifted whole-wheat flour. [after Sylvester *Graham*, 1794–1851, U.S. vegetarian]

grail (grāl) *n.* In medieval legend, the cup or dish used at the Last Supper by Jesus Christ, in which some of the blood shed at the Crucifixion was caught. Also called *Holy Grail*. [< OF < Med.L *gradalis*]

grain (grān) *n.* **1.** A hard seed or kernel; esp., that of any of the cereal plants, as wheat, oats, etc. **2.** The harvested seeds of these plants. **3.** These plants collectively. **4.** Any very small, hard mass. **5.** The smallest possible quantity of anything: a *grain* of truth. **6.** The smallest unit of weight used in several systems in the U.S. and Great Britain. Abbr. *g., G., gr.* See table front of book. **7.** The direction or arrangement of the fibers or fibrous particles in various kinds of wood; also, the resulting markings or pattern. **8.** The side of a piece of leather from which the hair has been removed; also, the characteristic texture or patterned markings of this side. **9.** A paint, stamp, or pattern used to imitate the characteristic markings of leather, wood, etc. **10.** The comparative size or texture of the particles composing a substance, surface, or pattern: marble of fine *grain*. **11.** The direction of cleavage of a mineral substance, as diamond, coal, etc. **12.** A state of crystallization. **13.** Natural disposition or temperament. — **against the grain** Contrary to one's temperament or inclinations. — *v.t.* **1.** To form into grains; granulate. **2.** To paint or stain in imitation of the grain of wood, marble, etc. **3.** To give a roughened or granular appearance or texture to. **4.** In leathermaking: **a** To scrape the hair from. **b** To soften or raise the grain or pattern of. — *v.i.* **5.** To form grains. [< OF < L *granum* seed] — **grain′er** *n.* — **grain′less** *adj.*

grain alcohol Ethanol.

grain elevator *U.S.* A building designed to store grain.

grain·y (grā′nē) *adj.* **grain·i·er, grain·i·est** **1.** Full of or consisting of grains or kernels. **2.** Having a granular texture. **3.** Resembling the grain in wood. — **grain′i·ness** *n.*

gram (gram) *n.* The unit of mass or weight in the metric system, equivalent to 15.432 grains, or one thousandth of a kilogram. Also **gramme.** Abbr. *g, g., gm., gr.* See table front of book. [< F < LL < Gk. *gramma* small weight]

-gram[1] *combining form* Something written or drawn: *telegram.* [< Gk. *gramma* letter, writing < *graphein* to write]

-gram[2] *combining form* A gram: used in the metric system: *kilogram.* [< GRAM]

gram atom *Chem.* The quantity of an element, expressed in grams, that is equal to the atomic weight of that element. Also **gram′-a·tom′ic weight** (-ə·tom′ik).

gram·mar (gram′ər) *n.* **1.** The scientific study and description of the morphology and syntax of a language or dialect. **2.** A system of morphologic and syntactic rules for the regulation of a given language. **3.** A treatise or book dealing with grammatical matters. **4.** Speech or writing considered with regard to current standards of correctness. **5.** The elements of any science or art, or a book or treatise dealing with them. [< OF < L < Gk. *grammatikē* (*technē*) literary (art) < *grammata* literature]

gram·mar·i·an (grə·mâr′ē·ən) *n.* A specialist in grammar.

grammar school **1.** An elementary school. **2.** *Brit.* A secondary school.

gram·mat·i·cal (grə·mat′i·kəl) *adj.* **1.** Of or pertaining to grammar. **2.** Conforming to the usage of standard speech or writing. — **gram·mat′i·cal·ly** *adv.* — **gram·mat′i·cal·ness** *n.*

gram molecule *Chem.* The quantity of a compound, expressed in grams, that is equal to the molecular weight of that compound: also called *mole.* Also **gram′-mo·lec′u·lar weight** (-mə·lek′yə·lər).

gram·o·phone (gram′ə·fōn) *n.* *Chiefly Brit.* A record player. [< *Gramophone*, a trade name]

gram·pus (gram′pəs) *n. pl.* **-pus·es** A large, dolphinlike cetacean of Atlantic and Pacific waters. [Alter. of obs. *grapeys* < OF < Med.L *crassus piscis* fat fish]

gran·a·ry (gran′ər·ē, grā′nər-) *n. pl.* **-ries** **1.** A storehouse for threshed grain. **2.** A region where grain grows in abundance. [< L *granum* grain]

grand (grand) *adj.* **1.** Impressive because of great size, extent, or splendor. **2.** In literature and the arts, lofty or sublime in subject or treatment. **3.** Majestic; stately. **4.** Worthy of respect because of age, experience, or dignity: often with *old:* the *grand* old man of politics. **5.** Of high or highest rank or official position: a *grand* duke; the *grand* jury. **6.** Principal; main: the *grand* ballroom. **7.** Characterized by pomp or luxury. **8.** Conscious of one's wealth or importance. **9.** Comprehensive; all-inclusive: the *grand* total. **10.** Having a family relationship one degree more distant than: used in combination: *grandson.* **11.** *Informal* Highly satisfactory; excellent. — *n.* **1.** A grand piano. **2.** *U.S. Slang* A thousand dollars. [< OF < L *grandis*] — **grand′ly** *adv.* — **grand′ness** *n.*

gran·dam (gran′dam, -dəm) *n. Archaic* A grandmother; an old woman. Also **gran′dame** (-dām, -dəm). [< AF *graund dame*]

Grand Army of the Republic An organization of Union veterans of the Civil War, founded in 1866. Abbr. *G.A.R.*

grand·aunt (grand′ant′, -änt′) *n.* A great-aunt.

Grand Canyon State Nickname of Arizona.

grand·child (grand′chīld′) *n. pl.* **-chil·dren** (-chil′drən) A child of one's son or daughter.

grand·dad (gran′dad′) *n. Informal* Grandfather. Also **grand′dad·dy.**

grand·daugh·ter (gran′dô′tər, grand′-) *n.* A daughter of one's son or daughter.

grand duchess **1.** The wife or widow of a grand duke. **2.** A woman who is sovereign of a grand duchy. **3.** Formerly, in Russia, a daughter of a czar.

grand duchy The territory under the rule of a grand duke or grand duchess.

grand duke **1.** The sovereign of a grand duchy, holding a rank just below king. **2.** Formerly, in Russia, a ruler of a principality; later, a son or grandson of a czar.

gran·dee (gran·dē′) *n.* **1.** A Spanish or Portuguese nobleman of the highest rank. **2.** Any person of high rank or great importance. [< Sp. *grande* great]

gran·deur (gran′jər, -jōōr) *n.* **1.** The quality or condition of being grand; magnificence. **2.** Greatness of character.

grand·fa·ther (grand′fä′thər) *n.* **1.** The father of one's father or mother. **2.** An ancestor. — **grand′fa′ther·ly** *adv.*

grandfather clock A clock having a pendulum and enclosed in a tall cabinet. Also **grandfather's clock.**

gran·dil·o·quent (gran·dil′ə·kwənt) *adj.* Speaking in or characterized by a pompous or bombastic style. [< L *grandis* great + *loqui* to speak] — **gran·dil′o·quence** *n.*

gran·di·ose (gran′dē·ōs, gran′dē·ōs′) *adj.* **1.** Producing an effect of grandeur; imposing. **2.** Pretentiously grand; pompous; bombastic. [< F < Ital. < L *grandis* great] — **gran′di·ose′ly** *adv.* — **gran·di·os·i·ty** (gran′dē·os′ə·tē) *n.*

grand jury A body of persons called to hear complaints of the commission of offenses and to ascertain whether there is prima-facie evidence for an indictment.

Grand Lama The Dalai Lama.

grand·ma (grand′mä′, gran′mä′, gram′mä, gram′ə) *n. Informal* Grandmother. Also **grand·ma·ma** (grand′mə·mä′, -mä′mə), **grand′mam·ma′.**

grand mal (grän mäl′) *Pathol.* A type of epilepsy characterized by severe convulsions and loss of consciousness: distinguished from *petit mal.* [< F, lit., great sickness]

grand·moth·er (grand′muth′ər) *n.* **1.** The mother of one's father or mother. **2.** A female ancestor.

grand·neph·ew (grand′nef′yōō, -nev′-, gran′-) *n.* A son of one's nephew or niece.

grand·niece (grand′nēs′, gran′-) *n.* A daughter of one's nephew or niece.

Grand Old Party In U.S. politics, the Republican Party.

grand opera A form of opera, usu. having a serious and complex plot, in which the entire text is set to music.

grand·pa (grand′pä′, gram′pä′, gram′pə) *n. Informal* Grandfather. Also **grand′pa·pa′** (-pə·pä′, -pä′pə).

grand·par·ent (grand′pâr′ənt, gran′-) *n.* A grandmother or grandfather.

grand piano A large piano having strings arranged horizontally in a curved, wooden case.

grand·sire (grand′sīr′, -sər) *n. Archaic* 1. A grandfather. 2. An ancestor. 3. Any venerable old man.

grand slam In bridge, the winning, by the declarer, of all thirteen tricks in a round of play; also, a bid to do so.

grand·son (grand′sun′, gran′-) *n.* A son of one's child.

grand·stand (grand′stand′, gran′-) *n.* A raised series of seats for spectators at a racetrack, sports stadium, etc.

grand tour 1. Formerly, an extended journey through the chief cities of continental Europe. 2. Any extended trip.

grand·un·cle (grand′ung′kəl) *n.* A great-uncle.

grange (grānj) *n.* 1. *Often cap. U.S.* Any subsidiary lodge or branch of the Grange. 2. *Brit.* A farm, with its dwelling house, barns, etc.; esp., the residence of a gentleman farmer. [< AF, OF < Med.L < L *granum* grain]

Grange (grānj) *n.* The order of Patrons of Husbandry, an association of U.S. farmers founded in 1867.

grang·er (grān′jər) *n.* 1. *Often cap. U.S.* A member of a grange. 2. A farmer. — **grang′er·ism** *n.*

grani- *combining form* Grain. [< L *granum* grain]

gran·ite (gran′it) *n.* 1. A hard, coarse-grained, igneous rock composed principally of quartz, feldspar, and mica, much used as a building material, in sculpture, etc. 2. Great hardness, firmness, endurance, etc. [< Ital. < L *granum* seed] — **gra·nit·ic** (grə·nit′ik) *adj.*

Granite State Nickname of New Hampshire.

gran·ite·ware (gran′it·wâr′) *n.* 1. A variety of ironware coated with hard enamel. 2. A type of fine, hard pottery.

gra·niv·o·rous (grə·niv′ər·əs) *adj.* Feeding on grain.

gran·ny (gran′ē) *n. pl.* **·nies** 1. Grandmother: used familiarly. 2. An old woman. 3. *Informal* A fussy, interfering person. 4. A granny knot. Also **gran′nie.**

granny knot A knot resembling the square knot but crossed in such a way as to form an insecure fastening. For illus. see KNOT. Also **granny's knot, granny's bend.**

grant (grant, gränt) *v.t.* 1. To confer or bestow, as a privilege, charter, etc. 2. To allow (someone) to have; give, as permission. 3. To accede to; yield to, as a request. 4. To admit as true, as for the sake of argument. 5. To transfer (property), esp. by deed. — *n.* 1. The act of granting. 2. That which is granted, as a piece of property, a sum of money, or a special privilege. — **to take for granted** 1. To assume to be true. 2. To accept as one's due. [< AF, ult. < L *credere* to believe]

gran·tee (gran·tē′, grän-) *n.* The recipient of a grant.

grant·or (gran′tər, gran·tôr′, grän-) *n.* The person by whom a grant is made.

gran·u·lar (gran′yə·lər) *adj.* 1. Composed of, like, or containing grains or granules. 2. Having a granulated surface. — **gran·u·lar′i·ty** (-lar′ə·tē) *n.* — **gran′u·lar·ly** *adv.*

gran·u·late (gran′yə·lāt) *v.t. & v.i.* **·lat·ed, ·lat·ing** 1. To make or become granular; form into grains. 2. To become or cause to become roughened, as by the formation of granules. — **gran′u·la′tion** *n.* — **gran′u·la′tive** *adj.*

gran·ule (gran′yool) *n.* A small grain or particle; tiny pellet. [< LL *granulum*, dim. of L *granum* grain]

grape (grāp) *n.* 1. One of the smooth-skinned, juicy, edible berries borne in clusters by various climbing vines or small shrubs, cultivated in many species as a fruit and for making wine. 2. Any of the vines bearing these berries. 3. A dark, purplish blue color. 4. Grapeshot. [< OF, bunch of grapes]

grape·fruit (grāp′frōot′) *n.* 1. A large, round citrus fruit having a pale yellow rind and tart, juicy pulp. 2. The tree bearing this fruit.

grape·shot (grāp′shot′) *n.* A kind of shot consisting of a cluster of iron balls, formerly fired from cannons.

grape·stone (grāp′stōn′) *n.* A seed of a grape.

grape sugar Dextrose.

grape·vine (grāp′vīn′) *n.* 1. Any of the climbing vines that bear grapes. 2. *U.S.* A secret or unofficial means of relaying information, usu. from person to person.

graph (graf, gräf) *n.* A diagram representing variations in the relationship between two or more factors by means of a series of connected points, or by bars, curves, lines, etc. — *v.t.* To express or represent in the form of a graph.

-graph *combining form* 1. That which writes or records: *seismograph.* 2. A writing or record: *autograph.* [< F < L < Gk. *graphein* to write]

-grapher *combining form* Forming nouns of agency corresponding to words in *-graph* or *-graphy*: *photographer.*

graph·ic (graf′ik) *adj.* 1. Describing in full detail; vivid. 2. Of, pertaining to, or illustrated by graphs or diagrams. 3. Pertaining to, consisting of, or expressed by writing. 4. Of, pertaining to, or characteristic of the graphic arts. Also **graph′i·cal.** [< L < Gk. *graphē* writing] — **graph′·i·cal·ly** or **graph′ic·ly** *adv.*

-graphic *combining form* Forming adjectives corresponding to nouns ending in *-graph*: *photographic.* Also **-graphical.**

graphic arts 1. Those visual arts involving the use of lines or strokes on a flat surface, as painting, drawing, engraving, etc. 2. In recent usage, those arts that involve impressions or reproductions taken from blocks, plates, type, or the like.

graph·ite (graf′īt) *n.* A soft, black variety of carbon having a metallic luster and a slippery texture, used as a lubricant and in making pencils, etc. Also called *black lead.* [< G < Gk. *graphein* to write + -ITE¹] — **gra·phit′ic** (-fit′ik) *adj.*

grapho- *combining form* Of or pertaining to writing. Also, before vowels, **graph-.** [< Gk. *graphein* to write]

graph·ol·o·gy (gra·fol′ə·jē) *n.* The study of handwriting, esp. as a method of estimating the writer's character. — **graph·o·log·i·cal** (graf′ə·loj′i·kəl) *adj.* — **graph·ol′o·gist** *n.*

-graphy *combining form* 1. A writing, recording, or process of representation: *biography, photography.* 2. A descriptive science: *petrography.* [< Gk. *graphein* to write]

grap·nel (grap′nəl) *n.* 1. A small anchor with several flukes at the end of the shank. 2. Any of various devices consisting of a hook or arrangement of hooked parts, used to grasp and hold objects. [ME *grapenel*, dim. of OF *grapin* hook]

grap·ple (grap′əl) *v.* **·pled, ·pling** *v.t.* 1. To seize or take hold of with or as with a grapnel. — *v.i.* 2. To struggle in close combat, as in wrestling. 3. To struggle or contend: with *with.* 4. To use a grapnel. — *n.* 1. A grapnel. 2. The act of grappling. 3. A grip or close hold, as in wrestling. [< OF *grappil* grapnel] — **grap′pler** *n.*

grappling iron A grapnel. Also **grappling hook.**

grasp (grasp, gräsp) *v.t.* 1. To seize firmly with or as with the hand; grip. 2. To grab. 3. To comprehend. — *v.i.* 4. To make the motion of grasping or clutching. — **to grasp at** 1. To try to seize. 2. To accept eagerly, as an offer or suggestion. — *n.* 1. The act of grasping; also, a grip of the hand. 2. The power or ability to seize; reach. 3. Absolute domination: the tyrant's *grasp.* 4. Intellectual comprehension or mastery. [ME *graspen,* metathetic var. of *grapsen* < LG] — **grasp′a·ble** *adj.* — **grasp′er** *n.*

grasp·ing (gras′ping, gräs′-) *adj.* 1. Greedy. 2. That grasps. — **grasp′ing·ly** *adv.* — **grasp′ing·ness** *n.*

grass (gras, gräs) *n.* 1. Any plant of a large family having rounded and hollow jointed stems, narrow, sheathing leaves, flowers borne in spikes or panicles, and hard, grainlike seeds. 2. Herbage generally; esp., the herbaceous plants eaten by grazing animals. 3. Any of numerous plants with grasslike foliage. 4. Ground on which grass is growing. 5. Grazing ground; pasture. 6. *pl.* Stalks or sprays of grass. — **to let the grass grow under one's feet** To let opportunity go by. — *v.t.* 1. To cover with grass or turf. 2. To feed with grass. 3. To spread (cloth, etc.) on the grass, for bleaching. — *v.i.* 4. To graze. 5. To become grassy. [OE *græs*]

grass·hop·per (gras′hop′ər, gräs′-) *n.* 1. Any of several insects, as the locust and katydid, with powerful hind legs adapted for leaping, many species of which are destructive to crops and vegetation. 2. *U.S. Slang* Any small, light airplane, used for dusting crops, military observation, etc.

grass·land (gras′land′, gräs′-) *n.* 1. Land reserved for pasturage or mowing. 2. Land in which grasses are the predominant vegetation, as the American prairies.

grass·roots (gras′rōots′, -rŏŏts, gräs′-) *U.S. Informal n.pl.* The common people, thought of as having practical and highly independent views or interests. — *adj.* 1. Coming from, pertaining to, or directed toward such people. 2. Basic. Also **grass′-roots′.**

grass widow A woman who is divorced, separated, or lives apart from her husband.

grass widower A man who is divorced, separated, or lives apart from his wife.

grass·y (gras′ē, gräs′ē) *adj.* **grass·i·er, grass·i·est** 1. Covered with or abounding in grass. 2. Of or containing grass. 3. Like grass. — **grass′i·ly** *adv.* — **grass′i·ness** *n.*

grate¹ (grāt) *v.* **grat·ed, grat·ing** *v.t.* 1. To reduce to fine pieces or powder by rubbing against a rough or sharp surface. 2. To rub or grind to produce a harsh sound. — *v.i.* 3. To have an irritating effect: with *on* or *upon.* 4. To produce a harsh sound. [< OF *grater* < Gmc.] — **grat′er** *n.*

grate² (grāt) *n.* 1. A framework of crossed or parallel bars placed over a window, drain, etc. 2. A metal framework to hold burning fuel in a furnace, etc. 3. A fireplace. — *v.t.* **grat·ed, grat·ing** To fit with a grate or grates. [< Ital. < L *cratis* lattice]

grate·ful (grāt′fəl) *adj.* 1. Thankful for benefits or kindnesses; appreciative; also, expressing gratitude. 2. Giving pleasure; welcome; agreeable. [< L *gratus* pleasing] — **grate′ful·ly** *adv.* — **grate′ful·ness** *n.*

grat·i·fi·ca·tion (grat′ə·fə·kā′shən) *n.* 1. The act of gratifying, or the state of being gratified. 2. That which gratifies.

grat·i·fy (grat′ə·fī) *v.t.* **·fied, ·fy·ing** 1. To give pleasure or satisfaction to. 2. To satisfy, humor, or indulge. — **Syn.** See SATISFY. [< MF < L *gratus* pleasing + *facere* to make] — **grat′i·fi′er** *n.* — **grat′i·fy′ing** *adj.* — **grat′i·fy′ing·ly** *adv.*

grat·ing[1] (grā'ting) *n.* **1.** An arrangement of bars or slats used as a cover or screen. **2.** *Physics* A diffraction grating.
grat·ing[2] (grā'ting) *adj.* **1.** Harsh or disagreeable in sound; rasping. **2.** Irritating; annoying. — **grat'ing·ly** *adv.*
gra·tis (grā'tis, grat'is) *adv.* Without requiring payment. — *adj.* Free of charge. [< L, var. of *gratiis* out of kindness]
grat·i·tude (grat'ə·tōōd, -tyōōd) *n.* Appreciation for favors, kindness, etc. [< F < L *gratus* pleasing]
gra·tu·i·tous (grə·tōō'ə·tas, -tyōō'-) *adj.* **1.** Given or obtained without payment or return; free. **2.** Lacking cause or justification; uncalled-for. [< L *gratuitus*] — **gra·tu'i·tous·ly** *adv.* — **gra·tu'i·tous·ness** *n.*
gra·tu·i·ty (grə·tōō'ə·tē, -tyōō'-) *n. pl.* **·ties** A gift, usu. of money, given in return for services rendered; tip.
gra·va·men (grə·vā'men) *n. pl.* **·vam·i·na** (-vam'ə·nə) **1.** *Law* The burden or gist of a charge. **2.** A grievance. [< LL < L < *gravis* heavy]
grave[1] (grāv) *adj.* **1.** Of great importance; weighty: a *grave* responsibility. **2.** Filled with danger; critical: a *grave* situation. **3.** Solemn and dignified; sober. **4.** Somber, as colors. **5.** *Music* Slow and solemn. **6.** *Phonet.* **a** Having the tonal quality indicated by the grave accent; also, marked with this accent. **b** Unaccented, as a syllable. — *n.* A mark (ˋ) used in French to indicate open *e*, or to make a distinction, as in *ou*, *où*: also **grave accent**. [< F < L *gravis* heavy] — **grave'ly** *adv.* — **grave'ness** *n.*
grave[2] (grāv) *n.* **1.** A burial place for a dead body, usu. a hole in the earth. **2.** A sepulcher; tomb. **3.** Death. **4.** Any place or state regarded as an end or final loss. — **to have one foot in the grave** **1.** To be very old or frail. **2.** To be dangerously ill. — **to turn (over) in one's grave** To be presumably uneasy after one's death because of the behavior of the living. [OE *græf*] — **grave'less** *adj.*
grave[3] (grāv) *v.t.* **graved, grav·en, grav·ing** **1.** To carve or sculpt. **2.** To engrave or incise. **3.** To impress firmly, as on the memory. [OE *grafan* to dig] — **grav'er** *n.*
grave·dig·ger (grāv'dig'ər) *n.* One who digs graves.
grav·el (grav'əl) *n.* **1.** A mixture of small, rounded pebbles or fragments of stone, often with sand. **2.** *Pathol.* **a** A deposit of sandlike crystals formed in the kidneys. **b** The disease of which these are characteristic. — *v.t.* **grav·eled** or **·elled, grav·el·ing** or **·el·ling** **1.** To cover or pave with gravel. **2.** To confound; baffle. [< OF *gravele* beach] — **grav'el·ly** *adj.*
grave·stone (grāv'stōn') *n.* A stone marking a grave.
grave·yard (grāv'yärd') *n.* A burial place; cemetery.
graveyard shift *U.S. Informal* A work shift during the night, generally beginning at midnight.
grav·i·met·ric (grav'ə·met'rik) *adj. Chem.* **1.** Determined by weight, as the constituents of a compound. **2.** Pertaining to measurement by weight. Also **grav'i·met'ri·cal.** — **grav'i·met'ri·cal·ly** *adv.*
gra·vim·e·try (grə·vim'ə·trē) *n.* The measurement of weight, density, or specific gravity.
grav·i·tate (grav'ə·tāt) *v.i.* **·tat·ed, ·tat·ing** **1.** To move or tend to move as a result of the force of gravity. **2.** To move as though from a force or natural impulse. **3.** To sink or settle to a lower level. [< NL < L *gravis* heavy] — **grav'·i·tat'er** *n.* — **grav'i·ta·tive** *adj.*
grav·i·ta·tion (grav'ə·tā'shən) *n.* **1.** *Physics* The force whereby any two bodies attract each other. **2.** The act or process of gravitating. — **grav'i·ta'tion·al** *adj.* — **grav'i·ta'tion·al·ly** *adv.*
grav·i·ty (grav'ə·tē) *n. pl.* **·ties** **1.** *Physics* Gravitation as manifested by the tendency of material bodies to fall toward the center of the earth. **2.** Gravitation in general. **3.** Weight; heaviness. **4.** Great importance; seriousness. **5.** Solemnity; dignified reserve. **6.** Lowness of pitch, as of music. [< F < L *gravitas* heaviness]
gra·vure (grə·vyōōr', grāv'yər) *n.* **1.** A process of printing or engraving by photographically prepared plates. **2.** A plate, usu. copper or wood, used in this process; also, a print made from such a plate. [< F < *graver* to engrave]
gra·vy (grā'vē) *n. pl.* **·vies** **1.** The juice, exuded by cooking meat; also, a sauce made from it. **2.** *U.S. Slang* Money or profit easily acquired. [ME *gravey*]
gray (grā) *adj.* **1.** Of a color produced by a mixture of black and white. **2.** Dark or dull, as from insufficient light; dismal. **3.** Having gray hair. **4.** Characteristic of old age; old. — *n.* **1.** A color consisting of a mixture of black and white. **2.** Something gray, as an animal. **3.** The state of being unbleached or undyed: said of fabrics. — *v.t. & v.i.* To make or become gray. Also, *esp. Brit.*, **grey**. [OE *græg*] — **gray'ly** *adv.* — **gray'ness** *n.*
gray·beard (grā'bird') *n.* An old man.
gray·ling (grā'ling) *n. pl.* **·ling** or **·lings** **1.** A troutlike fish having a large, colorful dorsal fin. **2.** Any of several North American butterflies having gray and brown markings.

gray matter **1.** *Anat.* The reddish gray nervous tissue of the brain and spinal cord, composed largely of nerve cells and nerve fibers. **2.** *Informal* Brains; intelligence.
graze[1] (grāz) *v.* **grazed, graz·ing** *v.i.* **1.** To feed upon growing grass or herbage. — *v.t.* **2.** To put (livestock) to feed on grass, pasturage, etc. **3.** To tend at pasture. **4.** To cause (a field, etc.) to be fed on. [OE *græs* grass] — **graz'er** *n.*
graze[2] (grāz) *v.* **grazed, graz·ing** *v.t.* **1.** To brush against lightly in passing. **2.** To scrape or abrade slightly: The bullet *grazed* his arm. — *v.i.* **3.** To move so as to scrape lightly against something. — *n.* **1.** A grazing. **2.** A scrape made by grazing. — **graz'ing·ly** *adv.*
graz·ing (grā'zing) *n.* Pasturage.
gra·zi·o·so (grä·tsyō'sō) *Music adj.* Graceful; elegant. — *adv.* Gracefully; elegantly. [Ital.]
grease (*n.* grēs; *v.* grēs, grēz) *n.* **1.** Animal fat in a soft state, as after melting or rendering. **2.** Any thick fatty or oily substance, as a lubricant. — *v.t.* **greased, greas'ing** To smear or lubricate with grease or fat. [< OF < L *crassus* fat] — **greas'er** *n.*
grease paint A waxy substance used for theater make-up.
grease·wood (grēs'wōōd') *n.* A stunted, prickly shrub of the SW U.S. Also **grease'bush.**
greas·y (grē'sē, -zē) *adj.* **greas·i·er, greas·i·est** **1.** Smeared or spotted with grease. **2.** Containing grease or fat; oily. **3.** Appearing or feeling like grease; smooth; slick. — **greas'i·ly** *adv.* — **greas'i·ness** *n.*
great (grāt) *adj.* **1.** Very large in bulk, volume, expanse, etc.; immense; big. **2.** Large in quantity or number: a *great* army. **3.** Prolonged in duration or extent; a *great* distance. **4.** More than ordinary; considerable: *great* pain. **5.** Of unusual importance; momentous; also, renowned: a *great* victory. **6.** Marked by nobility of thought, action, etc.: *great* deeds. **7.** Unusual in ability or achievement; highly gifted. **8.** Impressive; remarkable. **9.** Favored; popular. **10.** Absorbed or enthusiastic; also, proficient; skillful. **11.** Being of a relationship more remote by a single generation: used in combination: *great-uncle.* — *n.* **1.** Those who are eminent, powerful, etc.: preceded by *the.* **2.** *Usu. pl. Informal* An outstanding person: one of baseball's *greats.* — *adv. Informal* Very well; splendidly. [OE *grēat*] — **great'ness** *n.*
great-aunt (grāt'ant', -änt') *n.* An aunt of either of one's parents; grandaunt.
Great Bear The constellation Ursa Major.
great circle *Geom.* A circle formed on the surface of a sphere by a plane that passes through the center of the sphere.
Great Dane One of a breed of large, smooth-haired dogs.
great·er (grāt'ər) Comparative of GREAT. — *adj. Usu. cap.* Comprising a (specified) city and suburbs: *Greater* London.
great-grand·child (grāt'grand'chīld') *n.* A child of a grandchild.
great-grand·daugh·ter (grāt'gran'dô'tər) *n.* A daughter of a grandchild.
great-grand·fa·ther (grāt'grand'fä'thər) *n.* The father of a grandparent.
great-grand·moth·er (grāt'grand'muth'ər) *n.* The mother of a grandparent.
great-grand·par·ent (grāt'grand'pâr'ənt) *n.* The father or mother of a grandparent.
great-grand·son (grāt'grand'sun') *n.* A son of a grandchild.
great gross Twelve gross, a unit of quantity.
great·heart·ed (grāt'här'tid) *adj.* **1.** Noble or generous in spirit; magnanimous. **2.** High-spirited; courageous.
great horned owl A large owl having tufts of feathers that resemble horns, found chiefly in North America.
great·ly (grāt'lē) *adv.* **1.** To a great degree; very much. **2.** In a way characteristic of or befitting greatness.
great-neph·ew (grāt'nef'yōō, -nev'-) *n.* A grandnephew.
great-niece (grāt'nēs') *n.* A grandniece.
Great Rebellion The Civil War in England. See table under WAR.
Great Russian *adj.* Of or pertaining to Great Russia. — *n.* **1.** A native of Great Russia. **2.** The East Slavic language of the Great Russians.
great seal *Often cap.* The chief seal of a government.
great-un·cle (grāt'ung'kəl) *n.* An uncle of either of one's parents; granduncle.
Great White Way The brightly lighted theater district of New York City near Broadway and Times Square.
grebe (grēb) *n.* Any of a family of swimming and diving birds having partially webbed feet and very short tails; esp., the **pied-billed grebe** or **dabchick**. [< F *grèbe*]
Gre·cian (grē'shən) *adj.* Greek. — *n.* **1.** A Greek. **2.** One learned in the language or literature of Greece.
Gre·cism (grē'siz·əm) *n.* **1.** A Greek idiom. **2.** The style or spirit of Greek art, culture, etc. Also spelled *Graecism.*
Gre·cize (grē'sīz) *v.* **·cized, ·ciz·ing** *v.t.* **1.** To make Greek

in form, character, etc.; Hellenize. **2.** To translate into Greek. — *v.i.* **3.** To adopt or imitate Greek customs, speech, etc. Also spelled *Graecize*. [< F < L *Graecus* a Greek]

Greco- *combining form* Greek. Also spelled *Graeco-*.

Greco-Persian Wars See table for WAR.

Gre·co-Ro·man (grē′kō·rō′mən) *adj.* Of or pertaining to Greece and Rome together: also *Graeco-Roman*.

greed (grēd) *n.* Selfish and grasping desire for possession, esp. of wealth; avarice, covetousness. [< GREEDY]

greed·y (grē′dē) *adj.* **greed·i·er, greed·i·est 1.** Excessively eager for acquisition or gain; covetous; grasping. **2.** Having an excessive appetite for food and drink; voracious; gluttonous. [OE *grǣdig*] — **greed′i·ly** *adv.* — **greed′i·ness** *n.*

Greek (grēk) *adj.* **1.** Of or pertaining to Greece, or its people, language, or culture. **2.** Of or pertaining to the Greek Church. — *n.* **1.** One of the people of ancient or modern Greece. **2.** The Indo-European language of ancient or modern Greece. — **Late Greek** The Greek language from about A.D. 200 to 600. — **Medieval Greek** The Greek language of the Byzantine period, from 600 to 1500. — **Modern Greek** The language of Greece since 1500: also called *Romaic*, especially in its spoken form. **3.** Language or information that is unintelligible. **4.** *U.S. Slang* A member of a fraternity. [< L < Gk. *Graikos* Greek]

Greek Catholic 1. A member of the Eastern Orthodox Church. **2.** A member of a Uniat Church.

Greek Church 1. The Eastern Church. **2.** Loosely, the Eastern Orthodox Church,

Greek fire An incendiary substance first used by the Byzantine Greeks in naval warfare.

Greek Orthodox Church The established church of Greece, a branch of the Eastern Orthodox Church.

green (grēn) *adj.* **1.** Of the color between blue and yellow in the spectrum, as in the foliage of growing plants. **2.** Covered with or abounding in grass, growing plants, etc. **3.** Consisting of edible green leaves or plant parts: a *green* salad. **4.** Not fully developed; immature. **5.** Not cured or ready for use. **6.** Lacking training or skill; inexperienced. **7.** *adv.* — *n.* **1.** The color between blue and yellow in the spectrum, characteristic of the foliage of growing plants. **2.** A green pigment, dye, or substance. **3.** Green material, clothing, etc. **4.** A smooth grassy area or plot: the village *green.* **5.** In golf, the area of smooth, clipped grass surrounding the hole. **6.** *pl.* Freshly cut leaves, branches, vines, etc. **7.** *pl.* The edible leaves and stems of certain plants, as spinach, beets, etc. — *v.t. & v.i.* To make or become green. [OE *grēne*] — **green′ly** *adv.* — **green′ness** *n.*

green algae A class of algae in which the cells containing chlorophyll are dominant.

green·back (grēn′bak′) *n.* One of a class of U.S. notes used as legal tender.

green bean A string bean.

green·bri·er (grēn′brī′ər) A thorny vine having small, greenish flowers.

green·er·y (grē′nər·ē) *n. pl.* **·er·ies 1.** Green plants; verdure. **2.** A place where plants are grown or kept.

green-eyed (grēn′īd′) *adj.* **1.** Having green eyes. **2.** Jealous.

green·gage (grēn′gāj′) *n.* A variety of sweet plum.

green·gro·cer (grēn′grō′sər) *n. Brit.* A shopkeeper dealing in fresh vegetables, fruit, etc. — **green′gro′cer·y** (-sər·ē) *n.*

green·horn (grēn′hôrn′) *n.* **1.** An inexperienced person; beginner. **2.** One easily imposed upon or duped.

green·house (grēn′hous′) *n.* A heated shed or building constructed chiefly of glass, in which tender or exotic plants are grown or sheltered; hothouse.

green·ing (grē′ning) *n.* One of several varieties of apples having a green skin when ripe.

green·ish (grē′nish) *adj.* Somewhat green.

green light 1. A green signal light indicating that vehicles, pedestrians, etc., may proceed. **2.** *Informal* Approval or authorization to proceed.

Green Mountain State Nickname of Vermont.

green pepper 1. The unripe fruit of the sweet pepper. **2.** The unripe fruit of the red pepper, used in pickling.

green·room (grēn′rōōm′, -rōōm′) *n.* The waiting room in a theater used by performers when they are off-stage.

green soap A soap made from linseed oil and the hydroxides of potassium and sodium, used for skin diseases.

green·sward (grēn′swôrd′) *n.* Turf green with grass.

green tea Tea from tea leaves that have been heated, withered, and rolled without undergoing fermentation.

green thumb A special knack for making plants thrive.

green vitriol Copperas.

Greenwich mean time Time as reckoned from the meridian at Greenwich, England. Also **Greenwich time.**

green·wood (grēn′wood′) *n.* A forest in leaf.

greet (grēt) *v.t.* **1.** To express friendly recognition or courteous respect to, as upon meeting. **2.** To meet or receive in a specified manner. **3.** To present itself to; be evident to:

The warmth of a fire *greeted* us. — *v.i.* **4.** To offer a salutation upon meeting. [OE *grētan*] — **greet′er** *n.*

greet·ing (grē′ting) *n.* **1.** The act of one who greets; salutation; welcome. **2.** A friendly or complimentary message.

gre·gar·i·ous (gri·gâr′ē·əs) *adj.* **1.** Habitually associating with others, as in flocks, herds, or groups. **2.** Enjoying or seeking others; sociable. **3.** Of or characteristic of a flock, crowd, or aggregation. **4.** *Bot.* Growing in compact groups; clustered. [< L *grex, gregis* flock] — **gre·gar′i·ous·ly** *adv.* — **gre·gar′i·ous·ness** *n.*

Gre·go·ri·an (gri·gôr′ē·ən, -gō′rē-) *adj.* Of, pertaining to, or associated with Pope Gregory I or Pope Gregory XIII.

Gregorian Chant The system of plainsong associated with the liturgical reforms made by Pope Gregory I.

grem·lin (grem′lin) *n.* A mischievous, imaginary creature jokingly said to cause mechanical trouble in airplanes; also, any similar gnomelike troublemaker. [Origin uncertain]

gre·nade (gri·nād′) *n.* **1.** A small explosive or incendiary bomb designed either to be thrown by hand or projected from a rifle. **2.** A glass container that shatters and diffuses its volatile contents when thrown. [< F, pomegranate]

gren·a·dier (gren′ə·dir′) *n.* **1.** Formerly, a soldier assigned to throw grenades. **2.** A member of a special corps or regiment, as the British Grenadier Guards. [See GRENADE.]

gren·a·dine¹ (gren′ə·dēn′, gren′ə·dēn) *n.* A silk, wool, or cotton fabric of loose, open weave. [< F, ? after *Granada*]

gren·a·dine² (gren′ə·dēn′, gren′ə·dēn) *n.* A syrup made from pomegranates or red currants, used for flavoring.

Gresh·am's law (gresh′əmz) *Econ.* The principle stating that of two forms of currency, the less valuable form tends to drive the other from circulation, owing to the hoarding of the preferred form. Also **Gresham's theorem.** [after Sir Thomas Gresham, 1519–79, English merchant]

grew (grōō) Past tense of GROW.

grew·some (grōō′səm) See GRUESOME.

grey (grā) See GRAY.

grey·hound (grā′hound′) *n.* **1.** One of a breed of tall, slender, smooth-coated dogs noted for their speed. **2.** A fast ocean vessel. Also, *Rare, grayhound.* [OE *grīghund*]

grid (grid) *n.* **1.** An arrangement of regularly spaced parallel or intersecting bars, wires, etc.; grating; gridiron. **2.** A system of intersecting parallel lines dividing a map, chart, etc., into squares. **3.** A network of high-tension wires transmitting electric power over a wide area. **4.** *Electr.* A perforated or grooved metal plate in a storage cell or battery. **5.** *Electronics* An electrode, between the cathode and anode of an electron tube that controls the flow of electrons. [Back formation < GRIDIRON]

GREYHOUND
(28 inches high at shoulder)

grid·dle (grid′l) *n.* A flat pan used for cooking pancakes, etc. — *v.t.* **·dled, ·dling** To cook on a griddle. [< AF *gredil*]

grid·dle·cake (grid′l·kāk′) *n.* A pancake baked on a griddle: also, *U.S., flapjack.*

grid·i·ron (grid′ī′ərn) *n.* **1.** A football field. **2.** A metal grating set in a frame, used for broiling meat, fish, etc. **3.** Something resembling a cooking gridiron. [ME *gredire*, var. of *gredile* griddle]

grief (grēf) *n.* **1.** Deep sorrow or mental distress caused by loss, remorse, affliction, etc. **2.** A cause of such sorrow. — **to come to grief** To end badly; meet with disaster; fail.

grief-strick·en (grēf′strik′ən) *adj.* Overwhelmed by grief.

griev·ance (grē′vəns) *n.* **1.** A real or imaginary wrong regarded as cause for complaint or resentment. **2.** A feeling of resentment arising from a sense of having been wronged.

grieve (grēv) *v.* **grieved, griev·ing** *v.t.* **1.** To cause to feel sorrow or grief. — *v.i.* **2.** To feel sorrow or grief. [< L *gravis* heavy] — **griev′er** *n.* — **griev′ing·ly** *adv.*

griev·ous (grē′vəs) *adj.* **1.** Causing grief, sorrow, or misfortune. **2.** Meriting severe punishment or censure: a *grievous* sin. **3.** Expressing grief or sorrow. **4.** Causing physical suffering. — **griev′ous·ly** *adv.* — **griev′ous·ness** *n.*

grif·fin (grif′ən) *n.* In Greek mythology, a creature with the head and wings of an eagle and the body of a lion: also spelled *gryphon*. Also **grif′fon.** [< OF < L < Gk. *gryps*]

grift·er (grif′tər) *n. U.S. Slang* A petty swindler or confidence man; esp., one who operates a dishonest game of chance at a carnival or circus. [? < GRAFTER]

grill (gril) *v.t.* **1.** To cook on a gridiron or similar utensil. **2.** To subject to or torment with extreme heat. **3.** *U.S. Informal* To question or cross-examine persistently and searchingly. — *v.i.* **4.** To undergo grilling. — *n.* **1.** A gridiron or similar cooking utensil. **2.** A meal or portion of grilled food. **3.** A grillroom. **4.** A grille. [< F *gril,* var. of *grille* grating] — **grilled** *adj.* — **grill′er** *n.*

gril·lage (gril′ij) *n.* A framework of crossed timbers or steel beams serving as a foundation, esp. on soft ground.

grille (gril) *n.* A grating, often of decorative, open metalwork, used as a screen, divider, etc.: also spelled *grill.* [< OF, ult. < L *craticula,* dim. of *cratis* grating, lattice]

grill·room (gril'rŏŏm', -rŏŏm') *n.* A restaurant or eating place where grilled foods are prepared and served.

grilse (grils) *n. pl.* **grilse** (*Rare* **grils·es**) A young salmon that has returned for the first time from the sea to fresh water. [Origin unknown]

grim (grim) *adj.* **grim·mer, grim·mest 1.** Stern or forbidding in appearance or character. **2.** Unyielding; relentless. **3.** Sinisterly ironic; ghastly: a *grim* joke. **4.** Savagely destructive; fierce. [OE] **— grim'ly** *adv.* **— grim'ness** *n.*

gri·mace (gri·mās') *n.* A distorted facial expression, usu. indicative of pain, annoyance, disgust, etc. **—** *v.i.* **·maced, ·mac·ing** To distort the features; make faces. [< MF < Sp. *grimazo,* prob. < Gmc.] **— gri·mac'er** *n.*

gri·mal·kin (gri·mal'kin, -môl'-) *n.* **1.** A cat, particularly an old female cat. **2.** A shrewish old woman.

grime (grīm) *n.* Dirt, esp. soot, rubbed into or coating a surface. **—** *v.t.* **grimed, grim·ing** To make dirty; begrime. [< Flemish *grijm*]

grim·y (grī'mē) *adj.* **grim·i·er, grim·i·est** Full of or covered with grime; dirty. **— grim'i·ly** *adv.* **— grim'i·ness** *n.*

grin (grin) *v.* **grinned, grin·ning** *v.i.* **1.** To smile broadly. **2.** To draw back the lips so as to show the teeth, as in a snarl or a grimace of pain, rage, etc. **—** *v.t.* **3.** To express by grinning. **—** *n.* **1.** The act of grinning. **2.** A facial expression produced by grinning, as a broad smile. **— Syn.** See SMILE. [OE *grennian*] **— grin'ner** *n.* **— grin'ning·ly** *adv.*

grind (grīnd) *v.* **ground, grind·ing** *v.t.* **1.** To reduce to fine particles, as by crushing; pulverize. **2.** To sharpen, polish, or wear down by friction or abrasion. **3.** To rub together or press down with a scraping or turning motion: to *grind* the teeth. **4.** To oppress; crush. **5.** To operate by or as by turning a crank, as a coffee mill. **6.** To produce by or as by grinding. **7.** To produce mechanically or laboriously: followed by *out.* **8.** To teach or instill with great and constant effort: with *into.* **—** *v.i.* **9.** To perform the operation or action of grinding. **10.** To undergo grinding. **11.** To scrape; grate. **12.** *Informal* To study or work steadily and laboriously. **—** *n.* **1.** The act of grinding. **2.** The sound made by grinding. **3.** A specified state of pulverization, as of coffee. **4.** *Informal* Prolonged and laborious work or study. **5.** *U.S. Informal* A student who studies constantly. [OE *grindan*] **— grind'ing·ly** *adv.*

grind·er (grīn'dər) *n.* **1.** One who grinds; esp., one who sharpens tools, etc. **2.** A device used for grinding, as a coffee mill, etc. **3.** A molar. **4.** *pl. Informal* The teeth.

grind·stone (grīnd'stōn') *n.* **1.** A flat, circular stone rotated on an axle, used for sharpening tools, abrading, polishing, etc. **2.** A millstone. **— to keep** (or **have**) **one's nose to the grindstone** To work hard and continuously.

grin·go (grĭng'gō) *n. pl.* **·gos** In Latin America, a foreigner, esp. one from any country where English is the official language: an offensive term. [< Am. Sp., gibberish]

grip[1] (grip) *n.* **1.** The act of seizing and holding firmly. **2.** The ability to seize or maintain a hold; grasping power. **3.** Control; domination. **4.** Mental or intellectual grasp. **5.** The manner of grasping or holding something, as a tool or implement. **6.** A distinctive handclasp, as one used by members of a fraternal organization in greeting one another. **7.** The handle of an object. **8.** A device or mechanical part that seizes or holds something. **9.** The strength of the hand in grasping. **10.** *U.S.* A suitcase or valise. **11.** *U.S.* A stagehand. **— to come to grips 1.** To struggle in hand-to-hand combat. **2.** To deal decisively or energetically, as with a problem. **—** *v.* **gripped** or **gript, grip·ping** *v.t.* **1.** To seize; grasp firmly. **2.** To capture, as the mind or imagination; attract and hold the interest of. **3.** To join or attach securely with a grip or similar device. **—** *v.i.* **4.** To take firm hold. **5.** To capture the imagination or attention. [OE *gripan* to seize] **— grip'per** *n.* **— grip'ping·ly** *adv.*

grip[2] (grip) *n.* Influenza.

gripe (grīp) *v.* **griped, grip·ing** *v.t.* **1.** *U.S. Informal* To annoy; anger. **2.** To cause sharp pain or cramps in the bowels of. **—** *v.i.* **3.** *U.S. Informal* To complain; grumble. **4.** To cause or experience sharp pains in the bowels. **—** *n.* **1.** *U.S. Informal* A grievance. **2.** *Usu. pl.* Spasmodic pain in the bowels. [OE *gripan*] **— grip'er** *n.*

grippe (grip) *n.* Influenza. [< F *gripper* to seize] **— grip'py** *adj.*

grip·sack (grip'sak') *n. U.S.* A traveling bag; valise.

gris·ly (griz'lē) *adj.* **·li·er, ·li·est** Inspiring horror; gruesome. [OE *grislic*] **— gris'li·ness** *n.*

grist (grist) *n.* **1.** Grain that is to be ground; also, a batch of such grain. **2.** Ground grain. **— grist for one's mill** Something that can be used to one's advantage. [OE *grindan* to grind]

gris·tle (gris'əl) *n.* Cartilage, esp. in meat. [OE]

gris·tly (gris'lē) *adj.* **1.** Pertaining to or resembling gristle. **2.** Consisting of or containing gristle. **— gris'tli·ness** *n.*

grist·mill (grist'mil') *n.* A mill for grinding grain.

grit (grit) *n.* **1.** Small, rough, hard particles, as of sand, stone, etc. **2.** A hard, coarse-grained sandstone. **3.** Resolute spirit; pluck. **—** *v.* **grit·ted, grit·ting** *v.t.* **1.** To grind or press together, as the teeth. **2.** To cover with grit. **—** *v.i.* **3.** To make a grating sound. [OE *grēot*]

grits (grits) *n.pl.* **1.** Coarse meal. **2.** *U.S.* Coarsely ground hominy: also called *hominy grits.* [OE *grytte*]

grit·ty (grit'ē) *adj.* **·ti·er, ·ti·est 1.** Like, containing, or consisting of grit. **2.** Courageous; plucky. **— grit'ti·ly** *adv.* **— grit'ti·ness** *n.*

griz·zle (griz'əl) *v.t. & v.i.* **·zled, ·zling** To become or cause to become gray. **—** *n.* **1.** The color gray, esp. when produced by intermixed hairs, specks, etc., of black and white. **2.** Gray or graying hair. **—** *adj.* Gray. [< OF *gris* gray] **— griz'zled** *adj.*

griz·zly (griz'lē) *adj.* **·zli·er, ·zli·est** Grayish; grizzled. **—** *n. pl.* **·zlies** A grizzly bear.

grizzly bear A large bear of western North America.

groan (grōn) *v.i.* **1.** To utter a low, prolonged sound of or as of pain, disapproval, etc. **2.** To make a noise resembling such a sound; creak harshly. **3.** To suffer, as from cruel or unfair treatment: usu. with *under* or *beneath.* **4.** To be overburdened. **—** *v.t.* **5.** To utter or express with or as with a groan. **—** *n.* **1.** A low moaning or murmuring sound expressing pain, derision, etc. **2.** A creaking or roaring sound. [OE *grānian*] **— groan'er** *n.* **— groan'ing·ly** *adv.*

groat (grōt) *n.* **1.** A former English silver coin, worth fourpence. **2.** A tiny sum. [< MDu. *groot,* orig., large]

groats (grōts) *n.pl.* Hulled, usu. coarsely crushed grain, as barley, oats, or wheat. [OE *grotan*]

gro·cer (grō'sər) *n.* One who deals in foodstuffs and various household supplies. [< OF < Med.L < LL *grossus* gross]

gro·cer·y (grō'sər·ē, grōs'rē) *n. pl.* **·cer·ies 1.** *U.S.* A store in which foodstuffs and household supplies are sold. **2.** *pl.* The merchandise sold by a grocer.

grog (grog) *n.* Any alcoholic liquor, esp. rum, mixed with water. [after Old *Grog,* nickname of Admiral E. Vernon, 1684–1757, who first rationed it to English sailors]

grog·gy (grog'ē) *adj.* **·gi·er, ·gi·est** *Informal* **1.** Dazed or not fully conscious, as from a blow or exhaustion. **2.** Drunk. [< GROG] **— grog'gi·ly** *adv.* **— grog'gi·ness** *n.*

grog·ram (grog'rəm) *n.* A loosely woven, sometimes stiffened, fabric of coarse silk, or silk mixed with mohair or wool. [< F *gros grain* coarse grain]

groin (groin) *n.* **1.** *Anat.* The fold or crease formed at the juncture of either of the thighs with the abdomen. **2.** *Archit.* The curve formed by the intersection of two vaults. For illus. see VAULT. **—** *v.t.* To build with or form into groins. [? OE *grynde* abyss, hollow]

groin rib *Archit.* A rib covering a groin.

grom·met (grom'it) *n.* **1.** A reinforcing eyelet of metal or other material, through which a rope, cord, or fastening may be passed. **2.** *Naut.* A ring of rope or metal used to secure the edge of a sail. [< F < *gourmer* to curb]

GROIN RIBS IN
GROIN VAULTING

groom (grŏŏm, grŏŏm) *n.* **1.** A man or boy employed to tend horses; stableman. **2.** A bridegroom. **3.** One of several honorary functionaries in the British royal household. **—** *v.t.* **1.** To attend to the neatness or appearance of. **2.** To take care of (a horse) by cleaning, currying, etc. **3.** *U.S.* To prepare by giving special training or attention to, as for a political office. [ME *grom.*]

grooms·man (grŏŏmz'mən, grŏŏms'-) *n. pl.* **·men** (-mən) The best man at a wedding.

groove (grŏŏv) *n.* **1.** A long, narrow indentation or furrow cut into a surface, esp. by a tool. **2.** Any narrow depression, channel, or rut. **3.** A fixed, settled routine or habit. **4.** *Anat.* Any of various furrows or depressions in an organ or part of the body. **— in the groove** *U.S. Slang* Operating or performing expertly or smoothly. **—** *v.t.* **grooved, groov·ing** To form a groove in. [< Du. *groeve*]

groov·y (grŏŏ'vē) *adj.* **groov·i·er, groov·i·est** *U.S. Slang* Satisfying; delightful; great: a *groovy* feeling.

grope (grōp) *v.* **groped, grop·ing** *v.i.* **1.** To feel about with or as with the hands, as in the dark; feel one's way. **2.** To search bewilderedly or uncertainly. **—** *v.t.* **3.** To seek out or find by or as by groping. **—** *n.* The act of groping. [OE *grāpian*] **— grop'er** *n.* **— grop'ing·ly** *adv.*

gros·beak (grōs'bēk') *n.* Any of various finchlike birds having a short, stout beak. [< F < *gros* large + *bec* beak]

gros·grain (grō'grān) *n.* A strong, horizontally corded silk or rayon fabric, usu. woven as ribbon.

gross (grōs) *adj.* **1.** Undiminished by deductions; total: distinguished from *net*: *gross* income. **2.** Conspicuously bad or wrong: *gross* errors. **3.** Excessively fat or large. **4.**

Coarse in composition, structure, or texture. **5.** Coarse or obscene in character. **6.** Insensitive; dull. **7.** Dense; thick. **8.** *Anat.* or *Pathol.* Visible without the aid of a microscope: a *gross* lesion. — *n. pl.* **gross** for def. 1, **gross·es** for def. 2 A unit of quantity comprising twelve dozen. **2.** The entire amount; bulk. — **in the gross. 1.** In bulk; all together. **2.** Wholesale. — *v.t.* To earn or produce as total income or profit, before deductions for expenses. etc. [< OF < LL *grossus* thick] — **gross'ly** *adv.* — **gross'ness** *n.*

gross weight Total weight. Abbr. *gr. wt.*

grosz (grôsh) *n. pl.* **grosz·y** (grôsh/ē) A monetary denomination of Poland, the hundredth part of a zloty.

gro·tesque (grō·tesk/) *adj.* **1.** Distorted, incongruous, or fantastically ugly in appearance or style; outlandish. **2.** Characterized by fantastic combinations of human and animal figures with conventional design forms. — *n.* **1.** One who or that which is grotesque. **2.** Grotesque style or quality. [< F < Ital. *grotta* excavation; from art found in excavations] — **gro·tesque'ly** *adv.* — **gro·tesque'ness** *n.*

grot·to (grot/ō) *n. pl.* **·toes** or **·tos 1.** A cave. **2.** An artificial cavelike structure, as for a recreational retreat, shrine, etc. [< Ital. *grotta* < L *crypta*]

grouch (grouch) *U.S. Informal v.i.* To be surly, grumble. — *n.* **1.** A discontented, grumbling person. **2.** A grumbling, sulky mood. [< OF *groucher* to murmur]

grouch·y (grou/chē) *adj.* **grouch·i·er, grouch·i·est** *U.S. Informal* Ill-humored. — **grouch'i·ly** *adv.* — **grouch'i·ness** *n.*

ground¹ (ground) *n.* **1.** The layer of solid substances constituting the surface of the earth; land. **2.** Soil, sand, etc., at or near the earth's surface. **3.** *Sometimes pl.* An area or tract of land; esp., one reserved or used for a specific purpose: a burial *ground.* **4.** *pl.* Private land, as the surrounding premises of a dwelling, public institution, etc. **5.** *Usu. pl.* The fundamental cause, reason, or motive for an action, belief, etc.: *grounds* for suspicion: when plural, often construed as singular. **6.** A subject; topic. **7.** *Often pl.* A foundation or basis, as for a decision, argument, or relationship; footing: when plural, often construed as singular. **8.** *pl.* Sediment; dregs; esp., the particles remaining after a beverage has been brewed. **9.** The solid bottom of a body of water. **10.** In various arts and crafts, the background against which colors, designs, etc., are placed. **11.** *Electr.* The connection of an electrical current or circuit with the earth through a conductor. **12.** *Music* A ground bass. — **Syn.** See REASON. — **from the ground up** In every detail; thoroughly. — **on home (or on one's own) ground 1.** In accustomed circumstances or surroundings. **2.** Dealing with a thoroughly familiar subject. — **to break ground 1.** To dig into or cut through the soil, as in plowing, excavating a building site, etc. **2.** To make a start in any undertaking. **3.** *Naut.* To be raised or loosened from the bottom, as an anchor. — **to cover ground 1.** To move or travel, esp. over a considerable distance. **2.** To make progress. — **to gain ground 1.** To advance; make headway. **2.** To increase in favor, influence, etc. — **to give ground** To yield a position or advantage; retreat. — **to hold (or stand) one's ground** To refuse to yield or retreat. — **to lose ground 1.** To fail to maintain an advantage or gain. **2.** To decline in favor, influence, etc. — **to shift one's ground** To change one's point of view, as in an argument or discussion. — *adj.* **1.** Being on, near, or at a level with the ground. **2.** Living, growing, or active on or in the ground. — *v.t.* **1.** To place on the ground. **2.** To base on or as on a foundation; establish; found. **3.** To teach fundamentals to. **4.** *Aeron.* To confine (an aircraft, pilot, etc.) to the ground. **5.** *Electr.* To place in connection with the earth or a ground, as a circuit. **6.** *Naut.* To run (a vessel) aground. **7.** To supply with a ground or background. — *v.i.* **8.** To come or fall to the ground. **9.** In baseball, to hit a ground ball. **10.** *Naut.* To run aground. [OE *grund*]

ground² (ground) Past tense and past participle of GRIND.

ground alert *Mil.* A state of preparedness in which airplanes and their crews stand ready for a quick takeoff.

ground ball In baseball, etc., a batted ball that rolls or bounces along the ground. Also **ground·er** (groun/dər).

ground bass *Music* A short melodic phrase in the bass, repeated continually with varied melody and harmony.

ground crew *Aeron.* A group of workers responsible for the servicing and maintenance of aircraft on the ground.

ground floor In a building, the floor that is level or almost level with the ground. — **to get in on the ground floor** *U.S. Informal* To enter upon a project at its beginning.

ground glass 1. Glass of which the surface has been treated so that it is not fully transparent. **2.** Finely powdered glass.

ground hog The woodchuck.

ground-hog day (ground/hôg/, -hog/) February 2, on which, allegedly, if the ground hog sees his shadow, he goes underground again for six more weeks of winter.

ground·less (ground/lis) *adj.* Having no reason or cause, baseless. — **ground'less·ly** *adv.* — **ground'less·ness** *n.*

ground·ling (ground/ling) *n.* **1.** A plant or animal living, growing, or remaining on or close to the ground. **2.** A fish

that keeps close to the bottom of the water. **3.** A person of crude or undiscriminating tastes.

ground·nut (ground/nut/) A plant bearing edible tubers or underground nutlike seed pods, as the peanut.

ground pine Any of various creeping, evergreen plants of the club moss family.

ground plan 1. A diagrammatic plan of any floor of a building. **2.** Any preliminary plan or basic outline.

ground·sel (ground/səl) *n.* A common herb of the composite family having numerous yellow flowers. [OE *gundæswelge*, lit., that swallows pus (with ref. to its use in poultices)]

ground·sill (ground/sil/) *n.* The lowest horizontal timber in a frame building. Also **ground/sel.**

ground squirrel One of several small, terrestrial rodents of the squirrel family, as the gopher or chipmunk.

ground swell A billowing of the ocean in broad, deep waves caused by a prolonged storm, earthquake, etc.

ground water Underground water, accumulating by seepage, and serving as the source of springs, wells, etc.

ground wire *Electr.* The wire connecting an electrical apparatus with the ground or with a grounded object.

ground·work (ground/wûrk/) *n.* A foundation; basis.

ground zero The point on the ground vertically beneath or above the point of detonation of an atomic or thermonuclear bomb: also called *hypocenter.*

group (groop) *n.* **1.** A collection or assemblage of persons or things, considered as a unit; aggregation; cluster. **2.** A number of persons or things having in common certain characteristics, interests, etc. **3.** *Biol.* A number of plants or animals considered to be related because of certain common characteristics. **4.** In painting or sculpture, two or more figures or objects forming a harmonious unit or design. **5.** In the U.S. Air Force, a subdivision of a wing, designated for a specific purpose. **6.** *Chem.* An arrangement of atoms constituting part of a molecule; a radical. — *v.t.* **1.** To arrange or classify in a group or groups. — *v.i.* **2.** To form or be part of a group. [< F < Ital. *groppo* knot, lump]

group captain In the Commonwealth air forces, a commissioned officer. See table at GRADE.

group·er (groo/pər) *n.* A food fish related to the sea basses, esp. the **red grouper.** [< Pg. *garupa,* appar. < S. Am. Ind.]

grouse¹ (grous) *n. pl.* **grouse** Any of a family of game birds characterized by rounded bodies and mottled plumage, as the ruffed grouse. [Origin uncertain]

grouse² (grous) *Informal v.i.* **groused, grous·ing** To grumble. — *n.* A complaint. [? < OF *grousser* to murmur]

grove (grōv) *n.* A small wood or group of trees, esp. when cleared of underbrush. [OE *grāf*]

grov·el (gruv/əl, grov/-) *v.i.* **grov·eled** or **·elled, grov·el·ing** or **·el·ling 1.** To lie prostrate or crawl face downward, as in abjection, fear, etc. **2.** To act with abject humility. **3.** To take pleasure in what is base or sensual. [Back formation < GROVELING] — **grov'el·er** or **grov'el·ler** *n.*

grov·el·ing (gruv/əl·ing, grov/-) *adj.* **1.** Lying or crawling in an abject, prostrate position. **2.** Abjectly humble. **3.** Low; sordid. Also **grov·el·ling.** [ME *grovelynge,* adv. < *on gruff* face down + -LING²] — **grov'el·ing·ly** *adv.*

grow (grō) *v.* **grew, grown, grow·ing** *v.i.* **1.** To increase in size by the assimilation of nutriment; progress toward maturity. **2.** To germinate and develop to maturity, as from a seed or spore; originate, as from a basic source or cause. **3.** To flourish; thrive. **4.** To increase in size, amount, or degree. **5.** To become: She *grew* angry. **6.** To become joined or attached by or as by growth. — *v.t.* **7.** To cause to grow; cultivate. **8.** To produce by a natural process: to *grow* hair. **9.** To cover with a growth: used in the passive. — **to grow on** To become increasingly acceptable, pleasing, or necessary to. — **to grow out of 1.** To outgrow. **2.** To result from. [OE *grōwan*] — **grow'er** *n.*

growl (groul) *v.i.* **1.** To utter a deep, guttural sound, as that made by a hostile or agitated animal. **2.** To speak gruffly and angrily. **3.** To rumble, as distant thunder. — *v.t.* **4.** To utter or express by growling. — *n.* **1.** A deep, sustained, guttural sound uttered by a hostile or agitated animal. **2.** Any sound resembling this. **3.** A gruff, angry utterance. [? < OF *grouler* to mumble < Gmc.] — **growl'er** *n.*

grown (grōn) Past participle of GROW. — *adj.* Arrived at full physical growth or stature; mature; adult.

grown-up (grōn/up/) *n.* A mature person; adult.

grown-up (grōn/up/) *adj.* **1.** Physically or mentally mature; adult. **2.** Characteristic of or appropriate to an adult.

growth (grōth) *n.* **1.** The act or process of growing. **2.** A gradual increase in size, influence, etc. **3.** Something grown or in the process of growing: a *growth* of timber. **4.** Origin; source. **5.** *Pathol.* An abnormal formation of tissue.

grub (grub) *v.* **grubbed, grub·bing** *v.i.* **1.** To dig in the ground. **2.** To lead a dreary or miserable existence; drudge. **3.** To make careful or plodding search; rummage. — *v.t.* **4.** To dig from the ground; root out: often with *up* or *out.* **5.** To clear (ground) of roots, stumps, etc. **6.** *U.S. Slang* To scrounge. — *n.* **1.** The wormlike larva of certain insects, as of the June beetle. **2.** A drudge. **3.** *Slang* Food. [ME *grubben*] **— grub'ber** *n.*

grub·by (grub'ē) *adj.* **·bi·er, ·bi·est 1.** Dirty; sloppy. **2.** Infested with grubs. **— grub'bi·ly** *adv.* **— grub'bi·ness** *n.*

grub·stake (grub'stāk') *U.S. Informal n.* **1.** Money, supplies, or equipment provided a prospector on condition that he share his finds with the donor. **2.** Money or assistance furnished to advance any venture. **— v.t. ·staked, ·stak·ing** To supply with a grubstake.

grudge (gruj) *n.* A feeling of ill will, rancor, or enmity, harbored for a remembered wrong, etc. **— v. grudged, grudg·ing** *v.t.* **1.** To be displeased or resentful because of the possessions, good fortune, etc. of (another): They *grudge* him his wealth. **2.** To give or allow unwillingly and resentfully. [< OF *groucher*] **— grudg'er** *n.* **— grudg'ing·ly** *adv.*

gru·el (grōō'əl) *n.* A semiliquid food made by boiling meal in water or milk. **— v.t. gru·eled** or **·elled, gru·el·ing** or **·el·ling** To disable or exhaust by hard work, punishment, relentless questioning, etc. [< OF, ult. < Med.L *grutum* coarse meal < Gmc.] **— gru'el·er** or **gru'el·ler** *n.*

gru·el·ing (grōō'əl·ing) *adj.* Causing strain or exhaustion. **— n.** Any grueling experience. Also **gru'el·ling.**

grue·some (grōō'səm) *adj.* Inspiring repugnance; frightful; also spelled *grewsome.* [< Scot. *grue* to shudder + -SOME¹] **— grue'some·ly** *adv.* **— grue'some·ness** *n.*

gruff (gruf) *adj.* **1.** Brusque and rough in manner or speech. **2.** Hoarse and guttural; harsh. [< Du. *grof* rough] **— gruff'ly** *adv.* **— gruff'ness** *n.*

grum·ble (grum'bəl) *v.* **·bled, ·bling** *v.i.* **1.** To complain in a surly manner. **2.** To utter low, throaty sounds; growl. **3.** To rumble. **— v.t. 4.** To utter or express by grumbling. **— n.** **1.** A low, muttered complaint. **2.** A rumble. [Cf. Du. *grommelen* < *grommen* to growl] **— grum'bler** *n.* **— grum'bling·ly** *adv.* **— grum'bly** *adj.*

grump·y (grum'pē) *adj.* **grump·i·er, grump·i·est** Ill-tempered; cranky; surly. Also **grump'ish.** [? Blend of GRUNT and DUMP] **— grump'i·ly** *adv.* **— grump'i·ness** *n.*

grunt (grunt) *v.i.* **1.** To make the deep, guttural sound of a hog. **2.** To make a similar sound, as in annoyance, assent, effort, etc. **— v.t. 3.** To utter or express by grunting. **— n.** **1.** A short, deep, guttural sound, as of a hog. **2.** A food fish of warm American seas. [OE *grunnettan*] **— grunt'er** *n.*

Gru·yère cheese (grē·yâr', grōō-; *Fr.* grü·yâr') *n.* A light yellow, whole-milk Swiss cheese having a firm texture and few or no holes. [after *Gruyère*, a town in Switzerland]

G-string (jē'string') *n.* **1.** A narrow loincloth supported by a waistband. **2.** A similar garment worn by stripteasers. **3.** On musical instruments, a string tuned to G.

gua·no (gwä'nō) *n. pl.* **·nos 1.** The excrement of sea birds, found on the Peruvian coast, and used as a fertilizer. **2.** Any similar fertilizer. [< Sp. < Quechua *huanu* dung]

Gua·ra·ni (gwä'rä·nē') *n. pl.* **·nis** or **·ni 1.** A member of a South American Indian tribe, formerly occupying the valleys of the Paraná and the Uruguay. **2.** The Tupian language of these tribes. [< Tupi, *warrior*]

guar·an·tee (gar'ən·tē') *n.* **1.** A pledge or formal promise that something will meet stated specifications or that a specified act will be performed or continued: also called *warranty.* **2.** A guaranty (def. 2). **3.** A guarantor. **4.** One who receives a guaranty. **— v.t. 1.** To certify; vouch for: We *guarantee* our work. **2.** To accept responsibility for. **3.** To give security to (a person or thing), as against loss, damage, injury, etc. [Var. of GUARANTY]

guar·an·tor (gar'ən·tər, -tôr') *n.* One who makes or gives a guaranty.

guar·an·ty (gar'ən·tē) *n. pl.* **·ties 1.** A pledge or promise to be responsible for the contract, debt, or duty of another person in case of his default or miscarriage. **2.** Something given or taken as security. **3.** A guarantor. **— v.t. ·tied, ·ty·ing** To guarantee. [< OF *guarant* warrant < Gmc.]

guard (gärd) *v.t.* **1.** To watch over or care for; protect. **2.** To watch over so as to prevent escape, etc. **3.** To control or prevent exit or entry through. **4.** To maintain cautious control over. **5.** To furnish (something) with a protective device or shield. **— v.i. 6.** To take precautions: often followed by *against.* **7.** To serve as a guard. **— n.** **1.** One who guards; as: **a** A warder; keeper. **b** One who has control over a point of entry exit, etc. **2.** A group of persons serving as a ceremonial escort. **3.** The act of guarding. **4.** That which provides protection. **5.** A defensive posture or stance, as in boxing or fencing. **6.** In football, one of two linemen whose position in the front line is usually between one of the tackles and the center. **7.** In basketball, one of two players who direct the offense and are in the front line of defense. **— off (one's) guard** Unprepared. **— on (one's) guard** Watchful, cautious. **— to mount guard** To go on duty as a sentry. **— to stand guard** To maintain a protective watch. **2.** To serve as a sentry. [< OF *guarder*] **— guard'er** *n.*

guard·ed (gär'did) *adj.* **1.** Cautious; prudent; reserved: *guarded* criticism. **2.** Closely defended or kept under surveillance by a guard. **— guard'ed·ly** *adv.* **— guard'ed·ness** *n.*

guard·house (gärd'hous') *n.* **1.** The quarters and headquarters for military guards. **2.** A jail confining military personnel convicted of minor offenses, etc.

guard·i·an (gär'dē·ən) *n.* **1.** One who guards or watches over something. **2.** One who is legally assigned care of the person, property, etc., esp. of an infant or minor. ◆ Collateral adjective: *custodial.* **— adj.** Keeping guard; protecting. **— guard'i·an·ship** *n.*

guard·room (gärd'rōōm', -rŏŏm') *n.* A room for the use and accommodation of military or other guards.

guards·man (gärdz'mən) *n. pl.* **·men** (-mən) **1.** A guard. **2.** *U.S.* A member of the National Guard.

gua·va (gwä'və) *n.* **1.** A tree or shrub of the myrtle family, native to tropical America. **2.** Its small, pear-shaped edible fruit. [< Sp. *guayaba.*]

gu·ber·na·to·ri·al (gōō'bər·nə·tôr'ē·əl, -tō'rē, gyōō'-) *adj.* Of or pertaining to a governor. [< L *gubernator* governor]

guck (guk) *n. U.S. & Canadian Slang* Goo; muck.

gudg·eon (guj'ən) *n.* **1.** A small, carplike, fresh-water fish of Europe. **2.** A minnow. **3.** A bait or enticement. **— v.t.** To cheat; dupe. [< OF < L *gobio* small fish]

guer·don (gûr'dən) *Poetic n.* Reward; recompense. **— v.t.** To reward. [< OF < Med.L < OHG < *widar* in turn + *lōn* reward] **— guer'don·er** *n.*

guern·sey (gûrn'zē) *n. pl.* **·seys** A closely fitting knitted woolen shirt or sweater worn by seamen.

Guern·sey (gûrn'zē) *n. pl.* **·seys** One of a breed of dairy cattle having fawn and white coloration.

guer·ril·la (gə·ril'ə) *n.* One of a combatant band often operating in rear of the enemy. **— adj.** Of guerrillas or their warfare. Also **gue·ril'la.** [< Sp., dim. of *guerra* war]

guess (ges) *v.t.* **1.** To form a judgment or opinion of (some quantity, fact, etc.) on uncertain or incomplete knowledge. **2.** To conjecture correctly. **3.** *U.S.* To believe: I *guess* we'll be late. **— v.i. 4.** To form a judgment or opinion on uncertain or incomplete knowledge: often with *at.* **5.** To conjecture correctly: How did you *guess?* **— n.** **1.** An opinion or conclusion arrived at by guessing. **2.** The act of guessing. [ME *gessen*] **— guess'er** *n.*

guess·ti·mate (ges'tə·mit) *n. Slang* An estimate that is little better than a guess. [Blend of GUESS and ESTIMATE]

guess·work (ges'wûrk') *n.* **1.** The process of guessing. **2.** Something based on a guess or guesses, as an opinion.

guest (gest) *n.* **1.** One who is received and entertained by another or others, as at a party or meal, or for a visit, etc. **2.** One who pays for lodging, etc., as at a hotel. **— adj. 1.** Intended for guests. **2.** Acting on invitation. [OE *giest*]

guff (guf) *n. Slang* Empty talk; nonsense; baloney. [Imit.]

guf·faw (gə·fô') *n.* A loud burst of boisterous laughter. **— v.i.** To utter such a laugh. [Imit.]

guid·ance (gīd'ns) *n.* **1.** The act, process, or result of guiding. **2.** Something that guides.

guide (gīd) *v.* **guid·ed, guid·ing** *v.t.* **1.** To lead or direct, as to a destination. **2.** To direct the motion or physical progress of, as a vehicle, tool, animal, etc. **3.** To lead or direct the affairs, standards, opinions, etc., of. **— v.i. 4.** To act as a guide. **— n.** **1.** A person who guides; esp., one who conducts others on trips, through museums, on sight-seeing tours, etc. **2.** One who or that which is taken as a model. **3.** A book that guides or explains; esp., a guidebook. **4.** *Mech.* Any device that regulates or controls the operation of a part. [< OF *guider*] **— guid'a·ble** *adj.* **— guid'er** *n.*

guide·book (gīd'bŏŏk') *n.* A handbook containing directions and other information for tourists, visitors, etc.

guid·ed missile (gī'did) *Mil.* An unmanned aerial missile whose course can be altered during flight by mechanisms that are preset, self-reacting, or actuated by radio signals.

guide·line (gīd'līn') *n.* **1.** A line, as a rope, for guiding. **2.** Any suggestion, rule, etc., intended as a guide.

guide·post (gīd'pōst') *n.* **1.** A post on which directions for travelers are given. **2.** A guideline.

gui·don (gī'don, gīd'n) *n. Mil.* A small flag for unit identification. [< F < Ital. *guidone*]

guild (gild) *n.* **1.** In medieval times, an association of artisans or merchants, formed for mutual aid, etc. **2.** Any similar association or fellowship. Also spelled *gild.* [Fusion of OE *gild* payment and *gegyld* guild]

guil·der (gil'dər) *n.* The basic monetary unit of the Netherlands: in 1960 worth about 27 U.S. cents. Also called *gulden:* also spelled *gilder.* [< Du. *gulden* golden]

guild·hall (gild'hôl') *n. Brit.* **1.** The hall where a guild meets. **2.** A town hall.

guilds·man (gildz'mən) *n. pl.* **·men** (-mən) A member of a guild.

guild socialism An English theory of socialism that advo-

cates ownership of all industry by the state with guilds of workers exercising the powers of management and control.
guile (gīl) *n.* Treacherous cunning or craft; deceit. [< OF < Gmc.]
guile·ful (gīl/fəl) *adj.* Full of guile; treacherous; deceitful. — **guile/ful·ly** *adv.* — **guile/ful·ness** *n.*
guile·less (gīl/lis) *adj.* Free from guile; sincere. — **Syn.** See INGENUOUS. — **guile/less·ly** *adv.* — **guile/less·ness** *n.*
guil·le·mot (gil/ə·mot) *n.* Any of several narrow-billed auks found in northern latitudes. [< F, dim. of *Guillaume* William]
guil·lo·tine (*n.* gil/ə·tēn, gē/ə·tēn; *v.* gil/ə·tēn/, gil/ə·tēn) *n.*
1. The instrument of capital punishment in France, consisting of a weighted blade that slides down between two vertical guides and beheads the victim. 2. A similar machine for cutting paper, etc. — *v.t.* **·tined, ·tin·ing** To behead with the guillotine. [< F, after J. I. *Guillotin,* 1738–1814, French physician who advocated a humane means of execution]
guilt (gilt) *n.* 1. The fact or condition of having committed a legal or moral offense. 2. A feeling of remorse arising from a real or imagined commission of an offense. 3. Guilty conduct. [OE *gylt*]
guilt·less (gilt/lis) *adj.* 1. Free from guilt; innocent. 2. Lacking knowledge or experience: with *of.* — **guilt/less·ly** *adv.* — **guilt/less·ness** *n.*
guilt·y (gil/tē) *adj.* **guilt·i·er, guilt·i·est** 1. Deserving of blame for some offense. 2. Convicted of some offense. 3. Involving, pertaining to, or showing guilt. — **guilt/i·ly** *adv.* — **guilt/i·ness** *n.*
guimpe (gimp, gamp) *n.* A short blouse. [< F]
guin·ea (gin/ē) *n.* 1. Formerly, an English gold coin. 2. A British money of account, equal to 21 shillings. 3. The guinea fowl. 4. *U.S. Slang* A person of Italian descent: an offensive term.
guinea fowl A gallinaceous bird of African origin, having dark gray plumage speckled with white spots, long domesticated in Europe and America. Also **guinea, guinea hen.**
guinea pig 1. A small, domesticated rodent, usu. white, having a short tail and widely used in biological and medical experiments. 2. Any person used in experimentation.
Guinea worm A threadlike aquatic worm of tropical Africa and Asia, whose larvae infect the legs and lower trunk of men and animals.
Guin·e·vere (gwin/ə·vir) In Arthurian legend, Arthur's unfaithful queen and the mistress of Lancelot.
guise (gīz) *n.* 1. External appearance or aspect; semblance. 2. Assumed or false appearance; pretense. [< OF < Gmc.]
gui·tar (gi·tär/) *n.* A musical instrument having a fretted fingerboard, a large sound box with indented sides, and strings, usu. six, that are plucked with the fingers or plectrum. [< Sp. *guitarra*] — **gui·tar/ist** *n.*
gu·lar (gōō/lər, gyōō/-) *adj.* Of or pertaining to the throat; pharyngeal. [< L *gula* throat]
gulch (gulch) *n. U.S.* A deep, narrow ravine cut out by a rushing stream. [? < dial. *gulch* to swallow greedily]
gul·den (gōōl/dən) *n.* The guilder. [< Du., lit., *golden*]
gules (gyōōlz) *n.* 1. The color red. 2. *Heraldry* The tincture red. [< OF *gueules* red-dyed ermine fur]
gulf (gulf) *n.* 1. A large area of ocean or sea partially enclosed by an extended sweep of land. 2. An abyss; chasm; gorge. 3. A wide or impassable separation, as in social position, education, etc. — *v.t.* To swallow up; engulf. [< OF < Ital. < LGk. < Gk. *kolpos* bay]
Gulf Stream A warm ocean current flowing NE along the eastern coast of North America toward Europe.
gulf·weed (gulf/wēd/) *n.* Sargasso.
gull¹ (gul) *n.* A long-winged, web-footed sea bird, usu. white and gray, and having the upper mandible hooked. [ME]
gull² (gul) *n. Archaic* A person easily tricked. — *v.t. Archaic* To deceive; swindle; cheat. [? < obs. *gull* swallow]
Gul·lah (gul/ə) *n.* 1. One of a group of Negroes dwelling on a narrow coastal strip of South Carolina, Georgia, and NE Florida, or on islands lying off this coast. 2. The mixed (English and African) language of these people.
gul·let (gul/it) *n.* 1. The passage from the mouth to the stomach; esophagus. 2. The throat; pharynx; also, anything resembling a throat. [< OF < L *gula*]
gul·li·ble (gul/ə·bəl) *adj.* Easily cheated or fooled; credulous. — **gul/li·bil/i·ty** *n.* — **gul/li·bly** *adv.*
Gul·li·ver (gul/ə·vər), **Lemuel** The hero of Jonathan Swift's satire *Gulliver's Travels* (1726).
gul·ly (gul/ē) *n. pl.* **·lies** A channel, ravine, or ditch; esp., a ravine cut in the earth by running water. — *v.t.* **·lied, ·ly·ing** To cut or wear a gully in. [Var. of GULLET]
gulp (gulp) *v.t.* 1. To swallow greedily or in large amounts. 2. To choke back or stifle. — *v.i.* 3. To swallow convul-

sively as a sign of surprise, etc. — *n.* 1. The act of gulping. 2. The amount swallowed in gulping. [< Du. *gulpen*] — **gulp/er** *n.* — **gulp/ing·ly** *adv.*
gum¹ (gum) *n.* 1. A sticky, viscid substance exuded from various trees and plants, soluble in water and hardening on exposure to air. 2. Any similar substance, as resin. 3. A preparation made from gum and used in art, industry, etc. 4. Chewing gum. 5. Mucilage; glue. 6. The gum tree. 7. Rubber. 8. *U.S. Dial. pl.* Rubber overshoes. — *v.* **gummed, gum·ming** *v.t.* 1. To smear, stiffen, or clog with gum. 2. To glue or stick together with gum. — *v.i.* 3. To exude or form gum. 4. To become sticky or clogged with gum. — **to gum up** *Slang* To bungle. [< OF < L < Gk. *kommi*]
gum² (gum) *n. Often pl.* The fleshy tissue that covers the arches of the jaws and surrounds the necks of the teeth. — *v.t. & v.i.* **gummed, gum·ming** *U.S. Dial.* To chew without teeth. [OE *goma* inside of the mouth]
gum ammoniac Ammoniac².
gum arabic The gum from various species of acacia, used in medicine, candy, ink, etc.
gum·bo (gum/bō) *n. pl.* **·bos** 1. The okra or its edible, slippery pods. 2. A thick soup or stew containing okra pods. 3. *U.S. & Canadian* In the West, a type of fine, silty soil. Also **gumbo soil.** 4. A patois of French spoken by Negroes in Louisiana. [< Bantu (Angola)]
gum·boil (gum/boil/) *n.* A small boil or abscess on the gum.
gum·drop (gum/drop/) *n. U.S.* A small, round piece of jellylike candy, usu. colored and coated with sugar.
gum·my (gum/ē) *adj.* **·mi·er, ·mi·est** 1. Of or like gum; sticky; viscid. 2. Covered or clogged with gum or a gum-like substance. 3. Exuding gum. — **gum/mi·ness** *n.*
gump·tion (gump/shən) *n. Informal* 1. Bold, energetic initiative. 2. Shrewd common sense. [< dial. E (Scot.)]
gum resin A mixture of gum and resin that exudes as a milky juice from incisions in certain plants.
gum·shoe (gum/shōō/) *n. U.S.* 1. A rubber shoe or overshoe. 2. *pl.* Sneakers. 3. *Slang* A detective. — *v.i.* **·shoed, ·shoe·ing** *Slang* To go stealthily and noiselessly; sneak.
gum tree Any of various trees that produce gum.
gun (gun) *n.* 1. A weapon or projectile device from which a missile is thrown by the force of an explosive, by compressed air, by a spring, etc. 2. Loosely, any portable firearm. 3. *Mil.* **a** Any of various cannons with a flat trajectory, high muzzle velocity, and a barrel of over .25 caliber: anti-tank *gun.* **b** Any of various automatic weapons: machine *gun.* 4. Any device resembling a gun: grease *gun.* 5. The discharging of a firearm. 6. *U.S. Slang* The throttle controlling an engine. 7. *U.S. Slang* A gunman. — **big gun** *Slang* A person of influence. — **to give it (or her) the gun** *Slang* 1. To increase sharply the speed of a motor. 2. To give added speed, efficiency, etc., to some action. — **to go great guns** *U.S. Slang* To work or perform with great skill, speed, etc. — **to spike (someone's) guns** To destroy or make ineffective someone's plans, ideas, etc. — **to stick to one's guns** To continue in one's actions, plans, opinions, etc., in spite of opposition. — *v.* **gunned, gun·ning** *v.i.* 1. To go shooting or hunting with a gun. — *v.t. U.S. Slang* 2. To open the throttle of (an engine). 3. To shoot (a person) with a gun. — **to gun for (or after)** *U.S. Slang* 1. To seek with intent to injure or kill. 2. To seek out in order to win favor, etc. [ME *gonne, gunne*]
gun·boat (gun/bōt/) *n.* A small, armed naval vessel, used for patrolling rivers and coastal waters.
gun carriage The mechanical structure, often wheeled, upon which a cannon is mounted for firing or maneuvering.
gun·cot·ton (gun/kot/n) *n.* A type of cellulose nitrate used as an explosive.
gun·fire (gun/fīr/) *n.* 1. The firing of a gun or guns. 2. *Mil.* The use of artillery or small arms in warfare.
gung ho (gung/hō/) *U.S. Slang* Eager; enthusiastic; zealous: *gung ho* about army life. [< Chinese]
gun·lock (gun/lok/) *n.* The mechanism in certain guns by which the hammer is driven and the charge exploded.
gun·man (gun/mən) *n. pl.* **·men** (-mən) 1. A man armed with a gun; esp., an armed criminal. 2. A gunsmith.
gun·met·al (gun/met/l) *adj.* Of the color of gun metal.
gun metal 1. A bronze made of copper, tin, and zinc. 2. Any of various metal alloys of a dark bluish gray color, used for metal novelties. 3. A dark bluish gray color.
gun moll *U.S. Slang* 1. A female associate or accomplice of criminals. 2. A female thief.
gun·nel¹ (gun/əl) See GUNWALE.
gun·nel² (gun/əl) *n. pl.* **·nels** or **·nel** A fish of the blenny family, found in North Atlantic waters.
gun·ner (gun/ər) *n.* 1. One who operates a gun. 2. In the U.S. Navy and Marine Corps, a warrant officer whose duties were traditionally connected with ordnance. 3. In the U.S. Army, a noncommissioned officer who does the actual firing of a gun. 4. *Brit. Mil.* An artilleryman.
gun·ner·y (gun/ər·ē) *n.* 1. The science and art of constructing and operating guns. 2. Guns collectively.

GUILLOTINE
b Basket for body.
r Receptacle for head.

gun·ning (gun'ing) *n.* The art or act of hunting with a gun.

gun·ny (gun'ē) *n. pl.* **·nies** 1. A coarse, heavy material made of jute or hemp, used for making sacks, etc. 2. A bag or sack made from this material: also **gunny bag, gunny sack.** [< Hind. *gonī* gunny sack]

gun·pow·der (gun'pou'dər) *n.* An explosive mixture of potassium nitrate, charcoal, and sulfur, used in blasting and fireworks, and still occasionally as a propellant in guns.

gun·run·ning (gun'run'ing) *n.* The smuggling of guns and ammunition into a country. — **gun'run'ner** *n.*

gun·shot (gun'shot') *n.* 1. The range or reach of a gun. 2. The shooting of a gun; also, the noise or the shot. — *adj.* Caused by a gunshot.

gun·shy (gun'shī') *adj.* Afraid of a gun or of its sound.

gun·smith (gun'smith') *n.* One who makes or repairs guns.

gun·stock (gun'stok') *n.* The wooden stock of a gun.

gun·wale (gun'əl) *n. Naut.* The upper edge of the side of a boat: also spelled **gunnel.** [< GUN + WALE (plank)]

gup·py (gup'ē) *n. pl.* **·pies** A small, tropical, fresh-water fish, valued as an aquarium fish because of its coloring. [after R. J. L. *Guppy,* British scientist]

gur·gle (gûr'gəl) *v.* **·gled, ·gling** *v.i.* 1. To flow irregularly, with a bubbling sound, as water issuing from a bottle. 2. To make such a sound. — *v.t.* 3. To utter with a gurgling sound. — *n.* 1. The act of gurgling. 2. The sound of gurgling. [Var. of GARGLE] — **gur'gling·ly** *adv.*

gur·nard (gûr'nərd) *n. pl.* **·nards** or **·nard** Any of various marine fishes having a spiny head. Also **gur'net** (-nit). [< OF *grognard* grumbler]

gu·ru (gōō'rōō) *n.* In the East, a spiritual teacher or guide. [< Hind.]

gush (gush) *v.i.* 1. To pour out in volume and with sudden force. 2. To emit a sudden flow, as of blood, tears, etc. 3. *Informal* To be overly enthusiastic. — *v.t.* 4. To pour forth (blood, tears, words, etc.). — *n.* 1. A sudden flow or outburst. 2. *Informal* An extravagant effusion of emotion, praise, etc. [ME *guschen*] — **gush'ing·ly** *adv.*

gush·er (gush'ər) *n.* 1. One who gushes. 2. An oil well that spurts oil without the need of pumps.

gush·y (gush'ē) *adj.* **gush·i·er, gush·i·est** *Informal* Overly enthusiastic. — **gush'i·ness** *n.*

gus·set (gus'it) *n.* 1. A triangular piece inserted into a garment, glove, shoe, etc., for added strength or roomier fit. 2. A bracket used to strengthen a corner or angle of a structure. — *v.t.* To furnish with a gusset. [< OF *gousse* pod]

gust (gust) *n.* 1. A sudden, violent rush of wind or air. 2. A sudden burst or outpouring of fire, sound, water, etc. 3. A brief outburst of emotion. [< ON *gustr*]

gus·ta·to·ry (gus'tə·tôr'ē, -tō'rē) *adj.* Of or pertaining to the sense of taste or the act of tasting.

gus·to (gus'tō) *n.* 1. Keen enjoyment or enthusiasm; relish. 2. Individual taste or preference. 3. In art, a characteristic style or treatment. [< Ital. < L *gustus* taste]

gust·y (gus'tē) *adj.* **gust·i·er, gust·i·est** 1. Characterized by fitful gusts of wind or rain; blustery. 2. Given to sudden outbursts of feeling, etc. — **gust'i·ly** *adv.* — **gust'i·ness** *n.*

gut (gut) *n.* 1. The alimentary canal or any part of it; esp., the stomach or intestine. 2. *pl.* Bowels; entrails. 3. The specially prepared intestines of certain animals, used as strings for musical instruments, surgical sutures, etc. 4. *pl. Slang* **a** Courage; stamina; grit. **b** Effrontery. 5. A narrow passage, as a strait. — *v.t.* **gut·ted, gut·ting** 1. To take out the intestines of. 2. To plunder. 3. To destroy the contents of. [OE *guttas*]

gut·ta-per·cha (gut'ə·pûr'chə) *n.* A coagulated, rubber-like material, formed from the juice of various Malayan trees, used in electrical insulation, in the arts, as a dental plastic, etc. [< Malay *getah* gum + *percha* gum tree]

gut·ter (gut'ər) *n.* 1. A channel or ditch at the side of a street, for carrying off surface water. 2. A furrow or ditch formed by running water. 3. A trough, fixed below or along the eaves of a house, for carrying off rain water from the roof. 4. A state or condition of life, marked by poverty, filth, etc. 5. Any groove or channel. — *v.t.* 1. To form channels or grooves in. 2. To furnish with gutters, as a house. — *v.i.* 3. To flow in channels, as water. 4. To melt rapidly: said of lighted candles. [< OF < *goute* drop]

gut·ter·snipe (gut'ər·snīp') *n.* A neglected child, usu. of the slums, who spends much time in the streets.

gut·tur·al (gut'ər·əl) *adj.* 1. Pertaining to the throat. 2. Having a harsh, or muffled, grating quality. 3. *Phonet.* Velar. — *n. Phonet.* A velar sound. [< NL < L *guttur* throat] — **gut'tur·al·i·ty** *n.* — **gut'tur·al·ly** *adv.*

guy[1] (gī) *n.* 1. *Informal* A man or boy; fellow. 2. *Brit.* A person of grotesque appearance. — *v.t.* **guyed, guy·ing** *Informal* To ridicule. [after *Guy* Fawkes, leader of an abortive conspiracy in 1605 to assassinate King James I]

guy[2] (gī) *n.* A rope, cable, wire, etc., used to steady, guide,

or secure something. — *v.t.* To secure, steady, or guide with a guy. [< OF *guider* to guide]

guz·zle (guz'əl) *v.t. & v.i.* **·zled, ·zling** To drink greedily or to excess. [? < OF *gosier* throat] — **guz'zler** *n.*

gym (jim) *n. U.S. Informal* 1. A gymnasium. 2. A course in physical training. [Short for GYMNASIUM]

gym·na·si·um (jim·nā'zē·əm) *n. pl.* **·si·ums** or **·si·a** (-zē·ə) 1. A building or room equipped for certain athletic activities. 2. A place where ancient Greek youths met for physical exercise and discussion. [< L < Gk. *gymnazein* to exercise]

Gym·na·si·um (gim·nä'zē·ŏŏm) *n.* In Europe, esp. Germany, a secondary school to prepare students for the universities.

gym·nast (jim'nast) *n.* One skilled in gymnastics.

gym·nas·tic (jim·nas'tik) *adj.* Of or pertaining to gymnastics. Also **gym·nas'ti·cal.** — **gym·nas'ti·cal·ly** *adv.*

gym·nas·tics (jim·nas'tiks) *n.pl.* 1. Any physical exercises designed to improve strength, agility, etc. 2. (construed as *sing.*) The art or practice of such exercises.

gym·no·sperm (jim'nə·spûrm') *n.* One of a class of plants whose ovules and seeds are not enclosed in a case, as certain evergreens. [< Gk. *gymnos* naked + *sperma* seed] — **gym'no·sper'mous** *adj.*

gyneco- *combining form* Female; pertaining to women. Also, before vowels, **gynec-.** [< Gk. *gynē, gynaikos* woman]

gy·ne·col·o·gy (gī'nə·kol'ə·jē, jī'nə-, jin'ə-) *n.* That branch of medicine dealing with the functions and diseases peculiar to women. — **gy·ne·co·log·i·cal** (gī'nə·kə·loj'i·kəl, jī'nə-, jin'ə-) *adj.* — **gy'ne·col'o·gist** *n.*

gyno- *combining form* 1. Woman; female. 2. *Bot. & Med.* Female reproductive organ; ovary; pistil. Also, before vowels, **gyn-.** [< Gk. *gynē* woman]

gy·noe·ci·um (jī·nē'sē·əm, ji-) *n. pl.* **·ci·a** (-sē·ə) *Bot.* The female parts of a flower collectively; the pistil or pistils taken as a unit. Also **gy·nae'ce·um, gy·nae'ci·um, gy·ne'ci·um.**

-gynous *combining form* 1. Female; of women. 2. *Biol.* Having or pertaining to female organs or pistils: *androgynous.* [< Gk. *gynē* woman]

gyp (jip) *U.S. Informal v.t. & v.i.* **gypped, gyp·ping** To cheat, swindle, or defraud. — *n.* A fraud. [? < GYPSY]

gyp·sum (jip'səm) *n.* A mineral, hydrous calcium sulfate, $CaSO_4 \cdot 2H_2O$, used in plaster of Paris, fertilizer, etc. [< L < Gk. *gypsos* chalk]

gyp·sy (jip'sē) *n. pl.* **·sies** A person who looks like, or leads the life of, a Gypsy. — *adj.* Of, pertaining to, or like a gypsy or the Gypsies. — *v.i.* **·sied, ·sy·ing** To live or wander like a gypsy or the Gypsies. Also spelled *gipsy.*

Gyp·sy (jip'sē) *n. pl.* **·sies** 1. A member of a wandering, dark-haired, dark-skinned Caucasian people believed to have migrated to Europe from India in the 15th century, and known as fortunetellers, musicians, etc. 2. Romany (def. 2). Also spelled *Gipsy.* [Var. of *Egyptian* Egyptian]

gypsy moth A moth having larvae destructive to foliage.

gy·rate (jī'rāt) *v.i.* **·rat·ed, ·rat·ing** 1. To rotate or revolve, usu. around a fixed point or axis. 2. To turn in a spiral motion. — *adj.* Winding or coiled about; convolute. [< L *gyrare* to gyrate < Gk. *gyros*] — **gy·ra·tor** (jī'rā'tər, jī·rā'-) *n.* — **gy'ra·to'ry** *adj.*

gy·ra·tion (jī·rā'shən) *n.* 1. The act of gyrating; a spiral or whirling motion. 2. A single whorl of a spiral shell.

gyre (jīr) *n.* A spiral or round form, as a ring or vortex; also, whirling motion. [< L < Gk. *gyros* circle] — **gy'ral** *adj.*

gyr·fal·con (jûr'fal'kən, -fôl'-, -fô'-) See GERFALCON.

gy·ro (jī'rō) *n.* A gyroscope or gyrocompass.

gyro- *combining form* 1. Rotating. 2. Spiral. Also, before vowels, **gyr-.** [< Gk. *gyros* circle]

gy·ro·com·pass (jī'rō·kum'pəs, -kom'-) *n.* A compass that employs a motor-driven gyroscope so mounted that its axis of rotation maintains a constant position with reference to the true or geographic north.

gyro pilot *Aeron.* An automatic pilot.

gy·ro·plane (jī'rə·plān') *n.* An aircraft that obtains its lift from rotating airfoils, as a helicopter.

gy·ro·scope (jī'rə·skōp) *n.* Any of a class of devices consisting essentially of a heavy wheel, so mounted that when set to rotate at high speeds it resists all forces tending to change the angular position of its axis of rotation. [< F] — **gy'ro·scop'ic** (-skop'ik) *adj.*

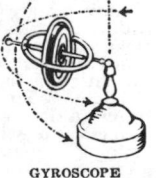

GYROSCOPE
Showing possible directional movements.

gy·ro·sta·bi·liz·er (jī'rō·stā'bə·lī'zər) *n.* A gyroscopic device designed to reduce the rolling motion of ships.

gy·ro·stat·ics (jī'rə·stat'iks) *n.pl.* (construed as *sing.*) The branch of physics that investigates the laws governing the rotation of solid bodies. — **gy'ro·stat'ic** *adj.* — **gy'ro·stat'i·cal·ly** *adv.*

H

h, H (āch) *n. pl.* **h's** or **hs, H's** or **Hs, aitch·es** (ā′chiz) **1.** The eighth letter of the English alphabet. **2.** The sound represented by the letter *h*, a voiceless, glottal fricative. In a few English words of French origin, as *heir, honor, hour,* etc., the letter *h* has no phonetic value. **3.** Anything shaped like an H. **4.** *U.S. Slang* Heroin. — *symbol* **1.** *Chem.* Hydrogen. **2.** *Physics* Strength or intensity of magnetic field (symbol H). **3.** *Electr.* Henry (symbol H).

ha (hä) *n. & interj.* An exclamation or sound expressing surprise, discovery, triumph, laughter, etc. Also spelled *hah.*

ha·ba·ne·ra (ä′bä·nā′rä) *n.* **1.** A slow, Cuban dance of African origin. **2.** Music for it. [< Sp., of Havana]

ha·be·as cor·pus (hā′bē·əs kôr′pəs) *Law* A writ commanding a person who detains another to produce the detained person before a court, esp. in order to determine the lawfulness of the detention. [< L, (you) have the body]

hab·er·dash·er (hab′ər·dash′ər) *n. U.S.* A shopkeeper who deals in men's furnishings, as shirts, hats, socks, etc. [Prob. < AF *hapertas,* kind of fabric]

hab·er·dash·er·y (hab′ər·dash′ər·ē) *n. pl.* **·er·ies 1.** The goods sold by haberdashers. **2.** A haberdasher's shop.

ha·bil·i·ment (hə·bil′ə·mənt) *n. Usu. pl.* Clothing; attire. [< OF < L *habilis* fit, apt]

ha·bil·i·tate (hə·bil′ə·tāt) *v.t.* **·tat·ed, ·tat·ing** *U.S.* In the West, to supply (a mine) with money, equipment, etc. [< L *habilis* fit] — **ha·bil′i·ta′tion** *n.*

hab·it (hab′it) *n.* **1.** An act or practice so frequently repeated as to become almost automatic. **2.** A tendency or disposition to act consistently or to repeat. **3.** An addiction: the drug *habit.* **4.** Mental or moral disposition: the scholar's *habit* of mind. **5.** A characteristic appearance or condition of the body. **6.** The clothing associated with a particular profession, etc.: a monk's *habit.* **7.** *Biol.* A characteristic action, aspect, or mode of growth of a plant or animal. — *v.t.* To clothe; dress. [< OF < L *habitus* condition, dress]

hab·it·a·ble (hab′it·ə·bəl) *adj.* Suitable for habitation. [< L *habitare* to inhabit] — **hab′it·a·bil′i·ty, hab′it·a·ble·ness** *n.* — **hab′it·a·bly** *adv.*

hab·i·tant (hab′ə·tənt) *n.* **1.** An inhabitant. **2.** A French farmer in Canada or Louisiana. [< F < L *habitare* to dwell]

hab·i·tat (hab′ə·tat) *n.* **1.** The region or environment where a plant or animal is normally found, as salt water, desert, equatorial forest, etc. **2.** The place where a person or thing usu. resides or is found. [< NL, it dwells]

hab·i·ta·tion (hab′ə·tā′shən) *n.* **1.** A place of abode; residence. **2.** The act of dwelling or inhabiting.

ha·bit·u·al (hə·bich′ōō·əl) *adj.* **1.** Practiced or recurring by habit; customary: *habitual* courtesy; also, occurring constantly. **2.** Given to or addicted to a practice. **3.** Expected from habit or usage: her *habitual* place. [< Med.L < L *habitus*] — **ha·bit′u·al·ly** *adv.* — **ha·bit′u·al·ness** *n.*

hab·it-form·ing (hab′it-fôr′ming) *adj.* Producing or resulting in a habitual practice or addiction.

ha·bit·u·ate (hə·bich′ōō·āt) *v.t.* **·at·ed, ·at·ing** To accustom (oneself, an animal, etc.) to a condition by repetition. [< LL *habituare* to condition] — **ha·bit′u·a′tion** *n.*

hab·i·tude (hab′ə·tōōd, -tyōōd) *n.* **1.** Customary or characteristic state of mind or body. **2.** A usual course of action.

ha·bit·u·é (hə·bich′ōō·ā, hə·bich′ōō·ā′; *Fr.* á·bē·tü·ā′) *n.* One who frequents a specific restaurant, club, etc. [< F *habituer* to accustom]

ha·chure (*n.* ha·shōōr′, hash′ōōr) *n.* One of the short, parallel lines used in drawing and mapmaking. [< F < *hacher*]

ha·ci·en·da (hä′sē·en′də, *Sp.* ä·syen′dä) *n.* In Spanish America: **a** A landed estate; a country house. **b** A farming, mining, or manufacturing establishment in the country. [< Am. Sp. < L *facienda* things to be done]

hack¹ (hak) *v.t.* **1.** To cut or chop crudely or irregularly, as with an ax, cleaver, etc. **2.** In basketball, to strike (an opposing player) on the arm. — *v.i.* **3.** To make cuts or notches with heavy, crude blows. **4.** To emit short, dry coughs. — *n.* **1.** A gash, cut, or nick made as by a sharp instrument. **2.** An ax, hoe, or tool for hacking. **3.** A short, dry cough. [OE *haccian* to cut] — **hack·er** *n.*

hack² (hak) *n.* **1.** A horse for hire, as a saddle horse. **2.** An old, worn-out horse; jade. **3.** A person hired to do routine work, esp. literary work. **4.** *U.S.* A hackney coach. **5.** *U.S. Informal* A taxicab. — *v.t.* **1.** To let out for hire, as a horse. **2.** To use or employ as a hack. **3.** To make stale or trite by constant use; hackney. **4.** *U.S. Informal* To drive a taxicab. **5.** To ride on horseback at a jog. — *adj.* **1.** Of or for hack: a *hack* stand. **2.** For hire as a hack: a *hack* writer. **3.** Of a routine, mercenary, or hackneyed nature.

hack³ (hak) *n.* A frame or rack on which to dry bricks, cheese, fish, etc. — *v.t.* To set on hacks to dry.

hack·ber·ry (hak′ber′ē, -bər·ē) *n. pl.* **·ries 1.** An American tree resembling the elm and having small, sweet, edible fruit. **2.** The fruit or wood. [< ON < *neggr* hedge + BERRY]

hack·ie (hak′ē) *n. U.S. Slang* The driver of a taxicab.

hack·le (hak′əl) *n.* **1.** One of the long, narrow feathers on the neck of a rooster, pigeon, etc.; also, such feathers collectively. **2.** In angling: A tuft of these used in a **hack′le fly. 3.** *pl.* The hairs on the neck and back of a dog, that rise in anger, etc. — **to make (someone's) hackles rise** To make angry; infuriate. — *v.t.* **led, ·ling** To furnish (a fly) with a hackle. [Var. of *hatchel* a comb for flax]

hack·ma·tack (hak′mə·tak) *n. U.S. & Canadian* **1.** The tamarack. **2.** The wood of this tree. [< N. Am. Ind.]

hack·ney (hak′nē) *n. pl.* **·neys 1.** A horse of medium size used for ordinary driving and riding. **2.** A carriage for hire. [< OF *haquenee* horse]

hack·neyed (hak′nēd) *adj.* Made commonplace by frequent use; trite. — **Syn.** See TRITE.

hack·saw (hak′sô′) *n.* A saw with a fine-toothed, narrow blade set in a frame, used for cutting metal. Also **hack saw.**

HACKSAW

had (had) Past tense and past participle of HAVE.

had·dock (had′ək) *n. pl.* **·dock** or **·docks** A food fish of the North Atlantic, allied to but smaller than the cod. [ME]

Ha·des (hā′dēz) **1.** In Greek mythology: **a** The brother of Zeus, god of the underworld, identified with the Greek and Roman *Pluto.* **b** The underground kingdom of the dead. **2.** In the New Testament, the condition or the abode of the dead. [< Gk. *a-* not + *idein* to see]

ha·des (hā′dēz) *n. Often cap. Informal* Hell: a euphemism.

hadj (haj) *n.* The pilgrimage to Mecca required of every Moslem at least once in his life. [< Turkish < Arabic *hājj* pilgrimage. Akin to HEGIRA.]

hadj·i (haj′ē) *n.* A Moslem who has made his hadj: used also as a title. Also **hadj′ee.**

hae (hā, ha) *v.t. Scot.* To have.

haem-, haemo- See HEMO-.

haema- See HEMA-.

haemat-, haemato- See HEMATO-.

-haemia See -EMIA.

haf·ni·um (haf′nē·əm) *n.* A metallic element (symbol Hf) found in zirconium minerals. See ELEMENT. [< NL, from L *Hafnia* Copenhagen]

haft (haft, häft) *n.* A handle of a knife, sword, etc. — *v.t.* To fit with a haft. [OE *hæft* handle]

hag (hag) *n.* **1.** A repulsive, usu. malicious old woman. **2.** A witch; sorceress. [OE *hægtes* witch]

Ha·gar (hā′gər) Abraham's concubine. *Gen.* xvi 1.

hag·fish (hag′fish′) *n. pl.* **·fish** or **·fish·es** A primitive eel-like, marine fish allied to the lamprey, that bores its way into the bodies of living fishes by means of a rasping mouth.

Hag·ga·dah (hə·gä′də, *Hebrew* hä·gô′dô) *n. pl.* **·doth** (-dôth) **1.** The nonlegal elements of Talmudic literature, consisting of fables, proverbs, etc. **2.** The story of the Exodus read at Passover. **3.** A book containing this story. Also **Ha·ga′dah, Hag·ga′da.** [< Hebrew < *higgid* to tell]

Hag·ga·i (hag′ē·ī, hag′ī) Sixth-century B.C. Hebrew prophet. — *n.* A book of the Old Testament written by him. Also, in the Douai Bible, *Aggeus.*

hag·gard (hag′ərd) *adj.* **1.** Having a worn, gaunt, or wild look, as from fatigue, worry, hunger, etc. **2.** Wild or intractable. [< OF *hagard* wild] — **hag′gard·ly** *adv.*

hag·gish (hag′ish) *adj.* Characteristic of a hag; haglike. — **hag′gish·ly** *adv.* — **hag′gish·ness** *n.*

hag·gle (hag′əl) *v.* **gled, gling** *v.i.* **1.** To argue or bargain in a petty, mean way, esp. about price or terms. — *v.t.* **2.** To cut unskillfully; hack; mangle. **3.** To tire or harass, as by wrangling. — *n.* The act of haggling. — **hag′gler** *n.*

hagio- *combining form* Sacred: *hagiography*. Also, before vowels, **hagi-**. [< Gk. *hagios* sacred]

Hag·i·og·ra·pha (hag′ē·og′rə·fə, hā′jē-) *n.pl.* The third of the three ancient divisions of the Old Testament, containing all those books not found in the Pentateuch or the Prophets. The Hagiographa consist of the following books (names in the Douai Bible, when different, are given in parentheses): I Chronicles (I Parlipomenon), II Chronicles (II Paralipomenon), Ruth, Ezra (I Esdras), Nehemiah (II Esdras), Esther, Job, Psalms, Proverbs, Ecclesiastes, Song of Solomon (Canticle of Canticles), Lamentations, Daniel. [< Gk. < *hagios* sacred + *graphein* to write]

hag·i·og·ra·pher (hag′ē·og′rə·fər, hā′jē-) *n.* **1.** A writer of or authority on the lives of saints. **2.** Any writer on sacred subjects; esp., one of the authors of the Hagiographa.

hag·i·og·ra·phy (hag′ē·og′rə·fē, hā′jē-) *n.* *pl.* **·phies 1.** The study of the lives of saints. **2.** A book of such studies. — **hag·i·o·graph·ic** (hag′ē·ə·graf′ik, hā′jē-) or **·i·cal** *adj.*

hag·i·ol·o·gy (hag′ē·ol′ə·jē, hā′jē-) *n.* *pl.* **·gies 1.** That part of literature dealing with the lives of the saints. **2.** A book on saints' lives. **3.** A list of saints. — **hag·i·o·log·ic** (hag′ē·ə·loj′ik, hā′jē-) or **·i·cal** *adj.* — **hag′i·ol′o·gist** *n.*

hah (hä) See HA.

ha-ha (hä′hä′, hä′hä′) *n. & interj.* A sound imitating laughter. — *v.i.* To laugh. Also spelled *haw-haw*. [Imit.]

hai·ku (hī′kōō) *n.* *pl.* **·ku** A Japanese verse form in three short lines. Also called *hokku*. [< Japanese]

hail¹ (hāl) *n.* **1.** Small lumps of ice that fall from the sky during a storm; hailstones. **2.** A rapid or heavy showering: a *hail* of blows. — *v.i.* **1.** To pour down hail. **2.** To fall like hail. — *v.t.* **3.** To hurl or pour like hail. [OE *hægel*]

hail² (hāl) *v.t.* **1.** To call loudly to in greeting. **2.** To call to so as to attract attention. **3.** To name as; designate. — *v.i.* **4.** To call out to, esp. between ships. — **to hail from** To come from, as a birthplace, residence, etc. — *n.* **1.** The act of hailing. **2.** A shout, as of greeting or for attention. **3.** The distance a shout can be heard; earshot: within *hail*. [ME < ON < *heill* whole, hale] — **hail′er** *n.*

hail fellow A pleasant companion. Also **hail fellow well met.**

hair (hâr) *n.* **1.** One of the fine, threadlike structures that grow from the skin of most mammals. ◆ Collateral adjective: *capillary*. **2.** Such structures collectively, esp. those that grow on the human head and on the skin of most mammals. **3.** *Bot.* A hairlike outgrowth of the epidermis in plants. **4.** Material woven of hair. **5.** Any exceedingly minute measure, etc. — **not to turn a hair** To show or reveal no sign of embarrassment, etc. — **to a hair** With the utmost exactness; in minute detail. — **to get in one's hair** *Slang* To vex or annoy one. — **to let one's hair down** *U.S. Slang* To discard one's reserve. — **to make one's hair stand on end** To horrify one. — **to split hairs** To make trivial distinctions. — *adj.* **1.** Like, or made of, hair. **2.** For the hair: *hair* oil. [OE *hær*] — **hair′less** *adj.*

hair·ball (hâr′bôl′) *n.* A rounded mass of hair often found in stomachs of animals that groom themselves by licking.

hair·breadth (hâr′bredth′, -bretth′) *n.* An extremely small space or margin. — *adj.* Very narrow or close: *hairbreadth* escape. Also **hair's′-breadth′** (hârz′/-), **hairs′breadth′.**

hair·brush (hâr′brush′) *n.* A brush for grooming the hair.

hair·cloth (hâr′klôth′, -kloth′) *n.* A stiff fabric of horsehair.

hair·cut (hâr′kut′) *n.* The act of cutting the hair or the style in which it is cut.

hair·do (hâr′dōō′) *n.* *pl.* **·dos 1.** A style of dressing or arranging a woman's hair. **2.** The hair so arranged.

hair·dress·er (hâr′dres′ər) *n.* One who cuts or arranges the hair, esp. women's hair.

hair·dres·sing (hâr′dres′ing) *n.* **1.** The act of arranging or dressing the hair. **2.** A preparation used in dressing the hair.

haired (hârd) *adj.* Having or characterized by a (specified kind of) hair: used in combination: *gray-haired*.

hair·line (hâr′līn′) *n.* **1.** The edge of the growth of hair on the head. **2.** A very thin line. **3.** *Printing* A very thin line on a type face; also, a style of type.

hair·pin (hâr′pin′) *n.* A thin, U-shaped piece of metal, bone, etc., used by women to hold the hair or a headdress in place. — *adj.* Bending sharply in a U: a *hairpin* curve.

hair·rais·er (hâr′rā′zər) *n.* *Informal* Something that causes excitement or fear. — **hair′-rais′ing** *adj.*

hair shirt A girdle or shirt made of haircloth, worn next to the skin by religious ascetics as a penance or mortification.

hair space *Printing* The thinnest of the metal spaces for separating letters or words.

hair·split·ting (hâr′split′ing) *n.* Insistence upon minute or trivial distinctions. — *adj.* Characterized by petty or overly fine distinctions. — **hair′split′ter** *n.*

hair·spring (hâr′spring′) *n.* The fine spring that regulates the movement of the balance wheel in a watch or clock.

hair trigger A trigger so delicately adjusted that it discharges the firearm at the slightest pressure.

hair-trig·ger (hâr′trig′ər) *adj.* *Informal* Stimulated or set in operation by the slightest provocation.

hair·y (hâr′ē) *adj.* **hair·i·er, hair·i·est 1.** Covered with or having much hair. **2.** Made of hair. — **hair′i·ness** *n.*

Hai·ti·an (hā′tē·ən, -shən) *adj.* Of or pertaining to Haiti, its people, or their culture. — *n.* **1.** A native or inhabitant of Haiti. **2.** A French patois spoken by the Haitians: also **Haitian Creole.** Also spelled *Haytian*.

hake (hāk) *n.* *pl.* **hake** or **hakes 1.** A marine food fish related to the cod. **2.** The codling¹ (def. 2). [OE *haca* hook]

ha·kim (hä′kēm) *n.* In Moslem countries: **1.** A judge or governor. **2.** A physician. [< Arabic *hakīm* wise]

hal- Var. of HALO-.

hal·berd (hal′bərd; *earlier* hôl′-, hô′-) *n.* A weapon used in the 15th and 16th centuries, an ax and spear combined. [< OF < MHG *helm* handle + *barte* broadax]

hal·cy·on (hal′sē·ən) *n.* A legendary bird supposed to calm the wind and the sea at the winter solstice so as to be able to breed on the water. — *adj.* **1.** Calm; peaceful. **2.** Of the halcyon. [< L < Gk. *alkyōn* kingfisher]

halcyon days 1. The seven days before and the seven days after the winter solstice. **2.** Any period of peace and quiet.

hale¹ (hāl) *v.t.* **haled, hal·ing** To compel to go: to *hale* into court. [Var. of HAUL] — **hal′er** *n.*

hale² (hāl) *adj.* Having sound and vigorous health; robust. [OE *hāl*] — **hale′ness** *n.*

half (haf, häf) *n.* *pl.* **halves** (havz, hävz) **1.** Either of two equal or approximately equal parts or quantities into which a thing may be divided. **2.** In sports: **a** In basketball, football, etc., either of two periods into which a game is divided between which play is suspended. **b** *Informal* In football, a halfback. — **better half** *Informal* One's wife or husband. — *adj.* **1.** Being either of two equal parts of a thing, amount, value, etc. **2.** Not complete; partial; imperfect. — *adv.* **1.** To the extent of half or approximately half. **2.** To a considerable extent; very nearly. **3.** *Informal* To any extent; at all: used with *not*: not *half* bad. [OE *healf*]

half-and-half (haf′ənd-haf′, häf′ənd-häf′) *n.* **1.** A mixture of half one thing and half another. **2.** A mixture of two malt liquors, esp. of porter and ale. — *adj.* Half of one thing and half of another. — *adv.* In two equal parts.

half·back (haf′bak′, häf′-) *n.* **1.** In football, either of two players who with the quarterback and fullback make up the backfield; also, his position. **2.** In other sports, as field hockey and soccer, a player behind the forward line.

half-baked (haf′bākt′, häf′-) *adj.* **1.** Incompletely baked; doughy. **2.** *Informal* Stupid; half-witted. **3.** *Informal* Imperfectly planned or conceived: a *half-baked* venture.

half blood 1. The relationship between persons with one parent in common; also, a person in such a relationship. **2.** A half-breed. **3.** A half-blooded animal. Also **half-blood** (haf′blud′, häf′-). — **half′-blood′ed** *adj.*

half-breed (haf′brēd′, häf′-) *n.* One having parents of different races; esp., the offspring of a white person and an American Indian. — *adj.* Hybrid: also **half-bred** (-bred′).

half brother A brother related through only one parent.

half-caste (haf′kast′, häf′käst′) *n.* **1.** A person having one Asian and one European parent; Eurasian. **2.** A halfbreed. — *adj.* Of or pertaining to mixed racial stock.

half cock In a firearm, the position of the hammer when raised halfway and so locked. — **to go off at half cock 1.** To discharge too soon. **2.** *Informal* To act or speak too hastily. Also **to go off half-cocked** (haf′kokt′, häf′-).

half crown An English silver coin worth 2½ shillings.

half dollar A U.S. silver coin worth fifty cents.

half gainer A dive in which one springs forward off the board, twists about, and plunges into the water head first.

half-heart·ed (haf′härt′id, häf′-) *adj.* Possessing or showing little interest, enthusiasm, etc. — **half′heart′ed·ly** *adv.* — **half′heart′ed·ness** *n.*

half hitch A knot made by passing the end of a rope once around the rope, then through the loop, and then drawing the end tight. For illus. see HITCH.

half-hour (haf′our′, häf′-) *n.* **1.** Thirty minutes. **2.** Thirty minutes past the beginning of an hour. — *adj.* **1.** Lasting for a half-hour. **2.** Occurring at the half-hour. — **half′-hour′ly** *adj. & adv.*

half life *Physics* The period of time during which half the atoms of a radioactive element or isotope will disintegrate.

half-mast (haf′mast′, häf′mäst′) *n.* The position of a flag flown about halfway up the staff, used in public mourning. — *v.t.* To put (a flag, etc.) at half-mast. Also *half-staff*.

half-moon (haf′mōōn′, häf′-) *n.* **1.** The moon when only half its disk is brightly illuminated. **2.** Something similar in shape to a half-moon. — *adj.* Shaped like a half-moon.

half nel·son (nel′sən) A wrestling hold in which one arm is passed under the opponent's armpit, usu. from behind, and the hand pressed against the back of his neck.

half note *Music* A note having one half the time value of a whole note. Also, *esp. Brit.*, **minim.**

half·pen·ny (hā′pən·ē, hāp′nē) *n. pl.* **half·pence** (hā′pəns) or **half·pen·nies** (hā′pən·ēz, hāp′nēz) **1.** The sum of one half of a penny. **2.** A British bronze coin equivalent to such a sum. — *adj.* **1.** Costing a halfpenny. **2.** Of little value.

half pint **1.** A measure of capacity equal to one half of a pint. **2.** *U.S. Slang* A person of short stature.

half sister A sister related through only one parent.

half-sole (haf′sōl′, häf′-) *v.t.* **·soled**, **·sol·ing** To repair (a shoe, boot, etc.) by attaching a half sole.

half sole The part of the sole of a boot or shoe extending from the shank or arch to the toe.

half step **1.** *Music* A semitone. **2.** *Mil.* A step of fifteen inches at quick time; in double time, one of eighteen inches.

half·tone (haf′tōn′, häf′-) *n.* **1.** In photoengraving: **a** A picture whose lights and shadows are composed of minute dots obtained by photographing the original through a finely lined screen. **b** The process by which such pictures are made. **2.** In art, photography, etc., any tone or shading halfway between a highlight and a deep shadow.

half tone *Music* A semitone (which see).

half-track (haf′trak′, häf′-) *n.* A vehicle propelled by caterpillar treads in the rear and wheels in front.

half·way (haf′wā′, häf′-) *adv.* **1.** At or to half the distance. **2.** Incompletely; partially. — *adj.* **1.** Midway between two points. **2.** Partial; inadequate.

half-wit (haf′wit′, häf′-) *n.* A feeble-minded person.

half-wit·ted (haf′wit′id, häf′-) *adj.* **1.** Feeble-minded. **2.** Frivolous. — **half′-wit′ted·ly** *adv.* — **half′-wit′ted·ness** *n.*

hal·i·but (hal′ə·bət, hol′-) *n. pl.* **·but** or **·buts** Either of two large flatfishes of northern seas, much esteemed as food. [ME *halybutte*, OE *halig* holy + BUT²]

hal·ide (hal′īd, -id; hā′līd, -lid) *n. Chem.* Any compound of a halogen with an element or radical. Also **hal·id** (hal′id).

hal·ite (hal′īt, hā′līt) *n.* A massive or granular, white or variously colored sodium chloride: also called *rock salt*.

hal·i·to·sis (hal′ə·tō′sis) *n.* Offensive or foul-smelling breath. [< NL < L *halitus* breath + -OSIS]

hall (hôl) *n.* **1.** A passage or corridor in a building. **2.** A vestibule; lobby. **3.** A large building or room used for public business or entertainment. **4.** In a university or college, a large building used for various purposes, as for dormitories, classrooms, etc. **5.** In British universities: **a** A college dining room; also, the dinner. **b** A building where university students reside. **6.** The main house on an estate. **7.** In medieval times, the large main room of a castle. [OE *heall*]

hal·le·lu·jah (hal′ə·lōō′yə) *interj.* Praise ye the Lord! — *n.* A musical composition of praise. Also **hal′le·lu′iah.** [< Hebrew *hallelū* praise + *yāh* Jehovah]

hal·liard (hal′yərd) See HALYARD.

hall·mark (hôl′märk′) *n.* **1.** An official mark stamped on gold and silver articles in England to guarantee their purity. **2.** Any proof of excellence. — *v.t.* To stamp with a hallmark. [< *Goldsmiths' Hall*, London, where the assaying and stamping were formerly exclusively done + MARK]

hal·loo (hə·lōō′) *interj.* A shout to attract attention, etc. — *n.* A cry of "halloo." — *v.i.* **1.** To shout "halloo"; cry out. — *v.t.* **2.** To incite with shouts. **3.** To shout to; hail. **4.** To shout (something). Also **hal·lo** (hə·lō′), **hal·loa** (hə·lō′), **hal·low** (hə·lō). [< OF *halloer* to pursue noisily]

hal·low (hal′ō) *v.t.* **1.** To make holy; consecrate. **2.** To look upon as holy; reverence. [OE *hālig* holy]

hal·lowed (hal′ōd, *in liturgical use* hal′ō·id) *adj.* **1.** Made holy. **2.** Honored as holy. — **hal′lowed·ness** *n.*

Hal·low·een (hal′ō·ēn′, hol′-) *n.* The evening of Oct. 31, vigil of All Saints' Day, celebrated by children with masquerading. Also **Hal′low·e′en′.** [< (ALL)HALLOW(S)E(V)EN]

hal·lu·ci·nate (hə·lōō′sə·nāt) *v.t.* **·nat·ed**, **·nat·ing** To affect with hallucinations. [< L *hallucinari* to wander mentally]

hal·lu·ci·na·tion (hə·lōō′sə·nā′shən) *n.* **1.** *Psychol.* Any of numerous auditory, visual, or tactile perceptions that have no external cause or stimulus. **2.** A mistaken notion.

hal·lu·ci·na·to·ry (hə·lōō′sə·nə·tôr′ē, -tō′rē) *adj.* Of, characterized by, or causing hallucination.

hal·lu·ci·no·gen (hə·lōō′sin·ə·jən) *n.* Any drug or chemical capable of inducing hallucinations.

hal·lu·ci·no·gen·ic (hə·lōō′sə·nə·jen′ik) *adj.* **1.** Causing or having to do with hallucinations or with a distortion of perception. **2.** Of or pertaining to hallucinogens.

hall·way (hôl′wā′) *n. U.S.* **1.** A hall or corridor. **2.** A passage or room leading into the main part of a building.

ha·lo (hā′lō) *n. pl.* **·los** or **·loes** **1.** In art, a disk or ring of light surrounding the head of a deity or holy person; nimbus. **2.** A splendor investing a person or thing held in reverence, etc. **3.** *Meteorol.* A luminous circle around the sun or moon. — *v.t.* **1.** To enclose with a halo. — *v.t.* **2.** To form a halo. [< L < Gk. *halōs* circular threshing floor]

halo- *combining form* **1.** Of or relating to salt. **2.** Of the

sea. **3.** Related to or containing a halogen. Also, before vowels, **hal-**. [< Gk. *hals, halos* salt, the sea]

hal·o·gen (hal′ə·jən) *n. Chem.* Any of the group of nonmetallic elements, fluorine, chlorine, bromine, iodine, and astatine. [< Gk. *hals* sea, salt + -GEN]

hal·oid (hal′oid, hā′loid) *adj.* Of, like, or derived from a halogen. — *n.* A salt formed from a halogen and a metal.

halt¹ (hôlt) *n.* A complete but temporary stop in any activity or movement. — *v.t. & v.i.* To bring or come to a halt. [< F < G *halten* to stop] — **halt′er** *n.*

halt² (hôlt) *v.i.* **1.** To be imperfect or defective in some way. **2.** To be in doubt; waver. — **the halt** Lame or crippled persons. [OE *healt* lame] — **halt′er** *n.*

hal·ter¹ (hôl′tər) *n.* **1.** A strap or rope to lead or secure a horse, cow, etc. **2.** A woman's upper garment designed to leave the arms and back bare, and held up by a band around the neck. **3.** A rope with a noose for hanging a person. **4.** Death by hanging. — *v.t.* **1.** To secure with a halter. **2.** To hang (someone). [OE *hælftre*]

hal·ter² (hal′tər) *n. pl.* **hal·te·res** (hal·tir′ēz) *Entomol.* One of a pair of appendages on each side of a winged insect, used to give balance in flight. [< NL < Gk. *haltēres* weights used in jumping]

ha·lutz (khä·lōōts′) *n. pl.* **ha·lu·tzim** (khä·lōō·tsēm′) A pioneer Jewish farmer in Palestine or Israel. [< Hebrew]

halve (hav, häv) *v.t.* **halved, halv·ing** **1.** To divide into two equal parts; share equally. **2.** To lessen by half; take away half of. **3.** In golf, to play (a match or hole) in the same number of strokes as one's opponent. [< HALF]

halves (havz, hävz) Plural of HALF. — **by halves** **1.** Imperfectly. **2.** Half-heartedly.

hal·yard (hal′yərd) *n. Naut.* A rope for hoisting or lowering a sail, a yard, or a flag: also spelled *halliard, haulyard.*

ham (ham) *n.* **1.** The thigh of an animal, as of the hog. **2.** The meat of a hog's thigh, used for food. **3.** *pl.* The back of the thigh together with the buttocks. **4.** That part of the leg behind the knee joint. **5.** *Slang* An actor who overacts or exaggerates. **6.** *Informal* An amateur radio operator. — *v.t. & v.i.* **hammed, ham·ming** *Slang* To act in an exaggerated manner. [OE *hamm*] — **ham′my** *adj.*

Ha·man (hā′mən) In the Bible, a Persian minister who was hanged when his plot to destroy the Jews was disclosed by Esther to King Ahasuerus (*Esth.* iii–vii).

ham·burg (ham′bûrg) *n.* Hamburger.

ham·burg·er (ham′bûr′gər) *n.* **1.** Ground or chopped beef. Also **hamburger steak.** **2.** A sandwich consisting of such meat placed between the halves of a round roll. [after *Hamburg*, Germany]

Ham·ite (ham′īt) *n.* **1.** A descendant of Ham, one of the sons of Noah. **2.** A member of an ethnic group that includes the ancient Egyptians, inhabiting NE Africa.

Ha·mit·ic (ha·mit′ik) *adj.* **1.** Of or pertaining to Ham or the Hamites. **2.** Designating a group of languages spoken by the Hamites. — *n.* A North African subfamily of the Hamito-Semitic family of languages, including ancient Egyptian, the modern Berber dialects, etc.

ham·let (ham′lit) *n.* **1.** A little village. **2.** *Brit.* A village without a church. [< OF < LL *hamellum* village]

Ham·let (ham′lit) In Shakespeare's play of this name, the hero, a Danish prince.

ham·mer (ham′ər) *n.* **1.** A tool usu. consisting of a handle with a metal head set crosswise at one end, used for driving nails, etc. **2.** Any object or machine that serves the same function as or resembles such a tool. **3.** A mechanical part that operates by striking; as: **a** The part of a gunlock that strikes the primer or firing pin. **b** One of the levers that strike the strings of a piano. **c** A piece that strikes a bell or gong. **4.** *Anat.* The malleus, a small bone of the middle ear. For illus. see EAR. **5.** An auctioneer's mallet. **6.** A metal ball attached to a flexible handle, thrown for distance in athletic contests. — **to go** (or **come**) **under the hammer** To be for sale at an auction. — *v.t.* **1.** To strike, beat, or drive with or as with a hammer. **2.** To produce or shape with or as with hammer blows. **3.** To join by hammering, as with nails. **4.** To force, impress, etc., by emphatic repetition. — *v.i.* **5.** To strike blows with or as with a hammer. **6.** To have the sound or feeling of rapid pounding: My heart *hammers.* **7.** To work at persistently: to *hammer* away at a task. [OE *hamer*] — **ham′mer·er** *n.*

ham·mer·head (ham′ər·hed′) *n.* A voracious shark of warm seas, having a transversely elongated head with the eyes at each end.

hammer lock A wrestling hold in which an opponent's arm is twisted behind his back and upward.

ham·mock (ham′ək) *n.* A hanging bed or couch of sturdy cloth or netting, suspended from a support at each end. [< Sp. *hamaca* < native West Indian name]

ham·per¹ (ham′pər) *v.t.* To interfere with the movements of; impede. [ME *hampren*]

ham·per² (ham′pər) *n.* A large, usu. covered basket, often used to store soiled laundry. [< OF *hanapier* a cup case]

ham·ster (ham'stər) *n.* Any of various burrowing rodents, used as a laboratory animal. [< G < OHG *hamastro*]

ham·string (ham'string') *n.* **1.** One of the tendons at the back of the human knee. **2.** The large sinew at the back of the hock of a quadruped. — *v.t.* **·strung, ·string·ing 1.** To cripple by cutting the hamstring of. **2.** To frustrate.

hand (hand) *n.* **1.** In man and other primates, the end of the forearm beyond the wrist, comprising the palm, fingers, and thumb. ◆ Collateral adjective: *manual.* **2.** In other organisms, a part that serves a similar function. **3.** An action performed by the hand or as by the hand: to die by one's own *hand.* **4.** The use of the hand or hands: to launder by *hand.* **5.** A characteristic mark, or kind of work: the *hand* of a master. **6.** A part or role: We all had a *hand* in it **7.** Assistance: to give a *hand.* **8.** *Usu. pl.* Supervisory care: in God's *hands.* **9.** A pledge or promise, often of marriage. **10.** A position to the side: on the right *hand.* **11.** One of two or more sides, aspects, or viewpoints: usu. with *on:* on the one *hand.* **12.** A source of information, etc.: at second *hand.* **13.** A person, considered as producing something. **14.** A person, considered with reference to his skill. **15.** A manual laborer: a stage *hand.* **16.** Style of handwriting. **17.** A person's signature. **18.** Show of approval by clapping. **19.** Something that resembles a hand in function, as the pointer of a clock. **20.** A unit of measurement four inches long, used to state the height of horses. **21.** In card games: **a** The cards held by a player in one round of a game. **b** The player. **c** The complete playing of all the cards given out at one deal. **— at hand 1.** Near by; readily available. **2.** About to occur. **— at the hand** (or **hands**) **of** By the action of. **— clean hands** Freedom from guilt. **— from hand to hand** Into the possession of one person after another. **— from hand to mouth** Using or spending immediately all of one's income, provisions, etc. **— hand and foot 1.** So as to satisfy all needs or wishes. **2.** So as to be unable to move the hands and feet. **— hand in** (or **and**) **glove** In close alliance or connection. **— hand in hand** Each holding the hand of the other; in close association. **— hands down** With ease; effortlessly. **— Hands off!** A command not to touch or interfere. **— Hands up!** A command to raise the hands, intended to forestall resistance. **— in hand 1.** In one's immediate grasp or possession. **2.** Under control. **3.** In process of execution. **— off one's hands** Out of one's care or responsibility. **— on hand 1.** In one's possession; available for use. **2.** *U.S.* Present. **— on one's hands** In one's care or responsibility. **— out of hand 1.** Unruly; uncontrollable. **2.** Immediately. **3.** Finished and done with. **— to hand 1.** Within reach; readily accessible. **2.** In one's possession. **— to have one's hands full** To be engaged in a great or excessive amount of work. **— to keep one's hand in** To continue an activity or interest so as not to lose skill or knowledge. **— to lay hands on 1.** To do physical harm to. **2.** To bless, consecrate, ordain, etc. **— to show one's hand** To disclose one's involvement or intentions. **— to turn** (or **put**) **one's hand to** To engage in; undertake. **— to throw up one's hands** To give up in despair. **— to wash one's hands of** To refuse further responsibility for. **— upper hand** The controlling advantage. **— with a heavy hand 1.** In a clumsy manner or style. **2.** In an overbearing manner. **— with a high hand** In an arrogant, tyrannical manner. — *v.t.* To give, offer, assist, or transmit with the hand or hands. **— to hand down 1.** To transmit to one's heirs. **2.** To deliver or announce the decision or verdict of a court. **— to hand in** To give to a person or persons in authority; submit. **— to hand it to** *Slang* To give deserved praise or recognition to. **— to hand on** To give to the next in succession. **— to hand out** To distribute. **— to hand over** To give up possession of. *adj.* Of or pertaining to the hand or hands; as: **a** Suitable for carrying in the hand. **b** Operated by hand. **c** Executed by hand: *hand* embroidery. [OE *hand*]

hand·bag (hand'bag') *n.* **1.** A woman's purse or other bag for carrying small articles. **2.** A small suitcase.

hand·ball (hand'bôl') *n.* A game in which the players hit a ball with their hand against the wall of a court.

hand·bar·row (hand'bar'ō) *n.* A flat framework for carrying loads, having handles at either end for the bearers.

hand·bill (hand'bil') *n.* A printed advertisement or notice.

hand·book (hand'book') *n.* **1.** A small guidebook or book of instructions. **2.** *U.S.* A place away from a racetrack where bets are made; also, the record of such bets.

hand·breadth (hand'bredth', -bretth') *n.* A unit of measurement, usually 2½ to 4 inches: also *hand's breadth.*

hand·car (hand'kär') *n.* A small, open railroad car propelled by a hand pump or a crank.

hand·cart (hand'kärt') *n.* A cart pushed or pulled by hand.

hand·clasp (hand'klasp', -kläsp') *n.* The act of clasping a person's hand, as in greeting, an introduction, etc.

hand·cuff (hand'kuf') *n. Usu. pl.* One of a pair of metal rings joined by a chain, designed to lock around the wrist or wrists; a manacle. — *v.t.* To fetter with handcuffs.

hand·ed (han'did) *adj.* **1.** Characterized by or designed for the use of a (specified) hand: a *left-handed* batter. **2.** Having or characterized by a (specified kind of) hand or (a specified number of) hands: *four-handed; empty-handed.*

hand·ful (hand'fŏŏl') *n. pl.* **·fuls 1.** As much or as many as a hand can hold at once. **2.** A small number or quantity. **3.** *Informal* Something or someone difficult to control.

hand·i·cap (han'dē·kap) *n.* **1.** A race or contest in which disadvantages are imposed on superior contestants or advantages given to those of inferior ability, so that each may have an equal chance of winning. **2.** One of the conditions stipulated; esp., a disadvantage. **3.** Any disadvantage. — *v.t.* **·capped, ·cap·ping 1.** To serve as a hindrance or disadvantage to. **2.** To assign handicaps in a race. [? < *hand in cap*, a lottery game] **— hand'i·cap·per** *n.*

hand·i·craft (han'dē·kraft', -kräft') *n.* **1.** Skill and expertness in working with the hands. **2.** An occupation requiring such skill. Also *U.S.* **hand'craft'.** [OE *handcræft*]

hand·i·ly (han'də·lē) *adv.* **1.** In a handy manner; dexterously; easily. **2.** Conveniently.

hand·i·ness (han'dē·nis) *n.* **1.** Manual skill; expertness. **2.** Convenience. **— Syn.** See DEXTERITY.

hand·i·work (han'dē·wûrk') *n.* **1.** Work done by the hands; any article or articles made by hand. **2.** The result or product of working or action. [OE *handgeweorc*]

hand·ker·chief (hang'kər·chif) *n.* A piece of cloth, usu. square, used for wiping the nose or face.

han·dle (han'dəl) *v.* **·dled, ·dling** *v.t.* **1.** To touch, hold, or move with the hand or hands. **2.** To use the hands upon; manipulate: to *handle* clay. **3.** To have control over. **4.** To dispose of; deal with. **5.** To treat of or discuss. **6.** To act or behave toward. **7.** To trade or deal in as a commodity. — *v.i.* **8.** To respond to manipulation or control. — *n.* **1.** That part of an object designed to be grasped in the hand. **2.** Something that resembles or serves as a handle. **3.** That which serves as an opportunity in achieving a desired end. **4.** *Informal* A title added to a person's name. **— to fly off the handle** To become angry. [OE *handle*, *hand*]

han·dle·bar (han'dəl·bär') *n. Usu. pl.* **1.** The curved steering bar of a bicycle, etc. **2.** *U.S. Informal* A luxuriant mustache resembling handlebars: also **handlebar mustache.**

han·dler (hand'lər) *n.* **1.** One who handles. **2.** In sports, one who trains or manages animals, boxers, etc.

hand·made (hand'mad') *adj.* Made by hand.

hand·me-down (hand'mē·doun') *n. Informal* A worn or outgrown garment passed on to another person.

hand organ A large music box played by turning a hand crank; barrel organ.

hand·out (hand'out') *n.* **1.** Any free ration of food, money, apparel, etc. **2.** A prepared, distributed statement.

hand·pick (hand'pik') *v.t.* **1.** To gather by hand. **2.** To choose with care. **3.** To select for a particular purpose or job.

hand·rail (hand'rāl') *n.* A railing of a height for grasping in the hand, used at a staircase, balcony, etc.

hand·saw (hand'sô') *n.* A saw used with one hand.

hand's breadth A handbreadth.

hand·sel (hand'səl, han'-) *n.* A gift given at the start of a new year, enterprise, or situation in life. — *v.t.* **hand·seled** or **·selled, hand·sel·ing** or **·sel·ling** To give a handsel to. Also spelled *hansel.* [OE *hand + selen* gift]

hand·set (hand'set') *n.* A telephone receiver and transmitter combined in a unit that may be held in one hand.

hand·shake (hand'shāk') *n.* The act of clasping and shaking a person's hand, as in greeting, agreement, parting, etc.

hand·some (han'səm) *adj.* **1.** Pleasing or well-proportioned in appearance, form, feature, etc. **2.** Considerable; ample. **3.** Generous; gracious. [< HAND + -SOME "easy to handle"] **— hand'some·ly** *adv.* **— hand'some·ness** *n.*

hand·spike (hand'spīk') *n.* A bar used as a lever for moving heavy objects.

hand·spring (hand'spring') *n.* An acrobatic turn in which the body is supported by one or both hands while the feet are quickly passed in an arc over the head.

hand-to-hand (hand'tə·hand') *adj.* At close quarters.

hand-to-mouth (hand'tə·mouth') *adj.* Consuming immediately what is obtained; improvident or impoverished.

hand·work (hand'wûrk') *n.* Work done by hand.

hand·writ·ing (hand'rī'ting) *n.* **1.** Writing done by hand, as distinct from printing, typing, etc.; calligraphy. **2.** A characteristic style or form of writing. **— to see the handwriting on the wall** To sense or be aware beforehand of impending misfortune, etc.

hand·y (han'dē) *adj.* **hand·i·er, hand·i·est 1.** Ready at hand; available; nearby. **2.** Skillful. **3.** Useful.

hand·y·man (han'dē·man') *n. pl.* **·men** (-men') A man employed to perform odd jobs. Also **handy man.**

---

hang (hang) *v.* **hung** or (*esp. for defs 3, 12*) **hanged, hang·ing** *v.t.* **1.** To fasten, attach, or support from above only. **2.** To attach by means of a hinge, etc. **3.** To put to death on a gallows, cross, etc. **4.** To cause to bend downward; to *hang* one's head. **5.** To decorate or cover with things suspended; also, to fasten (wallpaper) to a wall. **6.** To suspend (pictures, etc.) in a gallery for display. **7.** *U.S.* To cause (a jury, etc.) to be unable to reach a decision. **8.** To damn: used as a mild oath. — *v.i.* **9.** To be suspended from above; dangle. **10.** To be attached so as to swing easily. **11.** To fall, drape, or fit. **12.** To be put to death or to die by hanging. **13.** To bend or project downward; droop. **14.** To keep one's hold; cling: with *on* or *onto.* **15.** To hover; float in the air. **16.** To be imminent; threaten: with *over.* **17.** To depend; be contingent: with *on* or *upon.* **18.** To be in a state of uncertainty or indecision. **19.** To pay close attention: He *hung* on her words. **— to be hung up** *U.S. Slang* To be halted or impeded, usu. temporarily. **— to hang around** (or **about**) *Informal* To loiter or linger about. **— to hang back** To be reluctant or unwilling. **— to hang in the balance** To be undecided or doubtful. **— to hang on** To be tenacious; persist. **— to hang one on** *U.S. Slang* **1.** To get very drunk. **2.** To strike (someone) with the fist. **— to hang out 1.** To lean out, as through a window. **2.** *Slang* To spend one's time. **— to hang together 1.** To remain in close association. **2.** To be coherent or consistent. **— to hang up 1.** *Chiefly U.S.* To end a telephone conversation. **2.** To delay or suspend the progress of. **—** *n.* **1.** The way in which a thing hangs. **2.** *Informal* A bit; a rap: I don't give a *hang.* **— to get the hang of** *U.S. Informal* **1.** To acquire the knack of. **2.** To understand the basic idea of. [Fusion of ME *hangen* and ME *henge* to cause to hang]
han·gar (hang′ər) *n.* A shelter, esp. one for aircraft. [< F]
hang·dog (hang′dôg′, -dog′) *adj.* Sneaky, furtive, or degraded in manner or appearance. — *n.* A low sneak.
hang·er (hang′ər) *n.* **1.** A device on or from which something may be hung; esp., a hooked frame of shoulder width for garments. **2.** One who hangs something.
hang·er-on (hang′ər·on′, -ôn′) *n. pl.* **hang·ers-on** (hang′ərz-) A clinging or self-seeking follower; parasite.
hang·fire (hang′fīr′) *n.* A delay in the explosion of a propelling charge, igniter, or the like.
hang·ing (hang′ing) *adj.* **1.** Suspended from something. **2.** Leaning or inclining downward. **3.** Lying on a steep slope: a *hanging* meadow. **4.** Worthy of or involving capital punishment. **5.** Undecided: The matter was left *hanging.* — *n.* **1.** The act of suspending, or the state of being suspended. **2.** Execution by being hanged from the neck. **3.** *Usu. pl.* Something hung on a wall, window, etc.
hang·man (hang′mən) *n. pl.* **·men** (-mən) A public executioner who hangs condemned persons.
hang·nail (hang′nāl′) *n.* Skin partially torn loose at the side or root of a fingernail.
hang·out (hang′out′) *n. Slang* A habitual loitering or dwelling place of some person or group: a thieves' *hangout.*
hang·o·ver (hang′ō′vər) *n. U.S. Informal* **1.** The headache following overindulgence in alcoholic liquor. **2.** Something or someone remaining from a past era or regime.
hang-up (hang′up′) *n. Slang* **1.** A psychological difficulty, esp. an obsession. **2.** Any block or obstacle to a process.
hank (hangk) *n.* **1.** A skein of yarn or thread. **2.** A measure of yarn or thread. **3.** A loop or curl, as of hair. [ME]
han·ker (hang′kər) *v.i.* To yearn; have desire: with *after, for,* or an infinitive. [Cf. Flemish *hankeren* to long for.]
hank·er·ing (hang′kər·ing) *n.* A yearning; craving.
han·ky-pan·ky (hang′kē-pang′kē) *n. Slang* **1.** Deceitful or mischievous behavior. **2.** Foolish talk; blather. [? Formed on analogy with HOCUS-POCUS]
Hanse (hans) *n.* The Hanseatic League.
Han·se·at·ic League (han′sē·at′ik) A medieval league of free towns in northern Germany and neighboring countries for mutual protection and trade advantages.
han·sel (han′səl) See HANDSEL.
Han·sen's disease (han′sənz) Leprosy. [after Gerhart *Hansen,* 1841–1912, Norwegian physician]
han·som (han′səm) *n.* A low, two-wheeled, one-horse carriage, with the driver seated behind and above the cab: also **hansom cab.** [after J. A *Hansom,* 1803–82, English inventor]
Ha·nuk·kah (khä′noo̅·kə, hä′-) *n.* A Jewish festival, lasting eight days from Kislev 25 (early December), in memory of the rededication of the temple at Jerusalem under the Maccabees in 164 B.C.: also *Chanukah.* Also **Ha′nu·kah.** [< Hebrew *hanukkah* dedication]

HANSOM

hap·haz·ard (hap′haz′ərd) *adj.* Dependent upon or happening by chance; accidental; random. — *n.* Mere chance; hazard. — *adv.* By chance; at random. — **hap′haz′ard·ly** *adv.* — **hap′haz′ard·ness** *n.*

hap·less (hap′lis) *adj.* Having no luck; unfortunate; unlucky. — **hap′less·ly** *adv.* — **hap′less·ness** *n.*
haplo- *combining form* Simple; single: also, before vowels, **hapl-.** [< Gk. *haploos* simple]
hap·loid (hap′loid) *adj. Biol.* Having only one set of unpaired chromosomes, as a germ cell, in contradistinction to the normal diploid number as found in somatic cells. Also **hap·loid′ic.** — *n.* A haploid organism or cell.
hap·pen (hap′ən) *v.i.* **1.** To take place or occur; come to pass. **2.** To occur by chance rather than by design. **3.** To chance: We *happened* to hear him sing. **4.** To come by chance: with *on* or *upon.* **5.** To come or go by chance: with *in, along, by,* etc. **— to happen to 1.** To befall. **2.** To become of: What *happened to* your old friend? [ME *happenen*]
hap·pen·ing (hap′ən·ing) *n.* **1.** An event; occurrence. **2.** A staged event, usu. partly improvised and often spectacular.
hap·pen·stance (hap′ən·stans, -stəns) *n. U.S. Informal* A chance occurrence; accident.
hap·py (hap′ē) *adj.* **·pi·er, ·pi·est 1.** Enjoying, showing, or characterized by pleasure; joyous; contented. **2.** Attended with good fortune; lucky. **3.** Produced or uttered with skill and aptness; felicitous: a *happy* phrase. [ME *happi* < *hap* an occurrence] — **hap′pi·ly** *adv.* — **hap′pi·ness** *n.*
hap·py-go-luck·y (hap′ē·gō-luk′ē) *adj.* Trusting habitually to luck; cheerful; unconcerned; easygoing.
ha·ri-ki·ri (har′ə-kir′ē; hä′rä-kē′rē) *n.* Suicide by disembowelment, traditionally practiced by high-ranking Japanese when disgraced: also *hari-kari.* Also **ha′ra-ka′ri** (-kä′rē). [< Japanese *hara* belly + *kiri* cut]
ha·rangue (hə-rang′) *n.* A lengthy, loud, and vehement speech; tirade. — *v.* **·rangued, ·rangu·ing** *v.t.* **1.** To address in a harangue. — *v.i.* **2.** To deliver a harangue. [< F < Med.L < OHG *hari* army, host + *hringa* ring] — **ha·rangu′er** *n.*
har·ass (har′əs, hə-ras′) *v.t.* **1.** To trouble or pursue relentlessly with cares, annoyances, etc.; torment. **2.** *Mil.* To worry (an enemy) by raids and small attacks. [< OF < *harer* to set dogs on] — **har′ass·er** *n.* — **har′ass·ment** *n.*
har·bin·ger (här′bin·jər) *n.* One who or that which goes before and announces the coming of something; herald. — *v.t.* To act as a harbinger to; presage; herald. [< OF < *herberge* shelter < Gmc.]
har·bor (här′bər) *n.* **1.** A sheltered place, natural or artificial, on the coast of a sea, lake, etc., used to provide protection and anchorage for ships; port. **2.** Any place of refuge or rest. — *v.t.* **1.** To give refuge to; shelter; esp., to conceal or be hospitable to harmful persons or things: to *harbor* thieves. **2.** To entertain in the mind; cherish: to *harbor* a grudge. — *v.i.* **3.** To take shelter in or as in a harbor. Also *Brit.* **har′bour.** [ME < OE *here* army + *beorg* refuge]
har·bor·age (här′bər·ij) *n.* **1.** A port or place of anchorage for ships. **2.** Shelter; lodging; entertainment.
har·bor·mas·ter (här′bər·mas′tər, -mäs′-) *n.* An officer in charge of enforcing the regulations of a harbor.
hard (härd) *adj.* **1.** Resisting indentation or compression; solid; firm; unyielding. **2.** Requiring vigorous mental or physical effort to do, solve, understand, explain, etc.; difficult. **3.** Energetic and steady; industrious: a *hard* worker. **4.** Showing little mercy or feeling; stern: a *hard* judge. **5.** Strict or exacting in terms: a *hard* bargain. **6.** Having force or intensity; severe; violent: a *hard* knock. **7.** Involving or inflicting sorrow, discomfort, pain, poverty, etc.: *hard* times. **8.** *U.S. Informal* Verified and specific: said of facts, information, etc. **9.** Given to shrewdness, practicality, and obstinacy: a *hard* head. **10.** Too harsh, brilliant, or penetrating: a *hard* light. **11.** *U.S. Informal* Menacing, cruel, or disreputable in character or appearance; tough: a *hard* face. **12.** Containing certain mineral salts that interfere with the cleansing action of soap: said of water. **13.** *U.S.* Containing much alcohol; strong: *hard* cider. **14.** *Agric.* High in gluten content: said of wheat. **15.** *Phonet.* Denoting (c) or (g) when articulated as a stop, as in *cod* or *god,* and not as a fricative or affricate. **16.** *Physics* Denoting radiant energy of great penetrating power, as gamma rays. **— hard and fast** Fixed and unalterable. **— hard of hearing** Deaf or partially deaf. **— hard up** *Informal* **1.** Poor; broke. **2.** In need of (something): with *for.* **— to be hard on** To be severe, cruel, or damaging to. — *adv.* **1.** With great energy or force; vigorously: to work *hard.* **2.** Intently; earnestly: to look *hard* for something. **3.** With effort or difficulty: to breathe *hard.* **4.** With resistance; reluctantly: to die *hard.* **5.** Securely; tightly: to hold on *hard.* **6.** So as to become firm or solid: to freeze *hard.* **7.** In close proximity; near: with *after, by,* or *upon.* **8.** *Naut.* To the extreme limit; fully: *Hard* aport. **— to be hard put** To have great difficulty. **— to go hard with** To be very painful and harsh for. [OE *heard*] **— hard′ness** *n.*
hard-bit·ten (härd′bit′n) *adj.* Tough; unyielding.
hard-boiled (härd′boild′) *adj.* **1.** Boiled until cooked through: said of an egg. **2.** *Informal* Callous; tough.
hard cash Actual money; cash on hand.

hard cider Cider that has fermented.
hard coal Anthracite.
hard-core (härd′kôr′, -kōr′) *adj. U.S.* Unlikely to change; inflexible; rigid: a *hard-core* radical.
hard·en (här′dən) *v.t. & v.i.* To make or become hard in various senses. — **hard′en·er** *n.*
hard-fist·ed (härd′fis′tid) *adj.* 1. Stingy; miserly. 2. Having hard hands, as a laborer. — **hard′-fist′ed·ness** *n.*
hard·head (härd′hed′) *n. pl.* **·heads** 1. A shrewd and practical person. 2. An obstinate person.
hard·head·ed (härd′hed′id) *adj.* 1. Having a shrewd and practical mind. 2. Having a stubborn character; obstinate. — **hard′head′ed·ly** *adv.* — **hard′head′ed·ness** *n.*
hard-heart·ed (härd′här′tid) *adj.* Lacking pity; unfeeling. — **hard′heart′ed·ly** *adv.* — **hard′heart′ed·ness** *n.*
har·di·hood (här′dē-hŏŏd) *n.* 1. Resolute courage; boldness; daring. 2. Audacity; impudence.
hard labor Compulsory physical labor imposed upon imprisoned criminals as part of their punishment.
hard·ly (härd′lē) *adv.* 1. Scarcely; barely; only just: I *hardly* felt it. 2. Not quite; not: That is *hardly* enough.
hard-nosed (härd′nōzd′) *adj. Slang* Hard-bitten; unyielding.
hard·pan (härd′pan′) *n. U.S.* 1. A layer of very hard, often claylike matter under soft soil. 2. Solid, unbroken ground. 3. The firm foundation of anything.
hard rubber Vulcanite.
hard sauce Butter, sugar, and flavorings creamed together and eaten on puddings, etc.
hard-shell (härd′shel′) *adj.* 1. Having a hard shell. 2. *U.S. Informal* Rigidly orthodox; inflexible.
hard·ship (härd′ship) *n.* 1. A difficult, painful condition, as from privation, suffering, etc. 2. An instance of this.
hard·tack (härd′tack′) *n.* Hard, crackerlike biscuit.
hard·top (härd′top′) *n.* An automobile with the body design of a convertible, but with a rigid top.
hard·ware (härd′wâr′) *n.* 1. Manufactured articles of metal, as utensils or tools. 2. Weapons: military *hardware*. 3. Any of the machinery that makes up a digital computer installation: distinguished from *software*.
hard·wood (härd′wŏŏd′) *n.* 1. Wood from deciduous trees, as oak, maple, etc., as distinguished from the wood of coniferous trees. 2. Any hard, compact, heavy wood. 3. A tree yielding such wood.
har·dy¹ (här′dē) *adj.* **·di·er, ·di·est** 1. Able to endure hardship, fatigue, privation, etc.; robust; tough. 2. Having courage and valor. 3. Foolhardy; rash. 4. Able to survive the winter outdoors: said of plants. [< OF < OHG *hartjan* to make hard] — **har′di·ly** *adv.* — **har′di·ness** *n.*
har·dy² (här′dē) *n. pl.* **·dies** A square-shanked chisel or fuller for insertion in a square hole (**hardy hole**) in a blacksmith's anvil.
hare (hâr) *n. pl.* **hares** or **hare** 1. A mammal allied to but larger than the rabbit, having long ears and long hind legs. ◆ Collateral adjective: *leporine*. 2. The common American rabbit. [OE *hara*]
hare·bell (hâr′bel′) *n.* A perennial herb with blue, bell-shaped flowers. Also called *bluebell*.
hare·brained (hâr′brānd′) *adj.* Foolish; flighty; giddy.
hare·lip (hâr′lip′) *n.* A congenital fissure of the upper lip, resembling the cleft lip of a hare. — **hare′lipped′** *adj.*
har·em (hâr′əm, har′-) *n.* 1. The apartments of a Moslem household reserved for females. 2. The women occupying the harem. [< Arabic < *harama* to forbid]
har·i·cot (har′ə-kō) *n.* 1. A stew of meat, esp. mutton, and vegetables; ragout. 2. The kidney bean or its pods. [< F]
ha·ri·ka·ri (har′ē-kar′ē; hä/rē-kä/rē) *n.* Hara-kiri.
hark (härk) *v.i.* To listen; harken: usu. in the imperative.
— **to hark back** To return to some previous point; revert.
— *n.* A cry used to urge on or guide hounds. [ME *herkien*]
hark·en (här′kən) *v.i. Poetic* To listen; give heed. Also spelled *hearken*. [OE *heorcnian*]
har·le·quin (här′lə·kwin, -kin) *n.* A buffoon. — *adj.* 1. Parti-colored; motley, like the dress of a Harlequin. 2. Designating eyeglasses with frames slanting upward like the eyes of a Harlequin's mask. [< MF < Ital. *arlecchino*, prob. akin to OF *Herlequin*, a devil in medieval legend]
Har·le·quin (här′lə·kwin, -kin) *n.* A pantomime character traditionally dressed in parti-colored tights, with masked face, and bearing a wooden sword.
har·lot (här′lət) *n.* A prostitute. [< OF, rogue]
har·lot·ry (här′lət·rē) *n. pl.* **·ries** Prostitution.
harm (härm) *n.* 1. Injury; damage; hurt. 2. Wrong; evil. — *v.t.* To do harm to; damage; hurt. [OE *hearm* an insult]
harm·ful (härm′fəl) *adj.* Having power to injure or do harm. — **harm′ful·ly** *adv.* — **harm′ful·ness** *n.*
harm·less (härm′lis) *adj.* Inflicting no injury; not harmful; innocuous. — **harm′less·ly** *adv.* — **harm′less·ness** *n.*
har·mon·ic (här·mon′ik) *adj.* 1. Producing, characterized

by, or pertaining to harmony; consonant; harmonious. 2. *Music* **a** Pertaining to harmony in musical sounds. **b** Pertaining to a tone whose rate of vibration is an integral multiple of a given primary tone. 3. *Physics* Designating or characterized by a harmonic. — *n.* 1. *Music* **a** A tone on a stringed instrument produced by touching a string lightly at a point. **b** A partial tone with a vibration rate that is an integral multiple of a given primary tone. 2. *Physics* Any component of a periodic quantity that is an integral multiple of a given fundamental frequency. [< L < Gk. < *harmonia* harmony] — **har·mon′i·cal·ly** *adv.*
har·mon·i·ca (här·mon′i·kə) *n.* 1. A musical instrument consisting of metal reeds fixed in slots in a small oblong frame, and played by blowing and inhaling through the slots: also called *mouth organ*. 2. An instrument composed of glass or metal strips, struck by hammers.
har·mon·ics (här·mon′iks) *n.pl.* (construed as sing. in def. 1) 1. The branch of acoustics dealing with musical sounds. 2. *Music* The overtones of a fundamental.
har·mo·ni·ous (här·mō′nē·əs) *adj.* 1. Made up of sounds, colors, or other elements that combine agreeably: a *harmonious* pattern. 2. Manifesting agreement and concord in views, attitudes, feelings, etc. 3. Pleasing to the ear; euphonious. — **har·mo′ni·ous·ly** *adv.* — **har·mo′ni·ous·ness** *n.*
har·mo·ni·um (här·mō′nē·əm) *n.* A type of reed organ in which air is compressed in the bellows, then driven out through the reeds; melodeon. [< F < L *harmonia*]
har·mo·nize (här′mə·nīz) *v.t. & v.i.* **·nized, ·niz·ing** 1. To make or become harmonious, suitable, or agreeable. 2. To arrange or sing in musical harmony. 3. To show the harmony or agreement of, as the Gospels. Also *Brit.* **har′mo·nise.** — **har′mo·ni·za′tion** *n.* — **har′mo·niz′er** *n.*
har·mo·ny (här′mə·nē) *n. pl.* **·nies** 1. Accord or agreement in feeling, manner, action, etc.; to live in *harmony*. 2. A state of order, agreement, or esthetically pleasing relationships among the elements of a whole. 3. Pleasing sounds; music. 4. *Music* **a** A simultaneous combination of tones or a group of melodic tones that suggest a simultaneous combination. **b** Musical structure in terms of the relations between successive harmonies. **c** The science or study of this structure. 5. A scholarly work displaying the similarities, etc., of different books or passages: a *harmony* of the Gospels. [< OF < L < Gk. < *harmozein* to join]
— **Syn.** 1, 2. Concord, accord, consonance, congruity.
har·ness (här′nis) *n.* 1. The combination of traces, straps, etc., forming the gear of a draft animal and used to attach it to a wheeled vehicle or plow. 2. Any similar arrangement of straps, cords, etc.; esp., one used for attaching something, as a parachute, to the body. — **in harness** Working at one's routine job. — *v.t.* 1. To put harness on (a horse, etc.). 2. To make use of the power or potential of: to *harness* a waterfall. [< OF *harneis*; ult. origin unknown] — **har′ness·er** *n.*
harp (härp) *n.* 1. A stringed musical instrument that in its present form is upright and triangular in shape, and is played by plucking with the fingers. 2. A harplike object or device. — **to harp on** (or **upon**) To talk or write about persistently and vexatiously. [OE *hearpe*] — **harp′er** *n.*
harp·ist (här′pist) *n.* One who plays the harp.
har·poon (här·pōōn′) *n.* A barbed missile weapon, carrying a long cord, for striking whales or large fish. — *v.t.* To strike, take, or kill with or as with a harpoon. [< F < *harpe* claw] — **har·poon′er, har·poon·eer′** (ir′) *n.*
harpoon gun A gun that fires a harpoon, used in whaling.
harp·si·chord (härp′sə·kôrd) *n.* A keyboard instrument widely used from the 16th to the 18th century and revived in the 20th, having the strings plucked by quills or leather points instead of struck. [< MF *harpechorde* < Ital. < LL *harpa* harp + *chorda* string]
har·py (här′pē) *n. pl.* **·pies** 1. A rapacious, predatory person, esp. a woman. 2. A large, crested, voracious tropical American eagle: also **harpy eagle.** [< HARPY]
Har·py (här′pē) *n. pl.* **·pies** In Greek mythology, one of several winged monsters with the head of a woman and the body of a bird, who carried off the souls of the dead, etc. [< F *Harpie* < L < Gk. < *harpazein* to seize]
har·que·bus (här′kwə·bəs) *n.* An early portable firearm, in its later form having a matchlock and fired from a forked rest: also *arquebus*. [< F < MLG *hakebusse* hooked gun]
har·ri·dan (har′ə·dən) *n.* A hateful old woman; vicious hag. [< OF *haridelle* jade]
har·ri·er (har′ē·ər) *n.* 1. A small hound used for hunting hares. 2. A cross-country runner.
har·row (har′ō) *n.* A farm implement set with spikes or disks, for leveling plowed ground, breaking clods, etc. For illus. see DISK HARROW. — *v.t.* 1. To draw a harrow over (a field, etc.). 2. To disturb the mind or feelings of painfully; distress. — *v.i.* 3. To undergo harrowing. [ME *harwe*, prob. < Scand.] — **har′row·er** *n.*

har·row·ing (har'ō·ing) *adj.* Lacerating or tormenting to the feelings. **— har'row·ing·ly** *adv.*

har·ry (har'ē) *v.* **·ried, ·ry·ing** *v.t.* **1.** To lay waste, as in war or invasion; pillage; sack. **2.** To harass in any way. — *v.i.* **3.** To make raids. [OE *hergian* to ravage]

harsh (härsh) *adj.* **1.** Grating, rough, or unpleasant to any of the senses: a *harsh* tone; a *harsh* light. **2.** Unpleasing to the mind or the artistic sense; ungraceful; crude. **3.** Manifesting severity; cruel: a *harsh* punishment. [ME *harsk*, prob. < Scand.] **— harsh'ly** *adv.* **— harsh'ness** *n.*

hart (härt) *n.* The male of the red deer, esp. after it has passed its fifth year. [OE *heort*]

harte·beest (härt'bēst, här'tə-) *n.* A large, grayish brown antelope of Africa. Also **hart'beest.** [< Afrikaans < Du. *hert* hart + *beest* beast]

harts·horn (härts'hôrn') *n.* **1.** The antler of a hart, **2.** Ammonium carbonate or a preparation made from it.

har·um-scar·um (hâr'əm·skâr'əm) *adj.* Reckless and wild; harebrained; irresponsible. — *adv.* In a wild, unrestrained manner. — *n.* **1.** A reckless person. **2.** Wild and heedless behavior. [prob. < obs. *hare* to frighten + SCARE]

har·vest (här'vist) *n.* **1.** The act of gathering or collecting a ripened crop of grain, fruit, vegetables, etc. **2.** The yield of such a crop; also, the crop itself. **3.** The time of year when such crops are gathered. **4.** The products of any effort. — *v.t. & v.i.* **1.** To gather (a crop). **2.** To gather the crop of (a field, hive, etc.). **3.** To reap or suffer (consequences, etc.). [OE *harfest* autumn, harvest]

har·vest·er (här'vis·ter) *n.* **1.** One who harvests. **2.** A reaping machine.

har·vest·man (här'vist·mən) *n.* *pl.* **·men** (-mən) **1.** One who labors in the harvest. **2.** A daddy-longlegs.

harvest moon The full moon that occurs near the autumnal equinox.

has (haz) Present indicative, third person singular, of HAVE.

has-been (haz'bin') *n. Informal* One who or that which is no longer popular or effective.

ha·sen·pfef·fer (hä'sən·fef'ər) *n.* A highly seasoned dish made of marinated rabbit, braised and simmered. [< G < *hase* rabbit, hare + *pfeffer* pepper]

hash (hash) *n.* **1.** A dish of chopped meat and potatoes or other vegetables, usu. sautéed, then baked or browned. **2.** A mess; jumble; mishmash. **— to make a hash of** *Informal* **1.** To bungle; spoil; mess up. **2.** To destroy or overcome (an argument, adversary, etc.). **— to settle** (or **fix**) **one's hash** *Informal* To deal with punitively; to subdue. — *v.t.* **1.** To cut or chop into small pieces; mince. **2.** *U.S. Informal* To discuss at length: often with *over.* **3.** *U.S. Informal* To make a mess of things. [< OF *hacher* to chop]

hash house *U.S. Slang* A cheap restaurant.

hash·ish (hash'ēsh, -ish) *n.* The tops and sprouts of hemp, used as a narcotic and intoxicant. Also called *bhang.* Also **hash'eesh.** [< Arabic *hashīsh* hemp]

hash mark *Mil. Slang* A service stripe.

Has·i·dim (has'i·dim, *Hebrew* khä·sē'dim) See CHASSIDIM.

has·n't (haz'ənt) Has not.

hasp (hasp, häsp) *n.* A hinged fastening for a door, lid, etc., esp. one that passes over a staple and is secured by a padlock. — *v.t.* To shut or fasten with or as with a hasp. [OE *hæpse*]

has·sle (has'əl) *n. U.S. Slang* An argument; squabble; fight. Also **has'sel.** [? < HAGGLE + TUSSLE]

has·sock (has'ək) *n.* **1.** An upholstered stool or cushion, used for kneeling or as a footstool. **2.** A rank tuft of coarse or boggy grass. [OE *hassuc* coarse grass, ? < Celtic]

hast (hast) *Archaic* or *poetic* second person singular, present tense, of HAVE: used with *thou.*

haste (hāst) *n.* **1.** Swiftness of movement or action; rapidity. **2.** Undue or reckless hurry. **3.** The necessity to act quickly; urgency. **— to make haste** To hurry. — *v.t. & v.i.* **hast·ed, hast·ing** *Poetic* To hasten. [< OF < Gmc.]

has·ten (hā'sən) *v.i.* **1.** To move or act with speed; be quick; hurry. — *v.t.* **2.** To cause to hurry or move quickly; expedite. **— has'ten·er** *n.*

hast·y (hās'tē) *adj.* **hast·i·er, hast·i·est 1.** Speedy; quick; rapid. **2.** Acting or made with excessive speed; rash. **3.** Manifesting anger: *hasty* words. **4.** Easily excited to anger. **— hast'i·ly** *adv.* **— hast'i·ness** *n.*

hasty pudding 1. A dish made of meal, seasoning, and boiling water or milk. **2.** *U.S.* A mush made with cornmeal.

hat (hat) *n.* A covering for the head, esp. one with a crown and brim. **— to pass the hat** To solicit and collect contributions of money. **— to talk through one's hat** *Informal* To talk nonsense; also, to bluff. **— to throw** (**toss,** etc.) **one's hat into the ring** To enter a contest or competition, esp. a contest for political office. **— under one's hat** *U.S. Informal* Secret; private. — *v.t.* **hat·ted, hat·ting** To provide or cover with a hat. [OE *hæt*]

hat·band (hat'band') *n.* A ribbon or band of cloth around a hat just above the brim.

hatch¹ (hach) *n.* **1.** An opening in a floor, deck, etc., giving access to spaces beneath: also called *hatchway.* **2.** A cover

or grating over such an opening: also **hatch cover. 3.** A door or gate with an opening above; also, the lower half of a door that is divided into two independently swinging parts. **4.** A floodgate (def. 1). **— Down the hatch!** *U.S. Slang* Drink up! [OE *hæc* grating]

hatch² (hach) *v.t.* **1.** To bring forth (young) from the egg by incubation. **2.** To bring forth young from (the egg). **3.** To devise, as a plan or plot. — *v.i.* **4.** To emerge from the egg. — *n.* **1.** The act of hatching. **2.** The brood hatched at one time. **3.** The result or outcome of any plan. [ME *hacchen*] **— hatch'er** *n.*

hatch³ (hach) *v.t.* To mark with close parallel or crossed lines in order to produce shading effects, etc. — *n.* Any of these lines. [< OF *hache* an ax < Gmc.] **— hatch'ing** *n.*

hatch·er·y (hach'ər·ē) *n.* *pl.* **·er·ies** A place for hatching eggs, esp. those of poultry or fish.

hatch·et (hach'it) *n.* **1.** A small, short-handled ax, for use with one hand. **2.** A tomahawk. **— to bury the hatchet.** To make peace. [< F, dim. of *hache* an ax]

hatch·way (hach'wā') *n.* Hatch¹ (def. 1).

hate (hāt) *v.* **hat·ed, hat·ing** *v.t.* **1.** To regard with extreme aversion; detest. **2.** To dislike: I *hate* doing that. — *v.i.* **3.** To feel hatred. — *n.* **1.** An extreme feeling of dislike or animosity; hatred. **2.** A person or thing detested. [OE *hatian*] **— hat'a·ble** or **hate'a·ble** *adj.* **— hat'er** *n.*

— Syn. (verb) **1.** *Hate* frequently refers to a deep, personal feeling actuated by enmity or malice; Iago *hated* Othello. *Loathe* and *abhor* both suggest aversion or disgust; *loathe* pictures that which causes a nauseating repugnance, and *abhor*, that from which we turn or shrink away. *Abominate* is used of things *hated* for moral reasons, and often indicates a righteous indignation.

hate·ful (hāt'fəl) *adj.* Arousing or worthy of hatred; detestable. **— hate'ful·ly** *adv.* **— hate'ful·ness** *n.*

hath (hath) Archaic or poetic third person singular, present tense, of HAVE.

ha·tred (hā'trid) *n.* Intense dislike or aversion; animosity; enmity. [ME < *hate* + *-red* < OE *-ræden* state]

haugh·ty (hô'tē) *adj.* **·ti·er, ·ti·est** Exhibiting great disdain for others; supercilious. [< OF *haut* high] **— haugh'ti·ly** *adv.* **— haugh'ti·ness** *n.*

haul (hôl) *v.t.* **1.** To pull or draw strongly; drag; tug. **2.** To transport or carry, as in a truck, car, etc. **3.** *Naut.* To change the course of (a ship), esp. so as to sail closer to the wind. — *v.i.* **4.** To pull or drag; tug. **5.** To change direction: said of the wind. **6.** To change one's views or course of action. **7.** *Naut.* To change course; especially, to steer nearer the wind. **— to haul off** To draw back the arm so as to punch. **— to haul up 1.** To compel to go: I was *hauled up* before the court. **2.** To come to a stop. **3.** *Naut.* To sail nearer the wind. — *n.* **1.** A strong pull; tug. **2.** That which is caught, won, taken, etc., at one time: a good *haul* of fish. **3.** The distance over which something is hauled. **4.** That which is hauled. [< OF *haler* < Gmc.] **— haul'er** *n.*

haul·age (hô'lij) *n.* **1.** The act or operation of hauling. **2.** A charge for hauling. **3.** Force expended in hauling.

haul·yard (hôl'yərd) See HALYARD.

haunch (hônch, hänch) *n.* **1.** In man and animals, the upper thigh, including the hip and buttock. **2.** The leg and loin of an animal, considered as meat. [< OF *hanche*]

haunch bone The innominate bone.

haunt (hônt, hänt) *v.t.* **1.** To visit or resort to (a person or place) repeatedly; esp., to do so, as a ghost or spirit. **2.** To recur persistently to the mind or memory of: The tune *haunts* me. **3.** To linger about; pervade. — *v.i.* **4.** To appear or recur often, esp. as a ghost. — *n.* A place often visited; resort; habitat. [< OF *hanter*] **— haunt'er** *n.*

haunt·ed (hôn'tid, hän'-) *adj.* Supposedly visited by ghosts.

haunt·ing (hôn'ting, hän'-) *adj.* Recurring to the mind; difficult to forget: a *haunting* tune. **— haunt'ing·ly** *adv.*

haut·boy (hō'boi, ō'-) *n.* An oboe. [< F *haut* high (in tone) + *bois* wood]

hau·teur (hō·tûr', *Fr.* ō·tœr') *n.* Haughtiness. [< F]

haut monde (ō mônd') *French* High society.

have (hav) *v.t.* Present indicative: I, you, we, they **have** (*Archaic* thou **hast**), he, she, it **has** (*Archaic* **hath**); past indicative **had** (*Archaic* thou **hadst**); present subjunctive **have;** past subjunctive **had;** *pp.* **had;** *ppr.* **hav·ing. 1.** To possess as property; own. **2.** To be connected with; be possessed of: to *have* a good government. **3.** To bear or possess as an attribute, quality, etc. **4.** To hold in the mind or among the feelings; entertain. **5.** To receive, take, or acquire. **6.** To achieve mastery of: Now I *have* it. **7.** To suffer from: to *have* boils. **8.** To engage in: to *have* a quarrel. **9.** To undergo or experience: to *have* a bad fright. **10.** To plan, arrange, and carry out: to *have* a party. **11.** To give birth to. **12.** To manifest or exercise: to *have* patience. **13.** To cause to, or cause to be: *Have* it cleaned. **14.** To allow; tolerate. **15.** To maintain; declare: So rumor *has* it. **16.** *Informal* To catch (someone) at a disadvantage in a game, etc. **17.** *Informal* To cheat; trick. **18.** *Informal* To perform the sexual act with. **19.** As an auxiliary, *have* is used: **a** With past participles to form perfect tenses expressing completed action: I *have* gone. **b** With the infinitive to express obligation or compulsion: I *have* to go. **— to have at** To attack. **— to have done** To stop; desist. **— to have it in for** *Informal* To hold a grudge against. **— to have it out** To continue a fight or discussion to a final settlement. **— to have on** To be dressed in. **— to let someone have it** *Informal* To attack or assault someone. **—** *n. Informal* A relatively wealthy person or country: the *haves* and the have-nots. [OE *habban*]

ha·ven (hā′vən) *n.* **1.** A harbor; port. **2.** A refuge; shelter. **—** *v.t.* To shelter in or as in a haven. [OE *hæfen*]

have-not (hav′not′) *n. Informal* A person or country relatively lacking in wealth: the haves and *have-nots*.

have·n't (hav′ənt) Have not.

hav·er·sack (hav′ər-sak) *n.* A bag for carrying rations, etc., on a march or hike. [< F < G *habersack* oat sack]

hav·oc (hav′ək) *n.* General carnage or destruction; ruin. **— to cry havoc** To give the signal for pillage and destruction. **— to play havoc with** To ruin; destroy; devastate. [< OF *havot* to plunder < Gmc.]

haw[1] (hô) *v.i.* To hesitate in speaking: to hem and *haw*. **—** *n. & interj.* A hesitating sound made by a speaker.

haw[2] (hô) *n.* The hawthorn or its fruit. [OE *haga*]

haw[3] (hô) *n. & interj.* An order to turn to the left or near side in driving horses: opposed to *gee*. **—** *v.t. & v.i.* To turn to the left. [Origin uncertain]

Ha·wai·ian (hə-wī′yən) *adj.* Of or pertaining to Hawaii, the Hawaiians, or their language. **—** *n.* **1.** A native or inhabitant of Hawaii. **2.** The Polynesian language of Hawaii.

Hawaiian guitar A guitar played horizontally, the chords being selected by a metal bar sliding on the strings.

haw-haw (hô′hô′) See HA-HA.

hawk[1] (hôk) *n.* **1.** Any of a large and widely distributed family of birds of prey, having broad, rounded wings, a long tail, and powerful talons. **2.** Any of various related birds, as the gerfalcon, kestrel, and osprey. **3.** A person who preys on others. **—** *v.i.* **1.** To hunt game with hawks. **2.** To fly in search of prey, as a hawk. [OE *hafoc, hafuc*]

hawk[2] (hôk) *v.t. & v.i.* To cry (goods) for sale in the streets; peddle. [Back formation < HAWKER]

hawk[3] (hôk) *v.t.* **1.** To cough up (phlegm). **—** *v.i.* **2.** To clear the throat with a coughing sound. **—** *n.* An effort to clear phlegm from the throat; also, the sound of this. [Imit.]

hawk·er (hô′kər) *n.* One who peddles goods in the street. [< MLG *hoker* peddler, huckster]

Hawk-eye (hôk′ī′) *n.* A native or inhabitant of Iowa.

hawk-eyed (hôk′īd′) *adj.* Having very keen eyesight.

Hawkeye State Nickname of Iowa.

hawk moth A large, stout-bodied moth that flies by twilight and sucks nectar from flowers.

hawks·bill (hôks′bil′) *n.* A tropical turtle that furnishes the best grade of tortoise shell used in commerce. Also **hawk's′-bill′, hawksbill turtle.**

hawk·weed (hôk′wēd′) *n.* A weedy perennial herb having small red, yellow, or orange flowers.

hawse (hôz) *n. Naut.* **1.** The part of a ship's bow where the hawseholes are located. **2.** *pl.* Hawseholes. **3.** The space between the bow of a moored ship and her anchor. [< ON *hals* neck, bow of a ship]

hawse·hole (hôz′hōl′) *n. Naut.* A hole in the bow of a ship, through which cables and hawsers pass.

haw·ser (hô′zər) *n. Naut.* A rope or cable used for mooring, towing, etc. [< OF *haucier* to lift]

haw·thorn (hô′thôrn) *n.* A shrub or tree of the rose family having a white or pink flower and a small pome fruit called *haw*: the State flower of Missouri. [OE *haguthorn*]

hay (hā) *n.* Grass, clover, or the like, cut and dried for fodder. **— not hay** *U.S. Slang* Not a small sum of money. **— to hit the hay** *U.S. Slang* To go to bed. **— to make hay while the sun shines** To take full advantage of an opportunity. **—** *v.i.* **1.** To mow, cure, gather, and store hay. **—** *v.t.* **2.** To make (grass, etc.) into hay. **3.** To feed with hay. **4.** To sow (land, etc.) with hay plants. [OE *hēg*]

hay·cock (hā′kok′) *n.* A dome-shaped pile of hay in the field.

hay fever *Pathol.* An allergic reaction to pollen of certain plants, characterized by sneezing, running nose, etc.

hay·loft (hā′lôft′, -loft′) *n.* An open upper section of a barn or stable, used for storing hay.

hay·mak·er (hā′mā′kər) *n.* **1.** One who makes hay. **2.** *Slang* A powerful punch. **— hay′mak′ing** *n.*

hay·mow (hā′mou′) *n.* **1.** A mass of hay, esp. one stored in a loft or bay. **2.** A hayloft.

hay·rack (hā′rak′) *n.* **1.** A frame or rack mounted on a wagon body, in which hay is hauled; also, a wagon so equipped. **2.** A framework for holding hay to feed livestock.

hay·seed (hā′sēd′) *n.* **1.** Grass seed that has shaken loose from hay. **2.** The chaff, seeds, etc., that fall from hay. **3.** *U.S.* A hick; rustic; yokel.

hay·wire (hā′wīr′) *adj. U.S. Slang* **1.** Broken; broken down; dilapidated. **2.** Crazy; nutty. **— to go haywire** *Informal* To act or become crazy.

haz·ard (haz′ərd) *n.* **1.** Danger of loss, injury, etc.; peril. **2.** Chance; accident. **3.** A gambling game played with dice. **4.** An obstacle or trap on a golf course. **5.** In tennis, any of various winning openings. **—** *v.t.* **1.** To put in danger; risk. **2.** To venture (a statement, opinion, etc.). **3.** To gamble on. [< OF < Arabic *al-zahr* a die]

haz·ard·ous (haz′ər-dəs) *adj.* **1.** Exposed to or involving danger, risk, loss, etc. **2.** Dependent on chance; fortuitous. **— haz′ard·ous·ly** *adv.* **— haz′ard·ous·ness** *n.*

haze[1] (hāz) *n.* **1.** A light suspension of water vapor, smoke, dust, etc., in the air. **2.** Mental confusion. [< HAZY]

haze[2] (hāz) *v.t.* hazed, haz·ing *U.S.* To subject (newcomers or initiates) to pranks and humiliating horseplay. [< OF *haser* to irritate] **— haz′er** *n.* **— haz′ing** *n.*

ha·zel (hā′zəl) *n.* **1.** A bushy shrub or small tree of the birch family; also, the wood of this tree. **2.** The hazelnut. **3.** A medium yellowish brown. **—** *adj.* **1.** Of or pertaining to the hazel. **2.** Of the color hazel. [OE *hæsel*]

ha·zel·nut (hā′zəl-nut′) *n.* The edible nut of the hazel.

haz·y (hā′zē) *adj.* haz·i·er, haz·i·est **1.** Misty. **2.** Lacking clarity; vague. **— haz′i·ly** *adv.* **— haz′i·ness** *n.*

H-bomb (āch′bom′) *n.* A hydrogen bomb.

he (hē) *pron., possessive* **his,** *objective* **him;** *pl. nominative* **they,** *possessive* **their** or **theirs,** *objective* **them 1.** The nominative singular pronoun of the third person, used of the male person. **2.** That person; anyone; one: *He* who hesitates is lost. **—** *n. pl.* **hes** A male person or animal. [OE *hē*]

he- *combining form* Male; masculine: used in hyphenated compounds: *he-goat*. [< HE]

head (hed) *n. pl.* **heads** or *for def. 15* **head 1.** The part of a vertebrate animal situated at the top or front of the spinal column, containing the brain, eyes, ears, nose, and mouth. ◆ Collateral adjective: *cephalic*. **2.** The analogous part of other animals and organisms. **3.** A part like a head: the *head* of a pin. **4.** A representation of the head. **5.** A leader or chief person. **6.** The position or rank of a leader. **7.** The front or beginning part of something. **8.** The highest part of something. **9.** The superior part of something. **10.** The source, as of a river. **11.** The part of a bomb or other missile that contains the explosive. **12.** Mind; intelligence. **13.** Self-control; self-possession. **14.** A person: two dollars a *head*. **15.** Of animals, a single specimen. **16.** The length of a head. **17.** A newspaper headline. **18.** A subject: He had much to say on that *head*. **19.** The side of a coin on which a face is struck. **20.** The tip or point of a boil, abscess, etc. **21.** Progress; headway. **22.** A climax, culmination, or crisis. **23.** A compact cluster of leaves or leaf stalks. **24.** The foam on the surface of beer or ale. **25.** An amount of stored-up pressure. **26.** A projecting, usu. high, piece of land on a coast. **27.** The taut, sounding membrane of a drum, tambourine, etc. **28.** The part of a tape recorder that imparts magnetic patterns to the tape or removes them from it. **29.** *Naut.* A toilet. **— head and shoulders above** (or **over**) Much better than. **— head over heels 1.** End over end. **2.** Rashly; impetuously. **2.** Entirely; totally. **— Heads up!** *U.S. Informal* Watch out! **— one's head off** *Informal* Excessively; vigorously: to yell *one's head off*. **— out of** (or **off**) **one's head** *Informal* **1.** Crazy; deluded. **2.** Delirious. **— over one's head 1.** Too difficult to understand. **2.** Beyond one's power to cope with or manage. **3.** To a higher authority. **— to come to a head 1.** Of boils, etc., to form a core or tip of pus. **2.** To reach a crisis. **— to give someone his head** To give someone freedom of action or unrestricted authority. **— to go to one's head 1.** To decrease one's sobriety, etc. **2.** To make one conceited. **— to have a head** *Informal* To have a bad headache. **— to have rocks** (or **holes**) **in the head** *U.S. Slang* **1.** To be crazy. **2.** To be stupid. **— to keep one's head above water 1.** To keep afloat. **2.** To manage to exist, keep out of debt, etc. **— to make head or tail of** To understand: usu. used in the negative. **— to take it into one's head** To do or originate something on one's own initiative. **— to turn one's head** To spoil or make vain by praising. **—** *v.t.* **1.** To be first or most prominent on: to *head* the list. **2.** To command; preside over. **3.** To direct the course of. **4.** To furnish with a head. **5.** To cut off the head or top of. **—** *v.i.* **6.** To move in a specified direction or toward a specified point. **7.** To come to or form a head. **8.** To originate: said of streams. **— to head off** To intercept the course of. **—** *adj.* **1.** Principal; chief. **2.** Situated at the front. **3.** Bearing against the front: a *head* wind. [OE *hēafod*]

head·ache (hed′āk′) *n.* **1.** A pain in the head. **2.** *U.S. Informal* A difficulty or vexation. **— head′ach′y** *adj.*

head·board (hed′bôrd′, -bōrd′) *n.* A board at the head end of a bed, grave, etc.

head·cheese (hed′chēz′) n. U.S. A cooked and jellied cheeselike meat made of the head and feet of a hog or calf.
head·dress (hed′dress′) n. 1. A covering or ornament for the head. 2. The style in which the hair is arranged; coiffure.
head·ed (hed′id) adj. 1. Having a head. 2. Having or characterized by a (specified kind of) head or (a specified number of) heads: clear-headed; two-headed.
head·er (hed′ər) n. 1. One who or that which makes or puts on heads, as of nails, rivets, etc. 2. Agric. A harvesting machine that cuts off the ripe ends of the grain. 3. Informal A fall or plunge: now only in the phrase to take a header.
head·first (hed′fûrst′) adv. 1. With the head first. 2. Without deliberation; recklessly. Also head′fore′most′.
head·gear (hed′gir′) n. 1. A hat, headdress, etc. 2. The parts of the harness placed about the horse's head.
head·hunt·ing (hed′hun′ting) n. Among certain savage tribes, the custom of decapitating slain enemies and preserving the heads as trophies. — head′-hunt′er n.
head·ing (hed′ing) n. 1. A caption or title, as of a chapter. 2. A section or division of a subject or discourse. 3. Something serving as the front or top part of anything. 4. Naut. & Aeron. Direction; course.
head·land (hed′lənd for def. 1; hed′land′ for def. 2) n. 1. A cliff projecting into the water. 2. A strip of unplowed land.
head·less (hed′lis) adj. 1. Having no head; decapitated. 2. Having no leader. 3. Stupid; erratic; brainless.
head·light (hed′līt′) n. A powerful light, as at the front of a locomotive, motor vehicle, etc.
head·line (hed′līn′) n. 1. A summarizing word or words set in bold type, as in a newspaper. 2. A line at the head of a page, containing title, page number, etc. — v.t. head·lined, head·lin·ing 1. To provide with a headline, as a news story. 2. To be a headliner in (a show, etc.).
head·lin·er (hed′lī′nər) n. One billed as the main attraction or star of a theatrical performance.
head·long (hed′lông′, -long′) adv. 1. Headfirst. 2. Without deliberation; recklessly; rashly. 3. With unbridled speed or force. — adj. 1. Made with the head foremost. 2. Advancing impetuously; rash. 3. Rare Steep.
head·mas·ter (hed′mas′tər, -mäs′-) n. The principal of a school, esp. a private school. Also head master.
head·mis·tress (hed′mis′tris) n.fem. The female principal of a school. Also head mistress.
head·most (hed′mōst′) adj. Most advanced; foremost.
head·on (hed′on′, -ôn′) adj. & adv. Front end to front end: a head-on collision; to collide head-on.
head·phone (hed′fōn′) n. An earphone, usu. attached by a band passing over the head.
head·piece (hed′pēs′) n. 1. A hat, helmet, or other covering for the head. 2. The head; intelligence. 3. A headset.
head·quar·ters (hed′kwôr′tərz) n.pl. (construed as sing. or pl.) 1. The place from which a chief or leader directs the operations of a military unit, police force, etc. 2. Any center of operations; also, the persons working there.
head·set (hed′set′) n. A pair of headphones.
head·ship (hed′ship) n. The position or function of a chief authority; command.
heads·man (hedz′mən) n. pl. ·men (-mən) A public executioner who carries out the death sentence by decapitation.
head·stall (hed′stôl′) n. The part of a bridle that fits over the horse's head.
head start An advance start; also, an advantage.
head·stock (hed′stok′) n. Mech. One of various machine parts that support or hold some revolving part.
head·stone (hed′stōn′) n. 1. The memorial stone at the head of a grave. 2. The cornerstone or keystone of a structure: also head stone.
head·strong (hed′strông′, -strong′) adj. 1. Stubbornly bent on having one's own way; obstinate; determined. 2. Proceeding from willfulness or obstinacy.
head·wait·er (hed′wā′tər) n. A restaurant employee who supervises waiters, seats guests, makes reservations, etc.
head·wa·ters (hed′wô′tərz, -wot′ərz) n.pl. The tributaries or other waters that form the source of a river.
head·way (hed′wā′) n. 1. Forward motion; progress. 2. The space or time interval between two trains, ships, etc., traveling over the same route. 3. Overhead clearance.
head wind A wind from ahead, blowing directly opposite to the course of a ship, aircraft, etc.
head·y (hed′ē) adj. head·i·er, head·i·est 1. Tending to affect the senses; intoxicating: a heady fragrance. 2. Headstrong; obstinate. — head′i·ly adv. — head′i·ness n.
heal (hēl) v.t. 1. To restore to health or soundness. 2. To bring about the remedy or cure of. 3. To remedy or mend (a quarrel, breach, etc.). 4. To cleanse of sin, grief, worry, etc. — v.i. 5. To become well. 6. To perform a cure or cures. [OE hǣlan] — heal′er n. — heal′a·ble adj.
health (helth) n. 1. Freedom from defect or disease. 2. General condition of body or mind. 3. A toast wishing health or happiness. — adj. Of, pertaining to, connected with, or conducive to health. [OE hǣlth < hāl whole]

Health, Education and Welfare, Department of An executive department of the U.S. government (established 1953), administering Social Security and other services.
health·ful (helth′fəl) adj. 1. Promoting health; salubrious. 2. Having or manifesting health; healthy. — health′ful·ly adv. — health′ful·ness n.
health·y (hel′thē) adj. health·i·er, health·i·est 1. Having good health. 2. Conducive to health. 3. Indicative or characteristic of sound condition. — health′i·ly adv. — health′i·ness n.
heap (hēp) n. 1. A collection of things piled up; a pile. 2. Informal A large number; lot. — v.t. 1. To pile into a heap. 2. To fill or pile (a container) full or more than full. 3. To bestow in great quantities: to heap insults on someone. — v.i. 4. To form or rise in a heap or pile. [OE hēap crowd]
hear (hir) v. heard (hûrd), hear·ing v.t. 1. To perceive by means of the ear. 2. To listen to; give ear to. 3. To be informed of: to hear good news. 4. To attend (an opera, concert, recitation, etc.). 5. To listen officially or judicially: hear a case. 6. To respond or accede to: to hear a prayer. — v.i. 7. To perceive sound. 8. To be informed or made aware. — to hear of To approve of: usu. in the negative: He won't hear of it. [OE hēran] — hear′er n.
hear·ing (hir′ing) n. 1. The capacity to hear. 2. The act of perceiving sound. 3. Reach or range within which sound may be heard. 4. An opportunity to be heard, as in a court. 5. Law a The examination of an accused person. b A judicial trial, esp. without a jury.
heark·en (här′kən) See HARKEN.
hear·say (hir′sā′) n. Common talk; report; rumor.
hearse (hûrs) n. A vehicle for conveying a dead person to the place of burial. [< F herse harrow]
heart (härt) n. 1. Anat. The primary organ of the circulatory system of animals, a hollow muscular structure that maintains the circulation of the blood by alternate contraction and dilatation. ◆ Collateral adjective: cardiac. 2. The seat of emotion. 3. Tenderness; affection; love. 4. The capacity for kindness. 5. Courage. 6. One's inmost thoughts or feelings. 7. Enthusiasm; energy. 8. State of mind; mood. 9. A person, esp. a dear one. 10. The central or inner part of anything. 11. The vital or essential part. 12. Anything represented as or shaped like a heart. 13. A playing card bearing red, heart-shaped spots. 14. pl. The suit of such playing cards. 15. pl. A game of cards. — after one's own heart Suiting one's taste. — at heart In one's deepest thoughts or feelings. — by heart By memory. — from (the bottom of) one's heart With all sincerity. — heart and soul With complete sincerity. — one's heart of hearts The deepest and most intimate part of one's being. — to break the heart of To cause deep disappointment and sorrow to. — to eat one's heart out 1. To endure great remorse or grief. 2. To have a great longing. — to have a heart To be sympathetic and generous. — to have a change of heart To change one's opinions, attitudes, etc. — to have one's heart in one's mouth To be excessively excited or frightened. — to have the heart To be callous or cruel enough: usually in the negative. — to lose heart To become discouraged. — to lose one's heart (to) To fall in love (with). — to set one's heart on To long for; crave. — to take to heart 1. To consider seriously. 2. To be concerned or anxious about. — to wear one's heart on one's sleeve To show one's feelings openly. — with all one's heart 1. With great willingness. 2. With great sincerity. [OE heorte]

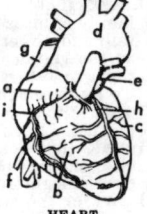

HEART
a Right atrium. b Right ventricle. c Left ventricle. d Aorta. e Pulmonary artery. f Inferior vena cava. g Superior vena cava. h Anterior coronary artery. i Posterior coronary artery.

heart·ache (härt′āk′) n. Mental anguish; grief; sorrow.
heart·beat (härt′bēt′) n. Physiol. A pulsation of the heart consisting of one full systole and diastole.
heart·break (härt′brāk′) n. Deep grief; overwhelming sorrow. — heart′break′er n. — heart′break′ing adj. & n.
heart·bro·ken (härt′brō′kən) adj. Overwhelmingly grieved. — heart′bro′ken·ly adv. — heart′bro′ken·ness n.
heart·burn (härt′bûrn′) n. 1. Pathol. A burning sensation in the esophagus due to acidity. 2. Discontent; jealousy.
heart·burn·ing (härt′bûrn′ing) n. Gnawing discontent, as from envy or jealousy. — adj. Deeply felt; distressful.
heart·ed (här′tid) adj. Having or characterized by a (specified kind of) heart: used in combination: lighthearted.
heart·en (här′tən) v.t. To give heart or courage to.
heart·felt (härt′felt′) adj. Deeply felt; most sincere.
hearth (härth) n. 1. The floor of a fireplace, furnace, or the like. 2. The fireside; home. 3. In a blast furnace, the lowest part, through which the melted metal flows. [OE heorth]
hearth·stone (härth′stōn′) n. 1. A stone forming a hearth. 2. The fireside; home.

heart·i·ly (härʹtə·lē) *adv.* **1.** With sincerity or cordiality. **2.** Abundantly and with good appetite. **3.** Completely; thoroughly: to be *heartily* disgusted.

heart·land (härtʹland/) *n.* In geopolitics, any central, strategically important area.

heart·less (härtʹlis) *adj.* **1.** Having no sympathy or kindness; pitiless. **2.** Having little courage or enthusiasm; dispirited. — **heartʹless·ly** *adv.* — **heartʹless·ness** *n.*

heart-rend·ing (härtʹren/ding) *adj.* Causing great distress or emotional anguish; grievous.

hearts·ease (härts/ēz/) *n.* Freedom from sorrow or care. Also **heartʹs/ease/**.

heart·sick (härtʹsik/) *adj.* Deeply disappointed or despondent. Also **heartʹsore/** (-sôr/, -sōr/).

heart-strick·en (härtʹstrik/ən) *adj.* Overwhelmed with grief or fear. Also **heartʹ-struck/** (-struk/).

heart·strings (härtʹstringz/) *n.pl.* The strongest feelings or affections.

heart-to-heart (härtʹtə·härtʹ) *adj.* Marked by frankness, intimacy, and sincerity.

heart·wood (härtʹwŏŏd/) *n. Bot.* The duramen.

heart·y (härʹtē) *adj.* **heart·i·er**, **heart·i·est 1.** Full of affectionate warmth or cordiality. **2.** Strongly felt; unrestrained. **3.** Healthy and strong. **4.** Supplying or enjoying abundant nourishment: a *hearty* meal; a *hearty* appetite. — *n. pl.* **heart·ies** A hearty fellow. — **heartʹi·ness** *n.*

heat (hēt) *n.* **1.** The state or quality of being hot; hotness; also, degree of hotness. **2.** That which raises the temperature; also, the rise itself. **3.** *Physics* A form of energy associated with and proportional to the molecular motions of a substance or body. ◆ Collateral adjective: *thermal.* **4.** The sensation produced by hotness. **5.** Condition, appearance, or color indicating high temperature. **6.** Hot weather or climate. **7.** Warmth supplied for a building, room, etc. **8.** *Metall.* A single heating or smelting operation, as in working iron or steel. **9.** A single effort or trial, esp. in a race. **10.** Great intensity of feeling: the *heat* of debate. **11.** The highest point of excitement or fury: the *heat* of battle. **12.** *Zool.* **a** Sexual excitement. **b** The period of sexual excitement. **13.** *U.S. Slang* **a** Any vigorous activity. **b** In the underworld, pressure applied to obtain information; also, intensive police action. — *v.t. & v.i.* **1.** To make or become hot or warm. **2.** To excite or become excited. [OE *hǣtu*] — **heatʹed** *adj.* — **heatʹed·ly** *adv.*

heat·er (hēʹtər) *n.* An apparatus for producing heat.

heat exhaustion A mild form of heat stroke.

heath (hēth) *n.* **1.** Any of a large genus of hardy evergreen shrubs, including the arbutus, azalea, and rhododendron. **2.** The common heather. **3.** *Brit.* An area of open land overgrown with heath or coarse herbage. [OE *hǣth*]

hea·then (hēʹthən) *n. pl.* **·thens** or **·then 1.** One who has not adopted Christianity, Judaism, or Islam. **2.** In the Old Testament, a non-Jew; Gentile. **3.** Any irreligious or uncultivated person. — *adj.* **1.** Unbelieving; irreligious. **2.** Of or pertaining to heathen peoples. [OE *hǣthen.* Akin to HEATH.] — **heaʹthen·dom** *n.* — **heaʹthen·ish** *adj.* — **heaʹthen·ish·ly** *adv.* — **heaʹthen·ish·ness** *n.* — **heaʹthen·ism** *n.*

heath·er (hethʹər) *n.* **1.** A hardy evergreen shrub related to the heath and having pinkish flowers. **2.** A dull, grayish red color. [ME *hadder*] — **heathʹer·y** *adj.*

heath grouse A grouse found in Great Britain, the male of which is mostly black: also called *black grouse.* Also **heath·bird** (hēthʹbûrd/), **heath cock.**

heat lightning A fitful play of lightning without thunder, sometimes seen near the horizon on hot evenings.

heat prostration Heat exhaustion.

heat stroke A state of exhaustion or collapse, usu. accompanied by fever, caused by excessive heat.

heat wave A period of very hot weather.

heave (hēv) *v.* **heaved** or (*esp. Naut.*) **hove, heav·ing** *v.t.* **1.** To throw or hurl, esp. with great effort. **2.** To raise with effort. **3.** To cause to rise or bulge. **4.** To utter painfully. **5.** *Naut.* **a** To pull or haul on (a rope, cable, etc.). **b** To cause (a ship) to move in a specified direction by or as by hauling on cables or ropes. — *v.i.* **6.** To rise or swell up; bulge. **7.** To rise and fall repeatedly. **8.** To vomit; retch. **9.** *Naut.* **a** To move or proceed: said of ships. **b** To haul or pull, as on a rope. — **heave, ho!** *Naut.* Pull (or push) hard together! — **to heave in** (or **into**) **sight** To appear to rise into view. — **to heave to 1.** To bring (a ship) to a standstill by heading into the wind with the sails hauled in or shortened. **2.** To cause a ship to lie to, as in a storm. — *n.* The act or exertion of heaving. [OE *hebban* to lift] — **heavʹer** *n.*

heav·en (hevʹən) *n.* **1.** *Theol.* The abode of God and his angels, where virtuous souls receive eternal reward after death. **2.** In various religious systems, any supernatural region inhabited by a deity or deities, slain heroes, etc. **3.**

Usu. pl. The regions around and above the earth; sky. **4.** Any condition of great happiness. **5.** Any place resembling heaven. [OE *heofon*] — **heavʹen·li·ness** *n.*

Heav·en (hevʹən) God or the celestial powers.

heav·en·ly (hevʹən·lē) *adj.* **1.** Of or belonging to the heaven of God. **2.** Of or pertaining to the sky. **3.** Full of the beauty and peace befitting heaven. — **heavʹen·li·ness** *n.*

heav·en·ward (hevʹən·wərd) *adv.* Toward heaven. Also **heavʹen·wards.** — *adj.* Directed toward heaven.

heav·i·er-than-air (hevʹē·ər-thən-âr/) *adj.* Having a weight greater than that of the air it displaces: said of airplanes, etc.

Heav·i·side layer (hevʹi·sīd) The lower region of the ionosphere, about 60 miles above the earth, that reflects radio waves of relatively low frequency back to the earth. [after O. *Heaviside*, 1850–1925, English physicist]

heav·y (hevʹē) *adj.* **heav·i·er, heav·i·est 1.** Having great weight; hard to move. **2.** Having relatively great weight in relation to size: the *heavy* metals. **3.** Having more than usual quantity, volume, etc.: a *heavy* snowfall. **4.** Practicing or indulging on a large scale: a *heavy* smoker. **5.** Having force and severity: a *heavy* blow. **6.** Exceeding the usual weight: *heavy* woolens. **7.** Having great importance; grave; serious: a *heavy* responsibility. **8.** Hard to do or accomplish: *heavy* labor. **9.** Hard to endure or bear; oppressive: *heavy* taxes. **10.** Of food, not easily digested. **11.** Of bread, pastry, etc., dense in texture; poorly leavened. **12.** Giving an impression of weight or ponderousness; thick: *heavy* lines. **13.** Despondent: a *heavy* heart. **14.** Lacking animation and grace; tedious: a *heavy* prose style. **15.** Lacking precision and delicacy: a *heavy* hand. **16.** Permeating and strong: a *heavy* odor. **17.** Profound; unbroken: a *heavy* silence. **18.** Showing fatigue: *heavy* eyes. **19.** Producing massive or basic goods: *heavy* industry. **20.** Weighted down. **21.** Pregnant. **22.** In the theater, designating a serious or tragic role, or the role of a villain. **23.** *Physics* Designating an isotope having a mass greater than that of others occurring in the same element: *heavy* hydrogen. **24.** *Mil.* **a** Designating the more massive types of weapons. **b** Formerly, designating troops or units with relatively massive equipment. — *adv.* Heavily. — **to hang heavy** To drag by tediously, as time. — *n. pl.* **heav·ies 1.** In the theater, the role of a villainous or tragic personage; also, the actor portraying him. **2.** *U.S. Informal* In sports, a heavyweight. [OE *hefig*] — **heavʹi·ly** *adv.* — **heavʹi·ness** *n.*

heav·y-du·ty (hevʹē·dōōʹtē, -dyōōʹ-) *adj.* Strongly constructed for long strain, hard use, etc.

heav·y-hand·ed (hevʹē·han/did) *adj.* **1.** Bungling; clumsy. **2.** Oppressive; domineering; cruel. — **heavʹy-hand/ed·ly** *adv.* — **heavʹy-hand/ed·ness** *n.*

heav·y-heart·ed (hevʹē·här/tid) *adj.* Melancholy; sad. — **heavʹy-heart/ed·ly** *adv.* — **heavʹy-heart/ed·ness** *n.*

heavy hydrogen Deuterium.

heav·y-lad·en (hevʹē·lād/n) *adj.* **1.** Bearing a heavy burden. **2.** Troubled; oppressed.

heavy spar Barite.

heavy water Deuterium oxide, D_2O, the compound of oxygen and the heavy isotope of hydrogen.

heav·y·weight (hevʹē·wāt/) *n.* **1.** A person or animal of much more than average weight. **2.** A boxer or wrestler over 175 pounds in weight. — *adj.* Of more than average weight or thickness.

heb·dom·a·dal (heb·domʹə·dəl) *adj.* Weekly. Also **heb·domʹa·dar/y** (-der/ē). — **heb·domʹa·dal·ly** *adv.*

He·be (hēʹbē) In Greek mythology, the goddess of youth and spring, cupbearer to the gods.

He·bra·ic (hi·brāʹik) *adj.* Relating to or characteristic of the Hebrew people and their culture and language. Also **He·braʹi·cal.** [< LL < Gk. *Hebraios* a Hebrew] — **He·braʹi·cal·ly** *adv.*

He·bra·ism (hēʹbrā·iz/əm, -brə-) *n.* **1.** A Hebrew idiom. **2.** Hebrew thought, character, practice, etc. **3.** The religion of the Hebrews; Judaism. — **Heʹbra·ist, Heʹbrew·ist** *n.* — **Heʹbra·isʹtic** or **·ti·cal** *adj.*

He·brew (hēʹbrōō) *n.* **1.** A member of that group of Semitic peoples claiming descent from the house of Abraham; Israelite; Jew. **2.** The ancient Semitic language of the Israelites as used in much of the Old Testament. **3.** The modern Hebrew language: official language of the republic of Israel. — **Epistle to the Hebrews** A book of the New Testament addressed to Hebrew Christians: also **Hebrews.** — *adj.* Hebraic; Jewish. [< OF < L < Gk. < Hebrew *'ibhri*, lit., one from beyond (Jordan)]

Hebrew calendar See (Hebrew) CALENDAR.

Hec·a·te (hekʹə·tē) In Greek mythology, a goddess of earth, moon, and underworld: also spelled *Hekate.*

heck (hek) *interj. Slang* Darn: a euphemism for *hell.*

heck·le (hekʹəl) *v.t.* **·led, ·ling** To try to annoy with taunts, questions, etc. [ME *hechelen*] — **heckʹler** *n.*

---

hec·tare (hek′târ) *n.* A unit of area in the metric system: also spelled *hektare.* Abbr. *ha.* See table front of book.

hec·tic (hek′tik) *adj.* 1. Characterized by great excitement, turmoil, haste, etc.: a *hectic* trip. 2. Denoting a condition of body, as in wasting diseases. 3. Designating the fever accompanying wasting diseases. Also **hec′ti·cal.** [< F < LL < Gk. *hektikos* consumptive] — **hec′ti·cal·ly** *adv.*

hecto- *combining form* In the metric system and in technical usage, a hundred times (a specified unit). Also spelled *hekto-.* Also, before vowels, **hect-.** [< F < Gk. *hekaton* hundred]

hec·to·gram (hek′tə-gram) *n.* In the metric system, a measure of weight: also spelled *hektogram.* Also **hec′to·gramme.** Abbr. *hg.* See table front of book.

hec·to·graph (hek′tə-graf, -gräf) *n.* A gelatin pad for making multiple copies of a writing or drawing. — *v.t.* To copy by hectograph. — **hec′to·graph′ic** *adj.*

hec·to·li·ter (hek′tə-lē′tər) *n.* In the metric system, a measure of capacity. Also *esp. Brit.* **hec′to·li′tre.** Abbr. *hl, hl.* See table front of book.

hec·to·me·ter (hek′tə-mē′tər, hek·tom′ə-tər) *n.* In the metric system, a measure of length. Also *esp. Brit.* **hec′to·me′tre.** Abbr. *hm., hm* See table front of book.

hec·tor (hek′tər) *v.t. & v.i.* 1. To bully; bluster; rant. 2. To tease; torment. — *n.* A bully. [after *Hector*]

Hec·tor (hek′tər) In the *Iliad,* a Trojan hero, son of Priam and Hecuba: killed by Achilles.

Hec·u·ba (hek′yŏŏ-bə) In the *Iliad,* the wife of Priam and mother of Hector, Troilus, Paris, Cassandra, and others.

he'd (hēd) 1. He had. 2. He would.

hedge (hej) *n.* 1. A fence or barrier formed of privet or other bushes set close together; also, any boundary or barrier. 2. The act of hedging a bet, risk, etc.; also, that which is used to hedge. — *v.* **hedged, hedg·ing** *v.t.* 1. To border or separate with a hedge. 2. To set barriers and restrictions to, so as to hinder freedom of movement or action; hem: often with *in* or *about.* 3. To guard against undue loss from (a bet, investment, etc.) by making compensatory bets, etc. — *v.i.* 4. To make compensatory bets, etc., in order to restrict losses. 5. To avoid forthright statement or action. [OE *hegg*] — **hedg′er** *n.* — **hedg′y** *adj.*

hedge·hog (hej′hôg′, -hog′) *n.* 1. A small, nocturnal, insectivorous mammal of Europe, having stout spines on the back and sides. 2. *U.S.* The porcupine. 3. *Mil.* An obstacle made of barbed wire on frames.

EUROPEAN HEDGEHOG (About 10 inches long)

hedge·hop (hej′hop′) *v.i.* **·hopped, ·hop·ping** To fly close to the ground in an airplane. — **hedge′hop′per** *n.*

hedge·row (hej′rō′) *n.* A dense row of bushes, trees, etc., planted as a hedge.

he·don·ism (hēd′n-iz′əm) *n.* 1. The doctrine that pleasure is the only proper goal of moral endeavor. 2. The pursuit of pleasure. [< Gk. *hēdonē* pleasure] — **he′don·ist** *n.* — **he′don·is′tic** *adj.* — **he′don·is′ti·cal·ly** *adv.*

-hedral *combining form* Having (a specified number of) sides or faces: *octahedral.*

-hedron *combining form* A figure having (a specified number of) sides or faces: *octahedron.* [< Gk. *hedra* surface]

heed (hēd) *v.t.* 1. To pay attention to; take more than casual notice of. — *v.i.* 2. To pay attention; listen. — *n.* Careful attention. [OE *hēdan*] — **heed′er** *n.*

heed·ful (hēd′fəl) *adj.* Giving heed; attentive; mindful. — **heed′ful·ly** *adv.* — **heed′ful·ness** *n.*

heed·less (hēd′lis) *adj.* Not showing any heed or attention; reckless. — **heed′less·ly** *adv.* — **heed′less·ness** *n.*

hee·haw (hē′hô′) *n.* The braying sound of a donkey. — *v.i.* To bray. [Imit.]

heel[1] (hēl) *n.* 1. In man, the rounded posterior part of the foot under and in back of the ankle; also, the rounded part of the palm of the hand nearest the wrist. 2. The analogous part of the hind foot of an animal. 3. That part of a shoe, stocking, etc., covering the heel. 4. In a shoe or boot, the built-up portion on which the rear of the foot rests. 5. Something analogous to the human heel, as the rounded end of a loaf of bread. 6. *Slang* A habitually dishonorable person; contemptible chiseler. — **at heel** Close behind. — **down at the heel** 1. Having the heels of one's shoes worn down. 2. Shabby; rundown. — **on** (or **upon**) **the heels of** 1. Right behind. 2. Close after; quickly following. — **to cool one's heels** To be kept waiting. — **to heel** 1. To an attendant position close behind one. 2. To submission; under control. — **to kick up one's heels** 1. To have a good time. 2. To let oneself go. — **to take to one's heels** To run away; flee. — *v.t.* 1. To supply with a heel, as a shoe. 2. To pursue closely. 3. *U.S. Slang* To supply with something, esp. with money or a weapon. — *v.i.* 4. To move the heels. 5. To follow at one's heels. [OE *hēla*] — **heel′less** *adj.*

heel[2] (hēl) *Naut. v.t. & v.i.* To lean or cause to lean to one side; cant, as a ship. — *n.* The act of heeling; a cant; list: also **heel′ing.** [Earlier *heeld,* OE *hieldan*]

heel bone The calcaneus.

heeled (hēld) *adj.* 1. Having heels: *high-heeled.* 2. *U.S. Slang* Supplied with money or a weapon.

heel·er (hē′lər) *n.* 1. One who heels shoes. 2. *U.S. Slang* A ward heeler.

heel·tap (hēl′tap′) *n.* 1. A thickness of leather on the heel of a shoe. 2. A small quantity of liquor left in a glass.

heft (heft) *Informal v.t.* 1. To test or gauge the weight of by lifting. 2. To lift up; heave. — *v.i.* 3. To weigh. — *n.* 1. Weight. 2. *U.S.* The bulk or gist. [Akin to HEAVE]

heft·y (hef′tē) *adj.* **heft·i·er, heft·i·est** *Informal* 1. Heavy; weighty. 2. Big and powerful; muscular.

He·ge·li·an·ism (hə-gā′lē-ən-iz′əm) *n.* The philosophical doctrine of Hegel that dialectic reasoning, a process whereby thought passes repeatedly in ascending stages from thesis to antithesis to synthesis, can unravel the order of development in which human consciousness and reality participate. Also **He·gel·ism** (hā′gəl-iz′əm). — **He·ge′lian** *n. & adj.*

he·gem·o·ny (hə-jem′ə-nē, hej′ə-mō′nē, hē′jə-) *n. pl.* **·nies** Domination or leadership; esp., the predominant influence of one state over others. [< Gk. *hēgeesthai* to lead] — **heg·e·mon·ic** (hej′ə-mon′ik) *adj.*

he·gi·ra (hi-jī′rə, hej′ə-rə) *n.* Any precipitate departure: also spelled *hejira.* [< Med.L < Arabic *hijrah* departure]

He·gi·ra (hi-jī′rə, hej′ə-rə) *n.* 1. The flight of Mohammed from Mecca to Medina in 622, now taken as the beginning of the Moslem era. 2. The Moslem era. Also spelled *Hejira.*

heif·er (hef′ər) *n.* A young cow that has not produced a calf. [OE *heahfore*]

height (hīt) *n.* 1. The state or quality of being high or relatively high. 2. The distance from the base to the top; altitude. 3. The distance above a given level, as the sea or horizon. 4. *Often pl.* A lofty or high place; eminence. 5. The highest part of anything; summit. 6. The highest degree: the *height* of quality. [OE *hīehtho*]

height·en (hīt′n) *v.t. & v.i.* 1. To make or become high or higher; raise or lift. 2. To make or become more in degree, amount, size, etc.; intensify. — **height′en·er** *n.*

heil (hīl) *German interj.* Hail! — *v.t.* To salute with "heil."

hei·nous (hā′nəs) *adj.* Extremely wicked; atrocious; odious. [< OF *haine* hatred < *hair* to hate] — **hei′nous·ly** *adv.* — **hei′nous·ness** *n.*

heir (âr) *n.* 1. Anyone inheriting rank or property from a deceased person; also, anyone likely to inherit upon the death of an incumbent or holder. 2. One who or that which takes over or displays the qualities of some forerunner. [< OF < L *heres*] — **heir′ess** *n.fem.* — **heir′less** *adj.*

heir apparent *pl.* **heirs apparent** *Law* One who must by course of law become the heir if he survives his ancestor.

heir·dom (âr′dəm) *n.* Heirship; inheritance.

heir·loom (âr′lōōm) *n.* 1. Anything that has been handed down in a family for generations. 2. *Law* Those chattels and articles that descend to an heir along with the estate.

heir presumptive *pl.* **heirs presumptive** *Law* An heir whose claim to an estate may become void by the birth of a nearer relative.

heir·ship (âr′ship) *n.* 1. The state or condition of being an heir. 2. The right to inheritance.

heist (hīst) *v.t. U.S. Slang* To steal. [Var. of HOIST]

he·ji·ra (hi-jī′rə, hej′ə-rə) See HEGIRA.

He·ji·ra (hi-jī′rə, hej′ə-rə) See HEGIRA.

Hek·a·te (hek′ə-tē) See HECATE.

hek·tare (hek′târ), **hek·to·gram** (hek′tə-gram), etc. See HECTARE, etc.

hekto- See HECTO-.

held (held) Past tense of HOLD.

Helen of Troy In Greek mythology, the beautiful wife of Menelaus, king of Sparta. Her elopement to Troy with Paris caused the Trojan War.

hel·i·cal (hel′i-kəl) *adj.* Pertaining to or shaped like a helix.

hel·i·ces (hel′ə-sēz) Alternative plural of HELIX.

helico- *combining form* Spiral; helical. Also, before vowels, **helic-.** [< Gk. *helix* spiral]

hel·i·coid (hel′ə-koid) *adj.* Coiled spirally, as certain univalve shells. Also **hel′i·coid′al.** — *n. Geom.* A surface generated by a straight line moving along a fixed helix in such a way as to maintain a constant angle with its axis. [< Gk. *helikoeidēs* spiral-shaped] — **hel′i·coi′dal·ly** *adv.*

hel·i·con (hel′i-kon, -kən) *n. Music* A large, circular tuba. [< HELICON; infl. by HELIX]

Hel·i·con (hel′i-kon, -kən) A mountain in Greece, legendary home of the Muses. — **Hel·i·co·ni·an** (hel′i-kō′nē·ən) *adj.*

hel·i·cop·ter (hel′ə-kop′tər, hē′lə-) *n. Aeron.* A type of aircraft whose aerodynamic support is obtained from engine-driven airfoil blades rotating around a vertical axis, and that is capable of rising and descending vertically. [< F < Gk. *helix, -ikos* spiral + *pteron* wing]

helio- *combining form* Sun; of the sun. Also, before vowels, **heli-.** [< Gk. *hēlios* the sun]

he·li·o·cen·tric (hē′lē·ə-sen′trik) *adj.* Having or regarding the sun as the center. Also **he′li·o·cen′tri·cal.**

he·li·o·graph (hē′lē-ə-graf′, -gräf′) n. 1. Astron. An instrument for taking photographs of the sun. 2. A mirror for signaling by flashes of light. Also **he′li·o** (-lē-ō). — v.t. & v.i. To signal with a heliograph. — **he·li·og·ra·pher** (hē′lē-og′rə-fər) n. — **he′li·o·graph′ic** adj. — **he′li·og′ra·phy** n.

He·li·os (hē′lē-os) In Greek mythology, the sun god.

he·li·o·scope (hē′lē-ə-skōp′) n. Astron. A device within a telescope by which the eyes are protected from pain or injury while observing the sun.

he·li·o·ther·a·py (hē′lē-ō-ther′ə-pē) n. Med. Exposure to the sun for purposes of treatment.

he·li·o·trope (hē′lē-ə-trōp′, hēl′yə-) n. 1. An herb of the borage family, with white or purplish fragrant flowers. 2. Any plant that turns toward the sun. 3. The bloodstone. 4. A soft, rosy purple. [< F < L < Gk. < hēlios sun + trepein to turn]

he·li·ot·ro·pism (hē′lē-ot′rə-piz′əm) n. Biol. The tendency of some organisms to move or turn toward or away from the sun. Also **he′li·o′tro·py.** — **he′li·o·trop′ic** adj.

hel·i·port (hel′ə-pôrt′, -pōrt′, hē′lə-) n. An airport for helicopters.

he·li·um (hē′lē-əm) n. An inert, odorless, nonflammable, gaseous element (symbol He) that is found chiefly in certain natural gas deposits, used to inflate balloons, dirigibles, etc. See ELEMENT. [< NL < Gk. hēlios sun]

he·lix (hē′liks) n. pl. **he·lix·es** or **hel·i·ces** (hel′ə-sēz) 1. A line, thread, wire, or the like, curved as if wound in a single layer round a cylinder; a form like a screw thread. 2. Any spiral. 3. Anat. The recurved border of the external ear. 4. Archit. A small volute. [< L, spiral < Gk.]

hell (hel) n. 1. Sometimes cap. In various religions, the abode of the dead or the place of punishment for the wicked after death; the abode of evil spirits. 2. Any condition of great mental or physical suffering; also, anything causing such suffering. — **a** (or **one**) **hell of a** Slang A remarkably bad, good, difficult, etc. (thing). — **like hell** Slang 1. Very much, very fast, very bad, etc.: He ran like hell. 2. Not at all; never. Like hell he will! — **to be hell on** Slang 1. To be damaging or harmful to. 2. To be unpleasant or difficult for. 3. To be very harsh or strict with. — **to catch** (or **get**) **hell** U.S. Slang To be roundly scolded or punished, as for a misdeed. — **to give** (**someone**) **hell** Slang To upbraid or punish (someone) severely. — **to raise hell** Slang To create a disturbance. — interj. An exclamation used as an imprecation or an expression of anger or impatience. [OE hel]

he′ll (hēl) He will.

Hel·las (hel′əs) Ancient or modern Greece. [< Gk.]

hell·bend·er (hel′ben′dər) n. U.S. A large aquatic salamander common to the Ohio River Valley.

hell-bent (hel′bent′) adj. U.S. Slang Determined to have or do; recklessly eager: hell-bent for home.

hell·cat (hel′kat′) n. 1. A shrewish woman. 2. A witch.

hel·le·bore (hel′ə-bôr, -bōr) n. 1. A perennial herb of the crowfoot family, having serrated leaves and large flowers; esp. the **black hellebore** of Europe, the root of which is a powerful cathartic. [< L < Gk. helleboros]

Hel·lene (hel′ēn) n. 1. A Greek. Also **Hel·le′ni·an.** [< Gk.]

Hel·len·ic (he-len′ik, -lē′nik) adj. Greek; Grecian. — n. A group of Indo-European languages, including Greek.

Hel·len·ism (hel′ə-niz′əm) n. 1. Ancient Greek character, ideals, or civilization. 2. An idiom or turn of phrase peculiar to Greek. 3. Assimilation of Greek speech, ideas, and culture. — **Hel′le·nist** n.

Hel·le·nis·tic (hel′ə-nis′tik) adj. 1. Pertaining to, resembling, or characteristic of the Hellenists or Hellenism. 2. Of or pertaining to the period that began with the conquests of Alexander the Great and ended about 300 years later, characterized by the spread of Greek language and culture throughout the Near East. Also **Hel′le·nis′ti·cal.**

Hel·le·nize (hel′ə-nīz) v.t. & v.i. **·nized, ·niz·ing** To make or become Greek; adopt or imbue with Greek language or customs. — **Hel′le·ni·za′tion** n. — **Hel′le·niz′er** n.

Hel·les·pont (hel′əs-pont) The ancient name for the DARDANELLES.

hell·fire (hel′fīr′) n. The flames or the punishment of hell.

hel·lion (hel′yən) n. Informal A person who delights in deviltry; a mischief-maker. [< HELL]

hell·ish (hel′ish) adj. 1. Of, like, or pertaining to hell. 2. Fiendish; horrible. — **hell′ish·ly** adv. — **hell′ish·ness** n.

hel·lo (hə-lō′) interj. 1. An exclamation of greeting, esp. over the telephone. 2. An exclamation used to gain attention. 3. An exclamation of surprise. — n. pl. **·loes** The saying or calling of "hello." — v.t. & v.i. **·loed, ·lo·ing** To call or say "hello" to.

helm (helm) n. 1. Naut. The steering apparatus of a vessel, esp. the tiller or wheel. 2. Any place of control or responsibility; administration. — v.t. To manage the helm of; steer; direct. [OE helma rudder]

hel·met (hel′mit) n. 1. Any of a number of protective coverings for the head; as: **a** The topmost piece of a suit of medieval or ancient armor. **b** The metal headguard worn by modern soldiers. **c** The leather or plastic headgear used by football players. **d** A head protector, as worn by firemen, welders, divers, etc. **e** A pith sun hat worn in hot countries. 2. Something resembling a helmet in appearance or position. [< OF, dim. of helme helmet < Gmc.] — **hel′met·ed** adj.

hel·minth (hel′minth) n. A worm; esp., a parasitic intestinal worm. [< Gk. helmins, -inthos worm]

helms·man (helmz′mən) n. pl. **·men** (-mən) A steersman; one who guides a ship.

hel·ot (hel′ət, hē′lət) n. 1. A slave; serf. 2. Usu. cap. One of a class of serfs in ancient Sparta. [< L < Gk., appar. < Helos, a Laconian town enslaved by Sparta] — **hel′ot·ry** n.

help (help) v.t. 1. To assist (someone) in doing something; cooperate with. 2. To assist (someone or something) in some action, change, etc.: with onto, into, out of, up, down, etc. 3. To provide aid or relief to. 4. To be, or be considered, responsible for: He can't help being lame. 5. To refrain from: I couldn't help laughing. 6. To remedy; alleviate. 7. To contribute to. 8. To serve; wait on, as a salesclerk. — v.i. 9. To give assistance. — **cannot help but** Cannot avoid; be obliged to. — **to help oneself** 1. To serve oneself, as with food. 2. To take without requesting or being offered. — n. 1. The act of helping. 2. Remedy; relief. 3. One who or that which gives assistance. 4. Any hired worker or helper. [OE helpan] — **help′er** n.

help·ful (help′fəl) adj. Affording help; giving service; beneficial. — **help′ful·ly** adv. — **help′ful·ness** n.

help·ing (hel′ping) n. 1. The act of assisting or aiding. 2. A single portion of food served at table.

help·less (help′lis) adj. 1. Unable to help oneself; dependent; feeble. 2. Incompetent; incapable. 3. Without recourse to help. — **help′less·ly** adv. — **help′less·ness** n.

help·mate (help′māt′) n. 1. A helper; partner. 2. A wife. Also **help·meet** (help′mēt′).

hel·ter-skel·ter (hel′tər-skel′tər) adv. In a hurried and confused manner. — adj. Hurried and confused. — n. Disorderly hurry; confused and hasty action. [Imit.]

helve (helv) n. The handle, as of an ax or hatchet. — v.t. **helved, helv·ing** To furnish with a helve. [OE helfe]

Hel·ve·tia (hel-vē′shə) 1. A country of Roman times including a large part of what is now Switzerland. 2. The Latin name for SWITZERLAND. — **Hel·ve′tian** adj. & n.

hem[1] (hem) n. 1. A finished edge made on a piece of fabric or a garment by turning the raw edge under and sewing it down. 2. Any similar border or edging. — v.t. **hemmed, hem·ming** 1. To provide with a hem. 2. To shut in; enclose; restrict: usu. with in, about, etc. [OE] — **hem′mer** n.

hem[2] (hem) interj. A sound made as in clearing the throat to attract attention, cover embarrassment, etc.; ahem. — v.i. **hemmed, hem·ming** 1. To make the sound "hem." 2. To hesitate in speaking. — **to hem and haw** To hesitate in speaking so as to keep from being explicit. [Imit.]

hem- See also words beginning HAEM-.

hem- See HEMO-.

hema- combining form Blood. Also spelled haema-. [< Gk. haima blood]

he·mal (hē′məl) adj. 1. Pertaining to blood or the vascular system. 2. Pertaining to or situated on the side of the body that contains the heart. Also spelled haemal.

he-man (hē′man′) n. pl. **·men** (-men′) Informal A virile, muscular man.

hem·a·tite (hem′ə-tīt, hē′mə-) n. Red ferric oxide, Fe_2O_3, an ore of iron, occurring in masses and crystallizing in the hexagonal system: also called ferric oxide. Also spelled haematite. [< L < Gk. < haima blood] — **hem·a·tit·ic** (hem′ə-tit′ik, hē′mə-) adj.

hemato- combining form Blood. Also, before vowels, **hemat-.** Also spelled haemato-. [< Gk. haima, haimatos, blood]

he·ma·tol·o·gy (hē′mə-tol′ə-jē, hem′ə-) n. The branch of biology that treats of the blood and its diseases. Also **he′ma·to·lo′gi·a** (-tə-lō′jē-ə). — **he′ma·tol′o·gist** n.

he·ma·tol·y·sis (hē′mə-tol′ə-sis, hem′ə-) n. Hemolysis.

he·ma·to·ma (hē′mə-tō′mə, hem′ə-) n. pl. **·to·ma·ta** (-tō′mə-tə) Pathol. A tumor or swelling formed by the effusion of blood.

hemi- prefix Half: hemisphere. Also, before vowels, **hem-.** [< Gk., half]

-hemia See -EMIA.

he·mic (hē′mik, hem′ik) adj. Of or pertaining to blood.

hem·i·dem·i·sem·i·qua·ver (hem′ē-dem′ē-sem′ē-kwā′vər) n. Music Chiefly Brit. A sixty-fourth note.

hem·i·ple·gi·a (hem′i-plē′jē-ə) n. Pathol. Paralysis of one side of the body. — **hem′i·ple′gic** (-plē′jik, -plej′ik) adj.

he·mip·ter·ous (hi-mip′tər-əs) adj. Of an order of insects generally having sucking mouth parts and four wings, including the cicadas, crickets, etc. [< NL < Gk. *hēmi*- half + *pteron* wing] — **hem·ip′ter·an** *adj. & n.*

hem·i·sphere (hem′ə·sfir) *n.* 1. A half-sphere formed by a plane passing through the center of the sphere. 2. A half of the terrestrial or celestial globe, or a map or projection of one. The world is usu. divided either at the equator into the **Northern** and **Southern Hemispheres,** or at some meridian between Europe and America into the **Eastern** and **Western Hemispheres.** [< F < L < Gk. *hēmi*- half + *sphaira* sphere] — **hem·i·spher·ic** (hem/ə·sfir′ik, -sfer-) *adj.*

hem·i·stich (hem′i·stik) *n.* Half a line of verse.

hem·line (hem′līn′) *n.* The line formed by the lower edge of a garment, as a dress or coat.

hem·lock (hem′lok) *n.* 1. One of several North American. or Asian evergreen trees of the pine family, having coarse, nonresinous wood used for paper pulp. Also **hemlock spruce.** 2. A large, biennial herb of the parsley family, yielding a poison: also **poison hemlock.** [OE *hymlice*]

hemo- *combining form* Blood. Also, before vowels, **hem-.** Also spelled *haemo-*. [< Gk. *haima* blood]

he·mo·glo·bin (hē′mə·glō′bin, hem′ə-) *n. Biochem.* The respiratory pigment in red blood corpuscles, composed of globin and heme, and serving as a carrier of oxygen.

he·mol·y·sis (hi·mol′ə·sis) *n.* Breakdown of red blood corpuscles with liberation of hemoglobin: also called *hematolysis*. — **he·mo·lyt·ic** (hē′mə·lit′ik, hem′ə-) *adj.*

he·mo·phil·i·a (hē′mə·fil′ē·ə, -fil′yə, hem′ə-) *n. Pathol.* A disorder characterized by immoderate bleeding even from slight injuries. [< NL < Gk. *haima* blood + *philia* fondness] — **he/mo·phil/i·ac, he/mo·phile/** (-fīl, -fil) *n.*

he·mo·phil·ic (hē′mə·fil′ik, hem′ə-) *adj.* 1. Of hemophilia. 2. Thriving in blood, as certain bacteria.

hem·or·rhage (hem′ər·ij, hem′rij) *n.* Copious discharge of blood from a ruptured blood vessel. — *v.i.* **·rhaged, ·rhag·ing** To bleed copiously. [< L < Gk. *haima* blood + *rhēgnynai* to burst] — **hem·or·rhag·ic** (hem/ə·raj′ik) *adj.*

hem·or·rhoid (hem′ə·roid) *n. Pathol.* A tumor or dilation of a vein in the anal region, usu. painful: also, in the plural, *piles.* [< F < L < Gk. < *haima* blood + *rheein* to flow] — **hem·or·rhoi·dal** (hem/ə·roid′l) *adj.*

he·mo·stat (hē′mə·stat, hem′ə-) *n. Med.* A device or drug for checking the flow of blood from a ruptured vessel.

he·mo·stat·ic (hē′mə·stat′ik, hem′ə-) *Med. adj.* 1. Stopping the flow of blood. 2. Preventive of bleeding.

hemp (hemp) *n.* 1. A tall, annual herb of the mulberry family, native in Asia but cultivated elsewhere. 2. The tough, strong fiber from this plant, used for cloth and cordage. 3. A narcotic prepared from the plant. [OE *henep*]

hemp·en (hem′pən) *adj.* Made of or like hemp.

hem·stitch (hem′stich′) *n.* The ornamental finishing of a hem, made by pulling out several threads and drawing the cross threads together in groups. — *v.t.* To embroider with a hemstitch. — **hem′stitch′er** *n.*

hen (hen) *n.* 1. The mature female of the domestic fowl and related birds. 2. The female of the lobster. [OE *henn*]

hen·bane (hen′bān) *n.* A poisonous Old World herb of the nightshade family, with sticky, malodorous foliage.

hence (hens) *adv.* 1. As a consequence; therefore; thus. 2. From this time or date: a week *hence*; also, ever afterwards; henceforth. 3. Away from this place. — *interj. Archaic & Poetic* Go! Depart! [ME < OE *heonan* from here]

hence·forth (hens′fôrth′, -fōrth′; hens/fôrth′, -fōrth′) *adv.* From this time on. Also **hence/for/ward** (-fôr′wərd).

hench·man (hench′mən) *n. pl.* **·men** (-mən) 1. A faithful follower. 2. *U.S.* A political supporter who works chiefly for personal gain. [ME < OE *hengst* horse + *man* groom]

hen·e·quen (hen/ə·kin) *n.* 1. A tough fiber obtained from the leaves of a Mexican plant. 2. The plant. Also **hen/e·quin.** [< Sp. < Taino]

hen·na (hen′ə) *n.* 1. An ornamental Oriental shrub or small tree. 2. A cosmetic made from its leaves, used for dyeing the hair, fingernails, etc. 3. A color varying from reddish orange to coppery brown. — *v.* **hen·naed, hen·na·ing** *v.t.* To dye with henna. [< Arabic *henna*]

hen·ner·y (hen/ər·ē) *n. pl.* **·ner·ies** A place where hens are kept.

hen·peck (hen′pek′) *v.t.* To domineer over or harass (one's husband) by nagging, ill temper, and petty annoyances.

hen·pecked (hen′pekt′) *adj.* Dominated by one's wife.

hen·ry (hen′rē) *n. pl.* **·ries** or **·rys** *Electr.* The unit equal to the inductance of a circuit in which the variation of a current at the rate of one ampere per second induces an electromotive force of one volt. [after Joseph *Henry*, 1797–1878, U.S. physicist]

hep·a·rin (hep′ə·rin) *n. Biochem.* A substance found in liver and other tissues, having the power to prevent coagulation of blood, used in medicine. [< Gk. *hēpar* liver]

he·pat·ic (hi·pat′ik) *adj.* 1. Of or like the liver. 2. Acting upon the liver. 3. Liver-colored. — *n.* A drug acting upon the liver. Also **he·pat/i·cal.** [< L < Gk. *hepar* liver]

he·pat·i·ca (hi·pat′ə·kə) *n. pl.* **·cas** or **·cae** (-sē) A small perennial herb with delicate flowers: also called *liverwort.* [< NL < L *hepaticus* of the liver]

hepatico- *combining form* Hepato-.

hep·a·ti·tis (hep′ə·tī′tis) *n. Pathol.* Inflammation of the liver.

hepato- *combining form* Pertaining to the liver. Also, before vowels, **hepat-.** [< Gk. *hēpar, hēpatos* the liver]

Hep·ple·white (hep′əl·hwīt) *adj.* Denoting an English style of furniture characterized by graceful curves and light, slender woodwork, developed in the reign of George III. [after G. *Hepplewhite*, died 1786, the designer]

hepta- *combining form* Seven. Also, before vowels, **hept-.** [< Gk. *hepta* seven]

hep·ta·gon (hep′tə·gon) *n.* A polygon having seven sides and seven angles. — **hep·tag·o·nal** (hep·tag′ə·nəl) *adj.*

hep·tam·e·ter (hep·tam′ə·tər) *n.* In prosody, a line of verse consisting of seven metrical feet.

hep·tane (hep′tān) *n. Chem.* A colorless flammable liquid hydrocarbon of the methane series, C_7H_{16}, used as a solvent and in the determination of the octane number of motor fules.

HEPPLEWHITE CHAIR

her (hûr) *pron.* The objective case of the pronoun *she.* — *pronominal adj.* The possessive case of *she.* [OE *hire*]

He·ra (hir′ə) In Greek mythology, the queen of the gods and goddess of women and marriage, sister and wife of Zeus: identified with the Roman *Juno.* Also spelled *Here.*

Her·a·cles (her′ə·klēz) Hercules. Also **Her/a·kles.**

her·ald (her′əld) *n.* 1. Any bearer of important news; messenger. 2. One who or that which shows what is to follow; harbinger. 3. *Brit.* An official whose duty is to grant or record arms, trace genealogies, etc. 4. Formerly, an officer who carried messages, arranged tournaments, etc. — *v.t.* To announce or proclaim publicly. [< OF < OHG *heren* to call] — **he·ral·dic** (hi·ral′dik) *adj.*

her·ald·ry (her′əl·drē) *n. pl.* **·ries** 1. The art or science that treats of armorial bearings, genealogies, etc., as in heraldic symbolism. 2. The office or function of a herald.

herb (ûrb, hûrb) *n.* 1. A plant without woody tissue, that withers and dies after flowering. 2. Any such plant as a medicine, seasoning, scent, etc. [< L *herba* grass, herbage]

her·ba·ceous (hûr·bā′shəs) *adj.* 1. Like herbs. 2. Having the semblance, color, or structure of a leaf.

herb·age (ûr′bij, hûr′-) *n.* 1. Herbs collectively, esp. pasturage. 2. The succulent parts of herbaceous plants.

herb·al (hûr′bəl, ûr′-) *adj.* Of or pertaining to herbs. — *n.* Formerly, a treatise on herbs or plants.

herb·al·ist (hûr′bəl·ist, ûr′-) *n.* A dealer in herbs.

her·bar·i·um (hûr·bâr′ē·əm) *n. pl.* **·bar·i·ums** or **·bar·i·a** (-bâr′ē·ə). 1. A collection of dried plants scientifically arranged. 2. A room or building containing such a collection.

her·biv·o·rous (hûr·biv′ər·əs) *adj.* 1. Feeding on vegetable matter; plant-eating. 2. Belonging to a group of mammals that feed mainly on herbage, as cows, horses, camels, etc. [< L *herba* grass] — **her·biv′o·rous·ly** *adv.*

her·cu·le·an (hûr·kyōō′lē·ən, hûr′kyə·lē′ən) *adj.* 1. Having great strength. 2. Requiring great strength.

Her·cu·le·an (hûr·kyōō′lē·ən, hûr′kyə·lē′ən) *adj.* Of or pertaining to Hercules (Heracles); Heraclean.

Her·cu·les (hûr′kyə·lēz) In classical mythology, the son of Zeus, renowned for his great strength: also called *Heracles.* — *n.* 1. Any man of great strength. 2. A constellation.

herd (hûrd) *n.* 1. A number of cattle or other animals feeding, moving about, or kept together. 2. A large crowd of people: a contemptuous term. — *v.t. & v.i.* To bring or drive together in a herd. — **Syn.** See FLOCK. [OE *heord*]

-herd *combining form* Herdsman: *swineherd, cowherd,* etc. [OE *hierde* herdsman]

herds·man (hûrdz′mən) *n. pl.* **·men** (-mən) *Brit.* One who owns or tends a herd. Also **herd/er, herd/man.**

here (hir) *adv.* 1. In, at, or about this place: opposed to *there.* Also used to indicate or emphasize: George *here* is a good swimmer. 2. To this place; hither. 3. At this point in time, in an action, etc.: *Here* you begin; *Here* are my reasons. 4. In the present life: distinguished from *hereafter.* — *interj.* An exclamation used to answer a roll call, attract attention, call an animal, etc. — **here and there** 1. Irregularly scattered. 2. Hither and thither. — **here goes!** For better or worse, I start now! — **neither here nor there** Beside the point; irrelevant. — *n.* 1. This place. 2. This time; this life: the *here* and now. [OE *hēr*]

He·re (hir′ē) See HERA.

here·a·bout (hir/ə·bout′) *adv.* About this place; in this vicinity. Also **here/a·bouts/.**

here·af·ter (hir·af′tər, -äf′-) *adv.* 1. At some future time. 2. From this time forth. 3. In the state of life after death. — *n.* A future state or existence. [OE *hēræfter*]

here·at (hir·at′) *adv.* 1. At this time. 2. Because of this.

here·by (hir·bī′) *adv.* By means or by virtue of this.

he·red·i·ta·ble (hə·red′i·tə·bəl) *adj.* Heritable. [< MF *héréditable*] — **he·red′i·ta·bil′i·ty** *n.* — **he·red′i·ta·bly** *adv.*

her·e·dit·a·ment (her′ə·dit′ə·mənt) *n. Law* Every kind of property capable of being inherited.

he·red·i·tar·y (hə·red′ə·ter′ē) *adj.* **1.** Derived from ancestors; inherited. **2.** Of or pertaining to heredity or inheritance. **3.** *Biol.* Transmitted or transmissible directly from an animal or plant to its offspring: distinguished from *congenital.* **4.** *Law* **a** Passing by inheritance to an heir. **b** Holding possession or title through inheritance. — **he·red′i·tar′i·ly** *adv.* — **he·red′i·tar′i·ness** *n.*

he·red·i·ty (hə·red′ə·tē) *n. pl.* **·ties** *Biol.* **1.** Transmission of characteristics from parents to offspring. **2.** The tendency manifested by an organism to develop in the likeness of a progenitor. **3.** The sum total of an individual's inherited characteristics. [< F < L *hereditas, -tatis* inheritance]

Her·e·ford (her′ə·fərd, *U.S.* hûr′fərd) *n.* One of a breed of beef cattle having a white face and a red and white coat.

here·in (hir·in′) *adv.* **1.** In or into this place; in this. **2.** In this case, circumstance, matter, etc. [OE *hērinne*]

here·in·af·ter (hir′in·af′tər, -äf′-) *adv.* In a subsequent part of this document, deed, contract, etc.

here·in·be·fore (hir′in·bi·fôr′, -fōr′) *adv.* In a preceding part of this document, deed, contract, etc.

here·in·to (hir·in′tōō) *adv.* **1.** Into this place. **2.** Into this case, circumstance, matter, etc.

here·of (hir·uv′, -ov′) *adv.* **1.** Of this. **2.** In regard to this.

here·on (hir·on′, -ôn′) *adv.* On this; hereupon.

her·e·sy (her′ə·sē) *n. pl.* **·sies** **1.** A belief contrary to the established doctrines of a church or religious system. **2.** Any belief contrary to established doctrine. **3.** The holding of such a belief or opinion. [< OF < Gk. *hairesis* sect]

her·e·tic (her′ə·tik) *n.* **1.** One who holds beliefs or opinions contrary to the established doctrines of his religion. **2.** One who maintains unorthodox opinions on any subject.

he·ret·i·cal (hə·ret′i·kəl) *adj.* Of, pertaining to, or characterized by heresy. — **he·ret′i·cal·ly** *adv.*

here·to (hir·tōō′) *adv.* To this thing, matter, etc.

here·to·fore (hir′tə·fôr′, -fōr′) *adv.* Before now; previously.

here·un·der (hir·un′dər) *adv.* **1.** Under this heading, etc. **2.** Under the terms of this statement, etc.

here·un·to (hir′un·tōō′) *adv.* To this; hereto.

here·up·on (hir′ə·pon′, -pôn′) *adv.* Immediately resulting from or following this; upon this.

here·with (hir·with′, -with′) *adv.* **1.** Along with this. **2.** By means of or through this.

her·i·ta·ble (her′ə·tə·bəl) *adj.* **1.** That can be inherited. **2.** *Rare* Capable of inheriting. [< OF < *heriter* to inherit] — **her′i·ta·bil′i·ty** *n.* — **her′i·ta·bly** *adv.*

her·i·tage (her′ə·tij) *n.* **1.** That which is inherited. **2.** A cultural tradition, body of knowledge, etc., handed down from past times. **3.** *Law* Property that is or can be inherited by descendants. [< OF *heriter* to inherit]

her·i·tor (her′ə·tər) *n.* An inheritor. — **her′e·trix** or **her′i·trix** (-triks) or **her′i·tress** (-tris) *n.fem.*

her·maph·ro·dite (hûr·maf′rə·dīt) *n.* **1.** An individual having both male and female reproductive organs. **2.** *Bot.* A plant having both stamens and pistils. — *adj.* Hermaphroditic. [after *Hermaphroditus,* son of Hermes, who became united with a nymph in a single body]

hermaphrodite brig *Naut.* A brigantine.

her·maph·ro·dit·ic (hûr·maf′rə·dit′ik) *adj.* Of, pertaining to, or characteristic of a hermaphrodite.

her·maph·ro·dit·ism (hûr·maf′rə·dīt·iz′əm) *n.* The state or condition of being a hermaphrodite.

Her·mes (hûr′mēz) In Greek mythology, the messenger of the gods, usually depicted with winged sandals, a hat, and a caduceus: identified with the Roman *Mercury.*

her·met·ic (hûr·met′ik) *adj.* **1.** Made impervious to air and liquids; airtight. **2.** Of or relating to alchemy; occult; magical. Also **her·met′i·cal.** [< Med.L *hermeticus*] — **her·met′i·cal·ly** *adv.*

her·mit (hûr′mit) *n.* **1.** One who abandons society and lives in seclusion, often for religious reasons. **2.** A molasses cooky. [< OF < LL < Gk. *erēmia* desert] — **her·mit′ic** or **·i·cal** *adj.* — **her·mit′i·cal·ly** *adv.*

her·mit·age (hûr′mə·tij) *n.* **1.** The retreat or dwelling of a hermit. **2.** Any secluded dwelling place.

hermit crab Any of various soft-bodied crustaceans that live in the empty shells of snails, etc.

her·ni·a (hûr′nē·ə) *n. pl.* **·ni·as** or **·ni·ae** (-nē-ē) *Pathol.* The protrusion of an organ or part of an organ, as of the intestine, through an opening in the wall surrounding it; rupture. [< L] — **her′ni·al** *adj.*

hernio- *combining form* Hernia.

he·ro (hir′ō, hē′rō) *n. pl.* **·roes** **1.** A man distinguished for exceptional courage, fortitude, or bold enterprise. **2.** One

idealized for superior qualities or deeds of any kind. **3.** The principal male character in a drama, fictional work, etc. **4.** In classical mythology and legend, a man of great nobility or physical prowess, often the son of a god and a mortal. **5.** *U.S.* A sandwich made with a loaf of bread cut lengthwise. [< L < Gk. *hēros*]

He·ro (hir′ō) In Greek legend, a priestess whose lover, Leander, nightly swam the Hellespont to join her. Finding him drowned one night, she cast herself into the sea.

he·ro·ic (hi·rō′ik) *adj.* **1.** Characteristic of or befitting a hero. **2.** Resembling a hero. **3.** Showing great daring or boldness; extreme in action or effect: a *heroic* attempt. **4.** Of or pertaining to the heroes of antiquity. **5.** Relating to or describing a hero or heroic deeds; epic: *heroic* poetry. **6.** Grandiose in style or language. **7.** Of sculpture, considerably larger than life size. Also **he·ro′i·cal.** — *n.* **1.** *Often pl.* Heroic verse. **2.** *pl.* Melodramatic or extravagant language, action, or ideas. — **he·ro′i·cal·ly** *adv.*

heroic couplet An English verse form consisting of two rhyming lines of iambic pentameter.

heroic verse One of several verse forms used especially in epic and dramatic poetry, as the iambic pentameter of the English heroic couplet and blank verse.

her·o·in (her′ō·in) *n.* A white, odorless, crystalline derivative of morphine, $C_{21}H_{23}O_5N$, a powerful, habit-forming narcotic. [< G]

her·o·ine (her′ō·in) *n.fem.* **1.** A girl or woman of heroic character. **2.** The principal female character of a drama, fictional work, etc. [< L < Gk. *hērōinē*]

her·o·ism (her′ō·iz′əm) *n.* **1.** The character or qualities of a hero or heroine. **2.** Heroic behavior.

her·on (her′ən) *n.* **1.** Any of several wading birds, having a long neck, a long, slender bill, and long legs. **2.** Any of various similar or related birds, as the egret or the bittern. [< OF *hairon,* ult. < Gmc.]

her·on·ry (her′ən·rē) *n. pl.* **·ries** A place where herons congregate and breed.

hero worship Enthusiastic or extravagant admiration for heroes or other persons. — **hero worshiper**

her·pes (hûr′pēz) *n. Pathol.* A virus infection of the skin and mucous membranes, characterized by the eruption of blisters. [< L < Gk. *herpein* to creep]

herpes zos·ter (zos′tər) *Pathol.* Shingles. [< L, herpes + *zoster* (< Gk. girdle, belt)]

her·pe·tol·o·gy (hûr′pə·tol′ə·jē) *n.* The branch of zoology that treats of reptiles and amphibians. [< Gk. *herpeton* reptile + -LOGY] — **her·pe·to·log′i·cal** (hûr′pə·tə·loj′i·kəl) *adj.* — **her′pe·tol′o·gist** *n.*

Herr (her) *n. pl.* **Her·ren** (her′ən) *German* A title of address equivalent oo the English *Mister.* Abbr. *Hr.*

her·ring (her′ing) *n. pl.* **·rings** or **·ring** **1.** A small food fish frequenting the North Atlantic, the young of which are canned as sardines, and the adults smoked, pickled, or salted. **2.** Any of various fish allied to the herring, as the shad, sardine, etc. [OE *hæring*]

her·ring·bone (her′ing·bōn′) *n.* **1.** A pattern utilizing a design, often repeated, resembling the spinal structure of a herring, in which the ribs form slanting parallel lines on either side of the spine. **2.** Something made in or consisting of such a pattern. — *adj.* Having or forming the pattern of a herringbone. — *v.* **·boned, ·bon·ing** *v.t.* **1.** To ornament with or arrange in a herringbone pattern. — *v.i.* **2.** To produce a herringbone pattern. **3.** In skiing, to walk up an incline with the skis pointed outward.

hers (hûrz) *pron.* **1.** The possessive case of the pronoun *she,* used predicatively: That book is *hers.* **2.** The one or ones belonging to or relating to her. — **of hers** Belonging or relating to her. [OE *hire* + -*s* (after *his*)]

her·self (hər·self′) *pron.* A form of the third person singular feminine pronoun, used: **1.** As a reflexive or as object of a preposition in a reflexive sense: She excused *herself*; She talks to *herself.* **2.** As an emphatic or intensive form of *she*: She *herself* called the police. **3.** As a designation of a normal or usual state: After her illness, she was *herself* again. **4.** *Irish* As a pronoun meaning *she*: How is *herself*?

Hertz·i·an wave (hert′sē·ən, hûrt′-) An electromagnetic wave in the radio and radar range, artificially produced. [after H. R. *Hertz*]

he's (hēz) **1.** He is. **2.** He has.

Hesh·wan (hesh·vän′, hesh′van) *n.* The second month of the Hebrew year. Also **Hesh·van′.** See (Hebrew) CALENDAR.

hes·i·tan·cy (hez′ə·tən·sē) *n. pl.* **·cies** The act or condition of hesitating; hesitation; uncertainty. Also **hes′i·tance.**

hes·i·tant (hes′ə·tənt) *adj.* Lacking certainty or decisiveness; hesitating; irresolute. — **hes′i·tant·ly** *adv.*

hes·i·tate (hez′ə·tāt) v.i. **·tat·ed, ·tat·ing** 1. To be slow or doubtful in acting, making a decision, etc.; be uncertain; waver. 2. To be reluctant. 3. To pause or falter. 4. To falter in speech. [< L haesitare, freq. of haerere to stick]

hes·i·ta·tion (hez′ə·tā′shən) n. 1. The act of hesitating. 2. A pause or delay caused by indecision or uncertainty. 3. A pause or faltering in speech. — **hes′i·ta·tive** adj.

Hes·pe·ri·an (hes·pir′ē·ən) adj. 1. Poetic In or of the west. 2. Of the Hesperides. [< L < Gk. hesperios western]

Hes·per·i·des (hes·per′ə·dēz) n.pl. 1. In Greek mythology, the daughters of Atlas who, together with a dragon, guarded the golden apples given to Hera. 2. The garden where these apples grew. [< Gk. hesperis western]

Hes·pe·rus (hes′pər·əs) n. The evening star, esp. Venus. Also Poetic **Hes′per.** [< L < Gk. Hesperos]

Hes·sian (hesh′ən) n. 1. A native of Hesse. 2. A soldier from Hesse hired by the British to fight in the American Revolution. — adj. Of Hesse or its inhabitants.

Hessian fly A small, blackish fly, whose larvae are very destructive to wheat, barley, and rye.

het (het) Dial. Past tense and past participle of HEAT. — **het up** Excited; angry.

he·tae·ra (hi·tir′ə, -tī′rə) n. pl. **·tae·rae** (-tir′ē, -tī′rē) In ancient Greece, a professional courtesan or concubine. Also **he·tae·ra** (hi·tī′rə). [< Gk. hetaira companion]

hetero- combining form Other; different: opposed to homo-. Also, before vowels, **heter-.** [< Gk. hetero- < heteros other]

het·er·o·cy·clic (het′ər·ə·sī′klik, -sik′lik) adj. Chem. Pertaining to or designating an organic ring compound containing atoms of one or more elements other than carbon.

het·er·o·dox (het′ər·ə·doks′) adj. 1. At variance with accepted or established doctrines or beliefs, esp. in religion. 2. Holding unorthodox beliefs or opinions. [< Gk. hetero- other + doxa opinion] — **het′er·o·dox′y** n.

het·er·o·dyne (het′ər·ə·dīn′) adj. Telecom. Denoting a radio circuit, receiver, etc., in which the incoming signal is combined with a signal of fixed frequency and the signal resulting from their beats is used as the amplifier input. — v.i. **·dyned, ·dyn·ing** To modify a signal in this manner.

het·er·o·ge·ne·i·ty (het′ər·ə·jə·nē′ə·tē) n. pl. **·ties** The state of being heterogeneous; dissimilarity.

het·er·o·ge·ne·ous (het′ər·ə·jē′nē·əs) adj. 1. Consisting of parts or elements that are dissimilar or unrelated; not homogeneous. 2. Differing in nature or kind; unlike. [< Med.L < Gk. < hetero- other + genos kind] — **het′er·o·ge′ne·ous·ly** adv. — **het′er·o·ge′ne·ous·ness** n.

het·er·og·e·nous (het′ə·roj′ə·nəs) adj. Biol. Originating outside the organism.

het·er·o·nym (het′ər·ə·nim′) n. A word spelled like another, but having a different sound and meaning, as bass, a male voice, and bass, a fish. Compare HOMOGRAPH. [< HETER(O)- + Gk. onyma name; on analogy with synonym] — **het·er·on·y·mous** (het′ə·ron′ə·məs) adj.

het·er·op·ter·ous (het′ə·rop′tər·es) adj. Designating a suborder of hemipterous insects that includes the true bugs. [< NL < Gk. hetero- other + pteron wing]

het·er·o·sex·u·al (het′ər·ə·sek′shōō·əl) adj. 1. Of, or having sexual desire for those of the opposite sex. 2. Biol. Of or pertaining to the opposite sex or to both sexes. — n. A heterosexual individual. — **het′er·o·sex′u·al′i·ty** (-al·ə·tē) n.

het·er·o·zy·gote (het′ər·ə·zī′gōt, -zig′ōt) n. Biol. A hybrid that carries different alleles of the same character and that does not breed true. — **het′er·o·zy′gous** (-zī′gəs) adj.

heu·ris·tic (hyŏŏ·ris′tik) adj. 1. Aiding or guiding in discovery. 2. Designating an educational method by which a pupil is stimulated to make his own investigations and discoveries. [< Gk. heuriskein to find out]

hew (hyōō) v. **hewed, hewn** or **hewed, hew·ing** v.t. 1. To make or shape with or as with blows of an ax or other cutting tool. 2. To cut or strike with an ax, sword, etc. 3. To fell with or as with ax blows. — v.i. 4. To make cutting and repeated blows, as with an ax or sword. 5. To conform, as to a principle. [OE hēawan] — **hew′er** n.

hex (heks) U.S. Dial. or Informal n. 1. An evil spell. 2. A witch. — v.t. To bewitch. [< G hexe witch]

hexa- combining form Six. Also, before vowels, **hex-.** [< Gk. hexa- < hex six]

hex·a·gon (hek′sə·gon) n. Geom. A polygon having six sides and six angles. [< L < Gk. hex six + gonia angle] — **hex·ag·o·nal** (hek·sag′ə·nəl) adj. — **hex·ag′o·nal·ly** adv.

hex·a·gram (hek′sə·gram) n. 1. A six-pointed star made by or as by completing the equilateral triangles based on the sides of a regular hexagon. 2. Any of various figures formed by six intersecting lines.

hex·am·e·ter (hek·sam′ə·tər) n. 1. In prosody, a line of verse consisting of six metrical feet. 2. The dactylic verse of Greek and Latin epics. — adj. Having six metrical feet. [< L < Gk. hex- ametros] — **hex·a·met·ric** (hek′sə·met′rik), **hex·am′e·tral** (-ə·trəl), **hex·a·met′ri·cal** adj.

hex·a·pod (hek′sə·pod) n. One of the true or six-legged insects. — adj. Having six feet. [< Gk. hexapous, -podos six-footed] — **hex·ap·o·dous** (hek·sap′ə·dəs) adj.

hex·ose (hek′sōs) n. Biochem. Any simple sugar, as glucose or fructose, containing six carbon atoms to the molecule.

hey (hā) interj. An exclamation calling for attention or expressing surprise, pleasure, inquiry, etc. [ME hei]

hey·day (hā′dā′) n. 1. Period of greatest vigor; height, as of power. 2. Exuberance; ardor. [Prob. < HIGH DAY]

H-hour (āch′our′) n. The hour appointed for a military operation to begin: also called zero hour.

hi (hī) interj. 1. U.S. An exclamation of greeting. 2. Brit. A call to attract attention. [Var. of HEY]

hi·a·tus (hī·ā′təs) n. pl. **·tus·es** or **·tus** 1. A gap or space from which something is missing, as in a manuscript; lacuna. 2. Any break or interruption. 3. A pause due to the coming together in a word or successive words of two separately pronounced vowels without an intervening consonant. [< L]

Hi·a·wath·a (hī′ə·woth′ə, -wô′thə, hē′ə-) 1. A Mohawk chief credited with organizing the Five Nations. 2. The hero of Longfellow's poem The Song of Hiawatha (1855).

hi·ba·chi (hi·bä′chē) n. pl. **·chis** A deep container to hold burning coals, used for heating and cooking. [< Japanese]

hi·ber·nal (hī·bûr′nəl) adj. Of or pertaining to winter; wintry. [< L hibernus wintry]

hi·ber·nate (hī′bər·nāt) v.i. **·nat·ed, ·nat·ing** 1. To pass the winter in a dormant state, as certain animals. 2. To remain inactive or secluded. [< L hibernare] — **hi′ber·na′tion** n.

Hi·ber·ni·a (hī·bûr′nē·ə) Latin and poetic name for Ireland. [< L, alter. of Iverna] — **Hi·ber′ni·an** n. & adj.

hi·bis·cus (hi·bis′kəs,‚hī-) n. A shrub or tree of the mallow family, having large, showy flowers: the state flower of Hawaii. [< L < Gk. hibiskos mallow]

hic·cup (hik′əp) n. 1. An involuntary contraction of the diaphragm, causing a sudden, audible inspiration of breath checked by a spasmodic closure of the glottis. 2. pl. A condition characterized by repetition of such spasms. — v. **·cuped** or **·cupped, ·cup·ing** or **·cup·ping** — v.i. 1. To make a sound of or as of a hiccup. — v.t. 2. To utter with hiccups. Also **hic·cough** (hik′əp). [Imit.]

hic ja·cet (hik jā′set) Latin Here lies: often inscribed on tombstones.

hick (hik) n. Informal One having the clumsy, unsophisticated manners, etc. supposedly typical of rural areas; bumpkin. — adj. Of or typical of hicks. [Alter. of Richard]

hick·ey (hik′ē) n. pl. **·eys** U.S. Informal 1. Any gadget or contrivance. 2. A pimple or blemish. [Origin unknown]

hick·o·ry (hik′ər·ē, hik′rē) n. pl. **·ries** 1. A North American tree of the walnut family, having hard, durable wood and yielding edible nuts. 2. The wood of such trees. 3. A switch made of this wood. [< Algonquian pawcohiccora]

hid (hid) Past tense and alternative past participle of HIDE[1].

hi·dal·go (hi·dal′gō, Sp. ē·thäl′gō) n. pl. **·gos** (-gōz, Sp. -gōs) A Spanish nobleman of lower rank than a grandee. [< Sp. < hijo de algo son of something]

hid·den (hid′n) Past participle of HIDE[1]. — adj. Not seen or known; concealed; obscure; mysterious.

hide[1] (hīd) v. **hid, hid·den** or **hid, hid·ing** v.t. 1. To put or keep out of sight; conceal. 2. To keep secret; withhold from knowledge. 3. To block or obstruct the sight of. — v.i. 4. To keep oneself out of sight; remain concealed. — **to hide out** U.S. Informal To remain in concealment, esp. as a fugitive. [OE hȳdan] — **hid′er** n.
— Syn. 1. Hide, conceal, and secrete mean to put or keep out of sight. We may hide without intention, but we conceal intentionally. An object is hidden or concealed when covered from view, when disguised as something else, or when buried out of reach. It is secreted when put into some private, secret place.

hide[2] (hīd) n. 1. The skin of an animal, esp. when stripped from the carcass or made into leather. 2. Informal The human skin. — v.t. **hid·ed, hid·ing** Informal To flog severely; whip. [OE hȳd skin]

hide-and-seek (hīd′n·sēk′) n. A children's game in which those who hide are sought by one who is "it." Also **hide′-and-go-seek′.**

hide·a·way (hīd′ə·wā′) n. A place of concealment.

hide·bound (hīd′bound′) adj. 1. Obstinately fixed in opinion; narrow-minded; bigoted. 2. Having the skin too tightly adhering to the back and ribs: said of cattle, etc.

hid·e·ous (hid′ē·əs) adj. 1. Extremely ugly: a hideous sight. 2. Morally odious or detestable; shocking. [< AF < OF hisde, hide fright] — **hid′e·ous·ly** adv. — **hid′e·ous·ness** n.

hide·out (hīd′out′) n. Informal A place of concealment or refuge, especially from legal authority. Also **hide′out′.**

hid·ing[1] (hī′ding) n. 1. The act of one who or that which hides. 2. A state or place of concealment.

hid·ing[2] (hī′ding) n. Informal A flogging; whipping.

hie (hī) v.t. & v.i. **hied, hie·ing** or **hy·ing** To hasten; hurry: often reflexive: I hied myself home. [OE hīgian]

hi·er·arch (hī′ə·rärk) n. A high priest or prelate. [< Med.L < Gk. hierarchēs sacred + hieros ruler]

hi·er·ar·chi·cal (hī′ə·rär′ki·kəl) *adj.* Of, belonging to, or characteristic of a hierarchy. Also **hi′er·ar′chic, hi/er·ar′·chal. — hi/er·ar′chi·cal·ly** *adv.*

hi·er·ar·chy (hī′ə·rär′kē) *n. pl.* **·chies** 1. Any group of persons or things arranged in successive orders or classes, each of which is subject to or dependent on the one above it. 2. A body of ecclesiastics so arranged. 3. Government or rule by such a body of ecclesiastics. 4. In science and logic, a series of systematic groupings in graded order.

hi·er·at·ic (hī′ə·rat′ik) *adj.* 1. Of or pertaining to priests or priestly usage. 2. Of or pertaining to a shortened form of hieroglyphic writing used by priests in ancient Egypt.

hiero- *combining form* Sacred; divine. Also, before vowels, **hier-**. [< Gk. *hieros* sacred]

hi·er·o·glyph·ic (hī′ər·ə·glif′ik, hī′rə·glif′ik) *n.* 1. *Usu. pl.* A picture or symbol representing an object, idea, or sound, as in the writing system of the ancient Egyptians. 2. *pl.* A system of writing using such pictures or symbols. 3. Any symbol or character having an obscure or hidden meaning. 4. *pl.* Illegible writing. Also **hi·er·o·glyph** (hī′ər·ə·glif′, hī′rə·glif). — *adj.* 1. Pertaining to, consisting of, or resembling hieroglyphics. 2. Written in or inscribed with hieroglyphics. 3. Difficult to decipher. Also **hi/er·o·glyph/i·cal.** [< LL < Gk. < *hieros* sacred + *glyphein* to carve] — **hi/er·o·glyph/i·cal·ly** *adv.* — **hi·er·og/ly·phist** (hī′ər·og′lə·fist, hī·rog′-) *n.*

hi-fi (hī′fī′) *n.* 1. High fidelity. 2. Radio, phonograph, or recording equipment capable of reproducing sound with high fidelity. — *adj.* Of or pertaining to high fidelity.

hig·gle (hig′əl) *v.i.* **·gled, ·gling** To argue over terms, prices, etc.; haggle. [Var. of HAGGLE] — **hig/gler** *n.*

hig·gle·dy-pig·gle·dy (hig′əl·dē-pig′əl·dē) *adj.* Disordered or confused; jumbled; topsy-turvy. — *adv.* In chaotic confusion or disorder. — *n.* Great confusion; muddle. [< obs. *higle-pigle*, a varied reduplication]

high (hī) *adj.* 1. Reaching or extending upward to some great or considerable distance; lofty; tall. 2. Having a specified elevation: ten feet *high.* 3. Located at some distance above the ground or other horizontal. 4. Reaching to the height of: used in combination: *knee-high.* 5. Produced or extending to or from a height: a *high* jump. 6. Greater or more than is usual or normal in degree, amount, etc.: *high* fever; *high* speed. 7. Superior, lofty, or exalted in quality, rank, kind, etc.: a *high* official. 8. Most important; main. 9. Having serious consequences: *high* treason. 10. Elated; joyful: *high* spirits. 11. *Informal* Feeling the effects of liquor, drugs, etc.; intoxicated. 12. Expensive; costly. 13. Luxurious or fashionable: *high* living. 14. Advanced to the fullest extent or degree: *high* tide. 15. Complex; advanced: usu. in the comparative degree: *higher* mathematics. 16. Strict or extreme in opinion, doctrine, etc.: *high* Tory. 17. Arrogant; haughty. 18. Slightly decomposed; gamy: said of meat. 19. Of sounds, having relatively short wavelengths; shrill. 20. *Music* **a** Having relatively short wavelengths: said of vocal or instrumental tones. **b** Being above the proper or indicated pitch; sharp. 21. *Mech.* Denoting a gear arrangement, as in a transmission, yielding the most rapid output speed. 22. *Phonet.* Of vowel sounds, produced with the tongue raised close to the roof of the mouth, as (ē) in *bead:* opposed to *low.* — **high and dry** 1. Completely above water level. 2. Stranded; helpless. — **high and mighty** *Informal* Overbearing; haughty. — *adv.* 1. To or at a high level, position, degree, price, rank, etc. 2. In a high manner. — **high and low** Everywhere. — *n.* 1. A high level, position, etc. 2. *Mech.* A gear arrangement yielding the most rapid output speed. 3. *Meteorol.* An area of high barometric pressure. [OE *hēah*]

high·ball¹ (hī′bôl′) *n. U.S.* A drink of whisky or other liquor mixed with soda, ginger ale, etc., and served with ice in a tall glass. [Prob. < HIGH + *ball*, obs., a drink of whisky]

high·ball² (hī′bôl′) *n.* A railroad signal to go ahead. — *v.i. U.S. Slang* To go at great speed. [From a large ball once used as a semaphore]

high·born (hī′bôrn′) *adj.* Of noble birth or ancestry.

high·boy (hī′boi′) *n.* A tall chest of drawers, built in two sections, the lower one mounted on legs. [Origin unknown]

high·bred (hī′bred′) *adj.* 1. Descended from fine stock; well-born. 2. Characteristic of or indicating good breeding.

high·brow (hī′brou′) *Informal n.* One who has or claims to have intellectually superior tastes: sometimes a term of derision. — *adj.* Of, pertaining to, or suitable for a highbrow: also **high/browed′.** — **high/brow/ism** *n.*

high·chair (hī′châr′) *n.* A baby's chair standing on tall legs and equipped with an eating tray. Also **high chair.**

High-Church (hī′chûrch′) *adj.* Of or pertaining to a group (**High Church**) in the Anglican Church that stresses authority and ritual. — **High′-Church/man** *n.*

high-class (hī′klas′, -kläs′) *adj. Slang* High or superior in quality, condition, status, etc.

high comedy Comedy dealing with the world of polite society and relying chiefly on witty dialogue for its effect.

high·er-up (hī′ər·up′) *n. Informal* A person of superior rank or position.

high·fa·lu·tin (hī′fə·lōōt′n) *adj. Informal* Extravagant, pompous, or high-flown in manner, speech, etc. Also **high′·fa·lu/ting.** [? < HIGH-FLOWN]

high fidelity *Electronics* The reproduction of a signal or sound with a minimum of distortion, esp. by phonographic equipment: also called *hi-fi.*

high·fli·er (hī′flī′ər) *n.* 1. One who or that which flies high. 2. *Informal* One having extravagantly pretentious or unrealistic ambitions, opinions, tastes, etc. Also **high/fly/er.**

high-flown (hī′flōn′) *adj.* 1. Extravagant or bombastic in style, language, etc. 2. Pretentious: *high-flown* tastes.

high frequency *Telecom.* A radio frequency in the band from 3 to 30 megacycles.

High German See under GERMAN.

high-grade (hī′grād′) *adj.* Of superior quality.

high·hand·ed (hī′han′did) *adj.* Arbitrary and overbearing. — **high/hand/ed·ly** *adv.* — **high/hand/ed·ness** *n.*

high hat A top hat.

high-hat (hī′hat′) *Informal v.t.* **·hat·ted, ·hat·ting** To snub. — *adj.* 1. Snobbish. 2. Fashionable. — *n.* A snob.

high·jack (hī′jak′) See HIJACK.

high jinks (jingks) Boisterous fun or roughhousing.

high jump In athletics, a jump for height.

high·land (hī′lənd) *n.* 1. Elevated land, as a plateau or promontory. 2. *Usu. pl.* A hilly or mountainous region. — *adj.* Of, pertaining to, or of the nature of a highland.

High·land·er (hī′lən·dər) *n.* 1. A native or inhabitant of the Highlands. 2. A soldier of a Highlands regiment.

Highland fling A lively Scottish dance.

high·light (hī′līt′) *n.* 1. An area or point in a painting, photograph, etc., showing or representing a brightly lighted part. 2. An event, detail, etc., of special importance. — *v.t.* 1. *Informal* To give special emphasis to; feature. 2. To provide or emphasize with a highlight or highlights.

high·ly (hī′lē) *adv.* 1. In or to a high degree; extremely. 2. With great approval or appreciation. 3. In a high position or rank. 4. At a high price or rate.

High Mass *Eccl.* A Mass celebrated with full ceremony, music, incense, etc.

high-mind·ed (hī′mīn′did) *adj.* Possessing or manifesting noble thoughts or sentiments. — **high/-mind/ed·ly** *adv.*

high·ness (hī′nis) *n.* The state or quality of being high.

High·ness (hī′nis) *n.* A title or form of address for persons of royal rank: often preceded by *His, Her, Your,* etc.

high-pitched (hī′picht′) *adj.* 1. High in pitch; shrill. 2. Of a roof, having a steep slope. 3. Lofty or exalted.

high-pres·sure (hī′presh′ər) *adj.* 1. Using or sustaining high steam pressure, as an engine. 2. Having or showing high barometric pressure. 3. *Informal* Exerting vigorously persuasive methods or tactics. — *v.t.* **·sured, ·sur·ing** *Informal* To persuade by aggressive or insistent methods.

high priest A chief priest.

high-rise (hī′rīz′) *adj.* Describing a relatively tall building or structure. — *n.* A tall building: also **high rise.**

high·road (hī′rōd′) *n.* 1. A main road. 2. An easy or sure method or course: the *highroad* to fame.

high school A school following elementary school or junior high school, in the U.S. typically comprising grades 9 to 12.

high seas The open waters of an ocean or sea that are beyond the territorial jurisdiction of any one nation.

high-sound·ing (hī′soun′ding) *adj.* Pretentious or imposing in sound or implication: *high-sounding* praise.

high-spir·it·ed (hī′spir′it·ed) *adj.* Having a courageous, vigorous, or fiery spirit; mettlesome.

high-ten·sion (hī′ten′shən) *adj. Electr.* Pertaining to, characterized by, or operating under very high voltage.

high-test (hī′test′) *adj.* 1. Designating a substance or product that has passed severe tests for fitness, quality, etc. 2. Denoting a grade of gasoline with a low boiling point.

high tide 1. The maximum level reached by the incoming tide. 2. The time that this occurs. 3. A culminating point.

high time 1. So late as to be almost past the proper time. 2. *Informal* A hilarious and enjoyable time.

high-toned (hī′tōnd′) *adj.* 1. *U.S. Informal* Stylish; modish. 2. Characterized by a lofty character, high principles, etc.: often used ironically. 3. High in tone or pitch.

high treason Treason against the sovereign or state.

high-up (hī′up′) *Informal adj.* Of high rank or position. — *n.* One who is in a high rank or position.

high water **1.** High tide. **2.** The condition of a body of water at its time of highest elevation, as during a flood.

high·wa·ter mark (hī′wô′tər, -wot′ər) **1.** The highest point reached by a body of water, as during high tide, a flood, etc. **2.** A mark left by such waters after receding. **3.** A point of highest achievement or development.

high·way (hī′wā′) *n.* **1.** A road or thoroughfare; esp., a main or principal road of some length that is open to the public. **2.** A main route on land or water. **3.** An ordinary, natural, or direct course of action, progress, etc.

high·way·man (hī′wā′mən) *n. pl.* **·men** (-mən) Formerly, a robber who waylaid travelers on highways.

hi·jack (hī′jak′) *v.t. U.S. Slang* **1.** To seize illegally while in transit, as cargo, vehicles, etc. **2.** To hold up and rob (a truck, etc.). **3.** To seize or steal valuables from (a person). **4.** To coerce or compel (someone). Also spelled *highjack.* [Orig. from hoboes who hailed their victim with "Hi Jack"]

hike (hīk) *v.* **hiked, hik·ing** *v.i.* **1.** To walk for a considerable distance, esp. through rugged terrain, woods, etc. **2.** To rise or be uneven, as part of a garment: often with *up.* — *v.t.* **3.** *Informal* To raise or lift: usu. with *up.* **4.** *Informal* To increase (prices, etc.): usu. with *up.* — *n.* **1.** A long walk or march. **2.** *Informal* An increase. [? Var. of HITCH] — **hi′ker** *n.*

hi·lar·i·ous (hi·lâr′ē·əs, hī-) *adj.* Boisterously gay or cheerful. — **hi·lar′i·ous·ly** *adv.* — **hi·lar′i·ous·ness** *n.*

hi·lar·i·ty (hi·lar′ə·tē, hī-) *n. pl.* **·ties** Noisy, exuberant gaiety. [< OF < L < Gk. *hilaros* cheerful]

hill (hil) *n.* **1.** A conspicuous, usu. rounded, elevation of the earth's surface, not as high as a mountain. **2.** A heap or pile: often used in combination: a *molehill.* **3.** A small mound of earth placed over or around certain plants and tubers. **4.** A plant or group of plants thus covered. — *v.t.* **1.** To surround or cover with hills, as potatoes. **2.** To form a hill or heap of. [OE *hyll*] — **hill′er** *n.*

hill·bil·ly (hil′bil′ē) *n. pl.* **·lies** *U.S. Informal* A person coming from or living in the mountains or a backwoods area, esp. of the southern U.S.: originally a disparaging term.

hill·ock (hil′ək) *n.* A small hill or mound. — **hill′ock·y** *adj.*

hill·side (hil′sīd′) *n.* The side or slope of a hill.

hill·top (hil′top′) *n.* The summit of a hill.

hill·y (hil′ē) *adj.* **hill·i·er, hill·i·est** **1.** Having many hills. **2.** Resembling a hill; steep. — **hill′i·ness** *n.*

hilt (hilt) *n.* The handle of a sword, dagger, etc. — **to the hilt** Thoroughly; fully. — *v.t.* To provide with a hilt. [OE]

hi·lum (hī′ləm) *n. pl.* **·la** (-lə) *Bot.* The scar on a seed at the point where it was attached to the placenta. [< L, a trifle]

him (him) *pron.* The objective case of the pronoun *he.*

him·self (him·self′) *pron.* A form of the third person singular masculine pronoun, used: **1.** As a reflexive or as object of a preposition in a reflexive sense: He cut *himself.* **2.** As an intensive form of *he:* He *himself* will do it. **3.** As a designation of a normal or usual state: He is not *himself.*

hind¹ (hīnd) *adj.* **hind·er, hind·most** or **hind·er·most** Situated at or toward the rear part; posterior. [OE *hindan*]

hind² (hīnd) *n.* The female of the red deer, esp. when fully grown. [OE]

hind·brain (hīnd′brān′) *n. Anat.* The rhombencephalon.

hind·er¹ (hin′dər) *v.t.* **1.** To interfere with the progress of; retard. **2.** To prevent from acting or occurring; deter; thwart. — *v.i.* **3.** To be an impediment or obstacle. [OE *hinder* behind] — **hin′der·er** *n.*

hind·er² (hīn′dər) Comparative of HIND¹. — *adj.* Pertaining to or situated at the rear or posterior end. [OE]

Hin·di (hin′dē) *n.* **1.** The principal language of northern India, belonging to the Indic branch of the Indo-Iranian languages, usu. divided into **Western Hindi,** of which Hindustani is the major dialect, and **Eastern Hindi. 2.** A form of literary Hindustani used by Hindus. [< Hind. < Persian < OPersian < Skt. *sindhu* river, the Indus]

hind·most (hīnd′mōst′) Superlative of HIND¹. Also **hind′· er·most′** (hīn′dər-).

hind·quar·ter (hīnd′kwôr′tər) *n.* **1.** One of the two back quarters of a carcass of beef, lamb, etc. **2.** *pl.* The rump.

hin·drance (hin′drəns) *n.* **1.** The act of hindering. **2.** One who or that which hinders.

hind·sight (hīnd′sīt′) *n.* **1.** The understanding of an event after it has happened. **2.** The rear sight of a gun, rifle, etc.

Hin·du (hin′dōō) *n.* **1.** A native of India who speaks one of the Indic languages. **2.** One whose religion is Hinduism. **3.** Loosely, a native of Hindustan. — *adj.* Of, pertaining to, or characteristic of the Hindus or Hinduism. Also **Hin′doo.**

Hin·du·ism (hin′dōō·iz′əm) *n.* The religion of the Hindus of India, characterized by worship of Brahma.

Hin·du·sta·ni (hin′dōō·stä′nē, -stan′ē) *n.* The major dialect of Hindi, the official language and general medium of communication in India. See URDU. — *adj.* **1.** Of or pertaining to Hindustan or its people. **2.** Of or pertaining to Hindustani. *Abbr.* Hind.

hinge (hinj) *n.* **1.** A device consisting of two parts, usu.

metal plates, connected by a pin inserted into interlocking grooves, and constituting a movable joint on which a door, gate, lid, etc., swings or turns. **2.** A natural movable joint connecting two parts, as the shells of a bivalve. **3.** That on which something turns or depends. — *v.* **hinged, hing·ing** *v.t.* **1.** To attach by or equip with a hinge or hinges. — *v.i.* **2.** To hang or turn on or as on a hinge. **3.** To depend or be contingent: with *on.* [ME, prob. < ON *hengja* to hang]

hin·ny (hin′ē) *n. pl.* **·nies** The hybrid offspring of a stallion and a she-ass. Compare MULE¹. [< L < Gk. *ginnos*]

hint (hint) *n.* **1.** An indirect suggestion or implication. **2.** A slight indication or trace. — *v.t.* **1.** To suggest indirectly; imply. — *v.i.* **2.** To show one's wishes, intentions, etc., by a hint or hints. **3.** To give a slight indication or suggestion: with *at.* [OE *hentan*]

hin·ter·land (hin′tər·land′) *n.* **1.** An inland region immediately adjacent to a coastal area. **2.** A region remote from urban areas; back country. **3.** An area adjacent to and dependent upon a port or other urban center. [< G]

hip¹ (hip) *n.* **1.** The part of the human body projecting below the waist on either side, formed by the edge of the pelvis and the upper part of the femur. **2.** An analogous part in animals. **3.** *Archit.* The angle at the juncture of adjacent sloping sides of a roof. — *v.t.* **hipped, hip·ping** *Archit.* To build (a roof) with a hip or hips. [OE *hype*]

hip² (hip) *n.* The ripened fruit of a rose. [OE *hēope*]

hip³ (hip) *adj. U.S. Slang* Aware; informed.

hip·bone (hip′bōn′) *n.* The innominate bone.

hipped¹ (hipt) *adj.* **1.** Having or characterized by (a specified kind of) hips: used in combination: *slim-hipped.* **2.** *Archit.* Having a hip or hips, as a roof.

hipped² (hipt) *adj. U.S. Slang* Fanatically interested or concerned; obsessed: followed by *on: hipped* on modern art.

hip·pet·y-hop (hip′ə·tē·hop′) *adv. Informal* With a jerky gait or motion. Also **hip·pet·y-hop·pet·y** (-hop′ə·tē).

hip·pie (hip′ē) *n.* One of a group of chiefly young people whose unconventional dress and behavior and use of drugs express withdrawal from middle-class life and indifference to its values. [Var. of HIPSTER]

hip·po (hip′ō) *n. pl.* **·pos** *Informal* A hippopotamus.

hippo- *combining form* Horse. Also, before vowels, **hipp-.** [< Gk. *hippos* horse]

Hip·po·crat·ic oath (hip′ə·krat′ik) An oath, attributed to Hippocrates, incorporating a code of ethics for physicians and administered to those about to receive a medical degree.

hip·po·drome (hip′ə·drōm) *n.* **1.** An arena or similar structure for horse shows, circuses, etc. **2.** In ancient Greece and Rome, a course or track for horse races and chariot races. [< F < L < Gk. < *hippos* horse + *dromos* running, course]

hip·po·pot·a·mus (hip′ə·pot′ə·məs) *n. pl.* **·mus·es** or **·mi** (-mī) A large, chiefly aquatic, herbivorous mammal, native to Africa, and having short legs, a massive, thick-skinned, hairless body, and a very broad muzzle. [< L < Gk. < *hippos* horse + *potamos* river]

-hippus *combining form Paleontol.* Horse. [< Gk. *hippos* horse]

hip roof *Archit.* A roof having sloping ends and sides.

hip·ster (hip′stər) *n. U.S. Slang* One who is hip; esp., one versed in jazz music. [< HIP³ + -STER]

hire (hīr) *v.t.* **hired, hir·ing** **1.** To obtain the services of (a person) for compensation. **2.** To acquire the use of (a thing) for a fee; rent. **3.** To grant the use or services of (someone or something) in return for payment: often with *out.* — **to hire out** To provide one's services in return for compensation. — *n.* **1.** Compensation paid for labor, services, etc. **2.** The act of hiring, or the condition of being hired. [OE *hŷr*] — **hir′a·ble** or **hire′a·ble** *adj.* — **hir′er** *n.*

hire·ling (hīr′ling) *n.* One who serves for hire; esp., one who does something unpleasant or reprehensible for mercenary motives: usu. a contemptuous term.

hir·sute (hûr′sōōt, hûr·sōōt′) *adj.* Covered with hair. [< L *hirsutus* rough] — **hir′sute·ness** *n.*

his (hiz) *pron.* **1.** The possessive case of the pronoun *he,* used predicatively: This room is *his.* **2.** The one or ones belonging or pertaining to him: Her book is better than *his.* — **of his** Belonging or pertaining to him: a double possessive. — *pronominal adj.* The possessive case of the pronoun *he,* used attributively: *his* book. [OE]

His·pa·ni·a (his·pā′nē·ə, -nyə, -pä′-) **1.** The Latin name for the region comprising modern Spain and Portugal. **2.** *Poetic* Spain. — **His·pan·ic** (his·pan′ik) *adj.*

hiss (his) *v.i.* **1.** To utter or produce a prolonged, sibilant sound, as that of *ss,* of air or steam escaping under pressure, etc. **2.** To utter such a sound as an expression of disapproval or derision. — *v.t.* **3.** To utter with a hiss. **4.** To express disapproval of by hissing. **5.** To rout or silence by hissing: with *off, down,* etc. — *n.* The sound produced by hissing. [ME *hissen,* imit.] — **hiss′er** *n.*

his·ta·mine (his′tə·mēn, -min) *n. Biochem.* A white, crystalline substance, $C_5H_9N_3$, found in plant and animal tissues. It reduces blood pressure, has a contracting action on the uterus, and is released in allergic reactions. **—his·ta·min·ic** (his'tə·min'ik) *adj.*

histo- *combining form* Tissue. Also, before vowels, **hist-**. [< Gk *histos* web]

his·tol·o·gy (his·tol'ə·jē) *n. pl.* **·gies** 1. The branch of biology that treats of the microscopic structure of tissues. 2. The tissue structure of an organism, part, etc. **—his·to·log·i·cal** (his'tə·loj'i·kəl) *adj.* **—his·tol'o·gist** *n.*

his·to·ri·an (his·tôr'ē·ən, -tō'rē-) *n.* 1. A writer of or authority on history. 2. A compiler of a record, esp. for a specific group or purpose: the class *historian*.

his·tor·ic (his·tôr'ik, -tor'-) *adj.* 1. Important or famous in history. 2. Memorable; significant. 3. Historical.

his·tor·i·cal (his·tôr'i·kəl, -tor'-) *adj.* 1. Constituting, belonging to, or of the nature of history. 2. Pertaining to, concerned with, or treating of events of history: a *historical* account. 3. Of, pertaining to, or based on known facts as distinct from legendary or fictitious accounts. 4. Serving as a source for knowledge of the past. 5. Historic. **—his·tor'i·cal·ly** *adv.* **—his·tor'i·cal·ness** *n.*

historical present *Gram.* The present tense used to narrate a past event.

his·to·ri·og·ra·pher (his·tôr'ē·og'rə·fər, -tō'rē-) *n.* A historian or chronicler, esp. one officially associated with a group or public institution. **—his·to'ri·og'ra·phy** *n.*

his·to·ry (his'tə·rē, his'trē) *n. pl.* **·ries** 1. That branch of knowledge concerned with past events, esp. those involving human affairs. 2. A record or account, usu. written and in chronological order, of past events, esp. those concerning a particular nation, people, field of knowledge or activity, etc. 3. A connected or related series of facts, events, etc., esp. those concerning a specific group or subject: the *history* of a political party. 4. Past events in general. 5. Something in the past. 6. An unusual or noteworthy past: That house has a *history*. 7. A drama depicting historical events. 8. A long narrative or story. [< L < Gk. *histōr* knowing]

his·tri·on·ic (his'trē·on'ik) *adj.* 1. Of or pertaining to actors or acting. 2. Overly dramatic. Also **his'tri·on'i·cal**. [< L *histrio, -onis* actor] **—his'tri·on'i·cal·ly** *adv.*

his·tri·on·ics (his'trē·on'iks) *n.pl.* (*construed as sing. in def. 1*) 1. Theatrical art or representation; dramatics. 2. Feigned emotional display; affectation in manner, speech, etc.

hit (hit) *v.* **hit, hit·ting** *v.t.* 1. To give a blow to; strike forcibly. 2. To reach or strike with or as with a missile, hurled or falling object, etc. 3. To come forcibly in contact with; collide with. 4. To cause (something) to make forcible contact: often with *on, against,* etc. 5. To inflict (a blow, etc.) on: I *hit* him a tremendous blow. 6. To set in motion or propel by striking. 7. To arrive at, achieve, or discover. 8. To accord with; suit. 9. To affect adversely; cause to suffer. 10. To attack; beset. 11. In baseball, to succeed in making (a specified kind of base hit). 12. *U.S. Informal* To begin to journey on: to *hit* the road. 13. *U.S. Informal* To arrive in or reach (a place). **—v.i.** 14. To deliver a blow; strike. 15. To make forcible contact; bump: often with *against, on,* etc. 16. To come or light; happen: followed by *on* or *upon*: to *hit* on the right answer. **— to hit it off** To be friendly; get along well. **— to hit on** (a specified number of) **cylinders** To function by or as by firing the charge in the cylinders: said originally of an internal-combustion engine. **—n.** 1. A blow, stroke, shot, etc., that reaches the objective aimed at. 2. A forceful impact; collision. 3. A popular or obvious success. 4. A fortunate chance or circumstance. 5. An apt or telling remark, witticism, piece of sarcasm, etc. 6. In baseball, a base hit. [OE < ON *hitta* to come upon] **—hit'ter** *n.*

hit-and-run (hit'n·run') *adj.* Designating or caused by the driver of a vehicle who illegally continues on his way after hitting a pedestrian or another vehicle.

hitch (hich) *v.t.* 1. To fasten or tie, esp. temporarily, with a knotted rope, strap, etc. 2. To harness to a vehicle: sometimes with *up*. 3. To move, pull, raise, etc., with a jerk: often with *up*: He *hitched* his pants up. 4. *Informal* To marry. 5. *U.S. Slang* To obtain (a ride) by hitchhiking. **—v.i.** 6. To move with a jerk or limp: to *hitch* forward. 7. To become fastened, caught, or entangled. 8. *U.S. Slang* To travel by hitchhiking. **—n.** 1. An obstacle; halt; delay. 2. A sudden, jerking movement; tug. 3. A limp or hobble. 4. A fastening or device used to fasten. 5. Any of various knots used for quick, temporary fastening. 6. *U.S. Informal* A period of enlistment in military service, esp. in the navy. 7. *U.S. Slang* In hitchhiking, a ride. [ME *hicchen*]

hitch·hike (hich'hīk') *v.i.* **·hiked, ·hik·ing** To travel by signaling for rides in passing vehicles. **— hitch'hik'er** *n.*

hitch·ing post (hich'ing) A post to which a horse, etc., may be hitched.

hith·er (hith'ər) *adv.* To or toward this place: Come *hither*. **—adj.** Situated toward this side; nearer. [OE *hider*]

hith·er·most (hith'ər·mōst') *adj.* Nearest to this place.

hith·er·to (hith'ər·tōō', hith'ər·tōō') *adv.* Until this time.

hit or miss Without regard for the outcome; at random.

hit-or-miss (hit'ər·mis') *adj.* Haphazard; careless.

Hit·tite (hit'īt) *n.* 1. One of an ancient people who established a powerful empire in Asia Minor and northern Syria about 2000–1200 B.C. 2. Their language. **—adj.** Of or relating to the Hittites or their language. [< Hebrew *Hittīm*]

hive (hīv) *n.* 1. An artificial structure serving as a habitation for honeybees; beehive. 2. A colony of bees inhabiting a hive; swarm. 3. A place astir with industrious activity. 4. A teeming multitude; throng. **—v.** **hived, hiv·ing** *v.t.* 1. To induce (bees) to enter into or collect in a hive. 2. To house or shelter in or as in a hive. 3. To store (honey) in a hive. 4. To store or hoard for future use. **—v.i.** 5. To enter a hive. 6. To dwell in or as in a hive. [OE *hȳf*]

hives (hīvz) *n.* Any of various skin disorders characterized by swellings, itching, etc., as urticaria. [Origin unknown]

ho (hō) *interj.* 1. An exclamation, often repeated, expressing exultation, derision, etc. 2. A call to attract attention.

Ho *Chem.* Holmium.

hoar (hôr, hōr) *adj.* 1. Having white or gray hair. 2. Ancient. 3. White or grayish, as with frost. **—n.** Hoariness. [OE *hār* gray-haired]

hoard (hôrd, hōrd) *n.* An accumulation of something stored away for safekeeping or future use. **—v.t.** 1. To amass and store or hide (money, valuables, etc.). **—v.i.** 2. To amass and store. [OE *hord* treasure] **—hoard'er** *n.*

hoard·ing[1] (hôr'ding, hōr'-) *n.* 1. The act of one who hoards. 2. *Usu. pl.* That which is hoarded.

hoard·ing[2] (hôr'ding, hōr'-) *n. Brit.* 1. A temporary fence. 2. A billboard. [< OF *hourd* palisade]

hoar·frost (hôr'frôst', -frost', hōr'-) *n.* Frost whitening the surface on which it is formed.

hoar·hound (hôr'hound', hōr'-) See HOREHOUND.

hoarse (hôrs, hōrs) *adj.* 1. Deep, harsh, and grating in sound. 2. Having a husky, gruff, or croaking voice. [OE *hā(r)s*] **—hoarse'ly** *adv.* **—hoarse'ness** *n.*

hoars·en (hôr'sən, hōr'-) *v.t. & v.i.* To make or become hoarse.

hoar·y (hôr'ē, hōr'ē) *adj.* **hoar·i·er, hoar·i·est** 1. Ancient; aged; venerable. 2. Gray or white with age. 3. White or whitish in color. **—hoar'i·ness** *n.*

hoax (hōks) *n.* A trick or deception, usu. on the public. **—v.t.** To deceive by a hoax. **—hoax'er** *n.*

hob[1] (hob) *n.* A projection at the interior of a fireplace, serving as a shelf on which to keep things warm.

hob[2] (hob) *n.* A hobgoblin or elf. **— to play** (or **raise**) **hob** To cause mischief or confusion. [Orig. a nickname for *Robert, Robin*]

hob·ble (hob'əl) *v.* **·bled, ·bling** *v.i.* 1. To walk with a limp. 2. To progress clumsily or irregularly. **—v.t.** 3. To hamper the free movement of, as a horse, by fettering the legs. 4. To cause to move lamely or awkwardly. **—n.** 1. An awkward or limping gait. 2. A rope, etc., used to hobble the legs of an animal. **—hob'bler** *n.*

hob·ble·de·hoy (hob'əl·dē·hoi') *n.* An adolescent boy, esp. when awkward and gawky. [Origin uncertain]

hob·by (hob'ē) *n. pl.* **·bies** A pursuit of interest, undertaken for pleasure during one's leisure; avocation. [after *Robin*, a personal name]

hob·by·horse (hob'ē·hôrs') *n.* 1. A rocking horse. 2. A toy consisting of a stick surmounted by a horse's head.

hob·gob·lin (hob'gob'lin) *n.* 1. An imaginary cause of terror or dread. 2. A mischievous imp.

hob·nail (hob'nāl') *n.* A nail used to stud the soles of heavy shoes against wear or slipping. **—hob'nailed'** *adj.*

hob·nob (hob'nob') *v.i.* **·nobbed, ·nob·bing** 1. To associate in a friendly manner; be on intimate terms. 2. To drink together. [OE *habban* to have + *nabban* to have not]

ho·bo (hō'bō) *n. pl.* **·boes** or **·bos** *U.S.* 1. A tramp. 2. An itinerant, usu. unskilled worker. [< *Hey, Bo*, a vagabond's greeting] **—ho'bo·ism** *n.*

Hob·son's choice (hob'sənz) A choice in which one must take what is offered or nothing. [after Thomas *Hobson*, 1544?–1631, English liveryman, who required each customer to take the horse nearest the door]

hock[1] (hok) *n.* 1. The joint of the hind leg in the horse, ox, etc., corresponding to the ankle in man. 2. The corresponding joint in a fowl. **—v.t.** To disable by cutting the tendons of the hock; hamstring. [OE *hōh* heel]

hock[2] (hok) *n.* Any white Rhine wine: originally **Hoch·hei·mer** (hok'hī·mər). [*Hochheim*, a German town]

hock[3] (hok) *U.S. Informal v.t.* To pawn. **—n.** The state

HITCHES
a Half-hitch.
b Clove-hitch.
c Rolling-hitch.

of being in pawn. — **in hock** *Informal* **1.** In pawn. **2.** In prison. **3.** In debt. [< Du. *hok* prison, debt]

hock·ey (hok′ē) *n.* **1.** A game played on ice (*ice hockey*), in which players, wearing skates and wielding sticks, try to drive a disk (puck) into the opponent's goal. **2.** A similar game played on a field (*field hockey*), in which a small ball is used instead of a puck. [< *hock* bent stick, var. of HOOK]

hockey stick A stick having a characteristic curve or bend at one end, used to move the ball or puck in hockey.

hock·shop (hok′shop′) *n. U.S. Informal* A pawnshop. Also **hock shop.**

ho·cus (hō′kəs) *v.t.* ·cused or ·cussed, ·cus·ing or ·cus·sing **1.** To deceive by a trick; dupe; cheat. **2.** To drug, as a drink. [Abbr. of HOCUS-POCUS]

ho·cus-po·cus (hō′kəs·pō′kəs) *n.* **1.** A verbal formula used in conjuring or sleight of hand. **2.** Deceptive skill. **3.** Any trickery or deception, as misleading gestures. — *v.t. & v.i.* ·po·cused or ·cussed, ·po·cus·ing or ·cus·sing To trick; cheat. [A sham Latin phrase]

hod (hod) *n.* **1.** A trough rested on the shoulder, to carry bricks, etc. **2.** A coalscuttle. [< OF *hotte* pannier]

hodge·podge (hoj′poj′) *n.* **1.** A jumbled mixture or collection; conglomeration. **2.** A stew. Also *hotchpotch.*

Hodg·kin's disease (hoj′kinz) *Pathol.* A generally fatal disease characterized by progressive enlargement of the lymph nodes, lymphoid tissue, and spleen. [after Dr. Thomas *Hodgkin*, 1798–1866, English physician, who described it]

hoe (hō) *n.* An implement as for weeding, having a flat blade attached to a long handle. — *v.t. & v.i.* **hoed, hoe·ing** To dig with a hoe. [< OF < OHG *houwan* to cut]

hoe·cake (hō′kāk′) *n. Southern U.S.* A thin, flat cake made from cornmeal, originally baked on a hoe.

hoe-down (hō′doun′) *n. U.S. Informal* A lively country dance or square dance; also, its music. [Origin uncertain]

hog (hog, hôg) *n.* **1.** A pig, esp. one weighing more than 120 pounds and raised for the market. **2.** An animal related to the pig, as the peccary. **3.** *Informal* A gluttonous or filthy person. — *v.* **hogged, hog·ging** *v.t.* *Slang* To take more than one's share of; grab selfishly. [OE *hog*]

hog·back (hog′bak′, hôg′-) *n. Geol.* A sandy or rocky ridge caused by unequal erosion on the edges of tilted strata.

hog·gish (hog′ish, hôg′-) *adj.* **1.** Of or like a hog. **2.** Greedy or dirty; piggish. — **hog′gish·ly** *adv.*

hog·nose (hog′nōz′, hôg′-) *n.* Any of several American nonvenomous snakes with flat heads and prominent snouts.

hogs·head (hogz′hed′, hôgz′-) *n.* **1.** A large cask, esp. one with a capacity of 63 to 140 gallons. **2.** A liquid measure, esp. one equal to 63 gallons, or 8.42 cubic feet.

hog-tie (hog′tī′, hôg′-) *v.t.* -tied, -ty·ing or -tie·ing **1.** To tie together four feet, or the hands and feet of. **2.** *Informal* To render (a person) ineffective, as by tying. Also **hog′tie′.**

hog·wash (hog′wosh′, -wôsh′, hôg′-) *n.* **1.** Kitchen refuse, etc., fed hogs. **2.** Any nonsense; insincere talk.

hoicks (hoiks) *interj.* A cry to the hounds in hunting. Also **yoicks.**

hoi pol·loi (hoi′ pə·loi′) The common people; the masses: usu. used contemptuously. [< Gk., the many]

hoist (hoist) *v.t.* To raise, lift, or heave up, esp. by mechanical means. — *n.* **1.** Any machine for raising large objects; a lift. **2.** The act of hoisting. [? < Du. *hijschen*]

hoi·ty-toi·ty (hoi′tē·toi′tē) *interj.* An exclamation of disapproval. — *adj.* **1.** Self-important; haughty. **2.** Flighty; giddy. **3.** Easily offended. — *n.* *pl.* -toi·ties **1.** Arrogance. **2.** Flighty behavior. [Obs. *hoit* to romp]

ho·kum (hō′kəm) *n. U.S. Slang* **1.** The devices used by a performer, etc., to get a response. **2.** Meaningless bunk. **3.** Insincere flattery. [Alter. of HOCUS]

hold[1] (hōld) *v.* **held, held, hold·ing** *v.t.* **1.** To take and keep in the hand, arms, etc.; clasp. **2.** To sustain or keep, as in position; support: to *hold* one's head high. **3.** To contain or enclose: The barrel *holds* ten gallons. **4.** To keep under control; restrain; also, to retain possession of. **5.** To keep in reserve; designate for future use. **6.** To have the benefit or responsibilities of: to *hold* office. **7.** To regard in a specified manner: to *hold* someone dear. **8.** To bind by contract or duty: *Hold* him to his agreement. **9.** *Music* To prolong or sustain (a tone). **10.** *Law* a To adjudge; decide. b To have title to. **11.** To maintain in the mind; harbor: to *hold* a grudge. **12.** To engage in; carry on: to *hold* a conference. — *v.i.* **13.** To maintain a grip or grasp. **14.** To withstand strain or remain unbroken: The rope *holds*. **15.** To continue in a state: the breeze *held*. **16.** To remain true: This decision *holds*. **17.** To adhere, as to a principle or purpose; cling. — **to hold back** **1.** To keep in check; restrain. **2.** To refrain. **3.** To retain. — **to hold down** **1.** To suppress; keep under control. **2.** *Informal* To be employed at (a job). — **to hold forth** To preach or speak at great length. — **to hold in 1.** To keep in check; curb. **2.** To conceal (one's feelings, etc.). — **to hold off 1.** To keep at a distance, as from attacking. **2.** To refrain from doing something. — **to hold on 1.** To maintain a grip or

hold. **2.** To persist or continue. **3.** *Informal* To stop or wait. — **to hold one's own** To maintain one's position, as in a contest. — **to hold out 1.** To stretch forth; offer. **2.** To last; endure: Our supplies *held out*. **3.** To continue resistance. **4.** *Slang* To refuse something anticipated or due. — **to hold over 1.** To put off to a later time. **2.** To remain or retain beyond the expected limit, as in office. **3.** To use as a means of controlling. — **to hold up 1.** To support; prop. **2.** To exhibit to view. **3.** To delay; stop. **4.** *Informal* To endure; remain firm. **5.** *Informal* To stop so as to rob. **6.** *Informal* To charge too high a price. — **to hold water 1.** To contain without leaking. **2.** *Informal* To be credible or sound, as an argument. — **to hold with** To approve of. — *n.* **1.** The act or method of grasping, as with the hands. **2.** Something grasped, held, or seized for support. **3.** A controlling force or influence. **4.** *Law* A holding or tenure: used in combination: *freehold*. **5.** *Music* a The holding of a note or rest beyond its time value. b The symbol (⌢) indicating this: also called *pause*. [OE *haldan*]

hold[2] (hōld) *n. Naut.* The space below the decks of a vessel, where cargo is stowed. [< HOLE or < MDu. *hol*]

hold·er (hōl′dər) *n.* **1.** One who or that which holds. **2.** An object used as an aid in holding. **3.** An owner; possessor: chiefly in compounds: *householder*. **4.** *Law* One who has a check, etc., for which he is entitled to payment.

hold·ing (hōl′ding) *n.* **1.** The act of one who or that which holds. **2.** A piece of land rented. **3.** *Often pl.* Property held by legal right, esp. stocks or bonds.

holding company A company that invests in the stocks of one or more other corporations, which it may thus control.

hold·o·ver (hōld′ō′vər) *n. Informal* **1.** One who or that which remains from a previous time or situation. **2.** An incumbent continuing in office after his term has expired.

hold·up (hōld′up′) *n.* **1.** Stoppage or delay. **2.** *Informal* A waylaying and robbing.

hole (hōl) *n.* **1.** A cavity in a solid mass or body; pit. **2.** An opening in anything; aperture. **3.** An animal's burrow or enclosed hiding place. **4.** Any small, crowded, squalid place, esp. a dwelling; also, a prison cell. **5.** A defect; fault. **6.** *Informal* An awkward situation. **7.** In golf: **a** A small cavity into which the ball is played. **b** A division of the course, usu. one of nine or eighteen. **8.** *U.S.* A deep, wide place in a creek, etc.; also, a cove. — **hole in one** In golf, the act of sinking the ball into a hole with one drive from the tee. — **in the hole** *Informal* In debt. — *v.* **holed, hol·ing** *v.t.* **1.** To make a hole in; perforate. **2.** To drive (a ball, etc.) into a hole. **3.** To dig (a shaft, tunnel, etc.). — *v.i.* **4.** To make a hole or holes. — **to hole out** In golf, to hit the ball into a hole. — **to hole up** To hide away; isolate oneself. [OE *hol*] — **hole′y** *adj.*

hol·i·day (hol′ə·dā) *n.* **1.** A day appointed by law for suspension of business in commemoration of some event. **2.** Any day of rest. **3.** A day for special religious observance. **4.** *pl. Chiefly Brit.* A vacation. — *v.i. Chiefly Brit.* To spend a holiday or vacation. [OE *hālig dæg* holy day]

ho·li·er-than-thou (hō′lē·ər·than·thou′) *adj. Informal* Affecting an attitude of superior goodness or virtue.

ho·li·ly (hō′lə·lē) *adv.* In a holy manner; piously; sacredly.

ho·li·ness (hō′lē·nis) *n.* The state or quality of being holy.

Ho·li·ness (hō′lē·nis) *n.* A title or form of address for the Pope: preceded by *His* or *Your.*

hol·land (hol′ənd) *n.* A cotton or linen fabric, often glazed, used for making window shades, upholstery, etc.

hol·lan·daise sauce (hol′ən·dāz′) A creamy sauce of butter, egg yolks, and lemon juice served with vegetables, etc. [< F, fem. of *hollandais* of Holland]

Hol·land·er (hol′ən·dər) *n.* A native or citizen of the Netherlands; a Dutchman.

Hol·lands (hol′əndz) *n.* Gin in which juniper is added to the mash instead of to the spirits. Also **Holland gin.**

hol·ler (hol′ər) *U.S. Informal v.t. & v.i.* To call out loudly; shout; yell. — *n.* A loud shout; yell.

hol·low (hol′ō) *adj.* **1.** Having a cavity within; enclosing an empty space. **2.** Having a deep opening; concave. **3.** Sunken; fallen: *hollow* cheeks. **4.** Deep or muffled in tone: a *hollow* groan. **5.** Not genuine; meaningless; empty. **6.** Hungry. — *n.* **1.** A cavity or empty space in anything; depression; hole. **2.** A valley. — *v.t. & v.i.* To make or become hollow: usu. with *out*. — *adv. Informal* Completely: used in the phrase **to beat (all) hollow**. [OE *holh*] — **hol′low·ly** *adv.* — **hol′low·ness** *n.*

hol·low·ware (hol′ō·wâr′) *n.* Utensils, serving dishes, etc., esp. of silver, that are hollow.

hol·ly (hol′ē) *n. pl.* ·lies A tree or shrub having dark green leaves edged with spines, and scarlet berries. [OE *holen*]

hol·ly·hock (hol′ē·hok) *n.* A tall, cultivated plant of the mallow family, having spikes of showy flowers. [ME *holi* holy + *hoc* mallow]

hol·mi·um (hōl′mē·əm) *n.* A metallic element (symbol Ho) of the lanthanide series, found in gadolinite. See ELEMENT. [after *Holmia*, Latinized name of Stockholm, Sweden]

hol·o·caust (hol′ə-kôst) n. 1. Wholesale destruction and loss of life, esp. by fire. 2. A sacrificial offering that is wholly consumed by fire. [< F < LL < Gk. < *holos* whole + *kaustos* burnt] — **hol′o·caus′tal, hol′o·caus′tic** adj.

hol·o·graph (hol′ə-graf, -gräf) adj. Denoting a document, as a will, in the handwriting of the person whose signature it bears. — n. A document so written. [< F < Gk. < *holos* entire + *graphein* to write] — **hol′o·graph′ic** or **·i·cal** adj.

Hol·stein (hōl′stīn, -stēn) n. A breed of black-and-white cattle. Also **Hol′stein-Frie′sian** (-frē′zhən).

hol·ster (hōl′stər) n. A leather case for a pistol, generally worn on a belt or attached to a saddle. [< Du.]

ho·ly (hō′lē) adj. **·li·er, ·li·est** 1. Regarded with or characterized by reverence because associated with God; having a divine origin; sacred. 2. Having spiritual and moral worth. 3. Designated for religious worship; consecrated. 4. Evoking or meriting reverence or awe. — n. pl. **·lies** A sacred or holy place. [OE *hālig*]

Holy City A city considered sacred by the members of a particular religion.

Holy Communion The Eucharist.

ho·ly·day (hō′lē-dā′) n. A day designated as a religious festival: sometimes called *holiday*. Also **holy day.**

Holy Father A title of the Pope.

Holy Ghost The third person of the Trinity. Also **Holy Spirit.**

Holy Grail The Grail.

Holy Land Palestine.

holy of holies 1. The innermost shrine of the Jewish tabernacle and temple, in which the ark of the covenant was kept. 2. Any very sacred place. Also called *sanctum sanctorum.*

holy orders *Eccl.* 1. The rite of admission to the priesthood or ministry; ordination. 2. The rank of the ministry.

Holy Roman Empire An empire in central and western Europe, 962–1806, regarded as the reestablishment of the Western Roman Empire under the Pope.

ho·ly·stone (hō′lē-stōn′) n. A piece of sandstone used to scour the decks of a ship. — v.t. **·stoned, ·ston·ing** To scrub with a stone. [Said to be used to clean decks for Sunday]

Holy Week The week before Easter Sunday.

Holy Writ The Scriptures.

hom·age (hom′ij, om′-) n. 1. Respect or honor given or shown, esp. by action. 2. A payment, etc., indicating allegiance. [< OF < LL *homo* vassal, man]

hom·bre (om′brā, om′brē) n. *U.S. Slang* Man. [< Sp.]

Hom·burg (hom′bûrg) n. A felt hat having a brim slightly turned up at the sides, and the crown indented lengthwise. Also **hom′burg.** [after *Homburg*, Germany]

home (hōm) n. 1. A house, apartment, or other dwelling serving as the abode of a person or household; residence. 2. A family or other group dwelling together: a happy *home.* 3. The country, region, city, etc., where one lives. 4. One's birthplace or residence during formative years. 5. A place natural or dear because of personal relationships or feelings of comfort and security. 6. A peaceful or restful place; haven. 7. The natural environment of an animal. 8. The place in which something originates or is found: New Orleans is the *home* of jazz. 9. A shelter for care of the orphaned, needy, infirm, etc. 10. In some games, esp. baseball, the goal or base that must be reached in order to win or score. — **at home** 1. In one's own residence, town, country, etc. 2. At one's ease, as if in one's residence. 3. Having a knowledge of; conversant: *at home* in the sciences. 4. Prepared to receive callers. 5. An informal social gathering at one's home. — adj. 1. Of or pertaining to one's home, country, etc.; domestic. 2. Being at the base of operations or place of origin: the *home* office. 3. Going straight to the point; effective. — adv. 1. To or at one's home. 2. To the place or point intended; to the mark. 3. Deeply and intimately; to the heart. — v. **homed, hom·ing** v.t. 1. To cause (an aircraft or guided missile) to proceed toward a target by means of radio waves, radar, or automatic timing devices. 2. To furnish with a home. — v.i. 3. To go home; return home. 4. To be directed toward a target by automatic devices: said of guided missiles: usu. with *in* or *in on.* 5. To have residence. [OE *hām*] — **home′less** adj.

home·bod·y (hōm′bod′ē) n. pl. **·ies** One who prefers to stay at home or whose main interest is in the home.

home·bred (hōm′bred′) adj. 1. Bred at home. 2. Uncultivated; unsophisticated. 3. *Canadian Slang* A home-brew.

home-brew (hōm′brōō′) n. An alcoholic beverage made at home, as for home use. — **home′-brewed′** adj.

home·com·ing (hōm′kum′ing) n. 1. A return to one's home. 2. *U.S.* In colleges, an annual alumni celebration.

home economics The science of home management, as of food, clothing, children, budgets, etc.

home·land (hōm′land′) n. The country of one's birth or allegiance.

home·ly (hōm′lē) adj. **·li·er, ·li·est** 1. Having a familiar, everyday character. 2. Having plain or ugly features. 3. Lacking in refinement. — **home′li·ness** n.

home·made (hōm′mād′) adj. 1. Made at home. 2. Simply or crudely fashioned.

home·mak·er (hōm′mā′kər) n. One in charge of managing her own home; housewife. — **home′mak′ing** n.

homeo- *combining form* Like; similar: *homeomorphism:* also spelled *homoeo-, homoio-.* [< Gk. *homoios* similar]

ho·me·op·a·thist (hō′mē-op′ə-thist, hom′ē-) n. One who practices homeopathy. Also **ho·me·o·path** (hō′mē-ə-path′).

ho·me·op·a·thy (hō′mē-op′ə-thē, hom′ē-) n. A system of therapy using minute doses of medicines that produce the symptoms of the disease treated. — **ho′me·o·path′ic** adj. — **ho′me·o·path′i·cal·ly** adv.

ho·me·o·sta·sis (hō′mē-ə-stā′sis, hom′ē-) n. *Biol.* The tendency of an organism to maintain a uniform and beneficial physiological stability within and between its parts; organic equilibrium. — **ho′me·o·stat′ic** (-stat′ik) adj.

home plate In baseball, the marker at which a player stands when batting, and to which he returns in scoring a run.

hom·er (hō′mər) n. *U.S. Informal* 1. In baseball, a home run. 2. A homing pigeon.

Ho·mer·ic (hō-mer′ik) adj. Of, pertaining to, or suggestive of Homer or his epic poetry. Also **Ho·mer′i·cal.**

home rule Self-government in local affairs within the framework of state or national laws. — **home ruler**

home run In baseball, a hit that cannot be fielded, thus permitting the batter to touch all the bases and score a run.

home·sick (hōm′sik′) adj. Unhappy or ill through longing for home; nostalgic. — **home′sick′ness** n.

home·spun (hōm′spun′) adj. 1. Spun at home. 2. Plain and simple; unsophisticated. 3. Made of homespun. — n. 1. Fabric woven at home or by hand. 2. A rough, loosely woven fabric similar to this.

home·stead (hōm′sted) n. 1. A house and its land, etc. 2. *U.S.* A tract of land occupied under the Homestead Act. — v.i. 1. *U.S.* To occupy land under the Homestead Act. — v.t. 2. *U.S.* To settle on (land) under the Homestead Act. — **home′stead′er** n.

Homestead Act *U.S.* A Congressional enactment of 1862 that provided a settler with 160 acres of free public land for cultivation and eventual ownership.

homestead law *U.S.* A law exempting up to a certain amount a dwelling and its land from certain liabilities incurred by the owner. Also **homestead exemption law.**

home-stretch (hōm′strech′) n. 1. The straight portion of a racetrack forming the final approach to the finish. 2. The last stage of any journey or endeavor.

home·ward (hōm′wərd) adv. Toward home. Also **home′wards** (-wərdz). — adj. Directed toward home.

home·work (hōm′wûrk′) n. Work done at home, esp. school work.

home·y (hō′mē) adj. **hom·i·er, hom·i·est** Suggesting the comforts of home. — **home′y·ness** or **hom′i·ness** n.

hom·i·ci·dal (hom′ə-sīd′l, hō′mə-) adj. 1. Of homicide. 2. Tending to homicide; murderous. — **hom′i·ci′dal·ly** adv.

hom·i·cide (hom′ə-sīd, hō′mə-) n. 1. The killing of any human being by another. 2. A person who has killed another. [< F < L *homo* man + *caedere* to cut, kill]

hom·i·let·ic (hom′ə-let′ik) adj. 1. Pertaining to or having the nature of a sermon or homily. 2. Of or pertaining to homiletics. Also **hom′i·let′i·cal.** — **hom′i·let′i·cal·ly** adv.

hom·i·let·ics (hom′ə-let′iks) n.pl. (construed as sing.) The branch of theological study that treats of the art of writing and delivering sermons. [< Gk. *homilētikos* sociable]

hom·i·ly (hom′ə-lē) n. pl. **·lies** 1. A sermon, especially one based on a Biblical text. 2. A solemn discourse or lengthy reproof, especially on morals or conduct. [< OF < LL < Gk. *homilos* assembly] — **hom′i·list** n.

hom·ing (hō′ming) adj. 1. Returning home. 2. Helping or causing an aircraft, missile, etc., to home.

homing pigeon A pigeon capable of making its way home from great distances: also called *carrier pigeon.*

hom·i·noid (hom′ə-noid, hō′mə-) adj. Like or related to man. — n. An animal resembling man. [< NL < L *homo, hominis* man]

hom·i·ny (hom′ə-nē) n. Kernels of dried, hulled white corn, prepared as a food by boiling. [< Algonquian *rockahominie* parched corn]

hominy grits Grits (def. 2).

homo- *combining form* Same; like: opposed to *hetero-.* [< Gk. *homos* < *homos* same]

homoeo- See HOMEO-.

ho·mo·ge·ne·i·ty (hō′mə-jə-nē′ə-tē, hom′ə-) n. The quality or condition of being homogeneous.

ho·mo·ge·ne·ous (hō′mə-jē′nē-əs, hom′ə-) adj. 1. Having the same composition, structure, or character throughout;

uniform. **2.** Similar or identical in nature or form; like. [< Med.L < Gk. < *homos* same + *genos* race] **— ho'mo·ge'ne·ous·ly** *adv.* **— ho'mo·ge'ne·ous·ness** *n.*

ho·mog·en·ize (hə·mojʹə·nīz, hōʹmə·jə·nīz') *v.t.* **·ized, ·iz·ing 1.** To make or render homogeneous. **2.** To process, as milk, so as to break up fat globules and disperse them uniformly. **— ho·mog'en·i·za'tion** *n.* **— ho·mog'en·iz'er** *n.*

hom·o·graph (homʹə·graf, -gräf, hōʹmə-) *n.* A word identical with another in spelling, but differing from it in origin and meaning and sometimes in pronunciation, as *wind*, an air current, and *wind*, to coil: also called *homonym.* [< Gk. < *homos* same + *graphein* to write] **— hom'o·graph'ic** *adj.*

homoio- See HOMEO-.

ho·mol·o·gize (hō·molʹə·jīz) *v.* **·gized, ·giz·ing** *v.t.* **1.** To make or demonstrate to be homologous. **—** *v.i.* **2.** To be homologous; have correspondence.

ho·mol·o·gous (hō·molʹə·gəs) *adj.* **1.** Similar or related in structure, position, proportion, value, etc.; corresponding in nature or relationship. **2.** *Biol.* Corresponding in structure or origin, as an organ or part of one animal to a similar organ or part of another: The foreleg of a horse and the wing of a bird are *homologous*: distinguished from *analagous.* [< Gk. < *homos* same + *logos* measure, proportion]

ho·mol·o·gy (hō·molʹə·jē) *n. pl.* **·gies 1.** The state or quality of being homologous. **2.** A homologous relationship.

ho·mo·mor·phism (hōʹmə·môrʹfiz·əm, homʹə-) *n. Biol.* Resemblance between unrelated parts or organisms. Also **ho'mo·mor'phy. — ho'mo·mor'phic, ho'mo·mor'phous** *adj.*

hom·o·nym (homʹə·nim, hōʹmə-) *n.* **1.** A word identical with another in pronunciation but differing from it in origin, spelling, and meaning, as *fair* and *fare, read* and *reed*: also called *homophone.* **2.** A word identical with another in spelling and pronunciation, but differing from it in origin and meaning, as *butter*, the food, and *butter*, one who butts. **3.** A homograph. [< Gk. *homos* same + *onyma* name] **— hom·o·nym·ic** (homʹə·nimʹik, hōʹmə-), **ho·mon·y·mous** (hō·monʹə·məs) *adj.*

hom·o·phone (homʹə·fōn, hōʹmə-) *n.* A homonym (def. 1). [< Gk. *homos* same + *phōnē* sound]

hom·o·phon·ic (homʹə·fonʹik, hōʹmə-) *adj.* **1.** Of, pertaining to, or having the same sound. **2.** *Music* Having one predominant part carrying the melody, with the other parts used for harmonic effect: opposed to *polyphonic.* **— ho·moph·o·ny** (hō·mofʹə·nē) *n.*

ho·mop·ter·ous (hō·mopʹtər·əs) *adj.* Of or pertaining to insects with sucking mouth parts and usu. two pairs of wings. [< NL < Gk. *homos* same + *pteron* wing] **— ho·mop'ter·an** *adj. & n.*

Homo sa·pi·ens (sāʹpē·enz) The scientific name for modern man. [< NL < L *homo* man + *sapiens* wise]

ho·mo·sex·u·al (hōʹmə·sekʹshōō·əl, homʹə-) *adj.* Of or having sexual desire for persons of the same sex. **—** *n.* A homosexual individual. **— ho'mo·sex'u·al'i·ty** (-alʹə·tē) *n.*

ho·mun·cu·lus (hō·mungʹkyə·ləs) *n. pl.* **·li** (-lī) A midget; dwarf. [< L *homo* man] **— ho·mun'cu·lar** *adj.*

hone (hōn) *n.* A fine, compact whetstone used for sharpening edged tools, razors, etc. **—** *v.t.* **honed, hon·ing** To sharpen, as a razor, on a hone. [OE *hān* stone]

hon·est (onʹist) *adj.* **1.** Not given to lying, cheating, stealing, etc. **2.** Not characterized by falsehood or intent to mislead: an *honest* statement. **3.** Giving or having full worth or value. **4.** Performed or earned in a conscientious manner. **5.** Sincere; frank. [< OF < L *honos* honor]

hon·est·ly (onʹist·lē) *adv.* **1.** In an honest manner. **2.** Really; truly; indeed: used for emphasis: *Honestly*, I'll go.

hon·es·ty (onʹis·tē) *n.* **1.** The state or quality of being honest. **2.** Truthfulness; sincerity; fairness.

hon·ey (hunʹē) *n. pl.* **hon·eys 1.** A sweet, viscous substance made by bees from nectar gathered from flowers. **2.** Anything resembling honey. **3.** Sweetness. **4.** Darling: a term of endearment. **5.** *U.S. Slang* Something regarded as a superior example of its kind: a *honey* of a car. **—** *v.* **hon·eyed** or **hon·ied, hon·ey·ing** *v.t.* **1.** To sweeten with or as with honey. **2.** To talk in a loving or flattering manner to. **—** *adj.* Of or like honey; sweet. [OE *hunig*]

honey bag The receptacle or dilatation of the esophagus in which the bee produces honey. Also **honey sac.**

hon·ey·bee (hunʹē·bē') *n.* A bee that produces honey.

hon·ey·comb (hunʹē·kōm') *n.* **1.** A structure consisting of series of hexagonal, wax cells, made by bees for the storage of honey, pollen, or their eggs. **2.** Anything like a honeycomb. **—** *v.t.* **1.** To fill with small holes or cavities; riddle. **2.** To penetrate or pervade so as to undermine or weaken. **—** *adj.* Like a honeycomb.

hon·ey·dew (hunʹē·dōō', -dyōō') *n.* **1.** A sweet fluid exuded by the leaves of various plants during warm weather. **2.** A sweetish substance secreted by certain insects.

honeydew melon A variety of melon having a smooth, white skin and sweet, greenish pulp.

hon·eyed (hunʹēd) *adj.* **1.** Full of, consisting of, or resembling honey. **2.** Sweet, soothing, or flattering.

honey locust A large, thorny North American tree bearing long pods with a sweet pulp between the seeds.

hon·ey·moon (hunʹē·mōōn') *n.* **1.** A vacation spent by a newly-married couple. **2.** The first, happy period of a marriage. **3.** *U.S. Informal* The early and easy period of any relationship. **—** *v.i.* To spend one's honeymoon.

hon·ey·suck·le (hunʹē·suk'əl) *n.* **1.** A climbing shrub having white, buff, or crimson flowers. **2.** Any of a number of similar fragrant plants. [OE *hunisūce*]

honk (hôngk, hongk) *n.* **1.** The sound made by a goose. **2.** A sound resembling this, as that of an automobile horn. **—** *v.i.* **1.** To make the sound of the goose. **2.** To make the sound of an automobile horn. **—** *v.t.* **3.** To cause (an automobile horn) to sound. [Imit.] **— honk'er** *n.*

hon·ky-tonk (hôngʹkē·tôngk', hongʹkē·tongk') *n. U.S. Slang* A noisy, squalid barroom or tavern. [Prob. imit.]

hon·or (onʹər) *n.* **1.** High regard, respect, or esteem. **2.** Glory; fame; credit. **3.** *Usu. pl.* An outward token, sign, act, etc., of regard or esteem. **4.** A strong sense of what is right. **5.** A reputation for high standards of conduct. **6.** A cause or source of esteem or pride: to be an *honor* to one's profession. **7.** A privilege or pleasure: May I have the *honor* of this dance? **8.** *Usu. pl.* Special recognition given to a student for superior scholarship, etc. **9.** Chastity in women. **10.** In bridge, one of the five highest cards of a suit. **11.** In golf, the privilege of playing first from the tee. **— to do honor to 1.** To pay homage to. **2.** To bring respect or credit to. **— to do the honors 1.** To act as host or hostess. **2.** To perform any of various social courtesies, as proposing toasts, etc. **—** *v.t.* **1.** To regard with honor or respect. **2.** To treat with courtesy. **3.** To confer an honor upon; dignify. **4.** To accept or pay, as a check or draft. Also *Brit.* **hon'our.** [< OF < L] **— hon'or·er** *n.*

Hon·or (onʹər) *n.* A title or form of address for a judge, mayor, etc.: preceded by *Your*, *His*, or *Her*.

hon·or·a·ble (onʹər·ə·bəl) *adj.* **1.** Worthy of honor or respect. **2.** Conferring honor or credit. **3.** Having eminence or high rank. **4.** Possessing or according to high moral principles. **5.** Accompanied by marks of honor. Also *Brit.* **hon'·our·a·ble. — hon'or·a·ble·ness** *n.* **— hon'or·a·bly** *adv.*

Hon·or·a·ble (onʹər·ə·bəl) *adj.* A formal title of courtesy for certain important officials, as cabinet members, justices of the Supreme Court, etc.: preceded by *The.*

hon·o·rar·i·um (onʹə·rârʹē·əm) *n. pl.* **·rar·i·ums** or **·rar·i·a** (-rârʹē·ə) A payment given, as to a professional man, for services rendered when law or propriety forbids a set fee. [< L *honorarium* honorary]

hon·or·ar·y (onʹə·rer'ē) *adj.* **1.** Designating an office, title, etc., bestowed as an honor, without the customary powers, duties, or salaries. **2.** Having such a title, office, etc.: an *honorary* chairman. **3.** Bringing, conferred in, or denoting honor: an *honorary* membership. [< L *honorarius*]

hon·or·if·ic (onʹə·rifʹik) *adj.* **1.** Conferring or implying honor or respect. **2.** Denoting certain phrases, words, or word elements, as in Oriental languages, used in respectful address. **—** *n.* Any honorific title, word, phrase, etc. [< L < *honor* honor + *facere* to make] **— hon'or·if'i·cal·ly** *adv.*

honors system In some colleges, a plan for selected students to undertake individual, specialized work.

honor system In some colleges, schools, etc., a system of government without immediate supervision.

hooch (hōōch) *n. U.S. Slang* Alcoholic liquor, esp. illegally distilled whisky. [< *hoochinoo*, alter. of *Hutanuwu*, name of Alaskan Indian tribe that made liquor]

hood[1] (hōōd) *n.* **1.** A covering for the head and back of the neck, sometimes forming part of a garment. **2.** Anything resmbling a hood in form or use: as **a** *U.S.* The movable metal cover protecting the engine of an automobile. **b** A projecting cover for a hearth, ventilator, etc. **3.** In falconry, a cover for the head and eyes of a hawk when it is not hunting. **4.** *Zool.* In certain animals, as the cobra, the folds of skin near the head, capable of expansion. **—** *v.t.* To cover or furnish with or as with a hood. [OE *hōd*] **— hood'ed** *adj.*

hood[2] (hōōd) *n. U.S. Slang* A hoodlum. [< HOODLUM]

-hood *suffix of nouns* **1.** Condition or quality of: state of being: *babyhood, falsehood.* **2.** Class or totality of those having a certain character: *priesthood.* [OE *hād* state, condition]

hood·lum (hōōdʹləm) *n. U.S.* **1.** A young street rowdy or tough. **2.** A thug or ruffian. [? < dia. G *hodalum* rowdy]

hoo·doo (hōōʹdōō) *n.* **1.** Voodoo. **2.** *Informal* One who or that which brings bad luck; a jinx. **3.** *Informal* Bad luck. **—** *v.t. Informal* To bring bad luck to. [Var. of VOODOO]

hood·wink (hōōdʹwingk') *v.t.* **1.** To blindfold. **2.** To trick; cheat. **3.** To conceal or hide. **— hood'wink'er** *n.*

hoo·ey (hōōʹē) *n. & interj. U.S. Slang* Nonsense.

hoof (hōōf, hōōf) *n. pl.* **hoofs** or **hooves** (hōōvz) **1.** The horny sheath incasing the foot in various mammals, as horses, cattle, swine, etc. ◆ Collateral adjective: *ungular.* **2.** The entire foot of such an animal. **3.** An animal with hoofs, especially as a unit of a herd. **4.** The human foot: a humorous usage. **— on the hoof** Alive; not butchered: said of cattle. — *v.t.* & *v.i.* **1.** To trample with the hoofs. **2.** *Informal* To walk or dance: usually with *it*. [OE *hōf*]

hoof·beat (hŏŏf'bēt', hōōf'-) *n.* The sound made by a hoofed animal in walking, trotting, etc.

hoof·er (hŏŏf'ər, hōōf'ər) *n.* *U.S. Slang* A professional dancer, esp. a tap dancer.

hoof·print (hŏŏf'print', hōōf'-) *n.* One of the tracks left by a hoofed animal.

hook (hŏŏk) *n.* **1.** A curved or bent piece of metal, wood, bone, etc., having one free end that serves to hold up, fasten, or drag something. **2.** A fishhook. **3.** A curved cutting tool. **4.** The fixed half of a hinge from which a door, gate, etc., swings. **5.** Something that ensnares; a trap. **6.** Something resembling a hook; as: **a** A recurved organ or part of an animal or plant. **b** A curved point of land. **c** A bend in a river. **d** A hook-shaped part of a letter. **7.** In baseball, a curve. **8.** In boxing, a short, swinging blow, with the elbow bent. **9.** In golf, a stroke that sends the ball curving to his left. **10.** *Music* One of the lines at the end of the stem of a note, used to indicate the note's value. **11.** *Naut. Slang* An anchor. — **by hook or by crook** In one way or another. — **hook, line, and sinker** *Informal* Entirely; unreservedly. — **off the hook** *Slang* Free from a troublesome situation, obligation, etc. — **on one's own hook** *Informal* By one's own efforts. — *v.t.* **1.** To fasten, attach, or take hold of with or as with a hook. **2.** To catch on a hook, as fish. **3.** To make into the shape of a hook. **4.** To catch on or wound with the horns, as those of a bull. **5.** To make (a rug, mat, etc.) by looping yarn through a backing of canvas or burlap. **6.** In baseball, to pitch (the ball) in a curve. **7.** In boxing, to strike with a short, swinging blow. **8.** In golf, to drive (the ball) to one's left. **9.** In hockey, to check illegally with the stick. **10.** *Informal* To trick; dupe. **11.** *Slang* To pilfer; steal. — *v.i.* **12.** To curve like a hook; bend. **13.** To be fastened or caught with or as with a hook or hooks. — **to hook up 1.** To fasten or attach with a hook or hooks. **2.** To put together or connect. — **to hook up with** *Slang* **1.** To become a companion of. **2.** To marry. [OE *hōc*] — **hook'y** *adj.*

hook·ah (hŏŏk'ə) *n.* An Oriental tobacco pipe having a long, flexible tube that passes through a vessel of water, thus cooling the smoke. Also **hook'a**. [< Arabic *huqqah*]

hook and eye A fastening for clothes, consisting of a small hook that passes through a loop of metal or thread.

hooked (hŏŏkt) *adj.* **1.** Curved like a hook. **2.** Supplied with a hook or hooks. **3.** Made by means of a hook, as a rug. **4.** *Slang* Married. **5.** *Slang* Addicted to a habit or practice, especially a harmful one. — **hook·ed·ness** (hŏŏk'id·nis) *n.*

hooked rug A rug made by looping yarn or strips of cloth with a hooked tool through a backing of burlap or canvas.

hook·nose (hŏŏk'nōz') *n.* A nose with a downward curve; aquiline nose. — **hook'-nosed'** (-nōzd') *adj.*

hook·up (hŏŏk'up') *n.* **1.** *Telecom.* The arrangement of the apparatus and connections used for a radio broadcast or other electrical transmission. **2.** *Informal* A relationship or connection, as between countries, persons, etc.

hook·worm (hŏŏk'wûrm') *n.* A nematode worm with hooked mouth parts, parasitic in the intestines and causing ancylostomiasis in man.

hookworm disease Ancylostomiasis.

hook·y (hŏŏk'ē) *n.* *U.S. Informal* Absence without leave, as from school: now only in the phrase **to play hooky**, to be a truant. [< HOOK, in dial. sense of "make off"]

hoo·li·gan (hōō'lə·gən) *n.* *Slang* A young hoodlum; petty gangster. [after *Hooligan*, name of an Irish family]

hoop (hōōp, hŏŏp) *n.* **1.** A circular band of metal, wood, etc.; esp., such a band used to confine the staves of a barrel, etc. **2.** A child's toy in the shape of a large ring. **3.** One of the rings of flexible metal, whalebone, etc., used to make a woman's skirt stand out from her body. **4.** The band of a finger ring. — *v.t.* **1.** To surround or fasten with a hoop or hoops. **2.** To encircle. [OE *hōp*]

hoop·er (hōō'pər, hŏŏp'ər) *n.* A cooper.

hoop·la (hōōp'lä) *n.* *U.S. Slang* Noise and excitement.

hoo·poe (hōō'pōō) *n.* An Old World bird having a long bill and an erectile crest. Also **hoo'poo**. [< F < L *upupa*]

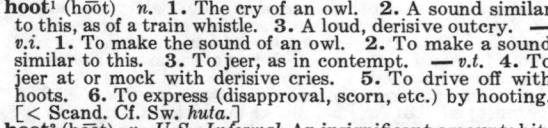

HOOPOE
(About 12 inch-
es long; bill
2½ inches)

hoop skirt 1. A bell-shaped structure made from several hoops of graduated sizes, used to expand a woman's skirt. **2.** The skirt worn over this.

hoo·ray (hŏŏ·rā', hə-, hōō-) See HURRAH.

hoose·gow (hōōs'gou) *n.* *U.S. Slang* Jail or prison. Also **hoos'gow**. [< Sp. *juzgado* tribunal]

Hoo·sier (hōō'zhər) *n.* *U.S.* A native or resident of Indiana. [Prob. < dial. *hoosier* mountaineer]

Hoosier State A nickname of Indiana.

hoot¹ (hōōt) *n.* **1.** The cry of an owl. **2.** A sound similar to this, as of a train whistle. **3.** A loud, derisive outcry. — *v.i.* **1.** To make the sound of an owl. **2.** To make a sound similar to this. **3.** To jeer, as in contempt. — *v.t.* **4.** To jeer at or mock with derisive cries. **5.** To drive off with hoots. **6.** To express (disapproval, scorn, etc.) by hooting. [< Scand. Cf. Sw. *huta*.]

hoot² (hōōt) *n.* *U.S. Informal* An insignificant amount; bit: commonly in the expression **I don't give a hoot,** I don't care a bit. [Earlier *hooter*, ? alter. of *iota*. Cf. JOT.]

hoot·en·an·ny (hōōt'n·an'ē) *n. pl.* **·nies 1.** *U.S.* A gathering of folk singers, especially for a public performance. **2.** *Informal* A gadget; thingamajig. Also **hoot·nan·ny** (hōōt'nan'ē). [Origin unknown]

hooves (hōōvz, hŏŏvz) Alternative plural of HOOF.

hop¹ (hop) *v.* **hopped, hop·ping** *v.i.* **1.** To move by making short leaps on one foot. **2.** To move in short leaps on both feet or on all four feet. **3.** To limp. **4.** *Informal* To dance. **5.** *Informal* To go, especially by airplane. — *v.t.* **6.** To jump over, as a fence. **7.** *Informal* To get on or board. — **to hop off** To leave the ground in flight, as an airplane. — *n.* **1.** The act of hopping. **2.** *Informal* A dance or dancing party. **3.** *Informal* A trip in an airplane. [OE *hoppian*]

hop² (hop) *n.* **1.** A perennial climbing herb with scaly fruit. **2.** *pl.* The dried cones, used medicinally, and as a flavoring in beer. [< MDu. *hoppe*]

hope (hōp) *v.* **hoped, hop·ing** *v.t.* **1.** To desire with expectation of fulfillment. **2.** To wish; want. — *v.i.* **3.** To have desire or expectation: usually with *for*. — **to hope against hope** To continue hoping even when it may be in vain. — *n.* **1.** Desire accompanied by expectation of fulfillment. **2.** Confident expectation. **3.** That which is desired. **4.** One who or that which is a cause of hopeful expectation. [OE *hopa*]

hope chest A box or chest used by young women to hold linen, clothing, etc., in anticipation of marriage.

hope·ful (hōp'fəl) *adj.* **1.** Full of or manifesting hope: a *hopeful* attitude. **2.** Affording grounds for hope; promising: a *hopeful* situation. — *n.* A young person who seems likely to succeed. — **hope'ful·ly** *adv.* — **hope'ful·ness** *n.*

hope·less (hōp'lis) *adj.* **1.** Without hope; despairing: a *hopeless* feeling. **2.** Affording no ground for hope: a *hopeless* predicament. — **hope'less·ly** *adv.* — **hope'less·ness** *n.*

Ho·pi (hō'pē) *n.* **1.** One of a group of North American Pueblo Indians of Shoshonean stock, now on a reservation in NE Arizona. **2.** Their Shoshonean language. [< Hopi *hópitu*, lit., peaceful ones]

hopped-up (hopt'up') *adj.* *U.S. Slang* **1.** Stimulated by narcotics; drugged. **2.** Supercharged, as an engine.

hop·per (hop'ər) *n.* **1.** One who or that which hops. **2.** A jumping insect or larva. **3.** Any of various funnel-shaped receptacles in which coal, sand, grain, etc., may be kept until ready for discharge through the bottom.

hop·scotch (hop'skoch') *n.* A children's game in which the player hops on one foot over the lines of a diagram, so as to recover a block or pebble.

ho·ral (hō'rəl) *adj.* Hourly. [< L *hora* hour]

Ho·ra·tian (hə·rā'shən) *adj.* Of or pertaining to Horace.

horde (hôrd, hōrd) *n.* **1.** A multitude, pack, or swarm, as of people, animals, etc. **2.** A tribe of nomadic Mongols. **3.** Any nomadic tribe. — *v.i.* **hord·ed, hord·ing** To gather in or live in a horde. [< F < G < Polish *horda*]

hore·hound (hôr'hound', hōr'-) *n.* **1.** A whitish, bitter, perennial herb of the mint family. **2.** The juice or extract of this plant. **3.** A candy or cough remedy flavored with this extract. Also spelled *hoarhound*. [OE *hārhūne*]

ho·ri·zon (hə·rī'zən) *n.* **1.** The line of the apparent meeting of the sky with the earth or sea. **2.** The bounds or limits of one's observation, knowledge, or experience. [< OF < L < Gk. *horizein* to bound]

hor·i·zon·tal (hôr'ə·zon'təl, hor'-) *adj.* **1.** Of, pertaining to, or close to the horizon. **2.** Parallel to the horizon; level: opposed to *vertical*. **3.** Equal and uniform: a *horizontal* tariff. — *n.* A line, plane, etc., assumed to be parallel with the horizon. — **Syn.** See LEVEL. — **hor'i·zon'tal·ly** *adv.*

horizontal union A craft union.

hor·mone (hôr'mōn) *n.* **1.** *Physiol.* An internal secretion produced by one of the endocrine glands, as the pituitary, thyroid, adrenals, etc., and carried by the blood stream to other parts of the body where it has a specific effect. **2.** *Bot.* A similar substance in plants. [< Gk. *hormaein* to excite] — **hor·mo·nal** (hôr·mō'nəl), **hor·mon·ic** (hôr·mon'ik) *adj.*

horn (hôrn) *n.* **1.** A hard, bonelike, permanent growth of epidermal tissue, usu. occurring in pairs and projecting from the head in various hoofed animals, as in oxen, sheep, cattle, etc. **2.** Either of the two antlers of a deer, shed annually. **3.** Any outgrowth projecting naturally from the head of an animal. **4.** The substance of which animal horn is made. **5.** The appendage like an animal's horn attributed to demons,

deities, etc.　**6.** In the Bible, a symbol of glory and power.
7. *Usu. pl.* The imaginary projections from the forehead of a
cuckold.　**8.** A vessel or implement formed from or shaped
like a horn: a powder *horn*.　**9.** One of the extremities of the
crescent moon.　**10.** The pommel of a saddle.　**11.** A device
for sounding warning signals: an automobile *horn*.　**12.** A
cornucopia.　**13.** Any pointed or tapering projection, as the
point of an anvil.　**14.** One of the two or more alternatives
of a dilemma.　**15.** *Music* **a** Any of the various brass instruments, formerly made from animal horns, in the shape of a
long, coiled tube widening out into a bell at one end. **b** The
French horn.　**16.** *Informal* Any musical wind instrument.
17. *Electronics* A hollow, tubular device terminating in a
cone of varying cross section, for collecting sound waves, as
in a loudspeaker.　**18.** *Geog.* **a** One of the branches forming
the delta of a stream or river. **b** A cape or peninsula. — **to
blow one's own horn** To brag. — **to haul** (or **pull** or **draw**)
in one's horns To check one's anger, zeal, etc.　**2.** To retract or withdraw, as a previous statement. — *adj.* Of or
like horn. — *v.t.* **1.** To provide with horns.　**2.** To shape
like a horn.　**3.** To attack with the horns; gore. — **to horn
in** *Slang* To intrude or enter without being invited.　[OE]
horn·bill (hôrn′bil′) *n.* A tropical bird, having a large bill
surmounted by a hornlike extension.
horn·blende (hôrn′blend) *n.* A common variety of amphi-
bole, greenish black or black, containing iron and silicate of
magnesium, calcium, and aluminum. — **horn′blend′ic** *adj.*
horn·book (hôrn′bo͝ok′) *n.* **1.** A leaf or page containing a
printed alphabet, etc., covered with transparent horn and
framed, formerly used in teaching reading to children.　**2.** A
primer or book of rudimentary knowledge.
horned (hôrnd, *Poetic* hôr′nid) *adj.* **1.** Having a horn or
horns.　**2.** Having a projection or process resembling a horn.
horned owl Any of various American owls with conspicuous
ear tufts; esp. the screech owl.
horned toad A flat-bodied, spiny lizard with a short tail and
toadlike appearance, common in semiarid regions of the
western U.S. Also **horn toad.**
horned viper A venomous African or Indian viper with a
hornlike growth over each eye.
hor·net (hôr′nit) *n.* Any of various wasps capable of inflicting a severe sting.　[OE *hyrnet*]
horn of plenty A cornucopia.
horn·pipe (hôrn′pīp′) *n.* **1.** An obsolete musical instrument resembling the clarinet.　**2.** A lively English dance for
one or more performers.　**3.** The music for such a dance.
horn·y (hôr′nē) *adj.* **horn·i·er, horn·i·est** **1.** Made of horn
or a similar substance.　**2.** Having horns or projections resembling horns.　**3.** Hard as horn; tough. — **horn′i·ness** *n.*
hor·o·loge (hôr′ə·lōj, hor′-) *n.* A timepiece, as a watch,
clock, etc.　[< OF < L < Gk. < *hōra* time + *legein* to tell]
ho·rol·o·ger (hô·rol′ə·jər, hō-) *n.* One skilled in horology;
also, one who makes or sells timepieces. Also **ho·rol′o·gist.**
ho·rol·o·gy (hô·rol′ə·jē, hō-) *n.* The science of the measurement of time or of the construction of timepieces. — **hor·o·
log′ic** (hôr′ə·loj′ik, hor′-) or **·i·cal** *adj.*
hor·o·scope (hôr′ə·skōp, hor′-) *n.* **1.** In astrology, the aspect of the heavens, with special reference to the positions of
the planets at any specific instant, esp. at a person's birth.
2. The diagram of the twelve divisions or houses of the heavens, used in predicting the future.　[< L < Gk. < *hōra* hour
+ *skopos* watcher] — **ho·ros·co·py** (hô·ros′kə·pē) *n.*
hor·ren·dous (hô·ren′dəs, ho-) *adj.* Horrible; frightful.
[< L *horrere* to bristle] — **hor·ren′dous·ly** *adv.*
hor·ri·ble (hôr′ə·bəl, hor′-) *adj.* **1.** Exciting or tending to
excite horror; shocking.　**2.** *Informal* Inordinate; excessive:
a horrible liar.　**3.** *Informal* Unpleasant; ugly.　[< F < L
horrere to bristle] — **hor′ri·ble·ness** *n.* — **hor′ri·bly** *adj.*
hor·rid (hôr′id, hor′-) *adj.* **1.** Causing great aversion or horror; dreadful.　**2.** *Informal* Very objectionable; offensive. —
hor′rid·ly *adv.* — **hor′rid·ness** *n.*
hor·ri·fy (hôr′ə·fī, hor′-) *v.t.* **·fied, ·fy·ing** **1.** To affect or fill
with horror.　**2.** *Informal* To shock or surprise painfully;
startle. — **hor′ri·fi·ca′tion** *n.*
hor·ror (hôr′ər, hor′-) *n.* **1.** A painful, strong emotion caused
by extreme fear, dread, repugnance, etc.　**2.** One who or that
which excites such an emotion.　**3.** *Often pl.* A quality that
excites horror: the *horrors* of crime.　**4.** Great aversion;
loathing.　**5.** *Informal* Something disagreeable, ugly, etc.
[< L]
hors d'oeuvre (ôr dûrv′, *Fr.* ôr dœ′vr′) *Usu. pl.* An appetizer, as olives, celery, etc.　[< F]
horse (hôrs) *n.* *pl.* **hors·es** or **horse** **1.** A large, strong, herbivorous mammal with solid hoofs and a long mane and tail,
employed in the domestic state as a draft or pack animal or
for riding.　◆ Collateral adjective: *equine.*　**2.** The full-grown
male horse as contrasted with the mare; a gelding or stallion.
3. Mounted soldiers; cavalry.　**4.** A device, generally having four legs, for holding or supporting something: often in
combination: *clotheshorse.*　**5.** In gymnastics, a wooden
leather-covered block on four legs, used for vaulting and

other exercises.　**6.** *Informal* In chess, a knight. — **a horse
of another** (or **a different**) **color** A completely different matter. — **out of** (or **straight from**) **the horse's mouth** From
the most direct and reliable source. — **to be** (or **get**) **on
one's high horse** *Informal* To act haughtily or scornfully.
— **to hold one's horses** *Slang* To restrain one's impetuosity
or impatience. — **To horse!** A command for cavalry troops
to mount. — *v.* **horsed, hors·ing** *v.t.* **1.** To furnish with a
horse or horses.　**2.** To put on horseback.　**3.** *U.S. Slang* To
subject to horseplay or ridicule. — *v.i.* **4.** To mount or ride
on a horse.　**5.** *Slang* To engage in horseplay: often with
around. — *adj.* **1.** Of or pertaining to a horse or horses.
2. Mounted on horses.　**3.** Large for its kind.　[OE *hors*]
horse·back (hôrs′bak′) *n.* **1.** A horse's back.　**2.** A ridge
of earth or rock; hogback. — *adv.* On a horse's back.
horse·car (hôrs′kär′)　**1.** A tramcar drawn by horses.　**2.**
A car for transporting horses.
horse chestnut **1.** A tree having digitate leaves, clusters of
flowers, and chestnutlike fruits.　**2.** The fruit of this tree.
horse·flesh (hôrs′flesh′) *n.* Horses collectively.
horse·fly (hôrs′flī′) *n.* *pl.* **·flies** A large fly, the female of
which sucks the blood of horses, cattle, etc.
horse·hair (hôrs′hâr′) *n.* **1.** The hair of horses, esp. that of
their manes and tails.　**2.** A fabric made of such hair; haircloth. — *adj.* Covered, stuffed, or made of horsehair.
horse·hide (hôrs′hīd′) *n.* **1.** The hide of a horse.　**2.** Leather
made from a horse's hide.
horse latitudes *Naut.* A belt at about 35° north or south
latitude, characterized by calms and light variable winds,
with diminishing to prevailing westerlies toward the poles
and trade winds toward the equator.
horse·laugh (hôrs′laf′, -läf′) *n.* A loud, scornful laugh.
horse·man (hôrs′mən) *n.* *pl.* **·men** (-mən) **1.** A man who
rides a horse.　**2.** A cavalryman. — **horse′man·ship** *n.*
horse pistol A large pistol formerly carried by horsemen.
horse·play (hôrs′plā′) *n.* Rough, boisterous play or fun.
horse·pow·er (hôrs′pou′ər) *n.* *Mech.* A unit of the rate of
work, equal to 550 pounds lifted one foot in one second.
horse·rad·ish (hôrs′rad′ish) *n.* **1.** A garden herb of the
mustard family.　**2.** A condiment made from its root.
horse sense *Informal* Innate common sense.
horse·shoe (hôrs′shōō′, hôrs′-) *n.* **1.** A piece of metal, U-
shaped to fit the edge of a horse's hoof, to which it is nailed
as a protective device.　**2.** Something resembling a horseshoe in shape.　**3.** *pl.* A game similar to quoits, in which the
object is to throw horseshoes over or near a stake. — *v.t.*
·shoed, ·shoe·ing To furnish with horseshoes.
horseshoe crab A large marine arthropod having a horse-
shoe-shaped carapace and a long telson: also called *king crab.*
horse·tail (hôrs′tāl′) *n.* **1.** The tail of a horse.　**2.** A perennial flowerless plant of wide distribution.
horse·whip (hôrs′hwip′) *n.* A whip for managing horses.
— *v.t.* **·whipped, ·whip·ping** To flog with a horsewhip.
horse·wom·an (hôrs′wŏŏm′ən) *n.* *pl.* **·wom·en** (-wim′in)
1. A woman who rides on horseback.　**2.** A woman who is
skilled in riding or managing horses.
hors·y (hôr′sē) *adj.* **hors·i·er, hors·i·est** **1.** Pertaining to,
suggestive of, or having the nature of a horse or horses.　**2.**
Associated with or devoted to horses, horseracing, fox hunting, etc. Also **hors′ey.** — **hors′i·ly** *adv.* — **hors′i·ness** *n.*
hor·ta·to·ry (hôr′tə·tôr′ē, -tō′rē) *adj.* Of, characterized by,
or giving exhortation or encouragement. Also **hor′ta·tive.**
[< L *hortatorius*] — **hor′ta·tive·ly** *adv.*
hor·ti·cul·ture (hôr′tə·kul′chər) *n.* **1.** The cultivation of a
garden.　**2.** The art or science of growing garden vegetables,
fruits, flowers, etc.　[< L *hortus* garden + *cultura* cultiva-
tion] — **hor′ti·cul′tur·al** *adj.* — **hor′ti·cul′tur·ist** *n.*
ho·san·na (hō·zan′ə) *interj.* Praised be the Lord. — *n.* **1.**
A cry of "hosanna."　**2.** Any exultant praise.　[< LL < Gk.
< Hebrew *hōshī āhnnā* save, we pray]
hose (hōz) *n.* *pl.* **hose** (*Archaic* **hos·en**) *for defs.* 1, 2; **hos·es**
for def. 3 **1.** *pl.* Stockings or socks.　**2.** *pl.* Formerly, a garment worn by men for covering the legs and lower part of the
body like tight trousers.　**3.** A flexible tube of rubber, plastic, etc., for conveying water and other fluids. — *v.t.* **hosed,
hos·ing** **1.** To water, drench, or douse with a hose.　**2.**
Canadian Slang To cheat or defeat.　[OE *hosa*]
Ho·se·a (hō·zē′ə, -zā′ə) Eighth-century B.C. Hebrew prophet. — *n.* A book of the Old Testament bearing his name:
also, in the Douai Bible, *Osee.*
ho·sier·y (hō′zhər·ē) *n.* Stockings and socks of all types.
hos·pice (hos′pis) *n.* A place of rest or shelter, usu. maintained by a religious order for pilgrims, travelers, etc.　[<
L *hospitium* inn, hospitality]
hos·pi·ta·ble (hos′pi·tə·bəl, hos·pit′ə·bəl) *adj.* **1.** Behaving
in a kind and generous manner toward guests.　**2.** Affording
or expressing welcome and generosity toward guests.　**3.**
Receptive in mind.　[< OF < L *hospitare* to entertain] —
hos′pi·ta·ble·ness *n.* — **hos′pi·ta·bly** *adv.*
hos·pi·tal (hos′pi·təl) *n.* An institution that provides medical, surgical, or psychiatric treatment and nursing care for

the ill or injured temporarily lodged there; also, the building used for this purpose. [< OF < L *hospes* guest]

hos·pi·tal·i·ty (hos/pə·tal/ə·tē) *n. pl.* **·ties** The spirit, practice, or act of being hospitable.

hos·pi·tal·ize (hos/pi·təl·īz/) *v.t.* **·ized, ·iz·ing** To put in a hospital for treatment and care.

hos·pi·tal·i·za·tion (hos/pi·təl·ə·zā/shən, -ī·zā/shən) *n.* **1.** The act of hospitalizing. **2.** *U.S.* A form of insurance that guarantees all or partial payment of hospital expenses: also **hospital insurance.**

host¹ (hōst) *n.* **1.** A man who extends hospitality to others, usu. to guests in his own home. **2.** *Biol.* Any living organism from which a parasite obtains nourishment and protection. — *v.t. Informal* To conduct or entertain in the role of host. [< OF < L *hospes* guest, host]

host² (hōst) *n.* **1.** A large number of men or things; a multitude. **2.** An army. [< OF < L *hostis* enemy]

host³ (hōst) *n. Eccl. Sometimes cap.* The Eucharistic bread or wafer. [< OF < L *hostia* sacrificial victim]

hos·tage (hos/tij) *n.* **1.** A person given or held as a pledge until specified conditions are met, as in war. **2.** The state of any person so treated. **3.** A pledge or security. [< OF]

hos·tel (hos/təl) *n.* One of a chain of supervised lodging houses for young people on bicycle or hiking trips.

hos·tel·ry (hos/təl·rē) *n. pl.* **·ries** *Archaic* A lodging place; inn. — **hos/tel·er, hos/tel·ler** *n.*

host·ess (hōs/tis) *n.* **1.** A woman who performs the duties of a host. **2.** A woman employed in a restaurant, etc., to greet and serve guests. **3.** A woman paid to dance with the patrons of a public dance hall. **4.** A female innkeeper.

hos·tile (hos/təl, *esp. Brit.* -tīl) *adj.* **1.** Having or expressing enmity or opposition; unfriendly. **2.** Of, pertaining to, or characteristic of an enemy: *hostile* acts; *hostile* forces. [< F < L *hostilis*] — **hos/tile·ly** *adv.*

hos·til·i·ty (hos·til/ə·tē) *n. pl.* **·ties** **1.** The state of being hostile. **2.** A hostile act. **3.** *pl.* War or acts of war.

hos·tler (hos/lər, os/-) *n.* A stableman; groom: also spelled *ostler.* [< OF *hostelier* innkeeper]

hot (hot) *adj.* **hot·ter, hot·test** **1.** Having or giving off great heat; having a high temperature. **2.** Having a relatively high degree of heat; very warm. **3.** Feeling or showing abnormal bodily warmth. **4.** Giving the sensation of heat or burning to the tongue or skin: *hot* pepper. **5.** Carrying an electric current, esp. one of high voltage. **6.** Dangerously radioactive. **7.** Constantly in action or use: War news kept the wires *hot.* **8.** In hunting, strong or fresh, as a scent. **9.** Not far behind: in *hot* pursuit. **10.** Marked by or showing strong or violent emotion: *hot* words. **11.** Marked by intense activity; raging; violent: a *hot* battle. **12.** *Slang* Lustful; sexy. **13.** *Slang* Strongly disposed toward; eager: often with *for.* **14.** *Informal* Controversial: a *hot* issue. **15.** *Informal* So new as not to have lost its currency, excitement, etc.: a *hot* item. **16.** *Slang* Excellent, skillful, etc.: He is not so *hot* tonight. **17.** *U.S. Slang* Recently stolen or illegally procured. **18.** *Music Slang* a Designating jazz marked by a fast tempo, heavily accented beat, exciting improvisations, etc. **b** Playing or performing such jazz: a *hot* trumpet. — **in hot water** *Informal* In trouble. — **to make it hot for** *Informal* To make the situation extremely uncomfortable for. — *adv.* In a hot manner. [OE *hāt*] — **hot/ly** *adv.*

hot air *Slang* Empty or pretentious talk; exaggeration.

hot·bed (hot/bed/) *n.* **1.** A bed of rich earth, protected by glass and warmed usu. by fermenting manure, used to promote the growth of plants in advance of their season. **2.** A place or condition favoring rapid growth or great activity.

hot-blood·ed (hot/blud/id) *adj.* Easily moved or excited.

hot cake A pancake or griddlecake. — **to go** (or **sell**) **like hot cakes** *Informal* To be disposed of quickly.

hot cross bun A circular cake or bun marked with a cross of frosting, eaten esp. during Lent.

hot dog *Informal* A cooked frankfurter, usu. grilled, served in a split roll, and garnished with mustard, relish, etc.

ho·tel (hō·tel/) *n.* **1.** An establishment or building providing lodging, food, etc., to travelers and long-term residents. **2.** *Canadian* Beer parlor. [< F < OF *hostel* inn]

hot·foot (hot/foot/) *v.i. Informal* To hurry: often with *it.*

hot·head (hot/hed/) *n.* A hotheaded person.

hot·head·ed (hot/hed/id) *adj.* **1.** Quick-tempered. **2.** Impetuous. — **hot/head/ed·ly** *adv.* — **hot/head/ed·ness** *n.*

hot·house (hot/hous/) *n.* A greenhouse kept warm artificially for the growth of out-of-season or delicate plants.

hot line A direct means of communication, esp. a telephone line for emergency use between Washington, D.C. and Moscow.

hot plate A small portable gas or electric stove.

hot rod *U.S. Slang* An automobile, usu. an older model, modified for high speeds.

hot spring A natural spring emitting waters with a temperature of 98° F. or above: also called *thermal spring.*

Hot·ten·tot (hot/ən·tot) *n.* **1.** A member of a South African people believed to be related to both the Bantus and the Bushmen. **2.** The language of this people. — *adj.* Of or pertaining to the Hottentots or their language.

hou·dah (hou/də) See HOWDAH.

hound (hound) *n.* **1.** A dog of any of several breeds kept for hunting, esp. one that hunts by scent and in a pack. **2.** A dog of any breed. **3.** A mean, detestable man. — **to follow** (or **ride to**) **the hounds** To engage in hunting (a fox, etc.) on horseback and with a pack of hounds. — *v.t.* **1.** To hunt with or as with hounds. **2.** To incite to pursue. **3.** *Informal* To nag persistently; pester. [OE *hund* dog]

hour (our) *n.* **1.** A space of time equal to ⅟₂₄ of a day; sixty minutes. ◆ Collateral adjective: *horal.* **2.** Any one of the twelve points on a timepiece indicating such a space of time. **3.** A definite time of day as shown in hours and minutes by a timepiece: The *hour* is 6:15. **4.** An indefinite, but usu. short, period of time: The happiest *hour* of one's life. **5.** A particular or regularly fixed time for some activity. **6.** *pl.* A set period of time for work or other regular pursuits: school *hours.* **7.** *pl.* One's usual time of rising and of going to bed: to keep regular *hours.* **8.** The present time or current situation. **9.** Distance calculated by the time ordinarily required to cover it: an *hour* away from home. **10.** In education, a single class session or period, usu. 50 minutes long. **11.** *Eccl.* **a** The canonical hours. **b** The office or prayers recited or sung at these hours. **12.** *Astron.* An angular measure of right ascension or longitude, being 15 degrees or the 24th part of a great circle of the sphere. — **the small** (or **wee**) **hours** The early hours of the morning. [< L < Gk. *hōra* time, period]

hour·glass (our/glas/, -gläs/) *n.* An old device for measuring time, consisting of two globular glass vessels connected by a narrow neck through which a quantity of sand, mercury, or water runs from the upper vessel to the lower during a stated interval of time, usu. an hour.

hou·ri (hoo/rē, hour/ē) *n.* In Moslem belief, one of the beautiful virgins allotted to those who attain Paradise. [< F < Persian < Arabic *hūrīyah* black-eyed woman]

HOURGLASS

hour·ly (our/lē) *adj.* **1.** Of, happening, or performed every hour. **2.** Occurring or accomplished in the course of an hour. **3.** Frequent. — *adv.* **1.** At intervals of an hour. **2.** Hour by hour. **3.** Frequently; often.

house (*n.* hous; *v.* houz) *n. pl.* **hous·es** (hou/zəz) **1.** A building intended as a dwelling for human beings, esp. one used as the residence of a family or single tenant. **2.** A household; family. **3.** The abode of a fraternity, religious community, or other group living together as a unit. **4.** A dormitory or resident hall, esp. in a college or university. **5.** *Brit.* A college in a university. **6.** Anything providing shelter or protection to an animal, as the shell of a snail. **7.** A structure for storing or sheltering something, as goods, plants, etc. **8.** A building used for any of various purposes: a *house* of correction. **9.** A place of worship. **10.** A theater or other place of entertainment. **11.** The audience in such a place of entertainment. **12.** *Govt.* **a** A legislative or deliberative body: *House* of Representatives. **b** A quorum of such a body. **c** The chamber or building such a body occupies. **13.** *Often cap.* A line of ancestors and descendants regarded as forming a single family: the *House* of Stuart. **14.** A business firm or establishment: a publishing *house.* **15.** In astrology: **a** One of the twelve divisions of the heavens. **b** A sign of the zodiac considered as the seat of greatest influence of a particular planet. — **like a house on fire** Very quickly and vigorously. — **on the house** At the expense of the proprietor. — **to bring down the house** To receive loud and enthusiastic applause. — **to clean house** *U.S. Slang* To get rid of undesirable conditions or persons, as in an organization. — **to keep house** To manage the affairs or work of a home. — **to put** (or **set**) **one's house in order** To tidy up one's personal or business affairs. — *v.* **housed, hous·ing** *v.t.* **1.** To take or put into a house; lodge. **2.** To store in a house or building. **3.** In carpentry, to fit into a mortise, joint, etc. — *v.i.* **4.** To take shelter or lodgings; dwell. [OE *hūs*] — **house/ful** *n.* — **house/less** *adj.*

house·boat (hous/bōt/) *n.* A barge or flat-bottomed boat fitted out as a dwelling and used in quiet waters.

house·break·ing (hous/brā/king) *n.* The act of breaking into and entering another's home with intent to commit theft or some other felony. — **house/break/er** *n.*

house·bro·ken (hous/brō/kən) *adj.* Trained to urinate and defecate outdoors or in a specific place, as a dog.

house·coat (hous/kōt/) *n.* A woman's garment, usu. long with a loose skirt, for informal wear within the house.

house·dress (hous/dres/) *n.* A dress, usu. of printed cotton fabric, worn esp. during household chores.

house·fly (hous'flī') *n. pl.* **·flies** The common fly, found in nearly all parts of the world.

house·hold (hous'hōld') *n.* **1.** A number of persons dwelling as a unit under one roof; esp., a family living together, including servants, etc. **2.** A home or the various domestic affairs of a home. — *adj.* Of or pertaining to the home.

house·hold·er (hous'hōl'dər) *n.* **1.** One who owns or occupies a house. **2.** The head of a family.

household word A person, product, place, etc., that is known or familiar to many people. Also **household name**.

house·keep·er (hous'kē'pər) *n.* **1.** One who performs the tasks of maintaining a home, as a housewife. **2.** A paid manager of a home. — **house'keep'ing** *n.*

house·maid (hous'mād') *n.* A girl or woman employed to do housework.

housemaid's knee *Pathol.* A chronic inflammation of the bursa in front of the knee, afflicting housemaids, etc.

house·mas·ter (hous'mas'tər, -mäs'-) *n. Chiefly Brit.* A teacher in charge of one of the houses of a boys' school.

house·moth·er (hous'muth'ər) *n.* A woman acting as a supervisor for a group of people living together.

House of Commons 1. The lower house of the British Parliament, the members of which are elected. **2.** The lower house of the Canadian Parliament.

house of correction An institution confining those given short-term sentences for minor offenses and considered to be capable of rehabilitation.

House of Lords The upper and nonelective house of the British Parliament, made up of the peerage and the highest ranking clergy.

House of Representatives 1. The lower, larger branch of the United States Congress, and of many State legislatures, composed of members elected on the basis of population. **2.** A similar legislative body, as in Australia, Mexico, etc.

house organ A publication regularly issued by a business organization for its employees and customers.

house party An entertainment of a group of guests for several days, usu. in a house or a college fraternity.

house physician A physician resident by appointment in a hospital, hotel, or other institution.

house·top (hous'top') *n.* The roof of a house. — **to shout** (or **cry**) **from the housetops** To give wide publicity to.

house·wares (hous'wârz') *n.* Kitchen utensils, dishes, glassware, and other wares used in the home.

house·warm·ing (hous'wôr'ming) *n.* A party held by or for those who have just moved into new living quarters.

house·wife (hous'wīf' *for def. 1*, huz'if *for def. 2*) *n. pl.* **house·wives** (hous'wīvz') *for def. 1*; **house·wifes** (huz'ifs) or **house·wives** (huz'ivz) *for def. 2* **1.** A married woman who manages her own household and does not work for a living. **2.** *Chiefly Brit.* A kit holding sewing articles. — **house'·wife'ly** *adj. & adv.*

house·wife·ry (hous'wī'fər·ē, -wīf'rē) *n.* The duties of a housewife; housekeeping.

house·work (hous'wûrk') *n.* The chores involved in keeping house, washing, cooking, etc.

hous·ing¹ (hou'zing) *n.* **1.** The act of providing shelter or lodging; also, the shelter or lodging so provided. **2.** The providing of houses on a large scale. **3.** Houses or dwellings collectively. **4.** That which serves as a shelter, cover, etc.: a bamboo *housing* for plants. **5.** *Mech.* **a** Something that holds part of a machine in place, as a frame or set of brackets. **b** A casing or cover for a machine or part of a machine.

hous·ing² (hou'zing) *n.* **1.** An ornamental cover for a horse. **2.** *Usu. pl.* Trappings. [< OF *houce*, prob. < Gmc.]

hove (hōv) Past tense of HEAVE.

hov·el (huv'əl, hov'-) *n.* **1.** A small, wretched dwelling. **2.** A low, open shed for sheltering cattle, tools, etc. — *v.t.* **hov·eled** or **·elled, hov·el·ing** or **·el·ling** To shelter or lodge in a hovel. [? Dim. of OE *hof* building]

hov·er (huv'ər, hov'-) *v.i.* **1.** To remain suspended in or near one place in the air. **2.** To linger or remain nearby, as if watching: with *around, near*, etc. **3.** To remain in an uncertain or irresolute state: with *between*. — *n.* The act or state of hovering. [< obs. *hove* to float] — **hov'er·er** *n.*

Hov·er·craft (huv'ər·kraft', hov'-, -kräft') *n.* A vehicle designed to travel just above the surface of land or water on a cushion of air generated by powerful fans: a trade name. Also **hov'er·craft.**

how (hou) *adv.* **1.** In what way or manner. **2.** To what degree, extent, or amount. **3.** In what state, or condition. **4.** For what reason or purpose. **5.** At what price: *How* is the stock selling today? **6.** With what meaning: *How* is that remark to be taken? **7.** By what name or designation. **8.** *Informal* What: *How* about having lunch? — *n.* A manner or means of doing. [OE *hū*]

how·be·it (hou·bē'it) *adv. Archaic* Be that as it may.

how·dah (hou'də) *n.* A seat for riders on an elephant or camel, often fitted with a canopy. [< Hind. *haudah*]

how-do-you-do (hou'də·yə·dōō') *n. Informal* An embarrassing or difficult situation: usu. preceded by *fine, pretty*, etc.

How do you do? What is the state of your health?: used as a formal greeting when being introduced to a person.

how·dy (hou'dē) *interj. Informal* An expression of greeting.

how·ev·er (hou·ev'ər) *adv.* **1.** In whatever manner; by whatever means. **2.** To whatever degree or extent: Spend *however* much it costs. — *conj.* Nevertheless; in spite of; still; yet. — **Syn.** See BUT¹. Also **how·e'er'** (-âr').

how·it·zer (hou'it·sər) *n.* A cannon with a barrel of medium length and operating at a relatively high angle of fire. [< Du., ult. < Czechoslovakian *houfnice* catapult]

howl (houl) *v.i.* **1.** To utter the loud, mournful wail of a dog, wolf, or other animal. **2.** To utter such a cry in pain, grief, or rage. **3.** To make a sound similar to this. **4.** To laugh loudly. — *v.t.* **5.** To utter or express with howling. **6.** To condemn, suppress, or drive away by howling: often with *down*. — *n.* **1.** The wailing cry of a wolf, dog, or other animal. **2.** Any howling sound. [ME *houlen*]

howl·er (hou'lər) *n.* **1.** One who or that which howls. **2.** A monkey of Central and South America, having a long, grasping tail and making loud howling sounds. **3.** *Informal* An absurd blunder in speaking or writing.

howl·ing (hou'ling) *adj.* **1.** Producing or uttering howls. **2.** Characterized by or filled with howls: the *howling* wilderness. **3.** *Slang* Very great; tremendous: a *howling* success.

how·so·ev·er (hou'sō·ev'ər) *adv.* **1.** In whatever manner. **2.** To whatever degree or extent.

hoy·den (hoid'n) *n.* A boisterous or ill-mannered girl. — *adj.* Boisterous. — *v.i.* To act like a hoyden. [Origin uncertain] — **hoy'den·ish** *adj.* — **hoy'den·ish·ness** *n.*

Hoyle (hoil) *n.* A book of rules and instructions for indoor games, esp. card games. [after Sir Edmund *Hoyle*, 1672–1769, English writer on card games]

hub (hub) *n.* **1.** The center part of a wheel into which the axle is inserted. **2.** Any center of great activity or interest.

hub·bub (hub'ub) *n.* **1.** A loud, confused noise, as of many voices shouting or talking. **2.** Uproar. [Origin unknown]

huck·le·ber·ry (huk'əl·ber'ē) *n. pl.* **·ries 1.** The edible black or dark blue berry of any of various North American shrubs. **2.** A shrub yielding this berry.

huck·ster (huk'stər) *n.* **1.** A peddler of wares, esp. fruits and vegetables. **2.** A petty, greedy tradesman. **3.** *U.S. Slang* One engaged in the advertising business. — *v.t.* **1.** To sell; peddle. **2.** To haggle. [< MDu. *heuken* to retail]

hud·dle (hud'l) *v.* **·dled, ·dling** *v.i.* **1.** To crowd or nestle together closely, as from fear or cold. **2.** To draw or hunch oneself together. **3.** In football, to gather in a huddle. — *v.t.* **4.** To bring or crowd together closely. **5.** To draw (oneself) together: often with *up*. **6.** To make or do hurriedly or confusedly, as dressing. — *n.* **1.** A number of persons or things crowded together. **2.** A state of confusion or disorder. **3.** In football, the grouping of a team before play. **4.** *U.S. Informal* Any small conference. [Origin uncertain]

hue¹ (hyōō) *n.* **1.** The attribute of a color that determines its position in the spectrum and differentiates it from an achromatic color of the same brightness. **2.** Color: the autumnal *hues*. **3.** A particular tint or shade of color. [OE *hīw* appearance] — **hued** *adj.*

hue² (hyōō) *n.* A loud clamor; shouting. — **hue and cry** Any great public stir. [< OF *huer* to shout after]

huff (huf) *n.* A fit of sudden anger or irritation. — *v.t.* **1.** To offend; make angry. — *v.i.* **2.** To take offense. **3.** To puff; blow. — **huf'fish** *adj.*

huf·fy (huf'ē) *adj.* **huff·i·er, huff·i·est 1.** Touchy. **2.** Petulant; sulky. — **huff'i·ly** *adv.* — **huff'i·ness** *n.*

hug (hug) *v.* **hugged, hug·ging** *v.t.* **1.** To take and clasp affectionately within the arms; press in close embrace. **2.** To squeeze between the forepaws, as a bear. **3.** To cherish or cling to, as a belief. **4.** To keep close to. — *v.i.* **5.** To crowd closely together; snuggle. — *n.* **1.** A close, affectionate embrace. **2.** A tight clasp with the arms, as in wrestling. **3.** A bear's grip. [Prob. < ON *hugga* to console]

huge (hyōōj) *adj.* Very great in size, quantity, extent, etc. [< OF *ahuge* high] — **huge'ly** *adv.* — **huge'ness** *n.*

hug·ger·mug·ger (hug'ər·mug'ər) *n.* Disorder; confusion. — *adj.* **1.** Secret; sly. **2.** Disorderly; slovenly.

Hu·gue·not (hyōō'gə·not) *n.* Any French Protestant of the 16th and 17th centuries. [< F < G *eidgenoss* confederate]

huh (hu) *interj.* An exclamation of inquiry, surprise, etc.

hu·la (hōō'lə) *n.* A Hawaiian dance characterized by sinuous arm movements that tell a story in pantomime. Also **hu·la-hu·la.** [< Hawaiian]

hulk (hulk) *n.* **1.** The body of an old, wrecked, or dismantled ship. **2.** *Often pl.* An old ship used for a prison, etc. **3.** Any bulky, unwieldy object or person. — *v.i.* **1.** To rise or loom bulkily: usu. with *up*. **2.** *Dial.* To lounge or slouch about. [OE, prob. < Med.L < Gk. *helkein* to drag]

hulk·ing (hul'king) *adj.* Big and unwieldy, bulky, or clumsy: a great *hulking* fellow. Also **hulk'y.**

hull (hul) *n.* **1.** The outer covering of certain fruits or seeds. **2.** The calyx of some fruits, as the strawberry. **3.** Any outer covering. **4.** *Naut.* The body of a ship, exclusive of the masts, etc. — *v.t.* **1.** To remove the hull of. **2.** To strike or pierce the hull of (a ship). [OE *hulu*]

hul·la·ba·loo (hul′ə·bə·lōō′) *n.* A loud, confused noise; uproar. Also **hul′la·bal·loo′.** [Imit. reduplication of HULLO]

hum¹ (hum) *v.* **hummed, hum·ming** *v.i.* **1.** To make a low, murmuring or droning sound. **2.** To sing with the lips closed. **3.** To give forth an indistinct sound: The streets *hummed* with traffic. **4.** To mumble indistinctly, as from confusion; hem. **5.** *Informal* To be very busy or active: The office *hummed.* — *v.t.* **6.** To sing with closed lips without words. **7.** To put into a state by humming: to *hum* a child to sleep. — *n.* The act or sound of humming. [ME *hummer*] — **hum′mer** *n.*

hum² *interj.* A nasal, murmuring sound made to express mental concentration, deliberation, hesitation, etc.

hu·man (hyōō′mən) *adj.* **1.** Of or characteristic of man. **2.** Having the nature or attributes of a man. **3.** Consisting of a man or men: *human* race. — *n.* A human being. [< OF < L *humanus*] — **hu′man·ness** *n.*

human being A man, woman, or child; a person.

hu·mane (hyōō·mān′) *adj.* **1.** Having kindness, sympathy, etc.; benevolent. **2.** Tending to refine or civilize: *humane* learning. — **hu·mane′ly** *adv.* — **hu·mane′ness** *n.*

hu·man·ism (hyōō′mən·iz′əm) *n.* **1.** The character or quality of being human. **2.** A system or attitude in thought, religion, etc., in which human ideals and the perfection of personality are made central. **3.** The study of the humanities.

Hu·man·ism (hyōō′mən·iz′əm) *n.* The intellectual and literary movement of the Renaissance, characterized by the study of Greek and Roman classics and by an emphasis on human interests rather than on religion.

hu·man·ist (hyōō′mən·ist) *n.* **1.** One learned in or devoted to the study of the humanities; esp., a classical scholar. **2.** One who subscribes to humanism (def. 2). — **hu′man·is′tic** *adj.* — **hu′man·is′ti·cal·ly** *adv.*

hu·man·i·tar·i·an (hyōō·man′ə·târ′ē·ən) *n.* One who seeks to promote the welfare of mankind; philanthropist. — *adj.* Pertaining to humanitarians. — **hu·man′i·tar′i·an·ism** *n.*

hu·man·i·ty (hyōō·man′ə·tē) *n.* *pl.* **·ties 1.** The human race; mankind. **2.** The state of being human; human nature. **3.** The state of being humane; benevolence. — **the humanities 1.** The study of classical Greek and Latin literature. **2.** Literature, philosophy, the fine arts, etc., as distinguished from the sciences. [< OF < L *humanus* human]

hu·man·ize (hyōō′mən·īz) *v.* **·ized, ·iz·ing** *v.t.* **1.** To make human; give human characteristics to. **2.** To make gentle, kindly, etc. — *v.i.* **3.** To become human or humane. — **hu′man·i·za′tion** (-ə·zā′shən, -ī·zā′-) *n.* — **hu′man·iz′er** *n.*

hu·man·kind (hyōō′mən·kīnd′) *n.* The human race; people.

hu·man·ly (hyōō′mən·lē) *adv.* **1.** In a human manner. **2.** Within human power or ability: Is this *humanly* possible? **3.** In accordance with man's experience or knowledge.

hum·ble (hum′bəl) *adj.* **·bler, ·blest 1.** Free from pride or vanity; modest. **2.** Lowly in station, condition, etc.; unpretentious. **3.** Servile; fawning. **4.** Respectful. — *v.t.* **·bled, ·bling 1.** To reduce the pride of. **2.** To lower in rank or dignity. [< F < L *humus* ground] — **hum′ble·ness** *n.* — **hum′bler** *n.* — **hum′bly** *adv.*

humble pie Formerly, a pie containing the inner and less choice parts (**humbles**) of a deer and given to the servants at hunting feasts: also spelled *umble pie.* — **to eat humble pie** To be forced to apologize. [< OF < LL *lumbus* loin]

hum·bug (hum′bug) *n.* **1.** Anything intended or used to delude; fraud. **2.** One who seeks to deceive others. **3.** The quality or practice of deceiving. — *v.* **·bugged, ·bug·ging** *v.t.* **1.** To delude; trick. — *v.i.* **2.** To practice deception. [Origin unknown] — **hum′bug·ger** *n.* — **hum′bug·ger·y** *n.*

hum·ding·er (hum·ding′ər) *n. Slang* One who or that which is remarkable or out of the ordinary.

hum·drum (hum′drum′) *adj.* Lacking interest, variety, or excitement; dull. — *n.* **1.** That which is tedious or dull. **2.** A tiresome person; bore. [Reduplication of HUM]

hu·mer·us (hyōō′mər·əs) *n.* *pl.* **·mer·i** (-mər·ī) *Anat.* The bone of the upper part of the arm, from shoulder to elbow. For illus. see SKELETON. [< L, shoulder] — **hu′mer·al** *adj.*

hu·mid (hyōō′mid) *adj.* Containing vapor or water; moist; damp. [< L *humere* to be moist] — **hu′mid·ly** *adv.*

hu·mid·i·fy (hyōō·mid′ə·fī) *v.t.* **·fied, ·fy·ing** To make moist or humid. — **hu·mid′i·fi·ca′tion** *n.* — **hu·mid′i·fi′er** *n.*

hu·mid·i·ty (hyōō·mid′ə·tē) *n.* Moisture; dampness, esp. of the atmosphere. — **relative humidity** The ratio of the amount of water vapor actually in the air to the total amount it could hold at the same temperature.

hu·mi·dor (hyōō′mə·dôr) *n.* A container in which moisture is retained, used for cigars, etc.

hu·mil·i·ate (hyōō·mil′ē·āt) *v.t.* **·at·ed, ·at·ing** To lower the pride or self-esteem of; mortify. [< L *humilis* lowly] — **hu·mil′i·a·to′ry** (-ə·tôr′ē, -ə·tō′rē) *adj.* — **hu·mil′i·a′tion** *n.*

hu·mil·i·ty (hyōō·mil′ə·tē) *n.* *pl.* **·ties** The state or quality of being humble. [< L *humilitas* lowness]

hum·ming·bird (hum′ing·bûrd′) *n.* Any of a family of very small birds of the New World, having a long, slender bill for sipping nectar from flowers, and rapidly vibrating wings that produce a humming sound during flight.

hum·mock (hum′ək) *n.* **1.** A low mound of earth or rock; hillock. **2.** Wooded land above a marsh. **3.** A ridge or pile in an ice field. [Origin unknown] — **hum′mock·y** *adj.*

hu·mor (hyōō′mər, yōō′-) *n.* **1.** The quality of anything that is funny or appeals to the comic sense. **2.** The ability to appreciate or express what is amusing, comic, etc. **3.** Speech, writing, or actions that are amusing or comic. **4.** A temporary mood: to be in a good *humor.* **5.** Temperament; disposition. **6.** A sudden liking, etc.; whim; caprice. **7.** *Physiol.* **a** A liquid or semiliquid substance of the body, as blood, bile, lymph, etc. **b** The aqueous humor of the eye. **8.** In ancient physiology, one of the four principal bodily fluids (**cardinal humors**), blood, phlegm, choler (yellow bile), and melancholy (black bile), which, according to their proportions in the body, were believed to influence health and temperament. — *v.t.* **1.** To comply with the moods of; indulge. **2.** To adapt oneself to the nature of (something). Also *Brit.* **hu′mour.** [< OF < L *umere* to be moist]

hu·mor·esque (hyōō′mə·resk′, yōō′-) *n.* A playful, lively musical composition; caprice. [< G *humoreske*]

hu·mor·ist (hyōō′mər·ist, yōō′-) *n.* **1.** One who exercises a sense of humor; joker; wag. **2.** A professional writer, entertainer, etc., in humor or jokes. — **hu′mor·is′tic** *adj.*

hu·mor·ous (hyōō′mər·əs, yōō′-) *adj.* **1.** Full of or characterized by humor; laughable; funny. **2.** Displaying or using humor. — **hu′mor·ous·ly** *adv.* — **hu′mor·ous·ness** *n.* — **Syn.** Comical, droll, witty.

hump (hump) *n.* **1.** A rounded protuberance, esp. on the back, as in the camel, bison, etc., or the deformity produced in man by a curvature of the spine. **2.** A low mound; hummock. — **over the hump** Beyond the most critical point. — *v.t.* To round into a hump; hunch. [Akin to LG *hump*]

hump·back (hump′bak′) *n.* **1.** A back with a hump. **2.** A person having a back with a hump; hunchback. **3.** A large whale. — **hump′backed′** *adj.*

humph (humf) *interj.* An exclamation of dissatisfaction.

Hump·ty Dump·ty (hump′tē dump′tē) A character in a nursery rhyme and riddle personifying an egg that fell from a wall and could not be pieced together again.

hump·y (hum′pē) *adj.* **hump·i·er, hump·i·est 1.** Covered with or full of humps. **2.** Like a hump.

hu·mus (hyōō′məs) *n.* The black or brown substance of the soil, formed by the decay of animal and vegetable matter, and providing nutrition for plant life. [< L, ground]

Hun (hun) *n.* **1.** One of a barbarous Asian people who invaded Europe in the fourth and fifth centuries, led by Attila. **2.** Any barbarous or destructive person. [OE < LL *Hunnus*] — **Hun′nish** *adj.* — **Hun′nish·ness** *n.*

hunch (hunch) *n.* **1.** *U.S. Informal* A premonition of some coming event. **2.** A hump. **3.** A lump or hunk. — *v.t.* **1.** To bend or draw up so as to form a hump. — *v.i.* **2.** To move or thrust forward jerkily. [Origin unknown]

hunch·back (hunch′bak′) *n.* **1.** A deformed back with a hump. **2.** A person so deformed. — **hunch′backed′** *adj.*

hun·dred (hun′drid) *n.* **1.** The sum of ninety and ten, written as 100, c, or C: a cardinal number. **2.** Anything consisting of a hundred units. — *adj.* Being ten more than ninety. [OE] — **hun·dredth** (hun′dridth) *adj.* & *n.*

hun·dred·fold (hun′drid·fōld′) *n.* An amount or number a hundred times as great as a given unit. — *adv.* So as to be a hundred times as many or as great. — *adj.* **1.** Consisting of one hundred parts. **2.** One hundred times as great.

hun·dred·weight (hun′drid·wāt′) *n.* A unit of weight commonly reckoned in the United States at 100 pounds avoirdupois, in England at 112 pounds.

Hundred Years' War See table for WAR.

hung (hung) Past tense and past participle of HANG.

Hun·gar·i·an (hung·gâr′ē·ən) *adj.* Of Hungary, its people, or their language. — *n.* **1.** A native or citizen of Hungary; esp., a Magyar. **2.** The Finno-Ugric language of the Hungarians: also called *Magyar.* [< Med.L *Hungarus*]

hun·ger (hung′gər) *n.* **1.** The state of discomfort or weakness caused by lack of food. **2.** A desire or need for food. **3.** Any strong desire or craving. — *v.i.* **1.** To be hungry. **2.** To have a desire or craving: with *for* or *after.* — *v.t.* **3.** To cause to undergo hunger; starve. [OE *hungor*]

hunger strike A self-imposed fast, as by a prisoner, political or religious leader, etc., as a means of protest.

hun·gry (hung′grē) *adj.* **·gri·er, ·gri·est 1.** Desiring or in need of food. **2.** Eagerly craving: *hungry* for applause. **3.** Indicating hunger: a *hungry* look. **4.** Not fertile. [OE *hungor*] — **hun′gri·ly** *adv.* — **hun′gri·ness** *n.*

---

hunk (hungk) *n. Informal* A large piece or lump; chunk: a *hunk* of meat. [Prob. < Flemish *hunke*]

hun·ky-do·ry (hung′kē-dôr′ē, -dō′rē) *adj. U.S. Slang* Fully satisfactory; all right. Also **hunk′y.**

hunt (hunt) *v.t.* **1.** To pursue (game) for the purpose of killing or catching. **2.** To range over (an area) in search of game. **3.** To use in the chase, as hounds. **4.** To chase, drive away, or pursue with hostility, violence, etc. **5.** To search for eagerly; seek: to *hunt* the truth. **6.** To search (a place) thoroughly. — *v.i.* **7.** To seek or pursue game. **8.** To search or seek: often with *for* or *after*. — **to hunt down 1.** To pursue until caught or killed. **2.** To search for until found. — *n.* **1.** The act of hunting game; chase. **2.** A group of huntsmen. **3.** A search; pursuit. **4.** An area used for hunting. [OE *huntian*]

hunt·er (hun′tər) *n.* **1.** One who hunts. **2.** An animal used in hunting, as a dog or horse.

hunt·ing (hun′ting) *n.* The act of one who or that which hunts. — *adj.* Of or used for hunting.

hunt·ress (hun′tris) *n.* A woman who hunts.

hunts·man (hunts′mən) *n. pl.* **·men** (-mən) **1.** One who hunts game; hunter. **2.** One who directs a hunt, hounds, etc.

Hu·pa (hōō′pə) *n.* **1.** One of a tribe of North American Indians in NW California. **2.** The language of this tribe.

hur·dle (hûr′dəl) *n.* **1.** A light, portable barrier for horses or runners to leap over in races. **2.** *pl.* A race in which such barriers are used: often with *the.* **3.** An obstacle or difficulty to be surmounted. — *v.* **·dled, ·dling** *v.t.* **1.** To leap over (a barrier) in a race. **2.** To make, cover, or enclose with hurdles. **3.** To surmount or overcome (a difficulty, etc.). — *v.i.* **4.** To leap over hurdles, etc. [OE *hyrdel*] — **hur′dler** *n.*

hur·dy-gur·dy (hûr′dē-gûr′dē) *n. pl.* **·dies** Musical instruments played by turning a crank, as the barrel organ.

hurl (hûrl) *v.t.* **1.** To throw, fling, or send with force. **2.** To throw down; overthrow. **3.** To utter with vehemence. — *v.i.* **4.** To throw something. — *n.* The act of hurling; also, a forceful throw. [ME *hurlen*] — **hurl′er** *n.*

hurl·ing (hûr′ling) *n.* An Irish game resembling field hockey. Also **hur′ley.** [< HURL]

hur·ly-bur·ly (hûr′lē-bûr′lē) *n. pl.* **·lies** Tumult; confusion; turmoil. — *adj.* Full of turmoil and confusion; tumultuous. [< earlier *hurling and burling*]

Hu·ron (hyŏŏr′ən, -on) *n.* A member of any of four tribes of North American Indians of Iroquoian stock, formerly between Lakes Huron and Ontario. [< F, ruffian]

hur·rah (hŏŏ·rô′, hə·rä′) *n. & interj.* An exclamation expressing triumph, joy, encouragement, etc. — *v.i.* **1.** To shout a hurrah or hurrahs. — *v.t.* **2.** To cheer with hurrahs. Also spelled *hooray.* Also **hur·ray′** (-rā′). [? < G *hurra*]

hur·ri·cane (hûr′ə·kān) *n.* **1.** *Meteorol.* A tropical cyclone, esp. one originating in the West Indies and often covering a wide area, having a wind velocity exceeding 75 miles per hour. **2.** Anything suggesting a hurricane in violence or speed. [< Sp. *huracán* < Carib.]

hurricane deck A light, upper deck on a passenger vessel.

hur·ried (hûr′ēd) *adj.* **1.** Urged or forced to move, act, etc., in haste. **2.** Done or carried on in great or too great haste; a *hurried* decision. — **hur′ried·ly** *adv.* — **hur′ried·ness** *n.*

hur·ry (hûr′ē) *v.* **·ried, ·ry·ing** *v.i.* **1.** To act or move rapidly or in haste; hasten. — *v.t.* **2.** To cause or urge to act or move more rapidly. **3.** To hasten the progress, etc., of, often unduly. — *n. pl.* **·ries 1.** The act of hurrying; haste. **2.** Eagerness to move, act, etc. [ME *horyen*]

hur·ry-scur·ry (hûr′ē·skûr′ē) *n. pl.* **·ries** A hasty, confused bustling about. — *v.i.* **·ried, ·ry·ing** To rush pell-mell. — *adv.* In disorderly haste. — *adj.* Hurried; confused. Also **hur′ry-skur′ry.**

hurt (hûrt) *v.* **hurt, hurt·ing** *v.t.* **1.** To cause physical harm or pain to; injure. **2.** To impair in some way: to *hurt* one's reputation. **3.** To grieve or distress; cause mental suffering to. — *v.i.* **4.** To cause discomfort, suffering, or damage. **5.** To give out a feeling of pain. — *n.* **1.** Any injury, wound, etc. **2.** Damage; impairment. **3.** An injury to the feelings; affront. [< OF *hurter* to hit] — **hurt′er** *n.*

hurt·ful (hûrt′fəl) *adj.* Causing hurt; injurious. — **hurt′ful·ly** *adv.* — **hurt′ful·ness** *n.*

hur·tle (hûr′təl) *v.* **·tled, ·tling** *v.i.* **1.** To collide or strike violently; clash. **2.** To rush headlong or impetuously. **3.** To make a rushing or crashing sound. — *v.t.* **4.** To hurl, throw, or drive violently. [Freq. of ME *hurten* to hit, hurt]

hus·band (huz′bənd) *n.* A man joined to a woman in lawful wedlock. — *v.t.* To use or spend wisely; conserve: to *husband* one's forces. [OE *hūs* house + *bonda* freeholder]

hus·band·ry (huz′bən·drē) *n.* **1.** The occupation or business of farming. **2.** Careful management; economy; thrift. **3.** Management of household affairs, expenditures, etc.

hush (hush) *v.t.* **1.** To make silent; cause to be quiet. **2.** To keep hidden or secret: usu. with *up*. **3.** To soothe or allay, as fears. — *v.i.* **4.** To be or become quiet or still. — *n.* Deep silence; quiet. — *interj.* Be quiet! [Back formation < ME *husht* quiet]

hush·a·by (hush′ə·bī′) *interj.* Go to sleep.

hush-hush (hush′hush′) *adj. Informal* Done in secrecy.

hush money A bribe to secure silence or secrecy.

hush-pup·py (hush′pup′ē) *n. pl.* **·pies** *Southern U.S.* A small fried ball of cornmeal dough.

husk (husk) *n.* **1.** The outer coating of certain fruits or seeds, esp. of an ear of corn. **2.** Any outer covering, esp. when comparatively worthless. — *v.t.* To remove the husk or outer covering of. [ME, prob. < Du. *huus* house]

husk·ing bee (hus′king) *U.S.* A cornhusking.

husk·y¹ (hus′kē) *adj.* **husk·i·er, husk·i·est 1.** Rough, or coarse in vocal quality. **2.** Full of or made of husks. **3.** Like a husk. [< HUSK] — **husk′i·ly** *adv.* — **husk′i·ness** *n.*

husk·y² (hus′kē) *U.S. Informal adj.* **husk·i·er, husk·i·est** Physically strong; burly. — *n. pl.* **husk·ies** A strong or powerful person. [HUSKY¹, with ref. to toughness of husks]

Hus·ky (hus′kē) *n. pl.* **Husk·ies** *U.S. & Canadian* **1.** A heavily furred Eskimo dog. Also **husk′y. 2.** An Eskimo. **3.** The Eskimo language. [? Alter. of ESKIMO]

hus·sar (hŏŏ·zär′) *n.* A member of a cavalry regiment found in some European armies and usu. distinguished by brilliant dress uniforms. [< Hungarian < Serbian < Ital. < Med.L *corsarius*]

hus·sy (huz′ē, hus′ē) *n. pl.* **·sies 1.** A woman of questionable behavior or reputation. **2.** A pert or forward girl; minx. [Alter. of HOUSEWIFE]

hust·ings (hus′tingz) *n.pl.* (*usu. construed as sing.*) **1.** The proceedings at an election. **2.** Any place where political speeches are made. [OE < ON *hūs* house + *thing* assembly]

hus·tle (hus′əl) *v.* **·tled, ·tling** *v.t.* **1.** To push about or crowd roughly; jostle. **2.** To force, push, or thrust hurriedly. **3.** *U.S. Informal* To cause to proceed rapidly or too rapidly; hurry. **4.** *U.S. Slang* To sell or solicit (something) in an aggressive or unethical manner. — *v.i.* **5.** To push or shove; elbow. **6.** *U.S. Informal* To move or work with great energy. **7.** *U.S. Slang* To make money by clever or unscrupulous means. — *n.* **1.** The act of hustling. **2.** *U.S. Informal* Energetic activity; drive; push. [< Du. *hutselen* to shake, toss] — **hus′tler** *n.*

hut (hut) *n.* A small, rude house or cabin; hovel. — *v.t. & v.i.* **hut·ted, hut·ting** To shelter or live in a hut. [< OF OHG *hutta*]

hutch (huch) *n.* **1.** A coop or pen for small animals: rabbit *hutch.* **2.** A chest, locker, or bin in which to store things; also, a cupboard for dishes. **3.** A small hut or cabin. **4.** A trough, as used by bakers for kneading dough. — *v.t.* To store up or hoard, as in a chest. [< F < LL *hutica*]

hutz·pah (hŏŏts′pə, kḥŏŏts′-) See CHUTZPAH.

huz·za (hə·zä′) *Archaic n. & interj.* An exclamation of joy, triumph, etc. — *v.* **·zaed, za·ing** *v.i.* **1.** To shout huzzas. — *v.t.* **2.** To cheer with huzzas. [Origin uncertain]

hwan (hwän) *n. pl.* **hwan** The monetary unit of South Korea: in 1960 worth about ⁹⁄₁₀ of a U.S. cent.

hy·a·cinth (hī′ə·sinth) *n.* **1.** A plant of the lily family, having clusters of fragrant, bell-shaped flowers. **2.** The bulb or flower of this plant. **3.** A brownish, reddish, or orange zircon: also called *jacinth.* **4.** In ancient times, a bluish or purplish gem, probably the sapphire or amethyst. **5.** A blue or purplish blue color. [< OF < L < Gk. *hyakinthos*.] — **hy·a·cin′thine** (-thin, -thīn) *adj.*

hy·ae·na (hī·ē′nə) See HYENA.

hy·a·line (hī′ə·lin, -līn) *adj.* Resembling glass; transparent. — *n.* Something transparent, like glass. [< L < Gk. *hyalos* glass]

hy·brid (hī′brid) *n.* **1.** An animal or plant produced by a male and female of different species, varieties, or breeds. **2.** Anything of mixed origin. **3.** *Ling.* A word composed of elements from more than one language. — *adj.* Of, pertaining to, or like a hybrid. [< L *hybrida* offspring of tame sow and wild boar] — **hy′brid·ism, hy·brid·i·ty** (hī·brid′ə·tē).

hy·brid·ize (hī′brid·īz) *v.t. & v.i.* **·ized, ·iz·ing** To produce or cause to produce hybrids. Also *Brit.* **hy′brid·ise.** — **hy·brid·i·za·tion** (hī′brid·ə·zā′shən, -ī·zā′-) *n.* — **hy′brid·iz′er** *n.*

hydr- Var. of HYDRO-.

hy·dra (hī′drə) *n. pl.* **·dras** or **·drae** (-drē) **1.** Any of various small, fresh-water polyps characterized by a long, slender body and tentacles. **2.** An evil that persists or reappears.

Hy·dra (hī′drə) *n.* **1.** In Greek mythology, a nine-headed serpent that grew two heads for each cut off. **2.** A constellation, the Hydra. [< Gk. *hydra* water serpent]

hy·dran·ge·a (hī·drān′jē·ə, -jə) *n.* A tree or shrub, having large clusters of white, blue, or pink flowers. [< NL < Gk. *hydōr* water + *angeion* vessel]

hy·drant (hī′drənt) *n.* A large, upright pipe connected to a water main, used for firefighting; fireplug. [< Gk. *hydōr* water + -ANT]

hy·drar·gy·rum (hī·drär′jə·rəm) *n. Chem.* Mercury. [< NL < L < Gk. *hydōr* water + *argyros* silver] — **hy′drar·gy′ric** (-jir′ik) *adj.*

hy·drate (hī′drāt) *Chem. n.* Any of a class of compounds associated with water in definite proportions. — *v.t.* **·drat·ed, ·drat·ing** To form a hydrate. — **hy·dra′tion** *n.*

hy·drau·lic (hī-drô′lik) *adj.* **1.** Of or pertaining to hydraulics. **2.** Operated by water or other liquid under pressure. **3.** Hardening under water: *hydraulic* cement. [< L < Gk. *hydōr* water + *aulos* pipe] — **hy·drau′li·cal·ly** *adv.*

hy·drau·lics (hī-drô′liks) *n.pl.* (construed as sing.) The science of the laws governing the motion of water and other liquids and of their practical applications in engineering.

hy·dra·zine (hī′drə-zēn, -zin) *n. Chem.* A colorless fuming liquid, N_2H_4, used esp. as a rocket or jet fuel.

hy·dric (hī′drik) *adj.* Of or containing hydrogen.

hy·dride (hī′drīd, -drid) *n. Chem.* A compound of hydrogen with another element or radical. Also **hy′drid** (-drid).

hy·dro (hī′drō) *Canadian adj.* Hydroelectric.

hydro- *combining form* **1.** Water; of, related to, or resembling water. **2.** *Chem.* Denoting a compound of hydrogen. Also, before vowels, *hydr-*. [< Gk. *hydōr* water]

hy·dro·car·bon (hī′drə-kär′bən) *n. Chem.* One of a large and important group of organic compounds that contain hydrogen and carbon only, as benzene, ethylene, methane, etc.

hy·dro·ceph·a·lus (hī′drə-sef′ə-ləs) *n. Pathol.* A condition characterized by the accumulation of fluid within the brain, causing abnormal enlargement of the head. Also **hy·dro·ceph′a·ly.** [< HYDRO- + Gk. *kephalē* head] — **hy′dro·ceph′a·loid** (-loid), **hy′dro·ceph′a·lous** *adj.*

hy·dro·chlo·ric acid (hī′drə-klôr′ik, -klō′rik) *Chem.* An aqueous solution of hydrogen chloride, widely used in industry, medicine, and the arts: also called *muriatic acid.*

hy·dro·chlo·ride (hī′drə-klôr′īd, -klō′rīd) *n. Chem.* A salt of hydrochloric acid with an organic base.

hy·dro·cy·an·ic acid (hī′drō-sī-an′ik) *Chem.* An aqueous solution of hydrogen cyanide, a colorless, volatile, very poisonous liquid with a bitter odor: also called *prussic acid.*

hy·dro·dy·nam·ic (hī′drō-dī-nam′ik) *adj.* **1.** Of or pertaining to the force or motion of water and other fluids. **2.** Of or pertaining to hydrodynamics. Also **hy′dro·dy·nam′i·cal.**

hy·dro·dy·nam·ics (hī′drō-dī-nam′iks) *n.pl.* (construed as *sing.*) The branch of dynamics that treats of the motions and forces of liquids, especially water.

hy·dro·e·lec·tric (hī′drō-i·lek′trik) *adj.* Of or pertaining to electricity generated by the energy of water. — **hy·dro·e·lec·tric·i·ty** (hī′drō-i·lek′tris′ə-tē, -ē′lek-) *n.*

hy·dro·flu·or·ic acid (hī′drə-floo-ôr′ik, -or′-, -flōōr′ik) *Chem.* An aqueous solution of hydrogen fluoride, used for etching glass, treating metals, etc.

hy·dro·foil (hī′drə-foil) *n.* **1.** A streamlined surface designed to provide support in the water through which it moves, as an attachment to a boat. **2.** A horizontal rudder used in raising or submerging a submarine.

hy·dro·gen (hī′drə-jən) *n.* The lightest of the elements (symbol H), an odorless, colorless, flammable gas, occurring chiefly in combination. See ELEMENT. [< F < Gk. *hydōr* water + -GEN] — **hy·drog·e·nous** (hī-droj′ə-nəs) *adj.*

hy·dro·gen·ate (hī′drə-jə-nāt′, hī-droj′ə-nāt) *v.t.* **·at·ed, ·at·ing** *Chem.* To combine with, treat with, or expose to the chemical action of hydrogen. — **hy′dro·gen·a′tion** *n.*

hydrogen bomb A very destructive thermonuclear bomb having no theoretical limit in size and power, releasing energy by the fusion, under extremely high temperatures, of light elements, as hydrogen isotopes: also called *H-bomb.*

hydrogen chloride *Chem.* A corrosive, pungent, gaseous compound of hydrogen and chlorine, HCl.

hydrogen cyanide *Chem.* An unstable, colorless, intensely poisonous gas, HCN, used chiefly as an extermination agent.

hydrogen ion The positively charged ion (H^+) present in all acid solutions.

hydrogen peroxide *Chem.* An unstable, colorless, syrupy liquid, H_2O_2, used for bleaching, etc.

hydrogen sulfide *Chem.* A colorless, gaseous, poisonous compound, H_2S, having a characteristic odor of rotten eggs.

hy·drog·ra·phy (hī-drog′rə-fē) *n.* The science of surveying, describing, and mapping seas, lakes, rivers, etc. — **hy·drog′·ra·pher** *n.* — **hy′dro·graph′ic** or **·i·cal** *adj.* — **hy′dro·graph′i·cal·ly** *adv.*

hy·droid (hī′droid) *Zool. adj.* **1.** Pertaining or belonging to a group of hydrozoans. **2.** Designating a stage in the development of hydrozoans, characterized by the budding of polyps. — *n.* A hydroid coelenterate, esp. a polyp.

hy·dro·ki·net·ics (hī′drō-ki-net′iks) *n.pl.* (construed as *sing.*) The branch of hydrodynamics dealing with the laws governing fluids in motion. — **hy′dro·ki·net′ic** *adj.*

hy·drol·o·gy (hī-drol′ə-jē) *n.* The branch of physical geography that deals with the waters of the earth, their distribution, characteristics, and effects in relation to human activities. — **hy·dro·log·ic** (hī′drə-loj′ik) or **·i·cal** *adj.* — **hy′dro·log′i·cal·ly** *adv.* — **hy·drol′o·gist** *n.*

hy·drol·y·sis (hī-drol′ə-sis) *n. pl.* **·ses** (-sēz) *Chem.* **1.** Action between the ions of water (H^+ and OH^-) and those of a salt to form an acid and a base. **2.** The decomposition of a compound by water. — **hy·dro·lyt·ic** (hī′drə-lit′ik) *adj.*

hy·dro·lyte (hī′drə-līt) *n.* Any substance affected by hydrolysis.

hy·dro·lyze (hī′drə-līz) *v.t. & v.i.* **·lyzed, ·lyz·ing** To undergo or cause to undergo hydrolysis. — **hy′dro·lyz′a·ble** *adj.* — **hy·dro·ly·za·tion** (hī′drə-lə-zā′shən, -lī-zā′-) *n.*

hy·drom·e·ter (hī-drom′ə-tər) *n.* A sealed tube marked with a graduated scale and weighted at one end, that determines the specific gravity or density of a liquid. — **hy·dro·met·ric** (hī′drə-met′rik) or **·ri·cal** *adj.* — **hy·drom′e·try** *n.*

hy·drop·a·thy (hī-drop′ə-thē) *n.* A treatment that professes to cure diseases by the use of water both internally and externally: also called *water cure.* — **hy·dro·path·ic** (hī′drə-path′ik) or **·i·cal** *adj.* — **hy·drop′a·thist, hy′dro·path** *n.*

hy·dro·pho·bi·a (hī′drə-fō′bē-ə) *n.* **1.** Rabies. **2.** Any morbid fear of water. [< L < Gk., *hydōr* water + *phobos* fear] — **hy′dro·pho′bic** (hī′drə-fō′bik, -fob′ik) *adj.*

hy·dro·phyte (hī′drə-fīt) *n. Bot.* A plant growing in water or in wet ground. — **hy·dro·phyt·ic** (hī′drə-fit′ik) *adj.*

hy·dro·plane (hī′drə-plān′) *n.* **1.** A seaplane. **2.** A type of motor boat designed so that its hull is raised partially out of the water when driven at high speeds. **3.** A hydrofoil (def. 2). — *v.i.* **·planed, ·plan·ing** To move at great speed on the water.

hy·dro·pon·ics (hī′drə-pon′iks) *n.pl.* (construed as *sing.*) The science of growing plants with their roots in nutrient solutions rather than in soil: also called *tank farming.* [< HYDRO- + Gk. *ponos* labor] — **hy′dro·pon′ic** *adj.*

hy·dro·sphere (hī′drə-sfir) *n.* **1.** The total water on the surface of the earth. **2.** The moisture in the earth's atmosphere. — **hy′dro·spher′ic** (-sfir′ik, -sfer′-) *adj.*

hy·dro·stat (hī′drə-stat) *n.* **1.** A device for preventing the explosion of a steam boiler due to lack of water. **2.** An electrical device for detecting the presence of water.

hy·dro·stat·ics (hī′drə-stat′iks) *n.pl.* (construed as *sing.*) The science that deals with the pressure and equilibrium of fluids, especially of liquids. — **hy′dro·stat′ic** or **·i·cal** *adj.* — **hy′dro·stat′i·cal·ly** *adv.*

hy·dro·sul·fide (hī′drə-sul′fīd) *n. Chem.* A compound derived from hydrogen sulfide by replacing one of the hydrogen atoms with a basic radical or a base.

hy·dro·sul·fu·rous acid (hī′drō-sul-fyōōr′əs, hī′drə-sul′fər-əs) Hyposulfurous acid.

hy·dro·ther·a·peu·tics (hī′drō-ther′ə-pyōō′tiks) *n.pl.* (construed as *sing.*) Hydrotherapy. — **hy′dro·ther′a·peu′tic** *adj.*

hy·dro·ther·a·py (hī′drō-ther′ə-pē) *n. Med.* The scientific use of water in the treatment of various diseases.

hy·drot·ro·pism (hī-drot′rə-piz′əm) *n. Biol.* A tropism in response to water. — **hy·dro·trop·ic** (hī′drə-trop′ik) *adj.*

hy·drous (hī′drəs) *adj.* **1.** Watery. **2.** *Chem.* Containing water of crystallization or hydration.

hy·drox·ide (hī-drok′sīd) *n. Chem.* A compound containing the **hydroxyl ion,** which consists of one atom each of oxygen and hydrogen and bears a charge of − 1.

hy·dro·zo·an (hī′drə-zō′ən) *adj. Zool.* Pertaining or belonging to a class of freshwater and marine coelenterates, including the hydra, certain jellyfishes and corals, etc. — *n.* A hydrozoan organism.

hy·e·na (hī-ē′nə) *n.* Any of a group of wolflike, carnivorous mammals of Africa and Asia, feeding chiefly on carrion, with short hind legs, a bristly mane, and strong teeth. Also *hyaena.* [< L < Gk. *hyaina* sow]

Hy·ge·ia (hī-jē′ə) In Greek mythology, the goddess of health. [< Gk. *hygieia* health]

hy·giene (hī′jēn, -ji-ēn) *n.* The science of health. [< F < Gk. *hygieinos* healthful]

hy·gi·en·ic (hī′jē-en′ik, hī-jē′nik, -jen′ik) *adj.* **1.** Of or pertaining to hygiene. **2.** Sanitary. — **hy′gi·en′i·cal·ly** *adv.*

hy·gi·en·ics (hī′jē-en′iks, hī-jē′niks) *n.pl.* (construed as *sing.*) The science of preserving or promoting health; hygiene.

hy·gi·en·ist (hī′jē-ən-ist) *n.* One who studies or is versed in the principles of hygiene. Also **hy′ge·ist** (-jē-ist), **hy′gi·e·ist.**

hygro- *combining form* Wet; moist. Also, before vowels, **hygr-.** [< Gk. *hygros* wet, moist]

hy·grom·e·ter (hī-grom′ə-tər) *n.* An instrument for measuring the humidity or moisture in the atmosphere. — **hy·gro·met·ric** (hī′grə-met′rik) *adj.*

hy·grom·e·try (hī-grom′ə-trē) *n.* The branch of physics that deals with the measurement of moisture in the air.

hy·gro·scope (hī′grə-skōp) *n.* A device for indicating the approximate humidity of the air.

hy·gro·scop·ic (hī′grə-skop′ik) *adj.* **1.** Pertaining to the hygroscope. **2.** Absorbing moisture from the air.

hy·la (hī′lə) *n.* Any of a genus of amphibians, esp. the tree frog. [< NL < Gk. *hylē* wood]

hy·men (hī′mən) *n. Anat.* A thin mucous membrane partially covering the external entrance of the vagina in a virgin. [< Gk. *hymēn* skin, membrane]

Hy·men (hī′mən) In Greek mythology, the god of marriage.

hy·me·ne·al (hī′mə-nē′əl) *adj.* Of or pertaining to marriage or a wedding. — *n.* A wedding song or poem.

hy·men·op·ter·on (hī′mən-op′tər-on) *n. pl.* **·ter·a** (-tər-ə) A hymenopterous insect. Also **hy′men·op′ter.**

hy·men·op·ter·ous (hī′mən-op′tər-əs) *adj. Entomol.* Of or belonging to an order of insects, typically having four wings, including bees, wasps, sawflies, etc. [< NL < Gk. *hymēn* membrane + *pteron* wing] — **hy·men·op·ter·an** (hī′mən-op′tə-rən) *adj. & n.*

hymn (him) *n.* A song of praise, adoration, thanksgiving, etc., esp. one sung at a religious service. — *v.i.* 1. To praise or express with a hymn. — *v.i.* 2. To sing hymns. [< LL < Gk. *hymnos* song, ode] — **hym′nic** (-nik) *adj.*

hym·nal (him′nəl) *n.* A book of hymns. Also *Canadian* **hym′na·ry** (-nə-rē), **hymn′book′** (-bo͝ok′). — *adj.* Of or relating to a hymn or hymns.

hym·nist (him′nist) *n.* A writer of hymns.

hym·nol·o·gy (him-nol′ə-jē) *n.* 1. The study of hymns. 2. The writing of hymns. 3. Hymns collectively. — **hym·no·log·ic** (him′nə-loj′ik) or **·i·cal** *adj.* — **hym·nol′o·gist** *n.*

hy·oid (hī′oid) *n. Anat.* In man, a U-shaped bone at the base of the tongue. Also **hyoid bone.** For illus. see MOUTH. — *adj.* Pertaining to the hyoid bone. [< F *hyoïde*]

hyp·aes·the·si·a (hip′is-thē′zhə, -zhē-ə) See HYPESTHESIA.

hyper- *prefix* 1. Over; above; excessive: *hypercritical.* 2. *Med.* Denoting an abnormal state of excess: *hypertension*: opposed to *hypo-.* 3. *Chem.* Denoting the highest in a series of compounds: now generally replaced by *per-.* [< Gk. *hyper* above]

hy·per·a·cid·i·ty (hī′pər-ə-sid′ə-tē) *n. Med.* An excess of acidity, as of the gastric juice.

hy·per·bar·ism (hī′per′bə-riz′əm) *n. Med.* A disturbed condition caused by atmospheric pressure greater than the pressure within the body: opposed to *hypobarism.* [< HYPER- + Gk. *baros* weight] — **hy′per·bar′ic** adj.

hy·per·bo·la (hī-pûr′bə-lə) *n. Math.* The curve produced by the intersection of a plane with the surface of a cone, the plane intersecting both nappes. [< NL < Gk. *hyperbolē* a throwing beyond, excess]

hy·per·bo·le (hī-pûr′bə-lē) *n.* An exaggeration or overstatement intended to produce an effect without being taken literally, as: *He was centuries old.* [< L < Gk. *hyperbolē* a throwing beyond, excess] — **hy·per′bo·lism** *n.*

hy·per·bol·ic (hī′pər-bol′ik) *adj.* 1. Of, pertaining to, or using hyperbole. 2. *Math.* Of or pertaining to the hyperbola. Also **hy′per·bol′i·cal.** — **hy′per·bol′i·cal·ly** *adv.*

hy·per·bo·lize (hī-pûr′bə-līz) *v.t. & v.i.* **·lized, ·liz·ing** To express in or use hyperbole; exaggerate.

hy·per·bo·re·an (hī′pər-bôr′ē-ən, -bō′rē-) *adj.* Of or pertaining to the far north; frigid; arctic.

Hy·per·bo·re·an (hī′pər-bôr′ē-ən, -bō′rē-) *n.* In Greek mythology, one of the people who lived in the far north in a land of everlasting peace and sunshine. [< L < Gk. *hyper-* beyond + *Boreas* north wind]

hy·per·crit·i·cal (hī′pər-krit′i-kəl) *adj.* Excessively critical or carping; faultfinding. — **hy′per·crit′i·cal·ly** *adv.* — **hy′per·crit′i·cism** (-siz′əm) *n.*

hy·per·gol·ic (hī′pər-gol′ik) *adj. Aerospace* Denoting a type of rocket propellant that ignites spontaneously on contact with an oxidizer. [< HYPER- + G *gola*, a code word used in German rocketry]

Hy·pe·ri·on (hī-pir′ē-on) In Greek mythology: **a** A Titan, the son of Uranus. **b** Helios. **c** In later use, Apollo.

hy·per·me·tro·pi·a (hī′pər-mə-trō′pē-ə) *n. Pathol.* Farsightedness. Also **hy′per·met′ro·py** (-met′rə-pē). [< NL < Gk. *hypermetros* excessive + *ōps* eye] — **hy′per·me·trop′ic** (-mə-trop′ik, -trō′pik) *adj.*

hy·per·on (hī′per-on) *n. Physics* Any of a class of atomic particles having a mass intermediate between that of a neutron and a deuteron.

hy·per·sen·si·tive (hī′pər-sen′sə-tiv) *adj.* 1. Excessively sensitive. 2. Allergic. — **hy′per·sen′si·tive·ness, hy′per·sen′si·tiv′i·ty** (-sen′sə-tiv′ə-tē) *n.*

hy·per·sen·si·tize (hī′pər-sen′sə-tīz) *v.t.* **·tized, ·tiz·ing** *Photog.* To increase the sensitiveness or speed of, as a film.

hy·per·son·ic (hī′pər-son′ik) *adj.* Of, pertaining to, or characterized by supersonic speeds of mach 5 or greater.

hy·per·son·ics (hī′pər-son′iks) *n.pl.* (construed as sing.) The branch of dynamics concerned with the design, performance, etc., of objects moving at hypersonic speeds.

hy·per·ten·sion (hī′pər-ten′shən) *n. Pathol.* High blood pressure. — **hy′per·ten′sive** (-siv) *adj.*

hy·per·thy·roid·ism (hī′pər-thī′roid-iz′əm) *n. Pathol.* 1. Excessive activity of the thyroid gland. 2. Any disorder caused by this. — **hy′per·thy′roid** *adj. & n.*

hy·per·tro·phy (hī-pûr′trə-fē) *n. Pathol.* 1. The excessive development of an organ or part. 2. The enlargement resulting from such a condition. — *v.i. & v.t.* **·phied, ·phy·ing** To grow or cause to grow excessively. — **hy·per·troph·ic** (hī′pər-trof′ik, -trō′fik) or **·i·cal** *adj.*

hyp·es·the·sia (hip′is-thē′zhə, -zhē-ə) *n. Pathol.* Diminished sensitiveness; partial loss of sensation: also spelled *hypaesthesia.* — **hyp′es·the′sic** (-sik) or **·thet′ic** (-thet′ik) *adj.*

hy·pha (hī′fə) *n. pl.* **·phae** (-fē) *Bot.* One of the long, threadlike, branching bodies that constitute the mycelium of a fungus. [< NL < Gk. *hyphē* web] — **hy′phal** *adj.*

hy·phen (hī′fən) *n.* A mark (- or - or ⸗) used to connect the elements of certain compound words or to show division of a word at the end of a line. — *v.t.* To hyphenate. [< LL < Gk. *hyph′* hen under one, together < *hypo-* under + *hen* one]

hy·phen·ate (hī′fən-āt) *v.t.* **·at·ed, ·at·ing** 1. To connect by a hyphen. 2. To write with a hyphen. — **hy′phen·a′tion** *n.*

hypno- *combining form* Sleep; of or related to sleep. Also, before vowels, **hypn-.** [< Gk. *hypnos* sleep]

hyp·noi·dal (hip-noid′l) *adj. Psychiatry* Resembling light hypnosis. Also **hyp·noid′.**

hyp·nol·o·gy (hip-nol′ə-jē) *n.* The science of sleep.

hyp·no·sis (hip-nō′sis) *n. pl.* **·ses** (-sēz) *Psychol.* A trancelike condition that can be artificially induced, characterized by an increased responsiveness to suggestion.

hyp·no·ther·a·py (hip′nō-ther′ə-pē) *n. Med.* The use of hypnotism in treating disease, esp. mental disease.

hyp·not·ic (hip-not′ik) *adj.* 1. Pertaining to hypnosis or hypnotism. 2. Readily hypnotized. 3. Tending to produce sleep. — *n.* 1. A drug or other agent producing sleep. 2. A hypnotized person or one susceptible to hypnosis. [< Gk. *hypnos* sleep] — **hyp·not′i·cal·ly** *adv.*

hyp·no·tism (hip′nə-tiz′əm) *n.* 1. The act or practice of inducing hypnosis. 2. The study of the techniques of hypnosis. 3. Hypnosis. — **hyp′no·tist** *n.*

hyp·no·tize (hip′nə-tīz) *v.t.* **·tized, ·tiz·ing** 1. To produce hypnosis in. 2. To fascinate; charm. Also *Brit.* **hyp′no·tise.** — **hyp′no·tiz′a·ble** *adj.* — **hyp′no·ti·za′tion** (-tə-zā′shən, -tī-zā′-) *n.* — **hyp′no·tiz′er** *n.*

hy·po[1] (hī′pō) *n. Photog.* Sodium thiosulfate (formerly called *sodium hyposulfite*), used as a fixing agent.

hy·po[2] (hī′pō) *n. pl.* **·pos** *Informal* A hypodermic injection.

hy·po[3] (hī′pō) *n. pl.* **·pos** *Slang* A hypochondriac.

hypo- *prefix* 1. Under; beneath. 2. Less than. 3. *Med.* Denoting a lack of or deficiency in: opposed to *hyper-.* 4. *Chem.* Indicating the lowest member in a series of compounds (that is, the lowest degree of oxidation). Also, before vowels, **hyp-.** [< Gk. < *hypo* under]

hy·po·bar·ism (hī′pə-bär′iz-əm) *n. Med.* A condition brought about when the atmospheric pressure is less than that of the gases within the body: opposed to *hyperbarism.* [< HYPO- + Gk. *baros* weight] — **hy′po·bar′ic** *adj.*

hy·po·cen·ter (hī′pə-sen′tər) *n.* Ground zero.

hy·po·chlo·rite (hī′pə-klôr′īt, -klō′rīt) *n. Chem.* A salt of hypochlorous acid.

hy·po·chlo·rous acid (hī′pə-klôr′əs, -klō′rəs) *Chem.* An unstable acid, HClO, used in aqueous solution as an oxidizer and bleach.

hy·po·chon·dri·a (hī′pə-kon′drē-ə, hip′ə-) *n.* A persistent anxiety about one's health, often with imagined symptoms of illness. Also **hy·po·chon·dri·a·sis** (hī′pō-kən-drī′ə-sis). [< L, abdomen (once taken to be the seat of this condition)]

hy·po·chon·dri·ac (hī′pə-kon′drē-ak, hip′ə-) *adj.* 1. Pertaining to or affected with hypochondria. 2. Of, pertaining to, or situated in the hypochondrium. Also **hy·po·chon·dri·a·cal** (hī′pō-kən-drī′ə-kəl). — *n.* A person subject to or affected with hypochondria. — **hy′po·chon·dri′a·cal·ly** *adv.*

hy·po·chon·dri·um (hī′pə-kon′drē-əm, hip′ə-) *n. pl.* **·dri·a** (-drē-ə) *Anat.* The region of the abdomen situated on either side of the body, under the short ribs. [< NL < Gk.]

hy·po·cot·yl (hī′pə-kot′l) *n. Bot.* The part of the axis of a seedling below the seed leaves or cotyledons. — **hy′po·cot′y·lous** *adj.*

hy·poc·ri·sy (hi-pok′rə-sē) *n. pl.* **·sies** The pretense of having feelings or characteristics one does not possess; esp., the deceitful assumption of virtue. [< OF < L < Gk. *hypokrinesthai* to play a part, act]

hyp·o·crite (hip′ə-krit) *n.* One who practices hypocrisy. — **hyp′o·crit′i·cal** *adj.* — **hyp′o·crit′i·cal·ly** *adv.*

hy·po·derm (hī′pə-dûrm) *n. Zool.* The layer that secretes the outer skin of an arthropod: also called *hypodermis.*

hy·po·der·ma (hī′pə-dûr′mə) *n. Bot.* The distinct sheath of tissue beneath the epidermis of stems in plants. [< NL < Gk. *hypo-* under + *derma* skin]

hy·po·der·mic (hī′pə-dûr′mik) *adj.* 1. Of or pertaining to the area under the skin. 2. Injected under the skin. — *n.* A hypodermic injection or syringe.

hypodermic syringe A syringe having a sharp, hollow needle for injection of substances beneath the skin.

hy·po·der·mis (hī′pə-dûr′mis) *n. Zool.* The hypoderm.

hy·po·gas·tric (hī′pə-gas′trik) *adj.* Pertaining to or situated in the hypogastrium.

hy·po·gas·tri·um (hī′pə-gas′trē-əm) *n. pl.* **·tri·a** (-trē-ə)

Anat. The region at the lower part of the abdomen on the middle line. [< NL < Gk. *hypo-* below + *gastēr* belly]

hy·po·sul·fite (hī′pə·sul′fīt) *n. Chem.* **1.** Sodium thiosulfate. **2.** A salt of hyposulfurous acid.

hy·po·sul·fu·rous acid (hī′pō·sul·fyŏor′əs, hī′pə·sul′fər·əs) *Chem.* An unstable acid, $H_2S_2O_4$, of strong reducing and bleaching properties: also called *hydrosulfurous acid.*

hy·pot·e·nuse (hī·pot′ə·nōōs, -nyōōs, hi-) *n. Geom.* The side of a right triangle opposite the right angle. Also **hy·poth′e·nuse** (-poth′-). [< L < Gk. *hypo-* under + *teinein* to stretch]

hy·po·thal·a·mus (hī′pə·thal′ə·məs, hip′ə-) *n. pl.* **·mi** *Anat.* A group of structures forming part of the diencephalon, controlling visceral activities, regulating body temperature and many metabolic processes, and influencing certain emotional states. — **hy·po·tha·lam·ic** (hī′pə·thə·lam′ik) *adj.*

hy·poth·e·cate (hī·poth′ə·kāt, hi-) *v.t.* **·cat·ed, ·cat·ing** *Law* To pledge (personal property) as security for debt without transfer of possession. [< Med.L < LL *hypotheca* pledge] — **hy·poth′e·ca′tion** *n.* — **hy·poth′e·ca′tor** *n.*

hy·poth·e·sis (hī·poth′ə·sis, hi-) *n. pl.* **·ses** (-sēz) **1.** An unproved scientific conclusion drawn from known facts. **2.** An assumption or set of assumptions provisionally accepted. [< NL < Gk., foundation, supposition]
— **Syn.** In science, a *hypothesis* is a proposition advanced as possibly true, and consistent with known data, but requiring further investigation; a *theory* is a *hypothesis* so well substantiated as to be generally accepted. *Supposition* and *assumption* are propositions accepted with less assurance than a *hypothesis.* A *conjecture* is a conclusion drawn from admittedly insufficient data; it differs from a guess only in not being wholly random and uninformed.

hy·poth·e·size (hī·poth′ə·sīz, hi-) *v.* **·sized, ·siz·ing** *v.t.* **1.**

To offer or assume as a hypothesis. — *v.i.* **2.** To make a hypothesis; theorize.

hy·po·thet·i·cal (hī′pə·thet′i·kəl) *adj.* **1.** Pertaining to or of the nature of a hypothesis. **2.** Based on hypothesis; theoretical. **3.** Characterized by the use of hypotheses. **4.** *Logic* Denoting a proposition based on another proposition; conditional. Also **hy′po·thet′ic.** — **hy′po·thet′i·cal·ly** *adv.*

hy·po·thy·roid·ism (hī′pō·thī′roid·iz′əm) *n. Pathol.* **1.** Deficient functioning of the thyroid gland. **2.** A disorder resulting from this, as goiter. — **hy′po·thy′roid** *adj. & n.*

hy·son (hī′sən) *n.* A green tea from China. [< Chinese]

hys·sop (his′əp) *n.* **1.** A bushy, medicinal herb of the mint family, with small clusters of blue flowers. **2.** In the Bible, an unidentified plant furnishing the twigs used in the Mosaic rites, etc. [OE and OF < L < Gk. *hyssōpos*]

hys·ter·ec·to·my (his′tə·rek′tə·mē) *n. pl.* **·mies** *Surg.* Complete removal of part or all of the uterus.

hys·te·ri·a (his·tir′ē·ə, -ter′-) *n.* **1.** Abnormal excitement; wild emotionalism; frenzy. **2.** *Psychiatry* A psychoneurotic condition characterized by violent emotional paroxysms and disturbances in the sensory and motor functions. — **Syn.** See FRENZY. [< NL < Gk. *hystera* the womb]

hys·ter·ic (his·ter′ik) *adj.* Hysterical. — *n.* **1.** One who is subject to hysteria. **2.** *pl.* A fit of hysteria.

hys·ter·i·cal (his·ter′i·kəl) *adj.* **1.** Resembling hysteria; uncontrolled; violent. **2.** Characterized or caused by hysteria. **3.** Inclined to hysteria. — **hys·ter′i·cal·ly** *adv.*

hystero- *combining form* **1.** The womb; uterine. **2.** Hysteria. Also, before vowels, **hyster-.** [< Gk. *hystera* the womb]

hys·ter·ot·o·my (his′tə·rot′ə·mē) *n. pl.* **·mies** *Surg.* **1.** The operation of cutting into the womb. **2.** Cesarean section.

I

i, I (ī) *n. pl.* **i's** or **is, I's** or **Is, eyes** (īz) **1.** The ninth letter of the English alphabet. **2.** Any sound represented by the letter *i.* — *symbol* **I.** The Roman numeral for 1: written I or i. **2.** *Chem.* Iodine (symbol I).

i-¹ Reduced var. of IN-¹.

i-² See Y-.

I (ī) *pron., possessive* **my** or **mine,** *objective* **me**; *pl. nominative* **we,** *possessive* **our** or **ours,** *objective* **us** The nominative singular pronoun of the first person, used by a speaker or writer in referring to himself. — *n. pl.* **I's 1.** The pronoun *I* used as a noun: His talk was full of *I's.* **2.** *Philos.* The ego. [OE *ic*]

-ia¹ *suffix of nouns* Occurring in: **1.** *Geog.* Names of countries: *Australia.* **2.** *Pathol.* Names of diseases and related terms: *hysteria.* **3.** *Bot.* Names of genera: *Lobelia.* **4.** Words borrowed directly from Latin or Greek: *militia.* [< L and Gk. *-ia,* suffix of fem. nouns]

-ia² *suffix of nouns* Occurring in: **1.** *Biol.* Names of classes: *Mammalia.* **2.** Names of classical festivals: *Bacchanalia.* **3.** Words, usu. collectives, borrowed from Latin or Greek: *regalia.* [< L and Gk. *-ia,* plural suffix of neut. nouns]

I·a·go (ē·ä′gō) The villain of Shakespeare's *Othello.*

-ial *suffix of adjectives* Var. of -AL¹, with connective *-i-,* as in *filial, nuptial.*

i·amb (ī′amb) *n.* **1.** In prosody, a metrical foot consisting of an unaccented syllable followed by an accented one (˘ ¯). **2.** A line of verse made up of such feet: Thĕ bĭrd | wăs grēen | ănd gōld | ĕn ĭn | thĕ sūn. [< L < Gk. *iambos*]

i·am·bic (ī·am′bik) *adj.* Consisting of, using, or like iambs. — *n.* **1.** A foot, line, or stanza consisting of an iamb or iambs. **2.** Iambic verse.

i·am·bus (ī·am′bəs) *n. pl.* **·bi** (-bī) or **·bus·es** An iamb.

-ian *suffix of adjectives and nouns* Var. of -AN, with *-i-* of the stem or as a connective: *amphibian, Bostonian.*

-iana See -ANA.

-iasis *suffix Med.* Denoting a process and its results, esp. in diseased conditions: *psoriasis.* [Var. of -OSIS]

-iatrics *combining form* Medical treatment: *pediatrics.* [< Gk. *iatrikos* pertaining to the art of healing]

iatro- *combining form* Medicine and. [< Gk. *iatros* physician]

-iatry *combining form* Medical or curative treatment: *psychiatry.* [< Gk. *iatreia* healing]

I-beam (ī′bēm′) *n.* A beam or joist that in cross section has the shape of the letter I.

I·be·ri·an (ī·bir′ē·ən) *adj.* Of, pertaining to, or characteristic of the Iberian Peninsula, its people, or their culture. — *n.* **1.** One of the ancient or modern inhabitants of the Iberian Peninsula. **2.** The unclassified language of the Iberian Peninsula. [< Gk. *Iberes* Spaniards]

i·bex (ī′beks) *n. pl.* **i·bex·es** or **i·bi·ces** (ī′bə·sēz, ib′ə-) One of various wild goats of Europe and Asia, with long, recurved horns.

i·bi·dem (i·bī′dem) *adv. Latin* In the same place; in the work, chapter, etc., just mentioned. Abbr. *ib., ibid.*

i·bis (ī′bis) *n. pl.* **i·bis·es** or **i·bis** One of various wading birds related to the heron. [< Egyptian]

-ible See -ABLE.

-ic *suffix* **1.** Forming adjectives with the meanings: **a** Of, pertaining to, or connected with: *volcanic.* **b** Of the nature of; resembling: *angelic.* **c** Produced by or in the manner of: *Homeric.* **d** Consisting of; containing: *alcoholic.* **e** *Chem.* Having a higher valence than that indicated by *-ous*: said of elements in compounds: *sulfuric* acid. **2.** Forming nouns by the substantive use of adjectives in *-ic*: *classic, lunatic.* **3.** Occurring in nouns derived from Latin and Greek nouns formed from adjectives: *stoic, music.* See note under -ICS. [< F *-ique* or L *-icus* or Gk. *-ikos*]

-ical *suffix* **1.** Forming parallel adjectives from adjectives in *-ic,* often in the same sense, as *alphabetic, alphabetical,* but sometimes with extended or special senses, as *economic, economical.* **2.** Forming adjectives from nouns in *-ic* or *-ics*: *musical, mathematical.* [< LL *-icalis* < *-icus* + *-alis*]

Ic·a·rus (ik′ə·rəs, ī′kə-) In Greek mythology, the son of Daedalus, who, by means of artificial wings, flew so high that the sun melted the wax that fastened the wings and he fell into the sea and drowned.

ice (īs) *n.* **1.** Congealed or frozen water. ◆ Collateral adjective: *glacial.* **2.** The frozen surface of a body of water. **3.** Something resembling ice. **4.** A frozen dessert made without cream. **5.** Icing for cake. **6.** *Slang* A diamond. — **to break the ice 1.** To dispel reserve or formality, esp. at a social gathering. **2.** To make a start. — **to cut no ice** *U.S. Informal* To have no influence. — **on ice** *U.S. Slang* **1.** Set aside; in reserve. **2.** Certain to be achieved or won. **3.** Incommunicado. — *v.* **iced, ic·ing** *v.t.* **1.** To cause to turn to ice; freeze. **2.** To cover or surround with ice. **3.** To chill with ice. **4.** To decorate with icing. **5.** In hockey, to put (a team) on the ice. — *v.i.* **6.** To turn to ice. [OE *īs*]

-ice *suffix of nouns* Condition, quality, or act: *cowardice, notice.* [< OF *-ice* < L *-itius, -itia, -itium*]

ice bag   A flexible, waterproof container designed to hold ice, applied to parts of the body: also called *ice pack.*

ice·berg (īs/bûrg/) *n.* A thick mass of ice separated from a glacier and floating in the ocean. [Prob. < Du. *ijsberg*]

ice·boat (īs/bōt/) *n.* **1.** A framework with skatelike runners and sails for sailing over ice. **2.** An icebreaker (def. 1).

ice·bound (īs/bound/) *adj.* Surrounded or obstructed by ice.

ice·box (īs/boks/) *n. U.S.* A cabinet for holding ice, in which food or other perishables are stored.

ice·break·er (īs/brā/kər) *n.* **1.** A vessel used to break up ice in waterways and harbors. **2.** A structure for deflecting floating ice from the base of a bridge, a pier, etc.

ice·cap (īs/kap/) *n.* A covering of ice and snow permanently overlying an extensive tract of land.

ice cream   A mixture of cream, butterfat, or milk, flavoring, sweetening, and often egg whites, beaten to a uniform consistency and frozen. [Orig., *iced cream*]

iced (īst) *adj.* **1.** Coated or covered with ice or sleet. **2.** Made cold with ice. **3.** Covered with icing, as a cake.

ice field   A large, flat expanse of floating ice. Also **ice floe.**

ice hockey   Hockey played by skaters on ice.

ice·house (īs/hous/) *n.* A building in which ice is stored.

Ice·land·er (īs/lan/dər) *n.* A native or citizen of Iceland.

Ice·land·ic (īs-lan/dik) *adj.* Of or pertaining to Iceland, its inhabitants, or their language. — *n.* The North Germanic language of Iceland. — **Old Icelandic** The language of Iceland before the 16th century: sometimes called *Old Norse.*

Iceland spar *Mineral.* A transparent variety of calcite exhibiting double refraction and polarizing light.

ice·man (īs/man/, -mən) *n. pl.* **·men** (men/, -mən) One who supplies or delivers ice to consumers.

ice pack **1.** A large expanse of floating ice cakes jammed together and frozen into a single mass. **2.** An ice bag.

ice pick   An awllike tool for breaking ice into small pieces.

ich·neu·mon (ik-nōō/mən, -nyōō/-) *n.* **1.** An Egyptian species of mongoose. **2.** An ichneumon fly. [< L < Gk. *ichneumōn*, lit., tracker]

ichneumon fly   A hymenopterous insect whose larvae feed upon caterpillars or other larvae.

i·chor (ī/kôr, ī/kər) *n.* **1.** In classical mythology, the ethereal fluid supposed to flow in the veins of the gods. **2.** *Pathol.* A watery, acrid fluid discharged from sores. [< Gk. *ichōr*] — **i·chor·ous** (ī/kər-əs) *adj.*

ichthyo- *combining form* Fish. Also, before vowels, **ichthy-.** [< Gk. *ichthys* fish]

ich·thy·ol·o·gy (ik/thē-ol/ə-jē) *n.* The branch of zoology that treats of fishes. — **ich·thy·o·log·ic** (ik/thē-ə-loj/ik) or **·i·cal** *adj.* — **ich·thy·ol/o·gist** *n.*

ich·thy·o·saur (ik/thē-ə-sôr/) *n. Paleontol.* Any of an order of extinct marine reptiles of the Mesozoic era, having a porpoiselike form. [< ICHTHYO- + Gk. *sauros* lizard]

ich·thy·o·sau·rus (ik/thē-ə-sôr/əs) *n. pl.* **·sau·ri** (-sôr/ī) An ichthyosaur.

-ician *suffix of nouns* One skilled in or engaged in some specified field: *musician, beautician.* [< F *-icien*]

i·ci·cle (ī/si·kel) *n.* A hanging, tapering rod of ice formed by dripping water. [OE *īsgicel*] — **i/ci·cled** *adj.*

i·ci·ly (ī/sə·lē) *adv.* In an icy manner.

i·ci·ness (ī/sē·nis) *n.* **1.** The state or quality of being frozen or extremely cold. **2.** Marked aloofness of manner.

ic·ing (ī/sing) *n.* **1.** A coating made of sugar, usu. mixed with egg whites or cream, used to cover cakes, pastry, etc. **2.** The formation of ice on the surface of an aircraft.

i·con (ī/kon) *n. pl.* **i·cons** or **i·co·nes** (ī/kə·nēz) **1.** In the Eastern Orthodox Church, a pictorial representation of Jesus Christ, the Virgin Mary, or some other sacred figure. **2.** An image; likeness; picture. Also spelled *ikon.* [< Gk. *eikōn* image] — **i·con/ic** *adj.*

icono- *combining form* Image. Also, before vowels, **icon-.** [< Gk. *eikōn* image]

i·con·o·clast (ī·kon/ə·klast) *n.* **1.** One who attacks conventional or cherished beliefs and institutions. [< LL < G,. *eikōn* image + *-klastēs* breaker] — **i·con/o·clasm/** *n.* — **i·con/o·clas/tic** *adj.*

i·con·o·scope (ī·kon/ə·skōp) *n. Telecom.* The part of a television camera that converts the image to be transmitted into electrical impulses.

-ics *suffix of nouns* **1.** An art or a field of study: *mathematics.* **2.** Methods, practices, or activities: *athletics.* [See -IC]

i·cy (ī/sē) *adj.* **i·ci·er, i·ci·est 1.** Consisting of, containing, or covered with ice. **2.** Resembling or having the characteristics of ice: *icy* green. **3.** Extremely cold. **4.** Forbiddingly aloof: an *icy* greeting. [OE *īsig*]

id (id) *n. Psychoanal.* The unconscious part of the psyche, but actuated by fundamental impulses toward fulfilling in-

stinctual needs; the reservoir of psychic energy or libido. [< NL < L *id* it, trans. of G *es*]

-id[1] *suffix of nouns* **1.** Offspring of: often occurring in names from classical mythology: *Danaid, Nereid.* **2.** An epic about a specified person or subject: *Aeneid.* **3.** *Zool.* **a** A member of a family: *leporid.* **b** A member of a class: *arachnid.* **4.** *Astron.* A meteor seeming to originate in a specified constellation: *Perseid.* [< L *-is, -idis* < Gk. *-is, -idos,* suffix of patronymics]

-id[2] *suffix of adjectives* Having a particular quality, or existing in a particular state: *humid, fluid.* [< F *-ide* < L *-idus*; or directly < L]

-id[3] *Chem.* Var. of -IDE.

I'd (īd) **1.** I would. **2.** I should. **3.** I had.

-idae *suffix Zool.* Forming the names of families: *Canidae.* [< NL *-idae* < L < Gk. *-idai,* plural patronymic suffix]

-ide *suffix Chem.* Used in the names of compounds, usu. binary, and attached to the electronegative element or radical: sodium *chloride.* Also spelled *-id.* [< F *-ide.* See -ID[2].]

i·de·a (ī·dē/ə) *n.* **1.** That which is conceived in the mind; a thought. **2.** An impression or notion. **3.** A conviction; opinion; belief. **4.** An intention; plan. **5.** Vague knowledge; inkling: I had an *idea* you might come. **6.** A passing fancy; whim. **7.** *Informal* Significance; meaning: Do you get the *idea?* **8.** *Philos.* The Platonic concept of an archetype or fundamental example, of which an existing thing is but a representation. [< L < Gk. < *ideein* to see] — **Syn.** Concept, conception, thought, notion, image.

i·de·al (ī·dē/əl, ī·dēl/) *n.* **1.** A concept or standard of supreme perfection. **2.** A person or thing taken as a standard of perfection. **3.** A high principle; lofty aim. **4.** That which exists only as a concept of the mind. — *adj.* **1.** Conforming to an absolute standard of excellence. **2.** Completely satisfactory: an *ideal* situation. **3.** Capable of existing as a mental concept only; utopian; imaginary. **4.** Pertaining to or existing in the form of an idea or ideas. **5.** *Philos.* Pertaining to or existing as a Platonic idea. [< F < L *idealis*]

i·de·al·ism (ī·dē/əl·iz/əm) *n.* **1.** The envisioning of things as they should be or are wished to be rather than as they are. **2.** Pursuit of an ideal. **3.** That which is idealized. **4.** In literature and art, the imaginative treatment of subject matter in accordance with preconceived standards of perfection: opposed to *realism.* **5.** *Philos.* Any of several theories that there is no reality, no world of objects or thing in itself apart from a reacting mind or consciousness and therefore that reality is essentially spiritual or mental.

i·de·al·ist (ī·dē/əl·ist) *n.* **1.** One who formulates or attempts to live in accordance with ideals. **2.** An impractical dreamer. **3.** An exponent of idealism in literature, art, or philosophy.

i·de·al·is·tic (ī/dē·əl·is/tik, ī·dē/əl-) *adj.* Of, pertaining to, or characteristic of idealists or idealism. Also **i/de·al·is/ti·cal·ly** *adv.*

i·de·al·ize (ī·dē/əl·īz) *v.* **·ized, ·iz·ing** *v.t.* **1.** To consider to be ideal; hold in high esteem. **2.** To glorify. — *v.i.* **3.** To form an ideal or ideals. **4.** To consider or represent things in their ideal form. Also *Brit.* **i·de/al·ise.** — **i·de/al·i·za/tion** *n.* — **i·de/al·iz/er** *n.*

i·de·al·ly (ī·dē/əl·ē, ī·dēl/ē) *adv.* **1.** In conformance with an ideal; perfectly. **2.** As conceived in the mind.

i·de·ate (ī·dē/āt) *v.t. & v.i.* **·at·ed, ·at·ing** To form an idea or ideas of something; think.

i·de·a·tion (ī/dē·ā/shən) *n.* Thinking. — **i/de·a/tion·al** *adj.*

i·dée fixe (ē·dā/ fēks/) *French* A fixed idea; obsession.

i·dem (ī/dem) *pron. & adj. Latin* The same: used as a reference to what has been previously mentioned. Abbr. *id.*

i·den·ti·cal (ī·den/ti·kəl) *adj.* **1.** One and the same; the very same. **2.** Alike in every respect. **3.** *Genetics* Designating human twins that develop from a single fertilized ovum: distinguished from *fraternal.* [< Med.L *idem* the same] — **i·den/ti·cal·ness** *n.*

i·den·ti·fi·ca·tion (ī·den/tə·fə·kā/shən) *n.* **1.** The act of identifying, or the state of being identified. **2.** Anything by which identity can be established.

i·den·ti·fy (ī·den/tə·fī) *v.* **·fied, ·fy·ing** *v.t.* **1.** To establish as being a particular person or thing; recognize. **2.** To regard as the same. **3.** To serve as a means of recognizing; be characteristic of. **4.** To associate closely. **5.** To consider (oneself) as one with another person. **6.** *Psychol.* To imagine (oneself) to be thinking or behaving like a person with whom one has formed a strong emotional tie. — *v.i.* **7.** To put oneself in the place of another. [< LL *identificare*] — **i·den/ti·fi/a·ble** *adj.* — **i·den/ti·fi/er** *n.*

i·den·ti·ty (ī·den/tə·tē) *n. pl.* **·ties 1.** The state of being identical. **2.** The state of being a specific person or thing and no other. **3.** The distinctive character belonging to an individual. [< F < LL < L *idem* the same]

ideo- *combining form* Idea. [< Gk. *idea* form, idea]

id·e·o·graph (id/ē·ō·graf/, -gräf/, ī/dē-) *n.* **1.** A pictorial symbol of an object or idea. **2.** A graphic symbol, as +, —, ¶, 4, $. Also **id·e·o·gram** (id/ē·ə·gram/, ī/dē-). — **id/e·o·graph/ic** or **·i·cal** *adj.* — **id/e·o·graph/i·cal·ly** *adv.*

i·de·ol·o·gist (ī′dē·ol′ə·jist, id′ē-) *n.* **1.** One who formulates or supports an ideology. **2.** One who studies or is expert in ideology or ideologies. **3.** A visionary.

i·de·ol·o·gy (ī′dē·ol′ə·jē, id′ē-) *n. pl.* **·gies** **1.** The ideas and objectives that influence a whole group or national culture, shaping their political and social procedure. **2.** The science that treats of the origin, evolution, and expression of human ideas. **3.** Fanciful or visionary speculation. **— i·de·o·log·ic** (ī′dē·ə·loj′ik, id′ē-) or **·i·cal** *adj.* **— i′de·o·log′i·cal·ly** *adv.*

ides (īdz) *n.pl.* In the ancient Roman calendar, the 15th of March, May, July, and October, and the 13th of the other months. [< OF < L *idus*]

id est (id est) *Latin* That is. Abbr. *i.e.*

idio- *combining form* One's own; peculiar to a person or thing; individual: *idiosyncrasy.* [< Gk. *idios* own, private]

id·i·o·cy (id′ē·ə·sē) *n. pl.* **·cies** **1.** The condition of being an idiot. **2.** Extreme stupidity or foolishness.

id·i·om (id′ē·əm) *n.* **1.** An expression peculiar to a language, not readily understandable from the meaning of its parts, as *to put up with* (tolerate, endure). **2.** The language or dialect of a region or people. **3.** The special terminology of a class, occupational group, etc. **4.** The distinctive character of a specific language. **5.** Typical style, form, or character, as in art, literature, or music. [< F < L *idios* one's own]

id·i·o·mat·ic (id′ē·ə·mat′ik) *adj.* **1.** Characteristic of a specific language. **2.** Of the nature of an idiom. **3.** Employing many idioms. Also **id′i·o·mat′i·cal.** **— id′i·o·mat′i·cal·ly** *adv.*

id·i·o·mor·phic (id′ē·ō·môr′fik) *adj.* **1.** Having its own distinctive form. **2.** *Mineral.* Possessing crystal faces: said of minerals of a rock. **— id′i·o·mor′phi·cal·ly** *adv.*

id·i·o·syn·cras·y (id′ē·ō·sing′krə·sē) *n. pl.* **·sies** **1.** A habit, mannerism, expression, etc., peculiar to an individual; oddity. **2.** The distinctive physical or psychological constitution of an individual. [< Gk. *syn* together + *krasis* mixing] **— id′i·o·syn·crat′ic** (-sin·krat′ik) *adj.* **— id′i·o·syn·crat′i·cal·ly** *adv.*

id·i·ot (id′ē·ət) *n.* **1.** A person exhibiting mental deficiency in its most severe form. **2.** An extremely foolish or stupid person. [< OF < L < Gk. *idios* one's own]
— Syn. The *idiot* is incapable of learning, and is completely helpless. An *imbecile* may learn to communicate, but is incapable of earning his own living. A *moron* may take a normal place in society, but needs constant supervision.

id·i·ot·ic (id′ē·ot′ik) *adj.* Of or characteristic of an idiot; senseless; stupid. Also **id′i·ot′i·cal.** **— id′i·ot′i·cal·ly** *adv.*

i·dle (īd′l) *adj.* **i·dler** (īd′lər), **i·dlest** (īd′list) **1.** Not engaged in work. **2.** Not being used; not operating. **3.** Unwilling to work; avoiding effort; lazy. **4.** Spent in inactivity; reserved for leisure: *idle* moments. **5.** Having no effectiveness; fruitless: *idle* threats. **6.** Of little value; frivolous; trifling. **7.** Having no basis; unfounded. **— v. i·dled, i·dling** *v.i.* **1.** To be engaged in trivial or useless activities; loaf. **2.** To move or progress lazily or aimlessly; linger. **3.** *Mech.* To operate without transmitting power, usu. at reduced speed: said of motors or machines. **— v.t. 4.** To spend (time) wastefully; fritter: often with *away.* **5.** *U.S. Informal* To cause to be idle. **6.** To cause to idle, as a motor. [OE *īdel* empty, useless] **— i′dle·ness** *n.* **— i′dly** *adv.*

i·dler (īd′lər) *n.* **1.** One who idles; a lazy person; loafer. **2.** An idle wheel or pulley.

i·dol (īd′l) *n.* **1.** An image representing a god, and worshiped as divine. **2.** In the Christian and Jewish religions, a false or nonexistent god; object of heathen worship. **3.** One who is loved or admired to an excessive degree; object of infatuation. **4.** A false or misleading idea. [< OF < L < Gk. *eidos* form, shape]

i·dol·a·ter (ī·dol′ə·tər) *n.* **1.** One who worships an idol or idols. **2.** A blindly devoted admirer. [< OF < LL < Gk. *eidōlatrēs*] **— i·dol′a·tress** (-tris) *n. fem.*

i·dol·a·trous (ī·dol′ə·trəs) *adj.* **1.** Of or characterized by worship of idols. **2.** Blindly devoted. **— i·dol′a·trous·ly** *adv.* **— i·dol′a·trous·ness** *n.*

i·dol·a·try (ī·dol′ə·trē) *n. pl.* **·tries** **1.** The worship of idols. **2.** Excessive admiration or veneration; blind infatuation. [< OF < LL < Gk. < *eidolon* idol + *latreia* worship]

i·dol·ize (īd′l·īz) *v.* **·ized, ·iz·ing** *v.t.* **1.** To love or admire blindly or to excess; adore. **2.** To worship as an idol. **— v.i. 3.** To worship idols. **— i·dol·i·za′tion** *n.* **— i′dol·iz′er** *n.*

i·dyl (īd′l) *n.* **1.** A poem or prose piece, usu. short, depicting simple scenes of pastoral, domestic, or country life. **2.** An event, scene, etc., suitable for an idyl. Also *Brit.* **i′dyll.** [< L < Gk. *eidyllion* form]

i·dyl·lic (ī·dil′ik) *adj.* **1.** Of or having the qualities of an idyl. **2.** Charmingly simple or picturesque. Also **i·dyl′li·cal.** **— i·dyl′li·cal·ly** *adv.*

-ie *suffix* Little; dear: used affectionately: *birdie.*

-ier *suffix of nouns* One who is concerned with or works with: *cashier.* Also, after *w*, **-yer**, as in *lawyer.* [< F]

if (if) *conj.* **1.** In the event that; in case: We shall turn back *if* it rains. **2.** On condition that; provided that. **3.** Allowing the possibility that; granting that: *If* I am wrong, I'm sorry. ◆ In the preceding senses, *if* is often used in elliptical constructions: I'll do it *if* possible; He's sixty, *if* a day. **4.** Whether: See *if* the mail has come. **5.** Even though; although: Her clothes are neat, *if* not stylish. **— n.** A possibility or condition. [OE *gif*]

ig·loo (ig′lōō) *n. pl.* **·loos** A dome-shaped hut used by Eskimos, usu. built of blocks of snow. [< Eskimo *igdlu* house]

ig·ne·ous (ig′nē·əs) *adj.* **1.** *Geol.* Formed by the action of great heat within the earth, as rocks consolidated from a molten state. **2.** Of or like fire. [< L *ignis* fire]

ig·nis fat·u·us (ig′nis fach′ōō·əs) *pl.* **ig·nes fat·u·i** (ig′nēz fach′ōō·ī) **1.** A flickering, phosphorescent light sometimes seen over marshes, thought to be caused by the spontaneous combustion of marsh gas: also called *will-o'-the-wisp.* **2.** A deceptive attraction. [< Med.L, foolish fire]

ig·nite (ig·nīt′) *v.* **·nit·ed, ·nit·ing** *v.t.* **1.** To set on fire; make burn. **2.** To enkindle; arouse. **3.** *Chem.* To cause to glow with intense heat; bring to combustion. **— v.i. 4.** To start to burn. [< L *ignire* to burn] **— ig·nit′a·ble** or **ig·nit′i·ble** *adj.* **— ig·nit′a·bil′i·ty** or **ig·nit′i·bil′i·ty** *n.*

ig·nit·er (ig·nī′tər) *n.* **1.** One who or that which ignites. **2.** A detonator (def. 1). Also **ig·ni′tor.**

ig·ni·tion (ig·nish′ən) *n.* **1.** The act of igniting, or the state of being ignited. **2.** The process of igniting the explosive mixture of fuel and air in a cylinder of an internal-combustion engine. **3.** The device or system that fires this mixture. [< Med.L < L *ignire* to burn]

ig·no·ble (ig·nō′bəl) *adj.* **1.** Dishonorable in purpose or character; base. **2.** Not of noble rank. **3.** Of low quality; inferior. [< F < L < *in-* not + *gnobilis* known] **— ig·no·bil·i·ty** (ig′nō·bil′ə·tē), **ig·no′ble·ness** *n.* **— ig·no′bly** *adv.*

ig·no·min·i·ous (ig′nə·min′ē·əs) *adj.* **1.** Marked by or involving dishonor or disgrace; shameful. **2.** Meriting disgrace; despicable. **3.** Tending to diminish one's self-respect. **— ig′no·min′i·ous·ly** *adv.* **— ig′no·min′i·ous·ness** *n.*

ig·no·min·y (ig′nə·min′ē) *n. pl.* **·min·ies** **1.** Disgrace; dishonor. **2.** That which causes disgrace; dishonorable conduct. [< L < *in-* not + *gnomen* name, reputation]

ig·no·ra·mus (ig′nə·rā′məs, -ram′əs) *n.* An ignorant person. [< L, we do not know]

ig·no·rance (ig′nər·əns) *n.* The state of being ignorant; lack of knowledge, information, or awareness. [< F < L *ignorantia*]

ig·no·rant (ig′nər·ənt) *adj.* **1.** Having no learning or education; unenlightened. **2.** Lacking awareness: with *of:* *ignorant* of the facts. **3.** Uninformed; inexperienced: with *in.* [< OF < L *ignorare.* See IGNORE.] **— ig′no·rant·ly** *adv.*

ig·nore (ig·nôr′, -nōr′) *v.t.* **·nored, ·nor·ing** **1.** To refuse to notice or recognize; disregard. **2.** *Law* To reject (a bill of indictment) for insufficient evidence. [< F < L *in-* not + *gnoscere* to know] **— ig·nor′er** *n.* **— ig·nor′a·ble** (-ə-bəl) *adj.*

i·gua·na (i·gwä′nə) *n.* Any of several tropical American lizards that sometimes attain a length of 6 feet. [< Sp. < Carib]

IHS A monogram of the name Jesus, derived from the Greek IH(ΣΟΤ)Σ, Jesus.

i·kon (ī′kon) See ICON.

il- Assimilated var. of IN-¹ and IN-².

-ile *suffix* Found in adjectives derived from French and Latin, and in nouns based on such adjectives: *docile, agile, juvenile.* Also, sometimes, **-il,** as in *civil, fossil.* [< F < L *-ilis,* suffix of adjectives; or directly < L]

il·e·um (il′ē·əm) *n. pl.* **il·e·a** (il′ē·ə) *Anat.* The lowest of the three divisions of the small intestine. For illus. see IN-TESTINE. [< LL < L *ileum* groin, small intestine] **— il·e·ac** (il′ē·ak) *adj.*

i·lex (ī′leks) *n.* Any tree or shrub of the holly family. [< L, holm oak]

Il·i·ad (il′ē·əd) An ancient Greek epic poem ascribed to Homer, describing the siege of Troy. **— n.** Any similar long narrative poem. [< L < Gk. *Ilion* Ilium (Troy)]

il·i·um (il′ē·əm) *n. pl.* **il·i·a** (il′ē·ə) *Anat.* The large upper portion of bones of the pelvis. For illus. see PELVIS. [< NL < L *ilia* loins, belly] **— il′i·ac** (-ak) *adj.*

Il·i·um (il′ē·əm) See TROY. Also **Il·i·on** (-ən).

ilk (ilk) *n.* Breed; sort; class: Smith and others of his *ilk.* [OE *ilca* same]

ill (il) *adj.* **worse, worst** **1.** Not in good health; suffering from a disorder; sick. **2.** Destructive in effect; harmful. **3.** Hostile or malevolent; unfriendly; spiteful. **4.** Portending danger or disaster; unfavorable. **5.** Morally bad; evil. **6.** Contrary to accepted standards; improper. **— Syn.** See SICK¹. **— n. 1.** Evil; wrong. **2.** Injury; harm: I wish him no *ill.* **3.** A cause of unhappiness, misfortune, etc. **4.** Disaster; trouble: to bode *ill.* **5.** A malady; sickness. **— adv.**

1. Not well; badly. **2.** With difficulty; hardly. **3.** Unsuitably; poorly. [ME < ON *illr*]

Ill may be used in combination. Such combinations are hyphenated when they appear before the words they modify, as in *ill-concealed* envy, but are not hyphenated when used predicatively, as in: His envy was *ill concealed*.

I'll (il) **1.** I will. **2.** I shall.

ill-ad·vised (il′əd-vīzd′) *adj.* Undertaken or acting in accordance with poor or insufficient advice; injudicious; rash.

ill-bred (il′bred′) *adj.* Unmannerly; impolite; rude.

ill-con·sid·ered (il′kən-sid′ərd) *adj.* Done with insufficient deliberation or forethought; thoughtless; unwise.

ill-dis·posed (il′dis-pōzd′) *adj.* **1.** Having an unpleasant disposition; unfriendly. **2.** Disinclined; averse. — **ill′-dis·pos′ed·ly** (-əd-lē) *adv.* — **ill′-dis·pos′ed·ness** (-əd-nes) *n.*

il·le·gal (i-lē′gəl) *adj.* **1.** Not legal; contrary to law. **2.** Violating official rules. — **il·le′gal·ly** *adv.*

il·le·gal·i·ty (il′ē-gal′ə-tē) *n. pl.* **·ties 1.** The state or quality of being illegal; unlawfulness. **2.** An illegal act.

il·leg·i·ble (i-lej′ə-bəl) *adj.* Not legible; incapable of being read. — **il·leg′i·bil′i·ty, il·leg′i·ble·ness** *n.* — **il·leg′i·bly** *adv.*

il·le·git·i·ma·cy (il′i-jit′ə-mə-sē) *n. pl.* **·cies** The state or quality of being illegitimate; esp., the status or condition of a person born out of wedlock.

il·le·git·i·mate (il′i-jit′ə-mit) *adj.* **1.** Born out of wedlock. **2.** Not according to law; unlawful. **3.** Contrary to good usage; incorrect. **4.** Contrary to logic; unsound. [< L < *in-* not + *legitimus* lawful] — **il·le·git′i·mate·ly** *adv.*

ill fame Bad repute. — **house of ill fame** A brothel.

ill-fa·vored (il′fā′vərd) *adj.* **1.** Unpleasant in appearance; ugly. **2.** Objectionable; disagreeable. — **ill′-fa′vored·ly** *adv.* — **ill′-fa′vored·ness** *n.*

ill-found·ed (il′foun′did) *adj.* Based on weak or incorrect evidence or premises; unsupported.

ill-got·ten (il′got′n) *adj.* Obtained illegally or evilly.

ill humor A disagreeable mood; ill temper; sullenness.

ill-hu·mored (il′hyōō′mərd) *adj.* Irritable; cross. — **ill′-hu′mored·ly** *adv.* — **ill′-hu′mored·ness** *n.*

il·lib·er·al (i-lib′ər-əl) *adj.* **1.** Not generous in giving; stingy. **2.** Narrow-minded; intolerant. **3.** Lacking breadth of culture; provincial. — **il·lib′er·al′i·ty** *n.* — **il·lib′er·al·ly** *adv.*

il·lic·it (i-lis′it) *adj.* Not permitted; unlawful; unauthorized. [< L < *in-* not + *licitus*] — **il·lic′it·ly** *adv.* — **il·lic′it·ness** *n.*

il·lim·it·a·ble (i-lim′it-ə-bəl) *adj.* Incapable of being limited; limitless; boundless. — **il·lim′it·a·bil′i·ty, il·lim′it·a·ble·ness** *n.* — **il·lim′it·a·bly** *adv.*

Il·li·nois (il′ə-noi′, -noiz′) *n. pl.* **·nois** A North American Indian of a tribe belonging to a confederacy of Algonquian tribes. [< F < N.Am.Ind.]

il·lit·er·a·cy (i-lit′ər-ə-sē) *n. pl.* **·cies 1.** The state of being illiterate; esp., inability to read and write. **2.** An error in speaking or writing indicative of lack of education.

il·lit·er·ate (i-lit′ər-it) *adj.* **1.** Lacking education; esp., unable to read and write. **2.** Of language, characteristic of the uneducated. — *n.* An illiterate person. [< L *in-* not + *litteratus* lettered] — **il·lit′er·ate·ly** *adv.* — **il·lit′er·ate·ness** *n.*

ill-man·nered (il′man′ərd) *adj.* Characterized by bad manners; discourteous; rude. — **ill-man′nered·ly** *adv.*

ill nature Unpleasant or spiteful disposition; surliness. — **ill′-na′tured** *adj.* — **ill′-na′tured·ly** *adv.*

ill·ness (il′nis) *n.* **1.** The state of being in poor health; sickness. **2.** An ailment; disease.

il·log·i·cal (i-loj′i-kəl) *adj.* Not logical; neglectful of reason. — **il·log′i·cal′i·ty, il·log′i·cal·ness** *n.* — **il·log′i·cal·ly** *adv.*

ill repute Evil reputation. — **house of ill repute** Brothel.

ill-spent (il′spent′) *adj.* Wasted; misspent.

ill-starred (il′stärd′) *adj.* Unlucky, as if under the influence of an evil star.

ill temper Cross disposition; irritable mood. — **ill′-tem′pered** *adj.* — **ill′-tem′pered·ly** *adv.*

ill-timed (il′tīmd′) *adj.* Occurring at an unsuitable time.

ill-treat (il′trēt′) *v.t.* To act cruelly toward; maltreat.

il·lu·mi·nant (i-lōō′mə-nənt) *n.* Something that gives light. [< L *illuminare* to give light]

il·lu·mi·nate (i-lōō′mə-nāt) *v.* **·nat·ed, ·nat·ing** *v.t.* **1.** To give light to; light up. **2.** To shed light upon; clarify. **3.** To enlighten, as the mind. **4.** To make illustrious; glorify. **5.** To decorate with lights. **6.** To decorate, as a manuscript, with ornamental borders, figures, etc., often of gold. — *v.i.* **7.** To shed light; become lighted. [< L < *in-* thoroughly + *luminare* to light] — **il·lu′mi·na′tor** *n.*

il·lu·mi·na·tion (i-lōō′mə-nā′shən) *n.* **1.** The act of illuminating, or the state of being illuminated. **2.** An amount or source of light. **3.** Decoration by means of lighting. **4.** Mental or spiritual enlightenment. **5.** Embellishment, as of a manuscript, by means of gold or colored decorations, letters, etc.; also, a letter, ornament, etc., so used.

il·lu·mi·na·tive (i-lōō′mə-nā′tiv) *adj.* Capable of illuminating; serving to illuminate.

il·lu·mine (i-lōō′min) *v.t. & v.i.* **·mined, ·min·ing** To illuminate or be illuminated. [< F < L *illuminare* to illuminate]

ill-use (*v.* il′yōōz′; *n.* il′yōōs′) *v.t.* **-used, -us·ing** To treat cruelly or unjustly; abuse. — *n.* Bad or unjust treatment: also **ill′-us′age** (-yōō′sij, -yōō′zij) *n.*

il·lu·sion (i-lōō′zhən) *n.* **1.** A false, misleading, or overly optimistic idea: youthful *illusions*. **2.** A general impression not consistent with fact: Red gives an *illusion* of heat. **3.** A delicate, transparent, netted fabric. [< OF < L *illudere* to make sport of < *in-* toward, against + *ludere* to play] — **il·lu′sion·al** (-əl), **il·lu′sion·ar·y** (-er-ē) *adj.*

il·lu·sive (i-lōō′siv) *adj.* Deceptive; unreal; illusory. — **il·lu′sive·ly** *adv.* — **il·lu′sive·ness** *n.*

il·lu·so·ry (i-lōō′sər-ē) *adj.* Of the nature of illusion; deceptive. — **il·lu′so·ri·ly** *adv.* — **il·lu′so·ri·ness** *n.*

il·lus·trate (il′ə-strāt, i-lus′trāt) *v.t.* **·trat·ed, ·trat·ing 1.** To explain or make clear by means of examples, comparisons, etc. **2.** To supply or accompany (a book, etc.) with pictures, as for instruction or decoration. [< L < *in-* thoroughly + *lustrare* to illuminate] — **il′lus·tra′tor** *n.*

il·lus·tra·tion (il′ə-strā′shən) *n.* **1.** An example, comparison, anecdote, etc., by which a statement is explained. **2.** A print, drawing, or picture in written or printed text. **3.** The act or art of illustrating. [< L *illustratio*]

il·lus·tra·tive (i-lus′trə-tiv, il′ə-strā′tiv) *adj.* Serving to illustrate. — **il·lus′tra·tive·ly** *adv.*

il·lus·tri·ous (i-lus′trē-əs) *adj.* **1.** Greatly distinguished; renowned. **2.** Conferring greatness or glory. [< L < *in-* + *lustrum* light] — **il·lus′tri·ous·ly** *adv.* — **il·lus′tri·ous·ness** *n.*

ill will Hostile feeling; malevolence.

il·ly (il′lē) *adv.* Not well; badly; ill. ♦ While *illy* is regularly formed from the adjective *ill*, the form *ill* is preferred for the adverb as well.

Il·lyr·i·a (i-lir′ē-ə) An ancient country bordering the east coast of the Adriatic. — **Il·lyr′i·an** *adj.*

im-[1] Var. of EM-[1].

im-[2] Assimilated var. of IN-[1] and IN-[2].

I'm (īm) I am.

im·age (im′ij) *n.* **1.** A representation or likeness of a real or imaginary person, creature, or object. **2.** A mental representation of something not perceived at the moment through the senses; mental picture. **3.** The way in which a person or thing is popularly perceived or regarded; public impression: a politician's *image*. **4.** A person or thing that closely resembles another. **5.** A sculptured likeness, as a statue. **6.** A representative example; embodiment. **7.** A literary device that evokes a mental picture, as a figure of speech. **8.** *Optics* The counterpart of an object produced by reflection, refraction, or the passage of rays through a small aperture. **9.** The optical replica of a scene reproduced by a television camera. — *v.t.* **·aged, ·ag·ing 1.** To form a mental picture of. **2.** To make a visible representation of; portray. **3.** To mirror; reflect. **4.** To describe effectively or vividly. **5.** To symbolize. [< OF < L *imitari* to imitate]

im·age·ry (im′ij·rē) *n. pl.* **·ries 1.** Mental images collectively. **2.** The act or process of forming mental images. **3.** The use of vivid descriptions or figures of speech in speaking or writing. **4.** Images used in art or decoration.

im·ag·i·nar·y (i-maj′ə-ner′ē) *adj.* Existing in the imagination only; unreal. — **im·ag′i·nar′i·ly** *adv.* — **im·ag′i·nar′i·ness** *n.*

im·ag·i·na·tion (i-maj′ə-nā′shən) *n.* **1.** The process of forming mental images of the objects of perception or thought in the absence of the concrete external stimuli. **2.** The mental ability to reproduce the images of memory. **3.** The mental ability to create original and striking images and concepts; the creative faculty. **4.** A creation of the mind; mental image. **5.** An absurd fancy. — **im·ag′i·na′tion·al** *adj.*

im·ag·i·na·tive (i-maj′ə-nə-tiv, -nā′tiv) *adj.* **1.** Endowed with imagination. **2.** Given to flights of fancy. **3.** Of or characterized by the creative imagination: *imaginative* poetry. — **im·ag′i·na·tive·ly** *adv.* — **im·ag′i·na·tive·ness** *n.*

im·ag·ine (i-maj′in) *v.* **·ined, ·in·ing 1.** To form a mental picture or idea of. **2.** To suppose; guess: I *imagine* he will be elected. — *v.i.* **3.** To use the imagination. **4.** To suppose; guess. [< L *imago* image] — **im·ag′i·na·ble** *adj.*

im·a·gism (im′ə-jiz′əm) *n.* A movement in poetry characterized by precise images and freedom in form. [< F *Des Imagistes*, the title of the first anthology of imagist poetry] — **im′a·gist** *n. & adj.* — **im′a·gis′tic** *adj.*

i·ma·go (i-mā′gō) *n. pl.* **i·ma·goes** or **i·mag·i·nes** (i-maj′ə-nēz) (**1**) *Entomol.* An insect in its adult, sexually mature stage. **2.** *Psychoanal.* An infantile, unconscious concept of a parent or other loved one persisting in the adult. [< L]

im·bal·ance (im-bal′əns) *n.* **1.** The state of being out of balance. **2.** *Physiol.* Any defective coordination.

im·be·cile (im′bə-sil) *n.* **1.** A person exhibiting a degree of mental deficiency between that of the idiot and the moron. **2.** A foolish or stupid person. — **Syn.** See IDIOT. — *adj.* **1.** Mentally deficient. **2.** Stupid; senseless. [< F < L *imbecillus* weak, feeble] — **im′be·cil′i·ty** *n.*

im·bibe (im-bīb′) *v.* **·bibed, ·bib·ing** *v.t.* **1.** To drink. **2.**

To suck up; absorb. **3.** To take in mentally: to *imbibe* learning. —*v.i.* **4.** To drink. [< F < L *in-* in + *bibere* to drink] —**im·bib′er** *n.*

im·bri·cate (*adj.* im′brə·kit; *v.* im′brə·kāt) *adj.* **1.** Arranged in a regular pattern with overlapping edges, as shingles on a roof. **2.** Covered or decorated with a design resembling overlapping scales, leaves, etc. Also **im′bri·ca′tive** (-kā′tiv). —*v.t. &. v.i.* **·cat·ed, ·cat·ing** To overlap in a regular arrangement. [< L *imbrex* gutter tile < *imber* rain]

im·bro·glio (im·brōl′yō) *n. pl.* **·glios 1.** A confused state of affairs. **2.** A confused heap or tangle. [< Ital.]

im·brue (im·brōō′) *v.t.* **·brued, ·bru·ing** To stain or drench, esp. with blood. [< OF < L *in-* in + *bibere* to drink]

im·bue (im·byōō′) *v.t.* **·bued, ·bu·ing 1.** To pervade or permeate (with emotions, ideals, etc.). **2.** To wet thoroughly; saturate, as with color. [< L *imbuere* to wet, soak]

im·i·ta·ble (im′ə·tə·bəl) *adj.* Capable of being imitated.

im·i·tate (im′ə·tāt) *v.t.* **·tat·ed, ·tat·ing 1.** To behave or attempt to behave in the same way as; follow the example of. **2.** To mimic or impersonate. **3.** To make a copy or reproduction of. **4.** To have or take on the appearance of. [< L *imitari* to imitate] —**im′i·ta′tor** *n.*

im·i·ta·tion (im′ə·tā′shən) *n.* **1.** The act of imitating. **2.** That which is done by or results from imitating; copy. **3.** *Biol.* Mimicry. —*adj.* Resembling or made to resemble something superior; not genuine. [< L *imitatio, -onis*]

im·i·ta·tive (im′ə·tā′tiv) *adj.* **1.** Tending to imitate; characterized by imitation. **2.** Patterned after or reproducing the characteristics of an original. **3.** Not genuine; spurious. **4.** *Ling.* Designating words that resemble natural sounds, as *buzz, swish.* —**im′i·ta′tive·ly** *adv.* —**im′i·ta′tive·ness** *n.*

im·mac·u·late (i·mak′yə·lit) *adj.* **1.** Without spot or stain; unsullied. **2.** Without sin; pure. **3.** Without error or blemish; faultless; flawless. [< L < *in-* not + *macula* spot] —**im·mac′u·late·ly** *adv.* —**im·mac′u·late·ness** *n.*

Immaculate Conception *Theol.* The doctrine that the Virgin Mary was conceived without original sin.

im·ma·nent (im′ə·nənt) *adj.* **1.** Existing or remaining within; indwelling. **2.** Of God, pervading all creation. [< L < *in-* in + *manere* to stay] —**im′ma·nence, im′ma·nen·cy** *n.* —**im′ma·nent·ly** *adv.*

Im·man·u·el (i·man′yōō·əl) A name of the Messiah. *Isa.* vii 14; *Matt.* i 23. Also *Emmanuel.*

im·ma·te·ri·al (im′ə·tir′ē·əl) *adj.* **1.** Of little or no importance; inconsequential; irrelevant. **2.** Not consisting of material substance. [< Med.L < *in-* not + *materia* matter] —**im′ma·te′ri·al·ly** *adv.* —**im′ma·te′ri·al·ness** *n.*

im·ma·ture (im′ə·chŏŏr′, -tyŏŏr′, -tŏŏr′) *adj.* **1.** Not mature or ripe. **2.** *Geog.* In an early stage of development. [< L < *in-* not + *maturus* mature] —**im′ma·ture′ly** *adv.* —**im′ma·ture′ness, im′ma·tur′i·ty** *n.*

im·meas·ur·a·ble (i·mezh′ər·ə·bəl) *adj.* Not capable of being measured; without limit; immense. —**im′meas′ur·a·bly** *adv.* —**im′meas′ur·a·bil′i·ty, im·meas′ur·a·ble·ness** *n.*

im·me·di·a·cy (i·mē′dē·ə·sē) *n.* **1.** The state or quality of being immediate; direct relationship. **2.** Intuitive knowledge as distinguished from that arrived at by reasoning.

im·me·di·ate (i·mē′dē·it) *adj.* **1.** Done or occurring without delay or lapse of time; instant. **2.** Pertaining to the present moment: We have no *immediate* vacancies. **3.** Separated by no appreciable interval of time or space: the *immediate* future. **4.** Very close in rank or relationship: the *immediate* family. **5.** Occurring or acting directly or without an intervening agency or cause. [< Med.L < *in-* not + *mediare* to stand between] —**im·me′di·ate·ness** *n.*

im·me·di·ate·ly (i·mē′dē·it·lē) *adv.* **1.** Without lapse of time; instantly; at once. **2.** In direct or close succession. **3.** Without an intervening agency or cause; directly. —*conj.* As soon as; at the instant that.

im·me·mo·ri·al (im′ə·môr′ē·əl, -mō′rē-) *adj.* Reaching back beyond memory; ancient. —**im′me·mo′ri·al·ly** *adv.*

im·mense (i·mens′) *adj.* **1.** Of great size, degree, or extent; huge. **2.** Having no limits; infinite. **3.** *Slang* Excellent; admirable. [< F < L < *in-* not + *mensus,* pp. of *metiri* to measure] —**im·mense′ly** *adv.* —**im·mense′ness** *n.*

im·men·si·ty (i·men′sə·tē) *n. pl.* **·ties 1.** The condition or quality of being immense; vastness. **2.** Boundless space.

im·men·sur·a·ble (i·men′shŏŏr·ə·bəl, -sə·rə-) *adj.* Immeasurable. [< MF < L < *in-* not + *mensurare* to measure] —**im·men′sur·a·bil′i·ty** *n.*

im·merge (i·mûrj′) *v.* **·merged, ·merg·ing** *v.t.* **1.** To immerse. —*v.i.* **2.** To plunge or sink into a liquid. [< L < *in-* in + *mergere* to dip] —**im·mer′gence** *n.*

im·merse (i·mûrs′) *v.t.* **·mersed, ·mers·ing 1.** To plunge or dip into water or other fluid so as to cover completely. **2.** To involve deeply; engross. **3.** To baptize by plunging the entire body under water. [< L *immersus,* pp. of *immergere* to dip] —**im·mer′sion** *n.*

im·mi·grant (im′ə·grənt) *adj.* Coming into a country or region of which one is not a native in order to settle there. Compare EMIGRANT. —*n.* A person who immigrates.

im·mi·grate (im′ə·grāt) *v.* **·grat·ed, ·grat·ing** *v.i.* **1.** To come into a country or region of which one is not a native in order to settle there. —*v.t.* **2.** To bring in as immigrants. —Syn. See MIGRATE. [< L < *in-* in + *migrare* to migrate]

im·mi·gra·tion (im′ə·grā′shən) *n.* **1.** The act of immigrating. **2.** The total number of immigrants entering a country during a stated period. **3.** Immigrants collectively. —**im·mi·gra·to·ry** (im′ə·grə·tôr′ē, -tō′rē) *adj.*

im·mi·nence (im′ə·nəns) *n.* **1.** The state or quality of being imminent. **2.** That which is imminent; esp., impending disaster. Also **im′mi·nen·cy.**

im·mi·nent (im′ə·nənt) *adj.* About to happen; impending; threatening: said esp. of danger or catastrophe. [< L < *in-* on + *-minere* so project] —**im′mi·nent·ly** *adv.*

im·mis·ci·ble (i·mis′ə·bəl) *adj.* Not capable of being mixed, as oil and water. [< L *in-* not + *miscere* to mix] —**im·mis′ci·bil′i·ty** *n.* —**im·mis′ci·bly** *adv.*

im·mo·bile (i·mō′bəl, -bēl) *adj.* **1.** Incapable of being moved. **2.** Not moving; motionless. [< OF < LL < L *in-* not + *movere* to move] —**im′mo·bil′i·ty** *n.*

im·mo·bil·ize (i·mō′bə·līz) *v.t.* **·lized, ·liz·ing 1.** To make immovable; fix in place. **2.** To make unable to move or mobilize, as a body of troops. —**im·mo′bi·li·za·tion** *n.*

im·mod·er·ate (i·mod′ər·it) *adj.* Not moderate; exceeding reasonable or proper bounds. —**im·mod′er·ate·ly** *adv.* —**im·mod′er·ate·ness** *n.* —**im·mod′er·a′tion** *n.*

im·mod·est (i·mod′ist) *adj.* **1.** Without sense of decency; improper. **2.** Lacking humility; bold. —**im·mod′est·ly** *adv.* —**im·mod′es·ty** *n.*

im·mo·late (im′ə·lāt) *v.t.* **·lat·ed, ·lat·ing** To sacrifice; esp., to kill as a sacrificial victim. [< L < *in-* on + *mola* meal] —**im′mo·la′tion** *n.* —**im′mo·la′tor** *n.*

im·mor·al (i·môr′əl, i·mor′-) *adj.* **1.** Violating the moral law; contrary to conscience or public morality. **2.** Sexually impure; licentious. —**im·mor′al·ly** *adv.*
—Syn. **1.** The *immoral* person violates moral principles knowingly; he is consciously wicked, dissolute, evil, etc. The *amoral* person lacks the sense of right and wrong, and thus may violate morality without evil intent. *Unmoral* and *nonmoral* mean not within the realm of morality; a baby is *unmoral.*

im·mo·ral·i·ty (im′ə·ral′ə·tē, -ôr·al′-) *n. pl.* **·ties 1.** The state or quality of being immoral; wickedness; dissoluteness. **2.** Sexual impurity or misconduct. **3.** An immoral act.

im·mor·tal (i·môr′təl) *adj.* **1.** Not subject to death; living forever; deathless. **2.** Having unending existence; eternal. **3.** Pertaining to immortality or to beings or concepts that are immortal; divine. **4.** Of enduring fame; memorable. —*n.* **1.** An immortal being. **2.** *pl.* The gods of classical mythology. **3.** A person who has gained enduring fame. —**im·mor′tal·ly** *adv.*

im·mor·tal·i·ty (im′ôr·tal′ə·tē) *n.* **1.** Unending existence; eternal life. **2.** Eternal fame.

im·mor·tal·ize (i·môr′tal·īz) *v.t.* **·ized, ·iz·ing** To make immortal; endow with perpetual fame. Also *Brit.* **im·mor′tal·ise.** —**im·mor′tal·iz′er** *n.* —**im·mor′tal·i·za·tion** *n.*

im·mor·telle (im′ôr·tel′) *n.* An everlasting (def. 2). [< F]

im·mov·a·ble (i·mōō′və·bəl) *adj.* **1.** Incapable of being moved; stable. **2.** Unable to move; stationary. **3.** Firm of purpose or opinion; unyielding. **4.** Not easily aroused emotionally; impassive. —*n.pl. Law* Real property. —**im·mov′a·bil′i·ty, im·mov′a·ble·ness** *n.* —**im·mov′a·bly** *adv.*

im·mune (i·myōōn′) *adj.* **1.** Protected against a disease, poison, or the like, as by inoculation. **2.** Not susceptible to harmful influence. **3.** Not subject to obligation, penalty, etc. —*n.* One who is immune, esp. to a disease.

im·mu·ni·ty (i·myōō′nə·tē) *n. pl.* **·ties 1.** Protection against or lack of susceptibility to a disease, poison, infection, or the like. **2.** Resistance to harmful influence. **3.** Exemption from civil obligations or jurisdiction. [< OF < L < *in-* not + *munis* serviceable]

im·mu·nize (im′yə·nīz) *v.t.* **·nized, ·niz·ing** To make immune; esp., to protect against a disease by inoculation. —**im′mu·ni·za′tion** *n.*

im·mu·nol·o·gy (im′yə·nol′ə·jē) *n.* The branch of medical science that deals with immunity to disease. —**im·mu·no·log·i·cal** (i·myōō′nə·loj′i·kəl) *adj.* —**im′mu·nol′o·gist** *n.*

im·mure (i·myŏŏr′) *v.t.* **·mured, ·mur·ing 1.** To enclose within walls; imprison. **2.** To place in seclusion; confine. **3.** To entomb within a wall. [< Med.L < *in-* in + LL *murare* to wall] —**im·mure′ment** *n.*

im·mu·ta·ble (i·myōō′tə·bəl) *adj.* Not mutable; unchanging; unalterable. —**im·mu′ta·bil′i·ty, im·mu′ta·ble·ness** *n.* —**im·mu′ta·bly** *adv.*

imp (imp) *n.* **1.** An evil spirit; small or minor demon. **2.** A mischievous or unruly child. [OE *impian* to ingraft]

---

im·pact (*n.* im′pakt; *v.* im·pakt′) *n.* **1.** A striking together; collision. **2.** The forcible momentary contact of a moving body with another either moving or at rest. **3.** Strong influence; powerful effect.   — *v.t.* To press or drive firmly into something. [< L *impactus*, pp. of *impingere* to impinge]

im·pact·ed (im·pak′tid) *adj. Dent.* Denoting a tooth unable to emerge through the gum.

im·pac·tion (im·pak′shən) *n.* **1.** The act of impacting, or the state of being impacted. **2.** *Dent.* An impacted tooth.

im·pair (im·pâr′) *v.t.* To cause to become less in quality, power, or value; make worse. [< OF < LL *in-* thoroughly + *pejorare* to make worse]   — **im·pair′ment** *n.*

im·pale (im·pāl′) *v.t.* **·paled**, **·pal·ing 1.** To fix upon a pale or sharp stake. **2.** To torture or put to death by thrusting a sharp stake through the body. **3.** To make helpless as if by fixing upon a stake. [< OF < LL < *in-* + *palus* stake] — **im·pale′ment** *n.* — **im·pal′er** *n.*

im·pal·pa·ble (im·pal′pə·bəl) *adj.* **1.** Not capable of being perceived by the sense of touch. **2.** Not capable of being distinguished by the mind. — **im·pal′pa·bil′i·ty** *n.* — **im·pal′pa·bly** *adv.*

im·pan·el (im·pan′əl) *v.t.* **·pan·eled** or **·elled**, **·pan·el·ing** or **·el·ling 1.** To enroll upon a panel or list, as for jury duty. **2.** To choose (members of a jury, etc.) from such a list. Also spelled *empanel*. — **im·pan′el·ment** *n.*

im·part (im·pärt′) *v.t.* **1.** To make known; disclose. **2.** To bestow a measure or quantity of: to *impart* happiness. [< OF < L *in-* in + *partire* to share] — **im·par·ta·tion** (im′pär·tā′shən), **im·part′ment** *n.* — **im·part′er** *n.*

im·par·tial (im·pär′shəl) *adj.* Not favoring one above another; free from bias; disinterested. — **im·par′tial·ly** *adv.* — **im·par′tial·ness** *n.*

im·par·ti·al·i·ty (im′pär·shē·al′ə·tē, im·pär′-) *n.* Freedom from bias; fairness.

im·pass·a·ble (im·pas′ə·bəl, -päs′-) *adj.* That cannot be traveled over or through: an *impassable* jungle. — **im·pass′a·bil′i·ty, im·pass′a·ble·ness** *n.* — **im·pass′a·bly** *adv.*

im·passe (im′pas, im·pas′; *Fr.* aṅ·päs′) *n.* **1.** A situation in which no further progress is possible; deadlock. **2.** A way or passage open at one end only; blind alley. [< F]

im·pas·si·ble (im·pas′ə·bəl) *adj.* **1.** Incapable of emotion; unfeeling. **2.** Incapable of suffering pain. **3.** Invulnerable. [< OF < Med.L < *in-* not + *pati* to suffer] — **im·pas′si·bil′i·ty, im·pas′si·ble·ness** *n.* — **im·pas′si·bly** *adv.*

im·pas·sion (im·pash′ən) *v.t.* To fill with passion; inflame.

im·pas·sioned (im·pash′ənd) *adj.* Filled with passion or strong feeling; fervent. — **im·pas′sioned·ly** *adv.*

im·pas·sive (im·pas′iv) *adj.* **1.** Not feeling emotion; unmoved. **2.** Calm; serene. **3.** Unconscious. — **im·pas′sive·ly** *adv.* — **im·pas′sive·ness, im·pas·siv·i·ty** (im′pa·siv′ə·tē) *n.*

im·pa·ti·ens (im·pā′shē·enz) *n.* An herb with stems enlarged at the joints and irregular flowers, as the jewelweed: also called *touch-me-not*. [< L, impatient; because the ripe seed pods burst open at a touch.]

im·pa·tient (im·pā′shənt) *adj.* **1.** Lacking patience; easily annoyed at delay, discomfort, etc.; irritable. **2.** Unwilling to tolerate: with *of*. **3.** Restlessly eager: *impatient* for success. **4.** Exhibiting lack of patience: an *impatient* gesture. — **im·pa′tience** *n.* — **im·pa′tient·ly** *adv.*

im·peach (im·pēch′) *v.t.* **1.** To charge (a high public official) before a legally constituted tribunal with crime or misdemeanor in office. **2.** To challenge or bring discredit upon the honesty or validity of. [< OF < LL < *in-* in + *pedica* fetter] — **im·peach′a·bil′i·ty** *n.* — **im·peach′a·ble** *adj.* — **im·peach′ment** *n.*

im·pec·ca·ble (im·pek′ə·bəl) *adj.* **1.** Free from error, fault, or flaw. **2.** Incapable of doing wrong; unerring. — *n.* An impeccable person. [< LL < L *in-* not + *peccare* to sin] — **im·pec′ca·bil′i·ty** *n.* — **im·pec′ca·bly** *adv.*

im·pe·cu·ni·ous (im′pə·kyōō′nē·əs) *adj.* Having no money; penniless. Also **im·pe·cu·ni·ar·y** (im′pə·kyōō′nē·er′ē). [< F < L *in-* not + *pecunia* money] — **im·pe·cu′ni·ous·ly** *adv.* — **im·pe·cu′ni·ous·ness, im·pe·cu′ni·os′i·ty** (-os′ə·tē) *n.*

im·ped·ance (im·pēd′ns) *n. Electr.* The total opposition to an alternating current presented by a circuit.

im·pede (im·pēd′) *v.t.* **·ped·ed**, **·ped·ing** To retard or hinder in progress or action; put obstacles in the way of. [< L *impedire*, lit., to shackle the feet < *in-* in + *pes, pedis* foot] — **im·ped′er** *n.* — **im·ped′ing·ly** *adv.*

im·pe·di·ent (im·pē′dē·ənt) *adj.* That impedes. — *n.* That which impedes.

im·ped·i·ment (im·ped′ə·mənt) *n.* **1.** That which hinders or obstructs; an obstacle. **2.** A physical handicap, esp. a speech defect. **3.** *Law* **a** A disability that prevents the making of a valid contract, as infancy, insanity, etc. **b** A disability that affects the validity of a marriage. — **im·ped′i·men′tal** (-men′təl), **im·ped′i·men·ta·ry** (-men′tər·ē) *adj.*

im·ped·i·men·ta (im·ped′ə·men′tə) *n.pl.* **1.** The baggage, supplies, and equipment carried by an army. **2.** Cumbersome baggage or equipment; also, any drawbacks or burdens. **3.** *Law* Impediments. [< L]

im·pel (im·pel′) *v.t.* **·pelled**, **·pel·ling 1.** To force or drive to an action; move by an impulse; urge on. **2.** To drive or push forward. — **Syn.** See ACTUATE. [< L < *in-* on + *pellere* to drive] — **im·pel′lent** *adj. & n.* — **im·pel′ler** *n.*

im·pend (im·pend′) *v.i.* **1.** To be about to occur; be imminent. **2.** To be suspended: with *over*. [< L < *in-* on + *pendere* to hang] — **im·pen′dent** *adj.* — **im·pen′dence** *n.*

im·pend·ing (im·pen′ding) *adj.* **1.** About to occur; imminent; threatening. **2.** Overhanging.

im·pen·e·tra·bil·i·ty (im·pen′ə·trə·bil′ə·tē) *n.* **1.** The state or quality of being impenetrable. **2.** *Physics* The property of matter that makes impossible the occupation of the same space by two bodies at the same time.

im·pen·e·tra·ble (im·pen′ə·trə·bəl) *adj.* **1.** Incapable of being penetrated; that cannot be pierced, entered, seen through, etc.; impervious. **2.** Incapable of being understood. **3.** Inaccessible to intellectual or moral influences. **4.** *Physics* Possessing impenetrability. [< OF < L < *in-* not + *penetrare* to put within] — **im·pen′e·tra·bil′i·ty, im·pen′e·tra·ble·ness** *n.* — **im·pen′e·tra·bly** *adv.*

im·pen·i·tent (im·pen′ə·tənt) *adj.* Not penitent; obdurate. — **im·pen′i·tence, im·pen′i·ten·cy** *n.* — **im·pen′i·tent·ly** *adv.* — **im·pen′i·tent·ness** *n.*

im·per·a·tive (im·per′ə·tiv) *adj.* **1.** Urgently necessary; obligatory. **2.** Having the nature of or expressing a command. **3.** *Gram.* Designating the mood used to express commands, requests, exhortations, etc. — *n.* **1.** That which is imperative. **2.** *Gram.* The mood used to express command, exhortation, etc., or a verb or verb form in this mood. [< LL *imperare* to command] — **im·per′a·tive·ly** *adv.* — **im·per′a·tive·ness** *n.*

im·per·cep·ti·ble (im′pər·sep′tə·bəl) *adj.* **1.** That can barely be perceived, as by reason of smallness, extreme delicacy, subtlety, etc. **2.** Not discernible by the mind or senses. — **im′per·cep′ti·ble·ness, im′per·cep′ti·bil′i·ty** *n.* — **im′per·cep′ti·bly** *adv.*

im·per·cep·tive (im′pər·sep′tiv) *adj.* Not perceptive; lacking the power of perception. — **im·per·cep·tiv·i·ty** (im′pər·sep·tiv′ə·tē), **im′per·cep′tive·ness** *n.*

im·per·fect (im·pûr′fikt) *adj.* **1.** Falling short of perfection; faulty: an *imperfect* performance. **2.** Wanting in completeness; deficient. **3.** Denoting a tense that indicates action, usu. past action, as uncompleted, continuing, or synchronous with some other action. — *n. Gram.* The imperfect tense, or a verb or verb form in this tense, as *was speaking* in *He was speaking when I entered*. — **im·per′fect·ly** *adv.* — **im·per′fect·ness** *n.*

im·per·fec·tion (im′pər·fek′shən) *n.* **1.** The state or quality of being imperfect. **2.** A defect; flaw. [< OF < LL < L *imperfectus* incomplete.]

im·per·fo·rate (im·pûr′fər·it) *adj.* **1.** Without perforations; not perforated. **2.** Not separated by lines of perforations: said of stamps. Also **im·per′fo·rat′ed** (-rā′tid). — *n.* An imperforated stamp. — **im·per′fo·ra′tion** *n.*

im·pe·ri·al (im·pir′ē·əl) *adj.* **1.** Of or pertaining to an empire. **2.** Designating a nation having sovereign power over colonies or dependencies. **3.** Pertaining to or suitable to the rank of an emperor or supreme ruler. **4.** Possessing commanding power or dignity; majestic; magnificent. **5.** Exercising the authority of or having the manner of a supreme ruler or commander; overbearing. **6.** Superior in size or quality. **7.** Designating or conforming to the legal standards of weights and measures of the United Kingdom. — *n.* **1.** A pointed tuft of hair on the chin. **2.** An article of more than usual size or of superior excellence. **3.** A size of paper: in the U.S. 23 x 31 inches. [< OF < L < *imperium* rule, power] — **im·pe′ri·al·ly** *adv.* — **im·pe′ri·al·ness** *n.*

im·pe·ri·al·ism (im·pir′ē·əl·iz′əm) *n.* **1.** The creation, maintenance, or extension of an empire, comprising many nations and areas, all controlled by a central government. **2.** A system of imperial government. **3.** Imperial character, authority, or spirit. — **im·pe′ri·al·ist** *n. & adj.* — **im·pe′ri·al·is′tic** *adj.* — **im·pe′ri·al·is′ti·cal·ly** *adv.*

im·per·il (im·per′il) *v.t.* **·per·iled** or **·illed**, **·per·il·ing** or **·il·ling** To place in peril; endanger.

im·pe·ri·ous (im·pir′ē·əs) *adj.* **1.** Characterized by an attitude of command; domineering; arrogant. **2.** Urgent; imperative. [< L *imperium*] — **im·pe′ri·ous·ly** *adv.* — **im·pe′ri·ous·ness** *n.*

im·per·ish·a·ble (im·per′ish·ə·bəl) *adj.* Not perishable; not subject to decay; enduring; everlasting. — **im·per′ish·a·bil′i·ty, im·per′ish·a·ble·ness** *n.* — **im·per′ish·a·bly** *adv.*

im·per·ma·nent (im·pûr′mə·nənt) *adj.* Not permanent; fleeting. — **im·per′ma·nence, im·per′ma·nen·cy** *n.*

im·per·me·a·ble (im·pûr′mē·ə·bəl) *adj.* **1.** Not permitting passage or penetration. **2.** Impervious to moisture. — **im·per′me·a·bil′i·ty, im·per′me·a·ble·ness** *n.* — **im·per′me·a·bly** *adv.*

im·per·mis·si·ble (im′pər·mis′ə·bəl) *adj.* Not to be permitted. — **im′per·mis′si·bil′i·ty** *n.* — **im′per·mis′si·bly** *adv.*

im·per·son·al (im·pûr′sən·əl) *adj.* **1.** Not personal; objective: an *impersonal* observation. **2.** Not having the characteristics of a person: an *impersonal* deity. **3.** *Gram.* Of a verb, having no specific subject: in English the word *it* is usu. used with such verbs. — *n. Gram.* An impersonal verb. — **im·per′son·al′i·ty** (-al′ə-tē) *n.* — **im·per′son·al·ly** *adv.*

im·per·son·ate (*v.* im·pûr′sən·āt; *adj.* im·pûr′sən·it) *v.t.* **·at·ed, ·at·ing 1.** To adopt or mimic the appearance, mannerisms, etc., of. **2.** To act or play the part of. **3.** *Archaic* To represent in human form. — *adj.* Embodied in one person. — **im·per′son·a′tion** *n.* — **im·per′son·a′tor** *n.*

im·per·ti·nence (im·pûr′tə·nəns) *n.* **1.** Deliberate disrespectfulness; rudeness. **2.** Irrelevancy. **3.** Unsuitability; inappropriateness; incongruity. **4.** An impertinent remark, act, etc. Also **im·per′ti·nen·cy.**

im·per·ti·nent (im·pûr′tə·nənt) *adj.* **1.** Deliberately disrespectful or unmannerly; impudent. **2.** Not pertinent; irrelevant. **3.** Not suitable; inappropriate; incongruous. — **im·per′ti·nent·ly** *adv.*

im·per·turb·a·ble (im′pər·tûr′bə·bəl) *adj.* Incapable of being disturbed or agitated; calm. — **im′per·turb′a·bil′i·ty, im′per·turb′a·ble·ness** *n.* — **im′per·turb′a·bly** *adv.*

im·per·vi·ous (im·pûr′vē·əs) *adj.* **1.** Incapable of being passed through, as by moisture or light rays; impermeable. **2.** Not open; unreceptive: a mind *impervious* to reason. Also **im·per′vi·a·ble.** [< L < *in-* not + *per-* through + *via* way, road] — **im·per′vi·ous·ly** *adv.* — **im·per′vi·ous·ness** *n.*

im·pe·ti·go (im′pə·tī′gō) *n. Pathol.* A contagious skin disease marked by pustules. [< L < *impetere* to attack]

im·pet·u·os·i·ty (im·pech′ōō·os′ə·tē) *n. pl.* **·ties 1.** The quality of being impetuous. **2.** An impetuous action.

im·pet·u·ous (im·pech′ōō·əs) *adj.* **1.** Tending to act on sudden impulse and without forethought. **2.** Resulting from sudden impulse; rashly hasty. **3.** Moving with violent force: an *impetuous* wind. [< MF < L < *impetere* to attack] — **im·pet′u·ous·ly** *adv.* — **im·pet′u·ous·ness** *n.*

— **Syn. 1.** impulsive, reckless, rash. **2.** sudden, spontaneous, precipitate, swift, headlong. — **Ant.** deliberate.

im·pe·tus (im′pə·təs) *n.* **1.** The force that sets a body in motion; also, the energy with which a body moves or is driven. **2.** Any motivating force; stimulus; incentive. [< L < *in-* upon + *petere* to seek]

im·pi·e·ty (im·pī′ə·tē) *n. pl.* **·ties 1.** Lack of reverence for God; ungodliness. **2.** Lack of respect for those to whom respect is due; undutifulness. **3.** An impious act.

im·pinge (im·pinj′) *v.i.* **·pinged, ·ping·ing 1.** To strike; fall: with *on, upon,* or *against.* **2.** To encroach; infringe: with *on* or *upon.* [< L < *in-* against + *pangere* to strike] — **im·pinge′ment** *n.* — **im·ping′er** *n.*

im·pi·ous (im′pē·əs) *adj.* **1.** Lacking in reverence for God; ungodly; blasphemous. **2.** Lacking in due respect, as for one's parents. [< L < *in-* not + *pius* reverent] — **im′pi·ous·ly** *adv.* — **im′pi·ous·ness** *n.*

imp·ish (imp′ish) *adj.* Characteristic of or resembling an imp; mischievous. — **imp′ish·ly** *adv.* — **imp′ish·ness** *n.*

im·pla·ca·ble (im·plā′kə·bəl, -plak′ə-) *adj.* That cannot be appeased or pacified. [< F < L < *in-* not + *placere* to please] — **im·pla′ca·bil′i·ty, im·pla′ca·ble·ness** *n.* — **im·pla′ca·bly** *adv.*

im·plant (*v.* im·plant′, -plänt′; *n.* im′plant′, -plänt′) *v.t.* **1.** To fix firmly, as in the ground; plant; embed. **2.** To instill in the mind: to *implant* new ideas; inculcate. **3.** *Med.* To insert or embed in (living tissue). — *n. Med.* **1.** A tissue implanted in the body. **2.** A small tube containing radioactive material, embedded in tissue for therapeutic or remedial purposes. [< F *implanter*] — **im′plan·ta′tion** *n.*

im·plau·si·ble (im·plô′zə·bəl) *adj.* Not plausible; lacking the appearance of truth or trustworthiness. — **im·plau′si·bil′i·ty, im·plau′si·ble·ness** *n.* — **im·plau′si·bly** *adv.*

im·ple·ment (*n.* im′plə·mənt; *v.* im′plə·ment) *n.* **1.** A piece of equipment used in some form of work or activity; tool; instrument; utensil. **2.** Any means or agent for the accomplishment of a purpose. — *v.t.* **1.** To provide for the accomplishment or carrying into effect of. **2.** To accomplish; fulfill. **3.** To furnish with implements. [< L < *in-* in + *plere* to fill] — **im′ple·men′tal** *adj.* — **im′ple·men·ta′tion** *n.*

im·pli·cate (im′plə·kāt) *v.t.* **·cat·ed, ·cat·ing 1.** To show to be involved or concerned, as in a plot or crime. **2.** To indicate as something to be inferred; imply. **3.** To fold or twist together; intertwine. [< L < *in-* in + *plicare* to fold]

im·pli·ca·tion (im′plə·kā′shən) *n.* **1.** The act of involving, or the state of being involved. **2.** The act of implying, or the state of being implied. **3.** That which is implied.

im·pli·ca·tive (im′plə·kā′tiv) *adj.* Tending to implicate. Also **im·pli·ca·to·ry** (im′pli·kə·tôr′ē, -tō′rē). — **im′pli·ca′tive·ly** *adv.*

im·plic·it (im·plis′it) *adj.* **1.** Unreserved; absolute. **2.** Implied or understood, but not specifically expressed: *implicit* agreement. **3.** Essentially contained, but not apparent; in-

herent: with *in:* The man is *implicit* in the child. [< F < L *implicare* to involve] — **im·plic′it·ly** *adv.* — **im·plic′it·ness** *n.*

im·plied (im·plīd′) *adj.* Understood, suggested, or included without being specifically expressed. — **im·plied′ly** *adv.*

im·plore (im·plôr′, -plōr′) *v.* **·plored, ·plor·ing** *v.t.* **1.** To call upon in humble or urgent entreaty; beseech. **2.** To beg for urgently. — *v.i.* **3.** To make urgent supplication. [< L < *in-* thoroughly + *plorare* to cry out] — **im·plo·ra·tion** (im′plə·rā′shən) *n.* — **im·plor′er** *n.* — **im·plor′ing·ly** *adv.*

im·ply (im·plī′) *v.t.* **·plied, ·ply·ing 1.** To involve necessarily as a circumstance, condition, effect, etc.: An action *implies* an agent. **2.** To indicate or suggest without stating; hint at; intimate. **3.** To signify. ◆ See note at INFER. [< OF < L < *in-* in + *plicare* to fold]

im·po·lite (im′pə·līt′) *adj.* Lacking in politeness; discourteous; rude. — **im′po·lite′ly** *adv.* — **im′po·lite′ness** *n.*

im·pol·i·tic (im·pol′ə·tik) *adj.* Not in keeping with good policy; not prudent; inexpedient; injudicious. — **im·pol′i·tic·ly** *adv.* — **im·pol′i·tic·ness** *n.*

im·pon·der·a·ble (im·pon′dər·ə·bəl) *adj.* Incapable of being estimated, calculated, or valued. — *n.* An imponderable factor or circumstance. — **im·pon′der·a·bil′i·ty, im·pon′der·a·ble·ness** *n.* — **im·pon′der·a·bly** *adv.*

im·port (*v.* im·pôrt′, -pōrt′, im′pôrt, -pōrt; *n.* im′pôrt, -pōrt) *v.t.* **1.** To bring or cause to be brought into a country from abroad for commercial purposes, as merchandise. **2.** To bring in from an outside source or another relationship; introduce. **3.** To have as its meaning; signify. — *n.* **1.** An imported commodity. **2.** The act of importing. **3.** That which is implied; meaning. [< F < L < *in-* + *portare* to carry] — **im·port′a·ble** *adj.* — **im·port′a·bil′i·ty** *n.*

im·port (*n.* im′pôrt, -pōrt; *v.* im·pôrt′, -pōrt′) *n.* Importance: a matter of no *import.* — *v.t.* To be of consequence; matter. [< F < Ital. < Med.L *importare* to be important]

im·por·tance (im·pôr′təns) *n.* **1.** The quality of being important; consequence; significance. **2.** Worthiness of esteem; standing: a man of *importance.* **3.** Pretentiousness.

im·por·tant (im·pôr′tənt) *adj.* **1.** Having much significance, value, or influence; outstanding; great. **2.** Deserving of special notice or attention; noteworthy. **3.** Having special relevance; mattering greatly: with *to.* **4.** Considering oneself worthy of high esteem or special attention; pompous. — **im·por′tant·ly** *adv.*

im·por·ta·tion (im′pôr·tā′shən, -pōr-) *n.* **1.** The act of importing. **2.** That which is imported.

im·port·er (im·pôr′tər, -pōr′-) *n.* One who is in the business of importing merchandise.

im·por·tu·nate (im·pôr′chə·nit) *adj.* **1.** Urgently or stubbornly persistent in demand; insistent: an *importunate* creditor. **2.** Of a demand or request, repeatedly made; pressing. — **im·por′tu·nate·ly** *adv.* — **im·por′tu·nate·ness** *n.*

im·por·tune (im′pôr·tōōn′, -tyōōn′, im·pôr′chən) *v.* **·tuned, ·tun·ing** *v.t.* **1.** To harass with persistent demands or requests. **2.** To ask or beg for persistently or urgently. — *v.i.* **3.** To make persistent requests or demands. — *adj.* Importunate. [< F < L *importunus* not blowing towards port (of a wind), hence unfavorable] — **im′por·tune′ly** *adv.* — **im′por·tun′er** *n.*

im·por·tu·ni·ty (im′pôr·tōō′nə·tē, -tyōō′-) *n. pl.* **·ties 1.** Persistence in making demands or requests. **2.** *pl.* Repeated demands or requests.

im·pose (im·pōz′) *v.t.* **·posed, ·pos·ing 1.** To establish by authority as an obligation, penalty, etc.: to *impose* a fine. **2.** To inflict or enforce in an arbitrary or authoritarian manner. **3.** To force (oneself, one's company, etc.) upon others. **4.** To palm off as true or genuine; foist. **5.** *Eccl.* To lay on (hands), as in confirmation. **6.** *Printing* To arrange in correct order in a form, as pages of type. — **to impose on** (or **upon**) **1.** To take advantage of; make unwarranted or unfair use of. **2.** To deceive; cheat. [< F *im-* on + *poser* to put down] — **im·pos′a·ble** *adj.* — **im·pos′er** *n.*

im·pos·ing (im·pō′zing) *adj.* Impressive in appearance or manner; grand; stately. — **im·pos′ing·ly** *adv.*

im·po·si·tion (im′pə·zish′ən) *n.* **1.** The act of imposing or imposing on. **2.** That which is imposed, as a tax or an excessive requirement. **3.** An act of trickery or deception. **4.** The laying on of hands, as in the religious ceremonies. [< L *impositio, -onis* < *impositus.* See IMPOST.]

im·pos·si·bil·i·ty (im·pos′ə·bil′ə·tē) *n. pl.* **·ties 1.** The quality of being impossible. **2.** Something impossible.

im·pos·si·ble (im·pos′ə·bəl) *adj.* **1.** Incapable of existing or taking place. **2.** Incapable of being done or put into practice. **3.** Contrary to fact or reality; inconceivable. **4.** Not acceptable; objectionable; intolerable. [< F. See POSSIBLE.] — **im·pos′si·bly** *adv.*

im·post (im′pōst) *n.* A tax or customs duty. — *v.t.* To classify (imported goods) for the purpose of determining customs duties. [< OF < L < *in-* on + *ponere* to lay, place]

im·post[2] (im'pōst) *n. Archit.* The top section of a pillar or wall, serving as support for an arch. [See IMPOST.[1]]

im·pos·tor (im·pos'tər) *n.* One who deceives; esp., one who assumes the name of another. [< F < LL *impostor*]

im·pos·ture (im·pos'chər) *n.* Deception by means of false pretenses; esp., the act of posing under a false name.

im·po·tence (im'pə·təns) *n.* The condition or quality of being impotent; esp., an incapacity for sexual intercourse: said of males. **—im'po·ten·cy.** [< OF < L *impotentia*]

im·po·tent (im'pə·tənt) *adj.* 1. Powerless to act or to accomplish anything. 2. Physically weak. 3. Incapable of sexual intercourse: said of males. **—im'po·tent·ly** *adv.*

im·pound (im·pound') *v.t.* 1. To shut up in a pound, as a stray dog. 2. To place in legal custody. 3. To collect (water) for irrigation. **—im·pound'age** (-poun'dij) *n.*

im·pov·er·ish (im·pov'ər·ish) *v.t.* 1. To reduce to poverty. 2. To exhaust the fertility of, as soil. [< OF < L *pauperare* to impoverish] **—im·pov'er·ish·ment** *n.*

im·pow·er (im·pou'ər) See EMPOWER.

im·prac·ti·ca·ble (im·prak'ti·kə·bəl) *adj.* 1. Incapable of being carried out or put into effect; not feasible. 2. Incapable of being used for an intended purpose. 3. Hard to get on with; intractable. **—im·prac'ti·ca·bil'i·ty, im·prac'ti·ca·ble·ness** *n.* **—im·prac'ti·ca·bly** *adv.*

im·prac·ti·cal (im·prak'ti·kəl) *adj.* Not practical. **—im·prac'ti·cal'i·ty** (-kal'ə·tē) *n.*

im·pre·cate (im'prə·kāt) *v.t.* **·cat·ed, ·cat·ing** To invoke or call down (some curse or calamity): to *imprecate* evil upon a person. [< L < *in-* on + *precari* to pray] **—im'pre·ca'tor** *n.* **—im'pre·ca·to'ry** (-kə·tôr'ē, -tō'rē) *adj.*

im·pre·ca·tion (im'prə·kā'shən) *n.* 1. The act of imprecating. 2. A malediction; curse.

im·preg·na·ble (im·preg'nə·bəl) *adj.* 1. Incapable of being taken by force. 2. Incapable of being overcome; unyielding. [< OF < *im-* not + *prendre* to take] **—im·preg'na·bil'i·ty** *n.* **—im·preg'na·bly** *adv.*

im·preg·nate (im·preg'nāt) *v.t.* **·nat·ed, ·nat·ing** 1. To make pregnant. 2. To fertilize, as an ovum. 3. To saturate or permeate. 4. To fill or imbue, as with ideas, etc. *—adj.* Made pregnant. [< LL < L *in-* in + *praegnans* pregnant] **—im'preg·na'tion** *n.* **—im·preg'na·tor** *n.*

im·pre·sa·ri·o (im'prə·sä'rē·ō) *n. pl.* **·sa·ri·os** or **·sa·ri** (-sä'rē) One who manages or sponsors performers or performances for entertainment. [< Ital. *impresa* enterprise]

im·press[1] (*v.* im·pres'; *n.* im'pres) *v.t.* 1. To produce a marked effect upon the mind or feelings of; influence. 2. To establish firmly in the mind, as ideas, beliefs, etc. 3. To form or make (an imprint or mark) by pressure; stamp. 4. To form or make an imprint or mark upon. 5. *Electr.* To establish (a voltage) in a conductor or circuit. *—n.* 1. The act or process of impressing. 2. A mark, indentation, or design produced by pressure. 3. Distinctive character or mark; stamp. [< L < *in-* on + *premere* to press] **—im·press'er** *n.*

im·press[2] (*v.* im·pres'; *n.* im'pres) *v.t.* 1. To force to enter public service, esp. naval service. 2. To seize (property) for public use. *—n.* The act of impressing; impressment. **—im·press'er** *n.* **—im·press'ment** *n.*

im·press·i·ble (im·pres'ə·bəl) *adj.* Capable of being impressed or of receiving an impression; susceptible. **—im·press'i·bil'i·ty, im·press'i·ble·ness** *n.* **—im·press'i·bly** *adv.*

im·pres·sion (im·presh'ən) *n.* 1. An effect produced on the mind, the senses, or the feelings. 2. A vague remembrance or uncertain belief. 3. A material change produced by any agency. 4. A mark made by pressure. 5. The act or process of impressing. 6. *Printing* **a** The act or result of pressing type or plates to paper. **b** The total number of copies of a publication printed at one time; also, a single copy: distinguished from *edition*. [< OF < L *impressio, -onis*]

im·pres·sion·a·ble (im·presh'ən·ə·bəl) *adj.* Highly receptive to impressions; readily influenced or molded; sensitive. [< F] **—im·pres'sion·a·bil'i·ty, im·pres'sion·a·ble·ness** *n.*

im·pres·sion·ism (im·presh'ən·iz'əm) *n.* 1. In art, a theory of painting, developed in the 19th century, that attempted to produce, by simulating the appearance of light, etc., the impressions made by the subject on the artist. 2. In literature, the presenting of the most arresting aspects of character, emotion, etc., with relatively little realistic detail. 3. In music, a style of composition, developed by Debussy and Ravel, that attempted to create impressions or moods. **—im·pres'sion·ist** *n. & adj.* **—im·pres'sion·is'tic** *adj.*

im·pres·sive (im·pres'iv) *adj.* Producing or tending to produce an impression; exciting emotion or admiration. **—im·pres'sive·ly** *adv.* **—im·pres'sive·ness** *n.*

im·pri·ma·tur (im'pri·mā'tər, -mä'-) *n.* 1. Official license or approval for publication of a literary work, esp. that granted by a censor or by the Roman Catholic Church. 2. Authorization in general. [< L, let it be printed.]

im·print (*v.* im·print'; *n.* im'print) *v.t.* 1. To produce (a figure, mark, etc.) by pressure. 2. To mark or produce a mark on, as with a stamp or seal. 3. To fix firmly in the heart, mind, etc. *—n.* 1. A mark or indentation made by

printing, stamping, or pressing. 2. Characteristic effect; impression; stamp. 3. The name of the publisher, place of publication, date of issue, etc., printed in a book usu. on the title page. [< OF < L < *in-* in + *premere* to press]

im·pris·on (im·priz'ən) *v.t.* 1. To put into a prison; hold in confinement. 2. To confine or restrain forcibly, as in a small space, tight garment etc. **—im·pris'on·ment** *n.*

im·prob·a·bil·i·ty (im'prob·ə·bil'ə·tē, im·prob'-) *n. pl.* **·ties** 1. The quality of being improbable; unlikelihood. 2. An unlikely circumstance, event, or result.

im·prob·a·ble (im·prob'ə·bəl) *adj.* Not probable; not likely to be true or not reasonably to be expected. **—im·prob'a·ble·ness** *n.* **—im·prob'a·bly** *adv.*

im·promp·tu (im·promp'tōō, -tyōō) *adj.* Made, done, or uttered on the spur of the moment. *— n.* Anything produced on the impulse of the moment. *—adv.* Without preparation. [< F < L *in promptu* in readiness]

im·prop·er (im·prop'ər) *adj.* 1. Deviating from fact, truth, or established usage. 2. Not conforming to accepted standards of conduct or good taste. 3. Unsuitable. **—im·prop'er·ly** *adv.* **—im·prop'er·ness** *n.*

improper fraction *Math.* A fraction in which the numerator exceeds the denominator.

im·pro·pri·e·ty (im'prə·prī'ə·tē) *n. pl.* **·ties** 1. The quality of being improper. 2. An improper action. 3. An improper usage in speech or writing.

im·prove (im·prōōv') *v.* **·proved, ·prov·ing** *v.t.* 1. To raise to a higher or more desirable quality, value, or condition; make better. 2. *U.S.* To increase the value or profit of, as land. 3. To use to good advantage; utilize. *—v.i.* 4. To become better. **— to improve on** (or **upon**) To do or produce something better than. [< AF < OF *en-* into + *prou* profit] **—im·prov'a·bil'i·ty, im·prov'a·ble·ness** *n.* **—im·prov'a·ble** *adj.* **—im·prov'a·bly** *adv.* **—im·prov'er** *n.*

im·prove·ment (im·prōōv'mənt) *n.* 1. The act of making better, or the state of becoming better. 2. A modification or addition by means of which a thing's excellence or value is increased. 3. A person, thing, or process that constitutes an advance in excellence. 4. Advantageous use.

im·prov·i·dent (im·prov'ə·dənt) *adj.* 1. Lacking foresight; incautious; rash. 2. Taking no thought of future needs; thriftless. **—im·prov'i·dence** *n.* **—im·prov'i·dent·ly** *adv.*

im·pro·vi·sa·to·ry (im'prə·vī'zə·tôr'ē, -tō'rē) *adj.* 1. Of or pertaining to an improviser. 2. Of the nature of improvisation. Also **im·prov'i·sa·to·ri·al** (im·prov'ə·zə·tôr'ē·əl, -tō'rē-).

im·pro·vise (im'prə·vīz) *v.* **·vised, ·vis·ing** *v.t.* 1. To produce (music, verse, drama, etc.) without previous thought or preparation. 2. To contrive or construct from whatever comes to hand. *—v.i.* 3. To produce anything extemporaneously. [< F < Ital. < L < *in-* not + *providere* to foresee] **—im·pro·vi·sa·tion** (im'prə·vī·zā'shən, im'prov·ə-) *n.* **—im·pro'vi·sa'tion·al** *adj.* **—im·pro·vis'er, im·prov'i·sa·tor** (im·prov'ə·zā'tər, im'prə·vī-) *n.*

im·pru·dent (im·prōōd'nt) *adj.* Not prudent; lacking discretion; unwise. **—im·pru'dence** *n.*

im·pu·dence (im'pyə·dəns) *n.* 1. The quality of being impudent; offensive boldness. 2. Impudent speech or conduct. Also **im'pu·den·cy.**

im·pu·dent (im'pyə·dənt) *adj.* Offensively bold; insolently assured; saucy; brazen. [< OF < L < *in-* not + *pudens* modest] **—im'pu·dent·ly** *adv.*

im·pugn (im·pyōōn') *v.t.* To attack (a statement, motives, etc.) with criticism or arguments; dispute the truth of. [< OF < L *in-* against + *pugnare* to strike, fight] **—im·pugn'a·ble** *adj.* **—im·pug·na·tion** (im'pəg·nā'shən), **im·pugn'ment** *n.* **—im·pugn'er** (im·pyōō'nər) *n.*

im·pulse (im'puls) *n.* 1. A brief exertion or communication of force tending to produce motion. 2. The motion produced. 3. A sudden, unreasoned inclination to action, often induced by an emotion, etc. 4. *Physiol.* The transference of a stimulus through a nerve fiber. [See IMPEL.]

im·pul·sion (im·pul'shən) *n.* 1. The act of impelling, or the state of being impelled. 2. An impelling force.

im·pul·sive (im·pul'siv) *adj.* 1. Actuated by impulse rather than by reflection. 2. Prompted by impulse; spontaneous; unpremeditated. 3. Having the power of inciting to action. **—im·pul'sive·ly** *adv.* **—im·pul'sive·ness** *n.*

im·pu·ni·ty (im·pyōō'nə·tē) *n. pl.* **·ties** Freedom or exemption from punishment, harm, or unpleasant consequence. [< L *in-* not + *poena* punishment]

im·pure (im·pyōōr') *adj.* 1. Containing something offensive or contaminating. 2. Mixed with an inferior or worthless substance, adulterated. 3. Contrary to moral purity; sinful. 4. Not for religious use. 5. Having the characteristics of more than one style, period, color, language, etc.; mixed. **—im·pure'ly** *adv.* **—im·pure'ness** *n.*

im·pu·ri·ty (im·pyōōr'ə·tē) *n. pl.* **·ties** 1. The state or quality of being impure. 2. That which is impure.

im·put·a·ble (im·pyōō'tə·bəl) *adj.* Capable of being imputed; ascribable; chargeable. **—im·put'a·bil'i·ty, im·put'a·ble·ness** *n.* **—im·put'a·bly** *adv.*

im·pu·ta·tion (im′pyŏŏ·tā′shən)　*n.*　**1.** The act of imputing; accusation.　**2.** That which is imputed or charged.

im·pu·ta·tive (im·pyŏŏ′ta·tiv)　*adj.*　**1.** Transferred or transmitted by imputation; imputed.　**2.** Tending to impute. — **im·pu′ta·tive·ly** *adv.*

im·pute (im·pyŏŏt′)　*v.t.* **·put·ed, ·put·ing**　**1.** To attribute (a fault, crime, etc.) to a person; charge.　**2.** To consider as the cause or source of; ascribe: with *to*. — **Syn.** See ATTRIBUTE.　[< OF < L < *in-* in + *putare* to reckon]

in (in)　*prep.*　**1.** Held by or within the confines of; enclosed by: apples *in* a bag.　**2.** Surrounded by; amidst: buried *in* the mud.　**3.** Within the limits of: sightseeing *in* Paris.　**4.** Within the range or scope of: He said it *in* my hearing.　**5.** Within the category, class, or number of; included as a member of; belonging to: twelve inches *in* a foot; *in* the best society.　**6.** Existing as a part, characteristic, or property of: *in* the works of Shaw.　**7.** Affecting: dust *in* one's eye.　**8.** Wearing; covered by; decorated with: a man *in* a straw hat.　**9.** Made of a specified color, style, or material.　**10.** Arranged, disposed, or proceeding so as to form: trees *in* a row.　**11.** Engaged at; occupied by: *in* business.　**12.** For the purpose of: to run *in* pursuit.　**13.** By means of: speaking *in* whispers.　**14.** According to: *In* my opinion.　**15.** With regard or respect to: Students vary *in* talent.　**16.** Affected by; under the influence of: to shout *in* rage.　**17.** During: a concert given *in* the evening. — **Syn.** See AT. — **in that** For the reason that; because; since. — *adv.*　**1.** To or toward the inside from the outside: Please come *in.*　**2.** In one's home, place of business, etc.: We stayed *in* all day.　**3.** In or into some activity or office; to join *in.*　**4.** Into some place, condition, or position: Tuck the baby *in.*　**5.** Into some understood substance, object, etc.: Blend *in* the oil. — **to be in for** *Informal* To be certain to experience (usu. something unpleasant). — **to have it in for** *Informal* To hold a grudge against. — *adj.*　**1.** That is in or remains within.　**2.** That has gained power or control: the *in* group.　**3.** Coming or leading in: the *in* door. — *n.*　**1.** A member of the group in power or at an advantage.　**2.** *Informal* A means of entrance or access; also, a position of favor or influence: to have an *in.* — **ins and outs** The full complexities or particulars: the *ins and outs* of a business. — *v.t.* **inned, in·ning** To enclose, as land.　[OE]

in-[1]　*prefix* Not; without; un-; non-. Also: *i-* before *gn*, as in *ignore*; *il-* before *l*, as in *illiterate*; *im-* before *b, m, p*, as in *imbalance, immiscible, impecunious*; *ir-* before *r*, as in *irresistible.* ◆ See note under UN-[2].　[< L]

in-[2]　*prefix* In; into; on; within; toward: *include, incur, invade*: also used intensively, as in *inflame*, or without perceptible force. Also *il-* before *l*, as in *illuminate*; *im-* before *b, m, p*, as in *imbibe, immigrate, impress*; *ir-* before *r*, as in *irradiate.*　[< OE *in*; sometimes < L *in-* in, prep.]

-in　*suffix Chem.* Occasionally used to denote neutral compounds, as fats, proteins, and glycerides: *stearin, albumin, lecithin.* Also *-ein.*　[Var. of -INE[2]]

in·a·bil·i·ty (in′ə·bil′ə·tē)　*n.* The state or quality of being unable; lack of the necessary power or means.

in ab·sen·ti·a (in ab·sen′shē·ə, -shə)　*Latin* In absence (of the person concerned).

in·ac·ces·si·ble (in′ak·ses′ə·bəl)　*adj.* Not accessible; incapable of being reached or closely approached. — **in′ac·ces′si·bil′i·ty, in′ac·ces′i·ble·ness** *n.* — **in′ac·ces′si·bly** *adv.*

in·ac·cu·ra·cy (in·ak′yər·ə·sē)　*n. pl.* **·cies**　**1.** The state or quality of being inaccurate.　**2.** An error; mistake.

in·ac·cu·rate (in·ak′yər·it)　*adj.* Not accurate; inexact; incorrect. — **in·ac′cu·rate·ly** *adv.* — **in·ac′cu·rate·ness** *n.*

in·ac·tion (in·ak′shən)　*n.* Absence of action; idleness.

in·ac·ti·vate (in·ak′tə·vāt)　*v.t.* **·vat·ed, ·vat·ing** To make inactive. — **in·ac′ti·va′tion** *n.*

in·ac·tive (in·ak′tiv)　*adj.*　**1.** Characterized by inaction; idle; inert.　**2.** Marked by absence of effort or action; indolent.　**3.** *Mil.* Not mobilized. — **in·ac′tive·ly** *adv.* — **in·ac·tiv·i·ty** (in·ak·tiv′ə·tē), **in·ac′tive·ness** *n.*

in·ad·e·qua·cy (in·ad′ə·kwə·sē)　*n. pl.* **·cies**　**1.** The state or quality of being inadequate; insufficiency.　**2.** A defect.

in·ad·e·quate (in·ad′ə·kwit)　*adj.* Not adequate; not equal to that which is required; insufficient. — **in·ad′e·quate·ly** *adv.* — **in·ad′e·quate·ness** *n.*

in·ad·mis·si·ble (in′əd·mis′ə·bəl)　*adj.* Not admissible; not to be considered, approved, or allowed. — **in′ad·mis′si·bil′i·ty** *n.* — **in′ad·mis′si·bly** *adv.*

in·ad·ver·tence (in′əd·vûr′təns)　*n.*　**1.** The fact or quality of being inadvertent; lack of due care or attention.　**2.** A result of inattention; oversight. Also **in′ad·ver′ten·cy.**

in·ad·ver·tent (in′əd·vûr′tənt)　*adj.*　**1.** Not exercising due care or consideration; negligent.　**2.** Resulting from inattention or oversight; unintentional. — **in′ad·ver′tent·ly** *adv.*

in·ad·vis·a·ble (in′əd·vī′zə·bəl)　*adj.* Not advisable; injudicious; unwise. — **in′ad·vis′a·bil′i·ty** *n.*

-inae　*suffix Zool.* Used in the names of subfamilies: *Cervinae.*　[< NL < L, fem. pl. of *-inus*, adj. suffix]

in·al·ien·a·ble (in·āl′yən·ə·bəl)　*adj.* Not transferable; that cannot be rightfully taken away. — **in·al′ien·a·bil′i·ty** *n.* — **in·al′ien·a·bly** *adv.*

in·am·o·ra·ta (in·am′ə·rä′tə, in′am-)　*n. pl.* **·tas** A woman who is loved or in love.　[< Ital. < *in-* in + *amore* love]

in·ane (in·ān′)　*adj.*　**1.** Lacking in sense; empty-headed; silly.　**2.** Empty of meaning; pointless.　[< L *inanis* empty] — **in·ane′ly** *adv.*

in·an·i·mate (in·an′ə·mit)　*adj.*　**1.** Not living or animate.　**2.** Lacking animation; torpid; spiritless. — **in·an′i·mate·ly** *adv.* — **in·an′i·mate·ness** *n.*

in·a·ni·tion (in′ə·nish′ən)　*n.*　**1.** Exhaustion caused by lack of nourishment or inability to assimilate food.　**2.** Emptiness.　[< F < LL < L *inanire* to empty]

in·an·i·ty (in·an′ə·tē)　*n. pl.* **·ties**　**1.** Lack of sense or meaning; silliness; foolishness.　**2.** A foolish remark, action, etc.　**3.** Emptiness.　[< OF < L *inanis* empty]

in·ap·pli·ca·ble (in·ap′li·kə·bəl)　*adj.* Not applicable; irrelevant; unsuitable. — **in·ap′pli·ca·bil′i·ty, in·ap′pli·ca·ble·ness** *n.* — **in·ap′pli·ca·bly** *adv.*

in·ap·po·site (in·ap′ə·zit)　*adj.* Not pertinent or suitable. — **in·ap′po·site·ly** *adv.*

in·ap·pre·ci·a·ble (in′ə·prē′shē·ə·bəl, -shə·bəl)　*adj.* Imperceptible; unnoticeable. — **in′ap·pre′ci·a·bly** *adv.*

in·ap·pro·pri·ate (in′ə·prō′prē·it)　*adj.* Not appropriate; unsuitable; unfitting. — **in′ap·pro′pri·ate·ly** *adv.* — **in′ap·pro′pri·ate·ness** *n.*

in·apt (in·apt′)　*adj.*　**1.** Not apt or fit.　**2.** Lacking skill or aptitude; inept; clumsy. — **in·apt′ly** *adv.* — **in·apt′ness** *n.*

in·ap·ti·tude (in·ap′tə·tōōd, -tyōōd)　*n.*　**1.** Lack of skill.　**2.** Unsuitability.

in·ar·tic·u·late (in′är·tik′yə·lit)　*adj.*　**1.** Uttered without the distinct sounds of spoken language: *inarticulate* cries.　**2.** Incapable of speech; dumb.　**3.** Unable to speak coherently.　**4.** Unspoken; unexpressed: *inarticulate* grief.　**5.** *Zool.* Not segmented, as certain worms. — **in′ar·tic′u·late·ly** *adv.* — **in′ar·tic′u·late·ness** *n.*

in·ar·tis·tic (in′är·tis′tik)　*adj.*　**1.** Contrary to the principles of art; made or done without skill or taste.　**2.** Lacking in artistic ability. — **in′ar·tis′ti·cal·ly** *adv.*

in·as·much as (in′əz·much′)　**1.** Considering the fact that; seeing that; because.　**2.** Insofar as; according as.

in·at·ten·tion (in′ə·ten′shən)　*n.* Lack of attention.

in·at·ten·tive (in′ə·ten′tiv)　*adj.* Not attentive; heedless. — **in′at·ten′tive·ly** *adv.* — **in′at·ten′tive·ness** *n.*

in·au·di·ble (in·ô′də·bəl)　*adj.* Incapable of being heard. — **in·au′di·bil′i·ty, in·au′di·ble·ness** *n.* — **in·au′di·bly** *adv.*

in·au·gu·ral (in·ô′gyər·əl)　*adj.* Of or pertaining to an inauguration. — *n.* A speech made at an inauguration.

in·au·gu·rate (in·ô′gyə·rāt)　*v.t.* **·rat·ed, ·rat·ing**　**1.** To begin or commence upon formally; initiate.　**2.** To induct into office with formal ceremony.　**3.** To celebrate the public opening of.　[< L *inaugurare* to take omens, consecrate, install] — **in·au′gu·ra′tion** *n.* — **in·au′gu·ra′tor** *n.*

Inauguration Day The day (January 20th) on which the inauguration of the President of the United States takes place.

in·aus·pi·cious (in′ô·spish′əs)　*adj.* Not auspicious; ill-omened; unfavorable. — **in′aus·pi′cious·ly** *adv.* — **in′aus·pi′cious·ness** *n.*

in·board (in′bôrd′, -bōrd′)　*adj. & adv.*　**1.** *Naut.* **a** Inside the hull. **b** Toward the center line of a vessel.　**2.** *Aeron.* Inward from the tip of an airfoil; close to the fuselage.

in·born (in′bôrn′)　*adj.* Implanted by nature; existing from birth; natural; inherent.

in·bound (in′bound′)　*adj.* Approaching a destination.

in·bred (in′bred′; *for def. 2, also* in′bred′)　*adj.*　**1.** Inborn; innate.　**2.** Produced by inbreeding; also, bred in-and-in.

in·breed (in′brēd′, in′brēd′)　*v.t.* **·bred, ·breed·ing** To breed by continual mating of closely related stock.

In·ca (ing′kə)　*n.* A member of a group of Quechuan Indian tribes dominant in Peru at the time of the Spanish conquest.　[< Sp. < Quechua *ynca* royal prince]

in·cal·cu·la·ble (in·kal′kyə·lə·bəl)　*adj.*　**1.** Incapable of being calculated.　**2.** Unpredictable. — **in·cal′cu·la·bil′i·ty** *n.* — **in·cal′cu·la·bly** *adv.*

in cam·er·a (in kam′ər·ə)　In closed or secret session; privately.　[< L, in a room]

In·can (ing′kən)　*adj.* Of or pertaining to the Incas, their culture, or their empire. — *n.*　**1.** An Inca.　**2.** The language of the Incas; Quechua.

in·can·desce (in′kən·des′)　*v.t. & v.i.* **·desced, ·desc·ing** To be or become, or cause to become, luminous with heat.

in·can·des·cent (in′kən·des′ənt)　*adj.*　**1.** Luminous or glowing with intense heat.　**2.** Shining with intense brilliance. — **in′can·des′cence, in′can·des′cen·cy** *n.* — **in′can·des′cent·ly** *adv.*

incandescent lamp   A lamp having a filament that is heated to incandescence by an electric current.

in·can·ta·tion (in/kan·tā/shən) *n.* **1.** The uttering or intoning of words or syllables supposed to produce magical results. **2.** The magic words or formula so uttered. [< F < L *incantare* to make an incantation]

in·ca·pa·ble (in·kā/pə·bəl) *adj.* **1.** Lacking in natural ability, power, or capacity; incompetent. **2.** *Law* Not legally qualified. **— incapable of 1.** Lacking the necessary ability or fitness for. **2.** Of such a nature or condition as not to allow or admit of: *incapable of* deceit. **3.** A totally incompetent person. **— in·ca/pa·bil/i·ty, in·ca/pa·ble·ness** *n.* **— in·ca/pa·bly** *adv.*

in·ca·pac·i·tate (in/kə·pas/ə·tāt) *v.t.* **·tat·ed, ·tat·ing 1.** To disable, as for normal physical activity. **2.** *Law* To deprive of legal capacity; disqualify. **— in/ca·pac/i·ta/tion** *n.*

in·ca·pac·i·ty (in/kə·pas/ə·tē) *n., pl.* **·ties 1.** Lack of ability, power, or fitness; disability. **2.** *Law* A condition or circumstance that legally disqualifies.

in·cap·su·late (in·kap/sə·lāt, -syoō-) *v.t.* **·lat·ed, ·lat·ing** To enclose as in a capsule.

in·car·cer·ate (*v.* in·kär/sə·rāt; *adj.* in·kär/sər·it, -sə·rāt) *v.t.* **·at·ed, ·at·ing 1.** To put in prison; imprison. **2.** To confine; enclose. **— adj.** Imprisoned. [< Med.L < L *in-* in + *carcer* jail] **— in·car/cer·a/tion** *n.* **— in·car/cer·a/tor** *n.*

in·car·na·dine (in·kär/nə·dīn, -dīn) *adj.* **1.** Flesh-colored; pale red; pink. **2.** Blood-red; crimson. **— n.** An incarnadine color. **— v.t. ·dined, ·din·ing** To color deep red or flesh-color. [< F < Ital. *incarnato* flesh-colored]

in·car·nate (*adj.* in·kär/nit; *v.* in·kär/nāt) *adj.* **1.** Embodied in flesh, esp. in human form: a fiend *incarnate.* **2.** Personified; exemplified: cruelty *incarnate.* **— v.t. ·nat·ed, ·nat·ing 1.** To give bodily form to. **2.** To invest with concrete shape or form. [< LL < L *in-* in + *caro, carnis* flesh]

in·car·na·tion (in/kär·nā/shən) *n.* **1.** The assumption of bodily form, esp. human form. **2.** *Often cap.* The assumption by Jesus Christ of the human form and condition. **3.** The bodily form assumed by a deity. **4.** A person, animal, or thing in which some ideal or quality is incarnated.

in·case (in·kās/) *v.t.* **·cased, ·cas·ing** To enclose in or as in a case: also spelled *encase.* **— in·case/ment** *n.*

in·cau·tion (in·kô/shən) *n.* Lack of caution; carelessness.

in·cau·tious (in·kô/shəs) *adj.* Lacking in caution; heedless; imprudent. **— in·cau/tious·ly** *adv.* **— in·cau/tious·ness** *n.*

in·cen·di·ar·y (in·sen/dē·er/ē) *adj.* **1.** Of or pertaining to the malicious burning of property. **2.** Inciting to riot, rebellion, etc.; inflammatory. **3.** Capable of generating intense heat. **— n., pl. ·ar·ies 1.** One who maliciously sets fire to property. **2.** One who stirs up mob violence, etc. **3.** An incendiary bomb. [< L *incendere* to set on fire] **— in·cen/di·a·rism** (-ə·riz·əm) *n.*

incendiary bomb   A bomb designed to start a fire.

in·cense¹ (in·sens/) *v.t.* **·censed, ·cens·ing** To inflame with anger; enrage. [< OF < L *incendere* to set on fire]

in·cense² (in/sens) *n.* **1.** An aromatic substance that gives off an agreeable odor when burned. **2.** The odor or smoke produced in burning such a substance. **3.** Any pleasant fragrance or aroma. **— v. ·censed, ·cens·ing v.t. 1.** To perfume with incense. **2.** To burn incense to. **— v.i. 3.** To burn incense. [< OF < L *incendere* to set on fire]

in·cen·tive (in·sen/tiv) *n.* That which incites, or tends to incite, to action; motivating force. **— adj.** Serving to incite to action. [< L *in-* on + *canere* to sing]

in·cep·tion (in·sep/shən) *n.* Beginning, as of an undertaking; start. [< L *incipere* to begin]

in·cep·tive (in·sep/tiv) *adj.* **1.** Beginning; incipient; initial. **2.** *Gram.* Denoting the beginning of an action, as certain verbs. **— n.** *Gram.* An inceptive word or construction.

in·cer·ti·tude (in·sûr/tə·tōōd, -tyōōd) *n.* **1.** Uncertainty; doubtfulness; indecisiveness. **2.** Insecurity.

in·ces·sant (in·ses/ənt) *adj.* Continuing without interruption; never ceasing. [< LL < L *in-* not + *cessare* to cease] **— in·ces/san·cy** *n.* **— in·ces/sant·ly** *adv.*

in·cest (in/sest) *n.* Sexual intercourse between persons so closely related that marriage between them is forbidden by law or taboo. [< L *in-* not + *castus* chaste]

in·ces·tu·ous (in·ses/chōō·əs) *adj.* **1.** Guilty of incest. **2.** Involving incest. **— in·ces/tu·ous·ly** *adv.*

inch (inch) *n.* **1.** A measure of length equal to the twelfth part of a foot: symbol ". Abbr. *in.* See table front of book. **2.** *Meteorol.* **a** The amount of rainfall or snowfall capable of covering a level surface to the depth of one inch. **b** A unit of atmospheric pressure expressed by an inch of the mercury column of a barometer. **3.** A very small distance, quantity, or degree. **— every inch** In every way; completely. **— v.t. & v.i.** To move or advance by inches or small degrees. [OE < L *uncia* the twelfth part, inch, ounce]

inch·meal (inch/mēl/) *adv.* Inch by inch.

in·cho·ate (in·kō/it) *adj.* **1.** In an early or rudimentary stage. **2.** Lacking order, form, coherence, etc. [< L *in-cohare* to begin] **— in·cho/ate·ly** *adv.* **— in·cho/ate·ness** *n.*

in·cho·a·tive (in·kō/ə·tiv) *adj.* **1.** *Gram.* Inceptive. **2.** *Rare* Inchoate. **— n.** *Gram.* An inceptive.

inch·worm (inch/wûrm/) *n.* A measuring worm.

in·ci·dence (in/sə·dəns) *n.* **1.** The degree of occurrence or effect: a high *incidence* of illiteracy. **2.** The act or manner of falling on, impinging upon, or affecting something.

in·ci·dent (in/sə·dənt) *n.* **1.** A distinct event or piece of action. **2.** A minor episode or event. **— adj. 1.** Naturally or usu. appertaining or attending: with *to*: the dangers *incident* to travel. **2.** Attached as a subsidiary. **3.** Falling or striking: *incident* rays of light. [< F < L *in-* on + *cadere* to fall]

in·ci·den·tal (in/sə·den/təl) *adj.* **1.** Occurring in the course of something. **2.** Naturally or usually attending: with *to*: problems *incidental* to adolescence. **3.** Minor; secondary: *incidental* expenses. **— n. 1.** An incidental circumstance or event. **2.** *pl.* Minor or casual expenses or items.

in·ci·den·tal·ly (in/sə·den/təl·ē; *for def. 2, also* in/sə·dent/lē) *adv.* **1.** As a subordinate, casual, or chance occurrence along with something else: The book *incidentally* contains some valuable references. **2.** By the by; by the way.

in·cin·er·ate (in·sin/ə·rāt) *v.t.* **·at·ed, ·at·ing** To consume with fire; reduce to ashes; cremate. [< Med.L < *in-* in + *cinis, cineris* ashes] **— in·cin/er·a/tion** *n.*

in·cin·er·a·tor (in·sin/ə·rā/tər) *n.* An apparatus for burning refuse or for cremating.

in·cip·i·ent (in·sip/ē·ənt) *adj.* Coming into existence; just beginning to appear. [< L *incipere* to begin] **— in·cip/i·ence, in·cip/i·en·cy** *n.* **— in·cip/i·ent·ly** *adv.*

in·cise (in·sīz/) *v.t.* **·cised, ·cis·ing 1.** To cut into, or cut marks upon, with a sharp instrument. **2.** To engrave; carve. [< OF < L *in-* in + *caedere* to cut] **— in·cised/** *adj.*

in·ci·sion (in·sizh/ən) *n.* **1.** The act of incising. **2.** A cut; gash. **3.** *Surg.* A cut made in soft tissue. **4.** Incisive quality; acuteness. [< OF < L *incisio, -onis*]

in·ci·sive (in·sī/siv) *adj.* **1.** Sharp; keen; penetrating: an *incisive* mind. **2.** Cutting; biting; sarcastic. [< Med.L *incisivus*] **— in·ci/sive·ly** *adv.* **— in·ci/sive·ness** *n.*

in·ci·sor (in·sī/zər) *n.* A front tooth adapted for cutting; in man, one of eight such teeth, four in each jaw. For illus. see TOOTH. [< NL]

in·cite (in·sīt/) *v.t.* **·cit·ed, ·cit·ing** To spur to action; urge on; instigate. [< OF < L < *in-* thoroughly + *citare* to rouse] **— in·ci/ta·tion** *n.* **— in·cite/ment** *n.* **— in·cit/er** *n.*

in·ci·vil·i·ty (in/sə·vil/ə·tē) *n., pl.* **·ties 1.** The state or quality of being uncivil; discourtesy. **2.** An uncivil or rude act.

in·clem·ent (in·klem/ənt) *adj.* **1.** Of the weather, severe; stormy. **2.** Without mercy; harsh. [< L *inclemens, -entis*] **— in·clem/en·cy** (-ən·sē) *n.* **— in·clem/ent·ly** *adv.*

in·cli·na·tion (in/klə·nā/shən) *n.* **1.** A personal leaning or bent; liking. **2.** A tendency toward a state or condition; trend. **3.** An activity, state, etc., toward which one is inclined. **4.** The act of inclining, or the state of being inclined. **5.** Deviation or degree of deviation from the vertical or horizontal; slope. **6.** A sloping surface. **7.** *Geom.* The angle formed between two intersecting lines, planes, etc. **— in/cli·na/tion·al, in·cli·na·to·ry** (in·klī/nə·tôr/ē) *adj.*

in·cline (*v.* in·klīn/; *n.* in/klīn, in·klīn/) *v.* **·clined, ·clin·ing v.i. 1.** To diverge from the horizontal or vertical; slant; slope. **2.** To have a bent or preference; be disposed. **3.** To tend in some quality or degree: purple *inclining* toward blue. **4.** To bend the head or body, as in courtesy; bow. **— v.t. 5.** To cause to bend, lean, or slope. **6.** To impart a tendency or leaning to (a person); dispose; influence. **7.** To bow or nod, as the head. **— n.** An inclined plane or surface; gradient; slope. [< OF < L < *in-* on + *clinare* to lean] **— in·clin/a·ble** *adj.* **— in·clin/er** *n.*

in·clined (in·klīnd/) *adj.* **1.** Having a tendency or inclination; disposed. **2.** Sloping; bent. **3.** Bending or intersecting so as to form an angle with another line, plane, etc.

inclined plane   A plane forming any but a right angle with a horizontal plane.

in·cli·nom·e·ter (in/klə·nom/ə·tər) *n.* An instrument for measuring the attitude or tilt of an aircraft, ship, etc., with relation to the horizontal.

in·close (in·klōz/), **in·clo·sure** (in·klō/zhər) See ENCLOSE, etc.

in·clude (in·klōōd/) *v.t.* **·clud·ed, ·clud·ing 1.** To have as a component part or parts; comprise; contain. **2.** To place in a general category, group, etc.; consider in a reckoning. **3.** To have or involve as a subordinate part, quality, etc.; imply. [< L < *in-* in + *claudere* to shut] **— in·clud/a·ble** or **in·clud/i·ble** *adj.*

in·clu·sion (in·klōō/zhən) *n.* **1.** The act of including, or the state of being included. **2.** That which is included.

in·clu·sive (in·klōō/siv) *adj.* **1.** Including: with *of*. **2.** Including the limits specified: from 1959 to 1964 *inclusive*. **3.** Comprehensive: an *inclusive* report. [< Med.L *inclusivus*] **— in·clu/sive·ly** *adv.* **— in·clu/sive·ness** *n.*

in·cog·ni·to (in·kog/nə·tō, in/kog·nē/tō) *adj. & adv.* Under an assumed name or identity, esp. so as to avoid recognition or attention; in disguise. **— n., pl. ·tos** (-tōz) **1.** The state of being incognito. **2.** The name or disguise assumed by one who is incognito. **3.** One who takes on an assumed name or identity. [< Ital. < L < *in-* not + *cognitus*, pp. of *cognoscere* to know] **—in·cog′ni·ta** (-tə) *n. & adj. fem.*

in·cog·ni·zant (in·kog′nə·zənt) *adj.* Not cognizant; unaware; with *of.* **—in·cog′ni·zance** *n.*

in·co·her·ence (in′kō·hir′əns) *n.* **1.** The state of being incoherent. **2.** That which is incoherent. Also **in′co·her′en·cy.**

in·co·her·ent (in′kō·hir′ənt) *adj.* **1.** Lacking in logical connection; confused: an *incoherent* speech. **2.** Unable to think clearly or express oneself logically. **3.** Consisting of parts or ingredients that do not stick together; loose: an *incoherent* mass. **4.** Lacking in agreement or harmony; disorganized. **—in′co·her′ent·ly** *adv.* **—in′co·her′ent·ness** *n.*

in·com·bus·ti·ble (in′kəm·bus′tə·bəl) *adj.* Incapable of being burned; not flammable. **—** *n.* An incombustible substance or material. **—in′com·bus′ti·bil′i·ty, in′com·bus′ti·ble·ness** *n.* **—in′com·bus′ti·bly** *adv.*

in·come (in′kum) *n.* Money, or sometimes its equivalent, received periodically by an individual, a corporation, etc., in return for labor or services rendered, or from property, etc.

income tax A tax levied on annual income over a specified amount and with certain legally permitted deductions.

in·com·ing (in′kum′ing) *adj.* Coming in or about to come in: *incoming* profits. **—** *n.* The act of coming in.

in·com·men·su·ra·ble (in′kə·men′shər·ə·bəl, -sər·ə-) *adj.* **1.** Lacking a common measure or standard of comparison. **2.** *Math.* Not expressible in terms of a common factor or divisor. **3.** Greatly out of proportion; not in accordance: conclusions *incommensurable* with the facts. **—** *n.* That which is incommensurable. **—in′com·men′su·ra·bil′i·ty, in′com·men′su·ra·ble·ness** *n.* **—in′com·men′su·ra·bly** *adv.*

in·com·men·su·rate (in′kə·men′shər·it) *adj.* **1.** Inadequate; disproportionate: a salary *incommensurate* with the position. **2.** Incommensurable. **—in′com·men′su·rate·ly** *adv.* **—in′com·men′su·rate·ness** *n.*

in·com·mode (in′kə·mōd′) *v.t.* **·mod·ed, ·mod·ing** To cause inconvenience to; disturb; bother. [< MF < L < *in-* not + *commodus* convenient]

in·com·mo·di·ous (in′kə·mō′dē·əs) *adj.* **1.** Uncomfortably small; cramped. **2.** Causing discomfort; inconvenient. **—in′com·mo′di·ous·ly** *adv.* **—in′com·mo′di·ous·ness** *n.*

in·com·mu·ni·ca·ble (in′kə·myōō′ni·kə·bəl) *adj.* Incapable of being communicated. **—in′com·mu′ni·ca·bil′i·ty** *n.*

in·com·mu·ni·ca·do (in′kə·myōō′nə·kä′dō) *adj. & adv.* Confined without means of communication. [< Sp., < L *in-* not + *communicare* to share]

in·com·mu·ni·ca·tive (in′kə·myōō′nə·kā′tiv, -kə·tiv) *adj.* Not communicative; taciturn; reserved. **—in′com·mu′ni·ca′tive·ly** *adv.* **—in′com·mu′ni·ca·tive·ness** *n.*

in·com·pa·ra·ble (in·kom′pər·ə·bəl) *adj.* **1.** Incapable of being equaled or surpassed; matchless. **2.** Lacking in qualities or characteristics that can be compared. **—in·com′pa·ra·bil′i·ty, in·com′pa·ra·ble·ness** *n.* **—in·com′pa·ra·bly** *adv.*

in·com·pat·i·ble (in′kəm·pat′ə·bəl) *adj.* **1.** Incapable of coexisting harmoniously. **2.** Disagreeing in nature; conflicting. **3.** Incapable of being held or occupied by one person at the same time, as more than one rank or office. **4.** *Med.* Having a harmful or undesirable effect when combined or used together. **—** *n.pl.* Incompatible persons, drugs, etc. **—in′com·pat′i·bil′i·ty** *n.* **—in′com·pat′i·ble·ness** *n.* **—in′·com·pat′i·bly** *adv.*

in·com·pe·tent (in·kom′pə·tənt) *adj.* **1.** Lacking in ability or skill; inadequate to the task; unfit. **2.** Reflecting a lack of ability or skill. **3.** *Law* Not legally qualified. **—** *n.* One who is incompetent. [< F < L *incompetentem*] **—in·com′pe·tence, in·com′pe·ten·cy** *n.* **—in·com′pe·tent·ly** *adv.*

in·com·plete (in′kəm·plēt′) *adj.* **1.** Not having all essential elements or parts; unfinished. **2.** Not fully developed; defective; imperfect: *incomplete* growth. **—in′com·plete′ly** *adv.* **—in′com·plete′ness, in′com·ple′tion** *n.*

in·com·pre·hen·si·ble (in′kom·pri·hen′sə·bəl, in·kom′-) *adj.* **1.** Incapable of being understood; unintelligible. **2.** *Archaic* Boundless. **—in′com·pre·hen′si·bil′i·ty, in′com·pre·hen′si·ble·ness** *n.* **—in′com·pre·hen′si·bly** *adv.*

in·com·pre·hen·sion (in′kom·pri·hen′shən, in·kom′-) *n.* Lack of understanding.

in·com·pre·hen·sive (in′kom·pri·hen′siv, in·kom′-) *adj.* Not comprehensive; limited in scope.

in·com·press·i·ble (in′kəm·pres′ə·bəl) *adj.* Incapable of being compressed. **—in′com·press′i·bil′i·ty** *n.*

in·con·ceiv·a·ble (in′kən·sē′və·bəl) *adj.* Incapable of being conceived by the mind; unbelievable. **—in′con·ceiv′a·bil′i·ty, in′con·ceiv′a·ble·ness** *n.* **—in′con·ceiv′a·bly** *adv.*

in·con·clu·sive (in′kən·klōō′siv) *adj.* **1.** Not leading to an ultimate conclusion; indeterminate; indecisive: *inconclusive* evidence. **2.** Not achieving a definite result; ineffective. **—in′con·clu′sive·ly** *adv.* **—in′con·clu′sive·ness** *n.*

in·con·gru·i·ty (in′kong·grōō′ə·tē, in′kən-) *n. pl.* **·ties 1.** The state or quality of being incongruous; unsuitableness; inappropriateness. **2.** That which is incongruous.

in·con·gru·ous (in·kong′grōō·əs) *adj.* **1.** Not suitable; inappropriate. **2.** Not corresponding or conforming; at odds: with *with* or *to.* **3.** Consisting of elements or qualities not properly belonging together. [< L < *in-* not + *congruus* agreeing] **—in·con′gru·ous·ly** *adv.* **—in·con′gru·ous·ness** *n.*

in·con·se·quent (in·kon′sə·kwənt) *adj.* **1.** Not following from the premises; contrary to logical inference. **2.** Not proceeding according to the usual course; irrelevant; disconnected. **3.** Illogical in thought or action; eccentric. **—in·con′se·quence** *n.* **—in·con′se·quent·ly** *adv.*

in·con·se·quen·tial (in·kon′sə·kwen′shəl, in·kon′-) *adj.* **1.** Having little or no consequence; unimportant; trivial. **2.** Inconsequent. **—** *n.* A thing of no importance. **—in·con′se·quen′ti·al′i·ty** (-kwen′shē·al′ə·tē), **in′con·se·quen′tial·ness** *n.* **—in·con′se·quen′tial·ly** *adv.*

in·con·sid·er·a·ble (in′kən·sid′ər·ə·bəl) *adj.* **1.** Small in quantity, size, or value. **2.** Not worth considering; trivial. **—in′con·sid′er·a·ble·ness** *n.* **—in′con·sid′er·a·bly** *adv.*

in·con·sid·er·ate (in′kən·sid′ər·it) *adj.* **1.** Lacking in concern for the rights or needs of others; thoughtless. **2.** Not carefully considered or thought out. **—in′con·sid′er·ate·ly** *adv.* **—in′con·sid′er·ate·ness, in′con·sid·er·a′tion** *n.*

in·con·sis·ten·cy (in′kən·sis′tən·sē) *n. pl.* **·cies 1.** The quality of being inconsistent. **2.** Something that is inconsistent. Also **in′con·sis′tence.**

in·con·sis·tent (in′kən·sis′tənt) *adj.* **1.** Lacking in agreement or compatibility; inconsonant; at variance. **2.** Containing contradictory elements or parts. **3.** Lacking uniformity in behavior or thought; erratic; changeable. **—in′·con·sis′tent·ly** *adv.*

in·con·sol·a·ble (in′kən·sō′lə·bəl) *adj.* Not to be consoled; disconsolate; dejected. **—in′con·sol′a·bil′i·ty, in′con·sol′a·ble·ness** *n.* **—in′con·sol′a·bly** *adv.*

in·con·so·nant (in·kon′sə·nənt) *adj.* Not consonant; not in accord. **—in·con′so·nance** *n.* **—in·con′so·nant·ly** *adv.*

in·con·spic·u·ous (in′kən·spik′yōō·əs) *adj.* **1.** Not conspicuous; not prominent or striking. **2.** Not attracting attention to oneself; shrinking from or not meriting notice. **—in′con·spic′u·ous·ly** *adv.* **—in′con·spic′u·ous·ness** *n.*

in·con·stant (in·kon′stənt) *adj.* Not constant; variable; fickle. **—** *n.* One who or that which is inconstant. **—in·con′stan·cy** *n.* **—in·con′stant·ly** *adv.*

in·con·test·a·ble (in′kən·tes′tə·bəl) *adj.* Not admitting of question; unassailable: *incontestable* evidence. [< F] **—in′con·test′a·bil′i·ty, in′con·test′a·ble·ness** *n.* **—in′con·test′a·bly** *adv.*

in·con·ti·nence (in·kon′tə·nəns) *n.* **1.** The quality or condition of being incontinent. **2.** An instance of incontinence. Also **in·con′ti·nen·cy.**

in·con·ti·nent (in·kon′tə·nənt) *adj.* **1.** Exercising little control or restraint, esp. in sexual desires. **2.** Incapable of keeping back: often with *of.* **3.** Unrestrained; unchecked: an *incontinent* flow of abuse. **—in·con′ti·nent·ly** *adv.*

in·con·trol·la·ble (in′kən·trō′lə·bəl) *adj.* Incapable of being controlled; uncontrollable. **—in′con·trol′la·bly** *adv.*

in·con·tro·vert·i·ble (in′kon·trə·vûr′tə·bəl) *adj.* Not admitting of controversy; undeniable. **—in′con·tro·vert′i·bil′i·ty, in′con·tro·vert′i·ble·ness** *n.* **—in′con·tro·vert′i·bly** *adv.*

in·con·ven·ience (in′kən·vēn′yəns) *n.* **1.** The state or quality of being inconvenient. **2.** Something that is inconvenient. **—** *v.t.* **·ienced, ·ienc·ing** To cause inconvenience to.

in·con·ven·ient (in′kən·vēn′yənt) *adj.* Causing or lending itself to discomfort and difficulty; troublesome; awkward. **—in′con·ven′ient·ly** *adv.*

in·con·ver·sant (in·kon′vər·sənt, in′kən·vûr′sənt) *adj.* Not conversant or familiar: with *in* or *with.*

in·con·vert·i·ble (in′kən·vûr′tə·bəl) *adj.* Incapable of being changed, exchanged, or converted; esp., of paper money, not exchangeable for specie. **—in′con·vert′i·bil′i·ty, in′con·vert′i·ble·ness** *n.* **—in′con·vert′i·bly** *adv.*

in·con·vin·ci·ble (in′kən·vin′sə·bəl) *adj.* Not to be convinced; not convincible. **—in′con·vin′ci·bil′i·ty, in′con·vin′ci·ble·ness** *n.* **—in′con·vin′ci·bly** *adv.*

in·co·or·di·nate (in′kō·ôr′də·nit, -nāt) *adj.* Not coordinated. Also **in′co·or′di·nat′ed** (-nā′tid).

in·cor·po·rate (*v.* in·kôr′pə·rāt; *adj.* in·kôr′pə·rit) *v.* **·rat·ed, ·rat·ing** *v.i.* **1.** To form a legal corporation or other association capable of acting as an individual. **2.** To become incorporated. **—** *v.t.* **3.** To take in or include as part of a whole. **4.** To add or inject (an ingredient, certain elements, etc.). **5.** To form (persons, groups, etc.) into a legal corporation or other association. **6.** To combine or merge into a whole. **— Syn.** See ENROLL, MIX, UNITE. **—** *adj.* **1.** Joined or combined into a single unit or whole; closely blended. **2.** Legally incorporated.

[< LL < *in-* in + *corporare* to form into a body] —in·cor′po·ra′tive *n.* —in·cor′po·ra′tor *n.*

in·cor·po·rat·ed (in·kôr′pə·rā′tid) *adj.* 1. Forming one body or whole; combined. 2. Organized into a legal corporation. Abbr. (def. 2) *inc., incor., incorp.*

in·cor·po·ra·tion (in·kôr·pôr′ā′shən) *n.* 1. The act or process of incorporating. 2. A corporation.

in·cor·po·re·al (in′kôr·pôr′ē·əl, -pō′rē-) *adj.* 1. Not consisting of matter; insubstantial. 2. Of or pertaining to nonmaterial things; spiritual. 3. *Law* Having no material existence, but regarded as existing by the law: *incorporeal* rights. [< L < *in-* not + *corpus, -oris* body] —in′cor·po′·re·al′i·ty (-al′ə·tē) *n.* —in′cor·po′re·al·ly *adv.*

in·cor·rect (in′kə·rekt′) *adj.* 1. Inaccurate or untrue as to fact or usage; wrong. 2. Not proper or fitting; unsuitable: *incorrect* behavior. 3. Not conforming to known or accepted standards; faulty: an *incorrect* idea. [< L *incorrectus*] —in′cor·rect′ly *adv.* —in′cor·rect′ness *n.*

in·cor·ri·gi·ble (in·kôr′ə·jə·bəl, -kor′-) *adj.* 1. Incapable of being reformed or chastened. 2. Firmly implanted; ineradicable, as a bad habit. 3. Incapable of being corrected or amended. — *n.* One who is incorrigible. —in·cor′ri·gi·bil′i·ty, in·cor′ri·gi·ble·ness *n.* —in·cor′ri·gi·bly *adv.*

in·cor·rupt (in′kə·rupt′) *adj.* 1. Not morally corrupt; esp., not susceptible to bribery; honest; upright. 2. Not marred by decay or spoilage; untainted; fresh. 3. Free from errors or alterations, as language, a literary text, etc. Also **in′cor·rupt′ed.** —in′cor·rupt′ly *adv.* —in′cor·rupt′ness *n.*

in·cor·rupt·i·ble (in′kə·rup′tə·bəl) *adj.* 1. Not accessible to bribery; steadfastly honest. 2. Incapable of corruption; not subject to decay or spoilage. —in′cor·rupt′i·bil′i·ty, in′cor·rupt′i·ble·ness *n.* —in′cor·rupt′i·bly *adv.*

in·crease (*v.* in·krēs′, *n.* in′krēs) *v.* ·creased, ·creas·ing *v.i.* 1. To become greater, as in amount, size, degree, etc.; grow. 2. To grow in number, esp. by reproduction; multiply. — *v.t.* 3. To make greater, as in amount, size, degree, etc.; augment; enlarge. — *n.* 1. A growing or becoming greater, as in size, quantity, etc. 2. The amount of growth or augmentation; that which is added; increment. [< OF < L *in-* in + *crescere* to grow] —in·creas′a·ble *adj.* —in·creas′er *n.* —in·creas′ing·ly *adv.*
  — **Syn.** (verb) augment, enlarge, extend, multiply.

in·cred·i·ble (in·kred′ə·bəl) *adj.* 1. Not credible; impossible to believe; unbelievable. —in·cred′i·bil′i·ty, in·cred′i·ble·ness *n.* —in·cred′i·bly *adv.* 2. Amazing; wonderful.

in·cre·du·li·ty (in′krə·dōō′lə·tē, -dyōō′-) *n.* The quality or state of being incredulous; disbelief; skepticism.

in·cred·u·lous (in·krej′ə·ləs) *adj.* 1. Not willing or not disposed to believe; skeptical. 2. Characterized by or showing disbelief. [< L < *in-* not + *credulus* < *credere* to believe] —in·cred′u·lous·ly *adv.* —in·cred′u·lous·ness *n.*

in·cre·ment (in′krə·mənt) *n.* 1. A quantity added to another quantity. 2. The act of increasing; enlargement. [< L *increscere* to increase] —in′cre·men′tal *adj.*

in·crim·i·nate (in·krim′ə·nāt) *v.t.* ·nat·ed, ·nat·ing 1. To imply the wrongdoing or guilt of (a person, etc.). 2. To charge with a crime or fault. — **Syn.** See ACCUSE. [< Med.L < *in-* in + *criminare* to accuse one of a crime] —in·crim′i·na′tion *n.* —in·crim′i·na·to·ry (-nə·tôr′ē) *adj.*

in·crust (in·krust′) *v.t.* 1. To cover with or as with a crust or hard coating; form a crust on. 2. To decorate lavishly, as with jewels. Also spelled *encrust.* [< OF < L < *in-* on + *crustare* to form a crust] —in′crus·ta′tion *n.*

in·cu·bate (in′kyə·bāt, ing′-) *v.* ·bat·ed, ·bat·ing *v.t.* 1. To sit upon (eggs) in order to hatch them; brood. 2. To hatch (eggs) in this manner or by artificial heat. 3. To maintain under conditions favoring optimum growth or development, as bacterial cultures. — *v.i.* 4. To sit on eggs; brood. 5. To undergo incubation. [< L < *in-* on + *cubare* to lie] —in′cu·ba′tive *adj.*

in·cu·ba·tion (in′kyə·bā′shən, ing′-) *n.* 1. The act of incubating, or the state of being incubated. 2. *Med.* The period between the time of exposure to an infectious disease and the appearance of the symptoms. [< L *incubatio, -onis*]

in·cu·ba·tor (in′kyə·bā′tər, ing′-) *n.* 1. An apparatus kept at a uniform warmth for artificial hatching of eggs. 2. *Bacteriol.* A device for the artificial development of microorganisms. 3. An apparatus for keeping warm a prematurely born baby. [< L, a hatcher]

in·cu·bus (in′kyə·bəs, ing′-) *n.* *pl.* ·bus·es or ·bi (-bī) 1. Anything that tends to oppress or discourage. 2. A nightmare. 3. In folklore, a male demon that has sexual intercourse with sleeping women. [< Med.L < LL, nightmare < L *incubare* to lie on]

in·cul·cate (in·kul′kāt, in′kul-) *v.t.* ·cat·ed, ·cat·ing To impress upon the mind by frequent repetition or forceful admonition; instill. [< L < *in-* on + *calcare* to tread] —in′cul·ca′tion *n.* —in′cul·ca′tor *n.*

in·cul·pate (in·kul′pāt, in′kul-) *v.t.* ·pat·ed, ·pat·ing To involve in an accusation; incriminate. [< Med.L < *in-* in + *culpa* fault] —in′cul·pa′tion *n.*

in·cum·ben·cy (in·kum′bən·sē) *n. pl.* ·cies 1. The state or quality of being incumbent. 2. That which is incumbent. 3. The holding of an office or the period in which it is held.

in·cum·bent (in·kum′bənt) *adj.* 1. Resting upon one as a moral obligation, or as necessary under the circumstances; obligatory. 2. Resting, leaning, or weighing wholly or partly upon something. — *n.* One who holds an office or performs official duties. [< L < *in-* on + *cubare* to lie] —in·cum′bent·ly *adv.*

in·cum·ber (in·kum′bər), in·cum·brance (in·kum′brəns), etc. See ENCUMBER, etc.

in·cu·nab·u·la (in′kyōō·nab′yə·lə) *n. pl. of* in·cu·nab·u·lum (-ləm) 1. Specimens of early European printing from movable type; esp., books printed before A.D. 1500. 2. The earliest stages of development; beginnings. [< L < *in-* in + *cunabula,* dim. of *cunae* cradle] —in′cu·nab′u·lar *adj.*

in·cur (in·kûr′) *v.t.* ·curred, ·cur·ring To become subject to (unpleasant consequences); bring on oneself. [< L < *in-* in + *currere* to run] —in·cur′rence *n.*

in·cur·a·ble (in·kyōōr′ə·bəl) *adj.* Not curable or remediable. — *n.* One suffering from an incurable disease. —in·cur′a·bil′i·ty, in·cur′a·ble·ness *n.* —in·cur′a·bly *adv.*

in·cur·sion (in·kûr′zhən, -shən) *n.* 1. A hostile, often sudden entrance into a territory; an invasion; raid. 2. A running in or running against; encroachment. [< L < *in-* + *currere* to run] —in·cur′sive *adj.*

in·curve (*v.* in·kûrv′; *n.* in′kûrv) *v.i. & v.t.* To curve inward. — *n.* In baseball, a pitch that curves toward the batter.

in·cus (ing′kəs) *n.* *pl.* in·cu·des (in·kyōō′dēz) *Anat.* The anvil-shaped central bone of the group of three bones in the middle ear of mammals: also called *anvil.* [< L, anvil]

in·debt·ed (in·det′id) *adj.* 1. Legally obligated to pay for value received; in debt. 2. Morally obligated to acknowledge benefits or favors. [< OF < *en-* in + *dette* debt]

in·debt·ed·ness (in·det′id·nis) *n.* 1. The state of being indebted. 2. The amount of one's debts.

in·de·cen·cy (in·dē′sən·sē) *n.* *pl.* ·cies 1. The quality or condition of being indecent. 2. An indecent act, speech, etc.

in·de·cent (in·dē′sənt) *adj.* 1. Offensive to one's moral sense or modesty; immodest. 2. Contrary to propriety or good taste; indelicate; vulgar. —in·de′cent·ly *adv.*

in·de·ci·pher·a·ble (in′di·sī′fər·ə·bəl) *adj.* Not decipherable; unreadable. —in′de·ci′pher·a·bil′i·ty *n.*

in·de·ci·sion (in′di·sizh′ən) *n.* Inability to make decisions.

in·de·ci·sive (in′di·sī′siv) *adj.* 1. Not bringing about a definite conclusion, solution, etc. 2. Incapable of making decisions. —in′de·ci′sive·ly *adv.* —in′de·ci′sive·ness *n.*

in·dec·o·rous (in·dek′ər·əs, in′di·kôr′əs) *adj.* Not decorous; unseemly. —in·dec′o·rous·ly *adv.* —in·dec′o·rous·ness *n.*

in·de·cor·um (in′di·kôr′əm, -kō′rəm) *n.* Lack of propriety.

in·deed (in·dēd′) *adv.* In fact; in truth: used to emphasize an affirmation, to mark a qualifying word or clause, or to denote a concession. — *interj.* Is that true?

in·de·fat·i·ga·ble (in′də·fat′ə·gə·bəl) *adj.* Not yielding readily to fatigue; tireless; unflagging. [< MF < L < *in-* not + *de-,* intens. + *fatigare* to tire out] —in′de·fat′i·ga·bil′i·ty, in′de·fat′i·ga·ble·ness *n.* —in′de·fat′i·ga·bly *adv.*

in·de·fea·si·ble (in′də·fē′zə·bəl) *adj.* Incapable of being annulled, set aside, or made void. —in′de·feas′i·bil′i·ty *n.* —in′de·fea′si·bly *adv.*

in·de·fen·si·ble (in′di·fen′sə·bəl) *adj.* 1. Incapable of being justified. 2. Incapable of being defended. —in′de·fen′si·bil′i·ty, in′de·fen′si·ble·ness *n.* —in′de·fen′si·bly *adv.*

in·de·fin·a·ble (in′di·fī′nə·bəl) *adj.* Incapable of being defined or described; vague; subtle; ineffable. —in′de·fin′a·ble·ness *n.* —in′de·fin′a·bly *adv.*

in·def·i·nite (in·def′ə·nit) *adj.* 1. Not definite or precise; vague. 2. Without a fixed number; indeterminate. 3. *Gram.* Not definite or determining, as the *indefinite* article. —in·def′i·nite·ly *adv.* —in·def′i·nite·ness *n.*

indefinite pronoun *Gram.* A pronoun that represents an object indefinitely or generally, as *each, none, another.*

in·de·his·cent (in′də·his′ənt) *adj.* *Bot.* Not opening spontaneously when ripe, as certain grains and fruits. —in′de·his′cence *n.*

in·del·i·ble (in·del′ə·bəl) *adj.* 1. Incapable of being blotted out or effaced. 2. Leaving a mark or stain not easily erased. [< L < *in-* not + *delibilis* perishable] —in·del′i·bil′i·ty, in·del′i·ble·ness *n.* —in·del′i·bly *adv.*

in·del·i·ca·cy (in·del′ə·kə·sē) *n.* *pl.* ·cies 1. The quality of being indelicate; coarseness. 2. An indelicate thing, act, etc.

in·del·i·cate (in·del′ə·kit) *adj.* 1. Lacking or offending a sense of delicacy or good taste; crude. 2. Unconcerned about the feelings of others; tactless. —in·del′i·cate·ly *adv.*

in·dem·ni·fy (in·dem′nə·fī) *v.t.* ·fied, ·fy·ing 1. To compensate (a person, etc.) for loss or damage sustained. 2. To make good (a loss). 3. To give security against future losses or punishment. [< L *indemnis* unhurt (< *in-* not + *damnum* harm) + -FY] —in·dem′ni·fi·ca′tion *n.*

in·dem·ni·ty (in·dem′nə·tē) *n.* *pl.* ·ties 1. That which is given as compensation for a loss or for damage. 2. An agree-

ment to remunerate another for loss or protect him against liability. **3.** Exemption from penalties or liabilities.
in·dent¹ (in·dent′; *for n., also* in′dent) *v.t.* **1.** To set in from the margin, as the first line of a paragraph. **2.** To cut or mark the edge or border of with toothlike notches; serrate. **3.** To indenture, as an apprentice. — *v.i.* **4.** To be notched or cut; form a recess. **5.** To set a line, paragraph, etc., in from the margin. — *n.* **1.** A cut or notch on the edge of a thing. **2.** A space before the first word of a paragraph; indention. [< OF < Med.L < *in-* in + *dentis* tooth]
in·dent² (in·dent′; *for n., also* in′dent) *v.t.* **1.** To press or push in so as to form a dent or depression; impress. **2.** To make a dent in. — *n.* A dent or depression; indentation.
in·den·ta·tion (in′den·tā′shən) *n.* **1.** A notch or series of notches in an edge or border. **2.** The act of notching, or the condition of being notched. **3.** A dent. **4.** An indention.
in·den·tion (in·den′shən) *n.* **1.** *Printing* **a** The setting in of a line or body of type at the left side. **b** The space thus left blank. **2.** A dent; indentation.
in·den·ture (in·den′chər) *n.* **1.** *Law* A deed or contract made between two or more parties. **2.** *Usu. pl.* Such a contract between master and apprentice. **3.** The act of indenting, or the state of being indented. **4.** Indentation. — *v.t.* **·tured, ·tur·ing** **1.** To bind by indenture. **2.** To make an indentation in.
in·de·pen·dence (in′di·pen′dəns) *n.* **1.** The quality or condition of being independent. **2.** Sufficient income for one's needs; a competence.
Independence Day July 4, a holiday in the U.S. commemorating the adoption of the Declaration of Independence, July 4, 1776.
in·de·pen·den·cy (in′di·pen′dən·sē) *n. pl.* **·cies** **1.** Independence. **2.** An independent state or territory.
in·de·pen·dent (in′di·pen′dənt) *adj.* **1.** Not subject to the authority of another; autonomous. **2.** Not dependent on or part of some larger group, system, etc.: an *independent* union. **3.** Not an adherent of a party or faction: an *independent* voter. **4.** Not influenced or guided by others. **5.** Acting so as to manage one's own affairs; self-reliant. **6.** Self-supporting. **7.** Having a competence; also, constituting a competence: *independent* means. **8.** *Gram.* Constituting or capable of constituting a complete sentence: said of clauses. — *n.* One who or that which is independent, esp. one not an adherent of a party or faction. — **in′de·pen′dent·ly** *adv.*
independent clause *Gram.* A clause constituting or capable of constituting a sentence.
in·de·scrib·a·ble (in′di·skrī′bə·bəl) *adj.* Incapable of being described; esp., too complex, extreme, etc., to be described; ineffable. — **in′de·scrib′a·bil′i·ty, in′de·scrib′a·ble·ness** *n.* — **in′de·scrib′a·bly** *adv.*
in·de·struc·ti·ble (in′di·struk′tə·bəl) *adj.* Incapable of being destroyed; very tough and durable. — **in′de·struc′ti·bil′i·ty, in′de·struc′ti·ble·ness** *n.* — **in′de·struc′ti·bly** *adv.*
in·de·ter·mi·na·ble (in′di·tûr′mi·nə·bəl) *adj.* **1.** Incapable of being ascertained. **2.** Incapable of being decided. — **in′· de·ter′mi·na·ble·ness** *n.* — **in′de·ter′mi·na·bly** *adv.*
in·de·ter·mi·na·cy (in′di·tûr′mə·nə·sē) *n.* The state or quality of being indeterminate.
in·de·ter·mi·nate (in′di·tûr′mə·nit) *adj.* **1.** Not definite in extent, amount, or nature. **2.** Not clear or precise; vague. **3.** Not decided; unsettled. **4.** Not fixed; inconclusive. — **in′de·ter′mi·nate·ly** *adv.* — **in′de·ter′mi·nate·ness** *n.*
in·de·ter·mi·na·tion (in′di·tûr′mə·nā′shən) *n.* **1.** Lack of determination. **2.** The condition of being indeterminate.
in·dex (in′deks) *n. pl.* **·dex·es** *or* **·di·ces** (-də·sēz′) **1.** An alphabetical list, as at the end of a book or similar publication, of topics, names, etc., and the numbers of the pages where they occur in the text. **2.** A descriptive list, as of items in a collection. **3.** Anything that serves as an indicator, as the needle on the dial of scientific instruments. **4.** The index finger. **5.** Anything that indicates or gives evidence of; sign: Alertness is an *index* of intelligence. **6.** *Printing* A mark (☞) used to direct attention to a specific word, passage, etc.: also called *fist, hand.* **7.** A numerical expression of the ratio between one dimension or magnitude and another: the cephalic *index.* **8.** *Math.* A subscript or superscript. — *v.t.* **1.** To provide with an index, as a book. **2.** To enter in an index, as a subject. **3.** To indicate. [< L, forefinger, sign] — **in′dex·er** *n.* — **in·dex′i·cal** *adj.*
In·dex (in′deks) *n.* A list of books the Roman Catholic Church forbids its members to read except with special permission.
index finger The finger next to the thumb: also called *forefinger.*
index number *Stat.* A figure indicating the relative changes in costs, production, etc., at a given period of time, as compared with those of a specific period in the past represented by the number 100 and used as an arbitrary base.
India ink **1.** A black pigment composed of lampblack

mixed with a binding material and molded in sticks or cakes. **2.** A liquid ink made from this pigment.
In·di·an (in′dē·ən) *n.* **1.** A citizen of the Republic of India. **2.** A native of India or the East Indies. **3.** A member of the aboriginal races of North America, South America, and the West Indies. **4.** Loosely, any of the languages of the American Indian. — *adj.* **1.** Of or pertaining to India and the East Indies and their peoples. **2.** Of or pertaining to the aborigines of North America, South America, and the West Indies. **3.** Made by or used by Indians. [< L *India*]
Indian club A bottle-shaped wooden club used in gymnastics, usu. in pairs.
Indian corn Corn (def. 1).
Indian file Single file.
Indian giver *U.S. Informal* One who gives a present and then wants it back.
Indian hemp **1.** Hemp (def. 1). **2.** A perennial American herb of the dogbane family.
Indian meal Cornmeal.
Indian pipe An herb with one pipe-shaped white flower.
Indian pudding A pudding of cornmeal, milk, and molasses.
Indian summer A period of mild, warm weather occurring in late autumn, often after the first frost.
India paper A thin, yellowish, absorbent printing paper, used in taking the finest proofs from engraved plates.
India rubber Rubber (def. 1).
In·dic (in′dik) *adj.* Pertaining to India, its peoples, languages, and culture; Indian. — *n.* A branch of the Indo-Iranian subfamily of Indo-European languages, including Sanskrit, Hindi, etc.
in·di·cate (in′də·kāt) *v.t.* **·cat·ed, ·cat·ing** **1.** To be or give a sign of; signify. **2.** To direct attention to; point out. **3.** To express or make known. [< L < *in-* in + *dicare* to point out, proclaim]
in·di·ca·tion (in′də·kā′shən) *n.* **1.** The act of indicating. **2.** That which indicates; sign. **3.** A degree or quantity shown on a measuring instrument.
in·dic·a·tive (in·dik′ə·tiv) *adj.* **1.** Suggestive of; pointing out. **2.** *Gram.* Pertaining to or denoting a mood in which an act or condition is stated or questioned as an actual fact. — *n. Gram.* **a** The indicative mood. **b** A verb in this mood. — **in·dic′a·tive·ly** *adv.*
in·di·ca·tor (in′də·kā′tər) *n.* **1.** One who or that which indicates or points out. **2.** An instrument or device that measures or shows position; also, its pointer or needle.
in·di·ces (in′də·sēz) Alternative plural of INDEX.
in·dict (in·dīt′) *v.t. Law* **1.** To prefer an indictment against. **2.** To charge with a crime or offense. — *Syn.* See ACCUSE. [< AF *enditer* to make known, inform; later infl. in form by Med.L *dictare* to accuse] — **in·dict′a·ble** *adj.* — **in·dict·ee** (in·dī·tē′) *n.* — **in·dict′er, in·dict′or** *n.*
in·dict·ment (in·dīt′mənt) *n.* **1.** The act of indicting, or the state of being indicted. **2.** *Law* A formal written charge of crime, presented by a grand jury on oath to the court, as the basis for trial of the accused. [< AF *enditement*]
in·dif·fer·ence (in·dif′ər·əns) *n.* **1.** The state or quality of being indifferent. **2.** Unimportance; insignificance. **3.** Mediocrity. — *Syn.* See APATHY. Also **in·dif′fer·en·cy.**
in·dif·fer·ent (in·dif′ər·ənt) *adj.* **1.** Having no interest or feeling; unconcerned. **2.** Lacking in distinction; mediocre. **3.** Only average in size, amount, etc. **4.** Having little importance or significance. **5.** Showing no preference; unbiased. **6.** Not active; inert: said of chemical compounds, electrical or magnetic properties, etc. [< OF < L *indifferens*] — **in·dif′fer·ent·ly** *adv.*
in·di·gence (in′də·jəns) *n.* The state of being indigent; poverty. Also **in′di·gen·cy.**
in·dig·e·nous (in·dij′ə·nəs) *adj.* **1.** Originating or occurring naturally in the place specified; native. **2.** Innate; inherent. — *Syn.* See NATIVE. Also **in·dig′e·nal.** [< LL < L *indu-* within + *gignere* to be born] — **in·dig′e·nous·ly** *adv.*
in·di·gent (in′də·jənt) *adj.* Lacking means of subsistence; poor. [< F < L < *indu-* within + *egere* to need] — **in′di·gent·ly** *adv.*
in·di·gest·i·ble (in′də·jes′tə·bəl) *adj.* Difficult to digest; not digestible. — **in′di·gest′i·bil′i·ty, in′di·gest′i·ble·ness** *n.* — **in′di·gest′i·bly** *adv.*
in·di·ges·tion (in′də·jes′chən) *n.* Difficulty in digesting food. [< F]
in·dig·nant (in·dig′nənt) *adj.* Feeling or showing indignation. — **in·dig′nant·ly** *adv.*
in·dig·na·tion (in′dig·nā′shən) *n.* Anger aroused by injustice or baseness. [< OF < L < *in-* not + *dignus* worthy]
in·dig·ni·ty (in·dig′nə·tē) *n. pl.* **·ties** An act that humiliates, degrades, or injures self-respect.
in·di·go (in′də·gō) *n. pl.* **·gos** *or* **·goes** **1.** A blue coloring substance obtained from certain plants of the pea family or

made synthetically. **2.** A deep violet blue. Also **indigo blue.**
3. A plant yielding a blue dyestuff. — *adj.* Deep violet blue.
[< Sp. < L < Gk. *Indikon (pharmakon)* Indian (dye)]

in·di·go bunting   A finch of North America, the male of which is a brilliant indigo. Also **indigo bird.**

in·di·rect (in/də·rekt/) *adj.* **1.** Not following a direct line or path. **2.** Not straightforward or open; underhand. **3.** Not coming as an immediate result: *indirect* benefits. **4.** Not aimed directly: an *indirect* proof. **5.** Not proceeding through a direct line of succession, as an inheritance. **6.** *Gram.* Not expressed in the exact words of the source: an *indirect* question. — **in/di·rect/ly** *adv.* — **in/di·rect/ness** *n.*

in·di·rec·tion (in/də·rek/shən) *n.* **1.** Indirect method or practice. **2.** Dishonest dealing; deceit.

indirect lighting   Lighting that is reflected, as from a white ceiling, or diffused to give a minimum of glare and shadow.

indirect tax   A tax, the burden of which is ultimately passed on to another, as in the form of higher market prices.

in·dis·cern·i·ble (in/di·sûr/nə·bəl, -zûr/-) *adj.* Incapable of being discerned; imperceptible. — **in/dis·cern/i·bly** *adv.*

in·dis·cov·er·a·ble (in/dis·kuv/ər·ə·bəl) *adj.* Incapable of being discovered. — **in/dis·cov/er·a·bil/i·ty** *n.*

in·dis·creet (in/dis·krēt/) *adj.* Lacking discretion; imprudent. — **in/dis·creet/ly** *adv.* — **in/dis·creet/ness** *n.*

in·dis·crete (in/dis·krēt/) *adj.* Not discrete; not separated; unified. — **in/dis·crete/ly** *adv.* — **in/dis·crete/ness** *n.*

in·dis·cre·tion (in/dis·kresh/ən) *n.* **1.** The state or quality of being indiscreet. **2.** An indiscreet act, speech, etc.

in·dis·crim·i·nate (in/dis·krim/ə·nit) *adj.* **1.** Showing no discrimination; not perceiving differences. **2.** Confused; chaotic. — **in/dis·crim/i·nate·ly** *adv.* — **in/dis·crim/i·nate·ness** *n.* — **in/dis·crim/i·nat/ing** *adj.* — **in/dis·crim/i·na/tion** *n.* — **in/dis·crim/i·na/tive** *adj.*

in·dis·pen·sa·ble (in/dis·pen/sə·bəl) *adj.* **1.** Not to be dispensed with; essential. **2.** Not to be ignored: an *indispensable* responsibility. — *n.* An indispensable person or thing. — **in/dis·pen/sa·bil/i·ty, in/dis·pen/sa·ble·ness** *n.* — **in/dis·pen/sa·bly** *adv.*

in·dis·pose (in/dis·pōz/) *v.t.* **·posed, ·pos·ing** **1.** To render unwilling; disincline. **2.** To render unfit. **3.** To make slightly ill or ailing. — **in/dis·po·si/tion** *n.*

in·dis·posed (in/dis·pōzd/) *adj.* **1.** Mildly ill; unwell. **2.** Disinclined; not willing. — **Syn.** See SICK[1].

in·dis·put·a·ble (in/dis·pyōō/tə·bəl, in·dis/pyŏŏ·tə·bəl) *adj.* Incapable of being disputed. — **in/dis·put/a·bil/i·ty, in/dis·put/a·ble·ness** *n.* — **in/dis·put/a·bly** *adv.*

in·dis·sol·u·ble (in/di·sol/yə·bəl, in·dis/ə·lyə·bəl) *adj.* **1.** Incapable of being dissolved, separated into its elements, or destroyed. **2.** Binding; extremely durable. — **in/dis·sol/u·bil/i·ty, in/dis·sol/u·ble·ness** *n.* — **in/dis·sol/u·bly** *adv.*

in·dis·tinct (in/dis·tingkt/) *adj.* **1.** Not clearly perceptible; blurred. **2.** Not readily distinguishable from something else; confused. **3.** Not producing clear impressions, images, etc. — **in/dis·tinct/ly** *adv.* — **in/dis·tinct/ness** *n.*

in·dis·tin·guish·a·ble (in/di·sting/gwish·ə·bəl) *adj.* Incapable of being perceived. — **in/dis·tin/guish·a·ble·ness, in/dis·tin/guish·a·bil/i·ty** *n.* — **in/dis·tin/guish·a·bly** *adv.*

in·di·um (in/dē·əm) *n.* A soft, malleable, silver-white metallic element (symbol In). See ELEMENT. [< NL < *indicum* indigo; with ref. to its spectrum color]

in·di·vid·u·al (in/də·vij/ōō·əl) *adj.* **1.** Existing as a unit; single. **2.** Separate, as distinguished from others of the same kind. **3.** Pertaining to or meant for a single person, animal, etc.: an *individual* serving. **4.** Differentiated from others by distinctive characteristics. — *n.* **1.** A single human being as distinct from others. **2.** A person. [< Med.L < L < *in-* not + *dividere* to divide] — **in/di·vid/u·al·ly** *adv.*

in·di·vid·u·al·ism (in/də·vij/ōō·əl·iz/əm) *n.* **1.** Personal independence in action, thought, etc. **2.** The state of being individual. **3.** Self-interest; egoism. **4.** The social theory that emphasizes the importance of the individual.

in·di·vid·u·al·ist (in/də·vij/ōō·əl·ist) *n.* **1.** One who is independent in character, action, thought, etc. **2.** One who advocates individualism. — **in/di·vid/u·al·is/tic** *adj.*

in·di·vid·u·al·i·ty (in/də·vij/ōō·al/ə·tē) *n.* *pl.* **·ties** **1.** A quality or trait that distinguishes one person or thing from others. **2.** Strikingly distinctive character or personality. **3.** The state of having separate, independent existence.

in·di·vid·u·al·ize (in/də·vij/ōō·əl·īz/) *v.t.* **·ized, ·iz·ing** **1.** To make individual; distinguish. **2.** To treat, mention, or consider individually. — **in/di·vid/u·al·i·za/tion** *n.*

in·di·vis·i·ble (in/də·viz/ə·bəl) *adj.* Not divisible; incapable of being divided. — *n.* Something that is indivisible. — **in/di·vis/i·ble·ness, in/di·vis/i·bil/i·ty** *n.* — **in/di·vis/i·bly** *adv.*

In·do- *combining form* Indian. [< Gk. *Indos* Indian]

In·do-chi·nese (in/dō·chī·nēz/, -nēs/) *adj.* Of or pertaining to Indochina, its inhabitants, or their language. — *n.* *pl.* **·nese** **1.** A member of one of the Mongoloid peoples of Indochina. **2.** The Sino-Tibetan family of languages.

in·doc·tri·nate (in·dok/trə·nāt) *v.t.* **·nat·ed, ·nat·ing** To

instruct in doctrines; esp., to teach partisan or sectarian dogmas. [< Med.L *in-* into + *doctrinare* to teach < L *docere* to teach] — **in·doc/tri·na/tion** *n.*

In·do-Eu·ro·pe·an (in/dō-yŏŏr/ə·pē/ən) *n.* The largest family of languages in the world, comprising most of the languages of Europe and many languages of India and SW Asia, and including as subfamilies Hellenic, Italic, Celtic, Germanic, Indo-Iranian, Armenian, Albanian, and Balto-Slavic. — *adj.* Of or pertaining to the Indo-European family of languages, or to the peoples speaking them.

In·do-I·ra·ni·an (in/dō·ī·rā/nē·ən) *n.* A subfamily of the Indo-European family of languages, consisting of Indic and Iranian branches. — *adj.* Of or pertaining to this subfamily.

in·do·lent (in/də·lənt) *adj.* Averse to exertion or work; lazy. [< LL *in-* not + *dolere* to feel pain] — **in/do·lence** *n.* — **in/do·lent·ly** *adv.*

in·dom·i·ta·ble (in·dom/i·tə·bəl) *adj.* Not easily defeated or subdued. [< LL < L < *in-* not + *domitare* to tame] — **in·dom/i·ta·bly** *adv.*

In·do·ne·sian (in/dō·nē/zhən, -shən) *n.* **1.** A citizen of Indonesia. **2.** One of a small, light-brown-skinned people native throughout the Malay Peninsula and Archipelago, the Philippines, Sumatra, Java, etc. **3.** The languages spoken by these people, including Malay, Tagalog, etc.: also called *Malayan.* — *adj.* Of or pertaining to Indonesia, its peoples, or their languages.

in·door (in/dôr/, -dōr/) *adj.* **1.** Pertaining to or meant for the interior of a house or building. **2.** Located or performed within a house or building. [Earlier *within-door*]

in·doors (in/dôrz/, -dōrz/) *adv.* Inside or toward the inside of a building.

in·dorse (in·dôrs/), etc. See ENDORSE, etc.

in·du·bi·ta·ble (in·dōō/bə·tə·bəl, -dyōō/-) *adj.* Not to be doubted. — **in·du/bi·ta·ble·ness** *n.* — **in·du/bi·ta·bly** *adv.*

in·duce (in·dōōs/, -dyōōs/) *v.t.* **·duced, ·duc·ing** **1.** To cause to act, speak, etc., by convincing or other influence; persuade. **2.** To bring on; cause. **3.** To reach, as a conclusion, by inductive reasoning. [< L *in-* in + *ducere* to lead] — **in·duc/er** *n.* — **in·duc/i·ble** *adj.*

in·duce·ment (in·dōōs/mənt, -dyōōs/-) *n.* **1.** That which induces; incentive. **2.** The act of inducing.

in·duct (in·dukt/) *v.t.* **1.** *U.S.* To bring (a draftee) into military service. **2.** To install formally in an office, etc. **3.** To initiate in knowledge, experience, etc.: with *to.* **4.** *Physics* To produce by induction. [See INDUCE.]

in·duc·tance (in·duk/təns) *n.* *Electr.* The ability of a circuit to produce induction.

in·duc·tee (in·duk·tē/) *n.* One inducted or being inducted.

in·duc·tile (in·duk/təl, -til) *adj.* **1.** Not ductile; not malleable. **2.** Not submissive; unyielding. — **in·duc·til/i·ty** *n.*

in·duc·tion (in·duk/shən) *n.* **1.** The act of inducting, or state of being inducted. **2.** The act of inducing or causing. **3.** The bringing forward of separate facts as evidence in order to prove a general statement; also, the resulting statement. **4.** *Electr.* The production of magnetization or electrification in a body by the mere proximity of a magnetic field or electric charge, or of an electric current in a conductor by the variation of the magnetic field in its vicinity. [< OF < L *inductio, -onis*] — **in·duc/tion·al** *adj.*

induction coil   *Electr.* A device that changes a low steady voltage into a high intermittent alternating voltage by electromagnetic induction.

in·duc·tive (in·duk/tiv) *adj.* **1.** Pertaining to or resulting from induction: *inductive* reasoning. **2.** *Electr.* Produced by or causing induction or inductance. [< LL *inductivus*] — **in·duc/tive·ly** *adv.* — **in·duc/tive·ness** *n.*

in·duc·tiv·i·ty (in/duk·tiv/ə·tē) *n.* *Electr.* **1.** Specific capability for induction. **2.** Inductance.

in·duc·tor (in·duk/tər) *n.* **1.** One who or that which inducts. **2.** *Electr.* Any part of an electrical apparatus that acts inductively upon another.

in·dulge (in·dulj/) *v.* **·dulged, ·dulg·ing** *v.t.* **1.** To yield to or gratify, as desires or whims. **2.** To yield to or gratify the desires, whims, etc., of; humor. **3.** In business, to grant more time (to someone) for payment of a bill. — *v.i.* **4.** To gratify one's own desire. — **Syn.** See PAMPER. [< L *indulgere* to be kind to] — **in·dulg/er** *n.*

in·dul·gence (in·dul/jəns) *n.* **1.** The act of indulging, or state of being indulgent. **2.** That which is indulged in. **3.** Something granted as a favor. **4.** In business, permission to defer paying a bill, etc. **5.** In the Roman Catholic Church, remission of temporal punishment due for a sin after it has been forgiven through sacramental absolution. Also **in·dul/gen·cy.** [< OF < L *indulgentia*]

in·dul·gent (in·dul/jənt) *adj.* Prone to indulge; lenient. — **in·dul/gent·ly** *adv.*

in·du·rate (*v.* in/dōō·rāt, -dyōō-; *adj.* in/dōō·rit, -dyōō-) *v.t. & v.i.* **·rat·ed, ·rat·ing** **1.** To make or become hard or unfeeling. **2.** To make or become hardy. — *adj.* Hard; unfeeling: also **in/du·rat/ed.** [< L *indurare* to make hard] — **in/du·ra/tion** *n.* — **in/du·ra/tive** *adj.*

in·dus·tri·al (in·dus′trē·əl) *adj.* **1.** Of, characteristic of, or resulting from industry. **2.** Engaged in industry. **3.** Having many industries: an *industrial* area. **4.** Intended for use in industry. **5.** Relating to, affecting, or benefiting workers in industry. —*n.* *pl.* Stocks or securities of industrial enterprises. [< F *industriel* and Med.L *industrialis*] — **in·dus′tri·al·ly** *adv.*

industrial arts The technical skills used in industry, esp. as subjects of study in schools.

industrial design. The esthetic and practical design of industrial products; also, the study of such design.

industrial engineer An engineer who supervises production in factories, lays out machinery, etc.

in·dus·tri·al·ism (in·dus′trē·əl·iz′əm) *n.* An economic system based chiefly on large-scale industries and production of goods rather than on agriculture, foreign trade, etc.

in·dus·tri·al·ist (in·dus′trē·əl·ist) *n.* A person important in the ownership or management of industry.

in·dus·tri·al·ize (in·dus′trē·əl·īz′) *v.t.* **·ized**, **·iz·ing** **1.** To establish large-scale industries in. **2.** To make or form into an industry. — **in·dus′tri·al·i·za′tion** *n.*

industrial relations The relations between management and employees in industrial concerns.

industrial union A labor union to which all workers in a particular industry may belong: also called *vertical union*.

in·dus·tri·ous (in·dus′trē·əs) *adj.* Hard-working. — **in·dus′tri·ous·ly** *adv.* — **in·dus′tri·ous·ness** *n.*

in·dus·try (in′dəs·trē) *n.* *pl.* **·tries** **1.** Any specific branch of production or manufacture. **2.** Manufacturing and productive interests collectively. **3.** Diligent and regular application to work or tasks. [< MF < L *industrius* diligent]

in·dwell (in′dwel′) *v.* **·dwelt**, **·dwell·ing** *v.t.* **1.** To dwell in. —*v.i.* **2.** To dwell. — **in′dwell′er** *n.* — **in′dwell′ing** *n.*

-ine¹ *suffix* Like; pertaining to; of the nature of: *marine*, *canine*. [< L *-inus*, adj. suffix]

-ine² *suffix* **1.** *Chem.* **a** Used in the names of halogens: *bromine*. **b** Used to indicate an alkaloid or basic substance: *morphine*. **c** Var. of **-IN**. **2.** Used in names of commercial products: *brilliantine*. [Special use of **-INE¹**]

-ine³ *suffix* **1.** Used to form feminine words, names, and titles: *heroine*. **2.** Used to form originally feminine abstract nouns: *medicine*, *doctrine*. [< F < L *-ina*, suffix of fem. nouns < Gk. *-inē*; or directly < L or < Gk.]

-ine⁴ *suffix* Like; resembling: *crystalline*. [< L < Gk. *-inos*]

in·e·bri·ate (*v.* in·ē′brē·āt; *n. & adj.* in·ē′brē·it, -āt) *v.t.* **·at·ed**, **·at·ing** **1.** To make drunk; intoxicate. **2.** To exhilarate; excite. —*n.* A habitual drunkard. —*adj.* Intoxicated. [< L < *in-* thoroughly + *ebriare* to make drunk] — **in·e′bri·at′ed** *adj.* — **in·e′bri·a′tion** *n.*

in·ed·i·ble (in·ed′ə·bəl) *adj.* Not eatable. — **in·ed′i·bil′i·ty** *n.*

in·ef·fa·ble (in·ef′ə·bəl) *adj.* **1.** Too overpowering to be expressed in words. **2.** Too lofty or sacred to be uttered. **3.** Indescribable; indefinable. [< MF < L < *in-* not + *effabilis* utterable] — **in·ef′fa·bil′i·ty, in·ef′fa·ble·ness** *n.* — **in·ef′fa·bly** *adv.*

in·ef·fec·tive (in′i·fek′tiv) *adj.* **1.** Not effective. **2.** Incompetent. — **in′ef·fec′tive·ly** *adv.* — **in′ef·fec′tive·ness** *n.*

in·ef·fec·tu·al (in′i·fek′chōō·əl) *adj.* **1.** Not effectual. **2.** Unsuccessful; fruitless. — **in′ef·fec′tu·al′i·ty, in·ef′fec′tu·al·ness** *n.* — **in′ef·fec′tu·al·ly** *adv.*

in·ef·fi·ca·cious (in·ef′ə·kā′shəs) *adj.* Not producing the effect desired or intended, as a medicine. — **in′ef·fi·ca′cious·ly** *adv.* — **in′ef·fi·ca′cious·ness** *n.*

in·ef·fi·ca·cy (in·ef′ə·kə·sē) *n.* The state of being inefficacious.

in·ef·fi·cient (in′i·fish′ənt) *adj.* **1.** Not efficient; not performing a function economically; wasteful. **2.** Incompetent. — **in′ef·fi′cien·cy** *n.* — **in′ef·fi′cient·ly** *adv.*

in·e·las·tic (in′i·las′tik) *adj.* Not elastic; inflexible; unadaptable. — **in·e·las·tic′i·ty** (in′i·las·tis′ə·tē) *n.*

in·el·e·gance (in·el′ə·gəns) *n.* **1.** The quality of being inelegant. **2.** Something inelegant. — **in·el′e·gant·ly** *adv.*

in·el·e·gan·cy (in·el′ə·gən·sē) *n.* *pl.* **·cies** Inelegance.

in·el·e·gant (in·el′ə·gənt) *adj.* **1.** Not elegant. **2.** Coarse; crude. — **in·el′e·gant·ly** *adv.*

in·el·i·gi·ble (in·el′ə·jə·bəl) *adj.* Not eligible; not qualified or suitable. —*n.* One who is not eligible. — **in·el′i·gi·bil′i·ty** *n.* — **in·el′i·gi·bly** *adv.*

in·e·luc·ta·ble (in′i·luk′tə·bəl) *adj.* Not to be escaped from or avoided; inevitable. [< L < *in-* not + *eluctabilis* resistible] — **in·e·luc′ta·bil′i·ty** *n.* — **in·e·luc′ta·bly** *adv.*

in·ept (in·ept′) *adj.* **1.** Not suitable or appropriate. **2.** Clumsy; awkward. [< L < *in-* not + *aptus* fit] — **in·ept′ly** *adv.* — **in·ept′ness** *n.*

in·ep·ti·tude (in·ep′tə·tōōd, -tyōōd) *n.* **1.** The state or quality of being inept. **2.** An inept act or remark.

in·e·qual·i·ty (in′i·kwol′ə·tē) *n.* *pl.* **·ties** **1.** The state of being unequal. **2.** An instance of this. **3.** Lack of evenness of proportion; variableness. **4.** Disparity of social position, opportunity, justice, etc. [< OF < L *inaequalitas*]

in·eq·ui·ta·ble (in·ek′wə·tə·bəl) *adj.* Not equitable; unfair. — **in·eq′ui·ta·bly** *adv.*

in·eq·ui·ty (in·ek′wə·tē) *n.* *pl.* **·ties** **1.** Lack of equity; injustice. **2.** An unfair act or course of action.

in·e·rad·i·ca·ble (in′i·rad′ə·kə·bəl) *adj.* Not eradicable; impossible to remove or root out. — **in′e·rad′i·ca·bly** *adv.*

in·e·ras·a·ble (in′i·rā′sə·bəl) *adj.* Not erasable; impossible to erase or rub out. — **in′e·ras′a·bly** *adv.*

in·ert (in·ûrt′) *adj.* **1.** Lacking independent power to move or to resist applied force. **2.** Disinclined to move or act; sluggish. **3.** *Chem.* Devoid of active properties. [< L < *in-* not + *ars* art] — **in·ert′ly** *adv.* — **in·ert′ness** *n.*

in·er·tia (in·ûr′shə) *n.* **1.** The state of being inert; inactivity. **2.** *Physics* The property of matter by virtue of which any physical body persists in its state of rest or of uniform motion until acted upon by some external force. [< L, idleness] — **in·er′tial** *adj.*

in·es·cap·a·ble (in′ə·skā′pə·bəl) *adj.* Impossible to escape; unavoidable. — **in′es·cap′a·bly** *adv.*

in·es·ti·ma·ble (in·es′tə·mə·bəl) *adj.* **1.** Not to be estimated. **2.** Having great value. — **in·es′ti·ma·bly** *adv.*

in·ev·i·ta·ble (in·ev′ə·tə·bəl) *adj.* That cannot be avoided or prevented from happening. —*n.* Something inevitable. [< L < *in-* not + *evitare* to avoid] — **in·ev′i·ta·bil′i·ty, in·ev′i·ta·ble·ness** *n.* — **in·ev′i·ta·bly** *adv.*

in·ex·act (in′ig·zakt′) *adj.* Not exact; not completely accurate or true. — **in′ex·act′ly** *adv.* — **in′ex·act′ness** *n.*

in·ex·cus·a·ble (in′ik·skyōō′zə·bəl) *adj.* Not excusable; impossible to excuse or justify. — **in′ex·cus′a·ble·ness** *n.* — **in′ex·cus′a·bly** *adv.*

in·ex·haust·i·ble (in′ig·zôs′tə·bəl) *adj.* **1.** Incapable of being exhausted or used up. **2.** Incapable of fatigue; tireless. — **in′ex·haust′i·bil′i·ty, in′ex·haust′i·ble·ness** *n.* — **in′ex·haust′i·bly** *adv.*

in·ex·o·ra·ble (in·ek′sər·ə·bəl) *adj.* **1.** Not to be moved by entreaty or persuasion; unyielding. **2.** Unalterable; relentless. [< L *inexorabilis*] — **in·ex′o·ra·bil′i·ty, in·ex′o·ra·ble·ness** *n.* — **in·ex′o·ra·bly** *adv.*

in·ex·pe·di·ent (in′ik·spē′dē·ənt) *adj.* Not expedient; unsuited to a particular purpose; inadvisable. — **in′ex·pe′di·ence, in′ex·pe′di·en·cy** *n.* — **in′ex·pe′di·ent·ly** *adv.*

in·ex·pen·sive (in′ik·spen′siv) *adj.* Not expensive; costing little. — **in′ex·pen′sive·ly** *adv.* — **in′ex·pen′sive·ness** *n.*

in·ex·pe·ri·ence (in′ik·spir′ē·əns) *n.* Lack of experience.

in·ex·pe·ri·enced (in′ik·spir′ē·ənst) *adj.* Not experienced.

in·ex·pert (in·ek′spûrt) *adj.* Not expert; unskilled; inept. — **in·ex′pert·ly** *adv.* — **in·ex′pert·ness** *n.*

in·ex·pi·a·ble (in·ek′spē·ə·bəl) *adj.* Incapable of being expiated or atoned for; unpardonable.

in·ex·pli·ca·ble (in·eks′pli·kə·bəl, in′iks·plik′ə·bəl) *adj.* Not explicable; impossible to explain. — **in·ex′pli·ca·bil′i·ty, in·ex′pli·ca·ble·ness** *n.* — **in·ex′pli·ca·bly** *adv.*

in·ex·press·i·ble (in′ik·spres′ə·bəl) *adj.* Incapable of being expressed or put into words. — **in′ex·press′i·bil′i·ty, in′ex·press′i·ble·ness** *n.* — **in′ex·press′i·bly** *adv.*

in·ex·tin·guish·a·ble (in′ik·sting′gwish·ə·bəl) *adj.* Incapable of being extinguished; unquenchable. — **in′ex·tin′guish·a·ble·ness** *n.* — **in′ex·tin′guish·a·bly** *adv.*

in ex·tre·mis (in iks·trē′mis) *Latin* At the point of death.

in·ex·tri·ca·ble (in·eks′tri·kə·bəl) *adj.* **1.** Impossible to extricate oneself from. **2.** Impossible to disentangle or undo. **3.** Too intricate to be solved. — **in·ex′tri·ca·bil′i·ty, in·ex′tri·ca·ble·ness** *n.* — **in·ex′tri·ca·bly** *adv.*

in·fal·li·ble (in·fal′ə·bəl) *adj.* **1.** Exempt from fallacy or error of judgment. **2.** Not liable to fail; sure: an *infallible* remedy. **3.** In Roman Catholic doctrine, incapable of error in matters of faith and morals. —*n.* One who or that which is infallible. — **in·fal′li·bil′i·ty** *n.* — **in·fal′li·bly** *adv.*

in·fa·mous (in′fə·məs) *adj.* **1.** Having a vile reputation. **2.** Deserving or producing infamy; odious. [< Med.L < L < *in-* not + *fama* fame] — **in′fa·mous·ly** *adv.* — **in′fa·mous·ness** *n.*

in·fa·my (in′fə·mē) *n.* *pl.* **·mies** **1.** Dishonor; disgrace. **2.** The state of being infamous. **3.** An infamous act.

in·fan·cy (in′fən·sē) *n.* *pl.* **·cies** **1.** The state or period of being an infant; babyhood. **2.** The beginnings of anything. **3.** *Law* The years before attaining the age of legal majority.

in·fant (in′fənt) *n.* **1.** A child in the earliest stages of life; baby. **2.** *Law* One who has not attained the age of legal majority, usu. 21; a minor. —*adj.* **1.** Of or typical of infancy or infants. **2.** Beginning to exist or develop. [< OF < L < *in-* not + *fari* to speak.] — **in′fant·hood** *n.*

in·fan·ta (in·fän′tə) *n.* A daughter of a Spanish or Portuguese king. [< Sp., infant (fem.)]

in·fan·te (in·fän′tā) *n.* A son, except the eldest, of a Spanish or Portuguese king. [< Sp., infant (masc.)]

in·fan·ti·cide (in-fan'tə-sīd) n. 1. The killing of an infant, esp. at birth. 2. One who has killed an infant. [< F < LL < L *infans* child + *caedere* to kill]

in·fan·tile (in'fən-til, -til) adj. 1. Of infancy or infants. 2. Like or characteristic of infancy or infants; babyish. 3. Being at the earliest stage of development. Also **in'fan·tine** (-tīn, -tin). [< LL *infantilis*]

infantile paralysis Poliomyelitis.

in·fan·til·ism (in-fan'tə-liz·em) n. Abnormal persistence of infantile mental and physical characteristics into adult life.

in·fan·try (in'fən-trē) n. pl. **·tries** Soldiers, units, or a branch of an army trained and equipped to fight on foot. [< F < Ital. < L *infans, infantis* child]

in·fan·try·man (in'fən-trē-mən) n. pl. **·men** (-mən) A soldier of the infantry.

in·fat·u·ate (v. in-fach'o͞o·āt; for adj., also in-fach'o͞o·it) v.t. **·at·ed, ·at·ing** 1. To inspire with a foolish and unreasoning love or passion. 2. To make foolish or fatuous. —adj. Infatuated. [< L *infatuare* to make a fool of] —**in·fat'u·a'tion** n.

in·fat·u·at·ed (in-fach'o͞o·ā·tid) adj. 1. Possessed by a foolish passion, esp. for another person. 2. Made fatuous. —**in·fat'u·at·ed·ly** adv.

in·fect (in-fekt') v.t. 1. To affect or infuse with disease-producing organisms, as a wound. 2. To cause (a person, etc.) to contract a communicable disease. 3. To contaminate with impurities; pollute. 4. To affect or inspire, as with attitudes or beliefs, esp. harmfully. [< L *inficere* to dip into, stain] —**in·fec'tor** or **in·fect'er** n.

in·fec·tion (in-fek'shən) n. 1. An injurious invasion of body tissue by disease-producing organisms. 2. A disease or other harmful condition resulting from an invasion by injurious organisms. 3. The communication or transference of a disease, idea, mood, etc. [< OF]

in·fec·tious (in-fek'shəs) adj. 1. Liable to produce infection. 2. Denoting diseases communicable by infection. 3. Tending to excite similar reactions: *infectious* laughter. —**in·fec'tious·ly** adv. —**in·fec'tious·ness** n.

infectious mononucleosis Pathol. An acute communicable disease marked by fever, sore throat, a swelling of the lymph nodes and an increase in mononuclear cells.

in·fec·tive (in-fek'tiv) adj. Liable to produce infection.

in·fe·lic·i·tous (in'fə-lis'ə-təs) adj. Not felicitous or suitable. —**in'fe·lic'i·tous·ly** adv. —**in'fe·lic'i·tous·ness** n.

in·fe·lic·i·ty (in'fə-lis'ə-tē) n. pl. **·ties** 1. The state of being infelicitous. 2. That which is infelicitous, as an inappropriate remark, etc. [< L *infelicitas*]

in·fer (in-fûr') v. **·ferred, ·fer·ring** v.t. 1. To derive by reasoning; conclude or accept from evidence or premises. 2. To involve or imply as a conclusion: said of facts, statements, etc. —v.i. 3. To draw an inference. [< L *in-* in + *ferre* to bring, carry] —**in·fer'a·ble** adj. —**in·fer'a·bly** adv.

◆ **infer, imply** *Infer* means to derive or conclude by reasoning: I *inferred* from the noise that you were at home. *Imply* means to suggest implicitly something that might be *inferred* by an observer: The noise *implied* that you were at home. *Infer* stresses the use of reason, whereas *imply,* the more general term, may be applied also to conclusions that are suggested or presumed.

in·fer·ence (in'fər·əns) n. 1. That which is inferred; a conclusion. 2. The act or process of inferring.

in·fer·en·tial (in'fə-ren'shəl) adj. Deducible by inference. —**in'fer·en'tial·ly** adv.

in·fer·i·or (in-fir'ē·ər) adj. 1. Lower in quality, worth, or adequacy. 2. Lower in rank or importance. 3. Mediocre; ordinary: an *inferior* wine. 4. Astron. **a** Between the earth and the sun: an *inferior* planet. **b** Below the horizon. —n. A person inferior in rank or in attainments. [< L, lower]

in·fe·ri·or·i·ty (in-fir'ē·ôr'ə·tē, -or'-) n. pl. **·ties** The state or quality of being inferior.

in·fer·nal (in-fûr'nəl) adj. 1. Of or pertaining to the mythological world of the dead, or to hell. 2. Diabolical; hellish. 3. *Informal* Damnable; hateful. [< OF < L *infernus* situated below] —**in·fer'nal·ly** adv.

in·fer·no (in-fûr'nō) n. pl. **·nos** 1. The infernal regions; hell. 2. Any place comparable to hell. [< Ital.]

in·fer·tile (in-fûr'til) adj. Not fertile or productive; sterile.

in·fest (in-fest') v.t. To overrun or occur in large numbers so as to be annoying or dangerous. [< MF *infester* or L *infestare* to assail] —**in'fes·ta'tion** n. —**in·fest'er** n.

in·fi·del (in'fi·dəl) n. 1. One who rejects all religious belief; unbeliever. 2. Among Christians, one who is not a Christian. 3. Among Moslems, one who is not a Moslem. —adj. 1. Having no religious belief. 2. Rejecting a particular faith, esp. Christianity or Islam. 3. Of or relating to infidels or unbelief. [< MF < L < *in-* not + *fidelis* faithful]

in·fi·del·i·ty (in'fi·del'ə·tē) n. pl. **·ties** 1. Lack of fidelity. 2. A disloyal act. 3. Adultery. 4. Lack of belief in a particular religion, esp. Christianity or Islam.

in·field (in'fēld') n. In baseball: **a** The space within the base lines of the field, and some adjacent space beyond the second and third base lines. **b** The infielders collectively.

in·field·er (in'fēld'ər) n. In baseball, either the first baseman, second baseman, shortstop, or third baseman, or the pitcher or catcher considered as a fielder.

in·fil·trate (in-fil'trāt, in'fil-trāt) v. **·trat·ed, ·trat·ing** v.t. 1. To gain or seek control of (an organization, etc.) by secretly occupying positions of power. 2. To cause (a liquid or gas) to pass into or through pores. 3. To filter or move through or into. —v.i. 4. To pass into or through a substance. —n. That which infiltrates. —**in'fil·tra'tion** n.

in·fi·nite (in'fə-nit) adj. 1. Having no boundaries or limits; extending without end. 2. Very numerous or great; vast. 3. All-embracing; perfect: *infinite* wisdom. 4. *Math.* Of or designating a quantity conceived as always exceeding any other quantity in value. —n. 1. That which is infinite. 2. *Math.* An infinite quantity. —**the Infinite** God. [< OF < L < *in-* not + *finitus* finite] —**in'fi·nite·ly** adv. —**in'fi·nite·ness** n.

—**Syn.** (adj.) 1. *Infinite* is applied to those things which we believe to have no bounds. *Measureless, numberless, countless,* and *innumerable* often mean merely vast in dimension or number. *Eternal* means *infinite* in time, but is also used to mean continued for a very long time.

in·fin·i·tes·i·mal (in'fin·ə·tes'ə·məl) adj. 1. Infinitely small. 2. So small as to be incalculable. —n. An infinitesimal quantity. [< NL < *infinitus* infinite + *-esimus* (after *centesimus* hundredth)] —**in'fin·i·tes'i·mal·ly** adv.

in·fin·i·tive (in-fin'ə·tiv) Gram. adj. 1. Without limitation of person or number. 2. Of or pertaining to the infinitive. —n. A verb form generally used either as the principal verb of a verb phrase, most often without *to,* or as a noun, most often with *to.* [< Med.L *infinitivus*]

in·fin·i·tude (in-fin'ə·to͞od, -tyo͞od) n. 1. The quality of being infinite or boundless. 2. An unlimited quantity.

in·fin·i·ty (in-fin'ə·tē) n. pl. **·ties** 1. The state of being infinite. 2. Something considered infinite, as space or time. 3. A very large amount or number. [< OF < L < *in-* not + *finitus* finite]

in·firm (in-fûrm') adj. 1. Feeble or weak, as from old age. 2. Lacking firmness of purpose. [< OF < L *infirmus* < *in-* not + *firmus* firm] —**in·firm'ly** adv. —**in·firm'ness** n.

in·fir·ma·ry (in-fûr'mər·ē) n. pl. **·ries** A place for the treatment of the sick, esp. in a school, etc. [< Med.L < L *infirmus* infirm, indisposed]

in·fir·mi·ty (in-fûr'mə·tē) n. pl. **·ties** 1. The state of being infirm. 2. A physical or mental defect.

in·fix (in-fiks') v.t. 1. To set firmly or insert in. 2. To implant (an idea, fact, etc.) in the mind. 3. *Gram.* To insert (an infix) within a word. —n. *Gram.* A modifying addition inserted in the body of a word. —**in·fix'ion** n.

in·flame (in-flām') v. **·flamed, ·flam·ing** v.t. 1. To set on fire; kindle. 2. To excite to violent emotion or activity. 3. To increase or make more intense, as anger, passion, etc. 4. To produce heat, swelling, and soreness in. —v.i. 5. To catch fire. 6. To become excited or aroused. 7. To become inflamed. [< OF < L < *in-* in + *flamma* flame]

in·flam·ma·ble (in-flam'ə·bəl) adj. 1. Flammable. 2. Easily excited or aroused. —n. A flammable thing or substance. —**in·flam'ma·bil'i·ty, in·flam'ma·ble·ness** n. —**in·flam'ma·bly** adv.

in·flam·ma·tion (in'flə-mā'shən) n. 1. The act of inflaming, or the state of being inflamed. 2. *Pathol.* A diseased condition characterized by redness, swelling, and pain.

in·flam·ma·to·ry (in-flam'ə·tôr'ē, -tō'rē) adj. 1. Tending to arouse excitement, anger, etc. 2. *Med.* Characterized by or causing inflammation.

in·flat·a·ble (in-flā'tə·bəl) adj. Capable of being inflated.

in·flate (in-flāt') v. **·flat·ed, ·flat·ing** v.t. 1. To cause to expand by filling with or as with gas or air. 2. To enlarge excessively; puff up: to *inflate* one's ego. 3. *Econ.* To increase (prices, credit, etc.) in excess of usual or prior levels. —v.i. 4. To become inflated. [< L < *in-* in + *flare* to blow] —**in·flat'er** or **in·flat'or** n.

in·fla·tion (in-flā'shən) n. 1. The act or process of inflating, or the state of being inflated. 2. *Econ.* An unstable rise in price levels due to an increase in currency and a mounting demand for goods. —**in·fla'tion·ar'y** adj.

in·flect (in-flekt') v.t. 1. To vary the tone or pitch of (the voice) modulate. 2. To turn from a straight or usual course; bend. 3. *Gram.* To give the inflections of (a word) by conjugating or declining. [< L < *in-* in + *flectere* to bend]

in·flec·tion (in-flek'shən) n. 1. The act of inflecting, or the state of being inflected. 2. An angle or bend. 3. Modulation of the voice. 4. *Gram.* **a** A change in form undergone by words to express grammatical and syntactical relations, as of case, number, tense, etc. The inflection of nouns, pronouns, and adjectives is called *declension;* that of verbs, *conjugation.* **b** An inflected form. —**in·flec'tion·al** adj.

in·flex·i·ble (in-flek'sə·bəl) adj. 1. Incapable of being bent; rigid. 2. Unyielding; stubborn. 3. That cannot be altered;

fixed: the *inflexible* laws of nature. [< L *inflexibilis*] — **in·flex/i·bil/i·ty, in·flex/i·ble·ness** n. — **in·flex/i·bly** adv.

in·flict (in-flikt/) v.t. 1. To deal; lay on: to *inflict* a blow. 2. To impose. [< L < *in*- on + *fligere* to strike] — **in·flict/er** or **in·flic/tor** n. — **in·flic/tive** adj.

in·flic·tion (in-flik/shən) n. 1. The act of inflicting. 2. That which is inflicted, as pain, punishment, etc.

in·flo·res·cence (in/flə·res/əns) n. 1. A flowering; flourishing. 2. *Bot.* **a** The mode of arrangement of flowers in relation to the stem or axis. **b** A cluster of flowers. **c** A single flower. [< NL < LL *inflorescere* to come into flower] — **in/flo·res/cent** adj.

in·flow (in/flō/) n. 1. The act of flowing in. 2. That which flows in.

in·flu·ence (in/flōō·əns) n. 1. The power of persons or things to produce effects on others, esp. by indirect means. 2. Power resulting from social position, wealth, etc. 3. One who or that which possesses the power to affect others. — v.t. **·enced**, **·enc·ing** 1. To produce an effect upon the actions or thought of. 2. To have an effect upon. [< OF < LL < L < *in*- in + *fluere* to flow] — **in/flu·enc·er** n.

in·flu·en·tial (in/flōō·en/shəl) adj. 1. Having or exercising influence. 2. Wielding influence. — **in/flu·en/tial·ly** adv.

in·flu·en·za (in/flōō·en/zə) n. *Pathol.* A contagious, infectious virus disease characterized by respiratory inflammation and fever: also called *flu, grip, grippe*. [< Ital., (illness due to) the influence (of the stars)]

in·flux (in/fluks/) n. 1. A flowing in, as of a fluid. 2. A continuous coming, as of people. 3. The mouth of a river. [< MF < LL *influere* to flow in]

in·fold (in-fōld/) v.t. 1. To wrap in folds. 2. To embrace. 3. To turn or fold inward. Also spelled *enfold*.

in·form (in-fôrm/) v.t. 1. To notify. 2. To give character to: with *with* or *by*. — v.i. 3. To disclose information. [< OF < L *informare* to give form to]

in·for·mal (in-fôr/məl) adj. 1. Not in the usual or prescribed form; unofficial. 2. Without formality; relaxed; casual. 3. Not requiring formal attire. 4. Characteristic of or suitable to the language of ordinary conversation or familiar writing. ◆ Informal language is widely used by educated people and is not to be confused with nonstandard usage or slang. — **in·for/mal·ly** adv.

in·for·mal·i·ty (in/fôr·mal/ə·tē) n. pl. **·ties** 1. The state of being informal. 2. An informal act or proceeding.

in·form·ant (in-fôr/mənt) n. One who gives information.

in·for·ma·tion (in/fər·mā/shən) n. 1. Knowledge acquired or derived; facts. 2. Timely knowledge; news. 3. The act of informing, or the state of being informed. 4. A service or facility for providing facts: Call *information*. [< F < L *informatio, -onis*] — **in/for·ma/tion·al** adj.

in·form·a·tive (in-fôr/mə·tiv) adj. Affording information; instructive. Also **in·form/a·to·ry** (-tôr/ē, -tō/rē).

in·formed (in-fôrmd/) adj. Having a high degree of knowledge, information, or education.

in·form·er (in-fôr/mər) n. 1. One who informs against others; stool pigeon; tattletale. 2. An informant.

infra- prefix Below; beneath; on the lower part. [< L]

in·frac·tion (in-frak/shən) n. The act of breaking or violating (a pledge, law, etc.); infringement. [< L *infractio, -onis*]

in·fran·gi·ble (in-fran/jə·bəl) adj. 1. Not breakable or capable of being broken into parts. 2. Inviolable. — **in·fran/gi·bil/i·ty, in·fran/gi·ble·ness** n. — **in·fran/gi·bly** adv.

in·fra·red (in/frə·red/) adj. *Physics* Having a wavelength greater than that of visible red light, and radiating heat.

in·fre·quent (in-frē/kwənt) adj. Present or occurring at widely separated intervals; uncommon. — **in·fre/quence, in·fre/quen·cy** n. — **in·fre/quent·ly** adv.

in·fringe (in-frinj/) v.t. fringed, fring·ing To break or disregard the terms of, as a law; violate. — **to infringe on** (or upon) To transgress or trespass on rights or privileges. [< L < *in*- in + *frangere* to break] — **in·fring/er** n.

in·fringe·ment (in-frinj/mənt) n. 1. The act of infringing. 2. Any violation of a right, privilege, regulation, etc.

in·fu·ri·ate (v. in-fyoor/ē·āt) v.t. **·at·ed, ·at·ing** To make furious or very angry; enrage. [< Med.L *infuriare* to madden] — **in·fu/ri·ate·ly** adv. — **in·fu/ri·at/ing·ly** adv.

in·fuse (in-fyooz/) v.t. **·fused, ·fus·ing** 1. To instill or inculcate, as principles. 2. To inspire; imbue: with *with*. 3. To pour in. [< L < *in*- in + *fundere* to pour] — **in·fus/er** n.

in·fus·i·ble[1] (in-fyoo/zə·bəl) adj. Incapable of or resisting fusion or melting. — **in·fus/i·bil/i·ty, in·fus/i·ble·ness** n.

in·fus·i·ble[2] (in-fyoo/zə·bəl) adj. Capable of being infused or poured in. — **in·fus/i·bil/i·ty, in·fus/i·ble·ness** n.

in·fu·sion (in-fyoo/zhən) n. 1. The act of infusing. 2. That which is infused. 3. A liquid extract obtained by soaking a substance in water. [< OF or < L *infusio, -onis*]

in·fu·so·ri·an (in/fyoo·sôr/ē·ən, -sō/rē-) n. One of a class of one-celled animals. [< NL < L *infundere* to pour into]

-ing[1] suffix 1. The act or art of doing the action expressed in the root verb: *hunting*. 2. The product or result of an action: a *painting*. 3. Material for: *flooring*. 4. That which performs the action of the root verb: a *covering*. ◆ In formal writing when the *-ing* form of the verb (see *gerund*) is modified by a noun or pronoun the modifier appears in the possessive. Thus, "We objected to *his leaving*" is preferred to "We objected to *him leaving*." [OE, *-ung, -ing*]

-ing[2] suffix Used in the present participle of verbs and in participial adjectives: He is *talking*; an *eating* apple. [ME < OE *-ende*]

-ing[3] suffix of nouns 1. One having the quality of: *sweeting*. 2. Descendant of: *Browning*. 3. Small; little. [OE]

in·gen·ious (in-jēn/yəs) adj. 1. Showing ingenuity; cleverly conceived. 2. Having inventive and adaptive ability; clever. [< MF < L < *in*- in + *gignere* to beget] — **in·gen/ious·ly** adv. — **in·gen/ious·ness** n.

in·gé·nue (an/zhə·noo/, *Fr.* añ·zhā·nü/) n. pl. **·nues** (-nooz/, *Fr.* -nü/) The role of a young girl in a play, film, etc.; also, an actress who plays such roles. [< F]

in·ge·nu·i·ty (in/jə·noo/ə·tē, -nyoo/-) n. pl. **·ties** 1. Imaginative resources; inventiveness. 2. Originality of design or execution. 3. A cleverly conceived act, device, etc.

in·gen·u·ous (in-jen/yoo·əs) adj. 1. Straightforward; candid; frank. 2. Innocent and simple; naive. [< L *ingenuus* inborn, natural < *in*- in + *genus* birth, origin] — **in·gen/u·ous·ly** adv. — **in·gen/u·ous·ness** n.

in·gest (in-jest/) v.t. To take or put (food, etc.) into the body by or as by swallowing. [< L *ingerere* < *in*- in + *gerere* to carry] — **in·ges/tion** n. — **in·ges/tive** adj.

in·glo·ri·ous (in-glôr/ē·əs, -glō/rē-) adj. Not reflecting honor or courage; disgraceful. — **in·glo/ri·ous·ly** adv.

in·go·ing (in/gō/ing) adj. Entering; going in.

in·got (ing/gət) n. A mass of cast metal from the crucible or mold. [? ME < OE *in*- in + *geotan* to pour]

in·grain (v. in·grān/) v.t. To impress firmly on the mind.

in·grained (in-grānd/) adj. 1. Worked into the inmost texture; deep-rooted. 2. Thorough; inveterate.

in·grate (in/grāt) n. An ungrateful person. [< OF < L < *in*- not + *gratus* pleasing]

in·gra·ti·ate (in-grā/shē·āt) v.t. **·at·ed, ·at·ing** To bring (oneself) deliberately into the favor or confidence of others. — **in·gra/ti·a/tion** n. — **in·gra/ti·a·to/ry** (-ə·tôr/ē, -tō/rē) adj. [< L *in*-into + *gratia* favor]

in·grat·i·tude (in-grat/ə·tood, -tyood) n. Lack of gratitude; insensibility to kindness; thanklessness.

in·gre·di·ent (in-grē/dē·ənt) n. 1. Anything that enters into the composition of a mixture. 2. A component of anything. [< F < L < *in*- in + *gradi* to walk]

in·gress (in/gres) n. 1. A going in, as into a building. Also **in·gres·sion** (in-gresh/ən). 2. A place of entrance. [< L *ingredi* to enter] — **in·gres/sive** adj.

in-group (in/groop/) n. *Sociol.* Any group with strong feelings of mutual cohesiveness and identification.

in·grow·ing (in/grō/ing) adj. 1. Growing into the flesh: an *ingrowing* hair. 2. Growing within or into.

in·grown (in/grōn/) adj. 1. Grown into the flesh, as a toenail. 2. Grown within; innate: *ingrown* vice.

in·gui·nal (ing/gwə·nəl) adj. *Anat.* Of, pertaining to, or located in the groin. [< L *inguen, -inis* groin]

inguino- combining form In or related to the groin. Also, before vowels, **inguin-**. [< L *inguen, -inis* groin]

in·hab·it (in-hab/it) v.t. To live in; occupy as a home. [< OF < L < *in*- in + *habitare* to dwell] — **in·hab/it·a·bil/i·ty** n. — **in·hab/it·a·ble** adj. — **in·hab/it·er** n. — **in·hab/i·ta/tion** n.

in·hab·i·tant (in-hab/ə·tənt) n. One who or that which dwells permanently, as distinguished from a visitor.

in·ha·la·tion (in/hə·lā/shən) n. 1. The act of inhaling. 2. That which is inhaled.

in·ha·la·tor in/hə·lā/tər) n. A device for enabling one to inhale air, medicinal vapors, anesthetics, etc.

in·hale (in-hāl/) v. **·haled, ·hal·ing** v.t. 1. To draw into the lungs, as breath, tobacco smoke, etc.; breathe in. — v.i. 2. To draw breath, tobacco smoke, etc., into the lungs. Opposed to *exhale*. [< L < *in*- in + *halare* to breathe]

in·hal·er (in-hāl/ər) n. 1. One who inhales. 2. *Med.* An inhalator. 3. A respirator.

in·har·mo·ni·ous (in/här·mō/nē·əs) adj. Lacking harmony; discordant. Also **in/har·mon/ic** (-mon/ik), **in/har·mon/i·cal**. — **in/har·mo/ni·ous·ly** adv. — **in/har·mo/ni·ous·ness** n.

in·here (in-hir/) v.i. **·hered, ·her·ing** To be a permanent or essential part of: with *in*. [< L < *in*- to + *haerere* to stick] — **in·her/en·cy** n.

in·her·ent (in-hir/ənt, -her/-) adj. Forming an essential element or quality of something. — **in·her/ent·ly** adv.

in·her·it (in-her/it) v.t. 1. To receive (property, title, etc.) by legal succession or will. 2. To derive (traits, qualities,

etc.) from one's parents or ancestors. **3.** To receive from one's predecessors. — *v.i.* **4.** To take possession of an inheritance. [< OF < LL *inheréditáre* to appoint an heir]
in·her·it·a·ble (in-her′ə-tə-bəl) *adj.* **1.** Capable of being inherited. **2.** Entitled to inherit. — **in·her′it·a·bil′i·ty, in·her′it·a·ble·ness** *n.* — **in·her′it·a·bly** *adv.*
in·her·i·tance (in-her′ə-təns) *n.* **1.** The act of inheriting. **2.** That which is legally transmissible to an heir; legacy. **3.** Derivation of qualities from one's forebears. **4.** A property, quality, etc., derived from predecessors. **5.** Hereditary right. [< OF *enheritance*]
inheritance tax A tax imposed on an inherited estate.
in·her·i·tor (in-her′ə-tər) *n.* An heir. — **in·her′i·tress** (-tris), **in·her′i·trix** (-triks) *n.fem.*
in·hib·it (in-hib′it) *v.t.* To restrain or check (an impulse, action, etc.) [< L < in- + *habere* to have, hold] — **in·hib′i·ter** or **in·hib′i·tor** *n.* — **in·hib′it·a·ble** *adj.* — **in·hib′i·tive, in·hib′i·to·ry** (-tôr′ē, -tō′rē) *adj.*
in·hi·bi·tion (in′hi-bish′ən, in′i-) *n.* **1.** A checking or restraining; esp., a self-imposed restriction on one's behavior. **2.** *Psychol.* The blocking of one impulse by another.
in·hos·pi·ta·ble (in-hos′pi-tə-bəl, in′hos-pit′ə-bəl) *adj.* **1.** Not hospitable. **2.** Not affording shelter, comfort, etc. — **in·hos·pi·ta·ble·ness** (in-hos′pi-tə-bəl·nis, in′hos-pit′-) *n.* — **in·hos·pi·ta·bly** (in-hos′pi-tə-blē, in′hos-pit′-) *adv.* — **in·hos′pi·tal′i·ty** (-tal′ə-tē) *n.*
in·hu·man (in-hyōō′mən) *adj.* **1.** Not befitting human nature; bestial. **2.** Not of the ordinary human type.
in·hu·mane (in′hyōō-mān′) *adj.* Not humane; cruel.
in·hu·man·i·ty (in′hyōō-man′ə-tē) *n.* *pl.* **·ties** **1.** Lack of human or humane qualities. **2.** A cruel act, word, etc.
in·im·i·cal (in-im′i-kəl) *adj.* **1.** Characterized by harmful opposition; antagonistic. **2.** Behaving as an enemy; hostile. [< LL < L < *in-* not + *amicus* friend] — **in·im′i·cal′i·ty** (-kal′ə-tē) *n.* — **in·im′i·cal·ly** *adv.*
in·im·i·ta·ble (in-im′ə-tə-bəl) *adj.* Matchless; unique. — **in·im′i·ta·bil′i·ty, in·im′i·ta·ble·ness** *n.* — **in·im′i·ta·bly** *adv.*
in·iq·ui·tous (in-ik′wə-təs) *adj.* Characterized by iniquity; unjust. — **in·iq′ui·tous·ly** *adv.* — **in·iq′ui·tous·ness** *n.*
in·iq·ui·ty (in-ik′wə-tē) *n.* *pl.* **·ties** **1.** Grievous violation of right or justice; wickedness. **2.** A wrongful act; sin. [< OF < L < *in-* not + *aequus* equal]
in·i·tial (in-ish′əl) *adj.* **1.** Standing at the beginning. **2.** Of or pertaining to the beginning; first. — *n.* **1.** *pl.* The first letters of one's proper name. **2.** The first letter of a word, name, etc. — *v.t.* **·tialed** or **·tialled, ·tial·ing** or **·tial·ling** To mark or sign with initials. [< L *initialis* < *initium* beginning] — **in·i′tial·ly** *adv.*
Initial Teaching Alphabet An alphabet representing the sounds of English, used in teaching children to read: also called *Augmented Roman.* Abbr. *I.T.A.*
in·i·ti·ate (in-ish′ē-āt; *for adj. & n., also* in-ish′ē-it) *v.t.* **·at·ed, ·at·ing** **1.** To begin; commence; originate. **2.** To admit to membership in an organization, fraternity, cult, etc. **3.** To instruct in fundamentals. — *adj.* Initiated. — *n.* One who has been ritually admitted to an organization, cult, etc. [< L *initiare* to begin] — **in·i′ti·a·tor** *n.*
in·i·ti·a·tion (in-ish′ē-ā′shən) *n.* **1.** The act of initiating, or the state of being initiated. **2.** The rites admitting one to some position, society, knowledge, etc.
in·i·ti·a·tive (in-ish′ē-ə-tiv, -ē-ā′tiv, -ish′ə-tiv) *n.* **1.** The power or right to take the first step or the next step in some action. **2.** The action of commencing or originating. **3.** The spirit needed to originate action. **4.** In government: **a** The right or power to propose legislative measures. **b** The process by which the electorate acts to originate legislation. — **on one's own initiative** Without instruction or compulsion; freely. — *adj.* **1.** Of or pertaining to initiation. **2.** Serving to initiate. [< MF] — **in·i′ti·a·tive·ly** *adv.*
in·ject (in-jekt′) *v.t.* **1.** To drive (a fluid, drug, etc.) into a bodily cavity, blood vessel, etc. by means of a syringe, needle, etc. **2.** To introduce (some new element): with *into.* **3.** To throw in or introduce abruptly (a comment, etc.). [< L < *in-* in + *jacere* to throw] — **in·jec′tion** *n.*
in·ju·di·cious (in′jōō-dish′əs) *adj.* Not judicious; imprudent. — **in′ju·di′cious·ly** *adv.* — **in′ju·di′cious·ness** *n.*
in·junc·tion (in-jungk′shən) *n.* **1.** The act of enjoining. **2.** An authoritative order. **3.** *Law* A judicial order requiring the party to do or refrain from some specified action. [< LL *injungere* to join to, enjoin] — **in·junc′tive** *adj.*
in·jure (in′jər) *v.t.* **·jured, ·jur·ing** **1.** To harm, damage, or impair, especially physically; hurt. **2.** To wrong or offend. [Back formation < INJURY] — **in′jur·er** *n.*
in·ju·ri·ous (in-jŏŏr′ē-əs) *adj.* **1.** Causing damage or hurt; harmful. **2.** Slanderous; abusive. — **in·ju′ri·ous·ly** *adv.* — **in·ju′ri·ous·ness** *n.*
in·ju·ry (in′jər-ē) *n.* *pl.* **·ries** **1.** Harm, damage, or grievous distress inflicted or suffered. **2.** A particular instance of such harm. [< OF < L < *in-* not + *jus, juris* right]
in·jus·tice (in-jus′tis) *n.* **1.** The fact or quality of being unjust. **2.** An unjust act; wrong. [< OF < L *injustus* unjust]

ink (ingk) *n.* **1.** Any of various colored substances used in a fluid or viscous consistency for writing, drawing, and printing. **2.** The dark fluid ejected by cuttlefish, etc. — *v.t.* To spread ink upon; stain or color with ink. [< OF < LL *encaustum* purple ink] — **ink′er** *n.*
ink·horn (ingk′hôrn′) *n.* A small container for ink.
inkhorn term A bookish, pedantic word.
ink·ling (ingk′ling) *n.* **1.** A slight suggestion or hint. **2.** A vague idea or notion. [ME < OE *inca* suspicion]
ink·stand (ingk′stand′) *n.* **1.** A rack or device for holding ink, pens, etc. **2.** An inkwell.
ink·well (ingk′wel′) *n.* A container for ink.
ink·y (ing′kē) *adj.* **ink·i·er, ink·i·est** **1.** Resembling ink in color; dark; black. **2.** Of, pertaining to, or containing ink. **3.** Smeared or stained with ink. — **ink′i·ness** *n.*
in·laid (in′lād′, in·lād′) *adj.* **1.** Decorated with wood, ivory, or other material embedded flush with the surface. **2.** Inserted to form a flush embedded pattern.
in·land (in′lənd; *for n. and adv., also* in′land′) *adj.* **1.** Remote from the sea or the border. **2.** Pertaining to or located in the interior of a country: *inland* population. **3.** Not foreign; domestic: *inland* trade. — *n.* The interior of a country. — *adv.* In or towards the interior of a land.
in·land·er (in′lən·dər, -land′ər) *n.* One who lives inland.
in·law (in′lô′) *n.* *Informal* A close relative by marriage.
in·lay (*v.* in·lā′, in′lā′; *n.* in′lā′) *v.t.* **·laid, ·lay·ing** **1.** To set or embed (ivory, gold, etc.) flush into a surface so as to form a pattern. **2.** To decorate by inserting such designs. — *n.* **1.** That which is inlaid. **2.** A pattern or design so produced. **3.** *Dent.* A filling for a tooth. — **in·lay′er** *n.*
in·let (*n.* in′let, -lit; *v.* in·let′) *n.* **1.** A relatively narrow channel of water; as: **a** A stream or bay leading into land. **b** A passage between nearby islands, floes, etc. **c** An entry from one body of water into another. **2.** An opening.
in lo·co pa·ren·tis (in lō′kō pə·ren′tis) *Latin* In the place of a parent.
in·mate (in′māt′) *n.* **1.** One who is lodged or confined in a prison, asylum, hospital, etc. **2.** An inhabitant. **3.** One who dwells with another or others. [? < INN + MATE]
in me·di·as res (in mē′dē·əs rēz) *Latin* In the midst of things; in the middle of events and not at the beginning.
in me·mo·ri·am (in mə·môr′ē·əm, -mō′rē) *Latin* In memory (of); as a memorial (to).
in·most (in′mōst′, -məst) *adj.* **1.** Located farthest from the outside. **2.** Most private or intimate. [OE *innemest*]
inn (in) *n.* A hotel, etc., where travelers may obtain meals or lodging. [OE *inn* room, house]
in·nards (in′ərdz) *n.pl.* *Dial. & Informal* The internal organs or parts of the body, a machine, etc.; insides.
in·nate (i-nāt′, in′āt) *adj.* Inherent in one's nature; inborn; not acquired. [< L *in-* in + *nasci* to be born] — **in·nate′ly** *adv.* — **in·nate′ness** *n.*
in·ner (in′ər) *adj.* **1.** Located or occurring farther inside; internal; interior. **2.** Pertaining to the mind or spirit; subjective. **3.** More obscure; hidden; esoteric. [OE *innerra*, compar. of *inne* in (adv.)] — **in′ner·ly** *adv.* — **in′ner·ness** *n.*
in·ner·most (in′ər·mōst′) *adj.* Inmost; farthest within.
inner tube A flexible, inflatable tube, usu. of rubber, used inside a pneumatic tire.
in·ning (in′ing) *n.* **1.** In baseball, a division of the game during which each team has a turn to bat. **2.** *pl.* In cricket, the period during which one side bats. **3.** *Often pl.* A chance for action. [OE *innung*, gerund of *innian* to put in]
inn·keep·er (in′kē′pər) *n.* The proprietor or host of an inn.
in·no·cence (in′ə·səns) *n.* The quality or fact of being innocent. Also **in′no·cen·cy.**
in·no·cent (in′ə·sənt) *adj.* **1.** Not tainted with sin, evil, or moral wrong; pure. **2.** Free from blame or guilt, especially legally. **3.** Not tending to harm or injure: *innocent* pastimes. **4.** Not maliciously intended: an *innocent* lie. **5.** Lacking in worldly knowledge; naive. **6.** Devoid of; entirely lacking in: with *of*: *innocent* of grammar. — *n.* **1.** One who is free from evil or sin. **2.** A simple or unsuspecting person. [< OF < L < *in-* not + *nocere* to harm] — **in′no·cent·ly** *adv.*
in·noc·u·ous (i-nok′yōō-əs) *adj.* Having no harmful qualities or effects; harmless. [< L < *in-* not + *nocuus* harmful] — **in·noc′u·ous·ly** *adv.* — **in·noc′u·ous·ness** *n.*
in·nom·i·nate bone (i-nom′ə-nit) *Anat.* One of two large, irregular bones that form the sides of the pelvis: also called *haunch bone, hipbone.*
in·no·vate (in′ə·vāt) *v.* **·vat·ed, ·vat·ing** *v.t.* **1.** To introduce or bring in (something new). — *v.i.* **2.** To bring in new ideas, methods, etc. [< L *in-* in + *novare* to make new] — **in′no·va′tive** *adj.* — **in′no·va′tor** *n.*
in·no·va·tion (in′ə·vā′shən) *n.* **1.** Something newly introduced. **2.** The act of introducing something new. — **in′no·va′tion·al** *adj.* — **in′no·va′tion·ist** *n.*
in·nu·en·do (in′yōō·en′dō) *n.* *pl.* **·does** An oblique comment, hint, or suggestion, usu. derogatory. [< L < *in-* to + *-nuere* to nod]

in·nu·mer·a·ble (i·nōō′mər·ə·bəl, i·nyōō′-) *adj.* Too numerous to be counted; numberless. Also **in·nu′mer·ous.** — **Syn.** See INFINITE. — **in·nu′mer·a·bil′i·ty, in·nu′mer·a·ble·ness** *n.* — **in·nu′mer·a·bly** *adv.*

in·oc·u·late (in·ok′yə·lāt) *v.* **·lat·ed, ·lat·ing** *v.t.* **1.** To communicate a mild form of a disease to (a person, animal, etc.) so as to produce immunity; also, to implant (a disease, bacteria, etc.). **2.** To inject immunizing serums, vaccines, etc. into. **3.** To implant ideas, opinions, etc., in the mind of. — *v.i.* **4.** To perform inoculation. [< L *inoculare* to put an eye or bud into] — **in·oc′u·la′tion** *n.* — **in·oc′u·la′tive** (-lā′tiv) *adj.* — **in·oc′u·la′tor** (-lā′tər) *n.*

in·of·fen·sive (in′ə·fen′siv) *adj.* Giving no offense; innocuous. — **in′of·fen′sive·ly** *adv.* — **in′of·fen′sive·ness** *n.*

in·op·er·a·ble (in·op′ər·ə·bəl) *adj.* **1.** Incapable of being cured or improved by surgical operation: *inoperable cancer.* **2.** Not practicable; unworkable. — **in·op′er·a·bil′i·ty, in·op′er·a·ble·ness** *n.* — **in·op′er·a·bly** *adv.*

in·op·er·a·tive (in·op′ər·ə·tiv) *adj.* **1.** Not functioning. **2.** Not effectual or in effect. — **in·op′er·a·tive·ness** *n.*

in·op·por·tune (in·op·ər·tōōn′, -tyōōn′) *adj.* Untimely or inappropriate; unsuitable. — **in·op′por·tune′ly** *adv.*

in·or·di·nate (in·ôr′də·nit) *adj.* **1.** Exceeding proper limits; immoderate; excessive. **2.** Unrestrained: *inordinate passion.* — **in·or′di·na·cy** (-nə·sē), **in·or′di·nate·ness** *n.* — **in·or′di·nate·ly** *adv.*

in·or·gan·ic (in′ôr·gan′ik) *adj.* **1.** Not having the organized structure of animal or vegetable life; not living; inanimate. **2.** Not characterized by life processes. **3.** *Chem.* Of, pertaining to, or designating the branch of chemistry dealing with compounds lacking carbon or containing it only in the form of carbonates, carbides, and most cyanides.

in·pa·tient (in′pā′shənt) *n.* A patient who is lodged and fed as well as medically treated in a hospital, clinic, or the like.

in·put (in′pŏŏt′) *n.* **1.** The amount of energy delivered to a machine, storage battery, etc. **2.** *Electr.* The voltage, current, power, etc., delivered to a circuit. **3.** *Electronics* Information placed in an electronic computer for later use.

in·quest (in′kwest) *n.* **1.** A legal investigation into a special matter; esp., one undertaken before a jury or by a coroner. **2.** The body of men chosen to make such an inquiry; also, its findings. [See INQUIRE.]

in·qui·e·tude (in·kwī′ə·tōōd, -tyōōd) *n.* **1.** A state of restlessness; uneasiness. **2.** *pl.* Anxieties; disquieting thoughts. — **in·qui′et** *adj.* — **in·qui′et·ly** *adv.*

in·quire (in·kwīr′) *v.* **·quired, ·quir·ing** *v.i.* **1.** To seek information by asking questions; ask. **2.** To make an investigation: with *into.* — *v.t.* **3.** To ask information about: They *inquired* the way. Also spelled *enquire.* — **Syn.** See ASK. [< OF < L < *in-* into + *quaerere* to seek] — **in·quir′er** *n.* — **in·quir′ing·ly** *adv.*

in·quir·y (in·kwīr′ē, in′kwər·ē) *n.* *pl.* **·quir·ies 1.** The act of inquiring or seeking. **2.** Investigation; research. **3.** A question; query. Also spelled *enquiry.* [ME *enquery*]

in·qui·si·tion (in′kwə·zish′ən) *n.* **1.** An investigation of the beliefs and activities of individuals, political groups, etc., for the ultimate purpose of enforcing orthodoxy. **2.** The act of inquiring or searching out. **3.** An inquest. — **in′qui·si′tion·ist, in·quis·i·tor** (in·kwiz′ə·tər) *n.*

In·qui·si·tion (in′kwə·zish′ən) *n.* A former judicial system of the Roman Catholic Church for the discovery, examination, and punishment of heretics: also called *Holy Office.*

in·qui·si·tion·al (in′kwə·zish′ən·əl) *adj.* **1.** Of or pertaining to an inquisition or the Inquisition. **2.** Characterized by questioning, prying, etc. — **in′qui·si′tion·al·ly** *adv.*

in·quis·i·tive (in·kwiz′ə·tiv) *adj.* **1.** Somewhat too curious; unduly questioning; prying. **2.** Eager for knowledge or learning. [< OF < LL *inquisitivus*] — **in·quis′i·tive·ly** *adv.* — **in·quis′i·tive·ness** *n.*

in·quis·i·tor (in·kwiz′ə·tər) *n.* **1.** One who inquires, investigates, or examines. **2.** A member of the Inquisition. [< OF < L *inquisitor*]

in·quis·i·to·ri·al (in·kwiz′ə·tôr′ē·əl, -tō′rē, in′kwiz-) *adj.* **1.** Of, pertaining to, or resembling an inquisitor or inquisition; offensively curious. **2.** Acting as an inquisitor. — **in·quis′i·to′ri·al·ly** *adv.* — **in·quis′i·to′ri·al·ness** *n.*

in re (in rē′) *Law* In the matter (of); concerning. [< L]

I.N.R.I. Jesus of Nazareth, King of the Jews (L *Iesus Nazarenus, Rex Iudaeorum*).

in·road (in′rōd′) *n.* **1.** *Usu. pl.* A serious encroachment; harmful trespass: with *on* or *upon: inroads* on one's happiness. **2.** A hostile raid or foray. [< IN-² + obs. *road* riding]

in·rush (in′rush′) *n.* A sudden rushing in; invasion.

in·sa·lu·bri·ous (in′sə·lōō′brē·əs) *adj.* Not wholesome; not healthful. [< L *insalubris*] — **in′sa·lu′bri·ous·ly** *adv.*

in·sane (in·sān′) *adj.* **1.** Not sane; mentally deranged or unsound. **2.** Characteristic of one who is not sane. **3.** Extremely foolish; hare-brained. **4.** Set apart for demented

persons: *insane* asylum. [< L *in-* not + *sanus* whole] — **in·sane′ly** *adv.* — **in·sane′ness** *n.*

in·san·i·tar·y (in·san′ə·ter·ē) *adj.* Not sanitary; dangerous to health; unhygienic. — **in·san′i·ta′tion** *n.*

in·san·i·ty (in·san′ə·tē) *n.* *pl.* **·ties 1.** The state of being insane: not a technical term in medicine or psychiatry. **2.** *Law* A defect or weakness of mind that releases a person from legal responsibility. **3.** Extreme folly.

in·sa·tia·ble (in·sā′shə·bəl, -shē·ə·bəl) *adj.* Incapable of being sated or satisfied; extremely greedy. Also **in·sa·ti·ate** (in·sā′shē·it). — **in·sa′tia·bil′i·ty, in·sa′tia·ble·ness** *n.* — **in·sa′tia·bly, in·sa′ti·ate·ly** *adv.* — **in·sa′ti·ate·ness** *n.*

in·scribe (in·skrīb′) *v.t.* **·scribed, ·scrib·ing 1.** To write, mark, or engrave (words, names, characters, etc.). **2.** To mark (a document, tablet, etc.) with writing or engraving. **3.** To enter (a name) on a formal or official list. **4.** To sign or dedicate (a book, photograph, etc.) for presentation. **5.** *Geom.* To draw (one figure) in another so that the latter circumscribes the former. [< L < *in-* on, in + *scribere* to write] — **in·scrib′er** *n.*

in·scrip·tion (in·skrip′shən) *n.* **1.** That which is inscribed; also, the act of inscribing. **2.** A durable marking or engraving on a solid object. **3.** An informal written dedication. — **in·scrip′tion·al, in·scrip′tive** *adj.*

in·scru·ta·ble (in·skrōō′tə·bəl) *adj.* That cannot be searched into or understood; incomprehensible. — **Syn.** See MYSTERIOUS. [< LL < *in-* not + *scrutare* to explore] — **in·scru′ta·bil′i·ty, in·scru′ta·ble·ness** *n.* — **in·scru′ta·bly** *adv.*

in·sect (in′sekt) *n.* **1.** *Zool.* Any of a large, cosmopolitan class of small to minute air-breathing invertebrate animals, usu. having six legs, a body divided into a head, thorax, and abdomen, and one or two pairs of wings or none. **2.** Loosely, any small, air-breathing invertebrate resembling an insect, as spiders, centipedes, ticks, etc. [< L (*animal*) *insectum* (animal) notched, alluding to their segmented bodies]

in·sec·ti·cide (in·sek′tə·sīd) *n.* A substance used or prepared for killing insects.

in·sec·ti·val (in′sek·tī′vəl, in·sek′tə-) *adj.* Of, pertaining to, or resembling an insect.

in·sec·tiv·o·rous (in′sek·tiv′ər·əs) *adj.* Feeding or subsisting upon insects, as shrews, moles, hedgehogs, etc.

in·se·cure (in′sə·kyŏŏr′) *adj.* **1.** Liable to break, fail, collapse, etc.; unsafe. **2.** Troubled by anxiety and apprehensiveness; threatened. [< Med.L *insecurus*] — **in′se·cure′ly** *adv.* — **in′se·cure′ness** *n.*

in·se·cu·ri·ty (in′sə·kyŏŏr′ə·tē) *n.* *pl.* **·ties 1.** The state or quality of being unsafe or liable to injury, failure, loss, etc. **2.** A condition of anxiety and apprehensiveness; sense of being unsafe and threatened. **3.** *Often pl.* An instance of insecurity. [< Med.L *insecuritas*]

in·sem·i·nate (in·sem′ə·nāt) *v.t.* **·nat·ed, ·nat·ing 1.** To make pregnant; inject semen into the vagina of. **2.** To sow (seed); also, to implant (ideas, etc.). **3.** To sow seed in; implant in. [< L < *in-* in + *seminare* to sow] — **in·sem′i·na′tion** *n.*

in·sen·sate (in·sen′sāt, -sit) *adj.* **1.** Showing a lack of humane feeling; unmoved; brutish. **2.** Stupid; foolish. **3.** Lacking physical sensation; inanimate. [< LL *insensatus*] — **in·sen′sate·ly** *adv.* — **in·sen′sate·ness** *n.*

in·sen·si·ble (in·sen′sə·bəl) *adj.* **1.** Deprived of consciousness; unconscious. **2.** Incapable of feeling or perceiving; indifferent: *insensible* to pain. **3.** So slight or gradual as to escape notice; imperceptible. [< LL *insensibilis*] — **in·sen′si·bil′i·ty** *n.* — **in·sen′si·bly** *adv.*

in·sen·si·tive (in·sen′sə·tiv) *adj.* **1.** Not keenly responsive in feeling or reaction. **2.** Without physical feeling or sensation. **3.** Not affected by physical agencies: *insensitive* to light. — **in·sen′si·tiv′i·ty, in·sen′si·tive·ness** *n.* — **in·sen′si·tive·ly** *adv.*

in·sen·ti·ent (in·sen′shē·ənt, -shənt) *adj.* Lacking senses or consciousness; inanimate. — **in·sen′ti·ence** *n.*

in·sep·a·ra·ble (in·sep′ər·ə·bəl) *adj.* Incapable of being separated or parted. — *n. Usu. pl.* Persons or things that are always together. — **in·sep′a·ra·bil′i·ty, in·sep′a·ra·ble·ness** *n.* — **in·sep′a·ra·bly** *adv.*

in·sert (*v.* in·sûrt′; *n.* in′sûrt) *v.t.* **1.** To put in; place; set. **2.** To introduce into a body of printed matter. — *n.* **1.** That which is inserted. **2.** In bookbinding, illustrations, maps, etc., not part of the printed text, bound into the finished book: also called *inset.* **3.** *U.S.* A circular, pamphlet, etc., set within a newspaper, magazine, or book for mailing. [< L *in-* in + *serere* to join, plant] — **in·sert′er** *n.*

in·ser·tion (in·sûr′shən) *n.* **1.** The act of inserting. **2.** That which is inserted; as: **a** A word, sentence, etc. **b** A strip of lace or embroidery sewn into plain cloth. **c** Each appearance of an advertisement, as in a newspaper.

in·set (*v.* in·set′; *n.* in′set) *v.t.* **·set, ·set·ting** To set in; insert; implant. — *n.* **1.** In bookbinding, an insert. **2.** A small diagram, map, etc., inserted in the border of a larger one. **3.** A piece of material let or set into a garment.

in·sheathe (in-shēth′) *v.t.* **·sheathed, ·sheath·ing** To place in or as in a sheath.

in·shore (in′shōr′, -shôr′) *adj.* Near or coming toward the shore. — *adv.* Toward the shore.

in·shrine (in-shrīn′) See ENSHRINE.

in·side (*n. & adj.* in′sīd′, -sīd′; *adv. & prep.* in′sīd′) *n.* **1.** The part, surface, space, etc., that lies within; interior. **2.** The internal nature or workings that are concealed. **3.** *pl. Informal* The inner parts of the body or a machine; innards. — **inside out** Reversed so that the inside is exposed. — *adj.* **1.** Situated within; inner; internal; interior. **2.** Restricted to a few; confidential. **3.** In baseball, passing too close to the batter: said of pitches. **4.** Suitable for, used, or working indoors; indoor. — *adv.* **1.** In or into the interior; within. **2.** Indoors. — *prep.* In or into the interior of. — **inside of** *Informal* **1.** Within; enclosed by. **2.** Within the time or distance specified: *inside of* a year.

in·sid·er (in′sī′dər) *n.* **1.** A member of a given group, club, etc. **2.** One close to a source, as of knowledge or influence.

inside track 1. The shortest path around a race track. **2.** *Informal* A position of special advantage.

in·sid·i·ous (in-sid′ē-əs) *adj.* **1.** Subtly cunning or deceitful; treacherous; wily. **2.** Progressing imperceptibly but harmfully: *insidious* disease. [< L *insidere* to sit in, lie in wait] — **in·sid′i·ous·ly** *adv.* — **in·sid′i·ous·ness** *n.*

in·sight (in′sīt′) *n.* Perception into the inner nature or real character of a thing. — **Syn.** See ACUMEN.

in·sig·ni·a (in-sig′nē-ə) *n. pl.* of **in·sig·ne** (in-sig′nē) **1.** Badges, emblems, brassards, and the like, used as marks of membership, office, or honor: the royal *insignia.* **2.** Marks betokening anything: the *insignia* of grief. [< L]

in·sig·nif·i·cance (in′sig-nif′ə-kəns) *n.* The quality or state of being insignificant; unimportance.

in·sig·nif·i·can·cy (in′sig-nif′ə-kən-sē) *n. pl.* **·cies 1.** Insignificance. **2.** An insignificant person or thing.

in·sig·nif·i·cant (in′sig-nif′ə-kənt) *adj.* **1.** Having no importance; trivial; trifling. **2.** Meaningless. **3.** Lacking size or quantity. **4.** Of persons, lacking distinction, character, etc. — **in′sig·nif′i·cant·ly** *adv.*

in·sin·cere (in′sin-sir′) *adj.* Not sincere; hypocritical. — **in′sin·cere′ly** *adv.* — **in′sin·cer′i·ty** (-ser′ə-tē) *n.*

in·sin·u·ate (in-sin′yōo-āt) *v.* **·at·ed, ·at·ing** *v.t.* **1.** To suggest by innuendo; hint. **2.** To introduce subtly and gradually. — *v.i.* **3.** To give sly and indirect intimations. [< L *in-* in + *sinuare* to curve] — **in·sin′u·at′ing·ly** *adv.* — **in·sin′u·a′tive** *adj.* — **in·sin′u·a′tor** *n.*

in·sin·u·a·tion (in-sin′yōo-ā′shən) *n.* **1.** That which is insinuated; a sly hint. **2.** The act of insinuating.

in·sip·id (in-sip′id) *adj.* **1.** Lacking spirit and vivacity; vapid; dull. **2.** Lacking flavor or savor; tasteless; flat; bland. [< L < *in-* not + *sapidus* savory] — **in·si·pid·i·ty** (in′si-pid′ə-tē), **in·sip′id·ness** *n.* — **in·sip′id·ly** *adv.*

in·sist (in-sist′) *v.i.* **1.** To demand or assert firmly and forcefully: with *on* or *upon.* **2.** To dwell on or repeatedly emphasize something: with *on* or *upon.* — *v.t.* **3.** To demand or maintain forcefully: with a noun clause as object: He *insisted* that the gate be opened. [< OF < L *insistere* to stand on, tread on] — **in·sis′tence, in·sis′ten·cy** *n.*

in·sis·tent (in-sis′tənt) *adj.* **1.** Insisting; persistent; urgent. **2.** Demanding attention. — **in·sis′tent·ly** *adv.*

in·snare (in-snâr′) See ENSNARE.

in·so·bri·e·ty (in′sə-brī′ə-tē) *n. pl.* **·ties** Lack of sobriety; intemperance, esp. in drinking.

in·so·far (in′sō-fär′) *adv.* To such an extent; in such measure: followed by *as.* Also **in so far.**

in·sole (in′sōl′) *n.* **1.** The fixed inner sole of a shoe or boot. **2.** A removable inner sole placed in a shoe to improve its fit or to protect against dampness.

in·so·lence (in′sə-ləns) *n.* **1.** The character or quality of being insolent. **2.** An insult.

in·so·lent (in′sə-lənt) *adj.* Overbearing or offensively impertinent in conduct or speech; insulting; disrespectful. — *n.* An insolent person. [< L *insolens, -entis* unusual, haughty] — **in′so·lent·ly** *adv.*

in·sol·u·ble (in-sol′yə-bəl) *adj.* **1.** Not soluble; incapable of being dissolved. **2.** Not solvable; incapable of being solved. — **in·sol′u·bil′i·ty, in·sol′u·ble·ness** *n.* — **in·sol′u·bly** *adv.*

in·solv·a·ble (in-sol′və-bəl) *adj.* Not solvable.

in·sol·ven·cy (in-sol′vən-sē) *n. pl.* **·cies** The state of being insolvent; bankruptcy.

in·sol·vent (in-sol′vənt) *adj. Law* **1.** Unable to meet the claims of creditors; bankrupt. **2.** Insufficient for the payment of debts. **3.** Of insolvency. — *n.* An insolvent person.

in·som·ni·a (in-som′nē-ə) *n.* Chronic inability to sleep. [< L < *in-* without + *somnus* sleep] — **in·som′ni·ac** *n.* — **in·som′ni·ous** *adj.*

in·so·much (in′sō-much′) *adv.* **1.** To such a degree: with *that* or *as.* **2.** Inasmuch: with *as.*

in·sou·ci·ant (in-sōō′sē-ənt, *Fr.* aṅ-sōō-syäṅ′) *adj.* Light-

hearted; carefree; unconcerned. [< F] — **in·sou′ci·ance** *n.* — **in·sou′ci·ant·ly** (in-sōō′sē-ənt-lē) *adv.*

in·spect (in-spekt′) *v.t.* **1.** To look at or examine carefully; esp., to examine for faults or defects. **2.** To examine or review officially and with ceremony, as troops. [< L < *in-* into + *specere* to look]

in·spec·tion (in-spek′shən) *n.* **1.** The act of inspecting; careful or critical examination. **2.** An official examination, check, or review, as of troops. — **in·spec′tion·al** *adj.*

in·spec·tor (in-spek′tər) *n.* **1.** One who inspects. **2.** An official examiner or checker. **3.** An officer of police usu. ranking next below the superintendent. [< L] — **in·spec′to·ral, in·spec·to′ri·al** (-tô′rē-əl, -tō′rē-əl) *adj.* — **in·spec′tor·ate, in·spec′tor·ship** *n.*

in·spi·ra·tion (in′spə-rā′shən) *n.* **1.** The infusion or arousal within the mind of some idea, feeling, or impulse, esp. one that leads to creative action. **2.** The state or quality of being inspired. **3.** One who or that which acts as an inspiring influence. **4.** Something that results from being inspired, as an idea, etc. **5.** *Theol.* Divine influence exerted upon the mind or spirit. **6.** The act of drawing in the breath; inhalation. — **in′spi·ra′tion·al** *adj.* — **in′spi·ra′tion·al·ly** *adv.*

in·spire (in-spīr′) *v.* **·spired, ·spir·ing** *v.t.* **1.** To exert an invigorative influence upon (a person); animate; stir. **2.** To move (a person) to a particular feeling, idea, etc.: It *inspires* me with hope. **3.** To arouse or create (a feeling, idea, etc.); generate: to *inspire* fear. **4.** To direct or guide, as by special divine influence. **5.** To breathe in; inhale: opposed to *expire.* — *v.i.* **6.** To inhale. **7.** To give or provide inspiration. [< OF < L < *in-* into + *spirare* to breathe] — **in·spir′a·ble** *adj.* — **in·spir′er** *n.*

in·spir·it (in-spir′it) *v.t.* To fill with renewed spirit or life; animate; exhilarate; enliven. — **in·spir′it·ing·ly** *adv.*

in·spis·sate (in-spis′āt) *v.t. & v.i.* **·sat·ed, ·sat·ing** To thicken, as by evaporation. [< L < *in-* thoroughly + *spissare* to thicken] — **in·spis·sa·tion** (in′spi-sā′shən) *n.* — **in·spis·sa·tor** (in′spi-sā′tər) *n.*

in·sta·bil·i·ty (in′stə-bil′ə-tē) *n. pl.* **·ties 1.** Lack of stability. **2.** Unsteadiness of character; unreliability.

in·sta·ble (in-stā′bəl) *adj.* Unstable.

in·stall (in-stôl′) *v.t.* **1.** To fix in position and adjust for service or use: to *install* a hot-water system. **2.** To place in any office, rank, etc. **3.** To establish in a place or position; settle. Also *Chiefly Brit.* **in·stal′.** [< MF < Med.L < *in-* in + *stallum* seat < OHG *stal* seat] — **in·stall′er** *n.*

in·stal·la·tion (in′stə-lā′shən) *n.* **1.** Any device or system, esp. mechanical, set in place and readied for use. **2.** The act of installing, or the state of being installed. **3.** *Mil.* Any large, fixed base or facility of the armed service.

in·stall·ment[1] (in-stôl′mənt) *n.* **1.** A portion of a debt or sum of money made payable in specified amounts at specified intervals. **2.** One of several parts, as of a serial in a newspaper or magazine. Also *Brit.* **in·stal′ment.**

in·stall·ment[2] (in-stôl′mənt) *n.* Installation.

installment plan A system of paying for goods or services by fixed, periodic amounts.

in·stance (in′stəns) *n.* **1.** A case or example. **2.** A step in proceedings: in the first *instance.* — **at the instance of** At the request or urging of. — **for instance** For example. — *v.t.* **·stanced, ·stanc·ing** To cite as an example. [< OF < L *instantia* presence, urgent pleading]

in·stant (in′stənt) *n.* **1.** A very short time; moment; twinkling. **2.** A specific point in time: at the same *instant.* — *adj.* **1.** Instantaneous; immediate: *instant* recognition. **2.** Pressing; urgent. **3.** Prepared quickly by the addition of water, milk, etc.: *instant* coffee. — *adv. Poetic* Instantaneously; instantly. [< OF < L < *in-* upon + *stare* to stand]

in·stan·ta·ne·ous (in′stən-tā′nē-əs) *adj.* **1.** Happening with no delay; immediate. **2.** Acting or completed within a moment. [< INSTANT, on analogy with *simultaneous*] — **in′stan·ta·ne·ous·ly** *adv.* — **in′stan·ta·ne·ous·ness** *n.*

in·stant·er (in-stan′tər) *adv.* Immediately; at once. [< L]

in·stant·ly (in′stənt-lē) *adv.* **1.** Without delay; at once. **2.** *Archaic* With urgency. — *conj.* As soon as.

in·stead (in-sted′) *adv.* **1.** In place or lieu; rather than: with *of:* a friend *instead* of an enemy. **2.** In the place of that just mentioned: to look for silver and find gold *instead.*

in·step (in′step′) *n.* **1.** *Anat.* The arched upper part of the human foot, extending from the toes to the ankle. **2.** The part of a shoe or stocking covering this.

in·sti·gate (in′stə-gāt) *v.t.* **·gat·ed, ·gat·ing 1.** To spur on or goad to some drastic course or deed; incite. **2.** To bring about by inciting; foment; provoke: to *instigate* treason. [< L < *in-* against + the root *stig-* to prick, goad] — **in′sti·ga′tion** *n.* — **in′sti·ga′tive** *adj.* — **in′sti·ga′tor** *n.*

in·still (in-stil′) *v.t.* **1.** To introduce (a quality, feeling, idea, etc.) gradually or by degrees: to *instill* courage. **2.** To pour in gradually by drops. Also *Brit.* **in·stil′.** [< L < *in-* + *stillare* to drop] — **in·stil·la·tion** (in′stə-lā′shən) *n.* — **in·still′er** *n.* — **in·still′ment** or **in·stil′ment** *n.*

in·stinct (*n.* in′stingkt; *adj.* in-stingkt′) *n.* **1.** *Biol. & Psy-*

chol. An innate tendency or response of a given species to act in ways that are essential to its existence, development, and preservation. **2.** A natural aptitude; knack. — *adj.* Animated from within; alive: usu. with *with.* [< L *instinctus,* pp. of *instinguere* to impel] — **in·stinc′tu·al** (-chōō-əl) *adj.*

in·stinc·tive (in-stingk′tiv) *adj.* **1.** Arising from or as from instinct: an *instinctive* fear. **2.** Of or pertaining to instinct. — **in·stinc′tive·ly** *adv.*

in·sti·tute (in′stə-tōōt, -tyōōt) *v.t.* **·tut·ed, ·tut·ing 1.** To set up or establish; found. **2.** To set in operation; initiate; start. **3.** *Eccl.* To place (a clergyman) in spiritual charge of a parish: with *in* or *into.* — *n.* **1.** A group or society devoted to the promotion of some particular field, often of a learned nature: an art *institute;* also, the building or buildings housing such a society. **2.** In education: **a** *Usu. cap.* A college for specialized instruction, often technical. **b** A center for postgraduate study and research. **3.** Something instituted, as an established principle, rule, or order. [< L *in-* in, on + *statuere* to set up] — **in′sti·tut′er, in′sti·tu′tor** *n.*

in·sti·tu·tion (in′stə-tōō′shən, -tyōō′-) *n.* **1.** A principle, custom, etc., that forms part of a society or civilization: the *institution* of slavery. **2.** A corporate body organized to perform some particular function, often in education, research, charity, etc.; also, the building or buildings housing such a body. **3.** A mental hospital, prison, or other place of confinement: a euphemistic use. **4.** *Informal* A familiar and characteristic object, custom, or person. **5.** The act of instituting, establishing, or setting in operation.

in·sti·tu·tion·al (in′stə-tōō′shən-əl, -tyōō′-) *adj.* **1.** Of, pertaining to, or characteristic of an institution. **2.** Designating a form of advertising intended to promote good will and prestige. — **in′sti·tu′tion·al·ly** *adv.*

in·sti·tu·tion·al·ize (in′stə-tōō′shən-əl-īz′, -tyōō′-) *v.t.* **·ized, ·iz·ing 1.** To make institutional. **2.** To turn into or regard as an institution. **3.** *U.S. Informal* To put (someone) in an institution, as for the aged. — **in′sti·tu′tion·al·i·za′tion** *n.*

in·struct (in-strukt′) *v.t.* **1.** To impart knowledge or skill to, esp. by systematic method; educate; teach. **2.** To give specific orders or directions to; order — **Syn.** See TEACH. [< L < *in-* in + *struere* to build]

in·struc·tion (in-struk′shən) *n.* **1.** The act of instructing or teaching. **2.** Knowledge or factual matter imparted; also, an item of such knowledge taught, as a rule, precept, or lesson. **3.** *pl.* Directions; orders. — **in·struc′tion·al** *adj.*

in·struc·tive (in-struk′tiv) *adj.* Serving to instruct; informative. — **in·struc′tive·ly** *adv.* — **in·struc′tive·ness** *n.*

in·struc·tor (in-struk′tər) *n.* **1.** One who instructs; teacher. **2.** *U.S.* A college teacher not having professorial rank. [< L] — **in·struc′tor·ship** *n.* — **in·struc′tress** *n. fem.*

in·stru·ment (*n.* in′strə-mənt; *v.* in′strə-ment) *n.* **1.** A tool or implement, esp. one used for exacting work: a surgical *instrument.* **2.** A device for producing musical sounds. **3.** An apparatus for measuring or recording; as: **a** A gauge or device for indicating engine performance, etc., in aircraft, refineries, and other complex systems. **b** A system or device used for navigation and control in aircraft, ships, rockets, etc. **4.** Anything serving to accomplish a purpose; means; agency. **5.** A person doing the will of another; dupe. **6.** *Law* A formal legal document, as a contract, deed, etc. — **on instruments** *Aeron.* Flying, landing, or navigating by means of instruments rather than by visual observation of the horizon, ground objects, etc. — **Syn.** See TOOL. — *v.t.* To provide instrumentation for (an aircraft, missile, or other apparatus). [See INSTRUCT]

in·stru·men·tal (in′strə-men′təl) *adj.* **1.** Serving as a means or instrument; useful; helpful. **2.** Of or pertaining to an instrument or tool. **3.** Of, pertaining to, composed for, or performed on musical instruments. — **in′stru·men′tal·ly** *adv.* [< Med.L *instrumentum*]

in·stru·men·tal·ist (in′strə-men′təl-ist) *n.* One who plays a musical instrument.

in·stru·men·tal·i·ty (in′strə-men-tal′ə-tē) *n. pl.* **·ties 1.** Anything serving to accomplish a purpose; means; agency. **2.** The condition of being instrumental.

in·stru·men·ta·tion (in′strə-men-tā′shən) *n.* **1.** The use of instruments; work performed with instruments. **2.** *Music* **a** The study of the characteristics and groupings of instruments. **b** Loosely, orchestration. **3.** A branch of engineering concerned with the use of instruments in military, technical, and scientific operations; also, an assembly of instruments, considered as a unit. **4.** Instrumentality.

instrument panel The panel holding the gauges and other indicators of performance in an automobile, airplane, engine room, etc. Also **instrument board.**

in·sub·or·di·nate (in′sə-bôr′də-nit) *adj.* Not subordinate or obedient; rebellious. — *n.* An insubordinate person. — **in′sub·or′di·nate·ly** *adv.* — **in′sub·or′di·na′tion** *n.*

in·sub·stan·tial (in′səb-stan′shəl) *adj.* **1.** Not real; imaginary; illusive. **2.** Not substantial, solid, or firm; flimsy. — **in′sub·stan′ti·al′i·ty** (-shē-al′ə-tē) *n.*

in·suf·fer·a·ble (in-suf′ər-ə-bəl) *adj.* Not to be endured; intolerable. — **in·suf′fer·a·ble·ness** *n.* — **in·suf′fer·a·bly** *adv.*

in·suf·fi·cien·cy (in′sə-fish′ən-sē) *n. pl.* **·cies** Lack of adequate effectiveness, amount, quality, etc.; inadequacy.

in·suf·fi·cient (in′sə-fish′ənt) *adj.* Not enough; inadequate; deficient. — **in′suf·fi′cient·ly** *adv.*

in·su·lar (in′sə-lar, -syə-) *adj.* **1.** Of or like an island. **2.** Dwelling or situated on an island. **3.** Composing or forming an island. **4.** Narrow or limited in customs, opinions, etc.; provincial. — *n.* An islander. [< L *insula* island] — **in′su·lar·ism, in·su·lar·i·ty** (in′sə-lar′ə-tē, -syə-) *n.*

in·su·late (in′sə-lāt, -syə-) *v.t.* **·lat·ed, ·lat·ing 1.** To surround or separate with nonconducting material in order to prevent or lessen the leakage of electricity, heat, sound, radiation, etc. **2.** To isolate. [< L *insula* island]

in·su·la·tion (in′sə-lā′shən, -syə-) *n.* **1.** Nonconducting material used for insulating. **2.** The act of insulating, or the state of being insulated.

in·su·la·tor (in′sə-lā′tər, -syə-) *n.* **1.** *Electr.* A device made of dielectric material, as glass, and used to insulate and support a conductor. **2.** One who or that which insulates.

in·su·lin (in′sə-lin, -syə-) *n.* *Biochem.* **1.** A hormone secreted by the pancreas, essential in regulating the metabolism of sugar. **2.** A preparation of this hormone, used in treating diabetes. [< L *insula* island (of Langerhans) + -IN]

in·sult (*v.* in-sult′; *n.* in′sult) *v.t.* To treat with insolence or contempt; disparage; abuse; affront. — **Syn.** See OFFEND. — *n.* An act, remark, etc., that offends or affronts. [< MF < L < *in-* on + *salire* to leap] — **in·sult′er** *n.* — **in·sult′ing** *adj.* — **in·sult′ing·ly** *adv.*

in·su·per·a·ble (in-sōō′pər-ə-bəl) *adj.* Not to be surmounted or overcome. [< L *insuperabilis*] — **in·su·per·a·bil′i·ty, in·su′per·a·ble·ness** *n.* — **in·su′per·a·bly** *adv.*

in·sup·port·a·ble (in′sə-pôr′tə-bəl, -pōr′-) *adj.* **1.** Not bearable; insufferable. **2.** Having no grounds; unjustifiable. — **in′sup·port′a·ble·ness** *n.* — **in′sup·port′a·bly** *adv.*

in·sur·ance (in-shōōr′əns) *n.* **1.** Protection against risk, loss, or ruin, by a contract in which an insurer or underwriter guarantees to pay a sum of money to the insured or the beneficiary in the event of death, accident, fire, etc., in return for the payment of premiums; also, the business of providing this protection. **2.** A contract guaranteeing such protection. Also **insurance policy. 3.** The payment made by the insured party. **4.** The amount for which anything is insured. **5.** Any safeguard against risk or harm.

in·sure (in-shōōr′) *v.* **·sured, ·sur·ing** *v.t.* **1.** To guarantee against loss of (life, property, etc.) with insurance. **2.** To ensure. — *v.i.* **3.** To issue or buy insurance. [< AF < *en-* in + *seur* sure] — **in·sur′a·bil′i·ty** *n.* — **in·sur′a·ble** *adj.*

in·sured (in-shōōrd′) *n.* The person protected by insurance.

in·sur·er (in-shōōr′ər) *n.* A person or company that insures against specified loss or damage.

in·sur·gence (in-sûr′jəns) *n.* The act of rising in insurrection; revolt; uprising. Also **in·sur′gen·cy.**

in·sur·gent (in-sûr′jənt) *adj.* Rising in revolt against established authority; rebellious. — *n.* An insurgent person. [< L < *in-* against + *surgere* to rise]

in·sur·mount·a·ble (in′sər-moun′tə-bəl) *adj.* Incapable of being surmounted or overcome. — **in′sur·mount′a·bly** *adv.*

in·sur·rec·tion (in′sə-rek′shən) *n.* An organized resistance to established government. [< F < LL < L *insurrectus,* pp. of *insurgere* to rise up against] — **in′sur·rec′tion·al** *adj.* — **in′sur·rec′tion·ar′y** *adj. & n.* — **in′sur·rec′tion·ist** *n.*

in·sus·cep·ti·ble (in′sə-sep′tə-bəl) *adj.* Incapable of being affected or infected; immune. — **in′sus·cep′ti·bil′i·ty** *n.*

in·tact (in-takt′) *adj.* Remaining whole, unchanged, and undamaged; unimpaired. [< L < *in-* not + *tactus,* pp. of *tangere* to touch] — **in·tact′ness** *n.*

in·ta·glio (in-tal′yō, *Ital.* ēn-tä′lyō) *n. pl.* **·glios** or **·gli** (-lyē) **1.** Incised carving; a sunken design. **2.** The art of making such designs. **3.** A work, esp. a gem, with incised carving. [< Ital. < *in-* in + *tagliare* to cut]

in·take (in′tāk′) *n.* **1.** The act of taking in or absorbing. **2.** That which is taken in: the annual *intake.* **3.** The amount or quantity absorbed. **4.** The place where water is drawn into a pipe, channel, or conduit.

in·tan·gi·ble (in-tan′jə-bəl) *adj.* **1.** Incapable of being perceived by touch; impalpable. **2.** Indefinite or vague to the mind. — *n.* That which is intangible; esp., any incorporeal asset, as good will. [< Med.L *intangibilis*] — **in·tan′gi·bil′i·ty, in·tan′gi·ble·ness** *n.* — **in·tan′gi·bly** *adv.*

in·te·ger (in′tə-jər) *n.* **1.** Any of the numbers 1, 2, 3, etc., as distinguished from a fraction or mixed number: also called *whole number.* **2.** A whole entity. [< L, untouched < *in-* not + root *tag-,* of *tangere* to touch]

in·te·gral (in′tə-grəl) *adj.* **1.** Being an indispensable part of a whole; essential; constituent.   2. Formed of parts that together constitute a unity: an *integral* whole.   3. Whole; entire; complete.   4. *Math.* **a** Pertaining to an integer. **b** Produced by integration. — *n.* 1. An entire thing; a whole.   2. *Math.* The result of integration.   [< LL *integralis*] —**in′te·gral′i·ty** (-gral′ə-tē) *n.* — **in′te·gral·ly** *adv.*

in·te·grate (in′tə-grāt)   *v.* **·grat·ed**, **·grat·ing** *v.t.* 1. To bring together into a whole; unify.   2. *U.S.* To make the use or occupancy of (a school, neighborhood, etc.) available to persons of all races.   3. To make whole or complete by the addition of necessary parts.   4. *Math.* To determine a function from its derivatives: opposed to *differentiate.* — *v.i.* 5. *U.S.* To become available to persons of all races, as a school, etc.   [< *integratus*, pp. of *integrare* to make whole, renew]   —**in′te·gra′tion** *n.* — **in′te·gra′tor** *n.*

in·teg·ri·ty (in·teg′rə-tē)   *n.* *pl.* **·ties** 1. Uprightness of character; honesty.   2. The condition or quality of being unimpaired or sound.   3. The state of being complete or undivided: [< L *integer* untouched]

in·teg·u·ment (in·teg′yə-mənt)   *n.* A covering or outer coating; esp., a natural covering or envelope, as the skin of an animal, coat of a seed, etc.   [< L < *in-* thoroughly + *tegere* to cover]   —**in·teg′u·men′ta·ry** *adj.*

in·tel·lect (in′tə-lekt)   *n.* 1. The power of the mind to grasp ideas and relations, and to exercise dispassionate reason and rational judgment; reason.   2. A mind or intelligence, especially a strong or brilliant one.   3. An intelligent person.   4. Mental power collectively: the *intellect* of the nation.   [< L *intellectus,* pp. of < *intelligere* to understand]
   —**Syn.** 1. *Intellect* refers to the powers of knowing and thinking, as distinguished from those of feeling and willing, while *mind* is the sum of all these powers or faculties. *Reason* is the ability to think, or at its simplest the ability to elaborate sense impressions into concepts. *Intelligence* is chiefly used to mean the capacity to learn or to deal with new situations.

in·tel·lec·tu·al (in′tə-lek′chōō-əl)   *adj.* 1. Of or pertaining to the intellect; mental.   2. Engaging, or requiring the use of, the intellect.   3. Possessing or showing intellect, esp. of a high order. — *n.* 1. One who pursues and enjoys matters of the intellect and of refined taste.   2. One whose work requires primarily the use of the intellect.   [< L *intellectualis*]   —**in′tel·lec′tu·al′i·ty** *n.* — **in′tel·lec′tu·al·ly** *adv.*

in·tel·lec·tu·al·ism (in′tə-lek′chōō-əl·iz′əm)   *n.* 1. Devotion to intellectual interests.   2. The exercise of the intellect.   —**in′tel·lec′tu·al·ist** *n.* — **in′tel·lec′tu·al·is′tic** *adj.*

in·tel·lec·tu·al·ize (in′tə-lek′chōō-əl·īz)   *v.* **·ized**, **·iz·ing** *v.t.* 1. To make intellectual; view or express intellectually. — *v.i.* 2. To think; reason.

in·tel·li·gence (in·tel′ə-jəns)   *n.* 1. The faculty of perceiving and comprehending meaning; active intellect; understanding.   2. The ability to adapt to new situations.   3. The collection of secret information, as by police or military authorities.   4. Information that has been so collected; also, the persons so occupied. — **Syn.** See INTELLECT.

intelligence quotient   *Psychol.* A number indicating the level of a person's mental development, obtained by multiplying his mental age by 100, and dividing by his chronological age.

intelligence test   *Psychol.* Any standardized test, or series of tests, designed to determine relative mental capacity.

in·tel·li·gent (in·tel′ə-jənt)   *adj.* 1. Having an active, discerning mind; acute: an *intelligent* reader.   2. Marked or characterized by intelligence.   3. Endowed with intellect or understanding; reasoning.   [< L < *inter-* between + *legere* to choose]   —**in·tel′li·gent·ly** *adv.*

in·tel·li·gent·si·a (in·tel′ə·jent′sē-ə, -gent′-)   *n.pl.* Intellectual or educated people collectively, esp. those with a broad and informed point of view.   [< Russian, ? < Ital. < L *intelligentia*]

in·tel·li·gi·ble (in·tel′ə·jə·bəl)   *adj.* Capable of being understood.   [< L *intelligibilis*]   —**in·tel′li·gi·bil′i·ty** *n.* — **in·tel′li·gi·bly** *adv.*

in·tem·per·ance (in·tem′pər·əns)   *n.* Lack of temperance or moderation; esp., excessive use of alcoholic drinks.

in·tem·per·ate (in·tem′pər·it)   *adj.* 1. Lacking moderation; unrestrained.   2. Given to excessive use of alcoholic drinks.   3. Excessive or extreme, as climate or the weather. — **in·tem′per·ate·ly** *adv.* — **in·tem′per·ate·ness** *n.*

in·tend (in·tend′)   *v.t.* 1. To have as a specific aim or purpose; plan.   2. To make, design, or destine for a purpose, use, etc.: a dress *intended* for summer.   3. To mean or signify; indicate. — *v.i.* 4. To have a purpose or plan.   [< OF < L < *in-* in, at + *tendere* to stretch]

in·ten·dan·cy (in·ten′dən·sē)   *n. pl.* **·cies** The office or work of an intendant; intendants collectively.

in·ten·dant (in·ten′dənt)   *n.* A superintendent; provincial administrator, as under the Bourbons in France.   [< F]

in·tend·ed (in·ton′did)   *adj.* 1. Planned; proposed: the *intended* results.   2. Prospective: one's *intended* wife. — *n.* *Informal* Prospective husband or wife.

in·tense (in·tens′)   *adj.* 1. Having great force; overpower-

ing: *intense* feelings.   2. Performed strenuously and steadily: *intense* study.   3. Expressing strong emotion: an *intense* look; also, characterized by strong and earnest feelings: an *intense* person.   4. Having its quality strongly concentrated.   [< OF < L *intensus,* pp. of *intendere* to stretch out] — **in·tense′ly** *adv.* — **in·tense′ness** *n.*

in·ten·si·fy (in·ten′sə-fī)   *v.* **·fied**, **·fy·ing** *v.t.* 1. To make more intense or acute; aggravate; also, to make intense.   2. *Photog.* To increase the contrast of (a negative or print). — *v.i.* 3. To become more intense; become intense. — **in·ten′si·fi·ca′tion, in·ten′si·fi′er** *n.*

in·ten·si·ty (in·ten′sə-tē)   *n. pl.* **·ties** 1. The state or quality of being intense; extreme force, brightness, concentration, etc.   2. The strength or degree of some action, quality, feeling, etc.: pain of low *intensity.*   3. Power and vehemence of thought or feeling; also, extreme effort and concentration.

in·ten·sive (in·ten′siv)   *adj.* 1. Of, pertaining to, or marked by intensity.   2. Intensifying.   3. *Agric.* Pertaining to a method of farming whereby much capital and labor are expended upon making a small area highly productive.   4. *Gram.* Adding emphasis or force. — *n.* 1. That which gives intensity or emphasis.   2. *Gram.* An intensive particle, word, or phrase.   [< F < Med.L *intensivus*]   — **in·ten′sive·ly** *adv.* — **in·ten′sive·ness** *n.*

in·tent (in·tent′)   *n.* 1. Purpose; aim; goal; design.   2. The act of intending.   3. *Law* The state of mind in which or the purpose with which one does an act; also, the character that the law imputes to an act. — *adj.* 1. Firmly directed or fixed: an *intent* stare.   2. Directing one's mind or efforts steadfastly: with *on* or *upon.*   [< OF < L *intendere* to stretch out, endeavor] — **in·tent′ly** *adv.* — **in·tent′ness** *n.*

in·ten·tion (in·ten′shən)   *n.* 1. Purpose, either ultimate or immediate; aim; goal.   2. The act of intending.   3. *pl. Informal* Purpose with regard to marriage.

in·ten·tion·al (in·ten′shən·əl)   *adj.* Resulting from purpose; deliberate; intended. — **in·ten′tion·al·ly** *adv.*

in·ten·tioned (in·ten′shənd)   *adj.* Having or characterized by (a specified kind of) intention or intentions: used in combination: *well-intentioned.*

in·ter (in·tûr′)   *v.t.* **·terred**, **·ter·ring** To place in a grave; bury.   [< OF < LL < *in-* in + *terra* earth]

inter-   *prefix* 1. With each other; together: *intertwine.*   2. Mutual; mutually: *intercommunicate.*   3. Between (the units signified): *intercollegiate.*   4. Occurring or situated between: *interlinear.*   [< L *inter-* < *inter* between, among]

in·ter·act (in′tər-akt′)   *v.i.* To act on each other. — **in′ter·ac′tion** *n.* — **in′ter·ac′tive** *adj.* — **in′ter·ac·tiv′i·ty** *n.*

in·ter·brain (in′tər-brān′)   *n. Anat.* The diencephalon.

in·ter·breed (in′tər-brēd′)   *v.* **·bred**, **·breed·ing** *v.t.* 1. To breed (different stocks) together; crossbreed.   2. To produce (offspring) by crossbreeding. — *v.i.* 3. To breed genetically dissimilar stocks or individuals.

in·ter·ca·lar·y (in·tûr′kə·ler′ē)   *adj.* 1. Added to the calendar.   2. Having an added day or month.   3. Interpolated.

in·ter·ca·late (in·tûr′kə·lāt)   *v.t.* **·lat·ed**, **·lat·ing** 1. To insert or interpolate.   2. To insert, as an additional day or month, into the calendar.   [< L < *inter-* between + *calare* to proclaim, call] — **in·ter′ca·la′tion** *n.*

in·ter·cede (in′tər-sēd′)   *v.i.* **·ced·ed**, **·ced·ing** 1. To plead or petition in behalf of another or others.   2. To come between parties in a dispute; mediate.   [< L < *inter-* between + *cedere* to pass, go] — **in′ter·ced′er** *n.*

in·ter·cel·lu·lar (in′tər·sel′yə·lər)   *adj. Biol.* Situated between or among cells.

in·ter·cept (*v.* in′tər·sept′; *n.* in′tər·sept)   *v.t.* 1. To seize or stop on the way; prevent from reaching the destination.   2. To meet, as a moving person, ship, etc.   3. To interrupt the course of; obstruct: to *intercept* the light.   4. *Math.* To mark off or bound a line, plane, surface, or solid. — *n.* 1. In the U.S. Air Force, an act or instance of interception.   2. *Math.* **a** An intercepted part. **b** A point of interception.   [< L < *inter-* between + *capere* to seize] — **in′ter·cep′tion** *n.* — **in′ter·cep′tive** *adj.*

in·ter·cep·tor (in′tər·sep′tər)   *n.* 1. One who or that which intercepts.   2. An airplane designed for the pursuit and interception of enemy aircraft. Also **in·ter′cept′er.**   [< L]

in·ter·ces·sion (in′tər·sesh′ən)   *n.* The act of interceding; entreaty or prayer in behalf of others.   [< L < *intercessus,* pp. of *intercedere* to come between] — **in′ter·ces′sion·al** *adj.*

in·ter·ces·sor (in′tər·ses′ər)   *n.* One who intercedes; a mediator.   [< L] — **in′ter·ces′so·ry** *adj.*

in·ter·change (in′tər·chānj′)   *v.* **·changed**, **·chang·ing** *v.t.* 1. To put each of (two things) in the place of the other.   2. To cause to alternate.   3. To give and receive in return, as gifts. — *v.i.* 4. To change places one with the other. — *n.* 1. A reciprocal giving in exchange.   2. An exchanging of places.   3. Alternation.   4. An intersection of a superhighway with another highway, so designed that vehicles may enter or turn off without obstructing traffic.   [< OF < *entre-* between + *changier* to exchange] — **in′ter·chang′er** *n.*

in·ter·change·a·ble (in′tər·chān′jə·bəl)   *adj.* Capable of being interchanged or substituted one for the other; permitting transposition. **— in′ter·change′a·bil′i·ty, in′ter·change′a·ble·ness** n. **— in′ter·change′a·bly** adv.

in·ter·col·le·giate (in′tər·kə·lē′jit, -jē·it) adj. Pertaining to or involving two or more colleges: intercollegiate sports.

in·ter·com (in′tər·kom′) n. Informal A telephone or radio system for intercommunication.

in·ter·com·mu·ni·cate (in′tər·kə·myōō′nə·kāt) v.i. **·cat·ed, ·cat·ing** To communicate with one another; esp., by a telephone system. **— in′ter·com′mu′ni·ca′tion** n. **— in′ter·com·mu′ni·ca′tive** adj. **— in′ter·com·mun′i·ca·tor** n.

in·ter·con·nect (in′tər·kə·nekt′) v.t. & v.i. To connect or be connected one with the other. **— in′ter·con·nec′tion** n.

in·ter·con·ti·nen·tal (in′tər·kon′tə·nen′tal) adj. Reaching or capable of reaching from one continent to another; also, pertaining to or involving two or more continents.

in·ter·cos·tal (in′tər·kos′tal) adj. Anat. Situated or occurring between the ribs. [< NL < L inter- between + costa rib] **— in′ter·cos′tal·ly** adv.

in·ter·course (in′tər·kôrs, -kōrs) n. 1. Mutual exchange; commerce. 2. The interchange of ideas. 3. Sexual connection; coitus. [< OF < L < inter- between + currere to run]

in·ter·de·nom·i·na·tion·al (in′tər·di·nom′ə·nā′shən·əl) adj. Of or pertaining to two or more religious denominations.

in·ter·de·pen·dent (in·tər·di·pen′dənt) adj. Dependent one on another; reciprocally dependent. **— in′ter·de·pend′ence, in′ter·de·pend′en·cy** n. **— in′ter·de·pend′ent·ly** adv.

in·ter·dict (in′tər·dikt′) v.t. 1. To prohibit or debar (some action, right of use, etc.) authoritatively; also, to forbid (a person or persons) to have or do something. 2. Eccl. To exclude (a place or certain persons) from participation in rites and services. **—** n. In the Roman Catholic Church, a ban forbidding the sacraments and solemn services to a place or to certain church members, but not imposing excommunication. [< OF < L < inter- between + dicere to say] **— in′ter·dic′tion** n. **— in′ter·dic′tive, in′ter·dic′to·ry** (-tə·rē) adj. **— in′ter·dic′tive·ly** adv. **— in′ter·dic′tor** n.

in·ter·est (in′tər·ist, -trist) n. 1. A feeling of curiosity or attentiveness. 2. The power to arouse curiosity or attentiveness; also, something that has such power: Tennis is his chief interest. 3. That which is of advantage; benefit. 4. Involvement or concern in something; also, selfish concern. 5. Payment for the use of money or credit, usu. expressed as a percentage of the amount owed or used, and depending also on the duration of the debt. 6. Something added in making a return: to give back a blow with interest. 7. Legal or financial right, claim, or share, as in a business or estate; also, that in which one has such a right, claim, or share. 8. Usu. pl. A group of persons involved in a particular business, cause, etc.: the dairy interests. **— in the interest** (or **interests**) **of** In behalf of. **—** v.t. 1. To excite or hold the curiosity or attention of. 2. To cause to be concerned in; involve: with in. [< OF < L < inter- between + esse to be]

in·ter·est·ed (in′tər·is·tid, -tris-, -tə·res′-) adj. 1. Having or displaying curiosity; having the attention involved. 2. Having a concern or wish for something. 3. Having a right or share in. 4. Seeking personal advantage; biased. **— in′ter·est·ed·ly** adv. **— in′ter·est·ed·ness** n.

in·ter·est·ing (in′tər·is·ting, -tris-, -tris·, -tə·res′-) adj. Exciting interest, attention, or curiosity; attractive. **— in′ter·est·ing·ly** adv. **— in′ter·est·ing·ness** n.

in·ter·fere (in′tər·fir′) v.i. **·fered, ·fer·ing** 1. To get in the way; be an obstacle or obstruction; impede: often with with. 2. To intervene and take part in the affairs of others; esp., to interpose oneself without invitation or warrant; meddle. 3. In sports, to obstruct the play of an opponent illegally. 4. Physics To cause interference. [< OF < L inter- between + ferire to strike] **— in′ter·fer′er** n. **— in′ter·fer′ing·ly** adv.

in·ter·fer·ence (in′tər·fir′əns) n. 1. The act of interfering. 2. In sports, illegal obstruction of the play of an opponent. 3. In football, the protection given the ball carrier from opposing tacklers. 4. Physics The effect produced by two or more sets of waves, as of light or sound, that on meeting tend to neutralize or augment each other by a combination of dissimilar or like phases. 5. Telecom. A disturbance in the reception of radio, etc., due to conflict with undesired signals.

in·ter·fold (in′tər·fōld′) v.t. & v.i. To fold together or one within another.

in·ter·fuse (in′tər·fyōōz′) v. **·fused, ·fus·ing** v.t. 1. To cause to permeate or spread throughout, as a fluid. 2. To spread through or permeate with something. 3. To intermix. **—** v.i. 4. To become intermixed. **— in′ter·fu′sion** n.

in·ter·im (in′tər·im) n. A time between periods or events; an intervening time. **—** adj. For an intervening period of time; temporary. [< L, meanwhile]

in·te·ri·or (in·tir′ē·ər) adj. 1. Of or situated on the inside; inner. 2. Remote from the coast or border; inland. 3. Pertaining to the internal affairs of a country. 4. Not exposed to view; private. **—** n. 1. The internal part; the inside. 2. The inland region of a country, continent, etc. 3. The domestic affairs of a country. 4. The inner nature of a person or thing. 5. A representation of the inside of a building or room. **— Department of the Interior** An executive department of the U.S. government (established 1849), headed by the Secretary of the Interior, that controls Indian affairs and conservation of natural resources. [< OF < L interior, compar. of inter within] **— in·te′ri·or′i·ty** (-ôr′ə·tē, -or′-) n. **— in·te′ri·or·ly** adv.

interior decoration The decorating and furnishing of interiors, as homes, offices, etc.; also, this occupation.

in·ter·ject (in′tər·jekt′) v.t. To throw in between other things: to interject a comment. [< L < inter- between + jacere to throw]

in·ter·jec·tion (in′tər·jek′shən) n. 1. The act of interjecting. 2. That which is interjected. 3. Gram. An exclamation lacking any grammatical connection, as Oh!, Alas! **— in′ter·jec′tion·al** adj. **— in′ter·jec′tion·al·ly** adv.

in·ter·lace (in′tər·lās′) v. **·laced, ·lac·ing** v.t. 1. To join by or as by weaving together; intertwine. 2. To blend; combine. 3. To vary or relieve the sameness of. **—** v.i. 4. To interlock or alternate with one another. [< OF entrelacier]

in·ter·lard (in′tər·lärd′) v.t. 1. To vary by interjecting something different: to interlard speech with profanity. 2. To occur frequently in. [< MF entrelarder to lard]

in·ter·lay (in′tər·lā′) v.t. **·laid, ·lay·ing** 1. To place between. 2. To decorate with something put or laid between.

in·ter·leaf (in′tər·lēf′) n. pl. **·leaves** (-lēvz′) An extra leaf, usu. blank, inserted between the regular leaves of a book.

in·ter·leave (in′tər·lēv′) v.t. **·leaved, ·leaving** To insert interleaves into (a book).

in·ter·line[1] (in′tər·līn′) v.t. **·lined, ·lin·ing** 1. To insert (words, phrases, etc.) between written or printed lines. 2. To annotate between the lines. [< OF < Med.L < L inter- between + linea line] **— in′ter·lin′er** n.

in·ter·line[2] (in′tər·līn′) v.t. **·lined, ·lin·ing** To put a lining between the usual lining and the outer fabric of (a garment).

in·ter·lin·e·ar (in′tər·lin′ē·ər) adj. 1. Situated or written between the lines. 2. Having lines inserted between the lines. Also **in′ter·lin′e·al.** [< Med.L interlinearis]

in·ter·lin·ing (in′tər·lī′ning) n. 1. An intermediate lining placed between the usual lining and the outer fabric of a garment. 2. The material of which such a lining is made.

in·ter·lock (v. in′tər·lok′) v.t. & v.i. To join firmly. **— in′ter·lock′er** n.

interlocking directorates Econ. Boards of directors that control separate corporations by overlapping membership.

in·ter·loc·u·tor (in′tər·lok′yə·tər) n. One who takes part in a conversation. [< L interloqui to speak between, converse] **— in′ter·loc′u·tress** (-tris) n.fem.

in·ter·loc·u·to·ry (in′tər·lok′yə·tôr′ē, -tō′rē) adj. 1. Pertaining to or having the nature of dialogue. 2. Interposed, as in a conversation. 3. Law Pronounced while a suit is pending; provisional.

in·ter·lope (in′tər·lōp′) v.i. To intrude in the affairs of others; meddle. [< INTER- + lope < Du. loopen to run] **— in′ter·lo′per** n.

in·ter·lude (in′tər·lōōd) n. 1. A period that occurs in and divides some longer process. 2. In English drama, a separate episode, usu. light or humorous, introduced between the acts or parts of a longer performance. 3. A short passage of instrumental music played between the stanzas of a hymn, etc. [< Med.L < L inter- between + ludus game, play]

in·ter·lu·nar (in′tər·lōō′nər) adj. Astron. Pertaining to the period between old and new moon, during which the moon is invisible. Also **in′ter·lu′na·ry.**

in·ter·mar·ry (in′tər·mar′ē) v.i. **·ried, ·ry·ing** 1. To marry someone not a member of one's own religion, race, class, etc. 2. To become connected through the marriage of members: said of different families, etc. **— in′ter·mar′riage** n.

in·ter·me·di·ar·y (in′tər·mē′dē·er′ē) adj. 1. Situated, acting, or coming between; intermediate. 2. Acting as a mediator. **—** n. pl. **·ar·ies** 1. One who acts as a mediator; go-between. 2. An intermediate form, stage, or product.

in·ter·me·di·ate[1] (in′tər·mē′dē·it) adj. Situated or occurring between two points, places, levels, etc. **—** n. Something intermediate. [< L < inter- between + medius middle] **— in′ter·me′di·ate·ly** adv. **— in′ter·me′di·ate·ness** n.

in·ter·me·di·ate[2] (in′tər·mē′dē·āt) v.i. **·at·ed, ·at·ing** To act as an intermediary; mediate. **— in′ter·me′di·a′tion** n. **— in′ter·me′di·a′tor** n.

in·ter·ment (in·tûr′mənt) n. The act of interring; burial.

in·ter·mez·zo (in′tər·met′sō, -med′zō) n. pl. **·zos** or **·zi** (-sē, -zē) 1. A short musical offering given between the acts of a play or opera. 2. Music A short movement connecting the main divisions of a large musical composition. [< Ital. < L intermedius intermediate]

in·ter·mi·na·ble (in·tûr′mə·nə·bəl) *adj.* Having no apparent end or limit; continuing for a very long time; endless. [< OF] **—in·ter′mi·na·bly** *adv.*

in·ter·min·gle (in′tər·ming′gəl) *v.t. & v.i.* **·gled, ·gling** To mingle together; mix.

in·ter·mis·sion (in′tər·mish′ən) *n.* **1.** An interval of time between events or activities; recess. **2.** The act of intermitting, or the state of being intermitted. **3.** *U.S.* The time between acts of a play, opera, etc. **—in·ter·mis′sive** *adj.*

in·ter·mit (in′tər·mit′) *v.t. & v.i.* **·mit·ted, ·mit·ting** To stop temporarily or at intervals; pause. [< L < *inter-* between + *mittere* to send, put] **—in·ter·mit′tence** *n.*

in·ter·mit·tent (in′tər·mit′ənt) *adj.* Ceasing from time to time; coming at intervals. **—in·ter·mit′tent·ly** *adv.*

in·ter·mix (in′tər·miks′) *v.t. & v.i.* To mix together. **in′·ter·mix′ture** *n.*

in·tern (*n.* in′tûrn; *v.* in·tûrn′) *n.* **1.** A medical graduate serving in and living at a hospital for clinical training before being licensed to practice medicine. **2.** One who is interned; internee. Also spelled *interne.* **—v.t. 1.** To confine or detain during wartime. **—v.i. 2.** To serve as an intern. [< F < L *internus* internal] **—in·tern′ment** *n.*

in·ter·nal (in·tûr′nəl) *adj.* **1.** Of or situated on the inside; inner. **2.** Belonging to or derived from the inside: *internal* evidence. **3.** Pertaining to the inner self or the mind. **4.** Pertaining to the domestic affairs of a country: *internal* revenue. **5.** Relating to or affecting the inside of the body. **6.** Intended to be taken or applied inwardly, as medication. **7.** *Anat.* Situated relatively nearer to the axis of the body. [< LL *internus*] **—in·ter′nal·ly** *adv.*

in·ter·nal-com·bus·tion (in·tûr′nəl·kəm·bus′chən) *adj.* Designating a heat engine in which the fuel burns inside the engine itself, most often in a cylinder.

internal medicine The branch of medicine that is concerned with the diseases of the internal organs.

internal revenue Revenue (def. 1).

in·ter·na·tion·al (in′tər·nash′ən·əl) *adj.* **1.** Existing or conducted among nations. **2.** Of or affecting various nations and their peoples. **3.** A person having ties with more than one nation. **—in·ter′na·tion·al·ly** *adv.*

in·ter·na·tion·al (in′tər·nash′ən·əl) *n.* Any of several international socialistic organizations of the late 19th and early 20th centuries. **— First International** A federation of trade unions founded in London in 1864 by Karl Marx and Friedrich Engels. **— Second International** An organization formed at Paris in 1889 to unite Socialist Party groups. **— Third International** The Comintern.

International Court of Justice The principal judicial organ of the United Nations. Also called *World Court.*

International Date Line See DATE LINE (def. 2).

in·ter·na·tion·al·ism (in′tər·nash′ən·əl·iz′əm) *n.* **1.** The belief that cooperation among nations will advance the common welfare. **2.** The state of being international. **—in′·ter·na′tion·al·ist** *n.* **—in·ter·na′tion·al′i·ty** *n.*

in·ter·na·tion·al·ize (in′tər·nash′ən·əl·īz′) *v.t.* **·ized, ·iz·ing** To place under international control; make international.

International Phonetic Alphabet An alphabet in which each symbol represents a specific sound defined as to place and manner of articulation.

in·terne (in′tûrn) See INTERN.

in·ter·ne·cine (in′tər·ne′sin, -sīn) *adj.* **1.** Destructive to both sides. **2.** Involving great slaughter. [< L < *inter-* among + *necare* to kill]

in·tern·ee (in′tûr·nē′) *n.* An interned person.

in·ter·nist (in·tûr′nist) *n.* A specialist in internal medicine.

in·ter·pel·late (in′tər·pel′āt, in·tûr′pə·lāt) *v.t.* **·lat·ed, ·lat·ing** To subject (a member of the government) to a demand for an explanation of an official act or policy. [< L < *inter-* between + *pellere* to drive] **—in·ter·pel·la′tion** *n.*

in·ter·pen·e·trate (in′tər·pen′ə·trāt) *v.* **·trat·ed, ·trat·ing** *v.t.* **1.** To penetrate thoroughly or mutually. **—v.i. 2.** To penetrate each other. **—in′ter·pen′e·tra′tion** *n.* **—in′ter·pen′e·tra′tive** *adj.*

in·ter·plan·e·tar·y (in′tər·plan′ə·ter′ē) *adj.* **1.** Between or among planets. **2.** Situated or occurring in the solar system, but not within the atmosphere of the sun or any other planet.

in·ter·play (in′tər·plā′) *n.* Reciprocal action, movement, or influence. **—v.i.** To act on each other; interact.

in·ter·po·late (in·tûr′pə·lāt) *v.* **·lat·ed, ·lat·ing** *v.t.* **1.** To introduce (additions, comments, etc.) into a discourse, process, or series. **2.** To interrupt with additions. **3.** *Math.* **a** To compute intermediate values in (a series): distinguished from *extrapolate.* **b** To insert (intermediate values) into a series. **—v.i. 4.** To make additions, insertions, interruptions, etc. [< L < *inter-* between + root of *polire* to polish] **—in·ter′po·la′ter, in·ter′po·la′tor** *n.* **—in·ter′po·la′tion** *n.*

in·ter·pose (in′tər·pōz′) *v.* **·posed, ·pos·ing** *v.t.* **1.** To put between other things, esp. as a separation or barrier. **2.** To put in or inject (a comment, etc.) in the course of speech or argument. **3.** To exercise (authority, action, etc.) in order to intervene. **—v.i. 4.** To come between; intervene. **5.**

To put in a remark. [< F *interposer* to place between] **—in′ter·po′sal** *n.* **—in·ter·pos′er** *n.* **—in·ter·po·si′tion** *n.*

in·ter·pret (in·tûr′prit) *v.* **·pret·ed, ·pret·ing** *v.t.* **1.** To give the meaning of; explain. **2.** To judge (persons, events, etc.) in a personal way. **3.** To convey the meaning of (an experience, a play, etc.) by artistic representation or performance. **—v.i. 4.** To explain or construe. **5.** To restate orally in one language what is said in another. [< F < L *interpres* agent, interpreter] **—in·ter′pret·a·ble** *adj.* **—in·ter′pret·a·bil′i·ty, in·ter′pret·a·ble·ness** *n.*

in·ter·pre·ta·tion (in·tûr′prə·tā′shən) *n.* **1.** The process of interpreting. **2.** The sense arrived at in interpreting; the explanation given. **3.** The meaning assigned to actions, intentions, works of art, etc. **—in·ter′pre·ta′tion·al** *adj.*

in·ter·pre·ta·tive (in·tûr′prə·tā′tiv) *adj.* **1.** Of or pertaining to interpretation. **2.** Providing an interpretation; explanatory. Also **in·ter′pre·tive.** **—in·ter′pre·ta′tive·ly** *adv.*

in·ter·pret·er (in·tûr′prit·ər) *n.* One who interprets; esp., one who serves as oral translator between people speaking different languages.

in·ter·ra·cial (in′tər·rā′shəl) *adj.* **1.** Of or for members of different races. **2.** Between, among, or affecting different races, or persons of different races.

in·ter·reg·num (in′tər·reg′nəm) *n.* **1.** An interval between the end of a sovereign's reign and the accession of his lawful successor. **2.** Any suspension of the usual ruling powers of a state. **3.** Any break in continuity. [< L < *inter*-between + *regnum* reign]

in·ter·re·lat·ed (in′tər·ri·lā′tid) *adj.* Reciprocally related.

in·ter·re·la·tion (in′tər·ri·lā′shən) *n.* Mutual or reciprocal relation. **—in′ter·re·la′tion·ship** *n.*

in·ter·ro·gate (in·ter′ə·gāt) *v.* **·gat·ed, ·gat·ing** *v.t.* **1.** To examine formally by questioning. **—v.i. 2.** To ask questions. **— Syn.** See ASK. [< L *inter-* between + *rogare* to ask] **—in·ter′ro·ga′tor** *n.*

in·ter·ro·ga·tion (in·ter′ə·gā′shən) *n.* **1.** The act of interrogating or questioning. **2.** A question; query.

interrogation point A question mark (?). Also **interrogation mark.**

in·ter·rog·a·tive (in′tə·rog′ə·tiv) *adj.* **1.** Asking or having the nature of a question. **2.** *Gram.* Used to ask or indicate a question. **—n.** *Gram.* An interrogative word, phrase, etc. [< L *interrogativus*] **—in·ter·rog′a·tive·ly** *adv.*

interrogative pronoun *Gram.* A pronoun that is used to introduce a question, as *which, whose, what.*

in·ter·rog·a·to·ry (in′tə·rog′ə·tôr′ē, -tō′rē) *adj.* Of, expressing, or implying a question. **—n.** *pl.* **·tor·ies** A question. **—in·ter·rog′a·to′ri·ly** (-tôr′ə·lē, -tō′rə-) *adv.*

in·ter·rupt (in′tə·rupt′) *v.t.* **1.** To break the continuity or regularity of. **2.** To hinder or stop (someone talking, working, etc.) by intervening. **—v.i. 3.** To intervene abruptly. [< L *inter-* between + *rumpere* to break] **—in′ter·rup′tive** *adj.* **—in·ter·rup′tive·ly** *adv.*

in·ter·rupt·ed (in′tə·rup′tid) *adj.* **1.** Lacking continuity. **2.** *Bot.* Exhibiting an abrupt change, as the alternation of leaflets with larger leaves. **—in′ter·rupt′ed·ly** *adv.*

in·ter·rup·tion (in′tə·rup′shən) *n.* **1.** The act of interrupting, or the state of being interrupted. **2.** That which interrupts. **3.** A temporary cessation; intermission; interval.

in·ter·scho·las·tic (in′tər·skə·las′tik) *adj.* Between or among schools, esp. elementary and secondary schools.

in·ter·sect (in′tər·sekt′) *v.t.* **1.** To divide by cutting or passing across. **—v.i. 2.** To cross each other. [< L < *inter-*between + *secare* to cut]

in·ter·sec·tion (in′tər·sek′shən) *n.* **1.** A place of crossing; esp., a place where streets or roads cross. **2.** The act of intersecting, or the state of being intersected.

in·ter·sperse (in′tər·spûrs′) *v.t.* **·spersed, ·spers·ing 1.** To scatter among other things. **2.** To diversify or adorn with other things; interlard. [< L < *inter-* among + *spargere* to scatter] **—in′ter·spers′ed·ly** *adv.* **—in·ter·sper′sion** (-spûr′zhən) *n.*

in·ter·state (in′tər·stāt) *adj.* Between, among, or involving different States of the U.S., or their citizens.

in·ter·stel·lar (in′tər·stel′ər) *adj.* Among the stars.

in·ter·stice (in·tûr′stis) *n.* *pl.* **·sti·ces** (-stə·sēz) A narrow opening or crack. [< F < L *intersistere* to stand between] **—in·ter·sti′tial** (-stish′əl) *adj.* **—in·ter·sti′tial·ly** *adv.*

in·ter·twine (in′tər·twīn′) *v.t. & v.i.* **·twined, ·twin·ing** To unite by twisting together or interlacing; intertwist. **—in′·ter·twine′ment** *n.* **—in′ter·twin′ing·ly** *adv.*

in·ter·ur·ban (in′tər·ûr′bən) *adj.* Between or among cities. **—n.** An interurban railroad, electric trolley line, etc.

in·ter·val (in′tər·vəl) *n.* **1.** The time coming between two events, points in time, etc. **2.** A space between two objects or distance between two points. **3.** A break in the continuity or course of something. **4.** *Brit.* An intermission, as in a play or concert. **5.** *Music* The difference in pitch between two tones. [< OF < L *inter-* between + *vallum* rampart]

in·ter·vene (in′tər·vēn′) *v.i.* **·vened, ·ven·ing 1.** To interfere or take a decisive role, esp. to correct or settle something.

2. To occur so as to modify an action, expectation, etc. **3.** To be located between. **4.** To take place between other events or times: Many years *intervened*. [< L < *inter-* between + *venire* to come] — **in'ter·ven'er** *n.*

in·ter·ven·tion (in'tər·ven'shən) *n.* **1.** The act of intervening. **2.** Interference with the acts of others. — **in'ter·ven'tion·ist** *adj. & n.*

in·ter·view (in'tər·vyōō) *n.* **1.** A conversation conducted, as by a reporter, with a person from whom information is sought; also, the record of such a conversation. **2.** A meeting with a person applying for a job. — *v.t.* To have an interview with. [< MF < L *inter-* between + *videre* to see] — **in'ter·view'er** *n.*

in·ter·weave (in'tər·wēv') *v.t. & v.i.* **·wove** or **·weaved, ·wo·ven, ·weav·ing** To weave together; blend.

in·tes·tate (in·tes'tāt, -tit) *adj.* **1.** Not having made a will or a valid will before death. **2.** Not legally disposed of by will. — *n.* One who dies intestate. [< L < *in-* not + *testari* to make a will] — **in·tes'ta·cy** (-tə·sē) *n.*

in·tes·ti·nal (in·tes'tə·nəl) *adj.* Of, found in, or affecting the intestine. — **in·tes'ti·nal·ly** *adv.*

in·tes·tine (in·tes'tin) *n. Anat. Often pl.* The section of the alimentary canal extending from the pylorus to the anus, consisting of the **small intestine**, including the duodenum, jejunum, and ileum; and the **large intestine**, including the cecum and vermiform appendix, the colon, and the rectum. — *adj.* Domestic; civil. [< L *intestinus* internal]

INTESTINES

a Duodenum. *b* Small intestine. *c* Large intestine. *d* Appendix. *e* Jejunum. *f* Ileum. *g* Cecum. *h* Rectum. *A* Ascending colon. *B* Transverse colon. *C* Descending colon.

in·ti·ma·cy (in'tə·mə·sē) *n. pl.* **·cies** **1.** The state of being intimate. **2.** An instance of this. **3.** *Usu. pl.* Sexual relations, esp. when illicit.

in·ti·mate[1] (in'tə·mit) *adj.* **1.** Characterized by pronounced closeness of friendship or association. **2.** Deeply personal; private: *intimate* thoughts. **3.** Having illicit sexual relations: with *with*: a euphemism. **4.** Resulting from close study. — *n.* A close or confidential friend. [< F < L *intimus*, superl. of *intus* within] — **in'ti·mate·ly** *adv.* — **in'ti·mate·ness** *n.*

in·ti·mate[2] (in'tə·māt) *v.t.* **·mat·ed, ·mat·ing** To make known without direct statement; hint. [< L *intimus*, superl. of *intus* within]

in·ti·ma·tion (in'tə·mā'shən) *n.* **1.** Information given indirectly; a hint. **2.** A declaration or notification. [< F]

in·tim·i·date (in·tim'ə·dāt) *v.t.* **·dat·ed, ·dat·ing** **1.** To make timid; scare. **2.** To discourage from acting by threats or violence: to *intimidate* a witness. [< Med.L < L *in-* very + *timidus* afraid] — **in·tim'i·da'tion** *n.* — **in·tim'i·da'tor** *n.*

in·to (in'tōō) *prep.* **1.** To or toward the inside of from outside: to go *into* the forest. **2.** To a time in the midst of: on *into* the night. **3.** To the form or condition of: to change water *into* steam. **4.** Dividing: Two *into* six is three. [OE]

in·tol·er·a·ble (in·tol'ər·ə·bəl) *adj.* Not tolerable; that cannot be borne or endured; insufferable. — **in·tol'er·a·bil'i·ty, in·tol'er·a·ble·ness** *n.* — **in·tol'er·a·bly** *adv.*

in·tol·er·ance (in·tol'ər·əns) *n.* **1.** The state of being intolerant. **2.** Incapacity or unwillingness to tolerate.

in·tol·er·ant (in·tol'ər·ənt) *adj.* **1.** Not tolerant, esp. of beliefs, racial or social types, etc., different from one's own; bigoted. **2.** Unable or unwilling to bear or endure. — *n.* One who is intolerant. — **in·tol'er·ant·ly** *adv.*

in·tomb (in·tōōm'), **in·tomb·ment** (in·tōōm'mənt), etc. See ENTOMB, etc.

in·to·na·tion (in'tō·nā'shən) *n.* **1.** Way of speaking a language or utterance; esp., the meaning and melody given to speech by changing levels of pitch. **2.** The act of intoning. **3.** *Music* **a** The production of tones of accurate pitch. **b** Pitch or the accuracy of pitch.

in·tone (in·tōn') *v.* **·toned, ·ton·ing** *v.t.* **1.** To utter or recite in a musical monotone; chant. **2.** To give particular tones or intonation to. **3.** To sing the opening notes of (a plainsong, psalm, etc.). — *v.i.* **4.** To speak or sing in a monotone. **5.** To emit a slow, protracted sound. [< MF < Med.L *intonare* to intone, thunder] — **in·ton'er** *n.*

in to·to (in tō'tō) *Latin* In the whole; altogether; entirely.

in·tox·i·cant (in·tok'sə·kənt) *n.* That which intoxicates. — *adj.* Intoxicating.

in·tox·i·cate (in·tok'sə·kāt) *v.* **·cat·ed, ·cat·ing** *v.t.* **1.** To make drunk. **2.** To elate or excite to a degree of frenzy. **3.** *Med.* To poison. — *v.i.* **4.** To possess intoxicating properties. [< Med.L < L *toxicum* poison] — **in·tox'i·ca'tion** *n.* — **in·tox'i·ca'tive** *adj.* — **in·tox'i·ca'tor** *n.*

in·tra- *prefix* Situated or occurring within; inside of: **intra-**

abdominal; intracollegiate; intra-urban. [< L *intra-* < *intra* within]

in·trac·ta·ble (in·trak'tə·bəl) *adj.* **1.** Not tractable; unruly. **2.** Difficult to manipulate, treat, or work. — **in·trac'ta·bil'i·ty, in·trac'ta·ble·ness** *n.* — **in·trac'ta·bly** *adv.*

in·tra·dos (in·trā'dos) *n.* The interior curved surface of an arch or vault. [< F < L *intra-* within + *dorsum* back]

in·tra·mu·ral (in'trə·myōō'rəl) *adj.* **1.** Taking place within a school, college, etc.: *intramural* football. **2.** Situated or occurring within the walls or limits of a city, building, organization, etc. — **in'tra·mu'ral·ly** *adv.*

in·tra·mus·cu·lar (in'trə·mus'kyə·lər) *adj.* Situated in or affecting the inside of a muscle. — **in'tra·mus'cu·lar·ly** *adv.*

in·tran·si·gent (in·tran'sə·jənt) *adj.* Refusing to compromise or come to terms, esp. in politics; unbending. — *n.* One who is intransigent: also **in·tran'si·gent·ist.** [< F < Sp. < L *in-* not + *transigere* to agree] — **in·tran'si·gence, in·tran'si·gen·cy** *n.* — **in·tran'si·gent·ly** *adv.*

in·tran·si·tive (in·tran'sə·tiv) *Gram. adj.* Of or pertaining to intransitive verbs. — *n.* An intransitive verb. — **in·tran'si·tive·ly** *adv.*

intransitive verb *Gram.* A verb that has or needs no complement to complete its meaning.

in·tra·state (in'trə·stāt') *adj.* Confined within or pertaining to a single state, esp. of the U.S.

in·tra·ve·nous (in'trə·vē'nəs) *adj.* Situated in or affecting the inside of a vein: an *intravenous* injection.

in·treat (in·trēt') See ENTREAT.

in·trep·id (in·trep'id) *adj.* Unshaken by fear; bold. [< L < *in-* not + *trepidus* agitated] — **in·tre·pid·i·ty** (in'trə·pid'ə·tē) *n.* — **in·trep'id·ly** *adv.*

in·tri·ca·cy (in'tri·kə·sē) *n. pl.* **·cies** **1.** The state or quality of being intricate. **2.** That which is intricate.

in·tri·cate (in'tri·kit) *adj.* **1.** Perplexingly entangled, complicated, or involved. **2.** Difficult to follow or understand; puzzling. [< L < *in-* in + *tricae* difficulties] — **in'tri·cate·ly** *adv.* — **in'tri·cate·ness** *n.*

in·trigue (in·trēg'; *for n.*, also in·trēg') *v.* **·trigued, ·tri·guing** *v.t.* **1.** To arouse the interest or curiosity of; fascinate; beguile. — *v.i.* **2.** To use secret or underhand means; plot; conspire. **3.** To carry on a secret or illicit love affair. — *n.* **1.** A plotting or scheming by secret or underhand means. **2.** A plot or scheme. **3.** A secret or illicit love affair. **4.** The quality or power of arousing curiosity or interest. [< F < Ital. < L *intricare* to entangle] — **in·tri'guer** *n.*

in·trin·sic (in·trin'sik) *adj.* Belonging to or arising from the true or fundamental nature of a thing; essential; inherent. Also **in·trin'si·cal.** [< OF < Med.L < L *intrinsecus* internally] — **in·trin'si·cal·ly** *adv.* — **in·trin'si·cal·ness** *n.*

intro- *prefix* In; within: *introvert.* [< L < *intro* inwardly]

in·tro·duce (in'trə·dōōs', -dyōōs') *v.t.* **·duced, ·duc·ing** **1.** To make (a person or persons) acquainted face to face, usu. in a formal manner: often with *to*. **2.** To bring into use or notice first; launch: to *introduce* a new technique. **3.** To broach or propose: to *introduce* an idea. **4.** To bring in as something added; establish as a new element. **5.** To present (a person, product, etc.) to a specific group or the general public. **6.** To bring (a person or persons) to first knowledge of something: with *to*: to *introduce* a class to algebra. **7.** To put in; insert. **8.** To bring forward for official notice or action. **9.** To begin; open. [< L < *intro-* within + *ducere* to lead] — **in'tro·duc'er** *n.* — **in'tro·duc'i·ble** *adj.*

in·tro·duc·tion (in'trə·duk'shən) *n.* **1.** The act of introducing. **2.** First knowledge or acquaintance; initiation. **3.** The presentation of a person to another, to a group, etc.; also, a means of acquainting persons, as a letter, etc. **4.** Something that leads up to what follows, as the first part of a book, etc. **5.** An elementary treatise in any branch of study. **6.** Something introduced.

in·tro·duc·to·ry (in'trə·duk'tər·ē) *adj.* Serving as an introduction; preliminary. Also **in'tro·duc'tive.** — **in'tro·duc'to·ri·ly** *adv.*

in·tro·it (in·trō'it) *n. Eccl.* **1.** In the Roman Catholic Church, the opening act of worship in the Mass, consisting usu. of a part of a psalm followed by the Gloria Patri. **2.** In the Anglican Church, a hymn sung at the beginning of public worship. [< F < L < *intro-* in + *ire* to go] — **in·tro'i·tal** (-təl) *adj.*

in·tro·spect (in'trə·spekt') *v.i.* To practice introspection or self-examination. [< L *intro-* within + *specere* to look]

in·tro·spec·tion (in'trə·spek'shən) *n.* The observation and analysis of one's own mental processes and emotional states. — **in'tro·spec'tive** *adj.* — **in'tro·spec'tive·ly** *adv.*

in·tro·ver·sion (in'trə·vûr'zhən, -shən) *n.* **1.** The act of introverting, or the state of being introverted. **2.** *Psychol.* The turning of one's interest inward upon the self rather than toward external objects. — **in'tro·ver'sive** (-vûr'siv) *adj.*

in·tro·vert (in'trə·vûrt) *n.* **1.** *Psychol.* A person whose interest is directed primarily toward the self. **2.** One who is sober, reserved, and withdrawn. **— v.t. 1.** To turn inward; cause to bend in an inward direction. **2.** To turn (the mind or thoughts) toward the self. **— adj.** Characterized by or tending to introversion. [< INTRO- + L *vertere* to turn]

in·trude (in·trōōd′) *v.* **·trud·ed, ·trud·ing v.t. 1.** To thrust or force in. **2.** *Geol.* To cause to enter by intrusion. **— v.i. 3.** To come in without leave or invitation: often with *upon*. [< L < *in-* in + *trudere* to thrust] **— in·trud′er** *n.*

in·tru·sion (in·trōō′zhən) *n.* **1.** The act or condition of intruding; encroachment. **2.** That which intrudes. **3.** *Geol.* **a** The movement of molten rock into an earlier solid rock formation. **b** An intrusive rock.

in·tru·sive (in·trōō′siv) *adj.* **1.** Coming or thrusting in without warrant; obtrusive. **2.** Prone to intrude. **3.** *Geol.* Formed by intrusion. **4.** *Phonet.* Denoting speech sounds that result from the adjustment of the vocal organs to the sounds preceding and following and have no etymological basis, as the (d) in *spindle* (Old English *spinel*). [See IN-TRUDE.] **— in·tru′sive·ly** *adv.* **— in·tru′sive·ness** *n.*

in·trust (in·trust′) See ENTRUST.

in·tu·it (in·tōō′it, -tōō′-) *v.t. & v.i.* **·tu·it·ed, ·tu·it·ing** To know or discover by intuition.

in·tu·i·tion (in′tōō·ish′ən, -tyōō-) *n.* **1.** A direct knowledge or awareness of something without conscious attention or reasoning. **2.** Anything perceived or learned without conscious attention, reasoning, concentration, etc. **3.** The ability or quality of perceiving without conscious attention or reasoning. [< Med.L < *in-* on + *tueri* to look] **— in′tu·i′tion·al** *adj.* **— in′tu·i′tion·al·ly** *adv.*

in·tu·i·tive (in·tōō′ə·tiv, -tyōō′-) *adj.* **1.** Perceived or learned by intuition; proceeding from intuition. **2.** Characterized by, or knowing through intuition. **— in·tu′i·tive·ly** *adv.* **— in·tu′i·tive·ness** *n.*

in·turn (in′tûrn′) *n.* A turning inward, as of the toes.

in·twine (in·twīn′) See ENTWINE.

in·un·dant (in·un′dənt) *adj.* Inundating; overflowing.

in·un·date (in′un·dāt) *v.t.* **·dat·ed, ·dat·ing 1.** To cover by overflowing; flood. **2.** To overwhelm with abundance or excess. [< L < *in-* in, on + *undare* to overflow] **— in′un·da′tion** *n.* **— in·un·da′tor** *n.* **— in·un·da·to·ry** (in·un′də·tôr′ē, -tō′rē) *adj.*

in·ure (in·yōōr′) *v.* **·ured, ·ur·ing v.t. 1.** To cause to accept or tolerate by use or exercise; accustom; habituate. **— v.i. 2.** *Rare* To have or take effect. [< IN-² + obs. *ure* work < OF < L *opera* work] **— in·ure′ment** *n.*

in va·cu·o (in vak′yōō·ō) *Latin* In a vacuum.

in·vade (in·vād′) *v.* **·vad·ed, ·vad·ing v.t. 1.** To enter by force with the intent of conquering or plundering. **2.** To rush or swarm into as if to occupy or overrun. **3.** To trespass upon; intrude upon: to *invade* privacy. **4.** To penetrate and spread through injuriously. **— v.i. 5.** To make an invasion. [< L < *in-* in + *vadere* to go] **— in·vad′er** *n.*

in·vag·i·nate (in·vaj′ə·nāt) *v.* **·nat·ed, ·nat·ing v.t. 1.** To put into or as into a sheath; ensheathe. **2.** To infold so as to form a depression or pouch. **— v.i. 3.** To undergo invagination. [< L < *in-* in + *vagina* sheath + -ATE²] **— in·vag′i·na·ble** (-nə·bəl) *adj.* **— in·vag′i·na′tion** *n.*

in·va·lid¹ (in′və·lid) *n.* A sickly or bedridden person; one disabled by injury or chronic disease. **— adj.** Enfeebled by ill health. **2.** Of or pertaining to disabled persons. **— v.t. 1.** To cause to become an invalid; disable. **2.** *Chiefly Brit.* To release or classify (a soldier, sailor, etc.) as unfit for duty because of ill health. **— v.i. 3.** To become an invalid. [< F < L *invalidus* not strong] **— in′va·lid·ism** *n.*

in·va·lid² (in·val′id) *adj.* Not valid; having no force, weight, or cogency; null; void. [< L *invalidus*] **— in·val′id·ly** *adv.*

in·val·i·date (in·val′ə·dāt) *v.t.* **·dat·ed, ·dat·ing** To weaken or destroy the validity of; render invalid; annul. **— in·val′i·da′tion** *n.* **— in·val′i·da′tor** *n.*

in·va·lid·i·ty (in′və·lid′ə·tē) *n.* Lack of validity.

in·val·u·a·ble (in·val′yōō·ə·bəl, -yōō·bəl) *adj.* Having a value beyond estimation; priceless. **— in·val′u·a·bly** *adv.*

in·var·i·a·ble (in·vâr′ē·ə·bəl) *adj.* Not variable; not subject to alteration; unchangeable; constant. **— in·var′i·a·bil′i·ty, in·var′i·a·ble·ness** *n.* **— in·var′i·a·bly** *adv.*

in·var·i·ant (in·vâr′ē·ənt) *adj.* Not subject to change or variation; constant. **— n.** *Math.* A quantity that remains unchanged; constant. **— in·var′i·ance, in·var′i·an·cy** *n.*

in·va·sion (in·vā′zhən) *n.* **1.** The act of invading with hostile armed forces; a military inroad. **2.** Any attack or onset of something injurious or disagreeable, as a disease. **3.** Encroachment by intrusion or trespass. **4.** Entrance with intent to overrun or occupy. **— in·va′sive** *adj.*

in·vec·tive (in·vek′tiv) *n.* Violent accusation or denunciation; abuse. **— adj.** Using or characterized by vituperation or abuse. [< OF < LL < L *invectus*, pp. of *invehere* to carry into] **— in·vec′tive·ly** *adv.* **— in·vec′tive·ness** *n.*

in·veigh (in·vā′) *v.i.* To utter vehement censure or invective: with *against*. [< L < *in-* into + *vehere* to carry] **— in·veigh′er** *n.*

in·vei·gle (in·vē′gəl, -vā-) *v.t.* **·gled, ·gling** To entice or induce by guile or flattery; draw; cajole: often with *into*. [< F *aveugle* blind, ult. < L *ab-* without + *oculus* eye] **— in·vei′gler** *n.*

in·vent (in·vent′) *v.t.* **1.** To devise or create by original effort; esp., to conceive or make originally (some mechanical, electrical, or other device). **2.** To make up, as something untrue or contrary to fact: to *invent* an excuse. [< L < *in-* on + *venire* to come] **— in·vent′i·ble** *adj.*

in·ven·tion (in·ven′shən) *n.* **1.** The act or process of inventing. **2.** A device or useful contrivance conceived or made by original effort. **3.** The skill or ingenuity needed for inventing or contriving; inventive powers. **4.** A mental fabrication or concoction. **— in·ven′tion·al** *adj.*

in·ven·tive (in·ven′tiv) *adj.* **1.** Skillful at invention or contrivance; ingenious. **2.** Characterized by or created by invention. **3.** Pertaining to invention. **— in·ven′tive·ly** *adv.* **— in·ven′tive·ness** *n.*

in·ven·tor (in·ven′tər) *n.* One who invents; esp., one who has originated some method, process, etc. Also **in·vent′er**.

in·ven·to·ry (in′vən·tôr′ē, -tō′rē) *n. pl.* **·ries 1.** A list of articles, with the description and quantity of each. **2.** A list of all finished goods in stock, goods in the process of manufacture, and the raw materials used, made annually by a business concern. **3.** The process of making such a list. **4.** The value of the goods or stock of a business. **— v.t.** **·ried, ·ry·ing 1.** To make an inventory of. **2.** To insert in an inventory. [< Med.L < L *inventorium*] **— in′ven·to′ri·al** (-tôr′ē·əl, -tō′rē) *adj.* **— in′ven·to′ri·al·ly** *adv.*

in·ver·ness (in′vər·nes′) *n. Often cap.* **1.** A type of overcoat having a detachable cape. **2.** The cape itself: also called **Inverness cape**. [after *Inverness*, Scotland]

in·verse (in·vûrs′, in′vûrs) *adj.* **1.** Reversed or opposite in order, effect, etc. **2.** Turned upside down; inverted. **— n.** That which is in direct contrast or opposition; the reverse; opposite. **— in·verse′ly** *adv.*

in·ver·sion (in·vûr′zhən, -shən) *n.* **1.** The act of inverting, or the state of being inverted. **2.** That which is inverted. **3.** In grammar and rhetoric, a reversing of the usual word order in a phrase, clause, or sentence. **— in·ver′sive** *adj.*

in·vert (*v.* in·vûrt′; *adj. & n.* in′vûrt) *v.t.* **1.** To turn upside down; turn completely over. **2.** To reverse the order, effect, or operation of. **3.** To alter by inversion, as in chemistry, music, etc. **— v.i. 4.** To undergo inversion. **— adj.** *Chem.* Inverted. **— n. 1.** One who or that which is inverted. **2.** *Psychiatry* A homosexual. [< L < *in-* in + *vertere* to turn] **— in·vert′er** *n.* **— in·vert′i·ble** *adj.*

in·ver·te·brate (in·vûr′tə·brit, -brāt) *adj.* **1.** *Zool.* Not vertebrate; lacking a backbone or spinal column. **2.** Lacking firmness or character; irresolute. Also **in·ver′te·bral** (-brəl). **— n. 1.** An invertebrate animal. **2.** One who lacks firmness of character.

in·vest (in·vest′) *v.t.* **1.** To commit or use (money, capital, etc.) for the purchase of property, securities, a business, etc., with the expectation of profit. **2.** To spend or use (money, time, effort, etc.) for: often with *in*. **3.** To place in office formally; install. **4.** To give power, authority, or rank to. **5.** To cover or surround as if with a garment; shroud. **6.** To provide or endow with qualities or traits: to *invest* a hero with glory. **7.** *Mil.* To surround or hem in; besiege. **— v.i. 8.** To make an investment or investments. [< L < *in-* on + *vestire* to clothe] **— in·ves′tor** *n.*

in·ves·ti·gate (in·ves′tə·gāt) *v.* **·gat·ed, ·gat·ing v.t. 1.** To search or inquire into; make a formal or official examination of. **— v.i. 2.** To make an investigation. [< L < *in-* in + *vestigare* to trace] **— in·ves′ti·ga·ble** (-gə·bəl) *adj.* **— in·ves′ti·ga′tive** *adj.* **— in·ves′ti·ga·to·ry** (-gə·tôr′ē, -tō′rē) *adj.*

in·ves·ti·ga·tion (in·ves′tə·gā′shən) *n.* **1.** A formal or official examination or study, as by the police or a governmental body. **2.** The act of investigating. [< F]

in·ves·ti·ga·tor (in·ves′tə·gā′tər) *n.* **1.** A detective, esp. a private detective. **2.** One who investigates. **— in·ves′ti·ga·to′ri·al** (-tôr′ē·əl, -tō′rē·əl) *adj.*

in·ves·ti·tive (in·ves′tə·tiv) *adj.* **1.** Of or pertaining to investiture. **2.** Having the function of investing.

in·ves·ti·ture (in·ves′tə·chər) *n.* **1.** The act or ceremony of investing with an office, authority, or right. **2.** An investing or clothing, as with a quality, garment, etc.

in·vest·ment (in·vest′mənt) *n.* **1.** The investing of money or capital to gain interest or income. **2.** Money or capital so invested. **3.** The form of property in which one invests. **4.** The act of investing, or the state of being invested. **5.** Investiture. **6.** *Biol.* An outer covering of an animal, plant, organ, or part. **7.** *Mil.* The surrounding of a fort or town to create a state of siege; blockade.

in·vet·er·ate (in·vet′ər·it) *adj.* **1.** Firmly established by long continuance; deep-rooted. **2.** Confirmed or hardened in a particular character, habit, or opinion: an *inveterate* bigot. [< L < *in-* very + *vetus* old] **— in·vet′er·a·cy** *n.* **— in·vet′er·ate·ly** *adv.* **— in·vet′er·ate·ness** *n.*

in·vid·i·ous (in·vid′ē·əs) *adj.* **1.** Exciting or creating ill will or dislike; offensive: *invidious* remarks. **2.** Provoking anger or resentment by unjust discrimination. [< L < *invidia* envy.] **—in·vid′i·ous·ly** *adv.* **—in·vid′i·ous·ness** *n.*

in·vig·or·ate (in·vig′ər·āt) *v.t.* **·at·ed, ·at·ing** To give vigor and energy to; animate. [< L *in-* in + *vigor* vigor + -ATE²] **—in·vig′or·at′ing·ly** *adv.* **—in·vig′or·a′tion** *n.* **—in·vig′or·a′tive** *adj.* **—in·vig′or·a′tive·ly** *adv.* **—in·vig′or·a′tor** *n.*

in·vin·ci·ble (in·vin′sə·bəl) *adj.* Not to be overcome; unconquerable. [< F < L *invincibilis*] **—in·vin′ci·bil′i·ty, in·vin′ci·ble·ness** *n.* **—in·vin′ci·bly** *adv.*

in·vi·o·la·ble (in·vī′ə·lə·bəl) *adj.* **1.** Not to be profaned, defiled, etc.; sacrosanct. **2.** Not to be violated or broken. **—in·vi′o·la·bil′i·ty, in·vi′o·la·ble·ness** *n.* **—in·vi′o·la·bly** *adv.*

in·vi·o·late (in·vī′ə·lit) *adj.* **1.** Not violated; not profaned or broken; intact. **2.** Inviolable. **—in·vi′o·la·cy** *n.* **—in·vi′o·late·ly** *adv.* **—in·vi′o·late·ness** *n.*

in·vis·i·ble (in·viz′ə·bəl) *adj.* **1.** Not visible; not capable of being seen. **2.** Not in sight; concealed. **3.** Not publicly or openly acknowledged. **4.** *Econ.* Not appearing in regular processes or financial statements: *invisible* assets. — *n.* One who or that which is invisible. [< OF] **—in·vis′i·bil′i·ty, in·vis′i·ble·ness** *n.* **—in·vis′i·bly** *adv.*

in·vi·ta·tion (in′və·tā′shən) *n.* **1.** The act of inviting. **2.** The means or words by which one invites or is invited: a written *invitation*. **3.** The act of alluring or inducing; enticement. **—in′vi·ta′tion·al** *adj.*

in·vite (*v.* in·vīt′; *n.* in′vīt) *v.* **·vit·ed, ·vit·ing** *v.t.* **1.** To ask (someone) courteously to be present in some place, to attend some event, or to perform some action. **2.** To make formal or polite request for: to *invite* suggestions. **3.** To present opportunity or inducement for; attract: his opinions *invite* criticism. **4.** To tempt; entice. — *v.i.* **5.** To give invitation; entice. — *n. Slang* An invitation. [< F < L *invitare* to entertain] **—in·vit′er** *n.*

in·vit·ing (in·vī′ting) *adj.* That invites or allures; attractive. **—in·vit′ing·ly** *adv.* **—in·vit′ing·ness** *n.*

in·vo·ca·tion (in′və·kā′shən) *n.* **1.** The act of invoking or appealing to a deity, or other agent for help, inspiration, witness, etc. **2.** A prayer, as at the opening of a ceremony. **3.** An appeal for assistance to the Muses or some divine being at the beginning of an epic or other poem. **4.** The act of conjuring an evil spirit. **—in·voc·a·tive** (in·vok′ə·tiv), **in·voc·a·to·ry** (in·vok′ə·tôr′ē, -tō′rē) *adj.*

in·voice (in′vois) *n.* **1.** A descriptive list of merchandise sent or services rendered to a purchaser, including quantities, prices, shipping and other costs, etc. **2.** The merchandise or services so itemized. — *v.t.* **·voiced, ·voic·ing** To make an invoice; list on an invoice. [< F *envoyer* to send.]

in·voke (in·vōk′) *v.t.* **·voked, ·vok·ing 1.** To call upon for aid, protection, witness, etc. **2.** To declare relevant and operative, as a law, power, right, etc.: to *invoke* the Fifth Amendment. **3.** To appeal to for confirmation; quote as an authority. **4.** To summon or conjure by incantation. **5.** To call or petition for: to *invoke* a blessing. [< F < L < *in-* on + *vocare* to call] **—in·vok′er** *n.*

in·vo·lu·cre (in′və·loo′kər) *n. Bot.* A ring of bracts at the base of a compound flower. [< F < L < *involvere* to roll up] **—in′vo·lu′cral** (-krəl) *adj.*

in·vol·un·tar·y (in·vol′ən·ter′ē) *adj.* **1.** Done or occurring without one's consent or choice; unintentional. **2.** *Physiol.* Functioning without conscious control: *involuntary* muscles. **—in·vol′un·tar′i·ly** *adv.* **—in·vol′un·tar′i·ness** *n.*

in·vo·lute (in′və·loot) *adj.* **1.** Having complications and intricacies; involved. **2.** *Bot.* Having the edges rolled inward, as a leaf. **3.** *Zool.* Having the whorls nearly or entirely concealing the axis, as a shell. Also **in′vo·lut′ed.** [< L *involutus*, pp. of *involvere* to involve]

in·vo·lu·tion (in′və·loo′shən) **1.** A complicating or intertwining; entanglement. **2.** Something involved or complicated. **3.** *Biol.* Arrest and reversal of development; degeneration. **4.** In rhetoric, complicated or cumbrous arrangement of words, clauses, or phrases. **—in′vo·lu′tion·al** *adj.*

in·volve (in·volv′) *v.t.* **·volved, ·volv·ing 1.** To include as a relevant or necessary aspect. **2.** To have effect on; affect by drawing in or spreading. **3.** To implicate; associate significantly: usu. with *in* or *with*: He is *involved* in the scandal. **4.** To absorb or engross: usu. with *in.* **5.** To make intricate or tangled. **6.** To envelop: to *involve* an issue in obscurity. [< L < *in-* in + *volvere* to roll] **—in·volve′ment** *n.*

in·volved (in·volvd′) *adj.* Complicated; intricate. **—in·volv·ed·ness** (in·vol′vid·nis) *n.*

in·vul·ner·a·ble (in·vul′nər·ə·bəl) *adj.* **1.** Not capable of being wounded or physically injured. **2.** Not to be overcome or damaged by attack; unconquerable. **—in·vul′ner·a·bil′i·ty,** and **in·vul′ner·a·ble·ness** *n.* **—in·vul′ner·a·bly** *adv.*

in·ward (in′wərd) *adv.* **1.** Toward the inside, center, or interior. **2.** In or into the mind or thoughts. Also *inwards.* — *adj.* **1.** Situated within, esp. with reference to the body; in-

ternal. **2.** Pertaining to the mind or spirit. **3.** Proceeding toward the inside: an *inward* thrust. **4.** Inland. **5.** Inherent; intrinsic. — *n.* The inner part. [OE *inweard*]

in·ward·ly (in′wərd·lē) *adv.* **1.** Within the mind or heart; secretly: *inwardly* anxious. **2.** On the inside; within. **3.** Toward the center or interior. **4.** Essentially; intrinsically.

in·ward·ness (in′wərd·nis) *n.* **1.** The state of being inward; existence within. **2.** Inner quality or meaning; essence. **3.** Intensity of feeling. **4.** Unworldliness.

in·wards (in′wərdz; *for n., also* in′ərdz) *adv.* Inward. — *n.pl.* The entrails.

in·weave (in·wēv′) *v.t.* **·wove** or **·weaved, ·wo·ven** or *less frequently* **·wove, ·weav·ing** To weave in or together.

in·wrap (in·rap′) See ENWRAP.

in·wrought (in·rôt′) *adj.* **1.** Worked into a fabric, metal, etc., as a pattern. **2.** Decorated with such a pattern or design. **3.** Closely combined with something; blended in.

i·o·dide (ī′ə·dīd) *n. Chem.* A compound of iodine and one other element. Also **i′o·did** (-did).

i·o·dine (ī′ə·dīn, -din; *in technical usage* ī′ə·dēn) *n.* **1.** A grayish black non-metallic element (symbol I), yielding, when heated, corrosive fumes of a rich violet color, used in medicine as an antiseptic and also in photography and organic synthesis. See ELEMENT. **2.** *Informal* A solution of iodine used as an antiseptic. Also **i·o·din** (ī′ə·din). [< F < Gk. *iōdēs* violetlike (< *ion* a violet + *eidos* form) + -INE²]

i·o·dize (ī′ə·dīz) *v.t.* **·dized, ·diz·ing** To treat with, combine with, or expose to the vapor of iodine. **—i′o·diz′er** *n.*

i·o·do·form (ī·ō′də·fôrm) *n. Chem.* A light yellow crystalline compound, CHI₃, used in medicine as an antiseptic.

i·on (ī′ən, ī′on) *n. Physics* An electrically charged atom, radical, or molecule, resulting from the action of an electrolyte, electric fields, high temperatures, various forms of radiation, etc., in adding or removing electrons. [< Gk. *ion*, neut. of *iōn*, ppr. of *ienai* to go] **—i·on′ic** *adj.*

-ion *suffix of nouns* **1.** Action, state, quality, or process of: *communion.* **2.** State or result of being: *union.* Also *-ation, -tion.* [< F < L *-io, -ionis*]

ion exchange *Chem.* A process whereby ions may be reversibly interchanged at the boundary of a liquid and solid in contact, the composition of the solid not being altered.

I·o·ni·a (ī·ō′nē·ə) The ancient coastal region of western Asia Minor, colonized by the Greeks in the 11th century B.C. **—I·o′ni·an** *adj. & n.*

I·on·ic (ī·on′ik) *adj.* **1.** Ionian. **2.** *Archit.* Of or pertaining to an order of Greek architecture characterized by a capital having typical scroll-like ornaments. — *n.* A dialect of ancient Greek. [< L < Gk. *Iōnikos*]

i·o·ni·um (ī·ō′nē·əm) *n.* A radioactive isotope of thorium, of mass 230 and a half life of about 80,000 years. [< ION + (URAN)IUM; from its ionizing action]

i·on·ize (ī′ən·īz) *v.t. & v.i.* **·ized, ·iz·ing** To convert or become converted, totally or in part, into ions. **—i′on·i·za′tion** *n.* **—i′on·iz′er** *n.*

i·on·o·sphere (ī·on′ə·sfir) *n.* A region of the earth's atmosphere above the mesosphere, consisting of several layers subject to ionization, with seasonal variations. **—i·on·o·spher′ic** (-sfir′ik, -sfer′-) *adj.*

i·o·ta (ī·ō′tə) *n.* **1.** The ninth letter in the Greek alphabet (I, ι), corresponding to English *i.* See ALPHABET. **2.** A very small or insignificant amount. [< L < Gk. *iōta*].

IOU A written acknowledgment of indebtedness having on it these letters (meaning *I owe you*). Also **I.O.U.**

-ious *suffix of adjectives* Characterized by; full of: occurring esp. in adjectives formed from nouns ending in *-ion: suspicious, cautious.* [< L *-iosus* full of]

ip·e·cac (ip′ə·kak) *n.* **1.** Either of two plants of the madder family, yielding a medicinal alkaloid. **2.** The dried root of either of these plants. **3.** An extract of this root, used as an emetic or cathartic. Also **ip·e·cac·u·an·ha** (ip′ə·kak′yoo·ä′nə). [< Pg. < Tupi < *ipe* little + *kaa* tree, herb]

Iph·i·ge·ni·a (if′ə·jə·nī′ə) In Greek legend, a daughter of Agamemnon and Clytemnestra who was offered as a sacrifice to Artemis so that the Greek fleet might sail on to Troy.

ip·se dix·it (ip′sē dik′sit) *Latin* **1.** Literally, he himself said (it). **2.** An improved or dogmatic assertion.

ip·so fac·to (ip′sō fak′tō) *Latin* By the fact itself; by that very fact or act: outlawed *ipso facto*².

ir- Assimilated var. of IN-¹ and IN-².

I·ra·ni·an (i·rā′nē·ən) *adj.* Of or pertaining to Iran, its people, or their language. — *n.* **1.** A native or inhabitant of Iran; a Persian. **2.** A branch of the Indo-Iranian subfamily of Indo-European languages, including Modern Persian, Kurdish, and Pashto, and such ancient languages as Old Persian and Scythian. **3.** Modern Persian.

I·ra·qi (i·rä′kē) *adj.* Of or pertaining to Iraq, its people, or their language. — *n.* **1.** A native or inhabitant of Iraq. **2.** The dialect of Arabic spoken in Iraq.

---

i·ras·ci·ble (i·ras/ə·bəl, ĭ·ras/-) *adj.* **1.** Easily provoked to anger; quick-tempered. **2.** Resulting from or characterized by anger or irritability. [< OF < LL *irasci* to be angry] — **i·ras/ci·bil/i·ty, i·ras/ci·ble·ness** *n.* — **i·ras/ci·bly** *adv.*

i·rate (ī/rāt, ī·rāt/) *adj.* Angry; enraged. [< L *iratus*, pp. of *irasci* to be angry] — **i/rate·ly** *adv.*

IRBM The intermediate range ballistic missile, having a range between 200 and 1500 miles.

ire (īr) *n.* Wrath; anger. [< OF < L *ira* anger]

ire·ful (īr/fəl) *adj.* Full of ire; wrathful; angry. — **ire/ful·ly** *adv.* — **ire/ful·ness** *n.*

ir·i·des·cent (ir/ə·des/ənt) *adj.* Displaying the colors of the rainbow in shifting hues and patterns, as soap bubbles, mother-of-pearl, etc. [< Gk. *iris, iridos* rainbow] — **ir/i·des/cence** *adj.* — **ir/i·des/cent·ly** *adv.*

i·rid·i·um (i·rid/ē·əm, ī·rid/-) *n.* A hard, brittle, silver-gray metallic element (symbol Ir) of the platinum group, used in certain alloys for making penpoints, jewelry, etc. See ELEMENT. [< NL < L < Gk. *iris* rainbow + -IUM]

irido- *combining form* The iris of the eye. Also, before vowels, **irid-.** [< Gk. *iris, iridos* iris]

ir·i·dos·mine (ir/ə·doz/min, -dos/-, ī/rə-) *n.* Osmiridium. Also **ir/i·dos/mi·um** (-mē·əm). [< IRID(IUM) + OSMIUM]

i·ris (ī/ris) *n.* *pl.* **i·ris·es** or **ir·i·des** (ir/ə·dēz, ī/rə-) **1.** *Anat.* The colored, circular, contractile membrane between the cornea and the lens of the eye, having the pupil as its central aperture. For illus. see EYE. **2.** *Bot.* A plant with sword-shaped leaves and large handsome flowers, as the crocus, gladiolus, etc. [< L < Gk. *iris*]

I·ris (ī/ris) In Greek mythology, the goddess of the rainbow and a messenger of the gods.

I·rish (ī/rish) *adj.* Of or pertaining to Ireland, its people, or their language. — *n.* **1.** The people of Ireland or of Irish ancestry: preceded by *the.* **2.** The ancient or modern language of Ireland, belonging to the Goidelic branch of the Celtic languages: also called *Irish Gaelic:* sometimes called *Erse.* **3.** The dialect of English spoken in Ireland: also called *Irish English.* [ME *Irisc* < OE *Ir- + -isc*]

Irish English Irish (def. 3).

Irish Gaelic Irish (def. 2).

I·rish·man (ī/rish·mən) *n.* *pl.* **·men** (-mən) A man of Irish birth or ancestry.

Irish moss Carrageen, a seaweed.

Irish potato The common or white potato.

Irish setter A reddish brown variety of setter.

Irish terrier A small terrier having a wiry, reddish coat.

Irish wolfhound A large, powerful hunting dog of an ancient breed, characterized by a hard, rough coat.

irk (ûrk) *v.t.* To annoy or weary; vex. [ME *irken*]

irk·some (ûrk/səm) *adj.* Troublesome; tiresome; tedious. — **irk/some·ly** *adv.* — **irk/some·ness** *n.*

i·ron (ī/ərn) *n.* **1.** A tough, abundant, malleable, easily oxidized and strongly magnetic metallic element (symbol Fe): also called *Ferrum.* See ELEMENT. **2.** That which is firm, harsh, unyielding, or indestructible. **3.** An implement or tool made of iron. **4.** A metal implement or appliance having a smooth, flat undersurface and a handle, heated either by direct contact with fire or by electric current, and used to press or smooth cloth, etc. **5.** *pl.* Chains used to confine a prisoner; shackles. **6.** A golf club having a metal head with an angled face. **7.** *Slang* A pistol or similar firearm: also called *shooting iron.* **8.** *Med.* A preparation containing iron. — **to have irons in the fire** To be engaged in various enterprises. — **to strike while the iron is hot** To act at the right moment. — *adj.* **1.** Made of or consisting of iron. **2.** Resembling iron. **3.** Inexorable; unyielding; firm. **4.** Grim; pitiless. — *v.t.* **1.** To smooth or press, as with a heated flatiron. **2.** To add or apply iron to. **3.** To put in chains; shackle. — *v.i.* To press clothes, etc., with an iron. — **to iron out** To remove, as difficulties. [OE *īrenisen, īsern*]

Iron Age The most recent and advanced of three early stages of human progress, following the Stone Age and the Bronze Age.

i·ron·bound (ī/ərn·bound/) *adj.* **1.** Bound with iron. **2.** Surrounded with rocks, as a seacoast. **3.** Unyielding.

i·ron·clad (ī/ərn·klad/) *adj.* **1.** Covered by or in armor. **2.** Strict; unbreakable, as a rule, etc. — *n.* Formerly, a warship sheathed with armor.

iron curtain An impenetrable barrier of censorship and secrecy imposed by the Soviet Union between its sphere of influence and the rest of the world.

i·ron·er (ī/ərn·ər) *n.* One who or that which irons.

i·ron·hand·ed (ī/ərn·han/did) *adj.* Exerting severe discipline or rigorous control; despotic.

i·ron·ic (i·ron/ik) *adj.* **1.** Of the nature of or characterized by irony. **2.** Given to the use of irony. Also **i·ron/i·cal.** — **i·ron/i·cal·ly** *adv.* — **i·ron/i·cal·ness** *n.*

i·ron·ing board (ī/ərn·ing) A board or folding table, usu. padded, on which articles of clothing, etc., are ironed.

iron lung A cabinetlike enclosure in which the respiration of a patient is artificially maintained.

i·ron·mon·ger (ī/ərn·mung/gər, -mong/-) *n.* *Brit.* One who sells iron articles; a hardware dealer. — **i/ron·mon/ger·y** *n.*

iron pyrites Pyrite.

I·ron·sides (ī/ərn·sīdz/) Nickname of Oliver Cromwell. — *n.pl.* Any of Cromwell's soldiers.

i·ron·stone (ī/ərn·stōn/) *n.* Glazed, usu. white pottery.

i·ron·ware (ī/ərn·wâr/) *n.* Articles made of iron; hardware.

i·ron·weed (ī/ərn·wēd/) *n.* An herb or shrub having mostly purple or reddish flowers.

i·ron·wood (ī/ərn·wŏŏd/) *n.* Any of various trees having unusually hard wood; also, the wood.

i·ron·work (ī/ərn·wûrk/) *n.* **1.** Parts or objects made of iron, as parts of a building. **2.** The act of working in iron. — **i/ron·work/er** *n.*

i·ron·works (ī/ərn·wûrks/) *n.pl.* (*often construed as sing.*) An establishment where iron or ironwork is made.

i·ro·ny (ī/rə·nē) *n.* *pl.* **·nies** **1.** A sarcastic or humorous manner of discourse in which what is said is meant to express its opposite, as when "That's very good" means "That's very bad". **2.** A result, ending, etc., the reverse of what was expected. **3.** A situation, event, pairing, etc., in which main elements are rationally or emotionally incompatible because of contrast, conflict, or surprise. **4.** The use of irony in literature, art, etc. **5.** The feigning of ignorance as a tehnique in argument; Socratic irony. — *Syn.* See SARCASM. [< L < Gk. *eirōn* dissembler]

Ir·o·quoi·an (ir/ə·kwoi/ən) *n.* **1.** A family of North American Indian languages, including Cayuga, Cherokee, Conestoga, Erie, Mohawk, Oneida, Seneca and other languages. **2.** A member of a tribe speaking these languages. — *adj.* Of the Iroquois Indians or their languages.

Ir·o·quois (ir/ə·kwoi, -kwoiz) *n.* *pl.* **·quois** **1.** A member of any of the North American Indian tribes known as the Five Nations; also, these tribes collectively. See FIVE NATIONS. **2.** A member of a tribe speaking an Iroquoian language. — *adj.* Of or pertaining to the Iroquois. [< F < Algonquian *Irinakoiw*, lit., real adders]

ir·ra·di·ant (i·rā/dē·ənt) *adj.* Sending forth light; shining. — **ir·ra/di·ance, ir·ra/di·an·cy** *n.*

ir·ra·di·ate (*v.* i·rā/dē·āt; *adj.* i·rā/dē·it, -āt) *v.* **·at·ed, ·at·ing** *v.t.* **1.** To light up; illuminate. **2.** To make clear or understandable. **3.** To send forth in or as in rays of light. **4.** To subject to X-rays, ultraviolet light, or similar rays. **5.** To expose to radiant energy. — *v.i.* **6.** To be radiant; shine. — *adj.* Made bright; illuminated. [< L *in-* thoroughly + *radiare* to shine] — **ir·ra/di·a/tion** *n.* — **ir·ra/di·a/tive** *adj.*

ir·ra·tion·al (i·rash/ən·əl) *adj.* **1.** Incapable of exercising the power of reason. **2.** Contrary to reason; absurd. **3.** *Math.* Denoting a number that cannot be expressed as an integer or a quotient of integers. [< L *irrationalis*] — **ir·ra/tion·al·ism** *n.* — **ir·ra/tion·al·ly** *adv.* — **ir·ra/tion·al·ness** *n.*

ir·ra·tion·al·i·ty (i·rash/ən·al/ə·tē) *n.* *pl.* **·ties** **1.** The state of being irrational. **2.** That which is irrational.

ir·re·claim·a·ble (ir/i·klā/mə·bəl) *adj.* Incapable of being reclaimed. — **ir/re·claim/a·bil/i·ty, ir/re·claim/a·ble·ness** *n.* — **ir/re·claim/a·bly** *adv.*

ir·rec·on·cil·a·ble (i·rek/ən·sī/lə·bəl, i·rek/ən·sī/lə·bəl) *adj.* Not able or willing to be reconciled or brought into accord. — *n.* **1.** One who refuses to yield or compromise. **2.** *pl.* Incompatible ideas. — **ir·rec/on·cil/a·bil/i·ty, ir·rec/on·cil/a·ble·ness** *n.* — **ir·rec/on·cil/a·bly** *adv.*

ir·re·cov·er·a·ble (ir/i·kuv/ər·ə·bəl) *adj.* **1.** Incapable of being recovered. **2.** Incapable of being remedied. — **ir/re·cov/er·a·ble·ness** *n.* — **ir/re·cov/er·a·bly** *adv.*

ir·re·deem·a·ble (ir/i·dē/mə·bəl) *adj.* **1.** Incapable of being recovered, bought back, or paid off. **2.** Not to be converted into coin: said of some types of paper money. **3.** Beyond redemption or change; incorrigible. — **ir/re·deem/a·bly** *adv.*

ir·re·den·tist (ir/i·den/tist) *n.* *Usu. cap.* A member of a party formed in Italy about 1878, that had as its aim the acquisition of certain regions subject to other governments but having an Italian-speaking population. — *adj.* Of or pertaining to the irredentists or their policies. [< Ital. < L *in-* not + *redemptus* redeemed] — **ir·re/den/tism** (-tiz·əm) *n.*

ir·re·duc·i·ble (ir/i·dōo/sə·bəl, -dyōō/-) *adj.* Incapable of being decreased or diminished. **2.** Incapable of being converted to a simpler or more basic form. — **ir/re·duc/i·bil/i·ty** *n.* — **ir/re·duc/i·bly** *adv.*

ir·ref·ra·ga·ble (i·ref/rə·gə·bəl) *adj.* That cannot be refuted or disproved. [< LL < L *in-* not + *refragari* to oppose] — **ir·ref/ra·ga·bil/i·ty** *n.* — **ir·ref/ra·ga·bly** *adv.*

ir·ref·u·ta·ble (i·ref/yŏo·tə·bəl, ir/i·fyōō/tə·bəl) *adj.* Incapable of being disproved. — **ir·ref·u·ta·bil/i·ty** (i·ref/yə·tə·bil/ə·tē, ir/i·fyōō/-) *n.* — **ir·ref/u·ta·bly** (i·ref/yə·tə·blē, ir/i·fyōō/-) *adv.*

IRIS
a Bearded.
b Japanese.
c Siberian.

ir·re·gard·less (ir/i·gärd/lis) *adv.* Regardless: a nonstandard or humorous usage.

ir·reg·u·lar (i·reg/yə·lər) *adj.* **1.** Lacking symmetry or uniformity. **2.** Occurring at unequal intervals: an *irregular* pulse. **3.** Not according to established rules or procedure. **4.** Not conforming to accepted standards of conduct. **5.** *Gram.* Not conforming to the usual pattern of inflection or conjugation. **6.** *Mil.* Of troops, not belonging to a regularly organized military force. — *n.* One who or that which is irregular. [< OF < Med.L *irregularis*] — **ir·reg/u·lar·ly** *adv.*

ir·reg·u·lar·i·ty (i·reg/yə·lar/ə·tē) *n. pl.* **·ties** **1.** The state or quality of being irregular. **2.** That which is irregular.

ir·rel·a·tive (i·rel/ə·tiv) *adj.* Irrelevant. — **ir·rel/a·tive·ly** *adv.* — **ir·rel/a·tive·ness** *n.*

ir·rel·e·vant (i·rel/ə·vənt) *adj.* Not relevant; not pertinent; inapplicable. — **ir·rel/e·vance, ir·rel/e·van·cy** *n.* — **ir·rel/e·vant·ly** *adv.*

ir·re·lig·ion (ir/i·lij/ən) *n.* **1.** Lack of religious faith. **2.** Indifference or hostility toward religion. — **ir/re·lig·ion·ist** *n.*

ir·re·lig·ious (ir/i·lij/əs) *adj.* **1.** Lacking in religious faith or piety. **2.** Profane. — **ir/re·lig/ious·ly** *adv.*

ir·re·me·di·a·ble (ir/i·mē/dē·ə·bəl) *adj.* Incapable of being remedied; incurable; irreparable. [< L *irremediabilis*] — **ir/re·me/di·a·ble·ness** *n.* — **ir/re·me/di·a·bly** *adv.*

ir·re·mis·si·ble (ir/i·mis/ə·bəl) *adj.* Not remissible; unpardonable, as a sin. — **ir/re·mis/si·bil/i·ty, ir/re·mis/si·ble·ness** *n.* — **ir/re·mis/si·bly** *adv.*

ir·re·mov·a·ble (ir/i·mōō/və·bəl) *adj.* Not removable.

ir·rep·a·ra·ble (i·rep/ər·ə·bəl) *adj.* Incapable of being repaired, rectified, remedied, or made good. — **ir·rep/a·ra·bil/i·ty, ir·rep/a·ra·ble·ness** *n.* — **ir·rep/a·ra·bly** *adv.*

ir·re·place·a·ble (ir/i·plā/sə·bəl) *adj.* Not replaceable.

ir·re·pres·si·ble (ir/i·pres/ə·bəl) *adj.* Not repressible; incapable of being controlled or restrained. — **ir/re·pres/si·bil/i·ty, ir/re·pres/si·ble·ness** *n.* — **ir/re·pres/si·bly** *adv.*

ir·re·proach·a·ble (ir/i·prō/chə·bəl) *adj.* Not meriting reproach; blameless. [< F *irréprochable*] — **ir/re·proach/a·ble·ness** *n.* — **ir/re·proach/a·bly** *adv.*

ir·re·sis·ti·ble (ir/i·zis/tə·bəl) *adj.* **1.** Not resistible. **2.** Completely fascinating or enchanting. — **ir/re·sis/ti·bil/i·ty, ir/re·sis/ti·ble·ness** *n.* — **ir/re·sis/ti·bly** *adv.*

ir·res·o·lute (i·rez/ə·lōōt) *adj.* Not resolute or resolved; lacking firmness of purpose; wavering; hesitating. — **ir·res/o·lute·ly** *adv.* — **ir·res/o·lute/ness, ir·res/o·lu/tion** *n.*

ir·re·spec·tive (ir/i·spek/tiv) *adj.* Existing without relationship to something else: now chiefly in the phrase **irrespective of,** regardless of. — **ir/re·spec/tive·ly** *adv.*

ir·re·spon·si·ble (ir/i·spon/sə·bəl) *adj.* **1.** Lacking in responsibility; unreliable. **2.** Free from or incapable of responsibility. — *n.* One who is irresponsible. — **ir/re·spon/si·bil/i·ty, ir/re·spon/si·ble·ness** *n.* — **ir/re·spon/si·bly** *adv.*

ir·re·spon·sive (ir/i·spon/siv) *adj.* Not responsive. — **ir/re·spon/sive·ness** *n.*

ir·re·trace·a·ble (ir/i·trā/sə·bəl) *adj.* Incapable of being retraced, as a path, footsteps, etc.

ir·re·triev·a·ble (ir/i·trē/və·bəl) *adj.* Not retrievable; irrecoverable; irreparable. — **ir/re·triev/a·bil/i·ty, ir/re·triev/a·ble·ness** *n.* — **ir/re·triev/a·bly** *adv.*

ir·rev·er·ence (i·rev/ər·əns) *n.* **1.** Lack of awe, veneration, or respect. **2.** Behavior or utterance indicative of this.

ir·rev·er·ent (i·rev/ər·ənt) *adj.* Characterized by or showing irreverence. — **ir·rev/er·ent·ly** *adv.*

ir·re·vers·i·ble (ir/i·vûr/sə·bəl) *adj.* **1.** Incapable of being turned in the opposite direction. **2.** Incapable of being annulled, repealed, or undone. — **ir/re·vers/i·bil/i·ty, ir/re·vers/i·ble·ness** *n.* — **ir/re·vers/i·bly** *adv.*

ir·rev·o·ca·ble (i·rev/ə·kə·bəl) *adj.* **1.** Incapable of being revoked. **2.** Incapable of being brought back. — **ir·rev/o·ca·bil/i·ty, ir·rev/o·ca·ble·ness** *n.* — **ir·rev/o·ca·bly** *adv.*

ir·ri·ga·ble (ir/ə·gə·bəl) *adj.* Capable of being irrigated.

ir·ri·gate (ir/ə·gāt) *v.t.* **·gat·ed, ·gat·ing** **1.** To supply (land) with water, as by means of ditches. **2.** To revitalize or refresh by or as if by watering. **3.** *Med.* To moisten or wash out with water. [< L < *in-* to + *rigare* to water] — **ir/ri·ga/tion** *n.* — **ir/ri·ga/tion·al** *adj.* — **ir/ri·ga/tor** *n.*

ir·ri·ta·bil·i·ty (ir/ə·tə·bil/ə·tē) *n. pl.* **·ties** The state or quality of being irritable.

ir·ri·ta·ble (ir/ə·tə·bəl) *adj.* **1.** Easily annoyed or angered. **2.** *Biol.* Responding to stimuli. **3.** *Pathol.* Influenced abnormally by the action of stimulants. — **ir/ri·ta·ble·ness** *n.* — **ir/ri·ta·bly** *adv.*

ir·ri·tant (ir/ə·tənt) *n.* That which irritates or causes irritation. — *adj.* Causing irritation. — **ir/ri·tan·cy** *n.*

ir·ri·tate (ir/ə·tāt) *v.t.* **·tat·ed, ·tat·ing** **1.** To excite annoyance, impatience, or ill temper in; vex. **2.** To make sore or inflamed. **3.** *Biol.* To stimulate (a cell, tissue, or organ) to a characteristic function or action. [< L *irritare* to irritate] — **ir/ri·ta/tive** *adj.* — **ir/ri·ta/tor** *n.*

ir·ri·tat·ing (ir/ə·tā/ting) *adj.* Causing irritation. — **ir/ri·tat/ing·ly** *adv.*

ir·ri·ta·tion (ir/ə·tā/shən) *n.* **1.** The act of irritating, or the state of being irritated; annoyance. **2.** *Pathol.* A condition of abnormal excitability or sensitivity in an organ or part.

ir·rup·tion (i·rup/shən) *n.* **1.** A breaking or rushing in. **2.** A violent, sudden invasion. [< L < *in-* in + *rumpere* to break] — **ir·rup/tive** *adj.*

is (iz) Present indicative, third person singular of BE. [OE]

is- Var. of ISO-.

I·saac (ī/zək) A Hebrew patriarch, son of Abraham and Sarah. *Gen.* xxi 3. [< Hebrew *ṣahaq* to laugh]

i·sa·go·ge (ī/sə·gō/jē) *n.* An introduction, as to a field of study. [< L < Gk. *eisagōgē* < *eisagein* to introduce < *eis-* into + *agein* to lead] — **i/sa·gog/ic** (-goj/ik) *adj.*

I·sa·iah (ī·zā/ə, ī·zī/ə) Eighth-century B.C. Hebrew prophet. — *n.* A book of the Old Testament attributed to him. Also, in the Douai Bible, **I·sai/as** (-əs). [< Hebrew *yesha'yāhu* Salvation of God]

Is·car·i·ot (is·kar/ē·ət) See JUDAS ISCARIOT.

is·che·mi·a (is·kē/mē·ə) *n.* *Pathol.* A localized anemia, due to a contracted blood vessel. Also **is·chae/mi·a.** [< NL < Gk. *ischein* to hold + *haima* blood] — **is·che/mic** *adj.*

is·chi·at·ic (is·kē·at/ik) *adj.* Of or pertaining to the ischium. Also **is/chi·ad/ic** (-ad/ik), **is·chi·al** (is/kē·əl).

is·chi·um (is/kē·əm) *n. pl.* **·chi·a** (-kē·ə) *Anat.* The lowest of the three sections composing the hipbone. For illus. see PELVIS. [< L < Gk. *ischion* hip, hip joint]

-ise Var. of -IZE.

I·seult (i·sōōlt/) In medieval romance Iseult the Beautiful of Ireland, married to King Mark and beloved of Tristan. See TRISTAN. Also called *Isolde, Isolt, Yseult.*

-ish[1] *suffix of adjectives* **1.** Of or belonging to (a specified national group): *Danish.* **2.** Of the nature of; like: *boyish.* **3.** Having the bad qualities of: *selfish.* **4.** Tending toward; inclined to: *bookish.* **5.** Somewhat: *tallish.* **6.** *Informal* Approximately: *fortyish.* [OE *-isc*, adjectival suffix]

-ish[2] *suffix of verbs* Appearing chiefly in verbs of French origin: *brandish, establish.* [< OF *-iss-*, stem ending of *-ir* verbs]

Ish·ma·el (ish/mē·əl) In the Bible, the son of Abraham and Hagar, banished with his mother. *Gen.* xxi 9–21. — *n.* An outcast. [< Hebrew *Yishmā'ēl* God heareth]

Ish·ma·el·ite (ish/mē·əl·īt/) *n.* **1.** A descendant of Ishmael. **2.** A wanderer. — **Ish/ma·el·it/ish** (-ī/tish) *adj.*

i·sin·glass (ī/zing·glas/, -gläs/, ī/zən-) *n.* **1.** A preparation of nearly pure gelatin made from the swim bladders of certain fishes. **2.** Mica, chiefly in the form of thin sheets. [Prob. < MDu. *huysenblas* sturgeon bladder]

I·sis (ī/sis) In Egyptian mythology, the goddess of fertility.

Is·lam (is·läm/, is/ləm, iz/-) *n.* **1.** The religion of the Muslims, that maintains that there is but one God, Allah, and that Mohammed is his prophet: also called *Mohammedanism, Muslimism.* Also **Is·lam·ism** (is/ləm·iz/əm, iz/ləm-). **2.** Muslims collectively. **3.** The areas of the world where Islam is the main religion. [< Arabic *islām* submission]

Is·lam·ic (is·lam/ik, -läm/-, iz-) *adj.* Muslim. Also **Is/lam·it/ic** (-it/ik).

Is·lam·ite (is/ləm·īt, iz/-) *n.* A Muslim.

Is·lam·ize (is/ləm·īz, iz/-) *v.t. & v.i.* **·ized, ·i·zing** To convert or adapt to Islam.

is·land (ī/lənd) *n.* **1.** A tract of land entirely surrounded by water. The major continental land masses are not usually considered islands. **2.** Something resembling an island and set apart from its surroundings. **3.** *Anat.* Any of various isolated cells of the body differentiated from those of the surrounding tissues. — *v.t.* To cause to become or resemble an island; isolate. [OE < *īg, īeg* island + *land*]

is·land·er (ī/lən·dər) *n.* A native or inhabitant of an island.

isle (īl) *n.* An island, esp. one of comparatively small size: used in place names, as the British *Isles*, or poetically. — *v. isled, isl·ing* *v.t.* **1.** To island. — *v.i.* **2.** To live on an isle or island. [< OF < L *insula*]

is·let (ī/lit) *n.* A small island. [< OF *islette*, dim. of *isle*]

ism (iz/əm) *n.* A distinctive theory, doctrine, or system: usually used disparagingly. [< -ISM]

-ism *suffix of nouns* **1.** The act, process, or result of: *ostracism.* **2.** The condition of being: *skepticism.* **3.** The characteristic action or behavior of: *heroism.* **4.** The beliefs, teachings, or system of: *Calvinism.* **5.** Devotion to; adherence to the teachings of: *nationalism.* **6.** A characteristic or peculiarity of: said especially of a language or idiom: *Americanism.* **7.** *Med.* An abnormal condition resulting from an excess of: *alcoholism.* [< L *-ismus* < Gk. *-ismos*]

is·n't (iz/ənt) Is not.

iso- *combining form* **1.** Equal; the same; identical. **2.** *Chem.* Isomeric with, or an isomer of. Also, before vowels, *is-*. [< Gk. *isos* equal]

i·so·bar (ī/sə·bär) *n.* **1.** *Meteorol.* A line drawn on a weather map connecting all points having the same barometric pressure for a given time or period.   **2.** *Physics* Any of two or more atoms having the same mass number but different atomic numbers.   [< Gk. *isos* equal + *baros* weight] — **i·so·bar·ic** (ī'sə-bar'ik) *adj.*

i·so·cline (ī'sə-klīn)   *n.*   *Geol.* An anticline or syncline in which the strata are so closely folded that they have the same dip.   [< ISO- + Gk. *klinein* to bend] — **i·so·cli·nal,** **i·so·clin·ic** (-klin'ik) *adj.*

i·so·gon·ic (ī'sə-gon'ik)   *adj.*   **1.** Having equal angles.   **2.** Denoting a line on the earth's surface such that all points on it have equal magnetic declination. Also **i·sog·o·nal** (ī-sog'ə-nəl). — *n.* An isogonic line.   [< Gk. *isogōnios* equiangular]

i·so·gram (ī'sə-gram)   *n.* A line on a map, chart, diagram, etc., such that all points on it have equal value with respect to a given geographical feature, physical condition, etc.

i·so·late (ī'sə-lāt, is'ə-)   *v.t.* **·lat·ed, ·lat·ing**   **1.** To set apart, as from a mass, group, or situation; cause to be alone.   **2.** *Chem.* To obtain (an element or substance) in a free or uncombined state.   [< Ital. *isolare* to isolate] — **i'so·la·ble** *adj.* — **i'so·la'tor** *n.*

i·so·la·tion (ī'sə-lā'shən, is'ə-)   *n.*   **1.** The act of isolating.   **2.** The state of being isolated; aloneness; solitude.

i·so·la·tion·ism (ī'sə-lā'shən·iz'əm, is'ə-)   *n.* A national policy advocating freedom from foreign political and economic alliances. — **i'so·la'tion·ist** *adj. & n.*

I·solde (i-sōld', *Ger.* i-zôl'də)   See ISEULT.

i·sol·o·gous (ī-sol'ə-gəs)   *adj. Chem.* Having similar molecular structure but different atoms of the same valence.

i·so·mer (ī'sə-mər)   *n.*   **1.** *Chem.* One of two or more compounds identical in composition, but having different structural arrangements and different properties.   **2.** *Physics* One of two or more nuclides having the same mass and atomic number but differing in energy characteristics.   [< Gk. < *isos* equal + *meros* part] — **i·so·mer·ic** (-mer'ik) *adj.*

i·som·er·ism (ī-som'ə·riz'əm)   *n. Chem.* The condition of being isomeric.

i·som·er·ous (ī-som'ər·əs)   *adj.*   **1.** Having an equal number of parts, organs, markings, etc.   **2.** *Bot.* Equal in number, as the members of successive whorls of flowers.

i·so·met·ric (ī'sə·met'rik)   *adj.*   **1.** Pertaining to or characterized by equality in dimensions or measurements.   **2.** Based upon contraction of muscles against resistance without shortening muscle fibers: *isometric* exercises. — **i'so·met'ri·cal·ly** *adv.*

i·so·mor·phic (ī'sə·môr'fik)   *adj.* Having similar form or appearance but of different ancestry, genetic constitution, or chemical composition.

i·so·mor·phism (ī'sə·môr'fiz·əm)   *n.* A similarity in form shown by substances of different composition, or by organisms belonging to different groups. — **i'so·morph** *n.*

i·so·oc·tane (ī'sō-ok'tān)   *n. Chem.* Trimethylpentane.

i·so·prene (ī'sə-prēn)   *n. Chem.* A volatile liquid hydrocarbon, C₅H₈, of the terpene group, obtained when crude rubber is subjected to pyrolysis. [Appar. an arbitrary coinage]

i·sos·ce·les (ī-sos'ə·lēz)   *adj. Geom.* Of a triangle, having two sides of equal length.   [< LL < Gk. *isos* equal + *skelos* leg]

i·sos·ta·sy (ī-sos'tə·sē)   *n.*   **1.** *Geol.* The equilibrium that the earth's crust tends to assume as a result of the action of terrestrial gravitation upon rock masses.   **2.** Equilibrium resulting from equal pressure on all sides.   [< ISO- + Gk. *stasis* standing] — **i·so·stat·ic** (ī'sə-stat'ik) *adj.*

ISOSCELES TRIANGLE
AB = CB

i·so·therm (ī'sə-thûrm)   *n. Meteorol.* A line drawn on a weather map connecting all points having the same mean temperature.   [< ISO- + Gk. *thermē* heat] — **i'so·ther'mal** *adj. & n.*

i·so·ton·ic (ī'sə-ton'ik)   *adj. Physiol.* Having the same osmotic pressure on opposite sides of a membrane: said of solutions, esp. blood or plasma.   [< Gk. < *isos* equal + *tonos* accent]

i·so·tope (ī'sə-tōp)   *n. Physics* Any of two or more forms of an element having the same atomic number and similar chemical properties but differing in mass number and radioactive behavior.   [< ISO- + Gk. *topos* place] — **i·so·top·ic** (ī'sə-top'ik) *adj.* — **i·sot·o·py** (ī-sot'ə-pē) *n.*

i·so·trop·ic (ī'sə-trop'ik, -trō'pik)   *adj. Physics* Exhibiting the same physical properties in every direction. Also **i·sot·ro·pous** (ī-sot'rə·pəs).

Is·ra·el (iz'rē·əl)   The patriarch Jacob. *Gen.* xxxii 28. — *n.* The Jewish people, regarded as descended from Jacob.   [< Hebrew *Yisrā'ēl* God persevereth]

Is·rae·li (iz-rā'lē)   *adj.* Of modern Israel, its people, or their culture. — *n. pl.* **·lis** A native or inhabitant of Israel.

Is·ra·el·ite (iz'rē·əl·īt)   *n.* Any of the people of Israel or their descendants; a Hebrew; a Jew. — *adj.* Of or pertaining to the Hebrews; Jewish: also **Is'ra·el·it'ish** (-ī'tish), **Is'·ra·el·it'ic** (-it'ik).

Is·sei (ēs·sā')   *n. pl.* **·sei** or **·seis** A Japanese who emigrated

to the U.S. after 1907, and was not legally eligible to become an American citizen.   [< Japanese *is* first + *sei* generation]

is·su·ance (ish'ōō·əns, -yōō-)   *n.* The act or procedure of issuing; promulgation. — **is'su·ant** *adj.*

is·sue (ish'ōō, -yōō)   *n.*   **1.** The act of giving out or publishing, esp. from an official source.   **2.** An item or set of items, as stamps, magazines, etc., published at a single time.   **3.** A result; consequence; outcome.   **4.** A matter of importance to be resolved.   **5.** An outflow; discharge.   **6.** A point of egress; outlet; exit.   **7.** Offspring; progeny.   **8.** Profits; proceeds, as from property.   **9.** *Med.* A discharge, as of blood or pus. — **at issue** In question; in controversy. — **to join issue** To enter into a controversy. — **to take issue** To disagree. — *v.* **·sued, ·su·ing** *v.i.*   **1.** To come forth; flow out; emerge.   **2.** To be derived or descended; originate.   **3.** To come as a consequence; result.   **4.** To terminate: often followed by *in.*   **5.** To be circulated or published; appear.   **6.** To be produced as profit. — *v.t.*   **7.** To publish; announce.   **8.** To give out; distribute, as supplies.   [< OF < L < *ex-* out of + *ire* to go] — **is'su·a·ble** *adj.* — **is'su·er** *n.*

-ist   *suffix of nouns*   **1.** One who or that which does or has to do with: *catechist.*   **2.** One whose profession is: *pharmacist.*   **3.** A student or devotee of: *genealogist.*   **4.** One who advocates or adheres to: *socialist.*   [< F < L < Gk. *-istēs*]

isth·mus (is'məs, isth'-)   *n. pl.* **·mus·es** or **·mi** (-mī)   A narrow piece of land extending into a body of water and connecting two larger land masses.   [< L < Gk. *isthmos* narrow passage] — **isth'mi·an** *adj. & n.*

-istic   *suffix of adjectives*   Having the qualities of: formed from nouns ending in *-ist* or *-ism: communistic.*

is·tle (is'lē, ist'lē)   *n.* A fiber derived from an agave plant, used for carpets, etc.

it (it)   *pron., possessive* **its;** *pl. nominative* **they,** *possessive* **their** or **theirs,** *objective* **them** The nominative and objective singular neuter pronoun of the third person, used: **1.** As a substitute for a specific noun or name when referring to things or places or to infants or animals of unspecified sex.   **2.** To represent some implied idea, condition, action, or situation: How was *it*?   **3.** As the subject or predicate nominative of a verb whose logical subject is anticipated: Who is *it*?   **4.** As the subject of an impersonal verb: *It* rained yesterday.   **5.** As the indefinite subject of a verb introducing a clause or a phrase: *It* seems that he knew.   **6.** As the indefinite object after certain verbs in idiomatic expressions: to brazen *it* out. — *n.* In certain children's games, the player required to perform some specified act.   [OE *hit*]

I.T.A.   Initial Teaching Alphabet.

I·tal·ian (i-tal'yən)   *adj.* Of Italy, its people, or their language. — *n.*   **1.** A native or naturalized inhabitant of Italy.   **2.** The Romance language of Italy.

i·tal·ic (i-tal'ik)   *n. Usu. pl.* A style of type in which the letters slant, often used to denote emphasis: *These words are printed in italics.* — *adj.* Designating or printed in italics.

I·tal·ic (i-tal'ik)   *adj.* Relating to any of the peoples of ancient Italy. — *n.* A subfamily of the Indo-European languages, comprising three branches, and including Latin and the Romance languages.

i·tal·i·cize (i-tal'ə·sīz)   *v.* **·cized, ·ciz·ing** *v.t.*   **1.** To print in italics.   **2.** To underscore to indicate italics. — *v.i.*   **3.** To use or indicate the use of italics. — **i·tal'i·ci·za'tion** *n.*

itch (ich)   *v.i.*   **1.** To experience or produce an irritation that causes a desire to scratch or rub the affected area.   **2.** To have a restless or unsatisfied desire to do something; hanker. — *n.*   **1.** An itching sensation or irritation.   **2.** Any of various usu. contagious skin diseases accompanied by itching.   **3.** A restless desire or yearning.   [ME < OE *giccan*]

itch·y (ich'ē)   *adj.* **itch·i·er, itch·i·est** Having or producing an itching sensation. — **itch'i·ness** *n.*

-ite¹   *suffix of nouns*   **1.** A native or inhabitant of: *suburbanite.*   **2.** A follower of or sympathizer with: *Pre-Raphaelite.*   **3.** A descendant of: *Israelite.*   **4.** Resembling or related to: *dynamite.*   **5.** *Mineral.* A rock or mineral: *graphite.*   **6.** *Paleontol.* A fossil: *trilobite.*   **7.** *Zool.* A part of the body or of an organ: *dendrite.*   [< F < L < Gk. *-ītēs*]

-ite²   *suffix Chem.* A salt or ester of an acid having a name that ends in *-ous: sulfite.*   [< F *-ite*]

-ite³   *suffix* Derived from the past participial form of certain Latin verbs and occurring in: **1.** Adjectives: *infinite, polite.*   **2.** Verbs: *unite.*   **3.** Nouns: *appetite.*   [< L *-itus*]

i·tem (ī'təm)   *n.*   **1.** A single unit or article included in a category, series, or enumeration.   **2.** An entry in an account.   **3.** A brief article of news, etc., as in a newspaper. — *v.t.* To record or take note of as an item. — *adv.* Likewise; also: used to introduce an entry in a list or series.   [< L, thus]

i·tem·ize (ī'təm·īz)   *v.t.* **·ized, ·iz·ing** To set down or specify by items. — **i'tem·i·za'tion** *n.* — **i'tem·iz'er** *n.*

it·er·ate (it'ə·rāt)   *v.t.* **·at·ed, ·at·ing** To state or utter again or repeatedly.   [< L *iterum* again] — **it'er·a'tion** *n.* — **it'·er·a·tive** *adj.*

i·tin·er·an·cy (ī·tin'ər·ən·sē, i·tin'-)   *n.* The act or state of being itinerant. Also **i·tin'er·a·cy** (-ə·sē).

i·tin·er·ant (ĭ·tĭn′ər·ənt, ĭ·tĭn′-) *adj.* **1.** Going from place to place; wandering. **2.** Traveling to a series of places in order to fulfill official duties. — *n.* One who travels from place to place. [< LL *itineris* journey, route] — **i·tin·er·ant·ly** *adv.*

i·tin·er·ar·y (ĭ·tĭn′ə·rer′ē, ĭ·tĭn′-) *n. pl.* **·ar·ies 1.** A route followed in traveling. **2.** A plan for or graphic representation of a journey. **3.** A detailed account or record of a journey. **4.** A guidebook for travelers. — *adj.* Pertaining to travel or routes of travel. [< LL *iter, itineris* journey, route]

-ition *suffix of nouns* **1.** Condition or quality: *ambition.* **2.** Act or process, or the result of an act or process: *audition.* [< L *-itio, -onis*]

-itious *suffix of adjectives* Characterized by; having the quality of: *ambitious.* [< L *-icius, -itius*]

-itis *suffix Pathol.* Inflammation of: *peritonitis.* [< Gk.]

it'll (ĭt′l) **1.** It will. **2.** It shall.

-itol *suffix Chem.* Denoting a class of alcohols containing two or more hydroxyl radicals.

its (ĭts) *pronominal adjective* The possessive case of the pronoun *it,* used attributively: *its* leaves. [< IT + *'s,* possessive case ending; written *it's* until the 19th century]

it's (ĭts) **1.** It is. **2.** It has.

it·self (ĭt·sĕlf′) *pron.* A form of the third person singular neuter pronoun, used: **a** As a reflexive or as object of a preposition in a reflexive sense: The motor started by *itself.* **b** As an intensifier or to give emphasis: simplicity *itself.* **c** As a designation for a normal or usual state: The house isn't *itself* with the children gone.

-ity *suffix of nouns* State or quality [< F < L *-itas*]

-ium *suffix Chem.* Denoting certain elements or compounds: *titanium.* [< L]

I've (īv) I have.

-ive *suffix of adjectives* **1.** Having a tendency or predisposition to: *disruptive.* **2.** Having the nature, character, or quality of: *massive.* Also *-ative.* [< F < L *-ivus*]

i·vied (ī′vēd) *adj.* Covered or overgrown with ivy.

i·vo·ry (ī′vər·ē) *n. pl.* **·ries 1.** A hard, white, smooth-textured dentine, the chief substance of the tusks of elephants, walruses, etc. **2.** Any substance resembling ivory. **3.** The creamy white color of ivory. **4.** *Usu. pl.* Articles made of ivory. **5.** Any form of dentine. **6.** A tusk, esp. of an elephant. **7.** *pl. Slang* **a** The teeth. **b** The keys of a piano. **c** Dice. — *adj.* **1.** Made of or resembling ivory. **2.** Of the color ivory. [< OF < L *ebur, -oris* ivory]

ivory tower A condition or attitude of withdrawal from the world and reality.

i·vy (ī′vē) *n. pl.* **i·vies** A climbing plant, having glossy, evergreen leaves: also **English ivy.** [OE *ĭfig*]

Ivy League An association of colleges in the NE U.S. (Brown, Columbia, Cornell, Dartmouth, Harvard, Princeton, the University of Pennsylvania, and Yale).

Iy·yar (ē·yär′, ē′yär) *n.* The eighth month of the Hebrew year. Also **I·yar′.** See (Hebrew) CALENDAR.

-ization *suffix* Used to form nouns from verbs in *-ize,* and denoting a condition, act, process, or result: *civilization.*

-ize *suffix of verbs* **1.** To cause to become or resemble: *Christianize.* **2.** To subject to the action of: *oxidize.* **3.** To change into: *mineralize.* **4.** To act in the manner of: *sympathize.* Also *-ise.* [< F < LL < Gk. *-izein*] ◆ The spelling of this suffix varies in British and American usage; *-ize* is the preferred spelling in the United States, while *-ise* is preferred in England. However, certain words, as *advise,* are always spelled with *-ise,* whereas others, as *baptize,* are always spelled with *-ize.*

iz·zard (ĭz′ərd) *n. Archaic* The letter Z. — **from A to izzard** From beginning to end. [< earlier *ezed,* var. of ZED]

J

j, J (jā) *n. pl.* **j's** or **js, J's** or **Js, jays** (jāz) **1.** The tenth letter of the English alphabet. **2.** The sound represented by the letter *j.*

jab (jab) *v.t. & v.i.* **jabbed, jab·bing 1.** To poke or thrust sharply. **2.** To punch or strike with short blows. — *n.* **1.** A sharp thrust. **2.** A rapid punch.

jab·ber (jab′ər) *v.t. & v.i.* To speak rapidly or without making sense. — *n.* Rapid or unintelligible talk; chatter. — **jab′ber·er** *n.*

ja·bot (zhā·bō′, *Fr.* zhà·bō′) *n. pl.* **·bots** (-bōz′, *Fr.* -bō′) A ruffle or similar decoration falling from the neckline or at the front of a blouse, shirt, or bodice. [< F, lit., gizzard]

ja·cinth (jā′sĭnth, jas′ĭnth) *n.* Hyacinth. [< OF < L *hyacinthus*]

jack (jak) *n.* **1.** *Sometimes cap.* A man or boy; fellow; esp.: **a** A manual laborer: usu. in combination: *jack-of-all-trades; lumberjack.* **b** A sailor. **2.** Any of various devices that perform an operation formerly done by a man or boy: often used in combinations: *bootjack.* **3.** Any of various devices used for raising heavy weights through short distances, usu. by means of a lever. **4.** In names or designations of animals: **a** Male: sometimes used in combination: *jackass.* **b** Any of various kinds of animals, birds, or fish: often in combination: *jackdaw; jack* rabbit. **5.** A playing card showing the picture of a young man; the knave. **6.** A flag, flown at the bow of a ship as a signal or as an indication of nationality when in port. **7.** *U.S. Slang* Money. **8.** A jackstone. **9.** *Electr.* A metallic connecting device with spring clips to which the wires of a circuit may be attached. — *v.t.* **1.** To raise or lift with or as with a jack: usu. with *up.* **2.** *Informal* To increase, as a price or charge: with *up.* [after *Jack,* a nickname for John]

jack·al (jak′əl, -ôl) *n.* **1.** Any of various African or Asian doglike carnivorous mammals. **2.** One who does menial work to serve another. [< Turkish < Persian *shaghal*]

jack·a·napes (jak′ə·nāps) *n.* An impertinent fellow; an upstart. [< *Jack Napes,* nickname of William de la Pole, 15th c. Duke of Suffolk]

jack·ass (jak′as) *n.* **1.** A male ass. **2.** A stupid person.

jack·boot (jak′boot′) *n.* A heavy topboot reaching above the knee.

jack·daw (jak′dô′) *n.* A glossy, black, crowlike bird of Europe, sometimes tamed as a pet.

jack·et (jak′ĭt) *n.* **1.** A short coat, usu. not extending below the hips. **2.** An outer covering or case, as the removable paper cover for a bound book, the skin of a cooked potato, etc. — *v.t.* To cover or surround with or as with a jacket. [< OF *jaque* short jacket]

Jack Frost A personification of frost or winter weather.

jack-in-the-box (jak′ĭn·thə·boks′) *n.* A toy consisting of a box containing a grotesque figure that springs up when the lid is unfastened: also **jack′-in-a-box′.**

jack-in-the-pul·pit (jak′ĭn·thə·pool′pĭt) *n.* A common American herb of the arum family, growing from a turnip-shaped bulb.

jack·knife (jak′nīf′) *n. pl.* **·knives** (-nīvz′) **1.** A large pocketknife. **2.** A dive in which the body is doubled forward with the knees unbent and the hands touching the ankles, and then straightened before entering the water. — *v.t. & v.i.* **knifed, knif·ing** To double up in the manner of a jackknife.

jack-of-all-trades (jak′əv·ôl′trādz′) *n.* One who is able to do many kinds of work.

jack-o'-lan·tern (jak′ə·lan′tərn) *n.* **1.** A lantern made of a pumpkin hollowed and carved into a grotesque face. **2.** A will-o'-the-wisp.

jack·pot (jak′pot′) *n.* **1.** In poker, a pot that accumulates until a player is dealt a pair of jacks or better with which he may open the betting. **2.** Any pot, pool, or prize in which the amount won is cumulative. — **to hit the jackpot** *U.S. Informal* **1.** To win the biggest possible prize. **2.** To achieve a major success.

jack rabbit A large American hare with long hind legs and long ears.

jacks (jaks) *n.pl.* (construed *as sing.*) The game of jackstones.

jack·stone (jak′stōn′) *n.* **1.** A stone or knobbed metal piece used in a children's game in which the pieces are tossed and picked up in a variety of ways: also called *jack.* **2.** *pl.* (construed *as sing.*) The game itself. [Var. of earlier *checkstone*]

jack·straw (jak′strô′) *n.* **1.** One of a set of thin strips of

JACK-IN-THE-PULPIT
a Flower.
b Fruit.

wood, bone, etc., used in a game in which the players attempt to pick up each strip without moving any of the others. **2.** *pl.* (*construed as sing.*) The game itself.

Ja·cob (jā′kəb) The second son of Isaac and father of the founders of the twelve Hebrew tribes. Also *Israel*. [< Hebrew *Ya‘aqob* he grasps the heel. Cf. *Gen.* xxv 26.]

Jac·o·be·an (jak′ə·bē′ən) *adj.* Of or pertaining to James I of England or the period in which he reigned. — *n.* A notable person of the Jacobean era. [< LL < *Jacobus* James]

Jac·o·bin (jak′ə·bin) *n.* During the French Revolution, a member of a French political society that inaugurated the Reign of Terror. [< OF *Jacobin* of St. James; with ref. to the church of St. James, in Paris, where the society first met]

Jac·o·bite (jak′ə·bīt) *n.* An adherent of James II of England after his abdication in 1688. — *adj.* Of the Jacobites: also **Jac·o·bit·ic** (jak′ə·bit′ik) or **-i·cal**. [< L *Jacobus* James]

Jacob's ladder 1. A ladder from earth to heaven that Jacob saw in a dream. *Gen.* xxviii 12. **2.** *Naut.* A rope ladder, often with wooden rungs.

jade¹ (jād) *n.* **1.** A hard, translucent mineral, usu. green, used as a gemstone. **2.** A green color characteristic of jade. [< F < Sp. (*piedra de*) *ijada* (stone) of the side; because supposed to cure pain in the side]

jade² (jād) *n.* **1.** An old, worthless, or unmanageable horse. **2.** A disreputable, ill-tempered, or perverse woman; hussy. — *v.t.* & *v.i.* **jad·ed, jad·ing** To weary or become weary through hard work or overuse; tire. [Origin uncertain]

jad·ed (jā′did) *adj.* **1.** Worn-out; exhausted. **2.** Dulled, as from overindulgence. — **jad′ed·ly** *adv.* — **jad′ed·ness** *n.*

jae·ger (yā′gər, jā′-) *n.* Any of a group of sea birds that pursue and harass gulls and terns until they drop or disgorge their prey. Also **jä′ger**. [< G, hunter]

jag¹ (jag) *n.* A sharp, projecting point; notch; tooth. — *v.t.* **1.** To cut notches or jags in. **2.** To cut unevenly or with slashing strokes. Also **jagg**. [ME *jagge*]

jag² (jag) *n.* *Slang* **1.** A period of unrestrained activity: a crying *jag*. **2.** A drunken spree.

jag·ged (jag′id) *adj.* Having jags or notches; serrate. — **Syn.** See ROUGH. — **jag′ged·ly** *adv.* — **jag′ged·ness** *n.*

jag·uar (jag′wär, jag′yōō·är) *n.* A large, spotted feline of Central and South America. [< Pg. < Tupi *jaguara*]

jai a·lai (hī ə·lī′) A game popular in Latin America, similar to handball but played with a long, curved, wicker basket strapped to the arm. [< Sp. < Basque, jolly festival]

jail (jāl) *n.* **1.** A place of confinement for those guilty of minor offenses or those awaiting trial. **2.** Loosely, any prison. — *v.t.* To put or hold in jail; imprison. Also, *Brit.*, *gaol*. [< OF *jaiole*, ult. < L *cavea* cave]

jail·bird (jāl′bûrd′) *n.* *Informal* A prisoner or ex-prisoner.

jail·er (jā′lər) *n.* The officer in charge of a jail: also, *Brit.*, *gaoler*. Also **jail′or**.

Jain·ism (jī′niz·əm) *n.* A religion of India, founded about 500 B.C., having elements of Brahmanism and Buddhism.

jal·ap (jal′əp) *n.* **1.** The dried root of any of several Mexican plants used as a purgative. **2.** Any allied plant yielding a similar drug. [< Sp. (*purga de*) *Jalapa* (medicine from) Jalapa] — **ja·lap·ic** (jə·lap′ik) *adj.*

ja·lop·y (jə·lop′ē) *n.* *pl.* **·lop·ies** *U.S. Informal* A decrepit automobile. Also **ja·lop′py**. [Origin uncertain]

ja·lou·sie (jal′ōō·sē, zhal′ōō·zē′) *n.* A window blind or shutter of overlapping horizontal slats or strips that may be tilted to keep out sun and rain while admitting air and some light. [< F, lit., jealousy]

jam¹ (jam) *v.* **jammed, jam·ming** *v.t.* **1.** To force or ram into or against something. **2.** To pack and block up by crowding. **3.** To cause (a machine, door, etc.) to become wedged or stuck. **4.** To interfere electronically with (a radio broadcast, etc.). **5.** To bruise or crush. — *v.i.* **6.** To become wedged; stick fast. **7.** To cease operation, as a machine, gun, etc., because parts have stuck or wedged together. **8.** To take part in a jam session. — *n.* **1.** A crowding together, as of people, cars, etc. **2.** The act of jamming. **3.** *Informal* An embarrassing or dangerous predicament. [Akin to CHAMP¹]

jam² (jam) *n.* A pulpy, sweet conserve of whole fruit boiled with sugar. [? < JAM¹, v.]

Ja·mai·can (jə·mā′kən) *adj.* Of or pertaining to Jamaica and its people. — *n.* A native or inhabitant of Jamaica.

jamb (jam) *n.* A side post or side of a doorway, window, etc. [< OF < LL *gamba* hoof, leg]

jam·bo·ree (jam′bə·rē′) *n.* **1.** *Informal* A boisterous frolic. **2.** A large, esp. international, assembly of Boy Scouts.

James (jāmz) One of the brothers of Jesus: called **Saint James**. — *n.* A book of the New Testament consisting of the epistle attributed to him.

jam session An informal gathering of jazz musicians performing informally on various themes.

jan·gle (jang′gəl) *v.* **·gled, ·gling** *v.i.* **1.** To make harsh, unmusical sounds. **2.** To wrangle; bicker. — *v.t.* **3.** To cause to sound discordantly. — *n.* **1.** A discordant sound. **2.** A quarrel; wrangling. [< OF *jangler*] — **jan′gler** *n.*

jan·i·tor (jan′i·tər) *n.* **1.** One who is employed to care for a building, etc. **2.** A doorkeeper; porter. [< L *janua* door] — **jan′i·to′ri·al** (-tôr′ē·əl) *adj.* — **jan′i·tress** *n.fem.*

jan·i·zar·y (jan′ə·zer′ē) *n.* *pl.* **·zar·ies** *Often cap.* **1.** A soldier in the Turkish sultan's army before 1826. **2.** Any Turkish soldier. Also **jan′i·sar·y, jan′is·sar·y** (-ser′ē). [< F < Turkish *yenicheri* new army]

Jan·u·ar·y (jan′yōō·er′ē) *n.* *pl.* **·ar·ies** or **·ar·ys** The first month of the year, containing 31 days. [< L *Januarius* < *Janus* Janus]

Ja·nus (jā′nəs) In Roman mythology, the god of portals and of beginnings and endings, usu. depicted as having two faces looking in opposite directions.

Ja·nus-faced (jā′nəs·fāst′) *adj.* Two-faced; deceitful.

Jap (jap) *adj.* & *n.* *Slang* Japanese: an offensive term.

ja·pan (jə·pan′) *n.* **1.** Any of various glossy black lacquers or varnishes, used for coating objects. **2.** A glossy, black, vitreous enamel baked onto machine parts, etc. **3.** Ornamental objects decorated or lacquered in the Japanese manner. — *adj.* Pertaining to, enameled with, or lacquered with japan. — *v.t.* **·panned, ·pan·ning** To enamel or lacquer with or as with japan. [< JAPAN]

Jap·a·nese (jap′ə·nēz′, -nēs′) *adj.* Of or pertaining to Japan, its people, or their language. — *n.* *pl.* **·nese 1.** A native of Japan, or a person of Japanese ancestry. **2.** The language of Japan.

Japanese beetle A destructive beetle introduced to the U.S. from Japan. The adults eat the leaves and fruits of various plants, and the larvae feed on grass roots.

jape (jāp) *Archaic v.* **japed, jap·ing** *v.i.* **1.** To joke; make jests. — *v.t.* **2.** To mock; jibe at. — *n.* A jest; jibe. [ME *jappen*] — **jap′er** *n.* — **jap′er·y** *n.*

Ja·pheth (jā′fith) Third and youngest son of Noah. *Gen.* v 32. Also **Ja′phet** (-fit). [< Hebrew *Yepheth*, lit., extension]

ja·pon·i·ca (jə·pon′i·kə) *n.* **1.** An Asian shrub with red flowers. **2.** The camellia. [< NL, Japanese]

jar¹ (jär) *n.* **1.** A wide-mouthed vessel of glass or earthenware, usu. deep and cylindrical. **2.** The quantity a jar contains: also **jar′ful** (-fŏŏl′). [< F < Arabic *jarrah*]

jar² (jär) *v.* **jarred, jar·ring** *v.t.* **1.** To strike against or bump so as to cause shaking, movement, etc.; jolt. **2.** To affect (one's nerves, feelings, etc.) unpleasantly or painfully. — *v.i.* **3.** To have an unpleasant or painful effect: with *on* or *upon*. **4.** To disagree or conflict; clash. **5.** To bump or jolt: with *against*. **6.** To make or have a disagreeable sound. — *n.* **1.** A shaking, shock, or jolt. **2.** A disagreeable sound or jumble of sounds; discord. **3.** A painful or irritating shock to the feelings. [Imit.]

jar·di·nière (jär′də·nir′, *Fr.* zhàr·dē·nyâr′) *n.* An ornamental pot or stand for flowers or plants. [< F, fem. of *jardinier* gardener]

jar·gon (jär′gən) *n.* **1.** Confused, unintelligible speech; gibberish. **2.** A language, dialect, or form of speech regarded as meaningless or confusing. **3.** The technical or specialized vocabulary or phraseology used among themselves by the members of a particular profession, sect, or similarly restricted group: legal *jargon*. **4.** A mixture of two or more dissimilar languages, often serving as a lingua franca; pidgin. — *v.i.* To speak in jargon. [< OF, a chattering]

jar·gon·ize (jär′gən·īz) *v.* **·ized, ·iz·ing** *v.t.* **1.** To translate into jargon. — *v.i.* **2.** To express oneself in jargon.

jas·mine (jas′min, jaz′-) *n.* **1.** An ornamental plant of the olive family, with fragrant, generally white flowers. **2.** Any of various other similar plants. Also called *jessamine*. [< F < Persian *yāsmin*]

Ja·son (jā′sən) In Greek legend, a prince who led the Argonauts in search of the Golden Fleece, and who married Medea. [< Gk., healer]

jas·per (jas′pər) *n.* **1.** An opaque, usu. red, brown, or yellow variety of quartz, admitting of a high polish: also **jas′per·ite**. **2.** In the Bible, one of the twelve stones in the breastplate of the high priest. *Ex.* xxviii 20. [< MF < L *jaspis* < Gk. < Semitic] — **jas·pid′e·an** (-pid′ē·ən), **jas·pid′e·ous** (-pid′ē·əs) *adj.*

jaun·dice (jôn′dis, jän′-) *n.* **1.** *Pathol.* A diseased condition of the liver due to the presence of bile pigments in the blood and characterized by yellowness of the skin and eyeballs. **2.** A state of mind, feeling, perception, etc., that distorts the judgment. — *v.t.* **·diced, ·dic·ing 1.** To affect with jaundice. **2.** To alter or influence (the mind, feelings, etc.) so as to affect the judgment. [< OF *jaune* < L *galbus* yellow]

jaunt (jônt, jänt) *n.* A short journey, esp. for pleasure. — *v.i.* To make such a journey. [Origin unknown]

jaunt·y (jôn′tē, jän′-) *adj.* **jaunt·i·er, jaunt·i·est 1.** Having a lively and self-confident air or manner; cheerfully brisk. **2.** Trim; dashing; a *jaunty* hat. [< F *gentil* genteel] — **jaunt′i·ly** *adv.* — **jaunt′i·ness** *n.*

ja·va (jä′və, jav′ə) *n.* *Sometimes cap. U.S. Slang* Coffee. [after *Java*]

Ja·va (jav′ə, jä′və) *n.* A type of coffee. [after *Java*]

Java man Pithecanthropus.

Jav·a·nese (jav′ə·nēz′, -nēs′) *adj.* Of or pertaining to Java, its language, or its people. — *n. pl.* **·nese 1.** A native or naturalized inhabitant of Java. **2.** The Indonesian language of central Java, closely related to Malay.

jave·lin (jav′lin, jav′ə·lin) *n.* **1.** A light spear thrown as a weapon. **2.** A long spear with a wooden shaft, thrown for distance in an athletic contest. [< F, prob. < Celtic]

jaw (jô) *n.* **1.** *Anat.* **a** Either of the two bony structures forming the framework of the mouth and holding the teeth, consisting of the **upper jaw** or maxilla, and the **lower jaw** or mandible. **b** *pl.* The mouth and its associated parts. **2.** One of a pair of gripping parts capable of opening and closing, as of a tool. **3.** Anything suggesting the action of the jaws: the *jaws* of death. **4.** *pl.* The narrow entrance of a gorge, canyon, etc. **5.** *Informal* A talk; chat. **6.** *Informal* Impudent talk. — *v.i.* **1.** *Informal* To talk; jabber. — *v.t.* **2.** *Informal* To scold or abuse. [ME < F *joue* cheek]

jaw·bone (jô′bōn′) *n.* One of the bones of the jaw, esp. that of the lower jaw.

jaw·break·er (jô′brā′kər) *n.* **1.** *U.S. Informal* A type of very hard candy. **2.** A machine that crushes ore: also **jaw′crush′er** (-krush′ər). **3.** *Informal* A word hard to pronounce.

jay (jā) *n.* Any of various corvine birds, usu. of brilliant coloring, as the blue jay. [< OF < Med.L *gaius*]

jay·hawk·er (jā′hô′kər) *n.* **1.** A guerrilla raider of the Civil War period in Kansas; also, any freebooting guerrilla. **2.** *Usu. cap.* A Kansan. [Origin uncertain]

jay·walk (jā′wôk′) *v.i. Informal* To cross a street recklessly, violating traffic regulations or signals. — **jay′walk′er** *n.*

jazz (jaz) *n.* **1.** A kind of music, chiefly extemporaneous but sometimes arranged, characterized by melodic, harmonic, and rhythmic variation, syncopation, flatted thirds and sevenths, and a melody played against various chord patterns. **2.** Loosely, any contemporary popular dance music. **3.** *U.S. Slang* Lying and exaggerated talk; also, idle and foolish talk. **4.** *U.S. Slang* Liveliness and animation. — *adj.* Of or pertaining to jazz. — *v.t.* **1.** *U.S. Slang* To quicken the tempo of; speed up. **2.** To play or arrange (music) as jazz. — **to jazz up** *U.S. Slang* To make more exciting. [< Creole *jass* coition; from its origin in the brothels of New Orleans] — **jazz′y** *adj.* — **jazz′i·ly** *adv.*

jeal·ous (jel′əs) *adj.* **1.** Fearful or suspicious of being displaced by a rival in affection or favors. **2.** Vindictive toward another because of supposed or actual rivalry. **3.** Vigilant in guarding: to be *jealous* of a privilege. **4.** Resulting or arising from jealousy: *jealous* fears. **5.** Demanding exclusive worship and love: a *jealous* God. [< OF < Med.L LL < Gk. *zēlos* zeal] — **jeal′ous·ly** *adv.* — **jeal′ous·ness** *n.*

jeal·ous·y (jel′əs·ē) *n. pl.* **·ous·ies 1.** The state or quality of being jealous. **2.** The fact of being jealous.

jean (jēn, jān) *n.* **1.** A sturdy, twilled cotton cloth used in workclothes. **2.** *pl.* Trousers or overalls made of this material. [after F *Gênes* Genoa, where it was made]

jee (jē) See GEE.

jeep (jēp) *n.* A small, military and civilian motorcar equipped with four-wheel drive. [< G(ENERAL) P(URPOSE) (VEHICLE)]

jeer (jir) *v.i.* **1.** To speak or shout in a derisive, mocking manner; scoff. — *v.t.* **2.** To treat with derision or mockery; scoff at. — *n.* A derisive and flouting word or remark. [Origin unknown] — **jeer′er** *n.* — **jeer′ing·ly** *adv.*

Jef·fer·so·ni·an (jef′ər·sō′nē·ən) *adj.* Of, pertaining to, or characteristic of Thomas Jefferson or his political ideas and beliefs. — *n.* An adherent of Jefferson or his school of thought. — **Jef′fer·so′ni·an·ism** *n.*

Je·hosh·a·phat (ji·hosh′ə·fat, -hos′-) Ninth-century B.C. king of Judah. I *Kings* xxii 41.

Je·ho·vah (ji·hō′və) In the Old Testament, God; the Lord. See YAHWEH. [< Hebrew *JHVH* Yahweh, either Creator or Eternal] — **Je·ho′vi·an, Je·ho′vic** *adj.*

Jehovah's Witnesses A Christian sect opposed to war and the authority of the government in matters of conscience.

je·june (ji·jōōn′) *adj.* **1.** Lacking in substance or nourishment; barren. **2.** Lacking interest; insipid; dry. [< L *jejunus* hungry] — **je·june′ly** *adv.* — **je·june′ness** *n.*

je·ju·num (ji·jōō′nəm) *n. pl.* **·na** (-nə) *Anat.* That portion of the small intestine that extends from the duodenum to the ileum. [< NL < L *jejunus* hungry]

jell (jel) *v.t. & v.i. U.S. Informal* **1.** To jelly; congeal. **2.** To assume or cause to assume definite form. [< JELLY]

jel·lied (jel′ēd) *adj.* **1.** Made gelatinous, as by chilling: *jellied* consommé. **2.** Covered with or prepared in jelly.

jel·li·fy (jel′ə·fī) *v.t. & v.i.* **·fied, ·fy·ing** To make into or become a jelly. — **jel′li·fi·ca′tion** *n.*

jel·lo (jel′ō) *n.* A fruit-flavored gelatin dessert. [< *Jell-O*, a trade name]

jel·ly (jel′ē) *n. pl.* **·lies 1.** Any food preparation made with gelatin or pectin, and having a consistency such that it quivers when shaken; esp., such a food made of boiled and sweet-

ened fruit juice and used as a spread or filler. **2.** Any gelatinous substance. — *v.* **·lied, ·ly·ing** *v.t.* **1.** To make into a jelly. **2.** To cover or fill with jelly. — *v.i.* **3.** To become jelly. [< OF < L *gelata*, pp. of *gelare* to freeze]

jel·ly·bean (jel′ē·bēn′) *n. U.S.* A bean-shaped candy having a hard, colored coating over a gelatinous center.

jel·ly·fish (jel′ē·fish′) *n. pl.* **·fish** or **·fish·es 1.** Any of a number of marine animals of jellylike substance, often having umbrella-shaped bodies with trailing tentacles. **2.** *Informal* One lacking determination or stamina; weakling.

je ne sais quoi (zhən se kwä′) *French* An indefinable something; literally, I know not what.

jen·net (jen′it) *n.* A breed of small Spanish horses. Also spelled *genet*. [< OF < Sp. *jinete* a light horseman.

jen·ny (jen′ē) *n. pl.* **·nies 1.** A spinning jenny. **2.** The female of some birds and animals: *jenny* wren; *jenny* ass. [after *Jenny*, a personal name]

jeop·ard·ize (jep′ər·dīz) *v.t.* **·ized, ·iz·ing** To put in jeopardy; expose to loss or injury; imperil. Also **jeop′ard**.

jeop·ar·dy (jep′ər·dē) *n.* **1.** Danger of death, loss, or injury; peril. **2.** *Law* The peril in which a defendant is put when placed on trial for a crime. [< OF < L *jocus partitus* divided play]

jer·bo·a (jər·bō′ə) *n.* Any of various nocturnal rodents of Asia and North Africa, with very long hind legs adapted for leaping. [< NL < Arabic *yarbu*′]

jer·e·mi·ad (jer′ə·mī′ad) *n.* A lament or tale of woe; complaint. [< F *Jérémie* Jeremiah]

Jer·e·mi·ah (jer′ə·mī′ə) Seventh-century B.C. Hebrew prophet. — *n.* The Old Testament book containing his prophecies. Also, in the Douai Bible, **Jer′e·mi′as** (-əs). [< Hebrew *Yirměyāhū*, lit., God looseneth (from the womb)]

jerk¹ (jûrk) *v.t.* **1.** To give a sharp, sudden pull or twist to. **2.** To throw, move, or thrust with a sharp, suddenly arrested motion. **3.** To utter in a gasping or broken manner: with *out*. — *v.i.* **4.** To give a jerk or jerks. **5.** To move with sharp, sudden motions; twitch. — *n.* **1.** A sudden sharp pull, twist, or thrust. **2.** *Physiol.* An involuntary contraction of a muscle caused by reflex action. **3.** *Slang* A stupid man. [? Var. of archaic *yerk*] — **jerk′y** *adv.* — **jerk′i·ly** *adv.* — **jerk′i·ness** *n.*

jerk² (jûrk) *v.t.* To cure (meat) by cutting into strips and drying. — *n.* Jerked meat, esp. beef. [< Sp. *charqui* < Quechua *echarqui* dried beef]

jer·kin (jûr′kin) *n.* **1.** A close-fitting jacket or vest, usu. sleeveless. **2.** Formerly, such a garment, often of leather, worn in the 16th and 17th centuries. [Origin unknown]

jerk·wa·ter (jûrk′wô′tər, -wot′ər) *U.S. Informal adj.* **1.** Not on the main line: a *jerkwater* town. **2.** Insignificant; small. — *n.* A train serving a branch line.

jer·ry·build (jer′ē·bild′) *v.t.* **·built, ·build·ing** To build flimsily and with inferior materials. [Origin unknown]

jer·sey (jûr′zē) *n. pl.* **·seys 1.** A ribbed elastic fabric of wool, cotton, etc., used for clothing. Also **jersey cloth. 2.** A close-fitting knit upper garment.

Jer·sey (jûr′zē) *n. pl.* **·seys** One of a breed of small cattle, usu. fawn-colored, originating in the island of Jersey and noted for milk rich in butterfat.

jes·sa·mine (jes′ə·min) *n.* Jasmine, a plant.

jest (jest) *n.* **1.** Something said or done to provoke laughter; joke. **2.** Playfulness; fun: to speak in *jest*. **3.** An object of laughter; laughingstock. — *v.i.* **1.** To make amusing remarks; tell jokes; quip. **2.** To speak or act in a playful way; trifle. [< OF < L *gesta* deeds]

jest·er (jes′tər) *n.* One who jests; esp., a court fool.

jest·ing (jes′ting) *n.* The action of one who jokes. — *adj.* Of the nature of a jest; prone to jest. — **jest′ing·ly** *adv.*

Jes·u·it (jezh′ōō·it, jez′yōō-) *n.* **1.** A member of the Society of Jesus, a religious order founded in 1534 by Ignatius Loyola to combat the Reformation and propagate the faith among the heathen. **2.** A crafty or scheming person; an equivocator: a derogatory term. [< NL < L *Jesus* Jesus] — **Jes′u·it′ic** or **·i·cal** *adj.* — **Jes′u·it′i·cal·ly** *adv.*

Jes·u·it·ize (jezh′ōō·it·īz′, jez′yōō-) *v.t. & v.i.* **·ized, ·iz·ing** To be or make Jesuitic.

Je·sus (jē′zəs) Founder of Christianity, 6? B.C.–29? A.D., son of Mary; regarded in the Christian faith as Christ, the Messiah. Also **Jesus Christ, Jesus of Nazareth.**

jet¹ (jet) *n.* **1.** A hard black lignite, taking a high polish, used for jewelry, buttons, etc. **2.** A deep, glossy black. — *adj.* **1.** Made of or resembling jet. **2.** Black as jet; jetblack. [< OF < L < Gk. *gagatēs*, after *Gagai*, a Lycian town where it was mined]

jet² (jet) *n.* **1.** A sudden spurt or gush of liquid or gas emitted from a narrow orifice. **2.** Liquid or gas that spurts from an orifice. **3.** A spout or nozzle. **4.** A jet-propelled aircraft. — *v.t. & v.i.* **jet·ted, ·ting** To spurt forth or emit in a stream. [< F, ult. < L *jactare*, freq. of *jacere* to throw]

Jet, meaning operating by, of, or relating to jet propulsion, may appear as a combining form or as the first element in two-word phrases; as in:

jet aircraft	jet bomber	jet pilot
jet airplane	jet fighter	jet plane
jet aviation	jetliner	jet-propelled

jet-black (jet'black') *adj. & n.* Deep black, like jet.
jet engine A reaction and heat engine that takes in outside air to oxidize fuel that it converts into the energy of a powerful jet of heated gas expelled to the rear under high pressure.
jet propulsion 1. Propulsion by means of a jet of gas or other fluid. 2. *Aeron.* Propulsion by means of jet engines.
jet·sam (jet'səm) *n.* 1. Goods thrown into the sea to lighten an imperiled vessel. 2. Such goods washed ashore. [Earlier *jetson*, short for JETTISON]
jet stream 1. The strong flow of gas or other fluid expelled from a jet engine, rocket motor, and the like. 2. *Meteorol.* A high-velocity wind circulating, usu. from west to east, near the base of the stratosphere.
jet·ti·son (jet'ə-sən) *v.t.* 1. To throw overboard (goods or cargo). 2. To discard (something that hampers). — *n.* 1. The act of jettisoning. 2. Jetsam. [< AF < L < *jactare* to throw]
jet·ty (jet'ē) *n. pl.* ·ties 1. A structure of piling, rocks, etc., extending out into a body of water to protect a harbor, etc. 2. A wharf or pier. [< OF *jeter* to throw]
jeu d'es·prit (zhœ des·prē') *pl.* jeux d'esprit (zhœ) A witticism. [< F]
Jew (jōō) *n.* 1. A member or descendant of the Hebrew people. 2. Any person professing Judaism. 3. Originally, a member of the tribe or the kingdom of Judah. — *adj.* Jewish: an offensive usage. [< OF < L < Gk. < Hebrew *y'hudi* descendant of Judah] — **Jew'ess** *n.fem.*
jew·el (jōō'əl) *n.* 1. A precious stone; gem. 2. An article for personal adornment, esp. one made of cut gems and precious metal. 3. A person or thing of rare excellence or value. 4. A bit of gem, crystal, glass, etc., used to form a durable bearing, as in a watch. — *v.t.* **jew·eled** or ·**elled**, **jew·el·ing** or ·**el·ling** To adorn with jewels; set jewels in. [< OF ult. < L *jocus* a joke, sport]
jew·el·er (jōō'əl-ər) *n.* A dealer in or maker of jewelry. Also **jew'el·ler.**
jew·el·ry (jōō'əl-rē) *n.* Jewels, collectively. Also *Brit.* **jew'el·ler·y.**
jew·el·weed (jōō'əl-wēd') *n.* A species of touch-me-not having deep yellow flowers.
Jew·ish (jōō'ish) *adj.* Of, pertaining to, or resembling the Jews, their customs, religion, etc. — *n.* Loosely, Yiddish.
Jewish holidays See HANUKKAH, PASSOVER, ROSH HA-SHANA, SUKKOTH, and YOM KIPPUR.
Jew·ry (jōō'rē) *n.* The Jewish people.
jew's-harp (jōōz'härp') *n.* A small musical instrument that is held between the teeth when played and consists of a lyre-shaped frame with a flexible steel tongue that is plucked with the finger. Also **jews'-harp.**
Jez·e·bel (jez'ə-bəl) The wife of Ahab, notorious for her evil actions. I *Kings* xvi 31. — *n.* A bold, vicious woman.
jib¹ (jib) *n.* 1. *Naut.* A triangular sail, set on a stay and extending from the foretopmast head to the jib boom or the bowsprit. For illus. see SCHOONER. 2. The boom of a crane or derrick. — *v.t. & v.i.* **jibbed, jib·bing** *Naut.* To jibe. [? Short for GIBBET]
jib² (jib) *v.i.* **jibbed, jib·bing** 1. To move restively sideways or backward, as a horse. 2. To balk. — *n.* A horse that jibs: also **jib'ber.** [Cf. OF *giber* kick]
jib boom *Naut.* A spar forming a continuation of the bowsprit and holding a jib.
jibe¹ (jīb) *v.* **jibed, jib·ing** *v.i.* 1. *Naut.* To swing from one side of a vessel to the other: said of a fore-and-aft sail or its boom. 2. To change course so that the sails shift in this manner. — *v.t.* 3. To cause to swing from one side of a vessel to the other. Also spelled *gibe, jib.* [< Du. *gijben*]
jibe² (jīb) See GIBE¹.
jibe³ (jīb) *v.i.* **jibed, jib·ing** *U.S. Informal* To agree; be in accordance. [Origin uncertain]
jif·fy (jif'ē) *n. pl.* ·**fies** *Informal* An instant; moment. Also **jiff.** [Origin unknown]
jig (jig) *n.* 1. A fast, lively dance; also, the music for such a dance. 2. *Mech.* A device for holding the material being worked or for guiding a tool. 3. In fishing, any of various combinations of hooks, spoons, etc., that are agitated in the water to attract and catch fish. 4. *Mining* A wire sieve or other device for separating or cleaning coal by jolting and shaking in water. — **the jig is up** *Slang* All hope of success is gone. — *v.* **jigged, jig·ging** *v.i.* 1. To dance or play a jig. 2. To move jerkily, esp. up and down; bob. 3. To use or operate a jig in working. 4. To fish with a jig. — *v.t.* 5. To jerk up and down or to and fro; jiggle. 6. To hold, form, process, etc., with a jig. 7. To catch (fish) with a jig. [Cf. OF *gigue* a fiddle]
jig·ger (jig'ər) *n.* 1. One who or that which jigs. 2. A

small glass or cup for measuring liquor, holding about one and one half ounces; also, the amount of liquor so measured. 3. A jig used in catching fish. 4. *Mech.* A jig. 5. Any of various types of jolting mechanisms, as an apparatus for separating ores, a potter's wheel, etc. 6. *Naut.* **a** A small sail set in the stern of a sailing craft, as a yawl. **b** A light tackle used on board ship. **c** A jigger mast. 7. *Informal* Any small device or thing one is unable to name definitely.
jigger mast *Naut.* The aftermost mast of a four- or five-masted vessel.
jig·gle (jig'əl) *v.t. & v.i.* ·**gled, ·gling** To move unsteadily up and down or backwards and forwards with slight, quick jerks. — *n.* A jerky, unsteady movement. [Freq. of JIG, v.]
jig·saw (jig'sô') *n.* A saw having a slim blade set vertically in a frame and operated with a reciprocating motion, used for cutting curved or irregular lines.
jigsaw puzzle A puzzle consisting of a picture mounted on wood or cardboard and then cut or stamped into irregular interlocking pieces for reassembly.
jilt (jilt) *v.t.* To cast off or discard (a previously favored lover or sweetheart). — *n.* A woman or girl who discards a lover. [Cf. dial. E (Scottish) *jillet* giddy girl] — **jilt'er** *n.*
jim-crow (jim'krō') *U.S. Slang adj.* Serving to segregate Negroes: *jim-crow* laws. — *v.t.* To subject (Negroes) to segregation or discrimination. Also **Jim'-Crow'.**
Jim Crow *U.S. Slang* 1. A Negro: an offensive term. 2. The segregation of Negroes. — **Jim-Crow'ism** *n.*
jim·my (jim'ē) *n. pl.* ·**mies** A burglar's crowbar. — *v.t.* ·**mied, ·my·ing** To break or pry open with or as with a jimmy. [after *Jimmy*, dim. of *James*, a personal name]
jim·son·weed (jim'sən-wēd') *n.* A tall, coarse, evil-smelling, poisonous annual weed of the nightshade family, yielding atropine and scopolamine: also called *stramonium.* Also **Jimson weed.** [Alter. of *Jamestown weed* Jamestown, Va.]
jin·gle (jin'gəl) *v.* ·**gled, ·gling** *v.i.* 1. To make light ringing or tinkling sounds. 2. To have an intrusive rhyme or rhythm: said of writing or music, often in deprecation. — *v.t.* 3. To cause to make ringing or tinkling sounds. — *n.* 1. A tinkling, clinking, or rapidly ringing sound. 2. A catchy short song or poem, esp. one used for advertising. 3. Rapid repetition in rhyme, rhythm, alliteration, etc. [Imit.] — **jin'gly** *adj.*
jin·go (jing'gō) *n. pl.* ·**goes** One who boasts of his patriotism and favors an aggressive foreign policy. — *adj.* Of, pertaining to, or characteristic of the jingoes. [Originally a magician's nonsense word] — **jin'go·ish** *adj.* — **jin'go·ism** *n.* — **jing·o'ist** *n.* — **jin'go·is'tic** *adj.*
jin·ni (jin'ē, ji·nē') *n. pl.* **jinn** (jin) In Moslem mythology, one of the supernatural beings able to assume human or animal form and often at the service of men: sometimes spelled *djinni, genie.* Also **jin·nee'.** [< Arabic *jinnī*]
jin·rik·sha (jin·rik'shə, -shô) *n.* A small oriental two-wheeled carriage drawn by one or two men: also called *rickshaw, ricksha.* Also **jin·rick'sha, jin·rik'i·sha.** [< Japanese *jin* man + *riki* power + *sha* carriage]
jinx (jingks) *Slang n.* A person or thing supposed to bring bad luck. — *v.t.* To bring bad luck to. [< earlier *jynx* < Gk. *iynx* the wryneck (a bird anciently used in witchcraft)]
jit·ney (jit'nē) *n. U.S.* 1. A motor vehicle that carries passengers for a small fare. 2. *Obs. Slang* A small coin.
jit·ter (jit'ər) *n. U.S. Slang* To be nervous. — **the jitters** *Slang* Intense nervousness. — **jit'ter·y** *adj.*
jit·ter·bug (jit'ər·bug') *U.S. Slang n.* One who dances rapidly and spasmodically to jazz. — *v.i.* ·**bugged, ·bug·ging** To dance to jazz in a fast, violent way.
jiu·jit·su (jōō·jit'sōō), **jiu·jut·su** (jōō·jit'sōō, -jōōt'sōō) See JUJITSU.
jive (jīv) *n. Slang* 1. The jargon of jazz music and musicians. 2. Jazz music. [Origin unknown]
job (job) *n.* 1. Anything that is to be done, esp. a definite single piece of work done for a set fee; also, the thing worked on. 2. A position or situation of employment. 3. Something done ostensibly for the public good, but actually for private profit. 4. *Informal* An affair; circumstance. 5. *Slang* A robbery or other criminal act. — **odd job** A piece of occasional or miscellaneous work. — **on the job** *Informal* 1. During working hours. 2. Attending strictly to the matter at hand. — **to lie (or lay) down on the job** *Informal* To evade work or responsibility. — *v.* **jobbed, job·bing** *v.i.* 1. To work by the job or piece. 2. To be a jobber or middleman. 3. To use a position of public trust for private advantage. — *v.t.* 4. To buy in bulk and resell in lots to dealers. 5. To sublet (work) among separate contractors. [Origin uncertain] — **job'less** *adj.* — **job'less·ness** *n.*
Job (jōb) In the Bible, the chief character in the Book of Job, who, despite great suffering and adversity, kept his faith in God. — *n.* The book itself.
job·ber (job'ər) *n.* 1. One who buys goods in bulk from the manufacturer or importer and sells to the retailer; wholesaler. 2. One who works by the job, or on small jobs; pieceworker.

job·ber·y (job/ər-ē) *n. pl.* **·ber·ies** Corrupt use of a public office or trust for private or partisan gain.

job·hold·er (job/hōl/dər) *n.* One who has a steady job.

job lot 1. A collection of miscellaneous goods sold to a retailer. 2. Any collection of things inferior in quality.

Jo·cas·ta (jō-kas/tə) In Greek legend, the queen who unwittingly marries her own son Oedipus.

jock·ey (jok/ē) *n. p.* **·eys** One employed to ride horses in races. — *v.t. & v.i.* 1. To maneuver for an advantageous position. 2. To ride (a horse) in a race. 3. To cheat; trick. [Dim. of JOCK] — **jock/ey·ing** *n.* — **jock/ey·ism** *n.*

jo·cose (jō-kōs/) *adj.* Humorous; playful; joking. [< L *jocus* joke] — **jo·cose/ly** *adv.* — **jo·cose/ness,** **jo/cos·i·ty** (-kos/ə·tē) *n.*

joc·u·lar (jok/yə-lər) *adj.* Given to joking; also, like a joke. Also **joc/u·la·to·ry** (-tôr/ē, -tō/rē). [< L *jocus* joke] — **joc/u·lar/i·ty** (-lar/ə·tē) *n.* — **joc/u·lar·ly** *adv.*

jo·cund (jok/ənd, jō/kənd) *adj.* Cheerful; gay; jovial. [< OF < LL *juvare* to delight] — **jo·cun·di·ty** (jō-kun/də·tē) *n.* — **joc/und·ly** *adv.* — **joc/und·ness** *n.*

jodh·purs (jod/pərz) *n.pl.* Wide riding breeches, close-fitting from knee to ankle. [after *Jodhpur,* India]

Jo·el (jō/əl) A Hebrew prophet. — *n.* A book of the Old Testament by this prophet. [< Hebrew, the Lord is God]

jog (jog) *v.* **jogged, jog·ging** *v.i.* 1. To proceed slowly or monotonously: with *on* or *along.* — *v.t.* 2. To push or touch lightly: esp. to nudge (someone). 3. To stimulate: to *jog* the memory. — *n.* 1. The act of jogging. 2. A nudge. 3. A slow, jolting motion or pace. 4. *U.S.* An angle or projection in a surface, as in a wall; jag. 5. *U.S.* A sudden temporary turning or veering in a road, course, etc. [Prob. imit. Akin to SHOG.] — **jog/ger** *n.*

jog·gle (jog/əl) *v.* **·gled, ·gling** *v.t.* 1. To shake slightly; jog. 2. To fasten or join together by a joggle or joggles. — *v.i.* 3. To move with an irregular or jolting motion; shake. — *n.* 1. The act of joggling. 2. A projection formed on a piece, as of stone, timber, etc., that serves to fit it firmly to an adjoining piece having a corresponding notch. 3. A dowel. [Freq. of JOG, v.]

jog trot 1. A slow, easy trot, as of a horse. 2. A slow, humdrum habit of living or doing the daily tasks.

john (jon) *n. Slang* A toilet.

John (jon) One of the twelve apostles, son of Zebedee and brother of James: called **Saint John the Evangelist, Saint John the Divine.** — *n.* 1. The fourth Gospel of the New Testament, attributed to him. 2. One of the three New Testament epistles that bear his name.

John Bull 1. The English people. 2. A typical Englishman. Also **Johnny Bull.** [after a character in a satire (1712) by Dr. John Arbuthnot] — **John-Bul·lism** (jon/bŏŏl/iz·əm) *n.*

John Doe (dō) A name to designate a fictitious or real personage in any legal transaction or proceeding.

John Han·cock (han/kok) *U.S. Informal* A person's autograph. [after *John Hancock*]

john·ny·cake (jon/ē·kāk/) *n. U.S.* A flat cake of cornmeal, baked on a griddle. [? < obs. *jonikin,* a type of bread]

john·ny·jump·up (jon/ē·jump/up/) *n.* 1. Any of various American spring violets. 2. The wild pansy.

John·son·ese (jon/sən·ēz/, -ēs/) *n.* A ponderous and elaborate literary style similar to that of Samuel Johnson.

John·so·ni·an (jon·sō/nē·ən) *adj.* Pertaining to or resembling Samuel Johnson or his work. — *n.* An admirer of Dr. Johnson, esp. a student of his life and work.

John the Baptist, 6? B.C.–A.D. 30?, forerunner and baptizer of Jesus; beheaded by Herod Antipas.

joie de vi·vre (zhwȧ də vēv/r') *French* Joy of living.

join (join) *v.t.* 1. To become a member of, as a club, party, staff, etc. 2. To come to as a companion or participant. 3. To unite in act or purpose. 4. To come to a junction with. 5. To connect. 6. To unite in marriage. 7. To take a place with, in, or among. 8. *Informal* To adjoin. — *v.i.* 9. To enter into association or agreement: often with *with.* 10. To take part: usually with *in.* 11. To come together; connect; unite. — **to join battle** To engage in a battle or conflict. — **to join up** *Informal* To enlist. — *n.* A joint or seam. [< OF < L *jungere* to join]

join·der (join/dər) *n.* 1. The act of joining. 2. *Law* **a** A joining of causes of action or defense. **b** A joining of parties in an action. **c** The acceptance of an issue tendered.

join·er (joi/nər) *n.* 1. One who or that which joins. 2. *U.S. Informal* One who joins many clubs, lodges, etc.

join·er·y (joi/nər·ē) *n.* 1. The art or skill of a joiner. 2. The articles constructed by a joiner.

joint (joint) *n.* 1. A place or point at which two or more parts of the same thing are joined together. 2. *Anat.* A place of union between two separate bones, usu. permitting movement; articulation. 3. *Bot.* The portion of the stem of a plant from which branches grow; a node. 4. A large cut of

meat from a shoulder or leg containing the bone, used for roasting. 5. *Slang* **a** A place of low repute, as for drinking, gambling, etc. **b** Any place of dwelling or gathering. — **out of joint** 1. Dislocated. 2. Disordered; disorganized. — *adj.* 1. Belonging to or used by two or more: *joint* bank account. 2. Sharing with another: *joint* owner. 3. Produced by combined action: a *joint* literary effort. — *v.t.* 1. To fasten by means of a joint or joints. 2. To form or shape with a joint or joints, as a board. 3. To cut at the joints, as meat. [< OF < L *jungere* to join]

joint account A bank account in the name of two or more persons, each of whom may deposit and withdraw funds.

Joint Chiefs of Staff *U.S.* A body within the Department of Defense, consisting of a military chairman, the Chief of Staff of the Army, the Chief of Naval Operations, and the Chief of Staff of the Air Force.

joint·ed (join/tid) *adj.* 1. Having a joint or joints. 2. Having a (specified kind of) joint: *short-jointed.*

joint·ly (joint/lē) *adv.* In a joint manner; unitedly.

joint resolution *U.S.* A resolution passed by both houses of Congress, becoming a law if signed by the President.

joint-stock company (joint/stok/) An unincorporated business association of many persons, each of whom owns shares of stock which he may sell or transfer at will.

join·ture (join/chər) *n. Law* A settlement of property made to a woman by her husband after his death; also, the property. — *v.t.* **·tured, ·tur·ing** To settle a jointure on. [< F < L *jungere* to join]

joist (joist) *n.* Any of the parallel beams placed horizontally from wall to wall, to which the boards of a floor or the laths of a ceiling are fastened. — *v.t.* To furnish with joists. [< OF < L *jacere* to lie]

joke (jōk) *n.* 1. Something said or done to amuse; esp., a funny story. 2. Something said or done in fun rather than in earnest. 3. One who or that which excites mirth. 4. A trifling matter. — *v.* **joked, jok·ing** *v.i.* 1. To tell or make jokes; jest. 2. To say something in fun and not in earnest. [< L *jocus*] — **jok/ing·ly** *adv.*

jok·er (jō/kər) *n.* 1. One who jokes. 2. In a deck of cards, an extra card used in certain games. 3. *U.S.* An unobtrusive clause in a legislative bill, etc., that undermines or nullifies its original purpose. 4. Any hidden difficulty.

jol·li·fy (jol/ə·fī) *v.t. & v.i.* **·fied, ·fy·ing** *Informal* To be or cause to be merry or jolly. — **jol/li·fi·ca/tion** *n.*

jol·li·ty (jol/ə·tē) *n. pl.* **·ties** 1. The state or quality of being jolly; gaiety. 2. *Brit.* A festive occasion or gathering.

jol·ly (jol/ē) *adj.* **·li·er, ·li·est** 1. Full of good humor and high spirits. 2. Festive; merry. 3. *Brit. Informal* Extraordinary: a *jolly* bore. — *v.t.* **·lied, ·ly·ing** *Informal* 1. To attempt to put or keep in good humor: often with *along* or *up.* 2. To make fun of. — *n. pl.* **·lies** 1. *Brit. Informal* A merry or festive gathering. 2. *Brit. Slang* A sailor. — *adv. Brit. Informal* Extremely; very: *jolly* ugly. [< OF *joli*] — **jol/li·ly** *adv.* — **jol/li·ness** *n.*

jolly boat A small boat belonging to a ship. [< Dan. *jolle* yawl + BOAT]

Jolly Roger The pirate flag bearing the skull and crossbones.

jolt (jōlt) *v.t.* 1. To strike or knock against; jar; jostle. 2. To shake up or about with a blow or bump. — *v.i.* 3. To move with a series of irregular bumps or jars, as over a rough road. — *n.* 1. A sudden bump or jar as from a blow. 2. An unexpected surprise or emotional shock. [ME *jot* bump and *joll* bump] — **jolt/er** *n.* — **jolt/y** *adj.*

Jo·nah (jō/nə) Eighth- or ninth-century B.C. Hebrew prophet, who, cast overboard during a storm, was swallowed by a great fish and then cast up on the shore alive three days later. — *n.* 1. A book of the Old Testament containing his story: also, in the Douai Bible, **Jo/nas** (-nəs). 2. Any person bringing bad luck. [< Hebrew *Yōnāh,* lit., dove]

jon·gleur (jong/glər, *Fr.* zhôn·glœr/) *n.* A wandering minstrel of medieval England and France. [< OF < L *joculator.* See JUGGLER.]

jon·quil (jon/kwil, jong/-) *n.* 1. A species of narcissus related to the daffodil, having fragrant, white or yellow flowers. 2. The flower. [< F < L *juncus* a rush]

Jordan almond A large Spanish almond, frequently sugar-coated as a confection. [ME *jardyne almaunde*]

Jo·seph (jō/zəf) In the Old Testament, a son of Jacob and Rachel, sold into slavery in Egypt by his brothers. *Gen.* xxx 24. [< Hebrew *Yōsēph,* lit., He will add]

Joseph Husband of Mary, the mother of Jesus. *Matt.* i 18.

Joseph of Ar·i·ma·the·a (ar/ə·mə·thē/ə) A wealthy disciple of Christ who provided a tomb for his burial. *Matt.* xxvii 57–60.

josh (josh) *U.S. Slang v.t. & v.i.* To make good-humored fun of (someone); tease; banter. — *n.* A good-natured joke. [Blend of JOKE and BOSH] — **josh/er** *n.*

Josh·u·a (josh′ōō-ə) Israelite leader and successor of Moses. — *n.* The book of the Old Testament bearing his name. [< Hebrew *Yehōshua'* God is salvation]

joss (jos) *n.* A Chinese god. [Pidgin English < Pg. *deos* God]

joss house A Chinese temple or place for religious images.

joss paper Paper burnt by the Chinese at funerals, etc.

joss stick A stick of perfumed paste burnt by the Chinese.

jos·tle (jos′əl) *v.t. & v.i.* **·tled, ·tling** To push or crowd roughly so as to shake up; elbow; shove. — *n.* A shoving or colliding against; jostling. [Freq. of JOUST] — **jos′tler** *n.*

jot (jot) *v.t.* **jot·ted, jot·ting** To make a hasty and brief note of: usually with *down.* — *n.* The least bit; iota. [< IOTA]

jot·ting (jot′ing) *n.* That which is jotted down; short note.

joule (joul, jōōl) *n. Physics* A unit of work equal to 10,000,-000 ergs or 0.737324 foot-pounds. [after J. P. Joule, 1818–1889, English physicist]

jounce (jouns) *v.t. & v.i.* **jounced, jounc·ing** To bounce; jolt. — *n.* A shake; a bump. [Origin unknown]

jour·nal (jûr′nəl) *n.* **1.** A diary or record of daily occurrences; esp. a ship's log. **2.** A newspaper, esp. one published daily. **3.** Any periodical or magazine. **4.** An official record of the daily proceedings of a legislature. **5.** In bookkeeping: **a** A daybook. **b** In double entry, a book in which daily transactions are entered to facilitate later posting in the ledger. **6.** *Mech.* The part of a shaft or axle that rotates in or against a bearing. [< OF < L *diurnalis* daily]

journal box *Mech.* The box or bearing for a journal.

jour·nal·ese (jûr′nəl-ēz′, -ēs′) *n.* The style of writing supposedly characteristic of newspapers, magazines, etc.: a derogatory term.

jour·nal·ism (jûr′nəl-iz′əm) *n.* The occupation, practice, and academic field concerned with writing, editing, and publishing newspapers and other periodicals.

jour·nal·ist (jûr′nəl-ist) *n.* One whose occupation is writing, editing, and publishing newspapers, etc. — **jour·nal·is·tic** (jûr′nəl-is′tik) *adj.* — **jour′nal·is′ti·cal·ly** *adv.*

jour·nal·ize (jûr′nəl-īz) *v.* **·ized, ·iz·ing** *v.t.* **1.** To enter in a journal or diary. — *v.i.* **2.** To keep a journal or diary.

jour·ney (jûr′nē) *n.* **1.** Travel from one place to another. **2.** The distance traveled. — *v.i.* To make a trip; travel. [< OF *journee* a day's travel] — **jour′ney·er** *n.*

jour·ney·man (jûr′nē-mən) *n. pl.* **·men** (-mən) A worker who has completed his apprenticeship in a skilled trade.

joust (just, joust, jōōst) *n.* **1.** A formal combat between two mounted knights armed with lances; tilt. **2.** *pl.* Tournament. — *v.i.* To engage in a joust. Also spelled *just.* [< OF < LL *juxtare* to approach] — **joust′er** *n.*

Jove (jōv) Jupiter. — **by Jove!** A mild oath expressing surprise, emphasis, etc. — **Jo′vi·an** *adj.*

jo·vi·al (jō′vē·əl) *adj.* Good-natured; convivial; jolly. [< F < LL *Jovialis* born under the influence of Jupiter] — **jo′vi·al·ly** *adv.* — **jo′vi·al·ness** *n.*

jo·vi·al·i·ty (jō′vē·al′ə·tē) *n.* The quality or state of being jovial; conviviality; merriment. Also **jo·vi·al·ty** (jō′vē·əl·tē).

jowl[1] (joul, jōl) *n.* The fleshy part under the lower jaw, esp. when fat; double chin. [ME *cholle* < OE *ceolu* throat]

jowl[2] (joul, jōl) *n.* **1.** The jaw, esp. the lower jaw. **2.** The cheek. [ME *chavel* < OE *ceafl*]

joy (joi) *n.* **1.** A strong feeling of happiness; gladness; delight. **2.** A state of contentment or satisfaction. **3.** Anything that causes delight or gladness. — *v.i.* To be glad; rejoice. [< OF < L *gaudere* to rejoice]

joy·ful (joi′fəl) *adj.* **1.** Full of joy. **2.** Showing or causing joy. — **joy′ful·ly** *adv.* — **joy′ful·ness** *n.*

joy·less (joi′lis) *adj.* Completely lacking in joy; causing no joy; dreary; sad. — **joy′less·ly** *adv.* — **joy′less·ness** *n.*

joy·ous (joi′əs) *adj.* Joyful. — **joy′ous·ly** *adv.* — **joy′ous·ness** *n.*

joy ride *Informal* **1.** A ride taken for pleasure. **2.** A reckless ride in a stolen vehicle. — **joy rider** — **joy riding**

joy stick *Informal* The control stick of an airplane.

ju·bi·lant (jōō′bə·lənt) *adj.* Exultingly joyful or triumphant. [< L *jubilare* to exult] — **ju′bi·lance, ju′bi·lan·cy** *n.* — **ju′bi·lant·ly** *adv.*

ju·bi·late (jōō′bə·lāt) *v.t. & v.i.* **·lat·ed, ·lat·ing** To rejoice.

ju·bi·la·tion (jōō′bə·lā′shən) *n.* Rejoicing; exultation.

ju·bi·lee (jōō′bə·lē) *n.* **1.** In Jewish history, a celebration (*Lev.* xxv 8–17) observed every fiftieth year, at which time slaves were freed, alienated lands returned, and the fields left uncultivated. **2.** In the Roman Catholic Church, a year of special indulgence occurring usu. every twenty-fifth year. **3.** A special anniversary of an event. **4.** Any time of rejoicing. Also **ju′bi·le.** [< OF < LL < Gk. < Hebrew *yōbēl* ram's horn, trumpet]

Judaeo- See JUDEO-.

Judah (jōō′də) In the Old Testament, a son of Jacob and Leah. *Gen.* xxix 35. — *n.* The tribe of Israel descended from him. [< Hebrew *Yehūdāh* praised]

Ju·da·ic (jōō·dā′ik) *adj.* Of or pertaining to the Jews. Also **Ju·da′i·cal.** [< L *Judaicus*] — **Ju·da′i·cal·ly** *adv.*

Ju·da·ism (jōō′dē·iz′əm) *n.* **1.** The religious beliefs or practices of the Jews. **2.** The observance of Jewish rites or practices. See CONSERVATIVE JUDAISM, ORTHODOX JUDAISM, REFORM JUDAISM. — **Ju′da·ist** *n.* — **Ju′da·is′tic** *adj.*

Ju·da·ize (jōō′dē·īz) *v.* **·ized, ·iz·ing** *v.t.* **1.** To bring into conformity with Judaism. — *v.i.* **2.** To accept Judaism.

Ju·das (jōō′dəs) **1.** The disciple of Jesus who betrayed him with a kiss: also **Judas Is·car·i·ot** (is·kar′ē·ət). **2.** Jude. — *n.* One who betrays another under the guise of friendship.

Judas tree A tree with reddish purple flowers. [from a tradition that Judas hanged himself upon a tree of this kind]

Jude (jōōd) **1.** One of the twelve apostles: called *Judas* (not Iscariot). *Luke* vi 16, *Acts* i 13, *John* xiv 22. **2.** The author of a book of the New Testament, possibly the brother of James and Jesus: called *Judas*. *Matt.* xiii 55, *Mark* vi 3. — *n.* A book of the New Testament by this author.

Ju·de·a (jōō·dē′ə) The southern part of ancient Palestine under Persian, Greek, and Roman dominion: also **Ju·dae′a.** — **Ju·de′an, Ju·dae′an** *n. & adj.*

Judeo- *combining form* Jewish. Also spelled *Judaeo-.* [< L *Judaeus*]

judge (juj) *n.* **1.** A public officer invested with the power to administer justice by hearing cases in a court of law. **2.** One appointed to make decisions. **3.** One considered competent to make critical evaluations: a *judge* of music. **4.** In Jewish history, one of the rulers of Israel before the kings. — *v.* **judged, judg·ing** *v.t.* **1.** To hear and decide the merits of (a case) or the guilt of (a person). **2.** To decide authoritatively, as a contest. **3.** To hold as judgment or opinion. **4.** To form an opinion or judgment concerning. **5.** To govern: said of the ancient Hebrew judges. — *v.i.* **6.** To act as a judge. **7.** To make a judgment or decision. [< OF < L *judex, -icis* < *ius* right + *dicere* to speak]

judge advocate *Mil.* **1.** A commissioned officer in the U.S. Army belonging to the Judge Advocate General's Corps. **2.** The legal staff officer for a commander.

Judge Advocate General A major general in the U.S. Army or the U.S. Air Force, serving as head of the Judge Advocate General's Department and supervising military justice and other legal matters.

Judg·es (juj′iz) *n.pl.* (*construed as sing.*) A book of the Old Testament, containing a history of the Jewish people.

judg·ment (juj′mənt) *n.* **1.** The act of judging. **2.** The decision or opinion reached through judging. **3.** The ability to judge wisely. **4.** *Law* **a** The sentence or decision. **b** A debt resulting from such a decision. **c** The record of such a decision. **5.** A disaster or misfortune regarded as inflicted by God. **judge′ment.**

Judgment Day *Theol.* The day or time of the Last Judgment: also *Day of Judgment.*

ju·di·ca·tor (jōō′də·kā·tər) *n.* One who acts as judge.

ju·di·ca·to·ry (jōō′də·kə·tôr′ē, -tō′rē) *adj.* Pertaining to the administration of justice. — *n. pl.* **·ries** **1.** Any tribunal. **2.** The judicial process.

ju·di·ca·ture (jōō′də·kə·chŏŏr) *n.* **1.** The action or function of administering justice, as in courts of law. **2.** The right, power, or authority of administering justice; jurisdiction. **3.** A court of law; also, judges collectively.

ju·di·cial (jōō·dish′əl) *adj.* **1.** Of or pertaining to the administering of justice, to courts of law or to judges. **2.** Decreed or enforced by a court of law. **3.** Of or befitting a judge. **4.** Inclined to make judgments; discriminating; critical. [< L *judex, -icis* judge] — **ju·di′cial·ly** *adv.*

ju·di·ci·ar·y (jōō·dish′ē·er′ē, -dish′ə·rē) *adj.* Of or pertaining to courts, judges, or judgments. — *n. pl.* **·ar·ies** **1.** The department of government that administers the law. **2.** The system of courts set up to carry out this function. **3.** The judges collectively.

ju·di·cious (jōō·dish′əs) *adj.* Having, showing, or exercising good judgment; prudent. [< F < L *judicium* judgment] — **ju·di′cious·ly** *adv.* — **ju·di′cious·ness** *n.*

Ju·dith (jōō′dith) **1.** A book in the Old Testament Apocrypha and the Douai Bible. **2.** A Jewish woman, heroine of this book, who rescued her countrymen by slaying the Assyrian general, Holofernes. [< Hebrew *Jehūdhith*]

ju·do (jōō′dō) *n.* A system of physical conditioning devised in Japan in 1882, based on jujitsu. [< Japanese *ju* gentle, pliant + *do* way of life]

jug[1] (jug) *n.* **1.** A pitcher or similar vessel for holding liquids. **2.** *Slang* A prison or jail. — *v.t.* **jugged, jug·ging** **1.** To put into a jug. **2.** *Slang* To imprison; jail. [after *Jug*, a nickname for *Joan*]

jug[2] (jug) *n.* The sound of a nightingale's note. — *v.i.* **jugged, jug·ging** To make the sound of the nightingale.

ju·gate (jōō′git, -gāt) *adj.* **1.** *Biol.* Occurring in pairs. **2.** *Bot.* Having paired leaflets. [< L *jugare* to bind together]

jug·ger·naut (jug′ər·nôt) *n.* Any slow and irresistible destructive force.

Jug·ger·naut (jug′ər·nôt) The eighth avatar of Vishnu whose idol at Puri, India, is annually drawn on a heavy car under the wheels of which devotees are said to have thrown themselves. [< Skt. *jagannātha* lord of the universe]

jug·gle (jug/əl) v. **·gled**, **·gling** v.t. **1.** To keep (two or more balls or other objects) continuously moving from the hand into the air. **2.** To manipulate dishonestly. — v.i. **3.** To perform as a juggler. **4.** To practice deception or fraud. — n. **1.** An act of juggling. **2.** A trick or deception. [< OF < L joculari to jest] — **jug/gler** n.

jug·gler·y (jug/lər-ē) n. pl. **·gler·ies 1.** The juggler's art; legerdemain. **2.** Deception; fraud.

jug·u·lar (jug/yə-lər, jōō/gyə-) adj. Anat. Of or pertaining to the throat or the jugular vein. — n. Anat. A jugular vein. [< NL < L jugulum collar bone]

jugular vein Anat. One of the large veins on either side of the neck that returns blood from the brain, face, and neck.

juice (jōōs) n. **1.** The liquid part of a vegetable, fruit, or animal. **2.** Usually pl. The fluids of the body. **3.** U.S. Slang Electricity. **4.** U.S. Slang Gasoline. **5.** U.S. Slang Vital force; strength. [< OF jus < L]

juic·er (jōō/sər) n. A device for extracting juice.

juic·y (jōō/sē) adj. **juic·i·er**, **juic·i·est 1.** Abounding with juice; moist. **2.** Full of interest; colorful; spicy. — **juic/i·ly** adv. — **juic/i·ness** n.

ju·jit·su (jōō·jit/sōō) n. A Japanese system of hand-to-hand fighting in which surprise and a knowledge of anatomy and leverage are used: also spelled jiujitsu, jiujutsu. Also **ju·jut·su** (jōō·jit/sōō, -jōōt/sōō). Compare JUDO. [< Japanese ju pliant + jutsu art]

ju·jube (jōō/jōōb; for def. 1, also jōō/jōō·bē) n. **1.** A gelatinous candy lozenge. **2.** An Old World tree or shrub of the buckthorn family. [< F or < Med.L jujuba]

juke box (jōōk) A large automatic phonograph, usu. coin-operated and permitting selection of the records to be played.

juke joint U.S. Slang A roadhouse or barroom for drinking and dancing. [< Gullah jook disorderly, wicked]

ju·lep (jōō/lip) n. **1.** A mint julep. **2.** A sweetened, syrupy drink. [< OF < Persian < gul rose + āb water]

Jul·ian (jōōl/yən) adj. Of, pertaining to, or named after Julius Caesar.

ju·li·enne (jōō/lē·en/, Fr. zhü·lyen/) n. A clear meat soup containing vegetables chopped or cut into thin strips. — adj. Cut into thin strips: julienne potatoes. [< F]

Ju·li·et (jōō/lē·et, jōōl/yit) The heroine of Shakespeare's Romeo and Juliet.

Ju·ly (jōō·lī/, jōō-) pl. **·lys** The seventh month of the calendar year, having 31 days. [< AF < L (mensis) Julius (month) of Julius Caesar]

jum·ble (jum/bəl) v. **·bled**, **·bling** v.t. **1.** To mix in a confused mass; put or throw together without order. **2.** To mix up in the mind; muddle. — v.i. **3.** To meet or unite confusedly. — n. **1.** A confused mixture or collection; hodgepodge: also **jum/ble·ment. 2.** A thin sweet cake. **3.** Any of various hairless bees. [Imit.]

jum·bo (jum/bō) n. pl. **·bos** A very large person, animal, or thing. — adj. Very large. [after Jumbo, an unusually large elephant exhibited by P. T. Barnum < ? W African]

jump (jump) v.i. **1.** To spring from the ground, floor, etc., by using the foot and leg muscles; leap; bound. **2.** To move or be moved jerkily; bob; bounce. **3.** To rise abruptly: Prices jumped. **4.** To pass suddenly, as if by leaping: to jump to a conclusion. **5.** To start in astonishment. **6.** To spring down from or out of a window, ladder, airplane, etc. **7.** In checkers, to capture a piece by passing another over it to a vacant square beyond. **8.** In bridge, to bid so as to exceed the preceding bid by more than the minimum. — v.t. **9.** To leap over or across. **10.** To cause to leap over or across: to jump a horse. **11.** To increase (prices, demands, etc.). **12.** To pass over; skip; omit. **13.** In bridge, to cause (a bid) to exceed the preceding bid by more than the minimum. **14.** U.S. To leave or quit abruptly: to jump town. **15.** Informal To get onto; board: to jump a train. **16.** Informal To attack suddenly or by surprise. — **to jump a claim** To take possession of another's mining or land claim by force and fraud. — **to jump at** To accept hastily. — **to jump bail** U.S. To forfeit one's bail bond by failing to appear when legally summoned. — **to jump off** Mil. To begin an attack. — **to jump on** (or **all over**) Informal To assail with abuse; scold. — **to jump ship** Naut. To end one's service in a ship's crew by desertion. — **to jump the gun** Slang **1.** To begin before the starting signal is given. **2.** To start prematurely. — **to jump the track** Of a train, etc., to leave the rails. — n. **1.** The act of jumping; a leap; spring; bound. **2.** An abrupt movement upward or outward; a jerk. **3.** A sudden rise or transition. **4.** The length or height of a leap. **5.** Something that is jumped over or across, as a hurdle, obstacle, or fence. **6.** A leap by parachute from an airplane. **7.** In sports, a competition in jumping: broad jump. — **on the jump** Informal Working or moving about at top speed; very busy. — **to get** (or **have**) **the jump on** U.S. Slang To get or have a head start

on or an advantage over. — adj. **1.** Mil. Of or pertaining to paratroops. **2.** U.S. Slang Of popular music, having a fast, excited tempo. [Cf. Scand. gumpa to jump]

jump·er¹ (jum/pər) n. **1.** One who or that which jumps. **2.** A piece of mechanism having a jumping motion. **3.** Electr. A short wire used to bypass or join parts of a circuit.

jump·er² (jum/pər) n. **1.** A sleeveless dress, usu. worn over a blouse or sweater. **2.** A loose jacket or smock worn over other clothes. [Prob. alter. of OF juppe jacket]

jump·ing bean (jump/ing) The seed of certain Mexican shrubs of the spurge family, that jumps about owing to the movements of a small larva inside.

jumping jack A toy figure of a man, whose jointed limbs are moved by strings.

jump·y (jum/pē) adj. **jump·i·er**, **jump·i·est 1.** Subject to sudden changes; fluctuating. **2.** Given to startled movements; nervous; apprehensive. — **jump/i·ness** n.

jun·co (jung/kō) n. pl. **·cos** Any of various small birds of North America, commonly seen in flocks during winter: also called snowbird. [< Sp. < L juncus rush]

junc·tion (jungk/shən) n. **1.** The act of joining, or the state of being joined. **2.** The place where lines or routes, as roads, railways, streams, etc., come together or cross.

junc·ture (jungk/chər) n. **1.** The act of joining, or the state of being joined; junction. **2.** A point or line of junction; a joint or seam. **3.** A point in time. **4.** A crisis; emergency. [< L junctura < jungere to join]

June (jōōn) The sixth month of the calendar year, having 30 days. [OE < L, or ME < OF Juin < L (mensis) Junius (month) of the Junii, a Roman family]

June bug A large, brightly colored beetle that flies in June. Also **June beetle.**

jun·gle (jung/gəl) n. **1.** A dense tropical thicket of high grass, reeds, vines, brush, or trees, usu. inhabited by wild animals. **2.** Any similar tangled growth. **3.** U.S. Slang A camp for hoboes. [< Hind. jangal forest] — **jun/gly** adj.

jun·ior (jōōn/yər) adj. **1.** Younger in years or lower in rank. **2.** Denoting the younger of two. **3.** Belonging to youth or earlier life. **4.** Later in effect or tenure. **5.** Pertaining to the third year of a high-school or collegiate course of four years. — n. **1.** The younger of two. **2.** One later or lower in service or standing. **3.** A student in the third or junior year. Abbr. jr., Jr. [< L junior, compar. of juvenis young]

junior college A school giving college courses up to and including the sophomore year.

junior high school A school intermediate between grammar school and high school, in the U.S. typically comprising grades 7 and 8, and sometimes grade 9.

Junior League A local branch of the Association of the Junior Leagues of America, Inc., composed of young society women engaged in volunteer welfare work.

ju·ni·per (jōō/nə·pər) n. **1.** An evergreen pinaceous shrub of Europe and America. **2.** The dark blue berry of this shrub, used in making gin and as a diuretic. [< L juniperus]

junk¹ (jungk) n. **1.** Castoff material, as scrap iron, old bottles, or paper. **2.** Informal Worthless matter; rubbish; trash. **3.** Slang Narcotics; dope. **4.** Naut. Old cable or cordage used for making gaskets, oakum, etc. — v.t. Informal To discard as trash; scrap. [ME jonke]

junk² (jungk) n. A large Chinese vessel with high poop, prominent stem, and battened lugsails. [< Sp. and Pg. junco < Malay djong ship]

CHINESE JUNK

Jun·ker (yŏŏng/kər) n. One of the landed aristocracy of Prussia. [< G jung young + herr master] — **Jun/ker·dom** n. — **Jun/ker·ism** n.

jun·ket (jung/kit) n. **1.** A feast, banquet, picnic, or pleasure trip. **2.** U.S. A trip taken by a public official with all expenses paid from public funds. **3.** A delicacy made of curds or of sweetened milk and rennet. — v.i. **1.** To have a feast; banquet. **2.** U.S. To go on a trip, esp. at public expense. — v.i. **3.** To entertain by feasting; regale. [< It. < L juncus rush] — **jun/ket·er** n.

junk·ie (jung/kē) n. Slang A dope addict. Also **junk/y.**

junk·man (jungk/man/) n. pl. **·men** (-men/) One who purchases, collects, and sells junk. Also **junk/deal/er** (-dē/lər).

Ju·no (jōō/nō) In Roman mythology, the wife of Jupiter, queen of the gods and goddess of marriage: identified with the Greek Hera. — n. A woman of queenly beauty.

Ju·no·esque (jōō/nō·esk/) adj. Stately and beautiful.

jun·ta (jun/tə, Sp. hōōn/tä) n. **1.** A Central or South American legislative council. **2.** A body of men engaged in secret, usu. political intrigue: also **jun/to** (-tō). [< Sp. < L jungere to join]

Ju·pi·ter (jōō/pə·tər) In Roman mythology, the god ruling over all other gods and all men: identified with the Greek *Zeus*: also called *Jove*. — *n.* The largest planet of the solar system, fifth in order from the sun. See PLANET.

Ju·ras·sic (jŏŏ·ras′ik) *Geol. adj.* Of or pertaining to a period of the Mesozoic era succeeding the Triassic and followed by the Cretaceous. See chart for GEOLOGY. — *n.* The Jurassic period or rock system. [< F *jurassique*, after *Jura*]

ju·rid·i·cal (jŏŏ·rid′i·kəl) *adj.* Pertaining to the law and to the administration of justice. Also **ju·rid′ic.** [< L *juris* law + *dicere* to say, speak] — **ju·rid′i·cal·ly** *adv.*

ju·ris·dic·tion (jŏŏr′is·dik′shən) *n.* **1.** Lawful right to exercise authority, whether executive, legislative, or judicial. **2.** Those things over which such authority may be exercised. **3.** Power in general; authority. [< OF < L *juris* law + *dicere* to say, speak] — **ju′ris·dic′tion·al** *adj.*

ju·ris·pru·dence (jŏŏr′is·prōōd′ns) *n.* **1.** The philosophy or science of law. **2.** A system of laws. [< L *juris* law + *prudentia* knowledge] — **ju′ris·pru·den′tial** (-prōō·den′·shəl) *adj.*

ju·ris·pru·dent (jŏŏr′is·prōōd′nt) *adj.* Skilled in the law. — *n.* One skilled in the law.

ju·rist (jŏŏr′ist) *n.* One versed in the law.

ju·ris·tic (jŏŏ·ris′tik) *adj.* Of or pertaining to a jurist or the profession of law. Also **ju·ris′ti·cal.** — **ju·ris′ti·cal·ly** *adv.*

ju·ror (jŏŏr′ər) *n.* **1.** One who serves on a jury. **2.** One who takes an oath. [< AF < L *jurare* to swear]

ju·ry¹ (jŏŏr′ē) *n. pl.* **·ries 1.** A body of legally qualified persons summoned to serve on a judicial tribunal and give a verdict according to the evidence. See GRAND JURY, PETIT JURY. **2.** A committee of award in a competition. [< AF < L *jurare* to swear]

ju·ry² (jŏŏr′ē) *adj. Naut.* Rigged up temporarily: a *jury* mast. [Prob. < OF *ajurie* aid < L *adjutare* to help]

ju·ry·man (jŏŏr′ē·mən) *n. pl.* **·men** (-mən) A juror.

just¹ (just) *adj.* **1.** Fair and impartial in acting or judging. **2.** Upright; honest. **3.** Legally valid; legitimate. **4.** Merited; deserved. **5.** True; correct; accurate. **6.** Fitting; proper. **7.** *Archaic* Righteous in the sight of God. — *adv.* **1.** To the exact point; precisely: *just* right. **2.** Exactly now: He is *just* leaving. **3.** A moment ago: He *just* left. **4.** By very little; barely: It *just* missed. **5.** Only; merely: *just* a layman. **6.** *Informal* Simply; really; very: It's *just* lovely. [< OF < L *jus* law] — **just′ly** *adv.* — **just′ness** *n.*

just² (just) See JOUST.

jus·tice (jus′tis) *n.* **1.** The quality of being just. **2.** The rendering of what is due or merited; also, that which is due or merited. **3.** Conformity to the law. **4.** The administration of law. **5.** A judge. **6.** *Theol.* An attribute of God, and of his laws and judgments. **7.** The abstract principle by which right and wrong are defined. — **Department of Justice** An executive department of the U.S. government, head-

ed by the Attorney General, that represents the government in legal matters, enforces antitrust laws, civil rights laws, etc., and supervises internal security and immigration. — **to bring to justice** To arrest and try (a wrongdoer). — **to do justice to** To show appreciation of. [See JUST¹.]

justice of the peace A local magistrate of limited jurisdiction with authority to fine and imprison in minor cases, commit to a higher court, perform marriages, etc.

jus·ti·fi·a·ble (jus′tə·fī′ə·bəl) *adj.* Capable of being justified; defensible. — **jus′ti·fi′a·bil′i·ty, jus′ti·fi′a·ble·ness** *n.* — **jus′ti·fi′a·bly** *adv.*

jus·ti·fi·ca·tion (jus′tə·fə·kā′shən) *n.* **1.** The act of justifying, or the state of being justified. **2.** The ground of justifying, or that which justifies. — **jus′ti·fi·ca′tive** *adj.*

jus·ti·fi·er (jus′tə·fī′ər) *n.* One who justifies.

jus·ti·fy (jus′tə·fī) *v.* **·fied, ·fy·ing** *v.t.* **1.** To show to be just, right, or reasonable; vindicate. **2.** To declare guiltless; absolve. **3.** To provide adequate grounds for; warrant. **4.** *Printing* To adjust (lines) to the proper length by spacing. — *v.i.* **5.** *Printing* To be properly spaced; fit. [< OF < LL < L *justus* just + *facere* to make]

jus·tle (jus′əl) See JOSTLE.

jut (jut) *v.i.* **jut·ted, jut·ting** To extend beyond the main portion; protrude; project: often with *out*. — *n.* Anything that juts; a projection. [Var. of JET²]

jute (jōōt) *n.* **1.** A tall annual Asian herb of the linden family. **2.** The tough fiber obtained from the inner bark of this plant, used for bags, cordage, etc. [< Bengali < Skt. *jūta* braid of hair]

Jute (jōōt) *n.* A member of a Germanic tribe, some of whom invaded Britain in the fifth century. [< LL *Jutae* the Jutes] — **Jut·ish** (jōō′tish) *adj.*

ju·ve·nes·cent (jōō′və·nes′ənt) *adj.* **1.** Becoming young; growing young again. **2.** Making young; rejuvenating. [< L *juvenescere* to grow younger] — **ju′ve·nes′cence** *n.*

ju·ve·nile (jōō′və·nəl, -nīl) *adj.* **1.** Young; youthful; also, immature. **2.** Designed for young persons: *juvenile* books. — *n.* **1.** A young person. **2.** An actor of youthful roles. **3.** A book for young persons. [< L *juvenis* young person] — **ju′ve·nile·ly** *adv.* — **ju′ve·nile·ness, ju′ve·nil′i·ty** *n.*

juvenile court A court that has jurisdiction in cases involving dependent, neglected, and delinquent children.

juvenile delinquent One who is guilty of antisocial behavior or of violations of the law, but is too young to be punished as an adult criminal. — **juvenile delinquency**

ju·ve·nil·i·a (jōō′və·nil′ē·ə, -nil′yə) *n.pl.* Works produced in youth, esp. writings or paintings.

juxta- *prefix* Near; next to. [< L *juxta* near]

jux·ta·pose (juks′tə·pōz′) *v.t.* **·posed, ·pos·ing** To place together; put side by side. [< F < L *juxta* near + *poser* to put down] — **jux·ta·po·si·tion** (juks′tə·pə·zish′ən) *n.*

K

k, K (kā) *n. pl.* **k's** or **ks, K's** or **Ks, kays** (kāz) **1.** The eleventh letter of the English alphabet. **2.** The sound represented by the letter. It normally has no phonetic value when initial before *n*, as in *knee, knight, know*, etc. — *symbol Chem.* Potassium (K for *kalium*).

Ka·a·ba (kä′ə·bə, kä′bə) *n.* The Moslem shrine at Mecca enclosing a sacred black stone, supposedly given to Abraham by the angel Gabriel, toward which worshipers face when praying: also spelled *Caaba*. [< Arabic *ka'b* cube]

kab·a·la (kab′ə·lə, kə·bä′lə), **kab·ba·la** See CABALA.

ka·bu·ki (kä·bōō′kē) *n.* A form of Japanese play on popular or comic themes, employing elaborate costume, stylized gesture, music, and dancing. [< Japanese]

Kad·dish (kä′dish) *n.* In Judaism, a prayer recited by mourners and part of the daily service. [< Aramaic, holy]

kaf·fee·klatsch (kôf′ē·kläch′, *Ger.* käf′ā·kläch′) *n. Sometimes cap.* An informal conversational gathering where coffee is drunk. [< G < *kaffee* coffee + *klatsch* chitchat]

kaf·fir (kaf′ər) *n.* A variety of sorghum grown in dry regions as a grain and forage plant. Also **kaffir corn.** [after *Kaffir*]

Kaf·fir (kaf′ər) *n.* **1.** A member of a powerful group of South African Bantu tribes. **2.** Xhosa, the language of these tribes. Also **Kaf′ir.** [< Arabic *kafir* unbeliever]

kaf·tan (kaf′tən, käf·tän′) See CAFTAN.

kai·ak (kī′ak) See KAYAK.

kai·ser (kī′zər) *n.* Emperor. [< G < L *Caesar* Caesar]

Kai·ser (kī′zər) Title of the emperors of the Holy Roman Empire, 962–1806; the Austrian emperors, 1804–1918; and the German emperors, 1871–1918.

kale (kāl) *n.* **1.** A variety of headless cabbage. **2.** *U.S. Slang* Money. [Var. of COLE]

ka·lei·do·scope (kə·lī′də·skōp) *n.* **1.** A tube-shaped optical toy that shows constantly changing symmetrical patterns as loose bits of colored glass are moved about under a set of mirrors. **2.** A swiftly changing scene, pattern, etc. [< Gk. *kalos* beautiful + *eidos* form + -SCOPE]

ka·lei·do·scop·ic (kə·lī′də·skop′ik) *adj.* **1.** Of or pertaining to a kaleidoscope. **2.** Rapidly changing and intricate. Also **ka·lei′do·scop′i·cal.** — **ka·lei′do·scop′i·cal·ly** *adv.*

kal·ends (kal′əndz) See CALENDS.

ka·lif (kā′lif, kal′if), **ka·liph** See CALIPH.

Kal·muck (kal′muk) *n.* **1.** A member of one of the Buddhistic Mongol tribes inhabiting a region extending from western China to the Volga river. **2.** The Mongolian language of these tribes. Also **Kal′muk, Kal·myk** (kal′mik).

kal·so·mine (kal′sə·mīn) See CALCIMINE.

kan·ga·roo (kang′gə·rōō′) *n. pl.* **·roos** A herbivorous marsupial of Australia and Tasmania, having short, weak forelimbs, stout tails, and powerful hind limbs adapted for leaping. [< Australian]

kangaroo court *U.S.* An unauthorized court in which the law is disregarded or willfully misinterpreted.

kangaroo rat A pouched rodent of the SW U.S. and Mexico having elongated hind limbs and tail.

Kant·i·an (kan′tē·ən) *adj.* Of or pertaining to Kant or his philosophy. — *n.* A follower of Kantianism.

Kant·i·an·ism (kan′tē·ən·iz′əm) *n.* The philosophy of Immanuel Kant, stating that man experiences the material world through sense perception, but its reality is determined by mental forms and categories. Also **Kant′ism.**

ka·o·lin (kā′ə·lin) *n.* A claylike hydrous aluminum silicate used in making porcelain. Also **ka′o·line** (-lin). [< F < Chinese *Kao-ling* mountain where first mined]

ka·pok (kā′pok) *n.* A cottony or silky fiber covering the seeds of the kapok tree, used for mattresses, life preservers, insulation material, etc. [< Malay *kāpoq*]

kapok tree A tropical tree having seeds covered with silky fiber. Also called *silk-cotton tree.*

kap·pa (kap′ə) *n.* The tenth letter in the Greek alphabet (Κ, κ), corresponding to the English *k.* See **ALPHABET.**

ka·put (kä·pŏŏt′) *adj. Slang* Ruined; done for. [< G]

kar·a·kul (kar′ə·kəl) *n.* **1.** A breed of sheep raised in the Soviet Union, Iran, Iraq, etc. **2.** The black or gray, loosely curled fur made from the pelt of the karakul lamb. Also spelled *caracul.* [after *Kara Kul,* a lake in Bukhara]

kar·at (kar′ət) *n.* **1.** The twenty-fourth part by weight of gold in an article: 18-*karat* gold has 18/24 or 3/4 gold by weight. **2.** Loosely, a carat. [Var. of CARAT]

ka·ra·te (kä·rä′tā, -tē) *n.* An Oriental method of hand-to-hand combat utilizing a variety of sudden, forceful blows, as with the side of the hand or the fingertips. [< Japanese]

kar·roo (kə·rōō′, ka-) *n. pl.* **·roos** A dry plateau or tableland of South Africa. Also **ka·roo′.** [< Hottentot]

karyo- *combining form Biol.* Nucleus: also spelled *caryo-.* Also, before vowels, **kary-.** [< Gk. *karyon* nut]

kar·y·o·tin (kar′ē·ō′tin) *n. Biol.* Chromatin.

Kas·bah (käz′bä) See CASBAH.

Kash·mi·ri (kash·mir′ē) *n.* The Indic language of the Kashmirians.

Kash·mi·ri·an (kash·mir′ē·ən) *adj.* Of or pertaining to Kashmir or its people. — *n.* A native of Kashmir.

kata- See CATA-.

ka·tal·y·sis (kə·tal′ə·sis) See CATALYSIS.

ka·thar·sis (kə·thär′sis) See CATHARSIS.

kath·ode (kath′ōd) See CATHODE.

kat·i·on (kat′ī′ən) See CATION.

ka·ty·did (kā′tē·did) *n.* A green, arboreal insect allied to the grasshoppers and crickets. [Imit., from sound produced by the males]

kau·ri (kou′rē) *n.* **1.** A large timber tree of New Zealand. **2.** Its wood. **3.** Kauri gum. Also **kau′ry.** [< Maori]

kauri gum A resinous exudation of the kauri tree, used in varnishes, for linoleum, etc. Also **kauri copal, kauri resin.**

kay·ak (kī′ak) *n. U.S. & Canadian* The hunting canoe of arctic America, made of seal skins stretched over a frame, with a hole amidships where the user sits. [< Eskimo]

kay·o (kā′ō) *Slang v.t.* **kay·oed, kay·o·ing** In boxing, to knock out. — *n.* In boxing, a knockout. Also **K.O., KO, k.o.** [< *k(nock) o(ut)*]

kedge (kej) *Naut. n.* A light anchor used in warping, freeing a vessel from shoals, etc.: also **kedge anchor.** — *v.* **kedged, kedg·ing** *v.i.* **1.** To move a vessel by hauling up to a kedge that has been dropped at a distance. **2.** Of a vessel, to be moved in this way. — *v.t.* **3.** To move (a vessel) in this way. [Origin uncertain]

keel (kēl) *n.* **1.** *Naut.* The main structural member of a vessel, running fore and aft along the bottom, to which all the crosswise members are solidly fixed; the backbone of a ship. **2.** A ship. **3.** Any part or object resembling a keel in shape or function. **4.** *Aeron.* **a** A vertical fin extending longitudinally at the bottom of an airship. **b** The center bottom of an airplane fuselage. **5.** *Biol.* A longitudinal ridge or process, as of the breastbone of a fowl. — **on an even keel** In equilibrium; steady. — *v.t. & v.i.* To turn over with the keel uppermost; capsize. — **to keel over 1.** To turn bottom up; capsize. **2.** To fall over or be felled, as from an injury. [< ON *kjölr* or OHG *kiol*]

keel·haul (kēl′hôl′) *v.t.* **1.** *Naut.* To haul (a man) under the keel of a ship as punishment. **2.** To reprove severely; castigate. Also **keel·hale** (kēl′hāl′). [< Du. *kielhalen*]

keel·son (kēl′sən) *n. Naut.* A beam running above the keel of a ship: also spelled *kelson.* [Akin to KEEL]

keen¹ (kēn) *adj.* **1.** Able to cut or penetrate readily; very sharp. **2.** Having mental acuteness, refined perception, etc. **3.** Manifesting intense absorption or eagerness: a *keen* interest. **4.** Of senses or sense organs, having great acuity and sensitivity. **5.** Having a piercing, intense quality or impact. **6.** Eager; enthusiastic: with *about, for, on,* or an infinitive. **7.** *U.S. Slang* Fine; excellent. [ME < OE *cēne*] — **keen′ly** *adv.* — **keen′ness** *n.*

keen² (kēn) *n.* A wailing lamentation for the dead. — *v.i.* To wail loudly over the dead. [< Irish *caoinim* I wail] — **keen′er** *n.*

keep (kēp) *v.* **kept, keep·ing** *v.t.* **1.** To retain possession or control of; avoid releasing or giving away: to *keep* one's earnings; to *keep* a secret. **2.** To hold or continue to hold in some specified state, relation, place, etc.: *Keep* your hands off; *Keep* the car in repair. **3.** To store, hold, or confine in a regular place. **4.** To maintain: to *keep* the peace. **5.** To be faithful to or abide by (a promise, vow, etc.). **6.** To do the required work of; manage: to *keep* house. **7.** To defend from harm. **8.** To care for; tend: to *keep* the flocks. **9.** To detain. **10.** To prevent: with *from.* **11.** To observe, as with rites or ceremony: to *keep* the Sabbath. **12.** To be the support of; maintain in food, clothing, etc. **13.** To write down and preserve in good order: to *keep* a diary. **14.** To stay in or on: *Keep* your seat. **15.** To have regularly for sale. **16.** To maintain for use or employ for service: to *keep* a butler. **17.** To preserve in good condition, as foods. — *v.i.* **18.** To persist in; continue: often with *on:* to *keep* on working. **19.** To remain; stay: *Keep* away; *Keep* indoors. **20.** To stay in good condition. **21.** To remain good for a later time: The news will *keep.* — **to keep back 1.** To restrain. **2.** To withhold. — **to keep in with** *Informal* To remain in the good graces of. — **to keep to oneself 1.** To remain solitary. **2.** To avoid revealing. — **to keep track of** (or **tabs on**) To continue to be informed about. — **to keep up 1.** To hold the pace. **2.** To maintain in good condition. **3.** To cause to continue: *Keep up* the good work. **4.** To cause to stay awake or out of bed. — **to keep up with** To stay abreast of (someone or something). — *n.* **1.** Means of subsistence: to earn one's *keep.* **2.** Guard or custody: They are in my *keep.* **3.** The donjon or strongest building of a castle; also, a castle or fortress. — **for keeps 1.** Very seriously; not for mere amusement. **2.** Permanently. [OE *cēpan* to observe]

keep·er (kē′pər) *n.* **1.** One who keeps or guards; as: **a** A guardian or protector. **b** The overseer of a prison. **c** The caretaker of a wild animal. **2.** One in charge of (a specified place, thing, etc.): used in combination: *gatekeeper.*

keep·ing (kē′ping) *n.* **1.** The act of one who keeps. **2.** Custody, charge, or possession. **3.** Maintenance; support. — **in keeping** (with) In right relation or proportion (to).

keep·sake (kēp′sāk′) *n.* Anything kept, or given to be kept, for the sake of the giver; a memento.

keg (keg) *n.* A small, strong barrel, usu. holding 5 to 10 gallons. [ME *cag,* prob. < ON *kaggi*]

keg·ler (keg′lər) *n. Informal* A bowler. [< G *kegel* ninepin]

kelp (kelp) *n.* **1.** Any of various large, coarse, brown algae; esp., the **giant kelp,** found mainly on the Pacific coast. **2.** The ashes of such algae, a source of iodine. [ME *culp*]

kel·pie (kel′pē) *n. Scot.* A water sprite in the form of a horse, supposed to be an omen of drowning. Also **kel′py.**

kel·son (kel′sən) See KEELSON.

Kelt (kelt), **Kelt·ic** (kel′tik) See CELT, CELTIC.

Kelvin scale (kel′vin) *Physics* The absolute scale of temperature, in which zero is equal to −273° Celsius or −459.4° Fahrenheit. [after William Thompson, 1824–1907, Lord *Kelvin,* English physicist]

ken (ken) *v.* **kenned** or **kent, ken·ning** *v.t.* **1.** *Scot.* To know. **2.** *Archaic* To see. — *v.i.* **3.** *Scot. & Brit. Dial.* To have knowledge or understanding. — *n.* Range of sight or knowledge. [OE *cennan,* infl. by ON *kenna*]

ken·nel (ken′əl) *n.* **1.** A house for a dog or for a pack of hounds. **2.** *Often pl.* An establishment where dogs are bred for sale, boarded, trained, etc. **3.** A pack of hounds. **4.** The hole or lair of a fox or like beast. **5.** A vile lodging. — *v.* **ken·neled** or **·nelled, ken·nel·ing** or **·nel·ling** — *v.t.* **1.** To keep or confine in or as in a kennel. — *v.i.* **2.** To lodge or take shelter in a kennel. [< MF < L *canis* dog]

Ken·nel·ly-Heav·i·side layer (ken′əl·ē-hev′ē·sīd) The Heaviside layer.

ken·o·tron (ken′ə·tron) *n. Electronics* A two-electrode electron tube used as a rectifier. [< Gk. *kenōsis* an emptying + (ELEC)TRON]

kept (kept) Past tense and past participle of KEEP.

ker·a·tin (ker′ə·tin) *n. Biochem.* An albuminous compound that forms the essential ingredient of horny tissue, as of horns, claws, and nails. — **ke·rat·i·nous** (kə·rat′ə·nəs) *adj.* [< Gk. *keras, -atos* horn + -IN]

ker·a·ti·tis (ker′ə·tī′tis) *n. Pathol.* Inflammation of the cornea.

kerb (kûrb) *n. Brit.* Curb (def. 2).

ker·chief (kûr′chif) *n.* A square of fabric used to cover the head or neck, or as a handkerchief. [ME < OF < *covrir* to cover + *chef* head]

ker·mes (kûr′mēz) *n.* The dried bodies of the females of a scale insect, used as a red dyestuff. [< Arabic *qirmiz*]

ker·mis (kûr′mis) *n.* **1.** In Flanders, etc., a periodical out-

---

door festival. **2.** An indoor or outdoor festival imitative of this. [< Du < *kerk* church + *miss* mass]

kern (kûrn) *Printing n.* The part of the face of a type that projects beyond the shaft or shank. — *v.t.* To form (type) with a kern. [< F < L *cardo, -inis* hinge]

ker·nel (kûr′nəl) *n.* **1.** The entire contents of a seed or grain within its coating. **2.** The edible part of a nut. **3.** The central part of anything; nucleus; gist. — *v.i.* **ker·neled** or **·nelled, ker·nel·ing** or **·nel·ling** To envelop as a kernel. [OE *cyrnel,* dim. of *corn* seed]

ker·o·sene (ker′ə·sēn, ker′ə·sēn′) *n.* A mixture of hydrocarbons distilled from crude petroleum and used for burning in lamps, stoves, and some engines: also called *coal oil.* Also **ker·o·sine** (ker′ə·sēn, ker′ə·sēn′). [< Gk. *kēros* wax + -ENE]

ker·sey (kûr′zē) *n.* A coarse, ribbed, closely napped woolen cloth. [after *Kersey,* village in Suffolk, England]

kes·trel (kes′trəl) *n.* A European falcon resembling the American sparrow hawk. [ME < OF *cresserelle*]

ketch (kech) *n.* A fore-and-aft rigged, two-masted vessel similar to a yawl but having the mizzen or jiggermast forward of the rudder post. [ME *cache,* prob. < CATCH, v., because used as a pursuit vessel]

ketch·up (kech′əp) *n.* A spicy sauce or condiment for meat, fish, etc., of which the base is tomatoes, or sometimes mushrooms or walnuts: also spelled *catchup, catsup.* [< Malay *kēchap,* ? ult. < Chinese *ke-tsiap* brine of pickled fish]

ke·tone (kē′tōn) *n. Chem.* One of a class of organic compounds in which the carbonyl radical unites with two hydrocarbon radicals. The simplest member is acetone. [< G, var. of F *acétone* acetone] — **ke·ton·ic** (ki·ton′ik) *adj.*

ket·tle (ket′l) *n.* **1.** A metallic vessel for boiling or stewing. **2.** A teakettle. **3.** A kettle-shaped cavity, as in rock or glacial drift: also **kettle hole. 4.** A kettledrum. — **kettle of fish** A trying or difficult situation. [OE < L *catillus,* dim. of *catinus* a deep vessel]

ket·tle·drum (ket′l·drum′) *n.* A large drum having a brass hemispherical shell and a parchment head that can be tuned through a small range of definite pitches; timpano.

Kew·pie (kyōō′pē) *n.* A chubby, cherubic doll, made of plastic, etc.: a trade name. Also **kew′pie doll.**

key[1] (kē) *n. pl.* **keys 1.** An instrument for moving the bolt or tumblers of a lock in order to lock or unlock. **2.** An instrument for holding and turning a screw, nut, valve, or the like, as for winding a clock. **3.** Anything serving to disclose, open, or solve something. **4.** Something that opens or prepares a way: the *key* to the situation. **5.** A gloss, table, or group of notes interpreting certain symbols, ciphers, problems, etc. **6.** Any one of the finger levers in typewriters, computers, etc. **7.** *Telecom.* A circuit breaker or opener operated by the fingers, as in a telegraph or radiotelegraph sending apparatus. **8.** *Music* **a** In musical instruments, a lever to be pressed by the finger or thumb. **b** A system of tones in which a piece of music is written or performed, where all the tones bear a definite relationship to some specific tone (the keynote or tonic): the *key* of C. **9.** The tone or pitch of the voice. **10.** Level of intensity of expression, feeling, or artistic execution: He writes in a high *key.* **11.** *Mech.* **a** A wedge, cotter, bolt, or pin used to secure various parts. **b** One of various instruments for fixing a collar to a shaft. **12.** *Archit.* A keystone. **13.** *Bot.* A key fruit. — *v.t.* **keyed, key·ing 1.** To fasten with or as with a key. **2.** To wedge tightly or support firmly with a key, wedge, etc. **3.** To complete (an arch) by adding the keystone. **4.** To provide with a key or keys. **5.** To provide with a cross-reference or a system of cross-references. **6.** To provide with a solution. **7.** *Music* To regulate the pitch or tone of. — **to key up** To cause excitement, expectancy, etc., in. — *adj.* Of chief and decisive importance: a *key* figure. [OE *cǣg*]

key[2] (kē) *n. pl.* **keys** A low island, esp. one of coral, along a coast; cay. [< Sp. < Taino, islet]

key·board (kē′bôrd′, -bōrd′) *n.* A row or rows of keys as in a piano or typewriter.

key·hole (kē′hōl′) *n.* A hole for a key, as in a door or lock.

key·note (kē′nōt′) *n.* **1.** The basic idea or principle of a philosophy, political platform, literary work, etc. **2.** *Music* The tonic of a key, from which it is named: also **key tone.** — *v.t.* **·not·ed, ·not·ing** To sound the keynote of.

keynote address *U.S.* An opening address, esp. at a political convention, presenting the basic issues and partisan principles. Also **keynote speech.**

key plug The part of a cylinder lock that receives the key. For illus. see LOCK.

key signature *Music* The sharps or flats following the clef sign at the beginning of each staff, placed so as to apply to specific tones whenever they occur.

key·stone (kē′stōn′) *n.* **1.** *Archit.* The uppermost and last-set stone of an arch, that completes it and locks its members together. **2.** The fundamental element, as of a science.

Keystone State Nickname of Pennsylvania.

khak·i (kak′ē, kä′kē; *in Canada, often* kär′kē) *n. pl.* **khak·is 1.** A color ranging from light sand to medium brown. **2.** A stout cotton cloth of this color used for uniforms. **3.** *pl.* A uniform made of khaki. — *adj.* Of the color khaki. [< Hind. < Persian *khāk* dust]

kha·lif (kā′lif, kal′if) See CALIPH.

khan (kän, kan) *n.* **1.** The title of the imperial successors to the Mongol conqueror Genghis Khan. **2.** A title for rulers, officials, or dignitaries in Central Asia, Iran, etc. [< Turkic *khān* lord, prince] — **khan′ate** (-āt) *n.*

kib·butz (ki·boots′) *n. pl.* **·but·zim** (-boot·sēm′) A cooperative or collective farm in Israel. [< Hebrew, gathering]

kib·itz (kib′its) *v.i. Informal* To act as a kibitzer. [Back formation < KIBITZER]

kib·itz·er (kib′it·sər) *n. Informal* One who meddles in the affairs of others; esp., a spectator who gives gratuitous advice to card players. [< Yiddish < G *kiebitzen* to look on]

kick (kik) *v.i.* **1.** To strike out with the foot or feet, as in swimming, propelling a ball, etc. **2.** To strike out habitually with the foot, hooves, etc. **3.** Of firearms, to recoil. **4.** In football, to punt, try for an extra point or field goal by kicking, etc. **5.** *U.S. Informal* To object or complain. — *v.t.* **6.** To strike with the foot. **7.** To drive or impel by striking with the foot. **8.** In football, to score (an extra point or a field goal) by kicking the ball. **9.** Of firearms, to strike in recoiling. — **to kick around** *U.S. Informal* **1.** To abuse; neglect. **2.** To roam from place to place. **3.** To give thought to; discuss. — **to kick back 1.** To recoil violently or unexpectedly, as a gun. **2.** *U.S. Slang* To pay back (part of a salary, fee, etc.) to someone in a position to grant favors, usu. as a bribe. — **to kick in** *U.S. Informal* To contribute or participate by contributing. — **to kick off 1.** In football, to put the ball in play by kicking it toward the opposing team. **2.** *U.S. Slang* To die. — **to kick out** *U.S. Informal* To exclude or eject violently or suddenly, as with a kick. — **to kick the bucket** *Slang* To die. — **to kick up** *U.S. Slang* To make or stir up (trouble, confusion, etc.). — *n.* **1.** A blow or thrust with the foot. **2.** *U.S. Informal* An objection or complaint. **3.** *U.S. Slang* Power to stimulate, excite, or intoxicate: whisky with a *kick.* **4.** *U.S. Slang* A pleasant and exciting sensation; thrill. **5.** *U.S. Slang* Energy; pep. **6.** The recoil of a firearm. **7.** In football, a kicking of the ball; esp., a punt. [ME *kike*] — **kick′er** *n.*

kick·back (kik′bak′) *n.* **1.** *Informal* A strong reaction; recoil; repercussion. **2.** *U.S. Slang* A paying back of part of a salary, fee, etc., also, the money so paid.

kick·off (kik′ôf′, -of′) *n.* **1.** In football, the kick with which play is begun. **2.** Any beginning: the *kickoff* of a political campaign.

kid (kid) *n.* **1.** A young goat. **2.** Leather made from the skin of a kid. **3.** *pl.* Gloves or shoes made of kidskin. **4.** The meat of a young goat. **5.** *Informal* A child; youngster. — *adj. Informal* Younger: my *kid* brother. — *v.t. & v.i.* **kid·ded, kid·ding 1.** *Slang* To make fun of (someone); to tease. **2.** *Slang* To deceive or try to deceive (someone); fool. **3.** Of a goat, to give birth. [ME < ON *kith*] — **kid′der** *n.*

kid·dy (kid′ē) *n. pl.* **·dies** *Slang* A small child. Also **kid′die.**

kid glove A glove made of kidskin or similar material. — **to handle with kid gloves** To treat tactfully or gingerly.

kid·nap (kid′nap) *v.t.* **kid·naped** or **·napped, kid·nap·ing** or **·nap·ping 1.** To seize and carry off (someone) by force or fraud, usu. so as to demand a ransom. **2.** To steal (a child). [< KID (def. 5) + *nap,* dial. var. of NAB] — **kid′nap·er** or **kid′nap·per** *n.*

kid·ney (kid′nē) *n. pl.* **·neys 1.** *Anat.* Either of two glandular organs situated at the back of the abdominal cavity close to the spinal column in vertebrates, serving to separate waste products from the blood and to excrete them as urine. ◆ Collateral adjective: *renal.* **2.** The meat of the kidney of certain animals, used as food. **3.** Temperament, nature, or type: a man of my own *kidney.* [Origin unknown]

kidney bean 1. A kidney-shaped bean. **2.** The bean of the scarlet runner.

kidney stone *Pathol.* A hard mineral concretion formed in the kidney; renal calculus.

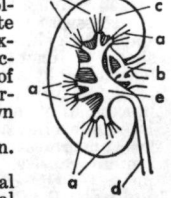

HUMAN KIDNEY

a Pyramid.
b Papillae.
c Cortex. *d* Ureter. *e* Pelvis.

kid·skin (kid′skin′) *n.* Leather tanned from the skin of a young goat, used for gloves, shoes, etc.

kill[1] (kil) *v.t.* **1.** To cause the death of. **2.** To slaughter for food; butcher. **3.** To bring to an end; destroy. **4.** *U.S. Slang* To make a strong emotional impression upon, as of amusement. **5.** To destroy the active qualities of; neutralize. **6.** To cancel by contrast, as a color. **7.** In printing, to delete. **8.** To turn off or stop (a motor, live circuit, etc.). **9.** To pass (time) aimlessly. **10.** To veto or quash (legislation). — *v.i.* **11.** To cause death. **12.** To murder; slay. **13.** To undergo death; die. — *n.* **1.** The act of killing, esp. in hunting. **2.** An animal or animals killed as prey. [ME *cullen, killen*]

—Syn. (verb) **1.** *Kill* is the general term applicable to all organisms, and frequently extended to inanimate things: frost *killed* the buds, to *kill* a story. *Murder*, *assassinate*, and *execute* are said only of persons. *Murder* refers to a deliberate, often premeditated, killing; *assassinate* is often applied to political killings. *Execute* refers to the carrying out of a legal sentence of death.

kill² (kil) *n.* A creek, stream, or channel: an element in geographical names: Schuylkill. [< Du. < MDu. *kille*]

kill·deer (kil′dir) *n. pl.* **·deers** or **·deer** A North American wading bird of the plover family, having a loud cry. Also **kill′dee** (-dē). [Imit., from its cry]

kill·er (kil′ər) *n.* One who or that which kills.

killer whale A voracious whale related to the dolphins.

kill·ing (kil′ing) *n.* **1.** Homicide. **2.** The act of one who or that which kills. **— to make a killing** To get or win a large amount of money. **— adj. 1.** Used to kill. **2.** Likely to kill. **3.** Resulting in death; fatal.

kill·joy (kil′joi′) *n.* One who spoils pleasure for others.

kiln (kil, kiln) *n.* An oven or furnace for baking, burning, or drying bricks, pottery, etc. [OE < L *culina* kitchen]

kil·o (kil′ō, kē′lō) *n. pl.* **kil·os 1.** A kilogram. **2.** A kilometer.

kilo- *prefix* In the metric system, a thousand times (a specified unit): *kilogram*. [< F < Gk. *chilioi* a thousand]

kil·o·cy·cle (kil′ə·sī′kəl) *n.* **1.** *Telecom.* A unit of electromagnetic wave frequency of 1,000 cycles per second. **2.** One thousand cycles. Abbr. *kc, kc.*

kil·o·gram (kil′ə·gram) *n.* In the metric system, a thousand grams. Also **kil′o·gramme**. [< F *kilogramme*] Abbr. *k., K., kg, kg., kilo.* See table front of book.

kil·o·gram-me·ter (kil′ə·gram-mē′tər) *n.* A unit of work, the equivalent of the force expended in raising a mass of one kilogram one meter against gravity, about 7.2 foot-pounds.

kil·o·li·ter (kil′ə-lē′tər) *n.* In the metric system, a thousand liters. Abbr. *kl, kl.* See table front of book.

kil·o·me·ter (kil′ə-mē′tər, ki-lom′ə-tər) *n.* In the metric system, a thousand meters. Abbr. *km, km., kilo.* See table front of book. **— kil′o·met′ric** or **·ri·cal** *adj.*

kil·o·ton (kil′ə-tun′) *n.* **1.** A weight of 1,000 tons. **2.** A unit equivalent to the explosive power of 1,000 tons of TNT.

kil·o·watt (kil′ə-wät) *n.* *Electr.* A unit of power equal to 1,000 watts. Abbr. *kw, kw.*

kil·o·watt-hour (kil′ə-wät-our′) *n.* The work done or the energy resulting from one kilowatt acting for one hour, equal to approximately 1.34 horsepower-hours.

kilt (kilt) *n.* A short pleated skirt worn by Scottish Highland men and Irishmen. **— v.t.** To make broad, vertical pleats in; pleat. [ME; prob. < Scand.] **— kilt′ing** *n.*

kil·ter (kil′tər) *n. Informal* Proper or working order: now only in the phrase **out of kilter**, out or order. [Origin uncertain]

ki·mo·no (ki-mō′nə, ki-mō′nō) *n. pl.* **·nos 1.** A loose robe fastened with a wide sash, worn in Japan as an outer garment. **2.** A woman's negligee. [< Japanese]

KILT
a Tartan.
b Kilt.
c Sporran.
d Brooch.

kin (kin) *n.* One's relatives by blood, collectively; one's family. **— next of kin** In law, one's nearest relative or relatives. **— adj. 1.** Related by blood. **2.** Similar; kindred; alike. [OE *cyn*]

-kin *suffix* Little; small: *lambkin*. [< MDu. -*kijn*, -*ken*]

kind¹ (kīnd) *adj.* **1.** Gentle and considerate; goodhearted. **2.** Proceeding from goodheartedness. [OE *gecynde*]

kind² (kīnd) *n.* **1.** A class or grouping; type. **2.** The distinguishing character of something: They differ in *kind.* **— in kind 1.** With a thing of the same sort: to return an insult *in kind.* **2.** In produce instead of money: to pay taxes *in kind.* **— kind of** *Informal* In a way; somewhat. **— of a kind** Inferior in quality. [OE *gecynd*]

kin·der·gar·ten (kin′dər-gär′tən) *n.* A school or class for young children, usu. from the ages of four to six. [< G]

kind·heart·ed (kīnd′här′tid) *adj.* Having or showing a kind nature. **— kind′heart′ed·ly** *adv.* **— kind′heart′ed·ness** *n.*

kin·dle (kin′dəl) *v.* **·dled**, **·dling** *v.t.* **1.** To cause to burn; ignite. **2.** To excite, as the feelings. **3.** To make bright or glowing as if with flame. **— v.i. 4.** To take fire. **5.** To become excited or inflamed. **6.** To become bright or glowing. [ME < ON *kynda*] **— kin·dler** *n.*

kin·dling (kind′ling) *n.* **1.** Sticks, wood chips, etc., with which a fire is started. **2.** The act of one who kindles.

kind·ly (kīnd′lē) *adj.* **·i·er**, **·li·est 1.** Having or showing kindness; sympathetic. **2.** Having a favorable effect. **— adv. 1.** In a kind manner; good-naturedly. **2.** Enthusiastically; heartily. **— to take kindly to 1.** To accept with liking. **2.** To be naturally attracted to. **— kind′li·ness** *n.*

kind·ness (kīnd′nis) *n.* **1.** The quality of being kind. **2.** A kind act or service; a favor. **3.** A kindly feeling.

kin·dred (kin′drid) *adj.* **1.** Related by blood; akin. **2.**

Having a like nature; similar. **— n.** One's relatives by blood. [ME < OE *cynn* kin + *rǣden* condition]

kine (kīn) *n. Archaic* Cattle: plural of COW¹.

kin·e·mat·ics (kin′ə-mat′iks) *n.pl.* (construed as sing.) The branch of physics treating of motion without reference to particular forces or bodies. [< Gk. < *kineein* to move] **— kin′e·mat′ic** or **·i·cal** *adj.* **— kin′e·mat′i·cal·ly** *adv.*

kin·e·mat·o·graph (kin′ə-mat′ə-graf, -gräf) See CINEMATO-GRAPH.

kin·e·scope (kin′ə-skōp) *n.* **1.** The cathode-ray tube of a television set, which reproduces by the action of an electron beam upon a fluorescent screen, the image impinging upon a similar tube in the television camera: also called *picture tube.* **2.** A filmed record of a television program: also **kin·e** (kin′ē).

kinesi- *combining form* A movement. [< Gk. *kinēsis* motion]

-kinesis *combining form* A movement; motion. [< Gk. *kinēsis* motion]

kin·es·the·si·a (kin′is-thē′zhə, -zhē-ə) *n. Physiol.* The perception of muscular movement, tension, etc., derived from the functioning of afferent nerves connected with muscle tissue, skin, joints, and tendons. Also **kin′es·the′sis** (-thē′sis). [< NL < Gk. *kineein* to move + *aisthēsis* perception] **— kin′es·thet′ic** (-thet′ik) *adj.*

ki·net·ic (ki-net′ik) *adj.* **1.** Of or pertaining to motion. **2.** Producing or caused by motion: *kinetic* energy. [< Gk. < *kineein* to move]

ki·net·ics (ki-net′iks) *n.pl.* (construed as sing.) The branch of physics dealing with the effect of forces in the production or modification of motion in bodies.

kin·folk (kin′fōk′) *n.pl. Informal* Kinsfolk. Also **kin′folks′.**

king (king) *n.* **1.** The sovereign male ruler of a kingdom; monarch. ◆ Collateral adjective: *regal.* **2.** One who is preeminent: a cattle *king.* **3.** A playing card bearing the likeness of a king. **4.** In chess, the principal piece, for whose defense all the moves of the other pieces are made. **5.** In checkers, a piece that, having reached the opponent's last rank of squares, is then crowned and may move in any direction. Abbr. *k., K.* [OE *cyng, cyning*]

King Arthur See ARTHUR.

king·bird (king′bûrd′) *n.* Any of various North American flycatchers.

king·bolt (king′bōlt′) *n.* A vertical central bolt usu. attaching the body of a wagon or similar vehicle to the fore axle, and serving as a pivot in turning: also called *kingpin.*

king crab 1. The horseshoe crab. **2.** Any of a genus of usu. large crablike crustaceans common in the north Pacific, with a small, triangular body and very long legs.

king·dom (king′dəm) *n.* **1.** The territory, people, state, or realm ruled by a king or a queen; monarchy. **2.** Any place or area thought of as a sovereign domain. **3.** Any of the three primary divisions of natural objects known as the *animal, vegetable,* and *mineral kingdoms.* **4.** The spiritual dominion of God. [OE *cyningdom*]

king·fish (king′fish′) *n. pl.* **·fish** or **·fish·es** Any of various American food fishes.

king·fish·er (king′fish′ər) *n.* Any of several nonpasserine birds of world-wide distribution, that feed on fish.

King James Bible An English translation of the Bible from Hebrew and Greek, proposed by James I and completed in 1611. Also **Authorized Version.** Complete revisions were published in England in 1885 (**Revised Version**) and in the U.S. in 1901 (**American Standard Version**) and in 1952 (**Revised Standard Version**).

king·let (king′lit) *n.* **1.** A young or insignificant king. **2.** Any of several small birds, resembling the warblers.

king·ly (king′lē) *adj.* **·li·er**, **·li·est** Of or worthy of a king; regal. **— adv.** In a kingly way. **— king′li·ness** *n.*

king·pin (king′pin′) *n.* **1.** In bowling or tenpins, the foremost pin of a set arranged in order for playing. **2.** In ninepins, the center pin. **3.** A kingbolt. **4.** *Informal* The person of central importance in a group, etc.

king post In carpentry, a single vertical strut supporting the apex of a triangular truss and resting on a crossbeam. For illustration see ROOF. Also **king·post** (king′pōst′)

Kings (kingz) *n.pl.* (construed as sing.) **1.** Either of two books, I Kings and II Kings, of the Old Testament, recounting the histories of the Hebrew kings after David. **2.** In the Douai version of the Old Testament, a group of four books, comprising I Samuel, II Samuel, I Kings, and II Kings.

king's English Standard English considered as set by official authority: also called *queen's English.*

king·ship (king′ship) *n.* **1.** The state, power, office, or dignity of a king. **2.** The monarchical type of government. **3.** As a title, the person of a king: his royal *kingship.*

king-size (king′sīz′) *adj. Informal* Greater in length or size than is usual. Also **king′sized′.**

king snake A large, harmless snake of the southern U.S. that feeds on rats and mice.

kink (kingk) *n.* **1.** An abrupt bend, curl, loop, or tangle in a line, wire, hair, etc. **2.** A mental quirk. **3.** A sharp, painful muscular spasm; crick. — *v.i. & v.t.* To form or cause to form a kink or kinks. [< Du., twist, curl]

kink·a·jou (king'kə-jōō) *n.* An arboreal, carnivorous mammal of Central and South America, having large eyes, soft woolly fur, and a long tail. [< F *quincajou* < Tupi]

kink·y (kingk'ē) *adj.* **kink·i·er, kink·i·est** Kinked; frizzy. — **kink'i·ness** *n.*

kins·folk (kinz'fōk') *n.pl.* One's relatives or family; kin: also, *Informal*, kinfolk.

kin·ship (kin'ship) *n.* Relationship, esp. by blood. — **Syn.** See RELATIONSHIP.

kins·man (kinz'mən) *n. pl.* **·men** (-mən) A male blood relation. — **kins'wom'an** (-wŏŏm'ən) *n.fem.*

ki·osk (kē·osk', kē'osk, kī'-) *n.* **1.** In Turkey, a lightly constructed, open summerhouse or pavilion. **2.** A similar structure, used as a booth, newsstand, etc. [< F < Turkish < Persian *kūskh* palace]

kip[1] (kip) *n.* **1.** The untanned skin of a calf, a lamb, or an adult of any small breed of cattle. **2.** A collection of such skins. Also **kip'skin'** (-skin'). [ME < Du.]

kip[2] (kip) *n. pl.* **kip** The monetary unit of Laos: in 1960 worth about one U.S. cent.

kip·per (kip'ər) *n.* **1.** A salmon or herring cured by kippering. **2.** The male salmon during the spawning season. — *v.t.* To cure (fish) by splitting, salting, and drying or smoking. [? OE *cypera* spawning salmon]

kirk (kûrk) *n. Scot & Brit. Dial.* A church.

kir·mess (kûr'mis) See KERMIS.

kir·tle (kûrt'l) *n. Archaic* **1.** A woman's skirt. **2.** A man's outer garment. [OE < L *curtus* short] — **kir'tled** *adj.*

Kis·lew (kis·lef', kis'lef) *n.* The third month of the Hebrew year. Also **Kish'lev, Kis'lev.** See (Hebrew) CALENDAR.

kis·met (kiz'met, kis'-) *n.* Appointed lot; fate. [< Turkish < Arabic *qasama* to divide]

kiss (kis) *v.t. & v.i.* **1.** To touch or caress with the lips as a sign of greeting, love, etc. **2.** To meet or touch lightly. — *n.* **1.** A touch or caress with the lips. **2.** A light meeting or touching. **3.** A small candy. [OE *cyssan*]

kiss·er (kis'ər) *n.* **1.** One who kisses. **2.** *Slang* The mouth or the face.

kit (kit) *n.* **1.** A collection of articles, tools, etc., for a special purpose. **2.** A set of parts, etc., from which something is to be made. **3.** One's effects or outfit, esp. for traveling. **4.** A box, bag, knapsack, etc. **5.** *Informal* A collection of persons or things. [ME < MDu. *kitte* jug, vessel]

kitch·en (kich'ən) *n.* **1.** A room set apart and equipped for cooking food. **2.** A culinary department; cuisine. [OE < L *coquere* to cook]

kitch·en·ette (kich'ən·et') *n.* A small, compactly arranged kitchen. Also **kitch'en·et'.**

kitchen police *Mil.* Enlisted men detailed to perform routine kitchen chores; also, such duty.

kitch·en·ware (kich'ən·wâr') *n.* Kitchen utensils.

kite (kīt) *n.* **1.** A lightweight structure of wood and paper, flown in the wind at the end of a long string. **2.** A predatory bird of the hawk family (*Falconidae*) with long, pointed wings. **3.** *Naut.* One of several light sails to use in a light wind. **4.** In commerce, any negotiable paper not representing a genuine transaction, employed to obtain money, sustain credit, etc. — *v.* **kit·ed, kit·ing** *v.i.* **1.** To soar or fly like a kite. **2.** To obtain money, etc., by the use of kites. — *v.t.* **3.** In commerce, to issue, as a kite. [OE *cȳta*]

kith (kith) *n. Archaic* One's friends, acquaintances, or associates: now only in **kith and kin.** [OE *cūth* known]

kit·ten (kit'ən) *n.* A young cat. [ME < OF *chaton* kitten]

kit·ten·ish (kit'ən·ish) *adj.* Playfully coy. — **kit'ten·ish·ly** *adv.* — **kit'ten·ish·ness** *n.*

kit·ti·wake (kit'ē·wāk) *n.* A gull of northern seas, having a rudimentary hind toe. [Imit.]

kit·ty[1] (kit'ē) *n. pl.* **·ties** **1.** Money pooled, as by card players, for any specific purpose. **2.** In certain card games, a hand or part of a hand left over after a deal; a widow. [Origin uncertain]

kit·ty[2] (kit'ē) *n. pl.* **·ties** **1.** A kitten or cat. **2.** A pet name for a cat.

kit·ty-cor·nered (kit'ē-kôr'nərd) *adj.* Cater-cornered.

Ki·wa·nis (kə·wä'nis, -wô'-) An international chain of men's clubs to promote higher business standards and to provide service to the community. [< N. Am. Ind. *keewanis* to make oneself known] — **Ki·wa'ni·an** *adj. & n.*

ki·wi (kē'wē) *n.* A flightless bird of New Zealand, the apteryx. [< Maori]

Klan (klan) The Ku Klux Klan. — **Klans'man** *n.*

klep·to·ma·ni·a (klep'tə·mā'nē·ə) *n.* An obsessive impulse to steal. [< Gk. *kleptēs* thief + -MANIA] — **klep'to·ma'ni·ac** (-mā'nē·ak) *n.*

klieg light (klēg) A powerful arc floodlight, used in making motion pictures. [after the *Kliegl* brothers, lighting pioneers born in Germany]

knack (nak) *n.* **1.** The ability to do something readily and well. **2.** Cleverness; adroitness. [ME *knak, knekke*]

knap·sack (nap'sak') *n.* A case or bag worn strapped across the shoulders, for carrying equipment or supplies; rucksack. [< Du < *knappen* to bite, eat + *zak* sack]

knave (nāv) *n.* **1.** A dishonest person; rogue. **2.** A playing card, the jack. [OE *cnafa* youth]

knav·er·y (nā'vər·ē) *n. pl.* **·er·ies** **1.** Deceitfulness; trickery; rascality. **2.** An act of trickery or deceit.

knav·ish (nā'vish) *adj.* Of, pertaining to, or characteristic of a knave. — **knav'ish·ly** *adv.* — **knav'ish·ness** *n.*

knead (nēd) *v.t.* **1.** To mix and work (dough, clay, etc.) into a uniform mass, usu. by pressing and pulling with the hands. **2.** To work upon by squeezes of the hands; massage. **3.** To make by kneading. [OE *cnedan*] — **knead'er** *n.*

knee (nē) *n.* **1.** *Anat.* The joint of the human leg that articulates the femur with the tibia and fibula and includes the patella. **2.** *Zool.* A part homologous to the human knee, as the stifle joint in horses, dogs, etc. **3.** Something like a bent knee, as a bent piece of metal or wood used in construction, etc. **4.** The part of a garment covering the knee. — *v.t.* To touch or strike with the knee. [OE *cnēow*]

knee·cap (nē'kap') *n.* The patella. Also **knee'pan'.**

knee-deep (nē'dēp') *adj.* Rising or sunk to the knee.

knee·hole (nē'hōl') *n.* A space for the knees, as in a desk.

kneel (nēl) *v.i.* **knelt** or **kneeled, kneel·ing** To fall or rest on the bent knee or knees. [OE *cnēowlian*] — **kneel'er** *n.*

knell (nel) *n.* **1.** The tolling of a bell, esp. one announcing a death. **2.** Any sad or doleful sound. — *v.i.* **1.** To sound a knell. **2.** To toll mournfully. — *v.t.* **3.** To proclaim by or as by a knell. [OE *cynllan* to knock]

knelt (nelt) Past tense and past participle of KNEEL.

knew (nōō, nyōō) Past tense of KNOW.

Knick·er·bock·er (nik'ər·bok'ər) *n.* **1.** A descendant of one of the early Dutch settlers in New York State. **2.** A New Yorker. [after Diedrich *Knickerbocker*, fictitious Dutch author of Washington Irving's *History of New York*]

knick·er·bock·ers (nik'ər·bok'erz) *n.pl.* Wide short breeches gathered below the knee: also **knick·ers** (nik'ərz).

knick·knack (nik'nak) *n.* A trifling article; trinket; trifle: also spelled nicknack. [Reduplication of KNACK]

knife (nīf) *n. pl.* **knives** (nīvz) **1.** An instrument for cutting, piercing, or spreading, with one or more sharp-edged, often pointed, blades, commonly set in a handle. **2.** A blade forming a part of an implement or machine. **3.** A weapon, such as a dagger. — *v.t.* **knifed, knif·ing** **1.** To stab or cut with a knife. **2.** *U.S. Slang* To discredit or betray behind one's back. [OE *cnīf*]

knight (nīt) *n.* **1.** In medieval times: **a** A feudal tenant serving his superior as a mounted soldier. **b** A gentleman, usu. of the nobility, trained for mounted combat and raised to the order of chivalry. **2.** In Great Britain, the holder of a nonhereditary dignity below the rank of baronet, conferred by the sovereign as a reward for personal merit or for service to the country. The holder is entitled to use *Sir* before his given name. **3.** In chess, a piece bearing a horse's head. — *v.t.* To make (a man) a knight. [OE *cniht* boy, military attendant] — **knight'ly** *adv.*

knight errant *pl.* **knights errant** A wandering knight who went forth to redress wrongs or seek adventures.

knight-er·rant·ry (nīt'er'ən·trē) *n. pl.* **·ries** **1.** The customs and practices of the knights errant; chivalry. **2.** Quixotic behavior or action.

knight·hood (nīt'hŏŏd) *n.* **1.** The character, rank, or vocation of a knight. **2.** Knights collectively.

Knights of Columbus A fraternal society of American Roman Catholic men, founded 1882.

Knight Templar *pl.* **Knights Templars** *for def. 1,* **Knights Templar** *for def. 2.* **1.** A member of a military and religious order founded in 1119 by the Crusaders for the protection of pilgrims. **2.** A Freemason of an order claiming descent from the medieval order of Knights Templars.

knit (nit) *v.* **knit** or **knit·ted, knit·ting** *v.t.* **1.** To form (a fabric or garment) by interlocking loops of a single yarn or thread by means of needles. **2.** To fasten or unite closely and firmly. **3.** To draw (the brows) together into wrinkles. — *v.i.* **4.** To make a fabric by interlocking loops of yarn or thread. **5.** To grow together, as broken bones. **6.** To come together in wrinkles; contract. — *n.* The fabric made by knitting. [OE *cnyttan*] — **knit'ter** *n.*

knit·ting (nit'ing) *n.* **1.** The act of one who or that which knits. **2.** The fabric produced by knitting.

knitting needle A slender, pointed rod, used in knitting.

knives (nīvz) Plural of KNIFE.

knob (nob) *n.* **1.** A rounded protuberance, bunch, or lump. **2.** A rounded handle, as of a door. **3.** A rounded mountain; knoll. [ME < MLG *knobbe*]

knob·by (nob'ē) *adj.* **·bi·er, ·bi·est** **1.** Full of knobs. **2.** Resembling a knob.

knock (nok) *v.t.* **1.** To deal a blow to; hit. **2.** To strike together. **3.** To drive or move by hitting. **4.** To make by striking or pounding: to *knock* a hole in the wall. **5.** To strike or push so as to make fall: with *down, over, off,* etc. **6.** *U.S. Slang* To find fault with; disparage. — *v.i.* **7.** To strike a blow or blows; rap: to *knock* at a door. **8.** To come into collision; bump. **9.** To make a pounding or clanking noise, as an engine. **— to knock around (or about)** **1.** *Informal* To wander from place to place. **2.** To treat roughly; abuse. **— to knock down 1.** To take apart for shipping or storing. **2.** At auctions, to sell to the highest bidder. **— to knock off 1.** *Informal* To stop or leave off (work, talking, etc.). **2.** To deduct. **3.** *Informal* To do or make quickly or easily. **4.** *U.S. Slang* To kill; also, to overwhelm or defeat. **— to knock (oneself) out** *U.S. Slang* **1.** To make a great effort; work very hard. **2.** To become exhausted. **— to knock out 1.** In boxing, to defeat (an opponent) by knocking to the canvas for a count of ten. **2.** To make unconscious. **3.** *U.S. Slang* To tire greatly. **— to knock together** To build or make roughly or hurriedly. — *n.* **1.** A sharp blow; rap. **2.** A noise made by an engine in faulty condition. **3.** A misfortune, setback, or reversal. **4.** *U.S. Slang* Hostile criticism; disparagement. [OE *cnocian*]

knock·a·bout (nok′ə·bout′) *n. Naut.* A small sailboat rigged like a sloop. — *adj.* **1.** Marked by roughness. **2.** Suitable for rough or casual occasions.

knock·down (nok′doun′) *adj.* **1.** Powerful enough to upset or overthrow. **2.** Made so as to be easily taken apart or put together: a *knockdown* chair. — *n.* **1.** A felling or upsetting, esp. by a blow. **2.** An article made for easy assembly.

knock·er (nok′ər) *n.* **1.** One who or that which knocks. **2.** A hinged metal hammer fastened to a door for knocking.

knock-knee (nok′nē′) *n.* **1.** An inward curvature of the legs that causes the knees to knock or rub together in walking. **2.** *pl.* Legs so curved.

knock-kneed (nok′nēd′) *adj.* Having knock-knees.

knock·out (nok′out′) *adj.* Forcible enough and so placed as to render unconscious. — *n.* **1.** A knocking unconscious or a knocking out of action. **2.** In boxing, a flooring of one fighter for a count of ten; a kayo. **3.** *Slang* A remarkably impressive person or thing.

knoll (nōl) *n.* A small round hill; a mound. [OE *cnoll* hill]

knot (not) *n.* **1.** An intertwining of rope, string, etc., one free end being passed through a loop and drawn tight; also, the lump thus made. **2.** An ornamental bow of silk, lace, braid, etc. **3.** A hard, gnarled portion of the trunk of a tree, or the round mark on sawed lumber left by this. **4.** A cluster or group of persons or things. **5.** A bond or union. **6.** An enlargement in a muscle, of a gland, etc. resembling a knot. **7.** Something not easily solved; problem. **8.** *Naut.* **a** A speed of a nautical mile in an hour, equivalent to 1.1516 statute miles per hour. **b** A nautical mile. — *v.* **knot·ted, knot·ting** *v.t.* **1.** To tie in a knot. **2.** To secure or fasten by a knot. **3.** To form knobs, bosses, etc., in. — *v.i.* **4.** To form a knot or knots. **5.** To become knotted or tangled. [OE *cnotta*]

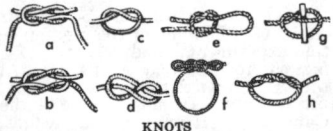

KNOTS

a Square or reef. *b* Granny. *c* Overhand. *d* Figure-eight. *e* Slipknot. *f* Double bowknot. *g* Boat. *h* Surgeon's.

knot·grass (not′gras′, -gräs′) *n.* A widely distributed herb with jointed stems.

knot·hole (not′hōl′) *n.* A hole in a plank or board left by the falling out of a knot.

knot·ty (not′ē) *adj.* **·ti·er, ·ti·est** **1.** Full of or tied in knots. **2.** Difficult or intricate; puzzling. **— knot′ti·ness** *n.*

knout (nout) *n.* A whip or scourge formerly used for flogging in Russia. — *v.t.* To flog with the knout. [< Russian < ON *knūtr, knūta* knot]

know (nō) *v.* **knew, known, know·ing** *v.t.* **1.** To be cognizant of; have a concept of in the mind. **2.** To be certain of; apprehend as true. **3.** To be acquainted or familiar with. **4.** To be sure about the identity of; recognize. **5.** To have a practical grasp of through instruction, study, etc.: to *know* French. **6.** To be able: with *how*: to *know* how to swim. **7.** To distinguish between: to *know* good from bad. **8.** To have memorized: The actor *knows* his lines. **9.** To have experienced: We *know* poverty. — *v.i.* **10.** To have awareness; apprehend. **11.** To have understanding or certainty; be sure. **— to know better** To be aware of something truer or more correct than what one says or does. — *n. Informal* The fact of knowing: now only in the phrase **to be in the know,** to have inside or secret information. [OE *cnāwan*] **— know′a·ble** *adj.* **— know′er** *n.*

know-how (nō′hou′) *n. Informal* Mastery of a complicated operation or procedure; technical skill.

know·ing (nō′ing) *adj.* **1.** Perceptive; astute; also, hinting at having sly or secret knowledge concerning something. **2.** Conscious; intentional. **3.** Having knowledge or information. **— know′ing·ly** *adv.* **— know′ing·ness** *n.*

knowl·edge (nol′ij) *n.* **1.** A result or product of knowing; information or understanding acquired through experience; practical ability, or skill. **2.** Deep and extensive learning; erudition. **3.** The cumulative culture of the human race. **4.** A sure conviction; certainty. **5.** The act, process, or state of knowing; cognition. **6.** Any object of knowing or mental apprehension; that which is or may be known. **7.** Specific information; notice. **8.** *Archaic* Sexual intercourse: often preceded by *carnal.* [ME < OE *cnāwlǣc* acknowledgement] **— Syn. 2.** Comprehension, apprehension, comprehension.

knowl·edge·a·ble (nol′ij·ə·bəl) *adj.* Having knowledge; well-informed; intelligent.

known (nōn) Past participle of KNOW. — *adj.* Recognized by all as the truth; understood; axiomatic: *known* facts.

know-noth·ing (nō′nuth′ing) *n.* An ignoramus.

knuck·le (nuk′əl) *n.* **1.** One of the joints of the fingers, or the region about it; esp., one of the joints connecting the fingers to the hand. **2.** The protuberance formed by one of these joints when the finger is bent. **3.** The carpal joint of the pig, calf, etc., the flesh of which is used as food. **4.** *pl.* Brass knuckles. — *v.* **knuck·led, knuck·ling** *v.t.* **1.** To rub, press, or hit with the knuckles. — *v.i.* **2.** To hold the knuckles on the ground in shooting a marble. **— to knuckle down** To apply oneself seriously and assiduously. **— to knuckle under** To yield; submit; give in. [ME *knokel*]

knuck·le·bone (nuk′əl·bōn′) *n.* **1.** In man, one of the bones forming a knuckle. **2.** In certain animals, as sheep, a leg bone with a knob at the end; also, this knob.

knuck·le·dus·ters (nuk′əl·dus′tərz) *n.pl.* Brass knuckles.

knurl (nûrl) *n.* **1.** A protuberance; lump. **2.** One of a series of small ridges on the edge of a metal object, as a coin, thumbscrew, etc. — *v.t.* To ridge or mill, as the edge of a coin. [? Dim. of KNUR] **— knurl′y** *adj.*

KO or **K.O.** or **k.o.** Knockout (boxing).

ko·a·la (kō·ä′lə) An arboreal marsupial having gray, woolly fur and no tail, and feeding on the leaves of the eucalyptus. [< native Australian name]

Ko·dak (kō′dak) *n.* A small portable camera carrying a roll of sensitized film: a trade name. Also **ko′dak.**

Ko·di·ak bear (kō′dē·ak) A very large brown bear found on Kodiak Island and adjacent islands off the Alaskan coast.

Koh·i·noor (kō′i·nōōr′) *n.* A famous Indian diamond weighing when cut about 106 carats, a British crown jewel since 1849. Also **Koh′i·nor′, Koh′i·nur′.** [< Persian *kōhinūr,* lit., mountain of light]

KOALAS (28 to 32 inches long)

kohl·ra·bi (kōl′rä·bē, kōl·rä′-) *n. pl.* **·bies** A variety of cabbage with a turnip-shaped stem. [< G < Ital. < L *caulis* cabbage + *rapa* turnip]

ko·la (kō′lə), **kola nut tree** See COLA.

kola nut See COLA NUT.

ko·lin·sky (kə·lin′skē, kō-) *n. pl.* **·skies 1.** Any of several minks of Asia and Russia. **2.** The fur of any of these animals, often dyed to resemble sable. Also called *Tartar mink.* [< Russian *kolinski* of Kola]

kol·khoz (kōl·khôz′) *n.* A collective farm in the Soviet Union. Also **kol·hoz′, kol·khos′.** [< Russian *kol(lektivnoe)* collective + *khoz(yaistvo)* farm, household]

ko·peck (kō′pek) *n.* A Russian bronze coin, the hundredth part of a ruble: also spelled *copeck.* Also **ko′pek.** Abbr. *k., K., kop.* [< Russian *kopye* lance]

Ko·ran (kō·rän′, -ran′) *n.* The sacred book of the Moslems, recording in Arabic the revelations of Allah (God) to Mohammed: also *Alcoran, Alkoran.* [< Arabic *Qur′ān,* lit., recitation < *qar′ā* to read]

Ko·re·an (kô·rē′ən, kō-) *adj.* Of or pertaining to Korea, its inhabitants, or their language. — *n.* **1.** A native of Korea, or a person of Korean ancestry. **2.** The language of Korea.

Korean War See table for WAR.

ko·ru·na (kô′rōō·nä) *n. pl.* **ko·ru·ny** (kô′rōō·nē) or **ko·run** (kô′rōōn) The monetary unit of Czechoslovakia: in 1960 worth about 14 U.S. cents. Also called *crown.* [< Czechoslovakian < L *corona* crown]

ko·sher (kō′shər) *adj.* **1.** Permitted to or conforming to Jewish (ceremonial) law: most often said of food. **2.** *Slang* Legitimate; proper. — *n.* Kosher food. — *v.t.* To make kosher. [< Hebrew *kāshēr* fit, proper]

kou·miss (kōō′mis), **kou·mys** See KUMISS.

kow·tow (kou′tou, kō′-) *v.i.* **1.** To behave in an obsequious,

servile manner. **2.** To strike the forehead on the ground as a sign of reverence, etc. — *n.* The act of kowtowing. [< Chinese *k'o-t'ou,* lit., to knock the head] — **kow'tow'er** *n.*
kraal (kräl) *n.* **1.** In South Africa, a village or group of native huts, usu. surrounded by a stockade. **2.** A fenced enclosure for cattle or sheep, esp. in South or central Africa. [< Afrikaans < Pg. *curral* pen for cattle]
krait (krīt) *n.* Any of several venomous snakes of Asia, esp. India. [< Hind. *karait*]
K ration A highly condensed, packaged emergency ration provided for soldiers of the U.S. Army in World War II.
Krem·lin (krem'lin) **1.** The walled citadel of Moscow containing the government offices of the Soviet Union. **2.** The government of the Soviet Union. [< Russian *kreml'* citadel]
kris (krēs) *n.* A Malay dagger or short sword with a wavy-edged blade: also spelled *crease, creese.* [< Malay]
Krish·na (krish'nə) A widely worshiped Hindu god, the eighth avatar of Vishnu. — **Krish'na·ism** *n.*
Kriss Krin·gle (kris kring'gəl) St. Nicholas; Santa Claus. [< G *Christkindl,* dim. of *Christkind* Christ child]
krô·na[1] (krō'nə) *n.* *pl.* **·nur** (-nər) The monetary unit of Iceland: also called *crown.* [< Icel.]
kro·na[2] (krō'nə, *Sw.* krōō'nä) *n.* *pl.* **·nor** (-nôr) The monetary unit of Sweden; also, a Swedish silver coin of this value. Also called *crown.* [< Sw.]
kro·ne (krō'ne) *n.* *pl.* **·ner** (-ner) **1.** The monetary unit of Denmark. **2.** The monetary unit of Norway. **3.** A Danish or Norwegian silver coin of this denomination. [< Dan.]
kryp·ton (krip'ton) *n.* A colorless, gaseous element (symbol Kr), present in minute amounts in the atmosphere, used

as a filler in incandescent and fluorescent electric lamps. See ELEMENT. [< Gk., neut. of *kryptos* hidden]
ku·chen (kōō'khən) *n.* A yeast-dough coffee cake usu. containing fruits and nuts, and covered with sugar. [< G]
ku·dos (kyōō'dos, kōō-) *n.* Glory; credit; praise: used only in the singular. [< Gk. *kydos* glory]
Ku Klux Klan (kōō' kluks' klan', kyōō') **1.** A secret society formed in the South after the Civil War to prevent Negro equality. **2.** An anti-Negro, anti-Catholic, and anti-Jewish secret society founded in Georgia in 1915 and most active during the 1920's. — **Ku' Klux' Klan'ner**
ku·lak (kōō·läk') *n.* In Russia, a wealthy peasant who employed labor, and opposed the Soviet collectivization of farms. [< Russian, lit., fist, tight-fisted man]
ku·miss (kōō'mis) *n.* Fermented mare's or camel's milk, used as a beverage by the nomads of central Asia. Also **ku'mys** [< Russian < Tatar *kumiz*]
küm·mel (kim'əl, *Ger.* kü'məl) *n.* A liqueur flavored with aniseed, cumin, or caraway. [< G, caraway seed]
kum·quat (kum'kwot) *n.* **1.** A small, round orange fruit with a sour pulp and edible rind, used in making preserves or confections. **2.** The tree bearing this fruit. [Cantonese alter. of Pekinese *chin-chü,* lit., golden orange]
Kuo·min·tang (kwō'min'tang') *n.* The nationalist party of China. [< Chinese *kuo* nationalist + *min* people's + *tang* party]
Kurd (kûrd, kŏŏrd) *n.* A member of a nomadic Moslem people dwelling chiefly in Kurdistan. — **Kurd'ish** *adj.*
kvass (kväs, kvas) *n.* A Russian fermented drink resembling sour beer, made from rye, barley, etc. [< Russian *kvas*]

L

l, L (el) *n.* *pl.* **l's** or **ls, L's** or **Ls, ells** (elz) **1.** The twelfth letter of the English alphabet. **2.** The sound represented by the letter *l.* **3.** Anything shaped like the letter L. — *symbol* The Roman numeral 50.
la[1] (lä) *n.* *Music* The sixth syllable used in solmization; the sixth degree of a major scale; also, the tone A.
la[2] (lä, lô) *interj.* An exclamation expressing surprise, emphasis; also spelled *law.* [OE *lā*]
lab (lab) *n.* *U.S. Informal* Laboratory.
la·bel (lā'bəl) *n.* **1.** A slip of paper, printed legend, etc., on a container or article showing its nature, producer, destination, etc. **2.** A term or phrase used to classify or describe persons, schools of thought, etc. — *v.t.* **la·beled** or **·belled, la·bel·ing** or **·bel·ling** **1.** To mark with a label. **2.** To classify. [< OF, ribbon] — **la'bel·er** or **la'bel·ler** *n.*
la·bi·a (lā'bē·ə) Plural of LABIUM.
la·bi·al (lā'bē·əl) *adj.* **1.** Of or pertaining to a labium or the lips. **2.** *Phonet.* Articulated or modified by the lips, as are (p), (b), (m), (w), or the rounded vowels (ō) and (ōō). — *n.* A labial sound. [< Med.L < L *labium* lip]
la·bi·ate (lā'bē·āt, -it) *adj.* Having lips or liplike parts. Also **la'bi·at/ed.** [< NL < L *labium* lip]
la·bile (lā'bil) *adj.* Liable to lapse or change; unstable. [< L < *labi* to slip, fall] — **la·bil'i·ty** *n.*
labio- *combining form* Related to, or formed by the lips and (another organ): *labiodental.* [< L *labium* lip]
la·bi·o·den·tal (lā'bē·ō·den'təl) *Phonet. adj.* Formed with the lower lip and the upper front teeth, as (f) and (v) in English. — *n.* A sound so formed.
la·bi·um (lā'bē·əm) *n.* *pl.* **·bi·a** (-bē·ə) *Anat.* **1.** A lip or liplike part. **2.** One of the four folds of the vulva, comprising the two outer folds of skin (**labia majora**) and the two inner folds of mucous membrane (**labia minora**). [< L, lip]
la·bor (lā'bər) *n.* **1.** Physical or manual work done for hire in economic production. **2.** Arduous physical or mental exertion; toil. **3.** The working class collectively, esp. as organized into labor unions. **4.** A piece of work; task. **5.** *Med.* The pain and stress of childbirth; esp., the uterine contractions prior to giving birth. — **Department of Labor** An executive department of the U.S. government (established 1913), headed by the Secretary of Labor, that carries out policies regarding wages, unemployment, etc. — *v.i.* **1.** To work hard physically or mentally. **2.** To progress with great effort or painful exertion. **3.** To suffer the pangs of childbirth. **4.** To be oppressed or hampered. — *v.t.* **5.** To work out laboriously; overwork: to *labor* an argument. Also *Brit.* **la'bour.** [< OF < L *labor* toil, distress]

lab·o·ra·to·ry (lab'rə·tôr'ē, -tō'rē; *Brit.* lə·bor'ə·trē) *n.* *pl.* **·ries** **1.** A building or room equipped for conducting scientific experiments, analyses, etc. **2.** A department, as in a factory, for research, testing, etc. Also, *Informal,* **lab.** [< Med.L < L *labor* toil]
Labor Day In most States of the United States and in Canada, a legal holiday, usu. the first Monday in September.
la·bored (lā'bôrd) *adj.* **1.** Performed laboriously; difficult: *labored* breathing. **2.** Overelaborate: *labored* prose.
la·bor·er (lā'bər·ər) *n.* One who performs physical or manual labor, esp. unskilled labor.
la·bo·ri·ous (lə·bôr'ē·əs, -bō'rē-) *adj.* **1.** Requiring much labor; toilsome. **2.** Diligent; industrious. — **la·bo'ri·ous·ly** *adv.* — **la·bo'ri·ous·ness** *n.* [< OF < L *labor* labor, toil]
la·bor·ite (lā'bər·īt) *n.* One who supports labor interests, esp. in politics. Also *Brit.* **la'bour·ite.**
la·bor·sav·ing (lā'bər·sā'ving) *adv.* Doing away with, or diminishing the need for, manual work: *laborsaving* devices.
labor union An association of workers organized to improve and advance mutual interests: also called *trade union.*
La·bour·ite (lā'bər·īt) *n.* A member of a Labour party in Great Britain or in one of the Commonwealth nations.
Labour Party **1.** In Great Britain, a political party drawing its chief support from labor and trade unions and committed to socialist reforms. **2.** A similar party in other members of the British Commonwealth of Nations.
la·bur·num (lə·bûr'nəm) *n.* Any of a group of leguminous Old World trees yielding a poisonous alkaloid, with pendulous yellow flowers and hard, dark wood. [< NL < L]
lab·y·rinth (lab'ə·rinth) *n.* **1.** A system of winding, intricate passages or paths designed to confuse whoever tries to go through and find the exit; maze. **2.** Anything resembling a labyrinth, as a confusing network of streets. **3.** Any intricate or perplexing set of difficulties. **4.** *Anat.* The winding passages of the inner ear.
Lab·y·rinth (lab'ə·rinth) In Greek mythology, the maze used to confine the Minotaur, constructed by Daedalus for Minos of Crete. [< L < Gk.]
lab·y·rin·thine (lab'ə·rin'thin, -thēn) *adj.* Of, pertaining to, or like a labyrinth. Also **lab'y·rin'thi·an, lab'y·rin'thic.**
lac (lak) *n.* A resinous deposit left on certain trees by the lac insect and used in making varnishes, paints, etc. [< Hind. < Prakrit < Skt. *lākshā*]
lace (lās) *n.* **1.** A cord or string passed through eyelets or over hooks for fastening together the edges of a shoe, garment, etc. **2.** A delicate openwork fabric or network, made by hand or on a machine, of linen, silk, cotton, etc. **3.** A

silver or gold braid used to decorate uniforms, hats, etc. — *v.* **laced, lac·ing** *v.t.* 1. To fasten or draw together by tying the lace or laces of. 2. To pass (a cord or string) through eyelets or over hooks as a lace. 3. To trim with or as with lace. 4. To compress the waist of (a person) by tightening laces of a corset. 5. To intertwine or interlace. 6. To streak with lines or colors. — *v.i.* 7. To be fastened by means of laces. **— to lace into** *Informal* 1. To strike or attack. 2. To scold; berate. [< OF < L *laqueus* noose, trap]
lac·er·ate (las′ər·āt) *v.t.* **·at·ed, ·at·ing** 1. To tear raggedly; esp., to wound the flesh by tearing. 2. To injure: to *lacerate* one's feelings. — *adj.* 1. Jagged; torn. 2. Harrowed; distressed. 3. *Biol.* Having the edges jagged or irregularly cleft. [< L *lacer* mangled] — **lac′er·a·ble** *adj.*
lac·er·a·tion (las′ər·ā′shən) *n.* 1. The act of lacerating. 2. The wound or jagged tear resulting from lacerating.
lace·wing (lās′wing′) *n.* An insect with four lacy wings.
lace·work (lās′wûrk′) *n.* 1. Lace. 2. Any decorative openwork resembling lace.
lach·es (lach′iz) *n. Law* Unreasonable delay in asserting a right, so that the court is warranted in refusing relief. [< AF, OF < L *laxus* lax]
Lach·e·sis (lak′ə·sis) One of the three Fates.
lach·ry·mal (lak′rə·məl) *adj.* Of, pertaining to, or producing tears. — *n. pl.* The organs secreting tears: also **lachrymal glands.** [< Med.L < L *lacrima* tear]
lach·ry·ma·to·ry (lak′rə·mə·tôr′ē, -tō′rē) *n. pl.* **·ries** A small bottle found in ancient tombs, formerly supposed to have held the tears of mourners. — *adj.* Of or producing tears. [< Med.L < L *lacrima* tear]
lach·ry·mose (lak′rə·mōs) *adj.* 1. Tearful. 2. Provoking tears; sad. — **lach′ry·mose′ly** *adv.*
lac·ing (lā′sing) *n.* 1. The act of one who or that which laces. 2. A cord or string for holding together opposite parts of a shoe, etc.; lace. 3. A fastening made with lacing. 4. *Informal* A thrashing; beating. 5. An ornamental braid.
lac insect Any of a family of insects, esp. an Indian species, the females of which exude lac.
lack (lak) *n.* 1. Deficiency or complete absence of something. 2. That which is absent or deficient; need. — *v.t.* 1. To be without. 2. To be short by. — *v.i.* 3. To be wanting or deficient. [ME, prob. < MLG *lak* deficiency]
lack·a·dai·si·cal (lak′ə·dā′zi·kəl) *adj.* Affectedly pensive or melancholy; listless. — **lack·a·dai′si·cal·ly** *adv.*
lack·ey (lak′ē) *n. pl.* **·eys** 1. A male servant of low status, usu. in livery; footman. 2. Any servile follower. — *v.t. & v.i.* To attend or act as a lackey. [< OF < Sp. *lacayo*]
lack·lus·ter (lak′lus′tər) *adj.* 1. Lacking sheen and brightness; dull. 2. Lacking spirit; mediocre: a *lackluster* performance. — *n.* A lack of brightness. Also **lack′lus′tre.**
la·con·ic (lə·kon′ik) *adj.* Brief and concise in expression. Also **la·con′i·cal.** [< L < Gk. *Lakōn* a Spartan; with ref. to the terseness of Spartan speech] — **la·con′i·cal·ly** *adv.*
lac·quer (lak′ər) *n.* 1. A transparent varnish made from various resins, dissolved in volatile solvent. 2. A resinous varnish obtained from the lacquer tree of China and Japan, and used to impart a high polish to wood. 3. Decorative woodwork or articles of wood painted with this lacquer: also **lac′quer·work′** (-wûrk′). — *v.t.* To coat with or as with lacquer. [< MF *lacre* a kind of sealing wax < Pg. *lacca* gum lac] — **lac′quer·er** *n.*
la·crosse (lə·krôs′, -kros′) *n. U.S. & Canadian* A ball game of American Indian origin, played with long, racketlike implements by two teams of ten men each, the object being to advance the ball into the opponents' goal. [< dial. F (Canadian) *la crosse*, lit., the crozier, hooked stick]
lact- Var. of LACTO-.
lac·tate (lak′tāt) *v.i.* **·tat·ed, ·tat·ing** 1. To form or secrete milk. 2. To suckle young. — *n.* A salt or ester of lactic acid. [< L *lactare* to suckle]
lac·ta·tion (lak·tā′shən) *n.* 1. The mammalian formation or secretion of milk. 2. The period during which milk is produced. 3. The act of suckling young.
lac·te·al (lak′tē·əl) *adj.* 1. Of, pertaining to, or resembling milk; milky. 2. Carrying chyle. Also **lac′te·an, lac′te·ous.** — *n. Anat.* Any of the lymphatic vessels that carry chyle from the small intestine to the blood. [< L *lac, lactis* milk]
lac·tic (lak′tik) *adj.* Of, pertaining to, or derived from milk.
lactic acid *Chem.* A limpid, syrupy acid, $C_3H_6O_3$, with a bitter taste, present in sour milk.
lacto- *combining form* Milk. Also, before vowels, *lact-*. [< L *lac, lactis* milk]
lac·to·fla·vin (lak′tō·flā′vin) *n.* Riboflavin.
lac·tose (lak′tōs) *n. Biochem.* A white, odorless, crystalline sugar, $C_{12}H_{22}O_{11}$, present in milk.
la·cu·na (lə·kyōō′nə) *n. pl.* **·nas** or **·nae** (-nē) 1. A space from which something is missing or has been omitted, esp. in a manuscript; hiatus. 2. *Anat.* Any of the minute cavities in bone containing bone cells. Also **la·cune′** (-kyōōn′). [< L *lacus* basin, pond] — **la·cu′nal, la·cu′nar, lac·u·nar·y** (lak′yōō·ner′ē) *adj.*
lac·y (lā′sē) *adj.* **lac·i·er, lac·i·est** Made of or resembling lace. — **lac′i·ly** *adv.* — **lac′i·ness** *n.*
lad (lad) *n.* 1. A boy or youth; stripling. 2. Familiarly, any male. [< ME *ladde*, ? ult. < ON]
lad·der (lad′ər) *n.* A device of wood, metal, rope, etc., for climbing and descending, usu. consisting of two parallel side pieces connected by a series of rungs, or rounds, placed at regular intervals to serve as footholds. [OE *hlæd(d)er*]
lad·die (lad′ē) *n.* A lad.
lade (lād) *v.* **lad·ed, lad·ed** or **lad·en, lad·ing** *v.t.* 1. To load with a cargo or burden; also, to load as a cargo. 2. To dip or lift (a liquid) in or out, as with a ladle. — *v.i.* 3. To receive cargo. 4. To dip or lift a liquid. [OE *hladan* to load]
lad·en[1] (lād′n) Alternative past participle of LADE. — *adj.* 1. Burdened; oppressed. 2. Weighed down; loaded.
lad·en[2] (lād′n) *v.t. & v.i.* **lad·ened, lad·en·ing** To lade.
lad·ing (lā′ding) *n.* 1. The act of one who or that which lades. 2. A load or cargo.
la·dle (lād′l) *n.* A cup-shaped vessel with a long handle, for dipping or conveying liquids. — *v.t.* **·dled, ·dling** To dip up or carry in a ladle. [OE *hladan* to lade] — **la′dler** *n.*
la·dy (lā′dē) *n. pl.* **·dies** 1. A woman showing refinement, gentility, and tact. 2. A woman of superior position in society. 3. A term of reference or address for any woman. 4. A woman at the head of a domestic establishment: now only in the phrase **the lady of the house.** 5. The woman a man loves. 6. A wife. — *adj.* 1. Of or pertaining to a lady; ladylike. 2. Denoting a female: a *lady* doctor. ◆ *Woman* doctor is preferable here. [OE *hlǣfdīge*, lit., bread-kneader < *hlāf* bread, loaf + *-dige*, a stem akin to *dah* dough]
La·dy (lā′dē) 1. In Great Britain a title given to women of various ranks. 2. The Virgin Mary: usu. with *Our.*
la·dy·bird (lā′dē·bûrd′) *n.* Any of a family of brightly colored beetles, usu. red spotted with black, that feeds on aphids and other insects. Also **lady beetle, la′dy·bug′.**
Lady Day 1. March 25, the church festival of the Annunciation. 2. Formerly, a day honoring the Virgin Mary.
la·dy·fin·ger (lā′dē·fing′gər) *n.* A small sponge cake of about the size and shape of a finger. Also **la′dys·fin′ger** (lā′dēz-).
lady in waiting *pl.* **ladies in waiting** A lady appointed to attend upon a queen or princess.
la·dy·kill·er (lā′dē·kil′ər) *n. Slang* A man supposed to be unusually fascinating to women. — **la′dy-kill′ing** *adj. & n.*
la·dy·like (lā′dē·līk′) *adj.* 1. Like or suitable to a lady; gentle; delicate. 2. Effeminate.
la·dy·love (lā′dē·luv′) *n.* A woman beloved; sweetheart.
la·dy·ship (lā′dē·ship) *n.* The rank or condition of a lady: used as a title, with *Her* or *Your.*
lady's man A man attentive to and fond of the company of women. Also **ladies' man.**
lady's-slipper (lā′dēz·slip′ər) *n.* An orchid having a flower that suggests a slipper in shape. Also **la′dy·slip′per** (lā′dē-).
laevo- See LEVO-.
lag (lag) *v.i.* **lagged, lag·ging** 1. To move slowly; stay or fall behind; straggle: sometimes followed by *behind.* 2. In marbles, to throw one's taw as near as possible to a line on the ground to decide the order of play. — *n.* 1. The condition or act of retardation or falling behind. 2. The amount or period of retardation. 3. In marbles, an act of lagging. [? < Scand.] — **lag′ger** *n.*
lag·an (lag′ən) *n.* In maritime law, goods cast from a vessel in peril, but to which a buoy or float is attached as evidence of ownership: also called *ligan.* [< AF < Gmc.]
la·ger (lä′gər) *n.* A beer stored for sedimentation before use. Also **lager beer.** [< G < *lager* storehouse + *bier* beer]
lag·gard (lag′ərd) *n.* One who lags; straggler. — *adj.* Falling behind; loitering; slow. — **lag′gard·ly** *adv.*
la·gniappe (lan·yap′, lan′yap) *n.* 1. *Southern U.S.* A small present given to the purchaser of an article by a merchant or storekeeper. 2. *Informal* Anything given beyond strict obligation; an extra. Also **la·gnappe′.** [< dial. F (Creole) F *la* the + Sp. *ñapa* lagniappe < Quechua *yapa*]
la·goon (lə·gōōn′) *n.* A body of shallow water, as a bay, inlet, pond, or lake, usu. connecting with a river, larger lake, or the sea; esp., the water within a coral atoll. Also **la·gune′.** [< F < Ital. < L *lacuna* pool]
la·ic (lā′ik) *adj.* Lay[2]. — *n.* A layman. [< LL < Gk. *laikos* < *laos* the people] — **la′i·cal·ly** *adv.*
la·i·cize (lā′ə·sīz) *v.t.* **·cized, ·ciz·ing** To remove from ecclesiastical control; secularize. — **la′i·ci·za′tion** *n.*
laid (lād) Past tense and past participle of LAY[1].
lain (lān) Past participle of LIE[1].
lair (lâr) *n.* A resting place or den, esp. that of a wild animal. — *v.i.* 1. To live or rest in a lair. — *v.t.* 2. To place in a lair. 3. To serve as a lair for. [OE *leger* bed]

laird (lârd) *n. Scot.* The proprietor of a landed estate. [Northern ME *laverd, lard*] — **laird′ly** *adj.* — **laird′ship** *n.*
lais·sez faire (les′ā-fâr′) **1.** In economics, the theory that the state should exercise as little control as possible in trade and industrial affairs. **2.** Noninterference or indifference. Also **lais′ser faire′.** [< F, lit., let do < *laisser* to let + *faire* to do, make]
la·i·ty (lā′ə-tē) *n. pl.* **·ties 1.** The people collectively; laymen: distinguished from *clergy.* **2.** All of those outside a specific profession or occupation.
La·i·us (lā′yəs) In Greek legend, a king of Thebes, husband of Jocasta, who was unwittingly killed by his son Oedipus.
lake¹ (lāk) *n.* **1.** A sizable inland body of either salt or fresh water. **2.** A large pool of any liquid: a *lake* of pitch. [Fusion of OE *lacu* stream, pool and OF *lac* basin, lake]
lake² (lāk) *n.* **1.** A deep red pigment made by combining cochineal with a metallic oxide. **2.** The color of this pigment. **3.** Any metallic compound yielding pigments by the interaction of mordant and dye. [Var. of LAC]
lake dwelling A habitation built on piles over the surface of a lake, esp. in prehistoric times. — **lake dweller**
lake herring A whitefish of the Great Lakes.
lake trout A salmonoid fish of the Great Lakes region of North America, somewhat resembling the brook trout.
la·la·pa·loo·za (lol′ə-pə-lōō′zə) See LOLLAPALOOZA. Also **lal′la·pa·loo′za.**
lam (lam) *Slang v.* **lammed, lam·ming** *v.i.* **1.** To run away, esp. to avoid arrest; flee. — *v.t.* **2.** To beat; thrash. — *n.* Sudden flight or escape. — **on the lam** In flight; fleeing. [? < ON *lemja* to thrash]
la·ma (lä′mə) *n.* A priest or monk of Lamaism. See DALAI LAMA. [< Tibetan *blama*]
La·ma·ism (lä′mə·iz′əm) *n.* The form of Buddhism practiced in Tibet and Mongolia, characterized by a complex hierarchy and Shamanistic beliefs and practices. — **La′ma·ist** *n.* — **La′ma·is′tic** *adj.*
La·marck·ism (lə-märk′iz-əm) *n. Biol.* The theory of organic evolution holding that species have developed through the inheritance of acquired characteristics. [after Chevalier de *Lamarck,* 1744–1829, French naturalist]
la·ma·ser·y (lä′mə-ser′ē) *n. pl.* **·ser·ies** A Lamaist monastery. [< F]
lamb (lam) *n.* **1.** A young sheep. **2.** The meat of a lamb used as food. **3.** Lambskin. **4.** Any gentle or innocent person, esp. a child. **5.** A gullible person. — **the Lamb** Christ. — *v.i.* To give birth: said of a ewe. [OE]
lam·baste (lam-bāst′) *v.t.* **·bast·ed, ·bast·ing** *Slang* **1.** To beat or thrash. **2.** To scold; castigate. — **lam·bast′ing** *n.*
lamb·da (lam′də) *n.* The eleventh letter in the Greek alphabet (Λ, λ), corresponding to the English *l.* See ALPHABET. [< Gk. < Phoenician *lamed*]
lam·bent (lam′bənt) *adj.* **1.** Playing over a surface with a soft, undulatory movement; flickering; licking: a *lambent* flame. **2.** Softly radiant. **3.** Lightly and playfully brilliant: *lambent* wit. [< L *lambens, -entis,* ppr. of *lambere* to lick] — **lam′ben·cy** *n.* — **lam′bent·ly** *adv.*
lamb·kin (lam′kin) *n.* **1.** A little lamb. **2.** A small child: a term of affection. Also **lamb′ie.** [Dim. of LAMB]
Lamb of God Christ, as the Paschal Lamb. *John* i 29.
lam·bre·quin (lam′bər-kin, -brə-) *n.* **1.** *U.S.* A draped strip of cloth, leather, etc., hanging from the casing above a window or doorway, and covering the upper half of the opening. **2.** In medieval times, a covering of heavy fabric for a helmet. [< F < Du. *lamperkin,* dim. of *lamper* veil]
lamb·skin (lam′skin) *n.* **1.** The dressed hide and wool of a lamb. **2.** Dressed leather made from a lamb's hide.
lame (lām) *adj.* **lam·er, lam·est 1.** Crippled or disabled, esp. in the legs or feet. **2.** Sore; painful: a *lame* back. **3.** Weak; ineffective: a *lame* effort. — *v.t.* **lamed, lam·ing** To make lame. [OE *lama*] — **lame′ly** *adv.* — **lame′ness** *n.*
la·mé (la-mā′) *n.* A fabric woven of flat gold or silver thread, sometimes mixed with silk or other fiber. [< F]
lame duck *Informal* **1.** *U.S.* An officeholder whose term continues for a time after his defeat for reelection. **2.** On the stock exchange, one who cannot fulfill his contracts. **3.** An ineffectual or disabled person.
la·mel·la (lə-mel′ə) *n. pl.* **·mel·lae** (-mel′ē) A thin plate, scale, or layer, as in bone or the gills of bivalves. [< NL < L, dim. of *lamina* plate, leaf] — **lam·el·lar** (lə-mel′ər, lam′ə-lər), **lam′el·late** *adj.*
la·mel·li·branch (lə-mel′i·brangk) *n. Zool.* One of a class of bivalve mollusks including clams, mussels, and oysters. [< NL < L *lamella* plate + Gk. *branchia* gills] — **la·mel′li·bran′chi·ate** (-brank′kē-āt, -it) *adj. & n.*
la·ment (lə-ment′) *v.t.* To feel remorse or regret over. — *v.i.* To feel or express sorrow, grief, or regret. — *n.* **1.** An expression of grief; lamentation. **2.** An elegiac melody or writing. [< L *lamentum* wailing, weeping] — **la·ment′er** *n.*
lam·en·ta·ble (lam′ən-tə-bəl, lə-men′tə-) *adj.* **1.** That warrants lamenting; deplorable: a *lamentable* failure. **2.** *Archaic* Expressing grief; mournful. — **lam′en·ta·bly** *adv.*

lam·en·ta·tion (lam′ən-tā′shən) *n.* **1.** The act of lamenting or bewailing. **2.** A lament; wail; moan.
Lam·en·ta·tions (lam′ən-tā′shənz) *n.pl. (construed as sing.)* A lyrical poetic book of the Old Testament, attributed to Jeremiah the prophet.
lam·ent·ed (lə-men′təd) *adj.* Mourned for; grieved over: usu. said of one who has died.
lam·i·na (lam′ə-nə) *n. pl.* **·nae** (-nē) or **·nas 1.** A thin scale or sheet. **2.** A layer or coat lying over another, as in bone, minerals, armor, etc. **3.** *Bot.* The blade or flat expanded portion of a leaf, or the blade of a petal. [< L]
lam·i·nate (lam′ə-nāt) *v.* **·nat·ed, ·nat·ing** *v.t.* **1.** To beat, roll, or press (metal) into thin sheets. **2.** To separate or cut into thin sheets. **3.** To make of layers united by the action of heat and pressure. **4.** To cover with thin sheets or laminae. — *v.i.* **5.** To separate into sheets. — *adj.* Laminated. [< NL < L *lamina* leaf] — **lam′i·na′tion** *n.*
lam·i·nat·ed (lam′ə-nā′təd) *adj.* Made up of or arranged in thin sheets; laminate.
lam·i·nose (lam′ə-nōs) *adj.* Laminate.
lamp (lamp) *n.* **1.** A device for holding one or more electric light bulbs and directing their light; also, an electric light bulb. **2.** Any of various devices for producing light by combustion, incandescence, electric arc, or fluorescence. **3.** A vessel in which oil or alcohol is burned through a wick to produce light or heat. **4.** Any of several devices for producing therapeutic heat or rays: sun *lamp.* [< OF < L < Gk. *lampein* to shine]
lamp·black (lamp′blak′) *n.* A black pigment consisting of fine carbon deposited from the smoke of burning oil or gas.
lamp·light (lamp′līt′) *n.* Light from lamps; artificial light.
lamp·light·er (lamp′lī′tər) *n.* **1.** One whose work is lighting lamps, esp. street lamps. **2.** Anything by which a lamp is lighted, as a torch, electric device, etc.
lam·poon (lam-pōōn′) *n.* A scurrilous, but often humorous, attack in prose or verse directed against a person. — *v.t.* To satirize in a lampoon. [< MF *lampons* let's drink (a song refrain)] — **lam·poon′er, lam·poon′ist** *n.* — **lam·poon′er·y** *n.*
lamp·post (lamp′pōst′) *n.* A post supporting a lamp.
lam·prey (lam′prē) *n. pl.* **·preys** An eellike, carnivorous, aquatic animal having a circular suctorial mouth with sharp rasping teeth on its inner surface. Also **lam·per eel** (lam′pər). [< OF < Med.L *lampreda lampetra*]
Lan·cas·ter (lang′kəs·tər), **House of** A royal house of England, reigning from 1399 to 1461. — **Lan·cas′tri·an** *adj. & n.*
lance (lans, läns) *n.* **1.** A spearlike weapon used by mounted soldiers or knights. **2.** One who is armed with a lance; lancer. **3.** Any of various long, slender weapons resembling a lance, as a whaler's spear, etc. **4.** A lancet. — *v.t.* **lanced, lanc·ing 1.** To pierce with a lance. **2.** To cut or open with a lancet. [ME < OF < L *lancea* light spear]
lance corporal 1. *Mil.* In the U.S. Marine Corps, an enlisted man. See table at GRADE. **2.** *Brit. Mil.* A private acting as a corporal, usu. without increased pay.
lance·let (lans′lit, läns′-) *n.* A small, fishlike animal having primitive vertebrate characteristics, and living in the sand: also called *amphioxus.* [Dim. of LANCE]
Lan·ce·lot of the Lake (lan′sə-lot, län′-) In Arthurian romance, the bravest and ablest of the knights of the Round Table. Also **Lancelot du Lac** (dü läk). [< F, servant]
lan·ce·o·late (lan′sē·ə-lit, -lāt) *adj.* **1.** Shaped like the head of a lance. **2.** *Bot.* Narrowing to a point; tapering, as certain leaves. [< LL < *lanceola* small lance]
lanc·er (lan′sər, län′-) *n.* A calvaryman armed with a lance.
lance sergeant *Brit. Mil.* A corporal acting temporarily as a sergeant without additional pay.
lan·cet (lan′sit, län′-) *n.* A small, two-edged, usu. pointed surgical knife, used to open abscesses, boils, etc. [< F *lancette,* dim. of *lance* < OF < L *lancea* light spear]
lancet arch *Archit.* A narrow, acutely pointed arch.
lancet window A narrow, acutely pointed window.
lance·wood (lans′wood′, läns′-) *n.* **1.** A tough, elastic wood used for carriage shafts, fishing rods, billiard cues, etc. **2.** Any of various tropical American trees yielding this wood.
land (land) *n.* **1.** The solid, exposed surface of the earth as distinguished from the waters of the seas. **2.** A country or region, esp. considered as a place of human habitation. **3.** The people of such a country or region. **4.** Ground considered with reference to its uses, location, character, etc.: pasture *land.* **5.** *Law* **a** Any tract of ground whatever that may be owned as goods together with all its appurtenances, as water, forests, buildings, etc. **b** A share or interest in such land. **6.** Rural places as distinguished from cities or towns. **7.** *Econ.* Natural resources as used in production. — *v.t.* **1.** To transfer from a vessel to the shore; put ashore. **2.** To bring (something in flight) down to rest. **3.** To bring to some point, condition, or state: His words *landed* him in trouble. **4.** To pull (a fish) out of the water; catch. **5.** *Informal* To obtain; win: to *land* a job. **6.** *Informal* To de-

liver (a blow) —*v.i.* **7.** To go or come ashore from a ship or boat. **8.** To touch at a port; come to land. **9.** To descend and come to rest after a flight or jump. **10.** To come to some place or state; end up: to *land* in jail. [OE]

-land *combining form* **1.** A region of a certain kind: *woodland*. **2.** The country of: *Scotland*. [< LAND]

lan·dau (lan′dô, -dou) *n.* **1.** A former type of closed sedan having a back seat with a collapsible top. **2.** A four-wheeled carriage with a collapsible top. [after *Landau*, a Bavarian city where it was first made]

land bank *U.S.* A bank making mortgage loans on land or other real property.

land·ed (lan′did) *adj.* **1.** Having an estate in land: *landed* gentry. **2.** Consisting in land: *landed* property.

-land·er *combining form* From or of a land. [< LAND]

land·fall (land′fôl′) *n.* A sighting of or coming to land; also, the land so sighted or reached.

land grant Government land granted to a railroad, educational institution, etc.

land-grant (land′grant) *adj.* Denoting a State college or university that received grants of land from the Federal government under the Morrill Act of 1862.

land·grave (land′grāv′) *n.* **1.** In medieval and Renaissance Germany, a count having jurisdiction over a specified territory. **2.** Later, the title of any of various German princes. [< MHG < *lant, land* land + *grave, graf* count]

land·hold·er (land′hōl′dər) *n.* An owner or occupant of land.

land·ing (lan′ding) *n.* **1.** The act of going or placing ashore from any kind of craft or vessel. **2.** The place where a craft or vessel lands; wharf; pier. **3.** The act of descending and settling on the ground after a flight, leap, etc. **4.** *Archit.* The platform or floor at the top of a flight of stairs, between flights of stairs, or interrupting a flight of stairs.

landing field A tract of ground selected or prepared for the landing and takeoff of aircraft.

land·la·dy (land′lā′dē) *n. pl.* **·dies 1.** A woman who owns and rents out real estate. **2.** The wife of a landlord. **3.** A woman who keeps an inn.

länd·ler (lent′lər) *n.* **1.** A slow Austrian country dance. **2.** Music for or in the manner of this dance, in triple meter. [< G < dial. G *Landl* upper Austria]

land·less (land′lis) *adj.* Owning no land.

land·locked (land′lokt′) *adj.* **1.** Surrounded by land; having no seacoast. **2.** Living in landlocked water: said esp. of a normally anadromous fish: *landlocked* salmon.

land·lord (land′lôrd′) *n.* **1.** A man who owns and rents out real estate. **2.** An innkeeper. **3.** *Brit.* The lord of a manor. [OE < *land* land + *hlaford* lord]

land·lub·ber (land′lub′ər) *n.* An awkward or inexperienced person on board a ship.

land·mark (land′märk′) *n.* **1.** A fixed object serving as a boundary mark to a tract of land, as a guide to travelers, etc. **2.** A prominent object in the landscape. **3.** A distinguishing fact, event, etc. [OE *land* land + *mearc* boundary]

land mine *Mil.* An explosive bomb placed in the ground.

land office A government office for the transaction of business pertaining to the public lands.

land-of·fice business (land′ô′fis, -of′is) *U.S. Informal* Business conducted at a rapid pace.

Land of Enchantment Nickname of New Mexico.

Land of Opportunity Nickname of Arkansas.

Land of Promise See PROMISED LAND.

Land of the Midnight Sun Norway.

Land of the Rising Sun Japan.

land·own·er (land′ō′nər) *n.* One who owns real estate. — **land′own′er·ship** *n.* — **land′own′ing** *n. & adj.*

land·scape (land′skāp) *n.* **1.** A stretch of inland natural scenery as seen from a single point. **2.** A picture representing such scenery. **3.** The branch of painting, photography, etc., that deals with inland natural scenery. —*v.* **·scaped**, **·scap·ing** *v.t.* **1.** To improve or change the features or appearance of a park, garden, etc. —*v.i.* **2.** To be a landscape gardener. [< Du. < *land* land + *-schap* -ship]

landscape architect One whose profession is to plan the decorative arrangement of outdoor features.

landscape gardener One who plans and carries out the arrangement of plants, trees, etc. — **landscape gardening**

land·scap·ist (land′skā′pist) *n.* A painter of landscapes.

land·slide (land′slīd′) *n.* **1.** The slipping down of a mass of soil, rock, and debris on a mountain side or other steep slope. **2.** The mass of soil, rock, etc., slipping down. Also *Chiefly Brit.*, **land′slip′** (-slip′). **3.** An overwhelming plurality of votes for one political party or candidate in an election.

lands·man (landz′mən) *n. pl.* **·men** (-mən) One who lives and works on land: distinguished from *seaman*.

land·ward (land′wərd) *adj. & adv.* Being, facing, or going toward the land. Also **land′wards** (-wərdz).

lane (lān) *n.* **1.** A narrow rural path or way, confined between fences, walls, hedges, or similar boundaries; also, a narrow city street. **2.** Any narrow way, passage, or similar course. **3.** A prescribed route for transoceanic shipping or for aircraft. **4.** A marked division of a highway or road for traffic moving in the same direction. **5.** In sports, any of a set of parallel courses for contestants in races. [OE *lanu*]

Lang·er·hans (läng′ər-häns), **islands of** See ISLANDS OF LANGERHANS.

lang·lauf (läng′louf) *n.* A cross-country ski run. [< G < *lang* long + *lauf* course] — **lang′läuf·er** (-loi-fər) *n.*

lang·syne (lang′sīn′, -zīn′) *adv. Scot.* Long since; long ago.

lan·guage (lang′gwij) *n.* **1.** The expression and communication of emotions or ideas between human beings by means of speech and hearing. **2.** Transmission of emotions or ideas between any living creatures by any means. **3.** The words used in communication among members of a single nation or group at a given period. **4.** The impulses, capacities, and powers that induce and make possible the creation and use of language. **5.** The vocabulary used in a specific business, science, etc. **6.** One's characteristic manner of expression or use of speech. [< OF < L *lingua* tongue, language]

language arts Reading, spelling, literature, and composition, considered as basic language skills.

lan·guid (lang′gwid) *adj.* **1.** Indisposed toward physical exertion; affected by weakness or fatigue. **2.** Feeling little interest in or inclination toward anything; listless. **3.** Lacking in activity or quickness of movement. [< L *languere* to languish] — **lan′guid·ly** *adv.* — **lan′guid·ness** *n.*

lan·guish (lang′gwish) *v.i.* **1.** To become weak or feeble; fail in health or vitality; grow listless. **2.** To droop gradually from restless longing; pine. **3.** To pass through a period of external discomfort and mental anguish: to *languish* in prison. **4.** To adopt a look of sentimental longing or melancholy. [< OF < L *languescere*, inceptive of *languere* to be weary, languish] — **lan′guish·er** *n.* — **lan′guish·ment** *n.*

lan·guish·ing (lang′gwish·ing) *adj.* **1.** Lacking alertness or force. **2.** Sentimentally pensive or melancholy. **3.** Becoming weak or listless. — **lan′guish·ing·ly** *adv.*

lan·guor (lang′gər) *n.* **1.** Lassitude of body; weakness; fatigue. **2.** A lack of energy or enthusiasm. **3.** A mood of tenderness or sentimental dreaminess. **4.** The absence of activity; stagnation. **5.** Oppressiveness; stillness.

lan·guor·ous (lang′gər-əs) *adj.* **1.** Languid. **2.** Producing languor. — **lan′guor·ous·ly** *adv.* — **lan′guor·ous·ness** *n.*

lan·gur (lung-goor′) *n.* A slender, long-tailed Asian monkey. [< Hind. < Skt. *lāṅgūlin*, lit., having a tail]

lan·iard (lan′yərd) See LANYARD.

lank (langk) *adj.* **1.** Lean; shrunken. **2.** Long, flat, and straight; not curly: *lank* hair. [OE *hlanc* flexible] — **lank′ly** *adv.* — **lank′ness** *n.*

lank·y (lang′kē) *adj.* **lank·i·er, lank·i·est** Ungracefully tall and thin; loose-jointed. — **lank′i·ly** *adv.* — **lank′i·ness** *n.*

lan·o·lin (lan′ə-lin) *n.* A fatty substance obtained from the wool of sheep and used in ointments, cosmetics, soaps, etc.; also called *wool fat*. Also **lan′o·line** (-lin, -lēn). [< L *lan(a)* wool + *ol(eum)* oil + -IN]

lan·tern (lan′tərn) *n.* **1.** A protective, usu. portable, case with transparent or translucent sides for enclosing a light. **2.** *Archit.* An open structure built on top of a building to admit light and air. **3.** A lighthouse, esp. the top that protects the light. **4.** *Archaic* A slide projector. [< F < L < Gk. *lampein* to shine]

lantern jaws Long, sunken jaws that make the face appear thin. — **lan′tern-jawed** (-jôd′) *adj.*

lan·tha·nide series (lan′thə·nīd) *Physics* The rare-earth elements beginning with lanthanum (according to some authorities, with cerium) and ending with lutetium. [< LANTHAN(UM) + -ide, var. of -ID²]

lan·tha·num (lan′thə·nəm) *n.* A dark lead gray metallic element (symbol La) chemically related to aluminum. See ELEMENT. [< NL < Gk. *lanthanein* to lie concealed]

lan·yard (lan′yərd) *n.* **1.** *Naut.* A small, usu. four-stranded hemp rope used on a ship for fastening riggings, etc. **2.** A cord used in firing certain types of cannon. **3.** A cord worn around the neck, used by sailors for attaching a knife. Also spelled *laniard*. [Alter. of obs. *lanyer* < OF *lasniere* thong]

La·o (lä′ō) *n. pl.* **La·o 1.** A Buddhistic people living in Laos and parts of Thailand. **2.** Their Thai language.

La·oc·o·on (lā-ok′ə·won, -ō·won) In Greek legend, a Trojan priest who warned against the wooden horse and was destroyed with his two sons by two serpents.

La·o·tian (lou′shən, lā-ō′shən, lä-ō′shən) *adj.* Of or pertaining to Laos. —*n.* A native or inhabitant of Laos.

lap¹ (lap) *n.* **1.** The chairlike place formed by the lower torso and thighs of a person seated; also, the clothing that covers this part. **2.** The front part of a skirt when lifted up. **3.** A place of nurture or fostering: fortune's *lap*. **4.** Control, care, or custody: in the *lap* of the gods. **— to throw into someone's lap** To give over the responsibility or control of something to someone else. [OE *læppa*]

lap² (lap)   *n.*   **1.** The state of overlapping.   **2.** A rotating disk used for grinding and polishing gems, etc.   **3.** One circuit of a race course.   **4.** The part of one thing that lies over another.   *— v.t.*   **1.** To fold or wrap about something.   **2.** To lay (one thing) partly over or beyond another.   **3.** To extend over or beyond; overlap.   **4.** To grind or polish with a lap.   **5.** To surround with love, etc.: now only in the passive: to be *lapped* in maternal tenderness.   *— v.i.*   **6.** To be folded.   **7.** To overlap.   **8.** To project beyond or into something else.   [ME *lappen* to fold]

lap³ (lap)   *v.t. & v.i.* **lapped, lap·ping**   **1.** To drink (a liquid) by taking it up with the tongue, as an animal does.   **2.** To wash against (the shore, etc.) with a sound resembling that of lapping.   *— n.*   **1.** The act of one who or that which laps.   **2.** The sound of lapping.   **— to lap up   1.** To drink by lapping.   **2.** *Informal* To eat or drink gluttonously.   **3.** To listen to eagerly.   [OE *lapian* to lap]   **— lap′per** *n.*

lap dog   A dog small enough to be held on the lap.

la·pel (lə-pel′)   *n.*   The front of a coat, jacket, etc., that is folded back to form an extension of the collar.   [< LAP¹]

lap·ful (lap′fŏŏl′)   *n.*   As much as the lap can hold.

lap·i·dar·y (lap′ə·der′ē)   *n.*   *pl.* **·dar·ies**   One whose work is to cut, engrave, or polish precious stones.   *— adj.* Pertaining to the art of cutting or engraving precious stones.   [< L *lapidarius* of stone]

lap·in (lap′in, *Fr.* là·pán′)   *n.*   **1.** A rabbit.   **2.** Rabbit fur, usu. dyed to resemble more expensive furs.   [< F]

lap·is laz·u·li (lap′is laz′yŏŏ·lī)   **1.** A bluish violet variety of lazurite valued as a gemstone.   **2.** The color of lapis lazuli.   Also **lap′is.**   [< NL < L *lapis* stone + Med.L *lazulus* azure]

lap joint   A joint in which a layer of material laps over another, as in shingling.   **— lap-joint·ed** (lap′join′tid) *adj.*

Lapp (lap)   *n.*   **1.** A member of a formerly nomadic Mongoloid people of Lapland, now settled largely in Sweden and Norway.   Also **Lap·land·er** (lap′lan·dər).   **2.** The Finno-Ugric language of the Lapps: also **Lap′pish.**   [< Sw.]

lap·pet (lap′it)   *n.*   **1.** A flap or fold on a headdress or garment.   **2.** A loose or pendent flap of flesh, as the lobe of the ear, the wattle of a bird, etc.   [Dim. of LAP¹]

lapse (laps)   *n.*   **1.** A gradual passing away, as of time.   **2.** A pronounced fall into ruin, decay, or disuse.   **3.** A slip or mistake, usually trivial.   **4.** A fault or negligence: a *lapse* of justice.   **5.** *Law* A forfeiture brought about by the failure to perform some necessary act.   *— v.i.* **lapsed, laps·ing   1.** To sink slowly; slip: to *lapse* into a coma.   **2.** To fall into ruin or a state of neglect.   **3.** To deviate from one's principles or beliefs.   **4.** To become void, usually by failure to meet obligations.   **5.** *Law* To pass or be forfeited to another because of negligence, failure, or death of the holder.   **6.** To pass away, as time.   [< L *labi* to glide, slip]   **— laps′a·ble, laps′i·ble** *adj.*   **— laps′er** *n.*

lap·wing (lap′wing′)   *n.* A ploverlike bird of the Old World, noted for its flopping flight and shrill cry.   [OE *hleapan* to leap + *wince*, prob. < *wancol* unsteady]

lar·board (lär′bərd, -bôrd′, -bōrd′)   *Naut. adj.* Being on or toward the left side of the ship as one faces the bow.   *— n.* The left-hand side of a ship: now replaced by *port*.   [ME *laddebord*, lit., prob., lading side]

lar·ce·ny (lär′sə·nē)   *n.*   *pl.* **·nies**   *Law* The unlawful removal of the personal goods of another with intent to defraud the owner; theft.   The distinction between **grand larceny** and **petty** (or **petit**) **larceny** is based on the value of the stolen property.   **— Syn.** See THEFT.   [< OF < L *latrocinari* to rob]   **— lar′ce·ner, lar′cen·ist** *n.*   **— lar′ce·nous** *adj.*   **— lar′ce·nous·ly** *adv.*

larch (lärch)   *n.*   Any of several coniferous, deciduous trees of the pine family; also, the wood.   [< G < L *larix, laricis*]

lard (lärd)   *n.*   The semisolid fat of a hog after rendering.   *— v.t.*   **1.** To cover or smear with lard.   **2.** To prepare (lean meat or poultry) by inserting strips of fat before cooking.   **3.** To intersperse (speech or writing) with embellishments, quotations, etc.   [< OF, < L *lardum* lard]   **— lard′y** *adj.*

lar·der (lär′dər)   *n.*   **1.** A room or cupboard where articles of food are stored.   **2.** The provisions of a household.   [< AF < Med.L *lardum* lard]

lar·es (lâr′ēz, lā′rēz)   *n.pl.* of **lar** (lär)   In ancient Rome, tutelary dieties, esp. those presiding over the household.   **lares and pe·na·tes** (pə·nā′tēz)   **1.** The household gods.   **2.** The cherished belongings of one's household.

large (lärj)   *adj.* **larg·er, larg·est   1.** Having considerable size, quantity, capacity, extent, etc.; big.   **2.** Bigger than another.   **3.** Sympathetic and broad in scope: to take a *large* view.   *— adv.* In a size greater than usual: Print *large*.   **— at large   1.** Free; at liberty: The maniac is *at large*.   **2.** In general: the people *at large*.   **3.** Elected from the whole State.   **4.** Exhaustively; fully.   [< OF < L *larga*, fem. of *largus* abundant]   **— large′ness** *n.*

large-heart·ed (lärj′här′tid)   *adj.* Generous; openhanded.   **— large′heart′ed·ness** *n.*

large·ly (lärj′lē)   *adv.*   **1.** To a great extent; mainly; chiefly.   **2.** On a big scale; extensively; abundantly.

large-scale (lärj′skāl′)   *adj.*   **1.** Of large size or scope.   **2.** Made according to a large scale: said of maps.

lar·gess (lär·jes′; lär′jis, -jes)   *n.*   Liberal giving; also, something liberally given.   Also **lar′gesse.**   [< F *largesse*]

lar·ghet·to (lär·get′ō)   *Music adj.* Moderately slow.   *— adv.* In a moderately slow tempo.   *— n.*   *pl.* **·tos** A moderately slow movement.   [< Ital., dim. of *largo*. See LARGO.]

lar·go (lär′go)   *Music adj.* Slow; broad.   *— adv.* In a slow tempo.   *— n.*   *pl.* **·gos** A slow movement or passage.   [< Ital., slow, large]

lar·i·at (lar′ē·ət)   *n.*   **1.** A rope for tethering animals.   **2.** A lasso.   *— v.t.* To fasten or catch with a lariat.   [< Sp. *la reata* < *la* the + *reata* rope]

lark¹ (lärk)   *n.*   **1.** Any of numerous small singing birds, as the skylark.   **2.** Any similar bird, as the meadowlark.   [ME < OE *láferce, lǽwerce*]

lark² (lärk)   *n.*   *Informal* A hilarious time.   *— v.t.*   **1.** To jump (a fence) on horseback.   *— v.i.*   **2.** To play pranks.   [Origin uncertain]   **— lark′er** *n.*   **— lark′some** *adj.*

lark·spur (lärk′spûr)   *n.*   Any of several showy herbs of the crowfoot family with clusters of white, pink, blue, or red flowers.

lar·ri·gan (lar′ə·gən)   *n.*   *Canadian* A high moccasin, worn by lumbermen, trappers, etc.   [Origin unknown]

lar·rup (lar′əp)   *Informal v.t.* To beat; thrash.   *— n.* A blow.   [< dial. E, ? < Du. *larpen* to thrash]

lar·va (lär′və)   *n.*   *pl.* **·vae** (-vē)   **1.** *Entomol.* The first stage of an insect after leaving the egg, as the maggot.   **2.** *Zool.* The immature form of any animal that must undergo metamorphosis.   [< L, ghost, mask]   **— lar′val** *adj.*

la·ryn·ge·al (lə·rin′jē·əl, -jəl)   *adj.* Of, pertaining to, or near the larynx.   Also **la·ryn·gal** (lə·ring′gəl).   [< NL < Gk. *larynx, laryngos* larynx]

lar·yn·gi·tis (lar′ən·jī′tis)   *n.* *Pathol.* Inflammation of the larynx.   **— lar′yn·git′ic** (-jit′ik) *adj.*

laryngo-   *combining form*   The larynx; pertaining to the larynx.   Also, before vowels, **laryng-.**   [< Gk. *larynx, laryngos* larynx]

la·ryn·go·scope (lə·ring′gə·skōp)   *n.*   An instrument for examining the larynx.   **— la·ryn′go·scop′ic** (-skop′ik) *adj.*   **— lar′yn·gos′co·py** (-gos′kə·pē) *n.*

lar·ynx (lar′ingks)   *n. pl.* **la·ryn·ges** (lə·rin′jēz) or **lar·ynx·es**   *Anat.* An organ of the respiratory tract situated at the upper part of the trachea, and consisting of a cartilaginous box containing the valvelike vocal cords. See illus. at LUNG.   [< NL < Gk. *larynx* larynx]

la·sa·gna (lə·zän′yə)   *n.* Broad, flat noodles, often served baked in a meat and tomato sauce. Also **la·sa′gne.** [< Ital.]

las·civ·i·ous (lə·siv′ē·əs)   *adj.* Having, manifesting, or arousing sensual desires; lustful.   [< L *lascivus* lustful]   **— las·civ′i·ous·ly** *adv.*   **— las·civ′i·ous·ness** *n.*

la·ser (lā′zər)   *n.*   *Physics* A maser that can generate or amplify light waves: also called *optical maser*.   [< *l(ight) a(mplification by) s(timulated) e(mission of) r(adiation)*]

lash¹ (lash)   *n.*   **1.** A whip or scourge.   **2.** A single whip stroke.   **3.** Anything that wounds the feelings.   **4.** An eyelash.   *— v.t.*   **1.** To strike, punish, or command with or as with a whip; flog.   **2.** To switch spasmodically: The lion *lashes* his tail.   **3.** To beat or dash against violently.   **4.** To assail sharply in speech or writing.   **5.** To incite.   *— v.i.*   **6.** To deliver a whip stroke or strokes.   **7.** To switch or wriggle rapidly.   **— to lash out   1.** To hit out suddenly and violently.   **2.** To break into angry verbal abuse.   [< Prob. fusion of MLG *lasch* flap and OF *laz* cord]   **— lash′er** *n.*

lash² (lash)   *v.t.* To bind or tie with rope or cord.   [< OF < L *laqueus* noose]   **— lash′er** *n.*

lash·ing¹ (lash′ing)   *n.*   **1.** The act of one who or that which lashes.   **2.** A flogging; whipping.   **3.** A berating; scolding.

lash·ing² (lash′ing)   *n.* The act of lashing with a rope, etc.; also, the rope.

lass (las)   *n.*   **1.** A young woman; girl.   **2.** A sweetheart.   **3.** *Scot.* A servant girl; maid.   [< Scand.]

las·sie (las′ē)   *n.* A little girl; lass.   [Dim. of LASS]

las·si·tude (las′ə·tōōd, -tyōōd)   *n.* A state of weariness or fatigue; languor.   [< F < L *lassus* faint]

las·so (las′ō)   *n.*   *pl.* **·sos** or **·soes**   A long rope with a running noose, used for catching horses, etc.   *— v.t.* To catch with a lasso.   [< Sp. < L *laqueus* snare]   **— las′so·er** *n.*

last¹ (last, läst)   *adj.*   **1.** Coming after all others; final in order, sequence, or time: the *last* page.   **2.** Being the only one remaining: his *last* dime.   **3.** Most recent: *last* year.   **4.** Least probable or suitable: the *last* man for the job.   **5.** Newest; most fashionable.   **6.** Conclusive; final: the *last* word.   **7.** *Rare* Least: the *last* of nations.   **8.** *Rare* Ultimate; utmost: to the *last* degree.   *— adv.*   **1.** After all others in time or order.   **2.** At a time next preceding the present: He was *last* seen going west.   **3.** In conclusion; finally.   *— n.*

1. The end; final part or portion. **2.** The final appearance, experience, or mention: We'll never hear the *last* of this. **— at last** At length; finally. [OE *latost,* superl. of *læt* slow]

last² (last, läst) *v.i.* **1.** To remain in existence; continue to be; endure. **2.** To continue unimpaired or unaltered. **3.** To hold out: Will our supplies *last*? [OE *læstan,* to follow a track, continue, accomplish] **— last′er** *n.*

last³ (last, läst) *n.* A shaped form, usu. of wood, on which to make a shoe or boot. **—** *v.t.* To fit to or form on a last. **— to stick to one's last** To attend to one's own business. [OE *læste, läst* footstep, track] **— last′er** *n.*

Las·tex (las′teks) *n.* Rubber manufactured in fine strands and wound with rayon, cotton, silk, or wool: a trade name. Also **las′tex.** [< (E)LAS(TIC) + TEX(TILE)]

last·ing (las′ting, läs′-) *adj.* Continuing; durable; permanent. **—** *n.* Endurance; continuance. [< LAST²] **— last′ing·ly** *adv.* **— last′ing·ness** *n.*

Last Judgment *Theol.* **a** The final trial and sentencing by God of all mankind. **b** The time of this.

last·ly (last′lē, läst′-) *adv.* In the last place; in conclusion.

last rites *Eccl.* Sacraments administered to persons in peril of death.

Last Supper The last meal of Jesus Christ and his disciples before the Crucifixion: also called *Lord's Supper.*

last word 1. The final and most authoritative utterance. **2.** *Informal* The most fashionable thing.

latch (lach) *n.* **1.** A fastening for a door or gate, usu. a movable bar that falls or slides into a notch. **2.** Any similar fastening. **— Syn.** See LOCK¹. **—** *v.t. & v.i.* To fasten by means of a latch; close. **— to latch on to** *U.S. Slang* To obtain, esp. something desirable. [OE *laeccean* to seize]

latch·key (lach′kē′) *n.* A key for releasing a latch.

latch·string (lach′string′) *n.* A string on the outside of a door, used for lifting the latch.

late (lāt) *adj.* **lat·er** or **lat·ter, lat·est** or **last 1.** Appearing or coming after the expected time; tardy. **2.** Occurring at an unusually advanced time: a *late* hour. **3.** Beginning at or continuing to an advanced hour. **4.** Recent or comparatively recent: the *late* war. **5.** Deceased: the *late* king. **—** *adv.* **1.** After the expected time; tardily. **2.** At or until an advanced time of the day, month, year, etc. **3.** *Archaic* Recently. **— of late** Recently. [OE *læt*] **— late′ness** *n.*

la·teen (la·tēn′) *adj. Naut.* Designating a rig common in the Mediterranean, having a triangular sail (**lateen sail**) suspended from a long yard set obliquely to the mast. [< F *(voile) latine* Latin (sail)]

la·tent (lā′tənt) *adj.* Not visible or apparent, but capable of developing or being expressed; dormant. [< L *latere* to be hidden] **— la′ten·cy** *n.* **— la′tent·ly** *adv.*

lat·er (lā′tər) *adv.* At a subsequent time; after some time.

lat·er·al (lat′ər·əl) *adj.* Pertaining to the side or sides; situated at, occurring, or coming from the side. **—** *n.* **1.** Something occurring at or on the side. **2.** In football, a lateral pass. [< L *latus, lateris* side] **— lat′er·al·ly** *adv.*

lateral pass In football, a pass that travels across the field or toward the passer's goal line, rather than forward.

Lat·er·an (lat′ər·ən) **1.** The basilica of St. John Lateran, the cathedral church of the pope as bishop of Rome. **2.** The adjoining palace. [< name of a Roman family]

la·tes·cent (lə·tes′ənt) *adj.* Becoming obscure, latent, or hidden. [< L *latere* to be hidden] **— la·tes′cence** *n.*

la·tex (lā′teks) *n. pl.* **lat·i·ces** (lat′ə·sēz) or **la·tex·es** The sticky emulsion secreted by certain plants, as the rubber tree, milkweed, etc., that coagulates on exposure to air and is the basis of natural rubber. [< L, liquid]

lath (lath, läth) *n.* **1.** Any of a number of thin strips of wood, etc., nailed to studs or joists to support a coat of plaster, or on rafters to support shingles or slates. **2.** Other similar materials used to support plaster, tiles, etc. **3.** Laths collectively: also **lath′work′** (-wûrk′). **—** *v.t.* To cover or line with laths. [Prob. fusion of OE *laett* and OE *laethth* (assumed)] **— lath′er** *n.*

lathe (lāth) *n.* A machine that holds and spins pieces of wood, metal, plastic, etc., so that they are cut and shaped when the operator holds cutting tools against them. **—** *v.t.* **lathed, lath·ing** To form on a lathe. [< MDu. *lade*]

lath·er (lath′ər) *n.* **1.** The suds or foam formed by soap or detergents and water. **2.** The foam of profuse sweating, as of a horse. **— in a lather** *U.S. Slang* In a state of intense excitement or agitation. **—** *v.t.* **1.** To cover with lather. **2.** *Informal* To flog; thrash. **—** *v.i.* **3.** To form lather. **4.** To become covered with lather, as a horse. [OE *lēathor* washing soda, soap] **— lath′er·er** *n.* **— lath′er·y** *adj.*

lath·ing (lath′ing, läth′-) *n.* **1.** The act or process of covering with laths. **2.** Laths collectively.

lat·i·ces (lat′ə·sēz) Plural of LATEX.

Lat·in (lat′n) *adj.* **1.** Pertaining to ancient Latium, its inhabitants, culture, or language. **2.** Pertaining to or denot-

ing the peoples or countries of France, Italy, and Spain. **3.** Of or belonging to the Western or Roman Catholic Church. **—** *n.* **1.** The Indo-European, Italic language of ancient Latium and Rome, extensively used in western Europe until modern times as the language of learning, and still the official language of the Roman Catholic Church. **2.** A member of one of the modern Latin peoples. **3.** A member of the Western or Roman Catholic Church. **4.** One of the people of ancient Latium. **— Old Latin** The language before the first century B.C., as preserved in inscriptions and the comedies of Plautus. **— Classical Latin** The literary and rhetorical language of the period 80 B.C. to A.D. 200. **— Late Latin** The language from 200–600. **— Low Latin** The language of any period after the classical, such as Medieval Latin. **— Medieval Latin** The language used by the writers of the Middle Ages, from 600–1500: also called *Middle Latin.* **— New** (or **Neo-**) **Latin** A form of the language based on Latin and Greek elements, now used chiefly for scientific and taxonomic terms. **— Vulgar Latin** The popular speech of the Romans from about A.D. 200 through the medieval period. [< L *Latinus* Latin]

Latin America The countries of the western hemisphere south of the Rio Grande, in which the official languages are derived from Latin. See SPANISH AMERICA. **— Lat·in-A·mer·i·can** (lat′n·ə·mer′ə·kən) *adj.* **— Latin American**

Lat·in·ate (lat′ən·āt) *adj.* Of, like, or from Latin.

Latin Church The Roman Catholic Church.

Latin cross A cross in which the upright is longer than the beam that crosses it near the top.

Lat·in·ism (lat′ən·iz′əm) *n.* An idiom in another language taken from or imitating Latin.

Lat·in·ist (lat′ən·ist) *n.* One versed or learned in Latin.

Lat·in·ize (lat′ən·īz) *v.* **·ized, ·iz·ing** *v.t.* **1.** To translate into Latin. **2.** To make Latin in customs, thought, etc. **—** *v.i.* **3.** To use Latin words, forms, etc. **— Lat·in·i·za′-tion** *n.* **— Lat′in·iz′er** *n.*

Latin Quarter A section of Paris on the south bank of the Seine, known for its many artists and students.

lat·i·tude (lat′ə·tood, -tyood) *n.* **1.** *Geog.* Angular distance on the earth's surface northward or southward of the equator, measured in degrees along a meridian. **2.** *Often pl.* A region or place considered with reference to its distance from the equator. **3.** Freedom from narrow restrictions. **4.** *Astron.* The angular distance of a heavenly body from the ecliptic (**celestial latitude**). [< L *latitudo* breadth]

lat·i·tu·din·al (lat′ə·tood′də·nəl, -tyood′-) *adj.* Of or pertaining to latitude. **— lat′i·tu′di·nal·ly** *adv.*

lat·i·tu·di·nar·i·an (lat′ə·tood′də·nâr′ē·ən, -tyood′-) *adj.* Characterized by or tolerant of liberal or unorthodox attitudes, beliefs, etc., esp. in matters of religion. **—** *n.* One who is latitudinarian. **— lat′i·tu′di·nar′i·an·ism** *n.*

La·ti·um (lā′shē·əm) An ancient country in central Italy.

la·trine (lə·trēn′) *n.* A public toilet, as in a camp, barracks, etc. [< F < L *latrina* bath, privy]

-latry *combining form* Worship of; excessive devotion to. [< Gk. *latreia* worship]

lat·ter (lat′ər) *adj.* **1.** Being the second of two persons or things referred to: often preceded by *the:* The *latter* statement is truer than the former. **2.** Later or nearer to the end: His *latter* years were happy. [OE *lætra,* compar. of *læt* late]

lat·ter-day (lat′ər-dā′) *adj.* Modern: a *latter-day* martyr.

Latter-day Saint A Mormon.

lat·ter·ly (lat′ər·lē) *adv.* **1.** Recently; lately. **2.** At a later time; toward the end.

lat·tice (lat′is) *n.* **1.** A structure consisting of strips of metal, wood, etc., crossed or interlaced to form regularly spaced openings. **2.** A window, screen, gate, etc., made from or consisting of such a structure. **—** *v.t.* **·ticed, ·tic·ing 1.** To furnish or enclose with a lattice. **2.** To form into or arrange like a lattice. [< OF *latte* lath]

lat·tice·work (lat′is·wûrk′) *n.* Openwork made from or resembling a lattice. Also **lat′-tic·ing.**

LATTICE

Lat·vi·an (lat′vē·ən) *adj.* Of or pertaining to Latvia, its people, or their language; Lettish. **—** *n.* **1.** A native or inhabitant of Latvia; a Lett. **2.** The Lettish language.

laud (lôd) *v.t.* To praise highly; extol. **— Syn.** See PRAISE. **—** *n. pl. Eccl.* The prescribed prayers immediately following matins, the two offices together constituting the first of the seven canonical hours. [< OF < L *laus, laudis* praise]

laud·a·ble (lô′də·bəl) *adj.* Deserving approbation. **— laud′-a·bil′i·ty, laud′a·ble·ness** *n.* **— laud′a·bly** *adv.*

lau·da·num (lô′də·nəm) *n.* **1.** Tincture of opium. **2.** Formerly, any opium preparation. [< NL < L *ladanum*]

laud·a·tion (lô·dā′shən) *n.* The act of lauding; praise.

laud·a·to·ry (lô′də·tôr′ē, -tō′rē) *adj.* Expressing or containing praise; complimentary. Also **laud′a·tive.**

laugh (laf, läf) *v.i.* **1.** To produce the characteristic physical manifestations expressive of merriment, elation, etc. **2.** To express or experience amusement, satisfaction, etc. — *v.t.* **3.** To express or utter with laughter. **4.** To induce, persuade, or bring about by or as by laughing: I *laughed* myself sick. — **to laugh at 1.** To express amusement at. **2.** To ridicule; mock. **3.** To make light of. — **to laugh away** To dispel or minimize with laughter. — **to laugh off** To rid one's self of or dismiss laughingly. — **to laugh up (or in) one's sleeve** To be covertly amused or exultant. — *n.* **1.** An act or sound of laughing. **2.** *Informal* A cause for provocation to laughter. — **to have the last laugh** To triumph or succeed after seeming at a disadvantage. [OE *hliehhan, hlæhhan*] — **laugh′er** *n.*

laugh·a·ble (laf′ə-bəl, läf′-) *adj.* Provoking laughter; amusing. — **laugh′a·ble·ness** *n.* — **laugh′a·bly** *adv.*

laugh·ing (laf′ing, läf′-) *adj.* **1.** Like or expressing laughter. **2.** Causing laughter. — *n.* Laughter. — **laugh′ing·ly** *adv.*

laughing gas Nitrous oxide.

laugh·ing·stock (laf′ing-stok′, läf′-) *n.* One who or that which provokes ridicule; a butt.

laugh·ter (laf′tər, läf′-) *n.* **1.** The sound, expression, or action of laughing. **2.** A cause of laughing.

Laun·ce·lot (lôn′sə-lot, län′-) See LANCELOT.

launch[1] (lônch, länch) *v.t.* **1.** To move or push (a vessel, etc.) into the water, esp. for the first time. **2.** To set in flight or motion, as a rocket, missile, etc. **3.** To start (a person, etc.) on a career or course of action. **4.** To initiate; open: to *launch* a campaign. **5.** To hurl; fling. — *v.i.* **6.** To make a beginning; start: usu. with *out* or *forth.* **7.** To begin (an action, speech, etc.) vehemently or impetuously: usu. with *into.* — *n.* The action of launching a vessel, missile, etc. [< AF *lancher* to launch] — **launch′er** *n.*

launch[2] (lônch, länch) *n.* **1.** An open or half-decked motor boat. **2.** Formerly, the largest of the boats carried by a ship. [< Sp. < Malay *lanca* three-masted boat]

launching pad *Aerospace* The platform from which a rocket or guided missile is fired. Also **launch pad.**

laun·der (lôn′dər, län′-) *v.t.* **1.** To wash (clothing, linens, etc.). **2.** To wash and prepare for use by or as by ironing. — *v.i.* **3.** To do the work of washing and ironing. **4.** To undergo washing: Nylon *launders* easily. [< OF < LL *lavare* to wash] — **laun′der·er** *n.*

laun·dress (lôn′dris, län′-) *n.* A woman paid or employed to do laundry; washerwoman.

laun·dro·mat (lôn′drə·mat, län′-) *n.* *U.S.* A place where laundry is washed and dried in coin-operated automatic machines. [< *Laundromat,* a trade name]

laun·dry (lôn′drē, län′-) *n.* *pl.* **·dries 1.** A room, commercial establishment, etc., where laundering is done. **2.** Articles to be laundered. **3.** The work of laundering.

laun·dry·man (lôn′drē-mən, län′-) *n.* *pl.* **·men** (-mən) **1.** A man who works in or manages a commercial laundry. **2.** A man who calls for and delivers laundry.

laun·dry·wom·an (lôn′drē-wŏom′ən, län′-) *n.* *pl.* **·wom·en,** (-wim′ən) A laundress.

lau·re·ate (lô′rē·it; *v.* -āt) *adj.* **1.** Singled out for special honor. **2.** Crowned or decked with laurel as a mark of honor. — *n.* **1.** A person honored with a prize or award. **2.** A poet laureate (which see). — *v.t.* **·at·ed, ·at·ing 1.** To crown with or as with laurel. **2.** To confer the title of poet laureate upon. [< L *laureatus* crowned with laurel]

lau·rel (lôr′əl, lor′-) *n.* **1.** An evergreen tree or shrub typifying a family that includes cinnamon, sassafras, etc. **2.** Any of various similar trees and shrubs. **3.** *Often pl.* A crown or wreath of laurel leaves, conferred as a symbol of honor, achievement, etc. **4.** *pl.* Honor or distinction gained by outstanding achievement. — **to look to one's laurels** To be on guard against losing a position of eminence, honor, etc. — **to rest on one's laurels** To be content with what one has already achieved. — *v.t.* **lau·reled** or **·relled, lau·rel·ing** or **·rel·ling 1.** To honor by or as by crowning with laurel. **2.** To adorn with laurel. [< OF < L *laurus*]

la·va (lä′və, lav′ə) *n.* **1.** Molten rock that issues from an active volcano or through a fissure in the earth's crust. **2.** Rock formed by the solidifying of this substance. [< Ital., orig., a stream formed by rain < *lavare* to wash]

lav·a·liere (lav′ə-lir′) *n.* An ornamental pendant worn on a thin chain around the neck. Also **lav′a·lier′,** *French* **la·val·lière** (là·và·lyâr′). [< F *la vallière* a type of necktie, ? after Louise de *La Vallière,* 1644–1710, mistress of Louis XIV]

lav·a·to·ry (lav′ə-tôr′ē, -tō′rē) *n.* *pl.* **·ries 1.** A room equipped with washing and usu. toilet facilities. **2.** A basin, sink, etc., used for washing. [< LL < L *lavare* to wash]

lav·en·der (lav′ən-dər) *n.* **1.** An Old World plant of the mint family, having spikes of fragrant, pale violet flowers; esp., the **true lavender,** of which the dried flowers and aromatic oil (**oil of lavender**) are much used in perfumery. **2.** The dried flowers and foliage of this plant, used to scent linen, clothing, etc. **3.** A pale, reddish violet color. — *adj.*

Pale reddish violet. — *v.t.* To perfume with lavender. [< AF < Med.L, ? < L *lividus* blue]

la·ver (lā′vər) *n.* In the ancient Jewish Temple, a large ceremonial vessel for washing. [< OF < LL *lavatorium*]

lav·ish (lav′ish) *adj.* **1.** Generous and unrestrained in giving, spending, etc.; prodigal. **2.** Provided or expended in great abundance. — *v.t.* To give or bestow generously. [< OF *lavasse, lavacho* downpour of rain] — **lav′ish·er** *n.* — **lav′ish·ly** *adv.* — **lav′ish·ness** *n.*

law (lô) *n.* **1.** A rule of conduct, recognized by custom or decreed by formal enactment, considered as binding on the members of a community, nation, etc. **2.** A system or body of such rules. **3.** The condition of society when such rules are observed: to establish *law* and order. **4.** The body of authoritatively established rules relating to a specified subject or activity: criminal *law.* **5.** Remedial justice as administered by legal authorities: to resort to the *law.* **6.** The branch of knowledge concerned with jurisprudence. **7.** The vocation of an attorney, etc.; the legal profession. **8.** The rules and principles of common law and statute law, as distinguished from equity. **9.** An authoritative rule or command: His will is *law.* **10.** *Often cap.* Divine will, command, or precept; also, a body of rules having such divine origin. **11.** Any generally accepted rule, procedure, or principle governing a specified area of conduct, body of knowledge, etc. **12.** In science and philosophy, a formal statement of the manner or order in which a set of natural phenomena occur under certain conditions. **13.** *Math.* A rule or formula governing a function or operation. — **the law. 1.** The legal authorities; the police. **2.** *Informal* A policeman. — **the Law 1.** The Mosaic Law. **2.** The Torah. — **to go to law** To engage in litigation. — **to lay down the law** To utter one's wishes, instructions, etc., in an authoritative manner. [OE < ON *lag* something laid or fixed, in pl., law]

law·a·bid·ing (lô′ə·bī′ding) *adj.* Obedient to the law.

law·break·er (lô′brā′kər) *n.* One who violates the law. — **law′break′ing** *n. & adj.*

law·ful (lô′fəl) *adj.* **1.** Permitted by law. **2.** Recognized by the law: *lawful* debts. **3.** Valid, authentic, etc., according to law: *lawful* marriage. — **law′ful·ly** *adv.* — **law′ful·ness** *n.*

law·giv·er (lô′giv′ər) *n.* One who originates or institutes a law or system of laws. — **law′giv′ing** *n. & adj.*

law·less (lô′lis) *adj.* **1.** Not controlled by law, authority, discipline, etc. **2.** Contrary to law. — **law′less·ly** *adv.* — **law′less·ness** *n.*

law·mak·er (lô′mā′kər) *n.* One who enacts or helps to enact laws; a legislator. — **law′mak′ing** *n. & adj.*

lawn[1] (lôn) *n.* A stretch of grassy land; esp., an area of closely mown grass near a house, in a park, etc. [*Obs. laund* < OF *launde* heath] — **lawn′y** *adj.*

lawn[2] (lôn) *n.* A fine, thin linen or cotton fabric. [after *Laon,* France, where it was formerly made] — **lawn′y** *adj.*

lawn mower A machine operated by a motor or propelled by hand, used to cut the grass of lawns.

Law of Moses The Mosaic Law.

law·ren·ci·um (lô-ren′sē·əm) *n.* A very short-lived radioactive element (symbol Lw), originally produced by bombarding californium with the nuclei of a boron isotope. See ELEMENT. [after E. O. *Lawrence,* 1901–58, U.S. physicist]

law·suit (lô′sōōt′) *n.* A case, action, or proceeding brought to a court of law for settlement.

law·yer (lô′yər) *n.* A member of any branch of the legal profession; esp., one who advises and acts for clients or pleads in court.

lax (laks) *adj.* **1.** Lacking strictness or disciplinary control. **2.** Lacking precision; vague. **3.** Lacking firmness or rigidity. [< L *laxus* loose] — **lax′ly** *adv.* — **lax′ness** *n.*

lax·a·tive (lak′sə-tiv) *n.* A medicine taken to produce evacuation of the bowels. — *adj.* **1.** Loosening or producing evacuation of the bowels. **2.** Characterized by or having loose bowel movements. [< F, fem. of *laxatif*]

lax·i·ty (lak′sə-tē) *n.* The state or quality of being lax.

lay[1] (lā) *v.* **laid, lay·ing 1.** To cause to lie; deposit; esp., to place in a horizontal, reclining, or low position. **2.** To put or place; esp., to cause to be in a specified place or condition. **3.** To construct or establish as a basis or support: to *lay* the groundwork. **4.** To place or arrange in proper position: to *lay* bricks. **5.** To produce internally and deposit (an egg or eggs). **6.** To think out; devise: to *lay* plans. **7.** To attribute or ascribe: to *lay* the blame. **8.** To impose as a penalty, obligation, etc.: to *lay* a fine. **9.** To set forth; present: to *lay* one's claim before a court. **10.** To cause to fall; knock down. **11.** To cause to settle, subside, or lie level: to *lay* the dust. **12.** To render ineffective; quell, as a rumor. **13.** To bury, as in a grave; inter. **14.** To apply in or as in a layer; spread, as paint. **15.** To set or prepare (a trap, etc.). **16.** To prepare (a table, etc.) for use by setting out the necessary equipment. **17.** To set or locate (a scene, action, etc.). **18.** To strike or inflict blows

with. **19.** To offer or stake as a bet. **20.** To twist strands so as to produce (rope, cable, etc.). — *v.i.* **21.** To produce and deposit eggs. **22.** To make a bet or bets. **23.** *Naut.* To move to a specified place or position: to *lay* aloft. **— to lay away 1.** To store up; save. **2.** To bury in or as in a grave. **— to lay down 1.** To place or put aside, in a low position. etc. **2.** To give up; sacrifice: to *lay down* one's life. **3.** To state authoritatively or dogmatically: to *lay down* the rules. **4.** To bet. **— to lay for** *U.S. Informal* To await an opportunity to attack or harm (someone). — to **lay in** To procure and store. **— to lay into** To attack vigorously. **— to lay it on** *Informal* To be extravagant, lavish, or exorbitant, esp. in praise or flattery. **— to lay low 1.** To strike down; prostrate. **2.** *U.S. Slang* To go into hiding. **— to lay off 1.** To mark out; plan. **2.** *U.S.* To dismiss from a job, usu. temporarily. **3.** *U.S. Informal* To stop working; take a rest. **4.** *U.S. Slang* To stop or cease. — **to lay out 1.** To arrange or display for use, inspection, etc. **2.** To arrange according to a plan; map. **3.** To spend or supply (a sum of money). **4.** To prepare (a corpse) for burial. **5.** *Informal* To strike down; prostrate. **— to lay over 1.** To overlay. **2.** *U.S. Informal* To stop for a time in the course of a journey. **— to lay to 1.** To work vigorously at. **2.** *Naut.* To maintain a vessel facing into the wind in a stationary or nearly stationary position. **— to lay up 1.** To make a store of. **2.** To incapacitate or confine, as by illness, injury, etc. — *n.* The manner in which something lies or is placed. [OE pt. of *licyan* to lie, recline]
◆ **lay, lie** Formal writing demands a distinction between these two words. *Lay* takes an object: We *lay* the papers on his desk every morning. *Lie*, meaning recline or be situated, does not take an object: The papers *lie* on the desk. The past tenses of these verbs are particularly liable to misuse and should be handled carefully: We *laid* the papers on his desk, and they *lay* there until he arrived.
lay² (lā) *adj.* **1.** Of or belonging to the laity; secular. **2.** Not belonging to or learned a learned profession: a *lay* opinion. [< OF < Med.L < Gk. *laos* the people]
lay³ (lā) Past tense of LIE¹.
lay⁴ (lā) *n.* **1.** A song, ballad, or narrative poem. **2.** A melody. [< OF *lai*]
lay·er (lā′ər) *n.* **1.** A single thickness, coating, covering, etc. **2.** One who or that which lays; esp., a hen considered as an egg producer. **3.** A shoot or twig constituting part of a growing plant, of which a part is placed in the ground for rooting. — *v.t. & v.i.* **1.** To form a layer or layers. **2.** To propagate (a plant) by means of a layer or layers.
layer cake A cake, usu. frosted, made in layers having a sweetened filling between them.
lay·ette (lā′et′) *n.* The supply of clothing, bedding, etc., provided for a newborn infant. [< F, dim. of *laie* packing box, drawer < Flemish < MDu. *lade* chest, trunk]
lay·man (lā′mən) *n. pl.* **·men** (mən) **1.** One without training or skill in a profession or branch of knowledge. **2.** A man belonging to the laity, as distinguished from the clergy.
lay·off (lā′ôf′, -of′) *n. U.S.* **1.** The temporary dismissal of employees. **2.** A period of enforced unemployment.
lay·out (lā′out′) *n.* **1.** A planned arrangement, as: **a** The relative positions of streets, rooms, etc. **b** Written matter, illustrations, etc., arranged for printing. **2.** That which is laid out or provided, as equipment.
lay·o·ver (lā′ō′vər) *n.* A break in a journey; a stopover.
la·zar (lā′zər, laz′ər) *n. Archaic* A beggar or pauper afflicted with a loathsome disease; esp., a leper. [< Med.L *lazarus*, after *Lazarus* (*Luke* xvi 20)]
laz·a·ret·to (laz′ə·ret′ō) *n. pl.* **·tos 1.** A hospital for the treatment of contagious diseases, as leprosy. Also **lazar house. 2.** A ship or building used as a place of quarantine. **3.** *Naut.* A storage space between decks in the stern of a vessel: also **laz·a·ret′**, **laz·a·rette′** (-ret′) [< Ital. dial. (Venetian) *lazareto*, *nazareto* (Santa Madonna di) *Nazaret*, Venetian church formerly used as a hospital]
Laz·a·rus (laz′ə·rəs) In the New Testament: **a** A brother of Martha and Mary, raised from the dead by Christ. *John* xi 1. **b** A sick beggar in the parable of the rich and the poor man. *Luke* xvi 20.
laze (lāz) *v.* **lazed**, **laz·ing** *v.i.* **1.** To be lazy; loaf; idle. — *v.t.* **2.** To pass (time) in idleness. [< LAZY]
laz·u·rite (laz′yŏō·rīt) *n.* A deep blue silicate of sodium and aluminum containing sulfur, the principal constituent of lapis lazuli. [< Med.L *lazur* azure]
la·zy (lā′zē) *adj.* **·zi·er**, **·zi·est 1.** Unwilling to work or engage in energetic activity; slothful. **2.** Moving or acting slowly or heavily. **3.** Characterized by idleness or languor. [Prob. < MLG *lasich* loose, feeble] — **la′zi·ly** *adv.* — **la′zi·ness** *n.*
la·zy·bones (lā′zē·bōnz′) *n. pl.* **·bones** *Informal* A lazy person.

Lazy Susan A revolving tray, often divided into compartments, used to hold condiments, etc. Also **lazy Susan.**
lea (lē) *n. Chiefly Poetic* A grassy field or tract; meadow. [OE *lēah*, orig., open ground in a wood]
leach (lēch) *v.t.* **1.** To cause (a liquid) to percolate or filter through something. **2.** To subject to the filtering action of a liquid. **3.** To remove or dissolve by or as by filtering. — *v.i.* **4.** To be removed or dissolved by percolation or filtration. — *n.* **1.** The process of leaching. **2.** A solution obtained from leaching. [OE *leccan* to wet, irrigate] — **leach′er** *n.*
lead¹ (lēd) *v.* **led**, **lead·ing** *v.t.* **1.** To go with or ahead of so as to show the way; guide. **2.** To cause to progress by or as by pulling or holding: to *lead* a child by the hand. **3.** To serve as or indicate a route for: The path *led* him to the hut. **4.** To control the actions or affairs of; direct. **5.** To influence the ideas, conduct, or actions of. **6.** To be first among. **7.** To be the principal participant in: to *lead* a discussion. **8.** To conduct the performance of (musicians or music). **9.** To experience or live; also, to cause to experience or go through: to *lead* a merry life; They *led* him a wild chase. **10.** To direct or effect the course of (water, conduits, cable, etc.). **11.** In card games, to begin a round by playing (a specified card). — *v.i.* **12.** To act as guide; conduct. **13.** To be led; yield readily to being pulled or guided. **14.** To afford a way or passage: The road *leads* through a swamp. **15.** To be conducive; tend: followed by *to*: Delinquency *leads* to crime. **16.** To have control or command. **17.** To be first or in advance. **18.** In card games, to make the first play. **— to lead off 1.** To make a start; begin. **2.** In baseball, to be the first batter in a line-up or inning. **— to lead on 1.** To entice or tempt, esp. to wrongdoing. **2.** To go first or in advance. — *n.* **1.** Position in advance or at the head. **2.** The distance or interval by which someone or something leads. **3.** Position of primary importance, responsibility, etc. **4.** Guidance; leadership; example: Follow his *lead.* **5.** Indication; clue: Give me a *lead.* **6.** In dramatic presentations: **a** A starring role. **b** A performer having such a role. **7.** In journalism, the introductory portion or paragraph of a news story. **8.** In card games: **a** The right or obligation to play first in a game or round. **b** The card, suit, etc., thus played. **9.** In baseball, a position taken by a runner part of the way between the base he has attained and the next base. **10.** *Electr.* A short wire or conductor, used as a connection to a source of current. **11.** A cord, leash etc., for leading an animal. [OE *lǣden* to cause to go]
lead² (led) *n.* **1.** A soft, heavy, malleable, dull gray metallic element (symbol Pb), occurring most commonly in the sulfide mineral galena. See ELEMENT. **2.** Any of various objects made of lead or similar metal; esp., a weight suspended from a line, used in sounding, etc. **3.** Graphite, esp. in the form of thin rods, used as the writing material in pencils. **4.** Bullets, shot, etc. **5.** White lead. **6.** *Printing* A thin strip of type metal used to provide space between printed lines. — *v.t.* **1.** To cover, weight, fasten, treat, or fill with lead. **2.** *Printing* To separate or space (lines of type) with leads. [OE *lead*]
lead·en (led′n) *adj.* **1.** Dull gray, as lead. **2.** Made of lead. **3.** Weighty; inert: a *leaden* mass. **4.** Heavy or labored in movement, etc., sluggish. **5.** Oppressive; gloomy. — **lead′·en·ly** *adv.* — **lead′en·ness** *n.*
lead·er (lē′dər) *n.* **1.** One who or that which goes ahead or in advance. **2.** One who acts as a guiding force, commander, etc. **3.** An article of merchandise offered at a special low price to attract customers. **4.** A pipe for draining a liquid, as rainwater. **5.** In fishing, a length of gut, etc., used for attaching a hook or lure to the line. **6.** *pl. Printing* Dots or hyphens in a horizontal row, serving to guide the eye across a page, column, etc.
lead·er·ship (lē′dər·ship′) *n.* **1.** The office, position, or capacity of a leader; guidance. **2.** Ability to lead, exert authority, etc. **3.** A group of leaders.
lead-in (lēd′in′) *n. Telecom.* A wire connecting a radio receiving set with its antenna.
lead·ing¹ (lē′ding) *adj.* **1.** Having the capacity or effect of controlling, influencing, guiding, etc. **2.** Most important; chief. **3.** Situated or going at the head; first. — *n.* The act of one who or that which leads; guidance.
lead·ing² (led′ing) *n.* **1.** The act or process of filling, covering, or separating with lead. **2.** A border of lead. **3.** *Printing* Spacing between lines.
leading question (lē′ding) A question having the intention or effect of eliciting the reply desired by the questioner.
lead-off (lēd′ôf′, -of′) *n.* **1.** A beginning action, move, etc., as the opening play in a competitive game. **2.** A player or participant who begins the action in a game or competition.
lead pencil (led) A pencil having a thin stick of graphite as its writing material.

PRONUNCIATION KEY: add, āce, câre, pälm; end, ēven; it, īce; odd, ōpen, ôrder; tŏŏk, pōōl; up, bûrn; ə = a in *above*, e in *sicken*, i in *flexible*, o in *melon*, u in *focus*; yōō = u in *fuse*; oil; pout; check; go; ring; thin; this; zh, vision.

lead poisoning (led) *Pathol.* Poisoning caused by the absorption of lead by the tissues.

leaf (lēf) *n. pl.* **leaves** (lēvz) 1. One of the outgrowths from the stem of a plant, commonly flat, thin, and green in color, and functioning as the principal area of photosynthesis. 2. Foliage collectively; leafage. 3. Loosely, a petal. 4. A product, as tobacco, tea, etc., in the form of gathered leaves. 5. One of the sheets of paper in a book, etc., each side being a single page. 6. A flat piece, hinged or otherwise movable, constituting part of a table, gate, etc. 7. Metal in a very thin sheet or plate: gold *leaf.* — **to turn over a new leaf** To begin anew, esp. with the intention of improving one's ways. — *v.i.* To put forth or produce leaves. [OE *lēaf*]

leaf·age (lē′fij) *n.* Leaves collectively; foliage.

leaf·less (lēf′lis) *adj.* Having or bearing no leaves. — **leaf′·less·ness** *n.*

leaf·let (lēf′lit) *n.* 1. One of the divisions of a compound leaf. 2. A small printed sheet or circular, often folded. 3. A little leaf or leaflike part.

leaf·stalk (lēf′stôk) *n.* A petiole (def. 1).

leaf·y (lē′fē) *adj.* **leaf·i·er, leaf·i·est** 1. Bearing, covered with, or characterized by a profusion of leaves. 2. Consisting of or resembling leaves. — **leaf′i·ness** *n.*

league¹ (lēg) *n.* A measure of distance varying from about 2.42 to 4.6 statute miles, but usu. reckoned as approximately 3 miles. [< OF < LL *leuga, leuca* Gaulish mile]

league² (lēg) *n.* 1. An association or confederation of persons, organizations, or states. 2. A compact or covenant binding such a union. 3. An association of athletic teams. — **in league** In close alliance. — *v.t. & v.i.* **leagued, lea·guing** To unite in a league. [< OF < Ital. *legare* to bind]

League of Nations An international organization established in 1920, primarily for the preservation of world peace, and formally dissolved in 1946.

Le·ah (lē′ə) In the Old Testament, Rachel's elder sister, who became the first wife of Jacob. *Gen.* xxix 16.

leak (lēk) *n.* 1. An opening, as a crack, permitting an undesirable escape or entrance of fluid, light, etc. 2. Any condition or agency by which something is let through or escapes: a *leak* in the security system. 3. An act or instance of leaking; leakage. — *v.i.* 1. To let a fluid, etc., pass or escape through a hole, crack, or similar opening. 2. To pass, flow, or escape through a hole, crack, etc. 3. To be divulged despite secrecy: The plans *leaked* out. — *v.t.* 4. To let (a liquid, etc.) escape. 5. To disclose (information, etc.) without authorization. [< ON *leka* to drip]

leak·age (lē′kij) *n.* 1. The act or circumstance of leaking. 2. That which escapes or passes through by leaking.

leak·y (lē′kē) *adj.* **leak·i·er, leak·i·est** Having a leak; permitting leakage. — **leak′i·ness** *n.*

lean¹ (lēn) *v.* **leaned** or **leant** (lent), **lean·ing** *v.i.* 1. To rest or incline for support: usu. with *against* or *on.* 2. To bend or slant from an erect position. 3. To have a tendency, preference, etc.: to *lean* toward conservatism. 4. To depend for support, etc.; rely. — *v.t.* 5. To cause to incline. 6. To place or rest (something) so as to be supported by something else: usu. with *against, on,* or *upon.* — *n.* The act or condition of leaning; slant. [OE *hleonian, hlinian*]

lean² (lēn) *adj.* 1. Not fat or plump; thin; spare. 2. Not containing fat: *lean* meat. 3. Not rich, plentiful, or satisfying; meager. — *n.* Meat or flesh having little or no fat. [OE *hlǣne* thin] — **lean′ly** *adv.* — **lean′ness** *n.*

Le·an·der (lē·an′dər) In Greek legend, the lover of Hero.

lean·ing (lē′ning) *n.* 1. An inclination; tendency; predisposition. 2. The act of one who or that which leans.

lean-to (lēn′tōō′) *n. pl.* **-tos** (-tōōz′) 1. A crude hut of branches, etc., sloping to the ground from a raised support. 2. A shed or extension of a building having a sloping roof and supported by an adjoining wall or structure.

leap (lēp) *v.* **leaped** or **leapt** (lept, lēpt), **leap·ing** *v.i.* 1. To rise or project oneself by a sudden thrust from the ground; jump; spring. 2. To move, react, etc., suddenly or impulsively. 3. To make an abrupt transition: to *leap* to a conclusion. — *v.t.* 4. To traverse by a jump. 5. To cause to jump. — *n.* 1. The act of leaping. 2. The space traversed by leaping. 3. A place from which a leap may be made. 4. An abrupt transition. [OE *hlēapan*] — **leap′er** *n.*

leap·frog (lēp′frog′, -frôg′) *n.* A game in which each player puts his hands on the back of another, who is bending over, and leaps over him in a straddling position.

leap year A year of 366 days, in which a 29th day is added to February. Every year divisible by 4 (as 1964) is a leap year, except those completing a century, which must be divisible by 400 (as 2000).

Lear (lir) Hero of Shakespeare's tragedy *King Lear.*

learn (lûrn) *v.* **learned** or **learnt, learn·ing** *v.t.* 1. To acquire knowledge of or skill in by study, practice, etc. 2. To find out; become aware of. 3. To commit to memory; memorize. 4. To acquire by experience or example. — *v.i.* 5. To gain knowledge or acquire skill. 6. To become informed; know: with *of* or *about.* [OE *leornian*] — **learn′er** *n.*

learn·ed (lûr′nid) *adj.* 1. Having profound or extensive knowledge. 2. Characterized by or devoted to scholarship.

learn·ing (lûr′ning) *n.* 1. Knowledge obtained by study; erudition. 2. The act of acquiring knowledge or skill.

lease (lēs) *n.* 1. A contract for the temporary occupation or use of premises, property, etc., in exchange for payment of rent. 2. The period of such occupation or use. — *v.t.* 1. To grant use of under a lease. 2. To hold under a lease. [< AF, OF < L *laxus* loose] — **leas′a·ble** *adj.*

leash (lēsh) *n.* 1. A thong, cord, etc., by which a dog or other animal is led or restrained. 2. Restraint; control. — *v.t.* To hold or secure by a leash. [< OF < L *laxus* loose]

least (lēst) Alternative superlative of LITTLE. — *adj.* Smallest in degree, value, size, etc.; most insignificant; slightest. — *n.* That which is smallest, slightest, or most insignificant. — **at least** 1. By the lowest possible estimate. 2. At any rate. — **in the least** In the slightest degree; at all. — *adv.* In the lowest or smallest degree. [OE *lǣssa* less]

least·wise (lēst′wīz′) *adv. Informal* At least; at any rate. Also *Dial.* **least′ways** (-wāz′).

leath·er (leth′ər) *n.* 1. Animal skin, usu. with the hair removed, prepared for use by tanning. 2. An article made of leather. — *v.t.* To cover or equip with leather. [OE *lether*]

leath·ern (leth′ərn) *adj. Archaic* 1. Made of leather. 2. Resembling leather; leathery. [OE *lether* leather]

leath·er·neck (leth′ər·nek′) *n. U.S. Slang* A marine.

leath·er·y (leth′ər·ē) *adj.* Resembling leather in texture or appearance; tough. — **leath′er·i·ness** *n.*

leave¹ (lēv) *v.* **left, leav·ing** *v.t.* 1. To go or depart from. 2. To allow to remain behind or in a specified place, condition, etc. 3. To have or cause as an aftermath: Oil *leaves* stains. 4. To cause to be made available in one's absence: *Leave* your name at the desk. 5. To commit for action, etc.; entrust: *Leave* it to me. 6. To terminate one's connection or association with. 7. To abandon; forsake. 8. To have remaining after one's death. 9. To transmit as a legacy; bequeath. 10. To have as a remainder as the result of an arithmetic operation. — *v.i.* 11. To go away; set out. — **to leave alone** 1. To refrain from interfering with, etc. 2. To allow to remain solitary. — **to leave off** To stop; cease. — **to leave out** 1. To omit. 2. To exclude. [OE *lǣfan,* lit., to let remain] — **leav′er** *n.*

◆ **leave, let** *Leave* means to depart or to permit to remain (*He left the room; He left the book on the table*), as distinguished from *let,* which means simply to permit (*Let him stay*). *Let* can be followed by the infinitive without *to; leave* cannot. *Leave it to him to decide* and *Let him decide* are standard, but *Leave him decide* is nonstandard.

leave² (lēv) *n.* 1. Permission to do something. 2. Permission to be absent; esp., **a** Official permission to be absent from duty. **b** The period covered by such permission: also **leave of absence.** 3. Formal farewell: usu. in the phrase **to take (one's) leave.** — **on leave** Absent from work or duty with permission. [OE *lēaf* permission]

leave³ (lēv) *v.i.* **leaved, leav·ing** To put forth leaves; leaf.

leaved (lēvd) *adj.* 1. Having a leaf or leaves. 2. Having or characterized by (a specified kind or number of) leaves.

leav·en (lev′ən) *n.* 1. An agent of fermentation, as yeast, added to dough or batter to produce a light texture. 2. A portion of fermented dough used for this purpose. 3. Any pervasive influence that produces a significant change. Also **leav′en·ing.** — *v.t.* 1. To cause fermentation in. 2. To affect in character; temper. [< OF < L *levare* to raise]

leaves (lēvz) Plural of LEAF.

leave-tak·ing (lēv′tā′king) *n.* An act of departure.

leav·ings (lē′vingz) *n.pl.* Unused portion; remnants.

Leb·a·nese (leb′ə·nēz′, -nēs′) *adj.* Of or pertaining to Lebanon or its people. — *n.* A native or citizen of Lebanon.

Le·bens·raum (lā′bəns·roum′) *n. German* Territory claimed by a nation as necessary for its economic independence or growth; literally, space for living.

lech·er (lech′ər) *n.* A lewd and prurient man. [< OF < OHG *leccōn* to lick]

lech·er·ous (lech′ər·əs) *adj.* Given to lewdness or inciting to lust. — **lech′er·ous·ly** *adv.* — **lech′er·ous·ness** *n.*

lech·er·y (lech′ər·ē) *n. pl.* **·ries** Unconstrained sexual indulgence.

lec·tern (lek′tərn) *n.* 1. A stand on which a speaker, instructor, etc., may place books or papers. 2. In some churches, a reading desk from which certain parts of the service are read. [< OF < LL < L *legere* to read]

lec·ture (lek′chər) *n.* 1. A discourse on a specific subject, delivered to an audience for instruction or information. 2. A formal reproof or lengthy reprimand. — *v.* **·tured, ·tur·ing** *v.i.* 1. To deliver a lecture or lectures. — *v.t.* 2. To deliver a lecture to. 3. To rebuke sternly or at length. [< L *legere* to read] — **lec′tur·er** *n.*

led (led) Past tense and past participle of LEAD¹.

Le·da (lē′də) In Greek mythology, the mother of Clytemnestra, Castor, Pollux, and Helen, of which the latter three were fathered by Zeus in the form of a swan.

ledge (lej) *n.* **1.** A narrow, shelflike projection along the side of a rocky formation. **2.** A shelf or sill projecting from or forming the top of a wall, etc. **3.** An underwater or coastal ridge. **4.** *Mining* A metal-bearing rock stratum; vein. [ME *legge*] — **ledg′y** *adj.*

led·ger (lej′ər) *n.* An account book in which all final entries of business transactions are recorded. [ME *legger*]

ledger line *Music* A short line added above or below the staff: also spelled *leger line.*

lee (lē) *n.* **1.** Shelter or protection, esp. from the wind. **2.** *Chiefly Naut.* **a** The side sheltered from the wind. **b** The direction opposite that from which the wind is blowing. — *adj. Chiefly Naut.* Pertaining to or being on the lee: opposed to *weather.* [OE *hlēo* shelter]

leech[1] (lēch) *n.* **1.** Any of a class of carnivorous or bloodsucking, chiefly aquatic annelid worms; esp. the *medicinal leech,* formerly used for bloodletting. **2.** One who clings to another for gain; a parasite. **3.** *Archaic* A physician. — *v.t. Archaic* To treat with leeches. [OE *lǣce,* orig., physician]

leech[2] (lēch) *n. Naut.* **1.** Either of the side edges of a square sail. **2.** The after edge of a fore-and-aft sail. [ME *leche*]

leek (lēk) *n.* **1.** A culinary herb of the lily family, closely allied to the onion but having a narrow bulb and broader, dark green leaves: the national emblem of Wales. **2.** Any of various related plants. [OE *lēac*]

leer (lir) *n.* A sly look or sidewise glance expressing salacious desire, malicious intent, knowing complicity, etc. — *v.i.* To look with a leer. [OE *hlēor* cheek, face]

leer·y (lir′ē) *adj. Informal* **1.** Suspicious; wary. **2.** Sly.

lees (lēz) *n.pl.* Sediment, esp. in wine or liquor; dregs. [Pl. of obs. *lee* < OF *lie*]

lee·ward (lē′wərd, *Naut.* lōō′ərd) *adj.* **1.** Of or pertaining to the direction toward which the wind is blowing. **2.** Being on or toward the side sheltered from the wind. — *n.* The side or direction toward which the wind is blowing. — *adv.* Toward the lee. Opposed to *windward.*

lee·way (lē′wā′) *n.* **1.** Additional space, time, range, etc., providing greater freedom of action. **2.** *Naut.* The lateral drift of a vessel or an aircraft in motion.

left[1] (left) Past tense and past participle of LEAVE[1].

left[2] (left) *adj.* **1.** Pertaining to, designating, or being on the side of the body that is toward the north when one faces east, and usu. having the weaker and less dominant hand, etc. **2.** Pertaining to or situated on the corresponding side of anything. **3.** Nearest to or tending in the direction of the left side. **4.** Worn on a left hand, foot, etc. **5.** *Sometimes cap.* Designating a person, party, faction, etc., having liberal, democratic, socialistic, or laborite views and policies. — *n.* **1.** Any part, area, etc., on or toward the left side. **2.** *Often cap.* A group, party, etc., whose views and policies are left (*adj.* def. 5); esp., in Europe, such parties whose members sit to the presiding officer's left in a deliberative assembly. **3.** In boxing: **a** A blow with the left hand. **b** The left hand. — *adv.* On, to, or toward the left. [ME (Kentish) var. of presumed OE *lyft* weak]

left face In military drill, a 90-degree pivot to the left, using the ball of the right foot and the heel of the left.

left-hand (left′hand′) *adj.* **1.** Of, for, pertaining to, or situated on the left side or the left hand. **2.** Turning, opening, or swinging to the left.

left-hand·ed (left′han′did) *adj.* **1.** Using the left hand habitually and more easily than the right. **2.** Done with the left hand. **3.** Adapted or intended for use by the left hand. **4.** Turning or moving from right to left, or counterclockwise. **5.** Ironical or insincere in intent or effect: a *left-handed* compliment. **6.** Clumsy. — *adv.* With the left hand. — **left′-hand′ed·ly** *adv.* — **left′-hand′ed·ness** *n.*

left·ist (lef′tist) *n.* One whose views and policies are left (*adj.* def. 5). — *adj.* Left (*adj.* def. 5). — **left′ism** *n.*

left-o·ver (left′ō′vər) *n. Usu. pl.* An unused part or remnant, esp. of prepared food. — *adj.* Left as a remnant.

left wing **1.** *Sometimes cap.* A party, group, faction, etc., having leftist policies. **2.** The wing, part, etc., on the left side. — **left-wing** (left′wing′) *adj.* — **left′-wing′er** *n.*

leg (leg) *n.* **1.** One of the limbs or appendages serving as a means of support and locomotion in animals and man. **2.** *Anat.* **a** A lower limb of the human body, extending from the hip to the ankle. **b** The part of the lower limb between the knee and the ankle. **3.** A support resembling a leg in shape, position, or function. **4.** The portion of an article of clothing, as hose, trousers, etc., that covers a leg. **5.** A division or section of a course or journey. **6.** One of the divisions of an angled or forked object, as a pair of compasses. **7.** *Geom.* Either of the sides of a triangle adjacent to the base or the hypotenuse. **8.** *Naut.* The distance traveled by a vessel in a single direction while tacking. — **on one's last legs** On the verge of collapse or death. — **to have not a leg to stand on** To have no sound or logical basis, as for argument, justifica-

tion, etc. — **to pull one's leg** *Informal* To make fun of; fool. — **to shake a leg** *Slang* **1.** To hurry. **2.** To dance. — *v.i.* **legged, leg·ging** *Informal* To walk or run: usu. followed by *it.* [< ON *leggr*]

leg·a·cy (leg′ə-sē) *n. pl.* **·cies** **1.** Personal property, money, etc., bequeathed by will; a bequest. **2.** Anything received from or passed on by an ancestor, predecessor, or earlier era. [< OF < Med.L *legatia* the district of a legate]

le·gal (lē′gəl) *adj.* **1.** Of, pertaining to, or concerned with law: *legal* documents. **2.** Established or authorized by law. **3.** Conforming with or permitted by law. **4.** According to, determined by, or coming under the jurisdiction of statute law, rather than equity. **5.** Characteristic of or appropriate to those who practice law. — **Syn.** See LAWFUL. [< OF < L *lex, legis* law] — **le′gal·ly** *adv.*

legal age Age (*n.* def. 3).

legal holiday *U.S.* A day on which banks are closed and official business is suspended or limited by law.

le·gal·ism (lē′gəl·iz′əm) *n.* Strict conformity to law; esp., the stressing of the letter and forms of the law rather than the spirit of justice. — **le′gal·ist** *n.* — **le·gal·is′tic** *adj.*

le·gal·i·ty (li·gal′ə·tē) *n. pl.* **·ties** **1.** The condition or quality of being legal; lawfulness. **2.** Adherence to law.

le·gal·ize (lē′gəl·īz) *v.t.* **·ized, ·iz·ing** To make legal. Also *Brit.* **le′gal·ise.** — **le′gal·i·za′tion** (-ə-zā′shən, -ī-zā′-) *n.*

legal medicine Medical jurisprudence.

legal tender Coin or other money that may be legally offered in payment of a debt, and that a creditor must accept.

leg·ate (leg′it) *n.* **1.** An ecclesiastic appointed as an official representative of the Pope. **2.** An official envoy, usu. acting as a diplomatic representative of a government. — **Syn.** See AMBASSADOR. [< OF < L *legare* to send as a deputy] — **leg·a·tine** (leg′ə·tin, -tīn) *adj.* — **leg′ate·ship** *n.*

leg·a·tee (leg′ə·tē′) *n.* One to whom a legacy is bequeathed.

le·ga·tion (li·gā′shən) *n.* **1.** The official residence or business premises of a diplomatic minister or envoy of lower rank than an ambassador. **2.** The official staff of a foreign envoy or diplomatic mission. **3.** The position or rank of a legate.

le·ga·to (li·gä′tō) *Music adj.* Smooth and flowing, with unbroken transition between successive notes. — *adv.* In a legato manner. — *n. pl.* **·tos** A smooth, connected style, performance, or passage. [< Ital., lit., bound]

leg·a·tor (li·gā′tər, leg′ə·tôr′) *n.* One who makes a will.

leg·end (lej′ənd) *n.* **1.** An unauthenticated story from earlier times, preserved by tradition and popularly thought to be historical. **2.** A body of such stories, as those connected with a people or culture. **3.** An inscription or motto, as on a coin, banner, etc. **4.** A caption or explanatory description accompanying an illustration, chart, etc. [< OF < Med.L < L *legere* to read]

leg·en·dar·y (lej′ən·der′ē) *adj.* **1.** Of, presented in, or of the nature of a legend. **2.** Famous; celebrated.

leg·end·ry (lej′ən·drē) *n.* Legends collectively; legend.

le·ger line (lej′ər) See LEDGER LINE.

leg·er·de·main (lej′ər·də·mān′) *n.* **1.** Sleight of hand. **2.** Any artful trickery or deception. [ME < MF *léger de main,* lit., light of hand] — **leg′er·de·main′ist** *n.*

le·ges (lē′jēz) Plural of LEX.

leg·ged (leg′id, legd) *adj.* Having or characterized by (a specified kind or number of) legs: *bow-legged; two-legged.*

leg·ging (leg′ing) *n.* A gaiter or similar covering for the leg, usu. extending from the knee to the instep.

leg·gy (leg′ē) *adj.* **·gi·er, ·gi·est** **1.** Having disproportionately long legs. **2.** *Informal* Having or displaying attractive, shapely legs. — **leg′gi·ness** *n.*

leg·horn (leg′hôrn, -ərn) *n.* **1.** Finely plaited wheat straw. **2.** A hat made from this straw. **3.** *Usu. cap.* One of a breed of small, hardy domestic fowl. [after *Leghorn*]

leg·i·ble (lej′ə·bəl) *adj.* **1.** Capable of being read or deciphered; easy to read. **2.** Readily perceived or discovered from apparent signs or evidence. [< LL < L *legere* to read] — **leg′i·bil′i·ty, leg′i·ble·ness** *n.* — **leg′i·bly** *adv.*

le·gion (lē′jən) *n.* **1.** In ancient Rome, a major military unit consisting primarily of infantry troops with an auxiliary force of cavalry, altogether comprising between 4,200 and 6,000 men. **2.** *Usu. pl.* Any large military force; army. **3.** A great number; multitude. ◆ Sometimes used predicatively with the adjectival sense *innumerable,* as in Their members are *legion.* **4.** *Usu. cap.* Any of various military or honorary organizations, usu. national in character. [< OF < L *legere* to choose, levy troops]

le·gion·ar·y (lē′jən·er′ē) *adj.* Of, or pertaining to a legion. — *n. pl.* **·ar·ies** A soldier or member of a legion.

le·gion·naire (lē′jən·âr′) *n. Often cap.* A member of a legion (def. 4). [< F *légionnaire*]

Legion of Merit *U.S.* A military decoration awarded for exceptionally meritorious conduct in the performance of outstanding services. See DECORATION.

leg·is·late (lej′is·lāt) v. ·lat·ed, ·lat·ing v.i. 1. To make a law or laws. — v.t. 2. To cause to be in a specified state by legislation: often with *into* or *out of*. [Back formation < LEGISLATOR]

leg·is·la·tion (lej′is·lā′shən) n. 1. The act or procedures of enacting laws. 2. An officially enacted law or laws.

leg·is·la·tive (lej′is·lā′tiv) adj. 1. Of, pertaining to, or involved in legislation. 2. Having the power to legislate: the *legislative* branch of the government: distinguished from *executive, judicial.* 3. Of or pertaining to a legislature. 4. Enacted by or resulting from legislation. — n. The legislative branch of a government. — **leg′is·la′tive·ly** adv.

leg·is·la·tor (lej′is·lā′tər) n. 1. One active in the formation and enactment of laws; a lawmaker. 2. A member of a legislature. [< L < *lex, legis* law + *lator* bearer, proposer] — **leg′is·la′tress** (-tris), **leg′is·la′trix** (-triks) n. *fem.*

leg·is·la·ture (lej′is·lā′chər) n. A body of persons officially constituted and empowered to make and enact the laws of a nation or state; esp., in the U.S., the lawmaking body of a State, Territory, etc., as distinguished from Congress.

le·git (lə·jit′) *Slang* n. Legitimate drama, theatrical productions, etc. — adj. Legitimate.

le·git·i·ma·cy (lə·jit′ə·mə·sē) n. The state or condition of being legitimate.

le·git·i·mate (adj. lə·jit′ə·mit; v. lə·jit′ə·māt) adj. 1. In accordance with law; lawful. 2. Based on or resulting from orderly, rational deduction or inference. 3. Authentic; valid. 4. Born in wedlock. 5. According to or based on strict hereditary right. 6. In the theater, denoting drama performed by living actors before an audience as distinguished from motion pictures, television, etc. — v.t. ·mat·ed, ·mat·ing 1. To make or establish as legitimate. 2. To show reason or authorization for. [< Med.L < L *legitimus* lawful < *lex, legis* law] — **le·git′i·mate·ly** adv. — **le·git′i·mate·ness** n. — **le·git′i·ma′tion** (-mā′shən) n.

le·git·i·mist (lə·jit′ə·mist) n. An advocate of rule or authority based on hereditary right; esp., of claims to a monarchy. — **le·git′i·mism** n. — **le·git′i·mis′tic** adj.

le·git·i·mize (lə·jit′ə·mīz) v.t. ·mized, ·miz·ing To legitimate. Also **le·git′i·ma·tize** (-mə·tīz). — **le·git′i·mi·za′tion** n.

leg·less (leg′lis) adj. Having no legs.

leg-of-mut·ton (leg′ə·mut′n) adj. Having the characteristically triangular or tapering shape of a haunch of mutton.

leg-of-mutton sleeve A sleeve puffed on the upper arm and fitting closely on the forearm: also called *gigot.*

leg·ume (leg′yōōm, lə·gyōōm′) n. 1. The fruit or seed of any leguminous plant, esp. when used as food or fodder. 2. Any leguminous plant. 3. *Bot.* The characteristic, sutured seed vessel of such a plant; a pod. [< F < L *legumen*, lit., something gathered < *legere* to gather]

le·gu·mi·nous (lə·gyōō′mə·nəs) adj. Of or belonging to a large family of plants including peas, beans, etc.

leg·work (leg′wûrk′) n. *Informal* Chores, errands, etc., accomplished by or as by going about on foot.

lei (lā, lā′ē) n. pl. **leis** A festival garland of blossoms, feathers, etc., as worn in Hawaii. [< Hawaiian]

lei·sure (lē′zhər, lezh′ər) n. 1. Freedom from the demands of work or duty. 2. Time available for recreation or relaxation. — **at leisure** 1. Free from pressing necessity or obligation; having time to spare. 2. Unoccupied; not employed. 3. When one has time or opportunity: also **at one's leisure.** — adj. 1. Not spent in work or necessary activity: *leisure* time. 2. Having considerable leisure: the *leisure* classes. [< OF < L *licere* to be permitted]

lei·sure·ly (lē′zhər·lē, lezh′ər-) adj. Free from exertion or pressure; relaxed and unhurried. Also **lei′sured** (-zhərd). — adv. In a leisurely manner. — **lei′sure·li·ness** n.

leit·mo·tif (līt′mō·tēf′) n. *Music* A theme used for a certain person, event, or idea throughout an opera, etc. Also **leit′mo·tiv′** (-tēf′). [< G < *leiten* to lead + *motiv* motive]

lem·ming (lem′ing) n. Any of several small arctic rodents, having a short tail and furry feet; esp., a European species, noted for recurrent mass migrations often terminated by drowning in the ocean. [< Norw.]

lem·on (lem′ən) n. 1. The oval, citrus fruit of an evergreen tree, having juicy, acid pulp and a yellow rind yielding an essential oil (**lemon oil**) used as a flavoring and perfuming agent. 2. The tree. 3. A bright, clear yellow. 4. *Slang* Something or someone disappointing or unattractive. — adj. Bright, clear yellow. [< OF < Sp. < Arabic < Persian *limūn*]

lem·on·ade (lem′ən·ād′) n. A drink made of lemon juice, water, and sugar.

le·mur (lē′mər) n. Any of various small, arboreal, mostly nocturnal mammals related to the monkeys; esp., one having a foxlike face and soft fur, found chiefly in Madagascar. [< NL < L *lemures* ghosts]

Len·a·pe (len′ə·pē) n. The generic name of the Delawares, an Algonquian people; also, their language: also called *Leni-*

Lenape, Lenni-Lenape. [Short for Algonquian (Lenape) *Leni-lenape*, lit., real man < *leni* real + *lenape* man]

lend (lend) v. **lent**, **lend·ing** v.t. 1. To grant the use or possession of with the understanding that the thing or its equivalent will be returned. 2. To grant the use of (money) at a stipulated rate of interest. 3. To impart, as an abstract quality. 4. To make available, as for aid or support. 5. To adapt or suit (itself or oneself) to a specific purpose. — v.i. 6. To make a loan or loans. [OE *lǣn* a loan] — **lend′er** n.

lending library A circulating library.

length (lengkth, length) n. 1. Linear extent from end to end; usu., the longest dimension of a thing, as distinguished from its width and thickness. 2. Extent from beginning to end, as of a period of time, series, book, word, etc. 3. The state or quality of being long or prolonged, either in time or space. 4. Duration or continuance, esp. in respect to time. 5. The measurement along, extent of, or distance equivalent to something specified: arm's *length*. 6. A piece or standard unit of something, measured longitudinally. 7. *Often pl.* The limit of one's efforts, ability, etc.: to go to great *lengths*. 8. In racing, the extent from front to back of a competing horse, boat, etc., used as a unit of estimating position. — **at length** 1. Finally. 2. In full. [OE *lengthu* < *lang* long]

length·en (lengk′thən, leng′-) v.t. & v.i. To make or become longer.

length·wise (lengkth′wīz′, length′-) adv. In the direction or dimension of length; longitudinally. Also **length′ways′** (-wāz′). — adj. According to length; longitudinal.

length·y (lengk′thē, leng′-) adj. **length·i·er, length·i·est** Unusually or unduly long. — **length′i·ly** adv. — **length′i·ness** n.

le·ni·en·cy (lē′nē·ən·sē, lēn′yən·sē) n. The state or quality of being lenient. Also **le′ni·ence.** — **Syn.** See MERCY.

le·ni·ent (lē′nē·ənt, lēn′yənt) adj. Gentle or merciful in disposition, effect, etc.; mild. [< L *leniens, -entis*, ppr. of *lenire* to soothe] — **le′ni·ent·ly** adv.

Len·i-Len·a·pe (len′ē·len′ə·pē) n. Lenape. Also **Len′ni-Len′a·pe.**

Len·in·ism (len′in·iz′əm) A modification of Marxism constituting the doctrine and practice of the Bolsheviks and the Communist Party in the Soviet Union under Lenin. — **Len′in·ist, Len′in·ite** n. & adj.

len·i·tive (len′ə·tiv) adj. Having the power or tendency to allay pain or distress; soothing. — n. That which soothes or mitigates. [< Med.L < L *lenitus*, pp. of *lenire* to soothe]

len·i·ty (len′ə·tē) n. The state or quality of being lenient. [< OF < L *lenitas, -tatis* softness]

lens (lenz) n. 1. *Optics* A piece of glass or other transparent substance, bounded by two curved surfaces or by one curved and one plane surface, by which rays of light are made to converge or diverge. See illus. for FOCUS. 2. Two or more such pieces in combination. 3. Any device that concentrates or disperses radiation, etc., other than light by action similar to that of an optical lens. 4. *Anat.* A transparent, biconvex body situated behind the iris of the eye and serving to focus an image on the retina. For illus. see EYE. [< L *lens, lentis* lentil; so called from the form]

lent (lent) Past tense and past participle of LEND.

Lent (lent) n. *Eccl.* The period of forty days, excluding Sundays, from Ash Wednesday to Easter, observed annually as a season of fasting, penitence, and self-denial. [Short for *Lenten* < OE *lencten, lengten* the spring]

Len·ten (len′tən) adj. Of, pertaining to, suitable for, or characteristic of Lent. Also **len′ten.**

len·til (len′təl) n. 1. A leguminous plant, having broad pods containing flattish, edible seeds. 2. The seed of this plant. [< F < L *lenticula*, dim. of *lens, lentis* lentil]

len·to (len′tō) *Music* adj. Slow. — adv. Slowly: a direction to the performer. — n. pl. ·**tos** A slow movement or passage. [< Ital. < L *lentus*]

l'en·voi (len′voi, Fr. län·vwà′) See ENVOY². Also **l'en′voy.**

Le·o (lē′ō) n. A constellation, the Lion; also, the fifth sign of the zodiac. See ZODIAC. [< NL < L]

Le·o Mi·nor (lē′ō mī′nər) A constellation, the Lesser Lion.

Le·o·nid (lē′ə·nid) n. pl. **Le·o·nids** or **Le·o·ni·des** (lē·on′ə·dēz) *Astron.* One of the meteors of a meteor shower having its radiant point in the constellation Leo, and appearing annually about November 14.

le·o·nine (lē′ə·nīn, -nin) adj. Pertaining to, resembling, or characteristic of a lion. [< L *leo, leonis* lion]

leop·ard (lep′ərd) n. 1. A large member of the cat family, native to Asia and Africa, having a tawny coat with dark brown or black spots grouped in rounded clusters: also called *panther.* 2. Any of various similar felines, as the cheetah, jaguar, or snow leopard. 3. The fur of a leopard. [< OF < LL < Gk. < *leōn* lion + *pardos* panther]

le·o·tard (lē′ə·tärd) n. *Often pl.* A close-fitting, stretchable garment worn by dancers, acrobats, etc. [after Jules *Léotard*, 19th c. French aerialist]

lep·er (lep′ər) n. One afflicted with leprosy. [< obs. *leper* leprosy < OF < L < Gk., orig. fem. of *lepros* scaly]

lep·i·dop·ter·ous (lep′ə·dop′tər·əs) adj. Belonging or per-

LEMMING
(To 6 inches long)

taining to an order of insects comprising the butterflies and moths, characterized by four wings covered with minute scales. [< NL < Gk. *lepis*, *-idos* scale + *pteron* wing] Also **lep′i·dop′ter·al.** — **lep′i·dop′ter·an** *n. & adj.*

lep·o·rine (lep′ə-rīn, -rin) *adj.* Pertaining to or characteristic of hares. [< L *lepus, leporis* hare]

lep·re·chaun (lep′rə-kôn) *n.* In Irish folklore, a tiny elfin cobbler supposed to own hidden treasure. [< Irish < OIrish < *lu* little + *corpán*, dim. of *corp* body < L *corpus, -oris*]

lep·ro·sy (lep′rə-sē) *n. Pathol.* A chronic, communicable disease caused by a microorganism and characterized by nodular skin lesions, nerve paralysis, and physical mutilation: also called *Hansen's disease.* [See LEPER.]

lep·rous (lep′rəs) *adj.* 1. Affected with leprosy. 2. Of or resembling leprosy. — **lep′rous·ly** *adv.*

-lepsy *combining form* Seizure; attack: *catalepsy.* Also **-lepsia.** [< Gk. *lepsis* seizure]

lep·ton (lep′ton) *n. pl.* **-tons** *Physics* An atomic particle of very small mass, as the electron, positron, or neutrino. [< Gk., neut. of *leptos* fine]

les·bi·an (lez′bē-ən) *Sometimes cap. n.* A homosexual woman. — *adj.* Pertaining to or characteristic of homosexual women. [< LESBIAN] — **les′bi·an·ism** *n.*

Les·bi·an (lez′bē-ən) *n.* 1. A native or inhabitant of Lesbos. 2. Sappho or one of her followers, alleged to have been homosexuals. — *adj.* 1. Of or pertaining to Lesbos or its inhabitants. 2. Of or pertaining to Sappho or her poetry. [< L < Gk. *Lesbos* Lesbos, the home of Sappho]

lese ma·jes·ty (lēz′ maj′is·tē) An offense against sovereign authority or a sovereign; treason. Also *Fr.* **lèse-ma·jes·té** (lez′mȧ·zhes·tā′). [< F < L < *laesa*, fem. of *laesus*, pp. of *laedere* to injure + *majestas* majesty]

le·sion (lē′zhən) *n.* 1. *Pathol.* Any abnormal or harmful change in the structure of an organ or tissue. 2. An injury; damage. [< F < L < *laesus*, pp. of *laedere* to injure]

less (les) Alternative comparative of LITTLE. — *adj.* 1. Not as great in quantity or degree; not as much. 2. Inferior in degree; smaller; lower: with *than.* — *adv.* To a smaller degree or extent; not as: followed by an adjective or adverb. — *n.* A smaller amount or part. — *prep.* With the subtraction of; minus. [OE *lǣs*]

-less *suffix of adjectives* 1. Devoid of; without: *blameless, harmless.* 2. Deprived of; lacking: *motherless, stemless.* 3. Not able to (do something): *restless;* not susceptible of (some action): *countless.* [OE *leas* free from]

les·see (les·ē′) *n.* One to whom a lease is granted. [< AF *lessee*, OF *lesse*, pp. of *lesser, laissier* to let, leave]

less·en (les′ən) *v.t.* 1. To decrease. 2. To make little of; disparage. — *v.i.* 3. To become less. — **Syn.** See DECREASE.

less·er (les′ər) *adj.* Not as large or important; minor.

Lesser Bear The constellation Ursa Minor.

lesser panda The panda (def. 1).

les·son (les′ən) *n.* 1. An instance or experience from which useful knowledge may be gained. 2. A division or portion of a course of study. 3. An assignment to be studied or learned, as by a student. 4. A reprimand; reproof. 5. A portion of the Bible read or designated to be read at a religious service. — *v.t. Rare* 1. To give a lesson or lessons to; instruct. 2. To admonish; rebuke. [< L *lectio, -ionis* a reading]

les·sor (les′ôr, les·ôr′) *n.* One who grants a lease; a landlord letting property under a lease. [See LESSEE]

lest (lest) *conj.* 1. In order to prevent the chance that (something might happen); for fear that. 2. That: after expressions denoting anxiety: We worried *lest* the money should not last. [OE (*thy*) *lǣs the* (by the) less that]

let¹ (let) *v.* **let, let·ting** *v.t.* 1. To allow; permit. 2. To permit to pass, come, go, etc.: followed by a preposition: *Let* him by. 3. To cause; make: with *know* or *hear: Let* me know when you arrive. 4. To grant or assign, as a contract for work to be performed. 5. An auxiliary verb, usu. in the imperative, signifying: **a** An exhortation or command: *Let's* go! **b** Acquiescence; inability to prevent the inevitable: *Let* it rain. **c** An assumption or suggestion: *Let* x equal the sum of two numbers. 6. *Chiefly Brit.* To rent (a house, room, etc.) to a tenant. 7. To cause to flow, as blood. — *v.i.* 8. *Chiefly Brit.* To be rented: rooms to *let.* — **let alone** *Informal* And surely not; not to say: He can't even float, *let alone* swim. — **to let down** 1. To cause to fall or descend; loosen, as hair. 2. To disappoint. — **to let in** To insert into the substance, material, or body of something. — **to let loose** To set free; release. — **to let off** 1. To emit; release, as from pressure or tension. 2. To discharge, dismiss, or excuse, as from work or obligation. 3. To allow to escape a punishment or penalty. — **to let on** *Informal* 1. To make it known; reveal. 2. To pretend. — **to let out** 1. To give vent to; emit. 2. To release or unfasten in order to make a garment, etc., wider or longer. — **to let up** 1. To grow less;

abate. 2. To reduce tension. — **to let up on** *Informal* To cease to subject to force or severe treatment. ◆ See note under LEAVE¹. [OE *lǣtan*]

let² (let) *n.* In tennis or similar games, a service, point, etc., that must be repeated because of some interruption or hindrance of playing conditions. — *v.t.* **let** or **let·ted, let·ting** *Archaic* To hinder; impede. [OE *lettan*, lit., to make late]

-let *suffix of nouns* 1. Small; little: *booklet.* 2. A band or ornament for (a specified part of the body): *anklet.* [< OF *-let, -lette < -el + -et*, dim. suffixes]

let·down (let′doun) *n.* 1. A decrease; slackening, as of speed, force, or energy. 2. *Informal* Disappointment.

le·thal (lē′thəl) *adj.* 1. Causing death; deadly; fatal. 2. Pertaining to or characteristic of death. [< L < *lethum, letum* death] — **le·thal·i·ty** (lē·thal′ə·tē) *n.*

le·thar·gic (li·thär′jik) *adj.* 1. Affected with or characterized by lethargy; drowsy; apathetic. 2. Pertaining to or causing lethargy. Also **le·thar′gi·cal.** — **le·thar′gi·cal·ly** *adv.*

leth·ar·gize (leth′ər·jīz) *v.t.* **·gized, ·giz·ing** To make lethargic.

leth·ar·gy (leth′ər·jē) *n. pl.* **·gies** 1. A state of indifference; apathy. 2. *Pathol.* Excessive drowsiness or abnormally deep sleep. [< OF < LL < Gk. *lēthargos* forgetful]

Le·the (lē′thē) *n.* 1. In Greek mythology, a river in Hades, a drink from which produced oblivion. 2. Oblivion. [< Gk. *lēthē* oblivion] — **Le·the·an** (lē·thē′ən) *adj.*

Lett (let) *n.* 1. A Latvian. 2. The Latvian language.

let·ter (let′ər) *n.* 1. A standardized sign or character used in writing or printing to represent a speech sound. 2. A written or printed message directed to a specified person or group of persons. 3. An official document granting certain rights or privileges to a specified person: a *letter* of credit. 4. Literal meaning: the *letter* of the law. 5. *pl.* Literature in general; literary profession; a man of *letters.* 6. *U.S.* An emblem in the form of the initial letter of a college, school, etc., conferred as an award for outstanding performance in athletics. — **to the letter** In accordance with the exact words or literal meaning. — *v.t.* 1. To inscribe letters on; mark with letters. 2. To print or inscribe by means of letters. — *v.i.* 3. To form letters, as by hand. [< OF < L *littera* letter of the alphabet, in pl., epistle] — **let′ter·er** *n.*

let·tered (let′ərd) *adj.* 1. Versed in letters; learned; literary; educated. 2. Inscribed or marked with letters.

let·ter·head (let′ər·hed′) *n.* A printed heading, as a name and address, on a sheet of writing paper; also, a sheet of paper bearing such a heading.

let·ter·ing (let′ər·ing) *n.* 1. The act or art of forming letters; process of marking or stamping with letters. 2. Letters collectively, esp. a single example.

letter of credit A letter issued by a bank and authorizing the bearer to draw a specified amount of money from other banks, etc.

let·ter·per·fect (let′ər·pûr′fikt) *adj.* 1. Perfect in memorization, as an actor. 2. Correct in all details, as a piece of writing. — *adv.* Perfectly: said of memorizing or writing.

let·ter·press (let′ər·pres′) *n. Printing* 1. Any printed matter, as distinguished from illustrations, etc. 2. Printing produced from type or similar raised surfaces.

letters patent *Law* The instrument granting a patent.

Let·tish (let′ish) *adj. & n.* Latvian.

let·tuce (let′is) *n.* A cultivated herb having crisp, edible leaves; also, the leaves. [< OF < L *lac, lactis* milk]

let·up (let′up′) *n. Informal* 1. A lessening or relaxation, as of force or intensity; lull. 2. A respite; pause; interlude.

leuco- *combining form* White; lacking color: also, before vowels, **leuc-.** Also **leuko-, leuk-.** [< Gk. *leukos* white]

leu·co·cyte (loo′kə·sīt) *n. Physiol.* A white or colorless blood corpuscle, constituting an important agent in protection against infectious diseases. Also spelled *leukocyte.*

leu·co·cyt·ic (loo′kə·sit′ik) *adj.* 1. Of or pertaining to leucocytes. 2. Characterized by an excess of leucocytes.

leuk- Var. of LEUCO-.

leu·ke·mi·a (loo·kē′mē·ə) *n. Pathol.* A generally fatal disease of the blood and bloodmaking tissues, characterized by a marked increase in the number of leucocytes, accompanied by anemia, exhaustion, etc. Also **leu·kae′mi·a.** [< LEUK- + Gk. *haima* blood]

leuko- See LEUCO-.

leu·ko·cyte (loo′kə·sīt) See LEUCOCYTE.

le·vant (lə·vant′) *n.* A kind of morocco leather having an irregularly grained surface. Also **Levant morocco.**

Levant (lə·vant′) *n.* The regions bordering the eastern Mediterranean, between western Greece and western Egypt: usu. preceded by *the.* [< F < L *levare* to raise] — **Le·van·tine** (lə·van′tin, lev′ən·tīn, -tēn) *adj. & n.*

le·va·tor (lə·vā′tər) *n. pl.* **le·va·to·res** (lev′ə·tôr′ēz, -tō′rēz) or **le·va·tors** *Anat.* A muscle that raises an organ or part. [< LL < L *levare* to raise]

lev·ee[1] (lev'ē) *n. U.S.* **1.** An embankment along the shore of a river, built for protection against floods. **2.** A landing place; wharf. [< F *lever* to raise < L *levare*]

lev·ee[2] (lev'ē, lə·vē') *n.* A reception or formal gathering of visitors, usu. held early in the day by a person of rank or distinction. [< F *levé* an arising]

lev·el (lev'əl) *n.* **1.** Relative place, degree, or stage: a high *level* of development. **2.** Position in the vertical dimension: the *level* of the lower branches. **3.** A horizontal line or surface: sea *level*. **4.** A flat expanse, as of land. **5.** Any of various devices used to find the conformity of a line or surface with the horizontal plane. **— on the level** *Informal* Without deception; fair and square. **— to find one's** (or **its**) **level** To come to the appropriate place on a vertical scale of distances, values, etc. *— adj.* **1.** Having a surface with no irregularities in height; even; flat. **2.** Conforming to a horizontal plane. **3.** Being in the same plane with or at the same height as something else. **4.** Measured so as to have a surface even with the edge of the container. **5.** Equal to something or someone else, as in importance, development, etc. **6.** Even, as in quality or tone. **— a level head** A calm and sensible mind. **— one's level best** *Informal* The best one can possibly do. *— v.* **lev·eled** or **·elled, lev·el·ing** or **·el·ling** *v.t.* **1.** To give an even or horizontal surface to. **2.** To destroy by or as by smashing to the ground. **3.** To knock down. **4.** To bring to a common state or condition. **5.** To aim or point as a weapon. **6.** To aim or direct (something) with force of emphasis: to *level* an accusation. *— v.i.* **7.** To bring persons or things to a common state or condition. **8.** To take measurements with a level. **9.** To aim a weapon at a target. **10.** *U.S. Slang* To be honest. *— adv.* In an even line or plane. [< OF < L *libra* a balance] **— lev'el·er** or **·el·ler** *n.* **— lev'el·ly** *adv.* **— lev'el·ness** *n.*

level crossing A grade crossing.

lev·el·head·ed (lev'əl·hed'id) *adj.* Characterized by common sense and cool judgment. **— lev'el·head'ed·ness** *n.*

level of usage *Ling.* A distinguishable variety of vocabulary, grammar, pronunciation, etc., considered appropriate for a class within the speech community.

lev·er (lev'ər, lē'vər) *n.* **1.** *Mech.* A device consisting of a rigid structure, often a straight bar, pivoting on a fixed support (the fulcrum), and serving to impart pressure or motion from a force or effort applied at one point to a resisting force at another point. **2.** Any of various tools, devices or parts operating on the above principle, as a crowbar. **3.** Any means of exerting effective power. *— v.t. & v.i.* To move or pry with or as with a lever. [< OF < L *levare* to raise]

lev·er·age (lev'ər·ij, lē'vər-) *n.* **1.** The use of a lever. **2.** The mechanical advantage gained by use of a lever.

lev·er·et (lev'ər·it) *n.* A young hare less than a year old. [< AF, OF *levre* hare]

Le·vi (lē'vī) In the Old Testament, a son of Jacob and Leah. *Gen.* xxix 34. *— n.* The tribe of Israel descended from him.

le·vi·a·than (lə·vī'ə·thən) *n.* **1.** A gigantic water beast mentioned in the Bible. **2.** Any enormous creature or thing.

Le·vis (lē'vīz) *n.pl.* Close-fitting, heavy denim trousers having rivets to reinforce points of greatest strain: a registered trade mark. [after *Levi* Strauss, U.S. manufacturer]

lev·i·tate (lev'ə·tāt) *v.* **·tat·ed, ·tat·ing** *v.i.* **1.** To rise and float in the air, as through buoyancy or supposed supernatural power. *— v.t.* **2.** To cause to rise and float in the air. [< L *levis* light, on analogy with *gravitate*] **— lev'i·ta'tor** *n.*

lev·i·ta·tion (lev'ə·tā'shən) *n.* **1.** The act of levitating, or the state of being levitated. **2.** The illusion of suspending a heavy object or the human body in the air without support.

Le·vite (lē'vīt) *n.* In Jewish history, one of the tribe of Levi, from whom were chosen those who assisted the priests.

Le·vit·i·cal (lə·vit'i·kəl) *adj.* **1.** Of or pertaining to the Levites. **2.** Of or pertaining to the book of Leviticus.

Le·vit·i·cus (lə·vit'i·kəs) The third book of the Old Testament, consisting chiefly of a compilation of ceremonial laws.

lev·i·ty (lev'ə·tē) *n. pl.* **·ties 1.** Lack of seriousness; inappropriate gaiety; frivolity. **2.** Fickleness; inconstancy. **3.** Lightness. [< L *levis* light]

levo- *combining form* Turned or turning to the left: used in chemistry and physics. Also spelled *laevo-*. [< L *laevus* left]

le·vo·ro·ta·to·ry (lē'vō·rō'tə·tôr'ē, -tō'rē) *adj. Optics* Causing the plane of polarization of light to rotate to the left, or counterclockwise: said of certain crystals: opposed to *dextrorotatory*.

lev·u·lose (lev'yə·lōs) *n. Biochem.* Fructose. [< L *laevus* left + -UL(E) + -OSE²]

lev·y (lev'ē) *v.* **lev·ied, lev·y·ing** *v.t.* **1.** To impose and collect by authority or force, as a tax, fine, etc. **2.** To enlist or

call up (troops, etc.) for military service. **3.** To prepare for, begin, or wage (war). *— v.i.* **4.** To make a levy. **5.** *Law* To seize property by judicial writ in order to fulfill a judgment: usu. with *on*. *— n. pl.* **lev·ies 1.** The act of levying. **2.** That which is levied, as money or troops. [< OF < L *levare* to raise] **— lev'i·er** *n.*

lewd (lood) *adj.* **1.** Characterized by or inciting to lust or debauchery. **2.** Obscene; ribald; bawdy. [OE *læwede* lay², unlearned] **— lewd'ly** *adv.* **— lewd'ness** *n.*

lew·is·ite (loo'is·īt) *n. Chem.* An oily liquid, $C_2H_2Cl_3As$, used in chemical warfare as a blistering agent. [after W. L. *Lewis*, 1878–1943, U.S. chemist]

lex (leks) *n. pl.* **le·ges** (lē'jēz) *Latin Law.*

lex·i·cog·ra·pher (lek'sə·kog'rə·fər) *n.* One who works at writing or compiling a dictionary.

lex·i·cog·ra·phy (lek'sə·kog'rə·fē) *n.* The practice or profession of compiling dictionaries. [< NL < Gk. < *lexikon* lexicon + *graphein* to write] **— lex'i·co·graph'ic** (-kō·graf'·ik) or **·i·cal** *adj.* **— lex'i·co·graph'i·cal·ly** *adv.*

lex·i·con (lek'sə·kon) *n.* **1.** A dictionary; esp., a dictionary of Latin, Greek, or Hebrew. **2.** A vocabulary or list of words relating to a particular subject, occupation, or activity. [< Gk. *lexikos* pertaining to words]

Leyden jar *Electr.* A device for accumulating a charge of static electricity, consisting principally of a glass jar coated with tinfoil inside and out. [after *Leyden*, earlier name of Leiden, where it was invented]

li·a·bil·i·ty (lī'ə·bil'ə·tē) *n. pl.* **·ties 1.** The state or condition of being liable. **2.** That for which one is liable, as a financial obligation or debt. **3.** *pl.* In accounting, the entries on a balance sheet showing the debts or obligations of a business: opposed to *assets*. **4.** Any obstacle or hindrance.

li·a·ble (lī'ə·bəl) *adj.* **1.** Justly or legally responsible, as for damages; answerable. **2.** Subject or susceptible, as to injury, illness, etc. **3.** Officially obligated to be available. **4.** *U.S. Informal* Likely. [< F < L *ligare* to bind]

li·ai·son (lē'ā·zon', lē·ā'zon, lē'ə·zon; *Fr.* lē·e·zôn') *n.* **1.** A means or agency for maintaining or furthering communication or unity, as between parts of an armed force or departments of a government. **2.** An illicit love affair. **3.** In spoken French and in many other languages, the carrying over of a final consonant to the initial vowel of a succeeding word, as in *il est arrivé* (ē le tà·rē·vā'). [< F < L *ligare* to bind]

li·ar (lī'ər) *n.* One who lies or utters falsehoods. [OE *lēogere*]

li·ba·tion (lī·bā'shən) *n.* **1.** A liquid ceremonially poured out, as in honor of a deity; also, the act of pouring such a liquid. **2.** Humorously, a drink. [< F < L *libare* to pour out (as an offering)]

li·bel (lī'bəl) *n.* **1.** *Law* **a** A written statement or graphic representation, esp. in published form, that damages a person's reputation. **b** The act or crime of publishing such a statement. **2.** Any defamatory or grossly unflattering statement. *— v.t.* **·beled** or **·belled, ·bel·ing** or **·bel·ling 1.** To publish or perpetrate a libel against. **2.** To defame or discredit, as by false or malicious statements. [< OF < L *libellus*, dim. of *liber* book] **— li'bel·er, li'bel·ler** *n.*

li·bel·ous (lī'bel·əs) *adj.* Constituting, containing, or like a libel. Also, *esp. Brit.*, **li'bel·lous. — li'bel·ous·ly** *adv.*

lib·er·al (lib'ər·əl, lib'rəl) *adj.* **1.** Characterized by or inclining toward opinions or policies favoring progress or reform, as in politics or religion. **2.** Not intolerant or prejudiced; broad-minded. **3.** Characterized by generosity or lavishness in giving. **4.** Given or yielded freely or in large quantity; ample. **5.** Not literal or strict: a *liberal* interpretation of the law. **6.** Suitable for persons of broad cultural interests: *liberal* arts. *— n.* One having liberal opinions or convictions, esp. in politics or religion. [< OF < L *liberalis* pertaining to a freeman] **— lib'er·al·ly** *adv.*

Lib·er·al (lib'ər·əl, lib'rəl) *adj.* Designating or belonging to one of various political parties, as the Liberal Party of Canada or Great Britain. *— n.* A member of such a party.

liberal arts A group of subjects or college courses including literature, philosophy, languages, history, etc., and distinguished from scientific, technical, or purely practical subjects; the arts, as in Bachelor of *Arts*; the humanities.

lib·er·al·ism (lib'ər·əl·iz'əm) *n.* **1.** Liberal beliefs or policies, esp. in regard to politics, social changes, religion, etc. **2.** *Sometimes cap.* The policies of the Liberal Party.

lib·er·al·i·ty (lib'ə·ral'ə·tē) *n. pl.* **·ties 1.** The quality of being liberal in giving; generosity. **2.** Broad-mindedness.

lib·er·al·ize (lib'ər·əl·īz') *v.t. & v.i.* **·ized, ·iz·ing** To make or become liberal. **— lib'er·al·i·za'tion** (lib'ər·əl·ə·zā'shən, -ī·zā'-, lib'rəl-) *n.* **— lib'er·al·iz'er** *n.*

Liberal Party 1. One of the principal political parties of Canada. **2.** In Great Britain, a Whiggish political party formed in the 1830's and the major opponent of the Conservative Party until after World War I.

lib·er·ate (lib'ə·rāt) *v.t.* **at·ed, at·ing 1.** To set free, as from bondage or confinement. **2.** To extricate, as from entanglement. **3.** To release from chemical combination, as a gas. [< L *liberatus*, pp. of *liberare* to free] **— lib'er·a'tion** *n.*

lib·er·a·tor (lib′ər·ā′tər) *n.* One who liberates; esp., one who emancipates a nation, people, etc.

lib·er·tine (lib′ər·tēn) *n.* One completely lacking in moral restraint; a profligate. — *adj.* Characteristic of a libertine. [< L *libertus* freedman] — **lib′er·tin·ism** *n.*

lib·er·ty (lib′ər·tē) *n.* *pl.* **·ties** 1. Freedom from oppression, tyranny, or the domination of a government not freely chosen. 2. The state of being free, as from confinement or slavery. 3. Freedom of thought or action, or exemption from forms of compulsion or indignity, regarded as a human right. 4. An overly free, familiar, or disrespectful act or manner. 5. Permission to be present in and make free use of a specified place: followed by *of.* 6. In the U.S. Navy and other maritime services, official permission to be absent from one's ship or place of duty, usu. for less than 48 hours. — **at liberty** 1. Free; authorized or permitted (to do something). 2. Not engaged in an activity or occupation; unemployed. 3. Able to move about freely. [< F < L < *liber* free]

Liberty Bell The bell in Independence Hall, Philadelphia, rung July 4, 1776, to celebrate the adoption of the Declaration of Independence, and cracked in 1835.

Liberty Ship A type of U.S. cargo ship built in large numbers during World War II.

li·bid·i·nous (li·bid′ə·nəs) *adj.* Characterized by or inclining toward excesses of sexual desire; lustful. — **li·bid′i·nous·ly** *adv.* — **li·bid′i·nous·ness** *n.*

li·bi·do (li·bē′dō, -bī-′) *n.* 1. Sexual desire or impulse. 2. *Psychoanal.* The instinctual craving or drive behind all human activities. [< L, lust] — **li·bid′i·nal** (-bid′ə·nəl) *adj.*

Li·bra (lī′brə, lē′-) *n.* A constellation, the Balance or Scales; also, the seventh sign of the zodiac. See ZODIAC. [< L]

li·brar·i·an (lī·brâr′ē·ən) *n.* 1. One who has charge of a library. 2. A person qualified by training for library service.

li·brar·y (lī′brer·ē, -brə·rē) *n.* *pl.* **·brar·ies** 1. A collection of books, pamphlets, etc.; esp., such a collection arranged to facilitate reference. 2. A building, room, etc., housing such a collection. 3. A commercial establishment that rents books. [< OF < L *liber, libri* book]

Library of Congress The national library of the U.S. in Washington, D.C., established in 1800.

li·brate (lī′brāt) *v.i.* **·brat·ed, ·brat·ing** 1. To move back and forth; oscillate. 2. To be poised; hover. [< L < *libra* balance] — **li·bra′tion** *n.* — **li′bra·to·ry** *adj.*

li·bret·tist (li·bret′ist) *n.* The writer of a libretto.

li·bret·to (li·bret′ō) *n.* *pl.* **·tos** or **·ti** (-tē) 1. The verbal text of an opera or other large-scale vocal work. 2. A book containing such a text. [< Ital., little book, dim. of *libro*]

Lib·y·an (lib′ē·ən) *adj.* Of or pertaining to Libya, its inhabitants, or their language. — *n.* 1. A native or inhabitant of Libya. 2. The Hamitic language of ancient Libya.

lice (līs) Plural of LOUSE.

li·cense (lī′səns) *n.* 1. An official document giving permission to engage in a specified activity, perform a specified act, etc. 2. Unrestrained liberty of action. 3. Abuse of freedom or privilege; laxity. 4. Deviation from or relaxation of established rules or standards, esp. for artistic effect: poetic *license.* — *v.t.* **·censed, ·cens·ing** To grant a license to or for; authorize. Also, *esp. Brit.,* **li′cence.** [< OF < L *licens, -entis,* ppr. of *licere* to be permitted] — **li′cens·a·ble** *adj.* — **li′cen·ser** or **li′cenc·er** or *Law* **li′cen·sor** *n.*

li·cen·see (lī′sən·sē′) *n.* One to whom a license has been granted. Also **li′cen·cee′.**

li·cen·ti·ate (lī·sen′shē·it, -āt) *n.* 1. A person licensed to practice a certain profession: a *licentiate* in dental surgery. 2. In some Continental universities, a person holding a degree intermediate between bachelor and doctor.

li·cen·tious (lī·sen′shəs) *adj.* Lacking in moral restraint; lewd. [< F < L *licentiosus*] — **li·cen′tious·ly** *adv.* — **li·cen′tious·ness** *n.*

li·chee (lē′chē) *n.* 1. The edible fruit of a tree native to China, having a hard seed and sweet pulp enclosed within a thin, brittle shell: also **lichee nut.** 2. The tree itself. [< Chinese *li-chih*]

li·chen (lī′kən) *n.* Any of various flowerless plants composed of fungi and algae, commonly growing in flat patches on rocks, trees, etc. [< L < Gk., prob. < *leichein* to lick] — **li′chen·ous, li′chen·ose** (-ōs) *adj.*

lic·it (lis′it) *adj.* Lawful. [< F ult. < L *licere* to be allowed] — **lic′it·ly** *adv.* — **lic′it·ness** *n.*

lick (lik) *v.t.* 1. To pass the tongue over the surface of. 2. To remove or consume by taking with the tongue: often followed by *up, off,* etc. 3. To move or pass lightly over or about: The flames *licked* the coals. 4. *Informal* To defeat. 5. *Informal* To thrash; beat. — *v.i.* 6. To move quickly or lightly; flicker. — **to lick into shape** To put in proper form or condition. — **to lick one's chops** To show pleased anticipation. — *n.* 1. A stroke of the tongue in licking. 2. A small amount. 3. *U.S.* A salt lick. 4. *Informal* A blow;

whack. 5. *Often pl. Informal* An opportunity to do something; a turn. 6. *Informal* A stroke; spell, as of work. — **a lick and a promise** *Informal* Hasty washing or cleaning. [OE *liccian*]

lick·e·ty·split (lik′ə·tē·split′) *adv. U.S. Informal* At full speed.

lick·ing (lik′ing) *n.* 1. The act of one who or that which licks. 2. *Informal* A whipping; beating.

lic·o·rice (lik′ə·ris, -rish) *n.* 1. A perennial leguminous herb of Europe. 2. The dried root of this plant, or an extract made from it, used in medicine and confections. 3. A confection flavored with this extract. Also, *esp. Brit.,* **liquorice.** [< AF, OF < LL < Gk. < *glykys* sweet + *rhiza* root]

lic·tor (lik′tər) *n.* In ancient Rome, one of the officers or guards who attended the chief magistrates, and who bore the fasces as a symbol of office. [< L, prob. < *ligare* to tie]

lid (lid) *n.* 1. A hinged or removable cover placed at the top of a receptacle or over an opening. 2. An eyelid. 3. *Bot.* A top, as of a pyxis, separating at a transverse dividing line; an operculum. [OE *hlid*] — **lid′ded** *adj.* — **lid′less** *adj.*

lie¹ (lī) *v.i.* **lay, lain, ly·ing** 1. To be in a recumbent or prostrate position. 2. To place oneself in a recumbent position; rest at full length: often with *down.* 3. To be placed upon or rest against a surface, esp. in a horizontal position. 4. To be buried, as in a grave or tomb. 5. To be or remain in a specified condition or state: to *lie* dormant. 6. To exist; be inherent: often followed by *in* or *within.* 7. To occupy a location; be situated. 8. To continue or extend: The future *lies* before us. ◆ See note under LAY¹. — **to lie in wait (for)** To wait in concealment so as to attack by surprise. — **to lie low** *Informal* To remain in concealment; conceal one's intentions. — **to lie with** To rest with; be up to: The choice *lies with* him. — *n.* 1. The position, manner, or situation in which something lies; aspect. 2. The resting place or haunt of an animal, bird, or fish. [OE *licgan*]

lie² (lī) *n.* 1. An untrue statement made with the intent of deceiving; a falsehood. 2. That which creates or is intended to produce a false impression. — **to give the lie (to)** To accuse (someone) of lying. 2. To expose as false. — **white lie** A false statement made with the intent of being polite or kind. — *v.* **lied, ly·ing** *v.i.* 1. To make an untrue statement or statements, esp. with intent to deceive. 2. To give an erroneous or misleading impression: Figures don't *lie.* — *v.t.* 3. To put or promote (oneself or someone) into a specified situation by telling lies. [OE *lyge*]

— **Syn.** (noun) A *lie* is a statement, known to be untrue, and made with the intent to deceive. *Falsehood* leaves open the question of intent to deceive, and *untruth* often implies error rather than malice; both *falsehood* and *untruth* are also used euphemistically for *lie.* *Fib* and *story* are almost exclusively used of *falsehoods* told by young children, and both are generally regarded as trivial.

lied (lēd, *Ger.* lēt) *n.* *pl.* **lied·er** (lē′dər) A German song; esp., a ballad or lyric poem set to music. [< G]

Lie·der·kranz (lē′dər·kränts) *n.* A soft cheese similar to but milder than Limburger: a trade name. Also **lie′der·kranz.** [< G, lit., garland of songs]

lie detector A polygraph (def. 3) used to establish the truth or falsity of an accused person's statements.

lief (lēf) *adv.* Willingly; readily: used chiefly in the phrase **would as lief.** — *adj. Archaic* 1. Dear; beloved. 2. Willing; inclined. [OE *lēof* dear]

liege (lēj) *n.* 1. A lord or sovereign to whom allegiance or feudal service is due. 2. A vassal or subject owing allegiance to a lord or sovereign. — *adj.* 1. Entitled to feudal allegiance, as of a vassal: now used chiefly in the phrase **liege lord.** 2. Bound in vassalage or owing allegiance to a lord or sovereign. [< OF < Med.L < *laeticus* free < OHG *ledig*]

lien (lēn, lē′ən) *n.* A legal right to claim or dispose of property in payment of or as security for a debt or charge. [< L *ligare* to tie]

lieu (lōō) *n.* Place; stead: now only in the phrase **in lieu of.** [ME *live* < OF < L *locus* place]

lieu·ten·an·cy (lōō·ten′ən·sē, *Brit.* lef·ten′ən·sē, or *Brit. Naval* lə·ten′-) *n.* The office, rank, or authority of a lieutenant.

lieu·ten·ant (lōō·ten′ənt, *Brit.* lef·ten′ənt, or *Brit. Naval* lə·ten′-) *n.* 1. *Mil.* A commissioned officer holding either of two ranks, **first** or **second lieutenant,** the former ranking next below a captain. See tables at GRADE. 2. *Naval* a *U.S.* A commissioned officer holding either of two ranks, **lieutenant** or **lieutenant (junior grade),** the former ranking next below a lieutenant commander and the latter next above an ensign. b *Brit. & Canadian* A commissioned officer ranking next below a lieutenant-commander. See tables at GRADE. 3. One deputized to perform the duties of a superior. [< F < *lieu* place + *tenant,* ppr. of *tenir* to hold]

lieutenant colonel *Mil.* An officer ranking next above a major. Also *Brit. & Canadian* **lieu·ten·ant-col·o·nel** (lef·ten′ənt·ker′nəl). See tables at GRADE.

lieutenant commander *Naval* An officer ranking next above a lieutenant and next below a commander. Also *Brit. & Canadian* **lieu·ten·ant-com·man·der** (lə-ten′ənt-kə-man′dər). See tables at GRADE.

lieutenant general *Mil.* An officer ranking next above a major general. Also *Brit. & Canadian* **lieu·ten·ant-gen·er·al** (lef·ten′ənt-gen′ər-əl). See tables at GRADE.

lieutenant governor 1. *U.S.* An elected official who performs the duties of the governor of a State during his absence or disability or who replaces him in case of death or resignation. 2. In the British Empire, a deputy governor of a territory under the jurisdiction of a governor general.

life (līf) *n.* *pl.* **lives** (līvz) 1. The form of existence that distinguishes animals and plants from inorganic substances and dead organisms, characterized by metabolism, growth, reproduction, irritability, etc. 2. The characteristic state of an organism that has not died. 3. Existence regarded as a desirable condition: *life*, liberty, and the pursuit of happiness. 4. A spiritual state regarded as a continuation or perfection of animate existence after death: eternal *life*. 5. Living organisms collectively. 6. A living being; person: to save a *life*. 7. The period of an individual's existence between birth and death; also, a specified portion of this period. 8. A biography. 9. The period during which something continues to be effective, useful, etc.: the *life* of an engine. 10. Human affairs or relationships: daily *life*. 11. Manner of existence; characteristic activities, as of a specified group, locality, etc.: city *life*. 12. Energetic force; animation: full of *life*. 13. A source of liveliness; animating spirit: the *life* of the party. 14. A living model; also, a representation of such a model. **— for dear life** With urgent effort, speed, etc. **— for life** For the remainder of one's existence. **— for the life of me** (him, etc.) Under any circumstances; at all: usu. with the negative. **— to bring to life** 1. To make vital; animate. 2. To recall vividly to the mind or senses. **— to come to life** 1. To regain consciousness. 2. To become animated. 3. To seem to be real or alive. **— to take life** To kill. [OE *līf*]

life belt A life preserver in the form of a belt.

life·blood (līf′blud′) *n.* 1. The blood necessary to life. 2. Anything indispensable to existence; vital force.

life·boat (līf′bōt′) *n.* A boat constructed and equipped for saving lives at sea in the event of shipwreck, storm, etc.; esp., such a boat carried on board a larger vessel.

life buoy A life preserver, often in the form of a ring.

life expectancy The probable length of life of an individual, esp. as predicted statistically.

life·guard (līf′gärd′) *n.* *U.S.* An expert swimmer employed at a beach, etc., to protect the safety of bathers.

life insurance Insurance on the life of an individual, providing payment to the beneficiary or beneficiaries upon the death of the insured or to the insured upon reaching a certain age. Also *Brit.* **life assurance.**

life jacket A life preserver in the form of a jacket or vest.

life·less (līf′lis) *adj.* 1. Not possessing the characteristics of living organisms. 2. Deprived of life; dead. 3. Not inhabited by or incapable of sustaining living organisms: a *lifeless* desert. 4. Lacking animation or vitality. 5. Exhibiting no signs of life. **— life′less·ly** *adv.* **— life′less·ness** *n.*

life·like (līf′līk′) *adj.* 1. Resembling actual life. 2. Accurately representing a person or thing. **— life′like′ness** *n.*

life line 1. A rope affording support to those in precarious situations. 2. Any route used for transporting vital supplies.

life·long (līf′lông′, -long′) *adj.* Lasting through life.

life net A strong net designed to rescue those who jump or fall from great heights, used by firemen, etc.

life preserver A buoyant device, either inflatable or filled with cork, kapok, etc., and made as a belt, jacket, or ring, used to keep afloat those in danger of drowning.

lif·er (lī′fər) *n.* *Slang* One sentenced to prison for life.

life raft A raftlike structure used as a rescue craft; esp., an inflatable rubber boat equipped with oars.

LIFE PRESERVERS
A Solid block cork.
B Cork ring buoy.
C Collar-type jacket.

life·sav·er (līf′sā′vər) *n.* 1. One who saves another's life. 2. A person trained to rescue those in danger of drowning. 3. *Informal* One who or that which provides aid, relief, etc., in time of need. **— life′sav′ing** *n. & adj.*

life-size (līf′sīz′) *adj.* Having the same size as the thing or person portrayed. Also **life′-sized′.**

life span The extreme length of life regarded as biologically possible in an organism or the group to which it belongs.

life·time (līf′tīm′) *n.* The period of animate existence; also, the period of effective functioning: the *lifetime* of the car.

life·work (līf′wûrk′) *n.* The work of a productive lifetime.

lift (lift) *v.t.* 1. To take hold of and raise to a higher place or position; hoist. 2. To move, direct, or cause to rise to a higher position or level. 3. To hold up. 4. To bring to a higher or more desirable degree or condition; exalt. 5. To emit in loud or clearly audible tones, as the voice: to *lift* a cry. 6. To subject (the face) to surgery in order to remove signs of age. 7. *Informal* To take surreptitiously; steal; also, to plagiarize. **—v.i.** 8. To exert effort in attempting to raise something. 9. To yield to upward pressure; rise. 10. To become dispersed or move away by or as by rising: the fog *lifted*. **— n.** 1. The act of lifting or raising. 2. The power or ability to lift or impart upward motion. 3. The height, distance, or degree to which something rises or is raised. 4. Assistance given by or as by raising. 5. A ride given to a traveler or in the direction of his destination. 6. A feeling of exaltation, exhilaration, or well-being. 7. Elevated or erect position, bearing, etc.: the *lift* of her chin. 8. A machine or device used in lifting or hoisting. 9. An amount lifted or capable of being lifted. 10. *Brit.* An elevator. 11. Any of the layers of leather, etc., constituting the heel of a shoe. 12. *Aeron.* The component of aerodynamic forces acting on an aircraft, exerted perpendicular to the relative wind and generally opposing the pull of gravity. [ME < ON *lypta* to raise in the air.] **— lift′er** *n.*

lift-off (lift′ôf′, -of′) *n. Aerospace* The vertical ascent of a rocket or spacecraft from its launching pad.

lig·a·ment (lig′ə-mənt) *n.* 1. *Anat.* A band of firm, fibrous tissue forming a connection between bones, or supporting an organ. 2. A bond or connecting tie. [< L *ligare* to bind] **— lig′a·men′tal, lig·a·men′ta·ry, lig′a·men′tous** *adj.*

li·gan (lī′gən) *n.* Lagan.

li·gate (lī′gāt) *v.t.* **gat·ed, gat·ing** To bind or constrict with a ligature. [< L *ligatus*, pp. of *ligare*, to bind, tie]

lig·a·ture (lig′ə-chŏŏr, -chər) *n.* 1. The act of tying up or constricting by binding. Also **li·ga·tion** (lī-gā′shən). 2. A band, strip, etc., used to tie, bind, or constrict. 3. In printing, a character consisting of two or more connected letters, as æ, fi, ffi. 4. *Music* A slur indicating a group of notes sung or played as a connected phrase; also, the group of notes thus indicated. **—v.t.** To ligate.

light¹ (līt) *n.* 1. *Physics* a The form of radiant energy that stimulates the organs of sight, having for normal human vision wavelengths ranging from about 3900 to 7700 angstroms and traveling at a speed of about 186,300 miles a second. b A closely related form of radiant energy not stimulating human vision; ultraviolet or infrared light. 2. The condition or medium that makes vision possible; illumination. 3. The sensation produced by stimulation of the organs of vision and visual centers of the brain. 4. Any source of brightness, as a lamp, the sun, etc. 5. An emission of brightness, esp. from a particular source or direction. 6. The daily illumination shed on the earth by the sun; daylight; also the period of daylight. 7. Mental or spiritual understanding or insight. 8. The state of being unhidden and observable: to come to *light*. 9. Way of being regarded; aspect: to see things in a new *light*. 10. *pl.* Ability and understanding: to live according to one's own *lights*. 11. A lively or intense expression on the face, esp. in the eyes. 12. An instance of kindling; ignition. 13. An opening admitting illumination, as a window. 14. In graphic arts: a The representation of light or atmosphere. b A part of a picture showing an illuminated area. 15. A person of authority or eminence; luminary: a lesser *light*. **— in the light of** In view of; considering. **— to see the light** 1. To come into being. 2. To be presented to public notice. 3. To become enlightened. **— to strike a light** To ignite something, as a match, by friction. **— adj.** 1. Full of light; bright. 2. Diluted or combined with white, as a color; pale. **— v. light·ed** or **lit, light·ing** *v.t.* 1. To ignite; kindle. 2. To illuminate or cause to illuminate. 3. To make bright, cheerful, animated, etc. 4. To guide or conduct with light. **—v.i.** 5. To become ignited. 6. To become luminous, radiant, or bright: often with *up*. [OE *lēoht*]

light² (līt) *adj.* 1. Having little weight; not heavy. 2. Having little weight in proportion to bulk or size; low in specific gravity. 3. Having less than standard or correct weight. 4. Not burdensome or oppressive. 5. Not difficult or arduous. 6. Having comparatively little effect; not intense, severe, etc. 7. Not great in degree or concentration; thin: a *light* fog. 8. Exerting little force or pressure; gentle: a *light* tap. 9. Characterized by buoyancy or ease in motion. 10. Moving or working swiftly and skillfully; deft. 11. Not clumsy, coarse, or massive in form or appearance; delicate. 12. Intended or enjoyed as entertainment; not lofty or heroic: *light* verse. 13. Slight in importance or consequence. 14. Frivolous; trivial. 15. Easily distracted or diverted; flighty. 16. Morally unrestrained; wanton. 17. Slightly faint or delirious; giddy. 18. Easily eaten or digested. 19. Comparatively low in alcoholic content: *light* wines. 20. Well-leavened; spongy or airy in texture: *light* biscuits. 21. Crumbly in texture; porous: *light* soil. 22. Relatively swift and maneuverable: a *light* cruiser. 23. *Mil.* a Designating the less massive types of weapons or equipment. b Formerly, designating troops or units with relatively less massive equipment: *light* cavalry. 24. *Meteorol.* Designating a breeze moving at 4 to 7 miles per hour. **25.** In phonetics, prosody, etc., designating an unaccented or unstressed syllable or vowel. **— to make light of** To treat or consider as trifling. — *v.i.* **light·ed** or **lit, light·ing 1.** To descend and settle down after flight, as a bird. **2.** To happen or come, as by chance: with *on* or *upon*. **3.** To get down, as from a horse or carriage. **4.** To fall; strike, as a blow. **— to light into** *U.S. Informal* To attack; assail. **— to light out** *U.S. Informal* To depart in haste. — *adv.* **1.** Lightly. **2.** Without encumbrance or excess equipment. [OE *lēoht, līht*]

light·en¹ (līt'n) *v.t.* **1.** To make light or bright; illuminate. — *v.i.* **2.** To become light; grow brighter. **3.** To glow with light; gleam. **4.** To emit or display lightning.

light·en² (līt'n) *v.t.* **1.** To reduce the weight or load of; make less heavy. **2.** To make less oppressive, troublesome, etc.; diminish the severity of. **3.** To relieve, as of distress, uneasiness, etc. — *v.i.* **4.** To become less heavy.

light·er¹ (līt'ər) *n.* One who or that which lights; esp., a device used to light cigarettes, cigars, etc.

light·er² (līt'ər) *Naut. n.* A bargelike vessel used in loading or unloading ships, or in transporting loads for short distances. — *v.t. & v.i.* To transport (goods) by lighter. [< Du. *lichten* to make light, unload]

light·er·age (līt'tər·ij) *n.* **1.** The removal or conveying of cargo by lighter. **2.** A price charged for this service.

light·er-than-air (līt'tər·thən·âr') *adj. Aeron.* Designating aircraft, as balloons, dirigibles, etc., that depend for flight on a specific gravity less than that of air.

light·face (līt'fās') *n. Printing* Type having characters formed of light, thin lines.

light-fin·gered (līt'fing'gərd) *adj.* Expert at picking pockets, etc. **— light'-fin'gered·ness** *n.*

light-foot·ed (līt'fŏŏt'id) *adj.* **1.** Stepping with buoyancy and grace. **2.** Running lightly and swiftly. Also *Poetic* **light'foot'.** **— light'-foot'ed·ly** *adv.* **— light'-foot'ed·ness** *n.*

light·head·ed (līt'hed'id) *adj.* **1.** Frivolous; giddy. **2.** Dizzy. **— light'head'ed·ly** *adv.* **— light'·head'ed·ness** *n.*

light·heart·ed (līt'här'tid) *adj.* Free from care; blithe; gay. **— light'heart'ed·ly** *adv.* **— light'heart'ed·ness** *n.*

light·house (līt'hous') *n.* A tower or similar structure equipped with a powerful beacon, erected at or near a dangerous place to serve as a warning or guide for ships.

light·ing (līt'ing) *n.* **1.** The providing of light or the state of being lighted. **2.** A system or apparatus supplying illumination, as in a public building, theater, etc. **3.** The arrangement or effect of lighted areas in a painting, etc.

light·ly (līt'lē) *adv.* **1.** With little weight or pressure; gently. **2.** To a slight degree; moderately. **3.** With a swift, buoyant step or motion. **4.** In a carefree manner or spirit. **5.** With insufficient seriousness or concern; frivolously; irresponsibly: often with the negative. **6.** With little esteem or appreciation; slightingly. **7.** *Archaic* Easily.

light-mind·ed (līt'mīn'did) *adj.* Thoughtless; frivolous. **— light'-mind'ed·ly** *adv.* **— light'-mind'ed·ness** *n.*

light·ness¹ (līt'nis) *n.* **1.** The state or quality of being illuminated or bright. **2.** Paleness of color.

light·ness² (līt'nis) *n.* **1.** The quality of having relatively little weight, force, etc. **2.** Buoyancy or ease of motion. **3.** Freedom from sorrow or care. **4.** Lack of seriousness.

light·ning (līt'ning) *n.* **1.** A sudden flash of light caused by the discharge of atmospheric electricity between electrified regions of cloud, or between a cloud and the earth. **2.** The discharge itself. [ME *lighten* to flash]

lightning bug *U.S.* A firefly.

lightning rod A pointed metal rod that protects buildings from lightning by grounding it harmlessly through a cable.

light opera Operetta.

light quantum *Physics* A photon.

lights (līts) *n.pl.* The lungs, esp. of animals used as food. [ME *lihtes*; so called from their light weight]

light·ship (līt'ship') *n.* A vessel equipped with warning lights, signals, etc., and moored in dangerous waters as a guide to ships.

light·some (līt'səm) *adj.* **1.** Untroubled by care; cheerful; gay. **2.** Buoyant, airy, or graceful. **3.** Frivolous; flighty. **— light'some·ly** *adv.* **— light'some·ness** *n.*

light·weight (līt'wāt') *n.* **1.** A person or animal of much less than average weight. **2.** A boxer or wrestler weighing between 127 and 135 pounds. **3.** *U.S. Informal* An unimportant, incompetent, or inadequate person. — *adj.* Of less than average or required weight.

light-year (līt'yir') *n. Astron.* A unit of interstellar space measurement equal to the distance traversed by light in one year, approximately six trillion miles.

lig·ne·ous (lig'nē·əs) *adj.* Having the composition, texture, or appearance of wood. [< L < *lignum* wood]

ligni- *combining form* Wood. Also, before vowels, **lign-.** Also **ligno-.** [< L *lignum* wood]

lig·nite (lig'nīt) *n.* A compact, carbonized, brownish vegetable substance often retaining a woodlike structure, forming a fuel intermediate between peat and bituminous coal. [< F] **— lig·nit'ic** (-nit'ik) *adj.*

lig·num vi·tae (lig'nəm vī'tē) **1.** A tree of tropical America, having hard, greenish brown wood. **2.** The wood of this tree. **3.** Any of various related or similar trees. [< NL < L, wood of life]

lik·a·ble (lī'kə·bəl) *adj.* Of a nature to be liked; attractive; pleasing. Also **like'a·ble.** **— lik'a·ble·ness** *n.*

like¹ (līk) *v.* **liked, lik·ing** *v.t.* **1.** To take pleasure in; enjoy. **2.** To feel affectionately toward; be fond of. **3.** To desire; prefer: I *like* that one. — *v.i.* **4.** To feel disposed; choose: Do as you *like.* — *n. Usu. pl.* Preference; inclination: chiefly in the phrase **likes and dislikes.** [OE *lician*]

like² (līk) *prep.* **1.** Having a close resemblance to; similar to. **2.** With the characteristics or qualities of: to smell *like* a rose. **3.** Characteristic or typical of: How *like* him to behave that way! **4.** Indicative of; likely to result in: It looks *like* rain. **5.** As though having the need for: with *feel*: to feel *like* resting. **6.** Such as: cities *like* London, Rome, New York. **7.** In the manner of: He used the board *like* a hammer. **— like anything** (or **blazes, mad, hell,** etc.) *Informal* With great intensity, force, effort, etc. — *adj.* **1.** Having the same or similar characteristics; related. **2.** Equal or nearly equal; equivalent. **3.** Similar to what is portrayed or represented, as a portrait. **— like . . . , like . . .** As (the one is), so (is the other): *Like* father, *like* son. — *adv.* **1.** *Dial.* or *Informal* Probably: *Like* enough he'll go. **2.** *Dial.* or *Illit.* To a certain degree; somewhat: I'm hungry *like.* **3.** *U.S. Slang* or *Illit.* A meaningless interpolation, as before adjectives, etc.: It's *like* cool. — *n.* **1.** Anything similar or in the same category: preceded by *the*: physics, chemistry, and the *like.* **2.** One of equal value, standing, etc.: We will not see his *like* again. — *conj.* **1.** *Informal* or *Illit.* As if; in the manner that: It turned out *like* you said. **2.** *Informal* As if: It looks *like* it's going to rain. [OE *gelic*]

-like *suffix of adjectives* **1.** Resembling or similar to: *wavelike.* **2.** Having the characteristics of: *childlike.* [< LIKE²]

◆ Compounds with *-like* are usu. solid, but are hyphenated when three *l*'s occur together, as in *shell-like.*

like·li·hood (līk'lē·hŏŏd) *n.* **1.** The state or quality of being probable; probability. **2.** Something probable.

like·ly (līk'lē) *adj.* **·li·er, ·li·est 1.** Having or showing an apparent tendency or possibility: He is *likely* to go. **2.** Seemingly about to happen; imminent; probable: His promotion is *likely.* **3.** Apparently true; plausible; believable. **4.** Suitable; appropriate: a *likely* spot. **5.** Capable; promising: a *likely* lad. — *adv.* Probably.

like-mind·ed (līk'mīn'did) *adj.* Having similar opinions, purposes, tastes, etc.

lik·en (lī'kən) *v.t.* To represent as similar; compare.

like·ness (līk'nis) *n.* **1.** The state or quality of being like; resemblance. **2.** A pictorial representation; portrait; image. **3.** Imitative form; guise: to take on the *likeness* of someone.

like·wise (līk'wīz') *adv.* **1.** Moreover; also; too. **2.** In like manner; similarly.

lik·ing (lī'king) *n.* **1.** Feeling of attraction or affection; fondness. **2.** Preference; taste.

li·lac (lī'lak, -lək, -lok) *n.* **1.** A flowering shrub of the olive family, having fragrant purplish or white flowers. **2.** A light pinkish purple color. — *adj.* Having a purplish color. [< F < Sp. < Arabic < Persian *līlak* bluish]

lil·i·a·ceous (lil'ē·ā'shəs) *adj.* Belonging to or characteristic of the lily family. [< LL < L *lilium* lily]

Lil·li·put (lil'ə·put, -pət) In Swift's *Gulliver's Travels* (1726), a country inhabited by a race of tiny people. **— Lil'li·pu'tian** *adj., n.*

lilt (lilt) *n.* **1.** A lively quality of speech, voice, song, etc., with pronounced variations of pitch. **2.** A light, buoyant motion or manner. — *v.i. & v.t.* To speak, sing, move, etc., in a cheerful rhythmic manner. [ME *lulte*]

lil·y (lil'ē) *n. pl.* **·ies 1.** Any of numerous wild or cultivated plants, having bulbous rootstocks and showy, usu. funnel-shaped flowers. **2.** Any of various other plants resembling a lily, as the calla or the water lily. — *adj.* Resembling a lily in whiteness, delicacy, beauty, etc. [OE < L *lilium*]

lil·y-liv·ered (lil'ē·liv'ərd) *adj.* Cowardly; fainthearted.

lil·y-of-the-val·ley (lil'ē·əv·thə·val'ē) *n. pl.* **lil·ies-of-the-valley** A perennial herb having small, fragrant white flowers. Also **lily of the valley.**

lily pad One of the large, floating leaves of the water lily.

li·ma bean (lī'mə) **1.** A species of the common bean, having large, flat, edible seeds. **2.** The seed of this plant, eaten as a vegetable. Also **Lima bean.** [after *Lima*, Peru]

limb¹ (lim) *n.* **1.** A part of the animal or human body attached to but distinct from the torso, as an arm, leg, or wing. **2.** One of the major divisions of a tree trunk; a large branch.

3. An extended or branching part, division, etc. **4.** A person or thing regarded as a part of a larger body, group, etc. **— out on a limb** *U.S. Informal* In a risky, vulnerable, or questionable position. [OE *lim*] **— limb′less** *adj.*

limb² (lim) *n. Astron.* The edge of the disk of the sun, moon, or other heavenly body. [< F < L *limbus* edge, border]

limbed (limd) *adj.* **1.** Having limbs. **2.** Having or characterized by a (specified kind of) limb or (a specified number of) limbs: used in combination: *strong-limbed; four-limbed.*

lim·ber¹ (lim′bər) *adj.* **1.** Pliant; flexible. **2.** Able to bend or move easily; lithe. **— v.t. 1.** To make pliant. **— v.i. 2.** To exercise so as to become limber: with *up.* [Origin uncertain] **— lim′ber·ly** *adv.* **— lim′ber·ness** *n.*

lim·ber² (lim′bər) *n. Mil.* A two-wheeled, detachable vehicle at the forepart of a gun carriage. **— v.t. & v.i.** To attach a limber to (a gun). [Origin uncertain]

lim·bo¹ (lim′bō) *n. pl.* **·bos 1.** *Theol.* A region on the edge of hell for the souls of the righteous who died before the coming of Christ, and those of infants who die before baptism. **2.** A place or condition for the relegation of unwanted or forgotten persons, things, etc. [< L *limbus* border]

lim·bo² (lim′bō) *n. pl.* **·bos** A dance popular in the West Indies, in which dancers pass under a bar placed at successively lower levels. [Origin uncertain]

Lim·burg·er cheese (lim′bûr′gər) A soft, white cheese having a strong odor and flavor. Also **Lim′burg cheese, Lim′burg·er.** Also **lim′burg·er.** [after *Limburg,* Belgium]

lime¹ (lim) *n.* A white, earthy substance, calcium oxide, CaO, prepared by calcining limestone or other forms of calcium carbonate, and used in mortars and cements. When dry it is called **quicklime** or **unslaked lime,** becoming **slaked lime** upon the addition of water. **— v.t. limed, lim·ing** To treat, mix, or spread with lime. [OE *lim*]

lime² (lim) *n.* **1.** A small, green, lemonlike citrus fruit whose juice is used for flavoring, in beverages, etc. **2.** The tropical tree yielding this fruit. [< F < Sp. *lima* < Arabic *limah*]

lime³ (lim) *n.* The European linden tree. [OE *lind* linden]

lime·kiln (lim′kil′, -kiln′) *n.* A kiln in which limestone, seashells, etc., are burned to produce lime.

lime·light (lim′lit′) *n.* **1.** Public attention or notice. **2.** A bright light used to illuminate a performer, stage area, etc., and originally produced by heating lime to incandescence.

lim·er·ick (lim′rik, -ə-rik) *n.* A humorous verse of five anapestic lines. Also **Lim′er·ick.** [? from the line "Will you come up to *Limerick,*"]

lime·stone (lim′stōn′) *n.* A sedimentary rock composed wholly or in part of calcium carbonate.

lime·wa·ter (lim′wô′tər, -wot′ər) *n.* An aqueous solution of calcium hydroxide, used in medicine.

lim·ey (li′mē) *n. pl.* **lime·ys** *U.S. Slang* **1.** A British sailor. **2.** Any Englishman. [from the former British maritime practice of drinking *lime* juice to prevent scurvy]

lim·it (lim′it) *n.* **1.** The furthest or utmost extent, range, degree, etc., beyond which an activity, power, or function cannot or may not proceed: one's *limit* of endurance. **2.** *Usu. pl.* The boundaries or extent of a specified area. **3.** An amount or quantity established as the greatest permissible: Four fish are the *limit.* **4.** *Math.* A definite quantity or value that a series is conceived or proved to approach but never reach. **— off limits** Forbidden to military personnel except on official business. **— the limit** *Informal* **1.** One who or that which tries one's patience, credulity, etc., to the utmost. **2.** To the utmost extent: usu. with *go.* **— v.t.** To set a bound or bounds to; confine; restrict. [< L *limes, limites*] **— lim′it·a·ble** *adj.* **— lim·i·ta·tive** (lim′ə·tā′tiv) *adj.* **— lim′it·er** *n.*

lim·i·ta·tion (lim′ə·tā′shən) *n.* **1.** That which limits; restriction; shortcoming. **2.** The act of limiting, or the state of being limited. **3.** *Law* **a** A restrictive condition. **b** A legally fixed period within which certain acts must be performed. [< L *limitatio, -onis*]

lim·it·ed (lim′it·id) *adj.* **1.** Confined within or defined by a limit or limits; restricted. **2.** Falling short of fullness or impressiveness: a *limited* success. **3.** Having powers restricted by constitutional law or authority, as a government. **4.** Of a train, bus, etc., making few stops. **5.** *Chiefly Brit. & Canadian* Restricted in liability to the amount invested by shareholders in its stock: a *limited* company. **— n.** A limited train, bus, etc. **— lim′i·ted·ly** *adv.* **— lim′i·ted·ness** *n.*

lim·it·ing (lim′it·ing) *adj. Gram.* Denoting adjectives that indicate the number or quantity of nouns rather than describe them, as *these* words, *seven* swans.

lim·it·less (lim′it·lis) *adj.* Having no limit; boundless.

limn (lim) *v.t.* To draw or paint; also, to describe in words. [ME < OF < L *illuminare*] **— lim·ner** (lim′nər) *n.*

Li·moges (lē·mōzh′, *Fr.* lē·môzh′) *n.* A type of fine porcelain manufactured at Limoges, France. Also **Limoges ware.**

lim·ou·sine (lim′ə·zēn′, lim′ə·zēn) *n.* **1.** A large automobile, originally having a closed compartment for passengers and an open driver's seat under a projecting roof. **2.** Any large, luxurious automobile. [< F]

limp¹ (limp) *v.i.* **1.** To walk with a halting or irregular step, as with an injured leg or foot. **2.** To progress in an irregular or labored manner. **— n.** The manner of walking of one who is lame. [OE *lemphealt* lame] **— limp′er** *n.*

limp² (limp) *adj.* **1.** Lacking stiffness or firmness; flabby. **2.** Lacking force or vigor; weak. [Origin uncertain] **— limp′ly** *adv.* **— limp′ness** *n.*

lim·pet (lim′pit) *n.* Any of various small marine animals having conical shells and noted for their ability to cling to rocks. [OE < LL *lampreda* limpet, lamprey]

lim·pid (lim′pid) *adj.* **1.** Characterized by crystalline clearness; transparent. **2.** Characterized by clarity, lucidity, or purity, as of style. **— Syn.** See CLEAR. [< L *limpidus* clear] **— lim·pid′i·ty, lim′pid·ness** *n.* **— lim′pid·ly** *adv.*

lim·y (li′mē) *adj.* **lim·i·er, lim·i·est** Containing or resembling lime.

lin·age (li′nij) *n.* **1.** The number of lines in a piece of written or printed matter. **2.** Alignment. Also *lineage.*

linch·pin (linch′pin′) *n.* A pin placed through the end of an axle in order to keep a wheel from sliding off. [OE *lynis*]

lin·den (lin′dən) *n.* Any of various shade trees having soft, white wood, heart-shaped leaves, and fragrant, cream-colored flowers: also called *basswood.* [OE *lind* linden]

line¹ (lin) *n.* **1.** A slender, continuous mark or indentation, as that drawn by a pen, pencil, or pointed tool. **2.** Any narrow band or strip resembling such a mark. **3.** A wrinkle or crease in the skin. **4.** Contour or profile, as of the edge of an area. **5.** A division or boundary between adjoining areas; border. **6.** A demarcation or limit separating contrasting concepts, kinds of behavior, etc. **7.** A row of persons or things. **8.** A chronological succession of persons: the royal *line.* **9.** A row of written or printed words. **10.** A short letter; note. **11.** A single row of words forming a verse, as of a stanza. **12.** Course of movement or progress; route: *line* of march. **13.** Course of action, thought, or performance: a *line* of thought. **14.** *Often pl.* General plan or concept, as of form, content, etc.: a work on heroic *lines.* **15.** Alignment; agreement; accord: to bring into *line.* **16.** Scope or field of activity, ability, etc.: that work is not in my *line.* **17.** Kind of work; occupation. **18.** Merchandise of a particular sort. **19.** *pl.* The words of an actor's or performer's part. **20.** *pl. Brit.* A certificate of marriage. **21.** *pl.* Lot in life; luck: hard *lines.* **23.** *U.S. Slang* A glib manner of speech intended to ingratiate or persuade. **24.** A pipe, conduit, or system of channels to convey liquids, gas, electricity, etc. **25.** In telephonic communication, etc.: **a** A wire or cable carrying power signals. **b** A system of such connections. **c** A connection or channel of communication: to keep a *line* open. **26.** Any system of public transportation over an established route or routes. **27.** The roadbed, track, or system of tracks of a railroad. **28.** A rope, string, cord, or the like, as used in fishing, measuring, etc. **29.** *Math.* The theoretical trace or course of a moving point, conceived of as having length, but no other dimension. **30.** In the arts: **a** The representation of form by the use of strokes, rather than by shading or coloring. **b** The distinctive form or contours of any artistic creation. **31.** *Mil.* **a** A trench or rampart. **b** A system of fortifications presenting an extended front. **c** *Often pl.* The disposition of troops: the front *lines.* **d** The combatant forces, as distinguished from the supporting services and the staff. **32.** In the naval services, those officers in charge of combat operations. **33.** In bridge, a horizontal division of the score, separating points counting toward game, written below it, and bonus points, written above it. **— in line 1.** So as to form a line or row. **2.** In accordance with accepted standards or limitations. **— in line for** Next in order for. **— on a line** At the same level; evenly aligned. **— on the line** Paid directly and promptly. **— out of line 1.** Not in conformity with accepted standards or practices. **2.** Insubordinate; unruly. **— to get a line on** *U.S. Informal* To acquire information about. **— to hold the line 1.** To maintain a defense or opposition. **2.** To wait while maintaining an open telephone connection. **3.** In football, to prevent the opposing team from gaining ground. **— v. lined, lining** *v.t.* **1.** To mark with lines. **2.** To place in a line. **3.** To form a row or line along; border. **4.** To indicate by or as by lines; sketch. **5.** In baseball, to bat (a ball, hit, etc.) in an approximately horizontal trajectory. **— v.i. 6.** To form a line; assume positions in a line: usually with *up.* **— to line out** In baseball, to be retired by hitting a line drive that is caught. **— to line up 1.** To form a line. **2.** To bring into alignment. **3.** To take a stand, as in support of something. **4.** To gather; marshal. **5.** To compare. [OE *line* cord]

line² (lin) *v.t.* **lined, lin·ing 1.** To put a covering or facing on the inner surface of. **2.** To constitute a covering or surface for: Tapestries *lined* the room. **3.** To fill or stuff, as with money, food, etc. [OE *lin* flax]

lin·e·age¹ (lin′ē·ij) *n.* **1.** Line of descent from a progenitor. **2.** Ancestry; family; stock. [< OF < L *linea* line]

line·age² (li′nij) See LINAGE.

lin·e·al (lin′ē·əl) *adj.* **1.** Being or occurring in the direct line of descent. **2.** Pertaining to or based upon direct descent. **3.** Consisting of lines; linear. — **lin′e·al·ly** *adv.*

lin·e·a·ment (lĭn′ē-ə-mənt) *n.* **1.** A facial contour or feature. **2.** A distinguishing characteristic.

lin·e·ar (lĭn′ē-ər) *adj.* **1.** Of or pertaining to a line or lines. **2.** Involving or pertaining to length. **3.** Composed of lines. **4.** Resembling a line. — **lin′e·ar·ly** *adv.*

Linear A, Linear B See under MINOAN.

linear measure 1. Measurement by length. **2.** A unit or system of units for measuring length. See table front of book.

line drive In baseball, a batted ball that travels in an approximately horizontal trajectory: also called *liner.*

line·man (lĭn′mən) *n.* *pl.* **·men** (-mən) **1.** A man who installs or repairs telephone or electric power lines: also *linesman.* **2.** A man who inspects a railroad track. **3.** In football, a center, guard, tackle, or end. **4.** In surveying, a man who holds the line, tape, or chain.

lin·en (lĭn′ən) *n.* **1.** A fabric woven from the fibers of flax. **2.** Articles or garments made of linen, or now often of cotton: bed *linen.* — *adj.* **1.** Made of the textile fiber of flax. **2.** Made of linen. [OE *linen* made of flax]

line of force *Physics* A hypothetical line in a field of force, coinciding at every point with the direction of the field.

lin·er[1] (lī′nər) *n.* **1.** A ship or airplane operated by a transportation line. **2.** In baseball, a line drive. **3.** One who or that which marks or produces lines.

lin·er[2] (lī′nər) *n.* **1.** One who makes or fits linings. **2.** Something used as a lining.

lines·man (līnz′mən) *n.* *pl.* **·men** (-mən) **1.** In certain games, as tennis, an official making decisions on play at the lines of the court. **2.** In football, the official marking the distances gained or lost in each play. **3.** A lineman (def. 1).

line-up (līn′ŭp′) *n.* **1.** An arrangement of persons or things in a line. **2.** In sports: **a** The formation of players drawn up for action. **b** The players. **c** A list of the team members playing at the start of a game. **3.** In police work, a row of possible criminal suspects. Also **line′up′.**

lin·ey (lī′nē) See LINY.

ling (lĭng) *n.* *pl.* **ling** or **lings** A codlike food fish of the North Atlantic. [? < Du. *leng*]

-ling[1] *suffix of nouns* **1.** Little; young: *duckling.* **2.** Minor; petty: often used contemptuously: *princeling.* **3.** A person or thing related to or characterized by: *worldling.* [OE]

-ling[2] *suffix* Forming adverbs and adjectives: **1.** (from nouns) Toward: *sideling.* **2.** (from adjectives) Being; becoming: *darkling.* Also **-lings.** [OE *-ling, -linga*]

lin·ger (lĭng′gər) *v.i.* **1.** To stay on as if reluctant to leave. **2.** To proceed in a slow manner; dawdle. **3.** To continue to live or exist; endure. **4.** To pause or dwell with interest, pleasure, etc.: usually with *over.* — *v.t.* **5.** To spend or waste (time, one's life, etc.) idly or wearisomely: with *away* or *out.* [Northern ME *lenger* to delay] — **lin′ger·er** *n.*

lin·ge·rie (län′zhə·rē, län′zhə·rā′, Fr. lăṅ·zhrē′) *n.* Women's light undergarments, nightgowns, etc. [< F]

lin·ger·ing (lĭng′gər·ing) *adj.* **1.** Protracted; drawn out. **2.** Long-lasting; enduring. **3.** Slow. — **lin′ger·ing·ly** *adv.*

lin·go (lĭng′gō) *n.* *pl.* **·goes 1.** Language: used contemptuously or humorously of a tongue one does not understand. **2.** The specialized vocabulary and idiom of a profession, class, etc.: medical *lingo.* [< Pg. < L *lingua* tongue]

lin·gua fran·ca (lĭng′gwə frăng′kə) **1.** Any jargon or pidgin used as a commercial or trade language, as pidgin English. **2.** A mixture of French, Spanish, Italian, Greek, and Arabic, spoken in Mediterranean ports. [< Ital., lit., language of the Franks]

lin·gual (lĭng′gwəl) *adj.* Of or pertaining to the tongue or a tonguelike part. [< Med.L < L *lingua* tongue]

lin·gui·form (lĭng′gwi·fôrm) *adj.* Tongue-shaped.

lin·guist (lĭng′gwist) *n.* **1.** One who is fluent in several languages. **2.** A student or specialist in linguistics.

lin·guis·tic (lĭng·gwis′tĭk) *adj.* Of or pertaining to language or linguistics. Also **lin·guis′ti·cal.** — **lin·guis′ti·cal·ly** *adv.*

lin·guis·tics (lĭng·gwis′tĭks) *n.pl.* (*construed as sing.*) The scientific study of language.

linguistic stock A family of languages, including a parent language together with all the languages derived from it.

lin·i·ment (lĭn′ə·mənt) *n.* A liquid rubbed on the skin to relieve pain and stiffness. [< L *linire* to anoint]

lin·ing (lī′nĭng) *n.* An inner surface or facing inserted in a garment, container, etc., as for protection, reinforcement, etc.; also, the material used.

link (lĭngk) *n.* **1.** One of the loops, rings, or interlocking parts constituting a chain. **2.** A single element in a series, sequence, or set: a weak *link* in his argument. **3.** That which joins or connects separate parts, concepts, etc. **4.** A single sausage. **5.** In surveying, etc., the hundredth part of a chain, equal to 7.92 inches. — *v.t.* & *v.i.* To join or connect by or as by links; interlock; couple; unite. — **Syn.** See UNITE. [ME *linke* < Scand.]

link·age (lĭng′kĭj) *n.* **1.** The act of linking, or the state of being linked. **2.** A system of links.

link·ing verb (lĭng′kĭng) *Gram.* A verb that merely connects the subject and predicate of a sentence without asserting action, esp. the verbs *be, appear, become, feel, look, seem, smell, sound,* and *taste*: also called *copula.*

links (lĭngks) *n.pl.* A golf course. [OE *hlinc* slope]

Lin·ne·an (lĭ·nē′ən) *adj.* Pertaining to Linnaeus or his system of classifying plants and animals. Also **Lin·nae′an.**

lin·net (lĭn′ĭt) *n.* A common songbird of Europe. [< OF < L *linum* flax; from its feeding on flax seeds]

li·no·le·um (lĭ·nō′lē·əm) *n.* A material used as a floor covering, etc., made from oxidized linseed oil and cork pressed upon canvas or burlap. [< L *linum* flax + *oleum* oil]

Li·no·type (lī′nə·tīp) *n.* A typesetting machine operated by a keyboard, and casting a complete line of type on a single metal piece: a trade name. Also **li′no·type.**

li·no·typ·er (lī′nə·tīp′ər) *n.* One who operates a Linotype. Also **li′no·typ·ist.**

lin·seed (lĭn′sēd′) *n.* Flaxseed. [OE *līnsǣd*]

linseed oil A yellowish oil made from flaxseed and used as a drying agent in the preparation of oil paints, linoleum, etc.

lin·sey-wool·sey (lĭn′zē·wŏŏl′zē) *n.* *pl.* **-wool·seys** A coarse cloth woven of linen and wool or cotton and wool threads. [ME *lin* linen + *saye* cloth + WOOL]

lint (lĭnt) *n.* **1.** Bits of thread, fluff, etc. **2.** A downy substance used as a surgical dressing. **3.** *U.S.* The fibers of seeds of unginned cotton. [ME *linnet* lint] — **lin′ty** *adj.*

lin·tel (lĭn′təl) *n.* A horizontal part above the opening of a door or window, supporting the structure above it. [< OF < LL *lintellus, limitellus,* dim. of *limes, limites* limit]

lint·ers (lĭn′tərz) *n.pl.* *U.S.* The short fibers adhering to cotton seeds after ginning.

lin·y (lī′nē) *adj.* **lin·i·er, lin·i·est 1.** Resembling a line; narrow. **2.** Marked with lines or streaks. Also *liney.*

li·on (lī′ən) *n.* **1.** A large, tawny or brownish gray carnivorous mammal of the cat family, native to Africa and SW Asia, the adult male having a shaggy mane. ◆ Collateral adjective: *leonine.* **2.** Any of various animals related or similar to the lion, as the mountain lion. **3.** One of noble courage, great strength, etc. **4.** A celebrity. — **the lion's share** The largest portion; an unduly large part. [< F < L *leo* < Gk. *leōn*] — **li′on·ess** (-ĭs) *n.fem.*

Li·on (lī′ən) *n.* The constellation and sign of the zodiac Leo.

li·on·heart·ed (lī′ən·härt′ĭd) *adj.* Admirably brave.

li·on·ize (lī′ə·nīz) *v.t.* **·ized, ·iz·ing** To treat or regard as a celebrity. — **li·on·i·za′tion** *n.* — **li′on·iz′er** *n.*

lip (lĭp) *n.* **1.** One of the two folds of flesh that bound the mouth and serve as organs of speech. ◆ Collateral adjective: *labial.* **2.** A marginal part or structure resembling this. **3.** The rim or edge of any opening or cavity. **4.** The flared edge of a pitcher, bell, etc. **5.** *Slang* Brash and impudent talk; sass. **6.** *Music* The shaping and control of the mouth in playing a wind instrument. **7.** *Anat.* A labium. **8.** *Bot.* Either of the two divisions, upper or lower, of a corolla or calyx. — **to button one's lip** *Slang* To stop talking; shut up. — **to hang on (someone's) lips** To listen to with rapt attention. — **to keep a stiff upper lip** To maintain one's fortitude. — **to smack one's lips** To express anticipatory or remembered gusto; gloat. — *v.t.* **lipped, lip·ping 1.** To touch with the lips; apply the lips to. **2.** *Music* In playing a wind instrument, to produce the correct pitch of (a tone) by adjusting the position of the lips. — *adj.* **1.** Of, pertaining to, or applied to the lips. **2.** Made or formed by the lips or a lip; labial. **3.** Insincere; hypocritical. [OE *lippa*]

lip·oid (lĭp′oid) *adj.* Resembling fat. — *n. Biochem.* A fatlike substance. [< Gk. *lipos* fat]

lipped (lĭpt) *adj.* Having a lip or lips.

lip·py (lĭp′ē) *adj.* **·pi·er, ·pi·est** *Slang* Sassy.

lip-read (lĭp′rēd′) *v.t.* & *v.i.* **-read** (rĕd), **-read·ing** (rēd′ĭng) To interpret (speech) by watching the movements of lips.

lip reading The interpretation of speech by watching the movement of the lips, as by the deaf. — **lip reader**

lip·stick (lĭp′stĭk′) *n.* A pastelike cosmetic, usu. in the form of a small cylinder, used to color the lips.

liq·ue·fac·tion (lĭk′wə·fak′shən) *n.* The process of liquefying, or the state of being liquid.

liq·ue·fi·er (lĭk′wə·fī′ər) *n.* **1.** One who or that which liquefies. **2.** An apparatus in which a gas is liquefied.

liq·ue·fy (lĭk′wə·fī) *v.t.* & *v.i.* **·fied, ·fy·ing** To convert into or become liquid. [< L *liquere* to be liquid + *facere* to make] — **liq′ue·fi′a·ble** *adj.*

li·ques·cent (lĭ·kwes′ənt) *adj.* Becoming or likely to become liquid; melting. [< L *liquere* to become liquid] — **li·ques′cence, li·ques′cen·cy** *n.*

li·queur (lĭ·kûr′) *n.* An alcoholic beverage usu. made by adding sugar syrup and flavoring to brandy: also called *cordial*. [< F < OF *licur*]

liq·uid (lik′wid) *adj.* **1.** Capable of flowing or of being poured. **2.** Clear and flowing, as sounds. **3.** Clear and bright; limpid. **4.** Free and facile, as movement; fluent. **5.** Consisting of or readily converted into cash. **6.** *Physics* Not gaseous or solid. **7.** *Phonet.* Of consonants, produced without friction; vowellike, as (l) and (r). — *n.* **1.** A substance in that state in which the molecules move freely among themselves but remain in one mass; a fluid that is not a gas. **2.** *Phonet.* The sound (l) or (r), or sometimes other sonorants. [< F < L < *liquere* to be liquid] — **li·quid·i·ty** (li·kwid′ə·tē), **liq′uid·ness** *n.* — **liq′uid·ly** *adv.*

liquid air An extremely cold, liquid mixture of nitrogen and oxygen, used chiefly as a refrigerant.

liq·ui·date (lik′wə·dāt) *v.* **·dat·ed, ·dat·ing** *v.t.* **1.** To pay off or settle, as an obligation or debt. **2.** To wind up the affairs of (a business firm, etc.) by using the assets to settle debts or obligations. **3.** To convert into cash, as securities. **4.** To do away with. **5.** *Slang* To kill or murder. — *v.i.* **6.** To settle one's debts. [< Med.L *liquidare* to make liquid]

liq·ui·da·tion (lik′wə·dā′shən) *n.* The act or procedure of liquidating, or the state of being liquidated. — **to go into liquidation** Of a business firm, to cease transacting business and to settle debts or discharge obligations.

liquid measure A unit or system of units for measuring liquids. See table front of book.

liquid oxygen Oxygen liquefied by a reduction of temperature and an increase of pressure, used extensively to oxidize other components of rocket fuels: also called *lox*.

liq·uor (lik′ər) *n.* **1.** Any alcoholic beverage; esp., distilled spirits, as whisky, brandy, etc. **2.** A liquid such as broth, juice, etc. — *v.t.* **1.** *Slang* To ply with alcoholic drink: usu. with *up*. — *v.i.* **2.** To drink liquor, esp. in large amounts: usu. with *up*. [< OF < L *liquor*]

liq·uo·rice (lik′ə·ris, -rish) See LICORICE.

li·ra (lir′ə, *Ital.* lē′rä) *n.* *pl.* **li·re** (lir′ə, *Ital.* lē′rä) or **li·ras** (lir′əz) The monetary unit of Italy equivalent to 100 centesimi: in 1960 worth about ⅙₅ of a U.S. cent; also a coin of this value. [< Ital. < L *libra* pound]

lisle (līl) *n.* **1.** A fine twisted cotton thread used in knitting hosiery, etc. Also **lisle thread.** **2.** A fabric, usu. knitted, made from such thread. [after *Lisle*, now Lille, France]

lisp (lisp) *n.* **1.** A speech defect or affectation in which the sibilants (s) and (z) are articulated like (th) in *thank* and (ᵺ) in *this*. **2.** The act or habit of speaking with a lisp. **3.** A sound resembling a lisp. — *v.t. & v.i.* **1.** To pronounce with a lisp. **2.** To speak in a childlike manner. [OE *āwlyspian*]

lis·some (lis′əm) *adj.* **1.** Flexible; pliant. **2.** Agile; lithe. Also **lis′som.** — **lis′some·ly** *adv.* — **lis′some·ness** *n.*

list[1] (list) *n.* **1.** An itemized series of names, words, etc., usu. recorded in a set order. **2.** A classification of persons or things belonging in the same category: usu. with *on*. — *v.t.* **1.** To place on or in a list. **2.** To include in a register, catalogue, etc. [< OF < OHG *lista*] — **list′a·ble** *adj.*

list[2] (list) *n.* **1.** A strip, edging, or selvage, as of cloth. **2.** Fabric consisting of or woven like a selvage. — *v.t.* To edge with list. [OE *līste*]

list[3] (list) *v.t. & v.i.* *Naut.* Of a vessel, to lean or tilt to one side. — *n.* A leaning or inclination to one side.

list[4] (list) *Poetic v.t.* **1.** To listen to; hear. — *v.i.* **2.** To listen. [OE *hlyst* hearing]

lis·ten (lis′ən) *v.i.* **1.** To make conscious use of the sense of hearing; be attentive in order to hear. **2.** To pay attention; give heed. **3.** To be influenced or persuaded. — **to listen in 1.** To participate in hearing (a broadcast, etc.). **2.** To eavesdrop. [OE *hlysnan*] — **lis′ten·er** *n.*

list·er (lis′tər) *n.* *U.S.* A plow with a double moldboard that produces a ridged furrow.

list·ing (lis′ting) *n.* **1.** The act of one who or that which lists. **2.** An entry in a list. A list.

list·less (list′lis) *adj.* Languidly indifferent; apathetic; lackadaisical. — **list′less·ly** *adv.* — **list′less·ness** *n.*

list price The retail price of merchandise, from which a discount is sometimes made.

lists (lists) *n.pl.* **1.** The barriers enclosing the jousting field of a medieval tournament. **2.** The field thus enclosed. **3.** Any arena or scene of conflict. — **to enter the lists** To engage in a contest or controversy. [OE *līste* border]

lit (lit) Alternative past tense and past participle of LIGHT[1] and LIGHT[2].

lit·a·ny (lit′ə·nē) *n.* *pl.* **·nies** *Eccl.* A liturgical form of prayer consisting of a series of supplications said by the clergy, to which the congregation repeat a fixed response. [OE < LL < Gk. *litaneuein* to pray]

-lite *combining form Mineral.* Stone; stonelike. [< F < Gk. *lithos* stone]

li·ter (lē′tər) *n.* In the metric system, a measure of capacity equal to the volume of one kilogram of water at 4° C. and normal atmospheric pressure, or to 1.0567 liquid quarts. Also, *esp. Brit., litre.* See table front of book.

lit·er·a·cy (lit′ər·ə·sē) *n.* The state of being literate.

lit·er·al (lit′ər·əl) *adj.* **1.** Restricted to the exact, stated meaning; not figurative: the *literal* sense of the Scriptures. **2.** Following the exact words and order of an original: a *literal* translation. **3.** Tending to recognize or accept stated meanings only; matter-of-fact. **4.** Free from figurative language, etc., as a literary style; factual. [< OF < LL < *littera* letter] — **lit·er·al·i·ty** (lit′ər·al′ə·tē), **lit′er·al·ness** *n.*

lit·er·al·ly (lit′ər·ə·lē) *adv.* **1.** In a literal manner; in the strictest sense. **2.** Actually; really. **3.** In effect; virtually.

lit·er·ar·y (lit′ə·rer′ē) *adj.* **1.** Of, pertaining to, or treating of literature. **2.** Characteristic of or appropriate to literature. **3.** Versed in or devoted to literature. **4.** Professionally engaged in the field of literature. [< L *litterarius*]

lit·er·ate (lit′ər·it) *adj.* **1.** Able to read and write. **2.** Educated; cultured. **3.** Literary. — *n.* **1.** One able to read and write. **2.** An educated person. [< L < *littera* letter]

lit·er·a·ti (lit′ə·rä′tē, -rä′tī) *n.pl.* **1.** Men of letters; scholars. **2.** Literate or educated persons collectively. [< L]

lit·er·a·tim (lit′ə·rä′tim, -rä′-) *adv.* Letter for letter; literally. [< L]

lit·er·a·ture (lit′ər·ə·choŏr, -chər, lit′rə·chər) *n.* **1.** Written works collectively, esp. those of enduring importance, exhibiting creative imagination and artistic skill. **2.** Poetry, fiction, essays, etc., as distinguished from factual writing. **3.** The writings of a particular period, language, etc.: Elizabethan *literature*. **4.** The writings pertaining to a particular subject. **5.** The occupation of a professional writer. **6.** *Informal* Any printed matter used or distributed for advertising. [< L *littera* letter]

lith- Var. of LITHO-.

-lith *combining form* Stone; rock. [< Gk. *lithos* stone]

lith·arge (lith′ärj, li·thärj′) *n.* A yellowish monoxide of lead, PbO, made by heating lead in air, and used in glassmaking, as a pigment, etc. [< F *litarge* < L *lithargyrus* < Gk. *lithargyros* silver scum < *lithos* stone + *argyros* silver]

lithe (liᵺ) *adj.* Bending easily or gracefully; supple; pliant; limber. [OE, soft] — **lithe′ly** *adv.* — **lithe′ness** *n.*

lithe·some (liᵺ′səm) *adj.* Lithe.

lith·i·a (lith′ē·ə) *n.* Lithium oxide, Li₂O, a white, caustic compound. [< NL < Gk. *lithos* stone]

-lithic *combining form* Pertaining to a (specified) anthropological stage in the use of stone implements: *Neolithic*.

lith·i·um (lith′ē·əm) *n.* A soft, silver-white element (symbol Li), the lightest of the metals, found only in combination. See ELEMENT. [< NL < Gk. *lithos* stone]

litho- *combining form* Stone. Also, before vowels, *lith-*. [< Gk. *lithos* stone]

lith·o·graph (lith′ə·graf, -gräf) *n.* A print produced by the process of lithography. — *v.t.* To produce or reproduce by lithography. — **li·thog·ra·pher** (li·thog′rə·fər) *n.* — **lith′o·graph′ic** or **·i·cal** *adj.* — **lith′o·graph′i·cal·ly** *adv.*

li·thog·ra·phy (li·thog′rə·fē) *n.* The art or process of producing printed matter from a flat stone or zinc or aluminum plate on which a drawing or design has been made in a greasy or water-repellent material.

lith·o·sphere (lith′ə·sfir) *n.* The solid crust of the earth, as distinguished from the atmosphere and the hydrosphere.

Lith·u·a·ni·an (lith′ōō·ā′nē·ən) *adj.* Of or pertaining to Lithuania, its people, or their language. — *n.* **1.** A native or inhabitant of Lithuania. **2.** The Balto-Slavic language of the Lithuanians.

lit·i·ga·ble (lit′ə·gə·bəl) *adj.* Subject to legal dispute.

lit·i·gant (lit′ə·gənt) *n.* A participant in a lawsuit. — *adj.* Engaged in litigation. [< F < L < *litigare* to litigate]

lit·i·gate (lit′ə·gāt) *v.* **·gat·ed, ·gat·ing** *v.t.* **1.** To bring (a dispute, claim, etc.) before a court of law for decision; contest at law. — *v.i.* **2.** To engage in a lawsuit. [< L < *litis* lawsuit + *agere* to do, act] — **lit′i·ga′tor** *n.*

lit·i·ga·tion (lit′ə·gā′shən) *n.* **1.** The act or process of engaging in legal action. **2.** A judicial contest; lawsuit.

li·ti·gious (li·tij′əs) *adj.* **1.** Inclined to litigation; quarrelsome. **2.** Subject to litigation. **3.** Of or pertaining to litigation. — **li·ti′gious·ly** *adv.* — **li·ti′gious·ness** *n.*

lit·mus (lit′məs) *n.* A blue dyestuff made from certain lichens. It is turned red by acids and remains blue when treated with an alkali. [< AF < ON < *litr* color + *mosi* moss]

litmus paper Paper dyed with litmus, used to test acidity.

li·tre (lē′tər) See LITER.

lit·ter (lit′ər) *n.* **1.** Waste materials, scraps, or objects carelessly strewn about. **2.** Untidy or chaotic condition; mess. **3.** The young brought forth at one birth by any mammal normally having several offspring at one time. **4.** A stretcher for carrying sick or wounded persons. **5.** A couch carried between shafts by men or beasts of burden. **6.** Straw, hay, etc., spread in animal pens, or over plants as protection. — *v.t.* **1.** To make untidy or unsightly by carelessly discarding trash, etc. **2.** To drop or scatter carelessly. **3.** To provide with litter, as for bedding. **4.** To give birth to (pups, kittens, etc.) — *v.i.* **5.** To give birth to a litter of young. **6.** To drop or scatter refuse. [< OF < Med.L < L *lectus* bed]

lit·ter·bug (lit′ər·bug′) *n. U.S. Slang* One who litters public places, roads, etc., with trash.

lit·tle (lit′l) *adj.* **lit·tler** or (for defs. 2 and 3) **less, lit·tlest** or (for defs. 2 and 3) **least** **1.** Small, or smaller compared to others, in physical size: a *little* house. **2.** Not long; short; brief: a *little* time; a *little* distance away. **3.** Small or relatively small in quantity or degree: *little* wealth; *little* probability. **4.** Having small force or effectiveness; weak: a *little* effort. **5.** Not having great influence, power, or significance; minor; trivial. **6.** Narrow or limited in viewpoint; petty: *little* minds. — *adv.* **less, least 1.** Only slightly; not much: He sleeps *little*. **2.** Not at all: used before a verb: She *little* suspects. — *n.* **1.** A small amount: Give me a *little*. **2.** An insignificant amount: *Little* can be done about it. **3.** A short while or distance. — **little by little** By small degrees; gradually. [OE < *lȳt* little] — **lit′tle·ness** *n.*

little theater An amateur or community theater group.

lit·to·ral (lit′ər·əl) *adj.* Of a shore or coastal region. — *n.* A shore and its adjacent areas. [< L < *lit(t)us, -oris* seashore]

li·tur·gi·cal (li·tûr′ji·kəl) *adj.* Of or associated with public worship, ritual, etc. Also **li·tur′gic.** — **li·tur′gi·cal·ly** *adv.*

lit·ur·gy (lit′ər·jē) *n. pl.* **·gies 1.** In various religions, the prescribed form for public worship; religious ritual. **2.** The rite of the Eucharist. [< Med.L < Gk. *leitourgia* public duty, ult. < *laos* people + *ergon* work]

liv·a·ble (liv′ə·bəl) *adj.* **1.** Suitable or agreeable for living in. **2.** Worth living; tolerable. **3.** Agreeable, as for companionship. Also **live′a·ble.**

live[1] (liv) *v.* **lived, liv·ing** *v.i.* **1.** To function as an animate organism; be alive. **2.** To remain alive: as long as you *live*. **3.** To remain or persist, as in the mind. **4.** To remain valid or operative; endure. **5.** To have as one's home; reside: with *in* or *at*. **6.** To use as one's sole or customary nourishment: with *on*: to *live* on air. **7.** To maintain or support oneself: with *on* or *by*: to *live* on one's income. **8.** To pass life in a specified manner: to *live* in peace. **9.** To regulate one's life, as in accordance with principles, etc.: to *live* by a strict code. **10.** To enjoy a varied or satisfying life. — *v.t.* **11.** To spend or pass (life, time, etc.). **12.** To put into practice: to *live* one's religion. — **to live down** To live or behave so as to expiate the memory of (an error, crime, etc.). — **to live in** To reside, as a domestic servant, at one's place of employment. — **to live through** To survive or withstand (an experience). — **to live up to 1.** To satisfy (an ideal, expectations, etc.). **2.** To fulfill (a bargain, obligation, etc.). [OE *libban, lifian*] — **Syn. 5.** Dwell, reside, abide.

live[2] (liv) *adj.* **1.** Functioning as an animate organism; alive. **2.** Pertaining to, characteristic of, or abounding in life. **3.** Of present interest and importance: a *live* issue. **4.** Forceful and energetic; dynamic. **5.** Burning or glowing: a *live* coal. **6.** Vivid or brilliant, as color. **7.** Charged with electricity: a *live* wire. **8.** Capable of being detonated, as a bomb. **9.** In television, radio, etc., consisting of or performed by persons present at the time of transmission. **10.** In mechanical use, having motion or the power to impart motion or force. **11.** In printing, publishing, etc., ready or retained for use: *live* copy. **12.** In sports, being in play, as a ball.

live·bear·er (liv′bâr′ər) *n.* An ovoviviparous fish, as a guppy. — **live′bear′ing** *adj.*

lived (livd) *adj.* Having a (specified kind of) life or life span: used in combination: *long-lived*.

live·li·hood (liv′lē·hŏŏd) *n.* Means of supporting or maintaining one's existence. [ME < OE < *līf* life + *lād* way]

live·long (liv′lông′, -long′) *adj.* Long or seemingly long in passing; entire: the *livelong* day. [ME *lefe longe*, lit., *lief long*; *lief*, here orig. intens., was later confused with *live*]

live·ly (liv′lē) *adj.* **·li·er, ·li·est 1.** Full of vigor or motion; energetic. **2.** Arousing activity or excitement: a *lively* tune. **3.** Vivid; keen: a *lively* imagination. **4.** Striking and forceful to the mind: a *lively* impression. **5.** Filled with activity: a *lively* day. **6.** Invigorating; brisk: a *lively* breeze. **7.** Bouncing readily, as a ball; resilient. — *adv.* In a lively manner; briskly: now usu. in the expression **to step lively,** to hurry up. [OE *līflīce*] — **live′li·ly** *adv.* — **live′li·ness** *n.*

li·ven (lī′vən) *v.t. & v.i.* To make or become lively or cheerful: often with *up*. — **liv′en·er** *n.*

live oak Any of several evergreen trees having hard, wood.

liv·er[1] (liv′ər) *n.* **1.** *Anat.* The largest glandular organ of vertebrates, secreting bile and active in metabolism, in man situated just under the diaphragm and on the right side. ◆ Collateral adjective: *hepatic*. **2.** A similar digestive gland in invertebrates. **3.** Food consisting of or prepared from the liver of certain animals. [OE *lifer*]

liv·er[2] (liv′ər) *n.* **1.** One who lives in a specified manner: a luxurious *liver*. **2.** A dweller.

liv·er·ied (liv′ər·ēd) *adj.* Dressed in livery, as a servant.

liv·er·ish (liv′ər·ish) *adj. Informal* Feeling or exhibiting supposed symptoms of disordered liver; bilious; irritable.

liv·er·wort (liv′ər·wûrt′) *n.* **1.** Any mosslike cryptogam forming mats in damp, shady places. **2.** A hepatica.

liv·er·wurst (liv′ər·wûrst′) *n.* A sausage made of or containing ground liver. [< G *leberwurst*]

liv·er·y (liv′ər·ē) *n. pl.* **·er·ies 1.** The distinctive clothing or uniform worn by male household servants. **2.** The distinguishing dress of an organization or group. **3.** Characteristic garb or outward appearance. **4.** The stabling and care of horses for pay. **5.** *U.S.* A livery stable. [< OF *livree* gift of clothes by a master to a servant < L *liber* free]

liv·er·y·man (liv′ər·ē·mən) *n. pl.* **·men** (-mən) A man who keeps or works in a livery stable.

livery stable A stable where horses and vehicles are cared for or kept for hire.

lives (līvz) Plural of LIFE.

live·stock (līv′stok′) *n.* Domestic farm animals, as cattle, horses, and sheep, esp. when raised for profit.

live wire 1. A wire carrying an electric current or potential. **2.** *Informal* An energetic, enterprising person; a go-getter.

liv·id (liv′id) *adj.* **1.** Having the skin abnormally discolored, as: **a** Flushed, purplish, etc., as from intense emotion. **b** Black-and-blue, as from contusion. **2.** Having a leaden pallor; bluish gray. **3.** *Informal* Furious; enraged. [< F < L *livere* to be livid] — **liv′id·ly** *adv.* — **liv′id·ness, li·vid·i·ty** (li·vid′ə·tē) *n.*

liv·ing (liv′ing) *adj.* **1.** Alive; animate; not dead. **2.** Of or characteristic of everyday life: *living* conditions. **3.** Used or intended for maintaining existence: a *living* wage. **4.** Having contemporary value, force, or application: *living* languages. **5.** Of or pertaining to those who are alive. **6.** Lifelike; real: the *living* image of his father. — *n.* **1.** The state of one who or that which lives. **2.** Those that are alive: preceded by *the*. **3.** Manner or conduct of life: virtuous *living*. **4.** Means of supporting existence; livelihood.

living death A prolonged painful experience.

living room A room designed and furnished for the general use, social activities, etc., of a household; sitting room.

liz·ard (liz′ərd) *n.* **1.** Any of various reptiles typically having elongate, scaly bodies, long tails, and four legs, as the chameleon, iguana, skink, etc. **2.** Loosely, any similar reptile or amphibian. **3.** Leather made from the skin of a lizard. [< OF < L *lacerta*]

-'ll Contracted form of SHALL or WILL (*v.*) or of TILL (*prep.*).

lla·ma (lä′mə) *n.* A camellike, humpless ruminant of South America, having thick, woolly hair, and frequently used as a beast of burden. [< Sp. < Quechua]

lla·no (lä′nō, *Sp.* lyä′nō) *n. pl.* **·nos** (-nōz, *Sp.* -nōs) A flat, treeless plain, as those of the SW U.S. and northern Latin America. [< Sp., plain, flat < L *planus*]

lo (lō) *interj.* See! observe!: *Lo* and behold! [OE *lā*]

loach (lōch) *n.* Any of various fresh-water fishes related to the carp and minnow. [< F *loche*]

LLAMA
(3½ to 4 feet high at shoulder)

load (lōd) *n.* **1.** The weight or quantity placed upon and sustained by a vehicle, bearer, surface, etc. **2.** A quantity borne or conveyed: often used in combination: *carload*. **3.** Something borne with difficulty; cause of physical or mental strain; burden. **4.** The charge or ammunition for a firearm. **5.** The hours or amount of work required of an employee. **6.** *pl. Informal* An ample amount; lots: *loads* of time. **7.** *Electr.* The power delivered by a generating system. **8.** *Mech.* The resistance overcome by a motor or engine in driving machinery. — **to get a load of** *U.S. Slang* To listen to or look at. — *v.t.* **1.** To place a large quantity, burden, cargo, etc., upon. **2.** To place or take (cargo, people, etc.) as on a conveyance. **3.** To burden, encumber, or oppress: often with *down*. **4.** To provide abundantly; heap: He was *loaded* with honors. **5.** To charge (a firearm, etc.) with explosive or ammunition. **6.** To put film or a photographic plate into (a camera). **7.** To tamper with, esp. by adding weight to: to *load* dice. **8.** To make prejudicial: to *load* the evidence. — *v.i.* **9.** To put on or receive a load or cargo. **10.** To charge a firearm, cartridge, etc., with ammunition. [OE *lād* way, journey] — **load′er** *n.*

load·star (lōd′stär′), **load·stone** (lōd′stōn′) See LODESTAR, LODESTONE.

loaf[1] (lōf) *v.i.* **1.** To loiter lazily or aimlessly. **2.** To shirk or dawdle over one's work. — *v.t.* **3.** To spend (time) idly: with *away*. [Back formation < LOAFER]

loaf[2] (lōf) *n. pl.* **loaves** (lōvz) **1.** A rounded or elongated mass of bread baked in a single piece. **2.** Any shaped mass of food, as of cake, chopped meat, etc. [OE *hlāf* bread]

loaf·er (lō′fər) *n.* **1.** One who loafs; an idler or slacker. **2.** A casual shoe resembling a moccasin.

loam (lōm) *n.* **1.** Loose-textured soil consisting of a mixture of sand and clay containing organic matter. **2.** A moistened mixture of clay, sand, and straw, used in plastering. — *v.t.* To coat or fill with loam. [OE *lām*] — **loam′y** *adj.*

loan (lōn) *n.* **1.** Something lent; esp., a sum of money lent at interest. **2.** The act of lending: the *loan* of a knife. — *v.t. & v.i.* To lend. [ME < ON *lān*]

loan shark *U.S. Informal* One who lends money at an excessively high or illegal rate of interest.

loan-word (lōn′wûrd′) *n.* A word adopted from another language and partly or completely naturalized, as the English word *chauffeur*, taken from the French. Also **loan word, loan′word′.** [< G *lehnwort*]

loath (lōth) *adj.* Strongly disinclined; reluctant; unwilling: often followed by *to.* Also spelled *loth.* [OE *lāth* hateful]

loathe (lōth) *v.t.* loathed, loath·ing To feel great hatred or disgust for; abhor; detest. — **Syn.** See HATE. [OE *lāthian* to be hateful] — **loath′er** *n.*

loath·ing (lō′thing) *n.* Extreme dislike; abhorrence. — **loath′ing·ly** *adv.*

loath·some (lōth′səm) *adj.* Causing revulsion or disgust; repulsive. — **loath′some·ly** *adv.* — **loath′some·ness** *n.*

loaves (lōvz) Plural of LOAF.

lob (lob) *v.* lobbed, lob·bing *v.t.* **1.** To pitch, or strike (a ball, etc.) in a high, arching curve. — *v.i.* **2.** To move clumsily or heavily. **3.** To lob a ball. — *n.* In tennis, a stroke that sends the ball high into the air. [ME]

lo·bar (lō′bər, -bär) *adj.* **1.** Of or pertaining to a lobe. **2.** Affecting one or more lobes of the lungs. [< NL *lobaris*]

lo·bate (lō′bāt) *adj.* **1.** Having or consisting of lobes. **2.** Resembling a lobe. Also **lo′bat·ed.** [< NL *lobatus*]

lo·ba·tion (lō-bā′shən) *n.* **1.** The condition of having or forming lobes. **2.** A lobe or lobelike part.

lob·by (lob′ē) *n. pl.* ·bies **1.** An entrance hall, vestibule, or public lounge in an apartment house, hotel, theater, etc. **2.** *U.S.* A group representing persons or organizations with a common interest, who attempt to influence the votes of legislators. — *v.* ·bied, ·by·ing *U.S. v.i.* **1.** To attempt to influence legislators in favor of some interest. — *v.t.* **2.** To attempt to influence (legislators, etc.). **3.** To exert influence for the passage of: often with *through.* [< Med.L *lobia*]

lob·by·ism (lob′ē-iz′əm) *n. U.S.* The practice of lobbying. — **lob′by·ist** *n.*

lobe (lōb) *n.* **1.** A rounded division, protuberance, or part, as of a leaf. **2.** The soft lower part of the human ear. **3.** *Anat.* Any of several well-defined, often symmetrical portions of an organ or part of the body, as of the brain, lungs, liver, etc. [< F < L < Gk. *lobos*] — **lobed** *adj.*

lo·be·li·a (lō-bē′lē·ə, -bēl′yə) *n.* Any of a genus of herbaceous plants having flowers usu. borne in racemes. [< NL, after Matthias de *Lobel*, 1538–1616, Flemish botanist]

lob·lol·ly (lob′lol·ē) *n. pl.* ·lies **1.** *U.S.* A pine of the southern U.S., having scaly bark and wood valuable as lumber. **2.** The wood of this tree. Also **loblolly pine.** [< dial. E *lob* bubble + *lolly* broth]

lo·bo (lō′bō) *n. pl.* ·bos The timber wolf of the western U.S. [< Sp., wolf < L *lupus*]

lo·bot·o·my (lō-bot′ə-mē) *n. pl.* ·mies *Surg.* The operation of cutting into or across a lobe of the brain, esp. in order to modify or eliminate some function associated with a mental disorder. [< Gk. *lobos* lobe + -TOMY]

lob·ster (lob′stər) *n.* **1.** Any of various ten-legged marine crustaceans having the first pair of legs modified as claws, and compound eyes on flexible stalks. **2.** Any of various similar crustaceans. **3.** The flesh of any of these crustaceans eaten as food. [OE < L *locusta* lobster, locust]

lob·ule (lob′yool) *n.* **1.** A small lobe. **2.** A subdivision of a lobe. [< NL < *lobus* lobe] — **lob′u·lar, lob′u·lose** *adj.*

lo·cal (lō′kəl) *adj.* **1.** Pertaining to, characteristic of, or confined to a relatively small area. **2.** Restricted, as by environmental influences, etc. **3.** Of or pertaining to a particular place or position in space: *local* time. **4.** Stopping at all stations along its run, as a train. **5.** *Med.* Relating to or affecting a specific part of the body. — *n.* **1.** A branch or chapter of an organization, as a trade union. **2.** A bus, train, etc., that stops at all stations. **3.** A news item of local interest. [< F < L < *locus* place] — **lo′cal·ly** *adv.*

local color The characteristic appearance, mannerisms, etc., of a place or period, esp. as presented in literature.

lo·cale (lō-kal′) *n.* **1.** A place or locality, esp. with reference to some event or circumstance. **2.** The setting of a literary, dramatic, or artistic work; scene. [< F]

lo·cal·ism (lō′kəl·iz′əm) *n.* **1.** A local custom or idiom. **2.** A word, meaning of a word, pronunciation, etc., peculiar to a locality. **3.** Narrowness; provincialism.

lo·cal·i·ty (lō-kal′ə-tē) *n. pl.* ·ties **1.** A place, region, etc. **2.** Position, esp. in relation to surroundings, etc. **3.** The state of being local. [< F < LL *localitas*]

lo·cal·ize (lō′kəl-īz) *v.t.* ·ized, ·iz·ing **1.** To make local; con-

fine or assign to a specific area. **2.** To determine the place of origin of. — **lo′cal·iz′a·ble** *adj.* — **lo′cal·i·za′tion** *n.*

local option The right of a county or town, etc., to restrict or prohibit certain activities, as the sale of liquor.

lo·cate (lō′kāt, lō-kāt′) *v.* ·cat·ed, ·cat·ing *v.t.* **1.** To discover the position of; find. **2.** To establish or place at a particular site: The store is *located* on the corner. **3.** To place hypothetically as to setting, a relative position, etc. **4.** *U.S.* To survey and fix the site or boundaries of (property, a mining claim, etc.). — *v.i.* **5.** *U.S. Informal* To settle. [< L < *locus* place] — **lo·cat′a·ble** *adj.* — **lo′ca·ter** *n.*

lo·ca·tion (lō-kā′shən) *n.* **1.** The act of locating, or the state of being located. **2.** A site or situation, esp. considered in regard to its surroundings. **3.** Exact position or place occupied. **4.** A motion picture or television locale away from the studio on location. **5.** *U.S.* A tract of land having established boundaries. [< L *locatio*]

loc·a·tive (lok′ə·tiv) *adj. Gram.* In certain inflected languages, as Latin, Greek, and Sanskrit, designating a noun case denoting place where or at which. — *n. Gram.* **1.** The locative case. **2.** A word in this case. [< L *locatus*]

loch (lokh, lok) *n. Scot.* **1.** A lake. **2.** An arm of the sea.

lo·ci (lō′sī) Plural of LOCUS.

lock¹ (lok) *n.* **1.** A mechanical fastening device having a bolt or combination of bolts secured or released by a key, dial, etc., and used to prevent unauthorized entry, access, or operation. **2.** Any part or device that fastens, secures, or holds something firmly in place. **3.** A section of a canal, etc., enclosed by gates, within which the water depth may be varied to raise or lower boats from level to level. **4.** The mechanism that explodes the charge of a gun. **5.** An interlocking, fastening, or jamming together of parts. **6.** A wrestling grip or hold. — **lock, stock, and barrel** Altogether; completely. — *v.t.* **1.** To fasten, or secure by means of a lock. **2.** To keep, confine, etc., in or as in a locked enclosure: with *in, up,* or *away.* **3.** To fit together securely; interlock. **4.** To clasp or grip in or as in a firm hold. **5.** To make immovable by or as by jamming or fastening together. **6.** To move (a vessel) through a waterway by means of locks. — *v.i.* **7.** To become locked. **8.** To become firmly joined or interlocked. — **to lock out 1.** To prevent (employees) from working by closing a factory, shop, etc. **2.** To keep out by locking. [OE *loc* fastening, enclosure] — **lock′a·ble** *adj.*

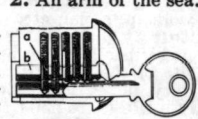

LOCK
Insertion of key raises tumblers (*a*), thus releasing key plug (*b*) and permitting key to turn.

lock² (lok) *n.* **1.** Strands of hair forming a curl. **2.** *pl.* The hair of the head. **3.** A tuft of wool, etc. [OE *locc*]

lock·er (lok′ər) *n.* **1.** A closet, cabinet, storage space, etc., fastened with a lock; as: **a** One of a series of metal cabinets, as in a school or gymnasium, in which clothes, equipment, etc., are kept. **b** A cabinet in which frozen foods are kept. **2.** A chest, etc., as on a ship, in which equipment or personal belongings are kept. **3.** One who or that which locks.

locker room A room having lockers for clothing, etc.

lock·et (lok′it) *n.* A small ornamental case for enclosing a picture or keepsake, usu. worn on a chain, ribbon, etc., around the neck. [< OF < *loc* latch < Gmc.]

lock·jaw (lok′jô′) *n. Pathol.* A form of tetanus causing rigid closure of the jaws: also called *trismus.*

lock·out (lok′out′) *n.* The closing of a place of business by an employer in order to make employees agree to terms.

lock·smith (lok′smith′) *n.* A maker or repairer of locks.

lock step A marching style in which each marcher follows as closely as possible the one in front of him.

lock·up (lok′up′) *n.* A jail or prison cell.

lo·co (lō′kō) *adj. U.S. Informal* Crazy; insane. — *n. pl.* ·cos Locoweed. — *v.t.* ·coed, ·co·ing **1.** To poison with locoweed. **2.** *U.S. Slang* To make insane. [< Sp., insane]

lo·co·mo·tion (lō′kə-mō′shən) *n.* The act or power of moving from one place to another. [< L *loco* from a place + *motio, -onis* movement]

lo·co·mo·tive (lō′kə-mō′tiv) *n.* An engine that moves by its own power, used to pull passenger or freight trains on a railroad. — *adj.* **1.** Of, pertaining to, or used in locomotion. **2.** Moving or able to move from one place to another. **3.** Capable of moving by its own power, as an engine.

lo·co·weed (lō′kō-wēd′) *n.* Any of several leguminous plants of the SW U.S., often poisonous to livestock.

lo·cus (lō′kəs) *n. pl.* ·ci (-sī) **1.** A place; locality; area. **2.** *Math.* **a** A surface or curve regarded as traced by a line or point moving under specified conditions. **b** Any figure made up wholly of points or lines that satisfy given conditions.

lo·cust¹ (lō′kəst) *n.* **1.** Any of a family of widely distributed winged insects resembling grasshoppers but having short antennae, including those of migratory habits that destroy vegetation. **2.** A cicada. [< OF < L *locusta*]

lo·cust² (lō′kəst) *n.* **1.** A leguminous tree of North America, having compound leaves and clusters of fragrant white flowers. **2.** The wood of this tree. **3.** Any of various similar trees, as the acacia and honey locust. [< L *locusta*]

lo·cu·tion (lō-kyōō′shən) *n.* **1.** A verbal expression or phrase. **2.** Manner of speech or expression; phraseology. [< L *locutio, -onis* a speaking < *loqui* to speak]

lode (lōd) *n. Mining* **1.** A deposit of metallic ore filling a fissure or series of fissures in native rock. **2.** Any deposit of ore located between definite boundaries of associated rock. Also called *vein.* [OE *lād* way, journey]

lode·star (lōd′stär′) *n.* **1.** A star used as a guide in navigation or travel; esp., the polestar. **2.** A guiding principle, etc. Also spelled *loadstar.* [ME *lode* course + STAR]

lode·stone (lōd′stōn′) *n.* **1.** A variety of magnetite exhibiting magnetism. **2.** Something that attracts by or as by magnetism. [ME *lode* course + STONE]

lodge (loj) *n.* **1.** A local branch of a secret or fraternal society; also, the meeting place of such a society. **2.** A small hut, cabin, etc., esp. one used as a base for outdoor activity. **3.** A small house on the grounds of an estate, etc., usu. serving as quarters for an employee. **4.** A North American Indian tepee or wigwam, etc.; also, a group living in such a dwelling. **5.** The characteristic den of certain animals, as beavers. — *v.* **lodged, lodg·ing** *v.t.* **1.** To furnish with temporary quarters; house. **2.** To rent a room or rooms to. **3.** To serve as a shelter or dwelling for. **4.** To place or implant firmly, as by thrusting or inserting. **5.** To deposit for safekeeping or storage. **6.** To submit or enter (a complaint, etc.) formally. **7.** To confer or invest (power, etc.): usu. with *in* or *with.* — *v.i.* **8.** To take temporary quarters. **9.** To live in a rented room or rooms. **10.** To become fixed or embedded. [< OF < Med.L < OHG *loub* foliage]

lodg·er (loj′ər) *n.* **1.** One who lives in a rented room or rooms in another's residence. **2.** Something fixed in place.

lodg·ing (loj′ing) *n.* **1.** A temporary dwelling place. **2.** *pl.* Living quarters consisting of a rented room or rooms in another's house. **3.** Accommodation for living and sleeping.

lodg·ment (loj′mənt) *n.* The act of lodging, or the state of being lodged. Also **lodge′ment.**

loess (lō′is, lœs) *n. Geol.* A pale, yellowish silt or clay forming finely powdered, usu. wind-borne deposits. [< G < *lösen* to pour, dissolve] — **loes′si·al** *adj.*

loft (lôft, loft) *n.* **1.** A floored space directly under a roof; attic. **2.** *U.S.* A large, open workroom or storeroom on an upper story of a commercial building. **3.** A hayloft. **4.** An upper section or gallery, as in a church: the choir *loft.* **5.** In golf: **a** The slope of the club face away from the vertical line of the shaft, intended to make a struck ball rise sharply in the air. **b** A stroke that causes the ball to rise sharply when struck. **c** The upward travel of a struck ball. — *v.t.* **1.** In sports, to strike (a ball) so that it travels in a high arc. **2.** To keep or store in a loft. — *v.i.* **3.** In golf, to strike a ball so that it rises in a high arc. [Late OE < ON, air, sky]

loft·y (lôf′tē, lof′-) *adj.* **loft·i·er, loft·i·est** **1.** Having great or imposing height. **2.** Elevated in character, quality, style, etc.; noble. **3.** Exalted in rank or position; eminent. **4.** Arrogant; haughty. — **loft′i·ly** *adv.* — **loft′i·ness** *n.*

log¹ (log, lôg) *n.* **1.** A full length or cut section of a felled tree trunk, limb, etc., stripped of branches. **2.** Something or someone inert, stupefied, etc. **3.** *Naut.* **a** A record of the daily progress of a vessel and of the events of a voyage. **b** Any of various devices for measuring the speed and mileage of a vessel. **4.** A record of operation or progress, as of an aircraft in flight. — *v.* **logged, log·ging** *v.t.* **1.** To cut down the trees of (a forest, etc.) for timber. **2.** To convert (timber) into logs. **3.** *Naut. & Aeron.* **a** To enter in a logbook. **b** To travel (a specified distance, etc.). **c** To travel at (a specified speed). — *v.i.* **4.** To engage in the operation of cutting and transporting timber. [ME *logge*]

log² (log, lôg) A logarithm.

log- Var. of LOGO-.

-log (log) Var. of -LOGUE.

lo·gan·ber·ry (lō′gən-ber′ē) *n. pl.* **·ries** **1.** A hybrid plant, obtained by crossing the red raspberry with the blackberry. **2.** The edible fruit of this plant. [after J. H. *Logan,* 1841–1928, U.S. horticulturist]

log·a·rithm (log′ə-rith′əm, lôg′-) *n. Math.* The power to which a fixed number, called the base, must be raised in order to produce a given number, the antilogarithm. [< NL < Gk. *logos* word, ratio + *arithmos* number] — **log′a·rith′mic** or **·mi·cal** *adj.* — **log′a·rith′mi·cal·ly** *adv.*

log·book (log′bŏŏk′, lôg′-) *n.* The book in which the official record of a ship, aircraft, etc., is entered. Also **log book.**

log chip *Naut.* A quadrant-shaped board weighted on the curved edge and suspended in the water from a moving vessel in order to measure its speed.

loge (lōzh) *n.* A box in a theater. [< F < OF]

log·ger (log′ər, lôg′-) *n.* **1.** A person engaged in logging; lumberjack. **2.** A machine for hauling and loading logs.

log·ger·head (log′ər-hed, lôg′-) *n.* A large marine turtle of tropical Atlantic waters. Also **loggerhead turtle.** — **at loggerheads** Engaged in a quarrel; unable to agree. [< dial. E *logger* log tied to a horse's leg + HEAD]

log·gi·a (loj′ē-ə, lô′jə; *Ital.* lôd′jä) *n.* A roofed gallery or portico that is open and supported by columns on one or more sides. [< Ital. < OF *loge*]

LOGGIA

log·ging (log′ing, lôg′-) *n.* The occupation of felling timber and transporting logs to a mill or market.

log·ic (loj′ik) *n.* **1.** The science concerned with the principles of valid reasoning and correct inference, either deductive or inductive. **2.** Method of reasoning, inference, etc.; esp., correct or sound reasoning. **3.** Effective force, influence, etc. **4.** The apparently inevitable chain of events involved in an outcome, etc. **5.** A system of or treatise on logic. [< F < L < Gk. < *logos* word, speech, thought]

log·i·cal (loj′i·kəl) *adj.* **1.** Relating to or of the nature of logic. **2.** Conforming to the laws of logic. **3.** Capable of or characterized by clear reasoning. — **log′i·cal′i·ty** (-kal′ə-tē), **log′i·cal·ness** *n.* — **log′i·cal·ly** *adv.*

-logical *combining form* Of or related to a (specified) science or study: *biological, geological.* Also **-logic.**

lo·gi·cian (lō-jish′ən) *n.* One versed in logic.

lo·gis·tics (lō-jis′tiks) *n.pl.* (*construed as sing.*) The branch of military science dealing with supplying, equipping, and moving troops. [< F *loger* to quarter] — **lo·gis′tic** *adj.*

logo- *combining form* Word; speech. Also, before vowels, *log-.* [< Gk. *logos* word, speech]

Log·os (log′os, lôg′-, lō′gōs) *n. Theol.* In the Christian religion, God, the incarnate second person of the Trinity, incarnate as Jesus Christ. *John* i 1–14.

log·roll (log′rōl′, lôg′-) *U.S. v.t.* To obtain passage of (a bill) by logrolling. — *v.i.* To engage in logrolling. Also **log′-roll′.** [Back formation < LOGROLLING]

log·roll·ing (log′rō′ling, lôg′-) *n. U.S.* **1.** The trading of votes and influence between politicians; also, any such trading of help or approval for one's own benefit. **2.** Birling. Also **log′-roll′ing.** — **log′roll′er** *n.*

-logue *combining form* Discourse; recitation: *monologue, prologue.* Also **-log.** [< OF < L < Gk. *logos* word, speech]

log·wood (log′wŏŏd′, lôg′-) *n.* **1.** The reddish wood of a Central American tree, used as a dyestuff. **2.** The tree itself.

lo·gy (lō′gē) *adj.* **·gi·er, ·gi·est** *U.S. Informal* Dull; heavy; lethargic. [Prob. < Du. *log* dull, heavy]

-logy *combining form* **1.** The science or study of. **2.** Speech; discourse. [< Gk. *logos* word, study]

Lo·hen·grin (lō′ən-grin) In medieval German legend, a knight of the Holy Grail and son of Parsifal.

loin (loin) *n. Usu. pl.* **1.** The part of the back and flanks between the lower ribs and the hipbone. ◆ Collateral adjective: *lumbar.* **2.** *pl. Chiefly Poetic* The lower back, thighs, and groin regarded as a zone to be clothed. **3.** The forepart of the hindquarters of beef, lamb, veal, etc., with the flank removed. — **to gird (up) one's loins** To prepare for action. [< OF *loigne, logne* < L *lumbus*]

loin·cloth (loin′klôth′, -kloth′) *n.* A garment consisting of a piece or strip of cloth worn about the loins and hips.

loi·ter (loi′tər) *v.i.* **1.** To linger idly or aimlessly; loaf. **2.** To dawdle. — *v.t.* **3.** To pass (time) idly: with *away.* [ME *lotere*] — **loi′ter·er** *n.*

Lo·ki (lō′kē) In Norse mythology, a god who created disorder and mischief. [< ON]

loll (lol) *v.i.* **1.** To lie or lean in a relaxed or languid manner; lounge. **2.** To hang loosely; droop. — *v.t.* **3.** To permit to droop or hang, as the tongue. — *n.* The act of lolling. [Cf. ME *lull,* MDu. *lollen* to sleep] — **loll′er** *n.*

lol·la·pa·loo·za (lol′ə-pə-lōō′zə) *n. U.S. Slang* Something extraordinary. Also **lol·la·pa·loo′sa.** [Origin unknown]

Lol·lard (lol′ərd) *n.* A follower of John Wycliffe, 14th-century English religious reformer. Also **Lol′ler.** [< MDu. *lollaerd* mumbler (of prayers)]

lol·li·pop (lol′ē-pop′) *n.* A lump or piece of candy on the end of a stick; also called *sucker.* Also **lol′ly·pop′.** [Prob. < dial. E *lolly* tongue + POP]

Lom·bard (lom′bərd, -bärd, lum′-) *n.* **1.** One of a Germanic tribe that established a kingdom in northern Italy in the sixth century. **2.** A native or inhabitant of Lombardy. — **Lom·bar′dic** *adj.*

London broil Broiled flank steak sliced thin.

lone (lōn) *adj.* **1.** Being without companions; solitary. **2.** Isolated. **3.** Unfrequented; deserted. [< ALONE]

lone·ly (lōn′lē) *adj.* **·li·er, ·li·est** **1.** Unfrequented by human beings; deserted; desolate. **2.** Sad from lack of companionship or sympathy; lonesome. **3.** Characterized by or inducing loneliness. — **lone′li·ly** *adv.* — **lone′li·ness** *n.*

lone·some (lōn′səm) *adj.* **1.** Depressed or uneasy because of being alone; lonely; forlorn. **2.** Inducing a feeling of loneliness. **3.** Unfrequented; secluded: a *lonesome* retreat. — **lone′some·ly** *adv.* — **lone·some·ness** *n.*

Lone Star State Nickname of Texas.

lone wolf *U.S. Informal* One who prefers to work, live, etc., by himself: also **lon·er** (lō′nər).

long[1] (lông, long) *adj.* **1.** Characterized by extent or measurement relatively great in proportion to breadth or width; not short. **2.** Having relatively great duration in time; prolonged. **3.** Having relatively great extension from beginning to end: a *long* tunnel. **4.** Being of a specified measurement in extent or duration: ten miles *long*; three hours *long*. **5.** Having more than the standard or usual quantity, extent, or duration: a *long* ton, a *long* play. **6.** Consisting of many items or entries, as a list. **7.** Slow; tedious. **8.** Extending far into time or space; having considerable range. **9.** Well supplied: *long* on excuses. **10.** In gambling: **a** Denoting odds indicating little likelihood of winning. **b** Denoting a bet, chance, guess, etc., characterized by such odds. **11.** In finance, holding considerable amounts of a stock, commodity, etc., in anticipation of a rise in its price. **12.** *Phonet.* Denoting the vowel sounds of *Dane, dean, dine, dome, dune* as contrasted with those of *Dan, den, din, don, duck.* **13.** In prosody, stressed, as in English verse. — **in the long run** As the ultimate result of inevitable consequences; eventually. — *adv.* **1.** For or during an extensive period of time: Will he stay *long?* **2.** For a time or period (to be specified): How *long* will he stay? **3.** For the whole extent or duration (of a specified period): It rained all day *long.* **4.** At a considerably distant time: *long* after midnight. — **as** (or **so**) **long as** **1.** For or during the time that. **2.** Inasmuch as; since. — *n.* **1.** Something relatively long. **2.** A long syllable or sound, as in phonetics, prosody, etc. — **before long** Soon. — **the long and the short** The entire sum and substance; the whole. [OE *long, lang*]

long[2] (lông, long) *v.i.* To have a strong or eager desire; wish earnestly; yearn. [OE *langian* to grow long]

long·boat (lông′bōt′, long′-) *n. Naut.* The largest boat carried by a sailing vessel.

long·bow (lông′bō′, long′-) *n.* A large bow drawn by hand and projecting long, feathered arrows.

long·cloth (lông′klôth′, long′kloth′) *n.* A fine, soft, cotton cloth used for making children's garments.

long-dis·tance (lông′dis′təns, long′-) *adj.* Connecting or covering relatively long distances or places. — *adv.* **1.** By long-distance telephone. **2.** At a distance.

long distance The telephone exchange, operator, or service that handles calls outside the immediate locality.

long division Arithmetical division, usu. with large numbers in which all the steps of the process are shown.

long-drawn (lông′drôn′, long′-) *adj.* Prolonged; protracted. Also **long′-drawn′-out′** (-out′).

lon·gev·i·ty (lon·jev′ə·tē) *n.* **1.** Great age or length of life. **2.** The tendency to live long. [< L < *longus* long + *aevum* age] — **lon·ge·vous** (lon·jē′vəs) *adj.*

long·hair (lông′hâr′, long′-) *U.S. Slang adj.* **1.** Of or pertaining to intellectuals or their tastes. **2.** Of or pertaining to serious rather than popular music. — *n.* **1.** A longhair person; intellectual. **2.** Longhair music. Also **long′-hair′.**

long·hand (lông′hand′, long′-) *n.* Ordinary handwriting with the words spelled in full.

long·head·ed (lông′hed′id, long′-) *adj.* **1.** Dolichocephalic. **2.** Characterized by shrewdness, foresight, etc. Also **long′-head′ed.** — **long′head′ed·ly** *adv.* — **long′head′ed·ness** *n.*

long·horn (lông′hôrn′, long′-) *n.* One of a breed of domestic cattle with long horns. Also **Texas longhorn.**

long house Among North American Indians, esp. the Iroquois, a council house or community dwelling.

longi- *combining form* Long. [< L *longus* long]

long·ing (lông′ing, long′-) *n.* A strong, earnest, persistent craving; desire. — *adj.* Having or showing such a craving. — **Syn.** See APPETITE. — **long′ing·ly** *adv.*

lon·gi·tude (lon′jə·tōōd, -tyōōd, long′gə-) *n.* **1.** *Geog.* Distance east or west on the earth's surface, usu. measured by the angle that the meridian through a particular place makes with the prime meridian that runs through Greenwich, England. Longitude may be expressed either in hours and minutes (**longitude in time**) or in degrees (**longitude in arc**). **2.** *Astron.* The angular distance eastward from the vernal equinox to the intersection with the ecliptic of the perpendicular from a heavenly body (**celestial longitude**). [< F < L *longus* long]

lon·gi·tu·di·nal (lon′jə·tōō′də·nəl, -tyōō′-, long′gə-) *adj.* **1.** Of or pertaining to longitude or length. **2.** Running lengthwise. — **lon′gi·tu′di·nal·ly** *adv.*

long-lived (lông′līvd′, -livd′, long′-) *adj.* Having a long life or period of existence. — **long′-lived′ness** *n.*

long measure Linear measure.

long-play·ing (lông′plā′ing, long′-) *adj.* LP.

long-range (lông′rānj′, long′-) *adj.* **1.** Designed to shoot or move over distances. **2.** Taking account of, or extending over, a long span of future time: *long-range* plans.

long·shore·man (lông′shôr′mən, -shōr′-, long′-) *n. pl.* **·men** (-mən) A man employed on the waterfront to load and unload vessels; stevedore. [< *alongshore* + MAN]

long shot *Informal* **1.** In betting, a race horse or other gambling choice, backed at great odds and having little chance of winning. **2.** Any similar venture, scheme, etc. — **not by a long shot** *Informal* Decidedly not; not at all.

long-sight·ed (lông′sī′tid, long′-) *adj.* **1.** Far-sighted. **2.** Characterized by or having foresight; sagacious. — **long′-sight′ed·ly** *adv.* — **long′-sight′ed·ness** *n.*

long-stand·ing (lông′stan′ding, long′-) *adj.* Having existed over a long period: a *long-standing* debt.

long-sta·ple (lông′stā′pəl, long′-) *adj.* Having a long fiber: said of fabrics, esp. cotton.

long-suf·fer·ing (lông′suf′ər·ing, long′-) *adj.* Patiently enduring injuries, misfortune, etc., for a long time. — *n.* Patient endurance of injuries, etc.: also **long′-suf′fer·ance.**

long-term (lông′tûrm′, long′-) *adj.* Involving or extending over a relatively long period of time: a *long-term* contract.

long-time (lông′tīm′, long′-) *adj.* Being such for a considerable period of time: a *long-time* friend.

long-wind·ed (lông′win′did, long′-) *adj.* **1.** Continuing for a long time in speaking or writing: a *long-winded* lecturer. **2.** Capable of vigorous activity without becoming short of breath. — **long′-wind′ed·ly** *adv.* — **long′-wind′ed·ness** *n.*

long·wise (lông′wīz′, long′-) *adv.* Lengthwise. Also **long′ways′** (-wāz′).

loo (lōō) *n. pl.* **loos** A game of cards in which each player deposits a forfeit in a pool. [< F *lanturelu*]

look (lōōk) *v.i.* **1.** To use one's sense of sight. **2.** To turn the eyes in a specified direction. **3.** To gaze so as to convey a specific feeling or meaning. **4.** To use one's eyes in order to examine, repair, etc.: Let's *look* at the engine. **5.** To consider: *Look* at his fine record. **6.** To seem: He *looks* reliable. **7.** To face in a specified direction. **8.** To expect: with an infinitive: I *look* to hear from you soon. — *v.t.* **9.** To express or influence by a glance or gaze: to *look* one's anger. — **it looks like 1.** It promises or suggests the coming of. **2.** *Informal* It seems as if: *It looks like* I'll have to move. — **to look after 1.** To take care of. **2.** To watch or follow with the eye. — **to look alive** *Informal* To be alert or attentive. — **to look back** To reflect on the past; recall. — **to look down on** (or **upon**) To regard with condescension or contempt. Also **to look down one's nose on** (or **upon**). — **to look for 1.** To search for. **2.** To anticipate; expect. — **to look forward to** To anticipate. — **to look in** (or **in on**) To make a short visit to. — **to look into 1.** To examine closely. **2.** To make inquiries about. — **to look on. 1.** To be a spectator. **2.** To consider; regard. — **to look oneself** To appear to be in a normal, usual, or healthy condition, etc. — **to look out for 1.** To protect: to *look out* for one's own interests. **2.** To be watchful; be on guard. — **to look over** To examine; scrutinize. — **to look the other way** To ignore or avoid an unpleasant or unfavorable situation, sight, etc. — **to look to 1.** To attend to. **2.** To turn to, as for help, advice, etc. **3.** To anticipate; expect. — **to look up 1.** *U.S.* To search for and find, as in a file, book, etc. **2.** *Informal* To discover the whereabouts of. **3.** *Informal* To improve; become better. — **to look up and down 1.** To inspect critically or appraisingly. **2.** To search everywhere. — **to look up to** To have respect for. — *n.* **1.** The act of looking. **2.** A search, examination, etc., by or as by means of one's eyes. **3.** Aspect or expression: a saintly *look.* **4.** *Often pl. Informal* General appearance: I like the *looks* of this place. **5.** *pl. Informal* Personal appearance: the *looks* of a model. — *interj.* **1.** See! **2.** Listen! [OE *lōcian*]

look·er (lōōk′ər) *n.* **1.** One who looks or watches. **2.** *U.S. Slang* A handsome or good-looking person.

look·er-on (lōōk′ər·on′, -ôn′) *n. pl.* **look·ers-on** A spectator; onlooker.

looking glass (lōōk′ing) A glass mirror.

look·out (lōōk′out′) *n.* **1.** The act of watching for someone or something. **2.** A place where such a watch is kept. **3.** The person or persons watching. **4.** *Naut.* A crow's-nest. **5.** *Informal* Concern; worry: It's your *lookout.*

look-see (lōōk′sē′) *n. Slang* A brief inspection or survey.

loom[1] (lōōm) *v.i.* **1.** To appear or come into view indistinctly, as through a mist. **2.** To appear to the mind as large or threatening. [Origin uncertain]

loom[2] (lōōm) *n.* Any of various machines on which thread or yarn is woven into fabric. [OE *gelōma* tool]

loon[1] (lōōn) *n.* Any of various diving, fish-eating waterfowl, having a weird, laughing cry. [Ult. < ON *lomr*]

loon[2] (lōōn) *n.* **1.** A stupid or crazy person. **2.** A worthless person; idler. [Cf. Du. *loen* stupid fellow]

loon·y (lōō′nē) *Informal adj.* **loon·i·er, loon·i·est** **1.** Lunatic or demented. **2.** Foolish; erratic; silly. — *n. pl.* **·ies** A demented or insane person. [< LUNATIC]

loop (lōōp) *n.* **1.** A folding or doubling over of one end of a piece of thread, rope, wire, etc., so as to form an oval opening. **2.** A ring or bent piece of metal, wood, thread, etc., serving as a fastener, staple, or the like. **3.** Something having or suggesting the shape of a loop. **4.** *Electr.* A complete magnetic or electrical circuit. **5.** *Aeron.* A complete circular turn made by an aircraft flying in a vertical plane. — *v.t.* **1.** To form a loop in or of. **2.** To fasten, connect, or encircle by means of a loop. **3.** *Aeron.* To fly (an aircraft) in a loop or loops. — *v.i.* **4.** To make a loop or loops. **5.** To move forward by forming loops. **— to loop the loop** To make a vertical circular turn in the air, esp. in an aircraft. [ME *loupe*] **— loop′y** *adj.*

loop·hole (loop′hōl′) *n.* **1.** A narrow slit in a wall, esp. one in a fortification. **2.** An opportunity for escaping or evading something. — *v.t.* **·holed, ·hol·ing** To furnish with loopholes.

loose (loos) *adj.* **loos·er, loos·est 1.** Not fastened or confined; unattached. **2.** Not taut; slack: a *loose* rein. **3.** Freed from bonds or restraint. **4.** Not firmly fitted or embedded. **5.** Not closely fitted, as clothing. **6.** Not bound or fastened together. **7.** Not compact, firm, or dense: *loose* soil. **8.** Not packaged: *loose* butter. **9.** Not constricted; open: said of lax bowels or a cough. **10.** Not properly controlled: a *loose* tongue. **11.** Dissolute; unchaste. **12.** Lacking in exactness or precision: a *loose* translation. **13.** *Informal* Not set aside for a specific use: *loose* funds. **— on the loose 1.** Not confined; at large. **2.** *Informal* Behaving in a free, uninhibited, and usu. dissolute manner. — *adv.* **1.** In a loose manner; loosely. **2.** So as to be or become loose: to break *loose*. **— to cut loose** *Informal* To behave in a free, uninhibited manner. — *v.* **loosed, loos·ing** *v.t.* **1.** To set free, as from bondage, penalty, etc. **2.** To untie or undo. **3.** To loosen. **4.** To make less strict; relax. **5.** To let fly; shoot, as an arrow. — *v.i.* **6.** To become loose. **7.** To loose something. [< ON *lauss*] **— loose′ly** *adv.* **— loose′ness** *n.*

loose end Something left undecided or undone, as a task, decision, etc. **— at loose ends 1.** In an unsettled state. **2.** Without a job.

loose-joint·ed (loos′join′tid) *adj.* **1.** Having joints not tightly articulated. **2.** Limber or flexible in movement.

loose-leaf (loos′lēf′) *adj.* Designed for or having pages that are easily inserted or removed: a *loose-leaf* notebook.

loos·en (loo′san) *v.t.* **1.** To untie or undo, as bonds. **2.** To set free; release. **3.** To make less tight, firm, or compact. — *v.i.* **4.** To become loose or looser. **— to loosen up** *Informal* **1.** To relax. **2.** To talk with ease; talk freely. **3.** To give more generously, as money. **— loos′en·er** *n.*

loose-strife (loos′strīf′) *n.* **1.** Any of various plants of the primrose family. **2.** Any of several related plants. [< LOOSE + STRIFE; direct trans. of L *lysimachia*]

loot (loot) *n.* **1.** Goods taken as booty by a victorious army from a sacked city, enemy forces, etc. **2.** Anything unlawfully taken. **3.** *U.S. Slang* Money. — *v.t.* **1.** To plunder; pillage. — *v.i.* **2.** To engage in plundering. [< Hind. *lūt* < Skt. *lunt*] **— loot′er** *n.*

lop¹ (lop) *v.t.* **lopped, lop·ping 1.** To cut or trim the branches, twigs, etc., from. **2.** To cut off, as branches, twigs, etc. — *n.* A part lopped off. [Origin unknown]

lop² (lop) *v.* **lopped, lop·ping** *v.i.* **1.** To droop or hang down loosely. **2.** To move about in an awkward manner. — *v.t.* **3.** To permit to droop or hang down loosely. — *adj.* Pendulous; drooping. [Origin unknown]

lope (lōp) *v.t. & v.i.* **loped, lop·ing** To run or cause to run with a steady, swinging stride or gallop. — *n.* A slow, easy stride or gallop. [< ON *hlaupa* to leap, run]

lop-eared (lop′ird′) *adj.* Having drooping ears.

lop·py (lop′ē) *adj.* **·pi·er, ·pi·est** Pendulous; limp.

lop·sid·ed (lop′sī′did) *adj.* Heavier, larger, or sagging on one side. **— lop′sid′ed·ly** *adv.* **— lop′sid′ed·ness** *n.*

lo·qua·cious (lō-kwā′shəs) *adj.* Characterized by continuous talking. [< L *loqui* to speak] **— lo·qua′cious·ly** *adv.* **— lo·qua′cious·ness** *n.*

lo·quac·i·ty (lō-kwas′ə-tē) *n.* *pl.* **·ties** Talkativeness.

lo·ran (lôr′an, lō′ran) *n.* A system in which the position of a ship or aircraft is determined by comparing the time intervals between radio signals from a network of synchronized ground stations. [< LO(NG) RA(NGE) N(AVIGATION)]

lord (lôrd) *n.* **1.** One possessing great power and authority. **2.** In Great Britain: **a** Any one of the noblemen or peers (**lords temporal**) having the title of marquis, earl, viscount, or baron and having seats in the House of Lords. **b** Any of the higher churchmen (**lords spiritual**) who are members of the House of Lords. **3.** In feudal law, the owner of a manor. — *v.t.* To invest with the title of lord. **— to lord it (over)** To act in a domineering or arrogant manner (toward). [OE *hlāford, hlāfweard,* lit., bread keeper]

Lord (lôrd) *n.* **1.** God: preceded by *the* except in direct address. **2.** Jesus Christ: also *Our Lord.* **3.** In Great Britain, a title of honor or nobility.

lord·ly (lôrd′lē) *adj.* **·li·er, ·li·est 1.** Befitting the rank and position of a lord. **2.** Noble; dignified. **3.** Arrogant; haughty. — *adv.* In a lordly manner. **— lord′li·ness** *n.*

lor·do·sis (lôr·dō′sis) *n.* *Pathol.* Inward curvature of the spine resulting in a hollow back. [< NL < Gk. *lordos* bent backward] **— lor·dot′ic** (-dot′ik) *adj.*

Lord's Day Sunday; the Sabbath.

lord·ship (lôrd′ship) *n.* **1.** The dominion, power, or authority of a lord. **2.** Sovereignty in general; supremacy. **3.** *Often cap.* In Great Britain, the title by which noblemen (excluding dukes), bishops, and judges are addressed or spoken of: preceded by *Your* or *His.* [OE *hlafordscipe.* See LORD.]

Lord's Prayer The prayer beginning *Our Father,* taught by Christ to his disciples. *Matt.* vi 9–13.

Lord's Supper, the 1. The Last Supper. **2.** The Eucharist; Holy Communion.

lore (lôr, lōr) *n.* **1.** The body of traditional, popular, often anecdotal knowledge about a particular subject: the *lore* of the woods. **2.** Learning or erudition. [OE *lār*]

Lo·re·lei (lôr′ə·lī, *Ger.* lō′rə·lī) In German romantic literature, a siren on a rock in the Rhine who lured boatmen to shipwreck by her singing. [< G]

lor·gnette (lôr·nyet′) *n.* **1.** A pair of eyeglasses with an ornamental handle. **2.** An opera glass with a long handle. [< F < *lorgner* to spy, peer]

lo·ris (lôr′is, lō′ris) *n.* *pl.* **·ris** or **·ris·es** A small, arboreal and nocturnal Asian lemur. [< F < Du. *loeres* booby]

lorn (lôrn) *adj.* *Archaic & Poetic* Abandoned; lonely; wretched; forlorn. [OE *loren,* pp. of *lēosan* to lose]

lor·ry (lôr′ē, lor′ē) *n.* *pl.* **·ries 1.** A low, four-wheeled wagon without sides. **2.** A motor truck. [Prob. dial. E *lurry* to pull]

lo·ry (lō′rē, lôr′ē) *n.* *pl.* **·ries** Any of a number of small parrots of Australia and the neighboring islands. [< Malay *lūrī*]

lose (looz) *v.* **lost, los·ing** *v.t.* **1.** To be unable to find; mislay. **2.** To fail to keep, control, or maintain: to *lose* one's footing. **3.** To be deprived of; suffer the loss of: to *lose* a leg. **4.** To fail to win. **5.** To fail to take advantage of; miss. **6.** To fail to see or hear. **7.** To fail to keep in sight, memory, etc. **8.** To occupy or absorb wholly; engross: usually in the passive. **9.** To cease to have: to *lose* one's courage. **10.** To squander; waste. **11.** To cause (someone or something) to be or become lost. **12.** To disappear: used reflexively: The river *loses* itself in the swamp. **13.** To outdistance or elude. **14.** To cause the loss of: His rashness *lost* him the election. **15.** To bring to destruction or death; ruin: usu. in the passive. — *v.i.* **16.** To suffer loss. **17.** To be defeated, as in battle or a contest. **— to lose oneself 1.** To lose one's way. **2.** To disappear or hide. **3.** To become engrossed or absorbed. **— to lose out** *Informal* To fail or be defeated. **— to lose out on** *Informal* To fail to secure; miss. [From OE *losian* to be lost and *lēosan* to lose] **— los′er** *n.*

los·ing (loo′zing) *n.* **1.** The act of one who or that which loses. **2.** *pl.* Money lost, esp. in gambling. — *adj.* **1.** Incurring loss: a *losing* business. **2.** Not winning.

loss (lôs, los) *n.* **1.** The act of losing or the state of being lost. **2.** One who or that which is lost. **3.** The harm, inconvenience, deprivation, etc., caused by losing something or someone. **4.** *pl. Mil.* **a** Casualties. **b** The number of casualties. **5.** In insurance: **a** Death, injury, property damage, etc., sustained by an insured. **b** The sum payable by the insurer on that account. **— at a loss** Perplexed. [ME]

loss leader An article that a retail store sells below or near cost to promote sales of other merchandise.

lost (lôst, lost) *adj.* **1.** Not to be found or recovered. **2.** No longer possessed, seen, or known: *lost* friends. **3.** Not won, gained, or secured. **4.** Having gone astray. **5.** Bewildered; perplexed. **6.** Helpless. **7.** Not used or taken advantage of; wasted. **8.** Destroyed; ruined. **9.** No longer known or practiced: a *lost* art. **— to be lost in** To be absorbed or engrossed in. **— to be lost to 1.** To no longer belong to. **2.** To be impervious or insensible to. **3.** To be no longer available to. **— to be lost upon** (or **on**) To have no effect upon.

lot (lot) *n.* **1.** That which is used in determining something by chance, as objects drawn at random from a container. **2.** The process of deciding something by this method. **3.** The decisions arrived at by such means. **4.** The share or portion that comes to one as a result of drawing lots. **5.** One's portion in life as ascribed to chance, fate, custom, etc. **6.** A number of things or persons considered as a single group. **7.** A job lot. **8.** A plot or quantity of land: a parking *lot.* **9.** *Informal* A (specified) type of person: He's a bad *lot.* **10.** In motion pictures, a studio and the adjacent area. **11.** *Often pl. Informal* A great deal: a *lot* of money; *lots* of trouble. **— Syn.** See DESTINY. **— a lot** (or **lots**) *Informal* Very much: He is *a lot* better; *lots* better. **— the lot** The whole of a certain number or quantity: He bought *the lot.* **— to cast** (or draw) **lots** To come to a decision or solution by the use of lots. **— to cast** (or **throw**) **in one's lot with** To join with and share the fortunes of. *— v.* **lot·ted, lot·ting** *v.t.* **1.** To apportion by lots; allot. **2.** To draw lots for. **3.** To divide, as land, into lots. *— v.i.* **4.** To cast lots. [OE *hlot*]

Lot (lot) In the Old Testament, a nephew of Abraham, whose wife was turned into a pillar of salt when she looked back upon the destruction of Sodom. *Gen.* xi 27, xix.

loth (lōth) See LOATH.

lo·tion (lō′shən) *n.* A liquid preparation used for external cleansing of the skin, eyes, etc. [< L < *lavare* to wash]

lot·ter·y (lot′ər·ē) *n.* *pl.* **·ter·ies** A method of distributing prizes in which numbered tickets are sold, the winning tickets being selected by lot. [< Ital. *lotto* lottery, lot]

lot·to (lot′ō) *n.* A game of chance played by drawing numbers from a container and covering with counters the corresponding numbers on cards, the winner being the first to cover a row of numbers. [< Ital.]

lo·tus (lō′təs) *n.* **1.** Any of various tropical water lilies noted for their large floating leaves and showy flowers; esp., the **white lotus** and the **blue lotus** of Egypt and the **sacred lotus** of India. **2.** A representation of any of these plants in art, architecture, sculpture, etc. **3.** Any of a genus of herbs of the bean family. Also **lo′tos**. [< L < Gk. *lōtos*]

lo·tus-eat·er (lō′təs·ē′tər) *n.* **1.** In the *Odyssey*, one of a people who lived a life of indolence induced by eating the fruit of the lotus tree. **2.** Anyone considered to be living an indolent, irresponsible existence.

lotus tree Any of a genus of Old World trees of the buckthorn family.

LOTUS
a Bud and leaf.
b Flower and leaf. *c* Stylized lotus in Egyptian architecture.

loud (loud) *adj.* **1.** Having great volume or intensity of sound: *loud* thunder. **2.** Making or uttering a great noise or sound: a *loud* trumpet. **3.** Emphatic or urgent; insistent: *loud* demands. **4.** *Informal* Crude; vulgar, as manners, persons, etc. **5.** *Informal* Excessively showy: a *loud* shirt. *— adv.* In a loud manner. [OE *hlūd*] **— loud′ly** *adv.* **— loud′ness** *n.*

loud-mouthed (loud′mouthd′, -moutht′) *adj.* Having a loud voice; offensively clamorous or talkative.

loud-speaker (loud′spē′kər) *n.* Any of various devices for converting an electric current into sound, as in a public-address system, radio, etc.: also called *speaker*.

lou·is d'or (lōō′ē dôr) *pl.* **lou·is d'or** **1.** A former French gold coin worth twenty francs. **2.** An old French coin, fluctuating in value, first minted in 1640. Also **lou′is**.

lounge (lounj) *v.* **lounged, loung·ing** *v.i.* **1.** To recline, walk, etc., in a relaxed, lazy manner. **2.** To pass time in doing nothing. *— v.t.* **3.** To spend or pass in idleness, as time. *— n.* **1.** A couch or sofa, esp. one with little or no back and a headrest at one end. **2.** A room in a hotel, club, train, etc., suitable for lounging and often having facilities for drinking. **3.** A lounging pace or gait. **4.** The act of lounging; also, a period of lounging. [Origin unknown] **— loung′er** *n.*

loupe (lōōp) *n.* A small magnifying glass, esp. one adapted as an eyepiece for jewelers or watchmakers. [< F]

louse (lous) *n.* *pl.* **lice** (līs) **1.** A small, flat-bodied, wingless insect living as an external parasite on man and some animals. **2.** Any of various other parasitic insects. **3.** *Slang* A contemptible person. *— v.t. & v.i.* **loused, lous·ing** *Slang* To ruin; bungle: with *up*. [OE *lūs*]

lous·y (lou′zē) *adj.* **lous·i·er, lous·i·est 1.** Infested with lice. **2.** *Slang* Contemptible; mean. **3.** *Slang* Worthless; inferior. **4.** *Slang* Having plenty (of): with *with*: *lousy* with money.

lout (lout) *n.* An awkward fellow; clown; boor. [? < ON *lutr* bent, stooped] **— lout′ish** *adj.*

lou·ver (lōō′vər) *n.* **1.** A window or opening, as in a gable, provided with louver boards; also, a louver board. **2.** One of several narrow openings serving as an outlet for heated air. [OF *lover*]

louver board One of a series of horizontal, overlapping slats in a window or opening, sloped downward to shed rain while admitting light and air. Also **louver boarding**.

LOUVER
a Construction.
b Set in gable.

Lou·vre (lōō′vr′) A royal palace in Paris, begun in 1554 and made into an art museum in the late 18th century.

lov·a·ble (luv′ə·bəl) *adj.* Worthy of love; amiable; also, evoking love. Also **love′a·ble**. **— lov′a·bil′i·ty, lov′a·ble·ness** *n.* **— lov′a·bly** *adv.*

love (luv) *n.* **1.** A deep devotion or affection for another person or persons: *love* for one's children. **2.** A strong sexual passion for another person. **3.** Sexual passion in general or the gratification of it. **4.** One who is beloved. **5.** A very great interest in, or enjoyment of, something; also, the thing so enjoyed. **6.** In tennis, a score of nothing. **— in love**

Experiencing love for someone or something. **— to fall in love** To conceive a love for someone or something. **— to make love** To kiss, embrace, etc., as lovers. *— v.* **loved, lov·ing** *v.t.* **1.** To feel love or affection for. **2.** To take pleasure or delight in: to *love* good food. **3.** To show love for by kissing or caressing. *— v.i.* **4.** To be in love. [OE *lufu*]

Love (luv) A personification of love; Cupid or Eros.

love apple A former name for the tomato.

love·bird (luv′bûrd′) *n.* One of several small parrots often kept as cage birds: so called from the affection they show.

love knot A knot tied in pledge of love and constancy; also, a representation of it, as in jewelry.

love·less (luv′lis) *adj.* **1.** Having no love. **2.** Receiving no love. **— love′less·ly** *adv.* **— love′less·ness** *n.*

love-lies-bleed·ing (luv′līz′blē′ding) *n.* A species of amaranth having crimson flowers.

love·lorn (luv′lôrn) *adj.* Pining for one's lover.

love·ly (luv′lē) *adj.* **·li·er, ·li·est 1.** Possessing qualities that inspire admiration or love. **2.** Beautiful: a *lovely* rose. **3.** *Informal* Delightful; pleasing. **— love′li·ness** *n.*

love potion A magic draft or drink designed to arouse love toward a certain person in the one who drinks.

lov·er (luv′ər) *n.* **1.** One who loves: a *lover* of humanity. **2.** One in love with or making love to a person of the opposite sex: in the singular now used only of the man. **3.** One who especially enjoys diversion, pursuit, etc.: a *lover* of golf. **— lov′er·ly** *adj. & adv.*

love seat A double chair or small sofa for two persons.

love·sick (luv′sik′) *adj.* **1.** Languishing with love. **2.** Indicating such a state: a *lovesick* serenade. **— love′sick′ness** *n.*

lov·ing (luv′ing) *adj.* **1.** Affectionate; devoted; kind. **2.** Indicative of love. **— lov′ing·ly** *adv.* **— lov′ing·ness** *n.*

loving cup A wine cup, usu. with two or more handles, formerly passed around a circle of friends at a banquet.

lov·ing-kind·ness (luv′ing·kīnd′nis) *n.* Kindness that comes from or indicates personal affection or regard.

low[1] (lō) *adj.* **1.** Having relatively little upward extension; not high or tall. **2.** Located or placed below the normal or usual level: a *low* marsh. **3.** Near the horizon: a *low* moon. **4.** Pertaining to latitudes nearest the equator. **5.** Relatively small in depth, height, amount, degree, etc. **6.** Of or producing sounds of relatively long wavelengths: a *low* pitch. **7.** Not loud; faint: a *low* rustle. **8.** Extending far downward; deep: a *low* bow. **9.** Exposing part of the wearer's shoulders, back, or chest: a *low* blouse. **10.** Melancholy or sad; depressed: *low* spirits. **11.** Lacking vigor; feeble. **12.** Not adequately provided with; short of: to be *low* on groceries. **13.** *Informal* Having little or no ready cash. **14.** Inexpensive: a *low* price. **15.** Poor, unfavorable, or disparaging: to have a *low* estimate of one's abilities. **16.** Humble or inferior, as in origin, rank, position, etc. **17.** Inferior in quality: a *low* grade of tobacco. **18.** Lacking in refinement; vulgar: *low* companions. **19.** Morally base or mean. **20.** Relatively recent, as a date. **21.** Relatively simple in structure, function, or organization: a *low* form of animal life. **22.** In the Anglican Church, of or pertaining to the Low Church. **23.** *Mech.* Denoting a gear arrangement, as in transmissions, yielding a slow or the slowest output speed. **24.** *Phonet.* Of vowel sounds, produced with the tongue depressed and flat, as (ä) in *large*: opposed to *high*. *— adv.* **1.** In or to a low level, position, degree, etc. **2.** In a low manner. **3.** Softly; quietly. **4.** With a low pitch. **5.** At a low price; cheaply. **6.** In or to a humble, poor, or degraded condition. *— n.* **1.** A low level, position, degree, etc. **2.** *Meteorol.* An area of low barometric pressure. **3.** *Mech.* An arrangement of gears that yields a slow or the slowest output speed. [Early ME *lah* < ON *lagr*] **— low′ness** *n.*

low[2] (lō) *v.i.* **1.** To make the hollow, bellowing sound of cattle; moo. *— v.t.* **2.** To utter by lowing. *— n.* The vocal sound made by cattle: also **low′ing**. [OE *hlōwan*]

low-born (lō′bôrn′) *adj.* Of humble birth.

low·boy (lō′boi) *n.* A short-legged chest of drawers of about table height, similar to the lower part of a highboy.

low·bred (lō′bred′) *adj.* **1.** Of humble or inferior origin or birth. **2.** Vulgar; coarse.

low·brow (lō′brou) *n.* *Informal* A person of uncultivated or vulgar tastes. *— adj.* Of or suitable for such a person: also **low′browed′**. **— low′brow·ism** *n.*

Low-Church (lō′chûrch′) *adj.* Of or belonging to a group (**Low Church**) in the Anglican Church that stresses evangelical doctrine and is, in general, opposed to extreme ritualism. **— Low′-Church′man** (-mən) *n.*

low comedy Comedy that is characterized by slapstick and lively physical action rather than by witty dialogue.

low-down[1] (lō′doun′) *n.* *Slang* The truth.

low-down[2] (lō′doun′) *adj.* *Informal* **1.** Unethical or mean. **2.** In jazz, slow, sad, or sensuous, as the blues.

low·er (lou′ər) *v.i.* **1.** To look sullen; scowl. **2.** To appear dark and threatening, as the weather. *— n.* **1.** A sullen look; a scowl. **2.** A dark, threatening look, as of the weather. [Cf. G *lauern* to lurk]

low·er² (lō′ər) Comparative of LOW. — *adj.* **1.** Inferior in rank, value, etc. **2.** Situated below something else. **3.** *Often cap. Geol.* Older; designating strata normally beneath the newer (and upper) rock formations. — *n.* That which is beneath something else; esp., a lower berth. — *v.t.* **1.** To bring to a lower position or level; let down, as a window. **2.** To reduce in degree, quality, amount, etc.: to *lower* prices. **3.** To undermine or weaken. **4.** To bring down in estimation, rank, etc. **5.** To change (a sound) to a lower pitch or volume. — *v.i.* **6.** To become less; decrease; sink.

low·er-case (lō′ər-kās′) *Printing adj.* Of, in, or indicating small letters, as distinguished from capitals. — *v.t.* **-cased, -cas·ing** To set as or change to lower-case letters.

lower case *Printing* **1.** In type cases, the lower tray, containing the small letters of the alphabet. See CASE². **2.** The small letters of the alphabet.

lower class The socially or economically inferior group in society. — **low·er-class** (lō′ər-klas′, -kläs′) *adj.*

low·er-class·man (lō′ər-klas′mən, -kläs′-) *n.* *pl.* **·men** (-mən) A student in either of the first two years of a four-year course; a freshman or sophomore.

Lower House The larger and more widely representative branch of a bicameral legislative body, as the House of Representatives in the U.S. Also **Lower Chamber**.

low·er·most (lō′ər-mōst′) *adj.* Lowest.

Lower Paleolithic See under PALEOLITHIC.

lower world **1.** The abode of the dead; hell; Hades; Sheol. Also **lower regions**. **2.** The earth.

low frequency *Telecom.* Radio waves having a frequency of from 30 to 300 kilocycles.

Low German See under GERMAN.

low·land (lō′lənd, -land′) *n.* *Usu. pl.* Land lying lower than the adjacent country. — *adj.* Of, pertaining to, or characteristic of a low or level country.

Low·land (lō′lənd, -land′) *n.* The speech or dialect of the Scottish Lowlands. — *adj.* Pertaining or belonging to the Scottish Lowlands.

Low Latin See under LATIN.

low·ly (lō′lē) *adj.* **·li·er, ·li·est** **1.** Humble or low in rank, origin, nature, etc. **2.** Full of humility; meek. **3.** Situated or lying low. — *adv.* **1.** In a low condition, manner, position, etc. **2.** Modestly; humbly. — **low′li·ness** *n.*

Low Mass A form of Mass celebrated without music and by one priest usu. assisted by a server or altar boy.

low-mind·ed (lō′mīn′did) *adj.* Having low, vulgar, or mean thoughts, sentiments, or motives. — **low′-mind′ed·ly** *adv.* — **low′-mind′ed·ness** *n.*

low-necked (lō′nekt′) *adj.* Having a low neckline.

low-pitched (lō′picht′) *adj.* **1.** Low in tone or range of tone. **2.** Having little slope, as a roof. **3.** *Music* Built for a pitch lower than standard pitch: said of instruments.

low-pres·sure (lō′presh′ər) *adj.* **1.** Having or operating under a low degree of pressure. **2.** *Meteorol.* Designating atmospheric pressure below that normal at sea level.

low relief Bas-relief.

low-spir·it·ed (lō′spir′it·id) *adj.* Despondent; melancholy. — **low′-spir′it·ed·ly** *adv.* — **low′-spir′it·ed·ness** *n.*

low tide **1.** The ebb tide at its lowest stage. **2.** The time this lowest stage occurs. **3.** The lowest point or level reached.

low water A very low level of water in a stream, etc.

lox¹ (loks) *n.* A salty, smoked salmon, often eaten with cream cheese, bagels, etc. [< Yiddish < G *lachs* salmon]

lox² (loks) *n.* Liquid oxygen.

loy·al (loi′əl) *adj.* **1.** Bearing true allegiance to a constituted authority, as to one's sovereign, government, etc. **2.** Constant and faithful in any relation or obligation implying trust, confidence, etc. **3.** Indicating or professing loyalty. [< OF < L *legalis*] — **loy′al·ism** *n.* — **loy′al·ly** *adv.*

loy·al·ist (loi′əl·ist) *n.* One who supports and defends his government, esp. in times of crisis or war.

Loy·al·ist (loi′əl·ist) *n.* **1.** In the American Revolution, a colonist who remained loyal to the British crown. **2.** In the Spanish Civil War, one who supported the government of the Republic against the uprising of Franco.

loy·al·ty (loi′əl·tē) *n.* *pl.* **·ties** The state, quality, or fact of being loyal; fidelity; allegiance.

loz·enge (loz′inj) *n.* **1.** A small sweetened tablet or candy, now usu. medicated. **2.** *Math.* A diamond-shaped figure. [< OF < L *lapis, -idis* stone]

LP (el′pē′) *adj.* Designating a phonograph record pressed with microgrooves and played at a speed of 33⅓ revolutions per minute: also *long-playing*. — *n.* An LP record: a trade mark. [< l(ong)-p(laying)]

LSD (el′es′dē′) *n.* A drug that produces states similar to those of schizophrenia, used in medicine and illicitly as a hallucinogen. See LYSERGIC ACID. Also **LSD-25**. [< *l(y)s*(ergic acid) d(iethylamide)]

lu·au (lōō·ou′) *n.* A Hawaiian feast with entertainment.

lub·ber (lub′ər) *n.* **1.** An awkward, ungainly fellow. **2.** A landlubber. [Origin uncertain] — **lub′ber·ly** *adj. & adv.*

lu·bri·cant (lōō′brə·kənt) *n.* A substance, as oil, grease, graphite, etc., used to coat moving parts in order to reduce friction and wear. — *adj.* Lubricating.

lu·bri·cate (lōō′brə·kāt) *v.t.* **·cat·ed, ·cat·ing** **1.** To apply a lubricant to. **2.** To make slippery or smooth. [< L < *lubricus* slippery] — **lu′bri·ca′tion** *n.* — **lu′bri·ca′tive** *adj.* — **lu′bri·ca′tor** *n.*

lu·bric·i·ty (lōō·bris′ə·tē) *n.* *pl.* **·ties** **1.** Lewdness; lasciviousness. **2.** Shiftiness; elusiveness. **3.** Slipperiness. [< F < L < *lubricus* slippery]

lu·cent (lōō′sənt) *adj.* **1.** Showing or giving off radiance. **2.** Transparent or semitransparent. [< L *lucens, -entis,* ppr. of *lucere* to shine] — **lu′cen·cy** *n.* — **lu′cent·ly** *adv.*

lu·cerne (lōō·sûrn′) *Brit.* Alfalfa. [< F]

lu·ces (lōō′sēz) Plural of LUX.

lu·cid (lōō′sid) *adj.* **1.** Easily understood; clear: a *lucid* explanation. **2.** Mentally sound, clear, or rational: a *lucid* interval. **3.** Shining; bright. [< L *lucere* to shine] — **lu·cid·i·ty** (lōō·sid′ə·tē), **lu′cid·ness** *n.* — **lu′cid·ly** *adv.*

Lu·ci·fer (lōō′sə·fər) *n.* **1.** The archangel who led the revolt of the angels and fell from Heaven: identified with Satan. **2.** The planet Venus when it appears as the morning star. [< L, light-bearer < *lux, lucis* light + *ferre* to bear]

Lu·cite (lōō′sīt) *n.* A transparent acrylic resin, easily machined into various shapes.

luck (luk) *n.* **1.** That which happens by chance; fortune; lot. **2.** Good fortune; success. **3.** Any object regarded as bringing good fortune. — **to be down on one's luck** To suffer failure, poverty, etc. — **to be in luck** To meet with success or good fortune. — **to be out of luck** To be unlucky. — **to try one's luck** To attempt to do something without any certainty of success. [Prob. < MDu. *luk, geluk*]

luck·less (luk′lis) *adj.* Having bad luck; unlucky. — **luck′less·ly** *adv.* — **luck′less·ness** *n.*

luck·y (luk′ē) *adj.* **luck·i·er, luck·i·est** **1.** Accompanied by or having good fortune. **2.** Bringing or resulting in good fortune. **3.** Believed to bring good fortune. — **luck′i·ly** *adv.* — **luck′i·ness** *n.*

lu·cra·tive (lōō′krə·tiv) *adj.* Producing or yielding gain, profit, or wealth; profitable. [< L < *lucratus,* pp. of *lucrari* to gain] — **lu′cra·tive·ly** *adv.* — **lu′cra·tive·ness** *n.*

lu·cre (lōō′kər) *n.* Money or riches: now chiefly in the humorous phrase: *filthy lucre.* [< F < L *lucrum* gain]

lu·cu·brate (lōō′kyōō·brāt) *v.i.* **·brat·ed, ·brat·ing** **1.** To study or write laboriously, esp. at night. **2.** To write in a learned manner. [< L *lucubrare* to work by candlelight]

lu·cu·bra·tion (lōō′kyōō·brā′shən) *n.* **1.** Earnest and labored study. **2.** The product of such study, esp. a pedantic literary composition. **3.** *pl.* Any literary effort. — **lu′cu·bra′tor** *n.* — **lu′cu·bra·to′ry** (-brə·tôr′ē, -tō′rē) *adj.*

lu·di·crous (lōō′də·krəs) *adj.* Exciting laughter or ridicule; ridiculous; absurd. [< L < *ludere* to play] — **lu′di·crous·ly** *adv.* — **lu′di·crous·ness** *n.*

luff (luf) *Naut. n.* **1.** The sailing of a ship close to the wind. **2.** The rounded and fullest part of a vessel's bow. **3.** The foremost edge of a fore-and-aft sail. — *v.i.* **1.** To bring the head of a vessel nearer the wind. **2.** To bring the head of a vessel into the wind, with the sails shaking. Also *loof.* [ME *lof, loven*]

Luft·waf·fe (lōōft′väf′ə) *n. German* The German air force during World War II.

lug¹ (lug) *n.* **1.** An earlike projection for holding or supporting something. **2.** *Mech.* A nut, closed at one end. **3.** *Slang* A fellow, esp. a clumsy one. [Origin uncertain]

lug² (lug) *v.* **lugged, lug·ging** *v.t.* **1.** To carry or pull with effort. — *v.i.* **2.** To pull or drag with effort; tug. — *n.* **1.** The act or exertion of lugging; also, that which is lugged. **2.** *Naut.* A lugsail. [Prob. Scand.]

lug³ (lug) *n.* A lugworm. [Origin uncertain]

lug·gage (lug′ij) *n.* Suitcases, trunks, etc., used for traveling; baggage. [< LUG²]

lug·ger (lug′ər) *n. Naut.* A one-, two-, or three-masted vessel having lugsails only. [< LUG(SAIL) + -ER²]

lug·sail (lug′səl, -sāl′) *n. Naut.* A four-cornered sail having no boom and bent to a yard that hangs obliquely on the mast: also called *lug.*

lu·gu·bri·ous (lōō·gōō′brē·əs, -gyōō′-) *adj.* Very sad, or mournful, esp. in a ludicrous manner. [< L < *lugere* to mourn] — **lu·gu′bri·ous·ly** *adv.* — **lu·gu′bri·ous·ness** *n.*

lug·worm (lug′wûrm′) *n.* An annelid worm with two rows of tufted gills on the back, living in the sand of seashores.

Luke (lōōk) Physician and companion of St. Paul; traditionally thought to be the author of the third Gospel: called **Saint Luke**. — *n.* The third Gospel of the New Testament.

luke·warm (lōōk′wôrm′) *adj.* **1.** Moderately warm; tepid. **2.** Lacking in ardor, enthusiasm, or conviction; indifferent:

a *lukewarm* greeting. [Prob. OE *hlēow* warm.] —**luke′· warm/ly** *adv.* —**luke/warm/ness** *n.*

lull (lul) *v.t.* **1.** To quiet or put to sleep by soothing sounds or motions. **2.** To calm or allay, esp. by deception: to *lull* someone's suspicions. —*v.i.* **3.** To become calm or quiet. —*n.* **1.** A brief interval of calm or quiet during noise or confusion. **2.** A period of diminished activity, prosperity, etc.: a *lull* in business. [Prob. imit.]

lull·a·by (lul/ə-bī) *n. pl.* **·bies 1.** A song to lull a child to sleep; a cradlesong. **2.** A piece of instrumental music in the manner of a lullaby. —*v.t.* **·bied, ·by·ing** *Rare* To soothe with a lullaby.

lum·ba·go (lum·bā/gō) *n.* Pain in the lumbar region of the back; backache, esp. in the small of the back.

lum·bar (lum/bər, -bär) *adj.* Pertaining to or situated near the loins. —*n.* A lumbar vertebra, nerve, artery, etc. [< NL < L *lumbus* loin]

lum·ber[1] (lum/bər) *n.* **1.** *U.S. & Canadian* Timber sawed into boards, planks, etc., of specified lengths. **2.** *Chiefly Brit.* Household articles no longer used and usu. stored away. —*adj.* Made of, pertaining to, or dealing in lumber. —*v.t.* **1.** *U.S. & Canadian* To cut down (timber); also, to cut down the timber of (an area). **2.** *Chiefly Brit.* To fill or obstruct with useless articles. —*v.i.* **3.** *U.S. & Canadian* To cut down or saw timber for marketing. [Var. of *Lombard* in obs. sense of "money-lender, pawnshop," hence, stored articles] —**lum/ber·er** *n.* —**lum/ber·ing** *n.*

lum·ber[2] (lum/bər) *v.i.* **1.** To move or proceed in a heavy or awkward manner. **2.** To move with a rumbling noise. —*n.* A rumbling noise. [ME *lomerer*] —**lum/ber·ing** *adj.* —**lum/ber·ing·ly** *adv.*

lum·ber·jack (lum/bər-jak) *n. U.S. & Canadian* A person who fells or transports timber; a logger. [< LUMBER[1] + *jack* man, boy]

lum·ber·man (lum/bər-mən) *n. pl.* **·men** (mən) *U.S. & Canadian* **1.** A lumberjack. **2.** One who is engaged in the business of lumbering.

lum·ber·yard (lum/bər-yärd) *n. U.S. & Canadian* A yard for the storage or sale of lumber.

lu·men (lōō/mən) *n. pl.* **·mens** or **·mi·na** (-mə-nə) **1.** *Anat.* The inner passage of a tubular organ, as a blood vessel. **2.** *Physics* A unit for measuring the flow of light, equal to the flow of one international candle. [< L, light]

lu·mi·nar·y (lōō/mə-ner/ē) *n. pl.* **·nar·ies 1.** Any body that gives light, esp. the sun or the moon. **2.** One who has achieved great eminence. [< OF < LL < *lumen* light]

lu·mi·nesce (lōō/mə-nes/) *v.i.* **·nesced, ·nesc·ing** To be or become luminescent.

lu·mi·nes·cence (lōō/mə-nes/əns) *n.* An emission of light, such as fluorescence and phosphorescence, not directly attributable to the heat that produces incandescence. [< L *lumen* light + -ESCENT] —**lu/mi·nes/cent** *adj.*

lumini- *combining form* Light; luminescence. Also **lumin-** (before vowels), **lumino-**. [< L *lumen, luminis* light]

lu·mi·nif·er·ous (lōō/mə-nif/ər-əs) *adj.* Producing light.

lu·mi·nous (lōō/mə-nəs) *adj.* **1.** Full of light. **2.** Giving off light; shining. **3.** Easily understood; clear. **4.** Brilliantly intelligent. [< L *lumen* light] —**lu/mi·nous·ly** *adv.* —**lu/mi·nous·ness, lu/mi·nos/i·ty** *n.*

lum·mox (lum/əks) *n. U.S. Informal* A stupid, clumsy person.

lump[1] (lump) *n.* **1.** A shapeless mass, esp. a small mass. **2.** A swelling. **3.** A mass of things thrown together; aggregate. **4.** A heavy, ungainly, and usu. stupid person. —**a lump in one's throat** A feeling of tightness in the throat, as from emotion. —**in** *s.* (or the) **lump** All together. —*adj.* Formed in a lump or lumps: *lump* sugar. —*v.t.* **1.** To put together in one mass, group, etc. **2.** To consider or treat as one mass, group, etc. **3.** To make lumps in or on. —*v.i.* **4.** To become lumpy. [< ME]

lump[2] (lump) *v.t. Informal* To put up with; endure: You can like it or *lump* it.

lump·ish (lum/pish) *adj.* **1.** Like a lump. **2.** Stupid; clumsy. —**lump/ish·ly** *adv.* —**lump/ish·ness** *n.*

lump sum A full or single sum of money paid at one time.

lump·y (lum/pē) *adj.* **lump·i·er, lump·i·est 1.** Full of lumps. **2.** Covered with lumps. **3.** Lumpish. **4.** Running in rough waves. —**lump/i·ly** *adv.* —**lump/i·ness** *n.*

Lu·na (lōō/nə) In Roman mythology, the goddess of the moon: identified with the Greek *Selene.* [< L]

lu·na·cy (lōō/nə·sē) *n. pl.* **·cies 1.** Irresponsible or senseless conduct. **2.** *Law* Insanity.

Luna moth A large North American moth having light green wings with long tails and lunate spots.

lu·nar (lōō/nər) *adj.* **1.** Of the moon. **2.** Round or crescentshaped like the moon. **3.** Measured by the revolutions of the moon: a *lunar* month. [< L < *luna* moon]

lunar month See under MONTH.

lunar year A period of twelve lunar months, one month being added at intervals to make the mean length of the astronomical year, as in the Hebrew calendar.

lu·nate (lōō/nāt) *adj.* Crescent-shaped. Also **lu′nat·ed.**

lu·na·tic (lōō/nə·tik) *adj.* **1.** Insane. **2.** Wildly foolish or irrational. **3.** Of or for the insane. Also **lu·nat·i·cal** (lōō-nat/i-kəl). —*n.* An insane person. [< LL < L *luna* moon]

lunatic fringe Those followers or devotees of a movement, idea, etc., who are extreme or fanatical in their enthusiasm.

lunch (lunch) *n.* **1.** A light meal, esp. the noonday meal. **2.** Food for a lunch. —*v.i.* To eat lunch. —**lunch/er** *n.*

lunch·eon (lun/chən) *n.* A noonday meal, esp. a formal one.

lunch·eon·ette (lun/chən-et/) *n.* A restaurant where light lunches and other meals may be obtained.

lunch·room (lunch/rōōm/, -rōōm/) *n.* A restaurant serving light lunches; luncheonette. Also **lunch room.**

lung (lung) *n. Anat.* **1.** Either of two saclike organs of respiration in the thorax of man and other airbreathing vertebrates. ◆ Collateral adjective: *pulmonary.* **2.** An analogous organ in certain invertebrates. [OE *lungen*]

lunge (lunj) *n.* **1.** A sudden pass or thrust, as with a sword, etc. **2.** A quick movement or plunge forward. —*v.* **lunged, lung·ing** —*v.i.* **1.** To make a lunge; thrust. **2.** To move with a lunge. —*v.t.* **3.** To cause to lunge. [< F < L *ad* to + *longus* long]

lung·wort (lung/wûrt/) *n.* Any of various plants of the borage family, esp., a European herb having white blotches on its leaves.

luni- *combining form* Of or pertaining to the moon; lunar. [< L *luna* moon]

lu·pine[1] (lōō/pīn) *adj.* **1.** Of, like, or related to a wolf or wolves. **2.** Fierce; ravenous. [< L < *lupus* wolf]

lu·pine[2] (lōō/pin) *n.* **1.** Any of various plants of the pea family, bearing mostly blue, white, or purple flowers, as the **white lupine** of Europe, whose seeds are edible. **2.** The seeds of the white lupine. [< F < L *lupinus* wolflike]

lu·pus (lōō/pəs) *n. Pathol.* Any of various forms of a tuberculous disease of the skin, characterized by brownish nodules or scaly red patches. [< L, wolf]

lurch[1] (lûrch) *v.i.* **1.** To roll suddenly to one side. **2.** To stagger. —*n.* **1.** A sudden swaying. **2.** A reeling.

lurch[2] (lûrch) *n.* **1.** An embarrassing or difficult position; predicament: now only in the phrase **to leave (someone) in the lurch. 2.** In cribbage, the state of a player who has made 30 points or less while his opponent has won with 61. [< F *lourche* deceived < Gmc.]

lure (lŏŏr, lyŏŏr) *n.* **1.** Anything that attracts or entices. **2.** In angling, an artificial bait. **3.** In falconry, a device consisting of a bunch of feathers and a bait, fastened to a long cord and used to recall a hawk. —*v.t.* **lured, lur·ing 1.** To attract or entice; allure. **2.** To recall (a hawk) with a lure. [< OF < MHG *luoder* to bait] —**lur/er** *n.*

lu·rid (lŏŏr/id, lyŏŏr-) *adj.* **1.** Shocking or sensational. **2.** Pale and sickly in color. **3.** Lighted up with a yellowish red glare or glow esp. in smoke or darkness. [< L *luridus* sallow] —**lu/rid·ly** *adv.* —**lu/rid·ness** *n.*

lurk (lûrk) *v.i.* **1.** To lie hidden, as in ambush. **2.** To exist unnoticed or unsuspected. **3.** To move secretly or furtively; slink. [ME *lurken*] —**lurk/ing·ly** *adv.*

lus·cious (lush/əs) *adj.* **1.** Very pleasurable to the sense of taste or smell. **2.** Pleasing to any sense. **3.** Excessively sweet; cloying. —**lus/cious·ly** *adv.* —**lus/cious·ness** *n.*

lush[1] (lush) *adj.* **1.** Abounding in vigorous growth: a *lush countryside.* **2.** Delicious and succulent. **3.** Elaborate in effects, etc. [< OF < L *laxus* loose] —**lush/ness** *n.*

lush[2] (lush) *Slang n.* A heavy drinker; drunkard.

lust (lust) *n.* **1.** Sexual appetite. **2.** Excessive sexual appetite, esp. that seeking immediate or ruthless satisfaction. **3.** An overwhelming desire: a *lust* for power. —*v.i.* To have passionate or inordinate desire, esp. sexual desire: often with *after* or *for.* [OE, pleasure]

lus·ter (lus/tər) *n.* **1.** Sheen; gloss. **2.** Brilliance of light; radiance. **3.** Splendor, glory, or distinction. **4.** A source or center of light, esp. a chandelier. **5.** Any of various substances used to give a polish to a surface. **6.** In ceramics, a glossy, metallic, and often iridescent finish given to the surface of an object. **7.** A fabric of mixed wool and cotton and having a glossy finish. **8.** *Mineral.* The surface appearance of a mineral as determined by the intensity or quality of the light it reflects. —*v.* **lus·tered** or *Brit.* **lus·tred, lus·ter·ing** or *Brit.* **·tring** *v.t.* **1.** To give a luster or gloss to. —*v.i.* **2.** To be or become lustrous. Also *Brit.* **lus/tre.** [< F < Ital. < L. < *lustrum* purification]

lus·ter·ware (lus/tər-wâr/) *n.* Pottery having a lustrous and often iridescent sheen.

lust·ful (lust′fəl) *adj.* Characterized or driven by lust. — **lust′ful·ly** *adv.* — **lust′ful·ness** *n.*

lus·trate (lus′trāt) *v.t.* ·trat·ed, ·trat·ing To purify by an offering or ceremony. [< L *lustrum* purification] — **lus·tra′tion** *n.* — **lus·tra·tive** (lus′trə·tiv) *adj.*

lus·trous (lus′trəs) *adj.* 1. Having a luster; glossy. 2. Brilliant; shining. — **lus′trous·ly** *adv.* — **lus′trous·ness** *n.*

lus·trum (lus′trəm) *n.* 1. A period of five years. 2. In ancient Rome, the solemn ceremony of purification of the entire people made every five years.

lust·y (lus′tē) *adj.* lust·i·er, lust·i·est 1. Full of vigor; robust. 2. Powerful. — **lust′i·ly** *adv.* — **lust′i·ness** *n.*

lu·ta·nist (loo′tə·nist, lyoo′-) *n.* One who plays the lute. Also **lu′te·nist.**

lute¹ (loot, lyoot) *n.* An old musical instrument having strings that are plucked by the fingers, a large body shaped like half of a pear, and a long, fretted neck usu. bent at a sharp angle just below the peg box. [< OF < Pg. < Arabic *al′ud* the piece of wood]

lute² (loot, lyoot) *n.* A composition of finely powdered clay, used as a sealing agent for joints of pipes, etc. Also **lut′ing.** — *v.t.* lut·ed, lut·ing To seal with lute. [< OF < L *lutum* mud]

LUTE

lu·te·ous (loo′tē·əs) *adj.* Light or moderate greenish yellow in color. [< L *luteus* < *lutum* weed used by dyers]

lu·te·ti·um (loo·tē′shē·əm, -tē′shəm) *n.* A metallic element (symbol Lu) of the lanthanide series, isolated from ytterbium. Also **lu·te′ci·um.** See ELEMENT.

Lu·ther·an (loo′thər·ən) *adj.* Of or pertaining to Martin Luther, his doctrines, or to the Lutheran Church. — *n.* A member of the Lutheran Church. — **Lu′ther·an·ism** *n.*

lu·tist (loo′tist) *n.* One who makes or plays lutes.

lux (luks) *n. pl.* **lux·es** or **lu·ces** (loo′sēz) *Physics* The unit of illumination in the metric system, equivalent to .0929 foot-candle, or 1 lumen per square meter. [< L, light]

lux·u·ri·ance (lug·zhoor′ē·əns, luk·shoor′-) *n.* The state or quality of being luxuriant. Also **lux·u′ri·an·cy.**

lux·u·ri·ant (lug·zhoor′ē·ənt, luk·shoor′-) *adj.* 1. Growing lushly and profusely, as vegetation. 2. Abundant, exuberant, or ornate, as in design, etc. — **lux·u′ri·ant·ly** *adv.*

lux·u·ri·ate (lug·zhoor′ē·āt, luk·shoor′-) *v.i.* ·at·ed, ·at·ing 1. To take great pleasure; indulge oneself fully: with *in.* 2. To live sumptuously. 3. To grow profusely. [See LUXURY.] — **lux·u′ri·a′tion** *n.*

lux·u·ri·ous (lug·zhoor′ē·əs, luk·shoor′-) *adj.* 1. Characterized by or conducive to luxury or extreme comfort; opulent; sumptuous. 2. Indulging in or given to luxury. — **lux·u′ri·ous·ly** *adv.* — **lux·u′ri·ous·ness** *n.*

lux·u·ry (luk′shər·ē, *occasionally* lug′zhər·ē) *n. pl.* ·ries 1. Anything, usu. expensive or rare, that ministers to comfort or pleasure but is not a necessity to life, health, etc. 2. Free indulgence in that which is expensive, rare, or extremely gratifying. [< OF < L *luxus* extravagance]

-ly¹ *suffix of adjectives* 1. Like; characteristic of; pertaining to: *manly, godly.* 2. Occurring every (specified interval): *weekly, daily.* Compare -LIKE. [OE -*līc*]

-ly² *suffix of adverbs* 1. In a (specified) manner: used to form adverbs from adjectives, or (rarely) from nouns: *brightly, busily.* 2. At every (specified interval): *hourly, yearly.* [OE -*lice* < -*lic* -ly¹]

ly·cée (lē·sā′) *n. French* In France, a secondary school financed by the government. [See LYCEUM.]

ly·ce·um (lī·sē′əm, lī′-) *n. pl.* ·ce·ums or ·ce·a (-sē′ə) 1. *U.S.* An organization providing popular instruction by lectures, concerts, etc.; also, its building. 2. A lycée.

Ly·ce·um (lī·sē′əm, lī′-) A grove near Athens in which Aristotle taught. [< L < Gk. *lykeios,* epithet of Apollo]

lyd·dite (lid′īt) *n.* A high explosive, composed chiefly of picric acid, used in shells. [after *Lydd,* a town in England]

Lyd·i·a (lid′ē·ə) An ancient country in western Asia Minor, famous for its wealth and luxury. — **Lyd′i·an** *adj. & n.*

lye (lī) *n.* 1. A solution leached from ashes, or derived from a substance containing alkali, used in making soap. 2. Any solution obtained by leaching. [OE *lēah*]

ly·ing (lī′ing) *n.* The act of telling lies; untruthfulness. — *adj.* Deceitful or false; untrue: a *lying* tongue.

ly·ing (lī′ing) *Present participle of* LIE¹.

ly·ing-in (lī′ing·in′) *n.* The confinement of women during childbirth. — *adj.* Of or pertaining to childbirth.

lymph (limf) *n. Physiol.* A yellowish alkaline fluid derived from the body tissues, consisting of lymphocytes and a plasma similar to that of blood. [< L *limpa* water]

lym·phat·ic (lim·fat′ik) *adj.* 1. Containing, conveying, or pertaining to lymph. 2. Caused by or affecting the lymph nodes. 3. Sluggish; indifferent. — *n.* A vessel that conveys lymph into the veins.

lymphato- *combining form* Lymphatic. Also, before vowels, **lymphat-.**

lymph node *Anat.* Any of numerous glandlike bodies found in the course of the lymphatic vessels and producing lymphocytes and monocytes. Also **lymph gland.**

lympho- *combining form* Lymph; of the lymph or the lymphatics. Also, before vowels, **lymph-.** [See LYMPH]

lym·pho·cyte (lim′fə·sīt) *n. Physiol.* A variety of nucleated, colorless leucocyte formed in the tissue of the lymph nodes and resembling white blood corpuscles. Also **lymph cell.**

lym·phoid (lim′foid) *adj.* Of, pertaining to, or resembling lymph or the tissues of a lymph node.

lynch (linch) *v.t.* To kill (a person accused of a crime) by mob action, as by hanging, without due process of law. [< LYNCH LAW] — **lynch′er** *n.* — **lynch′ing** *n.*

lynch law The practice of administering punishment by lynching. [? after Charles *Lynch,* 1736–96, or William *Lynch,* 1742–1820, Virginia magistrates]

lynx (lingks) *n. pl.* **lynx·es** or **lynx** A wildcat of Europe and North America having a short tail, tufted ears, and relatively long limbs. Also called *bobcat.* [< L < Gk. *lynx*]

lynx-eyed (lingks′īd′) *adj.* Having sharp sight.

ly·on·naise (lī′ə·nāz′, *Fr.* lē·ô·nez′) *adj.* Made with finely sliced onions; esp. designating a method of preparing potatoes with fried onions. [< F, fem. of *lyonnais* of Lyon]

ly·o·phil·ic (lī′ə·fil′ik) *adj. Chem.* Designating a colloidal system in which the solid particles attract and hold molecules of the dispersion medium. [< LYO- + Gk. *philos* loving]

ly·o·pho·bic (lī′ə·fō′bik) *adj. Chem.* Designating a colloidal system in which the solid particles are easily precipitated out of the dispersion medium. [< LYO- + Gk. *phobos* fear]

Ly·ra (lī′rə) *n.* A constellation, the Harp or the Lyre, containing the star Vega. [< L < Gk.]

ly·rate (lī′rāt) *adj.* Shaped like a lyre. Also **ly′rat·ed.** [< NL *lyratus*] — **ly′rate·ly** *adv.*

lyre (līr) *n.* An ancient harplike stringed instrument, used by the Greeks to accompany poetry and song. [< OF < L *lyra* < Gk.]

Lyre (līr) *n.* The constellation Lyra.

lyre·bird (līr′bûrd′) *n.* Either of two species of Australian birds, the male of which spreads its tail feathers into the shape of a lyre.

lyr·ic (lir′ik) *adj.* 1. Of poetry, expressing the poet's personal or inner feelings; also, pertaining to the method, personality, etc., of a writer of such verse. 2. Meant to be sung. 3. *Music* Having a singing voice of a light, flexible quality: a *lyric* soprano. 4. Pertaining to a lyre. Also **lyr′i·cal.** — *n.* 1. *Usu. pl.* The words of a song. 2. A lyric poem. [< L < Gk. *lyra* a lyre] — **lyr′i·cal·ly** *adv.*

lyr·i·cism (lir′ə·siz′əm) *n.* The quality of emotional self-expression in the arts.

lyr·i·cist (lir′ə·sist) *n.* 1. One who writes the words of a song or the lyrics for a musical play. 2. A lyric poet.

ly·ri·form (lī′rə·fôrm) *adj.* Shaped like a lyre.

lyse (līs) *v.t. & v.i.* lysed, lys·ing To undergo or cause to undergo lysis. [< Gk. *lysis* loosening]

ly·ser·gic acid (lī·sûr′jik) *n. Biochem.* A crystalline alkaloid derived from ergot and forming the base of **lysergic acid di·eth·yl·am·ide-25** (d′eth·əl·am′īd), or LSD. [< LYS- + *erg(ot)* + -IC]

lysi- *combining form* A loosening; dissolving: *lysergic acid, lysine.* Also, before vowels, **lys-.** [< Gk. *lysis* a loosening]

ly·sine (lī′sēn, -sin) *n. Biochem.* An amino acid $C_6H_{14}O_2N_2$, necessary to animal growth, produced by the hydrolysis of various proteins. Also **ly·sin.** [< LYS- + -INE²]

ly·sis (lī′sis) *n.* 1. *Med.* The gradual disappearing of the symptoms of a disease. 2. *Biochem.* The process of disintegration or destruction of cells, bacteria, etc. [< NL < Gk., < *lyein* to loosen]

-lysis *combining form* A loosing, dissolving, etc.: *hydrolysis, paralysis.* [< Gk., *loosening*]

Ly·sol (lī′sôl, -sōl, -sol) *n.* Proprietary name for a liquid disinfectant containing soap and cresol. Also **ly′sol.**

-lyte *combining form* A substance decomposed by a (specified) process: *electrolyte.* [< Gk. *lytos* loosened, dissolved]

ly·tic (lit′ik) *adj.* Of, relating to, or effecting lysis, esp., of cells. [See -LYTIC.]

-lytic *combining form* Loosing; dissolving: used in adjectives corresponding to nouns in -*lysis*: *hydrolytic, paralytic.* [< Gk. *lytikos* loosing < *lysis* a loosening]

-lyze *suffix of verbs* To perform, cause, or undergo: formed from nouns in -*lysis*: *electrolyze, paralyze.* Also *esp. Brit.* **-lyse.** [< -LYSIS]

M

m, M (em) *n. pl.* **m's** or **ms, M's** or **Ms** or **ems** (emz) **1.** The thirteenth letter of the English alphabet. **2.** The sound represented by the letter *m*, usually a bilabial nasal. — *symbol* **1.** The Roman numeral 1,000. **2.** *Printing* An em.

M-1 (em′wun′) **carbine** *U.S. Mil.* The carbine.

M-1 rifle *U.S. Mil.* A semiautomatic .30 caliber rifle adopted by the U.S. Army in World War II: also *Garand rifle.*

ma (mä, mô) *n. Informal & Dial.* Mama.

ma'am (mam, mäm, *unstressed* məm) *n.* **1.** A term of respectful address used to women; madam. **2.** *Brit.* A term of respectful address used to the queen or to a royal princess.

Mac- *prefix* In Scottish and Irish names, son of: *MacDougal*, son of Dougal: abbr. *Mc, Mᶜ,* or *M′*. See also **Mc-**. Compare FITZ-, O′. [< Scottish Gaelic and Irish, son]

ma·ca·bre (mə-kä′brə, -bər) *adj.* Suggesting death and decay; gruesome; ghastly. Also **ma·ca′ber.** [< F < OF *(danse) macabre* (dance) of death]

mac·ad·am (mə-kad′əm) *n.* **1.** A macadamized pavement or road. **2.** Broken stone used in macadamizing a road. [after John L. *McAdam*, 1756–1836, Scottish engineer]

mac·ad·am·ize (mə-kad′ə-mīz) *v.t.* **·ized, ·iz·ing** To pave by spreading and compacting small stones, often with tar or asphalt. — **mac·ad′am·i·za′tion** *n.* — **mac·ad′am·iz′er** *n.*

mac·a·ro·ni (mak′ə-rō′nē) *n.* **1.** A dried paste of wheat flour made into short tubes and prepared as a food by boiling. **2.** An 18th-century Italian dandy. Also **mac′ca·ro′ni.** [< Ital. *maccaroni* pl. of *macherone* groats]

mac·a·roon (mak′ə-rōōn′) *n.* A small cooky made of ground almonds or sometimes coconut, egg, and sugar. [< MF *macaron*]

ma·caw (mə-kô′) *n.* Any of various large tropical American parrots with a long tail, harsh voice, and brilliant plumage. [< Pg. *macao*, prob. < Tupi]

Mac·beth (mək·beth′), died 1057?, king of Scotland 1040–1057?; hero of Shakespeare's *Macbeth.*

Mac·ca·bees (mak′ə-bēz) The family of Jewish patriots who led a revolt against Syrian religious oppression. — *n.pl.* Four books in the Old Testament Apocrypha treating of oppression against the Jews from 222 to 135 B.C. [< LL < Gk. < Aramaic *maggābā* a hammer] — **Mac′ca·be′an** *adj.*

mace¹ (mās) *n.* **1.** A heavy medieval war club, usu. with a spiked metal head for use against armor. **2.** A club-shaped staff symbolic of office or authority. [< OF *masse, mace*]

mace² (mās) *n.* An aromatic spice ground from the covering between the husk and the seed of the nutmeg. [< OF < L < Gk. *maker* a spicy bark from India]

Mace (mās) *n.* A chemical solution similar to tear gas that temporarily blinds or incapacitates one when sprayed in the face, used as a weapon. — *v.t.* **Maced, Mac·ing** To spray with Mace. [< Chemical *Mace*, a trade name]

Mac·e·do·ni·a (mas′ə-dō′nē-ə) The ancient kingdom of **Mac·e·don** (mas′ə-don) that became a leading world power under Alexander the Great. — **Mac·e·do′ni·an** *adj. & n.*

mac·er·ate (mas′ə-rāt) *v.* **·at·ed, ·at·ing** *v.t.* **1.** To reduce (a solid substance) to a soft mass by soaking in liquid. **2.** To break down the structure of (food) in digestion. **3.** To cause to grow thin; emaciate. — *v.i.* **4.** To become macerated. [< L < *macerare* to make soft, knead] — **mac′er·a′ter** or **mac′er·a′tor** *n.* — **mac′er·a′tion** *n.*

mach (mäk) *n. Often cap.* A mach number.

ma·chet·e (mə·shet′ē, mə·shet′; *Sp.* mä·chā′tā) *n.* A heavy knife or cutlass used as an implement and a weapon in tropical America. [< Sp., dim. of *macho* an ax, hammer]

Mach·i·a·vel·li·an (mak′ē·ə·vel′ē·ən) *adj.* Pertaining to, resembling, or based upon the amoral principles for getting and keeping political power prescribed in Niccolò Machiavelli's *The Prince.* — *n.* A follower of Machiavelli's principles. Also **Mach′i·a·vel′i·an.** — **Mach′i·a·vel′li·an·ism, Mach′i·a·vel′ism** *n.* — **Mach′i·a·vel′list** *adj. & n.*

ma·chic·o·late (mə·chik′ə·lāt) *v.t.* **·lat·ed, ·lat·ing** *Archit.* To furnish with machicolations. [< Med.L < OF *macher* to crush + *couler* to flow]

ma·chic·o·la·tion (mə·chik′ə·lā′shən) *n.* **1.** *Archit.* An opening between the corbels of a projecting parapet, through which missiles or boiling liquids may be dropped. **2.** The act of dropping missiles through such openings.

mach·i·nate (mak′ə·nāt) *v.t. & v.i.* **·nat·ed, ·nat·ing** To

scheme or contrive. [< L *machinari* to contrive] — **mach′i·na′tor** *n.*

mach·i·na·tion (mak′ə·nā′shən) *n. Usu. pl.* A concealed working and scheming for some devious purpose.

ma·chine (mə·shēn′) *n.* **1.** Any combination of interrelated parts for using or applying energy to do work. **2.** The party organization of a city, county, or state: a derogatory term. **3.** The organization and operating principles of a complex structure: the human *machine.* **4.** An automobile. **5.** A person who behaves with machinelike precision, regularity, etc. **6.** In the ancient theater, a windlass used for the spectacular entrance and exit of gods, etc. — *adj.* **1.** Of or pertaining to a machine or machines. **2.** Produced by machine. **3.** Characterized by the use of machines: *machine age.* — *v.t.* **·chined, ·chin·ing** To shape, mill, make, etc., by machine. [< F < L < Gk. *mēchos* a contrivance] — **ma·chin′a·ble, ma·chin′al** *adj.* — **ma·chin′a·bil′i·ty** *n.*

ma·chine-gun (mə·shēn′gun′) *v.t.* **-gunned, -gun·ning** To fire at or shoot with a machine gun.

machine gun A rapid-firing automatic gun, usually mounted, that fires small-arms ammunition. — **machine gunner.**

ma·chin·er·y (mə·shē′nər·ē, -shēn′rē) *n.* **1.** A collection of machines or machine parts. **2.** The mechanism or operating parts and principles of a complex structure: the *machinery* of the law. **3.** In literary works, plot devices.

machine shop A shop where metal and other materials are cut, shaped, milled, finished, etc., with machine tools.

machine tool A power-driven tool, partly or wholly automatic in action, for cutting, shaping, boring, milling, etc.

ma·chin·ist (mə·shē′nist) *n.* **1.** One who is skilled in the operation or repair of machines or machine tools. **2.** In the U.S. Navy and Coast Guard, a warrant officer who is assistant to the engineer officer.

mach number A number representing the ratio between the speed of an object moving through a fluid medium, as air, and the speed of sound in the same medium. Also **Mach number.** [after Ernst *Mach*, 1838–1916, Austrian physicist]

ma·chree (mə·krē′) *n.* My heart; my love: an Anglo-Irish term of endearment. [< Irish < *mo* my + *croidhe* heart]

-machy *combining form* A fight between, or by means of. [< Gk. *-muchia* < *machē* a battle]

mac·in·tosh (mak′in·tosh) See MACKINTOSH.

mack·er·el (mak′ər·əl) *n.* **1.** A food fish of the Atlantic, steel blue with blackish bars above, and silvery beneath. **2.** Any of various fishes resembling it. [< OF *makerel*]

mackerel sky Cirrocumulus.

mack·i·naw (mak′ə·nô) A Mackinaw blanket, boat, or coat. [< dial. F (Canadian) *Mackinac* Mackinac Island]

Mackinaw blanket A thick, heavy blanket formerly used by Indians and traders of the western United States.

Mackinaw coat A thick, short, double-breasted woolen coat, commonly with a plaid pattern.

mack·in·tosh (mak′in·tosh) *n. Chiefly Brit.* **1.** A waterproof overgarment or cloak; raincoat. **2.** Thin, rubber-coated cloth. Also *macintosh.* [after Charles *Macintosh*, 1766–1843, Scottish chemist, inventor of the cloth]

macro- *combining form* **1.** *Pathol.* Enlarged or overdeveloped. **2.** Large or long in size or duration: *macrocosm.* Also, before vowels, **macr-.** [< Gk. *makros* large]

mac·ro·ceph·a·ly (mak′rō·sef′ə·lē) *n.* Abnormal largeness of the head. [< MACRO- + Gk. *kephalē* head] — **mac′ro·ce·phal′ic** (-sə·fal′ik) *adj. & n.* — **mac′ro·ceph′a·lous** (-ləs) *adj.*

mac·ro·cosm (mak′rə·koz′əm) *n.* The whole universe, esp. when regarded in contrast to man. [< OF < Med.L < Gk. *makros* long, great + *kosmos* world] — **mac′ro·cos′mic** *adj.*

ma·cron (mā′kran, -kron) *n.* A straight line (—) over a vowel letter to show that it represents a long sound, as *ā* in *made.* [< Gk. *makron*, neut. of *makros* long]

mac·u·la (mak′yə·lə) *n. pl.* **·lae** (-lē) A spot, as on the skin, the sun, etc. [< L, a spot]

mad (mad) *adj.* **mad·der, mad·dest** **1.** Suffering from or manifesting severe mental disorder; insane; psychotic. **2.** *Chiefly U.S. Informal* Feeling or showing anger; angry. **3.** Wildly foolish; rash: a *mad* project. **4.** Subject to an overpowering emotion: *mad* with grief. **5.** Turbulent and confused: a *mad* jumble. **6.** Of animals, suffering from hydrophobia; rabid. **7.** *Informal* Showing a passionate infatuation with or desire for: with *about, for,* or *over.* **8.** *Informal* Flamboyant; daring. **— like mad** *Informal* As if insane; frantically. **— mad as a hatter** (or **March hare**) Totally insane; crazy. **— mad money** *Slang* Money to be used by a girl to pay her way home from a date in case she quarrels with her escort. **—** *n. U.S. Informal* A fit of temper: now only in the phrase **to have a mad on,** to be angry. **—** *v.t. & v.i.* **mad·ded, mad·ding** *Rare* To make or become mad. [OE *gemād* insane] **— mad′ly** *adv.* **— mad′ness** *n.*

mad·am (mad′əm) *n. pl.* **mes·dames** (mā-däm′, *Fr.* mā-dàm′) *for def. 1*; **mad·ams** *for def. 2.* **1.** My lady; mistress: a title of courtesy. See MA′AM. **2.** A woman who manages a brothel. [< OF *ma dame* < *ma* my + *dame* lady]

mad·ame (mad′əm, *Fr.* mà·dàm′) *n. pl.* **mes·dames** (mā-däm′, *Fr.* mā-dàm′) The French title of courtesy for a married woman, equivalent to the English *Mrs.* Abbr. *Mme., Mme, Mdme.* [< F < OF *ma dame*]

mad·cap (mad′kap′) *adj.* Wild; rattlebrained. **—** *n.* One who acts wildly or rashly.

mad·den (mad′n) *v.t. & v.i.* To make or become mad or insane; inflame; infuriate. **— mad′den·ing·ly** *adv.*

mad·der[1] (mad′ər) Comparative of MAD.

mad·der[2] (mad′ər) *n.* **1.** Any of various perennial herbs, esp. an Old World species, the root of which yields a brilliant red extract. **2.** The red coloring matter. **3.** A brilliant red. **—** *v.t.* To dye with madder. [OE *mædere, mæddre*]

mad·ding (mad′ing) *adj.* Being or growing mad; delirious; raging. **— mad′ding·ly** *adv.*

made (mād) Past tense and past participle of MAKE. **—** *adj.* **1.** Produced by fabrication, invention, or skill; not occurring naturally. **2.** Assured of success or fortune. **— to have it made** *U.S. Slang* To be sure of success.

Ma·dei·ra (mə-dir′ə, *Pg.* mə-thā′rə) *n.* A fortified dessert wine made in the Madeira islands.

mad·e·moi·selle (mad′ə·mə·zel′, *Fr.* màd·mwà·zel′) *n. pl.* **mad·e·moi·selles,** *Fr.* **mes·de·moi·selles** (mād·mwà·zel′) **1.** The French title of courtesy for unmarried women, equivalent to the English *Miss.* **2.** A French nurse. [< F < *ma* my + *demoiselle* (< OF *dameisele* gentlewoman)]

made-to-order (mād′tōō-ôr′dər) *adj.* **1.** Made according to specific instructions. **2.** Perfectly adapted or useful.

made-up (mād′up′) *adj.* **1.** Devised by fabrication or invention; fictitious. **2.** Adorned or altered by cosmetics. **3.** Complete; finished: a *made-up* sample. **4.** Compensated for or provided: said of work, money, etc.

mad·house (mad′hous′) *n.* **1.** A hospital for the mentally ill; insane asylum. **2.** A place of confusion or uproar; bedlam.

mad·man (mad′man′) *n. pl.* **·men** (-men′) A maniac.

Ma·don·na (mə-don′ə) *n.* **1.** The Virgin Mary. **2.** A painting or statue of the Virgin Mary. [< Ital. < *ma* my + *donna* lady]

ma·dras (mə-dras′, -dräs′, mad′rəs) *n.* **1.** A cotton cloth with thick strands at intervals, giving either a striped, corded, or checked effect. **2.** A silk cloth, usually striped. [after *Madras,* India, because originally made there]

mad·re·pore (mad′rə·pôr, -pōr) *n. Zool.* Any of various stony corals that form reefs in tropical seas. [< NL < Ital. *madrepora,* lit., mother stone] **— mad′re·por′al** (-pôr′əl, -pō′rəl), **mad′re·po′ric** (-pôr′ik, -por′ik) *adj.*

mad·ri·gal (mad′rə·gəl) *n.* **1.** *Music* An unaccompanied part song, often in counterpoint, usu. for four to six voices, popular during the 16th and 17th centuries. **2.** A short lyric poem. **3.** Any song, esp. a part song. [< Ital. < LL *matricale* original, chief] **— mad′ri·gal·ist** *n.*

mad·wom·an (mad′wŏŏm′ən) *n. pl.* **·wom·en** (-wim′in) An insane woman; lunatic.

Mae·ce·nas (mī-sē′nəs) *n.* A patron, esp. of the arts. [after *Maecenas,* died 8 B.C., Roman patron of Horace and Vergil]

mael·strom (māl′strəm) *n.* **1.** Any dangerous and irresistible force, or a place where it prevails. **2.** A whirlpool. [< Du. < *malen* to whirl around + *stroom* stream]

Mael·strom (māl′strəm) A famous whirlpool in the Arctic Ocean off the NW coast of Norway.

mae·nad (mē′nad) *n.* **1.** A female votary or priestess of Dionysius, a bacchante. **2.** Any woman beside herself with frenzy. Also spelled *menad.* [< L < Gk. < *mainesthai* to rave] **— mae·nad′ic** *adj.* **— mae·nad′i·cal·ly** *adv.*

ma·es·to·so (mä′es-tō′sō) *Music adj.* Majestic; stately. **—** *adv.* In a stately manner. [< Ital., majestic]

ma·es·tro (mä·es′trō, mīs′trō) *n. pl.* **·tros** A master in any art, esp., an eminent conductor, composer, or performer of music. [< Ital., master]

Ma·fi·a (mä′fē·ä, maf′ē·ə) *n.* A secret criminal organization of Sicilians and Italians believed to exist in many countries, including the U.S. Also **Maf′fi·a.** [< Ital.]

mag·a·zine (mag′ə·zēn′, mag′ə·zēn) *n.* **1.** A periodical publication, usu. with a paper cover, containing articles,

stories, etc., by various writers. **2.** A warehouse or depot, esp. for military supplies. **3.** A building or storeroom for explosives and ammunition. **4.** A receptacle or part of a gun holding ammunition ready for chambering. **5.** A supply chamber in a battery, camera, etc. [< MF < OF < Arabic *makhāzin* storehouses]

mag·da·len (mag′də-lin) *n.* A reformed prostitute. Also **mag·da·lene** (-lēn). [after Mary *Magdalene*]

Mag·da·le·ni·an (mag′də-lē′nē-ən) *adj. Anthropol.* Of or pertaining to the most advanced culture stage of the Paleolithic period in Europe. [< F, after *La Madeleine* in west central France, where artifacts were found]

Mag·el·lan·ic cloud (maj′ə-lan′ik) *Astron.* Either of two aggregations of star clusters and nebulae near the south celestial pole.

ma·gen·ta (mə-jen′tə) *n.* **1.** Fuchsin, a dye. **2.** The purplish red color produced by fuchsin. [after *Magenta,* Italy]

mag·got (mag′ət) *n.* The legless larva of an insect, as the housefly, esp. one found in decaying matter. [Prob. alter. of ME < ON *mathkr* worm] **— mag′got·y** *adj.*

Ma·gi (mā′jī) *n. pl. of* **Ma·gus** (mā′gəs) **1.** The three "wise men from the east" who came to Bethlehem to pay homage to the infant Jesus. *Matt.* ii 1–12. **2.** The priestly caste of the Medes and Persians: also **ma′gi.** [< L < Gk. < Persian *magu* priest, magician] **— Ma·gi·an** (mā′jē·ən) *adj. & n.*

mag·ic (maj′ik) *n.* **1.** Seeming control over or foresight of natural events, forces, etc., through supernatural agencies. **2.** An overpowering influence: the *magic* of his voice. **3.** Sleight of hand; legerdemain. **—** *adj.* **1.** Of or used in magic. **2.** Producing the effects of magic. **3.** Mysteriously impressive; beautiful. [< OF < LL *magica* (*ars*) magic (art) < Gk. < *magikos* of the Magi]

mag·i·cal (maj′i-kəl) *adj.* Of, pertaining to, or produced by or as by magic. **— mag′i·cal·ly** *adv.*

ma·gi·cian (mə-jish′ən) *n.* One who performs magic; esp., an entertainer who uses illusion and legerdemain.

magic lantern *Archaic* A slide projector.

mag·is·te·ri·al (maj′is-tir′ē·əl) *adj.* **1.** Of or like a master. **2.** Dictatorial; domineering. **3.** Of or pertaining to a magistrate. **— mag′is·te′ri·al·ly** *adv.*

mag·is·tra·cy (maj′is-trə·sē) *n. pl.* **·cies** **1.** The office, function, or term of a magistrate. **2.** Magistrates collectively. **3.** The district under a magistrate's jurisdiction.

mag·is·trate (maj′is-trāt, -trit) *n.* **1.** A public official with the power to enforce the law. **2.** A minor judicial officer, as a justice of the peace. [< L < *magister* master]

mag·ma (mag′mə) *n. pl.* **·ma·ta** (-mə-tə) *Geol.* The molten, plastic mass of rock material from which igneous rocks are formed. [< L < Gk. < *massein* to knead]

Mag·na Car·ta (mag′nə kär′tə) **1.** The Great Charter of English liberties, delivered June 19, 1215, by King John on the demand of the English barons. **2.** Any document that secures liberty and rights. Also **Mag′na Char′ta.** [< Med.L, lit., Great Charter]

mag·na·nim·i·ty (mag′nə·nim′ə·tē) *n. pl.* **·ties** **1.** The quality of being magnanimous. **2.** A magnanimous act.

mag·nan·i·mous (mag·nan′ə·məs) *adj.* **1.** Manifesting generosity in forgiving insults or injuries. **2.** Characterized by magnanimity. [< L < *magnus* great + *animus* mind, soul] **— mag·nan′i·mous·ly** *adv.* **— mag·nan′i·mous·ness** *n.*

mag·nate (mag′nāt) *n.* One notable or powerful, esp. in industry: a railroad *magnate.* [< LL *magnus* great]

mag·ne·sia (mag·nē′zhə, -shə, -zē·ə) *n. Chem.* Magnesium oxide, MgO, a light, white powder used in medicine as an antacid and laxative, and in the manufacture of firebrick. [< Med.L < Gk. *Magnēsia* (*lithos*) (stone) of Magnesia]

mag·ne·si·um (mag·nē′zē·əm, -zhē-, -shē-) *n.* A light, silver-white, malleable and ductile metallic element (symbol Mg), that burns with a very hot, bright flame and is used in lightweight alloys. See ELEMENT. [< NL < *magnesia*]

mag·net (mag′nit) *n.* **1.** A body that has a magnetic field and therefore attracts iron and other magnetic material. **2.** A lodestone. **3.** One who or that which exercises a strong attraction. [< OF < L < Gk. *Magnēs* (*lithos*) Magnesian (stone), i.e., a magnet]

mag·net·ic (mag·net′ik) *adj.* **1.** Pertaining to magnetism or a magnet. **2.** Capable of setting up a magnetic field. **3.** Capable of being attracted by a magnet or a lodestone. **4.** Possessing personal magnetism. Also **mag·net′i·cal.** **— mag·net′i·cal·ly** *adv.*

magnetic field That region in the neighborhood of a magnet or current-carrying body in which magnetic forces are observable.

magnetic needle A freely movable magnetized needle that tends to point to the magnetic poles of the earth.

magnetic north The direction, usu. differing from true north, toward which the needle of a compass points.

magnetic pickup A phonograph pickup that employs a

magnet and coils to transform vibrations into electrical impulses.

magnetic pole 1. Either of the poles of a magnet. 2. Either of two points (**north magnetic pole** and **south magnetic pole**) on the surface of the earth where the lines of magnetic force converge and are vertical. These poles attract the compass needle, slowly change position, and do not coincide with the geographical poles.

magnetic tape *Electronics* A thin ribbon coated with magnetic particles that form patterns corresponding to the electromagnetic impulses generated by a tape recorder.

mag·net·ism (mag′nə·tiz′əm) *n.* 1. The specific properties of a magnet. 2. The science that treats of the laws and conditions of magnetic phenomena. Also **mag·net·ics** (mag·net′iks). 3. The amount of magnetic moment in a magnetized body. 4. A personal quality that attracts.

mag·net·ite (mag′nə·tīt) *n.* A massive black iron oxide, Fe₃O₄, that is strongly magnetic and is called *lodestone* when it has polarity. — **mag·net·it·ic** (-tit′ik) *adj.*

mag·net·ize (mag′nə·tiz) *v.t.* **·ized, ·iz·ing** 1. To communicate magnetic properties to. 2. To attract by personal influence. — **mag′net·i·za′tion** *n.* — **mag′net·iz′er** *n.*

mag·ne·to (mag·nē′tō) *n. pl.* **·tos** Any of various devices in which the rotation of a coil of wire between the poles of a permanent magnet induces an electric current in the coil; esp., such a device used to produce the ignition spark in some internal-combustion engines. Also **mag·ne·to·dy·na·mo** (mag·nē′tō·dī′nə·mō), **mag·ne·to·gen·er·a·tor** (mag·nē′tō·jen′ə·rā′tər). [Short for *magnetoelectric machine*]

magneto- *combining form* Magnetic; magnetism.

mag·ne·to·e·lec·tric·i·ty (mag·nē′tō·i·lek·tris′ə·tē) *n.* 1. Electricity generated by the inductive action of a magnet. 2. The science that treats of such electricity. — **mag·ne·to·e·lec′tric, mag·ne·to·e·lec′tri·cal** *adj.*

mag·ne·to·hy·dro·dy·nam·ics (mag·nē′tō·hī′drō·dī·nam′iks) *n.pl.* (*construed as sing.*) The branch of physics that treats of the interaction of electromagnetic, thermal, and hydrodynamic forces. — **mag·ne·to·hy′dro·dy·nam′ic** *adj.*

mag·ne·tom·e·ter (mag′nə·tom′ə·tər) *n.* An instrument for measuring the intensity and direction of magnetic forces.

mag·ne·to·sphere (mag·nē′tə·sfir, -net′ə-) *n. Physics* A region of the upper atmosphere forming a continuous band of ionized particles trapped by the earth's magnetic field.

magni- *combining form* Great; large; long. [< L *magnus* great]

mag·nif·ic (mag·nif′ik) *adj. Archaic* 1. Magnificent; sumptuous. 2. Pompous. Also **mag·nif′i·cal.** [< F < L < *magnus* great + *facere* to make] — **mag·nif′i·cal·ly** *adv.*

Mag·nif·i·cat (mag·nif′ə·kat) *n.* 1. The canticle of the Virgin Mary. *Luke* i 46–55. 2. A musical setting for this. [< L, it magnifies]

mag·ni·fi·ca·tion (mag′nə·fə·kā′shən) *n.* 1. The act, process, or degree of magnifying. 2. The state of being magnified. 3. The magnifying power of a lens or other optical device. 4. A magnified representation of an object, as in a drawing, photograph, etc. [< L < *magnificus* great]

mag·nif·i·cence (mag·nif′ə·səns) *n.* The state or quality of being magnificent; splendor; impressiveness.

mag·nif·i·cent (mag·nif′ə·sənt) *adj.* 1. Presenting an extraordinary imposing appearance; splendid; beautiful. 2. Exceptionally pleasing; superb. 3. Exalted or sublime in expression or concept. — **mag·nif′i·cent·ly** *adv.*

mag·nif·i·co (mag·nif′ə·kō) *n. pl.* **·coes** Any lordly personage. [< Ital.]

mag·ni·fy (mag′nə·fī) *v.* **·fied, ·fy·ing** *v.t.* 1. To increase the perceived size of, as by a lens. 2. To increase the size of; enlarge. 3. To cause to seem greater or more important; exaggerate. 4. *Archaic* To extol; exalt. — *v.i.* 5. To increase or have the power to increase the apparent size of an object, as a lens. [< OF < L < *magnificus* great] — **mag′ni·fi′a·ble** *adj.* — **mag′ni·fi′er** *n.*

mag·nil·o·quent (mag·nil′ə·kwənt) *adj.* Speaking or spoken in a grandiose style; grandiloquent. [< L *magnus* great + *loquens, -entis,* ppr. of *loqui* to speak] — **mag·nil′o·quence** *n.* — **mag·nil′o·quent·ly** *adv.*

mag·ni·tude (mag′nə·tōod, -tyōod) *n.* 1. Size or extent. 2. Greatness or importance: the *magnitude* of the achievement. 3. *Astron.* The relative brightness of a star, ranging from one for the brightest to six for those just visible to the naked eye. [< L *magnus* large]

mag·no·li·a (mag·nō′lē·ə, -nōl′yə) *n.* 1. An ornamental flowering shrub or tree with large fragrant flowers. 2. The fragrant white flower of the **evergreen magnolia,** the State flower of Louisiana and Mississippi. [< NL, genus name, after Pierre *Magnol,* 1638–1715, French botanist]

Magnolia State Nickname of Mississippi.

mag·num (mag′nəm) *n.* A wine bottle holding about two quarts; also, the quantity such a bottle will hold. [< L, neut. of *magnus* great]

magnum o·pus (ō′pəs) A great work; masterpiece; esp., the greatest single work of a writer, artist, etc. [< L]

mag·pie (mag′pī) *n.* 1. Any of various large, noisy corvine birds having a long tapering tail and black and white plumage: sometimes called *pie.* 2. A chatterbox. [< *Mag,* diminutive of MARGARET + PIE²]

mag·uey (mag′wā, *Sp.* mä·gā′ē) *n.* 1. Any of the agaves of Mexico with fleshy leaves, esp. the species yielding pulque, and the century plant. 2. The tough fibers taken from these plants and used in rope, etc. [< Sp., prob. < Taino]

Ma·gus (mā′gəs) Singular of MAGI.

Mag·yar (mag′yär, mäg′-; *Hungarian* mud′yär) *n.* 1. A member of the dominant group of the population of Hungary. 2. Hungarian, a Finno-Ugric language. — *adj.* Of or pertaining to the Magyars or their language.

ma·ha·ra·ja (mä′hə·rä′jə, *Hind.* mə·hä′rä′jə) *n.* A title of certain princes of India, particularly one ruling an Indian state. Also **ma′ha·ra′jah.** [< Hind. < Skt. < *maha* great + *rājā* king]

ma·ha·ra·ni (mä′hə·rä′nē, *Hind.* mə·hä′rä′nē) *n.* 1. The wife of a maharaja. 2. A sovereign princess of India. Also **ma′ha·ra′nee.** [< Hind. < *maha* great + *rāni* queen]

ma·hat·ma (mə·hat′mə, -hät′-) *n.* In theosophy and some Asian religions, one of a group of holy men possessed of special occult knowledge: often a title of respect. [< Skt. < *maha* great + *ātman* soul] — **ma·hat′ma·ism** *n.*

Ma·hi·can (mə·hē′kən) *n.* One of a tribe of North American Indians of Algonquian stock formerly occupying the territory from the Hudson River to Lake Champlain: also called *Mohican.* [< Algonquian, lit., wolf]

mah·jong (mä′zhong′, -zhông′) *n.* A game of Chinese origin, usu. played with 144 pieces or tiles. Also **mah′-jong′, mah′jongg′.** [< dial. Chinese < Chinese *ma ch'iao* house sparrow; from the design on one of the tiles]

ma·hog·a·ny (mə·hog′ə·nē) *n. pl.* **·nies** 1. Any of various tropical trees yielding fine-grained reddish hardwood much used for furniture and cabinet work. 2. The wood itself. 3. Any of various trees yielding a similar wood. 4. Any of the various shades of brownish red of the finished wood. — *adj.* Having a mahogany color. [< obs. Sp. *mahogani*]

Ma·hom·et (mə·hom′it) Mohammed.

Ma·hom·e·tan (mə·hom′ə·tən) *adj. & n.* Mohammedan.

ma·hout (mə·hout′) *n.* In India and the East Indies, the keeper and driver of an elephant. [< Hind. < Skt. *mahā-mātra,* lit., great in measure]

Mah·rat·i (mə·rat′ē) See MARATHI.

Mah·rat·ta (mə·rat′ə) *n.* One of a Hindu people of SW and central India: also *Maratha.* [< Hind. < Marathi < Skt. *Mahārāstra,* lit., great country]

Mai·a (mā′yə, mī′ə) In Greek mythology, the eldest of the Pleiades, mother by Zeus of Hermes.

maid (mād) *n.* 1. A young unmarried woman or girl; maiden. 2. A female servant. [Short for MAIDEN]

maid·en (mād′n) *n.* 1. An unmarried woman, esp. if young. 2. A virgin. — *adj.* 1. Of, pertaining to, or befitting a maiden. 2. Unmarried: said of women. 3. Of or pertaining to the first use, trial, or experience: *maiden* effort. 4. Untried. [OE *mægden,* prob. dim. of *mægeth* virgin]

maid·en·hair (mād′n·hâr′) *n.* A very delicate and graceful fern with an erect black stem, common in damp, rocky woods. Also **maidenhair fern.**

maid·en·head (mād′n·hed′) *n.* The hymen.

maid·en·hood (mād′n·hŏŏd) *n.* The state or time of being a maiden.

maid·en·ly (mād′n·lē) *adj.* Of, pertaining to, or befitting a maiden or young girl. — **maid′en·li·ness** *n.*

maiden name A woman's surname before marriage.

maid of honor 1. The chief unmarried attendant of a bride at a wedding. 2. An unmarried woman, usu. of noble birth, attendant upon an empress, queen, or princess.

maid·ser·vant (mād′sûr′vənt) *n.* A female servant.

mail¹ (māl) *n.* 1. Letters, printed matter, parcels, etc., sent or received through a governmental postal system. 2. The postal system itself. 3. Postal matter collected or delivered at a specified time: the morning *mail.* 4. A conveyance, as a train, plane, etc., for carrying postal matter. — *adj.* Pertaining to or used for the handling or conveyance of mail. — *v.t. U.S.* To send by mail, as letters; post. [< OF < OHG *malha* wallet] — **mail′a·ble** *adj.* — **mail′er** *n.*

mail² (māl) *n.* 1. Flexible armor made of interlinked rings or overlapping scales. 2. Loosely, any defensive armor. 3. A defensive covering, as a turtle's shell. — *v.t.* To cover with or as with mail. [< OF < L *macula* spot, mesh of a net]

mail·bag (māl′bag′) *n.* A bag in which mail is carried or shipped. Also **mail′pouch′** (-pouch′).

mail·box (māl′boks′) *n. U.S.* 1. A box in which letters, etc., are deposited for collection: also called *post box.* 2. A box into which private mail is delivered. Also **mail box.**

mail·man (māl′man′, -mən) *n. pl.* **·men** (-men′, -mən) One who carries and delivers letters: also called *postman.*

mail order An order for merchandise to be sent by mail.

mail-or·der house (māl′ôr′dər) A business enterprise that sells its merchandise wholly or in part by mail order.

maim (mām) *v.t.* **1.** To deprive of the use of a bodily part; mutilate; disable. **2.** To render imperfect; make defective. [< OF *mahaignier, mayner*] — **maim′er** *n.*

main¹ (mān) *adj.* **1.** First or chief in size, importance, etc.; leading: *main* event. **2.** Fully exerted; sheer: by *main* force. **3.** Of or pertaining to a broad expanse of land, sea, etc. — *n.* **1.** A principal conduit or pipe in a system conveying gas, water, etc. **2.** Utmost effort; force: now chiefly in the phrase **with might and main. 3.** The chief or most important point or part. **4.** *Naut.* The mainmast. — **in** (or **for**) **the main** For the most part; chiefly. [OE *mægen*]

main² (mān) *n.* In cockfighting, a match of several battles.

main clause *Gram.* An independent clause. See under CLAUSE.

main deck *Naut.* The chief deck of a vessel.

main·land (mān′land, -lənd) *n.* The main part of a continent, as distinguished from an island or peninsula.

main line The principal line of a railroad or highway.

main·ly (mān′lē) *adv.* Chiefly; principally.

main·mast (mān′məst, -mast′, -mäst′) *n. Naut.* **1.** The second mast from the bow in a schooner, brig, etc. **2.** The mast nearer the bow in a two-masted vessel.

main·sail (mān′səl, -sāl′) *Naut.* **1.** A sail bent to the main yard of a square-rigged vessel: also **main course. 2.** The principal sail on a mainmast.

main·sheet (mān′shēt′) *n. Naut.* The sheet by which the mainsail is trimmed and set.

main·spring (mān′spring′) *n.* **1.** The principal spring of a mechanism, as of a watch. **2.** The principal or most compelling cause or agency.

main·stay (mān′stā′) *n.* **1.** *Naut.* The rope from the mainmast head forward, used to steady the mast in that direction. **2.** A chief support: the *mainstay* of my old age.

main·stream (mān′strēm′) *n.* The main or middle course.

Main Street **1.** The principal business street of a town. **2.** The typical manners, customs, etc., of a small town.

main·tain (mān·tān′) *v.t.* **1.** To carry on or continue; keep in existence. **2.** To preserve or keep. **3.** To keep in proper condition. **4.** To supply with a livelihood; support. **5.** To claim to be true; uphold. **6.** To hold or defend (a position, place, etc.) against attack. [< OF < L < *manu*, ablative of *manus* hand + *tenere* to hold]

main·te·nance (mān′tə-nəns) *n.* **1.** The act of maintaining, or the state of being maintained. **2.** Means of support or subsistence; livelihood. **3.** The work of keeping roads, machines, buildings, etc., in good condition.

main·top (mān′top′) *n. Naut.* A platform at the head of the lower section of the mainmast.

main·top·mast (mān′top′məst) *n. Naut.* **1.** On a square-rigged vessel, the section of the mast above the maintopgallantmast. **2.** On a fore-and-aft-rigged ship, the section of the mast next above the mainmast.

main·top·sail (mān′top′səl) *n. Naut.* The sail set on the maintopmast.

main yard *Naut.* The lower yard on the mainmast.

maître d'hô·tel (me′tr′ dō·tel′) **1.** A headwaiter or steward. Also *U.S. Informal* **mai·tre d'** (mā′trə dē′). **2.** The proprietor or manager of a hotel. **3.** Having a sauce of melted butter, parsley, and lemon juice or vinegar. [< F]

maize (māz) *n.* **1.** Corn (def. 1). **2.** The deep shade of yellow of ripe corn. [< Sp. < Taino *mahiz*]

ma·jes·tic (mə·jes′tik) *adj.* Having or exhibiting majesty; stately; royal. Also **ma·jes′ti·cal.** — **ma·jes′ti·cal·ly** *adv.*

maj·es·ty (maj′is·tē) *n. pl.* **·ties 1.** Exalted dignity; stateliness; grandeur. **2.** Sovereign authority: the *majesty* of the law. [< OF < L *majestas, -tatis*]

Maj·es·ty (maj′is·tē) *n. pl.* **·ties** A title or form of address for a sovereign: preceded by *His, Her, Your*, etc. Abbr. *M.*

ma·jol·i·ca (mə·jol′i·kə, -yol′-) *n.* A kind of glazed and colorfully decorated Italian pottery. [< Ital., prob. < *Majorca*, where formerly made]

ma·jor (mā′jər) *adj.* **1.** Greater in quantity, number, or extent. **2.** Having primary or greater importance, excellence, rank, etc.: a *major* writer. **3.** Of, relating to, or making up a majority. **4.** *Music* **a** Denoting the larger of two similarly named intervals: *major* third. **b** Denoting a triad in which the third above the fundamental is major. **c** Denoting a type of diatonic scale, or a key based on this scale. Compare MINOR. **5.** *Logic* Having a greater degree of generality: *major* premise. **6.** *U.S.* In education, pertaining to the principal area of specialized study of a degree candidate in a college or university. **7.** Having attained the age of one's majority. — *n.* **1.** *Mil.* An officer ranking next above a captain. See tables at GRADE. **2.** *Music* A major interval, triad, or scale. **3.** *U.S.* The principal area of specialized study of a degree candidate in a college or university. **4.** One who has reached his majority or full legal age. **5.** One of superior status within a given group. **6.** *pl.*

U.S. The major leagues. — *v.i. U.S.* In education, to study as a major: with *in.* [< L, compar. of *magnus* great]

ma·jor-do·mo (mā′jər-dō′mō) *n. pl.* **·mos** The chief steward or butler, esp. of a royal or noble household. [< Sp. < Med.L < *major* an elder + *domus* house]

ma·jor·ette (mā′jər-et′) *n. U.S. Informal* A girl who marches and twirls a baton with a band, as in a parade.

major general *Mil.* An officer ranking next above a brigadier or brigadier general. Also *Brit. & Canadian* **ma·jor·gen·er·al** (mā′jər·jen′ər·əl). See tables at GRADE.

ma·jor·i·ty (mə·jôr′ə·tē, -jor′-) *n. pl.* **·ties 1.** More than half of a given number or group; the greater part. **2.** The number of jurors, voters, etc., in accord who compose more than half of the total group. **3.** The number of votes cast for a particular candidate, bill, etc., over and above the total number of remaining votes. Distinguished from *plurality*. **4.** The party or group having the most power. **5.** The age when full civil and personal rights may be legally exercised. **6.** The rank, commission, or office of a major. [< MF < L *majoritas, -tatis*]

major key A key based on a major scale. See SCALE².

major league In baseball, either of the two main groups of professional teams in the U.S., the **National League** or the **American League.**

major mode An arrangement of tones found in or characteristic of a major key or scale. See SCALE².

major premise *Logic* The more general premise in a syllogism. See SYLLOGISM.

major scale See under SCALE².

major suit In bridge, either spades or hearts.

major term *Logic* The predicate of both the major premise and the conclusion of a syllogism. See SYLLOGISM.

ma·jus·cule (mə·jus′kyōōl) *adj.* **1.** Large, as either capital or uncial letters. **2.** Written in such letters. — *n.* A majuscule letter. [< F < L *majuscula* (*littera*), fem. of *majusculus*, dim. of *major* major] — **ma·jus′cu·lar** *adj.*

make (māk) *v.* **made, mak·ing** *v.t.* **1.** To bring about the existence by shaping or combining of materials; produce; construct; fashion. **2.** To cause: Don't *make* trouble. **3.** To bring to some state: The wind *makes* him cold. **4.** To put into a specified rank or position: They *made* him president. **5.** To form or create in the mind, as a plan, conclusion, or judgment. **6.** To compose (a poem). **7.** To entertain mentally, as doubts, scruples, etc.: *Make* no mistake about it. **8.** To understand the meaning or significance; interpret: with *of*. **9.** To utter or express, as an announcement. **10.** To represent as being or appearing: That hat *makes* you look old. **11.** To put forward or proffer: to *make* friendly overtures. **12.** To engage in: to *make* war. **13.** To earn or acquire: to *make* a fortune. **14.** To act in such a way as to win or gain. **15.** To amount to; add up to. **16.** To bring the total to. **17.** To draw up, enact, or frame, as laws, treaties, etc. **18.** To effect or form, as an agreement or arrangement. **19.** To estimate to be; reckon. **20.** To prepare or arrange for use: to *make* a bed. **21.** To induce or force; compel. **22.** To be the essential element or determinant of: Nourishing food *makes* strong bodies. **23.** To afford or provide: Venison *makes* good eating. **24.** To become through development: He will *make* a good soldier. **25.** To cause the success of: His last book *made* him. **26.** To perform (a specific physical movement). **27.** To cover (distance) by traveling. **28.** To travel at the rate of. **29.** To arrive at; reach: to *make* Boston. **30.** To arrive in time for. **31.** In games and sports, to achieve as a score. **32.** *Electr.* To complete (a circuit). **33.** *U.S. Informal* To win a place or position, as on a team; also, to achieve the rank or status of: to *make* colonel. — *v.i.* **34.** To cause something to assume a specified condition: to *make* sure. **35.** To act or behave in a certain manner: to *make* merry. **36.** To start, or appear to start, to do something: They *made* to go. **37.** To be made: It *makes* easily. — **to make after** To pursue; follow. — **to make away with 1.** To carry off; steal. **2.** To kill. **3.** To get rid of; destroy. — **to make believe** To pretend; feign. — **to make do** To get along with what is available, esp. with an inferior substitute. — **to make for 1.** To go toward, esp. rapidly. **2.** To rush at in order to attack. — **to make it** *Informal* To succeed in doing something. — **to make off** To leave suddenly; run away. — **to make off with** To steal. — **to make or break** To bring about the success or failure of. — **to make out 1.** To see; discern. **2.** To comprehend. **3.** To establish by evidence. **4.** To fill out or draw up, as a document, bank check, etc. **5.** To succeed. **6.** To do well enough; get by. — **to make over 1.** To renovate; refashion. **2.** To transfer title or possession of. — **to make up 1.** To compose; compound, as a prescription. **2.** To be the parts of; constitute. **3.** To settle differences and become friendly again. **4.** To devise; fabricate. **5.** To supply what is lacking in. **6.** To compensate; atone. **7.** To settle; decide: to *make up* one's mind. **8.** *Printing* To arrange lines of type, illustrations, etc., for (a book, etc.). **9.** To put cosmetics on (the face). **10.** In education: **a** To repeat (an examination or course one has failed). **b** To take (an examination one has missed). — *n.* **1.** Style or type: a good *make* of car. **2.** The manner in which something is made. **3.** The quantity produced. **4.** The act of making. **5.** The closing of an electric circuit. — **on the make** *Informal* **1.** Greedy for profit or advancement. **2.** Eager for amorous conquest. [OE *macian*]

make-be·lieve (māk′bi-lēv′) *n.* **1.** Pretense; sham. **2.** One who pretends or feigns. — *adj.* Pretended; unreal.

mak·er (mā′kər) *n.* **1.** One who or that which makes. **2.** *Law* One who signs a promissory note.

Ma·ker (mā′kər) *n.* God, the creator.

make-shift (māk′shift′) *n.* A temporary means devised for an emergency; stopgap. — *adj.* Having the nature of or used as a temporary substitute: also **make′shift′y.**

make-up (māk′up′) *n.* **1.** The arrangement or combination of parts or qualities of which anything is composed. **2.** The cosmetics, etc., used by an actor in a specific role; also, the art of applying or assuming them. **3.** Cosmetics used by women. **4.** Physical or mental constitution. **5.** *Printing* The arranging of composed type and cuts into pages, columns, or forms. Also **make′up′.**

mak·ing (mā′king) *n.* **1.** The act of one who or that which makes, fashions, or constructs. **2.** That which contributes to improvement or success: Discipline is the *making* of a soldier. **3.** *Usu. pl.* The materials or qualities from which something can be made. **4.** A quantity made at one time; batch. **5.** *pl.* Paper and tobacco for cigarettes. — **in the making** In the process of being made.

mal- *prefix* **1.** Bad; ill; wrong: maladjustment. **2.** Defective; imperfect: malformation. [< F < L *malus* bad]

Ma·lac·ca (mə-lak′ə) *n.* The stem of a rattan palm, used for walking sticks, umbrella handles, etc. Also **Malacca cane.** [after *Malacca*, Malaya]

Mal·a·chi (mal′ə-kī) Fifth-century B.C. Hebrew prophet. — *n.* A book of the Old Testament containing his prophecies. Also, in the Douai Bible, **Ma·la·chi·as** (mal-ə-kī′əs).

mal·a·chite (mal′ə-kīt) *n.* A green basic copper carbonate, Cu_2CO_3 $(OH)_2$, a common ore of copper. [< OF, ult. < L < Gk. *malachē* mallow; so called because of its color]

mal·ad·just·ed (mal′ə-jus′tid) *adj.* **1.** Poorly adjusted. **2.** *Psychol.* Poorly adapted to one's environment through conflict between personal desires and external circumstances.

mal·ad·just·ment (mal′ə-just′mənt) *n.* Poor adjustment.

mal·a·droit (mal′ə-droit′) *adj.* Lacking skill; clumsy; blundering. [< F < *mal-* mal- + *adroit* clever] — **mal′a·droit′ly** *adv.* — **mal′a·droit′ness** *n.*

mal·a·dy (mal′ə-dē) *n.* *pl.* **·dies** **1.** A disease, esp. when chronic or deep-seated. **2.** Any disordered or disturbed condition. [< OF < LL < L *male* ill + *habere* to have]

Mal·a·ga (mal′ə-gə) *n.* **1.** A rich, sweet white wine made in Málaga, Spain. **2.** A white, sweet grape of the muscat variety, grown in Spain and California.

mal·aise (mal-āz′, *Fr.* mȧ·lez′) *n.* A feeling of vague discomfort or lassitude, sometimes indicating the beginning of an illness. [< F < *mal* ill + *aise* ease]

ma·la·mute (mä′lə-myōōt, mal′ə-) *n.* *U.S. & Canadian* A large Alaskan sled dog with a thick, long coat: also spelled *malemute, malemiut.* [Orig. name of an Innuit tribe, alter. of Eskimo *Mahlemut < Mahle,* the tribe's name + *mut* village]

Mal·a·prop (mal′ə-prop), **Mrs.** A character in Sheridan's play *The Rivals* (1775), who uses words in an absurdly inappropriate manner. [< MALAPROPOS]

mal·a·prop·ism (mal′ə-prop-iz′əm) *n.* **1.** The absurd misuse of words. **2.** An instance of this.

mal·ap·ro·pos (mal′ap-rə-pō′) *adj.* Not appropriate. — *adv.* Inappropriately. [< F *mal à propos* not to the point]

ma·lar·i·a (mə-lâr′ē-ə) *n.* **1.** *Pathol.* Any of several forms of a disease caused by certain parasitic protozoans introduced into the blood by the bite of the infected female anopheles mosquito and characterized by periodic attacks of chills, fever, and profuse sweating. **2.** Foul or noxious vapors; miasma. [< Ital. *mal′ aria, mala aria,* lit., bad air] — **ma·lar′i·al, ma·lar′i·ous** *adj.*

ma·lar·key (mə-lär′kē) *n.* *U.S. Slang* Insincere or senseless talk; bunk. Also **ma·lar′ky.** [Origin unknown]

Ma·lay (mā′lā, mə-lā′) *n.* **1.** A member of a people dominant in Malaysia; a Malayan. **2.** The language spoken on the Malay Peninsula and now adopted as the official language of Indonesia. **3.** A variety of domestic fowl. —*adj.* Of or pertaining to the Malays; Malayan.

Mal·a·ya·lam (mal′ə-yä′ləm) *n.* The Dravidian language of the Malabar Coast, India, related to Tamil.

Ma·lay·an (mo lā′ən) *adj.* **1.** Malay. **2.** Indonesian. — *n.* **1.** A Malay (def. 1). **2.** An Indonesian. **3.** The Indonesian subfamily of Austronesian languages.

Ma·lay·o-Pol·y·ne·sian (mə-lā′ō·pol′ə·nē′zhən, -shən) *adj. & n.* Austronesian.

mal·con·tent (mal′kən·tent) *adj.* Discontented or dissatisfied, esp. with a government or economic system. — *n.* One who is malcontent.

mal de mer (mȧl′ də mâr′) *French* Seasickness.

male (māl) *adj.* **1.** Of or belonging to the sex that begets young or produces sperm. **2.** Of, characteristic of, or suitable for members of this sex; masculine. **3.** Made up of men or boys. **4.** *Bot.* **a** Designating a plant having stamens but no pistil. **b** Adapted to fertilize, but not to produce fruit, as stamens **5.** *Mech.* Denoting a part, as in some electric plugs, etc., designed to be inserted into a correlated slot or bore known as *female.* — *n.* **1.** A male person or animal. **2.** *Bot.* A plant with only staminate flowers. [< OF < L *masculus*] — **male′ness** *n.*

mal·e·dic·tion (mal′ə-dik′shən) *n.* **1.** The pronouncing of a curse against someone. **2.** Slander; calumny. [< L < *male* ill + *dicere* to speak] — **mal′e·dic′to·ry** (-tər-ē) *adj.*

mal·e·fac·tor (mal′ə-fak′tər) *n.* **1.** One who commits a crime; criminal. **2.** An evildoer. [< L < *male* ill + *facere* to do] — **mal′e·fac′tion** *n.* — **mal′e·fac′tress** (-tris) *n.fem.*

ma·lef·i·cent (mə-lef′ə-sənt) *adj.* Causing or doing evil or mischief; harmful: opposed to *beneficent.*

ma·le·mute (mä′lə-myōōt, mal′ə-) See MALAMUTE. Also **ma′le·miut.**

ma·lev·o·lent (mə-lev′ə-lənt) *adj.* Wishing evil toward others; malicious. [< OF < L < *male* ill + *volens, -entis,* ppr. of *velle* to wish] — **ma·lev′o·lence** *n.* — **ma·lev′o·lent·ly** *adv.*

mal·fea·sance (mal-fē′zəns) *n.* *Law* The performance of some act that is wrongful or that one has specifically contracted not to perform: said usu. of official misconduct. [< AF < OF < L *malus* bad + *facere* to do] — **mal·fea′sant** *adj. & n.*

mal·for·ma·tion (mal′fôr·mā′shən) *n.* Defective structure, esp. in an organism.

mal·formed (mal-fôrmd′) *adj.* Badly formed; deformed.

mal·func·tion (mal′fungk′shən) *n.* **1.** Failure to function. **2.** Defective functioning. — *v.i.* **1.** To fail to function. **2.** To function improperly.

mal·ic (mal′ik, mā′lik) *adj.* Of, pertaining to, or made from apples. [< L < *malum* apple]

mal·ice (mal′is) *n.* **1.** An intention or desire to injure another; specific ill will; spite. **2.** *Law* A willfully formed design to do another an injury: also, **malice aforethought, malice prepense.** [< OF < L < *malus* evil]

ma·li·cious (mə-lish′əs) *adj.* **1.** Revealing or characterized by malice; spiteful. **2.** *Law* Resulting from or prompted by malice. — **ma·li′cious·ly** *adv.* — **ma·li′cious·ness** *n.*

ma·lign (mə-līn′) *v.t.* To speak slander of; defame. — *adj.* **1.** Having an evil disposition toward others; malevolent. **2.** Tending to injure; pernicious. [< OF < LL < L *malignus* ill-disposed] — **ma·lign′ly** *adv.* — **ma·lign′er** *n.*

ma·lig·nan·cy (mə-lig′nən-sē) *n.* *pl.* **·cies** **1.** The state of being malignant. **2.** A malignant tumor. Also **ma·lig′nance.**

ma·lig·nant (mə-lig′nənt) *adj.* **1.** *Pathol.* **a** Of tumors, rapidly growing and liable to metastasize: opposed to *benign.* **b** Becoming progressively worse; virulent. **2.** Tending to do great harm. **3.** Having an evil disposition toward others; malign. — *n.* A malcontent. [< LL < L *malignus* ill-disposed] — **ma·lig′nant·ly** *adv.*

ma·lig·ni·ty (mə-lig′nə-tē) *n.* *pl.* **·ties** **1.** The state or character of being malign; intense ill will. **2.** A harmful tendency; virulence. **3.** *Often pl.* Something evil.

ma·lines (mə-lēn′, *Fr.* mȧ·lēn′) *n.* A gauzelike veiling for trimming hats, etc.: also **ma·line′.** [< F, after *Malines* Mechlin]

ma·lin·ger (mə-ling′gər) *v.i.* To pretend sickness so as to avoid work or duty. [< F *malingre* sickly, ? < *mal* ill + OF *heingre* lean] — **ma·lin′ger·er** *n.*

mall¹ (môl, mal) See MAUL.

mall² (môl, mel, mel) *n.* **1.** A promenade or walk, usu. public and often shaded. **2.** *U.S. & Canadian* A street of shops closed off to vehicles and enhanced with trees, benches, etc. [Short for *Pall-Mall,* a street in London]

mal·lard (mal′ərd) *n.* *pl.* **·lards** or **·lard** **1.** A common wild duck, the ancestor of the domestic breeds, having brownish plumage, and, in the male, a bright green head. **2.** The male or drake of this duck. [< OF < *masle* male]

mal·le·a·ble (mal′ē-ə-bəl) *adj.* **1.** Capable of being hammered or rolled out without breaking: said esp. of metals. **2.** Capable of being shaped or molded; flexible; pliable. [< OF < L *malleare* to hammer] — **mal′le·a·bil′i·ty, mal′le·a·ble·ness** *n.* — **mal′le·a·bly** *adv.*

mal·let (mal′it) *n.* **1.** A hammer having a head of wood, rubber, etc. **2.** A long-handled wooden hammer used in the game of croquet. **3.** A wooden-headed flexible stick used in the game of polo. [< OF < L *malleus* hammer]

mal·le·us (mal′ē-əs) *n.* *pl.* **·le·i** (-lē-ī) *Anat.* The club-shaped bone of the middle ear, articulating with the incus: also called *hammer.* For illus. see EAR. [< L, hammer]

mal·low (mal′ō) *n.* **1.** Any of various herbs having roundish leaves, pale pink flowers, and disklike fruit. **2.** Any similar plant, as the hibiscus. [OE < L *malva*]

malm·sey (mäm′zē) *n. pl.* **·seys** A rich, sweet wine made in the Canary Islands, Madeira, etc.; also, the grape used for this wine. [< Med.L < Gk. *Monembasia* Monemvasia, Greece, a town formerly exporting wine]

mal·nu·tri·tion (mal′nōō-trish′ən, -nyōō-) *n.* Faulty or inadequate nutrition; undernourishment.

mal·o·dor·ous (mal-ō′dər-əs) *adj.* Having a disagreeable smell. — **mal·o′dor·ous·ly** *adv.* — **mal·o′dor·ous·ness** *n.*

mal·prac·tice (mal-prak′tis) *n.* **1.** In medicine or surgery, the improper, injurious, or negligent treatment of a patient. **2.** Improper or immoral conduct in a professional or public position. — **mal·prac·ti·tion·er** (mal′prak-tish′ən-ər) *n.*

malt (môlt) *n.* **1.** Grain, usu. barley, germinated by soaking and then kiln-dried. **2.** Liquor made with malt, as beer, ale, etc. — *v.t.* **1.** To cause (grain) to become malt. **2.** To treat or combine with malt or malt extract. — *v.i.* **3.** To become malt. **4.** To change grain into malt. [OE *mealt*] — **malt·y** (môl′tē) *adj.*

mal·ted milk (môl′tid) **1.** A beverage made of milk, a powder of malted cereals and dried milk, and usu. ice cream: also **malt′ed. 2.** The powder used in this beverage.

Mal·tese (môl·tēz′, -tēs′) *adj.* Of or pertaining to Malta, its inhabitants, or their language. — *n. pl.* **·tese 1.** A native or inhabitant of Malta. **2.** The language of Malta. **3.** A Maltese cat or dog.

Maltese cat A cat with long, silky, bluish gray hair.

Maltese cross An eight-pointed cross formed by four arrowheads joining at their points.

malt extract Wort (def. 2).

Mal·thu·si·an (mal-thōō′zē-ən, môl′-, -zhən) *adj.* Of or pertaining to the theory of T. R. Malthus that population tends to outrun its means of support, and will be checked by disaster unless restricted by sexual restraint. — *n.* A believer in the theories of Malthus. — **Mal·thu′si·an·ism** *n.*

malt·ose (môl′tōs) *n. Biochem.* A white, crystalline sugar, $C_{12}H_{22}O_{11}H_2O$, formed by the action of diastase on starch. Also **malt sugar.**

mal·treat (mal-trēt′) *v.t.* To treat badly, roughly or unkindly; abuse. [< F *maltraiter*] — **mal·treat′ment** *n.*

malt·ster (môlt′stər) *n.* A maker of or dealer in malt.

ma·ma (mä′mə, mə-mä′) *n.* Mother: used familiarly. [Repetition of infantile syllable *ma*]

mam·bo (mäm′bō) *n. pl.* **·bos** A dance resembling the rumba; also the syncopated four-beat music for this dance. — *v.i.* To dance the mambo. [< Haitian Creole]

mam·ma (mam′ə) *n. pl.* **·mae** (-mē) In mammals, the organ that secretes milk; a breast; udder. [< L, breast]

mam·mal (mam′əl) *n.* Any of a class of vertebrates whose females have mammae to nourish their young, including man, all warm-blooded quadrupeds, seals, etc. [< NL < LL < L *mamma* breast] — **mam·ma·li·an** (ma-mā′lē·ən, -māl′yən) *adj. & n.*

mam·ma·ry (mam′ər-ē) *adj.* Of, pertaining to, or of the nature of a mamma or breast, or the mammae.

mam·mon (mam′ən) *n.* **1.** Riches regarded as an evil influence and ignoble goal. **2.** Worldliness; avarice. [< LL < Gk. < Aramaic *māmōnā* riches] — **mam′mon·ish** *adj.*

Mam·mon (mam′ən) The personification of riches, avarice, and worldly gain.

mam·moth (mam′əth) *n. Paleontol.* A large, once very abundant, now extinct elephant having a thick hairy coat and long curved tusks. — *adj.* Huge; gigantic. [< Russian *mammot, mamant*]

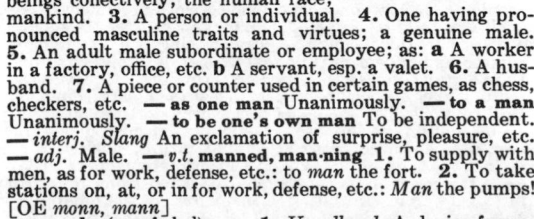

WOOLLY MAMMOTH
(9 to 12 feet high at shoulder)

mam·my (mam′ē) *n. pl.* **·mies 1.** Mother: used familiarly. **2.** *Southern U.S.* A Negro nurse or foster mother of white children. Also spelled **mammie.** [Dim. of MAMA]

man (man) *n. pl.* **men** (men) **1.** An adult male human being. **2.** Human beings collectively; the human race; mankind. **3.** A person or individual. **4.** One having pronounced masculine traits and virtues; a genuine male. **5.** An adult male subordinate or employee; as: **a** A worker in a factory, office, etc. **b** A servant, esp. a valet. **6.** A husband. **7.** A piece or counter used in certain games, as chess, checkers, etc. — **as one man** Unanimously. — **to a man** Unanimously. — **to be one's own man** To be independent. — *interj. Slang* An exclamation of surprise, pleasure, etc. — *adj.* Male. — *v.t.* **manned, man·ning 1.** To supply with men, as for work, defense, etc.: to *man* the fort. **2.** To take stations on, at, or in for work, defense, etc.: *Man* the pumps! [OE *mann, mann*]

man·a·cle (man′ə-kəl) *n.* **1.** *Usually pl.* A device for restraining the hands; shackle; handcuff. **2.** Anything that constrains. — *v.t.* **·cled, ·cling 1.** To put manacles on. **2.** To constrain or hamper. [< OF < L *manus* hand]

man·age (man′ij) *v.* **·aged, ·ag·ing** *v.t.* **1.** To direct or control the affairs or interests of: to *manage* a hotel. **2.** To arrange; contrive: usu. with an infinitive as object: He *managed* to stay. **3.** To control or guide the operation or performance of. **4.** To cause to do one's bidding: to *manage* a crowd. **5.** To handle or wield; use, as a weapon, etc. — *v.i.* **6.** To direct or control business, affairs, etc. **7.** To be able to continue or thrive. [< Ital. < L *manus* hand]

man·age·a·ble (man′ij-ə-bəl) *adj.* Capable of being managed. — **man′age·a·bil′i·ty, man′age·a·ble·ness** *n.* — **man′age·a·bly** *adv.*

managed currency (man′ijd) A monetary system in which the amount in circulation is regulated in an attempt to control prices, credit, etc.

man·age·ment (man′ij·mənt) *n.* **1.** The act, art, or practice of managing. **2.** The person or persons who manage a business, etc.. **3.** Managers collectively, esp. in their relations with labor unions. **4.** The skillful use of means.

man·ag·er (man′ij·ər) *n.* **1.** One who manages; esp., one who directs an enterprise, business, etc. **2.** One skilled in managing, esp. business affairs. — **man′ag·er·ship** *n.*

man·a·ge·ri·al (man′ə-jir′ē·əl) *adj.* Of or pertaining to a manager or management. — **man′a·ge′ri·al·ly** *adv.*

ma·ña·na (mä-nyä′nä) *n. & adv. Spanish* Tomorrow; some other time.

Ma·nas·seh (mə-nas′ə) In the Old Testament, a son of Joseph. *Gen.* xli 51. — *n.* The tribe of Israel descended from Manasseh. Also **Ma·nas·ses** (mə-nas′is).

man-at-arms (man′ət-ärmz′) *n. pl.* **men-at-arms** (men′-) A soldier; esp., an armed medieval mounted soldier.

man·a·tee (man′ə-tē′) *n.* A sluggish aquatic mammal of the coastal waters of Florida, the Gulf of Mexico, and the West Indies: also called *sea cow*. [< Sp. < Carib *manattoui*]

Man·chu (man·chōō′, man′chōō) *n.* **1.** One of a Mongoloid people that conquered China in 1643 and established the dynasty overthrown in 1912. **2.** The language of this people. — *adj.* Of or pertaining to Manchuria, its people, or its language. Also **Man·choo′.** [< Manchu, lit., pure]

-mancy *combining form* Divining or foretelling by means of: *necromancy*. [< OF < LL < Gk. *manteia* power of divination]

man·da·mus (man-dā′məs) *n. Law* A writ issued by a higher court to subordinate courts, corporations, etc., commanding them to do something. [< L, we command]

man·da·rin (man′də-rin) *n.* **1.** A member of any of the nine grades of well-educated officials of the Chinese Empire. **2.** A powerful person; esp., an intellectual arbiter. **3.** A tangerine: also **mandarin orange. 4.** An orange or reddish yellow dye. [< Pg. < Malay < Skt. *mantra* counsel]

Man·da·rin (man′də-rin) *n.* The Chinese language of north and west China, including the Peking dialect upon which the official language of the country is based.

man·da·tar·y (man′də-ter′ē) *n. pl.* **·tar·ies** One having or receiving a mandate.

man·date (man′dāt; *for n., also* -dit) *n.* **1.** In politics, an instruction from an electorate to its representative, expressed by the result of an election. **2.** Formerly, a charge to a nation from the League of Nations authorizing the administration of a territory, colony, etc.; also, the territory given in charge. **3.** An authoritative command; order. **4.** *Law* A judicial command issued by a higher court or official to a lower one. — *v.t.* **·dat·ed, ·dat·ing** To assign (a territory, etc.) to a specific nation under a mandate. [< L < *manus* hand + *dare* to give] — **man·da′tor** (-dā′tər) *n.*

man·da·to·ry (man′də-tôr′ē, -tō′rē) *adj.* **1.** Required by or as if by mandate or command; obligatory. **2.** Of or pertaining to a mandate. **3.** Holding a mandate. — *n. pl.* **·ries** A mandatary. — **man′da·to′ir·ly** *adv.*

man·di·ble (man′də-bəl) *n. Biol.* **1.** The lower jaw bone. **2.** Either part of the beak of a bird **3.** Either the upper or outer pair of jaws in an insect or other arthropod. [< L *mandere* to chew] — **man·dib·u·lar** (man-dib′yə-lər) *adj.*

man·do·lin (man′də-lin, man′də-lin′) *n.* A musical instrument with a fretted neck, a pear-shaped body, and eight metal strings. [< F < Ital. < L < Gk. *pandoura* lute]

man·drake (man′drāk) *n.* **1.** A short-stemmed Old World plant of the nightshade family with narcotic properties and fleshy forked roots sometimes resembling the human form. **2.** The May apple. Also **man·drag·o·ra** (man-drag′ə·rə). [< OE < LL < L < Gk. *mandragoras*]

man·drel (man′drəl) *n. Mech.* **1.** A shaft or spindle on which material may be fixed for working on a machine. **2.** A metal bar used as a core about which wire, glass, metal, etc., may be bent, forged, or shaped. Also **man′dril.** [Prob. alter. of F *mandrin* lathe]

man·drill (man′dril) *n.* A large, ferocious West African baboon.

mane (mān) *n.* The long hair growing on and about the neck of some animals, as the horse, lion, etc. [OE *manu*] — **maned** *adj.*

man-eat·er (man′ē′tər) *n.* **1.** A cannibal. **2.** An animal, as a tiger, shark, etc., that devours or is said to devour human flesh. — **man′-eat′ing** *adj.*

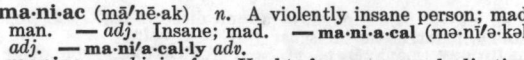

MANDRILL
(About 2½ feet high at shoulder; 3 to 4 feet long)

ma·nège (ma·nezh′) *n.* **1.** The art of training and riding horses; also, a school for horsemanship. **2.** The movements of a trained horse. Also **man·ege′**. [< F < Ital. *maneggiare* to handle, train horses]

ma·nes (mā′nāz) *n.pl. Often cap.* In ancient Roman religion, the spirits of the dead, esp. of ancestors. [< L]

ma·neu·ver (mə·nōō′vər, -nyōō′-) *n.* **1.** *Mil.* **a** A planned movement or shift, as of troops, warships, etc. **b** *pl.* Large-scale tactical exercises simulating war. **2.** Any skillful move or stroke. — *v.t.* **1.** To manage or conduct skillfully. **2.** To put (troops, vessels, etc.) through a maneuver or maneuvers. — *v.i.* **3.** To perform a maneuver or maneuvers. **4.** To use artful moves or strokes. Also, *esp. Brit.*, **manoeuver, manoeuvre.** [< F < OF < LL < L *manu operari* to work with the hand] — **ma·neu′ver·a·bil′i·ty** or **·vra·bil′i·ty** *n.* — **ma·neu′ver·a·ble** or **·vra·ble** *adj.* — **ma·neu′ver·er** *n.*

man Friday A person devoted or subservient to another, like Robinson Crusoe's servant of that name; a factotum.

man·ful (man′fəl) *adj.* Having a manly spirit; sturdy. — **man′ful·ly** *adv.* — **man′ful·ness** *n.*

man·ga·nese (mang′gə·nēs, -nēz) *n. Chem.* A hard, brittle, grayish white metallic element (symbol Mn), oxidizing readily and forming an important component of certain alloys. See ELEMENT. [< F < Ital., alter. of Med.L *magnesia*]

mange (mānj) *n. Vet.* An itching skin disease of dogs and other domestic animals, caused by parasitic mites. [< OF *manjue* an itch, eating]

man·ger (mān′jər) *n.* A trough or box for feeding horses or cattle. [< OF < L *manducare* to chew]

man·gle¹ (mang′gəl) *v.t.* **·gled, ·gling** **1.** To disfigure or mutilate by cutting, bruising, crushing, etc. **2.** To mar or ruin; spoil. [< AF, appar. freq. of OF *mahaignier*] — **man′gler** *n.*

man·gle² (mang′gəl) *n.* A machine for smoothing and pressing fabrics by passing them between rollers. — *v.t.* **·gled, ·gling** To smooth with a mangle. [< Du. < MDu. < Ital. < LL < Gk. *manganon* a pulley, a war machine]

man·go (mang′gō) *n. pl.* **·goes** or **·gos** **1.** An edible tropical fruit having a slightly acid taste. **2.** The tree producing this fruit. [< Pg. < Malay < Tamil < *mān* mango tree + *kāy* a fruit]

man·grove (mang′gōv, man′-) *n.* A tropical evergreen shrub or tree, sometimes having aerial roots, growing in marshy and coastal areas. [< Sp. *mangle* < Taino]

man·gy (mān′jē) *adj.* **·gi·er, ·gi·est** **1.** Affected with or resembling mange. **2.** Squalid; shabby. — **man′gi·ly** *adv.* — **man′gi·ness** *n.*

man·han·dle (man′han′dəl) *v.t.* **·dled, ·dling** **1.** To handle with rough force. **2.** To handle by manpower alone.

Man·hat·tan District (Man·hat′an, man-) In World War II, the project that developed the atomic bomb.

man·hole (man′hōl′) *n.* A usu. circular and covered opening by which a man may enter a sewer, boiler, etc.

man·hood (man′hŏŏd) *n.* **1.** The state of being an adult male human being. **2.** The masculine qualities collectively. **3.** Men collectively. **4.** The state of being human.

man-hour (man′our′) *n.* The amount of work a man can do in an hour.

ma·ni·a (mā′nē·ə, mān′yə) *n.* **1.** An extraordinary enthusiasm, craving, etc. **2.** *Psychiatry* An exaggerated sense of well-being with excessive but disordered mental and physical activity, often alternating with melancholia, as in manic-depressive psychosis. [< L < Gk., madness]

-mania *combining form* An exaggerated or irrational craving for or infatuation with. [< Gk. *mania* madness]
In the following list each entry denotes a mania for what is indicated:

acromania high places	**hodomania** travel
agoramania open places	**hylomania** woods
ailuromania cats	**hypnomania** sleep
anthomania flowers	**ichthyomania** fish
chionomania snow	**necromania** death or the dead
choreomania dancing	**noctimania** night
chrematomania money	**ophidiomania** reptiles
cynomania dogs	**ornithomania** birds
entomomania insects	**pedomania** children
gymnomania nakedness	**phonomania** noise
gynemania women	**thalassomania** ocean or sea
heliomania exposure to sun	**xenomania** strangers
hippomania horses	**zoomania** animals

ma·ni·ac (mā′nē·ak) *n.* A violently insane person; madman. — *adj.* Insane; mad. — **ma·ni·a·cal** (mə·nī′ə·kəl) *adj.* — **ma·ni·a·cal·ly** *adv.*

-maniac *combining form* Used to form nouns and adjectives from nouns ending in -mania: *kleptomaniac.*

man·ic (man′ik, mā′nik) *adj.* **1.** Extraordinarily animated or excited. **2.** *Psychiatry* Of or affected by mania.

man·ic-de·pres·sive (man′ik·di·pres′iv) *adj. Psychiatry* Denoting or characteristic of a mental disorder in which periods of depression alternate with periods of excitement. — *n.* One who suffers from this disorder.

man·i·cure (man′ə·kyŏŏr) *n.* The care of the hands and fingernails. — *v.t. & v.i.* **·cured, ·cur·ing** To treat (the nails, etc.). [< F < L *manus* hand + *cura* care]

man·i·cur·ist (man′ə·kyŏŏr′ist) *n.* One whose work is to care for the hands and fingernails.

man·i·fest (man′ə·fest) *adj.* Plainly apparent; obvious. — *v.t.* **1.** To reveal; show; display. **2.** To prove; be evidence of. **3.** To record in a manifest. — *n.* In transportation, an itemized account or list, as of passengers, cargo, etc. [< L *manifestus* evident, lit., struck by the hand] — **man′·i·fes′ta·ble** *adj.* — **man′i·fest′ly** *adv.* — **Syn.** (*adj.*) patent, visible, palpable, plain, evident.

man·i·fes·ta·tion (man′ə·fes·tā′shən) *n.* **1.** The act of manifesting, or the state of being manifested. **2.** A sign; indication.

man·i·fes·to (man′ə·fes′tō) *n. pl.* **·toes** or **·tos** A public and formal declaration or explanation of principles, intentions, etc., usually by a political faction or similar group.

man·i·fold (man′ə·fōld) *adj.* **1.** Having many and varied forms, types, instances, etc.: *manifold sorrows.* **2.** Having an assortment of features, etc. — **Syn.** See COMPLEX. — *n.* **1.** *Mech.* A pipe or chest having several or many openings, as for exhaust gas. **2.** A copy made by manifolding. **3.** Something that is manifold. — *v.t.* **1.** To make more than one copy of. **2.** To multiply. — *adv.* By many or by much: to increase *manifold.* [OE *manigfeald* varied, numerous] — **man′i·fold·ly** *adv.* — **man′i·fold·ness** *n.*

man·i·kin (man′ə·kin) *n.* **1.** A little man; dwarf. **2.** See MANNEQUIN. [< Du. *manneken*, dim. of *man* man]

ma·nil·a (mə·nil′ə) *n. Often cap.* The fiber of the abaca, a banana plant, used for making rope, etc. Also **ma·nil′a hemp.**

Manila paper A heavy, light brown paper, originally made of Manila hemp, now made of various fibers.

Manila rope Rope made of Manila hemp.

man in the street The common or ordinary person.

man·i·oc (man′ē·ok, mā′nē-) *n.* Cassava (def. 1). [< F < Tupi *mandioca* manioc root]

ma·nip·u·late (mə·nip′yə·lāt) *v.* **·lat·ed, ·lat·ing** *v.t.* **1.** To manage (persons, figures, stocks, etc.) shrewdly and deviously for one's own profit. **2.** To control, move, treat, etc., with or as with the hands; esp., to handle skillfully. — *v.i.* **3.** To perform manipulation. [Back formation < MANIPULATION] — **ma·nip′u·la·ble** *adj.* — **ma·nip′u·la·tive,** or **nip′u·la·to′ry** *adj.* — **ma·nip′u·la′tor** *n.*

ma·nip·u·la·tion (mə·nip′yə·lā′shən) *n.* **1.** The act of manipulating, or the state of being manipulated. **2.** *Surg.* A manual procedure, esp. in orthopedics or obstetrics. [< F, ult. < L < *manus* hand + *plere* to fill]

man·kind (man′kīnd′; *for def. 1, also* man′kīnd′) **1.** The whole human species. **2.** Men collectively, as distinguished from women.

man·ly (man′lē) *adj.* **·li·er, ·li·est** **1.** Pertaining to or appropriate for a man; virile: *manly* charm. **2.** Having the qualities and virtues of a man, as courage, determination, strength, etc. — **the manly art** Boxing. — *adv. Archaic* Manfully. — **man′li·ly** *adv.* — **man′li·ness** *n.*

man·na (man′ə) *n.* **1.** The food miraculously given to the Israelites in the wilderness as they fled from Egypt (*Ex.* xvi 14–36); also, any nourishment, help, etc., received as by divine bounty. **2.** A sweetish substance obtained from various plants, esp. from the flowering ash, and used as a mild laxative. [< LL < Gk. < Aramaic < Hebrew *mān* What is it?]

man·ne·quin (man′ə·kin) *n.* **1.** A full-sized model of a human figure used for cutting, fitting, or displaying garments. **2.** A woman who models clothing; model. Also spelled *manikin.* [< F < Du. *manneken.* See MANIKIN.]

man·ner (man′ər) *n.* **1.** A way of doing or a way in which something happens or is done. **2.** A style of speech and action: a grave *manner.* **3.** *pl.* Social conduct; etiquette; esp., polite and civil social behavior: to learn *manners* from Emily Post. **4.** *pl.* The modes of social behavior prevailing in a group, nation, period, etc. **5.** Typical or customary practice; esp., a characteristic style in literature, music, art, etc. — **in a manner of speaking** Approximately; more or less. — **to the manner born** Familiar or fitted from or as from birth. [< AF, OF, ult. < L *manuarius* of the hand]

man·nered (man′ərd) *adj.* **1.** Having (a specific kind of) manner or manners: used in combination: *mild-mannered.* **2.** Having mannerisms in writing, speaking, etc.

man·ner·ism (man′ər·iz′əm) *n.* **1.** Marked use of a distinctive style, as in writing. 2. A distinctive trait; idiosyncrasy. — **man′ner·ist** n. — **man′ner·is′tic** or **·ti·cal** adj.

man·ner·ly (man′ər·lē) adj. Well-behaved; polite. — adv. With good manners; politely. — **man′ner·li·ness** n.

man·ni·kin (man′ə·kin) See MANIKIN.

man·nish (man′ish) adj. Resembling a man; masculine; said of women. — **man′nish·ly** adv. — **man′nish·ness** n.

ma·noeu·ver (mə·nōō′vər, -nyōō′-), **ma·noeu·vre** See MANEUVER.

man of the world A worldly-wise and sophisticated man.

man-of-war (man′əv·wôr′, -ə·wôr′) n. pl. **men-of-war** (men′-) Chiefly Archaic An armed ship; warship.

man-of-war bird A frigate bird (which see). Also **man-of-war hawk.**

ma·nom·e·ter (mə·nom′ə·tər) n. Any of various instruments used to measure pressure, as of gases, liquids, vapors, etc. [< F < Gk. manos thin, rare + -mètre -meter] — **man·o·met·ric** (man′ə·met′rik) or **·ri·cal** adj.

man on horseback A military leader whose popularity is a threat to the civil government.

man·or (man′ər) n. 1. In England: a Formerly, a feudal domain. b A landed estate. 2. A manor house. 3. A mansion. 4. In colonial America, a landed estate with hereditary feudal rights. [< OF < L manere to dwell] — **ma·no·ri·al** (mə·nôr′ē·əl, -nō′rē-) adj.

manor house The residence of the lord of a manor.

man·pow·er (man′pou′ər) n. 1. The force of human physical strength. 2. The number of men whose strength and skill are available to a nation, army, project, etc.; personnel.

man·qué (män·kā′) adj. French Lacking fulfillment; in wish but not in fact: a writer manqué.

man·sard (man′särd) n. Archit. A curb roof having the lower slope almost vertical and the upper almost horizontal, with the same profile on all four sides of the building. [after F. Mansard, 1598–1666, French architect who revived it]

manse (mans) n. 1. A clergyman's house. 2. Archaic A manor house. [< Med.L mansa, pp. of L manere to dwell]

man·ser·vant (man′sûr′vənt) n. An adult male servant.

man·sion (man′shən) n. A large and impressive house, typically that of a wealthy person or family. [< OF < L mansio, -onis a dwelling]

man·slaugh·ter (man′slô′tər) n. 1. Law The unlawful killing of a human being without malice. 2. Slaying of men.

man·ta (man′tə) n. 1. Any of several very large rays common in tropical American waters: also called devilfish. Also **manta ray.** 2. A woman's shawl made of a coarse fabric. [< Sp., blanket < LL mantum cloak]

MANTA
(To 20 feet long)

man·teau (man′tō, Fr. män·tō′) n. pl. **·teaus** (-tōz) or **·teaux** (Fr. -tō′) A cloak or mantle. [< F. See MANTLE.]

man·tel (man′tel) n. 1. The shelf above a fireplace. 2. A facing of wood, brick, stone, etc., around a fireplace: also called chimney piece. Also **man′tel·piece′** (-pēs′). [< F manteau mantelpiece]

-mantic combining form Used to form adjectives from nouns ending in -mancy. [< Gk. mantikos prophetic]

man·til·la (man·til′ə) n. A light scarf often of black lace worn over the head and shoulders of women in Spain and Spanish America. [< Sp. dim. of manta. See MANTA.]

man·tis (man′tis) n. pl. **·tis·es** or **·tes** (-tēz) A carnivorous, long-bodied insect with large eyes and swiveling head, that stands with its forelegs folded as if in prayer: also called praying mantis. [< NL < Gk., a prophet]

man·tle (man′tel) n. 1. A loose and usu. sleeveless garment worn over other garments. 2. Anything that clothes, envelops, or conceals. 3. Zool. The variously modified flap or folds of the membranous covering of a mollusk. 4. A mantel. 5. A gas mantle. — v. **·tled, ·tling** v.t. 1. To cover with or as with a mantle; conceal. — v.i. 2. To overspread or cover the surface of something. 3. To be or become covered or suffused, as a blush, etc. [OE < OF < L mantellum]

man·tu·a (man′chōō·ə, -tōō·ə) n. A woman's cloak, worn about 1700. [Alter. of F manteau; infl. in form by Mantua]

man·u·al (man′yōō·əl) adj. Involving, used, or operated by the hands. — n. 1. A small book of instructions. 2. An organ keyboard. 3. A prescribed drill in manipulating a rifle, flag, etc. [< OF < L manus hand] — **man′u·al·ly** adv.

manual alphabet A series of manual signs or gestures used by the deaf and deaf-mutes as a substitute for vocal speech: sometimes called deaf-and-dumb alphabet.

manual training In U.S. schools, practical training in carpentry, woodworking, etc.

man·u·fac·ture (man′yə·fak′chər) v. **·tured, ·tur·ing** v.t. 1. To make or process a product, esp. on a large scale and with machinery. 2. To fabricate or invent (a lie, alibi, etc.). 3. To produce (poetry, art, etc.) mechanically. —

v.i. 4. To make or process something. — n. 1. The act or process of manufacturing. 2. Something that is manufactured. [< MF < L manus hand + factura a making] — **man′u·fac′tur·a·ble** adj. — **man′u·fac′tur·er** n.

man·u·mit (man′yə·mit′) v.t. **·mit·ted, ·mit·ting** To free from bondage, as a slave. [< L manumittere, lit., to send forth from one's hand] — **man′u·mis′sion** (-mish′ən) n.

ma·nure (mə·nōōr′, -nyōōr′) n. Dung, compost, etc., used to fertilize soil. — v.t. **·nured, ·nur·ing** To apply manure or other fertilizer to, as soil. [< AF maynoverer to work with the hands] — **ma·nur′er** n.

man·u·script (man′yə·skript) n. 1. A usu. typewritten copy of a book, article, document, etc., prepared or submitted for publication. 2. Something written by hand. — adj. Written by hand. [< Med.L < LL < L manus hand + scriptus, pp. of scribere to write]

Manx (mangks) adj. Of or pertaining to the Isle of Man, its people, or their language. — n. 1. The people of the Isle of Man. 2. The Gaelic language of the Manx, nearly extinct. [< Scand. ult. < Celtic Man Isle of Man]

Manx cat A type of domestic cat having no tail.

Manx·man (mangks′mən) n. pl. **·men** (-mən) A native of the Isle of Man.

man·y (men′ē) adj. **more, most** Adding up to a large number; numerous. — n. 1. A large number. 2. The masses: with the. — **a great many** Many: with plural verb. — **many a** (or **an** or **another**) Many: with singular noun. — pron. A large number of persons or things. [OE manig]

Mao·ism (mou′iz′əm) n. The communist doctrines or practices of Mao Tse-tung. — **Mao′ist** n., adj.

Ma·o·ri (mä′ō·rē, mou′rē) n. 1. One of an aboriginal, light brown people of New Zealand, chiefly Polynesian mixed with Melanesian. 2. The Polynesian language of these people. — adj. Of or pertaining to the Maoris or their language.

map (map) n. 1. A representation on a plane surface of any region, as of the earth's surface; a chart. 2. Anything resembling a map. 3. Slang The face. — **off the map** Out of existence. — v.t. **mapped, map·ping** 1. To make a map of. 2. To plan in detail: often with out. [< OF < Med.L mappa (mundi) map (of the world)]

ma·ple (mā′pəl) n. 1. Any of numerous deciduous trees of the north temperate zone, with opposite leaves and a fruit of two joined samaras, as the sugar maple, etc. 2. The wood of these trees. 3. The amber-yellow color of the finished wood. 4. The flavor of the sap of the sugar maple. [OE mapul (trēow) maple (tree)]

maple sugar Sugar made from the sap of the sugar maple.

maple syrup The refined sap of the sugar maple.

ma·quis (mà·kē′) n. A zone of shrubby, mostly evergreen plants in the Mediterranean region, known as cover for game, bandits, etc. [< F < Ital. macchia thicket]

Ma·quis (mà·kē′) n. pl. **·quis** 1. The French resistance movement against the Germans during World War II. 2. A member of this group. [< MAQUIS]

mar (mär) v.t. **marred, mar·ring** 1. To do harm to; damage. 2. To injure so as to deface. — n. A disfiguring mark; blemish. [OE mierran to hinder] — **mar′rer** n.

mar·a·bou (mar′ə·bōō) n. 1. A stork of Africa, whose soft, white, lower tail and wing feathers are used in millinery. 2. A plume from the marabou. 3. The adjutant (def. 2). Also **mar′a·bout** (-bōōt). [< F marabou, marabout hermit]

ma·ra·ca (mə·rä′kə, Pg. mä·rä·kä′) n. A percussion instrument made of a gourd or gourd-shaped rattle with beans or beads inside it. [< Pg maracá, ? < Tupi]

mar·a·schi·no (mar′ə·skē′nō) n. A cordial distilled from the fermented juice of a small wild cherry and flavored with the cracked pits. [< Ital. < marasca. See MARASCA.]

maraschino cherries Cherries preserved in a syrup usu. flavored with imitation maraschino.

mar·a·thon (mar′ə·thon) n. 1. A footrace of 26 miles, 385 yards: so called from a messenger's run from Marathon to Athens to announce the Athenian victory over the Persians, 490 B.C. 2. Any endurance contest.

Mar·a·thon (mar′ə·thon) A plain in Attica, Greece, scene of decisive victory of the Athenians over the Persians, 490 B.C.

ma·raud (mə·rôd′) v.i. 1. To rove in search of plunder. — v.t. 2. To invade for plunder. — n. A foray. [< F maraud rogue] — **ma·raud′er** n.

mar·ble (mär′bəl) n. 1. A compact, granular, partly crystallized limestone occurring in many colors, used for building, sculpture, etc. 2. A piece, block, statue, etc., of this stone. 3. A small ball of this stone, or of glass, porcelain, etc. 4. pl. A boys' game played with balls of glass, etc. — v. **·bled, ·bling** v.t. 1. To color or vein in imitation of marble, as book edges. — v.i. 2. To be flecked with fat: said of meat. — adj. 1. Made of or consisting of marble. 2. Resembling marble as to chilliness, lack of feeling, etc. [< OF < L < Gk. marmaros, lit., sparkling stone] — **mar′bly** adj.

marble cake A cake made of light and dark batter mixed to give a marblelike appearance.

mar·ble·ize (mär′bəl·īz) *v.t. & v.i.* **·ized, ·iz·ing** *U.S.* To marble.

mar·ca·site (mär′kə·sīt) *n.* **1.** A pale, bronze-yellow, iron disulfide, FeS$_2$: also called *white iron pyrites.* **2.** An ornament made of crystallized marcasite or of polished steel. [< Med.L *marcasita*]

mar·cel (mär·sel′) *v.t.* **·celled, ·cel·ling** To dress (the hair) in even, continuous waves by means of special irons. [after M. *Marcel*, 19th c. French hairdresser] **— mar·cel′ler** *n.*

march¹ (märch) *v.i.* **1.** To walk or proceed with measured, regular steps, as a soldier or body of troops. **2.** To walk in a solemn or dignified manner. **3.** To advance steadily. **—** *v.t.* **4.** To cause to march. **—** *n.* **1.** The act of marching. **2.** A regular, measured step, as of a body of troops. **3.** The distance passed over in marching: a full day's *march.* **4.** Onward progress: the *march* of events. **5.** A musical composition for marching. [< MF *marcher* to walk, orig., to trample] **— mar′cher** *n.*

march² (märch) *n.* A region or district lying along a boundary line; frontier. Also **march′land′** (-land′). [< OHG *marka* mark]

March (märch) The third month of the year, containing 31 days. [< AF, OF < L *Martius* (*mensis*) (month) of Mars < *Mars* Roman god of war]

mar·che·se (mär·kā′zā) *n. pl.* **·che·si** (-kā′zē) *Italian* A marquis. **— mar·che′sa** (-zä) *n.fem.*

Mar·ches·van (mär·kĥesh′vən) Heshwan. See (Hebrew) CALENDAR.

mar·chion·ess (mär′shən·is) *n.* **1.** The wife or widow of a marquis. **2.** A woman having in her own right the rank corresponding to that of a marquis. [< Med.L *marchionissa* < *marchio, -onis* captain of the marches]

march·pane (märch′pān) *n.* Marzipan. [< MF < Ital. *marzapane.* See MARZIPAN.]

Mar·di gras (mär′dē grä′) Shrove Tuesday, the last day before Lent, often a carnival. [< F, lit., fat Tuesday]

mare¹ (mâr) *n.* The female of the horse and other equine animals. [OE *miere*, fem. of *mearh* horse]

mar·e² (mâr′ē) *n. pl.* **mar·i·a** (mâr′ē·ə) Any of a number of dark, seemingly flat areas of the moon's surface. [< L, sea; because of their resemblance to seas]

mare's nest 1. A discovery that proves worthless or false. **2.** Loosely, a cluttered and confusing mess.

mare's-tail (mârz′tāl′) *n. Meteorol.* Long, fibrous, cirrus clouds, supposed to indicate rain.

mar·ga·rine (mär′jə·rin, -rēn, -gə-) *n.* **1.** A substitute for butter, made from vegetable oils and milk. **2.** Oleomargarine. Also **mar·ga·rin** (mär′jə·rin, -gə-). [< F]

mar·gin (mär′jin) *n.* **1.** The part of a page around the body of printed or written text. **2.** A bounding line or surface; border. **3.** An extra amount of something, as space, time, money, etc. **4.** A limiting or end point; limit. **5.** In commerce, the difference between the cost and selling price of a commodity. **6.** In the stock market, security deposited with a broker to protect him against loss in trading. **—** *v.t.* **1.** To furnish with a margin. **2.** To enter, place, or specify on the margin of a page, as a note. **3.** In the stock market, to deposit a margin upon. [< L *margo*]

mar·gi·nal (mär′jə·nəl) *adj.* **1.** Pertaining to or constituting a margin. **2.** Situated or written at or on a margin. Also *Archaic* **mar′gent** (-jənt). **3.** Having relatively low quality or value; meager. **4.** *Econ.* Barely profitable. [< F] **— mar′gin·al′i·ty** *n.* **mar′gin·al·ly** *adv.*

mar·gi·na·li·a (mär′jə·nā′lē·ə, -nāl′yə) *n.pl.* Marginal notes.

marginal land *Econ.* Land so poor as to remain unused until the lack of more desirable land forces its development.

mar·grave (mär′grāv) *n.* **1.** Formerly, the lord or governor of a German mark, march, or border. **2.** A hereditary title of certain princes of the Holy Roman Empire. [< MDu. *marke* march² + *graf* count]

mar·gra·vi·ate (mär·grā′vē·it) *n.* The territory of a margrave. Also **mar·gra·vate** (mär′grə·vāt).

mar·gue·rite (mär′gə·rēt′) *n.* Any of several flowers, esp. the oxeye daisy. [< F pearl, daisy]

Mar·i·an (mâr′ē·ən) *n.* A worshiper or devotee of the Virgin Mary. **—** *adj.* Of or pertaining to the Virgin Mary.

mar·i·gold (mar′ə·gōld) *n.* **1.** Any of several plants of the composite family with golden-yellow flowers. **2.** Any plant resembling these. [< Virgin *Mary* + GOLD]

mar·i·jua·na (mar′ə·wä′nə, *Sp.* mä/rē·hwä′nä) *n.* **1.** Hemp (def. 1). **2.** The dried leaves and flower tops of this plant, capable of producing disorienting or hallucinogenic effects when smoked in cigarettes or ingested. Also **ma′·ri·hua′na.** [< Am. Sp. *marihuana, mariguana*]

ma·rim·ba (mə·rim′bə) *n.* A form of xylophone having a resonator beneath each tuned bar. [< Bantu *marimba, ma-limba*, pl. of *limba*, kind of musical instrument]

ma·ri·na (mə·rē′nə) *n. U.S.* A docking area or basin for small vessels. [< Ital., seacoast < L *marinus*. See MARINE.]

mar·i·nade (mar′ə·nād′) *n.* **1.** A brine pickle sometimes flavored with wine, oil, spices, etc., in which meat or fish are soaked before cooking. **2.** Pickled meat or fish. **—** *v.t.* **·nad·ed, ·nad·ing** To marinate. [< F < Sp. *marinar* to pickle in brine]

mar·i·nate (mar′ə·nāt) *v.t.* **·nat·ed, ·nat·ing 1.** To soak (food) in marinade. **2.** To allow, as salad, to soak in French dressing before serving. [< Ital. *marinare*]

ma·rine (mə·rēn′) *adj.* **1.** Of, pertaining to, existing in, or formed by the sea. **2.** Pertaining to the navigation or handling of ships on the sea; nautical. **3.** Relating to the navy; naval. **4.** Used or intended for use at sea or in navigation. **5.** Serving aboard ship. **—** *n.* **1.** A soldier trained for service at sea and on land; a member of the Marine Corps: also **Ma·rine′. 2.** Shipping vessels, shipping, or the navy collectively. **3.** A seascape. **4.** The department of naval affairs in some countries. [< OF < L *mare, maris* sea] **— Syn.** (adj.) Maritime, nautical, naval.

Marine Corps A branch of the U.S. Navy, made up of combat troops, air forces, etc., under their own officers: officially, the *United States Marine Corps.*

mar·i·ner (mar′ə·nər) *n.* One who navigates or assists in navigating a ship; sailor; seaman. [< OF *marinier*]

mar·i·o·nette (mar′ē·ə·net′) *n.* A small jointed human or animal figure of wood, cloth, etc., used in shows and animated by manipulating strings: also called *puppet.* [< F *marionnette*, dim. of *Marion*, dim. of *Marie*]

Mar·i·po·sa lily (mar′ə·pō·sə, -zə) Any of various liliaceous Mexican and Californian plants. Also **Mariposa tulip.**

mar·i·tal (mar′ə·təl) *adj.* Of or pertaining to marriage. [< L *maritus* husband, orig., married] **— mar′i·tal·ly** *adv.*

mar·i·time (mar′ə·tīm) *adj.* **1.** Situated on or near the sea. **2.** Of or pertaining to the sea, its navigation, commerce, etc. **— Syn.** See MARINE. [< MF < L *mare, maris* sea]

Maritime Provinces New Brunswick, Nova Scotia, and Prince Edward Island on the Atlantic coast of Canada.

Mar·i·tim·er (mar′ə·tī′mər) *n.* A resident or native of the Maritime Provinces.

mar·jo·ram (mär′jər·əm) *n.* Any of several perennial herbs of the mint family, one of which, **sweet marjoram**, is used in cookery. [< OF *majorane*, ult. origin uncertain]

mark¹ (märk) *n.* **1.** A visible trace, impression, or figure on something, as a line, scratch, spot, or dot. **2.** An identifying symbol, seal, inscription, or label; trademark. **3.** A cross or other sign made by one who cannot write. **4.** A letter, number, or symbol used to indicate achievement, quality, defect, etc., as of a student's work. **5.** A symbol, written or printed. **6.** An object, point, sign, etc., serving to indicate, guide, or direct. **7.** That which indicates the presence of a thing, quality, process, etc.: a *mark* of distinction. **8.** A visible indication of some quality, trait, position, etc.: the *mark* of an outcast. **9.** That which is aimed at, or toward which effort is directed. **10.** A standard or criterion of quality, performance, etc. **11.** *Informal* A person easily duped or victimized: a *mark* for every schemer. **12.** In track sports, the starting line of the contest. **13.** *Naut.* A knot, twist, rag, etc., on a lead line at intervals to indicate fathoms of depth. **14.** Notice; attention; heed: worthy of *mark.* **— beside the mark 1.** Missing the point aimed at. **2.** Irrelevant. **— hit the mark 1.** To be accurate. **2.** To achieve one's goal. **— to leave** (or **make**) **a mark** To leave or make an impression; influence. **— to make one's mark** To succeed. **— of mark** Having, or worthy of distinction, renown, etc. **— up to the mark** Up to standard; in good health or condition, etc. **— wide of the mark 1.** Striking far from the point aimed at. **2.** Irrelevant. **—** *v.t.* **1.** To make a mark or marks on. **2.** To trace the boundaries of; set limits to: often with *out.* **3.** To indicate or show by a mark or sign. **4.** To characterize; distinguish: a year *marked* by great events. **5.** To designate, appoint, or select, as if by marking: to be *marked* for death. **6.** To pay attention to; notice; heed. **7.** To make known or clear; manifest; display. **8.** To apply or attach a price tag, identification label, etc., to an article. **9.** To evaluate by giving marks to. **10.** To keep (record or score) in various games. **11.** To produce by drawing, writing, etc. **—** *v.i.* **12.** To take notice; pay attention; consider. **13.** To make a mark or marks. **14.** To keep score in games. **— to mark down 1.** To note down by writing. **2.** To put a lower price on, as for sale. **— to mark time 1.** To keep time by moving the feet but not advancing. **2.** To pause in action or progress temporarily. **— to mark up 1.** To make marks on; scar. **2.** To increase the price of. [ME < OE *mearc*, orig., boundary] **— mark′er** *n.*

mark² (märk) *n.* The former standard monetary unit and silver coin of Germany, equivalent to 100 pfennigs, superseded after World War II by the deutschemark in West Germany and a deutschemark of different value in East Germany. [OE *marc* a unit of weight]

Mark (märk) The evangelist who wrote the second of the gospel narratives in the New Testament: called **Saint Mark.** **—** *n.* The second Gospel of the New Testament.

marked (märkt) *adj.* **1.** Clearly evident; noticeable. **2.** Having a mark or marks. **— a marked man** One singled out for vengeance, punishment, etc. **— mark·ed·ly** (mär′ked·lē) *adv.* **— mark′ed·ness** *n.*

mar·ket (mär′kit) *n.* **1.** Trade and commerce in a specific service or commodity: the boat *market*; also, trade and commerce generally: with *the*. **2.** A region where one can buy or sell; also, a category of persons, institutions, etc., considered as buyers: the college *market*. **3.** The state of trade: a brisk *market*. **4.** A place where something is offered for sale. **5.** A public gathering, often weekly, for buying and selling. **6.** Market value (which see). **— in the market** Seeking to buy. **— on the market** Up for sale. **—** *v.t.* **1.** To sell. **—** *v.i.* **2.** To deal in a market. **3.** To buy household provisions. [ME < AF < L < *merx, mercis* merchandise]

mar·ket·a·ble (mär′kit·ə·bəl) *adj.* Suitable for sale; in demand. **— mar′ket·a·bil′i·ty** *n.*

mar·ket·place (mär′kit·plās′) *n.* **1.** A market (def. 4). **2.** The imagined place where ideas, opinions, works, etc., are tested and traded. Also **market place.**

market value The amount that can be obtained for goods on the open market. Also **market price.**

mark·ing (mär′king) *n.* **1.** A mark or an arrangement of marks. **2.** *Often pl.* The color pattern on a bird, animal, etc. **3.** The act of making a mark.

mark·ka (märk′kä) *n.* The standard monetary unit of Finland, equivalent to 100 pennia. [< Finnish < Sw. *mark*]

marks·man (märks′mən) *n. pl.* **·men** (-mən) **1.** One skilled in hitting the mark, as with a rifle or other weapon. **2.** *Mil.* In the U.S. Army, the lowest of three grades for skill in the use of small arms. **— marks′man·ship** *n.* **— marks′wom·an** (-wŏŏm′ən) *n.fem.*

mark·up (märk′up′) *n.* **1.** A raising of price. **2.** The amount of price increase.

marl (märl) *n.* **1.** An earthy deposit containing lime, clay, and sand, used as fertilizer. **2.** A soft, crumbly soil. **3.** *Poetic* Earth. **—** *v.t.* To spread with marl. [< OF < LL < L *marga* marl] **— marl′y, mar·la′ceous** (lā′ɸhəs) *adj.*

mar·lin (mär′lin) *n.* Any of various deep-sea game fishes; esp., the **blue marlin** of the Atlantic, and the **striped marlin** of the Pacific. [< MARLINE(SPIKE); because of its shape]

mar·line (mär′lin) *n. Naut.* A small rope of two strands loosely twisted together, used for winding ropes, cables, etc. [< Du. *marren* to tie + *lijn* a line]

mar·line·spike (mär′lin·spīk′) *n. Naut.* A sharp-pointed iron pin used in splicing ropes. Also **mar′lin·spike′, mar′·ling·spike′** (-ling-).

mar·ma·lade (mär′mə·lād) *n.* A preserve made by boiling with sugar the pulp and rind of fruits, usu. citrus fruits, to the consistency of jam. [< MF < Pg *marmelada*]

mar·mo·re·al (mär·môr′ē·əl, -mō′rē-) *adj.* Pertaining to, made of, or resembling marble. Also **mar·mo′re·an** (-môr′ē-, -mō′rē-). [< L *marmoreus* < *marmor*. See MARBLE.]

mar·mo·set (mär′mə·zet) *n.* Any of various small Central and South American monkeys with soft, woolly hair and a long hairy tail. [< OF *marmouset* grotesque figure]

mar·mot (mär′mət) *n.* Any of various rodents, as the woodchuck or ground hog. [Fusion of OF *marmotte* monkey and Romansch *murmont* marmot]

ma·roon¹ (mə·rōōn′) *v.t.* **1.** To put ashore and abandon on a desolate island or coast. **2.** To abandon; leave helpless. **—** *n.* One of a class of Negroes, chiefly fugitive slaves or their descendants, living wild in the mountains of some West Indies islands and of Guiana. [< Am. Sp. *cimarron* wild]

ma·roon² (mə·rōōn′) *n.* A dull, dark red color. **—** *adj.* Having a dull, dark red color. [< F *marron* chestnut]

mar·quee (mär·kē′) *n.* **1.** A canopy used as a shelter over the sidewalk in front of a theater, hotel, etc. **2.** A large field tent, as one used at outdoor parties. [< *marquise* canopy]

mar·quess (mär′kwis) See MARQUIS.

mar·que·try (mär′kə·trē) *n.* Inlaid work of wood often interspersed with stones, ivory, etc., esp. as used in furniture. Also **mar′que·te·rie.** [< MF < *marqueter* to variegate]

mar·quis (mär′kwis, Fr. mår·kē′) *n.* The title of a nobleman next in rank below a duke. Also, *Brit., marquess.* [< OF < Med.L *markensis* commander of the marches]

Mar·quis (mär′kwis) *n.* An important variety of wheat, first developed in Canada.

mar·quis·ate (mär′kwiz·it) *n.* The rank of a marquis.

mar·quise (mär·kēz′) *n.* **1.** The wife or widow of a French marquis. **2.** An ornamental hood over a door; a marquee.

mar·qui·sette (mär′ki·zet′, -kwi-) *n.* A lightweight, open-mesh fabric of cotton, silk, rayon, or nylon, or a combination of these, used for curtains and women's and children's garments. [< F, dim. of *marquise* a marquise]

mar·riage (mar′ij) *n.* **1.** The state of being married; a legal contract, entered into by a man and a woman, to live together as husband and wife; wedlock. ♦ Collateral adjec-

tives: *hymeneal, marital.* **2.** The act of marrying; also, the accompanying rites or festivities; wedding; nuptials. **3.** Any close union. [< OF < L *maritare* to marry]

mar·riage·a·ble (mar′ij·ə·bəl) *adj.* Fitted or suitable for marriage. **— mar′riage·a·bil′i·ty, mar′riage·a·ble·ness** *n.*

mar·ried (mar′ēd) *adj.* **1.** United in matrimony; having a spouse. **2.** Of or pertaining to marriage or to persons united in marriage. **3.** Closely related or joined.

mar·ron (mar′ən, Fr. mà·rôn′) *n. Often pl.* A large variety of chestnut, esp. when preserved in syrup, etc. [< F]

mar·row (mar′ō) *n.* **1.** A soft, vascular tissue found in the central cavities of bones. **2.** The essence of anything; pith. **3.** Vitality. [OE *mearg*] **— mar′row·y** *adj.*

mar·row·bone (mar′ō·bōn′) *n.* **1.** A bone containing edible marrow. **2.** *pl.* One's knees: used humorously.

mar·row·fat (mar′ō·fat′) *n.* A variety of green pea, having a large, succulent seed. Also **marrow pea.**

mar·ry (mar′ē) *v.* **·ried, ·ry·ing** *v.t.* **1.** To accept as husband or wife; take in marriage. **2.** To join as husband and wife in marriage. **3.** To give in marriage. **4.** To unite closely. **—** *v.i.* **5.** To take a husband or wife. **6.** To join or unite closely. [< OF < L < *maritus* husband, married]

Mars (märz) In Roman mythology, the god of war: identified with the Greek *Ares.* **—** *n.* The seventh largest planet of the solar system and fourth from the sun. See PLANET.

Mar·sa·la (mär·sä′lä) *n.* A dark-colored, sweet, heavy wine, originally made in Marsala, Sicily.

Mar·seil·laise (mär′sə·lāz′, Fr. mår·sà·yez′) The national anthem of France, written in 1792 by Rouget de Lisle.

mar·seille (mär·sāl′) *n.* A thick cotton fabric. Also **mar·seilles** (mär·sālz′). [after *Marseille*, France]

marsh (märsh) *n.* A tract of low, wet land; swamp. [OE *mersc, merisc*]

mar·shal (mär′shəl) *n.* **1.** In various foreign countries, a military officer of high rank, usu. just below the commander in chief: a field *marshal.* **2.** *U.S.* **a** An officer of the Federal courts, assigned to a judicial district and having duties similar to those of a sheriff. **b** In some cities, the chief of the police or fire department. **3.** An officer authorized to organize or regulate processions, ceremonies, etc. **4.** A title of certain royal court or household officials, often in charge of matters of protocol. **—** *v.t.* **mar·shaled** or **·shalled, mar·shal·ing** or **·shal·ling** **1.** To arrange or dispose in order, as facts. **2.** To array or draw up, as troops for battle. **3.** To lead; usher. [< OF < Med.L < OHG < *marah* horse + *scalh* servant] **— mar′shal·cy, mar′shal·ship** *n.* **— mar′·shal·er, mar′shal·ler** *n.*

Marshal of the Royal Canadian Air Force In the Royal Canadian Air Force, a commissioned officer of the highest rank. See table at GRADE.

marsh gas Methane.

marsh hawk A marsh-dwelling American hawk having gray or brown plumage, a white rump, and rounded wings.

marsh·mal·low (märsh′mel′ō, -mal′ō) *n.* **1.** A confection made of starch, sugar, corn syrup, and gelatin, and coated with powdered sugar. **2.** A sweetmeat formerly made from the root of the marsh mallow.

marsh mallow A plant of the mallow family growing in marshy places.

marsh marigold A showy swamp plant of the crowfoot family, having yellow flowers: also called *cowslip.*

marsh·y (mär′shē) *adj.* **marsh·i·er, marsh·i·est** **1.** Of, pertaining to, or containing a marsh. **2.** Swampy; boggy. **3.** Growing or produced in a marsh. **— marsh′i·ness** *n.*

mar·su·pi·al (mär·sōō′pē·əl) *n.* Any member of an order of mammals, as the kangaroos, opossums, wombats, etc., whose females carry their undeveloped young in a marsupium. **—** *adj.* Having a marsupium or pouch. **— mar·su′pi·a′li·an** (-ā′lē·ən), **mar·su′pi·an** *adj. & n.*

mar·su·pi·um (mär·sōō′pē·əm) *n. pl.* **·pi·a** (-pē·ə) A pouchlike receptacle on the abdomen of female marsupials, containing the teats and used for carrying the young. [< L < Gk. *marsypion*, dim. of *marsipos* bag]

mart (märt) *n.* A market. [< MDu. < L *mercatus*]

mar·ten (mär′ten) *n.* **1.** A weasellike carnivorous mammal having arboreal habits, as the **pine marten** of eastern North America. **2.** The valuable, dark brown fur of a marten. [< OF *martrine* of the marten < WGmc.]

Mar·tha (mär′thə) A sister of Lazarus and Mary, who served Jesus at Bethany. *Luke* 38–41.

mar·tial (mär′shəl) *adj.* **1.** Of, pertaining to, or concerned with war or the military life. **2.** Suggestive of or suitable for war or military operations. **3.** Of or characteristic of a warrior. [< OF < L *martialis* pertaining to Mars] **— mar′tial·ism** *n.* **— mar′tial·ist** *n.* **— mar′tial·ly** *adv.*

martial law Temporary jurisdiction or rule by military forces over the citizens of an area where civil law and order no longer function or exist.

Mar·tian (mär′shən) *adj. Astron.* Of or pertaining to the planet Mars. — *n.* One of the supposed inhabitants of Mars. [< L *Martius*]

mar·tin (mär′tən) *n.* **1.** Any of certain birds of the swallow family, having a tail that is less forked than that of the common swallow; esp., the **house martin** of Europe, and the **purple martin** of North America. **2.** Any of various similar birds. [< F]

mar·ti·net (mär′tə·net′) *n.* **1.** A strict military disciplinarian. **2.** One who demands rigid adherence to rules, etc. [after General Jean *Martinet*, 17th c. French drillmaster]

mar·tin·gale (mär′tən·gāl) *n.* A forked strap that prevents a horse from rearing its head, connecting the head gear with the bellyband. Also **mar′tin·gal** (-gal). [< F < Provençal *martengalo*, appar. fem. of *martengo* an inhabitant of Martigues, miserly person < Sp. *almartaga* < Arabic]

mar·ti·ni (mär·tē′nē) *n. pl.* **·nis** A cocktail made of gin and dry vermouth, usu. served with an olive or lemon peel. [after *Martini* and Rossi, a company making vermouth]

mar·tyr (mär′tər) *n.* **1.** One who submits to death rather than renounce his religion. **2.** One who dies, suffers, or sacrifices everything for a principle, cause, etc. **3.** One who suffers much, as from ill health or misfortune. — *v.t.* **1.** To make a martyr of. **2.** To torture or persecute. [OE < LL < Gk. *martyr*, Aeolic form of *martyrs*, *martyros* witness] — **mar′tyr·dom** (-dəm) *n.*

mar·tyr·ize (mär′tər·īz) *v.* **·ized, ·iz·ing** *v.t.* **1.** To make a martyr of. — *v.i.* **2.** To become a martyr. — **mar′tyr·i·za′tion** *n.*

mar·vel (mär′vəl) *v.* **mar·veled** or **·velled, mar·vel·ing** or **·vel·ling** *v.i.* **1.** To be filled with wonder, surprise, etc. — *v.t.* **2.** To wonder at or about: with a clause as object. — *n.* That which excites wonder; a prodigy. [< OF < L *mirabilia* neut. pl. of *mirabilis* wonderful]

mar·vel·ous (mär′vəl·əs) *adj.* **1.** Causing astonishment and wonder; amazing; extraordinary. **2.** Miraculous; incredible. **3.** *Informal* Very good; excellent; admirable. Also **mar′vel·lous.** — **mar′vel·ous·ly** *adv.* — **mar′vel·ous·ness** *n.*

Marx·ism (märk′siz·əm) *n.* The body of socialist doctrines formulated by Karl Marx and Friedrich Engels, the basic tenets of which are dialectical materialism, the theory of class struggle, and the labor theory of value. — **Marx′ist, Marx′ian** (mark′sē·ən) *n. & adj.*

Marx·ism-Len·in·ism (märk′siz·əm-len′in·iz·əm) *n.* The modification of Marxist philosophy or doctrines attributed to Lenin. — **Marx′ist-Len′in·ist** *n., adj.*

Mar·y (mâr′ē) The mother of Jesus: also *Virgin Mary.*

Mary The sister of Lazarus and Martha. *Luke* x 39–42.

Mary Mag·da·lene (mag′də·lēn, mag′də·lē′nē) A woman from Magdala out of whom Jesus cast seven devils, often identified with the penitent sinner whom Jesus forgave.

mar·zi·pan (märt′sə·pan, mär′zə-) *n.* A confection of grated almonds, sugar, and white of eggs, usu. made into a paste and molded into various shapes: also called *marchpane.* [< G < Ital. < Med.L *matapanus* a Venetian coin]

-mas *combining form* Mass; a (specified) festival or its celebration: *Christmas.* [< MASS²]

mas·car·a (mas·kar′ə) *n.* A cosmetic preparation used to darken or tint the eyelashes and eyebrows. [< Sp. *mascara* mask < Arabic *maskharah* buffoon]

mas·cot (mas′kot, -kət) *n.* A person, animal, or object thought to bring good luck by its presence. [< F < Provençal *mascot*, dim. of *masco* sorcerer, lit., mask]

mas·cu·line (mas′kyə·lin) *adj.* **1.** Of or pertaining to the male sex; male. **2.** Of, pertaining to, typical of, or appropriate for men or boys: *masculine* sports. **3.** Mannish: said of a female. **4.** *Gram.* Applicable to males only or to persons or things classified, as in declension, as male. — *n. Gram.* **1.** The masculine gender. **2.** A word or form belonging to the masculine gender. [< OF < L < *masculus* male] — **mas′cu·line·ly** *adv.* — **mas′cu·lin′i·ty, mas′cu·line·ness** *n.*

masculine rhyme Rhyme in which the primary stress and the rhyme fall upon the final or only syllable, as in *breaks, takes,* and *alert, convert.*

ma·ser (mā′zər) *n. Physics* Any of various devices that generate or amplify electromagnetic waves of precise frequency without loss of frequency and phase, by using the excess energy of an atomic or molecular system. [< m(icro-wave) a(mplification by) s(timulated) e(mission of) r(adiation)]

mash (mash) *n.* **1.** A soft, pulpy mixture or mass. **2.** A mixture of meal, bran, etc., and water, fed warm to horses and cattle. **3.** Crushed or ground grain or malt, steeped in hot water to produce wort for making beer. — *v.t.* **1.** To crush into a mash or pulp. **2.** To steep (malt, grain meal, etc.) in hot water to produce wort. [OE *max-*, *māsc* (*wyrt*) mash (wort), infused malt]

mash·er (mash′ər) *n.* **1.** One who or that which mashes. **2.** *Slang* A man who flirts or attempts familiarities, usu. with women unknown to him.

mash·ie (mash′ē) *n.* In golf, a five iron. Also **mash′·y** [? Alter. of F *massue* club < Celtic]

mask (mask, mäsk) *n.* **1.** A covering used to conceal all or part of the face; esp.: **a** A covering, often grotesque or comic, worn at a masquerade, at Halloween, etc. **b** A large, headlike covering for an actor's face, used to represent a specific character or trait, as in Greek and Roman drama. **c** A covering made of heavy wire or other material, worn to protect the face from a fencing foil, baseball, glass, etc. **d** A gas mask. **2.** A cast of a face, usu. made of plaster. **3.** That which hides or conceals something from the sight or mind: under the *mask* of piety. **4.** One who wears a mask. **5.** A masquerade. **6.** See MASQUE. **7.** *Mil.* A screen or cover for concealing any military installation or operation. — *v.t.* **1.** To cover (the face, head, etc.) with a mask. **2.** To disguise. — *v.i.* **3.** To put on a mask; assume a disguise. [< F < Ital. < Arabic *maskharah* buffoon] — **masked** *adj.* — **mas′ker** *n.*

MASKS
a Greek tragedy. *b* Greek comedy. *c* Tibetan ceremonial. *d* Ancient Shinto. *e* Domino.

mask·ing tape (mas′king, mäs′-) An adhesive tape to cover those parts of a surface not to be painted, sprayed, etc.

mas·o·chism (mas′ə·kiz′əm) *n. Psychol.* A condition in which sexual gratification depends largely on undergoing physical pain or humiliation. **2.** A tendency to derive pleasure from one's own suffering. [after Leopold von Sacher-*Masoch*, 1835–95, Austrian novelist, who described this condition] — **mas′o·chist** *n.* — **mas′o·chis′tic** *adj.* — **mas′o·chis′ti·cal·ly** (-kə-lē, -klē) *adv.*

ma·son (mā′sən) *n.* **1.** One skilled in building with stone, brick, concrete, etc. **2.** A stonecutter. — *v.t.* To build of or strengthen with brick, stone, etc. [< OF < Med.L *matio, macio, -onis,* prob. < Gmc.]

Ma·son (mā′sən) *n.* Freemason. — **Ma′son·ry** *n.*

ma·son·ic (mə·son′ik) *adj.* **1.** *Usu. cap.* Of, pertaining to, or like Freemasons or Freemasonry. **2.** Of or pertaining to masons or masonry.

Ma·son·ite (mā′sən·īt) *n.* A tough fiberboard made from wood fibers, used as a building and construction material: a trade name. Also **ma′son·ite.**

Ma·son jar (mā′sən) A glass jar having a tightly fitting screw top, used for canning and preserving. [after John L. *Mason,* 19th c. American inventor]

ma·son·ry (mā′sən·rē) *n. pl.* **·ries 1.** The art or work of a mason. **2.** That which is built by masons.

masque (mask, mäsk) *n.* **1.** An elaborately staged dramatic performance, popular during the 16th and 17th centuries in England; also, something written for this. **2.** A masquerade. Also spelled *mask.* [See MASK.]

mas·quer·ade (mas′kə·rād′, mäs′-) *n.* **1.** A social gathering in which the guests are masked and dressed in fancy costumes. **2.** The costumes worn at such a gathering. **3.** A false show, disguise, or pretense. Also called *mask, masque.* — *v.i.* **·ad·ed, ·ad·ing 1.** To take part in a masquerade. **2.** To wear a mask or disguise. **3.** To disguise one's true character; assume a false appearance. [Alter. of F *mascarade* < Sp. < *máscara* mask] — **mas′quer·ad′er** *n.*

mass (mas, mäs) *n.* **1.** A body of matter having no definite shape but relatively large in size. **2.** An assemblage of individual parts or objects that collectively make up a single body. **3.** A great amount or number of anything. **4.** The principal or greater part of anything; majority. **5.** The volume or magnitude of a solid body; bulk; size. **6.** In painting, the solid, unified portions of color or light in a composition. **7.** *Physics* The measure of the inertia of a body, expressed as the quotient of the weight of the body divided by the acceleration due to gravity. — **the masses** The great body or majority of ordinary people. — *adj.* **1.** Attended by, designed for, characteristic of, or affecting a large mass of people. **2.** Done in a large-scale manner; produced in large amounts. **3.** Total; all-over: the *mass* effect. — *v.t. & v.i.* To form into a mass; assemble. [< OF < L *massa,* prob. < Gk. *maza* barley cake]

Mass (mas, mäs) *n. Eccl.* **1.** In the Roman Catholic and some Anglican churches, the eucharistic liturgy, consisting of various prayers and ritual ceremonies and regarded as a commemoration or repetition of Christ's sacrifice on the Cross. **2.** A celebration of this liturgy. **3.** A musical setting for some of the fixed portions of this liturgy. [OE < LL < L *missa,* pp. fem. of *mittere* to send, dismiss < *ite, missa est* go, you are dismissed; said by the priest]

Mas·sa·chu·set (mas′ə·chōō′sit) *n.* **1.** One of a large tribe of North American Indians of Algonquian stock, formerly inhabiting the region around Massachusetts Bay. **2.** Their language. Also **Mas′sa·chu′sett.** [< Algonquian (Massachuset) < *mass* big + *wadchu* hill + *es,* dim. + *et* at the]

mas·sa·cre (mas/ə·kər)　*n.*　**1.** A savage and indiscriminate killing of human beings, as in warfare, acts of persecution, revenge, etc.　**2.** *U.S. Informal* A crushing defeat, as in sports.　— *v.t.* **·cred** (-kərd), **·cring** **1.** To kill indiscriminately or in great numbers.　**2.** *U.S. Informal* To defeat severely, as in sports.　[< MF < OF, ? < *mache-col* butcher < *macher* to smash + *col* neck]　— **mas/sa·crer** *n.*
　— **Syn.** (noun) A *massacre* is the killing of those who are defenseless or unresisting, as in barbarous warfare. *Slaughter* may be used in the same sense, but frequently is applied to any great loss of life in battle, riot, etc. In a more restricted sense, *slaughter* is used of the killing of animals for food. *Carnage* retains much of its original sense of the heaped up bodies of the slain, and refers to the result rather than to the process of a *massacre* or *slaughter*.
mas·sage (mə·säzh/)　*n.* A manual or mechanical manipulation of parts of the body, as by rubbing, kneading, slapping or the like, used to promote circulation, relax muscles, etc.　— *v.t.* **·saged**, **·sag·ing** To treat by massage.　[< F < L, ? < Gk. *massein* to knead]　— **mas·sag/er, mas·sag/ist** *n.*　— **mas·sa·geuse** (mas/ə·zhœz/) *n.fem.*
mas·seur (ma·sûr/, *Fr.* mȧ·sœr/)　*n.* A man who practices or gives massage.　[< F]　— **mas·seuse** (ma·sōoz/, -sōos/; *Fr.* mȧ·sœz/) *n.fem.*
mas·sive (mas/iv)　*adj.* **1.** Forming or constituting a large mass; having great bulk and weight; ponderous.　**2.** Relatively large or heavy: a *massive* head.　**3.** Imposing or impressive in scale, scope, degree, etc.　**4.** *Mineral.* Lacking definite or externally observable crystalline form.　**5.** *Geol.* Homogeneous, as certain rock formations.　**6.** *Pathol.* Extending over or affecting a large area: a *massive* swelling.　[< F *massif*]　— **mas/sive·ly** *adv.*　— **mas/sive·ness** *n.*
mass media The various means of disseminating information to a wide public audience, as newspapers, radio, etc.
mass meeting A large public gathering for the discussion or promotion of some topic or cause, usu. political.
mass number *Physics* The total number of nucleons of an atom; the integer nearest the observed mass of an isotope.
mass production The manufacture or production, usu. by machinery, of goods or articles in great numbers or quantities.　— **mass-pro·duced** (mas/prə·dōost/, -dyōost/) *adj.*
mass ratio *Aerospace* The ratio of the mass of a rocket at the time of liftoff to its mass after the fuel has been used up.
mass spectrograph *Physics* An instrument for determining the relative masses of electrically charged particles by passing a stream of them through a magnetic field and noting the variable deflections from a straight path.
mass·y (mas/ē)　*adj.* **mass·i·er, mass·i·est** Massive.　— **mass/i·ness** *n.*
mast¹ (mast, mäst)　*n.* **1.** *Naut.* A pole or spar set upright in a sailing vessel to sustain the yards, sails, etc.　**2.** Any large, upright pole, as of a derrick, crane, etc.　— **before the mast** Serving as a common sailor.　— *v.t.* To furnish with a mast or masts.　[OE *mæst*]
mast² (mast, mäst)　*n.* The fruit of the oak, beech, etc., when used as food for swine.　[OE *mæst* mast, fodder]
mast- Var. of MASTO-.
mas·ta·ba (mas/tə·bə)　*n.* In ancient Egypt, an oblong building with sloping sides and a flat top, covering the mouth of a burial pit and used as a chapel and place of offering. Also **mas/ta·bah**.　[< Arabic *mastabah* bench]
mas·ter (mas/tər, mäs/-)　*n.* **1.** One who has control, direction, or authority over someone or something, as over a household, an animal, etc.　**2.** One exceptionally gifted or skilled in an art, science, etc.: a *master* of oratory.　**3.** A craftsman or worker whose skill or experience qualifies him to practice his craft on his own and to train apprentices.　**4.** One who has the ability to control or dispose of something to good advantage.　**5.** A teacher or leader in philosophy, religion, etc., who has followers or disciples.　**6.** *Chiefly Brit.* A male teacher.　**7.** One who has received a Master of Arts degree.　**8.** One who has charge of or presides over a place, institution, ceremony, etc.: a *master* of ceremonies.　**9.** Something considered as having the power to control or influence: Never let fear be your *master*.　**10.** Something, as a matrix, stencil, etc., from which copies or impressions are made.　**11.** *Usu. cap.* A youth or boy; also, a title prefixed to a boy's name.　**12.** *Usu. cap.* A title of respect for or of address, now generally replaced by *Mister*.　**13.** In the Scottish peerage, the title of the eldest son or heir apparent of a viscount or baron.　**14.** A victor or conqueror.　**15.** *Law* An officer of the court who assists the judge.　— *v.t.* **1.** To bring under control; defeat.　**2.** To become expert in: to *master* Greek.　**3.** To control or govern as a master.　— *adj.* **1.** Of, pertaining to, or characteristic of a master.　**2.** Having or exercising control.　**3.** Principal; main: the *master* plan.　**4.** Designating a device or mechanism that controls, operates, or acts as a pattern or norm for something else: a *master* switch.　[OE < L *magnus* great]　— **mas/ter·dom** *n.*　— **mas/ter·hood** *n.*

master builder **1.** An architect.　**2.** One who supervises building construction.
mas·ter·ful (mas/tər·fəl, mäs/-)　*adj.* **1.** Vigorously bold or authoritative in conduct, decision, manner, etc.　**2.** Domineering; imperious.　**3.** Having or displaying the skill of a master.　— **mas/ter·ful·ly** *adv.*　— **mas/ter·ful·ness** *n.*
master key A key that will unlock two or more locks, each of which has its own key that fits no other lock.
mas·ter·ly (mas/tər·lē, mäs/-)　*adj.* Characteristic of or befitting a master: a *masterly* performance.　— *adv.* In a masterly manner.　— **mas/ter·li·ness** *n.*
master mechanic An able, experienced mechanic.
mas·ter·mind (mas/tər·mīnd/, mäs/-)　*n.* A person of great executive ability; esp., one who plans and directs at the highest levels of policy and strategy.　— *v.t.* To plan and direct (a project, etc.) at the highest strategic level.
Master of Arts **1.** A degree given by a college or university to a person who has completed a prescribed course of graduate study of at least one year in the humanities, social sciences, etc.　**2.** A person who has received this degree.
master of ceremonies **1.** A person presiding over an entertainment or dinner and introducing the performers or speakers.　**2.** A person who supervises the ceremonies at a public or formal function. Also called *emcee*.
Master of Science **1.** A degree given by a college or university to a person who has completed a prescribed course of graduate study of at least one year in science.　**2.** A person who has received this degree.
mas·ter·piece (mas/tər·pēs/, mäs/-)　*n.* **1.** Something of notable excellence; an unusually brilliant achievement.　**2.** Something considered the greatest achievement of its creator. Also **mas/ter·work/**.　[Trans. of G *meisterstück*]
mas·ter·ship (mas/tər·ship, mäs/-)　*n.* **1.** The state of being a master or ruler.　**2.** The status or function of a master.　**3.** The skill, experience, or authority of a master.
mas·ter·stroke (mas/tər·strōk/, mäs/-)　*n.* A masterly or decisive action or achievement.
mas·ter·y (mas/tər·ē, mäs/-)　*n.* *pl.* **·ter·ies** **1.** Superior knowledge or skill.　**2.** Victory or superiority, as in a contest.　**3.** The act of mastering a craft, technique, etc.
mast·head (mast/hed/, mäst/-)　*n.* **1.** *Naut.* The top of a mast.　**2.** The part of a periodical that gives the names of the editors, staff, and owners.　— *v.t.* To display at the masthead.
mas·tic (mas/tik)　*n.* **1.** A small Mediterranean evergreen tree of the cashew family.　**2.** The resin obtained from this tree, used in varnishes and as a flavoring agent.　[< F < LL < Gk. *mastichē*]
mas·ti·cate (mas/tə·kāt)　*v.t.* **·cat·ed, ·cat·ing** **1.** To chew.　**2.** To reduce, as rubber, to a pulp by crushing or kneading.　[< LL < Gk. *mastichaein* to gnash the teeth]　— **mas/ti·ca/tion** *n.*　— **mas/ti·ca/tor** *n.*
mas·ti·ca·to·ry (mas/tə·kə·tôr/ē, -tō/rē)　*adj.* **1.** Of or pertaining to mastication.　**2.** Adapted for chewing.　— *n.* *pl.* **·ries** A substance chewed to increase salivation.
mas·tiff (mas/tif, mäs/-)　*n.* A breed of large hunting dogs, having a thickset, heavy body, drooping ears, and pendulous lips.　[< OF < L pp. of *mansuescere* to tame]
mas·ti·tis (mas·tī/tis)　*n.* *Pathol.* Inflammation of the breast.
masto- *combining form Med.* The breast or the mammary glands. Also, before vowels, **mast-**.　[< Gk. *mastos* breast]
mas·to·don (mas/tə·don)　*n.* *Paleontol.* Any of various large, extinct mammals resembling the elephant.　[< NL < MAST- + Gk. *odous, odontos* tooth]
mas·toid (mas/toid)　*adj.* **1.** *Anat.* Designating a nipple-shaped process of the temporal bone located behind the ear.　**2.** Having the shape of a breast or nipple.　— *n.* The mastoid process.　[< Gk. < *mastos* breast + *eidos* form]
mas·toid·i·tis (mas/toid·ī/tis)　*n.* *Pathol.* Inflammation of the mastoid process.
mas·tur·bate (mas/tər·bāt)　*v.i.* **·bat·ed, ·bat·ing** To perform masturbation.　[< L *masturbatus*, pp. of *masturbari*]
mas·tur·ba·tion (mas/tər·bā/shən)　*n.* Stimulation of the sexual organs, usu. by oneself: also called *onanism*.　— **mas/·tur·ba/tor** *n.*
ma·su·ri·um (mə·sŏor/ē·əm)　*n.* A supposed metallic element whose place in the periodic table is now occupied by technetium.　[after *Masuria*, where first found]
mat¹ (mat)　*n.* **1.** A flat piece of material made of fiber, rushes, rubber, etc., and used primarily to cover floors; also, a smaller piece of this material, used to sit or lie on.　**2.** A thickly padded piece of material placed on the floor for protection in various gymnastic sports.　**3.** A small, flat piece of material, as lace, straw, or plastic, used as a table protection, ornament, etc.　**4.** Any dense, twisted, or tangled mass, as of hair.　— *v.* **mat·ted, mat·ting** *v.t.* **1.** To cover with or as with a mat or mats.　**2.** To knot or entangle into a mat.　— *v.i.* **3.** To become entangled together.　[OE < LL *matta*]

mat² (mat)   *n.* **1.** A border of cardboard or other material, serving as the frame or part of the frame of a picture. **2.** *Printing* A matrix. **3.** A lusterless, dull, or roughened surface, as on metal or glass. — *v.t.* **mat·ted, mat·ting 1.** To produce a dull surface on, as on metal or glass. **2.** To furnish (a picture) with a mat. — *adj.* Having a lusterless surface. [OF, defeated]

mat·a·dor (mat′ə·dôr)   *n.* In bullfighting, the man who kills the bull after completing various maneuvers with a cape in order to tire the animal. [< Sp. < *matar* to slay]

match¹ (mach)   *n.* **1.** One who or that which is similar to another in some quality or characteristic. **2.** One who or that which is exactly equal to another. **3.** One who or that which is able to cope with or oppose another as an equal. **4.** Either of two things that harmonize or correspond with each other. **5.** A suitable or fit pair. **6.** A game or contest. **7.** A marriage or mating; also, an agreement to marry or mate. **8.** A possible partner in marriage. — *v.t.* **1.** To be similar to or in accord with in quality, degree, etc. **2.** To make, provide, or select as equals or as suitable for one another: to *match* pearls. **3.** To cause to correspond; adapt: *Match* your expenses to your income. **4.** To compare so as to decide superiority; test. **5.** To set (equal opponents) in opposition. **6.** To equal; oppose successfully. **7.** To flip (a coin or coins) so as to compare or bet on the faces that land upright; also, to flip coins in this manner with (another person). **8.** To place together as mates; marry. — *v.i.* **9.** To be equal or similar. **10.** To be married; mate. [OE *gemæcca* companion] — **match′a·ble** *adj.* — **match′er** *n.*

match² (mach)   *n.* **1.** A splinter of soft wood or a piece of waxed thread or cardboard tipped with a combustible composition that ignites by friction. **2.** A wick or cord formerly used for firing cannon. [< OF *mesche* wick]

match·box (mach′boks′)   *n.* A small box for matches.

match·less (mach′lis)   *adj.* Having no match or equal; peerless. — **match′less·ly** *adv.* — **match′less·ness** *n.*

match·lock (mach′lok′)   *n.* **1.** An old type of musket fired by igniting the powder with a slow-burning wick or match. **2.** The gunlock on such a musket.

match·mak·er¹ (mach′mā′kər)   *n.* **1.** One who tries to bring about a marriage between other persons. **2.** One who arranges an athletic match. — **match′mak′ing** *adj.* & *n.*

match·mak·er² (mach′mā′kər)   *n.* One who makes matches for lighting. — **match′mak′ing** *adj.* & *n.*

match play In golf, a form of competitive play in which the score is computed by totaling the number of holes won or lost by each side. Compare MEDAL PLAY.

mate¹ (māt)   *n.* **1.** Something matched, paired, or joined with another. **2.** A husband or wife. **3.** The male or female of two animals paired for propagation. **4.** A companion; comrade. **5.** An officer of a merchant vessel, ranking next below the captain. **6.** *Naval* A petty officer. — *v.* **mat·ed, mat·ing** *v.t.* **1.** To join together; pair. **2.** To join in marriage. **3.** To unite for breeding, as animals. — *v.i.* **4.** To marry. **5.** To pair. **6.** To consort; associate. [< MLG < *ge-* together + *mat* meat, food]

mate² (māt)   *v.t.* **mat·ed, mat·ing** In chess, to checkmate. — *n.* A checkmate. — *interj.* Checkmate.

ma·te³ (mä′tā, mat′ā)   *n.* **1.** An infusion of the leaves of a Brazilian holly, much used as a beverage in South America. **2.** The plant itself. [< Sp. < Quechua *mati* calabash]

ma·ter (mā′tər, mä′-)   *n. Brit. Informal* Mother. [< L]

ma·te·ri·al (mə·tir′ē·əl)   *n.* **1.** That of which anything is or may be composed or constructed. **2.** Anything that may be used in creating, working up, or developing something. **3.** *pl.* The tools, instruments, etc., for doing something. **4.** Cloth or fabric. — *adj.* **1.** Of, pertaining to, or composed of matter; physical. **2.** Of, related to, or affecting the body or sensual appetites: *material* well-being. **3.** Concerned with or devoted to things primarily physical rather than spiritual or intellectual. **4.** Substantial; important. **5.** Relevant; pertinent: with *to*. [< LL < L *materia* matter, stuff]

ma·te·ri·al·ism (mə·tir′ē·əl·iz′əm)   *n.* **1.** *Philos.* The doctrine that everything in the universe is reducible to matter and can be explained in terms of physical laws. **2.** Undue regard for the material rather than the spiritual or intellectual aspects of life. — **ma·te′ri·al·ist** *n.* — **ma·te′ri·al·is′tic** *adj.* — **ma·te′ri·al·is′ti·cal·ly** *adv.*

ma·te·ri·al·ize (mə·tir′ē·əl·īz′)   *v.* **·ized, ·iz·ing** *v.t.* **1.** To give material or actual form to. **2.** In spiritualism, to cause (a spirit, etc.) to appear in visible form. **3.** To make materialistic. — *v.i.* **4.** To assume material or visible form; appear. **5.** To take form or shape; be realized. — **ma·te′ri·al·i·za′tion** *n.* — **ma·te′ri·al·iz′er** *n.*

ma·te·ri·al·ly (mə·tir′ē·əl·ē)   *adv.* **1.** In an important manner or to a considerable degree. **2.** Physically. **3.** In respect to matter as distinguished from form.

ma·te·ri·a med·i·ca (mə·tir′ē·ə med′i·kə)   *Med.* **1.** Substances, as drugs, etc., employed as remedial agents. **2.** The branch of medicine that treats of these substances. [< Med.L < *materia* matter + *medica*, fem. of *medicus* medical]

ma·te·ri·el (mə·tir′ē·el′)   *n.* **1.** The equipment and supplies of a military force. **2.** The equipment of any organization. Also *Fr.* **ma·té·riel** (må·tā·ryel′). [< F, material]

ma·ter·nal (mə·tûr′nəl)   *adj.* **1.** Pertaining to a mother; motherly. **2.** Inherited from one's mother. **3.** Coming through the relationship of a mother. [< F < L < *mater* mother] — **ma·ter′nal·ly** *adv.*

ma·ter·ni·ty (mə·tûr′nə·tē)   *n. pl.* **·ties 1.** The state of being a mother. **2.** The qualities of a mother. — *adj.* **1.** Fashioned for pregnant women: *maternity* clothes. **2.** Designed to accommodate women and babies during and after childbirth: a *maternity* ward. [< F < L *maternitas*]

math (math)   *n. U.S. Informal* Mathematics.

math·e·mat·i·cal (math′ə·mat′i·kəl)   *adj.* **1.** Of, pertaining to, or like mathematics. **2.** Used in mathematics. **3.** Rigidly exact or precise. Also **math′e·mat′ic.** [< L < Gk. < *manthanein* to learn] — **math′e·mat′i·cal·ly** *adv.*

math·e·ma·ti·cian (math′ə·mə·tish′ən)   *n.* One who specializes or is expert in mathematics.

math·e·mat·ics (math′ə·mat′iks)   *n.pl.* (*construed as sing.*) The study of quantity, form, arrangement, and magnitude; esp., the methods and processes for disclosing the properties and relations of quantities and magnitudes.

mat·in (mat′in)   *n.* **1.** *pl. Eccl.* **a** The prescribed prayers that, with lauds, constitute the first of the seven canonical hours. **b** In the Anglican Church, the order for public worship in the morning. **2.** *Poetic* Any morning song. — *adj.* Of matins or the morning: also **mat′in·al.** Also spelled *mattin.* [< OF < L *matutinus* (*tempus*) (time) of the morning]

mat·i·nee (mat′ə·nā′)   *n.* A performance or entertainment, as a play, concert, etc., held in the daytime, usu. in the afternoon. Also **mat′i·née′.** [< F *matin* morning]

mat·ing (mā′ting)   *n.* The act of pairing or matching.

matri- *combining form* Mother. [< L *mater* mother]

ma·tri·arch (mā′trē·ärk)   *n.* A woman holding the position corresponding to that of a patriarch in her family or tribe. — **ma′tri·ar′chal, ma′tri·ar′chic** *adj.*

ma·tri·ar·chy (mā′trē·ar′kē)   *n. pl.* **·chies** A social organization having the mother as the head of the family, in which descent is traced through the mother.

mat·ri·cide (mat′rə·sīd)   *n.* **1.** The killing of one's mother. **2.** One who kills his mother. [< L < *mater* mother + *caedere* to kill] — **mat′ri·ci′dal** *adj.*

ma·tric·u·late (mə·trik′yə·lāt)   *v.t.* & *v.i.* **·lat·ed, ·lat·ing** To register or enroll in a college or university as a candidate for a degree. — *n.* One who is so enrolled. [< Med.L < *matriculare* to enroll < *matrix* womb] — **ma·tric′u·lant** *n.* — **ma·tric′u·la′tion** *n.* — **ma·tric′u·la′tor** *n.*

mat·ri·mo·ny (mat′rə·mō′nē)   *n. pl.* **·nies 1.** The state or condition of being married. **2.** The act, ceremony, or sacrament of marriage. [< L < *mater* mother] — **mat′ri·mo′ni·al** *adj.* — **mat′ri·mo′ni·al·ly** *adv.*

ma·trix (mā′triks)   *n. pl.* **ma·trix·es** or **ma·tri·ces** (mā′trə·sēz, mat′rə-) **1.** That in which anything originates, develops, takes shape, or is contained. **2.** The womb. **3.** A mold in or from which anything is cast or shaped. **4.** *Printing* **a** A mold in which the face of a type is cast. **b** In stereotyping, a papier-mâché or other impression of a form from which a plate for printing may be made. [< L, womb]

ma·tron (mā′trən)   *n.* **1.** A married woman or widow who is usu. a mother. **2.** A female attendant or guard, as in a woman's prison, rest room, etc. **3.** A female superintendent of an institution, etc. [< OF < L < *mater* mother] — **ma′tron·li·ness** *n.* — **ma′tron·ly** *adj.* & *adv.*

matron of honor A married woman acting as chief attendant to a bride at a wedding.

mat·ted (mat′id)   *adj.* **1.** Covered with or made from mats or matting. **2.** Tangled or twisted in a mass. **3.** Covered with a dense or twisted growth.

mat·ter (mat′ər)   *n.* **1.** That which makes up the substance of anything; constituent material. **2.** That which is material and physical, occupies space, and is perceived by the senses. **3.** A specific kind of substance: organic *matter.* **4.** A subject, event, or situation that is an object of discussion, concern, etc.: a *matter* of faith. **5.** Cause, occasion, or reason: usu. with *of* or *for*: a *matter* of great concern. **6.** Importance; consequence: It's of no *matter* what happens. **7.** Something of importance or consequence. **8.** A usu. unpleasant condition or circumstance: with *the*: What's the *matter* with you? **9.** The content or meaning of a book, etc., as distinguished from the style or form. **10.** An indefinite amount, quantity, etc.: a *matter* of a few dollars. **11.** Pus. **12.** That which is written, printed, etc.: *matter* for reading. **13.** Anything sent by mail: third-class *matter.* **14.** *Printing* **a** Type set up or composed. **b** Material to be set up; copy. — *v.i.* **1.** To be of concern; signify: It *matters* little. **2.** To form or discharge pus. [< OF < L *materia* stuff]

mat·ter-of-course (mat′ər·əv·kôrs′, -kōrs′)   *adj.* **1.** To be expected. **2.** Accepting things as a matter of course.

matter of course Something expected to follow as a natural or logical result.

MATHEMATICAL SYMBOLS

Symbol	Meaning	Symbol	Meaning
$+$	Plus; positive; sign of addition	Σ	Summation of
$-$	Minus; negative; sign of subtraction	$\sum_{1}^{n}$	Summation of n terms, one for each positive integer from 1 to n
$\pm$	Plus or minus	Π	Product of
$\mp$	Minus or plus	$\prod_{1}^{n}$	Product of n terms, one for each positive integer from 1 to n
$\times, \cdot$	Multiplied by	$\int$	Integral of
$\div, :$	Divided by	$\int_{b}^{a}$	Definite integral between limits a and b
$=, ::$	Equals	$\doteq, \rightarrow$	Approaches as a limit
$\cong$	Approximately equal; congruent	$f(x), F(x), \phi(x)$	Function of x
$>$	Greater than	Δ	Increment of, as Δy
$<$	Less than	d	Differential, as dx
$/$	Is not; does not: drawn through another symbol, as $a \neq b$, a is not equal to b	$\frac{dy}{dx}, f'(x)$	Derivative of $y = f(x)$ with respect to x
$\geqq$	Greater than or equal to	δ	Variation, as δy
$\leqq$	Less than or equal to	π	Pi; the ratio of the circumference and a diameter of the same circle; 3.14159...
$\sim$	Similar to; equivalent		
$\therefore$	Therefore	$n!, \underline{\lfloor n}$	n factorial; factorial n
$\because$	Since; because	$(), [], \{\}$	Indicate that the enclosed symbols are to be treated as a single number
$\equiv$	Identical; identically equal to	$-$	Indicates that the symbols below it are to be treated as a single number, as $\overline{PQ}^2$. See VINCULUM.
$\propto$	Directly proportional to; varies directly as		
∞	Infinity	$\angle$	Angle
i	Square root of minus one	$\parallel$	Parallel to
a_1, a_2, etc.	Particular values of a (a variable)	$\perp$	Perpendicular to; perpendicular
a^n	a multiplied by itself n times	$\triangle$	Triangle
$\frac{a}{b}$	a divided by b	$\llcorner$	Right angle
$\sqrt{a}$	Square root of a. See RADICAL SIGN.	$'$	Minutes of arc; prime
$\sqrt[n]{a}$	nth root of a	$''$	Seconds of arc; double prime
e, ϵ	Base of natural system of logarithms; 2.718...		

mat·ter-of-fact (mat'ər·əv·fakt') *adj.* Closely adhering to facts; not fanciful; unimaginative; practical.

Mat·thew (math'yōo) One of the twelve apostles and author of the first Gospel: called **Saint Matthew**. — *n.* The first Gospel of the New Testament.

mat·tin (mat'in) See MATIN.

mat·ting[1] (mat'ing) *n.* **1.** A woven fabric of fiber, straw, or other material, used as a floor covering, for packing, etc. **2.** The act of making mats. **3.** Mats collectively.

mat·ting[2] (mat'ing) *n.* **1.** A mat for framing a picture. **2.** A dull, lusterless surface, as on metal or glass.

mat·tock (mat'ək) *n.* Either of two tools resembling a pickax, having a blade on one end and a pick on the other, or a blade on each end. [OE *mattuc*]

mat·tress (mat'rəs) *n.* A large pad made of a strong fabric and filled with a resilient material, as cotton, rubber, hair, feathers, etc., used on or as a bed. [< OF < Ital. < Arabic *matrah* place where something is thrown]

MATTOCK

mat·u·rate (mach'ŏo·rāt, mat'yŏo-) *v.i.* **·rat·ed**, **·rat·ing** **1.** To form pus; suppurate. **2.** To ripen or mature. [< L *maturus* ripe, fully developed] — **mat'u·ra'tion** *n.* — **mat'u·ra'tive** *adj.*

ma·ture (mə·tyŏor', -tŏor', -chŏor') *adj.* **1.** Completely developed; fully ripe, as plants, fruit, animals, etc. **2.** Highly developed in intellect, outlook, etc.: a *mature* thinker. **3.** Thoroughly developed, perfected, etc.: a *mature* scheme. **4.** Due and payable: a *mature* bond. — *v.* **·tured**, **·tur·ing** *v.t.* **1.** To cause to ripen; bring to full development. **2.** To perfect; complete. — *v.i.* **3.** To come to full development. **4.** To become due, as a note. [< L *maturus* ripe, of full age] — **ma·ture'ly** *adv.* — **ma·ture'ness** *n.*

ma·tu·ri·ty (mə·tyŏor'ə·tē, -tŏor'-, -chŏor'-) *n.* **1.** The state of being mature. **2.** Full physical development. **3.** The time at which a note, etc., becomes due.

ma·tu·ti·nal (mə·tŏo'tə·nəl, -tyŏo'-, mach·ə·tī'nəl) *adj.* Of, pertaining to, or taking place in the morning; early. [< L *matutinus* early in the morning] — **ma·tu'ti·nal·ly** *adv.*

mat·zo (mät'sə) *n.*, *pl.* **·zos** or **·zot** (-sōt) or **·zoth** (-sōth, -sōt) A large, flat piece of unleavened bread, traditionally eaten during Passover. Also **mat'za**, **mat'zah**, **mat'zoh**. [< Hebrew *matstāh* unleavened bread]

maud·lin (môd'lin) *adj.* **1.** Excessively and tearfully emotional or sentimental. **2.** Overly sentimental or emotional from too much liquor. — *Syn.* See SENTIMENTAL. [< OF *Madeleine* (Mary) Magdalen, often depicted weeping]

maul (môl) *n.* A heavy mallet for driving wedges, piles, etc. — *v.t.* **1.** To beat and bruise. **2.** To handle roughly; manhandle; abuse. Also spelled *mall*. [< OF *mail* < L *malleus* hammer] — **maul'er** *n.*

Mau Mau (mou' mou') *pl.* **Mau Mau** or **Mau Maus** A member of a secret society of Kikuyu tribesmen in Kenya organized against European colonists. [< native name]

maun·der (môn'dər) *v.i.* **1.** To talk in a wandering or incoherent manner; drivel. **2.** To move dreamily or idly. [? Freq. of obs. *maund* to beg] — **maun'der·er** *n.*

Maun·dy Thursday (môn'dē) The day before Good Friday, commemorating the Last Supper of Christ. [< OF < L *mandatum* command]

Mau·ser (mou'zər) *n.* A magazine rifle having great range and velocity; also, a type of automatic pistol: a trade name. [after P. S. *Mauser*, 1838–1914, German inventor]

mau·so·le·um (mô'sə·lē'əm) *n.* *pl.* **·le·ums** or **·le·a** (-lē'ə) A large, stately tomb. [< L < Gk. *Mausōleion*, tomb of King Mausolus at Halicarnassus] — **mau'so·le'an** *adj.*

mauve (mōv) *n.* Any of various purplish rose shades. [< F, mallow]

mav·er·ick (mav'ər·ik) *n.* **1.** *U.S.* An unbranded or orphaned animal, as a calf, traditionally belonging to the first person to claim or brand it. **2.** *U.S. Informal* One who is unorthodox in his ideas, attitudes, etc. [after Samuel A. *Maverick*, 1803–70, Texas lawyer who did not brand his cattle]

ma·vour·neen (mə·vŏor'nēn, -vôr'-) *n.* My darling. Also **ma·vour'nin.** [< Irish *mo muirnin*]

maw (mô) *n.* **1.** The jaws, mouth, or gullet of a voracious mammal or fish. **2.** The craw of a bird. **3.** The stomach. [OE *maga* stomach]

mawk·ish (mô'kish) *adj.* **1.** Characterized by false or feeble sentimentality. **2.** Sickening or insipid. [< ON *mathkr* maggot] — **mawk'ish·ly** *adv.* — **mawk'ish·ness** *n.*

max·il·la (mak·sil′ə) *n. pl.* **max·il·lae** (mak·sil′ē) **1.** In vertebrates, the upper jaw or jawbone. **2.** *Zool.* In insects, crustaceans, etc., either of two pairs of jawlike appendages behind the mandibles. [< L *mala* jaw]

max·il·lar·y (mak′sə·ler′ē, mak·sil′ər·ē) *adj.* Of, pertaining to, or situated near the upper jaw or a maxilla. — *n. pl.* **·lar·ies** The upper jaw or a maxilla.

max·im (mak′sim) *n.* A brief statement of a general principle, truth, or rule of conduct. [< F < L *maxima* (*sententia, propositio*) greatest (authority, premise)]

max·i·mal (mak′sə·məl) *adj.* Of or being a maximum; greatest or highest possible. — **max′i·mal·ly** *adv.*

max·i·mize (mak′sə·mīz) *v.t.* **·mized, ·miz·ing** To make as great as possible; increase or intensify to the maximum.

max·i·mum (mak′sə·məm) *n. pl.* **·mums** or **·ma** (-mə) **1.** The greatest possible quantity, amount, or degree. **2.** The greatest quantity, degree, etc., reached or recorded. — *adj.* **1.** Consisting of the greatest amount or degree possible, permissible, attainable, etc. **2.** Of or pertaining to a maximum or maximums. [< L *magnus* great]

may¹ (mā) *v.* Present: *sing.* **may, may** (*Archaic* **may·est** or **mayst**), **may,** *pl.* **may;** past: **might** A defective verb now used only in the present and past tenses as an auxiliary followed by the infinitive without *to*, or elliptically with the infinitive understood, to express: **1.** Permission or allowance: *May* I go? **2.** Desire, prayer, or wish: *May* your tribe increase! **3.** Contingency, especially in clauses of result, concession, purpose, etc.: He died that we *might* live. **4.** Possibility: You *may* be right. **5.** *Law* Obligation or duty: the equivalent of *must* or *shall*. [OE *mæg*]

may² (mā) *n. Brit.* A species of hawthorn having white, rose, or crimson flowers. [< MAY, when it blooms]

May (mā) *n.* **1.** The fifth month of the year, containing 31 days. **2.** The prime of life; youth. **3.** May Day festivities. [< OF < L (*mensis*) *Maius* (month of) May]

Ma·ya¹ (mä′yə) *n.* In Hindu philosophy, illusion, often personified as a maiden: also **ma′ya.** [< Skt. *māyā* illusion]

Ma·ya² (mä′yə) *n.* **1.** One of a tribe of Central American Indians, having an early advanced civilization and still living in Yucatán, northern Guatemala, and British Honduras. **2.** The language of the Mayas. — *adj.* Of the Mayas, their culture, or their language. — **Ma′yan** *adj. & n.*

May·ap·ple A North American herb whose roots yield a purgative; also, its edible fruit. Also called *mandrake*.

may·be (mā′bē) *adv.* Perhaps; possibly. [< (*it*) *may be*]

May Day The first day of May, traditionally celebrated as a spring festival and, in recent times, celebrated in some countries by demonstrations commemorating labor.

may·est (mā′ist) May: archaic or poetic second person singular, present tense of MAY: used with *thou*. Also **mayst.**

may·flow·er (mā′flou′ər) *n.* Any of various plants that blossom in the spring; esp., in the U.S., the trailing arbutus, and in Great Britain, the hawthorn.

Mayflower The ship on which the Pilgrims came to America in 1620.

May fly Any of a large group of insects, having transparent forewings, a relatively long nymphal life, and a short-lived adult stage: also called *dayfly, ephemerid.* Also **may′fly** *n.*

may·hem (mā′hem) *n.* **1.** *Law* The offense of injuring a person's body so as to render him less able to defend himself. **2.** Any situation characterized by violence, confusion, noise, etc. [< OF *mehaing, mahaym*]

may·on·naise (mā′ə·nāz′, mī′-) *n.* **1.** A dressing, as for salads, made by beating together raw egg yolk, butter or olive oil, lemon juice or vinegar, and condiments. **2.** A dish, as of meat or fish, mixed with this dressing. [< F]

may·or (mā′ər, mâr) *n.* The chief magistrate of a city, borough, or municipal corporation. [< F < L *major* greater] — **may′or·al** *adj.*

may·or·al·ty (mā′ər·əl·tē, mâr′əl-) *n. pl.* **·ties** The office or term of service of a mayor. [< OF *mairalté*]

May·pole (mā′pōl′) *n.* A decorated pole around which dancing takes place on May Day. Also **may′pole′.**

May·time (mā′tīm′) *n.* The month of May. Also **May′·tide′** (-tīd′).

may tree *Brit.* The hawthorn.

maze (māz) *n.* **1.** An intricate network of paths or passages; a labyrinth. **2.** A state of bewilderment, uncertainty, or perplexity. [< AMAZE] — **ma′zy** *adj.* — **maz′i·ly** *adv*

ma·zur·ka (mə·zûr′kə, -zŏŏr′-) *n.* **1.** A lively Polish dance in 3/4 time. **2.** The music for such a dance. Also **ma·zour′·ka.** [< Polish, woman from Mazovia, a province]

maz·zard cherry (maz′ərd) The sweet cherry, esp. the fruit of a wild sweet cherry. [Earlier *mazer* maple wood]

Mc- See also MAC-.

Mc·Car·thy·ism (mə·kär′thē·iz′əm) *n.* The practice of making public accusations of disloyalty or corruption, usu. with little evidence, ostensibly to expose pro-Communist activity. [after Joseph *McCarthy*, 1909–57, U.S. Senator]

Mc·Coy (mə·koi′), **the (real)** *U.S. Slang* The authentic person or thing.

Mc·In·tosh (mak′ən·tosh) *n. U.S. & Canadian* A red, early autumn, eating apple. Also **McIntosh red.** [after John *McIntosh* of Ontario, who discovered it about 1796]

M-Day (em′dā′) *n. Mil.* Mobilization day, the day the Department of Defense orders mobilization for war.

me (mē) *pron.* The objective case of the pronoun *I.* [OE *mē*, dat. sing.]
◆ **It's me,** etc. Anyone who answers the question "Who's there?" by saying "It's me" is using acceptable informal idiom. Here *It is I* would seem stilted, although at the formal level of writing it is expected: They have warned me that *it is I*, and not he, who will have to bear the burden.

mead¹ (mēd) *n.* An alcoholic beverage of fermented honey and water to which yeast and spices are added. [OE *medu*]

mead² (mēd) *n. Poetic* A meadow. [OE *mǣd*]

mead·ow (med′ō) *n.* **1.** A tract of grassland, usu. used for grazing or for growing hay. **2.** A low or level piece of land, as near a river, used for growing grass or hay. [OE *mǣdwe*, oblique case of *mǣd*] — **mead′ow·y** *adj.*

mead·ow·lark (med′ō·lärk′) *n.* Any of various songbirds of North America, marked with black on a yellow breast.

mea·ger (mē′gər) *adj.* **1.** Deficient in quantity or quality; scanty; inadequate. **2.** Lacking in fertility, strength, or richness: *meager* soil. **3.** Thin; emaciated. Also *Brit.* **mea′·gre.** [< OF < L *macer* lean] — **mea′ger·ly** *adv.*

meal¹ (mēl) *n.* **1.** The edible seeds of any grain, coarsely ground and unbolted. **2.** Any powdery material. [OE *melu*]

meal² (mēl) *n.* **1.** The food served or eaten regularly at certain times during the day. **2.** The time or occasion of taking such food. [OE *mǣl* measure, time, meal]

meal·ie (mē′lē) *n.* In Africa: **a** An ear of corn (def. 1). **b** *pl.* Corn. [< Afrikaans *milje* < Pg. *milho* millet]

meal ticket 1. A ticket or card bought for a specified price and redeemable at a restaurant for food. **2.** *U.S. Slang* One who or that which provides a livelihood for another.

meal·time (mēl′tīm′) *n.* The habitual time for a meal.

meal·y (mē′lē) *adj.* **meal·i·er, meal·i·est 1.** Resembling meal; dry; powdery; soft. **2.** Containing meal. **3.** Springkled or covered with or as with meal. **4.** Anemic or pale in color, etc. **5.** Mealy-mouthed. — **meal′i·ness** *n.*

meal·y-mouthed (mē′lē·mouth′, -mouthd′) *adj.* Unwilling to express facts or opinions plainly and frankly.

mean¹ (mēn) *v.* **meant** (ment), **mean·ing** *v.t.* **1.** To have in mind as a purpose or intent. **2.** To intend or design for some purpose, destination, etc.: Was that remark *meant* for me? **3.** To intend to express or convey: That's not what I *meant.* **4.** To have as the particular sense or significance. — *v.i.* **5.** To have disposition or intention: He *means* well. **6.** To be of specified importance or influence: Her work *means* everything to her. [OE *mǣnan* to tell]

mean² (mēn) *adj.* **1.** Poor or inferior in grade or quality. **2.** Having little worth or consequence. **3.** Ignoble in mind or character. **4.** Miserly; stingy. **5.** Poor in appearance; shabby. **6.** Humble in birth, rank, or station. **7.** *Informal* Disagreeable; nasty; vicious. **8.** *Informal* Ashamed; humiliated. **9.** *U.S. Informal* Ill; out of sorts: to feel *mean*. **10.** *U.S. Informal* Difficult; troublesome. **11.** *U.S. Slang* Excellent; expert. [OE (*ge*) *mǣne* ordinary]

mean³ (mēn) *n.* **1.** *pl.* The medium, method, or instrument by which some end is or may be accomplished. **2.** *pl.* Money; wealth. **3.** The middle point or state between two extremes. **4.** Avoidance of excess; moderation. **5.** *Math.* **a** A number or quantity contained within the range of a set of numbers or quantities and representative of each of the set; an average. **b** Arithmetic mean (which see). **c** Geometric mean (which see). **d** The second or third term in a proportion containing four terms. — **by all means** Without hesitation; certainly. — **by any means** In any manner possible; at all; somehow. — **by means of** With the help of; through using. — **by no** (or **no manner of**) **means** Most certainly not; on no account whatever. — *adj.* **1.** Intermediate or average in size, degree, quality, etc.; medium. **2.** Halfway between extremes; average. [< OF < L *medianus* middle]

me·an·der (mē·an′dər) *v.i.* **1.** To wind and turn in a course. **2.** To wander aimlessly. — *n.* **1.** *Often pl.* A tortuous or winding course. **2.** Aimless wandering. [< L < Gk. *Maiandros*, the river Meander] — **me·an′der·er** *n.*

mean·ing (mē′ning) *n.* **1.** That which is intended or meant; aim; purpose; end. **2.** That which is signified; sense; import. **3.** Interpretation or significance. — *adj.* **1.** Having purpose or intention: usu. in combination: *well-meaning*. **2.** Significant; expressive. — **mean′ing·ly** *adv.*

mean·ing·ful (mē′ning·fəl) *adj.* Full of meaning. — **mean′·ing·ful·ness** *n.* — **mean′ing·ful·ly** *adv.*

mean·ing·less (mē′ning·lis) *adj.* Having no meaning, significance, or importance. — **mean′ing·less·ly** *adv.* — **mean′·ing·less·ness** *n.*

mean·ly (mēn′lē) *adv.* In a mean, poor, or ignoble manner.

mean·ness (mēn′nis) *n.* **1.** The state or quality of being mean. **2.** A mean act.

meant (ment) Past tense and past participle of MEAN[1].

mean·time (mēn′tīm′) *n.* Intervening time. —*adv.* **1.** In or during the intervening time. **2.** At the same time.

mean·while (mēn′hwīl′) *n. & adv.* Meantime.

mea·sles (mē′zǝlz) *n.pl. (construed as sing. or pl.)* **1.** An acute, highly contagious virus disease affecting children and sometimes adults, characterized by an extensive eruption of small red spots: also called *rubeola.* **2.** Any similar disease, as German measles. [ME *maseles*, pl. of *masel* blister]

mea·sly (mēz′lē) *adj.* ·sli·er, ·sli·est **1.** Affected with measles. **2.** *Slang* Contemptibly stingy, scanty, or petty.

meas·ur·a·ble (mezh′ǝr·ǝ·bǝl) *adj.* **1.** Capable of being measured or compared. **2.** Notable; significant. —**meas′- ur·a·bil′i·ty, meas′ur·a·ble·ness** *n.* —**meas′ur·a·bly** *adv.*

meas·ure (mezh′ǝr) *n.* **1.** The extent, range, dimensions, capacity, etc., of anything. **2.** A standard or unit of measurement, as a yard. **3.** Any standard of criticism or judgment. **4.** A system of measurements: liquid *measure.* **5.** An instrument for taking measurements. **6.** The act of measuring. **7.** A specific quantity: a full *measure.* **8.** A fixed or suitable limit or bound: talkative beyond all *measure.* **9.** A certain amount, extent, or degree of anything: a *measure* of freedom. **10.** *Often pl.* A specific action, step, or procedure. **11.** A legislative bill. **12.** Rhythmic movement or beat. **13.** *Music* **a** A group of beats marked off by regularly recurring primary accents. **b** The portion of music contained between two bar lines; bar. **14.** In prosody: **a** Meter (def. 1). **b** A metrical foot. —**for good measure** As something additional or extra. —**in a measure** To some degree or extent. —**to take one's measure** To estimate or form an opinion of one's character, skill, etc. —*v.* ·ured, ·ur·ing *v.t.* **1.** To take or ascertain the dimensions, quantity, capacity, etc., of. **2.** To set apart, mark off, allot, etc., by or as by measuring: often with *off* or *out.* **3.** To estimate; judge; weigh. **4.** To serve as the measure of. **5.** To bring into competition or comparison. **6.** To travel over. **7.** To adjust; regulate: *Measure* your actions to your aspirations. —*v.i.* **8.** To make or take measurements. **9.** To yield a specified measurement. **10.** To admit measurement. —**to measure one's length** To fall or lie prostrate at full length. —**to measure up to** To fulfill, or meet, as expectations. [< F < L *mensura* < *metiri* to measure] —**meas′ur·er** *n.*

meas·ured (mezh′ǝrd) *adj.* **1.** Determined by some standard. **2.** Slow and stately; rhythmical. **3.** Carefully considered or weighed; deliberate. **4.** Moderate. **5.** Metrical. —**meas′ured·ly** *adv.* —**meas′ured·ness** *n.*

meas·ure·less (mezh′ǝr·lis) *adj.* Incapable of being measured; very great; immense. —**Syn.** See INFINITE.

meas·ure·ment (mezh′ǝr·mǝnt) *n.* **1.** The act or process of measuring anything. **2.** The amount, capacity, or extent determined by measuring. **3.** A system of measures.

measuring worm The larva of a geometrid moth, that advances its body by a succession of loops: also *inchworm.*

meat (mēt) *n.* **1.** The flesh of animals used as food, esp. the flesh of mammals as opposed to fish or fowl. **2.** The edible part of anything. **3.** Anything eaten for nourishment, as in **meat and drink.** **4.** The essence, gist, or main idea of something. **5.** *Informal* Anything one particularly enjoys or does with ease. [OE *mete*] —**meat′less** *adj.*

meat packing *U.S.* The commercial slaughtering of meat-producing animals and the processing, packaging, and distribution of meat and meat products. —**meat packer**

me·a·tus (mē·ā′tǝs) *n. pl.* ·tus or ·tus·es *Anat.* A passage, duct, or canal: the auditory *meatus.* [< L, passage]

meat·y (mē′tē) *adj.* meat·i·er, meat·i·est **1.** Of, pertaining to, or like meat. **2.** Full of meat. **3.** Full of substance; significant. —**meat′i·ness** *n.*

mec·ca (mek′ǝ) *n.* **1.** A place or attraction visited by many people. **2.** The goal of one's aspirations. [after *Mecca*]

me·chan·ic (mǝ·kan′ik) *n.* One skilled in the making, operation, or repair of tools or machinery. —*adj.* **1.** Involving or pertaining to manual labor or skill. **2.** Mechanical. [< L < Gk. *mēchanē* machine]

me·chan·i·cal (mǝ·kan′i·kǝl) *adj.* **1.** Of, involving, or having to do with the construction, operation, design, etc., of machinery or tools. **2.** Operated or produced by a machine. **3.** Of, pertaining to, or in accordance with the science of mechanics. **4.** Made or performed without spontaneity or by force of habit; automatic; lifeless. —**me·chan′i·cal·ly** *adv.* —**me·chan′i·cal·ness** *n.*

mechanical drawing A drawing done with the aid of compasses, squares, etc.

mech·a·ni·cian (mek′ǝ·nish′ǝn) *n.* One who builds, operates, or repairs machines or tools.

me·chan·ics (mǝ·kan′iks) *n.pl. (construed as sing, in defs. 1 and 2)* **1.** The branch of physics that treats of motion and of the action of forces on material bodies. **2.** The body of knowledge dealing with the design, operation, and mainte-

nance of machinery. **3.** The technical aspects of anything.

mech·a·nism (mek′ǝ·niz′ǝm) *n.* **1.** The parts or arrangement of parts of a machine. **2.** Something similar to a machine. **3.** The process or technique by which something works. **4.** A theory that all natural phenomena can be explained by the laws of chemistry and physics.

mech·a·nist (mek′ǝ·nist) *n.* **1.** A mechanician. **2.** A believer in mechanism (def. 5). —*adj.* Mechanistic.

mech·a·nis·tic (mek′ǝ·nis′tik) *adj.* **1.** Of, pertaining to, or of the nature of mechanics. **2.** Pertaining to or based on mechanism (def. 4). —**mech′a·nis′ti·cal·ly** *adv.*

mech·a·nize (mek′ǝ·nīz) *v.t.* ·nized, ·niz·ing **1.** To make mechanical. **2.** To convert (an industry, etc.) to machine production. **3.** *Mil.* To equip with tanks, trucks, etc. —**mech′a·ni·za′tion** *n.*

med·al (med′l) *n.* A small piece of metal, bearing an image, inscription, etc., and often given as an award for some outstanding act or service. —*v.t.* **med·aled** or ·alled, **med·al·ing** or ·al·ling To confer a medal upon. [< F < Ital. < L *metallum* mine]

med·al·ist (med′l·ist) *n.* **1.** A collector or maker of medals. **2.** The recipient of a medal awarded for services or merit. **3.** In golf, the winner at medal play.

me·dal·lion (mǝ·dal′yǝn) *n.* **1.** A large medal. **2.** An ornamental subject usu. set in a circular or oval frame, and used as a decorative element. [< F *médaillon*]

Medal of Honor The highest U.S. military decoration, awarded to one who risked his life beyond the call of duty. Also called *Congressional Medal of Honor.* See DECORATION.

medal play In golf, a form of competitive play in which the score is computed by counting the strokes of each competitor in a round of play. Compare MATCH PLAY.

med·dle (med′l) *v.i.* ·dled, ·dling **1.** To participate or interfere officiously: often with *in* or *with.* **2.** To tamper. [< OF *medler* < L *miscere* to mix] —**med′dler** *n.*

med·dle·some (med′l·sǝm) *adj.* Inclined to meddle. —**med′dle·some·ly** *adv.* —**med′dle·some·ness** *n.*

Me·de·a (mǝ·dē′ǝ) In Greek legend, a sorceress of Colchis who helped Jason obtain the Golden Fleece.

me·di·a (mē′dē·ǝ) Alternative plural of MEDIUM.

me·di·ae·val (mē′dē·ē′vǝl, med′ē-), **me·di·ae·val·ism,** etc. See MEDIEVAL, etc.

me·di·al (mē′dē·ǝl) *adj.* **1.** Of, pertaining to, or situated in the middle. **2.** Of or pertaining to a mathematical average; mean. [< LL < L *medius* middle] —**me′di·al·ly** *adv.*

me·di·an (mē′dē·ǝn) *adj.* **1.** Pertaining to or situated in the middle; medial. **2.** *Stat.* Designating the middle point in a series of values: 8 is the *median* of 2, 5, 8, 10, 13. —*n.* A median point, line, or number. [< L < *medius* middle] —**me′di·an·ly** *adv.*

me·di·ate (*v.* mē′dē·āt; *adj.* -it) *v.* ·at·ed, ·at·ing *v.t.* **1.** To settle or reconcile (differences) by intervening as a peacemaker. **2.** To serve as the medium for effecting (a result) or conveying (an object, etc.). —*v.i.* **3.** To act between disputing parties to bring about a settlement, etc. **4.** To be in an intermediate position. —*adj.* **1.** Acting as an intervening agency. **2.** Occurring or effected as a result of indirect or median agency. [< LL < *mediare* to stand between] —**me′di·ate·ly** *adv.* —**me′di·a′tive** *adj.*

me·di·a·tion (mē′dē·ā′shǝn) *n.* The act of mediating; intercession; interposition. —**me′di·a′tor** *n.*

me·di·a·tor·y (mē′dē·ǝ·tôr′ē, -tō′rē) *adj.* **1.** Of or pertaining to mediation. **2.** Serving to mediate. Also **me′di·a·to′- ri·al** (-tôr′ē·ǝl, -tō′rē·ǝl). —**me·di·a·to′ri·al·ly** *adv.*

med·ic[1] (med′ik) *n.* Any of several cloverlike plants, esp. alfalfa. [< L < Gk. *Mēdikē* (*poa*) Median (grass)]

med·ic[2] (med′ik) *n. Informal* **1.** A physician or intern. **2.** A medical student. **3.** A corpsman.

med·i·ca·ble (med′ǝ·kǝ·bǝl) *adj.* Capable of being relieved by medical treatment; curable.

med·i·cal (med′i·kǝl) *adj.* **1.** Of or pertaining to medicine. **2.** Having curative properties.

medical jurisprudence The application of medical principles in law: also called *forensic medicine, legal medicine.*

med·i·ca·ment (med′ǝ·kǝ·mǝnt, mǝ·dik′ǝ-) *n.* Any substance for the cure of disease or the alleviation of pain.

med·i·care (med′i·kâr) *n. U.S. & Canadian* Government medical care or health insurance.

med·i·cate (med′ǝ·kāt) *v.t.* ·cat·ed, ·cat·ing **1.** To treat medicinally. **2.** To tincture or impregnate with medicine. [< L < *medicare* to heal] —**med′i·ca′tion** *n.* —**med′i·ca′- tive** *adj.*

me·dic·i·nal (mǝ·dis′ǝ·nǝl) *adj.* Pertaining to or having the properties of medicine; healing, curative, or alleviating.

med·i·cine (med′ǝ·sǝn, *Brit.* med′sǝn) *n.* **1.** Any substance used in the treatment of disease or in the relief of pain. **2.** The science of the preservation and restoration of health and of treating disease, esp., as distinguished from surgery. **3.**

The profession of medicine. **4.** Among American Indians, any magic spell or power. **— to take one's medicine** To endure punishment, etc. [< OF < L *medicus* physician]

med·i·cine ball A large, heavy, leather-covered ball, thrown and caught for physical exercise.

med·i·cine man Among North American Indians, one professing supernatural powers of healing, etc.; magician.

med·i·co (med′ə·kō) *n.* *pl.* **·cos** *Informal* A physician or a medical student. [< Ital. or Sp., physician]

medico- *combining form* Pertaining to medical science and: *medico-legal.* Also, before vowels, **medic-.** [< L *medicus* physician]

me·di·e·val (mē′dē·ē′vəl, med′ē-) *adj.* Of, like, or characteristic of the Middle Ages: also spelled *mediaeval.* [< L *medius* middle + *aevum* age] **— me·di·e′val·ly** *adv.*

me·di·e·val·ism (mē′dē·ē′vəl·iz′əm, med′ē-) *n.* **1.** The spirit, beliefs, customs, and practices of the Middle Ages. **2.** Devotion to the Middle Ages. **3.** Any custom, idea, etc., surviving from the Middle Ages. Also spelled *mediaevalism.*

me·di·e·val·ist (mē′dē·ē′vəl·ist, med′ē-) *n.* **1.** A scholar or specialist in medieval history, literature, or art. **2.** One devoted to the Middle Ages. Also spelled *mediaevalist.*

medio- *combining form* Middle. Also, before vowels, **medi-.** [< L *medius* middle]

me·di·o·cre (mē′dē·ō′kər, mē′dē·ō′kər) *adj.* Of only average quality; ordinary. [< F < L < *medius* middle]

me·di·oc·ri·ty (mē′dē·ok′rə·tē) *n.* *pl.* **·ties** **1.** The condition or quality of being mediocre. **2.** Mediocre ability or performance. **3.** A mediocre person.

med·i·tate (med′ə·tāt) *v.* **·tat·ed, ·tat·ing** *v.i.* **1.** To engage in continuous and contemplative thought; muse; cogitate. **— v.t. 2.** To think about doing; plan. [< L < *meditari* to muse, ponder] **— med′i·tat′er, med′i·ta′tor** *n.* **— med′i·ta′tive** *adj.* **— med′i·ta′tive·ly** *adv.*

med·i·ta·tion (med′ə·tā′shən) *n.* The act of meditating; reflection upon a subject; contemplation.

med·i·ter·ra·ne·an (med′ə·tə·rā′nē·ən) *adj.* Enclosed nearly or wholly by land. [< L *medius* middle + *terra* earth]

Med·i·ter·ra·ne·an (med′ə·tə·rā′nē·ən) *adj.* Of or pertaining to the Mediterranean Sea or its shores. **— n. 1.** The Mediterranean Sea. **2.** One who lives in a Mediterranean country, or belongs to the Mediterranean race.

Mediterranean fever Undulant fever.

me·di·um (mē′dē·əm) *n.* *pl.* **·di·ums** (always for def. 5) or **·di·a** (-ə) **1.** An intermediate degree or condition; mean. **2.** The surrounding or enveloping element; environment. **3.** An intervening substance in which something may act or an effect be produced. **4.** A means or agency; instrument: an advertising *medium.* **5.** One through whom the spirits of the dead are believed to communicate with the material world. **6.** An area or form of artistic expression, or the materials used. **7.** In painting, a liquid with which pigments are mixed to make them fluid enough to be applied. **8.** *Biol.* A culture medium. **— adj.** Intermediate in quantity, quality, size, etc. [< L, orig. neut. sing. of *medius* middle]

medium frequency *Telecom.* Radio waves ranging in frequency from 300 to 3000 kilocycles.

med·lar (med′lər) *n.* **1.** A small, European tree of the rose family. **2.** The fruit of this tree, eaten when it begins to decay. [< OF *mesle* fruit of the medlar]

med·ley (med′lē) *n.* **1.** A mingled and confused mass of elements; jumble. **2.** A musical composition made up of different airs or parts of songs. **— adj.** Made up of heterogeneous parts; jumbled; mixed. [< OF *medlee*, orig. fem. pp. of *medler* to meddle]

Mé·doc (mā·dôk′) *n.* A red wine made in Médoc, France.

me·dul·la (mə·dul′ə) *n.* *pl.* **·lae** (-lē) **1.** *Anat.* **a** The soft inner portion of an organ or part, such as the kidney. **b** The marrow of bones. **c** The medulla oblongata. **2.** *Bot.* Pith (def. 1). [< L, marrow, pith] **— med·ul·lar·y** (med′ə·ler·ē, mi·dul′ər·ē), **me·dul′lar** *adj.*

medulla ob·lon·ga·ta (ob′lông·gä′tə) *Anat.* The hindmost and lowest part of the brain, narrowing down into the spinal cord, and controlling breathing, circulation, etc.

me·du·sa (mə·dōō′sə, -zə, -dyōō′-) *n.* *pl.* **·sas** or **·sae** (-sē, -zē) A jellyfish. [< L] **— me·du′san, me·du′soid** *adj. & n.*

Me·du·sa (mə·dōō′sə, -zə, -dyōō′-) In Greek mythology, one of the Gorgons, killed by Perseus.

meek (mēk) *adj.* **1.** Having a patient, gentle disposition. **2.** Lacking spirit or backbone; submissive. [ME < ON *miukr* gentle, soft] **— meek′ly** *adv.* **— meek′ness** *n.*

meer·schaum (mir′shəm, -shôm, -shoum) *n.* **1.** A light, heat-resisting magnesium silicate, used for tobacco pipes, etc. **2.** A tobacco pipe made from this. [< G < *meer* sea + *schaum* foam]

meet[1] (mēt) *v.* **met, meet·ing** *v.t.* **1.** To come upon; encounter. **2.** To be at, or go to the place of arrival of: to *meet* him at the station. **3.** To make the acquaintance of. **4.** To come into the company of or in association with, as for a conference. **5.** To come into contact or conjunction with. **6.** To keep an appointment with. **7.** To come into the ob-

servation, perception, or recognition of (the eye, ear, etc.). **8.** To experience; undergo: to *meet* adversity. **9.** To oppose in battle. **10.** To answer (a blow, move, etc.) by another in return. **11.** To deal or cope with; handle. **12.** To comply or act in accordance with: to *meet* the requirements for a diploma. **13.** To pay (a bill, debt, etc.). **14.** To fulfill (an obligation, need, etc.). **— v.i. 15.** To come together; come face to face. **16.** To come together in conjunction, or union. **17.** To assemble. **18.** To make acquaintance or be introduced. **19.** To come together in conflict or opposition; contend. **— to meet with 1.** To come upon; encounter. **2.** To deal or confer with. **3.** To experience. **— n.** An assembling for a sport or an athletic contest; also, the persons so assembled, or the place of assembly. [OE *mētan*]

meet[2] (mēt) *adj.* Suitable; proper. [OE *gemǣte*] **— meet′ly** *adv.*

meet·ing (mē′ting) *n.* **1.** A coming together. **2.** An assembly or gathering of persons; also, the persons present. **3.** A joining or conjunction of things. **4.** An assembly of Quakers for religious services; also, their meeting house.

meeting house 1. A house used for public meetings. **2.** A place of worship used by the Quakers.

mega- *combining form* **1.** Great; large: *megaphone.* **2.** In the metric system, a million times (a specified unit): *megacycle.* Also, before vowels, **meg-.** [< Gk. *megas* large]

meg·a·cy·cle (meg′ə·sī′kəl) *n.* **1.** *Telecom.* A unit of electromagnetic wave frequency of 1,000,000 cycles per second. **2.** One million cycles.

megalo- *combining form* Big; indicating excessive or abnormal size. Also, before vowels, **megal-.** [< Gk. *megas, megalou* big]

meg·a·lo·ceph·a·ly (meg′ə·lō·sef′ə·lē) *n.* Unusual largeness of the head. Also **meg′a·lo·ce·pha′li·a** (-sə·fā′lē·ə). [< MEGALO- + Gk. *kephalē* head] **— meg′a·lo·ce·phal′ic** (-sə·fal′ik), **meg′a·lo·ceph′a·lous** *adj.*

meg·a·lo·ma·ni·a (meg′ə·lō·mā′nē·ə, -mān′yə) *n.* **1.** *Psychiatry* A mental disorder in which the subject thinks himself great or exalted. **2.** A tendency to magnify and exaggerate. **— meg′a·lo·ma′ni·ac** *adj. & n.*

meg·a·phone (meg′ə·fōn) *n.* A funnel-shaped device for amplifying or directing sound. **— v.t. & v.i. ·phoned, ·phon·ing** To speak through or as through a megaphone.

meg·a·ton (meg′ə·tun′) *n.* **1.** One million tons. **2.** A unit equal to the explosive power of one million tons of TNT.

me·grim (mē′grim) *n.* **1.** *pl.* Depression of spirits; dullness. **2.** Migraine. [< F < L < Gk. *hēmi* half + *krania* skull]

mei·o·sis (mī·ō′sis) *n.* *Biol.* The cell divisions leading to the formation of gametes in which the number of chromosomes is reduced by half. [< Gk. *meiōn* less] **— mei·ot′ic** (-ot′ik) *adj.*

Meis·ter·sing·er (mīs′tər·sing′ər, *Ger.* mīs′tər·zing′ər) *n.* *pl.* **·sing·er** *German* Any of the poets and musicians, mainly artisans and tradesmen, active in the principal cities of Germany between the 14th and 16th centuries.

mel·a·mine (mel′ə·mēn, -min) *n.* *Chem.* A crystalline nitrogen compound, $C_3N_2(NH_2)_3$, that reacts with formaldehyde to produce a high-grade thermosetting resin. [< *mel(am)*, a chemical compound + AMINE]

melan- Var. of MELANO-.

mel·an·cho·li·a (mel′ən·kō′lē·ə) *n.* *Psychiatry* Great depression of spirits and excessive brooding without apparent or sufficient cause. [< L] **— mel′an·cho′li·ac** *adj. & n.*

mel·an·chol·y (mel′ən·kol′ē) *adj.* **1.** Excessively gloomy; sad. **2.** Suggesting or promoting sadness: a *melancholy* day. **3.** Somberly thoughtful; pensive. **— n.** *pl.* **·chol·ies 1.** Low spirits; depression. **2.** Pensive or sober reflection. [< F < L < Gk. < *melas, -anos* black + *cholē* bile] **— mel′an·chol′ic** *adj.* **— mel′an·chol′li·cal·ly** *adv.*

Mel·a·ne·sian (mel′ə·nē′zhən, -shən) *adj.* Of or pertaining to Melanesia, its native inhabitants, or their languages. **— n. 1.** A member of any of the dark-skinned, kinky-haired peoples of Melanesia. **2.** Any of the languages of the Austronesian group spoken in Melanesia.

me·lange (mā·länzh′) *n.* *French* A mixture or medley.

mel·a·nin (mel′ə·nin) *n.* *Biochem.* A brownish black pigment contained in animal tissues, as the skin and hair.

melano- *combining form* Black; dark-colored. Also, before . vowels, **melan-.** [< Gk. *melas, melanos* black]

Mel·ba toast (mel′bə) Thinly sliced bread toasted until brown and crisp.

meld (meld) *v.t. & v.i.* In pinochle and other card games, to announce or declare (a combination of cards) for inclusion in one's total score. **— n.** A group of cards to be declared, or the act of declaring them. [< G *melden* to announce]

me·lee (mā′lā, mā·lā′) *n.* A confused, general hand-to-hand fight; affray. Also *Fr.* **me·lée** (me·lā′). [< F < OF *meslee,* var. of *medlee* medley]

mel·io·rate (mēl′yə·rāt) *v.t. & v.i.* **·rat·ed, ·rat·ing** To improve, as in quality or condition; ameliorate. [< LL < *melior* better] **— mel′io·ra·ble** *adj.* **— mel′io·ra′tion** *n.* **— mel′io·ra′tive** *adj.* **— mel′io·ra′tor** *n.*

mel·lif·er·ous (mə·lif'ər·əs) *adj.* Producing or bearing honey. Also **mel·lif'ic**. [< L < *mel* honey + *ferre* to bear]

mel·lif·lu·ent (mə·lif'lōō-ənt) *adj.* Mellifluous. — **mel·lif'lu·ence** *n.* — **mel·lif'lu·ent·ly** *adv.*

mel·lif·lu·ous (mə·lif'lōō-əs) *adj.* Sweetly or smoothly flowing: *mellifluous* speech. [< L < *mel* honey + *fluere* to flow] — **mel·lif'lu·ous·ly** *adv.* — **mel·lif'lu·ous·ness** *n.*

mel·low (mel'ō) *adj.* **1.** Soft, sweet, and full-flavored by reason of ripeness, as fruit. **2.** Well-matured, as wines. **3.** Rich and soft in quality, as colors or sounds. **4.** Made gentle and sympathetic by maturity or experience. **5.** Made jovial or genial by liquor. **6.** Soft and friable, as soil. — *v.t. & v.i.* To make or become mellow; soften. [ME, ? < OE *melu* meal] — **mel'low·ly** *adv.* — **mel'low·ness** *n.*

me·lo·de·on (mə·lō'dē·ən) *n.* A small reed organ or harmonium. [A pseudo-Greek formation < MELODY]

me·lod·ic (mə·lod'ik) *adj.* **1.** Pertaining to or containing melody. **2.** Melodious. — **me·lod'i·cal·ly** *adv.*

me·lo·di·ous (mə·lō'dē·əs) *adj.* **1.** Producing or characterized by melody; tuneful. **2.** Pleasant to hear. — **me·lo'di·ous·ly** *adv.* — **me·lo'di·ous·ness** *n.*

mel·o·dra·ma (mel'ə·drä'mə, -dram'ə) *n.* **1.** A play or drama in which the emotions displayed are violent or extravagantly sentimental, and the plot is made up of sensational incidents. **2.** Formerly, a romantic drama with sensational incidents, usu. including music and songs. **3.** Sensational and highly emotional behavior or language. [< F < Gk. *melos* song + *drama* drama] — **mel'o·dram'a·tist** *n.*

mel·o·dra·mat·ic (mel'ə·drə·mat'ik) *adj.* Of, pertaining to, or like melodrama; sensational; exaggerated. — **mel'o·dra·mat'i·cal·ly** *adv.*

mel·o·dra·mat·ics (mel'ə·drə·mat'iks) *n.pl.* Melodramatic behavior.

mel·o·dy (mel'ə·dē) *n.* *pl.* **·dies** **1.** Pleasing sounds, or an agreeable succession of such sounds. **2.** *Music* **a** An organized succession of tones, usu. in the same voice or instrument. **b** The leading part in a homophonic composition; the air. [< OF < LL < Gk. < *melos* song + *aoidos* singer]

mel·on (mel'ən) *n.* **1.** The large fruit of any of various plants of the gourd family, as the muskmelon and the watermelon. **2.** Any of these plants. [< F < LL *melo, melonis*]

Mel·pom·e·ne (mel·pom'ə·nē) In Greek mythology, the Muse of tragedy.

melt (melt) *v.t. & v.i.* **melt·ed, melt·ed** (*Archaic* **mol·ten** (mōl'tən), **melt·ing** **1.** To reduce or change from a solid to a liquid state by heat. **2.** To dissolve, as in water. **3.** To disappear or cause to disappear; dissipate: often with *away*. **4.** To blend by imperceptible degrees: often with *into*. **5.** To make or become softened in feeling or attitude. — *n.* **1.** Something melted. **2.** A single operation of fusing. **3.** The amount of a single fusing. [OE *meltan, mieltan*] — **melt'a·ble** *adj.* — **melt'a·bil'i·ty** *n.* — **melt'er** *n.*

melting point The temperature at which a specified solid substance melts or fuses.

melting pot **1.** A vessel in which a substance is melted. **2.** A country, city, or region in which immigrants of various racial and cultural backgrounds are assimilated.

mel·ton (mel'tən) *n.* A heavy woolen cloth with a short nap, used for overcoats. [after *Melton* Mowbray, England]

mem·ber (mem'bər) *n.* **1.** One who belongs to a society, club, party, etc. **2.** *Usu. cap.* One who belongs to a legislative body. **3.** *Biol.* A part or organ of an animal body, esp. a limb. **4.** A part or element of a structural or composite whole. **5.** *Math.* Either side of an algebraic equation. [< OF < L *membrum* limb]

mem·ber·ship (mem'bər·ship) *n.* **1.** The state or fact of being a member. **2.** The members of an organization, etc., collectively; also, the total number of members.

mem·brane (mem'brān) *n.* A thin, pliable, sheetlike layer of animal or vegetable tissue serving to cover or line an organ or part, separate adjoining cavities, or connect adjoining structures. [< L *membrana*, lit., limb coating]

mem·bra·nous (mem'brə·nəs) *adj.* **1.** Of, pertaining to, or like a membrane. **2.** Marked by the formation of a membrane. Also **mem·bra·na·ceous** (mem'brə·nā'shəs).

me·men·to (mə·men'tō) *n.* *pl.* **·tos** or **·toes** Anything that serves as a hint or reminder of the past; souvenir. [< L, remember, imperative of *meminisse* to remember]

memento mo·ri (môr'ī) *Latin* An emblem or reminder of death, as a skull, etc.: literally, remember that you must die.

mem·o (mem'ō) *n.* *pl.* **mem·os** *Informal* A memorandum.

mem·oir (mem'wär) *n.* **1.** *pl.* Personal reminiscences or records; esp., a narrative of events based on the writer's personal observations and experiences. **2.** A biography. **3.** *pl.* An account of the proceedings of a learned society. **4.** A monograph. [< F < L *memoria* memory]

mem·o·ra·bil·i·a (mem'ə·rə·bil'ē·ə) *n.pl.* Things or events worthy of remembrance and record. [< L]

mem·o·ra·ble (mem'ər·ə·bəl) *adj.* Worthy to be remembered; noteworthy. — **mem'o·ra·bil'i·ty, mem'o·ra·ble·ness** *n.* — **mem'o·ra·bly** *adv.*

mem·o·ran·dum (mem'ə·ran'dəm) *n.* *pl.* **·dums** or **·da** (-də) **1.** A brief note of a thing or things to be remembered. **2.** A record of transactions, etc., esp. for future use. **3.** An informal letter, usu. sent between departments in an office. **4.** *Law* A brief written outline of the terms of a transaction or contract. **5.** In business, a statement of goods sent from a consignor to a consignee. [< L, a thing to be remembered]

me·mo·ri·al (mə·môr'ē·əl, -mō'rē-) *adj.* **1.** Serving to keep in memory a deceased person or an event; commemorative. **2.** Of or pertaining to memory. — *n.* **1.** Something serving to keep in remembrance a person, event, etc. **2.** A written summary or presentation of facts addressed to a legislative body, official, etc., as the grounds for or in the form of a petition. [< OF < L < *memoria*]

Memorial Day *U.S.* A day set apart to honor the dead of any American war; in most states May 30. Also called *Decoration Day.*

me·mo·ri·al·ize (mə·môr'ē·əl·īz', -mō'rē-) *v.t.* **·ized, ·iz·ing** **1.** To commemorate. **2.** To present a memorial to; petition. Also *Brit.* **me·mo'ri·al·ise'**. — **me·mo'ri·al·i·za'tion** *n.*

mem·o·rize (mem'ə·rīz) *v.t.* **·rized, ·riz·ing** To commit to memory. — **mem'o·ri·za'tion** *n.* — **mem'o·riz'er** *n.*

mem·o·ry (mem'ər·ē) *n.* *pl.* **·ries** **1.** The mental function or capacity of recalling or recognizing previously learned behavior or past experience. **2.** The total of what is remembered. **3.** One who or that which is remembered. **4.** The period of time covered by the faculty of remembrance. **5.** The state of being remembered. **6.** Remembrance or commemoration. [< OF < L *memor* mindful]

mem·sah·ib (mem'sä·ib) *n.* *Anglo-Indian* A European lady: a name given by native servants. [< MA'AM + Hind. *sāhib* master < Arabic]

men (men) Plural of MAN.

men·ace (men'is) *v.* **·aced, ·ac·ing** *v.t.* **1.** To threaten with evil or harm. — *v.i.* **2.** To make threats; appear threatening. — *n.* **1.** A threat. **2.** *Informal* A troublesome person; pest. [< OF < L < *minax, -acis* threatening] — **men'ac·er** *n.* — **men'ac·ing·ly** *adv.*

me·nad (mē'nad), etc. See MAENAD, etc.

mé·nage (mā·nàzh', *Fr.* mā·nàzh') *n.* **1.** The persons of a household, collectively. **2.** Household management. Also **me·nage'**. [< F < L *mansio, -onis* house]

me·nag·er·ie (mə·naj'ər·ē) *n.* **1.** A collection of wild animals kept for exhibition. **2.** The enclosure in which they are kept. [< F]

mend (mend) *v.t.* **1.** To make sound or serviceable again by repairing. **2.** To correct errors or faults in; improve. *Mend* your ways. **3.** To correct (some defect). — *v.i.* **4.** To become better, as in health. **5.** To improve: said of conditions. — *n.* **1.** A repairing. **2.** A mended place, as on a garment. — **on the mend** Recovering health. [Var. of AMEND] — **mend'a·ble** *adj.* — **mend'er** *n.*

men·da·cious (men·dā'shəs) *adj.* **1.** Lying; deceitful. **2.** Untrue; false. [< L *mendax, -acis* lying] — **men·da'cious·ly** *adv.* — **men·da'cious·ness** *n.*

men·dac·i·ty (men·das'ə·tē) *n.* *pl.* **·ties** **1.** The quality of being mendacious. **2.** A lie; untruth.

men·de·le·vi·um (men'də·lē'vē·əm) *n.* A short-lived radioactive element (symbol Md). See ELEMENT. [after Dmitri Ivanovich *Mendeleyev*]

Mendel's laws *Genetics* Principles formulated by Gregor Mendel, stating that alternative unit characters of hybrids segregate from one another in transmission to offspring and that different pairs of such characters segregate independently of each other. — **Men·de·li·an** (men·dē'lē·ən) *adj.*

men·di·cant (men'də·kənt) *adj.* **1.** Begging; depending on alms for a living. **2.** Pertaining to or like a beggar. — *n.* **1.** A beggar. **2.** A begging friar. [< L < *mendicus* needy] — **men'di·can·cy, men·dic'i·ty** (men·dis'ə·tē) *n.*

Men·e·la·us (men'ə·lā'əs) In Greek legend, a king of Sparta and the husband of Helen of Troy.

men·ha·den (men·hād'n) *n.* A fish of North Atlantic and West Indian waters, used as a source of oil, as fertilizer, and as bait. [Alter. of Algonquian *munnawhat* fertilizer]

me·ni·al (mē'nē·əl, mēn'yəl) *adj.* **1** Pertaining to or appropriate to servants. **2.** Servile; abject. — *n.* **1.** A domestic servant. **2.** One who has a servile nature. [< AF < OF < LL < L *mansio* house] — **me'ni·al·ly** *adv.*

me·nin·ges (mə·nin'jēz) *n.* *pl.* of **me·ninx** (mē'ningks) *Anat.* The three membranes enveloping the brain and spinal cord. [< NL < Gk. *mēninx, mēningos* membrane] — **me·nin'ge·al** *adj.*

men·in·gi·tis (men'ən·jī'tis) *n.* *Pathol.* Inflammation of the meninges, esp. through infection. — **men'in·git'ic** (-jit'ik) *adj.*

me·nis·cus (mə-nis'kəs) *n. pl.* **·nis·cus·es** or **·nis·ci** (-nis'ī) 1. A crescent or crescent-shaped body. 2. *Optics* A lens concave on one side and convex on the other. 3. *Physics* The curved upper surface of a liquid column. [< L < Gk. *mēniskos* crescent, dim. of *mēnē* moon]

Men·non·ite (men'ən-īt) *n.* A member of a Protestant Christian sect founded in the 16th century, opposing the taking of oaths, the holding of public office, and military service. [after *Menno* Simons, 1492–1559, a leader of the sect]

Me·nom·i·nee (mə-nom'ə-nē) *n. pl.* **·nee** 1. One of an Algonquian tribe of North American Indians, inhabiting central Wisconsin. 2. The Algonquian language of this tribe. Also **Me·nom·i·ni** (-nē).

men·o·pause (men'ə-pôz) *n. Physiol.* The final cessation of menstruation, occurring normally between the ages of 45 and 50. [< Gk. *mēn* month + *pauein* to cause to cease]

Me·no·rah (mə-nôr'ə, -nō'rə) *n.* In the Jewish religion, a candelabrum having nine candles lighted in increasing numbers during Hannukah. [< Hebrew, candlestick]

men·ses (men'sēz) *n.pl. Physiol.* Menstruation. [< L, pl. of *mensis* month]

Men·she·vik (men'shə-vik) *n. pl.* **·vi·ki** (-vē'kē) or **·viks** A member of the conservative element in the Russian Social Democratic Party. Compare BOLSHEVIK. Also **Men'she·vist.** [< Russian *menshe* minority] — **Men'she·vism** *n.*

men·stru·al (men'strōō-əl) *adj.* 1. *Physiol.* Of or pertaining to menstruation. Also **men'stru·ous.** 2. Monthly. [< L < *menstruus* monthly]

men·stru·ate (men'strōō-āt) *v.i.* **·at·ed, ·at·ing** To undergo menstruation.

men·stru·a·tion (men'strōō-ā'shən) *n. Physiol.* 1. The periodical flow of bloody fluid from the uterus, occurring normally about every 28 days: also called *menses*. 2. An occurrence of this flow: also called *period*.

men·stru·um (men'strōō-əm) *n. pl.* **·stru·ums** or **·stru·a** (-strōō-ə) The medium in which a substance is dissolved.

men·su·ra·ble (men'shər-ə-bəl) *adj.* That can be measured. [< LL < *mensurare* to measure] — **men'su·ra·bil'i·ty** *n.*

men·su·ral (men'shər-əl) *adj.* Pertaining to measure.

men·su·ra·tion (men'shə-rā'shən) *n.* 1. The art, act, or process of measuring. 2. The branch of mathematics having to do with determining length, area, and volume.

-ment *suffix of nouns* 1. The product or result of: *achievement*. 2. The instrument or means of: *atonement*. 3. The process or action of: *government*. 4. The quality, condition, or state of being: *astonishment*. [< F < L *-mentum*]

men·tal (men'təl) *adj.* 1. Of or pertaining to the mind or intellect. 2. Effected by or taking place in the mind, esp. without the aid of written symbols: *mental calculations.* 3. Affected by mental illness: a *mental patient.* 4. For the care of the mentally ill: *mental hospital.* [< F < LL < L *mens, mentis* mind] — **men'tal·ly** *adv.*

mental age See under AGE.

mental deficiency *Psychol.* A condition characterized by subnormal intelligence to the extent that the individual is handicapped from participating fully in ordinary life.

mental healing The alleged curing of any disorder, ailment, or disease by mental concentration and suggestion.

mental hygiene The scientific study and application of methods to preserve and promote mental health.

men·tal·i·ty (men-tal'ə-tē) *n. pl.* **·ties** 1. The mental faculties or powers; mental activity. 2. Intellectual capacity or power: an average *mentality.* 3. Cast or habit of mind.

men·thol (men'thôl, -thōl, -thol) *n. Chem.* A white, waxy, crystalline alcohol, $C_{10}H_{19}OH$, obtained from and having the odor of oil of peppermint, used as a flavoring agent, in perfumery, and in medicine. [< G < L *mentha* mint + -OL]

men·tho·lat·ed (men'thə-lā'tid) *adj.* Treated with, containing, or impregnated with menthol.

men·tion (men'shən) *v.t.* To refer to incidentally, briefly, or in passing. — *n.* 1. The act of one who mentions. 2. Slight reference; casual allusion. [< OF < L *mens, mentis* mind] — **men'tion·a·ble** *adj.* — **men'tion·er** *n.*

men·tor (men'tər, -tôr) *n.* A wise and trusted teacher or guide. [< MENTOR] — **men·to'ri·al** (-tôr'ē-əl, -tō'rē-) *adj.*

Men·tor (men'tər, -tôr) In the *Odyssey*, the sage guardian appointed by Odysseus for Telemachus.

men·u (men'yōō, mān'-; *Fr.* mə·nü') *n.* A bill of fare; also, the dishes included in it. [< F < L *minutus* small, detailed]

me·ow (mē·ou', myou) *n.* The crying sound made by a cat. — *v.t.* To make the sound of a cat. [Imit.]

Meph·is·toph·e·les (mef'is·tof'ə·lēz) 1. In medieval legend, a devil to whom Faust sold his soul for wisdom and power. 2. A leading character in Marlowe's *Dr. Faustus*, Goethe's *Faust*, etc. — *n.* A diabolical or crafty person. Also **Me·phis·to** (mə·fis'tō). — **Me·phis·to·phe·le·an** (mə·fis'tə·fē'lē·ən), **Me·phis·to·phe·li·an** *adj.*

me·phit·ic (mə·fit'ik) *adj.* 1. Poisonous; foul. 2. Offensive to the sense of smell. Also **me·phit'i·cal.**

me·pro·ba·mate (mə·prō'bə·māt, me·prō'bə/māt) *n. Chem.* A white, nearly odorless, bitter powder, $C_9H_{18}N_2O_4$, used in

medicine as a tranquilizer. [< ME(THYL) + PRO(PANEDIOL) + (DI-) + (CAR)BAMATE]

mer·can·tile (mûr'kən·til, -tīl) *adj.* 1. Of, pertaining to, or characteristic of merchants or commerce. 2. Of or pertaining to the mercantile system. [< F < Ital. < L *mercans, -antis*, pp. of *mercari* to traffic]

mercantile system The theory in political economy that the wealth of a country consists in its quantity of gold and silver, and that the importation of precious metals, and the exportation of goods should be encouraged by the state. Also called **mer·can·til·ism** (mûr'kən·til·iz'əm).

Mer·ca·tor projection (mər·kā'tər) A map projection in which the earth is shown as projected on a cylinder, the meridians and parallels forming a rectangular grid, with areas and distances being less truly represented the farther they are from the equator. [after Gerardus *Mercator*, 1512–94, Flemish cartographer]

MERCATOR PROJECTION

mer·ce·nar·y (mûr'sə·ner'ē) *adj.* 1. Influenced by a desire for gain or reward. 2. Serving for pay: now said only of soldiers hired by a foreign state. — *n. pl.* **·nar·ies** A hireling; esp., a hired soldier in foreign service. [< L *merces* reward, hire] — **mer'ce·nar'i·ly** *adv.* — **mer'ce·nar'i·ness** *n.*

mer·cer·ize (mûr'sə·rīz) *v.t.* **ized, iz·ing** To treat (cotton fabrics) with caustic soda so as to increase strength, impart a gloss, and render more receptive to dyes. [after John *Mercer*, 1791–1866, English inventor. — **mer'cer·i·za'tion** *n.*

mer·chan·dise (mûr'chən·dīz, -dīs) *n.* Anything bought and sold for profit; goods; wares. — *v.t. & v.i.* **dised, dis·ing** 1. To buy and sell; trade. 2. To promote the sale of (goods) through advertising, etc. Also **mer'chan·dize.** [See MERCHANT.] — **mer'chan·dis'er** *n.*

mer·chant (mûr'chənt) *n.* 1. One who buys and sells commodities for profit. 2. A storekeeper. — *adj.* 1. Of or pertaining to merchants or trade. 2. Of or pertaining to the merchant marine. [< OF < L *mercari* to traffic, buy]

mer·chant·a·ble (mûr'chən·tə·bəl) *adj.* Marketable.

mer·chant·man (mûr'chənt·mən) *n. pl.* **·men** (-mən) A trading or merchant vessel.

merchant marine 1. All the merchant or trading vessels of a nation, collectively. 2. The officers and men employed on these vessels.

mer·ci (mer·sē') *interj. French* Thank you.

Mer·ci·a (mûr'shē·ə, -shə) An ancient Anglo-Saxon kingdom of central England. — **Mer'ci·an** *adj. & n.*

mer·ci·ful (mûr'sə·fəl) *adj.* 1. Full of or exercising mercy; compassionate. 2. Characterized by or indicating mercy: a *merciful* death. — **mer'ci·ful·ly** *adv.* — **mer'ci·ful·ness** *n.*

mer·ci·less (mûr'sə·lis) *adj.* Having or showing no mercy; pitiless. — **mer'ci·less·ly** *adv.* — **mer'ci·less·ness** *n.*

mer·cu·ri·al (mər·kyŏŏr'ē·əl) *adj.* 1. Lively; volatile; clever: a *mercurial* wit. 2. Of, pertaining to, containing, or caused by the action of mercury, or quicksilver. 3. *Often cap.* Of or pertaining to the god Mercury or the planet Mercury. — *n. Med.* A preparation containing mercury. — **mer·cu'ri·al·ly** *adv.* — **mer·cu'ri·al·ness** *n.*

mer·cu·ri·al·ism (mər·kyŏŏr'ē·əl·iz'əm) *n. Pathol.* Poisoning produced by excessive amounts of mercury.

mer·cu·ri·al·ize (mər·kyŏŏr'ē·əl·īz') *v.t.* **ized, iz·ing** 1. To make mercurial. 2. To treat with mercury. — **mer·cu'ri·al·i·za'tion** *n.*

mer·cu·ric (mər·kyŏŏr'ik) *adj. Chem.* Of, pertaining to, or containing mercury in its highest valence.

mercuric chloride *Chem.* A white, crystalline, very poisonous compound, $HgCl_2$, used in industry, the arts, and as a strong disinfectant: also called *bichloride of mercury, corrosive sublimate.* Also **mercuric chloride.**

mercuric sulfide Cinnabar.

mer·cu·rous (mər·kyŏŏr'əs) *adj. Chem.* Of, pertaining to, or containing mercury in its lowest valence.

mer·cu·ry (mûr'kyə·rē) *n. pl.* **·ries** 1. A heavy, silver-white metallic element (symbol Hg), liquid at ordinary temperatures: also called *hydrargyrum, quicksilver.* See ELEMENT. 2. The quicksilver in a thermometer or barometer, as indicating temperature, etc. 3. A messenger.

Mer·cu·ry (mûr'kyə·rē) In Roman mythology, the messenger of the gods, god of commerce, eloquence, and skill, and patron of travelers, merchants, and thieves: identified with the Greek *Hermes.* — *n.* The smallest planet of the solar system, and that nearest the sun. See PLANET.

mer·cy (mûr'sē) *n. pl.* **-cies** **1.** Kind or compassionate treatment of an offender, adversary, prisoner, etc., in one's power. **2.** A disposition to be kind, forgiving, or helpful. **3.** The power to show mercy or compassion. **4.** A thing to be thankful for. **— at the mercy of** Wholly in the power of. [< OF < L *merces, mercedis* payment, reward]
— **Syn. 1.** *Mercy* comes from compassion, kindness, or other ennobling sentiment. *Clemency* is a colder word, chiefly applied to moderation in the exercise of legal power to punish. *Leniency* denotes easygoing forbearance, sometimes with a suggestion of undue laxity or indulgence.

mercy killing Euthanasia.

mere (mir) *adj.* Being nothing more or less than: a *mere* trifle. [< L *merus* unmixed, bare]

-mere *combining form Zool.* A part or division. [< Gk. *meros* part]

mere·ly (mir'lē) *adv.* Nothing more than; solely; only.

mer·e·tri·cious (mer'ə·trish'əs) *adj.* Artificially and vulgarly attractive. [< L < *merere* to earn, gain] — **mer'e·tri'cious·ly** *adv.* — **mer'e·tri'cious·ness** *n.*

mer·gan·ser (mər·gan'sər) *n.* Any of several fish-eating, diving ducks having the head usu. crested. [< NL < L < *mergere* to plunge + *anser* goose]

merge (mûrj) *v.t. & v.i.* **merged, merg·ing** To combine or be combined so as to lose separate identity; blend. [< L *mergere* to dip, immerse] — **mer'gence** *n.*

merg·er (mûr'jər) *n.* **1.** The combining of two or more commercial interests into one. **2.** The act of merging.

me·rid·i·an (mə·rid'ē·ən) *n.* **1.** *Geog.* **a** A great circle drawn from any point on the earth's surface and passing through both poles. **b** Half of a circle so drawn between the poles. **2.** *Astron.* An imaginary great circle of the celestial sphere passing through its poles and the zenith of an observer at any point. **3.** The highest or culminating point; zenith. — *adj.* **1.** Of or pertaining to a meridian. **2.** Of or pertaining to midday. [< OF < L < *medius* middle + *dies* day]

me·ringue (mə·rang') *n.* **1.** The stiffly beaten white of eggs blended with sugar and usu. baked, used as a topping for pastry or pies. **2.** A small cake or tart shell made of this. [< F < G *meringe*, lit., cake of Mehringen (in Germany)]

me·ri·no (mə·rē'nō) *n. pl.* **-nos** **1.** A breed of sheep having fine, closely set, silky wool and heavy curled horns in the male; also, the wool of this sheep. **2.** A fine fabric originally made of merino wool. **3.** A type of fine yarn used for knitted underwear, hosiery, etc. — *adj.* Made of merino wool, yarn or cloth. [< Sp., roving from pasture to pasture, shepherd]

mer·it (mer'it) *n.* **1.** Worth or excellence; high quality. **2.** That which deserves esteem, praise, or reward. **3.** *Sometimes pl.* The quality or fact of being entitled to reward, praise, etc. **4.** *pl.* The actual rights or wrongs of a matter, esp. a legal matter. — *v.t.* To earn as a reward or punishment; deserve. [< OF < L < *merere* to deserve] — **mer'it·ed** *adj.*

mer·i·to·ri·ous (mer'ə·tôr'ē·əs, -tō'rē-) *adj.* Deserving of reward or praise. — **mer'i·to'ri·ous·ly** *adv.* — **mer'i·to'ri·ous·ness** *n.*

merit system A system adopted in the U.S. Civil Service whereby appointments and promotions are made on the basis of merit, ascertained through qualifying examinations.

merle (mûrl) *n.* The European blackbird. Also **merl.** [< F < L *merula* blackbird]

Mer·lin (mûr'lin) In the Arthurian cycle and other medieval legends, a magician and prophet. [< Med.L < Welsh *Myrrdin*, lit., sea fortress]

mer·maid (mûr'mād') *n.* A legendary marine creature having the head and upper body of a woman and the tail of a fish. Also **mer'maid'en** (-mād'n). [OE *mere* sea, lake + MAID]

mero- *combining form* Part; partial. Also, before vowels, **mer-**. [< Gk. *meros* part, division]

-merous *suffix Zool.* Having (a specified number or kind of) parts. [< Gk. *meros* part, division]

Mer·o·vin·gi·an (mer'ə·vin'jē·ən, -jən) *adj.* Of or pertaining to the first Frankish dynasty founded about A.D. 500 and lasting until 751. — *n.* A member of the Merovingian dynasty. Also **Mer'o·win'gi·an.** [< L *Merovingi*, descendants of Marovaeus, a legendary Frankish king]

mer·ri·ment (mer'i·mənt) *n.* Laughter; fun.

mer·ry (mer'ē) *adj.* **·ri·er, ·ri·est** **1.** Full of mirth and laughter; joyous; gay. **2.** Characterized by or conducive to mirth, cheerfulness, etc. [OE *myrige* pleasant] — **mer'ri·ly** *adv.* — **mer'ri·ness** *n.*

mer·ry-an·drew (mer'ē·an'drōō) *n.* A clown or buffoon.

mer·ry-go-round (mer'ē·gō·round') *n.* **1.** A revolving platform fitted with wooden horses, seats, etc., on which people, esp. children, ride for amusement; carousel. **2.** A whirl, as of business or pleasure. Also, *Brit.*, **roundabout.**

mer·ry·mak·ing (mer'ē·mā'king) *n.* The act of having fun and making merry. — *adj.* Festive. — **mer'ry·mak'er** *n.*

mes- Var. of MESO-.

me·sa (mā'sə, *Sp.* mä'sä) *n.* A high, flat tableland descending sharply to the surrounding plain, common in the SW U.S. [< Sp. < L *mensa* table]

mé·sal·li·ance (mā·zal'ē·əns, *Fr.* mā·zȧ·lyäns') *n.* A marriage with one of inferior position; misalliance. [< F]

mes·cal (mes·kal') *n.* **1.** A spineless cactus, native to the SW U.S. and northern Mexico, whose dried tops, **mescal buttons**, are chewed by the Indians for their narcotic effect: also called *peyote.* **2.** An intoxicating liquor distilled from certain species of agave. [< Sp. < Nahuatl *mexicalli*]

mes·dames (mā·dām', *Fr.* mā·dȧm') Plural of MADAME.

mes·de·moi·selles (mād·mwȧ·zel') *French* Plural of MADEMOISELLE.

me·seems (mē·sēmz') *v. impersonal Archaic* It seems to me.

mes·en·ceph·a·lon (mes'en·sef'ə·lon') *n. Anat.* One of the three principal divisions of the central nervous system of the embryo: also called *midbrain.* [< NL < MES- + ENCEPHALON] — **mes·en·ce·phal·ic** (mes·en'sə·fal'ik) *adj.*

mes·en·ter·y (mes'ən·ter'ē) *n. pl.* **·ter·ies** *Anat.* A membranous fold that invests an intestine and connects it with the posterior abdominal wall. Also **mes'en·te'ri·um** (-tir'ē·əm). [< Med.L < Gk. < *mesos* middle + *enteron* intestine] — **mes'en·ter'ic** *adj.*

mesh (mesh) *n.* **1.** One of the open spaces between the cords of a net or the wires of a screen. **2.** *pl.* The cords or wires bounding such a space or spaces. **3.** A net or network. **4.** *Usu. pl.* Anything that entangles or involves; a snare. **5.** *Mech.* The engagement of gear teeth. — *v.t. & v.i.* **1.** To make or become entangled, as in a net. **2.** To make or become engaged, as gear teeth. [< MDu. *maesche* mesh]

mesh·work (mesh'wûrk') *n.* Meshes; network.

mes·mer·ism (mes'mə·riz'əm, mez'-) *n.* Loosely, hypnotism: also called *animal magnetism.* [after Franz Anton *Mesmer*, 1733–1815, German physician] — **mes·mer·ic** (mes·mer'ik, mez-) *adj.* — **mes'mer·ist** *n.*

mes·mer·ize (mes'mə·rīz, mez'-) *v.t.* **·ized, ·iz·ing** To hypnotize. Also *Brit.* **mes'mer·ise.** — **mes'mer·i·za'tion** *n.*

meso- *combining form* **1.** Situated in the middle. **2.** Intermediate in size or degree. Also, before vowels, **mes-**. [< Gk. *mesos* middle]

mes·o·blast (mes'ə·blast, mē'sə-) *n. Biol.* The mesoderm in its early stages. [< MESO- + Gk. *blastos* sprout] — **mes'o·blas'tic** *adj.*

mes·o·carp (mes'ə·kärp, mē'sə-) *n. Bot.* The middle layer of a pericarp, as the fleshy part of certain fruits.

mes·o·derm (mes'ə·dûrm, mē'sə-) *n.* The middle of the three primary germ layers in the embryo of animals, developing into the skeletal and muscular systems.

Mes·o·lith·ic (mes'ə·lith'ik, mē'sə-) *adj. Anthropol.* Pertaining to or designating the period of human culture followed by the Neolithic and characterized by an economy transitional between food gathering and a settled agriculture.

mes·o·mor·phic (mes'ə·môr'fik, mē'sə-) *adj.* Designating a human body type characterized by a sturdy body structure. — **mes'o·morph** *n.* — **mes'o·mor'phy** *n.*

mes·on (mē'son, mes'on) *n. Physics* Any of a group of unstable nucleons having a mass intermediate between that of the electron and the proton. [< Gk. *mesos* middle]

mes·o·tho·ri·um (mes'ə·thôr'ē·əm, -thō'rē-; mē'sə-) *n.* Either of two isotopes resulting from the radioactive disintegration of thorium, intermediate between thorium and radiothorium.

Mes·o·zo·ic (mes'ə·zō'ik, mē'sə-) *Geol. adj.* Pertaining to the era between the Paleozoic and the Cenozoic. — *n.* This era, including the Triassic, Jurassic, and Cretaceous periods.

mes·quite (mes·kēt', mes'kēt) *n.* A spiny, leguminous shrub or small tree, found in SW U.S. and extending southward to Peru, that yields sweet pods used for cattle fodder: also called *honey mesquite.* Also spelled *mezquit, mezquite.* Also **mes·quit** (mes·kēt', mes'kēt). [< Sp. < Nahuatl *mizquitl*]

mess (mes) *n.* **1.** A state of disorder; esp., a condition of dirty or untidy confusion. **2.** A confusing, difficult, or embarrassing situation or condition; muddle. **3.** An unpleasant or confused mixture or collection; hodgepodge. **4.** A quantity of food sufficient for a meal or dish. **5.** A portion of soft, partly liquid food. **6.** A disagreeable or sloppy preparation of food. **7.** A number of persons who regularly take their meals together, as in the military; also, a meal taken by them. — *v.i.* **1.** To busy oneself; dabble: often with *around* or *about.* **2.** To make a mess; bungle: often with *up.* **3.** To interfere; meddle: often with *around.* **4.** To eat with as a member of a mess. — *v.t.* **5.** To make a mess of; botch: often with *up.* **6.** To make dirty: often with *up.* **7.** To provide meals for. [< OF < L *missus* course at a meal]

mes·sage (mes'ij) *n.* **1.** A communication sent by any of various means. **2.** An official or formal communication, as from a chief executive to a legislative body. **3.** A communication embodying important principles or counsel. [< OF < Med.L < *mittere* to send]

mes·sa·line (mes/ə-lēn′, mes/ə-lēn) *n.* A lightweight, lustrous, twilled silk fabric.

mes·sen·ger (mes/ən-jər) *n.* **1.** One sent with a message or on an errand; esp., one whose work is running errands. **2.** A bearer of official dispatches; courier. **3.** *Archaic* A harbinger. [ME < OF *messagier*. The *n* is nonhistoric.]

mess hall A place where a group of persons regularly take their meals, as in the army, navy, etc.

Mes·si·ah (mə-sī/ə) *n.* **1.** In Judaism, a deliverer of Israel promised by God and expected by the Jews. **2.** In Christianity, Jesus regarded as this deliverer. **3.** Any expected liberator of a country, people, etc. Also **Mes·si/as.** [< LL < Gk. < Aramaic *mĕshīhā*, Hebrew *māshīah* anointed] — **Mes·si/ah·ship** *n.* — **Mes·si·an·ic** (mes/ē·an/ik) *adj.*

mes·sieurs (mes/ərz, *Fr.* mā·syœ′) *n.pl.* of *Fr.* **mon·sieur** (mə·syœ′) Sirs; gentlemen: in English in the contracted form *Messrs.*, used as plural of *Mr.*

mess jacket A man's tailored jacket, usu. white and terminating at the waistline, worn on semiformal occasions.

mess kit A small, compact unit containing cooking and eating utensils, used by soldiers in the field and campers.

mess sergeant A noncommissioned officer who plans meals, issues rations, and superintends the company mess.

mess·y (mes/ē) *adj.* Being in or causing a condition of dirt or confusion; untidy. — **mess/i·ly** *adv.* — **mess/i·ness** *n.*

mes·ti·zo (mes·tē/zō) *n. pl.* **·zos** or **·zoes** Any one of mixed blood; in Mexico and the western U.S., a person of Spanish and Indian blood: also called *Ladino.* Also **mes·te/so, mes·ti/no** (-nō). [< Sp. < LL < L *mixtus*, pp. of *miscere* to mix] — **mes·ti/za** (-zə) *n.fem.*

met (met) Past tense and past participle of MEET[1].

met- Var. of META-.

meta- *prefix* **1.** Changed in place or form; reversed; altered. **2.** *Anat. & Zool.* Behind; after; on the farther side of; later: often equivalent to *post-* or *dorso-.* **3.** With; alongside. **4.** Beyond; over; transcending: *metaphysics, metapsychology.* **5.** *Chem.* **a** A modification of. Also, before vowels and *h*, **met-.** [< Gk. < *meta* after, beside, with]

met·a·bol·ic (met/ə·bol/ik) *adj. Biol. & Physiol.* Of, pertaining to, or having the nature of metabolism.

me·tab·o·lism (mə·tab/ə·liz/əm) *n. Biol. & Physiol.* The aggregate of all chemical processes constantly taking place in a living organism, including those that use energy to convert nutritive materials into protoplasm (anabolism) and those that release energy for vital processes in breaking down protoplasm into simpler substances (catabolism). [< Gk. < *meta-* beyond + *ballein* to throw]

me·tab·o·lize (mə·tab/ə·līz) *v.t. & v.i.* **·lized, ·liz·ing** To subject to or change by metabolism.

met·a·car·pus (met/ə·kär/pəs) *n. Anat.* The part of the forelimb between the carpus or wrist and the phalanges or bones of the finger. [< NL < Gk. < *meta-* beyond + *karpos* wrist] — **met·a·car/pal** *adj. & n.*

met·a·gal·ax·y (met/ə·gal/ək·sē) *n. pl.* **·ax·ies** *Astron.* The entire material universe, regarded esp. as a system including all the galaxies.

met·al (met/l) *n.* **1.** Any of a class of elements characterized by a distinctive luster, malleability, ductility, thermal and electrical conductivity, and capable of forming positive ions. **2.** A composition of such metallic elements; alloy. **3.** Molten glass. **4.** The constituent material of anything. — **white metal** Any one of the various white alloys, as pewter, Babbitt metal, etc., used for ornaments, castings, etc. — *v.t.* **met·aled** or **·alled, met·al·ing** or **·al·ling** To furnish or cover with metal. [< OF < L < Gk. *metallon*]

me·tal·lic (mə·tal/ik) *adj.* **1.** Of, pertaining to, or consisting of metal. **2.** Resembling or having the nature of metal: a *metallic* sound. **3.** Yielding or containing metal.

met·al·lif·er·ous (met/ə·lif/ər·əs) *adj.* Yielding or containing metal.

met·al·lur·gy (met/ə·lûr/jē) *n.* **1.** The art or science of extracting a metal or metals from ores. **2.** The art or science of working with metals and alloys for the purpose of their development, improvement, etc. [< NL < Gk. < *metallon* mine + *-ergos* working] — **met/al·lur/gic** or **·gi·cal** *adj.* — **met/al·lur/gi·cal·ly** *adv.* — **met/al·lur/gist** *n.*

met·al·work (met/l·wûrk′) *n.* **1.** Articles made of metal. **2.** The art of making such things. — **met/al·work/er** *n.* — **met/al·work/ing** *n.*

met·a·mor·phic (met/ə·môr/fik) *adj.* **1.** Of or pertaining to metamorphosis. **2.** *Geol.* Of, pertaining to, or exhibiting metamorphism. Also **met/a·mor/phous.**

met·a·mor·phism (met/ə·môr/fiz·əm) *n.* **1.** *Geol.* The changes in the composition and texture of rocks caused by force, heat, pressure, moisture, etc. **2.** Metamorphosis.

met·a·mor·phose (met/ə·môr/fōz) *v.t.* **·phosed, ·phos·ing** **1.** To change the form of. — *v.i.* **2.** To undergo metamorphosis. Also **met/a·mor/phize.** [< MF *métamorphoser*]

met·a·mor·pho·sis (met/ə·môr/fə·sis) *n. pl.* **·pho·ses** (-fə-

sēz) **1.** Change from one form, shape, or substance into another by any means. **2.** Complete transformation of character, purpose, circumstances, etc. **3.** One who or that which is metamorphosed. **4.** *Biol.* Any marked change in the form and structure of an animal in its development from embryo to adult, as from tadpole to frog. [< L < Gk. < *meta-* beyond + *morphē* form]

met·a·phor (met/ə·fôr, -fər) *n.* A figure of speech in which one object is likened to another by speaking of it as if it were that other, as *He was a lion in battle:* distinguished from *simile.* — **Syn.** See SIMILE. — **mixed metaphor** A figurative expression in which two or more incongruous metaphors are used, as *He kept a tight rein on his boiling passions.* [< F < L < Gk. < *meta-* beyond, over + *pherein* to carry] — **met/a·phor/ic** (-fôr/ik, -for/ik) or **·i·cal** *adj.* — **met/a·phor/i·cal·ly** *adv.*

met·a·phys·i·cal (met/ə·fiz/i·kəl) *adj.* **1.** Of, pertaining to, or of the nature of metaphysics. **2.** Highly abstruse; abstract. **3.** Of or designating certain English poets of the 17th century whose poetry is characterized by complex, intellectual imagery and paradox. [See METAPHYSICS.] — **met/a·phys/i·cal·ly** *adv.*

met·a·phys·ics (met/ə·fiz/iks) *n.pl.* (*construed as sing.*) **1.** The branch of philosophy that investigates principles of reality transcending those of any particular science, traditionally including cosmology and ontology. **2.** All speculative philosophy. [< Med.L < Med.Gk. < *ta meta ta physika* (the works) after the *Physics* of Aristotle]

me·tas·ta·sis (mə·tas/tə·sis) *n. pl.* **·ses** (-sēz) *Pathol.* **1.** The transfer of a disease from one part of the body to another, as in certain types of cancer. **2.** A site to which such a transfer has been made. [< L < Gk. < *meta-* after + *histanai* to place] — **met/a·stat/ic** (-stat/ik) *adj.* — **met/a·stat/i·cal·ly** *adv.*

me·tas·ta·size (mə·tas/tə·sīz) *v.i.* **·sized, ·siz·ing** *Pathol.* To shift or spread from one part of the body to another, as a malignant growth.

met·a·tar·sus (met/ə·tär/səs) *n. pl.* **·si** (-sī) *Anat.* **1.** In man, the part of the foot situated between the tarsus and the bones of the toes. **2.** An analogous part in the hind or pelvic limb of animals or birds. — **met/a·tar/sal** *adj. & n.*

me·tath·e·sis (mə·tath/ə·sis) *n. pl.* **·ses** (-sēz) The transposition of letters, syllables, or sounds in a word: Old English *bridd* became *bird* by *metathesis.* [< LL < Gk. < *meta-* over + *tithenai* to place] — **met·a·thet·ic** (met/ə·thet/ik) or **·i·cal** *adj.*

met·a·zo·an (met/ə·zō/ən) *n. Zool.* Any of a primary division of animals, whose bodies are made up of many cells. Also **met/a·zo/on.** — *adj.* Of the metazoans: also **met/a·zo/ic.** [< META- + Gk. *zōion* animal]

mete[1] (mēt) *v.t.* **met·ed, met·ing** To allot or distribute by or as by measure: usu. followed by *out.* [OE *metan* to measure]

mete[2] (mēt) *n.* A boundary line; limit: now chiefly in the phrase **metes and bounds.** [< OF < L *meta* goal, boundary]

me·tem·psy·cho·sis (mə·temp/sə·kō/sis, met/əm·sī-) *n.* Transmigration of souls. [< LL < Gk. < *meta-* over + *em-psychoein* to animate]

met·en·ceph·a·lon (met/en·sef/ə·lon) *n. pl.* **·la** (-lə) *Anat.* That part of the brain comprising the cerebellum and the pons Varolii: also called *afterbrain.* — **met/en·ce·phal/ic** (-sə·fal/ik) *adj.*

me·te·or (mē/tē·ər, -ôr) *n.* **1.** *Astron.* A meteoroid that on entering the earth's atmosphere at great speed is heated to luminosity and is visible as a streak of light: also called *shooting star.* **2.** Loosely, a meteorite or meteoroid. [< Med.L < Gk. < *meta-* beyond + *eōra* suspension]

me·te·or·ic (mē/tē·ôr/ik, -or/ik) *adj.* **1.** Of, pertaining to, or consisting of meteors. **2.** Resembling a meteor; brilliant, rapid, and dazzling: a *meteoric* career. **3.** Of or pertaining to atmospheric phenomena. — **me/te·or/i·cal·ly** *adv.*

me·te·or·ite (mē/tē·ə·rīt′) *n.* A portion of a meteor that has not been completely destroyed by combustion and has fallen to earth. — **me/te·or·it/ic** (-ə·rit/ik) *adj.*

me·te·or·oid (mē/tē·ə·roid′) *n. Astron.* One of the pieces of matter moving through outer space, that upon entering the earth's atmosphere form meteors.

me·te·or·ol·o·gy (mē/tē·ə·rol/ə·jē) *n.* **1.** The science that treats of atmospheric phenomena, esp. those that relate to weather. **2.** The weather conditions of any particular place. [< Gk. < *meteōros* high in the air + *logos* discourse] — **me/te·or·o·log/ic** (-ôr·ə·loj/ik) or **·i·cal** *adj.* — **me/te·or·o·log/i·cal·ly** *adv.* — **me/te·or·ol/o·gist** *n.*

meteor shower *Astron.* Any of various displays of meteors that recur at definite intervals and appear to radiate from a single point or region.

me·ter[1] (mē/tər) *n.* An instrument or device used to measure and indicate quantity or variation in amount, as of a liquid or gas, electric current, light, etc.; also, a similar device for measuring speed, time, distance, etc. — *v.t.* To measure or test by means of a meter. [< METE[1]]

me·ter[2] (mē/tər) *n.* **1.** A measured verbal rhythm constituting one of the chief characteristics of verse, and, in prosody, forming definite groups (feet) of accented and unaccented syllables, usu. of a specified number for each line. **2.** *Music* The combining of rhythmic pulses into successive groups having like arrangement and duration. Also, *esp. Brit.*, *metre*. [OE < L < Gk. *metron* a measure]

me·ter[3] (mē/tər) *n.* The basic unit of length in the metric system, equivalent to 39.37 inches. Also *metre*. See table front of book. [< F *mètre* < Gk. *metron*]

-meter *combining form* **1.** A device for measuring (a specified quality, thing, etc.). **2.** Division into (a specified number of) prosodic feet: *pentameter*. **3.** A (specified kind of) unit in the metric system: *kilometer*: also, *esp. Brit.*, -*metre*.

me·ter·age (mē/tər·ij) *n.* The process or result of measuring by or as by a meter.

me·ter-kil·o·gram-sec·ond (mē/tər·kil/ə·gram/sek/ənd) *adj.* See MKS.

meth- *combining form Chem.* Used to indicate the presence of a methyl group in a compound. Also, before consonants, *metho-*. [< METHYL]

meth·ane (meth/ān) *n. Chem.* A colorless, odorless, flammable gas, CH_4, the first member of the methane series, the chief constituent of firedamp and marsh gas, and commercially obtained from natural gas.

methane series *Chem.* A group of saturated hydrocarbons having the general formula C_nH_{2n+2}: also called *paraffin series*.

meth·a·nol (meth/ə·nōl, -nol) *n. Chem.* A colorless, flammable, highly toxic alcohol, CH_3OH, obtained by the destructive distillation of wood, and widely used in industry and the arts: also called *methyl alcohol, wood alcohol.*

me·thinks (mē·thingks/) *v. impersonal,* **me·thought** *Archaic & Poetic* It seems to me. [OE *thyncan* to seem]

metho- Var. of METH-.

meth·od (meth/əd) *n.* **1.** A way, means, or manner of proceeding; esp., a regular, systematic, or orderly way of doing anything. **2.** System, order, or regularity in action or thought. **3.** The techniques used in a particular field of knowledge, thought, practice, etc.: the scientific *method.* **4.** Systematic and orderly arrangement, as of ideas, facts, topics, etc. — **the method** A system or style of acting in which the actor makes a strong emotional identification with the role portrayed. [F < L < Gk. < *meta-* after + *hodos* way] — **meth/od·ism** *n.* — **meth/od·ist** *n.*

me·thod·i·cal (mə·thod/i·kəl) *adj.* **1.** Arranged in or performed in systematic order. **2.** Characterized by orderly or systematic habits, behavior, etc.: a *methodical* man. Also **me·thod/ic.** — **me·thod/i·cal·ly** *adv.* — **me·thod/i·cal·ness** *n.*

Meth·od·ist (meth/əd·ist) *n.* A member of any of the Protestant denominations having their origin in a religious movement begun in England in the first half of the 18th century by John and Charles Wesley and their followers. — *adj.* Pertaining to or characteristic of Methodism or Methodists. — **Meth/od·ism** *n.* — **Meth/od·is/tic** or -ti·cal *adj.*

meth·od·ize (meth/ə·diz) *v.t.* **·ized, ·iz·ing** To reduce to or arrange in accordance with a method. — **meth/od·i·za/tion** *n.*

meth·od·ol·o·gy (meth/ə·dol/ə·jē) *n. pl.* **·gies 1.** The principles, practices, etc., of orderly thought or procedure applied to a particular branch of learning. **2.** The branch of logic dealing with such procedures. [< Gk. *methodos* method + -LOGY] — **meth·od·o·log·i·cal** (meth/əd·ə·loj/i·kəl) *adj.* — **meth/od·o·log/i·cal·ly** *adv.*

me·thought (mē·thôt/) Past tense of METHINKS.

Me·thu·se·lah (mə·thōō/zə·lə) In the Old Testament, a Hebrew patriarch reputed to have lived 969 years. *Gen.* v 27. — *n.* A very old man.

meth·yl (meth/əl) *n. Chem.* A univalent organic radical, CH_3, existing chiefly in combination, as in methanol, etc. [< METHYLENE] — **me·thyl·ic** (mə·thil/ik) *adj.*

methyl alcohol *Chem.* Methanol.

meth·yl·ate (meth/əl·āt) *Chem. n.* A compound derived from methanol by replacing the hydroxyl group with a metal. — *v.t.* **·at·ed, ·at·ing 1.** To mix with methanol. **2.** To combine with the methyl radical. — **meth/yl·a/tion** *n.*

methylated spirit Denatured alcohol prepared by the admixture of methanol. Also **methylated spirits.**

me·tic·u·lous (mə·tik/yə·ləs) *adj.* Extremely or overly precise about details, esp. in minor or trivial matters. [< F < L *meticulosus* fearful] — **me·tic/u·los/i·ty** (-los/ə·tē), **me·tic/u·lous·ness** *n.* — **me·tic/u·lous·ly** *adv.*
  — **Syn.** Scrupulous, punctilious, fastidious.

mé·tier (mā·tyā/) *n.* **1.** One's occupation, trade, or profession. **2.** Work or activity for which one is esp. well suited. [< OF < L *ministerium* service, employment]

met·o·nym·i·cal (met/ə·nim/i·kəl) *adj.* **1.** Pertaining to or characterized by metonymy. **2.** Used in metonymy. Also **met/o·nym/ic.** — **met/o·nym/i·cal·ly** *adv.*

me·ton·y·my (mə·ton/ə·mē) *n.* A figure of speech that

consists in substituting an associated term for the name itself, as in "the *crown* decrees" for "the *ruler* decrees." [< L < Gk. < *meta-* altered + *onyma* name]

metr- Var. of METRO-.

Met·ra·zol (met/rə·zōl, -zol) *n.* Proprietary name of a synthetic drug, $C_6H_{10}N_4$, used in medicine as a heart stimulant and in the shock treatment of certain mental disorders. Also **met/ra·zol.**

me·tre[1] (mē/tər) See METER[1].

me·tre[2] (mē/tər) See METER[3].

-metre See -METER (def. 3).

met·ric (met/rik) *adj.* Of, pertaining to, or using the meter as a unit of measurement. [< F *métrique*]

met·ri·cal (met/ri·kəl) *adj.* **1.** Of, pertaining to, or characterized by meter; rhythmic. **2.** Composed in or constituting a unit of poetic meter. **3.** Of, pertaining to, or involving measurement. Also **met/ric.** — **met/ri·cal·ly** *adv.*

metric hundredweight A unit of weight equal to 50 kilograms.

met·rics (met/riks) *n.pl.* (construed as sing.) **1.** The art or branch of learning concerned with meter in prosody. **2.** The science or theory of measurement.

metric system A decimal system of weights and measures having as fundamental units the gram, the meter, and the liter. See table front of book.

metric ton A unit of weight equal to 1,000 kilograms, or 2,204.62 pounds avoirdupois.

met·rist (met/rist) *n.* One who is skillful in using poetic meter. Also **met/ri·cist** (-rə·sist). [< Med.L *metrista*]

met·ro (met/rō) *n. Often cap. Informal* An underground railroad; subway; esp., the subway system of Paris. Also **mé·tro** (mā·trō/). [< F *métro* < (*chemin de fer*) *métro-* (*politain*) metro(politan railroad)]

metro-[1] *combining form* The uterus; pertaining to the uterus. Also, before vowels, *metr-.* [< Gk. *metra* uterus]

metro-[2] *combining form* Measure. Also, before vowels, *metr-.* [< Gk. *metron* a measure]

met·ro·nome (met/rə·nōm) *n.* An instrument for indicating exact tempo in music, usu. producing audible clicks controlled by a reversed pendulum whose motion is regulated by a sliding weight. [< METRO-[2] + Gk. *nomos* law] — **met/ro·nom/ic** (-nom/ik) *adj.*

me·tro·nym·ic (mē/trə·nim/ik, met/rə-) *adj.* Derived from the name of one's mother or a female ancestor. — *n.* A metronymic name or designation. [< Gk. < *mētēr* mother + *onyma* name]

me·trop·o·lis (mə·trop/ə·lis) *n. pl.* **·lis·es 1.** The capital or the largest or most important city of a country, state, or area. **2.** An urban center of activity, culture, trade, etc. **3.** The see or city over which a metropolitan has authority. [< Gk. < *mētēr* mother + *polis* city]

METRONOME

met·ro·pol·i·tan (met/rə·pol/ə·tən) *adj.* **1.** Constituting a major urban center and its environs: the *metropolitan* area. **2.** Pertaining to or designating a bishop having authority over a metropolis (def. 3). — *n.* **1.** In various churches, an archbishop having authority over the bishops within his jurisdiction. **2.** One who lives in or has the viewpoint, etc., of one living in a metropolis.

-metry *combining form* The process, science, or art of measuring: *geometry.* [< Gk. *metria* < *metron* a measure]

met·tle (met/l) *n.* **1.** Character or temperament. **2.** Courage; pluck. — **on one's mettle** Aroused to one's best efforts. [Var. of METAL]

met·tle·some (met/l·səm) *adj.* Full of spirit; courageous; valiant. Also **met/tled** (met/əld).

mew[1] (myōō) *n.* **1.** A cage in which molting hawks are kept. **2.** *pl.* Stables built around a court or alley: so called from the royal stables in London. **3.** *pl.* (construed as sing.) *Chiefly Brit.* A narrow street or alley, often with dwellings converted from stables. — *v.t.* To confine in or as in a cage; often with *up.* [< OF *muer* to change, molt < L *mutare*]

mew[2] (myōō) *v.i.* To utter the high-pitched cry of a cat. — *n.* The high-pitched, plaintive cry of a cat. [Imit.]

mew[3] (myōō) *n.* A gull; esp. the common gull of Europe: also called *sea mew.* [OE *mǣw*]

mewl (myōōl) *v.i.* To whimper or cry feebly, as an infant. — *n.* A whimper or feeble cry. [Freq. of MEW[2]]

Mex·i·can (mek/sə·kən) *n.* **1.** A native or inhabitant of Mexico. **2.** A language indigenous to Mexico, as Nahuatl. — *adj.* Of Mexico, its inhabitants, or their language.

Mexican hairless One of a breed of small dogs, hairless except for a tuft on the head and the end of the tail.

Mexican War See table for WAR.

mez·cal (mez·kal/) See MESCAL.

---

mez·quit (mez·kēt′, mez′kēt), **mez·quite** See MESQUITE.

mez·za·nine (mez′ə·nēn, -nin) n. 1. An intermediate story, usu. not of full width, between two main floors. 2. In a theater, the first balcony, or the front rows of the balcony. [< F < Ital. *mezzanino* < L *medianus*]

mez·zo (met′sō, med′zō, mez′ō) adj. Half; medium; moderate: often used in combination: *mezzo-soprano.* — adv. *Music* Moderately: *mezzo forte.* — n. pl. **·zos** A mezzo-soprano. [< Ital., < L *medius* middle]

mez·zo-so·pran·o (met′sō·sə·pran′ō, -prä′nō, med′zō-, mez′ō-) n. pl. **·pran·os** or **·pra·ni** (-nē) 1. A female voice intermediate between a soprano and a contralto. 2. A person having such a voice. — adj. Of or pertaining to such a voice. [< Ital.]

mez·zo·tint (met′sō·tint′, med′zō-, mez′ō-) n. 1. A method of engraving in which the roughened surface of a copper or steel plate is scraped or burnished to produce effects of light and shade. 2. A print produced from such a plate. — v.t. To engrave by or represent in mezzotint. [< Ital. < *mezzo* middle + *tinto* painted] — **mez′zo·tint′er** n.

mi (mē) n. *Music* The third syllable used in solmization; the third tone of a major scale; also, the tone E.

Mi·am·i (mī·am′ē, -am′ə) n. pl. **Mi·am·i** or **Mi·am·is** A member of an Algonquian tribe of North American Indians formerly inhabiting a region in Wisconsin, Indiana, and Ohio. [< N.Am.Ind.]

mi·aou, mi·aow (mē·ou′) See MEOW.

mi·as·ma (mī·az′mə, mē-) n. pl. **·mas** or **·ma·ta** (-mə·tə) 1. Noxious or unwholesome influence, etc. 2. The poisonous effluvium once supposed to rise from swamps, etc. Also **mi′asm** (-az·əm). [< NL < Gk. < *miainein* to stain, defile] — **mi·as′mal, mi·as·mat·ic** (mī′əz·mat′ik), **mi·as′mic** adj.

mib (mib) n. *U.S. Dial.* 1. A marble. 2. pl. The game of marbles. [? Alter. of MARBLE]

mi·ca (mī′kə) n. Any of a class of silicate minerals, cleaving into tough, thin, often transparent and flexible laminae: sometimes called *isinglass.* [< L, crumb] — **mi·ca·ceous** (mī·kā′shəs) adj.

Mi·cah (mī′kə) Eighth-century B.C. Hebrew prophet. — n. A book of the Old Testament bearing his name. Also, in the Douai Bible, **Mi·che·as** (mī·kē′əs).

mice (mīs) Plural of MOUSE.

Mi·chael (mī′kəl) One of the archangels, represented as a militant protector and defender of the faithful: sometimes called *the Archangel. Dan.* x 10–12, *Rev.* xii 7–9.

Mich·ael·mas (mik′əl·məs) n. September 29, the church festival of the archangel Michael, in Great Britain serving as the fall quarter day. Also **Michaelmas Day.**

mick·ey (mik′ē) n. pl. **·eys** *U.S. Slang* A Mickey Finn.

Mick·ey Finn (mik′ē fin′) *U.S. Slang* An alcoholic drink secretly drugged so as to render the drinker unconscious. Also **mick′ey finn.** [Origin unknown]

Mic·mac (mik′mak) n. pl. **·mac** or **·macs** A member of an Algonquian tribe living in Nova Scotia, New Brunswick, and Newfoundland. [< N.Am.Ind., lit., allies]

mi·cra (mī′krə) Plural of MICRON.

micro- *combining form* 1. Very small; minute. 2. Enlarging or magnifying size or volume: *microscope.* 3. *Pathol.* Abnormally small or underdeveloped. 4. Of a science, depending on, using, or requiring a microscope: *microbiology.* 5. In the metric system and in technical usage, one millionth of (a specified unit): *microwatt.* Sometimes, before vowels, **micr-.** [< Gk. *mikros* small]

mi·crobe (mī′krōb) n. A microscopic organism; esp., one of the bacteria that cause disease. [< F < Gk. *mikros* small + *bios* life] — **mi·cro′bi·al, mi·cro′bi·an, mi·cro′bic** adj.

— **Syn.** *Microbe* was originally a general term, applied at first to protozoa, and then to *bacteria; germ* originally denoted a reproductive cell. Both words are now popularly used to refer to disease-producing *bacteria. Microorganism* developed as a general term for protozoa, bacteria, and *viruses. Bacteria* are unicellular organisms, distinguished from protozoa because they possess both plant and animal characteristics. *Bacillus* properly denotes one class only of *bacteria.* A *virus* is a complex protein molecule capable of invading the cells and there reproducing itself.

mi·cro·bi·ol·o·gy (mī′krō·bī·ol′ə·jē) n. The branch of biology concerned with the study of microorganisms. — **mi′cro·bi′o·log′i·cal** (-bī′ə·loj′i·kəl) adj. — **mi′cro·bi·ol′o·gist** n.

mi·cro·ceph·a·ly (mī′krō·sef′ə·lē) n. Abnormal smallness of the head and cranial capacity. [< MICRO- + Gk. *kephalē* head] — **mi′cro·ce·phal′ic** (-sə·fal′ik) adj. & n. — **mi′cro·ceph′a·lous** adj.

mi·cro·chem·is·try (mī′krō·kem′is·trē) n. A branch of chemistry dealing with minute quantities.

mi·cro·coc·cus (mī′krə·kok′əs) n. pl. **·coc·ci** (-kok′sī) Any member of a group of spherical bacteria that occur in irregular masses and are often pathogenic. [< NL]

mi·cro·cop·y (mī′krə·kop′ē) n. pl. **·cop·ies** A reduced photographic copy of a letter, manuscript, etc. — v.t. & v.i. **·cop·ied, ·cop·y·ing** To reproduce in the form of microcopy.

mi·cro·cosm (mī′krə·koz′əm) n. 1. A little world; the universe in miniature. 2. Man regraded as epitomizing the universe. Also **mi·cro·cos′mos** (-koz′məs). [< LL < Gk. *mikros cosmos*, lit., little world] — **mi′cro·cos′mic** adj.

mi·cro·film (mī′krə·film) n. A photographic reproduction on film of a printed page, document, or other object, highly reduced for ease in transmission and storage, and capable of reenlargement. — v.t. & v.i. To reproduce on microfilm.

mi·cro·gram (mī′krə·gram) n. In the metric system, one millionth of a gram. Also **mi′cro·gramme.**

mi·cro·groove (mī′krə·grōōv) n. An extremely fine groove cut in the surface of a long-playing phonograph record.

Mi·cro·groove (mī′krə·grōōv) n. A long-playing record: a trade name.

mi·crom·e·ter (mī·krom′ə·tər) n. 1. An instrument used for measuring very small distances or dimensions, as in conjunction with a microscope or telescope. 2. A micrometer caliper.

micrometer caliper A caliper or gauge having a micrometer screw, used for precise measurements.

micrometer screw A screw with a very finely cut thread and a graduated head, used in micrometers, etc.

mi·crom·e·try (mī·krom′ə·trē) n. Measurement by means of a micrometer. — **mi·cro·met·ric** (mī′krō·met′rik) or **·ri·cal** adj. — **mi′cro·met′ri·cal·ly** adv.

MICROMETER
a Frame. *b* Anvil.
c Movable spindle.
d Sleeve. *e* Thimble.

mi·cro·mil·li·me·ter (mī′krō·mil′ə·mē′tər) n. A millimicron. Also **mi′cro·mil′li·me′tre.**

mi·cron (mī′kron) n. pl. **·cra** (-krə) A unit of measurement equal to one thousandth of a millimeter. [< NL < Gk. *mikron*, neut. of *mikros* small]

Mi·cro·ne·sian (mī′krə·nē′zhən, -shən) adj. Of or pertaining to Micronesia, its people, or their languages. — n. 1. A native of Micronesia. 2. Any of the Austronesian languages spoken in Micronesia.

mi·cro·or·gan·ism (mī′krō·ôr′gən·iz′əm) n. Any microscopic or ultramicroscopic organism, as a bacterium or protozoan. Also **mi·cro·or′gan·ism.** — **Syn.** See MICROBE.

mi·cro·phone (mī′krə·fōn) n. A device for converting sound waves into electric currents, forming the principal element of a telephone transmitter or of any sound-reproducing system, as in broadcasting. — **mi·cro·phon′ic** (-fon′ik) adj.

mi·cro·pho·to·graph (mī′krō·fō′tə·graf, -gräf) n. 1. A very small or microscopic photograph, as on microfilm. 2. Loosely, a photomicrograph. — **mi′cro·pho′to·graph′ic** adj. — **mi′cro·pho·tog′ra·phy** (-fə·tog′rə·fē) n.

mi·cro·print (mī′krə·print) n. A microphotograph reproduced in a print that may be examined or read by means of a magnifying glass. — v.t. & v.i. To represent or reproduce by means of a microprint.

mi·cro·scope (mī′krə·skōp) n. An optical instrument used for magnifying objects too small to be seen or clearly observed by ordinary vision. [< NL *microscopium*]

mi·cro·scop·ic (mī′krə·skop′ik) adj. 1. So minute as to be visible only under a microscope. 2. Exceedingly small. 3. Of, pertaining to, or of the nature of a microscope or microscopy. 4. Performed with or depending on use of a microscope. 5. Characterized by or done with minute observation. Also **mi′cro·scop′i·cal.** — **mi′cro·scop′i·cal·ly** adv.

mi·cros·co·py (mī·kros′kə·pē, mī′krə·skō′pē) n. 1. The process or technique of using the microscope. 2. Investigation by means of the microscope. — **mi·cros·co·pist** (mī·kros′kə·pist, mī′krə·skō′pist) n.

mi·cro·tome (mī′krə·tōm) n. An instrument for cutting very thin sections of organic tissue, etc., for microscopic observations. — **mi′cro·tom′ic** (-tom′ik) or **·i·cal** adj.

mi·cro·wave (mī′krə·wāv) n. An electromagnetic wave having a frequency between about 1,000 and 30,000 megacycles. Compare RADIO WAVE.

mic·tu·rate (mik′chə·rāt) v.i. **·rat·ed, ·rat·ing** To urinate. [< L *micturire* to desire to urinate] — **mic′tu·ri′tion** (-rish′ən) n.

mid¹ (mid) adj. Being approximately in the middle; central. [OE *midd-*]

mid² (mid) prep. *Chiefly Poetic* Amid; among. Also **'mid.**

mid- *combining form* 1. Middle point or part of, as in: *midafternoon, mid-century.* 2. Being in the middle or center, as in: **midpoint; mid-position** 3. With adjectives, of or pertaining to the middle part of that which is modified or implied, as in: **mid-Asian, midmonthly.**

mid·air (mid′âr′) n. A point or region seemingly in the middle or midst of the air. Also **mid′-air′.**

Mi·das (mī′dəs) In Greek legend, a king of Phrygia who had the power of turning whatever he touched into gold.

mid·brain (mid′brān′) n. *Anat.* The mesencephalon.

mid·day (mid′dā′) n. The middle of the day; noon. — adj. Of, pertaining to, or occurring in the middle of the day.

mid·den (mid′n) n. *Brit. Dial.* A dunghill or heap of refuse. [ME *midding* < Scand.]

mid·dle (mid′l) *adj.* **1.** Equally distant from the extremes, periphery, etc.; central. **2.** Intermediate in position, status, etc. **3.** Intervening between the earlier part and the latter part of a sequence, period of time, etc. **4.** Moderate, as in size or effect. **5.** *Usu. cap.* Designating a language in a stage between an earlier and a recent form: *Middle* English. — *n.* **1.** The area or point equally distant from the extremes, etc. **2.** The intermediate section of anything. **3.** The middle part of the body; the waist. — *v.t.* **·dled, ·dling** To place in the middle. [OE *middel*]

middle age The time of life between youth and old age, usu. thought of as the years between 40 and 60. — **mid′dle-aged′** (mid′l·ājd′) *adj.*

Middle Ages The period in European history between classical antiquity and the Renaissance, usu. regarded as extending from the downfall of Rome, in 476, to about 1450.

Middle Atlantic States New York, New Jersey, and Pennsylvania.

middle C *Music* The note written on the first ledger line above the bass staff and the first ledger line below the treble staff; also, the corresponding tone.

middle class The part of a society occupying a social or economic position between the laboring class and the very wealthy or the nobility. — **mid′dle-class** *adj.*

middle ear *Anat.* The portion of the ear between the tympanic membrane and the opening of the Eustachian tube; also, the membrane itself: also called *tympanum.*

Middle East **1.** The region including Egypt and the countries of SW Asia west of Pakistan and India. **2.** *Brit.* This region with the exception of Turkey and including India, Pakistan, Burma, Tibet, Libya, Ethiopia, and Somaliland.

Middle Latin Medieval Latin. See under LATIN.

mid·dle·man (mid′l·man′) *n. pl.* **·men** (-men′) **1.** One who acts as an agent; go-between. **2.** One who buys in bulk from producers and sells to retailers or consumers.

mid·dle·most (mid′l·mōst′) *adj.* Situated exactly or most nearly in the middle: also *midmost.*

middle of the road A moderate position or course.

mid·dle-of-the-road·er (mid′l·əv·thə·rō′dər) *n.* One who endorses a moderate course, esp. in politics.

mid·dle·weight (mid′l·wāt′) *n.* **1.** A person or animal of average weight. **2.** A boxer or wrestler weighing between 147 and 160 pounds.

mid·dling (mid′ling) *adj.* **1.** Of middle size, quality, or condition; mediocre. **2.** *Informal* In fair health. — *adv. Informal* Fairly; moderately. — *n.* **1.** *pl.* Any of various commodities regarded as intermediate in quality, size, etc. **2.** *pl.* The coarser part of ground grain. — **mid′dling** *adv.*

mid·dy (mid′ē) *n. pl.* **·dies** *Informal* **1.** A midshipman. **2.** A middy blouse (which see).

middy blouse A loosely fitting blouse with a sailor collar.

midge (mij) *n.* **1.** A gnat or small fly; esp. any of various small, dipterous insects. **2.** An extremely small person or creature. [OE *mycge*]

mid·get (mij′it) *n.* **1.** A person of abnormally small size but of normal physical proportions. **2.** Anything very small of its kind. — *adj.* Very small; diminutive.

Mid·i·an·ite (mid′ē·ən·īt′) *n.* One of an ancient nomadic tribe of Arabia. *Gen.* xxv 2. [< *Midian* a son of Abraham]

mid·i·ron (mid′ī′ərn) *n.* In golf, a five iron.

mid·land (mid′lənd) *n.* The central or interior part of a country or region. — *adj.* Of, pertaining to, or situated in an inland or interior region.

Mid·land (mid′lənd) *n.* The dialects of Middle English spoken in London and the Midlands; esp., **East Midland**, the direct predecessor of Modern English.

mid·most (mid′mōst′) *adj.* Middlemost. — *adv.* In the midst or middle. [OE *mydmest*]

mid·night (mid′nīt′) *n.* The middle of the night; twelve o'clock at night. — *adj.* **1.** Of or occurring at midnight. **2.** Resembling midnight; very dark. — **to burn the midnight oil** To work or study late into the night.

midnight sun The sun visible at midnight during summer at latitudes greater than 70° north or south of the equator.

mid·rib (mid′rib′) *n. Bot.* The central vein of a leaf.

mid·riff (mid′rif′) *n.* The part of the body between the chest and the abdomen, in the region of the diaphragm; also, the diaphragm itself. [OE < *midd* mid + *hrif* belly]

mid·ship (mid′ship′) *adj. Naut.* Of, pertaining to, or situated in the middle of a ship.

mid·ship·man (mid′ship′mən) *n. pl.* **·men** (-mən) **1.** In the U.S. Navy, a student training to be commissioned as an officer, esp. at the U.S. Naval Academy at Annapolis. **2.** In the Commonwealth navies, an officer ranking between a naval cadet and the lowest commissioned officer. See table at GRADE. [< *amidshipman;* so called from being amidships when on duty]

mid·ships (mid′ships′) *Naut. adv.* Amidships.

midst (midst) *n.* **1.** The condition of being surrounded, as by people or things, engaged, as in an activity, or beset, as by troubles: used chiefly in the phrase **in the midst of.** **2.** The central part; middle. — **in our (your, their) midst** Among us (you, them). — *prep.* Amid. [ME *middest*]

mid·sum·mer (mid′sum′ər) *n.* The middle of summer.

mid·term (mid′tûrm′) *n.* **1.** The middle of a term. **2.** *U.S.* An examination given in the middle of a school term.

mid·Vic·to·ri·an (mid′vik·tôr′ē·ən, -tō′rē-) *adj.* **1.** Of or pertaining to the middle period of Queen Victoria's reign, about 1850–80. **2.** Characteristic of the popular moral attitudes, culture, etc., of this period; prudishly old-fashioned. — *n.* **1.** One who lived during this period. **2.** One having mid-Victorian tastes, standards, or ideas.

mid·way (mid′wā′; *for adj. and adv., also* mid′wā′) *adv.* In the middle of the way or distance. — *adj.* Being in the middle of the way or distance. — *n. U.S.* At a fair, exposition, etc., the area or mall where amusements, side shows, or exhibitions are situated. [OE *midweg*]

mid·week (mid′wēk′) *n.* The middle of the week.

mid·wife (mid′wīf′) *n. pl.* **·wives** (-wīvz′) A woman who assists women in childbirth. [OE *mid* with + *wīf* woman]

mid·wife·ry (mid′wī′fər·ē, -wīf′rē) *n.* The skill or practice of assisting women in childbirth; obstetrics.

mid·win·ter (mid′win′tər) *n.* The middle of winter.

mid·year (mid′yir′) *n.* **1.** The middle of the year. **2.** *U.S.* An examination given in the middle of a school year.

mien (mēn) *n.* Manner, bearing, expression, etc. [? Aphetic form of DEMEAN]

miff (mif) *Informal v.t.* **1.** To cause to be offended or annoyed. — *v.i.* **2.** To take offense. — *n.* **1.** An ill-tempered mood; huff. **2.** A minor quarrel; tiff.

mig (mig) *n. U.S. Dial.* **1.** A marble. **2.** *pl.* The game of marbles. Also **mig·gle** (mig′əl).

might[1] (mīt) Past tense of MAY[1].

might[2] (mīt) *n.* **1.** Power to dominate; force; strength. **2.** Physical strength. — **with (all one's) might and main** With all one's strength or ability. [OE *miht*]

might·y (mī′tē) *adj.* **might·i·er, might·i·est** **1.** Possessed of might; powerful. **2.** Of great size, importance, etc. — *adv. Informal* Very; exceedingly. — **might′i·ly** (mī′tə·lē) *adv.* — **might′i·ness** *n.*

mi·gnon·ette (min′yən·et′) *n.* A plant having racemes of fragrant, yellowish green flowers. Also called *reseda.* [< F]

mi·graine (mī′grān) *n.* A type of severe, recurrent headache, usu. in one side of the head: also called *hemicrania.* [< F < LL < Gk. < *hēmi* half + *kranion* skull]

mi·grant (mī′grənt) *adj.* Migratory. — *n.* One who or that which migrates, as a bird or animal, an itinerant worker, etc. [< L *migrare* to roam, wander]

mi·grate (mī′grāt) *v.i.* **·grat·ed, ·grat·ing** **1.** To move from one country, region, etc., to settle in another. **2.** To move seasonally from one climate or region to another, as birds or fish. [< L *migrare*] — **mi′gra·tor** *n.*

— **Syn.** **1.** One may *migrate* to or from a place, whether permanently or transiently. *Emigrate* and *immigrate* imply a more or less permanent change. They are both applied to the same action performed by the same person, but *emigrate* refers to the place of departure and *immigrate* to the new home.

mi·gra·tion (mī·grā′shən) *n.* **1.** An act or instance of migrating. **2.** Those participating in a single instance of migrating. **3.** *Chem.* **a** The shifting of one or more atoms from one position to another. **b** The movement of ions under the influence of electromotive force toward one or the other electrode. [< L *migratio*] — **mi·gra′tion·al** *adj.*

mi·gra·to·ry (mī′grə·tôr′ē, -tō′rē) *adj.* **1.** Characterized by migration. **2.** Pertaining to or characteristic of migration or those that migrate. **3.** Roving; nomadic.

mi·ka·do (mi·kä′dō) *n. pl.* **·dos** The emperor of Japan. [< Japanese *mi* august + *kado* door]

mike (mīk) *n. Informal* A microphone.

mil (mil) *n.* **1.** A unit of length or diameter, equal to one thousandth of an inch. See table front of book. **2.** *Mil.* **a** A unit of angular measure equal to 1/6400 of a circle, or about 0.0560 degree. **b** A unit of angular measure equal to 0.001 radian. [< L *mille* thousand]

mi·la·dy (mi·lā′dē) *n. pl.* **·dies** **1.** An English noblewoman or gentlewoman: a Continental term. **2.** A fashionable woman. Also **mi·la′di.** [< F < E *my lady*]

mil·age (mī′lij) See MILEAGE.

Mil·an·ese (mil′ən·ēz′, -ēs′) *adj.* Of or pertaining to Milan or its people. — *n. pl.* **·ese** A native or inhabitant of Milan.

milch (milch) *adj.* Giving milk, as a cow. [OE -*milc*]

mild (mīld) *adj.* **1.** Kind or amiable in disposition or manners. **2.** Gentle or moderate: *mild* words; *mild* weather. **3.** Not intense or strong: a *mild* flavor. [OE *milde*] — **mild′ly** *adv.* — **mild′ness** *n.*

mil·dew (mil′dōō, -dyōō) *n.* **1.** A disease of plants usu.

---

caused by a parasitic fungus that deposits a whitish or discolored coating. **2.** Any of the fungi causing such a disease. **— v.t. & v.i.** To affect or be affected with mildew. [OE *meledēaw* honeydew] **— mil′dew·y** *adj.*

mile (mīl) *n.* **1.** A measure of distance used in the U.S. and other English-speaking countries, equal to 5,280 feet, 1,760 yards, or 1,609.35 meters: also called *statute mile.* See table front of book. **2.** Any considerable distance or amount. **— geographical, nautical, or air mile** One sixtieth of a degree of the earth's equator, or 6,080.2 feet. **— international nautical mile** A unit of distance by sea equal to 1,852 meters or 6,076.103 feet. [OE < LL < L *mille* (*passuum*) thousand (paces)]

mile·age (mī′lij) *n.* **1.** Total length or distance expressed in miles. **2.** Number of miles traveled by an automobile, etc., as estimated for each gallon of fuel used. **3.** Period of usefulness, estimated by miles used or traveled. **4.** *U.S.A.* traveling allowance estimated at a fixed amount per mile. Also spelled *milage.*

mile·post (mīl′pōst′) *n.* A post or similar marker indicating distance in miles, as along a highway.

mil·er (mī′lər) *n.* A runner, racehorse, etc., trained to compete in mile races.

mile·stone (mīl′stōn′) *n.* **1.** A post or stone set up to indicate mileage from a given point. **2.** An important event or turning point.

mi·lieu (mē·lyœ′) *n.* Environment; surroundings. [< F < OF *mi* middle + *lieu* place]

mil·i·tant (mil′ə·tənt) *adj.* **1.** Combative or warlike; aggressive. **2.** Positive and forceful in action; resolute. **3.** Engaged in conflict; fighting. **— n.** One who is militant. [< L *militare* to be a soldier] **— mil′i·tan·cy** *n.* **— mil′i·tant·ly** *adv.*

mil·i·ta·rism (mil′ə·tə·riz′əm) *n.* **1.** The ideals characteristic of a military class; emphasis on martial qualities. **2.** A national policy that promotes a powerful military position. **— mil′i·ta·rist** *n.* **— mil′i·ta·ris′tic** *adj.*

mil·i·ta·rize (mil′ə·tə·rīz′) *v.t.* **·rized, ·riz·ing 1.** To convert to a military system or adapt for military purposes. **2.** To prepare for warfare. **— mil′i·ta·ri·za′tion** *n.*

mil·i·tar·y (mil′ə·ter′ē) *adj.* **1.** Of or pertaining to the armed forces. **2.** Of or characteristic of warfare. **3.** Characteristic of or befitting a soldier or soldiers. **— n.** Soldiers collectively; armed forces: preceded by *the.* [< F < L < *miles, militis* soldier] **— mil′i·tar′i·ly** *adv.*

military police Soldiers who perform police duty.

mil·i·tate (mil′ə·tāt) *v.i.* **·tat·ed, ·tat·ing** To have influence or effect: with *against,* or, more rarely, *for:* The evidence *militated* against him. [< L *miles, militis* soldier]

mi·li·tia (mə·lish′ə) *n.* A body of citizens enrolled and drilled in military organizations other than the regular military forces, and called out only in emergencies. [< L, military service]

mi·li·tia·men (mə·lish′ə·mən) *n.* *pl.* **·men** (mən) A member of the militia.

milk (milk) *n.* **1.** The opaque, whitish liquid secreted by the mammary glands of female mammals for the nourishment of their young; esp., cow's milk. **2.** Any of various liquids resembling this, as the sap of certain plants, or the liquid contained in a coconut. **— v.t. 1.** To draw or express milk from the mammary glands of. **2.** To draw off or drain by or as by milking. **3.** To draw or extract something from: to *milk* someone of information. **4.** To exploit; take advantage of: to *milk* a client. **— v.i. 5.** To milk (a cow, cows, etc.). **6.** To yield milk. [OE *meolc, milc*]

milk leg A painful swelling of the leg in women shortly after childbirth, resulting from phlebitis of the femoral vein.

milk·maid (milk′mād′) *n.* A woman or girl who milks cows or works in a dairy.

milk·man (milk′man′) *n.* *pl.* **·men** (-men′) A man who sells or delivers milk.

milk of magnesia A white, aqueous suspension of magnesium hydroxide, $Mg(OH)_2$, used as a laxative and antacid.

milk shake A drink made of chilled, flavored milk, and sometimes ice cream, shaken, beaten, or whipped.

milk snake A nonpoisonous snake of eastern North America, feeding on rodents, frogs, etc.

milk·sop (milk′sop′) *n.* A weak, timorous fellow; sissy.

milk sugar Lactose.

milk·toast (milk′tōst′) *n.* **1.** A dish of buttered toast served in hot milk. **2.** See MILQUETOAST.

milk tooth A temporary tooth of a young mammal.

milk·weed (milk′wēd′) *n.* Any of various herbs, shrubs, and vines having milky juice.

milk·y (mil′kē) *adj.* **milk·i·er, milk·i·est 1.** Resembling or suggestive of milk. **2.** Containing or yielding milk or a milklike substance. **3.** Very mild or bland. **— milk′i·ly** *adv.* **— milk′i·ness** *n.*

Milky Way A luminous band visible across the night sky, composed of distant stars and nebulae not separately distinguishable to the naked eye: also called the *Galaxy.*

mill¹ (mil) *n.* **1.** A machine or mechanical device by means of which a solid or coarse substance is ground, crushed, or reduced to a pulp. **2.** A device, machine, building, or establishment in which grain is ground. **3.** Any of various machines that process materials used in combination: *sawmill; windmill.* **4.** A manufacturing or industrial establishment; factory. **5.** A steel roller for impressing a design on a printing plate, etc. **6.** A trying experience; ordeal: used chiefly in the phrase **through the mill. — v.t. 1.** To grind, roll, shape, polish, etc., in or with a mill. **2.** To raise, indent, or ridge the edge of (a coin, etc.). **3.** To cause to move in a circle, as cattle. **— v.i. 4.** To move with a circular or surging motion, as cattle. [OE < LL < L *mola* millstone]

mill² (mil) *n.* A monetary denomination of the U.S., one tenth of a cent. [< L *mille* thousand]

mill·dam (mil′dam′) *n.* A dam constructed across a watercourse to raise its level sufficiently to turn a mill wheel.

mil·len·ni·um (mi·len′ē·əm) *n.* *pl.* **·ni·a** (-nē·ə) or **·ni·ums** **1.** A period of a thousand years. **2.** The thousand years during which Christ is to rule the world. *Rev.* xx 1–5. **3.** Any period of happiness, prosperity, etc. [< NL < *mille* thousand + *annus* year] **— mil·len′ni·al** *adj.*

mil·le·ped (mil′ə·ped), **mil·le·pede** (mil′ə·pēd) See MILLIPEDE.

mil·le·pore (mil′ə·pôr, -pōr) *n.* *Zool.* Any of a group of corals that form large branching structures containing numerous tiny surface cavities. [< F < *mille* thousand + *pore* pore]

mill·er (mil′ər) *n.* **1.** One who operates or tends a mill. **2.** A milling machine. **3.** Any of various moths having pale, dusty wings.

mil·let (mil′it) *n.* **1.** A grass cultivated in the U.S. for forage, and in many parts of the Old World for its small, edible seeds. **2.** Any of various similar grasses. **3.** The seed of these grasses. [< F, dim. of *mil* < L *milium*]

milli- *combining form* In the metric system and in technical use, one thousandth of (a specified unit), as in the following: **milliampere, millivolt.** [< L *mille* thousand]

mil·liard (mil′yərd) *n.* *Brit.* A thousand millions: called a *billion* in the U.S. [< F < Provençal *milhar* thousand]

mil·li·gram (mil′ə·gram) *n.* A unit of weight in the metric system, equal to one thousandth of a gram. Also **mil′li·gramme.** See table front of book.

mil·li·li·ter (mil′ə·lē′tər) *n.* A unit of capacity in the metric system, equal to one thousandth of a liter. Also **mil′li·li·tre.** See table front of book.

mil·li·me·ter (mil′ə·mē′tər) *n.* A unit of length in the metric system, equal to one thousandth of a meter. Also **mil′li·me′tre.** See table front of book.

mil·li·mi·cron (mil′ə·mī′kron) *n.* A unit of length equal to one thousandth of a micron: also called *micromillimeter.*

mil·li·ner (mil′ə·nər) *n.* One who makes or sells women's hats. [< *Milaner* an inhabitant of Milan, Italy]

mil·li·ner·y (mil′ə·ner′ē, -nər·ē) *n.* **1.** The articles made or sold by milliners. **2.** The business of a milliner.

mil·lion (mil′yən) *n.* **1.** A thousand thousands, written as 1,000,000: a cardinal number. **2.** A million units of money, as of dollars: He is worth a *million.* **3.** An indefinitely great number. **— adj. 1.** Being a million in number. **2.** Very many. [< OF < Ital. *millione* (now *milione*), aug. of *mille* thousand] **— mil′lionth** *n. & adj.*

mil·lion·aire (mil′yən·âr′) *n.* One whose wealth is valued at a million or more, as of dollars, pounds, etc. Also **mil′lion·naire′.** [< F *millionnaire*] **— mil′lion·air′ess** *n.fem.*

mil·li·pede (mil′ə·pēd) *n.* Any of various wormlike animals having a rounded body divided into numerous segments, nearly all of which bear two pairs of appendages: also called *wireworm:* also spelled *milliped, millepede.* Also **mil′li·ped** (-ped). [< L *mille* thousand + *pes, pedis* foot]

mill·pond (mil′pond′) *n.* A body of water dammed up to supply power for running a mill.

mill·race (mil′rās′) *n.* **1.** The current of water that operates a mill wheel. **2.** The channel in which it runs.

mill·stone (mil′stōn′) *n.* **1.** One of a pair of thick, heavy, stone disks used for grinding grain, etc. **2.** That which crushes or bears down. **3.** A heavy or burdensome weight.

mill·stream (mil′strēm′) *n.* **1.** A stream whose current is used to operate a mill. **2.** The water in a millrace.

mill wheel A water wheel that drives a mill.

mill·work (mil′wûrk′) *n.* Objects or material finished or processed in a mill; esp. woodwork ready for use.

mill·wright (mil′rīt′) *n.* One who plans, builds, or repairs mills or mill machinery.

mi·lord (mi·lôrd′) *n.* An English nobleman or gentleman: a Continental term. [< F < *my lord*]

milque·toast (milk′tōst′) *n.* A timid, meek, or very apologetic person: also spelled *milktoast.* [after Caspar *Milquetoast,* a creation by H. T. Webster, U.S. cartoonist]

milt (milt) *n.* **1.** Fish sperm. **2.** The reproductive organs of a male fish when filled with seminal fluid. **— v.t.** To impregnate (fish roe) with milt. [OE *milte*]

Mil·ton·ic (mil·ton/ik) *adj.* Of or like the poet Milton or his works; sublime. Also **Mil·to/ni·an** (-tō/nē·ən).

Mil·town (mil/toun) *n.* Proprietary name for a brand of meprobamate used in pill form as a tranquilizer.

mime (mīm) *n.* **1.** An actor, comedian, etc., who specializes in pantomime. **2.** In ancient Rome or Greece, a type of dramatic farce in which actual persons or events were ludicrously represented. **3.** An actor in such performances. — *v.* **mimed, mim·ing** — *v.i.* **1.** To play a part with gestures and, usu., without words. — *v.t.* **2.** To portray by pantomime. [< L < Gk. *mimos*] — **mim/er** *n.*

mim·e·o·graph (mim/ē·ə·graf/, -gräf/) *n.* **1.** A duplicating device that reproduces copies of written matter etc., by means of a stencil wrapped around a drum: also **Mim/e·o·graph/.** **2.** A copy so made. — *v.t. & v.i.* To reproduce by mimeograph. [< *Mimeograph*, a trade name]

mi·met·ic (mi·met/ik, mī-) *adj.* **1.** Tending to imitate or mimic; imitative. **2.** Pertaining to or like mimicry. **3.** Make-believe. [< Gk. < *mimēsis* imitation] — **mi·met/i·cal·ly** *adv.*

mim·ic (mim/ik) *v.t.* **·icked, ·ick·ing** **1.** To imitate the speech or actions of. **2.** To copy closely; ape. **3.** To have or assume the color, shape, etc., of. — *n.* **1.** One who mimics or imitates. **2.** A copy; imitation. — *adj.* **1.** Of the nature of mimicry; imitative; mimetic. **2.** Make-believe; simulated; mock. [< L < Gk. < *mimos* mime] — **mim/i·cal** *adj.* — **mim/ick·er** *n.*

mim·ic·ry (mim/ik·rē) *n. pl.* **·ries** **1.** The act, practice, or art of mimicking or imitating. **2.** *Biol.* A resemblance of an organism to another or to its environment, for purposes of concealment, etc.

mi·mo·sa (mi·mō/sə, -zə) *n.* Any of a group of leguminous tropical herbs, shrubs, or trees with feathery foliage, and small, often yellow, flowers. [< NL < L *mimus* mime]

min·a·ret (min/ə·ret/) *n.* A high, slender tower attached to a Moslem mosque and surrounded by balconies, from which a muezzin calls the summons to prayer. [< Sp. < Turkish < Arabic *manārah* lamp, lighthouse]

min·a·to·ry (min/ə·tôr/ē, -tō/rē) *adj.* Conveying or expressing a threat. Also **min/a·to/ri·al.** [< OF < LL < *minari* to threaten] — **min/a·to/ri·al·ly, min/a·to/ri·ly** *adv.*

mince (mins) *v.* **minced, minc·ing** *v.t.* **1.** To cut or chop into small bits, as food. **2.** To subdivide minutely. **3.** To moderate the force or strength of (language, ideas, etc.): He didn't *mince* words with her. **4.** To say or express with affected primness or elegance. — *v.i.* **5.** To walk with short steps or affected daintiness. **6.** To speak or behave with affected primness. — *n. Chiefly Brit.* Any finely chopped food, as mincemeat. [< OF < L *minuere* to lessen, make smaller] — **minc/er** *n.*

mince·meat (mins/mēt/) *n.* A mixture of chopped apples, raisins, spices, etc., used as a pie filling. — **to make mincemeat of** To cut up, destroy, or annihilate utterly.

mince pie A pie filled with mincemeat.

minc·ing (min/sing) *adj.* Affectedly precise, refined, or dainty, as in manner, gait, etc. — **minc/ing·ly** *adv.*

mind (mīnd) *n.* **1.** The aggregate of processes originating in or associated with the brain, involving conscious and subconscious thought, interpretation of perceptions, insight, imagination, etc. **2.** Memory: within the *mind* of man. **3.** Opinion; sentiment: to change one's *mind*. **4.** Desire; inclination: to have a *mind* to leave. **5.** Way or state of thinking or feeling: a logical *mind*. **6.** Intellectual power or capacity: He has the *mind* for such work. **7.** A highly intelligent individual. **8.** Sound mental condition; sanity. **9.** Attention: to keep one's *mind* on a subject. — **Syn.** See INTELLECT. — **a piece of one's mind** **1.** One's bluntly or candidly expressed opinion. **2.** A severe scolding. — **on one's mind** In one's thoughts, esp. so as to cause concern or worry. — **out of one's mind** **1.** Insane; mad. **2.** Distracted; frantic. — **to bear (or keep) in mind** To focus one's thoughts or attention on; remember. — **to be of one mind** To be in accord; agree. — **to have a good (or great) mind** To feel strongly disposed (to do something). — **to have in mind** To be thinking about. — **to make up one's mind** To decide; be determined. — *v.t.* **1.** To pay attention to. **2.** To be careful concerning: *Mind* your step. **3.** To obey: *Mind* your leaders. **4.** To look after; tend. **5.** To object to: Do you *mind* the noise? **6.** *Dial.* To notice; perceive. **7.** *Dial.* To remember. — *v.i.* **8.** To pay attention; heed: *Mind* you now, not a word. **9.** To be obedient. **10.** To be concerned; care; object: I don't *mind*. **11.** To be careful. [OE *gemynd*] — **mind/er** *n.*

mind·ed (mīn/did) *adj.* **1.** Having or characterized by a (specified kind of) mind: used in combination: *evil-minded.* **2.** Having an inclination; disposed: often with *to.*

mind·ful (mīnd/fəl) *adj.* Keeping in mind; heeding; aware. — **mind/ful·ly** *adv.* — **mind/ful·ness** *n.*

mind·less (mīnd/lis) *adj.* **1.** Devoid of intelligence; senseless. **2.** Not giving heed or attention; careless. — **mind/·less·ly** *adv.* — **mind/less·ness** *n.*

mind reader One supposedly able to perceive the thoughts of others. — **mind reading**

mine¹ (mīn) *n.* **1.** An excavation in the earth dug to obtain coal, precious stones, etc. **2.** The site of such an excavation, together with its buildings, equipment, etc. **3.** Any deposit of ore, coal, etc. **4.** Any source or abundant store of something: a *mine* of talent. **5.** *Mil.* **a** An encased explosive charge placed in the earth or water and designed to be actuated by contact, a time fuse, or remote control. **b** Formerly, an underground tunnel dug beneath an enemy's fortifications. — *v.* **mined, min·ing** *v.t.* **1.** To dig (coal, ores, etc.) from the earth. **2.** To dig into (the earth, etc.) for coal, ores, etc. **3.** To make by digging, as a tunnel. **4.** To obtain useful material or information from. **5.** To undermine by slow or secret means. **6.** To place an explosive mine in or under. — *v.i.* **7.** To dig in a mine for coal, ores, etc. **8.** To make a tunnel, etc., by digging. **9.** To place explosive mines. [< OF < Celtic. Cf. Irish *mein* vein of metal]

mine² (mīn) *pron.* **1.** The possessive case of the pronoun *I,* used predicatively: That book is *mine.* **2.** The one or ones belonging or relating to me: His work is better than *mine.* — **of mine** Belonging or relating to me; my. — *pronominal adj.* *Archaic* My: formerly used before a vowel or *h*: *mine* eyes. [OE *mīn*]

mine detector An electromagnetic device used to locate the position of explosive mines. — **mine detection**

mine·field (mīn/fēld/) *n.* An area on land or in water in which explosive mines have been systematically placed.

mine·lay·er (mīn/lā/ər) *n.* A vessel provided with special equipment for laying explosive mines.

min·er (mīn/ər) *n.* One who works in a mine.

min·er·al (min/ər·əl) *n.* **1.** A naturally ocurring inorganic substance having a characteristic set of physical properties, a definite range of chemical composition, and a molecular structure usu. expressed in crystalline form. **2.** Inorganic material, esp. as distinguished from animal or vegetable matter. — *adj.* Of, like, or containing a mineral or minerals. [< OF < Med.L < *mineralis* of a mine]

min·er·al·ize (min/ər·əl·īz/) *v.t.* **·ized, ·iz·ing** **1.** To convert (a metal) to a mineral. **2.** To convert to a mineral substance; petrify. **3.** To impregnate with minerals. — **min/·er·al·iz/er** *n.* — **min/er·al·i·za/tion** *n.*

min·er·al·o·gy (min/ə·ral/ə·jē, -rol/-) *n. pl.* **·gies** **1.** The science of minerals, embracing their origin, structure, characteristics, properties, and classification. **2.** A treatise on minerals. — **min/er·a·log/i·cal** (-ər·ə·loj/i·kəl) *adj.* — **min/·er·a·log/i·cal·ly** *adv.* — **min/er·al/o·gist** *n.*

mineral oil Any of various oils, esp. petroleum, derived from minerals and used as a fuel, in medicine, etc.

mineral spring A spring containing natural mineral water.

mineral water Any water naturally containing or artificially impregnated with mineral salts or gases.

mineral wool A fibrous, woollike material, used as packing and as insulation: also called *rock wool, slag wool.*

Mi·ner·va (mi·nûr/və) In Roman mythology, the goddess of wisdom and invention: identified with the Greek *Athena.*

min·e·stro·ne (min/ə·strō/nē, *Ital.* mē/nä·strō/nä) *n. Italian* A thick vegetable soup having a meat stock.

mine·sweep·er (mīn/swē/pər) *n.* A ship equipped to detect, destroy, and remove marine mines.

Ming (ming) *n.* In Chinese history, the last ruling dynasty (1368–1644) of truly Chinese origin, noted for its scholarly and artistic achievements, esp. for its porcelains.

min·gle (ming/gəl) *v.* **·gled, ·gling** *v.t.* **1.** To mix or unite together; blend. **2.** To make by combining. — *v.i.* **3.** To be or become mixed, united, or closely joined. **4.** To enter into company; mix or associate, as with a crowd. [OE *mengan*] — **min/gler** *n.*

min·i·a·ture (min/ē·ə·chər, min/ə·chər) *n.* **1.** A portrayal or representation of anything on a small scale. **2.** Reduced dimensions, form, or extent. **3.** In art: **a** A painting done on a very small scale. **b** The art of executing such paintings. — *adj.* On a very small or reduced scale. [< F < Ital. < L *miniatus* painted red; later infl. by L *minuere* to lessen]

min·i·a·tur·ize (min/ē·ə·chər·īz/, min/ə·chər·īz/) *v.t.* **·ized, ·iz·ing** To reduce the size of. — **min/i·a·tur/i·za/tion** *n.*

min·im (min/im) *n.* **1.** A small liquid measure, 1/60 of a fluid dram, or about one drop. See table front of book. **2.** *Music Chiefly Brit.* A half note. **3.** One who or that which is very small or insignificant. **4.** A small particle; jot. — *adj.* Extremely small. [< L *minimus* least, smallest]

min·i·mal (min/ə·məl) *adj.* Of a minimum amount, degree, etc.; least possible; smallest. — **min/i·mal·ly** *adv.*

min·i·mize (min/ə·mīz) *v.t.* **·mized, ·miz·ing** **1.** To reduce to the smallest amount or degree. **2.** To regard or represent as of the least possible importance, size, etc. Also *Brit.* **min'·i·mise.** — **min'i·mi·za'tion** *n.* — **min'i·miz'er** *n.*

min·i·mum (min'ə·məm) *n. pl.* **·mums** or **·ma** (-mə) **1.** The least possible quantity, amount, or degree. **2.** The lowest quantity, degree, number, etc., reached or recorded. — *adj.* **1.** Consisting of or showing the least amount or degree possible, permissible, attainable, etc. **2.** Of or pertaining to a minimum or minimums. [< L, neut. of *minimus*]

minimum wage The smallest wage, fixed by law or by agreement, an employer may offer an employee.

min·ing (mī'ning) *n.* The act, process, or business of extracting coal, ores, etc., from mines.

min·ion (min'yən) *n.* **1.** A servile favorite or follower. **2.** *Printing* A size of type, 7-point. [< F *mignon* darling]

min·is·ter (min'is·tər) *n.* **1.** One who is authorized to administer the sacraments, preach, etc., in a church; clergyman; pastor. **2.** One appointed to head an administrative department of a government. **3.** One authorized to represent his government to another government in diplomatic matters and ranking next below an ambassador. **4.** One who or that which acts as the agent of another person or thing: a *minister* of good. — **Syn.** See AMBASSADOR. — *v.i.* **1.** To provide for the wants or needs of someone. **2.** To be helpful or useful. — *v.t.* **3.** To administer or apply (a sacrament, medicine, etc.). [< OF < L *minister* attendant]

min·is·te·ri·al (min'is·tir'ē·əl) *adj.* **1.** Of, or pertaining to a minister or to the ministry. **2.** Administrative; executive. **3.** Contributive; instrumental. — **min'is·te'ri·al·ly** *adv.*

min·is·trant (min'is·trənt) *adj.* Ministering. — *n.* One who ministers. [< L < *ministrare* to serve]

min·is·tra·tion (min'is·trā'shən) *n.* **1.** The act of serving. **2.** *Often pl.* Help or aid. — **min'is·tra'tive** *adj.*

min·is·try (min'is·trē) *n. pl.* **·tries** **1.** The profession, duties, length of service, etc., of a minister of religion. **2.** The clergy. **3.** *Govt.* **a** An executive or administrative department presided over by a minister; also, its building. **b** A body of ministers collectively. **c** The duties of a minister; also, his term of office. **4.** The act of ministering.

min·i·track (min'i·track') *n. Aerospace* An electronic system for tracking earth satellites by the radio signals received from the satellite. Also **Min'i·track'.**

min·i·um (min'ē·əm) *n.* A vivid, opaque, red lead oxide Pb₃O₄, used chiefly as a pigment: also called *red lead.* [< L]

min·i·ver (min'ə·vər) *n.* **1.** A white or gray and white fur, used in the Middle Ages as trimming, etc. **2.** Any white fur, as ermine. [< OF *menu vair*, lit., little spotted (fur)]

mink (mingk) *n.* **1.** A semiaquatic, slender-bodied carnivorous mammal, resembling a weasel. **2.** The valuable, soft, brown fur of this mammal. [< Scand. Cf. Sw. *menk.*]

min·ne·sing·er (min'ə·sing'ər) *n.* A lyric poet and singer of medieval Germany. [< G < *minne* love + *singer* singer]

min·now (min'ō) *n. pl.* **min·nows** (*Rare* **min·now**) **1.** A small European cyprinoid fish of the carp family. **2.** Any of various related fishes. **3.** Any small fish. [ME *menawe*]

Mi·no·an (mi·nō'ən) *adj.* **1.** Of or pertaining to an advanced Bronze Age civilization that flourished in Crete from about 3000 to 1100 B.C. **2.** Designating two varieties of linear script, one (**Linear A**) deciphered in 1957, the other (**Linear B**) deciphered in 1952 and found to be an Achaean dialect of Greek.

mi·nor (mī'nər) *adj.* **1.** Less in quantity, number, or extent. **2.** Of secondary or lesser importance: a *minor* poet. **3.** Under legal age. **4.** *Music* **a** Denoting an interval smaller by a half step than the corresponding major interval. **b** Denoting a triad in which the third above the fundamental is minor. **c** Denoting a type of diatonic scale, or a key based on this scale. **5.** Sad or plaintive; mournful: said of a sound or voice. **6.** *U.S.* In education, of or pertaining to an area of specialized study usu. requiring fewer class hours than a major field of study. **7.** Of or constituting a minority — *n.* **1.** One who is below full legal age. **2.** *U.S.* In education, a minor subject or area of study. **3.** *Music* A minor chord, interval, scale, key, etc. — *v.i. U.S.* In education, to study as a minor subject: with *in*: to *minor* in philosophy. [< L]

mi·nor·i·ty (mə·nôr'ə·tē, -nor'-, mī-) *n. pl.* **·ties** **1.** The smaller in number of two parts or parties: opposed to *majority.* **2.** A racial, religious, political, or national group smaller than and usu. different in some ways from the larger group of which it is a part. **3.** The state or period of being under legal age. [< F *minorité* or L *minoritas*]

minor league *U.S.* Any professional sports league not having the standing of a major league. — **mi·nor-league** (mī'nər-lēg') *adj.*

minor suit In bridge, diamonds or clubs.

Mi·nos (mī'nəs, -nos) In Greek mythology: **a** A king of Crete who became a judge of the lower world after his death. **b** His grandson. [< Gk. *Mīnōs*]

Min·o·taur (min'ə·tôr) In Greek mythology, a monster with the body of a man and the head of a bull, confined in the Labyrinth until it was killed by Theseus. [< L < Gk. *Mīnōtauros*]

min·ster (min'stər) *n. Chiefly Brit.* **1.** A monastery church. **2.** A cathedral or large church. [OE *mynster*]

min·strel (min'strəl) *n.* **1.** In the Middle Ages, a wandering musician who made his living by singing and reciting poetry. **2.** A performer in a minstrel show. **3.** *Poetic* A poet, musician, etc. [< OF < LL *ministerialis* servant, jester]

minstrel show A comic variety show of songs, dances, jokes, etc., given by a company of performers in blackface.

min·strel·sy (min'strəl·sē) *n. pl.* **·sies** **1.** The art or occupation of a minstrel. **2.** Ballads or lyrics collectively, esp. those sung by minstrels. **3.** A troupe of minstrels.

mint¹ (mint) *n.* **1.** A place where the coin of a country is lawfully manufactured. **2.** An abundant supply, esp. of money. **3.** A source of manufacture or inspiration. — *v.t.* **1.** To make (money) by stamping; to coin. **2.** To invent or fabricate (a word, etc.). — *adj.* In original condition; unused. [OE < L *Moneta* epithet of Juno, whose temple at Rome was used as a mint] — **mint'er** *n.*

mint² (mint) *n.* **1.** Any of several aromatic herbs; esp. spearmint and peppermint, used as a flavoring, garnish, etc. **2.** A mint-flavored candy. [OE < L < Gk. *mintha*]

mint·age (min'tij) *n.* **1.** The act or process of minting. **2.** The money manufactured by a mint. **3.** The fee paid for coining. **4.** The authorized impression stamped upon a coin.

mint julep A drink made of bourbon mixed with crushed ice and sugar and flavored with sprigs of fresh mint.

min·u·end (min'yŏo·end) *n. Math.* The number from which another is to be subtracted. [< L *minuere* to lessen]

min·u·et (min'yŏo·et') *n.* **1.** A stately dance for couples, introduced in France in the 17th century. **2.** Music for or in the manner of this dance, in moderate triple meter. [< F < L *minutus*]

mi·nus (mī'nəs) *prep.* **1.** Lessened or reduced by; less. **2.** *Informal* Lacking; deprived of. — *adj.* **1.** Of or denoting subtraction. **2.** Negative: a *minus* value. **3.** Less in quality or value than: a C *minus.* **4.** *Informal* Non-existent; lacking: His chances were *minus.* — *n.* **1.** The minus sign (−). **2.** A minus quantity. **3.** A deficit or loss. [< L, neut. of *minor*]

mi·nus·cule (mi·nus'kyŏol, min'ə·skyŏol) *n.* Any small or lower-case letter. — *adj.* **1.** Of, pertaining to, like, or composed of minuscules. **2.** Very small; miniature. [< L *minusculus*, dim. of *minor* less]

minus sign A sign (−) denoting subtraction or a negative quantity.

min·ute¹ (min'it) *n.* **1.** The 60th part of an hour; 60 seconds. **2.** Any very brief period of time; moment. **3.** A specific instant of time. **4.** A unit of angular measure equal to the 60th part of a degree, indicated by the sign (') and called **a minute of arc.** **5.** A memorandum. **6.** *pl.* An official record of the business discussed and transacted at a meeting, conference, etc. — **up to the minute** In accord with the latest fashion, equipment, etc. — *v.t.* **·ut·ed, ·ut·ing** **1.** To make a minute or brief note of; record. **2.** To time to the minute. [< F < Med.L < LL *minutia* small]

mi·nute² (mī·nōot', -nyōot', mi-) *adj.* **1.** Exceedingly small; tiny. **2.** Having little importance or value. **3.** Demonstrating or characterized by careful, precise attention to small details. [< L *minutus* small] — **mi·nute'ness** *n.*

minute hand (min'it) The hand that indicates the minute on a clock or similar timepiece.

min·ute·ly¹ (min'it·lē) *adj. & adv.* At intervals of a minute.

mi·nute·ly² (mī·nōot'lē, -nyōot'-, mi-) *adv.* In a minute manner or degree; with great detail, precision, or exactness.

min·ute·man (min'it·man') *n. pl.* **·men** (·men') In the American Revolution, one of the armed citizens who volunteered to be ready for combat at a minute's notice.

minute steak (min'it) A small, thin cut of steak that can be cooked quickly.

mi·nu·ti·ae (mi·nōo'shi·ē, -nyōo'-) *n. pl. of* **mi·nu·ti·a** (-shē·ə, -shə) Small or unimportant details; trifles. [< L]

minx (mingks) *n.* A saucy, bold, or flirtatious girl. [Prob. < LG *minsk* impudent woman. Akin to G *mensch* person.]

Mi·o·cene (mī'ə·sēn) *adj.* Pertaining to or designating the fourth geological epoch of the Tertiary period. See chart for GEOLOGY. — *n.* The Miocene epoch or series. [< Gk. *meiōn* less + *kainos* recent]

mir·a·cle (mir'ə·kəl) *n.* **1.** An event that appears to be neither a part nor result of any known natural law or agency and is therefore often attributed to a supernatural source. **2.** Any wonderful or amazing thing, fact, or event. **3.** One who or that which is of surpassing merit or excellence. **4.** A miracle play. [< F < L < *mirari* to wonder]

miracle play A medieval play dealing with the lives of saints and with their miracles. Compare MYSTERY PLAY.

mi·rac·u·lous (mi·rak'yə·ləs) *adj.* **1.** Wonderful and amazing. **2.** Apparently caused by the direct intervention of a supernatural power. **3.** Having the power to work miracles. — **Syn.** See SUPERNATURAL. — **mi·rac'u·lous·ly** *adv.* **mi·rac'u·lous·ness** *n.*

mi·rage (mi·räzh') *n.* **1.** An optical illusion, as of a sheet of water, upside-down ship, etc., that sometimes appears in a desert or in the air, and is caused by reflection from layers of atmosphere having different densities. **2.** Anything that appears to be real but is not. [< F < L *mirari* to wonder at]

mire (mīr) *n.* **1.** An area of wet, yielding earth; swampy ground. **2.** Deep mud or slush. — *v.* **mired, mir·ing** *v.t.* **1.** To cause to sink or become stuck in mire. **2.** To smear or soil with mud; defile. **3.** To entangle or entrap. — *v.i.* **4.** To sink in mire; bog down. [< ON *mȳrr* swampy ground] — **mir′y** *adj.* — **mir′i·ness** *n.*

Mir·i·am (mir′ē·əm) Sister of Moses and Aaron. *Ex.* xv 20.

mirk (mûrk), **mirk·i·ly** (mûrk′i·lē), etc. See MURK, etc.

mir·ror (mir′ər) *n.* **1.** Any smooth reflecting surface, as of glass backed with a coating of silver, aluminum, etc. **2.** Whatever reflects or depicts truly. — *v.t.* To reflect or show an image of, as in a mirror. [< OF < LL < L *mirari* to wonder at, admire]

mirth (mûrth) *n.* Spirited gaiety; social merriment. [OE *myrig* pleasant, merry]

mirth·ful (mûrth′fəl) *adj.* Full of or characterized by mirth; merry. — **mirth′ful·ly** *adv.* — **mirth′ful·ness** *n.*

mis-¹ *prefix* Bad; amiss; badly; wrongly; unfavorably: used in combination, as in *miscalculate, miscolor, miscopy,* etc. [OE *mis-* wrong; infl. in meaning by ME *mes-* mis-²]

mis-² *prefix* Bad; amiss; not: found with negative or depreciatory force in words borrowed from Old French: *misadventure, miscreant.* [< OF *mes-* < L *minus* less]

mis-³ Var. of MISO-.

mis·ad·ven·ture (mis′əd·ven′chər) *n.* A disastrous event.

mis·ad·vise (mis′ad·vīz′) *v.t.* **·vised, ·vis·ing** To give bad advice or erroneous information or advice to.

mis·al·li·ance (mis′ə·lī′əns) *n.* An undesirable alliance or marriage. [< F *mésalliance*]

mis·al·ly (mis′ə·lī′) *v.t.* **·lied, ·ly·ing** To ally badly.

mis·an·thrope (mis′ən·thrōp, miz′-) *n.* One who hates or distrusts his fellow men. Also **mis·an·thro·pist** (mis·an′thrə·pist). [< Gk. < *misein* to hate + *anthrōpos* man]

mis·an·throp·ic (mis′ən·throp′ik) *adj.* Of, pertaining to, or like a misanthrope. Also **mis′an·throp′i·cal.** — **mis·an·throp′i·cal·ly** *adv.*

mis·an·thro·py (mis·an′thrə·pē) *n.* Hatred of mankind.

mis·ap·ply (mis′ə·plī′) *v.t.* **·plied, ·ply·ing** To use or apply incorrectly or wrongfully. — **mis·ap·pli·ca′tion** *n.*

mis·ap·pre·hend (mis′ap·ri·hend′) *v.t.* To apprehend or interpret wrongly. — **mis·ap·pre·hen′sion** *n.*

mis·ap·pro·pri·ate (mis′ə·prō′prē·āt) *v.t.* **·at·ed, ·at·ing** To use or take improperly or dishonestly; misapply. — **mis·ap·pro′pri·a′tion** *n.*

mis·be·come (mis′bi·kum′) *v.t.* **·came, ·come, ·com·ing** To be unbecoming or not appropriate to.

mis·be·have (mis′bi·hāv′) *v.i. & v.t.* **·haved, ·hav·ing** To behave badly. — **mis′be·hav′ior** *n.*

mis·be·lief (mis′bi·lēf′) *n.* False belief or opinion.

mis·be·lieve (mis′bi·lēv′) *v.* **·lieved, ·liev·ing** *v.i.* To hold a false, unorthodox, or heretical belief. — **mis′be·liev′er** *n.*

mis·cal·cu·late (mis·kal′kyə·lāt) *v.t. & v.i.* **·lat·ed, ·lat·ing** To calculate wrongly. — **mis′cal·cu·la′tion** *n.*

mis·call (mis·kôl′) *v.t.* To call by a wrong name.

mis·car·riage (mis·kar′ij) *n.* **1.** A premature delivery of a nonviable fetus. **2.** Failure to bring about a proper conclusion. **3.** Failure to reach an intended destination.

mis·car·ry (mis·kar′ē) *v.i.* **·ried, ·ry·ing** **1.** To fail; go wrong. **2.** To bring forth a fetus prematurely. **3.** To fail to reach an intended destination, as freight, mail, etc.

mis·cast (mis·kast′, -käst′) *v.t.* **·cast, ·cast·ing** To cast (a play, role, or an actor) inappropriately.

mis·ce·ge·na·tion (mis′i·jə·nā′shən) *n.* Interbreeding of ethnic stocks or races. [< L *miscere* to mix + *genus* race] — **mis′ce·ge·net′ic** (-jə·net′ik) *adj.*

mis·cel·la·ne·ous (mis′ə·lā′nē·əs) *adj.* **1.** Composed of various and diverse things or elements; mixed. **2.** Possessing diverse qualities or capabilities. [< L *miscellus* mixed] — **mis′cel·la′ne·ous·ly** *adv.* — **mis′cel·la′ne·ous·ness** *n.*

mis·cel·la·ny (mis′ə·lā′nē) *n. pl.* **·nies** A miscellaneous collection, esp. of literary works.

mis·chance (mis·chans′, -chäns′) *n.* Bad luck; also, an instance of bad luck; mishap.

mis·chief (mis′chif) *n.* **1.** Action, often playful, that causes some irritation, harm, or trouble. **2.** The disposition to annoy, tease, or disturb. **3.** Harm or injury: High winds can cause great *mischief.* **4.** A cause or source of damage, evil, etc. [< OF < *meschever* to come to grief]

mis·chief-mak·er (mis′chif·mā′kər) *n.* One who causes mischief. — **mis′chief-mak′ing** *adj. & n.*

mis·chie·vous (mis′chi·vəs) *adj.* **1.** Inclined to or full of mischief. **2.** Troubling or annoying. **3.** Having a playful, teasing nature or quality. **4.** Causing harm or injury. — **mis′chie·vous·ly** *adv.* — **mis′chie·vous·ness** *n.*

mis·ci·ble (mis′i·bəl) *adj.* Capable of being mixed. [< L *miscere* to mix] — **mis′ci·bil′i·ty** *n.*

mis·con·ceive (mis′kən·sēv′) *v.t. & v.i.* **·ceived, ·ceiv·ing** To conceive wrongly; misunderstand. — **mis′con·ceiv′er** *n.* — **mis′con·cep′tion** *n.*

mis·con·duct (*n.* mis·kon′dukt; *v.* mis′kən·dukt′) *n.* **1.** Improper or immoral behavior. **2.** Unlawful conduct. — *v.t.* **1.** To behave (oneself) improperly. **2.** To mismanage.

mis·con·strue (mis′kən·strōō′) *v.t.* **·strued, ·stru·ing** **1.** To interpret wrongly; misunderstand. **2.** *Gram.* To construe incorrectly. — **mis′con·struc′tion** *n.*

mis·count (mis·kount′) *v.t. & v.i.* To count incorrectly; miscalculate. — *n.* An incorrect count or reckoning.

mis·cre·ant (mis′krē·ənt) *n.* An unscrupulous wretch; evildoer. — *adj.* Villainous; vile. [< OF < *mes-* mis²- + *croire* to believe]

mis·cue (mis·kyōō′) *n.* **1.** In billiards, a stroke spoiled by a slipping of the cue. **2.** *Informal* An error; slip-up. — *v.i.* **·cued, ·cu·ing** **1.** To make a miscue. **2.** In the theater, etc., to miss one's cue or to answer another's cue.

mis·date (mis·dāt′) *v.t.* **·dat·ed, ·dat·ing** To date incorrectly; assign a wrong date to. — *n.* An incorrect date.

mis·deal (mis·dēl′) *v.t. & v.i.* **·dealt** (-delt′), **·deal·ing** In card games, to deal incorrectly or improperly. — *n.* An incorrect deal. — **mis·deal′er** *n.*

mis·deed (mis·dēd′) *n.* An evil or immoral act.

mis·de·mean·or (mis′di·mē′nər) *n. Law* Any offense less serious than a felony, or for which the punishment is less severe.

mis·di·rect (mis′di·rekt′, -dī·rekt′) *v.t.* To direct or guide wrongly, as a letter, person, etc. — **mis′di·rec′tion** *n.*

mis·do (mis·dōō′) *v.t. & v.i.* **·did, ·done, ·do·ing** To do wrongly. [OE *misdōn*] — **mis·do′er** *n.* — **mis·do′ing** *n.*

mis·em·ploy (mis′im·ploi′) *v.t.* To put to a wrong or improper use. — **mis′em·ploy′ment** *n.*

mi·ser (mī′zər) *n.* One who saves or hoards avariciously, often sacrificing his own comfort. [< L, wretched]

mis·er·a·ble (miz′ər·ə·bəl, miz′rə-) *adj.* **1.** Being in a state of misery, poverty, or wretched unhappiness. **2.** *Informal* In poor health; not well. **3.** Causing misery or extreme discomfort: a *miserable* headache. **4.** Proceeding from or exhibiting misery: a *miserable* life. **5.** Of inferior quality; worthless. **6.** Paltry or meager; skimpy. **7.** Deserving of pity: a *miserable* creature. **8.** Disreputable; shameful: a *miserable* scoundrel. [< OF < L < *miserari* to pity] — **mis′er·a·ble·ness** *n.* — **mis′er·a·bly** *adv.*

Mis·e·re·re (miz′ə·râr′ē, -rir′ē) *n.* **1.** The 51st Psalm (in the Vulgate and Douai versions, the 50th): from the opening word of the Latin version. **2.** A musical setting of this psalm. [< L, imperative of *miserēri* to have mercy]

mis·er·i·cor·di·a (miz′ə·ri·kôr′dē·ə) *n. Latin* Pity; mercy.

mi·ser·ly (mī′zər·lē) *adj.* Of, like, or characteristic of a miser; grasping; avaricious. — **mi′ser·li·ness** *n.*

mis·er·y (miz′ər·ē) *n. pl.* **·er·ies** **1.** A condition of great wretchedness or suffering, as caused by poverty, pain, etc. **2.** Intense mental or emotional anguish; extreme unhappiness. **3.** A cause or source of suffering or unhappiness. — **Syn.** See SUFFERING. [< OF < L < *miser* wretched]

mis·fea·sance (mis·fē′zəns) *n. Law* The performance of a lawful act in an unlawful or culpable manner. [< OF < *mes-* mis- + *faire* to do] — **mis·fea′sor** *n.*

mis·fire (*v.* mis·fīr′; *n.* mis′fīr′) *v.i.* **·fired, ·fir·ing** **1.** To fail to fire, ignite, or explode at the desired time, as a firearm, internal-combustion engine, etc. **2.** To fail in achieving the proper or desired effect. — *n.* An instance of misfiring.

mis·fit (mis·fit′; *for n. def. 2,* mis′fit′) *v.t. & v.i.* **·fit·ted, ·fit·ting** To fail to fit or make fit. — *n.* **1.** Something that fits badly. **2.** One who is not well adjusted to his environment. **3.** The act or condition of fitting badly.

mis·for·tune (mis·fôr′chən) *n.* **1.** Adverse or ill fortune; bad luck; adversity. **2.** A calamity; mishap.

mis·giv·ing (mis·giv′ing) *n.* A feeling of doubt, distrust, or apprehension.

mis·gov·ern (mis·guv′ərn) *v.t.* To govern badly; administer improperly. — **mis·gov′ern·ment** *n.*

mis·guide (mis·gīd′) *v.t.* **·guid·ed, ·guid·ing** To guide wrongly; mislead. — **mis·guid′ance** *n.* — **mis·guid′er** *n.*

mis·guid·ed (mis·gī′did) *adj.* Guided or led wrongly in thought or action. — **mis·guid′ed·ly** *adv.*

mis·han·dle (mis·han′dəl) *v.t.* **·dled, ·dling** To handle, treat, or manage badly; abuse.

mis·hap (mis′hap, mis·hap′) *n.* An unfortunate accident.

mish·mash (mish′mash′, -mosh′) *n.* A confused mixture or collection of things; hodgepodge. Also **mish′-mash.**

mis·in·form (mis′in·fôrm′) *v.t.* To give false or erroneous information to. — **mis′in·form′ant, mis′in·form′er** *n.* — **mis′in·for·ma′tion** *n.*

mis·in·ter·pret (mis′in·tûr′prit) *v.t.* To interpret or understand incorrectly. — **mis·in·ter·pre·ta·tion** n. — **mis·in·ter·pret·er** n.

mis·judge (mis-juj′) v.t. & v.i. **·judged, ·judg·ing** To judge wrongly or unfairly. — **mis·judg·ment** or Brit. **mis·judge·ment** n.

mis·lay (mis-lā′) v.t. **·laid, ·lay·ing** 1. To put or lay in a place not remembered; misplace. 2. To place or put down incorrectly: He mislaid the carpet. — **mis·lay·er** n.

mis·lead (mis-lēd′) v.t. **·led** (-led′), **·lead·ing** 1. To guide or lead in the wrong direction. 2. To lead into error, as of judgment or conduct. — **mis·lead·er** n. — **mis·lead·ing** adj. — **mis·lead·ing·ly** adv.

mis·man·age (mis-man′ij) v.t. & v.i. **·aged, ·ag·ing** To manage badly or improperly. — **mis·man·age·ment** n. — **mis·man·ag·er** n.

mis·match (mis-mach′) v.t. To match badly or inappropriately, as in marriage. — n. A bad or incongruous match.

mis·mate (mis-māt′) v.t. & v.i. **·mat·ed, ·mat·ing** To mate unsuitably.

mis·name (mis-nām′) v.t. **·named, ·nam·ing** To call by a wrong name.

mis·no·mer (mis-nō′mər) n. 1. A name wrongly applied to someone or something. 2. The act of misnaming, esp. in a legal document. [< AF < OF < mes- wrongly + nomer < L nominare to name]

miso- combining form Hating; hatred. Also, before vowels, **mis-**. [< Gk. misein to hate]

mis·og·a·my (mis-og′ə-mē) n. Hatred of marriage. — **mis·og′a·mist** n.

mis·og·y·ny (mis-oj′ə-nē) n. Hatred of women [< Gk. < misein to hate + gynē woman] — **mis·og′y·nist** n. — **mis·og′y·nous** adj.

mis·place (mis-plās′) v.t. **·placed, ·plac·ing** 1. To put in a wrong place. 2. To put (confidence, faith, trust, etc.) in an unworthy or unsuitable person, thing, or idea. 3. To mislay (def. 1). — **mis·place′ment** n.

mis·play (mis-plā′; for n., also mis′plā) v.t. & v.i. In games, to play badly or incorrectly. — n. A bad play or move.

mis·print (mis-print′; for n., also mis′print′) v.t. To print incorrectly. — n. An error in printing.

mis·pri·sion (mis-prizh′ən) n. Law 1. Concealment of a crime, esp. of treason or felony. 2. Misconduct of a public official. 3. A mistake; often, a clerical error. [< OF < mes- mis- + prendre to take]

mis·prize (mis-prīz′) v.t. **·prized, ·priz·ing** To fail to appreciate the worth of; undervalue; despise.

mis·pro·nounce (mis′prə-nouns′) v.t. & v.i. **·nounced, ·nounc·ing** To pronounce incorrectly or in an unorthodox manner. — **mis·pro·nun·ci·a·tion** (mis′prə-nun′sē-ā′shən) n.

mis·quote (mis-kwōt′) v.t. & v.i. **·quot·ed, ·quot·ing** To quote incorrectly. — **mis·quo·ta·tion** (mis′kwō-tā′shən) n.

mis·read (mis-rēd′) v.t. **·read** (-red′), **·read·ing** (-rē′ding) To read incorrectly or with the wrong sense; misinterpret.

mis·rep·re·sent (mis′rep·ri·zent′) v.t. 1. To give an incorrect or false representation of. 2. To represent inadequately or poorly. — **mis·rep·re·sen·ta·tion** n. — **mis·rep·re·sen′ta·tive** adj. & n. — **mis·rep·re·sent′er** n.

mis·rule (mis-rool′) v.t. **·ruled, ·rul·ing** To rule unwisely or unjustly; misgovern. — n. 1. Bad or unjust rule or government. 2. Disorder or confusion, as from lawlessness.

miss[1] (mis) v.t. 1. To fail to hit, reach, or land upon (a specified object). 2. To fail to meet or catch, as a train. 3. To fail to obtain, accomplish, or achieve: to miss the presidency by a few votes. 4. To fail to see, hear, perceive, etc. 5. To fail to attend, keep, perform, etc. 6. To overlook or fail to take advantage of. 7. To discover the absence of, usu. belatedly: to miss one's wallet. 8. To feel the loss or absence of. 9. To escape; avoid. — v.i. 10. To fail to hit; strike wide of the mark. 11. To be unsuccessful; fail. — n. A failure to hit, find, succeed, etc. [OE missan]

miss[2] (mis) n. 1. Often cap. A title used in speaking to an unmarried woman or girl: used without name. 2. A young girl: chiefly informal or trade usage. [Contr. of MISTRESS]

Miss (mis) n. A title of address used before the name of a girl or unmarried woman. ◆ In referring to two or more unmarried women bearing the same name, either the Misses Brown or the Miss Browns is acceptable.

mis·sal (mis′əl) n. 1. A book containing all the prayers, responses, etc., for celebrating Mass throughout the year. 2. Loosely, any prayer book. [< Med.L missale, neut. of missalis (liber) mass (book)]

mis·shape (mis-shāp′) v.t. **·shaped, ·shaped** or **·shap·en, ·shap·ing** To shape badly; deform. — **mis·shap′en** adj.

mis·sile (mis′əl, Brit. mis′īl) n. 1. An object, esp. a weapon, intended to be thrown or discharged, as a bullet, arrow, etc. 2. A guided missile. — adj. 1. Such as may be thrown or discharged. 2. Used or adapted for throwing or discharging missiles. [< L < missus, pp. of mittere to send]

mis·sil·ry (mis′əl-rē) n. The science and art of designing, building, and operating missiles, esp. rockets and guided missiles. Also **mis′sile·ry**.

miss·ing (mis′ing) adj. 1. Not present; absent; lacking. 2. Mil. Absent: said of one whose whereabouts or fate in battle has not been determined: also **missing in action**.

missing link 1. A hypothetical animal intermediate in development between man and the anthropoid apes. 2. Something needed to complete a chain or series.

mis·sion (mish′ən) n. 1. Any body of persons sent some place in order to perform or accomplish a specific work or service; esp., such a body sent to a foreign country to conduct business, negotiations, etc., on behalf of its own country. 2. The specific task or responsibility that a person or body of persons is assigned to do or fulfill. 3. A body of missionaries sent by a religious organization to a foreign country or region to convert, aid, or instruct the inhabitants. 4. pl. The organized work of such missionaries. 5. The place or establishment where missionaries carry on their work and often live; also, the entire district or locality that they serve. 6. A special program or series of religious services or exercises for stimulating piety or converting unbelievers. 7. U.S. The permanent foreign office of an ambassador or envoy; embassy. 8. The particular work or goal that one is or feels destined to do or accomplish; a calling. 9. Mil. A definite task or field of operation assigned to an individual or unit of the armed forces. 10. A flight operation of a single aircraft or formation, esp. in wartime. — adj. Pertaining or belonging to a mission. — v.t. 1. To send on a mission. 2. To establish a mission in or among. [< L < missus, pp. of mittere to send] — **mis′sion·er** n.

mis·sion·ar·y (mish′ən·er′ē) n. pl. **·ar·ies** 1. A person sent to propagate religion or to do educational or charitable work in some foreign country or region. 2. One who advocates or spreads any new system or doctrine. — adj. Of, pertaining to, or characteristic of missionaries.

mis·sis (mis′əz) n. Informal & Dial. 1. A wife: often with the. 2. The female head of a household: with the. Also **mis′sus**. [Alter. of MISTRESS]

Mis·sis·sip·pi·an (mis′ə-sip′ē-ən) adj. 1. Of or pertaining to the Mississippi River or to the State. 2. Geol. Relating to the earliest of two geological periods or systems in the American Carboniferous division of the Paleozoic era. See chart for GEOLOGY. — n. 1. One born or residing in Mississippi. 2. The Lower Carboniferous geological formation.

mis·sive (mis′iv) n. A letter, esp. one of an official nature. — adj. Sent or designed to be sent. [< Med.L < L missus, pp. of mittere to send]

Mis·sou·ri (mi-zŏŏr′ē, -zŏŏr′ə) n. pl. **·ri** One of a tribe of North American Indians of the Siouan family, formerly inhabiting northern Missouri.

mis·speak (mis-spēk′) v.t. & v.i. **·spoke, ·speak·ing** To speak or pronounce incorrectly.

mis·spell (mis-spel′) v.t. & v.i. **·spelled** or **·spelt, ·spell·ing** To spell incorrectly.

mis·spell·ing (mis-spel′ing) n. An incorrect spelling.

mis·spend (mis-spend′) v.t. **·spent, ·spend·ing** To spend wrongfully or wastefully.

mis·state (mis-stāt′) v.t. **·stat·ed, ·stat·ing** To state wrongly or falsely. — **mis·state′ment** n.

mis·step (mis-step′) n. 1. A false step; a stumble. 2. An error or blunder, as in conduct.

mist (mist) n. 1. An aggregation of fine drops of water suspended in the atmosphere at or near the earth's surface. 2. Meteorol. A very thin fog with a horizontal visibility arbitrarily set at not more than two kilometers. 3. Watery vapor condensed on and blurring a surface. 4. Any cloud of particles forming a haze, as of dust, smoke, etc. 5. A film or haze before the eyes that blurs one's vision. 6. Anything that clouds or obscures one's memory, perceptions, etc. — v.i. 1. To be or become dim or misty; blur. 2. To rain in very fine drops. — v.t. To make dim or misty. [OE]

mis·tak·a·ble (mis-tāk′ə-bəl) adj. Capable of being mistaken or misunderstood. — **mis·tak′a·bly** adv.

mis·take (mis-tāk′) n. An error or fault in action, judgment, perception, understanding, etc. — v. **·took, ·tak·en, ·tak·ing** v.t. 1. To understand wrongly; acquire a wrong conception of. 2. To take (a person or thing) to be another. — v.i. 3. To make a mistake. [< ON mistaka]

mis·tak·en (mis-tā′kən) adj. 1. Based on or arising from error, as of judgment, understanding, perception, etc. 2. Wrong in opinion, action, etc. — **mis·tak′en·ly** adv.

mis·ter (mis′tər) n. Informal Sir: used without the name. [Var. of MASTER]

Mis·ter (mis′tər) n. 1. Master: a title of address prefixed to the name and to some official titles of a man: commonly written Mr. 2. The official term of address for certain military and naval persons.

mis·time (mis-tīm′) v.t. **·timed, ·tim·ing** 1. To time wrongly or inappropriately. 2. To misjudge the time of.

mis·tle·toe (mis′əl-tō) n. 1. A European parasitic shrub, found growing on various deciduous trees and having yellowish green leaves, inconspicuous flowers, and glutinous white berries, used as a Christmas decoration. 2. A related American plant used as a Christmas decoration and the State flower of Oklahoma. [OE *misteltān* mistletoe twig]

mis·took (mis·tŏŏk′) Past tense of MISTAKE.

mis·tral (mis′trəl, *Fr.* mēs·trál′) *n.* A cold, dry, violent northerly wind blowing down the Rhône Valley through Southern France and adjacent areas. [< F < Provençal, lit., master wind < L < *magister* master]

mis·trans·late (mis′trans·lāt′, -tranz-, mis·trans′lāt, -tranz′-) *v.t.* ·lat·ed, ·lat·ing To translate incorrectly. — **mis′trans·la′tion** *n.*

mis·treat (mis·trēt′) *v.t.* To treat badly or improperly. — **mis·treat′ment** *n.*

mis·tress (mis′tris) *n.* **1.** A woman in a position of authority or control; as: **a** The head of a household, institution, or estate. **b** The head of a staff of servants. **c** The owner of an animal or slave. **2.** A woman who unlawfully cohabits with a man, usu. over an extended period of time. **3.** A woman having supreme control over anything. **4.** *Often cap.* Anything considered feminine that has actual or potential power over something else. **5.** A woman who has mastered a skill, craft, or branch of learning. **6.** *Chiefly Brit.* A female schoolteacher. [< OF *maistresse*, fem. of *maistre* master]

Mis·tress (mis′tris) *n.* Formerly, a title of address applied to women, now supplanted by *Mrs.* and *Miss.*

mis·tri·al (mis·trī′əl) *n. Law* **1.** A trial made void because of some legal errors or defects. **2.** A trial terminated by the jury's inability to agree on a verdict.

mis·trust (mis·trust′) *v.t.* **1.** To regard (someone or something) with suspicion or doubt; be skeptical of. — *v.i.* **2.** To be wary or suspicious. — *n.* Lack of trust or confidence. — **mis·trust′er** *n.* — **mis·trust′ing·ly** *adv.*

mis·trust·ful (mis·trust′fəl) *adj.* Full of mistrust; suspicious. — **mis·trust′ful·ly** *adv.* — **mis·trust′ful·ness** *n.*

mist·y (mis′tē) *adj.* ·i·er, ·i·est **1.** Consisting of, characterized by, or like mist. **2.** Dimmed or obscured. **3.** Lacking clarity; vague. — **mist′i·ly** *adv.* — **mist′i·ness** *n.*

mis·un·der·stand (mis′un·dər·stand′, mis·un′/-) *v.t. & v.i.* ·stood, ·stand·ing To understand wrongly; misinterpret.

mis·un·der·stand·ing (mis′un·dər·stan′ding, mis·un′/-) *n.* **1.** A failure to understand the meaning, motive, etc., of someone or something. **2.** A disagreement or quarrel.

mis·un·der·stood (mis′un·dər·stŏŏd′, mis·un′/-) *adj.* **1.** Wrongly understood. **2.** Not valued or appreciated.

mis·us·age (mis·yōō′sij, -zij) *n.* **1.** Incorrect or improper use, as of words. **2.** Ill-treatment.

mis·use (*n.* mis·yōōs′; *v.* mis·yōōz′) *n.* Erroneous or improper use; misapplication. — *v.t.* ·used, ·us·ing **1.** To use or apply wrongly or improperly. **2.** To treat badly; abuse; maltreat. — **mis·us′er** *n.*

mis·val·ue (mis·val′yōō) *v.t.* ·ued, ·u·ing To value wrongly.

mite¹ (mīt) *n.* Any of various small arachnids, many of which are parasitic on men, animals, and plants, and feed upon stored grain. [OE *mīte*] — **mit′y** *adj.*

mite² (mīt) *n.* **1.** A very small particle, object, or creature. **2.** Any very small coin or sum of money. [< Du. *mijt*]

mi·ter (mī′tər) *n.* **1.** A tall ornamental headdress, rising in peaks at the front and back, worn by popes, bishops, and abbots. **2.** The office or dignity of a bishop. **3.** In carpentry: **a** A miter joint. **b** The beveled edges that come together to form a miter joint. — *v.t.* **1.** To confer a miter upon; raise to the rank of bishop. **2.** To make or join with a miter joint. Also, *Brit.*, **mitre.** [< OF < L *mitra* < Gk., belt, turban] — **mi′ter·er** *n.*

mi·tered (mī′tərd) *adj.* **1.** Shaped like an ecclesiastical miter. **2.** Wearing or permitted to wear a miter.

miter joint A joint made of two pieces of material whose joined ends have been beveled at equal angles, as at the corner of a picture frame.

mit·i·gate (mit′ə·gāt) *v.t. & v.i.* ·gat·ed, ·gat·ing To make or become milder or less severe. [< L < *mitis* mild + *agere* to do, drive] — **mit′i·ga·ble** *adj.* — **mit′i·ga′tion** *n.* — **mit′i·ga′tor** *n.*

mit·i·ga·tive (mit′ə·gā′tiv) *adj.* Tending to mitigate. — *n.* Something that mitigates pain, discomfort, etc. Also **mit′i·gant** (-gənt), **mit′i·ga·to′ry** (-gə·tôr′ē, -tō′rē).

mi·to·chon·dri·a (mī′tə·kon′drē·ə) *n.pl. Biol.* Small granular bodies found in the cytoplasm of a cell, believed to function in certain phases of metabolism. For illus. see CELL. [< NL < Gk. *mitos* thread + *chondros* cartilage, granule]

mi·to·sis (mī·tō′sis) *n. Biol.* The series of changes in cell division by which the chromatin is modified into two sets of chromosomes, one set going to each pole before the cell divides into two mature daughter cells. [< NL < Gk. *mitos* thread + -OSIS] — **mi·tot·ic** (mī·tot′ik) *adj.* — **mi·tot′i·cal·ly** *adv.*

mi·tral (mī′trəl) *adj.* **1.** Pertaining to or resembling a miter. **2.** Of or pertaining to a mitral valve.

mitral valve *Anat.* A membranous valve between the left atrium and the left ventrical of the heart, that prevents the blood from flowing back into the atrium.

mi·tre (mī′tər), **mi·tred** (mī′tərd), etc. See MITER, etc.

mitt (mit) *n.* **1.** In baseball, a covering somewhat like a mitten, to protect the hand catching the ball. **2.** A woman's glove, sometimes extending to or above the elbow but without fully covering the fingers. **3.** A mitten (def. 1). **4.** *Slang Usu. pl.* A hand. **5.** *Slang* A boxing glove.

mit·ten (mit′n) *n.* A covering for the hand, encasing the four fingers together and the thumb separately. [< F *mitaine*]

mix (miks) *v.* **mixed** or **mixt, mix·ing** *v.t.* **1.** To combine or put together in one mass or compound so as to render the constituent parts wholly or partially indistinguishable from one another. **2.** To make by combining ingredients: to *mix* cake batter. **3.** To put or add, as an ingredient: to *mix* two eggs into the batter. **4.** To combine or join: to *mix* age with wisdom. **5.** To bring into contact with; cause to mingle. **6.** To crossbreed. — *v.i.* **7.** To become mixed or have the capacity to become mixed; mingle. **8.** To associate; get along: He does not *mix* well with others. **9.** To take part; become involved. **10.** To crossbreed. — **to mix up 1.** To mix or blend together. **2.** To confuse. **3.** To mistake for another or others: He *mixed up* the meanings of those two words. **4.** To implicate or involve. — *n.* **1.** The act or product of mixing. **2.** A mixture of ingredients, often prepared and sold commercially: a cake *mix.* **3.** A beverage, as water, soda, ginger ale, etc., used in making cocktails and other mixed drinks. **4.** Confusion or bewilderment; a mess. **5.** *Telecom.* The correct blending of the outputs of two or more microphones. [Back formation < MIXED] — **mix′a·ble** or **mix′i·ble** *adj.*

mixed (mikst) *adj.* **1.** Mingled or blended together in a single mass or compound. **2.** Composed of different, dissimilar, or incongruous elements, qualities, classes, races, etc.: *mixed* motives. **3.** Made up of or involving persons of both sexes. **4.** Mentally confused: followed by *up.* Also **mixt.** [< F < L *mixtus*, pp. of *miscere* to mix]

mixed marriage Marriage between persons of different religions or races.

mixed metaphor See under METAPHOR.

mixed number A number, as 3½, 5¾, that is the sum of an integer and a fraction.

mix·er (mik′sər) *n.* **1.** One who or that which mixes. **2.** *Informal* A person with ability to mix socially or get along well in various groups. **3.** *Informal* A dance or gathering for the purpose of getting acquainted. **4.** A mix (def. 3).

mix·ture (miks′chər) *n.* **1.** Something formed by or resulting from mixing. **2.** Anything composed of unlike or various elements; as: **a** A cloth made of several types or colors of yarn. **b** A blend of different kinds or qualities of tea, tobacco, etc. **3.** *Chem.* A commingling of two or more substances in varying proportions, in which the components retain their individual chemical properties: distinguished from *compound.* **4.** The act of mixing, or the state of being mixed. [< F < L *miscere* to mix]

mix-up (miks′up′) *n.* **1.** A state of confusion; also, an instance of this. **2.** *Informal* A fight.

miz·zen (miz′ən) *Naut. n.* **1.** A triangular sail set on the mizzenmast. **2.** A mizzenmast. — *adj.* Of or pertaining to the mizzen or mizzenmast. Also **miz′en.** [< F < Ital. *mezzana*, fem. of *mezzano* middle, ? < L *medianus*]

miz·zen·mast (miz′ən·mast′, -mast′, -mäst′) *n. Naut.* **1.** In a ship with three masts, the mast nearest the stern. **2.** In a ship having more than three masts, the third mast from the forward end of the ship. **3.** In a ketch or yawl, the shorter of the two masts. Also **miz′en·mast′.**

mks The meter-kilogram-second system of measurement in which the unit of length is the meter, the unit of mass is the kilogram, and the unit of time is one second. Also **m.k.s., MKS, M.K.S.**

mne·mon·ic (nē·mon′ik, ni-) *adj.* **1.** Aiding or designed to aid the memory. **2.** Of or relating to mnemonics or memory. Also **mne·mon′i·cal.** — *n.* **1.** A device to assist memory. **2.** Mnemonics. [< Gk. < *mnasthai* to remember]

mne·mon·ics (nē·mon′iks, ni-) *n.pl.* (*construed as sing.*) A system of principles and formulas designed to assist or improve the memory. Also **mne·mo·tech·nics** (nē′mō·tek′niks).

mo·a (mō′ə) *n.* Any of a family of extinct, flightless birds of New Zealand, resembling the ostrich and having very powerful legs. [< Maori]

Mo·ab (mō′ab) An ancient country east of the Dead Sea. — **Mo′ab·ite** *adj. & n.*

moan (mōn) *n.* **1.** A low, sustained, mournful sound, as from grief or pain. **2.** Any similar sound. — *v.i.* **1.** To utter moans. **2.** To make a low, mournful sound, as wind. **3.** To complain or lament. — *v.t.* **4.** To lament; bewail. **5.** To utter with moans. [Cf. OE *mǣnan* to lament, moan]

moat (mōt) *n.* A deep, wide, and usu. water-filled trench around a castle, fortress, or town, designed to discourage attempts at invasion. —*v.t.* To surround with or as with a moat. [< OF *mote* embankment]

mob (mob) *n.* 1. A disorderly or lawless crowd or throng; a rabble. 2. Any large assemblage, group, or class of individuals or things: the ruling *mob.* 3. The lower class or classes of people; the masses. 4. *Informal* A gang of thieves, hoodlums, etc. —*v.t.* **mobbed, mob·bing** 1. To attack in a mob. 2. To crowd around and jostle or molest, as from adulation or curiosity. 3. To attend or crowd into (a hall, theater, etc.). [< L *mob(ile vulgus)* movable crowd] — **mob′ber** *n.* — **mob′bish** *adj.* — **mob′bish·ly** *adv.*

mo·bile (*adj.* mō′bəl, -bēl; *n.* mō′bēl; *Brit.* mō′bīl) *adj.* 1. Characterized by freedom of movement. 2. Flowing freely: a *mobile* liquid. 3. Capable of changing or responding easily or quickly, as to emotions, etc. 4. Moving easily from one thing to another; versatile: a *mobile* mind. 5. Capable of being easily and quickly moved. 6. Capable of moving with relative ease from one social group or status to another. 7. Of, pertaining to, or like a mobile. — *n.* A form of freely moving sculpture consisting of parts that are suspended from rods, wires, etc. [< F < L *mobilis* movable] — **mo·bil′i·ty** *n.*

mo·bi·lize (mō′bə·līz) *v.* **·lized, ·liz·ing** *v.t.* 1. To make ready for war, as an army, industry, men, etc. 2. To assemble for use; organize. 3. To put into activity, circulation, or use: to *mobilize* one's talents. —*v.i.* 4. To undergo mobilization. Also *Brit.* **mo′bi·lise.** [< F *mobiliser*] — **mo′bi·li·za′tion** (-lə-zā′shən, -lī-zā′-) *n.*

mob·ster (mob′stər) *n. Slang* A gangster.

moc·ca·sin (mok′ə·sin) *n.* 1. A heelless foot covering, made of buckskin or of any soft leather and formerly worn by North American Indians. 2. A shoe or slipper resembling a moccasin. 3. The water moccasin. [< Algonquian *mohkisson*]

moccasin flower Any of certain lady's-slippers.

mo·cha (mō′kə) *n.* 1. A choice, pungent coffee, originally brought from Mocha, Arabia. 2. A flavoring made of an infusion of coffee or of coffee and chocolate. 3. A fine sheepskin leather used for making gloves.

mock (mok) *v.t.* 1. To treat or address scornfully or derisively. 2. To mimic, as in sport, derision, or contempt. 3. To deceive or disappoint; delude. 4. To defy; make futile or meaningless. 5. *Poetic* To imitate; counterfeit. —*v.i.* 6. To express or show ridicule or contempt; scoff. — *adj.* Merely imitating or resembling the reality; sham. — *n.* 1. An act of mocking or derision; a jeer. 2. One who or that which is mocked. 3. An imitation or counterfeit. [< OF *mocquer*] — **mock′er** *n.* — **mock′ing·ly** *adv.*

mock·er·y (mok′ər·ē) *n. pl.* **·er·ies** 1. Derision; ridicule. 2. A contemptuous or derisive speech or action. 3. An object of derision or ridicule. 4. A deceitful, impudent, or contemptible imitation: His trial was a *mockery.* 5. Something ludicrously futile, inadequate, or unsuitable.

mock-he·ro·ic (mok′hi·rō′ik) *adj.* Imitating or satirizing the heroic manner, style, attitude, or character. Also **mock′-he·ro′i·cal.**

mock·ing·bird (mok′ing·bûrd′) *n.* 1. A bird common in the southern U.S., noted for its ability to imitate the calls of other birds. 2. Any of various birds of the same family.

mock turtle soup A soup prepared from calf's head and other meat and seasoned to taste like green turtle soup.

mock-up (mok′up′) *n.* A model, usu. full-scale, of a proposed structure, machine, apparatus, etc.

mo·dal (mōd′l) *adj.* 1. Of or pertaining to mode or a mode. 2. *Gram.* **a** Of or pertaining to mood. **b** Conveying a meaning similar to those meanings conveyed by a mood. 3. *Music* Of or pertaining to the modes. 4. *Stat.* Typical. — **mo·dal′i·ty** (-dal′ə·tē) *n.* — **mo′dal·ly** *adv.*

mode (mōd) *n.* 1. Manner or form of being, doing, etc.; way. 2. Prevailing or current style or fashion, as in dress. 3. *Gram.* Mood. 4. *Music* Any of the arrangements of tones achieved by starting at various points in a given scale and proceeding through one octave; esp. the modes of the diatonic scale, as major mode, minor mode, etc. 5. *Philos.* The manner or form in which a basic substance is manifested. 6. *Stat.* The value, magnitude, or score that occurs the greatest number of times in a given series of observations: also called *norm.* [< L *modus* measure, manner]

mod·el (mod′l) *n.* 1. An object, usu. in miniature and often built according to scale, that represents something to be made or something already existing. 2. A pattern, example, or standard that is or may be used for imitation or comparison. 3. A representation in clay, plaster, etc., of something later to be reproduced in more permanent material. 4. One who or that which serves as a figure or pattern for an artist, sculptor, etc. 5. One who is employed to display or advertise merchandise; esp. one who displays articles of clothing by wearing them. 6. A representative style, plan, or design. 7. In merchandise, a particular style or design. —*v.* **mod·eled** or **·elled, mod·el·ing** or **·el·ling** *v.t.* 1. To plan or fashion after a model or pattern. 2. To make a model of. 3. To shape or fashion. 4. To display by wearing. —*v.i.* 5. To make a model or models. 6. To pose or serve as a model (defs. 4 & 5). — *adj.* 1. Serving or used as a model. 2. Worthy or suitable to be used as a model. [< F < Ital. < L *modus* measure, manner] — **mod′el·er** or **mod′el·ler** *n.*

mod·el·ing (mod′ling, -əl·ing) *n.* 1. The act or art of making a model, esp. a sculptor's clay or wax model. 2. In painting, drawing, etc., the representation of depth or three-dimensional solidity. 3. The surfaces or planes of a solid form or shape. 4. The act or occupation of being a model (defs. 4 & 5). Also **mod′el·ling.**

mod·er·ate (*adj.* & *n.* mod′ər·it; *v.* mod′ə·rāt) *adj.* 1. Keeping or kept within reasonable limits; temperate. 2. Holding or characterized by ideas or convictions that are not extreme or radical. 3. Of medium or average quality, quantity, scope, extent, etc. 4. *Meteorol.* Designating a breeze (No. 4) or a gale (No. 7) on the Beaufort scale. — *n.* One having moderate views or practices, esp. in politics or religion. — *v.* **·at·ed, ·at·ing** *v.t.* 1. To reduce the violence, severity, etc., of. 2. To preside over. —*v.i.* 3. To become less intense or violent. 4. To act as a moderator. [< L *moderare* to regulate] — **mod′er·ate·ly** *adv.* — **mod′er·ate·ness** *n.*

mod·er·a·tion (mod′ə·rā′shən) *n.* 1. The state or quality of being moderate. 2. The act of moderating. — **in moderation** Within reasonable limits; temperately.

mod·e·ra·to (mod′ə·rä′tō) *Music adj.* Moderate. — *adv.* In moderate time; moderately. — *n. pl.* **·tos** A moderate passage or movement. Abbr. *mod.* [< Ital.]

mod·er·a·tor (mod′ə·rā′tər) *n.* 1. One who or that which moderates. 2. One who presides over a meeting, forum, or debate. 3. The arbitrator of a dispute. 4. *Physics* A substance, as graphite or beryllium, used to slow down neutrons in an atomic-energy reactor. — **mod′er·a′tor·ship** *n.*

mod·ern (mod′ərn) *adj.* 1. Of or pertaining to the present or recent time. 2. Characteristic of or serving to express the current times; up-to-date. 3. *Usu. cap.* Of, pertaining to, or characteristic of the most recent period in the development of a language: *Modern* French. — *n.* 1. One who lives in modern times. 2. One who has opinions, habits, prejudices, etc., characteristic of modern times. 3. *Printing* A style of type face characterized by heavy stems and extremely thin serifs. [< LL *modernus* recent] — **mod′ern·ly** *adv.*

mod·ern·ism (mod′ərn·iz′əm) *n.* 1. The character or quality of thought, action, etc., that is peculiar to modern times. 2. Something characteristic of modern times, as an act, practice, idiom, attitude, etc. 3. *Often cap.* In religion, a movement to reinterpret the Bible and church teachings to make them consistent with modern science and philosophy. — **mod·ern·ist** (mod′ərn·ist) *n.* 1. One who is sympathetic with or has a preference for modern things, practices, ideas, etc. 2. *Often cap.* An advocate of religious modernism. — **mod·ern·is′tic** *adj.*

mo·der·ni·ty (mo-dûr′nə·tē) *n. pl.* **·ties** 1. The condition or quality of being modern. 2. Something modern.

mod·ern·ize (mod′ərn·īz) *v.* **·ized, ·iz·ing** *v.t.* 1. To make modern in method, style, character, etc.; bring up to date. —*v.i.* 2. To accept or adopt modern ways, ideas, idioms, etc. — **mod′ern·i·za′tion** *n.* — **mod′ern·iz′er** *n.*

mod·est (mod′ist) *adj.* 1. Having or displaying a moderate or unexaggerated regard for oneself or one's abilities, accomplishments, etc.; humble. 2. Not showy, gaudy, or ostentatious. 3. Not excessive or extreme; moderate. 4. Reserved in speech, manner, dress, etc. [< L *modestus* moderate] — **mod′est·ly** *adv.*

mod·es·ty (mod′is·tē) *n. pl.* **·ties** 1. Freedom from vanity or excessive pride. 2. Freedom from showiness or ostentation. 3. Propriety in speech, dress, etc. 4. Moderation.

mod·i·cum (mod′i·kəm) *n. pl.* **·cums** or **·ca** (-kə) A moderate or small amount. [< L *modus* measure]

mod·i·fi·ca·tion (mod′ə·fə·kā′shən) *n.* 1. The act of modifying, or the state of being modified. 2. That which results from modifying. 3. A small adjustment, alteration, or qualification. 4. *Biol.* A noninheritable change in an organism, resulting from its own activity or its environment.

mod·i·fi·er (mod′ə·fī′ər) *n.* 1. One who or that which modifies. 2. *Gram.* A word, phrase, or clause that restricts or qualifies the meaning of another word or group of words.

mod·i·fy (mod′ə·fī) *v.* **·fied, ·fy·ing** *v.t.* 1. To make somewhat different in form, character, etc. 2. To revise by making less extreme, severe, or uncompromising. 3. *Gram.* To qualify the meaning of; limit. —*v.i.* 4. To be or become modified. [< F < L < *modus* measure + *facere* to make] — **mod′i·fi′a·ble** *adj.*

mod·ish (mō′dish) *adj.* Conforming to the current mode or fashion; stylish. — **mod′ish·ly** *adv.* — **mod′ish·ness** *n.*

mo·diste (mō·dēst′) *n.* A woman who deals in fashionable women's clothing, esp. hats or dresses. [< F]

mod·u·lar (moj′ŏŏ·lər) *adj.* 1. Of, like, or pertaining to a module or modulus. 2. Composed of modules: *modular* homes.

mod·u·late (moj′ŏŏ-lāt) *v.* **·lat·ed**, **·lat·ing** *v.t.* **1.** To vary the tone, inflection, pitch, or volume of. **2.** To regulate or adjust; modify. **3.** To sing or intone, as a prayer. **4.** *Telecom.* To alter some characteristic of (a radio carrier wave). — *v.i.* **5.** *Music* To change from one key to another. **6.** *Telecom.* To alter some characteristic of a carrier wave. [< L *modulatus*, pp. of *modulari* to regulate] — **mod′u·la·tor** *n.* — **mod′u·la·to·ry** (-lə-tôr′ē, -tō′rē) *adj.*
mod·u·la·tion (moj′ŏŏ-lā′shən) *n.* **1.** The act of modulating, or the state of being modulated. **2.** *Music* A change from one key to another. **3.** A melodious or rhythmical inflection of the voice. **4.** A melodious use of language, as in prose or poetry. **5.** *Telecom.* **a** The process whereby some characteristic of one carrier wave is varied in accordance with another wave. **b** The result of this process.
mod·ule (moj′ŏŏl) *n.* **1.** A standard or unit of measurement. **2.** *Archit.* A unit of measure used to determine the proportion among parts of a classical order. **3.** A standard structural component repeatedly used, as in a building, computer, etc. **4.** A self-contained component or subassembly: a housing *module*. [< L *modulus*, dim. of *modus* measure]
mo·dus op·er·an·di (mō′dəs op′ə·ran′dī) *Latin* A manner of operating or proceeding.
modus vi·ven·di (vi·ven′dī) *Latin* **1.** A manner of living. **2.** A temporary agreement in a dispute.
Mo·gul (mō′gul, mō·gul′) *n.* **1.** One of the conquerors of India, who in 1526 founded a Moslem empire. **2.** Any of their descendants. **3.** A member of the Mongoloid race. — *adj.* Of or pertaining to the Moguls or their empire. Also spelled *Mughal, Mughul*: also **Mo·ghal′, Mo·ghul′**. [< Persian *mugal* Mongol]
mo·hair (mō′hâr) *n.* **1.** The hair of the Angora goat. **2.** A glossy, wiry fabric made of mohair and cotton in a plain or twill weave. **3.** A fabric having a mohair pile, used for upholstery. [Earlier *mocayare* < Arabic *mukhayyar*]
Mo·ham·me·dan (mō·ham′ə·dən) *adj.* Of or pertaining to Mohammed or to his religion and institutions. — *n.* A follower of Mohammed or a believer in Islam; a Muslim. Also *Mahometan, Muhammadan, Muhammedan.*
Mohammedan calendar See under CALENDAR.
Mo·ham·me·dan·ism (mō·ham′ə·dən·iz′əm) *n.* Islam.
Mo·ha·ve (mō·hä′vē) *n.* One of a tribe of North American Indians of Yuman stock, formerly living along the Colorado River: also spelled *Mojave.*
Mo·hawk (mō′hôk) *n.* **1.** One of a tribe of North American Indians of Iroquoian stock, one of the original Five Nations, formerly ranging from the Mohawk River to the St. Lawrence. **2.** The language of this tribe. [< N.Am.Ind.]
Mo·he·gan (mō·hē′gən) *n.* **1.** One of a tribe of North American Indians of Algonquian stock, formerly living along the Thames River in Connecticut. **2.** Loosely, Mahican. [< Algonquian *maingan* wolf]
Mo·hi·can (mō·hē′kən) *n.* A Mahican.
Mo·hole (mō′hōl′) *n.* A hole drilled or to be drilled through the ocean floor to the level of the Mohorovicic discontinuity.
Mo·ho·ro·vic·ic discontinuity (mə·hôr′ə·vis′ik, -vich′ik) *n. Geol.* A rock layer forming a boundary zone beneath the earth's crust at depths of from about 6 to 25 miles and believed to explain certain changes in the character and velocity of seismic waves. Also **Mo·ho** (mō′hō). [after Andrija *Mohorovičić*, Yugoslavian geologist]
Mohs scale (mōz) *Mineral.* A qualitative scale in which the hardness of a mineral is determined by its ability to scratch, or be scratched by, any one of 15 minerals arranged in order of increasing hardness from talc to diamond. [after Friedrich *Mohs*, 1773–1839, German mineralogist]
moi·e·ty (moi′ə·tē) *n. pl.* **·ties 1.** A half. **2.** Any portion, part, or share. **3.** *Anthropol.* Either of two basic groups that together constitute a tribe. [< F < L *medius* half]
moil (moil) *v.i.* **1.** To work hard; toil. **2.** To move about ceaselessly. — *v.t.* **3.** To make wet. — *n.* **1.** Toil; drudgery. **2.** Confusion; uproar. [< OF *moillier, muiller* to wet < L *mollis* soft] — **moil′er** *n.* — **moil′ing·ly** *adv.*
moi·ré (mwä·rā′) *adj.* Having a wavelike or watered appearance, as certain fabrics. — *n.* **1.** A ribbed fabric, usu. silk or rayon, having a wavy or watered pattern: also **moire** (mwär, môr). **2.** A wavy pattern produced on fabrics by engraved cylinders. [< F < *moire* watered silk]
moist (moist) *adj.* **1.** Slightly wet or damp. **2.** Saturated with or characterized by moisture or liquid. **3.** Tearful or tearfully sentimental. [< OF, a fusion of L *musteus* dew + *mucidus* moldy] — **moist′ly** *adv.* — **moist′ness** *n.*
mois·ten (mois′ən) *v.t. & v.i.* To make or become moist. — **mois′ten·er** *n.*
mois·ture (mois′chər) *n.* **1.** Water or other liquid diffused as a vapor in the air or as a liquid through or on the surface of objects. **2.** Dampness. [< OF *moisteur*]
Mo·ja·ve (mō·hä′vē) See MOHAVE.

mo·lar (mō′lər) *n.* A grinding tooth, of which there are 12 in man, situated behind the canine and incisor teeth and having a broad, flattened crown. For illus. see TOOTH. — *adj.* **1.** Grinding or adapted for grinding. **2.** Pertaining to a molar. [< L < *mola* mill]
mo·las·ses (mə·las′iz) *n. pl.* **mo·las·ses** Any of various thick, dark-colored syrups obtained from sugar, sorghum, etc., during the refining process: also, *Brit., treacle.* [< Pg. < L *mellaceus* honeylike]
mold¹ (mōld) *n.* **1.** A form or matrix that gives a particular shape to anything in a fluid or plastic condition. **2.** A frame or model on or around which something is shaped or made: a basket *mold.* **3.** That which is shaped or made in or on a mold. **4.** The shape or pattern rendered by a mold. **5.** General shape, form, or pattern. **6.** Distinctive nature, character, or type. **7.** *Archit.* A molding or set of moldings. — *v.t.* **1.** To work into a particular shape or form. **2.** To shape or form in or as in a mold. **3.** To influence, determine, or direct: to *mold* public sentiment. **4.** To follow the contours of; cling to. — *v.i.* **5.** To assume or come to fit a particular shape or pattern. Also, *Brit., mould.* [< OF < L < *modus* measure, limit] — **mold′a·ble** *adj.* — **mold′er** *n.*
mold² (mōld) *n.* **1.** Any of a variety of fungous growths commonly found on the surfaces of decaying food or in warm, moist places, and usu. having a woolly or furry texture. **2.** A fungus producing one of these growths. — *v.i.* To become moldy. Also *Brit., mould.* [< obs. *mouled*, pp. of *moulen* to grow moldy]
mold³ (mōld) *n.* Soft, loose earth that is esp. suitable for plants because it is rich in decaying organic matter. — *v.t.* To cover with mold. Also, *Brit., mould.* [OE *molde* earth]
mold·board (mōld′bôrd′, -bōrd′) *n.* The curved metal plate of a plow that digs into and turns over the soil.
mold·er (mōl′dər) *v.i.* **1.** To decay gradually and turn to dust; crumble. **2.** To atrophy from lack of use. — *v.t.* **3.** To cause to crumble. **4.** To waste or squander. Also, *Brit., moulder.* [Freq. of obs. *mold* to crumble]
mold·ing (mōl′ding) *n.* **1.** The act or process of one who or that which molds. **2.** That which is molded. **3.** *Archit.* **a** A cornice or other depressed or projecting member, used to decorate the surface or angle of a building, room, etc. **b** The decoratively molded surface of a cornice, jamb, etc. **4.** A strip of decoratively shaped wood or other material, used to decorate or finish walls, doors, etc. Also, *Brit., moulding.*
mold·y (mōl′dē) *adj.* **mold·i·er, mold·i·est 1.** Covered with or containing mold. **2.** Musty, as from age, lack of use, etc. Also, *Brit., mouldy.* — **mold′i·ness** *n.*
mole¹ (mōl) *n.* A small, permanent spot on the human skin, slightly protuberant and often dark and hairy. [OE *māl*]
mole² (mōl) *n.* Any of a number of small insectivorous mammals that live mainly underground and have soft fur, small eyes, and broad forefeet adapted for digging and burrowing: also called *taupe.* [ME *molle*]

COMMON MOLE
(6 to 8 inches long; tail 1 inch)

mole³ (mōl) *n.* **1.** A massive, usu. stone barricade in the sea, built to enclose an anchorage or harbor for which it acts as a breakwater or pier. **2.** An anchorage or harbor so enclosed. [< F < L < Gk. *mylē* millstone]
mole⁴ (mōl) *Chem.* The gram molecule: also spelled *mol.*
mo·lec·u·lar (mə·lek′yə·lər) *adj.* Pertaining to, consisting of, or caused by molecules. [< NL *molecularis*]
molecular weight *Chem.* The sum of the atomic weights of all the atoms in a molecule.
mol·e·cule (mol′ə·kyōōl) *n. Chem.* One or more atoms constituting the smallest part of an element or compound that can exist separately without losing its chemical properties. **2.** Any very small particle. [< F < NL *molecula*, dim. of L *moles* mass]
mole·hill (mōl′hil′) *n.* **1.** A small heap or mound of earth raised by a burrowing mole. **2.** Something trivial or inconsequential: to make a mountain out of a *molehill.*
mole·skin (mōl′skin′) *n.* **1.** The dark gray pelt of a mole, very soft and fragile and used as a fur. **2.** A heavy, twilled cotton fabric with a thick, soft nap on one side. **3.** *Usu. pl.* Items of clothing, esp. trousers, made of this fabric.
mo·lest (mə·lest′) *v.t.* **1.** To disturb or annoy by unwarranted, excessive, or malicious interference. **2.** To interfere with improperly or illicitly, esp. with a sexual motive. [< OF < L < *molestus* troublesome] — **mo·les·ta·tion** (mō′les-tā′shən, mol′es-) *n.* — **mo·lest′er** *n.*
moll (mol) *n. Slang* **1.** The girl friend of a gangster. **2.** A prostitute. [< *Moll*, dim. of *Mary*]
mol·lie (mol′ē) *n.* Any of a variety of tropical fishes often raised in aquariums. Also **mol′ly.**
mol·li·fy (mol′ə·fī) *v.t.* **·fied, ·fy·ing 1.** To make less angry, violent, or agitated; soothe. **2.** To reduce the harshness,

severity, or intensity of. [< F < LL < L *mollis* soft + *facere* to make] — **mol′li·fi′a·ble** *adj.* — **mol′li·fi·ca′tion** *n.* — **mol′li·fi′er** *n.* — **mol′li·fy·ing·ly** *adv.*

mol·lus·coid (mə·lus′koid) *adj.* Of or like a mollusk. Also **mol·lus·coi·dal** (mol′əs·koid′l).

mol·lusk (mol′əsk) *n. Zool.* A large group of unsegmented, soft-bodied invertebrates, usu. protected by a calcareous shell of one or more pieces, and including snails, mussels, oysters, clams, octopi, whelks, etc. Also **mol′lusc.** [< F < L *molluscus* (*nux*) soft, thin-shelled (nut)] — **mol·lus·can** (mə·lus′kən) *adj. & n.* — **mol′lus′cous** *adj.*

mol·ly·cod·dle (mol′ē·kod′l) *n.* Any overprotected or pampered person; also, an effeminate man or boy. — *v.t.* **·dled, ·dling** To pamper; coddle. [< *Molly* a personal name + CODDLE] — **mol′ly·cod′dler** *n.*

Mo·loch (mō′lok) In the Bible, a god of the Ammonites and Phoenicians to whom parents offered their children to be burnt in sacrifice. — *n.* Anything exacting merciless sacrifices. [< LL < Gk. < Hebrew *Mōlekh* a king]

molt (mōlt) *v.t. & v.i.* To cast off or shed (feathers, horns, skin, etc.) in preparation for periodic replacement by new growth. — *n.* **1.** The act or process of molting. **2.** That which is molted. Also, *Brit., moult.* [ME < OE < L *mutare* to change] — **molt′er** *n.*

mol·ten (mōl′tən) Archaic past participle of MELT. — *adj.* **1.** Made fluid by heat; melted: *molten* metal. **2.** Made by melting and casting in a mold: *molten* images.

mol·to (mōl′tō) *adv. Music* Much; very. [< Ital. < L *multum* much]

mo·lyb·de·nite (mə·lib′də·nīt) *n.* A soft, lead-gray molybdenum disulfide, MoS₂, the chief ore of molybdenum.

mo·lyb·de·num (mə·lib′də·nəm, mol′ib·dē′nəm) *n.* A hard, heavy, silver-white, metallic element (symbol Mo) of the chromium group, occurring only in combination, used to harden steel. See ELEMENT. [< NL < L < Gk. < *molybdos* lead]

mom (mom) *n.* Mother: used familiarly. [< MAMA]

mo·ment (mō′mənt) *n.* **1.** A very short or relatively short period of time. **2.** A particular point in time, usu. the present time. **3.** A particular period or stage in a series of events: a great *moment* in history. **4.** Importance; consequence: ·matters of great *moment*. **5.** A brief period of excellence, distinction, enjoyment, etc.. **6.** *Mech.* **a** The tendency to produce motion, esp. rotatory motion. **b** A measure of such a tendency. [< F < L *momentum* movement]

mo·men·tar·i·ly (mō′mən·ter′ə·lē, mō′mən·ter′ə·lē) *adv.* **1.** For a moment: *momentarily* at a loss. **2.** In a moment; at any moment. **3.** From moment to moment; progressively.

mo·men·tar·y (mō′mən·ter′ē) *adj.* **1.** Lasting no more than a moment; fleeting. **2.** Occurring or operating at every moment. — **mo′men·tar′i·ness** *n.*

mo·ment·ly (mō′mənt·lē) *adv.* **1.** From moment to moment; at any instant. **2.** For a moment.

mo·men·tous (mō·men′təs) *adj.* Of great importance or consequence. — **mo·men′tous·ly** *adv.* — **mo·men′tous·ness** *n.*

mo·men·tum (mō·men′təm) *n. pl.* **·ta** (-tə) or **·tums 1.** *Physics* The quantity of motion in a body as measured by the product of its mass and velocity. **2.** Impetus, as of a body in motion.

mon- *combining form* Var. of MONO-.

mon·ad (mon′ad, mō′nad) *n.* **1.** An indestructible unit; a simple and indivisible substance. **2.** *Biol.* A minute, simple, single-celled organism. **3.** *Chem.* An atom, radical, or element with a valence of one. — *adj.* Of, pertaining to, or consisting of a monad: also **mo·nad·ic** (mə·nad′ik) or **i·cal.** [< LL < Gk. *monas* unit]

mon·arch (mon′ərk) *n.* **1.** A hereditary constitutional ruler, as a king, queen, etc. **2.** Formerly, a sole ruler of a state. **3.** One who or that which surpasses others of the same kind. **4.** *Entomol.* A large, orange and brown butterfly whose larvae feed on milkweed. [< LL < Gk. < *monos* alone + *archein* to rule] — **mo·nar·chal** (mə·när′kəl) *adj.* — **mo·nar′chal·ly** *adv.*

mo·nar·chi·cal (mə·när′ki·kəl) *adj.* **1.** Of, pertaining to, or characteristic of a monarchy or monarch. **2.** Governed by or favoring a monarch or monarchy. Also **mo·nar′chi·al, mo·nar′chic.** — **mo·nar′chi·cal·ly** *adv.*

mon·arch·ism (mon′ərk·iz′əm) *n.* **1.** The principles or system of a monarchy. **2.** The advocacy of a monarchy. — **mon′arch·ist** *n.* — **mon′arch·is′tic** *adj.*

mon·ar·chy (mon′ər·kē) *n. pl.* **·chies 1.** Government by a monarch; sovereign control. **2.** A government or territory ruled by a monarch. — **absolute monarchy** A government in which the will of the monarch is positive law; a despotism. — **constitutional** or **limited monarchy** A monarchy in which the power and prerogative of the sovereign are limited by constitutional provisions.

mon·as·ter·y (mon′əs·ter′ē) *n. pl.* **·ter·ies 1.** A dwelling place occupied by monks living under religious vows and in seclusion. **2.** The monks living in such a place. [< LL < LGk. < Gk. < *monazein* to live alone]

mo·nas·tic (mə·nas′tik) *adj.* **1.** Of, pertaining to, or characteristic of monasteries or their inhabitants; ascetic. **2.** Characteristic of a life of religious seclusion. Also **mon·as·te·ri·al** (mon′əs·tir′ē·əl), **mo·nas′ti·cal.** — *n.* A monk or other religious recluse. [< F < LL < Gk. *monastikos*] — **mon·as′ti·cal·ly** *adv.*

mo·nas·ti·cism (mə·nas′tə·siz′əm) *n.* The monastic life or system.

mon·a·tom·ic (mon′ə·tom′ik) *adj. Chem.* Consisting of a single atom, as the molecules of certain elements.

mon·au·ral (män′ôr·əl, mōn′-) *adj.* **1.** Pertaining to or characterized by the perception of sound by one ear only. **2.** *Electronics* Designating a system of sound reproduction in which the sound is perceived as coming from one direction only.

mon·ax·i·al (mon·ak′sē·əl) *adj.* Having but one axis.

mon·a·zite (mon′ə·zīt) *n.* A resinous, brownish red or brown phosphate of the lanthanide metals, chiefly cerium, lanthanum, and didymium, an important source of thorium. [< G < Gk. *monazein* to live alone]

Mon·day (mun′dē, -dā) *n.* The second day of the week. [OE *mōn(an)dæg* day of the moon]

mo·ne·cious (mə·nē′shəs, mō-) See MONOECIOUS.

Mo·nel metal (mō·nel′) A corrosion-resistant nickel alloy containing copper, iron, and manganese, used for industrial equipment machine parts, etc.: a trade name. [after Ambrose *Monel*, d. 1921, U.S. manufacturer]

mon·e·tar·y (mon′ə·ter′ē, mun′-) *adj.* **1.** Of or pertaining to currency or coinage. **2.** Pertaining to or concerned with money. [< L *monetarius* of a mint] — **mon′e·tar′i·ly** *adv.*

mon·ey (mun′ē) *n. pl.* **mon·eys** or **mon·ies 1.** Officially issued coins and paper currency that serve as a medium of exchange and a measure of value and may be used as payment for goods and services and for settlement of debts. ◆ Collateral adjective: *pecuniary.* **2.** Any substance or object used similarly, as checks, wampum, etc. **3.** Property of any type having monetary value. **4.** Money of account. **5.** A system of coinage. **6.** *pl.* Sums of money. **7.** Pecuniary profits. — **to put money on** To place a bet on. [< OF < L *moneta* mint]

mon·ey·bag (mun′ē·bag) *n.* **1.** A bag for holding money. **2.** *pl. Slang* A wealthy person; also, wealth.

money belt A belt with pouches for carrying money.

mon·ey·chang·er (mun′ē·chān′jər) *n.* **1.** One whose business it is to change money at a prescribed rate. **2.** A device for holding and dispensing coins.

mon·eyed (mun′ēd) *adj.* **1.** Possessed of money; wealthy. **2.** Consisting of, arising from, or representing money or wealth: *moneyed* interests. Also spelled *monied.*

mon·ey·lend·er (mun′ē·len′dər) *n.* One whose business is the lending of money at interest.

mon·ey·mak·ing (mun′ē·mā′king) *adj.* Likely to bring in money; profitable. — *n.* The acquisition of money or wealth. — **mon′ey·mak′er** *n.*

money of account A monetary denomination used in keeping accounts, usu. not represented by a coin, as the U.S. mill.

money order An order for the payment of a specified sum of money; esp., such an order issued at one post office or telegraph office and payable at another.

mon·ger (mung′gər, mong′-) *n.* **1.** *Brit.* A dealer or trader: chiefly in combination: *fishmonger.* **2.** One who engages in discreditable matters: chiefly in compounds: a *scandalmonger.* [OE < L *mango* dealer]

Mon·gol (mong′gəl, -gol, -gōl) *n.* **1.** A member of any of the native tribes of Mongolia; esp., one inhabiting eastern Mongolia or a Kalmuck. **2.** Any of the Mongolian languages. **3.** A member of the Mongoloid ethnic division. — *adj.* Mongolian (def. 1). [< Mongolian *mong* brave]

Mon·go·li·an (mong·gō′lē·ən, -gōl′yən, mon-) *adj.* **1.** Of or pertaining to Mongolia, its people, or their languages. **2.** Exhibiting Mongolism. — *n.* **1.** A native of Mongolia. **2.** A subfamily of the Altaic languages, including the languages of the Mongols. **3.** A person afflicted with Mongolism.

Mon·gol·ism (mong′gəl·iz′əm) *n.* A form of congenital mental deficiency characterized by a broad flat face and skull, obliquely set, narrow eyes, etc.

Mon·go·loid (mong′gə·loid) *adj.* **1.** *Anthropol.* Of, pertaining to, or belonging to a major ethnic division of the human species, characterized by yellowish skin, slanting eyes, straight head hair, high cheek bones, etc. **2.** Resembling, related to, or characteristic of Mongols or Mongolians. **3.** Characterized by Mongolism. — *n.* A Mongoloid person.

mon·goose (mong′gōōs, mung′-) *n. pl.* **·goos·es** A small, ferretlike, carnivorous mammal that destroys rats and can kill venomous snakes without injury to itself. [< Marathi *mangus*]

MONGOOSE

(To 18 inches long; tail 18 inches)

mon·grel (mung′grəl, mong′-) *n.* **1.** The progeny produced by crossing different breeds or varieties of plants or animals; esp. a dog of mixed breed. **2.** Any incongruous mixture.

adj. Of mixed breed, origin, nature, etc.: often a contemptuous term: a *mongrel* language. [ME < obs. *mong* mixture + -*rel*, dim. suffix]

'mongst (mungst) *prep. Poetic* Amongst.

mon·ied (mun′ēd) See MONEYED.

mon·i·ker (mon′ə-kər) *n. Informal* A name, signature, or nickname. Also **mon′ick·er.** [Prob. blend of MONOGRAM and MARKER]

mon·ism (mon′iz-əm, mō′niz-əm) *n. Philos.* The doctrine that there is but one principle of being or ultimate substance, as mind or matter. [< NL < Gk. *monos* single] — **mon′ist** *n.* — **mo·nis′tic** or **·ti·cal** *adj.*

mo·ni·tion (mō-nish′ən) *n.* **1.** A warning or admonition, as of impending danger. **2.** An official, legal, or formal notice. [< OF < L *monitus,* pp. of *monere* to warn]

mon·i·tor (mon′ə-tər) *n.* **1.** In some schools, a student selected to perform certain duties in class, as helping to keep records, maintain order, etc. **2.** One who advises or cautions, esp. in matters of conduct. **3.** Something that warns or reminds. **4.** Formerly, an ironclad warship having a low, flat deck and low freeboard, and fitted with one or more revolving turrets carrying heavy guns. **5.** *Zool.* Any of several large, carnivorous lizards of Africa, Asia, and Australia. **6.** *Telecom.* A receiver, loudspeaker, or other apparatus used to check radio or television broadcasts for quality of transmission, frequency, compliance with laws, material transmitted, etc. — *v.t. & v.i.* **1.** *Telecom.* To listen to or watch (a broadcast) with a monitor. **2.** To act or supervise as a monitor (def. 1). [< L < *monere* to warn] — **mon′i·to′ri·al** (-tôr′ē·əl, -tō′rē-) *adj.* — **mon′i·tor·ship′** *n.*

mon·i·to·ry (mon′ə-tôr′ē, -tō′rē) *adj.* Conveying a warning; admonitory. — *n.* A monitory letter. [< L *monitor*]

monk (mungk) *n.* **1.** One who has taken the religious vows of poverty, chastity, and obedience, usu. a member of a monastic order. **2.** Formerly, a religious hermit. [OE < LL < LGk. < Gk. *monos* alone]

mon·key (mung′kē) *n.* **1.** Any of the primates, excluding the anthropoid apes, having elongate limbs, hands and feet adapted for grasping, and a highly developed nervous system; esp., the marmosets, baboons, macaques, etc. **2.** One who acts in a way suggestive of a monkey, as a mischievous child. — *v.i. Informal* To play or trifle; meddle; fool: often with *with* or *around.* [? < MLG *Moneke,* name of the son of Martin the Ape in *Reynard the Fox*]

monkey business *Slang* Foolish tricks; deceitful or mischievous behavior.

mon·key-shine (mung′kē-shīn′) *n. Usu. pl. Slang* A mischievous or playful trick, prank, or joke.

monkey wrench A wrench having an adjustable jaw for grasping nuts, bolts, etc., of various sizes. — **to throw a monkey wrench into** *U.S. Informal* To disrupt.

monk's cloth (mungks) A sturdy cotton fabric with a basket weave used for drapes, curtains, etc.

monks·hood (mungks′hŏŏd′) *n.* A plant having the upper sepal arched like a hood; esp., a poisonous variety: also called *aconite.*

mono- *combining form* **1.** Single; one: *monologue.* **2.** *Chem.* Denoting the presence in a compound of a single atom, or an equivalent of the element or radical to the name of which it is prefixed. Also, before vowels, **mon-.** [< Gk. *monos* single]

mon·o·ba·sic (mon′ə-bā′sik) *adj. Chem.* Possessing but a single hydrogen atom replaceable by a metal or positive radical: applied to acids.

mon·o·chrome (mon′ə-krōm) *n.* A painting or drawing in a single color or in various shades of the same color. [< L < Gk. *monos* single + *chrōma* color] — **mon′o·chro·mat′ic, mon′o·chro′mic** or **-i·cal** *adj.*

mon·o·cle (mon′ə-kəl) *n.* An eyeglass for one eye. [< F < LL < Gk. *monos* single + L *oculus* eye] — **mon′o·cled** *adj.*

mon·o·cli·nal (mon′ə-klī′nəl) *Geol. adj.* Having an inclination in only one direction, or composed of rock strata so inclined. — *n.* A monocline. — **mon′o·cli′nal·ly** *adv.*

mon·o·cline (mon′ə-klīn) *n. Geol.* A monoclinal rock structure. [< MONO- + Gk. *klinein* to incline]

mon·o·cli·nous (mon′ə-klī′nəs) *adj. Bot.* Containing both stamens and pistils in the same flower; hermaphrodite. [< MONO- + Gk. *klīnē* bed, couch]

mon·o·cot·y·le·don (mon′ə-kot′ə-lēd′n) *n. Bot.* Any seed plant bearing one cotyledon in the embryo. Also **mon′o·cot′.** [< NL] — **mon′o·cot′y·le′do·nous** *adj.*

mon·o·dy (mon′ə-dē) *n. pl.* **·dies** **1.** A poem in which the poet laments the death of another. **2.** An ode performed by one voice; esp., a lyric ode in a Greek tragedy; dirge. **3.** *Music* A composition in which there is only one vocal part; also, the style of such a composition. [< LL < Gk. *monos* alone + *aeidein* to sing] — **mo·nod′ic** (mə-nod′ik) or **·i·cal** *adj.* — **mo·nod′i·cal·ly** *adv.* — **mon′o·dist** *n.*

mo·noe·cious (mə-nē′shəs) *adj.* **1.** *Biol.* Hermaphroditic. **2.** *Bot.* Monoclinous. Also *monecious, monoicous.* Also **mo·ne′cian.** [< MON- + Gk. *oikos* house]

mo·nog·a·my (mə-nog′ə-mē) *n.* The condition or practice of having only one wife or husband at a time. [< F < LL < Gk. *monos* single + *gamos* marriage] — **mo·nog′a·mic** (mon′ə-gam′ik) *adj.* — **mo·nog′a·mist** *n.* — **mo·nog′a·mous** *adj.*

mon·o·gram (mon′ə-gram) *n.* Two or more letters intertwined into one; esp., the initials of one's name. — *v.t.* **mon·o·grammed** or **·grammed, mon·o·gram·ing** or **·gram·ming** To mark with a monogram. [< LL < Gk. *monos* single + *grammē* letter] — **mon′o·gram·mat′ic** (-grə-mat′ik) *adj.*

mon·o·graph (mon′ə-graf, -gräf) *n.* A book, pamphlet, or treatise on one subject or on a single aspect of a subject. — **mo·nog·ra·pher** (mə-nog′rə-fər) *n.* — **mon′o·graph′ic** *adj.*

mon·o·lith (mon′ə-lith) *n.* A single block of stone, usu. very large, used in architecture and sculpture. [< LL < Gk. < *mono-* + *lithos* stone]

mon·o·lith·ic (mon′ə-lith′ik) *adj.* **1.** Of or resembling a monolith. **2.** Having a massive, uniform structure that does not permit individual variations: a *monolithic* state.

mon·o·logue (mon′ə-lôg, -log) *n.* **1.** A lengthy speech by one person, esp. one that interferes with conversation. **2.** A play or dramatic composition for one actor only. **3.** A soliloquy. **4.** A poem, etc., written as a soliloquy. Also **mon′o·log.** [< F < Gk. < *monos* alone + *-logos* speech] — **mo·nol·o·gist** (mə-nol′ə-jist) *n.*

mon·o·ma·ni·a (mon′ə-mā′nē-ə, -mān′yə) *n.* **1.** A mental disorder in which a person, otherwise rational, is obsessed with one idea or subject. **2.** An exaggerated fondness or irrational enthusiasm for something; craze. [< NL] — **mon′o·ma′ni·ac** *n.* — **mon′o·ma·ni′a·cal** (-mə-nī′ə-kəl) *adj.*

mon·o·mer (mon′ə-mər) *n. Chem.* The structural unit of a polymer. [< MONO- + Gk. *meros* part]

mon·o·met·al·ism (mon′ō-met′əl-iz′əm) *n.* The theory or system of a single metallic standard in coinage. Also **mon′o·met′al·ist** *n.* — **mon′o·me·tal′lic** (-mə-tal′ik) *adj.*

mo·no·mi·al (mō-nō′mē-əl) *adj.* Consisting of a single word or term. — *n.* A monomial term or expression.

mon·o·nu·cle·ar (mon′ə-nōō′klē-ər, -nyōō′-) *adj.* Having only one nucleus, as certain cells of the body.

mon·o·nu·cle·o·sis (mon′ō-nōō′klē-ō′sis, -nyōō′-) *n. Pathol.* **1.** The presence in the blood of an abnormal number of mononuclear leucocytes. **2.** Infectious mononucleosis.

mon·o·plane (mon′ə-plān) *n. Aeron.* An airplane with only one wing or pair of wings.

mo·nop·o·lize (mə-nop′ə-līz) *v.t.* **·lized, ·liz·ing** **1.** To obtain a monopoly of. **2.** To assume exclusive possession or control of. — **mo·nop′o·li·za′tion** *n.* — **mo·nop′o·liz′er** *n.*

mo·nop·o·ly (mə-nop′ə-lē) *n. pl.* **·lies** **1.** The exclusive control of a commodity, service, or means of production in a particular market, with the resulting power to fix prices. **2.** *Law* An exclusive privilege, granted by a government, of buying, selling, making, or using anything. **3.** A company having a monopoly. **4.** The commodity, service, etc., controlled under a monopoly. **5.** Exclusive possession or control of anything. [< L < Gk. < *monos* alone + *pōlein* to sell] — **mo·nop′o·lism** *n.* — **mo·nop′o·list** *n. & adj.* — **mo·nop′o·lis′tic** *adj.*

mon·o·pro·pel·lant (mon′ō-prə-pel′ənt) *n. Aerospace* A liquid rocket propellant consisting of fuel and oxidizer mixed and ready for simultaneous ignition.

mon·o·rail (mon′ō-rāl′) *n.* **1.** A single rail serving as a track for cars either suspended from it or balanced upon it. **2.** A railway using such a track.

mon·o·sac·cha·ride (mon′ə-sak′ə-rīd, -rid) *n. Biochem.* Any of a class of simple sugars that cannot be decomposed by hydrolysis, as glucose and fructose.

mon·o·syl·la·bic (mon′ə-si-lab′ik) *adj.* **1.** Having only one syllable. **2.** Using or speaking in monosyllables. **3.** Composed of monosyllables. — **mon′o·syl·lab′i·cal·ly** *adv.*

mon·o·syl·la·ble (mon′ə-sil′ə-bəl) *n.* A word of one syllable, as *no.*

mon·o·the·ism (mon′ə-thē-iz′əm) *n.* The doctrine or belief that there is but one God. [< MONO- + Gk. *theos* god] — **mon′o·the′ist** *n.* — **mon′o·the·is′tic** or **·ti·cal** *adj.* — **mon′o·the·is′ti·cal·ly** *adv.*

mon·o·tone (mon′ə-tōn) *n.* **1.** The utterance of a succession of words, etc., in a single tone. **2.** Sameness in expression, style, color, etc. **3.** A single musical tone unvaried in pitch. [< LGk. < Gk. *monos* single + *tonos* tone]

mo·not·o·nous (mə-not′ə-nəs) *adj.* **1.** Unvaried in tone. **2.** Tiresome by reason of monotony. [< Gk. *monotonos*] — **mo·not′o·nous·ly** *adv.* — **mo·not′o·nous·ness** *n.*

mo·not·o·ny (mə-not′ə-nē) *n.* **1.** Tiresome uniformity; irksome sameness. **2.** Lack of variety in cadence, pitch, or inflection. [< LGk. < Gk. *monos* single + *tonos* tone]

---

mon·o·treme (mon′ə·trēm) *n.* A member of the lowest order of mammals, including the egg-laying platypuses and the echidnas, that have a single opening for the excretory and reproductive functions. [< MONO- + Gk. *trēma* hole] — **mon′o·trem′a·tous** (-trem′ə·təs) *adj.*

mon·o·type (mon′ə·tīp) *n. Printing* A print from a metal plate on which a design, painting, etc., has been made.

Mon·o·type (mon′ə·tīp) *n. Printing* A machine that casts and sets type in single characters or units: a trade name.

mon·o·typ·ic (mon′ə·tip′ik) *adj. Biol.* 1. Having only one type: a *monotypic* genus. 2. Being a monotype.

mon·o·va·lent (mon′ə·vā′lənt) *adj. Chem.* Univalent. — **mon′o·va′lence, mon′o·va′len·cy** *n.* [< MONO- + L *valere* to be strong]

mon·ox·ide (mon·ok′sīd, mə·nok′-) *n. Chem.* An oxide containing a single atom of oxygen in each molecule.

Monroe Doctrine The doctrine, essentially formulated by President Monroe, that any attempt by European powers to interfere in the affairs of the American countries or to acquire territory on the American continents would be regarded by the U.S. as an unfriendly act.

mons (monz) *n. pl.* **mon·tes** (mon′tēz) *Anat.* The rounded fatty swelling over the pubic symphysis, covered with hair in the adult; the **mons pu·bis** (pyōō′bis) of the male, or the **mons ven·er·is** (ven′ər·is) of the female. [< L, hill]

Mon·sei·gneur (mon·sēn′yər; *Fr.* môn·se·nyœr′) *n. pl.* **Mes·sei·gneurs** (me·se·nyœr′) 1. My lord: a French title given to the higher nobility, bishops, etc. 2. One having this title. [< F *mon* my + *seigneur* lord < L *senior* older]

mon·sieur (mə·syûr′, *Fr.* mə·syœ′) *n. pl.* **mes·sieurs** (mes′ərz, *Fr.* me·syœ′) The French title of courtesy for men, equivalent to *Mr.* and *sir.* [< F *mon* + *sieur*, short for *seigneur* lord]

Mon·si·gnor (mon·sēn′yər, *Ital.* môn′sēn·nyōr′) *n. pl.* **·gnors** or *Ital.* **·gno·ri** (-nyō′rē) 1. In the Roman Catholic Church, a title of honor of certain prelates. 2. One having this title. [< Ital. < F *monseigneur*]

mon·soon (mon·sōōn′) *n. Meteorol.* 1. A seasonal wind that blows along the Asian coast of the Pacific and from the Indian Ocean, in winter from the northeast, in summer from the southwest. 2. The summer monsoon, characterized by heavy rains. [< MDu. < Pg. < Arabic *mausim* season]

mon·ster (mon′stər) *n.* 1. One who or that which is abnormal, unnatural, or hideous in form. 2. An animal or plant that is malformed; monstrosity. 3. One who or that which inspires hate or horror because of cruelty, wickedness, etc. 4. A huge person or thing. 5. A fabulous creature, as a centaur, dragon, etc. — *adj.* Enormous; huge. [< OF < L *monstrum* divine warning < *monere* to warn]

mon·strance (mon′strəns) *n.* In Roman Catholic ritual, a vessel in which the consecrated Host is exposed for adoration. [< OF < Med.L < L *monstrare* to show]

mon·stros·i·ty (mon·stros′ə·tē) *n. pl.* **·ties** 1. One who or that which is monstrous; also, a monster. 2. The condition or character of being monstrous. [< L *monstrositas*]

mon·strous (mon′strəs) *adj.* 1. Deviating greatly from the natural in form, structure, or character. 2. Enormous; huge. 3. Hideous; horrible; atrocious. 4. Strikingly wrong; ridiculous; absurd. 5. Having the appearance or nature of a fabulous monster. [< OF < LL < L *monstrum*] — **mon′strous·ly** *adv.* — **mon′strous·ness** *n.*

mon·tage (mon·täzh′) *n.* 1. A picture made by superimposing or arranging a number of different pictorial elements; also, the art or process of making such a picture. 2. In motion pictures or television, a rapid sequence of images used to illustrate a group of associated ideas. 3. Similar techniques in radio and writing. [< F < *monter* to mount]

mon·te (mon′tē) *n.* A Spanish or Spanish-American gambling game of cards. Also **monte bank.** [< Sp., lit., mountain < L; in ref. to the pile of unplayed cards]

month (munth) *n.* 1. One of the twelve parts (**calendar month**) into which the calendar year is divided. 2. A period of thirty days or four weeks. 3. The twelfth part (**solar month**) of the solar year. 4. The period (**lunar month**), equivalent to 29.53 days, during which the moon makes a complete revolution. ◆ Collateral adjective *mensal.* [OE *mōnath*]

month·ly (munth′lē) *adj.* 1. Happening, done, appearing, etc., every month. 2. Of or pertaining to a month. 3. Pertaining to the menses. 4. Continuing or lasting for a month. — *adv.* Once a month. — *n. pl.* **·lies** 1. A periodical published once a month. 2. *pl.* Menstruation.

mon·u·ment (mon′yə·mənt) *n.* 1. A statue, pillar, plaque, etc., erected to perpetuate the memory of a person, event, or historical period. 2. A tombstone. 3. Any conspicuous or fine structure surviving from the past. 4. A work of art, scholarship, etc., regarded as having enduring value. 5. A stone boundary marker. [< L *monere* to remind]

mon·u·men·tal (mon′yə·men′təl) *adj.* 1. Of, pertaining to, or serving as a monument. 2. Like a monument; enduring; imposing; massive. 3. Having great significance: a

monumental study. 4. *Informal* Very large; huge. [< L *monumentalis*] — **mon′u·men′tal·ly** *adv.*

-mony *suffix of nouns* The condition, state, or thing resulting from: *parsimony.* [< L *-monia*]

moo (mōō) *v.i.* To make the deep, moaning sound of a cow; to low. — *n. pl.* **moos** The sound made by a cow. [Imit.]

mooch (mōōch) *Slang v.t.* 1. To obtain without paying; beg; cadge. 2. To steal. — *v.i.* 3. To loiter. 4. To skulk; sneak. [< OF *muchier* to hide, skulk] — **mooch′er** *n.*

mood¹ (mōōd) *n.* 1. A specific state of mind or feeling, esp. a temporary one. 2. *pl.* Fits of sullen or morose behavior. — **in the mood** Disposed; inclined. [OE *mōd* mind]

mood² (mōōd) *n. Gram.* The set of distinctive forms of a verb showing the attitude and understanding of the speaker regarding the action or condition expressed: also *mode.* See IMPERATIVE, INDICATIVE, SUBJUNCTIVE. [Var. of MODE]

mood·y (mōō′dē) *adj.* **mood·i·er, mood·i·est** 1. Given to sudden moods of moroseness. 2. Expressive of such moods. [OE *mōd* courage] — **mood′i·ly** *adv.* — **mood′i·ness** *n.*

moon (mōōn) *n.* 1. A celestial body revolving around the earth from west to east in a lunar month of 29.53 days, and accompanying the earth in its yearly revolution about the sun. 2. This celestial body at a specific time of the month: new *moon*; full *moon.* 3. Any satellite revolving about a planet. 4. A month; esp., a lunar month. 5. Something resembling a full moon or crescent. 6. Moonlight. — *v.i.* 1. *Informal* To stare or wander about abstractedly. — *v.t.* 2. To pass (time) in such a way. [OE *mōna*]

moon·beam (mōōn′bēm′) *n.* A ray of moonlight.

moon·calf (mōōn′kaf′, -käf′) *n.* An imbecile; idiot.

moon·light (mōōn′līt′) *n.* The light of the moon. — *adj.* Pertaining to, illuminated by, or performed by moonlight: a *moonlight* excursion. — **moon′lit′** (-lit′) *adj.*

moon·light·ing (mōōn′līt′ing) *n. Slang* The act of one who holds a job in addition to the regular day's work. — **moon′light′er** *n.*

moon·shine (mōōn′shīn′) *n.* 1. Moonlight. 2. Nonsense. 3. *Informal* Smuggled or illicitly distilled whisky, etc.

moon·shin·er (mōōn′shī′nər) *n. U.S. Informal* One who conducts an illegal trade by night, esp. distilling.

moon·stone (mōōn′stōn′) *n.* A pearly, opalescent variety of orthoclase and albite, valued as a gemstone.

moon·struck (mōōn′struk′) *adj.* Lunatic; deranged. Also **moon′strick′en** (-strik′ən).

moon·y (mōō′nē) *adj.* **moon·i·er, moon·i·est** *Informal* Absent-minded; dreamy.

moor¹ (mōōr) *n. Brit.* A tract of wasteland sometimes covered with heath, often elevated, marshy, and abounding in peat; a heath. [OE *mōr*]

moor² (mōōr) *v.t.* 1. To secure (a ship, etc.) in place by means of cables attached to shore, anchors, etc. 2. To secure; fix. — *v.i.* 3. To secure a ship, etc., in position. 4. To be secured by chains or cables. [ME < MDu. *māren* to fasten] — **moor′age** (-ij) *n.*

Moor (mōōr) *n.* 1. A Moslem of mixed Berber and Arab ancestry, esp. one of the Saracen invaders of Spain in the 8th century. 2. A native of Morocco. [< OF < L < Gk. *Mauros*, lit., dark] — **Moor′ish** *adj.*

moor cock The male of the red grouse.

moor·fowl (mōōr′foul′) *n.* The red grouse.

moor hen *n.* The female of the red grouse.

moor·ing (mōōr′ing) *n.* 1. *Chiefly pl.* A mooring place. 2. *Chiefly pl.* That which secures an object, as a cable.

mooring mast The tower to which a dirigible or blimp may be secured when not in flight. Also **mooring tower.**

moose (mōōs) *n. pl.* **moose** 1. A large, heavily built mammal of the deer family, found in northern U.S. and Canada, the male of which bears huge palmate antlers. 2. The elk (def. 1). [< Algonquian *moosu* he strips off; because it eats the bark of trees]

moot (mōōt) *adj.* Open to discussion: debatable: a *moot* point. — *v.t.* 1. To bring up for discussion or debate. 2. To argue (a case) in a moot court. — *n.* 1. Discussion or argument. 2. In early English history, a meeting of freemen to discuss local affairs. [OE *mōt* assembly, court] — **moot′er** *n.*

MOOSE
(To 7 feet high at shoulder)

moot court A court for the trial of hypothetical legal cases by law students.

mop¹ (mop) *n.* 1. A device for cleaning floors, consisting of a bunch of heavy cotton yarn attached to a handle. 2. Any loosely tangled bunch, esp. of hair. — *v.t.* **mopped, mop·ping** To rub or wipe with or as with a mop. — **to mop up** *Informal* To finish. [ME *mappe*]

mop² (mop) *n.* A wry mouth. — *v.i.* To make a wry face.

mope (mōp) *v.* **moped, mop·ing** *v.i.* To be gloomy, listless, or dispirited. — *v.t.* 1. One who mopes. 2. *pl.* Dejection; depression. — **mop′er** *n.* — **mop′ish** *adj.* — **mop′ish·ly** *adv.* — **mop′ish·ness** *n.*

mop·pet (mop′it) *n. Informal* A child. [Dim. of MOP¹]

mo·raine (mə·rān′, mō-) *n. Geol.* Debris in various topographic forms that has been carried by a glacier, either along its course, at its edges, or at its lower terminus. [< F < dial. *morēna*] **—mo·rain′al, mo·rain′ic** *adj.*

mor·al (môr′əl, mor′-) *adj.* 1. Of or related to conduct or character from the point of view of right and wrong: *moral* goodness. 2. Of good character; right or proper in behavior. 3. Sexually virtuous. 4. Teaching standards of right and wrong. 5. Capable of distinguishing between right and wrong: Man is a *moral* agent. 6. Concerned with the establishment and application of principles of right and wrong: *moral* theology. 7. Arising from a sense of duty and right conduct: a *moral* obligation. 8. Acting not by physical force but by appeal to character, etc.: *moral* support. 9. Based on probability rather than on objective evidence: *moral* certainty. **—n.** 1. The lesson or teaching contained in or implied by a fable, poem, etc. 2. *pl.* Conduct or behavior with regard to right and wrong, esp. in sexual matters. 3. A maxim. [< OF < L *mos* custom; in the pl., *mores* manners, morals] **—mor′al·ly** *adv.*
—Syn. (adj.) 2. ethical, conscientious, scrupulous, upright, just, honest. **—Ant.** See synonyms for IMMORAL.

mo·rale (mə·ral′, -räl′, mō-) *n.* State of mind with reference to confidence, courage, hope, zeal, etc. [< F]

mor·al·ist (môr′əl·ist, mor′-) *n.* 1. A teacher of morals. 2. One who practices morality. **—mor′al·is′tic** *adj.*

mo·ral·i·ty (mə·ral′ə·tē, mô-) *n. pl.* **·ties** 1. The quality of being morally right; virtue. 2. Conformity to standards of right conduct. 3. Virtuous conduct, often sexual virtue. 4. A system of the principles of right and wrong conduct; ethics. 5. A lesson in morals. 6. A morality play.

morality play A form of allegorical drama of the 15th and 16th centuries in which the characters were personified virtues, vices, mental attributes, etc.

mor·al·ize (môr′əl·īz, mor′-) *v.* **·ized, ·iz·ing** *v.i.* 1. To make moral reflections; talk about morality. **—v.t.** 2. To explain in a moral sense; derive a moral from. 3. To improve the morals of. [< MF *moralizer*] **—mor′al·i·za′tion** *n.* **—mor′al·iz′er** *n.*

mo·rass (mə·ras′, mô-, mō-) *n.* 1. A tract of low-lying, soft, wet ground; marsh; bog. 2. Anything that impedes, perplexes, or traps. [< Du. < OF *maresc* < Gmc.]

mor·a·to·ri·um (môr′ə·tôr′ē·əm, -tō′rē, mor′-) *n. pl.* **·ri·a** (-rē·ə) or **·ri·ums** 1. A legal authorization to a debtor to suspend payments for a given period. 2. The period during which such suspension is in effect. 3. Any authorized suspension or deferment of action. [< NL < LL < L *morari* to delay]

mor·a·to·ry (môr′ə·tôr′ē, -tō′rē, mor′-) *adj.* Pertaining to or intended to delay; especially, designating legislation authorizing a moratorium. [< LL < L *morari* to delay]

Mo·ra·vi·an (mô·rā′vē·ən, mō-) *adj.* Pertaining to Moravia, the Moravians, or the Moravian Church. **—n.** 1. A native of Moravia. 2. A member of the Moravian Church.

mo·ray (môr′ā, mō·rā′) *n.* A brightly colored, voracious eel inhabiting tropical and subtropical waters. Also **mo′ray eel**. [Origin uncertain]

mor·bid (môr′bid) *adj.* 1. Taking or showing an excessive interest in matters of a gruesome or unwholesome nature. 2. Grisly; gruesome: a *morbid* fantasy. 3. Pertaining to, arising from, or affected by disease. [< L < *morbus* disease] **—mor′bid·ly** *adv.* **—mor·bid′i·ty, mor′bid·ness** *n.*

mor·dant (môr′dənt) *adj.* 1. Biting; cutting; sarcastic: a *mordant* wit. 2. Acting to fix colors in dyeing. **—n.** 1. A substance that, by combining with a dyestuff, serves to produce a fixed color in a textile, leather, etc. 2. In etching, a corrosive used to bite into the lines traced on a metal plate. **—v.t.** To treat or imbue with a mordant. [< F, ppr. of OF *modre* to bite] **—mor′dan·cy** *n.*

Mor·de·cai (môr′də·kī, -kā·ī) In the Old Testament, Esther's cousin, instrumental in saving the Jews. *Esth.* ii 5.

mor·dent (môr′dənt) *n. Music* A trill-like melodic ornamentation; also, the symbol that indicates this. [< G < Ital. < *mordere* to bite]

more (môr, mōr) *adj. superlative* **most** 1. Greater in amount, extent, degree, or number: comparative of *much* and *many*. 2. Additional: *More* coffee, please. **—n.** 1. A greater or additional quantity, amount, etc. 2. That which exceeds or excels something else. **—adv.** 1. In or to a greater extent or degree: used to form the comparative of many adjectives and adverbs of two or more syllables: *more* beautiful. 2. In addition; further. **—more or less** 1. In some undetermined degree. 2. Approximately. [OE *māra*]

more·o·ver (môr·ō′vər, mōr′-) *adv.* Beyond what has been said; further; besides; likewise; in addition.

mo·res (môr′āz, mō′rāz, môr′ēz, mō′rēz) *n.pl. Sociol.* 1. The established, traditional customs regarded by a social group as essential to its preservation. 2. The accepted conventions of a group. [< L, pl. of *mos, moris* custom]

mor·ga·nat·ic (môr′gə·nat′ik) *adj.* Of or designating a form of legitimate marriage between a member of certain royal families of Europe and a person of inferior rank, in which the titles and estates are not shared by the inferior partner or their children. [< NL < LL < OHG *morgangeba* morning gift] **—mor′ga·nat′i·cal·ly** *adv.*

morgue (môrg) *n.* 1. A place where the bodies of unknown dead persons and of those killed in accidents are kept for identification. 2. In a newspaper editorial office, the department in charge of filed items and biographical material used for obituary notices, etc. [< F]

mor·i·bund (môr′ə·bund, -bənd, mor′-) *adj.* 1. At the point of death; dying. 2. Approaching extinction. [< L < *mori* to die] **—mor′i·bun′di·ty** *n.* **—mor′i·bund·ly** *adv.*

mo·ri·on (môr′ē·on, mō′rē-) *n.* An open, crested, visorless helmet, worn in the 16th and 17th centuries. [< MF < Sp. < *morra* crown of the head]

Mo·ris·co (mə·ris′kō) *adj.* Moorish. **—n.** *pl.* **·cos** or **·coes** A Moor, especially one of Spain. [< Sp. < *moro* Moor]

Mor·mon (môr′mən) *n.* 1. A member of the Mormon Church; a Latter-day Saint. 2. In Mormon belief, a prophet of the fourth century who wrote, on golden tablets, a history of the early American people. **—adj.** Of or pertaining to the Mormons or their religion. **—Mor′mon·ism** *n.*

Mormon Church The Church of Jesus Christ of Latter-day Saints, founded by Joseph Smith in 1830.

Mormon State Nickname of Utah.

morn (môrn) *n. Poetic* The morning. [OE *morne*]

morn·ing (môr′ning) *n.* 1. The early part of the day; the time from midnight to noon, or from sunrise to noon. 2. The early part or stage of anything. **—adj.** Pertaining to or occurring in the morning. ◆ Collateral adjective: *matutinal.* [ME *morwen* + *-ing* by analogy with evening]

morn·ing-glo·ry (môr′ning·glôr′ē, -glō′rē) *n.* Any of various twining plants with colored, funnel-shaped flowers.

morning star A planet, esp. Venus, when rising in the east shortly before the sun.

Mo·ro (môr′ō, mō′rō) *n. pl.* **·ros** 1. A member of any of the various Moslem Malay tribes of the southern Philippines. 2. The language of the Moros. **—adj.** Of or pertaining to the Moros or their language. [< Sp., Moor]

mo·roc·co (mə·rok′ō) *n.* 1. A fine flexible leather, made originally in Morocco from goatskin tanned with sumac. 2. Any soft, grained leather. Also **morocco leather**.

Mo·roc·can (mə·rok′ən) A native or inhabitant of Morocco. **—adj.** Of or pertaining to Morocco.

mo·ron (môr′on, mō′ron) *n.* 1. A person exhibiting the mildest degree of mental deficiency, permitting adequacy in simple activities. 2. Loosely, a very stupid person. **—Syn.** See IDIOT. [< Gk. < *mōros* stupid] **—mo·ron·ic** (mô·ron′ik, mō-) *adj.* **—mo·ron′i·cal·ly** *adv.*

mo·rose (mə·rōs′) *adj.* Ill-humored; sullen; gloomy, as a person, mood, etc. [< L < *mos, moris* manner, mood] **—mo·rose′ly** *adv.* **—mo·rose·ness** *n.*
—Syn. glum, dour, crabbed. **—Ant.** cheerful, genial.

-morph *combining form* Having the form or shape of: *allomorph.* [< Gk. *morphē* form]

mor·pheme (môr′fēm) *n. Ling.* The smallest meaningful unit of a language or dialect, whether a word, base, or affix. See ALLOMORPH. [< F < Gk. *morphē* form]

Mor·phe·us (môr′fē·əs, -fyōōs) In Greek mythology, the god of dreams. [< L < Gk. *morphē* form; from the shapes he calls up in dreams] **—Mor′phe·an** *adj.*

-morphic *combining form* Having the form or shape of: *anthropomorphic.* [< Gk.*morphē* form]

mor·phine (môr′fēn) *n. Chem.* A bitter, white crystalline compound, $C_{17}H_{19}NO_3$, the principal alkaloid of opium, used as an analgesic and narcotic. Also **mor′phin** (-fin). [< F < L *Morpheus* god of dreams]

morpho- *combining form* Form; shape. Also, before vowels, **morph-.** [< Gk. *morphē* form]

mor·phol·o·gy (môr·fol′ə·jē) *n. pl.* **·gies** 1. *Biol.* The study of the form and structure of plants and animals considered apart from function. 2. *Ling.* a The arrangement and interrelationship of morphemes in words. b The branch of linguistics dealing with this. **—mor·pho·log·ic** (môr′fə·loj′ik) or **·i·cal** *adj.* **—mor·phol′o·gist** *n.*

-morphous *combining form* Having a (specified) form: often equivalent to *-morphic*: *anamorphous.*

mor·ris (môr′is, mor′-) *n.* An old English dance, performed especially on May Day. [Earlier *morys, morish* Moorish]

Morris chair A large armchair with an adjustable back. [after William *Morris*, who invented it]

mor·ro (môr′ō, mor′ō; Sp. môr′rō) *n. pl.* **·ros** (-rōs) *mor′-; Sp. môr′rōs*) A round hill or promontory. [< Sp. *morra*]

mor·row (môr′ō, mor′ō) *n. Archaic & Poetic* 1. The next succeeding day. **2.** A time immediately following a specified event. **3.** Formerly, morning. [See MORNING]

Morse code A system of telegraphic signals invented by S.F.B. Morse, composed of dots and dashes or short and long flashes representing the letters of the alphabet, numerals, etc., and used in transmitting messages.

mor·sel (môr′səl) *n.* **1.** A small fragment or bite of food. **2.** A tempting dish; tidbit. **3.** A small piece or bit of something. — *v.t.* **mor·seled** or **·selled, mor·sel·ing** or **·sel·ling** To divide into small pieces. [< OF, dim. of *mors* bite]

mor·tal (môr′təl) *adj.* **1.** Subject to death. **2.** Of or pertaining to humanity as subject to death. **3.** Of or relating to this life or world. **4.** Causing or liable to cause death. **5.** Relating to or accompanying death. **6.** Grievous; dire: *mortal* terror. **7.** Likely to remain so until death; implacable: a *mortal* enemy. **8.** *Theol.* Incurring spiritual death unless repented of and forgiven: distinguished from *venial*: *mortal* sin. **9.** *Informal* Possible; conceivable: There's no *mortal* reason for his action. — *n.* One who is mortal; a human being. — *adv.* *Informal* Very; exceedingly. [< OF < L *mors, mortis* death]

mor·tal·i·ty (môr·tal′ə·tē) *n. pl.* **·ties 1.** The condition of being mortal or subject to death. **2.** Loss of life on a large scale, as caused by war, disease, etc. **3.** The frequency of death; death rate. **4.** Humanity; mankind.

mor·tal·ly (môr′təl·ē) *adv.* **1.** Fatally. **2.** After the manner of a mortal. **3.** Extremely: *mortally* offended.

mor·tar¹ (môr′tər) *n.* A bowl-shaped vessel in which substances are crushed with a pestle. For illustration see PESTLE. [OE < L *mortarium* mixing trough]

mor·tar² (môr′tər) *n.* A building material consisting of a mixture of lime, cement, etc., with sand and water, used in bricklaying, plastering walls, etc. [< OF < L *mortarium* trough, mixture of sand and lime]

mor·tar³ (môr′tər) *n. Mil.* A smooth-bored or rifled muzzleloading weapon, firing a relatively heavy shell, having a shorter range and higher trajectory than a howitzer. [< F *mortier*]

mor·tar·board (môr′tər·bôrd′, -bōrd′) *n.* **1.** A square board with a handle, on which a mason holds mortar. **2.** A type of academic cap topped by a stiff, flat, four-cornered piece, worn at graduations.

mort·gage (môr′gij) *n. Law* **1.** A transfer of property pledged as security for the repayment of a loan. **2.** The contract specifying such a pledge. — *v.t.* **·gaged, ·gag·ing 1.** To make over or pledge (property) by mortgage. **2.** To pledge; stake. [< OF, dead pledge]

mort·ga·gee (môr′gi·jē′) *n.* The holder of a mortgage.

mort·ga·gor (môr′gi·jər) *n.* One who mortgages his property to another as security for a loan. Also **mort′gag·er.**

mor·tice (môr′tis) *n.* A mortise. — *v.t.* **·ticed, ·tic·ing** To mortise.

mor·ti·cian (môr·tish′ən) *n. U.S.* A funeral director; undertaker. [< L *mors, mortis* death + -ICIAN]

mor·ti·fi·ca·tion (môr′tə·fə·kā′shən) *n.* **1.** A feeling of loss of self-esteem; humiliation; shame. **2.** That which causes such humiliation. **3.** The ascetic practice of subduing the appetites and strengthening the will by fasting, etc. **4.** *Pathol.* The death of a part by gangrene or necrosis.

mor·ti·fy (môr′tə·fī) *v.* **·fied, ·fy·ing** *v.t.* **1.** To humiliate. **2.** To discipline or punish (the body, appetites, etc.) by fasting or other ascetic practices. **3.** *Pathol.* To cause mortification in (part of an animal body). — *v.i.* **4.** To practice ascetic self-discipline. **5.** *Pathol.* To undergo mortification. [< OF < LL < L *mors, mortis* death + *facere* to make] — **mor′ti·fi′er** *n.* — **mor′ti·fy′ing·ly** *adv.*

mor·tise (môr′tis) *n.* A space hollowed out in a piece of timber, stone, etc., and shaped to fit a tenon to which it is to be joined. — *v.t.* **·tised, ·tis·ing 1.** To cut or make a mortise in. **2.** To join by a tenon and mortise. Also spelled *mortice.* [< F < Arabic *murtazz* joined, fixed in]

mort·main (môrt′mān) *n. Law* The holding of lands and buildings in perpetual ownership. [< OF < Med.L *mortua manus* dead hand]

mor·tu·ar·y (môr′chōō·er′ē) *n. pl.* **·ar·ies** A place for the temporary reception of the dead before burial. — *adj.* **1.** Of the burial of the dead. **2.** Relating to death. [< MF < L *mortuarius* of the dead]

MORTISE
(a) AND
TENON (b)

mo·sa·ic (mō·zā′ik) *n.* **1.** Inlaid work composed of bits of stone, glass, etc., forming a pattern or picture; also, the process of making this. **2.** A design, arrangement, etc., resembling such work. — *adj.* Of, pertaining to, or resembling mosaic. — *v.t.* **·icked, ·ick·ing 1.** To make by or as if by combining in a mosaic. **2.** To decorate with mosaic. [< OF < Med.L < Gk. *mouseios* of the Muses, artistic] — **mo·sa·i·cist** (mō·zā′ə·sist) *n.*

Mo·sa·ic (mō·zā′ik) *adj.* Of or pertaining to Moses or the laws attributed to him. Also **Mo·sa′i·cal.**

Mosaic Law The code of civil and religious laws contained in the Pentateuch and traditionally attributed to Moses: also called *Law of Moses, the Law.*

Mo·selle (mō·zel′) *n.* A light, dry wine made in the valley of the Moselle, chiefly in Luxembourg.

Mo·ses (mō′zis, -ziz) In the Old Testament, the leader who led the Israelites out of Egypt to the Promised Land and received the Ten Commandments from God. [< Hebrew *Mōsheh,* ? < Egyptian *mesu* son]

mo·sey (mō′zē) *v.i. U.S. Slang* **1.** To saunter, or stroll; shuffle along. **2.** To go away; move off. [Origin unknown]

Mos·lem (moz′ləm) *n.* A believer in Islam; Mohammedan. — *adj.* Of or pertaining to Islam or the Muslims. Also *Muslim, Muslem.* [< Arabic *muslim* one who submits]

Mos·lem·ism (moz′ləm·iz′əm) *n.* Islam.

mosque (mosk) *n.* A Moslem temple of worship. [< F < Ital. < Arabic *masjid* < *sajada* to worship, pray]

mos·qui·to (məs·kē′tō) *n. pl.* **·toes** or **·tos** Any of various winged insects, having in the female a long proboscis capable of puncturing the skin of man and animals for extracting blood, certain species of which transmit malaria, yellow fever, etc. [< Sp., dim. of *mosca* fly] — **mos·qui′tal** *adj.*

mosquito boat A patrol torpedo boat.

mosquito net A fine net or gauze (**mosquito netting**) placed over windows, beds, etc., to keep out mosquitoes.

moss (môs, mos) *n.* **1.** A delicate plant having a stem and distinct leaves, and growing in tufts or clusters on the ground, decaying wood, rocks, etc. **2.** A clump or tuft of such plants. **3.** Any of several similar plants, as certain lichens. **4.** *Chiefly Scot.* A peat bog. [OE *mos* marsh] — **moss′y** *adj.* — **moss′i·ness** *n.*

moss agate A variety of agate containing mineral oxides and showing patterns arranged in mosslike forms.

moss·back (môs′bak′, mos′-) *n.* **1.** An old fish or turtle on whose back is a growth of algae or the like. **2.** *U.S. Slang* A very conservative or old-fashioned person; fogy.

Möss·bau·er effect (mœs′bou′ər) The absorption of gamma rays emitted from a radioactive isotope by nuclei of the same isotope, both of which are anchored in crystals; used in the determination of wavelengths, and in testing various concepts of relativity and quantum theory. [after Rudolf L. *Mössbauer,* born 1929, U.S. physicist born in Germany.]

moss rose A cultivated variety of the rose with a mossy calyx and stem.

most (mōst) *adj.* **1.** Consisting of the greatest number: superlative of *many.* **2.** Consisting of the greatest amount or degree: superlative of *much.* **3.** In the greatest number of instances: *Most* people are honest. — **for the most part** Generally; mostly. — *n.* **1.** (*construed as pl.*) The greatest number; the largest part. **2.** (*construed as pl.*) The greatest number of persons: too difficult for *most.* **3.** The greatest amount, quantity or degree; utmost. — **at (the) most** Not more than; at the extreme point or limit. — **to make the most of 1.** To use to the fullest advantage. **2.** To exaggerate the importance of. — *adv.* **1.** In or to the greatest or highest degree, quantity, extent, etc.: used with adjectives and adverbs to form the superlative degree. **2.** Very. **3.** *Informal* Almost; nearly. [OE *mǣst, mǟst*]

-most *suffix* Most: added to adjectives and adverbs to form superlatives: *innermost; outmost.*

most·ly (mōst′lē) *adv.* For the most part; principally.

mot (mō) *n.* A witty or pithy saying: bon *mot.* [< F, word]

mote (mōt) *n.* A minute particle or speck, esp., of dust. [OE *mot* dust]

mo·tel (mō·tel′) *n. U.S.* A roadside hotel for motorists, often comprising private cabins that open on parking facilities: also called *motor court.*

mo·tet (mō·tet′) *n. Music* A polyphonic vocal composition of a sacred nature, usu. unaccompanied. [< OF]

moth (môth, moth) *n. pl.* **moths** (môthz, môths, mothz, moths) Any of a large group of insects, usu. nocturnal, distinguished from the butterflies by having smaller wings, stouter bodies, and duller coloring. [OE *moththe*]

moth-ball (môth′bôl′, moth′-) *Mil. & Nav. adj.* Designating ships or military equipment laid up in reserve and covered with protective materials. — *v.t.* To put in storage.

moth ball A small ball of camphor or naphthalene used to repel moths from clothing, etc., during storage.

moth-eat·en (môth′ēt′n, moth′-) *adj.* **1.** Eaten or damaged by moths. **2.** Worn out. **3.** Old-fashioned.

moth·er¹ (muth′ər) *n.* **1.** A female who has borne offspring. **2.** A female who adopts a child, or who otherwise holds a maternal relationship toward another. **3.** The characteristics regarded as belonging to a mother. **4.** Anything that creates, nurtures, or protects something else. **5.** *Usu. cap.* A title given to certain nuns. — *adj.* **1.** Native: *mother* tongue. **2.** Relating to or characteristic of a mother: *mother* love. **3.** Holding a maternal relation: the *mother* church. — *v.t.* **1.** To bring forth as a mother; produce; create. **2.** To care for or protect as a mother. **3.** To admit or claim parentage, authorship, etc., of. [OE *mōder*]

moth·er[2] (muth'ər) *n.* A slimy film composed of bacteria and yeast cells, active in the production of vinegar.

Mother Goose **1.** The imaginary narrator of a volume of folk tales, compiled in French by Charles Perrault in 1697. **2.** The imaginary writer of a collection of nursery rhymes of English folk origin, first published in London about 1790.

moth·er·hood (muth'ər·hŏŏd) *n.* **1.** The state of being a mother. **2.** The spirit or qualities of a mother. **3.** Mothers collectively.

Mother Hub·bard (hub'ard) A woman's loose, flowing gown, unconfined at the waist: also **mother hubbard**.

moth·er-in-law (muth'ər·in·lô') *n.* *pl.* **moth·ers-in-law** The mother of one's spouse.

moth·er·land (muth'ər·land') *n.* **1.** The land of one's birth; native land. **2.** The land of one's ancestors.

mother lode In mining, any principal or very rich vein.

moth·er·ly (muth'ər·lē) *adj.* Resembling, characteristic of, or like a mother. — *adv.* In the manner of a mother. — **moth·er·li·ness** *n.*

moth·er-of-pearl (muth'ər·əv·pûrl') *n.* The pearly, iridescent internal layer of certain shells, as those of the pearl oyster and abalone, used in ornamental work, for buttons, etc.: also called **nacre.** — *adj.* Of mother-of-pearl.

Moth·er's Day (muth'ərz) *U.S.* A memorial day in honor of mothers, observed annually on the second Sunday in May.

mother's helper *U.S.* A girl or woman hired to help a mother care for her children and do light housekeeping chores.

mother tongue **1.** One's native language. **2.** A parent language.

mother wit Inherent or native intelligence; common sense.

moth·y (môth'ē, moth'ē) *adj.* **moth·i·er, moth·i·est** **1.** Moth-eaten. **2.** Full of moths.

mo·tif (mō·tēf') *n.* **1.** The underlying theme or main element in a literary or artistic work. **2.** In decoration, a distinct element of design. **3.** *Music* The shortest intelligible melodic or rhythmic fragment of a theme. Also **motive.** [< F]

mo·tile (mō'til, -təl) *adj.* *Zool.* Having the power of motion, as certain minute organisms. [< L *motus*, pp. of *movere* to move] — **mo·til·i·ty** *n.*

mo·tion (mō'shən) *n.* **1.** The act or process of changing position; movement: also, an instance of this. **2.** Change of place or position in the body or any of its parts. **3.** A formal proposal or suggestion in an assembly or meeting: to second the *motion.* **4.** An impulse; inclination. — **in motion** Moving; in operation. — *v.i.* **1.** To make a gesture of direction or intent, as with the hand. — *v.t.* **2.** To direct or guide by a gesture. [< OF < L *movere* to move]

motion picture **1.** A sequence of pictures of moving objects photographed on a strip of film, that, when projected on a screen, gives the optical illusion of continuous movement. **2.** A specific drama, story, etc., made by means of such photographs: also called *cinema, film, movie, moving picture, photoplay, picture, screen play.*

motion sickness Nausea, dizziness, etc., caused by the effects of motion, as in travel on land, water, and in the air.

mo·ti·vate (mō'tə·vāt') *v.t.* **·vat·ed, ·vat·ing** To provide with a motive. [< F *motiver*] — **mo·ti·va·tion** *n.* — **mo'·ti·va·tion·al** *adj.*

mo·tive (mō'tiv) *n.* **1.** A conscious or unconscious need, drive, etc., that incites a person to some action or behavior; incentive; goal. **2.** A motif. — **Syn.** See REASON. — *adj.* **1.** Causing or having the power to cause motion. **2.** Relating to or acting as a motive. — *v.t.* To motivate. [< OF < Med.L *movere* to move]

mot·ley (mot'lē) *adj.* **1.** Made up of diverse elements; heterogeneous. **2.** Variegated in color. **3.** Clothed in vari-colored garments. — *n.* **1.** A heterogeneous mixture or collection. **2.** A woolen cloth of mixed colors worn between the 14th and 17th centuries. **3.** A garment of various colors such as formerly worn by court jesters. [ME *motteley*]

mo·tor (mō'tər) *n.* **1.** An engine; esp., an internal-combustion engine propelling an automobile, motor boat, etc. **2.** Something that imparts or produces motion. **3.** *Chiefly Brit.* An automotive vehicle. — *adj.* **1.** Causing, producing, or imparting motion. **2.** Equipped with or driven by a motor. **3.** Of, pertaining to, or for automotive vehicles. **4.** *Psychol.* Transmitting impulses from nerve centers to the muscles. **5.** *Psychol.* Relating to or involving the movements of muscles. — *v.i.* To travel or ride in an automobile. [< L < *motus*, pp. of *movere* to move]

mo·tor·bike (mō'tər·bīk') *n.* *Informal* **1.** A bicycle driven by a small motor. **2.** A motorcycle.

mo·tor·boat (mō'tər·bōt') *n.* A boat propelled by a motor: also called *power boat.*

mo·tor·bus (mō'tər·bus') *n.* A passenger bus powered by a motor. Also **motor bus, motor coach.**

mo·tor·cade (mō'tər·kād) *n.* A procession of automobiles.

mo·tor·car (mō'tər·kär') *n.* An automobile.

motor court A motel.

mo·tor·cy·cle (mō'tər·sī'kəl) *n.* A two-wheeled vehicle, larger and heavier than a bicycle, propelled by an internal-combustion engine. — *v.i.* **·cled, ·cling** To travel or ride on a motorcycle. — **mo'tor·cy'clist** *n.*

mo·tor·ist (mō'tər·ist) *n.* One who drives or travels by automobile.

mo·tor·ize (mō'tər·īz) *v.t.* **·ized, ·iz·ing** **1.** To equip with a motor. **2.** To equip with motor-propelled vehicles in place of horses or horse-drawn vehicles. — **mo'tor·i·za'tion** *n.*

mo·tor·man (mō'tər·mən) *n.* *pl.* **·men** (-mən) **1.** One who operates an electric street car or electric railway locomotive. **2.** One who operates a motor.

motor scooter A two-wheeled vehicle similar to a child's scooter, having a driver's seat and powered by an internal-combustion engine.

mot·tle (mot'l) *v.t.* **·tled, ·tling** To mark with spots or streaks of different colors or shades; blotch. — *n.* **1.** A spotted, blotched, or variegated appearance, as of skin or marble. **2.** A spot, blotch, etc. [back formation < MOTLEY]

mot·tled (mot'ld) *adj.* Marked with spots of different color or shade; blotched; spotted.

mot·to (mot'ō) *n.* *pl.* **·toes** or **·tos** **1.** A word or phrase expressing a rule of conduct, principle, etc.; a maxim. **2.** An appropriate or indicative phrase inscribed on something, prefixed to a literary work, etc. [< Ital. < F *mot* word]

mouch (mooch) See MOOCH.

mou·choir (moo·shwâr') *n.* *French* A pocket handkerchief.

moue (moo) *n.* A pouting grimace, as of disdain. [< F]

mou·jik (moo·zhēk') See MUZHIK.

mould (mōld), etc. See MOLD, etc.

moult (mōlt) See MOLT, etc.

mound (mound) *n.* **1.** A heap or pile of earth, debris, etc., either natural or artificial. **2.** A small natural elevation; a hillock. **3.** In baseball, the slightly raised ground from which the pitcher pitches. — *v.t.* **1.** To fortify or enclose with a mound. **2.** To heap up in a mound. [Origin unknown]

Mound Builder One of the prehistoric Indians who built the burial mounds and fortifications found in the Mississippi basin and adjoining regions.

mount[1] (mount) *v.t.* **1.** To ascend or climb (a slope, stairs, etc.). **2.** To get up on; climb upon. **3.** To put or set on horseback. **4.** To furnish with a horse. **5.** To set or place in an elevated position: to *mount* a picture on a wall. **6.** To set, fix, or secure in or on a support, frame, etc., as for exhibition or use: to *mount* a drawing; to *mount* a specimen on a microscope slide. **7.** To furnish with scenery, costumes, etc.: to *mount* a play. **8.** *Mil.* **a** To set or raise into position, as a gun. **b** To carry or be equipped with. **c** To stand or post (guard). **d** To prepare and begin: to *mount* an offensive. — *v.i.* **9.** To rise or ascend; go or come up. **10.** To increase in amount, number, or degree. **11.** To get up on something, as on a horse. — *n.* **1.** Anything on or in which an object is placed for use, preparation, display, etc., as part of a proper name. **2.** A horse or other animal used for riding. **3.** The act or style of mounting. **4.** The act of riding a horse. [< OF *monter* < L *mons, montis* mountain] — **mount'a·ble** *adj.* — **mount'er** *n.*

mount[2] (mount) *n.* A mountain or hill: used poetically or as part of a proper name. [OE < L *mons, montis* mountain]

moun·tain (moun'tən) *n.* **1.** A natural elevation of the earth's surface, typically having steep sides and a narrow summit, and rising higher than a hill. **2.** Any large heap or pile: a *mountain* of paper. **3.** Anything of great size: a *mountain* of a man. — *adj.* **1.** Of, pertaining to, or like a mountain. **2.** Living, growing, or situated in or on mountains. [< OF < L < *mons, montis* mountain]

mountain ash **1.** A small tree of the rose family, having white flowers and orange-red berries. **2.** Any of various related trees.

mountain cat **1.** The puma. **2.** The lynx.

moun·tain·eer (moun'tən·ir') *n.* **1.** An inhabitant of a mountainous district. **2.** One who climbs mountains. — *v.i.* To climb mountains.

mountain goat The Rocky Mountain goat.

mountain laurel A low-growing evergreen shrub of the eastern U.S., having white or pink flowers: the State flower of Connecticut and Pennsylvania.

mountain lion The puma.

moun·tain·ous (moun'tən·əs) *adj.* **1.** Full of mountains. **2.** Huge; gigantic. — **moun'tain·ous·ly** *adv.*

moun·te·bank (moun'tə·bangk') *n.* **1.** One who sells quack medicines at fairs after drawing a crowd with jokes, tricks, etc. **2.** Any charlatan. [< Ital. < *montare* to mount + *in* upon + *banco* bench]

mount·ed (moun'tid) *adj.* **1.** Riding or seated on a horse.

2. Serving on or equipped with horses for transportation: *mounted* police. **3.** Set into position or fitted for use.

Moun·ty (moun'tē) *n. pl.* **·ties** *Informal* A member of the Royal Canadian Mounted Police. Also **Mount'ie.**

mourn (môrn, mōrn) *v.i.* **1.** To feel or express grief or sorrow, esp. for the dead; grieve. — *v.t.* **2.** To lament or sorrow for (someone dead). **3.** To grieve over or bemoan (misfortune, failure, etc.). [OE *murnan*] — **mourn'er** *n.*

mourners' bench *U.S.* At revival meetings, a bench near the preacher, reserved for penitents.

mourn·ful (môrn'fəl, mōrn'-) *adj.* **1.** Indicating, expressing, or exciting grief. **2.** Doleful; melancholy; sad. — **mourn'ful·ly** *adv.* — **mourn'ful·ness** *n.*

mourn·ing (môr'ning, mōr'-) *n.* **1.** The act of one who expresses grief or sorrow, esp. for the dead. **2.** The manifestations of grief, as the wearing of black dress, etc. **3.** The period during which one mourns. — *adj.* Of or expressive of mourning. — **mourn'ing·ly** *adv.*

mourning dove A dove common in North America, having a mournful cry: also called *turtledove.*

mouse (n. mous; v. mouz) *n. pl.* **mice** (mīs) **1.** One of various small rodents frequenting human habitations throughout the world. ◆ Collateral adjective: *murine.* **2.** Any of various similar animals. **3.** *U.S. Informal* A timid person. **4.** *Slang* A black eye. — *v.i.* **moused, mous·ing 1.** To hunt or catch mice. **2.** To hunt for something cautiously and softly; prowl. [OE *mūs*]

mous·er (mou'zər) *n.* Any animal that catches mice.

mouse·trap (mous'trap') *n.* A trap for catching mice.

mousse (mōōs) *n.* Any of various light, frozen desserts made with whipped cream, egg white, etc., and sugar and flavoring. [< F < L *mulsus* sweetened with honey]

mous·tache (məs·tash', mus'tash) See MUSTACHE.

Mous·te·ri·an (mōō·stir'ē·ən) *adj. Anthropol.* Pertaining to or describing a culture stage of the Paleolithic, represented in western Europe by artifacts of stone and generally found associated with Neanderthal men. [< F < *Le Moustier,* a village in France where such remains were found]

mous·y (mou'sē, -zē) *adj.* **mous·i·er, mous·i·est 1.** Of or resembling a mouse. **2.** Characterized by timidity, shyness, drabness, etc. **3.** Infested with mice. Also **mous'ey.**

mouth (n. mouth; v. mouth) *n. pl.* **mouths** (mouthz) **1.** The opening at which food is taken into the body; also, the cavity between the lips and throat containing the lingual and masticating structures. ◆ Collateral adjective: *oral.* **2.** One who needs food: so many *mouths* to feed. **3.** The organ or instrument of speech: to shut one's *mouth.* **4.** Something resembling a mouth; as: **a** The part of a stream where its waters are discharged into another body of water. **b** The entrance or opening of a cave, mine, etc. **c** The opening of a container: the *mouth* of a jar. — **down in** (or **at**) **the mouth** *Informal* Disconsolate; dejected. — **to have a big mouth** *Informal* **1.** To speak loudly or rudely. **2.** To talk too much. — *v.t.* **1.** To speak in a forced or affected manner. **2.** To seize or take in the mouth. **3.** To caress or rub with the mouth. **4.** To form (words, etc.) silently with the lips and tongue. — *v.i.* **5.** To speak in an affected manner. [OE *mūth*] — **mouth'er** (mou'thər) *n.*

mouthed (mouthd, moutht) *adj.* **1.** Having a mouth or mouths. **2.** Having a (specified kind of) mouth or (a specified number of) mouths: used in combination: *evil-mouthed.*

mouth·ful (mouth'fōōl') *n. pl.* **·fuls** (-fōōlz') **1.** As much as can be held in the mouth. **2.** As much as is usu. taken or put in the mouth at one time. **3.** A small quantity. **4.** *Slang* An important or perceptive remark: chiefly in the phrase **to say a mouthful.**

mouth organ 1. A harmonica. **2.** A set of panpipes.

mouth·piece (mouth'pēs') *n.* **1.** That part of a musical instrument, telephone, etc., that is used in or near the mouth. **2.** One who acts as spokesman for an individual, group, belief, etc. **3.** *Slang* A criminal lawyer. **4.** A rubber guard placed in the mouth of a boxer.

mouth·wash (mouth'wosh', -wôsh') *n.* An antiseptic and scented solution used for cleaning the mouth.

mouth·y (mou'thē, -thē) *adj.* **mouth·i·er, mouth·i·est** Garrulous; bombastic. — **mouth'i·ly** *adv.* — **mouth'i·ness** *n.*

mou·ton (mōō'ton) *n.* Sheepskin processed to simulate beaver or seal, used for women's coats, etc. [< F, sheep]

mov·a·ble (mōō'və·bəl) *adj.* **1.** Capable of being moved. **2.** *Eccl.* Varying in date from year to year: *movable* feast. **3.** *Law* Pertaining to personal property as distinguished from real property. — *n.* **1.** *Usu. pl.* Anything that can be moved; esp., an article of furniture. **2.** *pl. Law* Personal property. Also **move'a·ble.** — **mov'a·bil'i·ty, mov'a·ble·ness** *n.* — **mov'a·bly** *adv.*

move (mōōv) *v.* **moved, mov·ing** *v.i.* **1.** To change place or position; go to or from a place. **2.** To change one's residence. **3.** To make progress; advance. **4.** To live or carry on one's life: to *move* in cultivated circles. **5.** To operate, work, revolve, etc., as a machine. **6.** To take or begin to take action; act. **7.** To be disposed of by sale. **8.** To make an application or proposal: to *move* for adjournment. **9.** To evacuate: said of the bowels. **10.** In checkers, chess, etc., to transfer a piece from one position to another. **11.** *Informal* To go fast. — *v.t.* **12.** To change the place or position of, as by carrying, pushing, pulling, etc. **13.** To set or keep in motion. **14.** To dislodge or force from a set position: to *move* him from his purpose. **15.** To couse, influence, or impel to some action: to *move* her to agree. **16.** To affect or arouse the emotions, sympathies, etc., of; touch. **17.** To propose for action, deliberation, etc. **18.** To cause (the bowels) to evacuate. **19.** In checkers, chess, etc., to transfer (a piece). — *n.* **1.** An act of moving; movement. **2.** An action for some purpose or design; step; maneuver. **3.** A change in residence. **4.** In checkers, chess, etc., the transfer of a piece. [< AF, OF < L *movere* to set in motion]

move·ment (mōōv'mənt) *n.* **1.** The act of moving; any change of place or position. **2.** A specific instance or manner of moving: a dance *movement.* **3.** A series of actions, plans, etc., tending toward some end: the temperance *movement;* also, organizations, persons, etc., of a particular tendency: the right-wing *movement.* **4.** An inclination or tendency. **5.** *Mech.* A particular arrangement of related moving parts. **6.** *Music* **a** One of the sections of a work, as of a symphony, string quartet, etc. **b** Tempo. **c** Rhythm. **7.** In prosody, rhythm or meter; cadence. **8.** An emptying of the bowels. **9.** *Mil.* A maneuver. [< OF < L *movere* to set in motion]

mov·er (mōō'vər) *n.* One who or that which moves; esp., one whose business is moving household goods.

mov·ie (mōō'vē) *Informal n.* **1.** A motion picture. **2.** A motion-picture theater. **3.** *pl.* The motion-picture industry. [Contr. of MOVING PICTURE]

mov·ing (mōō'ving) *adj.* **1.** Going or capable of going from place to place, position to position, etc. **2.** Causing or producing motion or change. **3.** That actuates, impels, or influences. **4.** Affecting, arousing, or touching the feelings or passions. **5.** Exciting or stirring up controversy, debate, etc. — **mov'ing·ly** *adv.* — **mov'ing·ness** *n.*

moving picture A motion picture.

moving staircase An escalator.

mow¹ (mō) *v.* **mowed, mowed** or **mown, mow·ing** *v.t.* **1.** To cut down (grain, grass, etc.) with a scythe or machine. **2.** To cut the grain or grass of (a field, lawn, etc.). **3.** *Informal* To cut down or kill rapidly or indiscriminately: with *down.* — *v.i.* **4.** To cut down grass or grain. [OE *māwan*] — **mow'er** *n.*

mow² (mou) *n.* Hay or grain stored in a barn; also, the place of storage. — *v.t.* To store in a mow. [OE *mūga*]

mowing machine A farm machine with cutting blades used for mowing hay, etc.

mox·ie (mok'sē) *n. Slang* Native shrewdness or common sense.

moz·za·rel·la (mōd'dzä·rel'lä) *n.* A soft Italian curd cheese that is very stringy when cooked. [< Ital.]

Mrs. (mis'iz) *n.* A title prefixed to the name of a married woman: a contracted form of *Mistress.*

mu (myōō, mōō) *n.* **1.** The twelfth letter in the Greek alphabet (M, μ), corresponding to the English *m.* See ALPHABET. **2.** The micron (symbol μ).

much (much) *adj.* **more, most** Great in quantity, amount, extent, etc.: much noise. — *n.* **1.** A considerable quantity or amount; a great deal. **2.** A remarkable or important thing: It isn't *much.* — **to make much of 1.** To treat as very important. **2.** To treat (someone) with great courtesy, regard, etc. — *adv.* **1.** Greatly: *much* obliged. **2.** For the most part; almost. [ME < OE *mycel*] — **much'ness** *n.*

mu·ci·lage (myōō'sə·lij) *n.* **1.** An aqueous solution of vegetable gum or the like, used as an adhesive. **2.** Any of various gummy or gelatinous substances found in some plants. [< F < LL *mucilago* musty juice]

mu·ci·lag·i·nous (myōō'si·laj'ə·nəs) *adj.* **1.** Of, pertaining to, or producing mucilage. **2.** Resembling or characteristic of mucilage; slimy and viscid. — **mu·ci·lag'i·nous·ness** *n.*

muck (muk) *n.* **1.** Any wet and clinging material that soils; esp., viscid mud. **2.** Moist dung mixed with decomposed vegetable matter, used as a soil fertilizer; manure. **3.** A dark brown to black soil consisting largely of decomposing peat and other vegetable materials. **4.** A confusing or uncertain state or condition; mess. — *v.t.* **1.** To fertilize with manure. **2.** *Informal* To make dirty; pollute. **3.** To remove manure, dirt, rocks, etc., from. [ME *muk*] — **muck'y** *adj.*

muck·rake (muk'rāk') *v.i.* **·raked, ·rak·ing** To search for or expose real or alleged corruption on the part of political officials, businessmen, etc. [Back formation < *muckrakes,*

HUMAN MOUTH
a Hard palate. *b* Pharynx. *c* Soft palate. *d* Uvula. *e* Tonsil. *f* Epiglottis. *g* Esophagus. *h* Trachea. *i* Tongue. *j* Hyoid bone. *k* Larynx.

slang term in late 19th c. U.S. politics] — **muck′rak′er** *n.* — **muck′rak′ing** *n.*

mu·cous (myōō′kəs) *adj.* **1.** Secreting mucus. **2.** Pertaining to, consisting of, or resembling mucus. Also **mu′cose** (-kōs). — **mu·cos′i·ty** (-kŏs′ə·tē) *n.*

mucous membrane *Anat.* A membrane secreting or producing mucus, that lines passages communicating with the exterior, as the alimentary and respiratory passages, etc.

mu·cus (myōō′kəs) *n. Biol.* A viscid substance secreted by the mucous membranes. [< L]

mud (mud) *n.* **1.** Soft and sticky wet earth. **2.** *Informal* The most degrading place or situation: to drag one into the *mud.* — **clear as mud** Absolutely incomprehensible. — *v.t.* **mud·ded, mud·ding** To soil or cover with or as with mud. [ME < MLG *mudde* or MDu. *modde*]

mud·der (mud′ər) *n.* A race horse that runs well on a muddy track.

mud·dle (mud′l) *v.* **·dled, ·dling** *v.t.* **1.** To mix in a confused or disordered way; jumble. **2.** To confuse or confound (the mind, speech, etc.). **3.** To mess up or mismanage; bungle. **4.** To make muddy or turbid. — *v.i.* **5.** To act or think in a confused or ineffective manner. — **to muddle through** *Chiefly Brit.* To achieve one's object despite confusion or mistakes. — *n.* **1.** A state or condition of confusion, disorder, or uncertainty. **2.** A state of mental or intellectual disorder. [< MUD + freq. suffix -*le*]

mud·dle·head·ed (mud′l·hed′id) *adj.* Mentally confused; addlebrained; stupid. — **mud′dle·head′ed·ness** *n.*

mud·dler (mud′lər) *n.* **1.** A stick for stirring liquids, esp. drinks. **2.** One who muddles.

mud·dy (mud′ē) *adj.* **·di·er, ·di·est** **1.** Covered, spattered, or filled with mud. **2.** Not clear, bright, or distinct, as color, liquid, etc. **3.** Confused or obscure in thought, expression, meaning, etc. — *v.t. & v.i.* **·died, ·dy·ing** To become or cause to become muddy. — **mud′di·ly** *adv.* — **mud′di·ness** *n.*

mud eel An eel-shaped amphibian, with no hind legs, that inhabits swamps of the southern U.S.: also called *siren.*

mud·fish (mud′fish′) *n. pl.* **fish** or **fish·es** Any of various fishes that inhabit mud or muddy waters.

mud flat A low-lying strip of muddy ground, esp. one between high and low tide.

mud puppy A tailed amphibian found in streams and lakes of North America.

mud·sling·er (mud′sling′ər) *n.* One who casts malicious slurs, esp. at a political opponent. — **mud′sling′ing** *n.*

mud·suck·er (mud′suk·er) *n.* A fish of California, commonly used as bait.

mud turtle Any of various turtles inhabiting muddy waters in North and Central America.

mu·ez·zin (myōō·ez′in) *n.* In Islam, a crier who calls the faithful to prayer, as from a minaret of a mosque. Also **mu·ed′din** (-ed′in). [< Arabic *mu′adhdhin* < *adhana* to call]

muff¹ (muf) *v.t. & v.i.* To perform (some act) clumsily; esp., to fail to catch (a ball). — *n.* An awkward action. [< MUFF²; prob. to handle as if wearing a muff]

muff² (muf) *n.* **1.** A pillowlike or tubular case of fur or cloth, open at the ends, into which the hands are put for warmth. **2.** A tuft of feathers on the head or legs of certain birds. [< Du. < F *moufle* mitten]

muf·fin (muf′in) *n.* A small, cup-shaped portion of light bread, usu. eaten hot with butter. [Origin uncertain]

muf·fle (muf′əl) *v.t.* **·fled, ·fling** **1.** To wrap up in a blanket, scarf, etc., as for warmth or concealment: often with *up.* **2.** To deaden the sound of by or as by wrapping. **3.** To deaden (a sound). **4.** To prevent (someone) from seeing, hearing, etc., by wrapping the head. — *n.* **1.** Something used for muffling. **2.** A chamber in a kiln or furnace that protects its contents from flame, gases, etc. [< F < *moufle* mitten]

muf·fler (muf′lər) *n.* **1.** A device to reduce noise, as from the exhaust of an engine. **2.** A heavy scarf worn about the neck for warmth. **3.** Anything that muffles. [< MUFFLE]

muf·ti¹ (muf′tē) *n.* In Islam, an expounder of religious law. [< Arabic, active participle of *aftā* to expound the law]

muf·ti² (muf′tē) *n.* Civilian dress; plain clothes, esp. when worn by one who normally wears a uniform. [< MUFTI¹]

mug¹ (mug) *n.* **1.** A large drinking cup. **2.** As much as will fill a mug. [Origin unknown]

mug² (mug) *Slang* *n.* **1.** The face, esp. the mouth and chin. **2.** *U.S.* A photograph of the face. Also **mug shot.** **3.** *U.S.* A man; guy. **4.** *U.S.* A criminal. — *v.* **mugged, mug·ging** *v.t.* **1.** *U.S.* To photograph (someone's face), esp. for police files. **2.** To assault viciously and rob. — *v.i.* **3.** To make funny faces; overact to win an audience. Also **mugg.** [< MUG¹] — **mug′ger** *n.*

mug·gy (mug′ē) *adj.* **·gi·er, ·gi·est** Warm, humid, and close; sultry. [< dial. F *mug* drizzle] — **mug′gi·ness** *n.*

Mu·ghal (mōō′gəl) *n. & adj.* Mogul. Also **Mu′ghul.**

mug·wump (mug′wump′) *n. U.S.* **1.** *Usu. cap.* A Republican who bolted the party in the presidential election of 1884. **2.** Anyone who is independent, esp. in politics. [< Algonquian *mugquomp* great man, chief] — **mug′wump′·er·y, mug′wump′ism** *n.*

Mu·ham·ma·dan (mōō·ham′ə·dən) *adj. & n.* Mohammedan. Also **Mu·ham′me·dan.**

mu·jik (mōō·zhēk′, mōō′zhik) See MUZHIK.

mu·lat·to (mə·lat′ō, myōō-, ·lä′tō) *n. pl.* **·toes** **1.** A person having one white and one Negro parent. **2.** Anyone having mixed white and Negro ancestry. — *adj.* Having the light brown color of a mulatto. [< Sp. < L *mulus* mule]

mul·ber·ry (mul′ber′ē, mul′bar·ē) *n. pl.* **·ries** **1.** Any of various trees whose leaves are valued for silkworm culture. **2.** The berrylike fruit of any of these trees. **3.** A purplish red color. [ME *mulberie*, var. of *murberie*, < OF < L *morum* mulberry + OE *berie* berry]

mulch (mulch) *n.* Any loose material, as straw, leaves, peat moss, etc., placed about the stalks of plants to protect their roots from drying, freezing, etc. — *v.t.* To cover with mulch. [ME *molsh* soft, OE *milisc*]

mulct (mulkt) *v.t.* **1.** To defraud or cheat (someone). **2.** To punish with a fine. — *n.* A fine or similar penalty. [< L *muleta, multa* fine]

mule¹ (myōōl) *n.* **1.** A hybrid between the ass and horse: esp., a hybrid between a jackass and mare. **2.** *Biol.* Any hybrid or cross, esp. one that is sterile: said usu. of the hybrid between the canary and a related bird. **3.** *U.S. Informal* A stubborn person. **4.** A textile machine that spins fibers into yarn and winds it on spindles: also called *spinning mule:* also **mule′jen′ny.** [< OF < L *mulus*]

mule² (myōōl) *n.* A backless lounging slipper. [< F < L *mulleus* reddish (shoe)]

mule skinner *U.S. Informal* One who drives mules.

mu·le·teer (myōō′lə·tir′) *n.* A mule driver. [< F < MF *mulet,* dim. of OF *mul* mule] — **mu′le·tress** (-tris) *n.fem.*

mule train A train of mules carrying packs; also, a train of freight wagons drawn by mules.

mul·ish (myōō′lish) *adj.* Resembling a mule; stubborn. — **mul′ish·ly** *adv.* — **mul′ish·ness** *n.*

mull¹ (mul) *v.t.* To heat and spice, as wine or cider. [Origin uncertain]

mull² (mul) *v.t.* To ponder: usu. with *over.* [ME *mullen* to pulverize]

mul·lah (mul′ə, mōōl′ə) *n.* A Moslem religious leader or teacher, or any man of learned reputation: a title of respect. Also **mul′la.** [< Turkish, Persian, and Hind. < Arabic *mawlā* master, sir]

mul·lein (mul′ən) *n.* Any of various herbs of the figwort family; esp., the **great mullein** and the **moth mullein.** Also **mul′len.** [< AF *moleine,* prob. < OF *mol* soft < L *mollis*]

mul·let (mul′it) *n. pl.* **·lets** or **·let** Any of various marine and fresh-water fish, as the **striped mullet** of the Atlantic and Pacific. [< OF < L *mullus* red mullet]

mul·li·gan stew (mul′i·gən) *U.S. Slang* A stew, originally made by tramps, composed of odds and ends of meat, vegetables, etc. Also **mul′li·gan.** [? from personal name]

mul·li·ga·taw·ny (mul′i·gə·tô′nē) *n.* A strongly flavored soup of the East Indies, made of meat and curry. [< Tamil *milagutannir* pepper water]

mul·lion (mul′yən) *n. Archit.* A vertical dividing piece in an opening, esp. in a window. — *v.t.* To furnish with or divide by means of mullions. [? Var. of *monial* < OF < L *medianus* medial]

mul·lock (mul′ək) *n.* Waste rock or earth left from mining. [ME *mull* dust + -OCK] — **mul′lock·y** *adj.*

multi- *combining form* **1.** Much; many; consisting of many; as in:

multiangular	multihued	multipurpose
multiblade	multimillion	multisection
multicellular	multimolecular	multistoried
multicolor	multipartisan	multisyllable
multidirectional	multipersonal	multivoiced
multifaced	multipointed	multivolumed

2. Having more than two (or more than one); as in:

multicuspid	multielectrode	multinucleate
multicylinder	multimammate	multispeed

3. Many times over: *multimillionaire.* **4.** *Med.* Affecting many: *multiglandular.* Also, before vowels, sometimes **mult-.** [< L *multus* much]

mul·ti·col·ored (mul′ti·kul′ərd) *adj.* Having many colors.

mul·ti·far·i·ous (mul′tə·fâr′ē·əs) *adj.* Having great diversity or variety. [< LL *multifarius*] — **mul′ti·far′i·ous·ly** *adv.* — **mul′ti·far′i·ous·ness** *n.*

mul·ti·fold (mul′tə·fōld) *adj.* Many times doubled.

mul·ti·form (mul′tə·fôrm) *adj.* Having many forms or appearances. — **mul′ti·for′mi·ty** *n.*

mul·ti·lat·er·al (mul′ti·lat′ər·əl) *adj.* **1.** Having many sides. **2.** *Govt.* Involving more than two nations: also *multi-partite.* **— mul'ti·lat'er·al·ly** *adv.*

mul·ti·lin·gual (mul'ti-ling'gwəl) *n. & adj.* Polyglot.

mul·ti·mil·lion·aire (mul'ti-mil'yən-âr') *n.* One having a fortune of many millions; a very rich person.

mul·ti·no·mi·al (mul'ti-nō'mē-əl) *adj.* Polynomial.

mul·tip·a·ra (mul·tip'ə-rə) *n. pl.* **·rae** (-rē) A woman who has borne more than one child, or who is bearing her second. [< NL < MULTI- + L *parere* to give birth]

mul·tip·a·rous (mul-tip'ə-rəs) *adj.* **1.** Giving birth to many at one time. **2.** Of or relating to a multipara.

mul·ti·par·tite (mul'ti-pär'tīt) *adj.* **1.** Divided into many parts. **2.** *Govt.* Multilateral (def. 2).

mul·ti·ple (mul'tə-pəl) *adj.* **1.** Having, consisting of, or relating to more than one part, aspect, individual, etc.; manifold. **2.** Happening more than once; repeated: *multiple* echoes. **3.** *Electr.* Denoting a circuit having two or more conductors arranged in parallel. **—** *n. Math.* Any of the products of a given number and some other number: 8 and 12 are *multiples* of 4. [< F]

mul·ti·ple-choice (mul'tə-pəl-chois') *adj.* Giving several answers from which the correct one is to be selected.

multiple sclerosis *Pathol.* Sclerosis occurring in various areas of the brain or spinal cord or both, and characterized by tremors, failure of coordination, etc.

mul·ti·plex (mul'tə-pleks) *adj.* **1.** Multiple; manifold. **2.** *Telecom.* Designating a system for the simultaneous transmission of two or more signals over the same wire or radio frequency channel. [< L *multus* much + *plicare* to fold]

mul·ti·pli·cand (mul'tə-plə-kand') *n. Math.* A number multiplied, or to be multiplied, by another. [< L *multiplicandus* to be multiplied]

mul·ti·pli·ca·tion (mul'tə-plə-kā'shən) *n.* **1.** The act of multiplying, or the state of being multiplied. **2.** *Math.* The process of finding the sum of a number repeated a given number of times.

multiplication sign The symbol (×) placed between two numbers or quantities to denote a multiplication of the first by the second, as 4 × 2 = 8.

mul·ti·plic·i·ty (mul'tə-plis'ə-tē) *n. pl.* **·ties** **1.** The condition or quality of being manifold or various. **2.** A large number. [< OF < LL < L *multiplicare* to multiply]

mul·ti·pli·er (mul'tə-plī'ər) *n.* **1.** One who or that which multiplies or causes multiplication. **2.** *Math.* The number by which a quantity is multiplied.

mul·ti·ply¹ (mul'tə-plī) *v.t.* **·plied, ·ply·ing** **1.** To increase the quantity, amount, or degree of. **2.** *Math.* To determine the product of by multiplication. **—** *v.i.* **3.** To become more in number, amount, or degree; increase. **4.** *Math.* To determine the product by multiplication. **5.** To grow in number by procreation; propagate. [< OF < L *multus* much + *plicare* to fold] **— mul'ti·pli'a·ble** *adj.*

mul·ti·ply² (mul'tə-plē) *adv.* So as to be multiple; in many ways.

mul·ti·pro·pel·lant (mul'ti-prə-pel'ənt) *Aerospace n.* A rocket propellant consisting of two or more chemicals separately fed into the combustion chamber.

mul·ti·stage (mul'ti-stāj) *adj.* **1.** Having or characterized by a number of definite stages in the completion of a process or action. **2.** *Aerospace* Having several sections, as in a rocket, each of which fulfills a given task before burnout.

mul·ti·tude (mul'tə-tōōd, -tyōōd) *n.* **1.** A great number. **2.** A large gathering of people. **3.** The quality of being many or numerous. **— the multitude** The common people. [< OF < L *multus* many]

mul·ti·tu·di·nous (mul'tə-tōō'də-nəs, -tyōō'-) *adj.* **1.** Existing in great numbers; numerous; myriad. **2.** Consisting of or exhibiting many parts, features, etc. **— mul'ti·tu'di·nous·ly** *adv.* **— mul'ti·tu'di·nous·ness** *n.*

mul·ti·va·lent (mul'ti-vā'lənt) *adj. Chem.* Having three or more valences: also *polyvalent.* **— mul'ti·va'lence** *n.*

mum¹ (mum) *adj.* Silent; saying nothing. **—** *interj.* Hush! **— mum's the word** Keep silent; be secretive. [Imit.]

mum² (mum) *v.i.* **mummed, mum·ming** To play or act in a mask or disguise. Also **mumm.** [Prob. < MUM¹]

mum³ (mum) *n. Informal* A chrysanthemum.

mum·ble (mum'bəl) *v.t. & v.i.* **·bled, ·bling** To speak low and indistinctly; mutter. **—** *n.* A low, indistinct speech or sound; mutter. [ME *momelen*] **— mum'bler** *n.*

mum·ble·ty-peg (mum'bəl-tē-peg') *n.* A game played by manipulating a jackknife in various ways so as to stick it into the ground. Also **mum'ble-peg', mum·ble-the-peg** (mum'bəl-thə-peg').

mum·bo jum·bo (mum'bō jum'bō) **1.** Meaningless, complicated, or obscure ritual, observance, incantation, etc. **2.** *Usu. cap.* In certain African tribes, a village god or idol who opposes evil and terrifies the women into subjection. [< Mandingo *mama dyambo* a tutelary god]

mum·mer (mum'ər) *n.* **1.** One who acts or makes sport in a mask or disguise. **2.** An actor.

mum·mer·y (mum'ər-ē) *n. pl.* **·mer·ies** **1.** A performance by mummers. **2.** A pretentious or hypocritical ritual. [< MF *mommerie* dumb show]

mum·mi·fy (mum'ə-fī) *v.* **·fied, ·fy·ing** *v.t.* **1.** To make a mummy of; preserve by embalming, drying, etc. **2.** To make dry and lifeless, as an idea, institution, etc. **—** *v.i.* **3.** To dry up; shrivel. **— mum'mi·fi·ca'tion** *n.*

mum·my (mum'ē) *n. pl.* **·mies** **1.** A human or animal body embalmed in the ancient Egyptian manner. **2.** Any corpse that has been well preserved, as by cold, special preparation, etc. **3.** One who is lifeless, withered, or torpid. **—** *v.t. & v.i.* **·mied, ·my·ing** To mummify. [< F < Med.L < Arabic < Persian *mum* wax] **— mum'mi·form** *adj.*

mumps (mumps) *n.pl.* (*construed as sing.*) *Pathol.* A contagious virus disease usu. occurring in childhood, characterized by fever and swelling of the parotid and other facial glands, and occasionally of the testicles. [Pl. of obs. *mump* grimace]

munch (munch) *v.t. & v.i.* To chew steadily with a crunching noise. [ME, ? < MF *manger*] **— munch'er** *n.*

mun·dane (mun'dān, mun-dān') *adj.* **1.** Pertaining to or characterized by that which is practical, routine, or ordinary: *mundane* concerns. **2.** Of or relating to the world or earth; earthly. [< F < L *mundus* world] **— mun·dane'ly** *adv.* **— mun·dane'ness** *n.*

Munich Pact A pact, signed in 1938 by Nazi Germany, Great Britain, France, and Italy, in which the Sudetenland was ceded to Germany. Also **Munich Agreement.**

mu·nic·i·pal (myōō-nis'ə-pəl) *adj.* **1.** Of or pertaining to a town or city or its local government. **2.** Having local self-government. [< L *municeps, -cipis* free citizen < *munia* duties + *capere* to take] **— mu·nic'i·pal·ly** *adv.*

municipal borough See under BOROUGH.

mu·nic·i·pal·i·ty (myōō-nis'ə-pal'ə-tē) *n. pl.* **·ties** An incorporated borough, town, or city.

mu·nic·i·pal·ize (myōō-nis'ə-pəl-īz') *v.t.* **·ized, ·iz·ing** **1.** To place within municipal authority or transfer to municipal ownership. **2.** To make a municipality of. **— mu·nic'i·pal·i·za'tion** *n.*

mu·nif·i·cent (myōō-nif'ə-sənt) *adj.* Extraordinarily generous or bountiful; liberal. [< L < *munus* gift + *facere* to make] **— mu·nif'i·cence** *n.* **— mu·nif'i·cent·ly** *adv.*

mu·ni·tion (myōō-nish'ən) *n. Usu. pl.* Ammunition and all other necessary war materiel. **—** *v.t.* To furnish with munitions. [< F < L < *munire* to fortify]

mu·ral (myōōr'əl) *n.* A painting or decoration applied to a wall or ceiling. **—** *adj.* **1.** Placed or executed on a wall: a *mural* painting. **2.** Of, pertaining to, or resembling a wall. [< F < L *murus* wall] **— mu'ral·ist** *n.*

mur·der (mûr'dər) *n.* **1.** The unlawful, malicious, and intentional killing of one human being by another. **2.** *U.S. Informal* Something exceedingly difficult, painful, or hazardous. **— to get away with murder** *U.S. Slang* To avoid or elude punishment or responsibility. **—** *v.t.* **1.** To kill (a human being) unlawfully and with deliberate malice. **2.** To kill or slaughter in a brutal manner, as in war. **3.** To spoil or mar by a bad performance, improper pronunciation, etc. **—** *v.i.* **4.** To commit murder. **— Syn.** See KILL. [< OE *morthor*] **— mur'der·er** *n.* **— mur'der·ess** *n.fem.*

mur·der·ous (mûr'dər-əs) *adj.* **1.** Of, pertaining to, or involving murder. **2.** Capable of or given to murder. **3.** Having the characteristics of or resembling murder; brutal; deadly. **4.** Extremely difficult or dangerous. **— mur'der·ous·ly** *adv.* **— mur'der·ous·ness** *n.*

mu·ri·at·ic acid (myōōr'ē-at'ik) *n.* Hydrochloric acid, esp. an impure grade used commercially. [< L *muriaticus* pickled < *muria* brine]

mu·rine (myōōr'īn, -in) *adj.* Of or pertaining to a family or a subfamily of rodents that includes the true mice and rats. **—** *n.* A murine rodent. [< L *mus, muris* mouse]

murk (mûrk) *n.* Darkness; gloom. Also spelled *mirk.* [OE *mirce*]

murk·y (mûr'kē) *adj.* **murk·i·er, murk·i·est** **1.** Dark, gloomy, or obscure: the murky depths. **2.** Hazy, thick, or misty, as atmosphere, color, etc. **3.** Not clear or distinct to the mind; confused; abstruse. Also *mirky.* **— murk'i·ly** *adv.* **— murk'i·ness** *n.*

mur·mur (mûr'mər) *n.* **1.** A low, indistinct, continuously repeated sound, as of many voices. **2.** An indistinct or mumbled complaint; grumbling. **3.** *Med.* A soft, low sound heard on auscultation of certain organs; esp., an abnormal, rasping sound produced within the heart. **—** *v.i.* **1.** To make a low, indistinct sound. **2.** To complain in low, muttered tones; grumble. **—** *v.t.* **3.** To mutter. [< OF < L *murmur,* ? ult. imit.] **— mur'mur·er** *n.* **— mur'mur·ing·ly** *adv.*

mur·mur·ous (mûr'mər-əs) *adj.* Characterized by, filled with, or making murmurs. **— mur'mur·ous·ly** *adv.* **— mur'mur·ous·ness** *n.*

mur·rain (mûr'in) *n.* Any of various contagious diseases affecting cattle. [< OF < L *mori* to die]

mur·rey (mûr'ē) *adj.* Of a purplish red color. **—** *n.* A dark purplish red. [< OF < L *morum* mulberry]

Mus·ca (mus′kə) *n.* A constellation, the Fly. [< NL]

mus·ca·dine (mus′kə-din, -dīn) *n.* A North American grape having a thick skin and a strong flavor. [Prob. < Provençal < LL *muscus* musk]

mus·cat (mus′kat, -kət) *n.* 1. Any of several varieties of musk-flavored Old World grapes. 2. A sweet wine made from such cultivated grapes. Also called *muscatel.* [< F< Provençal, smelling like musk < LL *muscus* musk]

mus·ca·tel (mus′kə-tel′) *n.* 1. A rich, sweet wine, made from the muscat grape. 2. The muscat grape. Also **mus′·ca·del′** (-del′).

mus·cle (mus′əl) *n.* 1. *Anat.* A contractile tissue composed of bundles of elongated fibers that function to produce bodily movements. 2. An organ or structure consisting of such tissue. 3. Muscular strength; brawn. —*v.i.* **·cled,** **·cling** *U.S. Slang* To force one's way by or as by sheer brawn: often with *in.* [< F < L *musculus,* lit., little mouse, dim. of *mus*] —**mus′cled** *adj.*

mus·cle-bound (mus′əl·bound′) *adj.* Having enlarged and inelastic muscles, as from excessive exercise.

Mus·co·vite (mus′kə-vīt) *n.* An inhabitant of Muscovy or of Moscow. —*adj.* 1. Of or pertaining to Muscovy.

Mus·co·vy (mus′kə-vē) Ancient Russia.

Muscovy duck A large, greenish black duck of Central and South America. [Alter. of MUSK DUCK]

mus·cu·lar (mus′kyə-lər) *adj.* 1. Pertaining to or composed of muscle. 2. Having strong muscles; brawny. —**mus′cu·lar′i·ty** (-lar′ə·tē) *n.* —**mus′cu·lar·ly** *adv.*

muscular dystrophy *Pathol.* One of various diseases characterized by a progressive degeneration of muscle tissue.

mus·cu·la·ture (mus′kyə·lə·choor) *n.* 1. The disposition or arrangement of muscles in a part or organ. 2. The muscle system as a whole. Also **mus′cu·la′tion.** [< F]

muse¹ (myōōz) *n.* A spirit or power regarded as inspiring artists, poets, etc. [< MUSE]

muse² (myōōz) *v.t.* & *v.i.* **mused, mus·ing** To consider thoughtfully or at length; ponder; meditate. [< OF *muser* to reflect] —**muse′ful** *adj.* —**muse′ful·ly** *adv.*

Muse (myōōz) *n.* In Greek mythology, any of the nine goddesses who preside over the arts and sciences. [< F < L < Gk. *Mousa* a Muse, eloquence, music]

mu·se·um (myōō·zē′əm) *n.* A place or building for preserving and exhibiting works of art, scientific objects, curiosities, etc. [< L < Gk. *mouseion* shrine of the Muses]

mush¹ (mush) *n.* 1. *U.S.* A thick porridge made with corn meal boiled in water or milk. 2. Anything soft and pulpy. 3. *Informal* Maudlin sentimentality. [Var. of MASH]

mush² (mush) *Chiefly Canadian v.i.* In arctic regions, to travel over snow with a dog sled. —*interj.* Get along!: a command to a dog team. [Prob. < F (Canadian) *marche,* the cry of voyageurs and trappers to their dogs]

mush·mel·on (mush′mel′ən) *n. U.S. Dial.* A muskmelon.

mush·room (mush′rōōm, -rōōm) *n.* 1. Any of various fleshy, rapidly growing, umbrella-shaped fungi, esp., the common edible **field mushroom** and certain poisonous varieties loosely called toadstools. 2. Anything resembling a mushroom in shape or rapid growth. —*v.i.* To grow or spread rapidly or in a mushroomlike shape. [ME *muscheron*]

mush·y (mush′ē) *adj.* **mush·i·er, mush·i·est** 1. Soft; pulpy. 2. *Informal* Mawkishly sentimental. —**mush′i·ly** *adv.* —**mush′i·ness** *n.*

mu·sic (myōō′zik) *n.* 1. The art of producing significant arrangements of sounds, usu. with reference to rhythm, pitch, and tone color. 2. A musical composition or body of compositions; also, a musical score. 3. A succession or combination of musical sounds, esp. if pleasing to the ear. —**program music** Music intended to be heard with reference to a story, idea, situation, event, etc. —**to face the music** To accept the consequences of one's acts. [< OF < L < Gk. *mousikē* (*technē*), lit., the art of the Muse]

mu·si·cal (myōō′zi·kəl) *adj.* 1. Of, pertaining to, or capable of creating music. 2. Having the nature or characteristics of music; melodious; harmonious. 3. Fond of or versed in music. 4. Set to music. —*n.* A musical comedy. —**mu′si·cal·ly** *adv.* —**mu′si·cal′i·ty, mu′si·cal·ness** *n.*

musical comedy A show with music, songs, dances, jokes, colorful staging, etc., often based on a tenuous plot.

mu·si·cale (myōō′zə·kal′) *n.* A private concert or recital, as in a home. [< F (*soirée*) *musicale*]

musical saw A handsaw that is played with a violin bow and produces musical tones by being bent or flexed.

music box A mechanism that plays tunes, usu. by means of pins that strike the tuned teeth of a comblike metal plate.

music hall 1. A public building for musical performances. 2. *Brit.* A vaudeville theatre.

mu·si·cian (myōō·zish′ən) *n.* 1. A professional performer or composer of music. 2. One skilled in performing or composing music. —**mu·si′cian·ly** *adj.* —**mu·si′cian·ship** *n.*

mu·si·col·o·gy (myōō′zə·kol′ə·jē) *n.* *pl.* **·gies** The scientific and historical study of the forms, theory, methods, etc., of music. —**mu·si·col′o·gist** *n.*

music stand A rack to hold music for a performer.

musk (musk) *n.* 1. A soft, powdery secretion with a penetrating odor, obtained from the sac (**musk bag**) of the male musk deer, and used in making perfumes and in medicine. 2. Any similar substance, either natural or synthetic. 3. The odor of musk. [< OF < LL < LGk. *moskos*]

musk deer A small, hornless deer of Asia, of which the male has a musk-secreting gland.

mus·kel·lunge (mus′kə·lunj) *n. pl.* **·lunge** or **·lung·es** A large North American pike, valued as a game fish. Also **mus′kal·lunge, mus′kie** (-kē). [< Algonquian < *mas* great + *kinong* pike]

mus·ket (mus′kit) *n.* An archaic smoothbore, usually muzzleloading, firearm designed to be fired from the shoulder. [< MF < Ital. *moschetto* crossbow, dart]

mus·ket·eer (mus′kə·tir′) *n.* Formerly, a soldier armed with a musket. [< F *mousquetaire*]

mus·ket·ry (mus′kit·rē) *n.* 1. Muskets collectively. 2. The technique of firing small arms.

Mus·kho·ge·an (mus·kō′gē·ən, mus′kō·gē′ən) *n.* One of the principal North American Indian linguistic stocks formerly inhabiting the SE U.S. Also **Mus·ko′gi·an.**

musk·mel·on (musk′mel′ən) *n.* Any of several varieties of juicy, edible fruits of the gourd family, as the cantaloupe; also, the plant.

musk ox A shaggy, hollow-horned ruminant of arctic America and Greenland, emitting a strong odor of musk.

musk·rat (musk′rat) *n. pl.* **·rats** or **·rat** 1. An aquatic rodent of North America, having dark, glossy brown fur and a musky odor: also called *water rat.* 2. The valuable fur of this rodent. [< Algonquian *musquash*]

musk·y (mus′kē) *adj.* **musk·i·er, musk·i·est** Resembling musk in odor or taste. —**musk′i·ly** *adv.* —**musk′i·ness** *n.*

MUSKRAT
(About 12 inches long; tail 10 inches)

Mus·lim (muz′lim, mōōz′-, mōōs′-) *n. pl.* **·lims** or **·lim** A believer in Islam; Mohammedan. —*adj.* Of or pertaining to Islam. Also called *Moslem:* also **Mus′·lem.** [< Arabic, one who submits < *aslama* to surrender (to God)]

Mus·lim·ism (muz′ləm·iz′əm, mōōz′-, mōōs′-) *n.* Islam.

mus·lin (muz′lin) *n.* Any of several plain-weave cotton fabrics of varying fineness. [< F < Ital. < *Mussolo* Mosul, city in Iraq, where it was made]

muss (mus) *U.S. Informal n.* 1. A state of disorder or untidiness; mess. 2. A commotion or tumult. —*v.t.* To make messy or untidy; rumple: often with *up.* [Alter. of MESS]

mus·sel (mus′əl) *n.* 1. A bivalve marine mollusk, esp. the edible **blue mussel.** 2. Any of several fresh-water mollusks. [OE < L *musculus,* dim. of *mus* mouse]

Mus·sel·man (mus′əl·mən) *n. pl.* **·mans** (-mənz) or **·men** (-mən) A Muslim. [< Persian and Turkish *musulmān*]

muss·y (mus′ē) *adj.* *U.S. Informal* **muss·i·er, muss·i·est** Rumpled; messy. —**muss′i·ly** *adv.* —**muss′i·ness** *n.*

must¹ (must) *v. Present 3rd person sing.* **must** A defective verb now used only as an auxiliary followed by the infinitive without *to,* or elliptically with the infinitive understood, to express: **a** Compulsion: *Must* you go? **b** Requirement: You *must* be healthy to be accepted. **c** Probability or supposition: You *must* be tired. **d** Conviction or certainty: War *must* follow. ◆ A past conditional is formed by placing the following verb in the perfect infinitive: *He must have gone.* —*n. Informal* Anything that is required or vital: Safety is a *must.* —*adj. Informal* Important and essential: a *must* book. [OE *mōtan* to be able, to be obliged to]

must² (must) *n.* Mustiness; mold. [< MUSTY]

must³ (must) *n.* The expressed unfermented juice of the grape or other fruit. [OE < L *mustum* (*vinum*) new (wine)]

mus·tache (məs·tash′, mus′tash) *n.* 1. The growth of hair on the upper lip. 2. The hair or bristles growing near the mouth of an animal. Also **mus·ta·chio** (məs·tä′shō). Also, *Chiefly Brit.,* **mous·tache.** [< F < Ital. *mostaccio* face] —**mus·tached** (məs·tasht′) *adj.*

mus·tang (mus′tang) *n.* A wild horse of the American plains. [< Sp. *mesteño* belonging to a cattlemen's association]

mus·tard (mus′tərd) *n.* 1. A pungent condiment prepared as a paste or powder from the seed of the mustard plant. 2. Any of several plants of a large family that includes broccoli, cabbage, cress, etc. 3. The yellowish or brownish color of ground mustard. [< MF *moustarde*]

mustard gas *Chem.* An oily amber liquid, $C_4H_8Cl_2S$, having an odor of mustard or garlic, and used in warfare because of its powerful blistering effect.

mustard plaster A mixture of powdered black mustard and a suitable adhesive, used as a counterirritant.

mus·ter (mus′tər) *v.t.* **1.** To summon or assemble (troops, etc.), for service, review, roll call, etc. **2.** To collect, gather, or summon: often with *up.* — *v.i.* **3.** To gather or assemble, as troops for service, review, etc. — **to muster in** (or *out*) To enlist in (or leave) military service. — *n.* **1.** An assembling or gathering, as of troops. **2.** An assemblage or collection, as of troops. **3.** An official list of officers and men in a military unit or ship's crew: also **muster roll.** [< OF < L *monstrare* to show]

must·y (mus′tē) *adj.* **must·i·er, must·i·est 1.** Having a moldy odor or flavor, as a close room. **2.** Dull or stale with age. **3.** Without vigor; lifeless. [? Alter. of obs. *moisty* < MOIST] — **must′i·ly** *adv.* — **must′i·ness** *n.*

mu·ta·ble (myoo′tə·bəl) *adj.* **1.** Capable of or subject to change. **2.** Liable to frequent change. [< L < *mutare* to change] — **mu′ta·ble·ness, mu′ta·bil′i·ty** *n.* — **mu′ta·bly** *adv.*

mu·ta·gen·ic (myoo′tə·jen′ik) *adj. Genetics* Having the power to produce mutations in plant or animal organisms, as X-rays, certain chemicals, etc. [< L *mutare* to change]

mu·tant (myoo′tənt) *n.* A plant or animal organism differing from its parents in one or more characteristics that are inheritable; mutation; sport. — *adj.* Pertaining to, resulting from, or undergoing mutation. [< L *mutare* to change]

mu·tate (myoo′tāt) *v.t. & v.i.* **·tat·ed, ·tat·ing** To undergo or subject to change or mutation. [< L < *mutare* to change] — **mu′ta·tive** (-tə·tiv) *adj.*

mu·ta·tion (myoo·tā′shən) *n.* **1.** The act or process of changing; alteration. **2.** A change or modification in form, structure, function, etc. **3.** *Biol.* **a** A sudden, transmissible variation in a plant or animal. **b** An individual, species, etc., resulting from such a variation. [< OF < L < *mutare* to change] — **mu·ta′tion·al** *adj.*

mute (myoot) *adj.* **1.** Not producing speech or sound; silent. **2.** Lacking the power of speech; dumb. **3.** Expressed or conveyed without speech; unspoken: a mute appeal. **4.** *Law* Deliberately refusing to plead on arraignment. **5.** *Phonet.* Not pronounced; silent, as the *e* in *gone.* — *n.* **1.** One who is unable to speak; esp. a deaf-mute. **2.** *Law* One who refuses to plead on arraignment. **3.** *Phonet.* **a** A silent letter. **b** A plosive. **4.** *Music* A device used to muffle the tone of an instrument. — *v.t.* **mut·ed, mut·ing 1.** To muffle or deaden the sound of (a musical instrument, etc.). **2.** In art, to soften (a color, a shade, etc.). [< L *mutus* dumb] — **mute′ly** *adv.* — **mute′ness** *n.*

mu·ti·late (myoo′tə·lāt) *v.t.* **·lat·ed, ·lat·ing 1.** To deprive (a person, animal, etc.) of a limb or essential part; maim. **2.** To damage or make imperfect: to *mutilate* a speech. [< L *mutilare* to maim] — **mu′ti·la′tion** *n.* — **mu′ti·la·tive** *adj.* — **mu′ti·la′tor** *n.*

mu·ti·neer (myoo′tə·nir′) *n.* One guilty of mutiny.

mu·ti·nous (myoo′tə·nəs) *adj.* **1.** Disposed to mutiny; seditious. **2.** Characterized by, expressing, or constituting mutiny. — **mu′ti·nous·ly** *adv.* — **mu′ti·nous·ness** *n.*

mu·ti·ny (myoo′tə·nē) *n. pl.* **·nies** Rebellion against constituted authority; insubordination; esp., a revolt of soldiers or sailors against their commanders. — *v.i.* **·nied, ·ny·ing** To take part in a mutiny. [< MF *mutin* rebellious < OF < Med.L < L *movere* to move]

mutt (mut) *n. Slang* **1.** A cur; mongrel dog. **2.** A stupid person; blockhead. Also **mut.** [< MUTT(ONHEAD)]

mut·ter (mut′ər) *v.i.* **1.** To speak in a low, indistinct tone, as in complaining. **2.** To complain; grumble. **3.** To make a low, rumbling sound. — *v.t.* **4.** To say in a low, indistinct tone. — *n.* A low, indistinct utterance or tone. [ME *muteren*] — **mut′ter·er** *n.* — **mut′ter·ing·ly** *adv.*

mut·ton (mut′n) *n.* The flesh of sheep used as food; esp. the flesh of mature sheep as distinguished from lambs. [< OF *molton* sheep] — **mut′ton·y** *adv.*

mutton chop A piece of mutton from the rib for broiling or frying.

mut·ton·chops (mut′n·chops′) *n.pl.* Side whiskers narrow at the temples and broad at the lower cheeks.

mut·ton·head (mut′n·hed′) *n. Slang* A stupid, dense person. — **mut′ton·head′ed** (-hed′id) *adj.*

mu·tu·al (myoo′choo·əl) *adj.* **1.** Felt, expressed, or performed for or toward each other; reciprocal: *mutual* dislike. **2.** Having the same attitude toward or relationship with each other or others: *mutual* friends. **3.** Possessed in common. [< OF < L *mutuus* borrowed, exchanged, reciprocal] — **mu′tu·al·ly** *adv.* — **mu·tu·al′i·ty** *n.*

muu·muu (moo′moo′) *n.* A loose, flowing gown for women, gathered from the neckline. [< Hawaiian]

mu·zhik (moo·zhēk′, moo′zhēk) *n.* A Russian peasant in Czarist times. Also **mu·zjik′.** [< Russian]

muz·zle (muz′əl) *n.* **1.** The projecting part of an animal's head, including the jaws, mouth, and snout. **2.** A guard or covering for the snout. **3.** The front end of the barrel of a firearm. — *v.t.* **·zled, ·zling 1.** To put a muzzle on (an

animal, etc.). **2.** To restrain from speaking, expressing opinions, etc.; gag. [< OF < Med.L *musus* snout]

muz·zle·load·er (muz′əl·lō′dər) *n.* A gun loaded through the muzzle. — **muz′zle·load′ing** *adj.*

MVD The Ministry of Internal Affairs of the Soviet Union; the secret police. Also **M.V.D.**

my (mī) *pronominal adj.* The possessive case of the pronoun *I,* used attributively: also used in certain forms of address: *my* lord; *my* good man. — *interj.* An exclamation of surprise, dismay, etc.: Oh, *my!* [OE *mīn*]

my- Var. of MYO-.

my·as·the·ni·a (mī′əs·thē′nē·ə) *n. Pathol.* Muscular debility, often accompanied by progressive exhaustion.

my·ce·li·um (mī·sē′lē·əm) *n. pl.* **·li·a** (-lē·ə) *Bot.* The thallus or vegetative portion of a fungus, consisting of hyphae. Also **my′cele** (-sēl). [< NL < Gk. *mykēs* fungus] — **my·ce′li·al, my·ce′li·an** *adj.* — **my·ce′li·oid, my·ce·loid** (mī′sə·loid) *adj.*

My·ce·nae (mī·sē′nē) An ancient city in the NE Peloponnesus, Greece; first excavated 1876–77. — **My′ce·nae′an** *adj. & n.*

-mycete *combining form Bot.* A member of a class of fungi, corresponding in use to class names in *-mycetes.*

-mycetes *combining form Bot.* Used to form class names of fungi. [< Gk. *mykētes,* pl. of *mykēs* fungus]

myco- *combining form* Fungus. Also, before vowels, **myc-.** [< Gk. *mykēs* fungus]

my·col·o·gy (mī·kol′ə·jē) *n. pl.* **·gies** The branch of botany dealing with fungi. — **my·co·log·ic** (mī′kə·loj′ik) or **·i·cal** *adj.* — **my·col′o·gist** *n.*

my·co·sis (mī·kō′sis) *n. Pathol.* **1.** A fungous growth within the body. **2.** A disease caused by such a growth, as ringworm. — **my·cot′ic** (-kot′ik) *adj.*

my·e·len·ceph·a·lon (mī′ə·len·sef′ə·lon) *n. Anat.* The posterior part of the rhombencephalon or that portion of the medulla oblongata lying behind the pons Varolii and cerebellum.

my·e·li·tis (mī′ə·lī′tis) *n. Pathol.* **1.** Inflammation of the spinal cord. **2.** Inflammation of the bone marrow.

myelo- *combining form Anat.* The spinal cord or bone marrow. Also, before vowels, **myel-.** [< Gk. *myelos* marrow]

my·na (mī′nə) *n.* One of the various starlinglike Oriental birds, some of which are taught to speak words: sometimes spelled *mina.* Also **my′nah.** [< Hind. *mainā*]

myn·heer (mīn·hâr′, -hir′) *n.* **1.** *Cap.* The Dutch equivalent of *Mr.* **2.** A title of courtesy, equivalent to *sir.* [< Du. < *mijn* my + *heer* lord, master]

myo- *combining form* Muscle. Also, before vowels, **my-.** [< Gk. *mys, myos* muscle]

my·o·car·di·al (mī′ō·kär′dē·əl) *adj. Anat.* Of or pertaining to the heart muscle. [< MYO- + Gk. *kardia* heart]

my·o·car·di·um (mī′ō·kär′dē·əm) *n. Anat.* The muscular tissue of the heart. [< MYO- + Gk. *kardia* heart]

my·o·pi·a (mī·ō′pē·ə) *n.* **1.** *Pathol.* A visual defect in which objects are seen clearly only when close to the eye; nearsightedness. **2.** Lack of insight or discernment; obtuseness. Also **my·o·py** (mī′ə·pē). [< NL] — **my·op′ic** (-op′ik) *adj.*

myria- *combining form* **1.** Very many; of great number. **2.** In the metric system, ten thousand. Also, before vowels, **myri-.** [< Gk. *myrios* numberless]

myr·i·ad (mir′ē·əd) *adj.* Countless; innumerable. — *n.* **1.** A vast indefinite number. **2.** A vast number of persons or things. **3.** Ten thousand. [< Gk. *myrios* numberless]

myr·i·a·pod (mir′ē·ə·pod) *n. Zool.* One of a group of arthropods whose bodies are made up of a certain number of segments, each of which bears one or two pairs of jointed appendages, including the centipedes. — **myr·i·ap·o·dan** (mir′ē·ap′o·dan) *adj.* & *n.* — **myr′i·ap·o·dous** *adj.*

myr·mi·don (mûr′ma·don, -dən) *n.* A faithful, unquestioning follower. [< MYRMIDON]

Myr·mi·don (mûr′ma·don, -dən) *n.* In Greek legend, one of a warlike people of Thessaly, followers of Achilles in the Trojan War. [< L < Gk., pl. *Myrmidones*]

myrrh (mûr) *n.* **1.** An aromatic gum resin that exudes from certain small trees of Arabia and eastern Africa, used as incense, perfume, and in medicine. **2.** Any shrub or tree that yields this gum. [OE < L < Gk. *myrra* < Hebrew *mōr, mar* bitter]

myr·tle (mûr′təl) *n.* Any of a group of shrubs with evergreen leaves, white or rose-colored flowers, and black berries. **2.** One of various other plants, as the periwinkle. [< F < Med.L *myrtillus* myrtle]

my·self (mī·self′) *pron.* A form of the first person singular pronoun, used: **1.** As a reflexive or as the object of a preposition in a reflexive sense: I saw *myself* in the mirror. **2.** As an emphatic or intensive form of *I:* I *myself* invented the yo-yo. **3.** Informally as part of a direct compound object of a verb, or as an emphatic form of *me.* He asked John and *myself* to come along; They saw *myself* on television. **4.** As a designation of a normal, proper, or usual state: Once out of uniform, I was *myself* again in no time. [OE *mē* + *sylf*]

mys·te·ri·ous (mis·tir′ē·əs) *adj.* **1.** Implying or characterized by mystery. **2.** Unexplained; puzzling. **— mys·te′ri·ous·ly** *adv.* **— mys·te′ri·ous·ness** *n.*
— Syn. A *mysterious* occurrence contains something unknown, but not necessarily unknowable, while something *obscure* is hidden but may be brought to light. *Inscrutable* refers to that which is quite beyond the power of perception; *abstruse*, to that which is difficult to understand because of its complexity or profundity. *Esoteric* suggests something that is understood only by a small and select group possessing special knowledge. *Occult* marks those things considered to belong to a realm beyond human experience.

mys·ter·y (mis′tər·ē) *n. pl.* **·ter·ies 1.** Something that is not or cannot be known, understood, or explained. **2.** Any action, affair, or thing that arouses curiosity or suspense because it is not fully revealed. **3.** A story, play, movie, etc., narrating or dramatizing such an affair. **4.** Obscurity or darkness: shrouded in *mystery*. **5.** Baffling character or property, as of a glance, gesture, etc. **6.** *Theol.* A truth that can be known only through divine revelation. **7.** *Eccl.* **a** A sacrament, esp. the Eucharist. **b** *pl.* The Eucharistic elements. **c** Any of fifteen events in the life of Christ. **8.** *Usu. pl.* In ancient times, one of certain religious cults. **9.** *Often pl.* A secret rite, doctrine, or practice. [< L < Gk. *mysterion* secret rite]

mystery play A medieval dramatic representation dealing with Scriptural events or characters and typically presented by a craft guild on a holiday. Compare MIRACLE PLAY.

mys·tic (mis′tik) *adj.* **1.** Of the nature of or pertaining to mysteries. **2.** Of or designating an occult or esoteric rite, practice, belief, religion, etc. **3.** Of or pertaining to mystics or mysticism. **4.** Baffling or enigmatic. **—** *n.* One who believes in mysticism, or professes to have had mystical experiences. [< L *mysticus* pertaining to secret rites]

mys·ti·cal (mis′ti·kəl) *adj.* **1.** Of the nature of a direct, intuitive, or subjective perception beyond the ordinary range of human experience, esp. one of a religious character.

2. Having a spiritual character or reality beyond human reason. **3.** Mystic (defs. 1, 2, & 3). **— mys′ti·cal/i·ty** (-kal′ə·tē), **mys′ti·cal·ness** *n.* **— mys′ti·cal·ly** *adv.*

mys·ti·cism (mis′tə·siz′əm) *n.* **1.** The doctrine or belief that through contemplation and love man can achieve a direct and immediate consciousness of God or of divine truth, etc., without the use of reason or of any of the ordinary senses. **2.** Any mystical theory. **3.** Vague thinking.

mys·ti·fy (mis′tə·fī) *v.t.* **·fied, ·fy·ing 1.** To confuse or perplex, esp. deliberately. **2.** To make obscure or mysterious. [< F < *mystique* mystic] **— mys′ti·fi·ca′tion** *n.* **— mys′ti·fi′er** *n.* **— mys′ti·fy′ing·ly** *adv.*

mys·tique (mis·tēk′) *n.* A body of attitudes, opinions, or ideas that become associated with a person, thing, institution, etc., and give it a superhuman or mythical status: the *mystique* of bullfighting. [< F]

myth (mith) *n.* **1.** A traditional story, usu. focusing on the deeds of gods or heroes, often in explanation of some natural phenomenon, as the origin of the sun, etc. **2.** A theme, motif, character type, etc., in modern literature. **3.** Myths collectively. **4.** An imaginary or fictitious person, thing, event, or story. **5.** A false opinion, belief, or ideal. [< LL *mythos* < Gk., word, speech, story]

myth·i·cal (mith′i·kəl) *adj.* **1.** Pertaining to or like a myth; **2.** Derived from or contained in a myth. **3.** Imaginary, fictitious. Also **myth′ic.** **— myth′i·cal·ly** *adv.*

mytho- *combining form* Myth. Also, before vowels, **myth-.** [< Gk. *mythos* story]

myth·o·log·i·cal (mith′ə·loj′i·kəl) *adj.* **1.** Of, pertaining to, or described in mythology. **2.** Imaginary. Also **myth′o·log′ic. — myth′o·log′i·cal·ly** *adv.*

my·thol·o·gy (mi·thol′ə·jē) *n. pl.* **·gies 1.** The collective myths and legends of a particular people, person, institution, etc. **2.** The scientific collection and study of myths. **3.** A volume of myths. [< F < LL < Gk. < *mythos* story + *logos* < *legein* to speak, tell] **— my·thol′o·gist** *n.*

N

ɪ, N (en) *n. pl.* **n's** or **ns, N's** or **Ns, ens** (enz) **1.** The fourteenth letter of the English alphabet. **2.** The sound represented by the letter *n*, a voiced, alveolar nasal. **—** *symbol* **1.** *Printing* An en. **2.** *Chem.* Nitrogen (symbol N). **3.** *Math.* An indefinite number.

nab (nab) *v.t.* **nabbed, nab·bing** *Informal* **1.** To catch or arrest, as a fugitive or criminal. **2.** To take or seize suddenly; snatch. [Prob. of Scand. origin]

na·bob (nā′bob) *n.* **1.** A European who has become rich in India. **2.** Any very rich or powerful man. [< Hind. *nawwāb* < Arabic *nuwwab*, pl. of *nā′ib* viceroy]

na·celle (nə·sel′) *n. Aeron.* A separate enclosure on an aircraft, esp. one for an engine. [< F, small boat]

na·cre (nā′kər) *n.* Mother-of-pearl. [< F < Ital. *naccara* < Arabic *naqqāra* drum]

na·cre·ous (nā′krē·əs) *adj.* **1.** Containing, resembling, or producing nacre. **2.** Iridescent; pearly.

Na-Dene (nə·dēn′) *n.* A group of related North American Indian languages. Also **Na-Dé·né′** (-dā·nā′).

na·dir (nā′dər, -dir) *n.* **1.** The point of the celestial sphere directly beneath the position of an observer, and opposite to the zenith. **2.** The lowest possible point: opposed to *zenith*. [< MF < Arabic *nazīr* (*as-samt*) opposite (the zenith)]

nae (nā) *adj. & adv. Scot.* No; not.

nag[1] (nag) *v.* **nagged, nag·ging** *v.t.* **1.** To bother or annoy by repeatedly urging, scolding, carping, etc. **—** *v.i.* **2.** To urge, scold, carp, etc., continually. **—** *n.* One who nags. [< Scand.] **— nag′ger** *n.* **— nag′ging·ly** *adv.*

nag[2] (nag) *n.* **1.** A pony or small horse used for riding. **2.** An old, broken-down, or worthless horse. [ME *nagge*]

Na·hua·tl (nä′wät′l) *n.* **1.** The Uto-Aztecan language of the Aztecs and certain other Indian peoples. **2.** The peoples whose native language is Nahuatl. **—** *adj.* Of or pertaining to Nahuatl or the people who speak it.

Na·hua·tlan (nä′wät·lən) *n.* **1.** A branch of the Uto-Aztecan linguistic family of North and Central American Indians, including the Aztec dialects. **2.** Nahuatl. **—** *adj.* Of or pertaining to Nahuatl or Nahuatlan.

Na·hum (nā′əm, -hum) Seventh-century B.C. Hebrew prophet. **—** *n.* A book of the Old Testament containing his prophecies. [< Hebrew, comfort]

nai·ad (nā′ad, nī′-) *n. pl.* **·ads** or **·a·des** (-ə·dēz) **1.** In classical mythology, one of the water nymphs believed to dwell in and preside over fountains, springs, rivers, lakes, and wells. **2.** *Entomol.* The aquatic nymphal stage in the life cycle of certain insects. [< L < Gk. *Naias, -ados.*]

na·if (nä·ēf′) *adj. French* Masculine form of NAIVE. Also **na·if′.**

nail (nāl) *n.* **1.** A slender piece of metal, usu. pointed at one end and broadened at the other, used for driving into or through wood, etc., so as to hold or fasten one piece to another or to project as a peg. **2.** Something resembling a nail in shape or function. **3.** A thin, horny plate growing on one side of the ends of the fingers and toes of men and other primates. **4.** An animal part corresponding to the nail of a primate, as a claw, talon, or hoof. **— hard as nails 1.** In good physical condition; rugged. **2.** Not to be moved by sentiment, pity, etc. **— to hit the nail on the head** To do or say something exactly to the point. **—** *v.t.* **1.** To fasten or fix in place with a nail or nails. **2.** To close up or shut in by means of nails: often with *up*. **3.** To secure or make certain through quick or decisive action: often with *down*. **4.** To fix firmly or immovably: Terror *nailed* him to the spot. **5.** *Slang* To catch or arrest; intercept. **6.** *Slang* To expose, as a lie or liar. [OE *nægl*, orig., fingernail.]

nail file A small, fine file for shaping the fingernails.

nail·fold (nāl′fōld′) *n. Anat.* The cuticle (def. 3).

nail polish A clear or colored lacquer or other substance applied to the nails to give a glossy finish. Also **nail enamel.**

nail·set (nāl′set′) *n.* A punch for driving the head of a nail below or even with a surface. Also **nail set.**

nain·sook (nān′sŏŏk, nan′-) *n.* A soft, lightweight cotton fabric. [< Hind. *nainsukh*, lit., pleasure of the eye]

na·ive (nä·ēv′) *adj.* **1.** Having an unaffected or simple nature that lacks worldly experience; artless. **2.** Lacking or revealing the lack of deliberate or careful analysis; uncriti-

cal: a *naive* idea.   3. Uninstructed: a *naive* observer.   Also
na·ive′.   [< F, fem. of *naif* < L *nativus* natural, inborn]
— na·ive′ly *adv.*   **— na·ive′ness** *n.*

na·ive·té (nä·ēv′tā′, nä·ēv′tā) *n.* **1.** The state or quality of
being naive.   **2.** An incident, remark, etc., of a naive character.   Also **na·ive′té**, **na·ïve·ty** (nä·ēv′tē).   [< F]

na·ked (nā′kid) *adj.* **1.** Having no clothes on; nude.   **2.**
Having no covering, or lacking the usual covering; exposed.
3. Bare or stripped, as of vegetation, furnishings, ornaments, etc.   **4.** Without addition, adornment, or qualification; stark: the *naked* truth.   **5.** Unaided by an optical instrument: the *naked* eye.   **6.** Open or exposed to view: a
naked sword.   **7.** Without defense or protection; vulnerable.
8. Being without means of sustenance; destitute.   **9.** *Bot.* **a**
Not enclosed in an ovary or case: said of seeds. **b** Without
protective scales: said of buds. **c** Without a perianth: said of
flowers. **d** Without leaves: said of stalks. **e** Having no hairs;
smooth: said of leaves.   **10.** *Zool.* Lacking fur, hair, feathers,
etc.   [OE *nacod*]   **— na′ked·ly** *adv.*   **— na′ked·ness** *n.*

nam·by-pam·by (nam′bē-pam′bē) *adj.* **1.** Full of or exhibiting weak sentimentality; insipid.   **2.** Timid and irresolute.
— n. *pl.* **·bies** One who is namby-pamby.   [< The title
of a satiric poem by Henry Carey, died 1743.]

name (nām) *n.* **1.** A word or group of words by which a
person, thing, animal, class, or concept is distinctively
known or referred to; esp., the proper appellation of a person
or family.   **2.** A usu. derogatory word or phrase evaluating
character or quality: to call someone *names*.   **3.** Popular or
general reputation.   **4.** A famous or important person, organization, or thing: a big *name* in industry.   **5.** Mere semblance or outward form: a wife in *name* only.   **6.** Fame or
distinction.   **— by the name of** Named.   **— in the name of**
1. For the sake of.   **2.** By the authority of.   **— to make a**
name for oneself To achieve distinction or fame.   **— to**
one's name Of one's own: He hasn't a friend *to his name*.
— v. named, nam·ing *v.t.* **1.** To give a name to; call.   **2.** To
mention or refer to by name; cite.   **3.** To identify.   **4.** To
fix or determine: to *name* the day.   **5.** To nominate; appoint.   **— adj. 1.** Having or known by a name.   **2.** *U.S.*
Informal Famous.   [OE *nama*]   **— nam′er** *n.*

name day The feast day of the saint for whom one is
named.

name·less (nām′lis) *adj.* **1.** Undistinguished or obscure:
a *nameless* multitude.   **2.** That cannot be named; indescribable: *nameless* terror.   **3.** Not fit to be spoken of; un-
mentionable: *nameless* atrocities.   **4.** Unmentioned by name.
5. Having no name; esp., having no legal name; illegitimate.
— name′less·ly *adv.*   **— name′less·ness** *n.*

name·ly (nām′lē) *adv.* That is to say; to wit.

name·sake (nām′sāk′) *n.* One who is named after or has
the same name as another.

nan·keen (nan-kēn′) *n.* **1.** A buff-colored Chinese cotton
fabric.   **2.** *pl.* Clothes made of nankeen.   Also **nan·kin′**
(-kēn′).   [after *Nanking*, where originally made]

nan·ny (nan′ē) *n.* *pl.* **·nies** **1.** *Informal* A female goat:
also **nanny goat**.   **2.** *Brit.* A child's nurse.   [after *Nanny*,
a personal name, dim. of *Ann*]

nano- *combining form* **1.** Exceedingly small.   **2.** In the metric system and in technical usage, one billionth of (a specified
unit).   Also, before vowels, **nan-**.   [< Gk. *nānos* dwarf]

Nantes, Edict of (nants, *Fr.* nänt)   An order granting political equality to the Huguenots, issued by Henry IV of France
in 1598 and revoked by Louis XIV in 1685.

Na·o·mi (nā·ō′mē, nā′ə·mē, -mī)   In the Bible, the mother-
in-law of Ruth.   *Ruth* i 2.   [< Hebrew, my delight]

nap¹ (nap) *n.* A short sleep; doze.   **— v.i. napped, nap·ping**
1. To take a nap; doze.   **2.** To be unprepared or off one's
guard.   [OE *hnappian* to doze]

nap² (nap) *n.* **1.** The short fibers forming a downy or fuzzy
surface on flannel and certain other fabrics.   **2.** A covering
resembling this, as upon some plants.   **— v.t. napped, nap·**
ping To raise a nap on.   [< MDu. *noppe*]

na·palm (nā′päm) *n.* A jellylike mixture that is combined
with gasoline to form an incendiary fuel, as in bombs, flame
throwers, etc.   [< *na*(*phthenic*) and *palm*(*itic*) acids, chemical compounds used in its manufacture]

nape (nāp) *n.* The back of the neck.   [Origin uncertain]

na·per·y (nā′pər·ē) *n.* *pl.* **·per·ies** Household linen, esp.
napkins, tablecloths, etc.   [See NAPKIN.]

Naph·ta·li (naf′tə·lī, -lē)   In the Old Testament, a son of Jacob and Bilhah, Rachel's maid.   *Gen.* xxx 7–8.   **— n. 1.** A
tribe of Israel.   **2.** The land occupied by the tribe of Naph-
tali.   [< Hebrew, my wrestling]

naph·tha (naf′thə, nap′-) *n.* **1.** A volatile, colorless petroleum distillate intermediate between gasoline and benzene,
used as a solvent, cleaning fluid, fuel, etc.   **2.** Any similar
substance obtained from another source, as from coal tar.   **3.**
Petroleum.   [< L < Gk. prob. < Persian *naft* petroleum]

naph·tha·lene (naf′thə·lēn, nap′-) *n.* *Chem.* A colorless,
odorous coal-tar compound, $C_{10}H_8$, used in the making of
dyes, moth balls, etc.   Also **naph′tha·line** (-lin, -lēn).

naph·thol (naf′thōl, -thol, nap′-) *n.* *Chem.* Either of two
compounds, $C_{10}H_7OH$, derived from naphthalene and used
in making dyes.   Also **naph·tol** (naf′tol, -tōl, nap′-).

nap·kin (nap′kin) *n.* **1.** A small, usu. square cloth or paper,
used at meals for wiping the hands and mouth or protecting
the clothes.   **2.** A small piece of toweling.   **3.** *Chiefly Brit.*
A diaper.   [ME *napekyn*, < L *mappa* a cloth]

na·po·le·on (nə·pō′lē·ən, *Fr.* nȧ·pô·lā·ôṅ′) *n.* **1.** A rich
pastry composed of layers of puff paste filled with cream,
custard, etc.   **2.** A former French gold coin.   **3.** A card game.
[after *Napoleon* Bonaparte]

Na·po·le·on·ic (nə·pō′lē·on′ik) *adj.* Characteristic of, pertaining to, or suggesting Napoleon Bonaparte.

Napoleonic Wars See table for WAR.

nappe (nap) *n.* **1.** The sheet of water overlying the top of a
weir.   **2.** *Geom.* In a cone, one of the two conical surfaces
divided by the vertex.   [< F, sheet]

nap·per¹ (nap′ər) *n.* One who takes naps.

nap·per² (nap′ər) *n.* One who or that which raises a nap.

nap·py¹ (nap′ē) *adj.* **·pi·er, ·pi·est 1.** Having or coated with
nap.   **2.** Having a coarse or kinky quality, as hair.

nap·py² (nap′ē) *n.* *pl.* **·pies** *Brit. Informal* A baby's
diaper.   Also **nap′pie**.   [< NAPKIN]

nar·cis·sism (när′sis·iz·əm, när·sis′iz·əm) *n.* **1.** Excessive
admiration for or fascination with oneself.   **2.** *Psychoanal.*
The infantile stage of development in which the self is the
object of one's erotic interest.   Also **nar·cism** (när′siz·əm).
[< NARCISSUS]   **— nar′cis·sist** *n.*   **— nar′cis·sis′tic** *adj.*

nar·cis·sus (när·sis′əs) *n.* *pl.* **·cis·sus·es** or **·cis·si** (-sis′ī)
Any of various bulbous flowering plants of the amaryllis
family, including the daffodil and jonquil.

Nar·cis·sus (när·sis′əs)   In Greek mythology, a youth who
fell in love with his own image in water and pined away for
it until he died and changed into the narcissus.

narco- *combining form* Torpor; insensibility.   Also, before
vowels, **narc-**.   [< Gk. *narkē* numbness]

nar·co·sis (när·kō′sis) *n.* Deep stupor produced by a drug.

nar·co·syn·the·sis (när′kō·sin′thə·sis) *n.* *Psychiatry* Therapy using narcotics to enable the patient to recall and relive
painful experiences and minimize their hidden effects.

nar·cot·ic (när·kot′ik) *n.* **1.** A drug, as opium or morphine,
that relieves pain and induces sleep, but may be habit-
forming.   **2.** One who is addicted to the use of narcotics.   **3.**
Anything that deadens or soothes.   **— adj. 1.** Capable of
producing narcosis or stupor.   **2.** Pertaining to, like, or induced by a narcotic or narcotics.   **3.** Of, relating to, or for
narcotic addicts or their treatment.   [< L < Gk. < *narkē*
torpor]   **— nar·cot′i·cal·ly** *adv.*

nar·co·tism (när′kə·tiz′əm) *n.* **1.** Addiction to narcotics.
2. Narcosis.

nar·co·tize (när′kə·tīz) *v.t.* **·tized, ·tiz·ing** To bring under
the influence of a narcotic; stupefy.   **— nar′co·ti·za′tion** *n.*

nard (närd) *n.* **1.** Spikenard.   **2.** Any of several aromatic
plants or roots formerly used in medicine.   [< OF < L <
Gk. *nardos*, prob. < Semitic]

nar·es (nâr′ēz) *n.* *pl. of* **nar·is** (nâr′is) *Anat.* Openings into
the nasal cavities; esp., the nostrils.   [< L, nostrils]   **—**
nar·i·al (nâr′ē·əl), **nar·ine** (nâr′in, -īn) *adj.*

nar·ghi·le (när′gə·lā) *n.* A hookah.   Also **nar′gi·le, nar′gi·**
leh.   [< F < Persian < *nārgil* coconut]

Nar·ra·gan·set (nar′ə·gan′sit) *n.* *pl.* **·set** or **·sets 1.** One
of a tribe of North American Indians of Algonquian stock,
formerly inhabiting Rhode Island.   **2.** The language of this
tribe.   Also **Nar′ra·gan′sett**.

nar·rate (na·rāt′, nar′āt) *v.* **·rat·ed, ·rat·ing** *v.t.* **1.** To tell
or relate, as a story.   **2.** To speak in accompaniment and explanation of (a motion picture, television program, etc.).   **—**
v.i. **3.** To tell a story, etc.   [< L *narratus*, pp. of *narrare* to
relate]   **— nar·ra·tor** or **nar·rat·er** (na·rāt′ər, nar′ā·tər) *n.*

nar·ra·tion (na·rā′shən) *n.* **1.** The act of narrating.   **2.** A
narrative.   **3.** An account that narrates, as in fiction, etc.

nar·ra·tive (nar′ə·tiv) *n.* **1.** Something narrated, as an
account, story, or tale.   **2.** The act, art, or process of narrating.   **— adj.** Of the nature of, pertaining to, or dealing with
narration: a *narrative* poem.   **— nar′ra·tive·ly** *adv.*

nar·row (nar′ō) *adj.* **1.** Having little width, esp. in comparison with length; not broad.   **2.** Limited or small, as in
extent or scope: *narrow* ambition.   **3.** Narrow-minded.   **4.**
Nearly unsuccessful or disastrous: a *narrow* escape.   **5.** Exhibiting or characterized by small means or resources.   **6.**
Minute or detailed; painstaking: *narrow* search.   **— v.t. & v.i.**
To make or become narrow or narrower, as in width or
scope.   **— n. 1.** *Usu. pl.* A narrow passage; esp., the nar-
rowest part of a strait, isthmus, etc.   **2.** A narrow or contracted part, as of a street or valley.   [OE *nearu*]   **— nar′·**
row·ness *n.*

nar·row-gauge (nar′ō·gāj′) *adj.* Designed for or having a
width of railroad track less than 56½ inches.   Also **nar′row·**
gage′, nar′row-gaged′, nar′row-gauged′.

narrow gauge A narrow-gauge railway, locomotive, or car.
Also **narrow gage.**

nar·row·ly (nar/ō-lē) *adv.* **1.** Barely; hardly. **2.** So as to be narrow. **3.** In a narrow manner.

nar·row-mind·ed (nar/ō-mīn/did) *adj.* Having or characterized by narrow views or sentiments; illiberal; bigoted. — **nar/row-mind/ed·ly** *adv.* — **nar/row-mind/ed·ness** *n.*

nar·whal (när/wəl -hwəl) *n.* A large, arctic cetacean having in the male a long, straight, spiral tusk, and valued for its oil and ivory. Also **nar/wal, nar·whale** (när/wäl/, -hwäl/). [< Dan. or Sw. *narhval*]

na·sal (nā/zəl) *adj.* **1.** Of or pertaining to the nose. **2.** *Phonet.* Produced with the voice passing partially or wholly through the nose, as (m), (n), and (ng), and the French nasal vowels. **3.** Characterized by or suggestive of a sound so produced. — *n.* **1.** *Phonet.* A nasal sound. **2.** *Anat.* A part of the nose, as a bone. [< NL < L *nasus* nose] — **na·sal·i·ty** (nā-zal/ə-tē) *n.* — **na/sal·ly** *adv.*

na·sal·ize (nā/zəl-īz) *v.* **·ized, ·iz·ing** *v.t.* **1.** To give a nasal sound to. — *v.i.* **2.** To produce nasal sounds instead of oral ones. — **na/sal·i·za/tion** *n.*

nas·cent (nā/sənt, nas/ənt) *adj.* **1.** Beginning to exist or develop; newly conceived. **2.** *Chem.* Of, pertaining to, or being in the nascent state. [< L *nascens, -centis,* ppr. of *nasci* to be born] — **nas/cence, nas/cen·cy** *n.*

nascent state *Chem.* The uncombined condition of an atom in its most active state at the moment of its liberation from a compound. Also **nascent condition.**

naso- *combining form* **1.** Nose. **2.** Nasal and. [< L *nasus* nose]

na·stur·tium (nə-stûr/shəm) *n.* **1.** Any of various garden plants with funnel-shaped flowers, commonly yellow, orange, or red. **2.** A rich yellow or reddish orange color. [< L, cress < *nasus* nose + *tortus,* pp. of *torquere* to twist]

nas·ty (nas/tē) *adj.* **·ti·er, ·ti·est 1.** Offensive to the sense of taste or smell; disgusting. **2.** Indecent; obscene: *nasty* language. **3.** Disagreeable; unpleasant: *nasty* weather. **4.** Mean, spiteful, or ill-natured: a *nasty* remark. **5.** Serious or painful: a *nasty* cut. [< Du. *nestig* or Sw. *naskug* filthy] — **nas/ti·ly** *adv.* — **nas/ti·ness** *n.*

-nasty *combining form Biol.* An automatic response to a (specified) stimulus, or in a (specified) direction or character. [< Gk. *nastos* close-pressed]

na·tal (nāt/l) *adj.* **1.** Of or pertaining to one's birth. **2.** *Poetic* Native: said of a place. [< L *nasci* to be born]

na·ta·to·ry (nā/tə-tôr/ē, -tō/rē) *adj.* Of, pertaining to, or adapted for swimming. Also **na/ta·to/ri·al.**

Natch·ez (nach/iz) *n. pl.* **Natch·ez** One of a tribe of North American Indians of Muskhogean stock, formerly inhabiting the lower Mississippi valley.

Na·than (nā/thən) In the Bible, a prophet who denounced David for the death of Uriah. II *Sam.* xii 1. [< Hebrew *nāthān* he gave]

Na·than·a·el (nə-than/ē-əl, -than/yəl) A disciple of Jesus. *John* xxi 1. [< Hebrew, gift of God]

na·tion (nā/shən) *n.* **1.** A body of persons associated with a particular territory, usu. organized under a government, and possessing a distinctive cultural and social way of life. **2.** A body of persons having a common origin and language. **3.** A tribe or federation, esp. of American Indians. [< F < L *nasci* to be born]
— **Syn. 1.** A *nation* is primarily the people under one government; a *state* is an independent *nation.* The words are often interchanged, but *nation* stresses ethnic unity, while *state* stresses political autonomy. We may speak of the many *nations* that made up the ancient Roman *state. Country* is primarily geographical, a region of the earth distinct from others by its topographical features or political character; Montenegro is a *country,* but no longer a *state.*

na·tion·al (nash/ən-əl, nash/nəl) *adj.* **1.** Of, belonging to, or representative of a nation as a whole. **2.** Characteristic of or peculiar to a particular nation. — *n.* A subject or citizen of a nation. [< F] — **na/tion·al·ly** *adv.*

national bank 1. *U.S.* A commercial bank organized by federal statute and chartered by the national government. **2.** A bank associated with the national finances.

National Guard An organized militia force of a State, a Territory, or the District of Columbia, maintained in part by the U.S. government and subject to federal service in national emergencies.

na·tion·al·ism (nash/ən-əl-is/əm, nash/nəl-) *n.* **1.** Devotion, often chauvinistic, to one's own nation. **2.** The belief or doctrine that among nations the common welfare is best served by independent rather than collective or cooperative action. **3.** A desire or movement for national independence. — **na/tion·al·ist** *adj. & n.* — **na/·tion·al·is/ti·cal·ly** *adv.*

na·tion·al·i·ty (nash/ən-al/ə-tē) *n. pl.* **·ties 1.** A body of people having the same traditions, language, or ethnic origin, and potentially or actually constituting a nation. **2.**

The state or fact of being related to a particular nation, as by birth or citizenship. **3.** National character or quality. **4.** The fact or quality of existing as a nation.

na·tion·al·ize (nash/ən-əl-īz/, nash/nəl-) *v.t.* **·ized, ·iz·ing 1.** To place (the industries, resources, etc., of a nation) under the control or ownership of the state. **2.** To make national, as in character or scope. **3.** To accept as a national; naturalize. Also *Brit.* **na/tion·al·ise/.** — **na/tion·al·i·za/tion** *n.* — **na/tion·al·iz/er** *n.*

National League See under MAJOR LEAGUE.

National Socialism See under NAZI.

Nation of Islam See under BLACK MUSLIM.

na·tion-wide (nā/shən-wīd/) *adj.* Extending throughout the nation.

na·tive (nā/tiv) *adj.* **1.** Born in a particular place or region: a *native* New Yorker. **2.** Linked to one by birth or by conditions existing at the time and place of one's birth: *native* language. **3.** Produced, originated, or grown in a particular region or country; indigenous. **4.** Of, pertaining to, or characteristic of any particular area or its inhabitants. **5.** Natural rather than acquired; inborn: *native* shrewdness. **6.** Of, pertaining to, or characteristic of the original inhabitants, chiefly nonwhites, of areas recently discovered or settled by foreigners: *native* ritual. **7.** Occurring in nature in a pure state: *native* copper. — *n.* **1.** A permanent or lifelong resident of a country or region. **2.** One who was born in a specified country or place. **3.** An original inhabitant of a country or region; aborigine. **4.** An animal, plant, or mineral found only in a specified country or place. [< F < L < *nasci* to be born.] — **na/tive·ly** *adv.* — **na/tive·ness** *n.*
— **Syn.** (adj.) **1, 3.** indigenous, endemic.

na·tive-born (nā/tiv-bôrn/) *adj.* Born in the region or country specified.

na·tiv·i·ty (nā-tiv/ə-tē, nə-) *n. pl.* **·ties 1.** Birth, esp. with regard to the time, place, or circumstances surrounding it. **2.** In astrology, a horoscope taken at the time of one's birth. [< OF < L *nativitas*]

Na·tiv·i·ty (nā-tiv/ə-tē, nə-) *n. pl.* **·ties 1.** The birth of Christ: with *the.* **2.** A representation in a painting, drama, etc., of the birth of Christ. **3.** Christmas Day.

NATO (nā/tō) North Atlantic Treaty Organization.

na·tri·um (nā/trē-əm) *n.* Sodium. [< NL < F, ult. < Gk. *nitron* niter]

nat·ty (nat/ē) *adj.* **·ti·er, ·ti·est** Neat and smart, as in dress or appearance: a *natty* vest. [? Akin to NEAT¹] — **nat/ti·ly** *adv.* — **nat/ti·ness** *n.*

nat·u·ral (nach/ər-əl, nach/rəl) *adj.* **1.** Produced by or existing in nature; not artificial. **2.** Of, pertaining to, or involving nature or the study of nature. **3.** Derived from or defined by nature: *natural* day. **4.** Belonging to or existing in one's nature; innate: *natural* talent. **5.** Being so because of one's inherent ability, disposition, etc.: a *natural* athlete. **6.** Conforming to nature or to its usual or expected course: death from *natural* causes. **7.** Closely resembling nature; lifelike: a *natural* pose. **8.** Untouched by man or by the influences of civilization; wild. **9.** Free from affectation or awkwardness: *natural* manner. **10.** Derived from or consistent with the nature or essence of a thing; expected: *natural* conclusion. **11.** *Music* **a** Not sharped or flatted. **b** Denoting a scale or mode that is unaltered by accidentals. **12.** Physical or actual, as distinguished from spiritual, etc.: *natural* man. **13.** Determined by innate moral conviction: *natural* rights. **14.** Related by blood rather than through adoption: *natural* mother. **15.** Founded upon reason rather than faith: *natural* religion. **16.** Born out of wedlock. — *n.* **1.** *Music* **a** A note that is affected by neither a sharp nor a flat. **b** A character (♮) that cancels a sharp or flat at a specific line or space on the staff. **2.** In keyboard musical instruments, a white key. **3.** *U.S. Informal* One who or that which is naturally gifted, esp., well suited to some purpose, or obviously destined for success. [< F < L < *natura* nature, character] — **nat/u·ral·ness** *n.*

natural gas A gas consisting chiefly of methane, generated naturally in underground oil deposits and used as a fuel.

natural history The observation and study of the phenomena of the material universe, esp. the biological and earth sciences.

nat·u·ral·ism (nach/ər-əl-iz/əm, nach/rəl-) *n.* **1.** Close adherence to nature or human life in literature, painting, etc. **2.** *Philos.* The doctrine that all phenomena are derived from natural causes and can be explained by scientific laws. **3.** Action or thought derived exclusively from natural desires and instincts.

nat·u·ral·ist (nach/ər-əl-ist, nach/rəl-) *n.* **1.** One who is versed in natural history, as a zoologist or botanist. **2.** An adherent of the doctrine of naturalism.

nat·u·ral·is·tic (nach/ər-əl-is/tik, nach/rəl-) *adj.* **1.** Of, according to, or characteristic of naturalism. **2.** In accordance with or closely resembling nature.   **3.** Of or pertaining to naturalists or natural history.

nat·u·ral·ize (nach′ər-əl-īz′, nach′rəl-) *v.* **·ized, ·iz·ing** *v.t.* **1.** To confer the rights and privileges of citizenship upon, as an alien.   **2.** To adopt (a foreign word, custom, etc.) into the common use of a country or area.   **3.** To adapt (a foreign plant, animal, etc.) to the environment of a country or area.   **4.** To explain by natural laws: to *naturalize* a miracle.   **5.** To make natural or lifelike.   — *v.i.* **6.** To become as if native; adapt.   **7.** To observe or study nature. Also *Brit.* **nat′u·ral·ise′**.   — **nat·u·ral·i·za′tion** *n.*

nat·u·ral·ly (nach′ər-əl-ē, nach′rəl-ē) *adv.* **1.** In a natural, normal, or expected manner.   **2.** By inherent nature.   **3.** Of course; certainly.

natural number *Math.* A positive integer, as 1, 2, 3, etc.

natural philosophy **1.** The study of nature in general.   **2.** The physical sciences collectively.

natural resource *Usu. pl.* **1.** A source of wealth provided by nature, as forests, minerals, and water supply.   **2.** Any natural ability or talent.

natural science **1.** The sciences collectively that deal with the physical universe.   **2.** Any one of these sciences, as biology, chemistry, or physics.

natural selection *Biol.* The process whereby individual variations advantageous to an organism in a certain environment tend to become perpetuated in later generations; survival of the fittest forms.

na·ture (nā′chər) *n.* **1.** The essential character of something: the *nature* of democracy.   **2.** *Sometimes cap.* The overall pattern or system of natural objects, existences, forces, events, etc.; also, the principle or power that appears to guide it: laws of *nature*.   **3.** The entire material universe and its phenomena.   **4.** The basic character or disposition of a person or animal.   **5.** *Sometimes cap.* A force, drive, or tendency that influences or determines the behavior or condition of a person or thing; instinct.   **6.** Sort; kind; variety: nothing of that *nature*.   **7.** A wild, naked, or uncivilized condition.   **8.** That which is within the accepted or legal limits of morality: an act against *nature*.   **9.** Natural aspect or appearance, as of a person or scene.   — **by nature** By birth or disposition.   [< OF < L < *nasci* to be born]

-natured *combining form* Possessing a (specified) nature, disposition, or temperament: *good-natured*.

naught (nôt) *n.* **1.** Nothing.   **2.** A cipher; zero; the character 0. Also spelled *nought*.   [OE < *nā* not + *wiht* thing]

naugh·ty (nô′tē) *adj.* **·ti·er, ·ti·est** **1.** Mischievous; disobedient; bad.   **2.** Indecent or improper: a *naughty* word.   — **naugh′ti·ly** *adv.*   — **naugh′ti·ness** *n.*

nau·se·a (nô′zē-ə, -zhə, -sē-ə, -shə) *n.* **1.** A sick feeling in the stomach accompanied by an impulse to vomit; queasiness.   **2.** Strong disgust or loathing.   [< L < Gk. *nausia, nautia* seasickness]

nau·se·ate (nô′zē-āt, -sē-, -zhē-, -shē-) *v.t. & v.i.* **·at·ed, ·at·ing** To affect with or feel nausea or disgust.

nau·seous (nô′shəs, -zhē-əs, -zē-əs, -sē-əs) *adj.* **1.** Affected with nausea; queasy; sick.   **2.** Nauseating; disgusting.   — **nau′seous·ly** *adv.*   — **nau′seous·ness** *n.*

nau·ti·cal (nô′ti-kəl) *adj.* Pertaining to or involving ships, seamen, or navigation.   — **Syn.** See MARINE.   [< L < Gk. < *naus* ship]   — **nau′ti·cal·ly** *adv.*

nau·ti·lus (nô′tə-ləs) *n.* *pl.* **·lus·es** or **·li** (-lī) **1.** Any of a group of mollusks with a spiral shell whose chambers are lined with mother-of-pearl; esp., the **chambered** or **pearly nautilus**.   **2.** The paper nautilus.   [< L < Gk. *nautilos* sailor]

Nav·a·ho (nav′ə-hō) *n.* *pl.* **·hos** or **·hoes** or **·ho** One of a tribe of North American Indians now living on reservations in Arizona, New Mexico, and Utah. Also **Nav′a·jo**.

na·val (nā′vəl) *adj.* **1.** Of, involving, or having a navy: a *naval* power.   **2.** Of or pertaining to ships: a *naval* convoy.   — **Syn.** See MARINE.   [< L < *navis* ship]

CHAMBERED NAUTILUS
(Cross-section; diameter to 10 inches)

nave¹ (nāv) *n.* *Archit.* The main body of a church, situated between the side aisles.   [< L *navis* ship]

nave² (nāv) *n.* The hub of a wheel.   [OE *nafu*]

na·vel (nā′vəl) *n.* **1.** The depression on the abdomen where the umbilical cord was attached; umbilicus.   **2.** A central part or point.   [OE < *nafu* nave²]

navel orange An orange, usu. seedless, having a navellike depression that contains a small, secondary fruit.

nav·i·cert (nav′ə-sûrt′) *n. Brit.* A safe-conduct authorizing a vessel of a friendly or neutral nation to pass through a naval blockade.

nav·i·ga·ble (nav′ə-gə-həl) *adj.* Capable of being navigated; as: **a** Broad or deep enough to admit of passage: said of a body of water. **b** Capable of being steered.   — **nav′i·ga·bil′i·ty, nav′i·ga·ble·ness** *n.*   — **nav′i·ga·bly** *adv.*

nav·i·gate (nav′ə-gāt) *v.* **·gat·ed, ·gat·ing** *v.t.* **1.** To travel or move across, over, on, or through, as by ship or aircraft.   **2.** To plot the course of (a ship, aircraft, etc.).   **3.** To manage or direct the course of; guide: to *navigate* a missile.   — *v.i.* **4.** To guide or steer a ship, aircraft, etc.   **5.** To compute and plot the course, position, etc., as of a ship or aircraft.   **6.** To travel by ship.   [< L < *navis* boat + *agere* to direct]

nav·i·ga·tion (nav′ə-gā′shən) *n.* **1.** The act or practice of navigating.   **2.** The art or science of charting the course of ships, aircraft, etc.   — **nav′i·ga′tion·al** *adj.*

navigation light *Aeron.* One of the colored lights on an aircraft, indicating its size, position, and course at night: also called *running light*.

nav·i·ga·tor (nav′ə-gā′tər) *n.* **1.** One who navigates.   **2.** One who is trained in or practices navigation.   [< L]

nav·vy (nav′ē) *n.* *pl.* **·vies** *Brit.* A laborer, esp. in construction work on railways, roads, etc.   [< NAVIGATOR]

na·vy (nā′vē) *n.* *pl.* **·vies** **1.** *Often cap.* The entire military sea force of a country, including vessels, servicemen, yards, etc.; also, the agency of government charged with its supervision.   **2.** The warships of a nation, taken collectively.   **3.** Navy blue.   [< OF < L *navis* ship]

navy bean A small, dried, white bean related to the common kidney bean.   [from its use in the U.S. Navy]

navy blue A very dark blue: also *navy*.

Navy Cross A decoration in the form of a bronze cross, awarded by the U.S. Navy for extraordinary heroism in action against the enemy. See DECORATION.

navy yard A government-owned dockyard for the building, repairing, docking, and equipping of warships.

nay (nā) *adv.* **1.** *Archaic* No.   **2.** Not exactly that, but rather: She is a pretty, *nay*, a beautiful woman.   — *n.* **1.** A negative vote or voter: opposed to *yea*.   **2.** A denial or refusal.   [ME < ON < *ne* not + *ei* ever]

Naz·a·rene (naz′ə-rēn′) *n.* **1.** A native or inhabitant of Nazareth.   **2.** A Christian.   **3.** One of a sect of early Christians of Jewish origin who continued to observe much of the Jewish ritual.   — **the Nazarene** Jesus Christ.   — *adj.* Of Nazareth or the Nazarenes. Also **Naz′a·re′an** (-rē′ən).

Naz·a·rite (naz′ə-rīt) *n.* An ancient Hebrew who took vows of abstinence. *Num.* vi. Also **Naz′i·rite.**   [< Hebrew < *nāzar* to abstain]

na·zi (nä′tsē, nat′sē, nä′zē) *Often cap. n.* *pl.* **·zis** One who advocates or practices Nazism.   — *adj.* Of the nature of, pertaining to, or involving Nazism.   [< NAZI]

Na·zi (nä′tsē, nat′sē, nä′zē) *n.* *pl.* **·zis** A member of the National Socialist German Workers' Party, founded in 1919, whose fascistic program (called **National Socialism**) was dominant in Germany from 1933 to 1945 under the dictatorship of Hitler.   — *adj.* **1.** Of or pertaining to the Nazis or their party.   **2.** Caused or committed by Nazis: *Nazi* atrocities.   [< G, short for *nationalsozialist* National Socialist]   — **Na′zism** or **Na′zi·ism** *n.*

Ne·an·der·thal (nē-an′dər-täl, -thôl, -thol; *Ger.* nā-än′dər-täl) *adj.* Of or characteristic of Neanderthal man.

Neanderthal man *Anthropol.* An extinct species of man that typifies the paleolithic cavedwellers preceding modern man.   [< G *Neanderthal*, Neander valley, Germany, where the first bones of this species were found]

neap (nēp) *adj.* Designating or pertaining to a neap tide.   — *n.* A neap tide.   [OE *nēp-* in *nēpflod* low tide]

Ne·a·pol·i·tan (nē′ə-pol′ə-tən) *adj.* Of, relating to, or characteristic of Naples.   — *n.* A native or resident of Naples.

neap tide The tide occurring shortly after the first and third quarters of the moon, when the rise and fall are minimal: also called *neap*.

near (nir) *adv.* **1.** At, to, or within a little distance; not remote in place, time, or degree.   **2.** Nearly; almost: a team of *near* championship caliber.   **3.** In a close relation; intimately.   **4.** Stingily or frugally.   — *adj.* **1.** Not distant in place, time, or degree.   **2.** Closely approximating; almost achieved: a *near* success.   **3.** Narrow; close: a *near* escape.   **4.** Closely related, as by blood: someone *near* and dear.   **5.** Closely touching one's interests or affections; intimate.   **6.** That saves distance or time; short; direct.   **7.** Stingy; miserly.   **8.** On the left: used in riding or driving: the *near* ox: opposed to *off*.   — *prep.* Close by or to.   — *v.t. & v.i.* To come or draw near (to); approach.   [OE *nēar*, compar. of *nēah* nigh]   — **near′ness** *n.*

near·by (nir′bī′) *adj. & adv.* Close by; near; adjacent.

Near East The countries lying east of the Mediterranean, mostly in SW Asia, including Turkey, Syria, Lebanon, Israel, Jordan, Saudi Arabia, etc., and sometimes the Balkans and Egypt.

near·ly (nir′lē) *adv.* **1.** Almost; practically.   **2.** Closely, as in distance, time, degree, similarity, etc.

near·sight·ed (nir′sī′tid) *adj.* Able to see distinctly at short distances only; myopic.   — **near′sight′ed·ly** *adv.*   — **near′sight′ed·ness** *n.*

neat (nēt) *adj.* **1.** Characterized by or in a state of orderliness, tidiness, and cleanliness.   **2.** Free from sloppiness, vagueness, or embellishment; precise. **3.** Ingeniously done or said; clever: a *neat trick*. **4.** Free from admixture; undiluted, as liquor. **5.** Remaining after all deductions; net. [< OF < L *nitidus* shining] — **neat'ly** *adv.* — **neat'ness** *n.*

'neath (nēth) *prep. Dial.* or *Poetic* Beneath. Also **neath.**

neat's-foot oil (nēts'fŏŏt') A pale yellow oil obtained by boiling the shinbones and feet of cattle, used as a lubricant and softening agent for leather.

Neb·u·chad·nez·zar (neb'yŏŏ·kəd·nez'ər), died 562 B.C., king of Babylonia 605–562 B.C.; conquered Jerusalem. II *Kings* xxiv and xxv. Also **Neb'u·chad·rez'zar** (-rez'ər).

neb·u·la (neb'yə·lə) *n. pl.* **·lae** (-lē) or **·las** *Astron.* Any interstellar mass of cloudlike appearance and vast extent, often luminous, and composed of gaseous matter. [< L, vapor, mist] — **neb'u·lar** *adj.*

nebular hypothesis *Astron.* The hypothesis that the solar system was formed from the consolidation of great masses of matter thrown off by a rotating nebula.

neb·u·lose (neb'yə·lōs) *adj.* Nebulous.

neb·u·los·i·ty (neb'yə·los'ə·tē) *n. pl.* **·ties 1.** The state or quality of being nebulous. **2.** A nebula.

neb·u·lous (neb'yə·ləs) *adj.* **1.** Vague or confused; hazy. **2.** Cloudlike; misty. **3.** Of, pertaining to, or like a nebula. — **neb'u·lous·ly** *adv.* — **neb'u·lous·ness** *n.*

nec·es·sar·i·ly (nes'ə·ser'ə·lē) *adv.* **1.** As a necessary consequence. **2.** Of necessity; unavoidably.

nec·es·sar·y (nes'ə·ser'ē) *adj.* **1.** Absolutely needed to accomplish a certain result; essential. **2.** Being of such a nature that it must exist or occur; inevitable: a *necessary* belief. **3.** Caused by or acting under obligation or compulsion; required. **4.** That cannot be logically denied. — *n. pl.* **·sar·ies** Often *pl.* That which is indispensable; an essential requisite: the *necessaries* of life.

ne·ces·si·tate (nə·ses'ə·tāt) *v.t.* **·tat·ed, ·tat·ing 1.** To make necessary. **2.** To compel or oblige: No man is *necessitated* to lie. — **ne·ces'si·ta'tion** *n.* — **ne·ces'si·ta'tive** *adj.*

ne·ces·si·tous (nə·ses'ə·təs) *adj.* **1.** Extremely needy; destitute; poverty-stricken. **2.** Urgent; compelling. — **ne·ces'si·tous·ly** *adv.* — **ne·ces'si·tous·ness** *n.*

ne·ces·si·ty (nə·ses'ə·tē) *n. pl.* **·ties 1.** Often *pl.* That which is indispensable or requisite, esp. toward the attainment of some end. **2.** The quality, conditon, or fact of being necessary. **3.** The conditions that make compulsory a particular course of action: to resign out of *necessity*. **4.** Urgent or desperate need, as because of poverty or accident; also, a time of such need. **5.** That which is unavoidable because it is part of an invariable process, as in nature, logic, etc.; also, the process itself. — **of necessity** By necessity; inevitably. [< OF < L *necessitas*]

neck (nek) *n.* **1.** *Anat.* **a** The part of an animal that connects the head with the trunk. **b** Any similarly constricted part of an organ, bone, etc.: the *neck* of the uterus. ◆ Collateral adjective: *cervical*. **2.** The narrowed part of an object, esp. if near one end: the *neck* of a bottle. **3.** Something likened to a neck; as: **a** A narrow passage of water between two larger bodies of water. **b** A narrow strip of land, as a peninsula, isthmus, or cape. **4.** The part of a garment close to or covering the neck. **5.** The part of a violin, guitar, etc., that carries the fingerboard and tuning pegs. **6.** *Archit.* The upper part of the shaft of a column, just below the capital. — **neck and neck** Abreast of one another, as horses in a race. — **neck of the woods** *U.S. Informal* A neighborhood or region. — **to save one's (own) neck** To extricate oneself from difficult or dangerous circumstances, often without concern for others. — *v.i.* **1.** *U.S. Slang* To kiss and caress in lovemaking. — *v.t.* **2.** *U.S. Slang* To make love to (someone) in such a manner. [OE *hnecca*]

neck·band (nek'band') *n.* **1.** The part of a garment that fits around the neck. **2.** A band around the neck.

necked (nekt) *adj.* **1.** Having a neck or necks. **2.** Having or characterized by (a specified kind of) neck or (a specified number of) necks: used in combination: *long-necked*.

neck·er·chief (nek'ər·chif) *n.* A kerchief for the neck.

neck·ing (nek'ing) *n. U.S. Slang* Kissing and caressing in lovemaking.

neck·lace (nek'lis) *n.* An ornament worn around the neck and usu. consisting of a string of beads, shells gems, etc.

neck·line (nek'līn') *n.* The line or contour formed by the fit of a garment around the neck.

neck·piece (nek'pēs') *n.* An article of clothing, usu. of fur, worn around the neck like a scarf.

neck·tie (nek'tī') *n.* **1.** A strip of material worn knotted around the neck or collar and hanging down the front of a shirt. **2.** Any bow or tie worn under the chin.

neck·wear (nek'wâr') *n.* Articles worn around the neck, as ties, collars, mufflers, etc.

necro- *combining form* Corpse; the dead; death. Also, before vowels, **necr-.** [< Gk. *nekros* corpse]

ne·crol·o·gy (ne·krol'ə·jē) *n. pl.* **·gies 1.** A list of persons who have died in a certain place or time. **2.** An obituary notice. — **nec·ro·log·ic** (nek'rə·loj'ik) or **·i·cal** *adj.* — **nec'ro·log'i·cal·ly** *adv.* — **ne·crol'o·gist** *n.*

nec·ro·man·cy (nek'rə·man'sē) *n.* **1.** The art of divining the future through alleged communication with the dead. **2.** Black magic; sorcery. [ME < OF < L < Gk. <*nekros* corpse + *manteia* divination] — **nec'ro·man'cer** *n.* — **nec'ro·man'tic** *adj.*

nec·ro·phil·i·a (nek'rō·fil'ē·ə) *n.* An abnormal attraction, esp. of an erotic nature, to corpses. — **nec·ro·phile** (nek'rə·fīl, -fil) *n.* — **nec'ro·phil'ic** *adj.*

ne·crop·o·lis (ne·krop'ə·lis) *n.* A cemetery. [< Gk. < *nekros* corpse + *polis* city]

ne·cro·sis (ne·krō'sis) *n.* **1.** *Pathol.* The death of tissue in a living animal, resulting from infection or burns; gangrene. **2.** *Bot.* A decay and death of plant tissue. [< Gk. *nekrōsis* death] — **ne·crot'ic** (-krot'ik) *adj.*

nec·tar (nek'tər) *n.* **1.** In Greek mythology, the drink of the gods. **2.** Any delicious drink. **3.** *Bot.* The saccharine secretion of plants, collected by bees to make honey. [< L < Gk. *nektar*] — **nec·tar·e·an** (nek·târ'ē·ən), **nec·tar·e·ous** (nek·târ'ē·əs), **nec·tar·ous** (nek'tər·əs) *adj.*

nec·tar·ine (nek'tə·rēn', nek'tə·rēn) *n.* A variety of peach having a smooth, waxy skin and a firm pulp.

nec·ta·ry (nek'tər·ē) *n. pl.* **·ries** *Bot.* A gland that secretes nectar.

née (nā) *adj.* Born with the name of: used chiefly to note the maiden name of a married woman: Mrs. Mary Lincoln, *née* Todd. Also **nee.** [< F, pp. fem. of *naître* to be born]

need (nēd) *v.t.* **1.** To have an urgent or essential use for (something lacking); want; require. — *v.i.* **2.** To be in want. **3.** To be obliged or compelled; have to: He need not go. — *n.* **1.** The fact, quality, or condition of lacking or feeling the lack of something necessary or desirable. **2.** A desire or longing: the *need* for revenge. **3.** Obligation; necessity: no *need* to be afraid. **4.** A condition of want, danger, or helplessness. **5.** Something wanted or required: modest *needs.* **6.** Poverty; hardship. — **Syn.** See POVERTY. [OE *nied, nēd*] — **need'er** *n.*

need·ful (nēd'fəl) *adj.* **1.** Needed; requisite; necessary. **2.** *Archaic* Needy. — **need'ful·ly** *adv.* — **need'ful·ness** *n.*

need·i·ness (nē'dē·nis, -di·nis) *n.* The state of being needy; poverty; want.

nee·dle (nēd'l) *n.* **1.** A small, slender, pointed instrument, usu. of steel, with an eye at one end to carry thread through fabric in sewing. **2.** A hypodermic needle. **3.** A pointer or index, as in a gauge or compass. **4.** A small, pointed instrument of steel, diamond, etc., that traverses the grooves of a phonograph record and transmits sound vibrations: sometimes called *stylus.* **5.** A slender, pointed rod of steel, bone, etc., used in knitting; also, a similar, hooked rod used in crocheting. **6.** A needleshaped leaf, as that of a pine tree. **7.** Any object suggesting a needle in shape. **8.** A fine-pointed instrument used in etching. **9.** *Mech.* A needle valve (which see). — **on the needle** *U.S. Slang* Addicted to narcotics. — *v.* **·dled, ·dling** *v.t.* **1.** To sew or pierce with a needle. **2.** *Informal* To tease or heckle repeatedly. **3.** *U.S. Informal* To increase the alcoholic content of: to *needle* the beer. — *v.i.* **4.** To sew or work with a needle. **5.** To crystallize in the form of needles. [OE *nædle*]

nee·dle·point (nēd'l·point') *n.* **1.** Embroidery on canvas, as in a tapestry; also, a single stitch. **2.** Lace made with a sewing needle on a paper pattern: also called *point lace.*

need·less (nēd'lis) *adj.* Not needed or necessary; useless. — **need'less·ly** *adv.* — **need'less·ness** *n.*

needle valve *Mech.* A valve having a needlelike plug capable of closely regulating the flow of a liquid or gas.

nee·dle·wom·an (nēd'l·wŏŏm'ən) *n. pl.* **·wom·en** (-wim'in) A seamstress.

nee·dle·work (nēd'l·wûrk') *n.* Work done with a needle.

need·n't (nēd'nt) Need not.

needs (nēdz) *adv. Archaic* Of necessity: often with *must*: He *needs* must go. [OE *nīedes*]

need·y (nē'dē) *adj.* **need·i·er, need·i·est** Being in need, want, or poverty; necessitous.

ne'er (nâr) *adv. Poetic* Never.

ne'er-do-well (nâr'dōō·wel') *n.* A worthless, unreliable person. — *adj.* Shiftless; good-for-nothing.

ne·far·i·ous (ni·fâr'ē·əs) *adj.* Extremely wicked; vile. [< L < *ne-* not + *fas* divine law] — **ne·far'i·ous·ly** *adv.* — **ne·far'i·ous·ness** *n.*

ne·gate (ni·gāt', nē'gāt) *v.t.* **gat·ed, ·gat·ing 1.** To render ineffective or void; nullify. **2.** To deny; contradict; rule out. [< L *negatus*, pp. of *negare* to deny]

ne·ga·tion (ni·gā'shən) *n.* **1.** The absence or opposite of something: Sleep is the *negation* of consciousness. **2.** The act of denying or contradicting. **3.** That which is negative.

neg·a·tive (neg′ə-tiv) *adj.* **1.** Expressing, containing, or characterized by negation, denial, or refusal. **2.** Marked by the absence of positive or affirmative qualities: a *negative* attitude. **3.** *Math.* Less than zero; to be subtracted; minus. **4.** *Electr.* Having the kind of electricity exhibited by a resinous object when rubbed with wool. **5.** *Med.* Not indicating the presence of a particular disease, organism, etc.: a *negative* blood test. **6.** *Photog.* Having the lights and darks reversed. — *n.* **1.** *Photog.* An image showing the lights and darks reversed; also, the film or plate on which it appears. **2.** An expression of denial or refusal. **3.** The side of a question that denies or contradicts what the other side affirms, as in a debate. **4.** *Math.* A negative symbol or quantity. **5.** *Electr.* A negative pole, plate, terminal, etc. **6.** *Gram.* A negative particle, as *not*. — *adv.* No; not so: a military usage. — **double negative** *Gram.* The use of two negatives in the same statement, as in "I didn't see nobody." ◆ This usage is now considered nonstandard. Such statements as "I am not unhappy," however, are standard English and have the effect of weak affirmatives. — **in the negative 1.** By or with an expression of refusal; no. **2.** On the negative or opposing side. — *v.t.* **-tived, -tiv·ing 1.** reject; veto. **2.** To deny; contradict. **3.** To prove to be false. **4.** To make ineffective. [< F < L *negare* to deny] — **neg′a·tive·ly** *adv.* — **neg′a·tive·ness, neg′a·tiv′i·ty** *n.*

neg·a·tiv·ism (neg′ə-tiv-iz′əm) *n.* **1.** An attitude characterized by the questioning of traditional beliefs; skepticism. **2.** A tendency to deny, contradict, etc. **3.** *Psychol.* An attitude characterized by resistance to suggestion. — **neg′a·tiv·ist** *n. & adj.* — **neg′a·tiv·is′tic** *adj.*

neg·lect (ni-glekt′) *v.t.* **1.** To fail to heed or take note of; disregard. **2.** To fail to give proper attention to: to *neglect* one's business. **3.** To fail to do or perform; leave undone. — *n.* **1.** Habitual want of attention or care; negligence. **2.** The act of neglecting, or the state of being neglected. **3.** An instance of neglect. [< L < *nec-* not + *legere* to gather] — **neg·lect′er** or **neg·lec′tor** *n.*

neg·lect·ful (ni-glekt′fəl) *adj.* Exhibiting or indicating neglect. — **neg·lect′ful·ly** *adv.* — **neg·lect′ful·ness** *n.*

neg·li·gee (neg′li-zhā′, neg′li-zhā) *n.* **1.** A loose, flowing, usu. decorative dressing gown worn by women. **2.** Any informal attire. Also **neg·li·gée′**, *French* **né·gli·gé** (nā-glē-zhā′). [< F *négligé*, pp. of *négliger* to neglect]

neg·li·gence (neg′lə-jəns) *n.* **1.** The state, quality, or fact of being negligent. **2.** A negligent act or omission. [< OF]

neg·li·gent (neg′lə-jənt) *adj.* **1.** Habitually neglecting to do what ought to be done; neglectful. **2.** Free-and-easy; informal; nonchalant. — **neg′li·gent·ly** *adv.*

neg·li·gi·ble (neg′lə-jə-bəl) *adj.* Not worth considering, as because of trifling size, amount, or extent. — **neg′li·gi·bil′i·ty, neg′li·gi·ble·ness** *n.* — **neg′li·gi·bly** *adv.*

ne·go·ti·a·ble (ni-gō′shē-ə-bəl, -shə-bəl) *adj.* **1.** Capable of being negotiated. **2.** Open to negotiation. **3.** That can be legally transferred to another party. — **ne·go′ti·a·bil′i·ty** *n.*

ne·go·ti·ate (ni-gō′shē-āt) *v.* **-at·ed, -at·ing** *v.i.* **1.** To confer with another party with the aim of reaching an agreement. — *v.t.* **2.** To arrange or conclude by negotiation. **3.** To transfer (a note, bond, etc.) to another for a value received; sell. **4.** To manage to execute, traverse, or cope with (something difficult): to *negotiate* a steep hill. [< L *negotiari* to do business] — **ne·go′ti·a·tor** *n.*

ne·go·ti·a·tion (ni-gō′shē-ā′shən) *n.* **1.** The act or process of negotiating. **2.** A conference or discussion designed to produce an agreement.

Ne·gri·to (ni-grē′tō) *n. pl.* **-tos** or **-toes** *Anthropol.* One of the Pygmy peoples of the Malay Peninsula, the Philippine Islands, central Africa, and southeast Asia. [< Sp., dim. of *negro* black]

ne·gri·tude (nē′grə-tōōd′, -tyōōd′) *n. Often cap.* **1.** Awareness of and pride in one's black African heritage. **2.** The fact of being a Negro; Negroness. Also *French* **né·gri·tude** (nā′grə-tüd′). [< F < L *niger* black]

Ne·gro (nē′grō) *n. pl.* **-groes 1.** A member of the Negroid ethnic division of mankind. **2.** One who is of Negroid stock or has Negro ancestors. — *adj.* **1.** Of, pertaining to, or having the characteristics of a Negro or Negroes. **2.** Of Negroid ethnic stock. Also **ne′gro.** [< Sp. < L *niger* black]

Ne·groid (nē′groid) *adj.* **1.** *Anthropol.* Of, pertaining to, or belonging to a major ethnic division of the human species characterized by skin color ranging from dark brown to almost black. **2.** Resembling, related to, or characteristic of Negroes. — *n.* A Negroid person.

Ne·gro·ness (nē′grō-nis) *n.* The fact of being a Negro.

Ne·he·mi·ah (nē′hə-mī′ə) Fifth-century B.C. Hebrew statesman and historian. — *n.* A book of the Old Testament: also, in the Douai Bible, II *Esdras.* [< Hebrew *Nehemyāh* Jehovah comforts]

neigh (nā) *v.i.* To utter the cry of a horse; whinny. — *n.* The cry of a horse. [OE *hnǣgan;* imit.]

neigh·bor (nā′bər) *n.* **1.** One who lives near another. **2.** One who or that which is near another. **3.** *Chiefly Dial.*

Friend; mister: a term of address. — *adj.* Living nearby. — *v.t. & v.i.* To live or be near to or next to; adjoin. Also *Brit.* **neigh′bour.** [OE < *nēah* near + *gebur* dweller]

neigh·bor·hood (nā′bər-hŏŏd) *n.* **1.** A comparatively small region possessing some specific quality or character. **2.** The people who live in such a region. **3.** Any region or area; vicinity. Also *Brit.* **neigh′bour·hood.** — **in the neighborhood of 1.** Near. **2.** *Informal* Approximately.

neigh·bor·ing (nā′bər-ing) *adj.* Situated or living nearby.

neigh·bor·ly (nā′bər-lē) *adj.* Like a good neighbor; kind, sociable, etc. — **neigh′bor·li·ness** *n.*

nei·ther (nē′thər, nī′-) *adj.* Not the one nor the other; not either. — *pron.* Not the one nor the other: *Neither* of the hats is becoming. — *conj.* **1.** Not either; not: used with the correlative *nor* to list alternatives and to signify their negation: He *neither* reads nor writes. **2.** Nor yet: He cannot write: *neither* can he read. ◆ See usage note under EITHER. [ME *naither, neyther* < OE *nāhwaether*]

nemato- *combining form* Thread; filament: also, before vowels, **nemat-.** Also **nema-.** [< Gk. *nēma, -matos* thread]

nem·a·tode (nem′ə-tōd) *Zool. adj.* Of or belonging to a phylum or class of roundworms, as the hookworm. — *n.* A nematode worm. [< NL *Nematoda*]

nem·e·sis (nem′ə-sis) *n. pl.* **-ses** (-sēz) **1.** An unusually tenacious opponent or antagonist. **2.** An instrument of vengeance. [< Gk., retributive justice]

Nem·e·sis (nem′ə-sis) In Greek mythology, the goddess of retributive justice or vengeance. [< NEMESIS]

neo- *combining form* New; recent; a modern or modified form of. Also, before vowels, usu. **ne-.** [< Gk. < *neos* new]

ne·o·clas·sic (nē′ō-klas′ik) *adj.* Of, pertaining to, or denoting a revival of classical style in literature, art, music, etc. Also **ne′o·clas′si·cal.** — **ne·o·clas′si·cism** *n.* — **ne′o·clas′si·cist** *n.*

ne·o·dym·i·um (nē′ō-dim′ē-əm) *n.* A metallic element (symbol Nd) forming rose-colored salts, found in combination with cerium, etc. See ELEMENT. [< NEO- + (DI)DYMIUM]

Ne·o·lith·ic (nē′ə-lith′ik) *adj. Anthropol.* Of or pertaining to the period of human culture following the Mesolithic, characterized by polished stone implements and a settled agriculture. [< Gk. *neos* new + *lithos* stone]

ne·ol·o·gism (nē-ol′ə-jiz′əm) *n.* **1.** A new word or phrase. **2.** The use of new words or of new meanings for old words. Also **ne·ol′o·gy.** [< F *néologisme*] — **ne·ol′o·gist** *n.* — **ne·ol′o·gis′tic** or **-ti·cal** *adj.*

ne·o·my·cin (nē′ō-mī′sin) *n.* An antibiotic related to streptomycin, used in the treatment of certain infections.

ne·on (nē′on) *n.* A gaseous element (symbol Ne) occurring in the atmosphere in very small amounts. See ELEMENT. — *adj.* **1.** Of or pertaining to neon. **2.** Composed of or employing neon. [< NL < Gk., neut. of *neos* new]

ne·o·phyte (nē′ə-fīt) *n.* **1.** A recent convert, esp. in the early Christian Church. **2.** Any beginner. [< LL < Gk. *neophytos* newly planted] — **ne′o·phyt′ic** (-fit′ik) *adj.*

ne·o·plasm (nē′ə-plaz′əm) *n. Pathol.* Any abnormal growth of tissue in the body; a tumor. — **ne′o·plas′tic** *adj.*

ne·o·prene (nē′ə-prēn) *n. Chem.* Any of various types of synthetic rubber. [< NEO- + (CHLORO)PRENE]

Nep·a·lese (nep′ə-lēz′, -lēs′) *adj.* Of Nepal, its people, or their culture. — *n.* A native or inhabitant of Nepal.

ne·pen·the (ni-pen′thē) *n.* **1.** A drug or potion supposed by the ancient Greeks to banish pain and sorrow. **2.** Anything causing oblivion. [< L < Gk. < *nē-* not + *penthos* sorrow]

neph·ew (nef′yōō, *esp. Brit.* nev′yōō) *n.* The son of a brother or brother-in-law or of a sister or sister-in-law. [< OF < L *nepos* grandson, nephew.]

nepho- *combining form* Cloud. Also, before vowels, **neph-.** [< Gk. *nephos* cloud]

neph·rite (nef′rīt) *n.* A very hard, compact, white to dark-green mineral formerly worn as a remedy for diseases of the kidney. [< G *nephrit* < Gk. *nephros* kidney]

ne·phrit·ic (ni-frit′ik) *adj.* **1.** Of or pertaining to the kidney or kidneys; renal: also **neph′ric. 2.** Of, pertaining to, or suffering from nephritis. Also **ne·phrit′i·cal.** — *n.* Any medicine applicable to disease of the kidney.

ne·phri·tis (ni-frī′tis) *n. Pathol.* Inflammation of the kidneys. [< LL < Gk. *nephros* kidney]

nephro- *combining form* A kidney. Also, before vowels, **nephr-.** [< Gk. *nephros* kidney]

ne·phro·sis (ni-frō′sis) *n. Pathol.* Disease of the kidney.

ne plus ul·tra (nē plus ul′trə) *Latin* The extreme or utmost point; perfection; literally, nothing more beyond.

nep·o·tism (nep′ə-tiz′əm) *n.* Favoritism; esp. governmental patronage to relatives. [< F < L *nepos, -potis* grandson, nephew] — **ne·pot·ic** (ni-pot′ik) *adj.* — **nep′o·tist** *n.*

Nep·tune (nep′tōōn, -tyōōn) In Roman mythology, the god of the sea: identified with the Greek *Poseidon.* — *n.* The fourth largest planet and eighth in order from the sun. See PLANET. [< L *Neptunus*] — **Nep·tu′ni·an** *adj.*

nep·tu·ni·um (nep-tōō′nē-əm, -tyōō′-) *n.* A radioactive element (symbol Np), artificially produced from a uranium isotope by neutron bombardment and decaying to plutonium by emission of a beta particle. See ELEMENT.

Ne·re·id (nir′ē·id) *pl.* **Ne·re·i·des** (ni·rē′ə·dēz) or **Ne·re·ids** In Greek mythology, one of the fifty daughters of Nereus.

Ne·reus (nir′ōōs, -ē·əs) In Greek mythology, a sea god, father of the Nereides.

nerve (nûrv) *n.* **1.** *Physiol.* Any of the cordlike bundles of fibers that convey impulses of sensation, etc., between the brain or spinal cord and other parts or organs. **2.** Courage or boldness; daring. **3.** *Informal* Arrogant assurance; brashness. **4.** *Usu. pl.* Unsteadiness of mind and muscle; nervousness: *a case of nerves.* **5.** Muscle; sinew: now only in the phrase **to strain every nerve. — to get on one's nerves** *Informal* To irritate; exasperate; upset. **— v.t. nerved, nerving** To provide with nerve or nerves. **— to nerve oneself** To summon up one's courage. [< L *nervus* sinew]

nerve cell *Physiol.* A neuron.

nerve center 1. *Physiol.* An aggregation of neurons having a specific function, as hearing, sight, etc. **2.** The focus of command and communication; headquarters.

nerve impulse *Physiol.* A wave of electrical disturbance along a nerve fiber and continuing until it has been discharged into the appropriate sensory or motor channels.

nerve·less (nûrv′lis) *adj.* **1.** Lacking force; feeble. **2.** Completely controlled and calm in crises; cool. **3.** *Anat.* Having no nerves. **— nerve′less·ly** *adv.* **— nerve′less·ness** *n.*

nerve-rack·ing (nûrv′rak′ing) *adj.* Extremely irritating; harrowing. Also **nerve′-wrack′ing.**

ner·vous (nûr′vəs) *adj.* **1.** Characterized by or exhibiting restlessness, anxiety, tension, etc.; high-strung; excitable. **2.** Neural. **3.** Caused by or acting on the nerves or nervous system. **— ner′vous·ly** *adv.* **— ner·vos′i·ty** (-vos′ə·tē), **ner′vous·ness** *n.*
— Syn. 1. uneasy, fidgety, jittery, skittish.

nervous breakdown Popularly, any severe mental or emotional disturbance, usu. requiring hospitalization.

nervous system *Physiol.* A system in animals that coordinates, controls, and regulates various organic activities by means of the reception and transmission of stimuli.

ner·vure (nûr′vyŏŏr) *n. Biol.* A vein, as on a leaf or an insect's wing. Also **ner′vule** (-vyŏŏl). [< F < L *nervus* sinew] **— ner·vu·ra·tion** (nûr′vyə·rā′shən) *n.*

nerv·y (nûr′vē) *adj.* **nerv·i·er, nerv·i·est 1.** *U.S. Informal* Brazen; impudent; brash. **2.** *Brit. Informal* Nervous; jumpy. **3.** Having or requiring courage.

nes·cience (nesh′əns, -ē·əns) *n.* Lack or absence of knowledge; ignorance. [< L < *ne-* not + < *scire* to know] **— nes′cient** *adj. & n.* **— nes′cient·ist** *n.*

-ness *suffix of nouns* **1.** State or quality of being: *darkness.* **2.** An example of this state or quality: to do someone a *kindness.* [OE *-nes(s), -nis(s)*]

nest (nest) *n.* **1.** The habitation prepared or the place selected by a bird for the hatching of its eggs and the rearing of its young. **2.** A place used by fishes, insects, turtles, etc., for laying eggs. **3.** The group of animals, birds, etc., occupying such a place. **4.** A cozy or snug place. **5.** A haunt or den; also, those occupying such a place: *a nest of thieves.* **6.** A series or set of similar things designed to fit into one another, as bowls, boxes, etc. **— v.t. 1.** To place in or as in a nest. **2.** To pack or place one inside another. **— v.i. 3.** To build or occupy a nest. **4.** To hunt for nests. [OE]

n'est-ce pas (nes pä′) *French* Isn't that so?

nest egg 1. A sum of money set aside for emergencies, etc. **2.** An artificial egg kept in a nest to induce a hen to lay eggs.

nes·tle (nes′əl) *v.* **tled, tling** *v.i.* **1.** To lie or press closely and snugly; cuddle; snuggle. **2.** To lie or be embedded, or half-hidden. **— v.t. 3.** To place or press snugly or lovingly. **4.** To place, or shelter in or as in a nest. [OE *nestlian* to nest] **— nes′tler** *n.*

nest·ling (nest′ling, nes′-) *n.* **1.** A bird too young to leave the nest. **2.** A young child. **— adj.** Recently hatched.

Nes·tor (nes′tər) In Greek legend, the oldest and wisest Greek chief in the Trojan War. **— n.** Any wise old man.

net¹ (net) *n.* **1.** A fabric of thread, cord, rope, etc., woven or knotted to form an open pattern or meshwork and used to catch fish, birds, etc. ◆ Collateral adjective: *reticular.* **2.** Anything that traps or entangles; a snare. **3.** A piece of fine lace. **4.** Any of various devices constructed with meshes: cargo *net*; tennis *net.* **5.** Something resembling a net. **— v.t. net·ted, net·ting 1.** To catch in or as in a net; ensnare. **2.** To make into a net. **3.** To cover, enclose, or shelter with a net. **4.** In tennis, etc., to hit (the ball) into the net. [OE]

net² (net) *adj.* **1.** Obtained after deducting all expenses, losses, taxes, etc.: distinguished from *gross: net* proceeds. **2.** Free from anything extraneous; fundamental; basic: *net* results. **— n.** A net profit, amount, weight, etc. **— v.t. net·ted, net·ting** To earn or yield as clear profit. [< F]

neth·er (neth′ər) *adj.* Situated beneath or below. [OE *nither* < Gmc.]

neth·er·most (neth′ər·mōst′) *adj.* Lowest.

nether world 1. The world of the dead. **2.** The world of punishment after death; hell.

net·ting (net′ing) *n.* **1.** A net; network. **2.** The act or operation of making net. **3.** The right of using fishing nets.

net·tle (net′l) *n.* **1.** An herb having minute stinging hairs. **2.** Any of various plants having some real or fancied resemblance to this herb. **— v.t. ·tled, ·tling 1.** To annoy or irritate; provoke. **2.** To sting like nettle. [OE *netle* < Gmc.]

nettle rash Urticaria. Also **nettle fever.**

net ton A short ton. See under TON¹.

net·work (net′wûrk′) *n.* **1.** A system of interlacing lines, tracks, or channels. **2.** An openwork fabric; netting. **3.** *Telecom.* A chain of broadcasting stations. **4.** Any interconnected system: an espionage *network.*

Neuf·châ·tel (nōō′shə·tel′, *Fr.* nœ·shä·tel′) *n.* A soft, white cheese produced in Neufchâtel, a town in northern France.

neu·ral (nŏŏr′əl, nyŏŏr′-) *adj.* Of or pertaining to the nerves or nervous system. [< Gk. *neuron* cord, sinew]

neu·ral·gi·a (nŏŏ·ral′jē·ə, -jə, nyŏŏ-) *n. Pathol.* Acute pain along the course of a nerve. **— neu·ral′gic** *adj.*

neu·ras·the·ni·a (nŏŏr′əs·thē′nē·ə, -then′yə, nyŏŏr′-) *n.* A condition marked by general debility, depression, and bodily disturbances, formerly believed to be due to weakness or exhaustion of the nervous system. [< NL < Gk. *neuron* cord, sinew + *astheneia* weakness] **— neu·ras·then′ic** (-then′ik) *adj. & n.*

neu·ri·tis (nŏŏ·rī′tis, nyŏŏ-) *n. Pathol.* Inflammation of a nerve. **— neu·rit′ic** (-rit′ik) *adj.*

neuro- *combining form* Nerve. Also **neur-** (before vowels), **neuri-**. [< Gk. *neuron* sinew]

neu·rol·o·gy (nŏŏ·rol′ə·jē, nyŏŏ-) *n.* The branch of medicine that deals with the nervous system and its disorders. [< NL *neurologia*] **— neu·ro·log·i·cal** (nŏŏr′ə·loj′i·kəl, nyŏŏr′-) *adj.* **— neu·rol′o·gist** *n.*

neu·ron (nŏŏr′on, nyŏŏr′-) *n. Physiol.* The fundamental cellular unit of the nervous system, consisting of a nucleus with all its processes and extensions: also called *nerve cell.* Also **neu′rone** (-ōn). [< NL < Gk. *neuron* sinew] **— neu·ron·ic** (nŏŏ·ron′ik, nyŏŏ-) *adj.*

neu·rop·ter·an (nŏŏ·rop′tər·ən, nyŏŏ-) *n.* A neuropterous insect. Also **neu·rop′ter, neu·rop′ter·on** (-on). **— adj.** Neuropterous. Also **neu·rop′ter·oid.**

neu·rop·ter·ous (nŏŏ·rop′tər·əs, nyŏŏ-) *adj.* Of or pertaining to an order of insects having two pairs of membranous net-veined wings and chewing mouth parts. Also **neu·rop′ter·al.** [< NL *Neuroptera*]

neu·ro·sis (nŏŏ·rō′sis, nyŏŏ-) *n. pl.* **·ses** (-sēz) *Psychiatry* Any of various emotional disturbances, less severe than the psychoses, and usu. involving anxiety, depression, and unresolved psychic conflicts: also called *psychoneurosis.* [< NL]

neu·rot·ic (nŏŏ·rot′ik, nyŏŏ-) *adj.* **1.** Pertaining to or suffering from neurosis. **2.** Neural. **— n.** A neurotic person.

neu·ter (nōō′tər, nyōō′-) *adj.* **1.** *Gram.* Neither masculine nor feminine in gender. **2.** *Biol.* Having nonfunctioning or imperfectly developed sex organs, as a worker bee. **— n. 1.** *Biol.* A neuter plant or animal. **2.** A castrated animal. **3.** *Gram.* **a** The neuter gender. **b** A word in this gender. [ult. < L < *ne-* not + *uter* either]

neu·tral (nōō′trəl, nyōō′-) *adj.* **1.** Not taking the part of either side in a dispute or war. **2.** Of or belonging to neither side in a dispute, war, etc.: *neutral* territory. **3.** Neither one thing nor the other; indefinite; middling. **4.** Having no decided hue or color; grayish. **5.** *Biol.* Neuter; esp., without stamens or pistils. **6.** *Chem.* Neither acid nor alkaline: a *neutral* solution. **7.** *Electr.* Neither positive nor negative. **8.** *Phonet.* Produced with the tongue in a relaxed, midcentral position, as the *a* in *about.* **— n. 1.** One who or that which is neutral. **2.** *Mech.* The state in which transmission gears are disengaged: a car in *neutral.* [< L < *neuter* neither] **— neu′tral·ly** *adv.*

neu·tral·ism (nōō′trəl·iz′əm, nyōō′-) *n.* In foreign affairs, the policy of not associating or aligning a nation with any side of a power conflict. **— neu′tral·ist** *adj. & n.*

neu·tral·i·ty (nōō·tral′ə·tē, nyōō-) *n. pl.* **·ties** Neutral condition, status, attitude, policy, etc., as of a nation during a war. [< F < Med.L *neutralitas*]

neu·tral·ize (nōō′trəl·īz, nyōō′-) *v.t.* **·ized, ·iz·ing 1.** To counteract or destroy the force, influence, effect, etc., of. **2.** To declare (a nation, area, etc.) neutral during a war. **3.** *Chem.* To make neutral or inert. **4.** *Electr.* To render electrically neutral by combining equal negative and positive units. [< F *neutraliser*] **— neu′tral·i·za′tion** (-ə·zā′shən, -ī·zā′-) *n.* **— neu′tral·iz′er** *n.*

neu·tri·no (nōō·trē′nō, nyōō-) *n. pl.* **·nos** *Physics* An atomic particle associated with the radioactive emission of beta rays, carrying no electric charge and having a mass approaching zero. [< Ital., little neutron]

neu·tron (nōō'tron, nyōō'-) *n. Physics* An electrically neutral particle of the atomic nucleus having a mass approximately equal to that of the proton.

neutron number *Physics* The number of neutrons in the nucleus of an atom.

nev·er (nev'ər) *adv.* **1.** Not at any time; not ever: also used in combination to form adjectives: *never-ending.* **2.** Not at all; positively not: *Never* fear. [OE *næfre*]

nev·er·more (nev'ər·môr', -mōr') *adv.* Never again.

nev·er·the·less (nev'ər·thə·les') *adv.* Nonetheless; however; yet. — **Syn.** See BUT¹.

ne·vus (nē'vəs) *n. pl.* **·vi** (-vī) A birthmark or congenital mole. [< L *naevus* blemish] — **ne'void** *adj.*

new (nōō, nyōō) *adj.* **new·er, new·est** **1.** Having recently been made, used, developed, etc. **2.** Having never existed, occurred, etc., before. **3.** Recently discovered, observed, etc.: a *new* river. **4.** Different from that which is older or previous: a *new* dispensation. **5.** Unfamiliar; strange. **6.** Not accustomed or experienced: *new* at the job. **7.** Having recently come into a certain place, condition, relationship, etc.: a *new* member. **8.** Built, made, etc., in place of something older: a *new* post office. **9.** Fresh; unspoiled. **10.** Repeated; renewed: a *new* plea. **11.** Additional; increased: a *new* supply. **12.** Rejuvenated; refreshed: a *new* man. **13.** Modern; current; fashionable. **14.** *Usu. cap.* Designating the most recent form or period: said of languages. — *adv.* Newly; freshly; recently. — *n.* That which is new. [OE *nīwe* < Gmc.] — **new'ish** *adj.* — **new'ness** *n.*

new·born (nōō'bôrn', nyōō'-) *adj.* **1.** Just lately born. **2.** Reborn. — *n.* A newborn infant or animal.

New·burg (nōō'bûrg, nyōō'-) See À LA NEWBURG.

new·com·er (nōō'kum'ər, nyōō'-) *n.* One who has recently arrived.

New Deal **1.** The political, economic, and social policies and principles of the administration under Franklin D. Roosevelt. **2.** The Roosevelt administration. — **New Dealer** *n.*

new·el (nōō'əl, nyōō'-) *n. Archit.* **1.** The post that terminates the handrail of a staircase. **2.** The central pillar or upright of a spiral staircase. Also **newel post.** [< OF < LL < L *nux* nut]

New England The NE section of the United States, including Maine, New Hampshire, Vermont, Massachusetts, Rhode Island, and Connecticut. — **New Englander** *n.*

new·fan·gled (nōō'fang'gəld, nyōō'-) *adj.* Lately come into fashion; novel: a derogatory term. [ME < *newe* new + *fangel* contrivance, prob. < *fōn* to seize, grasp]

New·found·land (nōō'fənd·lənd, nyōō'-) *n.* A large dog of a breed originating in Newfoundland, having a broad head, square muzzle, and thick, abundant, usu. black coat.

New·gate (nōō'git, -gāt, nyōō'-) Formerly, a London prison.

New Jerusalem The city of God; heaven. *Rev.* xxi 2.

New Latin See under LATIN.

new·ly (nōō'lē, nyōō'-) *adv.* **1.** Very recently; lately. **2.** Once more; anew; afresh. **3.** In a new or different way.

new·ly·wed (nōō'lē·wed', nyōō'-) *n.* A person recently married.

new moon **1.** The phase of the moon when it is directly between the earth and the sun, its disk then being invisible; also, the first visible crescent of the disk. **2.** The period when the moon is new.

new·mown (nōō'mōn', nyōō'-) *adj.* Recently mown, as hay.

New Neth·er·land (neth'ər·lənd) The Dutch colony in North America, 1613–1664, near the mouth of the Hudson River; capital, New Amsterdam.

new penny A penny (def. 3).

news (nōōz, nyōōz) *n.pl.* (*construed as sing.*) **1.** Information of a recent event, development, etc., esp. as reported in a newspaper, on the radio, etc. **2.** Any new or unfamiliar information. [< NEW]

news·boy (nōōz'boi', nyōōz'-) *n.* A boy who sells or delivers newspapers.

news·cast (nōōz'kast', -käst', nyōōz'-) *n.* A radio or television broadcast of news. — **news'cast·er** *n.*

news·let·ter (nōōz'let'ər, nyōōz'-) *n.* A brief, specialized, periodical news report or set of reports sent by mail.

news·mag·a·zine (nōōz'mag'ə·zēn, -mag'ə·zēn', nyōōz'-) *n.* A periodical, especially a weekly, that summarizes the news.

news·man (nōōz'man', -mən, nyōōz'-) *n. pl.* **·men** (-men', -mən) **1.** A news reporter. **2.** A newsdealer.

news·pa·per (nōōz'pā'pər, nyōōz'-) *n.* **1.** A printed publication usu. issued daily or weekly, containing news, editorials, advertisements, etc. **2.** Newsprint.

news·print (nōōz'print', -nyōōz'-) *n.* The thin, unsized paper on which the ordinary newspaper is printed.

news·reel (nōōz'rēl', nyōōz'-) *n.* A short motion picture showing current events.

news·stand (nōōz'stand', nyōōz'-) *n. U.S.* A stand or stall at which newspapers and periodicals are offered for sale.

New Style See (Gregorian) CALENDAR.

news·wor·thy (nōōz'wûr'thē, nyōōz'-) *adj.* Having sufficient importance to be reported in a newspaper or newscast.

news·y (nōō'zē, nyōō'-) *Informal adj.* **news·i·er, news·i·est** Full of news. — *n. pl.* **news·ies** *U.S.* A newsboy.

newt (nōōt, nyōōt) *n.* Any of various semiaquatic salamanders. [Earlier *ewt*; in ME *an ewt* was taken as *a newt*]

New Testament That portion of the Bible containing the life and teachings of Christ and his followers.

New World The Western Hemisphere.

New Year The first day of the year; in the Gregorian calendar, January 1. Also **New Year's Day** (yirz).

New Year's Eve The night of December 31.

New York·er (yôr'kər) An inhabitant of New York; esp., a native or resident of New York City.

New Zea·land·er (zē'lənd·ər) **1.** A resident of New Zealand. **2.** Formerly, a Maori.

next (nekst) *adj.* **1.** Coming directly after in time, order, position, etc. **2.** Nearest or closest in space. **3.** Adjacent or adjoining: in the *next* room. — *adv.* **1.** Immediately afterward. **2.** On the first succeeding occasion: when *next* we meet. — *prep.* Nearest to: *next* his heart. — **next door** **1.** The adjacent house, building, apartment, etc. **2.** In, at, or to the adjacent house, etc. — **next to** Almost; nearly: *next to* impossible. [OE *niehst,* superl. of *neah* near]

next of kin The person most closely related to one.

nex·us (nek'səs) *n. pl.* **·us·es** or **·us** **1.** A bond or tie between the several members of a group or series; link. **2.** A connected series. [< L, pp. of *nectere* to tie]

ni·a·cin (nī'ə·sin) *n.* Nicotinic acid.

nib (nib) *n.* **1.** The point of a pen. **2.** The projecting, pointed part of anything; tip. — *v.t.* **nibbed, nib·bing** To furnish with a nib. [Var. of NEB < OE *nebb* beak]

nib·ble (nib'əl) *v.* **·bled, ·bling** *v.t.* **1.** To eat with small, quick, gentle bites: to *nibble* grass. **2.** To take little, soft bites of: to *nibble* an ear. — *v.i.* **3.** To eat or bite, esp. with small, gentle bites: often with *at.* — *n.* **1.** A little bit or morsel. **2.** The act of one who or that which nibbles. [< Gmc] — **nib'bler** *n.*

Ni·be·lung (nē'bə·lŏŏng) *n. pl.* **·lungs** or **·lung·en** (-lŏŏng'ən) In Teutonic mythology, one of a dwarf people who held a magic ring and a hoard of gold, taken from them by Siegfried.

Ni·be·lung·en·lied (nē'bə·lŏŏng'ən·lēt') The lay of the Nibelungs, a Middle High German epic poem written by an unknown author during the early 13th century.

nib·lick (nib'lik) *n.* In golf, a nine iron. [? < Du. < *knep·pel* club]

Nic·a·ra·guan (nik'ə·rä'gwən) *adj.* Of or pertaining to Nicaragua. — *n.* A native of Nicaragua.

nice (nīs) *adj.* **nic·er, nic·est** **1.** Agreeable; pleasing; respectable; suitable. **2.** Friendly; kind. **3.** Characterized by, revealing, or demanding discrimination, delicacy, or subtlety: a *nice* distinction. **4.** Precise, accurate, or minute, as an instrument. — **nice and** Gratifyingly; properly: *nice and* dry. [< OF, innocent, foolish < L *nescius* ignorant] — **nice'ly** *adv.* — **nice'ness** *n.*

Ni·cene Creed (nī'sēn, nī·sēn') *Eccl.* **1.** A Christian confession of faith, adopted by the first Council of Nicaea, A.D. 325. **2.** Any of several other creeds later adopted by Christian churches. [after *Nicaea,* an ancient town in Asia Minor]

ni·ce·ty (nī'sə·tē) *n. pl.* **·ties** **1.** *Usu. pl.* A minute or subtle point, detail, or distinction. **2.** *Usu. pl.* A delicacy or refinement: *niceties* of living. **3.** The quality of requiring careful and delicate treatment. **4.** Precision or accuracy; exactness. **5.** The quality of being nice. — **to a nicety** Exactly.

niche (nich) *n.* **1.** A recessed space or hollow, usu. in a wall, for a statue or the like. **2.** Any position specially adapted to its occupant: to find one's *niche.* — *v.t.* **niched, nich·ing** To put in a niche. [Prob. < F, ult. < L *nidus* nest]

Nich·o·las, (nik'ə·ləs, -lus) **Saint** See SANTA CLAUS.

nick (nik) *n.* A slight cut, chip, or indentation on a surface or edge. — **in the nick of time** At the exact or crucial moment. — *v.t.* To make a nick in or on.

nick·el (nik'əl) *n.* **1.** A hard, ductile, malleable, silver-white metallic element (symbol Ni) having a wide variety of uses. See ELEMENT. **2.** A five-cent coin of the U.S., made of an alloy of nickel and copper. — *v.t.* **·eled** or **·elled, ·el·ing** or **·el·ling** To plate with nickel. [< Sw. < G < (*kupfer*)*nickel,* lit., copper demon; because its ore looks like copper]

NICHE

nick·el·o·de·on (nik'əl·ō'dē·ən) *n. U.S.* **1.** Formerly, a motion-picture theater charging an admission fee of five cents. **2.** Formerly, a jukebox or other automatic music machine. [< NICKEL (def. 2) + *odeon* < F *odéon* theater]

nick·el·plate (nik'əl·plāt') *v.t.* **·plat·ed, ·plat·ing** To cover with nickel by electroplating.

nickel plate A thin layer of nickel deposited on the surface of objects by electroplating.

nickel silver German silver.

nick·er (nik'ər) *n.* **1.** A neigh. **2.** A neighing laugh. — *v.i.* **1.** To neigh. **2.** To snicker. [Imit.]

nick·nack (nik'nak') See KNICKKNACK.

nick·name (nik'nām') *n.* **1.** A familiar form of a proper name, as *Tom* for *Thomas.* **2.** A descriptive name given instead of in addition to the actual name of a person, place, or thing, as *Honest Abe.* — *v.t.* **·named, ·nam·ing 1.** To give a nickname to or call by a nickname. **2.** To misname. [ME *ekename* surname, *an ekename* becoming a *nickname*]

nic·o·tine (nik'ə-tēn, -tin) *n.* An acrid, poisonous, oily alkaloid, $C_{11}H_{14}N_2$, contained in the leaves of tobacco. Also **nic'o·tin.** [< F, after Jean *Nicot*, 1530–1600, French courtier, who introduced tobacco into France from Portugal] — **nic·o·tin·ic** (nik'ə-tin'ik) *adj.*

nicotinic acid *Biochem.* A colorless, water-soluble compound, $C_6H_5NO_2$, prepared by the oxidation of nicotine and forming part of the vitamin B complex, used to prevent pellagra: also called *niacin.*

nic·ti·tate (nik'tə-tāt) *v.i.* **·tat·ed, ·tat·ing** To wink. Also **nic'tate.** [< Med.L, freq. of L *nictare* to wink] — **nic'ti·ta'tion** *n.*

nictitating membrane A transparent third eyelid at the inner corner of the eye in various birds, reptiles, etc.

niece (nēs) *n.* The daughter of a brother or sister. [< OF, ult. < L *neptis* niece, granddaughter]

Nie·tzsche·an (nē'chi-ən) *adj.* Of or relating to Friedrich Nietzsche, or to his philosophy. — *n.* A follower of Nietzsche, or of his philosophy. — **Nie'tzsche·an·ism, Nie'·tzsche·ism** *n.*

nif·ty (nif'tē) *adj.* **·ti·er, ·ti·est** *Slang* Stylish; pleasing.

nig·gard (nig'ərd) *n.* A stingy person. — *adj.* Niggardly. [? < AF, ? ult. < ON *hnøggr*]

nig·gard·ly (nig'ərd-lē) *adj.* **1.** Stingy; parsimonious. **2.** Meanly insufficient; scanty. — *adv.* In the manner of a niggard. — **nig'gard·li·ness** *n.*

nig·ger (nig'ər) *n.* A Negro or member of any dark-skinned people: a vulgar and offensive term. [See NEGRO.]

nig·gle (nig'əl) *v.i.* **·gled, ·gling** To occupy oneself with trifles; behave trivially. [Cf. dial. Norw. *nigla*]

nig·gling (nig'ling) *adj.* **1.** Fussy; overprecise. **2.** Mean; petty. **3.** Annoying; nagging. — *n.* Overelaborate or overprecise work or behavior. — **nig'gling·ly** *adv.*

nigh (nī) *Chiefly Archaic & Dial. adj.* **nigh·er, nigh·est** or **next 1.** Close; near. **2.** Convenient; direct. — *adv.* **1.** Near in time or place. **2.** Almost: often with *on* or *onto: nigh on* a year. — *prep.* Near. — *v.t. & v.i.* To draw near; approach. [OE *nēah, nēh*] — **nigh'ness** *n.*

night (nīt) *n.* **1.** The period from sunset to sunrise, esp. the part that is dark. ◆ Collateral adjective: *nocturnal.* **2.** The period of evening and darkness before midnight of a given day. **3.** Darkness; the dark. **4.** A condition of ignorance, gloom, painful confusion, etc. [OE *niht, neaht*]

night blindness Vision that is abnormally poor in dim light but normal in daylight.

night-bloom·ing ce·re·us (nīt'blōō'ming sir'ē·əs) A tall tropical cactus having large white flowers that open at night.

night·cap (nīt'kap') *n.* **1.** A cap to be worn in bed. **2.** *Informal* A drink of liquor taken just before going to bed.

night·clothes (nīt'klōz', -klōthz') *n.pl.* Clothes to be worn in bed.

night club A restaurant open until late at night, providing entertainment, food, and drink.

night crawler Any large earthworm that emerges at night.

night·fall (nīt'fôl') *n.* The close of day.

night-gown (nīt'goun') *n.* A loose gown worn in bed by women and children. Also **night/dress'** (-dres').

night·hawk (nīt'hôk') *n.* **1.** Any of various birds related to the whippoorwill. **2.** The nightjar.

night·in·gale (nī'tən-gāl, nī'ting-) *n.* A small, Old World migratory bird allied to the thrushes and noted for the melodious song of the male. [OE < *niht* night + *galan* to sing]

night·jar (nīt'jär') *n.* Any of various goatsuckers of Europe: also called *nighthawk.*

night letter A telegram sent at night, at reduced rates.

night-light (nīt'līt') *n.* A usu. dim light kept on at night.

night·long (nīt'lông', -long') *adj.* Lasting through the night. — *adv.* Through the whole night.

night·ly (nīt'lē) *adj.* **1.** Of, pertaining to, or occurring each night. **2.** Pertaining to or occurring at night. — *adv.* **1.** By night. **2.** Each night: to take place *nightly.*

night·mare (nīt'mâr') *n.* **1.** A horrible and frightening dream. **2.** Any experience or condition resembling a nightmare. [< NIGHT + MARE²] — **night'mar·ish** *adj.*

night owl One who stays up late.

nights (nīts) *adv. Informal* At night. [OE *nihtes*]

night school A school that holds classes during the evening, esp. for those who cannot attend day school.

night·shade (nīt'shād') *n.* **1.** Any of various flowering plants typical of a family that includes tobacco, pepper, jimsonweed, the potato, and the tomato. **2.** Belladonna.

night·shirt (nīt'shûrt') *n.* A long, loose garment worn in bed, usu. by men or boys.

night-spot (nīt'spot') *U.S. Informal* A night club.

night·stick (nīt'stik') *n. U.S.* A long, heavy club carried by policemen.

night table A bedside table or stand.

night·time (nīt'tīm') *n.* The time from sunset to sunrise, or from dark to dawn.

night-walk·er (nīt'wô'kər) *n.* A night crawler.

night watch 1. A watch or guard kept at night. **2.** A night watchman. **3.** A period of watch or guard.

night·wear (nīt'wâr') *n.* Nightclothes.

night·y (nī'tē) *n. pl.* **night·ies** *U.S. Informal* A nightgown.

nigri- *combining form* Black. Also, before vowels, **nigr-.** [< L *niger, nigris* black]

ni·hil·ism (nī'əl-iz'əm, nī'hil-) *n.* **1.** *Philos.* **a** A doctrine that denies existence. **b** A doctrine that denies any basis for knowledge or truth. **c** Total denial of all traditional principles, values, and institutions. **2.** In politics: **a** A doctrine advocating the destruction of all political, economic, and social institutions. **b** *Usu. cap.* A revolutionary movement in Russia in the 19th century advocating violence and terror. **3.** Any revolutionary movement advocating terror and violence. — **ni/hil·ist** *n.* — **ni/hil·is/tic** *adj.*

Ni·ke (nī'kē) In Greek mythology, the winged goddess of victory: identified with the Roman *Victoria.* — *n.* An antiaircraft guided missile. [< Gk. *Nikē* victory]

nil (nil) *n.* Nothing. [< L, contr. of *nihil* nothing]

Nile green Any of several light green tints.

nil·gai (nil'gī) *n.* A large, short-maned antelope of India. Also **nil/gau** (-gô), **nil/ghai, nil/ghau** (-gô). [< Hind. < *nīl* blue + *gāi* cow]

nim·ble (nim'bəl) *adj.* **·bler, ·blest 1.** Light and quick in movement; lively. **2.** Characterized by a quick and ready intellect. [OE *numel* quick at grasping] — **nim'ble·ness** *n.* — **nim'bly** *adv.*

nim·bo·stra·tus (nim'bō·strā'təs, -strat'əs) *n. Meteorol.* A low, formless, dark gray cloud layer, precipitating continuous rain or snow.

nim·bus (nim'bəs) *n. pl.* **·bus·es** or **·bi** (-bī) **1.** A luminous emanation believed to envelop a deity or holy person. **2.** Any atmosphere or aura, as of fame, glamor, etc. **3.** Formerly, a nimbostratus. [< L, cloud]

Nim·rod (nim'rod) Grandson of Ham, described as a mighty hunter. *Gen.* x 8. — *n.* A hunter. Also **nim'rod.**

Ni·ña (nē'nə, *Sp.* nē'nyä) *n.* One of the three ships of Columbus on his first voyage to America.

nin·com·poop (nin'kəm-pōōp) *n.* An idiot; fool. [Origin unknown]

nine (nīn) *n.* **1.** The sum of eight and one: a cardinal number. **2.** Any symbol of this number, as 9, ix, IX. **3.** Anything consisting of or representing nine units, as a baseball team, etc. — **the Nine** The Muses. — *adj.* Being one more than eight. [OE *nigon*] — **ninth** *adj. & n.*

nine iron In golf, an iron with an extremely slanted face, used for lofting the ball: also called *niblick.*

nine·pence (nīn'pəns) *n. Brit.* **1.** The sum of nine pennies. **2.** A coin of this value, no longer minted.

nine·pins (nīn'pinz') *n.pl.* (construed as *sing.*) A bowling game similar to tenpins, using nine large wooden pins.

nine·teen (nīn'tēn') *n.* **1.** The sum of eighteen and one: a cardinal number. **2.** Any symbol of this number, as 19, xix, XIX. **3.** Anything consisting of or representing nineteen units. — *adj.* Being one more than eighteen. [OE *nigontiene*] — **nine'teenth'** *adj. & n.*

nine·ty (nīn'tē) *n. pl.* **·ties 1.** The sum of eighty and ten: a cardinal number. **2.** Any symbol of this number, as 90, xc, XC. **3.** Anything consisting of or representing ninety units, as an organization, game token, etc. — *adj.* Being ten more than eighty. [OE *nigontig*] — **nine'ti·eth** *adj. & n.*

Nin·e·veh (nin'ə·və) An ancient city on the Tigris, capital of Assyria. — **Nin'e·vite** (-vīt) *n.*

Ni·o·be (nī'ə-bē) In Greek mythology, the mother whose children were killed by Apollo and Artemis after she had vaunted their superiority. She was turned by Zeus into a stone from which tears continued to flow.

ni·o·bi·um (nī-ō'bē·əm) *n.* A rare, steel gray, metallic element (symbol Nb), valuable as an alloy metal: formerly called *columbium.* See ELEMENT. [< NIOBE]

nip¹ (nip) *v.* **nipped, nip·ping** *v.t.* **1.** To pinch or compress between two surfaces; bite. **2.** To sever or remove by pinching, biting, or clipping: usually with *off.* **3.** To check, arrest, or destroy the growth or development of. **4.** To affect painfully or injuriously, as by cold. **5.** *Slang* To steal; pilfer. **6.** *Slang* To catch; take. — *v.i.* **7.** *Brit. Informal* To move nimbly or rapidly: with *off*, *away*, etc. — *n.* **1.** The act of one who or that which nips. **2.** That which is nipped off. **3.** Any small portion: a *nip* of tea. **4.** A sharp, stinging quality. **5.** Severe cold or frost. **6.** A cutting remark. **7.** A sharp, pungent flavor. — **nip and tuck** *U.S.* Very close or even; precariously uncertain. [Cf. Du. *nijpen* to pinch]

nip² (nip) *n.* A small quantity of liquor. — *v.t. & v.i.* To sip (liquor). [? < earlier *nipperkin* a small liquid measure]

nip·per (nip′ər) *n.* **1.** One who or that which nips. **2.** *pl.* Any of various implements used for nipping, as pliers, pincers, etc. **3.** The large claw of a crab or lobster. **4.** *pl. Slang* Handcuffs. **5.** *Brit. Informal* A small boy; lad.

nip·ple (nip′əl) *n.* **1.** The protuberance on the breasts of higher mammals, esp. that of the female; teat. **2.** The rubber teatlike mouthpiece of a nursing bottle. **3.** Something resembling a nipple, as a short pipe coupling with threaded ends. [Earlier *nible*, ? dim. of NIB]

nip·py (nip′ē) *adj.* **·pi·er**, **·pi·est** **1.** Biting or sharp, as cold weather. **2.** *Brit. Informal* Active; alert. — **nip′pi·ly** *adv.* — **nip′pi·ness** *n.*

nir·va·na (nir·vä′nə, nər·van′ə) *n.* **1.** In Buddhism, the state of absolute felicity attained through the annihilation of the self. **2.** Freedom from care and pain; bliss. [< Skt. *nirvāna* extinction]

Ni·san (nē·sän′, nis′ən) *n.* The seventh month of the Hebrew year. Also **Nis′san**. See (Hebrew) CALENDAR.

Ni·sei (nē·sā) *n. pl.* **·sei** or **·seis** A native American of immigrant Japanese parentage.

ni·si (nī′sī) *conj. Law* Unless: used after the word *order*, *rule*, *decree*, etc., signifying that it shall become effective at a certain time, unless modified or avoided. [< L]

Nis·sen hut (nis′ən, nēs′-) A prefabricated sheet steel building resembling a long half-cylinder lying flat on the ground. [after P. N. *Nissen*, 1871-1930, who invented it]

nit (nit) *n.* **1.** The egg of a louse or other parasitic insect. **2.** An immature louse. [OE *hnitu*] — **nit′ty** *adj.*

ni·ter (nī′tər) *n.* **1.** Potassium or sodium nitrate; saltpeter. **2.** *Obs.* Natron. Also **ni′tre**. [< OF < L < Gk. *nitron*]

ni·ton (nī′ton) *n.* Radon. [< L (*nit*)*ere* to shine) + -ON]

nit-pick (nit′pik′) *Informal v.t.* **1.** To fuss over or find fault with. — *v.i.* **2.** To engage in nit-picking. Also **nit′-pick**. [Back formation < NIT-PICKING] — **nit′-pick′er** *n.*

nit-pick·ing (nit′pik′ing) *n. Informal* A fussing over trivial details, often with the aim of finding fault.

ni·trate (nī′trāt) *Chem. n.* **1.** A salt or ester of nitric acid. **2.** Niter. — *v.t.* **·trat·ed**, **·trat·ing** To treat or combine with nitric acid or a compound. [See NITER.]

ni·tric (nī′trik) *adj. Chem.* **1.** Of, pertaining to, or obtained from nitrogen. **2.** Containing nitrogen in the higher valence.

nitric acid *Chem.* A colorless, highly corrosive liquid, HNO_3, having strong oxidizing properties.

ni·tride (nī′trīd, -trid) *n. Chem.* A compound of nitrogen with some more electropositive element. Also **ni′trid** (-trid).

ni·tri·fy (nī′trə·fī) *v.t.* **·fied**, **·fy·ing** *Chem.* **1.** To treat or combine with nitrogen. **2.** To convert, as ammonium salts in the soil, into nitrates or nitrites by oxidation. **3.** To treat or impregnate (soil, etc.) with nitrates. [< F *nitrifier*] — **ni′tri·fi′a·ble** *adj.* — **ni′tri·fi·ca′tion** *n.*

ni·trite (nī′trīt) *n. Chem.* A salt of nitrous acid.

nitro- *combining form Chem.* Containing the univalent radical NO_2. Also, before vowels, **nitr-**. Also **nitri-**. [< L *nitrum* < Gk. *nitron*]

ni·tro·ben·zene (nī′trō·ben′zēn, -ben·zēn′) *n. Chem.* A yellow, oily compound, $C_6H_5NO_2$, formed by the nitration of benzene and used in the making of aniline.

ni·tro·gen (nī′trə·jən) *n.* An odorless, colorless, gaseous element (symbol N) forming about four-fifths of the atmosphere by volume and playing a decisive role in the formation of compounds essential to life. See ELEMENT. [< F *nitrogène* < *nitro-* NITRO- + *-gène* -GEN]

nitrogen fixation **1.** The conversion of atmospheric nitrogen into nitrates by soil bacteria. **2.** The production of nitrogen compounds, as for fertilizers and explosives, by processes utilizing free nitrogen. — **ni′tro·gen-fix′ing** *adj.*

ni·trog·en·ize (nī·troj′ən·īz, nī′trə·jən·īz′) *v.t.* **·ized**, **·iz·ing** To treat or combine with nitrogen.

ni·trog·e·nous (nī·troj′ə·nəs) *adj.* Pertaining to or containing nitrogen. Also **ni·tro·ge·ne·ous** (nī′trō·jē′nē·əs).

ni·tro·glyc·er·in (nī′trō·glis′ər·in) *n. Chem.* A colorless to pale yellow, oily liquid, $C_3H_5(ONO_2)_3$, made by nitrating glycerol, used as an explosive and propellant, etc. Also **ni′tro, ni′tro·glyc′er·ine**. [< NITRO- + GLYCERIN]

nitro group *Chem.* The univalent NO_2 radical.

ni·trous (nī′trəs) *adj. Chem.* Of, pertaining to, or derived from nitrogen: esp. applied to those compounds containing less oxygen than the nitric compounds.

nitrous oxide A gas, N_2O, used as an anesthetic in dental surgery, etc., and sometimes having an exhilarating effect when inhaled: also called *laughing gas*.

nit·ty-grit·ty (nit′ē-grit′ē) *U.S. Slang n.* The basic questions or details; essence. — *adj.* Down-to-earth; basic.

nit·wit (nit′wit′) *n.* A silly or stupid person.

ni·val (nī′vəl) *adj.* Of or pertaining to the snow; also, growing under the snow. [< L *nivalis* < *nix*, *nivis* snow]

nix¹ (niks) *n.* In Germanic mythology, a water sprite.

nix² (niks) *Slang n.* **1.** Nothing. **2.** No. — *adv.* No. — *interj.* Stop! Watch out! — *v.t.* To forbid or disagree with: He *nixed* our suggestions. [< G *nichts* nothing]

Ni·zam (ni·zäm′, -zam′, nī-) *n.* The title of the former hereditary rulers of Hyderabad, India.

no¹ (nō) *adv.* **1.** Nay; not so. **2.** Not at all; not in any wise: *no* better than the other. **3.** Not: used to express an alternative after *or*: whether or *no*. — *n. pl.* **noes** **1.** A negative reply; a denial. **2.** A negative vote or voter: The *noes* have it. [OE *nā* < *ne* not + *ā* ever]

no² (nō) *adj.* Not any; not one. [OE < *ne* not + *ān* one]

no³ (nō) *n. pl.* **no** *Sometimes cap.* The classical drama of Japan, traditionally tragic or noble in theme, having music and dancing: also spelled *noh*. Also **nō**. Compare KABUKI.

No·ah (nō′ə) In the Old Testament, a patriarch who built an ark that saved him, his family, and every kind of animal from the Flood. *Gen.* v-ix. [< Hebrew]

nob¹ (nob) *n.* **1.** *Slang* The head. **2.** In cribbage, the jack of trumps. [Var. of KNOB]

nob² (nob) *n. Slang* One who is rich, influential, etc.

No·bel Prizes (nō·bel′) Any of five prizes founded by the will of Alfred Nobel and awarded annually in the fields of physics, chemistry, medicine, literature, and the furtherance of world peace.

no·be·li·um (nō·bē′lē·əm) *n.* An unstable radioactive element (symbol No) originally produced by the bombardment of curium by an isotope of carbon. See ELEMENT. [after A. B. *Nobel*]

no·bil·i·ty (nō·bil′ə·tē) *n. pl.* **·ties** **1.** A class in society composed of persons having hereditary title, rank, and privileges. **2.** In Great Britain, the peerage. **3.** The state or quality of being noble.

no·ble (nō′bəl) *adj.* **·bler**, **·blest** **1.** Having excellence or dignity; eminent; illustrious; worthy. **2.** Characterized by or displaying superior moral qualities. **3.** Magnificent and imposing in appearance; grand; stately. **4.** Of or pertaining to the nobility; aristocratic. **5.** Chemically inert. — *n.* **1.** A nobleman. **2.** In Great Britain, a peer. [< MF < L *nobilis* noble, well-known] — **no′ble·ness** *n.* — **no′bly** *adv.*

no·ble·man (nō′bəl·mən) *n. pl.* **·men** (-mən) A man of noble rank; in England, a peer.

no·blesse o·blige (nō·bles′ ō·blēzh′) *French* Those of high birth, wealth, or social position must behave generously or nobly toward others; literally, nobility obligates.

no·ble·wom·an (nō′bəl·wŏŏm′ən) *n. pl.* **·wom·en** (-wim′in) **1.** A woman of noble rank. **2.** In England, a peeress.

no·bod·y (nō′bod′ē, -bəd·ē) *pron.* Not anybody. — *n. pl.* **·bod·ies** A person of no importance or influence.

nock (nok) *n.* **1.** The notch for the bowstring on the butt end of an arrow. **2.** The notch on the horn of a bow for securing the bowstring. [ME *nocke*]

nocti- *combining form* By or at night. Also, before vowels, **noct-**. [< L *nox*, *noctis* night]

noc·tu·id (nok′chōō·id) *n.* Any of a large family of medium-sized moths, esp. those whose larvae are destructive. — *adj.* Of this family of moths. [< NL < L *noctua* night owl]

noc·tur·nal (nok·tûr′nəl) *adj.* **1.** Of, pertaining to, or occurring at night. **2.** *Biol.* Active, blooming, etc., by night. [< LL < L *nocturnus* nightly] — **noc·tur′nal·ly** *adv.*

noc·turne (nok′tûrn) *n.* **1.** In painting, a night scene. **2.** *Music* A composition of a pensive or romantic nature.

nod (nod) *v.* **nod·ded**, **nod·ding** *v.i.* **1.** To lower the head forward briefly, as in agreement, assent, invitation, etc. **2.** To let the head fall forward slightly and involuntarily, as when drowsy. **3.** To be inattentive or careless. **4.** To sway or bend the top or upper part, as trees. — *v.t.* **5.** To lower (the head) by nodding. **6.** To express or signify (assent, agreement, etc.) by nodding the head. — *n.* The act of one who or that which nods. — **to give** (or **get**) **the nod** *U.S. Slang* To give (or receive) the sign to go ahead, assent, approval, etc. [ME *nodden*] — **nod′der** *n.*

nod·dle (nod′l) *Informal n.* The head; noodle. — *v.t. & v.i.* **·dled**, **·dling** To nod frequently. [Freq. of NOD]

nod·dy (nod′ē) *n. pl.* **·dies** **1.** A dunce; a fool. **2.** One of several terns of the Atlantic coast. [< NOD]

node (nōd) *n.* **1.** A knot, knob, or swelling; protuberance. **2.** *Bot.* A joint or knob of a stem. **3.** *Math.* A point at which a curve crosses itself. **4.** *Astron.* Either of two points at which the orbit of a heavenly body intersects the ecliptic. **5.** *Physics* A point, line, or surface in a standing wave system at which some component wave has virtually zero amplitude. **6.** *Anat.* A swelling. [< L *nodus* knot] — **nod·al** (nōd′l) *adj.* — **nod′al·ly** *adv.*

nod·ule (noj′ool, nod′yool) *n.* **1.** A little knot or node. **2.** *Bot.* A tubercle. [< L < *nodus* knot] — **nod·u·lar** (noj′ŏŏ·lər), **nod′u·lose** (-lōs), **nod′u·lous** (-ləs) *adj.*

no·ël (nō·el′) *n.* A Christmas carol. Also **no·el′**.

No·ël (nō·el′) *n.* Christmas. Also **No·el′.** [< F < LL (*dies*) *natalis* birthday]
nog (nog) *n.* **1.** Eggnog (which see). **2.** *Brit. Dial.* A strong ale. Also **nogg.** [Origin unknown]
nog·gin (nog′in) *n.* **1.** *Informal* A person's head. **2.** A small mug or cup. **3.** A measure of liquor equal to about one fourth of a pint or a gill. [Origin unknown]
noh (nō) See NO³.
no·how (nō′hou′) *adv. Dial.* In no way; not by any means.
noise (noiz) *n.* **1.** Loud, confused, or disturbing sound of any kind. **2.** In communication theory, any random disturbance that causes a received signal to differ from what was transmitted. — *v.* **noised, nois·ing** *Rare v.t.* **1.** To spread, report, or rumor: often with *about* or *abroad.* — *v.i.* **2.** To be noisy; make a noise. [< OF, ? < L *nausea*]
— **Syn.** (noun) **1.** din, clamor, uproar, hubbub, racket, clatter, blare. See SOUND¹.
noise·less (noiz′lis) *adj.* Causing or making little or no noise; quiet; silent. — **noise′less·ly** *adv.* — **noise′less·ness** *n.*
noise·mak·er (noiz′mā′kər) *n.* A horn, bell, etc., for making noise at celebrations. — **noise′mak′ing** *n. & adj.*
noi·some (noi′səm) *adj.* **1.** Offensive or disgusting, esp. in smell; stinking. **2.** Injurious; noxious. [ME < *noy* annoyance + OE -*sum* like, resembling] — **noi′some·ly** *adv.* — **noi′some·ness** *n.*
nois·y (noi′zē) *adj.* **nois·i·er, nois·i·est** **1.** Making a loud noise. **2.** Characterized by or full of noise. — **nois′i·ly** *adv.* — **nois′i·ness** *n.*
no·li-me-tan·ge·re (nō′lī-mē-tan′jə-rē) *n.* A warning against touching or meddling. [< L, touch me not]
nol·le pros·e·qui (nol′ē pros′ə-kwī) *Law* An entry of record in a civil or criminal case, to signify that the plaintiff or prosecutor will not press it. [< L, to be unwilling to prosecute]
no·lo con·ten·de·re (nō′lō kən·ten′də·rē) *Law* A plea by a defendant in a criminal action that has the same legal effect as an admission of guilt but does not debar him from denying the truth of the charges in any other proceedings. [< L, I am unwilling to contend]
nol-pros (nol′pros′) *v.t.* **-prossed, -pros·sing** *Law* To subject to a nolle prosequi. [Short for NOLLE PROSEQUI]
no·mad (nō′mad, nom′ad) *n.* **1.** One of a group of people that habitually shifts its abode to find food, avoid drought, etc. **2.** One who constantly moves about, usu. without pur-

pose; a wanderer. — *adj.* Nomadic. [< L < Gk. *nomas* < *nemein* to graze] — **no′mad·ism** *n.*
no·mad·ic (nō·mad′ik) *adj.* Of, pertaining to, or like nomads. Also **no·mad′i·cal.** — **no·mad′i·cal·ly** *adv.*
no m̄an's land **1.** A tract of waste or unowned land. **2.** In war, the land between opposing armies. **3.** An area of human activity characterized by ambiguity or peril.
nom de guerre (nôn də gâr′) *French* A pseudonym; literally, a war name.
nom de plume (nom′ də plōōm′, Fr. nôn də plüm′) A pen name; a writer's assumed name. — **Syn.** See PSEUDONYM. [< F *nom* name + *de* of + *plume* pen]
no·men·cla·ture (nō′mən·klā′chər, nō·men′klə-) *n.* **1.** The system of names used to describe the various elements of a science, art, etc.; terminology. **2.** The specific names for the parts or stages of a device, process, etc.
nom·i·nal (nom′ə·nəl) *adj.* **1.** Existing in name only; not actual. **2.** Slight or inconsiderable; trifling. **3.** Of or like a name. **4.** *Gram.* Of, pertaining to, or like a noun. [< L < *nomen* name]
nom·i·nal·ism (nom′ə·nəl·iz′əm) *n. Philos.* The doctrine that universals (abstract concepts) exist only as names and without a basis in reality: opposed to *realism.* [< F *nominalisme*] — **nom′i·nal·ist** *adj. & n.*
nom·i·nal·ly (nom′ə·nəl-ē) *adv.* In name only; not actually.
nom·i·nate (nom′ə·nāt) *v.t.* **-nat·ed, -nat·ing** **1.** To name or propose as a candidate for elective office. **2.** To appoint to some office or duty. — *adj.* Having a particular or special name. [< L *nominare* to name] — **nom′i·na′tion** *n.* — **nom′i·na′tor** *n.*
nom·i·na·tive (nom′ə·nə·tiv, nom′ə·nā′-) *adj.* **1.** *Gram.* Designating the case of the subject of a finite verb, or of a word agreeing with or in apposition to the subject. **2.** Appointed by nomination; nominated. — *n. Gram.* **1.** The nominative case. **2.** A word in this case.
nom·i·nee (nom′ə·nē′) *n.* One who receives a nomination.
-nomy *combining form* The science or systematic study of: *astronomy, economy.* [< Gk. *nomos* law]
non- *prefix* Not. [< F < L *non* not]
◆ *Non-* is the Latin negative adverb adopted as an English prefix. It denotes in general simple negation or absence of, as in *nonheroic,* not heroic, *nonattendance,* lack of attendance. Numerous words beginning with *non-* are self-explaining, as in the list beginning below.

nonabsolute	nonassertive	noncerebral	noncompression	nonconventional	nonderivable
nonabsorbent	nonassignable	nonceremonial	noncompulsion	nonconvergent	nonderivative
nonabstainer	nonassimilation	noncertified	nonconcealment	nonconversant	nonderogatory
nonaccent	nonathletic	nonchargeable	nonconcentration	nonconversion	nondespotic
nonacceptance	nonatmospheric	nonchemical	nonconception	nonconvertible	nondestructive
nonaccomplishment	nonattached	nonchemical	nonconcurrence	nonconviction	nondetachable
nonacid	nonattendance	non-Chinese	noncondensation	nonconvivial	nondetonating
nonacquaintance	nonattention	non-Christian	nonconditioned	noncoordinating	nondevelopment
nonacquiescence	nonattributive	nonchurch	nonconducive	noncorrective	nondevotional
nonaction	nonaugmentative	noncitizen	nonconducting	noncorresponding	nondialectical
nonactive	nonauthoritative	noncivilized	nonconferrable	noncorroborative	nondictatorial
nonadherence	nonautomatic	nonclassifiable	nonconfidential	noncorrosive	nondifferentiation
nonadjacent	nonautomotive	nonclerical	nonconflicting	noncosmic	nondiffusing
nonadministrative	nonbacterial	nonclinical	nonconforming	noncreative	nondiplomatic
nonadmission	non-Baptist	nonclotting	noncongealing	noncreditor	nondirectional
nonadult	nonbasic	noncoagulating	noncongenital	noncriminal	nondirigible
nonadvantageous	nonbeliever	noncoalescing	noncongestion	noncritical	nondisappearing
nonadverbial	nonbelieving	noncoercive	non-Congressional	noncrucial	nondischarging
nonaffiliated	nonbelligerent	noncognition	nonconnective	noncrystalline	nondisciplinary
non-African	nonbenevolent	noncognitive	nonconnivance	noncrystallized	nondiscontinuance
nonaggression	non-Biblical	noncoherent	nonconnotative	nonculpable	nondiscountable
nonagreement	nonblending	noncohesive	nonconnubial	noncultivated	nondiscovery
nonagricultural	nonblooming	noncoincident	nonconscious	noncultivation	nondiscrimination
nonalcoholic	non-Bolshevik	noncollaborative	nonconsecutive	noncumulative	nondiscriminatory
nonalgebraic	non-Bolshevist	noncollapsible	nonconsent	noncurrency	nondisfranchised
nonaligned	nonbreakable	noncollectable	nonconsenting	nondamageable	nondisinterested
nonallergic	non-British	noncollegiate	nonconsequence	nondecaying	nondispersion
nonalphabetic	non-Buddhist	noncolonial	nonconservative	nondeceptive	nondisposal
nonamateur	nonbudding	noncombat	nonconsideration	nondefensive	nondisqualifying
nonamendable	nonbureaucratic	noncombining	nonconspiring	nondeferential	nondissenting
non-American	nonburnable	noncombustible	nonconstitutional	nondeferrable	nondistinctive
non-Anglican	nonbusiness	noncombustion	nonconstructive	nondefilement	nondistribution
nonantagonistic	noncaffeine	noncommendable	nonconsular	nondefining	nondistributive
nonapologetic	noncaking	noncommercial	nonconsultative	nondegeneration	nondivergence
nonapostolic	non-Calvinist	noncommunicable	nonconsumption	nondelineation	nondivergent
nonappearance	noncanonical	noncommunicating	noncontagious	nondelirious	nondivisible
nonappearing	noncapitalistic	noncommunist	noncontemporary	nondelivery	nondivision
nonapprehensive	noncarnivorous	non-Communist	noncontiguous	nondemand	nondoctrinal
nonaquatic	noncategorical	noncompensating	noncontinental	nondemocratic	nondocumentary
non-Arab	non-Catholic	noncompensation	noncontinuous	nondepartmental	nondogmatic
non-Arabic	non-Caucasian	noncompetent	noncontradiction	nondeparture	nondomesticated
nonaristocratic	noncelestial	noncompeting	noncontradictory	nondependence	nondramatic
nonarithmetical	noncellular	noncompetitive	noncontributing	nondepletion	nondrying
nonarrival	non-Celtic	noncomplaisant	noncontributory	nondeportation	nonearning
non-Aryan	noncensored	noncompletion	noncontrolled	nondepositor	nonecclesiastical
non-Asiatic	noncentral	noncomplying	noncontroversial	nondepreciating	noneconomic

non·age (non′ij, nō′nij) *n.* **1.** The period of legal minority. **2.** A period of immaturity. [< OF < *non* not + *age* age]

non·a·ge·nar·i·an (non′ə·jə·nâr′ē·ən, nō′nə-) *n.* A person between 90 and 100 years of age. — *adj.* **1.** Being ninety years old, or between 90 and 100. **2.** Of or pertaining to a nonagenarian. [< L *nonagenarius* of ninety]

non·a·gon (non′ə·gon) *n. Geom.* A polygon having nine sides and nine angles. [< L *nonus* ninth + Gk. *gōnia* angle]

nonce (nons) *n.* Present time or occasion: now chiefly in the phrase **for the nonce.** [ME *for then ones* for the one (occasion), misread as *for the nones*]

nonce word A word coined for a single occasion.

non·cha·lant (non′shə·lənt, non′shə·länt′) *adj.* Marked by or exhibiting a lack of interest or excitement; casually indifferent. [< F < L *non* not + *calere* to be warm, to be desirous] — **non′cha·lance** *n.* — **non′cha·lant·ly** *adv.*

non·com (non′kom′) *U.S. Informal n.* A noncommissioned officer. — *adj.* Noncommissioned.

non·com·bat·ant (non′kəm·bat′ənt, non′kom′bə·tənt, -kum′-) *n.* **1.** One whose duties as a member of a military force do not entail fighting, as a chaplain or medical officer. **2.** A civilian in wartime.

non·com·mis·sioned (non′kə·mish′ənd) *adj.* Not holding a commission: said of certain grades of the armed forces.

noncommissioned officer *Mil.* An enlisted man appointed to a noncommissioned grade, as from corporal to sergeant major in the U.S. Army. See table for GRADE.

non·com·mit·tal (non′kə·mit′l) *adj.* Not involving or revealing a commitment to any particular attitude, opinion, etc. — **non′com·mit′tal·ly** *adv.*

non·com·pli·ance (non′kəm·plī′əns) *n.* Failure or neglect to comply. — **non′com·pli′ant** *adj. & n.*

non com·pos men·tis (non kom′pəs men′tis) *Law* Not of sound mind; mentally unbalanced: often **non compos.** [< L]

non·con·duc·tor (non′kən·duk′tər) *n.* A substance that offers resistance to the passage of some form of energy, as of heat or electricity. — **non′con·duct′ing** *adj.*

non·con·form·ist (non′kən·fôr′mist) *n.* **1.** One who does not conform to an approved manner of behaving or thinking. **2.** *Often cap.* An English Protestant who refuses to conform to the Church of England. — **non′con·form′ing** *adj.* — **non′con·for′mi·ty** *n.*

non·co·op·er·a·tion (non′kō·op′ə·rā′shən) *n.* Failure to cooperate; esp., resistance to a government through civil disobedience, including the refusal to pay taxes. — **non′co·op′er·a′tion·ist** *n.* — **non′co·op′er·a·tive** (-kō·op′rə·tiv, -kō·op′ə·rā′tiv) *adj.* — **non′co·op′er·a′tor** *n.*

non·de·script (non′di·skript) *adj.* Not distinctive enough to be described; lacking individual character. — *n.* A nondescript person or thing: often used disparagingly. [< NON- + L *descriptus*, pp. of *describere* to describe]

none (nun) *pron.* (construed as *sing.* or *pl.*) **1.** Not one; no one. **2.** No or not one (specified person or thing); not any (of a class of things). **3.** No part or portion; not any: It is *none* of my business. — *adv.* By no means; not at all: He is *none* too bright. [OE < *ne* not + *an* one]

non·ef·fec·tive (non′i·fek′tiv) *adj.* **1.** Not effective. **2.** Unfit or unavailable for active service or duty, as in the army or navy. — *n.* A noneffective soldier, sailor, etc.

non·en·ti·ty (non·en′tə·tē) *n. pl.* **·ties 1.** One who or that which is of little or no account; a nothing. **2.** That which does not exist, or exists solely in the imagination. **3.** The negation of being; nonexistence.

nones (nōnz) *n.pl.* **1.** In the ancient Roman calendar, the ninth day before the ides. **2.** *Often cap. Eccl.* Prescribed prayers constituting the fifth of the seven canonical hours. [< OF < L *nonae*, fem. pl. of *nonus* ninth]

none·such (nun′such′) *n.* **1.** One who or that which has no equal; nonpareil. **2.** A variety of apple. Also *nonsuch.*

none·the·less (nun′thə·les′) *adv.* In spite of everything; nevertheless. Also **none the less.**

non·fea·sance (non·fē′zəns) *n. Law* The nonperformance of some act that one is legally bound to perform. — **non·fea′sor** *n.*

non·fer·rous (non·fer′əs) *adj.* Not containing iron; esp., pertaining to metals other than iron, as copper, tin, platinum, etc.

non·fic·tion (non·fik′shən) *n.* Prose literature other than fiction, as historical works, biographies, etc. — **non·fic′tion·al** *adj.* — **non·fic′tion·al·ly** *adv.*

non·flam·ma·ble (non·flam′ə·bəl) *adj.* Not flammable.

no·nil·lion (nō·nil′yən) *n.* **1.** *U.S.* A thousand octillions, written as 1 followed by thirty zeros: a cardinal number. **2.** *Brit.* A million octillions (def. 2), written as 1 followed by fifty-four zeros: a cardinal number. — *adj.* Being a nonillion in number. [< MF < L *nonus* ninth + F (*m*)*illion* million] — **no·nil′lionth** (-yənth) *adj. & n.*

non·in·ter·ven·tion (non′in·tər·ven′shən) *n.* **1.** The refusal or failure to intervene; esp., the policy or practice of a nation of not intervening in the affairs of other nations. **2.** An instance of this. — **non′in·ter·ven′tion·ist** *adj. & n.*

non·join·der (non·join′dər) *n. Law* An omission to join an action or suit, as by a person who should be a party to it.

non·ju·ror (non·jŏŏr′ər) *n.* One who refuses to take an oath, as of allegiance, supremacy, or abjuration. [< NON- + JUROR, in obs. sense "one who takes an oath"]

non·met·al (non·met′l) *n. Chem.* Any element, as nitrogen, carbon, or sulfur, that has acid rather than basic properties.

non·mor·al (non·môr′əl, -mor′-) *adj.* Having no relation to morals; neither moral nor immoral. — **non′mo·ral′i·ty** *n.*

non·ob·jec·tive (non′əb·jek′tiv) *adj.* Not objective; esp., denoting a style of nonrepresentational art.

non·pa·reil (non′pə·rel′) *adj.* Having no equal; unrivaled. — *n.* **1.** One who or that which has no equal; a paragon. **2.** Any of various brilliantly colored finches of the southern U.S. **3.** *Printing* A size of type, 6 points, between agate and minion. [< MF < *non* not + OF *pareil* equal]

non·par·ti·san (non·pär′tə·zən) *adj.* Not partisan; esp., not controlled by, associated with, or in support of the interests of any one political party. Also **non·par′ti·zan.**

non·plus (non·plus′, non′plus) *v.t.* **·plused** or **·plussed, ·plus·ing** or **·plus·sing** To cause to be at a loss; baffle; perplex. — *n.* A mental standstill; bewilderment, esp. as causing speechlessness or indecision. [< L *non plus* no further]

non·pro·duc·tive (non′prə·duk′tiv) *adj.* **1.** Not productive; esp., pertaining to that part of the labor force that does not directly contribute to the production of goods, as office workers, salesmen, etc. **2.** Unproductive. — **non′pro·duc′tive·ly** *adv.* — **non′pro·duc′tive·ness** *n.*

nonedible	nonesthetic	nonextensile	nonforfeiture	nonhumorous	noninheritable
noneditorial	noneternity	nonextension	nonformal	nonidentical	noninjurious
noneducable	nonethereal	nonextinct	nonfortuitous	nonidentity	noninjury
noneducational	nonethical	nonextinction	nonfraudulent	nonidiomatic	noninquiring
noneffervescent	nonethnological	nonextortion	nonfreezing	nonidolatrous	noninstruction
nonefficacious	non-Euclidean	nonextradition	non-French	nonignitible	noninstrumental
nonefficiency	noneugenic	nonextraneous	nonfulfillment	nonimaginary	noninsurance
nonefficient	non-European	nonfactual	nonfunctional	nonimitative	nonintellectual
nonelastic	nonevanescent	nonfading	nonfundamental	nonimmunity	nonintelligent
nonelective	nonevangelical	nonfanatical	nongaseous	nonimpairment	noninterchangeable
nonelectric	nonevasion	nonfanciful	nongelatinous	nonimperative	noninterference
nonelementary	nonevolutionary	non-Fascist	nongenealogical	nonimperial	nonintermittent
nonelimination	nonexcessive	nonfastidious	nongenerative	nonimportant	noninternational
nonemotional	nonexchangeable	nonfatal	nongenetic	nonimportation	noninterrupted
nonemphatic	nonexciting	nonfatalistic	non-Gentile	nonimpregnated	nonintersecting
nonempirical	nonexclusive	nonfederal	non-German	nonimprovement	nonintestinal
nonenforcement	nonexcusable	nonfederated	nongovernmental	nonincandescent	nonintrospective
non-English	nonexecution	nonfermented	nongranular	noninclusive	nonintuitive
nonentailed	nonexemplary	nonfertility	non-Greek	nonincrease	noninverted
nonenteric	nonexempt	nonfestive	nongregarious	nonindependent	nonionized
nonentry	nonexercise	nonfeudal	nonhabitable	non-Indian	nonirrigation
nonephemeral	nonexistence	nonfigurative	nonhabitual	nonindictable	nonirritant
nonepicurean	nonexisting	nonfilamentous	nonharmonious	nonindictment	non-Islamic
nonequal	nonexpansive	nonfinancial	nonhazardous	nonindividual	nonisolation
nonequation	nonexpendable	nonfinite	nonheathen	nonindividualistic	non-Japanese
nonequatorial	nonexperienced	nonfireproof	non-Hellenic	non-Indo-European	non-Israelite
nonequilateral	nonexperimental	nonfiscal	nonhereditary	nonindustrial	non-Italian
nonequilibrium	nonexpert	nonfissionable	nonheretic	noninfallible	non-Japanese
nonequivalent	nonexploitation	nonflowering	nonheritable	noninfection	non-Jew
nonequivocating	nonexplosive	nonflowing	nonheroic	noninfinite	non-Jewish
nonerasure	nonexportable	nonfluctuating	nonhistoric	noninflammatory	nonjudicial
nonerotic	nonexportation	nonflying	nonhomogeneous	noninflected	nonjuristic
nonerudite	nonextant	nonfocal	nonhostile	noninflectional	nonlaminated
nonessential	nonextended	nonforfeitable	nonhuman	noninformative	non-Latin

non·prof·it (non·prof′it) *adj.* Not organized or maintained for the making of a profit: *nonprofit* charities.

non·pros (non·pros′) *v.t.* **·prossed, ·pros·sing** *Law* To enter judgment against (a plaintiff who fails to prosecute). [Short for NON PROSEQUITUR]

non pro·seq·ui·tur (non prō·sek′wi·tər) *Law* A judgment entered against a plaintiff who fails to prosecute an action. [< L, lit., he does not prosecute]

non·rep·re·sen·ta·tion·al (non′rep′ri·zen·tā′shən·əl) *adj.* Not representational; esp., denoting a style of art that does not seek to represent objects as they appear in nature.

non·res·i·dent (non·rez′ə·dənt) *adj.* Not resident; esp., not residing permanently in the locality where one works, owns property, attends school, etc. —*n.* One who is nonresident. —**non·res′i·dence, non·res′i·den·cy** *n.*

non·re·sis·tant (non′ri·zis′tənt) *adj.* **1.** Not resistant; esp., incapable of resistance, as to infection. **2.** Of, pertaining to, or characteristic of a nonresistant. —*n.* One who is passive in the face of violence. —**non′re·sis′tance** *n.*

non·re·stric·tive (non′ri·strik′tiv) *adj.* **1.** Not restrictive. **2.** *Gram.* Denoting a word or word group, esp. an adjective clause, that describes its antecedent, but may be omitted without loss of essential meaning, as *which is for sale* in *Our house, which is for sale, needs repairs.*

non·sec·tar·i·an (non′sek·târ′ē·ən) *adj.* Not restricted to or associated with any one religion, sect, or faction.

non·sense (non′sens, -səns) *n.* **1.** That which is without sense, or without good sense; esp., words or actions that are meaningless or absurd. **2.** Things of no importance or use; trifles. **3.** Foolish or frivolous conduct. —**non·sen′si·cal** *adj.* —**non·sen′si·cal·ly** *adv.* —**non·sen′si·cal·ness** *n.*

non seq·ui·tur (non sek′wə·tər) **1.** *Logic* An inference that does not follow from the premises. **2.** Any comment not relevant to what has preceded it. [< L, it does not follow]

non·skid (non′skid′) *adj.* Having a surface that resists skidding.

non·stan·dard (non′stan′dərd) *adj.* **1.** Varying or deviating from the standard. **2.** *Ling.* Designating those usages or varieties of a language that differ from the standard.

nonstandard English *Ling.* Those usages in English that differ from standard English: also *substandard English.*

non·stop (non′stop′) *adj.* Making, having made, or scheduled to make no stops: a *nonstop* flight; *nonstop* train.

non·such (nun′such′) *See* NONESUCH.

non·suit (non′soot′) *Law v.t.* To order the dismissal of the suit of. —*n.* **1.** The abandonment of a suit. **2.** A judgment dismissing a suit, when the plaintiff either abandons it or fails to establish a cause of action.

non·sup·port (non′sə·pôrt′, -pôrt′) *n.* Failure to provide for the support of a legal dependent.

non trop·po (non trop′ō) *Music* Not too much. [< Ital.]

non·un·ion (non·yōon′yən) *adj.* **1.** Not belonging to or associated with a trade union. **2.** Not recognizing or contracting with any trade union; also, not employing the members of any union: *nonunion* shop. **3.** Not produced or maintained by union labor.

non·un·ion·ism (non·yōon′yən·iz′əm) *n.* Opposition to trade unions. —**non·un′ion·ist** *n.*

non·white (non′hwīt′) *n.* One who is not a member of the Caucasoid ethnic division of mankind. —*adj.* **1.** Of or pertaining to nonwhites. **2.** Not white.

noo·dle[1] (nōod′l) *n.* **1.** A simpleton. Also **noo′dle·head′** (-hed′). **2.** *Informal* The head. [? < NOD]

noo·dle[2] (nōod′l) *n.* A thin strip of dried dough, usu. containing egg, used in soup, etc. [< G *nudel*]

nook (nōok) *n.* **1.** An interior corner or angle, as in a room. **2.** Any narrow or retired place, as a recess. [ME *nok* corner]

noon (nōon) *n.* **1.** The middle of the day; twelve o'clock in the daytime. **2.** The highest or culminating point; zenith: the *noon* of life. —*adj.* Of, pertaining to, or ocurring at or about noon. [OE < L *nona* (*hora*) ninth (hour)]

noon·day (nōon′dā′) *n.* Noon. —*adj.* Of or at noon.

no one Not any person; nobody.

noon·time (nōon′tīm′) *n.* **1.** Midday. **2.** The culminating point or period. Also *Archaic* **noon′tide′.** [OE *nōntīd*]

noose (nōos) *n.* **1.** A loop furnished with a running knot, as in a hangman's halter or a snare. **2.** Anything that entraps, restrains, or binds. —*v.t.* **noosed, noos·ing 1.** To capture or secure with a noose. **2.** To make a noose in or with. [< Provençal < L *nodus* knot]

Noot·ka fir (nōot′kə) The Douglas fir.

no-par (nō′pär′) *adj.* Having no par or face value, as certain stock.

nope (nōp) *adv. Chiefly U.S. Slang* No.

nor (nôr) *conj.* And not; likewise not. ◆ *Nor* is used chiefly as a correlative of a preceding negative, as *neither, not,* or *never:* He is neither tall *nor* short; He has not come, *nor* will he. *Nor* is also used to introduce a clause following an affirmative clause: He hates me, *nor* does he hide it. [Contr. of ME *nother* neither]

Nor·dic (nôr′dik) *adj. Anthropol.* Pertaining or belonging to the tall, long-headed, blond-haired subdivision of the Caucasian ethnic stock, distributed mainly in NW Europe. —*n.* A Nordic person. [< NL *nordicus*]

nor′·east·er (nôr·ēs′tər), etc. *See* NORTHEASTER, etc.

Nor·folk jacket (nôr′fək) A loose-fitting men's jacket with a belt and two box pleats at the back and front.

no·ri·a (nō′rē·ə) *n.* An undershot water wheel having buckets on its rim to raise water, used in Spain and the Orient: also called *Persian wheel.* [< Sp. < Arabic *nā′ūrah*]

norm (nôrm) *n.* **1.** A pattern, model, or standard regarded as typical of a specified group. **2.** *Psychol.* The standard of performance in a given function or test, usu. the average achievement for the group concerned. **3.** *Stat.* The mode. [< L *norma* rule]

nor·mal (nôr′məl) *adj.* **1.** Conforming to or consisting of a pattern, process, or standard regarded as usual or typical; natural. **2.** *Psychol.* **a** Well adjusted; without

NORIA

nonlegal	nonmedical	nonnuclear	nonparental	nonplausible	nonproportional
nonlethal	nonmember	nonnucleated	nonparishioner	nonplutocratic	nonproprietary
nonlicensed	nonmercantile	nonnutrient	nonparliamentary	nonpoetic	nonprotection
nonlicentiate	nonmetaphysical	nonnutritious	nonparochial	nonpoisonous	nonprotective
nonlimiting	nonmeteoric	nonnutritive	nonparticipation	nonpolarizable	non-Protestant
nonliquefying	non-Methodist	nonobedient	nonpartisanship	non-Polish	non-Prussian
nonliquidation	nonmetrical	nonobligatory	nonpaternal	nonpolitical	nonpsychic
nonliterary	nonmetropolitan	nonobservable	nonpathogenic	nonporous	nonpublication
nonliturgical	nonmigratory	nonobservance	nonpaying	non-Portuguese	nonpulmonary
nonliving	nonmilitant	nonobservant	nonpayment	nonpredatory	nonpuncturable
nonlocal	nonmilitary	nonobstructive	nonpenalized	nonpredicative	nonpunishment
nonloving	nonmimetic	nonoccupational	nonperceptual	nonpredictable	nonpurulent
nonluminescent	nonmineral	nonoccurrence	nonperforated	nonpreferential	nonracial
nonluminosity	nonministerial	nonodorous	nonperforating	nonprehensile	nonradical
nonlustrous	nonmiraculous	nonoffensive	nonperformance	nonprejudicial	nonratable
non-Lutheran	nonmischievous	nonofficial	nonperiodical	nonprepositional	nonrated
nonmagnetic	nonmobile	nonoperating	nonperishable	non-Presbyterian	nonrational
non-Magyar	non-Mohammedan	nonoperative	nonpermanent	nonprescriptive	nonreactive
non-Malay	non-Mongolian	nonoptional	nonpermeability	nonpreservative	nonreality
nonmalignant	non-Moslem	nonorganic	nonpermeable	nonpresidential	nonreasonable
nonmalleable	nonmunicipal	non-Oriental	nonpermissible	nonpressure	nonreceptive
nonmarital	nonmuscular	nonorthodox	nonperpendicular	nonprevalent	nonreciprocal
nonmaritime	nonmystical	nonowner	nonperpetual	nonpriestly	nonrecognition
nonmarriageable	nonmythical	nonoxidizing	nonpersecution	nonproducer	nonrecourse
nonmarrying	nonnatural	nonoxygenated	nonperseverance	nonprofessional	nonrecoverable
nonmartial	nonnautical	nonpacific	nonpersistence	nonprofessorial	nonrectangular
nonmaterial	nonnaval	nonpagan	nonpersistent	nonproficiency	nonrecurrent
nonmaterialistic	nonnavigable	nonpalatal	nonphilanthropic	nonprofiteering	nonrecurring
nonmateriality	nonnecessity	nonpalatalization	nonphilosophical	nonprogressive	nonredeemable
nonmaternal	nonnegotiation	nonpapist	nonphysical	nonprohibitive	nonrefillable
nonmathematical	non-Negro	nonpar	nonphysiological	nonprolific	nonrefueling
nonmatrimonial	nonneutral	nonparallel	nonpigmented	nonpromiscuous	nonregenerating
nonmechanical	non-Norman	nonparalytic	nonplanetary	nonprophetic	nonregenerative
nonmechanistic	non-Norse	nonparasitic	nonplastic	nonpropitiation	nonregent

marked or persistent mental aberrations. **b** Of average skill, intelligence, etc. **3.** *Chem.* **a** Denoting a solution containing one gram equivalent weight of solute per liter: used as a unit, as *two normal*, *three normal*, etc. **b** Denoting a hydrocarbon having a straight, unbranched chain of carbon atoms: *normal* butane. **4.** *Math.* Perpendicular. — *n.* **1.** *Math.* A perpendicular; esp., a perpendicular to a tangent line or plane at the point of tangency. **2.** The common or natural condition, form, degree, etc. **3.** The usual or accepted rule or process. [< L < *norma* rule] — **nor′mal·cy, nor·mal·i·ty** (nôr·mal′ə·tē), **nor′mal·ness** *n.*

normal curve *Stat.* A bell-shaped curve representing the distribution of a series of values of a variable.

normal distribution *Stat.* A frequency distribution represented by a normal curve.

nor·mal·ize (nôr′məl·īz) *v.t.* **·ized, ·iz·ing** To bring into accord with a norm or standard form; make normal. — **nor′·mal·i·za′tion** *n.* — **nor′mal·iz′er** *n.*

nor·mal·ly (nôr′mə·lē) *adv.* **1.** As a rule; usually: The mail *normally* comes before noon. **2.** In a normal manner.

normal school A school that prepares secondary-school graduates to become teachers.

Nor·man (nôr′mən) *n.* **1.** One of the Scandinavian people who conquered Normandy in the tenth century. **2.** One of the people of mixed Scandinavian and French descent who conquered England in 1066. **3.** A resident of Normandy. **4.** Norman French. — *adj.* Of or pertaining to Normandy or the Normans. [< OF *Normans* Northmen]

Norman Conquest The subjugation of England by William the Conqueror in 1066. See table for WAR.

Norman French **1.** The dialect of French spoken by the Normans in the Middle Ages. **2.** The legal parlance of England from the Norman Conquest to the 17th century. **3.** The dialect of French spoken in Normandy. Also *Norman.*

nor·ma·tive (nôr′mə·tiv) *adj.* **1.** Of, pertaining to, or based upon a norm, esp. one regarded as a standard or rule of usage. **2.** Implying, supporting, or establishing a norm.

Norse (nôrs) *adj.* **1.** Scandinavian. **2.** Of or pertaining to Norway, Iceland, and the Faroe Islands; West Scandinavian. — *n.* **1.** The Scandinavians or West Scandinavians collectively: used with *the.* **2.** The Scandinavian or North Germanic group of the Germanic languages; esp., Norwegian. **3.** The West Scandinavian languages. — **Old Norse 1.** The ancestor of the North Germanic languages, best represented by Old Icelandic: also called *Old Scandinavian.* **2.** Old Icelandic: see under ICELANDIC. [< Du. < MDu. *nordsch, nortsch* northern]

Norse·man (nôrs′mən) *n. pl.* **·men** (-mən) A Scandinavian of Viking times.

north (nôrth) *n.* **1.** The direction along a meridian that falls to the left of an observer on earth facing the sun at sunrise. **2.** One of the four cardinal points of the compass, directly opposite *south* and 90° counterclockwise from *east.* See COMPASS CARD. **3.** Any direction near this point. **4.** *Sometimes cap.* Any region north of a specified point. — the **North** In the U.S.: **a** The population or territory of the northern or northeastern States; esp., the region north of Maryland, the Ohio River, and Missouri. **b** The Free States op-

posed to the Confederacy (*the South*) in the Civil War. — *adj.* **1.** To, toward, facing, or in the north. **2.** Coming from the north. — *adv.* In or toward the north. [OE]

North American Indian An Indian of any of the tribes formerly inhabiting North America north of Mexico, now the United States and Canada. *Abbr. N.Am.Ind.*

North Atlantic Drift The terminal current of the Gulf Stream system, flowing from near Newfoundland northeast to Western Europe. Also **North Atlantic Current.**

North Atlantic Treaty Organization A military and naval alliance of Belgium, Canada, Denmark, France, Greece, Iceland, Italy, Luxemburg, the Netherlands, Norway, Portugal, Turkey, the United Kingdom, the U.S., and West Germany, organized under the **North Atlantic Treaty** of Washington, Apr. 4, 1919. *Abbr. NATO*

north·bound (nôrth′bound′) *adj.* Going northward. Also **north′-bound′.**

north·east (nôrth′ēst′, *Naut.* nôr-ēst′) *n.* **1.** The direction midway between north and east. **2.** A point on the mariner's compass, four points or 45° clockwise from due north. See COMPASS CARD. **3.** Any region lying in or toward this point. — *adj.* **1.** To, toward, facing, or in the northeast. **2.** Coming from the northeast. — *adv.* In or toward the northeast. — **north′east′ern** *adj.*

north·east·er (nôrth′ēs′tər, *Naut.* nôr-ēs′tər) *n.* **1.** A gale or storm from the northeast. **2.** A sailor's hat with a sloping brim worn in stormy weather. Also spelled *nor′easter.*

north·east·er·ly (nôrth′ēs′tər·lē, *Naut.* nôr-ēs′tər·lē) *adj.* **1.** In, of, or toward the northeast. **2.** From the northeast, as a wind. — *adv.* Toward or from the northeast. — *n.* A wind or storm from the northeast. Aso spelled *nor′easterly.*

north·east·ward (nôrth′ēst′wərd, *Naut.* nôr-ēst′wərd) *adv.* Toward the northeast. Also **north′east′wards** (-wərdz). — *adj.* To, toward, facing, or in the northeast. — *n.* Northeast.

north·east·ward·ly (nôrth′ēst′wərd·lē, *Naut.* nôr-ēst′wərd·lē) *adj. & adv.* Toward or from the northeast.

north·er (nôr′thər) *n.* **1.** A gale or storm from the north. **2.** *U.S.* A violent, cold north wind blowing over the plains of the SW States.

north·er·ly (nôr′thər·lē) *adj.* **1.** In, of, toward, or pertaining to the north. **2.** From the north, as a wind. — *adv.* Toward or from the north. — *n.* A wind or storm from the north. — **north′er·li·ness** *n.*

north·ern (nôr′thərn) *adj.* **1.** To, toward, or in the north. **2.** Native to or inhabiting the north: a *northern* species. **3.** *Sometimes cap.* Of, pertaining to, or characteristic of the north or the North. **4.** From the north, as a wind.

north·ern·er (nôr′thər·nər) *n.* **1.** One who is native to or lives in the north. **2.** *Usu. cap.* One who lives in or comes from the North.

northern lights The aurora borealis.

north·ern·most (nôr′thərn·mōst′) *adj.* Farthest north.

Northern Spy A large, yellowish red variety of apple.

north·land (nôrth′lənd) *n.* A land or region in the north. [OE] — **north′land·er** *n.*

North·man (nôrth′mən) *n. pl.* **·men** (-mən) A Scandinavian; esp., a Scandinavian of the Viking period. [OE]

North Star Polaris.

nonregimented	nonrevertible	non-Semitic	nonspeculative	nonsymptomatic	nonunited
nonregistered	nonrevival	nonsensitive	nonspherical	nonsynchronous	nonuniversal
nonreigning	nonrevolving	nonsensitized	nonspiritual	nonsyntactical	nonuser
nonrelative	nonrhetorical	nonsensual	nonspontaneous	nonsynthesized	nonuterine
nonrelevant	nonrhymed	nonsensuous	nonstainable	nonsystematic	nonutilitarian
nonreligious	nonrhythmic	nonsentient	nonstandardized	nontarnishable	nonutilization
nonremunerative	nonritual	nonseparable	nonstarter	nontaxable	nonvalidity
nonrenewable	nonrival	nonservile	nonstarting	nonteachable	nonvascular
nonrepayable	non-Roman	nonsexual	nonstatic	nontechnical	nonvegetative
nonrepentant	nonromantic	non-Shakespearean	nonstationary	nontemporal	nonvenereal
nonrepetition	nonrotating	nonsharing	nonstatistical	nontemporizing	nonvenomous
nonrepetitive	nonroyal	nonshattering	nonstatutory	nonterminating	nonvenous
nonreprehensible	nonruminant	nonshatterproof	nonstimulating	nonterrestrial	nonverbal
nonrepresentative	nonrural	nonshrinkable	non-Stoic	nonterritorial	nonvesicular
nonreproductive	non-Russian	nonsignificant	nonstrategic	nontextual	nonviable
nonresemblance	nonrusting	nonsilver	nonstretchable	nontheatrical	nonvibratory
nonresidential	nonsacramental	nonsimplification	nonstriker	nontheological	nonviolation
nonresidual	nonsacred	nonsinkable	nonstriking	nontherapeutic	nonviolence
nonresinous	nonsacrificial	non-Slavic	nonstructural	nonthinking	nonvirulent
nonresisting	nonsalable	nonslipping	nonsubmissive	nontitular	nonviscous
nonresistive	nonsalaried	nonsmoker	nonsubscriber	nontoxic	nonvisiting
nonresolvable	nonsaturated	nonsmoking	nonsubstantial	nontraditional	nonvisual
nonresonant	non-Scandinavian	nonsocial	nonsuccessful	nontransferable	nonvitreous
nonrestraint	nonscheduled	nonsocialist	nonsuccessive	nontransitional	nonvocal
nonrestricted	nonscholastic	nonsocialistic	nonsulfurous	nontransparent	nonvocational
nonretention	nonscientific	nonsolid	nonsupporter	nontransposing	nonvolatile
nonretinal	nonscoring	nonsolvent	nonsupporting	nontributary	nonvolcanic
nonretiring	nonseasonal	nonsovereign	nonsustaining	nontropical	nonvolition
nonretraceable	nonsecretarial	nonsparing	non-Swedish	nontruth	nonvoluntary
nonretractile	nonsecretive	nonsparkling	nonsyllabic	nontuberculous	nonvortical
nonretrenchment	nonsecular	non-Spartan	nonsymbolic	nontypical	nonvoter
nonretroactive	nonsedentary	nonspecialized	nonsymmetrical	nontypographical	nonvoting
nonreturnable	nonseditious	nonspecific	nonsympathetic	nontyrannical	nonvulcanizable
nonrevealing	nonsegmented	nonspectacular	nonsympathizer	nonulcerous	nonworking
nonreversible	nonselective	nonspectral	nonsymphonic	non-Unitarian	nonyielding

North·um·bri·a (nôr·thum′brē·ə) An ancient Anglo-Saxon kingdom, extending from the Humber to the Firth of Forth.
North·um·bri·an (nôr·thum′brē·ən) *adj.* **1.** Of or pertaining to Northumbria or to its inhabitants. **2.** Of or pertaining to the Old English dialect used in Northumbria. — *n.* **1.** A native or inhabitant of Northumbria. **2.** The Old English Northumbrian dialect.
north·ward (nôrth′wərd, *Naut.* nôr′thərd) *adv.* Toward the north. Also **north′wards** (-wərdz). — *adj.* To, toward, facing, or in the north. — *n.* A northward direction or point; also, a northern part or region.
north·ward·ly (nôrth′wərd·lē, *Naut.* nôr′thərd·lē) *adj. & adv.* **1.** Toward the north. **2.** Coming from the north.
north·west (nôrth′west′, *Naut.* nôr·west′) *n.* **1.** The direction midway between north and west. **2.** A point on the mariner's compass, four points or 45° counterclockwise from due north. See COMPASS CARD. **3.** Any region, lying in or toward this point. — *adj.* **1.** To, facing, or in the northwest. **2.** Coming from the northwest. — *adv.* In or toward the northwest. — **north′west′ern** *adj.*
north·west·er (nôrth′wes′tər, *Naut.* nôr·wes′tər) *n.* A gale or storm from the northwest: also spelled *nor′wester.*
north·west·er·ly (nôrth′wes′tər·lē, *Naut.* nôr·wes′tər·lē) *adj.* **1.** In, of, or toward the northwest. **2.** From the northwest, as a wind. — *adv.* Toward or from the northwest.
north·west·ward (nôrth′west′wərd, *Naut.* nôr·west′wərd) *adv.* Toward the northwest. Also **north′west′wards.** — *adj.* To, toward, or in the northwest. — *n.* Northwest.
north·west·ward·ly (nôrth′west′wərd·lē, *Naut.* nôr·west′wərd·lē) *adj. & adv.* Toward or from the northwest.
Nor·way maple (nôr′wā) A tall European maple.
Nor·we·gian (nôr·wē′jən) *adj.* Of or pertaining to Norway, its people, or their language. — *n.* **1.** A native or inhabitant of Norway. **2.** The North Germanic language of Norway. [< Med.L < ON < *nor(thr)* north + *vegr* way]
nor′·west·er (nôr·wes′tər), etc. See NORTHWESTER, etc.
nose (nōz) *n.* **1.** The part of the face or forward end of an animal that contains the nostrils and the organ of smell, and that in man encloses cavities used in the respiratory process. ◆ Collateral adjectives: *nasal, rhinal.* **2.** The sense of smell or the power of smelling; scent. **3.** The ability to perceive or discover by or as if by the sense of smell: a *nose* for scandal. **4.** Something resembling a nose, as a spout or nozzle. **5.** *Aeron.* The forward part of an aircraft. **6.** The prow of a ship. **7.** *Informal* The nose (def. 1), considered as its owner's agent for prying or interfering: Keep your *nose* out of this. — **by a nose** *Slang* By a narrow margin. — **on the nose** *Slang* **1.** Designating a racing bet on a horse, etc., to win. **2.** Exactly; precisely. — **to pay through the nose** *Slang* To pay an excessively high price. — *v.* **nosed, nos·ing** *v.t.* **1.** To nuzzle. **2.** To make (one's way) carefully with the front end foremost. **3.** To perceive or discover by or as if by smell; scent. — *v.i.* **4.** To pry or interfere; snoop: with *around* or *about.* **5.** To move forward, esp. carefully. **6.** To smell; sniff. — **to nose out** To defeat by a narrow margin. [OE *nosu*]
nose·band (nōz′band′) *n.* The part of a bridle that passes over the nose of a horse: also called *nosepiece.*
nose·bleed (nōz′blēd′) *n.* Bleeding from the nose.
nose cone *Aerospace* The cone-shaped forward section of a rocket or missile, separable from the main body and carrying the payload, and able to withstand great heat.
nose-dive (nōz′dīv′) *v.i.* **-dived, -div·ing** To take a nose dive; plunge downward.
nose dive 1. A steep, downward plunge of an aircraft, nose end foremost. **2.** Any steep, sudden drop.
nose·gay (nōz′gā′) *n.* A small bunch of flowers; bouquet. [< NOSE + GAY, in obs. sense "a pretty thing"]
nose·piece (nōz′pēs′) *n.* **1.** Any piece or part, as of a helmet, that covers or protects the nose. **2.** A noseband.
nos·ey (nōz′ē) See NOSY.
nos·tal·gi·a (nos·tal′jə, -jē·ə) *n.* **1.** A longing for familiar or beloved circumstances that are now remote or irrecoverable. **2.** Any longing for something far away or long ago. **3.** Severe homesickness. [< NL < Gk. *nostos* return home + *algos* pain] — **nos·tal′gic** *adj.*
nos·tril (nos′trəl) *n.* One of the external openings of the nose. [OE < *nos(u)* nose + *thyrel* hole]
nos·trum (nos′trəm) *n.* **1.** A medicine of one's own preparation; also, a quack medicine. **2.** A favorite remedy or plan. **3.** A cure-all. [< L *noster* our own]
nos·y (nōz′ē) *adj.* **nos·i·er, nos·i·est** *Informal* Prying; snooping; inquisitive: also spelled *nosey.*
not (not) *adv.* In no way, or to no extent or degree: used to note the absence, reverse, or opposite of something or to express negation, prohibition, or refusal. [OE < *ne* not + *ā* ever + *wiht* thing however small]
not- Var. of NOTO-.

no·ta·ble (nō′tə·bəl) *adj.* Worthy of note; remarkable; distinguished. — *n.* One who is distinguished, famous, etc. [< OF < L *nota* mark] — **no′ta·bil′i·ty** *n.* — **no′ta·ble·ness** *n.* — **no′ta·bly** *adv.*
no·ta·rize (nō′tə·rīz) *v.t.* **·rized, ·riz·ing** To attest to or authenticate as a notary public. — **no′ta·ri·za′tion** *n.*
no·ta·ry public (nō′tə·rē) *pl.* **no·ta·ries public** One who is legally authorized to administer oaths, certify contracts, etc. Also **notary.** — **no·tar′i·al** (-târ′ē·əl) *adj.*
no·ta·tion (nō·tā′shən) *n.* **1.** A system of signs, figures, or abbreviations used for convenience in recording a quantity, relation, process, etc.: musical *notation*; algebraic *notation.* **2.** The act or process of using notation. **3.** A note or comment. [< L < *notare* to note] — **no·ta′tion·al** *adj.*
notch (noch) *n.* **1.** A V-shaped cut in a surface. **2.** A nick cut into a stick, etc., as for keeping count. **3.** A narrow passage between mountains; a defile. **4.** *Informal* A degree; level: He is a *notch* above the others. — *v.t.* **1.** To make a notch or notches in. **2.** To record by or as if by notches; score. [Prob. ME < OF *oschier* to notch]
note (nōt) *n.* **1.** *Often pl.* A brief record or summary of facts set down for future study or reference: to take *notes.* **2.** A brief account or jotting to aid the memory. **3.** *Music* **a** A symbol representing a tone or sound of a given duration and pitch. **b** A tone or sound of a definite pitch. **c** A key of the keyboard. **4.** Any more or less musical sound, as the call of a bird. **5.** Any distinctive vocal sound, as the cry of an animal. **6.** A distinctive mark: a *note* of sadness; a *note* of spring in the air. **7.** A piece of paper currency issued by a government or authorized bank and negotiable as money: a bank *note.* **8.** A promissory note (which see). **9.** A formal, written communication of an official or diplomatic nature. **10.** A brief letter, esp. of an informal character. **11.** *pl.* A record of impressions, observations, reflections, etc. **12.** A marginal comment amending, criticizing, or explaining a passage in a book, etc.; annotation. **13.** Distinction; importance; reputation: a gentleman of *note.* **14.** Notice; attention: worthy of *note.* **15.** *Archaic* or *Poetic* A melody or song. — *v.t.* **not·ed, not·ing 1.** To become aware of; observe. **2.** To pay attention to; heed carefully: to *note* well. **3.** To make special mention of. **4.** To set down for remembering; make a note of. **5.** To point out or indicate. [< OF < L < *nota* mark] — **no′ter** *n.*
note·book (nōt′bo͝ok′) *n.* **1.** A book with blank pages on which notes may be entered. **2.** A book in which notes of hand are registered; bill book.
not·ed (nō′tid) *adj.* **1.** Well known by reputation; famous. **2.** Taken note of. — **not′ed·ly** *adv.* — **not′ed·ness** *n.*
note paper Paper for writing notes or letters.
note·wor·thy (nōt′wûr′thē) *adj.* Remarkable; significant. — **note′wor′thi·ly** *adv.* — **note′wor′thi·ness** *n.*
noth·ing (nuth′ing) *n.* **1.** Not anything; naught. **2.** No part or element: He knew *nothing* of it. **3.** One who or that which is of little or no importance. **4.** Insignificance or unimportance: to rise from *nothing.* **5.** Zero. **6.** A state of nonexistence; also, that which is nonexistent. — **for nothing 1.** Without charge; free. **2.** To no avail. **3.** Without cause. — *adv.* In no degree; not at all: now only in the expression **nothing like.** [ME < OE *nān thing*]
noth·ing·ness (nuth′ing·nis) *n.* **1.** The condition, quality, or fact of being nothing; nonexistence. **2.** Utter worthlessness or insignificance. **3.** That which is petty, trivial, or nonexistent. **4.** Unconsciousness.
no·tice (nō′tis) *v.t.* **·ticed, ·tic·ing 1.** To pay attention to or become aware of. **2.** To refer to or comment on. **3.** To treat courteously or with favor. — *n.* **1.** The act of noticing or observing. **2.** Announcement; information; warning. **3.** A formal announcement: to give *notice.* **4.** A written or printed communication publicly displayed. **5.** A short advertisement or review. **6.** Respectful treatment; civility. [< OF < L *notitia* fame, renown]
no·tice·a·ble (nō′tis·ə·bəl) *adj.* **1.** That can be noticed; perceptible. **2.** Worthy of notice. — **no′tice·a·bly** *adv.*
no·ti·fi·ca·tion (nō′tə·fə·kā′shən) *n.* **1.** The act of notifying. **2.** Notice given. **3.** A sign, advertisement, etc., by which notice is conveyed.
no·ti·fy (nō′tə·fī) *v.t.* **·fied, ·fy·ing 1.** To give notice to; inform. **2.** *Chiefly Brit.* To make known. [< OF < L *notus* known + *facere* to make] — **no′ti·fi′er** *n.*
no·tion (nō′shən) *n.* **1.** A general idea or impression; a vague conception. **2.** An opinion, belief, or idea. **3.** Intention; inclination. **4.** *pl. U.S.* Small miscellaneous articles for sale. — **Syn.** See IDEA. [See NOTIFY.]
no·tion·al (nō′shən·əl) *adj.* **1.** Pertaining to, expressing, or consisting of notions or concepts. **2.** Existing in imagination only. — **no′tion·al·ly** *adv.*
noto- *combining form* Back. Also, before vowels, *not-.* [< Gk. *nōton* back]

no·to·chord (nō/tə·kôrd) *n. Biol.* In invertebrate embryos, a flexible rod of cells along the median line on the dorsal side, a precursor of the spinal column.

no·to·ri·e·ty (nō/tə·rī/ə·tē) *n. pl.* **·ties** 1. The state or character of being notorious. 2. One who or that which is notorious.

no·to·ri·ous (nō·tôr/ē·əs, -tō/rē-) *adj.* 1. Widely known and generally disapproved of or deplored. 2. Generally known; acknowledged. [< Med.L < *noscere* to know] — **no·to/ri·ous·ly** *adv.*

no-trump (nō/trump/) *n.* 1. In bridge, a bid calling for play without a trump suit. 2. Play without a trump suit. — *adj.* Of or denoting a bid or play of no-trump.

not·with·stand·ing (not/with·stan/ding, -with-) *prep.* In spite of: He left *notwithstanding* your orders. — *adv.* All the same; nevertheless: Though closely guarded, he escaped *notwithstanding*. — *conj.* In spite of the fact that; although. — **notwithstanding that** Although.

nou·gat (nōō/gət, *Fr.* nōō·gä/) *n.* A confection made with chopped almonds, pistachios, etc., mixed in a honey or sugar paste. [< F < Provençal]

nought (nôt) See NAUGHT.

noun (noun) *n. Gram.* 1. A word used as the name of a thing, quality, or action. 2. Anything that can be used either as subject, object, or appositive, as a noun clause. — *adj.* Of or pertaining to a noun or nouns: also **noun/al.** [< AF, OF < L *nomen* name] — **noun/al·ly** *adv.*

noun clause *Gram.* A dependent clause that functions as a noun in a sentence, as *Whoever finds my wallet* in *Whoever finds my wallet will be rewarded*.

nour·ish (nûr/ish) *v.t.* 1. To furnish food or other material to sustain the life and promote the growth of (a living plant or animal). 2. To support; maintain; foster. [< OF < L *nutrire* to nourish] — **nour/ish·a·ble** *adj.* — **nour/ish·er** *n.* — **nour/ish·ing·ly** *adv.*

nour·ish·ment (nûr/ish·mənt) *n.* 1. That which nourishes; nutriment. 2. The act of nourishing, or the state of being nourished.

nou·veau riche (nōō/vō/ rēsh/) *French pl.* **nou·veaux riches** (nōō/vō/ rēsh/) One who has recently become rich.

no·va (nō/və) *n. pl.* **·vae** (-vē) or **·vas** *Astron.* A star that suddenly flares up and fades away after a period of a few months or years. [< L, fem. of *novus* new]

nov·el (nov/əl) *adj.* New, strange, or unusual. — *n.* A fictional prose narrative of considerable length, usu. having an overall pattern or plot. [< F < Ital. < L *novus* new]

nov·el·ette (nov/əl·et/) *n.* A short novel: also *novella.*

nov·el·ist (nov/əl·ist) *n.* A writer of novels.

nov·el·is·tic (nov/əl·is/tik) *adj.* Of, pertaining to, characteristic of, or found in novels. — **nov/el·is/ti·cal·ly** *adv.*

nov·el·ize (nov/əl·īz) *v.t.* **·ized, ·iz·ing** To put into the form of a novel. — **nov/el·i·za/tion** *n.*

no·vel·la (nō·vel/ə, *Ital.* nō·vel/lä) *n. pl.* **·vel·las,** *Ital.* **·vel·le** (-vel/lä) 1. A short tale or narrative, usu. with a moral. 2. A novelette. [< Ital. See NOVEL.]

nov·el·ty (nov/əl·tē) *n. pl.* **·ties** 1. Something novel or unusual. 2. The quality of being novel or new. 3. *Usu. pl.* A small manufactured article.

No·vem·ber (nō·vem/bər) The eleventh month of the year, containing 30 days. [< L, ninth month (of the old Roman calendar) < *novem* nine]

no·ve·na (nō·vē/nə) *n.* In the Roman Catholic Church, devotions made on nine successive days, for some special religious purpose. [< Med.L < L *novem* nine]

nov·ice (nov/is) *n.* 1. A beginner in any occupation; an inexperienced person. 2. *Eccl.* One who enters a religious order or community on probation. [< F < L *novicius* new]
— **Syn.** 1. *Novice* is a general term, often used as the official designation for those who have yet to demonstrate proficiency in a game or sport. *Beginner* is a homelier synonym for *novice*, sometimes implying disparagement; even more depreciatory is *tyro*.

no·vi·ti·ate (nō·vish/ē·it, -āt) *n.* 1. The state or period of being a novice. 2. *Eccl.* **a** The period of probation of a novice in a religious order or community. **b** The quarters occupied by such novices. 3. A novice (defs. 1 and 2). Also **no·vi/ci·ate.** [< F *novicat* or Med.L *novitiatus*]

No·vo·cain (nō/və·kān) *n.* Proprietary name for a brand of procaine used as a local anesthetic, less toxic than cocaine. Also **no/vo·cain, no/vo·caine, No/vo·caine.**

now (nou) *adv.* 1. At once. 2. At or during the present time. 3. Nowadays. 4. In the immediate past: He said so just *now.* 5. In the immediate future: He is going just *now.* 6. In such circumstances: *Now* we can be sure of getting home. 7. At this point in the proceedings, narrative, etc.: The war was *now* virtually over. — *conj.* Seeing that; since: *Now* that you've come, stay a while. — *n.* The present time, moment, or occasion. — **now and then** From time to time; occasionally: also **now and again.** [OE *nū*]

now·a·days (nou/ə·dāz/) *adv.* In the present time or age.

no·way (nō/wā/) *adv.* 1. In no way, manner, or degree. 2. *U.S. Dial.* By any means. Also **no/ways/** (-wāz/).

no·where (nō/hwâr/) *adv.* In no place; not anywhere. — *n.* No place. Also *U.S. Dial.* **no/wheres/** (-hwârz/).

no·wise (nō/wīz/) *adv.* In no manner or degree.

nox·ious (nok/shəs) *adj.* Causing or tending to cause injury to health or morals; hurtful. — **Syn.** See PERNICIOUS. [< L < *noxa* harm] — **nox/ious·ly** *adv.* — **nox/ious·ness** *n.*

noz·zle (noz/əl) *n.* A projecting spout or pipe serving as an outlet, as of a teapot, hose, or rifle. [Dim. of NOSE]

nth (enth) *adj.* 1. *Math.* Representing an ordinal equivalent to *n.* 2. Infinitely or indefinitely large (or small); most extreme: to the *nth* degree.

nu (nū, nōō) *n.* The thirteenth letter in the Greek alphabet (N, ν), corresponding to English *n.* See ALPHABET.

nu·ance (nōō·äns/, nōō/äns, nyōō/-; *Fr.* nü·äns/) *n.* A fine or subtle variation, as in color, tone, or meaning; gradation. [< F < OF *nuer* to shade < *nue* cloud]

nub (nub) *n.* 1. A knob or protuberance. 2. A small piece, as of coal. 3. *U.S. Informal* Core; gist; point: the *nub* of the story. [Var. of KNOB] — **nub/by** *adj.*

nub·bin (nub/in) *n. U.S.* 1. An imperfectly developed fruit or ear of corn. 2. Anything small or stunted. [< NUB]

nub·ble (nub/əl) *n.* A small protuberance or lump; nub. [Dim. of NUB] — **nub/bly** *adj.*

Nu·bi·an (nōō/bē·ən, nyōō/-) *adj.* Of Nubia, its people, or their language. — *n.* 1. A native of Nubia; esp., a member of any of the tribes formerly ruling the territory between Egypt and Abyssinia. 2. The language of the Nubians.

nu·bile (nōō/bil, nyōō/-) *adj.* Ready or suitable for marriage: said of young women. [< L < *nubere* to wed] — **nu·bil/i·ty** *n.*

nu·cle·ar (nōō/klē·ər, nyōō/-) *adj.* 1. Of, pertaining to, or resembling a nucleus or nuclei. Also **nu/cle·al** (-klē·əl). 2. Of or using atomic energy: *nuclear* reactor. [< F *nucléaire*]

nuclear fission *Physics* Fission.

nuclear fusion *Physics* Fusion.

nuclear physics The branch of physics that investigates the structure and properties of the atomic nucleus.

nuclear reaction *Physics* A change in the properties of one or more atomic nuclei, esp. as a result of a collision between two nuclei.

nu·cle·ase (nōō/klē·ās, nyōō/-) *n. Biochem.* An enzyme that hydrolyzes nucleic acids.

nu·cle·ate (nōō/klē·āt, nyōō/-) *adj.* Having a nucleus. — *v.t. & v.i.* **·at·ed, ·at·ing** To form or gather into a nucleus. [< L *nucleare* to form a kernel] — **nu/cle·a/tion** *n.* — **nu/cle·a/tor** *n.*

nu·cle·ic acid (nōō·klē/ik, nyōō-) *Biochem.* Any of a group of complex noncrystalline acids derived from nucleoproteins and containing carbohydrates combined with phosphoric acids and bases derived from purine or pyrimidine.

nu·cle·in (nōō/klē·in, nyōō/-) *n. Biochem.* A colorless, amorphous protein containing nucleic acid, found as a normal constituent of cell nuclei.

nucleo- *combining form* Nucleus. [< L *nucleus* kernel]

nu·cle·o·late (nōō/klē·ə·lāt, nyōō/-) *adj.* Having a nucleolus or nucleoli. Also **nu/cle·o·lat/ed.**

nu·cle·o·lus (nōō·klē/ə·ləs, nyōō/-) *n. pl.* **·li** (-lī) *Biol.* A rounded body sometimes found within the nucleus of a cell. Also **nu/cle·ole** (-ōl). For illus. see CELL. [< L, dim. of NUCLEUS] — **nu·cle/o·lar** *adj.*

nu·cle·on (nōō/klē·on, nyōō/-) *n. Physics* Any of the particles composing the nucleus of an atom, as the proton, neutron, neutrino, etc.

nu·cle·on·ics (nōō/klē·on/iks, nyōō/-) *n.pl.* (*usually construed as sing.*) The practical applications of nuclear physics in any field of science, engineering, or technology. — **nu/cle·on/ic** *adj.*

nu·cle·o·plasm (nōō/klē·ə·plaz/əm, nyōō/-) *n. Biol.* The protoplasm of a cell nucleus. — **nu/cle·o·plas/mic** *adj.*

nu·cle·o·pro·te·in (nōō/klē·ə·prō/tē·in, -tēn, nyōō/-) *n. Biochem.* Any of a class of substances found in the nuclei of plant and animal cells, containing one or more protein molecules combined with nucleic acid.

nu·cle·us (nōō/klē·əs, nyōō/-) *n. pl.* **·cle·i** (-klē·ī) 1. A central point or part around which other things are gathered; core. 2. A center of growth or development. 3. *Biol.* A complex spherical body surrounded by a thin membrane and embedded in the protoplasm of most plant and animal cells, containing chromatin and essential to the processes of heredity and to other vital activities of the cell. For illus. see CELL. 4. *Astron.* The brightest portion in the head of a comet or in the center of a nebula. 5. *Physics* The central core of an atom, containing nucleons that provide its effective mass and carrying a positive electric charge balanced by the negative charge of the surrounding electrons. 6. *Chem.* A group or ring of atoms so related structurally that their fundamental arrangement remains intact through a series of chemical changes. [Contr. of L *nuculeus,* dim. of *nux, nucis* nut]

nu·clide (nōō/klīd, nyōō/-) *n. Physics* A specific, relatively stable atom as defined by the composition and properties of its nucleus.

nude (nōōd, nyōōd) *adj.* Without clothing or covering; naked. — *n.* **1.** A nude figure, esp. in painting, sculpture, etc. **2.** The state of being nude. [< L *nudus* naked, bare] — **nude′ly** *adv.* — **nude′ness** *n.*

nudge (nuj) *v.t.* **nudged, nudg·ing** To touch or push gently, as with the elbow, in order to attract attention, etc. — *n.* A gentle push, as with the elbow. [? < Scand.]

nudi- *combining form* Without covering; naked; bare. [< L *nudus* naked]

nud·ism (nōō′diz·əm, nyōō′-) *n.* The doctrine or practice of living in the state of nudity.

nud·ist (nōō′dist, nyōō′-) *n.* One who believes in or practices nudism. — *adj.* Of or pertaining to nudism.

nu·di·ty (nōō′də·tē, nyōō′-) *n.* *pl.* **·ties 1.** The state or fact of being nude. **2.** A naked part; anything uncovered.

nud·nik (nōōd′nik) *n.* *U.S. Slang* A pestiferous or annoying person. Also **nud′nick.** [< Yiddish]

nug·get (nug′it) *n.* A lump; esp., a lump of gold found in its native state. [? Dim. of dial. E *nug* lump]

nui·sance (nōō′səns, nyōō′-) *n.* Anything that annoys, bothers, or irritates. [< F < *nuire* to harm]

nuisance tax A tax on various consumer goods and services, etc., regarded as more of a bother than a burden.

null (nul) *adj.* **1.** Of no legal force or effect; void; invalid. **2.** Nonexistent; negative. **3.** Of no avail; useless. — **null and void** Without legal force or effect. [< L < *ne* not + *ullus* any]

nul·li·fi·ca·tion (nul′ə·fə·kā′shən) *n.* **1.** The act of nullifying, or the state of being nullified. **2.** In U.S. history, the refusal of a State to obey an act of Congress, or the doctrine that such refusal is legal.

nul·li·fy (nul′ə·fī) *v.t.* **·fied, ·fy·ing 1.** To make useless or ineffective; undo. **2.** To deprive of legal force or effect. — **Syn.** See ANNUL. [< LL < *nullus* none + *facere* to make] — **nul′li·fi′er** *n.*

nul·li·ty (nul′ə·tē) *n.* *pl.* **·ties 1.** The state of being null. **2.** That which is null.

numb (num) *adj.* **1.** Having no sensation; without feeling. **2.** Unable to move, — *v.t.* To make numb. [ME < OE < *niman* to take] — **numb′ly** *adv.* — **numb′ness** *n.*

num·ber (num′bər) *n.* **1.** A specific quantity or place in a sequence, usu. designated by one of a series of symbols or words called *numerals.* **2.** A symbol or word used to designate number; a numeral. **3.** *Often pl.* A sizable collection or grouping: *numbers* of people. **4.** An indefinite quantity or collection: a *number* of facts. **5.** A specific sum or total count. **6.** *pl.* A large group; multitude. **7.** One of a series of things to which numbers are assigned: the March *number* of a magazine. **8.** A part of a program of music or entertainment. **9.** Quantity, as composed of units. **10.** A particular group, esp. of a privileged character. **11.** *Gram.* The representation in a language, by inflection or otherwise, of singleness or plurality. English has the singular and the plural number. **12.** *pl.* In poetry, metrical feet or rhythm; also, verse or verses. **13.** *Informal* An item or article, as of merchandise. Symbol #. — **any number of** A good many; rather a lot. — **beyond (or without) number** Too numerous to be counted. — **to get (or have) one's number** *Informal* To have insight into a person's motives, character, etc. — *v.t.* **1.** To determine the total number of; reckon. **2.** To assign a number to. **3.** To include as one of a collection or group. **4.** To amount to; total. **5.** To set or limit the number of. **6.** To be (a number of years, etc.) old or older. — *v.i.* **7.** To make a count; total. **8.** To be included, as in a particular group. **9.** To count off or call out numbers. [< OF < L *numerus*] — **num′ber·er** *n.*

num·ber·less (num′bər·lis) *adj.* **1.** Very numerous; countless. **2.** Having no number.

Num·bers (num′bərz) *n.pl.* (construed as sing.) The fourth book of the Old Testament.

num·bles (num′bəlz) *n.pl. Archaic* The entrails of an animal, as a deer. [< OF, ult. < LL *lumbellus*, dim. of L *lumbus* loin]

numb·skull (num′skul′) See NUMSKULL.

nu·mer·a·ble (nōō′mər·ə·bəl, nyōō′-) *adj.* That can be numbered. [< L *numerare* to count]

nu·mer·al (nōō′mər·əl, nyōō′-) *n.* A symbol, letter, or word that is used alone or in combination with others to express a number. — *adj.* **1.** Used in expressing or representing a number. **2.** Of or pertaining to number. [< LL < *numerus* number] — **nu′mer·al·ly** *adv.*

nu·mer·ate (nōō′mə·rāt, nyōō′-) *v.t.* **·at·ed, ·at·ing 1.** To enumerate; count. **2.** To read, as a numerical expression. [< L *numerare* to count]

nu·mer·a·tion (nōō′mə·rā′shən, nyōō′-) *n.* **1.** The act, process, or system of reading or naming numbers. **2.** An instance or example of this.

nu·mer·a·tor (nōō′mə·rā′tər, nyōō′-) *n.* **1.** *Math.* The term

of a fraction indicating how many of the parts of a unit are to be taken. In a common fraction it appears above or to the left of the line. **2.** One who or that which numbers.

nu·mer·i·cal (nōō·mer′i·kəl, nyōō′-) *adj.* **1.** Of or denoting number. **2.** Numerable. **3.** Represented by or consisting of numbers or figures rather than letters. [< NL < L *numerus* number] — **nu·mer′i·cal·ly** *adv.*

nu·mer·ous (nōō′mər·əs, nyōō′-) *adj.* Consisting of a great number of units; being many. — **nu′mer·ous·ly** *adv.* — **nu′·mer·os′i·ty** (nōō′mə·ros′ə·tē, nyōō′-), **nu′mer·ous·ness** *n.*

Nu·mid·i·a (nōō·mid′ē·ə, nyōō-) An ancient kingdom and Roman province in northern Africa. — **Nu·mid′i·an** *adj. & n.*

nu·mis·mat·ics (nōō′miz·mat′iks, -mis-, nyōō′-) *n.pl.* (construed as sing.) The study of coins, medals, and related objects, as paper money. [< F < L *numisma* coin < Gk. < *nomos* law] — **nu′mis·mat′ic** *adj.* — **nu·mis′ma·tist** *n.*

num·skull (num′skul′) *n.* A blockhead; dunce: also spelled *numbskull.*

nun (nun) *n.* A woman belonging to a religious order and living in a convent under vows of poverty, chastity, and obedience. [OE < LL *nonna* child's nurse, fem. of *nonnus*, orig., old man] — **nun′nish** *adj.*

nun·ci·o (nun′shē·ō, -sē·ō, nōōn′-) *n.* *pl.* **·ci·os** A permanent diplomatic envoy of the Pope to a foreign government. — **Syn.** See AMBASSADOR. [< Ital. < L *nuntius* messenger]

nun·ner·y (nun′ər·ē) *n.* *pl.* **·ner·ies** A convent for nuns.

nun's veiling (nunz) A soft, thin fabric, usu. of worsted, used for veiling and as a dress material.

nup·tial (nup′shəl) *adj.* Of or pertaining to marriage or the marriage ceremony. — *n.* *Usu. pl.* A marriage or wedding. [< L *nubere* to marry] — **nup′tial·ly** *adv.*

nurse (nûrs) *n.* **1.** A person who cares for the sick, injured, or infirm; esp., one who is trained to do such work. **2.** One who is a graduate of a school of nursing. **3.** A nursemaid. **4.** One who or that which fosters, nourishes, protects, or promotes. — *v.* **nursed, nurs·ing** *v.t.* **1.** To take care of (the sick, injured, or infirm). **2.** To feed (an infant) at the breast; suckle. **3.** To promote the growth and development of; foster; cherish. **4.** To feed and care for, as a child. **5.** To take steps to cure. **6.** To use or operate carefully: to *nurse* a weak wrist. **7.** To preserve or prolong deliberately. **8.** To fondle. **9.** To suckle at the breast of. — *v.i.* **10.** To act or serve as a nurse. **11.** To take nourishment from the breast. **12.** To suckle an infant. [Earlier *nurice* < OF < LL < L *nutrix* nursing mother] — **nurs′er** *n.*

nurse·maid (nûrs′mād′) *n.* A woman employed to care for children. Also **nurs·er·y·maid** (nûr′sər·ē·mād′, nûrs′rē-).

nurs·er·y (nûr′sər·ē, nûrs′rē) *n.* *pl.* **·er·ies 1.** A place where trees, shrubs, etc., are raised, as for sale. **2.** A room or area set apart for the use of children. **3.** A nursery school. **4.** Anything that fosters, breeds, or develops.

nurs·er·y·man (nûr′sər·ē·mən, nûrs′rē-) *n.* *pl.* **·men** (-mən) One who raises or cultivates plants in a nursery.

nursery rhyme A simple story, riddle, proverb, etc., presented in rhymed verse or jingle for children.

nursery school A place where children of preschool age regularly meet for training and supervised play.

nursing home A residence for persons who are unable to care for themselves, as the aged or the infirm.

nurs·ling (nûrs′ling) *n.* **1.** An infant or animal in the stage of being nursed. **2.** Anything that is carefully tended or supervised. Also **nurse′ling.**

nur·ture (nûr′chər) *n.* **1.** That which nourishes; food; sustenance. **2.** Training; breeding; education. — *v.t.* **tured, ·tur·ing 1.** To feed or support; nourish; rear. **2.** To bring up or train; educate. [< OF < LL < L *nutrire* to nourish]

nut (nut) *n.* **1.** A dry fruit consisting of a kernel or seed enclosed in a woody shell, as a walnut, pecan, acorn, etc. **2.** The kernel of such fruit, esp. when edible. **3.** A small block of metal having an internal screw thread so that it may be fitted upon a bolt, screw, or the like. **4.** A person or matter difficult to deal with; a problem. **5.** *U.S. Slang* A crazy, irresponsible, or eccentric person. **6.** *Slang* The head. **7.** *Usu. pl. Slang* A testicle. — *v.i.* **nut·ted, nut·ting** To gather nuts. [OE *hnutu*] — **nut′ter** *n.*

nut-brown (nut′broun′) *adj.* Of a dark shade of brown suggesting the color of certain nuts, as the walnut.

nut·crack·er (nut′krak′ər) *n.* **1.** *Sometimes pl.* A device for cracking the hard shells of nuts. **2.** Any of certain crowlike birds, as the common nutcracker of Europe.

nut-gall (nut′gôl′) *n.* A nut-shaped gall, as on an oak tree.

nut·hatch (nut′hach′) *n.* A small, short-tailed bird related to the titmouse and feeding on nuts.

nut·meg (nut′meg) *n.* **1.** The aromatic kernel of the fruit of various tropical trees, esp. of the nutmeg tree of the Molucca Islands. **2.** The tree itself. [ME < OF < *nois* nut + *mugue* musk]

Nutmeg State Nickname of Connecticut.

nut·pick (nut′pik′)   *n.* A small, sharp-pointed instrument for picking out the kernels of nuts.

nu·tri·a (nōō′trē-ə, nyōō′-)   *n.* The soft brown fur of the coypu, often dyed to resemble beaver. [< Sp., otter]

nu·tri·ent (nōō′trē-ənt, nyōō′-)   *adj.* 1. Giving nourishment; nutritious. 2. Conveying nutriment. — *n.* Something that nourishes; food. [< L < *nutrire* to nourish]

nu·tri·ment (nōō′trə-mənt, nyōō′-)   *n.* 1. That which nourishes; food. 2. Anything that promotes development. [< L < *nutrire* to nourish] — **nu′tri·men′tal** *adj.*

nu·tri·tion (nōō-trish′ən, nyōō-)   *n.* 1. The act or process of nourishing; esp., the processes by which food is converted into tissue in living organisms. 2. That which nourishes. [< L < *nutrire* to nourish] — **nu·tri′tion·al** *adj.* — **nu·tri′tion·al·ly** *adv.* — **nu·tri′tion·ist** *n.*

nu·tri·tious (nōō-trish′əs, nyōō-)   *adj.* Promoting growth and repairing the waste of living organisms; nourishing. — **nu·tri′tious·ly** *adv.* — **nu·tri′tious·ness** *n.*

nu·tri·tive (nōō′trə-tiv, nyōō′-)   *adj.* 1. Having nutritious properties. 2. Of or relating to nutrition. — **nu′tri·tive·ly** *adv.* — **nu′tri·tive·ness** *n.*

nuts (nuts)   *Chiefly U.S. Slang adj.* 1. Crazy; demented; eccentric. 2. Extremely enthusiastic or in love: with *about.* — *interj.* An exclamation of contempt, disappointment, etc. [< pl. of NUT]

nut·shell (nut′shel′)   *n.* The shell of a nut. — **in a nutshell** In brief and concise statement or form.

nut·ty (nut′ē)   *adj.* **·ti·er**, **·ti·est** 1. Abounding in or producing nuts. 2. Having the flavor of nuts. 3. *Chiefly U.S. Slang* Crazy; nuts. — **nut′ti·ly** *adv.* — **nut′ti·ness** *n.*

nux vom·i·ca (nuks′ vom/i-kə)   1. The silky disklike seed of an Indian tree containing strychnine and other poisons. 2. The tree itself. [< L *nux* nut + *vomere* to vomit]

nuz·zle (nuz′əl)   *v.* **·zled, ·zling** *v.i.* 1. To rub, press, or dig with or as with the nose. 2. To nestle or snuggle; lie close. — *v.t.* 3. To push or rub the nose, etc., into or against. 4. To root up with the nose or snout. [Freq. of NOSE, v.]

nycto-   *combining form* Night; nocturnal. Also, before vowels, **nyct-**. Also **nycti-**. [< Gk. *nyx, nyktos* night]

ny·lon (nī′lon)   *n.* 1. A synthetic material yielding fibers and bristles of great toughness, strength, and elasticity; esp., cloth made from these fibers. 2. *pl. Informal* Stockings made of nylon. [< *Nylon,* a trade name]

nymph (nimf)   *n.* 1. In Greek and Roman mythology, any of a class of minor female divinities dwelling in groves, forests, fountains, etc. 2. *Chiefly Poetic.* A young woman or girl. 3. *Entomol.* The young of an insect undergoing incomplete metamorphosis, at which stage the wing pads are first evident: also **nym·pha** (nim′fə). [< OF < L < Gk. *nymphē* nymph, bride] — **nymph′al, nym·phe·an** (nim-fē′-ən) *adj.*

nympho-   *combining form* Nymph; bride. Also, before vowels, **nymph-**. [< Gk. *nymphē* bride, nymph]

nym·pho·ma·ni·a (nim′fə-mā′nē-ə, -mān′yə)   *n. Psychiatry* An extreme and ungovernable sexual desire in women. — **nym′pho·ma′ni·ac** *adj. & n.*

Nyx (niks)   In Greek mythology, the goddess of night.

O

o, O (ō)   *n. pl.* **o's** or **os, O's** or **Os, oes** (ōz) 1. The fifteenth letter of the English alphabet. 2. Any sound represented by the letter *o.* 3. Anything shaped like an *O.* — *symbol* 1. *Math.* Zero or nought. 2. *Chem.* Oxygen.

o' (ō, ə)   *prep.* Of: one o'clock, man-o′-war, jack-o′-lantern.

o-   Var. of OB-.

O (ō)   *interj.* 1. An exclamation used in direct address, as in prayer or invocation: *O Lord!* 2. An exclamation of surprise, disappointment, fear, longing, etc.: *O dear!* — *n. pl.* **O's** An exclamation or lamentation.

O' (ō)   A descendant of: *O'Conor:* a patronymic prefix commonly used in Irish surnames, equivalent to the English and Scandinavian suffixes -*son,* -*sen.* Compare FITZ-, MAC-.

oaf (ōf)   *n. pl.* **oafs** or *Rare* **oaves** (ōvz) A stupid, bungling person. [Earlier *auf* < ON *ālfr* elf] — **oaf′ish** *adj.* — **oaf′ish·ly** *adv.* — **oaf′ish·ness** *n.*

oak (ōk)   *n.* 1. An acorn-bearing tree or shrub of the beech family, valued for the hardness, strength, and durability of its timber. ◆ Collateral adjective: *quercine.* 2. The wood of the oak. 3. Any of various plants resembling the oak. [OE *āc*] — **oak′en** *adj.*

oak apple A rounded gall produced on an oak by an insect. Also **oak gall.**

oak leaf cluster A bronze decoration given to holders of certain U.S. military medals in recognition of further merit.

oak·um (ō′kəm)   *n.* Hemp fiber obtained by untwisting and picking out the fibers of old rope, used for caulking seams, etc. [OE *ācumba* < *ā-* out + *cemban* to comb]

oar (ôr, ōr)   *n.* 1. A wooden implement for propelling or steering a boat, consisting of a long shaft with a blade at one end. 2. A person using an oar. 3. An oarlike part or appendage, as in certain worms. — *v.t.* 1. To propel with or as with oars; row. 2. To make (one's way) or traverse (water) with or as with oars. — *v.i.* 3. To proceed by or as by rowing; row. [OE *ār*]

oared (ôrd, ōrd)   *adj.* Having or equipped with oars.

oar·lock (ôr′lok′, ōr′-)   *n.* A device on the side of a boat for keeping an oar in place. Also, *Brit.,* rowlock.

oars·man (ôrz′mən, ōrz′-)   *n. pl.* **·men** (-mən) One who rows.

o·a·sis (ō-ā′sis, ō′ə-sis)   *n. pl.* **·ses** (-sēz) An area in a desert made fertile by groundwater or by irrigation. [< L < Gk.]

oat (ōt)   *n.* 1. *Usu. pl.* A cereal grass widely cultivated for its edible grain. 2. *Usu. pl.* The grain itself. 3. Any similar grass, as the wild oat. 4. A musical pipe made from the stem of an oat. — **to feel one's oats** *Informal* 1. To be exuberant or high-spirited. 2. To feel bold or self-assured. — **to sow one's wild oats** *Informal* To experience the adventures and follies characteristic of youth. [OE *āte*] — **oat′en** *adj.*

oat·cake (ōt′kāk′)   *n.* A thin, hard cake of oatmeal.

oath (ōth)   *n. pl.* **oaths** (ōths, ōᵺs) 1. A formal declaration in support of a pledge or promise, usu. based on an appeal to God or some other higher institution or figure; also, the form of the declaration. 2. The careless or profane use of the name of God or other sacred person or thing. 3. A profane or vulgar utterance. [OE *āth*]

oat·meal (ōt′mēl′)   *n.* A cereal food made from the cooked meal of oats; also, the meal itself. Also **oat meal.**

ob-   *prefix* 1. Toward; to; facing: *obvert.* 2. Against; in opposition to: *object, obstruct.* 3. Over; upon: *obliterate.* 4. Completely; obdurate. 5. Inversely: prefixed to adjectives in scientific terms. Also: *o-* before *m,* as in *omit; oc-* before *c,* as in *occur; of-* before *f,* as in *offend; op-* before *p,* as in *oppress.* [< L *ob* toward, for, against]

O·ba·di·ah (ō′bə-dī′ə)   Sixth-century B.C. minor Hebrew prophet. — *n.* A book of the Old Testament containing his prophecies.

ob·bli·ga·to (ob′lə-gä′tō, *Ital.* ōb′blē-gä′tō)   *Music adj.* Denoting a part or accompaniment essential to the performance of a composition. — *n.* An obbligato part. Also spelled *obligato.* [< Ital. < L *obligare.* See OBLIGE.]

ob·du·rate (ob′dyə-rit, -rāt)   *adj.* 1. Unmoved by or hardened against human feelings or moral influence; hardhearted. 2. Difficult to handle or manage; intractable. [< L < *ob-* against + *durare* to harden] — **ob′du·rate·ly** *adv.* — **ob′du·ra·cy** (-rə-sē), **ob′du·rate·ness** *n.*

o·be·di·ence (ō-bē′dē-əns, ə-bē′-)   *n.* The act of obeying, or the condition of being obedient; submission; compliance.

o·be·di·ent (ō-bē′dē-ənt, ə-bē′-)   *adj.* 1. Complying with or conforming to a command, restraint, etc.; dutiful. 2. Deferring habitually to laws, superiors, etc.; docile; compliant. [See OBEY.] — **o·be′di·ent·ly** *adv.*

o·bei·sance (ō-bā′səns, ō-bē′-)   *n.* Courtesy, reverence, or homage; also, an act or gesture expressing this: chiefly in phrases **to do (make, or pay) obeisance.** [< OF < *obeissant,* ppr. of *obeir* to obey] — **o·bei′sant** *adj.*

ob·e·lisk (ob′ə-lisk)   *n.* 1. A square shaft of stone with a pyramidal top, usu. tapering, and often used as a monument in ancient Egypt. 2. *Printing* The dagger sign (†), used as a mark of reference: also **ob·e·lus** (ob′ə-ləs). [< L < Gk. *obelos* a spit, hence pointed pillar] — **ob′e·lis′cal, ob′e·lis′koid** (-koid) *adj.*

O·ber·on (ō′bə-ron)   In medieval legend and folklore, the king of the fairies, husband of Titania.

o·bese (ō-bēs′)   *adj.* Very fat or corpulent. [< L *obesus* fat] — **o·bese′ly** *adv.*

o·bes·i·ty (ō-bē′sə-tē, ō-bes′ə-)   *n.* The condition of being obese; corpulence. Also **o·bese′ness** *n.*

o·bey (ō-bā′, ə-bā′) *v.t.* **1.** To comply with or carry out the command, request, etc., of. **2.** To comply with or execute (a command, request, etc.). **3.** To be guided, controlled, or actuated by. — *v.i.* **4.** To be obedient; comply. [< OF < L *oboedire* to give ear, obey] — **o·bey′er** *n.*

ob·fus·cate (ob·fus′kāt, ob′fəs-) *v.t.* **·cat·ed, ·cat·ing 1.** To confuse or perplex; bewilder. **2.** To darken or obscure. [< L *obfuscare* to darken, obscure] — **ob′fus·ca′tion** *n.*

o·bi (ō′bē) *n.* A broad sash tied with a stylized bow or loop in the back, worn by Japanese women. [< Japanese *ōbi*]

o·bit (ō′bit, ob′it) *n. Informal* An obituary.

ob·i·ter dic·tum (ob′ə-tər dik′təm) *Latin pl.* **ob·i·ter dic·ta** (dik′tə) **1.** *Law* A judicial opinion that is not binding. **2.** Any incidental remark.

o·bit·u·ar·y (ō-bich′ōō-er′ē) *n. pl.* **·ar·ies** A published notice of a person's death, usu. including a biographical sketch. — *adj.* Of or recording a death. [< Med.L < L *obitus* a going down, death]

ob·ject[1] (əb-jekt′) *v.i.* **1.** To offer an argument in opposition or disagreement. **2.** To feel or state disapproval. — *v.t.* **3.** To offer in opposition or criticism. [< L < *ob-* towards, against + *jacere* to throw] — **ob·jec′tor** *n.*

ob·ject[2] (ob′jikt, -jekt) *n.* **1.** Anything that is or may be apprehended by the senses. **2.** The purpose or end of an action. **3.** One who or that which is the focus or center of thought, action, etc. **4.** *Gram.* **a** A substantive that receives or is affected by the action of the verb, called the **direct object** when it receives the direct action, as *pie* in *She gave him the pie,* and the **indirect object** when it receives the secondary action, as *him* in the same sentence. **b** A substantive following a preposition, as *mountain* in the phrase *on the mountain.* — **Syn.** See PURPOSE. [< Med.L *objectum* something thrown in the way]

object glass *Optics* An objective (*n.* def. 3).

ob·jec·ti·fy (əb-jek′tə-fī) *v.t.* **·fied, ·fy·ing** To make objective. — **ob·jec′ti·fi·ca′tion** *n.*

ob·jec·tion (əb-jek′shən) *n.* **1.** A statement or feeling of disagreement, opposition, etc. **2.** The cause or reason for disagreement, etc. **3.** The act of objecting.

ob·jec·tion·a·ble (əb-jek′shən-ə-bəl) *adj.* Deserving of disapproval; offensive. — **ob·jec′tion·a·bil′i·ty** *n.* — **ob·jec′tion·a·bly** *adv.*

ob·jec·tive (əb-jek′tiv) *adj.* **1.** Free from personal feelings, opinions, prejudice, etc.; unbiased. **2.** Pertaining to what is external to or independent of the mind; real: opposed to *subjective.* **3.** Treating of or stressing external or actual phenomena, as distinct from inner or imaginary feelings and thoughts. **4.** *Gram.* Denoting the case of the object of a transitive verb or preposition; accusative. **5.** Pertaining to a goal or end. — *n.* **1.** That which is striven for or aimed at; a goal; end. **2.** *Gram.* **a** The objective or accusative case. **b** A word in this case. **3.** *Optics* A lens or lenses, as in a telescope, that is nearest to the object being viewed: also called *object glass.* — **ob·jec′tive·ly** *adv.*

ob·jec·tiv·i·ty (ob′jek·tiv′ə-tē) *n.* **1.** The state or quality of being objective. **2.** Material reality. Also **ob·jec′tive·ness.**

object lesson An example of a principle or moral in a concrete form or striking instance.

ob·jet d'art (ob-zhe′ dar′) *French pl.* **ob·jets d'art** (ob·zhe′) Any work of artistic value.

ob·jur·gate (ob′jər-gāt, əb-jûr′-) *v.t.* **·gat·ed, ·gat·ing** To rebuke severely; scold sharply. [< L < *ob-* against + *jurgare* to scold] — **ob′jur·ga′tion** *n.* — **ob′jur·ga′tor** *n.* — **ob·jur·ga·to·ri·ly** (ob·jûr′gə-tôr′ə-lē, -tō′rə-lē) *adv.* — **ob·jur′ga·to·ry** (-tôr′ē, -tō′rē) *adj.*

ob·late[1] (ob′lāt, ob-lāt′) *adj.* Flattened at the poles. [< NL < L *ob-* towards + (*pro*)*latus* lengthened out] — **ob·late·ly** (ob′lāt·lē, ob-lāt′-) *adv.*

ob·late[2] (ob′lāt, ob-lāt′) *adj.* Consecrated or devoted to a religious life. — *n.* A person so devoted, as in a monastery. [< Med.L *oblatus* < L, pp. of *offerre* to present]

ob·la·tion (ob-lā′shən) *n.* **1.** The act of offering religious worship, sacrifice, etc., esp. in the Eucharist. **2.** That which is offered, esp. the elements of the Eucharist. **3.** Any solemn offering. [See OBLATE[2].] — **ob·la′tion·al** *adj.* — **ob·la·to·ry** (ob′lə-tôr′ē, -tō′rē) *adj.*

ob·li·gate (ob′lə-gāt; for *adj.,* also -git) *v.t.* **·gat·ed, ·gat·ing** To bind or compel, as by contract, conscience, promise, etc. — *adj.* Bound or restricted. — **ob′li·ga·tor** *n.*

ob·li·ga·tion (ob′lə-gā′shən) *n.* **1.** The act of obligating, or the state of being obligated. **2.** The duty, promise, contract, etc., by which one is bound. **3.** Any duty or requirement. **4.** The constraining or binding power of a law, promise, conscience, etc. **5.** What one owes in return for a service, favor, etc.; also, the service or favor itself. [< OF < LL < L *obligare.* See OBLIGE.]

ob·li·ga·tive (ob′lə-gā′tiv) *adj.* Implying or expressing obligation.

ob·li·ga·to (ob′lə-gä′tō, *Ital.* ôb′blē-gä′tō) See OBBLIGATO.

ob·lig·a·to·ry (ə-blig′ə-tôr′ē, -tō′rē, ob′lə-gə-) *adj.* Of the nature of or constituting a duty or obligation; imperative.

o·blige (ə-blīj′) *v.t.* **o·bliged, o·blig·ing 1.** To place (one) under obligation, as for a service, favor, etc.: with *to.* **2.** To compel, bind, or constrain, as by command, promise, etc. **3.** To do a favor or service for. [< OF < L *obligare,* orig., to tie around] — **o·blig′er** *n.*

o·blig·ing (ə-blī′jing) *adj.* Disposed to do favors; accommodating; kind. — **o·blig′ing·ly** *adv.* — **o·blig′ing·ness** *n.*

ob·lique (ə-blēk′, *in military usage* ə-blīk′) *adj.* **1.** Deviating from the perpendicular or horizontal; slanting. **2.** Not direct or straightforward in meaning, expression, etc.: *oblique* praise. **3.** Indirectly aimed at or attained. **4.** *Geom.* Having an acute or obtuse angle. **5.** Not in the direct line of descent; collateral. — *n.* **1.** An oblique thing, as a line. **2.** *Naut.* The act of veering less than ninety degrees. — *v.i.* **·liqued, ·li·quing** To deviate from the perpendicular or horizontal; slant. [< L *obliquus*] — **ob·lique′ly** *adv.* — **ob·liq·ui·ty** (ə-blik′wə-tē), **ob·lique′ness** *n.*

oblique angle *Geom.* An angle not a right angle; an acute or obtuse angle.

ob·lit·er·ate (ə-blit′ə-rāt) *v.t.* **·at·ed, ·at·ing 1.** To destroy utterly. **2.** To blot or wipe out, as writing. [< L < *obliterare* to efface] — **ob·lit′er·a′tion** *n.* — **ob·lit′er·a′tive** *adj.* — **ob·lit′er·a′tor** *n.*

ob·liv·i·on (ə-bliv′ē-ən) *n.* **1.** The state or fact of being completely forgotten. **2.** The state or fact of forgetting completely. [< OF < L < *oblivisci* to forget]

ob·liv·i·ous (ə-bliv′ē-əs) *adj.* **1.** Not conscious or aware; unmindful: with *of* or *to.* **2.** Forgetful or given to forgetfulness. [< L *obliviosus*] — **ob·liv′i·ous·ly** *adv.* — **ob·liv′i·ous·ness** *n.*

ob·long (ob′lông, -long) *adj.* Longer in one dimension than in another: said usually of rectangles. — *n.* An oblong figure, object, etc. [< L *oblongus* somewhat long]

ob·lo·quy (ob′lə-kwē) *n. pl.* **·quies 1.** Abusive and defamatory language, esp. by a large group of people; vilification. **2.** Disgrace resulting from such abuse. [< LL < *ob-* against + *loqui* to speak]

ob·nox·ious (əb-nok′shəs) *adj.* Highly disagreeable; objectionable; offensive. [< L < *ob-* towards + *noxius* harmful] — **ob·nox′ious·ly** *adv.* — **ob·nox′ious·ness** *n.*

o·boe (ō′bō, ō′boi) *n.* A double-reed woodwind instrument with a conical bore, having a high, penetrating tone. [< Ital. < F *hautbois.* See HAUTBOY.] — **o′bo·ist** *n.*

ob·scene (əb-sēn′, ob-) *adj.* **1.** Offensive or abhorrent to prevailing concepts of morality or decency; indecent; lewd. **2.** Disgusting; loathsome; foul. [< MF < L *obscenus* ill-omened, filthy] — **ob·scene′ly** *adv.* — **ob·scene′ness** *n.*

ob·scen·i·ty (əb-sen′ə-tē, -sē′nə-, ob-) *n. pl.* **·ties 1.** The quality or state of being obscene. **2.** Something obscene.

ob·scur·ant (əb-skyōōr′ənt) *n.* One who or that which obscures, esp. by opposing or hindering educational progress, free thought, etc. — *adj.* **1.** Causing obscurity. **2.** Of an obscurant. [< L < *obscurare* to darken]

ob·scur·ant·ism (əb-skyōōr′ən·tiz′əm) *n.* **1.** The act or principles of an obscurant. **2.** Opposition to learning and inquiry. — **ob·scur′ant·ist** *n. & adj.*

ob·scure (əb-skyōōr′) *adj.* **scur·er, scur·est 1.** Not clear or plain to the mind; hard to understand. **2.** Not clear or distinct to the senses, difficult to discern. **3.** Not readily discovered; hidden; remote. **4.** Without distinction or fame; inconspicuous. **5.** Having little or no light, dark. — *v.t.* **·scured, scur·ing 1.** To render obscure, vague, indefinite, etc. **2.** To cover or darken so as to make dim, indistinct, etc. [< OF < L *obscurus* covered over] — **ob·scure′ly** *adv.* — **ob·scure′ness** *n.*

ob·scu·ri·ty (əb-skyōōr′ə-tē) *n. pl.* **·ties 1.** The state or quality of being obscure. **2.** An obscure person or thing.

ob·se·quies (ob′sə-kwēz) *n.pl.* Funeral rites. [< OF *obseques* < Med.L *obsequiae,* pl. funeral rites]

ob·se·qui·ous (ob·sē′kwē-əs) *adj.* Excessively obedient or submissive; sycophantic; servile. [< L < *obsequi* to comply with] — **ob·se′qui·ous·ly** *adv.* — **ob·se′qui·ous·ness** *n.*

ob·serv·a·ble (əb-zûr′və-bəl) *adj.* **1.** Capable of being observed; noticeable. **2.** Worthy of notice or mention; noteworthy. **3.** That may or must be observed, as a holiday. — **ob·serv′a·bly** *adv.* — **ob·serv′a·ble·ness** *n.*

ob·serv·ance (əb-zûr′vəns) *n.* **1.** The act of observing a command, law, etc. **2.** The act of celebrating a holiday, ceremony, etc. **3.** A customary rite, ceremony, etc. **4.** Observation; notice; attention. **5.** *Eccl.* The rule or constitution of a religious order.

ob·ser·vant (əb-zûr′vənt) *adj.* **1.** Attentive or quick in observing; heedful; alert. **2.** Strict or careful in obeying or keeping a custom, law, ceremony, etc.: often with *of: observant* of ritual. — **ob·ser′vant·ly** *adv.*

ob·ser·va·tion (ob'zər·vā'shən) *n.* **1.** The act of observing, or the fact of being observed; also, that which is observed. **2.** Close examination for the purpose of scientific study. **3.** An opinion or judgment. **— to take** (or **work out**) **an observation** *Naut.* To calculate the latitude and longitude from the altitude and position of the sun or other celestial body. **— ob'ser·va'tion·al** *adj.* **— ob'ser·va'tion·al·ly** *adv.*

ob·ser·va·to·ry (əb·zûr'və·tôr'ē, -tō'rē) *n. pl.* **·ries 1.** A building or station for the systematic observation of natural phenomena; esp., one for astronomical observation. **2.** A place affording a panoramic view.

ob·serve (əb·zûrv') *v.* **·served, ·serv·ing** *v.t.* **1.** To see or notice; perceive. **2.** To watch attentively. **3.** To make careful observation of, esp. for scientific purposes. **4.** To say or comment; remark. **5.** To follow or comply with (a law, custom, etc.); abide by. **6.** To celebrate as a holiday. **— v.i. 7.** To make a remark; comment: often with *on* or *upon.* **8.** To take notice. **9.** To look on or attend without taking part, as at a meeting. [< OF < L *observare* to watch] **— ob·serv'er** *n.* **— ob·serv'ing·ly** *adv.*

ob·sess (əb·ses') *v.t.* To occupy or trouble the mind of to an excessive degree; preoccupy; harass; haunt. [< L *obsidere* to occupy, beseige] **— ob·ses'sive** *adj.* **— ob·ses'sor** *n.*

ob·ses·sion (əb·sesh'ən) *n.* **1.** That which obsesses, as a persistent idea or feeling. **2.** *Psychiatry* An unwanted or compulsive idea or emotion persistently coming to awareness. **3.** The act of obsessing, or the state of being obsessed.

ob·sid·i·an (əb·sid'ē·ən, ob-) *n.* A glassy volcanic rock, usu. black. [< L *obsidianus*]

ob·so·les·cent (ob'sə·les'ənt) *adj.* Growing obsolete. **— ob'so·les'cence** *n.* **— ob'so·les'cent·ly** *adv.*

ob·so·lete (ob'sə·lēt, ob'sə·lēt') *adj.* **1.** Gone out of fashion; out-of-date. **2.** No longer used or practiced. **3.** *Biol.* Imperfectly developed; atrophied or vestigial. [< L *obsolescere* to wear out] **— ob'so·lete'ly** *adv.* **— ob'so·lete'ness** *n.* **— ob'so·let'ism** *n.*
— Syn. 1. An *obsolete* word is no longer used either in speech or writing, usually because it has been supplanted by a different word. *Archaic* words were current at some time in the past, and appear in the works of Shakespeare, the Bible, etc., but unlike obsolete words they are still used for effect because they have an unmistakable flavor of their period or milieu. *Rare* words may be *archaic* or current, but are little used.

ob·sta·cle (ob'stə·kəl) *n.* That which stands in the way; a hindrance or obstruction. [< OF < L *ob-* before, against + *stare* to stand]

ob·stet·ric (əb·stet'rik) *adj.* Of or pertaining to obstetrics or childbirth. Also **ob·stet'ri·cal.** [< L *obstetrix, -icis* midwife, lit., one who stands by] **— ob·stet'ri·cal·ly** *adv.*

ob·ste·tri·cian (ob'stə·trish'ən) *n.* A medical and surgical specialist in obstetrics.

ob·stet·rics (əb·stet'riks) *n.pl.* (*construed as sing.*) The branch of medicine dealing with pregnancy and childbirth.

ob·sti·na·cy (ob'stə·nə·sē) *n. pl.* **·cies 1.** The state or quality of being obstinate. **2.** An obstinate act, feeling, etc.

ob·sti·nate (ob'stə·nit) *adj.* **1.** Unreasonably fixed in one's purpose or opinion; unyielding; stubborn. **2.** Difficult to overcome or cure: an *obstinate* habit. [< L *obstinare* to persist] **— ob'sti·nate·ly** *adv.* **— ob'sti·nate·ness** *n.*

ob·strep·er·ous (əb·strep'ər·əs) *adj.* Unruly, noisy, or boisterous, esp. in resistance to control, advice, etc. [< L *ob-* towards + *strepere* to make noise] **— ob·strep'er·ous·ly** *adv.* **— ob·strep'er·ous·ness** *n.*

ob·struct (əb·strukt') *v.t.* **1.** To stop or impede movement through (a way or passage) by obstacles or impediments; barricade. **2.** To block or retard the progress or way of; impede. **3.** To come or be in front of so as to prevent a clear view. [< L < *ob-* before + *struere* to pile, build] **— ob·struct'er** or **ob·struc'tor** *n.* **— ob·struc'tive** *adj.* **— ob·struc'tive·ly** *adv.* **— ob·struc'tive·ness** *n.*

ob·struc·tion (əb·struk'shən) *n.* **1.** That which obstructs. **2.** The act of obstructing, or the state of being obstructed.

ob·struc·tion·ist (əb·struk'shən·ist) *n.* One who makes a practice of obstructing, esp. in politics, one who obstructs debate, legislation, etc. **— ob·struc'tion·ism** *n.*

ob·tain (əb·tān') *v.t.* **1.** To gain possession of, esp. by effort; acquire; get. **— v.i. 2.** To be prevalent or in effect. **— Syn.** See GET. [< OF < L *ob-* towards + *tenere* to hold] **— ob·tain'a·ble** *adj.* **— ob·tain'er** *n.* **— ob·tain'ment** *n.*

ob·trude (əb·trōōd') *v.* **·trud·ed, ·trud·ing** *v.t.* **1.** To thrust or force (oneself, an opinion, etc.) upon another without request or warrant. **2.** To push forward or out; eject. **— v.i. 3.** To intrude oneself. [< L < *ob-* towards + *trudere* to thrust] **— ob·trud'er** *n.* **— ob·tru'sion** *n.*

ob·tru·sive (əb·trōō'siv) *adj.* Tending to obtrude. **— ob·tru'sive·ly** *adv.* **— ob·tru'sive·ness** *n.*

ob·tuse (əb·tōōs', -tyōōs') *adj.* **1.** Lacking acuteness of intellect or feeling; insensible. **2.** Not clear or distinct to the senses; dull, as a sound or pain. **3.** *Bot.* Blunt or rounded at the extremity, as a leaf or petal. [< L *obtusus* blunt, ¹ulled] **— ob·tuse'ly** *adv.* **— ob·tuse'ness** *n.*

obtuse angle *Geom.* An angle greater than a right angle and less than a straight angle.

ob·verse (ob'vûrs; *for adj., also* ob·vûrs') *adj.* **1.** Turned toward or facing one. **2.** Narrower at the base than at the apex: an *obverse* leaf. **3.** Constituting a counterpart. **— n. 1.** The front or principal side of anything; esp., the side of a coin bearing the main design or device: distinguished from *reverse.* **2.** A counterpart. [< L < *ob-* towards + *vertere* to turn] **— ob·verse'ly** *adv.*

ob·vi·ate (ob'vē·āt) *v.t.* **·at·ed, ·at·ing** To prevent or counter (an objection, difficulty, etc.) by effective measures; provide for. [< L *obviatus,* pp. of *obviare* to meet, withstand] **— Syn.** preclude, forestall, avert.

ob·vi·ous (ob'vē·əs) *adj.* **1.** Immediately evident; palpably true; manifest. **2.** Behaving without equivocation or subtlety. [< L < *ob-* before + *via* way] **— ob'vi·ous·ly** *adv.* **— ob'vi·ous·ness** *n.*

oc- Assimilated var. of OB-.

oc·a·ri·na (ok'ə·rē'nə) *n.* A small musical instrument in the shape of a sweet potato, with a mouthpiece and finger holes, and yielding soft, sonorous notes. [< Ital., dim. of *oca* goose < L *auca*; so called with ref. to its shape]

oc·ca·sion (ə·kā'zhən) *n.* **1.** The particular time of an event or occurrence; also, the event or occurrence itself. **2.** An important or extraordinary event. **3.** A favorable time or condition; opportunity. **4.** The immediate cause or grounds for some action or state: to give one *occasion* to complain. **5.** A need or requirement. **— on occasion** On suitable opportunity; now and then. **— to take the (this,** etc.**) occasion** To avail oneself of the (this, etc.) opportunity. **— v.t.** To cause or bring about, esp. in an accidental or incidental manner. [< L < *ob-* towards + *cadere* to fall]

oc·ca·sion·al (ə·kā'zhən·əl) *adj.* **1.** Occurring, appearing, etc., irregularly or now and then. **2.** Made, intended, or suitable for a particular occasion: *occasional* verse. **3.** Pertaining to or designating a small chair, table, etc., that is not part of a set. **— oc·ca'sion·al·ly** *adv.*

oc·ci·dent (ok'sə·dənt) *n.* The west: opposed to *orient.* [< OF < L *occidens, -entis* region where the sun sets.]

Oc·ci·dent (ok'sə·dənt) **1.** The countries west of Asia; esp., Europe. **2.** The western hemisphere.

oc·ci·den·tal (ok'sə·den'təl) *adj.* Of or belonging to the west, or to the countries constituting the Occident: distinguished from *oriental.* **— n.** One born or living in a western country. Also **Oc'ci·den'tal.**

oc·cip·i·tal (ok·sip'ə·təl) *adj.* Pertaining to the occiput. **— n.** The occipital bone.

occipital bone *Anat.* The hindmost bone of the skull, between the parietal and temporal bones.

oc·ci·put (ok'sə·put, -pət) *n. pl.* **oc·cip·i·ta** (ok·sip'ə·tə) *Anat.* The lower back part of the skull. [< L, back of the head < *ob-* against + *caput* head]

oc·clude (ə·klōōd') *v.* **·clud·ed, ·clud·ing** *v.t.* **1.** To shut up or close, as pores or openings. **2.** To shut in, out, or off. **3.** *Chem.* To take up, either on the surface or internally, but without change of properties. **4.** *Meteorol.* To displace, as a mass of warm air by an advancing front of cold air. **— v.i. 5.** *Dent.* To meet so that the corresponding cusps fit closely together: said of the teeth of the upper and lower jaws. [< L < *ob-* against + *claudere* to close] **— oc·clu'dent** *adj.* **— oc·clu·sion** (ə·klōō'zhən) *n.*

oc·clu·sive (ə·klōō'siv) *adj.* **1.** Characterized by or bringing about occlusion or closure. **2.** *Phonet.* Pertaining to a stop. **— n.** *Phonet.* A stop.

oc·cult (ə·kult', ok'ult) *adj.* **1.** Of or pertaining to various magical arts and practices, as astrology, alchemy, etc. **2.** Beyond human understanding; mysterious. **3.** Not divulged or disclosed; secret. **— Syn.** See MYSTERIOUS. **— n.** Occult arts or practices: usu. with *the.* **— v.t.** To hide or conceal from view. **— v.i.** To become hidden or concealed from view. [< L *occultus,* pp. of *occulere* to cover over, hide] **— oc·cult'ism** *n.* **— oc·cult'ist** *n.* **— oc·cult'ly** *adv.*

oc·cul·ta·tion (ok'ul·tā'shən) *n.* *Astron.* Concealment of one celestial body by another interposed in the line of vision.

oc·cu·pan·cy (ok'yə·pən·sē) *n. pl.* **·cies 1.** The act of occupying, or the state of being occupied. **2.** *Law* The act of taking possession of something previously unowned. **3.** The condition of being an occupant or tenant. **4.** The time during which something is occupied.

oc·cu·pant (ok'yə·pənt) *n.* **1.** One who occupies a place, position, etc. **2.** A tenant. [See OCCUPY.]

oc·cu·pa·tion (ok'yə·pā'shən) *n.* **1.** One's regular, principal, or immediate business or job. **2.** The act of occupying, or the state of being occupied. **3.** The taking and holding of land by a military force: the *occupation* of Germany.
— Syn. 1. *Occupation* and *vocation* are general terms, meaning little more than line of work. A *profession* requires special knowledge and training: Law and medicine are *professions*. A *business* is usually industrial, commercial, or mercantile, but may also be general: the clothing *business*, the *business* of government. A *trade* requires manual skill, as does a *craft*, but the latter suggests a

greater degree of skill and even artistic creation: the bricklayer's *trade*, the jeweler's *craft*.

oc·cu·pa·tion·al (ok/yə-pā'shən-əl) *adj.* Of, pertaining to, or caused by an occupation. **— oc'cu·pa'tion·al·ly** *adv.*

occupational therapy *Med.* The treatment of nervous, mental, or physical disabilities by means of work designed to promote recovery or readjustment.

oc·cu·py (ok/yə-pī) *v.t.* **·pied, ·py·ing 1.** To take and hold possession of, as by conquest. **2.** To fill or take up (space or time). **3.** To inhabit; dwell in. **4.** To hold; fill, as an office or position. **5.** To busy or engage; employ. [< OF < L < *ob-* against + *capere* to take] **— oc'cu·pi'er** *n.*

oc·cur (ə-kûr') *v.i.* **·curred, ·cur·ring 1.** To happen or take place; come about. **2.** To be found or met with; appear. **3.** To suggest itself; come to mind. [< L < *ob-* towards, against + *currere* to run]

oc·cur·rence (ə-kûr'əns) *n.* **1.** The act or fact of occurring. **2.** That which occurs; an event. **— oc·cur'rent** *adj.*

o·cean (ō'shən) *n.* **1.** The great body of salt water that covers about 70 percent of the earth's surface. **2.** *Often cap.* Any one of the divisions of this body of water, usu. reckoned as five, the Atlantic, Pacific, Indian, Arctic, and Antarctic. **3.** A very large expanse or quantity. [< OF < L < Gk. *ōkeanos*]

ocean current Any of a large number of riverlike masses of water flowing in all oceans, each having a characteristic direction, length, depth, speed, and temperature.

o·ce·an·ic (ō'shē-an'ik) *adj.* **1.** Of, relating to, or living in the ocean; pelagic. **2.** Resembling an ocean; vast.

O·ce·an·ic (ō'shē-an'ik) *n.* A subfamily of the Austronesian family of languages, including the Melanesian languages of the Solomon Islands, Fiji, New Caledonia, the New Hebrides, etc., and the Micronesian group of languages.

o·ce·an·og·ra·phy (ō'shē-ən-og'rə-fē, ō'shən-og'-) *n.* The branch of physical geography that treats of oceanic life and phenomena. **— o'ce·an·og'ra·pher** *n.* **— o'ce·an·o·graph'ic** (-ə-graf'ik) or **·i·cal** *adj.* **— o'ce·an·o·graph'i·cal·ly** *adv.*

oc·el·lat·ed (os'ə-lā'tid, ō·sel'ā-tid) *adj.* **1.** Having an ocellus or ocelli. **2.** Resembling an ocellus. **3.** Spotted. Also **oc·el·late** (os'ə-lāt, ō·sel'āt). [< L *ocellatus* small-eyed]

o·cel·lus (ō·sel'əs) *n.* *pl.* **·li** (-lī) **1.** *Biol.* A minute simple eye, as of many invertebrates. **2.** An eyelike spot, as in the tail of a peacock. [< L, dim. of *oculus* eye] **— o·cel'lar** *adj.*

o·ce·lot (ō'sə-lət, -lot, os'ə-) *n.* A large cat of Central and South America, having a spotted yellowish or reddish gray coat. [< F, short for Nahuatl *tlaocelotl* < *tlalli* field + *ocelotl* jaguar]

o·cher (ō'kər) *n.* **1.** A naturally occurring iron oxide mixed with various earthy materials and varying from light yellow to deep orange or red, largely used as a pigment. **2.** A dark yellow color derived from or resembling ocher. Also *Brit.* **o'chre.** [< OF < L < Gk. *ōchra* yellow ocher < *ōchros* pale yellow] **— o'cher·ous, o·chre·ous** (ō'krē-əs), **o'cher·y, o·chry** (ō'krē) *adj.*

-ock *suffix of nouns* Small: *hillock.* [OE *-oc, -uc*]

o'clock (ə-klok') Of or according to the clock: six *o'clock*.

oct-, octa- See OCTO-.

oc·ta·gon (ok'tə-gon) *n.* *Geom.* A polygon having eight sides and eight angles. [< L < Gk. < *oktō* eight + *gōnia* angle] **— oc·tag·o·nal** (ok·tag'ə-nəl) *adj.* **— oc·tag'o·nal·ly** *adv.*

oc·ta·he·dron (ok'tə-hē'drən) *n.* *pl.* **·dra** (-drə) *Geom.* A polyhedron bounded by eight plane faces. [< Gk. < *oktō* eight + *hedra* seat] **— oc'ta·he'dral** *adj.*

oc·tane (ok'tān) *n.* *Chem.* One of a group of saturated hydrocarbons that have the formula C_8H_{18}.

octane number A measure of the antiknock properties of gasoline, expressed as the percentage, by volume, of isooctane that must be blended with normal heptane until the mixture has the same knock rating as the gasoline under test.

oc·tant (ok'tənt) *n.* An eighth part of a circle; an arc subtending an angle of 45 degrees. [< LL *octans, -antis* an eighth part < L *octo* eight] **— oc·tant'al** (-tan'təl) *adj.*

oc·tave (ok'tiv, -tāv) *n.* **1.** *Music* **a** The interval between a tone and another having twice as many or half as many vibrations per second. **b** A tone at this interval above or below any other, considered in relation to that other. **c** Two tones at this interval, sounded together; also, the resulting consonance. **d** An organ stop giving tones an octave above those normally corresponding to the keys played. **2.** *Eccl.* The eighth day from a feast day, beginning with the feast day as one; also, the lengthening of a festival so as to include a period of eight days. **3.** Any group or series of eight. **4.** In prosody, an octet. **— adj. 1.** Composed of eight. **2.** *Music* Producing tones an octave higher. [< L *octavus* eighth < *octo* eight] **— oc·ta·val** (ok·tā'vəl, ok'tə-) *adj.*

oc·ta·vo (ok·tā'vō, -tā'-) *n.* *pl.* **·vos 1.** The page size (6 x 9½ inches except where otherwise specified) of a book made

up of printer's sheets folded into eight leaves. **2.** A book consisting of pages of this size. **— adj.** In octavo. Also *eightvo*. Also written **8vo** or **8°**. [< L *in octavo* in an eighth]

oc·tet (ok·tet') *n.* **1.** A musical composition for eight singers or instrumentalists. **2.** A group of eight singers or instrumentalists. **3.** Any group of eight. Also **oc·tette'.** [< Ital. < L *octo* eight]

oc·til·lion (ok·til'yən) *n.* **1.** *U.S.* A thousand septillions, written as 1 followed by 27 zeros: a cardinal number. **2.** *Brit.* A million septillions (def. 2), written as 1 followed by 48 zeros: a cardinal number. **— adj.** Being an octillion in number. [< MF < *octo* eight + F (*m*)*illion*]

octo- *combining form* Eight: also, before vowels, *oct-*. Also *octa-*. [< L *octo* and Gk. *oktō* eight]

Oc·to·ber (ok·tō'bər) The tenth month of the year, containing 31 days. [< L, eighth month of early Roman calendar < *octo* eight]

October Revolution See RUSSIAN REVOLUTION under REVOLUTION.

oc·to·dec·i·mo (ok'tə-des'ə-mō) *n.* *pl.* **·mos 1.** The page size (approximately 4 x 6½ inches) of a book made up of printer's sheets folded into 18 leaves. **2.** A book consisting of pages of this size. **— adj.** In octodecimo; consisting of pages of this size. Also *eighteenmo*. Also written **18mo** or **18°**. [< L *in octodecimo* in an eighteenth]

oc·to·ge·nar·i·an (ok'tə-jə-nâr'ē-ən) *adj.* Being eighty or from eighty to ninety years of age. **— n.** One between eighty and ninety years of age. Also **oc·tog·e·nar·y** (ok·toj'ə-ner'ē) *adj. & n.* [< L < *octoginta* eighty]

oc·to·pod (ok'tə-pod) *n. Zool.* Any of a group of eight-armed cephalopods, as the octopus.

oc·to·pus (ok'tə-pəs) *n.* *pl.* **·pus·es** or **·pi** (-pī) or **oc·top·o·des** (ok·top'ə-dēz) **1.** An eight-armed marine mollusk having a large oval head and rows of suckers along the arms; a devilfish. **2.** Any organized power regarded as far-reaching and potentially destructive; esp., a powerful business organization. [< NL < Gk. < *oktō* eight + *pous* foot]

oc·to·roon (ok'tə-rōon') *n.* A person who is one-eighth Negro. [< *octo* eight + (QUAD)ROON]

oc·u·lar (ok'yə-lər) *adj.* Of, like, or related to the eye or sight. **— n.** The lenses forming the eyepiece of an optical instrument. [< L < *oculus* eye] **— oc'u·lar·ly** *adv.*

oc·u·list (ok'yə-list) *n.* A physician skilled in treating diseases of the eye; ophthalmologist. [< MF < L *oculus* eye]

o·da·lisque (ō'də-lisk) *n.* A female slave or concubine in an Oriental harem. Also **o'da·lisk.** [< F < Turkish *ōdaliq* chambermaid]

odd (od) *adj.* **1.** Strange or unusual in appearance, behavior, etc.; peculiar; queer. **2.** Not part of what is regular, usual, required, etc.: an *odd* job. **3.** Constituting a member of an incomplete pair, set, etc.: an *odd* slipper. **4.** Forming a remainder when divided by two; not even: Five is an *odd* number; also, characterized by such a number. **5.** Additional to a specified round number: seventy *odd* dollars. [< ON *oddi* point, hence, third point of a triangle, hence, odd number] **— odd'ly** *adv.* **— odd'ness** *n.*

odd·i·ty (od'ə-tē) *n.* *pl.* **·ties 1.** One who or that which is odd. **2.** An odd or peculiar quality or trait; an eccentricity. **3.** The state of being odd; singularity; strangeness.

odd·ment (od'mənt) *n.* *Usu. pl.* A fragment, scrap, or leftover; odds and ends.

odds (odz) *n.pl.* (*sometimes construed as sing.*) **1.** An equalizing allowance or advantage given to a weaker opponent. **2.** The proportion by which one bet differs from that of another. **3.** The ratio between the probability for and the probability against something being true or happening. **4.** A difference to the advantage of one side. **— at odds** At variance; disagreeing. [< plural of ODD]

odds and ends Miscellaneous things; fragments; scraps.

ode (ōd) *n.* A lyric poem often in the form of an elaborate address and usually characterized by loftiness of tone, feeling, and style. [< MF < LL < Gk. *ōidē* song]

-ode¹ *combining form* Way; path: *anode, cathode.* [< Gk. *hodos* way]

-ode² *suffix* Like; resembling; having the nature of. [< Gk. *-ōdēs* < *eidos* form]

O·din (ō'din) In Norse mythology, the supreme deity, god of war, art, culture, and the dead.

o·di·ous (ō'dē-əs) *adj.* Exciting hate, repugnance, or disgust; offensive; abhorrent. [< OF < L < *odium* hatred] **— o'di·ous·ly** *adv.* **— o'di·ous·ness** *n.*

o·di·um (ō'dē-əm) *n.* **1.** The state of being odious. **2.** Extreme dislike or aversion; hatred. **3.** The reproach, disgrace, or stigma associated with something hateful; opprobrium. [< L, hatred]

o·dom·e·ter (ō·dom'ə-tər) *n.* A device for measuring distance traveled by a vehicle. [< Gk. < *hodos* way, road + *metron* a measure] **— o·dom'e·try** *n.*

-odont *combining form* Toothed. [< Gk. *odous, odontos* tooth]

odonto- *combining form* Tooth; of the teeth. Also, before vowels, **odont-**. [< Gk. *odous, odontos* tooth]

o·don·tol·o·gy (ō′don·tol′ə·jē) *n.* The body of scientific knowledge that relates to the structure, health, and growth of the teeth. — **o·don·to·log·i·cal** (ō·don′tə·loj′i·kəl) *adj.* — **o·don·to·log′i·cal·ly** *adv.* — **o′don·tol′o·gist** *n.*

o·dor (ō′dər) *n.* **1.** That quality of a substance that renders it perceptible to the sense of smell; smell; scent. **2.** Regard or estimation. **3.** A perfume; incense. — **Syn.** See SMELL. Also *Brit.* **o′dour.** [< OF < L] — **o′dored** *adj.*

o·dor·if·er·ous (ō′də·rif′ər·əs) *adj.* Having or giving off an odor, especially a pleasant odor. [< L < *odor* odor + *ferre* to bear] — **o′dor·if′er·ous·ly** *adv.* — **o′dor·if′er·ous·ness** *n.*

o·dor·less (ō′dər·lis) *adj.* Having no odor. — **o′dor·less·ly** *adv.* — **o′dor·less·ness** *n.*

o·dor·ous (ō′dər·əs) *adj.* Having an odor, esp. a fragrant odor. — **o′dor·ous·ly** *adv.* — **o′dor·ous·ness** *n.*

-odynia *combining form Med.* Pain; chronic pain in a (specified) part of the body. [< Gk. *odynē* pain]

O·dys·seus (ō·dis′yōōs, -ē·əs) In Greek legend, king of Ithaca, one of the Greek leaders in the Trojan War and hero of the *Odyssey*: Latin *Ulysses.*

Od·ys·sey (od′ə·sē) An ancient Greek epic poem attributed to Homer, describing the wanderings of Odysseus during the ten years after the fall of Troy. — *n.* A long, wandering journey: often **od′ys·sey.** —**Od′ys·sey′an** *adj.*

oe- See also words beginning E-.

oe·de·ma (i·dē′mə) See EDEMA.

Oed·i·pus (ed′ə·pəs, ē′də-) In Greek legend, the son of Laius and Jocasta, rulers of Thebes, who unwittingly killed his father and married his mother.

Oedipus complex *Psychoanal.* A strong, typically unconscious attachment of a child to the parent of the opposite sex, esp. of a son to his mother, with antagonism toward the other parent. —**Oed·i·pal** (ed′ə·pəl, ē′də-) *adj.*

o′er (ôr, ōr) *prep. & adv. Poetic* Over.

oe·soph·a·gus (i·sof′ə·gəs) See ESOPHAGUS.

oes·tro·gen (es′trə·jən, ēs′-) See ESTROGEN.

oes·trous (es′trəs, ēs′-) See ESTROUS.

of (uv, ov; *unstressed* əv) *prep.* **1.** Coming from: Anne *of* Cleves; an actor of noble birth. **2.** Included among: Is he *of* your party? **3.** Located at: the Leaning Tower *of* Pisa. **4.** Away or at a distance from: within six miles *of* home. **5.** Named; specified as: the city *of* Newark; a fall *of* ten feet. **6.** Characterized by: a man *of* strength. **7.** With reference to; as to: quick *of* wit. **8.** About; concerning: Good is said *of* him. **9.** Because of: dying *of* pneumonia. **10.** Possessing: a man *of* means. **11.** Belonging to: the lid *of* a box. **12.** Pertaining to: the majesty *of* the law. **13.** Composed of: a ship *of* steel. **14.** Containing: a glass *of* water. **15.** From the number or class of: six *of* the seven conspirators. **16.** So as to be without: relieved *of* anxiety. **17.** Produced by: the plays *of* Shakespeare. **18.** Directed toward; exerted upon: a love *of* opera. **19.** During, on, or at a specified time or occasion: *of* recent years. **20.** Set aside for or devoted to: a program *of* music. **21.** *U.S.* Before; until: used in telling time: ten minutes *of* ten. **22.** *Archaic* By: loved *of* all men. [OE, away from, off]

of- Assimilated var. of OB-.

of course **1.** In the usual order of procedure; naturally; as expected. **2.** Doubtless; certainly.

off (ôf, of) *adj.* **1.** Farther or more distant; remote: an *off* chance. **2.** In a (specified) circumstance or situation: to be well *off.* **3.** Not in accordance with the facts; wrong: Your reckoning is *off.* **4.** Not up to standard: an *off* season for roses. **5.** No longer considered active or effective: The deal is *off.* **6.** Away from work; not on duty: *off* hours. **7.** In riding or driving, on the right: opposed to *near*: Pass on the *off* side. **8.** *Naut.* Seaward. — *adv.* **1.** To a distance; so as to be away: My horse ran *off.* **2.** To or at a (specified) future time: to put it *off* for a week. **3.** To or at a (specified) distance: to stand five feet *off.* **4.** So as to be no longer in place, connection, etc.: Take *off* your hat. **5.** So as to be no longer functioning, continuing, or in operation: to break *off* talks. **6.** So as to be away from one's work, duties, etc.: to take the day *off.* **7.** So as to be completed, exhausted, etc.: to kill *off* one's enemies. **8.** So as to deviate from or be below what is regarded as standard: His game dropped *off.* **9.** *Naut.* Away from land, a ship, the wind, etc. — **off and on** Now and then; intermittently. — **to be off** **1.** To leave; depart. **2.** *Informal* To be insane. — *prep.* **1.** So as to be separated, detached, distant, or removed from (a position, source, etc.): twenty miles *off* course. **2.** Not engaged in or occupied with; relieved from: *off* duty. **3.** Extending away or out from; no longer on: *off* Broadway. **4.** So as to deviate from or be below (what is regarded as standard): to be *off* one's game. **5.** On or from (the material or substance of): living *off* nuts and berries. **6.** *Informal* No longer using, engaging in, or advocating: to be *off* drinking. **7.** *Naut.*

Opposite to and seaward of: the battle *off* the eastern cape. — **off of** *Informal* Off; from: He fell *off of* the horse. —*n.* The state or condition of being off. [ME]

of·fal (ô′fəl) *n.* **1.** The waste parts of a butchered animal. **2.** Rubbish or refuse of any kind. [ME *of all* < OFF + FALL]

off-beat (ôf′bēt′, of′-) *n. Music* Any secondary or weak beat in a measure. — *adj. U.S. Slang* Out of the ordinary; strange; unconventional; unusual.

off-Broad·way (ôf′brôd′wā) *adj.* **1.** Not situated in the Broadway entertainment district: an *off-Broadway* theater. **2.** Designating a play that is regarded as experimental, noncommercial, etc. — *n.* Any area in New York City in which off-Broadway plays are produced.

off·cast (ôf′kast′, -käst′, of′-) *adj.* Rejected; castoff. — *n.* Anything thrown away or rejected.

off chance A bare possibility.

off-col·or (ôf′kul′ər, of′-) *adj.* **1.** Unsatisfactory in color, as a gem. **2.** Indelicate or indecent; risqué.

of·fence (ə·fens′) See OFFENSE.

of·fend (ə·fend′) *v.t.* **1.** To give displeasure or offense to. **2.** To be disagreeable to (the sense of smell, sight, etc.). —*v.i.* **3.** To give displeasure or offense; be offensive. [< L < *ob-* against + *fendere* to hit] — **of·fend′er** *n.* — **Syn.** 1. Insult, affront, exasperate, outrage.

of·fense (ə·fens′; *for defs. 4 & 5, also* ô′fens, of′ens) *n.* **1.** Any violation of a rule, duty, propriety, etc.; esp., a breach of law. **2.** The act of offending or causing displeasure. **3.** That which offends: an *offense* to the ear. **4.** The act of attacking or assaulting; attack. **5.** In football, hockey, etc., the team possessing the ball or puck. — **to give offense** To offend or cause anger, resentment, etc. — **to take offense** To be offended; feel angry, hurt, etc. Also *esp. Brit.,* **offence.**

of·fen·sive (ə·fen′siv) *adj.* **1.** Unpleasant or disagreeable; obnoxious; disgusting. **2.** Causing anger, resentment, etc.; insulting. **3.** Of, pertaining to, or characterized by attack: distinguished from *defensive.* — *n.* The movement, attitude, or position of offense or attack. — **of·fen′sive·ly** *adv.* — **of·fen′sive·ness** *n.*

of·fer (ô′fər, of′ər) *v.t.* **1.** To present for acceptance or rejection. **2.** To suggest for consideration or action; propose. **3.** To make an offering of: often with *up.* **4.** To show readiness to do or attempt; propose or threaten: to *offer* battle. **5.** To attempt to do or inflict; also, to do or inflict. **6.** To suggest as payment; bid. **7.** To present for sale. — *v.i.* **8.** To present itself; appear. **9.** To make an offering in worship or sacrifice. — *n.* **1.** The act of offering. **2.** That which is offered, as a bid, suggestion, etc. [OE *offrian* < L < *ob-* before + *ferre* to bring] — **of′fer·er** or **of′fer·or** *n.*

of·fer·ing (ô′fər·ing, of′ər-) *n.* **1.** The act of making an offer. **2.** That which is offered, as a sacrifice or contribution.

of·fer·to·ry (ô′fər·tôr′ē, -tō′rē, of′ər-) *n. pl.* **·ries** *Eccl.* **1.** *Usu. cap.* A section of the eucharistic liturgy during which the bread and wine to be consecrated are offered, and the alms of the congregation are collected. **2.** Any collection taken during a religious service. **3.** An antiphon, hymn, or anthem sung during this service. **4.** A prayer of oblation said by the celebrant over the bread and wine to be consecrated. [< Med.L *offertorium* < LL, place of offerings]

off·hand (ôf′hand′, of′-) *adv.* Without preparation; unceremoniously; extempore. Also **off′hand′ed·ly.** — *adj.* **1.** Done, said, or made offhand. **2.** Casual; informal; curt. Also **off′hand′ed.**

of·fice (ô′fis, of′is) *n.* **1.** A place in which the business of an individual, corporation, government bureau, etc., is carried out; also, the staff and administrative officials working in such a place. **2.** *Usu. cap. U.S.* An executive branch of the federal government ranking below the departments. **3.** Any post or position held by a person; especially, a position of authority or trust in the government, a corporation, etc. **4.** The duty, charge, or trust of a person. **5.** Any act done or intended to be done for another; a service; favor: through his kind *offices.* **6.** *Eccl.* A prescribed religious or devotional service, as: **a** The canonical hours. **b** The Morning or Evening Prayer. **7.** Any ceremony or rite, esp., a rite for the dead. [< OF < L *officium* service]

of·fice·hold·er (ô′fis·hōl′dər, of′-) *n.* One who holds an office under a government.

of·fi·cer (ô′fə·sər, of′ə-) *n.* **1.** In the armed forces, one appointed to a certain rank and authority; esp., one holding a commission. **2.** One elected or appointed to a position of authority or trust in a corporation, government, institution, etc. **3.** On a merchant or passenger ship, the captain or any of the mates. **4.** One who enforces the law, as a policeman. —*v.t.* **1.** To furnish with officers. **2.** To command; direct; manage.

officer of the day At a military installation, the officer who on a given day is responsible for the performance of the guard, maintenance of order or security, etc.

of·fi·cial (ə·fish′əl, ō-) *adj.* **1.** Of or relating to an office or position of authority. **2.** Supported by or derived from authority. **3.** Authorized to carry out some special duty.

4. Formal: *official* banquets. **—** *n.* One who holds an office or position; esp., one who is authorized to act for a corporation, government agency, etc., in a subordinate capacity. **— of·fi'cial·ly** *adv.*

of·fi·cial·dom (ə-fish'əl-dəm, ō-) *n.* **1.** Officials collectively or as a class. **2.** Rigid adherence to official forms, routines, etc.: also **of·fi'cial·ism.**

of·fi·ci·ate (ə-fish'ē-āt, ō-) *v.i.* **·at·ed, ·at·ing 1.** To act or serve as a priest or minister. **2.** To perform the duties or functions of any office or position. **— of·fi'ci·a'tion** *n.* **— of·fi'ci·a'tor** *n.*

of·fic·i·nal (ə-fis'ə-nəl) *adj.* Prepared and kept in stock by a pharmacy. **—** *n.* Any drug or medicine kept ready for sale. [< Med.L < L *officina* workshop]

of·fi·cious (ə-fish'əs, ō-) *adj.* Unduly forward in offering one's services or advice; obtrusive; meddling. [< L *officiosus* obliging < *officium* service] **— of·fi'cious·ly** *adv.* **— of·fi'cious·ness** *n.*

off·ing (ô'fing, of'ing) *n.* **1.** That part of the visible sea offshore but beyond anchorage. **2.** A position some distance offshore. **— in the offing 1.** In sight and not very distant. **2.** Ready or soon to happen; arrive, etc.

off·ish (ô'fish, of'ish) *adj.* Inclined to be distant in manner; aloof. **— off'ish·ly** *adv.* **— off'ish·ness** *n.*

off·scour·ing (ô'fskour'ing, of'-) *n.* **1.** *Usu. pl.* Trash; garbage. **2.** A social outcast; wretch.

off·set (*n.* ô'fset', of'-; *v.* ô'fset', of'-) *n.* **1.** That which balances or compensates for something else. **2.** That which derives, develops, or springs from something else; offshoot. **3.** *Archit.* A ledge formed along a wall by a reduction in thickness above; setoff. **4.** *Printing* **a** Offset printing. **b** An impression made by offset printing. **5.** A bend or curve made in a pipe, rod, etc., to allow it to pass an obstacle. **—** *v.* **·set, ·set·ting** *v.t.* **1.** To balance or compensate for. **2.** *Printing* **a** To reproduce by offset printing. **b** To transfer (an impression) by offset printing. **3.** *Archit.* To make an offset in. **—** *v.i.* **4.** To branch off or project as an offset.

offset printing A method of printing in which the inked impression from a lithographic plate is transferred to a rubber-coated cylinder, and then onto the paper.

off·shoot (ô'fshoot', of'-) *n.* **1.** *Bot.* A lateral shoot or branch from the main stem of a plant. **2.** Anything that derives or branches off from a principal source, stock, etc.

off·shore (ô'fshôr', -shōr', of'-) *adj.* **1.** Moving or directed away from the shore. **2.** Situated or occurring at some distance from the shore. **—** *adv.* From or away from the shore.

off·side (ô'fsīd', of'-) *adj.* In football, in front of the ball before it is put into play: said of a player, team, or play. Also **off side.**

off·spring (ô'fspring', of'-) *n.* *pl.* **·spring** or **·springs 1.** The progeny or issue of a person, animal, or plant; descendant. **2.** Any result or product: the *offspring* of his mind.

off·stage (ô'fstāj', of'-) *n.* The area behind or to the side of a stage, out of the view of the audience. **—** *adj.* In or from this area: *off-stage* dialogue. **—** *adv.* To this area.

off·white (ô'fhwīt', of'-) *n.* Oyster white.

oft (ôft, oft) *adv.* Often: archaic or poetic except in certain combinations, as **oft-repeated, oft-recurring,** etc. [OE]

oft·en (ôf'ən, of'-) *adv.* Frequently or repeatedly. [Var. of ME *ofte*, OE *oft*]

oft·en·times (ôf'ən-tīmz', of'-) *adv.* *Archaic* Frequently; often. Also **oft·times** (ôf'tīmz', of'-).

o·gee (ō'jē, ō·jē') *n.* *Archit.* **1.** Any S-shaped curve used in a construction. **2.** An arch having two S-shaped curves meeting at the apex: also **ogee arch.** [OF *ogive*]

o·give (ō'jīv, ō·jīv') *n.* *Archit.* **1.** A diagonal rib of a vaulted arch or bay. **2.** A pointed arch. [< OF *ogive*]

o·gle (ō'gəl, og'əl) *v.* **o·gled, o·gling** *v.t.* **1.** To look at with admiring or impertinent glances. **2.** To stare at; eye. **—** *v.i.* **3.** To look or stare in an admiring or impertinent manner. **—** *n.* An amorous or coquettish look. [< LG *oegeln*, freq. of *oegen* to look at < *oege* eye] **— o'gler** *n.*

o·gre (ō'gər) *n.* **1.** In fairy tales, a man-eating giant or monster. **2.** One who is brutal, hideous, or feared. [< F] **— o·gre·ish** (ō'gər·ish), **o·grish** (ō'grish) *adj.* **— o'gress** (-grəs) *n.fem.*

oh (ō) *interj.* An exclamation expressing surprise, sudden emotion, etc. **—** *n.* The interjection *oh.*

ohm (ōm) *n.* The unit of electrical resistance, equal to the resistance of a conductor carrying a current of one ampere at a potential difference of one volt between the terminals.

ohm·age (ō'mij) *n.* Electrical resistance of a conductor, expressed in ohms.

ohm·me·ter (ōm'mē'tər) *n.* A galvanometer for measuring the resistance of a conductor in ohms.

o·ho (ō·hō') *interj.* An exclamation expressing astonishment, exultation, etc.

-oid *suffix* Like; resembling; having the form of: *ovoid, hydroid.* [< NL *-oides* < Gk. *-oeidēs* < *eidos* form]

oil (oil) *n.* **1.** A greasy or unctuous, sometimes combustible liquid of vegetable, animal, or mineral origin, soluble in alcohol and ether, but not in water, variously used as food, for lubricating, illuminating, and fuel, and in the manufacture of soap, candles, cosmetics, perfumery, etc. **2.** Petroleum. **3.** An oil color; also, an oil painting. **4.** Anything of an oily consistency. **—** *v.t.* **1.** To smear, lubricate, or supply with oil. **2.** To bribe; flatter. **—** *adj.* **1.** Of or resembling oil. **2.** Using, obtained from, or yielding oil. [< OF < L prob. < Gk. *elaion* olive oil]

oil burner A heating unit that operates on oil fuel.

oil cake The mass of pressed seeds of cotton, flax, etc., or coconut pulp from which oil has been expressed, used as food (**oil meal**) for livestock, etc.

oil·cloth (oil'klôth', -kloth') *n.* A fabric waterproofed with oils and pigments, used as a covering for tables, etc.

oil color A color or paint made of pigment ground in linseed or other oil, used chiefly by artists.

oil of vitriol Sulfuric acid.

oil painting 1. A painting done in pigments mixed in oil. **2.** The art of painting in oils.

oil·paper (oil'pā'pər) *n.* Paper treated with oil for transparency and resistance against moisture and dryness.

oil·skin (oil'skin') *n.* Cloth made waterproof with oil, or a garment of such material.

oil slick A smooth area on water caused by a film of oil.

oil·stone (oil'stōn') *n.* A whetstone moistened with oil.

oil well A well that is dug or drilled to obtain petroleum.

oil·y (oi'lē) *adj.* **oil·i·er, oil·i·est 1.** Of, pertaining to, or containing oil. **2.** Coated, smeared, or soaked with oil; greasy. **3.** Smooth or suave in behavior, speech, etc.; unctuous. **— oil'i·ly** *adv.* **— oil'i·ness** *n.*

oint·ment (oint'mənt) *n.* A fatty or unctuous preparation applied to the skin as a medicine or cosmetic; unguent. [< OF *oignement*, ult. < L *unguentum* < *ungere* to anoint]

O·jib·wa (ō-jib'wä, -wə) *n.* *pl.* **·wa** or **·was 1.** One of a tribe of North American Indians formerly inhabiting the regions around Lake Superior. **2.** Their Algonquian language. Also called *Chippewa:* also **O·jib'way.**

OK (*interj.*, *adj.*, *adv.* & *n.* ō'kā'; *v.* ō·kā') *interj.*, *adj.*, & *adv.* All correct; all right: used to express approval, agreement, etc. **—** *v.t.* To approve, endorse, or agree to; especially, to sign with an *OK.* **—** *n.* Approval; agreement; endorsement. Also **O.K., o'kay', o'keh'.** [? < *o(ll) k(orrect),* humorous misspelling of "all correct," reinforced by *O(ld) K(inderhook)* in the name of a political club (1840) supporting Martin Van Buren of Kinderhook, N.Y.]

o·ka·pi (ō·kä'pē) *n.* An African ruminant related to the giraffe, but with a smaller body and a shorter neck. [< native African name]

O·kie (ō'kē) *n.* *U.S. Slang* A migrant farmworker, originally one from Oklahoma.

o·kra (ō'krə) *n.* **1.** A tall annual herb of the mallow family. **2.** Its green mucilaginous pods, used in soups and stews, or as a vegetable. **3.** Gumbo. [< West African]

-ol¹ *suffix Chem.* Denoting an alcohol or phenol: *methanol, glycerol.* [< (ALCOH)OL]

-ol² *suffix Chem.* Var. of -OLE¹, as in *benzol.*

old (ōld) *adj.* **old·er** or **eld·er, old·est** or **eld·est 1.** Living, existing, made, known, etc., for a relatively long time. **2.** Exhibiting the characteristics of advanced life. **3.** Having a specified age or duration: a child two months old. **4.** Worn with age or repeated use; shabby. **5.** Familiar through long acquaintance or use: an *old* friend. **6.** Skilled through long experience: an *old* hand at politics. **7.** Belonging to or associated with a relatively remote period in history; ancient. **8.** *Usu. cap.* Denoting the earlier or earliest of two or more things, periods, developments, etc.; *Old* English: the *Old* Testament. **9.** *Informal* Good; cherished; dear: a general term of affection or endearment: *old* buddy of mine. **10.** *Informal* Plentiful; great; wonderful: used to express intense pleasure, excess, etc.: a grand *old* time. **11.** *Geog.* In a late stage of a cycle of development: said of topographic features, streams, etc. **—** *n.* Past time: days of old. [OE *ald*] **— old'ness** *n.*

— Syn. (adj.) **1.** *Old* and *aged* mean having lived a long time, but *old* more often suggests feebleness or senility than *aged.* An *elderly* man has passed middle age, but is generally regarded as younger than an *old* man, both in years and in vigor.

Old Bailey The central criminal court of London.

old country The native country of an immigrant, esp. a European country.

old·en (ōl'dən) *adj.* *Archaic & Poetic* Old; ancient.

Old English *Printing* Black letter.

old·fan·gled (ōld'fang'gəld) *adj.* Having a fondness for what is old-fashioned. [On analogy with NEWFANGLED]

old-fash·ioned (ōld'fash'ənd) *adj.* Of, pertaining to, characteristic of, or favoring former times, old customs, etc.
old fashioned A cocktail of whisky, sugar, fruit, etc.
old fo·gy (fō'gē) One who is extremely conservative or old-fashioned. Also **old fo'gey. — old'-fo'gy·ish** *adj.*
Old French See under FRENCH.
Old Glory The flag of the United States.
old guard The conservative element in a community, political party, etc.
old hat *U.S. Slang* Out of style; old-fashioned; obsolete.
Old Hickory Nickname of Andrew Jackson.
Old High German See under GERMAN.
Old Icelandic See under ICELANDIC.
old·ish (ōl'dish) *adj.* Somewhat old.
old lady *Slang* 1. One's mother. 2. One's wife.
old-line (ōld'līn') *adj.* 1. Traditional or conservative in action or thought. 2. Long-established; traditional.
Old Line State Nickname of Maryland.
old maid 1. A spinster. 2. *Informal* One who is prim, prudish, fastidious, etc.
old man *Slang* 1. One's father. 2. One's husband. 3. Any man in a position of authority, as an employer.
old master Any of the famous painters who lived between the 13th and 16th centuries, esp. in Italy and the Low Countries; also, any of their paintings.
Old Nick The devil.
Old Prussian See under PRUSSIAN.
old rose Any of various shades of grayish or purplish red.
old·ster (ōld'stər) *n. Informal* An old or elderly person.
Old Stone Age The Paleolithic period of human culture.
old-style (ōld'stīl') *adj.* Of a former or old-fashioned style.
old style *Printing* A style of type having the stems and the serifs of nearly the same thickness.
Old Style See (Gregorian) CALENDAR.
Old Testament The first of the two main divisions of the Bible, divided into the Pentateuch, the Prophets, and the Hagiographa.
old-time (ōld'tīm') *adj.* 1. Of or characteristic of a former time. 2. Of long standing; long-established.
old-tim·er (ōld'tī'mər) *n. Informal* 1. One who has been a member, resident, etc., for a long time. 2. An old-fashioned person.
Ol·du·vai Gorge (ōl'dōō-vī', ōl'dōō-vī') A gorge about 100 mi. SE of Lake Victoria in Tanzania; site of fossils of extinct mammals believed to be forerunners of early man.
old-wom·an·ish (ōld'wŏm'ən-ish) *adj.* Characteristic of or suitable for an old woman; fussy.
old-world (ōld'wûrld') *adj.* 1. Of or pertaining to the Old World or Eastern Hemisphere. 2. Ancient; antique.
Old World The Eastern Hemisphere, including Europe, Asia and Africa; esp., Europe.
-ole[1] *suffix Chem.* Denoting a closed-chain compound having a five-membered ring. Also spelled **-ol.** [< L *oleum* oil]
-ole[2] *suffix* Small; little: *nucleole.* [< L *-olus,* dim. suffix]
o·le·a·ceous (ō'lē-ā'shəs) *adj. Bot.* Pertaining or belonging to the olive family of plants and including the lilac, jasmine, and ash. [< NL *oleaceae* < L *olea* olive tree]
o·le·ag·i·nous (ō'lē-aj'ə-nəs) *adj.* Of or pertaining to oil; oily. [< F < L < *olea* olive tree] **— o'le·ag'i·nous·ly** *adv.*
o·le·an·der (ō'lē-an'dər) *n.* An Old World, evergreen shrub, having leaves that yield a poisonous glycoside and clusters of fragrant rose or white flowers. [< Med.L]
o·le·ate (ō'lē-āt) *n. Chem.* A salt or ester of oleic acid.
o·le·ic (ō-lē'ik, ō'lē-) *adj.* Of, pertaining to, or derived from oil. [< L *oleum* oil + -IC]
oleic acid *Chem.* An oily compound, $C_{17}H_{33}COOH$, contained as an ester in most mixed oils and fats.
o·le·o (ō'lē-ō) Short for OLEOMARGARINE.
oleo- *combining form* Oil; of oil. [< L *oleum* oil]
o·le·o·mar·ga·rine (ō'lē-ō-mär'jə-rin, -rēn) *n.* A substitute for butter made usu. from vegetable oils: also called *margarine.* Also **o'le·o·mar'ga·rin.**
o·le·o·res·in (ō'lē-ō-rez'in) *n.* 1. A naturally occurring compound of an essential oil and a resin. 2. A pharmaceutical preparation consisting of a resin and sometimes other active matter in solution with a fixed or volatile oil.
ol·fac·tion (ol-fak'shən) *n.* The act, sense, or process of smelling odors. [< L *olfactus.* See OLFACTORY.]
ol·fac·to·ry (ol-fak'tər-ē, -trē) *adj.* Of or pertaining to the sense of smell. **— n.** *pl.* **·ries** *Usu. pl.* The organ of smell. [< L < *olere* to have a smell + *facere* to make]
ol·i·garch (ol'ə-gärk) *n.* A ruler in an oligarchy.
ol·i·gar·chy (ol'ə-gär'kē) *n. pl.* **·chies** 1. A form of government in which power is restricted to a few; also, a state so governed. 2. The ruling oligarchs. [< Gk. < *oligos* few + *archein* to rule] **— ol'i·gar'chic, ol'i·gar'chal, ol'i·gar'chi·cal** *adj.*
Ol·i·go·cene (ol'ə-gō-sēn') *Geol. adj.* Pertaining to the third oldest of the epochs or series comprised in the Tertiary system. **— n.** This epoch, with its included rock series. [< OLIGO- + Gk. *kainos* new, recent]

o·li·o (ō'lē-ō) *n. pl.* **o·li·os** A miscellaneous collection, as of musical pieces or numbers. [< Sp. *olla* pot, stew]
ol·ive (ol'iv) *n.* 1. A small, oily fruit native to Southern Europe and the Middle East. 2. The evergreen tree yielding this fruit, having leathery leaves and hard yellow wood. 3. The dull, yellowish green color of the unripe olive: also **olive green. — adj.** 1. Pertaining to or characteristic of the olive. 2. Having a dull, yellowish green color. 3. Tinged with this color: an *olive* complexion. [< L *oliva*]
olive branch 1. A branch of the olive tree as an emblem of peace. 2. Any peace offering.
olive drab 1. Any of several shades of greenish brown. 2. A woolen material of this color, formerly used by the armed services of the U.S. for uniforms. 3. *Often pl.* A uniform or a pair of trousers made of this cloth.
olive oil Oil pressed from olives, used in cooking, etc.
Olives, Mount of A hill just east of Jerusalem: *Matt.* xvi 1. Also **Ol·i·vet** (ol'ə-vet, -vit).
o·li·vine (ol'ə-vēn, -vin) *n.* A vitreous, often transparent, magnesium-iron silicate, often used as a gemstone.
ol·la (ol'ə, *Sp.* ō'lyä, ō'yä) *n.* 1. A wide-mouthed pot or jar, usu. of earthenware. 2. A highly seasoned stew. [< Sp. < L *olla* pot]
ol·o·gy (ol'ə-jē) *n. pl.* **·gies** *Informal* A science or branch of learning: a humorous term. [< -LOGY] **— ol'o·gist** *n.*
O·lym·pi·a (ō-lim'pē-ə) An ancient city in the western Peloponnesus, Greece; scene of the Olympic games.
O·lym·pi·ad (ō-lim'pē-ad) *n.* 1. The interval of four years between two successive celebrations of the Olympic games. 2. The modern Olympic games.
O·lym·pi·an (ō-lim'pē-ən) *adj.* 1. Of or pertaining to the great gods of Olympus, or to Mount Olympus. 2. Godlike. 3. Of or pertaining to Olympia or the Olympic games. Also **O·lym·pic** (ō-lim'pik, ə-). **— n.** 1. One of the twelve higher gods who dwelt on Mount Olympus. 2. A contestant in the Olympic games. 3. A native of Olympia.
Olympic games 1. In ancient Greece, athletic games, races, and contests in poetry held every four years at the plain of Olympia in Elis in honor of Zeus. 2. A modern international revival of the ancient athletic games, held every four years at some city chosen for the event. Also **Olympian games, O·lym'pics.**
-oma *suffix Med.* Tumor: *carcinoma.* [< Gk. *-ōma*]
o·ma·sum (ō-mā'səm) *n. pl.* **·sa** (-sə) The third stomach of a ruminant. [< L]
om·buds·man (om-budz'mən) *n. pl.* **·men** (-mən) A government official appointed to receive and report grievances against the government. [< Sw.]
-ome *combining form Bot.* Group; mass. [< Gk. *-ōma*]
o·me·ga (ō-mē'gə, ō-meg'ə, ō'meg·ə) *n.* 1. The twenty-fourth and last letter in the Greek alphabet (Ω, ω), corresponding to English long *o.* See ALPHABET. ◆ In the etymologies in this dictionary, omega is transliterated as ō. 2. The end; the last. [< Gk. *ō mega* great o]
om·e·let (om'lit, om'ə-lit) *n.* A dish of eggs beaten together with milk and cooked in a frying pan, often with other ingredients. Also *Brit.* **om'e·lette.** [< F *omelette*]
o·men (ō'mən) *n.* A phenomenon or incident regarded as a prophetic sign. **— v.t.** To foretell as or by an omen. [< L] **— Syn.** (noun) portent, foretoken, augury, presage.
om·i·cron (om'ə-kron, ō'mə-) *n.* The fifteenth letter of the Greek alphabet (O, o), corresponding to English short *o.* Also **om'i·kron.** See ALPHABET. [< Gk. *o mikron* small o]
om·i·nous (om'ə-nəs) *adj.* 1. Of the nature of or fore-shadowed by an omen or by a presentiment of evil; threatening. 2. Serving as an omen; prognostic. [< L < *omen* omen] **— om'i·nous·ly** *adv.* **— om'i·nous·ness** *n.*
o·mis·si·ble (ō-mis'ə-bəl) *adj.* Capable of being omitted.
o·mis·sion (ō-mish'ən) *n.* 1. The act of omitting, or the state of being omitted. 2. Anything omitted or neglected.
o·mis·sive (ō-mis'iv) *adj.* Failing to do or include. **— o·mis'sive·ly** *adv.*
o·mit (ō-mit') *v.t.* **o·mit·ted, o·mit·ting** 1. To leave out; fail to include. 2. To fail to do, make, etc.; neglect. [< L *omittere* to let go < *ob-* to, towards + *mittere* to send]
omni- *combining form* All; totally: *omnipotent.* [< L *omnis* all]
om·ni·a vin·cit a·mor (om'nē-ə vin'sit ā'môr) *Latin* Love conquers all things.
om·ni·bus (om'nə-bəs, -bus) *n.* 1. A bus. 2. A printed anthology: a Conrad *omnibus.* **— adj.** Covering a full collection of objects or cases. [< F < L, for all]
om·nif·er·ous (om-nif'ər-əs) *adj.* Producing all kinds. [< L *omnifer* < *omnis* all + *ferre* to bear]
om·nip·o·tence (om-nip'ə-təns) *n.* 1. Unlimited and universal power, esp. as a divine attribute. 2. *Usu. cap.* God. 3. Unlimited power. Also **om·nip'o·ten·cy.**
om·nip·o·tent (om-nip'ə-tənt) *adj.* Almighty; not limited in authority or power. **— the Omnipotent** God. [< OF < L < *omnis* all + *potens, -entis* able, powerful] **— om·nip'·o·tent·ly** *adv.*

om·ni·pres·ence (om′nə-prez′əns) *n.* The quality of being everywhere present at the same time. [< Med.L < L *omnis* all + *praesens, -entis* present] —**om′ni·pres′ent** *adj.*

om·ni·range (om′nə-rānj′) *n. Aeron.* A network of very-high-frequency radio signals emitted simultaneously in all directions from a transmitting station, enabling aircraft pilots to plot their bearings from the station.

om·nis·cience (om-nish′əns) *n.* **1.** Infinite knowledge. **2.** *Usu. cap.* God. **3.** Extensive knowledge. Also **om·nis′cien·cy.**

om·nis·cient (om-nish′ənt) *adj.* Knowing all things; all-knowing. —**the Omniscient** God. [< NL < L *omnis* all + *sciens, -entis,* ppr. of *scire* to know] —**om·nis′cient·ly** *adv.*

om·ni·um-gath·er·um (om′nē-əm-gath′ər-əm) *n.* A miscellaneous collection: a humorous pseudo-Latin term.

om·niv·o·rous (om-niv′ər-əs) *adj.* **1.** Eating both animal and vegetable food. **2.** Eating food of all kinds indiscriminately. **3.** That assimilates everything: an *omnivorous* taste for literature. [< L < *omnis* all + *vorare* to devour] —**om·niv′o·rous·ly** *adv.* —**om·niv′o·rous·ness** *n.*

on (on, ôn) *prep.* **1.** Above and supported by. **2.** In contact with any surface or outer part of: a blow *on* the head. **3.** Attached to or suspended from: *on* a string. **4.** Directed or moving along the course of. **5.** Near; adjacent to. **6.** Within the duration of. **7.** At the occasion of; because of: *On* seeing her, I left. **8.** At the moment or point of: *on* the hour. **9.** In a state or condition of: *on* fire; *on* record. **10.** By means of: *on* wheels. **11.** Using as a means of sustenance, activity, etc.: living *on* fruit. **12.** In addition to: thousands *on* thousands. **13.** Sustained or confirmed by: *on* good authority. **14.** With reference to: to bet *on* a horse. **15.** Concerning; about: a work *on* economics. **16.** Engaged in; occupied with: *on* a journey; *on* duty. **17.** As a consequence or result of: making a profit *on* tips. **18.** In accordance with or relation to; in terms of. **19.** Directed, tending, or moving toward or against: making war *on* the enemy. **20.** Following after: disease *on* the heels of famine. **21.** *Informal* With, as about one's person: Do you have five dollars *on* you? **22.** *Informal* At the expense of: The joke is *on* them; drinks *on* the house. **23.** *Informal* So as to annoy or make difficulty for: The car stalled *on* me. —**Syn.** See AT. ◆ See note under UPON. —**to have something on** *U.S. Informal* To have knowledge, possess evidence, etc., against. —*adv.* **1.** In or into a position or condition of contact, adherence, covering, etc.: He put his hat *on*. **2.** In the direction of an activity, performance, etc.: He looked *on* while they played. **3.** In advance; ahead, in space or time: later *on*. **4.** In continuous course or succession: The music went *on*. **5.** In or into operation, performance, or existence. —**and so on** And like what has gone before; et cetera. —**on and on** Without interruption; continuously. —**to be on to** *Informal* To be aware of, informed about, or alert to. —*adj.* **1.** Being in operation, progress, or application. **2.** Near; located nearer. [OE *on, an*]

-on *suffix* **1.** *Physics* Atomic or charged particle: *meson.* **2.** *Chem.* Inert gas; *neon.* [< Gk., neuter *-on*]

o·nan·ism (ō′nən-iz′əm) *n.* **1.** Withdrawal before orgasm; incomplete coitus. **2.** Masturbation. [after *Onan.* Cf. *Gen.* xxxviii 9.] —**o′nan·ist** *n.* —**o′nan·is′tic** *adj.*

once (wuns) *adv.* **1.** One time; without repetition. **2.** At or during some past time. **3.** At any time; ever. —**once (and) for all** Finally. —**once in a while** Occasionally. —*adj.* Former; formerly existing; quondam. —*conj.* As soon as; whenever. —*n.* One time. —**all at once 1.** All at the same time. **2.** All of a sudden. —**at once 1.** Simultaneously. **2.** Immediately. [ME < OE *ānes,* genitive of *ān* one]

once-o·ver (wuns′ō′vər) *n. Slang* **1.** A quick glance or survey. **2.** A quick putting of things in order.

on·com·ing (on′kum′ing, ôn′-) *adj.* Approaching. —*n.* An approach.

one (wun) *adj.* **1.** Being a single individual, object, or unit. **2.** Being or designating an unspecified or not precisely identified individual, thing, or time. **3.** Designating a person, thing, or group as contrasted with another or others. **4.** Single in kind; the same; closely united or alike. —*n.* **1.** A single unit, the first and lowest integer in the numerical series, preceding two: a cardinal number. **2.** Any symbol of this number, as 1, i, I. **3.** A single person or thing. —*pron.* **1.** Someone or something; anyone or anything. **2.** An individual or thing among persons or things already mentioned. —**all one 1.** Of equal consequence. **2.** Unimportant; of no significance. —**at one** In harmony or accord. —**one another** Each other. —**one by one** Singly and in succession. [OE *ān*]

◆ Expressions like *one of those who* may be followed by a plural or a singular verb, either *one* or *those* being regarded as the antecedent of *who* according to the sense or emphasis of the idea expressed. One may say *He is one of those who never*

break rules or *He is one of those who is always sure of what he is doing.*

One must work at one's own pace and *One must work at his own pace* are both correct, but the latter form is more common in the U.S.

-one *suffix Chem.* Denoting an organic compound of the ketone group: *acetone.* [< Gk. *-ōnē,* fem. patronymic]

one-horse (wun′hôrs′) *adj.* **1.** Drawn or adapted to be worked by one horse. **2.** *Informal* Of inferior resources or capacity; small; unimportant: a *one-horse* town.

O·nei·da (ō-nī′də) *n.* A member of a tribe of North American Indians of Iroquoian stock.

one·ness (wun′nis) *n.* **1.** Singleness; unity; sameness. **2.** Agreement; concord. **3.** Quality of being unique.

on·er·ous (on′ər-əs) *adj.* **1.** Burdensome or oppressive. **2.** *Law* Legally subject to an obligation. [< OF < L < *onus* burden] —**on′er·ous·ly** *adv.* —**on′er·ous·ness** *n.*

one·self (wun′self′, wunz′-) *pron.* A form of the indefinite pronoun *one,* used as a reflexive or as object of a preposition. Also **one's self.**

one-sid·ed (wun′sī′did) *adj.* **1.** Having, involving, or on one side. **2.** Biased; unfair. **3.** Having unequal or unbalanced sides. —**one′-sid′ed·ly** *adv.* —**one′-sid′ed·ness** *n.*

on-the-job (on-thə-job′, ôn-) *adj.* Pertaining to skills acquired while actually doing the job: *on-the-job* training.

one-time (wun′tīm′) *adj.* Former: a *one-time* winner.

one-track (wun′trak′) *adj.* **1.** Having or consisting of a single track. **2.** *Informal* Limited to a single idea or pursuit: a *one-track* mind.

one-way (wun′wā′) *adj.* Moving, or permitting movement, in one direction only: *one-way* traffic.

on·ion (un′yən) *n.* **1.** The edible, succulent bulb of an herb of the lily family, having a pungent odor and taste. **2.** Any of various allied plants. [< OF < L *unio* pearl, onion]

on·ion·skin (un′yən-skin′) *n.* A thin, translucent paper.

on·look·er (on′lŏŏk′ər, ôn′-) *n.* One who looks on; a spectator. —**on′look′ing** *adj.*

on·ly (ōn′lē) *adv.* **1.** In one manner or for one purpose alone. **2.** Solely; exclusively. **3.** Merely; just. —*adj.* **1.** Alone in its class; sole; single. **2.** Standing alone by reason of superior excellence. —*conj.* Except that; but. [OE *ānlīc*]

on·o·mat·o·poe·ia (on′ə-mat′ə-pē′ə, ŏ-nom′ə-tə-) *n.* **1.** The formation of words in imitation of natural sounds, as *crack, splash,* or *bow-wow.* **2.** An imitative word. **3.** The use of such words. Also **on′o·mat·o·po·e′sis** (-pō-ē′sis), **on′o·mat′o·py** (-mat′ə-pē). [< L < Gk. < *onoma* name + *poieein* to make] —**on′o·mat′o·po·et′ic** or **-i·cal, on′o·mat′o·po·et′ic** (-pō-et′ik) *adj.* —**on′o·mat′o·po·et′i·cal·ly** *adv.*

On·on·da·ga (on′ən-dô′gə, -dä′-) *n. pl.* **-ga** or **-gas 1.** A tribe of North American Indians of Iroquoian stock formerly living in New York and Ontario. **2.** A member of this tribe.

on·rush (on′rush′, ôn′-) *n.* An onward rush or flow.

on·set (on′set′, ôn′-) *n.* **1.** An attack; assault. **2.** An initial stage, as of illness. **3.** A setting about; outset; start.

on·shore (on′shôr′, -shôr′, ôn′-) *adv. & adj.* To, toward, or on the shore.

on·slaught (on′slôt′, ôn′-) *n.* A violent, often hostile assault. [< Du. *annslag,* or < ON + ME *slaught* slaughter]

on·to (on′tōo, ôn′-) *prep.* **1.** Upon the top of; to and upon. **2.** *Informal* Aware of: I'm *onto* your tricks. Also **on to.**

onto- *combining form* Being; existence: *ontogeny.* Also, before vowels, **ont-.** [< Gk. *ōn, ontos,* ppr. of *einai* to be]

on·tog·e·ny (on-toj′ə-nē) *n. pl.* **·nies** *Biol.* The history of the development of the individual organism. Also **on·to·gen·e·sis** (on′tō-jen′ə-sis). —**on·to·ge·net·ic** (on′tō-jə-net′ik), **on·to·gen′ic** *adj.* —**on·to·gen′ist** *n.*

on·tol·o·gy (on-tol′ə-jē) *n. pl.* **·gies** The branch of metaphysics dealing with the philosophical theory of reality. —**on′to·log′i·cal** or **-ic.** —**on·tol′o·gist** *n.*

o·nus (ō′nəs) *n.* A burden or responsibility. [< L]

on·ward (on′wərd, ôn′-) *adv.* In the direction of progress; forward in space or time; ahead. Also **on′wards.** —*adj.* Moving or tending to be forward or ahead. [ME]

on·yx (on′iks) *n.* A variety of chalcedony having layers of different colors, used as a semiprecious gemstone. [< L < Gk., nail, onyx]

oo- *combining form* **1.** Egg; pertaining to eggs: *oology.* **2.** *Biol.* An ovum; *oogenesis.* [< Gk. *ōon* egg]

oo·dles (ōōd′lz) *n.pl. Informal* A great deal; many. [< dial. E *oodle,* var. of HUDDLE, n.]

o·o·lite (ō′ə-līt) *n.* A granular variety of limestone made up of round grains resembling the roe of a fish. [< F < Gk. *ōon* egg + *lithos* stone] —**o′o·lit′ic** (-lit′ik) *adj.*

o·ol·o·gy (ō-ol′ə-jē) *n.* The branch of ornithology that deals with the study of eggs. —**o·o·log′ic** (ō′ə-loj′ik) or **-i·cal** *adj.* —**o·ol′o·gist** *n.*

oo·long (ōō′lông) *n.* A dark tea that is partly fermented before being dried. [< Chinese *wu-lung* black dragon]

oo·mi·ak (ōō′mē·ak) See UMIAK.

oophoro- *combining form* Ovary; ovarian. Also, before vowels, **oophor-**. [< Gk. *ōophoros* egg-bearing]

ooze¹ (ōōz) *v.* **oozed, ooz·ing** *v.i.* 1. To flow or leak out slowly or gradually. 2. To exude moisture. 3. To escape or disappear little by little. — *v.t.* 4. To give off or exude in or as in droplets or a trickle. — *n.* 1. A slow, gradual leak. 2. That which oozes. [ME < OE *wāse* slimy mud]

ooze² (ōōz) *n.* 1. Slimy mud or moist, spongy soil. 2. A deposit of calcareous matter found on the ocean bottom and largely made up of the remains of foraminifers. 3. Muddy or marshy ground; bog; fen. [OE *wāse* slimy mud]

oo·zy¹ (ōō′zē) *adj.* **·zi·er, ·zi·est** Slowly leaking.

oo·zy² (ōō′zē) *adj.* **·zi·er, ·zi·est** Of or resembling mud or ooze; slimy. — **oo′zi·ly** *adv.* — **oo′zi·ness** *n.*

op- Assimilated var. of OB-.

o·pac·i·ty (ō·pas′ə·tē) *n.* *pl.* **·ties** 1. The state or quality of being opaque. 2. That which is opaque.

o·pal (ō′pəl) *n.* An amorphous, variously colored hydrous silica, including some iridescent varieties esteemed as gemstones. [< L < Gk. < Skt. *upala* precious stone]

o·pal·esce (ō′pəl·es′) *v.i.* **·esced, ·esc·ing** To exhibit opalescence.

o·pal·es·cence (ō′pəl·es′əns) *n.* An iridescent play of brilliant or milky colors, as in an opal. — **o′pal·es′cent** *adj.*

o·pal·ine (ō′pəl·ēn, -in) *adj.* Resembling or characteristic of an opal; opalescent. — *n.* A milky variety of glass.

o·paque (ō·pāk′) *adj.* 1. Impervious to light; not translucent or transparent. 2. Impervious to reason; unintelligent. 3. Impervious to radiant heat, electric radiation, etc. 4. Having no luster; dull. 5. Unintelligible; obscure. — *n.* 1. That which is opaque. 2. A pigment used to darken or eliminate portions of a print, photographic negative, etc. [ME *opake* < L *opacus* dark] — **o·paque′ly** *adv.* — **o·paque′ness** *n.*

op art (op) A style of art of the 1960's characterized by complex geometric patterns. [< *op(tical) art*]

o·pen (ō′pən) *adj.* 1. Affording approach, view, passage, or access. 2. Public; accessible to all. 3. Not secret or hidden: *open* hostility. 4. Expanded; unfolded: an *open* flower. 5. Not enclosed or covered: an *open* car. 6. Ready for business, appointment, etc. 7. Not settled or decided; pending: an *open* question. 8. Available: The job is still *open*. 9. Unbiased; receptive: often with *to*: an *open* mind; *open* to conviction. 10. Generous; liberal: an *open* hand. 11. *Phonet.* **a** Produced with a wide opening above the tongue; low: said of vowels, as the *a* in *father* and *calm*: opposed to *close*. **b** Ending in a vowel or diphthong: said of a syllable. 12. Not deceptive: an *open* face. 13. Eager or willing to receive: with *open* arms. 14. In hunting or fishing, without prohibition: *open* season. 15. Liable to attack, robbery, temptation, etc. 16. Having openings, holes, or perforations, as needlework. 17. *Music* **a** Not stopped by the finger, as a string. **b** Not produced by the stopping of a string or hole, or the use of a valve or slide; not fingered, as the tone of an instrument. **c** Not stopped by the hand or by a mute, as a brass instrument or its tone. 18. Unrestricted by union regulations in employment: an *open* shop. 19. *U.S. Informal* Permitting illicit activities, as gambling and prostitution: an *open* town. 20. Out of doors. 21. Not to be defended in war: *open* city. 22. Not restricted by rigid classes, control, etc.: an *open* society. — *v.t.* 1. To set open or ajar, as a door; unclose; unfasten. 2. To make passable; free from obstacles. 3. To make or force (a hole, passage, etc.). 4. To remove the covering, lid, etc., of. 5. To expand, as for viewing; unroll; unfold, as a map. 6. To make an opening or openings into: to *open* an abscess. 7. To make or declare ready for commerce, use, etc.: to *open* a store. 8. To make or declare public or free of access, as a park. 9. To make less compact; expand: to *open* ranks. 10. To make more receptive to ideas or sentiments; enlighten: to *open* the mind. 11. To bare the secrets of; divulge; reveal: to *open* one's heart. 12. To begin, as negotiations. 13. *Law* To undo or recall (a judgment or order) so as to permit its validity to be questioned. — *v.i.* 14. To become open. 15. To come apart or break open; rupture. 16. To come into view; spread out; unroll. 17. To afford access or view: The door *opened* on a courtyard. 18. To become receptive or enlightened. 19. To begin: The season *opened* with a ball. 20. In the theater, to begin a season or tour. — *n.* Any wide space not enclosed, obstructed, or covered, as by woods, rocks, etc.: usu. with the definite article: in the *open*. [OE] — **o′pen·er** *n.* — **o′pen·ly** *adv.* — **o′pen·ness** *n.*

open-air (ō′pən·âr′) *adj.* Occurring, done, etc., out of doors: an *open-air* concert.

open-and-shut (ō′pən·ən·shut′) *adj.* *Informal* Obvious; easily determined.

open door 1. The policy or practice of giving to all nations the same commercial privileges in a region or area open for trade or exploitation. 2. Admission to all without charge.

o·pen-door (ō′pən·dôr′, -dōr′) *adj.* Of or characterized by the commercial policies or practices of the open door.

o·pen-eyed (ō′pən·īd′) *adj.* 1. Having the eyes open; aware; watchful. 2. Amazed: in *open-eyed* wonder.

o·pen-faced (ō′pən·fāst′) *adj.* 1. Having an honest face. 2. Having a face or side uncovered.

o·pen-hand·ed (ō′pən·han′did) *adj.* Giving freely; liberal. — **o′pen·hand′ed·ly** *adv.* — **o′pen·hand′ed·ness** *n.*

o·pen-heart·ed (ō′pən·här′tid) *adj.* Disclosing the thoughts and intentions plainly; frank; candid. — **o′pen·heart′ed·ly** *adv.* — **o′pen·heart′ed·ness** *n.*

o·pen-hearth (ō′pən·härth′) *adj.* *Metall.* Designating a steel-making process in which the material is melted in a shallow furnace open at each end to admit fuel and air.

open house 1. A house or a social event in which hospitality is extended to all who wish to come. 2. An occasion when a school, factory, institution, etc., is open to visitors.

o·pen·ing (ō′pən·ing) *n.* 1. The act of becoming open or of causing to be open. 2. A vacant or unobstructed space, as a hole, passage, or gap. 3. An aperture in a wall, esp. one for the admission of light or air. 4. The first part or stage, as of a period, act, or process. 5. A first time for or the beginning of something: the play's *opening*. 6. In chess, checkers, etc., a specific series of opening moves. 7. An opportunity for action, esp. in business.

open market A market accessible to all buyers and sellers.

o·pen-mind·ed (ō′pən·mīn′did) *adj.* Free from prejudiced conclusions; amenable to reason; receptive. — **o′pen·mind′ed·ly** *adv.* **o′pen·mind′ed·ness** *n.*

o·pen-mouthed (ō′pən·mouthd′, -moutht′) *adj.* 1. Having the mouth open; gaping, as in wonder or surprise. 2. Noisy; clamorous. 3. Greedy; voracious.

open sesame An unfailing means or formula for opening secret doors and gaining entrance: an allusion to the tale of *Ali Baba and the Forty Thieves* in the *Arabian Nights*.

open shop 1. An establishment employing both union and nonunion labor. 2. An establishment whose policy is to hire only nonunion labor.

open stock In merchandising, extra or additional parts of a set, as of dishes, that are always kept in stock.

o·pen-work (ō′pən·wûrk′) *n.* Any product of art or handicraft containing numerous small openings.

op·er·a (op′ər·ə, op′rə) Plural of OPUS. — *n.* 1. A form of drama in which music is a dominant factor, made up of arias, recitatives, choruses, etc., with orchestral accompaniment, scenery, acting, and sometimes dance. 2. A particular musical drama or its music or libretto. 3. An opera house. [< Ital. < L, service, work < *opus* work] — **op·er·at·ic** (op′ə·rat′ik) *adj.* — **op′er·at′i·cal·ly** *adv.*

op·er·a·ble (op′ər·ə·bəl) *adj.* 1. Capable of treatment by surgical operation. 2. Practicable. — **op′er·a·bil′i·ty** *n.*

o·pé·ra bouffe (ô·pā·rä bōōf′) *French* A farcical comic opera. Also *Ital.* **o·pe·ra buf·fa** (ō′pā·rä bōōf′fä)

opera glass Small binoculars suitable for use at the theater. Also **opera glasses.**

opera hat A man's top hat, having a collapsible crown.

opera house A theater adapted for performance of operas.

op·er·ate (op′ə·rāt) *v.* **·at·ed, ·at·ing** *v.i.* 1. To act or function; work. 2. To bring about the proper or intended effect. 3. *Surg.* To perform an operation. 4. To carry on a military or naval operation: usu. with *against*. — *v.t.* 5. To control the working of, as a machine. 6. To manage or conduct the affairs of. 7. To bring about or cause; effect. [< L *operari* to work] — **op′er·at′a·ble** *adj.*

op·er·a·tion (op′ə·rā′shən) *n.* 1. The act or process of operating. 2. A method of operating; mode of action. 3. An act or transaction, esp. in the stock market. 4. A course or series of acts to effect a certain purpose; process. 5. The state of being in action: to be in *operation*. 6. *Surg.* Any manipulation upon or within the body, performed with or without instruments, to restore disunited or deficient parts, to remove diseased or injured parts, etc. 7. *Math.* **a** The act of making a change in the value or form of a quantity. **b** The change itself as indicated by symbols or rules. 8. A military or naval campaign.

op·er·a·tion·al (op′ə·rā′shən·əl) *adj.* 1. Pertaining to an operation. 2. Checked and serviced for ready operation.

operations research The application of scientific methods and skills to insure maximum efficiency in industry and government. Also called **operational research.**

op·er·a·tive (op′ər·ə·tiv, -ə·rā′tiv) *adj.* 1. Exerting force or influence. 2. Moving or working efficiently; effective. 3. Being in operation or in force. 4. Connected with surgical operations. 5. Concerned with practical work, mechanical or manual. — *n.* 1. A skilled worker, as in a mill or factory. 2. *Informal* A detective. — **op′er·a·tive·ly** *adv.*

op·er·a·tor (op′ə·rā′tər) *n.* 1. One who operates a machine or mechanism. 2. One who runs a commercial or industrial establishment. 3. A broker. 4. *Math.* A symbol that briefly indicates a mathematical process. 5. *Slang* One who craftily obtains things with little or no cost to himself.

o·per·cu·late (ō-pûr′kyōō-lit, -lāt) *adj.* Having an opercu-lum. Also **o·per′cu·lat′ed.**

o·per·cu·lum (ō-pûr′kyōō-ləm) *n.* *pl.* **·la** (-lə) *Biol.* A lidlike part or organ in certain plants, esp. one serving to close an aperture or provide protection. Also **o·per·cele** (ō-pûr′sēl), **o·per′cule** (-kyōōl). [< L, a covering, lid < *operire* to cover] — **o·per′cu·lar** *adj.*

o·pe·re ci·ta·to (ōp′ə-rē sī-tā′tō) *Latin* In the work cited, or quoted. Abbr. *o.c., op. cit.*

op·e·ret·ta (ōp′ə-ret′ə) *n.* A type of short, humorous opera with dialogue: also called *light opera.* [< Ital., dim. of *opera*]

o·phid·i·an (ō-fid′ē-ən) *n.* One of a group of limbless rep-tiles with jaws connected by elastic ligaments; a serpent or snake. — *adj.* Snakelike. [< NL < Gk. *ophis* serpent]

oph·thal·mi·a (of-thal′mē-ə) *n.* *Pathol.* Inflammation of the eye, its membranes, or its lids. Also **oph·thal′my** (-mē). [< LL < Gk. < *ophthalmos* eye] — **oph·thal′mic** *adj.*

oph·thal·mic (of-thal′mik) *adj.* Of or pertaining to the eye.

oph·thal·mi·tis (of′thal-mī′tis) *n.* *Pathol.* Inflammation of the eye, including the outer and internal structures.

ophthalmo- *combining form* Eye; pertaining to the eyes. [< Gk. *ophthalmos*]

oph·thal·mol·o·gy (of′thal-mol′ə-jē) *n.* The science deal-ing with the structure, functions, and diseases of the eye. — **oph·thal′mo·log′ic** (-mə-loj′ik) or **·i·cal** *adj.* — **oph′thal·mol′o·gist** *n.*

oph·thal·mo·scope (of-thal′mə-skōp) *n.* An optical instru-ment for illuminating and viewing the center of the eye. — **oph·thal′mo·scop′ic** (-skop′ik) or **·i·cal** *adj.* — **oph·thal·mos·co·py** (of′thal-mos′kə-pē) *n.*

-opia *combining form* *Med.* A (specified) defect of the eye, or condition of sight: *myopia.* Also spelled *-opy.* [< Gk. *-ōpia* < *ōps, ōpos* the eye]

o·pi·ate (*n.* & *adj.* ō′pē-it, -āt; *v.* ō′pē-āt) *n.* **1.** Medicine containing opium or one of its derivatives. **2.** Something inducing relaxation or sleep. — *adj.* **1.** Consisting of opi-um. **2.** Tending to induce sleep. — *v.t.* **·at·ed, ·at·ing** **1.** To treat with opium or an opiate. **2.** To deaden; dull.

o·pine (ō-pīn′) *v.t.* & *v.i.* **o·pined, o·pin·ing** To hold or ex-press as an opinion; think; conjecture: now usu. humorous. [< MF < L *opinari* to think, suppose]

o·pin·ion (ə-pin′yən, ō-) *n.* **1.** A conclusion or judgment held with confidence, but falling short of positive knowledge. **2.** An expert judgment given more or less formally. **3.** An evaluation. **4.** A prevailing sentiment: public *opinion.* **5.** *Law* The formal announcement of the conclusions of a court. [< OF < L *opinari* to think]

o·pin·ion·at·ed (ə-pin′yən-ā′tid, ō-) *adj.* Obstinately at-tached to one's own opinion. — **o·pin′ion·at′ed·ness** *n.*

o·pin·ion·a·tive (ə-pin′yən-ā′tiv, ō-) *adj.* **1.** Opinionated. **2.** Of the nature of opinion. — **o·pin′ion·a′tive·ly** *adv.* — **o·pin′ion·a′tive·ness** *n.*

o·pi·um (ō′pē-əm) *n.* A narcotic drug obtained from the unripe capsules of the **opium poppy,** containing a mixture of alkaloids, including morphine. [< L < Gk. *opion* opium, dim. of *opos* vegetable juice]

o·pos·sum (ə-pos′əm, pos′əm) *n.* An American marsupial of largely arboreal and nocturnal habits, having a prehensile tail and feet adapted for grasping. [< Algonquian]

op·po·nent (ə-pō′nənt) *n.* One who opposes another, as in battle; antagonist. — **Syn.** See ENEMY. — *adj.* **1.** Acting against something or someone; opposing. **2.** *Anat.* Bringing one part, as of a muscle, into opposition to another. **3.** Standing in front; opposite. [< L < *ob-* against + *ponere* to place] — **op·po′nen·cy** *n.*

op·por·tune (op′ər-tōōn′, -tyōōn′) *adj.* **1.** Meeting some need; esp. right or fit. **2.** Occurring at the right moment; timely. [< MF < L *opportunus* favorable, lit., (a wind) blowing towards port] — **op′por·tune′ly** *adv.* — **op′por·tune′ness** *n.*

op·por·tu·nist (op′ər-tōō′nist, -tyōō′-) *n.* One who uses every opportunity to contribute to the achievement of some end, and who is relatively uninfluenced by moral principles or sentiment. — **op′por·tu·nis′tic** *adj.* — **op′por·tu′nism** *n.*

op·por·tu·ni·ty (op′ər-tōō′nə-tē, -tyōō′-) *n.* *pl.* **·ties** A fit or convenient time; favorable occasion or circumstance.

op·pos·a·ble (ə-pō′zə-bəl) *adj.* **1.** Capable of being placed opposite something else: said esp. of the thumb. **2.** That can be opposed. — **op·pos′a·bil′i·ty** *n.*

op·pose (ə-pōz′) *v.* **·posed, ·pos·ing** *v.t.* **1.** To act or be in opposition to; resist; combat. **2.** To set in opposition or contrast: to *oppose* love to hatred. **3.** To place before or in front. — *v.i.* **4.** To act or be in opposition. [< OF < L < *ob-* against + *ponere* to place] — **op·pos′er** *n.* — **Syn. 1.** Combat, fight, resist, withstand, dispute, contradict, contravene.

op·po·site (op′ə-zit) *adj.* **1.** Situated or placed on the other side, or on each side, of an intervening space or thing. **2.**

Facing or moving the other way: *opposite* directions. **3.** Contrary in tendency or character: *opposite* opinions. **4.** *Bot.* **a** Arranged in pairs, as leaves on a stem. **b** Having one part or organ immediately before or vertically over another, as a stamen before a petal. — *n.* Something or someone that is opposite, opposed, or contrary. — *adv.* In an oppo-site or complementary direction or position. — *prep.* **1.** Across from; facing. **2.** Complementary to, as in theatrical roles: He played *opposite* her. [< OF < L *oppositus.* See OPPOSE.] — **op′po·site·ly** *adv.* — **op′po·site·ness** *n.*

op·po·si·tion (op′ə-zish′ən) *n.* **1.** The act of opposing or re-sisting. **2.** The state of being opposite or opposed; antithe-sis. **3.** A position confronting another or a placing in con-trast. **4.** That which is or furnishes an obstacle to some re-sult: The stream flows without *opposition.* **5.** *Often cap.* The political party opposed to the party or administration in power. — **op′po·si′tion·al** *adj.* — **op·po·si′tion·ist** *n.* — **op′po·si′tion·less** *adj.*

op·pos·i·tive (ə-poz′ə-tiv) *adj.* Placed or capable of being placed in contrast. — **op·pos′i·tive·ly** *adv.*

op·press (ə-pres′) *v.t.* **1.** To burden or keep down by harsh and unjust use of force or authority. **2.** To lie heavy upon physically or mentally. [< OF < Med.L *oppressare,* ult. < L *ob-* against + *premere* to press] — **op·pres′sor** *n.*

op·pres·sion (ə-presh′ən) *n.* **1.** The act of oppressing, or the state of being oppressed. **2.** A sense of weight or constric-tion; mental depression. **3.** That which oppresses.

op·pres·sive (ə-pres′iv) *adj.* **1.** Burdensome; tyrannical; harsh; cruel. **2.** Producing a state of oppression. — **op·pres′sive·ly** *adv.* — **op·pres′sive·ness** *n.*

op·pro·bri·ous (ə-prō′brē-əs) *adj.* **1.** Contemptuously abu-sive; imputing disgrace. **2.** Shameful; disgraceful. — **op·pro′bri·ous·ly** *adv.* — **op·pro′bri·ous·ness** *n.*

op·pro·bri·um (ə-prō′brē-əm) *n.* **1.** The state of being scornfully reproached; ignominy. **2.** Reproach mingled with disdain. **3.** A cause of disgrace or reproach. [< L < *ob-* against + *probum* disgrace] — **Syn. 1.** odium, obloquy, infamy, disgrace.

op·pugn (ə-pyōōn′) *v.t.* To assail or oppose with argument; call in question; controvert. [< L < *ob-* against + *pugnare* to fight] — **op·pugn′er** *n.*

-opsia *combining form* *Med.* A (specified) type or condition of sight. Also **-opsy.** [< NL < Gk. *opsis* aspect, sight]

opt (opt) *v.i.* To choose; decide. [< F < L *optare*]

op·ta·tive (op′tə-tiv) *adj.* **1.** Expressing desire or choice. **2.** *Gram.* Denoting the mood that expresses wish or desire. — *n. Gram.* **1.** The optative mood. **2.** A word or construc-tion in this mood. [< F < LL < L *optare* to wish] — **op′·ta·tive·ly** *adv.*

op·tic (op′tik) *adj.* Pertaining to the eye or vision. — *n. Informal* The eye. [< MF < Med.L < Gk. *optikos* < stem *op-* as in *opsomai* I shall see]

op·ti·cal (op′ti-kəl) *adj.* **1.** Pertaining to optics. **2.** Of or pertaining to eyesight. **3.** Designed to assist or improve vi-sion. — **op′ti·cal·ly** *adv.*

optical fiber Any of various fibers of glass or other clear plastic through which light may be conducted along any de-sired path and in compact bundles will transmit images of high fidelity and resolution.

optical maser *Physics* A laser.

op·ti·cian (op-tish′ən) *n.* One who makes or deals in opti-cal goods.

optic nerve *Anat.* The special nerve of vision, connecting the retina with the cerebral centers. For illus. see EYE.

op·tics (op′tiks) *n.pl.* (construed *as sing.*) The science that treats of the phenomena of light, vision, and sight.

op·ti·mal (op′tə-məl) *adj.* Most favorable; best.

op·ti·mism (op′tə-miz′əm) *n.* **1.** A disposition to look on the bright side of things. **2.** The doctrine that everything is ordered for the best. **3.** The doctrine that the universe is constantly tending toward a better state. [< F < L *opti-mus* best] — **op′ti·mist** *n.* — **op′ti·mis′tic** or **·ti·cal** *adj.* — **op′ti·mis′ti·cal·ly** *adv.*

op·ti·mum (op′tə-məm) *n.* *pl.* **·ma** (-mə) or **·mums** The condition or degree producing the best result. — *adj.* Pro-ducing or conducive to the best results. [< L, neut. of *opti-mus* best]

op·tion (op′shən) *n.* **1.** The right, power, or liberty of choosing; discretion. **2.** The act of opting or choosing. **3.** The purchased privilege of either buying or selling something at a specified price within a specified time. **4.** A thing that is or can be chosen. [< MF < L < *optare* to choose]

op·tion·al (op′shən-əl) *adj.* Left to one's preference; not re-quired; elective. — **op′tion·al·ly** *adv.*

op·tom·e·try (op-tom′ə-trē) *n.* The profession or occupa-tion of measuring vision and prescribing corrective lenses to compensate for visual defects. — **op·tom′e·trist** *n.*

op·u·lence (op′yə-ləns) *n.* **1.** Wealth; affluence. **2.** Lux-

uriance; abundance. Also **op′u·len·cy** (-lən·sē).
— **Syn. 1.** riches, fortune, means, prosperity.
op·u·lent (op′yə·lənt) *adj.* **1.** Possessing great wealth; rich; affluent. **2.** Plentiful; abundant; profuse. [< L *opulentus* < *ops, opis* power, wealth] — **op′u·lent·ly** *adv.*
o·pus (ō′pəs) *n. pl.* **op·er·a** (op′ər·ə, op′rə) A literary or musical work or composition. Abbr. *op.* [< L, work]
-opy See -OPIA.
or (ôr, *unstressed* ər) *conj.* **1.** Introducing an alternative: stop *or* go. **2.** Offering a choice of a series: Will you take milk *or* coffee *or* chocolate? **3.** Introducing an equivalent: the culinary art *or* art of cookery. **4.** Indicating uncertainty: He lives in Chicago *or* thereabouts. **5.** Introducing the second alternative of a choice limited to two: with *either* or *whether*: It must be either black *or* white; I don't care whether he goes *or* not. **6.** *Poetic* Either; whether: *or* in the heart *or* in the head. [ME contraction, of *other, auther* either, OE *ǣther*; infl. in meaning by OE *oththe* or]
-or¹ *suffix of nouns* The person or thing performing the action expressed in the root verb: *competitor.* ◆ See note under -ER¹. [< AF *-our,* OF *-or* < L *-or, -ator*]
-or² *suffix of nouns* Quality, state, or condition: *favor.* [< OF < L]
or·a·cle (ôr′ə·kəl, or′-) *n.* **1.** The seat of worship of some ancient divinity, as of Apollo at Delphi, where prophecies were given out by the priests in answer to inquiries. **2.** A prophecy thus given. **3.** The deity whose prophecies were given. **4.** A person of unquestioned wisdom or knowledge, or something regarded as of infallible authority. **5.** A wise saying. [< OF < L *oraculum* < *orare* to speak, pray]
o·rac·u·lar (ō·rak′yə·lər, ō-) *adj.* **1.** Of or pertaining to an oracle. **2.** Obscure; enigmatical. **3.** Prophetic; farseeing. — **o·rac′u·lar′i·ty** *n.* — **o·rac′u·lar·ly** *adv.*
o·ral (ôr′əl, ō′rəl) *adj.* **1.** Uttered through the mouth; spoken. **2.** Of or pertaining to the mouth; also, situated at or near the mouth. **3.** Of, pertaining to, or using speech. **4.** Taken or administered by mouth. — **Syn.** See VERBAL. — *n. Usu. pl.* An academic examination in which the student speaks his answers aloud. [< L *os, oris* mouth] — **o′ral·ly** *adv.*
o·rang (ō·rang′) *n.* An orang-utan.
or·ange (ôr′inj, or′-) *n.* **1.** A round, juicy fruit of a low, much-branched, evergreen tree with a reddish yellow rind enclosing membranous divisions and a refreshing, sweetish or subacid pulp. **2.** Any of the trees yielding this fruit. **3.** Any of many related species. **4.** A reddish yellow color; also, a pigment of this color. — *adj.* **1.** Reddish yellow. **2.** Of an orange. [< OF < Provençal < Sp. < Arabic < Persian *nārang*]
or·ange·ade (ôr′inj·ād′, or′-) *n.* A beverage made of orange juice, sugar, and water. [< F]
orange blossom The white, fragrant blossom of the orange tree, often worn by brides: State flower of Florida.
Or·ange·man (ôr′inj·mən, or′-) *n. pl.* **·men** (-mən) A member of a secret society founded in northern Ireland in 1795 for upholding Protestant ascendancy and succession in England. [named in honor of William III, king of England and Prince of Orange]
orange pekoe A black tea from India, Ceylon, and Java.
or·ange·wood (ôr′inj·wo͝od′, or′-) *n.* The fine-grained, yellowish wood of the orange tree, used in lathe work.
o·rang·u·tan (ō·rang′ə·tan, -o͝o·tan) *n. pl.* **·tans** or **·tan** A large, anthropoid ape of Borneo and Sumatra, having brownish red hair and extremely long arms: also called *orang, ourang.* Also **o·rang′-ou·tang** (-ə·tang, -o͝o·tang). [< Malay < *oran* man + *utan* forest]
o·rate (ôr′āt, ô·rāt′, ō′rāt, ō·rāt′) *v.i.* **o·rat·ed, o·rat·ing** To talk oratorically or pompously; speechify. [See ORATION.]
o·ra·tion (ô·rā′shən, ō·rā′-) *n.* An elaborate public speech, esp. one given at a formal occasion. [< L < *orare* to speak]
or·a·tor (ôr′ə·tər, or′-) *n.* **1.** One who delivers an oration; an eloquent public speaker. **2.** *Law* The complainant in a chancery proceeding. — **or′a·tor·ship′** *n.*
or·a·to·ri·o (ôr′ə·tôr′ē·ō, -tō′rē·ō, or′-) *n. pl.* **·os** A large musical composition for solo voices, chorus, and orchestra, usu. dramatizing a sacred story, but without scenery or acting. [< Ital. < LL. See ORATORY².]
or·a·to·ry¹ (ôr′ə·tôr′ē, -tō′rē, or′-) *n.* **1.** The art of public speaking; eloquence. **2.** Eloquent language. [< L *oratoria* (ars) the oratorical (art)] — **or′a·tor′i·cal** (-tôr′i·kəl, -tor′-) *adj.* — **or′a·tor′i·cal·ly** *adv.*
or·a·to·ry² (ôr′ə·tôr′ē, -tō′rē, or′-) *n. pl.* **·ries** A place for prayer; private chapel. [< LL *oratorium* (*templum*) (temple) for prayer < *orare* to pray]
orb (ôrb) *n.* **1.** A rounded mass; a sphere or globe. **2.** A circle or orbit; anything circular. **3.** A sphere topped by a cross, used as a symbol of royal power. **4.** *Poetic* The eye. — *v.t.* **1.** To shape into a sphere or circle. **2.** *Poetic* To enclose; encircle. [< L *orbis* circle]
or·bic·u·lar (ôr·bik′yə·lər) *adj.* **1.** Having the form of an orb or orbit. **2.** Well-rounded. **3.** *Bot.* Circular, as a leaf.

[< F, or < L < *orbiculus,* dim. of *orbis* circle] — **or·bic′u·lar′i·ty** (-lar′ə·tē) *n.* — **or·bic′u·lar·ly** *adv.*
or·bic·u·late (ôr·bik′yə·lit, -lāt) *adj.* Having a rounded form; orbicular. Also **or·bic′u·lat′ed.** — **or·bic′u·late·ly** *adv.*
or·bit (ôr′bit) *n.* **1.** The path in space along which a heavenly body or artificial satellite moves about its center of attraction. **2.** A range of influence or action: the *orbit* of imperialism. — *v.t.* **1.** To cause to move in an orbit, as an artificial satellite. **2.** To revolve around (the earth, etc.), as a satellite. — *v.i.* **3.** To move in or as in an orbit. [< L *orbita* track of a wheel < *orbis* wheel, circle] — **or′bi·tal** *adj.*
or·chard (ôr′chərd) *n.* A plantation of trees grown for their products, as fruit, nuts, oils, etc.; also, the enclosure or ground containing them. [OE < *ort-geard* garden]
or·ches·tra (ôr′kis·trə) *n.* **1.** A comparatively large group of musicians playing together; esp., a symphony orchestra; also, the instruments they play. **2.** *U.S.* In theaters, the place immediately before the stage, occupied by the musicians: also **orchestra pit. 3.** The main floor of a theater. [< L < Gk. *orchēstra* dancing space] — **or·ches·tral** (ôr·kes′trəl) *adj.* — **or·ches′tral·ly** *adv.*
or·ches·trate (ôr′kis·trāt) *v.t. & v.i.* **·trat·ed, ·trat·ing** To compose or arrange (music) for an orchestra. — **or′ches·tra′tion** *n.*
or·chid (ôr′kid) *n.* **1.** Any of a family of herbs of temperate regions, having bulbous roots and often very showy flowers. **2.** Any of various delicate, rosy purple colors. [< NL < L *orchis* orchid < Gk., orig., a testicle; so called because of the shape of its rootstocks]
orchio- *combining form* Testicle; pertaining to the testicles. Also, before vowels, **orchi-.** [< Gk. *orchis* testicle]
or·chis (ôr′kis) *n.* Any of various plants having dense spikes of small flowers. [< L, orchid]
or·dain (ôr·dān′) *v.t.* **1.** To order or decree; enact. **2.** To predestine; destine: said of God, fate, etc. **3.** To invest with ministerial or priestly functions. [< OF < L *ordinare* to set in order] — **or·dain′er** *n.*
or·deal (ôr·dēl′, -dē′əl, ôr′dēl) *n.* **1.** A severe test of character or endurance. **2.** A former method of judicial trial in which the accused was subjected to painful physical tests that were supposed to do him no harm if he were innocent. [OE *ordāl, ordēl* judgment < *or-* out + *dǣl* a deal]
or·der (ôr′dər) *n.* **1.** A condition in which there is a methodical, proper, or harmonious arrangement of things. **2.** The disposition or arrangement of things. **3.** Established method, procedure, or condition. **4.** A proper or working condition. **5.** A command, direction, or regulation. **6.** *Law* Any direction of a court, entered in the record but not included in the final judgment. **7.** A commission or instruction to supply, purchase, or sell something; also, that which is supplied or purchased. **8.** A body of persons united by some common bond: the *Order* of Odd Fellows. **9.** A monastic or religious body. **10.** A group of persons upon whom an honor has been conferred, entitling them to wear specific insignia; also, the insignia so worn. **11.** *Eccl.* **a** *Usu. pl.* Any of the various grades or degrees of the Christian ministry. **b** The rite or sacrament of ordination. **c** A liturgical form for a service or the performance of a rite. **12.** *Archit.* **a** A style of classical architecture, as Doric, Ionic, or Corinthian, usu. represented by the general character of its columns. **b** A column with its entablature. **13.** *Biol.* A taxonomic category ranking next below the class, and above the family. — **in order 1.** In accordance with rule or proper procedure. **2.** Neat; tidy. — **in order that** So that; to the end that. — **in order to** For the purpose of. — **in short order** Quickly; without delay. — **on order** Ordered but not yet delivered. — **on the order of** Similar to. — **out of order 1.** Not in working condition. **2.** Not in proper arrangement or sequence. **3.** Not according to rule. **4.** Not suitable or appropriate. — **to order** According to the buyer's specifications. — *v.t.* **1.** To give a command or direction to. **2.** To command to go, come, etc. **3.** To give an order that (something) be done. **4.** To give an order for. **5.** To put in orderly or systematic arrangement. **6.** To ordain. — *v.i.* **7.** To give an order or orders. — **to order arms** *Mil.* To bring a rifle against the right side, with the butt on the ground. [< OF < L *ordo, -inis* row, series, order] — **or′der·er** *n.*
or·der·ly (ôr′dər·lē) *adj.* **1.** Having regard for arrangement, method, or system. **2.** Peaceful. **3.** Characterized by neatness and order. **4.** Pertaining to orders. — *n. pl.* **·lies 1.** A hospital attendant. **2.** A soldier detailed to carry orders. — *adv.* Methodically; regularly. — **or′der·li·ness** *n.*
or·di·nal¹ (ôr′də·nəl) *adj.* **1.** Denoting position in an order or succession. **2.** Pertaining to an order, as of plants, animals, etc. [< LL < L *ordo, -inis* order]
or·di·nal² (ôr′də·nəl) *n. Eccl.* A book of rites for certain church services. [< Med.L < LL < L *ordo, -inis* order]
ordinal number *Math.* A number that shows the order of a unit in a given series, as first, second, third, etc.: distinguished from *cardinal number.*
or·di·nance (ôr′də·nəns) *n.* **1.** An order, decree, or law of

a municipal body. **2.** A religious rite or ceremony. [< OF < Med.L < L < *ordinare* to set in order]

or·di·nar·i·ly (ôr′də·ner′ə·lē, ôr′də·nâr′ə·lē) *adv.* **1.** In ordinary cases; usually. **2.** In the usual manner. **3.** To the usual extent; normally.

or·di·nar·y (ôr′də·ner′ē) *adj.* **1.** Of common or everyday occurrence; customary; usual. **2.** According to an established order; normal. **3.** Common in rank or degree; average; commonplace. — *n.* *pl.* **·nar·ies** **1.** That which is usual or common. **2.** *Brit.* **a** A meal provided regularly at a fixed price. **b** An eating house where such meals are served. **3.** *Law* One who exercises jurisdiction in his own right, and not by delegation. **4.** *Eccl.* **a** A rule or book prescribing the form for saying Mass. **b** The practically unchangeable part of the Mass: with *the*: distinguished from the *proper*. **— in ordinary 1.** In actual and constant service. **2.** *Naut.* Out of commission; laid up: said of a ship. **— out of the ordinary** Not common or usual; extraordinary. [< OF < L *ordinarius* regular, usual] **— or′di·nar′i·ness** *n.*

or·di·nate (ôr′də·nit) *adj.* Characterized by order; regular. — *n.* *Math.* **1.** The distance of any point from the X-axis, measured on a line parallel to the Y-axis in a coordinate system. **2.** The line or number indicating such distance.

or·di·na·tion (ôr′də·nā′shən) *n.* **1.** *Eccl.* The rite of consecration to the ministry. **2.** The state of being ordained, regulated, or settled.

ord·nance (ôrd′nəns) *n.* **1.** Military weapons, ammunition, and associated equipment and materiel. **2.** Cannon or artillery. [Contr. of ORDINANCE]

Or·do·vi·cian (ôr′də·vish′ən) *adj.* *Geol.* Of or designating a period of the Paleozoic era, following the Cambrian and preceding the Silurian. — *n.* An epoch of the Paleozoic era. See chart for GEOLOGY. [< L *Ordovices* the Ordovices, an ancient Celtic tribe]

or·dure (ôr′jər, -dyŏŏr) *n.* Excrement; feces. [< OF < *ord* foul, nasty < L *horridus* bristling]

ore (ôr, ōr) *n.* **1.** A natural substance, as a mineral or rock, containing a valuable metal. **2.** A natural substance containing a nonmetallic mineral: sulfur *ore*. [OE *ār, ǣr* brass, copper; infl. in meaning by OE *ōra* unwrought metal]

ö·re (œ′rə) *n.* *pl.* **ö·re** A coin or monetary unit equivalent to one hundredth of a krone in Denmark and Norway, and of a krona in Sweden. [< Norw., Dan., and Sw.]

o·reg·a·no (ō·reg′ə·nō) *n.* A perennial herb of the mint family, having aromatic leaves used as a seasoning. [< Sp. < L *origanum* wild marjoram]

Oregon grape An evergreen shrub having dark blue berry clusters resembling grapes: the State flower of Oregon.

O·res·tes (ō·res′tēz, ō-) In Greek legend, the son of Agamemnon and Clytemnestra who, together with his sister Electra, avenged his father's murder by killing his mother and her lover. [< L < Gk.]

or·fray (ôr′frā) See ORPHREY.

or·gan (ôr′gən) *n.* **1.** A musical instrument consisting of a collection of pipes and reeds made to sound by means of compressed air controlled by one or more keyboards and by various knobs used to vary registration: often called *pipe organ*. **2.** Any musical instrument resembling this, either in sound or in some aspect of its mechanism. **3.** Any part of a plant or animal, as a stamen, the heart, etc., performing some definite function. **4.** An instrument or agency of communication; esp., a newspaper or periodical published in the interest of a political party, religious denomination, etc. [< OE *organa*, or < OF < L < Gk. *organon* instrument]

or·gan·dy (ôr′gən·dē) *n.* *pl.* **·dies** A thin, crisp, transparent, cotton muslin, used for dresses, collars, cuffs, etc. Also **or′gan·die.** [< F *organdi*; ult. origin uncertain]

organ grinder A street musician playing a hand organ.

or·gan·ic (ôr·gan′ik) *adj.* **1.** Of, pertaining to, or of the nature of animals and plants. **2.** Affecting or altering the structure of an organ or part: *organic* disease: distinguished from *functional*. **3.** Serving the purpose of an organ. **4.** *Chem.* Of or pertaining to compounds containing carbon. **5.** Inherent in or pertaining to the fundamental structure of something; constitutional. **6.** Of or characterized by systematic coordination of parts; organized; systematized. **7.** *Law* Designating the system of laws or principles forming the foundation of a government. Also **or·gan′i·cal.** [< L < Gk. < *organon* instrument] **— or·gan′i·cal·ly** *adv.*

organic chemistry The branch of chemistry that relates to the structure, formation, and properties of compounds containing carbon.

organic disease *Pathol.* A disease that affects or alters the structure of some particular organ or part.

or·gan·ism (ôr′gən·iz′əm) *n.* **1.** An animal or plant considered as a totality of interdependent parts functioning to maintain vital activities. **2.** Anything that is analogous in structure and function to a living thing: the social *organism*.

or·gan·ist (ôr′gən·ist) *n.* One who plays the organ.

or·gan·i·za·tion (ôr′gən·ə·zā′shən, -ī·zā′-) *n.* **1.** The act of organizing, or the state of being organized; also, that which is organized. **2.** A number of individuals systematically united for some end or work. **3.** The officials, committeemen, etc., who control a political party. Also *Brit.* **or′gan·i·sa′tion.**

or·gan·ize (ôr′gən·īz) *v.* **·ized, ·iz·ing** *v.t.* **1.** To bring together or form as a whole or combination, as for a common objective. **2.** To arrange systematically; order. **3.** To furnish with organic structure. **4.** To enlist (workers) in a trade union. **5.** To unionize the workers of (a factory, etc.). — *v.i.* **6.** To form or join an organization. Also *Brit.* **or′gan·ise.** **— or′gan·iz′a·ble** *adj.* **— or′gan·iz′er** *n.*

organo- *combining form* **1.** *Biol.* Related to an organ or to the organs of the body. **2.** *Chem.* Organic. [< Gk. *organon* instrument, organ]

or·ga·no·me·tal·lic (ôr′gə·nō·mə·tal′ik) *adj.* *Chem.* Designating or pertaining to a compound of metal and carbon.

organ pipe One of the tubes of a pipe organ in which a column of air is made to vibrate so as to produce a tone.

or·gasm (ôr′gaz·əm) *n.* *Physiol.* The acme of excitement at the culmination of a sexual act. [< NL < Gk. *orgaein* to swell] **— or·gas·tic** (ôr·gas′tik) *adj.*

or·gi·as·tic (ôr′jē·as′tik) *adj.* **1.** Pertaining to or resembling an orgy. **2.** Marked by orgies.

or·gy (ôr′jē) *n.* *pl.* **·gies** **1.** Wild or wanton revelry. **2.** Any immoderate or excessive indulgence. **3.** *pl.* The secret rites in honor of certain Greek and Roman deities, marked by frenzied songs and dances. [Earlier *orgies*, pl. < MF < L *orgia* < Gk., secret rites]

o·ri·el (ôr′ē·əl, ō′rē-) *n.* *Archit.* A bay window, esp. one built out from a wall and resting on a bracket or similar support. [< OF *oriol* porch, gallery, ? < Med.L *oriolum*]

o·ri·ent (*n. & adj.* ôr′ē·ənt, ō′rē-, -ent; *v.* ôr′ē·ent, ō′rē-) *n.* **1.** The east: opposed to *occident*. **2.** The eastern sky; also, sunrise. — *v.t.* **1.** To cause to face or turn to the east. **2.** To place or adjust, as a map, in exact relation to the points of the compass. **3.** To adjust in relation to something else. Also *orientate*. — *adj.* **1.** Resembling sunrise; bright. **2.** Ascending; rising. [< OF < L (*sol*) *oriens, -entis* rising (sun), east, ppr. of *oriri* to rise]

O·ri·ent (ôr′ē·ənt, ō′rē-, -ent) **1.** The countries east of Europe; esp., eastern Asia. **2.** The eastern hemisphere.

o·ri·en·tal (ôr′ē·en′təl, ō′rē-) *adj.* **1.** Of or pertaining to the East, or to the countries constituting the Orient: distinguished from *occidental*. **2.** Very bright, clear, and pure: said of gems. **3.** Denoting a variety of precious corundum, esp. sapphire: an *oriental* topaz. **— o′ri·en′tal·ly** *adv.*

O·ri·en·tal (ôr′ē·en′təl, ō′rē-) *adj.* Of or pertaining to the Orient; Eastern. — *n.* An inhabitant of Asia; an Asian.

O·ri·en·tal·ism (ôr′ē·en′təl·iz′əm, ō′rē-) *n.* **1.** An Oriental quality, mannerism, characteristic, etc. **2.** Knowledge of or proficiency in Oriental languages, literature, etc. Also **o′ri·en′tal·ist.** **— O′ri·en′tal·ist** *n.*

Oriental rug **1.** A rug or carpet hand-woven in one piece in the Orient. **2.** Any rug having a design or texture resembling those made in the Orient.

o·ri·en·tate (ôr′ē·en·tāt′, ō′rē-) *v.* **·tat·ed, ·tat·ing** *v.t.* **1.** To orient. — *v.i.* **2.** To face or turn eastward or in some specified direction. **3.** To become adjusted or oriented.

o·ri·en·ta·tion (ôr′ē·en·tā′shən, ō′rē-) *n.* **1.** The act of orienting, or the state of being oriented. **2.** The determination or adjustment of one's position with reference to circumstances, ideals, etc.

or·i·fice (ôr′ə·fis, or′-) *n.* An opening into a cavity; aperture. [< MF < LL < L *os, oris* mouth + *facere* to make]

or·i·flamme (ôr′ə·flam, or′-) *n.* **1.** The red banner of the abbey of St. Denis, used as a battle standard by the kings of France until the 15th century. **2.** Any flag or standard. [< F < OF < *orie* golden (< L *aureus*) + *flambe* banner]

or·i·ga·mi (ôr′i·gä′mē) *n.* The ancient Japanese art of folding single sheets of paper into realistic animal forms, usu. without the aid of scissors or paste. [< Japanese]

or·i·gan (ôr′ə·gən, or′-) *n.* The wild marjoram. [< OF < L < Gk. *origanon*, an herb like marjoram]

or·i·gin (ôr′ə·jin, or′-) *n.* **1.** The beginning of the existence of anything. **2.** A primary source; cause. **3.** Parentage; ancestry. **4.** *Math.* **a** The point at which the axes of a Cartesian coordinate system intersect. **b** The point in a polar coordinate system where the radius vector equals zero. [< OF < L *origo, -inis* source, beginning]

o·rig·i·nal (ə·rij′ə·nəl) *adj.* **1.** Of or belonging to the beginning, origin, or first stage of existence of a thing. **2.** Produced by one's own mind and thought; not copied or imitative. **3.** Able to produce works requiring thought without copying or imitating others; creative; inventive. — *n.* **1.** The first form of anything. **2.** An original work, as a paint-

ing, sculpture, etc., as distinct from a reproduction or copy.
3. A person or thing represented in a painting, biography, etc.   **4.** A person of unique character or genius.   **5.** An eccentric.   — **Syn.** See NEW.

o·rig·i·nal·i·ty (ə·rij/ə·nal/ə·tē) *n.   pl.* **·ties 1.** The power of originating; inventiveness.   **2.** The quality of being original or novel.   **3.** Something original.

o·rig·i·nal·ly (ə·rij/ə·nəl·ē) *adv.* **1.** At the beginning.   **2.** In a new and striking manner.

original sin *Theol.* The corruption and depravity held to be inherent in all mankind as a consequence of Adam's first sinful disobedience.

o·rig·i·nate (ə·rij/ə·nāt) *v.* **·nat·ed, ·nat·ing** *v.t.* **1.** To bring into existence; create; initiate.   — *v.i.* **2.** To come into existence; have origin; arise.   — **o·rig/i·na/tion** *n.* — **o·rig/i·na/tive** *adj.* — **o·rig/i·na/tive·ly** *adv.* — **o·rig/i·na/tor** *n.*   — **Syn.** 1. institute, propagate, produce.

o·ri·ole (ôr/ē·ōl, ō/rē-) *n.* **1.** Any of a family of black and yellow birds of the Old World, related to the crows.   **2.** Any of various black and yellow American songbirds that build hanging nests; esp., the Baltimore oriole and the orchard oriole. [< OF < Med.L < L *aureolus,* dim. of *aureus* golden]

O·ri·on (ō·rī/ən) In Greek and Roman mythology, a giant hunter who pursued the Pleiades and was killed by Diana.   — *n.* A constellation. [< L < Gk.]

or·i·son (ôr/i·zən, or/-) *n.   Usu. pl.* A devotional prayer. [< OF < LL *oratio, -onis* prayer]

Or·lon (ôr/lon) *n.* A synthetic fiber woven from an acrylic resin, having high resistance to heat, light, and chemicals, widely used as a textile material: a trade name. Also **or/lon.**

or·mo·lu (ôr/mə·lōō) *n.* Any of various alloys of copper, tin, and zinc that resemble gold in appearance, used in furniture decorations, jewelry, etc. [< F < *or* gold + *moulu,* pp. of *moudre* to grind]

or·na·ment (*n.* ôr/nə·mənt; *v.* ôr/nə·ment) *n.* **1.** Something that adorns or beautifies; a decoration.   **2.** Ornaments, collectively.   **3.** A person regarded as a source of honor or credit.   **4.** The act of adorning, or the state of being adorned; ornamentation.   **5.** *Music* A tone or group of tones used to embellish a melody without materially affecting its harmonic content.   — *v.t.* **1.** To furnish with ornaments; decorate.   **2.** To be an ornament to.   [< OF < L < *ornare* to adorn]   — **or/na·ment/er** (-ment/ər) *n.*

or·na·men·tal (ôr/nə·men/təl) *adj.* Of the nature of or serving as an ornament.   — *n.* An ornamental object; esp., a plant used as decoration.   — **or/na·men/tal·ly** *adv.*

or·na·men·ta·tion (ôr/nə·men·tā/shən) *n.* **1.** The act or result of ornamenting.   **2.** The state of being ornamented.   **3.** That which ornaments; also, ornaments, collectively.

or·nate (ôr·nāt/) *adj.* **1.** Elaborately or excessively ornamented; overdecorative.   **2.** Florid or showy, as a style of writing. [< L *ornatus,* pp. of *ornare* to adorn]   — **or·nate/ly** *adv.* — **or·nate/ness** *n.*

or·ner·y (ôr/nər·ē, ôrn/rē) *adj. Dial.* **1.** *U.S.* Disposed to be contrary or stubborn.   **2.** *U.S.* Mean; ugly; low; snide: an *ornery* trick.   **3.** Ordinary; common. [Alter. of ORDINARY]   — **or/ner·i·ness** *n.*

ornitho- *combining form* Bird; of or relating to birds. Also, before vowels, **ornith-.** [< Gk. *ornis, onithos* bird]

or·ni·thol·o·gy (ôr/nə·thol/ə·jē) *n.* The branch of zoology that treats of birds.   [< NL < Gk. *ornithologos* treating of birds]   — **or/ni·tho·log/ic** (-thə·loj/ik) or **·i·cal** *adj.* — **or/ni·tho·log/i·cal·ly** *adv.* — **or/ni·thol/o·gist** *n.*

oro-[1] *combining form* Mouth; oral: *oropharynx.* [< L *os, oris* mouth]

oro-[2] *combining form Geol.* Mountain; of mountains. [< Gk. *oros* mountain]

o·ro·tund (ôr/ə·tund, ō/rə-) *adj.* **1.** Full, clear, rounded, and resonant: said of the voice.   **2.** Pompous; inflated, as a manner of speech.   [< L < *os, oris* mouth + *rotundus* round]   — **o·ro·tun·di·ty** (ôr/ə·tun/də·tē) *n.*

or·phan (ôr/fən) *n.* **1.** A child whose parents are dead; also, less commonly, a child with one surviving parent.   **2.** A cast-off or waif.   — *adj.* **1.** That is an orphan.   **2.** Of or for orphans.   — *v.t.* To make an orphan of.   [< L < Gk. *orphanos* orphaned]   — **or/phan·hood** (-hŏŏd) *n.*

or·phan·age (ôr/fən·ij) *n.* **1.** An institution for the care of orphans or other abandoned children.   **2.** The condition of being an orphan; also, orphans collectively.

Or·phe·us (ôr/fē·əs) In Greek mythology, the son of a Muse, whose singing to the lyre could charm beasts and even rocks and trees. When his wife Eurydice died he was permitted to lead her back from Hades provided he did not turn to look at her until they had arrived in the upper world, but he did look back and she was lost.   — **Or/phe·an** *adj.*

or·phic (ôr/fik) *adj. Sometimes cap.* Of a mystical nature; oracular. Also **or/phi·cal.**   — **or/phi·cal·ly** *adv.*

Or·phic (ôr/fik) *adj.* **1.** Of, pertaining to, or associated with Orpheus.   **2.** Having the quality of the music of Orpheus; enchanting. Also **Or/phi·cal.** [< L < Gk. < *Orpheus*]

or·pine (ôr/pin) *n.* Any of a large, widely distributed family

of plants including the sedums and houseleeks as the **common** or **garden orpine,** having succulent stems and leaves and clusters of whitish flowers. Also **or/pin.**

Or·ping·ton (ôr/ping·tən) *n.* Any of a variety of large domestic fowls having single combs and unfeathered legs. [after *Orpington,* a village in Kent, England]

or·ris (ôr/is, or/-) *n.* Any of the several species of iris having a scented root; esp. one whose dried rootstock is used in medicine, as a perfume, etc. Also **or/rice.** [Prob. alter. of Ital. *ireos* < L *iris* iris]

ort (ôrt) *n.   Usu. pl. Archaic* or *Dial.* A worthless scrap or leaving, as of food. [ME; ult. origin uncertain]

or·thi·con (ôr/thə·kon) *n.* A sensitive television camera tube using low-velocity electrons in scanning: also called *image orthicon.* Also **or·thi·con·o·scope** (ôr/thi·kon/ə·skōp).

ortho- *combining form* **1.** Straight; upright; in line: *orthodontics.*   **2.** At right angles; perpendicular: *orthorhombic.*   **3.** Correct; proper; right: *orthography.*   **4.** *Med.* The correction of irregularities or deformities of: *orthopedics.*   **5.** *Chem.* **a** Designating that one of a series of acids that is most fully hydrated: *orthophosphoric* acid: distinguished from *meta-.* **b** Noting a benzene derivative in which the substituted atoms or radicals occupy adjoining positions. Also, before vowels, **orth-.** [< Gk. *orthos* straight]

or·tho·clase (ôr/thō·klās, -klāz) *n.* A brittle, vitreous, potassium-aluminum silicate of the feldspar group, a constituent of many igneous rocks: also called *potash feldspar.* [< ORTHO- + Gk. *klasis* fracture]

or·tho·don·tics (ôr/thə·don/tiks) *n.* The branch of dentistry concerned with the prevention and correction of irregularities of the teeth. Also **or/tho·don/tia** (-don/sha, -shē·ə). [< NL < Gk. *orthos* right, straight + *odous, odontos* tooth]   — **or/tho·don/tic** *adj.* — **or/tho·don/tist** *n.*

or·tho·dox (ôr/thə·doks) *adj.* **1.** Holding the commonly accepted or established faith, esp. in religion; correct or sound in doctrine.   **2.** Conforming to the Christian faith as represented in the early ecumenical creeds.   **3.** Adhering to traditional practice or belief.   [< LL < Gk. < *orthos* right + *doxa* opinion]   — **or/tho·dox/ly** *adv.*

Or·tho·dox (ôr/thə·doks) *adj.* **1.** Of, belonging to, or characteristic of the Eastern Orthodox Church.   **2.** Designating any of the bodies in this Church.

Orthodox Church The Eastern Orthodox Church.

Orthodox Judaism The branch of Judaism that accepts the Mosaic Laws and their authoritative rabbinical interpretations in the Talmud and elsewhere as binding for today.

or·tho·dox·y (ôr/thə·dok/sē) *n.   pl.* **·dox·ies 1.** Orthodox belief or practice; also, an instance of it.   **2.** The quality or condition of being orthodox.   — **or/tho·dox/i·cal** *adj.*

or·thog·ra·phy (ôr·thog/rə·fē) *n.   pl.* **·phies 1.** A mode or system of spelling, esp. of spelling correctly.   **2.** The study dealing with letters and spelling. [< OF < L < Gk. < *orthographos*]   — **or·thog/ra·pher,** or **or·thog/ra·phist** *n.* — **or/tho·graph/ic** (ôr/thə·graf/ik), **or/tho·graph/i·cal** *adj.* — **or/tho·graph/i·cal·ly** *adv.*

or·tho·pe·dics (ôr/thə·pē/diks) *n.pl.* (*construed as sing.*) The branch of surgery concerned with the correction of deformities of the skeletal system. Also **or/tho·pae/dics,** or **or·tho·pe·dy** (ôr/thə·pē/dē). [< F < Gk. *orthos* right + *paideia* rearing of children]   — **or/tho·pe/dic** *adj.* — **or/tho·pe/dist** *n.*

or·thop·ter·on (ôr·thop/tə·ron) *n.* An orthopterous insect.

or·thop·ter·ous (ôr·thop/tər·əs) *adj.* Designating any of an order of insects with membranous hind wings and leathery, usually straight, fore wings, including locusts, crickets, grasshoppers, etc. [< NL < Gk. *orthos* straight + *pteron* wing]   — **or·thop/ter·an** *adj. & n.*

or·to·lan (ôr/tə·lən) *n.* A bunting of Europe, having an olive-green head and a yellow throat. [< F < Provençal < Ital. < L *hortulus,* dim. of *hortus* garden]

-ory[1] *suffix of nouns* A place or instrument for (performing the action of the main element): *dormitory, lavatory.* [< OF *-oir, -oire.* See -ORY[2].]

-ory[2] *suffix of adjectives* Related to; like; resembling: *amatory, laudatory.* [< F *-oir, -oire,* or < L *-orius, -oria, -orium*]

o·ryx (ôr/iks, or/-, ō/riks) *n.   pl.* **o·ryx·es** or **o·ryx** Any of several long-horned antelopes, as the **Arabian oryx** and the gemsbok. [< NL < L < Gk.]

os[1] (os) *n.   pl.* **o·ra** (ôr/ə, ō/rə) *Anat.* A mouth or opening. [< L]

os[2] (os) *n.   pl.* **os·sa** (os/ə) *Anat.* A bone. [< L]

O·sage (ō/sāj) *n.* **1.** One of a tribe of North American Indians of Siouan stock now living in Oklahoma.   **2.** The language of this tribe. [< Siouan *Wazhazhe* war people]

Osage orange 1. A showy tree of the mulberry family, native to Arkansas and adjacent regions, widely used as a hedge. **2.** Its orangelike fruit.

Os·car (os/kər) *n.* One of the gold statuettes awarded annually in the U.S. for outstanding achevements in motion pictures. [Origin uncertain]

os·cil·late (os/ə·lāt) *v.i.* **·lat·ed, ·lat·ing 1.** To swing back and forth, as a pendulum. **2.** To fluctuate between various courses of action or thought; waver. [< L *oscillare* to swing] — **os′cil·la′tor** *n.*

os·cil·la·tion (os′ə-lā′shən) *n.* **1.** The act or state of oscillating. **2.** A single swing of an oscillating body. **3.** *Physics* A periodic fluctuation between extreme values of a quantity or force. — **os′cil·la·to′ry** (-lə-tôr′ē, -tō/rē) *adj.*

os·cil·lo·graph (ə·sil′ə·graf, -gräf) *n.* A device for recording and measuring any oscillating system convertible into wave forms, as sound, light, heartbeats, etc.

os·cil·lo·scope (ə·sil′ə·skōp) *n.* Any of various electronic instruments for projecting the forms of electromagnetic waves on the fluorescent screen of a cathode-ray tube.

os·cine (os′in, -īn) *adj.* Of or belonging to a suborder of birds, including those having the most highly developed vocal ability, as thrushes, sparrows, etc. Also **os′ci·nine.** — *n.* An oscine bird. [< NL < L *oscen, oscinis* singing bird]

Os·co-Um·bri·an (os′kō-um′brē-ən) *n.* A branch of the Italic subfamily of Indo-European languages.

os·cu·late (os′kyə·lāt) *v.t. & v.i.* **·lat·ed, ·lat·ing 1.** To kiss: used humorously. **2.** To come into close contact or union. **3.** *Biol.* To have (characteristics) in common. [< L *osculari* to kiss]

os·cu·la·tion (os′kyə·lā′shən) *n.* The act of kissing; also, a kiss. — **os′cu·la·to′ry** (-lə-tôr′ē, -tō/rē) *adj.*

-ose¹ *suffix of adjectives* **1.** Full of or abounding in (the main element): *verbose.* **2.** Like; resembling (the main element): *grandiose.* Compare -OUS. [< L *-osus*]

-ose² *suffix Chem.* Indicating a sugar or other carbohydrate: *lactose, fructose.* [< (GLUC)OSE]

O·see (ō′zē, ō′sē) The Douai Bible name for HOSEA.

o·sier (ō′zhər) *n.* Any of various willows producing long, flexible shoots used in wickerwork. [< OF]

O·si·ris (o·sī′ris) In Egyptian mythology, the god of the underworld and lord of the dead, husband of his sister Isis.

-osis *suffix of nouns* **1.** The condition, process, or state of: *metamorphosis.* **2.** *Med.* **a** A diseased or abnormal condition of: *neurosis.* **b** A formation of: *sclerosis.* [< L < Gk. *-ōsis*; or directly < Gk.]

-osity *suffix of nouns* Forming nouns corresponding to adjectives in *-ose: verbosity.* [< F *-osité* < L *-ositas*; or directly < L]

Os·man·li (oz·man′lē, os-) *n. pl.* **·lis 1.** An Ottoman Turk. **2.** The language of the Ottoman Turks; Turkish. — *adj.* Ottoman. [< Turkish *Osman* Osman < Arabic *'Othmān*]

os·mi·rid·i·um (os′mə·rid′ē·əm, oz′-) *n.* A mixture of iridium and osmium that occurs naturally, used in pen points: also called *iridosmine, iridosmium.* [< OSM(IUM) + IRIDIUM]

os·mi·um (oz′mē·əm, os′-) *n.* A hard, brittle, extremely heavy, white, metallic element (symbol Os) of the platinum group. See ELEMENT. [< Gk. *osmē* odor]

os·mose (oz′mōs, os′-) *v.t. & v.i.* **·mosed, mos·ing** To subject to or undergo osmosis.

os·mo·sis (oz·mō′sis, os-) *n. Chem.* **1.** The diffusion of a fluid through a semipermeable membrane, resulting in equalization of the pressures on each side. **2.** The tendency of a fluid to act in such a manner. Also **os′mose.** [< Gk. *ōsmos* < *ōthein* to impel] — **os·mot·ic** (oz·mot′ik, os-) *adj.* — **os·mot′i·cal·ly** *adv.*

os·prey (os′prē) *n.* An American hawk, brown above and white below, that preys upon fish: also called *fish hawk.* [ME < L < *os, ossis* bone + *frangere* to break]

ossi- *combining form* Bone: *ossify.* [< L *os, ossis* bone]

Os·sian (osh′ən, os′ē·ən) A legendary Irish hero and bard of the third century. — **Os·si·an·ic** (os′ē·an′ik) *adj.*

os·sif·er·ous (o·sif′ər·əs) *adj.* Yielding or containing bones. [< L *os, ossi(s)* + -FEROUS]

os·si·fy (os′ə·fī) *v.t. & v.i.* **·fied, ·fy·ing 1.** To convert or be converted into bone. **2.** To make or become rigid or inflexible in habits, beliefs, etc.; harden. [< L *os, ossis* + *facere* to make] — **os·sif·ic** (o·sif′ik) *adj.* — **os′si·fi·ca′tion** *n.*

os·te·al (os′tē·əl) *adj.* Of, pertaining to, or like bone; bony. [< Gk. *osteon* bone]

os·ten·si·ble (os·ten′sə·bəl) *adj.* Offered as real or genuine; apparent. [< F < L *ostendere* to show] — **os·ten′si·bly** *adv.*

os·ten·sive (os·ten′siv) *adj.* Manifest; apparent; ostensible. — **os·ten′sive·ly** *adv.*

os·ten·ta·tion (os′tən·tā′shən) *n.* **1.** The act of displaying vainly or pretentiously in order to excite admiration, awe, etc. **2.** Excessive or uncalled-for exhibition; showiness. [< OF < L *ostendere* to show]

os·ten·ta·tious (os′tən·tā′shəs) *adj.* **1.** Intended to attract notice; showy. **2.** Marked by ostentation. — **os′ten·ta′tious·ly** *adv.* — **os′ten·ta′tious·ness** *n.*

osteo- *combining form* Bone; pertaining to bone or bones. Also, before vowels, **oste-.** [< Gk. *osteon* bone]

os·te·ol·o·gy (os′tē·ol′ə·jē) *n.* The study of the skeleton and

of the structure of bones. — **os′te·o·log′i·cal** (-ə·loj′i·kəl) *adj.* — **os′te·ol′o·gist** *n.*

os·te·o·ma (os′tē·ō′mə) *n. pl.* **·o·mas** or **·o·ma·ta** (-ō′mə·tə) *Pathol.* A tumor of bony tissue. [< OSTE(O)- + -OMA]

os·te·o·my·e·li·tis (os′tē·ō·mī′ə·lī′tis) *n. Pathol.* Suppurative inflammation of the bone, sometimes involving the marrow. [< OSTEO- + MYEL(O)- + -ITIS]

os·te·op·a·thy (os′tē·op′ə·thē) *n.* A system of healing based on the theory that most diseases are the result of structural abnormalities of the body and may be cured by manipulation of the affected parts. — **os′te·o·path′,** or **os·te·o·pa·thist** (os′·te·op′ə·thist) *n.* — **os·te·o·path·ic** (os′tē·ə·path′ik) *adj.*

Os·ti·a (os′tē·ə, *Ital.* ō′styä) An ancient port city of Rome.

ost·ler (os′lər) See HOSTLER.

os·tra·cism (os′trə·siz′əm) *n.* **1.** In ancient Greece, temporary banishment by popular vote. **2.** The act of ostracizing or the state of being ostracized.

os·tra·cize (os′trə·sīz) *v.t.* **·cized, ·ciz·ing 1.** To shut out or exclude, as from society or from a particular group; banish. **2.** To exile by ostracism. Also *Brit.* **os′tra·cise.** [< Gk. *ostrakizein* < *ostrakon* potsherd, shell, voting tablet]

os·trich (ôs′trich, os′-) *n. pl.* **·trich·es** or **·trich 1.** A large, two-toed, flightless bird of Africa and Arabia, the largest of existing birds, having long, powerful legs and a plumage highly valued for ornamental purposes. **2.** A rhea. [< OF < LL < L *avis* bird + LL *struthio* ostrich]

Os·tro·goth (os′trə·goth) *n.* A member of the eastern branch of the Goths, who established a kingdom in Italy from 493 to 555. [< LL *Ostrogothi*] — **Os′tro·goth′ic** *adj.*

Os·ty·ak (os′tē·ak) *n.* **1.** One of a Finno-Ugric people inhabiting western Siberia and the Ural Mountains. **2.** The Ugric language of these people. Also **Os′ti·ak.**

Os·we·go tea (os·wē′gō) A species of mint with bright red flowers, found in the eastern U.S. [after *Oswego,* city in New York State]

ot- Var. of OTO-.

O·thel·lo (ō·thel′ō, ə-) In Shakespeare's play of this name, the hero, a Moor of Venice, whose jealousy, inspired by Iago, provokes him to kill his innocent wife Desdemona.

oth·er (uth′ər) *adj.* **1.** Different from the one or ones specified or implied. **2.** Noting the remaining one of two persons or things: the *other* eye. **3.** Additional; more: Have you no *other* children? **4.** Alternate; second: every *other* day. **5.** Different: The truth is *other* than what you suppose. **6.** Former: in *other* times. — *pron.* **1.** Another or different person or thing. **2.** The other person or thing: this hand, not the *other.* — *adv.* Differently; otherwise: with *than.* [OE *ōther*] — **oth′er·ness** *n.*

oth·er·wise (uth′ər·wīz′) *adv.* **1.** In a different manner; by other means. **2.** In other circumstances or conditions. **3.** In all other respects: an *otherwise* sensible person. — *adj.* **1.** Other than supposed; different: The facts are *otherwise.* **2.** Other: He could not be *otherwise* than proud.

other world A world peopled by the dead.

oth·er·world·ly (uth′ər·wûrld′lē) *adj.* Concerned with matters of the spirit or intellect, esp. to the neglect of material things. — **oth′er·world′li·ness** *n.*

Oth·man (oth′mən, *Arabic* ōōth·män′) Ottoman.

-otic *suffix of adjectives* **1.** *Med.* Of, related to, or affected by; corresponding to nouns in *-osis: sclerotic.* **2.** Causing or producing: *narcotic.* [< Gk. *-ōtikos,* suffix of adjectives]

o·ti·ose (ō′shē·ōs, -tē-) *adj.* **1.** Being at rest; indolent; lazy. **2.** Having no use or effect; futile. [< L *otiosus* idle] — **o′ti·ose′ly** *adv.* — **o′ti·os′i·ty** (-os′ə·tē) *n.*

o·ti·tis (ō·tī′tis) *n. Pathol.* Inflammation of the ear. [< OT(O)- + -ITIS]

oto- *combining form* Ear; pertaining to the ear: *otology.* Also, before vowels, **ot-.** [< Gk. *ous, ōtos* ear]

o·tol·o·gy (ō·tol′ə·jē) *n.* The science of the ear and its diseases. — **o·to·log·i·cal** (ō′tə·loj′i·kəl) *adj.* — **o·tol′o·gist** *n.*

ot·ta·va (ōt·tä′vä) *n. Ital.* An octave.

ottava ri·ma (rē′mä) In prosody, a stanza form of Italian origin consisting of eight lines in iambic pentameter and rhyming in the pattern *ababbcc.* [< Ital., octave rhyme]

Ot·ta·wa (ot′ə·wə) *n.* One of a tribe of North American Indians of Algonquian stock, originally inhabiting the region around Georgian Bay, Lake Huron and Ontario. [< dial. F *otauan*; ult. < Algonquian. Akin to Cree *atāweu* a trader.]

ot·ter (ot′ər) *n.* **1.** Any of various web-footed mammals of aquatic habits, related to the weasel and having a long, flattened tail. **2.** Its valuable, dark brown fur. [OE *otor*]

ot·to·man (ot′ə·mən) *n.* **1.** An upholstered, armless seat or sofa, usu. without a back. **2.** A cushioned footrest. [< F *ottomane,* orig. fem. of *ottoman* Ottoman]

OSTRICH

(To about 8 feet high)

Ot·to·man (ŏt′ə·mən) *n. pl.* **·mans** A Turk: also *Othman.* — *adj.* Of or pertaining to the Turks. [< F < Ital. *Ottomano* < Med.L *Ottomanus* < Arabic *'Othmāni* of Osman]

Ottoman Empire A former empire (1300–1919) of the Turks in Asia Minor, NE Africa, and SE Europe; capital, Constantinople: also *Turkish Empire.*

ouch (ouch) *interj.* An exclamation of sudden pain.

ought[1] (ôt) *v. Present 3rd person sing.* **ought** An auxiliary followed by the infinitive with *to* expressed or understood, meaning: **1.** To have a moral duty: A person *ought* to keep his promises. **2.** To be advisable: You *ought* to be careful. **3.** To be expected as something probable, natural, or logical: The engine *ought* to run. ◆ A past is formed by placing the following verb in the perfect infinitive, as in *He ought to have been there.* [OE past tense of *āgan* to owe]

ought[2] (ôt) See AUGHT[1].

ought[3] (ôt) See AUGHT[2].

oui (wē) *adv. French* Yes.

oui·ja (wē′ja) *n.* a device consisting of a large board inscribed with the alphabet and other characters and over which moves a small rectangular board resting on three legs, the pointer of which is thought to spell out mediumistic communications. [< F *oui* yes + G *ja* yes]

ounce (ouns) *n.* **1.** A unit of weight; one sixteenth of a pound avoirdupois, or 28.349 grams; one twelfth of a pound troy, or 31.1 grams. See table front of book. **2.** A fluid ounce. **3.** A small quantity. [< OF < L *uncia* twelfth part (of a pound or foot)]

our (our) *pronominal adj.* The possessive case of the pronoun *we*, used attributively: *our* child. [OE *ūre*, gen. of *wē*]

ours (ourz) *pron.* **1.** The possessive case of the pronoun *we*, used predicatively: That dog is *ours.* **2.** The one or ones belonging or relating to us: their country and *ours.* — **of ours** Belonging or relating to us: a double possessive.

our·self (our·self′) *pron.* Myself or ourselves, considered collectively: used in formal or regal contexts.

our·selves (our·selvz′) *pron.pl.* A form of the first person plural pronoun, used: **1.** As a reflexive: We helped *ourselves.* **2.** As an emphatic or intensive form of *we*: We *ourselves* want to know. **3.** As a designation of a normal, proper, or usual state: We weren't *ourselves* then.

-ous *suffix of adjectives* **1.** Full of, having, given to, like: *joyous, glorious.* **2.** *Chem.* Having a lower valence than that indicated by *-ic*: said of elements in compounds: *nitrous* oxide. [< OF < L *-osus*]

ou·sel (ōō′zəl) See OUZEL.

oust (oust) *v.t.* To force out or remove, as from a place or position. [< AF < LL < *ob-* against + *stare* to stand]

oust·er (ous′tər) *n.* **1.** The act or condition of ousting. **2.** One who ousts. **3.** *Law* The act of putting one out of possession or occupancy of real property to which he is legally entitled; wrongful dispossession.

out (out) *adv.* **1.** Away from the inside or center: to branch *out.* **2.** In or into the open air: to go *out.* **3.** Away from a specified or usual place, as from one's home or place of business: *out* to lunch. **4.** From a receptacle or source: to pour *out* wine. **5.** From among others: to pick *out.* **6.** So as to remove, deplete, or exhaust: to sweep *out*; to dry *out.* **7.** Thoroughly: tired *out.* **8.** Into extinction or inactivity: The flame went *out*; The excitement died *out.* **9.** To a conclusion; to the end: Hear me *out.* **10.** Into being or activity, or into a state manifest to the senses: An epidemic broke *out*; The sun came *out.* **11.** Into or within the realm of public knowledge: The secret leaked *out.* **12.** In or into circulation: to bring *out* a new edition. **13.** Aloud and boldly: to speak *out.* **14.** So as to be extended or projecting: to lean *out.* **15.** Into the care or control of another or others: to deal *out* cards. **16.** From a state of composure to a state of tension, irritation, etc.: to be put *out* over trifles. **17.** In or into a condition of being out-of-date or retired from use: Latin went *out* as a spoken language. **18.** In baseball, etc., so as to be or count as an out. **19.** *Informal* Into unconsciousness: to pass *out.* — **out and away** By far; incomparably. — **out of 1.** From the inside of; from among. **2.** Beyond the limits, scope, or usual position of: *out of* sight; *out of* joint. **3.** From (a material, etc.): made *out of* tin. **4.** Inspired or caused by: *out of* pity. **5.** Without (any): *out of* breath. — **out to** With the intention of. — *adj.* **1.** External; exterior. **2.** Irregular: an *out* size. **3.** Not in effective working order: The bridge is *out.* **4.** At a financial loss: *out* five dollars. **5.** Not to be considered: That method is altogether *out.* **6.** Exposed, as by tears in the clothing: *out* at the seams. **7.** In error; mistaken: *out* in one's reckoning. **8.** Not in office or in power. **9.** No longer latched, as at a game. **10.** Distant; outlying. ◆ *Out* may also be used in many of its adverbial senses as a predicate adjective with a form of the verb *to be*, as in the following examples: *He is out to lunch* (adv., def. 3); *The fire is out* (adv., def. 8); *The stars are out* (adv. def. 10). — *prep.* From within; forth from: *out* the door. — *n.* **1.** One who or that which is out. **2.** A way of dodging responsibility or involvement: to look for an *out.* **3.** In baseball, etc., the retirement of a batter or base runner; also, a player so retired. **4.** In tennis, etc., a return that falls outside the court. — **on the outs** (or **at outs**) Involved in a disagreement; at odds. — *v.i.* **1.** To come out; be revealed: Murder will *out.* **2.** To go out or outside. — *v.t.* **3.** To put (someone or something) out. — *interj.* Get out! Away! [OE *ūt*]

out- *combining form* **1.** Living or situated outside; away from the center; detached: *outlying, outpatient.* **2.** Going forth; outward: *outbound, outstretch.* **3.** Denoting the time, place, or result of the action expressed by the root verb: *outcome, outcry.* **4.** To a greater extent; more; better.

Out is widely used to form compounds, as in the list below.

out-and-out (out′and-out′) *adj.* Unqualified; outright.

out·bid (out·bid′) *v.t.* **·bid, ·bid·den** or **·bid, ·bid·ding** To bid more than; offer a higher bid than: also *overbid.*

out·board (out′bôrd′, -bōrd′) *adj. & adv. Naut.* **1.** Outside the hull. **2.** Away from the center line of a vessel.

outboard motor A portable gasoline or electric motor for temporary attachment to the stern of a small boat.

out·bound (out′bound′) *adj.* Outward bound.

out·break (out′brāk′) *n.* A sudden bursting forth, as of an emotion or a disease; an eruption.

out·build·ing (out′bil′ding) *n.* A building separate from and subordinate to a main building, as a woodshed or barn: also called *outhouse.*

out·burst (out′bûrst′) *n.* A bursting out; esp., a sudden and violent display, as of anger.

out·cast (out′kast′, -käst′) *n.* **1.** One who is cast out or excluded. **2.** A homeless person or vagabond. **3.** Anything cast out, as refuse. — *adj.* Rejected; discarded; forlorn.

outact	outbuild	outfeel	outkeep	outpromise	outsit	outthreaten
outadd	outbully	outfight	outkiss	outpush	outskirmish	outthrob
outambush	outburn	outfigure	outlaugh	outquestion	outslander	outtower
outanswer	outcaper	outfind	outleap	outquibble	outsleep	outtrade
outargue	outcatch	outfire	outlearn	outquote	outsmile	outtravel
outask	outcavil	outflatter	outlie	outrace	outsmoke	outtrick
outbabble	outcharm	outfool	outlighten	outraise	outsnore	outtrot
outbake	outchatter	outfrown	outlinger	outrank	outsparkle	outtrump
outbalance	outcheat	outgabble	outlisten	outrave	outspell	outvalue
outbanter	outchide	outgain	outlove	outread	outsprint	outvaunt
outbargain	outclimb	outgallop	outmanage	outreason	outstare	outvoice
outbark	outcompete	outgamble	outmaneuver	outredden	outstart	outvote
outbawl	outcook	outgather	outmarch	outring	outstate	outwait
outbeam	outcrawl	outgive	outmatch	outrival	outstay	outwalk
outbeg	outcrow	outglare	outmove	outrear	outsteer	outwallop
outbeggar	outcurse	outglitter	outpaint	outrock	outstrain	outwar
outbellow	outdance	outglow	outpass	outroll	outstride	outwarble
outblaze	outdare	outgnaw	outperform	outrun	outstrive	outwaste
outbleat	outdazzle	outgrin	outpity	outsail	outstudy	outwatch
outbless	outdodge	outguess	outplan	outsatisfy	outstunt	outweary
outbloom	outdream	outguide	outplod	outsavor	outsuffer	outweep
outblossom	outdress	outhasten	outpoison	outscold	outsulk	outwhirl
outbluff	outdrink	outhear	outpopulate	outscorn	outswagger	outwile
outblunder	outdrive	outhit	outpractice	outscream	outswear	outwill
outblush	outdrop	outhowl	outpraise	outsee	outswim	outwish
outbluster	outeat	outhumor	outpray	outserve	outswindle	outwrangle
outboast	outecho	outinvent	outpreach	outshame	outtalk	outwrestle
outbox	outfable	outjinx	outpreen	outshout	outtask	outwriggle
outbrag	outfast	outjockey	outpress	outshriek	outthank	outyell
outbrazen	outfawn	outjourney	outprice	outsin	outthieve	outyelp
outbribe	outfeast	outjump	outproduce	outsing	outthink	outyield

out·class (out·klas′, -kläs′) *v.t.* To surpass decisively.

out·come (out′kum′) *n.* Consequence or result.

out crop (*n.* out′krop′; *v.* out·krop′) *Geol. n.* 1. The exposure at or above the surface of the ground of any rock stratum, vein, etc. 2. The rock so exposed. — *v.i.* **·cropped**, **·crop·ping** To crop out above the ground, as rocks.

out·cry (*n.* out′krī′; *v.* out·krī′) *n. pl.* **·cries** 1. A loud cry or clamor. 2. A vehement outburst of alarm, indignation, etc. — *v.t.* **·cried**, **·cry·ing** To surpass in noise or crying.

out·date (out·dāt′) *v.t.* **·dat·ed**, **·dat·ing** To make obsolete or out-of-date.

out·dat·ed (out·dā′tid) *adj.* Out-of-date; old-fashioned.

out·dis·tance (out·dis′təns) *v.t.* **·tanced**, **·tanc·ing** 1. To outrun, as in a race; outstrip. 2. To surpass completely.

out·do (out·do̅o̅′) *v.t.* **·did**, **·done**, **·do·ing** To exceed in performance; surpass. — **out·do′er** *n.*

out·done (out·dun′) *adj. U.S. Dial.* Provoked; exasperated.

out·door (out′dôr′, -dōr′) *adj.* 1. Being or done in the open air. 2. Intended for the outdoors. Also *out-of-door.*

out·doors (out·dôrz′, -dōrz′) *adv.* Outside of the house; in the open air. — *n.* The world beyond the house; the open air. Also *out-of-doors.*

out·er (ou′tər) *adj.* 1. Being on the exterior side. 2. Farther from a center or from something regarded as the inside.

out·er·most (ou′tər·mōst) *adj.* Most remote from the inside or inner part; farthest out.

outer space The space beyond the extreme limits of the earth's atmosphere; interplanetary and interstellar space.

out·face (out·fās′) *v.t.* **·faced**, **·fac·ing** 1. To face or stare down. 2. To defy or confront fearlessly or impudently.

out·field (out′fēld′) *n.* In baseball: **a** The space beyond the infield. **b** The outfielders collectively.

out·field·er (out′fēl′dər) *n.* In baseball, any of three players whose positions are in the outfield.

out·fit (out′fit′) *n.* 1. The tools or equipment needed for any particular purpose, as a trade, etc. 2. *U.S. Informal* A group of persons regarded as a unit; esp., a military unit. 3. *U.S. Informal* A set of clothing. — *v.t. & v.i.* **·fit·ted**, **·fit·ting** To provide with or acquire an outfit. — **out′fit′ter** *n.*

out·flank (out·flangk′) *v.t.* To get around and in back of the flank of (an opposing force or army); flank.

out·flow (out′flō′) *n.* 1. That which flows out. 2. The act or process of flowing out.

out·fox (out·foks′) *v.t. U.S. Informal* To outwit.

out·go (*v.* out·gō′; *n.* out′gō′) *v.t.* **·went**, **·gone**, **·go·ing** To go farther than; exceed. — *n. pl.* **·goes** 1. That which goes out; outlay. 2. The act of going out. — **out′go′er** *n.*

out·go·ing (out′gō′ing) *adj.* 1. Going out; leaving. 2. Friendly; expansive. — *n.* The act of going out.

out·group (out′gro̅o̅p′) *n. Sociol.* Those not in an in-group.

out·grow (out·grō′) *v.t.* **·grew**, **·grown**, **·grow·ing** 1. To grow too large for. 2. To lose or get rid of in the course of time or growth: to *outgrow* a habit. 3. To surpass in growth.

out·growth (out′grōth′) *n.* 1. That which grows out of something else; an excrescence. 2. A natural result or development. 3. The process of growing out.

out·house (out′hous′) *n.* 1. An outdoor privy or toilet. 2. An outbuilding.

out·ing (ou′ting) *n.* 1. A short pleasure trip; an excursion. 2. The act of going out; an airing.

out·land·er (out′lan′dər) *n.* 1. A foreigner. 2. A stranger.

out·land·ish (out·lan′dish) *adj.* 1. Strange or unfamiliar, as in appearance or manners. 2. *Informal* Freakish; crazy. 3. Far-off; remote. [OE *ūtland*] — **out·land′ish·ly** *adv.* — **out·land′ish·ness** *n.*

out·last (out·last′, -läst′) *v.t.* To last longer than.

out·law (out′lô′) *n.* 1. One who habitually breaks or defies the law; a criminal. 2. A person deprived of the protection or benefit of the law. — *v.t.* 1. To prohibit; ban. 2. To deprive of legal force or protection, as a contract. 3. To declare an outlaw. [OE < ON *ūtlagi*] — **out·law′ry** *n.*

out·lay (*n.* out′lā′; *v.* out·lā′) *n.* 1. The act of disbursing or spending. 2. The amount spent; expenditure. — *v.t.* **·laid**, **·lay·ing** To expend (money, etc.).

out·let (out′let) *n.* 1. A passage or vent for escape or discharge. 2. A channel of expression or escape: an *outlet* for creative energy. 3. In commerce, a market for any commodity; also, a store handling the goods of a particular manufacturer. 4. *Electr.* The point in a wiring system at which the current is taken to supply electrical apparatuses.

out·line (out′līn′) *n.* 1. *Sometimes pl.* A preliminary sketch showing the principal features of a thing; general plan. 2. A systematic statement of the structure or content of an essay, etc. 3. The bordering line that serves to define a figure. 4. A sketch made only of such lines. — *v.t.* **·lined**, **·lin·ing** 1. To make or give an outline of. 2. To draw the outline of.

out·live (out·liv′) *v.t.* **·lived**, **·liv·ing** 1. To live longer than (another). 2. To live through; survive.

out·look (out′lo̅o̅k′) *n.* 1. A point of view. 2. The prospect of a thing. 3. A place where something is viewed. 4. The expanse in view. 5. The act of looking out.

out·man (out·man′) *v.t.* **manned**, **·man·ning** 1. To surpass in number of men. 2. To excel in manliness.

out·mo·ded (out·mō′did) *adj.* Out of fashion.

out·most (out′mōst′) *adj.* Farthest out; outermost.

out-of-date (out′əv·dāt′) *adj.* Old-fashioned; archaic.

out-of-door (out′əv·dôr′, -dōr′) *adj.* Outdoor.

out-of-doors (out′əv·dôrz′, -dōrz′) *adv. & n.* Outdoors.

out-of-the-way (out′əv·thə·wā′) *adj.* 1. Remote; difficult to reach; secluded. 2. Out of the common range; odd.

out·pa·tient (out′pā′shənt) *n.* A patient treated at but not formally admitted to a hospital, dispensary, etc.

out·play (out·plā′) *v.t.* To play better than; defeat.

out·point (out·point′) *v.t.* 1. To score more points than. 2. *Naut.* To sail closer to the wind than.

out·post (out′pōst′) *n.* 1. A detachment of troops stationed at a distance from the main body as a guard against surprise attack. 2. The station occupied by such troops. 3. Any outlying settlement, as at a frontier.

out·pour (*v.* out·pôr′, -pōr′; *n.* out′pôr′, -pōr′) *v.t. & v.i.* To pour out. — *n.* A free outflow. — **out′pour′er** *n.*

out·put (out′po̅o̅t′) *n.* 1. The amount of anything produced in a given time, as by a mine, factory, mill, etc. 2. The effective work done by a machine. 3. *Electr.* The electrical energy delivered by a generator, circuit, amplifier, etc.

out·rage (*n.* out′rāj′; *v.* out·rāj′) *n.* 1. An act of shocking violence or cruelty. 2. A gross violation of morality or decency. 3. A profound insult or injury. — *v.t.* **·raged**, **·rag·ing** 1. To commit an outrage upon. 2. To subject to an outrage. 3. To rape. [ME < OF ult. < L *ultra* beyond] — **Syn.** (noun) 1. crime, atrocity. — (verb) See OFFEND.

out·ra·geous (out·rā′jəs) *adj.* 1. Of the nature of an outrage; awful; atrocious. 2. Heedless of authority or decency. — **out·ra′geous·ly** *adv.* — **out·ra′geous·ness** *n.*

ou·tré (o̅o̅·trā′) *adj. French* Strikingly odd; exaggerated.

out·reach (*v.* out·rēch′; *n.* out′rēch′) *v.t.* 1. To reach or go beyond; surpass. 2. To extend (something). — *v.i.* 3. To reach out. — *n.* The act or extent of reaching out.

out·ride (out·rīd′) *v.t.* **·rode**, **·rid·den**, **·rid·ing** To ride faster, farther, or better than.

out·rid·er (out′rī′dər) *n.* A mounted attendant who rides in advance or to one side of a carriage.

out·rig·ger (out′rig′ər) *n.* 1. A part built or arranged to project beyond a natural outline, as of a vessel or machine. 2. A projecting contrivance terminating in a boatlike float, braced to the side of a canoe to prevent capsizing. 3. A bracket projecting from the side of a narrow rowboat, and provided with a rowlock for an oar; also, a boat so equipped.

out·right (*adj.* out′rīt′; *adv.* out′rīt′) *adj.* 1. Free from reserve or restraint; downright. 2. Complete; entire. 3. Going straight on. — *adv.* 1. Without reservation or limitation; openly. 2. Entirely; utterly. 3. Without delay.

out·sell (out·sel′) *v.t.* **·sold**, **·sell·ing** 1. To sell more readily or for a higher price than. 2. To sell more goods than.

out·set (out′set′) *n.* A setting out; beginning.

out·shine (out·shīn′) *v.* **·shone**, **·shin·ing** *v.t.* 1. To shine brighter than. 2. To surpass. — *v.i.* 3. To shine forth.

out·side (*n., adj., & adv.* out′sīd′; *prep.* out′sīd′) *n.* 1. The outer or exterior surface or side. 2. The space beyond a bounding line or surface. 3. The part that is seen; outward appearance. 4. Something empty of significance or substance; mere outward display. — **at the outside** *Informal* At the farthest, longest, or most. — *adj.* 1. Pertaining to, located on, or restricted to the outside. 2. Originating, caused by, or situated beyond designated limits or boundaries. 3. Reaching the limit; extreme: an *outside* estimate. 4. Slight; slim: an *outside* possibility. — *adv.* 1. On or to the outside; externally. 2. Beyond the outside limits of. 3. In the open air; outdoors. — *prep.* 1. On or to the exterior of. 2. Beyond the limits of. — **outside of** 1. *U.S. Informal* Except: No one came *outside* of me. 2. Outside.

out·sid·er (out′sī′dər) *n.* One who is outside or excluded. — **Syn.** stranger, alien, foreigner.

out·size (out′sīz′) *n.* An irregular size, as of clothing; esp., an uncommonly large size. — *adj.* Being of an outsize: also **out′sized′**.

out·skirts (out′skûrts′) *n.pl.* A place remote from the main or central area; an outlying district.

out·smart (out·smärt′) *v.t. Informal* To outwit; fool.

out·spo·ken (out·spō′kən) *adj.* 1. Bold or free in speech; frank. 2. Spoken boldly or frankly. — **out′spo′ken·ly** *adv.* — **out′spo′ken·ness** *n.*

out·spread (*v.* out·spred′; *n.* out′spred′) *v.t. & v.i.* **·spread**, **·spread·ing** To spread out; extend. — *n.* The act of spreading out.

out·stand·ing (out·stan′ding) *adj.* 1. Prominent; excellent. **2.** Still standing or unsettled, as a debt. **3.** Projecting; abutting.

out·stretch (out-strech´) *v.t.* **1.** To stretch out; expand; extend. **2.** To extend beyond.

out·strip (out-strip´) *v.t.* **·stripped, ·strip·ping 1.** To leave behind; outrun. **2.** To excel; surpass.

out·ward (out´wərd) *adj.* **1.** Of or pertaining to the outside; external. **2.** Relating to the physical as distinguished from the mental or spiritual aspect. **3.** Readily apparent, esp. to sight: no *outward* sign of trouble. **4.** Superficially evident: *outward* display of wealth. **5.** Not inherent; extrinsic: *outward* grace. — *adv.* **1.** In an outward direction. **2.** In an outward manner. **3.** Away from a place regarded as central, as home. [OE *ūtweard*] — **out´ward·ness** *n.*

out·ward·ly (out´wərd-lē) *adv.* **1.** On or toward the outside. **2.** In outward form or aspect; seemingly.

out·wards (out´wərdz) *adv.* Outward.

out·wear (out-wâr´) *v.t.* **·wore, ·worn, ·wear·ing 1.** To wear or stand use longer than; outlast. **2.** To wear out.

out·weigh (out-wā´) *v.t.* **1.** To weigh more than. **2.** To exceed in importance, value, etc.

out·wit (out-wit´) *v.t.* **·wit·ted, ·wit·ting** To trick or baffle by superior ingenuity or cunning.

out·work¹ (out-wûrk´) *v.t.* **·worked** or **·wrought, ·work·ing** To work faster or better than.

out·work² (out´wûrk´) *n. Mil.* Any outer defense, as beyond the ditch of a fort.

out·worn (out-wôrn´) Past participle of OUTWEAR.

ou·zel (ōō´zəl) *n.* **1.** One of various European thrushes, as the blackbird. **2.** The water ouzel. Also spelled *ousel.* [OE *ōsle*]

o·va (ō´və) Plural of OVUM.

o·val (ō´vəl) *adj.* **1.** Having the shape of an egg. **2.** Resembling an ellipse. — *n.* An oval shape or figure. [< MF < L *ovum* egg] — **o´val·ly** *adv.* — **o´val·ness** *n.*

o·va·ry (ō´və-rē) *n. pl.* **·ries** *Zool.* The genital gland of female animals in which the ova are produced. **2.** *Bot.* In plants, that organ in which the ovules are contained. For illus. see FLOWER. [< NL < L *ovum* egg] — **o·var´i·an, o·var´i·al** *adj.*

o·vate (ō´vāt) *adj. Bot.* Egg-shaped: said of leaves. [< L *ovum*] — **o´vate·ly** *adv.*

o·va·tion (ō-vā´shən) *n.* A spontaneous acclamation of popularity; enthusiastic applause. [< L *ovare* to rejoice, exult] — **o·va´tion·al** *adj.*

ov·en (uv´ən) *n.* An enclosed chamber in which substances are heated in order to cook or dry them. [OE *ofen*]

ov·en·bird (uv´ən-bûrd´) *n.* A North American warbler with an olive-colored back and a golden crown, having a grassy nest suggesting an oven.

o·ver (ō´vər) *prep.* **1.** In or to a place or position above; higher than. **2.** So as to pass or extend across: walking *over* the bridge. **3.** On the other side of: lying *over* the ocean. **4.** Upon the surface or exterior of. **5.** Here and there upon or within; throughout all parts of: traveling *over* land and sea. **6.** At or up to a level higher than: The mud is *over* my boots. **7.** So as to close or cover: Put the lid *over* the jar. **8.** During: a diary kept *over* several years. **9.** Up to the end of and beyond: Stay *over* Christmas. **10.** More than; in excess of, as in amount, extent, etc.: *over* a million dollars. **11.** In preference to: chosen *over* all other candidates. **12.** In a position to guide or control: They want a strong man *over* them. **13.** Upon, as an effect: his influence *over* her. **14.** With regard to: time wasted *over* trifles. — **over all** From one end or aspect to the other. — **over and above** In addition to; besides. — *adv.* **1.** Above; overhead. **2.** To another or opposite side, or to a specified place; across: to leap *over* a puddle; to bring *over* a friend. **3.** At or on the other side; at a distance in a specified direction or place: *over* in France. **4.** From one side, opinion, or attitude to another. **5.** From one person, condition, or custody to another. **6.** So as to close, cover, or be covered: The pond froze *over.* **7.** From beginning to end: I'll think the matter *over.* **8.** So as to bring the underside upward: to turn *over* the boat. **9.** From an upright position: to topple *over.* **10.** Once more; again. **11.** So as to constitute a surplus; to have some left *over.* **12.** Beyond or until a stated time: Stay *over* until tomorrow. — **over again** Once more; anew. — **over against** Opposite to; as contrasted with. — **over and over** Time and again; repeatedly. — *adj.* **1.** Finished; done; past. **2.** On the other side; having got across. **3.** Outer; superior; upper. **4.** In excess or addition; extra. — *n.* **1.** Something remaining or in addition. **2.** *Mil.* A shot hitting or exploding beyond the target. [OE *ofer*]

over- *combining form* **1.** Above; superior: *overlord.* **2.** Passing above; going beyond the top or limit of: *overflow.* **3.** Moving or causing to move downward, as from above: *overturn.* **4.** Excessively; excessive; too much: *overcharge.* *Over-* is widely used to form compounds, as in the list beginning below.

---

overability	overblithe	overcloseness	overcunningly	overearnest	overfeatured
overable	overboastful	overcold	overcured	overearnestly	overfed
overabound	overbold	overcolor	overcurious	overeasily	overfeed
overabstemious	overboldly	overcommend	overcuriousness	overeasy	overfeminine
overabundance	overbookish	overcompetitive	overdaintiness	overeducate	overfierce
overabundant	overboorish	overcomplacency	overdainty	overelaborate	overfill
overabundantly	overborrow	overcomplacent	overdance	overelaboration	overflatten
overaccentuate	overbounteous	overcomplete	overdare	overelate	overflourish
overaccumulation	overbravely	overcomplex	overdaring	overelegant	overfluent
overactive	overbred	overcompliant	overdazzle	overembellish	overfond
overactivity	overbreed	overconcentration	overdear	overemotional	overfondle
overadvance	overbright	overconcern	overdeck	overemphasis	overfondly
overagitate	overbrilliant	overcondense	overdecorate	overemphasize	overfondness
overagitation	overbroaden	overconfidence	overdecorative	overemphatic	overfoolish
overambition	overbroil	overconfident	overdeepen	overempty	overforce
overambitious	overbrown	overconfidently	overdeeply	overenjoy	overforged
overambitiously	overbrush	overconscientious	overdeliberate	overenrich	overforward
overanalyze	overbrutal	overconscious	overdeliberation	overenter	overforwardness
overanxiety	overbulky	overconsciousness	overdelicate	overenthusiastic	overfoul
overanxious	overburdensome	overconservatism	overdelicately	overesteem	overfrail
overanxiously	overbusily	overconservative	overdelighted	overexcelling	overfrank
overapprehension	overbusy	overconsiderate	overdemand	overexcitable	overfraught
overapprehensive	overbuy	overconsideration	overdemocratic	overexcite	overfree
overapprehensively	overcapability	overconsume	overdepress	overexcitement	overfreedom
overapt	overcapable	overconsumption	overdepressive	overexercise	overfreely
overargue	overcapacity	overcontented	overdesirous	overexert	overfreight
overassert	overcaptious	overcontribute	overdestructive	overexertion	overfrequency
overassertion	overcaptiousness	overcook	overdestructiveness	overexpand	overfrequent
overassertive	overcareful	overcool	overdevoted	overexpansion	overfrighten
overassess	overcareless	overcoolly	overdevotion	overexpect	overfruitful
overassessment	overcaring	overcopious	overdiffuse	overexpectant	overfull
overassumption	overcarry	overcorrect	overdignified	overexpenditure	overfulness
overattached	overcasual	overcorrupt	overdiligence	overexpress	overfunctioning
overattention	overcaution	overcostly	overdiligent	overexuberant	overfurnish
overattentive	overcautious	overcount	overdilute	overfacile	overgamble
overattentively	overcautiously	overcourteous	overdiscipline	overfaithful	overgarrison
overattentiveness	overcautiousness	overcovetous	overdiscourage	overfamiliar	overgeneralize
overbake	overcentralization	overcoy	overdistant	overfamiliarly	overgenerous
overballast	overcharitable	overcram	overdiversification	overfanciful	overgenial
overbanked	overcheap	overcredit	overdiversify	overfast	overgentle
overbanked	overcherish	overcredulity	overdogmatic	overfastidious	overgifted
overbarren	overcherish	overcredulous	overdominate	overfastidiousness	overgird
overbarrier	overchildish	overcritical	overdoubt	overfasting	overglad
overbashful	overchill	overcriticize	overdramatic	overfat	overgloomy
overbashfully	overcivil	overcrowd	overdredge	overfatigue	overglorious
overbelief	overcivility	overcull	overdrink	overfatten	overgoad
overbet	overcivilized	overculi	overdry	overfaten	overgodly
overbig	overclean	overcultivate	overeager	overfavor	overgorge
overbitter	overclever	overcultivation	overeagerness	overfear	overgracious
overblame	overclose	overcunning		overfearful	

o·ver·act (ō′vər·akt′) *v.t. & v.i.* To act with exaggeration.

o·ver·age[1] (ō′ver·ij) *n.* In commerce, an amount of money or goods in excess of that which is listed as being on hand.

o·ver·age[2] (ō′vər·āj′) *adj.* 1. Over the usual or specified age. 2. Too old to be of use: *overage* guns.

o·ver·all (ō′vər·ôl′) *adj.* 1. From one end to the other. 2. Including or covering everything.

o·ver·alls (ō′vər·ôlz′) *n.pl.* Loose, coarse trousers, often with suspenders and a piece extending over the breast, worn over the clothing as protection against soiling and wear.

o·ver·arm (ō′vər·ärm′) *adj.* Done with the arm above the level of the shoulder, as a swimming stroke.

o·ver·awe (ō′vər·ô′) *v.t.* **awed**, **aw·ing** To subdue or restrain by awe.

o·ver·bal·ance (ō′vər·bal′əns) *v.* **·anced**, **·anc·ing** *v.t.* 1. To exceed in weight, importance, etc. 2. To cause to lose balance. — *v.i.* 3. To lose one's balance. — *n.* Excess of weight or value.

o·ver·bear (ō′vər·bâr′) *v.* **·bore**, **·borne**, **·bear·ing** *v.t.* 1. To crush or bear down by physical weight or force. 2. To prevail over; domineer. — *v.i.* 3. To be too fruitful.

o·ver·bear·ing (ō′vər·bâr′ing) *adj.* 1. Arrogant; domineering. 2. Overwhelming. — **o′ver·bear′ing·ly** *adv.*

o·ver·bid (ō′vər·bid′) *v.t. & v.i.* **·bid**, **·bid·den** or **·bid**, **·bid·ding** 1. To bid more than the value of (something). 2. To outbid (someone).

o·ver·blown (ō′vər·blōn′) *adj.* 1. Blown up or swollen, as with conceit or pretentiousness; inflated; bombastic. 2. Past full bloom, as a flower.

o·ver·board (ō′vər·bôrd′, -bōrd′) *adv.* Over the side of or out of a boat or ship. — **to go overboard** *U.S. Informal* To be extremely enthusiastic about someone or something.

o·ver·bur·den (ō′vər·bûr′dən) *v.t.* To load with too much weight, care, etc. — *n.* That which overburdens.

o·ver·cap·i·tal·ize (ō′vər·kap′i·təl·īz′) *v.t.* **·ized**, **·iz·ing** 1. To invest capital in to an extent not warranted by actual prospects. 2. To affix an unjustifiable or unlawful value to the nominal capital of (a corporation). 3. To estimate the value of (a property, company, etc.) too highly. — **o′ver·cap′i·tal·i·za′tion** *n.*

o·ver·cast (ō′vər·kast′, -käst′; *for v. defs. 1, 2, & 4, also* ō′vər·kast′, -käst′) *adj.* 1. Covered or obscured, as with clouds. 2. Gloomy; melancholy. 3. Sewn with long wrapping stitches to prevent raveling. — *n.* 1. A covering or mantle, as of clouds. 2. *Meteorol.* A cloud or clouds covering more than nine-tenths of the sky. — *v.* **·cast**, **·cast·ing** *v.t.* 1. To make overcast. 2. To cast beyond. 3. To sew with an overcast stitch. — *v.i.* 4. To become overcast.

o·ver·charge (*v.* ō′vər·chärj′; *n.* ō′vər·chärj′) *v.t.* **·charged**, **·charg·ing** 1. To charge (someone) too high a price. 2. To overburden. 3. To overdo. — *n.* An excessive charge.

o·ver·cloud (ō′vər·kloud′) *v.t.* 1. To cover with clouds; darken. 2. To make gloomy. — *v.i.* 3. To become cloudy.

o·ver·coat (ō′vər·kōt′) *n.* An outdoor coat worn over a suit, etc., esp. in cold weather.

o·ver·come (ō′vər·kum′) *v.t.* **·came**, **·come**, **·com·ing** 1. To get the better of in any conflict or struggle; defeat; conquer. 2. To prevail over or surmount, as difficulties, obstacles, etc. 3. To render (someone) helpless, as by emotion, sickness, etc. — *v.i.* 4. To gain mastery; win. [OE *ofercuman*]

o·ver·com·pen·sa·tion (ō′vər·kom′pən·sā′shən) *n.* *Psychol.* Excessive or abnormal reaction, esp. to compensate for the fact or feeling of inferiority.

o·ver·de·vel·op (ō′vər·di·vel′əp) *v.t.* 1. To develop excessively. 2. *Photog.* To develop (a plate or film) to too great a degree. — **o′ver·de·vel′op·ment** *n.*

o·ver·do (ō′vər·dōō′) *v.* **·did**, **·done**, **·do·ing** *v.t.* 1. To do excessively; exaggerate. 2. To overtax the strength of; exhaust. 3. To cook too much, as meat. [OE *oferdōn*]

o·ver·dose (*v.* ō′vər·dōs′; *n.* ō′vər·dōs′) *v.t.* **·dosed**, **·dos·ing** To dose to excess. — *n.* An excessive dose.

o·ver·draft (ō′vər·draft′, -dräft′) *n.* 1. The act of overdrawing an account, as at a bank. 2. The amount by which an account is overdrawn. Also **o′ver·draught′**.

o·ver·draw (ō′vər·drô′) *v.t.* **·drew**, **·drawn**, **·draw·ing** 1. To draw against (an account) beyond one's credit. 2. To draw or strain excessively, as a bow. 3. To exaggerate.

o·ver·drive (*v.* ō′vər·drīv′; *n.* ō′vər·drīv′) *v.t.* **·drove**, **·driv·en**, **·driv·ing** To drive too hard or too far. — *n.* *Mech.* A gearing device that turns a drive shaft at a speed greater than that of the engine, thus decreasing power output.

o·ver·due (ō′vər·dōō′, -dyōō′) *adj.* 1. Remaining unpaid after becoming due. 2. Past due: an *overdue* plane or train.

o·ver·eat (ō′vər·ēt′) *v.i.* **·ate** (-āt′, *Brit.* -et′) or *Archaic* **·eat** (-et′, -ēt′), **·eat·en**, **·eat·ing** To eat to excess.

o·ver·es·ti·mate (*v.* ō′vər·es′tə·māt; *n.* ō′vər·es′tə·mit) *v.t.* **·mat·ed**, **·mat·ing** To value or estimate too highly. — *n.* An estimate that is too high. — **o′ver·es′ti·ma′tion** *n.*

o·ver·ex·pose (ō′vər·ik·spōz′) *v.t.* **·posed**, **·pos·ing** 1. To expose excessively. 2. *Photog.* To expose (a film or plate) too long. — **o′ver·ex·po′sure** (-spō′zhər) *n.*

o·ver·flow (*v.* ō′vər·flō′; *n.* ō′vər·flō′) *v.* **flowed**, **flown**,

overgraciously	overidealistic	overlate	overmerry	overparticular	overprovident
overgrasping	overidle	overlaudatory	overmighty	overpassionate	overprovision
overgrateful	overillustrate	overlaunch	overmild	overpassionately	overprovocation
overgratify	overimaginative	overlavish	overminutely	overpatient	overprovoke
overgraze	overimitate	overlawful	overminuteness	overpatriotic	overpublic
overgreasy	overimitative	overlax	overmix	overpensive	overpublicity
overgreat	overimpress	overlaxness	overmodest	overpeople	overpunish
overgreatness	overimpressible	overlearnedness	overmodestly	overpessimistic	overpunishment
overgreediness	overinclination	overlet	overmodesty	overpicture	overquantity
overgreedy	overinclined	overlewd	overmoist	overpiteous	overquick
overgrieve	overindividualistic	overliberal	overmoisten	overplain	overquiet
overgross	overindulge	overliberality	overmoisture	overplausible	overquietness
overhandle	overindulgence	overliberally	overmortgage	overplease	overrank
overhappy	overindulgent	overlighted	overmournful	overplentiful	overrapturous
overharass	overindustrialize	overlinger	overmultiply	overplenty	overrash
overhard	overinflate	overliterary	overnarrow	overplump	overrational
overharden	overinflation	overliveliness	overnear	overply	overrationalize
overhardy	overinfluence	overlively	overneat	overpolemical	overreadily
overharsh	overinfluential	overload	overneglect	overpolish	overreadiness
overhaste	overinsistence	overloftly	overnegligence	overponderous	overready
overhastily	overinsistent	overlogical	overnegligent	overpopular	overrealism
overhastiness	overinsolent	overlong	overnervous	overpopulate	overrealistic
overhasty	overinstruct	overloud	overnervousness	overpopulated	overrefine
overhate	overinsure	overlove	overnew	overpopulation	overrefined
overhaughty	overintellectual	overloyal	overnice	overpopulous	overrefinement
overheap	overintense	overluscious	overnimble	overpositive	overreflection
overheartily	overinterest	overlustiness	overnotable	overpotent	overreflective
overhearty	overinventoried	overlusty	overnourish	overpowerful	overregulation
overheavy	overinvest	overluxuriant	overnumerous	overpraise	overrelax
overhelpful	overirrigate	overluxurious	overobedient	overprecise	overreliant
overhigh	overirrigation	overmagnify	overobese	overpreciseness	overreligious
overhold	overjealous	overmany	overoblige	overpreoccupation	overrepresent
overholy	overjocular	overmarch	overobsequious	overpress	overreserved
overhomely	overjoyful	overmasterful	overobsequiousness	overpresumptuous	overresolute
overhonest	overjoyous	overmasterfulness	overoffensive	overproductive	overrestrain
overhonor	overjudicious	overmature	overofficious	overproficient	overretention
overhope	overjust	overmeanness	overofficiousness	overprolific	overreward
overhot	overkeen	overmeasure	overoften	overprominent	overrich
overhotly	overkind	overmeddle	overoptimistic	overprompt	overrife
overhuman	overknowing	overmeek	overornamented	overpromptness	overrighteous
overhumanize	overlabor	overmellow	overpainful	overprosperous	overrighteousness
overhurriedly	overlactation	overmelt	overpamper	overprotract	overrigid
overhysterical	overlade	overmerciful	overpartial	overproud	overrigorous
overidealism	overlarge	overmerrily	overpartiality	overprovide	overripe

·**flow·ing** *v.i.* **1.** To flow or run over the brim or bank, as water, rivers, etc. **2.** To be filled beyond capacity; superabound. — *v.t.* **3.** To flow over the brim or bank of. **4.** To flow or spread over; cover; flood. **5.** To cause to overflow. — *n.* **1.** The act or process of overflowing. **2.** That which flows over. **3.** The amount by which a capacity is exceeded; surplus. **4.** An outlet for liquid. [OE *oferflōwan*]

o·ver·grow (ō′vər-grō′) *v.* ·**grew**, ·**grown**, ·**grow·ing** *v.t.* **1.** To grow over; cover with growth. **2.** To grow too big for; outgrow. — *v.i.* **3.** To increase excessively; grow too large.

o·ver·hand (ō′vər-hand′) *adj.* **1.** In baseball, etc., executed with the hand above the level of the elbow or the shoulder. Also **o′ver·hand′ed** (-han′did). **2.** In sewing, made by carrying the thread over both edges, as a seam. — *adv.* In an overhand manner. — *n.* **1.** An overhand stroke or delivery, as in tennis. **2.** A kind of knot. For illus. see KNOT¹.

o·ver·hang (ō′vər-hang′) *v.* ·**hung** (-hung′), ·**hang·ing** *v.t.* **1.** To hang or project over (something); jut over. **2.** To threaten; menace. **3.** To adorn with hangings. — *v.i.* **4.** To hang or jut over something. — *n.* An overhanging portion of a structure; also, the amount of such projection.

o·ver·haul (*v.* ō′vər-hôl′; *n.* ō′vər-hôl′) *v.t.* **1.** To examine carefully for needed repairs. **2.** To make all needed repairs in; renovate. **3.** To catch up with; gain on. — *n.* A thorough inspection and repair. Also **o′ver·haul′ing.**

o·ver·head (*adj. & n.* ō′vər-hed′; *adv.* ō′vər-hed′) *adj.* **1.** Situated or working above the level of one's head: an *overhead* light. **2.** Of or relating to the overhead of a business. — *n.* The operating expenses of a business, as rent, light, heat, taxes, etc. — *adv.* Over or above the head.

o·ver·hear (ō′vər-hir′) *v.t.* ·**heard** (-hûrd′), ·**hear·ing** To hear (something said or someone speaking) without the knowledge or intention of the speaker. — **o′ver·hear′er** *n.*

o·ver·joy (ō′vər-joi′) *v.t.* To delight or please greatly.

o·ver·kill (ō′vər-kil′) *n.* The military capacity for destruction far beyond the resources and population of an enemy.

o·ver·land (ō′vər-land′) *adj.* Proceeding over or accomplished by land. — *adv.* Across, over, or via land.

o·ver·lap (*v.* ō′vər-lap′; *n.* ō′vər-lap′) *v.t. & v.i.* ·**lapped**, ·**lap·ping** **1.** To lie or extend partly over or upon (another or each other); lap over. **2.** To cover and project beyond (something). — *n.* **1.** The state or extent of overlapping. **2.** The part that overlaps.

o·ver·lay (*v.* ō′vər-lā′; *n.* ō′vər-lā′) *v.t.* ·**laid**, ·**lay·ing** **1.** To spread something over, as with a decorative pattern or layer. **2.** To lay or place over or upon something else. **3.** To overburden. — *n.* **1.** *Printing* A piece of paper placed on the tympan of a press to make the impression heavier or to compensate for a depression. **2.** Anything that covers or partly covers something. **3.** An ornamental layer, as veneer, applied to wood, etc. **4.** A transparent sheet laid over a map to add or emphasize certain features.

o·ver·leaf (ō′vər-lēf′) *adv.* On the other side of a page.

o·ver·leap (ō′vər-lēp′) *v.t.* ·**leaped** or ·**leapt**, ·**leap·ing** **1.** To leap over or across. **2.** To omit; overlook. **3.** To leap farther than; outleap. — **to overleap oneself** To miss one's purpose by going too far. [OE *oferhlēapan*]

o·ver·lie (ō′vər-lī′) *v.t.* ·**lay** (-lā′), ·**lain** (-lān′), ·**ly·ing** **1.** To lie over or upon. **2.** To suffocate by lying upon.

o·ver·load (*v.* ō′vər-lōd′; *n.* ō′vər-lōd′) *v.t.* To load excessively; overburden. — *n.* **1.** An excessive burden. **2.** *Electr.* An amperage in excess of that which can be safely carried.

o·ver·look (*v.* ō·vər-look′; *n.* ō′vər-look′) *v.t.* **1.** To fail to see or notice; miss. **2.** To disregard purposely or indulgently; ignore. **3.** To look over or see from a higher place. **4.** To afford a view of: The castle *overlooks* the harbor. **5.** To supervise; oversee. **6.** To examine or inspect. — *n.* **1.** The act of looking over, as from a height; an inspection; survey. **2.** An elevated place affording a view.

o·ver·lord (ō′vər-lôrd′) *n.* **1.** A superior lord or chief. **2.** One who holds supremacy over others. — **o′ver·lord′ship** *n.*

o·ver·ly (ō′vər-lē) *adv. Chiefly U.S.* To an excessive degree; too much; too.

o·ver·man (ō′vər-man′) *v.t.* ·**manned**, ·**man·ning** To provide with more men than necessary.

o·ver·mas·ter (ō′vər-mas′tər, -mäs′-) *v.t.* To overcome; overpower. — **o′ver·mas′ter·ing** *adj.*

o·ver·match (*v.* ō′vər-mach′; *n.* ō′vər-mach′) *v.t.* To be more than a match for; surpass. — *n.* One who or that which is superior in strength, skill, etc.

o·ver·much (ō′vər-much′) *adj.* Excessive; too much. — *adv.* In too great a degree. — *n.* An excess; too much.

o·ver·night (*adj. & adv.* ō′vər-nīt′) *adj.* **1.** Done during the previous evening; lasting all night. **2.** Away from home for one night: *overnight* trip. **3.** Used for nighttime travel or for short visits: an *overnight* bag. — *adv.* **1.** During or through the night. **2.** On the previous evening.

o·ver·pass (*n.* ō′vər-pas′, -päs′; *v.* ō′vər-pas′, -päs′) *n.* An elevated section of highway crossing other lines of travel. — *v.t.* **1.** To pass over, across, or through; cross. **2.** To surpass. **3.** To overlook. **4.** To transgress.

o·ver·play (ō′vər-plā′) *v.t.* **1.** To play or act (a part or role) to excess. **2.** To rely too much on the strength or value of. **3.** In golf, to send (the ball) beyond the putting green.

o·ver·pow·er (ō′vər-pou′ər) *v.t.* **1.** To gain supremacy over; subdue. **2.** To render wholly helpless or ineffective; overcome. **3.** To supply with more power than necessary. — **o′ver·pow′er·ing** (ō′vər-pou′ər-ing) *adj.* **1.** That overpowers. **2.** Intense. — **o′ver·pow′er·ing·ly** *adv.*

o·ver·print (*v.* ō′vər-print′; *n.* ō′vər-print′) *v.t.* To print additional material of another color on (sheets already printed). — *n.* Any word, symbol, etc., printed on a postage stamp, changing its value or use.

o·ver·pro·duce (ō′vər-prə-dōōs′, -dyōōs′) *v.t.* ·**duced**, ·**duc·ing** To produce too much of or so as to exceed demand.

o·ver·pro·duc·tion (ō′vər-prə-duk′shən) *n.* Production in excess of demand, or of the possibility of profitable sale.

o·ver·rate (ō′vər-rāt′) *v.t.* ·**rat·ed**, ·**rat·ing** To rate or value too highly; credit with undue merit; overestimate.

o·ver·reach (ō′vər-rēch′) *v.t.* **1.** To reach over or beyond. **2.** To spread over; cover. **3.** To defeat (oneself), as by attempting something beyond one's capability. **4.** To miss by stretching or reaching too far. **5.** To outwit; cheat. — *v.i.* **6.** To reach too far. **7.** To cheat. — **o′ver·reach′er** *n.*

o·ver·ride (ō′vər-rīd′) *v.t.* ·**rode** (-rōd′), ·**rid·den** (-rid′ən), ·**rid·ing** **1.** To disregard summarily, as if trampling down; supersede. **2.** To ride (a horse, etc.) to exhaustion. **3.** To ride over. **4.** To trample down; suppress.

o·ver·rule (ō′vər-rōōl′) *v.t.* ·**ruled**, ·**rul·ing** **1.** To decide against or nullify; set aside; invalidate. **2.** To disallow the arguments of (someone). **3.** To have control over; rule. **4.** To prevail over.

o·ver·run (*v.* ō′vər-run′; *n.* ō′vər-run′) *v.* ·**ran** (-ran′), ·**run**, ·**run·ning** **1.** To spread or swarm over, as vermin or in-

overripen	overservile	oversophistication	overstress	overtax	overurge
overroast	oversettled	oversorrow	overstretch	overtaxation	overuse
overrough	oversevere	overspacious	overstrict	overteach	overvaluable
oversad	overseverely	oversparing	overstrident	overtechnical	overvaluation
oversale	overseverity	oversparingly	overstriving	overtedious	overvariety
oversalt	oversexual	overspecialization	overstrong	overtenacious	overvehement
oversanguine	oversharp	overspecialize	overstudious	overtender	overventilate
oversaturate	overshort	overspecific	overstudiousness	overtenderness	overventuresome
oversaturation	overshorten	overspeculate	overstudy	overtense	overventurous
oversaucy	overshrink	overspeculation	oversublime	overtension	overvigorous
oversave	oversick	overspeculative	oversubscribe	overthick	overviolent
overscare	oversilent	overspeed	oversubscription	overthin	overvote
overscented	oversimple	overspeedily	oversubtle	overthoughtful	overwarm
overscrub	oversimplicity	overspent	oversubtlety	overthrifty	overwarmed
overscrupulosity	oversimplification	overspin	oversufficient	overthrong	overwary
overscrupulous	oversimplify	oversqueamish	oversup	overthrust	overweak
overscrupulousness	overskeptical	oversqueamishness	oversuperstitious	overtight	overwealthy
overseason	overslander	overstale	oversupination	overtimid	overwet
overseasoned	overslight	overstaring	oversure	overtimorous	overwide
overseason	overslow	overstately	oversusceptible	overtinseled	overwilling
overseasoned	oversmall	oversteadfast	oversuspicious	overtire	overwily
oversecure	oversmooth	oversteadfastness	oversuspiciously	overtoil	overwise
overseed	oversoak	oversteady	oversweet	overtorture	overwoody
oversensible	oversoft	overstiff	oversystematic	overtrain	overworry
oversensitive	oversoftness	overstimulate	oversystematize	overtrim	overworship
oversensual	oversolemn	overstimulation	overtalkative	overtrust	overyoung
oversensuality	oversolicitous	overstir	overtalkativeness	overtrustful	overyouthful
oversententious	oversoon	overstore	overtame	overtruthful	overzeal
oversentimental	oversoothing	overstout	overtart	overunionized	overzealous
overserious	oversophisticated	overstrain	overtask	overurbanization	overzealously

vaders. **2.** To overflow. **3.** To spread rapidly across or throughout, as a fashion or fad. **4.** To run beyond; pass the limit of. **5.** *Printing* To shift or rearrange (words, lines of type, etc.) from one line, page, or column to another. — *v.i.* **6.** To run over; overflow. **7.** To pass the usual or desired limit. — *n.* An instance of overrunning; also, the amount of overrunning.

o·ver·score (ō′vər·skôr′, -skōr′) *v.t.* **·scored, ·scor·ing** To draw a line or lines over a word, letter, etc.

o·ver·seas (ō′vər·sēz′) *adv.* Beyond the sea; abroad. — *adj.* Situated, coming from, or for use beyond the sea; foreign: also **o′ver·sea′.**

o·ver·see (ō′vər·sē′) *v.t.* **·saw, ·seen, ·see·ing 1.** To direct; superintend. **2.** To survey; watch. [OE *ofersēon*]

o·ver·se·er (ō′vər·sē′ər, -sir′) *n.* A person who oversees; esp., one who superintends laborers at their work.

o·ver·sell (ō′vər·sel′) *v.t.* **·sold** (-sōld′), **·sell·ing 1.** To sell to excess. **2.** To sell more of (a stock, etc.) than one can provide.

o·ver·set (*v.* ō′vər·set′; *n.* ō′vər·set′) *v.* **·set, ·set·ting** *v.t.* **1.** To disconcert. **2.** *Printing* To set too much (type or copy). — *v.i.* **3.** To overturn; fall over. — *n.* **1.** A turning over; upset. **2.** *Printing* Excess of composed type.

o·ver·shad·ow (ō′vər·shad′ō) *v.t.* **1.** To render unimportant or insignificant by comparison; loom above; dominate. **2.** To throw a shadow over; obscure.

o·ver·shoe (ō′vər·shōō′) *n.* A shoe worn over another for protection against water, mud, cold, etc.; a galosh.

o·ver·shoot (ō′vər·shōōt′) *v.* **·shot, ·shoot·ing** *v.t.* **1.** To shoot or go over or beyond (the mark, target, etc.). **2.** To go beyond; exceed, as a limit. **3.** To drive or force (something) beyond the proper limit. — *v.i.* **4.** To shoot or go over or beyond the mark. **5.** To go too far.

o·ver·shot (ō′vər·shot′) *adj.* **1.** Surpassed in any way. **2.** Projecting, as the upper jaw beyond the lower jaw. **3.** Driven by water flowing over from above: an *overshot* wheel.

o·ver·sight (ō′vər·sīt′) *n.* **1.** An inadvertent mistake or omission. **2.** Watchful supervision; superintendence.

o·ver·size (ō′vər·sīz′) *adj.* Of a larger size than necessary or normal: also **o′ver·sized′.** — *n.* A large size.

o·ver·skirt (ō′vər·skûrt′) *n.* A skirt or drapery worn over the skirt of a dress.

o·ver·sleep (ō′vər·slēp′) *v.* **·slept, ·sleep·ing** *v.i.* To sleep too long.

o·ver·spread (ō′vər·spred′) *v.t.* **·spread, ·spread·ing** To spread or extend over; cover completely.

o·ver·state (ō′vər·stāt′) *v.t.* **·stat·ed, ·stat·ing** To state in too strong terms; exaggerate. — **o′ver·state′ment** *n.*

o·ver·stay (ō′vər·stā′) *v.t.* To stay beyond the limits or duration of.

o·ver·step (ō′vər·step′) *v.t.* **·stepped, ·step·ping** To step over or go beyond; exceed, as a limit or restriction.

o·ver·stock (*v.* ō′vər·stok′, *n.* ō′vər·stok′) *v.t.* To stock to excess. — *n.* An excessive supply.

o·ver·strung (ō′vər·strung′) *adj.* Too tense or sensitive.

o·ver·stuff (ō′vər·stuf′) *v.t.* **1.** To stuff to excess. **2.** To cover completely with deep upholstery: said of furniture.

o·ver·sup·ply (*n.* ō′vər·sə·plī′; *v.* ō′vər·sə·plī′) *n. pl.* **·plies** An excessive supply. — *v.t.* **·plied, ·ply·ing** To supply in excess.

o·vert (ō′vûrt, ō·vûrt′) *adj.* **1.** Open to view; observable. **2.** *Law* Done with criminal intent. [< OF, pp. of *ovrir* to open] — **o·vert·ly** (ō′vûrt·lē, ō·vûrt′lē) *adv.*
— **Syn. 1.** evident, plain, open. See MANIFEST. — **Ant.** covert, hidden, secret.

o·ver·take (ō′vər·tāk′) *v.t.* **·took** (-tōōk′), **·tak·en, ·tak·ing 1.** To catch up with. **2.** To come upon suddenly.

o·ver-the-count·er (ō′vər-thə-koun′tər) *adj.* Not sold on the floor of a stock exchange: said of stocks, bonds, etc.

o·ver·throw (*v.* ō′vər·thrō′; *n.* ō′vər·thrō′) *v.t.* **·threw** (-thrōō′), **·thrown, ·throw·ing 1.** To bring down or remove from power by force; defeat; ruin. **2.** To throw over or down; upset. — *n.* **1.** The act of overthrowing; destruction; demolition. **2.** In baseball, etc., a throwing of the ball over and beyond the player or base aimed at.

o·ver·time (*n., adj., & adv.* ō′vər·tīm′; *v.* ō′vər·tīm′) *n.* Time used in working beyond the specified hours. — *adj.* During or for extra working time: *overtime* pay. — *adv.* Beyond the stipulated time. — *v.t.* **timed, ·tim·ing** *Photog.* To expose too long, as a plate or film.

o·ver·tone (ō′vər·tōn′) *n.* **1.** *Music* An upper partial tone: so called because it is heard with and above the fundamental tone produced by a musical instrument. **2.** Connotations, implications, etc., of language, thoughts, etc.

o·ver·top (ō′vər·top′) *v.t.* **·topped, ·top·ping 1.** To rise above the top of; tower over. **2.** To surpass; excel.

o·ver·ture (ō′vər·chər) *n.* **1.** *Music* An instrumental prelude to an opera or other large work. **b** Any of various orchestral pieces, often having programmatic content. **2.** An act or proposal intended to initiate a relationship, negotiations, etc. — *v.t.* **·tured, ·tur·ing 1.** To offer as an overture or proposal. **2.** To introduce with or as an overture. [See OVERT.]

o·ver·turn (*v.* ō′vər·tûrn′; *n.* ō′vər·tûrn′) *v.t.* **1.** To turn or throw over; capsize; upset. **2.** To overthrow; defeat; ruin. — *v.i.* **3.** To turn over; capsize; upset. — *n.* **1.** The act of overturning, or the state of being overturned. **2.** A subversion or destruction. **3.** Turnover (def. 6).

o·ver·ween·ing (ō′vər·wē′ning) *adj.* **1.** Presumptiously proud or conceited. **2.** Excessive; exaggerated. [OE *oferwēnan* to become insolent] — **o′ver·ween′ing·ly** *adv.*

o·ver·weigh (ō′vər·wā′) *v.t.* **1.** To outweigh; overbalance. **2.** To overburden; oppress.

o·ver·weight (*n.* ō′vər·wāt′; *adj. & v.* ō′vər·wāt′) *n.* **1.** Excess weight, as beyond the legal or customary amount. **2.** Greater importance; preponderance. — *adj.* Being more than the usual or permitted weight. — *v.t.* To overburden.

o·ver·whelm (ō′vər·hwelm′) *v.t.* **1.** To bury or submerge completely, as with a wave or flood. **2.** To overcome or defeat; crush. [ME *oferwhelmen* to turn upside down]
— **Syn. 1.** inundate, bury. **2.** rout, vanquish.

o·ver·whelm·ing (ō′vər·hwel′ming) *adj.* Crushing by reason of force, weight, or numbers; irresistible. — **o′ver·whelm′ing·ly** *adv.*

o·ver·work (*v.* ō′vər·wûrk′; *n.* ō′vər·wûrk′) *v.* **·worked** (*Archaic* **·wrought**), **·work·ing** *v.t.* **1.** To cause to work too hard. **2.** To work on or elaborate excessively: to *overwork* an argument. — *v.i.* **3.** To work too hard; do too much work. — *n.* Excessive work. [OE *oferwiercan*]

o·ver·write (ō′vər·rīt′) *v.t. & v.i.* **·wrote** (-rōt′), **·writ·ten** (-rit′ən), **·writ·ing 1.** To write in too elaborate or labored a style. **2.** To write too much about (a subject) or at too great length. **3.** To write over other writing.

o·ver·wrought (ō′vər·rôt′) *adj.* **1.** Worked up or excited excessively; overstrained. **2.** Worked all over, as with embroidery. **3.** Worked too hard. **4.** Too elaborate.

ovi- *combining form* Egg; of or pertaining to eggs: *oviparous.* Also **ovo-.** [< L *ovum* egg]

o·vi·duct (ō′vi·dukt) *n. Anat.* A Fallopian tube.

o·vi·form (ō′vi·fôrm) *adj.* Shaped like an egg or ovum.

o·vip·a·ra (ō·vip′ər·ə) *n.pl.* Animals that lay eggs. [< NL < L < *ovum* egg + *-parus* < *parere* to bring forth]

o·vip·a·rous (ō·vip′ər·əs) *adj. Zool.* Producing eggs or ova that mature and are hatched outside the body, as birds, most fishes, and reptiles. — **o·vip′a·rous·ly** *adv.* — **o·vip′a·rous·ness** *n.*

o·vi·pos·i·tor (ō′vi·poz′ə·tər) *n. Entomol.* The tubular organ at the extremity of the abdomen in many insects by which the eggs are deposited. [< OVI- + L *ponere* to place]

o·void (ō′void) *adj.* Egg-shaped: also **o·voi′dal.** — *n.* An egg-shaped body.

o·vo·vi·vip·a·rous (ō′vō-vī·vip′ər·əs) *adj. Zool.* Producing eggs that are hatched within the parent's body, but without formation of a placenta, as some reptiles and fishes. — **o′vo·vi·vip′a·rous·ly** *adv.* — **o′vo·vi·vip′a·rous·ness** *n.*

o·vu·late (ō′vyə·lāt) *v.i.* **·lat·ed, ·lat·ing** To produce ova; discharge ova from an ovary. [See OVULE.]

o·vu·la·tion (ō′vyə·lā′shən) *n. Biol.* **1.** The formation and discharge of ova. **2.** The period when this occurs.

o·vule (ō′vyōōl) *n.* **1.** *Bot.* The body within the ovary that upon fertilization becomes the seed. For illus. see FLOWER. **2.** *Zool.* An immature ovum. [< F < NL *ovulum*, dim. of L *ovum* egg] — **o′vu·lar, o·vu·lar·y** (ō′vyə·ler′ē) *adj.*

o·vum (ō′vəm) *n. pl.* **o·va** (ō′və) *Biol.* The female reproductive cell of animals, produced in the ovary. [< L]

owe (ō) *v.* **owed** (*Obs.* **ought**), **ow·ing** *v.t.* **1.** To be indebted to the amount of. **2.** To be obligated to render or offer: to *owe* an apology. **3.** To have or possess by virtue of some condition or cause: with *to*: He *owes* his success to his own efforts. **4.** To cherish (a certain feeling) toward another. — *v.i.* **5.** To be in debt. [OE *āgan* to own]

ow·ing (ō′ing) *adj.* Due; yet to be paid. — **owing to** Attributable to; on account of; in consequence of.

owl (oul) *n.* **1.** A predatory nocturnal bird, having large eyes and head, short, sharply hooked bill, long powerful claws, and a circular facial disk of radiating feathers. **2.** A person with nocturnal habits. [OE *ūle*]

owl·et (ou′lit) *n.* A small or young owl.

owl·ish (ou′lish) *adj.* **1.** Like an owl. **2.** *Brit. Dial.* Stupid. — **owl′ish·ly** *adv.* — **owl′ish·ness** *n.*

own (ōn) *adj.* **1.** Belonging or relating to oneself: following the possessive (usu. a possessive pronoun) as an intensive or to indicate the exclusion of others: my *own* horse; his *own* idea. **2.** Being of the nearest degree: *own* cousin. — **to come into one's own 1.** To obtain possession of one's property. **2.** To receive one's reward. — **to hold one's own 1.** To maintain one's place or position. **2.** To keep up with one's work, or remain undefeated. **— on one's own** Entirely dependent on one's self for support or success. **—** *v.t.* **1.** To have or hold as one's own; possess. **2.** To admit or acknowledge. **—** *v.i.* **3.** To confess: with *to.* **— to own up** *Informal* To confess forthrightly and fully. **— Syn.** See CONFESS. [OE *āgan* to possess, have] **— own′a·ble** *adj.*

own·er (ō′nər) *n.* One who has the legal title or right to or has possession of a thing. **— own′er·less** *adj.*

own·er·ship (ō′nər·ship) *n.* The state of being an owner.

ox (oks) *n.* *pl.* **ox·en** (ok′sən) **1.** An adult castrated male of the genus *Bos,* used for draft and food. **2.** Any bovine quadruped, as a buffalo, bison, or yak. [OE *oxa*]

ox·al·ic acid (ok·sal′ik) *Chem.* A white, crystalline, poisonous compound, $C_2H_2O_4·2H_2O$, found in plant tissues and made artificially, used in bleaching, dyeing, etc.

ox·blood (oks′blud′) *n.* A deep red color.

ox·bow (oks′bō′) *n.* **1.** A bent piece of wood in an ox yoke, that forms a collar for the ox. **2.** A bend in a river shaped like this.

ox·eye (oks′ī′) *n.* **1.** Any of several plants of the composite family having large yellow heads. **2.** The oxeye daisy. **3.** Any of various shore birds, as the sandpiper. **4.** An oval dormer window.

ox-eyed (oks′īd) *adj.* Having large, calm eyes, as an ox.

ox·ford (oks′fərd) *n.* *U.S.* **1.** A low shoe laced at the instep. Also **oxford shoe. 2.** A cotton cloth of basket weave, used for men's shirts. Also **Oxford.** [after *Oxford*]

oxford gray 1. A very dark gray. **2.** A woolen fabric of this color.

ox·heart (oks′härt′) *n.* A variety of sweet cherry.

ox·i·da·tion (ok′sə·dā′shən) *n.* *Chem.* **1.** The process or state of undergoing combination with oxygen. **2.** The process by which atoms lose or are deprived of valence electrons, or begin sharing them with a more electronegative element.

ox·ide (ok′sīd, -sid) *n.* *Chem.* Any binary compound of oxygen with another element: iron *oxide.* Also **ox′id** (-sid). [< F < *ox(ygène)* oxygen + *(ac)ide* acid]

ox·i·dize (ok′sə·dīz) *v.* **·dized, ·diz·ing** *Chem.* *v.t.* **1.** To convert (an element) into its oxide; combine with oxygen. **2.** To increase the valence of an atom or group of atoms by the loss of electrons. **—** *v.i.* **3.** To become oxidized. Also **ox·i·date** (ok′sə·dāt). Also *Brit.* **ox′i·dise. — ox′i·diz′a·ble** *adj.*

ox·lip (oks′lip′) *n.* A species of primrose, closely resembling the cowslip: also called *five-fingers.* [OE < *oxa, oxan* ox + *slyppe* slime]

Ox·o·ni·an (ok·sō′nē·ən) *adj.* Of or pertaining to Oxford, England, or to its university. **—** *n.* A student or graduate of Oxford University. [< LL *Oxonia* Oxford]

ox·tail (oks′tāl′) *n.* The tail of an ox, esp. when skinned for use in soup.

oxy-[1] *combining form* **1.** Sharp; pointed; keen. **2.** Acid: *oxygen.* [< Gk. *oxys* sharp, acid]

oxy-[2] *combining form* *Chem.* **1.** Oxygen; of or containing oxygen, or one of its compounds. **2.** An oxidation product. **3.** Containing the hydroxyl group. [< OXYGEN]

ox·y·a·cet·y·lene (ok′sē·ə·set′ə·lēn) *adj.* Designating or pertaining to a mixture of acetylene and oxygen, used to obtain high temperatures, as in welding.

ox·y·gen (ok′sə·jin) *n.* A colorless, tasteless, odorless gaseous element (symbol O), occurring free in the atmosphere, of which it forms about one-fifth by volume. It is an abundant and active element, combining with hydrogen to form water, supporting combustion, and essential in the respiration of plants and animals. See ELEMENT. [< F < *oxy-* oxy-[1] + *-gène* -gen]

ox·y·gen·ate (ok′sə·jən·āt′) *v.t.* **·at·ed, ·at·ing** To treat, combine, or impregnate with oxygen. **— ox′y·gen·a′tion** *n.*

ox·y·gen·ize (ok′sə·jən·īz′) *v.t.* **·ized, ·iz·ing** To oxidize.

oxygen mask A device worn over the nose and mouth by means of which the user can inhale oxygen as an aid to breathing.

oxygen tent A tentlike canopy placed over a patient's head and shoulders, within which pure oxygen may be circulated for the purpose of facilitating respiration.

ox·y·hy·dro·gen (ok′si·hī′drə·jən) *n.* A mixture of oxygen and hydrogen.

ox·y·mo·ron (ok′si·môr′on, -mō′ron) *n.* *pl.* **·mo·ra** (-môr′ə, -mō′rə) A figure of speech in which contradictory terms are brought together, as in the phrase, "*O heavy lightness, serious vanity!*" [< Gk. < *oxys* sharp + *moros* foolish]

o·yez (ō′yes, ō′yez) *interj.* Hear! hear ye! an introductory word to call attention to a proclamation, as by a court crier: usu. repeated three times. Also **o′yes.** [< OF *oyez,* imperative of *oir,* ult. < L *audire* to hear]

oys·ter (ois′tər) *n.* **1.** A bivalve mollusk, found in salt and brackish water and moored by the shell to stones, other shells, etc.; esp., a common edible species of Europe and America. **2.** An analogous bivalve, as the **pearl oyster. 3.** Some delicacy; tidbit; prize. **—** *v.i.* To gather or farm oysters. [< OF < L < Gk. *ostreon*]

oyster bed A place where oysters breed or are grown.

oyster crab A smooth-bodied crab living nonparasitically in the mantle of the oyster.

oyster cracker A small biscuit or hard, salted cracker.

oyster plant Salsify.

oyster white Any of several very light gray tints.

O·zark State (ō′zärk) Nickname of Missouri.

o·zo·ce·rite (ō·zō′kə·rīt, -sə-, ō′zə·sī·rīt′) *n.* A waxy, translucent mixture of natural hydrocarbons, used in candles, etc. Also **o·zo′ke·rite.** [< G < Gk. *ozein* to smell + *keros* wax]

o·zone (ō′zōn) *n.* **1.** An unstable allotropic form of oxygen, O_3, with a pungent odor like that of chlorine, formed variously, as by the passage of electricity through the air. It is a powerful oxidizing agent, and is used for bleaching oils, waxes, ivory, flour, and starch, and for sterilizing drinking water. **2.** *Informal* Fresh air. [< F < Gk. *ozein* to smell] **— o·zon·ic** (ō·zon′ik, ō·zō′nik), **o·zo·nous** (ō′zə·nəs) *adj.*

o·zo·nize (ō′zō·nīz) *v.t.* **·nized, ·niz·ing 1.** To treat or charge with ozone. **2.** To convert (oxygen) into ozone. **— o′zo·ni·za′tion** *n.* **— o′zo·niz′er** *n.*

o·zon·o·sphere (ō·zon′ə·sfir) *n.* *Meteorol.* A narrow layer in the stratosphere, containing a high concentration of ozone. Also **ozone layer. — o·zon′o·spher′ic** or **·i·cal** *adj.*

P

p, P (pē) *n.* *pl.* **p's** or **ps, P's** or **Ps, pees** (pēz) **1.** The sixteenth letter of the English alphabet. **2.** The sound represented by the letter *p,* the voiceless bilabial stop. **— symbol 1.** *Chem.* Phosphorus (symbol P). **2.** *Genetics* The parental generation: followed by a subscript numeral, as P_1, P_2, to indicate the first, second, etc., parental generation. **— to mind one's P's and Q's** To be careful of one's behavior.

pa (pä) *n.* *Informal* Papa.

paba or **PABA** *Biochem.* Para-aminobenzoic acid.

pab·u·lum (pab′yə·ləm) *n.* Any substance giving nourishment; aliment. [< L *pabulum* fodder] **— pab′u·lar** *adj.*

pace (pās) *n.* **1.** A step in walking; also, the distance covered in one such movement. **2.** A conventional measure of length approximating the average length of stride in walking: usu. 3 feet, but sometimes making 5 paces to the rod. The U.S. Army **regulation pace** is 30 inches, quick time; 36 inches, double time. **3.** The manner or speed of movement in going on the legs; carriage and action, esp. of a horse. **4.** Rate of speed, as in movement, work, etc. **5.** A gait of a horse, etc., in which both feet on the same side are lifted and moved forward at once. **— to put (one) through his paces**

To test the abilities, speed, etc., of. **—** *v.* **paced, pac·ing** *v.t.* **1.** To walk back and forth across. **2.** To measure by paces. **3.** To set or make the pace for. **4.** To train to a certain gait or pace. **—** *v.i.* **5.** To walk with slow or regular steps. **6.** To move at a pace (def. 5). [< F < L *passus,* pp. of *pandere* to stretch.] **— pac′er** *n.*

paced (pāst) *adj.* **1.** Having a particular pace: used in compounds: slow-*paced.* **2.** Measured in paces or by pacing. **3.** Done after or with the help of a pacemaker.

pace·mak·er (pās′mā′kər) *n.* **1.** One who makes or sets the pace for another in a race. **2.** *Anat.* A mass of tissue in the right atrium of the heart that normally regulates the heartbeat. **— pace′mak′ing** *n. & adj.*

pa·cha (pə·shä′, pash′ə), **pa·cha·lic** (pə·shä′lik) See PASHA, PASHALIK.

pach·ou·li (pach′ōō·lē, pə·chōō′lē) See PATCHOULI.

pachy- *combining form* Thick; massive. [< Gk. *pachys* thick]

pach·y·derm (pak′ə·dûrm) *n.* **1.** Any of certain thick-skinned, nonruminant hoofed animals, esp. an elephant, hippopotamus, or rhinoceros. **2.** A thick-skinned, insensitive person. [< F < Gk. < *pachys* thick + *derma* skin] — **pach′y·der′ma·tous** (-dûr′mə·təs), **pach′y·der′mous** *adj.*

pa·cif·ic (pə·sif′ik) *adj.* 1. Tending or leading to peace or conciliation. 2. Peaceful. Also **pa·cif′i·cal.** [< MF < L < *pax, pacis* peace + *facere* to make] — **pa·cif′i·cal·ly** *adv.*

Pa·cif·ic (pə·sif′ik) *adj.* Pertaining to the Pacific Ocean.

pa·cif·i·cate (pə·sif′ə·kāt) *v.t.* **·cat·ed, ·cat·ing** To pacify; calm. — **pac·i·fi·ca·tion** (pas′ə·fə·kā′shən) *n.* — **pa·cif′i·ca′tor** *n.* — **pa·cif′i·ca·to′ry** (-kə·tôr′ē, -tō′rē) *adj.*

pac·i·fi·er (pas′ə·fī′ər) *n.* 1. One who or that which pacifies. 2. A rubber nipple or ring, for babies to suck or bite on.

pac·i·fist (pas′ə·fist) *n.* One who opposes war or military preparedness, and proposes that all disputes be settled by arbitration. — **pac′i·fism** *n.* — **pac′i·fis′tic** *adj.*

pac·i·fy (pas′ə·fī) *v.t.* **·fied, ·fy·ing** 1. To bring peace to (an area). 2. To allay the anger or agitation of; quiet; soothe. [< F < L < *pax, pacis* peace + *facere* to make]

pack¹ (pak) *n.* 1. A bundle or large package, esp. one to be carried on the back of a man or animal. 2. A collection of anything; heap. 3. A full set of like or associated things usu. handled collectively, as cards. 4. A group of dogs or wolves that hunt together. 5. Any gang or band, esp. a criminal gang. 6. An ice pack. 7. A cosmetic paste for the face. 8. A wrapping of sheets or blankets used in certain water-cure treatments; also, the sheets or blankets used. 9. A parachute, fully assembled and folded for use. 10. The quantity of something, as foods, put in containers for preservation at one time or in one season. — **Syn.** See FLOCK. — *v.t.* 1. To make a pack or bundle of. 2. To place compactly in a trunk, box, etc., for storing or carrying. 3. To fill compactly, as for storing or carrying. 4. To put up for preservation or sale. 5. To compress tightly; crowd together. 6. To fill completely or to overflowing; cram. 7. To cover, fill, or surround so as to prevent leakage, damage, etc.: to *pack* a piston rod. 8. To load with a pack; burden. 9. To carry or transport on the back or on pack animals. 10. To carry or wear habitually: to *pack* a gun. 11. To send or dispatch summarily: with *off* or *away*. 12. To treat with a pack (def. 7). 13. *Slang* To be able to inflict: He *packs* a wallop. *v.i.* 14. To place one's clothes and belongings in trunks, boxes, etc., for storing or carrying. 15. To be capable of being stowed or packed. 16. To crowd together. 17. To settle in a hard, firm mass 18. To leave in haste: often with *off* or *away*. — **to send packing** To send away or dismiss summarily. [ME *pakke*, appar. < LG *pak*] — **pack′er** *n.*

pack² (pak) *v.t.* To arrange, select, or manipulate to one's own advantage: to *pack* a jury. [? < PACK¹]

pack·age (pak′ij) *n.* 1. Something packed, wrapped up, or bound together, as for transportation. 2. A box, case, or other receptacle used for packing. 3. The act of packing. 4. A combination of items considered as a unit. — *v.t.* **·aged, ·ag·ing** To arrange or tie into a package.

package store *U.S.* A store that sells liquor by the bottle.

pack animal An animal used to carry packs or burdens.

pack·et (pak′it) *n.* 1. A small package; parcel. 2. A steamship for conveying mails, passengers, and freight at stated times: also **packet boat.** — *v.t.* To make into a packet or parcel. [< AF *pacquet*, dim. of ME *pakke*]

pack·ing (pak′ing) *n.* 1. The act or operation of one who or that which packs. 2. The canning or putting up of meat, fish, fruit, etc. 3. Any material used in packing, closing a joint, stopping a wound, etc.

packing box 1. A stout box in which goods are packed. Also **packing case.** 2. *Mech.* A stuffing box.

packing plant *U.S.* A factory where meats and meat products are processed and packed. Also *U.S.* **packing house.**

pack rat A North American rat that carries off and hides small articles in its nest.

pack·sad·dle (pak′sad′l) *n.* A saddle for a pack animal, to which the packs are fastened so as to balance evenly.

pack·thread (pak′thred′) *n.* Strong thread used for wrapping.

pact (pakt) *n.* An agreement; compact. [< OF < L *pactum* agreement]

pad¹ (pad) *n.* 1. A cushion; also, any stuffed, cushionlike thing serving to protect from jarring, friction, etc. 2. A number of sheets of paper gummed together at one edge; a tablet. 3. A large floating leaf of an aquatic plant: a lily *pad*. 4. A soft cushionlike enlargement of skin on the undersurface of the toes of many animals. 5. The foot of a fox, otter, etc. 6. The footprint of an animal. 7. A launching pad. — *v.t.* **pad·ded, pad·ding** 1. To stuff, line, or protect with pads or padding. 2. To lengthen (speech or writing) by inserting unnecessary matter. 3. To add to (an expense account, voting register, etc.) for fraudulent purposes. [Origin unknown]

pad² (pad) *v.i.* **pad·ded, pad·ding** 1. To travel by walking. 2. To move with soft, almost noiseless footsteps. — *n.* A dull, padded sound, as of a footstep. [Akin to PAD³]

pad³ (pad) *n.* 1. An easy-paced road horse. 2. A highwayman. [< LG *pad* path]

pad·ding (pad′ing) *n.* 1. The act of one who or that which pads. 2. Material with which to pad. 3. Extraneous matter used in writing, etc., merely to fill space.

pad·dle (pad′l) *n.* 1. A broad-bladed implement resembling a short oar, used without a rowlock in propelling a canoe or small boat. 2. The distance covered during one trip in a canoe over a given time. 3. A flat board for inflicting bodily punishment. 4. A small, rounded, flat piece of wood with a handle, used in table tennis. 5. The act of paddling. — *v.* **·dled, ·dling** *v.i.* 1. To move a canoe, etc., on or through water by means of a paddle. 2. To row gently or lightly. 3. To swim with short, downward strokes, as ducks do. 4. To play in water with the hands or feet; wade. — *v.t.* 5. To propel by means of a paddle or paddles. 6. To convey by paddling. 7. To beat with a paddle; spank. 8. To stir. — **to paddle one's own canoe** To be independent. [ME, ? var. of *patel* < L *patella* shallow pan] — **pad′dler** *n.*

paddle board One of the broad, paddlelike boards set on the circumference of a paddle wheel or water wheel.

pad·dle·fish (pad′l·fish′) *n.* *pl.* **·fish** or **·fish·es** A large fish having a scaleless body and paddle-shaped snout, found in the Mississippi Valley streams.

paddle wheel A wheel having projecting floats or boards for propelling a vessel.

pad·dling (pad′ling) *n.* 1. The act of propelling with a paddle. 2. A beating or spanking.

pad·dock (pad′ək) *n.* 1. A pasture, lot, or enclosure for exercising horses, adjoining a stable. 2. A grassed enclosure at a racecourse where horses are walked and saddled. — *v.t.* To confine in a paddock, as horses. [Alter. of dial. E *parrock*, OE *pearruc* enclosure]

pad·dy¹ (pad′ē) *n.* *pl.* **·dies** The ruddy duck. [after *Paddy*, a proper name]

pad·dy² (pad′ē) *n.* *pl.* **·dies** Rice in the husk, whether gathered or growing. [< Malay *pādī*]

paddy wagon *U.S. Slang* A patrol wagon.

pa·di·shah (pä′di·shä) *n.* Lord protector; chief ruler: a title of the shah of Iran. Also **pad·shah** (päd′shä). [< Persian < *pati* master + *shāh* king]

pad·lock (pad′lok′) *n.* A detachable lock, having a pivoted hasp to be passed through a staple or ring and then locked. — *v.t.* To fasten with or as with a padlock. [ME]

pa·dre (pä′drā) *n.* 1. Father: a title used in Italy, Spain, and Spanish America in addressing or speaking of priests. 2. An army or navy chaplain. [< L *pater, patris* father]

pae·an (pē′ən) *n.* A song of joy or exultation. Also spelled *pean*. [< L < Gk. *paian* hymn addressed to Apollo]

paed-, paedo- See PEDO-.

paed·e·rast (ped′ər·ast), etc. See PEDERAST, etc.

pa·gan (pā′gən) *n.* 1. One who is neither a Christian, a Jew, nor a Moslem; a heathen. 2. In early Christian use, an idol worshiper. 3. An irreligious person. — *adj.* Of, pertaining to, or like pagans; heathenish. [< LL < L, orig., villager < *pagus* the country] — **pa′gan·dom** *n.* — **pa′gan·ish** *adj.* — **pa′gan·ism** *n.*

pa·gan·ize (pā′gən·īz) *v.t. & v.i.* **·ized, ·iz·ing** To make or become pagan.

page¹ (pāj) *n.* 1. A male attendant; esp., in chivalry, a lad or young man in training for knighthood, or a youth attending a royal or princely personage. 2. In Congress or other legislatures, a boy who attends upon legislators while in session. 3. A boy employed in a hotel, club, etc., to perform light duties. — *v.t.* **paged, pag·ing** 1. To seek or summon (a person) by calling his name. 2. To wait on as a page. [< OF < Ital. < Gk., < *pais, paidos* boy]

page² (pāj) *n.* 1. One side of a leaf of a book, letter, etc. 2. The printing or the type used on one side. 3. Any event or events worthy of being noted or recorded: a sad *page* in history. 4. *Usu. pl.* Any source or record of knowledge. — *v.* **paged, pag·ing** *v.t.* 1. To mark the pages of with numbers. — *v.i.* 2. To turn pages: usu. with *through*. [< F < L *pagina* written page < *pangere* to fasten]

pag·eant (paj′ənt) *n.* 1. A community outdoor celebration presenting scenes from local history and tradition. 2. An exhibition or spectacular parade devised for a public celebration. 3. A theatrical spectacle. 4. Unsubstantial display. [< Med.L *pagina* scaffold of a stage]

pag·eant·ry (paj′ən·trē) *n.* *pl.* **·ries** 1. Pageants collectively. 2. Ceremonial splendor or display. 3. Empty or showy display.

pag·i·nate (paj′ə·nāt) *v.t.* **·nat·ed, ·nat·ing** To number the pages of (a book) consecutively. [< L *pagina* page + -ATE¹]

pag·i·na·tion (paj′ə·nā′shən) *n.* 1. The numbering of the pages, as of a book. 2. The system of figures and marks used in paging.

pa·go·da (pə·gō′də) *n.* In the Far East, a sacred tower or temple, usu. pyramidal. Also **pag·od** (pag′əd, pə·god′). [< Pg. < Tamil < Skt. *bhagavati* belonging to a deity]

paid (pād) Past tense and past participle of PAY.

pail (pāl) *n.* **1.** A cylindrical vessel for carrying liquids, etc., properly having a handle; bucket. **2.** The amount carried in this vessel. [OE *paegel* wine measure] — **pail′ful′** *n.*

pail·lasse (pal·yas′, pal′yas) *n.* A mattress of straw, excelsior, etc.: also spelled *palliasse*. [< MF < L *palea* chaff]

pain (pān) *n.* **1.** The unpleasant sensation or feeling resulting from or accompanying some injury, overstrain, or obstruction of the physical powers. **2.** Any distressing or afflicting emotion. **3.** *pl.* Care, effort, etc. expended on anything: with much *pains*. **4.** *pl.* The pangs of childbirth. — **on** (or **upon** or **under**) **pain** of With the penalty of (some specified punishment). — **to take pains** To be careful; to make an effort. — *v.t.* **1.** To cause pain to; hurt. — *v.i.* **2.** To cause pain. [< OF < L < Gk. *poinē* fine, penalty]

pained (pānd) *adj.* **1.** Hurt physically or mentally; distressed. **2.** Showing pain: a *pained* expression.

pain·ful (pān′fəl) *adj.* **1.** Giving pain; distressing. **2.** Requiring labor or care; arduous. **3.** Affected with pain: said of the body. — **pain′ful·ly** *adv.* — **pain′ful·ness** *n.*

pain·less (pān′lis) *adj.* Free from pain; causing no pain. — **pain′less·ly** *adv.* — **pain′less·ness** *n.*

pains·tak·ing (pānz′tā′king, pān′stā′-) *adj.* Careful; assiduous. — *n.* Careful effort. — **pains′tak′ing·ly** *adv.*

paint (pānt) *n.* **1.** A color or pigment, either dry or mixed with oil, water, etc. **2.** A cosmetic, as rouge. **3.** Grease paint. **4.** A film, layer, or coat of pigment applied to the surface of an object; also, the dry coating of such a pigment: cracked *paint*. — *v.t.* **1.** In art: **a** To make a representation of in paints or colors. **b** To make, as a picture, by applying paints or colors. **2.** To describe vividly, as in words. **3.** To cover, coat, or decorate with paint. **4.** To apply cosmetics to. **5.** To apply (medicine, etc.) with or as with a swab. — *v.i.* **6.** To practice the art of painting; paint pictures. **7.** To apply cosmetics to the face, etc. [< OF < L *pingere* to paint] — **paint·y** (pān′tē) *adj.*

paint·brush (pānt′brush′) *n.* A brush for applying paint.

paint·ed (pān′tid) *adj.* **1.** Coated with paint. **2.** Depicted in colors. **3.** Having no reality, truth, or value; artificial.

painted bunting A brilliantly colored finch widely distributed in the southern U.S. Also **painted finch.**

paint·er¹ (pān′tər) *n.* **1.** One who covers surfaces with a coat of paint. **2.** An artist who paints in oils, etc.

paint·er² (pān′tər) *n. Naut.* A rope with which to fasten a boat by its bow. [Prob. < OF < L *pendere* to suspend]

paint·er³ (pān′tər) *n. U.S. Dial.* The puma, or cougar. [Var. of PANTHER]

paint·ing (pān′ting) *n.* **1.** The act of laying on paints with a brush. **2.** The art of creating meaningful effects on a surface by the use of pigments. **3.** A picture.

pair (pâr) *v.t.* **1.** To bring together or arrange in a pair or pairs; match; couple; mate. — *v.i.* **2.** To come together as a couple or pair. **3.** To marry or mate. — **to pair off** **1.** To separate into couples. **2.** To arrange by pairs. — *n.* **1.** Two persons or things of a kind, that are joined, related, or associated; a couple; brace. **2.** A single thing having two correspondent parts dependent on each other: a *pair* of scissors. **3.** A married couple; also, two animals mated. **4.** In legislative bodies, two opposed members who agree to abstain from voting, and so offset each other. **5.** A set of similar things making a whole: a *pair* of pajamas. **6.** In some games of cards, two cards of the same denomination: a *pair* of queens. ◆ Current usage calls for *pair* in the plural after a numeral of two or more, as, four *pairs* of shoes, though informally the singular is often used, as, four *pair* of shoes. [< F < L neut. plural of *par* equal]

Pais·ley (pāz′lē) *adj.* Made of or resembling a patterned woolen fabric originally made in Paisley, Scotland. — *n.* **1.** Paisley fabric. **2.** A Paisley shawl.

pa·ja·mas (pə·jä′məz, -jam′əz) *n. pl.* of **pa·ja·ma** (-mə) **1.** A garment consisting of loose trousers of silk, cotton, etc., and an accompanying jacket or blouse, used for sleeping. **2.** In the Orient, similar trousers worn by both men and women Also, *Brit.*, *pyjamas*. [< Hind. < Persian *pāi* leg < *jāmāh* garment]

PAISLEY DESIGN

pal (pal) *Informal* *n.* A friend or chum. — *v.i.* **palled, pal·ling** To associate as pals. [< Romany ult. < Skt. *bharatr* brother]

pal·ace (pal′is) *n.* **1.** A royal residence, or the official residence of some high dignitary, as of a bishop. **2.** Any splendid residence or stately building. [< OF < L *Palatium* Palatine Hill at Rome, on which stood the palace of Caesar Augustus]

pal·a·din (pal′ə·din) *n.* **1.** Any of the twelve peers of Charlemagne. **2.** A paragon of knighthood. [< F < Ital. < L *palatium*. See PALACE.]

palae- Var. of PALEO-.

palaeo- See PALEO-.

pal·an·quin (pal′ən·kēn′) *n.* A type of covered litter used as a means of conveyance in the Orient, borne by poles on the shoulders of two or more men. Also **pal′an·keen′.** [< Pg. < Javanese < Skt. *palyanka*]

pal·at·a·ble (pal′it·ə·bəl) *adj.* **1.** Agreeable to the taste or palate; savory. **2.** Acceptable. — **pal′at·a·bil′i·ty, pal′at·a·ble·ness** *n.* — **pal′at·a·bly** *adv.*

pal·a·tal (pal′ə·təl) *adj.* **1.** Pertaining to the palate. **2.** *Phonet.* **a** Produced by placing the front (not the tip) of the tongue near or against the hard palate, as *y* in English *yoke*. **b** Produced with the blade of the tongue near the hard palate, as *ch* in *child*, *j* in *joy*. — *n. Anat.* **1.** A bone of the palate. **2.** *Phonet.* **a** A palatal consonant. **b** A front vowel. [< F < L *palatum* palate]

pal·a·tal·ize (pal′ə·təl·īz) *v.t. & v.i.* **·ized, ·iz·ing** *Phonet.* To change a nonpalatal sound to a palatal by assimilation, as (-yo̅o̅r) to (-shər) in *censure*. — **pal′a·tal·i·za′tion** *n.*

pal·ate (pal′it) *n.* **1.** *Anat.* The roof of the mouth, consisting of the anterior **hard palate**, having a bony skeleton, and the posterior **soft palate**, that is composed of muscular tissue. For illus. see MOUTH, THROAT. **2.** The sense of taste. [< L *palatum*.]

pa·la·tial (pə·lā′shəl) *adj.* Of, like, or befitting a palace; magnificent. — **pa·la′tial·ly** *adv.*

pa·lat·i·nate (pə·lat′ə·nāt, -nit) *n.* A political division ruled over by a prince possessing certain prerogatives of royalty within his own domain.

pal·a·tine¹ (pal′ə·tīn, -tin) *adj.* Of or pertaining to the palate. — *n. Anat.* Either of the two bones forming the hard palate. [< F < L *palatum* palate]

pal·a·tine² (pal′ə·tīn, -tin) *adj.* **1.** Of or pertaining to a royal palace or its officials. **2.** Possessing royal prerogatives: a count *palatine*. — *n.* **1.** A lord exercising sovereign power over a province. **2.** A vassal exercising royal privileges over his territory. **3.** The ruler of a palatinate or county palatine. [< F < L *palatium* palace]

pa·lav·er (pə·lav′ər) *n.* **1.** Empty talk, esp. that intended to flatter or deceive. **2.** A public discussion or conference. **3.** Originally, a parley with native or aboriginal inhabitants, as by explorers. — *v.t.* **1.** To flatter; cajole. — *v.i.* **2.** To talk idly and at length. [< Pg. < LL *parabola* story, word] — **pa·lav′er·er** *n.*

pale¹ (pāl) *n.* **1.** A pointed stick or stake. **2.** A fence enclosing a piece of ground. **3.** Any boundary or limit. **4.** That which is enclosed within bounds. — *v.t.* **paled, pal·ing** To enclose with pales; fence in. [< OF < L *palus* stake]

pale² (pāl) *adj.* **1.** Of a whitish or ashen appearance. **2.** Of a very light shade of any color; lacking in brightness or intensity of color. **3.** Feeble or weak. — *v.t. & v.i.* **paled, pal·ing** To make or turn pale; blanch. [< OF < L *pallere* to be pale] — **pale′ly** *adv.* — **pale′ness** *n.*

pale·face (pāl′fās′) *n.* A white person: a term allegedly originated by North American Indians.

paleo- *combining form* **1.** Ancient; old. **2.** Primitive. Also, before vowels, **pale-.** Also *palae-, palaeo-.* [< Gk. *palaios* old, ancient]

Pa·le·o·cene (pā′lē·ə·sēn′) *Geol. adj.* Of or pertaining to the oldest epoch of the Tertiary period, preceding the Eocene. — *n.* This epoch. See chart for GEOLOGY.

pa·le·og·ra·phy (pā′lē·og′rə·fē) *n.* **1.** An ancient mode of writing; ancient writings collectively. **2.** The science of describing or deciphering ancient writings. — **pa′le·og′ra·pher** *n.* — **pa′le·o·graph′ic** (-ə·graf′ik) or **·i·cal** *adj.*

Pa·le·o·lith·ic (pā′lē·ō·lith′ik) *adj. Anthropol.* Designating, pertaining to, or associated with a period of human culture preceding the Mesolithic and characterized by chipped or flaked stone implements, cave paintings, etc.

pa·le·ol·o·gy (pā′lē·ol′ə·jē) *n.* The study of antiquity or antiquities; archeology. — **pa′le·o·log′i·cal** (-ə·loj′i·kəl) *adj.* — **pa′le·ol′o·gist** *n.*

pa·le·on·tol·o·gy (pā′lē·on·tol′ə·jē) *n. pl.* **·gies** **1.** The science that treats of ancient forms of life or of fossil organisms. **2.** A work dealing with this subject. [< PALEO- + Gk. *ōn, ontos* being, ppr. of *einai* to be + -LOGY] — **pa′le·on′to·log′ic** (-on′tə·loj′ik) or **·i·cal** *adj.* — **pa′le·on·tol′o·gist** *n.*

Pa·le·o·zo·ic (pā′lē·ō·zō′ik) *adj. Geol.* Of or pertaining to the era following the Pre-Cambrian and preceding the Mesozoic. — *n.* The Paleozoic era, with its life forms and rock systems. See chart for GEOLOGY. [< PALEO- + Gk. *zōē* life]

Pal·es·tine (pal′is·tīn) In Biblical times, a territory on the eastern coast of the Mediterranean, the country of the Jews: Old Testament *Canaan*: also *Holy Land*. — **Pal′es·tin′i·an** (-tin′ē·ən) *adj. & n.*

pa·les·tra (pə·les′trə) *n. pl.* **·trae** (-trē) In ancient Greece, a school or practice place for athletics. [< L < Gk. < *palaiein* to wrestle] — **pa·les′tral, pa·les′tri·an** *adj.*

pal·ette (pal′it) *n.* **1.** A thin board or tablet with a hole for the thumb, upon which artists lay and mix their colors **2.** The range of colors characteristic of a particular artist, painting, etc. Also spelled *pallet*. [< F < L *pala* spade]

Pa·li (pä'lē) *n.* The sacred language of the early Buddhist writings, still surviving in the religious literature of Burma and Thailand. [< Skt. *pāli (bhasa)* canonical (language)]

pal·imp·sest (pal'imp·sest) *n.* A parchment, manuscript, etc., written upon two or three times, the earlier writing having been wholly or partially erased to make room for the next. [< L < Gk. < *palin* again + *psaein* to rub]

pal·in·drome (pal'in·drōm) *n.* A word, sentence, verse, etc., that is the same read forward or backward, as "Madam, I'm Adam." [< Gk. < *palin* again + *dromos* run]

pal·ing (pā'ling) *n.* 1. One of a series of upright pales forming a fence. 2. Pales or pickets collectively. 3. A fence or enclosure made of pales or pickets. 4. The act of erecting a fence with pales.

pal·i·sade (pal'ə·sād') *n.* 1. A barrier or fortification made of strong timbers set in the ground. 2. One of the stakes forming such a barrier. 3. *pl.* An extended cliff or rocky precipice. — *v.t.* **·sad·ed, ·sad·ing** To enclose or fortify with a palisade. [< MF < Provençal < L *palus* stake]

pal·ish (pāl'ish) *adj.* Somewhat pale.

pall[1] (pôl) *n.* 1. A covering, usu. of black cloth, thrown over a coffin or over a tomb. 2. A dark, heavy covering, cloud, etc. 3. A gloomy or oppressive atmosphere, effect, etc. 4. *Eccl.* **a** A chalice cover, consisting of a square piece of cardboard faced on both sides with lawn or linen. **b** An altar cloth. — *v.t.* To cover with or as with a pall. [OE < L *pallium* cloak]

pall[2] (pôl) *v.i.* 1. To become insipid or uninteresting. 2. To have a dulling or displeasing effect: followed by *on.* — *v.t.* 3. To satiate; cloy. [Appar. aphetic var. of APPALL]

Pal·la·di·an (pə·lā'dē·ən) *adj.* 1. Pertaining to or characteristic of the goddess Pallas. 2. Characterized by wisdom or learning. [< L < Gk. *Palladios* of Pallas]

pal·la·di·um[1] (pə·lā'dē·əm) *n.* *pl.* **·di·a** (-dē·ə) Any object considered essential to the safety of a community or organization; a safeguard. [< PALLADIUM]

pal·la·di·um[2] (pə·lā'dē·əm) *n.* A rare, silver-white, malleable and ductile metallic element (symbol Pd) occurring in combination with platinum, iridium, and rhodium. See ELEMENT. [< NL, after the asteroid *Pallas*]

Pal·la·di·um (pə·lā'dē·əm) In Greek and Roman legend, a statue of Pallas Athena, esp. one in Troy, on the preservation of which the safety of the city depended.

Pal·las (pal'əs) In Greek mythology, a name of Athena, the goddess of wisdom: often **Pallas Athena.** — *n.* The second largest asteroid. [< Gk., prob. orig. maiden]

pall·bear·er (pôl'bâr'ər) *n.* One who forms part of an escort for a coffin at a funeral.

pal·let[1] (pal'it) *n.* 1. *Mech.* **a** A click or pawl used to regulate the motion of a ratchet wheel, etc., as by converting reciprocating into rotary motion, or the reverse. **b** The lip or point of a pawl. 2. A paddle for mixing and shaping clay for crucibles, etc. 3. A tool used in gilding the backs of books or for taking up gold leaf. 4. A painter's palette. [< F < L *pala* spade]

pal·let[2] (pal'it) *n.* 1. A small, mean bed or mattress, usu. of straw. 2. A blanket laid on the floor for a bed. [< OF < L *palea* chaff, straw]

pal·liasse (pal·yas', pal'yas) See PAILLASSE.

pal·li·ate (pal'ē·āt) *v.t.* **·at·ed, ·at·ing** 1. To cause (a crime, fault, etc.) to appear less serious or offensive. 2. To relieve the symptoms or effects of (a disease, etc.) without curing. [< L *palliatus,* pp. of *palliare* to cloak] — **pal'li·a'tion** *n.* — **pal'li·a'tive** *adj. & n.* — **pal'li·a'tor** *n.*

pal·lid (pal'id) *adj.* Of a pale or wan appearance; weak or lacking in color. [< L < *pallere* to be pale] — **pal'lid·ly** *adv.* — **pal'lid·ness** *n.*

pal·lor (pal'ər) *n.* The state of being pale or pallid; paleness. [< L < *pallere* to be pale]

palm[1] (päm) *n.* 1. The inner surface of the hand between the wrist and the base of the fingers. 2. A linear measure equal to the approximate breadth (3 or 4 inches) or length (about 8½ inches) of the hand. 3. That which covers the palm, as part of a glove. 4. The flattened terminal portion of the antler of a moose, etc. 5. The flat, expanding end of any armlike projection, as the blade of an oar. — *v.t.* 1. To hide (cards, dice, etc.) in or about the hand, as in sleight of hand. 2. To handle or touch with the palm. — **to palm off** To pass off or impose fraudulently. [< F < OF < L *palma*]

palm[2] (päm) *n.* 1. Any of a large and varied group of tropical evergreen trees or shrubs usu. having an unbranched trunk topped by a crown of large palmate or pinnate leaves. 2. A leaf or branch of the palm, used as a symbol of victory or joy. 3. Triumph; victory. [OE < L *palma* palm tree]

pal·ma·ceous (pal·mā'shəs, pä·mā'-) *adj.* Belonging to or characteristic of the group of plants comprising the palms.

pal·mar (pal'mər, pä'mər) *adj.* Of, pertaining to, or similar to the palm of the hand.

pal·mate (pal'māt, pä'māt) *adj.* 1. Resembling an open hand. 2. Broad and flat, with fingerlike projections, as the antlers of the moose, or some corals. 3. *Bot.* Having lobes that diverge from the apex of the petiole: a *palmate* leaf. 4. *Zool.* Webbed, as a bird's foot. Also **pal'mat·ed.** [< L *palmatus,* pp. of *palmare* to mark with the palm of the hand] — **pal'mate·ly** *adv.* — **pal·ma'tion** *n.*

palm·er (pä'mər) *n.* In the Middle Ages, one who had visited Palestine and brought back a palm branch as a token of the pilgrimage.

pal·met·to (pal·met'ō) *n.* *pl.* **·tos** or **·toes** Any of various palms having fanlike foliage. [< Sp. *palmito,* dim. of *palma* palm tree < L]

Palmetto State Nickname of South Carolina.

palmi- *combining form* Palm. [< L *palma* palm]

palm·ist (pä'mist) *n.* One who practices palmistry.

palm·is·try (pä'mis·trē) *n.* The art or practice of supposedly discovering a person's past or future from the lines and marks in the palm of the hand. [ME < *palme* palm + *-estrie,* prob. < OF *maistrie* mastery]

palm oil A yellowish, butterlike oil obtained from the fruit of several varieties of palm, and used in the manufacture of soap, candles, etc.

palm sugar Sugar made from palm sap.

Palm Sunday The Sunday before Easter, being the last Sunday in Lent and the first day in Holy Week. [Named for Christ's triumphal entry into Jerusalem, when palm branches were strewn before him]

palm·y (pä'mē) *adj.* **palm·i·er, palm·i·est** 1. Marked by prosperity; flourishing. 2. Abounding in palms.

pal·my·ra (pal·mī'rə) *n.* An East Indian palm having large fan-shaped leaves. [< Pg. *palmeira* palm tree]

pal·o·mi·no (pal'ə·mē'nō) *n.* *pl.* **·nos** A light tan or golden brown horse with a cream-colored mane and tail. [< Am. Sp., orig., dove-colored horse < Sp. < L *palumbus* ringdove]

pa·loo·ka (pə·loō'kə) *n.* *U.S. Slang* 1. An inferior or bungling pugilist. 2. A lout; lummox. [Coined by Jack Conway, U.S. journalist, d. 1928; ult. origin uncertain]

palp (palp) *n.* A palpus. [< F < L *palpus* feeler]

pal·pa·ble (pal'pə·bəl) *adj.* 1. Capable of being touched or felt. 2. Readily perceived; obvious. 3. Perceptible by touching. [< LL < L *palpare* to touch] — **pal'pa·bil'i·ty, pal'pa·ble·ness** *n.* — **pal'pa·bly** *adv.*

pal·pate (pal'pāt) *v.t.* **·pat·ed, ·pat·ing** To feel or examine by touch, esp. for medical diagnosis. — *adj.* Having a palpus or palpi. [< L *palpare* to touch] — **pal·pa'tion** *n.*

pal·pi·tate (pal'pə·tāt) *v.i.* **·tat·ed, ·tat·ing** 1. To quiver; tremble. 2. To beat more rapidly than normal; flutter: said esp. of the heart. [< L *palpitatus,* pp. of *palpitare* to tremble, freq. of *palpare* to touch] — **pal'pi·ta'tion** *n.*

pal·pus (pal'pəs) *n.* *pl.* **·pi** (-pī) *Zool.* A feeler; esp., one of the jointed sense organs attached to the mouth parts of arthropods: also called *palp.* [< NL < L *palpus* feeler]

pal·sied (pôl'zēd) *adj.* Affected with palsy; trembling.

pal·sy (pôl'zē) *n.* *pl.* **·sies** 1. Paralysis. 2. Any impairment or loss of ability to control movement. — *v.t.* **·sied, ·sy·ing** 1. To paralyze. 2. To cause to tremble or become helpless, as from fear or rage. [< OF < L *paralysis*]

pal·ter (pôl'tər) *v.i.* 1. To speak or act insincerely; equivocate; lie. 2. To be fickle or capricious; trifle. 3. To haggle or quibble. [Origin unknown] — **pal'ter·er** *n.*

pal·try (pôl'trē) *adj.* **·tri·er, ·tri·est** 1. Having little or no worth or value; trifling; trivial. 2. Contemptible; petty. [< LG < *palte* rag.] — **pal'tri·ly** *adv.* — **pal'tri·ness** *n.*

pa·lu·dal (pə·loōd'l) *adj.* Pertaining to a marsh; swampy. [< L *palus, paludis* marsh]

pam·pas (pam'pəz, Sp. päm'päs) *n.pl.* The great treeless plains south of the Amazon river, extending from the Atlantic to the Andes. [< Sp. < Quechua *pampa* plain]

pam·pe·an (pam'pē·ən, pam·pē'ən) *adj.* Of or pertaining to the pampas or to their native inhabitants. — *n.* An Indian of the pampas.

pam·per (pam'pər) *v.t.* To treat very indulgently; gratify the whims or wishes of; coddle. [Appar. < LG < *pampen* to live luxuriously] — **pam'per·er** *n.*

pam·phlet (pam'flit) *n.* 1. A printed work stitched or pasted, but not permanently bound. 2. A brief treatise or essay, often on a subject of current interest, printed and published without a binding. [< OF *pamphilet,* dim. of *Pamphilus,* title of a 12th c. Latin love poem]

pam·phlet·eer (pam'flə·tir') *n.* One who writes pamphlets: sometimes a term of contempt. — *v.i.* To write and issue pamphlets.

pan[1] (pan) *n.* 1. A wide, shallow vessel, usu. of metal, used for holding liquids or in cooking. 2. Any similar receptacle or vessel, as one used for boiling and evaporating. 3. A circular iron dish with sloping sides, in which gold is separated. 4. The powder cavity of a flintlock. 5. The skull; brainpan.

6. Hardpan.   **7.** Either of the two receptacles on a pair of scales or a balance. — *v.* **panned, pan·ning** *v.t.* **1.** To separate (gold) by washing gold-bearing earth in a pan. **2.** To wash (earth, gravel, etc.) for this purpose. **3.** To cook and serve in a pan. **4.** *Informal* To criticize severely. — *v.i.* **5.** To search for gold by washing earth, gravel, etc., in a pan. **6.** To yield gold, as earth. — **to pan out** *U.S. Informal* To succeed. [OE < Gmc. < LL < L < Gk. *patanē*]

pan² (pan)   *v.t.* **panned, pan·ning** To move (a motion-picture or television camera) so as to photograph an entire scene, follow a particular character, etc. [< PANORAMA]

pan- *combining form* **1.** All; every; the whole: *panchromatic.* **2.** Comprising, including, or applying to all: usually capitalized when preceding proper nouns or adjectives, as in: **Pan-African, Pan-Asia, Pan-Arab.** [< Gk., neut. of *pas* all]

Pan (pan)   In Greek mythology, a god identified with the Roman *Faunus.*

pan·a·ce·a (pan′ə·sē′ə)   *n.* A remedy for all diseases or ills; a cure-all. [< L < Gk. < *pan*, neut. of *pas* all + *akos* cure] — **pan′a·ce′an** *adj.*

Panama hat   A hat woven from the leaves of a palmlike tree of Central and South America.

Pan·a·ma·ni·an (pan′ə·mā′nē·ən, -mä′-)   *adj.* Of or pertaining to the Isthmus of Panama or its inhabitants. — *n.* A native or naturalized inhabitant of Panama. Also **Pan·a·man** (pan′ə·män′).

Pan-A·mer·i·can (pan′ə·mer′ə·kən)   *adj.* Including or pertaining to the whole of America, both North and South, or to all Americans. Also **Pan American.**

Pan-A·mer·i·can·ism (pan′ə·mer′ə·kən·iz′əm)   *n.* The advocacy of a closer political and economic cooperation among the republics of the western hemisphere.

Pan American Union   A bureau established in Washington, D.C., in 1890, by the 21 American republics to promote mutual peace.

pan·a·tel·a (pan′ə·tel′ə)   See PANETELA.

pan-broil (pan′broil′)   *v.t. & v.i.* To cook in a heavy frying pan placed over direct heat, using little or no fat.

pan·cake (pan′kāk′)   *n.* **1.** A thin, flat cake made from batter fried in a pan or baked on a griddle. **2.** A cosmetic resembling face powder: also **pancake make-up.** **3.** *Aeron.* An abrupt landing in which an airplane is leveled off and stalled well above the surface so that it drops flat. — *v.i.* **·caked, ·cak·ing** *Aeron.* To make a pancake landing.

pan·chro·mat·ic (pan′krō·mat′ik)   *adj. Photog.* Sensitive to light of all colors of the spectrum, as film or a plate. — **pan·chro′ma·tism** (-krō′mə·tiz′əm) *n.*

pan·cre·as (pan′krē·əs, pang′-)   *n. Anat.* A large gland situated behind the lower part of the stomach, secreting digestive enzymes into the duodenum and producing insulin in the islands of Langerhans. [< NL < Gk. < *pan-* all + *kreas* flesh] — **pan′cre·at′ic** (-at′ik) *adj.*

pan·da (pan′də)   *n. pl.* **·das** or **·da** **1.** A small, raccoonlike carnivore of the southeastern Himalayas, with long reddish brown fur and ringed tail: also called *bearcat.* **2.** A large, bearlike mammal of Tibet and China, with black-and-white coat and rings around the eyes: also called *giant panda.* [Prob. < Nepalese]

GIANT PANDA
(5 feet long; 2 feet high at shoulder)

Pan·de·an (pan·dē′ən)   *adj.* Of or pertaining to the god Pan.

pan·dem·ic (pan·dem′ik)   *adj.* **1.** *Med.* Widely epidemic. **2.** Universal; general. — *n.* A pandemic disease. [< Gk. < *pan-* all + *dēmos* people]

pan·de·mo·ni·um (pan′də·mō′nē·əm)   *n.* **1.** The abode of all demons. **2.** Loosely, hell. **3.** A place marked by disorder and uproar. **4.** Riotous uproar. Also **pan′dae·mo′ni·um.** [< NL < Gk. *pan-* all + *daimōn* demon]

pan·der (pan′dər)   *n.* **1.** A go-between in sexual intrigues; pimp. **2.** One who ministers to the passions or base desires of others. Also **pan′der·er.** — *v.i.* **1.** To act as a pander. — *v.t.* **2.** To act as a pander for. [< L < Gk. *Pandaros*; orig. < *Pandare*, character in Chaucer's Troilus and Criseyde]

Pan·do·ra (pan·dôr′ə, -dō′rə)   In Greek mythology, the first mortal woman, who brought with her a box (**Pandora's box**) containing all human ills which, when she opened the lid, escaped into the world. [< Gk., all-gifted]

pan·dow·dy (pan·dou′dē)   *n. pl.* **·dies** *U.S.* A deep-dish pie or pudding make of baked sliced apples and having only a top crust. Also **apple pandowdy.** [Origin unknown]

pane (pān)   *n.* **1.** One of the sections of a window, door, etc., filled with a sheet of glass. **2.** A sheet of glass for such a section. **3.** One of the flat surfaces on an object having several sides, as a nut, bolthead, or cut diamond. **4.** A panel in a door, ceiling, etc. [< OF < L *pannus* piece of cloth]

pan·e·gyr·ic (pan′ə·jir′ik)   *n.* **1.** A formal public eulogy, either written or spoken. **2.** Elaborate praise; laudation. [< MF < L < Gk. < *pan-* all + *agyris* assembly] — **pan′·e·gyr′i·cal** *adj.*   **pan′e·gyr′i·cal·ly** *adv.*

pan·e·gyr·ist (pan′ə·jir′ist)   *n.* One who panegyrizes.

pan·e·gy·rize (pan′ə·jə·rīz′)   *v.* **·rized, ·riz·ing** *v.t.* **1.** To deliver or write a panegyric upon; eulogize. — *v.i.* **2.** To make panegyrics.

pan·el (pan′əl)   *n.* **1.** A rectangular or square piece forming part of a wainscot, ceiling, door, etc., usu. raised above or sunk below the general level, surrounded by a molding, etc. **2.** A window pane. **3.** One or more pieces of the same or different fabric inserted lengthwise in a woman's skirt. **4.** A tablet of wood used as the surface for an oil painting; also, the picture painted on such a tablet. **5.** A picture very long for its width. **6.** *Law* **a** The official list of persons summoned for jury duty. **b** The body of persons composing a jury **7.** A small group of persons selected to hold a discussion, judge a contest, etc. **8.** An instrument panel. — *v.t.* **pan·eled** or **·elled, pan·el·ing** or **·el·ling 1.** To fit, furnish, or adorn with panels. **2.** To divide into panels. [< OF < Med.L < L *pannus* piece of cloth]

panel discussion   A discussion before an audience of a specific topic by a group of selected speakers.

pan·el·ing (pan′əl·ing)   *n.* **1.** Wood or other materials used in making panels. **2.** Panels collectively. Also **pan′el·ling.**

pan·el·ist (pan′əl·ist)   *n.* A person serving on a panel.

pan·e·tel·a (pan′ə·tel′ə)   *n.* A long, slender cigar: also spelled *panatela.* Also **pan′e·tel′la.** [< Sp.]

pan fish   Any little fish that can be fried whole.

pang (pang)   *n.* **1.** A sudden sharp pain. **2.** A spasm of mental anguish. [Origin unknown]

pan·go·lin (pang·gō′lin)   *n.* A heavily armored, typically long-tailed toothless mammal of Asia and Africa: also called *scaly anteater.* [< Malay *peng-gōling* roller, in ref. to its power of rolling itself up]

pan·han·dle¹ (pan′han′dəl)   *v.i.* **·dled, ·dling** *U.S. Informal* To beg, esp. on the street. [PAN-HAN-DLER]

pan·han·dle² (pan′han′dəl)   *n.* **1.** The handle of a pan. **2.** *Usu. cap. U.S.* A narrow strip of land shaped like the handle of a pan, as in Texas or West Virginia.

pan·han·dler (pan′han′dlər)   *n. U.S. Informal* A beggar. [< PAN¹ (used to receive alms) + HANDLE, v.]

Pan-Hel·len·ic (pan′he·len′ik)   *adj.* **1.** Of or pertaining to all Greeks. **2.** Of college fraternities or sororities.

pan·ic (pan′ik)   *n.* **1.** A sudden, unreasonable, overpowering fear, esp. when affecting a large number simultaneously. **2.** An instance of such fear. — *adj.* **1.** Of the nature of or resulting from panic. **2.** *Usu. cap.* Of or pertaining to the Greek god Pan. — *v.t. & v.i.* **·icked, ·ick·ing** To affect or become affected with panic. [< MF < Gk. *panikos* of or for the god Pan, who was believed to cause sudden or groundless fear] — **pan′ick·y** *adj.*

pan·i·cle (pan′i·kəl)   *n. Bot.* A loose compound flower cluster, produced by irregular branching. [< L *panicula*, dim. of *panus* swelling]

pan·ic-strick·en (pan′ik·strik′ən)   *adj.* Overcome by panic. Also **pan′ic-struck′** (-struk′).

pa·nic·u·late (pə·nik′yə·lāt, -lit)   *adj. Bot.* Arranged in panicles. Also **pa·nic′u·lat′ed.** — **pa·nic′u·late·ly** *adv.*

pan·jan·drum (pan·jan′drəm)   *n.* A mock title for an official of exaggerated importance or great pretensions. [Coined by Samuel Foote, 1720–1777, English dramatist and actor]

pan·nier (pan′yər)   *n.* **1.** One of a pair of baskets adapted to be slung on both sides of a beast of burden. **2.** A basket for carrying a load on the back. **3.** A light framework for extending a woman's dress at the hips; also, a skirt or overskirt so extended. [< MF < L *panarium* bread basket]

pa·no·cha (pə·nō′chə)   *n.* A coarse Mexican sugar. Also **pa·no′che.** [< Am. Sp., dim. of Sp. *pan*]

pan·o·ply (pan′ə·plē)   *n. pl.* **·plies 1.** The complete equipment of a warrior. **2.** Any complete covering that protects or arrays. [< Gk. *panoplia* full armor] — **pan′o·plied** *adj.*

pan·o·ram·a (pan′ə·ram′ə, -rä′mə)   *n.* **1.** A series of pictures representing a continuous scene, arranged to unroll and pass before the spectator. **2.** A complete view in every direction; also, a complete or comprehensive view of a subject or of passing events. [< PAN- + Gk. *horama* sight] — **pan′o·ram′ic** *adj.* — **pan′o·ram′i·cal·ly** *adv.*

pan·pipe (pan′pīp′)   *n. Sometimes cap. Often pl.* An instrument consisting of a graduated series of short flutes, originally reeds, bound together in proper order to produce a scale.

Pan-Slav·ism (pan′slō′viz·əm)   *n.* The idea of uniting all Slavic peoples, esp. under the hegemony of Russia. — **Pan′-Slav′ic** *adj.* — **Pan′-slav′ist** *n.*

pan·sy (pan′zē)   *n. pl.* **·sies 1.** A garden violet having blossoms of a variety of colors. **2.** *U.S. Slang* An effeminate or homosexual man. [< MF *pensée* thought]

pant (pant)   *v.i.* **1.** To breathe rapidly or spasmodically; gasp for breath. **2.** To emit smoke, steam, etc., in loud puffs. **3.** To gasp with desire; yearn: with *for* or *after.* **4.** To beat or pulsate rapidly. — *v.t.* **5.** To breathe out or utter gaspingly. — *n.* **1.** The act of panting. **2.** A gasp. **3.** A throb, as of the heart. **4.** A puff, as from an engine. [Appar. < OF, ult. < L *phantasiare* to have a nightmare]

pant- Var. of PANTO-.

pan·ta·lets (pan′tə·lets′) *n.pl.* **1.** Formerly, long ruffled or embroidered drawers extending below the hem of the skirt **2.** Separate frilled leg coverings to be attached to drawers. Also **pan′ta·lettes′.** [Dim. of PANTALOON]

pan·ta·loon (pan′tə·lōōn′) *n. pl.* Formerly, a tight-fitting garment for the hips and legs; trousers. [< MF < Ital. *pantalone* clown < *Pantaleone*, popular Venetian saint]

Pan·ta·loon (pan′tə·lōōn′) In early Italian comedy, a skinny, foolish old man wearing pantaloons.

pan·the·ism (pan′thē·iz′əm) *n.* **1.** The doctrine that the whole universe is God, or that every part of the universe is a manifestation of God. **2.** Worship of all the gods. [<PAN- + Gk. *theos* god] **—pan′the·ist** *n.* **—pan′the·is′tic, pan′the·is′ti·cal** *adj.* **—pan′the·is′ti·cal·ly** *adv.*

pan·the·on (pan′thē·on) *n.* **1.** All the gods of a people collectively. **2.** A mausoleum or temple commemorating the great of a nation. [< L < Gk. < *pan-* all + *theios* of or sacred to a god]

Pan·the·on (pan′thē·on) A circular domed temple at Rome, dedicated to all the gods, built in 27 B.C., rebuilt A.D. 120–124, and since A.D. 609 used as a church.

pan·ther (pan′thər) *n.* **1.** A leopard, esp. the black variety of Asia. **2.** The puma or cougar. **3.** The jaguar. [< OF < L < Gk. *panthēr*] **—pan′ther·ess** *n.fem.*

pant·ies (pan′tēz) *n.pl.* A woman's or child's underpants.

panto- *combining form* All; every. Also, before vowels, *pant-*. [< Gk. *pantos*, genitive of *pas* all]

pan·to·graph (pan′tə·graf, -gräf) *n.* An instrument used for copying drawings, maps, etc., to any scale. **—pant′o·graph′ic** or **-i·cal** *adj.* **—pan·tog·ra·phy** (pan·tog′rə·fē) *n.*

pan·to·mime (pan′tə·mīm) *n.* **1.** Any play in which the actors express their meaning by action without dialogue. **2.** Gestures without speech. **3.** In ancient Roman drama, a part of a play in which the actor used only gestures to the accompaniment of the chorus. **—v.t. & v.i.** mimed, mim·ing To act or express in pantomime. [< F < L < Gk. < *panto(s)* of all + *mimos* imitator] **—pan′to·mim′ic** (-mim′ik) or **-i·cal** *adj.* **—pan′to·mi′mist** (-mī′mist) *n.*

pan·try (pan′trē) *n. pl.* **·tries** A room or closet for provisions, dishes, table linen, etc. [ME < OF < L *panis* bread]

pants (pants) *n.pl. Chiefly U.S.* **1.** Trousers. **2.** Drawers; underpants. [Short for PANTALOONS]

pan·ty·waist (pan′tē·wāst′) *n.* **1.** A child's waist on which to fasten short pants. **2.** *Slang* An effeminate young man.

pan·zer (pan′zər, *Ger.* pän′tsər) *adj.* Armored; also, using armored tanks or mechanized troops. [< G, armor plating < MHG < OF < Ital. *panzia* belly]

pap¹ (pap) *n. Archaic* A teat; nipple. [ME *pappe*]

pap² (pap) *n.* **1.** Any soft food for babies. **2.** *Slang* The fees and privileges of public office. [Prob. akin to L *pappa*]

pa·pa (pä′pə, pə·pä′) *n.* Father: used familiarly. [< F < L < Gk. *papas*, child's word for father]

pa·pa·cy (pā′pə·sē) *n. pl.* **·cies** **1.** The dignity, office, or jurisdiction of the pope. **2.** The succession of popes. **3.** The period during which a pope is in office. [< Med.L < Gk. *papas* father]

Pa·pa·cy (pā′pə·sē) *n.* The Roman Catholic system of church government.

pa·pal (pā′pəl) *adj.* **1.** Of, pertaining to, or ordered by the pope. **2.** Of or pertaining to the papacy. **3.** Of or pertaining to the Roman Catholic Church.

Papal cross A cross having three crossbars or transoms, the top one the shortest and the bottom one the longest.

pa·paw (pə·pô′, pô′pô) *n.* **1.** The fleshy, edible fruit of a North American shrub or small tree. **2.** The tree bearing this fruit. Also spelled *pawpaw.* [< PAPAYA]

pa·pa·ya (pä·pä′yä, pə·pä′yə) *n.* **1.** The yellow, melonlike fruit of a tropical American evergreen tree, valued for its flavor and nutritious qualities. **2.** The tree bearing this fruit. [< Sp. and Pg.; ult of Carib origin]

pa·per (pā′pər) *n.* **1.** A substance made from pulp obtained from rags, wood, bark, etc., usu. formed into thin sheets for writing, printing, wrapping, etc. **2.** A sheet of this material. **3.** Something similar in appearance to paper, as papier-mâché. **4.** Wallpaper. **5.** A small paper wrapper or card holding a limited number or amount: a *paper* of pins. **6.** A printed or written document. **7.** A newspaper. **8.** A written discourse or treatise. **9.** In schools and colleges, a piece of written work, as an assignment, a report, etc. **10.** *pl.* A collection of letters, diaries, and other writings, especially by one person. **11.** *pl.* Personal documents or identification; credentials. **12.** *pl.* A ship's papers. **13.** In business, written or printed pledges to pay, that are negotiable. **14.** *Slang* Free passes to a theater, etc.; also, an audience so admitted. **15.** *pl. U.S.* Documents leading to naturalization: see FIRST PAPERS, SECOND PAPERS. **— on paper 1.** In written or printed form. **2.** In theory, as

distinguished from fact. **—v.t. 1.** To cover with wallpaper. **2.** To fold or enclose in paper. **3.** To supply with paper. **4.** *Slang* To issue free tickets of admission to (a place of amusement). **—adj. 1.** Made of paper. **2.** Existing only in writing. [< OF < L *papyrus*] **—pa′per·y** *adj.*

pa·per·back (pā′pər·bak′) *adj.* Of books, having a flexible paper cover or binding. **—n.** A book so bound.

pa·per·hang·er (pā′pər·hang′ər) *n.* One whose business is to cover walls, etc., with paper. **—pa′per·hang′ing** *n.*

pa·per·knife (pā′pər·nif′) *n. pl.* **·knives** (-nīvz′) A dull blade for opening letters, leaves of books, etc.

paper money Currency consisting of paper imprinted with certain fixed values issued by a government or by authorized banks for circulation as a substitute for metallic money.

paper nautilus One of various eight-armed marine mollusks having delicate shells.

pa·per·weight (pā′pər·wāt′) *n.* A small, heavy object, often ornamental, placed on loose papers to secure them.

pap·er·work (pā′pər·wûrk′) *n.* Work involving the preparation or handling of reports, letters, forms, etc.

pa·pier-mâ·ché (pā′pər·mə·shā′, *Fr.* pá·pyā·mä·shā′) *n.* A material consisting of paper pulp mixed with size, paste, oil, resin, etc., that can be molded into various shapes when wet and that becomes hard when dry. [< F *papier* paper + *mâché,* pp. of *mâcher* to chew]

pa·pil·la (pə·pil′ə) *n. pl.* **·pil·lae** (-pil·ē) **1.** *Anat.* **a** The nipple. **b** Any small nipplelike process of connective tissue, as on the tongue or at the root of a hair. **2.** *Bot.* A small nipple-shaped projection. [< L] **—pap·il·la·ry** (pap′ə·ler′ē) *adj.*

pap·il·lo·ma (pap′ə·lō′mə) *n. pl.* **·ma·ta** (-mə·tə) *Pathol.* An abnormality of the skin or mucous membrane consisting of tumorous outgrowths, as corns, warts, etc. [< PAPILLA]

pap·il·lose (pap′ə·lōs) *adj.* Having many papillae. **—pap′il·los′i·ty** (-los′ə·tē) *n.*

pa·pist (pā′pist) *n.* An adherent of the papacy; a Roman Catholic: usu. a disparaging term. [See PAPACY.] **—pa·pis·ti·cal** (pə·pis′ti·kal), **pa·pis′tic** *adj.* **—pa′pis·try** *n.*

pa·poose (pa·pōōs′) *n.* A North American Indian infant or small child. Also **pap·poose′.** [< Algonquian *papoos*]

pap·pus (pap′əs) *n. pl.* **pap·pi** (pap′ī) *Bot.* A downy tuft of hairs, as in thistles, or on certain fruits. [< NL < Gk. *pappos* grandfather] **—pap′pose** (-ōs), **pap′pous** (-əs) *adj.*

pap·py (pap′ē) *n. pl.* **·pies** Papa; father. [Dim. of PAPA¹]

pa·pri·ka (pa·prē′kə, pap′rə·kə) *n.* A condiment made from the ripe fruit of a mild variety of red pepper. Also **pa·pri′ca.** [< Magyar, red pepper]

Pap·u·an (pä′pōō·ən, pap′ōō·ən) *adj.* Of or pertaining to the Island of Papua or to the Papuan peoples. **—n.** A member of any of the dark peoples inhabiting Melanesia.

pap·u·la (pap′yə·lə) *n. pl.* **·lae** (-lē) *Pathol.* A pimple. Also **pap′ule** (-yōōl). [< L, pimple] **—pap′u·lan** *adj.*

pa·py·rus (pə·pī′rəs) *n. pl.* **·ri** (-rī) **1.** A tall rushlike aquatic plant of the sedge family, formerly common in Egypt. **2.** A type of writing paper made by the ancient Egyptians from this plant. **3.** A manuscript written on this material. [< L < Gk. *papyros*]

par (pär) *n.* **1.** An accepted standard or level used for comparison: usu. preceded by *on* or *upon:* His work is on a *par* with that of the other students. **2.** The normal average in amount, quality, or degree: His health is up to *par.* **3.** In commerce, the state of equality between the nominal, or face, value and the market value of shares of stock, bonds, bills of exchange, etc: also *parity.* **4.** In golf, the number of strokes allotted to a hole or round when played perfectly. **—adj. 1.** Normal; average. **2.** In commerce, having the face value normal. [< L, equal]

para-¹ *prefix* **1.** Beside; nearby; along with: *paradigm.* **2.** Beyond; aside from: amiss: *paradox.* **3.** *Chem.* A modification of or a compound similar to (not necessarily isomeric or polymeric): *paramorphine.* **4.** *Med.* **a** A functionally disordered or diseased condition: *paraplegia.* **b** Similar to but not identical with a true condition or form: *paratyphoid.* Also, before vowels and *h,* usu. **par-.** [< Gk. *para* beside]

para-² *combining form* Shelter or protection against: *parasol.* [< Ital *para,* imperative of *parare* to defend]

par·a·a·mi·no·ben·zo·ic acid (par′ə·ə·mē′nō·ben·zō′ik, -am′ə·nō-) *Biochem.* A colorless crystalline compound, $C_7H_7NO_2$, forming part of the vitamin B complex, present in yeast and also made synthetically.

par·a·ble (par′ə·bəl) *n.* A short narrative making a moral or religious point by comparison with natural or homely things. [< OF < LL < Gk. *parabolē* a placing side by side]

pa·rab·o·la (pə·rab′ə·lə) *n. Math.* The curve formed by the edges of a plane when cutting through a right circular cone at an angle parallel to one of its sides. [< L < Gk. *parabolē* a placing side by side]

par·a·bol·ic (par′ə·bol′ik) *adj.* **1.** Pertaining to or having the nature of a parable. **2.** Pertaining to or like a parabola. Also **par′a·bol′i·cal.** — **par′a·bol′i·cal·ly** adv.

pa·rab·o·lize (pə-rab′ə-līz) v.t. **·lized, ·liz·ing 1.** To relate in parable form. **2.** Math. To give the form of a parabola to.

par·a·chute (par′ə-shōōt) n. A large, umbrella-shaped apparatus for retarding the speed of a body descending through the air, esp. from an airplane. — v, **·chut·ed, ·chut·ing** v.t. **1.** To land (troops, materiel, etc.) by means of parachutes. — v.i. **2.** To descend by parachute. [< F < PARA² + chute fall] — **par′a·chut′ist** n.

par·a·clete (par′ə-klēt) n. One called to the aid of another. — **the Paraclete** The Holy Spirit as a helper or comforter. [< OF < LL < LGk. paraklētos comforter, advocate]

pa·rade (pə-rād′) n. **1.** A procession or march for ceremony or display. **2.** A marshaling and maneuvering of troops for display or inspection. **3.** A ground where military reviews are held. **4.** A promenade or public walk; also, the persons promenading. **5.** Pompous show, ostentation. — **on parade** On display. — v. **·rad·ed, ·rad·ing** v.t. **1.** To walk or march through or about. **2.** To display ostentatiously; flaunt. **3.** To cause to assemble for military parade. — v.i. **4.** To march formally. **5.** To walk in public for the purpose of showing oneself. **6.** To assemble in military order for inspection or review. [< MF < Sp. parada stopping place, exercise ground] — **pa·rad′er** n.

par·a·digm (par′ə·dim, -dīm) n. Gram. **1.** A list or table of all the inflected forms of a word or class of words, as of a particular declension, conjugation, etc. **2.** Any pattern or example. [< LL < Gk. paradeigma pattern] — **par′a·dig·mat′ic** (-dig·mat′ik) adj.

par·a·dise (par′ə-dīs) n. **1.** Heaven. **2.** A place or state of great beauty or delight. [< F < LL < Gk. paradeisos park] — **par′a·di·sa′ic** (-di-sā′ik) or **·i·cal, par′a·dis′i·ac** (-dis′ē-ak) or **par·a·di·si·a·cal** (par′ə-di·sī′ə-kəl) adj.

Par·a·dise (par′ə-dīs) Eden or heaven.

par·a·dox (par′ə-doks) n. **1.** A statement seemingly absurd or contradictory, yet in fact true. **2.** A statement essentially self-contradictory, false, or absurd. **3.** One whose character or behavior is inconsistent or contradictory. [< F < L < Gk. paradoxos incredible] — **par′a·dox′i·cal** adj. — **par′a·dox′i·cal′i·ty** (-kal′ə-tē), **par′a·dox′i·cal·ness** n. — **par′a·dox′i·cal·ly** adv.

par·a·drop (par′ə-drop) n. Mil. The dropping of supplies equipment, etc., by parachute.

par·af·fin (par′ə-fin) n. Chem. **1.** A waxy mixture of hydrocarbons, distilled from petroleum and widely used for candles, as a preservative, etc. **2.** Any hydrocarbon of the methane series — v.t. To treat or impregnate with paraffin. Also **par′af·fine** (-fin, -fēn). [< G < L par(um) too little + affin(is) related to; so named because it has little affinity for other substances]

paraffin series Chem. The methane series.

paraffin wax Paraffin in its solid state.

par·a·gon (par′ə-gon) n. A model or pattern of excellence, esp. of a specific excellence: a paragon of manhood. [< OF < Ital. paragone touchstone, prob. < Gk. parakonan to sharpen one thing against another]

par·a·graph (par′ə-graf, -gräf) n. **1.** A distinct part or section of a written discourse, begun on a new and usu. indented line and generally containing a unified statement of a particular point. **2.** A short article, item, or comment, as in a newspaper. **3.** A mark (¶) used to indicate where a paragraph is to be begun. — v.t. **1.** To arrange in or into paragraphs. **2.** To comment on or express in a paragraph. [< OF < LL < Gk. < para beside + graphein to write] — **par′a·graph′er** n. — **par′a·graph′ic, par′a·graph′i·cal** adj.

par·a·keet (par′ə-kēt) n. Any of certain small parrots, with long, wedge-shaped tails: also spelled paraquet, paroquet, parrakeet, parroket, parroquet. [< OF < Ital. parrochetto]

Par·a·li·pom·e·non (par′ə-li·pom′ə-non) n. The Douai Bible name for CHRONICLES.

par·al·lax (par′ə-laks) n. The apparent displacement of an object, esp. of a star or other heavenly body, when it is viewed successively from two points not in the same line of sight. [< F < Gk. parallassein to deviate]

par·al·lel (par′ə-lel) adj. **1.** Being a uniform distance away or apart throughout a certain area or extent. **2.** Geom. Not meeting, however far extended: said of straight lines and of planes. **3.** Having a close resemblance. **4.** Music **a** Denoting consecutive identical or similar intervals in the same two voices. **b** Denoting consecutive identical chords. **5.** Electr. Connected between like terminals, as a group of cells, condensers, etc. — n. **1.** An object or surface equidistant from another. **2.** Geom. A parallel line or plane. **3.** Essential likeness. **4.** A counterpart; match. **5.** Comparison: to draw a parallel between two things. **6.** Geog. Any of the circles imagined as drawn upon the earth's surface at right angles to its axis, every point on which marks a given latitude north or south of the equator. **7.** Electr. Connection between like terminals: usu. in the phrase **in parallel:** also called multiple. — v.t. **·leled** or **·lelled, ·lel·ing**

or **·lel·ling 1.** To place in parallel; make parallel. **2.** To be, go, or extend parallel to. **3.** To furnish with a parallel or equal; find a parallel to. **4.** To be a parallel to; correspond to. **5.** To compare; liken. [< MF < L < Gk. < para beside + allēlos one another]

parallel bars Two horizontal crossbars, parallel to each other and supported by upright posts, used for gymnastics.

par·al·lel·e·pi·ped (par′ə-lel′ə-pī′pid, -pip′id) n. A prism with six faces, each of which is a parallelogram. Also **par′al·lel/o·pi′ped, par·al·lel′e·pip′e·don, par·al·lel/o·pip′e·don** (-pip′ə·don, -pī′pə-). [< Gk. < parallēlos parallel + epipedon a plane surface]

par·al·lel·ism (par′ə-lel·iz′əm) n. **1.** The state or quality of being parallel. **2.** Likeness; similarity. **3.** A comparison.

par·al·lel·o·gram (par′ə-lel′ə-gram) n. **1.** Geom. A four-sided plane figure whose opposite sides are parallel and equal. **2.** Any area or object having such form. [< MF < L < Gk. < parallēlos parallel + grammē line]

pa·ral·y·sis (pə-ral′ə-sis) n. pl. **·ses** (-sēz) **1.** Pathol. Partial or complete loss of motor function, esp., voluntary motion, resulting from injury to the nervous system or to a muscular mechanism. **2.** Cessation or crippling of normal activities. [< L < Gk. < paralyein to disable] — **par·a·lyt·ic** (par′ə·lit′ik) adj. & n.

par·a·lyze (par′ə·līz) v.t. **·lyzed, ·lyz·ing 1.** To bring about paralysis in; make paralytic. **2.** To render powerless, ineffective, or inactive. [< F paralyser, back formation < paralysie palsy] — **par′a·lyz′er** n. — **par′a·ly·za′tion** n.

par·a·me·ci·um (par′ə-mē′shē·əm, -sē·əm) n. pl. **·ci·a** (shē-ə, -sē-ə) Any of various species of ciliate protozoa having a flattened, elongate body, and feeding by a primitive oral groove. [< NL < Gk. paramēkēs oblong, oval]

pa·ram·e·ter (pə·ram′ə·tər) n. **1.** Math. A constant whose values determine the operation or characteristics of a system. **2.** A fixed limit or guideline. [< NL < Gk. para beside + metron measure]

par·a·mil·i·tar·y (par′ə·mil′ə·ter′ē) adj. Having a military structure although not officially military; capable of becoming, replacing, or supplementing a military force: said of certain political movements, etc. [< PARA-¹ + MILITARY]

par·a·mount (par′ə·mount) adj. **1.** Superior to all others; chief in importance. **2.** Having the highest authority or rank. — n. A supreme lord; highest ruler. [< AF < OF par by + à mont up, above] — **par′a·mount·ly** adv.

par·a·mour (par′ə·mŏŏr) n. A lover, esp. one who unlawfully takes the place of a husband or wife. [< OF par amour with love]

par·a·noi·a (par′ə·noi′ə) n. Psychiatry A form of mental disorder characterized by delusions of persecution or of grandeur. [< NL < Gk., < para beside + noos, nous mind]

par·a·noi·ac (par′ə·noi′ak) adj. Relating to or affected by paranoia. — n. One affected by paranoia.

par·a·noid (par′ə·noid) adj. Resembling or suggestive of paranoia. — n. One affected by paranoia.

par·a·pet (par′ə·pit, -pet) n. A low wall about the edge of a roof, terrace, bridge, etc. [< MF, or < Ital. parapetto] — **par′a·pet·ed** adj.

par·a·pher·na·li·a (par′ə·fər·nā′lē·ə, -nāl′yə, -fə-) n.pl. **1.** Personal effects. **2.** A group of articles, esp. as used in some activity; equipment; gear. [< Med.L paraphernalia (bona) a wife's own (goods)]

par·a·phrase (par′ə·frāz) n. A restatement of the meaning of a passage, work, etc., as for clarity. — v.t. & v.i. **·phrased, ·phras·ing** To express in or make a paraphrase. [< MF < L < Gk. < para beside + phrazein to tell] — **par′a·phras′er, par′a·phrast** (-frast) n. — **par′a·phras′tic** or **·ti·cal** adj. — **par′a·phras′ti·cal·ly** adv.

par·a·ple·gi·a (par′ə·plē′jē·ə) n. Pathol. Paralysis of the lower half of the body, due to disease or injury of the spinal cord. Also **par′a·ple′gy** (-plē′jē). [< NL < Gk. < para beside + plēssein to strike] — **par·a·ple′gic** adj. & n.

par·a·psy·chol·o·gy (par′ə-sī·kol′ə·jē) n. The study of extrasensory perception and related psychic phenomena.

pa·ra·quet (par′ə·kēt) See PARAKEET.

par·a·site (par′ə·sīt) n. **1.** Biol. An animal or plant that lives in or on another organism, the host, and from whom it obtains nourishment. **2.** One who lives at another's expense without making proper return. [< L < Gk. parasitos, lit., one who eats at another's table] — **par′a·sit′ic, par·a·sit′i·cal** adj. — **par·a·sit′i·cal·ly** adv.

par·a·sit·ism (par′ə-sī′tiz·əm) n. The condition of being a parasite; parasitic mode of existence.

par·a·sol (par′ə·sôl, -sol) n. A small, light umbrella carried by women, used as protection against the sun. [< MF < Ital. < para- para-² + sole sun]

par·a·sym·pa·thet·ic (par′ə·sim′pə·thet′ik) adj. Anat. Denoting a part of the nervous system originating in the cranial and sacral regions and having among its functions the constriction of the pupil, the slowing of the heart, the dilation of the blood vessels, and the stimulation of the digestive and genitourinary systems.

par·a·thy·roid (par′ə·thī′roid) *adj. Anat.* **1.** Lying near the thyroid gland. **2.** Of or pertaining to any of the several, usu. four, small glands found near the thyroid gland and serving to control the amount of calcium in the blood. — *n.* One of the parathyroid glands.

par·a·troops (par′ə·trōōps) *n.pl.* Troops trained and equipped to drop behind enemy lines by parachute. — **par′a·troop·er** *n.*

par·a·ty·phoid (par′ə·tī′foid) *Pathol. adj.* Of or pertaining to paratyphoid fever. — *n.* Paratyphoid fever.

paratyphoid fever *Pathol.* An infectious disease having symptoms resembling those of typhoid fever, but caused by a different bacterium.

par a·vi·on (par′ à·vyöṅ′) *French* By airmail.

par·boil (pär′boil′) *v.t.* **1.** To boil partially. **2.** To make uncomfortable with heat. [< OF < LL *perbullire* to boil thoroughly]

par·buck·le (pär′buk′əl) *n.* A sling for vertically raising a heavy object by passing a doubled rope around it, the free ends being pulled through the loop. — *v.t.* **·led, ·ling** To hoist or lower by means of a parbuckle. [Earlier *parbunkle*; origin uncertain]

par·cel (pär′səl) *n.* **1.** Something that is wrapped up; package. **2.** A quantity of some commodity put up for sale; lot. **3.** An indefinite number of persons or things. **4.** A distinct portion of land. — *v.t.* **par·celed** or **·celled, par·cel·ing** or **·cel·ling 1.** To divide or distribute in parts or shares: usu. with *out.* **2.** To make up a parcel or parcels. — *adj. & adv.* Part; partly. [< F < L *pars, partis* part]

parcel post A postal service for the conveying and delivering of parcels not exceeding a specified weight and size.

parch (pärch) *v.t.* **1.** To make extremely dry. **2.** To make very thirsty. **3.** To dry (corn, peas, etc.) by exposing to great heat. **4.** To dry up or shrivel by exposing to cold. — *v.i.* **5.** To become dry. **6.** To become dry with thirst. [ME *parchen*; ult. origin uncertain]

par·chee·si (pär·chē′zē) *n.* A board game derived from pachisi. Also **par·che′si, par·chi′si.**

parch·ment (pärch′mənt) *n.* **1.** The skin of sheep, goats, and other animals prepared and polished with pumice stone, used as a material for writing or painting upon. **2.** A writing on this material. **3.** Any of several types of paper made in imitation of parchment. [< OF < L *pergamenus* of Pergamum, the city where it was first used]

pard¹ (pärd) *n. Archaic* A leopard or panther. [< OF < L < Gk. *pardos*]

pard² (pärd) *n. Slang* A partner. [Short for PARDNER]

pard·ner (pärd′nər) *n. U.S. Dial* Chum; friend. [Alter. of PARTNER]

par·don (pär′dən) *v.t.* **1.** To remit the penalty of (an offense, insult, etc.). **2.** To forgive (a person) for an offense. **3.** To grant courteous allowance for or to. — *n.* **1.** The act of pardoning; forgiveness. **2.** An official warrant declaring such a remission. **3.** In the Roman Catholic Church, an indulgence. [< OF < LL < *per-* through + *donare* to give] — **par′don·a·ble** *adj.* — **par′don·a·bly** *adv.*

par·don·er (pär′dən·ər) *n.* **1.** One who pardons. **2.** In the Middle Ages, a layman who sold ecclesiastical indulgences.

pare (pâr) *v.t.* **pared, par·ing 1.** To cut off the covering layer or part of. **2.** To cut off or trim away (a covering layer or part): often with *off* or *away.* **3.** To diminish gradually. [< OF *parer* to prepare, trim] — **par′er** *n.*

par·e·gor·ic (par′ə·gôr′ik, ·gor′ik) *n. Med.* A camphorated tincture of opium, used primarily to treat diarrhea. [< LL < Gk. < *paregoros* soothing]

pa·ren·chy·ma (pə·reng′ki·mə) *n.* **1.** *Biol.* The essential functioning cellular substance of an animal organ, as distinguished from connective tissue. **2.** *Bot.* The soft cell tissue of higher plants, as found in stem pith or fruit pulp. Also **pa·ren′chyme** (·kīm). [< NL < Gk. < *para* beside + *enchyma* infusion] — **par·en·chym·a·tous** (par′eng·kim′ə·tes) *adj.*

par·ent (pâr′ənt) *n.* **1.** A father or mother. **2.** One exercising the functions of a father or mother. **3.** A progenitor; forefather. **4.** Any organism that generates another. **5.** Source; cause. [< OF < L *parere* to beget] — **pa·ren·tal** (pa·ren′tal) *adj.* — **pa·ren′tal·ly** *adv.* — **par′ent·hood** *n.*

par·ent·age (pâr′ən·tij) *n.* **1.** Descent or derivation from parents; lineage; origin. **2.** Derivation from a source or origin. **3.** Parenthood. [< OF]

pa·ren·the·sis (pə·ren′thə·sis) *n. pl.* **·ses** (·sēz) **1.** Either or both of the upright curved lines () used to enclose an interjected, explanatory, or qualifying remark, mathematical quantities, etc. **2.** *Gram.* A word, phrase, or clause inserted in a sentence that is grammatically complete without it, set off usu. by commas, dashes, or upright curved lines. **3.** An intervening episode or incident. [< Med. L < Gk. < *para* beside + *en* in + *tithenai* to place]

pa·ren·the·size (pə·ren′thə·sīz) *v.t.* **·sized, ·siz·ing 1.** To insert as a parenthetical statement. **2.** To insert parentheses in. **3.** To place within parentheses (def. 1).

par·en·thet·i·cal (par′ən·thet′i·kəl) *adj.* **1.** Thrown in; episodic. **2.** Abounding in or like parentheses; also, given to using parentheses. — **par′en·thet′i·cal·ly** *adv.*

pa·re·sis (pə·rē′sis, par′ə·sis) *n. Pathol.* **1.** Partial paralysis affecting muscular motion but not sensation. **2.** General paresis. [< NL < Gk., a letting go] — **pa·ret·ic** (pə·ret′ik, ·rē′tik) *adj.* — **pa·ret′i·cal·ly** *adv.*

par ex·cel·lence (pär ek′sə·läns, *Fr.* pår ek·se·läns′) Beyond comparison; preeminently. [< F, lit., by excellence]

par·fait (pär·fā′) *n.* A frozen dessert or confection made with eggs, sugar, whipped cream, and fruit or other flavoring. [< F, perfect]

par·he·li·on (pär·hē′lē·ən) *n. pl.* **·li·a** (·lē·ə) *Meteorol.* One of two bright images sometimes appearing on a solar halo. Also **par·he′li·um** (·əm). [< L < Gk. < *para* beside + *hēlios* sun] — **par·he′lic, par·he·li·a·cal** (pär′hi·lī′ə·kəl) *adj.*

pari- *combining form* Equal. [< L *par, paris* equal]

pa·ri·ah (pə·rī′ə, par′ē·ə) *n.* **1.** A member of an extensive low caste of southern India and Burma. **2.** A social outcast. [< Tamil *paraiyon*, lit., (hereditary) drummer]

pa·ri·e·tal (pə·rī′ə·tal) *adj.* **1.** *Anat.* **a** Of, pertaining to, or forming the walls of a cavity or hollow organ. **b** Of or pertaining to the parietal bones. **2.** *Bot.* Attached to the wall of the ovary. **3.** *U.S.* Pertaining to residence or authority within the walls of a college. — *n.* A parietal bone. [< MF < L *paries* wall]

parietal bone *Anat.* Either of two bones that form a part of the top and sides of the cranium.

par·i·mu·tu·el (par′i·myōō′chōō·əl) *n.* **1.** A system of betting at races in which those who have bet on the winners share in the total amount wagered. Also **par′i·mu′tu·el. 2.** A pari-mutuel machine. [< F, stake or mutual wager]

pari-mutuel machine A machine for recording pari-mutuel bets: also called *totalizator, totalizer.*

par·ing (pâr′ing) *n.* **1.** The act of one who pares. **2.** *Often pl.* The part pared off.

Par·is (par′is) In Greek mythology, a son of Priam whose abduction of Helen caused the Trojan War.

Paris green A poisonous compound prepared from copper acetate and arsenic trioxide, used chiefly as an insecticide.

par·ish (par′ish) *n.* **1.** *Eccl.* In the Anglican, Roman Catholic, and some other churches, a district with its own church. **2.** *U.S.* All those who worship at the same church. **3.** *Brit.* A political subdivision of a county. **4.** In Louisiana, a civil district corresponding to a county. **5.** The people of a parish. ◆ Collateral adjective: *parochial.* [< OF < LL < Gk. *paroikia*, orig., neighborhood, later diocese]

pa·rish·ion·er (pə·rish′ən·ər) *n.* A member of a parish.

Pa·ri·sian (pə·rizh′ən, ·riz′ē·ən) *adj.* Of or pertaining to the city of Paris. — *n.* A native or resident of Paris.

par·i·ty (par′ə·tē) *n. pl.* **·ties 1.** Equality, as of condition, rank, value, etc.; also, a like state or degree. **2.** The equivalence in legal weight and quality of the legal tender of one class of money to another. **3.** Par (def. 3). **4.** Equality between the currency or prices of commodities of two countries or cities. **5.** Perfect analogy; close resemblance. **6.** *U.S.* A level for farm prices that gives to the farmer the same purchasing power that he averaged during each year of a chosen base period. [< MF < *paritas* equality]

park (pärk) *n.* **1.** A tract of land for public use in or near a city. **2.** An open square in a city. **3.** A national park (which see). **4.** An amusement park (which see). **5.** A large tract of land surrounding a country estate. **6.** *Mil.* An open area where guns, trucks, etc., are assembled for servicing and storage. **7.** In English law, a tract of land held through royal grant or by prescription. — *v.t.* **1.** To place or leave (an automobile, etc.) standing for a time, as on a street. **2.** *U.S. Slang* To place; set. **3.** To assemble or mass together: to *park* artillery. **4.** To enclose in or as in a park. — *v.i.* **5.** To park an automobile, etc. [< OF *parc* game preserve]

par·ka (pär′kə) *n. U.S. & Canadian* **1.** A hooded outer garment of undressed skins worn by Eskimos. **2.** A similar garment worn for skiing and other winter sports. [< Aleut]

Par·kin·son's disease (pär′kən·sənz) *Pathol.* A form of paralysis characterized by muscular rigidity, tremor, and weakness. Also **Park·in·son·ism.** [after James *Parkinson,* 1755–1824, English physician]

park·land (pärk′land′) *n. Often pl.* **1.** Land used or designated as a park. **2.** Grassland with trees.

park·way (pärk′wā) *n.* A wide thoroughfare adorned with spaces planted with turf and trees.

par·lance (pär′ləns) *n.* Manner of speech; language: legal *parlance.* [< OF < *parler* to speak]

par·lay (pär·lā′, pär′lē) *v.t. & v.i.* To place (an original bet and its winnings) on a later race, contest, etc. — *n.* Such a bet. [< F < Ital *paroli* grand cast at dice]

par·ley (pär′lē) *n.* A conference, as with an enemy; a discussion of terms. — *v.i.* To hold a conference, esp. with an enemy. [< F *parlée*, fem. pp. of *parler* to speak]

par·lia·ment (pär′lə·mənt) *n.* **1.** An assembly for consultation and deliberation. **2.** A national legislature, esp. when composed of various estates. [< OF *parlement* speaking < *parler* to speak]

Par·lia·ment (pär′lə·mənt) *n.* **1.** The supreme legislature of Great Britain and Northern Ireland, composed of the House of Lords and the House of Commons. **2.** The legislature in any of Great Britain's colonies or dominions.

par·lia·men·tar·i·an (pär′lə·men·târ′ē·ən) *n.* One versed in parliamentary procedure or debate.

par·lia·men·ta·ry (pär′lə·men′tər·ē) *adj.* **1.** Of, pertaining to, or enacted by a parliament. **2.** According to the rules of a parliament: *parliamentary* procedure. **3.** Of a government, having a parliament.

parliamentary procedure The rules by which meetings of deliberative assemblies, societies, boards, clubs, etc., are formally conducted. Also **parliamentary law.**

par·lor (pär′lər) *n.* **1.** A room for reception of callers or entertainment of guests. **2.** A room in an inn, hotel, etc., for private conversation, appointments, etc. Also *Brit.* **par′lour.** [< AF < Med.L < ML *parabolare* to speak]

parlor car A railway car fitted with luxurious chairs, and run as a day coach: also called *chair car.*

par·lous (pär′ləs) *Archaic adj.* **1.** Dangerous or exciting. **2.** Shrewd. — *adv.* Exceedingly. [Var. of PERILOUS]

Par·me·san cheese (pär′mə·zan′) A hard, dry Italian cheese made from skim milk, grated and used to flavor spaghetti, soups, etc. [after *Parma,* a city in Italy]

Par·nas·sus (pär·nas′əs), **Mount** **1.** A mountain in central Greece, anciently regarded as sacred to Apollo and the Muses. **2.** The domain of poetry or of literature. **3.** A collection of poems or other literary works. — **Par·nas·si·an** (pär·nas′ē·ən) *adj.*

pa·ro·chi·al (pə·rō′kē·əl) *adj.* **1.** Pertaining to, supported by, or confined to a parish. **2.** Narrow; provincial; restricted in scope. [See PARISH.] — **pa·ro′chi·al·ism** *n.* — **pa·ro′chi·al·ly** *adv.*

parochial school A school, usu. elementary, supported and directed by the parish of a church.

par·o·dy (par′ə·dē) *n. pl.* **·dies** **1.** A humorous or burlesque imitation of a literary or musical work or style. **2.** An incompetent attempt to imitate another's work or style. — *v.t.* **·died, ·dy·ing** To make a parody of. [Ult. < Gk. *parōidia* burlesque poem or song] — **pa·rod·ic** (pə·rod′ik) or **·i·cal** *adj.* — **par′o·dist** *n.*

pa·rol (pə·rōl′) *n.* A word: now only in phrase **by parol,** by word of mouth. [< OF *parole* word]

pa·role (pə·rōl′) *n.* **1.** The conditional release of a prisoner before his sentence has expired. **2.** The duration of such conditional freedom. **3.** *Mil.* A pledge of honor by a prisoner of war that he will not seek to escape or will not serve against his captors until exchanged. — **on parole** Freed from prison under conditions of parole. — *v.t.* **·roled, ·rol·ing** To release (a prisoner) on parole. [< F *parole (d'honneur)* word (of honor)]

pa·rol·ee (pə·rō′lē) *n.* One released from prison on parole.

par·o·quet (par′ə·ket) See PARAKEET.

pa·rot·id (pə·rot′id) *Anat. adj.* **1.** Situated near the ear. **2.** Designating one of the paired salivary glands in front of and below the ear. — *n.* A parotid gland. [< F < L < Gk. *parōtis,* < *para-* beside + *ous, ōtos* ear]

par·ox·ysm (par′ək·siz′əm) *n.* **1.** A sudden and violent outburst, as of emotion or action: a *paroxysm* of tears. **2.** *Pathol.* A sudden intensification of the symptoms of a disease, usu. occurring at intervals. [< MF < Med.L < Gk. < *para-* beside + *oxynein* to goad < *oxys* sharp] — **par′ox·ys′mal** (-siz′məl) *adj.* — **par′ox·ys′mal·ly** *adv.*

par·quet (pär·kā′, -ket′) *n.* **1.** Flooring of parquetry. **2.** The main floor of a theater, esp. the section from the orchestra pit to the parquet circle: also called *orchestra.* — *v.t.* **·quet·ed** (-kād′, -ket′id), **·quet·ing** (-kā′ing, -ket′ing) To make (a floor, etc.) of parquetry. [< F < OF *parchet* small compartment, dim. of *parc*]

parquet circle The section of theater seats at the rear of the parquet and under the balcony.

par·quet·ry (pär′kit·rē) *n. pl.* **·ries** Inlaid mosaic of wood, used esp. for floors.

parr (pär) *n.* **1.** A young salmon before its first migration seaward. **2.** The young of some other fishes, as the cod or pollack. [? < dial. E (Scottish)]

PARQUETRY

par·ra·keet (par′ə·kēt) See PARAKEET.

par·ri·cide (par′ə·sīd) *n.* **1.** The killing of a parent. **2.** One who has killed a parent. [< F < L *paricida* killer of a relative] — **par′ri·ci′dal** *adj.* — **par′ri·ci′dal·ly** *adv.*

par·ro·ket (par′ə·ket) See PARAKEET.

par·ro·quet (par′ə·ket) See PARAKEET.

par·rot (par′ət) *n.* **1.** Any of certain birds native in warm regions, having a hooked bill, and often brilliant plumage, including the macaws, parakeets, etc., some of which imitate human speech and laughter. **2.** One who repeats without understanding. — *v.t.* To repeat or imitate by rote. [ME, var. of *Perrot* < F < LL *Petrus*] — **par′rot·er** *n.*

parrot fish Any of many small fishes inhabiting warm seas and having vivid coloring and beaklike jaws.

par·ry (par′ē) *v.* **·ried, ·ry·ing** *v.t.* **1.** To ward off (a thrust, blow, etc.) in fencing. **2.** To avoid or evade. — *v.i.* **3.** To ward off a thrust or blow. — *n. pl.* **·ries** **1.** A defensive movement, as in fencing. **2.** An evasion or diversion in a contest of wits. [< Ital. *parare* to ward off]

parse (pärs) *v.t.* **parsed, pars·ing** **1.** To analyze (a sentence) grammatically by giving the form, function, and syntactical relation of each of its words. **2.** To describe and analyze (a word) grammatically. [< L *pars, partis* part]

par·sec (pär′sek) *n. Astron.* A unit of length used in expressing stellar distances, corresponding to an annual parallax of one second of arc, or 3.26 light-years.

Par·see (pär′sē, pär·sē′) *n.* A member of a religious sect practicing a form of Zoroastrianism, descendants of Persians who fled to India in the eighth century to escape Moslem persecution. Also **Par′si.** [< Persian *Pārsī* a Persian] — **Par′see·ism, Par′si·ism, Par′sism** *n.*

Par·si·fal (pär′si·fäl, -fəl) A knight in Wagner's opera (1882) of this name.

par·si·mo·ni·ous (pär′sə·mō′nē·əs) *adj.* Characterized by or showing parsimony; penurious; niggardly. — **par′si·mo′ni·ous·ly** *adv.* — **par′si·mo′ni·ous·ness** *n.*

par·si·mo·ny (pär′sə·mō′nē) *n. pl.* **·nies** Undue sparingness in the expenditure of money; stinginess. [< L < *parsus,* pp. of *parcere* to spare]

pars·ley (pärs′lē) *n.* A cultivated herb, having aromatic leaves, widely used to garnish and flavor foods. [< OF < LL < L < Gk. < *petra* rock + *selinon* parsley]

pars·nip (pärs′nip) *n.* A European herb of the parsley family, with a large, sweetish, edible root. [ME < OF *pasnaie* + OE *nǣp* turnip]

par·son (pär′sən) *n.* **1.** A clergyman; minister. **2.** In the Anglican Church, a clergyman having full charge of a parish; a rector. [< OF < Med.L *persona* rector] — **par·son·i·cal** (pär·son′i·kəl), **par·son′ic** *adj.*

par·son·age (pär′sən·ij) *n.* **1.** A clergyman's dwelling; esp., a free official residence provided by the church. **2.** In English ecclesiastical law, the benefice of a parson.

part (pärt) *n.* **1.** A portion of a whole; segment. **2.** *Math.* One of a specified number of equal divisions; an aliquot division. **3.** A distinct piece or portion of a machine that fulfills a specific function in the working of the whole. **4.** Something less than the whole. **5.** An organ, member, or other portion of an animal or plant body. **6.** *Usu. pl.* A region; territory: in foreign *parts.* **7.** One's proper share, as of obligation or performance: to do one's *part.* **8.** Individual concern or participation in something. **9.** The role or lines assigned to an actor in a play. **10.** *Usu. pl.* An endowment of mind or character: a man of *parts.* **11.** *Music* **a** The melody intended for a single voice or instrument in a concerted piece: sometimes called *voice.* **b** The written or printed copy for the performer's use. **12.** Division, section, or installment of a literary work. **13.** The dividing line on the scalp made by combing sections of the hair in opposite directions. — **for one's part** As far as one is concerned. — **for the most part** To the greatest extent; in general. — **in good part** With good grace; good-naturedly. — **in part** Partly. — **part and parcel** An essential part: an emphatic phrase. — **to take part** To participate; share or cooperate: usu. with *in.* — **to take someone's part** To support someone in a contest or disagreement. — *v.t.* **1.** To divide or break (something) into parts. **2.** To sever or discontinue (a relationship or connection). **3.** To separate by being or coming between; keep or move apart. **4.** To comb (the hair) so as to leave a dividing line on the sides or elsewhere on the scalp. **5.** To separate (mingled substances) chemically or mechanically. — *v.i.* **6.** To become divided or broken into parts. **7.** To go away from each other; cease associating. **8.** To depart. — **to part from** To separate from; leave. — **to part with 1.** To give up; relinquish. **2.** To part from. — *adv.* To some extent; partly. [< OF and OE < L *pars, partis*]

par·take (pär·tāk′) *v.* **took, ·tak·en, ·tak·ing** *v.i.* **1.** To take part or have a share: with *in.* **2.** To receive or take a portion or share: with *of.* **3.** To have something of the quality or character: with *of.* — *v.t.* **4.** To take or have a part in; share. [Back formation < *partaker* < L < *pars, partis* part + *capere* to take] — **par·tak′er** *n.*

part·ed (pär'tid) *adj.* **1.** Situated or placed apart; separated. **2.** *Bot.* Cut almost but not quite to the base, as certain leaves. **3.** Divided into parts.

par·terre (pär·târ') *n.* **1.** A flower garden having beds arranged in a pattern. **2.** The part of a theater on the main floor under the balcony and behind the parquet. [< MF < L *per* through, all over + *terra* land]

par·the·no·gen·e·sis (pär'thə·nō·jen'ə·sis) *n. Biol.* Reproduction by means of unfertilized eggs, seeds, or spores, as in many rotifers, insects, and algae. Also **par'the·nog'e·ny** (-noj'ə·nē). [< Gk. *parthenos* virgin + GENESIS] — **par'·the·no·ge·net'ic** (-jə·net'ik), **par'the·no·gen'ic** *adj.* — **par'·the·no·ge·net'i·cal·ly** *adv.*

Par·the·non (pär'thə·non) The temple of Athena on the Acropolis at Athens, dedicated in 438 B.C., regarded as one of the finest examples of Doric architecture.

Par·thi·a (pär'thē·ə) An ancient kingdom occupying what is now NE Iran.

Par·thi·an (pär'thē·ən) *n.* An inhabitant of Parthia. — *adj.* Of or pertaining to Parthia or the Parthians. — **Parthian shot** Any aggressive remark or action made in leaving or fleeing, after the manner of Parthian cavalry who shot at their enemies while retreating.

par·tial (pär'shəl) *adj.* **1.** Pertaining to, constituting, or involving a part only. **2.** Favoring one side; biased. **3.** Having a special liking: usu. with *to.* — *n.* In acoustics, a partial tone. [< OF < LL < L *pars, partis* part] — **par'·tial·ly** *adv.*

partial eclipse *Astron.* An eclipse in which only part of the disk of a celestial body is obscured from view.

par·ti·al·i·ty (pär'shē·al'ə·tē) *n. pl.* **·ties** **1.** The state of being partial. **2.** Unfairness; bias. **3.** A particular fondness; predilection. Also **par'tial·ness** (-shəl·nis).

partial tone Any of the simple or pure tones that, taken collectively, constitute a complex tone

par·tic·i·pant (pär·tis'ə·pənt) *adj.* Sharing; taking part in. — *n.* One who participates; a sharer.

par·tic·i·pate (pär·tis'ə·pāt) *v.* **·pat·ed**, **·pat·ing** *v.i.* To take part or have a share in common with others: with *in.* [< L < *pars, partis* part + *capere* to take] — **par·tic'i·pa'tion, par·tic'i·pance** *n.* — **par·tic'i·pa'tor** *n.*

par·ti·cip·i·al (pär'tə·sip'ē·əl) *Gram. adj.* **1.** Having the nature, form, or use of a participle. **2.** Characterized by, consisting of, or based on a participle. — *n.* A participle. — **par'ti·cip'i·al·ly** *adv.*

par·ti·ci·ple (pär'tə·sip'əl) *n. Gram.* A verbal adjective, often retaining some of the attributes of a verb, such as tense and the power of taking an object, but often also having the adjectival function of qualifying nouns. The **present participle** ends in *-ing* and the **past participle** commonly in *-d, -ed, -en, -n,* or *-t.* — **dangling participle** A participle that modifies the wrong substantive, as in "*Opening the door, the room looked large.*" [< OF, var. of *participe* < L *participium* a sharing, partaking]

par·ti·cle (pär'ti·kəl) *n.* **1.** A minute part, piece, or portion, as of matter. **2.** A very small amount or slight degree. **3.** *Physics* One of the elementary components of an atom, as an electron, proton, neutron, meson, etc. **4.** *Gram.* **a** A short, uninflected part of speech, as an article, preposition, interjection, or conjunction. **b** A prefix or suffix. **5.** A small section or clause, as of a document. [< L *particula,* dim. of *pars, partis* part]

par·ti-col·ored (pär'tē·kul'ərd) *adj.* **1.** Differently colored in different parts. **2.** Diversified. Also spelled *party-colored.* [< F *partir,* to divide + COLORED]

par·tic·u·lar (pər·tik'yə·lər) *adj.* **1.** Peculiar or pertaining to a specified person, thing, time, or place; specific. **2.** Referring to one as distinguished from others. **3.** Especially noteworthy: of *particular* importance. **4.** Comprising all details or circumstances: a *particular* description. **5.** Requiring or giving minute attention to details; fastidious: *particular* in dress. **6.** *Logic* Including some, not all, of a class: opposed to *universal.* — *n.* **1.** *Usu. pl.* An item; detail. **2.** An individual instance; a single or separate case. **3.** *Logic* A particular proposition. — **in particular** Particularly. [< OF < LL *particularis* concerning a part]

par·tic·u·lar·i·ty (pər·tik'yə·lar'ə·tē) *n. pl.* **·ties** **1.** The state or quality of being particular, as: **a** Exactitude in description. **b** Strict or careful attention to details; fastidiousness. **2.** That which is particular, as: **a** A circumstance or detail. **b** A special characteristic; peculiarity.

par·tic·u·lar·ize (pər·tik'yə·lə·rīz') *v.* **·ized, ·iz·ing** *v.t.* **1.** To speak of or treat individually or in detail. — *v.i.* **2.** To give particular details; be specific. — **par·tic'u·lar·i·za'·tion** *n.* — **par·tic'u·lar·iz'er** *n.*

par·tic·u·lar·ly (pər·tik'yə·lər·lē) *adv.* **1.** With specific reference; distinctly. **2.** In an unusually great degree. **3.** Part by part; in detail. **4.** Severally; personally.

par·tic·u·late (pər·tik'yə·lāt) *adj.* Consisting of minute, separate particles.

part·ing (pär'ting) *adj.* **1.** Given or done at parting: a *parting* glance. **2.** Of or pertaining to a parting or a going away. **3.** Departing; declining. **4.** Separating; dividing. — *n.* **1.** The act of separating, or the state of being separated. **2.** A leave-taking; esp., a final separation. **3.** A place, line, or surface of separation. **4.** That which serves to part or separate objects.

parting shot Any retort or aggressive action made as one is leaving or fleeing. [< PARTHIAN SHOT by folk etymology]

par·ti·san (pär'tə·zən) *n.* **1.** One who supports or upholds a party, cause, etc.; esp., an overly zealous adherent or devotee. **2.** *Mil.* A member of a body of detached or irregular troops; a guerrilla. — *adj.* **1.** Of, relating to, or characteristic of a partisan. **2.** Advocated by or composed of members of one party. **3.** *Mil.* Of or carried on by partisans. Also **par'ti·zan.** — **Syn.** See ADHERENT. [< F < Ital. < L *pars, partis* part] — **par'ti·san·ship** *n.*

par·tite (pär'tīt) *adj.* Divided into or composed of parts: used in combination: *bipartite, tripartite.* [< L *partitus,* pp. of *partire* to divide]

par·ti·tion (pär·tish'ən) *n.* **1.** The act of dividing, separating, distributing; also, the state of being divided, etc. **2.** Something that divides or separates, as a light interior wall dividing a room, an enclosure, a septum in a plant or animal structure, etc. **3.** One of the parts, sections, compartments, etc., into which a thing is divided. — *v.t.* **1.** To divide into parts, sections, segments, etc. **2.** To separate by a partition: often with *off.* [< OF < L *partire* to divide] — **par·ti'tion·er** *n.* — **par·ti'tion·ment** *n.*

par·ti·tive (pär'tə·tiv) *adj.* **1.** Separating into integral parts or distinct divisions. **2.** *Gram.* Denoting a part as distinct from the whole. Example: *Of them* is the *partitive* genitive in the sentence "Many *of them* were there." — *n. Gram.* A partitive word or case. [< F *partitif* or L < *partitus,* pp. of *partire* to divide] — **par'ti·tive·ly** *adv.*

part·ly (pärt'lē) *adv.* In some part; partially.

part·ner (pärt'nər) *n.* One who is united or associated with another or others in some action, enterprise, etc.; as: **a** *Law* A member of a partnership. **b** A husband or wife; spouse. **c** One of a couple who dance together. **d** One of two or more players on the same side in a game. **e** A colleague or associate in some undertaking; a sharer. — *v.t. Rare* **1.** To make a partner. **2.** To be the partner of. [ME < fusion of *parcener* and *part*]

part·ner·ship (pärt'nər·ship) *n.* **1.** The state or relationship of being a partner; association. **2.** *Law* **a** A contractual relationship in which two or more persons combine capital, labor, etc., to carry on a business. **b** The contract that creates such a relationship. **c** The persons associated.

part of speech *Gram.* One of the eight traditional classes of words in English, noun, pronoun, verb, adverb, adjective, conjunction, preposition, and interjection.

par·took (pär·took') Past tense of PARTAKE.

par·tridge (pär'trij) *n.* **1.** Any of certain small, plump game birds of the Old World. **2.** Any of various similar birds, as the ruffed grouse or the bobwhite. [< OF < L < Gk. *perdix, -ikos* partridge]

part song A song of three or more parts; esp., a secular choral piece without accompaniment.

part-time (pärt'tīm') *adj.* For, during, or by part of the time: a *part-time* student.

par·tu·ri·ent (pär·tyŏŏr'ē·ənt, -tŏŏr'-) *adj.* **1.** Bringing forth or about to bring forth young. **2.** Of or pertaining to parturition. **3.** Producing or about to produce an idea, discovery, etc. [< L *parturiens, -entis,* ppr. of *parturire* to be in labor] — **par·tu'ri·en·cy** *n.*

par·tu·ri·tion (pär'tyŏŏ·rish'ən, -chŏŏ-) *n.* The act of bringing forth young; delivery; childbirth.

par·ty (pär'tē) *n. pl.* **·ties** **1.** A social gathering for pleasure or entertainment. **2.** A group of persons associated or gathered together for some common purpose; as: **a** A group united in promoting or maintaining a cause, policy, system, etc.; esp., a political group organized to gain control of a government through the election of its candidates to public office. **b** A small body of persons selected for some special mission or assignment: a demolition *party.* **c** A group formed for a sport or other diversion. **3.** *Law* Either of the persons or groups involved in legal proceedings. **4.** One who takes part or participates in an action, plan, etc.: a *party* to his crime. **5.** *Informal* A person. — *adj.* Of or pertaining to a party or parties. [< OF *partir* to divide]

par·ty-col·ored (pär'tē·kul'ərd) See PARTI-COLORED.

party line **1.** A telephone line or circuit serving two or more subscribers. Also **party wire.** **2.** A boundary line between the properties of two or more owners. **3.** The essential beliefs or policies of a political party.

PRONUNCIATION KEY: add, āce, câre, pälm; end, ēven; it, īce; odd, ōpen, ôrder; tōōk, pōōl; up, bûrn; ə = a in *above,* e in *sicken,* i in *flexible,* o in *melon,* u in *focus;* yōō = u in *fuse;* oil; pout; check; go; ring; thin; this; zh, vision.

party politics Policies and acts aimed at furthering the interests of one political party.

party whip A whip (def. 4).

par value The nominal or stated value of stock; face value: distinguished from *market value*.

par·ve·nu (pär′və-nōō, -nyōō) *n.* One who has risen above his class through the sudden attainment of wealth or position; an upstart. — *adj.* **1.** Being a parvenu. **2.** Characteristic of or resembling a parvenu. [< F, orig., pp. of *parvenir* to arrive < L *pervenire*]

pas (pä) *n.* A dance step. [< F < L *passus* step]

pas·chal (pas′kəl) *adj.* Pertaining to the Jewish Passover or to Easter: *paschal* sacrifice. [< OF < LL < Gk. < Hebrew *pesakh* a passing over]

paschal flower The pasqueflower.

Paschal Lamb **1.** Jesus Christ. **2.** Any symbolic representation of Christ.

pas de deux (pä də dœ′) *French* A dance or ballet figure for two persons.

pa·sha (pə-shä′, pash′ə, pä′shə) *n.* Formerly, a Turkish honorary title placed after the name of generals, governors of provinces, etc.: also *pacha*. [< Turkish *bāsh* head]

pa·sha·lik (pə-shä′lik) *n.* The province or jurisdiction of a pasha: also spelled *pachalic*. Also **pa·sha′lic**. [< Turkish]

Pash·to (push′tō) *n.* The Iranian language dominant in Afghanistan: also called *Afghan*: also *Pushtu*.

pasque·flow·er (pask′flou′ər) *n.* Any of several plants of the crowfoot family, having white, red, or purple flowers blooming about Easter, the State flower of South Dakota: also called *paschal flower*. Also **pasch′flow′er**.

pas·quin·ade (pas′kwin-ād′) *n.* An abusive or coarse personal satire posted in a public place. — *v.t.* **·ad·ed, ·ad·ing** To attack or ridicule in pasquinades; lampoon. [< Ital. < *Pasquino*, orig., a disinterred statue at Rome on which satirical verses were pasted] — **pas′quin·ad′er** *n.*

pass (pas, päs) *v.* **passed** (*Rare*, **past**), **passed** or **past**, **pass·ing** *v.t.* **1.** To go by or move past. **2.** To succeed in meeting the requirements of (a test, trial, etc.). **3.** To go beyond or surpass. **4.** To spend (a specified period of time). **5.** To cause or allow to move, go past, proceed, advance, etc.: to *pass* him through the ranks. **6.** To approve or sanction; enact: to *pass* a bill. **7.** To be approved or sanctioned by: The bill *passed* the senate. **8.** To cause or allow to get through (a test, trial, etc.). **9.** To convey or transfer from one to another; transmit: to *pass* a bad check. **10.** In football, hockey, etc., to transfer (the ball, etc.) to another player on the same team. **11.** In baseball, to walk (a batter). **12.** To utter or pronounce, esp. judicially: to *pass* sentence. **13.** To discharge or excrete (waste); void. **14.** To omit paying (a dividend). **15.** *Law* To transfer ownership or title of to another; make over. **16.** *Rare* To permit to go unnoticed or unmentioned. **17.** *Rare* To pledge or promise. — *v.i.* **18.** To go or move; proceed; advance. **19.** To go by or move past. **20.** To obtain or force a way: to *pass* through a crowd. **21.** To lead or extend; run: The river *passes* under a bridge. **22.** To go by or elapse: The years *passed* slowly. **23.** To come to an end; terminate. **24.** To die. **25.** To go about or circulate; be current. **26.** To change or move from one condition, place, form, etc., to another: to *pass* from hot to cold. **27.** To be mutually exchanged or transacted: Whispers *passed* between them. **28.** To take place; occur: It came to *pass*. **29.** To be allowed or permitted without challenge, censure, etc. **30.** To undergo a test, etc., successfully. **31.** To be approved, sanctioned, ratified, etc. **32.** To be excreted or voided. **33.** *Law* To give or pronounce sentence, judgment, etc.: with *on* or *upon*. **34.** In football, hockey, etc., to transfer the ball, etc., to another player on the same team. **35.** In fencing, to make a pass or thrust; lunge. **36.** In card games, to decline to make a play, bid, etc. — **to pass away 1.** To come to an end. **2.** To die. **3.** To allow (time) to elapse. — **to pass for** To be accepted or regarded as, usu. erroneously. — **to pass off 1.** To come to an end; disappear. **2.** To give out or circulate as genuine; palm off. **3.** To be emitted, as vapor. — **to pass out 1.** To distribute or circulate. **2.** *Informal* To faint. — **to pass over** To fail to notice or consider, as an applicant. — **to pass up** *U.S. Informal* **1.** To reject or fail to take advantage of, as an offer or opportunity. **2.** To pass over. — *n.* **1.** A way or opening through which one can pass; esp., a narrow passage between the peaks of a mountain range. **2.** A permit, order, or license giving the bearer authority to enter, move about, depart, etc., without the usual restrictions; as: **a** *Mil.* A written form granting permission to the holder to be absent from duty; also, the permission itself or the period of absence covered by it. **b** A ticket allowing one to enter a theater, movie, train, etc., free of charge. **3.** The passing of an examination or course. **4.** In magic, hypnotism, etc.: **a** A movement of the hand, a wand, etc., over a person or thing. **b** The manipulation of objects by sleight of hand. **5.** A state of affairs; situation: to bring events to a critical *pass*. **6.** In fencing, a thrust or

lunge. **7.** In cards, a refusal to bid or raise a bid. **8.** In baseball, a walk. — **to bring to pass** To cause to be fulfilled or accomplished. — **to come to pass** To happen. — **to make a pass 1.** To attempt to hit. **2.** *Slang* To invite intimacies; proposition. [< OF < L *passus* step]

pass·a·ble (pas′ə-bəl, päs′-) *adj.* **1.** Capable of being passed, penetrated, crossed, etc.: *passable* rivers. **2.** Fairly good or acceptable; tolerable. **3.** Fit for general circulation, as money. — **pass′a·ble·ness** *n.* — **pass′a·bly** *adv.*

pas·sage (pas′ij) *n.* **1.** A portion of a writing, speech, or musical composition, usu. of small or moderate length. **2.** *Music* A short section of a composition designed primarily to display the performer's skill, as a run or flourish. **3.** A way, channel, duct, etc., by which a person or thing may pass. **4.** A hall, corridor, etc., between apartments in a building. **5.** The act of passing, changing, etc.: esp., the transition from one state or period to another: the *passage* from winter to summer. **6.** A journey, esp. by sea: a stormy *passage*; also, the right or privilege of making a journey: to secure *passage*. **7.** The right, power, or freedom to pass. **8.** The passing or enactment of a legislative measure. **9.** An evacuation of the bowels. — *v.i.* **·saged, ·sag·ing** *Rare* **1.** To make a journey. **2.** To fight or quarrel. [< OF]

pas·sage·way (pas′ij-wā′) *n.* A way affording passage, esp. a hall or corridor.

pass·book (pas′bŏŏk′, päs′-) *n.* A bankbook.

pas·sé (pa-sā′, pas′ā; *Fr.* pà·sā′) *adj.* **1.** Past the prime; faded. **2.** Out-of-date; old-fashioned. [< F, orig., pp. of *passer* to pass] — **pas·sée′** *adj. fem.*

passed ball (past, päst) In baseball, a misplay charged to the catcher for allowing a runner to advance by failing to catch a pitch that passes reasonably close to him.

pas·sen·ger (pas′ən-jər) *n.* One who travels in a conveyance. [< MF *passager* < *passage* passage]

passe par·tout (pas pär-tōō′, *Fr.* päs pär·tōō′) In picture framing: **a** A light frame consisting of a glass, the picture, and a pasteboard back put together with strips of tape pasted around the edges. **b** The tape. [< MF < *passer* to pass + *partout* everywhere]

pas·ser-by (pas′ər-bī′, päs′-) *n. pl.* **pas·sers-by** One who passes by, usu. casually.

pas·ser·ine (pas′ər-ēn, -in) *adj.* **1.** Of or pertaining to an order of birds including all singing birds, and more than half of the living birds of various sizes. **2.** Resembling or characteristic of a sparrow. — *n.* A passerine bird. [< L *passer* sparrow + -INE[1]]

pas·sim (pas′im) *adv. Latin* Here and there; in various passages: a reference note in books.

pass·ing (pas′ing, päs′-) *adj.* **1.** Going by or away. **2.** Transitory; fleeting. **3.** Happening or occurring; current. **4.** Done, said, etc., in a cursory or casual manner. **5.** Fulfilling all requirements: a *passing* grade. — **Syn.** See TRANSIENT. — *n.* **1.** The act of one who or that which passes. **2.** A means or place of passing, as a ford. — **in passing** Incidentally. — *adv. Archaic* In a surpassing degree or manner.

pas·sion (pash′ən) *n.* **1.** Any intense, extreme, or overpowering emotion or feeling. **2.** Ardent affection or love. **3.** Intense sexual desire or lust. **4.** Overwhelming anger or rage. **5.** An outburst of strong feeling, esp. of violence or anger. **6.** A strong desire or affection for some object, cause, etc. **7.** The object of such a desire or affection. [< OF < L < *passus* pp. of *pati* to suffer] — **pas′sion·less** *adj.*

Pas·sion (pash′ən) *n.* **1.** The sufferings of Christ, esp. after the Last Supper and on the Cross. **2.** The part of the Gospels that relates the sufferings and death of Christ. **3.** A representation of Christ's sufferings in art, music, etc.

pas·sion·ate (pash′ən-it) *adj.* **1.** Capable of or inclined to strong passion; excitable. **2.** Easily moved to anger; quick-tempered. **3.** Expressing, displaying, or characterized by passion or strong emotion; ardent. **4.** Strong or vehement, as a feeling or emotion. — **Syn.** See ARDENT. — **pas′sion·ate·ly** *adv.* — **pas′sion·ate·ness** *n.*

pas·sion·flow·er (pash′ən-flou′ər) *n.* Any of various vines or shrubs having showy flowers and sometimes edible berries: so called from the fancied resemblance of certain parts to the wounds, crown of thorns, etc., of Christ. [Trans. of Med.L *flos passionis*]

passion fruit The berries of the passion flower.

Passion play A religious drama representing the Passion of Christ.

pas·sive (pas′iv) *adj.* **1.** Not acting, working, or operating; inactive; inert. **2.** Acted upon, affected, or influenced by something external. **3.** Receiving or receptive to an external force, etc. **4.** Submitting or yielding without resistance or opposition; submissive. **5.** *Gram.* Designating a voice of the verb that indicates that the subject is receiving the action, as *was killed* is in the passive voice in *Caesar was killed by Brutus*: distinguished from *active*. — *n. Gram.* **1.** The passive voice. **2.** A verb or construction in this voice. [< L *passus* pp. of *pati* to suffer] — **pas′sive·ly** *adv.* — **pas′sive·ness** *n.*

passive resistance A method of opposing some authority or law by nonviolent acts, as voluntary fasting, etc.

pas·siv·i·ty (pa·siv′ə·tē) *n.* The state of being passive.

pass·key (pas′kē′, päs′-) *n.* A master key.

Pass·o·ver (pas′ō′vər, päs′-) *n.* A Jewish feast commemorating the night when God, smiting the first-born of the Egyptians, "passed over" the houses of the children of Israel.

pass·port (pas′pôrt′, -pōrt′, päs′-) *n.* **1.** An official warrant certifying the citizenship of the bearer and affording protection to him when traveling abroad. **2.** A permit to travel or convey goods through a foreign country. **3.** Anything that enables one to gain entrance, acceptance, etc. [< MF < *passer* to pass + *port* harbor]

pass·word (pas′wûrd′, päs′-) *n.* **1.** A secret word or phrase enabling the speaker to pass a guard or sentry. **2.** Anything that gains entrance or access for one.

past (past, päst) *adj.* **1.** Ended or finished; done with. **2.** Having existed in or belonging to a former time: *past* civilizations. **3.** Just passed or gone by: the *past* few days. **4.** Having formerly served in a public office, committee, etc.: a *past* governor. — *n.* **1.** Past or antecedent time, conditions, or events: usu. with *the.* **2.** Something, as a former life or career, that is kept secret. **3.** *Gram.* **a** A verb tense denoting any action or condition that occurred at a former time. **b** A verb or construction in this tense. — *adv.* In such a manner as to go by: to run *past.* — *prep.* **1.** Beyond in time; after. **2.** Beyond in place or position; farther than. **3.** Beyond the reach, power, or influence of: *past* hope. **4.** Beyond in amount or degree. [Orig. pp. of PASS]

pas·ta (päs′tə) *n.* A noodlelike paste or dough, as spaghetti, macaroni, etc. [< Ital. < LL, dough, paste]

paste (pāst) *n.* **1.** A mixture, usu. of flour and water, used as an adhesive for paper, etc. **2.** Any of various soft, moist, smooth preparations used as foods, in cooking, etc.; as: **a** Dough used in making pastry. **b** A soft, creamy mass made from fish, fruit, etc. **3.** A vitreous composition used in making imitation gems; also, a gem made of this composition. — *v.t.* **past·ed, past·ing** **1.** To stick or fasten with or as with paste. **2.** To cover by applying pasted material. [< OF < LL < Gk. *pastē* barley porridge] — **past′er** *n.*

paste·board (pāst′bôrd′, -bōrd′) *n.* **1.** Paper pulp compressed, or paper pasted together and rolled into a stiff sheet. **2.** A board on which dough for pastry is rolled. **3.** *Informal* A visiting card; also, a playing card. — *adj.* Flimsy.

pas·tel (pas·tel′, pas′tel) *n.* **1.** A picture drawn with colored crayons. **2.** The art of drawing such pictures. **3.** A dried paste made of pipe clay, pigment, and gum water, used for crayons; also, a hard crayon made of this paste: also called *pastille.* **4.** A delicate, soft, or slightly grayish tint. — *adj.* **1.** Of or pertaining to a pastel. **2.** Having a delicate, soft, or slightly grayish tint. [See PASTE.] — **pas′tel·ist** or **pas′tel·list** *n.*

pas·tern (pas′tərn) *n.* **1.** The part of a horse's foot that is between the fetlock and the hoof. **2.** A hobble for a horse's foot. [< OF < *pasture* tether for a grazing animal]

pas·teur·i·za·tion (pas′tər·ə·zā′shən, -chər-) *n.* A process of arresting or preventing fermentation in liquids, as beer, milk, wine, etc., by heating so as to destroy the vitality of the ferment. Also *Brit.* **pas′teur·i·sa′tion.**

pas·teur·ize (pas′tə·rīz, -chə·rīz) *v.t.* **·ized, ·iz·ing** To treat by pasteurization. Also *Brit.* **pas′teur·ise.**

pas·tic·cio (päs·tē′chō) *n.* *pl.* **·ci** (-chē) A work of art, music, or literature made up of fragments from various sources. [< Ital., paste]

pas·tiche (pas·tēsh′, päs-) *n.* A pasticcio, esp. one imitating or satirizing the style of other artists. [< F]

pas·tille (pas·til′, -til′) *n.* **1.** A compound of aromatic substances with niter for fumigating. **2.** A troche; lozenge. **3.** A flavored confection. **4.** Pastel (def. 3). Also **pas·til** (pas′til). [< MF < L *pastillus* little loaf, lozenge]

pas·time (pas′tīm′, päs′-) *n.* Something that serves to make time pass agreeably. [Trans. of F *passe-temps*]

past master **1.** One who has held the office of master in certain social or benevolent organizations. **2.** One who has thorough experience in something; an expert; adept.

pas·tor (pas′tər, päs′-) *n.* A Christian clergyman who has a church or congregation under his charge. [< AF, OF < L *pastor, -oris* shepherd, lit., feeder] — **pas′tor·ship** *n.*

pas·tor·al (pas′tər·əl, päs′-) *adj.* **1.** Of or pertaining to shepherds, rustics, or rural life. **2.** Having the characteristics usu. associated with rural life, as innocence, simplicity, etc. **3.** Dealing with or portraying rural life. **4.** Pertaining to a clergyman or to his duties. — *n.* **1.** A literary work, esp. a poem, dealing with rural life, scenes, etc. **2.** A picture illustrating rural scenes. **3.** *Eccl.* A letter from a pastor or bishop to his diocese. [< L *pastor* shepherd] — **pas′tor·al·ism** *n.* — **pas′tor·al·ist** *n.* — **pas′tor·al·ly** *adv.*

pas·tor·ate (pas′tər·it, päs′-) *n.* **1.** The office or jurisdic-

tion of a pastor. **2.** The duration of a pastoral charge. **3.** Pastors collectively.

past participle See under PARTICIPLE.

past perfect *Gram.* The verb tense indicating an action completed prior to the occurrence of some other past action or specified past time, as *had finished* is the past perfect in *He had finished before the bell rang.* Also called *pluperfect.*

pas·tra·mi (pə·strä′mē) *n.* Heavily seasoned, smoked beef, usu. cut from the shoulder. [< Yiddish < Rumanian]

pas·try (pās′trē) *n.* *pl.* **·tries** Articles of food that are sweet, baked, and are usu. made with a crust of shortened dough, as pies, tarts, etc.; also, any sweet baked foods.

pas·tur·age (pas′chər·ij, päs′-) *n.* **1.** Grass and herbage for cattle. **2.** Ground used or suitable for grazing.

pas·ture (pas′chər, päs′-) *n.* **1.** Ground for the grazing of domestic animals. **2.** Grass or herbage that grazing domestic animals eat. — *v.t.* **·tured, ·tur·ing** **1.** To put in a pasture to graze. **2.** To graze on (grass, etc.). **3.** To provide pasturage for (cattle, etc): said of land. [< OF < LL < L < *pascere* to feed] — **pas′tur·a·ble** *adj.*

past·y¹ (pās′tē) *adj.* **past·i·er, past·i·est** Like paste. — **past′i·ness** *n.*

past·y² (pās′tē, *Brit.* pas′tē, päs′tē) *n.* *pl.* **pas·ties** A pie; esp., a meat pie. [< OF < LL *pasta* paste]

pat (pat) *v.* **pat·ted, pat·ting** *v.t.* **1.** To touch or tap lightly with something flat, esp. with the hand in caressing, etc. **2.** To shape or mold by a pat or pats. — *v.i.* **3.** To run or walk with light steps. — *n.* **1.** A light, caressing stroke; a gentle tap. **2.** The sound of patting or pattering. **3.** A small, molded mass, as of butter. — *adj.* **1.** Exactly suitable; apt. **2.** Needing no change: a *pat* hand in a card game. **3.** Glib; facile. — *adv. Informal* **1.** Firm; steadfast: to stand *pat.* **2.** Aptly. [ME *patte*] — **pat′ness** *n.* — **pat′ter** *n.*

patch (pach) *n.* **1.** A small piece of material used to repair a garment, etc. **2.** A piece of courtplaster or the like, applied to the skin to hide a blemish or to set off the complexion. **3.** A small piece of ground; also, the plants growing on it: a *patch* of corn. **4.** A piece of material worn over an injured eye. **5.** Any small part of a surface not sharing the general character of the whole. **6.** A shred or scrap. — *v.t.* **1.** To put a patch or patches on. **2.** To repair or put together, esp. hurriedly or crudely: often with *up* or *together.* **3.** To make of patches, as a quilt. [ME *pacche*] — **patch′a·ble** *adj.* — **patch′er** *n.*

patch·ou·li (pach′ōō·lē, pə·chōō′lē) *n.* **1.** An East Indian herb of the mint family. **2.** A perfume obtained from it. Also spelled *pachouli.* Also **patch′ou·ly.** [< F < Tamil < *paccu* green + *ilai* leaf]

patch pocket A pocket sewn to the outside of a garment.

patch·work (pach′wûrk′) *n.* **1.** A fabric made of patches of cloth, as for quilts, etc. **2.** Work made up of heterogeneous materials; work done hastily or carelessly; a jumble.

patch·y (pach′ē) *adj.* **patch·i·er, patch·i·est** **1.** Made up of or abounding in patches. **2.** Careless; jumbled. **3.** Peevish; irritable. — **patch′i·ly** *adv.* — **patch·i·ness** *n.*

pate (pāt) *n.* The head or top of the head; also, the brains or intellect: usu. humorous or derogatory. [ME]

pâ·té de foie gras (pä·tā′ də fwä grä′) *French* A paste of fat goose liver.

pa·tel·la (pə·tel′ə) *n.* *pl.* **·tel·lae** (-tel′ē) *Anat.* The flat, movable, oval bone in front of the knee joint; kneecap. For illus. see SKELETON. [< L, dim. of *patina* pan, bowl] — **pa·tel′lar** *adj.* — **pa·tel·late** (pə·tel′āt, -it) *adj.*

pat·en (pat′n) *n.* **1.** A plate; esp., a plate for the eucharistic bread: also called *patina:* also spelled *patin, patine.* **2.** A thin, metallic plate or disk. [< OF < L *patina* pan]

pa·ten·cy (pāt′n·sē) *n.* **1.** The condition of being patent or evident. **2.** *Chiefly Med.* The state of being open, spread, enlarged, or without obstruction.

pat·ent (pat′nt, *Brit.* pāt′nt; *for adj. defs. 1, 4, & 5, usu.* pāt′nt) *n.* **1.** A government protection to an inventor, securing to him for a specific time the exclusive right of manufacturing, exploiting, using, and selling an invention; also, the right granted. **2.** Any official document securing a right. **3.** That which is protected by a patent or its distinctive marks or features. — *v.t.* To obtain a patent on (an invention). — *adj.* **1.** Manifest or apparent to everybody. **2.** Protected or conferred by letters patent. **3.** Open for general inspection or use: letters *patent.* **4.** Expanded; spreading widely, as leaves from the stem of a plant. **5.** *Chiefly Med.* Open; unobstructed, as an intestine. [< F < L < *patere* to lie open] — **pat′ent·a·bil′i·ty** *n.* — **pat′ent·a·ble** *adj.*

pat·en·tee (pat′n·tē′) *n.* One who holds a patent.

patent leather Leather with a glossy, varnishlike finish.

pa·tent·ly (pāt′nt·lē, pat′nt-) *adv.* Manifestly; clearly.

patent medicine A medicine manufactured and sold under patent and usu. of secret composition.

pat·en·tor (pat′n·tər) *n.* One who grants a patent.

pa·ter (pä/tər) *n. Brit. Informal* Father. [< L]

pa·ter·fa·mil·i·as (pä/tər-fə-mil/ē-əs) *n.* The father of a family. [< L < *pater* father + *familia* family]

pa·ter·nal (pə-tûr/nəl) *adj.* **1.** Of, pertaining to, or characteristic of a father; fatherly. **2.** Derived from, related through, or connected with one's father. [< LL < L < *pater* father] **— pa·ter/nal·ly** *adv.*

pa·ter·nal·ism (pə-tûr/nəl-iz/əm) *n.* The care or control of a country, community, group of employees, etc., in a manner suggestive of a father looking after his children. **— pa·ter/·nal·is/tic** *adj.* **— pa·ter/nal·is/ti·cal·ly** *adv.*

pa·ter·ni·ty (pə-tûr/nə-tē) *n.* **1.** The condition of being a father. **2.** Parentage on the male side. **3.** Origin in general.

pa·ter·nos·ter (pä/tər-nos/tər) *n.* **1.** The Lord's Prayer. *Matt.* vi 9–13. Also **Pa/ter Nos/ter. 2.** A large bead of the rosary, indicating that a paternoster is to be recited. [< L *pater noster* our father]

path (path, päth) *n. pl.* **paths** (pathz, päthz, paths, päths) **1.** A walk or way used by man or animals on foot. **2.** A track or course. **3.** A course of life or action. [OE *pæth*]

Pa·than (pə-tän/, pət-hän/) *n.* An Afghan; esp., one of a people of Afghanistan of Indo-Iranian stock and Moslem religion. [< Hind. < Afghan *Pĕstŭn* an Afghan]

pa·thet·ic (pə-thet/ik) *adj.* Of the nature of, expressing, or arousing sadness, pity, tenderness, etc. Also **pa·thet/i·cal.** [< LL < Gk. < *pathos* suffering] **— pa·thet/i·cal·ly** *adv.* **— pa·thet/i·cal·ness** *n.*

pathetic fallacy The ascribing of human emotions and characteristics to nature or things of nature, as *a sad day.*

path·find·er (path/fīn/dər, päth/-) *n.* One skilled in leading or finding a way, esp. in unknown regions.

-pathia See -PATHY.

path·less (path/lis, päth/-) *adj.* Trackless; untrodden.

patho- *combining form* Suffering; disease. Also, before vowels, **path-.** [< Gk. *pathos* suffering]

path·o·gen (path/ə-jən) *n.* Any disease-producing bacterium or microorganism. Also **path/o·gene** (-jēn).

path·o·gen·e·sis (path/ə-jen/ə-sis) *n. Med.* The production or development of any diseased condition. Also **pa·thog·e·ny** (pə-thoj/ə-nē).

path·o·gen·ic (path/ə-jen/ik) *adj. Med.* Productive of or pertaining to the production of disease. Also **path/o·ge·net/·ic** (-jə-net/ik).

path·o·log·i·cal (path/ə-loj/i·kəl) *adj.* **1.** Of pathology. **2.** Related to, involving, concerned with, or caused by disease. Also **path/o·log/ic. — path/o·log/i·cal·ly** *adv.*

pa·thol·o·gist (pə-thol/ə-jist) *n.* One skilled in pathology.

pa·thol·o·gy (pə-thol/ə-jē) *n. pl.* **·gies 1.** The branch of medical science that treats of the origin, nature, causes, and development of disease. **2.** The sum of the conditions, processes, and effects in the course of a disease.

pa·thos (pä/thos) *n.* The quality, esp. in literature or art, that arouses feelings of pity, sorrow, compassion, etc. **— Syn.** See FEELING. [< Gk. < *pathein* to suffer]

path·way (path/wā/, päth/-) *n.* A path; footway.

-pathy *combining form* **1.** Suffering; affection. **2.** *Med.* Disease, or the treatment of disease: *psychopathy.* Also spelled *-pathia.* [< Gk. *pathos* suffering]

pa·tience (pā/shəns) *n.* **1.** The state, quality, or fact of being patient; also, the ability to be patient. **2.** *Chiefly Brit.* Solitaire (def. 2). [< OF < L *pati* to suffer]

pa·tient (pā/shənt) *adj.* **1.** Possessing or demonstrating quiet, uncomplaining endurance under distress or annoyance. **2.** Tolerant, tender, and forbearing. **3.** Capable of tranquilly awaiting results. **4.** Persevering; diligent. **—** *n.* A person undergoing treatment for disease or injury. [< OF < L < *pati* to suffer] **— pa/tient·ly** *adv.*

pat·in (pat/n) See PATEN (def. 1).

pat·i·na[1] (pat/ə-nə, pə-tē/nə) *n. pl.* **·nae** (-nē) **1.** An earthenware or metal bowl or basin used as a domestic utensil by the Romans. A paten (def. 1). [< L < Gk. *patanē*]

pat·i·na[2] (pat/ə-nə, pə-tē/nə) *n.* **1.** A green rust that covers ancient bronzes, copper coins, medals, etc. **2.** Any surface of antique appearance. Also called *patine.* [< F, prob. < L *patina* plate]

pat·ine (pə-tēn/ *for def.1*, pat/n *for def.2*) *n.* **1.** Patina². **2.** See PATEN (def. 1).

pa·ti·o (pä/tē-ō, pat/ē-ō; *Sp.* pä/tyō) *n. pl.* **·ti·os 1.** The open inner court of a Spanish or Spanish-American dwelling. **2.** *U.S.* A paved area adjoining a house, used for parties, barbecues, etc. [< Sp., ? < L *patere* to lie open]

pat·ois (pat/wä, *Fr.* pá·twä/) *n. pl.* **pat·ois** (pat/wäz, *Fr.* pá·twä/) A type of local dialect, esp. one that is rustic or illiterate. [< F; origin uncertain]

patri- *combining form* Father: *patricide.* [< L *pater, -tris* father]

pa·tri·arch (pā/trē-ärk) *n.* **1.** The leader of a family or tribe who rules by paternal right. **2.** One of the fathers of the Hebrew race, Abraham, Isaac, or Jacob. **3.** One of the twelve sons of Jacob considered as the progenitors of the tribes of Israel. **4.** A venerable man; esp., the founder of a religion, order, etc. **5.** *Eccl.* **a** In the primitive Christian church, any of the bishops of Antioch, Alexandria, Rome, Constantinople, or Jerusalem. **b** In the Greek Orthodox Church, any of the bishops of Constantinople, Alexandria, Antioch, or Jerusalem. [< OF < L < Gk. < *patria* family, clan + *archein* to rule]

pa·tri·ar·chal (pā/trē-är/kəl) *adj.* **1.** Of, pertaining to, or governed by a patriarch. **2.** Of the nature of a patriarchy. **3.** Having the nature or character of a patriarch. **— pa/tri·ar/chal·ly** *adv.*

pa·tri·ar·chate (pā/trē-är/kit) *n.* **1.** The office, dominion, or residence of a patriarch. **2.** A patriarchal system of government.

pa·tri·ar·chy (pā/trē-är/kē) *n. pl.* **·chies 1.** A system of government in which the father or the male heir of his choice rules. **2.** Government by men.

pa·tri·cian (pə-trish/ən) *adj.* **1.** Of or pertaining to the aristocracy. **2.** Noble or aristocratic. **—** *n.* **1.** An aristocrat; esp., in ancient Rome, a member of the hereditary aristocracy. **2.** Any one of the upper classes. **3.** An honorary title bestowed by the later Roman emperors. [< OF < L *pater, -tris* senator, lit., father] **— pa·tri/cian·ly** *adv.*

pat·ri·cide (pat/rə-sīd) *n.* **1.** The killing of one's father. **2.** One who has killed his father. [< LL *patricidium*] **— pat/·ri·ci/dal** *adj.*

pat·ri·lin·e·al (pat/rə-lin/ē-əl) *adj.* Derived from or descending through the male line.

pat·ri·mo·ny (pat/rə-mō/nē) *n. pl.* **·nies 1.** An inheritance from a father or an ancestor; also, anything inherited. **2.** An endowment, as of a church. [< OF < L < *pater, -tris* father] **— pat/ri·mo/ni·al** *adj.* **— pat/ri·mo/ni·al·ly** *adv.*

pa·tri·ot (pā/trē-ət, -ot) *n.* One who loves his country and zealously guards its welfare; esp., a defender of popular liberty. [< F < LL < Gk. *patris* fatherland] **— pa/tri·ot/ic** *adj.* **— pa/tri·ot/i·cal·ly** *adv.*

pa·tri·ot·ism (pā/trē-ə-tiz/əm) *n.* Devotion to one's country.

pa·tris·tic (pə-tris/tik) *adj.* Of or pertaining to the fathers of the Christian church or to their writings. Also **pa·tris/ti·cal. — pa·tris/ti·cal·ly** *adv.*

pa·trol (pə-trōl/) *v.t. & v.i.* **·trolled, ·trol·ling** To walk or go through or around (an area, town, etc.) for the purpose of guarding or inspecting. **—** *n.* **1.** One or more soldiers, policemen, etc., patrolling a district. **2.** A reconnaissance or combat group sent out from the main body in air, ground, or naval warfare. **3.** The act of patrolling. **4.** A division of a troop of Boy Scouts. [< MF < *patrouiller*, var. of *patouiller*, orig., to paddle in mud] **— pa·trol/ler** *n.*

patrol car A squad car.

pa·trol·man (pə-trōl/mən) *n. pl.* **·men** (-mən) **1.** One who patrols. **2.** *U.S.* A policeman assigned to a beat.

patrol torpedo boat A small, highly maneuverable vessel, armed with torpedoes for action against enemy shipping: also called *PT boat.*

patrol wagon *U.S.* A police wagon for conveying prisoners.

pa·tron (pā/trən) *n.* **1.** One who protects, fosters, or supports some person, thing, or enterprise. **2.** A regular customer. **3.** A patron saint. [< OF < L *patronus* protector] **— pa/tron·al** *adj.* **— pa/tron·ess** *n.fem.*

pa·tron·age (pā/trən-ij, pat/rən-) *n.* **1.** The protection, support, or position of a patron. **2.** In the public service, the power or right to distribute offices, esp. political offices; also, the offices so distributed. **3.** The financial support given by customers to a commercial establishment. **4.** An overly condescending manner.

pa·tron·ize (pā/trən-īz, pat/rən-) *v.t.* **·ized, ·iz·ing 1.** To act as a patron toward; give support to. **2.** To treat in a condescending manner. **3.** To trade with as a regular customer; frequent. **— pa/tron·iz·er** *n.* **— pa/tron·iz/ing·ly** *adv.*

patron saint A saint regarded as the special protector of a country, city, person, cause, etc.

pat·ro·nym·ic (pat/rə-nim/ik) *adj.* Pertaining to or derived from the name of one's father or paternal ancestor. **—** *n.* **1.** A family name. **2.** A name formed by adding a prefix or suffix to a proper name, as *Johnson*, son of John. [< L < Gk. < *patēr* father + *onoma* name] **— pat/ro·nym/i·cal·ly** *adv.*

pa·troon (pə-trōon/) *n.* Formerly, under the old Dutch law, a holder of entailed estates, having some manorial rights. [< Du. < F < L *patronus* protector]

pat·ter[1] (pat/ər) *v.i.* **1.** To make a succession of light, sharp sounds. **2.** To move with light, quick steps. **—** *v.t.* **3.** To cause to patter. **—** *n.* The act or sound of pattering. [Freq. of PAT[1]]

pat·ter[2] (pat/ər) *v.t. & v.i.* To speak or say glibly or rapidly; mumble mechanically or indistinctly. **—** *n.* **1.** Glib and rapid talk, as used by comedians, etc. **2.** Patois or dialect. **3.** Any professional jargon. **4.** Rapid speech set to music. [Short for PATERNOSTER] **— pat/ter·er** *n.*

pat·tern (pat/ərn) *n.* **1.** An original or model proposed for or worthy of imitation. **2.** Anything shaped or designed to serve as a model or guide in making something else. **3.** Any decorative design or figure; also, such design worked on something. **4.** Arrangement of natural or accidental markings: the *pattern* of a butterfly's wings. **5.** The stylistic composition or design of a work of art. **6.** A complex of integrated parts functioning as a whole: the behavior *pattern* of a five-year-old. **7.** A representative example, sample, or instance. — *v.t.* **1.** To make after a model or pattern: with *on, upon,* or *after.* **2.** To decorate or furnish with a pattern. [< F *patron* patron]

pat·ty (pat/ē) *n. pl.* **·ties 1.** A small, flat piece of chopped meat, fish, etc. **2.** A small pie. [Alter. of F *pâté*]

patty shell A small puff-paste shell in which creamed meat, fish, vegetables, or fruit are served.

pau·ci·ty (pô/sə·tē) *n.* **1.** Smallness of number or quantity. **2.** Scarcity; insufficiency. [< OF or < L *paucus* few]

Paul (pôl), died 67? A.D., one of the apostles; the chief early Christian missionary to the Gentiles; author of several New Testament epistles: original name *Saul.* Also **Saint Paul, Paul the Apostle, Saul of Tarsus.**

Paul Bunyan The famous hero lumberjack of American folklore, of superhuman size and strength.

Paul·ine (pô/lēn, -līn) *adj.* Of the apostle Paul, his teachings, or writings. — **Paul/in·ism** *n.* — **Paul/in·ist** *n.*

paunch (pônch) *n.* **1.** The abdomen or the belly, esp. if protruding. **2.** A rumen (def. 1). [< OF < L *pantex, -ticis* belly] — **paunch/y** *adj.* — **paunch/i·ness** *n.*

pau·per (pô/pər) *n.* **1.** One who receives, or is entitled to receive, public charity. **2.** Any very poor person. [< Med.L < *pauper* poor] — **pau/per·ism** *n.*

pau·per·ize (pô/pər·īz) *v.t.* **·ized, ·iz·ing** To make a pauper of.

pause (pôz) *v.i.* **paused, paus·ing 1.** To cease action or utterance temporarily; hesitate. **2.** To dwell or linger: with *on* or *upon.* — *n.* **1.** A temporary ceasing of action; rest. **2.** A holding back because of doubt or irresolution; hesitation. **3.** A momentary cessation in speaking or music for the sake of meaning or expression; also, a sign indicating such cessation. **4.** *Music* A hold. **5.** In prosody, a calculated interval of silence in a meter, or the place at which the voice naturally pauses in reading a verse: see CAESURA. [< OF < L < Gk. < *pauein* to stop] — **paus/er** *n.*

pav·an (pə·van/, -vän/) *n.* **1.** A slow, stately dance of the 16th and 17th centuries. **2.** Music for or in the manner of this dance. Also **pav·ane** (pə·van/, -vän/; *Fr.* pȧ·vȧn/). [< MF < Sp. ? < L *pavo, -onis* peacock]

pave (pāv) *v.t.* **paved, pav·ing** To cover or surface with asphalt, gravel, concrete, etc., as a road. — **to pave the way (for)** To make preparation (for); lead up to. [< OF < L *pavire* to ram down] — **pav/er** *n.*

pave·ment (pāv/mənt) *n.* **1.** A hard, solid, surface covering for a road or footway. **2.** A paved road or footway. **3.** The material with which a surface is paved.

pa·vil·ion (pə·vil/yən) *n.* **1.** A movable or open structure, as a large tent or summerhouse. **2.** A related or connected part of a principal building, as for hospital patients. **3.** A canopy. — *v.t.* **1.** To provide with a pavilion. **2.** To shelter by a pavilion. [< OF < L *papilio, -onis* butterfly, tent]

pav·ing (pā/ving) *n.* **1.** The laying of a pavement. **2.** A pavement; also, the material used for pavement.

Pa·vo (pā/vō) A constellation, the Peacock. [< L]

pav·o·nine (pav/ə·nīn, -nin) *adj.* **1.** Resembling or characteristic of the peacock. **2.** Iridescent like the tail of a peacock. [< L *pavo, -onis* peacock]

paw (pô) *n.* **1.** The foot of an animal having nails or claws. **2.** *Informal* A human hand. — *v.t. & v.i.* **1.** To strike or scrape with the feet or paws: to *paw* the air. **2.** *Informal* To handle or caress rudely or clumsily; maul. [< OF *powe,* prob. of Gmc. origin] — **paw/er** *n.*

pawl (pôl) *n. Mech.* A hinged or pivoted member shaped to engage with ratchet teeth, either to drive a ratchet wheel or to stop its reverse motion. [Origin uncertain]

pawn[1] (pôn) *n.* **1.** A chessman of lowest rank, that moves on file but captures diagonally. **2.** Any insignificant person used at another's will. [< AF, OF *peon* foot soldier]

pawn[2] (pôn) *n.* **1.** Something pledged as security for a loan. **2.** The condition of being held as a pledge for money loaned. **3.** The act of pawning. — *v.t.* **1.** To give as security for a loan. **2.** To risk or stake. [< OF *pan,* var. of early Frisian *pand* pledge] — **pawn/a·ble** *adj.* — **pawn/age** *n.* — **pawn/er, pawn/or** *n.*

pawn·brok·er (pôn/brō/kər) *n.* One engaged in the business of lending money at interest on pledged personal property.

Paw·nee (pô·nē/) *n. pl.* **·nees** or **·nee** A member of one of four tribes of North American Indians formerly inhabiting the region between the Arkansas River and the Platte River, Nebraska, now living in Oklahoma.

pawn·shop (pôn/shop/) *n.* The shop of a pawnbroker.

pawn ticket A receipt for goods pawned.

paw·paw (pô/pô) See PAPAW.

pay[1] (pā) *v.* **paid** or (*Obs.* except for def. 2 of *to pay out*) **payed, pay·ing** *v.t.* **1.** To give (someone) what is due for a debt, purchase, etc.; remunerate. **2.** To give (money, etc.) for a purchase, service rendered, etc. **3.** To provide or hand over the amount of, as a debt, bill, etc. **4.** To yield as return or recompense. **5.** To afford profit or benefit to. **6.** To defray, as expenses. **7.** To require, as for an insult. **8.** To render or give, as a compliment, attention, etc. **9.** To make, as a call or visit. — *v.i.* **10.** To make recompense or payment. **11.** To be worthwhile: It *pays* to be honest — **to pay back** To repay. — **to pay off 1.** To pay the entire amount of (a debt, mortgage, etc.). **2.** To pay the wages of and discharge. **3.** To gain revenge upon or for. **4.** *U.S. Informal* To afford full return. **5.** *Naut.* To turn or cause to turn to leeward. **6.** *U.S. Slang* To bribe. — **to pay out 1.** To disburse or expend. **2.** *Naut.* To let out by slackening, as a rope or cable. — **to pay up** To make full payment (of). — *n.* **1.** That which is given as a recompense; wages. **2.** The act of paying, or the state of being paid. **3.** Paid employment. **4.** Requital; reward; also, retribution. — *adj.* **1.** Of or pertaining to payments, persons who pay, or services paid for: *pay* day. **2.** Constructed so as to require payment on use. **3.** Yielding enough metal to be worth mining: *pay* dirt. [< OF < L *pacare* to appease] — **pay/er** *n.* — **Syn.** (verb) **1.** compensate, indemnify. **2.** spend, expend, disburse. **3.** settle, liquidate.

pay[2] (pā) *v.t.* **paid** or **payed, pay·ing** To coat with a waterproof substance, as pitch. [< AF < L < *pix, picis* pitch]

pay·a·ble (pā/ə·bəl) *adj.* **1.** Due and unpaid. **2.** That can or will be paid. **3.** Likely to be profitable. — **pay/a·bly** *adv.*

pay·day (pā/dā/) *n.* The day on which wages are distributed.

pay dirt 1. Soil containing enough metal, esp. gold, to be profitable to mine. **2.** Anything profitable.

pay·ee (pā·ē/) *n.* A person to whom money has been or is to be paid.

pay·load (pā/lōd/) *n.* **1.** That part of a cargo producing revenue. **2.** The warhead of a guided missile.

pay·mas·ter (pā/mas/tər, -mäs/-) *n.* One who has charge of paying employees. — **pay/mis/tress** (-mis/tris) *n.fem.*

pay·ment (pā/mənt) *n.* **1.** The act of paying, or that which is paid. **2.** Recompense. **3.** Punishment.

pay·off (pā/ôf/, -of/) *n.* **1.** *Informal* Any settlement, reward, or punishment. **2.** *Informal* The climax or outcome of an incident or narrative. **3.** *U.S. Slang* A bribe.

pay·roll (pā/rōl/) *n.* A list of those entitled to receive pay, with the amounts due them; also, the total sum of money needed to make the payments. Also **pay roll.**

pays (pās) See PAIS.

pea (pē) *n. pl.* **peas** or **pease 1.** A climbing annual leguminous herb having pinnate leaves and round, green, usu. edible seeds. **2.** The seed of any one of various related plants. [< PEASE, incorrectly taken as a plural]

peace (pēs) *n.* **1.** A state of mental or physical quiet or tranquillity; calm. **2.** The absence or cessation of war. **3.** Public order and tranquillity. **4.** A state of reconciliation after strife or enmity. **5.** Freedom from mental agitation or anxiety. — **at peace 1.** In a quiet state; tranquil. **2.** In a state or condition of order and harmony. — **to hold (or keep) one's peace** To be silent. — *v.i. Obs.* except as an *imperative* To be or become quiet. [< OF < L *pax, pacis*]

Peace Corps A U.S. government organization, established in 1961, that trains and sends volunteers to live in and aid underdeveloped countries by teaching, farming, building, etc.

peace·a·ble (pē/sə·bəl) *adj.* **1.** Inclined to peace. **2.** Peaceful; tranquil. — **peace/a·ble·ness** *n.* — **peace/a·bly** *adv.*

peace·ful (pēs/fəl) *adj.* **1.** Not in a state of war, riot, or commotion; undisturbed. **2.** Averse to strife. **3.** Inclined to or characteristic of peace. — **peace/ful·ly** *adv.* — **peace/ful·ness** *n.*

peace·mak·er (pēs/mā/kər) *n.* One who effects a reconciliation between unfriendly parties. — **peace/mak/ing** *n. & adj.*

peace pipe The calumet.

peace·time (pēs/tīm/) *n.* A time of peace. — *adj.* Of, characterized by, or used in such a time.

peach[1] (pēch) *n.* **1.** The edible fruit of a tree of the rose family, wildly cultivated in many varieties. **2.** The tree itself. **3.** The yellowish pink color characteristic of the fruit. **4.** *Slang* Any particularly beautiful, pleasing, or excellent person or thing. [< OF < LL < L < Gk. *Persikon (mēlon)* Persian (fruit)]

peach[2] (pēch) *v.i. Slang* To inform against an accomplice; turn informer. [Aphetic var. of obs. *appeach* to accuse]

peach·y (pē/chē) *adj.* **peach·i·er, peach·i·est 1.** Resembling a peach, esp. in color or downiness. **2.** *Slang* Delightfully pleasant, beautiful, etc. — **peach/i·ness** *n.*

pea·coat (pē/kōt/) *n.* A pea jacket. Also **pea coat.**

---

pea·cock (pē′kok′) *n.* The male of a gallinaceous crested bird having erectile, brilliantly iridescent tail coverts enormously elongated and marked with eyelike spots, and the neck and breast of a greenish blue. ◆ Collateral adjective: *pavonine.* —*v.i.* To strut vainly; make a display. [OE *pēa, pāwa* peacock (< L *pavo*) + COCK¹]

MALE PEACOCK
(Body to 36 inches long; tail coverts to 6 feet)

peacock blue A vivid greenish blue.
pea·fowl (pē′foul′) *n.* A peacock or pea-hen.
pea green A light yellowish green.
pea·hen (pē′hen′) *n.* A female peafowl.
pea jacket A short coat of thick woolen cloth, worn by seamen. Also called *peacoat.* [< Du. *pij* coat of coarse wool + JACKET]
peak (pēk) *n.* 1. A projecting point or edge; an end terminating in a point. 2. A conspicuous or precipitous mountain; also, the summit of such a mountain. 3. A point formed by the growth or cut of hair. 4. The maximum development, strength, value, etc., of something. 5. *Naut.* a The after upper corner of a fore-and-aft sail. b The upper end of a gaff. c The sharply narrowed part of a vessel at the bow or stern. —*v.t.* 1. *Naut.* To raise to or almost to a vertical position, as a gaff or yard. 2. To make into a peak or point. —*v.i.* 3. To assume the form of a peak. [Var. of PIKE⁴]
peak·ed (pē′kid, pēkt) *adj.* Having a thin or sickly appearance. [Origin uncertain]
peal (pēl) *n.* 1. A prolonged, sonorous sound, as of a bell or thunder. 2. A set of large bells. 3. A change rung on a set of bells. —*v.t. & v.i.* To sound with a peal or peals. [ME *pele,* aphetic var. of *apele* < OF *apeler* to appeal]
pe·an (pē′ən) See PAEAN.
pea·nut (pē′nut′) *n.* 1. The nutlike seed or seed pod of an annual herbaceous vine ripening underground from the flowers that bury themselves after fertilization. 2. The plant bearing this nut.
peanut brittle A hard candy containing roasted peanuts.
peanut butter A spread resembling butter in consistency, made from ground, roasted peanuts.
pear (pâr) *n.* 1. The juicy, edible, fleshy fruit of a tree of the rose family. 2. The tree bearing this fruit. [OE < W Gmc. < LL < L *pira,* pl. of *pirum* pear]
pearl¹ (pûrl) *n.* 1. A smooth, rounded, variously tinted nacreous concretion formed as a deposit around a foreign body in the shells of various mollusks, and largely used as a gem. 2. Something like or likened to such a jewel in form, luster, value, etc. 3. Nacre or mother-of-pearl. 4. A very pale bluish gray: also **pearl blue, pearl gray.** 5. *Printing* A size of type smaller than agate, 5 points. —*adj.* 1. Pertaining to, consisting of, set with, or made of pearl or mother-of-pearl. 2. Shaped like a pearl. —*v.i.* 1. To seek or fish for pearls. 2. To form beads like pearls. —*v.t.* 3. To adorn or set with or as with pearls. 4. To color or shape like pearls. 5. To make into small round grains, as barley. [< OF < Med.L *perna* pearl < L, mussel] —**pearl′y** *adj.*
pearl² (pûrl) See PURL².
pearl·ash (purl′ash) *n.* Commercial potassium carbonate.
peas·ant (pez′ənt) *n.* 1. In Europe, a farmer, farm laborer, or rustic workman. 2. *Informal* A boorish, uncouth, or simple-minded person. [< AF < OF *pais* country < LL < *pagus* district]
peas·ant·ry (pez′ən·trē) *n.* 1. The peasant class; a body of peasants. 2. Rusticity.
pease (pēz) Alternate plural of PEA: now used only in the collective sense. [OE < LL < L, pl. of *pisum* < Gk. < *pisos,* pulse, pease]
pease·cod (pēz′kod) *n.* A pea pod. Also **peas′cod.**
pea·soup·er (pē′sōop′ər) *n.* 1. *Canadian* A French Canadian. 2. *Brit.* A thick fog.
peat (pēt) *n.* 1. A substance consisting of partially carbonized vegetable material, found usu. in bogs. 2. A block of this substance, pressed and dried for fuel: also called *turf.* [ME < Med.L *peta* piece of peat] —**peat′y** *adj.*
peat bog A marsh with an accumulation of peat.
peat moss 1. A moss of which peat is largely composed. 2. *Brit.* A peat bog.
pea·vey (pē′vē) *n.* *pl.* **·veys** An iron-pointed lever fitted with a movable hook and used for handling logs. Also **pea′vy.** [after Joseph *Peavey,* its inventor]
peb·ble (peb′əl) *n.* 1. A small, rounded fragment of rock, shaped by the action of water, ice, etc. 2. Quartz crystal; also, a lens made of it. 3. Leather that has been pebbled. —*v.t.* **·bled, ·bling** 1. To impart a rough grain to (leather). 2. To cover or pelt with pebbles. [Back formation of OE *papol(stān)* pebble(stone)]
peb·bly (peb′lē, peb′əl·ē) *adj.* **·bli·er, ·bli·est** 1. Covered with or full of pebbles. 2. Having a texture resembling pebbles.
pe·can (pi·kan′, -kän′, pē′kan) *n.* 1. A large hickory of the central and southern U.S., with edible, oval, thin-shelled nuts. 2. The nut of this tree. [Earlier *paccan* < Algonquian (Cree) *pacan*]
pec·ca·dil·lo (pek′ə·dil′ō) *n.* *pl.* **·los** or **·loes** A slight or trifling sin. [< Sp., dim. of *pecado* sin < L < *peccare* to sin]
pec·cant (pek′ənt) *adj.* 1. Guilty of sin; sinful. 2. Corrupt and offensive. —**pec′can·cy** *n.* —**pec′cant·ly** *adv.*
pec·ca·ry (pek′ər·ē) *n.* *pl.* **·ries** A hoglike animal of Central and South America. [< Sp. < Carib *pakira*]
pec·ca·vi (pe·kä′vī, -kä′vē) *n.* *pl.* **·vis** *Latin* A confession of guilt; literally, I have sinned.
peck¹ (pek) *v.t.* 1. To strike with the beak, as a bird does, or with something pointed. 2. To make by striking thus: to *peck* a hole in a wall. 3. To pick up, as food, with the beak. —*v.i.* 4. To make strokes with the beak or with something pointed. 5. To eat in small amounts or without appetite: with *at.* —*n.* 1. A quick, sharp blow, as with a beak. 2. A mark or hole made by such a blow. 3. *Informal* A quick kiss. [ME. Var. of PICK.] —**peck′er** *n.*
peck² (pek) *n.* 1. A measure of capacity: the fourth of a bushel. See table front of book. 2. A vessel for measuring a peck. 3. *Slang* A great quantity. [< OF *pek*]
pec·tin (pek′tin) *n. Biochem.* Any of a class of carbohydrates contained in the cell walls of various fruits as apples, lemons, etc., used as the basis of fruit jellies.
pec·to·ral (pek′tər·əl) *adj.* 1. Of or pertaining to the breast or chest. 2. Of or for diseases of the lungs or chest. —*n.* 1. A pectoral organ, fin, or muscle. 2. Any medicine for ailments of the chest. [< L < *pectus, -oris* breast]
pectoral fin *Zool.* One of the anterior paired fins of fishes, homologous with the anterior limb of higher vertebrates.
pec·u·late (pek′yə·lāt) *v.t. & v.i.* **·lat·ed, ·lat·ing** To steal or appropriate wrongfully (funds, esp. public funds entrusted to one's care); embezzle. [< L *peculatus,* pp. of *peculari* to embezzle] —**pec′u·la′tion** *n.* —**pec′u·la′tor** *n.*
pe·cu·liar (pi·kyōol′yər) *adj.* 1. Having a character exclusively its own; specific. 2. Singular; strange. 3. Select or special; separate. 4. Belonging particularly or exclusively to one. —*n.* A person or thing that is peculiar; formerly, any private possession. [< MF *peculier* or < L < *peculium* private property] —**pe·cu′liar·ly** *adv.*
pe·cu·li·ar·i·ty (pi·kyōo′lē·ar′ə·tē, -kyōol′yar′-) *n.* *pl.* **·ties** 1. A characteristic. 2. The quality of being peculiar. —Syn. See CHARACTERISTIC.
pe·cu·ni·ar·y (pi·kyōo′nē·er′ē) *adj.* 1. Consisting of or relating to money. 2. Having a monetary penalty; entailing a fine. [< L < *pecunia* money < *pecus* cattle]
ped-¹ Var. of PEDI-¹.
ped-² Var. of PEDO-.
-ped Var. of -PEDE.
ped·a·gog·ic (ped′ə·goj′ik, -gō′jik) *adj.* 1. Of or pertaining to the science or art of teaching. 2. Of or belonging to a pedagogue; affected with a conceit of learning. Also **ped′a·gog′i·cal.** —**ped′a·gog′i·cal·ly** *adv.*
ped·a·gog·ism (ped′ə·gog′iz·əm, -gôg′-) *n.* The nature, character, or business of a teacher. Also **ped′a·gogu′ism.**
ped·a·gogue (ped′ə·gog, -gôg) *n.* 1. A schoolmaster; educator. 2. A pedantic, narrow-minded teacher. Also **ped′a·gog.** [< OF < L < Gk. < *pais, paidos* child + *agōgos* leader]
ped·a·go·gy (ped′ə·gō′jē, -goj′ē) *n.* 1. The science or profession of teaching. 2. The theory of how to teach.
ped·al (ped′l) *adj.* 1. Of or pertaining to a foot, feet, or a footlike part. 2. Of or pertaining to a pedal. —*n. Mech.* A lever operated by the foot and having various functions: a bicycle *pedal;* a piano *pedal.* —*v.t. & v.i.* **ped·aled** or **·alled, ped·al·ing** or **·al·ling** To move or operate by working pedals. [< L < *pes, pedis* foot]
ped·al-push·ers (ped′l·pŏosh′ərz) *n.pl.* Slacks that come to just below the knees, worn by women and girls.
ped·ant (ped′ənt) *n.* One who makes needless display of his learning, or who insists upon the importance of trifling points of scholarship. [< MF < Ital. *pedante,* prob. < Med.L *paedagogans, -antis,* ppr. of *paedagogare* to teach] —**pe·dan′tic** or **pe·dan′ti·cal·ly** *adv.*
ped·ant·ry (ped′ən·trē) *n.* *pl.* **·ries** 1. Ostentatious display of knowledge. 2. Slavish adherence to forms or rules.
ped·ate (ped′āt) *adj.* 1. Resembling or having the functions of a foot; also, having feet. 2. *Bot.* Divided or parted as a fan, the lateral divisions being subdivided: said esp. of leaves. [< L *pedatus* having feet] —**ped′ate·ly** *adv.*
ped·dle (ped′l) *v.* **·dled, ·dling** *v.i.* 1. To travel about selling small wares. 2. To piddle. —*v.t.* 3. To carry about and sell in small quantities. 4. To sell or dispense in small quantities. [Appar. back formation < ME *pedlere* peddler]
ped·dler (ped′lər) *n.* One who peddles; a hawker. [ME < *ped* basket] —**ped′dler·y** *n.*
-pede *combining form* Footed: *centipede.* Also spelled *-ped,* as in *quadruped.* [< L *pes, pedis* foot]
ped·er·ast (ped′ə·rast, pē′də-) *n.* One addicted to pederasty: also spelled *paederast.*

ped·er·as·ty (ped′ə·ras′tē, pē′də-) *n.* Sex relations between men, esp. between men and boys. [< NL < Gk. < *pais, paidos* boy + *erastēs* lover] — **ped′er·as′tic** *adj.*

ped·es·tal (ped′is·təl) *n.* **1.** A base or support for a column, statue, or vase. **2.** Any foundation or support. — **to put on a pedestal** To hold in high estimation; to put in the position of an idol or hero. — *v.t.* **·taled** or **·tailed**, **·tal·ing** or **·tal·ling** To place on a pedestal. [< MF < Ital. < *piè, piede* foot + *di* of + *stallo* stall, standing place]

pe·des·tri·an (pə·des′trē·ən) *adj.* **1.** Moving on foot; walking. **2.** Pertaining to common people; plebeian. **3.** Commonplace, prosaic, or dull, as prose. — *n.* One who journeys or moves from place to place on foot; a walker. [< L *pedester, -tris* on foot] — **pe·des′tri·an·ism** *n.*

pedi-¹ *combining form* Foot; related to the foot or feet. Also, before vowels, *ped-*. [< L *pes, pedis* foot]

pedi-² Var. of PEDO-.

pe·di·a·tri·cian (pē′dē·ə·trish′ən, ped′ē-) *n.* A physician specializing in pediatrics. Also **pe·di·at·rist** (pē′dē·at′rist).

pe·di·at·rics (pē′dē·at′riks, ped′ē-) *n.pl.* (*construed as sing.*) That branch of medicine dealing with the diseases and hygienic care of children: also spelled *paediatrics*. [< Gk. *pais, paidos* child + -IATRICS] — **pe′di·at′ric** *adj.*

ped·i·cab (ped′i·kab) *n.* A three-wheeled vehicle operated by pedaling and used for public hire, esp. in Asia.

ped·i·cel (ped′ə·sel) *n.* **1.** A stalk or supporting part. **2.** *Bot.* The stalk supporting a single flower in an inflorescence composed of flowers arranged upon a common peduncle. **3.** *Zool.* A footlike sucker or part. [< NL *pedicellus,* dim. of L *pediculus,* dim. of *pes, pedis* foot]

ped·i·cel·late (ped′ə·sə·lit, -lāt′) *adj.* On or having a pedicel.

ped·i·cle (ped′i·kəl) *n.* A pedicel.

pe·dic·u·lo·sis (pə·dik′yə·lō′sis) *n. Pathol.* The condition of being infested with lice; lousiness. [< L *pediculus* little louse + -OSIS] — **pe·dic′u·lous** *adj.*

ped·i·cure (ped′i·kyŏŏr) *n.* **1.** Chiropody. **2.** A chiropodist; podiatrist. **3.** The cosmetic treatment of the feet and toenails. [< F < L *pes, pedis* foot + *curare* to care for]

ped·i·gree (ped′ə·grē) *n.* **1.** A line of ancestors; lineage. **2.** A list or table of descent and relationship, esp. of an animal of pure breed. [< MF *pié de grue* a crane's foot; from a three line mark denoting succession in pedigrees] — **ped′i·greed** *adj.*

ped·i·ment (ped′ə·mənt) *n. Archit.* **1.** A broad triangular part above a portico or door. **2.** Any similar piece surmounting a door, screen, bookcase, etc. [Earlier *periment,* prob. alter. of PYRAMID; infl. in form by L *pes, pedis* foot] — **ped′i·men′tal** (-men′təl) *adj.*

ᴘᴇᴅɪᴍᴇɴᴛ
(Supreme Court Building, Washington, D.C.)

pedo- *combining form* Child; children; offspring: also, before vowels, *ped-,* as in *pedagogy.* Also spelled *paedo-*. [< Gk. *pais, paidos* child]

pe·dom·e·ter (pi·dom′ə·tər) *n.* An instrument that records the number of steps taken by the person who carries it. [< F < L *pes, pedis* foot + Gk. *metron* measure]

pe·dun·cle (pi·dung′kəl) *n.* **1.** *Bot.* The general stalk or support of an inflorescence. **2.** *Zool.* A stalk or stalklike part. [< NL *pedunculus* footstalk, dim. of *pes, pedis* foot] — **pe·dun′cu·lar** (-kyə·lər) *adj.* — **pe·dun′cu·late** (-kyə·lit, -lāt) *adj.*

peek (pēk) *v.i.* To look furtively, slyly, or quickly; peep. — *n.* A peep, glance. [ME *piken;* origin uncertain]

peek·a·boo (pēk′ə·boo′) *n.* A children's game in which one hides one's face and calls out "peekaboo!"

peel¹ (pēl) *n.* The natural coating of certain kinds of fruit, as oranges and lemons; skin; rind. — *v.t.* **1.** To strip off the bark, skin, etc., of. **2.** To strip off; remove. — *v.i.* **3.** To lose bark, skin, etc. **4.** To come off: said of bark, skin, etc. **5.** *Slang* To undress. — **to keep one's eye peeled** *Informal* To keep watch; be alert. — **to peel off** *Aeron.* To veer off from a flight formation so as to dive or prepare for a landing. [ME < L *pilare* to deprive of hair] — **peel′er** *n.*

peel² (pēl) *n.* A long-handled implement used in moving bread, etc., about an oven. [< OF < L *pala* shovel]

peel·ing (pē′ling) *n.* Something peeled off, as rind, skin, etc.

peen (pēn) *n.* The end of a hammer head opposite the flat, striking face, usu. shaped like a wedge. — *v.t.* To beat, bend, or shape with the peen. [< ON]

peep¹ (pēp) *v.i.* **1.** To utter the small, sharp cry of a young bird or chick; chirp; cheep. **2.** To speak in a weak, small voice. — *n.* **1.** The cry of a chick or small bird, or of a young frog; chirp. **2.** A small sandpiper. [ME *pepen;* imit.]

peep² (pēp) *v.i.* **1.** To look through a small hole, from concealment, etc.; peek. **2.** To look furtively or quickly; peek. **3.** To begin to appear; be just visible. — *n.* **1.** A furtive look; a glimpse or glance. **2.** A peephole. **3.** The earliest appearance: the *peep* of day. [Prob. alter. of PEEK]

peep·er¹ (pē′pər) *n.* An animal that peeps, as a chick or any of several tree frogs.

peep·er² (pē′pər) *n.* **1.** One who peeps or peeks; a spying person. **2.** *Slang* An eye.

peep·hole (pēp′hōl′) *n.* An aperture, as a hole or crack, through which one may peep; also, a small window in a door.

peep·ing Tom (pē′ping tom′) An overly inquisitive or prying person; esp., one who peeps in at windows.

Peeping Tom of Coventry In British legend, a curious tailor who peeped at Lady Godiva and was struck blind.

peep·show (pēp′shō′) *n.* An exhibition of pictures, etc., viewed through a small orifice fitted with a magnifying lens.

peer¹ (pir) *v.i.* **1.** To look narrowly or searchingly, as in an effort to see clearly. **2.** To come partially into view. **3.** *Poetic* To appear. [Origin uncertain]

peer² (pir) *n.* **1.** An equal, as in natural gifts or in social rank. **2.** An equal before the law. **3.** A noble, esp. a British duke, marquis, earl, viscount, or baron; also, a prelate in the House of Lords. [< OF < L *par* equal]

peer·age (pir′ij) *n.* **1.** The office or rank of a peer or nobleman. **2.** Peers collectively. **3.** A book containing a genealogical list of the nobility.

peer·ess (pir′is) *n.* A woman who holds a title of nobility, either in her own right or by marriage with a peer.

peer·less (pir′lis) *adj.* Of unequaled excellence. — **peer′less·ly** *adv.* — **peer′less·ness** *n.*

peer of the realm One of the lords of Parliament.

peeve (pēv) *v.t.* **peeved, peev·ing** *Informal* To make peevish. — *n. Informal* A complaint, annoyance, or grievance. [Back formation < PEEVISH]

pee·vish (pē′vish) *adj.* **1.** Irritable or querulous; cross. **2.** Showing discontent and vexation. [ME *pevische;* origin uncertain] — **pee′vish·ly** *adv.* — **pee′vish·ness** *n.*

pee·wee (pē′wē) *n.* **1.** See PEWEE. **2.** *Informal* Anything or anyone small or diminutive. — *adj.* Tiny. [Imit.]

peg (peg) *n.* **1.** A pin, usu. of wood or metal, used to fasten articles together, to stop a hole, etc. **2.** A projecting pin upon which something may be hung, or which may serve to keep a score, etc. **3.** In a stringed musical instrument, a pin for holding fast the end of a string and adjusting its tension. **4.** A reason or excuse. **5.** A degree or step, as in rank or estimation. **6.** *Brit.* A drink of brandy or whisky and soda. **7.** *Informal* A leg, often of wood. **8.** *Informal* A throw, as in baseball. — **to take** (one) **down a peg** To lower the self-esteem of (a person). — *v.* **pegged, peg·ging** *v.t.* **1.** To drive or force a peg into; fasten with pegs. **2.** To mark with pegs. **3.** To strike or pierce with a peg or sharp instrument. **4.** *Informal* To throw. — *v.i.* **5.** To work or strive hard and perseveringly: usu. with *away.* **6.** In croquet, to hit a peg. **7.** To mark the score with pegs. — *adj.* Peg-top. [ME < MDu. *pegge*]

Peg·a·sus (peg′ə·səs) In Greek mythology, a winged horse, symbol of poetic inspiration. — *n.* A constellation, the Winged Horse. [< L < Gk. *Pēgasos*]

peg·board (peg′bôrd) *n.* **1.** Any perforated board into which pegs may be inserted for holding things, keeping score, etc. **2.** *Brit.* A game in which a player arranges pegs in certain patterns on a perforated board: also called *solitaire.*

peg leg *Informal* **1.** An artificial leg of rodlike or tapering shape. **2.** A person with such a leg.

peg-top (peg′top′) *adj.* Wide at the hip and narrow at the ankle: said of trousers: also *peg.* Also **pegged.**

peg top A child's wooden spinning top, pear-shaped and having a sharp metal peg.

pei·gnoir (pān·wär′, pān′wär) *n.* A loose dressing gown or negligée worn by women. [< F < *peigner* to comb]

pe·jo·ra·tion (pē′jə·rā′shən, pej′ə-) *n.* The condition of becoming worse; deterioration.

pe·jo·ra·tive (pē′jə·rā′tiv, pej′ə-, pi·jôr′ə·tiv, -jor′-) *adj.* Having or giving a derogatory or disparaging meaning or sense: a *pejorative* statement. — *n.* A pejorative word. [< LL *pejorare* to make worse] — **pe′jo·ra′tive·ly** *adv.*

Pe·king·ese (pē′kə·nēz′ *for def.* 1; pē′king·ēz′ *for defs.* 2, 3) *n. pl.* **·ese 1.** A variety of a pug dog, having long, silky hair, snub nose, and short legs. **2.** A native or inhabitant of Peking. **3.** The dialect spoken in Peking. — *adj.* Of or pertaining to Peking. Also **Pe·kin·ese** (pē′kə·nēz′).

Pe·king man (pē′king′) *Paleontol.* An extinct manlike primate whose fossil remains were found near Peking, China.

pe·koe (pē′kō, *Brit.* pek′ō) *n.* A superior black tea of India, Ceylon, and Java, made from the downy tips of the young buds of the tea plant. [< dial. Chinese *pek* white + *ho* hair]

pe·lag·ic (pə-laj′ik) *adj.* Of, pertaining to, or inhabiting the sea or ocean far from land. [< L < Gk. < *pelagos* the sea]

pel·ar·go·ni·um (pel′är-gō′nē-əm) *n.* Any of a number of strong-scented, ornamental herbs or shrubs generally known as *geraniums*, having handsome, variously colored flowers. [< NL < Gk. *pelargos* stork]

pelf (pelf) *n.* Money; wealth, esp. if dishonestly acquired. [< OF *pelfre* booty; ult. origin uncertain]

pel·i·can (pel′i-kən) *n.* A large, gregarious, web-footed bird of warm regions, having a pouch on the lower jaw for the temporary storage of fish. [OE < LL < Gk. *pelekan*]

Pelican State Nickname of Louisiana.

pe·lisse (pə-lēs′) *n.* A long outer garment or cloak, originally made of fur or lined with fur. [< F < Med.L < L (*vestis*) *pellicia* (a garment) of skins or fur]

pel·la·gra (pə-lā′grə, -lag′rə) *n. Pathol.* A disease characterized by gastric disturbance, skin eruptions, etc., caused by a deficiency of nicotinic acid. [< NL, prob. < Ital. *pelle agra* rough skin] —**pel·la′grous** *adj.*

pel·let (pel′it) *n.* 1. A small round ball, as of wax, paper, etc. 2. A small bullet. 3. A very small pill. 4. A stone. 5. A cannonball. —*v.t.* 1. To make into pellets. 2. To strike or hit with pellets. [< OF < Med.L < L *pila* ball]

pell-mell (pel′mel′) *adv.* 1. In a confused or disordered way or manner. 2. With a headlong rush; in wild haste. —*adj.* Devoid of order or method; confused. —*n.* A jumble; disorder. Also **pell′mell′.** [< F *pêlemêle* < OF *pesle-mesle*]

pel·lu·cid (pə-lōō′sid) *adj.* 1. Permitting to a certain extent the passage of light. 2. Transparently clear and simple: a *pellucid* style. [< L < *per-* through + *lucere* to shine] —**pel·lu′cid·ly** *adv.* —**pel·lu′cid·ness, pel·lu·cid·i·ty** (pel′ōō-sid′ə-tē) *n.*

Pel·o·pon·ne·sian (pel′ə-pə-nē′zhən, -shən) *adj.* Of or pertaining to the Peloponnesus. —*n.* A native or inhabitant of the Peloponnesus.

Peloponnesian War See table for WAR.

pe·lo·ta (pe-lō′tä) *n.* A game popular among Basques, Spaniards, and Spanish Americans. It is played in a walled court with a hard rubber ball and a curved, wicker racquet. [< Sp., lit., a ball, aug. of *pella* < L *pila*]

pelt[1] (pelt) *n.* 1. The skin of an animal, usu. with the fur left on. 2. A garment made of skin. The human skin: a humorous term. [< OF < L *pellis* skin]

pelt[2] (pelt) *v.t.* 1. To strike repeatedly with or as with blows. 2. To throw or hurl (missiles). 3. To assail with words. —*v.i.* 4. To beat or descend with violence. 5. To move rapidly; hurry. —*n.* 1. A blow. 2. A swift pace. [ME *pelten*, ? var. of *pulten* to thrust] —**pelt′er** *n.*

pel·tate (pel′tāt) *adj. Bot.* Attached at or near the center of the lower surface, as a leaf. Also **pel′tat·ed.** [< L *peltatus* armed with a shield] —**pel′tate·ly** *adv.*

pelt·ry (pel′trē) *n. pl.* **·ries** 1. Pelts collectively. 2. A pelt. 3. A place for keeping or storing pelts.

pelvi- *combining form* Pelvis. [< L *pelvis* basin]

pel·vic (pel′vik) *adj.* Of, pertaining to, or near the pelvis.

pelvic arch *Anat.* In vertebrates, that part of the skeleton to which the hind limbs (in man, the lower limbs) are attached. Also **pelvic girdle.**

pel·vis (pel′vis) *n. pl.* **·ves** (-vēz) 1. *Anat.* a The part of the skeleton that forms a bony girdle joining the lower or hind limbs to the body, composed, in man, of the two innominate bones and the sacrum. b The hollow interior portion of the kidney, into which the urine is discharged. For illus. see KIDNEY. 2. A basinlike structure. [< L, basin]

pem·mi·can (pem′ə-kən) *n. U.S. & Canadian* 1. Lean meat, usu. venison, cut into strips, dried, pounded into paste with fat and a few berries, and pressed into cakes. 2. A similar concentrated and nutritious food made from beef and dried fruits, used by Arctic explorers, etc. Also **pem′i·can.** [< Algonquian (Cree) *pimekan* < *pime* fat]

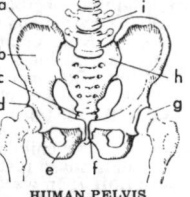

HUMAN PELVIS
a Crest of ilium. *b* Ilium. *c* Coccyx. *d* Acetabulum. *e* Ischium. *f* Pubic symphysis. *g* Head of femur. *h* Sacrum. *i* Lumbar vertebrae.

pen[1] (pen) *n.* 1. An instrument for writing with fluid ink, usu. a metal point split in the middle and fitted to a holder. 2. A ball-point pen. 3. The quality of one's penmanship. 4. The profession of writing. 5. The style of writing. 6. A writer. —*v.t.* **penned, pen·ning** To write with a pen. [< OF < LL < L, wing, feather] —**pen′ner** *n.*

pen[2] (pen) *n.* 1. A small enclosure, as for pigs; also, the animals contained in a pen. 2. Any small place of confinement. 3. *Slang* A penitentiary. —*v.t.* **penned** or **pent, pen·ning** To enclose in or as in a pen; confine. [OE *penn*]

pe·nal (pē′nəl) *adj.* 1. Of or pertaining to punishment. 2. Liable, or rendering liable, to punishment. 3. Enacting or prescribing punishment: a *penal* code. 4. Relating to the means, or place of punishment. [< OF < L *poena* penalty]

pe·nal·ize (pē′nəl-īz, pen′əl-) *v.t.* **·ized, ·iz·ing** 1. To subject to a penalty, as for a violation. 2. To declare, as an action, subject to a penalty. Also *Brit.* **pe′nal·ise.** —**pe′nal·i·za′tion** *n.*

pen·al·ty (pen′əl-tē) *n. pl.* **·ties** 1. The legal punishment for having violated a law. 2. A sum of money to be forfeited as punishment for illegal acts; fine. 3. The disadvantage, loss, or suffering incurred by some act, error, state of being, etc.: the *penalty* of sin. 4. In sports and games, any handicap imposed for a violation of rules.

pen·ance (pen′əns) *n.* 1. *Eccl.* A sacramental rite involving contrition, confession of sins to a priest, the acceptance of penalties, and absolution; also, the penalty imposed. 2. Any penalty, mortification, or act of piety voluntarily undertaken as an atonement for sin. —**to do penance** To perform an act or acts of penance. —*v.t.* **·anced, ·anc·ing** To impose a penance upon. [< OF < L *paenitere* to repent]

pence (pens) *Brit.* The plural of PENNY: used mostly in combination: *twopence.*

pen·chant (pen′chənt, *Fr.* päṅ-shäṅ′) *n.* A strong liking or inclination for something. [< F *pencher* to incline]

pen·cil (pen′səl) *n.* 1. A writing, drawing, or marking implement consisting of a stick or thin strip of graphite, colored chalk, slate, etc., encased in wood or inserted in a mechanically operated holder. 2. A pencillike instrument for applying cosmetics. 3. A small stick of some substance: a styptic *pencil.* 4. A set of rays, as of light, diverging from or converging upon a given point. 5. In drawing or painting, the artist's skill or style. —*v.t.* **pen·ciled** or **·cilled, pen·cil·ing** or **·cil·ling** 1. To mark, write, draw, or color with or as with a pencil. 2. To use a pencil on. [< OF < L *penicillum* paintbrush] —**pen′cil·er** or **pen′cil·ler** *n.*

pend (pend) *v.i.* 1. To await adjustment or settlement. 2. *Dial.* To hang; depend. [< MF < L *pendere* to hang]

pen·dant (pen′dənt) *n.* 1. Anything that hangs from something else, either for ornament or for use. 2. Something hanging from a chandelier, ceiling, lamp, etc., by which a light is turned on and off. 3. *Archit.* An ornament hanging from a ceiling, roof, etc. Also spelled *pendent.* —*adj.* See PENDENT. [See PEND.]

pen·dent (pen′dənt) *adj.* 1. Hanging downward; suspended. 2. Projecting; overhanging. 3. Undetermined; pending. Also spelled *pendant.* —*n.* See PENDANT. [Var. of PENDANT] —**pen′dent·ly** *adv.*

pend·ing (pen′ding) *adj.* 1. Remaining unfinished or undecided. 2. Imminent; impending. —*prep.* 1. During the process or continuance of. 2. While awaiting; until.

pen·drag·on (pen-drag′ən) *n.* In ancient Britain, a supreme ruler or chief. [< Welsh, a chief leader in war]

pen·du·lous (pen′jōō-ləs) *adj.* 1. Hanging, esp. so as to swing. 2. Undecided; wavering. [< L *pendere* to hang] —**pen′du·lous·ly** *adv.* —**pen′du·lous·ness** *n.*

pen·du·lum (pen′jōō-ləm, -də-) *n.* 1. A suspended body free to oscillate between two extremes. 2. Such a device serving to regulate the movement of a clock. 3. Something that changes often. [See PENDULOUS.]

Pe·nel·o·pe (pə-nel′ə-pē) In the *Odyssey,* the faithful wife of Odysseus, who, during his absence kept her many suitors in check under pretext of having to weave a shroud.

pen·e·tra·ble (pen′ə-trə-bəl) *adj.* That can be penetrated. —**pen′e·tra·bil′i·ty** *n.* —**pen′e·tra·bly** *adv.*

pen·e·trate (pen′ə-trāt) *v.t.* **·trat·ed, ·trat·ing** *v.t.* 1. To force a way into or through; pierce; enter. 2. To spread or diffuse itself throughout. 3. To perceive the meaning of; understand. 4. To affect or move profoundly. —*v.i.* 5. To enter or pass through something. 6. To have an effect on the mind or emotions. [< L *penetrare* to put within] —**pen′·e·tra·ble** (-trə-bəl) *adj.* —**pen′e·tra·bil′i·ty** *n.*

pen·e·trat·ing (pen′ə-trā′ting) *adj.* 1. Tending or having power to penetrate. 2. Acute; discerning: a *penetrating* mind. Also **pen′e·tra·tive.** —**pen′e·trat′ing·ly** *adv.* —**pen′e·trat′ing·ness** *n.*

pen·e·tra·tion (pen′ə-trā′shən) *n.* 1. The act or power of penetrating physically. 2. Ability to penetrate mentally; acuteness; discernment. 3. The depth to which a bullet sinks in a target.

pen·guin (pen′gwin, peng′-) *n.* A web-footed, flightless, aquatic bird of the southern hemisphere, with flipperlike wings and short legs. [< Welsh *pen* head + *gwyn* white]

pen·hold·er (pen′hōl′dər) *n.* 1. A handle with a device for inserting a metallic pen. 2. A rack for pens.

pen·i·cil·lin (pen′ə-sil′in) *n.* A powerful antibiotic found in a mold fungus, used to treat bacterial infections.

pen·i·cil·li·um (pen′ə-sil′ē-əm) *n. pl.* **·cil·li·a** (-sil′ē-ə) Any of various fungi growing on decaying fruits, ripening cheese, etc.; one of which is the principal source of penicillin. [< NL < L *penicillus* paintbrush]

pe·nin·su·la (pə-nin′sə-lə, -syə-) *n.* A piece of land almost surrounded by water, and connected with the mainland by an isthmus. [< L < *paene* almost + *insula* island] — **pe·nin′su·lar** *adj.*

Peninsula State A nickname for FLORIDA.

pe·nis (pē′nis) *n. pl.* **·nis·es** or **·nes** (-nēz) The copulatory organ of male animals. [< L, orig., tail] — **pe′ni·al** (-nē·əl), **pe′nile** (-nil, -nīl) *adj.*

pen·i·tence (pen′ə-təns) *n.* The state of being penitent; contrition. [< OF < L < *paenitere* to repent]

pen·i·tent (pen′ə-tənt) *adj.* Affected by a sense of one's own guilt, and resolved on amendment. — *n.* 1. One who is penitent. 2. One who confesses his sins to a priest and submits to the penance prescribed. — **pen′i·tent·ly** *adv.*

pen·i·ten·tial (pen′ə-ten′shəl) *adj.* Of or expressing penitence or penance. — *n.* A penitent. — **pen′i·ten′tial·ly** *adv.*

pen·i·ten·tia·ry (pen′ə-ten′shər-ē) *n. pl.* **·ries** A prison, esp. one operated by a state or federal government for those convicted of serious crimes. — *adj.* 1. Of or pertaining to penance. 2. Relating to or used for the punishment of criminals. 3. Rendering the offender liable to imprisonment. [See PENITENCE.]

pen·knife (pen′nīf′) *n. pl.* **·knives** (-nīvz′) A small pocket knife.

pen·man (pen′mən) *n. pl.* **·men** (-mən) 1. A person considered with regard to his handwriting. 2. An author.

pen·man·ship (pen′mən-ship) *n.* 1. The art of writing. 2. The style or quality of handwriting.

pen name An author's assumed name; pseudonym; nom de plume. — **Syn.** See PSEUDONYM.

pen·nant (pen′ənt) *n.* 1. A long, narrow flag, usu. triangular, used as a school emblem, etc. 2. A similar flag awarded to sports winners. [< PENNON]

pen·nate (pen′āt) *adj.* Having wings or feathers. Also **pen′nat·ed.** [< L *pennatus* winged < *penna* feather]

-pennate *combining form* Having wings or feathers.

pen·ni (pen′ē) *n. pl.* **pen·nis** or **pen·ni·a** (pen′ē·ə) A Finnish coin and monetary unit, the hundredth part of a markka. [< Finnish < G *pfennig* penny]

pen·ni·less (pen′i·lis) *adj.* Poverty-stricken.

pen·non (pen′ən) *n.* 1. A small, pointed flag, borne by medieval knights on their lances. 2. Any banner or flag. 3. A wing. [< OF *penon* streamer < L *penna* feather]

Pennsylvania Dutch 1. Descendants of immigrants from SW Germany and from Switzerland, who settled in Pennsylvania in the 17th and 18th centuries. 2. The language spoken by these people, a High German dialect with an admixture of English. [< early and dial. E *Dutch* (< G *Deutsch*) German] — **Penn′syl·va′ni·a-Dutch** *adj.*

Penn·syl·va·ni·an (pen′səl-vā′nē·ən, -vān′yən) *adj.* 1. Of or relating to the State of Pennsylvania. 2. *Geol.* Belonging to or denoting a Paleozoic period following the Mississippian and preceding the Permian periods. See table for GEOLOGY. — *n.* 1. A native or inhabitant of Pennsylvania. 2. *Geol.* The Pennsylvanian period or rock system.

pen·ny (pen′ē) *n. pl.* **pen·nies** or *Brit.* **pence** (pens) 1. In the U.S. and Canada, a cent. 2. A coin of Great Britain, Ireland, and various Commonwealth Nations, equivalent to ½ shilling. 3. In the United Kingdom, a coin equal in value to ⅟₁₀₀ pound: also *new penny.* 4. Money in general. — **a pretty penny** *Informal* A large or relatively large amount of money. [OE *penning, penig, pending*]

-penny *combining form* Costing (a specified number of) pennies: formerly designating the cost of nails per hundred, but now denoting their length, beginning at 1 inch for twopenny nails. [< PENNY]

penny ante 1. A poker game in which the ante is limited to one cent. 2. *Informal* Any piddling transaction.

penny pincher A parsimonious person. — **pen·ny-pinch·ing** (pen′ē-pinch′ing) *adj. & n.*

pen·ny·roy·al (pen′ē-roi′əl) *n.* A low, erect, strong-scented herb of North America yielding oil of **pennyroyal**, used in medicine. [Alter. of earlier *pulyole ryale*]

pen·ny·weight (pen′ē-wāt′) *n.* In troy weight, the twentieth part of an ounce, 24 grains, or 1.56 grams. See table front of book.

pen·ny-wise (pen′ē-wīz′) *adj.* Unduly economical in small matters. — **penny-wise and pound-foolish** Economical in small matters, but wasteful in large ones.

pen·ny·worth (pen′ē-wûrth′) *n.* 1. As much as can be bought for a penny. 2. A bargain. 3. A small amount.

Pe·nob·scot (pə-nob′skot) *n.* One of a tribe of North American Indians of the Algonquian confederacy of 1749.

pe·nol·o·gy (pē-nol′ə-jē) *n. pl.* **·gies** The science that treats of crime and of the management of prisons and reformatories. [< L *poena* penalty + -LOGY] — **pe·no·log·i·cal** (pē′nə-loj′i·kəl) *adj.* — **pe·nol′o·gist** *n.*

pen·sile (pen′sil) *adj.* 1. Hanging loosely. 2. Constructing pensile nests: said of birds. [< L < *pendere* to hang] — **pen′sile·ness, pen·sil′i·ty** *n.*

pen·sion¹ (pen′shən) *n.* 1. A periodic allowance to an individual or to his family, given when certain conditions, as age, length of service, etc., have been fulfilled. 2. A grant or allowance paid to someone of recognized ability in the arts or sciences. — *v.t.* 1. To grant a pension to. 2. To dismiss with a pension: with *off.* [< OF < L *pensio, -onis* payment] — **pen′sion·a·ble** *adj.*

pen·sion² (pen′shən, *Fr.* pän·syôn′) *n. French* A boarding house; also, a boarding school. [< OF, payment, rent]

pen·sion·ar·y (pen′shən·er′ē) *adj.* 1. Living by means of a pension. 2. Consisting of or like a pension. — *n. pl.* **·ar·ies** 1. A pensioner. 2. A hireling.

pen·sion·er (pen′shən·ər) *n.* 1. One who receives a pension or is dependent on the bounty of another. 2. At Cambridge University, a student who pays his own expenses. 3. A boarder, as in a convent or school.

pen·sive (pen′siv) *adj.* 1. Engaged in or addicted to serious, quiet reflection. 2. Expressive of, suggesting, or causing a melancholy thoughtfulness. [< OF < L *pensare* to think] — **pen′sive·ly** *adv.* — **pen′sive·ness** *n.*

pen·stock (pen′stok′) *n.* 1. A trough or conduit for carrying water to a water wheel. 2. A sluice or floodgate controlling the discharge of water, as from a pond.

pent (pent) Past participle of PEN². — *adj.* Penned up or in; closely confined.

penta- *combining form* Five: *pentagon.* Also, before vowels, **pent-.** [< Gk. *pente* five]

pen·ta·gon (pen′tə·gon) *n. Geom.* A polygon having five sides and five angles. [< L < Gk. < *pente* five + *gōnia* angle] — **pen·tag·o·nal** (pen·tag′ə·nəl) *adj.* — **pen·tag′o·nal·ly** *adv.*

Pentagon, the 1. A five-sided building in Arlington, Virginia, housing the U.S. Department of Defense and other offices. 2. The military leadership of the U.S.

pen·ta·he·dron (pen′tə·hē′drən) *n. pl.* **·dra** (-drə) *Geom.* A polyhedron bounded by five plane faces. — **pen′ta·he′dral** *adj.*

pen·tam·e·ter (pen·tam′ə·tər) *n.* 1. A line of verse consisting of five metrical feet. 2. Verse comprised of pentameters. — *adj.* Having five metrical feet. [< L < Gk. < *pente* five + *metron* a measure]

pen·tane (pen′tān) *n. Chem.* Any one of three isomeric, volatile, liquid hydrocarbons of the methane series, C_5H_{12}, two of which are contained in petroleum.

Pen·ta·teuch (pen′tə·tōōk, -tyōōk) *n.* The first five books of the Old Testament collectively, consisting of Genesis, Exodus, Leviticus, Numbers, and Deuteronomy. [< LL < Gk. < *pente* five + *teuchos* book] — **Pen′ta·teuch′al** *adj.*

pen·tath·lon (pen·tath′lən) *n.* An athletic contest consisting of five separate events, in all of which each contestant must participate. [< Gk. < *pente* five + *athlos* contest]

pen·ta·va·lent (pen′tə·vā′lənt, pen·tav′ə-) *adj. Chem.* Having a valence of five. [< PENTA- + L *valere* to have power or value]

Pen·te·cost (pen′tə·kôst, -kost) *n.* 1. A Christian festival, the seventh Sunday after Easter, commemorating the descent of the Holy Ghost upon the apostles (*Acts* ii): also called *Whitsunday.* 2. A Jewish festival, fifty days after the first day of Passover: also called *Shabuoth.* [< LL < Gk. *pentēkostē* (*hēmera*) the fiftieth (day)]

pen·te·cos·tal (pen′tə·kôs′təl, -kos′-) *adj. Often cap.* Of, pertaining to, or occurring at Pentecost.

pent·house (pent′hous′) *n.* An apartment or other structure on the roof of a building. [< OF, ? < LL *appendicium* appendage]

Pen·to·thal Sodium (pen′tə·thôl) A proprietary name for a brand of thiopental sodium.

pent-up (pent′up′) *adj.* Repressed: *pent-up* emotions.

pe·nuch·le (pē′nuk·əl), **pe·nuck·le** See PINOCHLE.

pe·nult (pē′nult, pi·nult′) *n.* The syllable next to the last in a word. Also **pe·nul·ti·ma** (pi·nul′tə·mə). [Short for *penultima* < L < *paene* almost + *ultimus* last]

pe·nul·ti·mate (pi·nul′tə·mit) *adj.* 1. Next to the last. 2. Of or belonging to the next to the last syllable. — *n.* A penultimate part. [< L *paene* almost + ULTIMATE]

pe·num·bra (pi·num′brə) *n. pl.* **·brae** (-brē) or **·bras** 1. A partial shadow, as in an eclipse, within which the rays of light from an illuminating body are partly but not wholly intercepted. 2. The dark fringe around the central part of a sunspot. [< NL < L *paene* almost + *umbra* shadow] — **pe·num′bral, pe·num′brous** (-brəs) *adj.*

pe·nu·ri·ous (pə-nŏŏr′ē·əs, -nyŏŏr′-) *adj.* 1. Excessively sparing in the use of money; stingy. 2. Extremely poor; needy. 3. Affording or yielding little; scanty. [< MF < Med.L < L *penuria* want, poverty] — **pe·nu′ri·ous·ly** *adv.* — **pe·nu′ri·ous·ness** *n.*

pen·u·ry (pen′yə·rē) *n.* Extreme poverty or want. [< OF < L *penuria* want]

pe·on (pē′ən) *n.* **1.** In Latin America, a laborer; servant. **2.** Formerly, a debtor kept in servitude until he had worked out of his debt. [< Sp. < LL *pedo, -onis* foot soldier < L *pes, pedis* foot]

pe·on·age (pē′ən·ij) *n.* **1.** The condition of being a peon. **2.** The system by which debtors are held in servitude until they have worked out their debt. Also **pe′on·ism** (-iz′əm).

pe·o·ny (pē′ə·nē) *n.* *pl.* **·nies 1.** A plant of the crowfoot family, having large crimson, rose, or white flowers. **2.** The flower. [OE < L < Gk. *Paion* Paeon, the Healer]

peo·ple (pē′pəl) *n.* *pl.* **peo·ple;** *for defs. 1 & 2, also* **peo·ples 1.** The entire body of human beings living in the same country, under the same government, and speaking the same language: the *people* of England. **2.** A body of human beings having the same history, culture, and traditions, and usu. speaking the same language: the Polish *people*. **3.** In a state or nation, the body of persons invested with political rights. **4.** A group of persons having the same interests, profession, condition of life, etc.: poor *people*. **5.** Persons considered collectively: *people* say. **6.** Ordinary persons; the populace: usu. with *the*. **7.** One's family or relatives. **8.** Human beings as distinguished from animals. **9.** Animals collectively: the ant *people*. —*v.t.* **pled, ·pling** To fill with inhabitants; populate. [< OF < L *populus* populace] — **peo′pler** *n.*

— **Syn.** A group having a common descent, language, culture, habitat, or government may be called a *people*. *Folk* is a homelier word for *people*, nearly as broad, and usu. stressing common traditions, customs, or behavior. A *nation* is a political entity, comprising the *people* (or *peoples*) under one government.

People's Party A political organization formed in the U.S. in 1891, advocating public control of railways, an income tax, and limitation of ownership of land.

pep (pep) *n.* *Informal* Energy and high spirits; vigorous activity. —*v.t.* **pepped, pep·ping** To fill or inspire with energy or pep: usu. with *up*. [Short for PEPPER]

pep·lum (pep′ləm) *n.* *pl.* **·lums** or **·la** (-lə) A short overskirt, ruffle, or flounce attached to a blouse or coat at the waist. [< L < Gk. *peplos* a woman's shawl]

pep·per (pep′ər) *n.* **1.** A pungent, aromatic condiment consisting of the dried immature berries of a plant. When ground entire it is **black pepper**, but when the outer coating of the seeds is removed, the product is **white pepper**. **2.** Any plant of the pepper family. **3.** Red pepper. **4.** Green pepper. —*v.t.* **1.** To sprinkle or season with pepper. **2.** To sprinkle freely. **3.** To shower, as with missiles; spatter; pelt. **4.** To make (speech or writing) vivid or pungent, as with humor, sarcasm, etc. —*v.i.* **5.** To discharge missiles at something. [OE, ult. < L < Gk. *peperi*]

pep·per-and-salt (pep′ər·ən·sôlt′) *adj.* Having or consisting of a mixture of white and black, so as to present a grayish appearance. — *n.* A pepper-and-salt cloth.

pep·per·box (pep′ər·boks′) *n.* **1.** A container for sprinkling pepper. **2.** A quick-tempered person.

pep·per·corn (pep′ər·kôrn′) *n.* **1.** A berry of the pepper plant. **2.** Anything trifling or insignificant.

pep·per·grass (pep′ər·gras′, -gräs′) *n.* A plant of the mustard family, having a pungent flavor, and used as a salad vegetable. Also **pep′per·wort** (-wûrt).

pepper mill A hand mill, often designed for table use, in which peppercorns are ground.

pep·per·mint (pep′ər·mint′) *n.* **1.** A pungent, aromatic herb used in medicine and confectionery. **2.** An oil made from this herb. **3.** A confection flavored with peppermint.

pepper pot 1. A pepperbox. **2.** A stew of meat or fish with vegetables, flavored with pepper, etc.

pepper tree A tree of Central and South America whose seeds are used as a spice.

pep·per·y (pep′ər·ē) *adj.* **1.** Pertaining to or like pepper; pungent. **2.** Quick-tempered; hasty. **3.** Spicy and vivid, as speech or writing. — **pep′per·i·ness** *n.*

pep·py (pep′ē) *adj.* **·pi·er, ·pi·est** *Informal* Full of energy; lively. — **pep′pi·ness** *n.*

pep·sin (pep′sin) *n.* **1.** *Biochem.* An enzyme secreted by the gastric juices that promotes the digestion of proteins. **2.** A medicinal preparation obtained from the stomachs of various animals, as the pig and the calf, used to aid digestion. Also **pep′sine** (-sin). [< G < Gk. *pepsis* digestion]

pep talk *Informal* A brief, vigorous talk meant to inspire.

pep·tic (pep′tik) *adj.* **1.** Of, pertaining to, or promotive of digestion. **2.** Of, pertaining to, or caused by pepsin. **3.** Able to digest. — *n.* An agent that promotes digestion. [< Gk. *pepsis* digestion]

pep·tone (pep′tōn) *n.* *Biochem.* Any of the soluble compounds into which proteins are converted when acted upon by pepsin, by acids and alkalis, by putrefaction, etc. [< G < Gk. *peptos* digested] — **pep·ton·ic** (pep·ton′ik) *adj.*

Pe·quot (pē′kwot) *n.* One of a tribe of Algonquian Indians, formerly inhabiting southern New England.

per (pûr) *prep.* **1.** By; by means of; through: used in commercial and business English: *per* bearer. **2.** To or for each: ten cents *per* yard. **3.** By the; every: esp. in Latin phrases: *per diem*. [< L, through, by]

per- *prefix* **1.** Through; throughout: *pervade, perennial*. **2.** Thoroughly: *perturb*. **3.** Away: *pervert*. **4.** Very: *perfervid*. **5.** *Chem.* Indicating an excess amount of a specified element in a compound: hydrogen *peroxide*. [< L *per* through]

per·ad·ven·ture (pûr′əd·ven′chər) *adv.* *Archaic* Perchance; perhaps. [< OF *par aventure* by chance]

per·am·bu·late (pə·ram′byə·lāt) *v.* **·lat·ed, ·lat·ing** *v.t.* **1.** To walk through or over. **2.** To walk through or around so as to inspect, etc. —*v.i.* **3.** To stroll. [< L < *per* through + *ambulare* to walk] — **per·am·bu·la·tion** (pə·ram′byə·lā′shən) *n.* — **per·am′bu·la·to·ry** (-tôr′ē, -tō′rē) *adj.*

per·am·bu·la·tor (pə·ram′byə·lā′tər) *n.* **1.** One who perambulates. **2.** *Chiefly Brit.* A baby carriage.

per an·num (pûr an′əm) *Latin* By the year.

per·cale (pər·kāl′, -kal′) *n.* A closely woven cotton fabric without gloss. [< F, prob. < Persian *pergālah*]

per cap·i·ta (pûr kap′ə·tə) *Latin* For each person; literally, by heads.

per·ceive (pər·sēv′) *v.t.* & *v.i.* **·ceived, ·ceiv·ing 1.** To become aware of (something) through the senses; see, hear, feel, taste, or smell. **2.** To come to understand; apprehend with the mind. [< OF < L < *per-* thoroughly + *capere* to take] — **per·ceiv′a·ble** *adj.* — **per·ceiv′a·bly** *adv.*

— **Syn. 1.** sense. Compare SEE, DISCERN. **2.** comprehend.

per·cent (pər·sent′) *n.* **1.** Number of parts in or to every hundred, often specified: fifty *percent* of the people. **2.** Amount or quantity commensurate with the number of units in proportion to one hundred: ten *percent* of fifty is five: symbol, %. **3.** *pl.* Securities bearing a certain percentage of interest. Also **per cent., per cent** [Short for L *per centum* by the hundred]

per·cent·age (pər·sen′tij) *n.* **1.** Rate per hundred, or proportion in a hundred parts. **2.** A proportion or part considered in its quantitative relation to the whole. **3.** In commerce, the allowance, commission, duty, or interest on a hundred. **4.** *Informal* Advantage; profit.

per·cen·tile (pər·sen′tīl, -til) *n.* *Stat.* Any of 100 points spaced at equal intervals within the range of a plotted variable, each point denoting that percentage of the total cases lying below it in the series. —*adj.* Of a percentile.

per·cept (pûr′sept) *n.* *Psychol.* **1.** Something perceived. **2.** Immediate knowledge derived from perceiving. [< L *percipere* to perceive]

per·cep·ti·ble (pər·sep′tə·bəl) *adj.* That can be perceived; appreciable. — **per·cep′ti·bil′i·ty** *n.* — **per·cep′ti·bly** *adv.*

per·cep·tion (pər·sep′shən) *n.* **1.** The act or process of perceiving. **2.** The result or effect of perceiving. **3.** Any insight, knowledge, etc., arrived at by or as by perceiving. **4.** The capacity for perceiving. — **per·cep′tion·al** *adj.* — **per·cep′tu·al** (-chōō·əl) *adj.*

per·cep·tive (pər·sep′tiv) *adj.* **1.** Having the power of perception. **2.** Having a quick capacity for perceiving. **3.** Of or pertaining to perception. — **per·cep′tive·ly** *adv.* — **per·cep·tiv·i·ty** (pûr′sep·tiv′ə·tē), **per·cep′tive·ness** *n.*

perch[1] (pûrch) *n.* **1.** A horizontal staff or pole used as a roost for poultry. **2.** Any place on which birds alight or rest. **3.** Any place for sitting or standing, esp. if elevated. **4.** A rod (def. 9). —*v.i.* **1.** To alight or sit on or as on a perch; roost. —*v.t.* **2.** To set on or as on a perch. [< OF < L *pertica* pole] — **perch·er** (pûr′chər) *n.*

perch[2] (pûrch) *n.* *pl.* **perch** or **perches 1.** A small, spiny-finned fresh-water food fish. **2.** Any of various other related fishes. [< OF < L < Gk. *perkē*]

per·chance (pər·chans′, -chäns′) *adv.* Possibly; perhaps. [< OF *par chance* by chance]

Per·che·ron (pûr′chə·ron, -shə-) *n.* A breed of large draft horses. [after *Perche*, a region of nothern France]

per·cip·i·ent (pər·sip′ē·ənt) *adj.* **1.** Having the power of perception. **2.** Perceiving rapidly or keenly. — *n.* One who or that which perceives. [< L < *per-* thoroughly + *capere* to take] — **per·cip′i·ence** or **·en·cy** *n.*

per·coid (pûr′koid) *adj.* Of or pertaining to an order of spiny-finned fishes, including the fresh-water perches; perch-like. — *n.* A percoid fish. Also **per·coi·de·an** (pər·koi′dē·ən). [< L *perca* perch[2] + -OID]

per·co·late (pûr′kə·lāt; *for n., also* pur′kə·lət) *v.t.* & *v.i.* **·lat·ed, ·lat·ing** Of a liquid, to pass or cause to pass through fine interstices; filter. — *n.* That which has percolated. [< L < *per-* through + *colare* to strain] — **per′co·la′tion** *n.*

per·co·la·tor (pûr′kə·lā′tər) *n.* A type of coffeepot in which boiling water rises to the top in a tube and then filters down through finely ground coffee to a container below.

per·cus·sion (pər·kush′ən) *n.* **1.** The sharp striking of one body against another. **2.** The shock, vibration, or sound produced by a striking of one body against another. **3.** *Med.* A light, quick tapping of the finger tips upon the back, chest, or abdomen, for determining by resonance the condition of the organ beneath. **4.** The act of striking the percussion cap in a firearm. **5.** *Music* Percussion instruments. — *adj.* Of, pertaining to, or operating by percussion. [< L < *per-* through + *quatere* to shake]

percussion cap A small cap of thin metal, containing mercury fulminate or some other detonator, formerly used in ammunition to explode the propelling charge.

percussion instruments Musical instruments whose tone is produced by striking, as the timpani, cymbals, piano, etc.

per·di·em (per dē′əm, dī′əm) **1.** By the day. **2.** An allowance for expenses each day. [< L]

per·di·tion (pər·dish′ən) *n.* **1.** Eternal damnation; the utter loss of a soul. **2.** The place of eternal damnation; hell. [< OF < L *per-* through, away + *dare* to give]

père (pâr) *n.* *French* Father: often used after a surname to distinguish father from son: Dumas *père*.

per·e·gri·nate (per′ə·gri·nāt′) *v.* **·nat·ed, ·nat·ing** *v.i.* **1.** To travel from place to place. — *v.t.* **2.** To travel through or along. [< L *peregrinari* to travel abroad] — **per′e·gri·na′·tion** *n.* — **per′e·gri·na′tor** *n.*

per·e·grine (per′ə·grin) *adj.* **1.** Coming from foreign regions. **2.** Wandering. — *n.* The peregrine falcon. [< L < *peregre* abroad < *per-* through + *ager* land]

peregrine falcon 1. A falcon generally blackish blue above and white or gray below, formerly much used in falconry. **2.** An American subspecies of this falcon.

per·emp·to·ry (pə·remp′tər·ē, per′əmp·tôr′ē, -tō′rē) *adj.* **1.** Not admitting of appeal; decisive; absolute. **2.** Positive in opinion, etc.; imperious. **3.** Intolerant of opposition; dictatorial. **4.** *Law* Precluding or putting an end to debate or discussion; final. [< L < *per-* entirely + *emere* to take] — **per·emp′to·ri·ly** *adv.* — **per·emp′to·ri·ness** *n.*

per·en·ni·al (pə·ren′ē·əl) *adj.* **1.** Continuing or enduring through the year or through many years. **2.** Perpetual; everlasting; unceasing. **3.** *Bot.* Lasting more than two years. — *n.* A plant that grows for three or more years, usu. blossoming and fructifying annually. [< L < *per-* through + *annus* year] — **per·en′ni·al·ly** *adv.*

per·fect (*adj. & n.* pûr′fikt; *v.* pər·fekt′) *adj.* **1.** Having all the elements or qualities requisite to its nature or kind; complete. **2.** Without defect; flawless: *perfect* weather. **3.** Thoroughly and completely skilled or informed: a *perfect* violinist. **4.** Accurately corresponding to a type or original; exact: a *perfect* replica. **5.** Thorough; utter: He made a *perfect* nuisance of himself. **6.** Completely effective: a *perfect* answer. **7.** *Informal* Very great: a *perfect* horror of spiders. **8.** *Gram.* Denoting the tense of a verb expressing action completed in the past. Grammarians note in English a present perfect, past perfect (or pluperfect), and a future perfect tense. **9.** *Music* a Denoting the three intervals whose accuracy of intonation the human ear can recognize within precise limits, the **perfect octave**, the **perfect fifth**, and the **perfect fourth**. b Complete: a *perfect* cadence. — *n. Gram.* The perfect tense; also, a verb in this tense. — *v.t.* **1.** To bring to perfection; complete. **2.** To make thoroughly skilled or accomplished: to *perfect* oneself in an art. [< OF < L < *per-* thoroughly + *facere* to do, make] — **per·fect′er** *n.* — **per′fect·ly** *adv.* — **per′fect·ness** *n.*

per·fect·i·ble (pər·fek′tə·bəl) *adj.* Capable of being made perfect or of arriving at perfection. — **per·fect′i·bil′i·ty** *n.*

per·fec·tion (pər·fek′shən) *n.* **1.** The state or quality of being perfect. **2.** The embodiment of something that is perfect: As a hostess, she is *perfection*. **3.** Any quality, characteristic, or trait considered to be perfect. **4.** The highest degree of something. **5.** The act or process of perfecting.

per·fec·tion·ist (pər·fek′shən·ist) *n.* One who demands of himself or of others an exceedingly high degree of excellence.

per·fec·tive (pər·fek′tiv) *adj.* Tending to make perfect. — **per·fec′tive·ly** *adv.* — **per·fec′tive·ness** *n.*

per·fec·to (pər·fek′tō) *n. pl.* **·tos** A cigar of medium size, shaped to taper at either end. [< Sp., perfect]

perfect participle Past participle.

perfect pitch Absolute pitch.

per·fer·vid (pər·fûr′vid) *adj.* Excessively fervid; ardent; zealous. [< NL < L *per-* thoroughly + *fervidus* burning] — **per·fer′vid·ly** *adv.* — **per·fid′i·ous·ness** *n.*

per·fid·i·ous (pər·fid′ē·əs) *adj.* Marked by or guilty of perfidy; treacherous. [< L *perfidia*] — **per·fid′i·ous·ly** *adv.* — **per·fid′i·ous·ness** *n.*

per·fi·dy (pûr′fə·dē) *n. pl.* **·dies** The act of violating faith, trust, or allegiance; treachery. [< MF < L < *per* through, under pretext of + *fides* faith]

per·fo·li·ate (pər·fō′lē·it, āt) *adj. Bot.* Growing so that the stem seems to pass through it, as a leaf. [< NL < L *per-* through + *folium* leaf] — **per·fo′li·a′tion** *n.*

per·fo·rate (*v.* pûr′fə·rāt; *adj.* pûr′fə·rit) *v.t.* **·rat·ed, ·rat·ing 1.** To make a hole or holes through, by or as by stamping or drilling. **2.** To pierce with holes in rows or patterns. — *adj.* Perforated. [< L < *per-* through + *forare* to bore]

— **per′fo·ra·ble** *adj.* — **per′fo·ra·tive, per′fo·ra·to·ry** (-rə·tôr′ē, -tō′rē) *adj.* — **per′fo·ra·tor** *n.*

per·fo·rat·ed (pûr′fə·rā′tid) *adj.* Pierced with a hole or holes; esp., pierced with lines of holes, as sheets of stamps.

per·fo·ra·tion (pûr′fə·rā′shən) *n.* **1.** The act of perforating, or the state of being perforated. **2.** A hole or series of holes drilled in or stamped through something.

per·force (pər·fôrs′, -fōrs′) *adv.* By or of necessity; necessarily. [< OF < *par* by (< L *per-*) + *force* force]

per·form (pər·fôrm′) *v.t.* **1.** To carry out in action; execute; do. **2.** To fulfill; discharge, as a duty or command. **3.** To act (a part) or give a performance of (a play, piece of music, etc.). — *v.i.* **4.** To carry through to completion an action, undertaking, etc. **5.** To give an exhibition or performance. [< OF < *par-* thoroughly (< L *per-*) + *fournir* to accomplish] — **per·form′a·ble** *adj.*

per·form·ance (pər·fôr′məns) *n.* **1.** An entertainment of some kind before an audience or spectators. **2.** A public presentation: The music had its first *performance* here. **3.** The act or manner of performing a play, part, piece of music, etc. **4.** Manner of operating or functioning: The car's *performance* improved. **5.** Any act, deed, or accomplishment.

per·form·er (pər·fôr′mər) *n.* One who performs; esp., an actor, musician, etc.

per·fume (pər·fyoom′; *for n., usu.* pûr′fyoom) *n.* **1.** A fragrant substance, usu. a volatile liquid, prepared to emit a pleasant odor; scent. **2.** A pleasant odor, as from flowers; fragrance. — **Syn.** See SMELL. — *v.t.* **·fumed, ·fum·ing** To fill or scent with a fragrant odor. [< MF < Ital. < *per-* through (< L) + *fumare* to smoke < LL *fumus* smoke]

per·fum·er (pər·fyoo′mər) *n.* **1.** One who makes or deals in perfumes. **2.** One who or that which perfumes.

per·fum·er·y (pər·fyoo′mər·ē) *n. pl.* **·er·ies 1.** The art or business of preparing perfumes. **2.** Perfumes in general, or a specific perfume. **3.** A place where perfumes are made.

per·func·to·ry (pər·fungk′tər·ē) *adj.* **1.** Done mechanically; careless; cursory. **2.** Having no zest or enthusiasm; dull. [< LL < L < *per-* through + *fungi* to perform] — **per·func′to·ri·ly** *adv.* — **per·func′to·ri·ness** *n.*

per·fuse (pər·fyooz′) *v.t.* **·fused, ·fus·ing 1.** To permeate, suffuse, or sprinkle with a liquid, color, etc. **2.** To spread (a liquid, etc.) over or through something; diffuse. [< L < *per-* throughout + *fundere* to pour] — **per·fu′sion** (-fyoo′zhən) *n.* — **per·fu′sive** (-fyoo′siv) *adj.*

per·go·la (pûr′gə·lə) *n.* An arbor or covered walk made of trelliswork covered with vegetation or flowers. [< Ital., arbor < L *pergula* projecting roof, arbor]

per·haps (pər·haps′) *adv.* Maybe; possibly. [< PER + *happes*, pl. of *hap* chance]

peri- *prefix* **1.** Around; encircling: *periphery*. **2.** Situated near; adjoining: *perihelion*. [< Gk. *peri* around]

per·i·anth (per′ē·anth) *n. Bot.* The envelope of a flower, esp. one in which the calyx and corolla are so alike as to be indistinguishable. [< F < NL < Gk. *peri-* around + *anthos* flower]

per·i·car·di·al (per′ə·kär′dē·əl) *adj.* Of or pertaining to the pericardium. Also **per′i·car′di·ac** (-ak), **per′i·car′di·an.**

per·i·car·di·tis (per′ə·kär·dī′tis) *n. Pathol.* Inflammation of the pericardium.

per·i·car·di·um (per′ə·kär′dē·əm) *n. pl.* **·di·a** (-dē·ə) *Anat.* A membranous bag that surrounds and protects the heart. [< NL < Gk. < *peri-* around + *kardia* heart]

per·i·carp (per′ə·kärp) *n. Bot.* The wall of a ripened ovary or fruit, usu. in three layers, the epicarp, mesocarp, and endocarp: also called *seedcase, seed vessel*. [< NL < Gk. < *peri-* around + *karpos* fruit] — **per′i·car′pi·al** *adj.*

Per·i·cle·an (per′ə·klē′ən) *adj.* Pertaining to, characteristic of, or named after Pericles, or the period of his supremacy, when Greek art, drama, and statesmanship are considered to have been at their height.

per·i·cra·ni·um (per′ə·krā′nē·əm) *n. pl.* **·ni·a** (-nē·ə) *Anat.* The periosteum of the external surface of the cranium. [< NL < Gk. < *peri-* around + *kranion* skull] — **per′i·cra′·ni·al** *adj.*

per·i·gee (per′ə·jē) *n. Astron.* The point in the orbit of the moon or of an artificial satellite at which it is nearest the earth: opposed to *apogee*. [< MF < Med.L < Gk. < *peri-*, near + *gē* earth] — **per′i·ge′al, per′i·ge′an** *adj.*

per·i·gon (per′ə·gon) *n. Geom.* An angle equal to two straight angles or 360 degrees.

per·i·he·li·on (per′ə·hē′lē·ən) *n. pl.* **·li·a** (-lē·ə) *Astron.* The point in the orbit of a planet or comet where it is nearest the sun: opposed to *aphelion*. [< NL < Gk. *peri-* around, near + *hēlios* sun]

per·il (per′əl) *n.* Exposure to the chance of injury; danger; risk. — *v.t.* **·iled** or **·illed, ·il·ing** or **·il·ling** To expose to danger; imperil. [< OF < L *periculum* trial, danger]

per·i·lous (per′əl·əs) *adj.* Involving, or attended with peril;

hazardous; risky. **—per′il·ous·ly** adv. **—per′il·ous·ness** n.

pe·rim·e·ter (pə·rim′ə·tər) n. **1.** The boundary line of any figure of two dimensions. **2.** The sum of the sides of a plane figure. [< L < Gk. < peri- around + metron measure] **— per·i·met·ric** (per′ə·met′rik) or **·ri·cal** adj.

per·i·ne·um (per′ə·nē′əm) n. pl. **·ne·a** (-nē′ə) Anat. **1.** The region of the body between the genital organs and the rectum. **2.** The entire region comprising the anus and the internal genitals. Also **per′i·nae′um**. [< LL < Gk. < peri- around + inein to empty out] **— per′i·ne′al** adj.

pe·ri·od (pir′ē·əd) n. **1.** A portion of time marked or defined by certain conditions, events, etc.: a period of rest. **2.** A portion or lapse of time, as in a process or development, a stage. **3.** A portion of time into which something is divided: Our new school day has seven periods. **4.** Astron. The time it takes a planet or satellite to revolve once about its primary. **5.** Geol. One of the divisions of geologic time. **6.** Physics The time that elapses between any two successive similar phases of an oscillation or other regularly repeated cyclical motion. **7.** A dot (.) placed on the line, used as a mark of punctuation after every complete declarative sentence, after most abbreviations, etc. **8.** The pause at the end of a sentence. **9.** Pathol. A stage distinguishable in the course of a disease. **10.** Menstruation. **11.** The completion of something. [< OF < L < Gk. < peri- around + hodos way]

pe·ri·od·ic (pir′ē·od′ik) adj. **1.** Of, pertaining to, or like a period. **2.** Recurring at regular intervals. **3.** Intermittent. **4.** Of or expressed in periodic sentences. **5.** Physics Recurring after a definite interval. **— pe′ri·od′i·cal·ly** adv.

pe·ri·od·i·cal (pir′ē·od′i·kəl) adj. **1.** Of or pertaining to publications that appear at fixed intervals of more than one day; also, published at regular intervals. **2.** Periodic. **—** n. A periodical publication.

pe·ri·o·dic·i·ty (pir′ē·ə·dis′ə·tē) n. The quality of being periodic or of recurring at definite intervals of time.

periodic law Chem. The statement that the physical and chemical properties of the elements are related to their atomic numbers, and that they recur periodically when the elements are arranged in the order of these numbers.

periodic sentence A sentence so constructed as to suspend completion of both sense and structure until the close.

periodic table Chem. A table in which the elements are arranged in groups as determined by the periodic law.

per·i·os·te·um (per′ē·os′tē·əm) n. Anat. A tough, fibrous vascular membrane that surrounds and nourishes the bones. [< NL < LL < Gk. < peri- around + osteon bone] **—per′·i·os′te·al, per′i·os′te·ous** adj.

per·i·pa·tet·ic (per′i·pə·tet′ik) adj. Walking about from place to place. **—** n. One given to walking about. [< MF < L < Gk. < peri- around + pateein to walk]

Per·i·pa·tet·ic (per′i·pə·tet′ik) adj. Of or pertaining to the philosophy of Aristotle, who lectured to his disciples while walking. **—** n. A disciple of Aristotle.

pe·riph·er·al (pə·rif′ər·əl) adj. **1.** Of or consisting of a periphery. **2.** Capable of perceiving images laterally that are not directly in one's line of sight: peripheral vision. **3.** Not central; marginal: of peripheral importance. **4.** Anat. Outer; external. **— pe·riph′er·al·ly** adv.

pe·riph·er·y (pə·rif′ər·ē) n. pl. **·er·ies 1.** The outer part surface, or boundary of something. **2.** A surrounding region, area, or country. [< OF < LL < Gk. < peri- around + pherein to carry]

pe·riph·ra·sis (pə·rif′rə·sis) n. pl. **·ses** (-sēz) A roundabout method or instance of expressing something; circumlocution. Also **per·i·phrase** (per′i·frāz′). [< L < Gk. < peri- around + phrazein to declare]

per·i·phras·tic (per′ə·fras′tik) adj. **1.** Of the nature of or involving periphrasis; circumlocutory. **2.** Gram. Denoting a construction in which a phrase is substituted for an inflected form, as, the hat of John for John's hat. Also **per′i·phras′ti·cal. — per′i·phras′ti·cal·ly** adv.

pe·rique (pə·rēk′) n. A dark, strongly flavored tobacco grown in Louisiana. [after nickname of Pierre Chenet, American tobacco grower who introduced this variety]

per·i·scope (per′ə·skōp) n. An instrument consisting of prisms or mirrors so arranged as to reflect light rays down a vertical tube, used to guide submarines, etc. [< Gk. peri- around + skopeein to look] **— per·i·scop·ic** (per′ə·skop′ik) or **·i·cal** adj.

per·ish (per′ish) v.i. **1.** To suffer a violent or untimely death. **2.** To pass from existence. [< OF < L < per- away + ire to go]

per·ish·a·ble (per′ish·ə·bəl) adj. **1.** Liable to perish. **2.** Liable to speedy decay, as fruit in transportation. **—** n. Usu. pl. Something liable to decay, as food. **— per′ish·a·ble·ness, per′ish·a·bil′i·ty** n. **— per′ish·a·bly** adv.

PERISCOPE

per·i·stal·sis (per′ə·stôl′sis, -stal′-) n. pl. **·ses** (-sēz) Physiol. A contractile muscular movement of any hollow organ, as of the alimentary canal, whereby the contents are gradually propelled toward the point of expulsion.

[< NL < Gk. < peri- around + stellein to place] **— per′i·stal′tic** adj.

per·i·style (per′ə·stīl) n. Archit. **1.** A system of columns about a building or an internal court. **2.** An area or space so enclosed. [< MF < L < Gk. < peri- around + stylos pillar] **— per′i·sty′lar** adj.

per·i·to·ne·um (per′ə·tə·nē′əm) n. pl. **·ne·a** (-nē′ə) Anat. A serous membrane that lines the abdominal cavity and is a more or less complete covering for the viscera. Also **per′i·to·nae′um**. [< LL < Gk. < peri- around + teinein to stretch] **— per′i·to·ne′al** or **·nae′al** adj.

per·i·to·ni·tis (per′ə·tə·nī′tis) n. Pathol. Inflammation of the peritoneum.

per·i·wig (per′ə·wig) n. A peruke or wig. [Earlier perwyke, alt. of perruck < MF perruque]

per·i·win·kle[1] (per′ə·wing′kəl) n. Any of several small marine snails, some of which are edible. [OE pinewincle, ? < L pina mussel + OE wincle a shellfish]

per·i·win·kle[2] (per′ə·wing′kəl) n. A plant having shining, evergreen leaves and blue or sometimes white flowers: also called myrtle. [OE < L pervinca]

per·jure (pûr′jər) v.t. **·jured, ·jur·ing 1.** To make (oneself) guilty of perjury. **2.** To find guilty of or involved in perjury. [< OF < L < per- thoroughly + jurare to swear] **— per′jur·er** n.

per·jured (pûr′jərd) adj. Guilty of or constituting perjury.

per·ju·ry (pûr′jə·rē) n. pl. **·ries** Law The wilful giving of false testimony or the withholding of material facts or evidence while under oath in a judicial proceeding.

perk[1] (pûrk) v.i. **1.** To recover one's spirits or vigor: with up. **2.** To carry oneself or lift one's head jauntily. **—** v.t. **3.** To raise quickly or smartly, as the ears: often with up. **4.** To make (oneself) trim and smart in appearance: often with up or out. **—** adj. Perky. [ME perken; ? var. of PERCH[1]]

perk[2] (pûrk) v.i. Informal To percolate.

perk·y (pûr′kē) adj. **perk·i·er, perk·i·est 1.** Jaunty; sprightly; pert. **2.** Spirited and self-assured. Also perk. **— perk′·i·ly** adv. **— perk′i·ness** n.

per·ma·frost (pûr′mə·frôst, -frost) n. The part of the earth's surface in arctic regions that is permanently frozen.

per·ma·nence (pûr′mə·nəns) n. The state or quality of being permanent.

per·ma·nen·cy (pûr′mə·nən·sē) n. pl. **·cies 1.** Permanence. **2.** Something permanent.

per·ma·nent (pûr′mə·nənt) adj. Continuing in the same state or without essential change; enduring; durable; fixed. **—** n. A permanent wave. [< L < per- through + manere to remain] **— per′ma·nent·ly** adv.

Permanent Court of International Justice An international tribunal established under the Covenant of the League of Nations (1921) and superseded in 1945 by the International Court of Justice: also called World Court.

permanent wave An artificial wave mechanically or chemically set in the hair and lasting several months.

per·man·ga·nate (pər·mang′gə·nāt) n. Chem. A dark purple salt of permanganic acid.

per·man·gan·ic acid (pûr′man·gan′ik) Chem. An acid, $HMnO_4$, that is a powerful oxidizer in aqueous solutions.

per·me·a·bil·i·ty (pûr′mē·ə·bil′ə·tē) n. The quality or condition of being permeable, as by liquids, gases, etc.

per·me·a·ble (pûr′mē·ə·bəl) adj. Allowing passage, esp. of fluids. **— per′me·a·bly** adv.

per·me·ance (pûr′mē·əns) n. **1.** The act of permeating. **2.** Electr. The ability to be traversed by magnetic lines of force.

per·me·ate (pûr′mē·āt) v. **·at·ed, ·at·ing** v.t. **1.** To spread thoroughly through; pervade. **2.** To pass through the pores or interstices of. **—** v.i. **3.** To spread itself. [< L < per- through + meare to pass] **— per′me·ant** adj. **— per′me·a′tion** n. **— per′me·a′tive** adj.

Per·mi·an (pûr′mē·ən) Geol. Of or pertaining to the latest period of the Paleozoic era. **—** n. The Permian rock system or period. See table for GEOLOGY. [after Perm, former E. Russian province]

per·mis·si·ble (pər·mis′ə·bəl) adj. That can be permitted; allowable. **— per·mis′si·bil′i·ty** n. **— per·mis′si·bly** adv.

per·mis·sion (pər·mish′ən) n. **1.** The act of permitting or allowing. **2.** Formal authorization or consent.

per·mis·sive (pər·mis′iv) adj. **1.** Permitting; granting permission. **2.** Permitted; optional. **3.** Not strict in discipline. **— per·mis′sive·ly** adv. **— per·mis′sive·ness** n.

per·mit (v. pər·mit′; n. pûr′mit) v. **·mit·ted, ·mit·ting** v.t. **1.** To allow the doing of; consent to. **2.** To give (someone) leave or consent; authorize. **3.** To afford opportunity for. **—** v.i. **4.** To afford possibility or opportunity. **5.** To allow. **—** n. **1.** Permission to do something. **2.** An official document or certificate authorizing performance of a specified activity; license. [< L < per- through + mittere to send, let go] **— per·mit′ter** n.

per·mut·a·ble (pər·myoo′tə·bəl) adj. Capable of being changed or of undergoing change or interchange.

per·mu·ta·tion (pûr′myŏŏ·tā′shən) *n.* **1.** The act of re-arranging; transformation. **2.** *Math.* Change in the order of sequence of elements or objects in a series; esp., the making of all possible changes of sequence, as *abc, acb, acb, bac,* etc.
per·mute (pər·myŏŏt′) *v.t.* **·mut·ed, ·mut·ing** To subject to permutation, esp., to change the order of. [< OF < L *per-* thoroughly + *mutare* to change]
per·ni·cious (pər·nish′əs) *adj.* **1.** Having the power of destroying or injuring; very injurious; deadly. **2.** Malicious; wicked. [< MF < L *per-* thoroughly + *nex, necis* death] — **per·ni′cious·ly** *adv.* — **per·ni′cious·ness** *n.*
— **Syn. 1.** Noxious, baneful, deleterious, detrimental.
pernicious anemia *Pathol.* Severe anemia characterized by inadequate development of red blood corpuscles and of progressive disturbances in the muscular, nervous, and gastrointestinal systems.
per·nick·e·ty (pər·nik′ə·tē) *adj.* Persnickety.
per·o·rate (per′ə·rāt) *v.i.* **·rat·ed, ·rat·ing 1.** To speak at length; harangue. **2.** To sum up or conclude a speech.
per·o·ra·tion (per′ə·rā′shən) *n.* The concluding portion of an oration or the summing up of an argument. [< L < *per-* through + *orare* to speak]
per·ox·ide (pə·rok′sīd) *n.* *Chem.* **1.** An oxide having the highest proportion of oxygen for a given series. **2.** Hydrogen peroxide. Also **per·ox′id** (-sid). — *v.t.* **·id·ed, ·id·ing** To bleach, as hair, with peroxide.
per·pen·dic·u·lar (pûr′pən·dik′yə·lər) *adj.* **1.** Being at right angles to the plane of the horizon; upright or vertical. **2.** *Math.* Meeting a given line or plane at right angles — *n.* **1.** A perpendicular line or plane. **2.** A plumb rule. **3.** A line at right angles to another line or to a plane. [< OF < L *perpendiculum* plumb line] — **per′pen·dic′u·lar′i·ty** (-lar′ə·tē) *n.* — **per′pen·dic′u·lar·ly** *adv.*
per·pe·trate (pûr′pə·trāt) *v.t.* **·trat·ed, ·trat·ing** To do, perform, or commit (a crime, etc.). [< L < *per-* thoroughly + *patrare* to accomplish] — **per′pe·tra′tion** *n.* — **per′pe·tra′tor** *n.*
per·pet·u·al (pər·pech′ŏŏ·əl) *adj.* **1.** Continuing or lasting forever or for an unlimited time. **2.** Incessant. [< OF < L < *per-* through + *petere* to seek] — **per·pet′u·al·ly** *adv.*
— **Syn.** (adj.) **1.** eternal, endless, interminable.
perpetual motion Continuous motion of a mechanism, conceived of as a capacity of doing work indefinitely by the energy supplied through its own operation.
per·pet·u·ate (pər·pech′ŏŏ·āt) *v.t.* **·at·ed, ·at·ing 1.** To make perpetual or enduring. **2.** To cause to remain known, current, etc.: to *perpetuate* a myth. [< L *perpetuare* to perpetuate] — **per·pet′u·a′tion** *n.* — **per·pet′u·a′tor** *n.*
per·pe·tu·i·ty (pûr′pə·tŏŏ′ə·tē, -tyŏŏ′-) *n. pl.* **·ties 1.** The quality or state of being perpetual. **2.** Something perpetual, as a perpetual annuity. **3.** Unending or unlimited time. [See PERPETUAL.]
per·plex (pər·pleks′) *v.t.* **1.** To cause to hesitate or become confused, as from doubt, difficulties encountered, etc.; puzzle. **2.** To make complicated, intricate, or confusing.
— **Syn. 1.** bewilder, mystify, confound. Compare BAFFLE.
per·plexed (pər·plekst′) *adj.* **1.** Confused; puzzled; bewildered. **2.** Of a complicated character; involved. [Appar. alter. of obs. *perplex,* adj., intricate < L *perplexus* involved] — **per·plex′ed·ly** (-plek′sid·lē) *adv.*
per·plex·ing (pər·plek′sing) *adj.* Confusing; puzzling. — **per·plex′ing·ly** *adv.*
per·plex·i·ty (pər·plek′sə·tē) *n. pl.* **·ties 1.** The state, quality, or condition of being perplexed; doubt; confusion; bewilderment. **2.** That which perplexes. **3.** The quality or condition of being intricate or complicated.
per·qui·site (pûr′kwə·zit) *n.* **1.** Any incidental profit, payment, etc., beyond what is earned as salary or wages. **2.** Any privilege or benefit owed or claimed as one's due. [< L *perquisitum* a thing diligently sought]
perse (pûrs) *adj.* Dark grayish blue. — *n.* A dark grayish blue. [< OF *pers* < LL *persus* < *Persicus* Persian]
per se (pûr sē′, sā′) *Latin* By itself; intrinsically.
per·se·cute (pûr′sə·kyŏŏt) *v.t.* **·cut·ed, ·cut·ing 1.** To annoy or harass persistently. **2.** To maltreat or oppress because of race, religion, or beliefs. [< F < L *persecutus,* pp. of *persequi* to pursue] — **per′se·cu′tion** *n.* — **per′se·cu′tive** *adj.* — **per′se·cu′tor** *n.*
Per·seph·o·ne (pər·sef′ə·nē) In Greek mythology, the daughter of Zeus and Demeter, abducted to the underworld by Pluto, but allowed to return to the earth for part of each year: identified with the Roman *Proserpine.*
Per·seus (pûr′syŏŏs, -sē·əs) In Greek mythology, the son of Zeus and Danae, slayer of Medusa and rescuer of Andromeda. — *n.* A northern constellation. See CONSTELLATION.
per·se·ver·ance (pûr′sə·vir′əns) *n.* **1.** The act or habit of persevering. **2.** *Theol.* In Calvinism, the continuance in grace and certain salvation of those chosen by God.

per·se·vere (pûr′sə·vir′) *v.i.* **·vered, ·ver·ing** To persist in any purpose or enterprise; strive in spite of difficulties, etc. [< OF < L *per-* thoroughly + *severus* strict] — **per′se·ver·ing** *adj.* — **per′se·ver′ing·ly** *adv.*
Per·sian (pûr′zhən, -shən) *adj.* Of or pertaining to Persia (now Iran), or its people, language, or culture. — *n.* **1.** A native or inhabitant of Persia or Iran. **2.** The Iranian language of the Persians. [< OF < L *Persia* Persia]
Persian Empire An empire of SW Asia, extending from the Indus to the Mediterranean, destroyed by Alexander the Great (331 B.C.).
Persian lamb 1. The lamb of the karakul sheep. **2.** Its black, gray, or brown curled fur.
Persian wheel A noria.
per·si·flage (pûr′sə·fläzh) *n.* A light, flippant style of conversation or writing. [< F < *persifler* to banter]
per·sim·mon (pər·sim′ən) *n.* **1.** Any of several trees having reddish orange fruit with an astringent taste when not ripe. **2.** The fruit of these trees. [< Algonquian]
per·sist (pər·sist′, -zist′) *v.i.* **1.** To continue firmly in some course, state, etc., esp. despite opposition or difficulties. **2.** To be insistent, as in repeating or continuing an action. **3.** To continue to exist; endure. [< L < *per-* thoroughly + *sistere* causative of *stare* to stand]
per·sis·tence (pər·sis′təns, -zis′-) *n.* **1.** The act, condition, or quality of persisting. **2.** Perseverance. **3.** The continuance of an effect longer than the cause that first produced it. Also **per·sis′ten·cy.**
per·sis·tent (pər·sis′tənt, -zis′-) *adj.* **1.** Persevering or stubborn in a course or resolve. **2.** Enduring; permanent. **3.** Constantly repeated. — **per·sis′tent·ly** *adv.*
per·snick·e·ty (pər·snik′ə·tē) *adj. Informal* **1.** Unduly fastidious; fussy. **2.** Demanding minute care or pains. Also *pernickety.* [< dial. E] — **per·snick′e·ti·ness** *n.*
per·son (pûr′sən) *n.* **1.** Any human being considered as a distinct entity or personality; an individual. **2.** The body of a human being. **3.** One's characteristic appearance or physical condition. **4.** *Law* Any human being, corporation, or body politic having legal rights and duties. **5.** *Theol.* One of the three individualities in the Trinity **6.** *Gram.* **a** A modification of the pronoun and verb that distinguishes the speaker (**first person**), the person or thing spoken to (**second person**), and the person or thing spoken of (**third person**). **b** Any of the forms or inflections indicating this, as *I* or *we, you, he, she, it.* — **in person 1.** Physically present. **2.** Acting for oneself. [< F < L *persona* actor's mask, character]
per·so·na (pər·sō′nə) *n. pl.* **·nae** (-nē) *Usu. pl.* A character in a drama, novel, etc. [L, person]
per·son·a·ble (pûr′sən·ə·bəl) *adj.* Attractive or pleasing in personal appearance. — **per′son·a·bly** *adv.*
per·son·age (pûr′sən·ij) *n.* **1.** A man or woman of importance or rank. **2.** A person; individual. **3.** A character in fiction, drama, history, etc.
per·so·na gra·ta (pər·sō′nə grä′tə, grā′tə) *Latin* An acceptable or welcome person.
per·son·al (pûr′sən·əl) *adj.* **1.** Pertaining to or concerning a particular person; not general or public. **2.** Relating to, having the qualities of, or constituting a person or persons. **3.** Done in person: a *personal* service. **4.** Of or pertaining to the body or appearance: *personal* beauty. **5.** Directly referring to an individual, esp. in a critical or disparaging manner: *personal* remarks. **6.** *Law* Pertaining to property regarded as movable or temporary: distinguished from *real.* **7.** *Gram.* Denoting or indicating person: *personal* pronouns. — *n.* **1.** *Law* A movable or temporary article or property; chattel. **2.** A paragraph or advertisement of personal reference or application. [< OF < LL < L *persona* a person]
per·son·al·i·ty (pûr′sən·al′ə·tē) *n. pl.* **·ties 1.** Distinctive qualities or characteristics of a person. **2.** A person of outstanding or distinctive qualities. **3.** That which constitutes a person; personal existence. **4.** *Often pl.* A remark or reference, often disparaging, of a personal nature.
per·son·al·ize (pûr′sən·əl·īz′) *v.t.* **·ized, ·iz·ing 1.** To make personal. **2.** To personify. **3.** To mark with one's name, initials, etc., as stationery or handkerchiefs.
per·son·al·ly (pûr′sən·əl·ē) *adv.* **1.** In person; not through an agent. **2.** As regards one's own opinions, tastes, etc. **3.** With regard to a person as an individual. **4.** As though intended for or directed toward oneself.
personal pronoun *Gram.* A pronoun that varies in form according to person, gender, case, and number, as *we, their, him.*
per·son·al·ty (pûr′sən·əl·tē) *n. pl.* **·ties** *Law* Personal property.
per·so·na non gra·ta (pər·sō′nə non grä′tə, grā′tə) *Latin* A person who is not welcome or acceptable.
per·son·ate (pûr′sən·āt) *v.t.* **·at·ed, ·at·ing 1.** To act the part of, as a character in a play. **2.** *Law* To impersonate

with intent to deceive. [See PERSON.] — **per'son·a'tion** n. — **per'son·a'tive** adj. — **per'son·a'tor** n.

per·son·i·fi·ca·tion (pər·son'ə·fə·kā'shən) n. 1. The figurative endowment of inanimate objects or qualities with personality or human attributes. 2. Exemplification of a quality or attribute in one's person; embodiment: She was the *personification* of joy. 3. Impersonation.

per·son·i·fy (pər·son'ə·fī) v.t. ·fied, ·fy·ing 1. To think of or represent as having life or human qualities. 2. To represent (an abstraction or inanimate object) as a person. 3. To be the embodiment of; typify. [< F < L *persona* mask, person + *facere* to make] — **per·son'i·fi'er** n.

per·son·nel (pûr'sə·nel') n. The persons employed in a business, in military service, etc. [See PERSONAL.]

per·spec·tive (pər·spek'tiv) n. 1. The art or theory of representing solid objects on a flat surface in such a way as to convey the impression of depth and distance. 2. The effect of distance upon the appearance of objects. 3. The relative importance of facts or matters from any special point of view. 4. Judgment of facts, circumstances, etc., with regard to their importance. 5. A distant view, vista, or prospect. — adj. Pertaining to, characterized by, or represented in perspective. [< Med.L < LL < L < *per-* through + *specere* to look] — **per·spec'tive·ly** adv.

per·spi·ca·cious (pûr'spə·kā'shəs) adj. 1. Keenly discerning or understanding. 2. Archaic Sharp-sighted. [< L *perspicax, -acis* sharp-sighted] — **per'spi·ca'cious·ly** adv. — **per'spi·ca'cious·ness** n.

per·spi·cac·i·ty (pûr'spə·kas'ə·tē) n. Keenness in mental penetration or discernment.

per·spi·cu·i·ty (pûr'spə·kyoo'ə·tē) n. 1. Clearness of expression or style; lucidity. 2. Perspicacity.

per·spic·u·ous (pər·spik'yoo·əs) adj. Having the quality of perspicuity; clear; lucid. — **per·spic'u·ous·ly** adv. — **per·spic'u·ous·ness** n.

per·spi·ra·tion (pûr'spə·rā'shən) n. 1. The act or process of perspiring. 2. The fluid excreted; sweat. 3. Arduous physical effort. — **per·spi·ra·to·ry** (pər·spī'rə·tôr'ē) adj.

per·spire (pər·spīr') v. ·spired, ·spir·ing v.i. 1. To give off a saline fluid through the pores of the skin; sweat. — v.t. 2. To give off through pores; exude. [< MF < L < *per-* through + *spirare* to breathe]

per·suade (pər·swād') v.t. ·suad·ed, ·suad·ing 1. To induce (someone) to do something. 2. To induce to a belief; convince. [< MF < L < *per-* thoroughly + *suadere* to advise] — **per·suad'a·ble** adj. — **per·suad'er** n.

per·sua·sion (pər·swā'zhən) n. 1. The act of persuading or of using persuasive methods. 2. Ability to persuade. 3. The state of being persuaded; settled opinion; conviction. 4. An accepted creed or belief. 5. A religious sect. 6. Party; group; faction.

per·sua·sive (pər·swā'siv) adj. Having power or tendency to persuade. — n. That which persuades or tends to persuade. — **per·sua'sive·ly** adv. — **per·sua'sive·ness** n.

pert (pûrt) adj. 1. Impertinent; saucy. 2. Dial. Handsome and lively. [Aphetic var. of ME *apert* < OF, open, impudent] — **pert'ly** adv. — **pert'ness** n.

per·tain (pər·tān') v.i. 1. To have reference; relate. 2. To belong as an adjunct, function, quality, etc. 3. To be fitting or appropriate. — **pertaining to** Having to do with; belonging or relating to. [< OF < L < *per-* through + *tenere* to hold]

per·ti·na·cious (pûr'tə·nā'shəs) adj. 1. Tenacious of purpose; adhering fixedly to a pursuit or opinion. 2. Stubbornly or doggedly persistent. [< L < *per-* thoroughly, very + *tenax, -acis* tenacious] — **per'ti·na'cious·ly** adv.

per·ti·nac·i·ty (pûr'tə·nas'ə·tē) n. pl. ·ties 1. Tenacity of purpose; unyielding adherence. 2. Obstinacy.

per·ti·nent (pûr'tə·nənt) adj. Related to or properly bearing upon the matter in hand; relevant. [See PERTAIN.] — **per'ti·nence, per'ti·nen·cy** n. — **per'ti·nent·ly** adv.

per·turb (pər·tûrb') v.t. 1. To disquiet or disturb greatly; alarm; agitate. 2. To throw into disorder; cause confusion in. [< OF < L < *per-* thoroughly + *turbare* to disturb] — **per·turb'a·ble** adj. — **per'tur·ba'tion** n.

pe·ruke (pə·rook') n. A wig; esp. one worn by men in the 17th and 18th centuries: also *periwig.* [< MF < *perruque* < Ital. *perrucca*]

pe·rus·al (pə·roo'zəl) n. The act or procedure of reading or examining carefully; a thorough reading or scrutiny.

pe·ruse (pə·rooz') v.t. ·rused, ·rus·ing 1. To read carefully or attentively. 2. To read. 3. To examine; scrutinize. [< PER- + USE, v.] — **pe·rus'a·ble** adj. — **pe·rus'er** n.

Pe·ru·vi·an (pə·roo'vē·ən) adj. Of or pertaining to Peru or its inhabitants, etc. — n. A native or inhabitant of Peru.

Peruvian bark Cinchona.

per·vade (pər·vād') v.t. ·vad·ed, ·vad·ing To spread through every part of; be diffused throughout; permeate. [< L < *per-* through + *vadere* to go] — **per·va'sion** (-zhən) n.

per·va·sive (pər·vā'siv) adj. Thoroughly penetrating or permeating. — **per·va'sive·ly** adv. — **per·va'sive·ness** n.

per·verse (pər·vûrs') adj. 1. Willfully deviating from acceptable or conventional behavior, opinion, etc. 2. Refractory; capricious. 3. Petulant; cranky. 4. Morally wrong or erring; wicked; perverted. [See PERVERT.] — **per·verse'·ly** adv. — **per·verse'ness** n.

per·ver·sion (pər·vûr'zhən, -shən) n. 1. The act of perverting, or the state of being perverted. 2. A perverted form, act, use, etc. 3. Deviation from the normal in sexual desires or activities.

per·ver·si·ty (pər·vûr'sə·tē) n. pl. ·ties 1. The state or quality of being perverse. 2. An instance of perverseness.

per·vert (v. pər·vûrt'; n. pûr'vərt) v.t. 1. To turn to an improper use or purpose; misapply. 2. To distort the meaning or intent of; misconstrue. 3. To turn from approved opinions or conduct; lead astray. 4. To deprave; debase; corrupt. — n. One characterized by or practicing sexual perversion. [< F < L < *per-* away + *vertere* to turn] — **per·vert'er** n. — **per·vert'i·ble** adj.

per·vert·ed (pər·vûr'tid) adj. 1. Deviating widely from what is right or acceptable; distorted. 2. Characterized by viciousness, sexual perversion, etc. — **per·vert'ed·ly** adv.

per·vi·ous (pûr'vē·əs) adj. 1. Capable of being penetrated. 2. Open to reason, suggestions, etc. [< L *pervius* having a way through] — **per'vi·ous·ly** adv. — **per'vi·ous·ness** n.

pe·se·ta (pə·sā'tə, Sp. pā·sā'tä) n. The standard monetary unit of Spain, equivalent to 100 centimos: in 1960 worth about 2 U.S. cents; also, a silver coin of this value. [< Sp., dim. of *pesa* weight]

pes·ky (pes'kē) adj. ·ki·er, ·ki·est U.S. Informal Annoying; troublesome. [Prob. < PEST + -Y²] — **pes'ki·ly** adv.

pe·so (pā'sō) n. pl. ·sos 1. The standard monetary unit of various Spanish-speaking countries, as Argentina, Mexico, or the Philippines, equivalent to 100 centavos. 2. A coin or note of this denomination. [< Sp., orig., a weight < L *pensum*, orig. pp. neut. of *pendere* to weigh]

pes·sa·ry (pes'ə·rē) n. pl. ·ries Med. 1. A device worn internally to remedy a uterine displacement. 2. A contraceptive device worn over or in the uterine cervix. [< Med.L < L < Gk. *pessos* oval stone]

pes·si·mism (pes'ə·miz'əm) n. 1. A disposition to take a gloomy or cynical view of affairs: opposed to *optimism.* 2. The doctrine that the world and life are essentially evil. [< L *pessimus* worst + -ISM] — **pes'si·mist** n. — **pes'si·mis'·tic** or **·ti·cal** adj. — **pes'si·mis'ti·cal·ly** adv.

pest (pest) n. 1. An annoying person or thing. 2. A destructive or injurious insect, plant, etc. 3. A virulent epidemic, esp. of plague. [< MF < L *pestis* plague]

pes·ter (pes'tər) v.t. To harass with petty and persistent annoyances; bother; plague. [< OF < *em-* in + LL *pastorium* foot shackles] — **pes'ter·er** n.

pest·hole (pest'hōl') n. A squalid or insanitary place in which disease is likely to occur and spread.

pes·ti·cide (pes'tə·sīd) n. A chemical or other substance used to destroy plant and animal pests. — **pes'ti·ci'dal** adj.

pes·tif·er·ous (pes·tif'ər·əs) adj. 1. Informal Annoying; bothersome. 2. Carrying or spreading infectious disease. 3. Having an evil or harmful influence. [< L < *pestis* plague + *ferre* to bear] — **pes·tif'er·ous·ly** adv. — **pes·tif'er·ous·ness** n.

pes·ti·lence (pes'tə·ləns) n. 1. Any widespread, often fatal infectious or contagious disease, as cholera or the bubonic plague. 2. A noxious or malign doctrine, influence, etc. — **pes'ti·len'tial** (-len/shəl) adj.

pes·ti·lent (pes'tə·lənt) adj. 1. Tending to produce infectious or epidemic disease. 2. Having a malign influence or effect. 3. Making trouble; vexatious. [< OF < L < *pestis* plague] — **pes'ti·lent·ly** adv.

pes·tle (pes'əl) n. 1. An implement used for crushing, pulverizing, or mixing substances in or as in a mortar. 2. A vertical moving bar employed in pounding, as in a stamp mill, etc. — v.t. & v.i. ·tled, ·tling To pound, grind, or mix with or as with a pestle. [< OF < L *pistus*, pp. of *pinsere* to pound]

PESTLE (a) IN MORTAR (b)

pet¹ (pet) n. 1. A tame animal treated lovingly or kept as a companion or playmate. 2. Any loved and cherished creature or thing. 3. A favorite: teacher's *pet.* — adj. 1. Tamed or kept as a pet. 2. Regarded as a favorite; cherished. — v. pet·ted, pet·ting — v.t. 1. To stroke or caress. 2. To treat indulgently; coddle. — v.i. 3. U.S. Slang To make love by kissing and caressing. [< dial. E (Scottish), ? < F *petit* little one]

pet² (pet) n. A fit of pique or ill temper. [Origin unknown]

pet·al (pet'l) n. Bot. One of the divisions or leaflike parts of a corolla. For illus. see FLOWER. [< NL < Gk. *petalon* leaf] — **pet'aled** or **pet'alled** adj.

-petal combining form Seeking: *centripetal.* [< L *petere* to seek]

pet·a·lif·er·ous (pet'ə·lif'ər·əs) adj. Bearing petals.

pe·tard (pi·tärd') n. 1. An explosive device formerly used to break through walls, gates, etc. 2. A small firecracker

exploding with a loud report. [< MF < OF < L *peditum*, orig. pp. neut. of *pedere* to break wind]
pet·cock (pet′cok′) *n. Mech.* A small valve or faucet, used for draining, releasing pressure, etc. Also **pet cock.** [? < obs. *pet* a fart + COCK¹]
pe·ter (pē′tər) *v.i. Informal* To diminish gradually and then cease or disappear: followed by *out*. [Orig. U.S. mining slang, ? < F *péter* (*dans la main*) to come to nothing]
Pe·ter (pē′tər) One of the twelve apostles, reputed author of two New Testament epistles: called **Saint Peter.** Also *Simon Peter.* — *n.* Either of the two books of the New Testament that bear his name. [< LL < Gk. *petros* stone]
Peter Pan The hero of J. M. Barrie's play (1904) of the same name, a little boy who remained perpetually a child.
Peter Pan collar A flat collar with rounded ends, used on girls' and women's blouses, dresses, etc.
pet·i·o·late (pet′ē·ə·lāt) *adj.* Having a petiole. Also **pet′i·o·lat′ed.**
pet·i·ole (pet′ē·ōl) *n.* 1. *Bot.* The stem or slender stalk of a leaf; a leafstalk. 2. *Anat.* A peduncle. [< L *petiolus*, orig. dim. of *pes, pedis* foot] — **pet′i·o·lar** *adj.*
pet·it (pet′ē) *adj. Law* Small; lesser; minor: *petit jury*: also spelled *petty*. [< OF, small]
pe·tite (pə·tēt′) *adj. fem.* Diminutive; little. [< F]
pet·it four (pet′ē fôr′, fōr′; *Fr.* pə·tē′fōōr′) *pl.* **pet·its fours** or **pet·it fours** (pet′ē fôrz′, fōrz′; *Fr.* pə·tē′fōōr′) A little, decoratively iced cake. [< F, lit., little oven]
pe·ti·tion (pə·tish′ən) *n.* 1. A formal request or prayer. 2. A formal request addressed to a person or group in authority and asking for some benefit, the redress of a grievance, etc. 3. *Law* A formal application in writing made to a court, requesting judicial action concerning some matter therein set forth. 4. Something formally requested or entreated. — *v.t.* 1. To make a petition to. 2. To ask for. — *v.i.* 3. To make a petition. [< OF < L < *petere* to seek] — **pe·ti′·tion·ar′y** *adj.* — **pe·ti′tion·er** *n.*
petit jury The jury that sits at a trial in civil and criminal cases: also called *trial jury*: also spelled *petty jury*.
petit larceny See under LARCENY.
pe·tit mal (pə·tē′ mäl′) *Pathol.* A mild form of epilepsy characterized by a momentary loss of consciousness: distinguished from *grand mal*. [< F, lit., little sickness]
pet·it point (pet′ē) 1. A fine tapestry stitch used in decorative needlework: also called *tent stitch*. 2. Needlework done in this stitch.
Pe·trar·chan sonnet (pə·trär′kən) A sonnet having the rhyme scheme *abbaabba* in the octave, and having in the sestet a set of two or three different, variously combined rhymes, as *cdcdcd*, or *cdecde*, etc.
pet·rel (pet′rəl) *n.* Any of various small sea birds as the storm petrel. [? < LL *Petrellus*, dim. of *Peter*, after St. Peter, in an allusion to his walking on the water. *Matt.* xiv 29]
pet·ri·fac·tion (pet′rə·fak′shən) *n.* 1. The act or process of petrifying, or the state of being petrified. 2. Anything petrified. Also **pet′ri·fi·ca′tion** (-fə·kā′shən). [< PETRIFY.] — **pet′ri·fac′tive** *adj.*
pet·ri·fy (pet′rə·fī) *v.* **·fied, ·fy·ing** *v.t.* 1. To convert (organic material) into a substance of stony character. 2. To make fixed and unyielding. 3. To daze or paralyze with fear, surprise, etc. — *v.i.* 4. To become stone or like stone. [< MF < L *petra* a rock + *facere* to make]
petro- *combining form* Rock; stone. Also, before vowels, **petr-.** [< F < L < Gk. *petra* rock and *petros* stone]
pet·ro·chem·is·try (pet′rō·kem′is·trē) *n.* The chemistry of petroleum and its derivatives, esp. the natural and synthetic hydrocarbons. — **pet′ro·chem′i·cal** *adj.* & *n.*
pe·trog·ra·phy (pə·trog′rə·fē) *n.* The systematic description and classification of rocks. — **pe·trog′ra·pher** *n.* — **pet·ro·graph·ic** (pet′rə·graf′ik) or **·i·cal** *adj.* — **pet′ro·graph′i·cal·ly** *adv.*
pet·rol (pet′rəl) *n. Brit.* Gasoline.
pet·ro·la·tum (pet′rə·lā′təm) *n.* A greasy, semisolid substance obtained from petroleum, used as a stabilizer for certain explosives and in ointments. Also **petroleum jelly.**
pe·tro·le·um (pə·trō′lē·əm) *n.* An oily, liquid mixture of numerous hydrocarbons, found in subterranean deposits, used in its natural state for heat and light, and as the source of gasoline, benzine, kerosene, paraffin, etc.: also called *naphtha, rock oil*. [< Med.L < L *petra* rock (< Gk.) + *oleum* oil]
petroleum ether *Chem.* A distillate of petroleum used as a solvent of fats, waxes, etc.
pe·trol·ic (pə·trol′ik) *adj.* Of or pertaining to petroleum.
pe·trol·o·gy (pə·trol′ə·jē) *n.* The science of the origin, structure, constitution, and characteristics of rocks. — **pet·ro·log·ic** (pet′rə·loj′ik) or **·i·cal** *adj.* — **pet′ro·log′i·cal·ly** *adv.* — **pe·trol′o·gist** *n.*
pet·ti·coat (pet′ē·kōt) *n.* 1. A skirt or skirtlike garment hanging from the waist; esp., a woman's underskirt. 2.

Something resembling a petticoat. 3. A woman: a humorous or disparaging term. 4. An electric insulator shaped like an inverted cup, for use on high-tension wires. — *adj.* Of or influenced by women: *petticoat* politics.
pet·ti·fog (pet′i·fog, -fôg) *v.i.* **·fogged, ·fog·ging** 1. To be unduly concerned over trivial matters; fuss. 2. To be a pettifogger. [Appar. back formation < PETTIFOGGER]
pet·ti·fog·ger (pet′i·fog′ər, -fôg′ər) *n.* 1. An inferior lawyer, esp. one dealing with insignificant cases, or resorting to tricks. 2. One who quibbles or fusses over trivialities. [Earlier *petty fogger* < PETTY + obs. *fogger* a trickster for gain] — **pet′ti·fog′ger·y** *n.*
pet·tish (pet′ish) *adj.* Capriciously ill-tempered; petulant; peevish. [Prob. < PET² + -ISH] — **pet′tish·ly** *adv.*
pet·ty (pet′ē) *adj.* **·ti·er, ·ti·est** 1. Having little worth or importance; trifling; insignificant. 2. Having little scope or generosity; narrow-minded. 3. Mean; spiteful. 4. Having a comparatively low rank or position; minor. 5. *Law* Petit. [< F *petit* small] — **pet′ti·ly** *adv.* — **pet′ti·ness** *n.*
petty cash A supply of money kept for minor expenses, as in a business office.
petty jury See PETIT JURY.
petty larceny See under LARCENY.
petty officer *Naval* Any of a class of noncommissioned officers. See table at GRADE.
pet·u·lant (pech′ōō·lənt) *adj.* Displaying or characterized by capricious fretfulness; peevish. [< OF < L *petulans, -antis* forward, ult. < *petere* to rush at] — **pet′u·lant·ly** *adv.* — **pet′u·lance, pet′u·lan·cy** *n.*
pe·tu·ni·a (pə·tōō′nē·ə, -tyōō′-) *n.* Any of various tropical American plants cultivated widely for their funnel-shaped, variously colored flowers. [< NL < F *petun* tobacco]
pew¹ (pyōō) *n.* 1. A bench for seating people in church, frequently with a kneeling rack attached. 2. Formerly, a boxlike enclosure with seats on three sides, occupied by a family attending church. [ME < OF < LL *podia*, pl. of *podium* height, balcony < Gk. *podion* base]
pew² (pyōō) *interj.* An expression of disgust or displeasure, as at a bad odor. [Origin unknown]
pe·wee (pē′wē) *n.* Any of various small, greenish gray flycatchers: also spelled *peewee*. [Imit.]
pe·wit (pē′wit, pyōō′it) *n.* Any of various birds having a high or shrill cry. [Imit.]
pew·ter (pyōō′tər) *n.* 1. An alloy, usu. of tin and lead, formerly much used for tableware. 2. Pewter articles collectively. 3. The characteristic dull gray of pewter. — *adj.* 1. Made of pewter. 2. Dull gray. [< OF *peutre, pialtre*]
pe·yo·te (pā·ō′tē, *Sp.* pā·yō′tā) *n.* Mescal. Also **pe·yo′tl** (-yot′l). [< Am. Sp. < Nahuatl *peyotl*, lit., caterpillar]
pfen·nig (pfen′ikh) *n. pl.* **·nigs** or **pfen·ni·ge** (pfen′i·gə) A small bronze coin of Germany, equivalent to one hundredth of a deutschemark. [< G, penny]
Phae·dra (fē′drə) In Greek mythology, the wife of Theseus, who fell in love with her stepson and killed herself because he spurned her. Also **Phæ′dra.**
Pha·e·thon (fā′ə·thon) In Greek mythology, the son of Helios, who borrowed his father's chariot of the sun, and would have set heaven and earth on fire by his careless driving if Zeus had not slain him with a thunderbolt.
pha·e·ton (fā′ə·tən, *esp. Brit.* fā′tən) *n.* 1. A light, four-wheeled carriage, open at the sides, and sometimes having a top. 2. An open automobile having front and back seats. [< F, ult. < Gk. *Phaethōn* Phaethon]
-phage *combining form* One who or that which eats or consumes: *bacteriophage*. [< Gk. *phagein* to eat]
phago- *combining form* Eating. Also, before vowels, **phag-.** [< Gk. *phagein* to eat]
phag·o·cyte (fag′ə·sīt) *n. Physiol.* A leucocyte that ingests and destroys harmful bacteria, etc., in the blood and tissues of the body. — **phag′o·cyt′ic** (-sit′ik) or **·i·cal** *adj.*
-phagous *combining form* Consuming; tending to eat. [< Gk. *phagein* to eat]
-phagy *combining form* The consumption or eating of. Also **-phagia.** [< Gk. *phagein* to eat]
phal·ange (fal′ənj, fə·lanj′) *n. Anat.* A phalanx.
pha·lan·ge·al (fə·lan′jē·əl) *adj.* Of, pertaining to, or resembling the phalanges of the fingers and toes. Also **pha·lan′gal** (-gəl), **pha·lan′ge·an.**
pha·lan·ger (fə·lan′jər) *n.* Any one of a family of small marsupials of Australia and New Guinea, having long, often prehensile tails. [< NL < *phalanges*, pl. of *phalanx* phalanx]
pha·lanx (fā′langks, *esp. Brit.* fal′angks) *n. pl.* **pha·lanx·es** (fə·lan′jēz) or **pha·lanx·es** 1. In ancient Greece, a marching order of heavy infantry, with close ranks and files, joined shields, and spears overlapping. 2. Any massed or compact body or corps. 3. *Anat.* One of the bones articulating with the joints of the fingers or toes: also called *phalange*. [< L < Gk. *phalanx, phalangos* line of battle]

phal·a·rope (fal′ə·rōp) *n.* Any of several swimming birds resembling the sandpiper, but having lobate toes. [< F < NL < Gk. *phalaris* coot + *pous* foot]

phal·lism (fal′iz·əm) *n.* Worship of the generative power in nature as symbolized by the phallus. Also **phal′li·cism.** — **phal′li·cist, phal′list** *n.*

phal·lus (fal′əs) *n.* *pl.* **·li** (-ī) **1.** A representation of the male generative organ, often used as a symbol of the generative power of nature. **2.** *Anat.* The penis or the clitoris. [< L < Gk. *phallos* penis] — **phal′lic** *adj.*

-phane *combining form* Something resembling or similar to (a specified substance or material): *cellophane.* [< Gk. *-phanēs* < *phainein* to show]

phan·tasm (fan′taz·əm) *n.* **1.** An imaginary appearance; phantom. **2.** A mental image; fancy. [< Gk. *phantasma*]

phan·tas·ma·go·ri·a (fan·taz′mə·gôr′ē·ə, -gō′rē·ə) *n.* **1.** A changing, incoherent series of apparitions or phantasms, as in a dream. **2.** An exhibition of pictures projected on a screen and made to increase or diminish in size rapidly while continuously in focus; also, any exhibition of optical effects. **3.** An apparition. Also **phan·tas′ma·go′ry.** [< NL < Gk. *phantasma* apparition + (prob.) *agora* crowd] — **phan·tas′ma·go′ri·al, phan·tas′ma·go′ric** (-gôr′ik, -gor′ik) or **·i·cal** *adj.*

phan·tas·mal (fan·taz′məl) *adj.* Of or like a phantasm; unreal or illusive; spectral. Also **phan·tas′mic.**

phan·ta·sy (fan′tə·sē, -zē) See FANTASY.

phan·tom (fan′təm) *n.* **1.** Something that exists only in appearance. **2.** An apparition; specter. **3.** The visible representative of an abstract state or incorporeal person. — *adj.* Illusive; ghostlike. Also spelled *fantom.* [< OF < L < Gk. *phantasma* apparition < *phainein* to show]

-phany *combining form* Appearance; manifestation: *epiphany.* [< Gk. < *phainein* to appear]

Phar·aoh (fâr′ō, fā′rō, fār′ē·ō) *n.* Any one of the monarchs of ancient Egypt. [< LL < Gk. < Hebrew < Egyptian *pr-‘ōh* the great house] — **Phar′a·on′ic** (-ē·on′ik) or **·i·cal** *adj.*

phar·i·sa·ic (far′ə·sā′ik) *adj.* **1.** Of or pertaining to the Pharisees. **2.** Observing the form, but neglecting the spirit, of religion; self-righteous. Also **phar′i·sa′i·cal** — **phar′i·sa′i·cal·ly** *adv.* — **phar′i·sa′i·cal·ness** *n.*

phar·i·sa·ism (far′ə·sā·iz′əm) *n.* **1.** *Often cap.* The principles of the Pharisees. **2.** Formality, self-righteousness, or hypocrisy. Also **phar′i·see·ism** (-sē·iz′əm).

Phar·i·see (far′ə·sē) *n.* **1.** A member of an ancient Jewish sect that accepted the Mosaic law and the oral traditions associated with it, and emphasized strict observance of ritual. **2.** A formal, sanctimonious, hypocritical person: also **phar′i·see.** [OE *fariseus,* infl. by OF *pharise,* both < L < Gk. < Aramaic *perishayā,* pl. of *perish*]

phar·ma·ceu·ti·cal (fär′mə·sōō′ti·kəl) *adj.* Pertaining to, using, or relating to pharmacy or the pharmacopoeia: also **phar·ma·cal** (fär′mə·kəl). Also **phar′ma·ceu′tic.** — *n.* A pharmaceutical product. [< L < Gk. < *pharmakon* drug] — **phar′ma·ceu′ti·cal·ly** *adv.* — **phar′ma·ceu′tist** *n.*

phar·ma·ceu·tics (fär′mə·sōō′tiks) *n.pl.* (*construed as sing.*) Pharmacy (def. 1).

phar·ma·cist (fär′mə·sist) *n.* A qualified druggist.

pharmaco- *combining form* A drug; of or pertaining to drugs. Also, before vowels, **pharmac-.** [< Gk. *pharmakon* drug]

phar·ma·col·o·gy (fär′mə·kol′ə·jē) *n.* The science of the nature, preparation, administration, and effects of drugs. — **phar′ma·co·log′ic** (-kə·loj′ik) or **·i·cal** *adj.* — **phar′ma·co·log′i·cal·ly** *adv.* — **phar′ma·col′o·gist** *n.*

phar·ma·co·poe·ia (fär′mə·kə·pē′ə) *n.* **1.** A book, usu. published by an authority, containing standard formulas and methods for the preparation of medicines, drugs, and other remedial substances. **2.** A collection of drugs. [< NL < Gk. < *pharmakon* drug + *poieein* to make] — **phar′ma·co·poe′ial** *adj.* — **phar′ma·co·poe′ist** *n.*

phar·ma·cy (fär′mə·sē) *n.* *pl.* **·cies 1.** The art or business of compounding and identifying drugs, and of compounding and dispensing medicines: also called *pharmaceutics.* **2.** A drugstore. [< OF < LL < Gk. < *pharmakon* drug]

pha·ryn·ge·al (fə·rin′jē·əl, far′in·jē′əl) *adj.* Of or pertaining to the pharynx. Also **pha·ryn′gal** (-gəl).

phar·yn·gi·tis (far′in·jī′tis) *n.* *Pathol.* Inflammation of the pharynx, as in diphtheria and sore throat.

pharyngo- *combining form* The throat; related to the throat. Also, before vowels, **pharyng-.** [< Gk. *pharynx* throat]

phar·ynx (far′ingks) *n.* *pl.* **pha·ryn·ges** (fə·rin′jēz) or **phar·ynx·es** *Anat.* The part of the alimentary canal between the palate and the esophagus, serving as a passage for air and food. For illus. see MOUTH, THROAT. [< NL < Gk. *pharynx, -yngos* throat]

phase (fāz) *n.* **1.** The view that anything presents to the eye; any one of varying distinctive manifestations of an object. **2.** *Astron.* One of the appearances or forms presented periodically by the moon and planets. **3.** *Physics* **a** Any particular stage in the complete cycle of a periodic system. **b**

The fraction of a cycle through which a wave has passed at any instant. **4.** *Chem.* Any homogeneous part of a material system separated from other parts by physical boundaries, as ice in water. **5.** *Biol.* Any characteristic or decisive stage in the growth, development, or life pattern of an organism. Also **pha·sis** (fā′sis). — **in phase** Reaching corresponding phases simultaneously, as two waves. — **to phase out** (or **in**) *U.S.* To plan and execute the orderly and gradual completion or initiation of an enterprise. [< NL < Gk. < *phainein* to show] — **pha·sic** (fā′zik) *adj.* — **Syn.** (noun) **1.** Aspect, side, fact.

-phasia *combining form* *Med.* Defect or malfunction of speech: *dysphasia.* Also **-phasy.** [< Gk. < *phanai* to speak]

pheas·ant (fez′ənt) *n.* **1.** A long-tailed, gallinaceous bird, originally of Asia, noted for the gorgeous plumage of the male; esp. the **ring-necked pheasant,** widely bred in the U.S. **2.** One of various other birds, as the ruffed grouse. [< AF < L < Gk. *Phasianos* (*ornis*) the Phasian (bird) < *Phasis* the Phasis, a river in the Georgian S.S.R.]

Phe·be (fē′bē) See PHOEBE.

phen- Var. of PHENO-.

phe·nac·e·tin (fə·nas′ə·tin) *n.* *Chem.* A white, crystalline, coal-tar compound, $C_{10}H_{13}NO_2$, used in medicine as an antipyretic. Also **phe·nac′e·tine.**

phe·nix (fē′niks) See PHOENIX.

pheno- *combining form* *Chem.* Related to benzene; a derivative of benzene. Also, before vowels, *phen-.* [< Gk. *phaino-* shining < *phainein* to show]

phe·no·bar·bi·tal (fē′nō·bär′bə·tal, -tôl) *n.* *Chem.* A white, odorless, slightly bitter, crystalline powder, $C_{12}H_{12}O_3N_2$, used as a sedative. Also **phe′no·bar′bi·tone** (-tōn).

phe·nol (fē′nōl, -nol) *n.* *Chem.* A white, crystalline, caustic compound, C_6H_5OH, derived from coal tar and used as a disinfectant: also called *carbolic acid.* [< Gk. *phaino-* shining < *phainein* to show + -OL¹]

phe·nol·phthal·ein (fē′nōl·thal′ēn, fē′nolf·thal′ē·in) *n.* *Chem.* A yellowish white derivative of phenol, $C_{20}H_{14}O_4$, used as a laxative, an indicator in acid-base titrations, etc.

phe·nom·e·na (fi·nom′ə·nə) Plural of PHENOMENON.

phe·nom·e·nal (fi·nom′ə·nəl) *adj.* **1.** Pertaining to phenomena. **2.** Extraordinary or marvelous. **3.** *Philos.* Perceptible through the senses. — **phe·nom′e·nal·ly** *adv.*

phe·nom·e·nal·ism (fi·nom′ə·nəl·iz′əm) *n.* *Philos.* The doctrine that denies either our knowledge or the existence of a reality beyond phenomena. — **phe·nom′e·nal·ist** *n.* — **phe·nom′e·nal·is′tic** *adj.* — **phe·nom′e·nal·is′ti·cal·ly** *adv.*

phe·nom·e·non (fi·nom′ə·non) *n.* *pl.* **phe·nom·e·na** (-nə); *for defs. 2 & 3, often* **phe·nom·e·nons 1.** Something visible or directly observable, as an appearance, action, change, etc. **2.** Any unusual occurrence; marvel. **3.** *Informal* A person having some remarkable talent, power, or ability; prodigy. **4.** *Med.* Any notable characteristic or disease. [< LL < Gk. < *phainein* to show]

phe·no·type (fē′nə·tīp) *n.* *Biol.* The aggregate of genetic characteristics visibly manifested by an organism. [< F < Gk. *phainein* to show + -TYPE] — **phe′no·typ′ic** (-tip′ik) or **·i·cal** *adj.* — **phe′no·typ′i·cal·ly** *adv.*

phen·yl (fen′əl, fē′nəl) *n.* *Chem.* The univalent radical C_6H_5, the basis of numerous aromatic compounds.

phew (fyōō, fōō) *interj.* An exclamation of disgust or surprise.

phi (fī, fē) *n.* The twenty-first letter in the Greek alphabet (Φ, φ): corresponding to English *ph* and *f.* See ALPHABET.

phi·al (fī′əl) See VIAL.

Phi Be·ta Kap·pa (fī bā′tə kap′ə, bē′tə) An American honorary society founded in 1776, having its membership based on conditions of high academic standing.

phil- Var. of PHILO-.

phi·lan·der (fi·lan′dər) *v.i.* To make love without serious intentions: said of a man. — *n.* A male flirt: also **phi·lan′der·er.** [< Gk. *philandros,* orig., loving men < *phileein* to love + *anēr, andros* man]

phi·lan·thro·py (fi·lan′thrə·pē) *n.* *pl.* **·pies 1.** The effort to promote the happiness or social elevation of mankind, as by making donations, etc. **2.** Love or benevolence toward mankind in general. [< LL < Gk. < *phileein* to love + *anthropos* man] — **phil·an·throp·ic** (fil′ən·throp′ik) or **·i·cal** *adj.* — **phil′an·throp′i·cal·ly** *adv.* — **phi·lan′thro·pist** *n.*

phi·lat·e·ly (fi·lat′ə·lē) *n.* The study and collection of postage stamps, stamped envelopes, etc.; stamp collecting. [< F < Gk. *philos* loving + *ateleia* exemption from tax as indicated by a stamp] — **phil·a·tel·ic** (fil′ə·tel′ik) or **·i·cal** *adj.* — **phil′a·tel′i·cal·ly** *adv.* — **phi·lat′e·list** (-lat′ə·list) *n.*

-phile *combining form* One who supports or is fond of; one devoted to: *bibliophile.* Also **-phil.** [< Gk. *-philos* loving]

Phi·le·mon (fi·lē′mən) A Greek of Colossae, converted to Christianity by Saint Paul. — *n.* A book of the New Testament consisting of an epistle addressed by Saint Paul to him.

phil·har·mon·ic (fil′här·mon′ik, -ər·mon′-) *adj.* *Sometimes cap.* Fond of music: often used in the names of musical societies. [< F < Ital. < Gk. *philos* loving + *harmonia* music]

-philia *combining form* **1.** A tendency toward: *hemophilia.* **2.** An excessive affection or fondness for: *necrophilia.* Also spelled *-phily.* [< Gk. *-philia* < *phileein* to love]

Phil·ip (fil′ip) One of the twelve apostles: called **Saint Philip.**

Phi·lip·pi (fi·lip′ī) An ancient town in northern Macedonia, Greece; scene of the defeat of Brutus and Cassius by Octavian and Antony, 42 B.C., and of Saint Paul's first preaching in Europe. *Acts* xvi 12. — **Phi·lip′pi·an** *adj. & n.*

Phi·lip·pi·ans (fi·lip′ē·ənz) *n.pl.* (*construed as sing.*) A book of the New Testament consisting of an epistle of Saint Paul addressed to Christians at Philippi.

phi·lip·pic (fi·lip′ik) *n.* An impassioned speech characterized by invective. — **the Philippics** A series of twelve speeches in which Demosthenes denounced Philip of Macedon. [< L < Gk. *Philippikos* pertaining to Philip]

Phi·lis·ti·a (fi·lis′tē·ə) An ancient region on the Mediterranean, SW Palestine. *Ps.* lx 8.

Phi·lis·tine (fi·lis′tin, -tēn, -tīn, fil′əs-) *n.* One of a warlike race of ancient Philistia. I *Sam.* xvii 23. [< F < LL < Gk. < Hebrew *p'lishtim*]

Phi·lis·tine (fi·lis′tin, -tēn, -tīn, fil′əs-) *n.* An ignorant, narrow-minded person, devoid of culture and indifferent to art. [< G student slang *Philister* one of the ancient Philistines] — **Phi·lis′tin·ism** *n.*

philo- *combining form* Loving; fond of. Also, before vowels, *phil-.* [< Gk. *philos* loving < *phileein* to love]

phil·o·den·dron (fil′ə·den′drən) *n.* Any of various climbing plants of the arum family, having glossy, evergreen leaves and cultivated as an ornamental house plant. [< NL < Gk., neut. of *philodendros* fond of trees.]

phi·log·y·ny (fi·loj′ə·nē) *n.* Fondness for or devotion to women. [< Gk. < *philos* loving + *gynē* woman] — **phi·log′y·nist** *n.* — **phi·log′y·nous** *adj.*

phi·lol·o·gy (fi·lol′ə·jē) *n.* **1.** The study of written records, chiefly literary works, to set up accurate texts and determine their meaning. **2.** Linguistics, esp. comparative and historical. [< F < L < Gk. *philologos* fond of argument or words.] — **phil·o·log·ic** (fil′ə·loj′ik) or **·i·cal** *adj.* — **phil′o·log′i·cal·ly** *adv.* — **phi·lol′o·gist, phi·lol′o·ger** *n.*

phil·o·mel (fil′ə·mel) *n. Poetic* The nightingale. Also **phil′o·me·la** (-mē′lə). [< F < L < Gk. ? < *philos* loving + *melos* song]

phi·los·o·pher (fi·los′ə·fər) *n.* **1.** A student of or specialist in philosophy. **2.** One who lives, makes judgments, etc., according to a philosophy. **3.** One who is calm and patient under all circumstances. [< OF < L < Gk. *philosophos* lover of wisdom]

philosopher's stone An imaginary stone or substance capable of transmuting the baser metals into gold.

phil·o·soph·i·cal (fil′ə·sof′i·kəl) *adj.* **1.** Of or founded on the principles of philosophy. **2.** Proper to or characteristic of a philosopher. **3.** Self-restrained; rational; thoughtful. Also **phil′o·soph′ic.** — **phil′o·soph′i·cal·ly** *adv.* — **phil′o·soph′i·cal·ness** *n.*

phi·los·o·phize (fi·los′ə·fīz) *v.i.* **·phized, ·phiz·ing** To speculate like a philosopher; moralize. — **phi·los′o·phiz′er** *n.*

phi·los·o·phy (fi·los′ə·fē) *n. pl.* **·phies 1.** The inquiry into the most comprehensive principles of reality in general, or of some sector of it, as human knowledge or human values. **2.** The love of wisdom, and the search for it. **3.** A philosophical system; also, a treatise on such a system. **4.** The general laws that furnish the rational explanation of anything: the *philosophy* of banking. **5.** Practical wisdom; fortitude. [< OF < L < Gk. *philosophos* lover of wisdom]

-philous *combining form* Loving; fond of. [< Gk. *-philos*]

phil·ter (fil′tər) *n.* **1.** A charmed draft supposed to have power to excite sexual love. **2.** Any magic potion. — *v.t.* To charm with a philter. Also **phil′tre.** [< MF < L < Gk. < *phileein* to love]

-phily Var. of -PHILIA.

phle·bi·tis (fli·bī′tis) *n. Pathol.* Inflammation of the inner membrane of a vein. [< NL < Gk. *phleps, phlebos* blood vessel + -ITIS] — **phle·bit′ic** (-bit′ik) *adj.*

phlebo- *combining form* Venous. Also, before vowels, **phleb-.** [< Gk. *phleps, phlebos* blood vessel]

phle·bot·o·mize (fli·bot′ə·mīz) *v.t.* **·mized, ·miz·ing** To treat by phlebotomy.

phle·bot·o·my (fli·bot′ə·mē) *n. Surg.* The practice of opening a vein for letting blood as a remedial measure; bloodletting. [< OF < L < Gk. *phleps, phlebos* blood vessel + *temnein* to cut] — **phleb·o·tom·ic** (fleb′ə·tom′ik) or **·i·cal** *adj.* — **phle·bot′o·mist** *n.*

phlegm (flem) *n.* **1.** *Physiol.* A viscid, stringy mucus secreted in the air passages, esp. when produced as a discharge through the mouth. **2.** Cold, undemonstrative temper. **3.** One of the four natural humors in ancient physiology. [< MF < LL < Gk., flame, phlegm < *phlegein* to burn]

phleg·mat·ic (fleg·mat′ik) *adj.* Not easily moved or excited. Also **phleg·mat′i·cal.** — **phleg·mat′i·cal·ly** *adv.*

phlo·em (flō′əm) *n. Bot.* The complex tissue serving for the conduction of the sap in plants. [< G < Gk. *phloos* bark]

phlo·gis·ton (flō·jis′tən) *n.* The hypothetical substance formerly assumed to be a necessary constituent of all combustible bodies, and to be given up by them in burning. [< NL < Gk., < *phlogizein* to set on fire]

phlox (floks) *n.* Any of various herbs with opposite leaves and clusters of variously colored flowers. [< NL < L < Gk., wallflower, lit., flame]

-phobe *combining form* One who fears or has an aversion to. [< LL < Gk. *phobeesthai* to fear]

pho·bi·a (fō′bē·ə) *n.* **1.** A compulsive and persistent fear of any specified type of object, stimulus, or situation. **2.** Any strong aversion or dislike. [< L < Gk. < *phobos* fear] — **pho′bic** (-bik) *adj.*

-phobia *combining form* An exaggerated and persistent dread of or aversion to. [< Gk. < *phobos* fear]

In the following list each entry denotes a phobia for what is indicated:

acrophobia	high places	**hemophobia**	blood
agoraphobia	open spaces	**musophobia**	mice
ailurophobia	cats	**necrophobia**	dead bodies
androphobia	men	**nyctophobia**	night, darkness
astraphobia	thunderstorms	**ophidiophobia**	reptiles
autophobia	self, being alone	**phonophobia**	noise
bathophobia	depths	**pyrophobia**	fire
cynophobia	dogs	**taphephobia**	being buried alive
demophobia	crowds	**thanatophobia**	death
gynophobia	women	**zoophobia**	animals

phoe·be (fē′bē) *n.* An American bird, a flycatcher, having grayish brown plumage and a slightly crested head. [Imit. of its cry; infl. in form by PHOEBE]

Phoe·be (fē′bē) In Greek mythology, Artemis as goddess of the moon. — *n. Poetic* The moon. Also spelled *Phebe.* [< L < Gk., bright]

Phoe·bus (fē′bəs) In Greek mythology, Apollo as god of the sun. Also **Phoebus Apollo.** — *n. Poetic* The sun.

Phoe·ni·cian (fə·nē′shən. -nish′ən) *adj.* Of ancient Phoenicia, its people, or its language. — *n.* **1.** One of the people of ancient Phoenicia or any of its colonies. **2.** The Northwest Semitic language of these people.

phoe·nix (fē′niks) *n.* In Egyptian mythology, a bird of great beauty, said to live for 500 or 600 years and then consume itself by fire, rising from its ashes to live through another cycle, often used as a symbol of immortality. Also spelled *phenix.* [OE < Med.L < L < Gk. *phoinix* phoenix, Phoenician, purple red, crimson]

phon- Var. of PHONO-.

pho·nate (fō′nāt) *v.i.* **·nat·ed, ·nat·ing** To make speech sounds. [< Gk. *phōnē* voice] — **pho·na′tion** *n.*

phone¹ (fōn) *Informal n.* A telephone. — *v.t. & v.i.* **phoned, phon·ing** To telephone. [Short for TELEPHONE]

phone² (fōn) *n. Phonet.* A sound used in human speech. [< Gk. *phōnē* a sound, voice]

-phone *combining form* Voice; sound: *microphone.* [< Gk. *phōnē* voice]

pho·neme (fō′nēm) *n. Ling.* A class of phonetically similar phones that alternate with each other according to phonetic environment and that function to distinguish utterances from one another, as /t/ and /p/ in the words *tin* and *pin.* See ALLOPHONE. [< F < Gk. *phōnēma* utterance]

pho·ne·mic (fə·nē′mik, fō-) *adj.* **1.** Of or referring to phonemes. **2.** Involving distinctive speech sounds: a *phonemic* difference. — **pho·ne′mi·cal·ly** *adv.*

pho·ne·mics (fə·nē′miks, fō-) *n.pl.* (*construed as sing.*) **1.** A phonemic system. **2.** The study of phonemic systems.

pho·net·ic (fə·net′ik, fō-) *adj.* **1.** Of or pertaining to phonetics, or to speech sounds and their production. **2.** Representing the sounds of speech. Also **pho·net′i·cal.** [< NL < Gk. *phōnē* sound] — **pho′net′i·cal·ly** *adv.*

pho·ne·ti·cian (fō′nə·tish′ən) *n.* A specialist in phonetics. Also **pho·net·i·cist** (fə·net′ə·sist), **pho′ne·tist.**

pho·net·ics (fə·net′iks, fō-) *n.pl.* (*construed as sing.*) **1.** The branch of linguistics dealing with the analysis, description, and classification of the sounds of speech. **2.** The system of sounds of a language: the *phonetics* of American English. **3.** Loosely, phonetic transcription.

pho·ney (fō′nē) See PHONY.

-phonia See -PHONY.

phon·ic (fon′ik, fō′nik) *adj.* Pertaining to or of the nature of sound, esp. speech sounds.

phon·ics (fon′iks, fō′niks) *n.pl.* (*construed as sing.*) **1.** The phonetic rudiments used in teaching reading and pronunciation. **2.** The science of sound; acoustics.

phono- *combining form* Sound; speech; voice. Also, before vowels, **phon-.** [< Gk. *phōnē* voice]

pho·no·gram (fō′nə·gram) *n.* A character symbolizing a speech sound, word, etc. — **pho′no·gram′ic** or ·**gram′mic** *adj.* — **pho′no·gram′i·cal·ly** or ·**gram′mi·cal·ly** *adv.*

pho·no·graph (fō′nə·graf, -gräf) *n.* A record player.

pho·no·graph·ic (fō′nə·graf′ik) *adj.* **1.** Pertaining to or produced by a phonograph. **2.** Pertaining to or written in phonography. — **pho′no·graph′i·cal·ly** *adv.*

phonograph record A grooved disk that reproduces sounds on a record player.

pho·nog·ra·phy (fō·nog′rə·fē, fə-) *n.* **1.** The art or science of representing words according to a system of sound elements; esp. a style of shorthand. **2.** The art of representing speech sounds by marks or letters.

pho·nol·o·gy (fō·nol′ə·jē) *n.* **1.** Phonemics. **2.** Phonemics and phonetics taken together. **3.** The history of the sound changes that have taken place in a language, or the study thereof. — **pho·no·log·ic** (fō′nə·loj′ik) or ·**i·cal** *adj.* — **pho′·no·log′i·cal·ly** *adv.* — **pho·nol′o·gist** *n.*

pho·ny (fō′nē) *U.S. Slang adj.* ·**ni·er**, ·**ni·est** Fake; false; spurious; counterfeit. — *n. pl.* ·**nies 1.** Something fake or not genuine. **2.** One who tries to be something he is not. Also spelled *phoney.* [? < British slang *fawney man* peddler of imitation jewelry, ult. < Irish *fainne* ring]

-phony *combining form* A (specified) type of sound or sounds: *cacophony.* Also *-phonia.* [< Gk. *phōnē* sound, voice]

-phore *combining form* A bearer or producer of: *semaphore.* [< NL < Gk. < *pherein* to bear]

-phorous *combining form* Bearing or producing: found in adjectives corresponding to nouns in *-phore.*

phos·gene (fos′jēn) *n. Chem.* A colorless, highly toxic gas, $COCl_2$, having a suffocating odor, used in organic chemistry and in warfare. [< Gk. *phōs* light + *-gene* -GEN]

phosph- Var. of PHOSPHO-.

phos·phate (fos′fāt) *n.* **1.** *Chem.* A salt or ester of phosphoric acid. **2.** *Agric.* Any fertilizer valued for its phosphoric acid. **3.** A beverage of carbonated water, containing small amounts of phosphoric acid. [< F]

phos·phat·ic (fos·fat′ik) *adj.* **1.** Relating to the phosphates. **2.** Containing some phosphate.

phos·phide (fos′fīd, -fid) *n. Chem.* A compound of phosphorus with a metal, as **calcium phosphide**, Ca_3P_2. Also **phos′phid** (-fid).

phos·phite (fos′fīt) *n.* A salt of phosphorous acid.

phospho- *combining form* Phosphorus; of or containing phosphorus, or any of its compounds. Also, before vowels, *phosph-.*

phos·phor (fos′fər) *n.* Any of a class of substances that will emit light under the action of certain chemicals or radiations. [< L < Gk. *phōs* light + *pherein* to bear]

Phos·phor (fos′fər) *n. Poetic* The morning star, esp. Venus. [< L *Phosphorus* morning star < Gk. *phōsphoros*]

phos·pho·rate (fos′fə·rāt′) *v.t.* ·**rat·ed**, ·**rat·ing** To combine with phosphorus.

phos·phor·esce (fos′fə·res′) *v.i.* ·**esced**, ·**esc·ing** To glow with a faint light unaccompanied by perceptible heat.

phos·phor·es·cence (fos′fə·res′əns) *n.* **1.** The emission of light without sensible heat; also, the light so emitted. **2.** The property of continuing to shine in the dark after exposure to light, shown by many mineral substances.

phos·phor·es·cent (fos′fə·res′ənt) *adj.* Exhibiting phosphorescence.

phos·phor·et·ed (fos′fə·ret′id) *adj. Chem.* Combined with phosphorus. Also **phos′phor·et′ted**, **phos′phu·ret′ed** (-fyə·ret′id) or ·**ret′ted.**

phos·phor·ic (fos·fôr′ik, -for′-) *adj. Chem.* Pertaining to or derived from phosphorus, esp. in its highest valence.

phosphoric acid *Chem.* One of three acids of phosphorus, esp. *orthophosphoric acid* (H_3PO_4), used as a reagent.

phos·pho·rous (fos′fər·əs, fos·fôr′əs, -fō′rəs) *adj. Chem.* Of, pertaining to, resembling, containing, or derived from phosphorus, esp. in its lower valence.

phosphorous acid *Chem.* A crystalline acid, H_3PO_3, with a garlic taste, obtained by the oxidation of phosphorus.

phos·pho·rus (fos′fər·əs) *n.* A soft, nonmetallic element (symbol P), found only in combination; white or yellow phosphorus is luminous in the dark, highly flammable, and poisonous; red phosphorus does not glow, is less flammable, and nonpoisonous. See ELEMENT. [< NL < L *Phosphorus* morning star < Gk. *phōs* light + *pherein* to bear]

pho·tic (fō′tik) *adj.* **1.** Of or relating to light or to the production of light. **2.** Designating those underwater regions penetrated by sunlight: the *photic* zone.

pho·to (fō′tō) *n. pl.* ·**tos** *Informal* A photograph.

photo- *combining form* **1.** Light; of, pertaining to, or produced by light. **2.** Photograph; photographic: *photoengrave.* [< Gk. *phōs* light]

pho·to·cell (fō′tō·sel′) *n.* A photoelectric cell.

pho·to·chem·is·try (fō′tō·kem′is·trē) *n.* The branch of chemistry dealing with chemical reactions produced or influenced by light. — **pho′to·chem′i·cal** *adj.*

pho·to·e·lec·tric (fō′tō·i·lek′trik) *adj.* Of or pertaining to the electrical or electronic effects due to the action of light. Also **pho′to·e·lec′tri·cal.**

photoelectric cell An electron tube, one of whose electrodes is sensitive to variations in the intensity of light, incorporated in electrical circuits as a controlling, testing, and counting device: also *electric eye, photocell, phototube.*

pho·to·e·lec·tron (fō′tō·i·lek′tron) *n.* An electron emitted from a metal surface when exposed to suitable radiation.

pho·to·en·grave (fō′tō·in·grāv′) *v.t.* ·**graved**, ·**grav·ing** To reproduce by photoengraving. — **pho′to·en·grav′er** *n.*

pho·to·en·grav·ing (fō′tō·in·grā′ving) *n.* **1.** The act or process of producing by the aid of photography a relief block or plate for printing. **2.** A plate or picture so produced.

photo finish 1. A race so closely contested that only a photograph of the finish can determine the winner. **2.** *Informal* Any race or competition decided by a slim margin.

pho·to·flash bulb (fō′tō·flash′) *Photog.* A flash bulb.

pho·to·flood lamp (fō′tō·flud′) *Photog.* An electric lamp operating at excess voltage to give high illumination.

pho·to·gen·ic (fō′tō·jen′ik) *adj.* **1.** Being a good subject for a photograph, esp. for esthetic reasons. **2.** *Biol.* Producing phosphorescence. — **pho′to·gen′i·cal·ly** *adv.*

pho·to·gram·me·try (fō′tō·gram′ə·trē) *n.* The art and technique of making surveys or maps by photographs.

pho·to·graph (fō′tə·graf, -gräf) *n.* A picture taken by photography. — *v.t.* **1.** To take a photograph of. — *v.i.* **2.** To practice photography. **3.** To be depicted in photographs: He *photographs* beautifully. — **pho·tog·ra·pher** (fə·tog′rə·fər) *n.*

pho·to·graph·ic (fō′tə·graf′ik) *adj.* **1.** Pertaining to, used in, or produced by photography. **2.** Of or like a photograph. Also **pho′to·graph′i·cal.** — **pho′to·graph′i·cal·ly** *adv.*

pho·tog·ra·phy (fə·tog′rə·fē) *n.* **1.** The process of forming and fixing an image of an object or objects by the chemical action of light and other forms of radiant energy on photosensitive surfaces. **2.** The art or business of producing and printing photographs.

pho·to·gra·vure (fō′tō·grə·vyŏŏr′, -grāv′yər) *n.* **1.** The process of making an intaglio plate from a photograph for use in printing. **2.** A picture so produced. [< F]

pho·to·lith·o·graph (fō′tō·lith′ə·graf, -gräf) *v.t.* To reproduce by photolithography. — *n.* A picture produced by photolithography.

pho·to·li·thog·ra·phy (fō′tō·li·thog′rə·fē) *n.* The art or operation of producing on stone, largely by photographic means, a printing surface from which impressions may be taken by a lithographic process. — **pho′to·lith′o·graph′ic** (-lith′ə·graf′ik) *adj.*

pho·tol·y·sis (fō·tol′ə·sis) *n.* Chemical or biological decomposition due to the action of light. [< NL < Gk. *phōs* light + *lyein* to loosen] — **pho·to·lyt·ic** (fō′tə·lit′ik) *adj.*

pho·to·map (fō′tō·map′) *n.* A map composed of one or more aerial photographs.

pho·tom·e·ter (fō·tom′ə·tər) *n.* Any instrument for measuring or comparing the intensity of light.

pho·tom·e·try (fō·tom′ə·trē) *n.* **1.** The measurement of the intensity of light, esp. with a photometer. **2.** The branch of optics that treats of such measurement. — **pho·to·met·ric** (fō′tə·met′rik) or ·**ri·cal** *adj.* — **pho·tom′e·trist** n.

pho·to·mi·cro·graph (fō′tō·mī′krə·graf, -gräf) *n.* A photograph taken through a microscope; a microphotograph. — **pho·to·mi·crog·ra·phy** (fō′tō·mī·krog′rə·fē) *n.*

pho·to·mon·tage (fō′tō·mon·täzh′, -môn-) *n.* Montage produced by photography.

pho·to·mu·ral (fō′tō·myŏŏr′əl) *n.* A photograph enlarged to a considerable size, used for wall decoration.

pho·ton (fō′ton) *n. Physics* A quantum of radiant energy moving with the velocity of light and an energy proportional to its frequency: also called *light quantum.* — **pho·ton′ic** *adj.*

pho·to·nu·cle·ar (fō′tō·nōō′klē·ər, -nyōō′-) *adj. Physics* Of, pertaining to, or designating a reaction initiated in an atomic nucleus by a photon.

pho·to·off·set (fō′tō·ôf′set, -of′-) *n.* Offset printing from a metal surface on which the text or design has been imprinted by photography.

pho·to·play (fō′tō·plā′) *n.* A play arranged for or presented in a motion-picture performance.

pho·to·sen·si·tive (fō′tō·sen′sə·tiv) *adj.* Sensitive to light. — **pho′to·sen′si·tiv′i·ty** *n.*

pho·to·sphere (fō′tə·sfir′) *n. Astron.* The visible shining surface of the sun. — **pho·to·spher′ic** (-sfir′ik, -sfer′-) *adj.*

pho·to·stat (fō′tə·stat) *v.t. & v.i.* ·**stat·ed** or ·**stat·ted**, ·**stat·ing** or ·**stat·ting** To make a reproduction (of) with a Photostat. — *n.* The reproduction so produced. — **pho′to·stat′ic** *adj.* — **pho′to·stat′i·cal·ly** *adv.*

Pho·to·stat (fō′tə·stat) *n.* A camera designed to reproduce facsimiles of documents, drawings, etc., directly as positives: a trade name. Also **pho′to·stat.**

pho·to·syn·the·sis (fō′tō·sin′thə·sis) *n. Biochem.* The process by which plants form carbohydrates from carbon dioxide, inorganic salts, and water through the agency of sunlight acting upon chlorophyll. — **pho′to·syn·thet′ic** (-sin·thet′ik) *adj.*

pho·to·tel·e·graph (fō′tō·tel′ə·graf, -gräf) *v.t. & v.i.* To transmit by phototelegraphy. — *n.* Something so transmitted.

pho·to·te·leg·ra·phy (fō′tō·tə·leg′rə·fē) *n.* The electrical or telegraphic transmission of messages, photographs, etc., by facsimile; telephotography. — **pho′to·tel′e·graph′ic** (-tel′ə·graf′ik) *adj.*

pho·to·trop·ic (fō′tə·trop′ik) *adj. Biol.* Turning in a particular direction under the influence of light. — **pho′to·trop′i·cal·ly** *adv.*

pho·tot·ro·pism (fō·tot′rə·piz′əm) *n. Biol.* Phototropic growth or response.

pho·to·tube (fō′tō·tōōb′, -tyōōb′) *n.* A photoelectric cell.

pho·to·type (fō′tə·tīp′) *n.* 1. A relief plate made for printing by photography. 2. The process by which it is produced: also **pho·to·typ·y** (fō′tō·tī′pē). 3. A picture printed from such a plate. — **pho′to·typ′ic** (-tip′ik) *adj.*

phrase (frāz) *n.* 1. *Gram.* A group of two or more associated words, not containing a subject and predicate: distinguished from *clause.* 2. A word or group of words spoken in one breath. 3. A concise, catchy expression. 4. *Music* A short division of time comprising several statements of one or more motifs. — *v.t. & v.i.* **·phrased, ·phras·ing** 1. To express in words or phrases. 2. To divide (a sentence, etc.) into phrases when speaking. 3. *Music* To divide (a melody) into phrases. [< LL < Gk. *phrazein* to point out] — **phras·al** (frā′zəl) *adj.* — **phras′ing** *n.*

phra·se·ol·o·gy (frā′zē·ol′ə·jē) *n. pl.* **·gies** 1. The choice and arrangement of words and phrases in expressing ideas. 2. A compilation or handbook of phrases. [< NL < Gk. *phrasis* speech + *logos* word] — **phra′se·o·log′i·cal** (-ə·loj′i·kəl) *adj.* — **phra′se·ol′o·gist** (-jist) *n.*

phren·ic (fren′ik) *adj.* 1. Of or pertaining to the mind. 2. *Anat.* Of or pertaining to the diaphragm: the *phrenic* nerve. [< NL < Gk. *phrēn, phrenos* diaphragm, mind]

phreno- *combining form* 1. Mind; brain. 2. Diaphragm; of or related to the diaphragm. Also, before vowels, **phren-.** [< Gk. *phrēn, phrenos* the diaphragm (thought to be the seat of intellect)]

phre·nol·o·gy (fri·nol′ə·jē) *n.* The doctrine that the conformation of the human skull allegedly indicates the degree of development of various mental faculties and characteristics. [< Gk. *phrēn, phrenos* mind + -LOGY] — **phren·o·log·ic** (fren′ə·loj′ik) or **·i·cal** *adj.* — **phre·nol′o·gist** *n.*

Phryg·i·a (frij′ē·ə) An ancient country in west central Asia Minor. — **Phryg′i·an** *n. & adj.*

phthal·e·in (thal′ē·in, -ēn, fthal′-) *n. Chem.* Any of a series of compounds formed by combining a phenol with phthalic acid or its anhydride, and yielding dyes in some derivatives. Also **phthal′e·ine.** [< PHTHAL(IC) + -*ein*, var. of -IN]

phthal·ic acid (thal′ik, fthal′-) *Chem.* One of three aromatic crystalline compounds, $C_8H_6O_4$, derived variously.

phthi·sis (thī′sis, fthī′-) *n. Pathol.* Tuberculosis of the lungs. Also **phthis·ic.** [< L < Gk., a wasting away < *phthinein* to decay] — **phthis′i·cal, phthis·ick·y** (fiz′ik·ē) *adj.*

-phyceae *combining form Bot.* Seaweed: used in the names of various classes of algae. [< Gk. *phykos* seaweed]

phyco- *combining form* Seaweed; of or related to seaweed. [< Gk. *phykos* seaweed]

phy·la (fī′lə) Plural of PHYLUM.

phy·lac·ter·y (fi·lak′tər·ē) *n. pl.* **·ter·ies** 1. In traditional Judaism, one of two small leather cases containing a strip or strips of parchment inscribed with Scriptural passages, and bound on the forehead or around the left arm during morning prayer. [< LL < Gk. *phylaktērion* safeguard]

phyllo- *combining form* Leaf; pertaining to a leaf. Also, before vowels, **phyll-.** [< Gk. *phyllon* leaf]

phyl·lo·tax·is (fil′ə·tak′sis) *n. Bot.* 1. The arrangement of leaves upon a stem. 2. The laws of this arrangement. Also **phyl′lo·tax′y.** [< NL < Gk. *phyllon* leaf + *taxis* arrangement] — **phyl′lo·tac′tic** (-tak′tik) *adj.*

-phyllous *combining form* Having (a specified kind or number of) leaves. [< Gk. *phyllon* leaf]

phylo- *combining form* Tribe; race; species. Also, before vowels, **phyl-.** [< Gk. *phylē, phylon* tribe]

phy·log·e·ny (fi·loj′ə·nē) *n. pl.* **·nies** 1. *Biol.* The history of the evolution of a species or group: distinguished from *ontogeny.* 2. Tribal or racial history. Also **phy·lo·gen·e·sis** (fī′lə·jen′ə·sis). [< Gk. *phylon* race + -*geneia* birth, origin] — **phy′lo·ge·net′ic** (-jə·net′ik) *adj.* — **phy′lo·ge·net′i·cal·ly** *adv.* — **phy′lo·gen′ic** *adj.*

phy·lum (fī′ləm) *n. pl.* **·la** (-lə) *Biol.* A great division of animals or plants of which the members are believed to have a common evolutionary ancestor. [< NL < Gk. *phylon* race]

-phyre *combining form Geol.* A porphyritic rock. [See PORPHYRY.]

physi- Var. of PHYSIO-.

phys·ic (fiz′ik) *n.* A cathartic; a purge. — *v.t.* **·icked, ·ick·ing** 1. To treat with medicine, esp. with a cathartic. 2. To cure or relieve. [< L < Gk. *physikē* (*epistēmē*) (the knowledge) of nature]

phys·i·cal (fiz′i·kəl) *adj.* 1. Of or relating to the human body, as distinguished from the mind or spirit. 2. Of the nature of or pertaining to matter or material things. 3. Of or relating to the material universe or to the sciences that treat of it. 4. Of or pertaining to physics: a *physical* law. 5. Apparent to the senses; external: *physical* changes. [See PHYSIC.] — **phys′i·cal·ly** *adv.*

physical chemistry The branch of chemistry that deals with the physical properties of substances, esp. with reference to the laws governing their quantitative energy transformations and chemical interactions.

physical education Athletic training and development of the human body; also, education in hygiene.

physical geography Geography dealing with the natural features of the earth, as vegetation, land forms, drainage, ocean currents, climate, etc.: also called *physiography.*

physical science Any of the sciences that treat of inanimate matter or energy, as physics, astronomy, chemistry, geology, etc.

physical therapy The treatment of disability, injury, and disease by external physical means, as by electricity, heat, light, massage, exercise, etc.: also called *physiotherapy.*

phy·si·cian (fi·zish′ən) *n.* 1. One who is legally authorized to practice medicine; a doctor. 2. A doctor engaged in general practice. 3. Any healer. [See PHYSIC.]

phys·i·cist (fiz′ə·sist) *n.* A specialist in physics.

physico- *combining form* Physics. [< Gk. *physikos* < *physis* nature. See PHYSIC.]

phys·i·co·chem·i·cal (fiz′i·kō·kem′i·kəl) *adj.* 1. Of or pertaining to the physical and chemical properties of matter. 2. Pertaining to physical chemistry.

phys·ics (fiz′iks) *n.pl.* (*construed as sing.*) The science that treats of motion, matter, and energy, and of their interactions.

physio- *combining form* Nature; related to natural functions or phenomena. Also, before vowels, **physi-.** [< Gk. *physis* nature. See PHYSIC.]

phys·i·og·no·my (fiz′ē·og′nə·mē, *esp. Brit.* fiz′ē·on′ə·mē) *n. pl.* **·mies** 1. The face or features considered as revealing character or disposition. 2. The outward look of a thing. 3. The practice of discerning character in the features of the face or form of the body. [< OF < Med.L *phisnomia* < Gk. *physiognōmonia* the judging of a man's nature (by his features)] — **phys′i·og·nom′ic** (-og·nom′ik, *esp. Brit.* -ə·nom′ik) or **·i·cal** *adj.* — **phys′i·og·nom′i·cal·ly** *adv.* — **phys′i·og′no·mist** *n.*

phys·i·og·ra·phy (fiz′ē·og′rə·fē) *n.* 1. A description of nature. 2. Physical geography. — **phys′i·og′ra·pher** *n.* — **phys′i·o·graph′ic** (-ə·graf′ik) or **·i·cal** *adj.* — **phys′i·o·graph′i·cal·ly** *adv.*

phys·i·ol·o·gy (fiz′ē·ol′ə·jē) *n. pl.* **·gies** 1. The science that treats of the processes and mechanisms by which living animals and plants function under varied conditions. 2. The aggregate of vital processes: the *physiology* of the frog. [< F < L < Gk. < *physiologos* speaker on nature] — **phys′i·o·log′i·cal, phys′i·o·log′ic** *adj.* — **phys′i·o·log′i·cal·ly** *adv.* — **phys′i·ol′o·gist** *n.*

phys·i·o·ther·a·py (fiz′ē·ō·ther′ə·pē) *n.* Physical therapy.

phy·sique (fi·zēk′) *n.* The structure, strength, or appearance of the body. [< F, orig. adj., physical]

-phyte *combining form* A (specified) kind of plant; a plant having a (specified) habitat. [< Gk. *phyton* plant]

phyto- *combining form* Plant; of or related to vegetation. Also, before vowels, **phyt-.** [< Gk. *phyton* plant]

pi¹ (pī) *n.* 1. The sixteenth letter in the Greek alphabet (Π, π): corresponding to English *p.* See ALPHABET. 2. *Math.* a This letter used to designate the ratio of the circumference of a circle to its diameter. b The ratio itself (3.14159 . . .). [def. 2 < Gk. *p(eripheria)* periphery]

pi² (pī) *n.* 1. *Printing* Type that has been thrown into disorder. 2. Any jumble or disorder. — *v.t.* **pied, pie·ing** To jumble or disorder, as type. Also spelled *pie.* [Var. of PIE¹]

pi·a ma·ter (pī′ə mā′tər) *Anat.* The delicate inner membrane that envelops the brain and spinal cord. [< Med.L, tender mother]

pi·a·nis·si·mo (pē′ə·nis′i·mō, *Ital.* pyä·nēs′sē·mo) *Music adj. & adv.* Very soft or very softly: a direction to the performer. — *n. pl.* **·mos** A passage so played. [< Ital. < L *planissimus*, superl. of *planus* soft]

pi·an·ist (pē·an′ist, pē′ə·nist) *n.* One who plays the piano; esp., an expert or professional performer on the piano. [< F *pianiste* and < Ital. *pianista*]

---

pi·an·o¹ (pē·an/ō) *n. pl.* **·os** A musical instrument having felt-covered hammers operated from a manual keyboard that strike upon steel wires to produce musical tones; a pianoforte. [< Ital., short for *pianoforte*. See PIANOFORTE.]

pi·a·no² (pē·ä/nō, *Ital.* pyä/nō) *Music adj. & adv.* Soft or softly: a direction to the performer. —*n. pl.* **·os** A passage so played. [< Ital. < L *planus* flat, soft]

pi·an·o·for·te (pē·an/ə·fôr/tā, -fōr/-, -fôrt/, -fōrt/) *n.* A piano. [< Ital. < *piano e forte* soft and loud]

pi·as·ter (pē·as/tər) *n.* **1.** A monetary unit of various countries, as Egypt, Libya, Sudan, and Syria: the hundredth part of a pound. **2.** A Turkish coin and monetary unit: also called *kurus*. **3.** The Spanish peso or dollar. Also **pi·as/tre**. [< F < Ital. *piastra*, lit., plate of metal]

pi·az·za (pē·az/ə, *Ital.* pyät/tsä) *n.* **1.** An open area or public square in a city or town, esp. in Italy. **2.** A covered outer walk or gallery. **3.** *Chiefly U.S.* A veranda or porch. [< Ital., square, market place]

pi·broch (pē/brokh) *n.* A martial air played on the bagpipe. [< Gaelic *piobaireachd* art of playing the bagpipe]

pi·ca (pī/kə) *n.* **1.** A size of type; 12-point; about ⅙ inch; also, a standard unit of measurement for thickness and length of leads, borders, etc. **2.** A size of typewriter type equivalent to 12-point, with 10 characters to the inch. [< Med.L, a book of church rules]

pic·a·dor (pik/ə·dôr, *Sp.* pē/kä·thôr/) *n.* In bullfighting, a horseman who seeks to weaken the bull by pricking him with a lance. [< Sp., lit., pricker < *picar* to prick]

pic·a·resque (pik/ə·resk/) *adj.* **1.** Of or involving rogues or vagabonds. **2.** Denoting a form of fiction involving rogues and vagabonds. [< Sp. *picaresco* roguish]

pic·a·roon (pik/ə·rōōn/) *n.* **1.** One who lives by cheating or robbery; a pirate, rogue, or adventurer. **2.** A pirate vessel. [< Sp. *picarón*, aug. of *picaro* rogue]

pic·a·yune (pik/i·yōōn/) *adj. U.S.* **1.** Of small value; paltry; contemptible. **2.** Petty; niggling; mean. Also **pic/a·yun/ish**. —*n.* **1.** *U.S.* A coin of little value. **2.** *U.S.* Anything of trifling value. [< F *picaillon* farthing]

pic·ca·lil·li (pik/ə·lil/ē) *n.* A relish of chopped vegetables.

pic·co·lo (pik/ə·lō) *n. pl.* **·los** A small flute pitched an octave higher than the ordinary flute. [< Ital., small]

pick¹ (pik) *v.t.* **1.** To choose; select, as from a group or number. **2.** To detach or pluck, as with the fingers. **3.** To clear (a field, tree, etc.) in such a manner. **4.** To clear of or harvest; gather. **5.** To prepare by removing the feathers, hulls, leaves, etc. **6.** To remove extraneous matter from (the teeth, etc.), as with the fingers or with a pointed instrument. **7.** To touch, irritate, or remove (something) with a fingernail, etc. **8.** To nibble at or peck. **9.** To eat in a dainty or overfastidious manner. **10.** To break up, penetrate, or indent with or as with a pointed instrument. **11.** To form in this manner: to *pick* a hole. **12.** To pull apart, as rags. **13.** To seek or point out critically: to *pick* flaws. **14.** To remove the contents of by stealth: to *pick* a pocket. **15.** To open (a lock) by means other than the key. **16.** To provoke: to *pick* a fight. —*v.i.* **17.** To work with a pick. **18.** To pluck or remove fruit, flowers, etc.; harvest. **19.** To eat daintily or without appetite; nibble. **20.** To select carefully. **21.** To steal. — **to pick apart** (or **to pieces**) **1.** To pull apart. **2.** To destroy by shrewd or critical analysis. — **to pick at 1.** To touch or toy with. **2.** To eat without appetite. **3.** *U.S. Informal* To nag at. — **to pick off 1.** To remove by picking. **2.** To hit, as with a bullet. **3.** In baseball, to catch (a base runner) off base. — **to pick on 1.** To determine on; choose. **2.** *Informal* To tease or annoy. — **to pick one's way** (or **steps**) To advance by careful selection of one's course. — **to pick out 1.** To choose or select. **2.** To distinguish (something) from its surroundings. **3.** To produce the notes of (a tune, etc.) singly or slowly, as by ear. — **to pick over** To examine carefully or one by one. — **to pick up 1.** To take up, as with the hand. **2.** To take up or receive into a group, vehicle, etc. **3.** To acquire casually or by chance. **4.** To gain speed; accelerate. **5.** To be able to perceive or receive, as a radio station. **6.** To break (ground, etc.) with a pick. **7.** *U.S.* To make (a room, etc.) tidy. **8.** *Informal* To recover spirits, health, etc.; improve. **9.** *Informal* To make the acquaintance of (a stranger, esp. of the opposite sex) under casual circumstances. —*n.* **1.** Right of selection; choice. **2.** That which is selected, esp. the choicest part. **3.** The quantity of certain crops that are picked by hand. **4.** The act of picking. [ME *piken, pikken* < OE *pican, pician*] — **pick/er** *n.*

pick² (pik) *n.* **1.** A double-headed, pointed metal tool mounted on a wooden handle, used for breaking ground, etc. **2.** Any of various implements for picking. **3.** A plectrum. [Appar. var. of PIKE¹]

pick·a·back (pik/ə·bak/) *adv.* Piggyback. [Earlier *pickback, pickpack*]

pick·a·nin·ny (pik/ə·nin/ē) *n. pl.* **·nies** A Negro child: a condescending or offensive term. Also **pic/ca·nin/ny**. [Dim. of Sp. *pequeño* little, small]

pick·ax (pik/aks/) *n.* A pick or mattock with one end of the head edged like a chisel and the other pointed; also, a pick with both ends pointed. Also **pick/axe/**.

picked (pikt) *adj.* **1.** Carefully selected. **2.** Cleaned by picking out refuse, stalks, etc.

picked-o·ver (pikt/ō/vər) *adj.* Handled; left after the best have been removed.

pick·er·el (pik/ər·əl, -rel) *n.* Any of various North American fresh-water fishes of the pike family, esp. the small species having a narrow snout and sharp teeth. [Dim. of PIKE¹]

pick·er·el·weed (pik/ər·əl·wēd/) *n.* Any of various perennial plants found in the shallows of North American lakes.

pick·et (pik/it) *n.* **1.** A pointed stick or post, used as a fence paling, tent peg, etc.; a stake. **2.** A person stationed at the outside of a place affected by a strike, for the purpose of publicizing alleged grievances, etc. **3.** A person engaged in publicly protesting a proposed law, policy, etc. **4.** *Mil.* A soldier or detachment of soldiers posted to guard a camp, army, etc. —*v.t.* **1.** To be a picket or station pickets outside of. **2.** To fence or fortify with pickets. **3.** To tie to a picket, as a horse. **4.** *Mil.* **a** To guard by means of a picket. **b** To post as a picket. —*v.i.* **5.** To act as a picket (defs. 2 & 3). [< F *piquet* pointed stake]

pick·et·er (pik/it·ər) *n.* A picket (defs. 2 & 3).

picket fence A fence made of upright pickets.

picket line A line of people picketing a business, etc.

pick·ing (pik/ing) *n.* **1.** The act of picking; also, that which is or may be picked. **2.** *pl.* That which is left: scanty *pickings*. **3.** *Usu. pl.* That which is taken by questionable means; spoils.

pick·le (pik/əl) *n.* **1.** A cucumber that has been preserved and flavored in a liquid solution, usu. of brine or vinegar. **2.** Any article of food so preserved or flavored. **3.** A liquid preservative, as brine or vinegar, sometimes spiced, for meat, fish, etc. **4.** Diluted acid used in cleaning metal castings, etc. **5.** *Informal* An embarrassing condition or position. —*v.t.* **led, ling 1.** To preserve or flavor in pickle. **2.** *Metall.* To treat with a pickle. [Appar. < MDu. *pekel, peeckel*]

pick·led (pik/əld) *adj.* **1.** Preserved in pickle. **2.** Of wood work, etc., having a bleached finish. **3.** *Slang* Drunk.

pick·lock (pik/lok/) *n.* **1.** A special implement for opening a lock. **2.** One who picks locks, esp. illegally.

pick-me-up (pik/mē/up/) *n. Informal* A drink, esp. an alcoholic drink, taken to renew one's energy or spirits.

pick·pock·et (pik/pok/it) *n.* One who steals from pockets.

pick·up (pik/up/) *n.* **1.** Acceleration, as in the speed of an automobile, engine, etc. **2.** *Electronics* A crystal, ceramic, or magnetic device that converts the oscillations of a needle in a record groove into electrical impulses. **3.** The tone arm of a record player. **4.** A small, usu. open truck for light loads. **5.** *Telecom.* **a** In radio, the location of microphones in relation to program elements. **b** The place where a broadcast originates. **c** In television, the scanning of an image by the electron beam. **d** The scanning apparatus. **6.** In baseball, the act of fielding a ball that has touched the ground. **7.** *Informal* A period of renewed or increased activity: a *pickup* in business. **8.** *Informal* Something that stimulates or renews in spirit. **9.** *Slang* A stranger with whom a casual acquaintance is made.

pic·nic (pik/nik) *n.* **1.** An outdoor social outing for which food is usu. provided by the people participating. **2.** *Slang* An easy or pleasant time or experience. —*v.i.* **·nicked, ·nick·ing** To have or attend a picnic. [< F *pique-nique*, prob. reduplication of *piquer* to pick, peck] — **pic/nick·er** *n.*

pico- *combining form* One trillionth (10⁻¹²) of a specified quantity or dimension. [< NL < Sp., small quantity]

pi·cot (pē/kō) *n.* A small thread loop on ornamental edging, ribbon, etc. —*v.t. & v.i.* **·coted** (-kōd). **·cot·ing** (-kō·ing) To sew with this edging. [< F, dim. of OF *pic* point]

pic·ric acid (pik/rik) *Chem.* A yellow, crystalline, bitter compound, $C_6H_2(NO_2)_3OH$, used in dyeing and in certain explosives.

picro- *combining form* Bitter. Also, before vowels, **picr-**. [< Gk. *pikros* bitter]

Pict (pikt) *n.* One of an ancient people of uncertain origin who inhabited Britain and the Scottish Highlands.

Pict·ish (pik/tish) *n.* The language of the Picts, of undetermined relationship. —*adj.* Of or pertaining to the Picts.

pic·to·graph (pik/tə·graf, -gräf) *n.* **1.** A picture representing an idea, as a hieroglyph. **2.** A record of such pictures. [< L *pictus* painted + -GRAPH] — **pic/to·graph/ic** *adj.* — **pic/to·graph/i·cal·ly** *adv.* — **pic·tog·ra·phy** (pik·tog/rə·fē) *n.*

pic·to·ri·al (pik·tôr/ē·əl, -tō/rē-) *adj.* **1.** Pertaining to, composed of, or concerned with pictures. **2.** Graphic; vivid. **3.** Containing or illustrated by pictures. —*n.* A periodical that devotes considerable space to pictures [< LL < L *pictus*, pp. of *pingere* to paint] — **pic·to/ri·al·ly** *adv.*

pic·ture (pik/chər) *n.* **1.** A visual representation of an object or scene upon a flat surface, as a painting, drawing, engraving, or photograph. **2.** A vivid or graphic verbal description. **3.** A mental image or impression of the nature of a situation, event, etc. **4.** An overall situation, esp. as perceived from a particular vantage point. **5.** One who or that which resembles or embodies another person or thing: *She is the picture of despair.* **6.** A motion picture. **7.** Something attractive or pleasant: *pretty as a picture.* — *v.t.* **·tured, ·tur·ing 1.** To form a mental image of. **2.** To describe graphically; depict verbally. **3.** To make a picture of. [< L *pictus*, pp. of *pingere* to paint]

picture gallery A room or hall for exhibiting pictures.

picture hat A woman's hat having a very wide brim and often trimmed with plumes.

pic·tur·esque (pik´chə·resk´) *adj.* **1.** Having a striking, irregular beauty, quaintness, or charm. **2.** Abounding in striking or original expression or imagery; richly graphic. **3.** Like or suitable for a picture; having pictorial quality. — **pic·tur·esque·ly** *adv.* — **pic·tur·esque·ness** *n.*

picture tube Kinescope.

picture window A large window consisting of a single pane of glass, designed to frame a view of the outside.

picture writing 1. The use of pictures or pictorial symbols in writing. **2.** A writing so made.

pid·dle (pid´l) *v.* **·dled, ·dling** *v.t.* **1.** To trifle; dawdle: usually with *away.* — *v.i.* **2.** To trifle; dawdle. **3.** To urinate. [Origin uncertain]

pid·dling (pid´ling) *adj.* Unimportant; trivial; trifling.

pidg·in (pij´in) *n.* A mixed language combining the vocabulary and grammar of dissimilar languages. [< Chinese pronun. of *business*]

Pidgin English A jargon composed of English and elements of local non-English dialects, used as the language of commerce in areas of China, Melanesia, Northern Australia, and West Africa. Also called **Pidgin.**

pie¹ (pī) *n.* **1.** A baked food consisting of one or two layers or crusts of pastry with a filling of fruit, custard, meat, etc. **2.** A layer cake filled with cream, jam, etc. **3.** See PI². **4.** *Slang* Anything very good or very easy. **5.** *Slang* Political graft. [? < PIE²; with ref. to the variety of objects collected by magpies]

pie² (pī) *n.* A magpie. [< OF < L *pica* magpie]

pie·bald (pī´bôld´) *adj.* Having spots, esp. of white and black. — *n.* A spotted or mottled animal, esp. a horse. [< PIE² + BALD; because like a magpie's plumage]

piece (pēs) *n.* **1.** A portion or quantity existing as an individual entity or mass: *a piece of paper.* **2.** A small portion considered as forming or having formed a distinct part of a whole. **3.** A coin: *a fifty cent piece.* **4.** An instance; example: *a piece of luck.* **5.** One of a class or group: *a piece of furniture.* **6.** A work of esthetic interest, as a literary or musical composition, a play, etc. **7.** Point of view; opinion: *to speak one's piece.* **8.** One of the disks or counters used in checkers, backgammon, etc. **9.** A quantity or length, as of wallpaper, in which an article is manufactured or sold. **10.** *Dial.* A short time, space, or distance: *to walk a piece.* **11.** *Dial.* A snack between regular meals. **12.** *Archaic or Dial.* A person; individual. — **a piece of one's mind** *Informal* Criticism or censure frankly expressed. — **of a** (or **one**) **piece 1.** Of the same kind, sort, or class. **2.** Of the same piece; undivided. — **to go to pieces 1.** To fall apart. **2.** *Informal* To lose moral or emotional self-control. — **to have a piece of** *U.S. Slang* To have a financial interest in. — *v.t.* **pieced, piec·ing 1.** To add or attach a piece or pieces to, as for enlargement. **2.** To unite or reunite the pieces of, as in mending. **3.** To unite (parts) into a whole. [< OF < Med.L *pecia*; ult. origin uncertain] — **piec´er** *n.*

pièce de ré·sis·tance (pyes də rā·zē·stäns´) *French* **1.** A principal or most important item. **2.** The chief dish of a dinner.

piece goods Fabrics made in standard lengths.

piece·meal (pēs´mēl´) *adv.* **1.** Piece by piece; gradually. **2.** In pieces. — *adj.* Made up of pieces. [ME < *pece* piece + *-mele* a part]

piece·work (pēs´wûrk´) *n.* Work done or paid for by the piece or quantity. — **piece´work´er** *n.*

pie chart *Stat.* A graph in the form of a circle divided into sectors.

pied (pīd) *adj.* Spotted; piebald; mottled. [< PIE²]

pied-à-terre (pyā·dä·târ´) *n. French* A temporary or secondary lodging; literally, foot on the ground.

pied·mont (pēd´mont) *adj. Geog.* At the foot of a mountain. [< L < *pes, pedis* foot + *mons, montis* mountain]

pie plant *U.S. Dial.* The common variety of rhubarb.

pier (pir) *n.* **1.** A structure extending over the water, secured by piles and serving as a landing place for vessels; wharf. **2.** A plain, detached mass of masonry, usu. serving as a support: the *pier* of a bridge. **3.** An upright projecting portion of a wall; a buttress. **4.** A solid portion of a wall between window openings, etc. [< OF *per* < Med.L *pera*]

pierce (pirs) *v.* **pierced, pierc·ing** *v.t.* To pass into or through, with or as if with a pointed instrument; puncture; stab. **2.** To force a way into or through: *to pierce the wilderness.* **3.** To make an opening or hole in, into, or through. **4.** To make or cut (an opening or hole) in or through something. **5.** To cut through as if stabbing; cleave. **6.** To affect sharply or deeply, as with emotion, pain, etc. **7.** To solve; understand: *to pierce a mystery.* — *v.i.* **8.** To enter; penetrate. [< OF *percer*] — **pierc´er** *n.* — **pierc´ing·ly** *adv.* — **pierc´ing·ness** *n.*

pier glass A large, high mirror intended to fill the space, or pier, between two windows.

Pi·e·ri·a (pī·ir´ē·ə) A coastal region of ancient Macedon, at the base of Mount Olympus, legendary birthplace of the nine Muses. — **Pi·e´ri·an** *adj.*

Pier·rot (pye·rō´) Formerly, a stock character in French pantomimes, wearing white pantaloons and a loose white jacket with big buttons. [< F, dim. of *Pierre* Peter]

Pie·tà (pyä·tä´) *n.* In painting, sculpture, etc., a representation of Mary mourning over the body of Christ in her arms. [< Ital., lit., pity]

pi·e·tism (pī´ə·tiz´əm) *n.* **1.** Piety or godliness; devotion. **2.** Affected or exaggerated piety. [< G *pietismus*] — **pi´e·tist** *n.* — **pi´e·tis´tic** or **·ti·cal** *adj.* — **pi·e·tis´ti·cal·ly** *adv.*

pi·e·ty (pī´ə·tē) *n. pl.* **·ties 1.** Reverence toward God or the gods. **2.** Honor and obedience due to parents, etc. **3.** A pious act, wish, etc. **4.** The state or quality of being pious. [< OF < L < *pius* dutiful]

piezo- *combining form* Pressure; related to or produced by pressure. [< Gk. *piezien* to press]

pi·e·zo·e·lec·tric·i·ty (pī·ē´zō·i·lek´tris´ə·tē, -ē´lik-) *n.* Electricity or electric phenomena resulting from pressure upon certain bodies, esp. crystals. — **pi·e´zo·e·lec´tric** or **·tri·cal** *adj.* — **pi·e´zo·e·lec´tri·cal·ly** *adv.*

pif·fle (pif´əl) *Informal v.i.* **·fled, ·fling** To talk nonsensically; babble. — *n.* Nonsense; babble. [? Blend of PIDDLE and TRIFLE]

pig (pig) *n.* **1.** A cloven-hoofed mammal having a long, mobile snout; esp., a small, young one: also called *hog, swine.* ◆ Collateral adjective: *porcine.* **2.** The flesh of a pig; pork. **3.** An oblong mass of metal, esp. iron or lead, just run from the smelter and cast in a rough mold; also, the mold. **4.** Pig iron or iron pigs in general. **5.** *Informal* A person who is filthy, gluttonous, or coarse. **6.** *Informal* A railroad locomotive. — *v.i.* **pigged, pig·ging 1.** To bring forth pigs. **2.** To act or live like pigs: with *it.* [ME *pigge*; ult. origin uncertain]

pig·eon (pij´ən) *n.* **1.** A bird having short legs, a small head and a sturdy body; esp., the domestic pigeon or rock dove. **2.** *Slang* One who is easily swindled. [< OF < LL *pipio, -onis* young chirping bird]

pigeon breast *Pathol.* A deformity in which the chest is narrow and pointed. — **pig´eon-breast´ed** *adj.*

pigeon hawk A small American falcon.

pig·eon-heart·ed (pij´ən-här´tid) *adj.* Timid; fearful.

pig·eon·hole (pij´ən-hōl´) *n.* **1.** A hole for pigeons to nest in. **2.** A small compartment, as in a desk, for filing papers. — *v.t.* **·holed, ·hol·ing 1.** To place in a pigeonhole; file. **2.** To file away and ignore. **3.** To place in categories.

pig·eon-toed (pij´ən-tōd´) *adj.* Having the toes or feet turned inward.

pig·ger·y (pig´ər·ē) *n. pl.* **·ger·ies** A place for keeping or raising pigs.

pig·gish (pig´ish) *adj.* Like a pig; greedy; dirty; selfish. — **pig´gish·ly** *adv.* — **pig´gish·ness** *n.*

pig·gy (pig´ē) *n. pl.* **·gies** A little pig. Also **pig´gie.**

pig·gy·back (pig´ē·bak´) *adv.* **1.** On the back or shoulders: *to ride piggyback:* also *pickaback.* **2.** On a railway flat car: *to ship trailers piggyback.* — **pig´gy·back´ing** *n.*

piggy bank A coin bank in the shape of a pig.

pig·head·ed (pig´hed´id) *adj.* Stupidly obstinate. — **pig´head´ed·ly** *adv.* — **pig´head´ed·ness** *n.*

pig iron Crude iron poured from a blast furnace into variously shaped molds or pigs of sand or the like.

pig latin A jargon in which the initial sound of a word is usu. transposed to the end and to which *-ay* (ā) is added, as in *Illkay the umbay* for *Kill the bum.* Also **pig Latin.**

pig·ment (pig´mənt) *n.* **1.** Any of a class of finely powdered, insoluble coloring matters suitable for making paints, enamels, etc. **2.** Any substance that imparts color to animal or vegetable tissues, as melanin and chlorophyll. [< L *pingere* to paint] — **pig´men·tar´y** (-ter´ē) *adj.*

pig·men·ta·tion (pig´mən·tā´shən) *n.* **1.** Coloration resulting from pigment. **2.** *Biol.* Deposition of pigment by cells.

pig·ment·ed (pig´mən·tid) *adj.* Having pigmentation.

pig·my (pig´mē) See PYGMY.

Pig·my (pig´mē) See PYGMY.

pig·nut (pig´nut´) *n.* **1.** The fruit of a species of hickory common in the U.S. **2.** The tree.

pig·pen (pig'pen') *n.* A pen or sty where pigs are kept.

pig·skin (pig'skin') *n.* **1.** The skin of a pig. **2.** Something made of this skin, as a saddle. **3.** *U.S. Informal* A football.

pig·sty (pig'stī') *n. pl.* **·sties** A sty or pen for pigs.

pig·tail (pig'tāl') *n.* **1.** A braid or plait of hair extending down from the back of the head. **2.** A twist of tobacco.

pike[1] (pīk) *n.* A long pole having a metal spearhead. —*v.t.* **piked, pik·ing** To run through or kill with a pike. [< MF *pique*]

pike[2] (pīk) *n.* **1.** A widely-distributed, voracious fresh-water food fish having a slender body and a long snout. **2.** Any of several other fishes resembling the pike. [< PIKE[5] with ref. to its pointed snout]

pike[3] (pīk) *n.* **1.** A turnpike. **2.** The fee for using a turnpike road. —*v.i.* **piked, pik·ing** *Slang* To go in haste: usu. with *along*. [Short for TURNPIKE]

pike[4] (pīk) *n. Brit. Dial.* A mountain peak or pointed hill.

pike[5] (pīk) *n.* A spike or sharp point, as the end of a spear.

piked (pīkt, pī'kid) *adj.* Having a pike; pointed. [< PIKE[5]]

pik·er (pī'kər) *n. U.S. Slang* **1.** One who bets or speculates in a small, niggardly way. **2.** One who acts in a petty or niggling way. [Origin uncertain]

pike·staff (pīk'staf', -stäf') *n. pl.* **·staves** (-stāvz') The wooden handle of a pike. [< PIKE[5] + STAFF[1]]

pi·laf (pi·läf') *n.* An Oriental dish of rice, raisins, spice, and a meat or fowl sauce. Also **pi·laff', pi·lau** (pi·lou', -lô'), **pi·law'** (-lô'). [< Persian and Turkish *pilāw*]

pi·lar (pī'lər) *adj.* Of, pertaining to, or covered with hair. [< NL < L *pilus* hair]

pi·las·ter (pi·las'tər) *n. Archit.* A rectangular column, with capital and base, engaged in a wall. [< MF < Ital. < L *pila* column]

pil·chard (pil'chərd) *n.* A small, herringlike food fish, the sardine of Mediterranean and European Atlantic waters. [Earlier *pilcher*; origin uncertain]

pile[1] (pīl) *n.* **1.** A quantity of anything gathered or thrown together in one place; a heap. **2.** A funeral pyre. **3.** A massive building or group of buildings. **4.** *Informal* A large accumulation, quantity, or number of something. **5.** *Physics* A reactor. **6.** *Slang* A large amount of money. —*v.* **piled, pil·ing** *v.t.* **1.** To make a heap or pile of: often with *up*. **2.** To cover or burden with a pile or piles: to *pile* a plate with food. —*v.i.* **3.** To form a heap or pile. **4.** To proceed or go in a confused mass: with *in, on, off, out,* etc. — **to pile up** To accumulate. [< OF < L *pila* pillar, pier]

PILASTER

pile[2] (pīl) *n.* **1.** A heavy timber forced into the earth to form a foundation for a building, pier, etc.: also called *spile*. **2.** Any similar supporting structure, as of steel or concrete. — *v.t.* **piled, pil·ing** **1.** To drive piles into. **2.** To furnish or strengthen with piles. [OE *pil* dart, pointed stake]

pile[3] (pīl) *n.* **1.** The cut or uncut loops that form the surface of certain fabrics, as velvets, plushes, and corduroys. **2.** The surface so formed. **3.** Hair collectively; fur; wool. **4.** Soft, fine hair; down. [< L *pilus* hair] —**piled** *adj.*

pi·le·at·ed (pī'lē·ā'tid, pil'ē-) *adj.* **1.** *Bot.* Provided with a pileus or cap. **2.** *Ornithol.* Having the feathers of the pileum elongated or conspicuous; crested. Also **pi'le·ate.** [< L *pileatus* capped]

pile driver A machine for driving piles.

pi·le·ous (pī'lē·əs) *adj.* Pilose.

piles (pīlz) *n.pl.* Hemorrhoids. [< LL *pila* ball]

pi·le·um (pī'lē·əm, pil'ē-) *n. pl.* **·le·a** (-lē·ə) *Ornithol.* The top of the head of a bird, from the base of the bill to the nape and above the eyes. [< L, var. of *pileus* felt cap]

pi·le·us (pī'lē·əs, pil'ē-) *n. pl.* **·le·i** (-lē·ī) *Bot.* The umbrella-shaped portion of a mushroom. [< L, felt cap]

pil·fer (pil'fər) *v.t. & v.i.* To steal in small quantities. [< OF *pelfrer* to rob] —**pil'fer·age** (-fər·ij) *n.* —**pil'fer·er** *n.*

pil·grim (pil'grim) *n.* **1.** One who journeys to some sacred place from religious motives. **2.** Any wanderer or wayfarer. [ME < OF < L *per-* through + *ager, agri* land]

Pil·grim (pil'grim) *n.* One of the English Puritans who founded Plymouth Colony in 1620.

pil·grim·age (pil'grə·mij) *n.* **1.** A journey made to a shrine or sacred place. **2.** Any long or arduous journey.

Pilgrim Fathers The founders of Plymouth Colony, Massachusetts, in 1620.

Pilgrim's Progress A religious allegory by John Bunyan.

pil·ing (pī'ling) *n.* **1.** Piles collectively. **2.** A structure formed of piles. **3.** The act or process of driving piles.

pill (pil) *n.* **1.** A pellet or globule containing medicine, convenient for swallowing whole. **2.** A disagreeable necessity. **3.** *Slang* A person difficult to bear with, a bore. **4.** *Slang* A ball or disk, as a baseball or golfball. — **the pill** or **the Pill** Any of various oral contraceptive drugs in tablet form, taken by women. —*v.t.* **1.** To form into pills. **2.** To dose with pills. [< L *pila* ball]

pil·lage (pil'ij) *n.* **1.** The act of taking money or property by open violence; looting. **2.** Spoil; booty. —*v.* **·laged, ·lag·ing** *v.t.* **1.** To plunder. **2.** To take as loot. —*v.i.* **3.** To take plunder. [< OF < *piller* to plunder] —**pil'lag·er** *n.*

pil·lar (pil'ər) *n.* **1.** A vertical, freestanding support, usu. slender in relation to its height; column; shaft. **2.** A structure of similar form used as a decoration or monument. **3.** Anything resembling a pillar in form or function. **4.** One who strongly supports a work or cause. — **from pillar to post** From one predicament to another. —*v.t.* To support or adorn with pillars. [< OF < LL < L *pila* pillar]

pill·box (pil'boks') *n.* **1.** A small box for pills. **2.** A small, round, concrete emplacement for a machine gun, antitank gun, etc. **3.** A small, round hat with a flat top.

pil·lion (pil'yən) *n.* A pad or seat behind the saddle of a horse or motorcycle for a second rider. [Appar. < Scottish Gaelic *pillean,* dim. of *pell* cushion]

pil·lo·ry (pil'ə·rē) *n. pl.* **·ries** A framework in which an offender was fastened by the neck and wrists and exposed to public scorn. —*v.t.* **·ried, ·ry·ing** **1.** To set in the pillory. **2.** To hold up to public scorn or ridicule. [< OF *pellori*]

pil·low (pil'ō) *n.* **1.** A case, usu. of cloth, filled with a soft or yielding material, as feathers or foam rubber, used to cushion the head, as during sleep. **2.** A small, usu. decorative cushion. **3.** Any body rest. **4.** Anything resembling a pillow. —*v.t.* **1.** To rest on or as on a pillow. **2.** To act as a pillow for. —*v.i.* **3.** To recline on or as on a pillow. [ME < OE < L *pulvinus* cushion] —**pil'low·y** *adj.*

pil·low·case (pil'ō·kās') *n.* A covering drawn over a pillow. Also **pillow slip.**

pi·lose (pī'lōs) *adj.* Hairy; also *pileous, pilous.* [< L *pilus* hair] —**pi·los·i·ty** (pī·lōs'ə·tē) *n.*

pi·lot (pī'lət) *n.* **1.** One who operates or guides an aircraft or spacecraft during flight. **2.** One who is trained and licensed to conduct ships in and out of port or through certain waters difficult to navigate. **3.** The helmsman of a ship. **4.** Any guide. **5.** *Mech.* A part that steadies or guides the action of a tool or other part. **6.** A pilot light (which see). —*v.t.* **1.** To act as the pilot of; steer. **2.** To guide or conduct, as through difficult circumstances. **3.** To serve as a pilot on, over, or in. —*adj.* **1.** Serving as a guide or control. **2.** Serving as a trial situation. **3.** Of or pertaining to a pilot or pilots. [< MF *pillotte, pilot* < Ital. *pilota*]

pi·lot·age (pī'lət·ij) *n.* **1.** The act of piloting a vessel or aircraft. **2.** The fee for such service.

pilot balloon A small balloon sent aloft to show the direction and velocity of the wind.

pilot fish An oceanic fish often seen in warm latitudes in company with sharks.

pi·lot·house (pī'lət·hous') *n.* An enclosed structure, usu. in the forward part of a ship, containing the steering wheel and compass: also called *wheelhouse.*

pilot lamp A small electric light that shows whether a given circuit, motor, etc., is functioning: also called *pilot light.*

pilot light **1.** A minute jet of gas kept burning for igniting an ordinary burner as soon as the gas is turned on: also **pilot burner.** **2.** A pilot lamp (which see).

pilot officer In the Royal, Royal Canadian, and other Commonwealth air forces, a commissioned officer ranking next below a flight officer. See table at GRADE.

pi·lous (pī'ləs) *adj.* Pilose.

pil·sner (pil'znər) *n. Often cap.* Beer of a kind originally brewed in Pilsen, Czechoslovakia. Also **pil'sen·er** (-zə·nər).

Pilt·down man (pilt'doun) A spurious type of early man postulated from skull fragments planted by a hoaxer near Piltdown, England.

Pi·ma (pē'mä) *n. pl.* **Pi·mas** or **Pi·ma** **1.** One of a tribe of North American Indians of southern Arizona and Northern Mexico. **2.** The Uto-Aztecan language of this tribe.

Pi·man (pē'mən) *n.* A branch of the Uto-Aztecan stock of North American Indians. —*adj.* Of or pertaining to this linguistic branch.

pi·men·to (pi·men'tō) *n. pl.* **·tos** **1.** The dried, unripe, aromatic berries of a West Indian tree of the myrtle family. **2.** Pimento, [< Sp. < Med.L *pigmentum* spiced drink, spice]

pimento cheese A cheese with pimentos added.

pi·mien·to (pi·myen'tō) *n. pl.* **·tos** A sweet pepper or its ripe fruit, used as a relish and as a stuffing in olives: also called *pimento.* [< Sp. < *pimienta* pepper]

pimp (pimp) *n.* A pander; esp., one who solicits for a prostitute in exchange for part of her earnings. —*v.i.* To act as a pimp. [? < F < MF < L *pipire* to murmur seductively]

pim·per·nel (pim'pər·nel) *n.* A plant of the primrose family, usu. with red flowers, as the common **scarlet pimpernel.** [< OF < Med.L < LL, ? < L *piper* pepper]

pim·ple (pim'pəl) *n.* A small swelling or elevation of the skin, with an inflamed base. [ME < OE *piplian* to break out in pimples] —**pim'pled, pim'ply** *adj.*

pin (pin) *n.* **1.** A short, stiff piece of wire with a sharp point and a round, usu. flattened head, used for fastening together parts of clothing, sheets of paper, etc. **2.** An ornament mounted on a pin or having a pin with a clasp. **3.** Anything resembling a pin in form or use, as a hairpin or clothespin. **4.** A peg or bar, as of metal or wood, used in fastening or supporting, as the bolt of a door, a linchpin, etc. **5.** A rolling pin. **6.** Something of no importance; a trifle. **7.** In bowling and other ball-throwing games, one of the rounded wooden clubs, that are set up as the target. **8.** In golf, a pole with a small flag attached to mark the position of a hole. **9.** *pl. Informal* The legs. **10.** *Music* A peg. **11.** *Naut.* **a** A belaying pin. **b** A thole. — **on pins and needles** Uneasy or anxious; nervous. — *v.t.* **pinned, pin·ning 1.** To fasten with or as with a pin or pins. **2.** To seize and hold firmly; make unable to move. **3.** To transfix with a pin, spear, etc. **4.** To force (someone) to make up his mind, follow a definite course of action, etc.: usu. with *down.* **5.** *U.S. Slang* In colleges and universities, to give one's fraternity pin to (a girl) as an expression of the intention to become engaged. **6.** *U.S. Slang* To hold responsible for (a wrongdoing, etc.); accuse of: with *on.* [OE *pinn* peg] — **pin′ner** *n.*

pi·na·ceous (pī·nā′shəs) *adj. Bot.* Pertaining or belonging to the pine family of widely distributed coniferous trees and shrubs having needlelike leaves and bearing hard, woody cones. [< NL < L *pinus* pine]

pin·a·fore (pin′ə·fôr, -fōr) *n.* A sleeveless apronlike garment, esp. one for protecting a child's dress.

pin·ball (pin′bôl′) *n.* A game in which a ball is propelled by a spring to the top of an inclined board, and in its descent touches any of various numbered pins, holes, etc., the contacts so made determining the player's score.

pince-nez (pans′nā′, pins′-, *Fr.* pans·nā′) *n. pl.* **pince-nez** Eyeglasses held upon the nose by a spring. [< F, lit., pinch-nose < *pincer* to pinch + *nez* nose]

pin·cer·like (pin′sər·līk′) *adj.* Resembling the action or form of one or both jaws of pincers: a *pincerlike* movement.

pin·cers (pin′sərz) *n.pl.* (*sometimes construed as sing.*) **1.** An instrument having two handles and a pair of jaws working on a pivot, used for holding objects. **2.** *Zool.* A nipperlike organ, as the claw of a lobster. Also **pinch·ers** (pin′chərz). [ME *pinsours,* appar. < AF *pincer* to pinch]

pinch (pinch) *v.t.* **1.** To squeeze between two hard edges or surfaces, as a finger and thumb, etc. **2.** To bend or compress painfully. **3.** To affect with pain or distress: The cold *pinched* his fingers. **4.** To contract or make thin, as from cold or hunger. **5.** To reduce in means; distress, as for lack of money. **6.** *Slang* To capture or arrest. **7.** *Slang* To steal. — *v.i.* **8.** To squeeze; hurt. **9.** To be careful with money; be stingy. — **to pinch pennies** To be economical or stingy — *n.* **1.** The act of pinching, or the state of being pinched. **2.** So much of a substance as can be taken between the finger and thumb; a small amount. **3.** An emergency. **4.** *Slang* A theft. **5.** *Slang* An arrest or raid. [< AF *pincher,* OF *pincier*] — **pinch′er** *n.*

pinch·beck (pinch′bek) *n.* **1.** An alloy of copper, zinc, and tin, forming a cheap imitation of gold. **2.** Anything spurious or pretentious. — *adj.* **1.** Made of pinchbeck. **2.** Cheap; spurious. [after Christopher *Pinchbeck,* 1670?–1732, English inventor]

pinch-hit (pinch′hit′) *v.i.* **-hit, -hit·ting 1.** In baseball, to go to bat in place of a regular player. **2.** *U.S. Informal* To substitute for another in an emergency. — **pinch hitter**

pin·cush·ion (pin′koosh′ən) *n.* A small cushion into which pins are stuck when they are not in use.

pine¹ (pīn) *n.* **1.** Any of various cone-bearing trees having needle-shaped evergreen leaves growing in clusters, and including many important timber trees. **2.** Loosely, any tree of the pine family. **3.** The wood of any pine tree. [Fusion of OE *pīn* and OF *pin,* both < L *pīnus* pine tree]

pine² (pīn) *v.* **pined, pin·ing** *v.i.* **1.** To grow thin or weak with longing, grief, etc. **2.** To have great longing; usu. with *for.* [OE *pīn* torment, ult. < L *poena* punishment]

pin·e·al (pin′ē·əl) *adj.* **1.** Shaped like a pine cone. **2.** Pertaining to the pineal body. [< F < L *pinea* pine cone]

pineal body *Anat.* A small, reddish gray, vascular, conical body of rudimentary glandular structure found in the brain and having no known function. Also **pineal gland.**

pine·ap·ple (pīn′ap′əl) *n.* **1.** A tropical American plant having spiny, recurved leaves and a cone-shaped fruit tipped with a rosette of spiked leaves. **2.** Its edible fruit. **3.** *Slang* A hand grenade.

pine cone The cone-shaped fruit of the pine tree.

pine needle The needle-shaped leaf of a pine tree.

pine tar A dark, viscous tar obtained by the destructive distillation of the wood of pine trees, used to treat skin ailments.

PINEAPPLE

Pine-Tree (pīn′trē′) State Nickname of Maine.

pine·y (pī′nē) See PINY.

pin·feath·er (pin′feth′ər) *n. Ornithol.* A rudimentary feather, esp. one just beginning to grow through the skin.

pin·fold (pin′fōld′) *n.* A pound for stray animals, esp. for cattle. — *v.t.* To shut in a pinfold. [OE *pundfald*]

ping (ping) *n.* A brief, sharp, high-pitched sound. — *v.i.* To make this sound. [Imit.]

ping-pong (ping′pong′, -pông′) *n.* The game of table tennis. [< *Ping Pong,* a trade name]

pin·head (pin′hed′) *n.* **1.** The head of a pin. **2.** Any small or insignificant object. **3.** A small minnow. **4.** A microcephalic. **5.** *Slang* A brainless or stupid person.

pin·hole (pin′hōl′) *n.* A minute puncture made by or as by a pin.

pin·ion¹ (pin′yən) *n.* **1.** The wing of a bird. **2.** A feather; quill. **3.** The outer segment of a bird's wing, bearing the flight feathers. **4.** The anterior border of the wing of an insect. — *v.t.* **1.** To cut off one pinion or bind the wings of (a bird) so as to prevent flight. **2.** To cut or bind (the wings) of a bird. **3.** To bind or hold the arms of (someone). **4.** To shackle; confine. [< OF < L *penna, pinna* feather]

pin·ion² (pin′yən) *n. Mech.* A toothed wheel driving or driven by a larger cogwheel. For illus. see DIFFERENTIAL GEAR. [< F < OF < L *pinna,* orig., pinnacle]

pink¹ (pingk) *n.* **1.** A pale hue of crimson. **2.** Any of several garden plants with narrow, grasslike leaves and fragrant flowers. **3.** The flower of any of these plants, as the carnation. **4.** The highest or best condition, degree, or example. **5.** *Informal* A person who holds somewhat radical economic or political views: a contemptuous term. — **in the pink (of condition)** *Informal* In excellent health. — *adj.* **1.** Being pink in color. **2.** *Informal* Moderately radical. [Origin uncertain] — **pink′ish** *adj.*

pink² (pingk) *v.t.* **1.** To prick or stab with a pointed weapon. **2.** To decorate, as cloth or leather, with a pattern of holes. **3.** To cut or finish the edges of (cloth) with a notched pattern, as to prevent raveling or for decoration. **4.** *Brit.* To adorn; deck. [ME *pynken*]

pink·eye (pingk′ī′) *n.* **1.** *Pathol.* An acute, contagious conjunctivitis marked by redness of the eyeball. **2.** *Vet.* A febrile, contagious keratitis of sheep.

pink·ie (pingk′ē) *n. U.S. Informal* The little or fifth finger. Also **pink′y.** [Prob. < obs. *pink* small]

pink·ing shears (pingk′ing) Shears with serrated blades for scalloping the edges of fabrics.

pink rhododendron A tall rhododendron having rosy purple flowers: State flower of Washington.

pin money 1. An allowance of money for minor incidental expenses. **2.** An allowance made by a husband to his wife for her personal expenses.

pin·na (pin′ə) *n. pl.* **pin·nae** (pin′ē) **1.** *Bot.* A single leaflet of a pinnate leaf. **2.** *Anat.* The auricle of the ear. **3.** *Zool.* A feather, wing, fin, or the like. [< NL < L *pinna, penna* feather] — **pin′nal** *adj.*

pin·nace (pin′is) *n. Naut.* **1.** Any ship's boat. **2.** Formerly, a small vessel used as a tender, scout, etc. [< OF < Ital. *pinaccia,* prob. < L *pinus* pine]

pin·na·cle (pin′ə·kəl) *n.* **1.** A small turret or tall ornament, as on a parapet. **2.** Anything resembling a pinnacle, as a mountain peak. **3.** The highest point or place; apex; summit. — *v.t.* **·cled, ·cling 1.** To place on or as on a pinnacle. **2.** To furnish with a pinnacle; crown. [< OF < LL *pinnaculum,* dim. of L *pinna* wing, pinnacle]

pin·nate (pin′āt, -it) *adj.* **1.** Like a feather. **2.** *Bot.* Having the shape or arrangement of a feather: said of compound leaves or leaflets arranged on each side of a common axis. Also **pin′nat·ed.** [< L < *pinna* feather, wing] — **pin′nate·ly** *adv.* — **pin·na′tion** *n.*

pinnati- *combining form* **1.** *Bot.* Feathered; resembling a feather. **2.** *Zool.* Pinni-. [< L *pinna* feather]

pinni- *combining form Zool.* Web; fin: *pinniped.* Also **pinnati.** [< L *pinna* feather]

pi·noch·le (pē′nuk·əl, -nok-) *n.* A card game for two, three, or four persons, played with a double deck of 48 cards with no card below a nine: also spelled *penuchle, penuckle.* Also **pi′noc·le.** [Origin uncertain]

pi·ñon (pin′yən, pēn′yōn; *Sp.* pē·nyōn′) *n.* **1.** Any of various pine trees of the southwestern U.S., having edible seeds: also spelled *pinyon.* **2.** A seed from such a tree. [< Sp. < L *pinea* pine cone]

pin·point (pin′point′) *n.* **1.** The point of a pin. **2.** Something extremely small. — *v.t.* To locate or define precisely.

pin·scher (pin′shər) *n.* A Doberman pinscher. [< G, terrier]

pint (pīnt) *n.* **1.** A dry and liquid measure of capacity equal to half a quart. See table front of book. **2.** A container having such a capacity. [< OF *pinte*]

Pin·ta (pin′tə, *Sp.* pēn′tä) *n.* One of the three ships of Columbus on his initial voyage to America.

pin·tail (pin′tāl′) *n.* **1.** A duck of the northern hemisphere, the male of which has a long, sharp tail. **2.** A sharp-tailed grouse of North America.

pin·tle (pin′təl) *n.* A pin upon which anything pivots, as a rudder, hinge, etc. [OE *pintel* penis]

pin·to (pin′tō) *adj. SW U.S.* Piebald; pied, as an animal. — *n. pl.* **·tos 1.** *SW U.S.* A pied animal: said esp. of a horse or pony. **2.** A kind of spotted bean of the southwestern U.S.: also **pinto bean.** [< Am. Sp. < Sp., lit., painted, ult. < L *pingere* to paint]

pin·up (pin′up′) *n. Slang* **1.** A picture of a sexually attractive young woman hung on a wall. **2.** A young woman who is the subject of such a picture. — *adj.* **1.** Capable of being affixed to a wall, etc.: a *pinup* lamp. **2.** *U.S. Slang* Having the qualities of or suitable for a pinup: a *pinup* girl.

pin·wheel (pin′hwēl′) *n.* **1.** A firework that revolves when ignited, forming a wheel of fire. **2.** A child's toy resembling a windmill, revolving on a pin attached to a stick.

pin·worm (pin′wûrm′) *n.* A nematode worm parasitic in the lower intestines and rectum of man, esp. of children.

pin·y (pī′nē) *adj.* **pin·i·er, pin·i·est** Pertaining to, suggestive of, or covered with pines: also spelled *piney*.

pin·yon (pin′yən) See PIÑON (def. 1).

pi·o·neer (pī′ə·nir′) *n.* **1.** One of the first explorers, settlers, or colonists of a new country or region. **2.** One of the first investigators or developers in a new field of research, enterprise, etc. **3.** *Mil.* An engineer who goes before the main body, building roads, bridges, etc. — *v.t.* **1.** To prepare (a way, etc.). **2.** To prepare the way for. **3.** To be a pioneer of. — *v.i.* **4.** To act as a pioneer. [< OF *peonier* foot soldier < ML < L *pes, pedis* foot]

pi·ous (pī′əs) *adj.* **1.** Actuated by reverence for a Supreme Being; religious; godly. **2.** Marked by a reverential spirit. **3.** Practiced in the name of religion. [< L *pius* dutiful, respectful] — **pi′ous·ly** *adv.* — **pi′ous·ness** *n.*

pip[1] (pip) *n.* The seed of an apple, orange, etc. [Short for PIPPIN]

pip[2] (pip) *n.* **1.** A spot, as on a playing card, domino, or die. **2.** A sharp audible or visible signal produced mechanically or electronically, as in radar. [< earlier *peep*; origin unknown]

pip[3] (pip) *v.* **pipped, pip·ping** *v.t.* **1.** To break through (the shell), as a chick in the egg. — *v.i.* **2.** To peep; chirp. [Prob. var. of PEEP[1]]

pip[4] (pip) *n.* **1.** *Vet.* A contagious disease of fowls marked by mucus in the throat or by a scale on the tongue. **2.** *Slang* A mild human ailment: used humorously. [< MDu. < LL < L *pituita* mucus, the pip]

pipe (pīp) *n.* **1.** An apparatus, usu. a small bowl with a hollow stem, for smoking tobacco, opium, etc. **2.** Enough tobacco to fill the bowl of a pipe. **3.** A long conducting passage of wood, metal, tiling, etc., for conveying a fluid. **4.** A single tube or long, hollow case. **5.** Any hollow or tubular part in an animal or plant body. **6.** *Music* **a** A tubular flute or woodwind instrument. **b** An organ pipe. **c** *pl.* The bagpipe. **7.** The voice; also, a bird's note or call. **8.** A large cask for wine; also, a liquid measure of half a tun. **9.** A boatswain's whistle. — *v.* **piped, pip·ing** *v.i.* **1.** To play on a pipe. **2.** To make a shrill sound. **3.** *Naut.* To signal the crew by means of a boatswain's pipe. — *v.t.* **4.** To convey by or as by means of pipes. **5.** To provide with pipes. **6.** To play, as a tune, on a pipe. **7.** To utter shrilly or in a high key. **8.** *Naut.* To call to order by means of a boatswain's pipe. **9.** To lead, entice, or bring by piping. **10.** To trim, as a dress, with piping. — **to pipe down** *Slang* To become silent; stop talking or making noise. — **to pipe up** **1.** To start playing or singing. **2.** To speak out, esp. in a shrill voice. [OE, ult. < L *pipare* to cheep]

pipe-clay (pīp′klā′) *v.t.* To whiten with pipe clay.

pipe clay A white clay used for pottery, for making tobacco pipes, and for whitening military accouterments.

pipe dream A groundless hope or wish; a daydream.

pipe·fit·ting (pīp′fit′ing) *n.* **1.** A piece of pipe used to connect two or more pipes together. **2.** The work of joining pipes together. — **pipe′fit′ter** *n.*

pipe·line (pīp′līn′) *n.* **1.** A line of pipe, as for the transmission of water, oil, etc. **2.** A channel for the transmission of information, usu. private or secret. — *v.t.* **lined, ·lin·ing** **1.** To convey by pipeline. **2.** To furnish with a pipeline.

pipe organ An organ having pipes, as distinguished from an electric organ, etc.

pip·er (pī′pər) *n.* **1.** One who plays upon a pipe, esp. a bagpipe. **2.** One who installs pipes.

pipe stem **1.** The stem of a tobacco pipe. **2.** Anything resembling this. Also **pipe-stem** (pīp′stem′).

pi·pette (pī·pet′, pi-) *n.* A small tube, often graduated, for removing or transferring measured quantities of a liquid. Also **pi·pet′.** [< F, dim. of *pipe* pipe]

pip·ing (pī′ping) *adj.* **1.** Playing on the pipe. **2.** Hissing or sizzling: *piping* hot. **3.** Having a shrill sound. **4.** Char-

acterized by peaceful rather than martial music. — *n.* **1.** The act of one who pipes. **2.** Music of or suggesting that of pipes; a wailing or whistling sound. **3.** A system of pipes, as for drainage. **4.** A narrow strip of cloth folded on the bias, used for trimming dresses, etc.

pip·it (pip′it) *n.* One of various larklike singing birds widely distributed in North America. [Prob. imit. of its call]

pip·kin (pip′kin) *n.* A small earthenware jar. [? Dim. of PIPE]

pip·pin (pip′in) *n.* **1.** An apple of many varieties. **2.** A seed; pip. [< OF *pepin* seed of a fruit]

pip·sis·se·wa (pip·sis′ə·wə) *n.* An evergreen of the heath family, with white or pink flowers and thick leaves, used in medicine as an astringent and diuretic. [< Algonquian]

pip-squeak (pip′skwēk′) *n.* **1.** A petty and contemptible person or thing. **2.** A small, insignificant person.

pip·y (pī′pē) *adj.* **pip·i·er, pip·i·est** **1.** Pipelike; tubular; containing pipes. **2.** Piping; thin and shrill.

pi·quant (pē′kənt, -känt, -kwənt, pē·känt′) *adj.* **1.** Having an agreeably pungent or tart taste. **2.** Tart; racy. **3.** Lively and interesting. — **Syn.** See RACY. [< F, orig. ppr. of *piquer* to sting]

pique (pēk) *n.* A feeling of irritation or resentment. — *v.t.* **piqued, pi·quing** **1.** To excite resentment in. **2.** To stimulate or arouse; provoke. **3.** To pride (oneself): with *on* or *upon*. [< MF < *piquer* to sting, prick] — **Syn.** (noun) displeasure, offense, umbrage, huff.

pi·qué (pē·kā′) *n.* A fabric of cotton, rayon, or silk, with raised cord or welts running lengthwise in the fabric. [< F, lit., quilted, orig. pp. of *piquer* to prick, backstitch]

pi·ra·cy (pī′rə·sē) *n. pl.* **·cies** **1.** Robbery on the high seas. **2.** The unauthorized publication, reproduction, or use of another's invention, idea, or literary creation.

pi·ra·nha (pi·rä′nyə) *n.* A small fish of tropical South America with massive jaws and sharp teeth, known to attack man and larger animals. [< Pg. (Brazilian) < Tupi, toothed fish]

pi·rate (pī′rit) *n.* **1.** A rover and robber on the high seas. **2.** A vessel engaged in piracy. **3.** A person who appropriates without right the work of another. — *v.t. & v.i.* **·rat·ed, ·rat·ing** **1.** To practice or commit piracy (upon). **2.** To plagiarize. [< L < Gk. *peiran* to attempt] — **pi·rat·ic** (pī·rat′ik) or **·i·cal** *adj.* — **pi·rat′i·cal·ly** *adv.*

pir·ou·ette (pir′ōo·et′) *n.* A rapid whirling upon the toes in dancing. — *v.i.* **·et·ted, ·et·ting** To make a pirouette. [< F spinning top, origin uncertain]

pis·ca·to·ri·al (pis′kə·tôr′ē·əl, -tō′rē-) *adj.* **1.** Pertaining to fishes or fishing. **2.** Engaged in fishing. Also **pis′ca·to′ry.** [< L < *piscator* fisherman] — **pis′ca·to′ri·al·ly** *adv.*

Pis·ces (pis′ēz, pī′sēz) *n.pl.* A constellation, the Fish or Fishes; also, the twelfth sign of the zodiac. See ZODIAC. [< L, pl. of *piscis* a fish]

Pis·cis Aus·tri·nus (pis′is ô·strī′nəs) A constellation containing the star Fomalhaut. [< L]

pisci- *combining form* Fish; of or related to fish. Also, before vowels, **pisc-.** [< L *piscis* fish]

pis·ci·cul·ture (pis′i·kul′chər) *n.* The hatching and rearing of fish. — **pis′ci·cul′tur·al** *adj.* — **pis′ci·cul′tur·ist** *n.*

pis·cine (pis′īn, -ēn, -in) *adj.* Of, pertaining to, or resembling a fish or fishes [< L *piscis* a fish + -INE[1]]

pis·civ·o·rous (pi·siv′ər·əs) *adj.* Feeding on fish.

pis·mire (pis′mīr) *n. Archaic & Dial.* An ant. Also **piss·ant** (pis′ant). [ME < *pisse* urine + *mire* an ant]

pis·ta·chi·o (pis·tä′shē·ō, -tash′ē·ō) *n. pl.* **·chi·os** **1.** A small tree of western Asia and the Levant. **2.** Its edible nut. **3.** The flavor produced by the pistachio nut. **4.** A delicate shade of green, the color of the pistachio nut. Also **pis·tache′** (-täsh′). [< L < Gk. < *pistakē* a pistachio tree, prob. < OPersian *pistah* a pistachio nut]

pis·til (pis′til) *n. Bot.* The seed-bearing organ of flowering plants, composed of the ovary, with its contained ovules, and the stigma, usu. with a style. For illus. see FLOWER. [< F < L *pistillum* pestle]

pis·til·late (pis′tə·lit, -lāt) *adj. Bot.* **1.** Having a pistil. **2.** Having pistils and no stamens. Also **pis′til·lar′y** (-ler′ē).

pis·tol (pis′təl) *n.* A small firearm having a stock to fit the hand, and a short barrel, and fired from one hand. — *v.t.* **pis·toled** or **·tolled, pis·tol·ing** or **·tol·ling** To shoot with a pistol. [< MF < MHG < Czechoslovakian *pišt'al*]

pis·tole (pis·tōl′) *n.* A former European gold coin of varying value. [< F, short for MF *pistolet* pistol]

pis·ton (pis′tən) *n.* **1.** *Mech.* A rigid disk fitted to slide in a cylinder, and connected with a rod for receiving the pressure of or exerting pressure upon a fluid in the cylinder. **2.** A valve in a wind instrument for altering the pitch of tones. [< F < Ital. < LL *pistare*, freq. of L *pinsere* to pound]

piston ring *Mech.* An adjustable metal ring fitted into a groove around the piston and designed to prevent leakage between the piston and the cylinder wall.

pit[1] (pit) *n.* **1.** A natural or artificial cavity in the ground, esp. when relatively wide and deep. **2.** A pitfall for snaring animals; snare. **3.** An abyss so deep that one cannot return from it, as the grave. **4.** Great distress or trouble. **5.** The main floor of the auditorium of a theater, esp. the rear part; also, the audience occupying this area. **6.** An enclosed space in which fighting cocks, etc., are pitted against each other. **7.** Any natural cavity or depression in the body: the *pit* of the stomach. **8.** Any slight depression or excavation, as a pockmark. **9.** That part of the floor of an exchange where a special line of trading is done: the wheat *pit*. **10.** A mining excavation, or the shaft of a mine. — *v.* **pit·ted, pit·ting** *v.t.* **1.** To mark with dents, pits, or hollows. **2.** To put, bury, or store in a pit. **3.** To match as antagonists; set in opposition. — *v.i.* **4.** To become marked with pits. [OE < *puteus* a well]

pit² (pit) *n.* The kernel of certain fruits, as the plum. — *v.t.* **pit·ted, pit·ting** To remove pits from, as fruits. [< Du.< MDu. *pitte* kernel, pith]

pit·a·pat (pit′ə·pat′) *v.i.* **·pat·ted, ·pat·ting** To move or sound with light, quick steps or pulsations. — *n.* A tapping or succession of taps, steps, or similar sounds. — *adv.* With a pitapat; flutteringly. Also *pitty-pat.* [Imit.]

pitch¹ (pich) *n.* **1.** A thick, viscous, dark substance obtained by boiling down tar from the residues of distilled turpentine, etc., used in coating seams. **2.** Any of a class of residues obtained from the refining of fats, oils, and greases. **3.** The resinous sap of pines. **4.** Bitumen or asphalt, esp. when unrefined. — *v.t.* To smear, cover, or treat with or as with pitch. [OE < L *pix, picis* pitch]

pitch² (pich) *v.t.* **1.** To throw or hurl; fling. **2.** To erect or set up (a tent, camp, etc.). **3.** To set the level, angle, degree, etc., of. **4.** To put in a definite place or position. **5.** To set in order; arrange: now chiefly in the phrase **pitched battle. 6.** In baseball, to deliver (the ball) to the batter. **7.** To set or be set in a pitch or key. — *v.i.* **8.** To fall or plunge forward or headlong. **9.** To lurch; stagger. **10.** To rise and fall alternately at the bow and stern, as a ship. **11.** To incline downward; slope. **12.** To encamp; settle. **13.** In baseball, to deliver the ball to the batter; act as pitcher. — **to pitch in** *Informal* **1.** To work together; cooperate. **2.** To start vigorously. — **to pitch into** To attack; assail. — *n.* **1.** Point or degree of elevation or depression. **2.** The extreme top or bottom point. **3.** The degree of descent of a declivity; also, a descent, slope, or inclination to the horizon. **4.** In building, the inclination of a roof. **5.** *Aeron.* The movement of an aircraft about its lateral axis. **6.** *Mech.* **a** The amount of advance of a screw thread in a single turn. **b** The distance between two corresponding points on the teeth of a gearwheel. **7.** *Physics* The dominant frequency of a sound wave perceived by the ear, ranging from a low tone of about 20 cycles per second to a maximum high approaching 30,000 cycles. **8.** *Music* **a** The sensory impression of the acuteness or gravity of a tone or sound. **b** The exact vibration frequency of a tone expressed in cycles per second. **9.** The act of pitching; a throw. **10.** In baseball: **a** The delivery of the ball by the pitcher. **b** The place of pitching. **c** The distance pitched. **11.** The act of dipping or plunging downward, as a ship. **12.** *U.S. Slang* A practiced talk or appeal intended to influence or persuade. [ME *picchen*]

pitch-black (pich′blak′) *adj.* Intensely black, as pitch.

pitch-blende (pich′blend′) *n.* A black or brown variety of a mineral occurring in the massive form and resembling pitch in luster, the chief source of uranium and radium. [< G < *pech* pitch¹ + *blende* blende]

pitch-dark (pich′därk′) *adj.* Very dark; as black as pitch.

pitch·er¹ (pich′ər) *n.* One who pitches; esp., in baseball, the player who delivers the ball to the batter. [< PITCH²]

pitch·er² (pich′ər) *n.* **1.** *Chiefly U.S.* A container with a spout and a handle, used for holding liquids to be poured out. **2.** A form of leaf suggestive of a pitcher. [< OF < LL < Gk. *bikos* wine jar]

pitcher plant Any of several carnivorous plants having tubular leaves arranged in the form of pitchers that function as insect traps.

pitch·fork (pich′fôrk′) *n.* A large fork with which to handle hay, straw, etc. — *v.t.* To lift and throw with or as with a pitchfork.

pitch·man (pich′mən) *n. pl.* **·men** (-mən) *Slang* One who sells small articles from a temporary stand, as at a fair, etc.; a sidewalk vender.

pitch pine Any of several American pines that yield pitch or turpentine.

pitch pipe *Music* A small pipe that sounds a particular tone when blown, used to adjust the pitch of a voice or instrument; also, a group of such pipes combined in a unit.

PITCHER PLANT
(About 2 feet tall)

pitch·y (pich′ē) *adj.* **pitch·i·er, pitch·i·est 1.** Resembling pitch; intensely dark; pitchlike. **2.** Full of or daubed with pitch. — **pitch′i·ly** *adv.* — **pitch′i·ness** *n.*

pit·e·ous (pit′ē·əs) *adj.* Exciting pity, sorrow, or sympathy. [See PITY] — **pit′e·ous·ly** *adv.* — **pit′e·ous·ness** *n.*

pit·fall (pit′fôl′) *n.* **1.** A hidden danger or unexpected difficulty. **2.** A pit for entrapping wild beasts or men. [ME < PIT¹ + *falle, fal* < OE *fealle* a trap]

pith (pith) *n.* **1.** *Bot.* The cylinder of soft, spongy tissue in the center of the stems and branches of certain plants. **2.** *Ornithol.* The spongy substance of the interior of the shaft of a feather. **3.** The marrow of bones or of the spinal cord. **4.** Concentrated force; vigor. **5.** The essential part; gist. — *v.t.* **1.** To destroy the central nervous system or spinal cord of (a frog, etc.) by passing a wire through the vertebral column. **2.** To remove the pith from. **3.** To kill (cattle) by severing the spinal cord. [OE *pitha*]

Pith·e·can·thro·pus (pith′ə·kan′thrə·pəs, -kan·thrō′pəs) *n. pl.* **·pi** (-pī) *n. Paleontol.* An extinct manlike primate represented by skeletal remains discovered in central Java: also called *Java man.* [< NL < Gk. *pithēkos* ape + *anthropos* man] — **pith′e·can′thro·pine** (-pēn, -pin) *adj.*

pith helmet A topi.

pith·less (pith′lis) *adj.* Having no pith; lacking force.

pith·y (pith′ē) *adj.* **pith·i·er, pith·i·est 1.** Consisting of pith; like pith. **2.** Forceful; effective: a *pithy* remark. — **Syn.** See TERSE. — **pith′i·ly** *adv.* — **pith′i·ness** *n.*

pit·i·a·ble (pit′ē·ə·bəl) *adj.* **1.** Arousing or meriting pity or compassion. **2.** Insignificant; contemptible. — **pit′i·a·ble·ness** *n.* — **pit′i·a·bly** *adv.*

pit·i·ful (pit′i·fəl) *adj.* **1.** Calling forth pity or compassion; wretched. **2.** Evoking a feeling of contempt. — **pit′i·ful·ly** *adv.* — **pit′i·ful·ness** *n.*

pit·i·less (pit′i·lis) *adj.* Having no pity; ruthless. — **pit′i·less·ly** *adv.* — **pit′i·less·ness** *n.*

pit·man (pit′mən) *n. pl.* **·men** (-mən) *for def 1,* **·mans** (-mənz) *for def. 2* **1.** One who works in a pit, as in a mine. **2.** *Mech.* A connecting rod.

pit·tance (pit′əns) *n.* A small allowance of money. [< OF *pitance,* monk's food allotment, pity]

pit·ter-pat·ter (pit′ər·pat′ər) *n.* A rapid series of light sounds or taps. [Varied reduplication of PATTER¹]

pit·ty-pat (pit′ē·pat′) See PITAPAT.

pi·tu·i·tar·y (pi·too′ə·ter′ē, -tyoo′-) *adj. Physiol.* **1.** Secreting mucus. **2.** *Anat.* Of the pituitary gland. — *n. pl.* **·tar·ies 1.** *Anat.* The pituitary gland. **2.** *Med.* Any of various preparations made from extracts of the pituitary gland. [< L < *pituita* mucus]

pituitary gland *Anat.* A small, rounded body at the base of the brain that secretes hormones affecting growth, metabolism, and other functions of the body. Also **pituitary body.**

pit viper Any of various venomous snakes, as the rattlesnake, bushmaster, copperhead, etc., characterized by a small depression between the nostril and the eye.

pit·y (pit′ē) *n. pl.* **pit·ies 1.** Grief or pain awakened by the misfortunes of others; compassion. **2.** That which arouses compassion; misfortune. — *v.t. & v.i.* **pit·ied, pit·y·ing** To feel pity (for). [< OF < L *pietas, -tatis* dutiful conduct] — **pit′i·er** *n.* — **pit′y·ing·ly** *adv.*

— **Syn.** (noun) **1.** Both *pity* and *compassion* are keen regret or sorrow, but *compassion* more strongly suggests the inclination to give aid or support, or to show mercy. *Sympathy* is a sharing of the feelings of another; it becomes akin to *pity* when those feelings are sorrow, chagrin, disappointment, etc.

più (pyoo) *adv. Music* More: a direction. [< Ital. < L *plus*]

piv·ot (piv′ət) *n.* **1.** *Mech.* Something upon which a related part turns, oscillates, or rotates, as a pin or short cylindrical bearing fixed on only one end, for carrying or rotating a swinging part. **2.** A person or thing upon which an important matter hinges or turns. — *v.t.* **1.** To place on, attach by, or provide with a pivot or pivots. — *v.i.* **2.** To turn on a pivot; swing. [< F, origin unknown] — **piv′ot·al** *adj.* — **piv′ot·al·ly** *adv.*

pix·i·la·ted (pik′sə·lā′tid) *adj.* **1.** Affected by the pixies; mentally unbalanced; fey. **2.** *Slang* Drunk. [Prob. alter. of dial. E (Cornish) *pixy-led* bewitched]

pix·y (pik′sē) *n. pl.* **pix·ies** A fairy or elf. Also **pix′ie.** [< dial. E *pixey,* origin uncertain]

piz·za (pēt′sə, *Ital.* pēt′sä) *n.* An Italian food comprising a doughy crust overlaid with a mixture of cheese, tomatoes, spices, etc., and baked. [< Ital.]

piz·ze·ri·a (pēt′sə·rē′ə) *n.* A place where pizzas are prepared, sold, and eaten. [< Ital. < *pizza* pizza]

piz·zi·ca·to (pit′sə·kä′tō, *Ital.* pēt′tsē·kä′tō) *Music adj.* Plucked with the fingers. — *adv.* In a pizzicato manner. — *n. pl.* **·ti** (-tē) A tone or passage played in a pizzicato manner. [< Ital., pp. of *pizzicare* to pluck, pinch]

pla·ca·ble (plā′kə·bəl, plak′ə-) *adj.* Appeasable; yielding; forgiving. [< OF < L < *placare* to appease] — **pla′·ca·bil′i·ty, pla′ca·ble·ness** *n.* — **pla′ca·bly** *adv.*

plac·ard (plak′ärd; *for v., also* plə·kärd′) *n.* 1. A paper publicly displayed, as a poster. 2. A tag or plate bearing the owner's name. — *v.t.* 1. To announce by means of placards. 2. To post placards on or in. [< F *plaquer* to veneer, plate]

pla·cate (plā′kāt, plak′āt, plak′ət) *v.t.* **·cat·ed, ·cat·ing** To appease the anger of; pacify. [< L < *placare* to appease] — **pla′cat·er** *n.* — **pla·ca′tion** *n.*

pla·ca·to·ry (plā′kə·tôr′ē, -tō′rē, plak′ə-) *adj.* Tending or intended to placate. Also **pla′ca·tive.**

place (plās) *n.* 1. A particular point or portion of space, esp. that part occupied by or belonging to a thing under consideration; a definite locality or location. 2. An occupied situation or building; space regarded as abode or quarters. 3. An open space or square in a city; also, a court or street. 4. Position in a sequence or series. 5. Station in life; rank. 6. An office, appointment, or employment; position. 7. Room for occupation. 8. Room; way: One thing gives *place* to another. 9. A particular passage or page in a book, etc. 10. The second position among the first three finishers in a race, as in a horse race. 11. *Math.* The position of a figure in relation to the other figures of a given arithmetical series or group. — **in place** 1. In a natural or suitable position. 2. In its original site. — **in place of** Instead of. — **out of place** Removed from or not situated in the natural or appropriate place, order, or relation. — **to take place** To happen; occur. — *v.* **placed, plac·ing** *v.t.* 1. To put in a particular place or position. 2. To put or arrange in a particular relation or sequence. 3. To find a place, situation, home, etc., for. 4. To appoint to a post or office. 5. To identify; classify. 6. To arrange for the satisfaction, handling, or disposition of. 7. To bestow or entrust. — *v.i.* 8. In racing: **a** To finish second: distinguished from *show, win.* **b** To finish among the first three finishers. [< OF, ult. < L < Gk. < *platys* wide]

pla·ce·bo (plə·sē′bō) *n.* *pl.* **·bos** *or* **·boes** 1. *Med.* Any harmless substance given to humor a patient or as a test in controlled experiments. 2. Anything said in order to flatter. [< L < *placere* to please]

place kick In football, a kick for a goal in which the ball is placed on the ground for kicking.

place mat A mat on which a table setting is placed.

place·ment (plās′mənt) *n.* 1. The act of placing, or the state of being placed. 2. Relative position; arrangement. 3. The business of placing persons in jobs. 4. In football, the setting of the ball for a place kick; also, the kick itself.

pla·cen·ta (plə·sen′tə) *n.* *pl.* **·tas** *or* **·tae** (-tē) 1. *Anat.* In higher mammals, the vascular, spongy organ of interlocking fetal and uterine structures by which the fetus is nourished in the uterus. 2. *Bot.* The part of the ovary that supports the ovules. [< L, cake < Gk. < *plax, plakos* flat object] — **pla·cen′tal, plac·en·tar·y** (plas′ən·ter′ē, plə·sen′tər·ē) *adj.*

pla·cen·tate (plə·sen′tāt) *adj.* Having a placenta.

plac·er¹ (plā′sər) *n.* One who or that which places.

plac·er² (plas′ər) *n.* *Mining* 1. An alluvial or glacial deposit of sand, gravel, etc., containing gold in particles large enough to be obtained by washing. 2. Any place where deposits are washed for valuable minerals. [Var. of Sp. *placel* sandbank < *plaza* place]

plac·id (plas′id) *adj.* Having a smooth surface or nature; unruffled; calm. [< L < *placere* to please] — **pla·cid·i·ty** (plə·sid′ə·tē), **plac′id·ness** *n.* — **plac′id·ly** *adv.*

plack·et (plak′it) *n.* The opening in the upper part of a dress, blouse, or skirt to make it easy to put on and take off. Also **placket hole.** [Origin unknown]

pla·gia·rism (plā′jə·riz′əm, -jē·ə-) *n.* 1. The act of plagiarizing. 2. Something plagiarized. — **pla′gia·rist** *n.* — **pla′gia·ris′tic** *adj.*

pla·gia·rize (plā′jə·rīz, -jē·ə-) *v.* **·rized, ·riz·ing** *v.t.* 1. To appropriate and pass off as one's own (the writings, ideas, etc., of another). 2. To appropriate and use passages, ideas, etc., from. — *v.i.* 3. To commit plagiarism. — **pla′gia·riz′er** *n.*

pla·gia·ry (plā′jər·ē, -jē·ər·ē) *n.* *pl.* **·ries** 1. The act or result of plagiarism. 2. One who plagiarizes; a plagiarist. [< L *plagium* kidnapping < Gk. *plagios* treacherous]

plagio- *combining form* Oblique; slanting. Also, before vowels, **plagi-.** [< Gk. *plagios* oblique]

pla·gi·o·clase (plā′jē·ə·klās′) *n.* Feldspar consisting chiefly of the silicates of sodium, calcium, and aluminum, and crystallizing in the triclinic system. [< PLAGIO- + Gk. *klasis* cleavage] — **pla′gi·o·clas′tic** (-klas′tik) *adj.*

plague (plāg) *n.* 1. Anything troublesome or harassing; affliction; calamity. 2. *Pathol.* Any of various forms of a virulent, febrile, highly contagious, and often pandemic disease, esp. the bubonic plague. 3. The Black Death. 4. *Informal* Nuisance; bother. — *v.t.* **plagued, pla·guing** 1. To vex; annoy. 2. To afflict with plague or disaster. [< OF < LL < L *plaga*, prob. < Gk. *plēssein* to strike]

pla·guy (plā′gē) *Informal adj.* Troublesome. — *adv.* Vexatiously; intolerably: also **pla′gui·ly.** Also **pla′guey.**

plaice (plās) *n.* 1. A flounder of European waters. 2. Any of various American flatfishes. [< OF < LL *platessa* flatfish, ult. < Gk. *platys* broad]

plaid (plad) *adj.* Having a tartan pattern; checkered. — *n.* An oblong woolen scarf of tartan or checkered pattern, worn in the Scottish Highlands as a cloak over one shoulder; also, any fabric of this pattern. [< Scottish Gaelic *plaide* blanket] — **plaid′ed** *adj.*

plain (plān) *adj.* 1. Flat; smooth. 2. Presenting few difficulties; easy. 3. Clear; understandable. 4. Straightforward; guileless. 5. Lowly in condition or station. 6. Unadorned; without ornamentation. 7. Not figured, twilled, or variegated: *plain* cloth. 8. Homely. 9. Not rich; simple: *plain* food. — *n.* An expanse of level land; a prairie. [< OF < L *planus* flat] — **plain′ly** *adv.* — **plain′ness** *n.*

plain·clothes man (plān′klōz′, -klōthz′) A member of a police force not in uniform; esp., a detective.

plains·man (plānz′mən) *n.* *pl.* **·men** (-mən) A dweller on the plains.

plain·song (plān′sông, -song) *n.* The old ecclesiastical chant, having simple melody, not governed by strict rules of meter but by accentuation of the words. Also **plain·chant** (plān′chant, -chänt). [Trans. of Med.L *cantus planus*]

plain-spo·ken (plān′spō′kən) *adj.* Candid; frank.

plaint (plānt) *n.* 1. A lamentation. 2. A complaint. [< OF < L *planger* to lament]

plain·tiff (plān′tif) *n.* *Law* The party that begins an action at law; the complaining party in an action: opposed to *defendant.* [< OF < L *plangere* to lament]

plain·tive (plān′tiv) *adj.* Expressing a subdued sadness; mournful. [< OF, fem. of *plaintif*] — **plain′tive·ly** *adv.* — **plain′tive·ness** *n.*

plait (plat, plāt) *v.t.* 1. To braid (hair, etc.). 2. To pleat. — *n.* 1. A braid, esp. of hair. 2. A pleat. [< OF < L *plicare* to fold]

plan (plan) *n.* 1. A scheme, method, or design for the attainment of some object. 2. A drawing showing the proportion and relation of parts, as of a building. 3. Any sketch; draft. 4. A mode of action. — *v.* **planned, plan·ning** *v.t.* 1. To form a scheme or method for doing, achieving, etc. 2. To make a plan of, as a building; design. 3. To have as an intention or purpose. — *v.i.* 4. To make plans. [< MF < OF < L < *planus* flat] — **plan′ner** *n.*

pla·nar·i·an (plə·nâr′ē·ən) *n.* *Zool.* Any of an order of chiefly aquatic flatworms having elongate flattened bodies, and the power of regenerating themselves when cut apart. [< NL < L *planus* flat]

plane¹ (plān) *n.* 1. *Geom.* A surface such that a straight line joining any two of its points lies wholly within the surface. 2. Any flat surface. 3. A grade of development; level: a *plane* of thought. 4. *Aeron.* A supporting surface of an airplane. 5. An airplane. — *adj.* 1. Lying in a plane. 2. Level; flat. 3. Dealing only with flat surfaces: *plane* geometry. [< L *planus* flat] — **pla·nar** (plā′nər) *adj.*

plane² (plān) *n.* A tool used for smoothing boards or other surfaces of wood. — *v.* **planed, plan·ing** *v.t.* 1. To make smooth or even with a plane. 2. To remove with a plane. — *v.i.* 3. To use a plane. 4. To do the work of a plane. [< F < LL < OF < L *planare* to level] — **plan·er** (plā′nər) *n.*

plane³ (plān) *v.i.* **planed, plan·ing** 1. To rise partly out of the water, as a power boat when driven at high speed. 2. To glide; soar. [< F < OF < L *planus* flat]

plan·et (plan′it) *n.* 1. *Astron.* One of the celestial bodies revolving around the sun and shining only by reflected light. Those within the Earth's orbit, Mercury and Venus, are called **inferior planets.** Those beyond it, the **superior planets,** are Mars, Jupiter, Saturn, Uranus, Neptune, and Pluto. Between Mars and Jupiter are the asteroids or **minor planets.** 2. In ancient astronomy, one of the seven heavenly bodies (the Sun, Moon, Mercury, Venus, Mars, Jupiter, and Saturn) having a motion relative to the fixed stars. 3. In astrology, a planet considered as an influence on human beings. [< OF < LL < Gk. < *planaesthai* to wander]

plan·e·tar·i·um (plan′ə·târ′ē·əm) *n.* *pl.* **·i·ums** *or* **·i·a** (-ē·ə) 1. An apparatus for exhibiting the features of the heavens as they exist at any time and for any place on earth, consisting of an array of suitably mounted stereopticons installed in a room having a circular dome. 2. A room or building having such an apparatus. 3. An apparatus or model representing the planetary system.

plan·e·tar·y (plan′ə·ter′ē) *adj.* 1. Of or pertaining to a planet or the planets. 2. Mundane; terrestrial. 3. Wandering; erratic. 4. *Mech.* Pertaining to or denoting a type of gearing in which one or more small wheels mesh with the toothed circumference of a larger wheel, around which they revolve, at the same time rotating axially.

plan·e·tes·i·mal (plan′ə·tes′ə·məl) *Astron. adj.* Of or pertaining to very small, solid, planetary bodies. — *n.* Any of such bodies.

TABLE OF PLANETS

Name	MERCURY	VENUS	EARTH	MARS	JUPITER	SATURN	URANUS	NEPTUNE	PLUTO
Symbol	☿	♀	⊕	♂	♃	♄	♅	Ψ	♇
Distance from sun, millions of miles	36	67	93	142	483	886	1780	2790	3670
Mean diameter, miles	3000	7600	7918	4200	87,000	72,000	33,200	31,000	4000
Period of sidereal revolution	88 days	225 days	365.25 days	687 days	12 years	29.5 years	84 years	165 years	248 years
Period of rotation	88 days	20–30 days?	23 hr., 56 min.	24 hr., 37 min.	9 hr., 50 min.	10 hr., 14 min.	10 hr., 45 min.	15 hr., 48 min.	?
No. of satellites	0	0	1	2	12	9	5	2	0
Mass, Earth considered as 1.	0.0543	0.8148	1.0000	0.1069	318.35	95.3	14.58	17.26	0.1?
Escape velocity, miles per second	2	6.3	6.95	3.1	37	22	13	15	?
Mean density, water = 1	5.3	4.95	5.52	3.95	1.33	0.69	1.56	2.27	5?
Surface gravity, Earth = 1	0.38	0.87	1.00	0.39	2.65	1.17	1.05	1.23	0.5?
Mean orbital velocity, miles per second	29.76	21.78	18.52	15.00	8.12	6.00	4.23	3.37	2.95

planetesimal hypothesis *Astron.* The hypothesis that the solar system developed from large masses of planetesimals that coalesced to form planets and satellites.

plan·et·fall (plan'it-fôl') *n.* The descent of a rocket or artificial satellite to the surface of a planet.

plan·e·toid (plan'ə-toid) *n. Astron.* An asteroid. **— plan'·e·toi'dal** *adj.*

plane tree Any of various large deciduous trees characterized by broad, lobed leaves and spreading growth. [< OF' < L < Gk. *platys* broad]

plan·et-struck (plan'it-struk') *adj.* Affected by the influence of planets. Also **plan'et-strick'en** (-strik'ən).

planet wheel One of the smaller wheels in an epicyclic train.

plan·gent (plan'jənt) *adj.* Dashing noisily; resounding, as the sound of bells. [< L *plangens, -entis,* ppr. of *plangere* to lament, strike] **— plan'gen·cy** *n.* **— plan'gent·ly** *adv.*

plan·gor·ous (plang'gər-əs) *adj.* Wailing; lamenting. [< L *plangor* lamentation < *plangere.* See PLANGENT.]

pla·ni·form (plā'nə-fôrm, plan'ə-) *adj.* Having the surfaces nearly flat.

pla·nim·e·ter (plə-nim'ə-tər) *n.* An instrument for measuring the area of any plane surface, however irregular, by moving a pointer around its boundary and reading the indications of a scale. [< F *planimètre*] **— pla·ni·met·ric** (plā'nə-met'rik, plan'ə-) or **·ri·cal** *adj.* **— pla·nim'e·try** *n.*

plan·i·sphere (plan'ə-sfir) *n.* A plane projection of the sphere; especially, a polar projection of the heavens on a chart, showing the stars visible at a given time. [< OF < Med.L *planisphaerium* < L *planus* flat + *sphaera* sphere] **— plan'i·spher'ic** (-sfir'ik, -sfer'-) *adj.*

plan·ish (plan'ish) *v.t.* To condense, smooth, toughen, or polish, as metal, by hammering, rolling, etc. [< MF < L *planus* flat]

plank (plangk) *n.* **1.** A broad piece of sawed timber, thicker than a board. **2.** A support. **3.** One of the principles of a political platform. **— to walk the plank** To walk off a plank projecting from the side of a ship, a method once used by pirates for executing prisoners. **— v.t. 1.** To cover, furnish, or lay with planks. **2.** To broil or bake and serve on a plank, as fish. **3.** *Informal* To put down forcibly. **4.** *Informal* To pay: with *out, down,* etc. [< OF < LL *planca*]

plank·ing (plangk'ing) *n.* **1.** The act of laying planks. **2.** Anything made of planks. **3.** Planks collectively.

plank·ton (plangk'tən) *n. Biol.* The marine animal and plant organisms that drift or float with currents, waves, etc., unable to influence their own course and ranging in size from microorganisms to jellyfish. [< G < Gk. *plazesthai* to wander] **— plank·ton'ic** *adj.*

plano-¹ *combining form* Roaming; wandering. Also, before vowels, **plan-.** [< Gk. *planos* wandering]

plano-² *combining form* Flat; level; plane: *plano-concave, planometer.* Also, before vowels, **plan-.** Also **plani-.** [< L *planus* flat]

pla·no-con·cave (plā'nō-kon'kāv) *adj.* Plane on one side and concave on the other.

pla·no-con·vex (plā'nō-kon'veks) *adj.* Plane on one side and convex on the other.

pla·nom·e·ter (plə-nom'ə-tər) *n.* A device for gauging a plane surface, especially as used in metalworking. [< PLANO-² + -METER] **— pla·nom'e·try** *n.*

plant (plant, plänt) *n.* **1.** A living organism belonging to the vegetable kingdom, as distinguished from the animal kingdom, having typically rigid cell walls and characterized by growth chiefly from the synthesis of simple, usually inorganic food materials from soil, water, and air. **2.** One of the smaller forms of vegetable life, as distinct from shrubs and trees. **3.** A set of machines, tools, apparatus, etc., necessary to conduct a manufacturing enterprise or other business: a chemical *plant.* **4.** The buildings, grounds, and permanent appliances needed for any institution, as a post office, college, etc. **5.** A slip or cutting from a tree or bush; sapling. **6.** A person placed in a theater audience to encourage applause, speak lines, or contribute to the action of a play. **7.** An apparently trivial passage early in a story or play that later becomes important in shaping the outcome of the action. **8.** *Slang* A trick; dodge; swindle. **— v.t. 1.** To set in the ground for growing. **2.** To furnish with plants or seed: to *plant* a field. **3.** To set or place firmly; put in position. **4.** To found; establish. **5.** To introduce into the mind; implant, as an idea or principle. **6.** To introduce into a country, as a breed of animal. **7.** To deposit (fish or spawn) in a body of water. **8.** To stock, as a river. **9.** To bed (oysters). **10.** *Slang* To deliver, as a blow. **11.** *Slang* To place or station for purposes of deception, observation, etc.: to *plant* evidence. **12.** *Slang* To hide; bury: Where did you *plant* the loot? [OE *plante* < L *planta* a sprout, cutting; ult. origin uncertain]

Plan·tag·e·net (plan·taj'i·net) A patronymic of the Angevin dynasty of English sovereigns from Henry II (1154) to the accession of the House of Tudor (1485). [< Med.L *planta genista* sprig of broom; with ref. to the habit of Geoffrey of Anjou, founder of the line, of wearing one]

plan·tain¹ (plan'tin) *n.* An annual or perennial herb (genus *Plantago*) widely distributed in temperate regions; especially, the **common** or **greater plantain** (*P. major*) with large, ovate, ribbed leaves. [< OF < L *plantago, -ginis* < *planta* sole of the foot; with ref. to the shape of the leaves]

plan·tain² (plan'tin) *n.* **1.** A tropical, perennial herb (*Musa paradisiaca*), sometimes growing to 30 feet. **2.** The long, bananalike fruit of this plant, edible when cooked. [< Sp. *plátano;* infl. in form by PLANTAIN¹]

plan·tar (plan′tər) *adj.* Pertaining to the sole of the foot. [< L *planta* sole of the foot]

plan·ta·tion (plan-tā′shən) *n.* **1.** Any place that is planted. **2.** A farm or estate of many acres, planted in cotton, tobacco, etc., worked by resident laborers. **3.** A colony. **4.** A grove cultivated for its wood. [< L < *plantare* to plant]

plant·er (plan′tər) *n.* **1.** One who plants. **2.** An early settler or colonizer. **3.** An owner of a plantation. **4.** An agricultural implement for dropping seed in soil. **5.** A decorative container in which shrubs and flowers are planted, especially outdoors. **6.** *Canadian* In Newfoundland, a trader who hires and provisions fishermen in return for a share of the catch.

plan·ti·grade (plan′tə·grād) *Zool. adj.* Walking on the whole sole of the foot: distinguished from *digitigrade.* [< F < L *planta* sole of the foot + *gradi* to walk]

plant louse **1.** An aphid. **2.** Any of a family of leaping insects that infest plants and suck their juices.

plaque (plak) *n.* **1.** A plate, disk, or slab of metal, porcelain, ivory, etc., artistically ornamented, as for wall decoration. **2.** A small disk or brooch worn as a badge of membership, etc. [< F < MDu. *placke* flat disk, tablet]

plash¹ (plash) *n.* A slight splash. — *v.t. & v.i.* To splash lightly, as water. [Prob. imit.] — **plash′y** *adj.*

plash² (plash) *n.* A small pool. [OE *plæsc* pool]

-plasia *combining form* Growth; development; formative action. Also **-plasis.** [< Gk. *plassein* to mold, form]

-plasm *combining form Biol.* The viscous material of an animal or vegetable cell: *protoplasm.* [< LL < Gk. *plassein* to mold, form]

plas·ma (plaz′mə) *n.* **1.** The liquid portion of nutritive animal fluids, as blood, lymph, or intercellular fluid. **2.** The clear, fluid portion of blood, freed from blood cells and used for transfusions. **3.** The viscous material of a cell; protoplasm. **4.** *Physics* **a** The region in a gas-discharge tube in which there are approximately equal numbers of positive ions and electrons. **b** Any gas composed of such particles. Also **plasm** (plaz′əm). [< LL < Gk. *plassein* to mold, form] — **plas·mat·ic** (plaz-mat′ik), **plas′mic** *adj.*

plasma engine A reaction engine producing a small but sustained thrust by emission of a plasma jet.

plasma jet *Physics* A beam of plasma ejected from a specially constructed generator that forms a brilliantly luminous jet of extremely high energy and temperature.

plasmo- *combining form* Plasma; of or pertaining to plasma. Also, before vowels, **plasm-.** [See -PLASM]

plas·mo·di·um (plaz-mō′dē·əm) *n. pl.* **-di·a** (-dē·ə) **1.** A mass of protoplasm resulting from the fusion of ameboid organisms, typical of the slime molds. **2.** Any of a genus of parasitic protozoans that include the causative agents of malaria. [< NL < PLASM(O)- + Gk. *eidos* form]

-plast *combining form* An organized living particle or cell. [< Gk. < *plassein* to form]

plas·ter (plas′tər, pläs′-) *n.* **1.** A composition of lime, sand, and water, sometimes mixed with hair, for coating walls and partitions. **2.** Plaster of Paris. **3.** A viscid substance spread on linen, silk, etc., and applied to some part of the body, used for healing. — *v.t.* **1.** To cover or overlay with or as with plaster. **2.** To apply a plaster to, as a part of the body. **3.** To apply like plaster or a plaster: to *plaster* posters on a fence. **4.** To cause to adhere or lay flat like plaster. [OE reinforced by OF *plastre* < LL < L < Gk. *emplessain* < *en* upon, into + *plassein* to mold] — **plas′ter·er** *n.* — **plas′·ter·ing** *n.* — **plas′ter·y** *adj.*

plas·ter·board (plas′tər·bôrd′, pläs′-, -bōrd′) *n.* A wallboard made of gypsum or plaster and fibrous paper.

plaster cast **1.** A cast or model of a person or object made by molding plaster of Paris. **2.** *Surg.* A cast.

plaster of Paris Calcined gypsum, setting readily when mixed with water, useful in making molds, casts, bandages, etc. [With ref. to use of gypsum from Paris]

plas·tic (plas′tik) *adj.* **1.** Giving form or fashion to matter. **2.** Capable of being molded; pliable. **3.** Pertaining to modeling or molding. **4.** *Surg.* Efficacious in recreating or remodeling injured or destroyed parts: *plastic* surgery. — *n.* **1.** Any substance or material that may be molded. **2.** *Chem.* One of a large class of synthetic organic compounds capable of being molded, extruded, cast, or otherwise fabricated into various shapes, or of being drawn into filaments for textiles. [< L < Gk. *plastikos* moldable] — **plas′ti·cal·ly** *adv.*

-plastic *combining form* Growing; developing; forming. [< Gk. *plastikos* moldable]

plas·tic·i·ty (plas-tis′ə·tē) *n.* **1.** The quality or state of being plastic. **2.** Capacity for being shaped or molded.

plas·ti·ciz·er (plas′tə·sī′zər) *n.* That which functions to make a substance plastic, preserve softness, etc.

plastic surgery Surgery that deals with the restoration or healing of lost, wounded, or deformed parts of the body.

plas·tid (plas′tid) *n. Biol.* **1.** A small, specialized mass in the cytoplasm of a cell. For illus. see CELL. **2.** An elementary organism, as a cell. [< G < Gk. < *plassein* to mold]

plas·tron (plas′trən) *n.* **1.** A leather shield worn on the breast by fencers. **2.** *Zool.* The ventral part of the shell of a turtle or tortoise: also **plas′trum.** [< F, < Ital. < *piastra* sheet of metal] — **plas′tral** (-trəl) *adj.*

-plasty *combining form Surg.* An operation involving: **a** A (specified) part of the body: *osteoplasty.* **b** Tissue from a (specified) source: *zooplasty.* **c** A (specified) process or formation: *neoplasty.* [< Gk. -*plastia* formation]

-plasy See -PLASIA.

plat (plat) *v.t.* **plat·ted, plat·ting** To plait or braid. — *n.* A plait; braid. [Var. of PLAIT]

plat- Var. of PLATY-.

plate (plāt) *n.* **1.** A flat, extended, rigid body of metal or any material of slight but even thickness. **2.** A shallow vessel made of crockery, wood, glass, etc., in which food is served or from which it is eaten at table. **3.** Household articles, as trays, carving sets, etc., that are plated with a precious metal. **4.** A portion of food served at table; plateful. **5.** A piece of flat metal bearing a design or inscription or intended for reproduction, as in a bookplate. **6.** Metal in sheets. **7.** An impression from an engraving, woodcut, etc., as reproduced in a book. **8.** An electrotype or stereotype. **9.** A horizontal timber laid on a wall to receive a framework. **10.** *Dent.* A piece of metal, vulcanite, or plastic fitted to the mouth and holding one or more artificial teeth. **11.** A thin part of the brisket or beef. **12.** *Photog.* A sensitized sheet of glass, metal, or the like, for taking photographs. **13.** In baseball, the home base. **14.** *Biol.* A platelike part or structure; a lamina. **15.** A dish used in taking up collections, as in churches; also, a collection. **16.** *Electronics* The principal anode in an electron tube. — *v.t.* **plat·ed, plat·ing 1.** To coat with a thin layer of gold, silver, etc. **2.** To cover or sheathe with metal plates for protection. **3.** In papermaking, to give a high gloss to (paper) by pressure between metal plates. **4.** *Printing* To make an electrotype or stereotype from. [< OF < LL *plattus* flat] — **plat′er** *n.*

pla·teau (pla·tō′, *esp. Brit.* plat′ō) *n. pl.* **·teaus** or **·teaux** (-tōz′) **1.** An extensive stretch of elevated and comparatively level land; mesa. **2.** A stage or period of leveling off in the development of something or in the process of learning. [< F < OF *plat* flat]

plat·ed (plā′tid) *adj.* **1.** Coated with a layer of gold, silver, etc.: often used in combination: *gold-plated.* **2.** Provided with plates, as of metal.

plate·ful (plāt′fool′) *n. pl.* **·fuls** The quantity that fills a plate.

plate glass Glass in clear, thick sheets, suitable for mirrors, display windows, etc.

plate·let (plāt′lit) *n.* **1.** A small, platelike object. **2.** *Physiol.* A blood platelet. [Dim. of PLATE]

plat·en (plat′n) *n. Mech.* **1.** The part of a printing press, typewriter, or the like, on which the paper is supported to receive the impression. **2.** In a machine tool, the adjustable table that carries the work. [See PLATE]

plat·form (plat′fôrm) *n.* **1.** Any floor or flat surface raised above the adjacent level, as a stage for public speaking or a raised walk upon which railroad passengers alight. **2.** A projecting stage at the end of a car or similar vehicle. **3.** A formal scheme of principles put forth by a religious, political, or other body; also, the document stating the principles of a political party. [< MF < *plate* flat + *forme* form]

plat·ing (plā′ting) *n.* **1.** A layer or coating of metal. **2.** A sheathing of metal plates, as armor. **3.** The act or process of sheathing or coating something with plates or metal.

pla·tin·ic (plə·tin′ik) *adj. Chem.* Of, pertaining to, or containing platinum, esp. in its higher valence.

plat·i·nize (plat′ə·nīz) *v.t.* **·nized, ·niz·ing** To coat or combine with platinum, esp. by electroplating.

platino- *combining form* Platinum; of or containing platinum. Also, before vowels, **platin-.** [< PLATINUM]

plat·i·nous (plat′ə·nəs) *adj. Chem.* Of, pertaining to, or containing platinum, esp. in its lower valence.

plat·i·num (plat′ə·nəm) *n.* **1.** A heavy, steel-gray, malleable and ductile metallic element (symbol Pt) that is very infusible, resistant to most acids, and that has a high electrical resistance. It is widely used as a catalyst, in industry and the arts, and in jewelry. See ELEMENT. **2.** A color resembling that of platinum. [< NL < Sp. *plata* silver]

platinum blond **1.** A very light, almost white blond. **2.** One having platinum blond hair.

plat·i·tude (plat′ə·tood, -tyood) *n.* **1.** A flat, dull, or commonplace statement; an obvious truism. **2.** Dullness; triteness. [< F *plat* flat] — **plat′i·tu′di·nous** *adj.*

plat·i·tu·di·nize (plat′ə·too′də·nīz, -tyoo′-) *v.i.* **·nized, ·niz·ing** To utter platitudes.

pla·ton·ic (plə·ton′ik) *adj. Often cap.* Purely spiritual, or devoid of sensual feeling. — **pla·ton′i·cal·ly** *adv.*

Pla·ton·ic (plə·ton′ik) *adj.* Of, pertaining to, or characteristic of Plato or of Platonism; academic; theoretical. Also **Pla·ton′i·cal.** — **Pla·ton′i·cal·ly** *adv.*

Pla·to·nism (plā′tə·niz′əm) *n.* The philosophy of Plato;

esp., the doctrine that objects are merely copies or images of eternal ideas and that these ideas are the ultimate realities. **— Pla′to·nist** *n.*

pla·toon (plə·tōōn′) *n.* **1.** A subdivision of a company, troop, or other military unit, commanded by a lieutenant. **2.** A company of people; esp., in football, a defensive or offensive unit. **— v.t.** In football, to use as or in a platoon. [< F *peloton* ball, group of men]

platoon sergeant In the U.S. Army, the senior noncommissioned officer in a platoon. See table for GRADE.

Platt·deutsch (plät′doich′) *n.* The low German vernacular of the north of Germany. [< G]

plat·ter (plat′ər) *n.* **1.** *Chiefly U.S.* An oblong shallow dish on which meat or fish is served. **2.** *Informal* A phonograph record. [< AF *plat* dish]

platy- *combining form* Flat. Also, before vowels, *plat-*. [< Gk. *platys* flat]

plat·y·pus (plat′ə·pəs) *n.* A burrowing, egg-laying, aquatic monotreme of Australia, having a ducklike bill: also called *duckbill.* [< NL < Gk. < *platus* flat + *pous* foot]

plau·dit (plô′dit) *n.* An expression of applause; praise bestowed. [< L *plaudite*, pl. imperative of *plaudere* to applaud]

plau·si·ble (plô′zə·bəl) *adj.* **1.** Seeming to be likely or probable, but open to doubt. **2.** Apparently trustworthy or believable. [< L *plausibilis* deserving applause] **— plau·si·bil′i·ty, plau′si·ble·ness** *n.* **— plau′si·bly** *adv.*

PLATYPUS
(To 2 feet long; tail about 5½ inches)

play (plā) *v.i.* **1.** To engage in sport or diversion; amuse oneself. **2.** To take part in a game of skill or chance. **3.** To act in a way that is not to be taken seriously. **4.** To act or behave in a specified manner: to *play* false. **5.** To behave lightly or insincerely: with *with*. **6.** To make love sportively. **7.** To move quickly or irregularly as if frolicking: lights *playing* along a wall. **8.** To discharge or be discharged freely or continuously: a fountain *playing* in the square. **9.** To perform on a musical instrument. **10.** To give forth musical sounds. **11.** To be performed or exhibited. **12.** To act on or as on a stage; perform. **13.** To move freely or loosely, esp. within limits, as part of a mechanism. **— v.t. 14.** To engage in (a game etc.). **15.** To imitate in play: to *play* cowboys and Indians. **16.** To perform sportively or wantonly: to *play* a trick. **17.** To oppose in a game or contest. **18.** To move or employ (a piece, card, etc.) in a game. **19.** To employ (someone) in a game as a player. **20.** To cause: to *play* havoc. **21.** To perform upon (a musical instrument). **22.** To perform or produce, as a piece of music, a play, etc. **23.** To act the part of on or as on the stage: to *play* the fool. **24.** To perform or act in: to *play* Chicago. **25.** To cause to move quickly or irregularly. **26.** To put into or maintain in action. **27.** In angling, to let (a hooked fish) tire itself by maintaining pressure on the line. **28.** To bet or bet on. **— to play at 1.** To take part in. **2.** To pretend to be doing; do half-heartedly. **— to play down** To minimize. **— to play into the hands of** To act to the advantage of (a rival or opponent). **— to play off 1.** To oppose against one another. **2.** To decide (a tie) by playing one more game. **— to play on 1.** To take unscrupulous advantage of (another's hopes, emotions, etc.) for one's own advantage. **2.** To continue. **— to play out 1.** To come to an end; be exhausted. **2.** To continue to the end. **— to play the game** To behave in a fair manner. **— to play up** *Informal* To emphasize. **— to play up to** *Informal* To try to win the favor of by flattery, etc. **— n. 1.** A dramatic composition; drama. **2.** The performance of such a composition. **3.** Exercise or action for recreation or diversion. **4.** A maneuver or turn in a game. **5.** Manner of playing: rough *play.* **6.** In sports, a state of being actively and legitimately in use or motion: in *play.* **7.** The act of playing a game, esp. gambling. **8.** Fun; joking: to say something in *play.* **9.** The active operation of something: the *play* of one's mind. **10.** Action or operation that is light, free, and unencumbered. **11.** Light, quick, fitful movement. **12.** Manner of acting toward or dealing with others: fair *play.* **— to make a play for** *Informal* **1.** To attempt to gain something, as a favor, votes, etc. **2.** To attempt to seduce. [OE *plegan*] **— play′a·ble** *adj.*

play·back (plā′bak′) *n.* **1.** The act of reproducing a sound recording, as from a record or tape. **2.** A method or machine for reproducing sound recordings.

play·bill (plā′bil′) *n.* **1.** A bill or poster advertising a play. **2.** A program of a play.

play·boy (plā′boi′) *n.* *Informal* One who constantly seeks pleasure at nightclubs, social gatherings, etc.

play-by-play (plā′bi·plā′) *adj.* Dealing with each play or event as it happens: a *play-by-play* report.

play·er (plā′ər) *n.* **1.** One who takes part or specializes in a game: a tennis *player.* **2.** An actor. **3.** A performer on a

musical instrument. **4.** A gambler. **5.** An automatic device for playing a musical instrument.

player piano A piano having a mechanical device by which it may be played automatically.

play·fel·low (plā′fel′ō) *n.* An associate in play; playmate.

play·ful (plā′fəl) *adj.* **1.** Lightly humorous; joking: a *playful* remark. **2.** Full of high spirits and play; frolicsome: a *playful* puppy. **— play′ful·ly** *adv.* **— play′ful·ness** *n.*

play·go·er (plā′gō′ər) *n.* One who goes often to the theater.

play·ground (plā′ground′) *n.* An area, usu. adjoining a school, used for playing games and for recreation.

play·house (plā′hous′) *n.* **1.** A theater. **2.** A small house for children to play in. **3.** A toy house.

playing card One of a pack of cards used in playing various games, the pack usu. consisting of four suits (spades, hearts, diamonds, clubs) of 13 cards each.

play·let (plā′lit′) *n.* A short play.

play·mate (plā′māt′) *n.* A companion in sports or in play.

play·off (plā′ôf′, -of′) *n.* In sports: **a** A decisive game or contest to break a tie. **b** A series of games to decide a championship, award, etc.

play·pen (plā′pen′) *n.* A small, usu. collapsible enclosure in which a baby or small child is left to amuse himself.

play·thing (plā′thing′) *n.* A thing to play with; a toy.

play upon words Words used with double meaning; a pun.

play·wright (plā′rīt′) *n.* A writer of plays.

pla·za (plä′zə, plaz′ə) *n.* An open square or market place in a town or city. [< Sp. < L *platea* wide street]

plea (plē) *n.* **1.** An appeal or entreaty. **2.** An excuse, pretext, or justification: the tyrant's *plea.* **3.** *Law* **a** An allegation made by either party in a cause: a pleading. **b** A statement made by or for the defendant concerning the charge or indictment against him. [< OF < L *placitum* opinion, orig. pp. of *placere* to please]

plead (plēd) *v.* **plead·ed** or **pled** (pled), **plead·ing** *v.i.* **1.** To make earnest entreaty; beg. **2.** *Law* **a** To advocate a case in court. **b** To file a pleading. **— v.t. 3.** To allege as an excuse or defense. **4.** *Law* To discuss or maintain (a case) by argument. [See PLEA.] **— plead′a·ble** *adj.* **— plead′er** *n.*

plead·ing (plē′ding) *n.* **1.** The act of making a plea. **2.** *Law* **a** The art, science, or system of preparing the formal written statements of the parties to an action. **b** *Usu. pl.* Any one of such statements. **— plead′ing·ly** *adv.*

pleas·ant (plez′ənt) *adj.* **1.** Giving or promoting pleasure; pleasing. **2.** Agreeable in manner, act, appearance, etc. **3.** Merry; gay. [< OF < L *placere* to please] **— pleas′ant·ly** *adv.* **— pleas′ant·ness** *n.*

pleas·an·try (plez′ən·trē) *n. pl.* **·tries 1.** A playful, amusing, or good-natured remark, jest, or trick. **2.** The quality or spirit of pleasant conversation or companionship.

please (plēz) *v.* **pleased, pleas·ing** *v.t.* **1.** To give pleasure to; be agreeable to. **2.** To be the wish or will of. **3.** To be so kind as to; be willing to: usu. in the imperative: *Please* pass the bread. **— v.i. 4.** To give satisfaction or pleasure. **5.** To have the will or preference; wish: Go when you *please.* [< OF < L *placere* to please]
— Syn. 1. cheer, gladden, delight, rejoice, exhilarate.

pleas·ing (plē′zing) *adj.* Affording pleasure or satisfaction; gratifying. **— pleas′ing·ly** *adv.* **— pleas′ing·ness** *n.*

pleas·ur·a·ble (plezh′ər·ə·bəl) *adj.* Gratifying; pleasant; satisfying. **— pleas′ur·a·ble·ness** *n.* **— pleas′ur·a·bly** *adv.*

pleas·ure (plezh′ər) *n.* **1.** An agreeable sensation or emotion; enjoyment. **2.** Something that gives a feeling of enjoyment, delight, or satisfaction. **3.** Amusement or diversion: a search for *pleasure.* **4.** Sensual gratification. **5.** One's preference; choice. [See PLEASE.]

pleat (plēt) *n.* A fold of cloth doubled on itself and pressed or sewn in place. **— v.t.** To make a pleat or pleats in. Also *plait.* [Var. of PLAIT] **— pleat′er** *n.*

plebe (plēb) *n.* *U.S.* A member of the freshman class in the U.S. Military Academy at West Point or the U.S. Naval Academy at Annapolis. [Short for PLEBEIAN]

ple·be·ian (pli·bē′ən) *adj.* **1.** Of or pertaining to the common people, esp. those of ancient Rome. **2.** Common or vulgar. **— n. 1.** One of the common people, esp. of ancient Rome. **2.** Anyone who is coarse or vulgar. [< L < *plebs* the common people] **— ple·be′ian·ism** *n.*

pleb·i·scite (pleb′ə·sīt, -sit) *n.* An expression of the popular will by means of a vote by the whole people, as to change a constitution. [< F < L < *plebs* common people + *scitum* decree] **— ple·bis·ci·tar·y** (plə·bis′ə·ter′ē) *adj.*

plec·trum (plek′trəm) *n. pl.* **·trums** or **·tra** (-trə) A small implement with which the player on a lyre, guitar, etc., picks or strikes the strings: also called *pick.* Also **plec′tron** (-tron). [< L < Gk. < *plessein* to strike]

pled (pled) Alternate past tense and past participle of PLEAD.

pledge (plej) *v.t.* **pledged, pledg·ing 1.** To give or deposit as security for a loan, etc. **2.** To bind by or as by a pledge.

3. To promise solemnly, as assistance. **4.** To offer (one's word, life, etc.) as a guaranty or forfeit. **5.** To drink a toast to. **6.** To promise to join (a fraternity). **7.** To accept (someone) as a pledge (def. 6). — *n.* **1.** A promise or agreement to perform or fulfill some act, contract, or duty. **2.** A formal promise to do or not to do something. **3.** The drinking of a toast to one's health, etc. **4.** Something given as security for a debt or obligation. **5.** The state of being given or held as security: to put property in *pledge.* **6.** One who has promised to join a fraternity but who has not yet been formally inducted. [< OF < Med.L *plebium,* prob. < Gmc.] — **pledg′er** *n.*

pledg·ee (plej·ē′) *n.* **1.** One to whom something is pledged. **2.** One with whom a pledge is deposited.

pledg·or (plej′ər) *n. Law* A pledger. Also **pledge′or.**

-plegia *combining form Pathol.* A (specified) kind of paralysis, or paralytic condition: *hemiplegia.* Also **-plegy.** [< Gk. *plēgē* stroke]

Plei·a·des (plē′ə·dēz, plī′-) *n.pl.* **1.** In Greek mythology, the seven daughters of Atlas, who were set by Zeus among the stars. **2.** *Astron.* A loose cluster of many hundred stars in the constellation Taurus, six of which are visible to ordinary sight.

Plei·o·cene (plī′ə·sēn) See PLIOCENE.

Pleis·to·cene (plīs′tə·sēn) *Geol. adj.* Of or pertaining to the earlier of the two epochs of the Quaternary, characterized by the glacial epoch of northern Asia, Europe, and North America. — *n.* The rock series of this epoch. See chart for GEOLOGY. [< Gk. *pleistos* most + *kainos* recent]

ple·na·ry (plē′nə·rē, plen′ə-) *adj.* **1.** Full in all respects or requisites; complete. **2.** Fully or completely attended, as an assembly. [< LL < L *plenus* full] — **ple′na·ri·ly** *adv.* — **ple′na·ri·ness** *n.*

plenary indulgence In the Roman Catholic Church, the remission of all temporal penalties incurred by sin.

plen·i·po·ten·ti·ar·y (plen′i·pə·ten′shē·er′ē, -sha·rē) *adj.* Possessing or conferring full powers. — *n. pl.* **·ar·ies** A person fully empowered to represent a government, as an ambassador, minister, or envoy. [< Med.L < LL < L *plenus* full + *potens* powerful < *potere* to be able]

plen·i·tude (plen′ə·tōōd, -tyōōd) *n.* The state of being full, complete, or abounding.

plen·te·ous (plen′tē·əs) *adj.* **1.** Characterized by plenty; amply sufficient. **2.** Yielding an abundance. — **plen′te·ous·ly** *adv.* — **plen′te·ous·ness** *n.*

plen·ti·ful (plen′ti·fəl) *adj.* **1.** Existing in great quantity; abundant. **2.** Yielding or containing plenty; affording ample supply. — **plen′ti·ful·ly** *adv.* — **plen′ti·ful·ness** *n.*

— **Syn. 1.** *Plentiful* suggests comparison with a need or demand, and can be applied to almost anything concrete: wheat is *plentiful* this year, aspirants for movie jobs are always *plentiful. Abundant* suggests, in the concrete, the works of nature rather than of man: *abundant* foliage. *Ample* means both just enough and more than enough, and so tends to imply an amount between enough and *plentiful.* — **Ant.** scanty, scarce.

plen·ty (plen′tē) *n.* **1.** The state of being sufficient and in abundance. **2.** As much as can be required; an abundance or sufficiency: I have *plenty.* — *adj.* Existing in abundance; plentiful. — *adv. Informal* In a sufficient degree: The house is *plenty* large enough. [< OF < L *plenus* full]

ple·o·nasm (plē′ə·naz′əm) *n.* **1.** The use of needless words; redundancy; also, an instance of it. **2.** A redundant word or phrase. **3.** Superabundance. [< L < Gk. < *pleōn* more] — **ple′o·nas′tic** (-nas′tik) *adj.* — **ple′o·nas′ti·cal·ly** *adv.*

pleth·o·ra (pleth′ər·ə) *n.* **1.** A state of excessive fullness; superfluity. **2.** *Med.* Superabundance of blood in the whole system or in an organ or part. [< LL < Gk. < *plēthein* to be full] — **ple·thor′ic** *adj.* — **ple·thor′i·cal·ly** *adv.*

pleu·ra (plōōr′ə) *n. pl.* **pleu·rae** (plōōr′ē) *Anat.* The serous membrane that envelops the lungs and is folded back upon the walls of the thorax and upon the diaphragm. [< Gk. *pleura* side] — **pleu′ral** *adj.*

pleu·ri·sy (plōōr′ə·sē) *n. Pathol.* Inflammation of the pleura, commonly attended with fever, pain in the chest, difficult breathing, exudation, etc. [< OF < LL < L < Gk. *pleura* side] — **pleu·rit·ic** (plōō·rit′ik) *adj.*

pleuro- *combining form* **1.** Of or pertaining to the side. **2.** *Med.* Of, related to, or affecting the pleura. Also, before vowels, **pleur-.** [< Gk. *pleura* side]

Plex·i·glas (plek′si·glas′, -gläs′) *n.* A lightweight thermoplastic acrylic resin, very weather-resistant and highly transparent: a trade name. Also **plex′i·glas, plex′i·glass.**

plex·us (plek′səs) *n. pl.* **plex·us·es** or **plex·us 1.** A network or complicated interlacing of parts. **2.** *Anat.* A network of cordlike structures, as blood vessels or nerves. [< L, pp. of *plectere* to intertwine]

pli·a·ble (plī′ə·bəl) *adj.* **1.** Easily bent or twisted; flexible. **2.** Easily persuaded or controlled; tractable. — **pli′a·bil′i·ty, pli′a·ble·ness** *n.* — **pli′a·bly** *adv.*

pli·an·cy (plī′ən·sē) *n.* The state or quality of being pliant.

pli·ant (plī′ənt) *adj.* **1.** Capable of being bent or twisted with ease. **2.** Easily yielding to influence; compliant. [< OF, ppr. of *plier* < L *plicare* to fold] — **pli′ant·ly** *adv.*

pli·cate (plī′kāt) *adj.* Folded or pleated, as a fan. Also **pli′cat·ed.** — **pli′cate·ness** *n.* — **pli′cate·ly** *adv.* — **pli·ca′tion, plic·a·ture** (plik′ə·chŏŏr) *n.*

pli·er (plī′ər) *n.* **1.** *pl.* Small pincers for bending, holding, or cutting: also **pair of pliers. 2.** One who or that which plies.

plight[1] (plīt) *n.* A condition, state, or circumstance, usu. of a dangerous or complicated nature. [< AF *plit* fold, condition < OF *pleit*]

plight[2] (plīt) *v.t.* **1.** To pledge (one's word, faith, etc.). **2.** To promise, as in marriage; betroth. — **to plight one's troth 1.** To pledge one's solemn word. **2.** To promise oneself in marriage. [OE *plihtan* to expose to danger] — **plight′er** *n.*

Plim·soll mark (plim′sol, -səl) A mark painted on the outside of the hull of a British vessel to show how deeply she may be loaded. Also **Plimsoll line.** [after Samuel *Plimsoll,* 1824–98, English statesman]

plinth (plinth) *n. Archit.* **1.** The slab, block, or stone, usu. square, on which a column, pedestal, or statue rests. **2.** A thin course, as of slabs, usu. projecting beneath a wall: also **plinth course.** [< L < Gk. *plinthos* brick]

Pli·o·cene (plī′ə·sēn) *Geol. adj.* Of or pertaining to the latest epoch of the Tertiary, and succeeded by the Pleistocene. — *n.* The Pliocene epoch or rock series. Also spelled *Pleiocene.* See chart for GEOLOGY. [< Gk. *pleiōn* more + *kainos* new] — **Pli′o·cen′ic** (-sen′ik) *adj.*

plod (plod) *v.* **plod·ded, plod·ding** *v.i.* **1.** To walk heavily or laboriously. **2.** To work in a steady, laborious manner. — *v.t.* **3.** To plod along heavily or laboriously. — *n.* **1.** The act or duration of plodding. **2.** The sound of a heavy step, as of a horse. [Imit.] — **plod′der** *n.* — **plod′ding·ly** *adv.*

-ploid *combining form Biol.* In cytology and genetics, having a (specified) number of chromosomes: *polyploid.* Corresponding nouns end in **-ploidy.** [< Gk. *-ploos* fold + -OID]

plop (plop) *v.t. & v.i.* **plopped, plop·ping** To drop with a sound like that of something striking the water without making a splash. — *n.* The act or sound of plopping. — *adv.* Suddenly with a plopping sound. [Imit.]

plo·sion (plō′zhən) *n. Phonet.* The sudden release of breath after closure of the oral passage in the articulation of a stop consonant, as after the *p* in *pat.* [< EXPLOSION]

plo·sive (plō′siv) *Phonet. adj.* Designating a sound produced by plosion. — *n.* A consonant so produced; a stop.

plot (plot) *n.* **1.** A piece or patch of ground, usu. used for some special purpose. **2.** A chart or diagram, as of a building, for showing certain data; also, a surveyor's map. **3.** A secret plan to accomplish some questionable purpose; conspiracy. **4.** The scheme or pattern of the events, incidents, or situations of a story, play, etc. — *v.* **plot·ted, plot·ting** *v.t.* **1.** To make a map, chart, or plan of, as of a ship's course, a building, etc. **2.** To plan for secretly. **3.** To arrange the plot of (a novel, etc.). **4.** *Math.* **a** To represent graphically the position of (a measured value) by a point located with reference to its coordinates on graph paper. **b** To draw (a curve) through a series of such points. — *v.i.* **5.** To form a plot; scheme. [OE] — **plot′ter** *n.*

plov·er (pluv′ər, plō′vər) *n.* **1.** Any of various shore birds, having long, pointed wings and a short tail. **2.** Any of certain related shore birds, as the **upland plover.** [< OF *plovier,* ult. < L *pluvia* rain]

plow (plou) *n.* **1.** An implement for cutting, turning over, stirring, or breaking up the soil, usu. drawn by horses or oxen, or by mechanical power. **2.** Any implement that operates like a plow: often in combination: a *snowplow.* — *v.t.* **1.** To turn up the surface of (land) with a plow. **2.** To make or form (a furrow, one's way, etc.) by or as by means of a plow. **3.** To furrow or score the surface of: Shot *plowed* the field. **4.** To dig out or remove with a plow: with *up* or *out.* **5.** To move or cut through (water). — *v.i.* **6.** To turn up soil with a plow. **7.** To undergo plowing in a specified way, as land. **8.** To move or proceed as a plow does: usu. with *through* or *into.* **9.** To advance laboriously; plod. — **to plow into** *Informal* **1.** To hit hard. **2.** To undertake vigorously to accomplish, finish, or solve (a meal, problem, etc.). Also, *esp. Brit.,* **plough.** [OE *plōh,* prob. < ON *plōgr*] — **plow′a·ble** *adj.*

plow·boy (plou′boi′) *n.* **1.** A boy who drives or guides a team in plowing. **2.** A country boy. Also **plough′boy′.**

plow·man (plou′mən) *n. pl.* **·men** (-mən) **1.** One who plows. **2.** A farmer; rustic. Also **plough′man.**

plow·share (plou′shâr′) *n.* The blade of a plow. Also **plough′share′.**

ploy (ploi) *n.* A maneuver or stratagem, as in a game or conversation. [< EMPLOY]

pluck (pluk) *v.t.* **1.** To pull out or off; pick. **2.** To pull with force; snatch or drag: with *off, away,* etc. **3.** To pull out the feathers, hair, etc., of. **4.** To give a twitch or pull to, as a sleeve. **5.** To cause the strings of (a musical instrument) to sound by quickly pulling or picking them. **6.** *Slang* To rob; swindle. — *v.i.* **7.** To give a sudden pull;

tug: with *at.* **— to pluck up** To rouse or summon (one's courage). **— n. 1.** Confidence and spirit in the face of difficulty or danger. **2.** A sudden pull; twitch. **— pluck′er** *n.* [OE *pluccian* to pick out, ? ult. < LL *pilus* hair]

pluck·y (pluk′ē) *adj.* **pluck·i·er, pluck·i·est** Brave and spirited; courageous. **— pluck′i·y** *adv.* **— pluck′i·ness** *n.*

plug (plug) *n.* **1.** Anything, as a piece of wood or a cork, used to stop a hole. **2.** *Electr.* A usu. two-pronged device attached to the end of a wire or cable and inserted in a socket or jack to make a connection. **3.** A spark plug. **4.** A fireplug. **5.** A flat cake of pressed or twisted tobacco. **6.** A piece of tobacco for chewing. **7.** *Informal* Anything useless or defective. **8.** *Informal* An old, worn-out horse. **9.** *Slang* A favorable word, recommendation, or piece of publicity for someone or something. **10.** *Geol.* A core of hard, igneous rock that has filled the neck of a volcano. **— v. plugged, plug·ging** *v.t.* **1.** To stop or close, as a hole, by inserting a plug; often with *up*. **2.** To insert as a plug. **3.** *Slang* To shoot a bullet into. **4.** *Slang* To hit or punch. **5.** *Slang* To advertise frequently or insistently. **— v.i. 6.** *Informal* To work doggedly. **7.** *Slang* To hit or shoot. **8.** *Slang* To favor or work for a cause, person, etc.: usu. with *for*. **— to plug in** To insert the plug of (a lamp, etc.) in an electrical outlet. [< MDu. *plugge*] **— plug′ger** *n.*

plug-ug·ly (plug′ug′lē) *n. pl.* **·lies** *U.S. Slang* A gangster, ruffian, or rowdy.

plum[1] (plum) *n.* **1.** The edible fruit of any of various trees of the rose family. **2.** The tree itself. **3.** The plumlike fruit of any of various other trees; also, a tree bearing such fruit. **4.** A raisin, esp. as used in cooking. **5.** Any of various shades of dark, reddish purple. **6.** The best or most choice part of anything. **7.** Something desirable, as a post or appointment. **8.** A sugarplum. [OE *plūme* < LL < L *prunum* < Gk. *prounon*]

plum[2] (plum) See PLUMB (*adj.* def. 2 and *adv.* def. 2).

plum·age (plōō′mij) *n.* **1.** The feathers of a bird; esp., a bird's entire covering of feathers. **2.** Gaudy costume or adornment. [< F < *plume* plume]

plumb (plum) *n.* A lead weight (*plumb bob*) on the end of a line (*plumb line*) used to find the exact perpendicular, to sound the depth of water, etc. **— off** (or **out of**) **plumb** Not exactly vertical; not in alignment. **— adj. 1.** Conforming to a true vertical or perpendicular. **2.** *Informal* Sheer; absolute; complete: also spelled *plum*. **— adv. 1.** In a line perpendicular to the plane of the horizon, vertically. **2.** *Informal* Utterly; completely; entirely: also spelled *plum*. **— v.t. 1.** To test the perpendicularity of with a plumb. **2.** To make vertical; straighten: usu. with *up*. **3.** To test the depth of; sound. **4.** To reach the lowest level or extent of: to *plumb* the depths of despair. [< F < L *plumbum* lead]

plumb- Var. of PLUMBO-.

plumb bob The weight used at the end of a plumb line.

plumb·er (plum′ər) *n.* One whose occupation is the installing or repairing of plumbing.

plumb·er's friend (plum′ərz) A plunger (def. 3).

plumb·ing (plum′ing) *n.* **1.** The art or trade of putting into buildings the tanks, pipes, etc., for water, gas, sewage, etc. **2.** The pipe system of a building. **3.** The act of sounding for depth, etc., with a plumb line.

plumb line 1. A cord by which a weight is suspended to test the perpendicularity or depth of something. **2.** Such a cord.

plumbo- *combining form* Lead; of or containing lead. Also, before vowels, **plumb-**. [< L *plumbum* lead]

plume (plōōm) *n.* **1.** A feather, esp. when long and ornamental. **2.** A large feather or tuft of feathers used as an ornament. **3.** *Biol.* A featherlike form or part. **4.** Plumage. **5.** Anything resembling a plume. **6.** A decoration of honor or achievement. **— v.t. plumed, plum·ing 1.** To adorn, dress, or furnish with or as with plumes. **2.** To smooth (itself or its feathers); preen. **3.** To congratulate or pride (oneself): with *on* or *upon*. [< F < L *pluma*]

plum·met (plum′it) *n.* **1.** A plumb bob. **2.** Something that oppresses or weighs down. **— v.i.** To drop straight down; plunge. [< OF *plom* < L *plumbum* lead]

plu·mose (plōō′mōs) *adj.* **1.** Bearing feathers or plumes. **2.** Plumelike; feathery. [< L *pluma* feather] **— plu′mose·ly** *adv.* **— plu·mos·i·ty** (plōō·mos′ə·tē) *n.*

plump[1] (plump) *adj.* **1.** Somewhat fat; chubby. **2.** Well filled or rounded out. **— v.t. & v.i.** To make or become plump: often with *up* or *out*. [< MDu., var. of *plomp* blunt] **— plump′ly** *adv.* **— plump′ness** *n.*

plump[2] (plump) *v.i.* **1.** To fall suddenly or heavily; drop with full impact. **2.** To give one's complete support: with

PLUMB BOB
a Plumb line.
b Plumb bob.
c Wall.

for. **3.** To come or go abruptly or in a hurry: with *in* or *out*. **— v.t. 4.** To drop or throw down heavily or all at once. **5.** To utter bluntly or abruptly: often with *out*. **— n. 1.** The act of plumbing or falling. **2.** The sound made by this. **— adj.** Containing no reservation or qualification; blunt; downright. **— adv. 1.** With a sudden impact or fall. **2.** Straightforwardly; bluntly. **3.** Straight down. [< MDu. *plompen*; ult. imit.] **— plump′er** *n.* **— plump′ly** *adv.*

plum·y (plōō′mē) *adj.* **plum·i·er, plum·i·est 1.** Made of, covered, or adorned with feathers. **2.** Like a plume or feather.

plun·der (plun′dər) *v.t.* **1.** To rob of goods or property by open violence, as in war; pillage. **2.** To despoil by robbery or fraud. **3.** To take as plunder. **— v.i. 4.** To take plunder. **— n. 1.** That which is taken by plundering; booty. **2.** The act of plundering or robbing. [< G < MHG *plundern*, orig., to remove household goods] **— plun′der·er** *n.*

plunge (plunj) *v.* **plunged, plung·ing** *v.t.* **1.** To thrust or force suddenly into a fluid, penetrable substance, hole, etc. **2.** To force into some condition or state: to *plunge* a nation into debt. **— v.i. 3.** To dive, jump, or fall into a fluid, chasm, etc. **4.** To move suddenly or with a rush. **5.** To move violently forward and downward, as a horse or ship. **6.** To descend abruptly or steeply, as a road or cliff. **7.** *Informal* To gamble or speculate heavily. **— n. 1.** The act of plunging; a leap; dive. **2.** A sudden and violent motion, as of a breaking wave. **3.** A place for diving or swimming. **4.** A swim. **5.** A heavy or extravagant bet, expenditure, or speculation. [< OF *plongier*, ult. < L *plumbum* lead]

plung·er (plun′jər) *n.* **1.** One who or that which plunges. **2.** *Informal* One who gambles recklessly. **3.** A cuplike device made of rubber and attached to a stick, used to clean out clogged drains, etc.: also called *plumber's friend*. **4.** *Mech.* Any appliance having a plunging motion, as a piston.

plunk (plungk) *Informal v.t.* **1.** To pluck, as a banjo or its strings; strum. **2.** To place or throw heavily and suddenly: with *down*. **— v.i. 3.** To emit a twanging sound. **4.** To fall heavily. **— n.** A heavy blow, or its sound. **— adv.** Directly; exactly: *plunk* in the middle. [Imit.]

plu·per·fect (plōō·pûr′fikt) *n. Gram.* The past perfect. [< L *plus quam perfectus*, lit., more than completed]

plu·ral (plōōr′əl) *adj.* **1.** Containing, consisting of, or designating more than one. **2.** *Gram.* Of or designating a linguistic form that denotes more than one (in languages that have dual number, as Sanskrit and Greek, more than two): distinguished from *dual*, *singular*. **— n.** *Gram.* The plural number or a word in this number. [< OF < L < *plus, pluris* more] **— plu′ral·ly** *adv.*

◆ English nouns regularly form their plurals by adding *s* to the singular. However, nouns that end in *y* preceded either by a consonant or by *qu* form their plurals by changing the *y* to *i* and adding *es*, as, body, *bodies*, city, *cities*, colloquy, *colloquies*; if the *y* is preceded by a vowel (other than *u*), the plural is formed by adding *s*, as, day, *days*, monkey, *monkeys*. Nouns ending in *ss*, *sh*, *ch*, *s*, *x*, and *zz* usually form their plurals by adding *es*, as, brass, *brasses*, crash, *crashes*, crutch, *crutches*, gas, *gases*, box, *boxes*, buzz, *buzzes*. Many nouns ending in *f* change the *f* to *v* and add *es*, as, wolf, *wolves*, half, *halves*. Nouns ending in *o* form their plurals by adding either *s* or *es*, and the preferable form will be found at the word entry. Some nouns of Old English origin have an irregular plural in *en*, as, child, *children*, and some form the plural by a vowel change, as mouse, *mice*; goose, *geese*; man, *men*. A few nouns retain the singular form unchanged in the plural, as, *deer*, *hose*, *moose*, *series*. Some such nouns, especially the names of animals, have also an alternative plural regularly formed, as fish, *fish* or *fishes*. *Fish* is the usual collective plural; *fishes* is used to indicate more than one genus, variety, species, etc. Many words of foreign derivation retain the plural forms peculiar to the languages from which they are derived, as, addendum, *addenda*; crisis, *crises*; datum, *data*. Many nouns of this class have also a plural of the regular English form, as, appendix, *appendixes* or *appendices*; beau, *beaus* or *beaux*; cherub, *cherubs* or *cherubim*; focus, *focuses* or *foci*. Compounds commonly form the plural regularly by adding *s* or *es* to the complete word, as, armful, *armfuls*; football, *footballs*. If the last element of the compound forms its plural irregularly, the same form usually appears in the plural of the compound, as, footman, *footmen*. Some nouns that end in *-man*, but are not compounds, form the plural regularly by adding *s*, as, Mussulman, *Mussulmans*. Hyphenated compounds in which the principal word forms the first element change that element to form the plural, as, father-in-law, *fathers-in-law*.

plu·ral·ism (plōōr′əl·iz′əm) *n.* **1.** The condition of being plural. **2.** A social condition in which disparate religious, ethnic, and racial groups are part of a common community. **3.** *Eccl.* The holding at the same time of more than one office. **4.** *Philos.* The doctrine that there are several ultimate substances. Compare DUALISM, MONISM. **— plu′ral·ist** *n.* **— plu′ral·is′tic** *adj.*

plu·ral·i·ty (plŏŏ-ral′ə-tē) *n. pl.* **·ties 1.** In U.S. politics: **a** The number of votes cast for a candidate over and above the number cast for his nearest opponent. **b** In a contest having more than two candidates, the greatest number of votes cast for any one candidate but not more than half the total number of votes cast. Distinguished from *majority.* **2.** The larger or greater portion of anything. **3.** The state or condition of being plural or numerous.

plu·ral·ize (plŏŏr′əl-īz) *v.t.* **·ized, ·iz·ing 1.** To make plural. **2.** To express in the plural. **— plu′ral·i·za′tion** *n.*

pluri- *combining form* More; many; several. [< L *plus, pluris* more]

plus (plus) *prep.* **1.** Added to: Three *plus* two equals five. **2.** Increased by: salary *plus* commission. **— adj. 1.** Of, pertaining to, or involving addition. **2.** Extra; supplemental. **3.** Denoting a value higher than ordinary in a specified grade: B *plus.* **4.** Positive: a *plus* quantity. **5.** *Informal* More of something than can be stated or described: He has personality *plus.* **6.** *Electr.* Positive. **— n. pl. plus·es 1.** The plus sign. **2.** An addition or an extra quantity. **3.** A positive quantity. **— adv. Electr.** Positively. [< L, more]

plus fours Knickerbockers cut very full and bagging below the knees. [Orig. tailor's cant; because they were four inches longer than ordinary knickerbockers]

plush (plush) *n.* A pile fabric of silk, rayon, mohair, etc., having a deeper pile than velvet. **— adj. 1.** Of plush. **2.** *Slang* Luxurious. [< MF < OF < Ital. < L *pilus* hair]

plush·y (plush′ē) *adj.* **plush·i·er, plush·i·est** Of or resembling plush. **— plush′i·ly** *adv.*

plus sign A sign (+) denoting addition or a positive quantity.

Plu·to (plŏŏ′tō) In Greek and Roman mythology, the god of the dead. **— n.** A planet of the solar system, ninth in order from the sun. See PLANET. [< L < Gk. *Ploutōn*]

plu·toc·ra·cy (plŏŏ-tok′rə-sē) *n. pl.* **·cies 1.** Government by the wealthy. **2.** A wealthy class that controls the government. [< Gk. *ploutos* wealth + *krateein* to rule]

plu·to·crat (plŏŏ′tə-krat) *n.* **1.** A member of a plutocracy. **2.** *Informal* Any wealthy person. **— plu′to·crat′ic, plu′to·crat′i·cal** *adj.* **— plu′to·crat′i·cal·ly** *adv.*

plu·ton·ic (plŏŏ-ton′ik) *adj. Geol.* Deeply subterranean in original position: said of igneous rocks. [< L *Pluto, -onis*]

plu·to·ni·um (plŏŏ-tō′nē-əm) *n.* A radioactive element (symbol Pu), formed in the bombardment of neptunium by deuterons. See ELEMENT. [< NL < *Pluto* (the planet)]

Plu·tus (plŏŏ′təs) In Greek mythology, the god of riches, blinded by Zeus. [< L < Gk. *Ploutos < ploutos* wealth]

plu·vi·al (plŏŏ′vē-əl) *adj.* **1.** Of or pertaining to rain. **2.** Caused by the action of rain. [< L *pluvia* rain]

pluvio- *combining form* Rain; pertaining to rain. Also before vowels, **pluvi-.** [< L *pluvia* rain]

ply[1] (plī) *v.t.* **plied, ply·ing** To bend; mold; shape. **— n. pl. plies 1.** A layer, fold, or thickness, as of cloth, etc. **2.** A strand of rope, yarn, thread, etc.; used in combination to mean (a certain) number of folds, twists, or strands: three-*ply* yarn. **3.** A bent; inclination. [< F < L *plicare* to fold]

ply[2] (plī) *v.* **plied, ply·ing** *v.t.* **1.** To use in working, fighting, etc.; wield; employ. **2.** To work at; be engaged in. **3.** To supply with or offer repeatedly: to *ply* a person with drink. **4.** To address (a person) repeatedly with questions, requests, etc. **5.** To strike or assail persistently: He *plied* the donkey with a whip. **6.** To traverse regularly: ferryboats that *ply* the river. **— v.i. 7.** To make regular trips; sail: usu. with *between.* **8.** To work steadily. **9.** To proceed; steer. **10.** *Naut.* To beat; tack. [< APPLY]

Plymouth Rock One of a breed of domestic fowls. [after *Plymouth Rock*]

ply·wood (plī′wŏŏd′) *n.* A structural material consisting of sheets or layers of wood glued together, the grains of adjoining layers usu. being at right angles to each other.

pneu·mat·ic (nŏŏ-mat′ik, nyŏŏ-) *adj.* **1.** Pertaining to pneumatics. **2.** Operated by compressed air. **3.** Pertaining to or containing air or gas. **4.** Spiritual. **5.** Containing air, as cavities in the bones of certain birds. Also **pneu·mat′i·cal.** **— n.** A tire inflated with compressed air. [< L < Gk. < *pneuma* breath, wind] **— pneu·mat′i·cal·ly** *adv.*

pneu·mat·ics (nŏŏ-mat′iks, nyŏŏ-) *n.pl. (construed as sing.)* The branch of physics that treats of the mechanical properties of air and other gases.

pneumato- *combining form* **1.** Air. **2.** Breath; breathing. **3.** Spirit; spirits. Also, before vowels, **pneumat-.** [< Gk. *pneuma, pneumatos* air, spirit, breath < *pneein* to blow]

pneu·ma·tol·o·gy (nŏŏ′mə-tol′ə-jē, nyŏŏ′-) *n. pl.* **·gies** The doctrine or study of the nature and operation of spirit and spiritual beings. **— pneu′ma·to·log′ic (-tə-loj′ik) or ·i·cal** *adj.* **— pneu′ma·tol′o·gist** *n.*

pneumo- *combining form* Lung; related to the lungs; respiratory. Also **pneum-** (before vowels), **pneumono-.** [< Gk. *pneumōn, pneumonos* a lung]

pneu·mo·coc·cus (nŏŏ′mə-kok′əs, nyŏŏ′-) *n. pl.* **·coc·ci** (-kok′sī) Any of a group of bacteria that inhabit the respiratory tract, some of which cause lobar pneumonia. **— pneu′·mo·coc′cal, pneu′mo·coc′cic** (-kok′sik) *adj.*

pneu·mo·nia (nŏŏ-mōn′yə, nyŏŏ-) *n. Pathol.* Inflammation of the lungs, a disease of bacterial or viral origin occurring in many forms, as **bronchial pneumonia** or **lobar pneumonia.** [< NL < Gk. < *pneumōn* lung]

pneu·mon·ic (nŏŏ-mon′ik, nyŏŏ-) *adj.* **1.** Of, pertaining to, or affected with pneumonia. **2.** Pulmonary. [< NL *pneumonicus* < Gk. *pneumonikos < pneumōn* lung]

poach[1] (pōch) *v.t.* To cook (eggs, fish, etc.) in boiling water, milk, or other liquid. [< OF *poche* pocket, pouch; because the egg white forms a pouch around the yolk]

poach[2] (pōch) *v.i.* **1.** To trespass on another's property, etc., esp. for the purpose of taking game or fish. **2.** To take game or fish unlawfully. **— v.t. 3.** To trespass on, as for taking game or fish. **4.** To take (game or fish) unlawfully. [< OF *pocher* to thrust, encroach upon] **— poach′er** *n.*

pock (pok) *n.* **1.** A pustule in an eruptive disease, as in smallpox. **2.** A pockmark. [OE *pocc*]

pock·et (pok′it) *n.* **1.** A small pouch inserted in a garment, for carrying money, etc. **2.** A small bag or pouch. **3.** Any opening, receptacle, or container. **4.** Money, means, or financial interests. **5.** *Mining* **a** A cavity containing ore. **b** An accumulation of ore. **6.** One of the pouches in a billiard or pool table. **7.** An air pocket (which see). **8.** A region or area, usu. small and differentiated in some way from the surrounding area. **— in one's pocket 1.** On terms of close intimacy. **2.** Under one's influence or control. **— adj. 1.** Diminutive, as if pocketable. **2.** Pertaining to, for, or carried in a pocket: *pocket* lining. **— v.t. 1.** To put into or confine in a pocket. **2.** To appropriate as one's own, esp. dishonestly. **3.** To enclose as if in a pocket. **4.** To conceal or suppress: *Pocket* your pride. **5.** To retain without signing. **6.** In billiards, etc., to drive (a ball) into a pocket. [< AF *pokete,* dim. of OF *poque, poche* pouch] **— pock′et·a·ble** *adj.*

pocket billiards Pool[2] (def. 5).

pock·et·book (pok′it-bŏŏk′) *n.* **1.** A wallet. **2.** A woman's purse or handbag. **3.** A book, usu. paperbound and smaller than standard size: also **pocket book.** **4.** Money or financial resources.

pock·et·ful (pok′it-fŏŏl′) *n. pl.* **·fuls** As much as a pocket will hold.

pock·et·knife (pok′it-nīf′) *n. pl.* **·knives** (-nīvz′) A knife having one or more blades that fold into the handle.

pocket money Money for small expenses.

pocket veto *U.S.* An act whereby the President, on being presented a bill by Congress for his signature of approval, retains ("pockets") it unsigned until the session has adjourned, thus causing it to fail without a direct veto.

pock·mark (pok′märk′) *n.* A pit or scar left on the skin by smallpox or a similar disease. **— pock′-marked′** *adj.*

pock·y (pok′ē) *adj.* **pock·i·er, pock·i·est 1.** Pertaining to, resembling, or affected with smallpox. **2.** Marked by pocks.

po·co (pō′kō) *adv. Music* Slightly; a little. [< Ital.]

pod[1] (pod) *n.* **1.** A seed vessel or capsule, esp. of a leguminous plant. **2.** *Aeron.* A separate enclosure on an aircraft, esp. one beneath the wing for a jet engine. **— v.i. pod·ded, pod·ding** To produce pods. [Origin unknown]

pod[2] (pod) *n.* A flock or collection of animals, esp. of seals, whales, or walruses. [Origin unknown]

-pod *combining form* **1.** One who or that which has (a specified number or kind of) feet: *arthropod.* **2.** A (specified kind of) foot. Also **-pode.** [< Gk. *pous, podos* foot]

-poda *combining form Zool.* Plural of -POD: used in names of phyla, orders, classes, etc.: *Arthropoda.*

podg·y (poj′ē) *adj.* **podg·i·er, podg·i·est** Pudgy. [< dial. *podge* to walk slowly and heavily] **— podg′i·ness** *n.*

po·di·a·try (pə-dī′ə-trē, pō-) *n.* Chiropody. [< Gk. *pous, podos* foot + -IATRY] **— po·di′a·trist** *n.*

po·di·um (pō′dē-əm) *n. pl.* **·di·ums** or **·di·a** (-dē-ə) **1.** A small platform or dais for the conductor of an orchestra, a speaker, etc. **2.** *Zool.* A foot, or any footlike structure. [< L < Gk. *podion,* dim. of *pous, podos* foot]

-podium *combining form* A footlike part. [< NL < Gk. *podion,* dim. of *pous, podos* a foot]

-podous *combining form* -footed: used in adjectives corresponding to nouns in -pod and -poda: *arthropodous.*

Po·dunk (pō′dungk) *n.* Any small town regarded as dull and nonprogressive. [? after *Podunk,* Massachusetts]

po·em (pō′əm) *n.* **1.** A composition in verse, characterized by the imaginative treatment of experience and a condensed use of language. **2.** Any composition in verse. **3.** Any composition or work of art characterized by intensity and beauty. [< F < L < Gk. *poiein* to make]

po·e·sy (pō′ə·sē, ·zē) *n. pl.* **·sies 1.** Poetic Poetry taken collectively. **2.** *Poetic* The art of writing poetry.

po·et (pō′it) *n.* **1.** One who writes poems. **2.** One esp. endowed with imagination and the creative faculty or power of artistic expression. **— po′et·ess** *n.fem.*

po·et·as·ter (pō′it·as′tər) *n.* An inferior poet. [< NL]

po·et·ic (pō·et′ik) *adj.* **1.** Of or pertaining to a poet or poetry. **2.** Having the nature or quality of or expressed in poetry: a *poetic* theme. **3.** Having or showing the sensibility, feelings, faculty, etc., of a poet. Also **po·et′i·cal.**

poetic justice The ideal distribution of rewards to the good and punishment to the evil as often represented in literature.

poetic license The departure from fact or rigid rule for the sake of an artistic effect.

po·et·ics (pō·et′iks) *n.pl.* (*usu. construed as sing.*) **1.** The nature, principles, and forms of poetry or, by extension, of any art. **2.** A treatise on poetry.

po·et·ize (pō′it·īz) *v.t. & v.i.* **·ized, ·iz·ing** To write or express in poetry. — **po′et·iz′er** *n.*

poet laureate *pl.* **poets laureate 1.** In Great Britain, the official poet of the realm, a member of the royal household charged with writing verses for particular occasions. **2.** A poet acclaimed as the most eminent in a locality.

po·et·ry (pō′it·rē) *n.* **1.** The art or craft of writing poems. **2.** Poems collectively. **3.** The quality, effect, or spirit of a poem or of anything poetic. **4.** Something that is poetic.

po·go stick (pō′gō) A stiltlike toy, with a spring at the base and fitted with two projections for the feet, on which a person may stand and propel himself in a series of hops.

po·grom (pō′grəm, pō·grom′) *n.* An organized and often officially instigated local massacre, esp. one directed against the Jews. [< Russian, destruction]

po·gy (pō′gē, pog′ē) *n. pl.* **·gies** or **·gy** The menhaden, a fish. [< Algonquian *pauhagen*]

poi (poi, pō′ē) *n.* A native Hawaiian food made from the root of the taro that is first cooked, ground to a paste, then fermented. [< Hawaiian]

-poietic *combining form* Making; producing; creating. [< Gk. *poiētikos* forming < *poieein* to make]

poign·ant (poin′yənt, poi′nənt) *adj.* **1.** Painful and afflicting to the feelings: *poignant* grief. **2.** Piercing, sharp, and cutting: *poignant* sarcasm. **3.** Penetrating and apt: *poignant* observations. [< OF, ppr. of *poindre* to prick] — **poign′an·cy** *n.* — **poign′ant·ly** *adv.*

poi·lu (pwä·lü′) *French adj.* Hairy. — *n.* A French soldier, esp. of World War I.

poin·ci·a·na (poin′sē·a′nə, -än′ə) *n.* **1.** A tropical tree or shrub of the bean family. **2.** A similar tree, the **royal poinciana,** having bright orange and scarlet flowers. [< N L, after M. de *Poinci*, a 17th c. governor of the West Indies]

poin·set·ti·a (poin·set′ē·ə) *n.* Any of various American plants of the spurge family, having large, showy red bracts. [after J. R. *Poinsett,* 1779–1851, U.S. statesman]

point (point) *n.* **1.** The sharp, tapering end of a thing. **2.** Something sharp or tapering, as a needle or dagger. **3.** In printing or writing, a dot, mark, etc. **4.** Any mark of punctuation, esp. a period. **5.** That which is conceived to have position, but not parts, dimension, or extent, as the extremity of a line. **6.** A spot, place, or locality. **7.** A tapering tract of land extending into water. **8.** A fixed place from which position and distance are reckoned. **9.** A particular degree, state, or limit reached or determined: the boiling *point.* **10.** One of the 32 equal divisions that indicate direction on a mariner's compass card, each division equal to an angular distance of 11° 15′, reckoning from north at 0°. For illustration see COMPASS CARD. **11.** A particular moment of time: on the *point* of starting; at the *point* of death. **12.** The important or main purpose or aim: the whole *point* of the inquiry. **13.** Advantage: What's the *point* of telling her? **14.** The main idea; gist: the *point* of the joke. **15.** An important, striking, or effective fact, idea, etc.: She has some good *points* in her argument. **16.** A tip, idea, or suggestion. **17.** Any single item or particular; detail. **18.** A prominent or distinguishing feature, attribute, or peculiarity. **19.** *pl.* The extremities of an animal, as a horse. **20.** A spike or prong on the antler of a deer. **21.** A unit, as in measuring, evaluating, rating, scoring, etc.: A touchdown equals six *points.* **22.** In schools and colleges, a unit of credit equal to a certain number of hours of academic work. **23.** *Printing* A unit of type size, about ½₂ of an inch. **24.** In commerce, one dollar, used in quoting prices of stocks, etc.: Wheat fell four *points.* **25.** The attitude of a pointer or setter when it finds game: The dog came to a *point.* **26.** *Electr.* **a** A contact or conducting part for making or breaking a circuit, as in a distributor, relay, etc. **b** *Brit.* An outlet or socket. **27.** *Brit.* In railroads, a movable rail that tapers to a point, as in a switch. **28.** *Mil.* The individual or group that goes ahead of an advance guard. **29.** The act of pointing. **30.** *Electr.* Any of a set of contacts determining the direction of current flow in a circuit. — **at** (or **on, upon**) **the point of** On the verge of. — **beside the point** Irrelevant. — **in point** Pertinent. — **in point of** In the matter of; as regards. — **to make a point of** To treat as vital or essential. — **to see the point**

To understand the purpose of a course of action; get the important meaning of a story, joke, etc. — **to stretch a point** To make an exception. — **to the point** Relevant; apt. — *v.t.* **1.** To direct or aim, as a finger or weapon. **2.** To indicate; direct attention to: often with *out:* to *point* the way; to *point* out errors. **3.** *Chiefly U.S.* To give force or point to, as a meaning or remark: often with *up.* **4.** To shape or sharpen to a point. **5.** To punctuate, as writing. **6.** To mark or separate with points, as decimal fractions: with *off.* **7.** In hunting, to indicate the presence or location of (game) by standing rigid and directing the muzzle toward it: said of dogs **8.** In masonry, to fill and finish the joints of (brickwork) with mortar. — *v.i.* **9.** To call attention or indicate direction by or as by extending the finger: usually with *at* or *to.* **10.** To direct the mind: Everything *points* to your being wrong. **11.** To be directed; have a specified direction; tend; face: with *to* or *toward.* **12.** To point game: said of hunting dogs. **13.** *Med.* To come to a head, as an abscess. **14.** *Naut.* To sail close to the wind. [< OF *point* dot and *pointe* sharp tip]

point·blank (point′blangk′) *adj.* **1.** Aimed directly at the mark; in gunnery, fired horizontally. **2.** Close enough to aim directly at the mark: *pointblank* range. **3.** Direct; plain: a *pointblank* question. — *n.* A shot with direct aim. — *adv.* **1.** In a straight line; from close range. **2.** Directly; without circumlocution. [? < F *de pointe en blanc* from a point into the white (of a target)]

point·ed (poin′tid) *adj.* **1.** Having a point. **2.** Sharply precise and cutting, as an epigram. **3.** Made clearly evident; emphasized. **4.** Directed or aimed, as at a particular person. — **point′ed·ly** *adv.* — **point′ed·ness** *n.*

point·er (poin′tər) *n.* **1.** One who or that which points. **2.** A hand, index finger, or other indicator, as on a clock or scale. **3.** A long tapering rod used in classrooms to point out things. **4.** One of a breed of smooth-haired dogs trained to scent and point out game. **5.** *Informal* A hint; tip.

pointes (points) *n.pl.* In ballet, dancing on tiptoe. [< F]

poin·til·lism (pwan′ta·liz′əm) *n.* In painting, a method of producing effects of light by placing small spots of varying hues close together on a surface. [< F < *pointiller* to mark with dots] — **point′til·list** *n.*

point lace Needlepoint (def. 2).

point·less (point′lis) *adj.* **1.** Having no point; blunt. **2.** Having no relevance or meaning. **3.** Having no force; ineffective. **4.** Having no points scored. — **point′less·ly** *adv.* — **point′less·ness** *n.*

point of honor Something that vitally affects one's honor.

point of no return That stage or position in any enterprise, course, action, etc., beyond which there can be no return to the starting point; a state of total commitment.

point of order A question as to whether or not the correct parliamentary procedure is being observed.

point of view 1. The place or position from which one views an object, situation etc. **2.** An attitude or viewpoint.

poise (poiz) *v.* **poised, pois·ing** *v.t.* **1.** To bring into or hold in balance; maintain in equilibrium. **2.** To hold; support, as in readiness. — *v.i.* **3.** To be balanced or suspended; hover. — *n.* **1.** The state or quality of being balanced; equilibrium. **2.** Repose and dignity of manner; self-possession. **3.** Physical ease or balance. **4.** Any condition of hovering or suspended motion. **5.** Indecision; suspense. [< OF < L *pendere* to weigh, suspend]

poi·son (poi′zən) *n.* **1.** Any substance that, either taken internally by or coming into contact with an organism, acts chemically upon the tissues in such a way as to harm or destroy. **2.** Anything that tends to harm, destroy, or corrupt. — *v.t.* **1.** To administer poison to; kill or injure with poison. **2.** To put poison into or on. **3.** To corrupt; pervert: to *poison* one's mind. — *adj.* Poisonous. [< OF < L *potio, -onis* drink, esp. a poisonous one] — **poi′son·er** *n.*

poison dogwood Poison sumac. Also **poison elder.**

poison ivy A climbing shrub related to sumac, having glossy, variously notched, trifoliate leaves, greenish flowers, whitish berries, and blistering poison.

poison oak 1. Any of various shrubs related to poison ivy or poison sumac. **2.** A species of poison ivy common in the western U.S.

poi·son·ous (poi′zən·əs) *adj.* **1.** Containing or being a poison. **2.** Having the effect of a poison; toxic. — **poi′son·ous·ly** *adv.* — **poi′son·ous·ness** *n.*

poison sumac A shrub or small tree growing in swamps in

POISON IVY (*a*) AND POISON SUMAC (*b*)

the U.S. and Canada, having smooth, entire leaflets, panicles of greenish yellow berries, and a strong poison.

poke¹ (pōk) *v.* **poked, pok·ing** *v.t.* **1.** To push or prod, as with the elbow; jab. **2.** To make by or as by thrusting. **3.** To thrust or push in, out, through, from, etc.: to *poke* one's head from a window. **4.** To stir (a fire, etc.) by prodding: often with *up.* — *v.i.* **5.** To make thrusts, as with a stick: often with *at.* **6.** To intrude or meddle. **7.** To go or look curiously; pry. **8.** To appear or show. **9.** To proceed slowly; dawdle; putter: often with *along.* — **to poke one's nose into** To meddle in. — **to poke fun at** To ridicule, esp. slyly. — *n.* **1.** A push; prod. **2.** One who moves sluggishly; a dawdler. **3.** *Informal* A punch. [< MLG *poken*]

poke² (pōk) *n.* A pocket or small bag. [< OF < Gmc.]

poke³ (pōk) *n.* A large bonnet with projecting front or brim. Also **poke bonnet.** [Prob. < POKE¹]

poke·ber·ry (pōk'ber'ē) *n.* *pl.* **·ries 1.** A berry of the pokeweed. **2.** The pokeweed plant.

pok·er¹ (pō'kər) *n.* **1.** One who or that which pokes. **2.** A metal rod for poking a fire.

pok·er² (pō'kər) *n.* Any of several games of cards in which the players bet on the value of the cards dealt to them, the winner being he whose hand contains the cards of highest value. [Cf. G *pochspiel,* lit., boast game < *pochen* to boast]

poker face *Informal* A face that reveals nothing: so called from the inscrutable faces of skillful poker players.

poke·weed (pōk'wēd') *n.* A stout perennial North American herb, having purple berries, edible shoots, and a medicinal root: also called *pokeberry.* Also **poke'root'** (-rōōt', -rŏot'). [< Algonquian (Virginian) *pakon* weed used for staining < *pak* blood]

pok·y (pō'kē) *adj.* **pok·i·er, pok·i·est** *Informal* **1.** Lacking briskness; dull; slow. **2.** Shabby or dowdy, as dress. **3.** Cramped; stuffy. Also **poke'y.**

Poland China An American mixed breed of large pigs.

po·lar (pō'lər) *adj.* **1.** Of the poles of a sphere, magnet, etc. **2.** Of, from, or near the North or South Pole. **3.** Directly opposite in character, etc. **4.** *Chem.* Exhibiting ionization. [< Med.L < L *polos* pivot, pole]

polar bear A large, white bear of arctic regions.

Po·lar·is (pō·lar'is, -lâr'-) *n.* One of the 20 brightest stars, 2.12 magnitude; Alpha in the constellation Ursa Minor: also called *Cynosure, polestar, North Star.* [< L]

po·lar·i·scope (pō·lar'ə·skōp) *n.* An optical instrument for exhibiting or measuring the polarization of light, or for examining substances in polarized light.

po·lar·i·ty (pō·lar'ə·tē, -lâr'-) *n.* *pl.* **·ties 1.** The quality or condition of having poles. **2.** *Physics* The possession by a body of two poles, the properties at one pole being of opposite or contrasting nature to the properties at the other pole, as in a magnet. **3.** The quality or condition of being attracted to one pole and repelled from the other. **4.** The possession of two contrary qualities, tendencies, etc.

po·lar·i·za·tion (pō'lər·ə·zā'shən, -ī·zā'-) *n.* **1.** The possession or bestowal of polarity. **2.** *Physics* A condition of electromagnetic waves, most noticeable in light, in which one component of its oscillation is limited to a certain plane, as by transmission through variously oriented crystals or other suitable media. **3.** *Electr.* A change in the potential of a cell due to the accumulation of liberated gases.

po·lar·ize (pō'lə·rīz) *v.* **·ized, ·iz·ing** *v.t.* **1.** To develop polarization in; give polarity to. — *v.i.* **2.** To acquire polarity. — **po'lar·iz'a·ble** *adj.* — **po'lar·iz'er** *n.*

Po·lar·oid (pō'lə·roid) *n.* A plastic capable of polarizing the light passing through: a trade name. Also **po'lar·oid.**

Polar Regions The areas within the Arctic and Antarctic circles.

pole¹ (pōl) *n.* **1.** Either of the two extremities of the axis of a sphere or any spheroidal body. **2.** One of the two points where the earth's axis of rotation meets the surface, called the North *Pole* and the South *Pole.* **3.** *Physics* One of the two points at which opposite qualities or forces are concentrated, as in a magnet. **4.** Either of two diametrically opposite forces, tendencies, etc. — **to be poles apart** (or **asunder**) To differ greatly. [< OF < L < Gk. *polos* pivot, pole]

pole² (pōl) *n.* **1.** A long, comparatively slender piece of wood or metal. **2.** A unit of linear measure, usu. equal to 16.5 feet. **3.** A unit of square measure equal to a square rod or 30.25 square yards. — *v.t. & v.i.* **poled, pol·ing** To propel or push (a boat, raft, etc.) with a pole. [OE < L *palus* stake]

Pole (pōl) *n.* A native or inhabitant of Poland.

pole·ax (pōl'aks') *n.* An ax, or a combined ax and pick, set on a long pole; a battle-ax. — *v.t.* To strike or fell with a poleax. Also **pole'axe'.** [ME *pol* poll + AX]

pole·cat (pōl'kat') *n.* **1.** A European carnivore allied to the weasel, noted for its offensive odor. **2.** *U.S.* A skunk. [< F *poule* pullet + CAT; from its predacity]

po·lem·ic (pō·lem'ik) *adj.* Of or pertaining to controversy; disputatious. Also **po·lem'i·cal.** — *n.* **1.** An argument or controversy. **2.** One who engages in argument or controversy. [< Gk. < *polemos* war]

po·lem·ics (pō·lem'iks) *n.pl.* (*construed as sing.*) The art or practice of disputation, esp., theological disputation. — **po·lem'i·cist** (-ə·sist) *n.*

pole·star (pōl'stär') *n.* Polaris.

pole-vault (pōl'vôlt') *v.i.* To perform a pole vault. — **pole'-vault'er** *n.*

pole vault An athletic event in which a vault or jump over a high, horizontal bar is made with the help of a long pole.

po·lice (pə·lēs') *n.* **1.** An official civil force or department organized to maintain order, prevent and detect crime, and enforce law. **2.** (*construed as pl.*) The members of such a force. **3.** In a community, the maintenance of order, law, health, safety, etc. **4.** In the U.S. Army: **a** The cleaning or keeping clean of a camp or garrison. **b** A group of soldiers assigned to some specific duty or duties: kitchen *police.* — *v.t.* **·liced, ·lic·ing 1.** To protect, regulate, or maintain order in (a city, etc.) with or as with police. **2.** *U.S.* To make clean or orderly, as a military camp. [< MF < LL < Gk. < *politēs* citizen < *polis* city]

police dog A German shepherd dog.

po·lice·man (pə·lēs'mən) *n.* *pl.* **·men** (-mən) A member of a police force.

police state A country whose citizens are rigidly supervised by a national police, often working secretly.

po·lice·wom·an (pə·lēs'wŏōm'ən) *n.* *pl.* **·wom·en** (-wim'-in) A woman member of a police force.

pol·i·clin·ic (pol'i·klin'ik) *n.* The department of a hospital in which outpatients are treated. Compare POLYCLINIC. [< G < Gk. *polis* city + *klinik* clinic]

pol·i·cy¹ (pol'ə·sē) *n.* *pl.* **·cies 1.** Any plan of action, esp. in governmental or business administration: a nation's foreign *policy.* **2.** Prudence, wisdom, or shrewdness, as in conduct or the management of one's affairs; also, any act or plan based on such principles: It was his *policy* always to be silent. [< OF < LL < Gk. *politeia* polity]

pol·i·cy² (pol'ə·sē) *n.* *pl.* **·cies** A written contract of insurance. [< MF < Ital. < Med.L < Gk. *apodeiknynai* to show forth] — **pol'i·cy·hol'der** *n.*

po·li·o (pō'lē·ō) *n. Informal* Poliomyelitis.

polio- *combining form Med.* Of or pertaining to the gray matter of the brain or the spinal cord. [< Gk. *polios* gray]

po·li·o·my·e·li·tis (pō'lē·ō·mī'ə·lī'tis, pō'lē-) *n. Pathol.* An acute, infectious virus disease, occurring esp. in children, and characterized by inflammation of the gray matter of the spinal cord, followed by paralysis and atrophy of various muscle groups: also called *infantile paralysis.* [< NL < Gk. *polios* gray + *myelos* marrow + -ITIS]

pol·ish (pol'ish) *n.* **1.** Smoothness or glossiness of surface. **2.** A substance used to produce a smooth or glossy surface. **3.** Refinement or elegance. **4.** The process of polishing. — *v.t.* **1.** To make smooth or lustrous, as by rubbing. **2.** To complete; perfect. **3.** To free from crudity, etc. — *v.i.* **4.** To take a gloss. **5.** To become elegant or refined. — **to polish off 1.** To do or finish completely. **2.** To dispose of. — **to polish up** To improve. [< OF < L *polire* to smooth] — **pol'ished** *adj.* — **pol'ish·er** *n.*

Po·lish (pō'lish) *adj.* Of or pertaining to Poland, its inhabitants, or their language. — *n.* The West Slavic language of the Poles.

Po·lit·bu·ro (pol'it·byŏōr'ō) *n.* The leading committee of the Communist party in the Soviet Union, replaced in 1952 by the Presidium. [< Russian *polit(icheskoe) buro*]

po·lite (pə·līt') *adj.* **·lit·er, ·lit·est 1.** Courteous; mannerly. **2.** Refined; cultured; polished: *polite* society. [< L *polire* to polish] — **po·lite'ly** *adv.* — **po·lite'ness** *n.*

— **Syn. 1.** *Polite* implies punctilious observance of the forms of speech and action customary among well-bred persons. *Civil* is weaker, implying little more than the avoidance of rudeness. To be *courteous* is to be *polite* while having also a warmer regard for the feelings and dignity of others. — **Ant.** impolite, rude, boorish.

po·li·tesse (pō·lē·tes') *n. French* Politeness; civility.

pol·i·tic (pol'ə·tik) *adj.* **1.** Skillful, ingenious, or shrewd. **2.** Crafty; sly; cunning. **3.** Wise, prudent, or expedient: a *politic* move. **4.** Political: see BODY POLITIC. [< OF < L < Gk. *politēs* citizen < *polis* city] — **pol'i·tic·ly** *adv.*

— **Syn. 1.** diplomatic, discreet. **2.** wily. **3.** See EXPEDIENT.

po·lit·i·cal (pə·lit'i·kəl) *adj.* **1.** Of or concerned with government. **2.** Of, relating to, or involved in politics. **3.** Characteristic of or similar to politics or politicians. **4.** Having an organized system of government. [< L < Gk. *politēs* citizen] — **po·lit'i·cal·ly** *adv.*

political economist A person skilled in political economy.

political economy Economics.

political science The science of the form, principles, and conduct of civil government.

pol·i·ti·cian (pol'ə·tish'ən) *n.* **1.** One who is engaged in politics, esp. professionally. **2.** One who engages in politics for personal or partisan aims. **3.** One who is skilled in the science of government or politics; a statesman.

po·lit·i·co (pə·lit'i·kō) *n.* *pl.* **·cos** A politician. [< Sp. < L *politicus*]

pol·i·tics (pol'ə·tiks) *n.pl.* (*Usu. construed as sing.*) **1.** The science or art of government. **2.** The affairs or activities of those engaged in controlling or seeking to control a government; also, the profession or area of activity of such persons. **3.** The principles, aims, or policies of a government. **4.** The acts or practices of those who seek any position of power or advantage. **5.** Political opinions. [< OF < L < Gk. *politēs* citizen]

pol·i·ty (pol'ə·tē) *n.* *pl.* **·ties 1.** The form or method of government of a nation, state, church, etc. **2.** Any community living under some definite form of government. [< MF < L < Gk. *politeia* polity]

pol·ka (pōl'kə, pō'-) *n.* **1.** A lively round dance consisting of three quick steps and a hop. **2.** Music for this dance, in duple meter. — *v.i.* **·kaed, ·ka·ing** To dance the polka. [< F < Czech *pulka* half step < *Polak* a Pole]

polka dot 1. One of a series of round dots decorating a textile fabric. **2.** A pattern or fabric made up of such dots.

poll (pōl) *n.* **1.** The voting at an election. **2.** The total number of votes cast or registered. **3.** *pl.* The place where votes are cast and counted. **4.** A survey of public opinion on a given subject, usu. obtained from a sample group. **5.** A list of persons. **6.** The head, esp. the top or back of the head where hair grows. — *v.t.* **1.** To receive (a specified number of votes). **2.** To enroll, as for taxation or voting; register. **3.** To cast (a vote) at the polls. **4.** To canvass in a poll (def. 4). **5.** To cut off or trim, as hair, horns, etc. **6.** To cut off or trim the hair, horns, top, etc.; of: to poll cattle. — *v.i.* **7.** To vote at the polls; cast one's vote. [< MDu. *polle* top of the head] — **poll'er** *n.*

pol·lack (pol'ək) *n.* A food fish of the North Atlantic: also spelled **pollock.** [< Scot. *podlok*]

pol·len (pol'ən) *n.* The male or fertilizing element in a seed plant, consisting of fine yellowish powder formed within the anther of the stamen. [< L, fine flour]

pollen count A measure of the relative concentration of pollen grains in the atmosphere at a given locality and date, usually expressed as the number of grains per cubic yard.

pol·li·nate (pol'ə·nāt) *v.t.* **·nat·ed, ·nat·ing** *Bot.* To supply or convey pollen to. Also **pol'len·ate.** — **pol'li·na'tion** *n.*

pol·li·wog (pol'ē·wog) *n.* A tadpole. Also **pol'ly·wog.** [ME *polwygle*]

poll·ster (pōl'stər) *n.* One who takes polls. Also **poll'ist.**

poll tax A tax on a person, as distinguished from that on property, esp. as a prerequisite for voting.

pol·lute (pə·lōōt') *v.t.* **·lut·ed, ·lut·ing** To make unclean or impure; dirty; corrupt; profane. [< L < *polluere* to defile] — **pol·lut'er** *n.* — **pol·lu'tion** *n.*

Pol·lux (pol'əks) In Greek mythology, the twin brother of Castor. See CASTOR AND POLLUX. — *n.* One of the 20 brightest stars, 1.21 magnitude; Beta in the constellation Gemini.

Pol·ly·an·na (pol'ē·an'ə) *n.* One who persistently finds good in everything. [after stories by Eleanor H. Porter, 1868–1920]

po·lo (pō'lō) *n.* **1.** A hockeylike game played on horseback, usu. with a light wooden ball and long-handled mallets. **2.** A similar game played on ice, roller skates, in the water, etc. [Prob. < Tibetan *pulu* ball] — **po'lo·ist** *n.*

pol·o·naise (pol'ə·nāz', pō'lə-) *n.* **1.** A stately, marchlike Polish dance. **2.** Music for this dance, in triple meter. [< F (*danse*) *polonaise* Polish (dance)]

po·lo·ni·um (pə·lō'nē·əm) *n.* A radioactive element (symbol Po) produced by the disintegration of various uranium minerals, discovered in 1898 by Pierre and Marie Sklodowska Curie. See ELEMENT. [< NL < Med.L *Polonia* Poland]

pol·ter·geist (pōl'tər·gīst) *n.* A ghost or spirit reputed to make much noise. [< G, lit., noisy ghost]

pol·troon (pol·trōōn') *n.* A mean-spirited coward; craven; dastard. — *adj.* Cowardly; contemptible. [< F < Ital. *poltrone* coward < *poltro* colt] — **pol·troon'er·y** *n.*

poly- *combining form* **1.** Many; several; much: *polygamy.* **2.** Excessive; abnormal. [< Gk. *polys* much, many]

pol·y·an·dry (pol'ē·an'drē) *n.* The condition of having more than one husband at the same time. [< Gk. < *poly-* many + *anēr, andros* man, husband] — **pol'y·an'drous** *adj.*

pol·y·cen·trism (pol'ē·sen'triz·əm) *n.* The existence of several centers of power in the Communist world, as Peking and Belgrade, where Moscow had formerly been the single undisputed center. — **pol'y·cen'trist** *n.* & *adj.*

pol·y·clin·ic (pol'i·klin'ik) *n.* A hospital or clinic in which all forms of diseases are treated. Compare POLICLINIC.

po·lyg·a·mous (pə·lig'ə·məs) *adj.* **1.** Of, pertaining to, practicing, or characterized by polygamy. **2.** *Bot.* Bearing unisexual and bisexual or hermaphrodite flowers on the same plant. — **po·lyg'a·mous·ly** *adv.*

po·lyg·a·my (pə·lig'ə·mē) *n.* **1.** The condition or practice of having more than one wife or husband at the same time.

2. *Zool.* The state of having more than one mate at the same time. [< F < LL < Gk. < *poly-* many + *gamos* marriage] — **po·lyg'a·mist** *n.*

pol·y·glot (pol'i·glot) *adj.* Expressed in several tongues or speaking several languages; multilingual. — *n.* **1.** A polyglot book or person. **2.** A mixture of several languages. [< Gk. < *poly-* many + *glōtta* tongue] — **pol'y·glot'ism** *n.*

pol·y·gon (pol'i·gon) *n.* *Geom.* A closed, usu. plane, figure bounded by straight lines or arcs, esp. by more than four. [< L < Gk. < *poly-* many + *gōnia* angle] — **po·lyg·o·nal** (pə·lig'ə·nəl), **pol·yg'o·nous** *adj.* — **po·lyg'o·nal·ly** *adv.*

pol·y·graph (pol'i·graf, -gräf) *n.* **1.** A device for multiplying or reproducing a drawing or writing. **2.** A versatile or prolific author. **3.** An electrical device for simultaneously recording variations in the heartbeat, blood pressure, muscle reflexes, and respiratory movements, sometimes used as a lie detector. [< Gk. *polygraphos* writing much] — **pol'y·graph'ic** or **·i·cal** *adj.* — **po·lyg·ra·phy** (pə·lig'rə·fē) *n.*

po·lyg·y·ny (pə·lij'ə·nē) *n.* The condition of having more than one wife at the same time. [< POLY- + Gk. *gynē* woman] — **po·lyg'y·nous** (pə·lij'ə·nəs) *adj.*

pol·y·he·dron (pol'i·hē'drən) *n.* *pl.* **·dra** (-drə) or **·drons** *Geom.* A solid bounded by plane faces, esp. by more than four. [< NL < Gk. < *poly-* many + *hedra* base, side] — **pol'y·he'dral** *adj.*

Pol·y·hym·ni·a (pol'i·him'nē·ə) The Muse of sacred song. Also **Po·lym·ni·a** (pə·lim'nē·ə).

pol·y·mer (pol'i·mər) *n.* *Chem.* Any of two or more compounds formed by polymerization. [< Gk. *polymerēs* manifold < *poly-* many + *meros* part]

pol·y·mer·ic (pol'i·mer'ik) *adj.* *Chem.* Having the same chemical composition but different molecular weights and different properties, as acetylene and benzene.

po·lym·er·ism (pə·lim'ə·riz'əm, pol'i·mə-) *n.* *Chem.* The condition of being polymeric.

po·lym·er·i·za·tion (pə·lim'ər·ə·zā'shən, pol'i·mər·ə-) *n.* *Chem.* The process of changing the molecular arrangement of a compound so as to form new compounds having the same percentage composition as the original, but of greater molecular weight and different properties.

po·lym·er·ize (pə·lim'ə·rīz, pol'i·mə·rīz') *v.t.* & *v.i.* **·ized, ·iz·ing** To subject to or undergo polymerization. Also *Brit.* **po·lym'er·ise.**

pol·y·morph (pol'i·môrf) *n.* A substance or organism that exhibits polymorphism. [< Gk. < *poly-* many + *morphē* form]

pol·y·morph·ism (pol'i·môr'fiz·əm) *n.* The property of having, assuming, or passing through several forms or characters. — **pol'y·mor'phic, pol'y·mor'phous** *adj.*

Pol·y·ne·sian (pol'i·nē'zhən, -shən) *n.* **1.** One of the native brown-skinned people of Polynesia. **2.** A subfamily of the Austronesian family of languages spoken by these people. — *adj.* Of or pertaining to Polynesia, its people, or their languages.

pol·y·no·mi·al (pol'i·nō'mē·əl) *adj.* Of, pertaining to, or consisting of many names or terms. — *n.* **1.** *Math.* An expression, as in algebra, containing two or more terms. **2.** *Biol.* A scientific name consisting of more than two terms. [< POLY- + *-nomial,* as in BINOMIAL]

pol·yp (pol'ip) *n.* **1.** *Pathol.* **a** A smooth growth of hypertrophied mucus found in mucous membrane, as in the nasal passages. **b** A tumor. **2.** *Zool.* **a** A single individual forming part of a colonial marine animal, esp. a hydrozoan. **b** A hydra. [< MF < L < Gk. < *poly-* many + *pou-* foot] — **pol'y·pous** *adj.*

pol·y·pet·al·ous (pol'i·pet'əl·əs) *adj.* *Bot.* Having the petals free and distinct. [< NL *polypetalus* < Gk. *poly-* many + *petalon* leaf]

pol·y·phase (pol'i·fāz) *adj.* *Electr.* Having or producing several phases, as an alternating current.

pol·y·phon·ic (pol'i·fon'ik) *adj.* **1.** Consisting of many sounds or voices. **2.** *Music* Designating or involving the simultaneous combination of two or more independent melodic parts. Also **po·lyph·o·nous** (pə·lif'ə·nəs). [< Gk. < *poly-* many + *phōnē* voice]

po·lyph·o·ny (pə·lif'ə·nē, pol'i·fō'nē) *n.* *pl.* **·nies 1.** Multiplicity of sounds, as in an echo. **2.** The representation by one written character or sign of more than one sound. **3.** Polyphonic music.

pol·y·ploid (pol'i·ploid') *adj.* *Genetics* Having more than twice the normal number of chromosomes. — *n.* An organism with more than two chromosome sets.

pol·y·pod (pol'i·pod) *adj.* **1.** Having many feet. **2.** *Zool.* Pertaining to many-footed organisms. — *n.* A myriapod. [< POLY- + -POD]

pol·y·pus (pol'i·pəs) *n.* *pl.* **·pi** (-pī) *Pathol.* A polyp.

pol·y·syl·lab·ic (pol'i·si·lab'ik) *adj.* **1.** Having or pertaining to several syllables, esp. to more than three. **2.** Characterized by words of more than three syllables. Also **pol·y·syl·lab·i·cal**. [< MF < Med.L < Gk. < *poly-* many + *syllabē* syllable]

pol·y·syl·la·ble (pol/i-sil/ə-bəl) *n*. A polysyllabic word. — **pol·y·syl·la·bism** or **-syl·lab·i·cism** (pol/i-si-lab/ə-siz/əm) *n*.

pol·y·tech·nic (pol/i-tek/nik) *adj*. Embracing many arts: also **pol·y·tech·ni·cal**. — *n*. A school of applied science and the industrial arts. [< F < Gk. < *poly-* many + *technē* craft, art]

pol·y·the·ism (pol/i-thē-iz/əm) *n*. The belief in and worship of more gods than one. [< F < Gk. < *poly-* many + *theos* god] — **pol/y·the/ist** *n*. — **pol/y·the·is/tic** or **·is/ti·cal** *adj*.

pol·y·va·lent (pol/i-vā/lənt) *adj*. **1.** *Bacteriol*. Designating a type of vaccine containing antibodies derived from two or more different strains of microorganisms. **2.** *Chem*. Multivalent. — **pol/y·va/lence** *n*.

pom·ace (pum/is) *n*. **1.** The pulpy substance of apples or similar fruit after grinding. **2.** The pulpy substance of anything ground. [< Med.L *pomacium* cider < L *pomum* apple]

po·ma·ceous (pō-mā/shəs) *adj*. **1.** Relating to or made of apples. **2.** Of or pertaining to a pome.

po·made (pō-mād/, -mäd/) *n*. A perfumed dressing for the hair or scalp. — *v.t.* **mad·ed, ·mad·ing** To anoint with pomade. [< MF < Ital. < L *pomum* apple]

pome (pōm) *n*. *Bot*. A fleshy fruit with a core, as an apple, quince, pear, or the like. [< OF, apple < L *pomum*]

pome·gran·ate (pom/gran·it, pum/-, pəm·gran/it) *n*. **1.** The fruit of a tropical Asian and African tree about the size of an orange and having many seeds. **2.** The tree itself. [< OF *pome* apple + *grenate* < L *granatum* seeded]

Pom·e·ra·ni·an (pom/ə·rā/nē·ən) *adj*. Relating to Pomerania or its inhabitants. — *n*. **1.** A native or inhabitant of Pomerania. **2.** One of a breed of small dog with pointed ears, a bushy tail, and long, straight, silky coat.

pom·mel (pum/əl, pom/-) *n*. **1.** A knob, as on the hilt of a sword, bayonet, etc. **2.** A knob at the front and on the top of a saddle. — *v.t.* **pom·meled** or **·melled, pom·mel·ing** or **·mel·ling** To beat with or as with the fists or a pommel. Also spelled *pummel*. [< OF *pomel* rounded knob]

po·mol·o·gy (pō-mol/ə·jē) *n*. The science that deals with fruits and fruit culture. [< NL < L *pomum* an apple, fruit + -LOGY] — **po·mo·log·i·cal** (pō/mə·loj/i·kəl) *adj*. — **po/mo·log/i·cal·ly** *adv*. — **po·mol/o·gist** *n*.

pomp (pomp) *n*. **1.** Magnificent or stately display; splendor. **2.** Ostentatious display; vain show. [< OF < L < Gk. *pompē* a sending, procession]

pom·pa·dour (pom/pə·dôr, -dŏor, -dōr) *n*. A style of arranging hair by puffing it over the forehead. [after the Marquise de *Pompadour*, 1721–64]

pom·pa·no (pom/pə·nō) *n*. *pl*. **·nos** Any of various spiny-finned food fishes of warm seas. [< Sp. *pámpano*]

pom·pon (pom/pon, *Fr*. pôn·pôn/) *n*. **1.** A tuft or ball, as of wool, ribbon, etc., worn on hats, on costumes, etc. **2.** A small, compact variety of chrysanthemum or dahlia. [< F]

pom·pos·i·ty (pom·pos/ə·tē) *n*. *pl*. **·ties** The state or quality of being pompous in manner or speech.

pom·pous (pom/pəs) *adj*. **1.** Marked by exaggerated dignity or self-importance. **2.** Bombastic and florid, as speech. **3.** Full of pomp. [See POMP.] — **pom/pous·ness** *n*. — **pom/pous·ly** *adv*.

pon·cho (pon/chō) *n*. *pl*. **·chos 1.** A South American cloak like a blanket with a hole in the middle for the head. **2.** A similar waterproofed garment, used as a raincoat. [< Sp.]

pond (pond) *n*. A body of still water, smaller than a lake. [ME *ponde*, var. of POUND[2]]

pon·der (pon/dər) *v.t.* **1.** To weigh in the mind; consider carefully. — *v.i.* **1.** To meditate; reflect. [< OF < L *ponderare* to weigh] — **pon/der·er** *n*.

pon·der·a·ble (pon/dər·ə·bəl) *adj*. Capable of being weighed; having appreciable weight. — **pon/der·a·bil/i·ty** *n*.

pon·der·ous (pon/dər·əs) *adj*. **1.** Having great weight; also, huge; bulky. **2.** Heavy to the extent of dullness; lumbering. [< F < L < *pondus, ponderis* weight] — **pon/der·os/i·ty** (-də·ros/ə·tē), **pon/der·ous·ness** *n*. — **pon/der·ous·ly** *adv*.

pond lily Any of various plants of the water-lily family.

pond scum Any of a group of free-floating, fresh-water green algae that form a scum on ponds.

pond·weed (pond/wēd/) *n*. Any of various perennial aquatic plants that grow in ponds and streams.

pone (pōn) *n*. *Southern U.S.* Corn pone.

pon·gee (pon·jē/) *n*. A thin, natural, unbleached silk with a rough weave, originally made in China from wild silkworms. [? < Chinese *pen chi* home loom]

pon·iard (pon/yərd) *n*. A dagger. — *v.t.* To stab with a poniard. [< MF < OF *poing* fist < L *pugnus*]

pons (ponz) *n*. *pl*. **pon·tes** (pon/tēz) **1.** A bridge: used in Latin phrases. **2.** The pons Varolii. [< L]

pons Va·ro·li·i (ponz və·rō/lē·ī) *Anat*. A broad band of nerve fibers that connect the cerebrum, cerebellum, and medulla oblongata. [< NL, bridge of Varoli; after Costanzo *Varoli*, 1543?–75, Italian anatomist]

pon·ti·fex (pon/tə·feks) *n*. *pl*. **pon·tif·i·ces** (pon·tif/ə·sēz) In ancient Rome, a priest belonging to the Pontifical College. [< L *pons, pontis* bridge + *facere* to make]

pon·tiff (pon/tif) *n*. **1.** In the Roman Catholic Church: **a** The Pope. **b** Any bishop. **2.** In ancient Rome, a pontifex. [< MF *pontife* < L *pontifex* pontifex] — **pon·tif/ic** *adj*.

pon·tif·i·cal (pon·tif/i·kəl) *adj*. **1.** Of, pertaining to, or suitable for a pope or bishop. **2.** Haughty; pompous; dogmatic. — **pon·tif/i·cal·ly** *adv*.

Pontifical College In ancient Rome, the highest priestly group that had supreme jurisdiction in religious matters.

pon·tif·i·cate (*n*. pon·tif/ə·kit, -kāt/; *v*. -kāt/) *v.i.* **·cat·ed, ·cat·ing 1.** To act or speak pompously or dogmatically. **2.** To perform the office of a pontiff. — *n*. The office or term of a pontiff.

pon·ton (pon/tən) *n*. *U.S. Mil*. A pontoon.

pon·toon (pon·tōon/) *n*. **1.** *Mil*. A flat-bottomed boat, air-tight metal cylinder, or the like, used in the construction of temporary floating bridges over rivers. **2.** A pontoon bridge. **3.** Either of the floats on the landing gear of a seaplane. [< MF < L *pons, pontis* bridge]

pontoon bridge A bridge supported on pontoons. Also **ponton bridge**.

po·ny (pō/nē) *n*. *pl*. **·nies 1.** A breed of very small horse, esp. one not over 14 hands high. **2.** Any small horse. **3.** *U.S. Slang* A translation used to prepare foreign language lessons: also called *trot*. **4.** Anything that is small for its kind. **5.** *Informal* **a** A very small glass for liquor or its contents. — *v.t.* & *v.i.* **·nied, ·ny·ing** *U.S. Slang* **1.** To translate lessons with the aid of a pony. **2.** To pay (money) that is due: with *up*. [< dial. E (Scottish) *powney*]

pony express A former postal system by which mail was relayed by riders mounted on swift ponies.

pooch (pōoch) *n*. *Slang* A dog; esp., a small mongrel. [? < dial. E and obs. *pooch*, var. of POUCH]

poo·dle (pōod/l) *n*. One of a breed of dogs of high intelligence, with long, curly, usu. white or black hair. [< G *pudel* < *pudeln* to splash in water]

pooh (pōo) *interj*. An exclamation of contempt, disdain, etc.

Pooh-Bah (pōo/bä/) *n*. *Informal* A pretentious, pompous official. [after a character in Gilbert and Sullivan's *The Mikado*]

pooh-pooh (pōo/pōo/) *v.t.* To reject or speak of disdainfully. [Reduplication of POOH]

pool[1] (pōol) *n*. **1.** A small body of fresh water, as a spring. **2.** A deep place in a stream. **3.** Any small, isolated body of liquid: a *pool* of blood. **4.** A swimming pool. [OE *pōl*]

pool[2] (pōol) *n*. **1.** In certain gambling games, a collective stake. **2.** In business, a combination whereby companies agree to fix prices in order to overcome competition. **3.** In finance, any combination formed for a speculative operation, as in stocks. **4.** Any combining of efforts or resources: a typists' *pool*. **5.** Any of various games played on a six-pocket billiard table: also *pocket billiards*. See BILLIARDS. — *v.t.* **1.** To combine in a mutual fund or pool. — *v.i.* **2.** To form a pool. [< F < L *pulla* stake]

pool·room (pōol/rōom/, -rŏom/) *n*. A commercial establishment or room equipped for the playing of pool, billiards, etc.

pool table A six-pocket billiard table for playing pool.

poop[1] (pōop) *Naut*. *n*. **1.** The after part or stern of a ship. **2.** A short deck built over the main deck at the stern of a ship: also **poop deck**. — *v.t.* **1.** To break over the stern or poop of: said of a wave. **2.** To take (a wave) over the stern. [< OF < OProvençal < L *puppis*]

poop[2] (pōop) *U.S. Slang v.t.* To tire: usu. in the passive: He was *pooped* by the long climb. [Origin unknown]

poor (pōor) *adj*. **1.** Lacking means of comfortable subsistence; needy. **2.** Characterized by poverty: a *poor* neighborhood. **3.** Lacking in abundance; scanty; meager: a *poor* crop. **4.** Lacking in fertility; sterile: *poor* soil. **5.** Inferior in workmanship or quality. **6.** Feeble; frail: *poor* health. **7.** Thin from bad feeding; lean, as cattle. **8.** Contemptible; mean. **9.** Lacking proper ability; unsatisfactory. **10.** Deserving of pity. — *n*. Indigent or needy people collectively: preceded by *the*. [< OF < L *pauper* poor] — **poor/ly** *adv*. & *adj*. — **poor/ness** *n*.

poor·house (pōor/hous/) *n*. A public establishment maintained as a dwelling for paupers.

poor-spir·it·ed (pōor/spir/it·ed) *adj*. Having little spirit or courage. — Syn. See COWARDLY. — **poor/-spir/it·ed·ness** *n*.

poor white In the southern U.S., a member of a class of poverty-stricken white farmers or laborers: an offensive term. Also **poor white trash**.

pop[1] (pop) *v*. **popped, pop·ping** *v.i.* **1.** To make a sharp, explosive sound. **2.** To burst open or explode with such a sound. **3.** To move or go suddenly or quickly: with *in, out*, etc. **4.** To bulge: His eyes *popped*. — *v.t.* **5.** To cause to burst or explode, as kernels of corn. **6.** To thrust or put suddenly: with *in, out*, etc. **7.** To fire (a gun, etc.). **8.** To shoot. — **to pop the question** *Informal* To make a proposal of marriage. — *n*. **1.** A sharp, explosive noise. **2.** A shot with a firearm. **3.** Soda (def. 2). — *adv.* **1.** Like, or with the sound of a pop. **2.** Suddenly. [Imit.]

pop² (pop) *n. Slang* **1.** Papa. **2.** A familiar term of address for an old man. [Short for *poppa*, var. of PAPA]

pop³ (pop) *n.* A concert of popular or light classical music. — *adj.* Featuring popular or light classical music: a *pop* concert; a *pop* orchestra. Also **pops.** [Short for POPULAR]

pop art *Sometimes cap.* A style of art of the 1960's influenced by popular commercial art.

pop·corn (pop′kôrn′) *n.* A variety of maize, the kernels of which explode when heated, forming large white balls; also, the corn after popping, eaten as a confection.

pope (pōp) *n. Often cap.* In the Roman Catholic Church, the bishop of Rome and the head of the Church. [OE < LL < LGk. < Gk. *pappas* father] — **pope′dom** *n.*

pop·er·y (pō′pər·ē) *n.* The practices, doctrines, etc., of the Roman Catholic Church: an offensive term.

pop·eyed (pop′īd′) *adj.* **1.** Having bulging or protruding eyes. **2.** Filled with astonishment; amazed.

pop·gun (pop′gun′) *n.* A child's toy gun that expels a pellet with a popping sound by compressed air.

pop·in·jay (pop′in·jā) *n.* A pretentious, conceited person. [< OF *papegai* < Sp. < Arabic *babaghā*]

pop·ish (pō′pish) *adj.* Pertaining to popes or popery: an offensive term. — **pop′ish·ly** *adv.* — **pop′ish·ness** *n.*

pop·lar (pop′lər) *n.* **1.** Any of a genus of dioecious trees and bushes of the willow family. **2.** The wood of any of these trees. [< OF < L *populus*]

pop·lin (pop′lin) *n.* A durable silk, cotton, or rayon fabric with a ribbed surface, used for dresses, etc. [< F < Ital. *papalina* papal; because made in Avignon, a papal residence]

pop·o·ver (pop′ō′vər) *n.* A very light egg muffin.

pop·per (pop′ər) *n.* **1.** One who or that which pops. **2.** A container or device for popping corn.

pop·pet valve (pop′it) *Mech.* A valve that rises and falls perpendicularly, used in gasoline engines.

pop·py (pop′ē) *n. pl.* **·pies 1.** Any of various plants having lobed or toothed leaves and showy red, violet, orange, or white flowers, as the opium poppy. **2.** A medicinal extract, as opium, from such a plant. **3.** The bright scarlet color of certain poppy blossoms: also **poppy red.** [OE < L *papaver*]

pop·py·cock (pop′ē·kok) *n. Informal* Pretentious talk; humbug; nonsense. [< Dial. Du. *pappekak*, lit., soft dung]

poppy seed The small, black seed of the poppy plant used to flavor and top rolls, bread, etc.

pop·u·lace (pop′yə·lis) *n.* The common people; the masses. [< MF < Ital. < L *populus* people]

pop·u·lar (pop′yə·lər) *adj.* **1.** Approved of, admired, or liked by most people: *popular* music. **2.** Having many friends. **3.** Of, pertaining to, or engaged in by the people at large: *popular* government. **4.** Suited to the intelligence of ordinary people. **5.** Prevalent among the people in general. **6.** Suited to the means of the people: *popular* prices. [< L *popularis* of the people] — **pop′u·lar·ly** *adv.*

popular front A coalition of leftist, labor, and liberal parties formed to combat fascism and promote reform.

pop·u·lar·i·ty (pop′yə·lar′ə·tē) *n.* The condition of being popular. [See POPULAR.]

pop·u·lar·ize (pop′yə·lə·rīz′) *v.t.* **·ized, ·iz·ing** To make popular. Also *Brit.* **pop′u·lar·ise′.** — **pop′u·lar·i·za′tion** *n.* — **pop′u·lar·iz′er** *n.*

pop·u·late (pop′yə·lāt) *v.t.* **·lat·ed, ·lat·ing 1.** To furnish with inhabitants, as by colonization; people. **2.** To inhabit. [< LL < L *populus* the people]

pop·u·la·tion (pop′yə·lā′shən) *n.* **1.** The total number of persons living in a country, city, or other specified area. **2.** The total number of persons of a particular group, class, race, etc., residing in a place. **3.** The act or process of populating or furnishing with inhabitants. **4.** *Stat.* A group of items or individuals. [< LL < L *populus* the people]

Pop·u·list (pop′yə·list) *adj.* Of or pertaining to the Populist or People's Party. — *n.* A member of the People's Party. — **Pop′u·lism** *n.* — **Pop′u·lis′tic** *adj.*

Populist Party People's Party.

pop·u·lous (pop′yə·ləs) *adj.* Containing many inhabitants; thickly settled. — **pop′u·lous·ly** *adv.* — **pop′u·lous·ness** *n.*

por·ce·lain (pôrs′lin, pōrs′-, pôr′sə-, pōr′-) *n.* **1.** A white, hard, translucent ceramic ware, usu. glazed; chinaware. **2.** An object made of this material. [< MF < Ital. *porcellana* shell < L *porcella*, dim. fem. of *porcus* pig] — **por·ce·la·ne·ous** (pôr′sə·lā′nē·əs, pōr′-) or **por′cel·la′ne·ous** *adj.*

porch (pôrch, pōrch) *n.* **1.** A covered structure or recessed space at the entrance to a building; a stoop. **2.** *U.S.* A veranda. **3.** A covered walk or portico. [< OF < L *porticus* colonnade < *porta* gate]

por·cine (pôr′sīn, -sin) *adj.* **1.** Of, pertaining to, or characteristic of swine. **2.** Swinish; hoggish; piggish. [< F, fem. of *porcin* < L < *porcus* pig]

por·cu·pine (pôr′kyə·pīn) *n.* Any of various large, clumsy rodents covered with erectile spines or quills used for defense: also, *U.S.* hedgehog. [< OF < OProvençal < It. < L *porcus* pig + *spina* thorn]

pore¹ (pôr, pōr) *v.i.* **pored, por·ing 1.** To gaze steadily or intently. **2.** To study or read with care and application: with *over:* to *pore* over one's accounts. **3.** To meditate; ponder: with *on, over,* or *upon.* [ME *pouren*]

pore² (pôr, pōr) *n.* **1.** A minute orifice or opening, as in the skin or a leaf, serving as an outlet for perspiration or as a means of absorption. **2.** Any similar opening, as in rock. [< OF < L < Gk. *poros* pore, passage]

por·gy (pôr′gē) *n. pl.* **·gies** or **·gy 1.** Any of various saltwater food fishes, esp. the red porgy of Mediterranean and European waters. **2.** Any of various related fishes, as the scup. [Origin uncertain]

pork (pôrk, pōrk) *n.* **1.** The flesh of swine used as food. **2.** *U.S. Slang* Government money, favors, etc., obtained through political patronage. [< OF < L *porcus* pig]

pork barrel *U.S. Slang* A federal appropriation for some local enterprise that will favorably impress a representative's constituents.

pork·er (pôr′kər, pōr′-) *n.* A pig or hog, esp. one fattened for slaughter.

pork·pie (pôrk′pī, pōrk′-) *n.* **1.** A pie filled with chopped pork and having a thick crust. **2.** A man's hat with a low, flat crown. Also **pork pie.**

pork·y (pôr′kē, pōr′-) *adj.* **pork·i·er, pork·i·est 1.** Of or like pork. **2.** Obese; fat, as from overeating.

por·nog·ra·phy (pôr·nog′rə·fē) *n. pl.* **·phies** Obscene literature or art. [< Gk. < *pornē* prostitute + *graphein* to write] — **por·no·graph·ic** (pôr′nə·graf′ik) *adj.*

po·ros·i·ty (pô·ros′ə·tē, pō-) *n. pl.* **·ties 1.** The property of being porous; porousness. **2.** A porous part or structure.

po·rous (pôr′əs, pō′rəs) *adj.* **1.** Having pores. **2.** Permeable by fluids or light. — **po′rous·ly** *adv.* — **po′rous·ness** *n.*

por·phy·ry (pôr′fə·rē) *n. pl.* **·ries** An igneous rock that has a groundmass enclosing crystals of feldspar or quartz. [< OF < Med.L < Gk. *porphyros* purple]

por·poise (pôr′pəs) *n. pl.* **·pois·es** or **·poise 1.** A dolphinlike animal with a blunt, rounded snout; esp., the **harbor porpoise** of the North Atlantic and Pacific, blackish above and white below. **2.** Loosely, any small cetacean, as the common dolphin. [< OF < L *porcus pisces,* lit., hog fish]

PORPOISE (def. 1)
(To 6 feet long)

por·ridge (pôr′ij, por-) *n.* **1.** *Chiefly Brit.* A soft food made by boiling oatmeal or other meal in water or milk until thickened. **2.** Originally, pottage. [Alter. of POTTAGE]

por·rin·ger (pôr′in·jər, por′-) *n.* A small, relatively shallow bowl for porridge or soup; esp., such a bowl used by small children. [Earlier *pottanger* < MF *potager* soup bowl]

port¹ (pôrt, pōrt) *n.* **1.** A city or place of customary entry and exit of ships, esp. for commerce. **2.** A harbor or haven. **3.** *Law* A port of entry. [OE < L *portus* harbor]

port² (pôrt, pōrt) *Naut. n.* The left side of a vessel as one faces the front or bow: formerly called *larboard:* opposed to *starboard.* — *v.t. & v.i.* To put or turn to the port or larboard side. — *adj.* Left: *port* side. [Prob. < PORT¹]

port³ (pôrt, pōrt) *n.* **1.** *Naut.* **a** A porthole. **b** A covering for a porthole. **2.** *Mech.* An orifice for the passage of air, gas, etc.: a steam *port.* [Prob. < OF < L *porta* gate, door]

port⁴ (pôrt, pōrt) *n.* A variety of sweet wine, usu. dark red. [Short for *Oporto* wine, after *Oporto,* Portugal]

port⁵ (pôrt, pōrt) *v.t. Mil.* To carry (a rifle, saber, etc.) diagonally across the body and sloping to the left shoulder. — *n.* **1.** *Mil.* The position of a rifle or other weapon when ported. **2.** The way in which one bears or carries himself. [< MF < L *portare* to carry]

port·a·ble (pôr′tə·bəl, pōr′-) *adj.* That can be readily carried or moved. — *n.* Something portable, as a typewriter or radio. [< MF < LL < L *portare* to carry] — **port′a·bil′i·ty, port′a·ble·ness** *n.* — **port′a·bly** *adv.*

port·age (pôr′tij, pōr′-) *n. U.S. & Canadian* **1.** The act of transporting (canoes, boats, and goods) from one navigable water to another; also, that which is transported. **2.** The route over which and the place where such transportation is made. **3.** The charge for transportation.

por·tal (pôr′təl, pōr′-) *n.* **1.** *Often pl.* An entrance, door, or gate, esp. one that is grand and imposing. **2.** The portal vein. — *adj.* Pertaining to the portal vein. [< MF < Med.L, ult. < L *porta* gate]

por·ta·tive (pôr′tə·tiv, pōr′-) *adj.* **1.** Of or pertaining to carrying; capable of carrying. **2.** Portable. [< OF < L *portatus,* pp. of *portare* to carry]

port authority Any official body having charge of the coordination of all rail and water traffic of a port.

port·cul·lis (pôrt·kul'is, pōrt-) *n.* A grating made of strong bars of wood or iron that can be let down suddenly to close the gateway of a fortified place. [< OF < *porte* gate + fem. of *coleis,* pp. of *couler* to slide]

Porte (pôrt, pōrt) *n.* The former Ottoman Turkish government: with *the.* [< F (*la Sublime*) Porte (the High) Gate, trans. of Turkish *Babi Ali*]

porte-co·chère (pôrt'kō-shâr', pōrt'-; *Fr.* pôrt·kô·shâr') *n.* 1. A large covered gateway for vehicles, leading into a courtyard. 2. A porch over a driveway at the entrance of a building for sheltering persons entering or leaving vehicles. [< F < *porte* gate + *cochère,* fem. adj. < *coche* coach]

por·tend (pôr·tend', pōr-) *v.t.* To warn of as an omen; forebode. [< L < *pro-* forth + *tendere* to stretch]

por·tent (pôr'tent, pōr'-) *n.* 1. An indication or sign of what is to happen, esp. of something momentous or calamitous. 2. Ominous significance. 3. A prodigy; marvel.

por·ten·tous (pôr·ten'təs, pōr-) *adj.* 1. Having the nature of a portent; foreboding. 2. Causing astonishment or awe; extraordinary. **—por·ten'tous·ly** *adv.* **—por·ten'tous·ness** *n.*

por·ter¹ (pôr'tər, pōr'-) *n.* 1. One who carries travelers' luggage, etc., for hire, as at a railroad station. 2. *U.S.* An attendant in a Pullman car. [< OF < LL *portator* to carry]

por·ter² (pôr'tər, pōr'-) *n.* A keeper of a door or gate; janitor. [< OF < LL < L *porta* gate, door]

por·ter³ (pôr'tər, pōr'-) *n.* A dark brown, heavy, English liquor resembling ale, formerly drunk chiefly by porters.

por·ter·house (pôr'tər·hous', pōr'-) *n.* 1. A place where porter, ale, etc., are retailed. 2. A restaurant; chophouse. 3. A choice cut of beefsteak including a part of the tenderloin, usu. next to the sirloin: also **porterhouse steak.**

port·fo·li·o (pôrt·fō'lē·ō, pōrt-) *n.* *pl.* **·li·os** 1. A portable case for holding drawings, papers, etc. 2. Such a case for carrying documents of a department of state. 3. The office of a minister of state or a cabinet member. 4. An itemized list of investments, securities, etc., of a bank or investor. [< Ital. < L *portare* to carry + *folium* leaf, sheet of paper]

port·hole (pôrt'hōl', pōrt'-) *n.* 1. A small opening in a ship's side for admitting light and air, for shooting a weapon through, or for loading cargo. 2. A loophole in the wall of a fort for shooting through; embrasure. 3. An opening into a furnace, engine, or the like, shaped like a porthole.

por·ti·co (pôr'ti·kō, pōr'-) *n.* *pl.* **·coes** or **·cos** An open space or ambulatory with roof upheld by columns; a porch. [< Ital. < L *porticus* < *porta* door] **—por'ti·coed** *adj.*

por·tière (pôr·tyâr', pōr-; *Fr.* pôr·tyâr') *n.* A curtain for a doorway, used instead of a door. Also **por·tiere'.** [< F]

por·tion (pôr'shən, pōr'-) *n.* 1. A part of a whole, whether separated from it or not. 2. An allotment or share. 3. The quantity of food usu. served to one person. 4. The part of an estate coming to an heir or next of kin. 5. A dowry (def. 1). **—** *v.t.* 1. To divide into shares for distribution; parcel: usu. with *out.* 2. To give a dowry or inheritance to. 3. To assign; allot. [< OF < L *portio, -onis*] **—por'tion·a·ble** *adj.* **—por'tion·less** *adj.*

—Syn. (noun) 1. *Portion, fraction,* and *section* denote a part of a whole. A *portion* was originally an alloted share, and so suggests a measured quantity: to devote a *portion* of one's time to study. A *fraction,* originally a very small part, now denotes a part taken away: the first *fraction* in the distillation of petroleum. Unlike the other synonyms, *fraction* has little or no suggestion of measurement. A *section* is the part lying between two cuts; hence, any clearly demarcated part: a *section* of a book.

por·tion·er (pôr'shən·ər, pōr'-) *n.* One who divides in shares or holds a share or shares.

port·ly (pôrt'lē, pōrt'-) *adj.* **·li·er, ·li·est** 1. Somewhat corpulent; stout. 2. Having a stately appearance and carriage; impressive. [< PORT⁵ + -LY] **—port'li·ness** *n.*

port·man·teau (pôrt·man'tō, pōrt-) *n.* *pl.* **·teaus** or **·teaux** (-tōz) *Chiefly Brit.* A large, leather suitcase hinged at the back to form two distinct compartments. [< MF < *porter* to carry + *manteau* coat < L *mantellum*]

port of call A port where vessels put in for supplies, repairs, discharge or taking on of cargo, etc.

port of entry *Law* A place, whether on the coast or inland, designated as a point at which persons or merchandise may enter or pass out of a country: also called *port.*

por·trait (pôr'trit, pōr'-, -trāt) *n.* 1. A likeness of a person, esp. of the face, produced, usu. from life, by an artist or photographer. 2. A vivid word description, esp. of a person. [See PORTRAY] **—por'trait·ist** *n.*

por·trai·ture (pôr'tri·chər, pōr'-) *n.* 1. The art or practice of making portraits. 2. A portrait. 3. Portraits collectively.

por·tray (pôr·trā', pōr-) *v.t.* 1. To represent by drawing, painting, etc. 2. To describe or depict in words. 3. To represent, as in a play; act. [< OF < Med.L < L < *pro-* forward + *trahere* to draw] **—por·tray'a·ble** *adj.* **—por·tray'al** *n.* **—por·tray'er** *n.*

por·tress (pôr'tris, pōr'-) *n.* A woman porter or doorkeeper. Also **por·ter·ess** (pôr'tris, -tər·is, pōr'-).

Por·tu·guese (pôr'chə·gēz', -gēs', pōr'-) *adj.* Pertaining to Portugal, its inhabitants, or their language. **—** *n.* 1. A native or inhabitant of Portugal. 2. The people of Portugal. 3. The Romance language of Portugal and Brazil.

Portuguese man-of-war Any of several large marine organisms, having long, stinging tentacles hanging down from a bladderlike float.

pose¹ (pōz) *n.* 1. The position of the whole or part of the body, esp. such a position assumed for or represented by an artist or photographer. 2. A mental attitude adopted for effect. **—** *v.* **posed, pos·ing** *v.i.* 1. To assume or hold an attitude or position, as for a portrait. 2. To affect mental attitudes. 3. To represent oneself: to *pose* as an expert. **—** *v.t.* 4. To cause to assume an attitude or position, as an artist's model. 5. To state or propound; put forward as a question, etc. [< OF, fusion of LL *pausare* to place < L, to pause and *pos-,* stem of L *ponere* to put]

pose² (pōz) *v.t.* **posed, pos·ing** To puzzle or confuse by asking a difficult question. [< obs. *appose,* var. of OPPOSE]

Po·sei·don (pō·sī'dən) In Greek mythology, brother of Zeus, god of the sea and of horses: identified with the Roman *Neptune.* **—Po'sei·do'ni·an** (-dō'nē·ən) *adj.*

pos·er¹ (pō'zər) *n.* One who poses. [< POSE¹, v.]

pos·er² (pō'zər) *n.* A question that baffles. [< POSE²]

po·seur (pō·zœr') *n.* One who affects a particular attitude to make an impression on others. [< F < *poser* to pose]

pos·it (poz'it) *v.t.* 1. To put in position; place. 2. To lay down or assume as a fact or basis of argument; postulate. [< L *positus,* pp. of *ponere* to place]

po·si·tion (pə·zish'ən) *n.* 1. The manner in which a thing is placed. 2. Disposition of the body or parts of the body. 3. The locality or place occupied by a person or thing. 4. *Med.* The placement or arrangement of the body of a patient in order to facilitate therapeutic, surgical, or obstetrical procedures. 5. The proper or appropriate place: in *position.* 6. State or situation in relation to other conditions: to be in a false *position.* 7. An attitude or point of view; stand. 8. Relative social standing; status; also, high social standing. 9. Employment; job. 10. In sports, the assignment of an area covered by a particular player. **— to be in a position** To have the means or opportunity to. **—** *v.t.* To place in a particular or appropriate position. [< OF < L < *ponere* to place] **—po·si'tion·al** *adj.*

—Syn. (noun) 1. See PLACE. 9. office, post, situation.

pos·i·tive (poz'ə·tiv) *adj.* 1. That is or may be directly affirmed; actual. 2. Expressing, containing, or characterized by affirmation: a *positive* attitude. 3. Inherent in a thing by and of itself, regardless of its relations to other things. 4. Openly and plainly expressed: a *positive* denial. 5. Imperative. 6. Not admitting of doubt or denial. 7. Noting one of two opposite directions, qualities, properties, etc., which is taken as primary, or as indicating increase or progression. 8. *Math.* Greater than zero; plus: said of quantities and usu. denoted by the sign ($+$). 9. *Med.* Denoting the presence of a specific condition or organism: a *positive* Wasserman reaction. 10. *Photog.* Having the lights and darks in their original relation, as in a print made from a negative. 11. *Biol.* Noting the response of an organism toward a stimulus: a *positive* tropism. 12. *Electr.* Having the kind of electricity exhibited by a glass object when rubbed with silk; characterized by a deficiency of electrons on a charged body. 13. *Chem.* Basic. 14. *Gram.* Denoting the simple, uncompared degree of the adjective or adverb. 15. *Stat.* Designating a correlation in which the values of two variables tend to increase or decrease together: also *direct.* **—** *n.* 1. That which is positive or capable of being directly or certainly affirmed. 2. *Math.* A positive symbol or quantity. 3. *Electr.* A positive pole, terminal, etc. 4. *Photog.* A positive picture or print. 5. *Gram.* The positive degree of an adjective or adverb; also, a word in this degree. [< OF, fem. of *positif* < L < *ponere* to place] **—pos'i·tive·ly** *adv.* **—pos'i·tive·ness** *n.*

pos·i·tiv·ism (poz'ə·tiv·iz'əm) *n.* 1. A way of thinking that regards nothing as ascertained or ascertainable beyond the facts of physical science or of sense. 2. *Philos.* A system of philosophy elaborated by Auguste Comte, holding that man can have no knowledge of anything but actual phenomena and facts and their interrelations. 3. Certitude, or the claim of certitude, in knowledge. **—pos'i·tiv·ist** *n.* **—pos'i·tiv·is'tic** *adj.*

pos·i·tron (poz'ə·tron) *n.* *Physics* The positive counterpart of an electron.

pos·se (pos'ē) *n.* 1. A posse comitatus. 2. A force of men; squad. [< Med.L, armed force < L, to be able]

pos·se com·i·ta·tus (pos'ē kom/ə·tā'təs) The body of men that a sheriff or other peace officer calls or may call to his assistance in the discharge of his official duty, as to quell a riot. [< Med.L < *posse* power | *comitatus* county]

pos·sess (pə·zes') *v.t.* 1. To have as property; own. 2. To have as a quality, attribute, etc. 3. To enter and exert control over; dominate: often used passively: The idea *possessed* him. 4. To maintain control over (oneself, one's mind, etc.). **5.** To put in possession, as of property, news, etc.: with *of*. **6.** To have knowledge of; gain mastery of, as a language. **7.** To imbue or impress, as with wonder or an idea: with *with*. **8.** To have sexual intercourse with. [< F < L < *potis* master + *sedere* to sit (as)]

pos·sessed (pə·zest′) *adj.* **1.** Having; owning: *possessed* of a ready tongue. **2.** Calm; cool: to be *possessed* in time of danger. **3.** Controlled by or as if by evil spirits; beyond self-control; frenzied.

pos·ses·sion (pə·zesh′ən) *n.* **1.** The act or fact of possessing. **2.** The state of being possessed. **3.** That which is possessed or owned. **4.** *pl.* Property; wealth. **5.** The state of being possessed by, or as by, evil spirits. **6.** Self-possession.

pos·ses·sive (pə·zes′iv) *adj.* **1.** Of or pertaining to possession or ownership. **2.** Having a strong desire for complete emotional domination of another person. **3.** *Gram.* Designating a case of the noun or pronoun that denotes possession, origin, or the like. In English, this is formed in nouns by adding 's to the singular and to irregular plurals: *John's* book; *men's* souls; and a simple apostrophe to the regular plural and sometimes to singulars and proper names ending in a sibilant: *boys'* shoes; *James'* (or *James's*) brother. Pronouns in the possessive case have special forms, as *my, mine, his, her, hers, its, our, ours, your, yours, their, theirs, whose.* — *n. Gram.* **1.** The possessive case. **2.** A possessive form or construction. — **pos·ses′sive·ness** *n.*

pos·set (pos′it) *n.* A drink of hot milk curdled with wine or ale, sweetened and spiced. [< ME *poshote, possot*]

pos·si·bil·i·ty (pos′ə·bil′ə·tē) *n. pl.* ·ties **1.** The fact or state of being possible. **2.** That which is possible.

pos·si·ble (pos′ə·bəl) *adj.* **1.** Capable of happening or proving true: not contrary to fact, natural laws, or experience. **2.** Capable of being done or of coming about; feasible. **3.** That may or may not happen. [< OF < L < *posse* to be able + *esse* to be] — **pos′si·bly** *adv.*

pos·sum (pos′əm) *n. Informal* An opossum. — **to play possum** To feign death, illness, etc. [< OPOSSUM.]

post¹ (pōst) *n.* An upright piece of timber or other material; as: **a** A support for a sign. **b** A bearing or framing member in a building. **c** An indicator of the starting or finishing point of a racecourse, etc. — *v.t.* **1.** To put up (a poster, etc.) in some public place. **2.** To fasten posters upon. **3.** To announce by or as by a poster: to *post* a reward. **4.** To publish the name of on a list. [OE < L *postis* door post]

post² (pōst) *n.* **1.** A position or employment, esp. a public office. **2.** *Mil.* **a** A place occupied by a detachment of troops. **b** The buildings and grounds of such a place. **3.** An assigned beat, position, or station, as of a sentry, policeman, etc. **4.** A trading post or settlement. **5.** *U.S.* A local unit of a veterans' organization. — *v.t.* To assign to a particular post; station, as a sentry. [< MF < Ital. < LL *postum*, contr. of L *positum*, pp. neut. of *ponere* to place]

post³ (pōst) *n.* **1.** *Chiefly Brit.* A single delivery of mail to a home, office, etc.; also, the mail itself. **2.** *Chiefly Brit.* An established, usu. government, system, for transporting the mails; also, a local post office. **3.** *Brit.* A mailbox. **4.** A rider or courier who carries mail over a fixed route. **5.** Any of the stations furnishing relays of men and horses on such a route. — *v.t.* **1.** *Chiefly Brit.* To place in a mailbox or post office; mail. **2.** To inform. **3.** In bookkeeping: **a** To transfer (items or accounts) to the ledger. **b** To make the proper entries in (a ledger). — *v.i.* **4.** To travel with post horses. **5.** To travel with speed; hasten. — *adv.* **1.** By post horses. **2.** Speedily; rapidly. [< MF < Ital. *posta*, orig., a station < LL, contr. of L *posita*, pp. fem. of *ponere* to place]

post- *prefix* **1.** After in time or order; following: *postdate, postwar*. **2.** Chiefly in scientific terms, after in position; behind. [< L *post* behind, after]

post·age (pōs′tij) *n.* **1.** The charge levied on mail matter. **2.** The act of going by post.

postage stamp A small, printed label issued and sold by a government to be affixed to letters, parcels, etc., in payment of postage.

pos·tal (pōs′tal) *adj.* Pertaining to the mails or to mail service. — *n.* A postal card.

postal card A card, issued officially, for carrying a written or printed message through the mails.

post-bel·lum (pōst′bel′əm) *adj.* Occurring after a war, esp. after the Civil War. [< L *post* after + *bellum* war]

post·box (pōst′boks′) *n.* A mailbox (def. 1).

post card **1.** A postal card. **2.** An unofficial card of any regulation size, usu. having a picture on one side, transmissible through the mails on prepayment of postage.

post chaise A closed carriage used for traveling and drawn by post horses.

post·date (pōst′dāt′) *v.t.* ·dat·ed, ·dat·ing **1.** To assign or fix a date later than the actual date to (a check, document, etc.). **2.** To follow in time.

post·er (pōs′tər) *n.* **1.** A placard or bill used for advertising, public information, etc., to be posted on a wall or other surface. **2.** A billposter. [< POST¹]

pos·te·ri·or (pos·tir′ē·ər) *adj.* **1.** Situated behind or toward the hinder part. **2.** Coming after another in a series. **3.** Subsequent in time; later. **4.** *Anat.* **a** In animals, pertaining to the tail end of the body. **b** In man, pertaining to the back side of the body. — *n. Sometimes pl.* The buttocks. [< L, compar. of *posterus* coming after < *post* after, behind] — **pos·te′ri·or′i·ty** (-ôr′ə·tē, -or′ə-) *n.* — **pos·te′ri·or·ly** *adv.*

pos·ter·i·ty (pos·ter′ə·tē) *n.* **1.** Future generations taken collectively. **2.** All of one's descendants. [< OF < L < *posterus* coming after]

pos·tern (pōs′tərn, pos′-) *n.* A small back gate or door, esp. in a fortification or castle. — *adj.* Situated at the back or side. [< OF < LL < *postera* back door, gate]

post exchange *Mil.* An establishment for the sale of merchandise and services to military personnel. Abbr. *PX*

post·grad·u·ate (pōst′graj′ōō·it, -āt) *adj.* Of or pertaining to studies pursued after the taking of an advanced degree. — *n.* One who pursues such studies.

post·haste (pōst′hāst′) *Archaic n.* Great haste or speed, like that of the post. — *adv.* With utmost speed.

post horse A horse kept at a post house.

post house A house where post horses were kept for relay; also, formerly, a post office.

post·hu·mous (pos′chōō·məs) *adj.* **1.** Denoting a child born after the father's death. **2.** Published after the author's death, as a book. **3.** Arising or continuing after one's death. [< LL < L *postumus* latest, last] — **post′hu·mous·ly** *adj.*

pos·til·ion (pōs·til′yən, pos-) *n.* One who guides a team drawing a carriage or other heavy vehicle by riding the near horse when one pair is used or the near horse of the leaders when two or more pairs are used. Also **pos·til′lion.** [< MF < Ital. < *posta* post, station]

post·im·pres·sion·ism (pōst′im·presh′ən·iz′əm) *n.* The theories and practice of a group of expressionist painters of the late 19th century, who rejected the objective naturalism of the Impressionists and emphasized the subjective point of view of the artist. — **post′im·pres′sion·ist** *n. & adj.* — **post′im·pres′sion·is′tic** *adj.*

post·lude (pōst′lōōd) *n. Music* **1.** An organ voluntary concluding a church service. **2.** Loosely, a coda.

post·man (pōst′mən) *n. pl.* ·men (-mən) A mailman.

post·mark (pōst′märk′) *n.* Any official mark stamped on mail to cancel stamps and to give the date and place of sending or receiving. — *v.t.* To stamp with a postmark.

post·mas·ter (pōst′mas′tər, -mäs′-) *n.* **1.** An official having charge of a post office. **2.** One who provides horses for posting. — **post′mis′tress** (-mis′tris) *n.fem.*

postmaster general *pl.* **postmasters general** The executive head of the postal service of a government.

post·me·rid·i·an (pōst′mə·rid′ē·ən) *adj.* Pertaining to or occurring in the afternoon. Also **post′me·rid′i·o·nal.** [< L < *post* after + *meridies* noon]

post me·rid·i·em (pōst mə·rid′ē·əm) After midday. Abbr. *p.m., P.M.* [< L]

post-mortem (pōst′môr′təm) *adj.* **1.** Happening or performed after death. **2.** Of or pertaining to a post-mortem examination. — *n.* **1.** A post-mortem examination. **2.** *Informal* An analysis or discussion of an accomplished fact. [< L *post mortem* after death]

post-mortem examination *Med.* A thorough examination of a human body after death: also called *autopsy*.

post·na·tal (pōst′nāt′l) *adj.* Occurring after birth.

post office **1.** The branch of the civil service of a government charged with carrying and delivering the mails. **2.** Any local office that receives, sorts, and delivers mail, sells stamps, etc. **3.** Any town or place having a post office.

post·op·er·a·tive (pōst′op′ər·ā·tiv, -ə·rā′-) *adj. Surg.* Occurring or done after a surgical operation: *postoperative* care.

post·paid (pōst′pād′) *adj.* Having postage prepaid.

post·par·tum (pōst′pär′təm) *adj. Med.* After childbirth. [< POST- + L *partus* childbirth < *parere* to bear]

post·pone (pōst·pōn′) *v.t.* ·poned, ·pon·ing **1.** To put off to a future time; defer; delay. **2.** To subordinate. [< L < *post-* after + *ponere* to put] — **post·pon′a·ble** *adj.* — **post·pone′ment** *n.* — **post·pon′er** *n.*
— **Syn. 1.** Delay, defer, procrastinate, adjourn, stay.

post·pran·di·al (pōst·pran′dē·əl) *adj.* After-dinner. [< POST- + L *prandium* lunch + -AL¹]

post road A road built for the transportation of mail, formerly having post houses at specified distances.

post·script (pōst′skript′) *n.* **1.** A sentence or paragraph added to a letter after the writer's signature. **2.** A supplemental addition to a written or printed document. Abbr. *p.s., P.S.* [< L *postscriptum*, pp. of *postscribere* to write after]

pos·tu·lant (pos′chə·lənt) *n.* **1.** One who presents a request. **2.** *Eccl.* An applicant for admission into a religious order. [< L < *postulare*, freq. of *poscere* to ask] — **pos′·tu·lant·ship** *n.*

pos·tu·late (*v.* pos′chə·lāt; *n.* pos′chə·lit) *v.t.* ·**lat·ed**, ·**lat·ing** **1.** To claim, demand, or require. **2.** To set forth as self-evident. **3.** To assume the truth or reality of. — *n.* **1.** A self-evident truth. **2.** A prerequisite. **3.** A fundamental principle. — **pos′tu·la′tion** *n.* — **pos′tu·la′tor** *n.*

pos·ture (pos′chər) *n.* **1.** The position or carriage of the body or parts of the body. **2.** Such a position assumed during posing for an artist, etc. **3.** The visible disposition of the various parts of a material thing. **4.** A mental attitude; frame of mind. **5.** A situation or condition, esp. if a consequence of policy: national defense posture. — *v.t.* **1.** To place (a person) in a specific position or pose. — *v.i.* **2.** To assume or adopt a bodily pose or a character not natural to one. [< F < L *positura* position] — **pos′tur·al** *adj.* — **pos′tur·er, pos′tur·ist** *n.*

pos·tur·ize (pos′chə·rīz) *v.t. & v.i.* ·**ized**, ·**iz·ing** To posture; pose.

post·war (pōst′wôr′) *adj.* After a war.

po·sy (pō′zē) *n.* *pl.* ·**sies** A single flower or a bouquet. [Contr. of POESY]

pot (pot) *n.* **1.** A round, fairly deep vessel of metal, earthenware, or glass, generally having a handle, used for cooking and other domestic purposes. **2.** Such a vessel and its contents. **3.** The amount a pot will hold. **4.** A large drinking cup, as a tankard; also, drink or liquor. **5.** In cardplaying, the amount of stakes wagered or played for, esp. in poker. **6.** *Informal* A large sum of money. **7.** In fishing, a basketlike trap for catching lobsters, eels, etc. — **to go to pot** To deteriorate. — *v.* pot·ted, pot·ting *v.t.* **1.** To put into a pot or pots: to *pot* plants. **2.** To preserve (meat, etc.) in pots or jars. **3.** To cook in a pot. **4.** To shoot (game) for food rather than for sport. **5.** To shoot or kill with a pot shot. **6.** *Informal* To secure, capture, or win; bag. — *v.i.* **7.** To take a pot shot; shoot. [OE *pott*]

po·ta·ble (pō′tə·bəl) *adj.* Suitable for drinking: said of water. — *n.* *Often pl.* Something drinkable; a drink. [< MF < LL < *potare* to drink]

po·tage (pō·täzh′) *n.* French Any thick soup.

pot·ash (pot′ash′) *n.* **1.** Potassium hydroxide. **2.** Crude potassium carbonate. **3.** The oxide of potassium, K_2O. [< Du. *potasch*]

po·tas·si·um (pə·tas′ē·əm) *n.* A bluish white, highly reactive, metallic element (symbol K), never found free in nature, but yielding many compounds of great practical value in industry, medicine, etc.: also called *kalium*. See ELEMENT. [< NL < *potass* potash] — **po·tas′sic** *adj.*

potassium bitartrate *Chem.* A white crystalline compound, $HKC_4H_4O_6$, having an acid taste; an ingredient of baking powder: also called *cream of tartar*.

potassium bromide *Chem.* A crystalline compound, KBr, used in photography, and in medicine as a sedative.

potassium carbonate *Chem.* A white, strongly alkaline compound, K_2CO_3, used in making soap and glass.

potassium cyanide *Chem.* An intensely poisonous compound, KCN, used in photography, and as a reagent.

potassium hydroxide *Chem.* A whitish deliquescent solid, KOH, yielding a strong caustic solution: used in saltmaking, electroplating, as a chemical reagent, etc. Also called *caustic potash, potash.*

potassium nitrate *Chem.* A crystalline white salt, KNO_3, used in gunpowder, fertilizers, and in medicine. Also called *niter, saltpeter.*

potassium permanganate *Chem.* A purple red crystalline salt, $KMnO_4$, used as an oxidizing agent in antiseptics and deodorizing substances.

potassium sulfate *Chem.* A salt, K_2SO_4, used in the manufacture of glass and alum, and in the crude state as a component of fertilizer.

po·ta·tion (pō·tā′shən) *n.* **1.** The act of drinking; also, a drink, esp. of an alcoholic beverage. **2.** A drinking bout. [< OF < L < *potare* to drink]

po·ta·to (pə·tā′tō) *n.* *pl.* ·**toes** **1.** One of the edible tubers of a plant of the nightshade family: also called *Irish potato, white potato.* **2.** The plant. **3.** The sweet potato. [< Sp. *patata* < Arawakan (Taino) *batata*]

potato beetle A beetle having long black stripes on the wing covers, that feeds on the leaves of the potato, tomato, and similar plants. Also **potato bug.**

potato chip *U.S.* A very thin slice of potato fried crisp and salted.

pot·bel·ly (pot′bel′ē) *n.* *pl.* ·**lies** **1.** A protuberant belly. **2.** An upright wood- or coal-burning stove with bulging sides: also **potbellied stove.** — **pot′bel′lied** *adj.*

pot·boil·er (pot′boi′lər) *n.* *Informal* A literary or artistic work produced simply to obtain the means of subsistence.

po·tent (pōt′nt) *adj.* **1.** Physically powerful. **2.** Having great authority. **3.** Exerting great influence on mind or morals; very convincing: a *potent* argument. **4.** Of a drug, liquor, etc., strong in its physical and chemical effects. **5.** Sexually competent: said of the male. [< L < *potis* able + *esse* to be] — **po′ten·cy, po′tence** *n.* — **po′tent·ly** *adv.* — **po′tent·ness** *n.*

po·ten·tate (pōt′n·tāt) *n.* One having great power or sway; a sovereign. [< LL *potentatus*]

po·ten·tial (pə·ten′chəl) *adj.* **1.** Possible but not actual. **2.** Having capacity for existence, but not yet existing; latent. **3.** *Gram.* Indicating possibility, power, or liberty, as a verb phrase including *may, can, must,* etc. — *n.* **1.** A possible development; potentiality. **2.** *Electr.* The charge on a body as referred to another body or to a given standard, as the earth, considered as having zero potential. [< LL *potentialis*] — **po·ten′tial·ly** *adv.*

po·ten·ti·al·i·ty (pə·ten′chē·al′ə·tē) *n.* *pl.* ·**ties** **1.** Inherent capacity for development or accomplishment. **2.** That which is potential ro capable of being realized.

poth·er (poth′ər) *n.* Excitement mingled with confusion; bustle; fuss. — *v.t. & v.i.* To worry; bother.

pot·herb (pot′ûrb′, -hûrb′) *n.* Any plant or herb, esp. greens, when cooked or used to flavor boiled foods.

pot·hole (pot′hōl′) *n.* A deep hole, as in a road.

pot·hook (pot′hook′) *n.* **1.** A curved or hooked piece of iron for lifting or hanging pots. **2.** A curved mark or elementary stroke used in teaching penmanship.

pot·house (pot′hous′) *Brit. n.* An alehouse; saloon.

po·tion (pō′shən) *n.* A draft, as a large dose of liquid medicine: often used of a magic or poisonous draft. [< OF < L < *potare* to drink]

pot·luck (pot′luk′) *n.* Whatever food may have been prepared for the family: usu. in the phrase **to take potluck.**

pot·pie (pot′pī′) *n.* **1.** A meat pie baked in a deep dish. **2.** Meat stewed with dumplings.

pot·pour·ri (pot·poor′ē, *Fr.* pō·pōō·rē′) *n.* **1.** A mixture of dried flower petals kept in a jar and used to perfume a room. **2.** A musical medley or literary miscellany. **3.** Any incongruous mixture. [< F, lit., rotten pot]

pot roast Meat braised and cooked in a covered pot.

pot·sherd (pot′shûrd) *n.* A bit of broken earthenware.

pot shot **1.** A shot fired to kill, without regard to the rules of sports. **2.** A shot fired, as from ambush, at a person or animal within easy range. **3.** A random shot.

pot·stone (pot′stōn′) *n.* A variety of steatite or soapstone.

pot·tage (pot′ij) *n.* A thick broth or stew of vegetables with or without meat. [< OF *pot*]

pot·ted (pot′id) *adj.* **1.** Placed or kept in a pot. **2.** Cooked or preserved in a pot. **3.** *Slang* Drunk.

pot·ter[1] (pot′ər) *v.t. & v.i. Chiefly Brit.* To putter. [Freq. of dial, *pote*] — **pot′ter·er** *n.*

pot·ter[2] (pot′ər) *n.* One who makes earthenware or porcelain vessels.

potter's field A piece of ground appropriated as a burial ground for the destitute and the unknown. *Matt.* xxvii 7.

potter's wheel A horizontal rotating disk used by potters for holding and manipulating prepared clay.

pot·ter·y (pot′ər·ē) *n.* *pl.* ·**ter·ies** **1.** Ware molded from clay and hardened by intense heat. **2.** The art of making earthenware or porcelain. **3.** A place where pottery is made. [< OF < Med.L *pot* pot]

pot·tle (pot′l) *n.* **1.** A drinking vessel, pot, or tankard holding about half a gallon. **2.** An old liquid measure of half a gallon. **3.** Liquor. [< OF *pot* pot]

pot·ty[1] (pot′ē) *adj. Brit. Informal* **1.** Insignificant. **2.** Slightly drunk; also, a little silly.

pot·ty[2] (pot′ē) *n.* *pl.* ·**ties** A receptacle that fits under a child's toilet seat; also, the toilet seat.

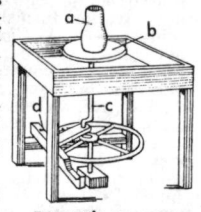

POTTER'S WHEEL
a Molding clay. *b* Rotating wheel. *c* Shaft. *d* Treadle.

pouch (pouch) *n.* **1.** A small bag, sack, or other container, used for carrying money, pipe tobacco, ammunition, etc. **2.** *Zool.* **a** A saclike part for temporarily containing food, as in gophers and pelicans. **b** A marsupium. **3.** *Bot.* Any baglike cavity, as the pod of the mustard plant. **4.** A mailbag. — *v.t.* **1.** To put in a pouch. **2.** To fashion in pouchlike form. — *v.i.* **3.** To form a pouchlike cavity. [< OF *poche*] — **pouch′y.** *adj.*

poul·tice (pōl′tis) *n.* A moist, mealy mass of flour, mustard, etc., applied hot to a sore part of the body. — *v.t.* ·**ticed**, ·**tic·ing** To cover with a poultice. [< L *puls* porridge]

poul·try (pōl′trē) *n.* Domestic fowls, generally or collectively, as hens, ducks, etc. [< OF *poule* hen]

pounce[1] (pouns) *v.i.* **pounced**, **pounc·ing** To swoop or spring in or as in seizing prey: with *on, upon,* or *at.* — *n.* **1.** A talon or claw of a bird of prey. **2.** The act of pouncing.

pounce[2] (pouns) *n.* **1.** A powder, as of cuttlebone, formerly used to absorb excess of ink, as on a manuscript.

2. A finely pulverized substance used in transferring designs. — *v.t.* To sprinkle, smooth, or rub with pounce. [< F < L *pumex* pumice]

pound¹ (pound) *n.* **1.** A unit of weight varying in different countries and at different periods. **2.** In Great Britain and the U.S., either of two legally fixed units, the avoirdupois pound and the troy pound. See table front of book. **3.** The standard monetary unit of the United Kingdom, equivalent to 20 shillings: in 1960 worth about $2.81: also **pound sterling.** Symbol £. **4.** A similar monetary unit of Ireland and several members of the Commonwealth of Nations. **5.** A standard monetary unit of various other countries; esp. Egypt, Israel, and Turkey. [OE < L *pondus* weight]

pound² (pound) *n.* **1.** A place, enclosed by authority, in which stray animals or distrained possessions are left until claimed or redeemed. **2.** A place of confinement for lawbreakers. **3.** A trap for wild animals. **4.** An area or place in which to catch or stow fish. — *v.t.* To confine in a pound; impound. [OE *pund-*]

pound³ (pound) *v.t.* **1.** To strike heavily and repeatedly; beat. **2.** To reduce to a pulp or powder by beating. — *v.i.* **3.** To strike heavy, repeated blows: with *on, at,* etc. **4.** To move or proceed heavily. **5.** To throb heavily or resoundingly. — *n.* **1.** A heavy blow. **2.** The act of pounding. [OE *pūnian* to bruise] — **pound′er** *n.*

pound·age (poun′dij) *n.* A rate on the pound sterling.

pound·al (poun′dəl) *n. Physics* A unit of force that, acting on a mass of one pound, imparts to it a velocity of one foot per second.

pound-cake (pound′kāk′) *n.* A rich cake having ingredients equal in weight, as a pound each of flour, butter, and sugar, with eggs added.

pound·er (poun′dər) *n.* **1.** Anything weighing a pound. **2.** One who or that which weighs, has, etc., a given number of pounds: used in combination: an eight-*pounder.*

pound-fool·ish (pound′fōō′lish) *adj.* Extravagant with large sums, but watching small sums closely.

pour (pôr, pōr) *v.t.* **1.** To cause to flow in a continuous stream, as water, sand, etc. **2.** To send forth, emit, or utter profusely or continuously — *v.i.* **3.** To flow in a continuous stream; gush. **4.** To rain heavily. **5.** To move in great numbers; swarm. — *n.* A pouring, flow, or downfall. [ME *pouren*] — **pour′er** *n.* — **pour′ing·ly** *adv.*

pour·boire (pōōr·bwär′) *n. French* A gratuitous gift of money, as a tip. [< F, lit., in order to drink]

pout¹ (pout) *v.i.* **1.** To thrust out the lips, esp. in ill humor. **2.** To be sullen; sulk. **3.** To swell out; protrude. — *v.t.* **4.** To thrust out (the lips, etc.). **5.** To utter with a pout. — *n.* **1.** A pushing out of the lips as in pouting. **2.** A fit of ill humor. [ME *pouten*]

pout² (pout) *n.* Any of various fresh-water catfishes. [OE (æle) *pūte* eelpout]

pout·er (pou′tər) *n.* **1.** One who pouts. **2.** A breed of pigeon having the habit of puffing out the crop.

pov·er·ty (pov′ər·tē) *n.* **1.** The condition or quality of being poor. **2.** Scantiness of supply: a *poverty* of imagination. **3.** Absence or scarcity of necessary qualities, elements, etc.: *poverty* of soil. [< OF < L < *pauper* poor] — **Syn. 1.** Privation, indigence, penury.

pov·er·ty-strick·en (pov′ər·tē-strik′ən) *adj.* Suffering from poverty; destitute.

pow·der (pou′dər) *n.* **1.** A finely ground or pulverized mass of loose particles formed from a solid substance in the dry state. **2.** Any of various substances prepared in this form, as a cosmetic, medicine, or explosive. — *v.t.* **1.** To reduce to powder; pulverize. **2.** To sprinkle or cover with or as with powder. — *v.i.* **3.** To be reduced to powder. **4.** To use powder as a cosmetic. [< OF < L *pulvis* dust] — **pow′der·er** *n.*

powder blue A soft medium blue.

powder horn The hollow horn of an ox or cow, formerly fitted with a cover and used for holding gunpowder.

powder puff A soft pad used to apply powder to the skin.

pow·der·y (pou′dər·ē) *adj.* **1.** Consisting of or like fine powder or dust. **2.** Covered with or as with powder; mealy; dusty. **3.** Capable of being easily powdered; friable.

pow·er (pou′ər) *n.* **1.** Ability to act; capability. **2.** Potential capacity. **3.** Strength or force actually put forth. **4.** The right, ability, or capacity to exercise control; legal authority. **5.** Any agent that exercises power, as in control or dominion: an important and influential sovereign nation. **6.** Great or telling force or effect. **7.** Often *pl.* A mental or physical faculty. **8.** Any form of energy available for doing work; esp., electrical energy. **9.** *Physics* The time rate at which energy is transferred, or converted into work. **10.** *Math.* **a** The product of a number multiplied by itself a given number of times: The third *power* of 2 is 8.

b An exponent. **11.** *Optics* Magnifying capacity, as of a lens. — *v.t.* To provide with means of propulsion. [< OF < LL < L *posse* to be able]

power boat A motorboat.

pow·er·ful (pou′ər·fəl) *adj.* **1.** Possessing great force or energy; strong. **2.** Exercising great authority, or manifesting high qualities. **3.** Having great effect on the mind. — *adv. Dial. & Informal* Very. — **pow′er·ful·ly** *adv.*

pow·er·house (pou′ər·hous′) *n. Electr.* A station where electricity is generated.

pow·er·less (pou′ər·lis) *adj.* **1.** Destitute of power; unable to accomplish an effect; impotent. **2.** Without authority. — **pow′er·less·ly** *adv.* — **pow′er·less·ness** *n.*

power of attorney *Law* **1.** The authority or power to act conferred upon an agent. **2.** The instrument or document by which that power or authority is conferred.

power politics The use or threatened use of superior force to exact international concessions.

pow·wow (pou′wou′) *U.S. n.* **1.** *Informal* Any meeting or conference. **2.** A North American Indian ceremony to cure the sick or effect success in war, etc. **3.** A conference with or of American Indians. — *v.i.* To hold a powwow. [< Algonquian (Massachusetts) *pauwaw*, lit., he dreams]

pox (poks) *n.* **1.** Any disease characterized by purulent eruptions: *chickenpox.* **2.** Syphilis. [Var. of *pocks,* pl. of POCK]

prac·ti·ca·ble (prak′ti·kə·bəl) *adj.* **1.** That can be put into practice; feasible. **2.** That can be used; usable. [< F < Med.L < LL < Gk. *prassein* to do] — **prac′ti·ca·bil′i·ty, prac′ti·ca·ble·ness** *n.* — **prac′ti·ca·bly** *adv.*

prac·ti·cal (prak′ti·kəl) *adj.* **1.** Pertaining to or governed by actual use and experience or action, as contrasted with speculation. **2.** Trained by or derived from practice or experience. **3.** Applicable to use. **4.** Manifested in practice. **5.** Being such to all intents and purposes; virtual. — **Syn.** See PRACTICABLE. [< MF < LL < Gk. *prassein* to do] — **prac′ti·cal·i·ty** (-kal′ə·tē), **prac′ti·cal·ness** *n.*

practical joke A trick having a victim or victims.

prac·ti·cal·ly (prak′tik·lē) *adv.* **1.** In a practical manner. **2.** To all intents and purposes; in fact or effect; virtually.

practical nurse One who has some training and practice in nursing but who is not a registered nurse.

prac·tice (prak′tis) *v.* **·ticed, ·tic·ing** *v.t.* **1.** To make use of habitually or often: to *practice* economy. **2.** To apply in action; make a practice of. **3.** To work at a profession. **4.** To do or perform repeatedly in order to acquire skill or training; rehearse. **5.** To instruct, as pupils, by repeated exercise or lessons. — *v.i.* **6.** To repeat or rehearse something in order to acquire skill or proficiency. **7.** To work at a profession. — *n.* **1.** Any customary action or proceeding; habit. **2.** An established custom or usage. **3.** The act of doing or performing: distinguished from *theory.* **4.** The regular prosecution of a profession. **5.** Frequent and repeated exercise in any matter. **6.** *pl.* Stratagems or schemes for bad purposes; tricks. **7.** The rules by which legal proceedings are governed. Also **prac′tise.** [< MF < Med.L < LL < Gk. *praktikos* < *prassein* to do] — **prac′tic·er** *n.* — **Syn.** (noun) **5.** *Practice* is the putting into action of what one has learned in theory, to gain skill and facility. *Exercise* is primarily physical action to acquire and maintain strength. *Drill* is systematic and rigorous *practice* under an instructor.

prac·ticed (prak′tist) *adj.* **1.** Expert by practice; experienced. **2.** Acquired by practice. Also **prac′tised.**

prac·ti·tion·er (prak·tish′ən·ər) *n.* One who practices an art or profession.

prae- See PRE-.

prae·fect (prē′fekt) See PREFECT.

prae·no·men (prē·nō′mən) *n. pl.* **·nom·i·na** (-nom′ə·nə) The first name of an ancient Roman; also, any given name: also spelled *prenomen.* [< L]

praeter- See PRETER-.

prae·tor (prē′tər) *n.* A city magistrate of ancient Rome; also spelled *pretor.* [< L < *praeire* to go before] — **prae·to·ri·al** (pri·tôr′ē·əl, -tō′rē-) *adj.* — **prae′tor·ship** *n.*

prae·to·ri·an (pri·tôr′ē·ən, -tō′rē-) *adj.* Of a praetor; praetorial. — *n.* A praetor or ex-praetor. Also spelled *pretorian.*

Prae·to·ri·an (pri·tôr′ē·ən, -tō′rē-) *adj.* Denoting the Praetorian Guard. — *n.* A soldier of the Praetorian Guard. Also spelled *Pretorian.*

Praetorian Guard 1. The bodyguard of the Roman emperors. **2.** A member of this bodyguard.

prag·mat·ic (prag·mat′ik) *adj.* **1.** Pertaining to the study of events with emphasis on cause and effect. **2.** *Philos.* Pertaining to pragmatism. **3.** Pragmatical. [< L < Gk. < *pragma, pragmatos* thing done < *prassein* to do]

prag·mat·i·cal (prag·mat′i·kəl) *adj.* Relating to everyday business; practical; commonplace.

---

prag·mat·i·cal·ly (prag·mat′i·kəl·ē) *adv.* In a pragmatic or pragmatical manner. **— prag·mat′i·cal·ness** *n.*

prag·ma·tism (prag′mə·tiz′əm) *n.* **1.** *Philos.* The doctrine that ideas have value only in terms of their practical consequences, and that results are the sole test of the validity or truth of one's beliefs. **2.** The quality or condition of being pragmatic. **— prag′ma·tist** *n.*

prai·rie (prâr′ē) *n.* *U.S. & Canadian* A tract of grassland; esp., the broad, grassy plain of central North America. [< F < L *pratum* meadow]

prairie chicken Either of two gallinaceous game birds inhabiting the plains of western North America. Also **prairie hen.**

prairie dog A burrowing rodent of the plains of North America. Also **prairie squirrel.**

prairie schooner *U.S.* A covered wagon for travel by pioneers.

Prairie State Nickname of ILLINOIS.

prairie wolf A coyote.

praise (prāz) *n.* **1.** An expression of approval or commendation. **2.** The glorifying and honoring of a god, ruler, hero, etc. **—** *v.t.* **praised, prais·ing** **1.** To express approval and commendation of; applaud. **2.** To express adoration of; glorify, esp. in song. [< OF < LL *pretiare* to prize] **— prais′er** *n.*

— Syn. (verb) **1.** *Praise* is a weak word, and may refer to the mere speaking of compliments. To *laud* is to *praise* highly. *Extol* stresses the intention to elevate or magnify a person or thing by praise. *Applaud* and *acclaim* point to a public show of approval, as by clapping the hands or shouting. **— Ant.** blame, decry.

praise·wor·thy (prāz′wûr′thē) *adj.* Worthy of praise. **— praise′wor′thi·ly** *adv.,* **— praise′wor·thi·ness** *n.*

Pra·krit (prä′krit) *n.* Any of several vernacular languages of ancient India. [< Skt. *prakrtā* natural]

pra·line (prä′lēn, prā′-) *n.* A confection made of pecans or other nuts browned in boiling sugar. [< F, after Marshal Duplessis-*Praslin*, 1598–1675, whose cook invented it]

pram (pram) *n.* *Chiefly Brit. Informal* A baby carriage. [Short for PERAMBULATOR]

prance (prans, präns) *v.* **pranced, pranc·ing** *v.i.* **1.** To move proudly with high steps, as a spirited horse; spring from the hind legs; also, to ride a horse moving thus. **2.** To move in an arrogant or elated manner; swagger. **3.** To gambol; caper. **—** *v.t.* **4.** To cause to prance. **—** *n.* The act of prancing; a high step; caper. [ME *prauncen*] **— pranc′er** *n.*

pran·di·al (pran′dē·əl) *adj.* Of or pertaining to a meal, esp. dinner. [< L *prandium* breakfast or lunch]

prank¹ (prangk) *v.t.* **1.** To decorate gaudily. **—** *v.i.* **2.** To make an ostentatious show. [Prob. < MLG *prank* pomp]

prank² (prangk) *n.* A mischievous or frolicsome act; a trick. **—** *v.i.* To play pranks or tricks. [Origin uncertain; ? < PRANK¹] **— prank′ish** *adj.*

pra·sco·dym·i·um (prā′zē·ō·dim′ē·əm, prā′sē-) *n.* A yellowish white metallic element (symbol Pr) of the lanthanide series, having olive-green salts. See ELEMENT. [< NL < Gk. *prasios* light green + (DI)DYMIUM]

prate (prāt) *v.* **prat·ed, prat·ing** *v.i.* **1.** To talk idly and at length; chatter. **—** *v.t.* **2.** To utter idly or emptily. **—** *n.* Idle talk; prattle. [< MDu.-MLG *praten*] **— prat′er** *n.* **— prat′ing·ly** *adv.*

prat·fall (prat′fôl′) *n.* *U.S. Slang* A fall on the buttocks.

prat·tle (prat′l) *v.* **·tled, ·tling** *v.i.* **1.** To talk foolishly or like a child. **—** *v.t.* **2.** To utter in a foolish or childish way. **—** *n.* **1.** Childish speech. **2.** Idle or foolish talk. [See PRATE.] **— prat′tler** *n.*

prawn (prôn) *n.* Any of various shrimplike crustaceans of tropical and temperate waters, used as food. **—** *v.i.* To fish for prawns. [ME *prane, prayne*]

pray (prā) *v.i.* **1.** To address prayers to a deity, idol, etc. **2.** To make earnest request or entreaty; beg. **—** *v.t.* **3.** To say prayers to. **4.** To ask (someone) earnestly; entreat. **5.** To ask for by prayers or entreaty. [< OF < LL < L *prex, precis* request, prayer] **— pray′er** *n.*

prayer (prâr) *n.* **1.** A devout request or petition to a deity. **2.** The act of praying, esp. to God. **3.** A set form of words used for a devout request, petition, etc. **4.** Spiritual and wordless communion with God. **5.** *Often pl.* A religious service. **6.** Something prayed for. **7.** Any earnest request.

prayer book **1.** A book of prayers for divine service. **2.** *Usu. cap.* The Book of Common Prayer.

prayer·ful (prâr′fəl) *adj.* Inclined or given to prayer; devotional. **— prayer′ful·ly** *adv.* **— prayer′ful·ness** *n.*

prayer wheel A wheel, cylinder, or vertical drum containing written prayers, used by the Buddhists of Tibet.

praying mantis The mantis (which see).

pre- *prefix* **1.** Before in time or order; prior to; preceding; as in: *preurrange, pre-Roman.* **2.** Before in position; anterior: chiefly in scientific terms; as in: *preabdomen, preanal.* **3.** Preliminary to; preparing for; as in: *precollege.* Also *prae-.* [< L *prae* before]

preach (prēch) *v.t.* **1.** To advocate or recommend urgently. **2.** To proclaim or expound upon: to *preach* the gospel. **3.** To deliver (a sermon, etc.). **—** *v.i.* **4.** To deliver a sermon. **5.** To give advice, esp. in an officious or moralizing manner. [< OF < L *praedicare* to proclaim]

preach·er (prē′chər) *n.* **1.** *Informal* A clergyman, esp. a Protestant minister. **2.** One who preaches.

preach·i·fy (prē′chə·fī) *v.i.* **·fied, ·fy·ing** *Informal* To preach or discourse tediously. **— preach′i·fi·ca′tion** *n.*

preach·ment (prēch′mənt) *n.* A sermon or moral lecture, esp. a tedious one.

preach·y (prē′chē) *adj.* **preach·i·er, preach·i·est** Given to preaching; sanctimonious.

pre·am·ble (prē′am·bəl) *n.* **1.** An introductory statement or preface, esp. to a formal document. **2.** An introductory act, event, fact, etc. [< OF < Med.L < L *prae-* before + *ambulare* to walk] **— pre·am′bu·lar′y** (-byə·ler′ē) *adj.*

pre·am·pli·fi·er (prē·am′plə·fī′ər) *n.* In a sound reproduction system, an auxiliary amplifier used to reinforce very weak signals before sending them into the main amplifier. Also **pre·amp** (prē′amp).

preb·end (preb′ənd) *n.* **1.** A stipend allotted from the revenues of a cathedral or conventual church to a clergyman. **2.** The land or tithe yielding the stipend. **3.** A prebendary. [< MF < Med.L < L *praebere* to supply] **— preb′en·dal** *adj.*

preb·en·dar·y (preb′ən·der′ē) *n. pl.* **·dar·ies** A canon or clergyman who holds a prebend. Also called *prebend.*

Pre-Cam·bri·an (prē·kam′brē·ən) *adj. Geol.* Of or pertaining to all geological time and rock formations preceding the Cambrian. See table for GEOLOGY. **—** *n.* Pre-Cambrian era or rocks.

pre·can·cel (prē·kan′səl) *v.t.* **·celed** or **·celled, ·cel·ing** or **·cel·ling** To cancel (stamps) before use on mail. **—** *n.* A precanceled stamp.

pre·car·i·ous (pri·kâr′ē·əs) *adj.* **1.** Subject to continued risk; uncertain. **2.** Subject or exposed to danger; hazardous. **— Syn.** See RISKY. **3.** Without foundation or basis. [< L *precarius* obtained by prayer]

pre·cau·tion (pri·kô′shən) *n.* **1.** A step or preparation taken to avoid a possible danger, evil, etc. **2.** Caution observed in preparation for a possible emergency. [< F < LL < L < *prae-* before + *cavere* to take care] **— pre·cau′tion·ar′y** *adj.*

pre·cau·tious (pri·kô′shəs) *adj.* Exercising precaution. **— pre·cau′tious·ly** *adv.* **— pre·cau′tious·ness** *n.*

pre·cede (pri·sēd′) *v.* **·ced·ed, ·ced·ing** *v.t.* **1.** To go or be before in order, place, rank, time, etc. **2.** To preface; introduce. **—** *v.i.* **3.** To go or be before; take precedence. [< F < L < *prae-* before + *cedere* to go]

prec·e·dence (pri·sēd′əns, pres′ə·dəns) *n* **1.** The act, right, or state of preceding in place, time, or rank. **2.** The ceremonial order observed by persons of different ranks on formal occasions. Also **prec·e·den·cy** (pri·sēd′ən·sē, pres′ə·dən·sē).

prec·e·dent (*n.* pres′ə·dənt; *adj.* pri·sēd′nt) *n.* An act or instance capable of being used as a guide or standard in evaluating future actions. **—** *adj.* Former; preceding. **— prec′e·den′tial** *adj.*

pre·ced·ing (pri·sē′ding) *adj.* Going before, as in time, place, or rank; earlier; foregoing. **— the preceding** That which precedes or has been mentioned before.

pre·cen·tor (pri·sen′tər) *n.* One who leads the singing of a church choir or congregation. [< LL < L < *prae-* before + *canere* to sing] **— pre·cen·to·ri·al** (prē′sen·tôr′ē·əl, -tō′rē-) *adj.* **— pre·cen′tor·ship** *n.*

pre·cept (prē′sept) *n.* **1.** A rule prescribing a particular kind of conduct or action. **2.** A proverbial standard or guide to morals; a maxim. [< L *praecipere* to prescribe]

pre·cep·tive (pri·sep′tiv) *adj.* **1.** Consisting of or expressing a precept or precepts. **2.** Pertaining to or of the nature of a precept.

pre·cep·tor (pri·sep′tər) *n.* A teacher; instructor. [< L *praeceptor*] **— pre·cep·to·ri·al** (prē′sep·tôr′ē·əl, -tō′rē-) *adj.* **— pre·cep′tress** (-tris) *n.fem.*

pre·ces·sion (pri·sesh′ən) *n.* The act of preceding. **— pre·ces′sion·al** *adj.*

pre·cinct (prē′singkt) *n.* **1.** *U.S.* An election district of a town, township, county, etc. **2.** *U.S.* **a** A subdivision of a city or town under the jurisdiction of a police unit. **b** The police station for such an area. **3.** A place marked off by fixed limits; also, the boundary of such a place. **4.** *pl.* Neighborhood; environs. **5.** A limited area of thought, action, etc. [< Med.L < L *praecingere* < *prae-* before + *cingere* to encircle]

pre·ci·os·i·ty (presh′ē·os′ə·tē) *n. pl.* **·ties** Extreme fastidiousness or affected refinement, as in speech, style, etc.

pre·cious (presh′əs) *adj.* **1.** Highly priced or prized; valuable. **2.** Greatly esteemed; truth is precious. **3.** Beloved; cherished. **4.** Affectedly delicate or sensitive, as a style of writing. **5.** *Informal* Flagrant; surpassing: a *pre-*

cious scoundrel. — *n.* Precious one; sweetheart. — *adv.* Extremely; very. [< OF < L < *pretium* price] — **pre'·cious·ly** *adv.* — **pre'cious·ness** *n.*

precious stone A valuable, rare gem, as the diamond, ruby, sapphire, or emerald.

prec·i·pice (pres'i·pis) *n.* 1. A high vertical or overhanging face of rock; the brink of a cliff. 2. A perilous situation. [< F < L < *prae-* before + *caput* head]

pre·cip·i·ta·ble (pri·sip'ə·tə·bəl) *adj. Chem.* Capable of being precipitated: a *precipitable* salt.

pre·cip·i·tant (pri·sip'ə·tənt) *adj.* 1. Rushing or falling quickly or heedlessly. 2. Rash; overhasty; impulsive. 3. Very sudden; abrupt. — *n. Chem.* Any substance that, when added to a solution, results in the formation of a precipitate. — **pre·cip'i·tance, pre·cip'i·tan·cy** *n.* — **pre·cip'i·tant·ly** *adv.*

pre·cip·i·tate (pri·sip'ə·tāt; *for adj. & n., also* pri·sip'ə·tit) *v.* **·tat·ed, ·tat·ing** *v.t.* 1. To hasten the occurrence of. 2. To hurl from or as from a height; throw headlong. 3. *Meteorol.* To cause (vapor, etc.) to condense and fall as dew, rain, etc. 4. *Chem.* To separate (a substance) in solid form, as from a solution. — *v.i.* 5. *Meteorol.* To fall as condensed vapor, etc. 6. *Chem.* To separate and settle, as a substance held in solution. 7. To fall headlong. — *adj.* 1. Moving speedily or hurriedly; rushing headlong. 2. Lacking due deliberation; hasty; rash. 3. Sudden and brief, as a disease. — *n. Chem.* A deposit of solid matter formed by precipitation. [< L *praeceps*. See PRECIPICE.] — **pre·cip'i·tate·ly** *adv.* — **pre·cip'i·tate·ness** *n.* — **pre·cip'i·ta'tive** *adj.* — **pre·cip'i·ta'tor** *n.*

pre·cip·i·ta·tion (pri·sip'ə·tā'shən) *n.* 1. *Meteorol.* a The depositing of moisture from the atmosphere upon the surface of the earth. b The amount of rain, snow, etc., deposited. 2. *Chem.* The process of separating any of the constituents of a solution. 3. The act of precipitating, or the state of being precipitated. 4. Rash haste or hurry.

pre·cip·i·tous (pri·sip'ə·təs) *adj.* 1. Consisting of or like a precipice; very steep. 2. Having many precipices. 3. Hasty. — **pre·cip'i·tous·ly** *adv.* — **pre·cip'i·tous·ness** *n.*

pré·cis (prā'sē, prā·sē') *n. pl.* **pré·cis** (prā'sēz, prā·sēz') A concise summary of a book, article, or document; abstract. — Syn. See ABRIDGMENT. [< F]

pre·cise (pri·sīs') *adj.* 1. Sharply and clearly determined or defined. 2. No more and no less than; exact in amount. 3. Noting or confined to a certain thing; particular. 4. Exact or distinct in sound, statement, etc. 5. Scrupulously observant of rule. [< F < L < *prae* before | *caedere* to cut] — **pre·cise'ly** *adv.* — **pre·cise'ness** *n.*

pre·ci·sion (pri·sizh'ən) *n.* The state or quality of being precise; accuracy; definition. — *adj.* 1. Designed for extremely accurate measurement: *precision* instruments. 2. Characterized by precision. — **pre·ci'sion·ist** *n.*

pre·clude (pri·klōōd') *v.t.* **·clud·ed, ·clud·ing** 1. To make impossible or ineffectual by prior action. 2. To shut out; exclude. — Syn. See PREVENT. [< L < *prae-* before + *claudere* to shut] — **pre·clu'sion** (-klōō'zhən) *n.* — **pre·clu'sive** (-klōō'siv) *adj.* — **pre·clu'sive·ly** *adv.*

pre·co·cious (pri·kō'shəs) *adj.* 1. Unusually developed or advanced for one's age. 2. Pertaining to or showing premature development. [< L < *prae-* beforehand, early + *coquere* to cook] — **pre·co'cious·ly** *adv.* — **pre·co'cious·ness, pre·coc'i·ty** (-kos'ə·tē) *n.*

pre·con·ceive (prē'kən·sēv') *v.t.* **·ceived, ·ceiv·ing** To conceive in advance; form an idea or opinion beforehand.

pre·con·cep·tion (prē'kən·sep'shən) *n.* 1. An idea or opinion formed or conceived in advance. 2. A prejudice or misconception; bias. — **pre'con·cep'tion·al** *adj.*

pre·con·di·tion (prē'kən·dish'ən) *n.* A condition that must be met before a certain result is attained; prerequisite.

pre·cur·sor (pri·kûr'sər) *n.* One who or that which precedes and suggests the course of future events. [< L < *prae-* before + *currere* to run]

pre·cur·so·ry (pri·kûr'sər·ē) *adj.* Going before as a precursor or harbinger; preliminary. Also **pre·cur'sive** (-kûr'siv).

pre·da·cious (pri·dā'shəs) *adj.* Living by preying upon others, as a beast or bird; raptorial: also *predatory*. Also **pre·da'ceous**. [< L *praeda* prey] — **pre·da'cious·ness, pre·dac'i·ty** (-das'ə·tē) *n.*

pre·date (prē'dāt') *v.t.* **·dat·ed, ·dat·ing** 1. To date before the actual time. 2. To precede in time.

pred·a·tor (pred'i·tər) *n.* A predatory person or animal.

pred·a·to·ry (pred'ə·tôr'ē, -tō'rē) *adj.* 1. Of, relating to, or characterized by plundering. 2. Accustomed to or living by pillaging. 3. Predacious. [< L *praeda* prey] — **pred'a·to'ri·ly** *adv.* — **pred'a·to'ri·ness** *n.*

pre·de·cease (prē'di·sēs') *v.t.* **·ceased, ·ceas·ing** To die before: She *predeceased* her husband by five years.

pred·e·ces·sor (pred'ə·ses'ər) *n.* 1. One who goes or has gone before another in point of time. 2. A thing succeeded

by something else. 3. An ancestor. [< OF < LL < *prae-* before + *decessor* withdrawer]

pre·des·ti·nate (prē·des'tə·nāt) *v.t.* **·nat·ed, ·nat·ing** 1. *Theol.* To foreordain by divine decree or purpose. 2. To predestine. [< L < *prae-* before + *destinare* to determine]

pre·des·ti·na·tion (prē·des'tə·nā'shən) *n.* 1. The act of predestining, or the state of being predestined; destiny; fate. 2. *Theol.* The foreordination of all things by God, including the salvation or damnation of men.

pre·des·tine (prē·des'tin) *v.t.* **·tined, ·tin·ing** To destine or decree beforehand; foreordain; predestinate.

pre·de·ter·mine (prē'di·tûr'min) *v.t.* **·mined, ·min·ing** 1. To determine beforehand; foreordain. 2. To urge to accept (a point of view, etc.) beforehand; influence. — **pre'de·ter'mi·nate** (-mə·nit, -nāt) *adj.* — **pre'de·ter'mi·na'tion** *n.*

pred·i·ca·ble (pred'i·kə·bəl) *adj.* Capable of being predicated or affirmed. — *n.* 1. Anything predicable. — **pred'i·ca·bil'i·ty, pred'i·ca·ble·ness** *n.*

pre·dic·a·ment (pri·dik'ə·mənt) *n.* 1. A trying or embarrassing situation; plight. 2. A specific state, position, or situation. [< LL < *praedicare* to proclaim. See PREACH.]

pred·i·cate (*v.* pred'i·kāt; *n. & adj.* pred'i·kit) *v.* **·cat·ed, ·cat·ing** *v.t.* 1. *U.S.* To found or base (an argument, proposition, etc.): with *on* or *upon*. 2. To affirm as a quality or attribute of something. 3. To imply or connote. 4. To declare; proclaim. 5. *Logic* To state or affirm concerning the subject of a proposition. — *v.i.* 6. To make a statement or affirmation. — *n.* 1. *Gram.* The verb in a sentence or clause together with its complements and modifiers. 2. *Logic* In a proposition, that which is stated about a subject. — *adj.* 1. That predicates. 2. *Gram.* Belonging to, relating to, or of the nature of a predicate. [< L < *praedicare* to proclaim] — **pred'i·ca'tive** *adj.* — **pred'i·ca'tive·ly** *adv.*

predicate adjective *Gram.* An adjective that describes the subject of a linking verb, as *sad* in *He is sad.*

predicate noun *Gram.* A noun that designates or identifies the subject of a linking verb, as *king* in *He was king.*

pred·i·ca·tion (pred'i·kā'shən) *n.* 1. The act of predicating. 2. Something predicated. — **pred'i·ca'tion·al** *adj.*

pre·dict (pri·dikt') *v.t.* 1. To make known beforehand; prophesy. 2. To assert on the basis of data, theory, or experience but in advance of proof. — *v.i.* 3. To make a prediction. [< L < *prae-* before + *dicere* to say] — **pre·dict'a·ble** *adj.* — **pre·dict'a·bly** *adv.* — **pre·dic'tor** *n.*

pre·dic·tion (pri·dik'shən) *n.* 1. The act of predicting. 2. Something predicted. — **pre·dic'tive** *adj.* — **pre·dic'tive·ly** *adv.*

pre·di·gest (prē'di·jest', -dī-) *v.t.* To treat (food) by a process of partial digestion before introduction into the stomach.

pre·di·lec·tion (prē'də·lek'shən, pred'ə-) *n.* A preference or bias in favor of something; a partiality: with *for.* [< F < Med.L < L *prae-* before + *diligere* to love, choose]

pre·dis·pose (prē'dis·pōz') *v.t.* **·posed, ·pos·ing** 1. To give a tendency or inclination to; make susceptible: Exhaustion *predisposes* one to sickness. 2. To dispose of beforehand.

pre·dom·i·nant (pri·dom'ə·nənt) *adj.* Superior in power, influence, effectiveness, number, or degree; prevailing over others. — **pre·dom'i·nance, pre·dom'i·nan·cy** *n.* — **pre·dom'i·nant·ly** *adv.*

pre·dom·i·nate (pri·dom'ə·nāt) *v.i.* **·nat·ed, ·nat·ing** 1. To have governing influence or control; be in control: often with *over.* 2. To be superior to all others. 3. To prevail. — **pre·dom'i·nat'ing·ly** *adv.* — **pre·dom'i·na'tion** *n.*

pre·em·i·nent (prē·em'ə·nənt) *adj.* Supremely eminent; distinguished above all others; outstanding; conspicuous. [< L < *prae-* before + *eminere* to stand out] — **pre·em'i·nent·ly** *adv.* — **pre·em'i·nence** *n.*

pre·empt (prē·empt') *v.t.* 1. To acquire or appropriate beforehand. 2. To occupy (public land) so as to acquire by preemption. — *v.i.* 3. In bridge, to make a preemptive bid. — **pre·emp'tor** *n.* — **pre·emp'to·ry** (-tər·ē) *adj.*

pre·emp·tion (prē·emp'shən) *n.* 1. The right to purchase something before others; also, the act of so purchasing. 2. Public land obtained by exercising this right. [< Med.L < L *prae-* before + *emptus*, pp. of *emere* to buy]

pre·emp·tive (prē·emp'tiv) *adj.* 1. Pertaining to or capable of preemption. 2. In bridge, designating a bid that is unnecessarily high, intended to discourage subsequent bidding.

preen (prēn) *v.t.* 1. To trim and dress (feathers, etc.) with the beak, as a bird. 2. To dress or adorn (oneself) carefully. 3. To pride or congratulate (oneself): with *on.* — *v.i.* 4. To primp; prink. [ME *proyne, preyn, prene*]

pre·ex·ist (prē'ig·zist') *v.t. & v.i.* To exist before. — **pre'·ex·is'tence** *n.* — **pre'ex·is'tent** *adj.*

pre·fab (prē'fab') *n.* A prefabricated structure or part.

pre·fab·ri·cate (prē·fab'rə·kāt) *v.t.* **·cat·ed, ·cat·ing** 1. To build beforehand. 2. To manufacture in standard sections that can be rapidly assembled. — **pre·fab'ri·ca'tion** *n.*

pref·ace (pref'is) *n.* **1.** A statement or brief essay, included in the front matter of a book, etc., and dealing primarily with the purpose and scope of the work. **2.** Any introductory speech, writing, etc. — *v.t.* **·aced, ·ac·ing 1.** To introduce or furnish with a preface. **2.** To serve as a preface for. [< OF < L < *prae-* before + *fari* to speak]

pref·a·to·ry (pref'ə·tôr'ē, -tō'rē) *adj.* Of the nature of a preface; introductory. Also **pref·a·to·ri·al.** — **pref'a·to'ri·ly** *adv.*

pre·fect (prē'fekt) *n.* **1.** In ancient Rome, any of various civil and military officials. **2.** Any magistrate, chief official, etc.; esp., in France: **a** The chief administrator of a department. **b** The head of the Paris police. **3.** The dean of certain private or religious schools. Also spelled *praefect.* [< OF < L *praefectus* to set over]

pre·fec·ture (prē'fek·chər) *n.* The office, jurisdiction, or province of a prefect. — **pre·fec'tur·al** *adj.*

pre·fer (pri·fûr') *v.t.* **·ferred, ·fer·ring 1.** To hold in higher regard or esteem; value more. **2.** To choose (something or someone) over another or others; like better. **3.** To give priority to, as certain securities over others. — **Syn.** See CHOOSE. [< F < L < *prae-* before + *ferre* to carry] — **pre·fer'rer** *n.*

pref·er·a·ble (pref'ər·ə·bəl) *adj.* That is preferred; more desirable; worthy of choice. — **pref'er·a·ble·ness, pref'er·a·bil'i·ty** *n.* — **pref'er·a·bly** *adv.*

pref·er·ence (pref'ər·əns) *n.* **1.** The choosing of one person or thing over another or others; also, the privilege of so choosing. **2.** One who or that which is preferred. **3.** The granting of special advantage to one over others, as to one country or group of countries. **4.** The act of preferring, or the state of being preferred.

pref·er·en·tial (pref'ə·ren'shəl) *adj.* **1.** Showing or arising from preference or partiality. **2.** Giving preference, as in tariffs. — **pref'er·en'tial·ism** *n.* — **pref'er·en'tial·ly** *adv.*

preferential shop A shop that gives preferential treatment to union members when hiring, laying off, promoting, etc.

pre·fer·ment (pri·fûr'mənt) *n.* **1.** The act of promoting to higher office; advancement. **2.** A position, rank, or office of social prestige or profit. **3.** The act of preferring.

preferred stock Stock on which dividends must be paid before dividends can be paid on common stocks, usu. also receiving preference in the distribution of assets on liquidation. Also *Brit.* **preference shares.**

pre·fig·u·ra·tion (prē·fig'yə·rā'shən) *n.* **1.** The act of prefiguring. **2.** That which prefigures; a prototype. — **pre·fig·ur·a·tive** (prē·fig'yər·ə·tiv) *adj.* — **pre·fig'ur·a·tive·ly** *adv.* — **pre·fig'ur·a·tive·ness** *n.*

pre·fig·ure (prē·fig'yər) *v.t.* **·ured, ·ur·ing 1.** To serve as an indication or suggestion of; foreshadow. **2.** To imagine or picture to oneself beforehand. [< LL < L *prae-* before + *figurare* to form]

pre·fix (*n.* prē'fiks; *v.* prē·fiks') *n.* **1.** *Gram.* A bound form affixed to the beginning of a base, stem, or root, altering or modifying its meaning, as *re-* in *renew.* Compare COMBINING FORM, SUFFIX. **2.** Something placed before, as a title before a name. — *v.t.* To put or attach before or at the beginning; add as a prefix. [< OF < L < *prae-* before + *figere* to fasten, fix] — **pre'fix·al·ly** *adv.* — **pre·fix·ion** (prē·fik'shən) *n.*

preg·na·ble (preg'nə·bəl) *adj.* **1.** Capable of being captured, as a fort. **2.** Open to attack; vulnerable; assailable. [< OF < L *prehendere* to seize] — **preg'na·bil'i·ty** *n.*

preg·nan·cy (preg'nən·sē) *n. pl.* **·cies** The state or quality of being pregnant.

preg·nant (preg'nənt) *adj.* **1.** Carrying a growing fetus in the uterus. **2.** Having considerable weight or significance; full of meaning. **3.** Teeming with ideas. **4.** Bearing issue or results; fruitful; prolific. [< L < *prae-* before + *gnasci* to be born] — **preg'nant·ly** *adv.*

pre·hen·si·ble (pri·hen'sə·bəl) *adj.* Capable of being grasped.

pre·hen·sile (pri·hen'sil) *adj.* Adapted for grasping or holding, as the tail of a monkey. [See PREHENSION.] — **pre·hen·sil·i·ty** (prē'hen·sil'ə·tē) *n.*

pre·hen·sion (pri·hen'shən) *n.* The act of grasping, physically or mentally. [< L *prehendere* to seize]

pre·his·tor·ic (prē'his·tôr'ik, -tor'-) *adj.* Of or belonging to the period before written history. Also **pre'his·tor'i·cal.** — **pre'his·tor'i·cal·ly** *adv.*

pre·his·to·ry (prē·his'tə·rē) *n. pl.* **·ries** The history of mankind in the period preceding written records.

pre·judge (prē·juj') *v.t.* **·judged, ·judg·ing** To judge beforehand or without proper inquiry. [< F < Med.L < *prae-* before + *judicare* to judge] — **pre·judg'er** *n.* — **pre·judg'ment** or **pre·judge'ment** *n.*

prej·u·dice (prej'oo·dis) *n.* **1.** A judgment or opinion formed before the facts are known; esp., an unfavorable, irrational opinion. **2.** The act or state of holding preconceived, irrational opinions. **3.** Hatred of or dislike for a particular group, race, religion, etc. **4.** Injury or damage to a person arising from a hasty and unfair judgment by others. — **in** (or **to**) **the prejudice of** To the injury or detriment of. — *v.t.* **·diced, ·dic·ing 1.** To cause to have a prejudice; bias; influence. **2.** To damage or impair by some act, judgment, etc. [< OF < L < *prae-* before + *judicium* judgment] — **Syn.** (noun) *Prejudice, bias,* and *partiality* are compared as they denote an attitude of mind that interferes with fair judgment. Only *prejudice* is necessarily a term of opprobrium; literally, it signifies prejudgment without adequate hearing or consideration, but it is chiefly used to refer to a strong emotional *bias.* A *bias* is an imbalance of mind, an inclination in some direction that prevents a fair weighing of issues. *Partiality* is an inclination to favor one person or view unfairly. A *bias* may be for or against someone or something, but *partiality* always implies favor.

prej·u·di·cial (prej'oo·dish'əl) *adj.* Tending to prejudice or injure; detrimental. — **prej'u·di'cial·ly** *adv.*

prel·a·cy (prel'ə·sē) *n. pl.* **·cies 1.** The system of church government by prelates: sometimes used disparagingly. **2.** The dignity or function of a prelate; also, prelates collectively: also **prel·a·ture** (prel'ə·chər).

prel·ate (prel'it) *n.* An ecclesiastic of high rank, as a bishop, archbishop, etc. [< OF *prelat* < L *praelatus* set over] — **prel'ate·ship** *n.* — **pre·lat·ic** (pri·lat'ik) or **·i·cal** *adj.*

pre·lim·i·nar·y (pri·lim'ə·ner'ē) *adj.* Before or introductory to the main event, proceeding, or business; prefatory; preparatory. — *n. pl.* **·nar·ies 1.** A preparatory step or act. **2.** A preliminary examination. **3.** In sports, a minor, introductory event, as a boxing match. [< F *pré-* pre- + *liminaire* prefatory] — **pre·lim'i·nar'i·ly** *adv.*

pre·lit·er·ate (prē·lit'ər·it) *adj.* Of a culture, lacking or predating the existence of written language or records.

prel·ude (prel'yood, prē'lood) *n.* **1.** *Music* **a** An instrumental composition of moderate length, in a free style. **b** An opening section or movement of a musical composition. **2.** Any introductory or opening performance or event. — *v.* **·ud·ed, ·ud·ing** *v.t.* **1.** To introduce with a prelude. **2.** To serve as a prelude to. — *v.i.* **3.** To serve as a prelude. **4.** To provide or play a prelude. [< Med.L < L < *prae-* before + *ludere* to play] — **pre·lud·er** (pri·loo'dər, prel'yə·dər) *n.* — **pre·lu·di·al** (pri·loo'dē·əl) *adj.*

pre·ma·ture (prē'mə·choor', -toor', -tyoor'; *Brit.* prem'ə·tyoor') *adj.* Existing, happening, or developed before the natural or proper period; untimely. [< L < *prae-* before + *maturus* ripe] — **pre'ma·ture'ly** *adv.* — **pre'ma·ture'ness, pre'ma·tu'ri·ty** *n.*

pre·med·i·cal (prē·med'i·kəl) *adj.* Preparatory to or preparing for the study of medicine. Also *Informal* **pre·med'.**

pre·med·i·tate (prē·med'ə·tāt) *v.t. & v.i.* **·tat·ed, ·tat·ing** To plan or consider beforehand. [< L < *prae-* before + *meditari* to muse, ponder] — **pre·med'i·tat'ed·ly** *adv.* — **pre·med'i·ta'tor** *n.*

pre·med·i·ta·tion (prē·med'ə·tā'shən) *n.* **1.** The act of premeditating. **2.** *Law* The deliberation and planning of a crime before its commission, showing intent to commit it.

pre·mi·er (prē'mē·ər, *esp. Brit.* prem'yər; *for n., also* pri·mir') *adj.* **1.** First in rank or position; principal. **2.** First in order of occurrence; senior. — *n.* **1.** Prime minister. **2.** In Canada, the head of a Provincial cabinet. [< F < L *primus* first] — **pre·mier·ship'** *n.*

pre·mière (pri·mir', *Fr.* prə·myâr') *n.* The first performance of a play, movie, etc. [< F, fem. of *premier* first]

pre·mil·len·ni·al (prē'mi·len'ē·əl) *adj.* Pertaining to or occurring before the millennium.

prem·ise (prem'is; *for v., also* pri·mīz') *n.* **1.** A proposition that serves as a ground for argument or for a conclusion. **2.** *pl.* A definite portion of real estate; land with its appurtenances; also, a building or part of a building. **3.** In a syllogism, either of the two propositions that combine to form a conclusion. **4.** *pl. Law* That part in a deed that sets forth the date, names of parties, the land or thing conveyed or granted, etc. Also **prem'iss.** — *v.* **·mised, ·mis·ing** *v.t.* **1.** To state beforehand, as by way of introduction or explanation. **2.** To state or assume as a premise or basis of argument. — *v.i.* **3.** To make a premise. [< MF < Med.L < L < *prae-* before + *mittere* to send]

pre·mi·um (prē'mē·əm) *n.* **1.** An object or service offered free as an inducement to buy, rent, or contract for another object or service. **2.** The amount paid or payable for insurance, usu. in periodical installments. **3.** An extra amount or bonus paid in addition to a fixed price, wage, etc. **4.** A price paid for a loan, usu. in addition to interest. **5.** The rate or price at which stocks, shares, or money are valued in excess of their nominal or par value: bank shares at a *premium* of five percent. **6.** High regard or value. **7.** A reward or prize awarded in a competition. — **at a premium 1.** Valuable and in demand. **2.** Above par. [< L ult. < *prae-* before + *emere* to take]

pre·mo·lar (prē·mō'lər) *Anat. n.* One of the teeth situated in front of the molars and behind the canines: also called *bicuspid.* — *adj.* Situated in front of the molar teeth.

pre·mo·ni·tion (prē'mə·nish'ən, prem'ə-) *n.* **1.** A presentiment of the future not based on information received; an instinctive foreboding. **2.** An actual warning of something yet to occur. [< LL < *prae-* before + *monere* to advise] — **pre·mon·i·to·ry** (pri·mon′ə·tôr′ē, -tō′rē) *adj.* — **pre·mon′·i·to·ri·ly** *adv.*

pre·na·tal (prē-nāt′l) *adj.* Prior to birth: *prenatal* care. — **pre·na′tal·ly** *adv.*

pre·no·men (prē-nō′mən) See PRAENOMEN.

pre·oc·cu·pied (prē-ok′yə·pīd) *adj.* **1.** Engrossed in thought or in some action. **2.** Previously occupied.

pre·oc·cu·py (prē-ok′yə·pī) *v.t.* **·pied, ·py·ing 1.** To engage fully; engross the mind. **2.** To occupy or take possession of first. [< L *praeoccupare* to seize beforehand] — **pre·oc′u·pan·cy** (-pən·sē), **pre·oc′cu·pa′tion** *n.*

pre·or·dain (prē′ôr·dān′) *v.t.* To ordain beforehand; foreordain. — **pre·or·di·na·tion** (prē′ôr·də·nā′shən) *n.*

prep (prep) *adj. Informal* Preparatory: a *prep* school.

pre·pack·age (prē·pak′ij) *v.t.* **·aged, ·ag·ing** To package (meats, etc.) before offering them for sale.

prep·a·ra·tion (prep′ə·rā′shən) *n.* **1.** The act or process of preparing. **2.** An act or proceeding undertaken in advance of some event; provision. **3.** The fact or state of being prepared. **4.** Something made or prepared, as a medicine.

pre·par·a·to·ry (pri·par′ə·tôr′ē, -tō′rē) *adj.* **1.** Serving as preparation. **2.** Occupied in preparation: a *preparatory* scholar. — *adv.* As a preparation: *Preparatory* to writing, I will consider this: also **pre·par′a·to′ri·ly.**

preparatory school A private school that prepares students for college admission.

pre·pare (pri·pâr′) *v.* **·pared, ·par·ing** *v.t.* **1.** To make ready, fit, or qualified; put in readiness. **2.** To provide with what is needed; equip: to *prepare* an expedition. **3.** To bring to a state of completeness: to *prepare* a meal. — *v.i.* **4.** To make preparations; get ready. [< F < L < *prae-* before + *parare* to produce] — **pre·par·ed·ly** (pri·pâr′id·lē) *adv.* — **pre·par′er** *n.*

pre·par·ed·ness (pri·pâr′id·nis, -pârd′-) *n.* Readiness; esp., a condition of military readiness for war.

pre·pay (prē-pā′) *v.t.* **·paid, ·pay·ing** To pay or pay for in advance. — **pre·pay′ment** *n.*

pre·pense (pri·pens′) *adj.* Considered beforehand; premeditated: chiefly in the phrase **malice prepense.** [< OF < L *pro-* ahead + *pensare* to think] — **pre·pense′ly** *adv.*

pre·pon·der·ant (pri·pon′dər·ənt) *adj.* Having superior force, weight, importance, quantity, etc.. — **pre·pon′der·ance, pre·pon′der·an·cy** *n.* — **pre·pon′der·ant·ly** *adv.*

pre·pon·der·ate (pri·pon′də·rāt) *v.i.* **·at·ed, ·at·ing 1.** To be of greater weight. **2.** To incline downward or descend, as the scale of a balance. **3.** To be of greater power, importance, quantity, etc.; predominate; prevail. [< L < *prae-* before + *ponderare* to weigh] — **pre·pon′der·a′tion** *n.*

prep·o·si·tion (prep′ə·zish′ən) *n. Gram.* **1.** In some languages, a word as *by, for, from,* functioning to indicate the relation of a substantive (the object of the preposition) to another substantive, verb, or adjective and usu. placed before its object. Together they constitute a prepositional phrase that serves as an adjectival or an adverbial modifier as: sitting *beside the fire*; a man *of honor.* **2.** Any word or construction that functions in a similar manner, as *in reference to* in *He telephoned in reference to your letter.*

◆ It was once maintained that a sentence should never end with a preposition, but natural English sentences often do. *What did you laugh at?* is good English. *At what did you laugh?* is awkward and unnatural. [< F < L < *prae-* before + *ponere* to place] — **prep′o·si′tion·al** *adj.* — **prep′o·si′tion·al·ly** *adv.*

pre·pos·sess (prē′pə·zes′) *v.t.* **1.** To preoccupy to the exclusion of other ideas, beliefs, etc.; prejudice; bias. **2.** To impress or influence beforehand or at once, esp. favorably. — **pre′pos·ses′sion** *n.*

pre·pos·sess·ing (prē′pə·zes′ing) *adj.* Inspiring a favorable opinion; pleasing. — **pre′pos·sess′ing·ly** *adv.*

pre·pos·ter·ous (pri·pos′tər·əs) *adj.* Contrary to nature, reason, or common sense; utterly absurd or impracticable. [< L < *prae* before + *posterus* last] — **pre·pos′ter·ous·ly** *adv.* — **pre·pos′ter·ous·ness** *n.*

pre·puce (prē′pyoōs) *n. Anat.* The fold of skin covering the glans of the penis or clitoris: also called *foreskin.* [< L *praeputium*] — **pre·pu·tial** (pri·pyoō′shəl) *adj.*

Pre-Raph·a·el·ite (prē·raf′ē·ə·līt, -rā′fē-) *n.* **1.** A follower of the **Pre-Raphaelite Brotherhood,** a society of artists formed in England, 1847–49, stressing characteristics supposedly typical of Italian art before the time of Raphael. **2.** Any modern artist with similar aims. — *adj.* Of or pertaining to the Pre-Raphaelites. — **Pre-Raph′a·el·it′ism** *n.*

pre·req·ui·site (prē·rek′wə·zit) *adj.* Required as an antecedent condition; necessary to something that follows. — *n.* Something prerequisite.

pre·rog·a·tive (pri·rog′ə·tiv) *n.* **1.** An exclusive and unquestionable right belonging to a person or body of persons; esp., a hereditary or official right. **2.** Any characteristic privilege peculiar to a person or class. **3.** Precedence; preeminence. — *adj.* Of, pertaining to, or possessing a prerogative. [< OF < L < *prae-* before + *rogare* to ask]

pres·age (*n.* pres′ij; *v.* pri·sāj′) *n.* **1.** An indication of something to come; omen. **2.** A presentiment; foreboding. **3.** Prophetic meaning or import. — *v.* **·saged, ·sag·ing** *v.t.* **1.** To give a presage or portent of; foreshadow. **2.** To have a presentiment of. **3.** To predict; foretell. — *v.i.* **4.** To make a prediction. [< MF < L < *prae-* before + *sagire* to perceive keenly] — **pre·sag′er** *n.*

pres·by·ter (prez′bə·tər, pres′-) *n. Eccl.* **1.** In the early Christian church, one of the elders of a church. **2.** In various hierarchical churches, a priest. **3.** In the Presbyterian Church: **a** An ordained clergyman: also called *teaching elder.* **b** A layman who is a member of the governing body of a congregation. [< LL < Gk. *presbyteros* elder, compar. of *presbys* old, important]

pres·by·ter·i·al (prez′bə·tir′ē·əl, pres′-) *adj.* Pertaining to a presbytery or a presbyter. Also **pres·byt′er·al.** — **pres′by·te′ri·al·ly** *adv.*

pres·by·te·ri·an (prez′bə·tir′ē·ən, pres′-) *adj.* Pertaining to or characterized by church government by presbyters. — **pres′by·te′ri·an·ism** *n.*

Pres·by·te·ri·an (prez′bə·tir′ē·ən, pres′-) *adj.* Pertaining to any of various Protestant churches that have church government by presbyters. — *n.* A member of a Presbyterian church. — **Pres′by·te′ri·an·ism** *n.*

pres·by·ter·y (prez′bə·ter′ē, pres′-) *n. pl.* **·ter·ies 1.** In the Presbyterian Church, a court composed of the ministers and one or two presbyters of each church in a district. **2.** Presbyters collectively. **3.** Government of a church by presbyters. **4.** That part of a church set apart for the clergy. [< OF < LL *presbyterium* assembly of elders]

pre·school (prē′skool′) *adj.* Of, intended for, or designating a child past infancy but under school age.

pre·sci·ence (prē′shē·əns, presh′ē-) *n.* Knowledge of events before they take place; foreknowledge. [< OF < L < *prae-* before + *scire* to know]

pre·sci·ent (prē′shē·ənt, presh′ē-) *adj.* Having prescience; farseeing. — **pre′sci·ent·ly** *adv.*

pre·scribe (pri·skrīb′) *v.* **·scribed, ·scrib·ing** *v.t.* **1.** To set down as a direction or rule to be followed; enjoin. **2.** *Med.* To order the use of (a medicine, treatment, etc.). — *v.i.* **3.** To lay down laws or rules; give directions. **4.** *Med.* To order a remedy; give prescriptions. [< L < *prae-* before + *scribere* to write] — **pre·scrib′er** *n.*

pre·script (prē′skript; *for adj., also* pri·skript′) *n.* Something prescribed; a rule or regulation, esp. a rule of conduct. — *adj.* Laid down, prescribed.

pre·scrip·tion (pri·skrip′shən) *n.* **1.** *Med.* **a** A physician's order for a medicine including directions for its use. **b** The remedy so prescribed. **2.** The act of prescribing. **3.** That which is prescribed; a prescript.

pre·scrip·tive (pri·skrip′tiv) *adj.* **1.** Making strict requirements or rules: *prescriptive* grammar. **2.** Sanctioned by custom or long use. — **pre·scrip′tive·ly** *adv.*

pres·ence (prez′əns) *n.* **1.** The state or fact of being present. **2.** The area immediately surrounding a person or thing; close proximity. **3.** The immediate vicinity of a person of superior rank, esp., a sovereign; also, the person or personality of a sovereign, ruler, etc. **4.** Personal appearance; bearing; esp., a pleasing or dignified bearing. **5.** An invisible spirit or influence felt to be near.

presence of mind Full command of one's faculties, esp. in an emergency; coolness, alertness, and readiness.

pres·ent¹ (prez′ənt) *adj.* **1.** Now going on; not past or future. **2.** Of or pertaining to time now occurring; current. **3.** Being in the place or company referred to or considered; being at hand. **4.** Being actually considered, written, discussed, etc.: the *present* issue. **5.** *Gram.* Denoting a tense or verb form that expresses a current or habitual action or state. — *n.* **1.** Present time; the time being; now. **2.** *Gram.* The present tense; also, a verb form denoting it. **3.** *pl. Law* Present writings: a term for the document in which the word occurs: Know all men by these *presents.* — **at present** Now. [< OF < L < *prae-* before + *esse* to be]

pre·sent² (*v.* pri·zent′; *n.* prez′ənt) *v.t.* **1.** To bring into the presence or acquaintance of another; introduce, esp. to one of higher rank. **2.** To exhibit to view or notice. **3.** To suggest to the mind: This *presents* a problem. **4.** To put forward for consideration or action; submit, as a petition. **5.** To make a gift or presentation of or to, usu. formally. **6.** To aim or level (a weapon, etc.). — **to present arms** *Mil.* To salute by holding a gun vertically in front of one's body with the muzzle up and the trigger facing forward. — *n.* Something presented or given; a gift. [< OF < L *praeesse* to be before] — **pre·sent'er** *n.*

pre·sent·a·ble (pri·zen'tə·bəl) *adj.* **1.** Fit to be presented; in suitable condition or attire for company. **2.** Capable of being offered, exhibited, or bestowed. — **pre·sent·a·bil'i·ty, pre·sent'a·ble·ness** *n.* — **pre·sent'a·bly** *adv.*

pres·en·ta·tion (prez'ən·tā'shən, prē'zən-) *n.* **1.** The act of presenting or proffering for acceptance, approval, etc., or the state of being presented. **2.** The formal offering of a complimentary gift. **3.** The act of introducing or bringing to notice, esp. to one of higher rank: *presentation* at court. **4.** An exhibition or representation, as of a play. **5.** *Med.* The position of the fetus at birth, designated by the part that is first presented at the mouth of the womb: breech *presentation*.

pres·ent-day (prez'ent·dā') *adj.* Modern; current.

pre·sen·ti·ment (pri·zen'tə·mənt) *n.* A prophetic sense of something to come; a foreboding. [< F < L < *prae-* before + *sentire* to perceive]

pres·ent·ly (prez'ənt·lē) *adv.* **1.** After a little time; shortly. **2.** At the present time; now.

pre·sent·ment (pri·zent'mənt) *n.* **1.** The act of presenting; also, the state or manner of being presented; presentation. **2.** Something represented or exhibited.

present participle See under PARTICIPLE.

present perfect *Gram.* The verb tense expressing an action completed by the present time, usu. constructed with a form of the verb *to have*, as *has finished* in *By now he has finished the task.*

present tense *Gram.* The verb tense marking present time, as *am* in *I am here*, or *are going* in *You are going home.*

pre·ser·va·tive (pri·zûr'və·tiv) *adj.* Serving or tending to preserve. — *n.* A preservative agent; esp., a chemical substance added to food to retard spoilage.

pre·serve (pri·zûrv') *v.* **·served, ·serv·ing** *v.t.* **1.** To keep in safety; guard: May the gods *preserve* you. **2.** To keep intact or unimpaired; maintain. **3.** To prepare (food) for future consumption, as by boiling with sugar or by salting. **4.** To keep from decomposition or change, as by chemical treatment. **5.** To keep for one's private hunting or fishing: to *preserve* foxes. — *v.i.* **6.** To make preserves, as of fruit. **7.** To maintain a game preserve. — *n.* **1.** *Usu. pl.* Fruit that has been cooked, usu. with sugar, to prevent its fermenting. **2.** Something that preserves or is preserved. **3.** An area set apart for the protection of wildlife, forests, etc.; also, such an area reserved for restricted or private hunting or fishing. [< OF < LL < L *prae-* before + *servare* to keep] — **pre·serv'a·bil'i·ty** *n.* — **pre·serv'a·ble** *adj.* — **pres·er·va'tion** (prez'ər·vā'shən) *n.* — **pre·serv'er** *n.*

pre-shrunk (prē'shrungk') *adj.* Shrunk during manufacture to minimize later shrinkage during washing or cleaning.

pre·side (pri·zīd') *v.i.* **·sid·ed, ·sid·ing** **1.** To sit in authority, as over a meeting; act as chairman or president. **2.** To exercise direction or control. **3.** To occupy a featured place, as an instrumentalist on a program. [< F < L < *prae-* before + *sedere* to sit] — **pre·sid'er** *n.*

pres·i·den·cy (prez'ə·dən·sē) *n. pl.* **·cies 1.** The office, function, or term of office of a president. **2.** *Often cap.* The office of president of the U.S.

pres·i·dent (prez'ə·dənt) *n.* **1.** One who is chosen to preside over an organized body. **2.** *Often cap.* The chief executive of a republic. **3.** The chief executive officer of a government department, corporation, society, or similar body. **4.** The chief officer of a college or university. **5.** The chairman of a meeting conducted under parliamentary rules. [< OF < L *praesidens, -entis*, ppr. of *praesidere* to preside] — **pres·i·den'tial** (prez'ə·den'shəl) *adj.* — **pres'i·dent·ship'** *n.*

pre·sid·i·o (pri·sid'ē·ō) *n. pl.* **·sid·i·os** A garrisoned post; fortified settlement; fort. [< Am. Sp. < L *praesidium*]

pre·sid·i·um (pri·sid'ē·əm) *n.* An executive committee in the Soviet Union serving as the permanent organ of a larger governmental body.

Pre·sid·i·um (pri·sid'ē·əm) *n.* **1.** A governmental body of the Soviet Union that exercises the powers of the Supreme Soviet between plenary sessions. **2.** The supreme policy-making committee of the Communist party of the Soviet Union, headed by the party secretary. See POLITBURO.

pre·sig·ni·fy (prē·sig'nə·fī) *v.t.* **·fied, ·fy·ing** To signify or give token of in advance; presage; foreshadow.

press[1] (pres) *v.t.* **1.** To act upon by weight or pressure: to *press* a button. **2.** To compress so as to extract the juice: to *press* grapes. **3.** To extract by pressure, as juice. **4.** To exert pressure upon so as to smooth, shape, make compact, etc. **5.** To smooth or shape by heat and pressure, as clothes; iron. **6.** To embrace closely; hug. **7.** To force or impel. **8.** To distress or harass; place in difficulty. **9.** To urge persistently; entreat: They *pressed* me for an answer. **10.** To advocate persistently; emphasize. **11.** To put forward insistently: to *press* a claim. **12.** To urge onward; hasten. **13.** To proceed further in, as a lawsuit. **14.** To produce (a phonograph record) from a matrix. — *v.i.* **15.** To ex-

ert pressure; bear heavily. **16.** To advance forcibly or with speed. **17.** To press clothes, etc. **18.** To crowd; cram. **19.** To be urgent or importunate. — *n.* **1.** Newspapers or periodical literature collectively, or the persons concerned with such publications, as editors, reporters, etc. **2.** Criticism, news, etc., in newspapers and periodicals. **3.** The place of business where printing is carried on. **4.** The art, process, or business of printing. **5.** A printing press. **6.** An apparatus by which pressure is applied, as for crushing grapes to make wine. **7.** The act of crowding together. **8.** Hurry or presures of affairs: the *press* of business. **9.** The proper creases and folds in a pressed garment. **10.** A movable upright closet. [< OF < L *pressare*, freq. of *premere* to press] — **press'er** *n.*

THE PRESIDENTS OF THE UNITED STATES

Number—Name	Birthplace—Inaugurated: year		Age
1 George Washington	Westmoreland Co., Va.	1789	57
2 John Adams	Quincy, Mass.	1797	61
3 Thomas Jefferson	Shadwell, Va.	1801	57
4 James Madison	Port Conway, Va.	1809	57
5 James Monroe	Westmoreland Co., Va.	1817	58
6 John Quincy Adams	Quincy, Mass.	1825	57
7 Andrew Jackson	Union Co., N.C.	1829	61
8 Martin Van Buren	Kinderhook, N.Y.	1837	54
9 William H. Harrison	Berkeley, Va.	1841	68
10 John Tyler	Greenway, Va.	1841	51
11 James K. Polk	Little Sugar Creek, N.C.	1845	49
12 Zachary Taylor	Orange Co., Va.	1849	64
13 Millard Fillmore	Summerhill, N.Y.	1850	50
14 Franklin Pierce	Hillsboro, N.H.	1853	48
15 James Buchanan	Cove Gap, Pa.	1857	65
16 Abraham Lincoln	Hardin Co., Ky.	1861	52
17 Andrew Johnson	Raleigh, N.C.	1865	56
18 Ulysses S. Grant	Point Pleasant, O.	1869	46
19 Rutherford B. Hayes	Delaware, O.	1877	54
20 James A. Garfield	Cuyahoga Co., O.	1881	49
21 Chester A. Arthur	Fairfield, Vt.	1881	50
22 Grover Cleveland	Caldwell, N.J.	1885	47
23 Benjamin Harrison	North Bend, O.	1889	55
24 Grover Cleveland	Caldwell, N.J.	1893	55
25 William McKinley	Niles, O.	1897	54
26 Theodore Roosevelt	New York, N.Y.	1901	42
27 William H. Taft	Cincinnati, O.	1909	51
28 Woodrow Wilson	Staunton, Va.	1913	56
29 Warren G. Harding	Corsica, O.	1921	55
30 Calvin Coolidge	Plymouth, Vt.	1923	51
31 Herbert C. Hoover	West Branch, Ia.	1929	55
32 Franklin D. Roosevelt	Hyde Park, N.Y.	1933	51
33 Harry S Truman	Lamar, Mo.	1945	60
34 Dwight D. Eisenhower	Denison, Tex.	1953	62
35 John F. Kennedy	Brookline, Mass.	1961	43
36 Lyndon B. Johnson	Stonewall, Tex.	1963	55
37 Richard M. Nixon	Yorba Linda, Calif.	1969	56
38 Gerald R. Ford	Omaha, Nebr.	1974	61
39 (James Earl) Jimmy Carter (Jr.)	Plains, Ga.	1977	52

press² (pres) *v.t.* **1.** To force into military or naval service. **2.** To put to use in a manner not intended or desired. — *n.* A commission to impress men into the public service; also, the impressment of men. [< obs. *prest* enlistment for advance pay < OF < L < *prae-* before + *stare* to stand]

press agent A person employed to advance the interests of an actor, singer, etc., by means of publicity.

press conference An interview granted by a celebrity, official, etc., to a number of journalists at the same time.

press gang A detachment of men detailed to press men into naval or military service. Also **press-gang** (pres'gang/).

press·ing (pres'ing) *adj.* **1.** Demanding immediate attention; urgent. **2.** Importunate. — **press'ing·ly** *adv.*

press·man (pres'mən) *n. pl.* **·men** (-mən) **1.** A man in charge of a press, as a printing press. **2.** *Brit.* A journalist.

press of canvas *Naut.* The maximum spread of sail that can be carried with safety. Also **press of sail.**

press·or (pres'ər) *adj. Physiol.* Increasing the functional activities of an organ, as a nerve. [< PRESS¹]

press release A bulletin prepared by a public relations department, etc., announcing an event, decision, etc.

pres·sure (presh'ər) *n.* **1.** The act of pressing, or the state of being pressed. **2.** Any force that acts against an opposing force. **3.** An impelling or constraining moral force. **4.** Urgent demands on one's time or strength. **5.** The oppressive influence or depressing effect of something hard to bear; weight. **6.** *Physics* The force acting upon a surface per unit of area. — *v.t.* **·sured, ·sur·ing** *Informal* To compel, as by forceful persuasion. [< OF < L < *premere* to press]

pressure cabin *Aeron.* An enclosed compartment in an aircraft in which air is pressurized.

pressure cooker A strong, airtight pot for cooking food at high temperature under pressure: also called *autoclave.*

pressure group A group that seeks to influence legislators and public opinion in behalf of its own special interests.

pres·sur·ize (presh'ər·īz) *v.t.* **·ized, ·iz·ing** **1.** To subject to high pressure. **2.** To establish (in an aircraft compartment, special suit, etc.) an air pressure higher than the low atmospheric pressure at high altitudes. — **pres'sur·i·za·tion** *n.*

press·work (pres'wûrk') *n.* **1.** The operating or management of a printing press. **2.** The work done by it.

pres·ti·dig·i·ta·tion (pres/tə·dij/ə·tā/shən) *n.* The practice of sleight of hand; legerdemain. [< F < Ital. < LL *praestus* nimble + L *digitus* finger] — **pres'ti·dig'i·ta'tor** *n.*

pres·tige (pres·tēzh/, pres/tij, pres·tēj/) *n.* **1.** Authority or importance based on past achievements, reputation, power, etc. **2.** Importance, respect, etc., due to the appearance of wealth or power. [< F < L *praestigium* illusion < *prae-* before + *stringere* to bind]

pres·ti·gious (pres·tij/əs, -tē/jəs) *adj.* Having a famous reputation or name; honored or well-known; illustrious. — **pres·ti'gious·ly** *adv.* — **pres·ti'gious·ness** *n.*

pres·to (pres/tō) *adj. Music* Quick; faster than allegro. — *adv.* **1.** *Music* In a presto manner: a direction to the performer. **2.** At once; speedily. — *n. Music* A presto movement or passage. [< Ital. < L *praesto* at hand]

pre·sum·a·ble (pri·zōōm/mə·bəl) *adj.* That may be assumed or presumed; reasonable. — **pre·sum'a·bly** *adv.*

pre·sume (pri·zōōm/) *v.* **·sumed, ·sum·ing** *v.t.* **1.** To take for granted; assume to be true until disproved. **2.** To take upon oneself without warrant or permission; venture: usu. with the infinitive. **3.** To indicate the probability of; seem to prove: A concealed weapon *presumes* the intent to commit a crime. — *v.i.* **4.** To act or proceed presumptuously or overconfidently. **5.** To make excessive demands: with *on* or *upon.* [< OF < L < *prae-* before + *sumere* to take] — **pre·sum·ed·ly** (pri·zōō/mid·lē) *adv.* — **pre·sum'er** *n.*

pre·sump·tion (pri·zump/shən) *n.* **1.** Offensively forward or arrogant conduct or speech; insolence. **2.** The act of presuming; also, something presumed. **3.** A ground or reason for presuming. **4.** That which may be logically assumed true until disproved. **5.** *Law* The inference of a fact from circumstances that usually or necessarily attend such a fact. — **Syn. 1.** arrogance, boldness, impudence, impertinence.

pre·sump·tive (pri·zump/tiv) *adj.* **1.** Creating or affording reasonable grounds for belief. **2.** Based upon presumption: an heir *presumptive.* — **pre·sump'tive·ly** *adv.*

pre·sump·tu·ous (pri·zump/chōō·əs) *adj.* Unduly confident or bold; audacious; arrogant. — **pre·sump'tu·ous·ly** *adv.* — **pre·sump'tu·ous·ness** *n.*

pre·sup·pose (prē/sə·pōz/) *v.t.* **·posed, ·pos·ing** **1.** To assume to start with. **2.** To imply as a necessary antecedent condition. — **pre·sup·po·si·tion** (prē/sup·ə·zish/ən) *n.*

pre·tend (pri·tend/) *v.t.* **1.** To assume or display a false appearance; feign. **2.** To claim or assert falsely. **3.** To feign in play; make believe. — *v.i.* **4.** To make believe, as in play or deception. **5.** To put forward a claim: with *to.* [< L < *prae-* before + *tendere* to spread out]

pre·tend·ed (pri·ten/did) *adj.* **1.** Alleged or asserted; professed. **2.** Deceptive; false. — **pre·tend'ed·ly** *adv.*

pre·tend·er (pri·ten/dər) *n.* **1.** One who advances a claim or title; a claimant to a throne. **2.** One who pretends.

pre·tense (pri·tens/, prē/tens) *n.* **1.** A pretended claim; pretext. **2.** A false assumption of a character or condition. **3.** The act or state of pretending. **4.** A right or title asserted. **5.** The condition of being a claimant. Also *Brit.* **pre·tence/.** [< AF < Med.L < L *praetendere* to pretend]

pre·ten·sion (pri·ten/shən) *n.* **1.** A claim put forward, as to an office, privilege, rank, etc. **2.** Affectation; display. **3.** A bold or presumptuous assertion.

pre·ten·tious (pri·ten/shəs) *adj.* **1.** Making an ambitious outward show; ostentatious. **2.** Making claims, esp. when exaggerated or false. [< F *prétentieux*] — **pre·ten'tious·ly** *adv.* — **pre·ten'tious·ness** *n.*

preter- *prefix* Beyond; past; more than: also spelled *praeter-.* [< L *praeter* beyond < *prae* before]

pret·er·it (pret/ər·it) *Gram. adj.* Signifying past time or completed past action. — *n.* The tense that expresses absolute past time; also, a verb in this tense. Also **pret'er·ite.** [< OF < L < *praeter-* beyond + *ire* to go]

pre·ter·i·tive (pri·ter/ə·tiv) *adj. Gram.* Used only in a past tense or past tenses: said of certain verbs.

pre·ter·mit (prē/tər·mit/) *v.t.* **·mit·ted, ·mit·ting** To fail or cease to do; neglect; omit. [< L < *praeter-* beyond + *mittere* to send] — **pre'ter·mis'sion** (-mish/ən) *n.*

pre·ter·nat·u·ral (prē/tər·nach/ər·əl) *adj.* **1.** Diverging from or exceeding the common order of nature, but not outside the natural order: distinguished from *supernatural.* **2.** Outside the natural order. — **Syn.** See SUPERNATURAL. — **pre'ter·nat'u·ral·ism** *n.* — **pre'ter·nat'u·ral·ly** *adv.*

pre·text (prē/tekst) *n.* **1.** A fictitious reason or motive advanced to conceal a real one. **2.** A specious excuse or explanation. [< F < L < *prae-* before + *texere* to weave]

pre·tor (prē/tər), **pre·to·ri·an** (pri·tôr/ē·ən, -tō/rē-), etc. See PRAETOR, etc.

pret·ti·fy (prit/i·fī) *v.t.* **·fied, ·fy·ing** To make pretty; embellish overmuch.

pret·ty (prit/ē) *adj.* **·ti·er, ·ti·est** **1.** Characterized by delicacy, gracefulness, or proportion rather than by striking beauty. **2.** Pleasant; attractive: a *pretty* melody. **3.** Decent; good; sufficient: often used ironically: A *pretty* mess you've made of it! **4.** *Informal* Rather large in size or degree; considerable. **5.** Foppish. — *adv.* To a fair extent; rather: He looked *pretty* well. — **sitting pretty** *Informal* In good circumstances. — *n. pl.* **·ties** (-tēz) A pretty person or thing. [OE *prættig* sly, cunning] — **pret'ti·ly** *adv.* — **pret'ti·ness** *n.*

pret·zel (pret/səl) *n.* A glazed, salted biscuit, usu. baked in the form of a loose knot. [< G *brezel*]

pre·vail (pri·vāl/) *v.i.* **1.** To gain mastery; triumph: with *over* or *against.* **2.** To be effective or efficacious. **3.** To use persuasion or influence successfully: with *on, upon,* or *with.* **4.** To be or become a predominant feature or quality; be prevalent. **5.** To have general or widespread use or acceptance. [< OF or L < *prae-* before + *valere* to be strong]

pre·vail·ing (pri·vā/ling) *adj.* **1.** Current; prevalent. **2.** Having effective power or influence; efficacious. — **pre·vail'ing·ly** *adv.* — **pre·vail'ing·ness** *n.*

prev·a·lent (prev/ə·lənt) *adj.* **1.** Of wide extent or frequent occurrence; common. **2.** Predominant; superior. **3.** Efficacious; effective. — **prev'a·lence** *n.* — **prev'a·lent·ly** *adv.*

pre·var·i·cate (pri·var/ə·kāt) *v.i.* **·cat·ed, ·cat·ing** To speak or act in a deceptive, ambiguous, or evasive manner; lie. [< L < *prae-* before + *varicare* to straddle] — **pre·var'i·ca'tion** *n.* — **pre·var'i·ca'tor** *n.*

pre·vent (pri·vent/) *v.t.* **1.** To keep from happening, as by previous measures or preparations; preclude; thwart. **2.** To keep from doing something; forestall; hinder. [< L < *prae-* before + *venire* to come] — **pre·vent'a·ble** or **pre·vent'i·ble** *adj.* — **pre·vent'a·bil'i·ty** or **pre·vent'i·bil'i·ty** *n.* — **pre·vent'er** *n.*
— **Syn. 1.** *Prevent* suggests forcible restraint and complete stoppage. The sense of anticipation, originally understood in *prevent,* is now to be found in *preclude* and *forestall.* An event is *precluded* by circumstances which make its occurrence impossible; to *forestall* is to make advance preparation to deal with, esp. to restrain. *Avert* suggests a warding off of something. — **Ant.** permit, facilitate.

pre·ven·tion (pri·ven/shən) *n.* **1.** The act of preventing. **2.** A hindrance; obstruction.

pre·ven·tive (pri·ven/tiv) *adj.* Intended or serving to ward off harm, disease, etc.: *preventive* medicine. — *n.* That which prevents or hinders. Also **pre·vent·a·tive** (pri·ven/tə·tiv). — **pre·ven'tive·ly** *adv.* — **pre·ven'tive·ness** *n.*

pre·view (prē/vyōō/) *n.* **1.** An advance showing of a motion picture, a fashion show, etc., to invited guests. **2.** Any advance display or viewing. — *v.t.* To view in advance. Also spelled *prevue*.

pre·vi·ous (prē′vē·əs) *adj.* **1.** Existing or taking place before something else in time or order; antecedent; prior to. **2.** *Informal* Acting or occurring too soon; premature. — **previous to** Antecedent to; before. [< L < *prae-* before + *via* way] — **pre′vi·ous·ly** *adv.* — **pre′vi·ous·ness** *n.*

pre·vise (prē·vīz′) *v.t.* **·vised, ·vis·ing 1.** To foresee. **2.** To notify beforehand. [< L < *prae-* before + *videre* to see]

pre·vi·sion (prē·vizh′ən) *n.* **1.** The act or power of foreseeing; prescience; foresight. **2.** An anticipatory vision.

pre·vue (prē′vyōō′) See PREVIEW.

pre·war (prē′wôr′) *adj.* Of or pertaining to a condition, arrangement, time, etc., before a war.

prex·y (prek′sē) *pl.* **·ies** *n.* *Slang* A president; esp., a college president. Also **prex.**

prey (prā) *n.* **1.** Any animal seized by another for food. **2.** A victim of a harmful or hostile person or influence. — *v.i.* **1.** To seek or take prey for food. **2.** To make someone a victim, as by cheating. **3.** To exert a wearing or harmful influence. Usu. with *on* or *upon*. [< OF < L *praeda* booty] — **prey′er** *n.*

Pri·am (prī′əm) In Greek legend, the father of Hector and Paris, the last king of Troy who was killed at the end of the Trojan War.

price (prīs) *n.* **1.** The amount of money, goods, etc., for which something is bought or sold. **2.** The cost at which something is obtained. **3.** Value; worth. **4.** A bribe, or anything used for a bribe. **5.** A reward for the capture or death of someone. — **beyond price 1.** Invaluable; priceless. **2.** Not bribable. — **to price out of the market** To lose one's share of a market by overpricing. — **to set a price on one's head** To offer a reward for the capture of a person, dead or alive. — *v.t.* **priced, pric·ing 1.** To set a price on; establish a price for. **2.** *Informal* To ask the price of. [< OF < L *pretium*]

price cutting The act of reducing the price of an article below the price at which it is usually advertised or sold.

price fixing 1. The establishment and maintenance of a scale of prices by specified groups of producers or distributors. **2.** The establishing by law of maximum or minimum or fixed prices for certain goods and services. **3.** The fixing of the retail price of a product by a manufacturer or producer. — *adj.* Pertaining to price fixing.

price·less (prīs′lis) *adj.* **1.** Beyond price or valuation; invaluable. **2.** *Informal* Wonderfully amusing or absurd.

price list A catalogue of goods listing their prices.

price rigging The concealed illegal fixing of prices.

prick (prik) *v.t.* **1.** To pierce slightly, as with a sharp point; puncture. **2.** To affect with sharp mental pain; sting; spur. **3.** To outline or indicate by punctures. **4.** To transplant (young plants) preparatory to later planting. **5.** To trace (a ship's course, etc.) on a chart: with *off*. **6.** To urge on with or as with a spur; goad. — *v.i.* **7.** To have or cause a stinging or piercing sensation. — **to prick up one's** (or its) **ears 1.** To raise the ears erect. **2.** To listen attentively. — *n.* **1.** The act of pricking; also, the sensation of being pricked. **2.** A mental sting or spur. **3.** A slender, sharp-pointed thing, as a thorn or weapon. **4.** A puncture; dot. [OE *prica* point, dot] — **prick′er** *n.*

prick·le (prik′əl) *n.* **1.** A small, sharp point, as on the bark of a plant. **2.** A tingling or stinging sensation. — *v.* **·led, ·ling** *v.t.* **1.** To prick; pierce. **2.** To cause a tingling or stinging sensation in. — *v.i.* **3.** To have a stinging sensation; tingle. [OE *pricel*]

prick·ly (prik′lē) *adj.* **1.** Furnished with prickles. **2.** Stinging, as if from a prick or sting: a *prickly* sensation.

prickly heat A rash characterized by redness, itching, and small eruptions: also called *heat rash.*

prickly pear 1. A flat-stemmed cactus bearing a pear-shaped and often prickly fruit. **2.** The fruit itself.

pride (prīd) *n.* **1.** An undue sense of one's own superiority; arrogance; conceit. **2.** A proper sense of personal dignity and worth. **3.** That of which one is justly proud. **4.** The most excellent part of anything: the nation's *pride.* **5.** The best time or the flowering of something: the *pride* of summer. **6.** A group or company: said of lions. — *v.t.* **prid·ed, prid·ing** To take pride in (oneself) for something: with *on* or *upon*. [OE *prūt* proud]

— **Syn.** (noun) **1.** *Pride* manifests itself in disdain or haughtiness toward others; *self-esteem*, in more deference to one's opinions than others grant. *Conceit* is an exaggerated opinion of one's ability or worth. *Vanity* is seen in an excessive desire for admiration, while *vainglory* points to undue boasting about one's accomplishments. **6.** See FLOCK. — **Ant.** humility, modesty.

pride·ful (prīd′fəl) *adj.* Full of pride; haughty; disdainful.

prio diou (prō dyoo′) *n.* A small deok with a shelf for a book, at which to kneel at prayers. [< F, *pray God*]

pri·er (prī′ər) *n.* One who pries: also spelled *pryer.*

priest (prēst) *n.* **1.** One esp. consecrated to the service of a divinity, and serving as mediator between the divinity and

his worshipers. **2.** In the Anglican, Greek, and Roman Catholic churches, a clergyman in the second order of the ministry, ranking next below a bishop, and having authority to administer the sacraments. [OE < L *presbyter*]

priest·craft (prēst′kraft′, -kräft′) *n.* **1.** Priestly arts and wiles: a disparaging term. **2.** The knowledge of priests.

priest·ess (prēs′tis) *n.* A woman or girl who exercises priestly functions.

priest·hood (prēst′hŏŏd) *n.* **1.** The priestly office or character. **2.** Priests collectively. [OE *prēosthad*]

priest·ly (prēst′lē) *adj.* Of, pertaining to, or befitting a priest or the priesthood. — **priest′li·ness** *n.*

priest·rid·den (prēst′rid′n) *adj.* Completely under the influence or domination of priests.

prig (prig) *n.* A formal and narrow-minded person who assumes superior virtue and wisdom. [Origin uncertain]

prig·gish (prig′ish) *adj.* Like a prig; smug. — **prig′gish·ly** *adv.* — **prig′gish·ness** *n.*

prim (prim) *adj.* Minutely or affectedly precise and formal; stiffly proper and neat. — *v.t.* **primmed, prim·ming** To fix (the face, mouth, etc.) in a precise or prim expression. [Origin uncertain] — **prim′ly** *adv.* — **prim′ness** *n.*

pri·ma·cy (prī′mə·sē) *n.* *pl.* **·cies 1.** The state of being first, as in rank or excellence. **2.** The office or province of a primate; archbishopric: also **pri′mate·ship** (-mit·ship). **3.** In the Roman Catholic Church, the office of the Pope. [< OF < Med.L < LL *primas, primatis* one of the first]

pri·ma don·na (prē′mə don′ə) **1.** A leading female singer, as in an opera company. **2.** *Informal* A temperamental or vain person. [< Ital., lit., first lady]

pri·ma fa·ci·e (prī′mə fā′shi·ē, fā′shē) *Latin* At first view; so far as at first appears. — **pri′ma-fa′ci·e** *adj.*

prima-facie evidence Evidence that, if unexplained or uncontradicted, would establish the fact alleged.

pri·mal (prī′məl) *adj.* **1.** Being at the beginning or foundation; first; original. **2.** Most important; chief. [< Med.L < L *primus*]

pri·ma·ri·ly (prī·mâr′ə·lē, prī′mə·rə·lē) *adv.* In the first place; originally; essentially.

pri·ma·ry (prī′mer·ē, -mər·ē) *adj.* **1.** First in time or origin; primitive. **2.** First in a series or sequence. **3.** First in rank or importance; chief. **4.** Constituting the fundamental or original elements of which a whole is composed; basic; elemental. **5.** Of the first stage of development; elementary; lowest: *primary* school. **6.** *Electr.* Of, pertaining to, or noting an inducing current or its circuit: a *primary* coil. **7.** *Chem.* **a** Having some characteristic in the first degree, as an initial replacement of one atom or radical. **b** Having a carbon atom directly joined to only one other carbon atom in a molecule. — *n.* *pl.* **·ries 1.** That which is first in rank, dignity, or importance. **2.** *Usu. pl.* A direct primary election. **3.** One of the primary colors. **4.** A primary cell. **5.** *Ornithol.* One of the large flight feathers of the pinion of a bird's wings. **6.** *Astron.* A body, as a planet, as distinguished from another body that revolves around it, as a satellite. [< L *primus* first]

primary cell *Electr.* Any of several devices consisting of two electrodes immersed in an electrolyte and capable of generating a current by chemical action when the electrodes are in contact through a conducting wire. Also called *voltaic cell.*

primary colors Any of several sets of colors considered basic to all other colors, as red, green, and blue (**physiological, fundamental,** or **additive primaries**); red, yellow, green, blue, black, and white (**psychological** or **subtractive primaries**); and red, yellow, and blue (**painting primaries**).

primary election A direct primary election.

primary school A school for very young pupils, usu. the first four grades of elementary school.

pri·mate (prī′mit, -māt) *n.* **1.** The prelate highest in rank in a nation or province. **2.** Any of an order of mammals, including the tarsiers, lemurs, marmosets, monkeys, apes, and man. [< OF < LL < L *primus*] — **pri·ma·tial** (prī·mā′shəl) *adj.*

pri·ma·tol·o·gy (prī′mə·tol′ə·jē) *n.* The study of the origin, structure, evolution, and classification of primates. — **pri′·ma·tol′o·gist** *n.*

prime[1] (prīm) *adj.* **1.** First in rank, dignity, or importance. **2.** First in value or quality; first-rate. **3.** First in time or order; original; primitive. **4.** *Math.* Divisible by no whole number except itself and unity. Two or more numbers are said to be *prime* to each other when they have no common factor except unity. **5.** Not derived; first. — *n.* **1.** The period of full vigor, beauty, and power succeeding youth and preceding age. **2.** The period of full perfection in anything. **3.** The beginning of anything; dawn; spring. **4.** The best of anything: a *prime* grade. **5.** *Math.* A prime number. **6.** A mark or accent (′) written above and to the right of a letter or figure; also, an inch, a minute, etc., as indicated by that sign. **7.** *Music* Unison. — *v.* **primed, prim·ing** *v.t.* **1.** To prepare; make ready. **2.** To put a primer into (a gun, etc.) preparatory to firing. **3.** To pour water into (a pump) so as to displace air and promote suction. **4.** To cover (a surface) with sizing, a first coat of paint, etc. **5.** To supply beforehand with facts, information, etc.; brief. — *v.i.* **6.** To make something ready, as for firing, pumping, etc. [< OF < L *primus*] — **prime′ly** *adv.* — **prime′ness** *n.*

prime² (prīm) *n. Often cap. Eccl.* The second of the seven canonical hours. [OE < LL *prima* (*hora*) first (hour)]

prime meridian A meridian from which longitude is reckoned, now, generally, the one that passes through Greenwich, England.

prime minister The chief minister and head of a cabinet, and often the chief executive of a government.

prim·er¹ (prim′ər) *n.* **1.** An elementary textbook; esp., a beginning reading book. **2.** *Printing* Either of two sizes of type, **great primer** (18-point) and **long primer** (10-point). [< Med.L < L *primus*]

prim·er² (prī′mər) *n.* **1.** Any device, as a cap, tube, etc., used to detonate the main charge of a gun, mine, etc. **2.** One who or that which primes.

pri·me·val (prī-mē′vəl) *adj.* Belonging to the first ages; primitive. [< L *primus* first + *aevum* age] — **pri·me′val·ly** *adv.*

primi- *combining form* First. [< L *primus* first]

pri·mi·ge·ni·al (prī′mə-jē′nē-əl) *adj.* Being the first or first-born; primal; original. [< L *primus* + *genus* kind]

prim·ing (prī′ming) *n.* **1.** That with which anything is primed. **2.** A combustible composition used to ignite an explosive charge. **3.** The first layer of paint laid on a surface.

prim·i·tive (prim′ə-tiv) *adj.* **1.** Pertaining to the beginning or origin; earliest; primary; not derived. **2.** Resembling the manners or style of early times; simple; crude. **3.** *Anthropol.* Of or pertaining to the earliest anthropological forms or civilizations. **4.** *Biol.* **a** Being or occurring at an early stage of development or growth; first-formed; rudimentary. **b** Not much changed by evolution: a *primitive* species. — *n.* **1.** An artist, or a work of art, belonging to an early period; also, a work resembling such art, or an artist producing it. **2.** One who or that which is primitive. [< F < L < *primus* first] — **prim′i·tive·ly** *adv.* — **prim′i·tive·ness, prim′i·tiv′i·ty** *n.*

prim·i·tiv·ism (prim′ə-tiv-iz′əm) *n.* Belief in or adherence to primitive forms and customs.

pri·mo·gen·i·tor (prī′mə-jen′ə-tər) *n.* An earliest ancestor; a forefather. [< Med.L < L *primo* first + *genitor* father]

pri·mo·gen·i·ture (prī′mə-jen′ə-chər) *n.* **1.** The state of being the first-born child. **2.** The exclusive right of the eldest son to inherit the property, title, etc., of a parent. [< Med.L < L *primo* first + *gignere* to beget]

pri·mor·di·al (prī-môr′dē-əl) *adj.* **1.** First in time; original; elemental. **2.** *Biol.* First in order or appearance in the growth or development of an organism. [< LL < L *primus* first + *ordiri* to begin a web] — **pri·mor′di·al·ly** *adv.*

primp (primp) *v.t. & v.i.* To prink; dress up, esp. with superfluous attention to detail.

prim·rose (prim′rōz) *n.* **1.** An early-blossoming perennial herb with tufted basal leaves and variously colored flowers. **2.** The evening primrose. **3.** A pale yellow color, named for the common primrose of England. — *adj.* **1.** Pertaining to a primrose. **2.** Of primrose color. **3.** Flowery; gay. [ME < OF < Med.L < L *primus* first]

prince (prins) *n.* **1.** A nonreigning male member of a royal family. **2.** A male monarch or sovereign. **3.** *Brit.* The son of a sovereign or of a son of the sovereign. **4.** One of a high order of nobility. **5.** The ruler of a small state. **6.** One of the highest rank of any class: a merchant *prince*. [< OF < L < *primus* first + stem of *capere* to take]

Prince Al·bert (al′bûrt) A long, double-breasted frock coat.

prince consort The husband of a reigning female sovereign.

prince·ling (prins′ling) *n.* **1.** A young prince. **2.** A subordinate prince. Also **prince′let** (-lit).

prince·ly (prins′lē) *adj.* **·li·er, ·li·est 1.** Liberal; generous. **2.** Like or suitable for a prince. **3.** Having the rank of a prince. — *adv.* In a princely manner. — **prince′li·ness** *n.*

Prince of Darkness Satan.

Prince of Peace Jesus Christ.

Prince of Wales The title conferred on the eldest son of the British sovereign, to make that son heir apparent.

prin·cess (prin′sis) *n.* **1.** A nonreigning female member of a royal family. **2.** The consort of a prince. **3.** Formerly, a female sovereign. **4.** *Brit.* A daughter of the sovereign or of a son of the sovereign. [< F *princesse*]

prin·cesse (prin-ses′, prin′sis) *adj.* Designating a woman's close-fitting garment hanging in an unbroken line from shoulder to flared hem. Also **prin′cess.** [< F, princess]

princess royal The eldest daughter of a sovereign.

prin·ci·pal (prin′sə-pəl) *adj.* First in rank, character, or importance. — *n.* **1.** One who takes a leading part in some action. **2.** *Law* An actor in a crime, or one present aiding and abetting. **b** The employer of one who acts as an agent. **c** One primarily liable for whom another has become surety. **d** The capital or body of an estate. **3.** One who is at the head of some body or society. **4.** The head teacher, master, or officer of a school. **5.** Property or capital, as opposed to interest or income. **6.** The chief truss or rafter of a roof. [< F < L *princeps* first, principal] — **prin′ci·pal·ly** *adv.* — **prin′ci·pal·ship′** *n.*

principal axis *Optics* The imaginary line passing through the center of a lens or mirror at right angles to each surface.

principal clause *Gram.* An independent clause. See under CLAUSE.

prin·ci·pal·i·ty (prin′sə-pal′ə-tē) *n. pl.* **·ties 1.** The territory of a reigning prince, or one that gives to a prince a title of courtesy. **2.** The state, office, or jurisdiction of a prince.

principal parts The inflected forms of a verb from which all other inflected forms may be derived. In English, the principal parts of a verb are the infinitive (*go, walk*), the past tense (*went, walked*), and the past participle (*gone, walked*). In this dictionary, when appropriate, the past, past participle, and present participle are shown (*gave, given, giving*). When, however, the principal parts are entirely regular in formation, adding *-ed* and *-ing* directly to the infinitive without spelling modification, they are not shown. In cases where the past tense and past participle are identical, only the one is shown (*behaved, behaving*).

prin·ci·ple (prin′sə-pəl) *n.* **1.** A general truth or law, basic to other truths. **2.** A rule of personal conduct. **3.** Moral standards collectively: a man of *principle*. **4.** That which is inherent in anything, determining its nature. **5.** A primary source or fundamental cause. **6.** An established mode of action or operation in natural phenomena: the *principle* of relativity. **7.** *Chem.* An essential constituent of a compound or substance. [< L *principium* a beginning]

prin·ci·pled (prin′sə-pəld) *adj.* Having or characterized by ethical principles: often in combination: *high-principled*.

prink (pringk) *v.t.* **1.** To dress (oneself) for show. — *v.i.* **2.** To dress oneself showily or fussily. — **prink′er** *n.*

print (print) *n.* **1.** An impression with ink from type, plates, etc.; printed characters collectively; also, any printed matter. **2.** Anything printed from an engraved plate or lithographic stone; a proof; also, a printed picture or design. **3.** An impression or mark made upon a substance by pressure; imprint: the *print* of a shoe in the snow. **4.** Any fabric stamped with a design. **5.** Any tool or device bearing a pattern or design, or that upon which it is impressed. **6.** *Photog.* A positive picture made from a negative. — **in print** Printed; also, for sale in printed form. — **out of print** No longer on sale, the edition being exhausted: said of books, etc. — *v.t.* **1.** To mark, as with inked type, a stamp, die, etc. **2.** To stamp or impress (a mark, seal, etc.) on or into a surface. **3.** To fix as if by impressing: The scene is *printed* on my memory. **4.** To produce (a book, newspaper, etc.) by the application of inked type, plates, etc., to paper or similar material. **5.** To cause to be put in print; publish. **6.** To write in letters similar to those used in print. **7.** *Photog.* To produce (a positive picture) by transmitting light through a negative onto a sensitized surface. — *v.i.* **8.** To be a printer. **9.** To take or give an impression in printing. **10.** To form letters similar to printed ones. [< OF < L *premere* to press] — **print′a·ble** *adj.* — **prin′ter** *n.*

printer's devil Devil (def. 7).

print·ing (prin′ting) *n.* **1.** The making and issuing of printed matter. **2.** The act of reproducing a design upon a surface. **3.** That which is printed. **4.** The number of copies of anything printed at one time. **5.** Writing that resembles printed matter. **6.** The act of one who or that which prints.

printing press A mechanism for printing from an inked surface, operating by pressure.

pri·or¹ (prī′ər) *adj.* Preceding in time, order, or importance. — **prior to** Before. [< L, earlier, superior]

pri·or² (prī′ər) *n.* A monastic officer next in rank below an abbot. [OE < L] — **pri′or·ate** (-it) *n.*

pri·or·ess (prī′ər·is) *n.* A woman holding a position corresponding to that of a prior; a nun next below an abbess.

pri·or·i·ty (prī-ôr′ə-tē, -or′-) *n. pl.* **·ties 1.** Antecedence; precedence. **2.** A first right established on emergency or need. **3.** A certificate giving a first right to a manufacturer or contractor.

pri·or·y (prī′ər·ē) *n. pl.* **·or·ies** A monastic house presided over by a prior or prioress. [< OF *priorie* < Med.L *prioria*]

prism (priz′əm) *n.* **1.** *Geom.* A solid whose bases or ends are any similar equal and parallel plane figures, and whose lateral faces are parallelograms. **2.** *Optics* A prism made of glass or other transparent substance and usually having triangular ends, used to produce a spectrum or to refract light beams. [< LL < Gk., < *prizein* to saw]

pris·mat·ic (priz-mat′ik) *adj.* **1.** Refracted or formed by a prism. **2.** Resembling the spectrum; exhibiting rainbow tints. **3.** Pertaining to or shaped like a prism. Also **pris·mat′i·cal. — pris·mat′i·cal·ly** *adv.*

pris·on (priz′ən) *n.* **1.** A public building for the safekeeping of persons in legal custody; a penitentiary. **2.** Any place of confinement. **3.** Imprisonment. **—** *v.t.* To imprison. [< OF < F < *prehendere* to seize]

pris·on·er (priz′ən·ər, priz′nər) *n.* **1.** One who is confined in a prison or whose liberty is forcibly restrained. **2.** A person confined for any reason. [< OF *prisonier*]

pris·sy (pris′ē) *Informal adj.* **·si·er, ·si·est** Effeminate; overprecise; prim. [Blend of PRIM or PRECISE + SISSY]

pris·tine (pris′tēn, -tĭn; *Brit.* pris′tīn) *adj.* **1.** Of or pertaining to the earliest state or time; primitive. **2.** Extremely pure; untouched; unspoiled. [< L *pristinus* primitive]

prith·ee (prith′ē) *interj. Archaic* I pray thee.

pri·va·cy (prī′və·sē) *n. pl.* **·cies 1.** The condition of being private; seclusion. **2.** The state of being secret; secrecy.

pri·vate (prī′vit) *adj.* **1.** Removed from public view; secluded. **2.** Not for public or common use. **3.** Having no official rank, character, office, etc.: a *private* citizen. **4.** Not generally known; secret. **5.** Not common or usual; special: a *private* interpretation. **6.** Individual; personal: one's *private* opinion. **—** *n.* **1.** *Mil.* An enlisted man ranking below a corporal. Abbr. *Pvt.* See table at GRADE. **2.** *pl.* The genitals. **— in private** In secret. [< L *privatus* apart from the state] **— pri′vate·ly** *adv.* **— pri′vate·ness** *n.*

private detective A detective employed by a private citizen, business enterprise, etc., rather than by a city or state.

private enterprise Free enterprise.

pri·va·teer (prī′və·tir′) *n.* **1.** A vessel owned and commanded by private persons, but carrying on maritime war under letters of marque. **2.** The commander or one of the crew of a privateer: also **pri′va·teers′man** (-tirz′mən). **—** *v.i.* To cruise in or as a privateer. **— pri′va·teer′ing** *n.*

private eye *Informal* A private detective.

private first class A soldier ranking next above a private and below a corporal. Abbr. *Pfc, Pfc.* See table at GRADE.

private school *U.S.* A school maintained under private or corporate management, usu. for profit.

private secretary A secretary who works for one individual only and is usu. entrusted with confidential matters.

pri·va·tion (prī·vā′shən) *n.* The state of lacking something necessary or desirable; esp., want of the common comforts of life. [< L *privare* to set apart]

priv·a·tive (priv′ə·tiv) *adj.* **1.** Causing privation, want, or destitution; depriving. **2.** *Gram.* Altering a word so as to express a negative instead of a positive meaning: *privative* particles (such prefixes and suffixes as *a-, an-, in-, -less*). **—** *n. Gram.* A privative prefix or suffix. [< L *privativus*] **— priv′a·tive·ly** *adv.* **— priv′a·tive·ness** *n.*

priv·et (priv′it) *n.* An ornamental, bushy shrub of the olive family, with white flowers and black berries, used for hedges. [Earlier *primet*; origin unknown]

priv·i·lege (priv′ə·lij) *n.* **1.** A special or peculiar benefit, favor, or advantage. **2.** An exemption or immunity by virtue of one's office or station. **3.** A fundamental or basic civil, legal, or political right; the *privilege* of voting. **—** *v.t.* **·leged, ·leg·ing 1.** To grant a privilege to. **2.** To exempt or free: with *from.* [< OF < L < *privus* one's own + *lex* law]

priv·i·leged (priv′ə·lijd) *adj.* Having or enjoying a privilege.

priv·y (priv′ē) *adj.* **1.** Participating with another or others in the knowledge of a secret transaction: with *to: privy* to the plot. **2.** *Archaic* Secret. **—** *n. pl.* **priv·ies 1.** *Law* One who is concerned with another in a matter affecting the interests of both. **2.** A small toilet or outhouse. [< F < L *privatus.* See PRIVATE.] **— priv′i·ly** *adv.*

privy council Any body of advisers or counselors, as appointed by a sovereign for his personal use.

Privy Council 1. In Great Britain, the sovereign's personal council whose duties have been largely assumed by the cabinet. **2.** In Canada, a body that advises the Governor General.

privy seal In Great Britain, the seal used by the sovereign on papers that later pass under the great seal or do not demand the great seal.

prix fixe (prē fēks′) A meal served at a fixed price; table d'hôte. Compare À LA CARTE. [< F, fixed price]

prize¹ (prīz) *n.* **1.** That which is offered or won as a reward for superiority or success, as in a contest. **2.** Anything to be striven for. **3.** Anything offered or won, as in a lottery, etc. **—** *adj.* **1.** Offered or awarded as a prize: a *prize* medal. **2.** Having drawn a prize; entitled to a prize. **3.** Highly valued or esteemed. **—** *v.t.* **prized, priz·ing 1.** To value highly. **2.** To estimate the value of; appraise. [Var. of PRICE.]

prize² (prīz) *n.* In international law, property, as a vessel and cargo, captured by a belligerent at sea in conformity with the laws of war. **—** *v.t.* **prized, priz·ing 1.** To seize as a prize, as a ship. **2.** To raise or force with a lever; pry: also spelled *prise.* [< F *prise* something taken, booty]

prize court A court sitting for the adjudication of prizes taken at sea in wartime.

prize fight A fight between professional boxers for a prize, a certain sum of money, etc., generally limited to a specified number of rounds. **— prize fighter — prize fighting**

prize ring A roped enclosure within which boxers fight.

pro¹ (prō) *n. pl.* **pros 1.** An argument or vote in favor of something: in the phrase *pros and cons.* **2.** *Usu. pl.* One who votes for or favors a proposal. **—** *adv.* In behalf of; in favor of; for: to argue *pro* and con. [< L, for]

pro² (prō) *n. pl.* **pros** *Informal* **1.** A professional athlete. **2.** Any expert in any field.

pro-¹ *prefix* **1.** Forward; to or toward the front from a position behind; forth: *produce*, to lead forth; *project*, to throw forth. **2.** Forth from its place; away: *profugate*, to flee away. **3.** To the front of; forward and down: *prolapse*, to slip forward and down. **4.** Forward in time or direction: *proceed*, to go forward. **5.** In behalf of: *prolocutor.* **6.** In place of; substituted for: *proconsul.* **7.** In favor of: *pro-Russian.* [< L *pro- < pro* before, forward, for]

pro-² *prefix* **1.** Prior; occurring earlier in time: *prognosis.* **2.** Situated in front; forward; before: *prognathous.* [< Gk. *pro- < pro* before, in front]

pro·a (prō′ə) *n.* A swift Malaysian vessel, propelled by sails or oars. Also called *prahu.* [< Malay *prāü*]

prob·a·bil·i·ty (prob′ə·bil′ə·tē) *n. pl.* **·ties 1.** The state or quality of being probable; likelihood. **2.** A probable event, statement, condition, etc.

prob·a·ble (prob′ə·bəl) *adj.* **1.** Likely to be true or to happen, but leaving room for doubt. **2.** That renders something worthy of belief, but falls short of demonstration: *probable* evidence. **— Syn.** See APPARENT. [< OF < L *probare* to prove, test]

prob·a·bly (prob′ə·blē) *adv.* In all probability.

pro·bate (prō′bāt) *adj.* **1.** Of or pertaining to a probate court. **2.** Pertaining to making proof. **—** *n.* **1.** Formal, legal proof, as of a will. **2.** The right or jurisdiction of proving wills. **—** *v.t.* **·bat·ed, ·bat·ing** To obtain probate of, as a will. [< L < *probare* to prove]

probate court A court having jurisdiction of the proof of wills, of guardianships, and of the settlement of estates.

pro·ba·tion (prō·bā′shən) *n.* **1.** *Law* A method of allowing a person convicted of a minor offense to go at large but usu. under the supervision of a probation officer. **2.** A proceeding or period designed to test character, qualifications, etc., as of a new employee. **3.** The status or condition of one being tried out, or free under suspension of sentence: to be on *probation.* **4.** The act of proving; also, proof. **— pro·ba′tion·al, pro·ba′tion·ar′y** *adj.*

pro·ba·tion·er (prō·bā′shən·ər) *n.* One on probation.

probation officer A person delegated to supervise an offender on suspended sentence.

pro·ba·tive (prō′bə·tiv) *adj.* **1.** Serving to prove or test. **2.** Pertaining to probation; proving. Also **pro·ba·to·ry** (prō′bə·tôr′ē, -tō′rē).

probe (prōb) *v.* **probed, prob·ing** *v.t.* **1.** To explore with a probe. **2.** To investigate or examine thoroughly. **—** *v.i.* **3.** To penetrate; search. **—** *n.* **1.** *Surg.* An instrument for exploring cavities, wounds, etc. **2.** That which proves or tests. **3.** *U.S.* A searching investigation or inquiry, esp. into crime. [< LL *proba* proof] **— prob′er** *n.*

pro·bi·ty (prō′bə·tē, prob′ə-) *n.* Virtue or integrity tested and confirmed. [< F < L < *probus* good, honest]

prob·lem (prob′ləm) *n.* **1.** A perplexing question or situation, esp. when difficult or uncertain of solution. **2.** Any puzzling or difficult circumstance or person. **3.** *Math.* A proposition in which some operation or construction is required, as to bisect an angle. **—** *adj.* **1.** Presenting and dealing with a problem. **2.** Being a problem. [< OF < L < Gk. < *pro-* forward + *ballein* to throw]

prob·lem·at·ic (prob′ləm·at′ik) *adj.* Constituting or involving a problem; questionable; contingent. Also **prob′lem·at′i·cal. — prob′lem·at′i·cal·ly** *adv.*

pro·bos·cis (prō·bos′is) *n. pl.* **·bos·cis·es** or **·bos·ci·des** (-bos′ə·dēz) **1.** *Zool.* **a** A long flexible snout, as of the tapir. **b** The trunk of an elephant. **2.** *Entomol.* Any of various tubular feeding structures of certain insects, as bees and mosquitoes. **3.** A human nose: a humorous term. [< L < Gk. < *pro-* before + *boskein* to feed]

pro·caine (prō·kān′, prō′kān) *n.* A white crystalline compound, C₁₃H₂₀O₂N₂, used chiefly in its hydrochloride form as a local anesthetic. [< PRO-¹ + (CO)CAINE]

pro·ce·dure (prə·sē′jər) *n.* **1.** A manner of proceeding or acting in any course of action. **2.** The methods or forms of conducting a business, parliamentary affairs, etc. **3.** A course of action; a proceeding. **— pro·ce′du·ral** *adj.*

pro·ceed (prə·sēd′) *v.i.* **1.** To go on or forward, esp. after a stop. **2.** To begin and carry on an action or process. **3.** To issue or come, as from some cause, source, or origin: with *from.* **4.** *Law* To institute and carry on legal proceedings. [< OF < L *pro-* forward + *cedere* to go] **— pro·ceed′er** *n.*

pro·ceed·ing (prə·sē′ding) *n.* **1.** An act or course of action; also, a particular act or course of action. **2.** The act of one

who or that which proceeds. **3.** *pl.* The records or minutes of the meetings of a society, etc. **4.** *Law* Any action instituted in a court.
pro·ceeds (prō′sēdz) *n.pl.* The amount derived from the disposal of goods, work, or the use of capital; return; yield.
proc·ess (pros′es, *esp. Brit.* prō′ses) *n.* **1.** A course or method of operations in the production of something. **2.** A series of continuous actions that bring about a particular result, end, or condition: the *process* of growth. **3.** A forward movement; advance; course. **4.** *Law* **a** Any judicial writ or order. **b** A writ issued to bring a defendant into court. **c** The whole course of proceedings in a cause. **5.** *Biol.* An accessory outgrowth or prominence of an organism or any of its parts: vertebral *process*. — *adj.* **1.** Produced by a special method: *process* butter; *process* cheese. **2.** Pertaining to, for, or made by a mechanical or chemical photographic process: a *process* illustration. — *v.t.* **1.** To subject to a routine procedure: to *process* an application. **2.** To treat or prepare by a special method. **3.** *Law* **a** To issue or serve a process on. **b** To proceed against. [See PROCEED.] — **proc′es·sor** or **proc′ess·er** *n.*
pro·ces·sion (prə-sesh′ən, prō-) *n.* **1.** An array, as of persons or vehicles, arranged in succession and moving in a formal manner; a parade; also, any continuous course: the *procession* of the stars. **2.** The act of proceeding or issuing forth: the *procession* of the Holy Ghost from the Father. — *v.i.* To march in procession. [See PROCEED.]
pro·ces·sion·al (prə-sesh′ən-əl) *adj.* Of, pertaining to, or moving in a procession. — *n.* **1.** A hymn sung at the opening of a church service, during the entrance of the choir, etc. **2.** The music played or sung during a procession. — **pro·ces′sion·al·ly** *adv.*
pro·claim (prō-klām′) *v.t.* **1.** To announce or make known publicly or officially; declare. **2.** To make plain; manifest. **3.** To outlaw, prohibit, or restrict by proclamation. [< L *pro-* before + *clamare* to call] — **pro·claim′er** *n.*
proc·la·ma·tion (prok′lə-mā′shən) *n.* **1.** The act of proclaiming. **2.** That which is proclaimed.
pro·cliv·i·ty (prō-kliv′ə-tē) *n.* *pl.* **·ties** Natural tendency: usu. with *to.* [< L < *pro-* before + *clivus* slope]
pro·con·sul (prō-kon′səl, prō′kon′-) *n.* **1.** In ancient Rome, an official who exercised authority over a province or an army. **2.** A governor of a dependency; a viceroy. [< L] — **pro·con′su·lar** (-sə-lər, -syə-) *adj.* — **pro·con′su·late** (-sə-lit, -syə-), **pro·con′sul·ship** *n.*
pro·cras·ti·nate (prō-kras′tə-nāt) *v.* **·nat·ed, ·nat·ing** *v.i.* **1.** To put off taking action until a future time; be dilatory. — *v.t.* **2.** To defer or postpone. [< L *procrastinare*] — **pro·cras′ti·na′tion** *n.* — **pro·cras′ti·na′tor** *n.*
pro·cre·ate (prō′krē-āt) *v.t.* **·at·ed, ·at·ing** **1.** To engender or beget (offspring). **2.** To originate; produce. [< L < *pro-* before + *creare* to create] — **pro′cre·ant** *adj.* — **pro′cre·a′tion** *n.* — **pro′cre·a′tor** *n.*
pro·cre·a·tive (prō′krē·ā′tiv) *adj.* **1.** Possessed of generative power; reproductive. **2.** Pertaining to procreation.
Pro·crus·te·an (prō-krus′tē-ən) *adj.* **1.** Pertaining to or characteristic of Procrustes. **2.** Ruthlessly or violently bringing about conformity.
Pro·crus·tes (prō-krus′tēz) In Greek mythology, a giant of Attica, who tied travelers to an iron bed and amputated or stretched their limbs until they fitted it.
procto- *combining form Med.* Related to or affecting the rectum. Also, before vowels, **proct-**. [< Gk. *proktos* anus]
proc·tol·o·gy (prok-tol′ə-jē) *n.* The branch of medicine that treats of the diseases of the rectum. — **proc·to·log·i·cal** (prok′tə-loj′i·kəl) *adj.* — **proc·tol′o·gist** *n.*
proc·tor (prok′tər) *n.* **1.** An agent acting for another; attorney; proxy. **2.** A university or college official charged with maintaining order, supervising examinations, etc. — *v.t. & v.i.* To supervise (an examination). [ME *proketour, procutour*] — **proc·to·ri·al** (prok-tôr′ē-əl, -tō′rē-) *adj.*
pro·cum·bent (prō-kum′bənt) *adj.* **1.** *Bot.* Lying on the ground; trailing, as certain vines and plants. **2.** Lying down or on the face; prone; prostrate. [< L *pro-* forward + *cumbere* to lie down]
pro·cur·a·ble (prō-kyoor′ə-bəl) *adj.* That can be procured.
pro·cur·ance (prō-kyoor′əns) *n.* The process of procuring.
proc·u·ra·tor (prok′yə-rā′tər) *n.* **1.** A person authorized to act for and manage the affairs of another. **2.** In ancient Rome, one who had charge of the imperial revenues or, in a province, was an administrator. [See PROCURE.] — **proc′u·ra·to·ri·al** (-rə-tôr′ē-əl, -tō′rē-) *adj.* — **proc′u·ra′tor·ship** *n.*
pro·cure (prō-kyoor′) *v.* **·cured, ·cur·ing** *v.t.* **1.** To obtain by some effort or means; acquire. **2.** To bring about; cause. **3.** To obtain (women) for the gratification of the lust of others. — *v.i.* **4.** To be a procurer or procuress. — **Syn.** See GET. [< OF < L < *pro-* on behalf of + *curare* to attend to] — **pro·cure′ment** *n.*

pro·cur·er (prō-kyoor′ər) *n.* One who procures for another, as to gratify lust; a pimp. — **pro·cur′ess** *n.fem.*
Pro·cy·on (prō′sē-on) *n.* One of the 20 brightest stars, 2.12 magnitude; Alpha in the constellation Canis Minor: also called *Dog Star.* [< L < Gk. *Prokyōn*]
prod (prod) *v.t.* **prod·ded, prod·ding** **1.** To punch or poke with or as with a pointed instrument. **2.** To arouse mentally; urge; goad. — *n.* **1.** Any pointed instrument used for prodding; a goad. **2.** A thrust or punch; a poke. **3.** A reminder. [Origin unknown] — **prod′der** *n.*
prod·i·gal (prod′ə-gəl) *adj.* **1.** Addicted to wasteful expenditure, as of money, time, or strength; extravagant. **2.** Yielding in profusion; bountiful. **3.** Lavish; profuse. — *n.* One who is wasteful or profligate; a spendthrift. [< L *prodigus* wasteful] — **prod′i·gal·ly** *adv.*
prod·i·gal·i·ty (prod′ə·gal′ə·tē) *n.* *pl.* **·ties** **1.** Extravagance; wastefulness. **2.** Great abundance; lavishness. **3.** Extreme generosity; bounteousness.
pro·dig·ious (prə-dij′əs) *adj.* **1.** Enormous or extraordinary in size, quantity, or degree; vast. **2.** Marvelous; amazing. [< L *prodigium* omen] — **pro·dig′ious·ly** *adv.* — **pro·dig′ious·ness** *n.*
prod·i·gy (prod′ə-jē) *n.* *pl.* **·gies** **1.** A person having remarkable qualities or powers: a violin *prodigy.* **2.** Something extraordinary. **3.** Something out of the ordinary course of nature; a monstrosity. [< L *prodigium*]
pro·duce (*v.* prə-dōōs′, -dyōōs′; *n.* prod′ōōs, -yōōs, prō′dōōs, -dyōōs) *v.* **·duced, ·duc·ing** *v.t.* **1.** To bring forth or bear; yield, as young or a natural product. **2.** To bring forth by mental effort; compose, write, etc. **3.** To bring about: His words *produced* a violent reaction. **4.** To bring to view; exhibit: to *produce* evidence. **5.** To manufacture; make. **6.** To bring to performance before the public, as a play. **7.** To extend or lengthen, as a line. **8.** *Econ.* To create (anything with exchangeable value). — *v.i.* **9.** To yield or generate an appropriate product or result. — *n.* That which is produced; a product; esp. farm products collectively. [< L *pro-* forward + *ducere* to lead] — **pro·duc′i·ble** *adj.*
pro·duc·er (prə-dōōs′ər, -dyōō′-) *n.* **1.** One who or that which produces, esp. one who makes things for sale and use. **2.** One who finances and generally controls the production of a play, concert, motion picture, etc.
prod·uct (prod′əkt, -ukt) *n.* **1.** Anything produced or obtained as a result of some operation or work, as by generation, growth, labor, study, or skill. **2.** A result. **3.** *Math.* The result obtained by multiplication.
pro·duc·tion (prə-duk′shən) *n.* **1.** The act or process of producing. **2.** That which is produced. **3.** Any tangible result of industrial, artistic, or literary effort.
pro·duc·tive (prə-duk′tiv) *adj.* **1.** Producing or tending to produce; fertile; creative, as of artistic things. **2.** Producing or tending to produce profits or increase in quantity, quality, or value. **3.** Causing; resulting in: with *of.* — **pro·duc′tive·ly** *adv.* — **pro·duc·tiv·i·ty** (prō′duk·tiv′ə·tē), **pro·duc′tive·ness** *n.*
pro·em (prō′əm) *n.* An introductory statement; preface. [< OF < L < Gk. *prooimion* overture] — **pro·e·mi·al** (prō·ē′mē·əl) *adj.*
prof·a·na·tion (prof′ə·nā′shən) *n.* **1.** The act of profaning; also, an instance of it. **2.** Abusive or improper treatment of anything.
pro·fane (prə-fān′, prō-) *v.t.* **·faned, ·fan·ing** **1.** To treat (something sacred) with irreverence or abuse; desecrate; pollute. **2.** To put to an unworthy or degrading use; debase. — *adj.* **1.** Manifesting irreverence or disrespect toward the Deity or sacred things. **2.** Not religious or concerned with religious things; secular. **3.** Vulgar; common; coarse. [< F < L < *profanus* before or outside the temple, hence, unsacred] — **pro·fan·a·to·ry** (prə-fan′ə-tôr′ē, -tō′rē) *adj.* — **pro·fane′ly** *adv.* — **pro·fan′er** *n.* — **pro·fane′ness** *n.*
pro·fan·i·ty (prə-fan′ə·tē) *n.* *pl.* **·ties** **1.** The state of being profane. **2.** Profane speech or action.
— **Syn.** **2.** *Profanity* may refer to irreverent use of a sacred name, as well as to the use of words considered lewd or coarse. *Blasphemy* is a much stronger word; *profanity* may be thoughtless or careless speech, but *blasphemy* denotes a degree of malicious insult to sacred things. *Cursing* and *swearing* are types of *profanity; cursing* involves the uttering of imprecations in the name of God, generally as an expression of rage or frustration, while *swearing* is the uttering of rash or empty oaths.
pro·fess (prə-fes′) *v.t.* **1.** To declare openly; avow; affirm. **2.** To assert, usu. insincerely: to *profess* remorse. **3.** To declare or affirm faith in. **4.** To have as one's profession: to *profess* the law. **5.** To receive into a religious order. **6.** To make open declaration; avow. **7.** To take the vows of a religious order. [< L *pro-* before + *fateri* to confess]
pro·fess·ed·ly (prə-fes′id·lē) *adv.* **1.** By open profession; avowedly. **2.** Pretendedly.

pro·fes·sion (prə·fesh′ən) *n.* **1.** An occupation that properly involves a liberal, scientific, or artistic education. **2.** The collective body of those following such occupations. **3.** The act of professing or declaring; declaration: *professions of good will.* **4.** That which is avowed or professed; a declaration. **5.** The act of binding oneself to a religious order; also, the condition of being so bound. **— Syn.** See OCCUPATION.

pro·fes·sion·al (prə·fesh′ən·əl) *adj.* **1.** Connected with, preparing for, engaged in, appropriate to, or conforming to a profession: *professional* courtesy. **2.** Of or pertaining to an occupation pursued for gain: a *professional* ball player. — *n.* **1.** One who pursues as a business some vocation or occupation. **2.** One who engages for money to compete in sports. **3.** One skilled in a profession, craft, or art. **— pro·fes′sion·al·ism** *n.* **— pro·fes′sion·al·ly** *adv.*

pro·fes·sor (prə·fes′ər) *n.* **1.** A teacher of the highest rank in a university or college, or in an institution where professional or technical studies are pursued. ◆ *Professor* may be abbreviated *Prof.* before the full name but is usu. written out before the surname, as *Professor Smith.* **2.** One who professes skill and offers instruction in some sport or art. **— pro·fes′sor·ship** *n.*

pro·fes·so·ri·al (prō′fə·sôr′ē·əl, -sō′rē-, prof′ə-) *adj.* Of, pertaining to, or characteristic of a professor; pedagogic; academic. **— pro·fes·so′ri·al·ly** *adv.*

prof·fer (prof′ər) *v.t.* To offer for acceptance. *— n.* The act of proffering, or that which is proffered. [< AF, OF < L *pro-* in behalf of + *offere* to offer] **— prof′fer·er** *n.*

pro·fi·cien·cy (prə·fish′ən·sē) *n.* *pl.* **·cies** A high state of attainment in some knowledge, art, or skill; expertness.

pro·fi·cient (prə·fish′ənt) *adj.* Thoroughly versed, as in an art or science. *— n.* An expert. [< L < *pro-* forward + *facere* to do] **— pro·fi′cient·ly** *adv.*

pro·file (prō′fil, *esp. Brit.* prō′fēl) *n.* **1.** The outline of a human face or figure as seen from the side; also, a drawing of this outline. **2.** Any outline or contour. **3.** A short biographical sketch vividly presenting the most striking characteristics of a personality. **4.** *Archit.* The outline of a perpendicular section of a building, etc., or the contour of an architectural member. **5.** *Geol.* A vertical section of the earth's crust. *— v.t.* **·filed, ·fil·ing 1.** To draw a profile of. **2.** To write or make a profile of. [< Ital. *profilare* to draw in outline < L *pro-* forward + *filum* thread, line]

prof·it (prof′it) *n.* **1.** Any advantage or gain; benefit. **2.** *Often pl.* Excess of returns over outlay or expenditure. **3.** The return from the employment of capital after deducting the amount paid for raw material and for wages, rent, interest, etc. **4.** That part of the amount received for goods which exceeds the sum originally paid for them with or without all secondary expenses involved. **— gross profit** The excess of receipts from sales over expenditures for production or purchase. **— net profit** The surplus remaining after all necessary deductions, as for interest, bad debts, etc. *— v.i.* **1.** To be of advantage or benefit. **2.** To derive gain or benefit. *— v.t.* **3.** To be of profit or advantage to. [< OF < L *profectus,* pp. of *proficere* to go forward] **— prof′it·less** *adj.*

prof·it·a·ble (prof′it·ə·bəl) *adj.* Bringing profit or gain; advantageous. **— prof′it·a·ble·ness** *n.* **— prof′it·a·bly** *adv.*

prof·i·teer (prof′ə·tir′) *v.i.* To seek or obtain excessive profits. *— n.* One who is given to making excessive profits, esp. to the detriment of others. **— prof′i·teer′ing** *n.*

profit sharing A system of remuneration by which workmen are given a share of the net profits of a business. **— prof·it·shar·ing** ((prof′it·shâr′ing) *adj.*

prof·li·ga·cy (prof′lə·gə·sē) *n.* *pl.* **·cies** The state or quality of being profligate.

prof·li·gate (prof′lə·git, -gāt) *adj.* **1.** Lost or insensible to principle, virtue, or decency. **2.** Recklessly extravagant; in great profusion. *— n.* **1.** A depraved or dissolute person. **2.** A reckless spendthrift. [< L, pp. of *profligare* to destroy < *pro-* forward + *fligere* to dash] **— prof′li·gate·ly** *adv.* **— prof′li·gate·ness** (-git·nis, -gāt′nis) *n.*

prof·lu·ent (prof′lōō·ənt) *adj.* Flowing smoothly or plentifully. [< L < *pro-* before + *fluere* to flow] **— prof′lu·ence** *n.*

pro·found (prə·found′, prō-) *adj.* **1.** Intellectually deep or penetrating. **2.** Reaching to, arising from, or affecting the depth of one's nature: *profound* respect. **3.** Situated far below the surface; unfathomable. **4.** Deep. **5.** Thorough; exhaustive: *profound* changes. *— n.* A fathomless depth. **2.** The ocean; the deep. [< OF < L < *pro-* very + *fundus* deep] **— pro·found′ly** *adv.* **— pro·found′ness** *n.*

pro·fun·di·ty (prə·fun′də·tē, prō-) *n.* *pl.* **·ties 1.** The state or quality of being profound, in any sense. **2.** A deep place or thing. **3.** A profound or abstruse statement, theory, etc.

pro·fuse (prə·fyōōs′, prō-) *adj.* **1.** Giving or given forth lavishly; liberal; extravagant. **2.** Copious; overflowing; abundant: *profuse* vegetation. [< L < *pro-* forward + *fundere* to pour] **— pro·fuse′ly** *adv.* **— pro·fuse′ness** *n.*

pro·fu·sion (prə·fyōō′zhən, prō-) *n.* **1.** A lavish supply or condition: a *profusion* of ornaments. **2.** The act of pouring forth or supplying in great abundance; prodigality.

pro·gen·i·tor (prō·jen′ə·tər) *n.* A forefather or parent. [< F < L < *pro-* forth + *gignere* to beget]

prog·e·ny (proj′ə·nē) *n.* *pl.* **·nies** Offspring.

pro·ges·ter·one (prō·jes′tə·rōn) *n.* *Biochem.* A female hormone, isolated as a white, crystalline compound, $C_{21}H_{30}O_2$, and also made synthetically. It is active in preparing the uterus for the fertilized ovum. Also **pro·ges·tin** (prō·jes′tin).

prog·na·thous (prog′nə·thəs, prog·nā′thəs) *adj.* Having abnormally projecting jaws. Also **prog·nath·ic** (prog·nath′ik). **— prog·na·thism** (prog′nə·thiz′əm) *n.*

prog·no·sis (prog·nō′sis) *n.* *pl.* **·ses** (-sēz) **1.** *Med.* **a** A prediction or conclusion regarding the course of a disease and the probability of recovery. **b** Likelihood of recovery: The *prognosis* is excellent. **2.** Any prediction or forecast. [< NL < Gk. < *pro-* before + *gignōskein* to know]

prog·nos·tic (prog·nos′tik) *adj.* **1.** Of, pertaining to, or serving as a prognosis. **2.** Predicting or foretelling. *— n.* **1.** A sign of some future occurrence; an omen. **2.** *Med.* A symptom indicative of the course of a disease.

prog·nos·ti·cate (prog·nos′tə·kāt) *v.t.* **·cat·ed, ·cat·ing 1.** To foretell (future events, etc.) by present indications. **2.** To indicate beforehand. **— prog·nos′ti·ca′tion** *n.* **— prog·nos′ti·ca′tor** *n.*

pro·gram (prō′gram, -grəm) *n.* **1.** A performance or show, esp. one given at a scheduled time on television or radio. **2.** A printed announcement or schedule of events, esp. one for a theatrical performance. **3.** Any prearranged, proposed, or desired plan or course of proceedings. **4.** *Electronics* A sequence of instructions set up on the control panels of an electronic computer as guides in the performance of a desired operation or group of operations. Also *Brit.* **pro′gramme.** *— v.t.* **·gramed** or **·grammed, ·gram·ing** or **·gram·ming 1.** To arrange or include in a program. **2.** To make up a program for (a radio station, a computer, etc.). [< LL < Gk. < *pro-* before + *graphein* to write] **— pro·gram·mat·ic** (prō′grə·mat′ik) or **pro′gram·at′ic** *adj.*

pro·gram·mer (prō′gram·ər) *n.* One who makes up a computer program. Also **pro′gram·er.**

program music See under MUSIC.

prog·ress (*n.* prog′res, *esp. Brit.* prō′gres; *v.* prə·gres′) *n.* **1.** A moving forward in space; movement forward nearer a goal. **2.** Advancement toward maturity or completion; improvement. *— v.i.* **1.** To move forward or onward. **2.** To advance toward completion or fuller development. [< L < *pro-* forward + *gradi* to walk]

pro·gres·sion (prə·gresh′ən) *n.* **1.** The act of progressing; advancement. **2.** *Math.* A sequence of numbers or quantities, each of which is derived from the preceding by a constant relationship. **3.** *Music* **a** A movement from one tone or chord to another. **b** A succession of tones, chords, etc. **4.** Course or lapse of time; passage. **— pro·gres′sion·al** *adj.* **— pro·gres′sion·ism** *n.*

pro·gres·sive (prə·gres′iv) *adj.* **1.** Moving forward; advancing. **2.** Proceeding gradually or step by step. **3.** Aiming at or characterized by progress. **4.** Spreading from one part to others; increasing: said of a disease: *progressive* paralysis. **5.** Striving for or favoring progress or reform, esp. social, political, educational, or religious. **6.** Denoting or pertaining to a tax or taxes in which the tax rate increases as the amount taxed increases. **7.** *Gram.* Designating an aspect of the verb that expresses the action as being in progress at some time in the past, present, or future: formed with any tense of the auxiliary *be* and the present participle; as, He *is speaking;* he *had been speaking;* he *will be speaking.* *— n.* **1.** One who believes in progress or in progressive methods; esp., one who favors or promotes reforms or changes, as in politics or religion. **2.** *Gram.* A progressive verb form. [< OF *progressif*] **— pro·gres′sive·ly** *adv.* **— pro·gres′sive·ness** *n.* **— pro·gres′siv·ism** *n.* **— pro·gres′siv·ist** *n.*

Pro·gres·sive-Con·ser·va·tive Party (prə·gres′iv·kən·sûr′və·tiv) In Canada, one of the principal political parties, formerly called the Conservative Party.

Progressive Party 1. A political party formed under the leadership of Theodore Roosevelt in 1912. **2.** A political party formed in 1924 under the leadership of Robert M. LaFollette. **3.** A political party formed in 1948, which nominated Henry A. Wallace for president.

pro·hib·it (prō·hib′it) *v.t.* **1.** To forbid, esp. by authority or law; interdict. **2.** To prevent or hinder. [< L < *pro-* before + *habere* to have] **— pro·hib′it·er** *n.*

pro·hi·bi·tion (prō′ə·bish′ən) *n.* **1.** The act of prohibiting, preventing, or stopping; also, a decree or order forbidding anything. **2.** The forbidding of the manufacture, transportation, and sale of alcoholic liquors as beverages.

pro·hi·bi·tion·ist (prō′ə·bish′ən·ist) *n.* One who favors legal prohibition of the manufacture and sale of alcoholic liquors.

pro·hib·i·tive (prō·hib′ə·tiv) *adj.* **1.** Prohibiting or tending to prohibit. **2.** Preventing the sale, purchase, etc., of something: *prohibitive* costs. Also **pro·hib′i·to·ry** (-tôr′ē, -tō′rē). **— pro·hib′i·tive·ly** *adv.*

proj·ect (*n.* proj′ekt; *v.* prə·jekt′) *n.* **1.** Something proposed or mapped out in the mind, as a course of action; a plan. **2.** In schools, a problem, task, or piece of work given to a student or group of students. **3.** A housing project. — *v.t.* **1.** To cause to extend forward or out. **2.** To throw forth or forward, as missiles. **3.** To visualize as an external reality. **4.** To cause (an image, shadow, etc.) to fall on a surface. **5.** To propose or plan. **6.** *Math.* **a** To make a projection (of a solid, etc.) on a plane. **b** To reproduce (a figure) by drawing lines from a vertex through every point (of the figure) to the corresponding point of the reproduction. **7.** To use or produce (one's voice, words, etc.) so as to be heard clearly and at a distance. — *v.i.* **8.** To protrude. **9.** *Psychol.* To attribute one's own ideas, impulses, etc., to others. **10.** To speak or sing so as to be heard clearly and at a distance. [< L < *pro-* before + *jacere* to throw]
pro·jec·tile (prə·jek′təl, *esp. Brit.* -tīl) *adj.* **1.** Projecting, or impelling forward. **2.** Capable of being or intended to be projected or shot forth. **3.** Protrusile. — *n.* **1.** A body projected or thrown forth by force. **2.** *Mil.* A missile for discharge from a gun or cannon. [< NL < L *projectus* thrown out]
pro·jec·tion (prə·jek′shən) *n.* **1.** The act of projecting; a jutting, throwing, or shooting out or forth. **2.** That which projects; a projecting part. **3.** A scheme; project. **4.** A system of lines drawn on a given fixed plane, as in a map, representing point for point a given terrestrial or celestial surface. **5.** *Psychol.* **a** The unconscious process of attributing one's own feelings, attitudes, etc., to others. **b** An instance of this process. **6.** *Photog.* **a** The process of exhibiting motion pictures or slides on a screen. **b** The picture so produced. — **pro·jec′tive** *adj.* — **pro·jec′tive·ly** *adv.*
pro·jec·tor (prə·jek′tər) *n.* **1.** An apparatus for throwing illuminated images or motion pictures upon a screen. **2.** A mirror or combination of lenses for projecting a beam of light. **3.** One who devises projects; schemer; promoter.
pro·lapse (prō·laps′) *Pathol.* *v.i.* **lapsed, laps·ing** To fall out of place, as an organ or part. — *n.* The falling down of an organ or part, as the uterus, from its normal position. Also **pro·lap·sus** (prō·lap′səs). [< L < *pro-* forward + *labi* to glide, fall]
pro·late (prō′lāt) *adj.* **1.** Extended lengthwise. **2.** Lengthened toward the poles, as a spheroid. [< L < *pro-* forward + *ferre* to carry]
pro·le·gom·e·non (prō′lə·gom′ə·non) *n.* *pl.* **·na** (-nə) Often *pl.* An introductory remark or remarks; a preface. [< Gk. < *pro-* before + *legein* to say] — **pro·le·gom′e·nous** *adj.*
pro·le·tar·i·an (prō′lə·târ′ē·ən) *adj.* Of or pertaining to the proletariat. — *n.* A member of the proletariat. [< L < *proles* offspring: so called because they served the Roman state only by having children] — **pro′le·tar′i·an·ism** *n.*
pro·le·tar·i·at (prō′lə·târ′ē·ət) *n.* **1.** Wageworkers collectively; the working class: a term used esp. in Marxism. **2.** In ancient Rome, the lowest class of the state.
pro·lif·er·ate (prō·lif′ə·rāt) *v.i. & v.t.* **·at·ed, ·at·ing** To produce, reproduce, or grow, esp. with rapidity, as cells in tissue formation. — **pro·lif′er·a′tion** *n.* — **pro·lif′er·a′tive** *adj.*
pro·lif·er·ous (prō·lif′ər·əs) *adj.* **1.** Producing offspring freely. **2.** *Bot.* **a** Developing buds, branches, and flowers from unusual places. **b** Bearing progeny in the way of offshoots, buds, etc. [< Med.L < L *proles, prolis* offspring + *ferre* to bear]
pro·lif·ic (prō·lif′ik) *adj.* **1.** Producing abundantly, as offspring or fruit; fertile. **2.** Producing results abundantly: a *prolific* writer. [< F < Med.L < L *proles, prolis* offspring + stem of *facere* to make] — **pro·lif′i·ca·cy** (-i·kə·sē), **pro·lif′ic·ness** *n.* — **pro·lif′i·cal·ly** *adv.*
— **Syn. 1.** fruitful, fecund. **2.** productive.
pro·lix (prō·liks′, prō′liks) *adj.* **1.** Unduly long and verbose, as an address. **2.** Indulging in long and wordy discourse. [< F < L < *pro-* before + stem of *liquere* to flow] — **pro·lix·i·ty** (prō·lik′sə·tē), **pro·lix′ness** *n.* — **pro′lix·ly** *adv.*
pro·logue (prō′lôg, -log) *n.* **1.** A prefatory statement to a poem, discourse, or performance; esp., an introduction, often in verse, spoken or sung before a play or opera. **2.** Any anticipatory act or event. — *v.t.* To introduce with a prologue or preface. Also **pro′log.** [< OF < L < Gk. < *pro-* before + *logos* discourse]
pro·lo·guize (prō′lôg·īz, -log-) *v.i.* **·ized, ·iz·ing** To make or utter a prologue. Also **pro′log·ize.** — **pro′lo·guiz′er** *n.*
pro·long (prə·lông′, -long′) *v.t.* To extend in time or space; continue; lengthen. Also **pro·lon′gate** (-lông′gāt, -long′-). [< OF < LL < L *pro-* forth + *longus* long] — **pro·lon·ga·tion** *n.* — **pro·long′er** *n.* — **pro·long′ment** *n.*
prom (prom) *n.* *U.S. Informal* A formal college or school dance or ball. [Short for *promenade*]
prom·e·nade (prom′ə·nād′, -näd′) *n.* **1.** A walk for amusement or exercise, or as part of a formal or social entertain-

ment. **2.** A place for promenading. **3.** A concert or ball opened with a formal march; also, the march. — *v.* **·nad·ed, ·nad·ing** *v.i.* **1.** To take a promenade. — *v.t.* **2.** To take a promenade through or along. **3.** To take or exhibit on or as on a promenade. [< MF < LL < *pro-* before + *minare* to drive (cattle)] — **prom′e·nad′er** *n.*
Pro·me·theus (prə·mē′thyōōs, -thē-əs) In Greek mythology, a Titan who stole fire from heaven for mankind and as a punishment was chained to a rock, where an eagle daily devoured his liver, which was made whole again at night. [< L < Gk. *Promētheus*] — **Pro·me′the·an** *adj. & n.*
pro·me·thi·um (prə·mē′thē·əm) *n.* A radioactive element (symbol Pm), separated from uranium fission products and belonging to the lanthanide series: formerly called *illinium*. See ELEMENT. [< NL < PROMETHEUS]
prom·i·nence (prom′ə·nəns) *n.* **1.** The state of being prominent. **2.** That which is prominent. **3.** *Astron.* One of the great tongues of flame shooting out from the sun's surface, seen during total eclipses. Also **prom′i·nen·cy.**
prom·i·nent (prom′ə·nənt) *adj.* **1.** Jutting out; projecting; protuberant. **2.** Conspicuous in position, character, or importance. **3.** Well-known; eminent. [< L < *prominere* to project] — **prom′i·nent·ly** *adv.*
pro·mis·cu·ous (prə·mis′kyōō·əs) *adj.* **1.** Composed of individuals or things confusedly or indiscriminately mingled. **2.** Indiscriminate, esp. in sexual relations. **3.** *Informal* Lacking plan or purpose; casual; irregular. [< L < *pro-* thoroughly + stem of *miscere* to mix] — **pro·mis·cu·i·ty** (prō′mis·kyōō′ə·tē, prom′is-) *n.* — **pro·mis′cu·ous·ly** *adv.* — **pro·mis′cu·ous·ness** *n.*
prom·ise (prom′is) *n.* **1.** An assurance given by one person to another that the former will or will not perform a specified act. **2.** Reasonable ground for hope or expectation, esp. of future excellence or satisfaction. **3.** Something promised. — *v.* **·ised, ·is·ing** *v.t.* **1.** To engage or pledge by a promise: used with the infinitive or a clause. **2.** To make a promise of (something) to someone. **3.** To give reason for expecting. **4.** *Informal* To assure (someone). — *v.i.* **5.** To make a promise. **6.** To give reason for expectation. [< L < *pro-* forth + *mittere* to send] — **prom′is·ee** *n.* — **prom′is·er** *n.*
Promised Land 1. Canaan, promised to Abraham by God. *Gen.* xv 18. **2.** Any longed-for place of happiness or improvement. **3.** Heaven; paradise. Also *Land of Promise.*
prom·is·ing (prom′is·ing) *adj.* Giving promise of good results: a *promising* sign. — **prom′is·ing·ly** *adv.*
prom·is·so·ry (prom′ə·sôr′ē, -sō′rē) *adj.* **1.** Containing or of the nature of a promise. **2.** Indicating what is to be required after the signing of an insurance contract.
promissory note A written promise by one party to pay another party a certain sum of money at a specified time, or upon demand.
prom·on·to·ry (prom′ən·tôr′ē, -tō′rē) *n.* *pl.* **·ries 1.** A high point of land extending into the sea; headland. **2.** *Anat.* A rounded projection or part. [< Med.L < L, ? < *prominere* to project]
pro·mote (prə·mōt′) *v.t.* **·mot·ed, ·mot·ing 1.** To contribute to the progress, development, or growth of; further; encourage. **2.** To advance to a higher position, grade, or honor. **3.** To work in behalf of; advocate actively. **4.** In education, to advance (a pupil) to the next higher school grade. **5.** To seek to make (a commercial product, business venture, etc.) popular or successful, as by securing capital or by advertising. [< L < *pro-* forward + *movere* to move] — **pro·mot′er** *n.* — **pro·mo′tion** *n.* — **pro·mo′tion·al** *adj.* — **pro·mo′tive** *adj.*
prompt (prompt) *v.t.* **1.** To incite to action; instigate. **2.** To suggest or inspire (an act, thought, etc.). **3.** To remind of something forgotten or next in order; give a cue to. — *v.i.* **4.** To give help or suggestions. — *adj.* **1.** Acting or ready to act at the moment; punctual. **2.** Done or rendered with readiness or alacrity; taking place at the appointed time. — *n.* **1.** An act of prompting. **2.** The information imparted by prompting. [< OF < L < *pro-* forth + *emere* to take] — **prompt′ness** *n.*
prompt·er (promp′tər) *n.* **1.** In a theater, one who follows the lines and prompts the actors. **2.** One who or that which prompts.
promp·ti·tude (promp′tə·tōod, -tyōod) *n.* The quality, habit, or fact of being prompt; promptness.
prompt·ly (prompt′lē) *adv.* In a prompt manner; at once.
pro·mul·gate (prō·mul′gāt, prom′əl·gāt) *v.t.* **·gat·ed, ·gat·ing** To make known or announce officially and formally; put into effect by public proclamation, as a law or dogma. [< L < *pro-* forth + *vulgus* people] — **pro′mul·ga′tion** *n.* — **pro·mul·ga·tor** (prō·mul′gā·tər, prom′əl-) *n.*
prone (prōn) *adj.* **1.** Lying flat, esp. with the face, front, or palm downward; prostrate. **2.** Leaning forward or downward; also, moving or sloping sharply downward. **3.** Men-

tally inclined or predisposed: with *to.* [< L *pronus* prostrate] — **prone'ly** *adv.* — **prone'ness** *n.*

prong (prông, prong) *n.* **1.** A pointed end of an instrument, as the tine of a fork. **2.** Any pointed, projecting part, as the end of an antler. — *v.t.* To prick or stab with or as with a prong. [Cf. LG *prange* pointed stick, Du. *prangen* to pinch]

prong·horn (prông'hôrn', prong'-) *n. pl.* **·horns** or **·horn** A ruminant of western North America, resembling an antelope, with deciduous branched horns.

pro·nom·i·nal (prō·nom'ə·nəl) *adj.* Of, pertaining to, or of the nature of a pronoun. — **pro·nom'i·nal·ly** *adv.*

pronominal adjective The possessive case of a personal pronoun used attributively, as *my, your, his, her,* etc.

pro·noun (prō'noun) *n. Gram.* A word that may be used instead of a noun or noun phrase, as an adjective, or to introduce a question. [< OF < L < *pro-* in place of + *nomen* name, noun]

pro·nounce (prə·nouns') *v.* **·nounced, ·nounc·ing** *v.t.* **1.** To utter or deliver officially or solemnly; proclaim: to *pronounce* judgment. **2.** To assert; declare, esp. as one's judgment. **3.** To enunciate or articulate (sounds). **4.** To utter the constituent sounds of (a word or phrase) in a particular sequence or with a particular accentual pattern. **5.** To utter (the sound of a letter). — *v.i.* **6.** To make a judgment or pronouncement. **7.** To articulate words; speak. [< OF < LL < L < *pro-* forth + *nuntiare* to announce] — **pro·nounce'a·ble** *adj.* — **pro·nounc'er** *n.*

pro·nounced (prə·nounst') *adj.* Of marked or clearly indicated character. — **pro·nounc·ed·ly** (prə·noun'sid·lē) *adv.*

pro·nounce·ment (prə·nouns'mənt) *n.* **1.** The act of pronouncing. **2.** A formal declaration or announcement.

pron·to (pron'tō) *adv. U.S. Informal* Quickly; promptly; instantly. [< Sp. < L *promptus* brought forth]

pro·nun·ci·a·men·to (prə·nun'sē·ə·men'tō, -shē·ə-) *n. pl.* **·tos** A public announcement; proclamation; manifesto. [< Sp. < L *pronuntiare* to pronounce]

pro·nun·ci·a·tion (prə·nun'sē·ā'shən) *n.* **1.** The act or manner of uttering words. **2.** Articulation.

proof (prōof) *n.* **1.** The act or process of proving; esp., the establishment of a fact by evidence or a truth by other truths. **2.** A trial of strength, truth, excellence, etc. **3.** Evidence and argument sufficient to induce belief. **4.** *Law* Anything that serves to determine a verdict. **5.** The state or quality of having successfully undergone a test. **6.** Impenetrability; also, impenetrable armor. **7.** The standard of strength of alcoholic liquors. **8.** *Printing* A printed trial sheet showing the contents or condition of matter in type or of a plate, or the like. **9.** In engraving and etching, a trial impression taken from an engraved plate, stone, or block; also, a perfect impression from such a plate, etc., when finished. **10.** *Photog.* A trial print from a negative. **11.** *Math.* A process to check a computation by using its result; also, a demonstration. **12.** In philately, an experimental printing of a stamp. — *adj.* **1.** Employed in or connected with proving or correcting. **2.** Capable of resisting successfully: with *against.* **3.** Of standard alcoholic strength, as liquors. [< OF < LL < *probare* to test]

-proof *combining form* **1.** Impervious to; able to withstand; not damaged by: *bombproof.* **2.** Protected against: *mothproof.* **3.** As strong as: *armorproof.* **4.** Resisting; showing no effects of: *panicproof.* Adjectives formed with *-proof* may also be used as verbs. [< PROOF, adj.]

proof·read (prōof'rēd') *v.t. & v.i.* **·read** (-red'), **·read·ing** (-rē'ding) To read and correct (printers' proofs). — **proof'·read'er** *n.* — **proof'read'ing** *n.*

proof spirit An alcoholic liquor that contains a standard amount of alcohol. In the U.S. 100 proof indicates a liquor half of whose volume is ethyl alcohol having a specific gravity of 0.7939 at 60° F.

prop¹ (prop) *n.* **1.** A rigid object, as a beam or pole, that bolsters or sustains an incumbent weight. **2.** One who gives support to an institution, organization, etc. — *v.t.* **propped, prop·ping 1.** To support or keep from falling with or as with a prop. **2.** To lean or place: usu. with *against.* **3.** To support; sustain. [< MDu. *proppe* a support]

prop² (prop) *n.* A property (def. 7.).

prop·a·ga·ble (prop'ə·gə·bəl) *adj.* That can be propagated.

prop·a·gan·da (prop'ə·gan'də) *n.* **1.** A systematic effort to persuade a body of people to support or adopt a particular opinion, attitude, or course of action. **2.** Any selection of facts, ideas, or allegations forming the basis of such an effort. **3.** An institution or scheme for propagating a doctrine or system. ◆ *Propaganda* is now often used in a disparaging sense, as of a body of distortions and half-truths calculated to bias one's judgment or opinions. [< PROPAGANDA] — **prop'a·gan'dism** *n.* — **prop'a·gan'dist** *n. & adj.*

Prop·a·gan·da (prop'ə·gan'də) *n.* In the Roman Catholic Church, a society of cardinals charged with overseeing the foreign missions. [< NL (*congregatio de*) *propaganda* (*fide*) (the council for) propagating (the faith)]

prop·a·gan·dize (prop'ə·gan'dīz) *v.* **·dized, ·diz·ing** *v.t.* **1.**

To spread by means of propaganda. **2.** To subject to propaganda. — *v.i.* **3.** To carry on or spread propaganda.

prop·a·gate (prop'ə·gāt) *v.* **·gat·ed, ·gat·ing** *v.t.* **1.** To cause (animals, plants, etc.) to multiply by natural reproduction. **2.** To spread from person to person, as a doctrine or belief; disseminate. **3.** To transmit through a medium: to *propagate* heat. **4.** To reproduce (itself), as a species of plant or animal. **5.** To pass on (traits, qualities, etc.) to one's offspring. — *v.i.* **6.** To have offspring; breed. [< L < *pro-* forth + *pag-* root of *pangere* to fasten] — **prop'a·ga'tion** *n.* — **prop'a·ga'tive** *adj.* — **prop'a·ga'tor** *n.*

pro·pane (prō'pān) *n. Chem.* A gaseous hydrocarbon of the methane series, C_3H_8, obtained from petroleum and sometimes used as a fuel gas.

pro pa·tri·a (prō pä'trē·ə) *Latin* For one's country.

pro·pel (prə·pel') *v.t.* **·pelled, ·pel·ling** To cause to move forward or ahead; drive or urge forward. [< L < *pro-* forward + *pellere* to drive]

pro·pel·lant (prə·pel'ənt) *n.* **1.** One who or that which propels. **2.** *Mil.* An explosive that upon ignition propels a projectile from a gun. **3.** A solid or liquid fuel that serves to propel a rocket, guided missile, etc.: also spelled *propellent.*

pro·pel·lent (prə·pel'ənt) *adj.* Able to propel; propelling. — *n.* See PROPELLANT.

pro·pel·ler (prə·pel'ər) *n.* **1.** One who or that which propels. **2.** Any device for propelling a craft through water or air; esp., one having blades mounted at an angle on a power-driven shaft and producing a thrust by their rotary action on the medium.

pro·pe·no·ic acid (prō'pə·nō'ik) *Chem.* Acrylic acid.

pro·pen·si·ty (prə·pen'sə·tē) *n. pl.* **·ties** A natural disposition or tendency; bent. [< L < *pro-* forward + *pendere* to hang]

prop·er (prop'ər) *adj.* **1.** Specially suited or adapted for some end; appropriate. **2.** Conforming to a prevalent standard of conduct or manners; fitting. **3.** Understood in a strict or literal sense: usu. following the noun modified: part of the book *proper.* **4.** Naturally belonging to a particular person, thing, or class: Crying is *proper* to babies. **5.** Modest; decent. **6.** *Gram.* Designating a particular person, place, or the like: a *proper* name. **7.** *Brit. Informal* Thorough; unmitigated: a *proper* bore. — *n. Sometimes cap. Eccl.* The portion of the breviary, missal, or Mass containing the prayers and collects suitable to special occasions or feasts: with *the:* distinguished from *ordinary.* [< OF < L *propius* one's own] — **prop'er·ly** *adv.* — **prop'er·ness** *n.*

proper fraction *Math.* A fraction in which the numerator is less than the denominator.

proper noun *Gram.* A noun that names a particular person, place, or thing, and is always capitalized, as *Paul, Venice, U.S.S. Nautilus:* distinguished from *common noun.*

prop·er·tied (prop'ər·tēd) *adj.* Owning property.

prop·er·ty (prop'ər·tē) *n. pl.* **·ties 1.** Any object of value that a person may lawfully acquire and hold; that which may be owned, as stocks, land, etc. **2.** The legal right to the possession, use, enjoyment, and disposal of a thing. **3.** Holdings, land, etc., owned; wealth. **4.** A parcel of land. **5.** Any of the qualities or characteristics that together make up the nature or basic structure of a thing. **6.** A quality or feature that belongs distinctively to a particular object or class; a peculiarity. **7.** In the theater, any portable article used in a performance other than scenery and the costumes, as books, dishes, etc.: also called *prop.* [< OF < L *proprius* one's own] — **prop'er·ty·less** *adj.*

— **Syn. 3.** chattels, goods, estate. **6.** See CHARACTERISTIC.

proph·e·cy (prof'ə·sē) *n. pl.* **·cies 1.** A prediction made under divine influence and direction. **2.** Any prediction. **3.** Discourse delivered by a prophet under divine inspiration. **4.** A book of prophecies. [< OF < LL < Gk. < *pro* before + *phanai* to speak]

proph·e·sy (prof'ə·sī) *v.* **·sied, ·sy·ing** *v.t.* **1.** To utter or foretell with or as with divine inspiration. **2.** To predict (a future event). **3.** To point out beforehand. — *v.i.* **4.** To speak by divine influence, or as a medium between God and man. **5.** To foretell the future. **6.** To explain or teach religious subjects; preach. [See PROPHECY] — **proph'e·si'er** *n.*

— **Syn. 1.** *Prophesy* and *foretell* are often interchangeable, but in Scriptural sense *prophesy* refers to the uttering of religious truths under divine inspiration, and does not necessarily include the prediction of future events. *Foretell* always bears the latter sense.

proph·et (prof'it) *n.* **1.** One who delivers divine messages or interprets the divine will. **2.** One who foretells the future; esp., an inspired predictor. **3.** A religious leader. **4.** An interpreter or spokesman for any cause. **5.** A mantis. — **the Prophet** According to Islam, Mohammed. — **the Prophets** The second of the three ancient divisions of the Old Testament, containing all those books not found in the Pentateuch or the Hagiographa. [< OF < LL < Gk. < *pro-* before + *phanai* to speak] — **proph'et·ess** *n.fem.*

pro·phet·ic (prə·fet'ik) *adj.* **1.** Of or pertaining to a prophet or prophecy. **2.** Pertaining to or involving prediction or presentiment; predictive. Also **pro·phet′i·cal. — pro·phet′i·cal·ly** *adv.* **— pro·phet′i·cal·ness** *n.*

pro·phy·lac·tic (prō′fə·lak′tik, prof′ə-) *adj.* Tending to protect against or ward off something, esp. disease; preventive. **— n.** A prophylactic medicine or appliance. [< Gk. < *pro-* before + *phylassein* to guard]

pro·phy·lax·is (prō′fə·lak′sis, prof′ə-) *n.* Preventive treatment for disease. [< NL < Gk. *pro-* before + *phylaxis* guarding]

pro·pin·qui·ty (prō·ping′kwə·tē) *n.* **1.** Nearness in place or time. **2.** Kinship. **— Syn.** See APPROXIMATION. [< L *prope* near]

pro·pi·ti·ate (prō·pish′ē·āt) *v.t.* **·at·ed, ·at·ing** To cause to be favorably disposed; conciliate. [See PROPITIOUS.] **— pro·pi·ti·a·ble** (prō·pish′ē·ə·bəl) *adj.* **— pro·pi′ti·at′ing·ly** *adv.* **— pro·pi′ti·a′tion** *n.* **— pro·pi′ti·a′tive** *adj.* **— pro·pi′ti·a′tor** *n.*

pro·pi·ti·a·to·ry (prō·pish′ē·ə·tôr′ē, -tō′rē) *adj.* Pertaining to or causing propitiation.

pro·pi·tious (prō·pish′əs) *adj.* **1.** Attended by favorable circumstances; auspicious. **2.** Kindly disposed; gracious. [< OF < L *propitious* favorable, ? < *pro-* before + *petere* to seek] **— pro·pi′tious·ly** *adv.* **— pro·pi′tious·ness** *n.*
— Syn. 1. *Propitious* may be applied to persons, while *auspicious* is not so used.

prop·jet (prop′jet′) *n.* *Aeron.* A turboprop.

pro·po·nent (prə·pō′nənt) *n.* **1.** One who makes a proposal or proposition. **2.** One who advocates or supports a cause or doctrine. [< L < *pro-* forth + *ponere* to put]

pro·por·tion (prə·pôr′shən, -pōr′-) *n.* **1.** Relative magnitude, number, or degree, as existing between parts, a part and a whole, etc. **2.** Fitness and harmony; symmetry. **3.** A proportionate or proper share. **4.** An equality or identity between ratios. **5.** *Math.* The relationship among four terms such that the product of the second and third terms is equal to the product of the first and fourth. **6.** *pl.* Size; dimensions. **— v.t. 1.** To adjust properly as to relative magnitude, amount, or degree. **2.** To form with a harmonious relation of parts. [< OF < L *pro-* for + *portio, -onis* share] **— pro·por′tion·a·ble** *adj.* **— pro·por′tion·a·bly** *adv.* **— pro·por′tion·er** *n.* **— pro·por′tion·ment** *n.*

pro·por·tion·al (prə·pôr′shən·əl, -pōr′-) *adj.* **1.** Of or being in proportion. **2.** *Math.* **a** Constituting the terms of a proportion. **b** Varying so that corresponding values form a proportion. **— n.** Any quantity or number in proportion to another or others. **— pro·por′tion·al·ly** *adv.* **— pro·por′tion·al′i·ty** (-al′ə·tē) *n.*

pro·por·tion·ate (*adj.* prə·pôr′shən·it, -pōr′-; *v.* prə·pôr′shən·āt, -pōr′-) *adj.* Being in due proportion; proportional. **— v.t. ·at·ed, ·at·ing** To make proportionate. **— pro·por′tion·ate·ly** *adv.* **— pro·por′tion·ate·ness** *n.*

pro·po·sal (prə·pō′zəl) *n.* **1.** An offer proposing something to be accepted or adopted. **2.** An offer of marriage. **3.** Something proposed, as a scheme or plan.

pro·pose (prə·pōz′) *v.* **·posed, ·pos·ing** *v.t.* **1.** To put forward for acceptance or consideration. **2.** To nominate, as for appointment. **3.** To intend; aim. **4.** To suggest the drinking of (a toast or health). **— v.i. 5.** To form or announce a plan or design. **6.** To make an offer, as of marriage. [< OF < *pro-* forth (< L) + *poser* to put down, rest] **— pro·pos′er** *n.*
— Syn. 3. What we *propose* to do is subject to further consideration. What we *purpose* to do is settled; the word suggests that the mind has been made up.

prop·o·si·tion (prop′ə·zish′ən) *n.* **1.** A scheme or proposal offered for consideration or acceptance. **2.** *U.S. Informal* Any matter or person to be dealt with. **3.** A subject or statement presented for discussion. **4.** *Logic* A statement in which something (the *subject*) is affirmed or denied in terms of something else (the *predicate*). **5.** *Math.* A statement of a truth to be demonstrated (a *theorem*) or of an operation to be performed (a *problem*). [< OF < L < *pro-* forth + *ponere* to put] **— prop′o·si′tion·al** *adj.* **— prop′o·si′tion·al·ly** *adv.*

pro·pound (prə·pound′) *v.t.* To put forward for consideration, solution, etc.; submit. [Earlier *propone* < L *proponere* to set forth] **— pro·pound′er** *n.*

pro·pri·e·tar·y (prə·prī′ə·ter′ē) *adj.* **1.** Of or belonging to a proprietor. **2.** Subject to exclusive ownership. **3.** Designating an article, as a medicine, protected by copyright, patent, secrecy, etc. **— n.** *pl.* **·tar·ies 1.** A proprietor or proprietors collectively. **2.** Proprietorship; ownership. [< LL < L *proprius* one's own]

pro·pri·e·tor (prə·prī′ə·tər) *n.* **1.** A person having the exclusive title to anything. **— pro·pri′e·tor·ship′** *n.* **— pro·pri′e·tress** *n.fem.*

pro·pri·e·ty (prə·prī′ə·tē) *n.* *pl.* **·ties** The character or quality of being proper; esp., accordance with recognized usage or principles. **— the proprieties** The standards of good society. [< OF *propriete* < L *proprius* one's own]

pro·pul·sion (prə·pul′shən) *n.* **1.** The act or operation of propelling. **2.** A propelling force. **— pro·pul′sive** (-siv) *adj.*

pro·pyl (prō′pil) *n.* *Chem.* The univalent radical, C_3H_7, derived from propane.

pro ra·ta (prō rā′tə, rat′ə, rä′tə) In proportion. [< L *pro rata (parte)* according to the calculated (share)]

pro·rate (prō·rāt′, prō′rāt′) *v.t. & v.i.* **·rat·ed, ·rat·ing** To distribute or divide proportionately. [< PRO RATA] **— pro·rat′a·ble** *adj.* **— pro·ra′tion** *n.*

pro·ro·ga·tion (prō′rə·gā′shən) *n.* **1.** The act of proroguing. **2.** The act of prolonging; also, continuance.

pro·rogue (prō·rōg′) *v.t.* **·rogued, ·ro·guing** To discontinue a session of (an assembly). [< MF < L < *pro-* forward + *rogare* to ask]

pro·sa·ic (prō·zā′ik) *adj.* **1.** Unimaginative; commonplace; dull. **2.** Of or like prose. Also **pro·sa′i·cal.** [< LL < L *prosa* prose] **— pro·sa′ic·ness** *n.*

pro·sce·ni·um (prō·sē′nē·əm) *n.* *pl.* **·ni·a** (-nē·ə) The part of a theater stage in front of the curtain, sometimes including the curtain and its arch. [< L < Gk. < *pro-* before + *skēnē* stage, tent]

pro·scribe (prō·skrīb′) *v.t.* **·scribed, ·scrib·ing 1.** To denounce or condemn; prohibit. **2.** To outlaw or banish. **3.** In ancient Rome, to publish the name of (one condemned or exiled). [< L *proscribere* to write publicly] **— pro·scrib′er** *n.* **— pro·scrip′tion** (-skrip′shən) *n.* **— pro·scrip′tive** *adj.*

prose (prōz) *n.* **1.** Speech or writing without metrical structure: distinguished from *verse.* **2.** Commonplace or tedious discourse. **— adj. 1.** Of or pertaining to prose. **2.** Tedious; tiresome. **— v.t. & v.i. prosed, pros·ing** To write or speak in prose. [< OF < L *prosa (oratio)* straightforward (discourse)]

pros·e·cute (pros′ə·kyōōt) *v.* **·cut·ed, ·cut·ing** *v.t.* **1.** To go on with so as to complete. **2.** To carry on or engage in, as a trade. **3.** *Law* **a** To bring suit against. **b** To seek to enforce, as a claim, by legal process. **— v.i. 4.** To begin and carry on a legal proceeding. **— Syn.** See PUSH. [< L < *pro-* forward + *sequi* to follow]

prosecuting attorney The attorney empowered to act in behalf of the state, county, or national government in prosecuting for penal offenses.

pros·e·cu·tion (pros′ə·kyōō′shən) *n.* **1.** The act or process of prosecuting. **2.** *Law* The instituting and carrying forward of a judicial or criminal proceeding. **3.** The party instituting and conducting it.

pros·e·cu·tor (pros′ə·kyōō′tər) *n.* **1.** One who prosecutes. **2.** *Law* **a** One who institutes and carries on a suit, esp. a criminal suit. **b** A prosecuting attorney.

pros·e·lyte (pros′ə·līt) *n.* One who has been brought over to any opinion, belief, sect, or party, esp. from one religious belief to another. **— v.t. & v.i. ·lyt·ed, ·lyt·ing** To proselytize. [< LL < Gk. *proselytos,* orig., a newcomer] **— pros′e·lyt′ism** (-lə·tiz′əm, -līt′iz·əm) *n.*

pros·e·lyt·ize (pros′ə·lit·īz′) *v.* **·ized, ·iz·ing** *v.i.* **1.** To make proselytes. **— v.t. 2.** To make a convert of. Also *proselyte:* also *Brit.* **·lyt·ise′.**

pros·en·ceph·a·lon (pros′en·sef′ə·lon) *n.* *Anat.* The anterior segment of the three divisions of the brain in embryos, developing into the cerebrum and the optic thalamus, with related structures: also called *forebrain.* [< NL < Gk. *pros* toward + *encephalon* brain] **— pros′en·ce·phal′ic** (-sə·fal′ik) *adj.*

Pros·er·pine (pros′ər·pīn, prō·sûr′pə·nē) In Roman mythology, the daughter of Ceres and wife of Pluto: identified with the Greek *Persephone.* Also **Pro·ser·pi·na** (prō·sûr′pə·nə).

pro·sit (prō′sit, *Ger.* prō′zit) *interj.* To your good health: used as a drinking toast, esp. by the Germans. Also **prost** (prōst). [< L, lit., may it benefit]

pro·slav·er·y (prō·slā′vər·ē, -slāv′rē) *adj.* In U.S. history, advocating Negro slavery.

pro·sod·ic (prō·sod′ik) *adj.* Of or pertaining to prosody. Also **pro·sod′i·cal.**

prosodic symbols In the scansion of verse, those signs used to indicate the various kinds of syllables, stresses, feet, etc.: these include the breve (˘), macron (—), acute (´), caesura (‖), and vertical bar (|).

pros·o·dy (pros′ə·dē) *n.* The science of poetical forms, including quantity and accent of syllables, meter, versification, and metrical composition. [< L < Gk. *prosōidia* a song sung to music] **— pro·so·di·ac** (prō·sō′dē·ak), **pro·so·di·al** (prō·sō′dē·əl) *adj.* **— pros′o·dist** *n.*

pros·pect (pros′pekt) *n.* **1.** A future probability; esp., often in the plural, the chance for future success. **2.** An extended view. **3.** An exposure; outlook. **4.** A prospective buyer. **— v.t. & v.i.** To explore (a region) for gold, oil, etc. [< L < *pro-* forward + *specere* to look]

pro·spec·tive (prə-spek′tiv) *adj.* **1.** Anticipated. **2.** Looking toward the future. — **pro·spec′tive·ly** *adv.*

pros·pec·tor (pros′pek·tər) *n.* One who searches or examines a region for mineral deposits or precious stones.

pro·spec·tus (prə-spek′təs) *n. pl.* **·tus·es 1.** A paper containing information of a proposed undertaking. **2.** A summary; outline. [< L < *pro-* forward + *specere* to look]

pros·per (pros′pər) *v.i.* To be prosperous; thrive; flourish. [< OF < L *prosperus* favorable, prosperous]

pros·per·i·ty (pros·per′ə·tē) *n. pl.* **·ties** The state of being prosperous; material well-being.

pros·per·ous (pros′pər·əs) *adj.* **1.** Successful; flourishing. **2.** Auspicious. **3.** Favorable. [< MF < L *prosperus* favorable] — **pros′per·ous·ly** *adv.* — **pros′per·ous·ness** *n.*

pros·tate (pros′tāt) *Anat. adj.* Of or designating the prostate gland. — *n.* The prostate gland. [< NL < Gk. *prostatēs* stander before < *pro-* before + *histanai* to set]

prostate gland *Anat.* A partly muscular gland at the base of the bladder and surrounding the urethra in male mammals, providing some of the chemicals necessary to maintain the sperm for reproduction. — **pro·stat·ic** (prō-stat′ik) *adj.*

pros·the·sis (pros′thə·sis) *n. pl.* **·ses** (-sēz) **1.** *Surg.* The fitting of artificial parts to the body. **2.** A part so fitted, as an artificial limb, false tooth, etc. [< L < Gk. < *pros-* to + *tithenai* to put] — **pros·thet·ic** (pros·thet′ik) *adj.*

pros·thet·ics (pros·thet′iks) *n.pl.* (*construed as sing.*) The branch of surgery that specializes in artificial parts. — **pros·the·tist** (pros′thə·tist) *n.*

pros·tho·don·tics (pros′thə·don′tiks) *n.* The branch of dentistry concerned with the making of crowns, bridges, dentures, and artificial teeth; dental prosthetics. Also **pros′·tho·don′ti·a.** (-thə·don′shē·ə). [< NL < Gk. *prosthesis* addition + *odous* tooth] — **pros·tho·don·tist** (pros′thə·don′tist) *n.*

pros·ti·tute (pros′tə·tōōt, -tyōōt) *n.* **1.** A woman who offers her body for hire for purposes of sexual intercourse. **2.** One who sells his services for unworthy purposes. — *v.t.* **·tut·ed, ·tut·ing 1.** To apply (talent, etc.) to unworthy purposes. **2.** To offer (oneself or another) for lewd purposes, esp. for hire. [< L < *pro-* forward + *statuere* to place] — **pros′ti·tu′tion** *n.* — **pros′ti·tu′tor** *n.*

pros·trate (pros′trāt) *adj.* **1.** Lying prone, or with the face to the ground. **2.** Brought low in mind or spirit. **3.** Lying at the mercy of another. **4.** *Bot.* Trailing along the ground. — *v.t.* **·trat·ed, ·trat·ing 1.** To bow or cast (oneself) down, as in adoration or pleading. **2.** To throw flat; lay on the ground. **3.** To overcome; make helpless. [< L < *pro-* before + *sternere* to stretch out] — **pros·tra′tion** *n.*

pros·y (prō′zē) *adj.* **pros·i·er, pros·i·est 1.** Like prose; prosaic. **2.** Dull; tedious. — **pros′i·ly** *adv.* — **pros′i·ness** *n.*

prot- Var. of PROTO-.

pro·tac·tin·i·um (prō′tak·tin′ē·əm) *n.* A radioactive metallic element (symbol Pa) of the actinide series, intermediate between thorium and uranium: also called *protoactinium.* See ELEMENT.

pro·tag·o·nist (prō·tag′ə·nist) *n.* **1.** The actor who played the chief part in a Greek drama. **2.** Any leading character, contender, etc. [< Gk. < *prōtos* first + *agōnistēs* actor]

pro·te·an (prō′tē·ən, prō·tē′ən) *adj.* Readily assuming different forms or various aspects; changeable. [< PROTEUS]

pro·te·ase (prō′tē·ās) *n. Biochem.* An enzyme that digests proteins.

pro·tect (prə·tekt′) *v.t.* **1.** To shield or defend from attack, harm, or injury. **2.** *Econ.* To assist (domestic industry) by means of protective tariffs. **3.** In commerce, to provide funds to guarantee payment of (a draft, etc.). [< L < *pro-* before + *tegere* to cover] — **pro·tect′ing·ly** *adv.*

pro·tec·tion (prə·tek′shən) *n.* **1.** The act of protecting, or the state of being protected. **2.** One who or that which protects. **3.** *Econ.* A system aiming to protect the industries of a country by imposing duties. See PROTECTIVE TARIFF. — **pro·tec′tive** *adj.* — **pro·tec′tive·ly** *adv.*

pro·tec·tion·ism (prə·tek′shən·iz′əm) *n.* The economic doctrine or system of protection. — **pro·tec′tion·ist** *n.*

protective tariff A tariff that is intended to insure protection of domestic industries against foreign competition.

pro·tec·tor (prə·tek′tər) *n.* **1.** One who protects; a defender. **2.** In English history, one appointed as a regent of the kingdom during minority or incapacity of the sovereign. Also **pro·tect′er.** — **pro·tec′tress** *n.fem.*

Pro·tec·tor (prə·tek′tər) *n.* The title borne by Oliver Cromwell, 1653–58, and by Richard Cromwell, his son, 1658–59 during the Protectorate: in full, **Lord Protector.**

pro·tec·tor·ate (prə·tek′tər·it) *n.* **1.** A relation of protection and partial control by a strong nation over a weaker power. **2.** A country or region under the protection of another. **3.** The office, or period of office, of a protector of a kingdom. Also **pro·tec′tor·ship.**

Pro·tec·tor·ate (prə·tek′tər·it) *n.* The English government during the rule of the Cromwells, 1653–59.

pro·té·gé (prō′tə·zhā, *Fr.* prô·tā·zhā′) *n.* One specially cared

for by another who is older or more powerful. [< F < L *protegere* to protect] — **pro′té·gée** *n.fem.*

pro·te·in (prō′tē·in, -tēn) *n. Biochem.* Any of a class of highly complex nitrogenous compounds originally synthesized by plants, and forming an essential constituent in the processes of animal metabolism. Also **pro′te·id** (-id). [< G < Gk. *prōtos* first]

pro tem·po·re (prō tem′pə·rē) *Latin* For the time being.

Prot·er·o·zo·ic (prot′ər·ə·zō′ik) *Geol. adj.* Of or designating the geological era following the Archeozoic and succeeded by the Paleozoic. See chart for GEOLOGY. — *n.* The Proterozoic era. [< Gk. *proteros* former + ZOIC]

pro·test (*n.* prō′test; *v.* prə·test′) *n.* **1.** A solemn or formal objection or declaration. **2.** A public expression of dissent. **3.** A formal notarial certificate attesting the fact that a note or bill of exchange has been presented for acceptance or payment and that it has been refused. **4.** The act of protesting. — *adj.* Of or relating to public protest: *protest* demonstrations. — *v.t.* **1.** To assert earnestly or positively. **2.** *U.S.* To make a protest against; object to. **3.** To declare formally that payment of (a promissory note, etc.) has been duly submitted and refused. — *v.i.* **4.** To make solemn affirmation. **5.** To make a protest; object. [< OF < L < *pro-* forth + *testari* to testify] — **pro·test′er** *n.* — **pro·test′ing·ly** *adv.*

prot·es·tant (prot′is·tənt, prə·tes′-) *n.* One who makes a protest. [< MF < L < *protestari*]

Prot·es·tant (prot′is·tənt) *n.* A member of one of those bodies of Christians that adhere to Protestantism, as distinguished from Roman Catholicism. — *adj.* Pertaining to Protestants or Protestantism.

Protestant Episcopal Church A religious body in the United States that is descended from the Church of England: also called *Episcopal Church.*

Prot·es·tant·ism (prot′is·tənt·iz′əm) *n.* **1.** The principles and common system of doctrines of the Protestants. **2.** The ecclesiastical system founded upon this faith; also, Protestants, collectively. **3.** The state of being a Protestant.

prot·es·ta·tion (prot′is·tā′shən) *n.* **1.** The act of protesting; also, that which is protested. **2.** A formal declaration of dissent. **3.** Any solemn or urgent avowal.

Pro·te·us (prō′tē·əs, -tyōōs) In Greek mythology, a sea god who had the power of assuming different forms.

pro·tist (prō′tist) *n. Biol.* Any member of a large division or kingdom of one-celled or noncellular plants and animals, including bacteria, flagellates, rhizopods, and ciliates. [< NL < Gk. *prōtos* first] — **pro·tis′tan** *adj. & n.* — **pro·tis′tic** *adj.*

pro·ti·um (prō′tē·əm) *n. Chem.* The hydrogen isotope of atomic mass 1 (symbol, H^1): sometimes so called in distinction from deuterium and tritium. [< NL < Gk. *prōtos* first]

proto- *combining form* **1.** First in rank or time; chief; typical. **2.** Primitive; original: *prototype.* Also, before vowels, *prot-.* [< Gk. *prōtos* first]

pro·to·ac·tin·i·um (prō′tō·ak·tin′ē·əm) *n.* Protactinium.

pro·to·col (prō′tə·kôl, -kol) *n.* **1.** The rules of diplomatic and state etiquette and ceremony. **2.** The preliminary draft of diplomatic negotiation or of an official document, as a treaty. — *v.i.* **·coled** or **·colled, ·col·ing** or **·col·ling** To write or form protocols. [< OF < Med.L < LGk. *prōtokollon* the first sheet glued to a papyrus roll enumerating the contents < *prōtos* first + *kolla* glue]

pro·ton (prō′ton) *n. Physics* One of the elementary particles in the nucleus of an atom, having a unitary positive charge and a mass of approximately 1.672×10^{-24} gram. [< NL < Gk. *prōtos* first]

pro·to·plasm (prō′tə·plaz′əm) *n. Biol.* The physicochemical basis of living matter, a viscid, grayish, translucent substance of complex composition that forms the essential part of plant and animal cells. [< G < Gk. *prōtos* first + *plasma* form] — **pro′to·plas′mic** *adj.*

pro·to·type (prō′tə·tīp) *n.* **1.** *Biol.* A primitive or ancestral organism; an archetype. **2.** An original model on which subsequent forms are to be based. [< F < NL < Gk. < *prōtos* first + *typos* form] — **pro′to·typ′al** (-tī′pəl), **pro′to·typ′ic** (-tip′ik), **pro′to·typ′i·cal** *adj.*

pro·to·zo·an (prō′tə·zō′ən) *n.* Any of a phylum of microscopic, single-celled organisms, largely aquatic and including many parasites. Also **pro′to·zo′on.** [< NL < Gk. *prōtos* first + *zōion* animal] — **pro′to·zo′al, pro′to·zo′ic** *adj.*

pro·tract (prō·trakt′) *v.t.* **1.** To extend in time; prolong. **2.** In surveying, to draw or map by means of a scale and protractor; plot. **3.** *Anat.* To protrude or extend. [< L < *pro-* forward + *trahere* to draw] — **pro·trac′tion** *n.* — **pro·trac′tive** *adj.*

pro·trac·tile (prō·trak′til) *adj.* Capable of being protracted or protruded.

pro·trac·tor (prō·trak′tər) *n.* **1.** One who protracts. **2.** An instrument for measuring and laying off angles. **3.** *Anat.* A muscle that extends a limb or moves it forward.

pro·trude (prō·trōōd′) *v.t. & v.i.* **·trud·ed, ·trud·ing** To push or thrust out; project outward. [< L < *pro-* forward + *trudere* to thrust] — **pro·tru'sion** (-trōō'zhən) *n.*

pro·tru·sile (prō-trōō'sil) *adj.* Adapted to being thrust out, as the tongue of an anteater. Also **pro·tru'si·ble.**

pro·tru·sive (prō-trōō'siv) *adj.* 1. Tending to protrude; protruding. 2. Pushing or driving forward. — **pro·tru'sive·ly** *adv.* — **pro·tru'sive·ness** *n.*

pro·tu·ber·ance (prō·tōō'bər·əns, -tyōō'-) *n.* 1. Something that protrudes; a knob; prominence. 2. The state of being protuberant. Also **pro·tu'ber·an·cy, pro·tu'ber·a'tion.**

pro·tu·ber·ant (prō·tōō'bər·ənt, -tyōō-) *adj.* Swelling out beyond the surrounding surface; bulging. [< LL < L *pro-* forth + *tuber* a swelling] — **pro·tu'ber·ant·ly** *adv.*

proud (proud) *adj.* 1. Actuated by, possessing, or manifesting pride; arrogant; also, self-respecting. 2. Sensible of honor and personal elation: generally followed by *of* or by a verb in the infinitive. 3. High-mettled, as a horse. 4. Proceeding from or inspired by pride. 5. Being a cause of honorable pride, as a distinction. — **to do oneself proud** To do extremely well. [OE < OF, prob. ult. < L < *pro-* for + *esse* to be] — **proud'ly** *adv.*

proud flesh *Pathol.* A granulated growth resembling flesh in a wound or sore. [So called from its swelling up]

prove (prōōv) *v.* **proved, proved** or **prov·en, prov·ing** *v.t.* 1. To show to be true or genuine, as by evidence or argument. 2. To determine the quality or genuineness of; test: to *prove* a gun. 3. To establish the authenticity or validity of, as a will. 4. *Math.* To verify the accuracy of (a calculation, etc.). — *v.i.* 5. To be shown to be by the result or outcome; turn out to be. [< OF < L < *probus* upright] — **prov'a·ble** *adj.* — **prov'er** *n.*

Pro·ven·çal (prō'vən·säl', *Fr.* prō·vän·sàl') *n.* 1. A native or resident of Provence, France. 2. The Roman language of Provence, used esp. in the 12th and 13th centuries in the lyric literature of the troubadours. — *adj.* Of or pertaining to Provence, its inhabitants, or their language.

prov·en·der (prov'ən·dər) *n.* 1. Food for cattle; esp., dry food, as hay. 2. *Rare* Provisions generally. — *v.t.* To provide with food, as cattle. [< OF < L *praebere* to supply]

prov·erb (prov'ərb) *n.* 1. A pithy saying, esp. one condensing the wisdom of experience; adage; saw; maxim. 2. An enigmatic saying. 3. A typical example; byword. [< OF < L < *pro-* before + *verbum* word]

— **Syn.** 1. A *proverb* is usually a homely illustration of a general truth, as: A rolling stone gathers no moss. An *adage* is a time-honored and generally accepted *proverb*, as: A man is known by the company he keeps. Any ancient and hackneyed *adage* is a *saw*, as: All that glitters is not gold.

pro·ver·bi·al (prə·vûr'bē·əl) *adj.* 1. Pertaining to, or like a proverb. 2. Well-known; notorious. — **pro·ver'bi·al·ly** *adv.*

Prov·erbs (prov'ərbz) *n.pl.* (construed as *sing.*) An Old Testament book of moral sayings.

pro·vide (prə·vīd') *v.* **·vid·ed, ·vid·ing** *v.t.* 1. To supply or furnish. 2. To afford; yield. 3. To prepare, make ready, or procure beforehand. 4. To set down as a condition; stipulate. — *v.i.* 5. To take measures in advance: with *for* or *against*. 6. To furnish means of subsistence: usu. with *for*. 7. To make a stipulation. [< L < *pro-* before + *videre* to see] — **pro·vid'er** *n.*

pro·vid·ed (prə·vī'did) *conj.* On condition; if: He will get the loan *provided* he offers good security.

prov·i·dence (prov'ə·dəns) *n.* 1. The care exercised by God over the universe. 2. An event or circumstance ascribable to divine interposition. 3. The exercise of foresight and care for the future. [< OF < L *providere* to foresee]

Prov·i·dence (prov'ə·dəns) God; the Deity.

prov·i·dent (prov'ə·dənt) *adj.* Anticipating and making ready for future wants. — **prov'i·dent·ly** *adv.*

prov·i·den·tial (prov'ə·den'shəl) *adj.* Resulting from or involving God's providence. — **prov'i·den'tial·ly** *adv.*

pro·vid·ing (prə·vī'ding) *conj.* On condition; provided.

prov·ince (prov'ins) *n.* 1. A country incorporated with a kingdom or empire and subject to central administration. 2. Any large administrative division of a country with a permanent local government. 3. *pl.* Regions lying at a distance from the capital or most populous part of a country. 4. A sphere of knowledge, activity, or endeavor. [< OF < L *provincia* province]

pro·vin·cial (prə·vin'shəl) *adj.* 1. Of or pertaining to a province. 2. Confined to a province; rustic; local. 3. Narrow; uncultured; illiberal. — *n.* 1. A native or inhabitant of a province. 2. One who is provincial. — **pro·vin'ci·al'i·ty** (-shē·al'ə·tē) *n.* — **pro·vin'cial·ly** *adv.*

pro·vin·cial·ism (prə·vin'shəl·iz'əm) *n.* 1. The quality of being provincial. 2. A provincial custom, esp. of speech.

pro·vi·sion (prə·vizh'ən) *n.* 1. The act of providing, or the state of being provided. 2. Measures taken or means made ready in advance. 3. *pl.* Food or a supply of food. 4. Something provided or prepared, as against future need. 5. The part of an agreement, instrument, etc., referring to one specific thing; a stipulation. — *v.t.* To provide with food or provisions. [< OF < L < *pro-* before + *videre* to see] — **pro·vi'sion·er** *n.*

pro·vi·sion·al (prə·vizh'ən·əl) *adj.* Provided for a present service or temporary necessity; adopted tentatively. Also **pro·vi'sion·ar'y.** — **pro·vi'sion·al·ly** *adv.*

pro·vi·so (prə·vī'zō) *n.* *pl.* **·sos** or **·soes** A stipulation or clause, as in a contract or statute, limiting, modifying, or rendering conditional its operation. [< Med.L *proviso* it being provided < L *providere* to foresee]

pro·vi·so·ry (prə·vī'zər·ē) *adj.* 1. Conditional. 2. Provisional. — **pro·vi'so·ri·ly** *adv.*

prov·o·ca·tion (prov'ə·kā'shən) *n.* 1. The act of provoking. 2. An incitement to action; stimulus.

pro·voc·a·tive (prə·vok'ə·tiv) *adj.* Serving to provoke; stimulating. — *n.* That which provokes or tends to provoke. — **pro·voc'a·tive·ly** *adv.* — **pro·voc'a·tive·ness** *n.*

pro·voke (prə·vōk') *v.t.* **·voked, ·vok·ing** 1. To stir to anger or resentment; irritate; vex. 2. To arouse or stimulate to some action. 3. To stir up or bring about: to *provoke* a quarrel. 4. To induce or cause; elicit: to *provoke* a smile. [< OF < L < *pro-* forth + *vocare* to call] — **pro·vok'ing·ly** *adv.* — **pro·vok'ing·ness** *n.*

prov·ost (prov'əst) *n.* 1. A person having charge or authority over others. 2. The chief magistrate of a Scottish city. 3. In some English and American colleges, the head of the faculty. 4. The head of a collegiate chapter or a cathedral; a dean. [< OE and OF, both < LL *propositus*, var. of L *praepositus* chief] — **prov'ost·ship** *n.*

pro·vost marshal (prō'vō) A military or naval officer exercising police functions: also called *provost*.

prow (prou) *n.* 1. The fore part of the hull of a vessel; the bow. 2. Any projection. [< MF < L < Gk. *prōira*]

prow·ess (prou'is) *n.* 1. Strength, skill, and courage, esp. in battle. 2. A daring and valiant deed. [< OF *prouesse*, *proece* < *prou* brave]

prowl (proul) *v.t.* & *v.i.* To roam about stealthily, as in search of prey or plunder. — *n.* The act of prowling. [ME *prollen* to search] — **prowl'er** *n.*

prowl car *U.S.* A police patrol car.

prox·i·mal (prok'sə·məl) *adj.* 1. *Anat.* Relatively nearer the central portion of the body or point of origin. 2. Proximate. — **prox'i·mal·ly** *adv.*

prox·i·mate (prok'sə·mit) *adj.* Being in immediate relation with something else; next: also *proximal.* [< LL < L *proximus*, superl. of *prope* near] — **prox'i·mate·ly** *adv.*

prox·im·i·ty (prok·sim'ə·tē) *n.* The state or fact of being near or next; nearness. [See PROXIMATE.]

proximity fuse A fuse in a projectile, usu. activated by an electronic device, that detonates by simple proximity to the target: also called *VT fuse.*

prox·i·mo (prok'sə·mō) *adv.* In or of the next or coming month. [See PROXIMATE.]

prox·y (prok'sē) *n.* *pl.* **prox·ies** 1. A person empowered by another to act for him. 2. The office or right to so act, or the instrument conferring it. [ME *prokecie*]

prude (prōōd) *n.* A person who makes an affected display of modesty and propriety, esp. in matters relating to sex. [< F *preude* (femme) strong, hence, modest (woman)] — **prud'ish** *adj.* — **prud'ish·ly** *adv.* — **prud'ish·ness** *n.*

pru·dence (prōōd'ns) *n.* The quality or state of being prudent; sagacity; discretion.

pru·dent (prōōd'nt) *adj.* 1. Cautious; worldly-wise. 2. Exercising sound judgment. 3. Not extravagant. 4. Decorously discreet. [< OF < L *prudens, -entis* knowing, foreseeing] — **pru'dent·ly** *adv.*

— **Syn.** 1. discreet, circumspect, wary. 3. thrifty, economical, frugal. — **Ant.** imprudent, indiscreet, rash, reckless.

pru·den·tial (prōō·den'shəl) *adj.* 1. Proceeding from or marked by prudence. 2. Exercising prudence and wisdom. — **pru·den'tial·ly** *adv.*

prud·er·y (prōō'dər·ē) *n.* *pl.* **·er·ies** 1. Extreme priggishness; primness. 2. Prudish action or language.

prune¹ (prōōn) *n.* The dried fruit of the plum. [< OF < LL < L *prunum*]

prune² (prōōn) *v.t.* & *v.i.* **pruned, prun·ing** 1. To trim or cut branches or parts (from) so as to improve growth, appearance, etc. 2. To cut off (branches or parts). [< OF *proöignier, proignier, ? < provaignier* to cut] — **prun'er** *n.*

pru·ri·ent (prōōr'ē·ənt) *adj.* 1. Having lustful cravings or desires. 2. Lewd. [< L *pruriens, -entis,* ppr. of *prurire* to itch] — **pru'ri·ence, pru'ri·en·cy** *n.* — **pru'ri·ent·ly** *adv.*

pru·ri·tus (prōō·rī'təs) *n.* *Pathol.* Intense itching. [< L < *prurire* to itch] — **pru·rit·ic** (-rit'ik) *adj.*

Prus·sian (prush'ən) *adj.* 1. Of or pertaining to Prussia, its inhabitants, or their language. 2. Characteristic of the

Junkers of Prussia; militaristic; overbearing. — *n.* A native or inhabitant of Prussia.

Prussian blue 1. *Chem.* Any one of a group of cyanogen compounds containing chiefly ferric ferrocyanide, formerly much used in dyeing. 2. A deep blue pigment.

prus·sic acid (prus/ik) Hydrocyanic acid.

pry[1] (prī) *v.i.* **pried, pry·ing** To look or peer carefully, curiously, or slyly; snoop. — *n. pl.* **pries** 1. A sly and searching inspection. 2. One who pries; an inquisitive, prying person. [ME *prien*] — **pry/ing·ly** *adv.*

pry[2] (prī) *v.t.* **pried, pry·ing** *Chiefly U.S.* 1. To raise, move, or open by means of a lever; prize. 2. To obtain by effort. — *n.* A lever, as a bar, stick, or beam; also, leverage. [Back formation < *prize* lever]

pry·er (prī/ər) See PRIER.

psalm (säm) *n.* 1. *Often cap.* A sacred song or lyric contained in the Old Testament Book of Psalms. 2. Any sacred song. — *v.t.* To celebrate or praise in psalms. [OE < LL < Gk. *psalmos* song accompanied by a harp]

psalm·ist (sä/mist) *n.* A maker or composer of psalms. — **the Psalmist** King David, as the traditional author of many of the Scriptural psalms.

psalm·o·dy (sä/mə·dē, sal/-) *n. pl.* **·dies** 1. The use of psalms in divine worship. 2. A collection of psalms. [< OF < LL < Gk. < *psalmos* psalm + *aeidein* to sing]

Psalms (sämz) A lyrical book of the Old Testament, containing 150 hymns. Also **Book of Psalms.**

psal·ter (sôl/tər) *n.* The psalms appointed to be read or sung at any given service. [See PSALTERY.] — **psal·te·ri·an** (sôl·tir/ē·ən, sal-) *adj.*

Psal·ter (sôl/tər) *n.* The Book of Psalms, esp. for use in religious services. Also **Psal/ter·y.**

psal·ter·y (sôl/tər·ē) *n. pl.* **·ter·ies** An ancient stringed musical instrument played by plucking with a plectrum. [< OF < L < Gk. < *psallein* to pluck]

pseu·do (sōo/dō) *adj.* Pretended; sham.

pseudo- *combining form* 1. False; pretended: *pseudonym.* 2. Counterfeit; not genuine. 3. Closely resembling: *pseudopodium.* 4. Illusory; apparent. 5. Abnormal; erratic. Also, before vowels, **pseud-.** [< Gk. < *pseudēs* false]

pseu·do·nym (sōo/də·nim) *n.* A fictitious name; pen name. [< F < Gk. < *pseudēs* false + *onoma* name] — **pseu·don·y·mous** (sōo·don/ə·məs) *adj.* — **pseu·don/y·mous·ly** *adv.* — **pseu·don/y·mous·ness, pseu/do·nym/i·ty** *n.*

— **Syn.** *Pseudonym, alias, pen name,* and *nom de plume* denote an assumed name. Pseudonym is the general term, including all the others. An *alias* is a name taken to conceal one's true identity, most often for some wrongful purpose. *Pen name* and *nom de plume* refer to a fictitious name signed to a literary work by its author.

pseu·do·po·di·um (sōo/də·pō/dē·əm) *n. pl.* **·di·a** (-dē-ə) *Zool.* A temporary extension of the protoplasm of a cell or of a protozoan, used for taking in food, locomotion, etc. Also **pseu/do·pod** (-pod), **pseu/do·pode** (-pōd). [< NL]

pshaw (shô) *interj.* An exclamation of annoyance, disapproval, disgust, or impatience. — *v.t. & v.i.* To exclaim *pshaw* at (a person or thing).

psi (sī, psī, psē) *n.* The twenty-third letter in the Greek alphabet (Ψ, ψ): equivalent to English *ps.* See ALPHABET.

psit·ta·co·sis (sit/ə·kō/sis) *n.* An acute, infectious virus disease of parrots and related birds, transmissible to man and resembling influenza: also called *parrot fever.* [< NL < Gk. *psittakos* parrot + -OSIS]

pso·ri·a·sis (sə·rī/ə·sis) *n. Pathol.* A noncontagious, inflammatory skin disease, chronic or acute, characterized by reddish patches and white scales. [< NL < Gk. *psōra* an itch] — **pso·ri·at·ic** (sôr/ē·at/ik, sō/rē-) *adj.*

psych- Var. of PSYCHO-.

psy·che (sī/kē) *n.* 1. The human soul. 2. *Psychoanal.* The mind, often regarded as an entity functioning apart from or independently of the body. [< Gk. *psyche* soul]

Psy·che (sī/kē) In Greek and Roman mythology, a maiden who is united with Eros and is a personification of the soul.

psy·che·del·ic (sī/kə·del/ik) *adj.* Causing or having to do with an abnormal stimulation of consciousness or perception. [< Gk. *psyche* soul + *del(os)* manifest + -IC]

psy·chi·a·trist (sī·kī/ə·trist, si-) *n.* A physician specializing in the practice of psychiatry.

psy·chi·a·try (sī·kī/ə·trē, si-) *n.* The branch of medicine that deals with the diagnosis and treatment of mental disorders. — **psy·chi·at·ric** (sī/kē·at/rik) or **·ri·cal** *adj.*

psy·chic (sī/kik) *adj.* 1. Pertaining to the mind. 2. Pertaining to mental phenomena that appear to be independent of normal sensory stimuli, as clairvoyance, telepathy, and extrasensory perception. 3. Caused by, proceeding from, or attributed to a nonmaterial or occult agency. 4. Sensitive to mental or occult phenomena. Also **psy/chi·cal.** — *n.* One sensitive to extrasensory phenomena. [See PSYCHE.] — **psy/chi·cal·ly** *adv.*

psycho- *combining form* Mind; soul; spirit: *psychosomatic.* Also, before vowels, **psych-.** [< Gk. *psychē.* See PSYCHE.]

psy·cho·a·nal·y·sis (sī/kō·ə·nal/ə·sis) *n.* A system of psy-

chotherapy that seeks to alleviate neuroses and other mental disorders by the analysis of unconscious factors as revealed in dreams, free association, lapses of memory, etc. — **psy/·cho·an/a·lyt/ic** (-an/ə·lit/ik) or **·i·cal** *adj.* — **psy/cho·an/·a·lyt/i·cal·ly** *adv.*

psy·cho·an·a·lyst (sī/kō·an/ə·list) *n.* One who practices psychoanalysis.

psy·cho·an·a·lyze (sī/kō·an/ə·līz) *v.t.* **·lyzed, ·lyz·ing** To treat by psychoanalysis. Also *Brit.* **psy/cho·an/a·lyse.**

psy·cho·chem·i·cal (sī/kō·kem/i·kəl) *n. Chem.* A drug or compound that affects consciousness and behavior. — *adj.* Consisting or of the nature of a psychochemical.

psy·cho·gen·ic (sī/kō·jen/ik) *adj.* Having mental origin, or being affected by mental conflicts and states.

psy·cho·log·i·cal (sī/kə·loj/i·kəl) *adj.* 1. Of or pertaining to psychology. 2. Of or in the mind. Also **psy/cho·log/ic.** — **psy/cho·log/i·cal·ly** *adv.*

psy·chol·o·gist (sī·kol/ə·jist) *n.* A student of or a specialist in psychology.

psy·chol·o·gize (sī·kol/ə·jīz) *v.i.* **·gized, ·giz·ing** 1. To study psychology. 2. To theorize on psychology.

psy·chol·o·gy (sī·kol/ə·jē) *n. pl.* **·gies** 1. The science of the human mind in any of its aspects, operations, powers, or functions. 2. The systematic investigation of mental phenomena, especially those associated with consciousness, behavior, and the problems of adjustment to the environment. 3. The behavior patterns regarded as characteristic of an individual, type, group, etc. 4. A work on psychology.

psy·cho·mo·tor (sī/kō·mō/tər) *adj. Physiol.* Of or pertaining to muscular movements resulting from mental processes.

psy·cho·neu·ro·sis (sī/kō·nŏŏ·rō/sis, -nyŏō-) *n. pl.* **·ses** (-sēz) *Psychiatry* Neurosis. — **psy/cho·neu·rot/ic** (-rot/ik) *adj. & n.*

psy·cho·path (sī/kō·path) *n.* One who is mentally unstable, esp. in a criminal or antisocial manner.

psy·cho·path·ic (sī/kō·path/ik) *adj.* Of or characterized by psychopathy.

psy·cho·pa·thol·o·gy (sī/kō·pə·thol/ə·jē) *n.* The pathology of the mind. — **psy/cho·path/o·log/i·cal** (-path/ə·loj/i·kəl) *adj.* — **psy/cho·pa·thol/o·gist** *n.*

psy·chop·a·thy (sī·kop/ə·thē) *n.* Mental disorder.

psy·cho·phar·ma·col·o·gy (sī/kō·fär/mə·kol/ə·jē) *n.* The branch of pharmacology dealing with drugs that affect the mind. — **psy/cho·phar/ma·co·log/ic** (-kə·loj/ik) *adj.*

psy·cho·sis (sī·kō/sis) *n. pl.* **·ses** (-sēz) *Psychiatry* A severe mental disorder, often involving disorganization of the total personality, with or without organic disease. [< NL < Gk. *psychōsis* giving of life < *psychoein* to animate]

psy·cho·so·mat·ic (sī/kō·sō·mat/ik) *adj.* 1. Of or pertaining to the effect of emotional states upon the body, with special reference to certain disorders. 2. Designating a branch of medicine that treats such disorders with a psychological approach.

psy·cho·ther·a·py (sī/kō·ther/ə·pē) *n. pl.* **·pies** The treatment of nervous and mental disorders, by psychological methods, as hypnosis, re-education, psychoanalysis, etc. Also **psy/cho·ther/a·peu/tics** (-ther/ə·pyōō/tiks). — **psy/·cho·ther/a·peu/tic** *adj.* — **psy/cho·ther/a·pist** *n.*

psy·chot·ic (sī·kot/ik) *n.* One suffering from a psychosis. — *adj.* Of or characterized by a psychosis.

psy·chot·o·mi·met·ic (sī·kot/ō·mi·met/ik, -mī·met/ik) *adj.* Designating a group of drugs capable of inducing altered states of consciousness and having possible therapeutic value.

psychro- *combining form* Cold. [< Gk. *psychros* cold]

ptar·mi·gan (tär/mə·gən) *n. pl.* **·gans** or **·gan** A grouse of the northern hemisphere, having a white winter plumage, and feathered toes. [< Scottish Gaelic *tarmachan*]

PT boat A patrol torpedo boat.

ptero- *combining form* Wing; feather; winglike. Also, before vowels, **pter-.** [< Gk. *pteron* wing]

pter·o·dac·tyl (ter/ə·dak/til) *n. Paleontol.* Any of a genus of extinct flying reptiles of the Jurassic period. [< NL < Gk. *pteron* wing + *daktylos* finger]

-pterous *combining form* Having (a specified number or kind of) wings: *dipterous.* [< Gk. *pteron* wing]

Ptol·e·ma·ic (tol/ə·mā/ik) *adj.* Of or pertaining to Ptolemy, the astronomer, or to the dynasty of Egyptian kings that began with Ptolemy I. [< Gk. *Ptolemaïkos*]

Ptolemaic system The ancient astronomical system of Ptolemy. It assumed that the earth was the central body around which the sun, planets, and celestial bodies revolved.

Ptol·e·ma·ist (tol/ə·mā/ist) *n.* A believer in or adherent of the Ptolemaic system.

pto·maine (tō/mān, tō·mān/) *n. Biochem.* Any of a class of basic nitrogenous compounds, some of which are poisonous, derived from decomposing animal or vegetable protein. Also **pto/main.** [< Ital. < Gk. *ptōma* corpse]

ptomaine poisoning An erroneous term for food poisoning.

pty·a·lin (tī/ə·lin) *n. Biochem.* An enzyme, contained in saliva, that converts starch into dextrin and maltose. [< Gk. *ptyalon* saliva < *ptuein* to spit + -IN]

pub (pub) *n. Brit. Informal* A public house; inn; tavern.
pu·ber·ty (pyōō'bər·tē) *n. pl.* **·ties** The period during which an individual becomes physiologically capable of reproduction. [< L < *pubes, puberis* an adult]
pu·bes (pyōō'bēz) *n.* **1.** *Anat.* The part of the lower abdomen covered with hair in the adult; the pubic region. **2.** The hair that appears on the body at puberty; esp., the hair on the pubic region. [< L, pubic hair]
pu·bes·cent (pyōō·bes'ənt) *adj.* **1.** Arriving or having arrived at puberty. **2.** Having a growth of soft, fine hairs, as certain plants. [< MF < L *pubescens, -entis*, ppr. of *pubescere* to grow hair, attain puberty] —**pu·bes'cence** *n.*
pu·bic (pyōō'bik) *adj.* Of or pertaining to the region in the lower part of the abdomen: the *pubic* bones.
pu·bis (pyōō'bis) *n. pl.* **·bes** (-bēz) *Anat.* Either of the two bones that join with a third to form an arch on either ventral side of the pelvis. [See PUBES.]
pub·lic (pub'lik) *adj.* **1.** Of, pertaining to, or affecting the people at large or the community. **2.** Maintained by or for the public: *public* parks. **3.** Participated in by the people: a *public* demonstration. **4.** For the use of the public: especially, for hire: a *public* cab, hall, etc. **5.** Well-known; open; notorious: a *public* scandal. **6.** Acting before or for the community: a *public* official. —*n.* **1.** Those who may be grouped together for any given purpose. **2.** An audience; esp., the admirers of an actor or other celebrity. —**the public** The people of a locality or nation. [< MF < L *publicus*] —**pub'lic·ly** *adv.* —**pub'lic·ness** *n.*
pub·lic-ad·dress system (pub'lik-ə-dres') An apparatus for the amplification of speech, music, etc., in public places.
pub·li·can (pub'lə·kən) *n.* **1.** In England, the keeper of a public house. **2.** In ancient Rome, a tax collector. [< OF < L < *publicum* public revenue, orig. neut. of *publicus*]
pub·li·ca·tion (pub'lə·kā'shən) *n.* **1.** The act of publishing or offering to public notice. **2.** Any printed work placed on sale or otherwise distributed or offered for distribution. **3.** Notification to people at large orally or by writing or print; promulgation; proclamation. [See PUBLISH.]
public domain Lands owned by a state or national government; public lands. —**in the public domain** Available for unrestricted use: said of material on which copyright or patent right has expired.
public enemy **1.** A person, esp. a criminal, regarded as a menace to the public. **2.** An enemy state.
public house **1.** An inn, tavern, or hotel. **2.** In England, a place licensed to sell intoxicating liquors; a saloon.
pub·li·cist (pub'lə·sist) *n.* **1.** A writer on international law or on topics of public interest. **2.** A public-relations man or publicity agent.
pub·lic·i·ty (pub·lis'ə·tē) *n.* **1.** Information or personal news intended to promote the interests of individuals, institutions, etc. **2.** The state of being public, or the act of making or becoming public; exposure; notoriety. **3.** The attention or interest of the public gained by any method.
pub·li·cize (pub'lə·sīz) *v.t.* **·cized, ·ciz·ing** To advertise.
public library **1.** A library maintained for the use of the public. **2.** The building in which it is contained.
public opinion The prevailing ideas, beliefs, and aims of the people, collectively.
public relations The activities and techniques used by organizations and individuals to establish favorable attitudes and responses in their behalf on the part of the general public or of special groups; also, the occupation of establishing such attitude and responses.
public school **1.** *U.S.* A school maintained by public funds for the free education of the children of the community, usu. covering elementary and secondary grades. **2.** *Brit.* A private or endowed school not run for profit, esp. one preparing students for the universities, as Eton, Harrow, etc.
public servant A government official.
public utility A business organization or industry that supplies water, electricity, gas, etc., to the public, and is subject to particular governmental regulations.
public works Architectural or engineering works or improvements built with public money, as parks, roads, etc.
pub·lish (pub'lish) *v.t.* **1.** To print and issue (a book, magazine, map, etc.) to the public. **2.** To make known or announce publicly; promulgate; proclaim. [See PUBLIC.] —**pub·lish·a·ble** *adj.*
pub·lish·er (pub'lish·ər) *n.* One who publishes; esp., one whose business is publishing books, etc.
puce (pyōōs) *adj.* Of a dark brown or purplish brown. [< F, flea color, flea < L *pulex, -icis* flea]
puck[1] (puk) *n.* An evil sprite or hobgoblin. [OE *pūca*]
puck[2] (puk) *n.* The black, hard, rubber disk used in playing ice hockey. [? < dial. E, to strike]
Puck (puk) A mischievous elf or goblin in Shakespeare's *A Midsummer Night's Dream.* [< PUCK[1]]

puck·a (puk'ə) See PUKKA.
puck·er (puk'ər) *v.t. & v.i.* To gather or draw up into small folds or wrinkles. —*n.* A wrinkle or group of wrinkles. [Appar. freq. of POKE[2]] —**puck'er·y** *adj.*
puck·ish (puk'ish) *adj.* Mischievous; impish.
pud·ding (pŏŏd'ing) *n.* **1.** A sweetened and flavored dessert of soft food, usu. made of milk, flavoring, a thickening agent, etc. **2.** A sausage of seasoned minced meat, blood, or the like, usu. boiled or broiled. [ME *poding*, orig., sausage, black pudding]
pud·dle (pud'l) *n.* **1.** A small pool of water, esp. dirty water. **2.** A small pool of any liquid. —*v.t.* **·dled, ·dling** **1.** *Metall.* To convert (molten pig iron) into wrought iron by melting and stirring in the presence of oxidizing substances. **2.** To mix (clay, etc.) with water so as to obtain a watertight paste. **3.** To make muddy; stir up. [ME *podel*, dim. of OE *pudd* ditch] —**pud'dly** *adj.*
pud·dle·ball (pud'l·bôl') *n. Metall.* A ball of iron reduced to a pasty condition in the puddling furnace and ready for hammering or rolling.
pud·dler (pud'lər) *n.* **1.** One who puddles. **2.** A device for stirring fused metal.
pud·dling (pud'ling) *n. Metall.* The operation or business of making wrought iron from pig iron in a puddling furnace.
puddling furnace A reverberatory furnace for puddling pig iron: also called **hearth.**
pudg·y (puj'ē) *adj.* **pudg·i·er, pudg·i·est** Short and fat; dumpy; chubby: also *podgy.* [< Scot.]
pueb·lo (pweb'lō *for def.* 1; pwā'blō *for def.* 2) *n. pl.* **·los** **1.** A communal adobe or stone building or group of buildings of the Indians of the SW U.S. **2.** A town or village of Indians or Spanish Americans, as in Mexico. [< Sp., village]
Pueb·lo (pweb'lō) *n.* A member of one of the Indian tribes of Mexico and the SW U.S., as a Zuni, Hopi, etc.
pu·er·ile (pyōō'ər·il, pyōō'rəl, -ril, pwer'əl, -īl) *adj.* **1.** Pertaining to or characteristic of childhood; juvenile. **2.** Immature; weak; silly: a *puerile* suggestion. [< L < *puer* boy, child] —**pu'er·ile·ly** *adv.* —**pu'er·ile·ness** *n.*
pu·er·il·i·ty (pyōō'ə·ril'ə·tē, pyōō·ril'-, pwer·il'-) *n. pl.* **·ties** **1.** Puerile state. **2.** A childish act or expression.
pu·er·per·al (pyōō·ûr'pər·əl) *adj. Med.* Of or connected with childbirth. [< L < *puer* child + *parere* to bear]
puff (puf) *n.* **1.** A breath emitted suddenly and with force; also, a sudden emission, as of air, smoke, or steam. **2.** A light, air-filled piece of pastry. **3.** A light ball, tuft, wad, or pad for dusting powder on the hair or skin. **4.** A loose roll of hair in a coiffure, or a light cushion over which it is rolled. **5.** A quilted bed coverlet; a comforter. **6.** In dressmaking, a part of a fabric so gathered as to produce a loose, fluffy distention. **7.** Excessive praise, as in a newspaper or advertisement. **8.** A puffball. —*v.i.* **1.** To blow in puffs, as the wind. **2.** To breathe hard, as after violent exertion. **3.** To emit smoke, steam, etc., in puffs. **4.** To smoke a cigar, etc., with puffs. **5.** To move, act, or exert oneself while emitting puffs: with *away, up*, etc. **6.** To swell, as with air or pride; dilate: often with *up* or *out.* —*v.t.* **7.** To send forth or emit with short puffs or breaths. **8.** To move, impel, or stir up with or in puffs. **9.** To smoke, as a pipe or cigar, with puffs. **10.** To swell or distend. **11.** To praise excessively. **12.** To arrange (hair, etc.) in a puff. [ME *puf*]
puff adder A large, sluggish, venomous African viper with a habit of violently puffing out its breath.
puff·ball (puf'bôl') *n.* Any of various globular fungi that puff out dustlike spores when broken open.
puff·er (puf'ər) *n.* One who or that which puffs.
puf·fin (puf'in) *n.* A sea bird allied to the auk and having a deep, compressed, highly colored bill. [ME *poffin*]
puff·y (puf'ē) *adj.* **puff·i·er, puff·i·est** **1.** Swollen with or as with air, etc. **2.** Inflated in manner; bombastic. **3.** Blowing in puffs. —**puff'i·ly** *adv.* —**puff'i·ness** *n.*
pug[1] (pug) *n.* Clay worked with water, for molding pottery or bricks. —*v.t.* **pugged, pug·ging** **1.** To knead or work (clay) with water, as in brickmaking. **2.** To fill in with clay, etc. [Orig. unknown]
pug[2] (pug) *n.* **1.** A breed of dog characterized by a short square body, upturned nose, curled tail, and short smooth coat. **2.** A pug nose. [Prob. alter. of PUCK]
pug[3] (pug) *n. Anglo-Indian* An animal's footprint; trail. [< Hind. *pag* foot]
pug[4] (pug) *n. Slang* A professional pugilist. [Short for PUGILIST]
pugh (pyōō, pōō) *interj.* An exclamation of disgust.
pu·gi·lism (pyōō'jə·liz'əm) *n.* The art or practice of boxing or fighting with the fists. [< L *pugil* boxer] —**pu'gi·list** *n.* —**pu'gi·lis'tic** *adj.*
pug·na·cious (pug·nā'shəs) *adj.* Disposed or inclined to fight; quarrelsome. [< L *pugnare* to fight] —**pug·na'·cious·ly** *adv.*

pug·nac·i·ty (pug·nas′ə·tē) *n.* *pl.* **·ties** The quality of being pugnacious; quarrelsome disposition; combativeness. Also **pug·na′cious·ness** (-nā′shəs·nis).

pug nose A short nose tilted upward at the end. [< PUG²] **— pug-nosed** (pug′nōzd′) *adj.*

puis·ne (pyōō′nē) *adj.* *Law* Junior as to rank; younger. [< OF < *puis* afterwards + *né* born]

pu·is·sant (pyōō′ə·sənt, pyōō·is′ənt, pwis′ənt) *adj.* Powerful; mighty. [< OF < L *posse* to be able] **— pu′is·sance** *n.* **— pu′is·sant·ly** *adv.*

puke (pyōōk) *v.t.* & *v.i.* **puked, puk·ing** To vomit or cause to vomit. **— n.** Vomit. [Origin unknown]

puk·ka (puk′ə) *adj.* *Anglo-Indian* 1. Made of good materials; substantial. 2. Genuine; superior. Also spelled *pucka*. [< Hind. *pakkā* substantial, cooked, ripe]

pul·chri·tude (pul′krə·tōōd, -tyōōd) *n.* Beauty; grace; physical charm. [< L *pulchritudo, -inis* < *pulcher* beautiful]

pul·chri·tu·di·nous (pul′krə·tōō′də·nəs, -tyōō′-) *adj.* Beautiful; lovely; esp., having physical beauty.

pule (pyōōl) *v.i.* **puled, pul·ing** To cry plaintively, as a child; whimper; whine. [Prob. imit.] **— pul′er** *n.*

Pul·itz·er Prize (pyōō′lit·sər, pōōl′it-) One of several annual awards for outstanding work in American journalism, letters, music, and art, established by Joseph Pulitzer, 1847–1911, U.S. journalist.

pull (pōōl) *v.t.* 1. To apply force so as to cause motion toward or in the direction of the source of force; drag; tug. 2. To draw or remove from a natural or fixed place. 3. To give a pull or tug to. 4. To pluck, as a fowl. 5. To rip; tear; rend. 6. To strain so as to cause injury. 7. In golf, etc., to strike (the ball) so that it curves obliquely from the direction in which the striker faces. 8. In baseball, to hit (the ball) to the field that the batter faces on completing his swing. 9. *Slang* To put into effect; carry out: often with *off*. 10. *Slang* To make a raid on; arrest. 11. *Slang* To draw out so as to use. 12. *Printing* To make or obtain by impression from type: to *pull* a proof. 13. In boxing, to deliver (a punch, etc.) with less than one's full strength. 14. In rowing: **a** To operate (an oar) by drawing toward one. **b** To propel or transport by rowing. **c** To be propelled by: The gig *pulls* four oars. **— v.i.** 15. To use force in hauling, dragging, moving, etc. 16. To move: with *out, in, away, ahead*, etc. 17. To drink or inhale deeply. 18. To propel a boat with oars; row. **— to pull for** 1. To strive in behalf of. 2. *Informal* To declare one's allegiance to. **— to pull oneself together** To regain one's composure. **— to pull out** To withdraw, as from established position. **— to pull through** To manage to succeed, recover, etc. **— to pull up** To come to a halt. **— to pull up with** To advance to a position even with. **— n.** 1. The act of pulling. 2. Something that is pulled, as the handle of a drawer. 3. An impression made by pulling the lever of a hand press. 4. A long swallow, or a deep puff. 5. Any steady, continuous effort. 6. *Slang* A means of influencing those in power; influence. 7. Attraction; appeal. 8. The amount of resistance met in drawing a bowstring, pulling a trigger or the like, usu. measured in pounds. [OE *pullian* to pluck] **— pull′er** *n.*

pull·back (pōōl′bak′) *n.* 1. A restraint or drawback. 2. A device for drawing or holding something back, as part of a dress, or a window.

pul·let (pōōl′it) *n.* A young hen, or one not fully grown. [< OF *polete, poulet,* dim. of *poule* hen]

pul·ley (pōōl′ē) *n.* *pl.* **·leys** 1. A wheel grooved to receive a rope, and usu. mounted in a block, used to increase the mechanical advantage of an applied force. 2. A block with its pulleys or tackle. 3. A wheel driving, carrying, or being driven by a belt. [< OF < Med.L *poleia,* prob. ult. < Gk. *polos* pivot, axis]

Pull·man (pōōl′mən) *n.* A sleeping car or chair car on a passenger train: a trade name. Also **Pullman car.** [after George M. *Pullman,* 1831–97, U.S. inventor]

pull·out (pōōl′out′) *n.* 1. A withdrawal, as of troops. 2. *Aeron.* The maneuver of an airplane in passing from a dive to horizontal flight.

pull·o·ver (pōōl′ō′vər) *adj.* Put on by being drawn over the head. **— n.** A garment so put on, as a sweater or shirt.

pulmo- *combining form Lung.* [< *pulmo, -onis* lung]

pul·mo·nar·y (pul′mə·ner′ē) *adj.* 1. Of, pertaining to, or affecting the lungs: also *pneumonic.* 2. Having lunglike organs. [< L *pulmo, -onis* lung]

pulmonary artery *Anat.* An artery that conveys venous blood from the right ventricle of the heart to the lungs.

pulmonary tuberculosis Tuberculosis.

pul·mon·ic (pul·mon′ik) *adj.* Pulmonary.

Pul·mo·tor (pul′mō′tər, pōōl′-) *n.* An apparatus for producing artificial respiration by forcing oxygen into the lungs: a trade name. Also **pul′mo′tor.** [< PUL(MO)- + MOTOR]

pulp (pulp) *n.* 1. A moist, soft, slightly cohering mass of matter, as the succulent part of fruit. 2. A mixture of wood fibers or rags reduced to a pulpy consistency and forming the substance of paper. 3. *Often pl.* A magazine printed on rough, unglazed paper, and usu. having contents of a cheap, sensational nature: distinguished from *slick.* 4. *Dent.* The soft tissue of vessels and nerves that fills the central cavity of a tooth. **— v.t.** 1. To reduce to pulp. 2. To remove the pulp or envelope from. **— v.i.** 3. To be or become of a pulpy consistency. [< MF < L *pulpa* flesh, pulp of fruit, pith]

pul·pit (pōōl′pit) *n.* 1. An elevated stand or desk for a preacher in a church. 2. The office or work of preaching. 3. The clergy as a class. [< L *pulpitum* scaffold, stage]

pulp·wood (pulp′wōōd′) *n.* The soft wood of certain trees, as the spruce, used in the manufacture of paper.

pulp·y (pul′pē) *adj.* **pulp·i·er, pulp·i·est** 1. Consisting of or resembling pulp. 2. Of a soft, juicy consistency. Also **pul′pous** (-pəs). **— pulp·i′ly** *adv.* **— pulp′i·ness** *n.*

pul·que (pul′kē, pōōl′-; *Sp.* pōōl′kā) *n.* A fermented drink made from various species of agave, esp. from the juice of the maguey. [< Am. Sp.]

pul·sate (pul′sāt) *v.i.* **·sat·ed, ·sat·ing** 1. To move or throb with rhythmical impulses, as the pulse or heart. 2. To vibrate; quiver. [< L *pellere* (pp. *pulsus*) to beat] **— pul·sa′tion** *n.* **— pul′sa·tive** (-sə-tiv) *adj.* **— pul·sa′tor** *n.* **— pul·sa·to·ry** (pul′sə·tôr′e) *adj.*

pulse¹ (puls) *n.* 1. *Physiol.* The rhythmical beating of the arteries resulting from the successive contractions of the heart. 2. Any throbbing or pulsation. 3. *Telecom.* A brief surge of electrical or electromagnetic energy, usu. transmitted as a signal in communication. 4. An indication of general opinion or sentiment. **— v.i.** **pulsed, puls·ing** To pulsate; throb. [< OF < L *pulsus* (*venarum*) the beating (of the veins)] **— pulse′less** *adj.*

pulse² (puls) *n.* Leguminous plants collectively, as peas, beans, etc.; also, their edible seeds. [< OF < L *puls* pottage of meal or pulse]

pulse·jet (puls′jet′) *n.* *Aeron.* A jet engine having movable vanes that intermittently take in air to develop power in rapid bursts. Also **pul′so·jet′** (-sō·jet′).

pul·som·e·ter (pul·som′ə·tər) *n.* A device for pumping liquids by steam pressure, consisting of two pear-shaped chambers connected by valves: also called *vacuum pump.*

pul·ver·ize (pul′və·rīz) *v.* **·ized, ·iz·ing** *v.t.* 1. To reduce to powder or dust, as by crushing. 2. To demolish; annihilate. **— v.i.** 3. To become reduced to powder or dust. Also *Brit.* **pul′ver·ise.** [< MF < LL < L *pulvis, pulveris* powder, dust] **— pul′ver·iz′a·ble** *adj.* **— pul′ver·i·za′tion** *n.* **— pul′ver·iz′er** *n.*

pu·ma (pyōō′mə) *n.* A reddish carnivore of the cat family, ranging from Canada to Patagonia: also called *cougar, mountain cat, mountain lion.* [< Sp. < Peruvian]

pum·ice (pum′is) *n.* Spongy volcanic lava, used as an abrasive and polishing material, esp. when powdered. Also **pumice stone.** **— v.t.** **·iced, ·ic·ing** To smooth, polish, or clean with pumice. [< OF < L *pumex, pumicis*] **— pu·mi·ceous** (pyōō·mish′əs) *adj.*

pum·mel (pum′əl) *v.t.* **·meled** or **·melled, ·mel·ing** or **·mel·ling** To pommel. **— n.** A pommel.

pump¹ (pump) *n.* A mechanical device for raising, circulating, exhausting, or compressing a liquid or gas by drawing or pressing it through openings and pipes. **— v.t.** 1. To raise with a pump, as water or other liquid. 2. To remove the water, etc., from. 3. To inflate with air by means of a pump. 4. To propel, discharge, force, etc., from or as if from a pump. 5. To obtain information from persistently or subtly: to *pump* a witness. 6. To obtain (information) in such a manner. **— v.i.** 7. To work a pump; raise water or other liquid with a pump. 8. To move up and down like a pump handle. [Prob. < MDu. *pompe*] **— pump′er** *n.*

pump² (pump) *n.* A low-cut shoe without a fastening, having either a high or a low heel. [Origin uncertain]

pum·per·nick·el (pum′pər·nik′əl) *n.* A coarse, dark, sour bread made from unsifted rye. [< G]

pump·kin (pump′kin, pung′-) *n.* 1. A large, round, edible, yellow-orange fruit borne by a coarse trailing vine with heart-shaped leaves. 2. The vine. 3. Any of several related European plants. [< MF < L < Gk. *pepon* melon]

pun (pun) *n.* The humorous use of two words having the same or similar sounds but different meanings, or of two different, more or less incongruous meanings of the same word. **— v.i.** **punned, pun·ning** To make a pun. [Origin uncertain] **— pun′ning·ly** *adv.*

punch¹ (punch) *n.* 1. A tool for perforating or indenting, or for driving out or in an object inserted in a hole, as a bolt or pin. 2. A machine for impressing a design or stamping a die. **— v.t.** To perforate, shape, indent, etc., with a punch. [Prob. short for PUNCHEON¹]

punch² (punch) *v.t.* 1. To strike sharply, esp. with the fist. 2. To poke with a stick; prod. 3. To operate; work; use: to *punch* a time clock. 4. *U.S.* In the West, to drive (cattle). **— n.** 1. A swift blow with the fist; also, a thrust or nudge. 2. *Slang* Vitality; force: an editorial with *punch.* [Prob. var. of POUNCE²] **— punch′er** *n.*

punch³ (punch) *n.* A beverage having wine or spirits, milk, tea, or fruit juices as a basic ingredient, sweetened, sometimes spiced, and diluted with water. [? < Hind. < Skt. *pañchan* five; from the five original ingredients]

Punch (punch) The quarrelsome, grotesque hero of a comic puppet show, **Punch and Judy**, who habitually fights with his wife, Judy. **— pleased as Punch** Extremely pleased; highly gratified. [Short for PUNCHINELLO]

punch card In data processing, a card marked by an arrangement of positions to record information indicated by the presence or absence of punched holes. Also **punched card.**

punch-drunk (punch′drungk′) *adj.* **1.** Groggy, slow in movement, speech, etc., from repeated blows to the head: said of prize fighters. **2.** Confused; dazed.

pun·cheon[1] (pun′chən) *n.* **1.** An upright supporting timber. **2.** A punch or perforating tool. **3.** A broad, heavy piece of roughly dressed timber. [< OF *poncon, poinchon* a punch]

pun·cheon[2] (pun′chən) *n.* **1.** A liquor cask of variable capacity, from 72 to 120 gallons. **2.** A liquor measure of varying amount. [< OF *ponçon, poinchon*]

Pun·chi·nel·lo (pun′chə·nel′ō) *n.* *pl.* **·los** or **·loes** A comic character; buffoon, esp. in an Italian puppet show. Also **pun′chi·nel′lo.** [< dial. Ital. (Neapolitan) *Polcenella*]

punch·ing bag (pun′ching) An inflated or stuffed ball, usu. suspended, that is punched with the fists for exercise.

punch press A machine equipped to cut or form metal.

punc·til·i·o (pungk·til′ē·ō) *n.* *pl.* **·til·i·os 1.** A fine point of etiquette. **2.** Preciseness in the observance of etiquette or ceremony. [< Sp. < Ital. < L *punctum* point]

punc·til·i·ous (pungk·til′ē·əs) *adj.* **1.** Very careful in the observance of forms of etiquette, etc. **2.** Very precise. **— punc·til′i·ous·ly** *adv.* **— punc·til′i·ous·ness** *n.*

punc·tu·al (pungk′chōō·əl) *adj.* **1.** Acting or arriving promptly. **2.** Done or made precisely at an appointed time. **3.** Punctilious; exact. [< Med.L < L *punctus* pricking, point] **— punc′tu·al·ly** *adv.*

punc·tu·al·i·ty (pungk′chōō·al′ə·tē) *n.* *pl.* **·ties** The quality, characteristic, act, or habit of being punctual.

punc·tu·ate (pungk′chōō·āt) *v.* **·at·ed, ·at·ing** *v.t.* **1.** To divide or mark with punctuation. **2.** To interrupt at intervals. **3.** To emphasize; stress. **—** *v.i.* **4.** To use punctuation. [< Med.L < L *punctus* point] **— punc′tu·a′tor** *n.*

punc·tu·a·tion (pungk′chōō·ā′shən) *n.* The use of points or marks in written or printed matter to indicate the separation of the words into sentences, clauses, and phrases, and to aid in the better comprehension of the meaning; also, the marks so used (**punctuation marks**). **— punc′tu·a′tive** *adj.* The chief punctuation marks are:

period	.	parentheses	( )
colon	:	brackets	[ ]
semicolon	;	dash (em-dash)	—
comma	,	(en-dash)	–
question mark	?	hyphen	-
(interrogation point)		quotation marks	" "
exclamation mark	!	virgule (virgil)	/

punc·ture (pungk′chər) *v.* **·tured, ·tur·ing** *v.t.* **1.** To pierce with a sharp point. **2.** To make by pricking, as a hole. **3.** To cause to collapse: to *puncture* a tire. **—** *v.i.* **4.** To be pierced or punctured. **—** *n.* **1.** A small hole made by piercing with a sharp point. **2.** A minute depression; pit. **3.** The act of puncturing. [< L < *pungere* to prick]

pun·dit (pun′dit) *n.* **1.** In India, one versed in Sanskrit lore and in the science, laws, and religion of the Hindus. **2.** Any learned man. [< Hind. < Skt. *pandita*]

pun·gent (pun′jənt) *adj.* **1.** Sharp or acrid to taste or smell; keen; penetrating: a *pungent* odor. **2.** Affecting the mind or feelings so as to cause pain; poignant. **3.** Caustic; biting: *pungent* sarcasm. [< L < *pungere* to prick] **— pun′gence** (-jəns), **pun′gen·cy** *n.* **— pun′gent·ly** *adv.*

Pu·nic (pyōō′nik) *adj.* **1.** Of or pertaining to ancient Carthage or the Carthaginians. **2.** Untrustworthy, as the Carthaginians. **—** *n.* The language of the Carthaginians. [< L < *Poenus* Carthaginian, Phoenician]

Punic Wars See table for WAR.

pun·ish (pun′ish) *v.t.* **1.** To subject (a person) to pain, confinement, or other penalty for a crime or fault. **2.** To impose a penalty on. **3.** To use roughly; injure. **4.** To deplete, as a stock of food. [< OF < L *punire* to punish] **— pun′ish·a·ble** *adj.* **— pun′ish·a·bil′i·ty** *n.* **— pun′ish·er** *n.*

pun·ish·ment (pun′ish·mənt) *n.* **1.** A penalty imposed, as for transgression of law. ◆ Collateral adjective: *penal.* **2.** Any ill suffered in consequence of wrongdoing. **3.** The act of punishing. **4.** *Informal* Rough handling, as in a prize fight.

pu·ni·tive (pyōō′nə·tiv) *adj.* **1.** Pertaining to or inflicting punishment: *punitive* measures. **2.** *Law* Of a character to punish or vindicate. Also **pu′ni·to′ry** (-tôr′ē, -tō′rē). **— pu′ni·tive·ly** *adv.* **— pu′ni·tive·ness** *n.*

Pun·ja·bi (pun·jä′bē) *n.* **1.** A native of the Punjab. **2.** The Sanskritic language of the Punjab: also spelled *Panjabi.*

punk[1] (pungk) *n.* **1.** Wood decayed through the action of a fungus, useful as tinder. **2.** An artificial preparation that will smolder without flame. [< Algonquian]

punk[2] (pungk) *U.S. Slang n.* **1.** Nonsense. **2.** A petty hoodlum. **3.** A young, inexperienced boy or man: a contemptuous term. **—** *adj.* **1.** Worthless. **2.** Unwell. [Origin uncertain]

pun·ka (pung′kə) *n.* A fan; esp., a rectangular strip of cloth, etc., swung from the ceiling and moved by a servant or by machinery. Also **pun′kah.** [< Hind. *pankhā* fan]

pun·ster (pun′stər) *n.* One who puns. Also **pun′ner.**

punt[1] (punt) *n.* A flat-bottomed, square-ended boat, often propelled by a pole, used in shallow waters. **—** *v.t.* **1.** To propel (a boat) by pushing with a pole against the bottom of a shallow stream, lake, etc. **2.** To convey in a punt. **—** *v.i.* **3.** To go or hunt in a punt. [OE < L *ponto, -onis* punt, pontoon] **— punt′er** *n.*

PUNT

punt[2] (punt) *v.i.* In certain card games, to gamble or bet, esp. against a bank. [< F < Sp. < L *punctum* point] **— punt′er** *n.*

punt[3] (punt) *n.* In football, a kick made by dropping the ball from the hands and kicking it before it strikes the ground. **—** *v.t. & v.i.* In football, to propel (the ball) with a punt. [? Var. of BUNT] **— punt′er** *n.*

pun·ty (pun′tē) *n.* *pl.* **·ties** An iron rod used in glassmaking to handle the hot glass. [< F *pontil*]

pu·ny (pyōō′nē) *adj.* **·ni·er, ·ni·est** Of small and feeble development or importance; weak and insignificant. [See PUISNE.] **— pu′ni·ly** *adv.* **— pu′ni·ness** *n.*

pup (pup) *n.* **1.** A puppy (def. 1). **2.** The young of the seal, the shark, and certain other animals. **—** *v.i.* **pupped, pupping** To bring forth pups. [Short for PUPPY]

pu·pa (pyōō′pə) *n.* *pl.* **·pae** (-pē) *Entomol.* **1.** The quiescent stage in the development of an insect, following the larval and preceding the adult stage. **2.** An insect in such a stage. [< NL < L, girl, doll, puppet] **— pu′pal** *adj.*

pu·pil[1] (pyōō′pəl) *n.* A person of any age under the care of a teacher; learner. **— Syn.** See STUDENT. [< OF < L *pupillus,* dim. of *pupus* boy and *pupilla,* dim. of *pupa* girl]

pu·pil[2] (pyōō′pəl) *n.* *Anat.* The contractile opening in the iris of the eye, through which light reaches the retina. [< OF < L *pupilla* pupil of the eye]

pup·pet (pup′it) *n.* **1.** A small figure of a person, animal, etc., and animated by the hand. **2.** A marionette. **3.** One slavishly subject to the will of another; a tool. **—** *adj.* **1.** Of or pertaining to puppets. **2.** Not autonomous: a *puppet* state. [< OF < L *pupa* girl, doll, puppet]

pup·pet·eer (pup′i·tir′) *n.* One who manipulates puppets.

puppet show A drama with puppets for the actors.

pup·py (pup′ē) *n.* *pl.* **·pies 1.** A young dog: also called *pup.* **2.** A pup (def. 2). [< OF < L *pupa* girl, doll] **— pup′py·ish** *adj.*

puppy love Sentimental, adolescent love or infatuation.

pup tent A shelter tent.

pur·blind (pûr′blīnd′) *adj.* **1.** Partly blind. **2.** Having little or no insight or understanding. [ME] **— pur′blind′ly** *adv.* **— pur′blind′ness** *n.*

pur·chase (pûr′chəs) *v.t.* **·chased, ·chas·ing 1.** To acquire by paying money or its equivalent; buy. **2.** To obtain by exertion, sacrifice, flattery, etc. **3.** To move, hoist, or hold by a mechanical purchase. **—** *n.* **1.** Something purchased. **2.** The act of purchasing. **3.** A device that holds or grips something so as to prevent slipping, etc. **4.** A device that gives a mechanical advantage, as a tackle or lever; also, leverage. **5.** Any means of increasing influence or advantage. **6.** Value; worth. [< OF *porchacier* to seek for] **— pur′chas·a·ble** *adj.* **— pur′chas·er** *n.*

pur·dah (pûr′də) *n.* *Anglo-Indian* **1.** A curtain or screen used to seclude women. **2.** The state or system of such seclusion. [< Urdu and Persian *pardah*]

pure (pyŏŏr) *adj.* **pur·er, pur·est 1.** Free from anything that weakens, impairs, or pollutes. **2.** Free from adulteration; clear; clean. **3.** Genuine; stainless: *pure* food; *pure* motives. **4.** Free from moral defilement; innocent; chaste. **5.** Free from foreign or imported elements, as a language. **6.** Free of harsh qualities, as music; also, correct in form or style; finished. **7.** Abstract; nonobjective: *pure* form. **8.** *Phonet.* Having a single, unvarying tone or sound: said of vowels. **9.** Concerned with fundamental research, as distinguished from practical application; theoretical: said of sciences. **10.** *Genetics* Breeding true with respect to one or more characters; purebred. **11.** Nothing but; sheer: *pure* luck. [< OF < L *purus* clean, pure] **— pure′ness** *n.*

pure·bred (*adj.* pyŏŏr′bred′; *n.* pyŏŏr′bred′) *adj.* *Biol.* Bred from stock having had no admixture for many generations: said especially of livestock. **—** *n.* A purebred animal.

pu·rée (pyŏŏ·rā′, pyŏŏr′ā; *Fr.* pü·rā′) *n.* A thick pulp, usu. of vegetables, boiled and strained. [< F < OF < L *purare* to purify]

pure·ly (pyŏŏr′lē) *adv.* 1. So as to be free from admixture, taint, or any harmful substance. 2. Chastely; innocently. 3. Completely; totally. 4. Merely; simply.

pur·ga·tion (pûr·gā′shən) *n.* The act of purging; catharsis.

pur·ga·tive (pûr′gə·tiv) *adj.* Tending to purge; esp., precipitating a bowel movement. — *n.* A purgative agent.

pur·ga·to·ry (pûr′gə·tôr′ē, -tō′rē) *n.* *pl.* **·ries** 1. In Roman Catholic theology, a state or place where the souls of those who have died penitent are made fit for paradise by expiating venial sins and undergoing any punishment remaining for previously forgiven sins. 2. Any place or state of temporary banishment, suffering, or punishment. [See PURGE.] — **pur′ga·to′ri·al** *adj.*

purge (pûrj) *v.* **purged, purg·ing** *v.t.* 1. To cleanse of what is impure or extraneous; purify. 2. To remove (impurities, etc.) in cleansing: with *away, off,* or *out.* 3. To rid (a group, nation, etc.) of elements regarded as undesirable or inimical, esp. by killing. 4. To cleanse or rid of sin, fault, or defilement. 5. *Med.* **a** To cause evacuation of (the bowels, etc.). **b** To induce evacuation of the bowels of. — *v.i.* 6. To become clean or pure. 7. *Med.* To have or induce evacuation of the bowels, etc. — *n.* 1. The act or process of purging. 2. That which purges, esp. a cathartic. [< OF < L *purgare* to cleanse < *purus* pure] — **purg′er** *n.* — **purg′ing** *n.*

pu·ri·fy (pyŏŏr′ə·fī) *v.* **·fied, ·fy·ing** *v.t.* 1. To make pure or clean. 2. To free from sin. 3. To free of foreign or debasing elements, as a language. — *v.i.* 4. To become pure or clean. [< OF < L < *purus* pure + *facere* to make] — **pu′ri·fi·ca′-tion** *n.* — **pu·rif·i·ca·to·ry** (pyŏŏ·rif′ə·kə·tôr′ē, -tō′rē) *adj.* — **pu′ri·fi′er** *n.*

Pu·rim (pŏŏr′im, pyŏŏr′im; *Hebrew* pōō·rēm′) *n.* A Jewish festival commemorating the defeat of Haman's plot to massacre the Jews (*Esth.* ix 26), observed about the first of March. [< Hebrew *pūrīm,* pl. of *pūr* lot]

pur·ist (pyŏŏr′ist) *n.* 1. One who believes in or practices exact or meticulous usage, as of a language, style, etc. 2. One who practices or advocates an art form in which primary stress is placed on structural simplicity, as in works of a geometric nature. — **pur′ism** *n.* — **pu·ris′tic** *adj.*

pu·ri·tan (pyŏŏr′ə·tən) *n.* *Sometimes cap.* One who is scrupulously strict or exacting in his religious or moral life: often used disparagingly. — *adj.* Puritanical. — **pu′ri·tan·ism** *n.*

Pu·ri·tan (pyŏŏr′ə·tən) *n.* One of a group of English Protestants who in the 16th and 17th centuries advocated simpler forms of creed and ritual in the Church of England. — *adj.* Of or pertaining to the Puritans or to their beliefs or customs. [< LL < L *purus* pure] — **Pu′ri·tan·ism** *n.*

pu·ri·tan·i·cal (pyŏŏr′ə·tan′i·kəl) *adj.* 1. Rigidly scrupulous or exacting in religious observance or morals; strict. 2. *Often cap.* Of or characteristic of the Puritans. Also **pu′ri·tan′ic.** — **pu′ri·tan′i·cal·ly** *adv.* — **pu′ri·tan′i·cal·ness** *n.*

pu·ri·ty (pyŏŏr′ə·tē) *n.* 1. The quality or state of being pure. 2. Saturation: said of a color.

purl¹ (pûrl) *v.i.* 1. To whirl; turn. 2. To flow with a bubbling sound. 3. To move in eddies. — *n.* 1. A circling movement of water; an eddy. 2. A gentle, continued murmur, as of a rippling stream. [Cf. Norw. *purla* to gush out]

purl² (pûrl) *v.t.* 1. In knitting, to make (a stitch) backward. 2. To edge with lace, embroidery, etc. Also spelled *pearl.* — *v.i.* 3. To do edging with lace, etc.: also spelled *pearl.* — *n.* 1. An edge of lace, embroidery, etc. 2. In knitting, the inversion of the knit stitch, giving a horizontal rib effect. Also spelled *pearl.* 3. A spiral of gold or silver wire used in lacework. [Earlier *pyrle* < *pyrl* twist]

pur·lieu (pûr′lōō) *n.* 1. *pl.* The outlying districts or outskirts of any place. 2. A place in which one is free to come and go. 3. Formerly, ground unlawfully taken for a royal forest, but afterward disafforested and restored to its rightful owners. [< AF < OF < *puraler* to go through]

pur·lin (pûr′lin) *n.* A horizontal timber supporting rafters. Also **pur′line** (-lin). For illus. see ROOF. [ME *purlyn*]

pur·loin (pûr·loin′) *v.t.* & *v.i.* To steal; filch. [< OF *porloigner* to remove, put far off] — **pur·loin′er** *n.*

pur·ple (pûr′pəl) *n.* 1. A color of mingled red and blue, between crimson and violet. 2. Cloth or a garment of this color, worn formerly by sovereigns. 3. Royal power or dignity: usu. in the phrase **born to the purple.** 4. The office of a cardinal, from the official red hat and robes. 5. The office of a bishop. — *v.t.* & *v.i.* **·pled, ·pling** To make or become purple. — *adj.* 1. Of the color of purple. 2. Imperial; regal. 3. Ornate; flowery: a *purple* passage of prose. [OE < OF < L *purpura,* orig., shellfish yielding Tyrian purple dye, or cloth dyed with it]

Purple Heart A decoration, the Order of the Purple Heart, awarded to members of the armed forces or to citizens of the U.S. honorably wounded in action. See DECORATION.

pur·plish (pûr′plish) *adj.* Somewhat purple.

pur·port (pûr′pôrt, -pōrt; *for v.,* also pər·pôrt′, -pōrt′) *v.t.*

1. To have or bear as its meaning; signify; imply. 2. To claim or profess (to be), esp. falsely. — *n.* 1. That which is conveyed or suggested to the mind as the meaning or intention; import. 2. The substance of a statement, etc., given in other than the exact words. [< AF or OF < L *pro*- forth + *portare* to carry] — **pur·port′ed·ly** *adv.*

pur·pose (pûr′pəs) *n.* 1. An idea or ideal kept before the mind as an end of effort or action; design; aim. 2. A particular thing to be effected or attained. 3. Practical advantage or result; use: words to little *purpose.* 4. Settled resolution; determination. 5. Purport; intent, as of spoken or written language. 6. A proposition; question at issue. — **on purpose** Intentionally. — *v.t.* & *v.i.* **·posed, ·pos·ing** To have the intention of doing or accomplishing (something); intend; aim. [< OF *pro*- forth + *poser* to put] — **pur′pose·ful** *adj.* — **pur′pose·ful·ly** *adv.* — **pur′pose·ful·ness** *n.* — **pur′pose·less** *adj.* — **pur′pose·less·ly** *adv.* — **Syn.** (noun) 1. Intent, intention, aim, goal, design, end.

pur·pose·ly (pûr′pəs·lē) *adv.* For a purpose; intentionally.

pur·po·sive (pûr′pə·siv) *adj.* 1. Pertaining to, having, or indicating purpose. 2. Functional; useful. — **pur′po·sive·ly** *adv.* — **pur′po·sive·ness** *n.*

purr (pûr) *n.* A murmuring sound, such as a cat makes when pleased. — *v.i.* 1. To make such a sound. — *v.t.* 2. To express by or as by purring. [Imit.]

purse (pûrs) *n.* 1. A small bag or pouch, esp. one for carrying money. 2. Available resources or means; treasury: the public *purse.* 3. A sum of money offered as a prize. — *v.t.* **pursed, purs·ing** To contract into wrinkles or folds: to *purse* the lips. [OE < LL < Gk. *byrsa* skin, hide]

purs·er (pûr′sər) *n.* 1. An officer having charge of the accounts, etc., of a vessel. 2. Formerly, a naval paymaster.

purs·lane (pûrs′lin, -lān) *n.* A common garden herb with reddish green stem and leaves and small yellow flowers, used as a salad: also called *pussley.* [< OF < L *porcilaca*]

pur·su·ance (pər·sōō′əns) *n.* The act of pursuing; a following up; prosecution: usu. in the phrase **in pursuance of.**

pur·su·ant (pər·sōō′ənt) *adj.* Done in accordance with or by reason of something; conformable. — *adv.* In accordance; conformably: usu. with *to:* also **pur·su′ant·ly.**

pur·sue (pər·sōō′) *v.* **·sued, ·su·ing** *v.t.* 1. To follow in an attempt to overtake or capture; chase. 2. To seek or attain. 3. To advance along the course of; keep to the direction or provisions of, as a path, plan, or system. 4. To apply one's energies to or have as one's profession or chief interest: to *pursue* one's studies. 5. To follow persistently; harass. — *v.i.* 6. To follow; chase. 7. To continue; persist. [< AF, OF < LL < L < *pro*- forth + *sequi* to follow] — **pur·su′a·ble** *adj.* — **pur·su′er** *n.*

pur·suit (pər·sōōt′) *n.* 1. The act of pursuing; a chase. 2. That which is followed as a continued employment, pastime, etc. — **Syn.** See OCCUPATION.

pursuit plane *Mil.* A fighter plane.

purs·y (pûr′sē) *adj.* **purs·i·er, purs·i·est** 1. Short-breathed; asthmatic. 2. Fat; hefty. [Earlier *pursive* < AF *pursif,* OF *polsif* < *polser* to pant, gasp] — **purs′i·ness** *n.*

pu·ru·lent (pyŏŏr′ə·lənt, -yə·lənt) *adj.* Consisting of or secreting pus; suppurating. [< L < *pus, puris* pus] — **pu′·ru·lence** or **·len·cy** *n.* — **pu′ru·lent·ly** *adv.*

pur·vey (pər·vā′) *v.t.* & *v.i.* To furnish (provisions, etc.). [< AF < L *providere*] — **pur·vey′or** *n.*

pur·vey·ance (pər·vā′əns) *n.* 1. The act of purveying. 2. That which is purveyed or supplied; provisions.

pur·view (pûr′vyōō) *n.* 1. Extent, sphere, or scope of anything, as of official authority. 2. Range of view, experience, or understanding; outlook. 3. *Law* The body or the scope or limit of a statute. [< AF *purveu* provided]

pus (pus) *n.* A yellowish secretion from inflamed tissues. [< L] — **pus·sy** (pus′ē) *adj.*

push (pŏŏsh) *v.t.* 1. To exert force upon or against (an object) for the purpose of moving. 2. To force (one's way), as through a crowd, jungle, etc. 3. To press forward, prosecute, or develop with vigor and persistence. 4. To urge, advocate, or promote vigorously and persistently: to *push* a new product. 5. To bear hard upon; harass: I am *pushed* for time. — *v.i.* 6. To exert steady pressure against something so as to move it. 7. To move or advance vigorously or persistently. 8. To exert great effort. — *n.* 1. The act of pushing; a shove. 2. *Informal* An extremity; exigency: at a *push* for money. 3. Determined activity; energy. 4. Anything pushed to cause action. 5. An influential clique. [< OF < L *pusare* to beat]

push button A button or knob that on being pushed opens or closes a circuit in an electric system. — **push-but·ton** (pŏŏsh′but′n) *adj.*

push·cart (pŏŏsh′kärt′) *n.* A two- or four-wheeled cart pushed by hand, used by fruit venders, peddlers, etc.

push·er (pŏŏsh′ər) *n.* 1. One who or that which pushes; esp., an active, energetic person. 2. *Aëron.* An airplane with the propeller in the rear of the wings. 3. *U.S. Slang* One who illegally sells narcotics to addicts.

push·ing (poosh'ing) *adj.* **1.** Possessing enterprise and energy. **2.** Aggressive; impertinent. **— push'ing·ly** *adv.*

push·o·ver (poosh'ō'vər) *n. Slang* **1.** One who is easily defeated, overcome, taken advantage of, etc.; an easy mark. **2.** Anything that can be done with little or no effort.

push·pin (poosh'pin') *n.* A pin with a large head, inserted by thumb pressure and used for mounting papers, etc.

push-pull (poosh'pool') *adj. Electronics* Designating a circuit or system that uses two similar components operating in opposite phase.

Push·tu (push'too) *n.* Pashto.

push·y (poosh'ē) *adj.* **·i·er**, **·i·est** *Informal* Offensively aggressive; bossy. **— push'i·ly** *adv.* **— push'i·ness** *n.*

pu·sil·lan·i·mous (pyoo'sə·lan'ə·məs) *adj.* **1.** Lacking courage, or spirit; cowardly. **2.** Characterized by weakness of purpose or lack of courage. [< LL < L *pusillus* very little + *animus* soul] **— pu'sil·la·nim'i·ty** (-lə·nim'ə·tē) *n.* — **pu'sil·lan'i·mous·ly** *adv.* **— pu'sil·lan'i·mous·ness** *n.*

puss¹ (poos) *n. Informal* **1.** A cat. **2.** A child or young woman: a term of affection. [< LG *puus*, name for a cat]

puss² (poos) *n. Slang* The mouth; face. [< Irish *pus* mouth]

puss·ley (pus'lē) *n.* Purslane. [Alter. of PURSLANE]

pus·sy (poos'ē) *n. pl.* **·sies** *Informal* **1.** A cat. **2.** A fuzzy catkin, as of a willow, birch, etc. [Dim. of PUSS¹]

pus·sy·foot (poos'ē·foot') *v.i.* **1.** To move softly and stealthily, as a cat does. **2.** To act or proceed without committing oneself or revealing one's intentions.

pus·sy willow (poos'ē) A small American willow with silky catkins in early spring.

pus·tu·late (pus'choo·lāt; *for adj. also* pus'·choo·lit) *v.t. & v.i.* **·lat·ed**, **·lat·ing** To form into or become pustules. *— adj.* Covered with pustules. [< L *pustulatus*, pp. of *pustulare* to blister] **— pus'tu·la'tion** *n.*

pus·tule (pus'chool) *n.* **1.** *Pathol.* A small elevation of the skin with an inflamed base containing pus. **2.** Any elevation resembling a pimple or a blister. [< L *pustula*] **— pus'tu·lar, pus'·tu·lous** *adj.*

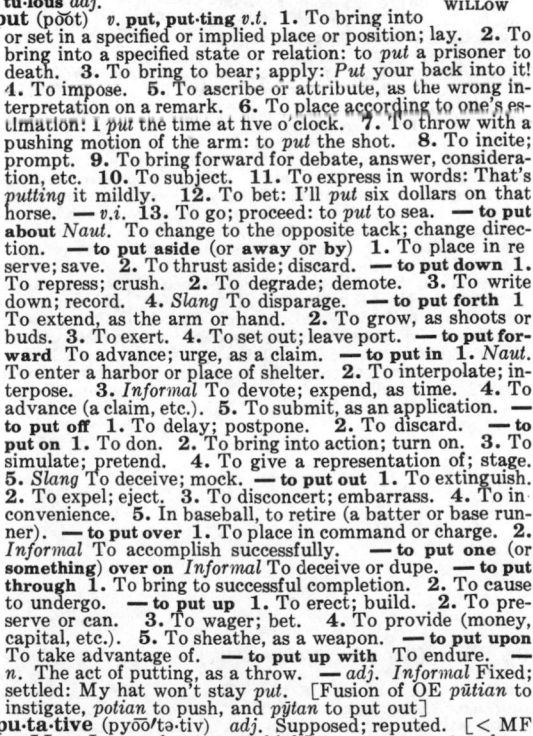

PUSSY
WILLOW

put (poot) *v.* **put, put·ting** *v.t.* **1.** To bring into or set in a specified or implied place or position; lay. **2.** To bring into a specified state or relation: to *put* a prisoner to death. **3.** To bring to bear; apply: *Put* your back into it! **4.** To impose. **5.** To ascribe or attribute, as the wrong interpretation on a remark. **6.** To place according to one's estimation: I *put* the time at five o'clock. **7.** To throw with a pushing motion of the arm: to *put* the shot. **8.** To incite; prompt. **9.** To bring forward for debate, answer, consideration, etc. **10.** To subject. **11.** To express in words: That's *putting* it mildly. **12.** To bet: I'll *put* six dollars on that horse. *— v.i.* **13.** To go; proceed: to *put* to sea. **— to put about** *Naut.* To change to the opposite tack; change direction. **— to put aside** (or **away** or **by**) **1.** To reserve; save. **2.** To thrust aside; discard. **— to put down 1.** To repress; crush. **2.** To degrade; demote. **3.** To write down; record. **4.** *Slang* To disparage. **— to put forth 1.** To extend, as the arm or hand. **2.** To grow, as shoots or buds. **3.** To exert. **4.** To set out; leave port. **— to put forward** To advance; urge, as a claim. **— to put in 1.** *Naut.* To enter a harbor or place of shelter. **2.** To interpolate; interpose. **3.** *Informal* To devote; expend, as time. **4.** To advance (a claim, etc.). **5.** To submit, as an application. **— to put off 1.** To delay; postpone. **2.** To discard. **— to put on 1.** To don. **2.** To bring into action; turn on. **3.** To simulate; pretend. **4.** To give a representation of; stage. **5.** *Slang* To deceive; mock. **— to put out 1.** To extinguish. **2.** To expel; eject. **3.** To disconcert; embarrass. **4.** To inconvenience. **5.** In baseball, to retire (a batter or base runner). **— to put over 1.** To place in command or charge. **2.** *Informal* To accomplish successfully. **— to put one** (or **something**) **over on** *Informal* To deceive or dupe. **— to put through 1.** To bring to successful completion. **2.** To cause to undergo. **— to put up 1.** To erect; build. **2.** To preserve or can. **3.** To wager; bet. **4.** To provide (money, capital, etc.). **5.** To sheathe, as a weapon. **— to put upon** To take advantage of. **— to put up with** To endure. *— n.* The act of putting, as a throw. *— adj. Informal* Fixed; settled: My hat won't stay *put.* [Fusion of OE *pūtian* to instigate, *potian* to push, and *pȳtan* to put out]

pu·ta·tive (pyoo'tə·tiv) *adj.* Supposed; reputed. [< MF or LL < L, pp. of *putare* to think] **— pu'ta·tive·ly** *adv.*

put·off (poot'ôf', -of') *n.* An evasion; excuse.

put-on (poot'on') *n. Slang* A hoax or deception.

put·out (poot'out') *n.* In baseball, the act of causing an out, as of a batter or base runner.

pu·tre·fac·tion (pyoo'trə·fak'shən) *n.* **1.** The decomposition of organic matter. **2.** The state of being putrefied. **3.** Putrescent or putrefied matter.

pu·tre·fac·tive (pyoo'trə·fak'tiv) *adj.* **1.** Of or pertaining to putrefaction. **2.** Producing putrefaction.

pu·tre·fy (pyoo'trə·fī) *v.t. & v.i.* **·fied**, **·fy·ing** **1.** To decay or cause to decay with a fetid odor; rot. **2.** To make or become gangrenous. **— Syn.** See DECAY. [< F < L < *putrere* to decay + *facere* to make] **— pu'tre·fi'er** *n.*

pu·tres·cent (pyoo·tres'ənt) *adj.* **1.** Becoming putrid; **2.** Pertaining to putrefaction. **— pu·tres'cence** *n.*

pu·trid (pyoo'trid) *adj.* **1.** Being in a state of putrefaction; rotten. **2.** Indicating or produced by putrefaction: a *putrid* smell. **3.** Rotten; corrupt. [< L *putrere* to decay] **— pu·trid'i·ty** *n.* **— pu'trid·ly** *adv.* **— pu'trid·ness** *n.*

Putsch (pooch) *n.* An outbreak or rebellion; an attempted *coup d'état.* [< G < dial. G (Swiss), lit., push, blow]

putt (put) *n.* In golf, a light stroke made on a putting green to place the ball in or near the hole. *— v.t. & v.i.* To strike (the ball) with such a stroke. [Var. of PUT]

put·tee (put'ē, pu·tē') *n.* A strip of cloth wound spirally about the leg from knee to ankle, used by soldiers, sportsmen, etc.; also, a leather gaiter strapped around the leg. Also **put'ty.** [< Hind. < Skt. *patta* strip of cloth]

put·ter¹ (put'ər) *n.* **1.** In golf, one who putts. **2.** An upright, stiff-shafted golf club used on the putting green.

put·ter² (put'ər) *v.i.* **1.** To act or work in a dawdling manner. *— v.t.* **2.** To waste (time, etc.) in dawdling or puttering. [Var. of POTTER¹]

put·ting green (put'ing) In golf: **a** Green (*n.* def. 5). **b** A place set aside for putting practice.

put·ty (put'ē) *n.* **1.** Whiting mixed with linseed oil to the consistency of dough, used for filling holes or cracks in wood surfaces, securing panes of glass in the sash, etc. **2.** Any of various similar substances. *— v.t.* **·tied**, **·ty·ing** To fill, stop, fasten, etc., with putty. [< OF *potée* calcined tin, lit., potful] **— put'ti·er** *n.*

putty knife A knife with a spatulalike blade, used in applying putty.

put-up (poot'up') *adj. Informal* Prearranged or contrived in an artful manner: a *put-up* job.

puz·zle (puz'əl) *v.* **·zled**, **·zling** *v.t.* **1.** To confuse or perplex. **2.** To solve by investigation and study, as something perplexing: with *out.* *— v.i.* **3.** To be perplexed or confused. **— to puzzle over** To attempt to understand or solve. *— n.* **1.** Something that puzzles; enigma. **2.** A toy, word game, etc., designed to test one's ingenuity or patience. **3.** The state of being puzzled; perplexity. [Origin unknown] **— puz'zler** *n.* **— puz'zle·ment** *n.*

— Syn. (verb) **1.** confound, bewilder, baffle, daze. — (noun) **1.** A *puzzle* is usually intricate but can be solved by ingenuity and patience; many *puzzles* are made for amusement. An *enigma* is something said or written whose meaning is hidden and can only be inferred from clues. A *conundrum* is a baffling question, the answer to which depends upon some trick of words. *Conundrums* are also *riddles,* but a *riddle* is usually less playful in character.

py- Var. of PYO-.

pyelo- *combining form* Pelvis. Also, before vowels, **pyel-.** [< Gk. *pyelos* pelvis, trough]

py·e·mi·a (pī·ē'mē·ə) *n. Pathol.* A type of blood poisoning characterized by many abscesses. [< NL < Gk. *pyon* pus + *haima* blood] **— py·e'mic** *adj.*

Pyg·ma·li·on (pig·mā'lē·ən, -māl'yən) In Greek mythology, a sculptor of Cyprus who fell in love with his statue, Galatea, which Aphrodite later brought to life.

pyg·my (pig'mē) *adj.* **1.** Diminutive; dwarfish. **2.** Trivial; unimportant. *— n. pl.* **·mies** A small person or thing regarded as insignificant. Also spelled *pigmy.* [< L < Gk. *pygmē* the length from elbow to knuckles]

Pyg·my (pig'mē) *n. pl.* **·mies** **1.** A member of a Negroid people of equatorial Africa, ranging in height from four to five feet. **2.** Any of the Negrito peoples of the Philippines, Andaman Islands, and Malaya.

py·ja·mas (pə·jä'məz, -jam'əz) See PAJAMAS.

py·lon (pī'lon) *n.* **1.** *Archit.* A monumental structure constituting an entrance to an Egyptian temple, consisting of a central gateway, flanked on each side by a truncated pyramidal tower. **2.** A stake marking the course in an airport or turning point in an air race. **3.** One of the steel towers supporting a high-tension electric power line. **4.** *Surg.* An artificial leg, usu. temporary. [< Gk. *pylōn* gateway]

py·lo·rus (pī·lôr'əs, -lō'rəs, pi-) *n. pl.* **·ri** (-rī) *Anat.* The opening between the stomach and the duodenum, surrounded by a sphincter. [< LL < Gk. < *pylē* gate + *ouros* watcher] **— py·lor'ic** (-lôr'ik, -lor'ik) *adj.*

pyo- *combining form* Pus; of or related to pus. Also, before vowels, **py-.** [< Gk. *pyon* pus]

py·or·rhe·a (pī'ə·rē'ə) *n. Pathol.* A continuous discharge of pus; esp., from the gums, with loosening of the teeth. [< NL < Gk. *pyon* pus + *rheein* to flow] **— py'or·rhe'al** *adj.*

pyr- Var. of PYRO-.

pyr·a·mid (pir′ə·mid) *n.* **1.** *Archit.* A structure of masonry typically having a square base and triangular sides meeting in an apex, sometimes vast in size, as those used as tombs or temples in ancient Egypt. **2.** Something pyramidal in form. **3.** *Geom.* A solid consisting of a polygonal base and triangular

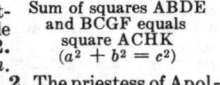

PYRAMIDS AT GIZA

sides, having a common vertex. **4.** *Mineral.* A crystal form consisting of three or more similar planes having a common point of intersection. — *v.t. & v.i.* **1.** To arrange or form in the shape of a pyramid. **2.** To buy or sell (stock) with paper profits, and to continue so buying or selling. [ME *piramis* (pl. *pyramids*) and later borrowing of F *pyramide*, both < L < Gk. *pyramis, -idos*] — **py·ram·i·dal** (pi·ram′ə·dal), **pyr′a·mid′ic** or **-i·cal** *adj.* — **py·ram′i·dal·ly** *adv.*

pyre (pīr) *n.* **1.** A heap of combustibles arranged for burning a dead body. **2.** Any pile or heap of combustible material. [< L *pyra* hearth, funeral pile < Gk. *pyr* fire]

py·reth·rum (pi·reth′rəm, -rē′thrəm) *n.* The powdered flowers of a chrysanthemum, used medically as an ointment, and as an insecticide. [< L, feverfew < Gk. *pyrethron*]

py·ret·ic (pi·ret′ik) *adj.* **1.** Affected with or relating to fever. **2.** Remedial in fevers. [< NL < Gk. *pyretos* fever]

Py·rex (pī′reks) *n.* A type of heat-resisting glass having a high silica content, with additions of soda, aluminum, and boron: a trade name. Also **py′rex**.

pyr·i·dox·ine (pir′ə·dok′sēn, -sin) *n. Biochem.* Vitamin B_6, a water-soluble compound, $C_8H_{10}NO_3$, occurring in cereal grains, vegetable oils, legumes, yeast, meats, and fish, and also made synthetically. [PYRID(INE) + OX(Y)-² + -INE²]

py·rite (pī′rīt) *n. pl.* **py·ri·tes** (pī·rī′tēz) A metallic, pale yellow iron disulfide, FeS_2, a source of sulfuric acid: also called *fool's gold, iron pyrites.* [< L < Gk. < *pyrités* (*lithos*) fire (stone)] — **py·rit′ic** (-rit′ik) or **-i·cal** *adj.*

py·ri·tes (pī·rī′tēz) *n.pl.* Any of various metallic sulfides.

pyro- *combining form* Fire; heat. Also, before vowels, *pyr-*. [< Gk. *pyr, pyros* fire]

py·ro·e·lec·tric (pī′rō·i·lek′trik, pir′ō-) *adj.* Of, pertaining to, or manifesting pyroelectricity; developing poles when heated. — *n.* A pyroelectric substance.

py·ro·e·lec·tric·i·ty (pī′rō·i·lek′tris′ə·tē, -ē′lek-, pir′ō-) *n.* Electrification or electric polarity developed in certain minerals by a change in temperature.

py·ro·gen·ic (pī′rə·jen′ik, pir′ə-) *adj.* **1.** Causing or produced by heat. **2.** Caused by or inducing fever. Also **py·rog·e·nous** (pī·roj′ə·nəs, pi-).

py·rog·ra·phy (pī·rog′rə·fē, pi-) *n.* The art or process of producing a design, as on wood or leather, by a red-hot point or fine flame. — **py·ro·graph** (pī′rə·graf, -gräf, pir′ə-) *n.* — **py·rog′ra·pher** *n.* — **py·ro·graph′ic** *adj.*

py·rol·y·sis (pī·rol′ə·sis) *n. Chem.* Decomposition of organic compounds or other substances by the action of heat. [< NL < Gk. *pyr, pyros* fire + *lysis* loosing] — **py·ro·lit·ic** (pī′rə·lit′ik, pir′ə-) *adj.*

py·ro·mag·net·ic (pī′rō·mag·net′ik, pir′ō-) *adj.* Of, per-

taining to, or produced by changes in magnetic properties caused by change of temperature.

py·ro·ma·ni·a (pī′rə·mā′nē·ə, -mān′yə, pir′ə-) *n.* A compulsion to set things on fire. — **py′ro·ma′ni·ac** (-ak) *adj. & n.* — **py·ro·ma·ni·a·cal** (pī′rō·mə·nī′ə·kəl, pir′ō-) *adj.*

py·rom·e·ter (pī·rom′ə·tər) *n.* An instrument for measuring high degrees of heat. — **py′ro·met′ric** (pī′rə·met′rik, pir′ə-) or **-ri·cal** *adj.* — **py·rom′e·try** *n.*

py·ro·tech·nic (pī′rə·tek′nik, pir′ə-) *adj.* Pertaining to fireworks or their manufacture. Also **py′ro·tech′ni·cal.**

py·ro·tech·nics (pī′rə·tek′niks, pir′ə-) *n.pl.* (*construed as sing. in defs. 1, 4*) **1.** The art of making or using fireworks. Also **py·ro·tech·ny** (pī′rə·tek′nē, pir′ə-) **2.** A display of fireworks. **3.** An ostentatious display, as of oratory. **4.** *Mil.* Rockets, flares, or the like, that produce flame or smoke for signaling, lighting, screening, etc. [< MF < Gk. *pyr, pyros* fire + *technē* art] — **py·ro·tech′nist** *n.*

py·ro·tox·in (pī′rə·tok′sin, pir′ə-) *n. Biochem.* Any of various toxins found in the body and inducing a rise of bodily temperature or symptoms of fever.

py·rox·y·lin (pī·rok′sə·lin) *n. Chem.* A cellulose nitrate mixture, less explosive than guncotton, and widely used in making Celluloid, collodion, lacquers, adhesives, etc. Also **py·rox′y·line** (-lēn, -lin). [< F < Gk. *pyr, pyros* fire + *xylon* wood + F -*in* -in]

Pyr·rhic victory (pir′ik) A victory gained at a ruinous loss, such as that of Pyrrhus over the Romans in 279 B.C. [after *Pyrrhus* king of Epirus]

Py·thag·o·re·an·ism (pi·thag′ə·rē′ən·iz′əm) *n.* The mystical philosophy taught by Pythagoras, including the idea that number is the essence of all things. — **Py·thag·o·re·an** (pi·thag′ə·rē′ən) *n. & adj.*

Pythagorean theorem *Geom.* The theorem that the sum of the squares of the legs of a right triangle is equal to the square of the hypotenuse.

PYTHAGOREAN THEOREM

Sum of squares ABDE and BCGF equals square ACHK
$(a^2 + b^2 = c^2)$

Pyth·i·an (pith′ē·ən) *adj.* **1.** Relating to Delphi, to Apollo's temple there, its oracle, or its priestess. **2.** Relating to the Pythian games. — *n.* **1.** A native or inhabitant of Delphi. **2.** The priestess of Apollo. **3.** An epithet of the Delphic Apollo. [< L *Pythius* < Gk. *Pythios*]

Pythian games In ancient Greece, games held every four years at Delphi in honor of Apollo.

Pyth·i·as (pith′ē·əs) See DAMON AND PYTHIAS.

py·thon (pī′thon, -thən) *n.* **1.** A large, nonvenomous serpent that crushes its prey. **2.** Any nonvenomous constrictor. [< L < Gk. *Python*, a serpent slain by Apollo]

py·tho·ness (pī′thə·nis, pith′ə-) *n.* **1.** The priestess of the Delphic oracle. **2.** Any woman supposed to be possessed of the spirit of prophecy.

pyx (piks) *n. Eccl.* A vessel or casket, usu. of precious metal, in which the Host is preserved. [< L < Gk. *pyxos* box tree]

pyx·i·di·um (pik·sid′ē·əm) *n. pl.* **·i·a** (-ē·ə) *Bot.* A seed vessel with two parts, the upper separating as a lid.

pyx·is (pik′sis) *n. pl.* **pyx·i·des** (pik′sə·dēz) **1.** A box or pyx; esp., an ancient form of ornamental jewel case or toilet box. **2.** An emollient ointment. **3.** *Bot.* A pyxidium. [< L]

Q

q, Q (kyoo) *n. pl.* **q's** or **qs, Q's** or **Qs, cues** (kyooz) **1.** The 17th letter of the English alphabet. **2.** The sound represented by the letter *q*. In English *q* is always followed by *u* and represents (kw), as in *quack, quest, quote, equal,* etc. In some words borrowed from French, however, English follows the French pronunciation with (k) alone, as in *appliqué, conquer, coquette, pique.* Final -*que* always represents (k), as in *antique, oblique, physique, unique,* etc.

qua (kwā, kwä) *adv.* In the capacity of; by virtue of being; insofar as. [< L, ablative sing. fem. of *qui* who]

quack¹ (kwak) *v.i.* To utter a harsh, croaking cry, as a duck. — *n.* The sound made by a duck, or a similar croaking noise. [Imit.]

quack² (kwak) *n.* **1.** A pretender to medical knowledge or skill. **2.** One who falsely poses as an expert; a charlatan. — *adj.* Of or pertaining to quacks or quackery. — *v.i.* To play

the quack. [Short for QUACKSALVER] — **quack′ish** *adj.* — **quack′ish·ly** *adv.*

quack·er·y (kwak′ər·ē) *n. pl.* **·er·ies** Ignorant or fraudulent practice. Also **quack′hood** (-hood), **quack′ism.**

quack·sal·ver (kwak′sal′vər) *n.* A medical quack. [< MDu. < *quacken* quack¹ + *salf* salve]

quad¹ (kwod) *n. Informal* A quadrangle, as of a college.

quad² (kwod) *n. Printing* A piece of type metal of less height than the letters, used for spacing: also called *quadrat.*

quad·ran·gle (kwod′rang·gəl) *n.* **1.** *Geom.* A plane figure having four sides and four angles. **2.** A court, either square or oblong; also, the building or buildings that surround such a court. [< OF < LL < L *quattuor* four + *angulus* angle] — **quad·ran′gu·lar** (-gyə·lər) *adj.*

quad·rant (kwod′rənt) *n.* **1.** A quarter section of a circle, subtending an arc of 90°; also, the arc subtended. **2.** An instrument having a graduated arc of 90°, with a movable radius for measuring angles on it, used in navigation, surveying, and astronomy for measuring altitudes. [< L *quattuor* four] — **quad·ran·tal** (kwod·ran′təl) *adj.*

quad·rat (kwod′rət) *n. Printing* A quad².

quad·rate (kwod′rāt; *for n., also* kwod′rit) *n.* **1.** In astrology, an aspect of two heavenly bodies in which they are distant from each other 90°. **2.** A cubical or square object. — *adj.* Square; four-sided. [< L *quadrare* to square]

quad·rat·ic (kwod·rat′ik) *adj.* **1.** Pertaining to or resembling a square. **2.** *Math.* Pertaining to or designating an equation, curve, surface, etc., of the second degree. — *n. Math.* A quadratic equation, curve, etc.

quad·rat·ics (kwod·rat′iks) *n.pl.* (*construed as sing.*) *Rare* The branch of algebra dealing with quadratic equations.

quad·ra·ture (kwod′rə·chər) *n.* **1.** The act or process of squaring. **2.** *Math.* The determination of the area of a surface, esp. one bounded by a curve.

quad·ren·ni·al (kwod·ren′ē·əl) *adj.* **1.** Occurring once in four years. **2.** Lasting four years. — **quad·ren′ni·al·ly** *adv.*

quadri- *combining form* Four: *quadrilateral.* Also *quadru-*: also **quadr-** (before vowels). [< L *quattuor* four]

quad·ri·lat·er·al (kwod′rə·lat′ər·əl) *adj.* Formed or bounded by four lines; four-sided. — *n. Geom.* A figure bounded by four straight lines terminated at four angles. [< L *quattuor* four + *latus* side]

qua·drille (kwə·dril′) *n.* **1.** A square dance for four couples, having five figures. **2.** Music for or in the manner of this dance. [< F < Sp. < L *quattuor* four]

quad·ril·lion (kwod·ril′yən) *n.* **1.** *U.S.* A thousand trillions, written as 1 followed by fifteen zeros: a cardinal number. **2.** *Brit.* A million trillions (def. 2), written as 1 followed by twenty-four zeros: a cardinal number. — *adj.* Being a quadrillion in number. [< MF < *quadri-* four + (*mi*)*llion* million] — **quad·ril′lionth** *adj. & n.*

quad·ri·no·mi·al (kwod′rə·nō′mē·əl) *n. Math.* An algebraic expression having four terms.

quad·ri·va·lent (kwod′rə·vā′lənt) *adj. Chem.* Having a valence of four, as carbon: also *tetratomic, tetravalent.* [< QUADRI- + L *valere* to be worth] — **quad′ri·va′lence, quad′ri·va·len·cy** *n.*

quad·roon (kwod·rōōn′) *n.* A person having one Negro grandparent. [< Sp. *cuarto* fourth]

quadru- Var. of QUADRI-.

quad·ru·ped (kwod′rōō·ped) *n.* An animal having four feet; esp., a four-footed mammal. — *adj.* Having four feet. [< L *quattuor* four + *pes* foot] — **quad·ru·pe·dal** (kwod·rōō′pə·dəl, kwod·rōō·ped′l) *adj.*

quad·ru·ple (kwod′rōō·pəl, kwod·rōō′pəl) *v.t. & v.i.* **·pled, ·pling** To multiply by four; make or become four times larger. — *adj.* **1.** Consisting of four. **2.** Multiplied by four. — *n.* A sum four times as great as another. — *adv.* So as to make four times larger. [< OF < L *quadruplus*]

quad·ru·plet (kwod′rōō·plit, kwod·rōō′-) *n.* **1.** A compound or combination of four things or objects. **2.** One of four offspring born of the same mother at one birth.

quad·ru·pli·cate (kwod·rōō′plə·kāt; *for adj. & n., also* kwod·rōō′plə-kit) *adj.* Quadruple; fourfold. — *n.* One of four like things. [< L *quattuor* four + stem of *plicare* to fold] — **quad·ru′pli·cate·ly** *adv.* — **quad·ru′pli·ca′tion** *n.*

quaff (kwaf, kwof, kwôf) *v.t. & v.i.* To drink, esp. copiously or with relish. — *n.* A drink; swallow. — **quaff′er** *n.*

quag·gy (kwag′ē, kwog′ē) *adj.* **·gi·er, ·gi·est** Yielding to or quaking under the foot, as soft, wet earth; boggy.

quag·mire (kwag′mīr′, kwog′-) *n.* **1.** Marshy ground that gives way under the foot. **2.** A difficult situation. [< obs. *quag* to shake + MIRE] — **quag′mired′, quag′mir′y** *adj.*

qua·hog (kwô′hôg, -hog, kwə·hôg′, -hog′) *n.* An edible American clam called *hard-shelled clam.* Also **qua′haug.** [< Algonquian (Narraganset) *poquauhock*]

quail¹ (kwāl) *n.* Any of various small American game birds related to the partridge, esp. the bobwhite. [< OF *quaille,* prob. of Gmc. origin]

quail² (kwāl) *v.i.* To shrink with fear; lose heart or courage. [ME *quailen*]

quaint (kwānt) *adj.* **1.** Combining an antique appearance with a pleasing oddity, fancifulness, or whimsicalness. **2.** Pleasingly odd or old-fashioned; fanciful. [< OF < L *cognoscere* to ascertain] — **quaint′ly** *adv.* — **quaint′ness** *n.*

quake (kwāk) *v.i.* **quaked, quak·ing 1.** To shake, as with violent emotion or cold. **2.** To shake or tremble, as earth during an earthquake. *Syn.* See SHAKE. — *n.* **1.** The act of quaking. **2.** An earthquake. [OE *cwacian* to shake]

Quak·er (kwā′kər) *n.* A member of the Society of Friends: originally a term of derision. [< QUAKE, v.; with ref. to their founder's admonition to tremble at the word of the Lord] — **Quak′er·ish** *adj.* — **Quak′er·ish·ly** *adv.* — **Quak·er·ism** (kwā′kə·riz′əm) *n.* — **Quak′er·ly** *adj. & adv.*

quak·y (kwā′kē) *adj.* **quak·i·er, quak·i·est** Shaky; tremulous. — **quak′i·ly** *adv.* — **quak′i·ness** *n.*

qual·i·fi·ca·tion (kwol′ə·fə·kā′shən) *n.* **1.** The act of qualifying, or the state of being qualified. **2.** Any ability, training, etc., that fits a person for a specific office, role, position, etc. **3.** A restriction: to accept without *qualification.*

qual·i·fied (kwol′ə·fīd) *adj.* **1.** Competent or fit, as for public office. **2.** Restricted or modified. — **qual′i·fied′ly** *adv.*

qual·i·fy (kwol′ə·fī) *v.* **·fied, ·fy·ing** *v.t.* **1.** To make fit or capable, as for an office, occupation, or privilege. **2.** To make legally capable. **3.** To limit or restrict. **4.** To attribute a quality to; describe; characterize. **5.** To make less strong or extreme. **6.** To change the strength or flavor of. **7.** *Gram.* To modify. — *v.i.* **8.** To be or become qualified or fit; meet the requirements, as for entering a race. [< MF < Med.L < L *qualis* of such a kind + *facere* to make] — **qual′i·fi′a·ble** *adj.* — **qual′i·fi′er** *n.*

qual·i·ta·tive (kwol′ə·tā′tiv) *adj.* Of or pertaining to quality: distinguished from *quantitative.* [< LL < L *qualis* of such a kind] — **qual′i·ta′tive·ly** *adv.*

qualitative analysis *Chem.* The process of determining the kind and number of ingredients present in a substance.

qual·i·ty (kwol′ə·tē) *n. pl.* **·ties 1.** That which makes something such as it is; a distinguishing element or characteristic. **2.** The basic or essential character, nature, etc., of something. **3.** Excellence: *quality* rather than quantity. **4.** The degree of excellence. **5.** A moral or personality trait or characteristic. **6.** *Music* The timbre of a voice or musical instrument. **7.** *Archaic* High or superior social rank or birth; also, persons of superior rank collectively. — *adj.* Of superior quality. [< F < L *qualis* of such a kind]

qualm (kwäm, kwôm) *n.* **1.** A feeling of sickness. **2.** A twinge of conscience; moral scruple. **3.** A sensation of fear or misgiving. [? OE *cwealm* death] — **qualm′ish** *adj.* — **qualm′ish·ly** *adv.* — **qualm′ish·ness** *n.* — **qualm′y** *adj.*

quan·da·ry (kwon′dər·ē, -drē) *n. pl.* **·da·ries** A state of hesitation or perplexity; predicament.

quan·ta (kwon′tə) Plural of QUANTUM.

quan·ti·ta·tive (kwon′tə·tā′tiv) *adj.* **1.** Of or pertaining to quantity. **2.** Having to do with quantities only: distinguished from *qualitative.* — **quan′ti·ta·tive·ly** *adv.* — **quan′ti·ta·tive·ness** *n.*

quantitative analysis *Chem.* The process of finding the amount or percentage of each element or ingredient present in a material or compound.

quan·ti·ty (kwon′tə·tē) *n. pl.* **·ties 1.** A specified or indefinite number, amount, weight, etc. **2.** The property of a thing that admits of exact measurement. **3.** *Often pl.* A large amount: abundance: *quantities* of food. **4.** Measure; amount: *quantity* rather than quality. **5.** *Math.* An entity regarded as possessing a certain determinable magnitude, as length, size, volume, or number. **6.** The relative length of a speech sound, prosodic syllable, or musical tone. **7.** *Electr.* The amount of current. [< OF < L *quantus* how much]

quan·tize (kwon′tīz) *v.t.* **·tized, ·tiz·ing** *Physics* **1.** To restrict the possible values of (an observable quantity or magnitude). **2.** To express as multiples of a given quantity or quantum. — **quan′ti·za′tion** *n.*

quan·tum (kwon′təm) *n. pl.* **·ta** (-tə) *Physics* A fundamental unit of energy as provided for in the quantum theory. [< L, neuter of *quantus* how much]

quantum theory *Physics* The theory that energy is not a smoothly flowing continuum but is manifested by the emission from radiating bodies of discrete particles or *quanta,* the values of which are expressed as the product of Planck's constant multiplied by the frequency of the given radiation.

quar·an·tine (kwôr′ən·tēn, kwor′-) *n.* **1.** The enforced isolation for a fixed period of time of persons, ships, or goods arriving from places infected with or exposed to contagious disease. **2.** A place designated for the enforcement of such interdiction. **3.** The enforced isolation of any person or place infected with contagious disease. **4.** Any enforced isolation. **5.** A period of forty days. — *v.t.* **·tined, ·tin·ing** To subject to or retain in quarantine; isolate by or as by quarantine. [< Ital. < ult. < L *quadraginta* forty]

quar·rel (kwôr′əl, kwor′-) *n.* **1.** An unfriendly, angry, or violent dispute. **2.** A falling out; breach of amity. **3.** The cause for dispute. — *v.i.* **quar·reled** or **·relled, quar·rel·ing** or **·rel·ling 1.** To engage in a quarrel. **2.** To break off a mutual friendship. **3.** To find fault. [< F < L *queri* to complain] — **quar′rel·er** or **quar′rel·ler** *n.* — *Syn.* (noun) **1.** Wrangle, bicker, squabble, altercation, scrap.

quar·rel·some (kwôr′əl·səm, kwor′-) *adj.* Inclined to quarrel. — **quar′rel·some·ly** *adv.* — **quar′rel·some·ness** *n.*

quar·ry¹ (kwôr′ē, kwor′ē) *n. pl.* **·ries 1.** A beast or bird hunted or killed, as in the chase. **2.** Anything hunted, slaughtered, or pursued. [< OF < L *corium* hide]

quar·ry² (kwôr′ē, kwor′ē) *n. pl.* **·ries** An excavation from which stone is taken by cutting, blasting, or the like. — *v.t.* ·ried, ·ry·ing 1. To cut, dig, or take from or as from a quarry. 2. To establish a quarry in. [< OF < L *quadrus* square] — **quar′ri·er** *n.*

quart (kwôrt) *n.* 1. A measure of capacity, the fourth part of a gallon, or two pints. In the U.S., the dry quart is equal to 1.10 liters and the liquid quart is equal to 0.946 liter. See table front of book. 2. A container having such a capacity. [< OF < L *quartus* fourth]

quar·ter (kwôr′tər) *n.* 1. One of four equal parts into which anything is or may be divided. 2. In the U.S. and Canada, a coin having the value of 25 cents. 3. Fifteen minutes or the fourth of an hour; also, the moment such a period begins or ends. 4. Three months or a fourth of a year. 5. A term of school, usu. one fourth of a year. 6. *Astron.* A fourth part of the moon's revolution about the earth. 7. One of the four periods into which a game, as football, is divided. 8. One of the four principal points of the compass. 9. A particular district or locality, as of a city: the native *quarter*. 10. A place or source from which something comes: on authority of the highest *quarter*. 11. *Usu. pl.* Proper or assigned station, as of officers and crew on a warship. 12. *pl.* A place of lodging or residence. 13. Mercy shown to a vanquished enemy. 14. Either of the four limbs of a quadruped, together with the adjacent parts. 15. *Naut.* The upper part of a vessel's side, near the stern. 16. *Heraldry* a Any of four equal divisions into which a shield is divided. b An ordinary occupying such a division. — **at close quarters** Close by; at close range. — *adj.* 1. Being one of four equal parts. 2. Having one fourth of a standard value. — *v.t.* 1. To divide into four equal parts. 2. To divide into a number of parts or pieces. 3. To cut the body of (an executed person) into four parts. 4. To range from one side to the other of (a field, etc.) while advancing. 5. To furnish with quarters or shelter; lodge. 6. *Heraldry* a To divide (a shield) into quarters. b To bear or arrange (different coats of arms) quarterly upon a shield. — *v.i.* 7. To be stationed or lodged. 8. To range from side to side of an area, as dogs in hunting. 9. *Naut.* To blow on a ship's quarter: said of the wind. [< OF < L *quartus* fourth]

quar·ter·back (kwôr′tər·bak′) *n.* In American football, one of the backfield, who often calls the signals.

quarter day Any of the four days of the year when quarterly payments are due.

quar·ter·deck (kwôr′tər·dek′) *n. Naut.* The rear part of a ship's upper deck, reserved for officers.

quar·tered (kwôr′tərd) *adj.* 1. Divided into four quarters. 2. Lodged; stationed; also, having quarters. 3. Quartersawed. 4. *Heraldry* Divided into quarters.

quar·ter·ly (kwôr′tər·lē) *adj.* 1. Containing or being a fourth part. 2. Occurring at intervals of three months. — *n. pl.* ·lies A publication issued once every three months. — *adv.* 1. Once in a quarter of a year. 2. In or by quarters.

quar·ter·mas·ter (kwôr′tər·mas′tər, ·mäs′-) *n.* 1. *Usu. cap. Mil.* An officer responsible for the supply of food, fuel, clothing, etc. 2. On shipboard, a petty officer responsible for steering and related functions.

quar·tern (kwôr′tərn) *n.* A fourth part of certain measures or weights, as of a peck or pound. [< OF < L < *quartus* fourth]

quarter note *Music* A note having one fourth the time value of a whole note: also called *crotchet*.

quar·ter·saw (kwôr′tər·sô′) *v.t.* ·sawed, ·sawed or ·sawn, ·saw·ing To saw (a log) lengthwise into quarters so that each face corresponds with one of the log's radii.

quarter section A tract of land half a mile square, containing one fourth of a square mile, or 160 acres.

quarter sessions A court held quarterly.

quar·ter·staff (kwôr′tər·staf′, ·stäf′) *n. pl.* ·staves (-stāvz′) A stout, iron-tipped staff about 6½ feet long, formerly used in England as a weapon; also, the use of the quarterstaff.

quarter tone *Music* Half of a semitone. Also **quar·ter·tone** (kwôr′tər·tōn′).

quar·tet (kwôr·tet′) *n.* 1. A composition for four voices or instruments. 2. The four persons who perform such compositions. 3. Any group or set of four things of a kind. Also **quar·tette′**. [< F *quartette* < Ital.]

quar·to (kwôr′tō) *adj.* Having four leaves or eight pages to the sheet: a *quarto* book. — *n. pl.* ·tos A book or pamphlet having pages the size of a fourth of a sheet: often written **4to** or **4°**. [< L (*in*) *quarto* (in) fourth]

quartz (kwôrts) *n.* Silicon dioxide, SiO_2, a hard, vitreous mineral occurring in many varieties, sometimes massive, as jasper and chalcedony, or sometimes in colorless and transparent or diversely colored forms crystallizing in the hexagonal system. [< G *quarz*; ult. origin uncertain]

quartz crystal A thin section of pure quartz, accurately ground and polished for use in certain optical instruments and as a high-frequency oscillator in some electron tubes.

quartz lamp A mercury-vapor lamp that is enclosed in a quartz tube and transmits ultraviolet wavelengths.

quash¹ (kwosh) *v.t. Law* To make void or set aside, as an indictment; annul. — **Syn.** See ANNUL. [< OF < L *quassare* to shatter; meaning infl. by SQUASH¹]

quash² (kwosh) *v.t.* To put down or suppress forcibly or summarily: to *quash* a rebellion. [< OF < L *quassare* to shatter]

quasi- *prefix* 1. (With nouns) Resembling; not genuine, as in *quasi-adult*, *quasi-insight*. 2. (With adjectives) Nearly; almost, as in *quasi-complex*, *quasi-official*. [< L, as if]

qua·si-ju·di·cial (kwä′sī·jōō·dish′əl, -zī-, kwä′sē-) *adj.* Exercising functions of a judicial nature as a guide for official action, as a committee investigating facts and drawing conclusions from them.

quas·si·a (kwosh′ē·ə, kwosh′ə) *n.* 1. The wood of either of two tropical American trees yielding a variety of economic products. 2. A bitter drug prepared from this wood, used in medicine as a tonic, etc. 3. The tree itself. [< NL, after Graman *Quassi* who discovered its use in 1730]

qua·ter·na·ry (kwə·tûr′nə·rē) *adj.* 1. Consisting of four. 2. Fourth in order. — *n. pl.* ·ries 1. The number four; a group of four things. 2. *Math.* A quantic function having four variables. [< L *quaternarius* < *quaterni* by fours]

Qua·ter·na·ry (kwə·tûr′nə·rē) *adj. Geol.* Of, pertaining to, or designating a geological period and system of the Cenozoic era, following the Tertiary and still continuing. See chart for GEOLOGY. — *n.* The Quaternary system or period.

qua·ter·ni·on (kwə·tûr′nē·ən) *n.* A set, system, or file of four. [< LL < *quattuor* four < L *quattor*]

quat·rain (kwot′rān) *n.* A stanza or poem of four lines. [< F < *quatre* four]

quat·re·foil (kat′ər·foil′, kat′rə-) *n.* 1. A leaf, etc., having four leaflets. 2. *Archit.* An ornament with four foils or lobes. [< OF *quatre* four + *foil* leaf]

quat·tro·cen·to (kwat′rō·chen′tō) *n.* The 15th century as connected with the revival of art and literature, esp. in Italy. — *adj.* Of or pertaining to the quattrocento. [< Ital.]

QUATREFOILS

qua·ver (kwā′vər) *v.i.* 1. To tremble or shake: said usu. of the voice. 2. To produce trills or quavers in singing or in playing a musical instrument. — *v.t.* 3. To utter or sing in a tremulous voice. — *n.* 1. A quivering or tremulous motion. 2. A shake or trill, as in singing. 3. *Music Chiefly Brit.* An eighth note. [Freq. of obs. *quave*, ME *cwafian* to tremble] — **qua′ver·y** *adj.*

quay (kē) *n.* A wharf or artificial landing place where vessels may load or unload. [< OF *cai* hedge, wall]

quean (kwēn) *n.* A brazen or ill-behaved woman; harlot; prostitute. [OE *cwene* prostitute]

quea·sy (kwē′zē) *adj.* **quea·si·er**, **quea·si·est** 1. Sick at the stomach. 2. Nauseating; also, caused by nausea. 3. Easily nauseated. 4. Fastidious; squeamish. 5. Requiring to be carefully treated; delicate. 6. Hazardous. [ME *coisy*; origin unknown] — **quea′si·ly** *adv.* — **quea′si·ness** *n.*

Quech·ua (kech′wä) *n.* 1. One of a tribe of South American Indians. 2. The language of the Quechuas: also called *Incan*. Also spelled *Kechua*. — **Quech′uan** (kech′wən) *adj. & n.*

queen (kwēn) *n.* 1. The wife of a king. 2. A female sovereign or monarch. 3. A woman preeminent in a given sphere. 4. In chess, the most powerful piece, capable of moving any number of squares in a straight or diagonal line. 5. A playing card bearing a conventional picture of a queen. 6. *Entomol.* The single fully developed female in a colony of social insects, as bees, ants, etc. — *v.t.* 1. To make a queen of. 2. In chess, to make a queen of (a pawn) by moving it to the eighth row. — *v.i.* 3. To reign as or play the part of a queen. — **to queen it** To act in a domineering, queenly manner. [OE *cwēn* woman, queen]

Queen Anne's lace The wild carrot.

Queen Anne's War See WAR OF THE SPANISH SUCCESSION in table for WAR.

queen consort The wife of a reigning king, who does not share his sovereignty.

queen dowager The widow of a king.

queen·ly (kwēn′lē) *adj.* **queen·li·er**, **queen·li·est** 1. Of or like a queen. 2. Fit for a queen. — *adv.* In the manner of a queen. — **queen′li·ness** *n.*

queen mother A queen dowager who is mother of a reigning sovereign.

queen olive A large variety of Spanish olive.

queen post One of two upright suspending or sustaining posts of compression members, as in a roof truss.

queen's English King's English.

queer (kwir) *adj.* 1. Unusual; singular; odd. 2. Of questionable character. 3. *Slang* Counterfeit. 4. *Slang* Homosexual. — *n. Slang* 1. Counterfeit money. 2. *Slang* A homosexual person. — *v.t. U.S. Slang* To jeopardize or spoil. [Origin unknown] — **queer′ly** *adv.* — **queer′ness** *n.*

quell (kwel) *v.t.* 1. To put down or suppress by force; extinguish. **2.** To quiet; allay, as pain. [OE *cwellan* to kill] — **Syn. 1.** subdue, crush. **2.** soothe, still.

quel·que chose (kel′kə shōz′) *French* A trifle; something.

quench (kwench) *v.t.* **1.** To put out or extinguish, as a fire. **2.** To put an end to. **3.** To slake or satisfy (thirst). **4.** To suppress or repress, as emotions. **5.** To cool, as heated iron or steel, by thrusting into water or other liquid. [OE *cwincan* to grow less, disappear] — **quench′a·ble** *adj.* — **quench′er** *n.* — **quench′less** *adj.*

quer·u·lous (kwer′ə·ləs, -yə·ləs) *adj.* **1.** Disposed to complain or be fretful; captious. **2.** Indicating or expressing a complaining or whining disposition. [< LL < *queri* to complain] — **quer′u·lous·ly** *adv.* — **quer′u·lous·ness** *n.*

que·ry (kwir′ē) *v.* **·ried**, **·ry·ing** *v.t.* **1.** To inquire into; ask about. **2.** To ask questions of; interrogate. **3.** To express doubt concerning the correctness or truth of. — *v.i.* **4.** To have or express doubt; question. — **Syn.** See ASK. — *n. pl.* **·ries 1.** An inquiry or question. **2.** A doubt; interrogation. [< L < *quaerere* to ask]

quest (kwest) *n.* **1.** The act of seeking or looking for something; a search. **2.** An adventure or expedition, as in medieval romance. **3.** The person or persons engaged in a quest. — *v.t. & v.i.* To go on a quest or to search for (something). [< OF < L < *quaerere* to ask, seek] — **quest′er** *n.*

ques·tion (kwes′chən) *n.* **1.** An interrogative sentence calling for an answer; an inquiry. **2.** A subject of inquiry or debate; a matter to be decided; problem. **3.** A subject of dispute; a controversy. **4.** A proposition under discussion in a deliberative assembly. **5.** Possibility of disagreement or dispute; doubt: no *question* about it. **6.** The act of asking or inquiring. — **beside the question** Irrelevant; not pertinent. — **beyond (all) question** Not open to dispute; settled. — **out of the question** Not to be thought of; impossible. — *v.t.* **1.** To put a question or questions to; interrogate. **2.** To be uncertain of; doubt. **3.** To make objection to; challenge; dispute. — *v.i.* **4.** To ask a question or questions. — **Syn.** See ASK. [< OF < L < *quaerere* to ask] — **ques′tion·er** *n.*

ques·tion·a·ble (kwes′chən·ə·bəl) *adj.* **1.** Characterized by doubtful integrity, honesty, respectability, etc. **2.** Liable to be called in question; debatable. **3.** Uncertain; difficult to decide. — **ques′tion·a·bil′i·ty**, **ques′tion·a·ble·ness** *n.* — **ques′tion·a·bly** *adv.*

question mark A mark of punctuation (?) indicating that the sentence it closes is a direct question: also called *interrogation point*.

ques·tion·naire (kwes′chə·nâr′) *n.* A written or printed form comprising a series of questions submitted to a number of persons to obtain data for a survey or report. [< F]

quet·zal (ket·säl′) *n. pl.* **·zal·es** (-sä′lās) **1.** A bird of long, brilliant plumage, the national symbol of Guatemala, regarded as a deity by the Mayas. **2.** The standard monetary unit of Guatemala: in 1962 worth about one U.S. dollar. Also **que·zal** (kā·säl′). [< Sp.]

queue (kyōō) *n.* **1.** A pigtail. **2.** A line of persons or vehicles. — *v.i.* **queued**, **queu·ing** *Brit.* To form a line: usu. with *up*. Also **cue**. [< MF < L *cauda* a tail]

quib·ble (kwib′əl) *n.* **1.** An evasion of a point or question. **2.** A trivial distinction or objection; cavil. — *v.i.* **·bled**, **·bling** To evade the truth or the point in question, as by raising trivial objections. [< obs. *quib* < L *quibus*, ablative pl. of *qui* who, which] — **quib′bler** *n.*

quick (kwik) *adj.* **1.** Done or occurring in a short time; rapid; swift. **2.** Responding readily or eagerly to impressions or instruction: a *quick* mind. **3.** Alert; sensitive; perceptive: a *quick* ear. **4.** Easily aroused or excited; hasty: a *quick* temper. **5.** Nimble: *quick* fingers. **6.** Pregnant; with child. **7.** Refreshing; bracing. **8.** Burning briskly. — *n.* **1.** Those who are alive: chiefly in the phrase **the quick and the dead. 2.** The living flesh, esp. the tender flesh under a fingernail. **3.** The feelings: cut to the *quick*. **4.** A plant suitable for hedges. — *adv.* Quickly; rapidly. [OE *cwic* alive] — **quick′ness** *n.*

quick bread Any bread, biscuits. etc., whose leavening agent makes immediate baking possible.

quick·en (kwik′ən) *v.t.* **1.** To cause to move more rapidly; hasten or accelerate. **2.** To give or restore life to. **3.** To excite or arouse; stimulate: to *quicken* the appetite. — *v.i.* **4.** To move or act more quickly; become more rapid. **5.** To come or return to life; revive. **6.** To begin to manifest signs of life: said of the fetus. — **quick′en·er** *n.*

quick-freeze (kwik′frēz′) *v.t.* **-froze, -fro·zen, -freez·ing** To subject (food) to rapid refrigeration for storing at or below freezing temperatures.

quick·ie (kwik′ē) *n. U.S. Slang* Anything done hastily, as by short cuts or makeshift methods.

quick·lime (kwik′līm′) *n.* See under LIME¹.

quick·ly (kwik′lē) *adv.* In a quick manner; rapidly; soon.

quick march A march in quick time; quickstep.

quick·sand (kwik′sand′) *n.* A bed of sand, often of considerable depth, so water-soaked as to engulf any object, person, or animal resting or moving upon it.

quick·set (kwik′set′) *n.* **1.** A plant suitable for hedges, esp. hawthorn. **2.** A hedge made of it.

quick·sil·ver (kwik′sil′vər) *n.* **1.** Mercury in its liquid form. **2.** An amalgam of tin, used for the backs of mirrors. [OE *cwicseolfor.* Trans. of L *argentum vivum.*]

quick·step (kwik′step′) *n.* A march or dance written in a rapid tempo; also, a quick march.

quick-tem·pered (kwik′tem′pərd) *adj.* Easily angered.

quick time A marching step of 120 paces a minute, each pace of 30 inches, used in military drills and ceremonies.

quick-wit·ted (kwik′wit′id) *adj.* Having a ready wit or quick discernment; keen; alert. — **quick′-wit′ted·ly** *adv.* — **quick′-wit′ted·ness** *n.*

quid¹ (kwid) *n.* **1.** A small portion of chewing tobacco. **2.** A cud, as of a cow. [OE *cwudu.* Var. of CUD.]

quid² (kwid) *n. pl.* **quid** *Brit. Slang* A pound sterling, or a sovereign. [? Suggested by L QUID PRO QUO]

quid·di·ty (kwid′ə·tē) *n. pl.* **·ties 1.** The essence of a thing. **2.** A quibble; cavil. [< LL < L *quid* which, what]

quid·nunc (kwid′nungk′) *n.* One who seeks to know all that is going on; a busybody. [< L *quid nunc* what now]

quid pro quo (kwid′ prō kwō′) *Latin* **1.** Something for something; an equivalent in return. **2.** A substitution.

qui·es·cent (kwī·es′ənt) *adj.* **1.** Being in a state of repose or inaction; quiet; still. **2.** Resting free from anxiety, emotion, or agitation. [< L *quiescere* to be quiet] — **qui·es′cence** *n.* — **qui·es′cent·ly** *adv.*

qui·et (kwī′ət) *adj.* **1.** Making little or no noise. **2.** Having little or no motion; still; calm. **3.** Characterized by silence; also, retired or secluded: a *quiet* nook. **4.** Free from excessive activity, turmoil, or vexation: a *quiet* day at the office. **5.** Gentle; mild: a *quiet* temperament. **6.** Restful to the eye; reposeful: a *quiet* scene. **7.** Not showy or pretentious; modest: *quiet* decorations. **8.** Not loud or brash; reserved: a *quiet* sense of humor. **9.** In commerce, not busy or active. — **Syn.** See CALM. — *n.* **1.** The quality or condition of being quiet. **2.** Peace; tranquillity; calmness. — *v.t. & v.i.* To make or become quiet: often with *down*. — *adv.* In a quiet or peaceful manner. [< OF < L *quies, quietis* rest, repose] — **qui′et·ly** *adv.* — **qui′et·ness** *n.*

qui·et·ism (kwī′ə·tiz′əm) *n.* **1.** A form of religious mysticism in which the will and the intellect fix themselves in a passive contemplation of God. **2.** A state of quiet.

qui·et·ist (kwī′ə·tist) *n.* **1.** An advocate or practicer of quietism. **2.** One who seeks or enjoys quiet.

qui·e·tude (kwī′ə·tōōd, -tyōōd) *n.* A state or condition of calm or tranquillity; repose; rest.

qui·e·tus (kwī·ē′təs) *n.* **1.** A silencing or suppressing, as of a rumor. **2.** Anything that kills, as a blow. **3.** A final discharge, as of a debt. [< L *quietus est* he is quit]

quill (kwil) *n.* **1.** *Ornithol.* One of the large, strong flight feathers or tail feathers of a bird. **2.** Something made from a quill, as a pen or plectrum. **3.** *Zool.* One of the large, sharp spines of a porcupine or hedgehog. [ME *quil*]

quilt (kwilt) *n.* **1.** A bedcover made by stitching together firmly two layers of cloth or patchwork with some soft and warm substance (as wool or cotton) between them. **2.** Any bedcover, esp. if thick. **3.** A quilted skirt or other quilted article. — *v.t.* **1.** To stitch together (two pieces of material) with a soft substance between. **2.** To stitch in ornamental patterns or crossing lines. **3.** To pad or line with something soft. — *v.i.* **4.** To make a quilt or quilted work. [< OF < L *culcita* bed, cushion]

quilt·ing (kwil′ting) *n.* **1.** The act or process of making a quilt, or of stitching as in making a quilt. **2.** Material for quiltwork. **3.** A quilting bee or party.

quilting bee A social gathering of women for working on a quilt or quilts. Also **quilting frolic, quilting party.**

quince (kwins) *n.* **1.** The hard, acid, applelike fruit of a small tree of the rose family, used for preserves. **2.** The tree. [< MF < OF *cooin* < L < Gk. *kydōnion*]

qui·nine (kwī′nīn, *esp. Brit.* kwi·nēn′) *n. Chem.* A white, amorphous or slightly crystalline, very bitter alkaloid, $C_{20}H_{24}N_2O_2$, contained in cinchona barks, the salts of which are used in medicine for their tonic and antipyretic qualities and in the treatment of malaria. Also **quin·in** (kwin′in). [< Sp. *quina* cinchona bark and its extract]

quinine water A carbonated beverage flavored with quinine: also called *tonic*.

quin·qua·ge·nar·i·an (kwin′kwə·jə·nâr′ē·ən) *adj.* Of or pertaining to the age of 50 years, or to the decade between 50 and 60 years of age. — *n.* One who is of this age.

Quin·qua·ges·i·ma Sunday (kwin′kwə·jes′ə·mə) The Sunday before Ash Wednesday: also called *Shrove Sunday.* [< L *quinquagesima (dies)* fiftieth (day)]

PRONUNCIATION KEY: add, āce, câre, pälm; end, ēven; it, īce; odd, ōpen, ôrder; tŏŏk, pōōl; up, bûrn; ə = a in *above*, e in *sicken*, i in *flexible*, o in *melon*, u in *focus*; yōō = u in *fuse*; oil; pout; check; go; ring; thin; this; zh, vision.

quinque- *combining form* Five: *quinquennial.* Also, before vowels, **quinqu-.** [< L *quinque* five]

quin·quen·ni·al (kwin-kwen′ē-əl) *adj.* Occurring every five years, or once in five years; also, lasting five years. —*n.* A quinquennial anniversary. [< L *quinque* five + *annus* year]

quin·sy (kwin′zē) *n. Pathol.* A suppurative inflammation of the tonsils. [< Med.L < Gk. *kynanchē* dog's collar]

quint (kwint) *n.* **1.** A fifth. **2.** A set of five. **3.** *Informal* A quintuplet. [< L *quintus* fifth]

quin·tal (kwin′təl) *n.* **1.** A measure of weight, a hundred-weight. **2.** In the metric system, 100 kilograms. [< MF < Med.L *quintale* < Arabic *quintar* < LL *centarium* one hundred pieces of gold]

quin·tes·sence (kwin-tes′əns) *n.* **1.** An extract from anything, containing in concentrated form its most essential principle. **2.** The purest and most essential part of anything. [< F < Med.L *quinta essentia* fifth essence] — **quin·tes·sen·tial** (kwin′tə-sen′shəl) *adj.*

quin·tet (kwin-tet′) *n.* **1.** A musical composition for five voices or instruments; also, the five persons performing it. **2.** Any group of five persons or things. Also **quin·tette′.** [< F < Ital. *quintetto,* dim. of *quinto* fifth]

quin·til·lion (kwin-til′yən) *n.* **1.** *U.S.* A thousand quadrillions, written as 1 followed by 18 zeros: a cardinal number. **2.** *Brit.* A million quadrillions (def. 2), written as 1 followed by 30 zeros: a cardinal number. —*adj.* Being a quintillion in number. [< *quinti-* five + *(mi)llion*] — **quin·til′lionth** *adj. & n.*

quin·tu·ple (kwin′tōō-pəl, -tyōō-, kwin-tōō′pəl, -tyōō′-) *v.t. & v.i.* **·pled, ·pling** To multiply by five; make or become five times as much or as large. —*adj.* **1.** Consisting of five things united or of five parts. **2.** Multiplied by five. —*n.* A number or a sum five times as great as another. [< F < LL *quintuplex* fivefold]

quin·tu·plet ((kwin′tōō-plit, -tyōō-, kwin-tōō′plit, -tyōō′-, -tup′lit) *n.* **1.** Five things of a kind used or occurring together. **2.** One of five born of the same mother at one birth.

quin·tu·pli·cate (*adj.* kwin-tōō′plə-kit, -tyōō′-; *v.* kwin-tōō′plə-kāt, -tyōō′-) *adj.* **1.** Fivefold. **2.** Raised to the fifth power. —*v.t. & v.i.* **·cat·ed, ·cat·ing** To multiply by five; quintuple. —*n.* One of five identical things. — **in quintuplicate** So as to have five identical copies. — **quin·tu′pli·cate·ly** *adv.* — **quin·tu′pli·ca′tion** *n.*

quip (kwip) *n.* **1.** A sarcastic or witty jest or retort. **2.** A quibble. **3.** An odd, fantastic action or object. —*v.i.* **quipped, quip·ping** To make a witty remark; jest. [Prob. < L *quippe* indeed] — **quip′pish** *adj.*

quip·ster (kwip′stər) *n.* One who makes quips.

quire (kwīr) *n.* **1.** The twentieth part of a ream of paper; 24 (or 25) sheets. **2.** A set of all the sheets necessary to make a book. —*v.t.* **quired, quir·ing** To fold or separate into quires. [< OF *quaer,* ult. < L *quaterni* a set of four]

Quir·i·nal (kwir′ə-nəl) *n.* **1.** One of the Seven Hills of Rome, containing the **Quirinal palace,** after 1870 the official residence of the kings of Italy. **2.** The monarchical or civil government of Italy: distinguished from the *Vatican.* —*adj.* Pertaining to or situated on the Quirinal.

quirk (kwûrk) *n.* **1.** A personal peculiarity, mannerism, or caprice. **2.** A quibble. **3.** A sharp turn or twist. **4.** A sudden curve or flourish, as in writing. **5.** A bright retort; quip. [Origin uncertain] — **quirk′y** *adj.*

quirt (kwûrt) *n.* A short-handled riding whip with a braided lash. —*v.t.* To strike with a quirt. [< Am. Sp. *cuarta*]

quis·ling (kwiz′ling) *n.* One who betrays his country to the enemy and is then given political power by the conquerors. [after Vidkun *Quisling,* 1887–1945, Norwegian Nazi party leader and traitor] — **quis′ling·ism** *n.*

quit (kwit) *v.* **quit** or **quit·ted, quit·ting** *v.t.* **1.** To cease or desist from; discontinue. **2.** To give up; renounce. **3.** To go away from; leave. **4.** To let go of (something held). —*v.i.* **5.** To stop; cease; discontinue. **6.** To leave; depart. **7.** *Informal* To resign from a position, etc. —*adj.* Released, relieved, or absolved from something; clear; free; rid. —*n.* The act of quitting. — **to be quits** To be even (with another). — **to cry quits** To declare (oneself) willing to stop competing. [< OF < Med.L < L *quietus* at rest]

quit·claim (kwit′klām′) *n. Law* A full release and acquittance given by one to another in regard to a certain demand, suit, or right of action. Also **quit′claim′ance** (-əns). —*v.t.* To relinquish or give up claim or title to; release from a claim. [< MF *quite clamer* to declare quit or free]

quite (kwīt) *adv.* **1.** To the fullest extent; totally: *quite dead.* **2.** Really; truly. **3.** *Informal* To a great or considerable extent; noticeably; very; *quite ill.* ◆ The phrase *quite a* is used in many idioms to indicate considerable but indefinite number, size, quantity, etc., as in *quite a lot* (a good deal), *quite a few* (many), *quite a while* (a long while). It is also used in informal expressions with the sense of "wonderful, great, etc.," as in *quite a guy.* [ME; var. of QUIT, adj.]

quit·rent (kwit′rent′) *n.* A fixed rent formerly paid by a freeholder, whereby he was released from feudal services.

quit·tance (kwit′ns) *n.* **1.** Discharge or release, as from a debt or obligation. **2.** A document or receipt certifying this. **3.** A recompense or repayment. [< OF < *quitter* to quit]

quit·ter (kwit′ər) *n.* One who quits needlessly; a shirker.

quiv·er[1] (kwiv′ər) *v.i.* To shake with a slight, tremulous motion; vibrate; tremble. —*n.* The act or fact of quivering; a trembling or shaking. [Var. of QUAVER]

quiv·er[2] (kwiv′ər) *n.* A portable case for arrows; also, its contents. [< AF *quivier,* OF *cuivre* < OHG *kochar*]

quix·ot·ic (kwik-sot′ik) *adj.* **1.** Of, pertaining to, or like Don Quixote. **2.** Ridiculously chivalrous or romantic; having high but impractical sentiments, aims, etc. — **quix·ot′i·cal·ly** *adv.* — **quix·ot·ism** (kwik′sə-tiz′əm) *n.*

quiz (kwiz) *n.* **1.** The act of questioning; esp., an informal oral or written examination of a class or individual. **2.** An eccentric person or thing. **3.** A hoax; practical joke. —*v.t.* **quizzed, quiz·zing** **1.** To examine by asking questions; question. **2.** *Brit.* To make fun of; ridicule. — **Syn.** See ASK. [Origin unknown] — **quiz′zer** *n.*

quiz·zi·cal (kwiz′i·kəl) *adj.* **1.** Given to chaffing or bantering. **2.** Queer; odd. **3.** Questioning; puzzled: a *quizzical* smile. — **quiz′zi·cal·ly** *adv.*

quoin (koin, kwoin) *n.* **1.** An external angle or corner of a building. **2.** A stone or stones forming such an angle. **3.** A wedge or wedgelike piece, as one of the stones in an arch. **4.** *Printing* A wedge or pair of wedges for locking type in a chase or galley. —*v.t.* To provide, secure, or support with a quoin or quoins. [Var. of COIN]

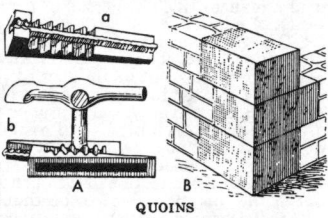

QUOINS

A Printer's: a Single quoin, *b* Pair ready for locking with key. *B* Quoins of dressed stone.

quoit (kwoit, *esp. Brit.* koit) *n.* **1.** A ring of metal, rope, etc., thrown in a game at a short stake, either encircling it or coming as close to it as possible. **2.** *pl.* (construed *as sing.*) The game so played. —*v.t.* To pitch as a quoit. [< MF *coite,* ? flat stone < OF *cuilte.* See QUILT.]

quon·dam (kwon′dəm) *adj.* Having been formerly; former. [< L]

Quon·set hut (kwon′sit) A prefabricated, metal structure the roof of which is half of a cylinder cut lengthwise and resting on the ground: a trade name. [after *Quonset,* Rhode Island, where first made]

quo·rum (kwôr′əm, kwō′rəm) *n.* The number of members of any deliberative or corporate body as is necessary for the legal transaction of business, commonly, a majority. [< L, genitive plural of *qui* who]

quo·ta (kwō′tə) *n.* A proportional part or share required from each person, group, state, etc., for making up a certain number or quantity. [< Med.L < L *quotus* how many]

quot·a·ble (kwō′tə·bəl) *adj.* Suitable for quotation. — **quot′a·bil′i·ty** *n.*

quo·ta·tion (kwō-tā′shən) *n.* **1.** The act of quoting. **2.** The words quoted or cited. **3.** A price quoted or current, as of securities, etc.: the *quotations* for wheat. — **quo·ta′tion·al** *adj.* — **quo·ta′tion·al·ly** *adv.* — **quo·ta′tion·ist** *n.*

quotation mark Either of the marks placed at the beginning and end of a word or passage that is an exact quotation of the original. In English usage, one or two inverted commas (' ") mark the beginning of a quotation, and correspondingly, one or two apostrophes (' ") the close, the single marks being used to set off a quotation within a quotation.

quote (kwōt) *v.* **quot·ed, quot·ing** *v.t.* **1.** To reproduce the words of. **2.** To repeat or cite (a rule, author, etc.), as for authority or illustration. **3.** In commerce: **a** To state (a price). **b** To give the current or market price of. **4.** *Printing* To enclose within quotation marks. —*v.i.* **5.** To make a quotation, as from a book. —*n.* **1.** Loosely, a quotation. **2.** A quotation mark. [< Med.L *quotare* to distinguish by number < L *quot* how many] — **quot′a·ble** *adj.* — **quot′er** *n.* — **quote′wor′thy** (-wûr′thē) *adj.* — **quot′ing·ly** *adv.*

quoth (kwōth) *v.t.* Said or spoke; uttered: the imperfect tense of the obsolete verb *queth,* used only in the first and third persons, the subject always following the verb: *quoth* he. [OE *cwæth,* pt. of *cwethan* to say]

quo·tid·i·an (kwō-tid′ē·ən) *adj.* Recurring or occurring every day. —*n.* A fever that returns every day. [< OF, or < L *quotidianus* daily]

quo·tient (kwō′shənt) *n. Math.* The result obtained by division; a number indicating how many times one quantity is contained in another. [< L *quotiens* how often]

quo war·ran·to (kwō wô-ran′tō, wo-) *Law* A proceeding, usu. criminal in form but in substance civil, by which a government or sovereign seeks to recover an office or franchise. [< L, by what warrant]

R

r, R (är) *n.* *pl.* **r's** or **rs, R's** or **Rs, ars** (ärz) **1.** The 18th letter of the English alphabet. **2.** The sound represented by the letter *r*. — *symbol* **1.** *Chem.* An alkyl group. **2.** *Math.* Ratio. **3.** *Electr.* Resistance. — **the three R's** Reading, writing, and arithmetic regarded as the essential elements of a primary education.

Ra (rä) The supreme Egyptian deity, the sun god, usu. represented as a hawk-headed man crowned with the solar disk and the sacred serpent: also *Re*.

rab·bet (rab′it) *n.* **1.** A recess or groove in or near the edge of one piece of wood, etc., cut so as to receive the edge of another piece. **2.** A joint so made. — *v.* **·bet·ed, ·bet·ing** *v.t.* **1.** To cut a rabbet in. **2.** To unite in a rabbet. — *v.i.* **3.** To be jointed by a rabbet. [< OF < *rabattre* to beat down]

RABBET JOINTS

rab·bi (rab′ī) *n.* *pl.* **·bis** or **·bies** In Judaism: **a** The spiritual head of a Jewish community, authorized to perform religious duties. **b** Master; teacher: a title for one learned in the Law. Also **rab′bin** (-in). [< Hebrew *rabbī* my master]

rab·bin·ate (rab′in·āt) *n.* **1.** The office or term of office of a rabbi. **2.** Rabbis collectively.

Rab·bin·ic (rə·bin′ik) *n.* The Hebrew language as used in late ancient and early medieval periods.

rab·bin·i·cal (rə·bin′i·kəl) *adj.* Pertaining to the rabbis or to their opinions, languages, or writings. Also **rab·bin′ic.** — **rab·bin′i·cal·ly** *adv.*

rab·bit (rab′it) *n.* **1.** Any of a family of various small, long-eared mammals allied to but smaller than the hare, as the common American cottontail. **2.** The pelt of a rabbit or hare. **3.** Welsh rabbit. — *v.i.* To hunt rabbits. [Akin to Walloon *robett*, Flemish *robbe*] — **rab′bit·er** *n.*

rabbit fever Tularemia.

rabbit foot The left hind foot of a rabbit, carried as a good-luck charm. Also **rab·bit's foot.**

rabbit hutch A coop in which domestic rabbits are bred.

rabbit punch A short chopping blow at the base of the skull or back of the neck.

rab·ble (rab′əl) *n.* A disorderly crowd or mob. — **the rabble** The populace or lower classes: a contemptuous term. — *adj.* Of, suited to, or characteristic of a rabble; disorderly. — *v.t.* **·bled, ·bling** To mob. [? < RABBLE³]

rab·ble-rous·er (rab′əl·rou′zər) *n.* One who tries to incite mobs by arousing prejudices and passions.

Rab·e·lai·si·an (rab′ə·lā′zē·ən, -zhən) *adj.* **1.** Of, pertaining to, or resembling Rabelais or his works. **2.** Bawdy and boisterous. — *n.* A student or imitator of Rabelais. — **Rab′e·lai′si·an·ism, Rab′e·la′ism** *n.*

rab·id (rab′id) *adj.* **1.** Affected with, arising from, or pertaining to rabies; mad. **2.** Unreasonably zealous; fanatical; violent. **3.** Furious; raging. Also **rab′ic.** [< L *rabere* to be mad] — **rab′id·ly** *adv.* — **rab′id·ness** *n.*

ra·bies (rā′bēz, -bi·ēz) *n.* An acute, infectious, usu. fatal disease of certain animals, esp. of dogs, readily transmissible to man by the bite of an affected animal: also called *hydrophobia*. [< L, madness] — **ra′bi·et′ic** (-et′ik) *adj.*

rac·coon (ra·kōōn′) *n.* **1.** A North American nocturnal carnivore, grayish brown with a black cheek patch and a black-and-white-ringed bushy tail. **2.** The fur of this animal. Also spelled **racoon.** [Alter. of Algonquian *arakunem* hand-scratcher]

race¹ (rās) *n.* **1.** One of the major zoological subdivisions of mankind, regarded as having a common origin and exhibiting a relatively constant set of physical traits, such as pigmentation, hair form, and facial and bodily proportions. **2.** Any group of people or any grouping of peoples having, or assumed to have, common characteristics, habits, appearance, etc. **3.** A nation: the German *race*. **4.** A genealogical or family stock; clan: the *race* of MacGregor. **5.** Pedigree; lineage: a noble *race*. **6.** Any class of beings having characteristics uniting them, or differentiating them from others: the *race* of lawyers. **7.** *Biol.* A group of plants or animals, having distinct characteristics that are passed on to offspring. [< MF < Ital. *razza*; origin uncertain]

race² (rās) *n.* **1.** A contest to determine the relative speed of the contestants. **2.** Any contest. **3.** Movement or progression, esp. when regular or swift. **4.** Duration of life; course; career. **5.** A swift current of water or its channel. **6.** A sluice or channel by which to conduct water to or from a water wheel or around a dam. **7.** Any groove along which some part of a machine slides or is guided. — *v.* **raced, racing** *v.i.* **1.** To take part in a contest of speed. **2.** To move at great or top speed. **3.** To move at an accelerated or too great speed: said of machinery. — *v.t.* **4.** To contend against in a race. **5.** To cause to race. [< ON *rás*]

race·course (rās′kôrs′, -kōrs′) *n.* A racetrack.

race·horse (rās′hôrs′) *n.* A horse bred and trained for contests of speed.

ra·ceme (rā·sēm′, rə-) *n.* **1.** *Bot.* An inflorescence in which the flowers are arranged singly at intervals on a common axis. **2.** *Chem.* A racemic compound. [< L *racemus* cluster]

ra·ce·mic (rā·sē′mik, -sem′ik, rə-) *adj.* **1.** *Bot.* Of, pertaining to, or contained in racemes. **2.** *Chem.* Indicating any compound that is optically inactive, but separable into two isomers, one dextrorotatory, the other levorotatory. Also **rac·e·moid** (ras′ə·moid).

rac·e·mose (ras′ə·mōs) *adj.* Like a raceme in form or nature. Also **rac′e·mous** (-məs). — **rac′e·mose·ly** *adv.*

rac·er (rā′sər) *n.* **1.** One who races. **2.** Anything designed or used for racing, as a car, yacht, etc. **3.** One of various colubrine snakes, as the blacksnake.

race riot A violent conflict between groups in the same community, based on differences of color or creed.

race suicide The slow reduction in numbers of a people through voluntary failure on the part of individuals to maintain the birth rate at or above the level of the death rate.

race·track (rās′trak′) *n.* A track or course over which a horse race, dog race, etc., is run: also called *racecourse*.

race·way (rās′wā′) *n.* **1.** A channel for conducting water. **2.** A tube for protecting wires, as in a subway. **3.** *U.S.* A racetrack for trotting horses.

Ra·chel (rā′chəl) The wife of Jacob; mother of Joseph and Benjamin. *Gen.* xxix 6. [< Hebrew, lit., ewe]

ra·chi·tis (rə·kī′tis) *n.* *Pathol.* Rickets. [< NL < Gk. < *rachis* spine] — **ra·chit′ic** (-kit′ik) *adj.*

ra·cial (rā′shəl) *adj.* Of, pertaining to, or characteristic of a race, races, or descent. — **ra′cial·ly** *adv.*

ra·cial·ism (rā′shəl·iz′əm) *n.* Racism. — **ra′cial·ist** *n.*

ra·cism (rā′siz·əm) *n.* **1.** An irrational belief in or advocacy of the superiority of a given group, people, or nation, usu. one's own, on the basis of racial differences having no scientific validity. **2.** Social action or government policy based upon such assumed differences. — **ra′cist** *n.*

rack¹ (rak) *n.* **1.** An open grating, framework, or the like, in or on which articles may be placed. **2.** A triangular frame for arranging the balls on a billiard table. **3.** A container or framework in an airplane for carrying bombs. **4.** *Mech.* A bar or the like having teeth that engage with those of a gearwheel, pinion, or worm gear. **5.** A machine for stretching or making tense; esp., an instrument of torture that stretches the limbs of victims. **6.** Torture or punishment as by the rack; also, intense mental or physical suffering. **7.** A wrenching or straining, as from a storm. — *v.t.* **1.** To place or arrange in or on a rack. **2.** To torture on the rack. **3.** To torment. **4.** To strain, as with the effort of thinking: to *rack* one's brains. **5.** To raise (rents) excessively. — **to rack up** *U.S. Informal* To achieve: to *rack up* a perfect score. [< MDu. < *recken* to stretch] — **rack′er** *n.*

rack² (rak) *n.* **1.** Thin, flying, or broken clouds. **2.** Any floating vapor. — *v.i.* To move rapidly; send, as clouds before the wind. Also spelled **wrack.** [< Scand.]

rack³ (rak) *n.* Destruction; wreck; demolition: now usu. in the phrase **rack and ruin.** — **to rack up** *U.S. Slang* To wreck. [Var. of WRACK²]

rack·et¹ (rak′it) *n.* **1.** A nearly elliptical hoop of bent wood, usu. strung with catgut or nylon, and having a handle, used in striking a tennis ball, etc. **2.** A large wooden sole or shoe to support the weight of a man or horse on swampy ground.

3. A snowshoe. **4.** An organ stop. **5.** *Often pl.* A game resembling court tennis, played in a court with four walls. Often *racquet.* [< MF < Arabic *rāha* palm of the hand]

rack·et² (rak'it) *n.* **1.** A clattering, vociferous, or confused noise. **2.** *Informal* A scheme for getting money or other benefits by fraud, intimidation, or other illegitimate means. **3.** *Slang* Any business or occupation. **4.** Social activity or excitement. — *v.i.* **1.** To make a loud, clattering noise. **2.** To indulge in noisy sport or diversion. [Prob. imit.]

rack·et·eer (rak'ə-tir') *n.* **1.** One engaged in a racket. **2.** Formerly, a bootlegger or rumrunner. — **rack'et·eer'ing** *n.*

rack·et·y (rak'it-ē) *adj.* Making a racket; noisy.

rac·on·teur (rak'on-tûr', *Fr.* rà-kôn'tœr') *n.* A skilled storyteller.

ra·coon (ra-kōōn') See RACCOON.

rac·quet (rak'it) See RACKET¹.

rac·y (rā'sē) *adj.* **rac·i·er, rac·i·est** **1.** Having a spirited or pungent interest; spicy; piquant. **2.** Having a characteristic flavor assumed to be indicative of origin, as wine; rich, fresh, or fragrant. **3.** Suggestive; slightly immodest: a *racy* story. [< RACE] — **rac'i·ly** *adv.* — **rac'i·ness** *n.*

ra·dar (rā'där) *n. Telecom.* An electronic device that locates objects by beaming radio-frequency impulses that are reflected back from the object, and determines its distance by a measurement of the time elapsed between transmission and reception of the impulses. [< *ra(dio) d(etection) a(nd) r(anging)*]

radar beacon *Telecom.* The part of a radar that transmits radio-frequency waves. Also **ra·con** (rā'kon).

ra·dar·scope (rā'där-skōp) *n. Telecom.* The oscilloscope of a radar set.

rad·dle (rad'l) *v.t.* **·dled, ·dling** To intertwine or weave together. [< OF < MHG *reidel* stout stick]

ra·di·al (rā'dē-əl) *adj.* **1.** Pertaining to, consisting of, or resembling a ray or radius. **2.** Extending from a center like rays. **3.** Of or pertaining to the radius or a radiating part. **4.** *Anat.* Denoting the radius. **5.** Developing uniformly on all sides. — *n.* A radiating part. — **ra'di·al·ly** *adv.*

radial engine A multicylinder internal-combustion engine having its cylinders arranged like the spokes in a wheel.

ra·di·an (rā'dē-ən) *n. Math.* **1.** An arc equal in length to the radius of the circle of which it is a part. **2.** The angle subtended by such an arc, equal to 57° 17′ 44.80625″ +.

ra·di·ance (rā'dē-əns) *n.* The quality or state of being radiant; brightness; effulgence. Also **ra'di·an·cy, ra'di·ant·ness.**

ra·di·ant (rā'dē-ənt) *adj.* **1.** Emitting rays of light or heat. **2.** Beaming with light or brightness, kindness, or love: a *radiant* smile. **3.** Resembling rays. **4.** Consisting of or transmitted by radiation: *radiant* heat. — *n.* **1.** A straight line proceeding from and conceived as revolving around a given point. **2.** *Astron.* That point in the heavens from which, during a meteoric shower, the meteors seem to shoot. **3.** The luminous point from which light proceeds or is made to radiate. **4.** That which radiates. [< L *radians, -antis,* ppr. of *radiare* to emit rays] — **ra'di·ant·ly** *adv.*

radiant energy *Physics* The energy associated with and transmitted in the form of waves, esp. those of electromagnetic frequencies, as heat, light, radio waves, X-rays, etc.

ra·di·ate (*v.* rā'dē-āt; *adj. & n.* rā'dē-it) *v.* **·at·ed, ·at·ing** *v.i.* **1.** To emit rays or radiation; be radiant. **2.** To issue forth in rays, as light from the sun. **3.** To spread out from a center, as the spokes of a wheel. — *v.t.* **4.** To send out or emit in rays. **5.** To cause to spread as if from a center; diffuse. **6.** To show as if shining with. — *adj.* Divided or separated into rays; having rays; radiating. — **ra'di·a·tive** *adj.*

ra·di·a·tion (rā'dē-ā'shən) *n.* **1.** The act of radiating, or the state of being radiated. **2.** *Physics* **a** The emission and propagation of radiant energy, esp. by radioactive substances capable of affecting living tissue. **b** The stages of emission, absorption, and transmission involved in this.

radiation sickness *Pathol.* A condition due to absorption of excess radiation and marked by fatigue, vomiting, internal hemorrhage, and progressive tissue breakdown.

ra·di·a·tor (rā'dē-ā'tər) *n.* **1.** That which radiates. **2.** A chamber, coil, or flat hollow vessel, through which is passed steam or hot water for warming a building or apartment. **3.** In engines, a nest of tubes for cooling water flowing through them. **4.** *Physics* Any source of radiant energy, whether in the form of particles or of electromagnetic waves. — **ra'di·a·to'ry** (-ə-tôr'ē, -tō'rē) *adj.*

rad·i·cal (rad'i-kəl) *adj.* **1.** Of, proceeding from, or pertaining to the root or foundation; fundamental. **2.** Thoroughgoing; extreme: *radical* measures. **3.** *Math.* Pertaining to the root or roots of a number. **4.** In etymology, belonging or referring to a root or a root syllable. **5.** *Chem.* Pertaining to a radical. **6.** Of or pertaining to political radicals. — *n.* **1.** One who carries his theories or convictions to their furthest application. **2.** In politics, one who advocates widespread governmental changes and reforms at the earliest opportunity. **3.** The primitive or underived part of a word; a root. **4.** *Math.* **a** A quantity that is the root of another quantity. **b** The radical sign. **5.** *Chem.* A group of atoms that acts as a unit in a compound and may pass unchanged through a series of reactions. [< LL *radicalis* having roots] — **rad'i·cal·ly** *adv.* — **rad'i·cal·ness** *n.*

rad·i·cal·ism (rad'i-kəl-iz'əm) *n.* **1.** The state of being radical. **2.** Advocacy of radical measures.

radical sign *Math.* The symbol √ placed before a quantity to indicate that a designated root is to be taken.

rad·i·cle (rad'i-kəl) *n.* **1.** *Bot.* **a** The embryonic root below the cotyledon of a plant. **b** A small root or rootlet. **2.** *Anat.* A rootlike part, as the initial fiber of a nerve. [< L *radicula,* dim. of *radix, -icis* root]

ra·di·i (rā'dē-ī) Plural of RADIUS.

ra·di·o (rā'dē-ō) *n. pl.* **·os** **1.** The science and technique of communicating by means of radio waves that have been modulated to carry information either in the form of sound or of a code. **2.** A radio program or broadcast. **3.** A receiver, transmitter, or other radio apparatus. **4.** A radio message or radiogram. **5.** The radio business and industry. — *adj.* Of, pertaining to, designating, employing, or produced by radiant energy, esp. in the form of electromagnetic waves. — *v.t. & v.i.* **ra·di·oed, ra·di·o·ing** To transmit (a message, etc.) or communicate with (someone) by radio. Also, *Brit., wireless.* [< RADIO(TELEGRAPHY)]

radio- *combining form* **1.** Radial. **2.** Radio; produced or obtained by or related to radio. **3.** Radioactive. **4.** Radiation. [< L *radius* ray]

ra·di·o·ac·tive (rā'dē-ō-ak'tiv) *adj.* Pertaining to, exhibiting, caused by, or characteristic of radioactivity.

radioactive series *Physics* The sequence of disintegration products through which a radioactive element passes before reaching a stable form as an isotope of lead. The three principal series are those of uranium, thorium, and actinium.

ra·di·o·ac·tiv·i·ty (rā'dē-ō-ak-tiv'ə-tē) *n. Physics* The spontaneous nuclear disintegration of certain elements and isotopes, with the emission of nucleons or of electromagnetic radiation; also, a particular form of such disintegration.

radio astronomy The branch of astronomy and astrophysics that studies celestial objects by the analysis of radio waves intercepted by radio telescopes.

radio beacon A stationary radio transmitter that sends out characteristic signals for the guidance of ships and aircraft.

radio beam *Aeron.* A continuous radio signal along an airway to guide aircraft.

ra·di·o·bi·ol·o·gy (rā'dē-ō-bī-ol'ə-jē) *n.* The study of the effects of radiation upon living organisms.

ra·di·o·broad·cast (rā'dē-ō-brôd'kast', -käst') *v.t. & v.i.* **·cast** or **·cast·ed, ·cast·ing** To broadcast by radio. — *n.* A broadcast. — **ra'di·o·broad'cast'er** *n.*

ra·di·o·car·bon (rā'dē-ō-kär'bən) *n. Physics* The radioactive isotope of carbon of mass 14 with a half life of about 5570 years, much used in the dating of fossils, artifacts, and certain kinds of geological formations: also called *carbon 14.*

radio compass *Aeron.* A directional radio receiver that indicates the bearing of a radio transmitting station.

ra·di·o·dat·ing (rā'dē-ō-dā'ting) *n.* The technique of dating objects by measuring their radioactivity.

ra·di·o·el·e·ment (rā'dē-ō-el'ə-mənt) *n. Physics* Any isotope or element exhibiting radioactivity.

radio fix The position of an aircraft, ship, or radio transmitter, as determined by use of radio signals.

radio frequency Any wave frequency lying between about 10 kilocycles and 30,000 megacycles.

ra·di·o·gram (rā'dē-ō-gram') *n.* **1.** A message sent by radio. **2.** A radiograph.

ra·di·o·graph (rā'dē-ō-graf', -gräf') *n.* A picture made by means of radioactivity; an X-ray photograph. — *v.t.* To make a radiograph of. — **ra·di·og'ra·pher** (-og'rə-fər) *n.* — **ra'di·o·graph'ic** or **·i·cal** *adj.* — **ra'di·og'ra·phy** *n.*

ra·di·o·i·so·tope (rā'dē-ō-ī'sə-tōp) *n. Physics* A radioactive isotope, usu. one produced artificially from a normally stable element, used in biological and physical research and in medicine for diagnostic and therapeutic purposes.

ra·di·ol·o·gy (rā'dē-ol'ə-jē) *n.* The branch of science that relates to radiant energy and its applications, especially in the diagnosis and treatment of disease. — **ra·di·o·log·i·cal** (rā'dē-ə-loj'i-kəl) or **ra'di·o·log'ic** *adj.* — **ra·di·ol'o·gist** *n.*

ra·di·om·e·ter (rā'dē-om'ə-tər) *n.* An instrument for detecting and measuring radiant energy by converting it into mechanical energy, as by the rotation of blackened vanes suspended in a vacuum and exposed to sunlight. — **ra'di·o·met'ric** (-met'rik) *adj.* — **ra'di·om'e·try** *n.*

ra·di·o·phone (rā'dē-ō-fōn') *n.* **1.** Any device for the production or transmission of sound by radiant energy. **2.** A radiotelephone. — **ra'di·o·phon'ic** (-fon'ik) *adj.* — **ra'di·oph'o·ny** (-of'ə-nē) *n.*

ra·di·o·pho·tog·ra·phy (rā'dē-ō-fə-tog'rə-fē) *n.* The transmission of a photograph by radio waves. — **ra'di·o·pho'to·graph** (-fō'tə-graf, -gräf) *n.*

radio pill *Med.* A tiny radio transmitter that can be introduced into the body to transmit physiological data.

ra·di·o·scope (rādē·ō·skōp′) *n.* An apparatus for detecting radioactivity or X-rays.

ra·di·os·co·py (rā′dē·os′kə·pē) *n.* Examination of opaque bodies with the aid of X-rays or some other form of radiant energy. — **ra′di·o·scop′ic** (-skop′ik) or **-i·cal** *adj.*

ra·di·o·sonde (rā′dē·ō·sond′) *n. Meteorol.* An airborne device, usu. attached to a balloon, that radios meteorological data to the ground. [< F < *radio* radio + *sonde* sounding]

radio spectrum The full range of frequencies pertaining to and associated with radiant energy; esp., the radio frequencies.

radio star Any of a large number of stars that may be identified and studied by means of the radio waves they emit.

radio station An installation of all the equipment needed for effective radio broadcasting, esp. when used for commercial or educational purposes and licensed to employ an assigned frequency and power.

ra·di·o·stron·tium (rā′dē·ō·stron′shəm, -tē·əm) *n. Physics* Strontium 90.

ra·di·o·tel·e·gram (rā′dē·ō·tel′ə·gram) *n.* A message sent by radiotelegraphy.

ra·di·o·te·leg·ra·phy (rā′dē·ō·tə·leg′rə·fē) *n.* Telegraphic communication using radio waves. — **ra′di·o·tel′e·graph′ic** (-tel′ə·graf′ik) — **ra′di·o·tel′e·graph** (-graf, -gräf) *n.*

ra·di·o·tel·e·phone (rā′dē·ō·tel′ə·fōn) *n.* A telephone that operates by means of radio waves. — **ra′di·o·tel′e·phon′ic** (-tel′ə·fon′ik) *adj.* — **ra′di·o·te·leph′o·ny** (-tə·lef′ə·nē) *n.*

radio telescope *Astron.* A highly sensitive radio receiver, designed to receive radio waves from outer space.

ra·di·o·ther·a·py (rā′dē·ō·ther′ə·pē) *n. Med.* The treatment of disease by X-rays and other forms of radioactivity.

ra·di·o·ther·my (rā′dē·ō·thûr′mē) *n. Med.* Diathermy.

ra·di·o·tho·ri·um (rā′dē·ō·thôr′ē·əm, -thō′rē·əm) *n.* A radioactive isotope of thorium, with a half life of 1.9 years.

radio tube An electron tube.

radio wave Any electromagnetic wave having a radio frequency; a Hertzian wave.

rad·ish (rad′ish) *n.* **1.** The pungent, edible root of a tall, branching herb of the mustard family. **2.** The herb yielding this root. [OE *rædic* < L *radix, radicis* root]

ra·di·um (rā′dē·əm) *n.* A powerfully radioactive metallic element (symbol Ra), obtained principally as a disintegration product of uranium. It has a half life of about 1,600 years, emitting alpha and beta particles and gamma rays in a succession of stages beginning with radon and continuing to radium G, a stable isotope of lead. See ELEMENT. [< NL < L *radius* ray + -IUM]

radium therapy The treatment of diseases, esp. cancer, by means of radium.

ra·di·us (rā′dē·əs) *n. pl.* **·di·i** (-dē·ī) **1.** A straight line from the center of a circle or sphere to the circumference or surface. **2.** *Anat.* The thicker and shorter bone of the forearm, on the same side as the thumb. **3.** *Zool.* A similar bone in the forelimb of other vertebrates. **4.** *Bot.* A ray floret of a composite flower. **5.** A ray or radiating part. **6.** A circular area or boundary measured by the length of its radius. **7.** Sphere, scope, or limit, as of activity. **8.** A fixed limit of travel or operation under specified conditions: the cruising *radius* of a ship. [< L, orig. rod, hence spoke of a wheel]

radius vector *pl.* **radius vectors** or **ra·di·i vec·to·res** (rā′dē·ī vek·tôr′ēz, -tō′rēz) *Math.* The straight-line distance from a fixed origin to any point of a curve.

ra·dix (rā′diks) *n. pl.* **rad·i·ces** (rad′ə·sēz, rā′də-) or **ra·dix·es 1.** *Math.* A number or symbol used as the basis of a scale of enumeration. **2.** *Bot.* The root of a plant. [< L, root]

ra·dome (rā′dōm) *n.* A protective housing for the antenna of a radar assembly. [< RA(DAR) + DOME]

ra·don (rā′don) *n.* A heavy, gaseous, radioactive element (symbol Rn), an emanation of radium with a half life of about 14 days: formerly called *niton*. See ELEMENT.

raff (raf) *n.* The rabble; riffraff. [< dial. *raff* to rake < OF *rafler* < *rafle*]

raf·fi·a (raf′ē·ə) *n.* **1.** A cultivated palm of Madagascar, the leafstalks of which furnish fiber for making hats, mats, baskets, etc. **2.** Its fiber. [< Malagasy]

raff·ish (raf′ish) *adj.* **1.** Tawdry; gaudy; flashy. **2.** Disreputable.

raf·fle (raf′əl) *n.* A form of lottery in which one buys a chance on an object. — *v.* **·fled, ·fling** *v.t.* **1.** To dispose of by a raffle: often with *off*. — *v.i.* **2.** To take part in a raffle. [< OF *rafle* a game of dice < Du. *rafelen*] — **raf′fler** *n.*

raft¹ (raft, räft) *n.* **1.** A float of logs, planks, etc., fastened together for transportation by water. **2.** A life raft. — *v.t.*

1. To transport on a raft. **2.** To form into a raft. **3.** To travel by, be employed on, or manage a raft. [< *raptr* rafter]

raft² (raft, räft) *n. Informal* A large number or indiscrinate collection of any kind. [< RAFF]

raft·er (raf′tər, räf′-) *n.* A beam giving form, slope, ar support to a roof. For illus. see ROOF. [OE *ræfter*]

rafts·man (rafts′mən, räfts′-) *n. pl.* **·men** (-mən) One wh manages or works on a raft.

rag¹ (rag) *v.t.* **ragged, rag·ging** *Slang* **1.** To tease or annoy. **2.** To scold. — *n. Brit.* A ragging. [Origin uncertain]

rag² (rag) *n.* **1.** A torn or discarded piece of cloth. **2.** A small cloth used for washing, cleaning, etc. **3.** A fragment of anything. **4.** *pl.* Cotton or linen textile remnants used in the making of rag paper. **5.** *pl.* Tattered or shabby clothing. **6.** Any clothing: a jocular usage. **7.** Anything resembling a rag in appearance or worth: used humorously or in disparagement. — **glad rags** *Slang* One's best clothes. — **to chew the rag** *Slang* To talk or argue at great length. [OE < ON *rögg* tuft]

rag³ (rag) *v.t.* **ragged, rag·ging** To compose or play in ragtime. — *n.* Ragtime.

rag·a·muf·fin (rag′ə·muf′in) *n.* Anyone, esp. a child, wearing very ragged clothes. [after *Ragamoffyn*, demon in William Langland's *Piers Plowman*, 1393]

rage (rāj) *n.* **1.** Violent anger; wrath; fury. **2.** Any great violence or intensity, as of a fever or a storm. **3.** Extreme eagerness or emotion; great enthusiasm. **4.** Something popular or in demand; a fad. — *v.i.* **raged, rag·ing 1.** To speak, act, or move with unrestrained anger. **2.** To act or proceed with great violence. **3.** To spread or prevail uncontrolled, as an epidemic. [< OF < LL < L *rabere* to rage] — **rag′ing·ly** *adv.*

rag·ged (rag′id) *adj.* **1.** Rent or worn into rags; frayed. **2.** Wearing worn, frayed, or shabby garments. **3.** Of rough or uneven character or aspect. **4.** Naturally of a rough or shaggy appearance. — **rag′ged·ly** *adv.* — **rag′ged·ness** *n.*

ragged edge *Informal* The extreme or precarious edge; the verge; the *ragged edge* of starvation. — **on the ragged edge** Dangerously near to losing one's self-control, sanity, etc.

rag·lan (rag′lən) *n.* An overcoat or topcoat, the sleeves of which extend in one piece up to the collar. — *adj.* Denoting a garment with such sleeves. [after Lord *Raglan*, 1788–1855, English field marshal]

rag·man (rag′man′, -mən) *n. pl.* **·men** (-men′, -mən) One who buys and sells old rags and other waste; a ragpicker.

ra·gout (ra·gōō′) *n.* A highly seasoned dish of stewed meat and vegetables. — *v.t.* **ra·gouted** (-gōōd′), **ra·gout·ing** (-gōō′ing) To make into a ragout. [< F]

rag·pick·er (rag′pik′ər) *n.* One who picks up rags and other junk for a livelihood.

rag·time (rag′tīm′) *n.* **1.** A kind of American dance music, developed from about 1890 to 1920, characterized by highly syncopated rhythm in fast time. **2.** The rhythm of this music. Also called *rag.* [< *ragged time*]

rag·weed (rag′wēd′) *n.* A coarse, very common annual or perennial herb, the pollen of which induces hay fever.

rag·wort (rag′wûrt′) *n.* Any of several herbs of the composite family, with bright yellow flowers.

rah (rä) *interj.* Hurrah: a cheer used chiefly in college yells.

raid (rād) *n.* **1.** A hostile or predatory incursion by a rapidly moving body of troops or an armed vessel; a foray. **2.** An air raid. **3.** Any sudden invasion, capture, or seizure. **4.** An attempt by speculators to lower stock prices. — *v.t.* **1.** To make a raid on. — *v.i.* **2.** To participate in a raid. [< Scottish form of OE *rād* a riding] — **raid′er** *n.*

rail¹ (rāl) *n.* **1.** A bar of wood, metal, etc., resting on supports, as in a fence, at the side of a stairway, or capping the bulwarks of a ship; a railing. **2.** One of a series of parallel bars of iron or steel, resting upon crossties and forming a support and guide for wheels, as of a railroad. **3.** A railroad considered as a means of transportation: to ship by *rail*. — *v.t.* To furnish or shut in with rails; fence. [< OF < L *regula* wooden ruler]

RAIL FENCE

rail² (rāl) *n.* Any of numerous marsh birds having very short wings, moderately long legs and toes, and a short turned-up tail. [< OF *raale*]

rail³ (rāl) *v.i.* **1.** To use scornful, insolent, or abusive language; scold: with *at* or *against*. — *v.t.* **2.** To drive or force by railing. [< MF < Provençal *ralhar* to jest at] — **rail′er** *n.*

rail·ing (rā′ling) *n.* **1.** A series of rails; a balustrade. **2.** Rails, or material from which rails are made.

rail·ler·y (rā′lər·ē) *n. pl.* **·ler·ies** Merry jesting or teasing; banter. [< F *raillerie* jesting]

rail·road (rāl′rōd′) *n.* **1.** A graded road having metal rails

RADIO
SONDE
a Instrument box.

pported by ties or sleepers, for the passage of trains or roll-
g stock drawn by locomotives. **2.** The system of tracks,
ations, etc., used in transportation by rail. **3.** The cor-
oration or persons owning or operating such a system. —
v.t. **1.** To transport by railroad. **2.** *U.S. Informal* To rush
or force with great speed or without deliberation: to *railroad*
a bill through Congress. **3.** *U.S. Slang* To cause to be imprisoned on false charges or without fair trial. — *v.i.* **4.** To
work on a railroad. — **rail′road′er** *n.* — **rail′road′ing** *n.*
rail-split·ter (rāl′split′ər) *n.* One who splits logs into fence
rails.
rail·way (rāl′wā′) *n.* **1.** *Chiefly Brit.* A railroad. **2.** Rails
similar to those of a railroad, as for streetcars. **3.** A track
or set of rails, as in a factory, for handling heavy articles, etc.
rai·ment (rā′mənt) *n.* *Archaic* Wearing apparel; clothing;
garb. [Aphetic var. of *arrayment* < ARRAY + -MENT]
rain (rān) *n.* **1.** The condensed water vapor of the atmosphere falling in drops. ◆ Collateral adjective: *pluvial.* **2.**
The fall of such drops. **3.** A fall or shower of anything in the
manner of rain. **4.** A rainstorm; shower. **5.** *pl.* The rainy
season, as in a tropical country. — *v.i.* **1.** To fall from the
clouds in drops of water: usu. with *it* as the subject. **2.** To
fall like rain, as tears. **3.** To send or pour down rain, as
clouds. — *v.t.* **4.** To send down like rain; shower. — **to
rain out** To cause (a game, outdoor event, etc.) to be canceled or postponed because of rain. [OE *regn*]
rain·bow (rān′bō′) *n.* **1.** An arch of prismatic colors formed
in the sky opposite the sun and caused by refraction, reflection, and dispersion of light in raindrops falling through the
air. **2.** Any similar display of color. [OE *regnboga*]
rain check *U.S.* **1.** The stub of a ticket to an outdoor
event, as a baseball game, entitling the holder to admission
at a future date if for any reason the event is called off. **2.** A
postponed invitation.
rain·coat (rān′kōt′) *n.* A coat, often waterproof, intended
to be worn in rainy weather. Also, *Brit., waterproof.*
rain·fall (rān′fôl′) *n.* **1.** A fall of rain. **2.** *Meteorol.* The
amount of water, measured in inches, precipitated in a given
region over a stated time, as rain, hail, snow, or the like.
rain gauge An instrument for measuring the amount of
rainfall at a given place or time. Also **rain gage.**
rain·mak·er (rān′mā′kər) *n.* One reputedly able to cause
rain; esp., among certain American Indians, one who uses
incantations to produce rain. — **rain′mak′ing** *n.*
rain·out (rān′out′) *n.* *Physics* Precipitation of radioactive
water droplets following an underwater nuclear explosion.
rain·proof (rān′prōōf′) *adj.* Shedding rain, as garments.
rain·storm (rān′stôrm′) *n.* A storm accompanied by rain.
rain·wa·ter (rān′wô′tər, -wot′-) *n.* Water that falls or has
fallen in the form of rain. Also **rain water.**
rain·y (rā′nē) *adj.* **rain·i·er, rain·i·est** Characterized by,
abounding in, or bringing rain. — **rain′i·ness** *n.*
rainy day A time of need; hard times.
raise (rāz) *v.* **raised, rais·ing** *v.t.* **1.** To cause to move upward or to a higher level; elevate. **2.** To place erect; set up.
3. To construct or build. **4.** To make greater in amount,
size, or value: to *raise* prices. **5.** To advance or elevate in
rank, estimation, etc. **6.** To increase the strength, intensity,
or degree of. **7.** To breed; grow: to *raise* tomatoes. **8.** *U.S.*
To rear (children, a family, etc.). **9.** To cause to be heard:
to *raise* a hue and cry. **10.** To cause; occasion, as a smile or
laugh. **11.** To stir to action or emotion. **12.** To waken;
animate or reanimate. **13.** To gather together; obtain or
collect, as an army, capital, etc. **14.** To bring up for consideration, as a question. **15.** To cause to swell or become
lighter; leaven. **16.** To put an end to, as a siege. **17.** In
poker, to bet more than. **18.** *Naut.* To cause to appear
above the horizon, as land or a ship, by approaching nearer.
— *v.i.* **19.** *Informal* To cough up phlegm. **20.** In poker, to
make a raise. — **to raise the devil** (or **the dickens, hell,
the roof, a rumpus,** etc.) *Informal* To make a great disturbance; stir up confusion. — *n.* **1.** The act of raising. **2.**
An increase, as of wages or a bet. ◆ In British usage, a *rise*
is an increase in wages. [< ON *risa* to rise] — **rais′er** *n.*
raised (rāzd) *adj.* **1.** Elevated in low relief. **2.** Made with
yeast or leaven.
rai·sin (rā′zən) *n.* A grape of a special sort dried in the sun
or in an oven. [< OF < L *racemus* bunch of grapes]
rai·son d′ê·tre (re·zôn′ de′tr′) *French* Reason or excuse for
existing; literally, reason for being.
raj (räj) *n.* In India, sovereignty; rule. [< Hind. *rāj*]
ra·jah (rä′jə) *n.* A Hindu prince or chief of a tribal state in
India; also, a Malay or Javanese ruler: often used as a courtesy title. Also **ra′ja.** [< Hind. < Skt. *rājan* king]
Raj·put (räj′pōōt) *n.* One of a powerful and warlike Hindu
caste. Also **Raj′poot.** [< Hind. < Skt. < *rājan* king +
putra son]
rake[1] (rāk) *n.* A toothed implement for drawing together
loose material, loosening the surface of the soil, etc. — *v.*
raked, rak·ing *v.t.* **1.** To scrape or gather together with or
as with a rake. **2.** To smooth, clean, or prepare with a rake.

3. To gather by diligent effort; scrape together. **4.** To
search or examine carefully. **5.** To direct heavy gunfire
along the length of, as a ship or column of troops; enfilade.
— *v.i.* **6.** To use a rake. **7.** To scrape or pass roughly or
violently: with *across, over,* etc. **8.** To make a search. — **to
rake in** *Informal* To earn or acquire (money, etc.) in large
quantities. [OE *raca*] — **rak′er** *n.*
rake[2] (rāk) *v.* **raked, rak·ing** *v.i.* **1.** To lean from the perpendicular, as a ship's masts. — *v.t.* **2.** To cause to lean;
incline. — *n.* Inclination from the perpendicular or horizontal, as of the edge of a cutting tool. [Origin uncertain]
rake[3] (rāk) *n.* A dissolute, lewd man; a roué. [Earlier *rake-
hell* < ME *rakel* rash, wild]
rake-off (rāk′ôf′, -of′) *n.* *U.S. Slang* **1.** A share, as of profits; commission. **2.** A rebate, usu. illegitimate.
rak·ish[1] (rā′kish) *adj.* **1.** Dashing; jaunty; smart. **2.** *Naut.*
Having the masts unusually inclined, so as to suggest speed.
[< RAKE[2]] — **rak′ish·ly** *adv.* — **rak′ish·ness** *n.*
rak·ish[2] (rā′kish) *adj.* Characteristic of a rake; dissolute;
profligate. — **rak′ish·ly** *adv.* — **rak′ish·ness** *n.*
râle (räl) *n.* *Pathol.* A sound additional to that of normal
respiration, heard on auscultation of the chest and indicative
of the presence, nature, or stage of a disease. [< F, rattle]
ral·len·tan·do (ral′ən·tan′dō, *Ital.* räl′len·tän′dō) *Music*
adj. & adv. Gradually slower. [< Ital.]
ral·ly[1] (ral′ē) *n. pl.* **·lies** **1.** A meeting or assembly of persons for a common purpose. **2.** A rapid recovery of a normal
condition as after exhaustion, depression, etc. **3.** A return,
as of scattered troops, to order or action. **4.** In tennis, the
interchange of several strokes before one side wins the point.
5. A driving competition or procession over a fixed, often extensive course, as for sports cars, antique automobiles, etc.
— *v.* **·lied, ·ly·ing** *v.t.* **1.** To bring together and restore to
effective discipline: to *rally* fleeing troops. **2.** To summon
up or revive: to *rally* one's spirits. **3.** To bring together for
common action. — *v.i.* **4.** To return to effective discipline
or action: The enemy *rallied.* **5.** To unite for common action. **6.** To make a partial or complete return to a normal
condition; improve. **7.** In tennis, to engage in a rally. [<
F < *re-* again + *allier* to join] — **ral′li·er** *n.*
ral·ly[2] (ral′ē) *v.t. & v.i.* **·lied, ·ly·ing** To mock or tease with
raillery; banter. [< F *railler* to banter] — **ral′li·er** *n.*
ram (ram) *n.* **1.** A male sheep. **2.** A device for driving,
forcing, or crushing by heavy blows or thrusts. **3.** A hydraulic ram. — *v.t.* **rammed, ram·ming** **1.** To strike with
or as with a ram; dash against. **2.** To drive or force down or
into something. **3.** To cram; stuff. [OE *ramm*] — **ram′·
mer** *n.* — **ram′mish** *adj.*
ram·ble (ram′bəl) *v.i.* **·bled, ·bling** **1.** To walk about freely
and aimlessly; roam. **2.** To write or talk aimlessly or without sequence of ideas. **3.** To proceed with turns and twists;
meander. — **Syn.** See WANDER. — *n.* **1.** The act of rambling; an aimless or leisurely stroll. **2.** A meandering path;
maze. [? ME *romblen,* freq. of *romen* to roam]
ram·bler (ram′blər) *n.* **1.** One who or that which rambles.
2. Any of several varieties of climbing roses, with clusters of
deep red flowers.
ram·bunc·tious (ram·bungk′shəs) *adj.* *U.S. Informal* Boisterous; rough. [Prob. var. of *robustious* < ROBUST]
ram·e·kin (ram′ə·kin) *n.* **1.** A seasoned dish of bread
crumbs with eggs and cheese, baked and served in a shallow
dish. **2.** A dish, usu. with a handle, in which ramekins are
baked. **3.** Any dish used both for baking and serving. Also
ram′e·quin. [< F *ramequin* < Du.]
ram·ie (ram′ē) *n.* The fiber yielded by a shrubby Chinese
and East Indian perennial of the nettle family, used for cordage and certain textiles. Also **ram′ee.** [< Malay *rami*]
ram·i·fi·ca·tion (ram′ə·fə·kā′shən) *n.* **1.** The act or process
of ramifying. **2.** An offshoot or subdivision. **3.** A result,
consequence, etc., stemming from a main source.
ram·i·form (ram′ə·fôrm) *adj.* **1.** Branch-shaped. **2.**
Branched. [< L *ramus* branch + -FORM]
ram·i·fy (ram′ə·fī) *v.t. & v.i.* **·fied, ·fy·ing** To divide or
spread out into or as into branches; branch out. [< F <
Med.L < L *ramus* branch + *facere* to make]
ram jet (ram′jet′) *n.* A type of jet engine that provides continuous jet propulsion.
ra·mose (rā′mōs, rə·mōs′) *adj.* **1.** Branching. **2.** Consisting of or having branches. [< L *ramus* branch]
ra·mous (rā′məs) *adj.* Of or like branches. **2.** Ramose.
[See RAMOSE.]
ramp[1] (ramp) *n.* **1.** An inclined passageway or roadway, as
between floors of a building. **2.** A movable stairway by
which passengers enter or leave an airplane. [< F < OF
ramper to climb]
ramp[2] (ramp) *v.i.* **1.** To rear up on the hind legs and stretch
out the forelegs, as a horse. **2.** To act in a violent or threatening manner; rampage. — *n.* The act of ramping. [< OF
ramper to climb]
ram·page (*n.* ram′pāj; *v.* ram·pāj′) *n.* Boisterous agitation
or excitement. — *v.i.* **·paged, ·pag·ing** **1.** To rush or act vi-

olently. **2.** To storm; rage. [Orig. Scot., ? < RAMP²] — **ram·pag′er** n. — **ram·pa′geous** adj.

ram·pant (ram′pənt) adj. **1.** Exceeding all bounds; wild. **2.** Widespread or unchecked, as an erroneous belief. **3.** Standing on the hind legs; rearing: said of a quadruped. **4.** Heraldry Standing on the hind legs, with both forelegs elevated. [< OF, ppr. of ramper. See RAMP².] — **ram′pan·cy** n. — **ram′pant·ly** adv.

ram·part (ram′pärt, -pərt) n. **1.** The embankment surrounding a fort, on which the parapet is raised. **2.** A bulwark or defense. — v.t. To supply with or as with ramparts; fortify. [< F remparer to fortify]

ram·rod (ram′rod′) n. **1.** A rod used to drive home the charge of a muzzleloading gun or pistol. **2.** A similar rod used for cleaning the barrel of a rifle, etc.

ram·shack·le (ram′shak′əl) adj. Likely to go to pieces, as from age or neglect. [< ransackle, freq. of RANSACK]

ran (ran) Past tense of RUN.

ranch (ranch) n. **1.** An establishment for raising or grazing cattle, sheep, horses, etc., in large herds. **2.** The buildings, personnel, and lands connected with it. **3.** A large farm. — v.i. To manage or work on a ranch. [< Sp. rancho soldiers' mess] — **ranch′er, ranch′man** n.

ranch house 1. The main building of a ranch **2.** U.S. A one-story house usu. having a low roof with a wide overhang.

ran·cid (ran′sid) adj. Having the unpleasant taste or smell of oily substances that have begun to spoil; rank; sour. [< L < rancere to be rank] — **ran·cid′i·ty, ran′cid·ness** n.

ran·cor (rang′kər) n. Bitter enmity; spitefulness. Also Brit. **ran′cour.** [< OF < LL < L rancere to be rank] — **ran′cor·ous** adj. — **ran′cor·ous·ly** adv. — **ran′cor·ous·ness** n.

rand (rand, ränd) n. The standard monetary unit of South Africa, worth in 1964 about $1.40. [< The Rand, or Witwatersrand, a region of Transvaal, South Africa]

ran·dom (ran′dəm) n. Lack of definite aim or intention: now chiefly in the phrase **at random,** without definite purpose or aim; haphazardly. — adj. Done at random. [< OF random rapidity, impetuosity] — **ran′dom·ly** adv.

ra·nee (rä′nē) See RANI.

rang (rang) Past tense of RING².

range (rānj) n. **1.** The area over which anything moves, operates, or is distributed. **2.** U.S. An extensive tract of land over which cattle, sheep, etc., roam and graze. **3.** Extent or scope: the whole range of politics. **4.** The extent to which any power can be made effective: range of influence. **5.** The extent of variation of anything: the temperature range. **6.** A line, row, or series, as of mountains. **7.** The maximum distance that an aircraft, ship, vehicle, etc., can travel before its fuel is exhausted; also, the maximum distance at which a weapon, transmitter, etc., is effective. **8.** A place for shooting at a mark: a rifle range. **9.** A large cooking stove. — adj. Of or pertaining to a range. — v. ranged, rang·ing v.t. **1.** To arrange in definite order, as in rows. **2.** To assign to a class, division, or category. **3.** To move about or over (a region, etc.). **4.** To put (cattle) to graze on a range. **5.** To adjust or train, as a telescope or gun. — v.i. **6.** To move over an area in a thorough, systematic manner. **7.** To rove; roam. **8.** To extend or proceed: The shot ranged to the right. **9.** To exhibit variation within specified limits. **10.** To lie in the same direction, line, etc. [< OF < ranc row]

range finder An instrument for determining the distance of an object from a given point.

rang·er (rān′jər) n. **1.** One who or that which ranges; a rover. **2.** One of an armed band designed to protect large tracts of country. **3.** One of a herd of cattle that feeds on a range. **4.** U.S. A warden employed in patrolling forest tracts. — **rang′er·ship** n.

Rang·er (rān′jər) n. One of a select group of U.S. soldiers trained for raiding action on enemy territory.

rang·y (rān′jē) adj. **rang·i·er, rang·i·est 1.** Disposed to roam, or adapted for roving, as cattle. **2.** Having long, slender limbs, as a person. **3.** Affording wide range; roomy. **4.** Resembling a mountain range.

ra·ni (rä′nē) n. **1.** The wife of a raja or prince. **2.** A reigning Hindu queen or princess. Also spelled ranee. [< Hind. < Skt. rājnī, fem. of rajan king]

rank¹ (rangk) n. **1.** A series of objects ranged in a line or row; a range. **2.** Degree of official standing, esp. in the armed forces. See table for GRADE. **3.** A line of soldiers drawn up side by side in close order. **4.** pl. An army; also, the mass of soldiery. **5.** Relative position or status; degree; grade. **6.** High degree or position: a lady of rank. — Syn. See CLASS. — v.t. **1.** To arrange in a rank or ranks. **2.** To place in a class, order, etc. **3.** To outrank: Sergeants rank corporals. — v.i. **4.** To hold a specified place or rank. **5.** To have the highest rank or grade. [< OF ranc]

rank² (rangk) adj. **1.** Very vigorous and flourishing in growth, as vegetation. **2.** Strong and disagreeable to the

taste or smell. **3.** Utter; complete: rank injustice. **4.** Producing a luxuriant growth; fertile. [OE ranc strong] — **rank′ly** adv. — **rank′ness** n.

rank and file 1. The common soldiers of an army, including all from the corporals downward. **2.** Those who form the bulk of any organization, as distinct from officers or leaders.

rank·ing (rangk′ing) adj. Superior in rank; taking precedence over others in the same category: a ranking senator.

ran·kle (rang′kəl) v. **·kled, ·kling** v.i. **1.** To cause continued resentment: The defeat rankles in his breast. **2.** To become irritated or inflamed; fester. — v.t. **3.** To irritate; embitter. [< OF rancler to fester]

ran·sack (ran′sak) v.t. **1.** To search through every part of. **2.** To search throughout for plunder; pillage. [< ON rannsaka to search a house] — **ran′sack·er** n.

ran·som (ran′səm) v.t. **1.** To secure the release of (a person, property, etc.) for a required price, as from captivity or detention. **2.** To set free on payment of ransom. — n. **1.** The payment for the release of a person or property detained. **2.** Release purchased. [< OF < L < re- back + emere to buy] — **ran′som·er** n.

rant (rant) v.i. **1.** To speak in loud, violent, or extravagant language; rave. — v.t. **2.** To utter in a ranting manner. — n. Declamatory and bombastic talk. [< MDu. ranten to rave] — **rant′er** n.

rap¹ (rap) v. **rapped, rap·ping** v.t. **1.** To strike sharply and quickly; hit. **2.** To utter in a sharp manner: with out. — v.i. **3.** To strike sharp, quick blows. — n. **1.** A sharp blow. **2.** A sound caused by or as by knocking. **3.** Slang A charge of wrongdoing; blame. [ME, prob. imit.] — **rap′per** n.

rap² (rap) n. The least bit: I don't care a rap. [< RAPT]

ra·pa·cious (rə·pā′shəs) adj. **1.** Given to plunder or rapine. **2.** Grasping; greedy. **3.** Subsisting on prey seized alive, as hawks, etc. [< L rapere to seize] — **ra·pa′cious·ly** adv. — **ra·pa′cious·ness** n. — **ra·pac′i·ty** (-pas′ə·tē) n.

rape¹ (rāp) v. **raped, rap·ing** v.t. **1.** To commit rape upon; ravish. **2.** Archaic To carry off by force. — n. **1.** The forcible and unlawful carnal knowledge of a woman against her will. **2.** Archaic A capturing or snatching away by force. [< AF < L rapere to seize] — **rap′ist** n.

rape² (rāp) n. A plant related to the cabbage, grown as a forage crop for sheep and hogs, and having seeds that yield rape oil. [< L rapum turnip]

rape oil An oil obtained from rapeseed, and used as a lubricant, etc.: also called colza oil.

rape·seed (rāp′sēd′) n. The seed of the rape.

Raph·a·el (raf′ē·əl, rā′fē-) One of the archangels.

rap·id (rap′id) adj. **1.** Having or moving with great speed; swift. **2.** Characterized by rapidity: a rapid style. **3.** Done or completed in a short time: rapid growth. — Syn. See SWIFT¹. — n. Usu. pl. A swift-running descent in a river. [< L rapere to seize, rush] — **ra·pid·i·ty** (rə·pid′ə·tē) n. — **rap′id·ly** adv. — **rap′id·ness** n.

rap·id-fire (rap′id·fīr′) adj. **1.** Firing or designed for firing shots in rapid succession. **2.** Characterized by speed: rapid-fire repartee. Also **rap′id-fir′ing.**

ra·pi·er (rā′pē·ər, rāp′yər) n. **1.** A long, straight, two-edged sword with a large cup hilt, used for dueling, chiefly for thrusting. **2.** A shorter straight sword without cutting edge and therefore used for thrusting only. [< MF rapière]

rap·ine (rap′in) n. The taking of property by force, as in war; spoliation; pillage. [< OF < L rapere to seize]

rap·port (rə·pôr′, -pōr′) n. Harmony or sympathy of relation; agreement; accord. — **en rapport** (äṅ rȧ·pôr′) French In close accord. [< F rapporter to bring back]

rap·proche·ment (rȧ·prôsh·mäṅ′) n. French A state of harmony or reconciliation; restoration of cordial relations.

rap·scal·lion (rap·skal′yən) n. A rogue; scamp; rascal. [< earlier rascallion, extension of RASCAL]

rapt (rapt) adj. **1.** Carried away with lofty emotion; enraptured; transported. **2.** Engrossed; intent; deeply engaged. [< L < rapere to seize]

rap·to·ri·al (rap·tôr′ē·əl, -tō′rē-) adj. **1.** Seizing and devouring living prey; predatory. **2.** Having talons adapted for seizing prey: said esp. of hawks, vultures, eagles, and other carnivorous birds. [< L < rapere to seize]

rap·ture (rap′chər) n. **1.** The state of being rapt or transported; ecstatic joy; ecstasy. **2.** Often pl. An act or expression of excessive delight. — v.t. **·tured, ·tur·ing** Poetic To enrapture. [< RAPT] — **rap′tur·ous** adj. — **rap′tur·ous·ly** adv. — **rap′tur·ous·ness** n.

rare¹ (râr) adj. **rar·er, rar·est 1.** Infrequent in occurrence, distribution, etc. **2.** Highly esteemed because of infrequency or uncommonness. **3.** Rarefied: now said chiefly of the atmosphere, etc. [< L rarus rare] — **rare′ness** n. — **Syn. 1.** scarce, unusual, exceptional. See OBSOLETE.

rare² (râr) adj. Not thoroughly cooked, as roasted or broiled meat retaining its redness and juices. [OE hrēre]

rare·bit (râr′bit) *n.* Welsh rabbit.

rare earth *Chem.* Any of the metallic oxides of the lanthanide series of elements.

rare-earth element (râr′ûrth′) *Chem.* Any of a group of metallic elements constituting the lanthanide series. Also **rare-earth metals.**

rar·e·fy (râr′ə·fī) *v.* **·fied, ·fy·ing** *v.t.* **1.** To make rare, thin, less solid, or less dense. **2.** To refine or purify. — *v.i.* **3.** To become rare, thin, or less solid. **4.** To become pure. [< F < L < *rarus* rare + *facere* to make] — **rar′e·fac′tion** (-fak′shən) *n.* — **rar′e·fac′tive** *adj.* — **rar′e·fi′a·ble** *adj.*

rare·ly (râr′lē) *adv.* **1.** Not often; infrequently. **2.** With unusual excellence or effect; finely **3.** Exceptionally.

rar·ing (râr′ing) *adj.* *U.S. Informal* Extremely eager or enthusiastic. [< Pres. part. of *rare,* dial. of REAR²]

rar·i·ty (râr′ə·tē) *n.* *pl.* **·ties 1.** That which is exceptionally valued because of scarceness. **2.** The state of being rare.

ras·cal (ras′kəl) *n.* An unprincipled fellow; rogue; knave: sometimes used playfully. — *adj.* *Obs.* Base; mean. [< OF, ult. < L *radere* to scratch] — **ras·cal′i·ty** (-kal′ə·tē) *n.* — **ras′cal·ly** *adj. & adv.*

rase (rāz) *v.t.* **rased, ras·ing** To raze.

rash¹ (rash) *adj.* **1.** Acting without due caution or regard of consequences; reckless. **2.** Exhibiting recklessness or precipitancy. [Prob. < MLG < OHG *rasc* lively] — **rash′ly** *adv.* — **rash′ness** *n.*

rash² (rash) *n.* A superficial eruption of the skin, often localized. [< OF, ult. < L *radere* to scratch]

rash·er (rash′ər) *n.* A thin slice of meat, esp. bacon.

rasp (rasp, räsp) *n.* **1.** A file having coarse pyramidal projections for abrasion. **2.** The act or sound of rasping. — *v.t.* **1.** To scrape or rub with or as with a rasp. **2.** To affect unpleasantly; irritate. **3.** To utter in a rough voice. — *v.i.* **4.** To grate; scrape. **5.** To make a rough, harsh sound. [< OF *rasper* to scrape] — **rasp′er** *n.* — **ras′py** *adj.*

rasp·ber·ry (raz′ber′ē, -bər·ē, räz′-) *n.* *pl.* **·ries 1.** The round fruit of certain brambles of the rose family, composed of drupes clustered around a fleshy receptacle. **2.** Any plant yielding this fruit. **3.** *Slang* A Bronx cheer: also spelled *razzberry.* [< earlier *raspis* (berry)]

rat (rat) *n.* **1.** A destructive and injurious rodent of worldwide distribution, larger and more aggressive than the mouse. **2.** *Slang* A cowardly or selfish person who deserts or betrays his associates. **3.** A pad over which a woman's hair is combed to give a coiffure body. — **to smell a rat** To suspect that something is wrong. — *v.i.* **rat·ted, rat·ting 1.** To hunt rats. **2.** *Slang* To desert one's party, etc. **3.** *Slang* To inform; betray: with *on.* [OE *ræt*]

rat·a·ble (rā′tə·bəl) *adj.* **1.** *Brit.* Legally liable to taxation. **2.** Estimated proportionally; pro rata: a *ratable* distribution. **3.** That may be rated or valued. Also **rate′a·ble.** — **rat′a·bil′i·ty, rat′a·ble·ness** *n.* — **rat′a·bly** *adv.*

ra·tan (ra·tan′) See RATTAN.

ratch·et (rach′it) *n.* **1.** A mechanism consisting of a notched wheel, the teeth of which engage with a pawl, permitting motion of the wheel in one direction only. **2.** The pawl or the wheel thus used. Also **ratchet wheel.** [< F *rochet* bobbin]

rate¹ (rāt) *n.* **1.** The measure of a variable in relation to some fixed unit: a *rate* of 5 miles per hour. **2.** Degree of value; price; also, the unit cost of a commodity or service. **3.** Comparative rank or class. **4.** *Brit.* A local tax on property. **5.** Proportion, as of an incidence, to some fixed number of cases: the death *rate* per 100,000 adults. **6.** A fixed allowance, amount, or ratio. — **at any rate** In any case; anyhow. — *v.* **rat·ed, rat·ing** *v.t.* **1.** To estimate the value or worth of; appraise. **2.** To place in a certain rank or grade. **3.** To consider; regard. **4.** To fix the rate for the transportation of (goods), as by rail. **5.** *Informal* To deserve. — *v.i.* **6.** To have rank, rating, or value. **7.** *Informal* To stand in comparison with others. [< OF < L < *reri* to calculate] — **rat′er** *n.*

rate² (rāt) *v.t. & v.i.* **rat·ed, rat·ing** To reprove with vehemence; rail at.

rath·er (rath′ər, rä′thər) *adv.* **1.** More willingly. **2.** With more reason, justice, wisdom, etc. **3.** More precisely, strictly, or accurately. **4.** Somewhat; in a greater or less degree: *rather* cold. **5.** On the contrary. **6.** *Brit.* Yes indeed! ◆ Both *had rather* and *would rather* are acceptable forms. [OE *hrathor,* compar. of *hrathe* soon, quickly]

raths·kel·ler (rath′skel·ər, räts′kel·ər) *n.* A beer hall or similar restaurant, usu. located in a cellar. [< G *rat* council, town hall + *keller* cellar]

rat·i·fy (rat′ə·fī) *v.t.* **·fied, ·fy·ing** To give sanction to, esp. official sanction; confirm. [< OF < Med.L < L *ratus* fixed, calculated + *facere* to make] — **rat′i·fi·ca′tion** (-fə·kā′shən) *n.* — **rat′i·fi′er** *n.*

— **Syn.** The U.S. Senate *ratifies* a proposed treaty; Congress *confirms* Presidential appointments; notarization *validates* a bill of sale. These words are chiefly used of governmental process.

rat·i·né (rat·ə·nā′) *n.* A heavy, loosely woven fabric with a nubby surface. [< F < *ratiner* to make nubby]

rat·ing (rā′ting) *n.* **1.** Classification according to a standard; grade; rank; status. **2.** An evaluation of the financial standing of a business firm or an individual. **3.** Any specialist grade held by an enlisted man or officer: the *rating* of pilot in the Air Force.

ra·tio (rā′shō, -shē·ō) *n.* *pl.* **·tios 1.** Relation of degree, number, etc.; proportion; rate. **2.** The relation of two quantities, esp. the quotient of the first divided by the second. A ratio of 3 to 5 is expressed as 3 : 5 or ⅗. [< L *reri* to think]

ra·ti·oc·i·nate (rash′ē·os′ə·nāt) *v.i.* **·nat·ed, ·nat·ing** To make a deduction from premises; reason. [< L *reri* to think] — **ra′ti·oc′i·na′tion** *n.* — **ra′ti·oc′i·na′tive** *adj.* — **ra′ti·oc′i·na′tor** *n.*

ra·tion (rash′ən, rā′shən) *n.* **1.** A portion; share. **2.** A fixed allowance or portion of food, etc., allotted in time of scarcity. **3.** *Mil.* Food for one person for one day. — *v.t.* **1.** To issue rations to, as an army. **2.** To give out or allot in rations. **3.** To restrict to limited rations. [< F < L *ratio, -onis*] — **ra′tion·ing** *n.*

ra·tion·al (rash′ən·əl) *adj.* **1.** Possessing the faculty of reasoning. **2.** Having full possession of one's mental faculties; sane. **3.** Conformable to reason; judicious; sensible. **4.** Attained by reasoning. **5.** *Math.* Denoting an algebraic expression containing no variables within irreducible radicals. [See RATIO.] — **ra·tion·al·i·ty** (rash′ən·al′ə·tē) *n.* — **ra′tion·al·ly** *adv.* — **ra′tion·al·ness** *n.*

ra·tion·ale (rash′ən·al′, -ä′lē, -ā′lē) *n.* **1.** The rational or logical basis of something. **2.** A rational explanation of principles.

ra·tion·al·ism (rash′ən·əl·iz′əm) *n.* **1.** The formation of opinions by reason alone, independently of authority or of revelation. **2.** *Philos.* The theory that truth and knowledge are attainable through reason rather than by empirical means. — **ra′tion·al·ist** *n.* — **ra′tion·al·is′tic** or **·ti·cal** *adj.* — **ra′tion·al·is′ti·cal·ly** *adv.*

ra·tion·al·ize (rash′ən·əl·īz′) *v.* **·ized, ·iz·ing** *v.t.* **1.** *Psychol.* To explain or base (one's behavior) on grounds ostensibly rational but not in accord with the actual or unconscious motives. **2.** To explain or treat from a rationalistic point of view. **3.** To make rational or reasonable. — *v.i.* **4.** To think in a rational or rationalistic manner. Also *Brit.* **ra′tion·al·ise′.** — **ra·tion·al·i·za·tion** (rash′ən·əl·ə·zā′shən, -ī·zā′shən) *n.* — **ra′tion·al·iz′er** *n.*

ra·tite (rat′īt) *adj.* Designating a group of flightless birds including ostriches, cassowaries, kiwis, emus, etc. — *n.* A ratite bird. [< L *ratis* raft + -ITE¹]

rat·line (rat′lin) *n.* *Naut.* **1.** One of the small ropes fastened across the shrouds of a ship, used as a ladder for going aloft or descending. **2.** The rope so used. Also **rat′lin** (-lin). [Origin unknown]

RA·TO (rā′tō) *n.* An airplane takeoff assisted by an auxiliary rocket motor or unit; also, the rocket motor or unit used. Also **ra′to.** [< *r(ocket)* + *a(ssisted)* + *t(ake)o(ff)*]

rat race *Slang* A frantic, usu. fruitless, struggle.

rats·bane (rats′bān′) *n.* Rat poison.

rat's nest *Informal* A cluttered and messy place.

rat·tan (ra·tan′) *n.* **1.** The long, tough, flexible stem of various tropical palms, used in making wickerwork, light furniture, etc. **2.** The palm itself. Also spelled *ratan.* [< Malay *rotan*]

rat·ter (rat′ər) *n.* **1.** A dog or cat that catches rats. **2.** *Slang* A deserter; traitor.

rat·tle (rat′l) *v.* **·tled, ·tling** *v.i.* **1.** To make a series of sharp noises in rapid succession, as of hard objects striking one another. **2.** To move or act with such noises; also, to make a gurgling sound in the throat. **3.** To talk rapidly and foolishly; chatter. — *v.t.* **4.** To cause to rattle: to *rattle* pennies in a tin cup. **5.** To utter or perform rapidly or noisily. **6.** *Informal* To confuse; disconcert; agitate. — *n.* **1.** A series of short, sharp sounds in rapid succession. **2.** A plaything, implement, etc., made to produce a rattling noise. **3.** Any of the jointed horny rings in the tail of a rattlesnake. **4.** Rapid and noisy talk; chatter. [Imit.]

rat·tle·brain (rat′l·brān′) *n.* A talkative, flighty person; foolish chatterer. Also **rat′tle·head′** (-hed′), **rat′tle·pate′** (-pāt′). — **rat′tle·brained′** *adj.*

rat·tler (rat′lər) *n.* **1.** One who or that which rattles. **2.** A rattlesnake.

rat·tle·snake (rat′l·snāk′) *n.* Any of several venomous American snakes with a tail ending in a series of horny, loosely connected, modified joints, that make a rattling noise when the tail is vibrated.

RATTLESNAKE
(To 8 feet long)

rat·tle·trap (rat′l·trap′) *n.* Any rickety, clattering, or worn-out vehicle or article.

rat·trap (rat′trap′) *n.* **1.** A trap for catching rats. **2.** Any hopeless or involved predicament.

rat·ty (rat′ē) *adj.* **·ti·er, ·ti·est 1.** Ratlike. **2.** Abounding in rats. **3.** *Slang* Disreputable; shabby.

rau·cous (rô′kəs) *adj.* **1.** Rough in sound; hoarse; harsh. **2.** Boisterous; unruly; disorderly. [< L *raucus*] **— rau′·cit·y** (-sə·tē), **rau′cous·ness** *n.* **— rau′cous·ly** *adv.*

rau·wol·fi·a (rou·wŏŏl′fē·ə) *n.* Any of a genus of tropical trees or shrubs, several of which contain alkaloids having valuable medicinal properties. [after Leonard *Rauwolf*, 17th c. German botanist]

rav·age (rav′ij) *v.* **·aged, ·ag·ing** *v.t.* **1.** To lay waste, as by pillaging or burning; despoil. **—** *v.i.* **2.** To wreak havoc; be destructive. **—** *n.* Violent and destructive action, or its result; ruin. [See RAVISH.] **— rav′ag·er** *n.*

rave (rāv) *v.* **raved, rav·ing** *v.i.* **1.** To speak wildly or incoherently. **2.** To speak with extravagant enthusiasm. **3.** To make a wild, roaring sound; rage. **—** *v.t.* **4.** To utter wildly or incoherently. **—** *n.* The act or state of raving; a frenzy. **—** *adj. Informal* Extravagantly enthusiastic: *rave* reviews. [< OF *raver* to wander, to be delirious]

rav·el (rav′əl) *v.* **rav·eled** or **·elled, rav·el·ing** or **·el·ling** *v.t.* **1.** To separate the threads or fibers of; unravel. **2.** To make clear or plain; explain: often with *out.* **—** *v.i.* **3.** To become separated, as threads or fibers; unravel; fray. **—** *n.* **1.** A broken or rejected thread. **2.** A raveling. [< MDu. *ravelen* to tangle] **— rav′el·er** or **rav′el·ler** *n.*

rav·el·ing (rav′əl·ing) *n.* A thread or threads raveled from a fabric. Also **rav′el·ling.**

ra·ven¹ (rā′vən) *n.* A large, omnivorous, widely distributed corvine bird, having lustrous black plumage. **—** *adj.* Black and shining, like a raven. [OE *hræfn*]

rav·en² (rav′ən) *v.t.* **1.** To devour hungrily or greedily. **2.** To take by force; ravage. **—** *v.i.* **3.** To search for prey or plunder. **4.** To eat voraciously. **—** *n.* The act of plundering; spoliation; pillage. [< OF *raviner* < L *rapina* < *rapere* to seize] **— rav′en·er** *n.*

Ra·ven (rā′vən) *n.* The constellation Corvus.

rav·en·ing (rav′ən·ing) *adj.* **1.** Seeking eagerly for prey; rapacious. **2.** Devouring; voracious. **3.** Mad.

rav·en·ous (rav′ən·əs) *adj.* **1.** Violently voracious or hungry. **2.** Extremely eager for gratification. [See RAVEN².] **— rav′en·ous·ly** *adv.* **— rav′en·ous·ness** *n.*

ra·vine (rə·vēn′) *n.* A deep gorge or gully, esp. one worn by a flow of water. [< F]

rav·ing (rā′ving) *adj.* **1.** Furious; delirious; frenzied. **2.** *Informal* Outstandingly attractive: a *raving* beauty. **—** *n.* A furious, incoherent, or irrational utterance.

ra·vi·o·li (rä·vyō′lē, rä′vē·ō′lē, rav′ē-) *n.pl.* Little envelopes of dough for encasing meat or cheese, boiled, and often served in a tomato sauce. [< Ital. pl. of *raviolo* little turnip]

rav·ish (rav′ish) *v.t.* **1.** To fill with strong emotion, esp. delight; enrapture. **2.** To commit a rape upon. **3.** *Archaic* To seize and carry off by force. [< OF < L *rapere* to seize] **— rav′ish·er** *n.* **— rav′ish·ment** *n.*

rav·ish·ing (rav′ish·ing) *adj.* Filling with delight; enchanting. **— rav′ish·ing·ly** *adv.*

raw (rô) *adj.* **1.** Not changed or prepared by cooking; uncooked. **2.** Having the skin irritated or abraded. **3.** Bleak; chilling: a *raw* wind. **4.** In a natural state; crude. **5.** Newly done; fresh: *raw* paint, *raw* work. **6.** Inexperienced; undisciplined. **7.** Obscene; coarse; off-color. **8.** Harshly unfair; ruthless. **—** *n.* A sore or abraded spot: with *the.* **— in the raw 1.** In a raw, unrefined, or untempered state. **2.**

U.S. Informal Naked; nude. [OE *hrēaw.*] **— raw′ly** *adv.* **— raw′ness** *n.*

raw-boned (rô′bônd′) *adj.* Bony; gaunt.

raw·hide (rô′hīd′) *n.* **1.** A hide dressed without tanning. **2.** A whip made of such hide.

ray¹ (rā) *n.* **1.** A narrow beam of light. **2.** Anything representing or suggesting this. **3.** A slight manifestation; glimmer; hint. **4.** *Geom.* One of several straight lines emerging from a point and unlimited in one direction. **5.** *Zool.* **a** One of the rods supporting the membrane of a fish's fin. **b** One of the radiating parts of a radiate animal, as a starfish. **6.** *Bot.* A ray flower. **7.** *Physics* **a** A line of propagation of any form of radiant energy. **b** A stream of particles spontaneously emitted by a radioactive substance. **—** *v.i.* **1.** To emit rays; shine. **2.** To issue forth as rays; radiate. **—** *v.t.* **3.** To send forth as rays. **4.** To mark with rays or radiating lines. **5.** To treat with X-rays, etc. [< OF < L *radius* rod]

ray² (rā) *n.* Any of various fishes having a flattened body with expanded pectoral fins and gill openings on the lower surface. [< OF < L *raia*]

ray flower *Bot.* Any of the flat marginal flowers surrounding the disk, as the daisy or sunflower. Also **ray floret.**

ray·on (rā′on) *n.* **1.** A synthetic fiber produced from cellulose, the material being forced through fine jets to produce threadlike filaments. **2.** A fabric made from such fibers. [Coined from RAY¹; prob. infl. by F *rayon* ray]

raze (rāz) *v.t.* **razed, raz·ing 1.** To demolish, as a building. **2.** *Rare* To scrape or shave off. Also spelled *rase.* **— Syn.** See DEMOLISH. [< OF < L *radere* to scrape]

ra·zor (rā′zər) *n.* A sharp cutting implement used for shaving off the beard or hair. [< OF < LL *rasorium* scraper]

ra·zor·back (rā′zər·bak′) *n.* **1.** The rorqual, a whale. **2.** A lean, long-legged, half-wild hog, common in the southeastern U.S. **3.** A hill with a sharp, narrow ridge.

razor blade A thin, metal blade, having either one or two sharpened edges, inserted in a safety razor.

razz (saz) *Slang* *n.* A Bronx cheer. **—** *v.t.* To heckle; deride. [< RAZZBERRY]

razz·ber·ry (raz′ber′ē, -bər·ē, räz′-) *n.* *pl.* **·ries** *U.S. Slang* A Bronx cheer. [< RASPBERRY]

raz·zle-daz·zle (raz′əl·daz′əl) *n.* *U.S. Slang* Bewildering, exciting, or dazzling activity or performance. Also **razz·ma·tazz** (raz′mə·taz′). [Varied reduplication of DAZZLE]

re¹ (rā) *n.* *Music* The second of the syllables used in solmization; the second degree of a major scale; also, the tone D. [< L *re(sonare).* See GAMUT.]

re² (rē) *prep.* Concerning; about; in the matter of: used in business letters, law, etc. [< L, ablative of *res* thing]

re- *prefix* **1.** Back: *rebound, remit.* **2.** Again; anew; again and again. [< L *re-, red-* back, again]

◆ Sense 2 of *re-* is freely used in forming words, particularly verbs or words derived from verbs. Some words thus formed are hyphenated to prevent confusion with similarly spelled words, as *recoil*, to spring back, and *re-coil*, to coil again, but in current usage most other words using *re-* as a prefix are written solid. However, many writers still prefer to hyphenate some combinations of *re-* and a word beginning with a vowel, especially *e*.

A list of self-explanatory words containing the prefix *re-* (def. 2) appears below.

reabandon	reappointment	reblossom	recondense	rediscover	reengage
reabsorb	reapportion	reboil	reconduct	rediscovery	reengagement
reabsorption	reapportionment	reborn	reconfirm	redissolve	reengrave
reaccept	reargue	rebuild	reconquer	redistill	reenjoy
reaccommodate	reargument	rebuilt	reconquest	redistribute	reenjoyment
reaccompany	reascend	rebury	reconsecrate	redivide	reenkindle
reaccuse	reascension	recapitalize	reconsolidate	redivision	reenlist
reacquire	reascent	recarry	reconvene	redo	reenlistment
readapt	reassemble	recelebrate	recopy	redraw	reenslave
readdress	reassembly	rechallenge	recoronation	redrive	reenter
readjourn	reassert	rechange	recross	redry	reentrance
readjournment	reassertion	recharge	recrown	redye	reerect
readjust	reassign	recharter	recrystallization	reecho	reestablish
readjustment	reassimilate	recheck	recrystallize	reedit	reestablishment
readmission	reassimilation	rechoose	recultivate	reelect	reexamination
readmit	reassociate	rechristen	recultivation	reelection	reexamine
readopt	reassume	recircle	rededicate	reelevate	reexchange
readorn	reassumption	recirculate	rededication	reembark	reexhibit
readvance	reattach	reclasp	redefeat	reembody	reexpel
reaffirm	reattack	reclean	redefine	reembrace	reexperience
reaffirmation	reattain	reclothe	redemand	reemerge	reexport
realign	reattempt	recoin	redemonstrate	reemergence	reexpulsion
realignment	reavow	recoinage	redeny	reemigrate	reface
reannex	reawake	recolonize	redeposit	reenact	refashion
reannoint	reawaken	recolor	redescend	reenaction	refasten
reappear	rebaptism	recombine	redescent	reenactment	refertilize
reappearance	rebaptize	recombination	redescribe	reencourage	refire
reapply	rebind	recommence	redetermine	reencouragement	reflow
reappoint	rebloom	recommission	redigest	reendow	reflower

reach (rēch) *v.t.* **1.** To stretch out or forth, as the hand; extend. **2.** To present or hand over. **3.** To be able to touch or grasp: Can you *reach* the top shelf? **4.** To arrive at or come to by motion or progress. **5.** To achieve communication with; gain access to. **6.** To amount to; total. **7.** To strike or hit, as with a blow or missile. — *v.i.* **8.** To stretch the hand, foot, etc., out or forth. **9.** To attempt to touch or grasp something: He *reached* for his wallet. **10.** To have extent in space, time, etc.: The ladder *reached* to the ceiling. **11.** *Naut.* To sail on a tack with the wind on or forward of the beam. — *n.* **1.** The act or power of reaching. **2.** The distance one is able to reach, as with the hand, an instrument, or missile. **3.** Extent of thought, influence, etc.; scope; range. **4.** An unbroken stretch, as of a stream; a vista or expanse. **5.** *Naut.* The sailing, or the distance sailed, by a vessel on one tack. [OE *rǣcan*] — **reach'er** *n.*

re-act (rē-akt/) *v.i.* **1.** To act in response, as to a stimulus. **2.** To act in a manner contrary to some preceding act. **3.** *Physics* To exert an opposite and equal force on an acting or impinging body. **4.** *Chem.* To undergo a reaction.

re-act (rē-akt/) *v.t.* To act again.

re-ac-tance (rē-ak/təns) *n. Electr.* In a circuit, the opposition to an alternating current caused by inductance and capacitance.

re-ac-tion (rē-ak/shən) *n.* **1.** Responsive action, attitude, etc. **2.** Tendency toward a former state of things; esp., a trend toward an earlier social, political, or economic policy or condition. **3.** The action of a muscle, nerve, organ, etc., in response to a stimulus; reflex action. **4.** *Psychol.* A response to an experience, situation, influence, etc. **5.** *Physics* **a** The equal and opposite force exerted on an agent by the body acted upon. **b** A nuclear reaction. **6.** *Chem.* The reciprocal action of substances subjected to chemical change. **7.** *Med.* The effect upon an organism of any foreign substance introduced for therapeutic purposes, or for testing, immunizing, etc.

re-ac-tion-ar-y (rē-ak/shən-er/ē) *adj.* Pertaining to, favoring, or characterized by reaction (def. 2). — *n. pl.* **·ar-ies** One who favors political or social reaction; one hostile toward change or progress. Also **re-ac/tion-ist.**

re-ac-ti-vate (rē-ak/tə-vāt) *v.t.* **·vat-ed, ·vat-ing** To make active or effective again. — **re-ac-ti-va/tion** *n.*

re-ac-tive (rē-ak/tiv) *adj.* **1.** Reacting or tending to react. **2.** Resulting from reaction. **3.** Responsive to a stimulus.

re-ac-tiv-i-ty (rē/ak-tiv/ə-tē) *n.* **1.** The state or quality of being reactive. **2.** *Chem.* The relative tendency of an element to enter into chemical reactions.

re-ac-tor (rē-ak/tər) *n.* **1.** One who or that which reacts. **2.** *Electr.* A device for introducing reactance into a circuit, as for starting motors, controlling current, etc. **3.** *Physics* Any of various assemblies for the generation and control of atomic energy: formerly called *pile.*

read (*v. & n.* rēd; *adj.* red) *v.* **read** (red), **read-ing** (rē/ding) *v.t.* **1.** To apprehend the meaning of (a book, writing, etc.) by perceiving the form and relation of the printed or written characters. **2.** To utter aloud (something printed or written). **3.** To understand the significance, intent, etc., of as if by reading: to *read* the sky. **4.** To apprehend the meaning of something written in (a foreign language). **5.** To make a study of: to *read* law. **6.** To discover the true nature of (a person, character, etc.) by observation or scrutiny. **7.** To interpret (something read) in a specified manner. **8.** To take as the meaning of something read. **9.** To have as its wording: The passage *reads* "principal," not "principle." **10.** To indicate or register, as an instrument or device. **11.** To bring into a specified condition by reading: I *read* her to sleep. — *v.i.* **12.** To apprehend written or printed characters, as of words, music, etc. **13.** To utter aloud the words or contents of a book, etc. **14.** To gain information by reading: with *of* or *about.* **15.** To learn by means of books; study. **16.** To have a specified wording: How does the contract *read?* **17.** To admit of being read in a specified manner: The first verse *reads* well. **18.** To have the quality of a specified style or manner of writing: His work *reads* like poetry. **19.** To give a public reading or recital. — **to read between the lines** To perceive or infer what is not expressed or obvious. — **to read out** **1.** To read aloud. **2.** To expel from a religious body, political party, etc., by proclamation or concerted action. — **to read up** (or **up on**) To learn by reading. — *adj.* Informed by books: well *read.* [OE *rǣdan* to read]

read-a-ble (rē/də-bəl) *adj.* **1.** Legible. **2.** Interesting or enjoyable to read. — **read/a-bil/i-ty, read/a-ble-ness** *n.* — **read/a-bly** *adv.*

read-er (rē/dər) *n.* **1.** One who reads. **2.** A professional reciter. **3.** One who reads and criticizes manuscripts offered to publishers. **4.** A textbook containing exercises in reading. **5.** *Eccl.* A church functionary authorized to read in church services.

read-ing (rē/ding) *n.* **1.** The act or practice of one who reads. **2.** A public or formal recital of something written. **3.** Literary research; study; scholarship. **4.** Matter that is read or is designed to be read. **5.** The indication of a meter, dial, graduated instrument, etc. **6.** The form in which any passage or word appears in any copy of a work. **7.** A specific interpretation. — *adj.* **1.** Pertaining to or suitable for reading. **2.** Of or pertaining to a reader or readers.

read-y (red/ē) *adj.* **read-i-er, read-i-est** **1.** Prepared for use or action. **2.** Prepared in mind; willing. **3.** Likely or liable: with *to:* ready to sink. **4.** Quick to act, follow, occur, or appear; prompt. **5.** Immediately available or at hand; convenient; handy. **6.** Designating the standard position in which a rifle is held just before aiming. **7.** Quick to perceive or understand; alert; facile: a *ready* wit. — *n.* The position in which a rifle is held before aiming. — *v.t.* **read-ied, read-y-ing** To make ready; prepare. [ME < OE *rǣde, gerǣde* + *ig*, suffix of adverbs] — **read/i-ly** *adv.* — **read/i-ness** *n.*

read-y-made (red/ē-mād/) *adj.* **1.** Not made to order; prepared or kept on hand for general demand: said especially of clothing. **2.** Prepared beforehand; not impromptu.

read-y-mix (red/ē-miks) *adj. U.S.* Ready to use after adding liquid, etc.: *ready-mix* pancake flour.

ready money Money on hand; cash.

read-y-to-wear (red/ē-tə-wâr/) *adj.* Ready-made: said of clothing.

---

refold	reinaugurate	reinvite	renavigate	repurify	restrive
reforge	reincite	reinvolve	renominate	repursue	restudy
reformulate	reincorporate	rejudge	renomination	requicken	resubject
refortification	reincur	rekindle	renotify	reradiate	resubjection
refortify	reinduce	relabel	renumber	reread	resummon
reframe	reinfect	relace	reobtain	rerecord	resummons
refreeze	reinfection	relaunch	reobtainable	rerise	resupply
refuel	reinflame	relaunder	reoccupation	reroll	resurvey
refurnish	reinform	relearn	reoccupy	reroute	reteach
regather	reinfuse	relight	reoccur	resaddle	retell
regear	reinhabit	reline	reoccurrence	resail	retest
regerminate	reinoculate	reliquidate	reopen	resalute	retie
regermination	reinoculation	reliquidation	reoppose	reseal	retranslate
regild	reinscribe	relive	reordain	reseed	retraverse
reglaze	reinsert	reload	reordination	reseek	retrim
reglorify	reinsertion	reloan	repacify	resegregate	retype
reglue	reinspect	relocate	repack	reseize	reuse
regrade	reinspection	relocation	repaint	reseizure	reutilize
regraft	reinspire	remade	repaper	resell	reutter
regrant	reinstall	remake	repass	resend	revaluate
regroup	reinstruct	remanufacture	repave	resettle	revalue
rehandle	reintegrate	remarriage	repenalize	resettlement	revarnish
rehear	reintegration	remarry	replant	reshape	reverification
rehearing	reinter	rematch	replantation	resharpen	reverify
reheat	reinterment	remeasure	replay	reshuffle	revictual
reheel	reinterrogate	remelt	repledge	resift	revictualment
rehire	reintrench	remerge	replunge	resolder	revindicate
reignite	reintroduce	remigrate	repolish	resolidify	revindication
reimplant	reintroduction	remigration	repopulate	resow	revisit
reimpose	reinundate	remilitarization	repopulation	respread	revitalize
reimposition	reinvent	remilitarize	repour	restack	rewarm
reimpregnate	reinvest	remix	reprocess	restipulate	rewash
reimpress	reinvestigate	remodification	reproclaim	restipulation	reweigh
reimprint	reinvestigation	remodify	republication	restrengthen	rewin
reimprison	reinvigorate	remold	republish	restrike	rewind
reimprisonment	reinvigoration	rename	repurchase	restring	rework

re·a·gent (rē·ā′jənt) *n. Chem.* Any substance used to ascertain the nature or composition of another by means of their reciprocal chemical action. [< RE- + AGENT]

real¹ (rēl, rē′əl) *adj.* 1. Having existence or actuality as a thing or state; not imaginary: a *real* event. 2. Not artificial or counterfeit; genuine. 3. Representing the true or actual, as opposed to the apparent or ostensible: the *real* reason. 4. Unaffected; unpretentious: a *real* person. 5. *Philos.* Having actual existence. 6. *Law* Pertaining to property regarded as immovable or permanent, as land or tenements: distinguished from *personal.* — *adv. Informal* Very; extremely: to be *real* glad. [< OF < LL *realis* < L *res* thing] — **real′ness** *n.*

re·al² (rē′əl, *Sp.* rä·äl′) *n. pl.* **re·als** or **re·a·les** (rä·ä′läs) *for def. 1,* **reis** (rās) *for def. 2* 1. A former small silver coin of Spain and various Latin-American countries. 2. A former Portuguese and Brazilian coin. [< Sp., lit., royal]

real estate Land, including whatever is made part of or attached to it by man or nature, as trees, houses, etc. — **real-es·tate** (rēl′ə·stāt′, rē′əl-) *adj.*

re·al·ism (rē′əl·iz′əm) *n.* 1. The tendency to be concerned with and act in accordance with actual facts rather than ideals, feelings, etc. 2. In literature and art, the treatment of subject matter in conformance with nature or real life and without idealization: opposed to *idealism.* 3. *Philos.* **a** The doctrine that abstract concepts have objective existence and are more real than concrete objects: opposed to *nominalism.* **b** The doctrine that things have reality apart from the conscious perception of them. — **re·al·ist** *n.* — **re·al·is·tic** *adj.* — **re·al·is·ti·cal·ly** *adv.*

re·al·i·ty (rē·al′ə·tē) *n. pl.* **·ties** 1. The fact, state, or quality of being real or genuine. 2. That which is real; an actual thing, situation, or event. 3. The sum or totality of real things. 4. *Philos.* The absolute or ultimate, as contrasted with the apparent. [< Med.L < L *realis* real]

re·al·ize (rē′əl·īz, rē′līz) *v.* **·ized, ·iz·ing** *v.t.* 1. To understand or appreciate fully. 2. To make real or concrete. 3. To cause to appear real. 4. To obtain as a profit or return. 5. To obtain money in return for: He *realized* his holdings for a profit. — *v.i.* 6. To sell property for cash. Also *Brit.* **re·al·ise.** — **re′al·iz′a·ble** *adj.* — **re′al·i·za′tion** *n.*

re·al-life (rē′əl·līf′, rēl′-) *adj. U.S. Informal* Actual; true.

real·ly (rē′ə·lē, rē′lē) *adv.* 1. In reality; as a matter of fact; actually; indeed. 2. Honestly; truly: used for emphasis: *Really*, the situation is impossible.

re·al·ly (rē′ə·lī′) *v.t. & v.i.* **·al·lied, ·al·ly·ing** To ally again.

realm (relm) *n.* 1. A kingdom or domain. 2. The scope or range of any power or influence: the *realm* of imagination. 3. A primary zoogeographical division of the globe. also called *region.* [< OF *realme*]

Re·al·tor (rē′əl·tor, -tôr) *n. U.S.* A realty broker who is a member of the National Association of Real Estate Boards: a trade name. Also **re′al·tor.** [< REALTY + -OR¹]

re·al·ty (rē′əl·tē) *n. pl.* **·ties** *U.S. Law* Real estate or real property in any form. [< REAL¹ (def. 6) + -TY¹]

real wages Wages evaluated in terms of purchasing power.

ream¹ (rēm) *n.* 1. A unit of quantity for sheets of paper consisting of twenty quires or 480 sheets (**short ream**), 500 sheets (**long ream**), or 516 sheets (**printer's** or **perfect ream**). 2. *pl. Informal* A prodigious amount of printed, written, or spoken material: *reams* of footnotes. [< OF < Sp. < Arabic *rizmah* bundle]

ream² (rēm) *v.t.* 1. To increase the size of (a hole). 2. To enlarge or taper (a hole) with a rotating cutter or reamer. 3. To get rid of (a defect) by reaming. [? OE *ryman* to enlarge]

ream·er (rē′mər) *n.* 1. One who or that which reams. 2. A finishing tool with a rotating cutting edge for reaming: sometimes called *rimmer.* 3. A device with a ridged cone for extracting juice from citrus fruits.

re·an·i·mate (rē·an′ə·māt) *v.t.* **·mat·ed, ·mat·ing** 1. To bring back to life; resuscitate. 2. To give renewed strength or vigor to; revive. — **re′an·i·ma′tion** *n.*

reap (rēp) *v.t.* 1. To harvest or gather (a crop) with a scythe, reaper, etc. 2. To cut the growth from or gather the fruit of, as a field. 3. To obtain as the result of action or effort; receive as a return or result. — *v.i.* 4. To harvest grain, etc. 5. To receive a return or result. [OE *rēopan, ripan*] — **reap′a·ble** *adj.*

reap·er (rē′pər) *n.* 1. One who reaps. 2. A reaping machine.

reap·ing machine (rē′ping) A machine for harvesting standing grain, often equipped with appliances for pressing, bundling, and binding the cut grain: also called *harvester.*

rear¹ (rir) *n.* 1. The back or hind part. 2. A place or position behind any person or thing. 3. The portion of a military force that is last or farthest from the front: opposed to *van.* — *adj.* Being in the rear. [Var. of ARREAR]

rear² (rir) *v.t.* 1. To place upright; raise. 2. To build; erect. 3. To care for and bring to maturity. 4. To breed or grow. — *v.i.* 5. To rise upon the hind legs, as a horse. 6. To rise high; tower, as a mountain. [OE *ræran,* causative of *rīsan* to rise] — **rear′er** *n.*

rear admiral *Naval* A commissioned officer ranking next below a vice admiral. Also *Brit. & Canadian* **rear-ad·mi·ral** (rir′ad′mər·əl). See tables at GRADE.

rear guard A body of troops to protect the rear of an army.

re·arm (rē·ärm′) *v.t. & v.i.* 1. To arm again. 2. To arm with more modern weapons. — **re·ar′ma·ment** *n.*

rear·most (rir′mōst′) *adj.* Coming or stationed last.

re·ar·range (rē′ə·rānj′) *v.t. & v.i.* **·ranged, ·rang·ing** To arrange again or in some new way. — **re′ar·range′ment** *n.*

rear·ward (rir′wərd) *adj.* Coming last or toward the rear; hindward. — *adv.* Toward or at the rear; backward: also **rear′wards.** — *n.* Hindward position; the rear; end.

rea·son (rē′zən) *n.* 1. A motive or cause for an action, belief, thought, etc. 2. An explanation for or defense of an action, belief, etc.; justification. 3. The faculty of thinking logically. 4. Good judgment; common sense. 5. A normal state of mind; sanity. — **by reason of** Because of. — **in reason** In accordance with reason or good sense. — **it stands to reason** It is logical or reasonable. — **with reason** Justifiably; properly. — *v.i.* 1. To think logically; obtain inferences or conclusions from known or presumed facts. 2. To talk or argue logically. — *v.t.* 3. To think out carefully and logically; analyze: with *out.* 4. To influence by means of reason; persuade or dissuade. 5. To argue; debate. [< OF *raison* < L < *reri* to think, reckon] — **rea′son·er** *n.* — **rea′son·less** *adj.*

— **Syn.** (noun) A *reason* seeks to explain or justify an action by citing facts, circumstances, inducement, and the like, together with the workings of the mind upon them. The *purpose* of an action is the effect that it is intended to produce; its *motive* is the inner impulse that sets it in motion and guides it. *Grounds* are the facts, data, etc., that the mind weighs in reaching a decision; and *argument* is the logical demonstration of how these facts and data determine the decision. 3. See INTELLECT.

rea·son·a·ble (rē′zən·ə·bəl) *adj.* 1. Conformable to reason; sensible. 2. Having the faculty of reason; rational. 3. Governed by reason. 4. Moderate, as in price; fair. — **rea′son·a·bil′i·ty, rea′son·a·ble·ness** *n.* — **rea′son·a·bly** *adv.*

rea·son·ing (rē′zən·ing) *n.* 1. The mental process of drawing conclusions from known or presumed facts. 2. The proofs, data, etc., employed in or resulting from this process.

re·as·sure (rē′ə·shŏŏr′) *v.t.* **·sured, ·sur·ing** 1. To restore to courage or confidence. 2. To assure again. 3. To reinsure. — **re′as·sur′ance** *n.* — **re′as·sur′ing·ly** *adv.*

re·bate (rē′bāt, ri·bāt′) *v.t.* **·bat·ed, ·bat·ing** 1. To allow as a deduction. 2. To make a deduction from. 3. *Obs.* To blunt, as an edge. — *n.* A deduction from a gross amount; discount: also **re·bate′ment.** [< OF *rabattre* to beat down < *re-* again + *abattre.* See ABATE.] — **re′bat·er** *n.*

re·bec (rē′bek) *n.* An early violinlike instrument. Also **re′beck.** [< F, alter. of OF *rebebe* < Arabic *rabāb*]

Re·bec·ca (ri·bek′ə) In the Bible, the wife of Isaac, and mother of Esau and Jacob. *Gen.* xxiv 15.

re·bel (*v.* ri·bel′; *n. & adj.* reb′əl) *v.i.* **·belled, ·bel·ling** 1. To rise in armed resistance against the established government or ruler of one's land. 2. To resist any authority or established usage. 3. To react with violent aversion: usu. with *at.* — *n.* One who rebels. — *adj.* Rebellious; refractory. [< OF < L < *re-* again + *bellare* to make war]

re·bel·lion (ri·bel′yən) *n.* 1. The act of rebelling. 2. Organized resistance to a lawful government or authority.

re·bel·lious (ri·bel′yəs) *adj.* 1. Being in a state of rebellion; insubordinate. 2. Of or pertaining to a rebel or rebellion. 3. Resisting control; refractory: *rebellious* curls. — **re·bel′lious·ly** *adv.* — **re·bel′lious·ness** *n.*

re·birth (rē·bûrth′, rē′bûrth′) *n.* 1. A new birth. 2. A revival or renaissance.

re·bound (ri·bound′; *for n.,* also rē′bound′) *v.i.* 1. To bound back; recoil. — *v.t.* 2. To cause to rebound. — *n.* 1. Recoil. 2. Something that rebounds or resounds. 3. *Informal* Reaction of feeling after a disappointment: to fall in love on the *rebound.* [< F < *re-* back + *bondir* to bound]

re·broad·cast (rē·brôd′kast′, -käst′) *v.t.* **·cast** or **·cast·ed, ·cast·ing** 1. To broadcast (the same program) more than once. 2. To broadcast (a program received from another station). — *n.* A program so transmitted.

re·buff (ri·buf′) *v.t.* 1. To reject or refuse abruptly or rudely. 2. To drive or beat back; repel. — *n.* 1. A sudden repulse; curt denial. 2. A sudden check; defeat. 3. A beating back. [< MF < Ital. *ribuffare* to reprimand]

re·buke (ri·byōōk′) *v.t.* **·buked, ·buk·ing** To reprove sharply; reprimand. — *n.* A strong expression of disapproval. [< AF < OF < *re-* back + *buchier* to beat] — **re·buk′a·ble** *adj.* — **re·buk′er** *n.*

re·bus (rē′bəs) *n. pl.* **·bus·es** A puzzle representing a word, phrase, sentence, etc., by letters, numerals, pictures, etc., whose names have the same sounds as the words represented. [< L, ablative pl. of *res* thing]

re·but (ri·but′) *v.t.* **·but·ted, ·but·ting** To refute by contrary evidence or proof, as in formal argument; disprove. — **Syn.** See REFUTE. [< OF < *re-* back + *bouter* to strike, push] — **re·but′ter** *n.*

re·but·tal (ri·but′l) *n.* The act of rebutting; refutation.

re·cal·ci·trant (ri·kal′sə·trənt) *adj.* Not complying; obstinate; rebellious; refractory. — *n.* One who is recalcitrant. [< L < *re-* back + *calcitrare* to kick < *calx* heel] — **re·cal′·ci·trance, re·cal′ci·tran·cy** *n.*

re·call (ri·kôl′; *for n., also* rē′kôl) *v.t.* **1.** To call back; order or summon to return. **2.** To summon back in awareness or attention. **3.** To recollect; remember. **4.** To take back; revoke. — *n.* **1.** A calling back or to mind. **2.** Revocation. **3.** A system whereby officials may be removed from office by popular vote.

re·cant (ri·kant′) *v.t.* **1.** To withdraw formally one's belief in (something previously believed or maintained). — *v.i.* **2.** To disavow an opinion or belief previously held. [< L < *re-* back + *cantare* to sing] — **re·can·ta·tion** (rē′kan·tā′·shən) *n.* — **re·cant′er** *n.*

re·cap (*v.* rē′kap′, rē·kap′; *n.* rē′kap′) *v.t.* **·capped, ·cap·ping** To recondition (an automobile tire) by vulcanizing new rubber onto the surface that comes in contact with the road. — *n.* A tire that has been recapped.

re·ca·pit·u·late (rē′kə·pich′ŏŏ·lāt) *v.t. & v.i.* **·lat·ed, ·lat·ing 1.** To review briefly; sum up. **2.** *Zool.* To reproduce (typical ancestral forms) in the course of embryonic development. [< LL < *re-* again + *capitulare* to draw up in chapters] — **re·ca·pit·u·la·tion** *n.* — **re′ca·pit′u·la·tive** (-lā′tiv), **re·ca·pit′u·la·to′ry** (-lə·tôr′ē, -tō′rē) *adj.*

re·cap·ture (rē·kap′chər) *v.t.* **·tured, ·tur·ing 1.** To capture again; obtain by recapture. **2.** To recall; remember. — *n.* **1.** The act of retaking. **2.** Anything recaptured.

re·cast (*v.* rē·kast′, -käst′; *n.* rē′kast′, -käst′) *v.t.* **·cast, ·cast·ing 1.** To form anew; cast again. **2.** To fashion anew by changing style, arrangement, etc., as a discourse. **3.** To calculate anew. — *n.* Something that has been recast.

re·cede (ri·sēd′) *v.i.* **·ced·ed, ·ced·ing 1.** To move back, as flood waters. **2.** To withdraw, as from an agreement, etc. **3.** To slope backward: a *receding* forehead. **4.** To become more distant. [< L < *re-* back + *cedere* to go]

re·cede (rē·sēd′) *v.t.* **·ced·ed, ·ced·ing** To cede back.

re·ceipt (ri·sēt′) *n.* **1.** The act or state of receiving anything. **2.** *Usu. pl.* That which is received: cash *receipts.* **3.** A written acknowledgment of the payment of money, of the delivery of goods, etc. **4.** A recipe. — *v.t.* **1.** To give a receipt for the payment of. **2.** To write acknowledgment of payment on, as a bill. [< OF < L < *re-* back + *capere* to take]

re·ceiv·a·ble (ri·sē′və·bəl) *adj.* **1.** Capable of being received; fit to be received, as legal tender. **2.** Maturing for payment: said of a bill. — *n. pl.* Outstanding accounts listed among the assets of a business.

re·ceive (ri·sēv′) *v.* **·ceived, ·ceiv·ing** *v.t.* **1.** To take into one's hand or possession (something given, delivered, etc.); acquire. **2.** To gain knowledge of: He *received* the news at breakfast. **3.** To take from another by hearing or listening: The king *received* his oath of fealty. **4.** To bear; support: These columns *receive* the weight of the building. **5.** To experience; meet with: to *receive* abuse. **6.** To undergo; suffer: He *received* a wound. **7.** To contain; hold. **8.** To allow entrance to; admit; greet. **9.** To accept as true, proven, etc. — *v.i.* **10.** To be a recipient. **11.** To welcome visitors or callers. **12.** *Telecom.* To convert radio waves into some useful form by means of a receiver. [< OF < L < *re-* back + *capere* to take]
— **Syn. 1.** *Receive* has no close synonym; he who *receives* takes what is given or what comes entirely passively. *Acquire* implies an active role, or some effort to obtain; the same is true of *get,* for the most part, but this word is broad enough to include some of the sense of *receive.*

re·ceiv·er (ri·sē′vər) *n.* **1.** One who receives; a recipient. **2.** An official assigned to receive money due. **3.** *Law* A person appointed by a court to take into his custody, control, and management the property or funds of another pending judicial action concerning them. **4.** Something that receives; a receptacle. **5.** *Telecom.* **a** An instrument serving to receive and reproduce signals transmitted from another part of a circuit: a telephone *receiver.* **b** Any of various electronic devices that convert radio waves into audio signals, video signals, etc., or into forms useful as a basis for observation, as in radio telescopes or radar: also **receiving set.**

re·ceiv·er·ship (ri·sē′vər·ship) *n.* **1.** The office and functions pertaining to a receiver under appointment of a court. **2.** The state of being in the hands of a receiver.

re·cent (rē′sənt) *adj.* Pertaining to, or formed, developed, or created in time not long past; modern. [< MF < L *recens*] — **re′cent·ly** *adv.* — **re′cen·cy, re′cent·ness** *n.*

Re·cent (rē′sənt) *adj. Geol.* Pertaining to or designating the present geological epoch, succeeding the Pleistocene. See chart for GEOLOGY.

re·cep·ta·cle (ri·sep′tə·kəl) *n.* **1.** Anything that serves to contain or hold something else. **2.** *Bot.* The base to which the parts of the flower, fruit, or seeds are fixed. For illus. see FLOWER. [< L < *re-* back + *capere* to take] — **re·cep·tac·u·lar** (rē′sep·tak′yə·lər) *adj.*
— **Syn. 1.** container, repository.

re·cep·tion (ri·sep′shən) *n.* **1.** The act of receiving, or the state of being received. **2.** A formal social entertainment of guests: a wedding *reception.* **3.** The manner of receiving a person or persons: a warm *reception.* **4.** *Telecom.* The act or process of receiving, or the quality of reproduction achieved. [< OF < L < *re-* back + *capere* to take]

re·cep·tion·ist (ri·sep′shən·ist) *n.* One employed to receive callers at the entrance to an office.

re·cep·tive (ri·sep′tiv) *adj.* **1.** Able or inclined to receive, as truths or impressions. **2.** Able to take in or hold. — **re·cep′tive·ly** *adv.* — **re·cep·tiv·i·ty** (rē′sep·tiv′ə·tē), **re·cep′·tive·ness** *n.*

re·cep·tor (ri·sep′tər) *n. Anat.* The terminal structure of a neuron, specialized to receive stimuli and transmit them to the spinal cord and brain. [< OF or L, receiver]

re·cess (*n.* ri·ses′, rē′ses; *for def. 2. usu.* rē′ses; *v.* ri·ses′) *n.* **1.** A depression or indentation in any otherwise continuous line or surface, esp. in a wall; niche. **2.** A time of cessation from employment or occupation: The school took a *recess.* **3.** *Usu. pl.* A secluded spot; withdrawn or inner place: the *recesses* of the mind. — *v.t.* **1.** To place in or as in a recess. **2.** To make a recess in. — *v.i.* **3.** To take a recess. [< L < *re-* back + *cedere* to go]

re·ces·sion (ri·sesh′ən) *n.* **1.** The act of receding; a withdrawal. **2.** The procession of the clergy, choir, etc., as they leave the chancel after a church service. **3.** An economic setback in commercial and industrial activity, esp. one occurring as a downward turn during a period of generally rising prosperity.

re·ces·sion (rē·sesh′ən) *n.* The act of ceding again; a giving back.

re·ces·sion·al (ri·sesh′ən·əl) *adj.* Of or pertaining to recession. — *n.* A hymn sung as the choir or clergy leave the chancel after service.

re·ces·sive (ri·ses′iv) *adj.* **1.** Having a tendency to recede or go back; receding. **2.** *Genetics* Designating one of a pair of hereditary characters that, appearing in a hybrid offspring, is masked by a contrasting character. — *n. Genetics* A recessive character. — **re·ces′sive·ly** *adv.*

re·cher·ché (rə·sher·shā′) *adj. French* **1.** Rare and exquisite; choice. **2.** Elegant and refined; also, overrefined.

rec·i·pe (res′ə·pē) *n.* **1.** A formula or list of ingredients of a mixture, giving proper directions for compounding, cooking, etc. **2.** A medical prescription: usu. abbreviated to ℞. **3.** A method prescribed for attaining a desired result. [< L < *re-* back + *capere* to take]

re·cip·i·ent (ri·sip′ē·ənt) *adj.* Receiving or ready to receive; receptive. — *n.* One who or that which receives. [< L < *re-* back + *capere* to take] — **re·cip′i·ence, re·cip′i·en·cy** *n.*

re·cip·ro·cal (ri·sip′rə·kəl) *adj.* **1.** Done or given by each of two to the other; mutual. **2.** Mutually interchangeable. **3.** Alternating; moving to and fro. **4.** Expressive of mutual relationship or action: used in connection with certain pronouns and verbs or their meaning. **5.** *Math.* Of or pertaining to various types of mutual relations between two quantities. — *n.* **1.** That which is reciprocal. **2.** *Math.* The quotient obtained by dividing unity by a number or expression, as ½ is the *reciprocal* of *x.* In a fraction, this reverses the numerator and denominator, as ⅗ is the *reciprocal* of ⅗. [< L *reciprocus*] — **re·cip·ro·cal·i·ty** (-kal′ə·tē), **re·cip′ro·cal·ness** *n.* — **re·cip′ro·cal·ly** *adv.*

reciprocal pronouns *Gram.* Pronouns or phrases denoting reciprocal action or relation, as *each other, one another.*

re·cip·ro·cate (ri·sip′rə·kāt) *v.* **·cat·ed, ·cat·ing** *v.t.* **1.** To cause to move backward and forward alternately. **2.** To give and receive mutually; interchange. **3.** To give, feel, do, etc., in return; requite, as an emotion. — *v.i.* **4.** To move backward and forward. **5.** To make a return in kind. **6.** To give and receive favors, gifts, etc., mutually. [< L < *reciprocus* reciprocal] — **re·cip′ro·ca′tion** *n.* — **re·cip′ro·ca·tive** *adj.* — **re·cip′ro·ca′tor** *n.* — **re·cip′ro·ca·to′ry** (-kə·tôr′ē, -tō′rē) *adj.*

rec·i·proc·i·ty (res′ə·pros′ə·tē) *n.* **1.** Reciprocal obligation, action, or relation. **2.** A trade relation between two countries by which each makes concessions favoring the importation of the other's products. [< F *réciprocité*]

re·cit·al (ri·sīt′l) *n.* **1.** A telling over in detail, or that which is thus told. **2.** A public delivery of something previously memorized. **3.** A musical program performed usu. by one person or several appearing as soloists.

rec·i·ta·tion (res′ə·tā′shən) *n.* **1.** The act of repeating from memory. **2.** The reciting of a lesson, or the meeting of a class for that purpose. **3.** That which is allotted for recital or actually recited. [< L < *re-* again + CITE]

rec·i·ta·tive (res/ə·tə·tēv/, rə·sit/ə·tiv) *n.* *Music* **1.** Language uttered in the phrasing of ordinary speech, but set to music. **2.** This style of singing, or a passage so rendered. Also *Italian* **re·ci·ta·ti·vo** (rā/chē·tä·tē/vō). [< Ital. *recitativo*]

re·cite (ri·sīt/) *v.* **·cit·ed, ·cit·ing** *v.t.* **1.** To declaim or say from memory, esp. formally, as a lesson in class. **2.** To tell in particular detail; relate. **3.** To enumerate. — *v.i.* **4.** To declaim or speak something from memory. **5.** To repeat or be examined in a lesson or part of a lesson in class. [< OF < L < *re-* again + CITE] — **re·cit/er** *n.*
— **Syn. 1.** repeat. **2.** recount, narrate, recapitulate.

reck (rek) *v.t.* & *v.i. Archaic* **1.** To have a care (for); heed; mind. **2.** To be of concern (to). [OE *reccan*]

reck·less (rek/lis) *adj.* **1.** Foolishly heedless of danger; rash. **2.** Proceeding from carelessness or rashness. [OE *recceléas*] — **reck/less·ly** *adv.* — **reck/less·ness** *n.*

reck·on (rek/ən) *v.t.* **1.** To count; compute; calculate. **2.** To look upon as being; regard: They *reckon* him a fool. — *v.i.* **3.** To make computation; count up. **4.** To rely or depend: with *on* or *upon*: to *reckon* on help. — **to reckon with 1.** To settle accounts with. **2.** To take into consideration. [OE *recenian* to explain] — **reck/on·er** *n.*

reck·on·ing (rek/ən·ing) *n.* **1.** The act of counting; computation; a settlement of accounts. **2.** Account; score; bill, as at a hotel. **3.** *Naut.* Dead reckoning (which see).

re·claim (ri·klām/) *v.t.* **1.** To bring (swamp, desert, etc.) into a condition to support cultivation or life, as by draining or irrigating. **2.** To obtain (a substance) from used or waste products. **3.** To cause to return from wrong or sinful ways of life. — *n.* The act of reclaiming, or state of being reclaimed. [< OF < L < *re-* back + *clamare* to cry out] — **re·claim/a·ble** *adj.* — **re·claim/ant, re·claim/er** *n.*

re·claim (rē·klām/) *v.t.* To claim again.

rec·la·ma·tion (rek/lə·mā/shən) *n.* **1.** The act of reclaiming. **2.** Restoration, as to usefulness or a moral life.

re·cline (ri·klīn/) *v.* **·clined, ·clin·ing** *v.i.* & *v.t.* To assume or cause to assume a recumbent position; lie or lay down or back. [< L < *re-* back + *clinare* to lean] — **rec·li·na·tion** (rek/lə·nā/shən) *n.* — **re·clin/er** *n.*

rec·luse (ri·klōōs/; *for n.*, also rek/lōōs) *n.* **1.** One who lives in retirement or seclusion. **2.** A religious devotee who lives voluntarily shut up in a cell. — *adj.* Secluded or retired from the world. [< OF < L < *re-* back + *claudere* to shut] — **re·clu/sion** *n.* — **re·clu/sive** *adj.*

rec·og·ni·tion (rek/əg·nish/ən) *n.* **1.** The act of recognizing, or the state of being recognized. **2.** Acknowledgment of a fact or claim. **3.** Friendly notice; salutation; attention. **4.** Acknowledgment and acceptance on the part of one government of the independence of another. [< L < *re-* again + *cognoscere* to know] — **re·cog·ni·to·ry** (ri·kog/nə·tôr/ē, tō/rē) **re·cog/ni·tive** *adj.*

re·cog·ni·zance (ri·kog/nə·zəns, -kon/ə-) *n. Law* **1.** An obligation of record, with condition to do some particular act, as to appear and answer. **2.** A sum of money deposited as surety for fulfillment of such act or obligation, and forfeited by its nonperformance. [< OF < L. See RECOGNITION] — **re·cog/ni·zant** *adj.*

rec·og·nize (rek/əg·nīz) *v.t.* **·nized, ·niz·ing** **1.** To perceive as identical with someone or something previously known. **2.** To identify, as by previous experience: I *recognize* poor poetry when I see it. **3.** To perceive as true; realize: to *recognize* the facts in a case. **4.** To acknowledge the independence and validity of, as a newly constituted government. **5.** To indicate appreciation or approval of. **6.** To regard as valid or genuine: to *recognize* a claim. **7.** To give (someone) permission to speak, as in a legislative body. **8.** To admit the acquaintance of; greet. [Back formation < RECOGNIZANCE] — **rec·og·niz·a·ble** (rek/əg·nī/zə·bəl) *adj.* — **rec/·og·niz/a·bly** *adv.* — **rec/og·niz/er** *n.*

re·coil (*v.* ri·koil/; *n.* rē/koil/) *v.i.* **1.** To start back, as in fear or loathing; shrink. **2.** To spring back, as from force of discharge or impact. **3.** To return to the source; react: with *on* or *upon*: Crime *recoils* upon its perpetrator. — *n.* A backward movement, as of a gun at the moment of firing; also, a shrinking. [< OF < *re-* backwards + *cul* backside < L *culus*] — **re·coil/er** *n.*

re·coil (rē/koil/) *v.t.* & *v.i.* To coil again.

rec·ol·lect (rek/ə·lekt/) *v.t.* **1.** To call back to the mind. — *v.i.* **2.** To have a recollection of something. [< L < *re-* again + COLLECT]

re·col·lect (rē/kə·lekt/) *v.t.* **1.** To collect again, as things scattered. **2.** To collect or compose (one's thoughts or nerves); compose or recover (oneself). — **re/·col·lec/tion** *n.*

rec·ol·lec·tion (rek/ə·lek/shən) *n.* **1.** The act or power of remembering. **2.** Something remembered. — **rec/ol·lec/·tive** *adj.* — **rec/ol·lec/tive·ly** *adv.*

rec·om·mend (rek/ə·mend/) *v.t.* **1.** To commend with favorable representations. **2.** To make attractive or acceptable. **3.** To advise; urge. **4.** To give in charge; commend. [< Med.L < L *re-* again + COMMEND] — **rec/om·mend/er** *n.*

rec·om·men·da·tion (rek/ə·men·dā/shən) *n.* **1.** The act of recommending, or of being recommended. **2.** A letter recommending a person.

re·com·mit (rē/kə·mit/) *v.t.* **·mit·ted, ·mit·ting** **1.** To commit again. **2.** To refer back to a committee, as a bill. — **re/com·mit/tal** *n.*

rec·om·pense (rek/əm·pens) *v.t.* **·pensed, ·pens·ing** **1.** To give compensation to; pay or repay; reward. **2.** To compensate for, as a loss. — *n.* **1.** An equivalent for anything given or done; payment. **2.** Compensation or reward. [< OF < LL < L *re-* again + *compensare.* See COMPENSATE.] — **Syn.** (verb) **1.** reimburse. **2.** indemnify.

rec·on·cil·a·ble (rek/ən·sī/lə·bəl) *adj.* Capable of being reconciled, adjusted, or harmonized. — **rec/on·cil/a·bil/i·ty, rec/on·cil/a·ble·ness** *n.* — **rec/on·cil/a·bly** *adv.*

rec·on·cile (rek/ən·sīl) *v.t.* **·ciled, ·cil·ing** **1.** To bring back to friendship after estrangement. **2.** To settle or adjust, as a quarrel. **3.** To bring to acquiescence, content, or submission. **4.** To make or show to be consistent or congruous; harmonize: often with *to* or *with*: Can he *reconcile* his statement with his conduct? [< OF < L < *re-* again + *conciliare* to unite] — **rec/on·cile/ment** *n.* — **rec/on·cil/er** *n.* — **rec·on·cil·i·a·tion** (rek/ən·sil/ē·ā/shən) *n.*

rec·on·dite (rek/ən·dīt, ri·kon/dīt) *adj.* **1.** Remote from ordinary or easy perception; abstruse; secret. **2.** Dealing in abstruse matters. **3.** Hidden. [< L < *recondere* to hide] — **rec/on·dite/ly** *adv.* — **rec/on·dite/ness** *n.*

re·con·di·tion (rē/kən·dish/ən) *v.t.* To put into good or working condition, as by making repairs; overhaul.

re·con·nais·sance (ri·kon/ə·səns, -säns) *n.* **1.** A reconnoitering; a preliminary examination or survey, as of the territory and resources of a country. **2.** *Mil.* The act of obtaining information of military value, especially regarding the position, strength, and movement of enemy forces. Also **re·con/nois·sance.** [< F]

re·con·noi·ter (rē/kə·noi/tər, rek/ə-) *v.t.* To examine or survey, as for military, engineering, or geological purposes. — *v.i.* To make a reconnaissance. [< OF < L < *re-* again + *cognoscere* to know] — **re/con·noi/ter·er** *n.*

re·con·sid·er (rē/kən·sid/ər) *v.t.* & *v.i.* To consider again, esp. with a view to a reversal of previous action. — **re/con·sid/er·a/tion** *n.*

re·con·sti·tute (rē·kon/stə·tōōt, -tyōōt) *v.t.* **·tut·ed, ·tut·ing** To constitute again; make over. — **re·con/sti·tu/tion** *n.*

re·con·struct (rē/kən·strukt/) *v.t.* To build again; rebuild.

re·con·struc·tion (rē/kən·struk/shən) *n.* **1.** The act of reconstructing, or the state of being reconstructed. **2.** *Often cap.* The restoration of the seceded States as members of the Union under the **Reconstruction Acts** of March 2 and 23, 1867. — **re/con·struc/tive** *adj.*

Reconstruction period *U.S.* The period following the Civil War during which the seceded Southern States were reorganized in accordance with the Congressional program.

re·con·vert (rē/kən·vûrt/) *v.t.* **1.** To change back to a state or form previously possessed. **2.** To convert back to a previously held religious belief. — **re/con·ver/sion** *n.*

rec·ord (*n.* & *adj.* rek/ərd; *v.* ri·kôrd/) *n.* **1.** An account in written or other permanent form serving as a memorial or authentic evidence of a fact or event. **2.** Something on which such an account is made, as a document or monument. **3.** Information preserved and handed down: the heaviest rainfall on *record.* **4.** The known career or performance of a person, animal, organization, etc. **5.** The best listed achievement, as in a competitive sport. **6.** *Law* A written account of an act, statement, or transaction made by an officer acting under authority of law, and intended as permanent evidence thereon. **b** An official written account of a judicial or legislative proceeding. **7.** A phonograph record. — **off the record 1.** Unofficial or unofficially. **2.** Not for quotation or publication, or not from a source to be identified. — *adj.* Surpassing any previously recorded achievement or performance of its kind. — *v.t.* **1.** To write down or otherwise inscribe, as for preserving a record. **2.** To indicate; register, esp. in permanent form, as a cardiograph does. **3.** To make a tape or phonograph record of. — *v.i.* **4.** To record something. [< OF < L *recordari* to remember]
— **Syn.** (noun) **1.** note, memorandum, register, roll, catalogue.

record changer A device on some record players that automatically feeds successive records onto the turntable.

re·cord·er (ri·kôr/dər) *n.* **1.** One who records. **2.** A magistrate having criminal jurisdiction in a city or borough. **3.** A registering apparatus. **4.** Any of a group of fipple flutes having eight finger holes, and various ranges. **5.** A tape or wire recorder. — **re·cord/er·ship** *n.*

re·cord·ing (ri·kôr′ding) *n.* **1.** *Telecom.* The process of registering a relatively permanent physical record of sounds or other communicable signals. **2.** A phonograph record.

record player A motor-driven turntable with a pickup attachment and auxiliary equipment for the playing of phonograph records: also called *gramophone, phonograph.*

re·count (ri·kount′) *v.t.* **1.** To relate the particulars of; narrate in detail. **2.** To enumerate; recite. [< OF *reconter* to relate]

re·count (rē·kount′; *for n., also* rē′kount′) *v.t.* To count again. — *n.* A repetition of a count; esp., a second count of votes cast. — **re·count′al** *n.*

re·coup (ri·kōōp′) *v.t.* **1.** To recover or obtain an equivalent for; make up, as a loss. **2.** To reimburse for a loss; indemnify. — *n.* The act or process of recouping. [< OF < *re-* back + *couper* to cut] — **re·coup′a·ble** *adj.* — **re·coup′ment** *n.*

re·course (rē′kôrs, -kōrs, ri·kôrs′, -kōrs′) *n.* **1.** Resort to or application for help or security. **2.** One who or that which is resorted to for help or supply. [< OF < L < *re-* back + *currere* to run]

re·cov·er (ri·kuv′ər) *v.t.* **1.** To regain after losing. **2.** To make up for; retrieve, as a loss. **3.** To restore (oneself) to natural balance, health, etc. **4.** To reclaim, as land. **5.** *Law* To gain or regain in legal proceedings. — *v.i.* **6.** To regain health, composure, etc. [< OF < L < *re-* back + *capere* to take] — **re·cov′er·a·ble** *adj.* — **re·cov′er·er** *n.*

re·cov·er (rē·kuv′ər) *v.t.* To cover again.

re·cov·er·y (ri·kuv′ər·ē) *n. pl.* **·er·ies** **1.** The act of recovering. **2.** The state of being or having recovered. **3.** Restoration from sickness or from a condition of evil. **4.** The extraction of valuable substances from original sources, by-products, waste, etc.

rec·re·ant (rek′rē·ənt) *adj.* **1.** Unfaithful to a cause or pledge; false. **2.** Craven; cowardly. — *n.* A cowardly or faithless person; also, a deserter. [< OF < Med.L < L *re-* back + *credere* to believe] — **rec′re·ance, rec′re·an·cy** *n.* — **rec′re·ant·ly** *adv.*

rec·re·ate (rek′rē·āt) *v.* **·at·ed, ·at·ing** *v.t.* **1.** To impart fresh vigor to; refresh. — *v.i.* **2.** To take recreation. [< L < *re-* again + *creare* to create] — **rec′re·a′tive** *adj.*

re·cre·ate (rē′krē·āt′) *v.t.* **·at·ed, ·at·ing** To create anew. — **re′-cre·a′tion** *n.*

rec·re·a·tion (rek′rē·ā′shən) *n.* **1.** Refreshment of body or mind; diversion; amusement. **2.** Any pleasurable exercise or occupation. — **rec′re·a′tion·al** *adj.*

re·crim·i·nate (ri·krim′ə·nāt) *v.* **·nat·ed, ·nat·ing** *v.t.* **1.** To accuse in return. — *v.i.* **2.** To repel one accusation by making another in return. [< Med.L < L *re-* again + *criminare* to accuse of crime] — **re·crim′i·na′tive, re·crim′i·na·to·ry** (ri·krim′ə·nə·tôr′ē, -tō′rē) *adj.* — **re·crim′i·na′tor** *n.*

re·crim·i·na·tion (ri·krim′ə·nā′shən) *n.* **1.** The act of recriminating. **2.** A countercharge.

re·cru·desce (rē′krōō·des′) *v.i.* **·desced, ·desc·ing** To break out afresh. [< L < *re-* again + *crudescere* to become raw] — **re′cru·des′cence** *n.* — **re′cru·des′cent** *adj.*

re·cruit (ri·krōōt′) *v.t.* **1.** To enlist (men) for military or naval service. **2.** To muster; raise, as an army, by enlistment. **3.** To supply with recruits. **4.** To regain or revive (lost health, strength, etc.). — *v.i.* **5.** To enlist new men for military or naval service. **6.** To regain lost health or strength. **7.** To gain or raise new supplies of anything lost or needed. — *n.* A newly enlisted member of an organization, esp. of the armed forces. See tables at GRADE. [< F < OF < L < *re-* again + *crescere* to grow] — **re·cruit′er** *n.* — **re·cruit′ment** *n.*

rec·tal (rek′tal) *adj. Anat.* Of, for, or in the rectum.

rec·tan·gle (rek′tang′gəl) *n.* A parallelogram with all its angles right angles. [< F < LL < L *rectus* straight + *angulus* angle]

rec·tan·gu·lar (rek·tang′gyə·lər) *adj.* **1.** Having one or more right angles. **2.** Resembling a rectangle in shape. — **rec·tan′gu·lar′i·ty** (-lar′ə·tē) *n.* — **rec·tan′gu·lar·ly** *adv.*

recti- *combining form* Straight: *rectilinear.* Also, before vowels, **rect-.** [< L *rectus* straight < *regere* to guide]

rec·ti·fi·er (rek′tə·fī′ər) *n.* **1.** One who or that which rectifies. **2.** *Electr.* A device used to convert an alternating current into a direct current.

rec·ti·fy (rek′tə·fī) *v.t.* **·fied, ·fy·ing** **1.** To make right; correct; amend. **2.** *Chem.* To refine and purify, as a liquid, by repeated distillations. **3.** *Electr.* To change (an alternating current) into a direct current. **4.** To allow for errors or inaccuracies in, as a compass reading. [< MF < LL < L *rectus* straight] — **rec′ti·fi′a·ble** *adj.* — **rec′ti·fi·ca′tion** (rek′·tə·fə·kā′shən) *n.*

rec·ti·lin·e·ar (rek′tə·lin′ē·ər) *adj.* Pertaining to, consisting of, moving in, or bounded by a straight line or lines; straight. Also **rec′ti·lin′e·al** (-ē·əl). — **rec′ti·lin′e·ar·ly** *adv.*

rec·ti·tude (rek′tə·tōōd, -tyōōd) *n.* **1** Uprightness in principles and conduct. **2.** Correctness, as of judgment. [< F < LL < L *rectus* straight]

rec·to (rek′tō) *n. pl.* **·toes** A right-hand page, as of a book: opposed to *verso.* [< L *recto* (*folio*) on the right (page)]

recto- *combining form Anat.* Rectal; pertaining to or located in the rectum. Also, before vowels **rect-**. [See RECTUM]

rec·tor (rek′tər) *n.* **1.** In the Church of England, a priest who has full charge of a parish, and receives the parochial tithes. **2.** In the Protestant Episcopal Church, a priest in charge of a parish. **3.** In the Roman Catholic Church: **a** A priest in charge of a congregation or church, esp. one not having parochial status. **b** The head of a seminary or religious house. **4.** In certain universities, colleges, and schools, the head or chief officer. [< L < *regere* to guide, rule] — **rec′tor·ate** (-it) *n.* — **rec·to·ri·al** (rek·tôr′ē·əl, -tō′rē-) *adj.*

rec·to·ry (rek′tər·ē) *n. pl.* **·ries** **1.** A rector's dwelling. **2.** In England, a parish church's buildings, revenue, etc.

rec·tum (rek′təm) *n. pl.* **·ta** (-tə) *Anat.* The terminal portion of the large intestine, connecting the colon with the anus. [< NL *rectum* (*intestinum*) straight (intestine)]

re·cum·bent (ri·kum′bənt) *adj.* **1.** Lying down, wholly or partly. **2.** *Biol.* Tending to rest upon or extend from a surface, as certain plant or animal organs. [< L < *re-* back + *-cumbere* < *cubare* to lie down] — **re·cum′bence, re·cum′ben·cy** *n.*

re·cu·per·ate (ri·kōō′pə·rāt, -kyōō′-) *v.* **·at·ed, ·at·ing** *v.i.* **1.** To regain health or strength. **2.** To recover from loss, as of money. — *v.t.* **3.** To obtain again after loss; recover. **4.** To restore to vigor and health. — *Syn.* See RECOVER. [< L < *re-* back + *capere* to take] — **re·cu′per·a′tion** *n.* — **re·cu′per·a′tive, re·cu′per·a·to·ry** (-pər·ə·tôr′ē, -tō′rē) *adj.* — **re·cu′per·a′tor** *n.*

re·cur (ri·kûr′) *v.i.* **·curred, ·cur·ring** **1.** To happen again or repeatedly, esp. at regular intervals. **2.** To come back or return; esp., to return to the mind or in recollection. [< L < *re-* back + *currere* to run]

re·cur·rent (ri·kûr′ənt) *adj.* **1.** Happening or appearing again or repeatedly; recurring. **2.** *Anat.* Running back: said of arteries and nerves. — **re·cur′rence, re·cur′ren·cy** *n.* — **re·cur′rent·ly** *adv.*

re·cur·vate (ri·kûr′vit, -vāt) *adj.* Bent back. — **re·cur′va·ture** (-və·chər) *n.*

re·curve (ri·kûrv′) *v.t. & v.i.* **·curved, ·curv·ing** To curve or bend back or down. [< L < *re-* back + *curvus* curved] — **re·cur·va·tion** (rē′kûr·vā′shən) *n.*

red (red) *adj.* **red·der, red·dest** **1.** Being of or having a bright color resembling that of blood. **2.** Communistic. — *n.* **1.** One of the primary colors, occurring at the opposite end of the spectrum from violet; the color of blood. **2.** Any pigment or dye having or giving this color. **3.** An ultraradical in political views, esp. a communist. **4.** A red object considered with reference to its color. — **in the red** *Informal* Operating at a loss; owing money. — **to see red** *Informal* To be very angry. [OE *rēad*] — **red′dish** *adj.* — **red′ly** *adv.* — **red′ness** *n.*

Red (red) *n.* **1.** A member of the Communist party of Russia. **2.** A member of the Communist party of any country. **3.** Any person who supports or approves of the aims of the Communist party. **4.** An ultraradical; anarchist.

re·dact (ri·dakt′) *v.t.* **1.** To prepare, as for publication; edit; revise. **2.** To draw up or frame, as a message or edict. [< L < *re-* back + *agere* to drive] — **re·dac′tion** *n.* — **re·dac′tor** *n.*

red algae Any of a class of algae of a red, brownish red, or purplish color.

Red Army The army of the Soviet Union.

red·bait·ing (red′bā′ting) *n.* The practice of denouncing groups or individuals as communist or sympathetic to communism, often with little evidence. — **red′bait′er** *n.*

red·bird (red′bûrd′) *n.* **1.** The cardinal (def. 2). **2.** The scarlet tanager.

red·blood·ed (red′blud′id) *adj.* Having vitality and vigor.

red·breast (red′brest′) *n.* A bird having a red breast, as the American or European robin.

red·cap (red′kap′) *n. U.S.* A railroad porter.

red cedar **1.** An American juniper tree of the cypress family, having a fine-grained, durable wood of a bright or dark red color resembling cedar. **2.** The wood of this tree.

Red Chamber The chamber of the Canadian Senate at Ottawa.

Red China *Informal* The People's Republic of China.

red·coat (red′kōt′) *n.* A British soldier of the period when a red coat was part of the uniform, esp. during the American Revolution and the War of 1812.

Red Cross An international organization for the care of the sick and wounded in war, formed in accordance with the international convention signed at Geneva in 1864, the members wearing a red Geneva cross as a badge of neutrality. These members are now national organizations, as the **American Red Cross**, and continue their activities in times of peace, as in fighting disease, etc.

red deer **1.** The common European and Asian stag. **2.** The white tailed deer in its rufous summer coat.

red·den (red′n) *v.t.* **1.** To make red. — *v.i.* **2.** To grow red; flush; blush.

re·dec·o·rate (ri-dek′ə-rāt) *v.t. & v.i.* **·rat·ed, ·rat·ing** To renovate or remodel, as an apartment. — **re′dec·o·ra′tion** *n.*

re·deem (ri-dēm′) *v.t.* **1.** To regain possession of by paying a price; esp., to recover, as mortgaged property. **2.** To pay off; receive back and satisfy, as a promissory note. **3.** To set free; ransom. **4.** *Theol.* To rescue from sin and its penalties. **5.** To fulfill, as an oath or promise. **6.** To compensate for: The play was *redeemed* by its acting. [< MF < L < *re*- back + *emere* to buy] — **re·deem′a·ble, re·demp′ti·ble** (-demp′tə-bəl) *adj.*

re·deem·er (ri-dē′mər) *n.* One who redeems. — **The Redeemer** Jesus Christ.

re·deem·ing (ri-dē′ming) *adj.* Compensating for faults, lacks, poor quality, etc.: the *redeeming* feature.

re·de·liv·er (rē′di·liv′ər) *v.t.* **1.** To deliver again, as a message or a speech. **2.** To give back; return; restore. — **re′·de·liv′er·ance, re′de·liv′er·y** *n.*

re·demp·tion (ri-demp′shən) *n.* **1.** The act of redeeming, or the state of being redeemed. **2.** The recovery of what is mortgaged or pledged. **3.** The payment of a debt or obligation; esp., the paying of the value of its notes, warrants, etc., by a government. [< OF < L < *redimere* to redeem.]

re·demp·tive (ri-demp′tiv) *adj.* Serving to redeem, or connected with redemption. Also **re·demp′to·ry** (-tər·ē).

Red Ensign The Canadian flag, bearing both the Union Jack and the arms of Canada.

re·de·vel·op (rē′di·vel′əp) *v.t.* **1.** To develop again. **2.** *Photog.* To intensify with chemicals and put through a second developing process. — *v.i.* **3.** To develop again. Also **re′de·vel′ope.** — **re′de·vel′op·er** *n.* — **re′de·vel′op·ment** *n.*

red·eye (red′ī′) *n.* **1.** *U.S. Informal* The danger signal in a railroad semaphore system. **2.** *U.S. Slang* Inferior whisky.

red·fin (red′fin′) *n. pl.* **·fins** or **·fin** One of various cyprinoid fishes; esp., the common shiner of eastern North America.

red-hand·ed (red′han′did) *adj.* **1.** Having just committed any crime. **2.** Caught in the act of doing some particular thing. — **red′hand′ed·ly** *adv.* — **red′-hand′ed·ness** *n.*

red·head (red′hed′) *n.* **1.** A person with red hair. **2.** An American duck, sometimes mistaken for the canvasback.

red herring 1. Herring dried and smoked to a reddish color. **2.** A diverting of attention from the main subject by introducing some irrelevant topic.

red-hot (red′hot′) *adj.* **1.** Heated to redness. **2.** New, as if just from the fire: *red-hot* news. **3.** Heated; excited.

red·in·gote (red′ing·gōt) *n.* An outer coat with long full skirts. [< F *rédingote*, alter. of E *riding coat*]

re·din·te·grate (ri·din′tə·grāt) *v.t.* **·grat·ed, ·grat·ing** To restore to a perfect state. — *adj.* Restored. [< L < *red*-again + *integrare* to make whole] — **re·din′te·gra′tion** *n.*

re·di·rect¹ (rē′di·rekt′) *v.t.* To direct again or anew: to *redirect* a letter. — **re′di·rec′tion** *n.*

re·di·rect² (rē′di·rekt′) *adj. Law* Designating the examination of a witness, after cross-examination, by the party who first examined him.

re·dis·trict (rē-dis′trikt) *v.t.* To district again; esp., to redraw the boundaries of the election districts of.

red lead (led) Minium.

red-let·ter day (red′let′ər) A memorable occasion: from the use on calendars of red letters to indicate holidays.

red light A red traffic or signal light meaning "stop."

red-light district (red′līt′) A part of a city or town in which brothels, often marked by a red light, are numerous.

red man An American Indian.

red·neck (red′nek′) *n.* In the rural South, a poor, uneducated white person: a disparaging term.

red oak 1. Any of several oaks having a dense, cross-grained wood. **2.** The wood of any of these oaks.

red·o·lent (red′ə·lənt) *adj.* Full of or diffusing a pleasant fragrance. [< OF < L < *red*- thoroughly + *olere* to smell] — **red′o·lence, red′o·len·cy** *n.* — **red′o·lent·ly** *adv.*

re·dou·ble (rē-dub′əl) *v.t. & v.i.* **·led, ·ling 1.** To make or become double. **2.** To increase greatly. **3.** To echo or reecho. **4.** To fold or turn back. **5.** In bridge, to double (an opponent's double). — *n.* In bridge, the doubling of an opponent's double.

re·doubt (ri-dout′) *n.* **1.** An enclosed fortification, esp. a temporary one of any form. **2.** An earthwork or simple fortification placed within the main rampart line of a permanent fortification. [< F < Ital. < Med.L < L *reductus* secret place, pp. of *reducere* to reduce]

re·doubt·a·ble (ri·dou′tə·bəl) *adj.* **1.** Inspiring fear; formidable. **2.** Deserving respect or deference. Also **re·doubt′ed** (-dou′tid). [< F, ult. < L *re*- thoroughly + *dubitare* to doubt] — **re·doubt′a·ble·ness** *n.* — **re·doubt′a·bly** *adv.*

re·dound (ri·dound′) *v.i.* To have an effect, as by reaction, to the credit, discredit, advantage, etc., of the original agent; accrue. — *n.* A return by way of consequence; requital. [< F < L < *red*- back + *undare* to surge]

red pepper A species of capsicum cultivated in many varieties and used as a condiment: also called *cayenne pepper.*

red·poll (red′pōl′) *n.* Any of various small finches of northern regions, having a reddish crown.

re·draft (*n.* rē′draft′, -dräft′; *v.* rē-draft′, -dräft′) *n.* **1.** A second draft or copy. **2.** A bill of exchange drawn by the holder of a protested bill on the drawer or endorsers for the reimbursement of the amount of the original bill with costs and charges. — *v.t. & v.i.* To make a redraft (of).

re·dress (ri·dres′; *for n., also* rē′dres) *v.t.* **1.** To set right, as a wrong, by compensation or by punishment of the wrongdoer; make reparation for. **2.** To make reparation to; compensate. **3.** To remedy; correct. **4.** To adjust, as balances. — *n.* **1.** Satisfaction for wrong done; reparation; amends. **2.** A restoration; correction. [< F < *re*- again + *dresser* to arrange] — **re·dress′er** or **re·dres′sor** *n.*

re·dress (rē·dres′) *v.t. & v.i.* To dress again.

red salmon The sockeye.

red·skin (red′skin′) *n.* A North American Indian.

red snapper A reddish fish found in Atlantic waters and esteemed as a food fish.

red·start (red′stärt′) *n.* **1.** A small European singing bird allied to the warblers; having a black throat, white forehead, and rust-red breast, sides, and tail. **2.** A small fly-catching warbler of eastern North America, with bright orange-red patches against black and white.

red tape Rigid official procedure involving delay or inaction: from the tying of public documents with red tape.

re·duce (ri·dōōs′, -dyōōs′) *v.* **·duced, ·duc·ing** *v.t.* **1.** To make less in size, amount, number, intensity, etc.; diminish. **2.** To bring to a lower condition; degrade. **3.** To bring to submission; conquer. **4.** To bring to a specified condition or state: with *to*: to *reduce* a person to desperation. **5.** To thin (paint, etc.) with oil or turpentine. **6.** *Math.* To change (an expression) to a more elementary form. **7.** *Surg.* To restore (displaced parts) to normal position. **8.** *Chem.* **a** To decrease the valence of (an atom or group of atoms) by adding electrons. **b** To remove oxygen from (a compound). **9.** *Metall.* To extract (a metal) from a combined state, as in an ore. — *v.i.* **10.** To become less in any way. **11.** To decrease one's weight, as by dieting. — **Syn.** See DECREASE. [< L < *re*- back + *ducere* to lead] — **re·duc′er** *n.* — **re·duc′i·bil′i·ty** *n.* — **re·duc′i·ble** *adj.* — **re·duc′i·bly** *adv.*

reducing agent *Chem.* A substance that effects reduction, while increasing its valence and becoming oxidized.

re·duc·ti·o ad ab·sur·dum (ri·duk′shē·ō ad ab·sûr′dəm) *Latin* Reduction to an absurdity; disposal of a proposition by showing that its logical conclusion is absurd.

re·duc·tion (ri·duk′shən) *n.* **1.** The act or process of reducing, or its results. **2.** *Chem.* **a** The process of depriving a compound of oxygen. **b** The process by which atoms gain valence electrons or cease to share them with a more electronegative element. — **re·duc′tion·al** *adj.* — **re·duc′tive** (-tiv) *adj.*

re·dun·dance (ri·dun′dəns) *n.* **1.** The condition or quality of being redundant. **2.** That which is redundant.

re·dun·dan·cy (ri·dun′dən·sē) *n. pl.* **·cies 1.** Redundance. **2.** In information theory, the extent to which a signal repeats the same message, reducing the probability of error and reducing the effective capacity of the channel.

re·dun·dant (ri·dun′dənt) *adj.* **1.** Being more than is required; constituting an excess. **2.** Unnecessarily verbose; tautological. [< L *redundans, -antis*, ppr. of *redundare* to overflow] — **re·dun′dant·ly** *adv.*

re·du·pli·cate (*v.* ri·dōō′plə·kāt, -dyōō′-; *adj.* ri·dōō′plə·kit, -dyōō′-) *v.* **·cat·ed, ·cat·ing** *v.t.* **1.** To repeat again and again; redouble; iterate. **2.** *Ling.* To affix a reduplication to. — *v.i.* **3.** To undergo reduplication. — *adj.* **1.** Repeated again and again; duplicated. **2.** *Bot.* Valvate with the margins reflexed. [< L < *re*- again + *duplicare* to double] — **re·du′pli·ca′tive** *adj.*

re·du·pli·ca·tion (ri·dōō′plə·kā′shən, -dyōō′-) *n.* **1.** The act of reduplicating, or the state of being reduplicated; a redoubling. **2.** *Ling.* The repetition of an initial element or elements in a word. **b** The doubling of all or part of a word, often with vowel or consonant change, as in *razzle-dazzle.*

red·wing (red′wing′) *n.* **1.** An American blackbird with bright scarlet patches on the wings of the male. Also **red′-winged′ blackbird. 2.** An Old World red-winged thrush, with bright reddish orange on the sides and underwings.

red·wood (red′wŏŏd′) *n.* **1.** A sequoia. **2.** Its durable reddish wood. **3.** Any of various similar trees.

re·ech·o (ri·ek′ō) *v.t.* **1.** To echo back, as a sound. **2.** To echo again; repeat, as an opinion. — *v.i.* **3.** To echo again; reverberate. — *n.* That which is reechoed.

reed (rēd) *n.* **1.** The slender, frequently jointed stem of certain tall grasses growing in wet places, or the grasses themselves. **2.** A thin, elastic plate of reed, wood, or metal nearly closing an opening, as in a pipe, used in reed organs, oboes, clarinets, etc., to produce a musical tone. **3.** A musical pipe made of the hollow stem of a plant. **4.** *Archit.* A semicylindrical ornamental molding or bead. **5.** An arrow. **6.** The abomasum. — *v.t.* **1.** To fashion into or decorate with reeds. **2.** To thatch with reeds. [OE *hrēod*]

reed·ing (rē′ding) *n.* **1.** Beading or semicylindrical moldings collectively. **2.** Ornamentation by such moldings. **3.** A molding of this kind. **4.** The knurling on the edge of a coin, as distinguished from milling.

reed organ A keyboard musical instrument sounding by means of free reeds vibrated by air currents.

reed pipe An organ pipe that acts as a resonator for a tuned reed. Compare FLUE PIPE.

re·ed·u·cate (rē·ej′oō-kāt) *v.t.* **·cat·ed, ·cat·ing 1.** To educate again. **2.** To rehabilitate, as a criminal, by education.

reed·y (rē′dē) *adj.* **reed·i·er, reed·i·est 1.** Full of reeds. **2.** Like a reed. **3.** Having a thin, sharp tone, like a reed instrument. — **reed′i·ness** *n.*

reef[1] (rēf) *n.* **1.** A ridge of sand or rocks, or esp. of coral, at or near the surface of the water. **2.** A lode, vein, or ledge. Compare SHOAL[1]. [< ON *rif*] — **reef′y** *adj.*

reef[2] (rēf) *Naut. n.* **1.** The part of a sail that is folded and secured or untied and let out in regulating its size on the mast. **2.** The tuck taken in a sail when reefed. — *v.t.* **1.** To reduce (a sail) by folding a part and fastening it to a yard or boom. **2.** To shorten or lower, as a topmast by taking part of it in. [< ON *rif* rib]

reef·er[1] (rē′fər) *n.* **1.** One who reefs. **2.** A close-fitting, often double-breasted coat or jacket of heavy material.

reef·er[2] (rē′fər) *n. U.S. Slang* A marihuana cigarette. [? from its resemblance to the reef of a sail]

reef knot A square knot.

reek (rēk) *v.i.* **1.** To give off smoke, vapor, etc. **2.** To give off a strong, offensive smell. **3.** To be pervaded with anything offensive. — *v.t.* **4.** To expose to smoke or its action. **5.** To give off or emit (fumes, an odor, etc.) [OE *rēocan* to smoke] — **reek′er** *n.* — **reek′y** *adv.*

reel[1] (rēl) *n.* **1.** A rotary device or frame for winding rope, film, or other flexible substance. **2.** Motion picture film wound on one reel, used as a unit of length. **3.** A wooden spool for wire, thread, etc. **4.** Material, as thread, paper, etc., wound on a reel. — *v.t.* **1.** To wind on a reel or bobbin, as a line. **2.** To pull by reeling a line: with *in*: to *reel* a fish in. **3.** To say, do, etc., easily and fluently: with *off*. [OE *hrēol*] — **reel′a·ble** *adj.* — **reel′er** *n.*

reel[2] (rēl) *v.i.* **1.** To stagger, sway, or lurch, as when giddy or drunk. **2.** To whirl round and round. **3.** To have a sensation of giddiness or whirling. **4.** To waver or fall back, as attacking troops. — *v.t.* **5.** To cause to reel. — *n.* A staggering motion; giddiness. [< REEL[1]] — **reel′er** *n.*

reel[3] (rēl) *n.* A lively dance, chiefly Scottish or Irish; also, the music for this dance. [? < REEL[1]]

re·en·force (rē′en-fôrs′, -fōrs′), **re·en·force·ment** (rē′en-fôrs′mənt, -fōrs′-), etc. See REINFORCE, etc.

re·en·try (rē-en′trē) *n. pl.* **·tries 1.** The act of entering again. **2.** In whist and bridge, an entry. **3.** *Aerospace* The return of a rocket or other object to the atmosphere of the earth after travel to very high altitudes.

re·e·val·u·ate (rē′i-val′yōō-āt) *v.t.* **·at·ed, ·at·ing** To evaluate or consider anew. — **re·e·val′u·a′tion** *n.*

reeve[1] (rēv) *v.t.* **reeved** or **rove, reev·ing** *Naut.* **1.** To pass, as a rope or rod, through a hole, block, or aperture. **2.** To fasten in such manner. **3.** To pass a rope, etc., through (a block or pulley). [Origin uncertain]

reeve[2] (rēv) *n.* **1.** In Canada, the elected head of a rural municipal council. **2.** In medieval England: **a** A high administrative officer. **b** A bailiff; steward. [OE *gerēfa*]

reeve[3] (rēv) *n.* The female of the ruff, a sandpiper.

re·fec·tion (ri-fek′shən) *n.* **1.** Refreshment with food and drink. **2.** A light meal. [< OF < L < *re-* again + *facere* to make]

re·fec·to·ry (ri-fek′tə-rē) *n. pl.* **·ries** A room or hall for eating, esp. in a religious house or college.

re·fer (ri-fûr′) *v.* **·ferred, ·fer·ring** *v.t.* **1.** To direct or send for information, assistance, etc. **2.** To hand over or submit for consideration, settlement, etc. **3.** To assign or attribute to a source, cause, class, period, etc. — *v.i.* **4.** To make reference; allude. **5.** To turn, as for information, help, or authority. — **Syn.** See ATTRIBUTE. [< OF < L < *re-* back *ferre* to carry] — **ref·er·a·ble** (ref′ər-ə-bəl), **re·fer′ra·ble** or **re·fer′ri·ble** *adj.* — **re·fer′ral** *n.* — **re·fer′rer** *n.*

ref·er·ee (ref′ə-rē′) *n.* **1.** A person to whom something is referred, esp. for settlement or arbitration. **2.** In certain sports, as football, a supervisory official. — **Syn.** See JUDGE. — *v.t. & v.i.* **·reed, ·ree·ing** To judge as a referee.

ref·er·ence (ref′ər-əns, ref′rəns) *n.* **1.** The act of referring. **2.** An incidental allusion or direction of the attention: *reference* to a recent event. **3.** A note or other indication in a

book, referring to some other book or passage. Compare CROSS-REFERENCE. **4.** One who or that which is or may be referred to. **5.** The state of being referred or related: used in the phrases **with** (or **in**) **reference to. 6.** The person or persons to whom one seeking employment may refer for recommendation. — **ref′er·enc·er** *n.*

ref·er·en·dum (ref′ə-ren′dəm) *n. pl.* **·dums** or **·da** (-də) **1.** The submission of a proposed public measure or law that has been passed upon by a legislature or convention to a vote of the people for ratification or rejection. **2.** The vote in such a procedure. [< L, gerund of *referre* to refer]

ref·er·ent (ref′ər-ənt) *n.* The object, concept, etc., to which reference is made in a statement or its symbolic equivalent.

re·fill (*v.* rē·fil′; *n.* rē′fil′) *v.t.* To fill again. — *n.* Any commodity packaged to fit and fill a container originally containing that commodity: a *refill* for a lipstick case.

re·fine (ri-fīn′) *v.* **·fined, ·fin·ing** *v.t.* **1.** To make fine or pure; free from impurities or extraneous matter. **2.** To make polished or cultured. **3.** To improve or change by subtle or precise alterations. — *v.i.* **4.** To become fine or pure. **5.** To become more polished or cultured. **6.** To make fine distinctions. [< RE- + FINE[1], v.] — **re·fin′er** *n.*

re·fined (ri-fīnd′) *adj.* **1.** Characterized by refinement; cultivated; polished. **2.** Free from impurity; purified. **3.** Exceedingly precise or exact; subtle.

re·fine·ment (ri-fīn′mənt) *n.* **1.** Fineness of thought, taste, language, etc.; freedom from coarseness or vulgarity; delicacy; culture. **2.** The act, effect, or process of refining. **3.** A nice distinction; subtlety. **4.** Fastidiousness.

— **Syn. 1.** *Refinement* implies not only the elimination of vulgarity and grossness but also the development of delicate perception and understanding. *Cultivation* is the self-discipline, study, and exercise that bring urbanity, learning, esthetic taste, etc. *Culture* primarily contrasts the enlightenment of the civilized man with that of a savage or a child; *breeding* suggests the training that manifests itself in good manners, tact, and consideration for others. — **Ant.** coarseness, grossness, vulgarity.

re·fin·er·y (ri-fī′nər-ē) *n. pl.* **·er·ies** A place where some crude material, as sugar or petroleum, is purified.

re·fit (rē·fit′) *v.t. & v.i.* **·fit·ted, ·fit·ting** To make or be made fit or ready again, as by repairs, replacing equipment, etc. — *n.* The repair of damages or wear, esp. of a ship.

re·flect (ri-flekt′) *v.t.* **1.** To turn or throw back, as waves of light, heat, or sound. **2.** To give back an image of; mirror. **3.** To cause as a result of one's actions, character, etc.; cast: He *reflects* credit on his teacher. **4.** To manifest as a result of influence, imitation, etc. — *v.i.* **5.** To send back rays, as of light or heat. **6.** To shine back. **7.** To give back an image; be mirrored. **8.** To think carefully; ponder. **9.** To bring blame, discredit, etc.: with *on* or *upon*. **10.** *Anat.* To fold back upon itself, as a membrane or tissue. [< OF < L < *re-* back + *flectere* to bend]

re·flec·tion (ri-flek′shən) *n.* **1.** The act of reflecting, or the state of being reflected. **2.** *Physics* The throwing off or back from a surface of impinging light, heat, sound, or any form of radiant energy. **3.** The result of reflecting; reflected rays or an image thrown by reflection. **4.** Meditation; careful consideration. **5.** An imputation of blame or censure. **6.** *Anat.* The folding of a part upon itself. Also **re·flex′ion.** — **re·flec′tion·al** or **re·flex′ion·al** *adj.*

— **Syn. 4.** rumination, reverie, thought. **5.** aspersion, animadversion.

re·flec·tive (ri-flek′tiv) *adj.* **1.** Given to reflection or thought; meditative. **2.** Of, pertaining to, or caused by reflection. **3.** Having the quality of throwing back light, heat, etc. — **re·flec′tive·ly** *adv.* — **re·flec′tive·ness** *n.* — **re′flec·tiv′i·ty** *n.*

re·flec·tor (ri-flek′tər) *n.* **1.** That which reflects. **2.** A polished surface for reflecting light, heat, sound, etc. **3.** A telescope that transmits an image from a reflecting surface to the eyepiece. **4.** *Physics* A substance placed around the core of a nuclear reactor for the purpose of maintaining the level of the chain reaction.

re·flex (*adj. & n.* rē′fleks; *v.* ri-fleks′) *adj.* **1.** *Physiol.* Of, pertaining to, or produced by involuntary response to a stimulus. **2.** Turned, thrown, or directed backward or in the opposite direction. **3.** Bent back; reflexed. — *n.* **1.** *Physiol.* An involuntary movement or response to a stimulus, as in winking, sneezing, shivering, etc.: also **reflex action. 2.** Reflection, or an image produced by reflection, as from a mirror or like surface. **3.** Light reflected from an illuminated surface to a shady one. — *v.t.* To bend back; turn back or reflect. [See REFLECT.]

reflex angle *Geom.* An angle greater than 180 degrees.

reflex arc *Physiol.* The entire path of a nerve impulse from the receptors to the nerve center, and thence to the effectors.

re·flex·ive (ri-flek′siv) *adj.* **1.** *Gram.* **a** Of verbs, having an object that is identical with the subject, as "dresses" in "He dresses himself." **b** Of pronouns in the objective case, being identical with the subject, as "herself" in "She hurt herself." **2.** Of or pertaining to a reflex or reflection. — *n. Gram.* A reflexive verb or pronoun. — **re·flex'ive·ly** *adv.* — **re·flex'·ive·ness, re·flex·iv·i·ty** (rē/flek·siv/ə·tē) *n.*

ref·lu·ent (ref/lōō·ənt) *adj.* Flowing back; ebbing, as the tide. [< L < *re-* back + *fluere* to flow] — **ref'lu·ence** *n.*

re·flux (rē/fluks') *n.* A flowing back; ebb: the flux and *reflux* of fortune. [< L *refluxus*, pp. of *refluere*. See REFLUENT.]

re·for·est (rē·fôr/ist, -for/-) *v.t. & v.i.* To replant (an area) with trees. — **re'for·es·ta'tion** *n.*

re·form (ri·fôrm') *v.t.* **1.** To make better by removing abuses, altering, etc. **2.** To improve morally; persuade or educate to a better life. **3.** To put an end to (an abuse, malpractice, etc.). — *v.i.* **4.** To give up sin or error; become better. — *n.* **1.** An act or result of reformation; change for the better, esp. in administration. **2.** Improvement in one's personal life, esp. by abandonment of bad habits. [< OF < L < *re-* again + *formare* to form] — **re·form'a·tive** *adj.* — **re·form'er, re·form'ist** *n.*

re·form (rē/fôrm') *v.t. & v.i.* To form again. — **re'-for·ma'tion** *n.*

ref·or·ma·tion (ref/ər·mā/shən) *n.* The act of reforming, or the state of being reformed; esp., moral improvement.

Ref·or·ma·tion (ref/ər·mā/shən) *n.* The 16th-century religious revolution that aimed at reforming Catholicism and ended with the establishment of Protestantism.

re·for·ma·to·ry (ri·fôr/mə·tôr/ē, -tō/rē) *n. pl.* **·ries** An institution for the reformation and instruction of juvenile offenders. Also **reform school.** — *adj.* Tending to reform.

re·formed (ri·fôrmd') *adj.* **1.** Restored to a better state; corrected or amended. **2.** Improved in conduct, habits, etc.

Reform Judaism The branch of Judaism that does not accept in entirety the Mosaic Laws, the Talmud, and rabbinical interpretations as binding in modern times.

re·fract (ri·frakt') *v.t.* **1.** To deflect (a ray) by refraction. **2.** *Optics* To determine the degree of refraction of (an eye or lens). [< L *refringere* to turn aside]

re·frac·tion (ri·frak/shən) *n.* **1.** *Physics* The change of direction of a ray, as of light or heat, in passage from one medium to another of different density. **2.** *Optics* The refracting of light rays by the eye so as to form an image upon the retina. — **re·frac'tive** *adj.* — **re·frac'tive·ly** *adv.* — **re·frac'tive·ness, re·frac·tiv·i·ty** (rē/frak·tiv/ə·tē) *n.*

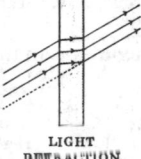

LIGHT REFRACTION

refractive index *Optics* The ratio of the velocity of a specific radiation in a vacuum to its velocity in a given medium.

re·frac·tor (ri·frak/tər) *n.* **1.** That which refracts. **2.** A refracting telescope. See under TELESCOPE.

re·frac·to·ry (ri·frak/tər·ē) *adj.* **1.** Not amenable to control; unmanageable; obstinate. **2.** Resisting heat or ordinary methods of reduction, as an ore. **3.** Resisting treatment, as a disease. — *n. pl.* **·ries 1.** One who or that which is refractory. **2.** Any of various materials highly resistant to the action of great heat, as fire clay. [See REFRACT.] — **re·frac'to·ri·ly** *adv.* — **re·frac'to·ri·ness** *n.*

re·frain[1] (ri·frān') *v.i.* To keep oneself back; abstain from action. [< OF < L *refrenare* to curb] — **re·frain'er** *n.*

re·frain[2] (ri·frān') *n.* **1.** A phrase or strain in a poem or song repeated at the end of each stanza. **2.** Any saying repeated over and over. [< OF < L *refringere* to turn aside]

re·fran·gi·ble (ri·fran/jə·bəl) *adj.* Capable of being refracted, as light. [< RE- + L *frangere* to break + -IBLE] — **re·fran'gi·bil'i·ty, re·fran'gi·ble·ness** *n.*

re·fresh (ri·fresh') *v.t.* **1.** To make fresh or vigorous again, as by food or rest; reinvigorate; revive. **2.** To make fresh, clean, cool, etc. **3.** To stimulate, as the memory. **4.** To renew or replenish with or as with new supplies. — *v.i.* **5.** To become fresh again; revive. **6.** To take refreshment. [< OF < *re-* again + *fres* fresh]

re·fresh·er (ri·fresh/ər) *adj.* Reviewing material previously studied. — *n.* One who or that which refreshes.

re·fresh·ing (ri·fresh/ing) *adj.* **1.** Serving to refresh. **2.** Enjoyably novel or unusual. — **re·fresh'ing·ly** *adv.*

re·fresh·ment (ri·fresh/mənt) *n.* **1.** The act of refreshing, or the state of being refreshed. **2.** That which refreshes, as food or drink. **3.** *pl.* Food, or food and drink.

re·frig·er·ant (ri·frij/ər·ənt) *adj.* **1.** Cooling or freezing. **2.** Allaying bodily heat or fever. — *n.* **1.** Any medicine or material, as ice, that reduces abnormal heat of the body. **2.** A substance used for obtaining and maintaining a low temperature, as frozen carbon dioxide or ammonia.

re·frig·er·ate (ri·frij/ə·rāt) *v.t.* **·at·ed, ·at·ing 1.** To keep or make cold. **2.** To freeze or chill (foodstuffs, etc.) for preservative purposes. [< L < *re-* thoroughly + *frigerare* to cool] — **re·frig'er·a'tion** *n.* — **re·frig'er·a'tive** *adj. & n.* — **re·frig'er·a·to·ry** (-tôr/ē, -tō/rē) *adj.*

re·frig·er·a·tor (ri·frij/ə·rā/tər) *n.* A box, cabinet, room,

railroad car, etc., equipped with a cooling apparatus for preserving perishable foods, etc.

reft (reft) Past tense and past participle of REAVE.

ref·uge (ref/yōōj) *n.* **1.** Shelter or protection, as from danger or distress. **2.** One who or that which shelters or protects. **3.** A safe place; asylum. [< OF < L < *re-* back + *fugere* to flee]

— **Syn.** (noun) **3.** sanctuary, retreat, haven.

ref·u·gee (ref/yōō·jē/, ref/yōō·jē/) *n.* One who flees from invasion, persecution, or political danger.

re·ful·gent (ri·ful/jənt) *adj.* Shining brilliantly; radiant. [< L < *re-* back + *fulgere* to shine] — **re·ful'gence, re·ful'gen·cy** *n.* — **re·ful'gent·ly** *adv.*

re·fund[1] (*v.* ri·fund'; *n.* rē/fund) *v.t.* **1.** To give or pay back (money, etc.). **2.** To repay; reimburse. — *v.i.* **3.** To make repayment. — *n.* A repayment; also, the amount repaid. [< OF < L < *re-* back + *fundere* to pour] — **re·fund'er** *n.*

re·fund[2] (rē·fund') *v.t.* To fund anew; replace (an old loan) by issuing new securities.

re·fur·bish (re·fûr/bish) *v.t.* To furbish again; renovate or freshen; polish up; brighten.

re·fus·al (ri·fyōō/zəl) *n.* **1.** The act of refusing; declination. **2.** The privilege of accepting or rejecting; option.

re·fuse[1] (ri·fyōōz') *v.* **·fused, ·fus·ing** *v.t.* **1.** To decline to do, permit, take, or yield. **2.** *Mil.* To turn back (the wing of a line of troops), so that it stands at an angle with the main body. **3.** To decline to jump over: said of a horse at a ditch, hedge, etc. — *v.i.* **4.** To decline to do, permit, take, or yield something. [< OF < L *refusus*, pp. of *refundere* to refund]

ref·use[2] (ref/yōōs) *n.* Anything worthless; rubbish. — *adj.* Rejected as worthless. [See REFUSE[1].]

re·fute (ri·fyōōt') *v.t.* **·fut·ed, ·fut·ing 1.** To prove the incorrectness or falsity of (a statement). **2.** To prove (a person) to be in error; confute. [< L *refutare* to repulse] — **re·fut'·a·bil'i·ty** *n.* — **re·fut'a·ble** *adj.* — **re·fut'a·bly** *adv.* — **ref·u·ta·tion** (ref/yōō·tā/shən), **re·fu'tal** *n.* — **re·fut'er** *n.*

— **Syn. 1.** *Refute, disprove, rebut,* and *confute* mean to show to be incorrect or fallacious. *Refute* emphasizes the fact of opposing a statement or argument; *disprove* emphasizes the result of such opposition. To *rebut* is to *refute* in formal debate, while to *confute* is to *disprove,* overthrow, or put to confusion; *confute* may include the use of ridicule, as well as of logical argument.

re·gain (ri·gān') *v.t.* **1.** To get possession of again, as something lost; recover. **2.** To reach again; get back to: He *regained* the street. [< MF *regaigner*] — **re·gain'er** *n.*

re·gal (rē/gəl) *adj.* **1.** Of a king; royal. **2.** Stately. [< OF < L *regalis* < *rex, regis* king] — **re'gal·ly** *adv.*

re·gale (ri·gāl') *v.* **·galed, ·gal·ing** *v.t.* **1.** To give unusual pleasure to; delight. **2.** To entertain sumptuously; feast. — *v.i.* **3.** To feast. [< F < *ré-* again + OF *gale* pleasure] — **re·gale'ment** *n.*

re·ga·li·a (ri·gā/lē·ə, -gāl/yə) *n.pl.* **1.** The insignia and emblems of royalty, as the crown, scepter, etc. **2.** The distinctive symbols, insignia, etc., of any society, order, or rank. **3.** Fine clothes; fancy trappings. [See REGAL.]

re·gard (ri·gärd') *v.t.* **1.** To look at or observe closely or attentively. **2.** To look on or think of in a certain or specified manner; consider: I *regard* him as a friend. **3.** To take into account; consider. **4.** To have relation or pertinence to; concern. — *v.i.* **5.** To pay attention. **6.** To gaze or look. — *n.* **1.** Careful attention or notice; heed; consideration. **2.** Esteem; respect. **3.** Reference; relation: in *regard* to this matter. **4.** A look or aspect. **5.** *Usu. pl.* Good wishes; affection. [< OF < *re-* again + *garder* to guard, heed]

re·gard·ful (ri·gärd/fəl) *adj.* **1.** Having or showing regard; heedful. **2.** Respectful; deferential. — **re·gard'ful·ly** *adv.*

re·gard·ing (ri·gär/ding) *prep.* In reference to; concerning.

re·gard·less (ri·gärd/lis) *adj.* Having no regard or consideration; heedless; negligent: often with *of.* — *adv. Informal* In spite of everything. — **re·gard'less·ly** *adv.*

re·gat·ta (ri·gat/ə, -gä/tə) *n.* **1.** A boat race, or a series of such races. **2.** Originally, a gondola race. [< Ital.]

re·gen·cy (rē/jən·sē) *n. pl.* **·cies 1.** The government or office of a regent or body of regents. **2.** The period during which a regent governs. **3.** A body of regents. **4.** The district under the rule of a regent. Also **re'gent·ship.**

re·gen·er·ate (*v.* ri·jen/ə·rāt; *adj.* ri·jen/ər·it) *v.* **·at·ed, ·at·ing** *v.t.* **1.** To cause complete moral and spiritual reformation or regeneration in. **2.** To produce or form anew; recreate; reproduce. **3.** To make use of (heat or other energy that might otherwise be wasted) by means of various devices. **4.** *Biol.* To grow or form by regeneration. **5.** *Telecom.* To return (part of the output of an amplifier) to the input in reinforcing phase to control gain, selectivity, etc. — *v.i.* **6.** To form anew; be reproduced. **7.** To become spiritually regenerate. **8.** To effect regeneration. — *adj.* **1.** Having new life; restored. **2.** Spiritually renewed; regenerated.

[< L < *re-* again + *generare* to generate] **—re·gen′er·a·cy,** **re·gen′er·a′tion** *n.* **—re·gen·er·a·tive** (ri·jen′ə·rā′tiv, -ər·ə· tiv) *adj.* **—re·gen′er·a′tive·ly** *adv.* **—regen′er·a′tor** *n.*

re·gent (rē′jənt) *n.* **1.** One who rules in the name and place of a sovereign. **2.** A resident master who takes part in the government of a university or college. **3.** One of various educational officers, as of a state. *— adj.* **1.** Exercising authority in another's place. **2.** Governing; ruling. [< OF < L < *regere* to rule]

reg·i·cide (rej′ə·sīd) *n.* **1.** The killing of a king or sovereign. **2.** One who has killed a king or sovereign. [< L *rex, regis* king + -CIDE] **—reg′i·ci′dal** *adj.*

re·gime (ri·zhēm′) *n.* **1.** System of government or administration. **2.** A social system. **3.** Regimen. Also **ré·gime** (rā·zhēm′). [< F < L < *regere* to rule, guide]

reg·i·men (rej′ə·mən) *n.* A systematized course of living, as to food, clothing, etc.: also *regime*. [< L *regere* to rule]

reg·i·ment (rej′ə·mənt) *n.* **1.** *Mil.* An administrative and tactical unit of infantry, artillery, etc., larger than a battalion and smaller than a division, usu. commanded by a colonel. **2.** Any large body of persons. *— v.t.* **1.** To form into a regiment or regiments; organize. **2.** To assign to a regiment. **3.** To form into well-defined units or groups; systematize. **4.** To make uniform. [< OF < LL < L *regere* to rule] **—reg′i·men′tal** *adj.* **—reg′i·men·ta′tion** *n.*

reg·i·men·tals (rej′ə·men′təlz) *n.pl.* **1.** A military uniform. **2.** The uniform worn by a regiment.

re·gion (rē′jən) *n.* **1.** An indefinite portion of territory or space, usu. of considerable extent. **2.** A particular area or place: the delta *region* of the Nile. **3.** General area; scope; province: in the *region* of literature. **4.** A portion of the body. **5.** A realm (def. 3). [< AF < L < *regere* to rule]

re·gion·al (rē′jən·əl) *adj.* **1.** Of or pertaining to a particular region; sectional; local: *regional* planning. **2.** Of or pertaining to an entire region or section. **—re′gion·al·ly** *adv.*

reg·is·ter (rej′is·tər) *n.* **1.** A formal or official record or account, as of names or transactions; also, a book containing such a record. **2.** An individual entry in a register. **3.** Any of various devices for counting or recording: a cash *register*. **4.** An official keeper of records; registrar. **5.** *Music* **a** A portion of the compass of a voice or instrument having tones of a relatively homogeneous timbre. **b** A full set of organ pipes or harpsichord strings controlled by a single stop. **6.** A device by which heated or cooled air is admitted to a room. **7.** *Printing* **a** Exact correspondence of the lines and margins on the opposite sides of a printed sheet. **b** Correct relation of the colors in color printing. **8.** The act of recording or registering; registry. *— v.t.* **1.** To enter in or as in a register; record officially or exactly. **2.** To indicate, as on a scale. **3.** To express; show: His face *registered* shock. **4.** To cause (mail) to be recorded, on payment of a fee, when deposited with the postal system, so as to insure delivery. **5.** *Printing* To effect the exact correspondence of; put in register. *— v.i.* **6.** To enter one's name in a register. **7.** To cause one's name to be included on a list of eligible voters by fulfilling certain requirements. **8.** *Informal* To have effect; make an impression. **9.** *Printing* To be in register. [< OF < Med.L < LL < L < *re-* back + *gerere* to carry] **—reg·is·tra·ble** (rej′is·trə·bəl) *adj.* **—reg′is·trant** *n.*

reg·is·tered (rej′is·tərd) *adj.* **1.** Recorded, as a birth, a voter, an animal's pedigree, etc. **2.** Having a required or official certificate, as a nurse.

registered nurse A graduate nurse licensed to practice by the appropriate State authority and entitled to add R.N. after her name.

reg·is·trar (rej′is·trär, rej′is·trär′) *n.* An authorized keeper of a register or of records; esp., a college or university officer who records the enrollment of students, their grades, etc.

reg·is·tra·tion (rej′is·trā′shən) *n.* **1.** The act of entering in a registry; also, such an entry. **2.** The registering of voters; also, the number of voters registered. **3.** Enrollment in a school, college, or university. **4.** *Music* The combination of stops used in playing a composition on the organ.

reg·is·try (rej′is·trē) *n.* *pl.* **·tries 1.** The act of registering; registration. **2.** A register, or the place where it is kept.

reg·nant (reg′nənt) *adj.* **1.** Reigning in one's own right. **2.** Dominant. [< L *regnum* reign] **—reg′nan·cy** *n.*

re·gorge (ri·gôrj′) *v.t.* **·gorged, ·gorg·ing** To vomit up; disgorge. [< F < *re-* again + *gorger* to gorge]

re·gress (*n.* rē′gres; *v.* ri·gres′) *n.* **1.** Passage back; return. **2.** The power or right of passing back. **3.** Withdrawal; retrogression. *— v.i.* To go back; move backward; return. [< L < *re-* back + *gradi* to walk] **—re·gres′sor** *n.*

re·gres·sion (ri·gresh′ən) *n.* **1.** The act of regressing. **2.** *Psychoanal.* A retreat of the libido to earlier and less mature forms of behavior. **3.** *Stat.* The return to a mean or average value. **4.** *Med.* The subsidence of a disease.

re·gres·sive (ri·gres′iv) *adj.* **1.** Tending to regress. **2.** Of or marked by regression. **3.** Denoting or pertaining to a tax or taxes in which the tax rate decreases as the amount taxed increases. **—re·gres′sive·ly** *adv.*

re·gret (ri·gret′) *v.t.* **·gret·ted, ·gret·ting 1.** To look back upon with a feeling of distress or loss. **2.** To feel sorrow or grief concerning. *— n.* **1.** Distress of mind over loss or circumstances beyond one's control. **2.** Remorseful sorrow; compunction. **3.** *pl.* A polite refusal in response to an invitation. [< OF *regreter* < Gmc.] **—re·gret′ta·ble** *adj.* **—re·gret′ta·bly** *adv.* **—re·gret′ter** *n.*

re·gret·ful (ri·gret′fəl) *adj.* Feeling, expressive of, or full of regret. **—re·gret′ful·ly** *adv.* **—re·gret′ful·ness** *n.*

reg·u·lar (reg′yə·lər) *adj.* **1.** Made according to rule; symmetrical; normal. **2.** Acting according to rule; methodical; orderly: *regular* habits. **3.** Constituted, appointed, or conducted in the proper manner; duly authorized: a *regular* meeting. **4.** *Gram.* Undergoing the inflection that is normal or most common to the class of words to which it belongs: said esp. of weak verbs. **5.** *Bot.* Having all the parts or organs of the same kind uniform in structure or shape and size: said mainly of flowers. **6.** *Eccl.* Bound by a religious rule. **7.** *Mil.* Pertaining or belonging to the permanent military services. **8.** In politics, adhering loyally to a party organization or platform. **9.** *Geom.* Having equal sides and angles. **10.** *Math.* Controlled or governed by one law or operation throughout: a *regular* equation. **11.** *Informal* Thorough; unmitigated; absolute. **12.** *U.S.* Designating the component of the armed services that consists of persons in continuous service on active duty in both peace and war: the *regular* Army. *— n.* **1.** A regular soldier. **2.** *Informal* One regularly employed or engaged; also, a habitual customer. **3.** *Eccl.* A member of a religious or monastic order. **4.** A person loyal to a certain political party. [< OF < L < *regula* rule] **—reg′u·lar·ly** *adv.* **—reg′u·lar·ness** *n.*

reg·u·lar·i·ty (reg′yə·lar′ə·tē) *n.* *pl.* **·ties** The state, quality, or character of being regular; also, an instance of this.

reg·u·lar·ize (reg′yə·lə·rīz′) *v.t.* **·ized, ·iz·ing** To make regular. Also *Brit.* **reg′u·lar·ise′.** **—reg′u·lar·i·za′tion** *n.*

reg·u·late (reg′yə·lāt) *v.t.* **·lat·ed, ·lat·ing 1.** To direct or control according to certain rules, principles, etc. **2.** To adjust according to a standard, degree, etc.: to *regulate* currency. **3.** To adjust to accurate operation. **4.** To put in order. [< LL < *regulare* to rule] **—reg′u·la′tive, reg′u·la·to′ry** *adj.*

reg·u·la·tion (reg′yə·lā′shən) *n.* **1.** The act of regulating, or the state of being regulated. **2.** A rule of conduct.

reg·u·la·tor (reg′yə·lā′tər) *n.* **1.** One who or that which regulates. **2.** A device for regulating the rate of a watch. **3.** *Mech.* A contrivance for regulating or equalizing motion or flow. **—reg′u·la·tor·ship** *n.*

Reg·u·lus (reg′yə·ləs) A white star, one of the 20 brightest, 1.34 magnitude; Alpha in the constellation Leo. [< L]

re·gur·gi·tate (ri·gûr′jə·tāt) *v.* **·tat·ed, ·tat·ing** *v.i.* **1.** To rush, pour, or surge back. *— v.t.* **2.** To cause to surge back, as partially digested food; vomit. [< Med.L < *re-* back + LL *gurgitare* to swallow, engulf] **—re·gur′gi·tant** *adj.* **—re·gur′gi·ta′tion** *n.*

re·ha·bil·i·tate (rē′hə·bil′ə·tāt) *v.t.* **·tat·ed, ·tat·ing 1.** To restore to a former state, capacity, privilege, rank, etc.; reinstate. **2.** To restore to a state of health, useful activity, etc., through training, therapy, guidance. [< Med.L < *re-* back + HABILITATE] **—re′ha·bil′i·ta′tion** *n.*

re·hash (*v.* rē·hash′; *n.* rē′hash′) *v.t.* To work into a new form; go over again. *— n.* Something hashed over, or made or served up from something used before.

re·hear·ing (rē·hir′ing) *n.* A new hearing, as in court.

re·hears·al (ri·hûr′səl) *n.* **1.** A practice session or performance of a play, etc. **2.** The act of practicing or drilling for public performance. **3.** The act of telling over again.

re·hearse (ri·hûrs′) *v.* **·hearsed, ·hears·ing** *v.t.* **1.** To perform privately in preparation for public performance, as a play or song. **2.** To instruct by rehearsal. **3.** To say over again; repeat aloud; recite. **4.** To give an account of; relate. *— v.i.* **5.** To rehearse a play, song, dance, etc. [< OF < *re-* again + *hercier* to harrow] **—re·hears′er** *n.*

Reich (rīkh) *n.* Germany or its government. **—First Reich** The Holy Roman Empire from its establishment in the ninth century to its collapse in 1806. **—Second Reich** Either of two German governments in the period 1871–1933. **—Third Reich** The Nazi state under Adolf Hitler, 1933–45. [< G, realm]

reichs·mark (rīkhs′märk′) *n.* A former standard monetary unit of Germany, worth about 24 U.S. cents.

Reichs·tag (rīkhs′täkh) *n.* The former legislative assembly of Germany. [< G]

reign (rān) *n.* **1.** The possession or exercise of supreme power, esp. royal power; sovereignty. **2.** The time or duration of a sovereign's rule. *— v.i.* **1.** To hold and exercise sovereign power. **2.** To hold sway; prevail: Winter *reigns*. [< F < L *regnum* rule]

Reign of Terror The period of the French Revolution from May, 1793, to August, 1794, during which thousands were guillotined, including Louis XVI and Marie Antoinette.

re·im·burse (rē′im·bûrs′) *v.t.* **·bursed, ·burs·ing 1.** To pay back (a person) an equivalent for what has been spent or lost; recompense; indemnify. **2.** To pay back; refund. [< RE- + obs. *imburse*] — **re′im·burs′a·ble** *adj.* — **re′im·burse′·ment** *n.* — **re′im·burs′er** *n.*

re·im·port (*v.* rē′im·pôrt′, -pōrt′, rē·im′pôrt, -pōrt; *n.* rē·im′·pôrt, -pōrt) *v.t.* To import (goods, etc., previously exported) again. — *n.* **1.** The act of importing again. **2.** That which is reimported. — **re′im·por·ta′tion** *n.*

rein (rān) *n.* **1.** *Usu. pl.* A strap attached to the bit to control a horse or other draft animal. **2.** Any means of restraint or control; a check. — *v.t.* **1.** To guide, check, or halt with or as with reins. **2.** To furnish with reins. — *v.i.* **3.** To check or halt a horse by means of reins: with *in* or *up.* [< AF < L *retinere* to retain]

re·in·car·nate (rē′in·kär′nāt) *v.t.* **·nat·ed, ·nat·ing** To cause to undergo reincarnation.

re·in·car·na·tion (rē′in·kär·nā′shən) *n.* **1.** A rebirth of the soul in successive bodies; also, the belief in such rebirth. **2.** In Vedic religions, the becoming of an avatar again.

rein·deer (rān′dir′) *n.* *pl.* **·deer** A deer of northern regions, having branched antlers in both sexes, long domesticated for its milk, hide, and flesh, and used as a pack animal. [< ON < *hreinn* reindeer + *dȳr* deer]

re·in·force (rē′in·fôrs′, -fōrs′) *v.t.* **·forced, ·forc·ing 1.** To give new force or strength to. **2.** *Mil.* To strengthen with additional personnel or equipment. **3.** To add some strengthening part or material to. **4.** *Psychol.* To strengthen (a response) by the addition of another stimulus, as a reward. Also spelled *reenforce.* [< RE- + *inforce*, var. of ENFORCE]

reinforced concrete Concrete containing metal bars, rods, or netting disposed through the mass to increase its tensile strength and durability: also called *ferro-concrete.*

re·in·force·ment (rē′in·fôrs′mənt, -fōrs′-) *n.* **1.** The act of reinforcing. **2.** *Often pl. Mil.* A fresh body of troops or additional vessels. Also spelled *reenforcement.*

re·in·state (rē′in·stāt′) *v.t.* **·stat·ed, ·stat·ing** To restore to a former state, position, etc. — **re′in·state′ment** *n.*

re·in·sure (rē′in·shoōr′) *v.t.* **·sured, ·sur·ing 1.** To protect (the risk on a policy already issued) by obtaining insurance from a second insurer: said of a first insurer. **2.** To insure anew. — **re′in·sur′ance** *n.* — **re′in·sur′er** *n.*

re·is·sue (rē·ish′ōō) *n.* **1.** A second or subsequent issue, as of a publication changed in form or price. **2.** A second printing of postage stamps from the same plates. — *v.t.* **·sued, ·su·ing** To issue again.

re·it·er·ate (rē·it′ə·rāt) *v.t.* **·at·ed, ·at·ing** To say or do again and again. [< L *re-* again + ITERATE] — **re·it′er·a′tion** *n.* — **re·it′er·a′tive** *adj.* — **re·it′er·a′tive·ly** *adv.*

re·ject (*v.* ri·jekt′; *n.* rē′jekt) *v.t.* **1.** To refuse to accept, recognize, believe, etc. **2.** To refuse to grant; deny, as a petition. **3.** To refuse (a person) recognition, acceptance, etc. **4.** To expel, as from the mouth; vomit. **5.** To cast away as worthless; discard. — *n.* One who or that which has been rejected. [< L < *re-* back + *jacere* to throw] — **re·ject′er** or **re·jec′tor** *n.* — **re·jec′tion** *n.*

re·joice (ri·jois′) *v.* **·joiced, ·joic·ing** *v.i.* **1.** To feel joyful; be glad. — *v.t.* **2.** To fill with joy; gladden. [< OF < *re-* again + *esjoir* to be joyous] — **re·joic′er** *n.*

re·joic·ing (ri·joi′sing) *adj.* Pertaining to or characterized by joyfulness. — *n.* The feeling or expression of joy.

re·join[1] (ri·join′) *v.t.* **1.** To say in reply; answer. — *v.i.* **2.** To answer; respond. [< F < *re-* again + *joindre* to join]

re·join[2] (rē′join′) *v.t.* **1.** To come again into company with. **2.** To join together again; reunite. — *v.i.* **3.** To come together again. [< RE- + JOIN]

re·join·der (ri·join′dər) *n.* **1.** An answer to a reply; also, any reply or retort. **2.** *Law* The answer filed by a defendant to a plaintiff's replication.

re·ju·ve·nate (ri·jōō′və·nāt) *v.t.* **·nat·ed, ·nat·ing** To give new vigor or youthfulness to. Also **re·ju′ve·nize.** [< RE- + L *juvenis* young + -ATE[1]] — **re·ju′ve·na′tion** *n.*

re·lapse (ri·laps′; *for n., also* rē′laps) *v.i.* **·lapsed, ·laps·ing 1.** To lapse back, as into a disease. **2.** To return to bad habits or ways; backslide. — *n.* The act or condition of relapsing. [< L < *re-* back + *labi* to slide] — **re·laps′er** *n.*

re·late (ri·lāt′) *v.* **·lat·ed, ·lat·ing** *v.t.* **1.** To tell the events or the particulars of; narrate. **2.** To bring into connection or relation. — *v.i.* **3.** To have relation: with *to.* **4.** To have reference: with *to.* [< F *relater*] — **re·lat′er, re·la′tor** *n.* — **Syn. 1.** report, recount, recite, rehearse, state. **3.** connect, link, join, associate. **3.** pertain, apply.

re·lat·ed (ri·lā′tid) *adj.* Standing in relation; connected. **2.** Connected by blood or marriage; of common ancestry; akin. **3.** Narrated; told. — **re·lat′ed·ness** *n.*

re·la·tion (ri·lā′shən) *n.* **1.** The fact or condition of being related or connected in some way. **2.** Connection by blood or marriage; kinship. **3.** A person connected by blood or marriage; kinsman. **4.** Reference; regard; allusion: as in *rela-*

tion to that matter. **5.** The position of one person with respect to another: the *relation* of ruler to subject. **6.** *pl.* Conditions or connections that bring an individual in touch with his fellows; also, any conditions or connections by which one country may come into contact with another politically and commercially. **7.** The act of narrating; also, that which is narrated. [< F < L. See REFER.] — **re·la′tion·al** *adj.*

re·la·tion·ship (ri·lā′shən·ship) *n.* The state of being related; connection.

— **Syn.** *Relationship, kinship, consanguinity,* and *affinity* are compared as they apply to persons of the same descent or family. *Relationship* is the most general term, embracing all the others and also the connection between things. *Kinship* is *relationship* by blood or marriage, and suggests mutual regard and affection. *Consanguinity* is *relationship* by blood only, and *affinity,* *relationship* by marriage only.

rel·a·tive (rel′ə·tiv) *adj.* **1.** Having connection; pertinent: an inquiry *relative* to one's health. **2.** Resulting from or depending upon relation; comparative: a *relative* truth. **3.** Intelligible only in relation to each other: the *relative* terms "father" and "son." **4.** Referring to, relating to, or qualifying an antecedent term: a *relative* pronoun. — *n.* **1.** One who is related; a kinsman. **2.** A relative word or term, esp. a relative pronoun. [< OF < Med.L < L *relatus*] — **rel′a·tive·ly** *adv.* — **rel′a·tive·ness** *n.*

relative clause *Gram.* An adjective clause.

relative pronoun *Gram.* A pronoun that relates to an antecedent and introduces a qualifying clause, as *who* in *We found a boatman who ferried us.*

rel·a·tiv·i·ty (rel′ə·tiv′ə·tē) *n.* **1.** The quality or condition of being relative. **2.** *Philos.* Existence only as an object of, or in relation to, a thinking mind. **3.** A condition of dependence or of close relation, as of the solar system on the sun. **4.** *Physics* The principle of the interdependence of matter, energy, space, and time, as mathematically formulated by Albert Einstein. The **special theory of relativity** states that the velocity of light is the maximum velocity possible in the universe, that it is constant and independent of the motion of its source, and that energy and mass are interconvertible in accordance with the equation *energy* = *mass* × *the square of the speed of light* or $E = mc^2$. The **general theory of relativity** extends these principles to the law of gravitation and the motions of the heavenly bodies.

re·lax (ri·laks′) *v.t.* **1.** To make lax or loose; make less tight or firm. **2.** To make less stringent or severe, as discipline. **3.** To abate; slacken, as efforts. **4.** To relieve from strain or effort. — *v.i.* **5.** To become lax or loose; loosen. **6.** To become less stringent or severe. **7.** To rest; repose. **8.** To become less formal; unbend. [< L < *re-* again + *laxare* to loosen] — **re·lax′a·ble** *adj.* — **re·lax·a′tion** *n.* — **re·lax′er** *n.*

re·lay (rē′lā, ri·lā′) *n.* **1.** A fresh set, as of men, horses, or dogs, to replace or relieve a tired set. **2.** A supply of anything kept in store for anticipated use or need. **3.** A relay race, or one of its laps or legs. **4.** *Electr.* A device that utilizes variations in the condition of a current in a circuit to effect the operation of similar devices in the same or another circuit. — *v.t.* **1.** To send onward by or as by relays. **2.** To provide with relays. **3.** *Electr.* To operate or retransmit by means of a relay. [< MF < L *relaxare* to loosen again]

re·lay (rē·lā′) *v.t.* **-laid, -lay·ing** To lay again.

relay race A race between teams each member of which races a set part of the course and is relieved by a teammate.

re·lease (ri·lēs′) *v.t.* **·leased, ·leas·ing 1.** To set free; liberate. **2.** To deliver from worry, pain, obligation, etc. **3.** To free from something that holds, binds, etc. **4.** To permit the circulation, sale, performance, etc., of, as a motion picture, phonograph record, or news item. — *n.* **1.** The act of releasing or the state of being released. **2.** A discharge from responsibility or penalty, as from a debt. **3.** *Law* An instrument of conveyance by which one surrenders and relinquishes all claim to something; quitclaim. **4.** Anything formally released to the public, as news, a motion picture, etc. **5.** *Mech.* Any catch or device to hold and release a mechanism, weights, etc. [< OF < L *relaxare* to relax] — **re·leas′er** *n.*

re·lease (rē′lēs′) *v.t.* **-leased, -leas·ing** To lease again.

released time *U.S.* A period during which school children are released from classes to receive religious instruction.

rel·e·gate (rel′ə·gāt) *v.t.* **·gat·ed, ·gat·ing 1.** To send off or consign, as to an obscure position or place. **2.** To assign, as to a particular class or sphere. **3.** To refer (a matter) to someone for decision **4.** To banish; exile. [< L < *re-* back + *legare* to send] — **rel′e·ga′tion** *n.*

re·lent (ri·lent′) *v.i.* To soften in temper; become more gentle or compassionate. [< L < *re-* again + *lentus* soft]

re·lent·less (ri·lent′lis) *adj.* **1.** Unremitting; continuous. **2.** Indifferent to the pain of others; pitiless. — **re·lent′less·ly** *adv.* — **re·lent′less·ness** *n.*

---

rel·e·vant (rel′ə-vənt) *adj.* Fitting or suiting given requirements; pertinent; applicable: usu. with *to.* [< Med.L ppr. of *relevare* to bear upon] **— rel′e·vance, rel′e·van·cy** *n.* **— rel′e·vant·ly** *adv.*

re·li·a·ble (ri-lī′ə-bəl) *adj.* That may be relied upon; worthy of confidence; trustworthy. **— re·li′a·bil′i·ty, re·li′a·ble·ness** *n.* **— re·li′a·bly** *adv.*

re·li·ance (ri-lī′əns) *n.* 1. The act of relying, or the condition of being reliant. 2. Something relied upon.

re·li·ant (ri-lī′ənt) *adj.* Manifesting reliance, esp. upon oneself. **— re·li′ant·ly** *adv.*

rel·ic (rel′ik) *n.* 1. Some remaining portion or fragment of that which has vanished or been destroyed. 2. A keepsake or memento. 3. The body or part of the body of a saint, or any sacred memento. 4. Any outworn custom, institution, etc. [< OF < L *reliquiae* remains, leavings.]

re·lief (ri-lēf′) *n.* 1. The act of relieving, or the state of being relieved. 2. That which relieves. 3. Charitable aid, as food or money. 4. The release, as of a sentinel or guard, from his post or duty, and the substitution of some other person or persons; also, the person or persons so substituted. 5. In architecture and sculpture, the projection of a figure, ornament, etc., from a surface: also, any such figure. 6. In painting, the apparent projection of forms and masses. 7. *Geog.* **a** The elevations and unevenness of land surface. **b** The parts of a map that portray the configuration of the district represented; contour lines. [See RELIEVE.]

re·li·er (ri-lī′ar) *n.* One who or that which relies.

re·lieve (ri-lēv′) *v.t.* **·lieved, ·liev·ing** 1. To free wholly or partly from pain, embarrassment, etc. 2. To lessen or alleviate, as pain or anxiety. 3. To give aid or assistance to. 4. To free from obligation, injustice, etc. 5. To release from duty, as a sentinel, by providing or serving as a substitute. 6. To make less monotonous, harsh, or unpleasant; vary. 7. To bring into relief or prominence. 8. To rid (oneself) of urine or excrement. [< OF < L < *re-* again + *levare* to lift, raise] **— re·liev′a·ble** *adj.* **— re·liev′er** *n.*

re·lig·ion (ri-lij′ən) *n.* 1. The beliefs, attitudes, emotions, behavior, etc., constituting man's relationship with the powers and principles of the universe, esp. with a deity or deities. 2. An object of conscientious devotion or scrupulous care: His work is a *religion* to him. [< OF < L < *re-* back + *ligare* to bind]

re·lig·i·os·i·ty (ri-lij′ē·os′ə·tē) *n.* *pl.* **·ties** Religiousness; also, pious sentimentality. [< Med.L *religiositas*]

re·lig·ious (ri-lij′əs) *adj.* 1. Feeling and manifesting religion; devout; pious 2. Of or pertaining to religion: a *religious* teacher. 3. Strict in performance; conscientious: a *religious* loyalty. 4. Belonging to the monastic life. **—** *n.* *pl.* **·ious** A person devoted to a life of piety; a monk or nun. [< OF < Med.L *religiosus*] **— re·lig′ious·ly** *adv.* **— re·lig′ious·ness** *n.*

re·lin·quish (ri-ling′kwish) *v.t.* 1. To give up; abandon. 2. To renounce: to *relinquish* a claim. 3. To let go (a hold, etc.). [< OF < L < *re-* back, from + *linquere* to leave] **— re·lin′quish·er** *n.* **— re·lin′quish·ment** *n.*

rel·i·quar·y (rel′ə·kwer′ē) *n.* *pl.* **·quar·ies** A repository for relics, as a casket, coffer, or shrine. [< F < L < *re-* back, from + *linquere* to leave]

rel·ish (rel′ish) *n.* 1. Appetite; appreciation; liking. 2. The flavor, esp. when agreeable, in food and drink. 3. The quality in anything that lends spice or zest: Danger gives *relish* to adventure. 4. Something taken with food to lend it flavor, as chopped pickles and spices. 5. A small but important characteristic; flavoring. **—** *v.t.* 1. To like the savor of; enjoy. 2. To give pleasant flavor to. **—** *v.i.* 3. To have an agreeable flavor; afford gratification. [ME < OF *relaissier* to leave behind] **— rel′ish·a·ble** *adj.*
— Syn. (noun) 1. gusto, zest.

re·luc·tance (ri-luk′təns) *n.* 1. The state of being reluctant. 2. *Electr.* Capacity for opposing magnetic induction. Also **re·luc′tan·cy.**
— Syn. 1. disinclination, unwillingness.

re·luc·tant (ri-luk′tənt) *adj.* 1. Marked by unwillingness or rendered unwillingly. 2. Disinclined to yield to some requirement. [< L < *re-* back + *luctari* to fight] **— re·luc′tant·ly** *adv.*
— Syn. 1. averse, hesitant, indisposed, loath.

rel·uc·tiv·i·ty (rel′ək·tiv′ə·tē) *n.* *pl.* **·ties** *Electr.* The specific electrical resistance to magnetization, of a given substance per unit of length or cross section.

re·ly (ri-lī′) *v.i.* **·lied, ·ly·ing** To place trust or confidence: with *on* or *upon.* [< OF < L < *re-* again + *ligare* to bind]

re·main (ri-mān′) *v.i.* 1. To stay or be left behind after the removal, departure, or destruction of other persons or things. 2. To continue in one place, condition, or character: He *remained* in office. 3. To be left as something to be done, dealt with, etc.: It *remains* to be proved. 4. To endure or last; abide. [< OF < L < *re-* back + *manere* to stay]

re·main·der (ri-mān′dər) *n.* 1. That which remains; something left after a subtraction, expenditure, or passing over of

a part. 2. *Math.* The quantity left after subtraction or division. 3. A copy or part of an edition of a book remaining with a publisher after sales have ceased. **—** *adj.* Left over. **—** *v.t.* To sell (books, etc.) as a remainder.

re·mains (ri-mānz′) *n.pl.* 1. That which is left after a part has been removed or destroyed. 2. The body of a deceased person. 3. Writings of an author published after his death. 4. Survivals of the past, as fossils, etc.

re·mand (ri-mand′, -mänd′) *v.t.* 1. To order or send back. 2. *Law* To recommit to custody, as an accused person after a preliminary examination. **—** *n.* 1. A remanding, or being remanded. 2. A remanded person. [< OF < LL < L *re-* back + *mandare* to order] **— re·mand′ment** *n.*

re·mark (ri-märk′) *n.* 1. An oral or written comment or saying; a casual observation. 2. The act of observing or noticing; observation; notice. **—** *v.t.* 1. To say or write by way of comment. 2. To take particular notice of. **—** *v.i.* 3. To make remarks: with *on* or *upon.* [< F < re- again + *marquer* to mark] **— re·mark′er** *n.*

re·mark·a·ble (ri-mär′kə·bəl) *adj.* 1. Worthy of notice. 2. Extraordinary; unusual; conspicuous; distinguished. **— re·mark′a·ble·ness** *n.* **— re·mark′a·bly** *adv.*

re·me·di·a·ble (ri-mē′dē·ə·bəl) *adj.* Capable of being cured or remedied. [< MF < L *remediabilis*] **— re·me′di·a·ble·ness** *n.* **— re·me′di·a·bly** *adv.*

re·me·di·al (ri-mē′dē·əl) *adj.* Of the nature of or adapted to be used as a remedy: *remedial* measures. [< L < *remediare* to remedy] **— re·me′di·al·ly** *adv.*

rem·e·dy (rem′ə·dē) *n.* *pl.* **·dies** 1. That which cures or affords relief to bodily disease or ailment; a medicine; also, remedial treatment. 2. A means of counteracting or removing an error, evil, etc. 3. *Law* A legal mode for enforcing a right or redressing or preventing a wrong. **—** *v.t.* **·died, ·dy·ing** 1. To cure or heal, as by medicinal treatment. 2. To make right; correct. 3. To overcome or remove (an evil, defect, etc.). [< AF < OF < L < *re-* again + *mederi* to heal]

re·mem·ber (ri-mem′bər) *v.t.* 1. To bring back or recall again to the mind or memory. 2. To keep in mind carefully, as for a purpose. 3. To bear in mind as worthy of a reward, gift, etc.: She *remembered* me in her will. 4. To reward; tip. **—** *v.i.* 5. To have or use one's memory. **— to remember (one) to** To inform a person of the regard of: *Remember* me *to* your wife. [< OF < LL < L re- again + *memorare* to bring to mind] **— re·mem′ber·er** *n.*

re·mem·brance (ri-mem′brəns) *n.* 1. The act or power of remembering, or the state of being remembered. 2. The period within which one can remember. 3. That which is remembered. 4. *Often pl.* A memento; keepsake. 5. Mindful regard. [< OF]

re·mind (ri-mīnd′) *v.t.* To bring to (someone's) mind; cause to remember. **— re·mind′er** *n.* **— re·mind′ful** *adj.*

rem·i·nisce (rem′ə·nis′) *v.i.* **·nisced, ·nisc·ing** *Chiefly U.S.* To recall incidents or events of the past; indulge in reminiscences. [Back formation < REMINISCENCE]

rem·i·nis·cence (rem′ə·nis′əns) *n.* 1. The recalling to mind of past incidents and events. 2. The narration of past experiences. 3. A feature, etc., serving as a reminder of something else. [< MF or LL < L < *re-* again + *memini* to remember] **— rem′i·nis′cent** *adj.* **— rem′i·nis′cent·ly** *adv.*

re·miss (ri-mis′) *adj.* Slack or careless in matters requiring attention; dilatory; negligent. [< L < *re-* back + *mittere* to send] **— re·miss′ness** *n.*

re·mis·si·ble (ri-mis′ə·bəl) *adj.* Capable of being remitted or pardoned, as sins. [< F *rémissible*] **— re·mis′si·bil′i·ty** *n.*

re·mis·sion (ri-mish′ən) *n.* 1. The act of remitting, or the state of being remitted. 2. Discharge from penalty; pardon; deliverance, as from a debt or obligation. 3. *Med.* Temporary abatement of a disease or pain. Also **re·mit′tal** (-mit′l). [See REMIT.]

re·mit (ri-mit′) *v.* **·mit·ted, ·mit·ting** *v.t.* 1. To send, as money in payment for goods; transmit. 2. To refrain from exacting or inflicting, as a penalty. 3. To pardon; forgive, as a sin or crime. 4. To abate; relax, as vigilance. 5. To refer or submit for judgment, settlement, etc., as to one in authority. 6. *Law* To refer (a legal proceeding) to a lower court for further consideration. 7. *Rare* To send back, as to prison. **—** *v.i.* 8. To send money, as in payment. 9. To diminish; abate. [< L < *re-* back + *mittere* to send] **— re·mit′ta·ble** *adj.* **— re·mit′ter** or **re·mit′tor** *n.*

re·mit·tance (ri-mit′əns) *n.* The act of sending money or credit; also, the money or credit so sent.

re·mit·tent (ri-mit′ənt) *adj.* Having temporary diminutions of energy or action, as a fever. **—** *n.* A remittent fever. **— re·mit′tence, re·mit′ten·cy** *n.* **— re·mit′tent·ly** *adv.*

rem·nant (rem′nənt) *n.* 1. That which remains of anything. 2. The piece of cloth, etc., left over after the last cutting. 3. Any small piece or quantity. **—** *adj.* Remaining. [< OF < L < *re-* back + *manere* to stay, remain]

re·mod·el (rē-mod′l) *v.t.* **·eled** or **·elled, ·el·ing** or **·el·ling** 1. To model again. 2. To make over or anew.

re·mon·e·tize (ri·mon′ə·tīz) *v.t.* **·tized, ·tiz·ing** To reinstate (esp. silver) as lawful money. — **re·mon′e·ti·za′tion** *n.*

re·mon·strance (ri·mon′strəns) *n.* **1.** The act of remonstrating; protest; expostulation. **2.** Expostulatory counsel.

re·mon·strant (ri·mon′strənt) *adj.* Having the character of a remonstrance; expostulatory. — *n.* One who presents or signs a remonstrance.

re·mon·strate (ri·mon′strāt) *v.* **·strat·ed, ·strat·ing** *v.t.* **1.** To say or plead in protest. — *v.i.* **2.** To urge strong reasons against any course or action; protest; object. [< Med.L < L < *re-* again + *monstrare* to show] — **re·mon·stra·tion** (rē′mon·strā′shən, rem′ən-) *n.* — **re·mon′stra·tive** (-strə·tiv) *adj.* — **re·mon′stra·tor** (-strā·tər) *n.*

re·morse (ri·môrs′) *n.* The keen or hopeless anguish caused by a sense of guilt; distressing self-reproach. [< OF < LL < L < *re-* again + *mordere* to bite] — **re·morse′ful** *adj.* — **re·morse′ful·ly** *adv.* — **re·morse′ful·ness** *n.* — **re·morse′less** *adj.* — **re·morse′less·ly** *adv.* — **re·morse′less·ness** *n.*

re·mote (ri·mōt′) *adj.* **·mot·er, ·mot·est** **1.** Located far from a specified place. **2.** Distant in time. **3.** Having slight relation or connection: a *remote* cousin. **4.** Not obvious; slight. **5.** Distant in manner; aloof. [< L < *re-* again + *movere* to move] — **re·mote′ly** *adv.* — **re·mote′ness** *n.*

remote control Control from a distance by electrical or radio circuits, as in the operation of a machine, aircraft, guided missile, etc.

re·mount (*v.* rē·mount′; *n.* rē′mount′) *v.t. & v.i.* To mount again. — *n.* **1.** A new setting or framing. **2.** A fresh riding horse. [< OF < *re-* again (< L) + *monter* to climb]

re·mov·a·ble (ri·mōō′və·bəl) *adj.* Capable of being removed. — **re·mov′a·bil′i·ty, re·mov′a·ble·ness** *n.* — **re·mov′a·bly** *adv.*

re·mov·al (ri·mōō′vəl) *n.* **1.** The act of removing, or the state of being removed. **2.** Dismissal, as from office. **3.** Changing of place, as of residence or business.

re·move (ri·mōōv′) *v.* **·moved, ·mov·ing** *v.t.* **1.** To take or move away, as from one place to another. **2.** To take off; doff, as a hat. **3.** To get rid of; do away with: to *remove* abuses. **4.** To kill. **5.** To displace or dismiss, as from office. **6.** To take out; extract: with *from.* — *v.i.* **7.** To change one's place of residence or business. **8.** *Poetic* To go away. — *n.* **1.** The act of removing, as one's business or belongings. **2.** The space moved over in changing an object from one position to another. **3.** A degree of difference; step: He is only one *remove* from a fool. [< OF < L < *re-* again + *movere* to move] — **re·mov′er** *n.*

— *Syn.* (verb) **1.** transfer, transplant, transpose. **3.** eliminate, obliterate, eradicate. **5.** depose, disestablish.

re·moved (ri·mōōvd′) *adj.* Separated, as by intervening space, time, or relationship, or by difference in kind: a cousin twice *removed.* — **re·mov·ed·ness** (ri·mōō′vid·nis) *n.*

re·mu·ner·ate (ri·myōō′nə·rāt) *v.t.* **·at·ed, ·at·ing** To make just or adequate return to or for; pay or pay for. [< L < *re-* again + *munus* gift] — **re·mu′ner·a·bil·i·ty** *n.* — **re·mu′ner·a·ble** *adj.* — **re·mu′ner·a′tion** *n.* — **re·mu′ner·a·tive** (-nə·rā′tiv, -nər·ə·tiv) *adj.* — **re·mu′ner·a′tive·ly** *adv.*

Re·mus (rē′məs) In Roman mythology, the twin brother of Romulus. See ROMULUS.

ren- Var. of RENI-.

ren·ais·sance (ren′ə·säns′, -zäns′, ri·nā′səns) *n.* A new birth; resurrection; renascence. [< F < L < *re-* again + *nasci* to be born]

Ren·ais·sance (ren′ə·säns′, -zäns′, ri·nā′səns; *Fr.* rə·ne·säns′) *n.* **1.** The revival of letters and art in Europe, marking the transition from medieval to modern history. **2.** The period of this revival, roughly from the 14th through the 16th century. **3.** The style of art, literature, etc., that was developed in and characteristic of this period. Also *Renascence.* — *adj.* **1.** Of the Renaissance. **2.** Pertaining to a style of architecture developed in Italy in the 15th century, and based on the classic Roman style.

re·nal (rē′nəl) *adj.* Of, pertaining to, affecting, or near the kidneys. [< F < LL < L *renes* kidneys]

Ren·ard (ren′ərd) See REYNARD.

re·nas·cence (ri·nas′əns) *n.* A rebirth; revival. [< L < *re-* again + *nasci* to be born] — **re·nas′cent** *adj.*

Re·nas·cence (ri·nas′əns) *n.* The Renaissance.

rend (rend) *v.* **rent** or **rend·ed, rend·ing** *v.t.* **1.** To tear apart forcibly. **2.** To pull or remove forcibly: with *away,*

RENAISSANCE
ARCHITECTURE

(Church of the Redentore, Venice, 1578–80)

from, off, etc. **3.** To pass through (the air) violently and noisily. **4.** To distress (the heart, etc.). — *v.i.* **5.** To split; part. [OE *rendan* to tear] — **rend′er** *n.*

ren·der (ren′dər) *v.t.* **1.** To give, present, or submit for action, approval, payment, etc. **2.** To provide; give: to *render* aid to the poor. **3.** To give as due: to *render* obedience. **4.** To perform; do: to *render* great service. **5.** To give or state formally. **6.** To give by way of requital: to *render* double for one's sins. **7.** To represent or depict, as in music or painting. **8.** To cause to be: to *render* a ship seaworthy. **9.** To translate. **10.** To melt and clarify, as lard. **11.** To give back; return: often with *back.* **12.** To surrender; give up. [< F < LL < L < *re-* back + *dare* to give] — **ren′der·a·ble** *adj.* — **ren′der·er** *n.*

ren·dez·vous (rän′dā·vōō, -də-; *Fr.* rän·dā·vōō′) *n.* *pl.* **·vous** (-vōōz, *Fr.* -vōō′) **1.** An appointed place of meeting. **2.** A meeting or an appointment to meet. — *v.t. & v.i.* **·voused** (-vōōd), **·vous·ing** (-vōō′ing) To assemble or cause to assemble at a certain place or time. [< F < *se rendre* to betake oneself]

ren·di·tion (ren·dish′ən) *n.* **1.** The interpretation of a text; a translation. **2.** Artistic, dramatic, or musical interpretation; also, the performance or execution of a dramatic or musical composition. **3.** The act of rendering; also, that which is rendered. [< obs. F < *rendre* to render]

ren·e·gade (ren′ə·gād) *n.* **1.** One who forsakes his faith, etc. **2.** A traitor; deserter. Also **ren′e·ga′do** (-gā′dō). — *adj.* Of or characteristic of a renegade; traitorous. [< Sp. < Med.L < L *re-* again + *negare* to deny]

re·nege (ri·nig′, -neg′, -nēg′) *v.i.* **neged, ·neg·ing** **1.** In card games, to fail to follow suit when able and required by the rules to do so; revoke. **2.** *Informal* To fail to fulfill a promise. [See RENEGADE.] — **re·neg′er** *n.*

re·new (ri·nōō′, -nyōō′) *v.t.* **1.** To make new or as if new again; restore to a former or sound condition. **2.** To begin again; resume. **3.** To repeat: to *renew* an oath. **4.** To regain (vigor, strength, etc.). **5.** To cause to continue in effect; extend. **6.** To revive; reestablish. **7.** To replenish or replace, as provisions. — *v.i.* **8.** To become new again. **9.** To begin or commence again. [< RE- + NEW] — **re·new′a·ble** *adj.* — **re·new′al** *n.* — **re·new′ed·ly** *adv.*

reni- *combining form* Kidney; of or related to the kidneys. Also **ren-** (before vowels): also **reno-.** [< L *ren, renis* kidney]

ren·i·form (ren′ə·fôrm, rē′nə-) *adj.* Kidney-shaped.

ren·net (ren′it) *n.* **1.** The mucous membrane lining the fourth stomach of a suckling calf or sheep. **2.** *Biochem.* A substance that yields rennin, obtained from the stomach of such an animal. [ME *rennen* to cause to run]

ren·nin (ren′in) *n.* *Biochem.* A milk-curdling enzyme present in rennet. [< RENN(ET) + -IN]

re·nounce (ri·nouns′) *v.* **·nounced, ·nounc·ing** *v.t.* **1.** To give up, esp., by formal statement. **2.** To disown; repudiate. [< F < L < *re-* back, against + *nuntiare* to report] — **re·nounce′ment** *n.* — **re·nounc′er** *n.*

— *Syn.* **1.** *Renounce* and *abjure* are often used in the general sense of put aside or abandon: to *renounce* one's citizenship, to *abjure* vice. *Forswear* has acquired an implication of perjury, esp. in the reflexive form: he *forswore* himself, that is, he swore falsely.

ren·o·vate (ren′ə·vāt) *v.t.* **·vat·ed, ·vat·ing** **1.** To make as good as new; repair. **2.** To renew; refresh. [< L < *re-* again + *novare* to make new] — **ren′o·va′tion** *n.* — **ren′o·va′tor** *n.*

re·nown (ri·noun′) *n.* Exalted reputation; celebrity; fame. [< AF < OF < L *re-* again + *nominare* to name]

re·nowned (ri·nound′) *adj.* Having renown; famous.

rent[1] (rent) *n.* **1.** Compensation made in any form by a tenant to a landlord or owner for the use of land, buildings, etc., esp., when paid in money at regular or specified intervals. **2.** Similar payment for the use of any property, movable or fixed. **3.** *Econ.* Income derived by the owner from the use or cultivation of his land or property. — **for rent** Available for use or occupancy by the paying of rent. — *v.t.* **1.** To obtain temporary possession and use of for a rent. **2.** To grant such temporary possession and use. — *v.i.* **3.** To be let for rent. [< OF < L < *re-* back + *dare* to give] — **rent′a·ble** *adj.* — **rent′er** *n.*

rent[2] (rent) Alternative past tense and past participle of REND. — *n.* **1.** A hole or slit made by rending or tearing; rip; fissure. **2.** A violent separation; schism.

rent·al (ren′tǝl) *n.* **1.** The revenue from rented property. **2.** A schedule of rents. — *adj.* Of or for rent. [< AF]

ren·tier (rän·tyā′) *n.* *French* One who owns or derives a fixed income from invested capital or lands.

re·nun·ci·a·tion (ri·nun′sē·ā′shən, -shē-) *n.* **1.** The act of renouncing or disclaiming; repudiation. **2.** A declaration or statement in which something is renounced. [< L *renunciatio, -onis* proclamation] — **re·nun′ci·a′tive** *adj.* — **re·nun′ci·a·to·ry** (ri·nun′sē·ə·tôr′ē, -tō′rē, -shē-) *adj.*

---

re·or·der (rē-ôr′dər) v.t. 1. To order (goods) again. 2. To put back into order. 3. To give a different order to; rearrange. — n. Goods ordered again.

re·or·gan·i·za·tion (rē′ôr-gən-ə-zā′shən, -ī-zā′-) n. 1. The act of reorganizing, or the condition of being reorganized. 2. The legal reconstruction of a corporation.

re·or·gan·ize (rē-ôr′gən-īz) v.t. & v.i. ·ized, ·iz·ing To organize anew. — re·or′gan·iz′er n.

rep¹ (rep) n. A silk, cotton, rayon, or wool fabric having a crosswise rib: also spelled repp. [< F reps, prob. < E ribs]

rep² (rep) n. Slang Reputation.

re·pair¹ (ri-pâr′) v.t. 1. To restore to sound or good condition after damage, decay, etc.; mend. 2. To make amends for (an injury); remedy. 3. To make up, as a loss; compensate for. — n. 1. The act or process of repairing. 2. Condition after use or after repairing: in good repair. [< OF < L < re- again + parare to prepare, make ready] — re·pair′er n.

re·pair² (ri-pâr′) v.i. To betake oneself; go: to repair to the garden. [< OF < LL < L re- again + patria native land]

re·pair·man (ri-pâr′man′, -mən) n. pl. ·men (-men′, -mən) A man whose work is to make repairs.

rep·a·ra·ble (rep′ər-ə-bəl) adj. Capable of being repaired. Also re·pair·a·ble (ri-pâr′ə-bəl). — rep′a·ra·bil′i·ty n. — rep′a·ra·bly adv.

rep·a·ra·tion (rep′ə-rā′shən) n. 1. The act of making amends; atonement. 2. That which is done by way of amends or satisfaction. 3. The act of repairing or the state of being repaired. 4. pl. Indemnities paid by defeated countries for acts of war. [< OF < LL < L. See REPAIR.¹] — re·par·a·tive (ri-par′ə-tiv) adj.

rep·ar·tee (rep′ər-tē′, -är-, -tā′) n. 1. Conversation marked by quick and witty replies. 2. Skill or quickness in such conversation. 3. A witty or quick reply; a sharp rejoinder. [< OF < repartir to depart again, reply]

re·past (ri-past′, -päst′) n. 1. Food taken at a meal. 2. A meal. [< OF < Med.L < LL < L re- again + pascere to feed]

re·pa·tri·ate (v. rē-pā′trē-āt; n. rē-pā′trē-it) v.t. ·at·ed, ·at·ing To send back to one's own country or to the place of citizenship. — n. One who has been repatriated. [< L re- again + patria native land] — re·pa′tri·a′tion n.

re·pay (ri-pā′) v. ·paid, ·pay·ing v.t. 1. To pay back; refund. 2. To pay back or refund something to. 3. To give a reward or inflict a penalty for; recompense or retaliate for. — v.i. 4. To make repayment or requital. [< OF repaier] — re·pay′a·ble adj. — re·pay′ment n.

re·peal (ri-pēl′) v.t. To rescind, as a law; revoke. — Syn. See ANNUL. — n. The act of repealing; revocation. [< OF < re- back, again + apeler to call, summon] — re·peal′a·ble adj. — re·peal′er n.

re·peat (ri-pēt′) v.t. 1. To say again; iterate. 2. To recite from memory. 3. To say (what another has just said) 4. To tell, as a secret, to another. 5. To do, make, or experience again. — v.i. 6. To say or do something again; esp., to vote more than once in an election. — n. 1. The act of repeating; a repetition. 2. Music A passage that is repeated; also, any notations indicating this. 3. Anything repeated. [< OF < L < re- again + petere to seek, demand]

re·peat·ed (ri-pē′tid) adj. Occurring or spoken again and again; reiterated. — re·peat′ed·ly adv.

re·peat·er (ri-pē′tər) n. 1. One who or that which repeats. 2. A repeating firearm. 3. U.S. One who votes, or attempts to vote, more than once at the same election. 4. One who has been repeatedly imprisoned.

re·peat·ing decimal (ri-pē′ting) A decimal in which a series of digits is repeated indefinitely, as 0.16353535. . ..

repeating firearm A gun, rifle, or pistol capable of shooting several bullets without reloading.

re·pel (ri-pel′) v. ·pelled, ·pel·ling v.t. 1. To force or drive back; repulse. 2. To reject; refuse, as a suggestion. 3. To cause to feel distaste or aversion. 4. To refuse to mix with or adhere to. 5. To push or keep away, esp. with invisible force. — v.i. 6. To act so as to drive something back or away. 7. To cause distaste or aversion. [< L < re- back + pellere to drive] — re·pel′ler n.

re·pel·lent (ri-pel′ənt) adj. 1. Serving, tending, or having power to repel. 2. Waterproof. 3. Repugnant; repulsive. — n. Something that repels, as a compound to repel insects. — re·pel′lence, re·pel′len·cy n.

re·pent (ri-pent′) v.i. 1. To feel remorse or regret, as for something one has done or failed to; be contrite. 2. To change one's mind concerning past action: with of: He repented of his generosity. — v.t. 3. To feel remorse or regret for (an action, sin, etc.). 4. To change one's mind concerning (a past action). [< OF < L re- again + poenitere to cause to repent] — re·pent′er n.

re·pen·tance (ri-pen′tons) n. The act of repenting or the condition of being repentant.

re·pen·tant (ri-pen′tənt) adj. Showing, feeling, or characterized by repentance. [< OF] — re·pen′tant·ly adv.

re·peo·ple (rē-pē′pəl) v.t. ·pled, ·pling 1. To people anew. 2. To provide again with animals; restock.

re·per·cus·sion (rē′pər-kush′ən) n. 1. The act of driving back, or the state of being driven back; repulse. 2. Echo; reverberation. 3. A stroke or blow given in return; also, the recoil after impact. 4. The indirect result of something; aftereffect. [< L < re- again + percutere to strike] — re′·per·cus′sive adj.

rep·er·toire (rep′ər-twär, -twôr) n. A list of songs, plays, operas, or the like, that a person or company is prepared to perform; also, such pieces collectively: also called repertory. [See REPERTORY.]

rep·er·to·ry (rep′ər-tôr′ē, -tō′rē) n. pl. ·ries 1. Repertoire. 2. A place where things are gathered together. 3. The things so gathered. [< LL repertorium inventory < L reperire to discover]

repertory company A theatrical group having a repertoire of productions, each typically running for a few weeks. Also repertory theater.

rep·e·ti·tion (rep′ə-tish′ən) n. 1. The act of repeating; the doing, making, or saying of something again. 2. Recital from memory. 3. That which is repeated; a copy. — re·pet·i·tive (ri-pet′ə-tiv) adj. — re·pet′i·tive·ly adv.

rep·e·ti·tious (rep′ə-tish′əs) adj. Characterized by or containing repetition, esp. useless or tedious repetition. — rep′·e·ti′tious·ly adv. — rep′e·ti′tious·ness n.

re·phrase (rē-frāz′) v.t. ·phrased, ·phras·ing To phrase again; esp., to express in a new way.

re·pine (ri-pīn′) v.i. ·pined, ·pin·ing To be discontented or fretful; complain; murmur. [< RE- + PINE²] — re·pin′er n.

re·place (ri-plās′) v.t. ·placed, ·plac·ing 1. To put back in place. 2. To take or fill the place of; supersede. 3. To refund; repay. — re·place′a·ble adj. — re·plac′er n.

re·place·ment (ri-plās′mənt) n. 1. One who or that which takes the place of another person or thing. 2. The act of replacing or the state of being replaced.

re·plen·ish (ri-plen′ish) v.t. 1. To fill again, as something wholly or partially emptied. 2. To bring back to fullness or completeness, as supplies. [< OF < L re- again + plenus full] — re·plen′ish·er n. — re·plen′ish·ment n.

re·plete (ri-plēt′) adj. 1. Full or supplied to the uttermost. 2. Gorged with food or drink; sated. [< OF < L < re- again + plere to fill] — re·ple′tion n.

re·plev·in (ri-plev′in) Law n. 1. An action to regain possession of personal property unlawfully retained, on giving security to try the title and respond to the judgment; also, recovery of property by such action 2. The writ or process by which such proceedings are instituted. — v.t. To recover (goods) by a writ of replevin. Also re·plev·y (ri-plev′ē). [< AF < OF < re- back + plevir to pledge]

rep·li·ca (rep′lə-kə) n. Any close copy or reproduction, esp. of a work of art, etc. [< Ital. < L replicare to reply]

rep·li·ca·tion (rep′lə-kā′shən) n. 1. A reply. 2. Law A plaintiff's reply to a defendant's plea or answer. [< OF < L < replicare to answer to] — rep/li·ca′tive adj.

re·ply (ri-plī′) v. ·plied, ·ply·ing v.i. 1. To give an answer orally or in writing. 2. To respond by some act, gesture, etc. 3. To bounce back, as a sound; echo. 4. Law To file a pleading in answer to the statement of the defense. — v.t. 5. To say in answer: often with a clause as object. — n. pl. ·plies Something said, written, or done by way of answer. [< OF < L replicare to fold back, answer to] — re·pli′er n.

re·port (ri-pôrt′, -pōrt′) v.t. 1. To make or give an account of, often formally. 2. To relate, as information obtained by investigation. 3. To repeat to another, as an answer. 4. To complain about, esp. to a superior. 5. To state the result of consideration concerning: The committee reported the bill. — v.i. 6. To make a report. 7. To act as a reporter. 8. To present oneself, as for duty. — n. 1. That which is reported. 2. A statement or record of an investigation, transaction, etc. 3. Common talk; rumor. 4. Fame, reputation, or character. 5. An explosive sound. [< OF < L < re- back + portare to carry] — re·port′a·ble adj.

report card U.S. A periodic statement of a pupil's scholastic record, which is presented to the parents or guardian.

re·port·ed·ly (ri-pôr′tid-lē, -pōr′-) adv. According to report.

re·port·er (ri-pôr′tər, -pōr′-) n. 1. One who reports; esp., one who reports news for a newspaper, magazine, etc. 2. One who reports cases in court for official publication. — rep·or·to·ri·al (rep′ər-tôr′ē-əl, -tō′rē-) adj.

re·pose¹ (ri-pōz′) n. 1. The act of taking rest or the state of being at rest. 2. Calm; peace. 3. Ease of manner; graceful and dignified calmness. 4. That which conduces to rest or calm. — v. ·posed, ·pos·ing v.t. 1. To lay or place in a position of rest. — v.i. 2. To lie at rest. 3. To rely; depend: with on, upon, or in. [< F < LL < re- again + pausare to pause] — re·pos′al n. — re·pose′ful adj. — re·pos′er n.

re·pose² (ri-pōz′) v.t. ·posed, ·pos·ing To place, as confidence or hope: with in. [ME < L reponere to put back] — re·pos′al n.

re·pos·i·to·ry (ri-poz′ə-tôr′ē, -tō′rē) *n. pl.* **·ries** **1.** A place in which goods are or may be stored. **2.** A person to whom a secret is entrusted **3.** A burial vault. **4.** A receptacle for relics. [< L < *re-* back, again + *ponere* to place]

re·pos·sess (rē′pə-zes′) *v.t.* **1.** To have possession of again; regain possession of. **2.** To give back possession or ownership to. — **re′pos·ses′sion** (-zesh′ən) *n.*

re·pous·sé (rə-pōō-sā′) *adj.* **1.** Formed in relief, as a design in metal. **2.** Adorned with such designs. [< F]

repp (rep) *n.* Rep, the fabric.

rep·re·hend (rep′ri-hend′) *v.t.* To criticize sharply; find fault with; blame. [< L < *re-* back + *prehendere* to hold]

rep·re·hen·si·ble (rep′ri-hen′sə-bəl) *adj.* Deserving blame or censure. — **rep′re·hen′si·bil′i·ty, rep′re·hen′si·ble·ness** *n.* — **rep′re·hen′si·bly** *adv.*

rep·re·hen·sion (rep′ri-hen′shən) *n.* The act of reprehending; also, an expression of blame; a rebuke. — **rep′re·hen′sive** *adj.* — **rep′re·hen′sive·ly** *adv.*

rep·re·sent (rep′ri-zent′) *v.t.* **1.** To serve as the symbol, expression, or designation of; symbolize. **2.** To express or symbolize in this manner. **3.** To depict; portray, as in painting or sculpture. **4.** To produce on the stage, as an opera. **5.** To act the part of; impersonate. **6.** To serve as or be the delegate, agent, etc., of. **7.** To describe: They *represented* him as a genius. **8.** To set forth in words; state; explain. **9.** To bring before the mind; present clearly. **10.** To serve as an example, specimen, type, etc., of. [< OF < L < *re-* again + PRESENT²] — **rep′re·sent′a·ble** *adj.* — **rep′re·sent′a·bil′i·ty** *n.*

re-present (rē′pri-zent′) *v.t.* To present again. — **re′-pre′sen·ta′tion** *n.*

rep·re·sen·ta·tion (rep′ri-zen-tā′shən) *n.* **1.** The act of representing or the state of being represented. **2.** Anything that represents, as a picture, a statue, etc. **3.** A dramatic performance. **4.** The right of acting authoritatively for others, esp. in a legislative body. **5.** Representatives collectively. **6.** A setting forth by statement or account, esp. to object or propose. [< OF]

rep·re·sen·ta·tion·al (rep′ri-zen-tā′shən-əl) *adj.* **1.** Serving to represent; esp., denoting a style of art that seeks to represent objects realistically. **2.** Of, pertaining to, or of the nature of representation.

rep·re·sen·ta·tive (rep′ri-zen′tə-tiv) *adj.* **1.** Typifying or typical of a group or class. **2.** Acting as a qualified agent. **3.** Made up of representatives. **4.** Based on or pertaining to the political principle of representation. **5.** Presenting, portraying, or representing, or capable of so doing — *n.* **1.** One who or that which is fit to stand as a type; a typical instance. **2.** One who is a qualified agent of any kind. **3.** A member of a legislative body, esp. a member of the lower house of Congress or of a State legislature. — **rep′re·sen′ta·tive·ly** *adv.* — **rep′re·sen′ta·tive·ness** *n.*

re·press (ri-pres′) *v.t.* **1.** To keep under restraint or control. **2.** To put down; quell, as a rebellion. **3.** *Psychoanal.* To effect the repression of, as fears, impulses, etc. [< L < *re-* back + PRESS] — **re·press′er** or **re·pres′sor** *n.* — **re·press′i·ble** *adj.*
— **Syn. 1.** check, curb, rein, restrain, subdue, suppress.

re-press (rē′pres′) *v.t. & v.i.* To press again.

re·pres·sion (ri-presh′ən) *n.* **1.** The act of repressing or the condition of being repressed. **2.** That which holds in check; a restraint. **3.** *Psychoanal.* The exclusion from consciousness of painful or unacceptable memories, etc.

re·pres·sive (ri-pres′iv) *adj.* **1.** Tending to repress. **2.** Capable of repressing. — **re·pres′sive·ly** *adv.* — **re·pres′sive·ness** *n.*

re·prieve (ri-prēv′) *v.t.* **·prieved, ·priev·ing** **1.** To suspend temporarily the execution of a sentence upon. **2.** To relieve for a time from suffering, danger, or trouble. — *n.* **1.** The temporary suspension of a sentence, or the instrument ordering such a suspension. **2.** Temporary relief or cessation of pain or ill. **3.** The act of reprieving or the state of being reprieved. [< earlier *repry* < F *repris*, pp. of *reprendre* to take back] — **re·priev′a·ble** *adj.*

rep·ri·mand (rep′rə-mand, -mänd) *v.t.* To reprove sharply or formally. — *n.* Severe reproof or censure. [< F *réprimande* reproof]

re·print (*n.* rē′print′; *v.* rē-print′) *n.* An edition of a printed work that is a verbatim copy of the original. — *v.t.* To print a new edition or copy of. — **re·print′er** *n.*

re·pri·sal (ri-prī′zəl) *n.* **1.** The application of force short of war by one nation against another in retaliation for acts committed; also, an instance of such use of force. **2.** Any act of retaliation. [< OF *reprendre* < L < *re-* back + *prehendere* to hold]

re·prise (rə-prēz′, -prīz′) *n. Music* A repeated phrase; esp., the repetition of or return to the subject after an intermediate movement. [See REPRISAL.]

re·proach (ri-prōch′) *v.t.* **1.** To charge with or blame for something wrong; rebuke; censure. **2.** To bring discredit and disgrace upon; to disgrace. — *n.* **1.** The act of reproaching, or the words of one who reproaches; censure; reproof; rebuke. **2.** A cause of blame or disgrace. **3.** Disgrace; discredit. [< F *reprocher*; ult. origin uncertain.] — **re·proach′a·bly** *adj.* — **re·proach′a·ble·ness** *n.* — **re·proach′a·bly** *adv.* — **re·proach′er** *n.*

re·proach·ful (ri-prōch′fəl) *adj.* Containing or full of reproach; expressing reproach. — **re·proach′ful·ly** *adv.* — **re·proach′ful·ness** *n.*

rep·ro·bate (rep′rə-bāt) *adj.* **1.** Having lost all sense of duty; depraved. **2.** Abandoned to punishment; condemned. — *n.* A depraved or profligate person. — *v.t.* **·bat·ed, ·bat·ing** To disapprove of heartily; condemn. [See REPROVE.] — **rep′ro·ba′tion** *n.* — **rep′ro·ba′tive** *adj.*

re·pro·duce (rē′prə-dōōs′, -dyōōs′) *v.* **·duced, ·duc·ing** *v.t.* **1.** To make a copy, image, or reproduction of. **2.** *Biol.* **a** To give rise to (offspring) by sexual or asexual generation. **b** To replace (a lost part or organ) by regeneration. **3.** To produce again. **4.** To recall to the mind; visualize again. — *v.i.* **5.** To produce offspring. **6.** To undergo copying, reproduction, etc. — **re′pro·duc′er** *n.* — **re′pro·duc′i·ble** *adj.*

re·pro·duc·tion (rē′prə-duk′shən) *n.* **1.** The act or power of reproducing. **2.** *Biol.* The process by which an animal or plant gives rise to another of its kind **3.** That which is reproduced, as a revival of a play or a copy of a picture.

re·pro·duc·tive (rē′prə-duk′tiv) *adj.* Pertaining to, employed in, or tending to reproduction. — **re′pro·duc′tive·ly** *adv.* — **re′pro·duc′tive·ness** *n.*

re·proof (ri-prōōf′) *n.* **1.** The act of reproving. **2.** A rebuke; blame; censure. Also **re·prov·al** (ri-prōō′vəl).

re·prove (ri′prōōv′) *v.t.* **·proved, ·prov·ing** **1.** To censure, as for a fault; rebuke. **2.** To express disapproval of (an act). [< OF < LL < *re-* again + *probare* to test] — **re·prov′a·ble** *adj.* — **re·prov′er** *n.* — **re·prov′ing·ly** *adv.*
— **Syn. 1.** chide, upbraid, reprimand.

re-prove (rē-prōōv′) *v.t.* **·proved, -prov·ing** To prove (a theory, assertion, etc.) anew.

rep·tile (rep′til, -tīl) *n.* **1.** Any of a class of cold-blooded, air-breathing vertebrates, including the snakes, crocodiles, lizards, and turtles. **2.** A groveling, abject person. — *adj.* **1.** Crawling on the belly. **2.** Groveling morally; sly and base; treacherous. **3.** Of or resembling a reptile [< LL < *reptus*, pp. of *repere* to creep]

rep·til·i·an (rep-til′ē-ən) *adj.* Of, pertaining to, or characteristic of a reptile or reptiles. — *n.* Any reptile.

re·pub·lic (ri-pub′lik) *n.* A state in which the sovereignty resides in the people and the legislative and administrative powers are lodged in officers elected by them; also, such a government. [< F < L *respublica* commonwealth]

re·pub·li·can (ri-pub′li-kən) *adj.* **1.** Of, like, or suitable for a republic. **2.** Supporting republican government. — *n.* One who advocates a republican form of government.

Re·pub·li·can (ri-pub′li-kən) *adj.* Pertaining to or belonging to the Republican Party of the U.S. — *n.* A member of the Republican Party.

Republican calendar See under CALENDAR.

re·pub·li·can·ism (ri-pub′li-kən-iz′əm) *n.* **1.** The theory or principles of republican government. **2.** Advocacy of or adherence to republican principles.

Re·pub·li·can·ism (ri-pub′li-kən-iz′əm) *n.* The policy and principles of the Republican Party of the U.S.

Republican Party One of the two major political parties of the United States, founded in 1854 in opposition to the extension of slavery.

re·pu·di·ate (ri-pyōō′dē-āt) *v.t.* **·at·ed, ·at·ing** **1.** To refuse to accept as valid or binding; reject. **2.** To refuse to acknowledge or pay. **3.** To cast off; disown, as a son. [< L < *repudiare* to divorce] — **re·pu′di·a′tion** *n.* — **re·pu′di·a′tive** *adj.* — **re·pu′di·a′tor** *n.*

re·pug·nance (ri-pug′nəns) *n.* The state of feeling aversion and resistance; antipathy. Also **re·pug′nan·cy.**

re·pug·nant (ri-pug′nənt) *adj.* **1.** Offensive to taste or feeling; exciting aversion or repulsion **2.** Being inconsistent or opposed; antagonistic. **3.** Hostile; resisting. [< OF < L < *re-* back + *pugnare* to fight]

re·pulse (ri-puls′) *v.t.* **·pulsed, ·puls·ing** **1.** To drive back; repel, as an attacking force. **2.** To repel by coldness, discourtesy, etc.; reject; rebuff. — *n.* **1.** The act of repulsing or the state of being repulsed. **2.** Rejection; refusal [< L *repulsus*, pp. of *repellere*. See REPEL.] — **re·puls′er** *n.*

re·pul·sion (ri-pul′shən) *n.* **1.** The act of repelling, or the state of being repelled. **2.** Aversion; repugnance **3.** *Physics* The mutual action of two bodies that tends to drive them apart.

re·pul·sive (ri-pul′siv) *adj.* **1.** Exciting feelings of dislike, disgust, or horror; grossly offensive. **2.** Such as to forbid approach or familiarity; forbidding. 3. Acting by repulsion: *repulsive* forces. — **re·pul′sive·ly** *adv.* — **re·pul′sive·ness** *n.*

rep·u·ta·ble (rep′yə·tə·bəl) *adj.* 1. Having a good reputation; estimable; honorable. 2. Consistent with proper usage, as words — **rep′u·ta·bil′i·ty** *n.* — **rep′u·ta·bly** *adv.*

rep·u·ta·tion (rep′yə·tā′shən) *n.* 1. The general estimation in which a person or thing is held by others. 2. The state of being in high regard or esteem 3. A particular credit or character ascribed to a person or thing: a *reputation* for honesty. [See REPUTE.]

re·pute (ri·pyōōt′) *v.t.* **-put·ed, -put·ing** To regard or consider to be as specified; esteem: usu. in the passive: They are *reputed* to be an intelligent people. — *n.* 1. Reputation (defs. 1 and 2). 2. Public opinion; general report. [< OF < L *reputare* to reckon, be reputed]

re·put·ed (ri·pyōō′tid) *adj.* Generally thought or supposed: a *reputed* criminal. — **re·put′ed·ly** *adv.*

re·quest (ri·kwest′) *v.t.* 1. To express a desire for. 2. To ask (a person) to do a favor, answer an inquiry, etc. — **Syn.** See ASK. — *n.* 1. The act of requesting; petition. 2. That which is requested. 3. The state of being in demand: in *request.* — *adj.* Having been asked for: a *request* program. [See REQUIRE.]

re·qui·em (rē′kwē·əm, rek′wē-) *n.* 1. Any musical composition, or service for the dead. 2. *Often cap. Eccl.* In the Roman Catholic Church, a solemn mass sung for the dead: also **Requiem mass.** 3. *Often cap.* A musical setting for such a mass. [< L *Requiem* (aeternam dona eis, Domine) rest (eternal give unto them, O Lord)]

req·ui·es·cat in pa·ce (rek′wē·es′kat in pä′sē) May he rest in peace Abbr. *R.I.P.* [< L]

re·quire (ri·kwīr′) *v.* **-quired, -quir·ing** *v.t.* 1. To have need of; find necessary. 2. To demand authoritatively; insist upon. — *v.i.* 3. To make demand or request. [< OF < L < *re-* again + *quaerere* to ask, seek] — **re·quir′a·ble** *adj.* — **re·quir′er** *n.* — **re·quire′ment** *n.*

req·ui·site (rek′wə·zit) *adj.* Required by the nature of things or by circumstances; indispensable. — *n.* That which cannot be dispensed with; a necessity. [See REQUEST.] — **req′ui·site·ly** *adv.* — **req′ui·site·ness** *n.*

req·ui·si·tion (rek′wə·zish′ən) *n.* 1. A formal request, summons, or demand, as for supplies. 2. A necessity or requirement. 3. The state of being required. — *v.t.* To make a requisition for or upon; demand or take upon requisition. [See REQUIRE.]

re·quite (ri·kwīt′) *v.t.* **-quit·ed, -quit·ing** 1. To make equivalent return for, as kindness, service, or injury; make up for. 2. To make return to; compensate or repay in kind. 3. To give or do in return. [< RE- + *quite*, obs. var. of QUIT] — **re·quit·al** (ri·kwīt′l) *adj.* — **re·quit′er** *n.*

rere·dos (rir′dos) *Chiefly Brit. n.* 1. An ornamental screen behind an altar. 2. The back of an open fire hearth. [< AF < *rere* rear + *dos* back]

re·run (*n.* rē′run; *v.* rē·run′) *n.* The presenting of a motion picture, play, etc., after its original run is over; also, the motion picture, play, etc., so presented. — *v.t.* **·ran, ·running** To run again or a second time.

re·sale (rē′sāl, rē·sāl′) *n.* The act of selling again.

re·scind (ri·sind′) *v.t.* To make void, as an act; abrogate; repeal. — **Syn.** See ANNUL. [< L < *re-* back + *scindere* to cut] — **re·scind′a·ble** *adj.* — **re·scind′er** *n.*

re·scis·sion (ri·sizh′ən) *n.* The act of rescinding or abrogating. — **re·scis′si·ble** (-sis′-) *adj.* — **re·scis′so·ry** *adj.*

re·script (rē′skript) *n.* 1. A formal answer to questions of state, law, morality, etc., as given by a Roman emperor or a Pope. 2. Any decree, edict or formal announcement. [< L < *re-* back + *scribere* to write]

res·cue (res′kyōō) *v.t.* **-cued, -cu·ing** 1. To save or free from danger, captivity, evil, etc.; deliver. 2. *Law* To remove forcibly from the custody of the law. — *n.* The act of rescuing; deliverance. [< OF *rescourre* < *re-* back + *escorre* to move, shake] — **res′cu·a·ble** *adj.* — **res′cu·er** *n.*

re·search (ri·sûrch′, rē′sûrch) *n.* 1. Diligent, protracted investigation; studious inquiry. 2. A systematic investigation of some phenomenon — *v.i.* To undertake research. [< F < *re-* back + *chercher* to seek] — **re·search′er** *n.*

re·seat (rē·sēt′) *v.t.* 1. To seat again. 2. To put a new seat or seats in or on.

re·sect (ri·sekt′) *v.t. Surg.* To cut or pare off. [< L < *re-* back + *secare* to cut] — **re·sec′tion** *n.*

re·sem·blance (ri·zem′bləns) *n.* 1. The quality of similarity in nature, form, etc.; likeness. 2. A semblance or likeness of a person or thing. — **Syn.** See ANALOGY.

re·sem·ble (ri·zem′bəl) *v.t.* **·bled, ·bling** To be similar to in appearance, quality, or character. [< OF < *re-* again + *sembler* to seem] — **re·sem′bler** *n.*

re·sent (ri·zent′) *v.t.* To feel or show resentment at; be indignant at. [< F < *re-* again + *sentir* to feel] — **re·sent′·ful** *adj.* — **re·sent′ful·ly** *adv.* — **re·sent′ful·ness** *n.*

re·sent·ment (ri·zent′mənt) *n.* Anger and ill will in view of real or fancied wrong or injury.

re·ser·pine (ri·sûr′pēn, -pin, res′ər-) *n.* A drug originally prepared from alkaloids found in rauwolfia, used as a tranquilizer. [< NL *Rauwolfia serpentina*, genus name + -INE]

res·er·va·tion (rez′ər·vā′shən) *n.* 1. The act of reserving. 2. That which is reserved, kept back, or withheld. 3. A qualification or condition, as to an opinion or commitment. 4. An agreement by which a seat on a train, hotel room, etc., is reserved in advance. 5. A tract of government land reserved for a special purpose, as for the use and occupancy of an Indian tribe, or for the preservation of forests, wildlife, etc. [< OF < LL *reservatio, -onis*]

re·serve (ri·zûrv′) *v.t.* **·served, ·serv·ing** 1. To hold back or set aside for special or future use. 2. To keep as one's own; retain. 3. To arrange for ahead of time; have set aside for one's use. — *n.* 1. Something stored up for future use or set apart for a particular purpose. 2. A reservation of land. 3. In banking, the amount of funds reserved in order to meet regular or emergent demands. 4. The act of reserving. 5. Silence or reticence as to one's feelings, opinions, or affairs. 6. A fighting force held back from action to meet possible emergencies. 7. A branch of the armed forces composed of persons trained for military service and subject to call in emergencies. — *adj.* Held in reserve; constituting a reserve. [< OF < L < *re-* back + *servare* to keep] — **re·serv′a·ble** *adj.* — **re·serv′er** *n.*

re·serve (rē·sûrv′) *v.t. & v.i.* **-served, -serv·ing** To serve again.

re·served (ri·zûrvd′) *adj.* 1. Characterized by reserve of manner; distant; undemonstrative. 2. Retained; kept back. — **re·serv·ed·ly** (ri·zûr′vid·lē) *adv.* — **re·serv′ed·ness** *n.*

Reserve Officers' Training Corps In the U.S., a military corps to train students at colleges and universities to qualify as officers in a reserve. Abbr. *ROTC, R.O.T.C.*

re·serv·ist (ri·zûr′vist) *n.* A member of a military reserve.

res·er·voir (rez′ər·vwôr, -vwär, -vôr) *n.* 1. A lake, either natural or artificial, for collecting and containing a supply of water, as for use in a city or for water power. 2. An attachment to a stove, machine, or instrument, for containing a fluid to be used in its operation. 3. An extra supply; a store of anything. [< F *réservoir*]

re·set (*v.* rē·set′; *n.* rē′set′) *v.t.* **·set, ·set·ting** To set again. — *n.* The act of resetting, or that which is reset.

re·ship (rē·ship′) *v.* **·shipped, ·ship·ping** *v.t.* 1. To ship again. 2. To transfer (oneself) to another vessel. — *v.i.* 3. To go on a vessel again. 4. To sign for another voyage as a crew member or a passenger. — **re·ship′ment** *n.*

re·side (ri·zīd′) *v.i.* **·sid·ed, ·sid·ing** 1. To dwell for a considerable time; make one's home; live. 2. To exist as an attribute or quality: with *in.* 3. To be vested: with *in.* — **Syn.** See LIVE. [< F < L *residere* to abide]

res·i·dence (rez′ə·dəns) *n.* 1. The place or the house where one resides. 2. The act of residing. 3. The fact of being officially present, esp. in the phrase *in residence.* 4. The seat of power of government. 5. The length of time one resides in a place. Also *residency.* [< OF < LL *residentia*]

res·i·den·cy (rez′ə·dən·sē) *n. pl.* **·cies** 1. Residence. 2. An official abode of the representative of a government. 3. *Med.* The period of clinical training served by a physician in his chosen specialty.

res·i·dent (rez′ə·dənt) *n.* 1. One who resides or dwells in a place. 2. A diplomatic representative residing at a foreign seat of government. 3. *Med.* One serving a residency. — *adj.* 1. Having a residence. 2. Abiding in a place in connection with one's official work: a *resident* physician. 3. Inherent: Pungency is *resident* in pepper. 4. Not migratory: said of certain birds.

res·i·den·tial (rez′ə·den′shəl) *adj.* 1. Of, pertaining to, or resulting from residence; having residence. 2. Of, consisting of, or suitable for residences or living quarters.

re·sid·u·al (ri·zij′ōō·əl) *adj.* 1. Pertaining to or having the nature of a residue or remainder. 2. Left over as a residue. — *n.* Something left over.

re·sid·u·ar·y (ri·zij′ōō·er′ē) *adj.* Of or pertaining to a residuum or remainder; residual.

res·i·due (rez′ə·dōō, -dyōō) *n.* 1. A remainder or surplus after a part has been separated or otherwise treated. 2. *Chem.* Insoluble matter left after filtration or separation from a liquid. 3. *Law* The portion of an estate that remains after all charges, debts, and particular bequests have been satisfied. Also **re·sid·u·um** (ri·zij′ōō·əm). [< OF < L < *re-* back + *sedere* to sit]

re·sign (ri·zīn′) *v.t.* 1. To give up, as a position, office, or trust. 2. To relinquish (a privilege, claim, etc.). 3. To give over (oneself, one's mind, etc.), as to fate or domination. — *v.i.* 4. To resign a position, etc. [< OF < L < *re-* back + *signare* to seal] — **re·sign′er** *n.*

re·sign (rē·sīn′) *v.t.* To sign again.

res·ig·na·tion (rez′ig·nā′shən) *n.* 1. The act of resigning, as a position or office. 2. A written statement declaring one's intention to resign. 3. The quality of being submissive or acquiescent.

re·signed (ri·zīnd′) *adj.* Characterized by resignation; submissive. — **re·sign·ed·ly** (ri·zī′nid·lē) *adv.*

re·sil·ience (ri·zil′yəns) *n.* The quality or power of being resilient; elasticity; rebound. Also **re·sil′ien·cy.**

re·sil·ient (ri·zil′yənt) *adj.* **1.** Springing back to a former shape or position. **2.** Capable of recoiling from pressure or shock unchanged or undamaged; buoyant. [< MF < L < re- back + salire to leap] — **re·sil′ient·ly** *adv.*

res·in (rez′in) *n.* **1.** An amorphous organic substance exuded from certain plants and trees, yellowish or dark in color. **2.** Any of a class of similar substances made by chemical synthesis, esp. those used in the making of plastics. **3.** Rosin (def. 1). — *v.t.* To apply resin to. [< OF < L < Gk. rhētinē] — **res·i·na·ceous** (rez′·ə·nā′shəs) *adj.*

res·i·nous (rez′ə·nəs) *adj.* **1.** Like or containing resin. **2.** Obtained from resin. Also **res·in·y** (rez′ən·ē).

re·sist (ri·zist′) *v.t.* **1.** To strive against; act counter to. **2.** To be proof against; withstand. — *v.i.* **3.** To offer opposition. [< OF < L resistere to withstand] — **re·sist′er** *n.*

re·sis·tance (ri·zis′təns) *n.* **1.** The act of resisting. **2.** Any force tending to hinder motion. **3.** *Electr.* The opposition that a conductor offers to the passage of a current, resulting from the conversion of energy into heat, light, etc. **4.** *Psychoanal.* The action of the ego in preventing the return to consciousness of unpleasant incidents and experiences. **5.** The underground and guerrilla movement opposing an occupying power. — **re·sis′tant** *n.*

re·sist·i·ble (ri·zis′tə·bəl) *adj.* Capable of being resisted. — **re·sist′i·bil′i·ty** *n.* — **re·sist′i·bly** *adv.*

re·sis·tive (ri·zis′tiv) *adj.* Having or exercising the power of resistance. — **re·sis′tive·ly** *adv.*

re·sis·tiv·i·ty (rē′zis·tiv′ə·tē) *n.* **1.** The capacity to resist, or the degree of that capacity. **2.** *Electr.* Specific resistance to electric or magnetic force of a substance as tested in a cube measuring one centimeter.

re·sist·less (ri·zist′lis) *adj.* **1.** Incapable of resisting; irresistible. **2.** Offering no resistance; powerless. — **re·sist′less·ly** *adv.* — **re·sist′less·ness** *n.*

re·sis·tor (ri·zis′tər) *n.* *Electr.* A device, as a coil of wire, for introducing resistance into an electrical circuit.

res·na·tron (rez′nə·tron) *n.* *Electronics* A tetrode electron tube operating on the resonance principle and capable of generating large power at high frequency and maximum efficiency. [< RES(O)NA(TOR) + -TRON]

re·sole (rē·sōl′) *v.t.* **soled, sol·ing** To sole (a shoe, etc.) again.

res·o·lute (rez′ə·loot) *adj.* **1.** Having a fixed purpose; determined. **2.** Bold; unflinching. [See RESOLVE.] — **res′o·lute·ly** *adv.* — **res′o·lute·ness** *n.*

res·o·lu·tion (rez′ə·loo′shən) *n.* **1.** The act of resolving or of reducing to a simpler form. **2.** The state of being resolute; active fortitude. **3.** The making of a resolve; also, the purpose or course resolved upon. **4.** The separation of anything into component parts. **5.** A proposition offered to or adopted by an assembly. **6.** *Med.* The termination of an abnormal condition. — **res′o·lu′tion·er, res′o·lu′tion·ist** *n.*

re·solve (ri·zolv′) *v.* **solved, solv·ing** *v.t.* **1.** To decide or determine (to do something). **2.** To cause to decide or determine. **3.** To separate or break down into constituent parts. **4.** To make clear; explain or solve, as a problem. **5.** To explain away; remove (doubts, etc.). **6.** To state or decide by vote, as in a legislative assembly. **7.** To transform; convert: He resolves his anger into pride. **8.** *Optics* To make distinguishable the structure or parts of, as in a microscope or telescope. — *v.i.* **9.** To make up one's mind; arrive at a decision: with on or upon. **10.** To become separated into constituent parts. — *n.* **1.** Fixity of purpose; resolution. **2.** A fixed determination; a resolution. **3.** The action of a deliberative body expressing formally its intention or purpose. [< L < re- again + solvere to loosen] — **re·solv′a·ble** *adj.* — **re·solv′a·bil′i·ty** *n.* — **re·solv′er** *n.*

re-solve (rē·solv′) *v.t.* **-solved, -solv·ing** To solve anew.

re·solved (ri·zolvd′) *adj.* Fixed or set in purpose; determined. — **re·solv·ed·ly** (ri·zol′vid·lē) *adv.*

res·o·nance (rez′ə·nəns) *n.* **1.** The state or quality of being resonant. **2.** *Physics* The property whereby any vibratory system responds with maximum amplitude to an applied force having a frequency equal or nearly equal to its own. **3.** *Electr.* The condition of an electric circuit in which maximum flow of current is obtained by impressing an electromotive force of given frequency.

res·o·nant (rez′ə·nənt) *adj.* **1.** Sending back or having the quality of sending back or prolonging sound. **2.** Resounding. **3.** Having resonance. [< L < re- again + sonare to sound] — **res′o·nant·ly** *adv.*

res·o·nate (rez′ə·nāt) *v.i.* **nat·ed, ·nat·ing** **1.** To exhibit resonance. **2.** To manifest sympathetic vibration, as a resonator. [< L resonatus, pp. of resonare. See RESONANT.]

res·o·na·tor (rez′ə·nā′tər) *n.* **1.** That which resounds. **2.** Any device utilizing the effects of resonance, esp. in connection with sound or electromagnetic waves. [< NL]

re·sorb (ri·sôrb′) *v.t.* To absorb again. [< L < re- back + sorbere to suck up] — **re·sorp·tion** (ri·sôrp′shən) *n.*

re·sor·cin·ol (ri·zôr′sin·ôl, -ol) *n.* *Chem.* A colorless crystalline compound, $C_6H_6O_2$, used as an antiseptic and in the making of dyes. Also **re·sor′cin·al** *adj.*

re·sort (ri·zôrt′) *v.i.* **1.** To go frequently or habitually; repair. **2.** To have recourse; apply or betake oneself for relief or aid: with to. — *n.* **1.** A place frequented for recreation or rest; health resort. **2.** The use of something as a means; a recourse. **3.** The act of frequenting a place. [< OF < re- again + sortir to go out] — **re·sort′er** *n.*

re-sort (rē·sôrt′) *v.t.* & *v.i.* To sort anew or again.

re·sound (ri·zound′) *v.i.* **1.** To be filled with sound; echo; reverberate. **2.** To make a loud, prolonged, or echoing sound. **3.** To ring; echo: said of sounds. — *v.t.* **4.** To give back (a sound, etc.); re·echo. **5.** *Poetic* To extol. [ME < OF < L resonare to echo]

re-sound (rē·sound′) *v.t.* & *v.i.* To sound again.

re·source (ri·sôrs′, -zôrs′, -sōrs′, rē′sôrs, -sōrs) *n.* **1.** That which is resorted to for aid or support; resort. **2.** *pl.* Available means or property; any natural advantages or products. **3.** Capacity for finding or adapting means; power of achievement. **4.** Fertility in expedients; skill or ingenuity in meeting any situation; resourcefulness. [< OF < re- again + sourdre < L surgere to rise]

re·source·ful (ri·sôrs′fəl, -sōrs′-, -zôrs′-) *adj.* **1.** Fertile in resources or expedients. **2.** Full of resources. — **re·source′ful·ly** *adv.* — **re·source′ful·ness** *n.*

re·spect (ri·spekt′) *v.t.* **1.** To have deferential regard for; esteem. **2.** To treat with propriety or consideration. **3.** To regard as inviolable; avoid intruding upon. **4.** To have relation or reference to; concern. — *n.* **1.** Regard for and appreciation of worth; honor and esteem. **2.** Demeanor or deportment indicating deference; courteous regard. **3.** *pl.* Expressions of consideration or esteem; compliments: to pay one's respects. **4.** Conformity to duty or obligation: respect for the law. **5.** The condition of being honored or respected. **6.** A specific aspect: In what respect is he wanting? **7.** Reference or relation: usu. with to: with respect to profits. [< L < re- again + specere to look] — **re·spect′er** *n.*

re·spect·a·ble (ri·spek′tə·bəl) *adj.* **1.** Deserving of respect; being of good name or repute; also, respected. **2.** Being of moderate excellence; average. **3.** Considerable in number, size, quality, etc. **4.** Having a good appearance; presentable. **5.** Conventionally correct or socially acceptable in conduct. — **re·spect′a·bil′i·ty** *n.* — **re·spect′a·bly** *adv.*

re·spect·ful (ri·spekt′fəl) *adj.* Marked by or manifesting respect. — **re·spect′ful·ly** *adv.* — **re·spect′ful·ness** *n.*

re·spect·ing (ri·spek′ting) *prep.* In relation to; regarding.

re·spec·tive (ri·spek′tiv) *adj.* Pertaining or relating severally to each of those under consideration; particular.

re·spec·tive·ly (ri·spek′tiv·lē) *adv.* As singly or severally considered; singly in the order designated: The first three go to John, James, and William respectively.

re·spell (rē·spel′) *v.t.* To spell again, esp. in a system whereby pronunciation is indicated.

res·pi·ra·tion (res′pə·rā′shən) *n.* **1.** The act of inhaling and exhaling; breathing. **2.** The process by which a plant or animal takes in oxygen from the air and gives off carbon dioxide and other products of oxidation. [< MF < L < re- again + spirare to breathe]

res·pi·ra·tor (res′pə·rā′tər) *n.* **1.** A screen, as of fine gauze, worn over the mouth or nose, as a protection against dust, etc. **2.** A device worn over the nose and mouth for the inhalation of medicated vapors, or of oxygen for lung patients. **3.** An apparatus for artificial respiration.

re·spir·a·to·ry (ri·spīr′ə·tôr′ē, -tō′rē, res′pər·ə-) *adj.* Of, pertaining to, used in, or caused by respiration.

res·pite (res′pit) *n.* **1.** Postponement; delay. **2.** Temporary intermission of labor or effort; an interval of rest. **3.** *Law* Temporary suspension of the execution of a sentence for a capital offense; reprieve. — *v.t.* **pit·ed, ·pit·ing 1.** To relieve by a pause or rest. **2.** To grant delay in the execution of (a penalty, sentence, etc.). **3.** To postpone. [< OF < L respectus regard, refuge]

re·splen·dent (ri·splen′dənt) *adj.* Shining with brilliant luster; vividly bright; splendid; gorgeous. [< L < re- back + splendere to shine] — **re·splen′dence, re·splen′den·cy** *n.* — **re·splen′dent·ly** *adv.*

re·spond (ri·spond′) *v.i.* **1.** To give an answer; reply. **2.** To act in reply or return; react. **3.** *Law* To be liable or answerable. — *v.t.* **4.** To say in answer; reply. — *n.* **1.** *Archit.* A pilaster or similar feature placed against a wall, to receive an arch. **2.** *Eccl.* A response (def. 2). [< L < re- back + spondere to pledge] — **re·spon′der** *n.*

re·spon·dence (ri·spon′dəns) *n.* **1.** The character or condition of being respondent. **2.** The act of responding. Also **re·spon′den·cy.**

re·spon·dent (ri·spon′dənt) *adj.* **1.** Giving response, or given as a response; answering; responsive. **2.** *Law* Occupying the position of defendant. — *n.* **1.** One who responds or answers. **2.** *Law* A defendant.

re·sponse (ri·spons′) *n.* **1.** The act of responding, or that which is responded; reply; reaction. **2.** *Eccl.* **a** A portion of a liturgy or church service said or sung by the congregation or choir in reply to the officiating priest. **b** An anthem sung or said during or after a reading. Also called *respond.* **3.** *Biol.* The behavior of an organism resulting from a stimulus or influence; a reaction. **4.** In bridge, the play of a high or low card in following suit, as a signal to one's partner.

re·spon·si·bil·i·ty (ri·spon′sə·bil′ə·tē) *n. pl.* **·ties** **1.** The state of being responsible or accountable. **2.** That for which one is answerable; a duty or trust. **3.** Ability to meet obligations or to act without superior authority or guidance. Also **re·spon′si·ble·ness.**

re·spon·si·ble (ri·spon′sə·bəl) *adj.* **1.** Answerable legally or morally for the discharge of a duty, trust, or debt. **2.** Having capacity to perceive the distinctions of right and wrong. **3.** Able to meet legitimate claims; having sufficient property or means for the payment of debts. **4.** Involving accountability or obligation. [See RESPOND.] — **re·spon′si·bly** *adv.*

re·spon·sive (ri·spon′siv) *adj.* **1.** Inclined or ready to respond; being or reacting in accord, sympathy, or harmony; responding. **2.** Constituting, or of the nature of, response or reply. **3.** Characterized by or containing responses. — **re·spon′sive·ly** *adv.* — **re·spon′sive·ness** *n.*

rest¹ (rest) *v.i.* **1.** To cease working, exerting oneself, etc., so as to refresh oneself. **2.** To cease from effort or activity for a time. **3.** To seek or obtain ease or refreshment by lying down, sleeping, etc. **4.** To sleep. **5.** To be at peace; be tranquil. **6.** To lie in death; be dead. **7.** To remain unchanged. **8.** To be supported; stand, lean, lie, or sit: with *against, on,* or *upon.* **9.** To be founded or based: with *on* or *upon.* **10.** To rely; depend: with *on* or *upon.* **11.** To be placed as a burden or responsibility: with *on* or *upon.* **12.** To be or lie in a specified place. **13.** To be directed; remain, as the gaze or eyes, on something. **14.** *Law* To cease presenting evidence in a case. **15.** *Agric.* To lie fallow. — *v.t.* **16.** To give rest to; refresh by rest. **17.** To put, lay, lean, etc., as for support or rest. **18.** To found; base. **19.** To direct (the gaze, eyes, etc.). **20.** *Law* To cease presenting evidence in (a case). — *n.* **1.** The act or state of resting; repose; quiet. **2.** Freedom from disturbance or disquiet; tranquillity. **3.** Sleep; also, death. **4.** That on which anything rests; a support. **5.** In billiards and pool, a support for a cue; a bridge. **6.** A place of repose or quiet; a stopping place; abode. **7.** *Music* A pause or interval of silence that corresponds to the time value of a note; also, the character indicating such a pause. **8.** In prosody, a pause in a verse; caesura. **9.** *Mil.* A command given troops, allowing them to relax. — **at rest** **1.** In a state of repose, as in sleep or death. **2.** Not in motion; still. **3.** Free from anxiety or worry: to set one's mind *at rest.* [OE *restan*] — **rest′er** *n.*

rest² (rest) *n.* **1.** That which remains or is left over; a remainder. **2.** (*construed as pl.*) Those remaining or not enumerated; the others. — *v.i.* To be and remain; stay: *Rest content.* [< L < re- back + *stare* to stand]

re·state (rē·stāt′) *v.t.* **·stat·ed, ·stat·ing** To state again or anew. — **re·state′ment** *n.*

res·tau·rant (res′tər·ənt, -tə·ränt) *n.* A place where refreshments or meals are provided; a public dining room. [< F, lit., restoring]

res·tau·ra·teur (res′tər·ə·tûr′, Fr. res·tō·rà·tœr′) *n.* The proprietor or keeper of a restaurant. [< F]

rest·ful (rest′fəl) *adj.* **1.** Full of or giving rest; affording freedom from disturbance, work, or trouble. **2.** Being at rest or in repose; quiet. — **rest′ful·ly** *adv.* — **rest′ful·ness** *n.*

rest·ing (res′ting) *adj.* **1.** In a state of rest; reposing; also, dead. **2.** *Bot.* Dormant: a *resting* spore.

res·ti·tu·tion (res′tə·tōō′shən, -tyōō′-) *n.* **1.** The act of restoring something that has been taken away or lost. **2.** The act of making good or rendering an equivalent for injury or loss. **3.** Restoration to, return to, or recovery of a former position or condition. **4.** *Physics* The tendency of elastic bodies to recover their shape after compression. [< OF < L < re- again + *statuere* to set up]

res·tive (res′tiv) *adj.* **1.** Impatient of control; unruly. **2.** Restless; fidgety. [< F < L *restare* to stand] — **res′tive·ly** *adv.* — **res′tive·ness** *n.*

rest·less (rest′lis) *adj.* **1.** Having no rest; never quiet. **2.** Unable or disinclined to rest. **3.** Constantly seeking change; discontented. **4.** Obtaining no rest or sleep; sleepless. — **rest′less·ly** *adv.* — **rest′less·ness** *n.*

re·stock (rē·stok′) *v.t.* To stock again or anew.

res·to·ra·tion (res′tə·rā′shən) *n.* **1.** The act of restoring a person or thing to a former place or condition. **2.** The state

of being restored; renewal. **3.** The reconstruction or repair of something so as to restore it to its original or former state; also, an object that has been so restored. — **the Restoration** The return of Charles II to the English throne in 1660, after the overthrow of the Protectorate; also, the following period until 1685.

re·sto·ra·tive (ri·stôr′ə·tiv, -stō′rə-) *adj.* **1.** Tending or able to restore. **2.** Pertaining to restoration. — *n.* That which restores; esp. something to restore consciousness.

re·store (ri·stôr′, -stōr′) *v.t.* **·stored, ·stor·ing** **1.** To bring into existence or effect again. **2.** To bring back to a former or original condition, appearance, etc., as a painting. **3.** To put back in a former place or position; reinstate, as a deposed monarch. **4.** To bring back to health and vigor. **5.** To give back (something lost or taken away). [< OF < L < re- again + -*staurare* to make firm] — **re·stor′er** *n.*

re-store (rē·stôr′, -stōr′) *v.t.* **·stored, ·stor·ing** To store again or anew.

re·strain (ri·strān′) *v.t.* **1.** To hold back from acting, proceeding, or advancing; repress. **2.** To deprive of freedom or liberty, as by placing in a prison. **3.** To restrict or limit. [< OF < L < re- back + *stringere* to draw tight] — **re·strain′a·ble** *adj.* — **re·strain′ed·ly** *adv.* — **re·strain′er** *n.*

re·straint (ri·strānt′) *n.* **1.** The act of restraining. **2.** The state of being restrained; confinement. **3.** That which restrains; a restriction. **4.** Self-repression; constraint.

restraint of trade Interference with the free flow of goods or with fair competition, as by price fixing.

re·strict (ri·strikt′) *v.t.* To hold or keep within limits or bounds. [< L *restrictus,* pp. of *restringere* to restrain]

re·strict·ed (ri·strik′tid) *adj.* **1.** Limited; confined. **2.** Not available to the general public; limited to a specific group: *restricted* information. **3.** Excluding people of certain races, religions, or nationalities. — **re·strict′ed·ly** *adv.*

re·stric·tion (ri·strik′shən) *n.* **1.** The act of restricting, or the state of being restricted. **2.** That which restricts.

re·stric·tive (ri·strik′tiv) *adj.* **1.** Serving, tending, or operating to restrict. **2.** *Gram.* Denoting a word or word group, esp. an adjective clause, that limits the identity of its antecedent and is therefore essential to the meaning of the sentence, as *who votes for Jones* in *Any man who votes for Jones is a fool.* — **re·stric′tive·ly** *adv.*

rest room A toilet and washroom in a public building.

re·sult (ri·zult′) *n.* **1.** The outcome of an action, course, process, or agency; consequence; effect; conclusion. **2.** *Math.* A quantity or value ascertained by calculation. — *v.i.* **1.** To be a result or outcome; be a physical or logical consequent; follow: with *from.* **2.** To have an issue; terminate; end: with *in.* [< L < re- back + *salire* to leap]

re·sul·tant (ri·zul′tənt) *adj.* Arising or following as a result. — *n.* **1.** That which results; a consequence. **2.** *Physics* A force, velocity, or other quantity, resulting from and equivalent in effect to the action of two or more quantities of the same kind.

re·sume (ri·zōōm′) *v.* **·sumed, ·sum·ing** *v.t.* **1.** To take up again after cessation or interruption; begin again. **2.** To take or occupy again. **3.** To take for oneself again: to *resume* a title. — *v.i.* **4.** To continue after cessation or interruption. [< MF < L < re- again + *sumere* to take] — **re·sum′a·ble** *adj.* — **re·sum′er** *n.*

ré·su·mé (rez′ōō·mā′, rez′ōō·mā) *n.* A summary, as of one's employment record. [< F]

re·sump·tion (ri·zump′shən) *n.* The act of resuming.

re·sur·face (rē·sûr′fis) *v.t.* **·faced, ·fac·ing** To provide with a new surface.

re·surge (ri·sûrj′) *v.i.* **·surged, ·surg·ing** **1.** To rise again; be resurrected. **2.** To surge or sweep back again, as the tide. [< L < re- again + *surgere* to rise]

re·sur·gent (ri·sûr′jənt) *adj.* **1.** Rising again. **2.** Surging back or again. — **re·sur′gence** *n.*

res·ur·rect (rez′ə·rekt′) *v.t.* **1.** To bring back to life; raise from the dead. **2.** To bring back into use or to notice. — *v.i.* **3.** To rise again from the dead. [Back formation < RESURRECTION]

res·ur·rec·tion (rez′ə·rek′shən) *n.* **1.** A rising again from the dead. **2.** The state of those who have risen from the dead. **3.** Any revival or renewal, as of a practice or custom, after disuse, decay, etc.; restoration. — **the Resurrection** *Theol.* **1.** The rising of Christ from the dead. **2.** The rising again of all the dead at the day of judgment. [See RESURGE.] — **res′ur·rec′tion·al** *adj.* — **res′ur·rec′tion·ar·y** *adj.*

re·sus·ci·tate (ri·sus′ə·tāt) *v.t. & v.i.* **·tat·ed, ·tat·ing** To bring or come back to life; revive from unconsciousness. [< L < re- again + *suscitare* to revive] — **re·sus′ci·ta′tion** *n.* — **re·sus′ci·ta′tive** *adj.* — **re·sus′ci·ta′tor** *n.*

ret (ret) *v.t.* **ret·ted, ret·ting** To steep or soak, as flax, to separate the fibers: also *rot.* [ME < MDu. *reten*]

re·tail (*n. & adj.* rē′tāl; *v.* ri·tāl′) *n.* The selling of goods in small quantities, esp. to the ultimate consumer: distinguished from *wholesale.* — *adj.* Pertaining to, involving, or engaged in the sale of goods at retail. — *v.t.* **1.** To sell at retail. **2.** To repeat, as gossip. — *v.i.* **3.** To be sold at retail. [< OF < *re-* back + *tailler* to cut] — **re'tail·er** *n.*

re·tain (ri·tān') *v.t.* **1.** To keep or continue to keep in one's possession; hold. **2.** To maintain in use, practice, etc. **3.** To keep in a fixed condition or place. **4.** To keep in mind; remember. **5.** To hire; also, to engage (an attorney or other representative) by paying a retainer. [< OF < L < *re-* back + *tenere* to hold] — **re·tain'a·ble** *adj.*

re·tain·er¹ (ri·tā'nər) *n.* **1.** A servant. **2.** One who retains or keeps. **3.** *Mech.* A device for holding the parts of ball or roller bearings in place.

re·tain·er² (ri·tā'nər) *n.* **1.** The fee paid, or the agreement made, to employ an attorney to serve in a suit; a retaining fee. **2.** A similar fee paid to anyone to retain his services. [< OF *retenir* to hold back, used as noun]

re·tain·ing wall (ri·tā'ning) A wall to prevent the material of an embankment or cut from sliding, as a revetment.

re·take (*v.* rē·tāk'; *n.* rē'tāk') *v.t.* **·took, ·tak·en, ·tak·ing 1.** To take back; receive again. **2.** To recapture. **3.** To photograph again. — *n.* A motion-picture or television scene, part of a musical or other recording, etc., done again.

re·tal·i·ate (ri·tal'ē·āt) *v.* **·at·ed, ·at·ing *v.i.* 1.** To return like for like; esp., to repay evil with evil. — *v.t.* **2.** To repay (an injury, wrong, etc.) in kind; revenge. [< L < *re-* back + *talio* punishment in kind] — **re·tal'i·a·tive** *adj.* — **re·tal'i·a·to·ry** *adj.*

re·tal·i·a·tion (ri·tal'ē·ā'shən) *n.* The act of retaliating; reprisal; requital. — **Syn.** See REVENGE.

re·tard (ri·tärd') *v.t.* **1.** To cause to move or proceed slowly; hinder the advance or course of; delay. — *v.i.* **2.** To be delayed. — *n.* The act of retarding; delay. [< MF < L < *re-* back + *tardare* to make slow] — **re·tard'ant** *n. & adj.* — **re·tar·da'tion** *n.* — **re·tard'a·tive** (-ə·tiv) *adj. & n.*

re·tard·ed (ri·tär'did) *adj. Psychol.* Slowed down or backward in mental development or school achievement.

re·tard·er (ri·tär'dər) *n.* **1.** One who or that which retards. **2.** *Chem.* A substance that slows a chemical reaction, usu. when added in small quantity: compare CATALYST.

retch (rech) *v.i.* To make an effort to vomit; strain; heave. [OE *hræcan* to clear one's throat]

re·ten·tion (ri·ten'shən) *n.* **1.** The act of retaining, or the state of being retained. **2.** The ability to remember. **3.** The capacity or ability to retain. **4.** *Med.* A retaining within the body of materials normally excreted, as urine.

re·ten·tive (ri·ten'tiv) *adj.* Having the power or tendency to retain. — **re·ten'tiv·i·ty** *n.* — **re·ten'tive·ness** *n.*

ret·i·cent (ret'ə·sənt) *adj.* Habitually silent or reserved in utterance. [< L < *re-* again + *tacere* to be silent] — **ret'i·cence, ret'i·cen·cy** *n.* — **ret'i·cent·ly** *adv.*

re·tic·u·lar (ri·tik'yə·lər) *adj.* Like a network; reticulate; intricate. Also **re·tic'u·lar'y.**

re·tic·u·late (ri·tik'yə·lāt; *for adj., also* ri·tik'yə·lit) *v.* **·lat·ed, ·lat·ing *v.t.* 1.** To make a network of. **2.** To cover with or as with lines of network. — *v.i.* **3.** To form a network. — *adj.* **1.** Having the form or appearance of a network. **2.** *Bot.* Having lines or veins crossing: also **re·tic'u·lat'ed.** — **re·tic'u·la'tion** *n.*

ret·i·cule (ret'ə·kyōōl) *n.* A small bag formerly used by women for carrying personal articles, etc. [See RETICULUM.]

re·tic·u·lum (ri·tik'yə·ləm) *n. pl.* **·la** (-lə) **1.** A netlike structure; network. **2.** *Zool.* The second stomach of a ruminant. [< L, dim. of *rete* net]

ret·i·na (ret'ə·nə, ret'nə) *n. pl.* **·nas** or **·nae** (-nē) *Anat.* The inner membrane at the back of the eyeball, containing light-sensitive rods and cones that transmit the image to the optic nerve. For illus. see EYE. [< Med.L < L *rete* net] — **ret'i·nal** *adj.*

ret·i·ni·tis (ret'ə·nī'tis) *n. Pathol.* Inflammation of the retina.

ret·i·nue (ret'ə·nōō, -nyōō) *n.* The body of retainers attending a person of rank; cortège. [< F < *retenir* to retain]

re·tire (ri·tīr') *v.* **·tired, ·tir·ing *v.i.* 1.** To go away or withdraw, as for privacy, shelter, or rest. **2.** To go to bed. **3.** To withdraw oneself from business, public life, or active service. **4.** To fall back; retreat, as troops under attack. **5.** To move back; recede or appear to recede. — *v.t.* **6.** To remove from active service. **7.** To pay off and withdraw from circulation: to *retire* bonds. **8.** To withdraw (troops, etc.) from action. **9.** In baseball, etc., to put out (a batter or side). [< MF < *re-* back + *tirer* to draw]

re·tired (ri·tīrd') *adj.* **1.** Withdrawn from public view; solitary; secluded: a *retired* life. **2.** Withdrawn from active service, business, office, etc. **3.** Due to or received by a person withdrawn from active service: *retired* pay.

re·tire·ment (ri·tīr'mənt) *n.* **1.** The act of retiring, or the state of being retired. **2.** A secluded place; a retreat.

re·tir·ing (ri·tīr'ing) *adj.* **1.** Shy; modest; reserved; unobtrusive. **2.** Pertaining to retirement: a *retiring* pension.

re·tort¹ (ri·tôrt') *v.t.* **1.** To direct (a word or deed) back upon the originator. **2.** To reply to, as an accusation or argument, by a similar accusation, etc. — *v.i.* **3.** To make answer, esp. sharply. — *n.* **1.** A keen rejoinder or retaliatory speech; caustic repartee. **2.** The act of retorting. [< L < *re-* back + *torquere* to twist] — **re·tort'er** *n.*

re·tort² (ri·tôrt') *n.* **1.** *Chem.* A vessel with a bent tube for the heating of substances, or for distillation. **2.** *Metall.* A vessel in which ore may be heated for the removal of its metal content. [< L *retortus* bent back.]

RETORTS
a Retort with receiver. *b* Common retort.

re·touch (rē·tuch'; *for n., also* rē'tuch) *v.t.* **1.** To add new touches to; modify; revise. **2.** *Photog.* To change or improve, as a print. — *n.* An additional touch, as to a picture, model, or other work of art. — **re·touch'er** *n.*

re·trace (ri·trās') *v.t.* **·traced, ·trac·ing 1.** To go back over; follow backward, as a path. **2.** To trace the whole story of, from the beginning. **3.** To go back over with the eyes or mind. [< F *retracer*] — **re·trace'a·ble** *adj.*

re·trace (rē·trās') *v.t.* **·traced, ·trac·ing** To trace again, as an engraving, drawing, or map.

re·tract (ri·trakt') *v.t. & v.i.* **1.** To take back (an assertion, admission, etc.); make a disavowal (of); recant. **2.** To draw back or in, as the claws of a cat. [< F < L < *re-* again + *tractare* to handle, freq. of *trahere* to draw] — **re·tract'a·ble** or **·i·ble** *adj.* — **re·trac·ta·tion** (rē'trak·tā'shən), **re·trac'·tion** *n.*

re·trac·tile (ri·trak'til) *adj. Zool.* Capable of being drawn back or in, as a cat's claws or the head of a tortoise. — **re·trac·til·i·ty** (rē'trak·til'ə·tē) *n.*

re·trac·tive (ri·trak'tiv) *adj.* Having the power or tendency to retract; retracting.

re·trac·tor (ri·trak'tər) *n.* **1.** One who or that which retracts. **2.** *Surg.* An instrument used to hold apart the edges of a wound, incision, etc.

re·tread (*n.* rē'tred'; *v.* rē·tred') *n.* A pneumatic tire furnished with a new tread. — *v.t.* **·tread·ed, ·tread·ing** To fit or furnish (an automobile tire) with a new tread.

re·tread (rē·tred') *v.t.* **·trod, -trod·den, -tread·ing** To tread again.

re·treat (ri·trēt') *v.i.* **1.** To go back or backward; withdraw; retire. **2.** To curve or slope backward. — *v.t.* **3.** In chess, to move (a piece) back. — *n.* **1.** The act of retreating. **2.** The retirement of a military force from a position of danger or from an enemy; also, a signal for retreating, made by a trumpet or drum. **3.** *Mil.* A signal, as by bugle, for the lowering of the flag at sunset. **4.** Retirement; seclusion; solitude. **5.** A place of retirement, quiet, or security; a refuge; haunt. **6.** Religious retirement; also, the time spent in religious retirement. — **to beat a retreat 1.** To give a signal for retreat, as by the beat of drums. **2.** To turn back; flee. [< OF < L < *re-* back + *trahere* to draw]

re·trench (ri·trench') *v.t.* **1.** To cut down or reduce; curtail (expenditures). **2.** To cut off or away; remove; omit. — *v.i.* **3.** To make retrenchments; economize. [< MF < *re-* back + *trencher* to cut]

re·trench·ment (ri·trench'mənt) *n.* **1.** The act of retrenching. **2.** Reduction, as of expenses, for the sake of economy. **3.** *Mil.* An interior fortification from which the enemy can be resisted should the outer line be taken.

re·tri·al (rē·trī'əl) *n.* A second or succeeding trial, as of a judicial case.

ret·ri·bu·tion (ret'rə·byōō'shən) *n.* **1.** The act of requiting; esp., impartial infliction of punishment. **2.** That which is done or given in requital, as a reward or punishment. [< OF < L < *re-* back + *tribuere* to divide, grant]

re·trib·u·tive (ri·trib'yə·tiv) *adj.* Tending to reward or punish. Also **re·trib'u·to·ry** (-tôr'ē, -tō'rē).

re·triev·al (ri·trē'vəl) *n.* **1.** The act or process of retrieving. **2.** Possibility of restoration or recovery.

re·trieve (ri·trēv') *v.* **·trieved, ·triev·ing *v.t.* 1.** To get back; regain. **2.** To restore; revive, as flagging spirits. **3.** To make up for. **4.** To call to mind. **5.** To find and bring in (wounded or dead game): said of dogs. **6.** *Electronics* To obtain or extract (specific information) from the storage unit of an electronic computer. — *v.i.* **7.** To retrieve game. — *n.* The act of retrieving; recovery. [ME < OF < *re-* again + *trouver* to find] — **re·triev'a·bil'i·ty** *n.* — **re·triev'a·ble** *adj.* — **re·triev'a·bly** *adv.*

re·triev·er (ri·trē'vər) *n.* **1.** A sporting dog specifically trained to retrieve game. **2.** One who retrieves.

retro- *prefix* **1.** Back; backward. **2.** Behind. [< L *retro* back, backward]

ret·ro·ac·tive (ret'rō·ak'tiv, rē'trō-) *adj.* Taking effect at a (usu. specified) time prior to its enactment, ratification, etc., as a provision in a law or contract; applying retrospectively. — **ret'ro·ac'tive·ly** *adv.* — **ret'ro·ac·tiv'i·ty** *n.*

ret·ro·cede (ret'rō·sēd') *v.* **·ced·ed, ·ced·ing** *v.t.* **1.** To cede or give back — *v.i.* **2.** To recede. [< L < *retro-* back + *cedere* to go] — **ret'ro·ces'sion** (-sesh'ən) *n.*

ret·ro·fire (ret'rə·fīr) *n. Aerospace* The operation or moment of firing a retrorocket.

ret·ro·flex (ret'rə·fleks) *adj.* Bent backward; reflexed: said esp. of the tongue. Also **ret·ro·flexed** (ret'rə·flexst). [< LL < L *retro-* back + *flectere* to bend]

ret·ro·grade (ret'rə·grād) *adj.* **1.** Going or tending backward; reversed. **2.** Declining to or toward a worse state or character. **3.** *Astron.* Apparently moving from east to west relative to the fixed stars. **4.** Reversed; inverted. — *v.* **·grad·ed, ·grad·ing** *v.i.* **1.** To move or appear to move backward. **2.** To degenerate. **3.** *Astron.* To have a retrograde motion. — *v.t.* **4.** To cause to move backward; reverse. [< L < *retro-* backward + *gradi* to walk] — **ret'ro·gra·da'tion** (-grā·dā'shən) *n.*

ret·ro·gress (ret'rə·gres) *v.i.* To go back to an earlier or worse state. [< L < *retro-* backward + *gradi* to walk] — **Syn.** In strict usage, *retrogress* suggests a return to a former place or condition, while *degenerate* implies a passing into a worse condition.

ret·ro·gres·sion (ret'rə·gresh'ən) *n.* **1.** The act or process of retrogressing. **2.** *Biol.* Return to or toward an earlier form or structure. — **ret'ro·gres'sive** *adj.*

ret·ro·rock·et (ret'rō·rok'it) *n. Aerospace* An auxiliary rocket whose reverse thrust decelerates a rocket or spaceship.

re·trorse (ri·trôrs') *adj.* Turned or directed backward. [< L *retrorsus*, contr. of *retroversus* < *retro-* backward + *versus*, pp. of *vertere* to turn] — **re·trorse'ly** *adv.*

ret·ro·spect (ret'rə·spekt) *n.* A view or contemplation of something past. [< L < *retro-* back + *specere* to look] — **ret'ro·spec'tion** *n.*

ret·ro·spec·tive (ret'rə·spek'tiv) *adj.* **1.** Looking back on the past. **2.** Looking or facing backward. **3.** Applying retroactively, as legislation. **4.** Characterized by retrospection. — **ret'ro·spec'tive·ly** *adv.*

ret·rous·sé (ret'rōō·sā', *Fr.* rə·trōō·sā') *adj.* Turned up at the end: said of a nose. [< F, pp. of *retrousser* to turn up]

re·try (rē·trī') *v.t.* **·tried, ·try·ing** To try again, as a judicial case.

re·turn (ri·tûrn') *v.i.* **1.** To come or go back, as to or toward a former place or condition. **2.** To come back or revert in thought or speech. **3.** To revert to a former owner. **4.** To answer; respond. — *v.t.* **5.** To bring, carry, send, or put back; replace. **6.** To give in return for something. **7.** To repay or requite, esp. with an equivalent: to *return* a compliment. **8.** To yield or produce, as a profit or interest. **9.** To send back; reflect, as light or sound. **10.** To render (a verdict, etc.). **11.** To submit, as a report or writ, to one in authority. **12.** To report or announce officially. **13.** In card games, to lead (a suit previously led by one's partner). — *n.* **1.** The act, process, state, or result of coming back or returning. **2.** That which is returned. **3.** That which accrues, as from investments, labor, or use; profit. **4.** A coming back, reappearance, or recurrence, as of a periodical event. **5.** A report, list, etc.; esp., a formal or official report. **6.** *pl.* A set of tabulated statistics: election *returns*. **7.** In card games, a lead in a suit formerly led, esp. by one's partner **8.** In tennis, etc., the act of returning a ball to one's opponent; also, the ball, etc., so returned. — *adj.* **1.** Of, pertaining to, or for a return: a *return* ticket. **2.** Given, taken, or done in return: a *return* visit. **3.** Occurring or presented a second time or again. **4.** Reversing direction; doubling back, as a U-shaped bend. [< OF < *re-* back + *torner* to turn] — **re·turn'a·ble** *adj.* — **re·turn'er** *n.*

re·turn (rē'tûrn') *v.t. & v.i.* To turn or fold back again.

return ticket A round-trip ticket.

Reu·ben (rōō'bin) In the Old Testament, the eldest son of Jacob and Leah. *Gen.* xxix 32. — *n.* The tribe of Israel descended from Reuben.

re·un·ion (rē·yōōn'yən) *n.* **1.** The act of reuniting. **2.** A gathering of persons who have been separated.

re·u·nite (rē'yōō·nīt') *v.t. & v.i.* **·nit·ed, ·nit·ing** To unite, cohere, or combine again after separation. — **re'u·nit'er** *n.*

Reu·ters (roi'tərz) *n.* A British organization for collecting news and distributing it to member newspapers. Also **Reuter's News Agency**. [after Baron P. J. von *Reuter*, 1816–99, born in Germany]

rev (rev) *n.* A revolution, as of a motor. — *v.t. & v.i.* **revved, rev·ving** To alter the speed of (a motor): with *up*.

re·vamp (rē·vamp') *v.t.* **1.** To patch up; make over; renovate. **2.** To vamp (a boot or shoe) anew.

re·veal (ri·vēl') *v.t.* **1.** To make known; disclose; divulge. **2.** To make visible; expose to view; show. [< OF < L to unveil < *re-* back + *velum* veil] — **re·veal'a·ble** *adj.* — **re·veal'er** *n.* — **re·veal'ment** *n.*

re·veil·le (rev'i·lē) *n.* **1.** A morning signal by drum or bugle, notifying soldiers or sailors to rise. **2.** The hour at which this signal is sounded. [< F, ult. < L < *re-* again + *vigilare* to keep watch]

rev·el (rev'əl) *v.i.* **rev·eled** or **·elled, rev·el·ing** or **·el·ling 1.** To take delight: with *in*: He *revels* in his freedom. **2.** To engage in boisterous festivities; make merry. — *n.* **1.** Merrymaking; carousing. **2.** *Often pl.* An occasion of boisterous festivity; a celebration. [< OF *reveler* to make an uproar < L *rebellare*] — **rev'el·er** or **rev'el·ler** *n.*

rev·e·la·tion (rev'ə·lā'shən) *n.* **1.** The act or process of revealing. **2.** That which is or has been revealed. **3.** *Theol.* **a** The act of revealing or communicating divine truth, esp. by divine agency. **b** That which has been so revealed, as concerning God in his relations to man.

Rev·e·la·tion (rev'ə·lā'shən) *n. Often pl.* The Apocalypse, or book of Revelation, the last book of the New Testament: in full, **The Revelation of Saint John the Divine.**

rev·el·ry (rev'əl·rē) *n. pl.* **·ries** Noisy or boisterous merriment.

re·venge (ri·venj') *v.* **·venged, ·veng·ing** *v.t.* **1.** To inflict punishment, injury, or loss in return for. **2.** To take or seek vengeance in behalf of. — *n.* **1.** The act of revenging. **2.** A means of avenging oneself or others. **3.** A desire for vengeance. [< OF < *re-* again + *vengier* to take vengeance] — **re·veng'er** *n.* — **Syn.** (noun) **1.** *Revenge* stresses personal bitterness that seeks relief in harming or humiliating an enemy. *Vengeance*, originally the indignant vindication of justice, is now applied to any furious and thoroughgoing return of *revenge*. *Retaliation* suggests the repayment of an act by a like act.

re·venge·ful (ri·venj'fəl) *adj.* Disposed to or full of revenge; vindictive. — **re·venge'ful·ly** *adv.* + **re·venge'ful·ness** *n.*

rev·e·nue (rev'ə·nyōō, -nōō) *n.* **1.** Total current income of a government, except duties on imports: also called *internal revenue*. **2.** Income from any form of property. **3.** A source of income. [< F < L < *re-* back + *venire* to come]

re·ver·ber·ant (ri·vûr'bər·ənt) *adj.* Reverberating.

re·ver·ber·ate (ri·vûr'bə·rāt) *v.* **·at·ed, ·at·ing** *v.i.* **1.** To resound or re-echo. **2.** To be reflected. **3.** To rebound or recoil. — *v.t.* **4.** To echo back (a sound); re-echo. **5.** To reflect. [< L < *re-* back + *verberare* to beat]

re·ver·ber·a·tion (ri·vûr'bə·rā'shən) *n.* **1.** The act or process of reverberating. **2.** That which is reverberated. **3.** The rebound or reflection of light, heat, or sound waves. — **re·ver'ber·a'tive** *adj.* — **re·ver'ber·a·to'ry** (-bər·ə·tôr'ē, -tō'rē) *adj.*

re·vere (ri·vir') *v.t.* **·vered, ·ver·ing** To regard with reverence; venerate. — **Syn.** See VENERATE. [< L < *re-* again + *vereri* to fear] — **re·ver'er** *n.*

rev·er·ence (rev'ər·əns) *n.* **1** A feeling of profound respect often mingled with awe and affection; veneration. **2.** An act of respect; an obeisance. — *v.t.* **·enced, ·enc·ing** To regard with reverence. — **Syn.** See VENERATE.

Rev·er·ence (rev'ər·əns) *n.* A title or form of address for clergymen: often preceded by *His, Your*, etc.

rev·er·end (rev'ər·ənd) *adj.* **1.** Worthy of reverence. **2.** *Often cap.* A title of respect often used with the name of a clergyman. — *n. Informal* A clergyman; minister. [See REVERE.]

rev·er·ent (rev'ər·ənt) *adj.* **1.** Feeling reverence. **2.** Expressing reverence. [See REVERE.] — **rev'er·ent·ly** *adv.*

rev·er·en·tial (rev'ə·ren'shəl) *adj.* Proceeding from or expressing reverence. — **rev'er·en'tial·ly** *adv.*

rev·er·ie (rev'ə·rē) *n. pl.* **·er·ies 1.** Abstracted musing; dreaming. **2.** A product of such musing. Also **rev'er·y.** [< F < MF *resver* to be delirious, dream]

re·vers (rə·vir', -vâr') *n. pl.* **·vers** (-virz', -vârz') A part of a garment folded over to show the inside, as the lapel of a coat. Also **re·vere'.** [< OF. See REVERSE.]

re·ver·sal (ri·vûr'səl) *n.* The act of reversing, or the state of being reversed.

re·verse (ri·vûrs') *adj.* **1.** Having a contrary or opposite direction, character, order, etc.; turned backward. **2.** Causing backward motion: the *reverse* gear of an automobile. — *n.* **1.** That which is directly opposite or contrary. **2.** The back or secondary side of anything: distinguished from *obverse*. **3.** A change to an opposite position, direction, or state. **4.** A change for the worse; a check or partial defeat. **5.** *Mech.* A reversing gear or movement. — *v.* **versed, ·vers·ing** *v.t.* **1.** To turn upside down or inside out. **2.** To turn in an opposite direction. **3.** To change into something different or opposite. **4.** To set aside; annul: to *reverse* a decree. **5.** *Mech.* To cause to have an opposite motion or effect. — *v.i.* **6.** To move or turn in the opposite direction. **7.** To reverse its action, as an engine. [< OF < L < *re-* back + *vertere* to turn] — **re·verse'ly** *adv.* — **re·vers'er** *n.*

re·vers·i·ble (ri·vûr'sə·bəl) *adj.* **1.** Capable of being reversed in direction or position. **2.** Capable of going either forward or backward, as a chemical reaction or physiological process. **3.** Capable of being used or worn inside out or backward, as a coat. **4.** Having the finish on both sides, as a fabric. — *n.* A reversible coat. — **re·vers′i·bil′i·ty, re·vers′i·ble·ness** *n.* — **re·vers′i·bly** *adv.*

re·ver·sion (ri·vûr′zhən, -shən) *n.* **1.** A return to or toward some former state, condition, practice, or belief. **2.** The act of reversing, or the state of being reversed. **3.** *Biol.* **a** The reappearance in an individual of characteristics that had not been evident for two or more generations: also called *atavism.* **b** An example of such reappearance. **4.** *Law* **a** The return of an estate to the grantor or his heirs after the expiration of the grant. **b** The right of succession to an estate. [See REVERT.] — **re·ver′sion·al,** — **re·ver′sion·ar′y** (-er′ē) *adj.*

re·vert (ri·vûrt′) *v.i.* **1.** To go or turn back to a former place, condition, attitude, etc. **2.** *Biol.* To return to or show characteristics of an earlier type. **3.** *Law* To return to the former owner or his heirs. [< OF < L < re- back + vertere to turn] — **re·vert′i·ble** *adj.* — **re·vert′ive** *adj.*

re·vet·ment (ri·vet′mənt) *n.* A facing or sheathing, as of masonry, for protecting earthworks, river banks, etc. [< F < OF < LL < L < re- again + vestire to clothe]

re·view¹ (ri·vyoō′) *v.t.* **1.** To go over or examine again; look at or study again. **2.** To look back upon; think of retrospectively. **3.** To make an inspection of, esp. formally. **4.** To write or make a critical review of, as a new book. **5.** *Law* To reexamine (something done or adjudged by a lower court). — *v.i.* **6.** To write a review or reviews, as for a magazine. [< RE- + VIEW]

re·view² (ri·vyoō′) *n.* **1.** A repeated or new view or study of something; a retrospective survey. **2.** A lesson studied or recited again. **3.** Critical study or examination. **4.** An article containing a critical discussion of some work. **5.** A periodical devoted to essays in criticism and on general subjects. **6.** A formal inspection, as of troops. **7.** *Law* A judicial revision by a superior court of the order or decree of a subordinate court. See REVUE. [< MF < L < re- again + videre to see]

re·view·al (ri·vyoō′əl) *n.* The act of reviewing; a review.

re·view·er (ri·vyoō′ər) *n.* One who reviews; esp., one who critically reviews new books, plays, movies, etc.

re·vile (ri·vīl′) *v.* ·**viled,** ·**vil·ing** *v.t.* **1.** To assail with abusive or contemptuous language; vilify; abuse. — *v.i.* **2.** To use abusive or contemptuous language. — **Syn.** See SCOLD. [< OF reviler to despise] — **re·vile′ment** *n.* — **re·vil′er** *n.* — **re·vil′ing·ly** *adv.*

re·vis·al (ri·vī′zəl) *n.* The act of revising; revision.

re·vise (ri·vīz′) *v.t.* ·**vised,** ·**vis·ing 1.** To read or read over so as to correct errors, suggest or make changes, etc. **2.** To change; alter. — *n.* **1.** The act or result of revising; a revision. **2.** A corrected proof after revision. [< MF < L < re- again + visere to scrutinize] — **re·vis′er** or **re·vi′sor** *n.*

re·vi·sion (ri·vizh′ən) *n.* **1.** The act or process of revising. **2.** Something revised, as a new version of a book. — **re·vi′sion·al, re·vi′sion·ar′y** *adj.*

re·vi·so·ry (ri·vī′zər·ē) *adj.* Effecting, or capable of effecting, revision; revising: *revisory* powers.

re·viv·al (ri·vī′vəl) *n.* **1.** The act of reviving or, the state of being revived. **2.** A recovery, as from depression. **3.** A restoration, as after neglect or obscurity. **4.** A renewal of interest in religion. **5.** A series of evangelical meetings to reawaken faith.

re·vi·val·ist (ri·vī′vəl·ist) *n.* A preacher or leader in a religious revival movement.

re·vive (ri·vīv′) *v.* ·**vived,** ·**viv·ing** *v.t.* **1.** To bring back to life or to consciousness. **2.** To give new health, etc., to. **3.** To bring back into use. **4.** To make effective or operative again. **5.** To renew in the mind or memory. **6.** To produce again, as an old play. — *v.i.* **7.** To come back to life again. **8.** To assume new vigor, health, etc. **9.** To come back into use. **10.** To become effective or operative again. [< MF < L < re- again + vivere to live] — **re·viv′er** *n.*

re·viv·i·fy (ri·viv′ə·fī) *v.t.* ·**fied,** ·**fy·ing** To give new life to; revive. [< L < re- again + vivus alive + facere to make] — **re·viv′i·fi·ca′tion** *n.*

rev·o·ca·ble (rev′ə·kə·bəl) *adj.* Capable of being revoked. Also **re·vok·a·ble** (ri·vō′kə·bəl). — **rev′o·ca·bil′i·ty** *n.* — **rev′o·ca·bly** *adv.*

rev·o·ca·tion (rev′ə·kā′shən) *n.* The act of revoking, or the state of being revoked; repeal; reversal; annulment.

re·voke (ri·vōk′) *v.* ·**voked,** ·**vok·ing** *v.t.* **1.** To annul or make void by recalling; cancel; rescind. — *v.i.* **2.** In card games, to fail to follow suit when possible and when required by the rules. — **Syn.** See ANNUL. — *n.* In card games, neglect to follow suit; a renege. [< OF < L < re- back + vocare to call] — **re·vok′er** *n.*

re·volt (ri·vōlt′) *n.* **1.** An uprising against authority; rebellion. **2.** An act of protest, refusal, or disgust. **3.** The state of a person or persons who revolt: to be in *revolt.* —

v.i. **1.** To rise in rebellion against constituted authority; mutiny. **2.** To turn away in disgust: with *against, at,* or *from.* — *v.t.* **3.** To cause to feel disgust; repel. [< MF < Ital. < L < re- back + volvere to roll] — **re·volt′er** *n.*

re·volt·ing (ri·vōl′ting) *adj.* Abhorrent; loathsome; nauseating. — **re·volt′ing·ly** *adv.*

rev·o·lu·tion (rev′ə·loō′shən) *n.* **1.** The act or state of revolving. **2.** A motion in a closed curve around a center, or a complete circuit made by a body in such a course. **3.** *Mech.* Rotation about an axis, as in a spiral, so as to come to a point corresponding to the starting point. **4.** *Astron.* The movement of a planet around the sun or of any celestial body around a center of attraction. **5.** A cycle of successive events or changes. **6.** The overthrow and replacement of a government or political system by those governed. **7.** A drastic change in a condition, method, idea, etc.: a *revolution* in industry. [< OF < LL < L < re- back + volvere to roll]

— **American Revolution** The war for independence carried on by the thirteen American colonies against Great Britain, 1775–83. Also *Revolutionary War.* See table for WAR.

— **Chinese Revolution** The events in China during the years 1911–12, inspired by Sun Yat-sen, that overthrew the Manchu Empire and established a republic.

— **English Revolution** The course of events in England in 1642–89 that brought about the execution of Charles I, the rise of the Commonwealth, the dethronement of James II, and the establishment of a constitutional government.

— **French Revolution** The revolution that began in France in 1789, overthrew the French monarchy, and culminated in the start of the Napoleonic era in 1799.

— **Russian Revolution** The conflict (1917–22), beginning in a Petrograd uprising on March 12, 1917, that resulted in a provisional moderate government and the abdication of Nicholas II. On November 6, the Bolsheviks under Lenin overthrew this government (the **October Revolution**), and in December, 1922, united the soviet states in the Union of Soviet Socialist Republics under Communist (Bolshevik) control.

rev·o·lu·tion·ar·y (rev′ə·loō′shən·er′ē) *adj.* **1.** Pertaining to or of the nature of revolution, esp. political; causing or tending to produce revolution. **2.** Rotating; revolving.

Revolutionary calendar See (Republican) CALENDAR.

Revolutionary War The American Revolution. See under REVOLUTION.

rev·o·lu·tion·ize (rev′ə·loō′shən·īz) *v.t.* ·**ized,** ·**iz·ing** To effect a radical change in the character, operation, etc., of.

re·volve (ri·volv′) *v.* ·**volved,** ·**volv·ing** *v.i.* **1.** To move in an orbit about a center. **2.** To spin around on an axis; rotate. **3.** To recur periodically. — *v.t.* **4.** To cause to move in a circle or orbit. **5.** To cause to rotate. **6.** To turn over mentally; consider. [< L < re- back + volvere to roll] — **re·volv′a·ble** *adj.*

re·volv·er (ri·vol′vər) *n.* **1.** A type of pistol having a revolving cylinder in the breech chambered to hold several cartridges that may be fired in succession without reloading. **2.** One who or that which revolves.

revolving door A door rotating like a turnstile about a central post and consisting of three or four adjustable leaves so encased in a doorway as to exclude drafts of air.

re·vue (ri·vyoō′) *n.* A musical show consisting of songs, dances, and skits that lampoon or burlesque contemporary people and events: also spelled *review.* [< F]

re·vul·sion (ri·vul′shən) *n.* **1.** A sudden change of or strong reaction in feeling. **2.** The drawing back from something; violent withdrawal or recoil. [< OF < L < re- back + vellere to pull] — **re·vul′sive** (-siv) *adj.*

re·ward (ri·wôrd′) *n.* **1.** Something given or done in return; esp., a gift, prize, etc., for merit, service, or achievement. **2.** Money offered for information, for the return of lost goods, etc. **3.** Profit; return. — *v.t.* **1.** To give a reward to or for. **2.** To be a reward for. [< OF < re- back (< L) + warder to guard] — **re·ward′er** *n.*

re·wire (rē·wīr′) *v.t.* ·**wired,** ·**wir·ing** To wire again, as a house or a machine.

re·word (rē·wûrd′) *v.t.* **1.** To say again in other words; express differently. **2.** To utter or say again in the same words.

re·write (*v.* rē·rīt′; *n.* rē′rīt′) *v.t.* ·**wrote,** ·**writ·ten,** ·**writ·ing 1.** To write over again. **2.** In American journalism, to put into publishable form (a story submitted by a reporter). — *n.* A news item written in this manner.

rex (reks) *n.* *pl.* **re·ges** (rē′jēs) *Usu. cap. Latin* King.

Reyn·ard (ren′ərd, rā′nərd) *n.* The fox, esp. as the personification of cunning: also spelled *Renard.* [< MDu. < OHG, name of fox in medieval legend]

-rhage, -rhagia, -rhagy See -RRHAGIA.

-rhaphy See -RRHAPHY.

rhap·so·dize (rap′sə·dīz) *v.t. & v.i.* ·**dized,** ·**diz·ing** To express or recite rhapsodically. — **rhap′so·dist** *n.*

rhap·so·dy (rap′sə·dē) *n.* *pl.* **·dies** **1.** A series of disconnected and often extravagant sentences, extracts, or utterances, gathered or composed under excitement. **2.** *Music* An instrumental composition of irregular form, often suggestive of improvisation. **3.** A miscellaneous collection. [< L < Gk. < *rhaptein* to stitch together + *ōidē* song] — **rhap·sod·ic** (rap·sod′ik) or **·i·cal** *adj.* — **rhap·sod′i·cal·ly** *adv.*

rhe·a (rē′ə) *n.* A flightless bird of the plains of South America, smaller than true ostriches, and having three toes: also called *ostrich.* [< NL < L < Gk.]

Rhe·a (rē′ə) In Greek mythology, the daughter of Uranus and Gaea and mother of Zeus.

-rhea See -RRHEA.

Rhen·ish (ren′ish) *adj.* Pertaining to the river Rhine, or to the adjacent lands. — *n.* Rhine wine. [< L *Rhenus* Rhine]

rhe·ni·um (rē′nē·əm) *n.* A heavy, lustrous, rare metallic element (symbol Re) of the manganese group. See ELEMENT. [< NL < L *Rhenus* Rhine]

rheo- *combining form* Current or flow, as of water or electricity. [< Gk. *rheos* a current]

rhe·o·stat (rē′ə·stat) *n.* *Electr.* A variable resistor used to control current and voltage strength in a circuit. [< RHEO- + Gk. *statos* standing] — **rhe′o·stat′ic** *adj.*

rhe·sus (rē′səs) *n.* A monkey with a short tail, common throughout India and widely used in biological and medical research. [< NL < Gk. *Rhēsos* Rhesus]

Rhe·sus factor (rē′səs) Rh factor.

rhet·o·ric (ret′ə·rik) *n.* **1.** The art of discourse, both written and spoken. **2.** The power of pleasing or persuading. **3.** Affected and exaggerated display in the use of language. **4.** The art of prose as distinct from verse. [< MF < Gk. < *rhētōr* public speaker]

rhe·tor·i·cal (ri·tôr′i·kəl, -tor′-) *adj.* **1.** Pertaining to rhetoric; oratorical. **2.** Designed for showy oratorical effect. — **rhe·tor′i·cal·ly** *adv.* — **rhe·tor′i·cal·ness** *n.*

rhetorical question A question put only for oratorical or literary effect, the answer being implied in the question.

rhet·o·ri·cian (ret′ə·rish′ən) *n.* **1.** A master of rhetoric. **2.** One who writes or speaks eloquently. [< F *rhétoricien*]

rheum (rōōm) *n.* *Pathol.* **1.** A thin, watery discharge from the nose and eyes. **2.** A cold. [< OF < L < Gk. *rheuma* stream < *rheein* to flow] — **rheum′y** *adj.*

rheu·mat·ic (rōō·mat′ik) *adj.* **1.** Of or relating to rheumatism. **2.** Affected with rheumatism. — *n.* One affected with rheumatism. [< OF < L < Gk. *rheuma* a stream]

rheumatic fever *Pathol.* An infectious disease chiefly affecting children, characterized by painful inflammation around the joints, typically intermittent fever, and inflammation of the pericardium and valves of the heart.

rheu·ma·tism (rōō′mə·tiz′əm) *n.* *Pathol.* **1.** A painful inflammation and stiffness of the muscles, joints, etc. **2.** Rheumatoid arthritis. [< L < Gk. *rheumatismos* < *rheuma* a stream]

rheu·ma·toid (rōō′mə·toid) *adj.* *Pathol.* **1.** Resembling rheumatism. **2.** Rheumatic. Also **rheu′ma·toi′dal** (-toid′l). — **rheu′ma·toi′dal·ly** *adv.*

rheumatoid arthritis *Pathol.* A persisting inflammatory disease of the joints, marked by atrophy, rarefaction of the bones, and deformities.

Rh factor *Biochem.* An agglutinogen present in the blood of most persons (who are said to be **Rh positive**) and that may cause hemolytic reactions under certain conditions, as during pregnancy or following transfusions with persons lacking this factor (who are said to be **Rh negative**): also called *Rhesus factor.*

rhin- Var. of RHINO-.

rhi·nal (rī′nəl) *adj.* Of or pertaining to the nose; nasal.

rhine·stone (rīn′stōn′) *n.* A refractive, colorless glass or paste, used as an imitation gemstone. [Trans. of F *caillou du Rhin;* so called because orig. made at Strasbourg]

Rhine wine **1.** Wine made from grapes grown in the neighborhood of the Rhine: also called *Rhenish.* **2.** Any of various white, dry, still wines.

rhi·ni·tis (rī·nī′tis) *n.* *Pathol.* Inflammation of the mucous membranes of the nose.

rhi·no¹ (rī′nō) *n.* *pl.* **·nos** A rhinoceros.

rhi·no² (rī′nō) *n.* *Slang* Money; cash. [Origin unknown]

rhino- *combining form* Nose; nasal. Also, before vowels, *rhin-.* [< Gk. *rhis, rhinos* nose]

rhi·noc·e·ros (rī·nos′ər·əs) *n.* *pl.* **·ros·es** or **·ros** A large, herbivorous mammal of Africa and Asia, having one or two horns on the snout and a very thick hide. [< LL < Gk. < *rhis, rhinos* nose + *keras* horn]

rhizo- *combining form* Root; pertaining to a root or roots. Also, before vowels, *rhiz-.* [< Gk. *rhiza* root]

rhi·zoid (rī′zoid) *adj.* Rootlike. — *n.* *Bot.* A hairlike, branching organ by which mosses and liverworts obtain nourishment and support. — **rhi·zoi′dal** (rī·zoid′l) *adj.*

rhi·zome (rī′zōm) *n.* *Bot.* A subterranean rootlike stem, producing roots from its lower surface and leaves or shoots from its upper surface: also called *rootstalk, rootstock.* Also

rhi·zo·ma (rī·zō′mə). [< NL *rhizoma* < Gk. *rhizōma*, ult. < *rhiza* root] — **rhi·zom·a·tous** (rī·zom′ə·təs, -zō′mə-) *adj.*

rhi·zo·pod (rī′zə·pod) *n.* Any of a class or subclass of protozoans with rootlike pseudopodia. — **rhi·zop·o·dan** (rī·zop′ə·dən) *adj. & n.* — **rhi·zop′o·dous** *adj.*

rho (rō) *n.* The seventeenth letter in the Greek alphabet (P, ρ), corresponding to the English *r* aspirated. See ALPHABET. [< Gk. *rhō*]

Rhode Island Red An American breed of domestic fowls, reddish and black in color, with yellow smooth legs.

Rhodes scholarships One of a number of scholarships at Oxford University, provided for in the will of Cecil Rhodes, for selected scholars (**Rhodes scholars**) from the U.S. and the British dominions and colonies.

Rho·di·an (rō′dē·ən) *adj.* Of or pertaining to the island of Rhodes. — *n.* A native of Rhodes.

rho·di·um (rō′dē·əm) *n.* A whitish gray, metallic element (symbol Rh) of the platinum group, whose salts are for the most part rose-colored, used in electroplating to prevent corrosion. See ELEMENT. [< NL < Gk. *rhodon* rose]

rho·do·den·dron (rō′də·den′drən) *n.* Any of a genus of evergreen shrubs or small trees of the heath family, with clusters of white, pink, or purple flowers: the State flower of West Virginia. [< L < Gk. < *rhodon* rose + *dendron* tree]

-rhoea See -RRHEA.

rhomb (rom, romb) *n.* A rhombus. [< F *rhombe*]

rhom·ben·ceph·a·lon (rom′ben·sef′ə·lon) *n.* *Anat.* A segment of the embryonic brain that divides into the metencephalon and myelencephalon: also called *hindbrain.* [< NL]

rhom·bic (rom′bik) *adj.* Pertaining to or having the shape of a rhombus. Also **rhom′bi·cal.**

rhom·boid (rom′boid) *n.* *Geom.* **1.** A parallelogram having opposite sides and opposite angles equal but having no right angle. **2.** A solid bounded by such parallelograms. — *adj.* **1.** Having the character or shape of a rhomboid. **2.** Having a shape approaching that of a rhombus. [< F *rhomboïde*] — **rhom·boi·dal** (rom·boid′l) *adj.*

rhom·bus (rom′bəs) *n.* *pl.* **·bus·es** or **·bi** (-bī) *Geom.* An equilateral parallelogram having the angles usu., but not necessarily, oblique. [< L < Gk. *rhombos* spinning top]

rhu·barb (rōō′bärb) *n.* **1.** A stout, coarse, perennial herb having large leaves and small clusters of flowers on tall stalks, esp. one whose acid leafstalks are used in cooking. **2.** *U.S. Slang* A heated argument or quarrel. [< MF < LL < Gk. *rha* rhubarb, ? < *Rha* the Volga River + L *barbarus* foreign]

rhumb (rum, rumb) *n.* *Naut.* **1.** One of the 32 points of the mariners' compass, separated by arcs of 11° 15′. **2.** One of these arcs or divisions. [< OF *rumb*]

rhum·ba (rum′bə) See RUMBA.

rhumb line A line or course along the surface of a sphere crossing successive meridians at the same angle.

rhyme (rīm) *n.* **1.** A correspondence of sounds in two or more words, esp. at the ends of lines of poetry. **2.** A verse whose lines have a correspondence of sounds in the end words. **3.** Poetry; verse. — *v.* **rhymed, rhym·ing** *v.i.* **1.** To make rhymes or verses. **2.** To correspond in sound or in terminal sounds. — *v.t.* **3.** To put or write in rhyme or verse. **4.** To use as a rhyme. Also spelled *rime.* [< OF *rime* < L *rhythmus* rhythm] — **rhym′er** *n.*

rhyme·ster (rīm′stər) *n.* A writer of jingles: also spelled *rimester.*

rhythm (rith′əm) *n.* **1.** The recurrence or repetition of stress, beat, sound, accent, motion, etc., usu. occurring in a regular or harmonious pattern or manner. **2.** *Music* **a** The relative duration and accent of musical sounds. **b** Any specific arrangement of the accents or durations of musical sounds. **3.** In poetry, the cadenced flow of sound as determined by the succession of long and short syllables (**classical rhythm**), or accented and unaccented syllables (**modern rhythm**). **4.** In painting, sculpture, etc., a regular or harmonious recurrence of lines, forms, colors, etc. [< MF < L < Gk. *rhythmos* < *rheein* to flow]

rhyth·mi·cal (rith′mə·kəl) *adj.* Of or possessing rhythm. Also **rhyth·mic** (rith′mik). — **rhyth′mi·cal·ly** *adv.*

rhythm method Birth control by sexual abstinence during the woman's estimated monthly period of fertility.

ri·al (rī′al) *n.* A standard monetary unit and coin of Iran: in 1961 worth about 13 U.S. cents. [< OF *rial, real* royal]

ri·al·to (rē·al′tō) *n.* *pl.* **·tos** A market or place of exchange. [< RIALTO]

Ri·al·to (rē·al′tō, *Ital.* rē·äl′tō) In New York City, the theater district. [after *Rialto,* the ancient business quarter of Venice]

rib (rib) *n.* **1.** *Anat.* One of the series of bony rods attached to the spine of most vertebrates, and nearly encircling the thoracic cavity. In man there are twelve ribs on each side, forming the walls of the thorax. For illus. see SKELETON. ◆ Collateral adjective: *costal.* **2.** Something likened to a rib: the *rib* of an umbrella. **3.** A curved side timber bending away from the keel in a boat or ship. **4.** A raised wale or stripe in cloth or knit goods. **5.** *Bot.* A vein of a leaf, esp. a central one. **6.** A cut of meat including one or more ribs. — *v.t.* **ribbed, rib·bing 1.** To make with ridges: to *rib* a piece of knitting. **2.** To strengthen or protect by or enclose within ribs. **3.** *Slang* To make fun of; tease. [OE]

rib·ald (rib′əl) *adj.* Pertaining to or indulging in coarse language or vulgar jokes. — *n.* One who uses coarse or abusive language. [< OF *ribauld* < Gmc.]

rib·ald·ry (rib′əl·drē) *n. pl.* **·ries** Ribald language.

rib·and (rib′ənd) *n. Archaic* A decorative ribbon.

rib·bing (rib′ing) *n.* An arrangement or collection of ribs, as in ribbed cloth, etc.

rib·bon (rib′ən) *n.* **1.** A narrow strip of fine fabric, usu. silk or satin, having finished edges and made in a variety of weaves, used as trimming. **2.** Something shaped like or suggesting a ribbon, as a watch spring. **3.** *Often pl.* A narrow strip; a shred: torn to *ribbons.* **4.** An ink-bearing strip of cloth for giving the impression in a typewriter or similar device. **5.** A colored strip of cloth worn to signify membership in an order, the award of a prize, or as a military badge. — *v.t.* To ornament with ribbons; also, to form or tear into ribbons. [< MF *riban* < Gmc.]

ri·bo·fla·vin (rī′bō·flā′vin) *n. Biochem.* A member of the vitamin B complex, vitamin B₂, an orange-yellow, crystalline compound, $C_{17}H_{22}N_4O_6$, found in milk, leafy vegetables, egg yolk, and meats, and also made synthetically: formerly called *lactoflavin, vitamin G.* [< RIBO(SE) + FLAVIN]

ri·bo·nu·cle·ase (rī′bō·nōō′klē·ās, -nyōō′-, -āz) *n. Biochem.* A pancreatic enzyme, effective in splitting ribonucleic acid.

ri·bo·nu·cle·ic acid (rī′bō·nōō·klē′ik, -nyōō-) *Biochem.* A nucleic acid of high molecular weight found in the cytoplasm and nuclei of cells and associated with DNA in the synthesis of cell proteins. *Abbr.* RNA

ri·bose (rī′bōs) *n. Chem.* A sugar, $C_5H_{10}O_5$, derived from pentose and occurring in certain nucleic acids. [< G *ribonsäure*, arbitrary alteration of ARABINOSE + *-säure* acid]

ri·bo·some (rī′bə·sōm) *n. Biol.* One of a class of minute protein particles found in the cytoplasm of plant and animal cells, associated with ribonucleic acid in the transmission of genetic characteristics. — **ri·bo·so·mal** (rī′bə·sō′məl) *adj.*

-ric *combining form* Realm or jurisdiction of: *bishopric.* [OE *rīce* kingdom, realm]

rice (rīs) *n.* **1.** The edible seeds of an annual cereal grass, rich in carbohydrates and forming a staple food throughout the world. **2.** The grass itself, cultivated in warm climates. [< OF < Ital. < L < Gk. *oryza*]

rice paper 1. Paper made from rice straw. **2.** A delicate vegetable paper made from the pith of a Chinese shrub, pared into thin rolls and flattened into sheets.

ric·er (rī′sər) *n.* A kitchen utensil consisting of a container perforated with small holes through which potatoes and other vegetables are pressed.

rich (rich) *adj.* **1.** Having large possessions, as of money, goods, or lands; wealthy; opulent. **2.** Composed of rare or precious materials; valuable; costly: *rich* fabrics. **3.** Luscious to the taste, often implying an excess of fats, flavoring, etc. **4.** Full, satisfying, and pleasing, as a tone, voice, color, etc. **5.** Luxuriant; abundant: *rich* hair; *rich* crops. **6.** Yielding abundant returns; fruitful. **7.** Abundantly supplied: often with *in* or *with.* **8.** Abounding in desirable qualities; of full strength, as blood. **9.** *Informal* Exceedingly humorous; amusing: a *rich* joke. **10.** Of a fuelair mixture, containing a relatively high ratio of fuel to air. [Fusion of OE *rice* powerful, rich and OF *riche* < Gmc.] — **rich′ly** *adv.* — **rich′ness** *n.*

rich·es (rich′iz) *n.pl.* **1.** Abundant possessions; wealth. **2.** Abundance of whatever is precious.

rick (rik) *n.* A stack, as of hay, having the top covered to protect the interior from rain. — *v.t.* To pile in ricks. [OE *hrēac*]

rick·ets (rik′its) *n. Pathol.* A disease of early childhood, chiefly due to a deficiency of calcium salts or vitamin D, characterized by softening of the bones and consequent deformity: also called *rachitis.* [? Alter. of Gk. *rachitis* inflammation of the spine]

rick·ett·si·a (rik·et′sē·ə) *n. pl.* **·si·ae** (-si·ē) Any of a genus of microorganisms typically parasitic in the bodies of certain ticks and lice, but transmissible to other animals and to man and the causative agent of typhus, Rocky Mountain spotted fever, etc. [after Howard T. *Ricketts,* 1871–1910, U.S. pathologist] — **rick·ett′si·al** *adj.*

rick·et·y (rik′it·ē) *adj.* **·et·i·er, ·et·i·est 1.** Ready to fall; tottering. **2.** Affected with or like rickets. **3.** Irregular, as motion. **4.** Feeble; infirm; unsteady. — **rick′et·i·ly** *adv.* — **rick′et·i·ness** *n.*

rick·ey (rik′ē) *n. pl.* **·eys** A cooling drink of which a liquor, as gin, lime juice, and carbonated water are the chief ingredients. [Said to be after a Colonel *Rickey*]

rick·rack (rik′rak′) *n.* Flat braid in zigzag form, made of cotton, rayon, silk, or wool; also, the openwork trimming made with this braid. [Reduplication of RACK¹]

rick·shaw (rik′shô) *n.* A jinriksha. Also **rick′sha.**

ric·o·chet (rik′ə·shā′, -shet′) *v.i.* **·cheted** (-shād′) or **·chetted** (-shet′id), **·chet·ing** (-shā′ing) or **·chet·ting** (-shet′ing) To glance from a surface, as a stone thrown over the water; make a series of skips or bounds. — *n.* **1.** A bounding, as of a projectile over or off a surface. **2.** A projectile so bounding. [< F; origin uncertain]

rid (rid) *v.t.* **rid** or **rid·ded, rid·ding** To free, as from a burden or annoyance: usu. with *of.* — *adj.* Free; clear; quit: with *of:* We are well *rid* of him. [< ON *rythja* to clear land]

rid·dance (rid′ns) *n.* A ridding of something undesirable, or the state of being rid. — **good riddance** A welcome deliverance from something undesirable.

rid·den (rid′n) Past participle of RIDE.

rid·dle¹ (rid′l) *v.t.* **·dled, ·dling 1.** To perforate in numerous places, as with shot. **2.** To sift through a coarse sieve. **3.** To damage, injure; criticize, etc., as if by perforating. — *n.* A coarse sieve. [OE *hriddel* sieve] — **rid′dler** *n.*

rid·dle² (rid′l) *n.* **1.** A puzzling question stated as a problem to be solved by clever ingenuity; a conundrum. **2.** Any puzzling object or person. — **Syn.** See PUZZLE. — *v.* **·dled, ·dling** *v.t.* **1.** To solve; explain. — *v.i.* **2.** To utter or solve riddles. [OE *rædels* advice, interpretation]

ride (rīd) *v.* **rode** (*Archaic* **rid**), **rid·den** (*Archaic* **rid**), **rid·ing** *v.i.* **1.** To sit on and be borne along by a horse or other animal. **2.** To be borne along as if on horseback. **3.** To travel or be carried on or in a vehicle or other conveyance. **4.** To be supported in moving: The wheel *rides* on the shaft. **5.** To support and carry a rider in a specified manner: This car *rides* easily. **6.** To seem to float in space, as a star. **7.** *Naut.* To lie at anchor, as a ship. **8.** To work or move upward out of place: with *up.* **9.** *Slang* To continue unchanged: Let it *ride.* — *v.t.* **10.** To sit on and control the motion of (a horse, bicycle, etc.). **11.** To move or be borne or supported upon. **12.** To overlap or overlie. **13.** To travel or traverse (an area, etc.) on horseback, in an automobile, etc. **14.** To control imperiously or oppressively: usually in the past participle: a king-*ridden* people. **15.** To accomplish by riding: to *ride* a race. **16.** To cause to ride. **17.** *Naut.* To keep at anchor. **18.** *Informal* To tease or harass by ridicule or petty criticisms; tyrannize. — **to ride out** To survive; endure successfully. — *n.* **1.** An excursion by any means of conveyance, as on horseback, by car, etc. **2.** A road intended for riding. [OE *rīdan*] — **rid′a·ble** *adj.*

rid·er (rī′dər) *n.* **1.** One who or that which rides. **2.** One who breaks in horses. **3.** Any device that rides upon or weighs down something else. **4.** A separate piece of writing or print added to a document, record, or the like. **5.** An addition or proposed addition to a legislative bill.

ridge (rij) *n.* **1.** An elevation long in proportion to its width and height and generally having sloping sides. **2.** A long, relatively narrow elevation of land. **3.** That part of a roof where the rafters meet the ridgepole. **4.** Any raised strip, as on fabric, etc. **5.** The back or backbone of an animal, especially of a whale. — *v.* **ridged, ridg·ing** *v.t.* **1.** To mark with ridges. **2.** To form into ridges. — *v.i.* **3.** To form ridges. [OE *hrycg*] — **ridg′y** *adj.*

ridge·pole (rij′pōl′) *n.* A horizontal timber at the ridge of a roof. Also **ridge beam, ridge piece, ridge plate.** For illus. see ROOF.

rid·i·cule (rid′ə·kyōōl) *n.* **1.** Language or actions calculated to make a person or thing the object of contemptuous or humorous derision or mockery. **2.** An object of mocking merriment; butt. — *v.t.* **·culed, ·cul·ing** To make fun of; deride. [< OF < L *ridiculum* a joke] — **rid′i·cul′er** *n.*

ri·dic·u·lous (ri·dik′yə·ləs) *adj.* Exciting ridicule; absurd and unworthy of consideration. — **ri·dic′u·lous·ly** *adv.* — **ri·dic′u·lous·ness** *n.*

rid·ing¹ (rī′ding) *n.* The act of one who rides; a ride. — *adj.* **1.** Suitable for riding. **2.** For use while at anchor.

rid·ing² (rī′ding) *n.* **1.** One of the three administrative divisions of Yorkshire, England. **2.** Any similar administrative division. **3.** In Canada, a political division represented by a member of parliament; constituency. [OE *thrithing* < ON *thrithjung* third part]

rife (rīf) *adj.* **1.** Great in number or quantity; plentiful; abundant. **2.** Prevalent; current. **3.** Containing in abundance: followed by *with.* [OE *rȳfe*]

riff (rif) *n.* In jazz music, a melodic phrase or motif, played repeatedly as background or used as the main theme. [? Back formation < RIFFLE, or ? < REFRAIN]

Riff (rif) *n.* One of a Berber tribe inhabiting the mountainous region of northern Morocco. — **Riff′i·an** *adj. & n.*

rif·fle (rif′əl) *n.* **1.** *U.S.* A shoal or rocky obstruction lying beneath the surface of a river or other stream. **2.** A stretch of shallow, choppy water caused by such a shoal. **3.** The act or a way of shuffling cards. — *v.t.* & *v.i.* **·fled, ·fling 1.** To cause or form a rapid. **2.** To shuffle (cards) by bending up adjacent corners of two halves of the pack, and permitting the cards to slip together as they are released. **3.** To thumb through (the pages of a book). [? Alter. of RUFFLE]

riff·raff (rif′raf′) *n.* **1.** The populace; rabble. **2.** Miscellaneous rubbish. [ME *riff and raff* one and all < OF *rif et raf*]

ri·fle[1] (rī′fəl) *n.* **1.** A firearm having a rifled or spirally grooved bore, fired from the shoulder. **2.** An artillery piece having a rifled bore. **3.** *pl.* A body of soldiers equipped with rifles. — *v.t.* **·fled, ·fling.** To cut a spirally grooved bore in (a firearm, etc.). [< *rifled gun* < OF *rifler* to file]

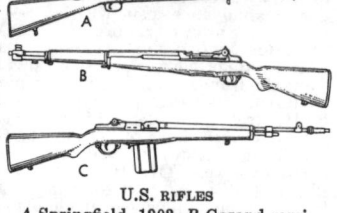

U.S. RIFLES
A Springfield, 1903. *B* Garand semi-automatic, World War II. *C* M-14 automatic, 1958.

ri·fle[2] (rī′fəl) *v.t.* **·fled, ·fling 1.** To search through and rob, as a safe. **2.** To search and rob (a person). **3.** To seize and take away by force. [< OF *rifler* to plunder] — **ri′fler** *n.*

ri·fle·man (rī′fəl-mən) *n. pl.* **·men** (-mən) One armed or skilled with the rifle.

rifle range An area used for shooting rifles at a target.

ri·fling (rī′fling) *n.* **1.** The operation of forming the grooves in a rifle. **2.** The grooves of a rifle collectively.

rift[1] (rift) *n.* **1.** An opening made by riving or splitting; a cleft; fissure. **2.** Any disagreement or lack of harmony, as between friends, nations, etc. — *v.t.* & *v.i.* To rive; burst open; split. [< Scand. Cf. Dan. *rift,* ON *rifa.*]

rift[2] (rift) *n.* A shallow place in a stream.

rig[1] (rig) *v.t.* **rigged, rig·ging 1.** To fit out; equip. **2.** *Naut.* **a** To fit, as a ship, with rigging. **b** To fit (sails, stays, etc.) to masts, yards, etc. **3.** *Informal* To dress; clothe, esp. in finery. **4.** To make or construct hurriedly: often with *up.* — *n.* **1.** *Naut.* The arrangement of sails, rigging, spars, etc., on a vessel. **2.** *Informal* A style of dress; costume. **3.** *U.S. Informal* A horse or horses and vehicle. **4.** Any apparatus, gear, or tackle: an oil-well *rig.* **5.** Fishing tackle. [< Scand. Cf. Norwegian and Sw. *rigga.*]

rig[2] (rig) *v.t.* **rigged, rig·ging** To control fraudulently; manipulate: to *rig* an election. [Origin uncertain]

rig·a·doon (rig′ə-dōōn′) *n.* **1.** A gay, quick dance for two, originating in Provence. **2.** Music for this dance. [< F]

Ri·gel (rī′jəl, -gəl) One of the 20 brightest stars, 0.34 magnitude; Beta in the constellation Orion. [< Arabic *rijl* foot]

rig·ger (rig′ər) *n.* **1.** One who rigs. **2.** One who fits the rigging of ships. **3.** A ship having a specified rig: used in combination: a *square-rigger.*

rig·ging (rig′ing) *n.* **1.** *Naut.* The entire cordage system of a vessel. **2.** Tackle used in logging. **3.** The act of one who or that which rigs.

right (rīt) *adj.* **1.** Done in accordance with or conformable to moral law or to some standard of rightness; equitable; just; righteous. **2.** Conformable to truth or fact. **3.** Conformable to a standard of propriety or to the conditions of the case; proper; fit; suitable. **4.** Most desirable or preferable; also, fortunate. **5.** Pertaining to, designating, or situated on the side of the body that is toward the south when one faces east. **6.** Holding one direction, as a line; straight; direct. **7.** Properly placed, disposed, or adjusted; well-regulated; orderly. **8.** Sound in mind or body; healthy; well. **9.** *Geom.* Formed with reference to a line or plane perpendicular to another line or plane: a *right* angle. **10.** Designed to be worn outward or when in use placed toward an observer: the *right* side of cloth. **11.** *Sometimes cap.* Designating a person, party, faction, etc., having absolutely or relatively conservative or reactionary views and policies. — **to rights** In a proper or orderly condition: to put a room *to rights.* — *adv.* **1.** In accordance with justice or moral principle. **2.** According to the fact or truth; correctly. **3.** In a straight line; directly. **4.** Very: used dialectally or in some titles: a *right* good time, *Right* Reverend. **5.** Suitably; properly. **6.** Precisely; just; also, immediately. **7.** Without delay or evasion. **8.** Toward the right. **9.** Completely or quite: The house burned *right* to the ground. — *n.* **1.** That which is right; moral rightness; also, justice. **2.** *Often pl.* A just and proper claim or title to anything. **3.** The right hand, side, or direction. **4.** Anything adapted for right-hand use or position. **5.** *Often cap.* A group, party, etc., whose views and policies are right (adj. def. 11) or, in Europe, whose members sit to the presiding officer's right in a deliberative assembly. **6.** In boxing, a blow delivered with the right hand. — *v.t.* **1.** To restore to an upright or normal position. **2.** To put in order; set right. **3.** To make

correct or in accord with facts. **4.** To make reparation for. **5.** To make reparation to (a person). — *v.i.* **6.** To regain an upright or normal position. [OE *riht*] — **right′er** *n.*

right·a·bout (rīt′ə-bout′) *n.* **1.** The opposite direction. **2.** A turning in or to the opposite direction.

right angle *Geom.* An angle whose sides are perpendicular to each other; an angle of 90°.

right-an·gled (rīt′ang′gəld) *adj.* Forming or containing a right angle or angles: a *right-angled* triangle.

right·eous (rī′chəs) *adj.* **1.** Conforming to a standard of right and justice; virtuous. **2.** Morally right; equitable: a *righteous* act. [OE < *riht* right + *wīs* wise] — **right′eous·ly** *adv.* — **right′eous·ness** *n.*

right face In military drill, a 90-degree pivot to the right, using the ball of the left foot and the heel of the right.

right·ful (rīt′fəl) *adj.* **1.** Characterized by or conforming to a right or just claim: *rightful* heritage. **2.** Consonant with moral right or with justice and truth. **3.** Proper. **4.** Upright; just. [OE *rihtful*] — **right′ful·ly** *adv.* — **right′ful·ness** *n.*

right-hand (rīt′hand′) *adj.* **1.** Of, for, pertaining to, or situated on the right side or right hand. **2.** Chiefly depended on: *right-hand* man. **3.** Toward the right.

right-hand·ed (rīt′han′did) *adj.* **1.** Using the right hand more easily than the left. **2.** Done with the right hand. **3.** Moving from left to right, as the hands of a clock. **4.** Adapted for use by the right hand. — **right′-hand′ed·ness** *n.*

right·ist (rī′tist) *n.* One whose views and policies are right (adj. def. 11). — *adj.* Right (adj. def. 11). — **right′ism** *n.*

right·ly (rīt′lē) *adv.* **1.** Correctly. **2.** Honestly; uprightly. **3.** Properly; aptly.

right-mind·ed (rīt′mīn′did) *adj.* Having right feelings or opinions. — **right′mind′ed·ly** *adv.* — **right′mind′ed·ness** *n.*

right·ness (rīt′nis) *n.* **1.** The quality or condition of being right. **2.** Rectitude. **3.** Correctness. **4.** Straightness.

right·o (rī′tō) *interj. Brit. Informal* Right; all right!

right of asylum In international law, the right to protection from arrest in a place recognized by law or custom.

right of search In international law, the right of a belligerent vessel in time of war to verify the nationality of a vessel and to ascertain, if neutral, whether it carries contraband goods. Also **right of visit and search.**

right of way 1. *Law* The right of a person to pass over the land of another; also, the path or piece of land. **2.** The strip of land over which a railroad lays its tracks, on which a public highway is built, or above which a high-tension power line is built. **3.** The legal or customary precedence which allows one vehicle or vessel to cross in front of another. Also **right-of-way** (rīt′əv-wā).

right triangle A triangle containing one right angle.

right whale Any of several whales of polar seas, having a large head and elastic whalebone plates in its mouth.

right wing 1. *Sometimes cap.* A party, group, faction, etc., having rightist policies. **2.** The wing, division, part, etc., on the right side. — **right-wing** (rīt′wing′) *adj.* — **right′-wing′er** *n.*

rig·id (rij′id) *adj.* **1.** Resisting change of form; stiff. **2.** Rigorous; inflexible; severe. **3.** Not moving; fixed. **4.** Strict; exact, as reasoning. **5.** *Aeron.* Designating a dirigible whose cells are enclosed within a rigid framework. [< L *rigere* to be stiff] — **rig′id·ly** *adv.* — **ri·gid′i·ty, rig′id·ness** *n.*

Rig·il Cen·tau·rus (rij′il ken-tôr′əs) *n.* One of the 20 brightest stars, 0.6 magnitude; Beta in the constellation Centaurus.

rig·ma·role (rig′mə·rōl) *n.* Incoherent talk or writing; nonsense. Also **rig′a·ma·role′** (-ə·mə-). [Alter. of *ragman roll* deed on parchment]

rig·or (rig′ər) *n.* **1.** The condition of being stiff or rigid. **2.** Stiffness of opinion or temper; harshness. **3.** Exactness without allowance or indulgence; inflexibility; strictness; severity. **4.** Inclemency, as of the weather; hardship. Also *Brit.* **rig′our.** [< OF < L < *rigere* to be stiff] — **rig′or·ist** *n.* — **rig′or·is′tic** *adj.*

rig·or mor·tis (rig′ər·môr′tis, rī′gər) The muscular rigidity that ensues shortly after death. [< L, stiffness of death]

rig·or·ous (rig′ər·əs) *adj.* **1.** Marked by or acting with rigor; uncompromising; severe. **2.** Logically accurate; exact; strict. **3.** Inclement; severe: a *rigorous* climate. — **rig′or·ous·ly** *adv.* — **rig′or·ous·ness** *n.*

rile (rīl) *v.t.* **riled, ril·ing** *Informal* or *Dial* **1.** To vex; irritate. **2.** To make (a liquid) muddy. Also *roil.* [Var. of ROIL]

rill (ril) *n.* **1.** A small stream. **2.** A long, narrow valley on the face of the moon: also **rille.** [Prob. < LG *rille*]

rim (rim) *n.* **1.** The edge of an object, usu. of a circular object. **2.** The peripheral part of a wheel, connected to the hub by spokes. **3.** The frame of a pair of spectacles, surrounding the lenses. — *v.t.* **rimmed, rim·ming 1.** To provide with a rim; border. **2.** In sports, to roll around the edge of (the basket, cup, etc.) without falling in. [OE *rima*]

rime[1] (rīm) See RHYME.

rime² (rīm)   *n.*   **1.** A milky white, granular deposit of ice formed on objects by fog or water vapor that has frozen.   **2.** Frost.   — *v.i.* & *v.t.* **rimed, rim·ing** To cover with or congeal into rime.   [OE *hrīm* frost]   — **rim′y** *adj.*

rim·er (rī′mər)   See RHYMER.

rime·ster (rīm′stər)   See RHYMESTER.

rim·mer (rim′ər)   *n.* A reamer (def. 2).

rind (rīnd)   *n.* The skin or outer coat that may be peeled or taken off, as of bacon, fruit, cheese, etc.   [OE *rind* bark]

rin·der·pest (rin′dər·pest)   *n.* *Vet.* An acute intestinal virus disease of cattle and sometimes of sheep.   [< G]

ring¹ (ring)   *n.*   **1.** Any circular object, line, mark, etc.   **2.** A circular band, usu. of precious metal, worn on a finger.   **3.** Any metal or wooden band used for holding or carrying something.   **4.** A group of persons or things in a circle; also, a circular movement.   **5.** A group of persons, as in business or politics; a clique.   **6.** One of a series of concentric layers of wood in the trunk of a tree, formed by annual growth.   **7.** An area or arena, usu. square, as that in which boxers fight; prize fighting in general.   **8.** Political competition or rivalry: He tossed his hat into the *ring.*   **9.** *Chem.* An arrangement of atoms in a closed chain: the benzene *ring.*   **10.** The space between two concentric circles.   — **to run rings around** *Informal* To be superior to in some way.   — *v.* **ringed, ring·ing** *v.t.*   **1.** To surround with a ring; encircle.   **2.** To form into a ring or rings.   **3.** To provide or decorate with a ring or rings.   **4.** To cut a ring of bark from (a branch or tree).   **5.** To hem in (cattle, etc.) by riding in a circle around them.   **6.** In certain games, to cast a ring over (a peg or pin).   — *v.i.*   **7.** To form a ring or rings.   **8.** To move or fly in rings or spirals; circle.   [OE *hring*]

ring² (ring)   *v.* **rang** (*Archaic* or *Dial.* **rung**), **rung, ring·ing** *v.i.*   **1.** To give forth a resonant, sonorous sound, as a bell when struck.   **2.** To sound loudly or be filled with sound or resonance; reverberate; resound.   **3.** To cause a bell or bells to sound.   **4.** To have or suggest a sound expressive of a specified quality: His story *rings* true.   **5.** To have a continued sensation of ringing or buzzing: My ears *ring.*   — *v.t.*   **6.** To cause (a bell, etc.) to ring.   **7.** To produce, as a sound, by or as by ringing.   **8.** To announce or proclaim by ringing: to *ring* the hour.   **9.** To summon, escort, usher, etc., in this manner: with *in* or *out*: to *ring* out the old year.   **10.** To call on the telephone: often with *up.*   — *n.*   **1.** The sound produced by a bell or other vibrating, sonorous body.   **2.** The act of sounding a bell.   **3.** A telephone call.   **4.** Any reverberating sound, as of acclamation.   **5.** Characteristic sound or impression: the *ring* of truth.   **6.** A set, chime, or peal of bells.   [OE *hringan*; imit.]

ring·bolt (ring′bolt′)   *n.* A bolt having a ring through an eye in its head.

ring·dove (ring′duv′)   *n.* One of several other pigeons having a black ring partially surrounding the neck.

ringed (ringd)   *adj.*   **1.** Having a wedding ring; lawfully married.   **2.** Encircled by raised or depressed lines or bands.   **3.** Marked by a ring or rings.   **4.** Composed of rings.

rin·gent (rin′jənt)   *adj.* *Biol.* Gaping, as a corolla in which the lips are widely separated.   [< L < *ringi* to gape]

ring·er¹ (ring′ər)   *n.*   **1.** One who or that which rings (a bell or chime).   **2.** *Slang* An athlete, horse, etc., illegally entered in a contest by concealing disqualifying facts, as age, professional status, etc.   **3.** *Slang* A person who bears a marked resemblance to another: You are a *ringer* for Jones.

ring·er² (ring′ər)   *n.*   **1.** One who or that which rings.   **2.** A quoit or horseshoe that falls around one of the posts.

ring·lead·er (ring′lē′dər)   *n.* A leader or organizer of any undertaking, esp. of an unlawful one, as a riot.

ring·let (ring′lit)   *n.*   **1.** A long, spiral lock of hair; a curl.   **2.** A small ring.

ring·mas·ter (ring′mas′tər, -mäs′-)   *n.* One who has charge of a circus ring and of the performances in it.

ring·side (ring′sīd′)   *n.* The space or seats immediately surrounding a ring, as at a prize fight.

ring·worm (ring′wûrm′)   *n.* *Pathol.* Any of several contagious skin diseases, caused by certain fungi, and marked by the appearance of discolored, scaly patches on the skin.

rink (ringk)   *n.*   **1.** A smooth, artificial surface of ice, used for ice-skating or hockey.   **2.** A smooth floor, used for roller-skating.   **3.** A building containing a surface for ice-skating or roller-skating.   [< Scot., course, race]

rinse (rins)   *v.t.* **rinsed, rins·ing**   **1.** To remove soap from by putting through clear water.   **2.** To wash lightly, as by dipping in water or by running water over or into.   **3.** To remove (dirt, etc.) by this process.   — *n.*   **1.** The act of rinsing, or the solution in which something is rinsed.   **2.** A hair coloring agent.   [< OF < L *recens* fresh]   — **rins′er** *n.*

rins·ing (rin′sing)   *n.*   **1.** A rinse.   **2.** The liquid in which anything is rinsed.   **3.** That which is removed by rinsing.

ri·ot (rī′ət)   *n.*   **1.** A disturbance consisting of wild and tur-

bulent conduct of a large number of persons, as a mob.   **2.** A brilliant or sometimes confusing display: a *riot* of color.   **3.** Boisterous festivity; revelry.   **4.** Loose or profligate living or activity.   **5.** *U.S. Slang* An uproariously amusing person, thing, or performance.   — **to run riot 1.** To act or move wildly and without restraint.   **2.** To grow profusely or luxuriantly, as vines.   — *v.i.*   **1.** To take part in a riot or public disorder.   **2.** To live a life of feasting, drinking, etc.   — *v.t.*   **3.** To spend (time, money, etc.) in riot or revelry.   [< OF < *rioter* to quarrel]   — **ri′ot·er** *n.*

riot act Any forceful or vigorous warning or reprimand.   — **to read the riot act to** To reprimand bluntly and severely.

ri·ot·ous (rī′ət·əs)   *adj.*   **1.** Of, pertaining to, or like a riot.   **2.** Engaged in a riot.   **3.** Loud; uproarious.   **4.** Profligate: *riotous* spending.   — **ri′ot·ous·ly** *adv.*   — **ri′ot·ous·ness** *n.*

riot squad A group of policemen specially trained, armed, and equipped to deal with riots.

rip¹ (rip)   *v.* **ripped, rip·ping** *v.t.*   **1.** To tear or cut apart roughly or violently; slash.   **2.** To tear or cut from something else in a rough or violent manner: with *off, away, out,* etc.   **3.** To saw or split (wood) in the direction of the grain.   — *v.i.*   **4.** To be torn or cut apart; split.   **5.** *Informal* To utter with vehemence: with *out.*   **6.** *Informal* To rush headlong.   — *n.*   **1.** A place torn or ripped open; a tear.   **2.** A ripsaw.   [Cf. MLG *reppen,* MDu. *rippen*]   — **rip′per** *n.*

rip² (rip)   *n.*   **1.** A ripple; a rapid in a river.   **2.** A riptide.   [? < RIP¹]

ri·par·i·an (ri·pâr′ē·ən, rī-)   *adj.* Of or growing on a bank of a river or stream.   [< L < *ripa* river bank]

rip·cord (rip′kôrd′)   *n.* *Aeron.* The cord, together with the handle and fastening pins, that when pulled releases a parachute from its pack.

ripe (rīp)   *adj.*   **1.** Grown to maturity and fit for food, as fruit or grain.   **2.** Brought by keeping and care to a condition for use, as wine or cheese.   **3.** Fully developed; matured.   **4.** Advanced in years.   **5.** In full readiness to do or try; prepared; ready.   **6.** Fit; opportune.   **7.** Resembling ripe fruit; rosy; luscious.   [OE *rīpe*]   — **ripe′ly** *adv.*   — **ripe′ness** *n.*

rip·en (rī′pən)   *v.t.* & *v.i.* To make or become ripe; mature.

ri·poste (ri·pōst′)   *n.*   **1.** A return thrust, as in fencing.   **2.** A quick, clever reply; repartee.   — *v.i.* **·post·ed, ·post·ing**   **1.** To make a riposte.   **2.** To reply quickly.   Also **ri·post′.**   [< F < Ital. *risposta* reply]

rip·ping (rip′ing)   *Brit. Slang*   *adj.* Splendid; excellent.   — *adv.* Very; extraordinarily: a *ripping* good time.

rip·ple (rip′əl)   *v.* **·pled, ·pling** *v.i.*   **1.** To become slightly agitated on the surface, as water blown on by a light breeze.   **2.** To flow with small waves or undulations on the surface.   **3.** To make a sound like water flowing in small waves.   — *v.t.*   **4.** To cause to form ripples.   — *n.*   **1.** One of the wavelets on the surface of water.   **2.** Any sound like that made by rippling.   **3.** Any appearance like a wavelet   [? Fusion of RIFFLE + RIP²]   — **rip′pler** *n.*   — **rip′ply** *adj.*

rip·plet (rip′lit)   *n.* A small ripple.

rip·roar·ing (rip′rôr′ing, -rōr′-)   *adj.* *U.S. Slang* Good and lively; boisterous.

rip·roar·i·ous (rip·rôr′ē·əs, -rōr′-)   *adj.* *U.S. Slang* Uproarious; boisterous; violent.   — **rip·roar′i·ous·ly** *adv.*

rip·saw (rip′sô′)   *n.* A coarse-toothed saw used for cutting wood in the direction of the grain: also called *rip.*

rip·snort·er (rip′snôr′tər)   *n.* *Archaic Slang* Any person or thing excessively noisy, violent, or striking.

rip·tide (rip′tīd′)   *n.* Water agitated and made dangerous for swimmers by conflicting tides or currents: also called *rip, tiderip.*

rise (rīz)   *v.* **rose, ris·en, ris·ing** *v.i.*   **1.** To move upward; go from a lower to a higher position.   **2.** To slope gradually upward.   **3.** To gain height or elevation: The city *rises* above the plain.   **4.** To gain elevation in rank, status, fortune, or reputation.   **5.** To swell up: Dough *rises.*   **6.** To become greater in force, intensity, height, etc.; also, to become higher in pitch, as the voice.   **7.** To become greater in amount, value, etc.   **8.** To become erect after lying down, sitting, etc.; stand up.   **9.** To get out of bed.   **10.** To return to life.   **11.** To revolt; rebel.   **12.** To adjourn.   **13.** To appear above the horizon: said of heavenly bodies.   **14.** To come to the surface, as a fish after a lure.   **15.** To have origin; begin.   **16.** To become perceptible to the mind or senses.   **17.** To occur; happen.   **18.** To be able to cope with an emergency, danger, etc.   — *v.t.*   **19.** To cause to rise.   — **to rise above** To prove superior to; show oneself indifferent to.   — *n.*   **1.** The act of rising; ascent.   **2.** Degree of ascent; elevation; also, an ascending course.   **3.** The act of beginning to be: the *rise* of a stream.   **4.** An elevated place; a small hill.   **5.** The act of appearing above the horizon.   **6.** Increase or advance, as in price or value.   **7.** Advance or elevation, as in rank, prosperity, or importance.   **8.** The spring or height of an arch above the impost level.   **9.** The height of a stair step.

10. Ascent in a musical scale; also, increase in volume of tone. **11.** The ascent of a fish to food or bait; also, the flying up of a game bird. **12.** *Informal* An emotional reaction; a response or retort. **13.** *Brit.* An increase in salary. [OE *rīsan*]

ris·en (riz'ən) Past participle of RISE.

ris·er (rī'zər) *n.* **1.** One who rises or gets up, as from bed: *He is an early riser.* **2.** The vertical part of a step or stair.

ris·i·bil·i·ty (riz'ə·bil'ə·tē) *n.* *pl.* **·ties** A tendency to laughter. **2.** *pl.* Impulses to laughter: also **ris/i·bles** (-bəlz).

ris·i·ble (riz'ə·bəl) *adj.* **1.** Having the power of laughing. **2.** Of a nature to excite laughter. **3.** Pertaining to laughter. [< F < LL < L *ridere* to laugh] — **ris/i·bly** *adv.*

ris·ing (rī'zing) *adj.* **1.** Increasing in wealth, power, or distinction. **2.** Ascending; also, sloping upward: a *rising* hill. **3.** Advancing to adult years or to a state of vigor and activity; growing: the *rising* generation. — *n.* **1.** The act of one who or that which rises. **2.** That which rises above the surrounding surface. **3.** An insurrection or revolt. **4.** Yeast or leaven used to make dough rise.

risk (risk) *n.* **1.** A chance of encountering harm or loss; hazard; danger. **2.** In insurance: **a** The hazard or chance of loss. **b** The degree of exposure to loss. **c** An insurance applicant who is considered a hazard to the insurer. — *v.t.* **1.** To expose to a chance of injury or loss. **2.** To incur the risk of. [< F < Ital. *risco*] — **risk/er** *n.*

risk·y (ris'kē) *adj.* **risk·i·er**, **risk·i·est** Attended with risk; hazardous; dangerous.

ri·sot·to (rē·sôt'tō) *n.* Rice cooked in broth and served with meat, cheese, etc. [< Ital. < *riso* rice]

ris·qué (ris·kā', *Fr.* rēs·kā') *adj.* Bordering on or suggestive of impropriety; bold; daring; off-color: a *risqué* story or play. [< F, pp. of *risquer* to risk] — **Syn.** racy, ribald, suggestive.

ris·sole (ris'ōl, *Fr.* rē·sôl') *n.* In cookery, a sausagelike roll consisting of minced meat or fish, enclosed in a thin puff paste and fried. [< F, ult. < LL *russeolus* reddish]

ri·tar·dan·do (rē'tär·dän'dō) *Music adj.* Slackening in tempo gradually; retarding. — *n. pl.* **·dos** A gradual slackening of tempo. [< Ital.]

rite (rīt) *n.* **1.** A solemn or religious ceremony performed in an established or prescribed manner, or the words or acts constituting or accompanying it. **2.** Any formal practice or custom. [< L *ritus*]

rit·u·al (rich'ōō·əl) *n.* **1.** A prescribed form or method for the performance of a religious or solemn ceremony; any body of rites or ceremonies. **2.** A book setting forth such a system of rites. — *adj.* Of, pertaining to, or practiced as a rite or rites. [< L *ritus* rite] — **rit/u·al·ly** *adv.*

rit·u·al·ism (rich'ōō·əl·iz'əm) *n.* **1.** Insistence upon ritual; adherence to ritual. **2.** The study of religious ritual. **3.** A love of ritual. — **rit/u·al·ist** *n.* — **rit/u·al·is/tic** *adj.* — **rit/u·al·is/ti·cal·ly** *adv.*

ritz·y (rit'sē) *adj.* **ritz·i·er**, **ritz·i·est** *U.S. Slang* Smart; elegant; classy. [< the *Ritz*-Carlton Hotel, New York; after César *Ritz*, 1850–1918, who founded it]

ri·val (rī'vəl) *n.* **1.** One who strives to equal or excel another, or is in pursuit of the same object as another; a competitor. **2.** One equaling or nearly equaling another, in any respect. — *v.* **ri·valed** or **·valled**, **ri·val·ing** or **·val·ling** *v.t.* **1.** To strive to equal or excel; compete with. **2.** To be the equal of or a match for. — *adj.* Being a rival; competing. [< L *rivalis*, pl. *rivales* those living near the same stream]

ri·val·ry (rī'vəl·rē) *n. pl.* **·ries** **1.** The act of rivaling. **2.** The state of being a rival or rivals; competition.

rive (rīv) *v.* **rived**, **rived** or **riv·en**, **riv·ing** *v.t.* **1.** To split asunder by force; cleave. **2.** To break (the heart, etc.). — *v.i.* **3.** To become split. [< ON *rifa*] — **riv·er** (rī'vər) *n.*

riv·er (riv'ər) *n.* **1.** A large, natural stream of water, usu. fed by converging tributaries along its course and discharging into a larger body of water, as the ocean, a lake, or another stream. ◆ Collateral adjective: *fluvial.* **2.** A large stream of any kind; copious flow — **to sell down the river** To betray the trust of; deceive. — **to send up the river** To send to the penitentiary. [< OF *rivière*]

river basin *Geog.* An extensive area of land drained by a river and its branches.

riv·er·ine (riv'ə·rīn, -ər·in) *adj.* Pertaining to or like a river; riparian.

riv·er·side (riv'ər·sīd') *n.* The space alongside of or adjacent to a river.

riv·et (riv'it) *n.* A short, soft metal bolt, having a head on one end, used to join objects, as metal plates, by passing the shank through holes and forming a new head by flattening out the other end. — *v.t.* **1.** To fasten with or as with a rivet. **2.** To batter the headless end of (a bolt, etc.) so as to make fast. **3.** To fasten firmly. **4.** To engross or attract (the eyes, attention, etc.). [< OF, prob. < MDu. *wriven* to cause to turn] — **riv/et·er** *n.*

riv·u·let (riv'yə·lit) *n.* A small stream or brook; streamlet. [< Ital. < L *rivulus*, dim. of *rivus* stream]

roach¹ (rōch) *n.* **1.** A European fresh-water fish of the carp family, with a greenish back. **2.** Any of various related fishes. [< OF *roche.*]

roach² (rōch) *n.* A cockroach.

road (rōd) *n.* **1.** An open way for public passage, esp. from one city, town, or village to another; a highway. **2.** Any way of advancing or progressing: the *road* to fame. **3.** *Usu. pl.* A roadstead: Hampton *Roads.* **4.** *U.S.* A railroad. — **on the road 1.** On tour: said of circuses, theatrical companies, etc. **2.** Traveling, as a canvasser or salesman. **3.** Living the life of a tramp or hobo. [OE *rād* journey < *rīdan* to ride]

road·bed (rōd'bed') *n.* **1.** The graded foundation of gravel, etc., on which the ties, rails, etc., of a railroad are laid. **2.** The graded foundation or surface of a road.

road·block (rōd'blok') *n.* **1.** An obstruction in a road. **2.** Any arrangement of men and materials for blocking passage, as of enemy troops.

road·house (rōd'hous') *n.* A restaurant, dance hall, etc., located at the side of the road in a rural area.

road metal Broken stone or the like, used for making or repairing roads.

road runner A long-tailed ground cuckoo inhabiting open regions of southwestern North America, and running with great swiftness.

road·side (rōd'sīd') *n.* The area along the side of a road. — *adj.* Situated on the side of a road.

road·stead (rōd'sted) *n.* *Naut.* A place of anchorage offshore, but less sheltered than a harbor. [< ROAD + *stead*, a place]

ROAD RUNNER
(Body to 24 inches; tail 12 inches)

road·ster (rōd'stər) *n.* A light, open automobile, usu. with a single seat for two people and a luggage compartment or rumble seat in the rear.

road·way (rōd'wā') *n.* A road, esp. that part over which vehicles pass.

roam (rōm) *v.i.* **1.** To move about purposelessly from place to place; rove. — *v.t.* **2.** To wander over; range. — *n.* The act of roaming. [ME *romen*] — **roam/er** *n.*

roan (rōn) *adj.* Of a horse, having a color consisting of bay, sorrel, or chestnut, thickly interspersed with gray or white. — *n.* **1.** A roan color. **2.** An animal of a roan color. [< MF < Sp. *roano.*]

roar (rôr, rōr) *v.i.* **1.** To utter a deep, prolonged cry, as of rage or distress. **2.** To make a loud noise or din, as the sea or a cannon. **3.** To laugh loudly. **4.** To move, proceed, or function with a roar, as an automobile. — *v.t.* **5.** To utter or express by roaring. — *n.* **1.** A full, deep, resonant cry, as of a beast, or of a human being in pain, grief, anger, etc. **2.** Any loud, prolonged sound, as of wind or waves. [OE *rārian*] — **roar/er** *n.*

roast (rōst) *v.t.* **1.** To cook (meat, etc.) by subjecting to the action of heat, as in an oven. **2.** To cook before an open fire, or by placing in hot ashes, embers, etc. **3.** To heat to an extreme degree. **4.** To dry and parch under the action of heat. **5.** *Metall.* To heat (ores) with access of air for the purpose of dehydration, purification, or oxidation. **6.** *Informal* To criticize or ridicule severely. — *v.i.* **7.** To roast food in an oven, etc. **8.** To be cooked or prepared by this method. **9.** To be uncomfortably hot. — *n.* **1.** Something roasted; esp., a piece of roasted meat. **2.** A piece of meat adapted or prepared for roasting. **3.** The act of roasting. — *adj.* Roasted. [< OF *rostir* < Gmc.]

roast·er (rōs'tər) *n.* **1.** One who or that which roasts. **2.** A pan or contrivance for roasting something. **3.** Something suitable for roasting, esp. a pig.

rob (rob) *v.* **robbed**, **rob·bing** *v.t.* **1.** To seize and carry off the property of by unlawful violence or threat of violence. **2.** To deprive of something belonging or due. **3.** To plunder; rifle, as a house. **4.** To steal. — *v.i.* **5.** To commit robbery. [< OF *robe* booty] — **rob/ber** (-ər) *n.*

robber baron *U.S.* One of the powerful and unscrupulous financial adventurers of the late 19th century.

rob·ber·y (rob'ər·ē) *n. pl.* **·ber·ies** The act of one who robs; the taking away of the property of another unlawfully, by force or fear. — **Syn.** See THEFT.

robe (rōb) *n.* **1.** A long, loose, flowing garment, worn over other dress; a gown. **2.** A bathrobe. **3.** *pl.* Such a garment worn as a badge of office or rank. **4.** Anything that covers in the manner of a robe. **5.** *U.S.* A blanket or covering, as for use in an automobile: lap *robe.* — *v.* **robed**, **rob·ing** *v.t.* **1.** To put a robe upon; dress. — *v.i.* **2.** To put on robes. [< OF, orig. booty < Gmc.]

rob·in (rob'in) *n.* **1.** A large North American thrush with black head and tail, grayish wings and sides, and reddish brown breast and underparts. **2.** A small European bird of the thrush family, with the cheeks, and breast yellowish red. Also **robin redbreast**. [< OF *Robin*, dim. of *Robert*]

Robin Hood A legendary medieval outlaw of England, famed for his chivalry and daring, who lived in Sherwood Forest and robbed from the rich to help the poor.

rob·in's-egg blue (rob′inz·eg′) A light greenish blue.

Rob·in·son Cru·soe (rob′in·sən krōō′sō) The hero of Defoe's *Robinson Crusoe* (1719), a sailor shipwrecked on a tropical island.

ro·bot (rō′bət, rob′ət) *n.* **1.** A mechanical man constructed to perform work in the place of human beings. **2.** One who works mechanically; automaton. **3.** Any mechanism or device that operates automatically or is remotely controlled. [< Czechoslovakian *robota* forced labor]

robot bomb A high-explosive bomb provided with a jet engine or rocket permitting it to travel under its own power after being launched on the target, as the German V-1 of World War II: also called *buzz bomb*.

ro·bust (rō·bust′, rō′bust) *adj.* **1.** Possessing or characterized by great strength or endurance; rugged. **2.** Requiring strength. **3.** Violent; rude. [< L < *robur* oak, hence strength] — **ro·bust′ly** *adv.* — **ro·bust′ness** *n.*

roc (rok) *n.* In Arabian and Persian legend, an enormous and powerful bird of prey. [< Arabic < Persian *rukh*]

Ro·chelle salt (rō·shel′) A white crystalline tartrate of potassium and sodium, $KNaC_4H_4O_6 \cdot 4H_2O$, used as a cathartic. [after La *Rochelle*]

rock¹ (rok) *n.* **1.** A large mass of stone or stony material. **2.** A fragment of rock small enough to be thrown; stone. **3.** *Geol.* The material forming the essential part of the earth's crust, classified principally according to mode of formation, as igneous or sedimentary. **4.** Something resembling or suggesting a rock, as a firm support, source of strength, etc. **5.** *U.S. Slang* A gemstone, esp. a large diamond. — **on the rocks** *U.S. Informal* **1.** Ruined; also, destitute or bankrupt. **2.** Served with ice cubes but without soda or water: said of whisky or other liquors. — *adj.* Made or composed of rock. [< OF *roque, roche*]

rock² (rok) *v.i.* **1.** To move backward and forward or from side to side; sway **2.** To sway, reel, or stagger, as from a blow; shake. — *v.t.* **3.** To move backward and forward or from side to side, esp. so as to soothe or put to sleep. **4.** To cause to sway or reel. — *n.* The act of rocking; a rocking motion. [OE *roccian*]

rock·a·by (rok′ə·bī) *interj.* Go to sleep: from a nursery song intended to lull a child to slumber. — *n.* A lullaby. Also **rock′a·bye, rock′-a-bye.**

rock-and-roll (rok′ən-rōl′) *adj.* Denoting a form of popular music derived from hillbilly styles, characterized by repetitious melody and rhythm and exaggerated vocal mannerisms. — *n.* Rock-and-roll music. Also **rock 'n' roll.**

rock bottom The very bottom; the lowest possible level: Prices hit *rock bottom*. — **rock-bot·tom** (rok′bot′əm) *adj.*

rock-bound (rok′bound′) *adj.* Encircled by or bordered with rocks.

rock candy Large crystals of sugar.

rock crystal Colorless transparent quartz.

rock dove The wild pigeon of Europe, the parent of domestic varieties.

rock·er (rok′ər) *n.* **1.** One who rocks, as a cradle or rocking chair. **2.** One of the curved pieces on which a rocking chair or a cradle rocks. **3.** A rocking chair. **4.** A rocking horse. — **off one's rocker** *Slang* Mentally unbalanced; nuts.

rock·et (rok′it) *n.* **1.** A firework, projectile, missile, or other device, usu. cylindrical in form, that is propelled by the reaction of escaping gases produced during flight. **2.** A type of vehicle operated by rocket propulsion and designed for space travel. — *v.i.* **1.** To move like a rocket. **2.** To fly straight up into the air, as a bird. — *v.t.* **3.** To propel by means of a rocket. [< Ital. *rocchetta*, dim. of *rocca* distaff < Gmc.]

rocket bomb A bomb delivered to its target by means of a rocket.

rock·et·eer (rok′ə·tir′) *n.* One who designs or launches rockets; a student of rocket flight.

rocket engine A reaction engine fueled by a liquid or solid propellant containing its own oxidizing agent.

rocket gun Any gunlike device used for the discharge of rocket projectiles, as a bazooka.

rock·et·ry (rok′it·rē) *n.* The science, art, and technology of rocket flight, design, construction, etc.

rock·et·sonde (rok′it·sond′) *n. Meteorol.* A radiosonde adapted for use on high-altitude rockets.

rock·fish (rok′fish′) *n. pl.* **fish** or **fish·es** Any of several spiny finned fishes of the Pacific coast of North America.

rock garden A garden with flowers and plants growing in rocky ground or among rocks.

rocking chair A chair having the legs set on rockers.

rocking horse A toy horse mounted on rockers, large enough to be ridden by a child: also called *hobbyhorse*.

rock lobster The spiny lobster.

rock maple The sugar maple.

rock oil Petroleum.

rock·oon (rok·ōōn′) *n.* A small rocket equipped with vari-

ous meteorological recording devices and attached to a balloon, from which it is released at predetermined altitudes. [< ROCK(ET) + (BALL)OON]

rock-ribbed (rok′ribd′) *adj.* **1.** Having rocky ridges. **2.** Unyielding; inflexible.

rock salt Halite.

rock·shaft (rok′shaft′, -shäft′) A shaft made to rock on its bearings; esp., such a shaft for operating a slide valve in an engine.

rock wool Mineral wool.

rock·y¹ (rok′ē) *adj.* **rock·i·er, rock·i·est** **1.** Consisting of, abounding in, or resembling rocks. **2.** Tough; unfeeling; hard. — **rock′i·ness** *n.*

rock·y² (rok′ē) *adj.* **rock·i·er, rock·i·est** **1.** Inclined to rock or shake; unsteady. **2.** *Informal* Dizzy or weak, as from dissipation. — **rock′i·ness** *n.*

Rocky Mountain goat A goatlike, shaggy white ruminant with short black horns, found in the mountains of NW North America: also called *mountain goat*.

Rocky Mountain sheep The bighorn.

Rocky Mountain spotted fever *Pathol.* An acute infectious disease caused by a microorganism transmitted by the bite of certain ticks, and marked by skin eruptions.

ro·co·co (rə·kō′kō, rō′kə·kō′) *n.* **1.** A style of art that developed in France in the 18th century and spread throughout Europe; esp., architecture and ornament characterized by curvilinear designs, often imitating shells, foliage, and scrolls in asymmetrical arrangements. **2.** *Music* The elegant, formal style of European music from about 1726 to 1775, immediately following the baroque. **3.** Florid, fantastic, or odd style, as in literature. — *adj.* **1.** In the rococo style. **2.** Overelaborate; florid. [< F, alter. of *rocaille* shellwork]

rod (rod) *n.* **1.** A straight, slim piece of wood, metal, or other material. **2.** A shoot or cane of any woody plant. **3.** A switch or several switches together, used as an instrument of punishment. **4.** Discipline; correction: with *the*. **5.** A scepter or badge of office; a wand. **6.** Dominion; power. **7.** A bar, typically of metal, forming part of a machine: a connecting *rod*. **8.** A light pole used to suspend and manipulate a fishing line. **9.** A measure of length, equal to 5.5 yards; also, a square rod: sometimes called *perch, pole*. See table front of book. **10.** A measuring rule. **11.** One of the rodlike bodies of the retina sensitive to faint light. **12.** A rod-shaped bacterium. **13.** In Biblical usage, a line of family descent. **14.** A lightning rod. **15.** The drawbar of a freight train. **16.** *U.S. Slang* A pistol. [OE *rodd*]

rode (rōd) Past tense of RIDE.

ro·dent (rōd′nt) *n.* Any of a large cosmopolitan order of gnawing mammals, having in each jaw two (rarely four) incisors growing continually from persistent pulps, and no canine teeth, as a squirrel, beaver, or rat. — *adj.* **1.** Gnawing; corroding. **2.** Of or pertaining to a rodent or rodents. [< L *rodens, -entis*, ppr. of *rodere* to gnaw]

rodent ulcer *Pathol.* A malignant ulcer that progressively destroys soft tissues and bones, especially of the face.

ro·de·o (rō′dē·ō, rō·dā′ō) *n. pl.* **·os** **1.** The driving of cattle together to be branded, counted, inspected, etc.; a roundup. **2.** A public spectacle in which the more exciting features of a roundup are presented, as the riding of broncos, branding, lariat throwing, etc. **3.** An enclosure for cattle. [< Sp. *rodear* to go around < L *rota* wheel]

roe¹ (rō) *n.* **1.** The spawn or eggs of female fish. **2.** The milt of male fish. **3.** The eggs of crustaceans. [Var. of dial. *roan*, appar. < ON *hrogn* or MDu. *roch*]

roe² (rō) *n.* A small, graceful deer of Europe and western Asia. Also **roe deer.** [OE *rā*]

roe·buck (rō′buk′) *n.* The male of the roe deer.

roent·gen (rent′gən, runt′-; *Ger.* rœnt′gən) *n.* A measure of the intensity of gamma or X-rays, being the quantity of radiation that will produce 1 electrostatic unit of electricity in 1 cubic centimeter of air at normal temperature and pressure: also spelled *röntgen*. [after Wilhelm Konrad *Roentgen*]

roent·gen·ize (rent′gən·iz, runt′-) *v.t.* **·ized, ·iz·ing** To subject to the action of X-rays. — **roent′gen·i·za′tion** *n.*

roentgeno- *combining form* X-rays; using, produced by, or producing X-rays. Also, before vowels, **roentgen-.** [< ROENTGEN]

roent·gen·o·gram (rent′gən·ə·gram′, runt′-) *n.* An X-ray photograph. Also **roent′gen·o·graph′** (-graf′, -gräf′).

roent·gen·og·ra·phy (rent′gən·og′rə·fē, runt′-) *n. Med.* Photography means of X-rays; radiography. — **roent′·gen·o·graph′ic** (-ə·graf′ik) *adj.* — **roent′gen·o·graph′i·cal·ly** *adv.*

Roentgen rays X-rays.

Ro·gal·lo wing (rō·gal′ō) *Aeron.* A kitelike triangular flexible wing that can be used on simple aircraft, as a kite, or type of parachute. [after F. M. *Rogallo*, U.S. engineer, the inventor]

ro·ga·tion (rō-gā′shən) *n. Often pl.* Litany; supplication, esp. as part of the rites of the Rogation Days. [< L < *roga-tus*, pp. of *rogare* to ask]

Rogation Days *Eccl.* The three days immediately preceding Ascension Day, observed as days of special supplication.

rog·er (roj′ər) *interj.* **1.** *Often cap.* Message received: used in radio communication. **2.** *Informal* All right; O.K. [after *Roger*, personal name representing *r* in telecommunication]

rogue (rōg) *n.* **1.** A dishonest and unprincipled person; rascal. **2.** One who is innocently mischievous or playful. **3.** *Biol.* A variation from a standard. **4.** A fierce and dangerous animal, as an elephant, separated from the herd. **5.** *Archaic* A vagrant. — *v.* **rogued, ro·guing** *v.t.* **1.** To practice roguery upon; defraud. **2.** *Bot.* To eliminate (inferior individuals) from a plot of plants undergoing selection. [Origin uncertain]

ro·guer·y (rō′gər·ē) *n. pl. ·guer·ies* **1.** Conduct characteristic of a rogue; trickery. **2.** A roguish act.

rogues' gallery A collection of photographs of criminals taken to aid the police in identification.

ro·guish (rō′gish) *adj.* **1.** Playfully mischievous. **2.** Knavish; dishonest. — **ro′guish·ly** *adv.* — **ro′guish·ness** *n.*

roil (roil) *v.t.* **1.** To make muddy or turbid, as by stirring up sediment. **2.** To vex; irritate; rile. [< F *rouiller, ruiler*]

roil·y (roi′lē) *adj.* **roil·i·er, roil·i·est** Turbid; muddy.

roist·er (rois′tər) *v.i.* **1.** To act in a blustery manner; swagger. **2.** To engage in tumultuous merrymaking; revel. [< OF < L *rusticus* rustic] — **roist′er·er** *n.*

Ro·land (rō′lənd, *Fr.* rô·län′) Legendary nephew of Charlemagne and hero of the medieval French epic *Chanson de Roland*, in which he dies fighting the Saracens.

role (rōl) *n.* **1.** A part or character taken by an actor. **2.** Any assumed character or function. Also **role.** [< F *rôle*]

roll (rōl) *v.i.* **1.** To move forward on a surface by turning round and round, as a ball or wheel. **2.** To move or be moved on wheels or rollers. **3.** To move or appear to move in undulations or swells, as waves. **4.** To assume the shape of a ball or cylinder by turning over and over upon itself, as a ball of yarn. **5.** To pass; elapse: with *on* or *by.* **6.** Of sounds: **a** To make a deep, prolonged sound, as thunder. **b** To trill, as a bird. **c** To produce a roll, as on a drum. **7.** To rotate wholly or partially: his eyes *rolled.* **8.** To sway or move from side to side, as a ship. **9.** To wander or travel about. **10.** To walk with a swaying motion; also, to stagger. **11.** To become spread or flat because of pressure applied by a roller, etc.: The metal *rolls* easily. **12.** To perform a periodic revolution or cycle, as the seasons. **13.** To move ahead; progress. — *v.t.* **14.** To cause to move along a surface by turning round and round, as a ball, log, etc. **15.** To move, push forward, etc. on wheels or rollers. **16.** To wrap round and round upon itself or on an axis: often with *up.* **17.** To cause to assume the shape of a ball or cylinder by means of rotation and pressure: to *roll* a cigarette. **18.** To impel or cause to move onward with a steady, surging motion. **19.** To spread or make flat by pressing with a roller or rollers, as dough. **20.** To impart a swaying motion to. **21.** To wrap or envelop in or as in a covering. **22.** To rotate, as the eyes. **23.** Of sounds: **a** To utter with a trilling sound: to *roll* one's r's. **b** To emit in a full and swelling manner. **c** To beat a roll upon (a drum, etc.). **24.** To cast (dice) in the game of craps. **25.** *Printing* To apply ink to (a form) by means of a roller or rollers. **26.** *U.S. Slang* To rob (a drunk or a person who is asleep). — **to roll back** In commerce, to cause (prices, wages, etc.) to return to a previous, lower level, as by government direction. — **to roll in** *Informal* **1.** To arrive, esp. in numbers; congregate. **2.** To wallow; luxuriate: to *roll in* money. — **to roll up** *Informal* **1.** To accumulate; amass, as profits. **2.** To arrive, as an automobile. — *n.* **1.** Anything rolled up in cylindrical form. **2.** A register or list of names. **3.** A roller; esp., a cylinder in fixed bearings used as a roller. **4.** A strip of material, as of ribbon or carpeting, that is rolled upon itself or upon a core, often of an agreed length for use as a measure. **5.** Any food rolled up in preparation for use; also, a small, individually shaped portion of bread. **6.** A rolling gait or movement, as of a ship. **7.** Of sounds: **a** reverberation, as of thunder. **b** A rapid sustained series of short sounds: a drum *roll.* **c** A trill, as of a bird. **8.** A swell or undulation of a surface, as of land or water. **9.** *U.S. Slang* **a** A wad of paper money. **b** Money in general. **10.** The act of rolling, or the state of being rolled. **11.** *Aeron.* A complete rotation of an airplane about its longitudinal axis without change in the direction of flight. [< OF < L *rotula* < *rota* wheel]

roll·a·way (rōl′ə·wā′) *adj.* Mounted on rollers for easy movement into storage: a *rollaway* bed.

roll call **1.** The act of calling a roll or list of the names of a number of persons, as soldiers, to determine which are present. **2.** The time of or signal for calling the roll.

roll·er (rō′lər) *n.* **1.** One who or that which rolls. **2.** Any of various cylindrical devices that roll or rotate. **3.** The wheel of a caster or roller skate. **4.** A rod on which a win-

dow shade, towel, map, etc., is rolled. **5.** A heavy cylinder for rolling, smoothing, or crushing something: a steam *roller.* **6.** *Surg.* A long rolled bandage. **7.** One of a series of long, swelling waves that break on a coast, esp. after a storm. **8.** *Ornithol.* **a** Any of various European birds having gaudy colors and remarkable for their rolling and tumbling flight. **b** A canary having a trilling song.

roller bearing A bearing employing steel rollers to lessen friction between the parts of a mechanism.

roller coaster *U.S.* A railway with small, open cars run over a route of steep inclines and sharp turns, common at amusement parks.

roller skate A skate having wheels instead of a runner.

rol·lick (rol′ik) *v.i.* To move or behave in a careless, frolicsome manner. [? Blend of ROLL and FROLIC]

rol·lick·ing (rol′ik·ing) *adj.* **1.** Acting in a carefree, swaggering manner. **2.** Jovial; light-hearted; merry. Also **rol′-lick·some** (-səm), **rol′lick·y.**

roll·ing (rō′ling) *adj.* **1.** Turning round and round, esp. so as to move forward on a surface. **2.** Having a succession of sloping elevations and depressions: *rolling* hills. **3.** Turning on or as if on wheels; rotating. **4.** Turned back or down as if over a roll: a *rolling* collar. **5.** Surging in puffs, billows, or waves, as smoke, water, etc. **6.** Of sounds: **a** Trilled. **b** Resounding; reverberating. **7.** Swaying from side to side. **8.** Recurring; elapsing. — *n.* The act of one who or that which rolls or is rolled.

rolling hitch A knot having one or more intermediate turns between the first and last hitch. For illus. see HITCH.

rolling mill **1.** An establishment in which metal is rolled into sheets, bars, etc. **2.** A machine used to roll metal.

rolling pin A cylindrical device, usu. of wood and with a handle at each end, for rolling out dough, etc.

rolling stock The wheeled transportation equipment of a railroad, as locomotives and passenger cars.

roll-top (rōl′top′) *adj.* Designating a type of desk having a flexible, slatted cover that rolls back out of the way.

ro·ly-po·ly (rō′lē·pō′lē) *adj.* Short and fat; pudgy; dumpy. — *n. pl. -pol·ies* **1.** A roly-poly person or thing. **2.** *Chiefly Brit.* A pudding made of pastry dough spread with fruit, preserves, etc., rolled up and cooked. [Reduplication of ROLL]

Ro·ma·ic (rō·mā′ik) *adj.* Pertaining to or characteristic of the language or people of modern Greece. — *n.* Modern Greek, esp. the popular spoken form. [< LL < Gk. *Rhōmaikos* Roman]

ro·maine (rō·mān′) *n.* A variety of lettuce characterized by long, crisp leaves. [< F, fem. of *romain* Roman]

ro·man (rō′mən) *Sometimes cap. n.* A common style of type or lettering characterized by serifs, perpendicularity, and thicker vertical strokes than horizontal strokes: This line is set in roman. — *adj.* Pertaining to, designating, or printed in roman. Distinguished from *italic.* [< ROMAN]

Ro·man (rō′mən) *adj.* **1.** Of, pertaining to, or characteristic of modern or ancient Rome or its people. **2.** Of or belonging to the Roman Catholic Church. **3.** Of, pertaining to, or characteristic of the language of ancient Rome; Latin. **4.** Of or pertaining to the Holy Roman Empire. — *n.* **1.** A native, resident, or citizen of ancient or modern Rome. **2.** The language of ancient Rome; Latin. **3.** *Informal* A Roman Catholic. [< OF < L *Roma* Rome]

Roman calendar See under CALENDAR.

Roman candle A firework consisting of a tube filled with a composition that discharges colored balls and sparks of fire.

Roman Catholic A member of the Roman Catholic Church. — **Roman Catholicism**

Roman Catholic Church The Christian church that recognizes the Pope as its supreme head: also called *Catholic Church, Church of Rome.*

ro·mance (rō·mans′; *for n., also* rō′mans) *n.* **1.** A love affair. **2.** A kind of love between the sexes, usu. youthful and nonmarital, characterized by high ideals of purity and devotion, strong ardor, etc. **3.** Adventurous, heroic, or picturesque character or nature: the *romance* of faraway places. **4.** A tendency toward the mysterious or adventurous. **5.** A long narrative, sometimes in verse, presenting chivalrous ideals and usu. involving heroes in strange adventures and affairs of love. **6.** Any long fictitious narrative embodying scenes and events filled with extravagant adventures. **7.** An extravagant or fanciful falsehood. — *v.* **-manced, -manc-ing** *v.i.* **1.** To tell or write romances. **2.** To think or act in a romantic manner. **3.** *Informal* To make love. — *v.t.* **4.** *Informal* To make love to; woo. [< OF *romans* story written in French < L < *Romanicus* Roman] — **ro·manc′er** *n.*

Ro·mance (rō·mans′, rō′mans) *adj.* Pertaining or belonging to one or more, or all, of the languages that have developed from Vulgar Latin and that exist now as French, Italian, Spanish, Portuguese, Catalan, Provençal, and Rumanian. — *n.* One or all collectively, of the Romance languages.

Roman Empire The empire of ancient Rome, established in 27 B.C. and continuing until A.D. 395.

Ro·man·esque (rō′mən·esk′) *adj.* Of, pertaining to, or designating a style of Western architecture that developed from Roman principles, prevailed from the 5th to the 12th century, and was characterized by round arches and general massiveness. — *n.* The Romanesque style of architecture.
Roman holiday 1. Enjoyment or profit derived from the suffering of others. 2. A day of gladiatorial and other contests in ancient Rome.
Ro·man·ic (rō·man′ik) *adj.* 1. Roman. 2. Romance.
Ro·man·ism (rō′mən·iz′əm) *n.* The dogmas, forms, etc., of the Roman Catholic Church: often used disparagingly. — **Ro′man·ist** *n.*
Ro·man·ize (rō′mən·īz) *v.t.* & *v.i.* ·ized, ·iz·ing 1. To make or become Roman or Roman Catholic. 2. To write in the Roman style, language, etc. — **Ro′man·i·za′tion** *n.*
Roman nose A nose that is somewhat aquiline.
Roman numerals The letters used by the ancient Romans as symbols in arithmetical notation. The basic letters are I(1), V(5), X(10), L(50), C(100), D(500), and M(1000), and intermediate and higher numbers are formed as follows: Any symbol following another of equal or greater value adds to its value, as II = 2, XI = 11; any symbol preceding one of greater value subtracts from its value, as IV = 4, IX = 9, XC = 90. When a symbol stands between two of greater value, it is subtracted from the second and the remainder added to the first, as XIV = 14, LIX = 59.
Ro·ma·nov (rō′mə·nôf, *Russian* rô·mä′nôf) A Russian dynasty founded in 1613, and ended in 1918 with the execution of Nicholas II. Also **Ro′ma·noff.**
Ro·mans (rō′mənz) *n.pl.* (*construed as sing.*) One of the books of the New Testament, a letter from the apostle Paul to the Christians at Rome: in full **Epistle to the Romans.**
ro·man·tic (rō·man′tik) *adj.* 1. Of, characterized by, or of the nature of romance. 2. Characterized by or given to feelings or thoughts of love or romance. 3. Suitable for or conducive to love or amorousness. 4. Visionary; impractical. 5. Not based on fact; imaginary; fictitious. 6. Of or pertaining to romanticism in art, literature, and music. — *n.* One who is romantic. [< F *romant* romance, novel] — **ro·man′ti·cal·ly** *adv.*
ro·man·ti·cism (rō·man′tə·siz′əm) *n.* 1. *Usu. cap.* A movement in art, music, and literature originating in Europe in the late 18th century, characterized by a revolt against the neoclassic adherence to rules, forms, and traditions, an exalting of the feelings, and a marked preference for individualism, etc.: distinguished from *classicism.* Also **Romantic Movement.** 2. Romantic quality. — **ro·man′ti·cist** *n.*
ro·man·ti·cize (rō·man′tə·sīz) *v.* ·cized, ·ciz·ing *v.t.* To regard or interpret in a romantic manner.
Rom·a·ny (rom′ə·nē, rō′mə-) *n.* *pl.* ·nies 1. A Gypsy (def. 1). 2. The Indic language of the Gypsies: also called *Gypsy.* — *adj.* Of or pertaining to the Gypsies or their language. Also **Rom′ma·ny** (rom′ə·nē). [< *Romany* < *rom* man]
Rome (rōm) 1. Capital of the former Roman republic, the Roman Empire, and the States of the Church: Italian and Latin *Roma.* 2. The Roman Catholic Church.
Ro·me·o (rō′mē·ō) The hero of Shakespeare's *Romeo and Juliet.*
romp (romp) *v.i.* 1. To play boisterously. 2. To win easily. — *n.* 1. One who romps, esp. a girl. 2. Noisy, exciting frolic or play. 3. *Informal* An easy win. — **romp′ish** *adj.* — **romp′ish·ly** *adv.* — **romp′ish·ness** *n.*
romp·er (rom′pər) *n.* 1. One who romps. 2. *pl.* A garment combining a waist and bloomers, worn by young children.
Rom·u·lus (rom′yə·ləs) In Roman mythology, a son of Mars and founder of Rome, who with his twin brother Remus was reared by a she-wolf. Later Romulus slew his brother to become the first ruler of Rome.
ron·deau (ron′dō, ron·dō′) *n.* *pl.* ·deaux (-dōz, -dōz′) A poem of thirteen (or sometimes ten) lines with only two rhymes, and in which the opening words are repeated in two places as an unrhymed refrain. [< F *rond* round]
ron·del (ron′dəl, -del) *n.* A verse form consisting of 13 or 14 lines, the first two lines being repeated, as a refrain, in the seventh and eighth lines, and again in the thirteenth and fourteenth. [< F *rond* round]
ron·do (ron′dō, ron·dō′) *n.* *Music* A composition or movement having a main theme and several contrasting episodes, the main theme being repeated after each subordinate theme. [< Ital. < F *rond* round]

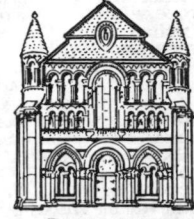
ROMANESQUE ARCHITECTURE
(Notre Dame de la Grande, Poitiers, France, 11th century)

rönt·gen (rent′gən, runt′-; *Ger.* rœnt′gən) See ROENTGEN.
rood (rōōd) *n.* 1. A cross or crucifix; esp., a large crucifix or representation of the Crucifixion over the altar screen of a church. 2. A land measure equivalent to one-fourth of an acre, or 40 square rods: also **square rood.** [OE *rōd* rod, measure of land, cross]
roof (rōōf, rŏŏf) *n.* 1. The exterior upper covering of a building. For other illustrations see GABLE ROOF, GAMBREL ROOF. 2. Any top covering, as of a car or oven. 3. The most elevated part of anything. — *v.t.* To cover with or as with a roof. [OE *hrōf*] — **roof′less** *adj.*
roof·er (rōō′fər, rŏŏf′ər) *n.* One who makes or repairs roofs.
roof garden 1. A garden on the roof of a building. 2. A space on a roof including a garden and used as a restaurant, etc.

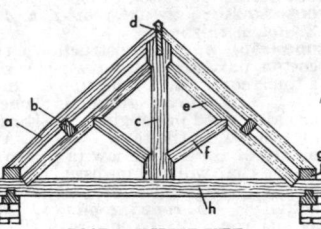
ROOF, KINGPOST TYPE
a Common rafter. *b* Purlin. *c* Kingpost. *d* Ridge beam. *e* Principal rafter. *f* Strut. *g* Pole plate. *h* Tie beam.

roof·ing (rōō′fing, rŏŏf′ing) *n.* 1. The act of covering with a roof. 2. Material for roofs. 3. A roof; covering.
roof·tree (rōōf′trē′, rŏŏf′-) *n.* 1. The ridgepole of a roof; also, the roof itself. 2. A home or dwelling.
rook¹ (rŏŏk) *n.* 1. An Old World crow noted for its gregariousness. 2. A trickster or cheat; a sharper. — *v.t.* & *v.i.* To cheat; defraud. [OE *hrōc*]
rook² (rŏŏk) *n.* A castle-shaped chessman that can move any number of unoccupied squares parallel to the sides of the board: also called *castle.* [< OF *roc* ult. < Persian *rukh*]
rook·er·y (rŏŏk′ər·ē) *n.* *pl.* ·er·ies 1. A colony or breeding place of rooks. 2. A breeding place of sea birds, seals, etc.
rook·ie (rŏŏk′ē) *n.* *Slang* 1. A raw recruit in the army, etc. 2. Any novice, as in baseball. [Prob. alter. of RECRUIT]
room (rōōm, rŏŏm) *n.* 1. An extent of space used for some implied or specified purpose. 2. A space for occupancy or use enclosed on all sides, as in a building. 3. *pl.* Lodgings. 4. Warrantable occasion; opportunity: *room* for doubt. — *v.i.* To occupy a room; lodge. [OE *rūm* space]
room·er (rōō′mər, rŏŏm′ər) *n.* A lodger; esp., one who rents a room and eats elsewhere.
room·ette (rōō·met′, rŏŏm·et′) *n.* A small compartment in a railroad sleeping car furnished with a folding bed.
room·ful (rōōm′fŏŏl′, rŏŏm′-) *n.* *pl.* ·fuls 1. As many or as much as a room will hold. 2. A number of persons present in a room.
room·ing house (rōō′ming, rŏŏm′ing) *U.S.* A house for roomers.
room·mate (rōōm′māt′, rŏŏm′-) *n.* *U.S.* One who shares lodgings with another or others.
room·y (rōō′mē, rŏŏm′ē) *adj.* room·i·er, room·i·est Having abundant room; spacious. — **room′i·ness** *n.*
roor·back (rōōr′bak) *n.* *U.S.* A slanderous report circulated for political purposes. [after *Roorback,* purported author of a (nonexistent) book of travel that was cited as authority for certain defamatory charges made against President Polk in the 1844 campaign]
roost (rōōst) *n.* 1. A perch upon which fowls rest at night; also, any place where birds resort to spend the night. 2. Any temporary resting place. — *v.i.* 1. To sit or perch upon a roost. 2. To come to rest; settle. [OE *hrōst*]
roost·er (rōōs′tər) *n.* The male of the chicken; cock.
root¹ (rōōt, rŏŏt) *n.* 1. The underground portion of a plant, that absorbs moisture, obtains or stores nourishment, and provides support. 2. Any underground growth, as a tuber or bulb. 3. That from which anything derives origin, growth, or support, or life and vigor: Money is the *root* of evil. 4. An ancestor. 5. A rootlike part of an organ or structure: the *root* of a tooth or nerve. 6. *Ling.* A base to which affixes and thematic vowels may be added to form words, as *know* in *unknown, knowable,* and *unknowingly.* See STEM. 7. *Math.* A quantity that, multiplied by itself a specified number of times, will give a given quantity: 3 is the square *root* of 9 and the cube *root* of 27. 8. *Music* The fundamental tone of a chord. — *v.i.* 1. To put forth roots and begin to grow. 2. To be or become firmly fixed. — *v.t.* 3. To fix by or as by roots. 4. To pull, dig, or tear up by or as by the roots: with *up* or *out.* [OE *rōt* < ON] — **root′less** *adj.* — **root′y** *adj.*
root² (rōōt, rŏŏt) *v.t.* 1. To dig with the snout, as swine. — *v.i.* 2. To turn up the earth with the snout. 3. To search; rummage. 4. To toil. [OE *wrōtan* to root up] — **root′er** *n.*

root³ (rōōt, rŏŏt) *v.i.* *U.S. Informal* To cheer for or encourage a contestant, team, etc., with *for.* [Prob. var. of ROUT²] — **root′er** *n.*

root beer A beverage made with yeast and root extracts.

root hair *Bot.* Hairlike outgrowths of plant roots, having an absorbent and protective function.

root·let (rōōt′lit, rŏŏt′-) *n.* A small root.

root·stalk (rōōt′stôk′, rŏŏt′-) *n. Bot.* A rhizome.

root·stock (rōōt′stok′, rŏŏt′-) *n.* **1.** Original source; origin. **2.** *Bot.* A rhizome.

rope (rōp) *n.* **1.** A construction of twisted fibers, as of hemp, cotton, flax, etc., so intertwined in several strands as to form a thick cord. **2.** A collection of things plaited or united in a line. **3.** A slimy or glutinous filament or thread. **4.** A cord or halter used in hanging. **5.** Execution or death by hanging: to die by the *rope.* **6.** *U.S.* A lasso. — **to give (one) plenty of rope** To allow (a person) to pursue unchecked a course that will end in disaster. — **to know the ropes** *Informal* To be familiar with all the conditions in any sphere of activity. — *v.* **roped, rop·ing** *v.t.* **1.** To tie or fasten with or as with rope. **2.** To enclose or divide with a rope: usu. with *off.* **3.** *U.S.* To catch with a lasso. — *v.i.* **4.** To become drawn out or extended into a filament or thread. [OE *rāp*]

rope·danc·er (rōp′dan/sər, -dän′-) *n.* A tightrope walker.

rope·walk (rōp′wôk′) *n.* A long alley or building used for the spinning of rope yarn.

rope·walk·er (rōp′wô/kər) *n.* A tightrope walker.

rop·y (rō′pē) *adj.* **rop·i·er, rop·i·est** **1.** That may be drawn into threads, as a glutinous substance; stringy. **2.** Resembling ropes or cordage. — **rop′i·ly** *adv.* — **rop′i·ness** *n.*

Roque·fort cheese (rōk′fərt, *Fr.* rôk·fôr′) A strong cheese with a blue mold, made from ewe's and goat's milk in the town of Roquefort, France.

ror·qual (rôr′kwəl) *n.* A whalebone whale of the Atlantic and Pacific oceans: also called *finback, razorback.* [< F < Norw. *röyrkval*]

Ror·schach test (rôr′shäk, -shäkh, rōr′-) *Psychol.* A test in which personality characteristics are made capable of analysis by the subject's interpretation of a series of standard inkblot patterns. [after Hermann *Rorschach,* 1884–1922, Swiss psychiatrist]

ro·sa·ceous (rō·zā′shəs) *adj.* **1.** *Bot.* Of, pertaining to, or designating the rose family of trees, shrubs, and herbs. **2.** Resembling a rose. [< L < *rosa* rose]

ro·sa·ry (rō′zə·rē) *n. pl.* **·ries** **1.** *Eccl.* **a** A series of prayers. **b** A string of beads for keeping count of these prayers. **2.** A garden or bed of roses. [< L *rosa* rose]

rose¹ (rōz) *n.* **1.** Any of a large genus of hardy, erect or climbing shrubs, with rodlike, prickly stems: the national flower of England and the State flower of New York, North Dakota, and Iowa. **2.** The flower of such a shrub, usu. having five sepals and exhibiting a wide range of colors, principally white, yellow, pink, or red. **3.** Any of various other plants or flowers likened to the true rose. **4.** A light pinkish red. **5.** An ornamental knot; a rosette. **6.** A form in which gems, esp. diamonds, are often cut; also, a diamond so cut. — **bed of roses** A peaceful or carefree time, place, or condition. — *v.t.* **rosed, ros·ing** To cause to blush; redden; flush. [OE < L *rosa,* prob. < Gk. *rhodea*]

rose² (rōz) Past tense of RISE.

ro·se·ate (rō′zē·it, -āt) *adj.* **1.** Rosy; rose-colored. **2.** Cheerful; optimistic. [< L *roseus*] — **ro′se·ate·ly** *adv.*

rose·bud (rōz′bud′) *n.* The bud of a rose.

rose·bush (rōz′bŏŏsh′) *n.* A rose-bearing shrub or vine.

rose campion An herbaceous plant, cultivated for its pink or crimson flowers.

rose chafer A hairy, fawn-colored beetle injurious to roses: also called *rose beetle.* Also **rose bug.**

rose-col·ored (rōz′kul′ərd) *adj.* Pink or crimson, as a rose. — **to see through rose-colored glasses** To see things in an unduly favorable light.

rose fever *Pathol.* A variety of hay fever, assumed to be caused by rose pollen. Also **rose cold.**

rose·mar·y (rōz′mâr′ē) *n. pl.* **·mar·ies** An evergreen, fragrant Old World shrub of the mint family, commonly with blue flowers, cultivated for use in making perfume and in cookery. [ME < L < *ros* dew + *marinus* of the sea]

rose of Sharon **1.** A hardy shrub of the mallow family: also called *shrub althea.* **2.** A species of St. Johnswort having large, yellow flowers.

rose quartz A semitransparent variety of quartz, pink or rose in color and often used for ornament and as a gemstone.

Ro·set·ta stone (rō·zet′ə) A tablet of basalt inscribed with two forms of Egyptian hieroglyphics and in Greek, found near Rosetta, Egypt, in 1799. It supplied the key to the ancient inscriptions of Egypt.

ro·sette (rō·zet′) *n.* **1.** An ornament or badge having some resemblance to a rose; esp., an architectural ornament with parts circularly arranged. **2.** A flowerlike cluster of leaves, organs, or markings, arranged in circles, as in certain plants. [< F, dim. of *rose*]

rose water A fragrant preparation made variously by the distillation of rose petals or rose oil with water, used as a toilet water and in cooking.

rose window A circular window filled with tracery, often radiating from the center like spokes.

rose·wood (rōz′wŏŏd′) *n.* **1.** A hard, close-grained, dark-colored, fragrant wood yielded by certain tropical American trees. **2.** Any of various other woods resembling true rosewood. **3.** Any tree yielding such a wood.

Rosh Ha·sha·na (rosh hə·shä′nə, rôsh) The Jewish New Year, celebrated in September or early October. Also **Rosh Ha·sho′nah** (-shō′-). [< Hebrew *rōsh* head + *hash-shānāh* of the year]

ros·in (roz′in) *n.* **1.** The hard, amber-colored resin forming the residue after the distillation of oil from crude turpentine: also called *resin.* **2.** Resin (defs. 1 & 2). — *v.t.* To apply rosin to. [Alter. of RESIN] — **ros′in·y** *adj.*

ros·ter (ros′tər) *n.* **1.** A list of officers and men enrolled for duty; also, a list of active military organizations. **2.** Any list of names. [< Du. *rooster* list, lit. gridiron]

ros·trum (ros′trəm) *n. pl.* **·trums** or **·tra** (-trə) *for defs. 1 & 3,* **·tra** *for def. 2* **1.** A pulpit or platform. **2.** In ancient Rome: **a** A beaklike part on the prow of a ship. **b** The orators' platform in the Roman forum, embellished with such parts. **3.** *Biol.* A beaklike process or part. [< L *rostrum* beak] — **ros′tral, ros′trate** (-trāt) *adj.*

ros·y (rō′zē) *adj.* **ros·i·er, ros·i·est** **1.** Like a rose; rose red; blushing. **2.** Bright, pleasing, or flattering. **3.** Made of or ornamented with roses. **4.** Auguring success; optimistic. — **ros′i·ly** *adv.* — **ros′i·ness** *n.*

rot (rot) *v.* **rot·ted, rot·ting** *v.i.* **1.** To undergo decomposition; decay. **2.** To become morally rotten. — *v.t.* **3.** To cause to decompose; decay. **4.** To ret. — **Syn.** See DECAY. — *n.* **1.** The process of rotting or the state of being rotten. **2.** That which is rotten. **3.** Any of various diseases involving decay in humans, plants, and animals, esp. sheep. **4.** *Informal* Trashy and nonsensical opinions or expressions. — *interj.* Nonsense. [OE *rotian*]

Ro·tar·i·an (rō·târ′ē·ən) *n.* A member of a Rotary Club. — *adj.* Of or pertaining to Rotary Clubs or their members. — **Ro·tar′i·an·ism** *n.*

ro·ta·ry (rō′tər·ē) *adj.* **1.** Turning or designed to turn around its axis, like a wheel. **2.** Having some part that turns on its axis. **3.** Characterized by movement around an axis; rotatory. — *n. pl.* **·ries** A rotary device or part. [< LL < L *rota* wheel]

Rotary Club A club belonging to an international association of clubs, **Rotary International,** whose aim is to improve civic service.

rotary engine *Mech.* **1.** An engine in which rotary motion is directly produced, as in a turbine. **2.** In internal-combustion engines, a radial engine revolving about a fixed crankshaft.

rotary press A printing press using curved type plates that revolve against the paper.

ro·tate (rō′tāt) *v.t.* & *v.i.* **tat·ed, ·tat·ing** **1.** To turn or cause to turn on or as on its axis. **2.** To alternate in a definite order or succession. [< L < *rotare* to turn < *rota* wheel] — **ro′tat·a·ble, ro·ta·tive** (rō′tə·tiv) *adj.* — **ro′ta·tor** *n.* — **Syn.** (verb) 1 spin, whirl, twirl, turn, gyrate. See REVOLVE.

ro·ta·tion (rō·tā′shən) *n.* **1.** The act or state of rotating; rotary motion. **2.** Change or alternation in a particular sequence; regular variation. [< L *rotatio, -onis*] — **ro·ta′tion·al** *adj.*

ro·ta·to·ry (rō′tə·tôr′ē, -tō′rē) *adj.* **1.** Having, pertaining to, or producing rotation. **2.** Following in succession. **3.** Alternating or recurring.

rote (rōt) *n.* **1.** Mechanical routine. **2.** Repetition of words as a means of learning them, with slight attention to the sense. — **by rote** Mechanically, without intelligent attention: to learn *by rote.* [ME; origin uncertain]

ro·te·none (rō′tə·nōn) *n. Chem.* A crystalline compound, $C_{23}H_{22}O_6$, the effective principle in insecticides and fish poisons, obtained from the roots of various plants. [Origin unknown]

rot·gut (rot′gut′) *U.S.* An inferior raw whisky.

ro·ti·fer (rō′tə·fər) *n.* One of a division of microscopic organisms usu. found in stagnant fresh water, having rings of cilia that in motion resemble revolving wheels. [< NL < L *rota* wheel + *ferre* to bear] — **ro·tif·er·al** (rō·tif′ər·əl), **ro·tif′er·ous** *adj.*

ro·tis·se·rie (rō·tis′ər·ē) *n.* **1.** A restaurant where patrons select uncooked food and have it roasted and served. **2.** A shop where food is roasted and sold. **3.** A rotating device for roasting meat, etc. [< F < *rôtir* to roast]

ro·to·gra·vure (rō′tə·grə·vyŏŏr′, -grāv′yər) *n.* **1.** The process of printing photographs, letters, etc., from cylinders etched from photographic plates and run through a rotary press. **2.** A picture printed by this process. **3.** The section of a newspaper containing such pictures. [< L *rota* wheel + GRAVURE]

ro·tor (rō′tər) *n.* **1.** The rotating section of a motor, dynamo, turbine, or other power generator: distinguished from *stator.* **2.** *Aeron.* The horizontally rotating unit of a helicopter or autogiro, consisting of the airfoils and hub. [Contraction of ROTATOR]

rot·ten (rot′n) *adj.* **1.** Decomposed by natural process; putrid. **2.** Untrustworthy; treacherous. **3.** Corrupt; venal. **4.** Liable to break; unsound. **5.** *Informal* Worthless. [< ON *rotinn*] **— rot′ten·ly** *adv.* **— rot′ten·ness** *n.* **— Syn. 1.** decayed, putrefied, putrescent, carious, fetid. Compare DECAY. **— Ant.** fresh, sweet, sound, wholesome, healthy.

rot·ter (rot′ər) *n. Chiefly Brit. Slang* A worthless or objectionable person; scoundrel.

ro·tund (rō·tund′) *adj.* **1.** Rounded out; spherical; plump. **2.** Full-toned, as a voice or utterance; sonorous. [< L *rotundus* round] **— ro·tun′di·ty** *n.* **— ro·tund′ly** *adv.* **— ro·tund′ness** *n.*

ro·tun·da (rō·tun′də) *n.* A circular building or an interior hall, surmounted with a dome. [< Ital. < L *rotundus.* See ROTUND.]

rou·ble (rōō′bəl) See RUBLE.

rou·é (rōō·ā′) *n.* A sensualist; debauchee. [< F < *rouer* to break on the wheel]

rouge (rōōzh) *n.* **1.** Any cosmetic used for coloring the cheeks or lips pink or red. **2.** A ferric oxide used in polishing metals and glass. **— v. rouged, roug·ing** *v.t.* **1.** To color with rouge. **— v.i. 2.** To apply rouge. [< F < L *rubeus* ruby]

rough (ruf) *adj.* **1.** Having an uneven surface; not smooth or polished. **2.** Coarse in texture; shabby. **3.** Disordered or ragged; shaggy. **4.** Having the surface broken; uneven. **5.** Characterized by rude or violent action. **6.** Boisterous or tempestuous; stormy. **7.** Characterized by harshness of spirit; brutal. **8.** Lacking the finish and polish bestowed by art or culture; crude. **9.** Done or made hastily and without attention to details, as a drawing. **10.** Harsh to the ear; grating; inharmonious. **— n. 1.** A low, rude, and violent fellow; a rowdy. **2.** A crude, incomplete, or unpolished object, material, or condition. **3.** Any part of a golf course on which tall grass, bushes, etc., grow. **— in the rough** In a crude or unpolished state. **— v.t. 1.** To make rough; roughen. **2.** To treat roughly. **3.** To make, cut, or sketch roughly: with *in* or *out.* **— v.i. 4.** To become rough. **5.** To behave roughly. **— to rough it** To live, camp, or travel under rough, hard, or impoverished conditions. **— adv.** In a rude manner, roughly. [OE *rūh*] **— rough′ly** *adv.* **— rough′ness** *n.*

rough·age (ruf′ij) *n.* **1.** Any coarse or tough substance. **2.** Food material containing a high percentage of indigestible constituents, as cellulose.

rough-and-read·y (ruf′ən·red′ē) *adj.* **1.** Characterized by or acting with rude but effective promptness. **2.** Unpolished but good enough.

rough-and-tum·ble (ruf′ən·tum′bəl) *adj.* **1.** Marked by the disregard of all rules, as a fight. **2.** Scrambling; disorderly. **— n.** A rough-and-tumble fight or scuffle.

rough·cast (ruf′kast′, -käst′) *v.t.* **·cast, ·cast·ing 1.** To shape or prepare in a preliminary or incomplete form. **2.** To coat, as a wall, with coarse plaster, and cover with thin mortar by dashing it on. **— n. 1.** Very coarse plaster for the outside of buildings. **2.** A form or model of something in its first rough stage. **— rough′cast′er** *n.*

rough-draw (ruf′drô′) *v.t.* **·drew, ·drawn, ·draw·ing** To sketch hastily or crudely.

rough-dry (ruf′drī′) *v.t.* **·dried, ·dry·ing** To dry without ironing, as washed clothes.

rough·en (ruf′ən) *v.t. & v.i.* To make or become rough.

rough-hew (ruf′hyōō′) *v.t.* **·hewed, ·hewed** or **·hewn, ·hew·ing 1.** To hew or shape roughly or irregularly. **2.** To make crudely; roughcast.

rough·house (ruf′hous′) *Slang n.* A noisy, boisterous, or violent game; rough play. **— v. ·housed, ·hous·ing — v.i. 1.** To make a disturbance; engage in horseplay or violence. **— v.t. 2.** To handle or treat roughly but without hostile intent.

rough·neck (ruf′nek′) *n. U.S. Slang* A rowdy.

rough·rid·er (ruf′rī′dər) *n. U.S.* One skilled in breaking broncos or performing dangerous feats in horsemanship.

Rough Riders The 1st U.S. Volunteer Cavalry in the Spanish-American War of 1898, mainly organized and subsequently commanded by Theodore Roosevelt.

rough·shod (ruf′shod′) *adj.* Shod with rough shoes to prevent slipping, as a horse. **— to ride roughshod (over)** To act overbearingly; domineer without consideration.

rou·lette (rōō·let′) *n.* **1.** A game played at a table divided into spaces numbered and colored red and black, and having a rotating disk (**roulette wheel**) on which a ball is rolled until it drops into one of 37 or 38 correspondingly marked spaces. **2.** An engraver's disk of tempered steel, as for tracing points on a copperplate; also, a draftsman's wheel for making dotted lines. **— v.t. ·let·ted, ·let·ting** To perforate or mark with a roulette. [< F < *roue* wheel]

round (round) *adj.* **1.** Having a contour that is circular or approximately so; spherical, ring-shaped, or cylindrical. **2.** Having a curved contour or surface; not angular or flat; convex or concave. **3.** Liberal; ample; large. **4.** Easy and free, as in motion; brisk. **5.** Of full cadence; well-balanced; full-toned. **6.** Made without reserve; outspoken. **7.** Open; just. **8.** Formed or moving in rotation or a circle. **9.** Returning to the point of departure: a *round* trip. **10.** Of a number, increased or decreased by a relatively small amount for the sake of simplicity: 3,992 is 4,000 in *round* numbers. **11.** Semicircular: a *round* arch. **12.** *Phonet.* Labialized; rounded. **— n. 1.** Something round, as a globe, ring, or cylinder, a rung of a ladder, a portion of the thigh of a beef, etc. **2.** *Often pl.* A circular course or range; circuit; beat. **3.** A single revolution; also revolving motion. **4.** A series of recurrent movements; routine; order: the daily *round* of life. **5.** One of a series of concerted actions performed in succession: a *round* of applause. **6.** One of the divisions of a boxing match; a bout. **7.** In golf, a number of holes or an interval of play in a match. **8.** *Music* A short canon in the octave or unison, in which each voice enters in turn and returns to the beginning upon reaching the end. **9.** A firing by a company or squad in which each soldier fires once; volley. **10.** A single shot or complete unit of ammunition. **11.** The state of being carved out on all sides: sculpture in the *round.* **12.** The state or condition of being circular; roundness. **13.** A thick slice from a haunch. **— to go** (or **make**) **the rounds 1.** To take a usual walk or tour, as of inspection. **2.** To pass from person to person of a certain group. **— v.t. 1.** To make round. **2.** To bring to completion; perfect: usually with *off* or *out.* **3.** To free of angularity; fill out to fullness of form. **4.** *Phonet.* To utter (a vowel) with the lips in a rounded position; labialize. **5.** To travel or go around; make a circuit of. **— v.i. 6.** To become round. **7.** To come to completeness or perfection. **8.** To fill out; become plump. **9.** To make a circuit; travel a circular course. **10.** To turn around. **— to round off 1.** To make round or rounded. **2.** To make into a round number. **— to round up 1.** To collect (cattle, etc.) in a herd, as for driving to market. **2.** *Informal* To assemble. **— adv. 1.** On all sides; in such a manner as to encircle. **2.** With a circular or rotating motion. **3.** Through a circle or circuit, as from person to person or point to point: provisions enough to go *round.* **4.** In circumference: a log 3 feet *round.* **5.** From one view or position to another; to and fro. **6.** In the vicinity: to hang *round.* **— prep. 1.** Enclosing; encircling. **2.** On every side of, or from every side toward; surrounding. **3.** Toward every side from; about. [< OF < L *rotundus* round] **— round′ish** *adj.* **— round′ish·ness** *n.* **— round′ness** *n.*

round·a·bout (round′ə·bout′) *adj.* **1.** Circuitous; indirect. **2.** Encircling. **— n. 1.** An outer garment reaching to the waist; a jacket. **2.** *Brit.* A merry-go-round.

round·ed (roun′did) *adj.* **1.** Round or spherical. **2.** *Phonet.* Formed or uttered with the lips rounded; labialized.

roun·de·lay (roun′də·lā) *n.* **1.** A simple melody. **2.** A musical setting of a poem with a recurrent refrain. [< OF < *rond* round]

round·er (roun′dər) *n.* **1.** A tool for rounding. **2.** *U.S. Slang* A drunkard, drifter, or petty criminal. **3.** *pl.* (*construed as sing.*) An English game somewhat resembling baseball.

Round·head (round′hed′) *n.* A member of the parliamentary party in England in the civil war of 1642–49.

round·house (round′hous′) *n.* **1.** A cabin on the after part of the quarter-deck of a vessel. **2.** A round building with a turntable in the center for housing and switching locomotives. **3.** In pinochle, a meld of four kings and four queens.

round·ly (round′lē) *adv.* **1.** In a round manner or form; circularly; spherically. **2.** Severely; vigorously: to be *roundly* denounced. **3.** Frankly; bluntly. **4.** Thoroughly.

round number A number expressed to the nearest ten, hundred, thousand, etc. Also **round figure.**

round robin 1. A tournament, as in tennis or chess, in which each player meets every other player. **2.** A letter circulated among the members of a group. **3.** A number of signatures, as to a petition, written in a circle so as to avoid giving prominence to any one name.

round-shoul·dered (round′shōl′dərd) *adj.* Having the back rounded or the shoulders stooping.

round table 1. A meeting place for conference. **2.** Any discussion group. **— round·ta·ble** (round′tā′bəl) *adj.*

Round Table 1. The table around which King Arthur and his knights sat. **2.** King Arthur and his knights.

round-the-clock (round′the·klok′) *adj.* Through all twenty-four hours of the day.

round trip A trip to a place and back again; a two-way trip. **— round'-trip'** *adj.*

round·up (round'up') *n. U.S.* **1.** The bringing together of cattle scattered over a range, as for inspection or branding. **2.** The cowboys, horses, etc., employed in this work. **3.** *Informal* A bringing together of persons or things.

round·worm (round'wûrm') *n.* A nematode worm, esp. one parasitic in the human intestines.

rouse (rouz) *v.* **roused, rous·ing** *v.t.* **1.** To cause to awaken from slumber, repose, unconsciousness, etc. **2.** To excite to vigorous thought or action; stir up. **3.** To startle or drive (game) from cover. — *v.i.* **4.** To awaken. **5.** To become active. **6.** To start from cover: said of game. — *n.* The act of rousing. [Orig. technical term in hawking and hunting] **— rous'er** *n.*

rous·ing (rou'zing) *adj.* **1.** Able to rouse or excite: a *rousing* speech. **2.** Lively; active; vigorous: a *rousing* trade. **3.** *Informal* Outrageous; astonishing: a *rousing* lie.

roust (roust) *v.t. & v.i. Informal* To arouse and drive (a person or thing); stir up: usu. with *out*. [< ROUSE]

roust·a·bout (roust'ə-bout') *n.* **1.** A laborer on river craft or on the waterfront. **2.** One who is employed for casual work; esp., a transient laborer on a cattle ranch, etc. **3.** A laborer in a circus.

rout¹ (rout) *n.* **1.** A disorderly and overwhelming defeat or flight. **2.** A boisterous crowd. — *v.t.* To defeat disastrously; put to flight. [< OF < L *rumpere* to break]

rout² (rout) *v.i.* **1.** To root, as swine. **2.** To search; rummage. — *v.t.* **3.** To dig or turn up with the snout. **4.** To turn up as if with the snout; disclose to view: with *out*. **5.** To hollow, gouge, or scrape, as with a scoop. **6.** To drive or force out. [Var. of ROOT²]

route (root, rout) *n.* **1.** A course, road, or way taken in traveling from one point to another. **2.** The specific course over which mail is sent. **3.** The territory covered by a newsboy. — *v.t.* **rout·ed, rout·ing** To dispatch or send by a certain way, as passengers, goods, etc. [< OF < L *rupta* (*via*) broken (road), fem. of *ruptus*. See ROUT¹.]

rout·er (rou'tər) *n.* **1.** One who scoops or routs. **2.** A tool for routing. **3.** A plane devised for working a molding around a circular sash. [< ROUT²]

rou·tine (rōō-tēn') *n.* **1.** A detailed method of procedure, regularly followed: an official *routine*. **2.** Habitual methods of action induced by circumstances. — *adj.* Customary; habitual. [< F < *route* way, road] **— rou·tine'ly** *adv.*

rou·tin·ism (rōō-tē'niz-əm) *n.* Adherence to routine or routine methods in general. **— rou·tin'ist** *n.*

rou·tin·ize (rōō-tē'nīz) *v.t.* **·ized, ·i·zing** To reduce or fit to a routine.

roux (rōō) *n. French* Butter and an equal portion of flour mixed and browned together, used for sauces, etc.

rove¹ (rōv) *v.* **roved, rov·ing** *v.i.* **1.** To wander from place to place; go or move without any definite destination. — *v.t.* **2.** To roam over, through, or about. — *n.* The act of roving; a ramble. [ME *roven*] **— rov'er** *n.*

rove² (rōv) Alternate past tense and past participle of REEVE¹.

row¹ (rō) *n.* **1.** An arrangement or series of persons or things in a continued line; a rank; file. **2.** A street lined with houses on both sides. **3.** A line of seats, as in a theater. **— a long row to hoe** A hard task or undertaking. — *v.t.* To arrange in a row: with *up*. [OE *rāw*, var. of *ræw* line]

row² (rō) *v.i.* **1.** To use oars, etc., in propelling a boat. — *v.t.* **2.** To propel across the surface of the water with oars, as a boat. **3.** To transport by rowing. **4.** To be propelled by (a specific number of oars): said of boats. **5.** To make use of (oars or rowers), esp. in a race. **6.** To row against in a race. — *n.* **1.** The act of rowing. **2.** A turn at the oars. **3.** A trip in a rowboat. [OE *rōwan*]

row³ (rou) *n.* **1.** A noisy disturbance or quarrel; a brawl. **2.** Any dispute or disturbance. — *v.t. & v.i.* To engage in a row or brawl. [Origin uncertain]

row·an (rō'ən, rou'-) A small tree native to Europe, having clusters of bright orange berries: also called *mountain ash*.

row·boat (rō'bōt') *n. U.S.* A boat propelled by oars.

row·dy (rou'dē) *n. pl.* **·dies** One inclined to create disturbances; a rough, disorderly person. — *adj.* **·di·er, ·di·est** Rough and loud; disorderly. [Origin unknown] **— row'dy·ish** *adj.* **— row'dy·ism, row'di·ness** *n.*

row·el (rou'əl) *n.* A spiked or toothed wheel, as on a spur. — *v.t.* **row·eled** or **·elled, row·el·ing** or **·el·ling** To prick with a rowel; spur. [< OF *roele* < L *rota* wheel]

row·lock (rō'lok') *n. Brit.* An oarlock.

roy·al (roi'əl) *adj.* **1.** Pertaining to a monarch; kingly. **2.** Under the patronage or authority of a king, or connected with a monarchical form of government: a *royal* governor. **3.** Like or befitting a king; regal. **4.** Of superior quality or size. **5.** *Informal* Extraordinarily good, large, impressive, etc. — *n.* **1.** A size of paper, 19 x 24 inches for writing, 20 x 25 inches for printing. **2.** *Naut.* A sail next above the topgallant. [< OF < L < *rex* king] **— roy'al·ly** *adv.*

royal blue A brilliant blue, often with reddish overtones.

Royal Canadian Mounted Police The federal police force of Canada.

roy·al·ist (roi'əl·ist) *n.* A supporter of a royal dynasty. — *adj.* Of or pertaining to royalists: also **roy'al·is'tic.**

Roy·al·ist (roi'əl·ist) *n.* **1.** In English history, a Cavalier or adherent of King Charles I. **2.** In French history, a supporter of the Bourbon or Orléans claims to the throne since 1793. **3.** In the American Revolution, a supporter of the king; Loyalist; Tory.

roy·al·mast (roi'əl·mast', -mäst') *n. Naut.* The section of a mast next above the topgallant mast.

royal palm Any of various palms native in tropical America, noted for their height and striking appearance.

royal purple **1.** A very deep violet color verging toward blue. **2.** Originally, a rich crimson.

roy·al·ty (roi'əl·tē) *n. pl.* **·ties** **1.** The rank, birth, or lineage of a king or queen. **2.** A royal personage; also, royal persons collectively. **3.** A share of proceeds paid to a proprietor, author, or inventor. **4.** A tax paid to the crown on the produce of royal mines, or on gold and silver coinage. **5.** A royal possession or domain. **6.** Any domain or province. [< OF *roialte*]

-rrhagia *combining form Pathol.* An abnormal or violent discharge or flow; an eruption: also *-rhage, -rhagia, -rhagy*. Also **-rrhage, -rrhagy.** Corresponding adjectives are formed with **-rrhagic.** [< Gk. < *rrhag-*, root of *rrhēgnynai* to burst]

-rrhaphy *combining form* A sewing together; a suture. [< F *-rrhaphie* < Gk. *rhaptein* to sew together]

-rrhea *combining form Pathol.* An abnormal or excessive flow or discharge: also spelled *-rhea, -rhoea.* Also **-rrhoea.** [< Gk. *-rrhoia* < *rhein* to flow]

rub (rub) *v.* **rubbed, rub·bing** *v.t.* **1.** To move or pass over the surface of with pressure and friction. **2.** To cause (something) to move or pass with friction; scrape; grate. **3.** To cause to become frayed, worn, or sore from friction. **4.** To clean, shine, burnish, etc., by means of pressure and friction. **5.** To apply or spread with pressure and friction. **6.** To remove or erase by friction: with *off* or *out*. — *v.i.* **7.** To move along a surface with friction; scrape. **8.** To exert pressure and friction. **9.** To become frayed, worn, or sore from friction; chafe. **10.** To undergo rubbing or removal by rubbing: with *off, out*, etc. **— to rub it in** *Slang* To harp on someone's errors, faults, etc. **— to rub out** *Slang* To kill. **— to rub the wrong way** *Slang* To irritate; annoy. — *n.* **1.** A rubbing; Give it a *rub*. **2.** A hindrance, doubt, etc.: There's the *rub*. **3.** Something that rubs or is rough to the feelings; a sarcasm. **4.** A roughness or unevenness of surface, quality, or character. [ME *rubben*, prob. < LG]

ru·ba·to (rōō-bä'tō) *Music adj.* Denoting the lengthening of one note at the expense of another. — *n. pl.* **·tos** A rubato modification. — *adv.* In a rubato manner. [< Ital., robbed]

rub·ber¹ (rub'ər) *n.* **1.** A resinous elastic material obtained by coagulating the milky latex of certain tropical plants, and also made synthetically: sometimes called *India rubber*. **2.** Anything used for rubbing, erasing, polishing, etc. **3.** An article made of rubber, as an elastic band or an overshoe. **4.** In baseball, the pitcher's plate. **5.** *Slang* A condom. **6.** One who or that which rubs. — *adj.* Made of rubber. [< RUB] **— rub'ber·y** *adj.*

rub·ber² (rub'ər) *n.* In bridge, whist, and other card games, a series of two or three games terminated when one side has won two games; also, the odd game that breaks a tie between the players. [Origin unknown]

rubber check *U.S. Slang* A worthless check.

rub·ber·ize (rub'ər·īz) *v.t.* **·ized, ·iz·ing** To coat, impregnate, or cover with a preparation of rubber.

rub·ber·neck (rub'ər·nek') *U.S. Slang n.* One who cranes his neck in order to see something; a sightseer; tourist. — *v.i.* To stretch or crane one's neck; gape.

rubber plant **1.** Any of several plants yielding rubber. **2.** A house plant of the mulberry family, having large, glossy, leathery leaves.

rub·ber-stamp (rub'ər·stamp') *v.t.* **1.** To endorse, initial, or approve with the mark made by a rubber stamping device. **2.** *Informal* To pass or approve as a matter of routine.

rub·bish (rub'ish) *n.* **1.** Waste refuse, or broken matter; trash. **2.** Nonsense; rot. [ME *rubbous*] **— rub'bish·y** *adj.*

rub·ble (rub'əl; *for def. 3, also* rōō'bəl) *n.* **1.** Rough, irregular pieces of broken stone. **2.** The debris to which buildings of brick, stone, etc., are reduced by violent actions, as by earthquakes or bombings. **3.** Rough pieces of stone for use in construction; also, masonry composed of such pieces. [Origin uncertain] **— rub'bly** *adj.*

rub·down (rub'doun') *n.* A type of massage.

rube (rōōb) *n. Slang* A farmer; rustic. [Abbreviation of *Reuben*, a personal name]

ru·bel·la (rōō-bel'ə) *n. Pathol.* German measles. [< NL, neut. pl. of L *rubellus* reddish, dim. of *ruber* red]

ru·be·o·la (roo-bē′ə-lə) *n. Pathol.* **1.** Measles (def. 1). **2.** German measles. [< NL, neut. pl. dim. of L *rubeus* red] — **ru·be′o·lar** *adj.*

Ru·bi·con (roo′bi·kon) A river in north central Italy, forming the boundary separating Caesar's province of Gaul from Italy, and by crossing it he committed himself to war with Pompey. **— to cross the Rubicon** To be committed definitely to some course of action.

ru·bi·cund (roo′bə·kənd) *adj.* Red, or inclined to redness; rosy. [< L *rubicundus* red] — **ru′bi·cun′di·ty** *n.*

ru·bid·i·um (roo·bid′ē·əm) *n.* A soft, rare, silvery white, metallic element (symbol Rb) resembling potassium. See ELEMENT. [< NL < L *rubidus* red]

ru·ble (roo′bəl) *n.* **1.** A standard monetary unit of the U.S.S.R.: in 1960 worth about 25 U.S. cents: also spelled *rouble.* **2.** Formerly, a Russian silver coin.

ru·bric (roo′brik) *n.* **1.** A part of an early manuscript or a book that appears in red, used to indicate initial letters, headings, etc. **2.** *Eccl.* A direction or rule printed in a devotional or liturgical office. **3.** A heading or title, as of a chapter, statute, etc. **4.** Any direction or rule of conduct. — *adj.* **1.** Red or reddish. **2.** Written in red. [< F < L *rubrica* red earth] — **ru′bri·cal** *adj.* — **ru′bri·cal·ly** *adv.*

ru·bri·cate (roo′brə·kāt) *v.t.* **·cat·ed, ·cat·ing** To mark or tint with red; illuminate with red, as a book. [< L *rubricare* to redden] — **ru′bri·ca′tion** *n.* — **ru′bri·ca′tor** *n.*

ru·by (roo′bē) *n. pl.* **·bies** **1.** A translucent, deep purplish red variety of corundum, highly valued as a gemstone: also called *Oriental ruby.* **2.** A rich red color like that of a ruby. — *adj.* Pertaining to or like a ruby; being of a rich crimson. — *v.t.* **·bied, ·by·ing** To tint with the color of a ruby; redden. [< OF *rubi*, ult. < L *rubeus* red]

ruche (roosh) *n.* A quilted or ruffled strip of fine fabric, worn about the neck or wrists of a woman's costume. [< F, beehive, frill]

ruch·ing (roo′shing) *n.* Material for ruches; also, ruches collectively.

ruck·sack (ruk′sak′, rook′-) *n.* A canvas knapsack. [< G < *rucken*, var. of *rücken* back + *sack* sack]

ruck·us (ruk′əs) *n. U.S. Slang* An uproar; commotion; rumpus. [Prob. blend of RUMPUS and RUCTION]

rud·der (rud′ər) *n.* **1.** *Naut.* A broad, flat, movable device hinged vertically at the stern of a vessel to direct its course. **2.** Anything that guides or directs a course. **3.** *Aeron.* A hinged or pivoted surface, used to control the position of an aircraft about its vertical axis. [OE *rothor* oar, scull]

rud·dy (rud′ē) *adj.* **·di·er, ·di·est** **1.** Tinged with red. **2.** Having a healthy glow; rosy: a *ruddy* complexion. **3.** *Brit. Slang* Bloody: a euphemism. [OE *rudig*] — **rud′di·ly** *adv.* — **rud′di·ness** *n.*

ruddy duck A small North American duck having stiffened tail feathers and, in the adult male, a bright chestnut-colored body.

rude (rood) *adj.* **rud·er, rud·est** **1.** Offensively blunt or uncivil; rough or abrupt; impudent. **2.** Characterized by lack of polish or refinement; uncultivated; uncouth. **3.** Unskillfully made or done; crude; rough. **4.** Robust; strong. **5.** Barbarous; savage. [< OF, or < L *rudis* rough] — **rude′ly** *adv.* — **rude′ness** *n.*

ru·di·ment (roo′də·mənt) *n.* **1.** A first principle, step, stage, or condition. **2.** That which is as yet undeveloped or only partially developed. **3.** *Biol.* An undeveloped or functionless organ or part. [< F < L *rudimentum* first attempt]

ru·di·men·ta·ry (roo′də·men′tər·ē) *adj.* **1.** Pertaining to or of the nature of a rudiment or first principle; elementary. **2.** Being or remaining in an imperfectly developed state; vestigial; abortive. Also **ru′di·men′tal.** — **ru′di·men′ta·ri·ly** *adv.* — **ru′di·men′ta·ri·ness** *n.*

rue¹ (roo) *v.* **rued, ru·ing** *v.t.* **1.** To feel sorrow or remorse for. — *v.i.* **2.** To feel sorrow or remorse; be regretful. — **Syn.** See MOURN. — *n.* Sorrowful remembrance; regret. [OE *hrēowan* to be sorry] — **ru′er** *n.*

rue² (roo) *n.* **1.** A small, bushy herb with bitter, acrid leaves, formerly much used in medicine. **2.** Any bitter draft. [< F < L *ruta* < Gk. *rhytē*]

rue·ful (roo′fəl) *adj.* **1.** Feeling or causing sorrow, regret, or pity; deplorable; sorrowful. **2.** Expressing sorrow or pity. — **rue′ful·ly** *adv.* — **rue′ful·ness** *n.*

ruff¹ (ruf) *n.* **1.** A pleated, round, heavily starched collar popular in the 16th century. **2.** Ruffle¹ (defs. 1 and 2). **3.** A natural collar of projecting feathers or hair around the neck of a bird or mammal. **4.** An Old World sandpiper of which the male in the breeding season has an erectile frill of feathers about the neck. [Short for RUFFLE¹]

ruff² (ruf) *n.* The playing of a trump upon another suit when one has no cards of that suit. — *v.t. & v.i.* To trump when unable to follow suit. [< OF *roffle, rouffle, ronfle*]

ruffed (ruft) *adj.* Having a ruff, ruffle, or frill; ruffled.

ruffed grouse A North American grouse: called *partridge* in the northern and *pheasant* in the southern U.S.

ruf·fi·an (ruf′ē·ən, ruf′yən) *n.* A lawless, brutal fellow; a tough. — *adj.* Lawlessly or recklessly brutal or cruel. [< OF *ruffian*] — **ruf′fi·an·ism** *n.* — **ruf′fi·an·ly** *adj.*

ruf·fle¹ (ruf′əl) *n.* **1.** A pleated strip or frill of fabric, lace, etc., used as trim or ornament. **2.** Anything resembling such a strip. Also called *ruff.* **3.** A temporary discomposure. **4.** A slight disturbance, as a ripple. — *v.* **·fled, ·fling** *v.t.* **1.** To disturb or destroy the smoothness or regularity of. **2.** To draw into folds or ruffles; gather. **3.** To furnish with ruffles. **4.** To erect (the feathers) in a ruff. **5.** To disturb or irritate; upset. **6.** To riffle (the pages of a book). **7.** To shuffle (cards). — *v.i.* **8.** To be or become rumpled or disordered. **9.** To become disturbed or irritated. [< RUFFLE²]

ruf·fle² (ruf′əl) *n.* A low continuous beat of a drum, not as loud as a roll. — *v.t.* **·fled, ·fling** To beat a ruffle upon, as a drum. [< earlier *ruff*; prob. imit.]

ru·fous (roo′fəs) *adj.* Dull red. [< L *rufus* red]

rug (rug) *n.* **1.** A heavy textile fabric, made in one piece, to cover a portion of a floor. **2.** A covering made from the skins of animals. **3.** *Chiefly Brit.* A heavy coverlet or lap robe. [< Scand. Cf. Norw. *rugga* coarse coverlet.]

rug·by football (rug′bē) **1.** *Usu. cap. Brit.* A form of football in which the ball is propelled toward the opponents' goal by kicking or carrying. **2.** *Canadian* Football (def. 3).

rug·ged (rug′id) *adj.* **1.** Having a surface full of abrupt inequalities; broken into irregular points or crags; rough; uneven. **2.** Shaggy; unkempt; ragged. **3.** Rough in temper, character, or action. **4.** Having strongly marked features; wrinkled. **5.** Lacking culture or refinement; rude. **6.** Rough to the ear; grating. **7.** Robust; sturdy; hale. **8.** Tempestuous; stormy. [< Scand.] — **rug′ged·ly** *adv.* — **rug′ged·ness** *n.*

ru·gose (roo′gōs) *adj.* Full of wrinkles, as some leaves. Also **ru′gous** (-gəs). [< L *ruga* wrinkle]

ru·in (roo′in) *n.* **1.** Total destruction of value or usefulness. **2.** Loss of honor, position, wealth, etc.; degradation. **3.** *Often pl.* That which remains of something demolished or decayed. **4.** A condition of desolation or destruction. **5.** That which causes destruction, downfall or injury. — *v.t.* **1.** To bring to ruin; destroy. **2.** To bring to bankruptcy or poverty. **3.** To deprive of chastity; seduce. — *v.i.* **4.** To fall into ruin. — **Syn.** See DEMOLISH. [< OF < L < *ruere* to fall] — **ru′in·a·ble** *adj.* — **ru′in·er** *n.*

ru·in·a·tion (roo′in·ā′shən) *n.* **1.** The act of ruining, or the state of being ruined. **2.** Something that ruins.

ru·in·ous (roo′in·əs) *adj.* **1.** Causing or tending to ruin. **2.** Falling to ruin; decayed. — **ru′in·ous·ly** *adv.* — **ru′in·ous·ness** *n.*

rule (rool) *n.* **1.** Controlling power, or its possession and exercise; government; dominion; authority. **2.** A method or principle of action: I make early rising my *rule.* **3.** An authoritative direction or enactment respecting the doing or method of doing something: the *rules* of a game. **4.** A regulation or body of directions laid down by or for a religious order. **5.** A prescribed form, method, or set of instructions for solving a given class of mathematical problems. **6.** An established usage or law, fixing the form or use of words or the construction of sentences. **7.** Something belonging to the ordinary course of events or condition of things. **8.** Regular or proper method; propriety, as of conduct; regularity. **9.** *Law* A judicial decision on some motion or special application: a *rule* to show cause. **10.** A straightedged instrument for use in measuring, or as a guide in drawing lines. **11.** *Printing* A strip of type-high metal for handling type or for printing a rule or line. **— as a rule** Ordinarily; usually. — *v.* **ruled, rul·ing** *v.t.* **1.** To have authority or control over; govern. **2.** To influence greatly; dominate. **3.** To decide or determine judicially or authoritatively. **4.** To restrain; keep in check. **5.** To mark with straight, parallel lines. **6.** To make (a straight line) with or as with a ruler. — *v.i.* **7.** To have authority or control; be in command. **8.** To maintain a standard of rates. **9.** To form and express a decision. [< OF < L *regula* ruler, rule] — **rul′a·ble** *adj.*

rule of thumb **1.** Measurement by the thumb. **2.** Roughly practical rather than scientifically accurate measure.

rul·er (roo′lər) *n.* **1.** One who rules or governs, as a sovereign. **2.** A straight-edged instrument for use in measuring, or as a guide in drawing lines, usu. marked in inches.

rul·ing (roo′ling) *adj.* Exercising dominion; controlling; predominant. — *n.* **1.** The act of one who rules or governs. **2.** A decision, as of a judge or presiding officer.

rum¹ (rum) *n.* **1.** An alcoholic liquor distilled from fermented molasses or cane juice. **2.** Any alcoholic liquor. [Origin uncertain; ? short for obs. *rumbullion* rum]

rum² (rum) *adj. Brit. Slang* Queer; strange; peculiar. [? < Romany *rom* man]

Ru·ma·ni·an (rōō·mā'nē·ən, -mān'yən) *adj.* Of Rumania, its people, or their language. — *n.* **1.** A native or inhabitant of Rumania. **2.** The Romance language of the Rumanians.

rum·ba (rum'bə, *Sp.* rōōm'bä) *n.* **1.** A dance having its origin among Cuban Negroes. **2.** A modern ballroom dance based on this; also, music for or in the manner of such a dance. Also spelled *rhumba.* [< Am.Sp.]

rum·ble (rum'bəl) *v.* **·bled, ·bling** *v.i.* **1.** To make a low, heavy, rolling sound, as thunder. **2.** To move or proceed with such a sound. — *v.t.* **3.** To cause to make a low, heavy, rolling sound. **4.** To utter with such a sound. — *n.* **1.** A continuous low, heavy, rolling sound. **2.** A seat or baggage compartment in the rear of a carriage. **3.** A folding seat in the back of a coupé or roadster: in full **rumble seat. 4.** *U.S. Slang* A gang fight, usu. involving teenagers. [ME *romblen*] — **rum'bler** *n.* — **rum'bling·ly** *adv.* — **rum'bly** *adj.*

ru·men (rōō'men) *n. pl.* **ru·mi·na** (rōō'mə·nə) The first stomach or the cud of a ruminant. [< L gullet]

ru·mi·nant (rōō'mə·nənt) *n.* One of a division or suborder of even-toed, cud-chewing mammals, as the deer, sheep, cow, camel, etc., having a stomach with four cavities, the rumen, reticulum, omasum, and abomasum. — *adj.* **1.** Chewing the cud. **2.** Of or pertaining to a ruminant. **3.** Meditative or contemplative. [< L < *ruminare* to chew over]

ru·mi·nate (rōō'mə·nāt) *v.t. & v.i.* **·nat·ed, ·nat·ing 1.** To chew (food previously swallowed and regurgitated) over again; chew (the cud). **2.** To meditate or reflect (upon); ponder. [See RUMINANT.] — **ru'mi·nat'ing·ly** *adv.* — **ru'mi·na'tion** *n.* — **ru'mi·na'tive** *adj.* — **ru'mi·na'tive·ly** *adv.* — **ru'mi·na'tor** *n.*

rum·mage (rum'ij) *v.* **·maged, ·mag·ing** *v.t.* **1.** To search through (a place, box, etc.) by turning over and disarranging the contents; ransack. **2.** To find or bring out by searching: with *out* or *up.* — *v.i.* **3.** To make a thorough search. — *n.* **1.** Any act of rummaging. **2.** An upheaval or stirring up; bustle. [< MF < *arrumer* to stow cargo] — **rum'mag·er** *n.*

rummage sale 1. A sale of second-hand objects to obtain money for some charitable purpose. **2.** A sale of unclaimed articles, or a sale for clearing out articles prior to restocking.

rum·my[1] (rum'ē) *n.* A card game in which each player draws a card and discards another card, the object being to combine or get rid of one's hand in sequences of three cards or more of the same suit. [? < Brit. slang *rummy,* queer]

rum·my[2] (rum'ē) *n. pl.* **·mies** *Slang* A drunkard. — *adj.* **·mi·er, ·mi·est** Of or resembling rum: a *rummy* flavor.

ru·mor (rōō'mər) *n.* **1.** An unverified or unfounded report, story, etc., circulating from person to person. **2.** Common gossip; hearsay. — *v.t.* To tell or spread as a rumor; noise about. Also *Brit.* **ru'mour.** [< OF < L]

rump (rump) *n.* **1.** The rounded or fleshy upper part of the hind quarters of an animal. **2.** The analogous region in man; the buttocks. **3.** A cut of beef between the loin and the round. **4.** A legislative group, representative body, etc., having only a remnant of its original membership, and therefore regarded as unauthoritative. **5.** A last, often undesirable remnant. [ME *rumpe* < Scand.]

rum·ple (rum'pəl) *v.t. & v.i.* **·pled, ·pling** To form into creases or folds; wrinkle; ruffle. — *n.* **1.** An irregular fold; untidy wrinkling. **2.** The condition of being rumpled. [< MDu. *rumpelen*]

rum·pus (rum'pəs) *n. Informal* A row; wrangle; to-do. [Origin uncertain]

rumpus room A room for games, informal gatherings, etc.

rum·run·ner (rum'run'ər) *n.* A person or ship illicitly transporting alcoholic liquors across a border.

run (run) *v.* **ran** (*Archaic* or *Dial.* **run**), **run, run·ning** *v.i.* **1.** To move by rapid steps, faster than walking, in such a manner that both feet are off the ground for a portion of each step. **2.** To move rapidly; go swiftly. **3.** To flee; take flight. **4.** To make a brief or rapid journey. **5.** To make regular trips; ply. **6.** To be a candidate or contestant. **7.** To finish a race in a specified position. **8.** To move or pass easily: The rope *runs* through the block. **9.** To elapse: The hours *run* by. **10.** To proceed in direction or extent: This road *runs* north. **11.** To move in or as in a stream; flow. **12.** To become liquid and flow, as wax; also, to spread or mingle confusedly, as colors when wet. **13.** To move or pass into a specified condition: to *run* into trouble. **14.** To climb or grow in long shoots, as vines. **15.** To become torn by unraveling, as a knitted fabric. **16.** To suppurate. **17.** To leak. **18.** To continue or proceed: The conversation *ran* on and on. **19.** To be in operation; be operative; work: Will the engine *run?* **20.** To continue in existence or effect; extend in time: Genius *runs* in her family. **21.** To be reported or expressed: The story *runs* as follows. **22.** To migrate, as salmon from the sea. **23.** To occur or return, as to the mind. **24.** To incline; tend: Her taste *runs* to luxuries. **25.** To be performed or repeated in continuous succession, as a play. **26.** To make a rapid succession of demands for payment, as on a bank. **27.** To continue unexpired or unpaid, as a debt;

become payable. — *v.t.* **28.** To go along by running, as a route, course, or path. **29.** To make one's way over, through, or past: to *run* rapids. **30.** To perform or accomplish by or as by running: to *run* an errand. **31.** To compete against in or as in a race. **32.** To enter (a horse, etc.) for a race. **33.** To present and support as a candidate. **34.** To hunt or chase, as game. **35.** To bring to a specified condition by or as by running: to *run* oneself out of breath. **36.** To drive or force: with *out of, off, into, through,* etc. **37.** To cause (a vessel) to move rapidly or freely. **38.** To move (the eye, hand, etc.) quickly or lightly. **39.** To cause to move, slide, etc., as into a specified position. **40.** To cause to go or ply: to *run* a train. **41.** To transport or convey in a vessel or vehicle. **42.** To smuggle. **43.** To cause to flow. **44.** To give forth a flow of, emit: Her eyes *ran* tears. **45.** To mold, as from melted metal. **46.** To sew or stitch in a continuous line. **47.** To maintain or control the motion or operation of, as a machine. **48.** To direct or control; manage; oversee. **49.** To allow to continue or mount up, as a bill: often with *up.* **50.** To become liable to; incur: to *run* a risk. **51.** In games, to make (a number of points, strokes, etc.) successively. **52.** To publish in a magazine or newspaper: to *run* an ad. **53.** To mark, set down, or trace, as a boundary line. **54.** To suffer from (a fever, etc.). — **to run across** To meet by chance. — **to run down 1.** To pursue and overtake, as a fugitive. **2.** To strike down while moving. **3.** To speak of disparagingly; decry. — **to run in 1.** To insert; include. **2.** *Printing* To print without a paragraph or break. **3.** *Slang* To arrest and place in confinement. — **to run into 1.** To meet by chance. **2.** To collide with. — **to run off 1.** To produce on a typewriter, printing press, etc. **2.** To decide (a tied race, game, etc.) by the outcome of another, subsequent race, game, etc. **3.** To flee or escape; elope. — **to run out** To come to an end; be exhausted, as supplies. — **run out of** To exhaust one's supply of. — **to run over 1.** To ride or drive over; run down. **2.** To overflow. **3.** To go over or examine hastily or quickly; rehearse. — **to run through 1.** To spend wastefully; squander. **2.** To stab or pierce. **3.** To run over (def. 3). — **to run up** To produce; make hurriedly, as on a sewing machine. — *n.* **1.** An act or instance of running or going rapidly. **2.** The movement or gait of running: to break into a *run.* **3.** A distance covered by running. **4.** A distance traveled between two points, as by a train or vessel. **5.** A rapid, brief journey. **6.** A course or route followed, as in reaching a destination. **7.** The privilege of free use or access: to have the *run* of the place. **8.** A series, succession, or sequence, as of playing cards in consecutive order. **9.** A continuous spell of a specified condition: a *run* of luck. **10.** A continuous period of consecutive performances, as of a theatrical production. **11.** A trend or tendency: the *run* of the market. **12.** A broadly inclusive category, type, or class: the general *run* of readers. **13.** A period of continuous operation, as of a machine or factory. **14.** The output during such a period. **15.** A continuous length or extent of something: a *run* of pipe. **16.** A lengthwise rip in knitted fabric. **17.** Characteristic direction, tendency, or linear form: the *run* of the grain in wood. **18.** Flowing movement, as of a stream. **19.** The period of such flow. **20.** A swift stream or current. **21.** Mass migration or movement of animals, esp. of fish to spawn. **22.** A trail, burrow, or terrain frequented by a specific kind of animal. **23.** An enclosure for animals or poultry. **24.** A steep course or runway, as for skiing or sledding. **25.** An unusually large number of demands for payment, as on a bank. **26.** Any great sustained demand, as for a commodity. **27.** *Music* A rapid succession of tones. **28.** In baseball, the scoring of a point by a player's making a complete circuit of the bases; also, a point so scored. **29.** In football, the ball carrier's attempt to run through or around the line of the opposing team. **30.** In cricket, the scoring of a point by both batsmen successfully reaching opposite popping creases after a hit. **31.** *Naut.* The after part of a ship's bottom. **32.** *Mining* A vein of ore or rock. **33.** An approach to a target made by a bombing plane: also *bomb run.* — **a run for one's money** A successful or satisfactory instance of activity, esp. in competition. — **in the long run** As the ultimate outcome of any train of circumstances. — *adj.* **1.** Made liquid; melted. **2.** Made by a process of melting and casting or molding: *run* metal; *run* butter. [OE *rinnan*]

run·a·bout (run'ə·bout') *n.* **1.** A small, open automobile. **2.** A light, open wagon. **3.** A small motorboat.

run·a·round (run'ə·round') *n.* **1.** *Slang* Artful deception; evasion. **2.** *Printing* Type set narrower than the body of the text, as around illustrations.

run·a·way (run'ə·wā') *adj.* **1.** Escaping or escaped from restraint or control; fugitive. **2.** Brought about by running away: a *runaway* marriage. **3.** Easily won as a horse race. **4.** Of, pertaining to, or characterized by a rapid price rise. — *n.* **1.** One who or that which runs away; also, a horse whose driver has lost control. **2.** An act of running away. **3.** *Informal* An easily won victory, as in a race.

run·down (run'doun')   *n.* A summary; resumé.
run·down (run'doun')   *adj.* **1.** Debilitated; physically weak; tired out. **2.** Dilapidated; shabby. **3.** Stopped because not wound: said of a timepiece.
rune (rōōn)   *n.* **1.** Any of the characters in the runic alphabet. **2.** A Finnish poem or one of its cantos. **3.** *pl.* Old Norse lore expressed in or as in runes. **4.** Any obscure or mystic song, poem, verse, or saying. [< OE and ON *rūn* mystery, secret conversation] — **ru'nic** *adj.*

RUNES
(Tomb inscription, Sweden, 11th century)

rung[1] (rung)   *n.* **1.** A round crosspiece forming one of the steps of a ladder. **2.** A crosspiece used in chairs to strengthen or support the legs or back. **3.** The spoke of a wheel. [OE *hrung* staff, pole]
rung[2] (rung)   Past participle of RING[2].
runic alphabet An old Germanic alphabet, probably originating in both the Latin and Greek, consisting originally of 24 characters, or runes.
run-in (*n.* run'in'; *adj.* run'in')   *n.* **1.** A quarrel; bicker. **2.** *Printing* Inserted or added matter. — *adj. Printing* Inserted or added.
run·nel (run'əl)   *n.* A rivulet. [OE *rynel* < *rinnan* to run]
run·ner (run'ər)   *n.* **1.** One who or that which runs, as one who runs a race. **2.** One who operates or manages anything. **3.** One who runs errands or goes about on any kind of business. **4.** That part on which an object runs or slides: the *runner* of a skate. **5.** *Mech.* A device to assist sliding motion. **6.** Any of various fishes of warm and temperate seas. **7.** *Bot.* **a** A slender, procumbent stem rooting at the end and nodes, as in the strawberry. **b** Any of various twining plants. **8.** A smuggler. **9.** A long, narrow rug or carpeting, used in hallways, etc. **10.** A narrow strip of cloth, used on tables, dressers, etc.
run·ner-up (run'ər-up')   *n.* A contestant or team finishing in second place.
run·ning (run'ing)   *adj.* **1.** Moving or going rapidly. **2.** Inclined or trained to run rather than to pace or trot: said of horses. **3.** Creeping or clinging, as a plant. **4.** Flowing: *running water.* **5.** Slipping or untying easily: a *running* knot. **6.** Moving or pulling easily and freely: a *running* rope. **7.** Being or able to be in operation: a *running* engine. **8.** Cursive: a *running* handwriting. **9.** Liquid or fluid. **10.** Discharging, as pus from a sore. **11.** In a straight line: three feet *running.* **12.** Current, as an account. **13.** Continuous; repeated: a *running* design. **14.** Kept up continuously. **15.** Passing; cursory: a *running* glance. **16.** Following one another without intermission; successive: He talked three hours *running.* **17.** Accomplished or performed with a run. **18.** Of or pertaining to a trip or run: the train's *running* time. — *n.* **1.** The act of one who or that which runs. **2.** That which runs or flows. **3.** The amount or quantity that runs. **4.** Ability or power to run. **5.** Competition or race: He is out of the *running.*
running board A footboard on the side of a locomotive, street car, automobile, etc.
running gear *Mech.* The wheels and axles of any vehicle and their immediate attachments, as distinguished from the body that they support.
running knot A knot made so as to slip along a noose and tighten when pulled upon: also called *slipknot.*
running light *Aeron.* A navigation light.
running mate The candidate for the lesser of two offices closely linked by constitutional provisions, as the vice-presidency with the presidency.
running title *Printing* A title or headline repeated at the head of every page or every other page throughout a book or chapter. Also **running head.**
Run·ny·mede (run'i-mēd)   A meadow in Surrey, England, where King John is said to have signed the Magna Carta.
run·off (run'ôf', -of')   *n.* **1.** The part of the rainfall that is not absorbed directly by the soil but is drained off in rills or streams. **2.** A special contest held to break a tie.
run-of-the-mill (run'əv-thə-mil')   *adj.* Not special in any way; average; ordinary. Also **run-of-the-mine.**
run-on (run'on', -ôn')   *n. Printing* Appended matter.
runt (runt)   *n.* **1.** An unusually small, weak, or stunted animal or plant. **2.** A small person: often a contemptuous term. [< Scot. *runt* old cow]
runt·y (run'tē)   *adj.* **runt·i·er, runt·i·est** Dwarfish; stunted. — **runt'i·ness** *n.*
run·way (run'wā')   *n.* **1.** A way or path over or through which something runs. **2.** A pathway extending from a

stage into the audience, used for certain types of theatrical entertainment. **3.** The channel or bed of a stream. **4.** In lumbering, a chute. **5.** Any track specially laid for wheeled vehicles. **6.** *Aeron.* An improved or unimproved roadlike surface, used for the takeoff and landing of aircraft.
ru·pee (rōō-pē')   *n.* **1.** The standard monetary unit of various countries; esp., the rupee of India and Pakistan, in 1960 worth about 21 U.S. cents. **2.** A coin of this denomination. [< Hind. < Skt. *rūpya* coined silver]
rup·ture (rup'chər)   *n.* **1.** The act of breaking apart, or the state of being broken apart. **2.** *Pathol.* Hernia. **3.** Breach of friendship or concord between individuals or nations. — *v.t. & v.i.* **·tured, ·tur·ing** **1.** To break apart; separate into parts. **2.** To affect with or suffer a rupture. [< Med.L *ruptura* < *rumpere* to break] — **rup'tur·a·ble** *adj.*
ru·ral (rōōr'əl)   *adj.* **1.** Of or pertaining to the country as distinguished from the city or the town; rustic. **2.** Of or pertaining to farming or agriculture. [< MF < L < *rus, ruris* country] — **ru'ral·ism** *n.* — **ru'ral·ist** *n.* — **ru'ral·ly** *adv.*
— **Syn. 1.** Rustic, pastoral, bucolic. — **Ant.** urban.
rural free delivery A government service of house-to-house free mail delivery in rural districts.
ru·ral·i·ty (rōō-ral'ə-tē)   *n. pl.* **·ties** **1.** The condition or quality of being rural. **2.** A rural characteristic.
ru·ral·ize (rōōr'əl-īz)   *v.* **·ized, ·iz·ing** *v.t.* **1.** To make rural. — *v.i.* **2.** To go into or live in the country; rusticate. — **ru'ral·i·za'tion** *n.*
ruse (rōōz)   *n.* An action intended to mislead or deceive; a stratagem; trick. [< MF *ruser* to turn aside.]
rush[1] (rush)   *v.i.* **1.** To move or go swiftly or with violence. **2.** To make an attack; charge: with *on* or *upon.* **3.** To proceed recklessly or rashly; plunge: with *in* or *into.* **4.** To come, surge, flow, etc., suddenly. — *v.t.* **5.** To drive or push with haste or violence; hurry. **6.** To do or perform hastily or hurriedly. **7.** To make a sudden assault upon; also, to capture by such an assault. **8.** *Slang* To seek the favor of with assiduous attentions. **9.** In football, to move (the ball) toward the goal of the other team by a run or rushes. **10.** *U.S.* To consider for membership in a fraternity or sorority. — *n.* **1.** The act of rushing; a sudden turbulent movement, drive, or onset. **2.** A state of pressed or impatient activity; hurry. **3.** A sudden surge, flow, or outpouring. **4.** A sudden pressing demand. **5.** A sudden or urgent press of traffic, business, etc. **6.** A sudden flocking of people to a new region, esp. to an area rumored to be rich in a precious mineral: a gold *rush.* **7.** *U.S.* A general contest or scrimmage between students, as between sophomores and freshmen. **8.** In football, an attempt to take the ball through the opposing linemen and toward the goal. **9.** *pl.* In motion pictures, the first film prints of a scene or series of scenes, before editing or selection. — *adj.* **1.** Requiring urgency or haste: a *rush* order. **2.** Characterized by much traffic, business, etc. **3.** *U.S.* Denoting a time or function set aside for fraternity or sorority members to meet new students to consider them for membership: *rush* week. [< AF < OF *ruser, reuser* to push back < L *recusare* to refuse] — **rush'er** *n.*
rush[2] (rush)   *n.* **1.** Any one of various grasslike, usu. aquatic herbs, growing in marshy ground and having pliant, cylindrical, leafless stems, often used for making mats, etc. **2.** A thing of little or no value. **3.** A rushlight. [OE *risc*]
rush hour A time when traffic or business is at its height. — **rush-hour** (rush'our') *adj.*
rush·light (rush'līt')   *n.* A candle made by dipping a rush in tallow. Also **rush candle.**
rush·y (rush'ē)   *adj.* **rush·i·er, rush·i·est** **1.** Abounding in, covered with, or made of rushes. **2.** Like a rush.
rusk (rusk)   *n.* **1.** A light, sweetened bread or biscuit. **2.** Bread or cake that has been crisped and browned in an oven. [< Sp. *rosca,* twisted loaf of bread]
rus·set (rus'it)   *n.* **1.** A reddish or yellowish brown. **2.** Coarse homespun cloth or clothing of this color. **3.** Russet leather. **4.** A winter apple of greenish color, mottled with brown. — *adj.* **1.** Of a reddish or yellowish brown color. **2.** Made of russet cloth; also, coarse; homespun. **3.** Finished, but not blacked: said of leather. [< OF < L *russus* red]
Rus·sian (rush'ən)   *adj.* Of or pertaining to Russia, its people, or their language. — *n.* **1.** A native or citizen of the Soviet Union or the former Russian Empire; esp., a Great Russian, Ukrainian, or Byelorussian. **2.** The East Slavic language of Russia, including Great Russian, Ukrainian, and Byelorussian.
Russian dressing Mayonnaise dressing to which chili sauce, pimientos, chopped pickles, etc., have been added.
Rus·sian·ize (rush'ən-īz)   *v.t.* **·ized, ·iz·ing** To make Russian in manner, character, etc.
Russian leather A smooth, well-tanned, high-grade leather of calfskin or light cattle hide, dressed with birch oil.

Russian Orthodox Church An autonomous branch of the Eastern Orthodox Church in the Soviet Union, under the patriarch of Moscow.

Russian Revolution See under REVOLUTION.

Russian roulette A suicidal stunt in which one aims a revolver containing one cartridge at one's head and pulls the trigger, with one chance in six of being shot.

Russian wolfhound The borzoi.

Russo- *combining form* Russia; pertaining to the Russians.

Russo-Japanese War (rus/ō·jap/ə·nēz/, -nēs/) See table for WAR.

Rus·so·pho·bi·a (rus/ə·fō/bē·ə) *n.* Fear of the policy or influence of Russia. — **Rus/so·phobe** *n.*

rust (rust) *n.* 1. The reddish or yellow coating formed on iron and steel by exposure to air and moisture, consisting of ferric hydroxide, $Fe(OH)_3$, and ferric oxide, Fe_2O_3. 2. Any film formed on the surface of a metal by oxidation. 3. A disease caused by a parasitic fungi living on the tissues of higher plants and characterized by the appearance of orange or reddish brown spots on the host plant. 4. Any coating or accretion formed by a corrosive or degenerative process. 5. A condition or tendency that destroys or weakens energy or active qualities: the *rust* of idleness. 6. Any of several shades of reddish brown, somewhat like the color of rust, but containing more orange. — *v.t. & v.i.* 1. To become or cause to become rusty. 2. To contract or cause to contract rust. 3. To become or cause to become weakened or impaired because of inactivity or disuse. 4. To make or become rust-colored. [OE *rūst*]

rus·tic (rus/tik) *adj.* 1. Typical of or appropriate to simple country life. 2. Plain; simple; homely: *rustic* garments. 3. Uncultured; rude; awkward. 4. Unaffected; artless: *rustic* simplicity. 5. Of or pertaining to any irregular style of work or decoration appropriate to the country; also, of or pertaining to work in natural, unpolished wood. — **Syn.** See RURAL. — *n.* 1. One who lives in the country. 2. A country person of simple manners or character; also, a coarse or clownish person. 3. Rusticwork. 4. Country dialect. [< L < *rus* country] — **rus/ti·cal·ly** *adv.*

rus·ti·cate (rus/tə·kāt) *v.* **·cat·ed**, **·cat·ing** *v.i.* 1. To go to the country. 2. To stay or live in the country. — *v.t.* 3. To send or banish to the country. 4. To make rustic. 5. To construct (masonry) with rusticwork. — **rus/ti·ca/tion** *n.* — **rus/ti·ca/tor** *n.*

rus·tic·i·ty (rus·tis/ə·tē) *n.*, *pl.* **·ties** 1. Rustic condition, character, or manners; simplicity; homeliness; awkwardness. 2. A rustic trait or peculiarity.

rus·tic·work (rus/tik·wûrk/) *n.* 1. Ashlar masonry having rough surfaces, and often deeply sunk grooves at the joints. 2. Furniture, etc., made of the natural limbs and roots of trees. Also **rustic work.**

rus·tle¹ (rus/əl) *v.t. & v.i.* **·tled**, **·tling** To fall, move, or cause to move with a quick succession of small, light, rubbing sounds, as dry leaves or sheets of paper. — *n.* A rustling sound. [ME *rustel*, alter. of OE *hruxlian* to make a noise] — **rus/tler** *n.* — **rus/tling·ly** *adv.*

rus·tle² (rus/əl) *v.t. & v.i.* **·tled**, **·tling** 1. *Informal* To act with or obtain by energetic or vigorous action. 2. *U.S. Informal* To steal (cattle, etc.). [Blend of RUSH and HUSTLE]

rus·tler (rus/lər) *n.* *U.S. Informal* 1. A cattle or horse thief. 2. A pushing, energetic person.

rust·y (rus/tē) *adj.* **rust·i·er**, **rust·i·est** 1. Covered or affected with rust. 2. Consisting of or produced by rust. 3. Having the reddish or yellowish appearance of rust: said often of salted fish or meat that has become rancid. 4. Impaired by inaction or want of exercise; also, stiff. 5. Ineffective or weakened through neglect; also, having lost skill for want of practice. 6. *Biol.* Appearing as if covered with rust; brownish red. — **rust/i·ly** *adv.* — **rust/i·ness** *n.*

rut¹ (rut) *n.* 1. A sunken track worn by a wheel, as in a road; also, a groove forming a path for anything. 2. A settled habit or course of procedure; routine. — *v.t.* **rut·ted, rut·ting** To wear or make a rut or ruts in. [Var. of ROUTE]

rut² (rut) *n.* 1. The sexual excitement of various animals, esp. of deer and other ruminants; estrus. 2. The period during which this excitement lasts. — *v.* **rut·ted, rut·ting** *v.i.* To be in rut. [< MF < L < *rugire* to roar]

ru·ta·ba·ga (rōō/tə·bā/gə) *n.* 1. A cultivated plant allied to the turnip. 2. Its edible root. [< dial. Sw. *rotabagge*]

ruth (rōōth) *n.* *Archaic* 1. Compassion; pity. 2. Grief; repentance; regret. [ME < OE *hrēow* sad]

Ruth (rōōth) A widow of Moab who left her own people and went with her mother-in-law Naomi to Bethlehem. — *n.* The book of the Old Testament in which this story is told.

Ru·the·ni·an (rōō·thē/nē·ən) *n.* 1. One of a group of Ukrainians living in eastern Czechoslovakia and the Transcarpathian Oblast, formerly Ruthenia. 2. The Ukrainian language. — *adj.* Of or pertaining to the Ruthenians or their language.

ru·the·ni·um (rōō·thē/nē·əm) *n.* A gray, brittle, rare metallic element (symbol Ru) of the platinum group. See ELEMENT. [< NL, after *Ruthenia*]

ruth·less (rōōth/lis) *adj.* Having no compassion; merciless. [< RUTH] — **ruth/less·ly** *adv.* — **ruth/less·ness** *n.*

rut·tish (rut/ish) *adj.* Disposed to rut; lustful; libidinous.

rut·ty (rut/ē) *adj.* **·ti·er**, **·ti·est** Full of ruts. — **rut/ti·ness** *n.*

-ry Var. of -ERY.

rye (rī) *n.* 1. The grain or seeds of a hardy cereal grass closely allied to wheat, used in the making of flour and whisky, and as a feed for livestock. 2. The plant. 3. Whisky distilled from rye or partly from rye. [OE *ryge*]

rye grass Darnel.

S

s, S (es) *n.*, *pl.* **s's** or **ss, S's** or **Ss, ess·es** (es/iz) 1. The 19th letter of the English alphabet. 2. The sound represented by the letter s, usu. a voiceless sibilant, but often voiced between vowels, as in *easy*. — *symbol* 1. Anything shaped like an S. 2. *Chem.* Sulfur (symbol S).

s- *Chem.* Symmetrical.

-s¹ A variant of *-es¹*, inflectional ending of the plurals of nouns, attached to nouns not ending in a sibilant or an affricate: *books, words, cars.* It represents (s) after a voiceless consonant, and (z) after a voiced consonant or a vowel. Compare -ES¹.

-s² An inflectional ending used to form the third person singular present indicative of verbs not ending in a sibilant, affricate, or vowel: *reads, walks, sings.* Compare -ES².

-s *suffix* On; of a; at: often used in adverbs without appreciable force: *nights, Mondays, always, towards.* [OE *-es*, forming adverbial genitives]

-'s¹ An inflectional ending used to form the possessive of singular nouns and of plural nouns not ending in *-s*: a *man's* world, *women's* fashions. In plurals ending in *-s* (or *-es*) a simple apostrophe is used as a sign of the possessive: a *girls'* school, the *churches'* steeples.

-'s² Contraction of: **a** Is: *He's* here. **b** Has: *She's* left. **c** Us: *Let's* go.

Sa *Chem.* Samarium.

Sab·ba·tar·i·an (sab/ə·târ/ē·ən) *adj.* Pertaining to the Sabbath or its strict observance. — *n.* 1. A Christian who observes Sunday strictly. 2. A Christian who observes the seventh day as the Sabbath. — **Sab/ba·tar/i·an·ism** *n.*

Sab·bath (sab/əth) *n.* 1. The seventh day of the week, appointed in the Decalogue as a day of rest to be observed by the Jews; now, Saturday. 2. The first day of the week as observed by Christians; Sunday. 3. The institution or observance of a day of rest; a time of rest, peace, or quiet. 4. The sabbatical year of the Jews. *Lev.* xxv 4. [Fusion of OE *sabat* and OF *sabbat, sabat*, both < L *sabbatum* < Gk. < Hebrew *shābath* to rest] — **Sab·bat/ic** or **·i·cal** *adj.* — **Sab·bat/i·cal·ly** *adv.*

sab·bat·i·cal (sə·bat/i·kəl) *adj.* Of the nature of the Sabbath as a day of rest; offering rest at regular intervals. Also **sab·bat/ic.** — *n.* A sabbatical year. [See SABBATH]

sabbatical year 1. In the ancient Jewish economy, every seventh year, in which the people were required to refrain from tillage. 2. A year's vacation awarded to teachers in some American educational institutions every seven years.

sa·ber (sā/bər) *n.* 1. A heavy one-edged cavalry sword, with a thick-backed blade, often curved. 2. In fencing, a light swordlike instrument, used for both thrusting and slashing, hits being scored with the point or either edge. — *v.t.* To strike, wound, or kill with a saber. Also, *Brit.*, **sabre.** [< F < G, prob. < Hung. *szabni* to cut]

Sa·bine (sā/bīn) *n.* One of an ancient central Italian people, conquered and absorbed by Rome in 290 B.C. — *adj.* Of or pertaining to the Sabines.

sa·ble (sā′bəl) *n.* **1.** A carnivore of northern Asia and Europe, related to the marten and prized for its valuable fur. **2.** The dressed fur of a sable, esp. of the Asian sable. **3.** *pl.* Garments made wholly or partly of this fur. **4.** The color black; also, mourning or a mourning garment. — *adj.* **1.** Black, esp. as the color of mourning. **2.** Made of or having the color of sable fur; dark brown. [< OF < Med.L *sabelum*]

sa·bot (sab′ō, *Fr.* sȧ·bō′) *n.* **1.** A wooden shoe. **2.** A shoe having a wooden sole but flexible shank. [< F < OF *savate*, ult. < Arabic *sabbat* sandal]

sab·o·tage (sab′ə·täzh, *Fr.* sȧ·bô·tȧzh′) *n.* An act of malicious damage or destruction, as one intended to obstruct the production of war materiel by the enemy. — *v.* **·taged, ·tag·ing** *v.i.* **1.** To engage in sabotage. — *v.t.* **2.** To damage or destroy by sabotage. [< F < *sabot* sabot; with ref. to damage done to machinery with sabots]

sab·o·teur (sab′ə·tûr′, *Fr.* sȧ·bô·tœr′) *n.* One who engages in sabotage. [< F]

sa·bra (sä′brə) *n.* A native Israeli. [< Hebrew, cactus]

sa·bre (sā′bər) See SABER.

sac (sak) *n. Biol.* A membranous pouch or receptacle in an animal or plant, as for containing a liquid: the ink *sac* of a squid. [< F < L *saccus* sack¹]

Sac (sak, sôk) See SAUK.

sac·cha·ride (sak′ə·rīd, -rid) *n. Chem.* Any of a large group of carbohydrates containing sugar, usu. classified as *monosaccharide, disaccharide,* etc.

sac·cha·rin (sak′ər·in) *n. Chem.* A white crystalline coal-tar compound, $C_7H_5O_3NS$, from 300 to 500 times sweeter than cane sugar, used as a noncaloric sweetening agent. [< L < Gk. ult. < Skt. *sharkarā* grit, sugar]

sac·cha·rine (sak′ər·in, -ə·rīn) *adj.* **1.** Of, pertaining to, or of the nature of sugar; sweet. **2.** Cloyingly sweet: a *saccharine* manner. — *n.* Saccharin. — **sac·cha·rine·ly** *adv.* — **sac′cha·rin′i·ty** *n.*

saccharo- *combining form* Sugar; of or pertaining to sugar. Also, before vowels, **sacchar-.** [See SACCHARIN]

sac·cha·rose (sak′ə·rōs) *n.* Sucrose.

sac·er·do·tal (sas′ər·dōt′l) *adj.* **1.** Pertaining to a priest or priesthood; priestly. **2.** Believing in the divine authority of the priesthood. [< MF < L *sacerdos, -dotis* priest] — **sac′er·do′tal·ly** *adv.*

sac·er·do·tal·ism (sas′ər·dōt′l·iz′əm) *n.* **1.** The character and methods of the priesthood, priestcraft. **2.** Zeal for priestly things.

sa·chem (sā′chəm) *n.* A North American Indian hereditary chief. [< Algonquian (Narraganset)]

sa·chet (sa·shā′, *esp. Brit.* sash′ā) *n.* A small ornamental bag for perfumed powder. [< MF, dim. of *sac* sack]

sack¹ (sak) *n.* **1.** A bag for holding bulky articles. **2.** A measure or weight of varying amount. **3.** A loose jacket-like garment, worn by women and babies: also **sacque.** **4.** *Slang* Dismissal: esp. in the phrases **to get the sack, to give (someone) the sack. 5.** In baseball slang, a base. **6.** *U.S. Slang* A bed; mattress. — **to hit the sack** *U.S. Slang* To go to bed. — **to sack out** *U.S. Slang* To go to bed. — *v.t.* **1.** To put into a sack or sacks. **2.** To dismiss, as a servant. [OE < L < Gk. < Hebrew *saq* sack, sackcloth]

sack² (sak) *v.t.* To plunder or pillage (a town or city) after capturing. — *n.* **1.** The pillaging of a captured town or city. **2.** Loot or booty obtained by pillage. [< MF *sac* < Ital. *sacco,* orig., plunder < Med.L < L *saccus* sack¹] — **sack′er** *n.*

sack³ (sak) *n.* Light-colored Spanish dry wine; also, any strong white wine from southern Europe. [Earlier (*wyne*) *seck* < F (*vin*) *sec* dry (wine) < L *siccus* dry]

sack·but (sak′but) *n.* **1.** An early instrument resembling the trombone. **2.** In the Bible, a stringed instrument. [< MF < OF *saquer* to draw + *bouter* to push]

sack·cloth (sak′klôth′, -kloth′) *n.* **1.** A coarse cloth used for making sacks. **2.** Coarse cloth or haircloth worn in penance. — **in sackcloth and ashes 1.** In the Bible, wearing garments of sackcloth and sprinkling ashes on one's head as marks of penance or sorrow. **2.** In any state of sorrow, penance, or self-abasement.

sack coat A short, loose-fitting coat with no waist seam.

sack·ful (sak′fool) *n. pl.* **·fuls** Enough to fill a sack.

sack·ing (sak′ing) *n.* A coarse cloth made of hemp or flax and used for sacks.

sack race A race run with the feet in a sack.

sa·cral¹ (sā′krəl) *adj.* Of, pertaining to, or situated near the sacrum. — *n.* A sacral vertebra or nerve.

sa·cral² (sā′krəl) *adj.* Pertaining to sacred rites. [< L *sacrum* rite < *sacer* sacred]

sac·ra·ment (sak′rə·mənt) *n.* **1.** *Eccl.* Any of certain rites ordained by Christ by the church, as baptism; the Eu-

charist, confirmation, etc. **2.** *Often cap. Eccl.* **a** The Eucharist; the Lord's Supper. **b** The consecrated bread and wine of the Eucharist: often with *the.* **3.** Any sign or token of a solemn covenant or pledge. **4.** Anything considered to have a secret or mysterious meaning. [< OF < L *sacrare* to consecrate]

sac·ra·men·tal (sak′rə·men′təl) *n.* **1.** One of certain rites, such as the use of holy water, oil, or salt, employed as adjuncts to sacraments, or regarded as analogous to a sacrament. **2.** *pl.* The objects, words, or ceremonies used in administering a sacrament. — *adj.* **1.** Of or pertaining to a sacrament. **2.** Constituting or composing a sacrament. **3.** Having the influence or efficacy of a sacrament. **4.** Consecrated, as by sacred vows. — **sac′ra·men′tal·ism** *n.* — **sac′ra·men′tal·ist** *n.* — **sac′ra·men′tal·ly** *adv.*

sa·cred (sā′krid) *adj.* **1.** Set apart or dedicated to religious use; hallowed. **2.** Pertaining or related to deity, religion, or hallowed places or things. **3.** Consecrated or dedicated to a person or purpose. **4.** Entitled to reverence or respect; not to be profaned; inviolable. [< OF < L *sacrare* to treat as sacred] — **sa′cred·ly** *adv.* — **sa′cred·ness** *n.*

Sacred College The College of Cardinals.

sacred cow 1. *U.S. Informal* Something or someone regarded as above criticism or reproach. **2.** A cow when considered sacred, as by the Hindus.

sac·ri·fice (sak′rə·fīs) *n.* **1.** The act of making an offering to a deity, in worship or atonement; also, that which is so offered. **2.** A giving up of some cherished or desired object, person, idea, etc., usu. for the sake of something else; also, that which is so given up. **3.** Loss incurred or suffered without return. **4.** A reduction of price that leaves little or no profit or involves loss. **5.** In baseball, a sacrifice hit. — *v.* **·ficed, ·fic·ing** *v.t.* **1.** To make an offering or sacrifice of, as to a god or deity. **2.** To give up, yield, permit injury to, or relinquish (something valued) for the sake of something else, as a person, thing, or idea. **3.** To sell at a reduced price; part with at a loss. **4.** In baseball, to advance (one or more runners) by means of a sacrifice hit. — *v.i.* **5.** To make a sacrifice. **6.** To make a sacrifice hit. [< OF < L *sacer* sacred + *facere* to perform, do] — **sac′ri·fic′er** *n.* — **sac′ri·fic′ing·ly** *adv.*

sacrifice fly In baseball, a fly ball hit with less than two out that enables a runner on third base to score after the catch.

sacrifice hit In baseball, a bunt made with less than two out that enables a runner or runners to advance a base while the batter is being retired. Also **sacrifice bunt.**

sac·ri·fi·cial (sak′rə·fish′əl) *adj.* Of, pertaining to, performing, or like a sacrifice. — **sac′ri·fi′cial·ly** *adv.*

sac·ri·lege (sak′rə·lij) *n.* The act of violating or profaning anything sacred, including sacramental vows. [< OF < L < *sacer, sacris* sacred + *legere* to gather, steal] — **sac′ri·le′gist** (-lē′jist) *n.*

sac·ri·le·gious (sak′rə·lij′əs, -lē′jəs) *adj.* **1.** Having committed sacrilege; impious. **2.** Of, pertaining to, or like sacrilege. — **sac′ri·le′gious·ly** *adv.* — **sac′ri·le′gious·ness** *n.*

sac·ris·tan (sak′ris·tən) *n.* An officer having charge of the sacristy of a church. [< Med.L < L *sacer, sacris* sacred]

sac·ris·ty (sak′ris·tē) *n. pl.* **·ties** A room in a religious house for the sacred vessels and vestments; vestry.

sacro- *combining form Med.* Near, or related to the sacrum. [< L (*os*) *sacrum* the sacral (bone)]

sac·ro·il·i·ac (sak′rō·il′ē·ak) *adj. Anat.* Pertaining to the sacrum and the ilium and to the joints or ligaments connecting them. [< SACRO- + ILIAC]

sac·ro·sanct (sak′rō·sangkt) *adj.* Peculiarly and exceedingly sacred; inviolable: sometimes used ironically. [< L < *sacro,* ablative of *sacrum* rite + *sanctus,* pp. of *sancire* to make holy, inviolable] — **sac′ro·sanc′ti·ty** *n.*

sa·crum (sā′krəm) *n. pl.* **·cra** (-krə) *Anat.* A composite bone formed by the union of the five vertebrae between the lumbar and caudal regions, constituting the dorsal part of the pelvis. For illus. see PELVIS. [< NL < L (*os*) *sacrum* sacred (bone); from its use in sacrifices]

sad (sad) *adj.* **sad·der, sad·dest 1.** Sorrowful or depressed in spirits. **2.** Causing sorrow or pity; unfortunate. **3.** *Informal* Pitifully inadequate; bad; contemptible. **4.** Dark-hued; somber. [OE *sæd,* orig., sated] — **sad′ly** *adv.* — **sad′ness** *n.*

sad·den (sad′n) *v.t. & v.i.* To make or become sad.

sad·dle (sad′l) *n.* **1.** A seat or pad for a rider, as on the back of a horse or on a bicycle. **2.** A padded cushion for a horse's back, used as part of a harness or to support a pack, etc. **3.** A part of an animal that is similar to a saddle in shape, position, etc.; esp., the lower part of the back of a fowl. **4.** The two hindquarters of a carcass, as of mutton, veal, or venison; also, the undivided loins of such a carcass. **5.** Something resembling a saddle in form or position, as a bearing for a car axle. — **in the saddle** In control. — *v.* **·dled, ·dling** *v.t.*

1. To put a saddle on. **2.** To load, as with a burden. **3.** To place as a burden or responsibility: with *upon*. — *v.i.* **4.** To get into a saddle. [OE *sadol*]

sad·dle-backed (sad′l·bakt) *adj.* **1.** Concave, as a saddle, in the back or upper part. **2.** Having a saddlelike mark, as some birds.

sad·dle-bag (sad′l·bag) *n.* One of a pair of pouches connected by a strap or band and slung over an animal's back or attached to a saddle.

sad·dle-cloth (sad′l·klôth′, -kloth′) *n.* A cloth placed under and attached to a saddle.

saddle horse A horse used with or trained for the saddle.

sad·dler (sad′lər) *n.* **1.** A maker of saddles, harness, etc. **2.** A saddle horse.

saddle roof A ridge roof having two gables.

sad·dler·y (sad′lər·ē) *n. pl.* **·dler·ies 1.** Saddles, harnesses, etc., collectively. **2.** A shop where such articles are sold. **3.** The craft or business of a saddler.

saddle shoe A white sport shoe having a dark band of leather across the instep.

saddle soap A softening and preserving soap for leather, containing pure white soap, as Castile, and neat's-foot oil.

Sad·du·cee (saj′ŏŏ-sē, sad′yŏŏ-sē) *n.* A member of an ancient Jewish sect that adhered to the written Mosaic law but repudiated oral tradition, rejecting the resurrection of the body, etc. Compare PHARISEE. [Appar. ult. after *Zadok*, a high priest (*Ezek.* xl 46)] — **Sad′du·ce′an, Sad′du·cae′an** *adj.* — **Sad′du·cee′ism** *n.*

sad·i·ron (sad′ī′ərn) *n.* An iron for pressing clothes.

sad·ism (sā′diz·əm, sad′iz·əm) *n.* **1.** *Psychol.* A condition in which sexual gratification depends largely on the infliction of pain upon others. **2.** A tendency to take delight in being cruel. Compare MASOCHISM. [after Comte Donatien de *Sade*, 1740–1814, who described such sexual aberrations in his writings] — **sad·ist** (sā′dist, sad′ist) *n. & adj.* — **sa·dis·tic** (sə-dis′tik, sā-) *adj.* — **sa·dis′ti·cal·ly** *adv.*

sad sack *U.S. Slang* A blundering, pitiable person.

sa·fa·ri (sə-fä′rē) *n. pl.* **·ris** An expedition or journey, often on foot, as for hunting. [< Swahili < Arabic *safara* to travel.]

safe (sāf) *adj.* **saf·er, saf·est 1.** Free or freed from danger or evil. **2.** Having escaped injury or damage; unharmed. **3.** Not involving risk or loss. **4.** Conferring safety. **5.** Prudent or trustworthy. **6.** Not likely to cause or do harm or injury. **7.** In baseball, having reached base without being retired. — *n.* **1.** A strong metal receptacle for protecting valuables. **2.** Any place of safe storage. [< OF < L *salvus* whole, healthy] — **safe′ly** *adv.* — **safe′ness** *n.*

safe·break·er (sāf′brā′kər) *n.* A safecracker.

safe·con·duct (sāf′kon′dukt) *n.* **1.** An official document assuring protection on a journey or voyage, as in time of war; a passport. **2.** The act of conducting in safety.

safe·crack·er (sāf′krak′ər) *n.* One who breaks into safes to rob them. — **safe′crack′ing** *n.*

safe-de·pos·it box (sāf′di·poz′it) A box or other fireproof receptacle for valuables, generally in a bank.

safe·guard (sāf′gärd′) *n.* One who or that which guards or protects against accident or injury. — *v.t.* To defend; protect; guard.

safe·keep·ing (sāf′kē′ping) *n.* The act or state of keeping or being kept in safety; protection.

safe·ty (sāf′tē) *n. pl.* **·ties 1.** Freedom from danger or injury. **2.** A device or catch designed as a safeguard, as in a firearm. **3.** In football, the act or play of touching the ball to the ground behind the player's own goal line when the impetus that sent the ball over the goal line was given to it by one of his own side. Also **safe′ty-touch′down′** (-tuch′-doun′). [< OF < Med.L < L *salvus* sound]

safety belt 1. A strap or strip of strong belting encircling the user and fastened to a fixed object, worn by linemen, window cleaners, etc., as a safeguard against falling. **2.** A strap fixed to the seat of an aircraft or vehicle, by which the occupant is secured against sudden shocks or turning movements: also called *seat belt*.

safety glass Two sheets of glass having a film of transparent, adhesive plastic tightly pressed between them: also called *shatterproof glass*.

safety lamp A miner's lamp having the flame surrounded by fine wire gauze that prevents the ignition of explosive gases: also called *davy*.

safety match A match that will ignite only when struck upon a chemically prepared surface.

safety pin A pin whose point springs into place within a protecting sheath.

safety razor A razor provided with a guard or guards for the blade to prevent accidental gashing of the skin.

safety valve 1. *Mech.* A valve in a steam boiler, etc., for automatically relieving excessive pressure. **2.** Any outlet for pent-up energy or emotion.

saf·fron (saf′rən) *n.* **1.** An autumn-flowering species of crocus. **2.** The dried orange-colored stigmas of this plant,

used for coloring confectionery, etc., and as a flavoring in cookery. **3.** A deep yellow-orange: also **saffron yellow.** — *adj.* Yellow-orange. [< OF < Med.L < Arabic *za′farān*]

sag (sag) *v.* **sagged, sag·ging** *v.i.* **1.** To bend or sink downward from weight or pressure, esp. in the middle. **2.** To hang unevenly. **3.** To lose firmness or determination; weaken, as from exhaustion, age, etc. **4.** To decline, as in price or value. — *v.t.* **5.** To cause to sag. — *n.* **1.** A sagging. **2.** A sagging or sunken place or part. [ME *saggen*]

sa·ga (sä′gə) *n.* **1.** A medieval Scandinavian prose narrative dealing with legendary or historical exploits, usu. of a single hero or family. **2.** A long story, sometimes poetic, often chronicling the history of a family. [< ON]

sa·ga·cious (sə-gā′shəs) *adj.* **1.** Characterized by discernment, shrewdness, and wisdom. **2.** Ready and apt to apprehend. [< L *sagax*] — **sa·ga′cious·ly** *adv.* — **sa·ga′cious·ness** *n.*

sa·gac·i·ty (sə-gas′ə·tē) *n.* The quality of being sagacious; discernment and judgment; shrewdness.

sag·a·more (sag′ə-môr, -mōr) *n.* A chief among the Algonquian Indians of North America, usu. inferior to sachem. [< Algonquian (Penobscot) *sagamo* he prevails]

sage[1] (sāj) *n.* A venerable man of recognized wisdom, experience, prudence, and foresight. — *adj.* **sag·er, sag·est 1.** Characterized by or proceeding from calm, far-seeing wisdom and prudence. **2.** Profound; learned. — **Syn.** See WISE[1]. [< OF, ult. < LL *sapius* prudent, wise] — **sage′ly** *adv.* — **sage′ness** *n.*

sage[2] (sāj) *n.* **1.** A plant of the mint family, having gray-green leaves used for flavoring meats. **2.** The leaves of this plant. **3.** The sagebrush. [< F < L *salvus* safe]

sage·brush (sāj′brush′) *n.* An aromatic, bitter, typically perennial herb or small shrub, widely distributed on the alkali plains of the western U.S.

Sagebrush State Nickname of Nevada.

sage hen A large grouse of the western U.S.

sag·it·tal (saj′ə·təl) *adj.* **1.** Of, pertaining to, or resembling an arrow or arrowhead. **2.** *Anat.* Of or pertaining to the longitudinal plane dividing an animal into right and left halves. [< L *sagitta* arrow] — **sag′it·tal·ly** *adv.*

Sag·it·ta·ri·us (saj′ə-târ′ē·əs) *n.* A constellation, the Archer; also, the ninth sign of the zodiac. See ZODIAC. [< L *sagitta* arrow]

sag·it·tate (saj′ə·tāt) *adj. Bot.* Shaped like an arrowhead, as certain leaves. [< L *sagitta* arrow]

sa·go (sā′gō) *n. pl.* **·gos 1.** Any of several varieties of East Indian palm. **2.** The pith of this palm, used as a thickening agent in puddings, etc. [< Malay *sāgū*]

sa·gua·ro (sə-gwä′rō, -wä′-) *n. pl.* **·ros** A large desert cactus with an erect, columnar trunk, strong spines, and flowering tops. Also **sa·hua′ro** (-wä′-). [< Sp. < Piman]

Sa·hib (sä′ib) *n.* Master; sir: used in India and Pakistan for people of rank and, esp. formerly, for Europeans. Also **Sa′heb.** [< Urdu < Arabic *sāhib* lord, companion]

said (sed) Past tense and past participle of SAY. — *adj. Law* Previously mentioned; aforesaid.

sail (sāl) *n. pl.* **sails;** *for def. 3, often* **sail 1.** *Naut.* A piece of canvas, or other strong material, attached to a vessel so that it may be spread to the wind and aid in the vessel's propulsion. **2.** Sails collectively. **3.** A sailing vessel or craft. **4.** A trip or passage in any watercraft. **5.** Anything resembling a sail in form or use, as the broad part of the arm of a windmill. — **to make sail 1.** To unfurl a sail or sails. **2.** To set out on a voyage. — **to set sail** To begin a voyage; get under way. — **under sail** Sailing; with sails spread. — *v.i.* **1.** To move across the surface of water by the action of wind or mechanical power. **2.** To travel over water in a ship or boat. **3.** To begin a voyage. **4.** To manage a sailing craft. **5.** To glide or float in the air. **6.** To move along in a stately or dignified manner. **7.** *Informal* To pass rapidly. **8.** *Informal* To proceed boldly into action: with *in*. — *v.t.* **9.** To move or travel across the surface of (a body of water) in a ship or boat. **10.** To navigate (a ship, etc.). — **to sail into 1.** To begin with energy. **2.** To attack violently. [OE *segl*] — **sail′a·ble** *adj.*

sail·boat (sāl′bōt′) *n. U.S.* A small boat propelled by a sail or sails.

sail·cloth (sāl′klôth′, -kloth′) *n.* A very strong, firmly woven cotton canvas suitable for sails.

sail·er (sā′lər) *n.* A vessel that sails; a ship having a specified sailing power: a fast *sailer.*

sail·fish (sāl′fish′) *n. pl.* **·fish** or **·fish·es** A marine fish allied to the spearfish, having a large or conspicuous dorsal fin likened to a sail.

sail·or (sā′lər) *n.* **1.** A seaman; mariner. **2.** A sailor hat.

sailor hat A low-crowned, flat-topped straw hat with a brim, worn by both sexes: also called *sailor.*

saint (sānt) *n.* **1.** A holy or godly person. **2.** In certain churches, such a person who has died and been canonized. **3.** Any one of the blessed in heaven. **4.** A very patient, unselfish person. — *v.t.* To canonize; venerate as a saint.

adj. Holy; canonized. [< OF < L *sancire* to make sacred]
— **saint'hood, saint'ship** *n.*

Saint For entries not found under *Saint*, see under ST.

Saint (sānt) *n.* A member of one of the religious bodies known as **Saints**: Latter-day *Saint*.

Saint Bernard A working dog of great size and strength, characterized by a massive head, and a thick, white, red, or brindled coat, used to rescue travelers by the hospice at Great St. Bernard Pass in the Swiss Alps.

saint·ed (sān'tid) *adj.* **1.** Canonized. **2.** Of holy character; saintly.

saint·ly (sānt'lē) *adj.* **·li·er, ·li·est** Like, concerned with, or suitable for a saint. — **saint'li·ness** *n.*

SAINT BERNARD
(About 27 inches high at shoulder)

Saint Patrick's Day March 17, a day traditionally celebrated by the Irish in honor of their patron saint.

Saint Valentine's Day February 14, the anniversary of the beheading of St. Valentine by the Romans, and also a day when valentines are exchanged.

saith (seth) *Archaic* Present indicative third person singular of SAY.

sake[1] (sāk) *n.* **1.** Purpose of obtaining or accomplishing: to speak slowly for the *sake* of clarity. **2.** Interest; account; advantage: for your own *sake*. [OE *sacu* lawsuit]
— **Syn. 2.** Something done for the *sake* of a person, or on his *behalf*, is intended to promote his welfare. But *sake* suggests the benevolence of a parent or friend, while *behalf* suggests a somewhat less personal relationship, as that of an attorney or patron.

sa·ke[2] (sä'kē) *n.* A fermented liquor made in Japan from rice. Also **sa'ki.** [< Japanese]

sal (sal) *n.* Salt. [< L]

sa·laam (sə·läm') *n.* An oriental salutation or obeisance made with a low bow, the palm of the right hand being held to the forehead; also, a respectful or ceremonious verbal greeting. — *v.t. & v.i.* To greet with or make a salaam. [< Arabic *salām* peace, a salutation]

sal·a·ble (sā'lə·bəl) *adj.* Such as can be sold; marketable: also spelled *saleable*. — **sal'a·bil'i·ty, sal'a·ble·ness** *n.*

sa·la·cious (sə·lā'shəs) *adj.* **1.** Lustful; lewd. **2.** Obscene: a *salacious* joke. [< L *salire* to leap] — **sa·la'cious·ly** *adv.* — **sa·la'cious·ness, sa·lac'i·ty** (-las'ə·tē) *n.*

sal·ad (sal'əd) *n.* Green herbs or vegetables, usu. uncooked and served with a dressing, sometimes mixed with chopped cold meat, fish, etc.; also, a similar dish made with fruit. [< OF < Provençal < L *sal* salt]

sal·a·man·der (sal'ə·man'dər) *n.* **1.** Any of a variety of tailed, lizardlike amphibians having a smooth, moist skin and two pairs of limbs. **2.** A mythical lizard or other creature fabled to live in fire. **3.** Any person or thing that can stand great heat. **4.** A large poker or other implement used around or in fire, or when red-hot. [< OF < L *salamandra* < Gk.] — **sal'a·man'drine** (-drin) *adj.*

sa·la·mi (sə·lä'mē) *n.* A salted, spiced sausage, originally Italian. [< Ital., < L *sal* salt]

sal ammoniac *Chem.* A white, crystalline, soluble compound, NH$_4$Cl, used in medicine and industry. [< L *sal Ammoniacum*, lit. salt of Ammon]

sal·a·ried (sal'ər·ēd, sal'rēd) *adj.* **1.** In receipt of a salary. **2.** Yielding a salary.

sal·a·ry (sal'ər·ē, sal'rē) *n.* *pl.* **·ries** A periodic, fixed payment for services, esp. for official or professional services as distinguished from manual or menial labor. — *v.t.* **·ried, ·ry·ing** To pay or allot a salary to. [< AF < L *salarium* money paid Roman soldiers for their salt]

sale (sāl) *n.* **1.** The act of selling; the exchange or transfer of property of any kind for money or its equivalent. **2.** An auction. **3.** The selling of something at bargain prices. **4.** Opportunity of selling; market. — **for sale** (or **on sale**) Offered or ready for sale. [OE *sala* < ON]

sale·a·ble (sā'lə·bəl) See SALABLE.

sal·e·ra·tus (sal'ə·rā'təs) *n.* Sodium bicarbonate, for use in cookery; baking soda. [< NL *sal aëratus* aerated salt]

sales·girl (sālz'gûrl') *n.* *U.S.* A woman or girl hired to sell merchandise, especially in a store.

sales·la·dy (sālz'lā'dē) *n.* *pl.* **·dies** *Informal* A woman or girl hired to sell merchandise, esp. in a store.

sales·man (sālz'mən) *n.* *pl.* **·men** (-mən) A man hired to sell goods, stock, etc., in a store or by canvassing.

sales·man·ship (sālz'mən·ship) *n.* **1.** The work or profession of a salesman. **2.** Ability or skill in selling.

sales·peo·ple (sālz'pē'pəl) *n.pl.* Salespersons.

sales·per·son (sālz'pûr'sən) *n.* A person hired to sell merchandise, esp. in a store.

sales resistance The ability to resist any attempts to induce one to buy certain goods or services.

sales·room (sālz'rōōm', -rŏŏm') *n.* A room where merchandise is displayed for sale.

sales tax A tax on money received from sales of goods.

sales·wom·an (sālz'wŏŏm'ən) *n.* *pl.* **·wom·en** (-wim'in) A woman or girl hired to sell merchandise, esp. in a store.

sal·ic (sal'ik) *adj.* *Geol.* Belonging to a group of igneous rocks composed chiefly of silica and alumina, as the feldspars, quartz, etc. [< S(ILICA) + AL(UMINUM) + -IC]

sal·i·cyl·ate (sal'ə·sil'āt, sə·lis'ə·lāt) *n.* *Chem.* A salt or ester of salicylic acid.

sal·i·cyl·ic acid (sal'ə·sil'ik) *Chem.* A white crystalline compound, C$_7$H$_6$O$_3$, occurring in many plants and also made synthetically, one acetyl form of which is widely known as aspirin. [< SALIC(IN) + -YL + -IC]

sa·li·ent (sā'lē·ənt) *adj.* **1.** Standing out prominently; striking; conspicuous. **2.** Protruding; projecting. **3.** Leaping; springing. — *n.* The part of a fortification, etc., that most protrudes towards the enemy. [< L < *salire* to leap] — **sa'li·ence** *n.* — **sa'li·ent·ly** *adv.* — **sa'li·ent·ness** *n.*

sa·line (sā'līn) *adj.* **1.** Of, constituting, or characteristic of salt. **2.** Containing salt; salty. — *n.* **1.** A metallic salt. **2.** A salt solution used in the investigation of biological and physiological processes, and also in medicine. [< F < LL < L *sal, salis* salt] — **sa·lin·i·ty** (sə·lin'ə·tē) *n.*

Salisbury steak Hamburger (def. 2).

sa·li·va (sə·lī'və) *n.* *Physiol.* The slightly alkaline fluid secreted by the glands of the mouth, considered a promoter of digestion. [< L] — **sal·i·var·y** (sal'ə·ver'ē) *adj.*

sal·i·vate (sal'ə·vāt) *v.* **·vat·ed, ·vat·ing** *v.i.* To secrete saliva. — *v.t.* To produce salivation in. [< L < *saliva* saliva] — **sal'i·va'tion** *n.*

sal·low (sal'ō) *adj.* Of an unhealthy yellowish color: said chiefly of the human skin. [OE *salu*] — **sal'low·ish** *adj.* — **sal'low·y** *adv.* — **sal'low·ness** *n.*

sal·ly (sal'ē) *v.i.* **·lied, ·ly·ing 1.** To rush out suddenly. **2.** To set out energetically. **3.** To go out, as from a room or building. — *n.* *pl.* **·lies 1.** A rushing forth, as of troops against besiegers; sortie. **2.** Any sudden rushing forth. **3.** A going forth, as on a walk. **4.** A bantering remark or witticism. [< OF < L *salire* to leap]

sal·ma·gun·di (sal'mə·gun'dē) *n.* **1.** A saladlike dish of chopped meat, anchovies, eggs, onions, oil, etc. **2.** Any medley or mixture. Also **sal'ma·gun'dy.** [< F *salmigondis*]

salm·on (sam'ən) *n.* **1.** Any of various food fishes inhabiting the North Atlantic coastal waters and ascending to adjacent rivers to spawn, having a brownish color above, silvery sides, black spots, and a delicate pink flesh. **2.** Any of various other salmonoid fishes. **3.** A reddish or pinkish orange color: also **salmon pink.** — *adj.* Having a salmon color. [< OF < L *salmo, -onis*, prob. akin to *salire* to leap] — **sal·mo·noid** (sal'mə·noid) *adj. & n.*

salmon trout 1. The European brown trout. **2.** The lake trout. **3.** The steelhead.

Sa·lo·me (sə·lō'mē) The daughter of Herodias, who asked Herod for the head of John the Baptist in return for her dancing. *Matt.* xiv 8.

sa·lon (sə·lon', *Fr.* sà·lôn') *n.* **1.** A room in which guests are received; a drawing room. **2.** The periodic gathering of noted persons, under the auspices of some distinguished figure. **3.** A hall or gallery used for exhibiting works of art. **4.** An establishment devoted to some specific purpose: a beauty *salon*. [< F < Ital. < L *sala* hall < Gmc.]

sa·loon (sə·lōōn') *n.* **1.** A place where alcoholic drinks are sold; a bar. **2.** A large apartment or room for assemblies, public functions, exhibitions, etc. **3.** The main cabin of a passenger ship. [< F *salon* salon]

sa·loon·keep·er (sə·lōōn'kē'pər) *n.* One who owns or manages a saloon (def. 1).

sal·si·fy (sal'sə·fē, -fī) *n.* *pl.* **·fies** An Old World plant with a white, edible root and an oysterlike flavor: also called *oyster plant*. [< F < Ital. *sassefrica*]

sal soda Sodium carbonate.

salt (sôlt) *n.* **1.** Sodium chloride, NaCl, a compound found in sea water and as a mineral, used as a seasoning and as a preservative. ◆ Collateral adjective: *saline*. **2.** *Chem.* Any compound consisting of the cation of a base and the anion of an acid, combined in proportions that give a balance of electropositive and electronegative charges. **3.** *pl.* A salt used as a laxative or cathartic; also, smelling salts. **4.** Piquant humor; dry wit; repartee. **5.** That which preserves or purifies. **6.** *Informal* A sailor: an old *salt*. **7.** A saltcellar. — **to take with a grain of salt** To have doubts about. — *adj.* **1.** Flavored with salt; briny. **2.** Cured or preserved with salt. **3.** Containing, or growing or living in or near, salt water. — *v.t.* **1.** To season with salt. **2.** To preserve or cure with salt. **3.** To furnish with salt: to *salt* cattle. **4.** To add zest or piquancy to. **5.** To add something to so as to increase the value fraudulently: to *salt* a mine with gold. — **to salt away**

1. To pack in salt for preserving. **2.** *Informal* To store up; save. [OE *sealt*] **— salt/ness** *n.*

salt·cel·lar (sôlt/sel'ər) *n.* A small receptacle for salt; a saltshaker. [ME < *salt* + F *salière* saltcellar]

salt·ed (sôl/tid) *adj.* **1.** Treated with salt; preserved. **2.** *Informal* Experienced or expert in some occupation.

sal·tine (sôl·tēn') *n.* A crisp, salty cracker.

salt lick A place to which animals go to lick salt from superficial deposits; a salt spring or dried salt pond.

salt·pe·ter (sôlt/pē'tər) *n.* Potassium nitrate. **— Chile saltpeter** Mineral sodium nitrate, found chiefly in Chile. [< OF < Med.L < L *sal* salt + *petra* a rock < Gk.]

salt·shak·er (sôlt/shā'kər) *n.* A container with small holes for sprinkling table salt.

salt·wa·ter (sôlt/wô'tər, -wot'ər) *adj.* Of, composed of, or living in salty water.

salt·works (sôlt/wûrks') *n. pl.* **·works** An establishment where salt is made on a commercial scale.

salt·wort (sôlt/wûrt') *n.* **1.** Any of various maritime plants of the goosefoot family. **2.** Any of various glassworts.

salt·y (sôl/tē) *adj.* **salt·i·er, salt·i·est 1.** Of, containing, or tasting like salt. **2.** Reminiscent of the sea; smelling of the sea. **3.** Piquant; sharp; pungent, as literature or speech. **— salt/i·ly** *adv.* **— salt/i·ness** *n.*

sa·lu·bri·ous (sə·lōō/brē·əs) *adj.* Conducive to health; healthful; wholesome. [< L *salus* health] **— sa·lu/bri·ous·ly** *adv.* **— sa·lu/bri·ous·ness, sal·u/bri·ty** *n.*

sal·u·tar·y (sal/yə·ter'ē) *adj.* **1.** Calculated to bring about a sound condition by correcting evil or promoting good; beneficial. **2.** Salubrious. [< F < L < *salus, salutis* health] **— sal/u·tar/i·ly** *adv.* **— sal/u·tar/i·ness** *n.*

sal·u·ta·tion (sal/yə·tā/shən, -yōō-) *n.* **1.** The act of saluting. **2.** Any form of greeting. **3.** The opening words of a letter, as *Dear Sir.* [< MF < L < *salus, salutis* health]

sa·lu·ta·to·ri·an (sə·lōō/tə·tôr/ē·ən, -tō/rē-) *n. U.S.* In schools, the graduating student, usu. receiving second highest honors, who delivers the salutatory. [< SALUTATORY]

sa·lu·ta·to·ry (sə·lōō/tə·tôr/ē, -tō/rē) *n. pl.* **·ries** An opening oration, as at a school commencement. *— adj.* Of or consisting in greeting; esp., relating to a salutatory address. [< L *salutare*. See SALUTE.]

sa·lute (sə·lōōt') *n.* **1.** A greeting by display of military or other official honors, as by presenting arms, firing cannon, etc. **2.** The act of or attitude assumed in giving a military salute. **3.** A gesture of greeting, compliment, etc. *— v.* **·lut·ed, ·lut·ing** *v.t.* **1.** To greet with a sign of welcome, respect, etc. **2.** To honor in some prescribed way, as by raising the hand to the cap. *— v.i.* **3.** To make a salute. [< F < L *salus, salutis* health] **— sa·lut/er** *n.*

sal·va·ble (sal/və·bəl) *adj.* Capable of being saved or salvaged. [< LL < L *salvus* safe] **— sal/va·bil/i·ty** *n.*

sal·vage (sal/vij) *v.t.* **·vaged, ·vag·ing** To save, as a ship or its cargo, from wreck, capture, etc. *— n.* **1.** The saving of a ship, cargo, etc., from loss. **2.** Any act of saving property. **3.** Compensation to persons who save a vessel, her cargo, or the lives of those belonging to her. **4.** That which is saved from a wrecked or abandoned vessel or from a fire. **5.** Anything saved from destruction. [< MF < Med.L < L *salvus* safe] **— sal/vage·a·ble** *adj.* **— sal/vag·er** *n.*

sal·va·tion (sal·vā/shən) *n.* **1.** The process or state of being saved. **2.** *Theol.* Deliverance from sin and penalty, realized in a future state. **3.** Any means of deliverance from danger, evil, or ruin. [< OF < LL < L *salvus* safe]

Salvation Army A religious and charitable organization on semimilitary lines, founded by William Booth in 1865.

salve¹ (sav, säv) *n.* **1.** A thick, adhesive ointment for local ailments. **2.** Anything that heals, soothes, or mollifies. **3.** Praise or flattery. *— v.t.* **salved, salv·ing 1.** To dress with ointment. **2.** To soothe; appease. [OE *sealf*]

salve² (salv) *v.t.* **salved, salv·ing** To save from loss; salvage. [< Med.L *salvare*]

sal·ve³ (sal/vē) *interj.* Hail. [< L < *salvere* to be well]

sal·ver (sal/vər) *n.* A tray, as of silver. [< OF < Sp. < *salvar* to taste]

sal·vi·a (sal/vē·ə) *n.* Any of a genus of ornamental plants of the mint family, as the sage. [< L. See SAGE².]

sal·vo (sal/vō) *n. pl.* **·vos** or **·voes 1.** A simultaneous discharge of artillery, or of two or more bombs. **2.** A salute given by firing all the guns. **3.** Any salute or simultaneous outburst: a *salvo* of applause. [< Ital. *salva* salute]

sal vo·lat·i·le (sal vō·lat/ə·lē) Ammonium carbonate; also, an aromatic solution of ammonium carbonate, used as smelling salts. [< NL, volatile salt < L]

sam·a·ra (sam/ər·ə, sə·mâr/ə) *n. Bot.* A one-seeded fruit, as of the elm, ash, or maple, provided with a membrane or wing. [< L, elm seed]

Sa·mar·i·a (sə·mâr/ē·ə) In the Bible, a city of Palestine, capital of the northern kingdom of Israel, or later, a restricted portion of central Palestine west of the Jordan occupied by the Samaritans.

Sa·mar·i·tan (sə·mar/ə·tən) *n.* **1.** One of the people of Sa-

maria. II *Kings* xvii. **2.** Good Samaritan (which see). *— adj.* Of or pertaining to Samaria.

sa·mar·i·um (sə·mâr/ē·əm) *n.* A hard, brittle, yellowish gray, metallic element (symbol Sm) of the lanthanide series. See ELEMENT. [< NL < *samarskite*, an orthorhombic, vitreous, black mineral]

sam·ba (sam/bə, säm/bä) *n.* **1.** A popular dance of Brazilian origin. **2.** Music for this dance, in duple meter. *— v.i.* To dance the samba. [< Pg. < native African name]

Sam Browne belt (sam/ broun') A military belt with a shoulder strap running diagonally across the chest. [after Sir *Samuel J. Browne*, 1824–1901, British general]

same (sām) *adj.* **1.** Having individual or specific identity or quality; identical; equal: with *the.* **2.** Similar in kind or quality. **3.** Similar in quantity or measure; equivalent. **4.** Aforesaid; identical: said of a person or thing just mentioned. **— all the same 1.** Nevertheless; yet. **2.** Equally acceptable or unacceptable. **— just the same 1.** Nevertheless; yet. **2.** Unchanged. *— pron.* The identical person, thing, etc. *— adv.* In like manner; equally: with *the.* [< ON *samr*]

same·ness (sām/nis) *n.* **1.** Lack of change or variety; monotony. **2.** Close similarity; likeness. **3.** Identity; unity.

Sam Hill (sam/ hil') *U.S. Slang* Hell: a euphemism.

sam·i·sen (sam/i·sen) *n.* A Japanese guitarlike instrument with three strings, played with a plectrum. [< Japanese < Chinese *san hsien* three strings]

SAMISEN

sa·mite (sā/mīt, sam/it) *n.* A rich medieval fabric of silk, often interwoven with gold or silver. [< OF < Med.L < Gk. *hex* six + *mitos* thread]

Sa·mo·an (sə·mō/ən) *adj.* Of or pertaining to Samoa, to its aboriginal Polynesian inhabitants, or to their language. *— n.* **1.** A native of the Samoan islands. **2.** The Polynesian language of the Samoans.

sam·o·var (sam/ə·vär, sam/ə·vär') *n.* A metal urn for heating water, as for making tea. [< Russian, lit., self-boiler]

Sam·o·yed (sam/ə·yed') *n.* **1.** One of a Mongoloid people inhabiting the Arctic coasts of Siberia. **2.** A large dog having a thick white coat of long hair. *— adj.* Of the Samoyeds or their language; Samoyedic. Also **Sam/o·yede/** (-yed'). [< Russian, lit., self-eater]

Sam·o·yed·ic (sam/ə·yed/ik) *adj.* Of or pertaining to the Samoyeds or their language. *— n.* A subfamily of the Uralic languages, including the language of the Samoyeds.

samp (samp) *n.* Coarse Indian corn; also, a porridge made of it. [< Algonquian *nasaump* softened with water]

sam·pan (sam/pan) *n.* A small flat-bottomed boat or skiff used along rivers and coasts of China and Japan. [< Chinese *san* three + *pan* board, plank]

sam·ple (sam/pəl) *n.* A portion, part, or piece taken or shown as a representative of the whole. *— v.t.* **·pled, ·pling** To test or examine by means of a sample. [See EXAMPLE.]

sam·pler¹ (sam/plər) *n.* One who tests by sampling.

sam·pler² (sam/plər) *n.* A piece of needlework, originally designed to show a beginner's skill. [See EXAMPLE.]

sam·pling (sam/pling) *n.* **1.** A small part of something or a number of items from a group selected for examination or analysis in order to estimate the quality or nature of the whole. **2.** The act or process of making such a selection.

Sam·son (sam/sən) A Hebrew judge of great strength, betrayed to the Philistines by Delilah. *Judges* xii–xvi.

Sam·u·el (sam/yōō·əl) A Hebrew judge and prophet. *— n.* Either of two historical books, I and II Samuel, of the Old Testament.

sam·u·rai (sam/ŏŏ·rī) *n. pl.* **·rai** Under the Japanese feudal system, a member of the soldier class of the lower nobility; also, the class itself. [< Japanese]

san·a·tive (san/ə·tiv) *adj.* Healing; sanatory; health-giving. [< OF < Med.L < L *sanare* to heal]

san·a·to·ri·um (san/ə·tôr/ē·əm, -tō/rē-) *n. pl.* **·ri·ums** or **·ri·a** (-tôr/ē·ə, -tō/rē·ə) **1.** An institution for the treatment and care of invalids and convalescents. **2.** A health resort. Also called *sanitarium.* [< NL < LL < L *sanare* to heal]

sanc·ti·fied (sangk/tə·fīd) *adj.* **1.** Made holy; freed from sin; consecrated. **2.** Sanctimonious; self-righteous.

sanc·ti·fy (sangk/tə·fī) *v.t.* **·fied, ·fy·ing 1.** To set apart as holy or for holy purposes; consecrate. **2.** To purify or make holy. **3.** To render sacred or inviolable, as a vow. [< OF < LL < L *sanctus* holy + *facere* to make] **— sanc/ti·fi·ca/tion** *n.* **— sanc/ti·fi/er** *n.*

sanc·ti·mo·ni·ous (sangk/tə·mō/nē·əs) *adj.* Making an ostentatious display or pretense of sanctity. **— sanc/ti·mo/ni·ous·ly** *adv.* **— sanc/ti·mo/ni·ous·ness** *n.*

sanc·ti·mo·ny (sangk/tə·mō/nē) *n.* Assumed or outward sanctity; a show of holiness or devoutness. [< OF < L *sanctimonia* holiness]

sanc·tion (sangk/shən) *v.t.* **1.** To approve authoritatively; confirm; ratify. **2.** To countenance; allow. *— n.* **1.** Final and authoritative confirmation or ratification. **2.** A formal decree. **3.** A provision for securing conformity to law, as by the enactment of rewards or penalties or both. **4.** *Usu. pl.* In international law, coercive measures adopted to force a nation that is violating international law to desist. **5.** In ethics, that which makes virtue morally obligatory. [< L < *sancire* to render sacred, inviolable]

sanc·ti·ty (sangk′tə·tē) *n. pl.* **·ties** **1.** The state of being sanctified; holiness. **2.** Sacredness; solemnity.

sanc·tu·ar·y (sangk′chōō·er′ē) *n. pl.* **·ar·ies** **1.** A holy or sacred place. **2.** The most sacred part of a place in a sacred structure. **3.** A place of refuge; asylum; also, immunity. [< OF < LL < L *sanctus* holy]

sanc·tum (sangk′təm) *n. pl.* **·tums** or **·ta** (-tə) **1.** A sacred place. **2.** A private room where one is not to be disturbed. [< L, neut. of *sanctus* holy]

sanc·tum sanc·to·rum (sangk′təm sangk·tôr′əm, -tō′rəm) **1.** The holy of holies. **2.** A place of great privacy: often used humorously.

Sanc·tus (sangk′təs) *n. Eccl.* **1.** An ascription of praise to God, occurring at the end of the Preface in many eucharistic liturgies. **2.** A musical setting for this. [< L *sanctus* holy]

sand (sand) *n.* **1.** A hard, granular rock material finer than gravel and coarser than dust. **2.** *pl.* Stretches of sandy beach, desert, etc. **3.** *pl.* Sandy grains in an hourglass. **4.** *pl.* Moments of time or life. **5.** A reddish yellow color. — *v.t.* **1.** To sprinkle or cover with sand. **2.** To smooth or abrade with sand or sandpaper. **3.** To mix sand with. **4.** To fill with sand. [OE] — **sand′er** *n.*

san·dal (san′dəl) *n.* **1.** A foot covering, consisting usu. of a sole only, held to the foot by thongs. **2.** A light slipper. **3.** An overshoe of rubber, cut very low. [< OF < Gk. *sandalon*] — **san′daled,** **san′dalled** *adj.*

san·dal·wood (san′dəl·wŏod′) *n.* **1.** The fine-grained, dense, fragrant wood of any of several East Indian trees. **2.** The similar wood of other trees, whose dark red wood is used as a dyestuff. [< Med.L < Skt. *çandana*]

sand·bag (sand′bag′) *n.* **1.** A bag filled with sand, used for building fortifications, for ballast, etc. **2.** A long, narrow bag filled with sand and used as a club or weapon. — *v.t.* **·bagged, ·bag·ging** **1.** To fill or surround with sandbags. **2.** To strike with a sandbag. — **sand′bag′ger** *n.*

sand·bar (sand′bär′) *n.* A ridge of silt or sand in rivers, along beaches, etc., formed by the action of currents or tides.

sand·blast (sand′blast′, -bläst′) *n.* **1.** A fine jet of sand, propelled under pressure and used to clean, grind, or decorate hard surfaces. **2.** The apparatus used in applying this blast. — *v.t.* To clean or engrave by means of a sandblast.

sand·box (sand′boks′) *n.* **1.** A box on a locomotive or streetcar filled with sand to be poured on the rail treads to prevent slipping. **2.** A box of sand for children to play in.

sand·cast (sand′kast′, -käst′) *v.t.* **-cast, -cast·ing** To make (a casting) by pouring metal into a mold of sand.

sand crack *Vet.* A crack running down from the coronet of a horse's hoof and apt to cause lameness if neglected.

sand flea Any of various fleas that live in sand, as the chigoe.

sand·hog (sand′hôg′, -hog′) *n.* One who works under air pressure, as in caisson sinking, tunnel building, etc.

sand·lot (sand′lot′) *adj.* Of or in a vacant lot in or near an urban area: *sand-lot* baseball.

sand·man (sand′man′) *n.* In nursery lore, a person supposed to make children sleepy by casting sand in their eyes.

sand painting A form of painting by the American Indians in which fine colored sand is trickled on a ground base.

sand·pa·per (sand′pā′pər) *n.* Heavy paper coated with sand for smoothing or polishing. — *v.t.* To rub or polish with sandpaper.

sand·pi·per (sand′pī′pər) *n.* Any of certain small wading birds related to the snipes and frequenting seashores. Also **sand′peep′** (-pēp′).

sand·stone (sand′stōn′) *n.* A rock consisting chiefly of quartz sand cemented with silica, feldspar, lime, or clay.

sand·storm (sand′stôrm′) *n.* A high wind by which sand or dust is carried along.

sand·wich (sand′wich, san′-) *n.* **1.** Two thin slices of bread, having between them meat, cheese, etc. **2.** Any combination of alternating dissimilar things pressed together. — *v.t.* **1.** To place between two layers or objects. **2.** To insert between dissimilar things. [after John Montagu, fourth Earl of *Sandwich,* 1718–92, who originated it in order to eat without leaving the gaming table]

sandwich man *n. pl.* **men** *Informal* A man carrying advertising boards (**sandwich boards**) slung in front and behind.

sand·y (san′dē) *adj.* **sand·i·er, sand·i·est** **1.** Consisting of or characterized by sand; containing, covered with, or full of sand. **2.** Yellowish red: a *sandy* beard. — **sand′i·ness** *n.*

sane (sān) *adj.* **1.** Mentally sound; not deranged. **2.** Proceeding from a sound mind. [< L *sanus* whole, healthy] — **sane′ly** *adv.* — **sane′ness** *n.*

San·for·ize (san′fə·rīz) *v.t.* **·ized, ·iz·ing** To treat (cloth) so as to prevent shrinkage: a trade name. Also **san′for·ize.** [after *Sanford* L. Cluett, born 1874, U.S. inventor]

sang (sang) Past tense of SING.

sang-froid (sän·frwä′) *n.* Calmness amid trying circumstances; coolness; composure. [< F, lit., cold blood]

sangui- *combining form* Blood. [< L *sanguis* blood]

san·gui·nar·y (sang′gwə·ner′ē) *adj.* **1.** Attended with bloodshed. **2.** Bloodthirsty. **3.** Consisting of blood. — **san′gui·nar′i·ly** *adv.* — **san′gui·nar′i·ness** *n.*

san·guine (sang′gwin) *adj.* **1.** Of cheerful, hopeful disposition. **2.** Ruddy; robust. **3.** Of, like, or full of blood. **4.** *Obs.* Bloodthirsty; sanguinary. [< OF < L *sanguis, -inis* blood] — **san′guine·ly** *adv.* — **san′guine·ness** *n.*

San·he·drin (san′hi·drin, san′i-, san·hē′drin, -hed′rin) *n.* **1.** In ancient times, the supreme council and highest court of the Jewish nation. Also **Great Sanhedrin.** **2.** Any council or assembly. Also **San′he·drim** (-drim). [< Hebrew < Gk. < *syn-* together + *hedra* a sitting]

san·i·tar·i·an (san′ə·târ′ē·ən) *adj.* Of or relating to sanitation or health. — *n.* An expert in public health.

san·i·tar·i·um (san′ə·târ′ē·əm) *n. pl.* **·tar·i·ums** or **·tar·i·a** (-târ′ē·ə) A sanatorium. [< NL < L *sanitas* health]

san·i·tar·y (san′ə·ter′ē) *adj.* **1.** Relating to the preservation of health. **2.** Favorable to health; hygienic. [< F < L *sanitas* health] — **san′i·tar′i·ly** *adv.*

sanitary napkin An absorbent pad worn by women during menstruation.

san·i·ta·tion (san′ə·tā′shən) *n.* The use and practical application of sanitary measures; the removal or neutralization of elements injurious to health.

san·i·ty (san′ə·tē) *n. pl.* **·ties** **1.** The state of being sane; soundness of mind. **2.** Sane moderation or reasonableness.

San Jo·sé scale (san′ hō·zā′) A scale insect destructive to various fruit trees.

sank (sangk) Past tense of SINK.

sans (sanz, *Fr.* sän) *prep.* Without. [< OF *sanz*]

sans-cu·lotte (sanz′kyōō·lot′, *Fr.* sän·kü·lôt′) *n.* **1.** A revolutionary: originally a term of contempt applied by the aristocrats to the French revolutionaries in 1789. **2.** Any revolutionary or radical. [< F, lit., without knee breeches] — **sans-cu·lot′tic** *adj.* — **sans′-cu·lot′tism** *n.*

San·sei (sän·sā) *n. pl.* **·sei** or **·seis** An American citizen of Japanese descent whose grandparents settled in the U.S. [< Japanese, third generation]

san·se·vi·e·ri·a (san′sə·vi·ir′ē·ə) *n.* Any of several perennial herbs of the lily family, cultivated as an ornamental plant. [after the Prince of *Sanseviero,* 1710–71]

San·skrit (san′skrit) *n.* The ancient and classical language of the Hindus of India, belonging to the Indic branch of the Indo-Iranian subfamily of Indo-European languages. Also **San′scrit.** [< Skt. *samskrita* artificial, highly cultivated]

San·skrit·ic (san·skrit′ik) *adj.* **1.** Of, pertaining to, or written in Sanskrit. **2.** Designating a group of some 30 to 40 ancient and modern languages and dialects of India.

sans ser·if (sanz ser′if) *Printing* A type face without serifs: also called *gothic.*

San·ta Claus (san′tə klôz′) In nursery lore, a fat, jolly old man who brings presents at Christmas time. [< Du. *Sant Nikolaas* Saint Nicholas]

San·ta Ma·ri·a (san′tə mə·rē′ə) One of the three ships of Columbus on his maiden voyage to America.

sap¹ (sap) *n.* **1.** The juices of plants, that contain and transport the materials necessary to growth. **2.** Any vital fluid; vitality. **3.** *Slang* A foolish or gullible person. [OE *sæp*]

sap² (sap) *v.* **sapped, sap·ping** *v.t.* **1.** To weaken or destroy gradually and insidiously; enervate; exhaust. **2.** To approach or undermine (an enemy fortification) by digging a sap. — *v.i.* **3.** To dig a sap or saps. — *n.* A deep, narrow trench or tunnel dug so as to approach or undermine a fortification. [< MF < Ital. *zappa* spade, goat]

sap·head (sap′hed′) *n. Slang* A simpleton; sap. — **sap·head′ed** *adj.*

sa·pi·ent (sā′pē·ənt) *adj.* Wise; sagacious: often used ironically. [< OF < L < *sapere* to have good taste] — **sa′pi·ence, sa′pi·en·cy** *n.* — **sa′pi·ent·ly** *adv.*

sap·less (sap′lis) *adj.* **1.** Destitute of sap; withered. **2.** Wanting vitality, spirit, or vivacity; insipid; dull.

sap·ling (sap′ling) *n.* **1.** A young tree. **2.** A youth. [Dim. of SAP¹]

sap·o·dil·la (sap′ə·dil′ə) *n.* **1.** A large evergreen tree of the West Indies and tropical America. **2.** Its edible, apple-shaped fruit, a source of chicle: also **sapodilla plum.** Also **sa·po·ta** (sə·pō′tə), **sap′a·dil′lo, sap′o·dil′lo.** [< Sp. < Nahuatl *tzapotl*]

sap·o·na·ceous (sap/ə·nā/shəs) *adj.* Soapy.
sa·pon·i·fy (sə·pon/ə·fī) *v.t.* **·fied, ·fy·ing** *Chem.* To convert (a fat or oil) into soap by the action of an alkali. [< F < L *sapo, saponis* soap + *facere* to make] — **sa·pon/i·fi/a·ble** *adj.* — **sa·pon·i·fi·ca·tion** (sə·pon/ə·fə·kā/shən) *n.* — **sa·pon/i·fi/er** *n.*
sap·per (sap/ər) *n.* **1.** One who or that which saps. **2.** A soldier employed in making a sap². [< SAP² + -ER]
Sap·phic (saf/ik) *adj.* **1.** Pertaining to or in the manner of Sappho. **2.** In prosody, denoting a line of trochaic pentameter with a dactyl in the third foot, much used by Sappho. [after *Sappho*]
sap·phire (saf/īr) *n.* **1.** Any of the hard, translucent, colored varieties of corundum other than the red variety, that when cut are used as gems; esp., a deep blue corundum. **2.** Deep pure blue. [< OF < L < Gk. *sappheiros*]
sap·py (sap/ē) *adj.* **·pi·er, ·pi·est** **1.** Full of sap; juicy. **2.** *Slang* Immature; silly. — **sap/pi·ly** *adv.* — **sap/pi·ness** *n.*
sapro- *combining form* **1.** Decomposition or putrefaction. **2.** Saprophytic. [< Gk. *sapros* rotten]
sap·ro·phyte (sap/rə·fīt) *n.* A vegetable organism that lives on dead or decaying organic matter, as certain funguses, various bacteria, etc. — **sap/ro·phyt/ic** (-fit/ik) *adj.*
sap·suck·er (sap/suk/ər) *n.* Any of various small black and white woodpeckers that damage orchard trees by exposing and drinking the sap.
sap·wood (sap/wŏŏd/) *n. Bot.* The new wood next to the bark of an exogenous tree.
sar·a·band (sar/ə·band) *n.* **1.** A slow, stately dance of the 17th and 18th centuries. **2.** Music for this dance, in triple meter. Also **sar/a·bande.** [< F < Sp. < Persian *sarband* a kind of dance and song]
Sar·a·cen (sar/ə·sən) *n.* **1.** Originally, a nomad Arab of the Syrian-Arabian desert. **2.** A Moslem, esp. during the Crusades. **3.** Any Arab. [< LL < LGk. *Sarakēnos*] — **Sar/a·cen/ic** (-sen/ik) or **·i·cal** *adj.*
Sar·ah (sâr/ə) The wife of Abraham. *Gen.* xvii 15.
sa·ran (sə·ran/) *n.* Any of a class of synthetic fibers and textile materials obtained by the polymerization of vinyl chloride. [Coined by Dow Chemical Co.]
sa·ra·pe (sə·räp/ē) See SERAPE.
Saratoga trunk A very large traveling trunk used formerly by ladies. [after *Saratoga* Springs]
sar·casm (sär/kaz·əm) *n.* **1.** An ironical or scornful utterance; contemptuous and taunting language. **2.** The use of biting gibes or cutting rebukes. [< LL < Gk. *sarkazein* to tear flesh, sneer < *sarx, sarkos* flesh]
— **Syn.** **1.** *Sarcasm* may describe a man's weakness in subtly pejorative terms, or may show the vanity of his pretensions, or his absurdity. *Irony* is more limited, and is sometimes regarded as one of the methods of *sarcasm*; it consists of the assertion of the opposite of what is really meant.
sar·cas·tic (sär·kas/tik) *adj.* **1.** Characterized by or of the nature of sarcasm; taunting. **2.** Given to the use of sarcasm. Also **sar·cas/ti·cal.** — **sar·cas/ti·cal·ly** *adv.*
sar·ce·net (särs/nit) See SARSENET.
sarco- *combining form* Flesh; of or related to flesh. Also, before vowels, **sarc-.** [< Gk. *sarx, sarkos* flesh]
sar·co·carp (sär/kō·kärp) *n. Bot.* The succulent part of a stone fruit, as the fleshy edible part of a plum or peach.
sar·co·ma (sär·kō/mə) *n. pl.* **·ma·ta** (-mə·tə) *Pathol.* A tumor, often malignant, made up of cells resembling those of embryonic connective tissue. [< Gk. < *sarx, sarkos* flesh] — **sar·co/ma·toid, sar·co/ma·tous** (-kō/mə·təs, -kom/ə-) *adj.*
sar·coph·a·gus (sär·kof/ə·gəs) *n. pl.* **·gi** (-jī) **1.** A stone coffin or tomb. **2.** A large ornamental coffin of marble or stone placed in a crypt or exposed to view. **3.** A kind of limestone, used by the Greeks for coffins. [< L < Gk. < *sarx, sarkos* flesh + *phagein* to eat]
sar·cous (sär/kəs) *adj.* Of, pertaining to, or composed of flesh or muscle. [< Gk. *sarx, sarkos* flesh]
sard (särd) *n.* The deep brownish red variety of chalcedony, used as a gem. [< OF < L < Gk. *Sardeis* Sardis]
sar·dine (sär·dēn/) *n.* **1.** A small, herringlike fish commonly preserved in oil as a food delicacy, esp. the pilchard. **2.** Any of various related fishes similarly preserved. [< OF < L < Gk. *sardēnē,* ? < *Sardo* Sardinia]
Sar·dis (sär/dis) An ancient city of Asia Minor, capital of Lydia; destroyed by Tamerlane. Also **Sar/des.**
sar·don·ic (sär·don/ik) *adj.* Scornful or derisive; mocking; cynical. [< F < L < Gk. *sardanios* bitter, scornful] — **sar·don/i·cal·ly** *adv.* — **sar·don/i·cism** *n.*
sar·do·nyx (sär/də·niks) *n.* A variety of chalcedony in bands varying from light to reddish brown, with other colors. [< L < Gk., appar. < *sardios* sard + *onyx* onyx]
sar·gas·so (sär·gas/ō) *n.* An olive-brown seaweed having small air bladders on its stalks, native in tropical American waters; also called *gulfweed.* Also **sar·gas/sum.** [< Pg. < *sarga,* ? < L *salicastrum*]
sa·ri (sä/rē) *n. pl.* **·ris** A long piece of cotton or silk cloth, constituting the principal garment of Hindu women, worn round the waist, one end falling to the feet, and the other crossed over the bosom and shoulder, and sometimes over the head. Also **sa·ree.** [< Hind. *sarī* < Skt. *śāṭī*]
sa·rong (sə·rong/) *n.* **1.** A skirtlike garment of colored silk or cotton cloth worn by both sexes in the Malay Archipelago, etc. **2.** The material used for this garment. [< Malay *sārung,* prob. < Skt. *sāraṅga* variegated]
sar·sa·pa·ril·la (sas/pə·ril/ə, sär/sə·pə·ril/ə) *n.* **1.** The dried roots of certain tropical American climbing plants of the lily family. **2.** A medicinal preparation or a beverage made from such roots. [< Sp. < *zarza* bramble + *parilla,* dim. of *parra* vine]
sarse·net (särs/nit) *n.* A fine, thin silk, used for linings: also spelled *sarcenet.* [< AF, prob. < ME *sarzin* Saracen]
sar·to·ri·al (sär·tôr/ē·əl, -tō/rē-) *adj.* **1.** Pertaining to a tailor or his work. **2.** Pertaining to men's clothes. [< L *sartor* patcher, mender] — **sar·to/ri·al·ly** *adv.*
sash¹ (sash) *n.* An ornamental band or scarf, worn as a girdle, or around the waist or over the shoulder. [Orig. *shash* < Arabic *shāsh* muslin, turban]
sash² (sash) *n.* A frame, as of a window, in which glass is set. — *v.t.* To furnish with a sash. [Alter. of CHASSIS, taken as a pl.]
sa·shay (sa·shā/) *v.i. U.S. Informal* To move with a swinging or gliding motion. [Alter. of *chassé,* a dance motion]
sass (sas) *Informal n.* Impudence; back talk. — *v.t.* To talk to impudently or disrespectfully. [Dial. alter. of SAUCE]
sas·sa·fras (sas/ə·fras) *n.* **1.** An aromatic, deciduous tree of the laurel family. **2.** The root bark of this tree, used for flavoring, and yielding a volatile oil. [< Sp. *sasafrás,* prob. < N. Am. Ind. name]
sas·sy¹ (sas/ē) *adj.* **·si·er, ·si·est** *U.S. Dial.* Saucy; impertinent; cheeky.
sas·sy² (sas/ē) *n.* A West African tree having a bark that yields a poisonous alkaloid. Also **sas/sy·bark/** (-bärk/), **sas/sy·wood/** (-wŏŏd/). [< native W. African name]
sat (sat) Past tense of SIT.
Sa·tan (sā/tən) In the Bible, the great adversary of God and tempter of mankind; the Devil: identified with *Lucifer. Luke* iv 5–8; *Rev.* xii 7–9. Also **Sa/than** (sā/tən), **Sath·a·nas** (sath/ə·nəs). [< Hebrew *sātān* enemy]
sa·tan·ic (sā·tan/ik) *adj.* Devilish; infernal; wicked. Also **sa·tan/i·cal.** — **sa·tan/i·cal·ly** *adv.*
satch·el (sach/əl) *n.* A small handbag or suitcase. [< OF < L *sacellus,* dim. of *saccus* sack]
sate (sāt) *v.t.* **sat·ed, sat·ing** To satisfy the appetite of; satiate. [Appar. alter. of obs. *sade* to sate, OE *sadian;* refashioned after L *sat, satis* enough]
sa·teen (sa·tēn/) *n.* A cotton fabric woven so as to give it a satin surface. [Alter. of SATIN]
sat·el·lite (sat/ə·līt) *n.* **1.** *Astron.* A smaller body attending upon and revolving round a larger one; a moon. **2.** One who attends upon a person in power. **3.** Any obsequious attendant. **4.** A small nation that is politically, economically, or militarily dependent on a great power. **5.** A town or community whose activities are largely determined by those of a neighboring metropolis. **6.** Any manmade object launched from and revolving around the earth. [< F < L *satelles, satellitis* attendant, guard]
sa·ti·a·ble (sā/shē·ə·bəl, -shə·bəl) *adj.* Capable of being satiated. — **sa/ti·a·bil/i·ty, sa/ti·a·ble·ness** *n.* — **sa/ti·a·bly** *adv.*
sa·ti·ate (sā/shē·āt) *v.t.* **·at·ed, ·at·ing** **1.** To satisfy the appetite or desire of; gratify. **2.** To fill or gratify beyond natural desire; glut. — **Syn.** See SATISFY. — *adj.* Filled to satiety; satiated. [< L < *satis* enough] — **sa/ti·a/tion** *n.*
sa·ti·e·ty (sə·tī/ə·tē) *n. pl.* **·ties** The state of being satiated.
sat·in (sat/ən) *n.* A silk, cotton, rayon, or acetate fabric of thick texture, with glossy face and dull back. — *adj.* Of or resembling satin; glossy; smooth. [< OF < Med.L *satinus, setinus,* ult. < L *seta* silk] — **sat/in·y** *adj.*
sat·i·net (sat/ə·net/) *n.* **1.** A strong fabric with cotton warp and woolen filling. **2.** A thin satin. Also **sat/i·nette/.** [< F, dim. of *satin* satin]
sat·in·wood (sat/ən·wŏŏd/) *n.* **1.** The satinlike wood of an East Indian tree of the mahogany family. **2.** The tree.
sat·ire (sat/īr) *n.* **1.** The use of sarcasm, irony, or wit in exposing abuses or follies; ridicule. **2.** A written composition in which vice, folly, etc., is held up to ridicule. [< MF < L *satira, satura* satire, orig. medley < (*lanx*) *satura* fruit salad, lit., full (dish), fem. of *satur* full]
— **Syn.** **1.** chaff, raillery, mockery, derision.
sa·tir·ic (sə·tir/ik) *adj.* Of, pertaining to, or resembling satire, esp. literary satire: *satiric* verse. Also *satirical.*
sa·tir·i·cal (sə·tir/i·kəl) *adj.* **1.** Given to or characterized by satire. **2.** Severely sarcastic; caustic: a *satirical* laugh. **3.** Satiric. — **sa·tir/i·cal·ly** *adv.* — **sa·tir/i·cal·ness** *n.*
sat·i·rist (sat/ə·rist) *n.* **1.** A writer of satire. **2.** A satirical person.
sat·i·rize (sat/ə·rīz) *v.t.* **·rized, ·riz·ing** To criticize by means of satire; subject to satire. — **sat/i·riz/er** *n.*

sat·is·fac·tion (sat/is·fak/shən) *n.* **1.** The act of satisfying or the state of being satisfied; gratification. **2.** The making of amends, reparation, or payment, as of a claim or obligation. **3.** That which satisfies; atonement; compensation.

sat·is·fac·to·ry (sat/is·fak/tər·ē) *adj.* **1.** Giving satisfaction; answering fully all desires, expectations, or requirements. **2.** Atoning; expiatory. — **Syn.** See ADEQUATE. — **sat/is·fac/to·ri·ly** *adv.* — **sat/is·fac/to·ri·ness** *n.*

sat·is·fy (sat/is·fī) *v.* **·fied, ·fy·ing** *v.t.* **1.** To supply fully with what is desired, expected, or needed; gratify. **2.** To free from doubt or anxiety; convince. **3.** To give what is due to. **4.** To pay or discharge (a debt, obligation, etc.). **5.** To answer sufficiently or convincingly, as a question or objection. **6.** To fulfill the conditions or requirements of, as an equation. **7.** To make reparation for; expiate. — *v.i.* **8.** To give satisfaction. [< OF < L < *satis* enough + *facere* to do] — **sat/is·fi/er** *n.* — **sat/is·fy/ing·ly** *adv.*
— **Syn. 1.** *Satisfy* suggests the giving of just enough, and no more, and a state of mind that is merely content. To *gratify* is to please, hence to give liberally, while *satiate* is now chiefly used to indicate an excess or oversupply.

sa·to·ri (sä·tôr/ē) *n.* The illumination of spirit sought by Zen Buddhists. [< Japanese]

sa·trap (sā/trap, sat/rap) *n.* **1.** A governor of a province in ancient Persia. **2.** A subordinate, often despotic, ruler or governor. [< L < Gk. < OPersian *shathraparan*, lit., protector of a province]

sa·trap·y (sā/trə·pē, sat/rə·pē) *n.* *pl.* **·trap·ies** The territory or the jurisdiction of a satrap. Also **sa·trap·ate** (sā/trə·pit, sat/rə·).

sat·u·rate (sach/ə·rāt; *for adj., also* sach/ə·rit) *v.t.* **·rat·ed, ·rat·ing 1.** To soak or imbue thoroughly. **2.** To fill, impregnate, or charge (a substance or material) to its full capacity. — *adj.* **1.** Filled to repletion; saturated. **2.** Very intense; deep: said of colors. [< L *saturatus*, pp. of *saturare* to fill up] — **sat·u·ra·ble** (sach/ər·ə·bəl) *adj.* — **sat/u·ra/ter** *or* **·tor** *n.* — **sat/u·ra/tion** *n.*

sat·u·rat·ed (sach/ə·rā/tid) *adj.* **1.** Incapable of holding more of a substance or material; completely satisfied; replete: *saturated* vapor. **2.** *Chem.* Designating an organic compound, as paraffin or methane, having no free valences and without double or triple bonds. **3.** Designating a color or hue exhibiting high saturation.

Sat·ur·day (sat/ər·dē, -dā) *n.* The seventh or last day of the week. [OE *Sæterdæg, Sæternesdæg*]

Sat·urn (sat/ərn) In Roman mythology, the god of agriculture: identified with the Greek *Cronus.* — *n.* The second largest planet of the solar system and sixth in order from the sun. See PLANET. [< L *Saturnus*] — **Sa·tur·ni·an** (sə·tûr/nē·ən) *adj.*

sat·ur·na·li·a (sat/ər·nā/lē·ə) *n.pl.* (*Usu. construed as sing.*) Any season or period of general license or revelry.

Sat·ur·na·li·a (sat/ər·nā/lē·ə) *n.pl.* The feast of Saturn, held at Rome in mid-December, and marked by wild reveling and licentious abandon. — **Sat/ur·na/li·an** *adj.*

sat·ur·nine (sat/ər·nīn) *adj.* Having a grave, gloomy, or morose disposition or character. [< OF < Med.L *Saturnus* lead, Saturn]

sat·yr (sat/ər, sā/tər) *n.* **1.** In Greek mythology, a lecherous woodland diety in human form, having pointed ears, goat's legs, and budding horns. **2.** A very lascivious man. [< L < Gk. *satyros*] — **sa·tyr·ic** (sə·tir/ik) *or* **·i·cal** *adj.*

sat·y·ri·a·sis (sat/ə·rī/ə·sis) *n.* *Psychiatry* An excessive and uncontrollable sexual desire in men. [< NL < Gk. < *satyros* satyr]

sauce (sôs) *n.* **1.** An appetizing dressing or liquid relish for food. **2.** Any appetizing garnish of a meal. **3.** Formerly, any condiment, as salt or pepper. **4.** A dish of fruit pulp stewed and sweetened. **5.** *Informal* Pert or impudent language. — *v.t.* **sauced, sauc·ing 1.** To flavor with sauce; season. **2.** To give zest or piquancy to. **3.** *Informal* To be saucy to. [< OF < LL *salsa*, orig. fem. of L *salsus* salted]

sauce·pan (sôs/pan/) *n.* A metal or enamel pan with projecting handle, for cooking food.

sau·cer (sô/sər) *n.* **1.** A small dish for holding a cup. **2.** Any small, round, shallow vessel of similar shape. [< OF < *sauce* sauce]

sau·cy (sô/sē) *adj.* **·ci·er, ·ci·est 1.** Disrespectful to superiors; impudent. **2.** Piquant; sprightly; amusing. — **sau/ci·ly** *adv.* — **sau/ci·ness** *n.*

sauer·bra·ten (sour/brätn, *Ger.* zou/ər·brätn/) *n.* Beef marinated in vinegar before being braised. [< G < *sauer* sour + *braten* to roast]

sauer·kraut (sour/krout/) *n.* Shredded and salted cabbage fermented in its own juice: also called *kraut.* [< G < *sauer* sour + *kraut* cabbage]

Sauk (sôk) *n.* One of a tribe of North American Indians of Algonquian stock, formerly occupying Michigan, later Wis-consin and the Mississippi valley, now on reservations in Oklahoma, Iowa, and Kansas. Also spelled *Sac.*

Saul (sôl) **1.** The first king of Israel. I *Sam.* ix 2. **2.** The Hebrew name of the Apostle Paul (*Acts* xiii 9): also **Saul of Tarsus.**

sau·na (sou/nə) *n.* A room or house for taking steam baths by the Finnish method, in steam produced by throwing water on hot stones; also, such a steam bath. [< Finnish]

saun·ter (sôn/tər) *v.i.* To walk in a leisurely or lounging way; stroll. — *n.* **1.** A slow, aimless manner of walking. **2.** An idle stroll. [ME *santren* to muse, meditate]

sau·ri·an (sôr/ē·ən) *n.* One of a suborder of reptiles, including the lizards, geckos, and chameleons. — *adj.* Pertaining to saurians. [< NL < Gk. *sauros* lizard]

sauro- *combining form* Lizard. Also, before vowels, **saur-**. [< Gk. *sauros* lizard]

-saurus *combining form Zool.* Lizard: used to form genus names: *Brontosaurus.* [< Gk. *sauros* lizard]

sau·sage (sô/sij) *n.* **1.** Finely chopped and highly seasoned meat, commonly stuffed into the cleaned entrails of some animal or into artificial casings. **2.** *Aeron.* A type of barrage or observation balloon, shaped like a sausage. [< AF < LL *salsicia*, ult. < L *salsus* salted]

sau·té (sō·tā/, sô-) *adj.* Fried quickly with little grease. — *v.t.* **·téed, ·té·ing** To fry quickly in a little fat. [< F, pp. of *sauter* to leap < L *saltare*]

sau·terne (sō·tûrn/, sô-; *Fr.* sō·tern/) *n.* A sweet, white French wine. Also **sau·ternes/.** [after *Sauternes*, district in SW France]

sav·age (sav/ij) *adj.* **1.** Having a wild and untamed nature; not domesticated. **2.** Ferocious; fierce. **3.** Living in or belonging to a primitive condition of human life and society; uncivilized: *savage* tribes. **4.** Vicious; cruel; furious. **5.** Rude; uncultivated; rough. — *n.* **1.** A primitive or uncivilized human being. **2.** A brutal, fierce, and cruel person; a barbarian. — *v.t.* **·aged, ·ag·ing** To attack savagely, esp. with the teeth. [< OF < L *salvaticus, silvaticus* < *silva* a wood] — **sav/age·ly** *adv.* — **sav/age·ness** *n.*

sav·age·ry (sav/ij·rē) *n.* *pl.* **·ries 1.** The state of being savage. **2.** Cruelty in disposition or action; a cruel or savage act. **3.** Savages collectively: also **sav/age·dom** (-dəm). Also **sav/ag·ism.**

sa·van·na (sə·van/ə) *n.* **1.** A tract of level land covered with low vegetation. **2.** Any large area of tropical or subtropical grassland, covered in part with trees and spiny shrubs. Also **sa·van/nah.** [Earlier *zavana* < Sp. < Carib]

sa·vant (sə·vänt/, sav/ənt; *Fr.* sȧ·vän/) *n.* A man of exceptional learning. [< F < L *sapere* to be wise]

save[1] (sāv) *v.* **saved, sav·ing** *v.t.* **1.** To preserve or rescue from danger, harm, etc. **2.** To keep from being spent, expended, or lost. **3.** To set aside for future use; accumulate: often with *up.* **4.** To treat carefully so as to avoid fatigue, harm, etc.: to *save* one's eyes. **5.** To prevent by timely action: A stitch in time *saves* nine. **6.** *Theol.* To deliver from spiritual death or the consequences of sin. — *v.i.* **7.** To avoid waste; be economical. **8.** To preserve something from danger, harm, etc. **9.** To admit of preservation, as food. [< OF < LL < L *salvus* safe] — **sav/a·ble** *or* **save/a·ble** *adj.* — **sav/a·ble·ness** *n.* — **sav/er** *n.*

save[2] (sāv) *prep.* Except; but. — *conj.* **1.** Except; but: usu. with *that.* **2.** *Archaic* Unless. [< OF *sauf* being excepted, orig., safe < L *salvus*]

sav·ing (sā/ving) *adj.* **1.** That saves; preserving, as from destruction. **2.** Redeeming; delivering. **3.** Avoiding needless waste or expense; economical; frugal. **4.** Incurring no loss, if not gainful: a *saving* investment. **5.** Holding in reserve; making an exception; qualifying: a *saving* clause. — *n.* **1.** Preservation from loss or danger. **2.** Avoidance of waste; economy. **3.** The extent of something saved: a *saving* of 16 percent. **4.** *pl.* Sums of money not expended. **5.** That which is saved. — *prep.* **1.** With the exception of; save. **2.** With due respect for: *saving* your presence. — *conj.* Save; but. — **sav/ing·ly** *adv.* — **sav/ing·ness** *n.*

savings account An account drawing interest at a bank.

savings bank 1. A bank whose chief functions are receiving and investing savings and paying interest on deposits. **2.** A container with a slot for depositing coins.

sav·ior (sāv/yər) *n.* One who saves. Also *Brit.* **sav/iour.** [< OF < LL < L *salvare* to save]

Sav·iour (sāv/yər) *n.* A title sometimes applied directly to God, but chiefly to Jesus Christ, as the Redeemer: usu. with *the.* Also **Sav/ior.**

sa·voir-faire (sȧ·vwȧr·fâr/) *French* Ability to say and do the right thing; tact; literally, to know how to act.

sa·vor (sā/vər) *n.* **1.** The quality of a thing that affects the sense of taste or smell, or both; flavor; odor. **2.** Specific or characteristic quality or approach to a quality; flavor. **3.** Relish; zest: The conversation had *savor.* — *v.i.* **1.** To have a specified savor; taste or smell: with *of*. **2.** To have a specified quality or character: with *of*. — *v.t.* **3.** To give flavor to; season. **4.** To taste or enjoy with pleasure; relish. **5.** To have the savor or character of. Also *Brit.* **sa′vour.** [< OF < L < *sapere* to taste, know] — **sa′vor·er** *n.* — **sa′·vor·ous** *adj.*

sa·vor·less (sā′vər-lis) *adj.* Tasteless; insipid.

sa·vor·y[1] (sā′vər-ē) *adj.* **1.** Of an agreeable taste and odor; appetizing. **2.** Piquant to the taste. **3.** In good repute; respectable. — *n. Brit.* A small, hot serving of food eaten at the end or beginning of a dinner. Also *Brit.* **sa′vour·y.** [< OF *savouré*, pp. of *savourer* to taste] — **sa′vor·i·ly** *adv.* — **sa′vor·i·ness** *n.*

sa·vor·y[2] (sā′vər-ē) *n.* A hardy, annual, aromatic herb of the mint family, used for seasoning. Also **summer savory.** [OE < *satureia*]

sa·voy (sə-voi′) *n.* A variety of cabbage with wrinkled leaves. [< F (*chou de*) *Savoie* (cabbage of) Savoy]

Sa·voy·ard (sə-voi′ərd, *Fr.* sȧ·vwä·yàr′) *n.* **1.** An actor or actress in the Gilbert and Sullivan operas. **2.** An admirer of these operas. [after the *Savoy* Theater in London]

sav·vy (sav′ē) *Slang v.i.* **·vied, ·vy·ing** To understand; comprehend. — *n.* Understanding; good sense. [Alter. of Sp. *¿ Sabe* (*usted*)? Do (you) know? < L *sapere* to know]

saw[1] (sô) *n.* **1.** A cutting instrument with pointed teeth arranged continuously along the edge of the blade, used to cut or divide wood, bone, metal, etc. **2.** A machine for operating a saw or gang of saws. **3.** Any tool or instrument without teeth used like a saw. — *v.* **sawed, sawed** or **sawn, saw·ing** *v.t.* **1.** To cut or divide with a saw. **2.** To shape or fashion with a saw. **3.** To cut or slice (the air, etc.) as if using a saw. **4.** To cause to move with a to-and-fro motion like that of a saw. — *v.i.* **5.** To use a saw. **6.** To cut: said of a saw. **7.** To be cut with a saw: This wood *saws* easily. [OE *sagu*] — **saw′er** *n.*

saw[2] (sô) *n.* A proverbial or familiar saying; old maxim. — **Syn.** See PROVERB. [OE *sagu*]

saw[3] (sô) Past tense of SEE[1].

saw·bones (sô′bōnz′) *n. Slang* A surgeon.

saw·buck (sô′buk′) *n.* **1.** A sawhorse consisting of two X-shaped ends joined by a connecting bar or bars. **2.** *U.S. Slang* A ten-dollar bill: so called from the resemblance of X, Roman numeral ten, to the ends of a sawbuck. [Trans. of Du. *zaagbok*]

saw·dust (sô′dust′) *n.* Small particles of wood produced by the action of sawing.

sawed-off (sôd′ôf′, -of′) *adj.* **1.** Having one end sawed off, as a shotgun. **2.** *U.S. Slang* Short; not of average height.

saw·fish (sô′fish′) *n.* *pl.* **·fish** or **·fish·es** Any of various elongate, sharklike tropical fish with the snout prolonged into a flat blade with teeth on each side.

saw·fly (sô′flī′) *n. pl.* **·flies** Any of various winged insects having in the female a sawlike ovipositor for piercing plants, soft wood, etc.

saw·horse (sô′hôrs′) *n.* A frame on which to rest wood, etc., for sawing, usu. consisting of a long wooden bar or plank supported by four extended legs.

saw log A log of suitable size for sawing.

saw·mill (sô′mil′) *n.* **1.** An establishment for sawing logs with power-driven machinery. **2.** A large sawing machine.

sawn (sôn) Alternative past participle of SAW[1].

saw-toothed (sô′tōōtht′) *adj.* Serrate; having teeth or toothlike processes similar to those of a saw.

saw·yer (sô′yər) *n.* **1.** One whose occupation is the sawing of wood, as in lumbering or in a sawmill. **2.** Any of various longicorn beetles having larvae that bore into wood, as the **pine sawyer.** [Alter. of SAWER]

sax (saks) *n. Informal* A saxophone.

sax·horn (saks′hôrn′) *n.* Any of a family of valved brass instruments resembling the bugle, made in a wide series of ranges. [after the inventor, Antoine Joseph *Sax* (called Adolphe), 1814–94, Belgian instrument maker + HORN]

sax·i·frage (sak′sə·frij) *n.* Any of a large, widely distributed genus of herbaceous plants growing in rocky places, bearing small white, yellow, or purplish flowers. [< OF < L (*herba*) *saxifraga*, lit., stone-breaking (herb)]

Sax·on (sak′sən) *n.* **1.** A member of a Germanic tribal group formerly inhabiting what is now Schleswig-Holstein. **2.** A member of any of the offshoots of this group, as those who, with the Angles and Jutes, invaded England in the fifth and sixth centuries A.D. **3.** An Anglo-Saxon. **4.** An inhabitant of Saxony. **5.** The modern High German dialect of Saxony. — **Old Saxon** The dialect of Low German current in the valley of the lower Elbe in the early Middle Ages. — *adj.* **1.** Of or pertaining to the Saxons or to their language. **2.** Anglo-Saxon; English. **3.** Of or pertaining to Saxony (Germany). [< F < L *Saxo, Saxonis* < WGmc.]

sax·o·phone (sak′sə·fōn) *n.* Any of a family of metal wind instruments having a single reed and conical bore, made in a wide series of ranges. [after A. J. *Sax* (see SAXHORN) + -PHONE] — **sax′o·phon′ist** *n.*

say (sā) *v.* **said, say·ing** *v.t.* **1.** To pronounce or utter; speak. **2.** To declare or express in words; tell; state. **3.** To state positively or as an opinion: *Say* which you prefer. **4.** To recite: to *say* one's prayers. **5.** To report; allege. **6.** To assume; suppose. — *v.i.* **7.** To make a statement; speak. — **that is to say** In other words. — *adv.* **1.** Approximately; at a guess: He is worth, *say*, a million. **2.** For example: Choose a number, *say*, ten. — *n.* **1.** What one has said or has to say; word. **2.** Right or turn to speak or choose: to have one's *say*. **3.** Authority: to have the *say*. — *interj.* *U.S. Informal* A hail or an exclamation to command attention: also *Brit.* **I say.** [OE *secgan*] — **say′er** *n.*

say·ing (sā′ing) *n.* **1.** A maxim; adage. **2.** Something said.

says (sez) Third person singular, present indicative of SAY.

say-so (sā′sō′) *n. Informal* **1.** An unsupported assertion or decision. **2.** Right or power to make decisions.

scab (skab) *n.* **1.** A crust formed on the surface of a wound or sore. **2.** *Vet.* Scabies. **3.** Any of certain plant diseases characterized by a roughened or warty appearance. **4.** *Slang* A mean, contemptible fellow. **5.** *Informal* A workman who will not join or act with a labor union; esp., a strikebreaker. — *v.i.* **scabbed, scab·bing 1.** To form or become covered with a scab. **2.** *Informal* To take the job of a striker. [Fusion of ON *skabbr* (assumed) and OE *sceabb*]

scab·bard (skab′ərd) *n.* A sheath for a weapon, as for a bayonet or a sword. — *v.t.* To sheathe in or furnish with a scabbard. [< OF *escalberc*, prob. < OHG *scar* sword + *bergan* to hide, protect]

scab·by (skab′ē) *adj.* **·bi·er, ·bi·est 1.** Having, consisting of, or resembling a scab or scabs. **2.** Having scabies. **3.** *Informal* Contemptible. — **scab′bi·ly** *adv.* — **scab′bi·ness** *n.*

sca·bi·es (skā′bi·ēz, -bēz) *n.* **1.** A skin disease caused by the itch mite; itch. **2.** *Vet.* A similar skin disease of sheep: also called *scab*. [< L, roughness, an itch < *scabere* to scratch, scrape.] — **sca·bi·et·ic** (skā′bē·et′ik) *adj.*

sca·bi·ous[1] (skā′bē·əs) *adj.* **1.** Pertaining to or resembling scabies. **2.** Having scabs.

sca·bi·ous[2] (skā′bē·əs) *n.* Any of a genus of herbs allied to the teasel, with heads of variously colored flowers. Also **sca′bi·o′sa** (-ō′sə). [< NL < Med.L (*herba*) *scabiosa*, fem. sing. of *scabiosus* scabious[1]]

sca·brous (skab′rəs, skā′brəs) *adj.* **1.** Roughened with minute points; scurfy. **2.** Off-color; risqué. **3.** Difficult to handle tactfully; knotty. [< LL < *scabere* to scratch] — **sca′·brous·ly** *adv.* — **sca′brous·ness** *n.*

scads (skadz) *n.pl. Informal* A large amount or quantity. [? Var. of dial E *scald* a large amount, great number]

scaf·fold (skaf′əld, -ōld) *n.* **1.** A temporary elevated structure for the support of workmen, materials, etc., as in building. **2.** Any raised wooden framework. **3.** A platform for the execution of criminals. — *v.t.* To furnish or support with a scaffold. [< OF (*e*)*schaffaut*]

scaf·fold·ing (skaf′əl·ding) *n.* A scaffold, or system of scaffolds, or the materials for constructing them. Also **scaf·fold·age** (skaf′əl·dij).

sca·lar (skā′lər) *Math. adj.* Definable by a number on a line or scale: said of a quantity having magnitude only, as a volume or mass: distinguished from *vector*. [< L < *scala* ladder]

scal·a·wag (skal′ə·wag) *n.* **1.** *Informal* A worthless fellow; scamp. **2.** *U.S.* During the Reconstruction period, a native Southern white Republican: a contemptuous term. Also called *scallywag*: also spelled *scallawag*. [Origin uncertain]

scald (skôld) *v.t.* **1.** To burn with or as with hot liquid or steam. **2.** To cleanse or treat with boiling water. **3.** To heat (a liquid) to a point just short of boiling. — *v.i.* **4.** To be or become scalded. — *n.* **1.** A burn or injury to the skin by a hot fluid. **2.** A destructive parasitic disease of plants. **3.** A discoloration of plant tissue due to improper conditions of growth, storage, etc. [< AF < LL < L < *ex-* very + *calidus* hot]

scale[1] (skāl) *n.* **1.** One of the thin, flat, horny, membranous or bony outgrowths of the skin of various animals, as most fishes, usu. overlapping and forming a nearly complete covering. **2.** Any similar thin, flat formation, piece, or part. **3.** A scab. **4.** A scale insect. **5.** *Bot.* A rudimentary or metamorphosed leaf, as of a pine cone. **6.** *Metall.* The coating of oxide that forms on heated iron, etc. **7.** An incrustation formed on the inside of boilers, etc. — *v.* **scaled, scal·ing** *v.t.* **1.** To strip or clear of scales. **2.** To form scales on. **3.** To take off in layers. — *v.i.* **4.** To come off in scales; peel. **5.** To shed scales. **6.** To become incrusted with scales. [< OF *escale* husk < Gmc.] — **scal′er** *n.*

scale[2] (skāl) *n.* **1.** Any instrument bearing accurately spaced lines or gradations for use in measurement. **2.** The series of marks so used. **3.** Any system of designating units of measurement: the Fahrenheit *scale*. **4.** A fixed proportion used in determining measurements or dimensions: a *scale* of one inch to the mile. **5.** Any progressive or graded classification: wage *scale*. **6.** Relative proportion, degree, scope, etc.: with *on*: to live on a grand *scale*. **7.** *Math.* A system of notation in which the successive places determine the value of the figures: the decimal *scale*. **8.** *Music* An arrangement of tones in ascending or descending order through the interval of an octave: a diatonic *scale*. — **major scale** *Music* A scale having semitones after the third and seventh steps, all the other intervals being whole tones. — **minor scale** A scale having semitones after the second and third steps (the natural form), or after the second, fifth, and seventh steps (the harmonic form), or after the second and seventh steps when ascending and the sixth and third when descending (the melodic form), all the other intervals being whole tones. — *v.* **scaled, scal·ing** *v.t.* **1.** To climb to the top of. **2.** To make according to a scale. **3.** To regulate or adjust according to a scale or ratio: with *up*, *down*, etc. — *v.i.* **4.** To climb; ascend. **5.** To rise in steps or stages. [< Ital. < L *scandere* to climb] — **scal'a·ble** *adj.* — **scal'er** *n.*

scale³ (skāl) *n.* **1.** Any weighing machine. **2.** A pan, scoop, platform, etc., that holds the object or material to be weighed in a weighing instrument or balance. **3.** *Usu. pl.* A balance (defs. 1 & 2). — **to turn the scales** To determine; decide. — *v.* **scaled, scal·ing** *v.t.* **1.** To weigh in scales. **2.** To amount to in weight. — *v.i.* **3.** To be weighed. [< ON *skāl* bowl, in pl., a weighing balance]

scale insect One of numerous small insects that feed on plants and as adults have a scalelike, protective shield.

sca·lene (skā·lēn′, skā·lēn′) *adj.* *Geom.* Designating a triangle having no two sides equal. [< LL < Gk. *skalēnos* uneven]

Scales (skālz) *n.pl.* The constellation and sign of the zodiac Libra.

scal·la·wag (skal′ə·wag) See SCALAWAG.

scal·lion (skal′yən) *n.* **1.** A young, tender onion with a small white bulb. **2.** A shallot or leek. [< OF < L (*caepa*) *Ascalonia* (onion) of Ashkelon, a Palestinian seaport]

scal·lop (skal′əp, skol′-) *n.* **1.** A bivalve mollusk having a rounded, ridged shell whose valves are snapped together in swimming. **2.** The edible adductor muscle of certain species of this mollusk. **3.** The shell of a scallop; esp., one in which seafood is cooked or served. **4.** One of a series of semicircular curves along an edge, as for ornament. — *v.t.* **1.** To shape the edge of with scallops. **2.** To bake (food) in a casserole with a sauce, often topped with bread crumbs. Also spelled *escallop, scollop.* [< OF *escalope* < Gmc.] — **scal'lop·er** *n.*

SCALLOP SHELL

scal·ly·wag (skal′ē·wag) *n.* A scalawag.

scalp (skalp) *n.* **1.** The skin of the top and back of the human skull, usu. covered with hair. **2.** A portion of this, formerly cut or torn away as a war trophy among certain North American Indians. — *v.t.* **1.** To cut or tear the scalp from. **2.** *Informal* To buy and resell (tickets) at prices exceeding the established rate. **3.** *Informal* To buy and sell again quickly in order to make a small profit. **4.** *Informal* To defeat utterly. — *v.i.* **5.** *Informal* To scalp bonds, tickets, etc. [ME, prob. < Scand.] — **scalp'er** *n.*

scal·pel (skal′pəl) *n.* A small pointed knife with a very sharp, thin blade, used in dissections and in surgery. [< L *scalpere* to cut]

scal·y (skā′lē) *adj.* **scal·i·er, scal·i·est** Having, resembling, or incrusted with scales. — **scal'i·ness** *n.*

scaly anteater A pangolin.

scamp¹ (skamp) *n.* A confirmed rogue; good-for-nothing fellow; rascal. [< obs. verb *scamp* to roam, contr. of SCAMPER] — **scamp'ish** *adj.*

scamp² (skamp) *v.t.* To perform (work) carelessly or dishonestly. [Orig. dial. E] — **scamp'er** *n.*

scam·per (skam′pər) *v.i.* To run quickly or hastily. — *n.* A hurried run or departure. [< OF, ult. < L *ex* out from + *campus* plain, battlefield] — **scam'per·er** *n.*

scan (skan) *v.* **scanned, scan·ning** *v.t.* **1.** To examine in detail; scrutinize closely. **2.** To pass the eyes over quickly; glance at. **3.** To separate (verse) into metrical feet; ascertain or indicate the rhythm of. **4.** *Telecom.* To pass a beam of light or electrons rapidly over every point of (a surface, etc.) for television, sound, or other reproduction. — *v.i.* **5.** To scan verse. **6.** To conform to metrical rules: said of verse. [< LL < L *scandere* climb] — **scan'na·ble** *adj.* — **scan'ner** *n.*

scan·dal (skan′dəl) *n.* **1.** Heedless or malicious gossip. **2.** Disgrace or reproach caused by outrageous or improper conduct. **3.** A discreditable circumstance, event, or action. **4.** Censure or open disapproval. **5.** One whose conduct results in disgrace or censure. [< AF < L < Gk. *skandalon* snare]

scan·dal·ize (skan′dəl·īz) *v.t.* **·ized, ·iz·ing** To shock the moral feelings of, as by improper, frivolous, or offensive conduct; outrage. — **scan'dal·i·za'tion** *n.* — **scan'dal·iz'er** *n.*

scan·dal·mong·er (skan′dəl·mung′gər, -mong′-) *n.* One who spreads or repeats scandal.

scan·dal·ous (skan′dəl·əs) *adj.* **1.** Causing or tending to cause scandal; disgraceful. **2.** Consisting of or spreading scandal. — **scan'dal·ous·ly** *adv.* — **scan'dal·ous·ness** *n.*

Scan·di·na·vi·an (skan′də·nā′vē·ən) *adj.* Of or pertaining to Scandinavia, its people, or their languages. — *n.* **1.** A native or inhabitant of Scandinavia. **2.** The North Germanic group of languages: see under GERMANIC. Also *Norse.* — **Old Scandinavian** Old Norse. See under NORSE.

scan·di·um (skan′dē·əm) *n.* A metallic element (symbol Sc) of the lanthanide series. See ELEMENT. [< NL < L *Scandia* Scandinavia]

scan·sion (skan′shən) *n.* The division or analysis of lines of verse according to a metrical pattern. Compare METER² (def. 1). [< F < LL < L *scandere* scan]

scant (skant) *adj.* **1.** Scarcely enough; meager in measure or quantity. **2.** Being just short of the measure specified: a *scant* half-hour; a *scant* five yards. **3.** Insufficiently supplied with: with *of*: We were *scant* of breath. — *v.t.* **1.** To restrict or limit in supply; stint. **2.** To treat briefly or inadequately. — *adv. Dial.* Scarcely; barely. [< ON *skammr* short] — **scant'ly** *adv.* — **scant'ness** *n.*

scant·ling (skant′ling) *n.* **1.** A piece of lumber of small or moderate cross section, used for studding, etc. **2.** Such lumber collectively. [< OF *eschantillon* cornerpiece]

scant·y (skan′tē) *adj.* **scant·i·er, scant·i·est** **1.** Limited in extent. **2.** Restricted in quantity or amount; scarcely sufficient; meager. — **scant'i·ly** *adv.* — **scant'i·ness** *n.*

scape (skāp) *Archaic v.t. & v.i.* To escape. — *n.* An escape or means of escape. Also **'scape.**

scape·goat (skāp′gōt) *n.* **1.** In the Bible, the goat upon whose head the high priest symbolically laid the sins of the people on the day of atonement, after which it was led away into the wilderness. *Lev.* xvi. **2.** An animal, person, or group that bears the blame or suffers for the errors or sins of others.

scape·grace (skāp′grās′) *n.* A mischievous or incorrigible person; rogue.

scapi- *combining form* A stalk, stem, or shaft. [< L *scapus* stalk]

scap·u·la (skap′yə·lə) *n.* *pl.* **·lae** (-lē) *Anat.* Either of a pair of large, flat, triangular bones in the back of the shoulder in man and having an analogous position in the skeleton of vertebrates: also called *shoulder blade.* [< LL < L *scapulae* shoulder blades]

scap·u·lar (skap′yə·lər) *n.* **1.** An outer garment consisting of two strips of cloth joined across the shoulders, worn by members of certain religious orders. **2.** A badge or sign of devotion worn about the neck by members of certain religious orders and groups. **3.** *pl. Ornithol.* The shoulder feathers of a bird. — *adj.* Of or pertaining to the scapula.

scap·u·lar·y (skap′yə·ler′ē) *n.* *pl.* **·ries** A scapular. — *adj.* Scapular.

scar (skär) *n.* **1.** The mark left on the skin after the healing of a wound or sore. **2.** Any mark, damage, or lasting effect resulting from past injury, stress, etc. — *v.t. & v.i.* **scarred, scar·ring** To mark or become marked with a scar. [< OF < LL *eschara* scab < Gk.]

scar·ab (skar′əb) *n.* **1.** A large, black beetle held sacred by the ancient Egyptians. **2.** A gem or ornament representing this beetle. [< MF < L *scarabaeus*]

scar·a·bae·us (skar′ə·bē′əs) *n.* *pl.* **·bae·us·es** or **·bae·i** (-bē′ī) A scarab. [< L]

scar·a·mouch (skar′ə·mouch, -mōōsh) *n.* A swaggering rascal. [< *Scaramouch*]

Scar·a·mouch (skar′ə·mouch, -mōōsh) In old Italian comedy, a stock character represented as a boastful, cowardly buffoon. [< F < Ital. *Scaramuccia*, lit., skirmish]

scarce (skârs) *adj.* **scarc·er, scarc·est** **1.** Rarely seen or found. **2.** Not plentiful; insufficient. — **to make oneself scarce** *Informal* To go away or stay away. [< OF, ult. < L < *ex-* out + *carpere* to pluck] — **scarce'ness** *n.*

scarce·ly (skârs′lē) *adv.* **1.** Only just; barely. **2.** Not quite; hardly.

scar·ci·ty (skâr′sə·tē) *n.* *pl.* **·ties** **1.** Inadequate supply; insufficiency; dearth. **2.** Infrequency of occurrence; rarity.

scare (skâr) *v.* **scared, scar·ing** *v.t.* **1.** To strike with sudden fear; frighten. **2.** To drive or force by frightening: with *off* or *away*. — *v.i.* **3.** To become scared. — **to scare up** *Informal* To get together or produce hurriedly. — *n.* **1.** Sudden fright, esp. from slight cause. **2.** Panic. [< ON < *skiarr* shy] — **scar'er** *n.* — **scar'ing·ly** *adv.*

scare·crow (skâr′krō′) *n.* **1.** Any effigy set up to scare crows and other birds away from growing crops. **2.** Something frightening but not dangerous. **3.** A person of ragged or disreputable appearance.

scare·head (skâr′hed′) *n. Informal* An exceptionally large newspaper headline giving news of sensational interest.

scarf¹ (skärf) *n. pl.* **scarfs** or **scarves** (skärvz) **1.** A band or square of cloth worn about the head, neck, etc., for warmth or protection, or as a decorative accessory. **2.** A necktie, cravat, kerchief, etc. **3.** A runner for a bureau or dresser. **4.** An official sash denoting rank. — *v.t.* To cover or decorate with or as with a scarf. [< OF *escharpe*]

scarf² (skärf) *n.* *pl.* **scarfs 1.** In carpentry, a lapped joint made by notching two timbers at the ends and joining them so as to form one continuous piece. Also **scarf joint. 2.** The notched end of a timber so cut. — *v.t.* **1.** To unite with a scarf joint. **2.** To cut a scarf in. [? < ON *skarfr* notch in a timber]

scar·i·fy (skar′ə·fī) *v.t.* **·fied, ·fy·ing 1.** To scratch or make slight incisions in, as the skin in surgery. **2.** To criticize severely. **3.** To stir or break up the surface of, as soil. [< MF < LL < L < Gk. *skariphos* stylus] — **scar′i·fi′er** *n.* — **scar′i·fi·ca′tion** *n.*

SCARF JOINTS

scar·la·ti·na (skär′lə·tē′nə) *n.* *Pathol.* **1.** Scarlet fever. **2.** A mild form of scarlet fever. [< Ital. See SCARLET.]

scar·let (skär′lit) *n.* **1.** A brilliant red, inclining to orange. **2.** Cloth or clothing of this color. — *adj.* **1.** Being scarlet in color. **2.** Unchaste; whorish. [< OF < Med.L, prob. < Arabic < Persian *saqalāt* a rich, scarlet cloth]

scarlet fever *Pathol.* An acute infectious bacterial disease characterized by a diffused scarlet rash followed by scaling of the skin.

scarlet runner A tall climbing bean of tropical America, having vivid red flowers and long seed pods.

scarlet tanager An American tanager, the male of which has brilliant red plumage with black wings and tail.

scarp (skärp) *n.* **1.** A steep slope. **2.** An embankment or wall at the outer part of a fortification. — *v.t.* To cut or form to a steep slope. [< AF < Ital. *scarpa*]

scarves (skärvz) Alternative plural of SCARF¹.

scar·y (skâr′ē) *adj.* **scar·i·er, scar·i·est** *Informal* **1.** Easily scared; timid. **2.** Causing fear or alarm; frightening.

scat (skat) *v.i.* **scat·ted, scat·ting** *Informal* To go away; depart: usu. in the imperative. [? < SCATTER]

scathe (skāth) *v.t.* **scathed, scath·ing 1.** To criticize severely. **2.** To injure severely; harm. — *n.* Severe injury; harm. [< ON < *skathi* to harm] — **scathe′ful** *adj.*

scathe·less (skāth′lis) *adj.* Free from harm.

scath·ing (skā′thing) *adj.* Mercilessly severe; blasting; withering: a *scathing* rebuke. — **scath′ing·ly** *adv.*

scato- *combining form* Dung; excrement. Also, before vowels, **scat-**. [< Gk. *skōr* dung]

scat·o·log·i·cal (skat′ə·loj′i·kəl) *adj.* Of or pertaining to scatology; obscene. Also **scat′o·log′ic.**

sca·tol·o·gy (skə·tol′ə·jē) *n.* The study of, or a preoccupation with, excrement. — **sca·tol′o·gist** *n.*

scat·ter (skat′ər) *v.t.* **1.** To throw about in various places; sprinkle. **2.** To separate and drive away in different directions; disperse. — *v.i.* **3.** To separate and go in different directions. [ME *scateren* to squander] — **scat′ter·er** *n.*

scat·ter·brain (skat′ər·brān′) *n.* A flighty or forgetful person. — **scat′ter·brained′** *adj.*

scatter rug A small rug used to cover only part of a floor.

scaup (skôp) *n.* A sea duck of northern regions, related to the canvasback, having the head and neck black in the male. Also **scaup duck.** [Var. of SCALP]

scav·enge (skav′inj) *v.* **·enged, ·eng·ing** *v.t.* **1.** To remove filth, rubbish, and refuse from, as streets. — *v.i.* **2.** To act as a scavenger. **3.** To search or rummage, as for food. [Back formation < SCAVENGER]

scav·en·ger (skav′in·jər) *n.* **1.** An animal that feeds on carrion, as the buzzard. **2.** One who searches refuse, garbage, etc., for usable material. **3.** A street cleaner. [ME < AF < Flemish *scauwen* to look]

sce·nar·i·o (si·nâr′ē·ō, -nä′rē·ō) *n.* *pl.* **·nar·i·os 1.** A summary or outline of the plot of a dramatic work. **2.** The written plot and arrangement of incidents of a motion picture. [< Ital. < LL < L < Gk. *skēnē* tent, stage]

sce·nar·ist (si·nâr′ist, -nä′rist) *n.* One who writes scenarios.

scene (sēn) *n.* **1.** A locality as presented to view. **2.** The place in which the action of a drama is supposed to occur; setting. **3.** The place and surroundings of any event: the *scene* of the crime. **4.** A division of an act of a play; one comprehensive event in a play. **5.** Any incident or episode that may serve as the subject of a description. **6.** The painted canvas screens for the background for a play. **7.** Any striking display; esp., a display of excited feeling. — **behind the scenes 1.** Out of sight of a theater audience. **2.** Privately; in secret. [< OF < L < Gk. *skēnē* tent, stage]

scen·er·y (sē′nər·ē) *n.* *pl.* **·er·ies 1.** The appearance or visible aspects of a landscape, locality, etc. **2.** The settings, backdrops, etc., of a theatrical production.

sce·nic (sē′nik, sen′ik) *adj.* **1.** Of or pertaining to natural scenery; picturesque. **2.** Relating to stage scenery. Also **sce′ni·cal.** — **sce′ni·cal·ly** *adv.*

scent (sent) *n.* **1.** A distinctive odor. **2.** A residual odor by which an animal can be tracked. **3.** A trail, trace, or clue aiding pursuit or investigation. **4.** A perfume. **5.** The sense of smell. — **Syn.** See SMELL. — *v.t.* **1.** To perceive by the sense of smell. **2.** To form a suspicion of. **3.** To cause to be fragrant; perfume. — *v.i.* **4.** To hunt by the sense of smell: said of hounds. [< OF *sentir* to discern by the senses, feel] — **scent′less** *adj.*

scep·ter (sep′tər) *n.* **1.** A staff carried as the badge of command or sovereignty. **2.** Kingly office or power. — *v.t.* To confer the scepter on; invest with royal power. Also *esp.* *Brit.* **scep′tre** (-tər). [< OF < L < Gk. *skēptron* staff]

scep·tic (skep′tik), **scep·ti·cal,** etc. See SKEPTIC, etc.

sched·ule (skej′ool, -əl, -ōō·əl; *Brit.* shed′yool) *n.* **1.** A written or printed statement specifying the details of some matter. **2.** A list; catalogue. **3.** A timetable, as for a transportation service. **4.** A detailed and timed plan; program. — *v.t.* **·uled, ·ul·ing 1.** To place in or on a schedule. **2.** To make a schedule of. **3.** To appoint or plan for a specified time or date. [ME < OF < LL < L *scida, scheda* leaf of paper]

sche·ma (skē′mə) *n.* *pl.* **·ma·ta** (-mə·tə) **1.** A scheme or summary. **2.** A plan or diagram, of a process, organization, etc. [< Gk. See SCHEME.] — **sche·mat′ic** (skē·mat′ik) or **·i·cal** *adj.* — **sche·mat′i·cal·ly** *adv.*

sche·ma·tism (skē′mə·tiz′əm) *n.* **1.** A particular form or disposition of anything. **2.** Orderly arrangement of parts.

sche·ma·tize (skē′mə·tīz) *v.t.* **·tized, ·tiz·ing** To form into or arrange according to a scheme or schema.

scheme (skēm) *n.* **1.** A plan of something to be done; a plot or device for the accomplishment of an object. **2.** A systematic arrangement, plan, or design. **3.** A secret or underhand plot or plan. **4.** An outline drawing or sketch; diagram. — *v.* **schemed, schem·ing** *v.t.* **1.** To make a scheme for; plan. **2.** To plan or plot in an underhand manner. — *v.i.* **3.** To make schemes; plan or plot. [< L < Gk. *schēma, -atos* a form, plan] — **schem′er** *n.*

scher·zan·do (sker·tsän′dō) *Music adv.* In a sportive or playful manner. — *adj.* Sportive; playful. [See SCHERZO.]

scher·zo (sker′tsō) *n.* *pl.* **·zos** or **·zi** (-tsē) *Music* A playful or satirical movement, often following a slow movement, as in a symphony or sonata. [< Ital., a jest < G *scherz*]

Schick test (shik) A test to determine the susceptibility of a person to diphtheria by the subcutaneous injection of a diluted diphtheria toxin. [after Dr. Béla *Schick*, born 1877, who devised it]

schil·ling (shil′ing) *n.* **1.** The standard monetary unit of Austria: in 1960 worth about 4 U.S. cents; also, a coin of this value. **2.** Formerly, a minor coin of Germany. [< G]

schism (siz′əm) *n.* **1.** A division of a church or other organized body into factions. **2.** The offense of causing such division. **3.** Any group, esp., an ecclesiastical one, separated from a larger body. [< OF < LL < Gk. *schizein* to split]

schis·mat·ic (siz·mat′ik) *adj.* Of, having the character of, implying, or promoting schism. Also **schis·mat′i·cal.** — *n.* One who makes or participates in a schism. — **schis·mat′i·cal·ly** *adv.* — **schis·mat′i·cal·ness** *n.*

schist (shist) *n.* *Geol.* Any rock that readily splits or cleaves into parallel layers: also spelled **shist.** [< F < L < Gk. < *schizein* to split] — **schist′ous, schist·ose** (shis′tōs) *adj.*

schizo- *combining form* Split; divided. Also, before vowels, **schiz-.** [< Gk. *schizein* to split]

schiz·o·carp (skiz′ə·kärp) *n.* *Bot.* A pericarp splitting at maturity into two or more one-seeded indehiscent portions. — **schiz′o·car′pous, schiz′o·car′pic** *adj.*

schiz·oid (skit′soid, skiz′oid) *Psychiatry n.* One who is abnormally shy and withdrawn. — *adj.* **1.** Of, pertaining to, or like a schizoid. **2.** Loosely, of or pertaining to schizophrenia. [< SCHIZ(OPHRENIA) + -OID]

schiz·o·phre·ni·a (skit′sō·frē′nē·ə, skiz′ō-) *n.* *Psychiatry* Any of a group of psychotic disorders characterized by delusions, withdrawal, conflicting emotions, and deterioration of the personality. [< NL < Gk. *schizein* to split + *phrēn* mind] — **schiz′o·phren′ic** (-fren′ik) *adj. & n.*

schle·miel (shlə·mēl′) *n.* *Slang* An inept, easily duped person; a bungler; dolt. Also **schle·mihl′.** [< Yiddish < Hebrew *Shelumiel*, a personal name]

schnapps (shnäps, shnaps) *n.* *pl.* **schnapps** Any strong liquor, esp. a type of gin. Also **schnaps.** [< G, < Du. *snaps* gulp, mouthful]

schnau·zer (shnou′zər) *n.* A terrier originally developed in Germany, having a wiry, black or pepper-and-salt coat. [< G *schnauzen* to growl, snarl]

schol·ar (skol′ər) *n.* **1.** A person eminent for learning, esp. in the humanities. **2.** One who does authoritative research and writing in some special field. **3.** The holder of a scholarship. **4.** A pupil. [See SCHOOL¹.]

schol·ar·ly (skol′ər·lē) *adj.* **1.** Of or befitting a scholar; *scholarly* methods. **2.** Having the qualities of a scholar. — *adv.* After the manner of a scholar.

schol·ar·ship (skol′ər·ship) *n.* **1.** The mental attainments and qualities of a scholar; learning; erudition. **2.** Scholarly inquiry or research. **3.** Maintenance or a stipend awarded to a student; also, the position of such a student.

scho·las·tic (skō·las′tik, skə-) *adj.* **1.** Of, or characteristic of scholars, education, or schools. **2.** Of, or characteristic of the medieval schoolmen. **3.** Precise; pedantic. Also **scho·las′ti·cal.** — *n.* **1.** *Often cap.* An advocate of scholasticism. **2.** A pedant. [< L < Gk. < *scholazein* to be at leisure, devote leisure to study] — **scho·las′ti·cal·ly** *adv.*

scho·las·ti·cism (skō·las′tə·siz′əm, skə-) *n.* **1.** *Often cap.* The systematized Christian logic, philosophy, and theology of medieval scholars. **2.** Any system of teaching that insists on traditional doctrines, etc.

school[1] (skōōl) *n.* **1.** Any institution devoted primarily to imparting knowledge or to developing certain skills or talents; esp., an educational institution for children. **2.** A place where formal instruction is given; a schoolhouse or schoolroom. **3.** A session or course of study at an educational institution. **4.** The pupils in an educational institution. **5.** A subdivision of a university: the *school* of medicine, law, etc. **6.** A body of disciples of a teacher or system; also, the system, methods, or opinions characteristic of those thus associated: a painting of the Flemish *school*. **7.** A general style of life, manners, etc.: a gentleman of the old *school*. **8.** Any sphere or means of instruction: the *school* of hard knocks. — *v.t.* **1.** To instruct in or as in a school; train; educate. **2.** To subject to rule or discipline. — **Syn.** See TEACH. [OE < L < Gk. *scholē* leisure, school]

school[2] (skōōl) *n.* A large number of fish, whales, etc., swimming together; shoal. — *v.i.* To swim together in a school. [< Du., a crowd, school of fishes]

school board A board of education.

school·book (skōōl′bŏŏk′) *n.* A book for use in school.

school·boy (skōōl′boi′) *n.* A boy attending school.

school·girl (skōōl′gûrl′) *n.* A girl attending school.

school·house (skōōl′hous′) *n.* A building in which a school is conducted.

school·ing (skōō′ling) *n.* **1.** Instruction given at school. **2.** The process of teaching or being taught in a school.

school·man (skōōl′mən) *n.* *pl.* **·men** (-mən) One of the theologians of the Middle Ages; a scholastic.

school·marm (skōōl′märm′) *n.* *Informal* A woman schoolteacher. Also **school′ma′am′** (-mäm′).

school·mas·ter (skōōl′mas′tər, -mäs′-) *n.* **1.** A man who teaches in or directs a school. **2.** Anything that instructs or disciplines: Necessity was his *schoolmaster.*

school·mate (skōōl′māt′) *n.* A fellow pupil.

school·mis·tress (skōōl′mis′tris) *n.* A woman who teaches school.

school·room (skōōl′rōōm′, -rŏŏm′) *n.* A room in which classes are held or instruction is given.

school·teach·er (skōōl′tē′chər) *n.* One who gives instruction in a school below the college level.

school year The part of the year during which a school or the schools of an educational system are in session.

schoon·er (skōō′nər) *n.* **1.** A fore-and-aft rigged vessel having two or more masts. **2.** A large beer glass. [New England < dial. *scoon* to skim on water]

schot·tische (shot′ish) *n.* **1.** A round dance similar to the polka, but slower. **2.** Music for this dance, in duple meter. [< G (*der*) *schottische* (*tanz*) (the) Scottish (dance)]

schwa (shwä, shvä) *n.* *Phonet.* A weak, neutral vowel sound occurring in most of the unstressed syllables in English speech, as the *a* in *alone*, the *e* in *happen*, or the *u* in *circus*: written ə. [< G < Hebrew *shewa*]

sci·at·ic (sī·at′ik) *adj.* Pertaining to or affecting the hip or its nerves. — *n.* A sciatic nerve or part. [< MF < Med.L < Gk. < *ischion* hip, hip joint]

sci·at·i·ca (sī·at′i·kə) *n.* *Pathol.* **1.** Neuralgia affecting the sciatic nerve. **2.** Any painful affection of the hip or adjoining areas. [See SCIATIC.]

sci·ence (sī′əns) *n.* **1.** Any department of knowledge in which the results of investigation have been logically arranged and systematized. **2.** Knowledge of facts, phenomena, laws, and proximate causes, gained and verified by exact observation, organized experiment, and ordered thinking. **3.** An orderly presentation of facts, reasonings, doctrines, and beliefs concerning some subject or group of subjects. **4.** Systematic knowledge in general. **5.** Expertness or skill resulting from knowledge. [< OF < L < *scire* to know]

science fiction Fiction in which facts or theories of contemporary science are imaginatively employed.

sci·en·tif·ic (sī′ən·tif′ik) *adj.* **1.** Of, discovered by, derived from, or used in science. **2.** Agreeing with the rules, principles, or methods of science; accurate; systematic; exact. **3.** Versed in science or a science; eminently learned or skillful. Also **sci′en·tif′i·cal.** [< LL < *scientia* knowledge + *facere* to make] — **sci′en·tif′i·cal·ly** *adv.*

sci·en·tist (sī′ən·tist) *n.* One versed in science or devoted to scientific study or investigation.

scil·i·cet (sil′ə·set) *adv.* Namely; to wit; that is to say. [< L *scire licet* it is permitted to know]

scim·i·tar (sim′ə·tər) *n.* A curved Oriental sword or saber. Also **scim′e·tar, scim′i·ter.** [< MF < Ital. *scimitarra*]

scin·til·la (sin·til′ə) *n.* A spark; trace; iota: a *scintilla* of truth. [< L]

scin·til·late (sin′tə·lāt) *v.* **·lat·ed, ·lat·ing** *v.i.* **1.** To give off sparks. **2.** To sparkle; glitter. **3.** To twinkle, as a star. — *v.t.* **4.** To give off as a spark or sparks. [< L < *scintilla* spark] — **scin′til·lant** *adj.* — **scin′til·lat′ing·ly** *adv.* — **scin′til·la′tion** *n.*

sci·o·lism (sī′ə·liz′əm) *n.* Superficial knowledge; charlatanism. [< L *scius* < *scire* to know] — **sci′o·lis′tic** *adj.*

sci·on (sī′ən) *n.* **1.** A child or descendant. **2.** See CION. [< OF < L *secare* to cut]

scis·sile (sis′il) *adj.* Capable of being cut or split easily and evenly. [< L *scindere* to cut]

scis·sion (sizh′ən, sish′-) *n.* **1.** The act of cutting or splitting, or the state of being cut. **2.** Any division. [< OF < LL < *scissus*, pp. of *scindere* to cut]

scis·sor (siz′ər) *v.t. & v.i.* To cut with scissors.

scis·sors (siz′ərz) *n.pl.* (*construed as sing. in defs. 2 & 3*) **1.** A cutting implement with handles and a pair of blades pivoted face to face so that the opposed edges may be brought together on the object to be cut. Also **pair of scissors.** **2.** In wrestling, a hold secured by clasping the legs about the body or head of the opponent. **3.** A gymnastic feat in which the movement of the legs suggests that of scissors. [< OF < LL *cisoria*, pl. of *cisorium* cutting instrument]

scissors kick In swimming, a kick performed usu. with the side stroke, in which both legs are thrust apart, the upper leg bent at the knee while the lower is kept straight, then brought sharply together.

scis·sor·tail (siz′ər·tāl′) *n.* A flycatcher of the SW U.S. and Mexico, having a scissorlike tail.

scis·sure (sizh′ər, sish′-) *n.* **1.** A lengthwise cut; fissure. **2.** Any division, rupture, or schism. [See SCISSION.]

scle·ra (sklir′ə) *n.* *Anat.* The hard, white, fibrous outer coat of the eyeball, continuous with the cornea. Also **scle·rot·i·ca** (sklə·rot′i·kə). For illus. see EYE. [< NL < Gk. *sklēros* hard]

scle·ren·chy·ma (sklə·reng′kə·mə) *n.* *Bot.* A tough, thick-walled tissue that protects and supports plants. [< NL < Gk. *sklēros* hard + *enchyma* infusion]

sclero- *combining form* Hardness; hard. Also, before vowels, **scler-.** [< Gk. *sklēros* hard]

scle·rosed (sklə·rōst′) *adj.* Affected with sclerosis; grown abnormally hard.

scle·ro·sis (sklə·rō′sis) *n.* *pl.* **·ses** (-sēz) **1.** *Pathol.* The thickening and hardening of a tissue or part. **2.** *Bot.* The hardening of a plant cell wall by the formation of lignin in it. [< Med.L < Gk. *sklēros* hard] — **scle·ro′sal** *adj.*

scle·rot·ic (sklə·rot′ik) *adj.* **1.** Dense; hard, as the sclera. **2.** Of or pertaining to the sclera. **3.** *Pathol.* Pertaining to or affected with sclerosis.

scle·rous (sklir′əs) *adj.* Hard or indurated; bony.

scoff (skôf, skof) *v.i.* **1.** To speak with contempt or derision; jeer: often with *at.* — *v.t.* **2.** To deride; mock. — *n.* An expression or an object of contempt or derision. [ME *scof*, prob. < Scand.] — **scoff′er** *n.* — **scoff′ing·ly** *adv.*

scoff·law (skôf′lô′, skof′-) *n.* One who scoffs at or flouts the law; esp., a habitual violator of traffic laws, etc.

scold (skōld) *v.t.* **1.** To find fault with harshly. — *v.i.* **2.** To find fault harshly or continuously. — *n.* One who scolds, esp. a shrewish woman. [Appar. < ON *skāld* poet, satirist] — **scold′er** *n.* — **scold′ing·ly** *adv.*

scol·lop (skol′əp), etc. See SCALLOP, etc.

scom·broid (skom′broid) *adj.* Of or pertaining to a widely distributed family of fishes, including mackerels. — *n.* A scombroid fish. [< NL < L < Gk. *skombros* mackerel]

sconce[1] (skons) *n.* **1.** A small earthwork or fort. **2.** A protective shelter, covering, or screen. [< Du. *schanz* fortress, wicker basket; infl. in form by SCONCE[2]]

sconce[2] (skons) *n.* An ornamental wall bracket for holding a candle or other light. [< OF < Med.L *sconsa* < L *abscondere* to hide]

scone (skōn, skon) *n.* A round tea cake or biscuit usu. eaten with butter. [? < MDu. *schoonbrot* fine bread]

scoop (skōōp) *n.* **1.** A shovellike instrument or large shovel with high sides. **2.** A small shovellike implement or ladle used by grocers, druggists, etc. **3.** An implement for bailing, as water from a boat. **4.** A spoon-shaped instrument for using in a cavity: a surgeons' *scoop*. **5.** An implement for dispensing uniform, spherical portions of ice cream, etc.; also, a portion thus dispensed. **6.** An act of scooping; a scooping movement. **7.** *Informal* A large gain, esp. in speculation. **8.** A bowl-shaped cavity. **9.** *Slang* In journalism, a news story obtained and published ahead of rival papers. **10.** *Slang* Any item of recent news. — *v.t.* **1.** To take or dip out with or as with a scoop. **2.** To hollow out, as with a scoop; excavate. **3.** To empty with a scoop. **4.** *Informal* To heap up or gather in or as in scoopfuls. **5.** *Slang* In journalism, to obtain and publish a news story before (a rival). [Fusion of MDu. *schope* vessel for bailing out water, and *schoppe* shovel] — **scoop′er** *n.*

scoot (sko͞ot) *v.i. Informal* To go quickly; dart off. — *n.* The act of scooting; a hurried darting off. [Prob. < Scand.]

scoot·er (sko͞o′tər) *n.* **1.** A child's vehicle consisting of a footboard mounted between two tandem wheels and steered by means of a long handle attached to the front axle. **2.** A motor scooter (which see). **3.** A sailboat with runners that may be used in water and on ice.

scope (skōp) *n.* **1.** Room for the exercise of faculties or function; capacity for achievement or effectiveness. **2.** Range of view or activity; outlook: a mind of limited *scope*. **3.** The area or sphere in which any activity takes place: the *scope* of a scientific work. **4.** *Naut.* The length or sweep of a cable at which a ship rides at anchor. **5.** *Informal* Any of various optical or detecting instruments, as a telescope. [< Ital. < L < Gk. < *skopein* to look at]

-scope *combining form* An instrument for viewing, observing, or indicating: *telescope*. [< Gk. *skopein* to watch]

sco·pol·a·mine (skō·pol′ə·mēn, -min, skō′pə·lam′ēn, -in) *n. Chem.* An alkaloid, $C_{17}H_{12}O_4N$, extracted from certain plants, the salts of which are used in medicine as a hypnotic and sedative. [< G < NL, after G. A. *Scopoli*, 1723–88, Italian naturalist]

-scopy *combining form* Observation; viewing: *microscopy*. [< Gk. *skopein* to watch]

scor·bu·tic (skôr·byo͞o′tik) *adj.* Relating to, characteristic of, or affected with scurvy: also **scor·bu′ti·cal.** [< NL < Med.L *scorbutus* scurvy] — **scor·bu′ti·cal·ly** *adv.*

scorch (skôrch) *v.t.* **1.** To change the color, taste, etc., of by slight burning; char the surface of. **2.** To wither or shrivel by heat. **3.** To criticize severely. — *v.i.* **4.** To become scorched. **5.** *Informal* To go at high speed. — *n.* **1.** A superficial burn. **2.** A mark caused by heat, as a slight burn. [Prob. akin to ME *skorken* < ON *skorpna* to dry up, shrivel] — **scorch′ing** *adj.* — **scorch′ing·ly** *adv.*

scorched-earth policy (skôrcht′ûrth′) The military policy of destroying all crops, industrial equipment, dwellings, etc., so as to leave nothing for the use of the enemy.

scorch·er (skôr′chər) *n.* **1.** One who or that which scorches. **2.** *Informal* An extremely hot day. **3.** *Informal* Severe or caustic criticism. **4.** *Informal* One who or that which moves at great speed.

score (skôr, skōr) *n.* **1.** The record of the winning points in a competition or game; also, the total of such points made by a player or a team. **2.** *Psychol.* A quantitative value assigned to an individual or group response to a test or series of tests. **3.** Grade or rating in a test or examination. **4.** Any record, esp. of indebtedness. **5.** A notch or groove cut in something for keeping a tally. **6.** Something charged or laid up against one: to settle old *scores*. **7.** A set of twenty. **8.** *pl.* An indefinitely large number. **9.** *Music* The complete notation for a composition, showing the various instrumental or vocal parts. — **to know the score** *Informal* To be aware of the real facts of a situation. — *v.* **scored, scor·ing** *v.t.* **1.** To mark with notches, cuts, or lines. **2.** To mark with cuts or lines for the purpose of keeping a tally or record. **3.** To obliterate or cross out by means of a line drawn through: with *out*. **4.** To make or gain, as points, runs, etc. **5.** To count for a score of, as in games. **6.** To rate or grade, as an examination paper. **7.** *Music* **a** To orchestrate. **b** To arrange or adapt for an instrument. **8.** *Informal* To criticize severely. **9.** In cooking, to make superficial cuts in (meat, etc.). — *v.i.* **10.** To make points, runs, etc., as in a game. **11.** To keep score. **12.** To make notches, cuts, etc. **13.** To win an advantage or success. [OE < ON *skor* notch, tally] — **scor′er** *n.*

sco·ri·a (skôr′ē·ə, skō′rē·ə) *n. pl.* **·ri·ae** (-ri·ē) **1.** Refuse or slag remaining after metal has been smelted. **2.** Loose, clinkerlike pieces of lava. [< L < Gk. *skōria* refuse] — **sco·ri·a·ceous** (-ā′shəs) *adj.*

sco·ri·fy (skôr′ə·fī, skō′rə-) *v.t.* **·fied, ·fy·ing** *Metall.* **1.** To separate, as gold or silver, from an ore by smelting with lead, borax, etc. **2.** To reduce to scoria or dross. — **sco′ri·fi·ca′tion** *n.*

scorn (skôrn) *n.* **1.** A feeling of contempt or loathing, as for someone or something deemed inferior or unworthy of attention; disdain. **2.** Behavior characterized by such a

feeling; derision. **3.** An expression of contempt or disdain. **4.** An object of contempt. — *v.t.* **1.** To hold in or treat with contempt; despise. **2.** To reject with scorn; disdain; spurn. [< OF < *escarnir* < Gmc.] — **scorn′er** *n.* — **scorn′ful** *adj.* — **scorn′ful·ly** *adv.* — **scorn′ful·ness** *n.*

Scor·pi·o (skôr′pē·ō) *n.* A constellation, the **Scorpion**, containing the bright star Antares; also, the eighth sign of the zodiac. Also **Scor′pi·us** (-əs). See ZODIAC. [< L]

scor·pi·on (skôr′pē·ən) *n.* **1.** One of an order of arachnids found chiefly in warmer regions, having an elongated, lobsterlike body and a segmented tail that bears a venomous sting. **2.** An instrument of chastisement; a whip or scourge. *I Kings* xii 11. [< OF < L < Gk. *skorpios*]

SCORPION
s Stinger.
(To 8 inches long)

scot (skot) *n.* An assessment or tax. [Fusion of ON *skot* and OF *escot*]

Scot (skot) *n.* **1.** A native of Scotland: also called *Scotsman*. **2.** Formerly, a Gaelic Highlander. **3.** One of a Gaelic people who migrated in the fifth century to northwestern Britain from Ireland. [OE *Scottas*, pl., the Irish < LL *Scotus, Scoti*]

scotch (skoch) *v.t.* **1.** To cut; scratch. **2.** To wound so as to maim or cripple. **3.** To put down; crush or suppress. — *n.* **1.** A superficial cut; a scratch; notch. **2.** A line traced on the ground, as for hopscotch. [Origin uncertain]

Scotch (skoch) *n.* **1.** The people of Scotland collectively: with *the*. **2.** One or all of the dialects spoken by the people of Scotland. **3.** Scotch whisky. — *adj.* Of or pertaining to Scotland, its inhabitants, or their language; Scottish; Scots.

Scotch·man (skoch′mən) *n. pl.* **·men** (-mən) A Scot; Scotsman. ◆ These forms are preferred to *Scotchman*.

Scotch tape A rolled strip of transparent cellulose tape having an adhesive on one side: a trade name.

Scotch terrier A Scottish terrier.

Scotch whisky Whisky made in Scotland from malted barley and having rather a smoky flavor.

sco·ter (skō′tər) *n.* Any of several dark sea ducks. [< dial. E *scote* scoot]

scot-free (skot′frē′) *adj.* **1.** Without injury or loss; unharmed; whole. **2.** Free from scot; untaxed.

Scot·land Yard (skot′lənd) The headquarters of the London Metropolitan Police and of the London Criminal Investigation Department, since 1890 located at the **New Scotland Yard** on the Thames Embankment.

Scots (skots) *adj.* Scottish. — *n.* The Scottish dialect of English. [Earlier *Scottis*, var. of SCOTTISH]

Scots·man (skots′mən) *n. pl.* **·men** (-mən) A Scot.

Scot·ti·cism (skot′ə·siz′əm) *n.* A form of expression or an idiom peculiar to the Scottish people.

Scot·tish (skot′ish) *adj.* Pertaining to or characteristic of Scotland, its inhabitants, or their language: also *Scots*. — *n.* **1.** The dialect of English spoken in Scotland, esp. in the Lowlands; Scots. **2.** The people of Scotland collectively: with *the*. [OE *Scottisc*]

Scottish Gaelic The Goidelic language of the Scottish Highlands: also called *Erse*.

Scottish terrier A small, short-legged terrier originating in Scotland, having a large head and a wiry coat: also *Scotch terrier*. Also *Informal* **Scot·tie** (skot′ē), **Scot′ty.**

scoun·drel (skoun′drəl) *n.* A mean, unprincipled rascal; a rogue. — *adj.* Of or characteristic of a scoundrel. [? < AF, OF < L *ex-* off + *condere* to hide] — **scoun′drel·ly** *adj.*

scour[1] (skour) *v.t.* **1.** To clean or brighten by thorough washing and rubbing, as with sand or steel wool. **2.** To remove dirt, etc., from; clean: to *scour* wool. **3.** To remove by or as by rubbing away. **4.** To clear by means of a strong current of water; flush. **5.** To purge the bowels of. **6.** To clean (wheat) before milling. — *v.i.* **7.** To rub something vigorously so as to clean or brighten it. **8.** To become bright or clean by rubbing. — *n.* **1.** The act of scouring. **2.** A place scoured, as by running water. **3.** A cleanser used in cleaning wool. **4.** *Usu. pl.* A watery diarrhea in cattle. [Prob. < MDu. < OF *escurer*, ult. < L *ex-* out + *curare* to take care of] — **scour′er** *n.*

scour[2] (skour) *v.t.* **1.** To range over or through, as in making a search. **2.** To move or run swiftly over or along. — *v.i.* **3.** To range about, as in making a search. **4.** To move swiftly. [ME *scoure*] — **scour′er** *n.*

scourge (skûrj) *n.* **1.** A whip for inflicting suffering or punishment. **2.** Any instrumentality or means for causing suffering or death. **3.** Severe punishment. **4.** A cause of suffering or trouble. — *v.t.* **scourged, scourg·ing** **1.** To whip severely; flog. **2.** To punish severely; afflict. [< AF < LL *excoriare* to flay] — **scourg′er** *n.*

scour·ings (skour′ingz) *n.pl.* **1.** The residue after scouring grain. **2.** Dirt or other residue left after any scouring.

scout[1] (skout) *n.* **1.** One who or that which is engaged in scouting; esp., a person sent out to observe and get information, as of a war enemy, rival team in sports, etc. **2.** The act of scouting. **3.** *Slang* A fellow or friend. **4.** A Boy or Girl

Scout. — v.t. **1.** To observe or spy upon for the purpose of gaining information. — v.i. **2.** To go or act as a scout. — **to scout around** To go in search. [< OF < L auscultare to listen] — **scout′er** n.

scout² (skout) v.t. & v.i. To mock; jeer. [< Scand.]

scout car An armored motor car for reconnaissance work.

scout·ing (skout′ing) n. The activities of a scout, esp. of a Boy Scout or Girl Scout.

scout·mas·ter (skout′mas′tər, -mäs′-) n. The leader of a troop of Boy Scouts.

scow (skou) n. A large boat with a flat bottom and square ends, chiefly used for freight and usually towed. [< Du. schouw boat propelled by a pole < MDu. schoude]

scowl (skoul) n. **1.** A lowering of the brows, as in anger, disapproval, or sullenness. **2.** Gloomy aspect. — v.i. **1.** To lower and contract the brows in anger, sullenness, or disapproval. **2.** To look threatening; lower. — v.t. **3.** To affect or express by scowling. [ME skoul, prob. < Scand.] — **scowl′er** n. — **scowl′ing·ly** adv.

scrab·ble (skrab′əl) v. ·bled, ·bling v.i. **1.** To scratch, scrape, or paw, as with the hands. **2.** To make irregular or meaningless marks; scribble. **3.** To struggle or strive. — v.t. **4.** To make meaningless marks on; scribble on. **5.** To gather hurriedly; scrape together. — n. **1.** The act of scrabbling or scrambling. **2.** A scrawling character, mark, etc.; scribble. **3.** A sparse growth, as of underbrush. [< Du. schrabbelen, freq. of schrabben to scratch]

scrag (skrag) v.t. scragged, scrag·ging Informal To use roughly; wring the neck of; esp., to kill by hanging. — n. **1.** Something thin or lean, as a person. **2.** Slang The human neck. **3.** A lean or bony piece of meat. [? < Scand.]

scrag·gly (skrag′lē) adj. ·gli·er, ·gli·est Unkempt; shaggy.

scrag·gy (skrag′ē) adj. ·gi·er, ·gi·est **1.** Rough. **2.** Lean; scrawny; bony. — **scrag′gi·ly** adv. — **scrag′gi·ness** n.

scram (skram) v.i. scrammed, scram·ming U.S. Slang To go away; leave quickly. [Prob. short for SCRAMBLE]

scram·ble (skram′bəl) v. ·bled, ·bling v.i. **1.** To move by clambering or crawling on hands and feet. **2.** To struggle with others in a disorderly manner; scuffle; also, to strive for something in such a manner. **3.** Aeron. To put interceptor aircraft into the air hurriedly to meet enemy aircraft. — v.t. **4.** To mix together haphazardly. **5.** To gather or collect hurriedly or confusedly. **6.** To fry (eggs) with the yolks and whites stirred together. **7.** Telecom. To alter or garble (a signal) so that a special receiving apparatus is needed to render it comprehensible. — n. **1.** The act of scrambling. **2.** A disorderly performance or struggle. **3.** A difficult climb or trek, as over rocks or rough terrain. [Prob. nasalized var. of SCRABBLE] — **scram′bler** n.

scrap¹ (skrap) n. **1.** A small piece cut or broken from something; fragment. **2.** A brief printed or written extract. **3.** pl. Pieces of crisp fat tissue after the oil has been expressed by cooking; also, any bits of food. **4.** Old or refuse metal. — v.t. scrapped, scrap·ping **1.** To break up into scrap. **2.** To discard. — adj. Having the form of scraps; discarded after use. [< ON skrapa to scrape]

scrap² (skrap) v.i. scrapped, scrap·ping Slang To fight; quarrel. — n. A quarrel, fight, or disagreement. [< SCRAPE (n. def. 2)] — **scrap′per** n.

scrap·book (skrap′bŏŏk′) n. **1.** A blank book in which to paste pictures, clippings, etc. **2.** A personal notebook.

scrape (skrāp) v. scraped, scrap·ing v.t. **1.** To rub, as with something rough or sharp, so as to abrade or to remove an outer layer or adherent matter. **2.** To remove thus: with off, away, etc. **3.** To rub (a rough or sharp object) across a surface. **4.** To rub roughly across or against (a surface). **5.** To dig or form by scratching or scraping. **6.** To gather or accumulate with effort or difficulty: usu. with up or together. — v.i. **7.** To scrape something. **8.** To rub with a grating noise. **9.** To emit or produce a grating noise. **10.** To draw the foot backward along the ground in bowing. **11.** To manage or get along with difficulty. **12.** To be very or overly economical. — n. **1.** The act or effect of scraping; also, the noise made by scraping. **2.** A difficult situation; predicament. **3.** A scraping or drawing back of the foot in bowing. [Prob. fusion of OE scrapian and ON skrapa to scrape, erase] — **scrap′er** n.

scrap·ing (skrā′ping) n. **1.** The act of someone or something that scrapes. **2.** The sound so produced. **3.** Often pl. That which is scraped off or together.

scrap iron Old pieces of iron suitable for reworking.

scrap·ple (skrap′əl) n. A mixture of meal or flour boiled with scraps of pork, seasoned, and allowed to set, usu. cooked by frying. [Dim. of SCRAP¹]

scrap·py¹ (skrap′ē) adj. ·pi·er, ·pi·est Composed of scraps; fragmentary. — **scrap′pi·ly** adv. — **scrap′pi·ness** n.

scrap·py² (skrap′ē) adj. ·pi·er, ·pi·est Pugnacious; given to picking fights. — **scrap′pi·ly** adv. — **scrap′pi·ness** n.

scratch (skrach) v.t. **1.** To tear or mark the surface of with something sharp or rough. **2.** To scrape or dig with something sharp or rough, as the claws or nails. **3.** To scrape lightly with the nails, etc., as to relieve itching. **4.** To rub with a grating sound; scrape. **5.** To write or draw awkwardly or hurriedly. **6.** To erase or cancel by or as by scratches or marks. **7.** To erase or cancel the name of (a candidate) from a political ticket, while supporting the rest of the ticket; also, to bolt (a ticket or party) in this way. **8.** To withdraw (an entry) from a race, game, etc. — v.i. **9.** To use the nails or claws, as in fighting or digging. **10.** To scrape the skin, etc., lightly, as to relieve itching. **11.** To make a harsh, grating noise. **12.** To manage or get along with difficulty. **13.** To withdraw from a game, race, etc. **14.** In billiards and pool, to make a scratch. — n. **1.** A mark or incision made on a surface by scratching; also, a quick mark or scribble, as made by a pencil. **2.** A slight flesh wound or cut. **3.** A harsh, grating sound. **4.** The act of scratching. **5.** The line from which contestants start, as in racing. **6.** The contestant who competes against an allowance. **7.** In billiards, a chance shot; also, a fluke; in billiards and pool, a shot resulting in a penalty. — **from scratch** From the beginning; from nothing. — **up to scratch** Informal Meeting the standard or requirement in courage, stamina, or performance. — adj. **1.** Done by chance; haphazard. **2.** In sports, without handicap or allowance. **3.** Used for quick notes, a memorandum, etc.: a scratch pad. **4.** Chosen at random or by chance. [Prob. blend of ME scratte to scratch and cracchen to scratch] — **scratch′er** n.

scratch test Med. A test to determine the substances to which a person is allergic by rubbing allergens in small scratches made in his skin.

scratch·y (skrach′ē) adj. scratch·i·er, scratch·i·est **1.** Characterized by or covered with scratches. **2.** Making a scratching noise. **3.** Straggling; shaggy; rough. **4.** That scratches or irritates. — **scratch′i·ly** adv. — **scratch′i·ness** n.

scrawl (skrôl) v.t. & v.i. To write hastily or illegibly. — n. Irregular or careless writing. [? < dial. E, var. of CRAWL]

scrawl·y (skrô′lē) adj. scrawl·i·er, scrawl·i·est Consisting of or characterized by ill-formed or irregular characters.

scraw·ny (skrô′nē) adj. ·ni·er, ·ni·est Skinny; thin. [< dial. E scranny, var. of SCRANNEL] — **scraw′ni·ness** n.

scream (skrēm) v.i. **1.** To utter a prolonged, piercing cry, as of pain, terror, or surprise. **2.** To make a prolonged, piercing sound. **3.** To laugh loudly or immoderately. **4.** To use heated, hysterical language. **5.** To have an odd or startling effect, as of screaming. — v.t. **6.** To utter with a scream. — n. **1.** A loud, shrill, prolonged cry or sound, generally denoting fear or pain. **2.** U.S. Slang A person or situation arousing great mirth. [ME scraemen]

scream·er (skrē′mər) n. **1.** One who or that which screams. **2.** Any of various birds of South America related to the ducks.

screech (skrēch) n. **1.** A shrill, harsh cry; shriek. **2.** Canadian Slang Cheap rum or wine. — v.t. **1.** To utter with or as with a screech. — v.i. **2.** To make a prolonged, harsh, piercing sound. [Var. of obs. scritch, prob. imit.] — **screech′er** n. — **screech′y** adv.

screech owl 1. Any of various owls common from Canada to Brazil; esp. a small, gray species of the eastern U.S. **2.** The barn owl of England.

screed (skrēd) n. **1.** A prolonged tirade; harangue. **2.** A long piece of discursive prose. — v.t. To rend or tear into shreds. [Var. of SHRED]

screen (skrēn) n. **1.** That which separates or cuts off, shelters, or protects, as a light partition. **2.** A network, as of wire, forming a partition or panel in a window, door, etc., to exclude insects and admit air. **3.** A sieve or riddle for sifting. **4.** A smooth surface, on which motion pictures, etc., may be shown. **5.** A motion picture or motion pictures collectively. — v.t. **1.** To shield from observation or annoyance with or as with a screen. **2.** To cause to pass through a screen or sieve; sift. **3.** To show or exhibit on a screen, as a motion picture. **4.** To determine the competence or eligibility of (an individual) for a specified task. — v.i. **5.** To be shown or be suitable for showing on a motion-picture screen. [Prob. < OF escren, escrin, prob. < OHG skirm] — **screen′a·ble** adj. — **screen′er** n.

screen·ing (skrē′ning) n. **1.** The act or instance of exhibiting a motion picture. **2.** The work of one who screens. **3.** Mesh, as of wire, fabric, or plastic, suitable for window screens and the like. **4.** pl. The residue of anything passed through a sieve; siftings.

screen play A motion picture.

screw (skrōō) n. **1.** A device resembling a nail but having a slotted head and a tapering grooved spiral for driving into wood with a screwdriver. **2.** A similar device of cylindrical form, for insertion into a corresponding grooved part: also

male or **external** screw. **3.** A cylindrical socket with a spiral groove: also **female** or **internal** screw. **4.** Anything having the form of a screw. **5.** A screw propeller. **6.** A turn of or as of a screw. **7.** Pressure; force. **8.** *Brit.* *Slang* Salary; pay. **9.** *Slang* A prison guard. **10.** A haggler over prices. **— to have a screw loose** *Slang* To be mentally deranged, eccentric, etc. **— to put the screws on** (or **to**) *Slang* To exert pressure or force upon. **— v.t. 1.** To tighten, fasten, attach, etc., by or as by a screw or screws. **2.** To turn or twist. **3.** To force as if by the pressure of a screw; urge: to *screw* one's courage to the sticking point. **4.** To twist out of shape; contort, as one's features. **5.** To practice oppression or extortion. **6.** To obtain by extortion. **— v.i. 7.** To turn or admit of being turned as a screw. **8.** To be attached or become detached by means of screws: with *on*, *off*, etc. **9.** To practice oppression or extortion. [Appar. < OF *escroue* nut, female screw] **— screw′er** *n.*

screw·ball (skrōō′bôl′) *n.* *U.S.* *Slang* An unconventional or erratic person.

screw·driv·er (skrōō′drī′vər) *n.* **1.** A tool with a flattened metal end that fits into the slot of a screw in order to turn it. **2.** A cocktail consisting of vodka and orange juice.

screw·pile (skrōō′pīl′) *n.* A pile having a strong metal base with a screw thread to ensure firm penetration of hard ground or bedrock.

screw propeller A mechanism consisting of a revolving shaft with radiating blades set at an angle to produce a spiral action, used in propelling ships, etc.

screw thread **1.** The projecting spiral ridge of uniform pitch on the outer or inner surface of a screw or nut. **2.** A complete revolution of any point on this ridge.

screw·y (skrōō′ē) *adj.* **screw·i·er, screw·i·est** *Slang* Extremely irrational; crazy.

scrib·ble (skrib′əl) *v.* **·bled, ·bling** *v.t.* **1.** To write hastily and carelessly. **2.** To cover with careless or illegible writing or marks. **— v.i. 3.** To write in a careless or hasty manner. **4.** To make illegible or meaningless marks. **— n. 1.** Hasty, careless writing. **2.** Any scrawl. [< Med.L *scribillare,* freq. of L *scribere* to write] **— scrib′bler** *n.*

scribe (skrīb) *n.* **1.** One who writes or copies manuscripts. **2.** A clerk, public writer, or amanuensis. **3.** An ancient Jewish teacher, interpreter, or writer of the Mosaic law. **— v. scribed, scrib·ing** *v.t.* **1.** To mark or scratch with a pointed instrument. **2.** To write, inscribe, or engrave. **— v.i. 3.** *Rare* To write; work as a scribe. [< L < *scribere* to write] **— scrib′al** *adj.*

scrim (skrim) *n.* **1.** A lightweight, open-mesh, cotton fabric, usu. white or ecru, used for draperies, etc. **2.** In the theater, a similar fabric, often painted, used as a transparency, to support artificial foliage, etc. [Origin unknown]

scrim·mage (skrim′ij) *n.* **1.** A rough-and-tumble contest; fracas. **2.** In American football, a mass play from the line of scrimmage after the ball has been placed on the ground and snapped back, the play ending when the ball is dead. **3.** In Rugby football, a scrummage. **4.** In football, a practice session or unofficial game played by opposing teams. **— line of scrimmage** In football, the hypothetic line on which the ball rests and along which the opposing linemen take position at the start of play. **— v.t. & v.i. ·maged, ·mag·ing** To engage in a scrimmage. Also *scrummage.* [Alter. of *scrimish,* var. of SKIRMISH]

scrimp (skrimp) *v.i.* **1.** To be very or overly economical. **— v.t. 2.** To be overly sparing with; skimp. **3.** To cut too small, narrow, etc. **— adj.** Scanty; scrimpy. [Prob. akin to OE *scrimman* to shrink, shrivel]

scrimp·y (skrim′pē) *adj.* **·i·er, ·i·est 1.** Scanty; skimpy; short. **2.** Tending to scrimp; niggardly. **— scrimp′i·ness** *n.*

scrip¹ (skrip) *n.* **1.** A scrap of paper, esp. one containing writing. **2.** A writing; a certificate, schedule, or written list. **3.** A piece of paper money less than a dollar, formerly issued in the U.S. [< SCRIPT]

scrip² (skrip) *n.* A provisional document (or documents collectively) certifying that the holder is entitled to receive something else, as shares of stock or land. [Short for obs. *subscription receipt*]

script (skript) *n.* **1.** Writing of the ordinary cursive form. **2.** Type, or printed or engraved matter, in imitation of handwriting. **3.** *Law* A writing, esp. an original. **4.** A piece of writing; esp., a prepared copy of a play or dramatic role, for the use of actors. **5.** Alphabet; writing system: phonetic *script.* **— v.t. & v.i. ** *U.S. Informal* To prepare a script for (a radio, television, or theatrical performance). [< OF < L *scribere* to write]

scrip·tur·al (skrip′chər·əl) *adj.* Relating to writing; written. **— scrip′tur·al·ly** *adv.* **— scrip′tur·al·ness** *n.*

Scrip·ture (skrip′chər) *n.* **1.** The books of the Old and New Testaments, including often the Apocrypha. **2.** A text or passage from the Bible. **— Scrip′tur·al** *adj.* **— Scrip′tur·al·ly** *adv.* **— Scrip′tur·al·ness** *n.*

script·writ·er (skript′rī′tər) *n.* A writer who prepares copy for the use of an actor or announcer.

scrive (skrīv) *v.t.* **scrived, scriv·ing** To engrave. [? < OF < L *scribere*]

scriv·en·er (skriv′ən·ər, skriv′nər) *n.* *Archaic* One who prepares deeds, contracts, and other writings; a clerk or scribe. [< obs. *scrivein* < OF < Ital. < L *scribere* to write]

scrod (skrod) *n.* A young codfish, esp. when split and prepared for broiling. [? < MDu. *schrode* piece cut off]

scrof·u·la (skrof′yə·lə) *n.* *Pathol.* A tuberculous condition of the lymphatic glands, characterized by enlargement, abscesses, and cheeselike degeneration: also called *struma.* [Orig. pl. < LL *scrofulae,* dim. pl. of *scrofa* breeding sow]

scrof·u·lous (skrof′yə·ləs) *adj.* **1.** Pertaining to, affected with, or of the nature of scrofula. **2.** Morally corrupt; degraded. **— scrof′u·lous·ly** *adv.* **— scrof′u·lous·ness** *n.*

scroll (skrōl) *n.* **1.** A roll of parchment, paper, or the like, esp. one containing or intended for writing; also, the writing on such a roll. **2.** Anything resembling or suggestive of a parchment roll; esp. a convoluted ornament or an ornamental space or tablet on sculptured work. [Earlier *scrowle,* alter. of obs. *scrow* < AF *escrowe*]

scroll saw A narrow-bladed hand or power saw for doing curved or irregular work.

scroll·work (skrōl′wûrk′) *n.* Ornamental work of scroll-like pattern.

Scrooge (skrōōj), **Ebenezer** In Dickens's *A Christmas Carol,* a miser whose hard nature is transformed on Christmas Eve.

scro·tum (skrō′təm) *n.* *pl.* **·ta** (-tə), **·tums** *Anat.* The pouch of skin that contains the testicles in most mammals. [< L] **— scro′tal** *adj.*

scrounge (skrounj) *v.t. & v.i.* **scrounged, scroung·ing** *Slang* **1.** To hunt about in order to take (something); pilfer. **2.** To mooch; sponge; beg. **— n.** One who scrounges: also **scroung′er.** [? < dial. E *scrunge* to steal]

scrub¹ (skrub) *v.* **scrubbed, scrub·bing** *v.t.* **1.** To rub vigorously in washing. **2.** To remove (dirt, etc.) by such action. **3.** *U.S.* *Slang* To cancel; call off. **— v.i. 4.** To rub something vigorously, as in washing. **— n.** The act of scrubbing. [? < Scand. Cf. Dan. *skrubbe,* MDu. *shrubben.*] **— scrub′ber** *n.*

scrub² (skrub) *n.* **1.** A stunted tree; also, such trees collectively. **2.** A thicket or group of stunted trees or shrubs. **3.** A domestic animal of inferior breed. **4.** A poor, insignificant person. **5.** In sports, a player not on the varsity or regular team. **— adj. 6.** Undersized or stunted-looking; inferior. [Dial. var. of SHRUB¹]

scrub·by (skrub′ē) *adj.* **·bi·er, ·bi·est 1.** Of stunted growth. **2.** Covered with or consisting of scrub or underbrush. **— scrub′bi·ness** *n.*

scrub·land (skrub′land′) *n.* Land covered with scrub.

scrub oak Any of various dwarf oaks of the United States.

scrub pine Any of several American pines having a tendency toward stunted or crowded growth.

scruff (skruf) *n.* The nape of the neck. [Earlier *scuff,* ? < ON *skopt* hair]

scrum·mage (skrum′ij) *v.t. & v.i.* **·maged, ·mag·ing** To scrimmage. **— n. 1.** A scrimmage. **2.** In Rugby football, a formation around the ball, out of which the ball is kicked to begin play. [Var. of SCRIMMAGE] **— scrum′mag·er** *n.*

scrump·tious (skrump′shəs) *adj.* *Slang* Elegant or stylish; fine; delightful; splendid. [Prob. alter. of SUMPTUOUS]

scrunch (skrunch) *v.t. & v.i.* To crush; squeeze; crunch. **— n.** A crunch. [Imit. alter. of CRUNCH]

scru·ple (skrōō′pəl) *n.* **1.** Doubt or uncertainty regarding a question of moral right or duty. **2.** An apothecaries' weight of twenty grains, or 1.296 grams (symbol: ℈). See table front of book. **3.** A minute quantity. **— v.t. & v.i. ·pled, ·pling** To have scruples (about). [< OF < L *scrupulus* small sharp stone]

scru·pu·lous (skrōō′pyə·ləs) *adj.* **1.** Cautious in action because of a wish to do right; nicely conscientious. **2.** Resulting from the exercise of scruples; exact; careful. **— Syn.** See METICULOUS. **— scru′pu·lous·ly** *adv.* **— scru·pu·los′i·ty** (-los′ə·tē), **scru′pu·lous·ness** *n.*

scru·ti·nize (skrōō′tə·nīz) *v.t.* **·nized, ·niz·ing** To observe carefully; examine in detail. Also *Brit.* **scru′ti·nise.** **— scru′ti·niz′er** *n.* **— scru′ti·niz′ing·ly** *adv.*

scru·ti·ny (skrōō′tə·nē) *n. pl.* **·nies 1.** The act of scrutinizing; close examination or investigation. **2.** A searching look or glance. [< OF < LL < L *scrutari* to examine]

scu·ba (skōō′bə, skyōō′-) *n. Sometimes cap.* An underwater breathing apparatus needing no connection with the surface, worn by divers. Also called *Aqua-Lung, aqualung.* [< s(elf)-c(ontained) u(nderwater) b(reathing) a(pparatus)]

scud (skud) *v.i.* **scud·ded, scud·ding 1.** To move, run, or fly swiftly. **2.** *Naut.* To run rapidly before the wind. **— n. 1.** The act of scudding or moving swiftly. **2.** Light clouds driven rapidly before the wind. [Prob. < Scand., ? infl. in mean-ing by scud, in earlier sense of "hare"]

scuff (skuf) *v.i.* **1.** To walk with a dragging movement of the feet; shuffle. **— v.t. 2.** To scrape (the floor, ground, etc.) with the feet. **3.** To roughen or wear down the surface of by rubbing or scraping. **—** *n.* **1.** The act of scuffing; also, the noise or mark so made. **2.** A flat slipper having no covering for the heel. [Prob. < ON *skūfa* to shove]

scuf·fle (skuf′əl) *v.i.* **·fled, ·fling 1.** To struggle roughly or confusedly. **2.** To drag one's feet; shuffle. **—** *n.* A disorderly struggle. [Prob. freq. of SCUFF] **— scuf′fler** *n.*

scull (skul) *n.* **1.** A long oar worked from side to side over the stern of a boat. **2.** A light, short-handled oar, used in pairs by one person. **3.** A small boat for sculling. **—** *v.t.* & *v.i.* To propel (a boat) by a scull or sculls. [ME *sculle, skulle;* origin unknown] **— scull′er** *n.*

scul·ler·y (skul′ər-ē) *n. pl.* **·ler·ies** A room where kitchen utensils are kept and cleaned, vegetables washed, etc. [< OF *escuelerie* care of dishes]

scul·lion (skul′yən) *n. Archaic* **1.** A servant who washes and scours dishes, pots, and kettles. **2.** A base, contemptible person. [< OF *escouillon* mop < *escouve* broom]

scul·pin (skul′pin) *n. pl.* **·pins** or **·pin** One of several broad-mouthed fishes with a large, spiny head. [Prob. alter. of F *escorpene* < L *scorpaena* scorpionlike fish]

sculpt (skulpt) *v.t.* & *v.i. Informal* To sculpture.

sculp·tor (skulp′tər) *n.* One who creates sculpture by carving wood, modeling clay or plastics, working metal, or chiseling stone, etc. **— sculp′tress** (-tris) *n.fem.*

sculp·ture (skulp′chər) *n.* **1.** The art of fashioning figures of wood, clay, plastics, metal, or stone. **2.** Figures or groups carved, cut, hewn, cast, or modeled in such materials. **3.** Raised or incised lines or markings, as upon a shell. **—** *v.t.* **·tured, ·tur·ing 1.** To fashion, as statuary, by modeling, carving, casting, or welding. **2.** To represent or portray in sculpture. **3.** To embellish with sculpture. **4.** To change, as the face of a valley or canyon, by erosion and deposition. [< L < *sculpere* to carve in stone] **— sculp′tur·al** *adj.*

sculp·tur·esque (skulp′chə·resk′) *adj.* Resembling sculpture; coldly, calmly, or grandly beautiful; statuesque.

scum (skum) *n.* **1.** Impure or extraneous matter that rises to the surface of boiling or fermenting liquids. **2.** Minute vegetation on stagnant water. **3.** Worthless element; refuse. **4.** A vile or worthless person or group of persons: often in the phrase **the scum of the earth.** **—** *v.* **scummed, scum·ming** *v.t.* **1.** To take scum from; skim. **—** *v.i.* **2.** To become covered with or form scum. [< MDu. *schuum*] **— scum′-mer** *n.*

scum·my (skum′ē) *adj.* **·mi·er, ·mi·est 1.** Covered with, containing, or resembling scum. **2.** Vile; contemptible.

scup (skup) *n. pl.* **scup** or **scups** A food fish of the eastern coast of the U.S.: also called *porgy.* Also **scup·paug** (skup′ôg, skə·pôg′). [< Algonquian (Narraganset) *mishcup* thick-scaled]

scup·per (skup′ər) *n. Naut.* A hole or gutter along the side of a ship's deck, to let water run off. [? Short for *scupper hole* < OF *escope* bailing scoop]

scup·per·nong (skup′ər·nông, -nŏng) *n.* **1.** A variety of muscadine grape cultivated in the southern United States. **2.** A sweet, straw-colored wine made from this grape. [after the *Scuppernong* River in North Carolina]

scurf (skûrf) *n.* **1.** Loose outer skin thrown off in minute scales, as in dandruff. **2.** Any scaly matter. [OE] **— scurf′y** *adj.*

scur·ril·i·ty (skə·ril′ə·tē) *n. pl.* **·ties 1.** A scurrilous remark. **2.** The quality of being obscenely jocular.

scur·ri·lous (skûr′ə·ləs) *adj.* **1.** Grossly and offensively abusive. **2.** Expressed with or given to coarse jocularity. Also **scur·rile** (skûr′il), **scur′ril.** [< L *scurrilis* buffoonlike] **— scur′ri·lous·ly** *adv.* **— scur′ri·lous·ness** *n.*

scur·ry (skûr′ē) *v.i.* **·ried, ·ry·ing** To move or go hurriedly; scamper. **—** *n. pl.* **·ries** The act or sound of scurrying. [Short for HURRY-SCURRY]

scur·vy (skûr′vē) *adj.* **·vi·er, ·vi·est 1.** Meanly low or contemptible; base. **2.** *Obs.* Scurfy; scabby. **—** *n. Pathol.* A disease caused by lack of vitamin C in the diet, and characterized by swollen and bleeding gums, and great weakness. [< SCURF] **— scur′vi·ly** *adv.* **— scur′vi·ness** *n.*

scut (skut) *n.* A short tail, as of a rabbit or deer. [ME, tail, hare, prob. < Scand. Cf. Icelandic *skott* fox's tail.]

scu·tate (skyōō′tāt) *adj.* **1.** *Zool.* Covered with horny, shieldlike plates or large scales. **2.** *Bot.* Shaped like a shield. [< L *scutatus* provided with a shield < *scutum* shield]

scutch·eon (skuch′ən) *n.* An escutcheon.

scu·tel·late (skyōō·tel′it, skyōō′tə·lāt) *adj. Zool.* **1.** Platterlike; shield-shaped. **2.** Covered with scales; scutate. Also **scu′tel·lat′ed** (-tə·lā′tid). [< NL *scutellatus* < L *scutella* platter, dim. of *scutra* tray] **— scu′tel·la′tion** *n.*

scu·tel·lum (skyōō·tel′əm) *n. pl.* **·la** (-lə) *Biol.* A small, shieldlike organ or part, as on the leg of a bird. [< NL, dim. of L *scutum* shield] **— scu·tel′lar** *adj.*

scut·tle¹ (skut′l) *n.* **1.** A small opening or hatchway with a movable lid or cover, esp. on the deck of a ship. **2.** The lid

closing such an opening. **3.** A sea cock in the bottom of a ship. **—** *v.t.* **·tled, ·tling** To sink (a ship) by making holes in the bottom or by opening the sea cocks. [< MF *escoutille* hatchway]

scut·tle² (skut′l) *n.* A metal vessel or hod for coal. [OE *scutel* dish, platter < L *scutella*]

scut·tle³ (skut′l) *v.i.* **·tled, ·tling** To run in haste; scurry. **—** *n.* A hurried run or departure. [? Var. of *scuddle*]

scut·tle·butt (skut′l·but) *n.* **1.** A drinking fountain aboard ship. **2.** Formerly, a cask containing the day's drinking water. **3.** *U.S. Slang* Rumor; gossip. [Orig. *scuttled butt* a lidded cask for drinking water]

scu·tum (skyōō′təm) *n. pl.* **·ta** (-tə) **1.** *Zool.* A platelike piece or part, as on a turtle. **2.** In ancient Rome, the large oval or rectangular shield of the legionaries. [< L]

Scyl·la (sil′ə) In Greek mythology, a six-headed sea monster who dwelt in a cave on the Italian coast opposite the whirlpool Charybdis. **— between Scylla and Charybdis** Between two dangers, where one cannot be avoided without incurring equally great peril from the other.

scythe (sīth, *sometimes* sī) *n.* An implement used for mowing, reaping, etc., consisting of a long, curved blade fixed at an angle to a long bent handle. **—** *v.t.* **scythed, scyth·ing** To cut or mow with or as with a scythe. [OE *sīthe*]

Scyth·i·a (sith′ē·ə) An ancient region of southern Europe, generally considered as lying north of the Black Sea. **— Scyth′i·an** *adj.* & *n.*

sea (sē) *n.* **1.** The great body of salt water covering the larger portion of the earth's surface; the ocean. **2.** A large body of oceanic water partly enclosed by land. **3.** A large inland body of water, salt or fresh. **4.** The swell or surface of the ocean: a calm *sea.* **5.** Anything that suggests the sea, as something vast. **6.** The occupation of a seaman. **— at sea 1.** On the ocean. **2.** At a loss; bewildered. **— to follow the sea** To follow the occupation of a sailor. **— to go to sea 1.** To become a sailor. **2.** To take an ocean voyage. **— to put to sea** To start on a voyage, as a ship. [OE *sǣ*]

sea anchor A large canvas bag or sail dragged from the stern of a ship to reduce yawing, as in a gale.

sea anemone Any of various marine animals that attach themselves to rocks, etc., suggesting flowers by their coloring and outspread tentacles.

sea bass 1. Any of various large-mouthed food fishes of Atlantic waters; esp., the **black sea bass. 2.** Any of various similar or related fishes.

Sea·bee (sē′bē′) *n.* A member of the Construction Battalions of the U.S. Navy, organized to build base facilities, airfields, etc. [< C(*on*struction) B(*attalion*)]

sea·board (sē′bôrd′, -bōrd′) *n.* The seashore or seacoast; also, the land or region bordering the sea. **—** *adj.* Bordering on the sea. [ME < SEA + *board* border, OE *bord*]

SEA ANEMONE

(3 to 5 inches high) a Tentacles contracted. b Tentacles extended.

sea breeze A cool breeze blowing inland from the ocean.

sea calf The harbor seal.

sea captain The captain of a seagoing vessel.

sea·coast (sē′kōst′) *n.* The seashore; seaboard.

sea cock A cock or valve controlling connection with the water through a vessel's hull.

sea coconut The very large and heavy seed of a palm native to islands of the Indian Ocean.

sea cow 1. Any aquatic mammal, as the manatee or the dugong. **2.** The walrus.

sea cucumber Any of a group of marine animals shaped like a cucumber and having long branched tentacles.

sea dog 1. The harbor seal. **2.** The sea lion. **3.** An old or experienced sailor.

sea·drome (sē′drōm′) *n. Aeron.* A floating airport for aircraft making overseas flights. [< SEA + -DROME]

sea duck Any of various diving ducks, esp. the eider.

sea·far·er (sē′fâr′ər) *n.* A seaman; a mariner.

sea·far·ing (sē′fâr′ing) *adj.* **1.** Following the sea as a calling. **2.** Traveling by sea. **—** *n.* **1.** Travel by sea. **2.** The profession of a seaman.

sea·flow·er (sē′flou′ər) *n.* A sea anemone.

sea foam 1. Foam of the ocean. **2.** Meerschaum. **3.** A fluffy candy made of spun sugar.

sea·food (sē′fōōd′) *n. U.S.* Edible marine fish or shellfish.

sea·fowl (sē′foul′) *n.* A sea bird, or sea birds collectively.

sea front Land or buildings that border on the sea.

sea·girt (sē′gûrt′) *adj.* Surrounded by waters of the sea.

sea·go·ing (sē′gō′ing) *adj.* **1.** Adapted for use on the ocean. **2.** Seafaring.

sea green A deep bluish green, like the color of sea water.

sea gull Any gull or large tern.

sea hog A porpoise.

sea horse   1. A marine fish, having a prehensile tail and a head resembling that of a horse. 2. A walrus. 3. A fabulous animal, half horse and half fish, driven by Neptune. 4. A large, white-crested wave.

Sea Islands   A chain of small islands off the coast of South Carolina, Georgia, and northern Florida.

sea king   A viking pirate king of the Middle Ages.

seal¹ (sēl)   n.   1. An instrument or device used for making an impression upon some plastic substance, as wax or a wafer; also, the impression made. 2. The wax, wafer, or similar token affixed to a document as a proof of authenticity; also, an impression, scroll, or mark on the paper. 3. A substance or device employed to secure a letter, door, etc., firmly or to prevent tampering. 4. Anything that confirms or ratifies; a pledge. 5. An ornamental stamp for packages, etc. — **under seal** Fastened or secured with an authoritative seal. — v.t. 1. To affix a seal to, as to prove authenticity or prevent tampering. 2. To stamp or impress a seal upon in order to attest to weight, quality, etc. 3. To fasten or close with or as with a seal. 4. To grant or assign under seal. 5. To establish or settle finally; determine. 6. In Mormon usage, to solemnize forever, as a marriage. 7. To secure, set, or fill up, as with plaster. 8. *Mech.* To supply with a device or trap for preventing a return flow of gas or air. [< OF < L *sigillum* small picture, seal] — **seal'a·ble** adj. — **seal'er** n.

seal² (sēl)   n.   1. Any of a group of aquatic carnivorous mammals mostly of northern latitudes. 2. The fur of a fur seal; sealskin. 3. Leather made from the hide of a seal. 4. Any fur prepared so as to look like sealskin. — v.i. To hunt seals. [OE *seolh*]

sea legs   *Informal* The ability to walk aboard ship, esp. in rough seas, without losing one's balance.

seal·er·y (sē'lər·ē)   n.   pl. **·er·ies** 1. The occupation of hunting seals. 2. A place where seals are regularly hunted.

sea lettuce   A green seaweed often used for food.

sea level   1. The assumed mean level of the ocean surface, esp. as used in determining elevation on maps, etc. 2. The actual mean level of the ocean surface.

sealing wax   A mixture of shellac and resin with turpentine and pigment that is fluid when heated but becomes solid as it cools, used for sealing papers, packages, etc.

sea lion   Any of various large, eared seals, esp., the **California sea lion**: also called *sea dog*.

seal ring   A finger ring containing an engraved stone or signet: also called *signet ring*.

seal·skin (sēl'skin')   n.   1. The under fur of the fur seal when prepared for use by removing the long hairs and dyeing dark brown or black. 2. A coat, etc., made of this fur. — adj. Made of this fur.

Sea·ly·ham terrier (sē'lē·ham, -əm)   A breed of terrier first developed at Sealyham, Wales, having short legs and a wiry, usu. white coat.

seam (sēm)   n.   1. A visible line of junction between parts, esp. the edges of two pieces of cloth sewn together. 2. A crack; fissure. 3. A ridge made in joining two pieces or left by a mold upon a casting. 4. A scar; also, a wrinkle. 5. A thin stratum of rock. — v.t. 1. To unite by means of a seam. 2. To mark with a cut, furrow, wrinkle, etc. 3. In knitting, to give the appearance of a seam to; purl. — v.i. 4. To crack open; become fissured. 5. In knitting, to form seams. [OE *sēam*] — **seam'er** n.

sea·man (sē'mən)   n.   pl. **·men** (-mən) 1. A sailor. 2. *Naval* An enlisted man of any of the lowest grades. See tables at GRADE. — **sea'man·like'** (-līk') adj. — **sea'man·ly** adj. & adv.

sea·man·ship (sē'mən·ship)   n.   The skill and ability of a seaman in the operation and handling of a boat or ship.

seam·less (sēm'lis)   adj.   Having no seam.

seam·stress (sēm'stris, *Brit.* sem'-)   n.   A woman skilled in needlework, esp. one whose occupation is sewing. Also **sempstress**. [< OE *sēamestre* seamster + -ESS]

seam·y (sē'mē)   adj.   **seam·i·er, seam·i·est** 1. Full of seams, as the wrong side of a garment. 2. Showing the worst aspect; distasteful: the *seamy* side. — **seam'i·ness** n.

sé·ance (sā'äns, *Fr.* sā·äns')   n.   1. A session or sitting. 2. A meeting of persons seeking spiritualistic manifestations. [< F < OF *seoir* to sit < L *sedere*]

sea onion   Squill¹.

sea otter   A large, nearly extinct marine animal of the North Pacific coast, having a valuable dark brown fur.

sea plane (sē'plān')   n   An airplane equipped to land on or take off from the water.

sea·port (sē'pôrt', -pōrt')   n.   1. A harbor or port on a coast accessible to seagoing ships. 2. A town located on such a harbor.

sea purse   *Zool.* The horny capsule enclosing the eggs of certain sharks, skates, and rays.

sea·quake (sē'kwāk')   n.   A seismic disturbance of the ocean floor.

sear (sir)   v.t.   1. To wither; dry up. 2. To burn the surface of; scorch. 3. To burn or cauterize, as with a hot iron; brand. 4. To make callous; harden. — v.i. 5. To cause dryness. — adj. *Poetic* Dried or blasted; withered. — n. A scar or brand. Also spelled *sere*. [OE *sēarian* to wither]

search (sûrch)   n.   1. The act of seeking or looking diligently. 2. Investigation; inquiry. 3. A critical examination or scrutiny. 4. *Law* Right of search. — v.t. 1. To look through or explore thoroughly in order to find something. 2. To subject (a person) to an examination, as for concealed weapons, etc. 3. To examine with close attention; probe. 4. To penetrate or pierce. 5. To learn by investigation: with *out*. — v.i. 6. To make a search. [< OF < L *circare* to go round, explore] — **search'a·ble** adj. — **search'er** n.

search·ing (sûr'ching)   adj.   1. Investigating minutely. 2. Keenly penetrating; observant: a *searching* gaze. — **search'ing·ly** adv. — **search'ing·ness** n.

search·light (sûrch'līt')   n.   1. An apparatus containing a reflector and an intensely brilliant light that may be thrown in various directions for search or signaling. 2. The beam of light from this apparatus.

search warrant   A warrant authorizing an officer to search a house or other specified place for things alleged to be unlawfully concealed there.

sea·scape (sē'skāp')   n.   1. An ocean view. 2. A picture presenting a marine view. [< SEA + (LAND)SCAPE]

sea·shell (sē'shel')   n.   The shell of any marine mollusk.

sea·shore (sē'shôr', -shōr')   n.   1. Land adjacent to or bordering on the ocean. 2. *Law* The ground between high- and low-water marks.

sea·sick (sē'sik')   adj.   Suffering from seasickness.

sea·sick·ness (sē'sik'nis)   n.   Nausea, dizziness, and prostration caused by the motion of a vessel at sea.

sea·side (sē'sīd')   n.   The seashore, esp. as a place of resort. — adj. Of or pertaining to the seashore.

sea·son (sē'zən)   n.   1. A division of the year as determined by the earth's position with respect to the sun, and as marked by the temperature, moisture, vegetation, etc. 2. A period of time. 3. Any of the periods into which the Christian year is divided. 4. A period of special activity: the hunting *season*. 5. A fit or suitable time. 6. That which imparts relish; seasoning. — **in season** 1. In condition and obtainable for use. 2. In good or sufficient time; opportunely. 3. Legally permitted to be killed or taken, as game. 4. Ready to mate or breed: said of animals. — v.t. 1. To increase the flavor or zest of (food), as by adding spices, etc. 2. To add zest or piquancy to. 3. To render more suitable for use. 4. To make accustomed or inured; harden. 5. To mitigate or soften. — v.i. 6. To become seasoned. [< OF < LL *satio, -onis* sowing time < L, a sowing] — **sea'son·er** n.

sea·son·a·ble (sē'zən·ə·bəl)   adj.   1. Being in keeping with the season. 2. Done at the proper time. — **sea'son·a·ble·ness** n. — **sea'son·a·bly** adv.

sea·son·al (sē'zən·əl)   adj.   Characteristic of, affected by, or occurring at a certain season. — **sea'son·al·ly** adv.

sea·son·ing (sē'zən·ing)   n.   1. The act or process by which something, as lumber, is rendered fit for use. 2. Something added to food to give relish; esp., a condiment. 3. Something added to increase enjoyment, zest, etc.

season ticket   A ticket or pass, usually at a reduced rate, entitling the holder to daily trips on a train for a certain period or to admission to a series of sporting events, etc.

seat (sēt)   n.   1. That on which one sits, as a chair, bench, or stool. 2. The part of a thing upon which one rests in sitting, or upon which an object or another part rests. 3. The buttocks; also, the portion of a garment covering them. 4. The place where anything is situated, settled, or established. 5. A place of abode. 6. The privilege or right of membership in a legislative body, stock exchange, etc. 7. The manner of sitting, as on horseback. 8. A surface or part upon which the base of anything rests. — v.t. 1. To place on a seat or seats; cause to sit down. 2. To have seats for. 3. To put or repair a seat on or in. 4. To locate, settle, or center: usually in the passive. 5. To fix or set firmly or in place. [< ON *sæti*. Akin to SIT.]

seat belt   A safety belt.

seat·ing (sē'ting)   n.   1. The act of providing with seats. 2. Fabric for upholstering seats. 3. The arrangement of seats, as in a room, auditorium, etc.

sea urchin   A marine animal having a soft rounded body covered with a shell bearing numerous movable spines.

sea wall   A wall or an embankment to prevent the encroachments of the sea, the erosion of the shore, etc.

sea·ward (sē'wərd)   adj.   1. Going toward the sea. 2. Blowing, as wind, from the sea. — adv. In the direction of the sea: also **sea'wards** (-wərdz).

sea·way (sē′wā′) *n.* **1.** A way or lane over the sea. **2.** An inland waterway that receives ocean shipping. **3.** The headway made by a ship. **4.** A rough sea: usu. in **in a seaway.**

sea·weed (sē′wēd′) *n.* **1.** Any of a widely distributed class of plants growing in the sea, including the kelps, rockweeds, dulse, etc. **2.** Any marine plant.

sea·wor·thy (sē′wûr′thē) *adj.* In fit condition for a voyage: said of a vessel. — **sea′wor′thi·ness** *n.*

se·ba·ceous (si·bā′shəs) *adj. Physiol.* **1.** Of, pertaining to, or like fat. **2.** Designating any of the glands in the skin that secrete sebum. [< NL *sebaceus* < L *sebum* tallow]

sebi- *combining form* Fat; fatty matter: also, before vowels, **seb-.** Also **sebo-.** [< L *sebum* tallow]

se·bum (sē′bəm) *n. Physiol.* A fatty matter secreted by the sebaceous glands. [< L, tallow]

sec (sek) *adj. French Dry:* said of wines.

se·cant (sē′kənt, -kant) *adj.* Cutting, esp. into two parts; intersecting. — *n.* **1.** *Geom.* **a** A straight line intersecting a given curve. **b** A line drawn from the center of a circle through one extremity of an arc to the tangent drawn from the other extremity of the same arc. **2.** *Trig.* A function of an acute angle, equal to the ratio of the hypotenuse to the side adjacent to the angle when the angle is included in a right triangle. [< L *secans, -antis,* ppr. of *secare* to cut]

se·cede (si·sēd′) *v.i.* **·ced·ed, ·ced·ing** To withdraw formally from a union, fellowship, or association, esp. from a political or religious organization. [< L < *se-* apart + *cedere* to go] — **se·ced′er** *n.*

se·ces·sion (si·sesh′ən) *n.* **1.** The act of seceding, esp. from political or religious association. **2.** *Usually cap.* The withdrawal of the Southern States from the Union in 1860–61. — **se·ces′sion·al** *adj.* — **se·ces′sion·ist** *adj. & n.*

Seck·el (sek′əl, sik′əl) *n.* A variety of small, sweet pear. [after the Pennsylvania farmer who introduced it]

se·clude (si·klōōd′) *v.t.* **·clud·ed, ·clud·ing 1.** To remove and keep apart from the company or society of others; isolate. **2.** To screen or shut off, as from view. [< L < *se-* apart + *claudere* to shut]

se·clud·ed (si·klōō′did) *adj.* **1.** Separated; withdrawn; living apart from others. **2.** Protected or screened. — **se·clud′ed·ly** *adv.* — **se·clud′ed·ness** *n.*

se·clu·sion (si·klōō′zhən) *n.* **1.** The act of secluding, or the state or condition of being secluded; solitude; retirement. **2.** A secluded place. — **se·clu′sive** *adj.* — **se·clu′sive·ly** *adv.* — **se·clu′sive·ness** *n.*

sec·ond¹ (sek′ənd) *n.* **1.** A unit of time, ⅟₆₀ of a minute. **2.** *Geom.* A unit of angular measure, ⅟₆₀ of a minute of arc. Symbol: ″. [< OF *seconde*]

sec·ond² (sek′ənd) *adj.* **1.** Next in order, authority, responsibility, etc., after the first: the ordinal of *two.* **2.** Ranking next to or below the first or best; secondary; subordinate. **3.** Identical in character with another or preceding one; another; other. **4.** *Music* Designating one of two parts for like instruments or voices, usu. the one lower in pitch or in some manner subordinate. — *n.* **1.** The one next after the first in position, rank, importance, or quality. **2.** An attendant who supports or aids another, as in a duel. **3.** *pl.* Articles of merchandise of imperfect manufacture or of inferior quality. **4.** *Music* **a** The interval between any note and the next above or below in the diatonic scale. **b** A note separated by this interval from any other. **c** Two notes at this interval written or sounded together. **d** A second or subordinate part, instrument, or voice. **5.** In parliamentary law, an utterance whereby a motion is seconded: Do I hear a *second?* — *v.t.* **1.** To act as a supporter or assistant of; promote; encourage. **2.** In deliberative bodies, to support formally, as a motion, resolution, etc. — *adv.* In the second order, place, or rank: also, in formal discourse, **sec′ond·ly.** [< OF < L *secundus* following]

sec·on·dar·y (sek′ən·der′ē) *adj.* **1.** Of second rank, grade, or influence; subordinate; auxiliary. **2.** Depending on what is primary or original: *secondary* sources. **3.** *Electr.* Of, pertaining to, or noting an induced current or its circuit, esp. in an induction coil. — *n. pl.* **·dar·ies 1.** One who acts in a secondary or subordinate capacity; an assistant. **2.** Anything of secondary size, position, or importance. **3.** *Ornithol.* One of the feathers that grow on the second joint or forearm of a bird's wing. — **sec′on·dar′i·ly** *adv.*

secondary accent See under ACCENT.

secondary cell *Electr.* A type of cell that can be recharged by the passage of direct current in reverse direction through the electrolyte: also called *storage cell.*

secondary education High school or preparatory school education between the elementary and college levels.

secondary school A high school or preparatory school intermediate between the elementary school and college.

second base In baseball, the base situated between first and third base.

second base·man (bās′mən) *n. pl.* **·men** (-mən) A baseball player stationed at or near second base.

sec·ond-best (sek′ənd·best′) *adj.* Next to the best.

second childhood Senility; dotage.

sec·ond-class (sek′ənd·klas′, -kläs′) *adj.* **1.** Ranking next below the first or best; inferior; mediocre. **2.** Of or pertaining to travel accommodations ranking between first class and third class. **3.** Of or pertaining to a class of mail including all printed periodicals. — *adv.* By second-class ticket or by using second-class conveniences.

Second Coming The expected second coming of Christ.

second estate The nobility.

second fiddle Any secondary or inferior status, esp. in the phrase **to be** (or **play**) **second fiddle.**

sec·ond-guess (sek′ənd·ges′) *v.t. & v.i.* To judge or conjecture about (something) after it has occurred.

sec·ond-hand (sek′ənd·hand′) *adj.* **1.** Having been previously owned, worn, or used by another; not new. **2.** Received from another: *secondhand* information. **3.** Handling or dealing in merchandise that is not new.

second hand The hand that marks the seconds on a clock or a watch.

second lieutenant *Mil.* The lowest grade of commissioned officer, ranking below first lieutenant.

second nature A disposition or character that is acquired and not innate; deep-seated habits that have become fixed.

second papers A popular name for a certificate of naturalization.

sec·ond-rate (sek′ənd·rāt′) *adj.* Second in quality, size, rank, importance, etc.; second-class. — **sec′ond-rat′er** *n.*

second sight The alleged power of seeing events occurring at distant places, in the future, etc.; clairvoyance.

sec·ond-sto·ry man (sek′ənd·stôr′ē, -stō′rē) *U.S. Slang* A burglar.

second-string (sek′ənd·string′) *adj. U.S. Informal* In sports, ranking next to the regular or starting player or team.

Second World War See WORLD WAR II in table for WAR.

se·cre·cy (sē′krə·sē) *n. pl.* **·cies 1.** The condition or quality of being secret or hidden; concealment. **2.** The character of being secretive; secretiveness. **3.** Privacy; retirement; solitude. Also **se·cret·ness** (sē′krit·nis).

se·cret (sē′krit) *adj.* **1.** Kept separate or hidden from view or knowledge; concealed; hidden. **2.** Beyond normal comprehension; obscure; recondite. **3.** Known or revealed only to the initiated: *secret* rites. **4.** Affording privacy; secluded. **5.** Good at keeping secrets; close-mouthed. **6.** *U.S. Mil.* Denoting the second highest category of security classification. Compare TOP-SECRET. — *n.* **1.** Something not to be told. **2.** A thing undiscovered or unknown. **3.** An underlying reason; that which, when known, explains; key. **4.** A secret contrivance. **5.** Secrecy. — **in secret** In privacy; in a hidden place. [< OF < L < *se-* apart + *cernere* to separate] — **se′cret·ly** *adv.*

sec·re·tar·i·at (sek′rə·târ′ē·it, -at) *n.* **1.** A secretary's position. **2.** The place where a secretary transacts his business. **3.** The executive department of an organization, esp. of the United Nations. **4.** The entire staff of secretaries in an office. Also **sec′re·tar′i·ate.**

sec·re·tar·y (sek′rə·ter′ē) *n. pl.* **·tar·ies 1.** A person employed to deal with correspondence, keep records, and handle clerical business for an individual, business, committee, etc. **2.** An executive officer presiding over and managing a department of government. **3.** A writing desk with a bookcase or cabinet. [< Med.L < L *secretum* secret] — **sec′re·tar′i·al** (-târ′ē·əl) *adj.*

secretary bird A South African bird that has long legs and a crest suggesting quill pens stuck behind the ear.

secretary general *pl.* **secretaries general** A chief secretary; an assistant to a governor general. — **sec′re·tar′y-gen′er·al·cy** (-jen′ər·əl·sē) *n.*

se·crete (si·krēt′) *v.t.* **·cret·ed, ·cret·ing 1.** To conceal; hide. **2.** *Physiol.* To produce (a secretion). [See SECRET.] — **se·cre′tor** *n.*

se·cre·tion (si·krē′shən) *n. Physiol.* **1.** The process, generally glandular, by which materials are separated from the blood and elaborated into new substances, as milk, etc. **2.** The substance secreted. [See SECRET.]

se·cre·tive (si·krē′tiv; *for def. 1, also* sē′krə·tiv) *adj.* **1.** Inclined to secrecy; reticent. **2.** *Physiol.* Producing or causing secretion. — **se·cre′tive·ly** *adv.* — **se·cre′tive·ness** *n.*

se·cre·to·ry (si·krē′tər·ē) *adj.* Of, or functioning as, a secretion. — *n. pl.* **·ries** A secreting organ or gland.

secret service 1. Investigation conducted secretly for a government. **2.** The secret or espionage work of various government agencies in time of war.

Secret Service A section of the Department of the Treasury concerned with the suppression of counterfeiting, the protection of the President of the United States, etc.

sect (sekt) *n.* **1.** A body of persons distinguished by peculiarities of faith and practice from other bodies adhering to the same general system, esp., the adherents of a particular religious creed. **2.** Any number of persons united in opinion, interest beliefs. [< OF < L < *sequi* to follow]

-sect *combining form* To cut; divide (in a specified manner): *vivisect, bisect*. [< L < *secare* to cut]

sec·tar·i·an (sek·târ'ē·ən) *adj.* **1.** Pertaining to or belonging to a particular sect. **2.** Adhering or confined to a specific group, party, etc.; partisan. — *n.* A member of a sect, esp. if bigoted. — **sec·tar'i·an·ism** *n.*

sec·ta·ry (sek'tər·ē) *n. pl.* **·ries 1.** A sectarian. **2.** A dissenter from an established church; a nonconformist. Also **sec'ta·rist.** [< MF or Med.L < L. See SECT.]

sec·tion (sek'shən) *n.* **1.** A separate part or division; as a portion of a book or a chapter. **2.** A distinct part of a country, community, etc. **3.** *U.S.* An area of land containing 640 acres, ⅟₃₆ of a township. **4.** Any of two or more trains, buses, airplanes, etc., represented by a single entry in a timetable or schedule. **5.** A portion of railroad track under the care of a particular set of men. **6.** In a sleeping car, a space containing two berths. **7.** A picture of a building, geological formation, etc., as if cut by an intersecting plane; also, the thing so viewed. **8.** The act of cutting; division by cutting. — **Syn.** See PORTION. — *v.t.* **1.** To cut or divide into sections. **2.** To shade (a drawing) so as to designate a section or sections. [< MF or L < *secare* to cut]

-section *combining form* The act or process of cutting or dividing: *vivisection*. [< L. See SECTION.]

sec·tion·al (sek'shən·əl) *adj.* **1.** Pertaining to a section, as of a country; local: a *sectional* dialect. **2.** Dividing or alienating one section from another. **3.** Made up of sections. — *n. U.S.* A long sofa having several separate units. — **sec'·tion·al·ly** *adv.*

sec·tion·al·ism (sek'shən·əl·iz'əm) *n.* Undue concern for a particular section of the country; intense consciousness of sectional differences. — **sec'tion·al·ist** *n.*

sec·tor (sek'tər) *n.* **1.** *Geom.* A part of a circle or ellipse bounded by two radii and the arc subtended by them. **2.** A part or portion: a wooded *sector* of land; the conservative *sector* of the population. **3.** *Mil.* A defined area for which a unit is responsible. — *v.t.* To divide into sectors. [< LL < L < *secare* to cut] — **sec·to·ri·al** (sek·tôr'ē·al) *adj.*

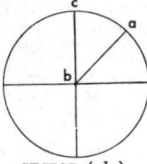

SECTOR (abc) OF A CIRCLE

sec·u·lar (sek'yə·lər) *adj.* **1.** Of this world or the present life; temporal; worldly: distinguished from *spiritual*. **2.** Not under the control of the church; civil. **3.** Not concerned with religion; not sacred. **4.** Not bound by monastic vows. — *n.* **1.** One in holy orders who is not bound by monastic vows. **2.** A layman. [< OF < LL < L *saeculum* generation, an age]

sec·u·lar·ism (sek'yə·lə·riz'əm) *n.* **1.** The belief that morality should be determined without reference to religious systems. **2.** The view that religion should not be introduced into public education or civil affairs. — **sec'u·lar·ist** *n.*

sec·u·lar·ize (sek'yə·lə·rīz') *v.t.* **·ized, ·iz·ing 1.** To convert from sacred to secular uses. **2.** To make worldly. — **sec'u·lar·i·za'tion** *n.*

se·cure (si·kyoor') *adj.* **1.** Guarded against or not likely to be exposed to danger; safe. **2.** Free from fear, apprehension, etc. **3.** Fixed or holding firmly in place. **4.** So strong or well-made as to render loss, escape, or failure impossible. **5.** Assured; certain; guaranteed. — *v.* **cured, ·cur·ing** *v.t.* **1.** To make secure; protect. **2.** To make firm or tight; fasten. **3.** To make certain; ensure. **4.** To obtain possession of; get. — *v.i.* **5.** To be or become secure; take precautions: with *against*, etc. [< L < *se-* without + *cura* care] — **se·cur'a·ble** *adj.* — **se·cure'ly** *adv.* — **se·cure'ment** *n.* — **se·cure'ness** *n.* — **se·cur'er** *n.*

se·cur·i·ty (si·kyoor'ə·tē) *n. pl.* **·ties 1.** The state of being secure; freedom from danger, poverty, etc. **2.** One who or that which secures or guarantees. **3.** Something deposited or pledged as a guarantee for payment. **4.** *pl.* Stocks, bonds, notes, etc. **5.** Protection of secrecy, as in wartime. — **Syn. 2, 3.** Both *security* and *surety* may mean property given as a guarantee or the person who gives it, but *security* is chiefly used in the first sense, and *surety* in the second. A *bond* is a written promise to pay compensation for loss, damage, etc.

Security Council A permanent organ of the United Nations charged with the maintenance of international peace.

security risk *U.S.* A person regarded as unfit for employment in government or in a job connected with national defense, as because of dubious associations.

se·dan (si·dan') *n.* **1.** A closed automobile having two or four doors and a front and back seat. **2.** A sedan chair. [? Ital. *sedere* to sit < L]

sedan chair A portable, enclosed chair, usu., for one passenger, carried by means of poles at the front and back.

se·date (si·dāt') *adj.* **1.** Characterized by habitual composure; unhurried; calm. **2.** Sober and decorous. [< L < *sedere* to sit] — **se·date'ly** *adv.* — **se·date'ness** *n.*

se·da·tion (si·dā'shən) *n. Med.* The act or process of reducing distress, irritation, excitement, etc., by administering sedatives.

sed·a·tive (sed'ə·tiv) *adj.* **1.** Having a soothing effect. **2.** *Med.* Allaying irritation; assuaging pain. — *n.* Any means, as a medicine, of soothing distress or allaying pain.

sed·en·tar·y (sed'ən·ter'ē) *adj.* **1.** Characterized by, requiring, or resulting from much sitting or a habitual sitting posture. **2.** Settled in one place, as certain tribes; sluggish; inactive. **3.** Accustomed to sitting. **4.** *Zool.* Remaining in one place; attached or fixed to an object. [< L *sedere* to sit] — **sed·en·tar'i·ly** *adv.* — **sed·en·tar'i·ness** *n.*

Se·der (sā'dər) *n. pl.* **Se·ders** or **Se·dar·im** (sə·där'im) In Judaism, the Passover feast commemorating the departure of the Israelites from Egypt. [< Hebrew *sedher* service]

sedge (sej) *n.* Any of various grasslike herbs widely distributed in marshy places. [OE *secg*] — **sedg'y** *adj.*

sed·i·ment (sed'ə·mənt) *n.* **1.** Matter that settles to the bottom of a liquid; settlings; dregs; lees. **2.** *Geol.* Fragmentary material deposited by water or air. — **Syn.** See WASTE. [< MF < L *sedere* to sit, settle] — **sed/i·men'ta·ry, sed/i·men'tal** *adj.*

se·di·tion (si·dish'ən) *n.* **1.** Language or conduct directed against public order and the safety of the state. **2.** The clandestine incitement of such disorder. **3.** Dissension; revolt. [< OF < L < *sed-* aside + *itio, -onis* a going] — **se·di'tion·ar·y, se·di'tion·ist** *adj. & n.*

se·di·tious (si·dish'əs) *adj.* **1.** Of, promoting, or having the character of sedition. **2.** Taking part in or guilty of sedition. [See SEDITION.] — **se·di'tious·ly** *adv.*

se·duce (si·dōos', -dyōos') *v.t.* **·duced, ·duc·ing 1.** To lead astray; entice into wrong, disloyalty, etc.; tempt. **2.** To induce to engage in illicit sexual intercourse, esp. for the first time. [< L < *se-* apart + *ducere* to lead] — **se·duc'er** *n.* — **se·duc'i·ble** or **se·duce'a·ble** *adj.*

se·duc·tion (si·duk'shən) *n.* **1.** The act of seducing. **2.** Something that seduces; an enticement. Also **se·duce·ment** (si·dōos'mənt, -dyōos'-). [See SEDUCE.]

se·duc·tive (si·duk'tiv) *adj.* Tending to seduce; enticing. — **se·duc'tive·ly** *adv.* — **se·duc'tive·ness** *n.*

se·du·li·ty (si·dōo'lə·tē, -dyōo'-) *n.* The state or character of being sedulous.

sed·u·lous (sej'ōo·ləs) *adj.* Constant in application or attention; assiduous. [< L *sedulus* careful] — **sed'u·lous·ly** *adv.* — **sed'u·lous·ness** *n.* — **Syn.** diligent, persevering. Compare BUSY.

se·dum (sē'dəm) *n.* Any of a large genus of chiefly perennial plants, having very thick leaves and usu. white, yellow, or pink flowers. [< L, houseleek]

see¹ (sē) *v.* **saw, seen, see·ing** *v.t.* **1.** To perceive with the eyes; gain knowledge or awareness of by means of one's vision. **2.** To perceive with the mind; understand. **3.** To find out or ascertain. **4.** To have experience or knowledge of. **5.** To encounter; chance to meet. **6.** To have a meeting or interview with; visit or receive as a guest, patient, etc. **7.** To attend as a spectator; view. **8.** To accompany; escort. **9.** To take care; be sure: *See* that you do it! **10.** In poker, to accept a bet by betting an equal sum. — *v.i.* **11.** To have or exercise the power of sight. **12.** To find out; inquire. **13.** To understand. **14.** To think; consider. — **to see about 1.** To inquire into the facts, causes, etc., of. **2.** To take care of; attend to. — **to see (someone) off** To accompany to a point of departure, as for a journey. — **to see (someone) through** To aid or protect, as throughout a period of difficulty or danger. — **to see through** To penetrate, as a disguise or deception. — **to see to** To be responsible for; give one's attention to. [OE *sēon*]

see² (sē) *n.* **1.** The local seat from which a bishop, archbishop, or pope exercises jurisdiction. **2.** Episcopal or papal jurisdiction, authority, rank, or office. — **Holy See** The Pope's jurisdiction or office. [< OF < L *sedes* seat]

seed (sēd) *n.* **1.** The ovule from which a plant may be reproduced; the fertilized ovule containing an embryo. **2.** That from which anything springs; source. **3.** Offspring; children. **4.** The male fertilizing element; semen; milt. **5.** Any small, usu. hard fruit; also, any part of a plant from which it may be propagated, as bulbs, tubers, etc. **6.** Seeds collectively. **7.** Ancestry; stock. — **to go to seed 1.** To develop and shed seed. **2.** To become shabby, useless, etc.; deteriorate. — *v.t.* **1.** To sow with seed. **2.** To sow (seed). **3.** To remove the seeds from. **4.** In sports, to arrange positions in a tournament, etc., so that the more skilled competitors meet only in the later events. **5.** To intersperse (clouds) with particles of silver iodide or other substances in order to produce rainfall. — *v.i.* **6.** To sow seed. **7.** To grow to maturity and produce or shed seed. [OE *sæd*] — **seed'er** *n.* — **seed'less** *adj.*

seed bud *Bot.* The germ within a seed; also, the ovule.

seed cake A sweet cake containing aromatic seeds.

seed·case (sēd'kās') *n. Bot.* A pericarp.

seed leaf *Bot.* A cotyledon.

seed·ling (sēd'ling) *n.* **1.** *Bot.* A plant grown from seed, as distinguished from one propagated by grafting. **2.** A very small or young tree or plant.

seed oyster A young oyster, esp. one transplanted to another bed.

seed pearl A small pearl, used in jewelry, embroidery, etc.

seeds·man (sēdz'mən) *n. pl.* **·men** (-mən) **1.** A dealer in seeds. **2.** A sower. Also **seed'man.**

seed vessel *Bot.* A pericarp.

seed·y (sē'dē) *adj.* **seed·i·er, seed·i·est 1.** Full of seeds. **2.** Gone to seed. **3.** Poor; shabby. **4.** *Informal* Feeling or looking wretched. — **seed'i·ly** *adv.* — **seed'i·ness** *n.*

see·ing (sē'ing) *n.* The act of seeing; vision; sight. — *conj.* Taking into consideration; since; in view of the fact.

seek (sēk) *v.* **sought, seek·ing** *v.t.* **1.** To go in search of; look for. **2.** To strive for; try to get or obtain. **3.** To endeavor or try: He *seeks* to mislead me. **4.** To ask or inquire for; request. **5.** To go to; betake oneself to: to *seek* a warmer climate. — *v.i.* **6.** To make a search or inquiry. [OE *sēcan*] — **seek'er** *n.*

seem (sēm) *v.i.* **1.** To give the impression of being; appear. **2.** To appear to oneself: I *seem* to hear strange voices. **3.** To appear to exist. **4.** To be evident or apparent: It *seems* to be raining. [ME < ON *sǣma* to conform to] — **seem'er** *n.*

seem·ing (sē'ming) *adj.* Having the appearance of reality; apparent but not necessarily actual. — *n.* Appearance; semblance; esp., false show. — **seem'ing·ly** *adv.* — **seem'ing·ness** *n.*

seem·ly (sēm'lē) *adj.* **·li·er, ·li·est** Befitting the proprieties; decorous. — *adv.* Becomingly; decently; appropriately. [< ON < *sǣmr* fitting] — **seem'li·ness** *n.*

seen (sēn) Past participle of SEE.

seep (sēp) *v.i.* To soak through pores or small interstices; percolate; ooze. — *n.* A small spring or a place out of which water, oil, etc., oozes. [Alter. of OE *sypian* to soak]

seep·age (sē'pij) *n.* **1.** The act or process of seeping or oozing. **2.** The fluid or moisture that oozes.

seer (sē'ər *for def. 1; also* sir *for defs. 2 and 3*) *n.* **1.** One who sees. **2.** A prophet. **3.** One believed to have second sight. [< SEE¹ + -ER] — **seer'ess** *n. fem.*

seer·suck·er (sir'suk'ər) *n.* A thin fabric of cotton, rayon, nylon, etc., usu. striped in colors, with a crinkled surface. [< Hind. < Persian *shīr o shakkar*, lit., milk and sugar]

see·saw (sē'sô') *n.* **1.** A balanced plank or board made to move alternately up and down by persons at opposite ends: also called *teeter.* **2.** The action or diversion of balancing on such a board. **3.** Any up-and-down or to-and-fro movement. — *v.t. & v.i.* **1.** To move or cause to move on or as if on a seesaw. **2.** To alternate; fluctuate. — *adj.* Moving to and fro; vacillating. [Reduplication of SAW¹]

seethe (sēth) *v.* **seethed, seethed, seeth·ing** *v.i.* **1.** To boil. **2.** To foam or bubble as if boiling. **3.** To be agitated, as by rage. — *v.t.* **4.** To soak in liquid; steep. — *n.* The act or condition of seething; turmoil. [OE *sēothan*]

seg·ment (seg'mənt) *n.* **1.** A part cut off or divided from the other parts of anything; a section. **2.** *Geom.* **a** A part of a figure, esp., of a circle, cut off by a line or plane. **b** A finite part of a line. — *v.t. & v.i.* To divide into segments. [< L < *secare* to cut] — **seg·men·ta·ry** (seg'mən·ter'ē) *adj.*

seg·men·tal (seg·men'təl) *adj.* **1.** Of a segment or segments. **2.** Divided into segments. — **seg·men'tal·ly** *adv.*

seg·men·ta·tion (seg'mən·tā'shən) *n.* **1.** The act of cutting or dividing into segments. **2.** The state of being so divided. **3.** *Biol.* The cleavage of a cell.

se·go (sē'gō) *n. pl.* **·gos 1.** A perennial herb of the lily family, having white flowers: the State flower of Utah. **2.** Its edible bulb. [< Shoshonean (Ute) *sigo*]

seg·re·gate (seg'rə·gāt; *for adj. also* seg'rə·git) *v.* **·gat·ed, ·gat·ing** *v.t.* **1.** To place apart from others or the rest; isolate. **2.** To subject to segregation. — *v.i.* **3.** To separate from a mass and gather about nuclei or along lines of fracture, as in crystallization. **4.** To undergo segregation. — *adj.* Set apart from others. [< L < *se-* apart + *grex, gregis* flock] — **seg're·ga'tive** *adj.* — **seg're·ga'tor** *n.*

seg·re·ga·tion (seg'rə·gā'shən) *n.* **1.** The act or process of segregating. **2.** The practice of requiring separate facilities, as in housing, schools, and transportation, for use by whites and nonwhites, esp. Negroes. — **seg're·ga'tion·ist** *n.*

Seid·litz powder (sed'lits) An aperient consisting of two separate parts, tartaric acid, and sodium bicarbonate mixed with Rochelle salt, dissolved separately and then combined. [after *Seidlitz*, a Czech village, site of a medicinal spring]

seign·ior (sēn'yər) *n.* **1.** A lord; noble. **2.** A title of respect equivalent to *Sir.* Also **sei·gneur** (sēn·yûr'). [< AF, OF < L *senior* older] — **sei·gnio·ri·al** (sēn·yôr'ē·əl, -yō'rē-) *adj.*

seign·ior·y (sēn'yər·ē) *n. pl.* **·ies 1.** The territory or juris-

diction of a seignior; a manor. **2.** Right belonging to feudal superiority. Also **sei'gneur·y.**

seine (sān) *n.* A long fishnet hanging vertically in the water and having floats at the top edge and weights at the bottom. — *v.t. & v.i.* **seined, sein·ing** To fish or catch with a seine. [OE < L < Gk. *sagēnē* fishnet]

seis·mic (sīz'mik, sīs'-) *adj.* Of, characteristic of, or produced by earthquakes. Also **seis'mal, seis'mi·cal, seis·mat·i·cal** (sīz·mat'ə·kəl, sīs-). [< Gk. < *seiein* to shake]

seismic sea wave A large and often destructive wave caused by a submarine earthquake; a tsunami.

seismo- *combining form* Earthquake. Also, before vowels, **seism-.** [< Gk. *seismos* earthquake]

seis·mo·gram (sīz'mə·gram, sīs'-) *n.* The record of an earthquake or earth tremor made by a seismograph.

seis·mo·graph (sīz'mə·graf, -gräf, sīs'-) *n.* An instrument for recording automatically the intensity, direction, and duration of an earthquake shock. — **seis'mo·graph'ic** *adj.* — **seis·mog·ra·pher** (sīz·mog'rə·fər, sīs-) *n.*

seis·mog·ra·phy (sīz·mog'rə·fē, sīs-) *n.* The study and recording of earthquake phenomena.

seis·mol·o·gy (sīz·mol'ə·jē, sīs-) *n.* The science of earthquake phenomena. — **seis·mo·log·ic** (sīz'mə·loj'ik, sīs'-) or **·i·cal** *adj.* — **seis'mo·log'i·cal·ly** *adv.* — **seis·mol'o·gist** *n.*

seize (sēz) *v.* **seized, seiz·ing** *v.t.* **1.** To take hold of suddenly and forcibly. **2.** To grasp mentally; comprehend. **3.** To take possession of by authority or right. **4.** To take possession of by force. **5.** To take prisoner; capture; arrest. **6.** To act upon with sudden and powerful effect: Terror *seized* the enemy. **7.** To take advantage of immediately, as an opportunity. **8.** *Law* To put into legal possession. **9.** *Naut.* To fasten or bind by turns of cord, etc. — *v.i.* **10.** To take a sudden or forcible hold. [< OF < Med.L (*ad propriam*) *sacire* to take (into one's own possession)] — **seiz'a·ble** *adj.* — **seiz'er** *n.*

sei·zure (sē'zhər) *n.* **1.** The act of seizing. **2.** A sudden or violent attack, as of epilepsy; fit; spell.

se·la·chi·an (si·lā'kē·ən) *adj.* Of or belonging to a group of fishes including the sharks, skates, and rays. — *n.* A selachian fish. [< NL < Gk. *selachos* shark]

se·lah (sē'lə) A word of unknown meaning occurring often at the end of a verse in the Psalms, usu. considered as a direction to readers or musicians. [< Hebrew *selāh*]

sel·dom (sel'dəm) *adv.* At widely separated intervals, as of time or space; infrequently. [OE *seldum*]

se·lect (si·lekt') *v.t.* **1.** To take in preference to another or others. — *v.i.* **2.** To make a choice. — *adj.* **1.** Chosen in preference to others; choice. **2.** Exclusive. **3.** Very particular in selecting. [< L < *se-* apart + *legere* to choose] — **se·lect'ness** *n.* — **se·lec'tor** *n.*

se·lec·tee (si·lek·tē') *n.* One selected; esp., one drafted for military or naval service.

se·lec·tion (si·lek'shən) *n.* **1.** Choice. **2.** Anything selected. **3.** A thing or collection of things chosen with care. **4.** *Biol.* The process by which certain organisms, or any of their characteristics, are favored in the struggle for survival.

se·lec·tive (si·lek'tiv) *adj.* **1.** Pertaining to selection; tending to select. **2.** Having or characterized by good selectivity.

selective service Compulsory military service according to specified conditions of age, fitness, etc.

se·lec·tiv·i·ty (si·lek'tiv'ə·tē) *n.* **1.** The state or quality of being selective. Also **se·lec'tive·ness. 2.** *Telecom.* That characteristic of a radio or television receiver, electrical circuit, etc., by which certain frequencies can be received to the exclusion of others.

se·lect·man (si·lekt'mən) *n. pl.* **·men** (-mən) In New England, one of a board of town officers, elected annually to exercise executive authority in local affairs.

Se·le·ne (si·lē'nē) In Greek mythology, goddess of the moon: identified with the Roman *Luna.* Also **Se·le'na** (-nə). [< Gk. *Selēnē,* lit., the moon]

sel·e·nite (sel'ə·nīt) *n.* A pearly, usu. transparent variety of gypsum. [< L < Gk. *selēnītēs* (*lithos*), lit., moonstone < *selēnē* the moon]

se·le·ni·um (si·lē'nē·əm) *n.* A gray, crystalline, nonmetallic element (symbol Se) of the sulfur group, varying greatly in electrical resistance under the influence of light. See ELEMENT. [< NL < Gk. *selēnē* the moon]

selenium cell A photoelectric cell in which plates of selenium respond to the action of light upon them.

seleno- *combining form* Moon; pertaining to the moon; lunar. Also, before vowels, **selen-.** [< Gk. *selēnē* the moon]

self (self) *n. pl.* **selves 1.** An individual known or considered as the subject of his own consciousness. **2.** Anything considered as having a distinct personality. **3.** Personal interest or advantage. **4.** Any thing, class, or attribute that, abstractly considered, maintains a distinct and characteristic individuality or identity. — *adj.* **1.** Being of the same color, substance, etc., throughout; uniform. **2.** Of a part, accessory, etc., made of the same material as that with which it is used. [OE]

◆ *Self* may appear as a combining form with various meanings as shown in the list below:

1. Of the self (the object of the root word); as in:

self-abandonment	self-disclosure	self-murderer
self-abasing	self-discovery	self-mutilation
self-abhorrence	self-disgrace	self-neglect
self-accusation	self-disparagement	self-neglectful
self-adaptive	self-display	self-nourishment
self-admiration	self-disposal	self-observation
self-admission	self-disquieting	self-offense
self-adornment	self-dissolution	self-opinion
self-adulation	self-doubt	self-painter
self-advancement	self-easing	self-paying
self-advertisement	self-enriching	self-perceiving
self-advertising	self-estimate	self-perceptive
self-affliction	self-evacuation	self-perfecting
self-analysis	self-exalting	self-perfection
self-annihilation	self-exculpation	self-perpetuating
self-applause	self-excuse	self-perpetuation
self-appreciation	self-expansion	self-persuasion
self-approbation	self-expatriation	self-pleasing
self-approval	self-exploiting	self-praise
self-asserting	self-exposure	self-praising
self-awareness	self-fearing	self-preparation
self-bedizenment	self-flatterer	self-presentation
self-betrayal	self-flattering	self-preserving
self-blame	self-flattery	self-projection
self-castigation	self-folding	self-protecting
self-chastisement	self-forgetful	self-protection
self-cognizance	self-formation	self-punishment
self-commendation	self-glorification	self-raising
self-committal	self-gratification	self-recollection
self-comparison	self-guidance	self-reconstruction
self-condemnation	self-harming	self-reduction
self-condemning	self-helpful	self-regulation
self-conditioning	self-humbling	self-representation
self-confinement	self-humiliation	self-repressing
self-confounding	self-hypnosis	self-repression
self-conquest	self-hypnotism	self-reproach
self-conservative	self-hypnotized	self-reproachful
self-conserving	self-idolatry	self-restriction
self-consideration	self-idolizing	self-revealing
self-consoling	self-ignorance	self-revelation
self-consuming	self-ignorant	self-ruin
self-contempt	self-imitation	self-satirist
self-contradicting	self-immolation	self-scrutinizing
self-conviction	self-immurement	self-scrutiny
self-correction	self-impairment	self-searching
self-corruption	self-indignation	self-slaughter
self-creation	self-indulging	self-soothing
self-criticism	self-inspection	self-study
self-cure	self-instruction	self-subjection
self-damnation	self-insurer	self-subordination
self-debasement	self-integration	self-suppression
self-deceit	self-intensifying	self-surrender
self-deceiving	self-interrogation	self-suspicious
self-dedication	self-introduction	self-taxation
self-defeating	self-judgment	self-teacher
self-deflation	self-justification	self-terminating
self-degradation	self-justifying	self-tolerant
self-deifying	self-laudatory	self-torment
self-dejection	self-limitation	self-torture
self-delusion	self-limiting	self-treatment
self-deprecating	self-loss	self-trust
self-depreciation	self-maceration	self-trusting
self-depreciative	self-maintenance	self-undoing
self-destroying	self-martyrdom	self-upbraiding
self-destruction	self-mastery	self-valuing
self-destructive	self-mistrust	self-vaunting
self-direction	self-mortification	self-vindication
self-disapproval	self-murder	self-worship

2. By oneself or itself; by one's own effort (the agent of the root word); as in self-employed.

self-abandoned	self-doomed	self-named
self-administered	self-elaborated	self-offered
self-approved	self-elected	self-ordained
self-authorized	self-explained	self-paid
self-balanced	self-exposed	self-pampered
self-beguiled	self-furnished	self-performed
self-betrayed	self-generated	self-perpetuated
self-blinded	self-honored	self-perplexed
self-caused	self-idolized	self-planted
self-chosen	self-illumined	self-posed
self-condemned	self-imposed	self-powered
self-conducted	self-incurred	self-proclaimed
self-constituted	self-initiated	self-professed
self-convicted	self-instructed	self-punished
self-corrupted	self-invited	self-renounced
self-declared	self-judged	self-repressed
self-defended	self-justified	self-restrained
self-deluded	self-kindled	self-revealed
self-deprived	self-limited	self-schooled
self-destroyed	self-maimed	self-sown
self-determined	self-matured	self-subdued
self-devised	self-misused	self-sustained
self-divided	self-mortified	self-tempted

3. To, toward, in, for, on, or with oneself; as in:

self-absorbed	self-desire	self-permission
self-aid	self-despair	self-pictured
self-aim	self-directed	self-pleased
self-amusement	self-direction	self-preference
self-application	self-disdain	self-prescribed
self-applied	self-disgust	self-pride
self-assumed	self-dislike	self-procured
self-assuming	self-dissatisfied	self-produced
self-benefit	self-elation	self-profit
self-care	self-enamored	self-purifying
self-comment	self-enclosed	self-reflection
self-communing	self-exultation	self-relation
self-compassion	self-focusing	self-relying
self-complacence	self-gain	self-repellent
self-complacency	self-helpfulness	self-repose
self-complacent	self-injurious	self-reproof
self-conflict	self-injury	self-repulsive
self-consistency	self-kindness	self-resentment
self-consistent	self-liking	self-resigned
self-content	self-loathing	self-respectful
self-contented	self-oblivious	self-rigorous
self-delight	self-occupied	self-sent
self-dependence	self-panegyrical	self-tenderness
self-dependent	self-penetration	self-vexation

4. From oneself or itself; from one's own nature or power; as in:

self-apparent	self-fruition	self-poise
self-arising	self-healing	self-poised
self-born	self-inclusive	self-refuting
self-coherence	self-initiative	self-renewing
self-complete	self-intelligible	self-resourceful
self-defining	self-issuing	self-resplendent
self-derived	self-luminous	self-restoring
self-desirable	self-manifestation	self-reward
self-developing	self-moving	self-rewarding
self-effort	self-operative	self-sprung
self-evolving	self-opinionated	self-stability
self-explaining	self-originating	self-stimulated
self-forbidden	self-perfect	self-warranting

5. Independent; as in:

self-agency	self-dominance	self-existence
self-authority	self-dominion	self-ownership
self-credit	self-entity	self-sovereignty

6. In technology, automatic or automatically; as in:

self-acting	self-cocking	self-moving
self-adapting	self-cooled	self-oiling
self-adjustable	self-defrosting	self-primer
self-adjusting	self-emptying	self-priming
self-aligning	self-feeder	self-recording
self-burning	self-feeding	self-registering
self-changing	self-filling	self-regulated
self-charging	self-inking	self-regulating
self-checking	self-lighting	self-righting
self-cleaning	self-locking	self-screwing
self-closing	self-lubricating	self-setting

self-a·base·ment (self'ə·bās'mənt) *n.* Abasement or degradation of oneself.

self-ab·ne·ga·tion (self'ab'ni·gā'shən) *n.* The complete putting aside of oneself and one's own claims for the sake of some other person or object; self-sacrifice.

self-ab·sorp·tion (self'ab·sôrp'shən, -zôrp'-) *n.* Absorption in or concentration on one's own affairs, work, interests, etc.

self-a·buse (self'ə·byōōs') *n.* **1.** The disparagement of one's own person or powers. **2.** Masturbation.

self-ad·dressed (self'ə·drest') *adj.* Addressed to oneself.

self-ap·point·ed (self'ə·poin'təd) *adj.* Appointed or designated by oneself rather than by others: a *self-appointed* boss.

self-as·ser·tion (self'ə·sûr'shən) *n.* The asserting or putting forward of oneself, one's opinions, claims, or rights. — **self'-as·ser'tive** *adj.* — **self'-as·ser'tive·ly** *adv.*

self-as·sured (self'ə·shŏŏrd') *adj.* Confident in one's own abilities; self-reliant. — **self'-as·sur'ance** *n.*

self-cen·tered (self'sen'tərd) *adj.* Concerned chiefly with one's own affairs and interests, often with a lack of consideration for others. Also *Brit.* **self'-cen'tred.** — **self'-cen'tered·ness** *n.* — **self'-cen'tered·ly** *adv.*

self-col·ored (self'kul'ərd) *adj.* **1.** Having the natural color. **2.** Of but one color or tint.

self-com·mand (self'kə·mand', -mänd') *n.* The state of having all the faculties and powers fully at command.

self-con·ceit (self'kən·sēt') *n.* An unduly high opinion of oneself; vanity. — **self'-con·ceit'ed** *adj.*

self-con·fi·dence (self'kon'fə·dəns) *n.* Confidence in oneself or in one's own unaided powers, judgment, etc. — **self'-con'fi·dent** *adj.* — **self'-con'fi·dent·ly** *adv.*

self-con·scious (self'kon'shəs) *adj.* **1.** Unduly conscious that one is observed by others; ill at ease. **2.** Manifesting embarrassment. — **self'-con'scious·ly** *adv.* — **self'-con'scious·ness** *n.*

self-con·tained (self'kən·tānd') *adj.* **1.** Keeping one's thoughts and feelings to oneself. **2.** Exercising self control. **3.** Complete and independent; self-sustaining. **4.** Having all parts needed for working order, as a machine bearing its own motor.

self·con·tra·dic·tion (self′kon′trə-dik′shən) *n.* **1.** The act or state of contradicting oneself or itself. **2.** That which contradicts itself. **— self′-con′tra·dic′to·ry** *adj.*

self·con·trol (self′kən-trōl′) *n.* The act, power, or habit of having one's faculties or energies under control of the will.

self·de·fense (self′di·fens′) *n.* Defense of oneself, one's property, or one's reputation. **— self′-de·fen′sive** *adj.*

self·de·ni·al (self′di-nī′əl) *n.* The act or power of denying oneself gratification. **— self′-de·ny′ing** *adj.* **— self′-de·ny′ing·ly** *adv.*

self·de·ter·mi·na·tion (self′di-tûr′mə-nā′shən) *n.* **1.** The principle of free will; decision by oneself. **2.** Decision by the people of a country or section as to its future political status. **— self′-de·ter′min·ing** *adj. & n.*

self·de·vo·tion (self′di-vō′shən) *n.* Devotion of oneself, with one's claims, wishes, or interests, to the service of a person or a cause. **— self′-de·vo′tion·al** *adj.*

self·dis·ci·pline (self′dis′ə-plin) *n.* The discipline or training of oneself, often for improvement.

self·ed·u·cat·ed (self′ej′ŏŏ-kā′tid) *adj.* **1.** Educated through one's own efforts without the aid of instructors. **2.** Educated at one's own expense. **— self′-ed′u·ca′tion** *n.*

self·ef·face·ment (self′i-fās′mənt) *n.* The keeping of oneself in the background through modesty, timidity, etc.

self·es·teem (self′ə-stēm′) *n.* A good opinion of oneself; an overestimate of oneself. **— Syn.** See PRIDE.

self·ev·i·dent (self′ev′ə-dənt) *adj.* Carrying its evidence or proof in itself; requiring no proof of its truth. **— self′-ev′i·dence** *n.* **— self′-ev′i·dent·ly** *adv.*

self·ex·am·i·na·tion (self′ig-zam′ə-nā′shən) *n.* Examination of one's own motives, desires, habits, etc.

self·ex·ist·ence (self′ig-zis′təns) *n.* Inherent, underived, independent existence. **— self′-ex·ist′ent** *adj.*

self·ex·plan·a·to·ry (self′ik-splan′ə-tôr′ē, -tō′rē) *adj.* Easily comprehended without explanation; obvious.

self·ex·pres·sion (self′ik-spresh′ən) *n.* Expression of one's own temperament or emotions, as in art.

self·fer·til·i·za·tion (self′fûr′təl-ə-zā′shən, -ī-zā′shən) *n. Biol.* Fertilization of an ovum by sperm from the same animal or of a plant ovule by its own pollen.

self·gov·ern·ment (self′guv′ərn-mənt, -ər-mənt) *n.* **1.** Government of a country or region by its own people. **2.** The state of being so governed. **3.** *Archaic* Self-control. **— self′-gov′erned, self′-gov′ern·ing** *adj.*

self·heal (self′hēl′) *n.* Any of various weedy, perennial herbs with violet flowers, formerly reputed to cure disease.

self·help (self′help′) *n.* The act or condition of getting along by one's own efforts without the aid of others.

self·hood (self′hŏŏd) *n.* **1.** The state of being an individual; personality. **2.** Selfishness; self-centeredness.

self·im·por·tance (self′im-pôr′təns) *n.* Pompous self-conceit. **— self′-im·por′tant** *adj.*

self·im·prove·ment (self′im-prōōv′mənt) *n.* Improvement of one's abilities or condition through one's own efforts.

self·in·duced (self′in-dōōst′, -dyōōst′) *adj.* **1.** Induced by oneself or itself. **2.** *Electr.* Produced by self-induction.

self·in·duc·tion (self′in-duk′shən) *n. Electr.* Induction within the same circuit, causing it to resist any change in the amount of current flowing in it. **— self′-in·duc′tive** *adj.*

self·in·dul·gence (self′in-dul′jəns) *n.* The indulgence or gratification of one's own desires, weaknesses, etc. **— self′-in·dul′gent** *adj.* **— self′-in·dul′gent·ly** *adv.*

self·in·flict·ed (self′in-flik′tid) *adj.* Inflicted on oneself by oneself: a *self-inflicted* wound. **— self′-in·flic′tion** *n.*

self·in·ter·est (self′in′tər-ist, -in′trist) *n.* Personal interest or advantage, or the pursuit of it; selfishness. **— self′-in′ter·est·ed** *adj.*

self·ish (sel′fish) *adj.* **1.** Caring chiefly for oneself or one's own interests or comfort, esp. to the point of disregarding the welfare or wishes of others. **2.** Proceeding from or characterized by undue love of self. **— self′ish·ly** *adv.*

self·ish·ness (sel′fish-nis) *n.* The quality of being selfish.

self·knowl·edge (self′nol′ij) *n.* Knowledge of one's own character, motives, limitations, etc.

self·less (self′lis) *adj.* Regardless of self; unselfish. **— self′less·ly** *adv.* **— self′less·ness** *n.*

self·load·ing (self′lō′ding) *adj.* Of firearms, utilizing a portion of the force of the exploding gas or of recoil to extract and eject the empty case and chamber the next round.

self·love (self′luv′) *n.* The desire or tendency that leads one to seek his own well-being. **— self′-lov′ing** *adj.*

self·made (self′mād′) *adj.* **1.** Having attained honor, wealth, etc., by one's own efforts. **2.** Made by oneself.

self·pit·y (self′pit′ē) *n.* The act or state of pitying oneself. **— self′-pit′y·ing** *adj.* **— self′-pit′y·ing·ly** *adv.*

self·pol·li·na·tion (self′pol′ə-nā′shən) *n. Bot.* The transfer of pollen from stamens to pistils of the same flower. **— self′-pol′li·nat·ed** *adj.*

self·pos·ses·sion (self′pə-zesh′ən) *n.* **1.** The full possession or control of one's powers or faculties. **2.** Presence of mind; self-command. **— self′-pos·sessed′** *adj.*

self·pres·er·va·tion (self′prez′ər-vā′shən) *n.* **1.** The protection of oneself from destruction. **2.** The urge to protect oneself, regarded as an instinct.

self·pro·nounc·ing (self′prə-noun′sing) *adj.* Having marks of pronunciation and stress applied to a word without phonetic alteration of the spelling.

self·pro·pelled (self′prə-peld′) *adj.* **1.** Able to propel itself. **2.** Having the means of propulsion contained within itself, as an automobile.

self·re·gard (self′ri-gärd′) *n.* **1.** Regard or consideration for oneself or one's own interests. **2.** Estimation of oneself.

self·re·li·ance (self′ri-lī′əns) *n.* Reliance on one's own abilities, resources, or judgment. **— self′-re·li′ant** *adj.*

self·re·spect (self′ri-spekt′) *n.* Proper respect for oneself and one's own character. **— self′-re·spect′ing** *adj.*

self·re·straint (self′ri-strānt′) *n.* Restraint, as of the passions, by the force of one's own will; self-control.

self·right·eous (self′rī′chəs) *adj.* Righteous in one's own estimation; pharisaic. **— self′-right′eous·ly** *adv.* **— self′-right′eous·ness** *n.*

self·ris·ing (self′rī′zing) *adj.* **1.** That rises of itself. **2.** Having the leaven already added, as some flours.

self·sac·ri·fice (self′sak′rə-fis) *n.* The sacrifice of one's self or one's personal welfare or wishes for the sake of duty or for the good of others. **— self′-sac′ri·fic′ing** *adj.*

self·same (self′sām′) *adj.* Exactly the same; identical. **— self′same′ness** *n.*

self·sat·is·fac·tion (self′sat′is-fak′shən) *n.* Satisfaction with one's own actions and characteristics; conceit; complacency. **— self′-sat′is·fied** *adj.* **— self′-sat′is·fy′ing** *adj.*

self·seek·ing (self′sē′king) *adj.* Exclusively seeking one's own interests or gain. **— n.** Actions, motives, etc., characteristic of a self-seeking person. **— self′-seek′er** *n.*

self·ser·vice (self′sûr′vis) *adj.* Designating a restaurant, store, etc., where patrons serve themselves.

self·ser·ving (self′sûr′ving) *adj.* Tending to advance one's own interests, often at the expense of others.

self·start·er (self′stär′tər) *n.* A starter (def. 3).

self·styled (self′stīld′) *adj.* Characterized (as such) by oneself: a *self-styled* gentleman.

self·suf·fi·cient (self′sə-fish′ənt) *adj.* **1.** Able to support or maintain oneself without aid or cooperation from others. **2.** Having overweening confidence in oneself. Also **self′-suf·fic′ing** (-sə-fī′sing). **— self′-suf·fi′cien·cy** *n.*

self·sup·port (self′sə-pôrt′, -pōrt′) *n.* The act or state of supporting oneself entirely by one's own efforts. **— self′-sup·port′ed, self′-sup·port′ing** *adj.*

self·sus·tain·ing (self′sə-stān′ing) *adj.* Sustaining oneself or itself without outside help; self-supporting.

self·taught (self′tôt′) *adj.* Taught by oneself or through one's own efforts, without the aid of formal instruction.

self·will (self′wil′) *n.* Strong or tenacious adherence to one's own will or wish, esp. with disregard of the wishes of others; obstinacy. **— self′-willed′** *adj.*

self·wind·ing (self′wīn′ding) *adj. Mech.* Having a device that automatically winds a clock or other mechanism.

sell (sel) *v.* **sold, sell·ing** *v.t.* **1.** To transfer (property) to another for money or for some other consideration. **2.** To deal in; offer for sale. **3.** To deliver, surrender, or betray for a price or reward: to *sell* one's honor. **4.** To promote the sale of: Good advertising *sells* many products. **5.** *Informal* To cause to accept or approve something: with *on*: They *sold* him on the scheme. **6.** *Informal* To cause the acceptance or approval of: He always *sold* himself well. **7.** *Slang* To deceive; cheat. **— v.i.** **8.** To transfer ownership for money, etc.; engage in selling. **9.** To be on sale; be sold. **10.** *Informal* To attract buyers: This item *sells* well. **11.** *Informal* To gain acceptance or approval: Will his plan *sell*? **— to sell off** To get rid of by selling. **— to sell out** **1.** To sell all one's merchandise, possessions, etc. **2.** *Slang* To betray. **— n.** **1.** On the stock exchange, a stock that ought to be sold. **2.** *Slang* A trick; joke; swindle. [OE *sellan* to give]

sell·er (sel′ər) *n.* **1.** One who sells. **2.** Something with a measure of salability: This book is a good *seller.*

sell·out (sel′out′) *n.* **1.** An act of selling out. **2.** *Informal* A performance for which all seats have been sold. **3.** *Slang* A betrayal through a secret bargain or agreement.

Selt·zer (selt′sər) *n.* An effervescing mineral water. Also **Seltzer water.** [Alter. of G *Selterser,* from *Nieder Selters,* a village in SW Prussia, its place of origin]

sel·vage (sel′vij) *n.* The edge of a woven fabric so finished that it will not ravel. Also **sel′vedge.** [< SELF + EDGE, trans. of MDu. *selfegghe*]

selves (selvz) Plural of SELF.

se·man·tic (si-man′tik) *adj.* **1.** Of or pertaining to meaning.   2. Of or relating to semantics.   [< Gk. *sēmainein* to signify]   — se·man'ti·cal·ly *adv.*

se·man·ti·cist (si·man'tə·sist) *n.* A specialist in semantics.

se·man·tics (si·man'tiks) *n.pl.* (*construed as sing.*) 1. *Ling.* The study of the meanings of speech forms, esp. of the development and changes in meaning of words and word groups. 2. *Logic* The relation between signs or symbols and what they signify or denote. 3. Loosely, verbal trickery.

sem·a·phore (sem'ə·fôr, -fōr) *n.* An apparatus for making signals, as with movable arms, disks, flags, or lanterns.   [< F < Gk. *sēma* a sign + -PHORE]   — sem'a·phor'ic (-fôr'ik, -for'ik) or ·i·cal *adj.*

sem·blance (sem'bləns) *n.* 1. A mere show without reality; pretense. 2. Outward appearance. 3. A likeness or resemblance.   [< OF < L *simulare, similare* to simulate]

se·men (sē'mən) *n.* The impregnating fluid of male animals that contains spermatozoa; seed.   [< L < *serere* to sow]

se·mes·ter (si·mes'tər) *n.* 1. A college half year. 2. In U.S. colleges and universities, a period of instruction, usu. lasting 17 or 18 months.   [< G < L (*cursus*) *semestris* (a period) of six months]   — se·mes'tral *adj.*

sem·i (sem'ī) 1. *U.S. Informal* A semitrailer. 2. *Canadian Slang* An American.

semi- *prefix* 1. Not fully; partially; partly: *semiautomatic, semicivilized.* 2. Exactly half: *semicircle.* 3. Occurring twice (in the periods specified): *semiweekly.*   [< L]

◆ *Semi*- (def. 1) appears as a prefix in many words, as in the following words and in the list below. It is pronounced sem'ē, sem'ə, or sometimes sem'ī.

semiacquaintance	semidivine	semiovoid
semiadherent	semidomestic	semipagan
semiaffectionate	semidomesticated	semipanic
semiagricultural	semidry	semiparallel
semialcoholic	semi-Empire	semiparalysis
semiallegiance	semienclosed	semipastoral
semianarchist	semierect	semipeace
semiangular	semieremitical	semiperfect
semianimal	semiexposed	semiperishable
semianimated	semiextinction	semipermanent
semiarborescent	semifailure	semiperspicuous
semiarchitectural	semifatalistic	semipinnate
semiarid	semifeudalism	semiplastic
semiatheist	semifictional	semipolitical
semiattached	semifinished	semipolitician
semiautonomous	semifit	semiporous
semiautonomy	semifitting	semipublic
semibald	semifixed	semiradical
semibarbarian	semiflexed	semiraw
semibarbaric	semifluctuating	semireactionary
semibarbarism	semiforeign	semirebellion
semibarbarous	semifriable	semireligious
semibarren	semifrontier	semiresolute
semibleached	semifunctional	semirespectability
semiblind	semigala	semirespectable
semiblunt	semigenuflection	semiretirement
semiboiled	semi-Gothic	semiriddle
semibourgeois	semigranulate	semi-Romanesque
semichannel	semihard	semi-Romanized
semichaotic	semihigh	semiroyal
semichivalrous	semihistorical	semirustic
semi-Christian	semihobo	semisacred
semiclerical	semihostile	semisatiric
semiclosed	semihumanitarian	semisatirical
semiclosure	semihumorous	semiscientific
semicoagulated	semi-idle	semisecrecy
semicollapsible	semi-idleness	semisecret
semicolonial	semi-incandescent	semiserious
semicoma	semi-independence	semiseriousness
semicomplete	semi-independent	semisocial
semiconceal	semi-intoxicated	semisocialism
semiconfident	semi-intoxication	semisoft
semiconfinement	semi-invalid	semispontaneity
semiconformist	semileafless	semispontaneous
semiconnection	semilegendary	semistagnant
semiconservative	semiliberal	semistagnation
semiconversion	semilined	semistarvation
semicooperation	semiliterate	semistarved
semicooperative	semilucent	semisuccess
semicured	semimilitary	semisuccessful
semicylindrical	semimobile	semisuspension
semidangerous	semimodern	semisymmetric
semidarkness	semimonastic	semisymmetrical
semideaf	semimonopoly	semitailored
semidelirious	semimute	semitechnical
semidenatured	semimystical	semitrained
semidependent	seminecessary	semitruth
semidestructive	seminervous	semivirtue
semideveloped	semioblivious	semivital
semidiaphanous	semiobscurity	semivoluntary
semidigested	semiopened	semiwarfare
semidirect	semiorganized	semiwild

sem·i·an·nu·al (sem'ē·an'yōō·əl) *adj.* Issued or occurring twice a year; half-yearly.   — *n.* A publication issued twice a year.   — sem'i·an·nu·al·ly *adv.*

sem·i·au·to·mat·ic (sem'ē·ô'tə·mat'ik) *adj.* 1. Partly au-

tomatic. 2. Of firearms, self-loading but firing once at each pull on the trigger.

sem·i·breve (sem'ē·brēv', -brev') *n. Chiefly Brit. Music* A whole note.

sem·i·cir·cle (sem'ē·sûr'kəl) *n.* 1. A half-circle; an arc or a segment of 180°. 2. Anything formed or arranged in a half-circle.   — sem'i·cir'cu·lar (-kyə·lər) *adj.*

semicircular canal *Anat.* One of the three tubular structures in the labyrinth of the ear, serving as the organ of equilibrium. For illus. see EAR.

sem·i·civ·i·lized (sem'ē·siv'ə·līzd) *adj.* Partly civilized.

sem·i·co·lon (sem'ē·kō'lən, sem'ə-) *n.* A mark (;) of punctuation, indicating a greater degree of separation than the comma.

sem·i·con·duc·tor (sem'ē·kən·duk'tər) *n. Physics* One of a class of substances whose electrical conductivity at ordinary temperatures is between that of a metal and an insulator, used in the manufacture of transistors.

sem·i·con·scious (sem'ē·kon'shəs) *adj.* Partly conscious.

sem·i·de·tached (sem'ē·di·tacht') *adj.* Joined to another on one side only; esp. designating a house having one wall in common with another house.

sem·i·fi·nal (sem'ē·fī'nəl) *n.* 1. In sports, a competition that precedes the final event. 2. One of two competitions in a tournament, the winners of each meeting in the final.   — *adj.* Next before the final.   — sem'i·fi'nal·ist *n.*

sem·i·flu·id (sem'ē·flōō'id) *adj.* Fluid, but thick and viscous. Also sem·i·flu·id·ic (-flōō·id'ik).   — *n.* A thick, viscous fluid.

sem·i·month·ly (sem'ē·munth'lē) *adj.* Taking place twice a month.   — *n. pl.* ·lies A publication issued twice a month.   — *adv.* At half-monthly intervals.

sem·i·nal (sem'ə·nəl) *adj.* 1. Of, pertaining to, or containing seeds or semen. 2. Having productive power; germinal. 3. Not developed; rudimentary. Also *seminary.*   [< OF < L < *semen, seminis* semen, seed]   — sem'i·nal·ly *adv.*

sem·i·nar (sem'ə·när) *n.* 1. A group of advanced students at a college or university, meeting regularly and informally with a professor for discussion of research problems. 2. The course thus conducted or the room where it meets.

sem·i·nar·y (sem'ə·ner'ē) *n. pl.* ·nar·ies 1. A special school, as of theology. 2. A school of higher education. 3. The place where anything is nurtured.   — *adj.* 1. Seminal. 2. Pertaining to a seminary.   [< L *seminarium* seed plot]

sem·i·na·tion (sem'ə·nā'shən) *n.* 1. The act of sowing or spreading; dispersion of seeds. 2. Propagation; reproduction.   [< L *seminare* to sow < *semen* seed]

sem·i·nif·er·ous (sem'ə·nif'ər·əs) *adj.* 1. Carrying or producing semen. 2. Bearing a seed or seeds.

Sem·i·nole (sem'ə·nōl) *n.* One of a Florida tribe of North American Indians of Muskhogean stock, an offshoot of the Creeks, now chiefly in Oklahoma.   [< Muskhogean (Creek) *Simanóle,* lit., separatist, runaway]

sem·i·of·fi·cial (sem'ē·ə·fish'əl) *adj.* Having some official authority or sanction; official to a certain extent.   — sem'i·of·fi'cial·ly *adv.*

sem·i·per·me·a·ble (sem'ē·pûr'mē·ə·bəl) *adj.* Partially permeable, as membranes that separate a solvent from the dissolved substance.

sem·i·pre·cious (sem'ē·presh'əs) *adj.* Of, pertaining to, or designating gemstones, as jade, garnet, opal, amethyst, etc., that are somewhat less rare or valuable than precious stones.

sem·i·pri·vate (sem'ē·prī'vit) *adj.* Partly but not wholly private, as a hospital room for two or several patients.

sem·i·pro·fes·sion·al (sem'ē·prə·fesh'ən·əl) *adj.* Engaged in a sport for profit, but not as a full-time occupation.   — *n.* A semiprofessional athlete. Also *Informal* sem'i·pro' (-prō').   — sem'i·pro·fes'sion·al·ly *adv.*

sem·i·qua·ver (sem'ē·kwā'vər) *n. Chiefly Brit. Music* A sixteenth note.

sem·i·rig·id (sem'ē·rij'id) *adj. Aeron.* Partly rigid, as an airship in which an exterior stiffener supports the load.   — *n.* A semirigid airship.

sem·i·skilled (sem'ē·skild') *adj.* Partly skilled.

sem·i·sol·id (sem'ē·sol'id) *adj.* Nearly solid; partly solid.

Sem·ite (sem'īt, sē'mīt) *n.* 1. One of a people of Caucasian stock, now represented by the Jews and Arabs, but originally including the ancient Babylonians, Assyrians, Arameans, Phoenicians, etc. 2. A person believed to be a descendant of Shem. Also *Shemite.*   [< NL < Gk. < Hebrew *Shēm*]

Se·mit·ic (sə·mit'ik) *adj.* Of or pertaining to the Semites, or to any of their languages.   — *n.* A subfamily of the Hamito-Semitic family of languages.

Sem·i·tism (sem'ə·tiz'əm) *n.* 1. A Semitic word or idiom. 2. Semitic practices, opinions, or customs. 3. Any policy favoring or thought to favor the Jews.

sem·i·tone (sem'ē·tōn') *n. Music* The smallest interval of the chromatic scale; a minor second; also called *half step, half tone.*   — sem'i·ton'ic (-ton'ik) *adj.*

sem·i·trail·er (sem'ē·trā'lər) *n.* A trailer having wheels only at the rear, the front end resting on the tractor.

sem·i·vow·el (sem′ē·vou/əl) *n. Phonet.* A vowellike sound used as a consonant, as (w), (y), and (r): also called *glide*.

sem·i·week·ly (sem/ē·wēk/lē) *adj.* Issued or occurring twice a week. — *n. pl.* **·lies** A publication issued twice a week. — *adv.* At half-weekly intervals.

sem·i·year·ly (sem/ē·yir/lē) *adj.* Issued or occurring twice a year. — *n. pl.* **·lies** A semiyearly occurrence. — *adv.* At half-yearly intervals.

sem·o·li·na (sem/ə·lē/nə) *n.* The gritty or grainlike portions of wheat retained in the bolting machine after the fine flour has been passed through. [< L *simila* fine flour]

sem·per fi·de·lis (sem/pər fi·dē/lis, fi·dā/lis) *Latin* Always faithful: motto of the U.S. Marine Corps.

sem·per pa·ra·tus (sem/pər pə·rā/təs) *Latin* Always prepared: motto of the U.S. Coast Guard.

sem·pi·ter·nal (sem/pə·tûr/nəl) *adj.* Eternal; everlasting. [< OF < L *sempiternus* everlasting] — **sem′pi·ter/ni·ty** *n.*

semp·stress (semp/stris, sem/′-) *n.* A seamstress.

sen (sen) *n. pl.* **sen** (sen) **1.** A former monetary unit and coin of Japan, equal to one hundredth of a yen. **2.** A monetary unit and coin of Indonesia.

sen·ate (sen/it) *n.* **1.** The governing body of some universities and institutions of learning. **2.** A council or legislative body. [< OF < L *senatus,* lit., council of old men]

Sen·ate (sen/it) *n.* **1.** The upper branch of national or state legislative bodies of the U.S., Canada, France, and other governments. The **United States Senate** is composed of two Senators elected by popular vote from each State. **2.** In ancient Rome, the state council.

sen·a·tor (sen/ə·tər) *n. Often cap.* A member of a senate.

sen·a·to·ri·al (sen/ə·tôr/ē·əl, -tō/rē-) *adj.* Of, pertaining to, or befitting a senator or senate. — **sen′a·to/ri·al·ly** *adv.*

send (send) *v.* **sent, send·ing** *v.t.* **1.** To cause or direct (a person or persons) to go; dispatch. **2.** To cause to be taken or directed to another place; transmit; forward: sometimes with *off.* **3.** To cause to issue; emit or discharge, as heat, light, smoke, etc. **4.** To throw or drive by force; impel. **5.** To cause to come, happen, etc.; grant. **6.** To bring into a specified state or condition. **7.** *U.S. Slang* To make rapturous with joy. — *v.i.* **8.** To dispatch an agent, messenger, or message. — **to send (someone) about his** (or **her**) **business** To dismiss with reproach or warning. — **to send down** *Brit.* To expel from a university. — **to send flying 1.** To scatter or knock violently away. **2.** To cause to flee. — **to send for** To summon by a message or messenger. — **to send packing** To dismiss quickly and forcefully. — **to send up** *Informal* To sentence to prison. [OE *sendan*] — **send/er** *n.*

send·off (send/ôf′, -of′) *n.* **1.** The act of sending off; a start. **2.** A farewell dinner or other celebration or demonstration at parting. **3.** Encouragement, as in starting a career.

Sen·e·ca (sen/ə·kə) *n.* One of a tribe of Indians of Iroquoian stock formerly inhabiting western New York. [< Du. *Sennacaas* the Five Nations < Algonquian *A'sinnika*]

Sen·e·ga·lese (sen/gə·lez′, -lēs) *adj.* Of or pertaining to Senegal, its inhabitants, customs, etc. — *n.* A native or inhabitant of Senegal.

se·nes·cent (si·nes/ənt) *adj.* **1.** Growing old. **2.** Characteristic of old age. [< L *senescere* to grow old] — **se·nes/cence** *n.*

sen·e·schal (sen/ə·shəl) *n.* **1.** An official in the household of a medieval prince or noble, having charge of feasts, etc.; a steward or major-domo. **2.** *Brit.* A cathedral official. [< OF < Gmc. Cf. OHG *siniskalk* old servant.]

se·nile (sē/nīl, -nil, sen/īl) *adj.* **1.** Pertaining to, proceeding from, or characteristic of old age. **2.** Infirm; weak; doting. **3.** *Geog.* Almost worn away to base level. [< L *senilis* < *senex* old] — **se/nile·ly** *adv.* — **se·nil/i·ty** (si·nil/ə·tē) *n.*

sen·ior (sēn/yər) *adj.* **1.** Older in years or higher in rank. **2.** Denoting the older of two: opposed to *junior.* ◆ The form used to distinguish a father from a son of the same name is usu. written *Albert Jones, Sr.* or *Albert Jones, senior.* **3.** Belonging to maturity or later life. **4.** Pertaining to the last year of a high-school or collegiate course of four years. — *n.* **1.** The older of two. **2.** One longer in service or higher in standing. **3.** A student in the senior year of a high-school, college, or university. [< L, comparative of *senex* old]

senior high school A high school, in the U.S. typically comprising grades 10, 11, and 12.

sen·ior·i·ty (sēn·yôr/ə·tē, -yor/′-) *n. pl.* **·ties 1.** The state of being senior; priority of age or rank. **2.** Precedence or priority due to length of service.

sen·na (sen/ə) *n.* **1.** The dried leaflets of any of several leguminous plants, used medicinally as purgatives. **2.** Any plant yielding senna. [< NL < Arabic *sanā*]

se·ñor (sā·nyôr′) *n. pl.* **·ño·res** (-nyō/rās) *Spanish* **1.** A gentleman. **2.** Sir; Mr.: used as a title of address.

se·ño·ra (sā·nyō/rä) *n. Spanish* **1.** A lady. **2.** Mrs.; madam.

se·ño·ri·ta (sā/nyō·rē/tä) *n. Spanish* **1.** A young, unmarried lady. **2.** Miss.

sen·sate (sen/sāt) *adj.* Perceived by the senses. Also **sen/sat·ed.** — *v.t.* **·sat·ed, ·sat·ing** To perceive by the senses. [< LL < L *sensus* sense]

sen·sa·tion (sen·sā/shən) *n.* **1.** The aspect of consciousness resulting from the stimulation of any of the sense organs, as hearing, taste, touch, smell, or sight. **2.** *Physiol.* The capacity to respond to such stimulation. **3.** That which produces great interest or excitement. **4.** An excited condition: to cause a *sensation.* [See SENSATE.]

sen·sa·tion·al (sen·sā/shən·əl) *adj.* **1.** Pertaining to emotional excitement. **2.** Of or pertaining to physical sensation. **3.** Causing excitement; startling; melodramatic. — **sen·sa/tion·al·ly** *adv.*

sen·sa·tion·al·ism (sen·sā/shən·əl·iz/əm) *n.* The use of sensational or melodramatic methods, words, etc. — **sen·sa/tion·al·ist** *n.* — **sen·sa/tion·al·is/tic** *adj.*

sense (sens) *n.* **1.** The faculty of sensation; sense perception. **2.** Any of certain agencies by or through which an individual receives impressions of the external world, as taste, touch, hearing, smell, or sight. **3.** *Physiol.* Any receptor, or group of receptors, specialized for the perception of external objects or internal bodily changes. **4.** Rational perception accompanied by feeling: a *sense* of wrong. **5.** *Often pl.* Normal power of mind or understanding; sound or natural judgment: She is coming to her *senses.* **6.** Signification; import; meaning. **7.** Opinion, view, or judgment of the majority. **8.** Sound reason or judgment; wisdom. **9.** Capacity to perceive or appreciate: a *sense* of color. — *v.t.* **sensed, sens·ing 1.** To become aware of through the senses. **2.** *Informal* To comprehend; understand. [< F < L *sensus* perception]

sense·less (sens/lis) *adj.* **1.** Devoid of sense; making no sense; irrational. **2.** Unconscious. **3.** Incapable of feeling or perception. — **sense/less·ly** *adv.* — **sense/less·ness** *n.*

sense organ A structure specialized to receive sense impressions, as the eye, nose, ear, etc.

sen·si·bil·i·ty (sen/sə·bil/ə·tē) *n. pl.* **·ties 1.** The capability of sensation; power to perceive or feel. **2.** The capacity of sensation and rational emotion, as distinguished from intellect and will. **3.** *Often pl.* Susceptibility or sensitiveness to outside influences or mental impressions. **4.** Appreciation accompanying mental apprehension; discerning judgment.

— **Syn. 1, 3.** *Sensibility* may be used of mere physical sensation, but more often denotes qualities of mind: *sensibility* to heat and cold, the *sensibility* of the artist to beauty. *Sensitivity* suggests great *sensibility,* and the readiness to be excited by small cause. *Susceptibility* is the capacity to receive, contain, or be influenced: *susceptibility* to colds. *Feeling* specifically refers to the tactile sense, but is also used in the sense of emotional response as a general, but less precise, substitute for the other words.

sen·si·ble (sen/sə·bəl) *adj.* **1.** Possessed of good practical judgment; exhibiting sound sense and understanding. **2.** Capable of physical sensation. **3.** Perceptible through the senses: *sensible* heat. **4.** Emotionally or mentally sensitive. **5.** Having a perception or cognition; fully aware; persuaded. **6.** Great enough to be perceived. [< OF < L *sentire* to feel, perceive] — **sen/si·ble·ness** *n.* — **sen/si·bly** *adv.*

sen·si·tive (sen/sə·tiv) *adj.* **1.** Easily affected by outside operations or influences; excitable or impressionable; touchy. **2.** Reacting readily to external agents or forces: paper *sensitive* to light. **3.** Pertaining to or depending on the senses or sensation. **4.** Closing or moving when touched or irritated, as certain plants. **5.** Liable to fluctuation. **6.** Capable of indicating minute changes or differences; delicate. [See SENSIBLE.] — **sen/si·tive·ly** *adv.* — **sen/si·tive·ness** *n.*

sensitive plant 1. A shrubby tropical herb whose leaves close at a touch. **2.** Any of various similar or related plants.

sen·si·tiv·i·ty (sen/sə·tiv/ə·tē) *n. pl.* **·ties** The state or degree of being sensitive. — **Syn.** See SENSIBILITY.

sen·si·tize (sen/sə·tīz) *v.t.* **·tized, ·tiz·ing 1.** To render sensitive. **2.** *Photog.* To make sensitive to light, as a plate or film. — **sen/si·ti·za/tion** *n.* — **sen/si·tiz/er** *n.*

sen·sor (sen/sər) *n.* That which receives and responds to a stimulus or signal; esp., an instrument or device designed to detect and respond to some force, change, or radiation.

sen·so·ri·um (sen·sôr/ē·əm, -sō/rē-) *n. pl.* **·ri·a** (-rē·ə) *Anat.* The nervous system, including the cerebrum, as the collective organ of sensation. **2.** *Biol.* The entire sensory apparatus. [< LL < L *sensus* sense]

sen·so·ry (sen/sər·ē) *adj.* **1.** Of or pertaining to sensation. **2.** Conveying or producing sense impulses. **3.** Pertaining to the sensorium. Also **sen·so·ri·al** (sen·sôr/ē·əl, -sō/rē-).

sen·su·al (sen/shoo·əl) *adj.* **1.** Unduly indulging the appetites or sexual pleasure; lewd. **2.** Pertaining to the body or to the physical senses; carnal. **3.** Pertaining to sensualism. ◆ See note under SENSUOUS. [< MF < LL < L *sensus* Sense] — **sen/su·al·ly** *adv.*

sen·su·al·ism (sen′shōo-əl-iz′əm) *n.* **1.** Sensuality. **2.** A system of ethics predicating the pleasures of sense to be the highest good. **— sen′su·al·ist** *n.* **— sen′su·al·is′tic** *adj.*

sen·su·al·i·ty (sen′shōo-al′ə-tē) *n. pl.* **·ties 1.** The state of being sensual, or sensual acts collectively. **2.** Sensual indulgence. Also called *sensualism:* also **sen′su·al·ness.**

sen·su·al·ize (sen′shōo-əl-īz′) *v.t.* **·ized, ·iz·ing** To make sensual. Also *Brit.* **sen′su·al·ise′. — sen′su·al·i·za′tion** *n.*

sen·su·ous (sen′shōo-əs) *adj.* **1.** Pertaining or appealing to or derived from the senses: used in a higher and purer signification than *sensual.* **2.** Keenly appreciative of and aroused by beauty, refinement, or luxury. **3.** Resembling imagery that appeals to the senses: a *sensuous* portrayal. **— sen′su·ous·ly** *adv.* **— sen′su·ous·ness** *n.*

◆ **sensuous, sensual** *Sensuous* refers not only to the physical senses but to any means of feeling, as intellectual or esthetic sensitivity, intuition, etc.: the *sensuous* pleasure of walking in the rain. *Sensual* is generally restricted to bodily sensations and to the satisfaction of physical appetites.

sent (sent) Past tense and past participle of SEND.

sen·tence (sen′təns) *n.* **1.** *Gram.* A group of words containing a subject and a predicate, as declarative, interrogative, imperative, and exclamatory sentences, or a single word in the case of the simple imperative. **— simple sentence** A sentence consisting of a subject and a predicate without any subordinate clauses. **— compound sentence** A sentence consisting of two or more independent clauses, usu. connected by a semicolon or a coordinating conjunction or both. **— complex sentence** A sentence consisting of an independent clause and one or more subordinate clauses. **2.** *Law* A penalty pronounced upon a person convicted. **3.** A formal determination or opinion. **—** *v.t.* **·tenced, ·tenc·ing** To pass sentence upon. [< OF < L *sentire* to feel, be of opinion] **— sen′tenc·er** *n.* **— sen·ten′tial** (sen-ten′shəl) *adj.*

sen·ten·tious (sen-ten′shəs) *adj.* **1.** Abounding in or giving terse expression to thought; axiomatic. **2.** Habitually using terse, laconic, or aphoristic language. **3.** Pompously formal; moralizing. [< L *sententia* < *sentire* to feel, be of an opinion] **— sen·ten′tious·ly** *adv.* **— sen·ten·ti·os·i·ty** (sen·ten′-shē·os′ə·tē), **sen·ten′tious·ness** *n.*

sen·ti·ent (sen′shē·ənt, -shənt) *adj.* Possessing powers of sense or sense perception; having sensation or feeling. **—** *n.* **1.** A sentient person or thing. **2.** The mind. [< L *sentiens, -entis,* ppr. of *sentire* to feel] **— sen′ti·ence, sen′ti·en·cy** *n.* **— sen′ti·ent·ly** *adv.*

sen·ti·ment (sen′tə·mənt) *n.* **1.** Noble, tender, or artistic feeling, or susceptibility to such feeling; sensibility. **2.** A verbal expression of such feeling. **3.** A mental attitude or response to a person, object, or idea, based on feeling instead of reason. **4.** An exaggerated emotional reaction. **5.** *Often pl.* An opinion or judgment. **6.** An expressive thought or idea in appropriate language [< OF < Med.L < L *sentire* to feel]

sen·ti·men·tal (sen′tə·men′təl) *adj.* **1.** Characterized by sentiment or emotion. **2.** Experiencing, displaying, or given to sentiment, often in an extravagant or mawkish manner: a *sentimental* novel. **— sen′ti·men′tal·ly** *adv.*

sen·ti·men·tal·i·ty (sen′tə·men·tal′ə·tē) *n. pl.* **·ties 1.** The state or quality of being mawkishly sentimental. **2.** Any expression of sentiment. Also **sen′ti·men′tal·ism** (-men′-təl·iz′əm). **— sen′ti·men′tal·ist** *n.*

sen·ti·men·tal·ize (sen′tə·men′təl·īz) *v.* **·ized, ·iz·ing** *v.t.* **1.** To make sentimental. **2.** To cherish sentimentally. **—** *v.i.* **3.** To behave sentimentally. Also *Brit.* **sen′ti·men′tal·ise.**

sen·ti·nel (sen′tə·nəl) *n.* **1.** A sentry. **2.** Any watcher or guard. **—** *v.t.* **·neled** or **·nelled, ·nel·ing** or **·nel·ling 1.** To watch over as a sentinel. **2.** To furnish with sentinels. **3.** To station or appoint as a sentinel. [< OF < Ital. < LL *sentinare* to avoid danger]

sen·try (sen′trē) *n. pl.* **·tries 1.** A soldier placed on guard to see that only authorized persons pass his post and to warn of danger. **2.** The watch or guard kept by a sentry. [? Short for obs. *centrenel,* var. of SENTINEL]

se·pal (sē′pəl) *n. Bot.* One of the individual leaves of a calyx. [< F < NL < L *sep(aratus)* separate + (*pet*)*alum* petal]

sep·a·ra·ble (sep′ər·ə·bəl, sep′rə-) *adj.* Capable of being separated. **— sep′a·ra·bil′i·ty, sep′a·ra·ble·ness** *n.* **— sep′-a·ra·bly** *adv.*

sep·a·rate (*v.* sep′ə·rāt; *adj.* sep′ər·it, sep′rit) *v.* **·rat·ed, ·rat·ing** *v.t.* **1.** To set asunder; disunite or disjoin; sever. **2.** To occupy a position between; serve to keep apart. **3.** To divide into components, parts, etc. **4.** To isolate or obtain from a compound, mixture, etc. **5.** To consider separately; distinguish between. **6.** *Law* To part by separation. **—** *v.i.* **7.** To be divided or disconnected; draw apart. **8.** To part company; withdraw from association or combination. **—** *adj.* **1.** Existing or considered apart from others; individual. **2.** Disunited from the body; disembodied. **3.** Separated; disjoined. [< L < *se-* apart + *parare* to prepare] **— sep′a·rate·ly** *adv.* **— sep′a·rate·ness** *n.* **— sep′a·ra′-**

tive, sep·a·ra·to·ry (sep′ər·ə·tôr′ē, -tō′rē, sep′rə-). **— sep′a·ra′tor** *n.*

sep·a·ra·tion (sep′ə·rā′shən) *n.* **1.** The act or process of separating; division. **2.** The state of being disconnected or apart. **3.** Something that separates. **4.** *Law* Relinquishment of cohabitation between husband and wife by mutual consent: distinguished from *divorce.*

separation center A central army or navy point that handles the discharging and releasing of personnel.

sep·a·ra·tist (sep′ər·ə·tist, sep′rə-) *n.* One who advocates or upholds separation, esp. one who secedes. Also **sep′a·ra′-tion·ist. — sep′a·ra·tism** *n.*

Se·phar·dim (si-fär′dim) *n.pl.* The Spanish and Portuguese Jews or their descendants. Also **Se·phar′a·dim** (-ə·dim). [< Hebrew *sephārādhîm*] **— Se·phar′dic** *adj.*

se·pi·a (sē′pē·ə) *n.* **1.** A reddish brown pigment prepared from the inky secretion of the cuttlefish. **2.** The color of this pigment. **3.** A picture done in this pigment. **—** *adj.* Executed in or colored like sepia; dark brown with a tinge of red. [< L < Gk. *sēpia* cuttlefish]

se·poy (sē′poi) *n.* A native Indian soldier who was employed in the former British Indian Army. [< Pg. *sipae* < Urdu *sipāhī* soldier < Persian *sipāh* army]

sep·pu·ku (sep·pōō-kōō) *n. Japanese* Hara-kiri.

sep·sis (sep′sis) *n. Pathol.* Infection by pathogenic microorganisms. [< NL < Gk. < *sēpein* to make putrid]

sep·ta (sep′tə) Plural of SEPTUM.

Sep·tem·ber (sep-tem′bər) The ninth month of the year, containing 30 days; the seventh month in the old Roman calendar. [< L *septem* seven]

sep·te·nar·y (sep′tə·ner′ē) *adj.* Consisting of, pertaining to, or being seven. **—** *n. pl.* **·nar·ies 1.** The number seven. **2.** Anything having a definite relation to the number seven. Also **sep′te·nar′i·us** (sep′tə·nâr′ē·əs). [< L *septem* seven]

sep·ten·ni·al (sep·ten′ē·əl) *adj.* **1.** Recurring every seven years. **2.** Continuing or capable of lasting seven years. [< L < *septem* seven + *annus* year] **— sep·ten′ni·al·ly** *adv.*

sep·tet (sep·tet′) *n.* **1.** A group of seven persons, things, etc. **2.** *Music* A composition for seven singers or instrumentalists. Also **sep·tette′.** [< G < L *septem* seven]

septi-[1] *combining form* Seven. Also, before vowels, **sept-.** [< L *septem* seven]

septi-[2] *combining form* A partition; fence. Also, before vowels, **sept-.** Also **septo-.** [< L *septum* enclosure, wall]

sep·tic (sep′tik) *adj.* **1.** Of, pertaining to, or caused by sepsis. **2.** Producing sepsis; infective. Also **sep′ti·cal. —** *n.* Any agent producing sepsis. [< LL < Gk. *sēpein* to putrefy] **— sep·tic·i·ty** (sep·tis′ə·tē) *n.*

sep·ti·ce·mi·a (sep′tə·sē′mē·ə) *n. Pathol.* An infection of the blood by pathogenic microorganisms; blood poisoning. Also **sep′ti·cae′mi·a.** [< NL < Gk. *sēptikos* putrefactive + *haima* blood] **— sep′ti·ce′mic** (-sē′mik) *adj.*

septic tank A tank in which sewage is allowed to remain until purified by the action of anaerobic bacteria.

sep·til·lion (sep·til′yən) *n.* **1.** *U.S.* A thousand sextillions, written as 1 followed by twenty-four zeros: a cardinal number. **2.** *Brit.* A million sextillions (def. 2), written as 1 followed by forty-two zeros: a cardinal number. **—** *adj.* Being a septillion in number. [< MF < *septi-* seven + (*mi*)*llion* million] **— sep·til′lionth** *adj.* & *n.*

sep·tu·a·ge·nar·i·an (sep′chōo·ə·jə·nâr′ē·ən, sep′tōo-) *n.* A person 70 years old, or between 70 and 80. **—** *adj.* **1.** Seventy years old, or between 70 and 80. **2.** Of or pertaining to a septuagenarian. [< L *septuaginta* seventy]

sep·tu·ag·e·nar·y (sep′chōo·aj′ə·ner′ē, sep′tōo-) *adj.* & *n.* Septuagenarian.

Sep·tu·a·ges·i·ma (sep′chōo·ə·jes′ə·mə, sep′tōo-) *n.* The third Sunday before Lent. Also **Septuagesima Sunday.** [< L, seventieth]

Sep·tu·a·gint (sep′chōo·ə·jint′, sep′tōo-) *n.* An old Greek version of the Old Testament Scriptures. [< L *septuaginta* seventy]

sep·tum (sep′təm) *n. pl.* **·ta** (-tə) *Biol.* **1.** A dividing wall between two cavities: the nasal *septum.* **2.** A partition, as in coral or in a spore. [< L < *sepire* to enclose] **— sep′tal, sep·tate** *adj.*

sep·ul·cher (sep′əl·kər) *n.* **1.** A burial place; tomb; vault. **2.** A receptacle for relics, esp. in an altar slab. **—** *v.t.* **·chered** or **·chred, ·cher·ing** or **·chring** To place in a sepulcher; bury. Also *Brit.* **sep′ul·chre** (-kər). [< OF < L *sepulcrum* burial place, tomb]

se·pul·chral (si-pul′krəl) *adj.* **1.** Pertaining to a sepulcher. **2.** Suggestive of the grave; dismal. **3.** Unnaturally low and hollow in tone, as a voice. **— se·pul′chral·ly** *adv.*

sep·ul·ture (sep′əl·chər) *n.* **1.** The act of entombing; burial. **2.** *Archaic* A sepulcher.

se·quel (sē′kwəl) *n.* **1.** Something that follows and serves as a continuation; a development from what went before. **2.** A narrative discourse that, though complete in itself, develops from a preceding one. **3.** A consequence; upshot; result. [< OF < L *sequela* < *sequi* to follow]

se·quence (sē′kwəns) *n.* **1.** The process or fact of following in space, time, or thought; succession or order: also **se′quen·cy**. **2.** Order of succession; arrangement. **3.** A number of things following one another, considered collectively; a series. **4.** An effect or consequence. **5.** In card games, a set of three or more cards next each other in value. **6.** A section of motion-picture film presenting a single episode, without time lapses or interruptions. **7.** *Math.* An ordered succession of quantities, as $2x$, $4x^2$, $8x^3$, $16x^4$. [< L < *sequi* to follow]

sequence of tenses   See under TENSE[2].

se·quent (sē′kwənt) *n.* That which follows; a consequence; result. — *adj.* **1.** Following in the order of time; succeeding. **2.** Consequent; resultant. [See SEQUENCE.]

se·quen·tial (si·kwen′shəl) *adj.* **1.** Characterized by or forming a sequence, as of parts. **2.** Sequent. — **se·quen·ti·al·i·ty** (si·kwen′shē·al′ə·tē) *n.* — **se·quen′tial·ly** *adv.*

se·ques·ter (si·kwes′tər) *v.t.* **1.** To place apart; separate. **2.** To seclude; withdraw: often used reflexively. **3.** *Law* To take (property) into custody until a controversy, claim, etc., is settled or satisfied. **4.** In international law, to confiscate and control (enemy property) by preemption. **5.** *Chem.* To render inactive, as by the process of chelation. [< OF < L *sequestrare* to remove, lay aside < *sequester* trustee] — **se·ques′tra·ble** *adj.* — **se·ques′tered** *adj.*

se·ques·trate (si·kwes′trāt) *v.t.* ·trat·ed, ·trat·ing **1.** To seize, esp. for the use of the government; confiscate. **2.** To take possession of for a time, with a view to the just settlement of the claims of creditors. **3.** To seclude; sequester. — **se·ques·tra·tion** (sē′kwes·trā′shən, sek′wəs-) *n.* — **se·ques·tra·tor** (sē′kwes·trā′tər, si·kwes′trā·tər) *n.*

se·quin (sē′kwin) *n.* A small coinlike ornament sewn on clothing. [< F < Ital. < Arabic *sikka* coining-die]

se·quoi·a (si·kwoi′ə) *n.* **1.** A gigantic evergreen tree of the western U.S., with spreading, lanceolate leaves and small cones: also called *redwood*. **2.** A closely related tree of the Sierra Nevada mountains of California, sometimes reaching a height of 300 feet. [< NL, after *Sequoyah*, 1770?–1843, a half-breed Cherokee Indian who invented the Cherokee alphabet]

ser (sir)   See SEER[2].

ser-   Var. of SERO.

se·ra (sir′ə)   Plural of SERUM.

se·ra·glio (si·ral′yō, -räl′-) *n.* **1.** The portion of a Moslem house reserved for the wives and concubines; a harem. **2.** Any residence of a sultan. Also **se·rail** (se·rāl′). [< Ital. *serraglio* enclosure, ult. < LL *serrare*, var. of L *serare* to lock up]

se·ra·pe (sə·räp′ē) *n.* A blanketlike outer garment worn in Latin America, esp. in Mexico: also *sarape*, *zarape*. [< Am. Sp.]

ser·aph (ser′əf) *n.* *pl.* **ser·aphs** or **ser·a·phim** (ser′ə·fim) A celestial being having three pairs of wings. *Isa.* vi 2. [Back formation < *Seraphim*, pl. < LL < Hebrew] — **se·raph·ic** (si·raf′ik), **se·raph′i·cal** *adj.* — **se·raph′i·cal·ly** *adv.*

ser·a·phim (ser′ə·fim) *n.* **1.** Plural of SERAPH. **2.** *pl.* **·phims** A seraph: an erroneous usage.

Ser·bo-Cro·a·tian (sûr′bō·krō·ā′shən) *n.* **1.** The South Slavic language of Yugoslavia, including all the old languages and dialects. **2.** One whose native tongue is Serbo-Croatian. Also **Ser′bo-Cro′at** (-krō′at, -ət). — *adj.* Of the Serbo-Croatian language or those who speak it.

sere[1] (sir)   See SEAR[1].

sere[2] (sir) *n.* *Ecol.* The series of changes found in a given plant formation from the initial to the ultimate stage. [Back formation < SERIES] — **ser′al** *adj.*

ser·e·nade (ser′ə·nād′) *n.* **1.** An evening song, usu. that of a lover beneath his sweetheart's window. **2.** Music performed in honor of some person in the open air at night. **3.** The music for such a song. **4.** *Music* A form of instrumental music similar to the suite, and usu. including a march and a minuet: also called *serenata*. — *v.t. & v.i.* ·nad·ed, ·nad·ing To entertain with a serenade. [< F < Ital. < L *serenus* clear, serene] — **ser′e·nad′er** *n.*

ser·e·na·ta (ser′ə·nä′tə) *n.* *pl.* **·tas**, **·te** (tä) *Music* **1.** A dramatic cantata on any imaginative or simple subject, often composed as a complimentary offering for a royal personage. **2.** A serenade. [< Ital. See SERENADE.]

ser·en·dip·i·ty (ser′ən·dip′ə·tē) *n.* The faculty of happening upon fortunate discoveries when not in search of them. [Coined by Horace Walpole (1754), in *The Three Princes of Serendip* (Ceylon)] — **ser′en·dip′i·tous** *adj.*

se·rene (si·rēn′) *adj.* **1.** Clear; calm: a *serene* sky. **2.** Marked by peaceful repose; tranquil; placid: a *serene* spirit. **3.** Of exalted rank: chiefly in the titles of certain European princes: His *Serene* Highness. — **Syn.** See CALM. [< L *serenus*] — **se·rene′ly** *adv.* — **se·rene′ness** *n.*

se·ren·i·ty (si·ren′ə·tē) *n.* *pl.* **·ties** **1.** The state or quality of being serene; peacefulness; repose. **2.** Clearness; brightness. **3.** *Usu. Cap.* A title of honor given to certain members of royal families: preceded by *His*, *Your*, etc.

serf (sûrf) *n.* **1.** In feudal times, a person bound in servitude on an estate. **2.** Anyone in servile subjection. [< OF < L *servus* slave] — **serf′age**, **serf′dom**, **serf′hood** *n.*

serge (sûrj) *n.* **1.** A strong twilled fabric made of wool yarns and characterized by a diagonal rib on both sides of the cloth. **2.** A rayon lining fabric. [< OF < L *serica (lana)* (wool) of the Seres < *Seres* the Seres, an eastern Asian people]

ser·geant (sär′jənt) *n.* **1.** *Mil.* Any of several noncommissioned officer grades. See tables at GRADE. **2.** A police officer ranking next below a captain (sometimes lieutenant) in the U.S., and next below an inspector in England. **3.** A sergeant at arms. **4.** A constable or bailiff. Also, *esp. Brit.*, **ser·jeant**. [< OF < L *serviens*, *-entis*, ppr. of *servire* to serve] — **ser′gean·cy**, **ser′geant·cy**, **ser′geant·ship** *n.*

sergeant at arms **1.** An executive officer in a legislative body who enforces order. **2.** The title of certain court or city officials who have ceremonial duties.

sergeant major A noncommissioned officer in the highest enlisted grade of the U.S. Army and Marine Corps. See table at GRADE.

Sergeant Major of the Army The highest enlisted rank in the U.S. Army. See table at GRADE.

se·ri·al (sir′ē·əl) *adj.* **1.** Of the nature of a series. **2.** Published in a series at regular intervals. **3.** Arranged in rows or ranks; successive: also **se·ri·ate** (sir′ē·it, -āt). — *n.* **1.** A novel or other story regularly presented in successive instalments, as in a magazine, on radio or television, or in motion pictures. **2.** *Brit.* A periodical. [< NL < L *series* row, order] — **se′ri·al·ly** *adv.*

se·ri·al·ize (sir′ē·əl·īz′) *v.t.* ·ized, ·iz·ing To arrange or publish in serial form. — **se′ri·al·i·za′tion** *n.*

serial number A number assigned to a person, object, item of merchandise, etc., as a means of identification.

se·ri·a·tim (sir′ē·ā′tim, ser′ē-) *adv.* One after another; serially. [< Med.L < L *series*, on analogy with *gradatim*]

ser·i·cul·ture (sir′ə·kul′chər) *n.* The raising and care of silkworms for the production of raw silk. [Contr. of F *sériciculture* < L *sericum* silk + *cultura* a raising, culture] — **ser′i·cul′tur·al** *adj.* — **ser′i·cul′tur·ist** *n.*

se·ries (sir′ēz) *n.* *pl.* **se·ries** **1.** An arrangement of one thing after another; a connected succession of persons, things, data, etc. on the basis of like relationships. **2.** *Math.* An ordered arrangement of terms the sum of which is indicated. **3.** *Electr.* **a** An arrangement of sources or utilizers of electricity in which the positive electrode of one is connected with the negative electrode of another. **b** The circuit so produced. [< L < *serere* to join, weave together]

series winding *Electr.* The winding of a dynamo or an electric motor in such a way that the field circuit is connected in series with the armature circuit. — **se·ries-wound** (sir′ēz·wound′) *adj.*

ser·if (ser′if) *n.* *Printing* A light line or stroke crossing or projecting from the end of a main line or stroke in a letter: also spelled *ceriph*. [Du. < L *scribere* to write]

se·ri·o·com·ic (sir′ē·ō·kom′ik) *adj.* Mingling the serious with the comic. Also **se′ri·o·com′i·cal**.

se·ri·ous (sir′ē·əs) *adj.* **1.** Grave and earnest in quality, feeling, or disposition; sober. **2.** Said, planned, or done with full practical intent; being or done in earnest. **3.** Of grave importance: a *serious* problem. **4.** Attended with considerable danger or loss: a *serious* accident. [< MF < LL < L *serius*] — **se′ri·ous·ly** *adv.* — **se′ri·ous·ness** *n.*

ser·jeant (sär′jənt)   See SERGEANT.

ser·mon (sûr′mən) *n.* **1.** A discourse based on a passage or text of the Bible, delivered as part of a church service. **2.** Any discourse intended for the pulpit. **3.** Any speech of a serious or solemn kind, as a formal exhortation. [< AF, OF < L *sermo*, *-onis* talk] — **ser·mon′ic** (-mon′ik) or **·i·cal** *adj.*

ser·mon·ize (sûr′mən·īz) *v.t. & v.i.* ·ized, ·iz·ing **1.** To compose or deliver a sermon or sermons (to). **2.** To address at length in a moralizing manner. — **ser′mon·iz′er** *n.*

Sermon on the Mount The discourse of Jesus found recorded in *Matt.* v, vi, vii: properly distinguished from the **Sermon on the Plain**, *Luke* vi 20–49.

sero- *combining form* Connected with or related to serum. Also spelled, **ser-**. [< Du. < L *serum* whey]

se·rol·o·gy (si·rol′ə·jē) *n.* The science of serums and their actions. — **se·ro·log·i·cal** (si·rə·loj′i·kəl) *adj.*

se·ro·to·nin (ser′ə·tō′nin) *n.* *Biochem.* A crystalline protein found in many body tissues but chiefly in the brain and blood, a powerful vasoconstrictor. [< SERO- + TON- + -IN]

ser·pent (sûr′pənt) *n.* **1.** A scaly, limbless reptile; a snake.

SEQUOIA
(To over 300 feet high)

2. Anything of serpentine form or appearance. **3.** An insinuating and treacherous person. **4.** Satan; the devil. [< OF < L < ppr. of *serpere* to creep]

ser·pen·tine (sûr'pən·tēn, -tīn) *adj.* **1.** Pertaining to or like a serpent; sinuous. **2.** Subtle; cunning. — *n.* A mottled green or yellow magnesium silicate, used as a source of asbestos, and as architecturally decorative stonework.

ser·rate (ser'āt, -it) *adj.* **1.** Toothed or notched like a saw. **2.** *Bot.* Having notched edges, as certain leaves. Also **ser'·rat·ed.** [< L *serratus*, ult. < *serra* saw]

ser·ra·tion (se·rā'shən) *n.* **1.** The state of being serrated. **2.** One of the projections of a serrate formation, or a series of such projections. Also **ser·ra·ture** (ser'ə·chər).

ser·ried (ser'ēd) *adj.* Compacted in rows or ranks, as soldiers in company formation. [Pp. of obs. *serry* to press close together in ranks < MF *serré*, pp. of *serrer* to tighten]

se·rum (sir'əm) *n.* *pl.* **se·rums** or **se·ra** (sir'ə) **1.** The clear, slightly yellow portion of an animal liquid after separation from its solid constituents, esp. that formed by the clotting of blood. **2.** Loosely, an antiserum. **3.** Serum of milk; whey. **4.** Any similar secretion. [< L, whey, watery fluid]

ser·val (sûr'vəl) *n.* An African wildcat, yellow with black spots and having a ringed tail and long legs. [< F < Pg. *lobo cerval* lynx < *lobo* wolf + *cerval* stag]

ser·vant (sûr'vənt) *n.* **1.** A person hired to assist in domestic matters, sometimes living within the employer's house; hired help. **2.** A person employed to work for another; an employee. **3.** A slave or bondman. **4.** A public servant.

serve (sûrv) *v.* **served, serv·ing** *v.t.* **1.** To work for, esp. as a servant; be in the service of. **2.** To be of service to; wait on. **3.** To promote the interests of; aid. **4.** To obey and give homage to: to *serve* God. **5.** To satisfy the requirements of. **6.** To perform the duties connected with, as a public office. **7.** To go through (a period of enlistment, etc.). **8.** To furnish or provide, as with a regular supply. **9.** To offer or bring food or drink to (a guest, etc.). **10.** To bring and place on the table or distribute among guests, as food or drink. **11.** To operate or handle: to *serve* a cannon. **12.** To copulate with: said of male animals. **13.** In tennis, etc., to put (the ball) in play by hitting it to one's opponent. **14.** *Law* **a** To deliver (a summons or writ) to a person. **b** To deliver a summons or writ to. **15.** *Naut.* To wrap (a rope, stay, etc.), as with marlin or spun yarn, so as to strengthen or protect. — *v.i.* **16.** To work as or perform the functions of a servant. **17.** To wait at table; distribute food or drink. **18.** To perform the duties of any employment, office, etc. **19.** To go through a term of service, as in the army or navy. **20.** To be suitable or usable, as for a purpose. **21.** In tennis, etc., to put the ball in play. — *n.* **1.** In tennis, etc., the delivering of the ball by striking it toward an opponent. **2.** The turn of the server. [< OF < L < *servus* slave]

serv·er (sûr'vər) *n.* **1.** One who serves. **2.** That which is used in serving, as a tray. **3.** The male of any domestic animal used for breeding. **4.** In games, the player who serves.

ser·vice (sûr'vis) *n.* **1.** Assistance or benefit afforded another. **2.** A useful result or product of labor that is not a tangible commodity. **3.** *pl.* Such products collectively, as distinguished from goods. **4.** The manner in which one is waited upon or served: The *service* in this restaurant is only fair. **5.** A system of labor and material aids for the public or a portion of it: telephone *service*. **6.** A division of public employment devoted to a particular function: the diplomatic *service*. **7.** Employment as a public servant in government. **8.** A public duty or function: jury *service*. **9.** Any branch of the armed forces. **10.** Military duty or assignment. **11.** Devotion to God, as demonstrated by obedience and good works. **12.** A formal and public exercise of worship. **13.** A ritual prescribed for a particular ministration or observance: a marriage *service*. **14.** The music for a liturgical office or rite. **15.** The state or position of a servant, esp. a domestic servant. **16.** A set of tableware for a specific purpose. **17.** Installation, maintenance, and repair of an article provided a buyer by a seller. **18.** *Law* The legal communication of a writ or process to a designated person. **19.** In tennis, etc., the act or manner of serving a ball. **20.** *Naut.* The protective cordage wrapped around a rope. **21.** In animal husbandry, the copulation or covering of a female. — *adj.* **1.** Pertaining to or for service. **2.** For the use of servants or tradespeople: a *service* entrance. **3.** Of, pertaining to, or belonging to a military service. — *v.t.* **·viced, ·vic·ing 1.** To maintain or repair. **2.** To supply service to. [< OF < L < *servus* slave]

ser·vice·a·ble (sûr'vis·ə·bəl) *adj.* **1.** That can be made of service; beneficial; usable. **2.** Capable of rendering long service; durable. — **ser'vice·a·bil'i·ty, ser'vice·a·ble·ness** *n.* — **ser'vice·a·bly** *adv.*

ser·vice·ber·ry (sûr'vis·ber'ē) *n.* *pl.* **·ries 1.** A small tree bearing racemes of white flowers and purple edible berries; also called *service tree, shadbush*. **2.** A berry from this tree.

service cap A military uniform cap with a visor.

ser·vice·man (sûr'vis·man') *n.* *pl.* **·men** (-men') **1.** A

member of one of the armed forces. **2.** A man who performs services of maintenance, supply, repair, etc. Also **service man.** — **ser'vice·wom'an** (-woom'ən) *n.fem.*

service ribbon A distinctively colored ribbon worn on the U.S. service uniform to indicate the wearer's right to the corresponding campaign medal or decoration.

service station A place for supplying automobiles, trucks, etc., with gasoline, oil, water, etc.

service tree 1. Either of two deciduous trees of Europe, having alternate pinnate leaves and panicled cream-colored flowers. **2.** The serviceberry.

ser·vi·ette (sûr'vē·et', -vyet') *n.* *Brit. & Canadian* A table napkin. [< MF, prob. < *servir* to serve]

ser·vile (sûr'vīl, -vil) *adj.* **1.** Having the spirit of a slave; abject: a *servile* flatterer. **2.** Pertaining to or appropriate for slaves or servants. **3.** Being in a condition of servitude. **4.** Obedient; subject: with *to*. [< L < *servus* slave] — **ser'vile·ly** *adv.* — **ser'vile·ness, ser·vil'i·ty** (sûr·vil'ə·tē) *n.*

serv·ing (sûr'ving) *n.* A portion of food for one person. — *adj.* Used for serving food at table: a *serving* platter.

ser·vi·tor (sûr'və·tər) *n.* One who waits upon and serves another; an attendant; servant. — **ser'vi·tor·ship'** *n.*

ser·vi·tude (sûr'və·tood, -tyood) *n.* **1.** The condition of a slave; bondage. **2.** Enforced service as a punishment for crime: penal *servitude*. **3.** A state of subjection to a person or thing. **4.** The condition or duties of a servant; menial service. **5.** *Law* A right that one man may have to use the land of another for a special purpose.

ser·vo (sûr'vō) *n.* *pl.* **·vos** Any of various relay devices used in the automatic control of a complex machine, instrument, operation, or process. Also **ser'vo·mech'a·nism** (-mek'-ə·niz'əm). [< L *servus* slave]

servo- *combining form* In technical use, auxiliary. [< L *servus* slave]

ser·vo·mo·tor (sûr'vō·mō'tər) *n.* An electric motor connected with and supplying power for a servo.

ses·a·me (ses'ə·mē) *n.* **1.** An East Indian plant. **2.** The seeds of this plant, used as food and as a source of **sesame oil,** an emollient. [< F < L < Gk. *sēsamon, sēsamē*]

sesqui- *prefix* One and a half; one and a half times: *sesquicentennial*. [< L < *semis* half + *que* and]

ses·qui·cen·ten·ni·al (ses'kwi·sen·ten'ē·əl) *adj.* Of or pertaining to a century and a half. — *n.* A 150th anniversary, or its celebration.

ses·sile (ses'il) *adj.* **1.** *Bot.* Attached by its base, without a stalk, as a leaf. **2.** *Zool.* Firmly or permanently attached; fixed. [< L < *sessus*, pp. of *sedere* to sit] — **ses·sil'i·ty** *n.*

ses·sion (sesh'ən) *n.* **1.** The sitting together of a legislative assembly, court, etc., for the transaction of business. **2.** A single meeting or series of meetings of a group of persons, convened for a specific purpose or activity. **3.** A division of a school year; term. **4.** A part of a day during which classes meet in a school. [< F < L *sessio, -onis* < *sedere* to sit] — **ses·sion·al** *adj.* — **ses·sion·al·ly** *adv.*

ses·tet (ses·tet') *n.* **1.** The last six lines of a sonnet; also, any six-line stanza. **2.** *Music* See SEXTET (def. 1). [< Ital. < *sesto* sixth (< L *sextus*) + *-etto*, dim. suffix]

set¹ (set) *v.* **set, set·ting** *v.t.* **1.** To put in a certain place or position; place. **2.** To put into a fixed or immovable position or state: to *set* one's jaw. **3.** To bring to a specified state: to *set* a boat adrift. **4.** To restore to proper position for healing, as a broken bone. **5.** To place in readiness for operation or use: to *set* a trap. **6.** To adjust according to a standard: to *set* a clock. **7.** To adjust (an instrument, dial, etc.) to a particular calibration or position. **8.** To place knives, forks, etc., on (a table) in preparing for a meal. **9.** To bend the teeth of (a saw) to either side alternately. **10.** To appoint or establish: to *set* a time. **11.** To fix or establish a time for. **12.** To assign for performance, completion, etc.; allot: to *set* a task. **13.** To assign to some specific duty or function; station: to *set* a guard. **14.** To cause to sit. **15.** To present or perform so as to be copied or emulated: to *set* a bad example. **16.** To direct: He *set* his course for the Azores. **17.** To put in place so as to catch the wind: to *set* the jib. **18.** To place in a mounting or frame, as a gem. **19.** To stud or adorn with gems. **20.** To arrange (hair) in waves, curls, etc., while moist. **21.** To place (a hen) on eggs to hatch them. **22.** To place (eggs) under a fowl or in an incubator for hatching. **23.** To place (a price or value): with *by* or *on*. **24.** To point (game): said of hunting dogs. **25.** *Printing* **a** To arrange (type) for printing; compose. **b** To put into type, as a sentence, manuscript, etc. **26.** *Music* **a** To arrange (music) for words. **b** To write (words) to accompany music. **27.** To describe (a scene) as taking place: to *set* the scene in Monaco. **28.** In the theater, to arrange (a stage) so as to depict a scene. **29.** In some games, as bridge, to defeat. **30.** *Dial.* or *Illit.* To sit. — *v.i.* **31.** To go or pass below the horizon, as the sun. **32.** To wane; decline. **33.** To sit on eggs, as fowl. **34.** To become hard or firm; congeal. **35.** To begin a journey; start: with *forth, out, off*, etc. **36.** To have a specified direction; tend. **37.** To hang or fit, as clothes. **38.** To point game: said of hunting dogs. **39.** *Bot.* To begin development or growth, as a rudimentary fruit. **40.** *Dial.* or *Illit.* To sit. **— to set about** To start doing; begin. **— to set against 1.** To balance; compare. **2.** To make unfriendly to. **— to set aside 1.** To place apart or to one side. **2.** To reject; dismiss. **3.** To declare null and void. **— to set back** To reverse; hinder. **— to set down 1.** To place on a surface. **2.** To write or print; record. **3.** To judge or consider. **4.** To attribute; ascribe. **— to set forth** To state or declare; express. **— to set in 1.** To begin to occur: Rigor mortis *set in.* **2.** To blow or flow toward shore, as wind or tide. **— to set off 1.** To put apart by itself. **2.** To serve as a contrast or foil for. **3.** To cause to explode. **— to set on** To incite or instigate; urge. **— to set out 1.** To present to view; exhibit. **2.** To establish the limits or boundaries of, as a town. **3.** To plant. **4.** To start a journey, enterprise, etc. **— to set to 1.** To start; begin. **2.** To start fighting. **— to set up 1.** To place in an upright position. **2.** To raise. **3.** To place in power, authority, etc. **4.** To construct or build; assemble. **5.** To establish. **6.** To provide with the means to start a new business. **7.** To cause to be heard: to *set up* a cry. **8.** *Informal* **a** To pay for the drinks, etc., of; treat. **b** To pay for (drinks, etc.). *— adj.* **1.** Established by authority or agreement; appointed: a *set* time; a *set* method. **2.** Customary; conventional: a *set* phrase. **3.** Deliberately and systematically conceived; formal: a *set* speech. **4.** Fixed and motionless; rigid. **5.** Fixed in opinion or disposition. **6.** Formed; made: with a qualifying adverb: deep-*set* eyes. **7.** Ready; prepared: to get *set.* *— n.* **1.** The act or condition of setting. **2.** Permanent change of form, as by chemical action, cooling, pressure, etc. **3.** The arrangement, tilt, or hang of a garment, sail, etc. **4.** Carriage or bearing: the *set* of his shoulders. **5.** The sinking of a heavenly body below the horizon. **6.** The direction of a current or wind. **7.** A young plant for setting out; a cutting, slip, or seedling. **8.** A group of games constituting a division of a tennis match. [OE *settan* to cause to sit]

set² (set) *n.* **1.** A number of persons regarded as associated through status, common interests, etc. **2.** A social group having some exclusive character; clique: the fast *set.* **3.** A number of things belonging together and customarily used together: a *set* of dishes. **4.** A number of specific things so grouped as to form a whole: a *set* of lyrics. **5.** A group of volumes issued together and related by common authorship or subject. **6.** In motion pictures, television, etc., the complete assembly of properties, structures, etc., required in a scene. **7.** Radio or television receiving equipment assembled for use. **8.** *Math.* An array of objects, quantities, magnitudes, etc., arranged in some particular way: the *set* of integers. [< OF < L *secta* sect]

se·ta (sē′tə) *n. pl.* **·tae** (-tē) *Biol.* **1.** A bristle, or slender, bristlelike part or process of an organism. **2.** A slender spine or prickle. **3.** A coarse, rigid hair. [< L]

se·ta·ceous (si·tā′shəs) *adj.* **1.** Bristly; more or less covered with bristles. **2.** Of the nature or form of setae. Also **se′tal** (sēt′l). [< NL < L *seta* bristle]

set·back (set′bak′) *n.* **1.** An unexpected reverse or relapse. **2.** *Archit.* In tall buildings, the stepping of upper sections so that they progressively recede from the street line.

Seth (seth) The third son of Adam. *Gen.* v 3.

seti- *combining form* A bristle. Also, before vowels, **set-**. [< L *seta* bristle]

set·off (set′ôf′, -of′) *n.* **1.** That which offsets or counterbalances; a counterpoise. **2.** A counterclaim or the discharge of a debt by a counterclaim.

set·screw (set′skrōō′) *n.* A screw used as a clamp, esp. one used to screw through one part and slightly into another to bind the parts tightly.

set·tee (se·tē′) *n.* **1.** A long wooden seat with a high back. **2.** A sofa suitable for two or three people. [< SETT¹ or SET- (TLE), n. + -ee, dim. suffix]

set·ter (set′ər) *n.* **1.** One who or that which sets. **2.** One of a breed of medium-sized, silky-coated, lithe hunting dogs trained to indicate the presence of game birds by standing rigid. See ENGLISH SETTER, GORDON SETTER, IRISH SETTER.

set·ting (set′ing) *n.* **1.** The act of anything that sets. **2.** An insertion. **3.** That in which something is set; a frame; environment. **4.** The act of indicating game like a setter. **5.** A number of eggs placed together for hatching. **6.** The music adapted to a song or poem. **7.** The scene or background of a play or narrative. **8.** The apparent sinking of the sun, etc., below the horizon. **9.** The tableware set out for one person.

set·tle (set′l) *v.* **·tled, ·tling** *v.t.* **1.** To put in order; set to rights. **2.** To put firmly in place: He *settled* himself on the couch. **3.** To free of agitation or disturbance; quiet: to *settle* one's nerves. **4.** To cause (sediment or dregs) to sink to the bottom. **5.** To cause to subside or come to rest; make

firm or compact: to *settle* dust or ashes. **6.** To make clear or transparent, as by causing sediment or dregs to sink. **7.** *Informal* To make quiet or orderly: One blow *settled* him. **8.** To decide or determine finally, as an argument or difference. **9.** To pay, as a debt; satisfy, as a claim. **10.** To establish residents or residence in (a country, town, etc.). **11.** To establish as residents. **12.** To establish in a permanent occupation, home, etc. **13.** To decide (a suit at law) by agreement between the litigants. **14.** *Law* To make over or assign (property) by legal act: with *on* or *upon.* *— v.i.* **15.** To come to rest, as after moving about or flying. **16.** To sink gradually; subside. **17.** To sink or come to rest, as dust or sediment. **18.** To become more firm or compact. **19.** To become clear or transparent, as by the sinking of sediment. **20.** To take up residence. **21.** To come to a decision; resolve: with *on, upon,* or *with.* **22.** To pay a bill, etc. **— settle down 1.** To start living a regular, orderly life, esp. after a period of wandering or irresponsibility. **2.** To apply steady effort or attention. *— n.* **1.** A long seat or bench, generally of wood, with a high back, often with arms and sometimes having a chest from seat to floor. **2.** A wide step; platform. [OE *setl* seat, *setlan* to seat]

set·tle·ment (set′l·mənt) *n.* **1.** The act of settling, or the state of being settled; esp., an adjustment of affairs by public authority. **2.** The settling of a new region; colonization. **3.** An area of country newly occupied by those who intend to live and labor there; a colony. **4.** A collection of frontier dwellings forming a community. **5.** *Brit.* A regular or settled place of living. **6.** An accounting; adjustment; liquidation in regard to amounts. **7.** The conveyance of property in such form as to provide for some future object, esp. the support of members of the settler's family; also, the property so settled. **8.** A welfare institution established in a congested part of a city, that conducts educational and recreational activities for the community: also **settlement house.**

set·tler (set′lər) *n.* **1.** One who settles; esp., one who establishes himself in a colony or new country; a colonist. **2.** One who or that which settles or decides something.

set-to (set′tōō′) *n. pl.* **-tos** A bout at fighting, fencing, arguing, or any other mode of contest.

set-up (set′up′) *n.* **1.** *U.S. Informal* The overall scheme or pattern of organization or construction; circumstances. **2.** *U.S. Slang* A contest or match arranged to result in an easy victory. **3.** *U.S. Informal* Ice, soda water, etc., provided for use in alcoholic drinks. **4.** *Physique;* physical build; make-up. **5.** Carriage of the body; bearing.

sev·en (sev′ən) *n.* **1.** The sum of six and one: a cardinal number. **2.** Any symbol of this number, as 7, vii, VII. **3.** Anything consisting of or representing seven units. *— adj.* Being one more than six. [OE *seofon*]

seven deadly sins *Often cap.* Pride, lust, envy, anger, covetousness, gluttony, and sloth: also called *cardinal sins.*

seven seas All the oceans of the world, now considered to be the North and South Atlantic, the North and South Pacific, the Indian, the Arctic, and the Antarctic oceans.

sev·en·teen (sev′ən·tēn′) *n.* **1.** The sum of sixteen and one: a cardinal number. **2.** Any symbol of this number, as 17, xvii, XVII. **3.** Anything consisting of or representing seventeen units. *— adj.* Being one more than sixteen. [OE *seofontiene*] **— sev′en·teenth′** *adj. & n.*

sev·en·teen-year locust (sev′ən·tēn′yir′) A dark-bodied, wedge-shaped cicada native to the eastern U.S., having an underground nymphal stage of from 13 to 17 years.

sev·enth (sev′ənth) *adj.* **1.** Next after the sixth: the ordinal of *seven.* **2.** Being one of seven equal parts. *— n.* **1.** One of seven equal parts. **2.** That which follows the sixth. **3.** *Music* **a** The interval between any tone and the seventh tone above it in the diatonic scale. **b** A tone separated by this interval from any other, considered with reference to that other. *— adv.* In the seventh order, place, or rank: also, in formal discourse, **sev′enth·ly.** [ME < *seven* + -TH, replacing OE *seofotha*]

sev·enth-day (sev′ənth-dā′) *adj.* **1.** Pertaining to the seventh day of the week. **2.** *Often cap.* Advocating the observance of this day as the Sabbath: a *Seventh-Day* Adventist.

seventh day Saturday: a Quaker term.

Seventh-Day Adventist See under ADVENTIST.

seventh heaven 1. A condition of great happiness. **2.** The highest heaven according to various ancient systems of astronomy or in certain theologies.

sev·en·ty (sev′ən·tē) *n. pl.* **·ties 1.** The sum of sixty and ten: a cardinal number. **2.** Any symbol of this number, as 70, lxx, LXX. **3.** Anything consisting of or representing seventy units. *— adj.* Being ten more than sixty. [OE (*hund-*) *seofontig*] **— sev′en·ti·eth** *adj. & n.*

Seven Wonders of the World The seven works of man considered the most remarkable in the ancient world: the Egyptian pyramids, the hanging gardens of Babylon, the temple of Diana at Ephesus, the statue of Zeus at Olympia, the mausoleum of King Mausolos at Halicarnassus, the Colossus of Rhodes, and the lighthouse of Alexandria.

Seven Years' War See table for WAR.

sev·er (sev′ər) *v.t.* **1.** To put or keep apart; separate. **2.** To cut or break into two or more parts. **3.** To break off; dissolve, as a relationship or tie. — *v.i.* **4.** To come or break apart or into pieces. **5.** To go away or apart; separate. [< AF, OF < L *separare* to separate] — **sev′er·a·ble** *adj.*

sev·er·al (sev′ər·əl, sev′rəl) *adj.* **1.** More than two, yet not many. **2.** Considered individually; single; separate. **3.** Individually different; various or diverse. — *n.* Several persons or things. [< AF < Med.L < L *separ* separate]

sev·er·al·ly (sev′ər·əl·ē, sev′rəl·ē) *adv.* **1.** Individually; separately. **2.** Respectively.

sev·er·ance (sev′ər·əns, sev′rəns) *n.* **1.** The act of severing, or the condition of being severed. **2.** Separation; partition.

se·vere (si·vir′) *adj.* **·ver·er, ·ver·est 1.** Rigorous in the treatment of others; unsparing. **2.** Conforming to rigid rules; accurate. **3.** Serious and austere in disposition or manner. **4.** Causing extreme anguish: a *severe* pain. **5.** Causing extreme hardship; harsh: a *severe* snowstorm. [< MF < L *severus*] — **se·vere′ly** *adv.* — **se·vere′ness** *n.*

se·ver·i·ty (si·ver′ə·tē) *n. pl.* **·ties 1.** The quality of being severe. **2.** Harshness or cruelty of disposition or treatment. **3.** Extreme strictness; rigor; exactness. **4.** Seriousness; austerity. **5.** Strict conformity to truth or law.

sew (sō) *v.* **sewed, sewed** or **sewn, sew·ing** *v.t.* **1.** To make, mend, or fasten with needle and thread. — *v.i.* **2.** To work with needle and thread. — **to sew up** *U.S. Informal* To conclude (a deal, etc.) successfully. [OE *siwian*] — **sew′er** *n.*

sew·age (sōō′ij) *n.* The waste matter from domestic, commercial, and industrial establishments carried off in sewers.

sew·er (sōō′ər) *n.* **1.** A conduit, usu. laid underground, to carry off drainage and excrement. ◆ Collateral adjective: *cloacal.* **2.** Any large public drain. [< OF, ult. < L *ex-* off + *aqua* water]

sew·er·age (sōō′ər·ij) *n.* **1.** A system of sewers. **2.** Systematic draining by sewers. **3.** Sewage.

sew·ing (sō′ing) *n.* **1.** The act or occupation of one who sews. **2.** That which is sewed.

sewing circle A group of women, meeting periodically to sew, usu. for some charitable purpose.

sewing machine A machine for stitching or sewing.

sewn (sōn) Alternative past participle of SEW.

sex (seks) *n.* **1.** Either of two divisions, male and female, by which organisms are distinguished with reference to the reproductive functions. **2.** The character of being male or female. **3.** The activity or phenomena of life concerned with sexual desire or reproduction. **4.** *Informal* Sexual gratification. [< OF < L, prob. orig. < *secare* to divide]

sex- *combining form* Six: also *sexi-*. [< L *sex* six]

sex·a·ge·nar·i·an (sek′sə·jə·nâr′ē·ən) *n.* A person between sixty and seventy years of age. — *adj.* Sixty years old, or between sixty and seventy. [< SEXAGENARY]

sex·ag·e·nar·y (seks·aj′ə·ner′ē) *adj.* Sexagenarian. — *n. pl.* **·nar·ies** A sexagenarian. [< L < *sexaginta* sixty]

sex appeal A physical quality that attracts sexual interest.

sex chromosome *Genetics* A chromosome whose presence in the reproductive cells of certain plants and animals is associated with the determination of the sex of offspring.

sex gland A gonad; either of the testes or ovaries.

sexi- Var. of SEX-.

sex·less (seks′lis) *adj.* **1.** Having or appearing to have no sex; neuter. **2.** Provoking or showing little sexual desire. — **sex′less·ly** *adv.* — **sex′less·ness** *n.*

sex linkage *Biol.* That type of inheritance that is associated with the transmission of genes attached to the sex chromosomes. — **sex-linked** (seks′ lingkt′) *adj.*

sex·ol·o·gy (seks·ol′ə·jē) *n.* The study of human sexual behavior. — **sex·o·log·ic** (sek′sə·loj′ik) or **·i·cal** *adj.* — **sex·ol′o·gist** *n.*

sext (sekst) *n. Often cap. Eccl.* Prescribed prayers constituting the fourth of the seven canonical hours. [< LL < L *sexta* (*hora*) the sixth (hour)]

sex·tant (seks′tənt) *n.* **1.** An instrument for measuring angular distance between two objects, as a heavenly body and the horizon, used esp. in determining latitude at sea. **2.** The sixth part of a circle; an arc of 60 degrees. [< L *sextus* sixth]

sex·tet (seks·tet′) *n.* **1.** *Music* A group of six singers or players; also, a musical composition for six performers: also called *sestet.* **2.** Any collection of six persons or things. Also **sex·tette′.** [Alter. of SESTET; refashioned after L *sex* six]

sex·til·lion (seks·til′yən) *n.* **1.** *U.S.* A thousand quintillions, written as 1 followed by twenty-one zeros: a cardinal number. **2.** *Brit.* A million quintillions (def. 2), written as 1 followed by thirty-six zeros: a cardinal number. — *adj.* Being a sextillion in number. [< MF < *sexti-* six + (*mi*)*lion* million] — **sex·til′lionth** *adj. & n.*

sex·to·dec·i·mo (seks′tō·des′ə·mō) *n. pl.* **·mos 1.** A page size made from a printer's sheet folded so as to have 16 leaves, usu. measuring 4½ x 6⅞ inches. **2.** A book or pamphlet having pages this size. — *adj.* Having or consisting of pages this size. Also *sixteenmo.* Also written **16mo., 16°** [< L < *sextus* sixth + *decimus* tenth]

sex·ton (seks′tən) *n.* A janitor of a church having charge also of ringing the bell, overseeing burials, etc. [< OF < Med.L *sacristanus*] — **sex′ton·ship** *n.*

sex·tu·ple (seks′tōō·pəl, -tyōō-, seks·tōō′-, -tyōō′-) *v.t.* **·pled, ·pling** To multiply by six. — *adj.* **1.** Consisting of six or of six parts. **2.** Multiplied by six. **3.** *Music* Having six beats to the measure. — *n.* A number or sum six times as great as another. [< L *sex* six, formed on analogy with *quadruple, quintuple,* etc.] — **sex′tu·ply** *adv.*

sex·tu·plet (seks′tōō·plit, -tyōō-, seks·tōō′-, -tyōō′-) *n.* **1.** A set of six similar things. **2.** One of six offspring produced at a single birth. [< SEXTUPLE on analogy with *triplet*]

sex·u·al (sek′shōō·əl) *adj.* **1.** Of, pertaining to, or characteristic of sex, the sexes, or the organs or functions of sex. **2.** Having sex. **3.** *Biol.* Designating a type of reproduction involving both sexes. [< LL < L *sexus* sex] — **sex′u·al′i·ty** (-al′ə·tē) *n.* — **sex′u·al·ly** *adv.*

sex·y (sek′sē) *adj.* **sex·i·er, sex·i·est** *Slang* **1.** Provocative of sexual desire. **2.** Concerned in large degree with sex.

sfor·zan·do (sfôr·tsän′dō) *Music adj.* Accented more forcibly than the rhythm requires. — *adv.* In a sforzando manner. Also **sfor·za′to** (-tsä′tō). [< Ital. *sforzare* to force]

shab·by (shab′ē) *adj.* **·bi·er, ·bi·est 1.** Threadbare; ragged. **2.** Wearing worn or seedy garments. **3.** Mean; paltry. [OE *sceabb* scab + -Y¹] — **shab′bi·ly** *adv.* — **shab′bi·ness** *n.*

Sha·bu·oth (shä·vōō′ōth, shə·vōō′əs) *n.pl.* The Jewish festival of Pentecost. [< Hebrew *shebuôth*, lit., weeks]

shack (shak) *n. U.S. & Canadian Informal* A rude cabin, as of logs. [? < dial. Sp. (Mexican) *jacal* wooden hut < Nahuatl *xacalli*]

shack·le (shak′əl) *n.* **1.** A ring, clasp, or braceletlike fastening for encircling and fettering a limb. **2.** Impediment or restraint. **3.** One of various forms of fastenings. — *v.t.* **·led, ·ling 1.** To restrain or confine with shackles. **2.** To keep or restrain from free action or speech. **3.** To connect or fasten with a shackle. [OE *sceacul*] — **shack′ler** *n.*

shack·o (shak′ō) See SHAKO.

shad (shad) *n. pl.* **shad** Any of several food fishes related to the herring. [OE *sceadd*]

shad·ber·ry (shad′ber′ē) *n. pl.* **·ries** The serviceberry.

shad·bush (shad′bōōsh′) *n.* **1.** The serviceberry (def. 1). **2.** Any of various other related plants. Also **shad′blow′** (-blō′). [< SHAD + BUSH¹; so called because it flowers when the shad appear in U.S. rivers]

shade (shād) *v.* **shad·ed, shad·ing** *v.t.* **1.** To screen from light by intercepting its rays. **2.** To make dim; darken. **3.** To screen or protect with or as with a shade. **4.** To cause to change by gradations. **5.** In graphic arts: **a** To represent (degrees of shade, colors, etc.) by gradations of light or dark lines or shading. **b** To represent varying shades, colors, etc., in (a picture, etc.) thus. **6.** To make slightly lower, as a price. — *v.i.* **7.** To change or vary by degrees. — *n.* **1.** Relative obscurity due to interception of the rays of light; darkness. **2.** The state of being outshone. **3.** A shady place; secluded retreat. **4.** *U.S.* A screen that shuts off light, heat, dust, etc. **5.** A gradation of color; also, slight degree; minute difference. **6.** The unilluminated part of a picture, etc. **7.** A disembodied spirit; ghost. — **the shades** The abode of departed spirits; Hades. [OE *sceadu*] — **shade′less** *adj.*

shad·ing (shā′ding) *n.* **1.** Protection against light or heat. **2.** The lines, dots, etc., by which degrees of darkness, color, or depth are represented in a picture. **3.** A slight variation.

shad·ow (shad′ō) *n.* **1.** A comparative darkness within an illuminated area, esp. that caused by the interception of light by a body. **2.** The dark image thus produced on a surface and representing the approximate shape of the intercepting body. **3.** The shaded portion of a picture. **4.** A mirrored image. **5.** A delusive image or semblance. **6.** A phantom; ghost; shade. **7.** A faint representation or indication; a symbol. **8.** A remnant; vestige. **9.** An insignificant trace or portion. **10.** Gloom; a saddening influence. **11.** An inseparable companion. **12.** One who trails another, as a detective. — *v.t.* **1.** To cast a shadow upon. **2.** To darken; make gloomy. **3.** To represent or foreshow dimly: with *forth* or *out.* **4.** To follow closely or secretly. **5.** To shade in painting, etc. [OE *sceadu* shade] — **shad′ow·er** *n.*

shad·ow·box (shad′ō·boks′) *v.i.* To spar with an imaginary opponent as a form of exercise. — **shad′ow·box′ing** *n.*

shad·ow·y (shad′ō·ē) *adj.* **·ow·i·er, ·ow·i·est 1.** Full of or affording shadow. **2.** Vague; dim. **3.** Unsubstantial or illusory. — **shad′ow·i·ness** *n.*

shad·y (shā′dē) *adj.* **shad·i·er, shad·i·est 1.** Full of shade; casting a shade. **2.** Shaded, sheltered, or hidden. **3.** *Informal* Questionable as to honesty or legality; dubious. —

on the shady side of Older than; past the age of. — shad/i·ly *adv.* — shad/i·ness *n.*

shaft¹ (shaft, shäft) *n.* 1. The long narrow rod of an arrow, spear, etc. 2. An arrow. 3. Anything resembling a missile in appearance or effect: *shafts* of ridicule. 4. A beam of light. 5. A long handle, as of a hammer, etc. 6. *Mech.* A long bar, esp. if rotating and transmitting motive power. 7. *Archit.* a The portion of a column between capital and base. b A slender column. 8. An obelisk or memorial column. 9. The stem of a feather. 10. One of two poles by which a horse is harnessed to a vehicle. [OE *sceat*]

shaft² (shaft, shäft) *n.* 1. A narrow, vertical or inclined, excavation connected with a mine. 2. The tunnel of a blast furnace. 3. An opening through the floors of a building, as for an elevator. [< LG *schacht* rod, shaft]

shag (shag) *n.* 1. A rough coat or mass, as of hair. 2. A wild growth, as of weeds. 3. A long nap on cloth. 4. Cloth having a rough or long nap. 5. A coarse, strong tobacco: also shag tobacco. — *v.* shagged, shag·ging *v.t.* To make shaggy; roughen. [OE *sceacga* rough hair, wool]

shag·bark (shag/bärk/) *n.* 1. A rough-barked hickory yielding high-grade, light-colored nuts. 2. Its tough, durable wood. Also called *shellbark.*

shag·gy (shag/ē) *adj.* ·gi·er, ·gi·est 1. Having, consisting of, or resembling rough hair or wool; rugged; rough. 2. Covered with any rough, tangled growth; fuzzy; scrubby. 3. Unkempt. — shag/gi·ly *adv.* — shag/gi·ness *n.*

sha·green (shə·grēn/) *n.* 1. The rough skin of various sharks and rays. 2. A rough-grained leather, usu. dyed green. [< F < Turkish *sāghrī* horse's hide]

shah (shä) *n.* An eastern king or ruler, esp. of Iran. [< Persian *shāh*]

shake (shāk) *v.* shook, shak·en, shak·ing *v.t.* 1. To cause to move to and fro or up and down with short, rapid movements. 2. To affect in a specified manner by or as by vigorous action: with *off, out, from,* etc. 3. To cause to tremble or quiver; vibrate. 4. To cause to stagger or totter. 5. To weaken or disturb: I could not shake his determination. 6. To agitate or rouse: often with *up.* 7. *Slang* To get rid of or away from. 8. *Music* To trill. — *v.i.* 9. To move to and fro or up and down in short, rapid movements. 10. To be affected in a specified way by vigorous action: with *off, out, from,* etc. 11. To tremble or quiver, as from cold or fear. 12. To become unsteady; totter. 13. *Music* To trill on a note, etc. — to shake down 1. To cause to fall by shaking; bring down. 2. To cause to settle. 3. *Slang* To extort money from. — to shake hands To clasp hands as a form of greeting, etc. — to shake off To rid oneself of by or as by shaking. — to shake up 1. To shake, mix, or stir. 2. *U.S. Informal* To shock or jar mentally or physically. — *n.* 1. A shaking; concussion; agitation; vibration; shock; jolt. 2. The state of being shaken. 3. *pl. Informal* The chill or ague of intermittent fever. 4. A frost or wind crack in timber; also, a tight fissure in rock. 5. An earthquake. 6. *Slang* An instant. 7. *Music* A trill. — no great shakes *Informal* Of no great importance; mediocre. [OE *scacan*] — shak/a·ble, shake/a·ble *adj.*

shake·down (shāk/doun/) *n. U.S. Slang* A swindle; extortion. — *adj. U.S. Informal* For the purpose of adjusting mechanical parts or habituating people: a *shakedown* cruise.

shak·er (shā/kər) *n.* 1. One who or that which shakes. 2. A container for shaking or pouring something: cocktail *shaker.*

Shak·er (shā/kər) *n.* A member of a sect practicing celibacy and communal living: so called from their characteristic bodily movements during religious meetings. — Shak/er·ism *n.*

Shake·spear·e·an (shāk·spir/ē·ən) *adj.* Of, pertaining to, or characteristic of Shakespeare, his work, or his style. — *n.* A specialist on Shakespeare or his writings. Also Shake·spear/i·an. — Shake·spear/e·an·ism *n.*

Shakespearean sonnet A sonnet having the rhyme scheme *ababcdcdefefgg*: also called *Elizabethan sonnet, English sonnet.*

shake·up (shāk/up/) *n.* A radical change of personnel or organization, as in a business office, etc.

shak·o (shak/ō) *n. pl.* ·os A kind of high, stiff military headdress, originally of fur, having a peak and an upright plume: also spelled *shacko.* [< F < Hungarian *csákó*]

shak·y (shā/kē) *adj.* shak·i·er, shak·i·est 1. Habitually shaking or tremulous; tottering; weak; unsound. 2. Wavering; unreliable. — shak/i·ly *adv.* — shak/i·ness *n.*

shale (shāl) *n.* A fissile claylike rock resembling slate, with fragile, uneven laminae. — shal/y *adj.*

shall (shal) *v.* Present 3rd person sing. shall; past should A defective verb having a past tense that is now used only as an auxiliary followed by

the infinitive without *to,* or elliptically without the infinitive, to express: 1. In the first person, simple futurity, with a matter-of-fact attitude toward the action or state projected: We *shall* take only the usual precautions. (But see usage note below.) 2. In the second and third persons, futurity combined with a mood or feeling of: a Determination: They *shall* not pass. b Promise: You *shall* have whatever you need. c Threat: You *shall* pay for this. d Command: No one *shall* twice be put in jeopardy. e Inevitability: When earthly time *shall* end, will life survive? 3. In all persons, indefinite future time in conditional statements: If and when you or we or the divers *shall* locate the treasure, it will (or, in legal use, the mandatory *shall*) be shared out according to the agreement. 4. In all persons, futurity involving ideal certainty, in clauses following expressions of anxiety, demand, or desire: They are anxious that you or I or both of us *shall* go, rather than any outsider. [OE *sceal* I am obliged]

◆ shall, will The formal view on the use of *shall* and *will* is that to indicate simple futurity *shall* is used in the first person, *will* in the second and third; their roles are reversed to express determination, command, inevitability, etc., while in questions the choice depends on the form expected in the answer. These rules apply to American usage only at the most formal level.

shal·lop (shal/əp) *n.* An open boat propelled by oars or sails. [< F < Du. *sloep.* See SLOOP.]

shal·lot (shə·lot/) *n.* 1. An onionlike vegetable allied to garlic but having milder bulbs that are used in seasoning and for pickles. 2. A small onion. [< OF *eschalotte*]

shal·low (shal/ō) *adj.* 1. Having the bottom not far below the surface; lacking depth. 2. Lacking intellectual depth; not wise; superficial. — *n.* A shallow place in a body of water; shoal. — *v.t. & v.i.* To make or become shallow. [ME *schalowe*] — shal/low·ly *adv.* — shal/low·ness *n.*

shalt (shalt) Archaic or poetic second person singular, present tense of SHALL: used with *thou.*

sham (sham) *v.* shammed, sham·ming *v.t.* 1. To assume or present the appearance of; counterfeit; feign. 2. To represent oneself as; pretend to be. — *v.i.* 3. To make false pretenses. — *adj.* False; counterfeit. — *n.* 1. A pretense; imposture; deception. 2. One who simulates a certain character; a pretender: also sham/mer. 3. A deceptive imitation. [Prob. dial. var. of SHAME]

sha·man (shä/mən, shā/-, sham/ən) *n.* 1. A priest of Shamanism; a magician. 2. A North American Indian medicine man. — *adj.* Of a shaman: also sha·man·ic (shə·man/ik). [< Russian < Tungusic < Skt. *śamana* ascetic]

Sha·man·ism (shä/mən·iz/əm, shā/-, sham/ən-) *n.* 1. A religion of NE Asia and Europe holding that gods and spirits work only through the shamans. 2. Any similar religion, as of certain Indians of the American Northwest. — Sha/man·ist *n. & n.* — Sha/man·is/tic *adj.*

sham·ble (sham/bəl) *v.i.* ·bled, ·bling To walk with shuffling or unsteady gait. — *n.* A shambling walk; shuffling gait. [Origin uncertain]

sham·bles (sham/bəlz) *n.pl.* (*usu. construed as sing.*) 1. A place where butchers kill animals; slaughterhouse. 2. Any place of carnage. 3. A place marked by great destruction or disorder. [OE < L < *scamnum* bench, stool]

shame (shām) *n.* 1. A painful sense of guilt or degradation caused by consciousness of guilt or of anything degrading, unworthy, or immodest. 2. Susceptibility to such feelings. 3. One who or that which brings reproach or disgrace. 4. A state of regret, dishonor, or disgrace. — to put to shame 1. To disgrace; make ashamed. 2. To surpass or eclipse. — *v.t.* shamed, sham·ing 1. To make ashamed; cause to feel shame. 2. To bring shame upon; disgrace. 3. To impel by a sense of shame: with *into* or *out of.* [OE *scamu*]

shame·faced (shām/fāst/) *adj.* Easily abashed; showing shame or bashfulness in one's face; modest; bashful. [< ME < OE *scamfæst* abashed] — shame·fac·ed·ly (shām/-fā/sid·lē, shām/fāst/lē) *adv.* — shame/fac/ed·ness *n.*

shame·ful (shām/fəl) *adj.* 1. Deserving or bringing shame or disgrace; disgraceful; scandalous. 2. Exciting shame; indecent. — shame/ful·ly *adv.* — shame/ful·ness *n.*

shame·less (shām/lis) *adj.* 1. Impudent; brazen; immodest. 2. Done without shame; indicating a want of pride or decency. — shame/less·ly *adv.* — shame/less·ness *n.*

sham·my (sham/ē), sham·ois (sham/ē) See CHAMOIS.

sham·poo (sham·pōo/) *n.* 1. Any of various liquid preparations of soap, chemical solvents, etc., used to cleanse the hair and scalp. 2. The act or process of shampooing. — *v.t.* To cleanse (the hair and scalp) with a shampoo. [< Hind. *chāmpnā* to press] — sham·poo/er *n.*

sham·rock (sham/rok) *n.* Any of several trifoliate plants, accepted as the national emblem of Ireland. [< Irish < *seamar* trefoil]

SHAKO

shang·hai (shang/hī, shang·hī/) *v.t.* ·haied, ·hai·ing 1. To drug or render unconscious and kidnap for service aboard a ship. **2.** To cause to do something by force or deception. [after *Shanghai*, China]

Shan·gri-la (shang'grĭ·lä') *n.* Any imaginary hidden utopia or paradise. [after the locale of *Lost Horizon*, a novel by James Hilton, 1900–54, English author]

shank (shangk) *n.* **1.** The part of the leg between the knee and the ankle. **2.** A cut of meat from the leg of an animal; the shin. **3.** Something resembling a leg. **4.** The part of a tool connecting the handle with the working part. **5.** The projecting piece or loop by which some forms of buttons are attached. **6.** The straight part of a hook. **7.** *Printing* The body of a type. **13.** The narrow part of a shoe sole. [OE *scanca*]

sha'nt (shant, shänt) Shall not. Also **shan't.**

shan·tey (shan'tē) See CHANTEY.

shan·tung (shan'tung, shan·tung') *n.* A fabric with a rough, nubby surface, originally made of wild silk, now often made of rayon combined with cotton. [after the Chinese town *Shantung*]

shan·ty[1] (shan'tē) *n. pl.* **·ties** A hastily built shack or cabin; a ramshackle or rickety dwelling. [< F (Canadian) *chantier* lumberer's shack]

shan·ty[2] (shan'tē) See CHANTEY.

shape (shāp) *n.* **1.** Outward form or construction; configuration; contour. **2.** A developed expression or definite formulation; embodiment; cast: to put an idea into *shape*. **3.** A phantom. **4.** The character or form in which a thing appears; guise; aspect. **5.** A pattern or mold; in millinery, a stiff frame. **6.** The lines of a person's body; figure. **7.** Manner of execution. **8.** Condition: Everything is in good *shape*. — **to take shape** To have or assume a definite form. — *v.* **shaped, shaped** (*Rare* **shap·en**), **shap·ing** *v.t.* **1.** To give shape to; mold. **2.** To adjust or adapt; modify. **3.** To devise; prepare. **4.** To give direction or character to. **5.** To put into or express in words. — *v.i.* **6.** To take shape; develop; form: often with *up* or *into*. — **to shape up** *Informal* **1.** To proceed satisfactorily or favorably. **2.** To develop proper form. [OE < *scieppan* to create] — **shap'er** *n.*

shaped (shāpt) *adj.* **1.** Formed. **2.** Resembling in shape: used in compounds: leaf-*shaped*.

shape·less (shāp'lĭs) *adj.* Having no definite shape; lacking symmetry. — **shape'less·ly** *adv.* — **shape'less·ness** *n.*

shape·ly (shāp'lē) *adj.* **·li·er, ·li·est** Having a pleasing shape; well-formed; graceful. — **shape'li·ness** *n.*

shard (shärd) *n.* **1.** A broken piece of a brittle substance, as of an earthen vessel; a potsherd; a fragment: also called *sherd.* **2.** A hard, thin shell, or a wing cover, of a beetle. [OE *sceard.* Related to SHEAR.]

share[1] (shâr) *n.* **1.** A portion; allotted or equitable part. **2.** One of the equal parts into which the capital stock of a company or corporation is divided. **3.** An equitable part of something enjoyed or suffered in common. — **to go shares** To partake equally, as in an enterprise. — *v.* **shared, shar·ing** *v.t.* **1.** To divide and give out in shares or portions; apportion. **2.** To enjoy or endure in common; participate in. — *v.i.* **3.** To have a part; participate: with *in*. [OE < *scieran* to shear] — **shar'er** *n.*

share[2] (shâr) *n.* A plowshare.

share·crop·per (shâr'krop'ər) *n.* A tenant farmer who pays a share of his crop as rent for his land.

share·hold·er (shâr'hōl'dər) *n.* An owner of a share or shares of a company's stock; a stockholder.

shark[1] (shärk) *n.* One of a group of fishes, mostly marine, of medium to large size, having dun-colored bodies covered with plate-like scales. Some species are dangerous to man. — *v.i.* To fish for sharks. [Origin uncertain]

shark[2] (shärk) *n.* A bold and dishonest person; a rapacious swindler. Also **shark'er.** — *v.i.* To live by trickery. [Prob. < G *schürke* scoundrel; infl. by SHARK[1]]

shark·skin (shärk'skin') *n.* **1.** The skin of a shark. **2.** A fabric with a smooth, almost shiny surface, made of acetate rayon and used for sports clothes.

sharp (shärp) *adj.* **1.** Having a keen edge or an acute point; capable of cutting or piercing. **2.** Coming to an acute angle; not obtuse; abrupt: a *sharp* peak. **3.** Keen of perception or discernment; also, shrewd in bargaining; artful; overreaching. **4.** Ardent; eager; keen; impetuous or fiery; attentive. **5.** Affecting the mind or senses, as if by cutting or piercing; poignant; acrimonious. **6.** Shrill. **7.** Pinching; cutting, as cold. **8.** Having an acrid or pungent taste. **9.** Distinct, as an outline. **10.** *Music* **a** Raised in pitch by a semitone. **b** Above the right, true pitch. **c** Having sharps in the key signature. **11.** Hard and rough; gritty. **12.** *Phonet.* Of consonants, voiceless: opposed to *flat*. — *adv.* **1.** In a sharp manner; sharply. **2.** Promptly; exactly: at 4 o'clock *sharp*. **3.** *Music* Above the proper pitch. — *n.* **1.** *Music* A sign (♯) placed before a note to indicate that the note is sharped; also, the note so altered. **2.** A cheat: a *cardsharp*. — *v.t. Music* To raise in pitch, as by [a] half step. [OE ǀ*scearp*] — **sharp'ly** *adv.* — **sharp'ness** *n.*

sharp·en (shär'pən) *v.t. & v.i.* To make or become sharp. — **sharp'en·er** *n.*

sharp·er (shär'pər) *n.* A swindler; cheat.

sharp-eyed (shärp'īd') *adj.* **1.** Having acute eyesight. **2.** Keenly observant; alert.

sharp·ie (shär'pē) *n.* A long, sharp, flat-bottomed sailboat having a centerboard and one or two masts, each having a triangular sail, originally used for fishing. [< SHARP]

sharp·shoot·er (shärp'shoo'tər) *n.* A skilled marksman, especially in the use of the rifle. — **sharp'shoot'ing** *n.*

sharp-tongued (shärp'tungd') *adj.* Bitter or caustic in speech.

sharp-wit·ted (shärp'wit'id) *adj.* Acute; intelligent. — **sharp'-wit'ted·ness** *n.*

shat·ter (shat'ər) *v.t.* **1.** To break into pieces suddenly, as by a blow. **2.** To break the health or tone of, as the body or mind; disorder; damage. — *v.i.* **3.** To break into pieces; burst. [ME *schateren*]

shave (shāv) *v.* **shaved, shaved** or **shav·en, shav·ing** *v.i.* **1.** To cut hair or beard close to the skin with a razor. — *v.t.* **2.** To remove hair or beard from (the face, head, etc.) with a razor. **3.** To cut (hair or beard) close to the skin with a razor: often with *off*. **4.** To trim closely: to *shave* a lawn. **5.** To cut thin slices from, as in preparing the surface; pare; plane. **6.** To cut into thin slices. **7.** To touch or scrape in passing; graze; come close to. — *n.* **1.** The act or operation of cutting off the beard with a razor. **2.** A knife or blade, mounted between two handles, as for shaving wood: also **draw shave, spoke shave. 3.** A shaving; thin slice. **4.** *Informal* The act of barely grazing something; a narrow escape: a close *shave*. [OE *scafan* to shave]

shave·ling (shāv'ling) *n.* **1.** One who is shaven; opprobriously, a monk or priest. **2.** A youth.

shav·en (shā'vən) Alternative past participle of SHAVE. — *adj.* **1.** Shaved; also, tonsured. **2.** Trimmed closely.

Sha·vi·an (shā'vē·ən) *n.* An admirer of George Bernard Shaw, his books, or his theories. — *adj.* Of, pertaining to, or like George Bernard Shaw, or his style and methods.

shav·ing (shā'ving) *n.* **1.** The act of one who or that which shaves. **2.** A thin paring shaved from anything, as a board.

shawl (shôl) *n.* A wrap, as a square cloth, or large scarf, worn over the upper part of the body. [< Persian *shāl*]

Shaw·nee (shô·nē') *n.* One of a tribe of North American Indians of Algonquian stock, now living in Oklahoma. [< Algonquian (Shawnee) *Shawunogi* southerners]

she (shē) *pron., possessive* **her** or **hers,** *objective* **her;** *pl. nominative* **they,** *possessive* **their** or **theirs,** *objective* **them 1.** The nominative singular pronoun of the third person, used of the female person or being previously mentioned or understood, or of things conventionally regarded as feminine, as ships, machines, etc. **2.** That woman or female; any woman: *She* who listens learns. — *n. pl.* **shes** A female person or being. [ME < OE *sēo, sīo,* fem. of *sē* the]

she- *combining form* Female; feminine: in hyphenated compounds: a *she*-lion; *she*-devil.

sheaf (shēf) *n. pl.* **sheaves** (shēvz) **1.** A quantity of the stalks of cut grain or the like, bound together. **2.** Any collection of things, as papers, tied together. **3.** A quiverful of arrows. — *v.t.* To bind in a sheaf. [OE *scēaf*]

shear (shir) *n.* **1.** A two-bladed cutting instrument; obsolete except in the plural. See SHEARS. **2.** *Physics* A deformation of a solid body, equivalent to a sliding over each other of adjacent laminar elements, with a progressive relative displacement; also **shearing stress. 3.** The act or result of shearing. **4.** A plowshare. — *v.* **sheared, sheared** or **shorn, shear·ing** *v.t.* **1.** To cut the hair, fleece, etc., from. **2.** To remove by cutting or clipping: to *shear* wool. **3.** To deprive; strip, as of wealth. **4.** To cut or clip with or as with shears. — *v.i.* **5.** To use shears. **6.** To slide or break from a shear (def. 2). **7.** To proceed by or as by cutting a way: with *through*. [OE < *scieran* to shear] — **shear'er** *n.*

shears (shirz) *n.pl.* **1.** Any large cutting or clipping instrument worked by the crossing of cutting edges. Also **pair of shears. 2.** The ways or guides, as of a lathe. [See SHEAR.]

shear·wa·ter (shir'wô'tər, -wot'ər) *n.* Any of various far-ranging sea birds related to the fulmars and petrels: so called because they skim close to the water.

sheath (shēth) *n. pl.* **sheaths** (shēthz, shēths) **1.** An envelope or case, as for a sword; scabbard. **2.** A covering in plants or animals resembling a sheath. **3.** A close-fitting dress having straight, unbroken lines. — *v.t.* To sheathe. [OE *scæth*] — **sheath'less** *adj.*

sheathe (shēth) *v.t.* **sheathed, sheath·ing 1.** To put into a sheath. **2.** To encase or protect with a covering. **3.** To draw in, as claws. [< SHEATH]

sheath·ing (shē'thing) *n.* **1.** A protective covering, as of a ship's hull; that which sheathes; also, the material used. **2.** The act of one who sheathes. **3.** The covering or waterproof material on outside walls or roofs.

sheave[1] (shēv) *v.t.* **sheaved, sheav·ing** To gather into sheaves; collect. [< SHEAF]

sheave² (shēv) *n.* A grooved pulley wheel; also, a pulley wheel and its block. [ME *schive*]

sheaves (shēvz) Plural of SHEAF¹.

She·ba (shē'bə), **Queen of** A queen who visited Solomon to test his wisdom. I *Kings* x 1–3.

she·bang (shi·bang') *n.* *U.S. Slang* **1.** A building, vehicle, etc. **2.** Matter; affair: tired of the whole *shebang.*

She·bat (shi·bät') *n.* The fifth month of the Hebrew year. Also spelled *Sebat.* See (Hebrew) CALENDAR.

shed¹ (shed) *v.* **shed, shed·ding** *v.t.* **1.** To pour forth in drops; emit, as tears. **2.** To cause to pour forth. **3.** To send forth; radiate. **4.** To throw off without allowing to penetrate, as rain; repel. **5.** To cast off by natural process, as hair, etc. **6.** To rid oneself of. — *v.i.* **7.** To cast off or lose skin, etc., by natural process. **8.** To fall or drop, as leaves. — **to shed blood** To kill. — *n.* **1.** That which sheds, as a sloping surface or watershed. **2.** That which has been shed. [OE *scēadan* to separate, part]

shed² (shed) *n.* **1.** A small low building, often with front or sides open; also, a lean-to: a wagon *shed.* **2.** *Brit.* A barn.

she'd (shēd) **1.** She had. **2.** She would.

shed·der (shed'ər) *n.* **1.** One who sheds. **2.** An animal that sheds or has lately shed its skin, as a snake.

sheen (shēn) *n.* **1.** A glistening brightness, as if from reflection. **2.** Shining attire. — *adj.* Shining; beautiful. — *v.i.* To shine; glisten. [OE *sciene* beautiful] — **sheen'y** *adj.*

sheep (shēp) *n.* *pl.* **sheep 1.** A medium-sized, domesticated, even-toed ruminant, bred in many varieties for its flesh, wool, and skin. ◆ Collateral adjective: *ovine.* **2.** Sheepskin. **3.** A meek, bashful, or timid person. [OE *scēap*]

sheep·cote (shēp'kōt') *n.* A small enclosure for the protection of sheep; a sheepfold. Also **sheep'cot'** (-kot').

sheep dip Any of several liquid disinfectants containing creosote, nicotine, arsenic, etc., used for dipping sheep.

sheep dog A dog trained to guard and control sheep, often a collie, but also an **old English sheep dog,** a rough-coated, heavy, bobtailed dog much used by drovers in England: also called *shepherd dog, shepherd's dog.*

sheep·fold (shēp'fōld') *n.* A pen for sheep.

sheep·herd·er (shēp'hûr'dər) *n.* A herder of sheep. — **sheep'herd'ing** *n.*

sheep·ish (shē'pish) *adj.* Foolish, as a sheep; awkwardly diffident; abashed. — **sheep'ish·ly** *adv.* — **sheep'ish·ness** *n.*

sheep ranch A ranch where sheep are bred and raised. Also *Brit.* **sheep·walk** (shēp'wôk'), *Austral.* **sheep run.**

sheep's eyes (shēps) Bashful or amorous glances.

sheep·skin (shēp'skin') *n.* **1.** The skin of a sheep, tanned or untanned, or anything made from it. **2.** A document written on parchment, as an academic diploma.

sheep sorrel An herb growing in dry places, and having leaves of an acrid taste.

sheer¹ (shir) *v.i.* To swerve from a course; turn aside. — *v.t.* To cause to swerve. — *n.* **1.** *Naut.* **a** The rise, or the amount of rise from a level, of the lengthwise lines of a vessel's hull. **b** A position of a vessel that enables it to swing clear of a single anchor. **2.** A swerving course. [< SHEAR]

sheer² (shir) *adj.* **1.** Having no modifying conditions; unmitigated; absolute: *sheer* folly. **2.** Exceedingly thin and fine: said of fabrics. **3.** Perpendicular; steep. **4.** Pure; pellucid. — *n.* Any very thin fabric used for clothes. — *adv.* Steeply; perpendicularly. [ME *schere*] — **sheer'ness** *n.* — **sheer'ly** *adv.*

sheet¹ (shēt) *n.* **1.** A very thin and broad piece of any substance; as: **a** A large rectangular piece of bed linen. **b** A piece of paper. **c** A newspaper. **d** A piece of metal or other substance hammered, rolled, fused, or cut very thin. **2.** A broad, flat surface; superficial expanse: a *sheet* of water. **3.** *Naut.* **a** A rope or chain from a lower corner of a sail to extend it or move it. **b** *pl.* In an open boat, the space at the bow and stern not occupied by the thwarts. **c** A sail. **4.** Any superficial deposit, as of gravel left by a glacier, or of soil or ice. **5.** The large, unseparated block of stamps printed by one impression of a plate. — **three sheets in the wind** *Slang* Tipsy; drunk. — *v.t.* **1.** To cover with a sheet. **2.** To furnish with sheets. [OE *scyte* linen cloth]

sheet anchor 1. One of two anchors for use only in emergency. **2.** One who or that which can be depended upon in danger or an emergency.

sheet bend *Naut.* A knot used to join two ropes' ends.

sheet·ing (shē'ting) *n.* **1.** The act of sheeting, in any sense. **2.** Cotton, muslin, etc., used for making sheets for beds.

sheet lightning Lightning appearing in sheetlike form as a momentary and broadly diffused radiance in the sky, caused by the reflection of a distant lightning flash.

sheet metal Metal rolled and pressed into sheets.

sheet music Music printed on unbound sheets of paper.

sheik (shēk, *Brit.* shāk) *n.* **1.** A Moslem high priest or a venerable man; also, the chief or head of an Arab tribe or

family. **2.** *Archaic Slang* A man who fascinates women. Also **sheikh.** [< Arabic *sheikh, shaykh,* lit., an elder, chief]

sheik·dom (shēk'dəm) *n.* The land ruled by a sheik. Also **sheikh'dom.**

shek·el (shek'əl) *n.* **1.** An Assyrian, Babylonian, and, later, Hebrew unit of weight and money; also, a coin having this weight. **2.** *pl. Slang* Money. [< Hebrew *shāqal* to weigh]

shel·drake (shel'drāk') *n.* **1.** A large Old World duck of southeastern Europe and North Africa. **2.** A merganser. [< dial. E *sheld* piebald, dappled + DRAKE]

shelf (shelf) *n.* *pl.* **shelves** (shelvz) **1.** A board or slab set horizontally against a wall, in a bookcase, etc., to support articles, as books. **2.** Contents of a shelf. **3.** Any flat projecting ledge, as of rock. **4.** A reef; shoal. **5.** A stratum of bedrock. — **on the shelf** No longer in use; discarded. [< LG *schelf* set of shelves]

shell (shel) *n.* **1.** Any of various hard structures encasing an animal, as a mollusk or other shellfish. **2.** The hard, relatively fragile outer coat of an egg. **3.** The relatively hard covering of a fruit, seed, or nut. **4.** The material composing a shell. **5.** A hollow structure or vessel, generally thin and weak; also, a case or mold for holding something: a pie *shell.* **6.** A very light, long, and narrow racing rowboat. **7.** A hollow metallic projectile filled with an explosive or chemical. **8.** A metallic or paper cartridge case for small arms. **9.** A shape or outline that merely simulates a reality; hollow form; external semblance. **10.** A reserved or impersonal attitude: to come out of one's *shell.* — *v.t.* **1.** To divest of or remove from a shell. **2.** To separate from the cob, as corn. **3.** To bombard with shells, as a fort. **4.** To cover with shells. — *v.i.* **5.** To shed the shell or pod. **6.** To fall off, as a shell. — **to shell out** *Informal* To hand over, as money. [OE *sciell* shell] — **shell'er** *n.* — **shell'y** *adj.*

she'll (shēl) She will.

shel·lac (shə·lak') *n.* **1.** A purified lac in the form of thin plates, extensively used in varnish, sealing wax, insulators, etc. **2.** A varnishlike solution of flake shellac dissolved in methylated spirit, used for coating floors, woodwork, etc. — *v.t.* **·lacked, ·lack·ing 1.** To cover or varnish with shellac. **2.** *Slang* To belabor; beat. **3.** *Slang* To defeat utterly. Also **shell'lac', shel·lack'.** [< SHELL + LAC¹]

shel·lack·ing (shə·lak'ing) *n.* *U.S. Slang* **1.** A beating; assault. **2.** A thorough defeat.

shell·back (shel'bak') *n.* A veteran sailor; an old salt; esp., one who has crossed the equator. [Prob. with reference to the shell of the sea turtle]

shell·bark (shel'bärk') *n.* The shagbark or one of its nuts.

shell·fire (shel'fīr') *n.* The firing of artillery shells.

shell·fish (shel'fish') *n.* *pl.* **·fish** or **·fish·es** Any aquatic animal having a shell, as a mollusk.

shell game 1. A swindling game in which the victim bets on the location of a pea covered by one of three nutshells. **2.** Any game in which the victim cannot win.

shell·proof (shel'pro͞of') *adj.* Built to resist the destructive effect of projectiles and bombs.

shell shock Formerly, combat fatigue. — **shell·shocked** (shel'shokt') *adj.*

shel·ter (shel'tər) *n.* **1.** That which covers or shields from exposure or danger; a place of safety. **2.** The state of being sheltered or protected. — *v.t.* **1.** To provide protection or shelter for; shield, as from danger or inclement weather. — *v.i.* **2.** To take shelter. [? Alter. of ME *scheltrum* < OE *sceld-truma* a body of men armed with shields, phalanx, protection] — **shel'ter·er** *n.* — **shel'ter·less** *adj.*

shelter tent *Mil.* A tent for two men, divided into two sections, each of which, called a **shelter half,** is carried as part of a soldier's field equipment: also called *pup tent.*

shelve (shelv) *v.* **shelved, shelv·ing** *v.t.* **1.** To place on a shelf. **2.** To postpone indefinitely; put aside. **3.** To retire. **4.** To provide or fit with shelves. — *v.i.* **5.** To incline gradually; slope. [< SHELF] — **shelv'y** *adj.*

shelves (shelvz) Plural of SHELF.

shelv·ing (shel'ving) *n.* **1.** Shelves collectively. **2.** Material for shelves.

Shem (shem) The eldest son of Noah. *Gen.* v 32.

Shem·ite (shem'īt) See SEMITE.

she·nan·i·gan (shi·nan'ə·gən) *n.* *Often pl. Informal* Trickery; foolery; nonsense; also, treacherous action or a treacherous act. [? < Irish *sionnach* fox]

she·ol (shē'ōl) *n.* Hell. [< Hebrew *she'ol* cave]

She·ol (shē'ōl) In the Old Testament, a place under the earth where the departed spirits were believed to go.

shep·herd (shep'ərd) *n.* **1.** A keeper or herder of sheep. **2.** A pastor, leader, or guide. — *v.t.* To watch and tend as a shepherd. [OE *scēaphyrde*] — **shep'herd·ess** (-is) *n.fem.*

shepherd dog A sheep dog. Also **shepherd's dog.**

shep·herd's-purse (shep'ərdz·pûrs') *n.* A weed bearing small white flowers and notched triangular pods.

Sher·a·ton (sher′ə·tən) *adj.* Denoting the graceful, straight-lined, classically chaste style of English furniture developed by Thomas Sheraton, 1751–1806, English furniture designer.

sher·bet (shûr′bit) *n.* **1.** A flavored water ice. **2.** *Brit.* A drink made of sweetened fruit juice and sometimes cooled with snow. [< Turkish *sherbet*]

sherd (shûrd) *n.* A fragment of pottery: often in combination: *potsherd*: also called *shard*. [Var. of SHARD]

she·rif (she·rēf′) *n.* **1.** A descendant of Mohammed through his daughter Fatima. **2.** An Arab chief. Also **she·reef′**. [< Arabic *sharif* noble]

sher·iff (sher′if) *n.* The chief administrative officer of a county, who executes the mandates of courts, enforces order, etc. [OE *scīr-gerēfa* shire reeve] — **sher′iff·dom** *n.*

she·root (shə·rōōt′) See CHEROOT.

Sher·pa (shûr′pə) *n.* One of a Tibetan tribe living on the southern slopes of the Himalayas in Nepal.

sher·ry (sher′ē) *n. pl.* **·ries** A fortified wine of Jerez, Spain; also, any similar wine. [after *Jerez*, Spain]

Sher·wood Forest (shûr′wōōd) A forest in Nottinghamshire, England, known as the home of Robin Hood.

she's (shēz) **1.** She is. **2.** She has.

Shet·land pony (shet′lənd) A small, hardy, shaggy breed of pony originally bred on the Shetland Islands.

shew (shō) *v.t. & v.i.* **shewed, shewn, shew·ing** *Archaic* To show. — **shew′er** *n.*

shew·bread (shō′bred′) *n.* Unleavened bread formerly displayed in the Jewish temple: also spelled *showbread*.

Shi·ah (shē′ə) *n.* **1.** One of the two great sects of Islam. Compare SUNNI. **2.** A Shiite. [< Arabic *shī′i* follower, sect]

shib·bo·leth (shib′ə·leth) *n.* **1.** A test word or pet phrase of a party; a watchword: from the Hebrew word *shibboleth*, given by Jephthah (*Judges* xii 4–6) as a test to distinguish his own men from the Ephraimites, who used the pronunciation *sibboleth*. **2.** A custom or use of language regarded as distinctive of a particular social class, profession, etc. [< Hebrew *shibbōleth* ear of grain]

shied (shīd) Past tense and past participle of SHY.

shield (shēld) *n.* **1.** A broad piece of defensive armor, commonly carried on the left arm. **2.** Something that protects or defends. **3.** Any device for covering or protecting something. **4.** *Heraldry* An escutcheon. **5.** A conventional figure having an oval bottom and a cusp at the top, used in flags, emblems, etc. — *v.t.* **1.** To protect from danger as with a shield; defend; guard. — *v.i.* **2.** To act as a shield or safeguard. [OE *scīld*] — **shield′er** *n.*

shi·er (shī′ər) Comparative of SHY. — *n.* A horse in the habit of shying. Also spelled **shyer**.

shift (shift) *v.t.* **1.** To change or move from one position, place, etc., to another. **2.** To change for another or others of the same class. **3.** To change (gears) from one arrangement to another. **4.** *Ling.* To alter as part of a systematic change. — *v.i.* **5.** To change position, place, etc. **6.** To evade; equivocate. **7.** To shift gears. — **to shift for oneself** To do the best one can to provide for one's needs. — *n.* **1.** The act of shifting. **2.** A dodge; artifice; trick; evasion; expedient: *We made* shift *to get along.* **3.** *Archaic or Dial.* An undergarment; chemise. **4.** A straight, loosely hanging woman's garment, as a dress. **5.** A change of position, place, direction, or form: *a* shift *in the wind.* **6.** A relay of workers; also, the working time of each group. **7.** *Physics* Any of various displacements of spectral lines caused by velocity of the light source, gravitational effect, etc. See DOPPLER EFFECT. **8.** *Geol.* The relative displacement of areas on opposite sides of a rock fault. [OE *sciftan* to divide] — **shift′er** *n.*

shift·less (shift′lis) *adj.* **1.** Unable or unwilling to shift for oneself; inefficient or lazy. **2.** Showing lack of energy or resource. — **shift′less·ly** *adv.* — **shift′less·ness** *n.*

shift·y (shif′tē) *adj.* **shift·i·er, shift·i·est** **1.** Artful; tricky; fickle. **2.** Full of expedients; alert; capable. — **shift′i·ly** *adv.* — **shift′i·ness** *n.*

Shi·ite (shē′īt) *n.* A Moslem of the Shiah sect: distinguished from Sunnite: also *Shiah*. Also **Shie′ite, Shi′ite**.

shill (shil) *n. Slang* The assistant of a sidewalk peddler or gambler, who makes a purchase or bet to encourage onlookers to buy or bet; a capper. [Origin unknown]

shil·le·lagh (shi·lā′lə, -lē) *n.* In Ireland, a stout cudgel made of oak or blackthorn. Also **shil·e′lah**. [after *Shillelagh*, a town in Ireland famed for its oaks]

shil·ling (shil′ing) *n.* **1.** A British monetary unit, since the Norman Conquest equivalent to 12 pence or ⅟₂₀ pound; also, a coin of this value, first issued in 1504. **2.** A similar monetary unit of various other countries. **3.** A former coin of colonial America. [OE *scilling*]

shil·ly-shal·ly (shil′ē·shal′ē) *v.i.* **·lied, ·ly·ing** **1.** To act with indecision; be irresolute; vacillate. **2.** To trifle. — *adj.* Weak; hesitating. — *n.* Weak or foolish vacillation; irresolution. — *adv.* In an irresolute manner. [Dissimilated reduplication of *shall I?*] — **shil′ly-shal′li·er** *n.*

shi·ly (shī′lē) See SHYLY.

shim (shim) *n.* A piece of metal or other material used to fill out space, for leveling, etc. — *v.t.* **shimmed, shim·ming** To wedge up or fill out by inserting a shim. [Origin unknown]

shim·mer (shim′ər) *v.i.* To shine faintly; glimmer. — *n.* A tremulous shining or gleaming; glimmer; gleam. [OE *scimerian*] — **shim′mer·y** *adj.*

shim·my (shim′ē) *n. pl.* **·mies** *U.S. Informal* A chemise. **2.** A former jazz dance accompanied by shaking movements. **3.** Unusual vibration, as in automobile wheels. — *v.i.* **·mied, ·my·ing** **1.** To vibrate or wobble. **2.** To dance the shimmy. [Alter. of CHEMISE]

shin (shin) *n.* **1.** The front part of the leg below the knee; also, the shinbone. **2.** The lower foreleg: *a* shin *of beef.* — *v.t. & v.i.* **shinned, shin·ning** **1.** To climb (a pole) by gripping with the hands or arms and the shins or legs: usu. with *up.* **2.** To kick (someone) in the shins. [OE *scinu*]

shin·bone (shin′bōn′) *n.* The tibia.

shin·dig (shin′dig) *n. U.S. Slang* A dance or noisy party. [< SHINDY, by folk etymology, suggesting *a dig on the shin*]

shine (shīn) *v.i.* **shone** or (*esp. for def. 5*) **shined, shin·ing** **1.** To emit light; beam; glow. **2.** To gleam, as by reflected light. **3.** To excel or be conspicuous in splendor, beauty, etc. — *v.t.* **4.** To cause to shine. **5.** To brighten by rubbing or polishing. — **to shine up to** *Slang* To try to please. — *n.* **1.** The state or quality of being bright or shining; radiance; luster; sheen. **2.** Fair weather; sunshine. **3.** *U.S. Informal* A liking or fancy. **4.** *U.S. Informal* A smart trick or prank. **5.** A shoeshine. — **to take a shine to** *U.S. Informal* To become fond of. [OE *scīnan*]

shin·er (shī′nər) *n.* **1.** One who or that which shines. **2.** One of various silvery fresh-water fishes related to the minnows. **3.** A silverfish, an insect. **4.** *Slang* A black eye.

shin·gle¹ (shing′gəl) *n.* **1.** A thin, tapering, oblong piece of wood or other material, used in courses to cover roofs. **2.** A small sign bearing the name of a doctor, lawyer, etc., and placed outside his office. **3.** A short haircut. — *v.t.* **·gled, ·gling** **1.** To cover (a roof, building, etc.) as or with shingles. **2.** To cut (the hair) short. [ME < L *scandula* shingle] — **shin′gler** *n.*

shin·gle² (shing′gəl) *n.* **1.** Rounded, waterworn gravel, found on the seashore. **2.** A place strewn with shingle, as a beach. [Cf. Norw. *singl* coarse gravel] — **shin′gly** *adj.*

shin·gles (shing′gəlz) *n.pl.* (*construed as sing. or pl.*) *Pathol.* An acute inflammatory virus disease characterized by blisters along the course of the affected nerve ganglia and accompanied by pain: also called *herpes zoster*. [Alter. of Med.L *cingulus* < L *cingulum* girdle < *cingere* to gird]

shin·ing (shī′ning) *adj.* **1.** Emitting or reflecting a continuous light; gleaming; luminous. **2.** Of unusual brilliance or excellence; conspicuous. — **shin′ing·ly** *adv.*

shin·ny¹ (shin′ē) *n.* **1.** A game resembling hockey; also, one of the sticks or clubs used by the players. **2.** *Canadian* Pond hockey. Also **shin′ney**. [< *shin ye*, a cry used in the game]

shin·ny² (shin′ē) *v.i.* **·nied, ·ny·ing** *U.S. Informal* To climb using one's shins: usually with *up.*

shin·plas·ter (shin′plas′tər, -pläs′-) *n.* **1.** *U.S.* Fractional currency issued by other than the constituted authorities. **2.** Any paper money issued by private enterprises. **3.** A plaster for a sore shin.

Shin·to (shin′tō) *n.* A religion of Japan, consisting chiefly in ancestor worship, nature worship, and, formerly, a belief in the divinity of the Emperor. Also **Shin′to·ism**. [< Japanese, way of the gods] — **Shin′to·ist** *n.*

shin·y (shī′nē) *adj.* **shin·i·er, shin·i·est** **1.** Glistening; glossy; polished. **2.** Bright; clear.

ship (ship) *n.* **1.** Any vessel suitable for deep-water navigation; also, its personnel. **2.** A large seagoing sailing vessel with at least three masts, carrying square-rigged sails on all three. **3.** An airship or airplane. — **when one's ship comes in** (or **home**) When one's fortune has been made or hopes realized. — *v.* **shipped, ship·ping** *v.t.* **1.** To transport by ship or other mode of conveyance. **2.** To hire and receive for service on board a vessel, as sailors. **3.** *Naut.* To receive over the side, as in rough weather: to *ship* a wave. **4.** *Informal* To get rid of. **5.** To set or fit in a prepared place on a boat or vessel, as a mast, or a rudder. — *v.i.* **6.** To go on board ship; embark. **7.** To undergo shipment: *Raspberries do not* ship *well.* **8.** To enlist as a seaman: usually with *out.* [OE *scip*]

-ship *suffix of nouns* **1.** The state, condition, or quality of: *friendship.* **2.** Office, rank, or dignity of: *kingship.* **3.** The art or skill of: *marksmanship.* [OE *-scipe*]

ship·board (ship′bôrd′, -bōrd′) *n.* **1.** The side or deck of a ship. **2.** A vessel: used only in the phrase **on shipboard**.

ship·build·er (ship′bil′dər) *n.* One whose work is the building of vessels. — **ship′build′ing** *adj. & n.*

ship canal A waterway deep enough for seagoing vessels.

ship chandler One who deals in supplies for vessels.

ship·load (ship′lōd′) *n.* The quantity that a ship carries or can carry; a cargo.

ship·mas·ter (ship/mas/tər, -mäs/-) n. The captain or master of a merchant ship.
ship·mate (ship/māt/) n. A fellow sailor.
ship·ment (ship/mənt) n. 1. The act of shipping. 2. That which is shipped.
ship of the line Formerly, a man-of-war large enough to take a position in a line of battle.
ship·own·er (ship/ō/nər) n. One owning a ship or ships.
ship·pa·ble (ship/ə·bəl) adj. That can be shipped or transported.
ship·per (ship/ər) n. One who ships goods.
ship·ping (ship/ing) n. 1. Ships collectively; also, tonnage. 2. The act of shipping.
ship·shape (ship/shāp/) adj. Well arranged, orderly, and neat, as on a ship, — adv. In an orderly manner; neatly.
ship's papers The documents required by international law to be carried by a ship.
ship·worm (ship/wûrm/) n. Any of various marine bivalves, resembling worms, that burrow into the timbers of ships, piers, wharfs, etc.
ship·wreck (ship/rek/) n. 1. The partial or total destruction of a ship at sea. 2. Utter or practical destruction; ruin. 3. Scattered remnants, as of a wrecked ship; wreckage. — v.t. 1. To wreck, as a vessel. 2. To bring to disaster; ruin.
ship·wright (ship/rīt/) n. One who builds or repairs ships.
ship·yard (ship/yärd/) n. A place where ships are built or repaired.
shire (shīr) n. A territorial division of Great Britain; a county. [OE *scīr*]
shirk (shûrk) v.t. 1. To avoid the doing of; evade doing (something that should be done). — v.i. 2. To avoid work or evade obligation. — n. One who shirks: also **shirk/er.** [? < G *schürke* rascal]
shirr (shûr) v.t. 1. To draw (material) into three or more parallel rows of gathers. 2. To bake with crumbs in a buttered dish, as eggs. — n. 1. A drawing of material into three or more parallel rows of gathers. 2. A rubber thread woven into a fabric to make it elastic. [Origin unknown]
shirt (shûrt) n. 1. A garment for the upper part of the body, usu. having collar and cuffs and a front closing. 2. A closely fitting undergarment. 3. A shirtwaist. — **to keep one's shirt on** *Slang* To remain calm. — **to lose one's shirt** *Slang* To lose everything. [OE *scyrte* shirt, short garment] — **shirt/less** adj.
shirt·ing (shûr/ting) n. Closely woven material of cotton, linen, silk, etc., used for making shirts, blouses, dresses, etc.
shirt·waist (shûrt/wāst/) n. 1. A woman's tailored, sleeved blouse or shirt, usu. worn tucked in under a skirt or slacks. 2. A woman's tailored dress having a bodice like a shirtwaist: also **shirtwaist dress.**
shish ke·bab (shish/kə·bob/) Meat roasted or broiled in small pieces on skewers and served with condiments. [< Turkish *shish* skewer + *kebap* roast meat]
shist (shist) See SCHIST.
Shi·va (shē/və) Siva, a Hindu god.
shiv·a·ree (shiv/ə·rē/) n. *U.S.* A charivari. [Alter. of CHARIVARI]
shiv·er¹ (shiv/ər) v.i. 1. To tremble; shake; quiver. — v.t. 2. *Naut.* To cause to flutter in the wind, as a sail. — n. The act of shivering; a tremble. [ME *chivere*] — **shiv/er·y** adj.
shiv·er² (shiv/ər) v.t. & v.i. To break suddenly into fragments; shatter. — n. A splinter; sliver. [ME *schivere*] — **shiv/er·y** adj.
shoal¹ (shōl) n. 1. A shallow place in any body of water. 2. A sandbank or bar, esp. one seen at low water. Compare REEF¹. — v.i. 1. To become shallow. — v.t. 2. To make shallow. 3. To sail into a lesser depth of (water): said of a ship. — adj. Shallow. [OE *sceald* shallow]
shoal² (shōl) n. 1. An assemblage or multitude; throng. 2. A school of fish. — v.i. 1. To throng in multitudes. 2. To school: said of fish. [OE *scolu* troop, multitude]
shoal·y (shō/lē) adj. shoal·i·er, shoal·i·est Abounding in shoals. — **shoal/i·ness** n.
shock¹ (shok) n. 1. A violent collision or concussion; impact; blow. 2. A sudden and violent sensation: a *shock* of paralysis. 3. A sudden and severe agitation of the mind or emotions, as in horror or great sorrow. 4. *Pathol.* Prostration of bodily functions, as from sudden injury. 5. The physical reactions produced by the passage of a strong electric current through the body, as involuntary muscular contractions. — v.t. 1. To shake by sudden collision; jar. 2. To disturb the emotions or mind of; horrify; disgust. 3. To give an electric shock to. [< F < *choquer* < Gmc.] — **shock/er** n.
shock² (shok) n. A number of sheaves of grain, stalks of maize, or the like, stacked for drying upright in a field. — v.t. & v.i. To gather (grain) into a shock or shocks. [ME *schokke* < Gmc. Cf. MLG *schok*.] — **shock/er** n.

shock³ (shok) adj. Shaggy; bushy. — n. A coarse, tangled mass, as of hair. [Back formation < *shock dog*]
shock absorber *Mech.* A device designed to absorb the force of shocks, as the springs of an automobile.
shock·ing (shok/ing) adj. 1. Causing a mental or emotional shock, as with horror or disgust. 2. *Informal* Terrible; awful. — **shock/ing·ly** adv. — **shock/ing·ness** n.
shock therapy *Psychiatry* The treatment of certain psychotic disorders by the injection of drugs, or by electrical shocks, both methods inducing coma, with or without convulsions.
shock troops *Mil.* Seasoned men selected to lead an attack.
shock wave *Physics* A compression wave following a sudden and violent disturbance of the transmitting medium, through which it is propagated with a velocity equal to or greater than that of sound.
shod (shod) Past tense and alternative past participle of SHOE.
shod·dy (shod/ē) n. pl. ·dies 1. Wool obtained by shredding discarded woolens or worsteds; also, cloth made of such wool. 2. Any inferior goods made to resemble those of better quality. — adj. shod·di·er, shod·di·est 1. Made of or containing shoddy. 2. Sham; inferior. [Origin uncertain] — **shod/di·ly** adv. — **shod/di·ness** n.
shoe (shoo) n. pl. shoes 1. An outer covering, usu. of leather, for the human foot. 2. Something resembling a shoe in position or use. 3. A rim or plate of iron to protect the hoof of an animal. 4. A strip of iron, steel, etc., fitted under a sleigh runner to receive friction. 5. The part of the brake that presses upon a wheel or drum. 6. The tread or outer covering of a pneumatic tire, as for an automobile. 7. The sliding contact plate on an electric car or locomotive by which it obtains current from the third rail. — v.t. shod, shod or shod·den, shoe·ing 1. To furnish with shoes or the like. 2. To furnish with a guard of metal, wood, etc., for protection, as against wear. [OE *scōh*]
shoe·black (shoo/blak/) n. One who cleans or polishes shoes as an occupation.
shoe·horn (shoo/hôrn/) n. A smooth curved implement of horn, metal, etc., used to help put on a shoe.
shoe·lace (shoo/lās/) n. A lace or cord for fastening shoes.
shoe·mak·er (shoo/mā/kər) n. One who makes or repairs shoes, boots, etc. — **shoe/mak/ing** n.
sho·er (shoo/ər) n. One who shoes horses.
shoe·shine (shoo/shīn/) n. 1. The waxing and polishing of a pair of shoes. 2. The polished look of shined shoes.
shoe·string (shoo/string/) n. A shoelace. — **on a shoestring** With a small sum of money with which to begin a business, etc.
shoe·tree (shoo/trē/) n. A form for inserting in a shoe to preserve its shape or to stretch it.
sho·far (shō/fär) n. A ram's horn used in Jewish ritual, sounded on solemn occasions and in war: also spelled *shophar.* [< Hebrew *shōphār*]
sho·gun (shō/gun, -goon) n. Any of the hereditary military dictators who ruled Japan until the 19th century and under whom the emperor was a figurehead. [< Japanese < Chinese *chiang-chün* leader of an army]
sho·ji (shō/jē) n. A translucent paper screen forming a partition, door, etc., in a Japanese house. [< Japanese]
shone (shōn, shon) Past tense and past participle of SHINE.
shoo (shoo) interj. Begone! be off!: used in driving away fowls, etc. — v.t. 1. To drive away, as by crying "shoo." — v.i. 2. To cry "shoo." [Imit.]
shoo·fly (shoo/flī) n. pl. ·flies *U.S.* 1. An enclosed child's rocker with sides representing horses, swans, etc. 2. A kind of pie with a syrupy filling made with molasses and brown sugar.
shoo-in (shoo/in/) *U.S. Informal* n. A contestant, candidate, etc., who is certain to win.
shook (shook) Past tense of SHAKE.
shoot (shoot) v. shot, shoot·ing v.t. 1. To hit, wound, or kill with a missile discharged from a weapon. 2. To discharge (a missile) from a bow, rifle, etc. 3. To discharge (a weapon): often with *off*: to *shoot* a cannon. 4. To take the altitude of with a sextant, etc.: to *shoot* the sun. 5. To send forth as if from a weapon, as questions, glances, etc. 6. To pass over or through swiftly: to *shoot* rapids. 7. To go over (an area) in hunting game. 8. To emit, as rays of light. 9. To photograph; film. 10. To cause to stick out or protrude; extend. 11. To put forth in growth; send forth (buds, leaves, etc.). 12. To push into or out of the fastening, as the bolt of a door. 13. To propel, discharge, or dump, as down a chute or from a container. 14. To variegate, as with streaks of color: usually in the past participle: His paintings are *shot* with pink and brown. 15. In games: **a** To score (a goal, point, etc.) by kicking or otherwise forcing the ball, etc., to the objective. **b** To play (golf, craps, pool, etc.). **c**

To play (marbles). **d** To cast (the dice). — *v.i.* **16.** To discharge a missile from a bow, firearm, etc. **17.** To go off; discharge. **18.** To move swiftly; dart. **19.** To hunt game. **20.** To jut out; extend or project. **21.** To put forth buds, leaves, etc.; germinate; sprout. **22.** To take a photograph. **23.** To start the cameras, as in motion pictures. **24.** In games, to make a play by propelling the ball, puck, etc., in a certain manner. — **to shoot at** (or **for**) *Informal* To strive for; attempt to attain or obtain. — **to shoot down** To bring to earth by shooting. — **to shoot off one's mouth** *Slang* To talk too freely or too much. — *n.* **1.** A young branch or sucker of a plant; offshoot. **2.** A narrow passage in a stream; a rapid. **3.** An inclined passage down which anything may be shot; a chute. **4.** The act of shooting; a shot. **5.** A shooting match, hunting party, etc. **6.** *U.S. Informal* A rocket or missile launching. **7.** The thrust of an arch. **8.** Any new growth, as a new antler. **9.** Shooting distance; range. [OE *scēotan*] — **shoot·er** *n.*

shoot·ing (shōō′ting) *n.* The act of one who or that which shoots.

shooting gallery A place, usu. enclosed, where one can shoot at targets.

shooting star 1. A meteor. **2.** Any of certain small perennial herbs, having clusters of white, rose, or crimson flowers.

shop (shop) *n.* **1.** A place for the sale of goods at retail. Also **shoppe. 2.** A place for making or repairing any article, or the carrying on of any artisan craft: a blacksmith's *shop*. **3.** One's own craft or business as a subject of conversation: to talk *shop*. — *v.i.* **shopped, shop·ping** To visit shops or stores to purchase or look at goods. [OE *sceoppa* booth]

shop·girl (shop′gûrl′) *n.* A girl who works in a shop.

sho·phar (shō′fär) See SHOFAR.

shop·keep·er (shop′kē′pər) *n.* One who runs a shop or store; a tradesman.

shop·lift·er (shop′lif′tər) *n.* One who steals goods exposed for sale in a shop. — **shop′lift′ing** *n.*

shop·per (shop′ər) *n.* **1.** One who shops. **2.** An employee of a store who compares the merchandise of competitors as to quality, price, etc. — **shop′ping** *n.*

shop steward A union worker chosen by fellow workers to represent them to management in seeking redress of grievances, etc. Also **shop chairman.**

shop·talk (shop′tôk′) *n.* Conversation limited to one's job or profession.

shop·walk·er (shop′wô′kər) *n. Brit.* A floorwalker.

shop·worn (shop′wôrn′, -wōrn′) *adj.* **1.** Soiled or otherwise deteriorated from having been handled or on display in a shop. **2.** Worn out, as from overuse; stale.

shore¹ (shôr, shōr) *n.* **1.** The coast or land adjacent to an ocean, sea, lake, or large river. ◆ Collateral adjective: *littoral.* **2.** Land: to be on *shore.* — **in shore** Near or toward the shore. — *v.t.* **shored, shor·ing 1.** To set on shore. **2.** To surround as with a shore. [ME *schore*]

— **Syn.** (noun) **1.** *Shore, coast, beach,* and *bank* denote the land adjacent to a body of water. *Shore* is the general term; we speak of the *shore* of the sea, of a lake, or of a river. *Coast* is the ocean *shore,* especially along a great extent of land: the *coast* of Florida. A *beach* is a low, gently sloping expanse of sand or gravel; a *bank* is a more or less steep slope: the *banks* of the Red River.

shore² (shôr, shōr) *v.t.* **shored, shor·ing** To prop, as a wall, by a vertical or sloping timber: usu., with *up.* — *n.* A beam set endwise as a prop or temporary support against the side of a building, a ship in drydock, etc. [Cf. Du. *schoor* prop, ON *skortha* stay]

shore·less (shôr′lis, shōr′-) *adj.* **1.** Having no shore. **2.** Boundless.

shore·line (shôr′līn′, shōr′-) *n.* The contour of a shore.

shore patrol A detail of the U.S. Navy, Coast Guard, or Marine Corps assigned to police duties ashore.

shore·ward (shôr′wərd, shōr′-) *adj. & adv.* Toward the shore. Also **shore′wards** (-wərdz).

shor·ing (shôr′ing, shō′ring) *n.* **1.** The operation of propping, as with shores. **2.** Shores, collectively.

shorn (shôrn, shōrn) Alternative past participle of SHEAR.

short (shôrt) *adj.* **1.** Having little linear extension; not long; of no great distance. **2.** Being below the average stature; not tall. **3.** Having little extension in time; of limited duration; brief. **4.** Abrupt in manner or spirit; cross. **5.** Not reaching or attaining a requirement, result, or mark; inadequate: often with *of.* **6.** Having a scant or insufficient amount: followed by *on.* **7.** Having little scope or breadth: a *short* view. **8.** In commerce: **a** Not having in possession when selling, but having to procure in time to deliver as contracted. **b** Of or pertaining to stocks or commodities not in possession of the seller: *short* sales. **9.** Not comprehensive or retentive; in error: a *short* memory. **10.** Breaking easily; crisp. **11.** *Phonet.* Denoting the vowel sounds of *Dun, den, din, don, duck,* as contrasted with those of *Dane, dean, dine, dome, dune.* **12.** In English prosody, unaccented. **13.** Less than: with *of.* **14.** Concise; compressed. — *n.* **1.** Anything that is short. **2.** A deficiency, as in a payment.

3. A short syllable or vowel. **4.** A short contract or sale; one who has sold short; a bear. **5.** *pl.* Bran mixed with coarse meal or flour. **6.** *pl.* Trousers with legs extending part way to the knees. **7.** *pl.* A man's undergarment covering the loins and often a portion of the legs. **8.** In baseball slang, shortstop. **9.** *Electr.* A short circuit. **10.** A short subject. — **for short** For brevity: Edward was called Ed *for short.* — **in short** In a word; briefly. — *adv.* **1.** Abruptly: to stop *short.* **2.** Curtly; crossly. **3.** So as not to reach or extend to a certain point, condition, etc.: to fall *short.* **4.** Without having in actual possession that which is sold: to sell *short.* — *v.t. & v.i.* To short-circuit. [OE *sort*] — **short′ness** *n.*

short·age (shôr′tij) *n.* The amount by which anything is short; deficiency.

short·bread (shôrt′bred′) *n.* A rich, dry cake or cooky made with shortening.

short·cake (shôrt′kāk′) *n.* **1.** A cake made short and crisp with butter or other shortening. **2.** Cake or biscuit served with fruit: strawberry *shortcake.*

short·change (shôrt′chānj′) *v.t.* **·changed, ·chang·ing** *Informal* To give less change than is due to; also, to cheat or swindle. — **short′chang′er** *n.*

short-cir·cuit (shôrt′sûr′kit) *v.t. & v.i.* To make a short circuit (in).

short circuit *Electr.* **1.** A path of low resistance established between any two points in an electric circuit, thus shortening the distance traveled by the current. **2.** Any defect in an electric circuit or apparatus that may result in a dangerous leakage of current.

short·com·ing (shôrt′kum′ing) *n.* A failure or deficiency in character, action, etc.

short·cut (shôrt′kut′) *v.t. & v.i.* **-cut, -cut·ting** To take a short cut (in).

short cut 1. A byway or path between two places that is shorter than the regular way. **2.** Any means or method that saves distance or time.

short·en (shôr′tən) *v.t.* **1.** To make short or shorter; curtail. **2.** To reduce; diminish; lessen. **3.** To furl or reef (a sail) so that less canvas is exposed to the wind. **4.** To make brittle or crisp, as pastry, by adding shortening. — *v.i.* **5.** To become short or shorter. — **short′en·er** *n.*

short·en·ing (shôr′tən·ing) *n.* **1.** A fat, such as lard or butter, used to make pastry crisp. **2.** An abbreviation. **3.** The act of one who shortens.

short·hand (shôrt′hand′) *n.* Any system of rapid writing, usu. employing symbols other than letters, words, etc. — *adj.* **1.** Written in shorthand. **2.** Using shorthand.

short·hand·ed (shôrt′han′did) *adj.* Not having a sufficient or the usual number of assistants, workmen, etc.

short·horn (shôrt′hôrn′) *n.* One of a breed of cattle with short horns, originally from northern England.

short-lived (shôrt′līvd′, -livd′) *adj.* Living or lasting but a short time.

short·ly (shôrt′lē) *adv.* **1.** In a short time; quickly; soon. **2.** In few words; briefly. **3.** Curtly; abruptly.

short order Food requiring little time to prepare. — **in short order** Without any delay; quickly; abruptly. — **short·or·der** (shôrt′ôr′dər) *adj.*

short shrift 1. A short time in which to confess before dying. **2.** Little or no mercy or delay, as in dealing with a person. — **to make short shrift of** To dispose of quickly.

short·sight·ed (shôrt′sī′tid) *adj.* **1.** Unable to see clearly at a distance; myopic; near-sighted. **2.** Lacking foresight. **3.** Resulting from or characterized by lack of foresight. — **short′-sight′ed·ly** *adv.* — **short′sight′ed·ness** *n.*

short-spo·ken (shôrt′spō′kən) *adj.* Characterized by shortness or curtness of speech or manner; abrupt; gruff.

short·stop (shôrt′stop′) *n.* In baseball, an infielder stationed between second and third bases; also, his position.

short story A narrative prose story shorter than a novel or novelette, usu. under 10,000 words.

short subject A motion picture of relatively short duration, often displayed between showings of the feature attraction on a program: also called *short.*

short-tem·pered (shôrt′tem′pərd) *adj.* Easily angered.

short-term (shôrt′tûrm′) *adj.* In finance, due or payable within a short time, usu. one year: said of loans, etc.

short ton See under TON¹.

short waves Electromagnetic waves that are 60 meters or less in length. — **short-wave** (shôrt′wāv′) *adj.*

short-wind·ed (shôrt′win′did) *adj.* Affected with difficulty of breathing; becoming easily out of breath.

Sho·sho·ne (shō·shō′nē) *n.* **1.** One of a large tribe of North American Indians of northern Shoshonean stock of the Uto-Aztecan family, formerly occupying parts of Wyoming, Idaho, Nevada, and Utah. **2.** The Shoshonean language of this tribe. Also **Sho·sho′ni.**

Sho·sho·ne·an (shō·shō′nē·ən, shō′shə·nē′ən) *n.* The largest branch of the Uto-Aztecan family of North American Indians, including the Comanche, Ute, and Shoshone plateau tribes, and the Hopi Indians. — *adj.* Of or pertaining to this linguistic branch. Also **Sho·sho'ni·an.**

shot[1] (shot) *n.* *pl.* **shots;** *for def.* 1 **shot** 1. A solid missile, as a ball of iron, or a bullet or pellet of lead, to be discharged from a firearm; also, such pellets collectively. 2. The act of shooting; any stroke, hit, or blow. 3. One who shoots; a marksman. 4. The distance traversed or that can be traversed by a projectile; range. 5. *U.S. Informal* The firing of a rocket, etc., that is directed toward a specific target: a moon *shot.* 6. A blast, as in mining. 7. A stroke, esp. in certain games, as in billiards. 8. A conjecture; guess. 9. An attempted performance or try. 10. A metal sphere that a competitor puts, pushes, or slings, in a distance contest. 11. *Informal* A hypodermic injection of a drug. 12. *Informal* A drink of liquor. 13. A single action or scene recorded on motion-picture or television film or tape. 14. A photograph or a snapshot. 15. *Naut.* A unit of chain length: in the U.S., 15 fathoms; in Great Britain, 12½ fathoms. — *v.t.* **shot·ted, shot·ting** 1. To load or weight with shot. 2. To clean, as bottles, by partially filling with shot and shaking. [OE *scot*]

shot[2] (shot) Past tense and past participle of SHOOT. — *adj.* 1. Of changeable color, as when warp and weft are of different colors; also, streaked or mixed irregularly with other colors: a sky *shot* with pink. 2. *Informal* Completely done for; ruined; also, worn out; completely broken.

shot[3] (shot) *n. Brit. & Canadian* A reckoning or charge, or a share of such a reckoning; scot. [Var. of SCOT]

shot effect *Electronics* The background noise resembling the patter of small shot, developed in an electron tube by the fluctuating emission of electrons from the heated filament. Also **shot noise.**

shot·gun (shot'gun') *n.* A light, smoothbore gun, either single or double barreled, adapted for the discharge of shot at short range. — *adj.* 1. Having a clear passageway straight through: a *shotgun* house. 2. Coerced with, or as with, a shotgun: a *shotgun* wedding.

shot-put (shot'poot') *n.* 1. An athletic contest in which a shot is thrown, or put, for distance. 2. A single put of the shot. — **shot'-put'ter** *n.*

shot·ten (shot'n) *adj.* Having spawned: said of a fish, esp. a herring. [Obs. pp. of SHOOT]

should (shood) Past tense of SHALL, but rarely a true past, rather chiefly used as a modal auxiliary that, while conveying varying shades of present and future time, expresses a wide range of subtly discriminated feelings and attitudes: 1. Obligation or propriety in varying degrees, but milder than *ought:* You *should* write that letter; *Should* we tell him the truth about his condition? 2. Condition: a Simple contingency, but involving less probability than *shall* or the present with future sense: If I *should* go, he would go too. b Assumption: *Should (Assuming that)* the space platform prove practicable, as seems almost certain, a trip to the moon will be easy. 3. Surprise at an unexpected event in the past: When I reached the station, whom *should* I run into but the detective! 4. Expectation: I *should* be at home by noon. 5. *U.S. Informal* Irony, in positive statement with negative force: He'll be fined heavily, but with all his money he *should* (*need not*) worry! ◆ In American usage the first person may be followed by either *should* or *would* in such expressions as I *should/would* be glad to see you. [OE *scolde,* pt. of *sculan* to owe]

shoul·der (shōl'dər) *n.* 1. The part of the trunk between the neck and the free portion of the arm or forelimb; also, the joint connecting the arm or forelimb with the body. 2. Anything that supports, bears up, or projects like a shoulder. 3. The forequarter of various animals. 4. An enlargement, projection, or offset, as for keeping something in place, or preventing movement past the projection. 5. Either edge of a road or highway. 6. The angle of a bastion included between a face and the adjacent flank; also **shoulder angle.** — **shoulder to shoulder** 1. Side by side and close together. 2. With united effort; in cooperation. — **straight from the shoulder** *Informal* Candidly; straightforwardly. — **to cry on (one's) shoulder** To seek sympathy and understanding from (one). — **to give the cold shoulder to** 1. To treat with scorn, contempt, or coldness. 2. To ignore, shun, or avoid. — **to put (one's) shoulder to the wheel** To work with great vigor and purpose. — *v.t.* 1. To assume as something to be borne; sustain; bear. 2. To push with or as with the shoulder or shoulders. 3. To fashion with a shoulder or abutment. — *v.i.* 4. To push with the shoulder or shoulders. — **to shoulder arms** To rest a rifle against the shoulder, holding the butt with the hand. [OE *sculdor*]

shoulder blade *Anat.* The scapula.

shoulder patch A cloth insignia worn on the upper part of the sleeve of a uniform to indicate one's branch or unit.

shoulder strap 1. A strap worn on or over the shoulder

to support an article of dress. 2. A strap of cloth marked with insignia of rank, worn by army and navy officers.

should·n't (shood'nt) Should not.

shouldst (shoodst) *Archaic* second person singular of SHALL: used with *thou.* Also **should·est** (shood'ist).

shout (shout) *n.* A sudden and loud outcry, often expressing joy, anger, etc., or used as a call or command. — *v.t.* 1. To utter with a shout; say or express loudly. — *v.i.* 2. To utter a shout. [Cf. ON *skúta* a taunt] — **shout'er** *n.*

shove (shuv) *v.t. & v.i.* **shoved, shov·ing** 1. To push, as along a surface. 2. To press forcibly (against); jostle. — **to shove off** 1. To push along or away, as a boat. 2. *Informal* To depart. — *n.* The act of pushing or shoving. [OE *scúfan*] — **shov'er** *n.*

shov·el (shuv'əl) *n.* A somewhat flattened scoop with a handle, as for digging, lifting earth, rock, snow, etc.; also, any large, usu. toothed device for extensive, heavy digging. — *v.* **shov·eled** or **·elled, shov·el·ing** or **·el·ling** *v.t.* 1. To take up and move with a shovel. 2. To toss hastily or in large quantities as if with a shovel. 3. To clear with a shovel, as a path. — *v.i.* 4. To work with a shovel. [OE *scofl*]

shov·el·board (shuv'əl·bôrd', -bōrd') *n.* Shuffleboard.

shov·el·er (shuv'əl·ər, shuv'lər) *n.* 1. One who or that which shovels. 2 A large river duck with a spatulate bill: also called *spoonbill:* also **shov·el·bill** (shuv'əl·bil'). Also **shov'el·ler.**

show (shō) *v.* **showed, shown** or, sometimes **showed, show·ing** *v.t.* 1. To cause or permit to be seen; exhibit, display. 2. To give in a marked or open manner; bestow: to *show* favor. 3. To cause or allow (something) to be understood or known; reveal; tell. 4. To cause (someone) to understand or see; teach. 5. *Law* To advance an allegation; plead: to *show* cause. 6. To make evident by logical process; demonstrate. 7. To guide; introduce, as into a room or building: with *in* or *up;* to *show* a caller in. 8. To indicate: The thermometer *shows* the temperature. 9. To enter in a show or exhibition. — *v.i.* 10. To become visible or known. 11. To seem. 12. To make one's or its appearance; be present. 13. *Informal* To give a theatrical performance; appear. 14. In racing, to finish third: distinguished from *place, win.* Also, *Archaic, shew.* — **to show off** 1. To exhibit proudly or ostentatiously. 2. To make an ostentatious display of oneself, or of one's accomplishments. — **to show up** 1. To expose or be exposed, as faults. 2. To be evident or prominent. 3. To make an appearance. 4. *Informal* To be better than; outdo. — *n.* 1. An entertainment or performance: a Broadway *show.* 2. Anything shown or manifested. 3. An elaborate display: a *show* of wealth. 4. A pretense or semblance: a *show* of piety. 5. Any public exhibition, contest, etc.: an art *show.* 6. An appearance: a bad *show.* 7. An indication; promise: a *show* of ore. 8. The third position among the first three winners of a race. 9. The act of showing. — **show of hands** A display of raised hands indicating the vote of a group. [OE *scēawian*] — **show'er** *n.*

show bill A poster announcing a play or show.

show·boat (shō'bōt') *n.* A boat on which a traveling troupe gives a theatrical performance.

show·bread (shō'bred') See SHEWBREAD.

show business The entertainment arts, esp. the theater, motion pictures, television, etc., collectively considered as an industry or profession.

show·case (shō'kās') *n.* A glass case for exhibiting and protecting articles for sale.

show·down (shō'doun') *n.* 1. In poker, the play in which the hands are laid on the table face up. 2. Any action or disclosure that brings an issue to a head.

show·er (shou'ər) *n.* 1. A fall of rain, hail, or sleet, esp. heavy rain of short duration within a local area. 2. A copious fall, as of tears, sparks, etc. 3. A shower bath. 4. An abundance or profusion of something. 5. A variety of fireworks for simulating a shower of stars. 6. A party for the bestowal of gifts, as to a bride; also, the gifts. — *v.t.* 1. To sprinkle or wet with or as with showers. 2. To discharge in a shower; pour out. 3. To bestow with liberality. — *v.i.* 4. To fall as in a shower. 5. To take a shower bath. [OE *scúr*] — **show'er·y** *adj.*

shower bath A bath in which water is sprayed on the body from an overhead, perforated nozzle; also, the area or room in which this is done.

show·ing (shō'ing) *n.* 1. A show or display, as of a quality. 2. A presentation or statement, as of a subject.

show·man (shō'mən) *n. pl.* **·men** (-mən) 1. One who exhibits or owns a show. 2. One who is skilled in presenting something. — **show'man·ship** *n.*

Show Me State Nickname of Missouri.

shown (shōn) Past participle of SHOW.

show·off (shō'ôf', -of') *n. Informal* 1. The act of showing off; ostentatious display. 2. One who shows off.

show·piece (shō′pēs′) *n.* **1.** A prized object considered worthy of special exhibit. **2.** An object on display.

show place A place exhibited for its beauty, historic interest, etc.

show room A room in which things, as merchandise, are displayed for sale or advertising.

show·y (shō′ē) *adj.* **show·i·er, show·i·est** **1.** Making a great or brilliant display. **2.** Given to cheap display; gaudy; ostentatious. — **show′i·ly** *adv.* — **show′i·ness** *n.*

shrank (shrangk) Past tense of SHRINK.

shrap·nel (shrap′nəl) *n. pl.* **·nel** *Mil.* **1.** A field artillery projectile for use against personnel, containing a quantity of metal balls and a time fuse and base charge that expel the balls in mid-air. **2.** Shell fragments. [after Henry *Shrapnel*, 1761–1842, British artillery officer]

shred (shred) *n.* **1.** A small irregular strip torn or cut off. **2.** A bit; fragment; particle. — *v.t.* **shred·ded** or **shred, shred·ding** To tear or cut into shreds. [OE *scrēade*] — **shred′der** *n.*

shrew (shrōō) *n.* **1.** Any of numerous diminutive, chiefly insectivorous mammals having a long pointed snout and soft fur, as the **long-tailed shrew** of North America. Also **shrew′mouse** (-mous′). **2.** A woman of vexatious, scolding, or nagging disposition. [OE *scrēawa*] — **Syn.** **2.** scold, vixen, termagant, virago.

shrewd (shrōōd) *adj.* **1.** Sharp or wise; sagacious. **2.** Artful; sly. [ME < *shrew* malicious person] — **shrewd′ly** *adv.* — **shrewd′ness** *n.*

shrew·ish (shrōō′ish) *adj.* Like a shrew; ill-tempered; nagging. — **shrew′ish·ly** *adv.* — **shrew′ish·ness** *n.*

shriek (shrēk) *n.* A sharp shrill outcry or scream. — *v.i.* **1.** To utter a shriek. — *v.t.* **2.** To utter with or in a shriek. [ME] — **shriek′er** *n.*

shrift (shrift) *n.* **1.** The act of shriving. **2.** Confession or absolution, as to or from a priest. [OE *scrift*]

shrike (shrīk) *n.* Any of numerous predatory birds with hooked bill, short wings, and long tail. [OE *scrīc* thrush]

shrill (shril) *adj.* **1.** Having a high-pitched and piercing tone quality. **2.** Emitting a sharp, piercing sound. — *v.t.* **1.** To cause to utter a shrill sound. — *v.i.* **2.** To make a shrill sound. — *adv.* Shrilly. [< Gmc.] — **shrill′ly** *adv.* — **shrill′ness** *n.*

shrimp (shrimp) *n. pl.* **shrimp** or **shrimps** *for def. 1*, **shrimps** *for def. 2* **1.** Any of numerous small, long-tailed, principally marine animals, some species of which are used as food. **2.** *Slang* A small or unimportant person. [Akin to OE *scrimman* to shrink, G *schrimpfen*]

shrine (shrīn) *n.* **1.** A receptacle for sacred relics. **2.** A place, as a tomb or a chapel, sacred to some holy personage. **3.** A thing or spot made sacred by historic or other association. — *v.t.* **shrined, shrin·ing** *Rare & Poetic* To enshrine. [OE < L *scrinium* case, chest]

SHRIMP
a Cephalothorax.
b Abdomen. *c* Tail. *t* Telson.

shrink (shringk) *v.* **shrank** or **shrunk, shrunk** or, sometimes, **shrunk·en, shrink·ing** *v.i.* **1.** To draw together; contract, as from heat, cold, etc. **2.** To diminish. **3.** To draw back, as from disgust, horror, or timidity; recoil: with *from*. **4.** To flinch; wince. — *v.t.* **5.** To cause to shrink, contract, or draw together. — *n.* The act of shrinking. [OE *scrincan*] — **shrink′a·ble** *adj.* — **shrink′er** *n.*

shrink·age (shringk′ij) *n.* **1.** The act or fact of shrinking; contraction. **2.** The amount lost by such shrinking. **3.** Decrease in value; depreciation.

shrive (shrīv) *v.* **shrove** or **shrived, shriv·en** or **shrived, shriv·ing** *v.t.* **1.** To receive the confession of and give absolution to. **2.** To obtain absolution for (oneself) by confessing one's sins and doing penance. — *v.i.* **3.** To make confession. **4.** To hear confession. [OE *scrīfan*, ult. < L *scribere* to write, prescribe] — **shriv′er** *n.*

shriv·el (shriv′əl) *v.t. & v.i.* **shriv·eled** or **·elled, shriv·el·ing** or **·el·ling** **1.** To contract into wrinkles; shrink and wrinkle: often with *up*. **2.** To make or become impotent; wither. [Origin uncertain]

shriv·en (shriv′ən) Alternative past participle of SHRIVE.

Shrop·shire (shrop′shir, -shər) *n.* A breed of black-faced, hornless sheep, noted for heavy fleece and superior mutton, originating in Shropshire.

shroud¹ (shroud) *n.* **1.** A dress or garment for the dead. **2.** Something that envelops or conceals like a garment: the *shroud* of night. — *v.t.* **1.** To dress for the grave; clothe in a shroud. **2.** To envelop, as with a garment. [OE *scrūd* garment] — **shroud′less** *adj.*

shroud² (shroud) *n. Naut.* One of a set of ropes, often of wire, stretched from a masthead to the sides of a ship, serving as means of ascent and as a support for the masts. **2.** *Usu. pl.* A guy, as a support for a smokestack. **3.** One of the supporting ropes attached to the edges of a parachute canopy. [< SHROUD¹]

shrove (shrōv) Alternative past tense of SHRIVE.

Shrove·tide (shrōv′tīd′) *n.* The three days immediately preceding Ash Wednesday, **Shrove Sunday** (Quinquagesima Sunday), **Shrove Monday, Shrove Tuesday**, on which confession is made in preparation for Lent. [ME *schroftide*]

shrub (shrub) *n.* A woody perennial plant of low stature, characterized by persistent stems and branches springing from the base. [OE *scrybb* brushwood]

shrub·ber·y (shrub′ər-ē) *n. pl.* **·ber·ies** **1.** Shrubs collectively. **2.** A collection of shrubs, as in a garden.

shrub·by (shrub′ē) *adj.* **·bi·er, ·bi·est** **1.** Containing many shrubs; covered with shrubs. **2.** Of, pertaining to, or like a shrub. — **shrub′bi·ness** *n.*

shrug (shrug) *v.t. & v.i.* **shrugged, shrug·ging** To draw up (the shoulders), as in displeasure, doubt, surprise, etc. — *n.* **1.** The act of shrugging the shoulders. **2.** A very short sweater or jacket, open in front. [ME *schrugge*]

shrunk (shrungk) Alternative past tense and past participle of SHRINK.

shrunk·en (shrungk′ən) Alternative past participle of SHRINK. — *adj.* Contracted and atrophied.

shuck (shuk) *n.* **1.** A husk, shell, or pod. **2.** A shell of an oyster or a clam. — *v.t.* **1.** To remove the husk or shell from (corn, oysters, etc.). **2.** *Informal* To take off or cast off, as clothes. [Origin unknown] — **shuck′er** *n.*

shucks (shuks) *interj. U.S. Informal* A mild ejaculation expressing annoyance, disgust, etc.

shud·der (shud′ər) *v.i.* To tremble or shake, as from fright or cold; shiver; quake. — *n.* The act of shuddering; a convulsive shiver, as from horror or fear; tremor. [ME *shodder*]

shuf·fle (shuf′əl) *n.* **1.** A mixing or changing of the order of things, as of cards in a pack before each deal. **2.** A hesitating, evasive, or tricky action; artifice. **3.** A scraping of the feet, as in walking; a slow, dragging gait. **4.** A dance, or the step used in it, where the dancer pushes his foot along the floor at each step. — *v.* **·fled, ·fling** *v.t.* **1.** To shift this way and that; mix; confuse; disorder; esp. to change the order of by mixing, as cards in a pack. **2.** To move (the feet) along the ground or floor with a dragging gait. **3.** To change from one place to another. **4.** To make up or remove fraudulently or hastily; also, to put aside carelessly: with *up, off,* or *out.* — *v.i.* **5.** To change position. **6.** To resort to indirect methods. **7.** To dance the shuffle. **8.** To scrape the feet along. **9.** To scrape or struggle along awkwardly. [Prob. < LG *schuffeln* to move with dragging feet, mix cards, etc.] — **shuf′fler** *n.*

shuf·fle·board (shuf′əl-bôrd′, -bōrd′) *n.* **1.** A game in which wooden or composition disks are slid by means of a pronged cue along a smooth surface toward numbered spaces. **2.** The board or surface on which the game is played. Also called *shovelboard.*

shun (shun) *v.t.* **shunned, shun·ning** To keep clear of; avoid; refrain from. [OE *scunian*] — **shun′ner** *n.*

shunt (shunt) *n.* **1.** The act of shunting. **2.** A railroad switch. **3.** *Electr.* A conductor joining two points in a circuit and serving to divert part of the current to an auxiliary circuit: also called *by-pass.* — *v.t.* **1.** To turn aside. **2.** To switch, as a train or car, from one track to another. **3.** *Electr.* To distribute by means of shunts. **4.** To evade by turning away from; put off on someone else, as a task. — *v.i.* **5.** To move to one side. **6.** *Electr.* To be diverted by a shunt: said of current. **7.** To shift or transfer one's views or course. [ME *schunten*] — **shunt′er** *n.*

shunt-wound (shunt′wound′) *adj. Electr.* Designating a type of direct-current motor in which the armature circuit and field circuit are connected in parallel.

shush (shush) *v.t.* To quiet, as by making the sound "sh."

shut (shut) *v.* **shut, shut·ting** *v.t.* **1.** To bring into such position as to close an opening or aperture; close, as a door, lid, or valve. **2.** To close (an opening, aperture, etc.) so as to prevent ingress or egress. **3.** To close and fasten securely, as with a latch or lock. **4.** To forbid entrance into or exit from. **5.** To keep from entering or leaving: with *in, out, from*, etc. **6.** To close, fold, or bring together, as extended, expanded, or unfolded parts: to shut an umbrella. **7.** To hide from view; obscure. — *v.i.* **8.** To be or become closed or in a closed position. — **to shut down** **1.** To cease from operating, as a factory or mine; close up; stop work. **2.** To lower; come down close: the fog *shut down*. **3.** *Informal* To suppress: with *on*. — **to shut one's eyes to** To ignore. — **to shut out** In sports, to keep (an opponent) from scoring during the course of a game. — **to shut up** **1.** *Informal* To stop talking or cause to stop talking. **2.** To close all the entrances to, as a house. **3.** To imprison; confine. — *adj.* **1.** Made fast or closed. **2.** Not sonorous; dull: said of sound. — *n.* **1.** The act of shutting. **2.** The time or place of shutting or closing. [OE *scyttan*]

shut-down (shut′doun′) *n.* The closing of or ceasing of work in a mine, mill, factory, or other industrial plant.

shut·eye (shut′ī) *n. Slang* Sleep.

shut-in (shut′in′) *n.* An invalid who is unable to go out. — *adj.* Obliged to stay at home.

shut·off (shut′ôf′, -of′)   *n.*   *Mech.* A device for shutting something off.

shut·out (shut′out′)   *n.*   **1.** A shutting out; esp., a lockout. **2.** In sports, a game in which one side is prevented from scoring.

shut·ter (shut′ər)   *n.*   **1.** One who or that which shuts. **2.** That which shuts out or excludes; esp., a cover or screen, usu. hinged, for closing a window. **3.** *Photog.* Any of various mechanisms for momentarily admitting light through a camera lens to the film or plate. — *v.t.* To furnish, close, or divide off with shutters.

shut·tle (shut′l)   *n.*   **1.** A device used in weaving to carry the weft to and fro between the warp threads. **2.** A similar rotating or other device in a sewing machine or used in tatting. **3.** A transport system operating between two nearby points. — *v.t. & v.i.* **·tled, ·tling** To move to and fro, like a shuttle. [OE *scytel* missile]

shut·tle·cock (shut′l·kok′)   *n.*   A rounded piece of cork, with a crown of feathers, used in badminton and battledore; also, the game of battledore. — *v.t.* To send or knock back and forth like a shuttlecock.

shy[1] (shī)   *v.i.*   **shied, shy·ing 1.** To start suddenly aside, as in fear: said of a horse. **2.** To draw back, as from doubt or caution: with *off* or *away*. — *adj.* **shi·er** or **shy·er, shi·est** or **shy·est 1.** Easily frightened or startled; timorous. **2.** Bashful; coy. **3.** Circumspect, as from motives of caution; wary: with *of*. **4.** Not easy to perceive, seize, or secure; elusive. **5.** Not prolific: said of plants, trees, or, rarely, birds. **6.** *Informal* Having less money than is called for or required: to be *shy* a dollar. **7.** *Informal* Short; lacking: often with *on*. — *n.* A starting aside, as in fear. [OE *scēoh* timid] — **shy′ness** *n.*

shy[2] (shī)   *v.t. & v.i.*   **shied, shy·ing** To throw with a swift sidelong motion. — *n. pl.* **shies** A careless throw or fling. [Origin unknown]

shy·er (shī′ər)   *n.*   **1.** One who shies. **2.** See SHIER.

Shy·lock (shī′lok)   In Shakespeare's *Merchant of Venice*, a revengeful usurer. — *n. Slang* Any relentless creditor.

shy·ly (shī′lē)   *adv.*   In a shy manner: also spelled *shily*.

shy·ster (shīs′tər)   *n. Slang* Anyone, esp. a lawyer, who conducts his business in an unscrupulous or tricky manner. [Origin uncertain]

si[1] (sē)   *n. Music* Formerly ti[1].

si[2] (sē)   *adv.*   Italian, Portuguese, Spanish, and sometimes French, for "yes." [< L *sic* thus]

Si *Chem.* Silicon.

sialo-   *combining form*   Saliva; pertaining to saliva. Also, before vowels, **sial-.** [< Gk. *sialon* saliva]

Si·a·mese (sī′ə·mēz′, -mēs′)   *adj.*   **1.** Pertaining to Thailand (Siam), its people, or their language. **2.** Closely connected; twin. — *n.* **1.** *pl.* **·mese** A native of Siam, belonging to the Thai stock. **2.** The Thai language of the people of Siam, now officially called *Thai*.

Siamese cat   A breed of short-haired cat, typically fawn-colored, with dark-tipped ears, tail, feet, and face, and blue, gently slanting eyes.

Siamese twins   Any twins joined together at birth. [after the two Chinese males, Eng and Chang, 1811–74, born in Siam, whose bodies were joined by a fleshy band]

sib (sib)   *Rare n.*   **1.** A blood relation; kinsman. **2.** Kinsmen collectively; relatives. — *adj.* **1.** Related by blood; akin. **2.** Related; similar. Also **sibb.** [OE *sibb*]

sib·bo·leth (sib′ə·leth)   See SHIBBOLETH.

sib·i·lant (sib′ə·lənt)   *adj.*   **1.** Hissing. **2.** *Phonet.* Denoting those consonants produced by the fricative passage of breath through a very narrow orifice, in the front part of the mouth, as (s), (z), (sh), and (zh). — *n. Phonet.* A sibilant consonant. [< L *sibilans, -antis*, ppr. of *sibilare* to hiss] — **sib′i·lance, sib′i·lan·cy** *n.* **sib′i·lant·ly** *adv.*

sib·ling (sib′ling)   *n.*   A brother or sister. [OE, a relative]

sib·yl (sib′əl)   *n.*   **1.** In ancient Greece and Rome, any of several women who prophesied under the supposed inspiration of some deity. **2.** A fortuneteller; sorceress. [< F < L *sibylla* < Gk.] — **sib′yl·line** (-īn, -ēn, in), **si·byl·ic** (si·bil′ik), **si·byl′lic** *adj.*

sic[1] (sik)   *adv.*   So; thus: inserted in brackets after a quotation to indicate that it is accurately reproduced even though it may seem questionable or incorrect. [< L]

sic[2] (sik)   *v.t.*   **sicked, sick·ing** To sick. See SICK[2].

Si·cil·i·an (si·sil′ē·ən, -sil′yən)   *adj.*   Of or pertaining to Sicily or its people: also **Si·ca′ni·an** (-kə′nē·ən). — *n.* An inhabitant or native of Sicily.

sick[1] (sik)   *adj.*   **1.** Affected with disease; ill. **2.** Of or used by ill persons: often used in combination: *sickroom*. **3.** Affected by nausea; desiring to vomit. **4.** Expressive of or experiencing disgust or unpleasant emotion. **5.** Impaired or unsound from any cause. **6.** Mentally unsound. **7.** Pallid; wan. **8.** Depressed and longing: *sick* for the sea. **9.** Disinclined by reason of satiety or disgust; surfeited: with *of*. **10.** Sadistic or macabre; morbid: *sick* jokes. — *n.* Sick people collectively: with *the*. [OE *sēoc*]

— **Syn. 2, 3.** In U.S. usage, *sick* is a general term that may refer to a slight ailment or the most severe illness; it may also mean nauseated, the sense it always bears in British usage. *Ill* is a close synonym but may refer to a greater variety of symptoms. *Unwell* is similar to *ill*, but is sometimes felt to be affected. *Ailing* and *indisposed* refer to slight illnesses. *Ailing* implies a minor, but chronic, condition; *indisposed* suggests a trivial or temporary illness that prevents normal activity.

sick[2] (sik)   *v.t.*   **1.** To attack: used in the imperative as an order to a dog. **2.** To urge to attack: I'll *sick* the dog on you. Also spelled *sic*. [Var. of SEEK]

sick·bay (sik′bā′)   *n.*   That part of a ship or of a naval base set aside for the care of the sick.

sick·bed (sik′bed′)   *n.*   The bed a sick person lies on.

sick call   *Mil.* **1.** The daily period during which all non-hospitalized sick or injured personnel report to the medical officer. **2.** The call or signal that announces this.

sick·en (sik′ən)   *v.t. & v.i.*   To make or become sick or disgusted. — **sick′en·er** *n.*

sick·en·ing (sik′ən·ing)   *adj.*   Disgusting; revolting; nauseating. — **sick′en·ing·ly** *adv.*

sick headache   Headache with nausea, esp., migraine.

sick·ish (sik′ish)   *adj.*   **1.** Somewhat sick. **2.** Slightly nauseating. — **sick′ish·ly** *adv.* — **sick′ish·ness** *n.*

sick·le (sik′əl)   *n.*   An implement with a curved or crescent-shaped blade mounted on a short handle, used for cutting tall grass, grains, etc. — *v.t.* **·led, ·ling** To cut with a sickle, as grass. [OE < L *secare* to cut]

sickle cell   A crescent-shaped red blood corpuscle containing a genetically transmitted type of hemoglobin in which the oxygen concentration is below normal, and causing an anemia (**sickle cell anemia**) occurring chiefly among Negroes.

sick·ly (sik′lē)   *adj.*   **·li·er, ·li·est 1.** Habitually indisposed; ailing; unhealthy. **2.** Marked by the prevalence of sickness: a *sickly* summer. **3.** Nauseating; disgusting. **4.** Pertaining to or characteristic of sickness: a *sickly* appearance. **5.** Weak; faint. — *adv.* In a sick manner; poorly; also **sick′li·ly.** — *v.t.* **·lied, ·ly·ing** To make sickly, as in color or complexion. — **sick′li·ness** *n.*

sick·ness (sik′nis)   *n.*   **1.** The state of being sick. **2.** A particular form of disease. **3.** Nausea.

sick·room (sik′rōōm′, -rŏŏm′)   *n.*   A room in which a sick person lies or stays.

side (sīd)   *n.*   **1.** Any one of the bounding lines of a surface or of the bounding surfaces of a solid object; also, a particular line or surface other than top or bottom: the *side* of a mountain. **2.** A lateral part of a surface or object, usu. designated as *right* or *left*. **3.** Either of the two surfaces of a piece of paper, cloth, etc.; also, a specific surface of something: the rough *side* of sandpaper. **4.** One of two or more contrasted directions, parts, or places: the east *side* of town. **5.** A distinct party or body of competitors or partisans. **6.** An opinion, aspect, or point of view: my *side* of the question. **7.** Family connection, esp. by descent through one parent. **8.** The lateral half of a slaughtered animal. **9.** Either half of the human body. **10.** The space beside someone. **11.** In billiards, a lateral spin given to the cue ball. **12.** In sports, a team. — **side by side** Beside or next to each other. — **to take sides** To support a particular opinion, point of view, etc. — *v.i.* See PHASE. — *adj.* **1.** Situated at or on one side: a *side* window. **2.** Being or viewed as if from one side: a *side* glance. **3.** Directed towards one side: a *side* blow. **4.** Not primary; subordinate: a *side* issue. — *v.t.* **sid·ed, sid·ing** To provide with sides, as a building. — **to side with** To support or take the part of. [OE *side*]

side·arm (sīd′ärm′)   *adj.*   Executed with the hand level with the elbow, as a pitch. — *adv.* In a sidearm manner.

side arms   Weapons worn at the side, as pistols, etc.

side·band (sīd′band′)   *n. Telecom.* One of the two bands immediately adjacent to a carrier frequency, corresponding to the band-width of the modulating signal.

side·board (sīd′bôrd′, -bōrd′)   *n.*   A piece of dining-room furniture for holding tableware.

side·burns (sīd′bûrnz′)   *n.pl. Chiefly U.S.* The hair growing on the sides of a man's face below the hairline, esp. when worn as whiskers. [Alter. of BURNSIDES]

side·car (sīd′kär′)   *n.*   A small, one-wheeled passenger car attached to the side of a motorcycle.

sid·ed (sī′did)   *adj.*   Having or characterized by (a specified kind or number of) sides: used in combination: *one-sided*.

SIAMESE CAT
(About 11 inches high at shoulder)

side effect A secondary, usu. injurious effect, as of a drug.

side·kick (sīd′kik′) *n.* *U.S. Slang* A close friend; buddy.

side·light (sīd′līt′) *n.* **1.** A side window. **2.** A light coming from the side. **3.** Incidental facts or information.

side·line (sīd′līn′) *n.* **1.** An auxiliary line of goods sold by a store or a commercial traveler. **2.** Any additional or secondary work differing from one's main job. **3.** In sports: **a** One of the lines bounding the two sides of a football field, tennis court, etc. **b** *Often pl.* The area just outside these lines. Also **side line.** —*v.t.* **·lined, ·lin·ing** To prevent or remove (someone) from active participation.

side·long (sīd′lông′, -long′) *adj.* **1.** Inclining, tending or directed to one side. **2.** Indirect; sly. —*adv.* In a lateral or oblique direction.

side·piece (sīd′pēs′) *n.* A piece at or forming a side.

si·de·re·al (sī·dir′ē·əl) *adj.* **1.** Of or pertaining to stars. **2.** Measured by means of the stars: *sidereal* year. [< L < *sidus* star] —**si·de′re·al·ly** *adv.*

sidereal year The period of 365 days, 6 hours, 9 minutes, and 9 seconds in which the sun apparently returns to the same position among the stars.

sidero-[1] *combining form* Iron; of or pertaining to iron. Also, before vowels, **sider-.** [< Gk. *sidēros* iron]

sidero-[2] *combining form* Star; stellar. Also, before vowels, **sider-.** [< L *sidus* star]

sid·er·o·lite (sid′ər·ə·līt′) *n.* A meteorite consisting of iron containing embedded grains of certain minerals.

side·sad·dle (sīd′sad′l) *n.* A woman's saddle having one stirrup and designed so that both legs of the rider are on the same side of the horse. —*adv.* On or as on a sidesaddle.

side show **1.** A small show incidental to but connected with a larger or more important one: a circus *side show.* **2.** Any subordinate issue or attraction.

side·slip (sīd′slip′) *v.i.* **·slipped, ·slip·ping** To slip or skid sideways. —*n.* **1.** A lateral skid. **2.** *Aeron.* A downward, sideways slipping of an airplane along the lateral axis.

side·split·ting (sīd′split′ing) *adj.* **1.** Hearty and uproarious, as laughter. **2.** Causing great laughter or hilarity.

side·step (sīd′step′) *v.* **·stepped, ·step·ping** *v.i.* **1.** To step to one side. **2.** To avoid responsibility, conflict, etc. —*v.t.* **3.** To avoid, as an issue, or postpone, as a decision; evade.

side step **1.** A step to one side, as of a pugilist. **2.** *Usu. pl.* One of a series of steps at the side of a building, etc.

side·swipe (sīd′swīp′) *n.* A sweeping blow along the side. —*v.t. & v.i.* **·swiped, ·swip·ing** To strike or collide with such a blow.

side·track (sīd′trak′) *v.t. & v.i.* **1.** To move to a siding, as a railroad train. **2.** To divert or distract from the main issue or subject. —*n.* A railroad siding; also, a branch line.

side·walk (sīd′wôk′) *n.* *U.S.* A path or pavement at the side of the street, for the use of pedestrians.

side·ward (sīd′wərd) *adj.* Directed or moving toward or from the side; lateral. —*adv.* Toward or from the side; laterally: also **side′wards** (-wərdz).

side·ways (sīd′wāz′) *adv.* **1.** From the side. **2.** So as to incline toward the side, or with the side forward: Hold it *sideways.* **3.** Toward one side; obliquely. —*adj.* Moving to or from one side. Also **side′way′, side′wise′** (-wīz′).

side wheel A wheel at the side; esp., one of two paddle wheels on either side of a steamboat. —**side·wheel** (sīd′-hwēl′) *adj.* —**side′-wheel′er** *n.*

sid·ing (sī′ding) *n.* **1.** A railway track by the side of the main track. **2.** The boarding that covers the side of a wooden house, etc.

si·dle (sīd′l) *v.i.* **·dled, ·dling** To move sideways, esp. in a cautious or stealthy manner. —*n.* A sideways movement. [Back formation < obs. *sidling* sidelong] —**si′dler** *n.*

siege (sēj) *n.* **1.** The act of surrounding any fortified area with the intention of capturing it. **2.** A steady attempt to win something. **3.** The time during which one undergoes a protracted illness or difficulty. —**to lay siege to** To attempt to capture or gain; besiege. —*v.t.* **sieged, sieg·ing** To lay siege to. [< OF < L *sedere* to sit]

Sieg·fried (sēg′frēd, *Ger.* zēkh′frēt) The hero of the *Nibelungenlied* and several other Germanic legends.

si·en·na (sē·en′ə) *n.* **1.** A brownish yellow clay containing oxides of iron and manganese, used as a pigment. **2.** The brownish yellow color of this pigment. [< Ital. (*terra di*) *Siena* (earth of) Siena]

si·er·ra (sē·er′ə) *n.* A mountain range or chain, esp. one having a jagged outline. [< Sp. < L *serra* saw]

si·es·ta (sē·es′tə) *n.* A midday or afternoon nap. [< Sp. < L *sexta* (*hora*) sixth (hour), noon]

sieve (siv) *n.* A utensil for straining or sifting, consisting of a frame with a bottom of wire mesh, etc. —*v.t. & v.i.* **sieved, siev·ing** To pass through a sieve. [OE *sife* sieve]

sift (sift) *v.t.* **1.** To pass through a sieve in order to separate the fine parts from the coarse. **2.** To scatter as by a sieve. **3.** To examine carefully. **4.** To separate; distinguish: to *sift* fact from fiction. —*v.i.* **5.** To use a sieve. **6.** To fall through or as through a sieve. [OE *siftan*] —**sift′er** *n.*

sigh (sī) *v.i.* **1.** To draw in and exhale a deep, audible breath, as in expressing sorrow, weariness, etc. **2.** To make a sound suggestive of a sigh, as the wind. **3.** To yearn; long. —*v.t.* **4.** To express with a sigh. —*n.* The act or sound of sighing. [Back formation < ME *sighte* < OE *sīcan* to sigh]

sight (sīt) *n.* **1.** The act or fact of seeing. **2.** That which is seen; a view. **3.** *pl.* Things worth seeing: the *sights* of the town. **4.** The faculty of seeing; vision. **5.** The range or scope of vision. **6.** A device to assist aim, as on a gun, etc. **7.** An aim or observation taken with a telescope or other sighting instrument. **8.** *Informal* Something unusual or ugly to look at: He was a *sight.* **9.** *Dial.* A great quantity or number: a *sight* of people. —**at** (or **on**) **sight** As soon as seen. —**not by a long sight** **1.** Never; not at all. **2.** Not nearly. —**sight unseen** Without ever having seen the object in question. —*v.t.* **1.** To perceive with the eyes; observe. **2.** To take a sight of. **3.** To furnish with sights, or adjust the sights of, as a gun. —*v.i.* **4.** To take aim. **5.** To make an observation or sight. [OE *gesiht*]

sight draft A draft or bill payable on presentation.

sight·less (sīt′lis) *adj.* **1.** Lacking sight; blind. **2.** Invisible. —**sight′less·ly** *adv.* —**sight′less·ness** *n.*

sight·ly (sīt′lē) *adj.* **·li·er, ·li·est** **1.** Pleasant to the view; comely. **2.** Affording a fine view. —**sight′li·ness** *n.*

sight·see·ing (sīt′sē′ing) *n.* The visiting of places of interest. —**sight·seer** (sīt′sē′ər) *n.*

sig·ma (sig′mə) *n.* The 18th letter in the Greek alphabet, written Σ (capital), σ (small initial or medial), or ς (small final), and corresponding to English *s* in *so.* See ALPHABET.

sig·moid (sig′moid) *adj.* Shaped like the Greek capital letter sigma (Σ), or like the letter S. Also **sig·moi·dal** (sig·moid′l). [< Gk. *sigmoeidēs*]

sign (sīn) *n.* **1.** A motion or action indicating a thought, desire, command, etc. **2.** A board, placard, etc., generally bearing an inscription conveying information of some kind: a street *sign*; an advertising *sign.* **3.** Any arbitrary mark, symbol, or token used to indicate a word, etc., or having its own specific meaning: a *sign* of mourning. **4.** Any indication, trace, or evidence: *signs* of poverty. **5.** A vestige; trace. **6.** Any omen or miraculous occurrence. **7.** One of the twelve equal divisions of the zodiac. —*v.t.* **1.** To write one's signature or initials on. **2.** *Law* To acknowledge an instrument by affixing a mark or seal to. **3.** To mark or consecrate with a sign, esp. with a cross. **4.** To engage by obtaining the signature of a contract; also, to hire (oneself) out for work: often with *on.* **5.** To dispose of or transfer title to by signature: with *off, over,* or *away.* **6.** To express or indicate with a sign. —*v.i.* **7.** To make signs or signals. **8.** To write one's signature or initials. —**to sign off** *Telecom.* To announce the close of a program from a broadcasting station and stop transmission. —**to sign up** To enlist, as in a military service. [< OF < L *signum*] —**sign′er** *n.*

sig·nal (sig′nəl) *n.* **1.** A sign or means of communication agreed upon or understood, and used to convey information, a command, etc. **2.** *Telecom.* An electromagnetic impulse that transmits information, whether direct or in code. **3.** Anything that incites to action or movement. **4.** In some card games, a lead or play that conveys certain information to one's partner. —*adj.* **1.** Notable; conspicuous. **2.** Used to signal. —*v.* **sig·naled** or **·nalled, sig·nal·ing** or **·nal·ling** *v.t.* **1.** To make signals to. **2.** To communicate by signals. —*v.i.* **3.** To make a signal or signals. [< F < L *signum* sign] —**sig′nal·er** or **sig′nal·ler** *n.*

Signal Corps A branch of the U.S. Army responsible for communications equipment and systems, photography, electronic reconnaissance devices, and related matters.

sig·nal·ize (sig′nəl·īz) *v.t.* **·ized, ·iz·ing** **1.** To render noteworthy. **2.** To point out with care.

sig·nal·ly (sig′nəl·ē) *adv.* In a signal manner; eminently.

sig·nal·man (sig′nəl·mən) *n.* *pl.* **·men** (-mən) One who makes or interprets signals, esp. railroad signals.

sig·na·to·ry (sig′nə·tôr′ē, -tō′rē) *adj.* Bound by the terms of a signed document; having signed: *signatory* powers. —*n.* One who has signed or is bound by a document; esp., a nation so bound. [< L < *signum* sign]

sig·na·ture (sig′nə·chər) *n.* **1.** The name of a person written by himself; also, the act of signing one's name. **2.** A distinctive mark, characteristic, etc. **3.** *Printing* **a** A distinguishing mark, letter, or number on the first page of each form or sheet of a book, as a guide to the binder. **b** The form or sheet on which this mark is placed. **c** A large printed sheet that, when folded, forms four, or a multiple of four, pages of a book. **4.** *Music* A symbol or group of symbols at the beginning of a staff, indicating meter or key. **5.** *Telecom.* The musical number or sound effect that introduces or closes a program. [< F < Med.L < L *signum* sign]

sign·board (sīn′bôrd′, -bōrd′) *n.* A board on which a sign, direction, or advertisement is displayed.

sig·net (sig′nit) *n.* **1.** A seal, esp. one used to authenticate documents, etc. **2.** An impression made by or as by a seal. [< F *signe* sign < L *signum*]

signet ring A seal ring.
sig·nif·i·cance (sig-nif′ə-kəns) *n.* **1.** The character or state of being significant. **2.** Meaning. **3.** Importance; consequence. Also **sig·nif′i·can·cy.**
sig·nif·i·cant (sig-nif′ə-kənt) *adj.* **1.** Having or expressing a meaning; bearing or embodying a meaning. **2.** Conveying or having some covert meaning: a *significant* look. **3.** Important; weighty; momentous. [< L < *signum* sign + *facere* to do, make] — **sig·nif′i·cant·ly** *adv.*
sig·ni·fi·ca·tion (sig′nə-fə-kā′shən) *n.* **1.** Meaning; sense; import. **2.** The act of signifying; communication. — **sig·nif·i·ca·tive** (sig-nif′ə-kā′tiv, -kə-tiv) *adj.*
sig·ni·fy (sig′nə-fī) *v.* **·fied, ·fy·ing** *v.t.* **1.** To make known by signs or words; express. **2.** To betoken in any way; import. **3.** To amount to; mean. — *v.i.* **4.** To have some meaning or importance; matter. — **sig′ni·fi′er** *n.*
sign language A system of communication by means of signs, largely manual.
si·gnor (sēn′yôr) *n.* An anglicized form of the Italian title *signore.* Also **si·gnor.**
si·gno·ra (sē-nyō′rä) *n. pl.* **·re** (-rā) *Italian* The Italian title of courtesy for a married woman, equivalent to *Mrs.*
si·gno·re (sē-nyō′rē) *n. pl.* **·ri** (-rē) The Italian title of courtesy for a man, equivalent to *Mr., sir.*
si·gno·ri·na (sē′nyō-rē′nä) *n. pl.* **·ne** (-nā) The Italian title of courtesy for an unmarried woman, equivalent to *Miss.*
sign·post (sīn′pōst′) *n.* **1.** A post bearing a sign. **2.** Any sign, clue, or indication.
Sig·urd (sig′oord) In German mythology, a hero who corresponds to Siegfried, the hero of the *Nibelungenlied.*
Sikh (sēk) *n.* One of a religious and military sect founded in India early in the 16th century. — *adj.* Of or pertaining to the Sikhs. [< Hind., lit., disciple] — **Sikh′ism** *n.*
si·lage (sī′lij) *n.* Ensilage. [< ENSILAGE]
si·lence (sī′ləns) *n.* **1.** The state or quality of being silent. **2.** Absence of sound or noise; stillness. **3.** A failure to mention or take note of something. — *v.t.* **·lenced, ·lenc·ing 1.** To make silent. **2.** To stop the motion or activity of. **3.** To force (guns, etc.) to cease firing, as by bombing, etc. — *interj.* Be silent. [< F < L *silere* to be silent]
si·lenc·er (sī′lən-sər) *n.* **1.** A tubular device attached to the muzzle of a firearm to reduce the sound of the report. **2.** *Chiefly Brit.* A muffler (def. 1). **3.** One who or that which silences.
si·lent (sī′lənt) *adj.* **1.** Not making any sound or noise; noiseless; still; mute. **2.** Not given to speech; taciturn. **3.** Making no mention or allusion. **4.** Unspoken or unuttered: *silent* grief. **5.** Free from activity, motion, or disturbance; calm; quiet: a *silent* retreat. [< L *silere* to be silent] — **si′lent·ly** *adv.* — **si′lent·ness** *n.*
silent butler A small receptacle with a handle and hinged lid, used for collecting refuse from ashtrays, etc.
silent partner One who has invested money in a business but does not participate in its management or its affairs.
si·lex (sī′leks) *n.* **1.** Silica. **2.** Glass that is resistant to heat. [< L, flint]
Si·lex (sī′leks) *n.* A coffee maker: a trade name. Also **si′lex.**
sil·hou·ette (sil′ōō-et′) *n.* **1.** A profile drawing or portrait having its outline filled in with uniform color, commonly black, and often cut out of paper, etc. **2.** The figure cast by a shadow; also, the outline of a solid figure. — *v.t.* **·et·ted, ·et·ting** To cause to appear in silhouette; outline; make a silhouette profile of. [after Étienne de *Silhouette*, 1709-67, French minister of finance]
silic- Var. of SILICO-.
sil·i·ca (sil′i-kə) *n.* A white or colorless, very hard, crystalline silicon dioxide, SiO₂, the principal constituent of quartz and sand: also called *silex*. [< NL < L *silex, silicis* flint]
sil·i·cate (sil′i-kit) *n. Chem.* A salt or ester of silicic acid.
si·li·ceous (si-lish′əs) *adj.* **1.** Pertaining to, resembling, or containing silica. **2.** Growing or living on soil rich in silica. Also **si·li′cious.** [< L < *silex, silicis* flint]
si·lic·ic (si-lis′ik) *adj.* Of, pertaining to, or derived from silica or silicon. [< SILIC- + -IC]
silicic acid *Chem.* Any of several gelatinous and easily decomposed compounds of silica and water; esp., H₄SiO₄, associated in the formation of many metallic silicates.
silico- *combining form* Silicon; of, related to, or containing silicon. Also, before vowels, *silic-.* [< L *silex, silicis* flint]
sil·i·con (sil′ə-kən, -kon) *n.* A widely distributed nonmetallic element (symbol Si) prepared as a dull brown amorphous powder, as shining metallic scales, or as a steel-gray crystalline mass. See ELEMENT. [< L *silex, silicis* flint]
sil·i·cone (sil′ə-kōn) *n. Chem.* Any of various compounds containing a silicon-carbon bond, used as lubricants, insulating resins, waterproofing materials, etc. [< SILICON]
sil·i·co·sis (sil′ə-kō′sis) *n. Pathol.* A pulmonary disease caused by the inhalation of finely powdered silica or quartz.

silk (silk) *n.* **1.** The creamy-white or yellowish, very fine natural fiber produced by the larvae of silkworms. **2.** A similar filamentous material spun by other insects. **3.** Cloth, thread, or garments made of silk. **4.** Anything resembling silk. — **to hit the silk** *Slang* To descend from an aircraft by parachute. — *adj.* **1.** Consisting of silk. **2.** Resembling silk. **3.** Of or pertaining to silk. — *v.t.* **1.** To clothe or cover with silk. — *v.i.* **2.** To produce the portion of the flower called silk: said of corn. [OE < L *sericus* silken]
silk cotton The silky seed covering of various tropical American trees; esp., kapok fiber.
silk·en (sil′kən) *adj.* **1.** Made of silk. **2.** Like silk; glossy; delicate; smooth. **3.** Dressed in silk. **4.** Luxurious.
silk hat A high cylindrical hat covered with fine silk plush, worn by men in dress clothes.
silk-screen process (silk′skrēn′) A stencil process that prints designs by forcing ink through the open meshes of a silk screen.
silk-stock·ing (silk′stok′ing) *adj.* **1.** Wearing silk stockings. **2.** Wealthy; luxurious. — *n.* One who wears silk stockings; a member of the wealthy class.
silk·worm (silk′wûrm′) *n.* The caterpillar of certain moths that spin a dense silken cocoon; esp., the **common silkworm,** yielding commercial silk.
silk·y (sil′kē) *adj.* **silk·i·er, silk·i·est 1.** Made of or resembling silk; soft; lustrous. **2.** Long and fine, as hairs, or covered with such hairs, as leaves. **3.** Gentle or insinuating in manner. — **silk′i·ly** *adv.* — **silk′i·ness** *n.*
sill (sil) *n.* **1.** *Archit.* A horizontal, lower member of something, as the bottom of a door or window casing. **2.** A timber in the frame of the floor of a railroad car: end *sill.* [OE *syll*]
sil·ly (sil′ē) *adj.* **·li·er, ·li·est 1.** Destitute of ordinary good sense; foolish. **2.** Stupid; absurd. **3.** *Informal* Stunned, as by a blow. — *n. pl.* **·lies** *Informal* A silly person. [OE *sæsig* happy] — **sil′li·ly** *adv.* — **sil′li·ness** *n.*
si·lo (sī′lō) *n. pl.* **·los** A pit or tower in which fodder, grain, or other food is stored green to be fermented and used as feed for cattle, etc. — *v.t.* **·loed, ·lo·ing** To put or preserve in a silo; turn into ensilage. [< Sp. < L < Gk. *siros* pit for corn]
silt (silt) *n.* An earthy sediment consisting of fine particles of rock and soil suspended in and carried by water. — *v.i.* **1.** To become filled or choked with silt: usu. with *up.* **2.** To ooze; drift. — *v.t.* **3.** To fill or choke with silt or mud: usually with *up.* [ME *cylte*] — **silt′y** *adj.*
Si·lu·ri·an (si-loor′ē-ən, sī-) *adj. Geol.* Of the period or rock system of the Paleozoic era. See chart for GEOLOGY. — *n. Geol.* The Silurian period or system.
sil·ver (sil′ver) *n.* **1.** A white, ductile, and very malleable metallic element (symbol Ag) of high electric conductivity, found native as well as in combination, and used in medicine, industry, and the arts: also called *argentum.* See ELEMENT. **2.** Silver regarded as a commodity or as a standard of currency. **3.** Silver coin; cash or change; money in general. **4.** Articles for domestic use made of silver or silver plate; silverware. **5.** A lustrous, pale gray color resembling that of silver. — *adj.* **1.** Made of or coated with silver. **2.** Of, containing, or producing silver. **3.** Having a silvery lustre. **4.** Having the soft, clear tones of a silver bell. **5.** Persuasive; eloquent. **6.** White or hoary, as the hair. **7.** Favoring the use of silver as a monetary standard. — *v.t.* **1.** To coat or plate with silver or with a silver-like substance. **2.** To make silvery. — *v.i.* **3.** To become silver or white. [OE *seolfor*] — **sil′ver·er** *n.*
silver anniversary A 25th anniversary.
silver certificate *U.S.* Paper currency representing one dollar in silver bullion on deposit in the U.S. treasury, and valid as full legal tender.
sil·ver·fish (sil′vər-fish′) *n. pl.* **·fish** or **·fish·es 1.** A silvery-white variety of the goldfish. **2.** Any of numerous flat-bodied, wingless insects that damage books, papers, etc.
silver fox 1. A color phase of the red fox of North America, having fur that is interspersed with white-tipped hairs. **2.** The fur of this animal.
silver gray A light, slightly bluish gray, the color of silver.
silver nitrate *Chem.* A crystalline, poisonous compound, AgNO₃, obtained by treating silver with nitric acid, widely used in industry, photography, and medicine.
silver plate Articles, as table utensils, made of silver or metal plated with silver.
sil·ver·smith (sil′vər-smith′) *n.* A worker in silver; a maker of silverware.
silver standard A monetary standard or system based on silver.

SILO
(Showing interior and pit)

Silver Star A U.S. military decoration, first issued in 1932, awarded for gallantry in action. See DECORATION.
Silver State Nickname of Nevada.
sil·ver·tongued (sil′vər·tungd′) *adj.* Eloquent.
sil·ver·ware (sil′vər·wâr′) *n.* Articles, esp., for table use, made of silver.
sil·ver·y (sil′vər·ē) *adj.* **1.** Containing or adorned with silver. **2.** Resembling silver, as in luster or hue. **3.** Soft and clear in sound. **— sil′ver·i·ness** *n.*
s'il vous plaît (sēl vōō plĕ′) *French* If you please; please.
Sim·chath To·rah (sim′khäs tō′rə) A Jewish holiday; literally, the rejoicing over the Law. Also **Sim′hath To′rah.**
Sim·e·on (sim′ē·ən) In the Old Testament, a son of Jacob and Leah. *Gen.* xxix 33. **—** *n.* The tribe of Israel descended from him.
sim·i·an (sim′ē·ən) *adj.* Pertaining to, resembling, or characteristic of apes and monkeys. **—** *n.* An ape or monkey. [< L *simia* ape]
sim·i·lar (sim′ə·lər) *adj.* **1.** Bearing resemblance to one another or to something else; like, but not completely identical. **2.** Of like characteristics, nature, or degree; of the same scope, order, or purpose. **3.** *Geom.* Shaped alike, as figures that may become congruent by the alteration of linear dimensions, the angles remaining unchanged. [< F < L *similis* like] **— sim′i·lar·ly** adv.
sim·i·lar·i·ty (sim′ə·lar′ə·tē) *n.* *pl.* **·ties 1.** The quality or state or being similar. **2.** The point in which the objects compared are similar. **3.** *pl.* Things that coincide with or resemble each other. **— Syn.** See ANALOGY.
sim·i·le (sim′ə·lē) *n.* A figure of speech expressing comparison or likeness by the use of such terms as *like, as, so,* etc.: distinguished from *metaphor.* [< L, neut. of *similis* similar] **— Syn.** *Simile* is a literary device to conjure up a vivid picture; "an Alpine peak like a frosted cake" is a *simile.* A *metaphor* omits "like" or "as", the words of comparison; "the silver pepper of the stars" is a *metaphor. A comparison* brings together things of the same kind or class.
si·mil·i·tude (si·mil′ə·tōōd, -tyōōd) *n.* **1.** Similarity. **2.** A counterpart or likeness. [< OF < L < *similis* like]
sim·mer (sim′ər) *v.i.* **1.** To boil gently or with a subdued sound; be or stay at or just below the boiling point. **2.** To be on the point of breaking forth, as with rage. **—** *v.t.* **3.** To keep at or just below the boiling point. **— to simmer down 1.** To reduce liquid content by boiling gently. **2.** *Informal* To subside from a state of anger or excitement. **—** *n.* The state or process of simmering. [< obs. *simper* to boil]
Si·mon Le·gree (sī′mən li·grē′) **1.** A cruel overseer of slaves in Harriet Beecher Stowe's *Uncle Tom's Cabin.* **2.** Any brutal master.
Simon Peter See PETER.
si·mon-pure (sī′mən-pyŏŏr′) *adj.* Real; genuine; authentic. [after *Simon Pure,* a character in the comedy *A Bold Stroke for a Wife* (1718), who is impersonated by a rival]
si·mo·ny (sī′mə·nē, sim′ə-) *n.* Traffic in sacred things; the purchase or sale of ecclesiastical preferment. [< Med.L < *Simon (Magus),* who offered Peter money for the gift of the Holy Spirit] **— si′mon·ist** *n.*
si·moom (si·mōōm′, sī-) *n. Meteorol.* A hot dry wind of the desert in northern Africa, Arabia, etc. Also **si·moon′** (-mōōn′). [< Arabic < *samma* poison]
sim·per (sim′pər) *v.i.* **1.** To smile in a silly, self-conscious manner; smirk. **—** *v.t.* **2.** To say with a simper. **—** *n.* A silly, self-conscious smile. [< Scand. Cf. Sw. and Norw. *semper* coy.] **— sim′per·er** *n.* **— sim′per·ing·ly** *adv.*
sim·ple (sim′pəl) *adj.* **·pler, ·plest 1.** Consisting of one thing; single; uncombined. **2.** Not complex or complicated; easy. **3.** Without embellishment; plain; unadorned. **4.** Free from affectation; sincere; artless. **5.** Of humble rank; lowly. **6.** Silly; feeble-minded. **7.** Insignificant; trifling. **8.** Lacking luxury; frugal. **9.** Having nothing added; mere. **10.** *Chem.* Of one element; also, unmixed. **11.** *Bot.* Not divided; entire. **—** *n.* **1.** That which is simple; an uncomplex, or natural thing. **2.** A simpleton. [< OF < L *simplex*]
simple fraction *Math.* A fraction in which both numerator and denominator are integers.
simple interest Interest computed on the original principal alone.
simple machine Any of certain elementary mechanical contrivances, as the lever, the wedge, the inclined plane, the screw, the wheel and axle, and the pulley.
sim·ple-mind·ed (sim′pəl·mīn′did) *adj.* **1.** Artless or unsophisticated. **2.** Mentally defective. **3.** Stupid; foolish. **— sim′ple-mind′ed·ly** *adv.* **— sim′ple-mind′ed·ness** *n.*
simple sentence See under SENTENCE.
sim·ple·ton (sim′pəl·tən) *n.* A weak-minded or silly person.
simplici- *combining form* Simple. Also, before vowels, **sim-plic-.** [< L *simpler, simplicis* simple]
sim·plic·i·ty (sim·plis′ə·tē) *n.* *pl.* **·ties 1.** The state of being simple; freedom from admixture, ostentation, subtlety, difficulty, etc. **2.** Sincerity; unaffectedness. **3.** Lack of intelligence or good sense. [< OF < L *simplicitas*]

sim·pli·fy (sim′plə·fī) *v.t.* **·fied, ·fy·ing** To make more simple or less complex. [< F < Med.L < L *simplex* simple + *facere* to make] **— sim′pli·fi·ca′tion** *n.* **— sim′pli·fi′er** *n.*
sim·plis·tic (sim-plis′tik) *adj.* Tending to ignore complications or details. **— sim′plism** *n.* **— sim-plis′ti·cal·ly** *adv.*
sim·ply (sim′plē) *adv.* **1.** In a simple manner; intelligibly. **2.** Without ostentation or extravagance. **3.** Without subtlety or affectation; unassumingly. **4.** Merely. **5.** Without sense or discretion; foolishly. **6.** Really; absolutely: *simply* charming: sometimes used ironically.
sim·u·la·crum (sim′yə·lā′krəm) *n.* *pl.* **·cra** (-krə) **1.** An image. **2.** An imaginary, visionary, or shadowy semblance. **3.** A sham. [See SIMULATE.]
sim·u·late (*v.* sim′yə·lāt; *for adj., also* -lit) *v.t.* **·lat·ed, ·lat·ing 1.** To have the appearance or form of, without the reality; counterfeit; imitate. **2.** To make a pretense of. **—** *adj.* Pretended. [< L < *similis* like] **— sim′u·la′tor** *n.*
sim·u·la·tion (sim′yə·lā′shən) *n.* **1.** The act of simulating; counterfeit; sham. **2.** The taking on of a particular aspect or form. **— sim′u·la′tive, sim′u·la·to′ry** (-lə·tôr′ē, -tō′rē) *adj.* **— sim′u·la′tive·ly** *adv.*
si·mul·cast (sī′məl·kast′, -käst′) *v.t.* **·cast, ·cast·ing** To broadcast by radio and television simultaneously. **—** *n.* A broadcast transmitted by radio and television simultaneously. [< SIMUL(TANEOUS) + (BROAD)CAST]
si·mul·ta·ne·ous (sī′məl·tā′nē·əs, sim′əl-) *adj.* Occurring, done, or existing at the same time. [< LL < L *simul* at the same time] **— si′mul·ta′ne·ous·ly** *adv.* **— si′mul·ta′ne·ous·ness, si′mul·ta·ne′i·ty** (-tə·nē′ə·tē) *n.*
sin (sin) *n.* **1.** A transgression, esp., when deliberate, of a law having divine authority. **2.** A particular instance of such transgression. **3.** Any offense against a standard: a literary *sin.* **—** *v.* **sinned, sin·ning** *v.i.* **1.** To commit sin; transgress the divine law. **2.** To violate any requirement of right, duty, etc.; do wrong. **—** *v.t.* **3.** To commit or do wrongfully. [OE *synn*]
Si·nai (sī′nī, -nē·ī′), **Mount** The mountain where Moses received the law from God. *Ex.* xix.
since (sins) *adv.* **1.** From a past time, mentioned or referred to, up to the present. **2.** At some time between a certain past time or event and the present. **3.** In time before the present; ago; before now. **—** *prep.* **1.** During or within the time after or later than: *since* you left. **2.** Continuously throughout the time after: *since* noon. **—** *conj.* **1.** During or within the time after which. **2.** Continuously from the time when. **3.** Because of or following upon the fact that; inasmuch as. [ME < OE *siththan* afterwards]
sin·cere (sin-sir′) *adj.* **1.** Being in reality as it is in appearance; genuine. **2.** Free from hypocrisy; honest. [< L < *sin*- without + stem of *caries* decay] **— sin·cere′ly** *adv.*
sin·cer·i·ty (sin-ser′ə·tē) *n.* *pl.* **·ties** The state or quality of being sincere; honesty of purpose or character; freedom from hypocrisy, deceit, or simulation. Also **sin·cere′ness.**
sine¹ (sīn) *n.* *Trig.* In a right triangle, a function of an acute angle, equal to the ratio of the side opposite the angle to the hypotenuse. [< L *sinus* a bend]
si·ne² (sī′nē) *prep. Latin* Without.
si·ne·cure (sī′nə·kyŏŏr, sin′ə-) *n.* **1.** An office or position for which recompense is received, but involving few or no duties. **2.** *Eccl.* A benefice without cure of souls. [< L *sine* without + *cura* care] **— si′ne·cur·ism** *n.* **— si′ne·cur·ist** *n.*
si·ne di·e (sī′nē dī′ē) *Latin* Without setting a day for reassembling; literally, without a day.
si·ne qua non (sī′nē kwä non′) *Latin* That which is indispensable; an essential; literally, without which not.
sin·ew (sin′yōō) *n.* **1.** A tendon or similar fibrous cord. **2.** Strength, or that which supplies strength. **—** *v.t.* To strengthen or knit together. [OE *seono*] **— sin′ew·less** *adj.*
sin·ew·y (sin′yōō·ē) *adj.* **1.** Characteristic or consisting of a sinew or sinews. **2.** Well supplied with sinews; strong; brawny. **3.** Forceful; vigorous: a *sinewy* style.
sin·ful (sin′fəl) *adj.* Characterized by, suggestive of, or tainted with sin; wicked; immoral. [OE *synfull*] **— sin′ful·ly** *adv.* **— sin′ful·ness** *n.*
sing (sing) *v.* **sang** *or (less commonly)* **sung, sung, sing·ing** *v.i.* **1.** To produce word sounds that differ from speech in that vowels are lengthened and pitches are clearly defined. **2.** To use the voice in this manner for musical rendition or performance. **3.** To produce melodious sounds, as a bird. **4.** To make a melodious sound suggestive of singing, as a teakettle. **5.** To buzz or hum; ring. **6.** To be suitable for singing. **7.** To relate something in verse. **—** *v.t.* **8.** To produce (a tone or tones) with the voice. **9.** To render (a song, etc.) by singing. **10.** To chant, intone, or utter in a songlike manner. **11.** To bring to a specified condition by singing: *Sing* me to sleep. **12.** To relate in or as in song; acclaim: they *sing* his fame. **— to sing out** *Informal* To call out loudly; shout. **—** *n.* **1.** A humming sound, as of a bullet in flight. **2.** *Informal* A gathering for general participation in singing. [OE *singan*] **— sing′a·ble** *adj.*
singe (sinj) *v.t.* **singed, singe·ing 1.** To burn slightly or su-

perficially; scorch. **2.** To remove bristles or feathers from by passing through flame. **3.** To burn the ends of (hair, etc.). — *n.* **1.** The act of singeing, esp. as performed by a barber. **2.** A superficial burn; scorch. [OE *sengan* to scorch, hiss, causative of *singan* to sing]

sing·er[1] (sing′ər) *n.* **1.** One who sings, esp. as a profession. **2.** That which produces a songlike utterance, as a songbird.

sing·er[2] (sinj′ər) *n.* One who or that which singes.

Sin·gha·lese (sing′gə·lēz′, -lēs′) *adj.* Of or pertaining to Ceylon, to a people constituting the majority of the inhabitants of Ceylon, or to their language. — *n.* **1.** One of the Singhalese people. **2.** The Indic language of the Singhalese. Also *Sinhalese*. [< Skt. *Sinhala* Ceylon]

sin·gle (sing′gəl) *adj.* **1.** Consisting of one only; individual. **2.** Having no companion or assistant; alone. **3.** Unmarried. **4.** Pertaining to the unmarried state. **5.** Consisting of only one part. **6.** Unswerving in purpose, intention, etc.; sincere. **7.** Designed for use by only one person or individual: a *single* bed. **8.** Engaged in by individuals in opposition to one another: *single* combat. — *n.* **1.** One who or that which is single; a unit. **2.** In baseball, a base hit that enables the batter to reach first base. **3.** A hotel room for one person. **4.** A golf match between two players only: opposed to *foursome*. **5.** In cricket, a hit that scores one run. **6.** *pl.* In tennis, etc., a game having one player on each side. — *v.* **·gled**, **·gling** *v.t.* **1.** To choose or select (one) from others: usu. with *out*. — *v.i.* **2.** To single-foot. **3.** In baseball, to make a one-base hit. [< OF < L *singulus*] — **sin′gle·ness** *n.*

single bed A bed wide enough for one person.

sin·gle-breast·ed (sing′gəl·bres′tid) *adj.* Having only one thickness of cloth over the breast and fastening in front with a single set of buttons, loops, etc., as a coat or jacket.

single file A line of people, animals, etc., disposed one behind the other, with no two abreast.

sin·gle-hand·ed (sing′gəl·han′did) *adj.* **1.** Having no assistance; unaided. **2.** Having or using but one hand. **3.** Capable of being used with a single hand. **4.** Having only one workman. — **sin′gle-hand′ed·ly** *adv.*

sin·gle-heart·ed (sing′gəl·här′tid) *adj.* Sincere; straightforward; loyal. — **sin′gle-heart′ed·ly** *adv.*

sin·gle-mind·ed (sing′gəl·mīn′did) *adj.* **1.** Having but one purpose or aim. **2.** Free from duplicity; ingenuous; sincere. — **sin′gle-mind′ed·ly** *adv.* — **sin′gle-mind′ed·ness** *n.*

sin·gle-phase (sing′gəl·fāz′) *adj. Electr.* Designating an alternating current circuit having one phase at any given instant.

sin·gle-stick (sing′gəl·stik′) *n.* **1.** A cudgel. **2.** A stick with a basket-shaped hilt, used in fencing. **3.** The art or practice of fencing with singlesticks.

single tax A tax to be obtained from a single source, esp. from a levy on land and natural resources, as a substitute for all other forms of taxation.

sin·gle·ton (sing′gəl·tən) *n.* **1.** In a hand of cards dealt to one player, a single card of a suit. **2.** Any single thing or individual, as distinguished from a pair or larger group.

sin·gle·tree (sing′gəl·trē′) *n.* A whiffletree.

sin·gly (sing′glē) *adv.* **1.** Without companions or associates; unaided, as an individual. **2.** One by one; one at a time.

sing·song (sing′sông′, -song′) *n.* **1.** Monotonous cadence in speaking or reading. **2.** Inferior verse; doggerel. — *adj.* Monotonous; droning, as verse, speech, etc.

sin·gu·lar (sing′gyə·lər) *adj.* **1.** Extraordinary; remarkable; uncommon. **2.** Odd; peculiar; not customary or usual. **3.** Representing the only one of its type; unique. **4.** *Gram.* Of or designating a word form that denotes one person or thing, or a class considered as a unit: distinguished from *dual*, *plural*. — *n. Gram.* The singular number, or a singular word form. [< OF < L < *singulus* single] — **sin·gu·lar′i·ty** (-lar′ə·tē) *n.* — **sin′gu·lar·ly** *adv.* — **sin′gu·lar·ness** *n.*

sin·gu·lar·ize (sing′gyə·lə·rīz′) *v.t.* **·ized**, **·iz·ing** To make or designate as singular.

Sin·ha·lese (sin′hə·lēz′, -lēs′) *adj. & n.* Singhalese.

sin·is·ter (sin′is·tər) *adj.* **1.** Underhandedly or suspiciously wrong or wicked. **2.** Malevolent; evil. **3.** Boding, tending toward, or attended with disaster; unlucky: often with *to*. **4.** *Heraldry* Being on the wearer's left, and hence on the observer's right: opposed to *dexter*. [< F < L *sinister* left] — **sin′is·ter·ly** *adv.* — **sin′is·ter·ness** *n.*

sin·is·tral (sin′is·trəl) *adj.* **1.** Of, pertaining to, or turned toward the left. **2.** Left-handed. — **sin′is·tral·ly** *adv.*

sin·is·trorse (sin′is·trôrs, sin′is·trôrs′) *adj. Bot.* Twining spirally toward the left, as certain climbing plants: opposed to *dextrorse*. Also **sin′is·tror′sal**. [< L, ult. < *sinister* left + *versum* turned] — **sin′is·tror′sal·ly** *adv.*

sink (singk) *v.* **sank** or (*less commonly*) **sunk**, **sunk** (*Obs.* **sunk·en**), **sink·ing** *v.i.* **1.** To go beneath the surface or to the bottom, as of a liquid. **2.** To descend to a lower level; go down, esp. slowly or by degrees. **3.** To descend toward or below the horizon, as the sun. **4.** To incline downward;

slope, as land. **5.** To pass into a specified state: to *sink* into a coma. **6.** To fail, as from ill health or lack of strength; approach death. **7.** To become less in force, volume, or degree: His voice *sank* to a whisper. **8.** To become less in value, price, etc. **9.** To decline in moral level, prestige, wealth, etc. **10.** To permeate: The oil *sank* into the wood. **11.** To become hollow; cave in, as the cheeks. **12.** To be impressed or fixed, as in the mind: with *in*. — *v.t.* **13.** To cause to go beneath the surface or to the bottom. **14.** To cause to fall or drop; lower. **15.** To force or drive into place: to *sink* a fence post. **16.** To make (a mine shaft, well, etc.) by digging or excavating. **17.** To reduce in force, volume, or degree. **18.** To debase or degrade, as one's character or honor. **19.** To suppress, hide, or omit. **20.** To defeat; ruin. **21.** To invest. **22.** To invest and subsequently lose. — *n.* **1.** A box-shaped or basinlike porcelain or metal receptacle with a drainpipe and usu. with a water supply. **2.** A cesspool, etc. **3.** A place where corruption and vice gather or are rampant. **4.** A natural pool, marsh, or basin in which a river terminates by evaporation or percolation. [OE *sincan*] — **sink′a·ble** *adj.*

sink·er (singk′ər) *n.* **1.** One who or that which sinks, or causes to sink. **2.** A weight for sinking a fishing line.

sink·hole (singk′hōl′) *n.* A natural cavity, esp. a drainage cavity, as a hole worn by water through a rock along a joint.

sinking fund A fund established and invested so that its gradual accumulations will wipe out a debt.

sin·less (sin′lis) *adj.* Having no sin; guiltless; innocent. — **sin′less·ly** *adv.* — **sin′less·ness** *n.*

sin·ner (sin′ər) *n.* One who has sinned; esp., one who has transgressed against religious laws or moral principles.

Sinn Fein (shin fān) An Irish political society that originated about 1905, having as its aims both independence and the cultural development of the Irish people. [< Irish, we ourselves] — **Sinn Fein′er** — **Sinn Fein′ism**

Sino- *combining form* Chinese; of or pertaining to the Chinese people, language, etc. Compare CHINO-. [< LL *Sinae* the Chinese]

Si·no-Ti·bet·an (sī′nō-ti·bet′n) *n.* A putative family of languages spoken over a wide area in central and SE Asia, comprising the two established subfamilies **Sino-Thai** (sī′nō-tī′) and **Tibeto-Burman**: also called *Indochinese*. — *adj.* Of these languages or the people who speak them.

sin·ter (sin′tər) *n. Metall.* Metal particles made cohesive by sintering. — *v.t. & v.i. Metall.* To make or become cohesive by the combined action of heat and pressure. [< G, dross of iron]

sin·u·ate (*adj.* sin′yōō·it, -āt; *v.* sin′yōō·āt) *adj.* **1.** Winding in and out; sinuous. **2.** *Bot.* Having a wavy or undulating margin, as a leaf. Also **sin′u·at·ed**. — *v.i.* **·at·ed**, **·at·ing** To curve in and out; wind. [< L *sinuatus*, pp. of *sinuare* to turn, wind] — **sin′u·ate·ly** *adv.* — **sin′u·a′tion** *n.*

sin·u·ous (sin′yōō·əs) *adj.* **1.** Characterized by bends, curves, or folds; winding; undulating. **2.** *Bot.* Sinuate. **3.** Devious; erring. [< L *sinus* bend] — **sin′u·os′i·ty** (-os′ə·tē) *n.* — **sin′u·ous·ly** *adv.* — **sin′u·ous·ness** *n.*

si·nus (sī′nəs) *n.* **1.** A recess formed by a bending or folding; an opening or cavity. **2.** *Anat.* **a** Any of the air-filled cavities in the cranial bones, communicating with the nostrils. **b** A channel or receptacle for venous blood. **c** A dilated part of a blood vessel. **3.** *Pathol.* Any narrow opening leading to an abscess. **4.** *Bot.* A recess or rounded curve between two projecting lobes or teeth of a leaf. [< L]

si·nu·si·tis (sī′nə·sī′tis) *n. Pathol.* Inflammation of a sinus or sinuses, esp. in the cranial bones.

-sion Var. of -TION.

Si·on (sī′ən) See ZION.

Siou·an (sōō′ən) *n.* A large family of North American Indian languages formerly spoken from the west banks of the Mississippi to the Rocky Mountains. — *adj.* Of or pertaining to this family of languages.

Sioux (sōō) *n. pl.* **Sioux** One of a group of North American Indian tribes formerly occupying the Dakotas and parts of Minnesota and Nebraska: also called *Dakota*.

sip (sip) *v.* **sipped**, **sip·ping** *v.t.* **1.** To drink by swallowing small quantities at a time. **2.** To drink from by sips. **3.** To imbibe. — *v.i.* **4.** To drink in sips. — *n.* **1.** A small amount of liquid swallowed at one time. **2.** The act of sipping. [ME < OE *sypian* to absorb] — **sip′per** *n.*

si·phon (sī′fən) *n.* **1.** A bent or flexible tube through which liquids may be passed from a higher to a lower level over an intervening elevation by making use of atmospheric pressure. **2.** A siphon bottle. **3.** *Zool.* A tubular structure in certain aquatic animals, as the squid, for drawing in or expelling liquids: for illus. see SQUID. — *v.t.* **1.** To draw off or cause to pass through or as through a siphon. — *v.i.* **2.** To pass through a siphon. Also spelled *syphon*. [< F < L < Gk. *siphōn*] — **si′phon·al** *adj.*

siphon bottle A bottle containing aerated or carbonated water that can be expelled by pressure on a valve through a bent tube in the neck of the bottle.

sir (sûr) *n.* The conventional term of respectful address to men, used absolutely, and not followed by a proper name. [< SIRE]

Sir (sûr) *n.* A title of baronets and knights, used before the Christian name or the full name.

sire (sīr) *n.* 1. A father; begetter: sometimes used in combination: *grandsire.* 2. The male parent of a mammal. 3. A form of address to a superior, now used in addressing a king or sovereign. — *v.t.* **sired, sir·ing** To beget: now used chiefly of domestic animals. [< OF < L *senior* older]

si·ren (sī′rən) *n.* 1. In Greek legend, one of a group of nymphs living on an island, who lured sailors to destruction by their sweet singing. 2. A fascinating, dangerous woman. 3. An acoustical device having a perforated rotating disk or disks through which sharp puffs of steam or compressed air are permitted to escape so as to produce a continued musical note or a loud whistle, often used as a warning signal. 4. *Zool.* Any of a family of eellike amphibians, as the mud eel. — *adj.* 1. Of or pertaining to a siren. 2. Alluring; dangerously fascinating. [< OF < L < Gk. *seirēn*]

Sir·i·us (sir′ē-əs) The brightest star, −1.58 magnitude; Alpha in the constellation Canis Major: also called *Dog Star.* [< Gk. *seirios* hot, scorching]

sir·loin (sûr′loin) *n.* A loin of beef, esp. the upper portion. [< OF < *sur-* over, above + *longe* loin]

si·roc·co (si-rok′ō) *n. pl.* **·cos** *Meteorol.* 1. A hot, dry, and dusty southerly wind blowing from the African coast to Italy, Sicily, and Spain. 2. A warm, sultry wind blowing from a warm region toward a center of low barometric pressure. [< Ital. < Arabic *sharq* the east, the rising sun]

sir·rah (sir′ə) *n. Archaic* Fellow; sir: a term of address expressing contempt or annoyance. [Var. of SIR]

sir·up (sir′əp) See SYRUP.

sis (sis) *n. Informal* Sister.

si·sal (sī′səl, sī′zəl, sis′əl, se′səl) *n.* 1. A strong fiber obtained from the leaves of an agave of the West Indies. 2. The plant yielding this fiber. Also **sisal grass, sisal hemp.** [after *Sisal,* town in Yucatán, Mexico]

sis·si·fied (sis′i-fīd) *adj. U.S. Informal* Effeminate.

sis·sy (sis′ē) *n. pl.* **·sies** *U.S. Informal* 1. An effeminate man or boy; a milksop. 2. A coward or weakling. [< SIS] — **sis′sy·ish** *adj.*

sis·ter (sis′tər) *n.* 1. A female having the same parents as another or others of either sex. 2. Something characterized as female, and closely associated with another of the same kind. 3. A member of a sisterhood; a nun. 4. *Brit.* A head nurse in the ward of a hospital; also, popularly, any nurse. — *adj.* Bearing the relationship of a sister or one suggestive of sisterhood. [OE *sweostor*]

sis·ter-ger·man (sis′tər-jûr′mən) *n. pl.* **sis·ters-ger·man** A full sister.

sis·ter·hood (sis′tər-hŏŏd) *n.* 1. The relationship of or state of being sisters, esp. by blood. 2. A body of women or girls united by some bond of fellowship or sympathy. 3. A community of women bound by monastic vows or pledged to works of mercy and faith.

sis·ter-in-law (sis′tər-in-lô′) *n. pl.* **sis·ters-in-law** 1. A sister of a husband or wife. 2. A brother's wife. 3. The wife of a wife's or husband's brother.

sis·ter·ly (sis′tər-lē) *adj.* Pertaining to or characteristic of a sister. — *adv.* As a sister. — **sis′ter·li·ness** *n.*

Sis·y·phus (sis′ə-fəs) In Greek mythology, a crafty, greedy king of Corinth, condemned in Hades forever to roll uphill a huge stone that always rolled down again.

sit (sit) *v.* **sat** (*Archaic* **sate**), **sat, sit·ting** *v.i.* 1. To rest with the buttocks on a supporting surface, with the body bent at the hips, and the spine nearly vertical. 2. To occupy a chair, bench, etc., in such a position. 3. To perch or roost, as a bird; also, to cover eggs so as to give warmth for hatching. 4. To be or remain in a seated or settled position. 5. To remain passive or inactive, or in a position of idleness or rest. 6. To assume an attitude or take a position for a special purpose; pose, as for a portrait. 7. To meet in assembly; hold a session. 8. To occupy or be entitled to a seat in a deliberative body. 9. To have or exercise judicial authority. 10. To fit or be adjusted; suit: That hat *sits* well. 11. To be suffered or borne, as a burden. 12. To be situated or located: The wind *sits* in the east. 13. To baby-sit, serve as company for someone ill, etc. — *v.t.* 14. To have or keep a seat or a good seat upon: to *sit* a horse. 15. To seat (oneself, etc.). — **to sit in (on)** *U.S.* To join or take part. — **to sit out** 1. To sit or remain quietly till the end of: to *sit out* an entertainment. 2. To sit aside during: They *sat out* a dance. 3. To stay longer than. — **to sit tight** *Informal* To wait for the next move. [OE *sittan*]

si·tar (si-tär′) *n.* An East Indian stringed instrument resembling a guitar. [< Hind. *sitār*]

sit-down strike (sit′doun′) A strike during which strikers refuse to leave their place of employment until agreement is reached. Also **sit′-down′.**

site (sīt) *n.* 1. Place of location. 2. A plot of ground set apart for some specific use. [< F < L *situs* position]

sit-in (sit′in′) *n.* A demonstration of protest, as by Negroes in the southern U.S., in which participants enter and remain seated in a public place, commercial establishment, etc., from which they are customarily excluded.

sito- *combining form* Food. [< Gk. *sitos* food]

sit·ter (sit′ər) *n.* 1. One who sits. 2. A baby sitter. 3. A person posing as a model. 4. A setting hen.

sit·ting (sit′ing) *adj.* 1. Being in a seated position. 2. Used for sitting: *sitting* room. — *n.* 1. The act or position of one who sits. 2. A seat; also, the place of or the right to a seat. 3. A single period of remaining seated for a specific purpose. 4. A session or term. 5. A period of hatching. 6. The number of eggs on which a bird sits at one incubation.

sitting duck *Informal* Any easy target.

sitting room A parlor; living room.

sit·u·ate (sich′ŏŏ-āt) *v.t.* **·at·ed, ·at·ing** 1. To fix a site for; locate. 2. To place in a certain position or under certain conditions or circumstances. [< Med.L *situatus,* pp. of *situare* to place]

sit·u·at·ed (sich′ŏŏ-ā′tid) *adj.* 1. Having a fixed place or location; placed. 2. Placed in (usu. specified) circumstances or conditions: He is *well* situated.

sit·u·a·tion (sich′ŏŏ-ā′shən) *n.* 1. Condition as modified or determined by surroundings or attendant circumstances; status. 2. A combination of circumstances, often leading to a complication, climax, or crisis. 3. The place in which something is situated; locality. 4. A salaried post of employment, usu. subordinate. — **sit·u·a·tion·al** *adj.*

Si·va (sē′və, shē′-) The Hindu god of destruction and reproduction, forming with Brahma and Vishnu the Hindu trinity: also *Shiva.* [< Hind. < Skt. *śivás* propitious] — **Si′va·ism** *n.* — **Si′va·ist** *n.* — **Si′va·is′tic** *adj.*

Si·van (sē-vän′) *n.* The ninth month of the Hebrew year. See (Hebrew) CALENDAR. Also **Si·wan′** (-vän′).

six (siks) *n.* 1. The sum of five and one: a cardinal number. 2. Any symbol of this number, as 6, vi, VI. 3. Anything consisting of or representing six units. — **at sixes and sevens** 1. In a state of confusion. 2. At odds; estranged. — **six of one, half-dozen of another** A situation offering no obvious choice. — *adj.* Being one more than five. [OE]

six·pence (siks′pəns) *n.* A British silver coin of the value of six pennies, equivalent to half a shilling.

six·pen·ny (siks′pen′ē, -pən-ē) *adj.* 1. Worth or sold for sixpence. 2. Paltry; trashy. 3. Denoting a size of nails.

six-shoot·er (siks′shŏŏ′tər) *n. Informal* A revolver that may be fired six times without reloading.

six·teen (siks′tēn′) *n.* 1. The sum of fifteen and one: a cardinal number. 2. Any symbol of this number, as 16, xvi, XVI. 3. Anything consisting of or representing sixteen units. — *adj.* Being one more than fifteen. [OE *sixtÿne*] — **six′teenth′** *adv. & n.*

six·teen·mo (siks′tēn′mō) *adj. & n.* Sextodecimo.

sixteenth note *Music* A note having one sixteenth the time value of a whole note: also, *chiefly Brit., semiquaver.*

sixth (siksth) *adj.* 1. Next after the fifth: the ordinal of *six.* 2. Being one of six equal parts. — *n.* 1. One of six equal parts. 2. That which follows the fifth. 3. *Music* a The interval between any tone and another tone five steps from it in a diatonic scale. b A tone separated by this interval from any other, considered with reference to that other; esp., the sixth above the keynote. — *adv.* In the sixth order, place, or rank: also, in formal discourse, **sixth′ly.**

sixth sense Intuitive perception supposedly independent of the five senses.

six·ty (siks′tē) *n. pl.* **·ties** 1. The sum of fifty and ten: a cardinal number. 2. Any symbol of this number, as 60, lx, LX. 3. Anything consisting of or representing sixty units. — *adj.* Being ten more than fifty. [OE *sixtig*] — **six′ti·eth** *adj. & n.*

six·ty-fourth note (siks′tē-fôrth′, -fôrth′) *Music* A note having one sixty-fourth the time value of a whole note: also, *chiefly Brit., hemidemisemiquaver.*

siz·a·ble (sī′zə-bəl) *adj.* Of comparatively large size. Also **size′a·ble.** — **siz′a·ble·ness** *n.* — **siz′a·bly** *adv.*

size¹ (sīz) *n.* 1. Measurement or extent of a thing as compared with some standard. 2. Comparative magnitude or bulk. 3. One of a series of graded measures, as of hats, shoes, etc. 4. A standard of measurement; specified quantity. 5. Mental caliber; character. 6. *Informal* State of affairs; true situation: That's the *size* of it. — *v.t.* **sized, siz·ing** 1. To estimate the size of. 2. To distribute or classify according to size. 3. To cut or otherwise shape (an article) to the required size. — **to size up** *Informal* 1. To form an estimate, judgment, or opinion of. 2. To meet specifications. [< F *assise* to assize]

size² (sīz) *n.* A solution of gelatinous material, usu. glue, casein, wax, or clay, used to glaze paper, coat wall surfaces, etc. **—** *v.t.* **sized, siz·ing** **1.** To treat with size. **2.** To make plastic, as clay. [< OItal. *sisa* painter's glue]

sized (sīzd) *adj.* Being of a definite or specified size: often used in combination: *good-sized.*

siz·ing (sī′zing) *n.* **1.** Size². **2.** The process of adding or applying size to a fabric, surface, etc.

siz·y (sī′zē) *adj.* **siz·i·er, siz·i·est** Glutinous. [< SIZE²]

siz·zle (siz′əl) *v.i.* **·zled, ·zling** **1.** To burn, fry, quench, etc., with or as with a hissing sound; emit a hissing sound under the action of heat. **2.** To be extremely hot. **—** *n.* A hissing sound as from frying or effervescence. [Imit.]

siz·zler (siz′lər) *n. Informal* Something extremely hot, as a summer day. [< SIZZLE]

skate¹ (skāt) *n.* **1.** A device consisting of a metal runner attached to the sole of a boot or shoe, enabling the wearer to glide over ice; also, such a runner. **2.** A roller skate. **—** *v.i.* **skat·ed, skat·ing** To glide or move over ice or some other smooth surface on or as on skates. [< earlier *skates* < Du. < OF *escache* stilt < Gmc.] **— skat′er** *n.*

skate² (skāt) *n.* Any of various ray fishes having large pectoral fins and a pointed snout. [< ON *skata*]

ske·dad·dle (ski·dad′l) *Informal v.i.* **·dled, ·dling** To flee in haste. **—** *n.* Hasty flight. [Origin unknown]

skeet (skēt) *n.* A variety of trapshooting in which a succession of targets simulating the flight of birds are fired at from various angles by the shooter. [Ult. < ON *skjota* to shoot]

skein (skān) *n.* **1.** A quantity of yarn, thread, etc., wound in a loose, elongated coil. **2.** Something resembling or suggestive of this. **3.** A flight of geese, etc. [< OF *escaigne*]

skel·e·ton (skel′ə·tən) *n.* **1.** The supporting or protective framework of a human or animal body, consisting of the bones and connective cartilage (endoskeleton) in man and the vertebrates, or of a hard outer structure (exoskeleton), as in crustaceans, insects, etc. **2.** A sketch or outline, as of a written work. **3.** A very thin or emaciated person or animal. **4.** A structure, group, etc., consisting of few parts, reduced numbers, or bare essentials. **— skeleton in the closet** A secret source of shame or discredit. **—** *adj.* **1.** Consisting merely of a framework, outline, or few parts or members. **2.** Resembling a skeleton in nature or appearance; meager; emaciated. [< NL < Gk. *skeleton* (*sōma*) dried (body), mummy < *skeletos* dried up] **— skel′e·tal** *adj.*

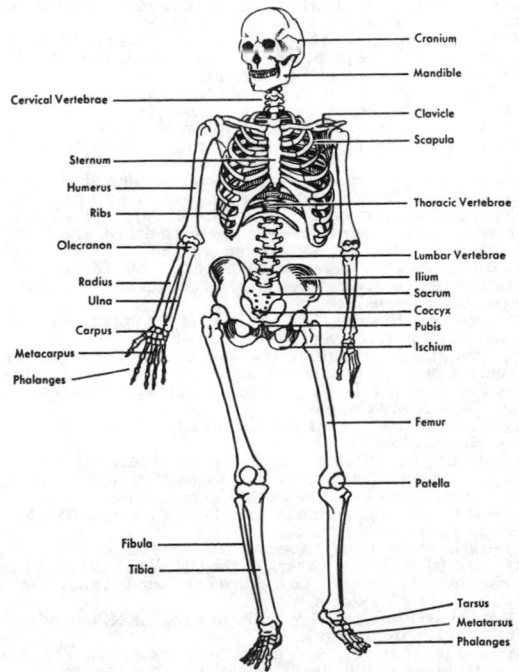

Cranium

Mandible

Cervical Vertebrae

Clavicle

Scapula

Sternum

Humerus

Thoracic Vertebrae

Ribs

Olecranon

Lumbar Vertebrae

Radius

Ilium

Ulna

Sacrum

Coccyx

Carpus

Pubis

Metacarpus

Ischium

Phalanges

Femur

Patella

Fibula

Tibia

Tarsus

Metatarsus

Phalanges

HUMAN SKELETON

skeleton crew A work crew barely sufficient for the job.

skel·e·ton·ize (skel′ə·tən·īz′) *v.t.* **·ized, ·iz·ing** **1.** To reduce to a skeleton, framework, or outline by removing soft tissues,

extraneous parts, etc. **2.** To reduce greatly in size or numbers. **3.** To draft in outline.

skeleton key A key filed to a slender shape, and used to open a number of different locks.

skep·tic (skep′tik) *n.* **1.** One who doubts, disbelieves, or disagrees with generally accepted ideas. **2.** One who by nature doubts or questions what he hears, reads, etc. **3.** One who questions the fundamental doctrines of a religion, esp. the Christian religion. **4.** *Sometimes cap.* An adherent of any philosophical school of skepticism. Also spelled *sceptic.* [< F < L < LGk. *skeptikos* reflective]

— Syn. *Skeptic* is a general term, and refers to a person who does not feel that the state of human knowledge, or the evidence available, is sufficient to establish the doctrine. A *freethinker* is one who refuses to accept a doctrine, especially a religious doctrine, simply on authority, and demands empiric proof. An *agnostic* rejects a doctrine because he believes that human knowledge is, and always will be, incapable of determining its truth or falsity.

Skep·tic (skep′tik) *n.* In ancient Greek philosophy, a member of a school of skepticism. [< SKEPTIC]

skep·ti·cal (skep′ti·kəl) *adj.* **1.** Doubting; questioning; disbelieving. **2.** Of, pertaining to, or characteristic of a skeptic or skepticism. Also spelled *sceptical.* **— skep′ti·cal·ly** *adv.* **— skep′ti·cal·ness** *n.*

skep·ti·cism (skep′tə·siz′əm) *n.* **1.** A doubting or incredulous state of mind; disbelieving attitude. **2.** *Philos.* The doctrine that absolute knowledge is unattainable and that judgments must be continually questioned and doubted. Also spelled *scepticism.*

sketch (skech) *n.* **1.** A rapid, incomplete, or hasty delineation or presentation, intended to give a general impression of a work, study, etc., to be completed; an outline. **2.** An artist's rough or rapid drawing or study. **3.** A short, slight, or unpretentious literary or dramatic composition. **4.** A short scene, play, or musical act in a revue, musical comedy, etc. **5.** *Informal* An amusing person; joker. **—** *v.t.* **1.** To make a sketch or sketches of; outline. **—** *v.i.* **2.** To make a sketch or sketches. **— to sketch in** To present or explain (details) in a rapid summary, way. **— to sketch out** To present or explain in a rapid, summary way. [< Du. < Ital. < L < Gk. *schedios* improvisation] **— sketch′a·ble** *adj.* **— sketch′er** *n.*

sketch·book (skech′book′) *n.* **1.** A book of paper used for sketching. **2.** A set or collection of literary sketches. Also **sketch book.**

sketch·y (skech′ē) *adj.* **sketch·i·er, sketch·i·est** **1.** Resembling or consisting of a sketch; roughly suggested without detail. **2.** Incomplete. **— sketch′i·ly** *adv.* **— sketch′i·ness** *n.*

skew (skyoō) *v.i.* **1.** To take an oblique direction; swerve. **2.** To look obliquely or askance; squint. **—** *v.t.* **3.** To give an oblique position, direction, or form to; make lopsided. **4.** To shift or twist the meaning or significance of; distort. **—** *adj.* **1.** Placed or turned obliquely; twisted to one side; lopsided. **2.** Distorted in effect or meaning. **—** *n.* A deviation from symmetry or straightness; oblique direction or position. [< AF *eskiuer*, OF *eschiuer* to shun < Gmc.]

skew·er (skyoō′ər) *n.* **1.** A long pin of wood, or metal, thrust into meat to hold it or keep it in shape while roasting or broiling. **2.** Any of various articles of similar shape or use. **—** *v.t.* To run through or fasten with or as with a skewer. [Var. of SKIVER]

ski (skē, *Norw.* shē) *n.* *pl.* **skis** or **ski** One of a pair of wooden or metal runners with turned-up points, attached to the feet and used in sliding over snow, esp. on slopes. **—** *v.i.* **skied** (skēd), **ski·ing** **1.** To glide or travel on skis. **2.** To engage in the sport of gliding over snow-covered inclines on skis. [< Norw. < ON *skith* snowshoe]

skid (skid) *n.* **1.** The act of skidding or slipping. **2.** A small frame or platform upon which merchandise is stacked to be moved about or temporarily stored. **3.** One of a pair of timbers used to support a heavy tilting or rolling object, or a log used as a track in sliding heavy articles about, or forming an inclined plane to ease their descent. **4.** In lumbering, one of several logs used to make a skid road or skidway. **5.** A shoe or drag on a wagon wheel. **6.** *Aeron.* A runner in an airplane's landing gear. **— on the skids** *U.S. Slang* Rapidly declining in prestige or power. **—** *v.* **skid·ded, skid·ding** *v.i.* **1.** To slide instead of revolving, as a wheel that does not rotate. **2.** Of a wheel, vehicle, etc., to slide or slip sideways because of loss of traction. **3.** *Aeron.* To move sideways, because of insufficient banking. **—** *v.t.* **4.** To furnish with skids; put, drag, or haul on skids. **5.** To brake or hold back with a skid. [? < ON *skith* piece of wood]

skid road A road or track along which logs are hauled.

skid row *U.S. Slang* An urban section inhabited by vagrants and derelicts. [< SKID ROAD]

ski·er (skē′ər) *n.* One who skis.

skiff (skif) *n.* A light rowboat or small, open sailing vessel light enough to be rowed with ease. [< F < Ital. < OHG *scif* ship, boat]

ski·ing (skē′ing) *n.* The act or sport of one who skis.

ski jump 1. A jump or leap made by a person wearing skis. 2. A course prepared for making such jumps.

ski lift Any of various devices, usu. an endless cable running on towers, with attached bars or chairs, used to transport skiers to the top of a slope or trail.

skill (skil) *n.* 1. Proficiency or technical ability in any art, science, handicraft, etc. 2. A specific art, trade, or technique. — **Syn.** See DEXTERITY. [< ON *skil* knowledge]

skilled (skild) *adj.* 1. Possessing or showing skill; proficient. 2. Having specialized ability or training, as a worker. 3. Requiring specialized ability or training, as a job.

skil·let (skil′it) *n.* A frying pan or similar cooking pot having a long handle. [ME *skelet*, ? < OF *esculette* dish]

skill·ful (skil′fəl) *adj.* 1. Having skill; clever; dexterous; able. 2. Characterized by or requiring skill. Also *Brit.* **skil′·ful. — skill′ful·ly** *adv.* **— skill′ful·ness** *n.*

skim (skim) *v.* **skimmed, skim·ming** *v.t.* 1. To remove floating matter from the surface of, as with a ladle: to *skim* milk. 2. To remove thus: to *skim* cream. 3. To cover with a thin film, as of ice. 4. To move lightly and quickly across or over. 5. To cause to pass swiftly and lightly, as a flat stone across a pond. 6. To read or glance over hastily or superficially. — *v.i.* 7. To move quickly and lightly across or near a surface; glide. 8. To make a hasty and superficial perusal; glance: with *over* or *through.* 9. To become covered with a thin film. — *n.* 1. The act of skimming. 2. That which has been skimmed, as skim milk. 3. A thin film or layer. — *adj.* Skimmed: *skim* milk. [Var. of SCUM]

skim·mer (skim′ər) *n.* 1. A flat ladle or other utensil for skimming. 2. One who or that which skims. 3. A hat having a shallow crown and a wide, round brim.

skim milk Milk from which the cream has been removed.

skimp (skimp) *v.t. & v.i.* To scrimp or scamp. — *adj.* Scant; meager. [Prob. < ON *skemma* to shorten]

skimp·y (skim′pē) *adj.* **skimp·i·er, skimp·i·est** 1. Insufficient in size, amount, etc. 2. Excessively saving or sparing. — **skimp′i·ly** *adv.* — **skimp′i·ness** *n.*

skin (skin) *n.* 1. The membranous tissue covering the body of an animal; the integument. ◆ Collateral adjectives: *cutaneous, dermal.* 2. The pelt of a small animal, removed from its body, whether raw or dressed. 3. A vessel for holding liquids, made of skin. 4. An outside layer, coat, or covering as the rind of a fruit, etc. 5. One's life: to save one's *skin.* **— by the skin of one's teeth** Very closely or narrowly; barely. **— to get under one's skin** 1. To be provoking or irritating. 2. To be an obsession. **— under the skin** In a close but not apparent figurative relationship: sisters *under the skin.* — *v.* **skinned, skin·ning** *v.t.* 1. To remove the skin of; flay; peel. 2. To cover with or as with skin. 3. To remove or peel off hastily. 4. *Slang* To cheat or swindle. — *v.i.* 5. To shed the skin. [< ON *skinn*]

skin-deep (skin′dēp′) *adj.* Superficial. — *adv.* Superficially.

skin-dive (skin′dīv′) *v.i.* **-dived** (*U.S. Informal* **-dove**), **-dived, -div·ing** To engage in skin diving.

skin diving Underwater swimming or exploration in which the swimmer is equipped with goggles and foot fins, and sometimes with a scuba or snorkel. **— skin diver**

skin·flint (skin′flint) *n.* A miser or niggardly person.

skin game 1. A crooked or rigged gambling game in which the players have no chance. 2. Any swindle.

skink (skingk) *n.* One of a group of lizards having smooth scales and short limbs. [< L < Gk. *skinkos* kind of lizard]

skin·ner (skin′ər) *n.* 1. One who flays or sells the skins of animals. 2. *U.S. Slang* A mule driver.

skin·ny (skin′ē) *adj.* **·ni·er, ·ni·est** 1. Very thin or emaciated; lean. 2. Consisting of or resembling skin. **— skin′·ni·ness** *n.*

skin·tight (skin′tīt′) *adj.* Fitting tightly to the skin.

skip (skip) *v.* **skipped, skip·ping** *v.i.* 1. To move with light springing steps; caper. 2. To bounce over, ricochet from, or skim a surface. 3. To pass from one point to another omitting or not noticing what lies between. 4. *Informal* To leave or depart hurriedly; flee. 5. To be advanced in school beyond the next grade in order. — *v.t.* 6. To leap lightly over. 7. To cause to skim or ricochet. 8. To pass over or by; omit. 9. *Informal* To leave (a place) hurriedly. — *n.* 1. A light bound or hop. 2. A passing over without notice. [Prob. < Scand. Cf. Sw. *skuppa* to skip.]

ski pants Long trousers that fit snugly, esp. at the ankles, worn for skiing, etc.

skip·jack (skip′jak′) *n.* Any of various fishes that leap from or skip along the surface of the water, as the bonito.

skip·per[1] (skip′ər) *n.* 1. One who or that which skips. 2. Any of a family of small butterflies.

skip·per[2] (skip′ər) *n.* 1. The captain of a ship. 2. One in a position of leadership. [< Du. *schip* ship]

skirl (skûrl, skirl) *Scot. v.i.* To produce a shrill sound, as a bagpipe. — *n.* A shrill cry or sound. [ME *scrille*]

skir·mish (skûr′mish) *v.i.* To fight in a preliminary or desultory way. — *n.* 1. A light engagement, as between small parties or groups. 2. Any encounter or action that evades the main contention or business. — **Syn.** See BATTLE. [< OF *eskermir* to fence, fight] — **skir′mish·er** *n.*

skirt (skûrt) *n.* 1. The part of a dress, gown, or robe that hangs from the waist downward. 2. A separate garment hanging from the waist and covering the lower portion of the body. 3. *pl.* The border, fringe, or edge of a particular area: on the *skirts* of the town. 4. One of the flaps or loose, hanging parts of a saddle. 5. *Slang* A woman or girl. — *v.t.* 1. To lie along or form the edge of; to border. 2. To surround or border: with *with.* 3. To pass around or about. 4. To evade or avoid (a subject, issue, etc.). — *v.i.* 5. To pass or be near the edge or border of something. [ON *skyrt* shirt]

skit (skit) *n.* 1. A short, usu. humorous dramatic scene or presentation. 2. A brief, humorous, often satirical piece of writing. [< Scand. Cf. ON *skjota* to shoot]

ski tow A type of ski lift consisting of an endless rope.

skit·ter (skit′ər) *v.i.* To glide or skim along, touching a surface at intervals. — *v.t.* To cause to skitter. [Freq. of SKITE]

skit·tish (skit′ish) *adj.* 1. Easily frightened, as a horse. 2. Capricious; uncertain; unreliable. 3. Tricky; deceitful. [< dial. E *skit* to caper, as a horse] — **skit′tish·ly** *adv.* — **skit′·tish·ness** *n.*

skit·tle (skit′l) *n.* 1. *pl.* A game of ninepins, in which a flattened ball or thick rounded disk is thrown to knock down the pins. 2. One of the pins used in this game. **— beer and skittles** Carefree existence; drink and play. [Prob. < Dan. *skyttel* a child's earthen ball]

skiv·vy (skiv′ē) *n. pl.* **·vies** *U.S. Slang* 1. A man's short-sleeved undershirt. Also **skivvy shirt.** 2. *pl.* Men's underwear. [Origin uncertain]

skoal (skōl) *interj.* To your good health: a toast in drinking, used esp. by Scandinavians. [< Scand.]

sku·a (skyōō′ə) *n.* A predatory gull-like bird of northern regions. [< Faroese *skúgver* < ON *skúfr*]

skul·dug·ger·y (skul-dug′ər-ē) *n. U.S.* Trickery; underhandedness. [Var. of dial. *sculduddery*; origin uncertain]

skulk (skulk) *v.i.* 1. To move about furtively; lie close or keep hidden. 2. To shirk; evade work or responsibility. — *n.* One who skulks. [< Scand.] — **skulk′er** *n.*

skull (skul) *n.* 1. The bony framework of the head of a vertebrate animal; the cranium. 2. The head considered as the seat of brain; the mind. [< Scand.]

skull and crossbones A representation of the human skull over two crossed bones, used as a symbol of death, as a warning label on poison, and as an emblem of piracy.

skull·cap (skul′kap′) *n.* A small, snug, brimless cap, often worn indoors.

skunk (skungk) *n.* 1. A carnivorous mammal of North America, usu. black with a white stripe and a bushy tail, and ejecting at will a malodorous liquid. 2. *Informal* A hateful or contemptible person. — *v.t. Slang* To defeat utterly in a game or contest. [< Algonquian *seganku*]

skunk cabbage A perennial plant of the arum family, emitting a strong odor, esp. when crushed or bruised. Also **skunk·weed** (skungk′wēd′).

sky (skī) *n. pl.* **skies** 1. The region of the upper air seen as a high vault or arch over the earth; the firmament. 2. *Often pl.* Atmospheric condition or appearance of the upper air: cloudy *skies.* 3. The celestial regions; heaven. — *v.t.* **skied, sky·ing** *Informal* To bat or throw (a ball, etc.) high into the air. [< ON *sky* cloup]

sky blue A blue like the color of the sky on a clear day. — **sky-blue** (skī′blōō′) *adj.*

sky·div·ing (skī′dī′ving) *n.* The sport of jumping from an airplane and performing various maneuvers and assuming various positions before opening the parachute.

Skye terrier (skī) A small terrier having a long body, short legs, and long, straight hair.

sky-high (skī′hī′) *adj. & adv.* Extremely high.

sky·lark (skī′lärk) *n.* A lark of the Old World that sings as it rises in flight. — *v.i.* To indulge in hilarious or boisterous frolic. — **sky′lark′er** *n.*

sky·light (skī′līt′) *n.* A window in a roof or ceiling, admitting daylight from above.

sky·line (skī′līn′) *n.* 1. The visible horizon. 2. The outline of a group of buildings, etc., seen against the sky.

sky pilot *Slang* A clergyman or a chaplain.

sky·rock·et (skī′rok′it) *n.* A rocket, as in a fireworks display, projected so as to explode high in the air. — *v.i.* To rise rapidly or suddenly.

sky·sail (skī′səl, -sāl′) *n. Naut.* A light sail above the royal in a square-rigged vessel.

sky·scrap·er (skī′skrā′pər) *n.* A very high building

sky·ward (skī′wərd) *adv.* Toward the sky. Also **sky′·wards.** — *adj.* Moving or directed toward the sky.

sky·way (skī′wā′) *n.* **1.** An air travel route. **2.** An elevated highway.

sky·writ·ing (skī′rī′ting) *n.* **1.** The forming of words in the air by the release of vapor from an airplane. **2.** The words or letters thus formed. **— sky′writ/er** *n.*

slab (slab) *n.* **1.** A flat plate, piece, mass, or slice, as of metal, stone, etc. **2.** The outside piece of a log sawed for lumber, often with the bark remaining on it. **3.** *U.S. Slang* In baseball, the pitcher's plate. *— v.t.* **slabbed, slab·bing 1.** To make or form into slabs. **2.** To cover with slabs. **3.** To saw slabs from, as a log. [ME. Origin uncertain.]

slack[1] (slak) *adj.* **1.** Hanging or extended loosely. **2.** Loose or careless in performance; remiss; slovenly. **3.** Flaccid; loose: a *slack* mouth. **4.** Lacking activity; not busy: a *slack* season. **5.** Listless; limp: a *slack* grip. **6.** Flowing or moving sluggishly, as wind, water, etc. *— v.t.* **1.** To slacken. **2.** To slake, as lime. *— v.i.* **3.** To be or become slack. **— to slack off** To slow down; be less diligent. *— n.* **1.** A part of a rope, sail, etc., that is slack or loose. **2.** Slack condition; looseness. **3.** A period of inactivity. **4.** An extent of water where there is no current. *— adv.* In a slack manner. [OE *sleac*] **— slack′ly** *adv.* **— slack′ness** *n.*

slack[2] (slak) *n.* Screenings or small pieces of coal. [Cf. Flemish *slecke*, LG *slacke*]

slack·en (slak′ən) *v.i.* **1.** To become less active, productive, etc. **2.** To become less tense or tight. **3.** To become slow or less intense. *— v.t.* **4.** To become slow, negligent, or remiss in: to *slacken* one's efforts. **5.** To make slack.

slack·er (slak′ər) *n.* One who shirks his duties or avoids military service in wartime; shirker.

slack-off (slak′ôf′) *n.* *Informal* A slowdown; abatement.

slacks (slaks) *n.pl.* Trousers worn by men or women for casual or sports wear.

slag (slag) *n.* **1.** *Metall.* The fused residue separated in the reduction of metals from their ores. **2.** Volcanic lava in small, cinderlike pieces. *— v.t. & v.i.* **slagged, slag·ging** To form into slag. [< MLG *slagge*] **— slag′gy** *adj.*

slain (slān) Past participle of SLAY.

slake (slāk) *v.* **slaked, slak·ing** *v.t.* **1.** To quench or satisfy, as thirst or an appetite. **2.** To lessen the force or intensity of. **3.** To moisten or refresh. **4.** To mix with water or moist air, as in the preparation of slaked lime. *— v.i.* **5.** To become disintegrated and hydrated, as lime. [OE *slacian* to retard < *sleac* slack[1]]

slaked lime See under LIME[1].

sla·lom (slä′ləm, slä′-) *n.* In skiing, a race or descent over a winding downhill course laid out between posts and marked with flags. *— v.i.* To ski in such a course. [< Norw.]

slam[1] (slam) *v.* **slammed, slam·ming** *v.t.* **1.** To shut or push to with violence and a loud noise. **2.** To put, dash, throw, etc., with violence and a loud noise; bang. **3.** *Slang* To hit or strike violently. **4.** *Slang* To disparage or criticize harshly. *— v.i.* **5.** To close, swing, etc., with force and noise. **6.** To make a noisy entrance. *— n.* **1.** The act or noise of slamming. **2.** *Slang* Harsh criticism; abuse. [< Scand. Cf. dial. Norw. *slamra* slam.]

slam[2] (slam) *n.* In bridge, the winning of all (grand slam) or all but one (little or small slam) of the tricks in a round of play; also, a bid to do so. [Origin uncertain]

slam-bang (slam′bang′) *adv.* Violently; noisily. *— v.i.* To move with noise and violence.

slan·der (slan′dər) *n.* **1.** *Law* **a** An oral statement of a false, malicious, or defamatory nature, tending to damage another's reputation, means of livelihood, etc. **b** The utterance of such a statement. **2.** A maliciously false tale or report. *— v.t.* **1.** To injure by maliciously uttering a false report. *— v.i.* **2.** To utter slander. [< AF < L *scandalum* cause of stumbling] **— slan′der·er** *n.*

slan·der·ous (slan′dər·əs) *adj.* **1.** Uttering or containing slander. **2.** Characterized by slander; calumnious. **— slan′der·ous·ly** *adv.* **— slan′der·ous·ness** *n.*

slang (slang) *n.* **1.** Language, words, or phrases of a vigorous, colorful, facetious, or taboo nature, invented for specific occasions or uses, or derived from the unconventional use of the standard vocabulary. **2.** The special vocabulary of a certain class, group, or profession: college *slang*. **3.** Formerly, the argot or jargon of thieves and vagrants. *— v.t. & v.i.* To address with or use slang. [Origin uncertain]

slang·y (slang′ē) *adj.* **slang·i·er, slang·i·est 1.** Like or consisting of slang. **2.** Using slang. **— slang′i·ly** *adv.* **— slang′i·ness** *n.*

slant (slant) *v.t.* **1.** To give an oblique or sloping direction to; incline. **2.** To write or edit (news or other literary matter) so as to express a special attitude, bias, or opinion. *— v.i.* **3.** To have or take an oblique direction; slope. **4.** To have a certain bias or attitude. *— Syn.* See TIP[1]. *— adj.* Lying at an angle; sloping. *— n.* **1.** A slanting direction, course, or plane; slope. **2.** A bent, bias, or leaning. **3.**

Point of view; attitude. [< earlier *slent* < Scand. Cf. Norw. *slenta* slope.] **— slant′ing·ly** *adv.*

slant·wise (slant′wīz′) *adj.* Slanting; oblique. *— adv.* At a slant or slope; obliquely. Also **slant′ways′** (-wāz′).

slap (slap) *n.* **1.** A blow delivered with the open hand or with something flat. **2.** A sharp rebuke; insult; slur. *— v.* **slapped, slap·ping** *v.t.* **1.** To hit or strike with the open hand or with something flat. **2.** To rebuff; insult. **3.** To put or place violently or carelessly. *— v.i.* **4.** To strike or beat as if with slaps. *— adv.* **1.** Suddenly and forcibly; abruptly. **2.** *Informal* Directly; straight. [< LG *slapp*] **— slap′per** *n.*

slap·dash (slap′dash′) *adj.* Done or acting in a dashing or reckless way; impetuous; careless. *— n.* Offhand or careless work, behavior, etc. *— adv.* In a careless manner.

slap·hap·py (slap′hap′ē) *adj.* **·pi·er, ·pi·est** *Slang* **1.** Dazed or giddy from or as from repeated blows. **2.** Silly; irresponsible. **— slap′hap′pi·ness** *n.*

slap·jack slap′jak′) *n.* *U.S.* A griddlecake; flapjack.

slap·stick (slap′stik′) *n.* **1.** Boisterous, loud comedy. **2.** A flexible paddle formerly used in farces and pantomimes to make a loud report when an actor was struck with it. *— adj.* Using or suggestive of slapstick: *slapstick* humor.

slash (slash) *v.t.* **1.** To strike or cut violently with or as with an edged instrument. **2.** To whip; lash. **3.** To make long gashes, cuts, or slits in. **4.** To cut slits in, as a garment, so as to expose lining. **5.** To criticize severely. **6.** To reduce sharply, as prices, wages, etc. *— v.i.* **7.** To make sweeping, violent, or haphazard strokes with or as with something sharp. *— n.* **1.** The act or result of slashing. **2.** A slit or gash, esp. an ornamental slit in a garment. **3.** An opening or gap left in a forest after logging, a destructive fire, or a high wind. **4.** *Printing* A virgule. [? < OF *esclachier* to break] **— slash′er** *n.*

slash·ing (slash′ing) *adj.* **1.** Aggressively or destructively severe; violent. **2.** *Informal* Very fine; splendid. *— n.* A slash. **— slash′ing·ly** *adv.*

slat (slat) *n.* A thin, narrow strip of wood or metal, as one of those in a crate, window blind, etc. *— v.t.* **slat·ted, slat·ting** To provide or make with slats. [< OF *esclat* splinter]

slate (slāt) *n.* **1.** A compact, fine-grained rock that splits readily into thin and even layers. **2.** A piece, slab, or plate of slate used for roofing, writing upon, etc. **3.** A record of one's past performance or behavior: a clean *slate*. **4.** A prearranged list, as of political candidates before their nomination or election. **5.** A dull bluish gray color resembling slate. *— adj.* **1.** Made of slate. **2.** Having the color of slate. *— v.t.* **slat·ed, slat·ing 1.** To roof with slate. **2.** To put on a political slate or a list of any sort. **3.** To designate or mark, as for a specific change in condition. [< OF *esclate*, fem. of *esclat* chip, splinter] **— slat′er** *n.* **— slat′y** *adj.*

slath·er (slath′ər) *Informal or Dial. v.t.* **1.** To daub thickly. **2.** To spend or use profusely. [Origin uncertain]

slat·tern (slat′ərn) *n.* An untidy or slovenly woman. *— adj.* Untidy; slovenly. [< dial. E *slatter* to slop, spill] **slat′tern·li·ness** *n.* **— slat′tern·ly** *adj. & adv.*

slaugh·ter (slô′tər) *n.* **1.** The act of killing; esp. the butchering of cattle and other animals for market. **2.** Wanton or savage killing, esp. of human beings; massacre; carnage. *— Syn.* See MASSACRE. *— v.t.* **1.** To kill for the market; butcher. **2.** To kill wantonly or savagely. [< ON *slâtr* butcher's meat] **— slaugh′ter·er** *n.* **— slaugh′ter·ous** *adj.* **— slaugh′ter·ous·ly** *adv.*

slaugh·ter·house (slô′tər·hous′) *n.* A place where animals are butchered; a scene of carnage.

Slav (släv, slav) *n.* A member of any of the Slavic-speaking peoples of northern or eastern Europe, comprising the Russians, Poles, Czechs, Moravians, Wends, Slovaks, Bulgarians, Serbians, Croats, Slovenes, etc.

slave (slāv) *n.* **1.** A person over whose life, liberty, and property someone has absolute control. **2.** A person in mental or moral subjection to a habit, vice, or influence. **3.** One who labors like a slave; a drudge. *— v.i.* **slaved, slav·ing** To work like a slave. [< F < Med.L *slavus, sclavus*]

slave driver 1. A person who oversees slaves at work. **2.** Any severe or exacting employer.

slave·hold·er (slāv′hōl′dər) *n.* An owner of slaves. **— slave′hold′ing** *adj. & n.*

slav·er[1] (slav′ər) *v.t.* **1.** To dribble saliva over. *— v.i.* **2.** To dribble saliva; drool. *— n.* Saliva issuing or dribbling from the mouth. [Prob. < ON *slafra*] **— slav′er·er** *n.*

slav·er[2] (slā′vər) *n.* A person or a vessel engaged in the slave trade.

slav·er·y (slā′vər·ē, slāv′rē) *n.* **1.** The holding of human beings as property or chattels; also, the condition of a slave. **2.** Mental, moral, or spiritual bondage. **3.** Slavish toil.

slave trade The business of dealing in slaves; esp. the bringing of Negro slaves to America. **— slave trader**

slav·ey (slā′vē, slav′ē) *n. pl.* **slav·eys** *Brit. Informal* A female servant, esp. a maid of all work.

Slav·ic (slä′vik, slav′ik) *adj.* Of or pertaining to the Slavs or their languages. — *n.* A branch of the Balto-Slavic sub-family of the Indo-European language family, consisting of the following groups: **East Slavic** (Russian, including Great Russian, Ukrainian, and Byelorussian); **West Slavic** (Czech, Slovak, Polish, Wendish); **South Slavic** (Serbo-Croatian, Bulgarian, Slovenian, Macedonian). — **Church Slavic** or **Church Slavonic** The liturgical language of the Eastern Orthodox Slavs and of certain Uniats: also called *Old Church Slavic, Old Church Slavonic, Old Slavic.*

slav·ish (slā′vish) *adj.* **1.** Pertaining to or befitting a slave; servile; base. **2.** Extremely hard or laborious. **3.** Dependent; imitative. — **slav′ish·ly** *adv.* — **slav′ish·ness** *n.*

Sla·von·ic (slə·von′ik) *adj. & n.* Slavic.

slaw (slô) *n.* Cole slaw.

slay (slā) *v.t.* **slew, slain, slay·ing** To kill, esp. by violence. [OE *slēan*] — **slay′er** *n.*

slea·zy (slē′zē, slā′-) *adj.* **·zi·er, ·zi·est 1.** Lacking firmness of texture or substance; poorly made. **2.** Cheap; shoddy. [Origin uncertain] — **slea′zi·ly** *adv.* — **slea′zi·ness** *n.*

sled (sled) *n.* **1.** A vehicle on runners, designed for carrying people or loads over snow and ice; a sledge. **2.** A small, light frame mounted on runners, used by children for sliding on snow and ice. — *v.* **sled·ded, sled·ding** *v.t.* **1.** To convey on a sled. — *v.i.* **2.** To ride on a sled. [< MLG *sledde*] — **sled′der** *n.*

sled·ding (sled′ing) *n.* **1.** The condition of roads for sleds. **2.** The act of using a sled. **3.** State or circumstances of progress, work, etc.: hard *sledding.*

sledge[1] (slej) *n.* A vehicle or sled for moving loads over snow and ice. — *v.t. & v.i.* **sledged, sledg·ing** To travel or convey on a sledge. [< MDu. *sleedse*]

sledge[2] (slej) *n.* A heavy hammer wielded with one or both hands, for blacksmiths' use, or for breaking stone, coal, etc.: also **sledge hammer.** — *v.t.* **sledged, sledg·ing** To hammer, break, or strike with a sledge. [OE *slecg*]

sleek (slēk) *adj.* **1.** Smooth and glossy; polished. **2.** Smooth-spoken; flattering; unctuous. — *v.t.* **1.** To make smooth, even, or glossy. **2.** To soothe; mollify. [Var. of SLICK] — **sleek′ly** *adv.* — **sleek′ness** *n.* — **sleek′y** *adj.*

sleep (slēp) *n.* **1.** A state or period of reduced activity, accompanied by a complete or partial unconsciousness. **2.** A period of slumber. **3.** Any condition of inactivity, torpor, or rest. — *v.* **slept, sleep·ing** *v.i.* **1.** To be or fall asleep; slumber. **2.** To be dormant, inactive or quiet, or to rest in death. — *v.t.* **3.** To rest or repose in: to *sleep* the sleep of the dead. **4.** To provide with sleeping quarters; lodge. — **to sleep away** (or **off** or **out**) To pass or get rid of by or as by sleep: to *sleep off* a hangover. — **to sleep on** To postpone a decision upon. [OE *slēp*]

sleep·er (slē′pər) *n.* **1.** One who or that which sleeps. **2.** A railroad sleeping car. **3.** *U.S. Informal* A play, motion picture, or book that achieves unexpected and striking success.

sleeping bag A large bag with a warm lining, used for sleeping, esp. out of doors.

sleeping car A passenger railroad car with accommodations for sleeping.

sleeping pill *Med.* A sedative; esp., one of the barbiturates taken to relieve acute or persistent insomnia.

sleeping sickness *Pathol.* The final stage of a disease prevalent in tropical Africa, marked by lethargy, fever and headaches and terminating in death.

sleep·less (slēp′lis) *adj.* Unable to sleep; wakeful; restless; unquiet. — **sleep′less·ly** *adv.* — **sleep′less·ness** *n.*

sleep·walk·ing (slēp′wô′king) *n.* The act or practice of one who walks while asleep. — **sleep′walk′er** *n.*

sleep·y (slē′pē) *adj.* **sleep·i·er, sleep·i·est 1.** Inclined to sleep. **2.** Drowsy; sluggish; dull; heavy. **3.** Conducive to sleep. — **sleep′i·ly** *adv.* — **sleep′i·ness** *n.*

sleep·y·head (slē′pē·hed′) *n.* A sleepy person. — **sleep′y·head′ed** *adj.*

sleet (slēt) *n.* **1.** A mixture of snow or hail and rain. **2.** A drizzle or shower of partly frozen rain. **3.** A thin coating of ice. — *v.i.* To pour or shed sleet. [Akin to MLG *slōte* hail] — **sleet′y** *adj.*

sleeve (slēv) *n.* **1.** The part of a garment that serves as a covering for the arm. **2.** *Mech.* A tube surrounding something, as a shaft, for protection or connection. — **up one's sleeve** Hidden but at hand. — *v.t.* **sleeved, sleev·ing** To furnish or fit with a sleeve or sleeves. [OE *slīefe*] — **sleeve′less** *adj.*

sleigh (slā) *n.* A light vehicle, usu. drawn by a horse with runners for use on snow and ice. — *v.i.* To ride or travel in a sleigh. [< Du. *slee,* contr. of *slode* slodge] — **sleigh′er** *n.* — **sleigh′ing** *n.*

sleight (slīt) *n.* **1.** The quality of being skillful in manipulation. **2.** Craft; cunning. [< ON *slǣgth* slyness]

sleight of hand 1. A juggler's or magician's trick so deftly done that the manner of performance escapes observation: also called *legerdemain.* **2.** The performance of such tricks.

slen·der (slen′dər) *adj.* **1.** Having a small diameter or circumference in proportion to the length or height; slim; thin. **2.** Having little strength or vigor; feeble; frail. **3.** Having slight basis or foundation; of little validity. **4.** Small or inadequate; moderate; insignificant. [ME *slendre*] — **slen′der·ly** *adv.* — **slen′der·ness** *n.*

slen·der·ize (slen′də·rīz) *v.t. & v.i.* **·ized, ·iz·ing** To make or become slender.

slept (slept) Past tense and past participle of SLEEP.

sleuth (slooth) *n.* **1.** *U.S. Informal* A detective. **2.** A bloodhound. — *v.t.* **1.** To follow; track. — *v.i.* **2.** To play the detective. [< ON *slōth* track, trail]

slew[1] (sloo) Past tense of SLAY.

slew[2] (sloo) See SLOUGH (def. 2).

slew[3] (sloo) *n.* *U.S. Informal* A large number, crowd, or amount; a lot: also spelled *slue.* [Cf. Irish *sluagh* crowd]

slew[4] (sloo) See SLUE[1].

slice (slīs) *n.* **1.** A thin, broad piece cut off from a larger piece. **2.** Any of various tools or devices having a broad, flat blade. **3.** In golf, a stroke that causes the ball to veer to the right. — *v.* **sliced, slic·ing** *v.t.* **1.** To cut or remove from a larger piece: often with *off.* **2.** To cut into broad, thin pieces; divide; apportion. **3.** In golf, to hit (the ball) with a slice. — *v.i.* **4.** In golf, to slice a ball. [< OF < OHG *slizan* to slit] — **slic′er** *n.*

slick (slik) *adj.* **1.** Smooth; slippery; sleek. **2.** Flattering; obsequious. **3.** *Informal* Dexterously done; cleverly said. **4.** Smart and clever, but often of little depth. **5.** Smooth; oily, as the surface of water. **6.** Glazed, as paper; also, printed on glazed paper: *slick* magazines. **7.** *Slang* Agreeable; excellent. — *n.* **1.** A smooth place on a surface of water, as from oil. **2.** A broad chisel for paring or slicking: also **slick chisel.** **3.** *Usu. pl. U.S.* A magazine printed on glazed paper: distinguished from *pulp.* — *adv. Slang* In a slick or smooth manner; deftly. — *v.t.* **1.** To make smooth, trim, glossy, or oily. **2.** *Informal* To trim up; make presentable: often with *up.* [ME *slike,* ? < OE *nīgslÿcod* glossy]

slick·er (slik′ər) *n.* **1.** *U.S.* A waterproof overcoat of oilskin, plastic, etc. **2.** *Informal* A clever, shifty person.

slide (slīd) *v.* **slid** (slid), **slid** or **slid·den** (slid′n), **slid·ing** *v.i.* **1.** To pass along over a surface with a smooth, slipping movement. **2.** To move easily or smoothly; pass gradually or imperceptibly. **3.** To proceed without being acted upon or directed: to let the matter *slide.* **4.** To lose one's equilibrium or foothold; slip. **5.** In baseball, to throw oneself along the ground toward a base. — *v.t.* **6.** To cause to slide, as over a surface. **7.** To move, put, enter, etc., with quietness or dexterity: with *in* or *into.* — *n.* **1.** An act of sliding. **2.** The slipping of a mass of earth, snow, etc., from a higher to a lower level; avalanche. **3.** An inclined plane or channel for sliding, as for children to slide upon. **4.** A small plate of glass on which a specimen is mounted and examined through a microscope. **5.** A small plate bearing a single image for projection on a screen. **6.** *Music* In a trumpet or trombone, a U-shaped portion of the tubing that is pushed in and out to vary the pitch. **7.** *Mech.* A sliding part. [OE *slīdan*] — **slid′er** *n.*

slide fastener A zipper.

slide projector An optical device for projecting magnified images from transparent slides onto a wall or screen.

slide rule A device consisting of a rigid ruler with a central sliding piece, both ruler and slide being graduated in a similar logarithmic scale to permit rapid calculations.

sliding door A door that opens and closes by moving sidewise along grooves.

sliding scale A schedule affecting imports, prices, or wages, varying under conditions of consumption, demand, or the market price of some article.

slight (slīt) *adj.* **1.** Of small importance; trifling. **2.** Small in quantity, intensity, or degree; inconsiderable. **3.** Slender; frail; delicate; flimsy. — *v.t.* **1.** To manifest neglect of or disregard for; ignore. **2.** To do imperfectly or thoughtlessly; shirk. **3.** To treat as trivial or insignificant. — *n.* An act or omission involving failure in courtesy or respect toward another. [ME] — **slight′ing** *adj.* — **slight′ing·ly** *adv.* — **slight′ly** *adv.* — **slight′ness** *n.*

sli·ly (slī′lē) See SLYLY.

slim (slim) *adj.* **slim·mer, slim·mest 1.** Small in thickness in proportion to height or length, as a human figure or a tree. **2.** Insufficient; meager: a *slim* attendance. — *v.t. & v.i.* **slimmed, slim·ming** To make or become thin or thinner. [< Du. *slim* bad] — **slim′ly** *adv.* — **slim′ness** *n.*

slime (slīm) *n.* **1.** Any soft, sticky, or dirty substance. **2.** Soft, moist, adhesive mud or earth; muck. **3.** A mucous exudation from the bodies of certain animals, as fishes and snails, and certain plants. — *v.* **slimed, slim·ing** *v.t.* **1.** To smear or cover with or as with slime. **2.** To remove slime from. [OE *slīm*]

SLEIGH

slim·y (slī′mē) *adj.* **slim·i·er, slim·i·est** **1.** Covered or bedaubed with slime. **2.** Containing slime. **3.** Slimelike; foul. **— slim′i·ly** *adv.* **— slim′i·ness** *n.*

sling¹ (sling) *n.* **1.** A strap or pocket usu. with a string attached to each end, for hurling a stone or other missile by whirling the whole and releasing one of the strings. **2.** Any of various ropes, straps, etc., for suspending or hoisting something, as for holding up an injured limb, carrying a rifle, etc. **3.** The act of slinging; a sudden throw; cast; fling. — *v.t.* **slung, sling·ing** **1.** To fling from or as from a sling; hurl. **2.** To place or hang up in or as in a sling; move or hoist, as by a rope or tackle. [OE *slingan*] **— sling′er** *n.*

sling² (sling) *n.* *U.S.* A drink of brandy, whisky, or gin, with sugar and nutmeg, lemon juice, and ice.

sling-shot (sling′shot′) *n.* A weapon or toy consisting of a forked stick with an elastic strap attached to the prongs for catapulting small missiles: also called *catapult.*

slink (slingk) *v.i.* **slunk, slunk, slink·ing** To creep or steal along furtively or stealthily, as in fear. [OE *slincan* to creep] **— slink′ing·ly** *adv.*

slink·y (slingk′ē) *adj.* **slink·i·er, slink·i·est** **1.** Sneaking; stealthy. **2.** *Slang* Sinuous or feline in movement or form.

slip¹ (slip) *v.* **slipped** or **slipt, slip·ping** *v.t.* **1.** To cause to move smoothly and easily; cause to glide or slide. **2.** To put on or off easily, as a loose garment. **3.** To convey slyly or secretly. **4.** To free oneself or itself from, as a fetter or bridle. **5.** To let loose; unleash, as hounds. **6.** To escape or pass unobserved: It *slipped* my mind. **7.** To overlook; omit negligently. — *v.i.* **8.** To slide so as to cause harm or inconvenience; lose one's footing; become misplaced by failing to hold. **9.** To fall into an error or fault; err. **10.** To escape, as a ship. **11.** To move smoothly and easily. **12.** To get free of restraint. **13.** To go or come stealthily or unnoticed: often with *off, away,* or *from.* **— to let slip** To say without intending to. **— to slip one over on** *Informal* To cheat; hoodwink. — *n.* **1.** An act of slipping; a sudden slide. **2.** A lapse or error in speech, writing, or conduct; a slight mistake. **3.** *U.S.* A narrow space between two wharves. **4.** An artificial pier sloping down to the water, serving as a landing place. **5.** An inclined plane leading down to the water, on which vessels are repaired or constructed. **6.** A woman's undergarment, usu. the length of a dress. **7.** A pillow case: also **pillow slip. 8.** A leash that permits quick release of the dog. **9.** *Geol.* A joint or fissure where two rock strata have moved upon each other. **— to give (someone) the slip** To elude (someone). [< MLC *slippen*]

slip² (slip) *n.* **1.** A cutting from a plant for planting or grafting; a cion. **2.** A small, slender person, esp. a youthful one. **3.** A small piece of something, as of paper or cloth, rather long relative to its width; a strip. **4.** A small piece of paper for jotting down memoranda, a record, etc. — *v.t.* **slipped, slip·ping** To cut off for planting; make a slip or slips of. [< MDu. *slippen* to cut]

slip-cov·er (slip′kuv′ər) *n.* A fitted cloth cover for a chair, sofa, etc., that can be readily removed.

slip-knot (slip′not′) *n.* **1.** A knot having part of the material drawn through in a loop so that it is easily untied. For illus. see KNOT. **2.** A running knot.

slip-on (slip′on′, -ôn′) *adj.* Easily donned or taken off. — *n.* A slip-on garment, as a blouse.

slip-o·ver (slip′ō′vər) *adj.* Easily donned by drawing over the head: a *slipover* shirt. — *n.* A slipover garment.

slip·per (slip′ər) *n.* A low, light shoe that is easily slipped on or off the foot. **— slip′pered** *adj.*

slip·per·y (slip′ər·ē) *adj.* **·per·i·er, ·per·i·est 1.** Having a surface so smooth that objects slip or slide easily on it. **2.** That evades one's grasp; tricky; elusive. **3.** Unreliable; undependable. **— slip′per·i·ly** *adv.* **— slip′per·i·ness** *n.*

slippery elm 1. A tree of eastern North America. **2.** Its mucilaginous inner bark, used in medicine.

slip·shod (slip′shod′) *adj.* **1.** Carelessly done or wrought; negligent; slovenly. **2.** Down at the heel; ragged; seedy.

slip-stream (slip′strēm′) *n.* *Aeron.* The stream of air driven backwards by the propeller of an aircraft.

slip-up (slip′up′) *n.* *Informal* A mistake; error.

slit (slit) *n.* A cut that is relatively straight and long; also, a long, narrow opening. — *v.t.* **slit, slit·ting 1.** To make a long incision in; slash. **2.** To cut lengthwise into strips. [ME *slitten* to cut] **— slit′ter** *n.*

slith·er (slith′ər) *v.i.* **1.** To slide; slip, as on a surface where footing is insecure. **2.** To glide, as a snake. — *v.t.* **3.** To cause to slither. [OE *slīdan* to slide] **— slith′er·y** *adj.*

sliv·er (sliv′ər) *n.* **1.** A slender piece cut or torn off lengthwise; a splinter. **2.** Corded textile fibers drawn into a fleecy strand. — *v.t. & v.i.* To cut or split into long thin pieces. [< dial. E *slive* to cleave < OE *tōflīfan*] **— sliv′er·er** *n.*

slob (slob) *n.* **1.** *Informal* A stupid, careless, or unclean person. **2.** *Irish* Mud; mire. [< Irish *slab*]

slob·ber (slob′ər) *v.t.* **1.** To wet and foul with, or as if with, liquids oozing from the mouth. — *v.i.* **2.** To drivel; slaver. **3.**To talk or act gushingly. — *n.* **1.** Liquid spilled as from the mouth; slaver. **2.** Gushing, sentimental talk. [Var. of SLABBER] **— slob′ber·er** *n.* **— slob′ber·y** *adj.*

sloe (slō) *n.* **1.** The blackthorn (defs. 1 & 2). **2.** Any of various related plants [OE *slāh*]

sloe-eyed (slō′īd′) *adj.* Having dark, velvety eyes.

sloe gin A cordial with a gin base, flavored with sloes.

slog (slog) *v.t. & v.i.* **slogged, slog·ging 1.** To strike hard; slug. **2.** To plod (one's way), as through deep mud. — *n.* A heavy blow. [Var. of SLUG] **— slog′ger** *n.*

slo·gan (slō′gən) *n.* **1.** A battle or rallying cry, originally of the Highland clans. **2.** A catchword or motto adopted by a group, as a political party. [< Scottish Gaelic *sluagh* army + *gairm* yell]

sloop (slōōp) *n.* *Naut.* A single-masted, fore-and-aft rigged sailing vessel carrying at least one jib, now used principally as a racing vessel. [< Du. *sloep*]

SLOOP

slop (slop) *v.* **slopped, slop·ping** *v.i.* **1.** To splash or spill. **2.** To walk or move through slush. — *v.t.* **3.** To cause (a liquid) to spill or splash. **4.** To spill a liquid upon. **— to slop over 1.** To overflow and splash. **2.** To do or say more than is necessary, because of excess zeal, sentimentality, etc. — *n.* **1.** Slush; watery mud. **2.** A puddle of liquid that has been slopped. **3.** An unappetizing liquid or watery food. **4.** Refuse liquid. **5.** *pl.* Waste food or swill, used to feed pigs, etc. [ME < OE *-sloppe*]

slope (slōp) *v.* **sloped, slop·ing** *v.i.* **1.** To be inclined from the level or the vertical; slant. — *v.t.* **2.** To cause to slope. **— Syn.** See TIP. — *n.* **1.** Any slanting surface or line. **2.** The degree of inclination of a line or surface from the plane of the horizon. [OE *āslūpan* to slip away] **— slop′er** *n.* **— slop′ing·ly** *adv.* **— slop′ing·ness** *n.*

slop·py (slop′ē) *adj.* **·pi·er, ·pi·est 1.** Slushy; splashy; wet. **2.** Watery or pulpy. **3.** Splashed with liquid or slops. **4.** *Informal* Messy; slovenly; untidy. **5.** *Informal* Slipshod; careless. **— slop′pi·ly** *adv.* **— slop′pi·ness** *n.*

slops (slops) *n.pl.* **1.** Articles of clothing, bedding, etc., supplied to sailors on shipboard. **2.** Cheap, ready-made clothes. [ME < OE *-slop*]

slosh (slosh) *v.t.* **1.** To throw about, as a liquid. — *v.i.* **2.** To splash; flounder: to *slosh* through a pool. — *n.* Slush. [Var. of SLUSH] **— slosh′y** *adj.*

slot (slot) *n.* **1.** A long narrow groove or opening; notch or slit: the coin *slot* of a vending machine; the *slot* of a mailbox. **2.** A job opening or a place in a sequence. — *v.t.* **slot·ted, slot·ting** To cut a slot in; groove. [< OF *esclot* the hollow between the breasts]

sloth (slōth, slôth, sloth) *n.* **1.** Disinclination to exertion; habitual indolence; laziness. **2.** A slow-moving, tree-dwelling mammal of tropical America. [< OE *slǣwth*]

sloth·ful (slōth′fəl, slôth′-, sloth′-) *adj.* Sluggish; lazy; indolent. **— sloth′ful·ly** *adv.* **— sloth′ful·ness** *n.*

slot machine A vending machine or gambling machine having a slot in which a coin is dropped to cause operation.

slouch (slouch) *v.i.* **1.** To have a downcast or drooping gait, look, or posture. **2.** To hang or droop in a careless manner, as a hat. — *v.t.* **3.** To cause to droop or hang down. — *n.* **1.** A drooping of the head and shoulders caused by depression, fatigue, etc. **2.** A drooping of the brim of a hat. **3.** An awkward, heavy, or incompetent person: usu. in the negative: He's no *slouch* at baseball. [Origin uncertain] **— slouch′y** *adj.* **— slouch′i·ness** *n.*

slough¹ (slou *for defs. 1 & 3*; slōō *for def. 2*) *n.* **1.** A place of deep mud or mire; bog. **2.** A stagnant swamp, backwater, bayou, inlet, or pond in which water backs up: also spelled *slew, slue.* **3.** A state or moral depravity or despair. [OE *slōh*] **— slough′y** *adj.*

slough² (sluf) *n.* **1.** Dead tissue separated and thrown off from the living parts, as in gangrene. **2.** The skin of a serpent that has been or is about to be shed. — *v.t.* **1.** To cast off, as dead from living tissue: with *off.* **2.** To discard; shed, as a habit: with *off.* — *v.i.* **3.** To be cast off. **4.** To cast off a slough or tissue. [ME *slouh*] **— slough′y** *adj.*

slough of despond (slōō) Deep despair or dejection; despondency. [after the *Slough of Despond* in John Bunyan's *Pilgrim's Progress*]

Slo·vak (slō′vak, slō-vak′) *n.* **1.** One of a Slavic people of eastern Czechoslovakia. **2.** The West Slavic language of the Slovaks. — *adj.* Of or pertaining to the Slovaks or to their language. Also **Slo·vak·i·an** (slō-vak′ē-ən, -vä′kē-ən). [< Czech *slovāk* Slav]

slov·en (sluv′ən) *n.* One who is careless of dress or of cleanliness; one habitually untidy.

Slo·vene (slō′vēn, slō·vēn′) *n.* One of a group of southern Slavs now living in NW Yugoslavia. — *adj.* Of or pertaining to the Slovenes or to their language. [< G *Slovene*]

Slo·ve·ni·an (slō·vē′nē·ən) *adj.* Of or pertaining to Slovenia, its people, or their language. — *n.* The South Slavic language of the Slovenes.

slov·en·ly (sluv′ən·lē) *adj.* **·li·er, ·li·est** 1. Having the habits of a sloven. 2. Careless or slipshod in manner of work, etc. — *adv.* In a slovenly manner. — **slov′en·li·ness** *n.*

slow (slō) *adj.* 1. Having relatively small velocity; not quick in motion, performance, or occurrence. 2. Behind the standard time: said of a timepiece. 3. Not precipitate or hasty: *slow* to anger. 4. Dull or tardy in comprehending; mentally sluggish. 5. Lacking promptness, spirit, or liveliness. 6. *Informal* Dull or tedious in character: a *slow* party. 7. Being in a condition that is not conducive to speed: a *slow* track. 8. Inactive: Business is *slow* today. — *v.t.* 1. To make slow or slower: often with *up* or *down.* — *v.i.* 2. To go or become slow or slower: often with *up* or *down.* — *adv.* In a slow or cautious manner or speed. [OE *slāw*] — **slow′ly** *adv.* — **slow′ness** *n.*

slow-mo·tion (slō′mō′shən) *adj.* Pertaining to or designating a motion picture filmed at greater than standard speed so that the action appears slow in normal projection.

slow·poke (slō′pōk′) *n. Informal* A person who works or moves at an exceedingly slow pace; a laggard.

sludge (sluj) *n.* 1. Soft, water-soaked mud; mire. 2. A slush of snow or broken ice. 3. Muddy or pasty refuse, as that produced by sewage purification. 4. The sediment in a water tank or boiler. [Earlier *slutch*] — **sludg′y** *adj.*

slue¹ (slōō) *v.* **slued, slu·ing** *v.t.* 1. To cause to move sideways, as if some portion were pivoted. — *v.i.* 2. To move sideways. — *n.* The act of sluing around sideways; also, the position of a body that has slued. Also spelled *slew.* [Origin unknown]

slue² (slōō) See SLEW³.

slue³ (slōō) See SLOUGH¹ (def. 2).

slug¹ (slug) *n.* 1. A bullet or shot of irregular or oblong shape. 2. *Printing* **a** A strip of type metal for spacing matter, etc. **b** A metal strip used as a compositor's mark. 3. Any often counterfeit small chunk of metal; esp., one used as a coin in automatic machines. [Origin uncertain]

slug² (slug) *n.* 1. Any of various mollusks related to the snail, having an elongated body and a rudimentary shell. 2. The larva of a sawfly or other insect, resembling a slug. 3. A sluggard. [ME *slugge* sluggard]

slug³ (slug) *Informal n.* 1. A heavy blow, as with the fist or a baseball bat. 2. A drink of undiluted liquor. — *v.t.* **slugged, slug·ging** To strike heavily or brutally, as with the fist or a baseball bat. [Origin uncertain] — **slug′ger** *n.*

slug·gard (slug′ərd) *n.* A person habitually lazy or idle; a drone. — *adj.* Lazy; sluggish.

slug·gish (slug′ish) *adj.* 1. Slow; inactive; torpid. 2. Habitually idle and lazy. 3. Not active; slow; stagnant: a *sluggish* season. — **slug′gish·ly** *adv.* — **slug′gish·ness** *n.*

sluice (slōōs) *n.* 1. An artificial channel for conducting water, equipped with a valve or gate (**sluice gate**) to regulate the flow. 2. The body of water so channeled. 3. Any artificial channel, esp. one for excess water. 4. A trough through which water is run to separate gold ore, to float logs, etc. 5. That through which anything issues or flows. — *v.* **sluiced, sluic·ing** *v.t.* 1. To wet, water, or irrigate by or as by means of a sluice. 2. To wash in or by a sluice. 3. To draw out or conduct by or through a sluice. 4. To send (logs) down a sluice. — *v.i.* 5. To flow out or issue from a sluice. [< OF < L *excludere* to shut out]

slum (slum) *n. Often pl.* A squalid, dirty, overcrowded section of a city, marked by poverty and poor living conditions. — *v.t.* **slummed, slum·ming** To visit slums for amusement or curiosity. [< cant, room] — **slum′mer** *n.*

slum·ber (slum′bər) *v.i.* 1. To sleep, esp. lightly or quietly. 2. To be inactive; stagnate. — *v.t.* 3. To spend or pass in sleeping. — *n.* 1. Sleep. 2. A state of inactivity or quiescence. [OE *slūma* slumber] — **slum′ber·er** *n.* — **slum′ber·ing·ly** *adv.* — **slum′ber·less** *adj.*

slum·ber·ous (slum′bər·əs) *adj.* 1. Inducing sleep. 2. Sleepy; drowsy. 3. Suggesting or resembling sleep. Also **slum′ber·y, slum·brous** (slum′brəs). — **slum′ber·ous·ly** *adv.* — **slum′ber·ous·ness** *n.*

slum·lord (slum′lôrd′) *n. U.S.* A landlord of slum property. [< SLUM + (LAND)LORD]

slump (slump) *v.i.* 1. To break through a crust and sink. 2. To slide with perceptible motion down a declivity: said of rock, etc. 3. To fall or fail suddenly, as in value or quality. 4. To stand or walk with a stooping posture. — *n.* The act of slumping; a collapsing fall; a failure; a decline.

slung (slung) Past tense and past participle of SLING.

slunk (slungk) Past tense and past participle of SLINK.

slur (slûr) *v.t.* **slurred, slur·ring** 1. To slight; disparage; depreciate. 2. To pass over lightly or hurriedly. 3. To weaken and elide (speech sounds) by hurried articulation.

4. *Music* **a** To sing or play as indicated by the slur. **b** To mark with a slur. — *n.* 1. A disparaging remark or insinuation. 2. *Music* **a** A curved line (‿ or ⌒) indicating that tones so tied are to be sung to the same syllable or performed without a break between them. **b** The legato effect indicated or produced by this mark. 3. A blur. 4. A slurred articulation. [< dial. E, orig., fluid mud]

slush (slush) *n.* 1. Soft, sloppy material, as melting snow or soft mud. 2. Grease. 3. Overly sentimental talk or writing; drivel. [? Scand. origin] — **slush′y** *adj.*

slush fund *U.S.* Money collected or spent for corrupt purposes, as bribery, etc.

slut (slut) *n.* 1. A slatternly woman. 2. A woman of loose character; hussy. 3. A female dog. [ME *slutte*] — **slut′tish** *adj.* — **slut′tish·ly** *adv.* — **slut′tish·ness** *n.*

sly (slī) *adj.* **sli·er** or **sly·er, sli·est** or **sly·est** 1. Artfully dexterous in doing things secretly; cunning in evading detection. 2. Playfully clever; mischievous. 3. Meanly or stealthily clever. 4. Done with or marked by artful secrecy: a *sly* trick. 5. Skillful; wise. — **on the sly** In a stealthy way; with concealment. [< ON *slœgr*] — **sly′ness** *n.*

sly·ly (slī′lē) *adv.* In a sly manner: also spelled *slily.*

smack¹ (smak) *n.* 1. A quick, sharp sound, as of the lips when separated rapidly. 2. A sounding blow or slap. 3. The sound of a blow, esp. with something flat. — *v.t. & v.i.* To give or make a smack, as in tasting, kissing, etc.

smack² (smak) *v.i.* 1. To have a taste or flavor, esp. as tested by smacking: usu. with *of.* 2. To have or disclose a slight suggestion: with *of.* — *n.* 1. A suggestive taste, or flavor. 2. A mere taste; smattering. [OE *smæc* the taste]

smack³ (smak) *n.* A small, decked or half-decked vessel of various rig used chiefly for fishing, esp. one having a well for fish in its hold. [< Du. *smak*]

smack·ing (smak′ing) *adj.* Brisk; lively: a *smacking* breeze.

small (smôl) *adj.* 1. Comparatively less in size, quantity, extent, etc.; diminutive. 2. Being of slight moment, weight, or importance. 3. Narrow; ignoble; mean; paltry. 4. Lacking in the qualities of greatness. 5. Acting or transacting business in a limited way. 6. Weak in characteristic properties: said of liquors: *small* beer. 7. Slender; fine; soft, as a voice. 8. Of low degree; obscure. 9. Lacking in power or strength. — *adv.* 1. In a low or faint tone. 2. Into small pieces. 3. In a small way; trivially; also, timidly. — *n.* 1. A small or slender part: the *small* of the back. 2. A small thing or quantity. [OE *smæl*] — **small′ness** *n.*

small arms Firearms of small caliber, as pistols, rifles, and machine guns.

small capital A capital letter cut slightly larger than the lower-case letters of a specified type size.

small change Coins of small denomination.

small craft Small boats or vessels collectively.

small fry 1. Small, young fish. 2. Young children. 3. Small or insignificant people or things.

small hours The early hours of the morning.

small letter A lower-case letter, as *a* in *Ra.*

small-mind·ed (smôl′mīn′did) *adj.* 1. Having a trivial, petty mind. 2. Narrow; intolerant; ungenerous. — **small′-mind′ed·ly** *adv.* — **small′-mind′ed·ness** *n.*

small potatoes *U.S. Informal* Insignificant persons or things.

small·pox (smôl′poks′) *n. Pathol.* An acute, highly contagious virus disease, characterized by inflammatory fever and the eruption of deep-seated pustules that usu. leave permanent scars: also called *variola.*

small talk Unimportant or trivial conversation.

small-time (smôl′tīm′) *adj. U.S. Slang* Petty; unimportant: a *smalltime* hoodlum.

smart (smärt) *v.i.* 1. To experience a stinging sensation, generally superficial, either bodily or mental. 2. To cause a stinging sensation. 3. To experience remorse. 4. To have one's feelings hurt. — *v.t.* 5. To cause to smart. — *adj.* 1. Quick in thought or action; bright; clever. 2. Impertinently witty: often used contemptuously. 3. Vigorous; emphatic; severe; brisk. 4. Causing a smarting sensation; stinging; pungent. 5. Sharp, as at trade; shrewd. 6. *Dial.* Large; considerable: a *smart* crop of wheat. 7. Sprucely dressed; showy. 8. Belonging to the stylish classes; fashionable. — *n.* 1. An acute stinging sensation, as from a scratch or an irritant. 2. Any distress; poignant mental suffering. [OE *smeortan*] — **smart′ly** *adv.* — **smart′ness** *n.*

smart al·eck (al′ik) *Informal* A cocky, offensively conceited person. — **smart-al·eck·y** (smärt′al′ik·ē) *adj.*

smart·en (smär′tən) *v.t.* 1. To improve in appearance; make smart: with *up.* 2. To make more alert or clever.

smart set Fashionable society.

smart·weed (smärt′wēd′) *n.* Any of several species of widely distributed marsh plants whose leaves cause itching.

smash (smash) *v.t.* 1. To break in many pieces suddenly, as by a blow, pressure, or collision. 2. To flatten; crush. 3. To dash or fling violently so as to crush or break. 4. To strike with a sudden, forceful blow. 5. To make bankrupt.

6. To destroy, as a theory.　**7.** In tennis, etc., to strike (the ball) with a hard, swift, overhand stroke.　—*v.i.* **8.** To go bankrupt; fail, as a business, etc.　**9.** To come into violent contact so as to crush or be crushed; collide.　**— to go to smash** *Informal* To be ruined; fail.　— *n.* **1.** An act or instance of smashing, or the state of being smashed.　**2.** Any disaster or sudden breakup: a *smash* in business.　**3.** In tennis, etc., a strong overhand shot.　**4.** *Informal* Something acclaimed by the public: a **smash hit**. [Prob. imit. Cf. Norw. *smaska*.]　**— smash′er** *n.*

smash·ing (smash′ing) *adj. Informal* Extremely impressive; overwhelmingly good: a *smashing* success.

smash-up (smash′up′)　*n.* A smash; a disastrous collision.

smat·ter (smat′ər)　*v.t.* To talk of, dabble in, study, or use superficially.　— *n.* A smattering. [ME *smateren*, ? < Scand.]　**— smat′ter·er** *n.*

smat·ter·ing (smat′ər·ing)　*n.* A superficial knowledge of something.　**— smat′ter·ing·ly** *adv.*

smear (smir)　*v.t.* **1.** To spread, rub, or cover with grease, paint, dirt, etc.; bedaub.　**2.** To spread or apply in a thick layer or coating: to *smear* grease on an axle.　**3.** To defame; slander.　**4.** *U.S. Slang* To defeat utterly.　—*v.i.* **5.** To be or become smeared.　— *n.* **1.** A soiled spot; stain.　**2.** A small quantity of material, as blood, sputum, etc., placed on a microscope slide for analysis.　**3.** A substance to be smeared on something, as a glaze for pottery.　**4.** A slanderous attack; defamation.　[OE < *smeoru* grease]

smear·y (smir′ē)　*adj.* **smear·i·er, smear·i·est** Greasy, viscous, or staining; also, smeared.　**— smear′i·ness** *n.*

smell (smel)　*v.* **smelled** or **smelt, smell·ing** *v.t.* **1.** To perceive by means of the nose and its olfactory nerves.　**2.** To perceive the odor of; scent.　**3.** To test by odor or smell.　**4.** To discover or detect as if by smelling: often with *out*.　—*v.i.* **5.** To emit an odor or perfume: frequently with *of*; also, to give indications of, as if by odor: to *smell* of treason.　**6.** To be malodorous.　**7.** To use the sense of smell.　**8.** To pry; investigate: with *about*.　— *n.* **1.** The special sense by means of which odors are perceived.　**2.** The sensation excited through the olfactory nerves.　**3.** That which is directly perceived by this sense; an odor.　**4.** A hint; trace.　**5.** An act of smelling.　[ME *smellen*]　**— smell′er** *n.*

— Syn. (noun) **3.** *Smell* often suggests a strong and slightly unpleasant sensation, and *odor*, a more delicate and pleasing one. *Scent* is always delicate. *Aroma, fragrance,* and *perfume* are pleasant. *Stench* and *stink* are sickening and unpleasant.

smelling salts Pungent or aromatic salts, or mixtures of such, often scented, used as stimulants by smelling.

smel·ly (smel′ē)　*adj.* **·li·er, ·li·est** *Informal* Having an unpleasant smell; malodorous.

smelt¹ (smelt)　*v.t. Metall.* **1.** To reduce (ores) by fusion in a furnace.　**2.** To obtain (a metal) from the ore by a process including fusion.　—*v.i.* **3.** To melt or fuse, as a metal. [< MDu. *smelten* to melt]

smelt² (smelt)　*n.* *pl.* **smelts** or **smelt** Any of various small silvery food fishes of north Atlantic and Pacific waters. [OE]

smelt³ (smelt)　Alternative past tense and past participle of SMELL.

smelt·er (smel′tər)　*n.* **1.** One engaged in smelting ore.　**2.** An establishment for smelting: also **smelt′er·y.**

smidg·en (smij′ən)　*n. U.S. Informal* A tiny bit or part.

smi·lax (smī′laks)　*n.* **1.** Any of various shrubby or herbaceous plants of the lily family, having thorny stems, flowers in umbels, and globular fruit, esp. one yielding sarsaparilla.　**2.** A delicate twining greenhouse plant of the lily family, with greenish flowers.　[< L < Gk. *smilax* yew]

smile (smīl)　*n.* **1.** A pleased or amused expression of the face, characterized by a raising up of the corners of the mouth.　**2.** A pleasant aspect: the *smile* of spring.　**3.** Propitious disposition; favor; blessing: the *smile* of fortune.　— *v.* **smiled, smil·ing** *v.i.* **1.** To give a smile; wear a cheerful aspect.　**2.** To show approval or favor: often with *upon*.　—*v.t.* **3.** To express by means of a smile. [ME *smilen,* prob. < LG]　**— smil′er** *n.*　**— smil′ing·ly** *adv.*　**— smil′ing·ness** *n.*

— Syn. (noun) **1.** In a *smile*, the mouth is closed or slightly opened; in a *grin* it is opened wide, displaying the teeth. A *smile* suggests pleasure, satisfaction, approval, or amity. A *grin* may denote amusement, triumph, or irony.

smirch (smûrch)　*v.t.* **1.** To soil, as with grime; smear.　**2.** To defame; degrade: to *smirch* a reputation.　— *n.* The act of smirching, or the state of being smirched; a smear; a moral stain or defect. [ME < OF *esmorcher* to hurt]

smirk (smûrk)　*v.i.* To smile in a silly, self-complacent, or affected manner.　— *n.* An affected or artificial smile. [OE *smearcian*]　**— smirk′er** *n.*　**— smirk′ing·ly** *adv.*

smite (smīt)　*v.* **smote, smit·ten** or **smit** or **smote, smit·ing** *v.t.* **1.** To strike (something).　**2.** To strike a blow with (something); cause to strike.　**3.** To cut, sever, or break by a blow: usually with *off* or *out*.　**4.** To strike with disaster; afflict.　**5.** To affect powerfully with sudden feeling.　**6.** To cause to feel regret or remorse.　**7.** To affect as if by a blow: The thought *smote* him.　**8.** To kill by a sudden blow.　—*v.i.* **9.** To come with sudden force; also, to knock against something.　[OE *smītan*]　**— smit′er** *n.*

smith (smith)　*n.* **1.** One who shapes metals by hammering: *goldsmith, tinsmith.*　**2.** A blacksmith.　[OE]

smith·er·eens (smith′ə·rēnz′)　*n.pl. Informal* Fragments produced as by an explosion. Also **smith′ers** (-ərz).　[Cf. dial. E (Irish) *smidirin* fragment]

smith·y (smith′ē, smith′ē)　*n.* *pl.* **smith·ies** A blacksmith's shop; a forge.　[< ON *smithja*]

smit·ten (smit′n)　Alternative past participle of SMITE.　— *adj.* **1.** Struck with sudden force; gravely afflicted.　**2.** Having the affections suddenly attracted.

smock (smok)　*n.* A loose outer garment of light material worn to protect one's clothes.　—*v.t.* **1.** To clothe in a smock.　**2.** To decorate with smocking. [OE *smoc*]

smock·ing (smok′ing)　*n.* Needlework in which the material is stitched into very small pleats or gathers, forming a kind of honeycomb ornamentation.

smog (smog)　*n.* A combination of smoke and fog, esp. as seen in thickly populated industrial and manufacturing areas. [Blend of SM(OKE) and (F)OG]

smoke (smōk)　*n.* **1.** The volatilized products of the combustion of organic substances, as coal, wood, etc., forming a suspension of carbon particles in a gas.　**2.** Anything transient and unsubstantial; a useless or ephemeral result.　**3.** The act of smoking a pipe, cigar, etc.　**4.** A period of time during which one smokes tobacco.　**5.** *Informal* A cigarette, cigar, or pipeful of tobacco.　— *v.* **smoked, smok·ing** *v.i.* **1.** To emit or give out smoke.　**2.** To inhale and exhale the smoke from a pipe, cigarette, etc.　—*v.t.* **3.** To inhale and exhale the smoke of (tobacco, opium, etc.); also, to use (a pipe, etc.) for this purpose.　**4.** To cure (meat, fish, etc.) by treating with smoke.　**5.** To apply smoke to (animals) in order to drive away: with *out*.　**6.** To force out of hiding (a criminal, etc.) or secrecy (information): with *out*. [OE *smoca*]

smoke·house (smōk′hous′)　*n.* A building or closed room in which meat, fish, hides, etc., are cured by smoke.

smoke·less (smōk′lis)　*adj.* Having or emitting little or no smoke: *smokeless* powder.

smok·er (smō′kər)　*n.* **1.** One who or that which smokes.　**2.** A smoking car.　**3.** A social gathering of men.

smoke screen A dense cloud of smoke used to prevent enemy observation of a place, force, or operation.　Also **smoke blanket, smoke curtain.**

smoke·stack (smōk′stak′)　*n.* **1.** An upright pipe, usu. of sheet or plate iron, through which combustion gases from a furnace are discharged into the air.　**2.** The funnel of a steamboat or locomotive, or the chimney of a factory, etc.

smoking jacket A short coat worn instead of a regular suit coat as a lounging jacket.

smok·y (smō′kē)　*adj.* **smok·i·er, smok·i·est 1.** Giving forth smoke.　**2.** Mixed with smoke: *smoky* air.　**3.** Emitting smoke improperly and unpleasantly, as from bad draft.　**4.** Discolored with smoke.　**5.** Smoke-colored; dark gray.　**6.** Covered with mist.　**— smok′i·ly** *adv.*　**— smok′i·ness** *n.*

smol·der (smōl′dər)　*v.i.* **1.** To burn and smoke with little smoke and no flame.　**2.** To exist in a latent state; to manifest suppressed feeling.　— *n.* Smoke. [ME *smoldren*]

smolt (smōlt)　*n.* A young salmon on its first descent from the river to the sea. [? Akin to SMELT²]

smooth (smooth)　*adj.* **1.** Having a surface without irregularities; not rough; continuously even.　**2.** Having no impediments or obstructions; easy; free from shocks or jolts.　**3.** Calm and unruffled; bland; mild.　**4.** Flowing melodiously: a *smooth* style.　**5.** Suave, as in speech; flattering: often implying deceit.　**6.** Free from hair; beardless.　**7.** Without lumps; having the elements perfectly blended.　**8.** Offering no resistance to a body sliding along its surface; without friction.　— *adv.* Calmly; evenly.　—*v.t.* **1.** To make smooth or even on the surface.　**2.** To make easy or less difficult: to *smooth* one's path.　**3.** To free from or remove obstructions.　**4.** To render less harsh or softer and more flowing.　**5.** To soften the worst features of; palliate: usu. with *over*.　**6.** To make calm; mollify.　—*v.i.* **7.** To become smooth.　**— to smooth (someone's) ruffled feathers** To mollify.　— *n.* **1.** The smooth portion or surface of anything.　**2.** The act of smoothing. [OE *smōth*]　**— smooth′er** *n.*　**— smooth′ly** *adv.*　**— smooth′ness** *n.*

smooth·bore (smooth′bôr′, -bōr′)　*n.* A firearm with an unrifled bore. Also **smooth bore.**　**— smooth′bored′** *adj.*

smooth breathing In classical Greek: **a** The absence of an aspirated sound. **b** The symbol (′) indicating this.

smooth·en (smoo′thən)　*v.t. & v.i.* To smooth.

smör·gås·bord (smôr′gəs·bôrd, *Sw.* smœr′gôs·bôrd)　*n.* **1.** Scandinavian hors d'oeuvres.　**2.** A buffet supper consisting of such hors d'oeuvres.   3. A restaurant serving smörgås-bord.   Also **smor·gas·bord.**   [< Sw.]

smote (smōt)   Past tense of SMITE.

smoth·er (smuth′ər)   *v.t.*   1. To prevent the respiration of; suffocate; stifle.   2. To cover, or cause to smolder, as a fire.   3. To hide or suppress: to *smother* one's feelings.   4. To cook in a covered dish or under some other substance.   — *v.i.*   5. To suffocate, as from lack of air, etc.   6. To be covered without air, as a fire.   7. To be hidden or suppressed, as wrath.   — *n.*   1. That which smothers, as stifling vapor or dust.   2. The state of being smothered; suppression.   [Earlier *smorther*]   — **smoth′er·y** *adj.*

smoul·der (smōl′dər)   See SMOLDER.

smudge (smuj)   *v.* **smudged, smudg·ing** *v.t.*   1. To smear; soil.   2. To protect (from frost, insects, etc.) by a heavy, smoky pall.   — *v.i.*   3. To cause a smudge.   4. To be smudged.   — *n.*   1. A soiling, as of dry dirt or soot; smear; stain.   2. A smoky fire or its smoke for driving away insects, preventing frost, etc.   [Var. of SMUTCH]

smudg·y (smuj′ē)   *adj.* **smudg·i·er, smudg·i·est** Full of or causing smudges.   — **smudg′i·ly** *adv.*   — **smudg′i·ness** *n.*

smug (smug)   *adj.* **smug·ger, smug·gest**   1. Characterized by a self-satisfied or complacent air.   2. Trim; spruce.   [Cf. LG *smuk* neat]   — **smug′ly** *adv.*   — **smug′ness** *n.*

smug·gle (smug′əl)   *v.* **·gled, ·gling** *v.t.*   1. To take (goods) into or out of a country without payment of lawful duties.   2. To bring in illicitly.   — *v.i.*   3. To practice smuggling.   [< LG *smuggeln*]   — **smug′gler** *n.*   — **smug′gling** *n.*

smut (smut)   *n.*   1. The blackening made by soot, smoke, etc.   2. Obscenity; obscene language.   3. Any of various fungus diseases of plants, in which the affected parts change into a dusty black powder.   4. Any of the fungi causing such a disease.   — *v.* **smut·ted, smut·ting** *v.t.*   1. To blacken or stain, as with soot or smoke.   2. To affect with smut, as growing grain.   3. To pollute; defame.   — *v.i.*   4. To give off smut.   5. To be or become stained.   [< LG *schmutt* dirt]

smutch (smuch)   *v.t.*   To smudge; soil.   — *n.*   A smear; smudge.   [Cf. MHG *smutzen* to smear]   — **smutch′y** *adj.*

smut·ty (smut′ē)   *adj.* **·ti·er, ·ti·est**   1. Soiled with smut; black; stained.   2. Affected with smut: *smutty* corn.   3. Obscene; coarse; indecent.   — **smut′ti·ly** *adv.*   — **smut′ti·ness** *n.*

snack (snak)   *n.*   1. A slight, hurried meal.   2. A share of something.   [< MDu. *snacken* to bite]

snaf·fle (snaf′əl)   *n.*   A horse's bit without a curb, jointed in the middle.   Also **snaf′fle·bit** (-bit′).   — *v.t.* **·fled, ·fling** To control with a snaffle.   [Cf. Du. *snavel* muzzle]

sna·fu (sna-fōō′, sna′fōō)   *Slang*   *adj.*   In a state of utter confusion.   — *v.t.* **·fued, ·fu·ing** To put into confusion.   [Acronym for "Situation normal, all fouled up"]

snag (snag)   *n.*   1. A jagged or stumpy knot or protuberance, esp. the stumpy base of a branch.   2. A broken or projecting tooth.   3. The trunk of a tree fixed in the bottom of a river, etc., by which boats are sometimes pierced.   4. Any obstacle or difficulty.   — *v.* **snagged, snag·ging** *v.t.*   1. To injure, destroy, or impede by or as by a snag.   2. To clear of snags.   — *v.i.*   3. To run upon a snag: said esp. of river craft.   [Prob. < Scand.]   — **snag′gy** *adj.*

snag·gle·tooth (snag′əl-tōōth′)   *n.* *pl.* **·teeth** A tooth that is broken, projecting, or out of alignment with the others.   — **snag′gle·toothed** (-tōōtht′, -tōōthd′) *adj.*

snail (snāl)   *n.*   1. Any of a large class of slow-moving mollusks of aquatic and terrestrial habits and having a spiral shell.   2. A slow or lazy person.   [OE *snægl*]

snail pace   A very slow gait or forward movement.   Also **snail's pace.**   — **snail-paced** (snāl′pāst′) *adj.*

snake (snāk)   *n.*   1. Any of a large order of scaly, legless reptiles with long, slim bodies and tapering tails; some kinds inject venom into the victim through tubular fangs.   2. A treacherous person.   3. A flexible, resilient wire used to clean clogged drains, etc.   — *v.* **snaked, snak·ing** *v.t.*   1. To drag by pulling forcibly from one end, as a log.   2. To pull with jerks.   — *v.i.*   3. To move like a snake.   [OE *snaca*]

SNAIL

snake·bite (snāk′bīt′)   *n.*   1. The bite of a snake.   2. Poisoning caused by the venom of a snake.

snake charmer   An entertainer who charms venomous snakes by rhythmic motions of his body and by music.

snake dance   1. A ceremonial dance of the Hopi Indians of Arizona.   2. A procession of persons moving in a winding or zigzag line to celebrate an athletic victory, etc.

snake·root (snāk′rōōt′, -rōōt′)   *n.*   1. Any of various plants having roots reputed to be effective against snakebite.   2. The root of any of these plants.

snak·y (snāk′ē)   *adj.* **snak·i·er, snak·i·est**   1. Of or like a snake; serpentine; winding.   2. Insinuating, cunning, treacherous.   3. Full of snakes.   — **snak′i·ly** *adv.*   — **snak′i·ness** *n.*

snap (snap)   *v.* **snapped, snap·ping** *v.i.*   1. To make a sharp, quick sound.   2. To break suddenly with a cracking noise.   3. To fly off or give way quickly, as when tension is suddenly relaxed.   4. To make the jaws come suddenly together in an effort to bite: often with *up* or *at.*   5. To seize or snatch suddenly: often with *up* or *at.*   6. To speak sharply, harshly, or irritably: often with *at.*   7. To emit, or seem to emit, a spark or flash of light: said of the eyes.   8. To close, fasten, etc., with a click.   9. To move or act with sudden, neat gestures: He *snapped* to attention.   — *v.t.*   10. To seize suddenly or eagerly, with or as with the teeth: often with *up.*   11. To sever with a snapping sound.   12. To utter, address, or interrupt harshly, abruptly, or irritably.   13. To cause to make a sharp, quick sound: to *snap* one's fingers.   14. To close, fasten, etc., with a snapping sound.   15. To cause to move suddenly, neatly, etc.   16. To photograph with a camera.   17. In football, to put in play.   — **to snap one's fingers at** To be unimpressed or unintimidated by.   — **to snap out of it** *Informal* 1. To recover quickly, as from a state of depression.   2. To change one's attitude.   — *n.*   1. The act of snapping, or a sharp, quick sound produced by it.   2. A sudden breaking of anything, or the sound so produced.   3. Any catch, fastener, or other similar device.   4. A sudden seizing or effort to seize with or as with the teeth.   5. A quick blow of the thumb sprung from the finger or of the finger from the thumb.   6. The sudden release of the tension of a spring or elastic cord.   7. A small, thin, crisp cake or cooky.   8. Brisk energy; vigor; vim; zip.   9. A brief spell; a sudden turn: said chiefly of cold weather.   10. *Informal* Any task or duty easy to perform.   11. A bit: It is not worth a *snap.*   12. A snapshot.   — *adj.*   1. Made or done suddenly and without consideration; offhand.   2. Fastening with a snap.   3. *Informal* Easy; requiring little work.   — *adv.* With a snap; quickly.   [< MDu. *snappen* to bite at]

snap·drag·on (snap′drag′ən)   *n.*   A plant of the figwort family having solitary flowers likened to dragons' heads.

snap·per (snap′ər)   *n.*   1. One who or that which snaps.   2. A large food fish of the Gulf Coast, as the **red snapper.**   3. A snapping turtle.

snapping turtle   A large, voracious, fresh-water turtle of North America, much used as food.

snap·pish (snap′ish)   *adj.*   1. Apt to speak crossly or tartly.   2. Disposed to snap, as a dog.   — **snap′pish·ly** *adv.*   — **snap′pish·ness** *n.*

snap·py (snap′ē)   *adj.* **·pi·er, ·pi·est**   1. *Informal* Brisk; energetic; vivacious.   2. *Informal* Smart or stylish in appearance.   3. Snappish.   — **make it snappy** *Informal* Hurry up!   — **snap′pi·ly** *adv.*   — **snap′pi·ness** *n.*

snap·shot (snap′shot′)   *n.*   1. A photograph taken with a small camera without timing.   2. A shot made without aim.

snare¹ (snâr)   *n.*   1. A device, as a noose, for catching birds or other animals; a trap.   2. Anything by which one is entangled or entrapped.   3. *Surg.* A loop of wire used to remove tumors and other growths from the body.   — *v.t.* **snared, snar·ing**   1. To catch with a snare.   2. To capture by trickery; entice.   [OE < ON *snara*]   — **snar′er** *n.*

snare² (snâr)   *n.*   1. One of the cords or wires stretched across one of the heads of a snare drum to increase the resonance.   2. A snare drum.   [< MDu., a string]

snare drum   A small drum having snares on one head.

snarl¹ (snärl)   *n.*   A sharp, harsh, angry growl; harsh or quarrelsome utterance.   — *v.i.*   1. To growl harshly, as a dog.   2. To speak angrily and resentfully.   — *v.t.*   3. To utter or express with a snarl.   [Freq. of obs. *snar* to growl]   — **snarl′er** *n.*   — **snarl′ing·ly** *adv.*   — **snarl′y** *adj.*

snarl² (snärl)   *n.*   1. A tangle, as of hair or yarn.   2. Any complication or entanglement.   3. *Informal* A quarrel.   — *v.i.*   1. To get into a snarl or tangle.   — *v.t.*   2. To put into a snarl or tangle.   3. To confuse; entangle mentally.   [< SNARE¹]   — **snarl′er** *n.*   — **snarl′y** *adj.*

snatch (snach)   *v.t.*   1. To seize or lay hold of suddenly, hastily, or eagerly.   2. To take or remove suddenly.   3. To take or obtain as the opportunity arises.   4. *Slang* To kidnap.   — *v.i.*   5. To attempt to seize swiftly and suddenly: with *at.*   6. To be eager to accept: with *at.*   — **Syn.** See STEAL.   — *n.*   1. An act of snatching.   2. A brief period.   3. A small amount.   4. *Slang* A kidnaping.   5. In weightlifting, a bringing of the weight from the floor to above the head in one motion.   [ME *snacchen*]   — **snatch′er** *n.*

snatch block   *Naut.*   A single block having an opening in one cheek to receive a rope.   For illus. see BLOCK¹.

snatch·y (snach′ē)   *adj.* **snatch·i·er, snatch·i·est**   Interrupted; spasmodic.

sneak (snēk)   *v.i.*   1. To move or go in a stealthy manner.   2. To act with cowardice or servility.   — *v.t.*   3. To put, give, transfer, move, etc., secretly or stealthily.   4. *Informal* To pilfer.   — *n.*   1. One who sneaks.   2. An act of sneaking.   — *adj.*   Stealthy; covert.   [OE *snīcan* to creep]

sneak·er (snē′kər)   *n.*   1. A sneak.   2. *pl. U.S. Informal* Rubber-soled canvas shoes, esp. for sports.

sneak·ing (snē′king)   *adj.*   1. Acting in an underhand way.   2. Secret: a *sneaking* suspicion.   — **sneak′ing·ly** *adv.*

sneak preview   *U.S.*   The showing of a new motion picture before its date of release.

sneak·y (snē′kē) *adj.* **sneak·i·er, sneak·i·est** Like a sneak; sneaking. **— sneak′i·ly** *adv.* **— sneak′i·ness** *n.*

sneer (snir) *n.* **1.** A grimace of contempt or derision made by slightly raising the upper lip. **2.** A mean insinuation. — *v.i.* **1.** To make or show a sneer. **2.** To express derision or contempt in speech, writing, etc. — *v.t.* **3.** To utter with a sneer or in a sneering manner. [ME *sneren*] **— sneer′er** *n.* **— sneer′ing·ly** *adv.*

sneeze (snēz) **sneezed, sneez·ing** *v.i.* To drive air forcibly and audibly out of the mouth and nose by a spasmodic involuntary action caused by irritation of the mucus membranes. **— not to be sneezed at** *Informal* Worthy of consideration. — *n.* An act of sneezing. [Alter. of ME *fnese*, OE *fnēosan* to sneeze] **— sneez′er** *n.* **— sneez′y** *adj.*

snell (snel) *n.* A short line of gut, horsehair, etc., bearing a fish hook, to be attached to a longer line. [Origin unknown]

snick (snik) *n.* A small cut; nick; snip. — *v.t.* To cut a nick in. [See SNICKERSNEE.]

snick·er (snik′ər) *n.* A half-suppressed or smothered laugh, often in derision. — *v.i.* **1.** To utter a snicker. — *v.t.* **2.** To utter or express with a snicker. [Imit.]

snick·er·snee (snik′ər-snē′) *n.* A swordlike knife. [Alter. of earlier *snick or snee* to thrust or cut]

snide (snīd) *adj.* Malicious or derogatory; nasty: *snide comments.* [Origin unknown]

sniff (snif) *v.i.* **1.** To breathe through the nose in short, quick, audible inhalations. **2.** To express contempt, etc., by or as by sniffing: often with *at.* — *v.t.* **3.** To breathe in through the nose; inhale. **4.** To smell with sniffs. **5.** To perceive as if by sniffs: to *sniff* peril. **6.** To express (contempt) by sniffs. — *n.* **1.** An act or the sound of sniffing. **2.** Perception by or as by sniffing. **3.** That which is inhaled by sniffing. [Appar. back formation < SNIVEL]

snif·fle (snif′əl) *v.i.* **·fled, ·fling** **1.** To breathe through the nose noisily. **2.** To snivel or whimper. — *n.* A snuffle. — **the sniffles** *Informal* A head cold or the sniffling that results. [Freq. of SNIFF]

snif·ter (snif′tər) *n.* **1.** A pear-shaped liquor glass. **2.** *U.S. Slang* A small drink of liquor. [< *snift*, var. of SNIFF]

snig·ger (snig′ər) *n.* A snicker. — *v.t. & v.i.* To snicker. [Var. of SNICKER.] **— snig′ger·er** *n.*

snip (snip) *v.* **snipped, snip·ping** *v.t.* **1.** To clip, remove, or cut with a light stroke of shears: often with *off.* — *v.i.* **2.** To cut with small, quick strokes. — *n.* **1.** An act of snipping. **2.** A small piece snipped off. **3.** *U.S. Informal* A small or insignificant person or thing. [< Du. *snippen*]

snipe (snīp) *n.* *pl.* **snipe** or **snipes** Any of various long-billed shore or marsh birds, allied to the woodcock. — *v.i.* **sniped, snip·ing 1.** To hunt or shoot snipe. **2.** To shoot at or pick off individual enemies from hiding. [< ON *snipa*]

snip·er (snī′pər) *n.* One who shoots an enemy from hiding.

snip·pet (snip′it) *n.* **1.** A small piece snipped off. **2.** A small portion or share.

snip·py (snip′ē) *adj.* **·pi·er, ·pi·est** *Informal* **1.** Pert; impertinent. **2.** Fragmentary; scrappy. Also **snip′pet·y** (-it-ē).

snitch (snich) *Slang v.t.* **1.** To grab quickly; steal; swipe. — *v.i.* **2.** To turn informer: with *on.* [Origin unknown]

sniv·el (sniv′əl) *v.* **·eled** or **·elled, ·el·ing** or **·el·ling** *v.i.* **1.** To cry in a snuffling manner. **2.** To whine. **3.** To run at the nose. — *v.t.* **4.** To utter with sniveling. — *n.* **1.** The act of sniveling. **2.** Nasal mucus. [OE *snyflung* mucus from the nose] **— sniv′el·er** or **sniv′el·ler** *n.*

snob (snob) *n.* **1.** One who makes birth, wealth, education, or intelligence the sole criterion of worth. **2.** Any pretender to gentility. [Origin uncertain] **— snob′ber·y** *n.*

snob·bish (snob′ish) *adj.* Characteristic of or befitting a snob or snobs. **— snob′bish·ly** *adv.* **— snob′bish·ness** *n.*

Sno·cat (snō′kat′) *n.* A trucklike vehicle used for traveling in arctic conditions: a trade name. Also **sno′cat.**

snood (snood) *n.* A small, meshlike cap or bag, worn by women to keep the hair in place. — *v.t.* To bind (hair) with a snood. [OE *snōd*]

snoop (snoop) *Informal v.i.* To look or pry into things with which one has no business. — *n.* One who snoops: also **snoop′er.** [< Du. *snoepen* to eat goodies on the sly]

snoop·y (snoo′pē) *adj.* **snoop·i·er, snoop·i·est** *Informal* Given to snooping.

snoot (snoot) *n.* *Informal* **1.** The nose or face. **2.** A wry face; a grimace. [Var. of SNOUT]

snoot·y (snoo′tē) *adj.* **snoot·i·er, snoot·i·est** *U.S. Informal* Conceited or supercilious.

snooze (snooz) *Informal v.i.* **snoozed, snooz·ing** To sleep lightly; doze. — *n.* A short nap. [Origin uncertain]

snore (snôr, snōr) *v.i.* **snored, snor·ing** To breathe in sleep with a hoarse, rough noise, usu. with an open mouth. — *n.* An act or the noise of snoring. [ME *snoren*] **— snor′er** *n.*

snor·kel (snôr′kəl) *n.* **1.** A mouth tube permitting a skin diver to breathe while swimming on the surface with his face under water. **2.** A tubelike apparatus for the ventilation of a submerged submarine. [< G *schnörkel*, lit., spiral]

snort (snôrt) *v.i.* **1.** To force air violently and noisily through the nostrils, as a horse. **2.** To express indignation, ridicule, etc., by a snort. **3.** *Informal* To laugh with a boisterous outburst. — *v.t.* **4.** To utter or express by snorting. — *n.* **1.** The act or sound of snorting. **2.** *Slang* A small drink. [ME *snorten*] **— snort′er** *n.*

snot (snot) *n.* **1.** Mucus from or in the nose: a vulgar term. **2.** *Slang* A low or mean fellow. [OE *gesnot*]

snot·ty (snot′ē) *adj.* **·ti·er, ·ti·est 1.** Dirtied with snot: a vulgar term. **2.** *Slang* Contemptible; mean; paltry. **3.** *Slang* Impudent; proudly conceited; saucy.

snout (snout) *n.* **1.** The forward projecting part of a beast's head. **2.** Something resembling a hog's snout. **3.** A person's nose: a contemptuous or humorous term. — *v.t.* To provide with a snout. [ME *snūte*] **— snout′ed** *adj.*

snow (snō) *n.* **1.** Water vapor in the air precipitated in the form of minute flakes when the temperature is below 32° F. ◆ Collateral adjective: *nival.* **2.** Anything resembling snow. **3.** A fall of snow; snowstorm. **4.** *Slang* Heroin or cocaine. **5.** The pattern of snowlike flecks appearing on a television screen. — *v.i.* **1.** To fall as snow. — *v.t.* **2.** To scatter or cause to fall as or like snow. **3.** To cover, enclose, or obstruct with or as with snow. **4.** *U.S. Slang* To subject to a snow job. [OE *snāw*]

snow·ball (snō′bôl′) *n.* A small round mass of snow compressed to be thrown, as in sport. — *v.i.* **1.** To throw snowballs. **2.** To gain in size, importance, etc., as a snowball that rolls over snow. — *v.t.* **3.** To throw snowballs at.

snow·bank (snō′bangk′) *n.* A large mound of snow.

snow·ber·ry (snō′ber′ē) *n.* *pl.* **·ries** A bushy American shrub having white berries: also called *waxberry.*

snow·bird (snō′bûrd′) *n.* **1.** The junco. **2.** *Slang* A cocaine or heroin addict.

snow blindness A temporary dimming of the sight caused by light reflected by snow. **— snow-blind** (snō′blīnd′) *adj.*

snow·bound (snō′bound′) *adj.* Hemmed in or forced to remain in a place because of heavy snow; snowed in.

snow bunting Any of various finches, the male of which in the breeding season is snow-white with black markings.

snow·cap (snō′kap′) *n.* A crest of snow, as on a mountain peak. **— snow′-capped′** *adj.*

snow·clad (snō′klad′) *adj.* Covered with snow.

snow·drift (snō′drift′) *n.* A snowbank made by the wind.

snow·drop (snō′drop′) *n.* A low, European, early blooming bulbous plant, bearing a single, white, drooping flower.

snow·fall (snō′fôl′) *n.* **1.** A fall of snow. **2.** The amount of snow that falls in a given period.

snow fence *U.S. & Canadian* Portable fencing of thin, closely placed slats, used to prevent the drifting of snow over roads, fields, etc., by causing it to drift elsewhere.

snow·flake (snō′flāk′) *n.* **1.** One of the small, feathery masses in which snow falls. **2.** Any of certain plants allied to and resembling the snowdrop.

snow job *U.S. Slang* An elaborate, insincere speech contrived to impress or persuade.

snow line The limit of perpetual snow on the sides of mountains. Also **snow limit.**

snow·mo·bile (snō′mō-bēl) *n.* An enclosed vehicle used for traveling over snow, ice, etc., often equipped with caterpillar treads. [< SNOW + (AUTO)MOBILE]

snow·plow (snō′plou′) *n.* Any plowlike device for turning fallen snow aside from a road or railroad, or for the removal of snow from surfaces. Also **snow′plough′.**

snow·shoe (snō′shoo′) *n.* A device, usu. a network of thongs in a wooden frame, fastened on the foot and worn in walking over snow. — *v.i.* **·shoed, ·shoe·ing** To walk on snowshoes. **— snow′sho′er** (-shoo′ər) *n.*

snow·storm (snō′stôrm′) *n.* A storm with a fall of snow.

snow·y (snō′ē) *adj.* **snow·i·er, snow·i·est 1.** Abounding in or full of snow. **2.** Pure; unblemished; spotless: *snowy* linen. **— snow′i·ly** *adv.* **— snow′i·ness** *n.*

snub (snub) *v.t.* **snubbed, snub·bing 1.** To treat with contempt or disdain, esp. by ignoring; slight. **2.** To rebuke with a cutting remark. **3.** To stop or check, as a rope in running out, by taking a turn about a post, etc.; also, to make fast (a boat, etc.) thus. — *adj.* Short; pug: said of the nose. — *n.* **1.** An act of snubbing; deliberate slight. **2.** A sudden checking, as of a running rope or cable. [< ON *snubba* to snub] **— snub′ber** *n.*

snub-nosed (snub′nōzd′) *adj.* Having a pug or snub nose.

snuff¹ (snuf) *v.t.* **1.** To draw in (air, etc.) through the nose. **2.** To smell; sniff. — *v.i.* **3.** To snort; sniff. — *n.* An act of snuffing. [< MDu. *snuffen*]

snuff² (snuf) *n.* The charred portion of a wick. — *v.t.* **1.** To extinguish: with *out.* **2.** To crop the snuff from (a wick). [Cf. G *schnuppe* snuff of a candle] **— snuf′fer** *n.*

snuff³ (snuf) *n.* Pulverized tobacco to be inhaled into the nostrils. **— up to snuff** *Informal* Meeting the usual standard, as in quality, health, etc. **—** *v.i.* To take snuff. [< Du. *snuf*] **— snuff′fer** *n.* **— snuff′y** *adj.* **— snuff′i·ness** *n.*

snuff·box (snuf′boks′) *n.* A small box for carrying snuff.

snuf·fle (snuf′əl) *v.* **·fled, ·fling** *v.t.* **1.** To sniffle. **2.** To breathe noisily, as a dog following a scent. **3.** To talk through the nose; snivel. **—** *v.t.* **4.** To utter in a nasal tone. **— n. 1.** An act of snuffing, or the sound made by it. **2.** An affected nasal or emotional voice or twang. [Freq. of SNUFF] **— snuf′fler** *n.* **— snuf′fly** *adj.*

snug (snug) *adj.* **snug·ger, snug·gest 1.** Closely and comfortably sheltered, covered, or situated. **2.** Close or compact; comfortable; cozy. **3.** Having everything closely secured; trim: said of a ship. **4.** Fitting closely but comfortably. **—** *v.* **snugged, snug·ging** *v.t.* **1.** To make snug. **—** *v.i.* **2,** To snuggle; move close. **— to snug down** To make a vessel ready for a storm by reducing sail, etc. [Prob. < LG. Cf. Du. *snugger* clean, smooth.] **— snug′ly** *adv.* **— snug′ness** *n.*

snug·gle (snug′əl) *v.t. & v.i.* **·gled, ·gling** To lie or draw close; cuddle: often with *up* or *together.*

so¹ (sō) *adv.* **1.** To this or that or such a degree; to this or that extent. **2.** In this, that, or such a manner; in the same way: often following a clause beginning with *as,* or preceding one beginning with *that:* As the twig is bent, *so* is the tree inclined. **3.** Just as said, directed, suggested or implied: Do it so; I will do so. **4.** According to fact: That is not *so.* **5.** *Informal* To an extreme degree; very. **6.** About as many or as much stated: I shall stay a day or *so.* **7.** According to the truth of what is sworn or averred: So help me God. **8.** To such an extent: used elliptically for *so much:* I love him *so!* **9.** Too: used in emphatic contradiction of a negative statement: You can so! **10.** Consequently; thus; therefore. **11.** *Informal* It seems that; can it be that; apparently: So you don't like it here! **12.** Let it be that way; very well. **— conj. 1.** With the purpose that; usu. with *that:* They left early *so that* they would avoid meeting him. **2.** As a consequence of which: He consented, *so* they left. **— interj. 1.** Is that so! **2.** Hold still! [OE *swā*]
◆ Careful writers use *so that* rather than the informal *so* (conj. def. 1) to introduce clauses of result or purpose, as in "I want to leave now *so that* I won't be late."

so² (sō) *n. Music* Sol.

soak (sōk) *v.t.* **1.** To place in liquid until thoroughly saturated; steep. **2.** To wet thoroughly; drench. **3.** To suck up; absorb: with *in* or *up.* **4.** To take in eagerly or readily: with *up:* to *soak* up knowledge. **5.** *Informal* To drink, esp. to excess: with *up.* **6.** *U.S. Slang* To overcharge. **7.** *U.S. Slang* To strike hard. **—** *v.i.* **8.** To remain or be placed in liquid till saturated. **9.** To penetrate; pass: with *in* or *into.* **10.** *U.S. Slang* To drink to excess. **— n. 1.** The act of soaking, or state of being soaked. **2.** Liquid in which something is soaked. **3.** *Slang* A hard drinker. [OE *socian*] **— soak′er** *n.*

so-and-so (sō′ən-sō′) *n.* **1.** An unnamed person or thing. **2.** *Informal* A euphemism for many offensive epithets.

soap (sōp) *n.* **1.** A cleansing agent made by decomposing the glyceryl esters of fats and oils with alkalis. **2.** A metallic salt of one of the fatty acids. **3.** *U.S. Slang* Money used for bribery. **— no soap** *U.S. Slang* **1.** No; not a chance. **2.** Futile. **—** *v.t.* To rub or treat with soap. [OE *sāpe*]

soap·ber·ry (sōp′ber′ē) *n.* *pl.* **·ries 1.** The fruit of any of mostly tropical trees and shrubs, sometimes used as a substitute for soap. **2.** A tree or shrub bearing this fruit.

soap·box (sōp′boks′) *n.* **1.** A box or crate for soap. **2.** Any box or crate used as a platform by street orators. Also **soap box. — soapbox oratory** Impromptu or crude oratory.

soapbox derby *U.S.* A race among unpowered racing cars, steered down a slope by the boys who have built them.

soap opera A daytime television or radio serial drama usu. dealing with highly emotional domestic themes.

soap·stone (sōp′stōn′) *n.* Steatite.

soap·suds (sōp′sudz′) *n. pl.* Suds of water and soap.

soap·y (sō′pē) *adj.* **soap·i·er, soap·i·est 1.** Resembling or consisting of soap. **2.** Smeared with soap. **3.** *Slang* Flattering; unctuous. **— soap′i·ly** *adv.* **— soap′i·ness** *n.*

soar (sôr, sōr) *v.i.* **1.** To rise high into the air. **2.** To sail through the air without perceptibly moving the wings, as a hawk or vulture. **3.** *Aeron.* To fly without power while gaining or holding altitude. **4.** To rise sharply above the usual level: Prices *soared.* **5.** To attain a lofty or exalted state. **— n.** The act of soaring; also, the height or range reached in soaring. [< F < L *ex* out + *aura* breeze, air] **— soar′er** *n.*

sob (sob) *v.* **sobbed, sob·bing** *v.i.* **1.** To weep with audible, convulsive catches of the breath. **2.** To make a sound like a sob. **—** *v.t.* **3.** To utter with sobs. **4.** To bring to a specified condition by sobbing: to *sob* oneself to sleep. **— n.** The act of sobbing. [ME *sobben*] **— sob′bing·ly** *adv.*

so·be·it (sō-bē′it) *conj. Archaic* If so; if only; provided.

so·ber (sō′bər) *adj.* **1.** Possessing or characterized by properly controlled faculties; well-balanced. **2.** Grave, sedate. **3.** Not drunk. **4.** Moderate or abstinent. **5.** Subdued or modest in color, manner of dress, etc. **—** *v.t. & v.i.* To make or become sober. [< OF < L *sobrius*] **— so′ber·ly** *adv.* **— so′ber·ness** *n.*

so·bri·e·ty (sō-brī′ə-tē) *n. pl.* **·ties** The state or quality of being sober. **2.** Moderateness in temper or conduct.

so·bri·quet (sō′bri-kā) *n.* A fanciful or humorous appellation; a nickname: also *soubriquet.* [< F]

sob story *Slang* A sad personal narrative told to elicit pity.

so-called (sō′kôld′) *adj.* Called as stated; generally styled thus: often implying a doubtful or incorrect designation.

soc·cer (sok′ər) *n.* A form of football in which the ball is propelled toward the opponents' goal by kicking or by striking with the body or head: officially called *association football.* [Alter. of ASSOCIATION]

so·cia·ble (sō′shə-bəl) *adj.* **1.** Inclined to seek company; social. **2.** Agreeable in company; genial. **3.** Characterized by or affording occasion for agreeable conversation and friendliness. **— n.** *U.S.* An informal social gathering: also called *social.* [< F < L *socius* friend] **— so′cia·bil′i·ty, so′cia·ble·ness** *n.* **— so′cia·bly** *adv.*

so·cial (sō′shəl) *adj.* **1.** Of or pertaining to society or its organization. **2.** Disposed to hold friendly intercourse with others; sociable; also, promoting friendly intercourse: a *social* club. **3.** Constituted to live in society: *social* beings. **4.** Of or pertaining to public welfare: *social* insurance. **5.** Of, pertaining to, or characteristic of persons considered aristocratic, fashionable, etc.: *social* register. **6.** Of animals or insects, living in communities. **7.** Venereal: *social* disease. **— n.** A sociable. [< L *socius* ally]

social disease A venereal disease.

so·cial·ism (sō′shəl-iz′əm) *n.* **1.** Public collective ownership or control of the basic means of production, distribution, and exchange, with the avowed aim of operating for use rather than for profit, and of assuring to each member of society an equitable share of goods, services, etc. **2.** The doctrines of those advocating this system.

so·cial·ist (sō′shəl-ist) *n.* An advocate of socialism. **— adj.** Socialistic.

so·cial·is·tic (sō′shəl-is′tik) *adj.* **1.** Of, pertaining to, or practicing socialism. **2.** Like or tending toward socialism.

Socialist Party The U.S. political party of socialism, formed in 1901 under the leadership of Eugene V. Debs.

so·cial·ite (sō′shəl-īt) *n. Informal* One who is prominent in fashionable society.

so·cial·i·ty (sō′shē·al′ə·tē) *n. pl.* **·ties** The state or character of being social; sociability.

so·cial·ize (sō′shəl-īz) *v.* **·ized, ·iz·ing** *v.t.* **1.** To place under group or government control. **2.** To make friendly, cooperative, or sociable. **3.** To convert or adapt to the needs of a social group. **—** *v.i.* **4.** *Informal* To take part in social activities. Also *Brit.* **so′cial·ise. — so′cial·i·za′tion** *n.*

socialized medicine A system proposing to supply the public with medical care at nominal cost, by regulating services and fees, by government subsidies to physicians, etc.

social register A directory of persons prominent in fashionable society.

social science 1. Sociology. **2.** Any field of knowledge dealing with human society, as economics, history, sociology, education, politics, ethics, etc.

social security *U.S.* A Federal program of old-age and unemployment insurance, public assistance to the blind, disabled, and dependent, and maternal and child welfare services.

social service Organized activity intended to advance human welfare. **— so·cial-ser·vice** (sō′shəl-sûr′vis) *adj.*

social studies *U.S.* In elementary and secondary schools, a course or unit of study based upon the social sciences.

social work Any clinical, social, or recreational service for improving community welfare, as through health clinics, recreational facilities, aid to the poor and the aged, etc.

so·ci·e·ty (sə-sī′ə-tē) *n. pl.* **·ties 1.** The system of community life in which individuals form a continuous and regulatory association for their mutual benefit and protection. **2.** The body of persons composing such a community; also, all people collectively. **3.** A number of persons regarded as having certain common interests, similar status, etc. **4.** The fashionable or aristocratic portion of a community. **5.** Association based on friendship or intimacy; companionship; also, one's friends or associates. [< OF *societe* < L *societas, -tatis* < *socius* friend] **— so·ci·e·tal** (sō·sī′ə·təl) *adj.*

Society of Friends A Christian religious group founded in England by George Fox about 1650, and characterized by the doctrine of "waiting upon the Spirit" for direct guidance and the repudiation of ritual, formal sacraments, oaths, and violence: commonly known as *Quakers.*

Society of Jesus The religious organization of the Jesuits.

socio- *combining form* **1.** Society; social. **2.** Sociology; sociological. [< F < L *socius* companion]

so·ci·o·ec·o·nom·ic (sō'sē·ō·ek'ə·nom'ik, sō'shē, -ē'kə-) *adj.* Social and economic: considered as a single factor: an upper *socioeconomic* group. — **so'ci·o·ec·o·nom'i·cal·ly** *adv.*

so·ci·ol·o·gy (sō'sē·ol'ə·jē, sō'shē-) *n.* The science that treats of the origin and evolution of human society and social phenomena. — **so·ci·o·log·ic** (sō'sē·ə·loj'ik) or **·i·cal** *adj.* — **so'ci·o·log'i·cal·ly** *adv.* — **so'ci·ol'o·gist** *n.*

so·ci·om·e·try (sō'sē·om'ə·trē, sō'shē-) *n.* The study of the interrelationships of individuals within a social group.

sock¹ (sok) *n.* *pl.* **socks**; *for def. 1 also* **sox** 1. A short stocking reaching above the ankle or just below the knee. 2. The light shoe worn by comic actors in the Greek and Roman drama. [OE < L *soccus* slipper]

sock² (sok) *Slang v.t.* To strike or hit, esp. with the fist; to punch. — *n.* A hard blow. [Origin unknown]

sock·et (sok'it) *n.* 1. *Mech.* A cavity or an opening adapted to receive and hold some corresponding piece or fixture. 2. *Anat.* A cavity or hollowed depression for the reception of an organ or part. — *v.t.* To furnish with, hold by, or put into a socket. [< AF *soket*, dim. of OF *soc* plowshare]

sock·eye (sok'ī') *n.* A salmon of the Pacific coast, highly valued as a food fish. [Alter. of Salishan *sukkegh*]

So·crat·ic (sō·krat'ik) *adj.* Pertaining to or characteristic of Socrates: also **So·crat'i·cal.** — **So·crat'i·cal·ly** *adv.*

Socratic method The dialectic method of instruction by questions and answers, as adopted by Socrates.

sod (sod) *n.* 1. A piece of grassy surface soil held together by the matted roots of grass and weeds; a turf or divot. 2. The surface of the earth. — *v.t.* **sod·ded, sod·ding** To cover with sod. [< MDu. *sode* piece of turf]

so·da (sō'də) *n.* 1. Any of several white, alkaline compounds widely used in medicine, industry, and the arts. 2. A soft drink containing soda water and flavoring; also **soda pop.** 3. A drink made from soda water, ice cream, and, sometimes, flavoring. [< Med.L, ? < Ital. *soda* (*cenere*) solid (ash) < L *solidus*]

soda ash Crude sodium carbonate, widely used in the manufacture of glass, soaps, paper, etc.

soda cracker A thin, crisp cracker made with yeast-leavened dough containing soda.

soda fountain 1. An apparatus from which soda water is drawn, usu. containing receptacles for syrups, ice cream, etc. 2. A counter at which soft drinks, etc., are dispensed.

soda jerk *U.S. Slang* A clerk at a soda fountain.

so·dal·i·ty (sō·dal'ə·tē) *n.* *pl.* **·ties** 1. Companionship. 2. A society; association. 3. In the Roman Catholic Church, a society organized for devotional and charitable purposes. [< L < *sodalis* companion]

soda water An effervescent drink consisting of water charged under pressure with purified carbon dioxide gas.

sod·den (sod'n) *adj.* 1. Soaked with moisture. 2. Doughy; soggy, as bread, biscuits, etc. 3. Flabby and pale, esp. from dissipation. 4. Dull; dreary. — *v.t. & v.i.* To make or become sodden. [ME *soden*, orig. pp. of SEETHE] — **sod'den·ly** *adv.* — **sod'den·ness** *n.*

so·di·um (sō'dē·əm) *n.* A silver-white, highly reactive, alkaline, metallic element (symbol Na) that is soft and malleable, and forms many compounds: also called *natrium.* See ELEMENT. [< NL < SODA]

sodium bicarbonate *Chem.* A white crystalline compound of alkaline taste, used in medicine and cookery: also called *baking soda, bicarbonate of soda.*

sodium carbonate *Chem.* A strongly alkaline compound that in crystalline hydrated form is known as washing soda, and in the anhydrous form as soda ash.

sodium chloride Common salt.

sodium hydroxide *Chem.* A strongly basic compound, NaOH, used for bleaching, etc.: also called *caustic soda.*

sodium nitrate *Chem.* A white compound used as a fertilizer and in explosives.

sodium Pen·to·thal (pen'tə·thôl, -thal) Proprietary name for a brand of thiopental sodium: also called *Pentothal sodium.* Also **sodium pent'o·thal.**

sodium thiosulfate *Chem.* A crystalline salt used industrially and medicinally and in photography as a fixing agent: also called *hypo.* Also **sodium hyposulfite.**

Sod·om (sod'əm) In the Bible, a city on the Dead Sea, destroyed with the city of Gomorrah because of the wickedness of the abide. *Gen.* xiii 10. — **Sod'om·ite** *n.*

sod·om·y (sod'əm·ē) *n.* Unnatural sexual relations, esp. between male persons or between a human being and an animal. [< OF < LL *Sodoma* Sodom, to whose people this practice was imputed] — **sod'om·ite** *n.*

so·ev·er (sō·ev'ər) *adv.* To or in some conceivable degree: often added to *who, which, what, when, how,* etc.

so·fa (sō'fə) *n.* A wide seat, upholstered and having a back and raised ends. [< F < Arabic *soffah* a part of a floor raised to form a seat]

soft (sôft, soft) *adj.* 1. Being or composed of a substance whose shape is changed easily by pressure, but without fracture; pliable, or malleable; easily worked: *soft* wood. 2. Smooth and delicate to the touch. 3. Gentle in its effect upon the ear; not loud or harsh. 4. Mild in any mode of physical action; bland: a *soft* breeze. 5. Of subdued coloring or delicate shading. 6. Expressing mildness, sympathy, etc.; gentle: *soft* words. 7. Giving or enjoying rest; placid: *soft* sleep. 8. Easily or too easily touched in feeling; tender: a *soft* heart. 9. Incapable of bearing hardship, strain, etc.; delicate: *soft* muscles. 10. Of yielding character; weak; effeminate. 11. *Informal* Involving little effort; easy: a *soft* job. 12. Free from mineral salts that prevent the detergent action of soap: said of water. 13. Bituminous, as opposed to anthracite: said of coal. 14. *Phonet.* **a** Describing *c* and *g* when articulated fricatively as in *cent* and *gibe*: opposed to *hard.* **b** Voiced and weakly articulated. 15. *Physics* Having relatively weak penetrating power: *soft* X-rays. — *n.* 1. That which is soft; a soft part or material. 2. *Informal* One who is soft or foolish; a softy. — *adv.* 1. Softly. 2. Quietly; gently. [OE *sōfte*] — **soft'ly** *adv. & interj.* — **soft'ness** *n.*

soft·ball (sôft'bôl', soft'-) *n.* 1. A variation of baseball, requiring a smaller diamond and a larger ball. 2. The ball used in this game.

soft-boiled (sôft'boild') *adj.* Boiled, as an egg, to an extent of incomplete coagulation of the albumen.

soft coal Bituminous coal.

soft drink A nonalcoholic drink, as ginger ale, etc.

sof·ten (sôf'ən, sof'-) *v.t. & v.i.* To make or become soft or softer. — **sof'ten·er** *n.*

soft·heart·ed (sôft'här'tid, soft'-) *adj.* Tender-hearted; merciful. — **soft'heart'ed·ly** *adv.* — **soft'heart'ed·ness** *n.*

soft-ped·al (sôft'ped'l, soft'-) *v.t.* **·aled** or **·alled, ·al·ing** or **·al·ling** 1. To mute the tone of by depressing the soft pedal. 2. *Informal* To render less emphatic; moderate.

soft pedal A pedal that mutes the tone, as in a piano.

soft-shell (sôft'shel', soft'-) *adj.* Having a soft shell, as certain clams, or a crab or lobster after shedding its shell: also **soft'-shelled'** (-sheld'). — *n.* A soft-shelled crab.

soft-shelled crab A crab of North America after it has molted.

soft-shelled turtle Any member of a family of turtles having a long snout and a soft, leathery shell.

soft-soap (sôft'sōp', soft'-) *v.t. Informal* To flatter; cajole. — **soft'-soap'er** *n.*

soft soap 1. Fluid or semifluid soap. 2. *Informal* Flattery.

soft-spo·ken (sôft'spō'kən) *adj.* 1. Speaking with a soft, low voice. 2. Ingratiating; suave: said of speech.

soft·ware (sôft'wâr', soft'-) *n.* Any of the programs used in operating a digital computer, as input and output programs: distinguished from *hardware* (def. 3).

soft·wood (sôft'wood', soft'-) *n.* 1. A coniferous tree or its wood. 2. Any soft wood, or any tree with soft wood.

soft·y (sôf'tē, sof'-) *n.* *pl.* **soft·ies** *Informal* 1. An extremely sentimental person. 2. A sissy.

sog·gy (sog'ē) *adj.* **·gi·er, ·gi·est** 1. Saturated with water or moisture; wet and heavy; soaked. 2. Heavy: said of pastry. 3. Soft; boggy: said of land. Also **sog·ged** (sog'id). [< dial. E *sog* a swamp, bog < Scand.] — **sog'gi·ly** *adv.* — **sog'gi·ness** *n.*

soil¹ (soil) *n.* 1. Finely divided rock mixed with vegetable or animal matter, constituting that portion of the surface of the earth in which plants grow. 2. Land; country: native *soil.* 3. A particular kind of earth. 4. A medium for development or growth: Slums are fertile *soil* for disease. [< OF < L < *solum* the ground]

soil² (soil) *v.t.* 1. To make dirty; smudge. 2. To disgrace; defile. — *v.i.* 3. To become dirty. — *n.* 1. The act of soiling or the state of being soiled. 2. A spot or stain. 3. Filth; sewage. 4. Manure used as fertilizer. [< OF, ult. < L *suculus,* dim. of *sus* pig]

soil·age (soi'lij) *n.* Green crops for feeding animals.

soi·ree (swä·rā', *Fr.* swȧ·rā') *n.* A party or reception given in the evening. Also **soi·rée**. [< F < *soir* evening]

so·ja (sō'jə, soi'yə) *n.* The soybean. [< NL < Du. *soya*]

so·journ (*v.* sō'jûrn, sō·jûrn'; *n.* sō'jûrn) *v.i.* To stay or dwell temporarily; abide for a time. — *n.* A temporary residence or stay, as of one in a foreign land. [< OF, ult. < L *sub-* under + *diurnus* daily] — **so'journ·er** *n.*

sol¹ (sōl) *n. Music* The fifth of the syllables used in solmization; the fifth tone of a major scale; also, the tone G: also **so.** [See GAMUT.]

sol² (sol, sōl) *n.* A colloidal suspension of a solid in a liquid.

Sol (sol) 1. The sun. 2. In Roman mythology, the god of the sun. [< L]

sol·ace (sol'is) *n.* Comfort in grief, trouble, or calamity; also, that which supplies such comfort: also **sol'ace·ment.**

— *v.t.* **·aced, ·ac·ing** **1.** To comfort or cheer in trouble, grief, or calamity. **2.** To alleviate, as grief; soothe. — **Syn.** See CONSOLE[1]. [< OF < L *solacium* comfort] — **sol'ac·er** *n.*
so·lar (sō'lər) *adj.* **1.** Pertaining to, proceeding from, or connected with the sun. **2.** Affected, determined, or measured by the sun. **3.** Operated by the action of the sun's rays: a *solar* engine. [< L *sol* sun]
solar battery An assembly of photovoltaic cells for the direct conversion of solar energy into electricity.
so·lar·i·um (sō-lâr'ē-əm) *n.* *pl.* **·i·a** (-ē-ə) or **·i·ums** A room or enclosed porch exposed to the sun's rays. [< L]
solar plexus **1.** *Anat.* The large network of nerves found behind the stomach, and serving the abdominal viscera. **2.** *Informal* The pit of the stomach.
solar system The sun together with the heavenly bodies that revolve about it.
sold (sōld) Past tense and past participle of SELL.
sol·der (sod'ər) *n.* **1.** A fusible metal or alloy used for joining metallic surfaces or margins, applied in a melted state. **2.** Anything that unites or cements. — *v.t.* **1.** To unite or repair with solder. **2.** To join together. — *v.i.* **3.** To work with solder. **4.** To be united by or as by solder. [< OF < L *solidus* firm, hard] — **sol'der·er** *n.*
sol·dier (sōl'jər) *n.* **1.** A person serving in an army. **2.** An enlisted man, as distinguished from a commissioned officer. **3.** A brave, skillful, or experienced warrior. **4.** One who serves loyally in any cause. **5.** *Entomol.* An asexual form of a termite or of certain ants, in which the head and jaws are largely developed to defend the colony. — *v.i.* To be a soldier. [< OF *soude* wages < LL *solidus* a gold coin] — **sol'dier·ly** *adj.*
soldier of fortune An adventurous, restless person who is willing to serve wherever his services are well paid.
Soldier's Medal A U.S. military decoration awarded to any member of the army, or of a military organization connected with it, for heroism not involving actual conflict with the enemy. See DECORATION.
sol·dier·y (sōl'jər·ē) *n.* *pl.* **·dier·ies** **1.** Soldiers collectively. **2.** Military service.
sole[1] (sōl) *n.* **1.** The bottom surface of the foot. ◆ Collateral adjective: *plantar.* **2.** The bottom surface of a shoe, boot, etc. **3.** The lower part of a thing, or the part on which it rests when standing; esp., the bottom part of a plowshare. **4.** The bottom part of the head of a golf club. — *v.t.* **soled, sol·ing** To furnish with a sole; resole, as a shoe. [< OF < Med.L *sola*, var. of L *solea* sandal]
sole[2] (sōl) *n.* **1.** Any of a family of flatfishes allied to the flounders, many of which are highly esteemed as food. **2.** One of various flounders of the Pacific coast of the U.S. [< OF < L *solea*]
sole[3] (sōl) *adj.* Being alone or the only one; only; individual. [< OF < L *solus* alone]
so·le·cism (sol'ə·siz'əm) *n.* **1.** A violation of grammatical rules or of the approved idiomatic usage of language. **2.** Any impropriety or incongruity. [< L < Gk. < *soloikos* speaking incorrectly < *Soloi*, a Cilician town whose people spoke a substandard Attic dialect] — **sol'e·cist** *n.* — **sol'e·cis'tic** or **·ti·cal** *adj.*
sole·ly (sōl'lē) *adv.* **1.** By oneself or itself alone; singly. **2.** Completely; entirely. **3.** Without exception; exclusively.
sol·emn (sol'əm) *adj.* **1.** Characterized by majesty, mystery, or power; impressive; awe-inspiring. **2.** Marked by gravity; serious. **3.** Characterized by ceremonial observances; sacred. **4.** *Law* Done in due form of law: a *solemn* protest. [< OF < L *solemnis*] — **sol'em·ness, sol'·emn·ness** *n.* — **sol'emn·ly** *adv.*
so·lem·ni·ty (sə·lem'nə·tē) *n.* *pl.* **·ties** **1.** The state or quality of being solemn; gravity; reverence. **2.** A rite expressive of religious reverence; also, any ceremonious observance. **3.** A thing of a solemn or serious nature.
sol·em·nize (sol'əm·nīz) *v.t.* **·nized, ·niz·ing** **1.** To perform as a ceremony or solemn rite, or according to legal or ritual forms: to *solemnize* a marriage. **2.** To dignify, as with a ceremony; celebrate. **3.** To make solemn, grave, or serious. Also *Brit.* **sol'em·nise.** — **Syn.** See CELEBRATE. — **sol'em·ni·za'tion** *n.* — **sol'em·niz'er** *n.*
so·le·noid (sō'lə·noid) *n.* *Electr.* A conducting wire in the form of a helix, capable of setting up a magnetic field by the passage through it of an electric current. [< F < Gk. *sōlēn* a channel + -OID] — **so'le·noi'dal** *adj.*
so·lic·it (sə·lis'it) *v.t.* **1.** To ask for earnestly; seek to obtain by persuasion or entreaty. **2.** To beg or entreat (a person) persistently. **3.** To tempt; esp., to entice (one) to an unlawful or immoral act. — *v.i.* **4.** To make petition or solicitation. — **Syn.** See ASK. [< OF < L *sollicitare* to agitate] — **so·lic'i·ta'tion** *n.*
so·lic·i·tor (sə·lis'ə·tər) *n.* **1.** A person who solicits; esp., one who solicits gifts of money or subscriptions to magazines. **2.** The legal advisor to certain branches of the public service. **3.** In England, a lawyer who may advise clients or prepare cases for presentation in court, but who may appear

as an advocate in the lower courts only: distinguished from *barrister.* Also **so·lic'i·ter.** — **so·lic'i·tor·ship'** *n.*
Solicitor General *pl.* **Solicitors General** **1.** In the U.S., an officer who ranks after the Attorney General. **2.** The principal law officer in some States, corresponding to the Attorney General in others.
so·lic·i·tous (sə·lis'ə·təs) *adj.* **1.** Full of anxiety or concern, as for the attainment of something: *solicitous* of our good will. **2.** Full of eager desire; willing. — **so·lic'i·tous·ly** *adv.* — **so·lic'i·tous·ness** *n.*
so·lic·i·tude (sə·lis'ə·tood, -tyood) *n.* **1.** The state of being solicitous; anxiety or concern. **2.** *Usu. pl.* That which makes one solicitous.
sol·id (sol'id) *adj.* **1.** Having definite shape and volume; not fluid. **2.** Substantial; firm and stable. **3.** Filling the whole of; not hollow. **4.** Having no aperture or crevice; compact. **5.** Manifesting strength and firmness; sound. **6.** Characterized by reality; substantial or satisfactory. **7.** Exhibiting united and unbroken characteristics, opinions, etc.; unanimous: a *solid* vote. **8.** Financially sound or safe. **9.** *U.S. Informal* Certain and safe in approval and support: They were *solid* with the boss. **10.** Having or relating to the three dimensions of length, breadth, and thickness. **11.** Written without a hyphen: said of a compound word. **12.** Cubic in shape: a *solid* yard. **13.** Unadulterated; unalloyed: *solid* gold. **14.** Carrying weight or conviction: a *solid* argument. **15.** Serious; reliable: a *solid* citizen. **16.** *Printing* Having no leads or slugs between the lines; not open. — *n.* **1.** A state of matter characterized by definite shape and volume. **2.** A magnitude that has length, breadth, and thickness, as a cone, cube, sphere, etc. [< F < L *solidus*] — **sol'id·ly** *adv.* — **sol'id·ness** *n.*
sol·i·dar·i·ty (sol'ə·dar'ə·tē) *n.* *pl.* **·ties** Coherence and oneness in nature, relations, or interests, as of a class.
solid fuel *Aerospace* A rocket fuel in solid, rather than liquid or gaseous, form. Also, **solid propellant.**
solid geometry The geometry that includes all three dimensions of space in its reasoning.
so·lid·i·fy (sə·lid'ə·fī) *v.t. & v.i.* **·fied, ·fy·ing** **1.** To make or become solid, hard, firm, or compact. **2.** To bring or come together in unity. — **so·lid'i·fi·ca'tion** *n.*
so·lid·i·ty (sə·lid'ə·tē) *n.* *pl.* **·ties** **1.** The quality or state of being solid; extension in the three dimensions of space. **2.** Mental, moral, or financial soundness; stability.
solid state physics The branch of physics that deals with the properties of solids, esp. at the atomic and molecular levels.
sol·i·dus (sol'ə·dəs) *n.* *pl.* **·di** (-dī) The sign (/) used to divide shillings from pence: 10/6 (10s. 6d.): sometimes also used to express fractions: 3/4. [< LL]
so·lil·o·quize (sə·lil'ə·kwīz) *v.i.* **·quized, ·quiz·ing** To talk to oneself; utter a soliloquy. Also *Brit.* **so·lil'o·quise.**
so·lil·o·quy (sə·lil'ə·kwē) *n.* *pl.* **·quies** A talking or discourse to oneself, as in a drama; a monologue. [< LL < L *solus* alone + *loqui* to talk]
sol·ip·sism (sol'ip·siz'əm) *n.* *Philos.* The theory that the self is the only thing really existent. [< L *solus* alone + *ipse* self] — **sol'ip·sist** *n.*
sol·i·taire (sol'ə·târ') *n.* **1.** A diamond or other gem set alone. **2.** *Chiefly U.S.* One of many games, esp. of cards, played by one person: also, *Brit.*, *patience.* **3.** *Brit.* Pegboard. [< F < L *solitarius* solitary]
sol·i·tar·y (sol'ə·ter'ē) *adj.* **1.** Living, being, or going alone. **2.** Made, done, or passed alone: a *solitary* life. **3.** Unfrequented by human beings; secluded. **4.** Lonesome; lonely. **5.** Single; sole: Not a *solitary* soul was there. — *n.* *pl.* **·tar·ies** **1.** One who lives alone; a recluse. **2.** *Informal* Solitary confinement. [< L < *solus* alone] — **sol'i·tar'i·ly** *adv.* — **sol'i·tar'i·ness** *n.*
solitary confinement The confining of a prisoner apart from other prisoners, usu. as punishment.
sol·i·tude (sol'ə·tood, -tyood) *n.* **1.** The state of being solitary; seclusion. **2.** A deserted or lonely place.
sol·mi·za·tion (sol'mə·zā'shən) *n.* *Music* The use of syllables, most commonly *do, re, mi, fa, sol, la, ti* (*si*), as names for the tones of a major scale, with vowel changes to indicate chromatic tones. [< SOL[1] + MI]
so·lo (sō'lō) *n.* *pl.* **·los** or **·li** (lē) **1.** A musical composition or passage for a single voice or instrument, with or without accompaniment. **2.** Any of several card games, esp. one in which one player may play alone against the other three. **3.** Any performance accomplished alone or without assistance. — *adj.* **1.** Composed or written for, or executed by, a single voice or instrument. **2.** Done by a single person alone: a *solo* flight. — *v.i.* **·loed, ·lo·ing** To fly an airplane alone, esp. for the first time. [< Ital. < L *solus* alone] — **so'lo·ist** *n.*
Sol·o·mon (sol'ə·mən) Tenth-century B.C. king of Israel; son of David and Bathsheba; noted for his wisdom.
Sol·o·mon's-seal (sol'ə·mənz-sēl') *n.* Any of several rather large perennial herbs having tubular flowers and rootstocks marked at intervals by circular scars.

sol·stice (sol′stis) *n.* **1.** *Astron.* The time of year when the sun is at its greatest distance from the celestial equator; either the **summer solstice**, about June 22 in the northern hemisphere, or the **winter solstice**, about Dec. 22. **2.** Either of the two points on the ecliptic marking these distances. **3.** A culminating or high point. [< F < L < *sol* sun + *sistere* to cause to stand] — **sol·sti·tial** (sol·stish′əl) *adj.*

sol·u·bil·i·ty (sol′yə·bil′ə·tē) *n.* *pl.* **·ties** The state of being soluble; capability of being dissolved. Also **sol′u·ble·ness.**

sol·u·ble (sol′yə·bəl) *adj.* **1.** Capable of being dissolved in a liquid. **2.** Susceptible of being solved or explained. [< OF < L < *solvere* to solve, dissolve] — **sol′u·bly** *adv.*

sol·ute (sol′yoot, sŏl′loot) *n.* The substance dissolved in a solution. — *adj.* Dissolved; in solution.

so·lu·tion (sə·loo′shən) *n.* **1.** A homogeneous mixture formed by dissolving one or more substances, whether solid, liquid, or gaseous, in another substance. **2.** The act or process by which such a mixture is made. **3.** The act or process of explaining, settling, or disposing, as of a difficulty, problem, or doubt. **4.** The answer to a problem; also, the method of finding the answer. **5.** Separation; disruption. [< OF < L *solutus*, pp. of *solvere* to dissolve]

So·lu·tre·an (sə·loo′trē·ən) *adj.* *Anthropol.* Pertaining to or characteristic of a Paleolithic culture preceding the Magdalenian and typified by a skilled technique in the making of flint implements. Also **So·lu′tri·an.** [after *Solutré*, a village in central France, where remains were found]

solv·a·ble (sol′və·bəl) *adj.* **1.** That may be solved. **2.** That may be dissolved. — **solv′a·bil′i·ty, solv′a·ble·ness** *n.*

solve (solv) *v.t.* **solved, solv·ing** To arrive at or work out the correct explanation or solution of; find the answer to; resolve. [< L *solvere* to solve, loosen] — **solv′er** *n.*

sol·vent (sol′vənt) *adj.* **1.** Having means sufficient to pay all debts. **2.** Having the power of dissolving. — *n.* **1.** That which solves. **2.** A substance, generally a liquid, capable of dissolving other substances. [< L *solvens, -entis*, ppr. of *solvere* to solve, loosen] — **sol′ven·cy** *n.*

-soma See **-SOME².**

So·ma·li (sō·mä′lē) *n.* **1.** A member of one of certain Hamitic tribes of Somalia, Kenya, Ethiopia, and French Somaliland. **2.** Their Hamitic language. Also **So·mal** (sō·mal′).

so·mat·ic (sō·mat′ik) *adj.* *Biol.* **1.** Of or relating to the body; physical; corporeal. **2.** Of or pertaining to the framework or walls of a body. [< Gk. *sōma* body]

somato- *combining form* Body; of, pertaining to, or denoting the body. Also, before vowels, **somat-.** [< Gk. *sōma, sōmatos* the body]

som·ber (som′bər) *adj.* **1.** Partially deprived of light or brightness; dusky; murky; gloomy. **2.** Somewhat melancholy; depressing. Also *Brit.* **som′bre,** *Archaic* **som′brous.** [< F *sombre*]

som·bre·ro (som·brâr′ō) *n.* *pl.* **·ros** A broad-brimmed hat, usu. of felt, much worn in Spain, Latin America, and the southwestern U.S. [< Sp. < *sombra* shade]

some (sum) *adj.* **1.** Of indeterminate or limited quantity, number, or amount. **2.** Conceived or thought of, but not definitely known: *some* person. **3.** Part (at least one) but not all of a class. **4.** *U.S. Informal* Worthy of notice: That was *some* cake. — *pron.* **1.** A certain undetermined quantity or part. **2.** Certain particular ones not definitely known or not specifically designated. — *adv.* **1.** In an approximate degree; about: *Some* eighty people were present. **2.** *Informal* or *Dial.* Somewhat. [OE *sum*]

-some¹ *suffix of adjectives* Characterized by, or tending to be (what is indicated by the main element): *blithesome, frolicsome.* [OE *-sum* like, resembling]

-some² *suffix of nouns* A body: *chromosome.* Also spelled **-soma.** [< Gk. *sōma* a body]

-some³ *suffix of nouns* A group consisting of (a specified number): *twosome, foursome.* [< SOME]

some·bod·y (sum′bod′ē, -bəd·ē) *pron.* A person unknown or unnamed. — *n. pl.* **·bod·ies** A person of consequence.

some·day (sum′dā′) *adv.* *U.S.* At some future time.

some·how (sum′hou′) *adv.* In some manner not explained.

some·one (sum′wun′, -wən) *pron.* Some person; somebody. — *n.* a somebody.

some·place (sum′plās′) *adv.* *Informal* Somewhere.

som·er·sault (sum′ər·sôlt) *n.* **1.** An acrobatic stunt in which a person either leaps or rolls from a sitting posture, turning heels over head. **2.** A complete reversal of opinion, attitude, etc. — *v.i.* To perform a somersault. Also spelled **summersault.** Also **som′er·set** (-set). [< OF, ult. < L *supra* above + *saltus* leap]

some·thing (sum′thing) *n.* **1.** A particular thing indefinitely conceived or stated. **2.** Some portion or quantity. **3.** A person or thing of importance. — *adv.* Somewhat: now only in the phrase **something like.**

some·time (sum′tīm′) *adv.* **1.** At some future time not precisely stated; eventually. **2.** At some indeterminate time or occasion. — *adj.* Former; quondam: a *sometime* student.

some·times (sum′tīmz′) *adv.* At times; occasionally.

some·way (sum′wā′) *adv.* In some way or other; somehow. Also **some way, someways** or **someway′s** (-wāz′).

some·what (sum′hwot′, -hwət) *n.* **1.** An uncertain quantity or degree; something. **2.** An individual or thing of consequence. — *adv.* In some degree.

some·where (sum′hwâr′) *adv.* **1.** In, at, or to some place unspecified or unknown. **2.** In one place or another. **3.** In or to some existent place. **4.** Approximately: with *about.* — *n.* An unspecified or unknown place.

some·wheres (sum′hwârz′) *adv.* *Chiefly Dial.* Somewhere.

som·nam·bu·late (som·nam′byə·lāt) *v.i.* **·lat·ed, ·lat·ing** To walk or wander about while asleep. [< L *somnus* sleep + AMBULATE]

som·nam·bu·lism (som·nam′byə·liz′əm) *n.* The act or state of walking during sleep; sleepwalking. Also **som·nam′·bu·la′tion.** — **som·nam′bu·lant** (-lənt) *adj.* — **som·nam′·bu·list** *n.* — **som·nam′bu·lis′tic** *adj.*

somni- *combining form* Sleep; of or pertaining to sleep: *somniferous.* [< L *somnus* sleep]

som·nif·er·ous (som·nif′ər·əs) *adj.* Tending to produce sleep; soporiferous; narcotic. Also **som·nif′ic.**

som·no·lence (som′nə·ləns) *n.* Oppressive drowsiness or inclination to sleep. Also **som′no·len·cy.**

som·no·lent (som′nə·lənt) *adj.* **1.** Inclined to sleep; drowsy. **2.** Tending to induce drowsiness. [< F < L < *somnus* sleep] — **som′no·lent·ly** *adv.*

son (sun) *n.* **1.** A male child considered with reference to either parent or to both parents. **2.** Any male descendant. **3.** One who occupies the place of a son, as by adoption, marriage, or regard. **4.** A person regarded as a native of a particular country or place. **5.** A male person representing some quality or character. [OE *sunu*] — **son′ship** *n.*

-son A descendant of: English and Scandinavian patronymic suffix: *Anderson.*

Son (sun) Jesus Christ; the second person of the Trinity.

so·nant (sō′nənt) *adj.* **1.** Sounding; resonant. **2.** *Phonet.* Voiced. — *n. Phonet.* **1.** A voiced speech sound. **2.** A syllabic sound. [< L *sonans, -antis*, ppr. of *sonare* to resound] — **so′nance** *n.*

so·nar (sō′när) *n.* A device using underwater sound waves for navigation, range finding, detection of submerged objects, communication, etc. — *adj.* Of, or pertaining to this device. [< SO(UND) NA(VIGATION AND) R(ANGING)]

so·na·ta (sə·nä′tä) *n. Music* A composition for one, two, or in older music, three or more instruments. [< Ital. < *sonare* to sound]

sonata form *Music* The outline upon which a movement, esp. the first, of a sonata, quartet, symphony, etc., is based.

so·na·ti·na (son′ə·tē′nə) *n. pl.* **·ti·nas** or **·ti·ne** (-tē′nā) *Music* A short or easy sonata. [< Ital., dim. of SONATA]

song (sông, song) *n.* **1.** A musical composition for one or more voices. **2.** The rendering of vocal music; more widely, any melodious utterance, as of a bird. **3.** A lyric or ballad. **4.** Poetry; verse. — **for a song** At a very low price. [OE]

song·bird (sông′bûrd′, song′-) *n.* A bird that utters a musical call.

song·ful (sông′fəl, song′-) *adj.* Full of song or melody.

Song of Solomon A book of the Old Testament consisting of a Hebrew dramatic love poem attributed to Solomon: also, in the Douai Bible, *Canticle of Canticles.* Also **Song of Songs.**

song sparrow A common sparrow of the eastern U.S. noted for its song.

song·ster (sông′stər, song′-) *n.* **1.** A person or bird given to singing. **2.** A poet. — **song′stress** *n.fem.*

song thrush A bird of the thrush family, native in Europe and having brown wings and a spotted breast.

song·writ·er (sông′rī′tər) *n.* One who writes music or lyrics, or both, for songs, esp. popular songs. Also **song writer.**

son·ic (son′ik) *adj.* **1.** Of, pertaining to, determined or affected by sound. **2.** Having a speed approaching that of sound. [< L *sonus* sound]

sonic barrier *Aeron.* The transonic barrier.

son-in-law (sun′in·lô′) *n. pl.* **sons-in-law** The husband of one's daughter.

son·net (son′it) *n.* A poem usu. of fourteen decasyllabic lines, properly expressing two successive phases of a single thought or idea. — *v.t.* **1.** To celebrate in sonnets. — *v.i.* **2.** To compose sonnets. [< F < Ital. < Provençal *sonet*, dim. of *son* sound < L *sonus*]

son·net·eer (son′ə·tir′) *n.* A composer of sonnets. — *v.i.* To compose sonnets.

son·ny (sun′ē) *n. Informal* Youngster: a familiar form of address to boys.

so·nor·ant (sə·nôr′ənt, -nō′rənt) *n. Phonet.* A voiced consonant of relatively high sonority, as (l), (r), (m), (n).

so·nor·i·ty (sə-nôr′ə-tē, -nŏr′-) *n. pl.* **·ties 1.** Sonorous quality or state; resonance; also **so·no′rous·ness. 2.** A sound.

so·no·rous (sə-nôr′əs, -nō′rəs, sŏn′ər-əs) *adj.* **1.** Productive or capable of sound vibrations. **2.** Loud and full-sounding; resonant. [< L *sonare* to resound] **— so·no′rous·ly** *adv.*

soon (sōōn) *adv.* **1.** At a future or subsequent time not long distant; shortly. **2.** Without delay; in a speedy manner. **3.** With ease; readily. **4.** With willingness or readiness: usu. preceded by *would as, had as,* etc. **5.** In good season; early. [OE *sōna* immediately]

Soon·er State (sōō′nər) Nickname for Oklahoma.

soot (sŏŏt, sōōt) *n.* A black substance, essentially carbon from the incomplete combustion of wood, coal, natural gas, etc., as deposited on the inside of chimneys and other surfaces. **—** *v.t.* To soil or cover with soot. [OE *sōt*]

sooth (sōōth) *Archaic adj.* True. **—** *n.* Truth. **— in sooth** In truth. [OE *sōth*] **— sooth′ly** *adv.*

soothe (sōōth) *v.* **soothed, sooth·ing** *v.t.* **1.** To restore to a quiet or normal state; calm. **2.** To mitigate, soften, or relieve, as pain or grief. **—** *v.i.* **3.** To have a calming or relieving effect. [OE *sōthian* to verify] **— sooth′er** *n.* **— sooth′ing** *adj.* **— sooth′ing·ly** *adv.*

sooth·say·er (sōōth′sā′ər) *n.* One who claims to be able to foretell events. **— sooth′say′ing** *n.*

soot·y (sŏŏt′ē, sōōt′ē) *adj.* **soot·i·er, soot·i·est 1.** Blackened or stained by soot. **2.** Producing or consisting of soot. **3.** Black like soot. **— soot′i·ly** *adv.* **— soot′i·ness** *n.*

sop (sŏp) *v.* **sopped, sop·ping** *v.t.* **1.** To dip or soak in a liquid. **2.** To drench. **3.** To take up by absorption: often with *up*. **—** *v.i.* **4.** To be absorbed; soak in. **5.** To be or become drenched. **—** *n.* **1.** Anything softened in liquid, as bread. **2.** Anything given to pacify, as a bribe. [OE *sopp*]

soph·ism (sŏf′iz·əm) *n.* **1.** A false argument intentionally used to deceive. **2.** The doctrine or method of the sophists. [< F or L < Gk., ult. < *sophos* wise]

soph·ist (sŏf′ist) *n.* **1.** A philosopher; a learned man. **2.** One who argues cleverly but fallaciously or unnecessarily minutely. **—** *adj.* Pertaining to the art or method of sophists, or to sophistry. [< L < Gk., ult. < *sophos* wise]

Soph·ist (sŏf′ist) *n.* **1.** A member of a school of early Greek philosophy, preceding the Socratic school. **2.** One of the later Greek teachers of philosophy and rhetoric, who showed great skill in subtle disputation under logical forms.

so·phis·tic (sə-fis′tik) *adj.* Pertaining to a Sophist, sophists, or sophistry. **—** *n.* The art or method of the Sophists. Also **so·phis′ti·cal. — so·phis′ti·cal·ly** *adv.* **— so·phis′ti·cal·ness** *n.*

so·phis·ti·cate (*v.* sə-fis′tə-kāt; *n.* sə-fis′tə-kit, -kāt) *v.* **·cat·ed, ·cat·ing** *v.t.* **1.** To make less simple or ingenuous in mind or manner; render worldly-wise. **2.** *Rare* To mislead or corrupt (a person). **3.** To increase the complexity and capability of. **—** *v.i.* **4.** To indulge in sophistry; be sophistic. **—** *n.* A sophisticated person. [< Med.L < L *sophisticus* sophistic] **— so·phis′ti·ca′tor** *n.*

so·phis·ti·cat·ed (sə-fis′tə-kā′tid) *adj.* **1.** Having fine or subtle perceptions; cultured. **2.** Appealing to the intellect; not suited to popular tastes. **3.** Worldly-wise; deprived of natural simplicity. **4.** Very complicated in design, capabilities, etc.: said of mechanical and electronic devices.

so·phis·ti·ca·tion (sə-fis′tə-kā′shən) *n.* **1.** Sophisticated ideas, attitudes, etc., derived from education and culture. **2.** The act of sophisticating. **3.** Adulteration; falsification.

soph·is·try (sŏf′is-trē) *n. pl.* **·tries 1.** Subtly fallacious reasoning or disputation. **2.** The art or methods of the Greek Sophists.

soph·o·more (sŏf′ə-môr, -mōr) *n.* In American high schools, colleges, and universities having a four-year course, a second-year student. [Earlier *sophumer* one who uses sophisms; later *soph.* in meaning by Gk. *sophos* wise + *mōros* fool]

soph·o·mor·ic (sŏf′ə-môr′ik, -mōr′-) *adj.* **1.** Of, pertaining to, or like a sophomore. **2.** Marked by a shallow assumption of learning or by empty grandiloquence; immature; callow. Also **soph′o·mor′i·cal. — soph′o·mor′i·cal·ly** *adv.*

Soph·o·ni·as (sŏf′ə-nī′əs) The Douai Bible name for ZEPHANIAH.

-sophy *combining form* Knowledge pertaining to a (specified) field: *theosophy.* [< Gk. *sophia* wisdom]

so·po·rif·ic (sō′pə-rif′ik, sŏp′ə-) *adj.* **1.** Causing or tending to cause sleep. **2.** Drowsy; sleepy. **—** *n.* A medicine that produces sleep. [< L *sopor* deep sleep]

sop·ping (sŏp′ing) *adj.* Wet through; drenched; soaking.

sop·py (sŏp′ē) *adj.* **·pi·er, ·pi·est 1.** Very wet. **2.** Rainy. **3.** *Brit. Slang* Mawkish; sentimental.

so·pran·o (sə-pran′ō, -prä′nō) *n. pl.* **so·pran·os** or **so·pra·ni** (-prä′nē) **1.** A voice of the highest range. **2.** The music intended for such a voice, or singing such a part. **—** *adj.* Of or pertaining to a soprano voice, part, etc. [< Ital. *sopra* above]

so·ra (sôr′ə, sō′rə) *n.* A small North American rail, esteemed as food. Also **sora rail.** [? < N.Am.Ind.]

Sorb (sôrb) *n.* A Wend.

Sor·bi·an (sôr′bē·ən) *adj.* Of or pertaining to the Sorbs or Wends or to their language. **—** *n.* **1.** A Sorb or Wend. **2.** The West Slavic language of the Sorbs; Wendish.

Sor·bonne (sôr-bôn′) The faculties of literature and science of the University of Paris.

sor·cer·er (sôr′sər·ər) *n.* A wizard; conjurer; magician. **— sor′cer·ess** *n.fem.*

sor·cer·y (sôr′sər·ē) *n. pl.* **·cer·ies** Alleged employment of supernatural agencies; witchcraft. [< OF < L *sors* fate] **— sor′cer·ous** *adj.* **— sor′cer·ous·ly** *adv.*

sor·did (sôr′did) *adj.* **1.** Filthy; dirty. **2.** Mercenary. **3.** Of degraded character; vile; base. [< L *sordes* filth] **— sor′did·ly** *adv.* **— sor′did·ness** *n.*

sore (sôr, sōr) *adj.* **sor·er, sor·est 1.** Painful or tender to the touch as an inflamed or injured part of the body. **2.** Grieved; distressed: a *sore* heart. **3.** Arousing painful feelings; irritating: a *sore* point. **4.** Extreme or severe: *sore* need. **5.** *Informal* Offended; aggrieved. **—** *n.* **1.** A place on the body where the skin or flesh is bruised, broken, or inflamed. **2.** A painful memory; grief. **—** *adv. Archaic* Sorely. [OE *sār*] **— sore′ness** *n.*

sore·head (sôr′hed′, sōr′-) *U.S. Slang n.* A disgruntled or offended person. **— sore′head·ed** *adj.*

sore·ly (sôr′lē, sōr′-) *adv.* **1.** Grievously; distressingly. **2.** Greatly; in high degree: His aid was *sorely* needed.

sor·ghum (sôr′gəm) *n.* **1.** Any of various stout, canelike tropical grasses cultivated for their saccharine juices and as fodder. **2.** Syrup prepared from their sweet juices of the plant. [< NL < Ital. *sorgo*]

so·ror·i·ty (sə-rôr′ə·tē, -ror′-) *n. pl.* **·ties** A sisterhood; esp., a women's national or local association having chapters in a secondary school, college, or university. [< Med.L < L *soror* sister]

sorp·tion (sôrp′shən) *n.* Any process by which one substance takes up and holds the molecules of another substance, as by absorption or adsorption. [< NL < L *sorbere*]

sor·rel[1] (sôr′əl, sor′-) *n.* Any of several herbs with acid leaves used in salads. [< F < OHG *sur* sour]

sor·rel[2] (sôr′əl, sor′-) *n.* **1.** A reddish or yellowish brown color. **2.** An animal of this color. [< OF *sor* hawk with red plumage]

sor·row (sôr′ō, sŏr′ō) *n.* **1.** Pain or distress of mind because of loss, injury, or misfortune. **2.** An event that causes pain or distress of mind. **3.** The expression of grief. **—** *v.i.* To feel sorrow; grieve. [OE *sorg*] **— sor′row·er** *n.*

sor·row·ful (sôr′ə·fəl, sŏr′-) *adj.* Sad; unhappy; mournful. **— sor′row·ful·ly** *adv.* **— sor′row·ful·ness** *n.*

sor·ry (sôr′ē, sŏr′ē) *adj.* **·ri·er, ·ri·est 1.** Grieved or pained; affected by sorrow from any cause. **2.** Causing sorrow; dismal. **3.** Pitiable or worthless; paltry. **4.** Painful; grievous. [OE *sār* sore] **— sor′ri·ly** *adv.* **— sor′ri·ness** *n.*

sort (sôrt) *n.* **1.** Any number or collection of persons or things characterized by the same or similar qualities; a kind; species; class; set. **2.** Form of being or acting; character; nature; quality; also, manner; style. **3.** *Usu. pl. Printing* A character or type considered as a portion of a font. **— of sorts** Originally, of various or different kinds; now, of a poor or unsatisfactory kind: an actor *of sorts*. **— out of sorts** *Informal* In an ill humor; irritable. **— sort of** *Informal* Somewhat. **—** *v.t.* To arrange or separate into grades, kinds, or sizes. [< OF < L *sors* lot, condition] **— sort′a·ble** *adj.* **— sort′a·bly** *adv.* **— sort′er** *n.*

sor·tie (sôr′tē) *n. Mil.* **1.** A sally of troops from a besieged place to attack the besiegers. **2.** A single trip of an aircraft on a military or naval mission. [< F *sortir* to go forth]

S O S (es′ō′es′) **1.** The code signal of distress adopted by the Radiotelegraphic Convention in 1912, and used by airplanes, ships, etc. **2.** Any call for assistance.

so-so (sō′sō′) *adj.* Passable; mediocre. **—** *adv.* Tolerably.

sot (sŏt) *n.* A habitual drunkard. [OE < OF < LL *sottus* drunkard] **— sot′tish** *adj.* **— sot′tish·ly** *adv.* **— sot′tish·ness** *n.*

sot·to vo·ce (sŏt′ō vō′chē, *Ital.* sôt′tō vō′chā) Softly; in an undertone; privately. [< Ital., under the (normal) voice]

sou (sōō) *n.* A former French coin of varying value. [< F < LL *solidus* a gold coin]

sou·brette (sōō-bret′) *n.* **1.** In light opera or comedy, the role of a pert, intriguing lady's maid. **2.** An actress playing such a role. **3.** Any frivolous or coquettish young woman character. [< F < Provençal *soubret* shy, coy] **— sou·bret′ish** *adj.*

sou·bri·quet (sōō′bri·kā) *n.* A sobriquet.

souf·flé (sōō-flā′) *adj.* Made light and frothy, and fixed in that condition by heat: also **souf·fléed′** (-flād′). **—** *n.* A light, baked dish made fluffy with beaten egg whites. [< F < L < *sub-* under + *flare* to blow]

sough (suf, sou) *v.i.* To make a sighing sound, as the wind. **—** *n.* A deep, murmuring sound. [OE *swōgan* to sound]

sought (sôt) Past tense and past participle of SEEK.

soul (sōl) *n.* **1.** The rational, emotional, and volitional faculties in man, conceived of as forming an entity distinct from the body. **2.** *Theol.* **a** The divine principle of life in man. **b** The moral or spiritual part of man as related to God. **3.** The emotional faculty of man as distinguished from the intellect: He puts his *soul* into his acting. **4.** Fervor; emotional force; heartiness; vitality. **5.** An essential or vital element: Justice is the *soul* of law. **6.** The leading figure or inspirer of a cause, movement, etc. **7.** A person considered as the embodiment of a quality or attribute: He is the *soul* of generosity. **8.** A living person: Every *soul* trembled at the sight. **9.** The disembodied spirit of one who has died; a ghost. [OE *sāwol*] — **souled** *adj.*

soul food Any of various Southern foods or dishes popular with American Negroes, as fried chicken, ham hocks, etc.
soul·ful (sōl'fəl) *adj.* Full or expressive of deep feeling: a *soulful* gaze. — **soul'ful·ly** *adv.* — **soul'ful·ness** *n.*
soul·less (sōl'lis) *adj.* **1.** Heartless; unemotional. **2.** Having no soul. — **soul'less·ly** *adv.* — **soul'less·ness** *n.*
sound[1] (sound) *n.* **1.** Any of a class of waves consisting of mechanical disturbances in an elastic system, esp. in air. **2.** The auditory stimulation produced by waves of this type having frequencies between about 20 and 20,000 cycles per second. **3.** An instance of this stimulation. **4.** A speech sound. **5.** Significance; implication: The story has a sinister *sound*. **6.** Sounding or hearing distance; earshot. **7.** Noise. — *v.i.* **1.** To give forth a sound or sounds. **2.** To give a specified impression; seem: The story *sounds* true. — *v.t.* **3.** To cause to give forth sound. **4.** To signal, order, announce or celebrate: to *sound* retreat, someone's praises, etc. **5.** To utter audibly; pronounce. **6.** To articulate a letter: to *sound* the *r* in *park*. **7.** To test or examine by sound; auscultate. [< OF < L *sonus*]
— **Syn.** (noun) **3.** *Sound* is the general term embracing aural sensations of all qualities. A *tone* is a *sound* of definite pitch, caused by vibrations, predominantly of one frequency. *Noise* is a *sound* lacking pitch, caused by vibrations of dissonant frequencies.
sound[2] (sound) *adj.* **1.** Having all the organs or faculties complete and in normal action and relation; healthy. **2.** Free from injury, flaw, mutilation, or decay: *sound* timber. **3.** Founded in truth; valid; legal. **4.** Correct in views or processes of thought. **5.** Solvent. **6.** Profound, as rest; deep; unbroken. **7.** Complete and effectual; thorough. **8.** Solid; stable; safe; also, trustworthy. **9.** Based on good judgment. [OE *gesund*] — **sound'ly** *adv.* — **sound'ness** *n.*
sound[3] (sound) *n.* **1.** A long and narrow body of water, more extensive than a strait, connecting larger bodies. **2.** The air bladder of a fish. [Fusion of OE and ON *sund*]
sound[4] (sound) *v.t.* **1.** To test or measure the depth of (water, etc.), esp., by means of a lead weight at the end of a line. **2.** To explore or examine (the bottom of the sea, etc.) by means of a sounding lead adapted for bringing up adhering particles. **3.** To discover or try to discover the views, beliefs, etc., of (a person) by means of conversation and roundabout questions: usu. with *out.* — *v.i.* **4.** To sound depth. **5.** To dive down suddenly and deeply. **6.** To investigate; inquire. — *n. Surg.* An instrument for exploring a cavity. [< OF < L *sub*- under + *unda* a wave] — **sound'a·ble** *adj.* — **sound'er** *n.*
sound barrier *Aeron.* The transonic barrier.
sound effects In motion pictures, radio, etc., the incidental and often mechanically produced sounds, as of rain, hoofbeats, explosions, etc., used to give the illusion of reality.
sound·ing[1] (soun'ding) *adj.* **1.** Giving forth a full sound; sonorous. **2.** Having much sound with little significance; noisy and empty. — **sound'ing·ly** *adv.*
sound·ing[2] (soun'ding) *n.* **1.** The act of one who or that which sounds. **2.** Measurement of the depth of water. **3.** *pl.* The depth of water as sounded; also, water of such depth that the bottom may be reached by sounding.
sounding board A structure or dome over a pulpit or speaker's platform to amplify and clarify the speaker's voice.
sound·less (sound'lis) *adj.* Having or making no sound; silent. — **sound'less·ly** *adv.* — **sound'less·ness** *n.*
sound·proof (sound'prōof') *adj.* Resistant to the penetration or spread of sound. — *v.t.* To make soundproof.
sound track The portion along the edge of a motion-picture film that carries the sound record.
soup (sōōp) *n.* **1.** Liquid food made by boiling meat, vegetables, etc., in water. **2.** *Slang* A thick overcast or fog. — **in the soup** *U.S. Slang* In difficulties. — **to soup up** *U.S. Slang* To supercharge or otherwise modify (an automobile) for high speed. [< F *soupe* < Gmc.]
soup·çon (sōōp-sôn') *n. French* A minute quantity; a taste; literally, a suspicion.
sour (sour) *adj.* **1.** Sharp to the taste; acid; tart, like vinegar. **2.** Having an acid or rancid taste as the result of fermentation. **3.** Having a rancid, acid smell or vapor; dank. **4.** Misanthropic and crabbed; cross; morose: a *sour* person.

5. Cold and wet; unpleasant. **6.** Acid: said of soil. — *v.t. & v.i.* To become or make sour. — *n.* **1.** Something sour or distasteful. **2.** An acid solution used in bleaching, etc. **3.** A sour or acid beverage: a whisky *sour*. [OE *sūr*] — **sour'ly** *adv.* — **sour'ness** *n.*
— **Syn.** (adj.) *Sour* and *acid* refer to the taste of vinegar, but *acid* stresses the natural composition and *sour* the result of fermentation or decay. *Bitter* suggests the taste of quinine or gall.
source (sôrs, sōrs) *n.* **1.** That from which any act, movement, or effect proceeds; a creator; origin. **2.** A place where something is found or whence it is taken or derived. **3.** The spring from which a stream of water proceeds; a fountain. **4.** A person, writing, or agency from which information is obtained. [< OF < L *surgere*]
sour·dough (sour'dō') *n.* **1.** *Dial.* Fermented dough for use as leaven in making bread. **2.** *U.S. & Canadian Slang* A pioneer or prospector.
sour grapes The attitude of affecting to despise something one cannot do or have: an allusion to a fable of Aesop.
sour·puss (sour'pŏos') *n. Slang* A person with a sullen, peevish expression or character.
souse (sous) *v.t. & v.i.* **soused, sous·ing 1.** To dip or steep in a liquid. **2.** To pickle. **3.** *Slang* To make or get drunk. — *n.* **1.** The act of sousing. **2.** Something steeped in pickle, esp., the feet and ears of a pig. **3.** A liquid used in pickling; brine. **4.** *Slang* A drunkard. [< OF < OHG *sulza* brine]
sou·tane (sōō-tän') *n.* A Roman Catholic priest's cassock. [< F < Ital. < *sotto* under < L *subtus*]
south (south) *n.* **1.** The direction along a meridian that falls to the right of an observer on earth facing the sun at sunrise. **2.** One of the four cardinal points of the compass, directly opposite *north* and 90° clockwise from *east*. See COMPASS CARD. **3.** Any direction near this point. **4.** *Sometimes cap.* Any region south of a specified point. — **the South** In the U.S.: **a** The population or territory of the southern or southeastern States. **b** The Confederacy. — *adj.* **1.** To, toward, facing, or in the south; southern. **2.** Coming from the south: the *south* wind. — *adv.* In or toward the south; southward. [OE *sūth*]
south·east (south'ēst', *Naut.* sou'ēst') *n.* **1.** The direction midway between south and east. **2.** A point on the mariner's compass, 12 points or 135° clockwise from due north. See COMPASS CARD. **3.** Any region lying in or toward this point. — *adj.* **1.** To, toward, facing, or in the southeast. **2.** Coming from the southeast. — *adv.* In or toward the southeast. — **south'east'** *adj.*
south·east·er (south'ēs'tər, *Naut.* sou'ēs'tər) *n.* A gale or storm from the southeast.
south·east·er·ly (south'ēs'tər·lē, *Naut.* sou'ēs'tər·lē) *adj.* **1.** In, of, or toward the southeast. **2.** From the southeast, as a wind. — *adv.* Toward or from the southeast.
south·east·ward (south'ēst'wərd, *Naut.* sou'ēst'wərd) *adv.* Toward the southeast. Also **south'east'wards.** — *adj.* To, toward, facing, or in the southeast. — *n.* Southeast.
south·east·ward·ly (south'ēst'wərd·lē, *Naut.* sou'ēst'wərd·lē) *adj. & adv.* Toward or from the southeast.
south·er (sou'thər) *n.* A gale or storm from the south.
south·er·ly (suth'ər·lē) *adj.* **1.** In, of, toward, or pertaining to the south. **2.** From the south, as a wind. — *adv.* Toward or from the south.
south·ern (suth'ərn) *adj.* **1.** To, toward, or in the south. **2.** Native to or inhabiting the south. **3.** *Sometimes cap.* Of, pertaining to, or characteristic of the south or South. **4.** From the south, as a wind. [OE *sūtherne*] — **south'ern·most** *adj.*
Southern Cross A southern constellation having four bright stars in the form of a cross.
south·ern·er (suth'ərn·ər) *n.* **1.** One who is native to or lives in the south. **2.** *Usu. cap.* One who lives in or comes from the southern United States.
Southern Hemisphere See under HEMISPHERE.
southern lights The aurora australis.
south·land (south'land') *n. Sometimes cap.* A land or region in the south or South. — **south'land'er** *n.*
south·paw (south'pô') *Informal n.* **1.** In baseball, a left-handed pitcher. **2.** Any left-handed person or player. — *adj.* Left-handed.
South Pole The southern extremity of the earth's axis.
south·south·east (south'south'ēst', *Naut.* sou'sou'ēst') *n.* **1.** The direction midway between south and southeast. **2.** A point on the mariner's compass, 14 points or 157° 30' clockwise from due north. See COMPASS CARD. — *adj. & adv.* In, toward, or from the south-southeast.
south·south·west (south'south'west', *Naut.* sou'sou'west') *n.* **1.** The direction midway between south and southwest. **2.** A point on the mariner's compass, 18 points or 202° 30' clockwise from due north. See COMPASS CARD. — *adj. & adv.* In, toward, or from the south-southwest.

south·ward (south'wərd, *Naut.* suth'ərd) *adv.* Toward the south. Also **south'wards.** — *adj.* To, toward, facing, or in the south. — *n.* A southward direction or point. — **south'ward·ly** *adj. & adv.*

south·west (south'west', *Naut.* sou'west') *n.* **1.** The direction midway between south and west. **2.** A point on the mariner's compass, 20 points or 225° clockwise from due north. See COMPASS CARD. **3.** Any region lying in or toward this point. — *adj.* **1.** To, toward, facing, or in the southwest. **2.** Coming from the southwest: a *southwest* wind. — *adv.* In or toward the southwest. — **south'west'ern** *adj.*

south·west·er (south'wes'tər, *Naut.* sou'wes'tər) *n.* **1.** A gale or storm from the southwest. **2.** A waterproof hat with a broad brim over the neck. Also **sou'·west'er.**

south·west·er·ly (south'wes'tər·lē, *Naut.* sou'wes'tər·lē) *adj.* **1.** In, of, or toward the southwest. **2.** From the southwest, as a wind. — *adv.* Toward or from the southwest.

south·west·ward (south'west'wərd, *Naut.* sou'west'wərd) *adv.* Toward the southwest. Also **south'west'wards.** — *adj.* To, toward, facing, or in the southwest. — *n.* Southwest. — **south'west'ward·ly** *adj. & adv.*

sou·ve·nir (sōō'və·nir', sōō'və·nir') *n.* A token of remembrance; memento. [< F < L *subvenire* to come to mind]

sov·er·eign (sov'rən, suv'-) *n.* **1.** A person, governing body, etc., in whom the supreme power or authority is vested; monarch; ruler. **2.** An English gold coin equivalent to one pound sterling or twenty shillings. — *adj.* **1.** Exercising or possessing supreme authority or jurisdiction. **2.** Independent, and free from external authority or influence: a *sovereign* state. **3.** Possessing supreme excellence or efficacy. [< OF, ult. < L *super* above] — **sov'er·eign·ly** *adv.*

sov·er·eign·ty (sov'rən·tē, suv'-) *n. pl.* **·ties 1.** The state of being sovereign; supreme authority. **2.** The supreme power in a state. **3.** A sovereign state, kingdom, etc. **4.** The status or dominion of a sovereign.

so·vi·et (sō'vē·et, -ət, sō'vē·et') *n.* **1.** In the Soviet Union, any of the legislative bodies existing at various governmental levels. See SUPREME SOVIET. **2.** Any of various similar legislative bodies. [< Russian *sovyet* council]

So·vi·et (sō'vē·et, -ət, sō'vē·et') *adj.* Of or pertaining to the Union of Soviet Socialist Republics.

so·vi·et·ism (sō'vē·ə·tiz'əm) *n.* The policies of or government by soviets, esp., as practiced in the Soviet Union. — **so'vi·et·ist** *n.* — **so'vi·et·is'tic** *adj.*

so·vi·et·ize (sō'vē·ə·tīz') *v.t.* **·ized, ·iz·ing** To bring under a soviet form of government. — **so'vi·et·i·za'tion** *n.*

sow¹ (sō) *v.* **sowed, sown** or **sowed, sow·ing** *v.t.* **1.** To scatter (seed) over land for growth. **2.** To scatter seed over (land). **3.** To spread abroad; disseminate; implant: to *sow* the seeds of distrust. **4.** To cover or sprinkle. — *v.i.* **5.** To scatter seed. [OE *sāwan*] — **sow'er** *n.*

sow² (sou) *n.* A female hog. [OE *sū, sugu*]

sow·bel·ly (sou'bel'ē) *n. U.S. Dial.* Salt pork.

soy (soi) *n.* **1.** The soybean. **2.** An Asian sauce prepared from soybeans fermented and steeped in brine: also **soy sauce.** [< Japanese, short for *shōyu*]

soy·bean (soi'bēn') *n.* **1.** An erect, leguminous herb native to China and India, and cultivated for forage. **2.** Its bean, a source of oil, flour, and other products. Also called *soy:* also **soy·a** (soi'ə). [< SOY + BEAN]

spa (spä) *n.* **1.** Any locality frequented for its mineral springs. **2.** A mineral spring. [from the Belgian town, *Spa*]

space (spās) *n.* **1.** That which is characterized by dimensions extending indefinitely in all directions from any given point, and within which all material bodies are located. **2.** An interval or area between or within points or objects. **3.** Area, room, or extent, as for some purpose: parking *space.* **4.** Outer space. **5.** An interval of time; period; while. **6.** An occasion or opportunity. **7.** *Printing* A piece of type metal used for spacing between words. **8.** A part of a musical staff included between two lines. **9.** Reserved accommodations, as on a train. **10.** Pages, linage, broadcasting time, etc., available for advertisements. — *v.t.* **spaced, spac·ing 1.** To separate by spaces. **2.** To divide into spaces. [< OF < L *spatium*] — **space'less** *adj.* — **spac'er** *n.*

space·craft (spās'kraft', -kräft') *n. Aerospace* Any vehicle, manned or unmanned, designed for research, exploration, or travel in outer space. Also **space·ship** (spās'ship').

space·flight (spās'flīt') *n.* Flight in outer space by a man-made object or vehicle.

space·man (spās'mən) *n. pl.* **·men** (-mən) *Aerospace* One who travels in outer space; an astronaut.

space medicine Aerospace medicine.

space·port (spās'pôrt', -pōrt') *n. Aerospace* A base for rockets and other spacecraft with supporting equipment.

space probe *Aerospace* An artificial satellite or other spacecraft equipped to obtain data in outer space.

space-time (spās'tīm') *n.* A four-dimensional continuum consisting of three spatial coordinates and one coordinate of time. Also **space-time continuum.**

spa·cial (spā'shəl) See SPATIAL.

spac·ing (spā'sing) *n.* **1.** The act, process, or result of arrangement by spaces. **2.** A space or spaces, as in print.

spa·cious (spā'shəs) *adj.* **1.** Of indefinite or vast extent. **2.** Affording ample room; capacious. — **spa'cious·ly** *adv.* — **spa'cious·ness** *n.*

spade¹ (spād) *n.* **1.** An implement used for digging, cutting turf, etc., heavier than a shovel and having a flatter blade. **2.** Any of various tools or implements resembling a spade. — **to call a spade a spade** To speak the plain, uncompromising truth. — *v.t.* **spad·ed, spad·ing** To dig or cut with a spade. [OE *spadu*] — **spad'er** *n.*

spade² (spād) *n.* **1.** A figure on playing cards, resembling a heart with a stalk or handle at the juncture of the lobes. **2.** A card so marked. **3.** *Usu. pl.* The suit of cards so marked. [< Sp. < L < Gk. *spathē* sword]

spade·work (spād'wûrk') *n.* **1.** Work done with a spade. **2.** Preliminary work necessary to get a project under way.

spa·dix (spā'diks) *n. pl.* **spa·di·ces** (spā-dī'sēz) *Bot.* A spike or head of flowers with a fleshy axis, usu. enclosed within a spathe. [< Gk. < *spaein* to break]

spa·ghet·ti (spə·get'ē) *n.* A food consisting of cordlike strands of flour paste. [< Ital., pl. dim. of *spago* cord]

spake (spāk) Archaic past tense of SPEAK.

span¹ (span) *v.t.* **spanned, span·ning 1.** To measure, esp. with the hand with thumb and little finger extended. **2.** To encircle or grasp with the hand, as in measuring. **3.** To stretch across: This road *spans* the continent. **4.** To provide with something that stretches across or extends over. — *n.* **1.** The extreme space over which the hand can be expanded, usu. considered as nine inches. **2.** Distance or extent between any two extremities. **3.** Any small interval or distance, in space or in time. **4.** That which spans, as a bridge. [OE *spann*] — **span'less** *adj.*

span² (span) Archaic past tense of SPIN.

span·drel (span'drəl) *n. Archit.* **a** The triangular space between the outer curve of an arch and the rectangular figure formed by the moldings or framework surrounding it. **b** The space between the shoulders of two adjoining arches. Also **span'dril.** [Dim. of AF *spaundre,* prob. < OF *espandre* to expand]

spang (spang) *adv. U.S. Informal* Directly; exactly; straight: He ran *spang* into the wall. [Origin uncertain]

span·gle (spang'gəl) *n.* **1.** A small bit of sparkling metal, plastic, etc., used for decoration in dress, as in theatrical costume. **2.** Any small sparkling object. — *v.* **·gled, ·gling** *v.t.* **1.** To adorn with or as with spangles; cause to glitter. — *v.i.* **2.** To sparkle as spangles; glitter. [Dim. of MDu. *spang* clasp, brooch] — **span'gly** *adj.*

Span·iard (span'yərd) *n.* A native or citizen of Spain.

span·iel (span'yəl) *n.* **1.** Any of various breeds of small or medium-sized dogs having large pendulous ears and usu. long silky hair. **2.** One who follows like a dog; an obsequious follower. [< OF *espaignol* Spanish (dog)]

Span·ish (span'ish) *adj.* Of or pertaining to Spain, its people, or their language. — *n.* **1.** The Romance language of Spain, Spanish America, and the Philippine Islands. **2.** The inhabitants of Spain collectively: with *the.*

Span·ish-A·mer·i·can (span'ish·ə·mer'ə·kən) *adj.* **1.** Of or pertaining to Spanish America. **2.** Designating or pertaining to the war between the U.S. and Spain, 1898. — *n.* One of Spanish origin living in America, esp. Central or South America; a citizen of a Spanish-American country.

Spanish-American War See table for WAR.

Spanish Main Loosely, the part of Caribbean through which Spanish merchant vessels formerly sailed.

Spanish moss A long, pendent plant that grows on trees of the southern U.S. near the seacoast.

spank (spangk) *v.t.* **1.** To slap or strike, esp. on the buttocks with the open hand as a punishment. — *v.i.* **2.** To move briskly. — *n.* A smack on the buttocks. [Imit.]

spank·er (spangk'ər) *n.* **1.** One who or that which spanks. **2.** *Naut.* A fore-and-aft sail extended by a boom and a gaff from the mizzenmast of a ship or boat. **3.** Any person or thing uncommonly large or fine.

spank·ing (spangk'ing) *adj.* **1.** Moving or blowing rapidly; swift; dashing; lively; strong. **2.** *Brit. Informal* Uncommonly large or fine. — *n.* A series of slaps on the buttocks given as punishment. — *adv. Informal* Very: *spanking* clean.

span·ner (span'ər) *n.* **1.** One who or that which spans. **2.** *Brit.* A hand tool used to turn nuts, bolts, etc. [< G]

spar¹ (spär) *n.* **1.** *Naut.* A round timber or pole for extending a sail, as a mast, yard, or boom. **2.** A similar pole forming part of a derrick, crane, etc. **3.** *Aeron.* Any principal lateral member of an airplane wing. — *v.t.* **sparred, spar·ring** To furnish with spars. [Cf. ON *sparri,* MDu. *sparre* beam]

spar² (spär) *v.i.* **sparred, spar·ring 1.** To box, esp. with care and adroitness. **2.** To bandy words; wrangle. — *n.* The act or practice of boxing. [? < OF < Ital. *sparare* to kick < L *parare* to prepare]

spar³ (spär) *n.* A vitreous, crystalline, easily cleavable, lustrous mineral of varied composition. [< MDu.]

Spar (spär) *n.* A member of the women's reserve of the U.S. Coast Guard. Also **SPAR**. [< L *s(emper) par(atus)* always ready, the motto of the U.S. Coast Guard]

spar deck *Naut.* The light upper deck of a vessel, extending from bow to stern.

spare (spâr) *v.* **spared, spar·ing** *v.t.* **1.** To refrain from injuring, molesting, or killing. **2.** To free or relieve (someone) from (pain, expense, etc.). **3.** To refrain from using or exercising; use frugally. **4.** To part with; do without: Can you *spare* a dime? — *v.i.* **5.** To be frugal. **6.** To be lenient or forgiving; show mercy. — *adj.* **spar·er, spar·est 1.** That can be spared or used at will; disposable; available. **2.** Held in reserve; extra. **3.** Having little flesh; lean. **4.** Not lavish or abundant; scanty. **5.** Economical; parsimonious. — *n.* **1.** That which has been saved or stored away. **2.** A duplicate item kept as a substitute in case the original breaks down, as an automobile tire. **3.** In bowling, the knocking down by a player of all the pins with the two bowls in any frame; also, the score so made. [OE *sparian*] — **spare′ly** *adv.* — **spare′ness** *n.* — **spar′er** *n.*

spare·rib (spâr′rib′) *n.* A cut of meat, esp. pork, consisting of closely trimmed ribs. [? Alter. of MLG *ribbespēr*]

spar·ing (spâr′ing) *adj.* **1.** Scanty; slight. **2.** Frugal. **3.** That spares. — **spar′ing·ly** *adv.* — **spar′ing·ness** *n.*

spark (spärk) *n.* **1.** An incandescent particle thrown off from a red-hot or burning substance or struck from a flint. **2.** Any glistening or brilliant point or transient luminous particle. **3.** Anything that kindles or animates. **4.** *Electr.* **a** The luminous effect of a disruptive electric discharge, or the discharge itself. **b** A small transient arc or an incandescent particle thrown off from such an arc. **5.** A small diamond or bit of diamond, as for cutting glass. **6.** A small trace or indication. — *v.i.* **1.** To give off sparks; scintillate. — *v.t.* **2.** To activate or cause: to *spark* a revolution. [OE *spearca*] — **spark′er** *n.*

spar·kle (spär′kəl) *v.i.* **·kled, ·kling 1.** To give off flashes of light; scintillate; glitter. **2.** To emit sparks. **3.** To bubble; effervesce. **4.** To be brilliant or vivacious. — *n.* A spark; gleam. [Freq. of SPARK¹]

spar·kler (spär′klər) *n.* **1.** Something that sparkles. **2.** A sparkling gem. **3.** A thin, rodlike firework that emits sparks.

spar·kling (spär′kling) *adj.* **1.** Giving out sparks or flashes; glittering. **2.** Brilliant; vivacious. — **spar′kling·ly** *adv.*

spark plug An electrical device for igniting the explosive gases in an internal-combustion engine by means of a spark passing between two terminals. Also *Brit.* **spark′ing plug.**

spar·ling (spär′ling) *n.* **1.** A smelt, parr, or other young fish. **2.** A young herring. [< OF *esperlinge* < Gmc.]

spar·row (spar′ō) *n.* **1.** A small hardy bird related to the finches, grosbeaks, and buntings, introduced into the U.S., where it is known as the **English sparrow. 2.** Any of several related North American birds. [OE *spearwa*]

sparrow hawk 1. A small American falcon that preys on other birds, mice, insects, etc. **2.** A small European hawk that preys on birds.

sparse (spärs) *adj.* Scattered at considerable distances apart; not dense. [< L *sparsus,* pp. of *spargere* to scatter] — **sparse′ly** *adv.* — **sparse′ness, spar′si·ty** *n.*

Spar·ta (spär′tə) An ancient city in the Peloponnesus, southern Greece; capital of ancient Laconia.

Spar·tan (spär′tən) *adj.* **1.** Of or pertaining to Sparta or the Spartans. **2.** Resembling the Spartans in character; courageous, hardy, austere, stoical, and rigorous. — *n.* **1.** A native or citizen of Sparta. **2.** A person of Spartan character. — **Spar′tan·ism** *n.*

spasm (spaz′əm) *n.* **1.** Any sudden, transient burst of energy or activity. **2.** *Pathol.* Any involuntary convulsive muscular contraction. When manifested by alternate contractions and relaxations it is a **clonic spasm;** when persistent and steady, it is a **tonic spasm.** [< L < Gk. < *span* to draw, pull]

spas·mod·ic (spaz·mod′ik) *adj.* **1.** Of the nature of a spasm; convulsive. **2.** Violent, or impulsive and transitory. Also **spas·mod′i·cal.** — **spas·mod′i·cal·ly** *adv.*

spas·tic (spas′tik) *adj.* Of, pertaining to, or characterized by spasms; spasmodic. — *n.* A person afflicted with cerebral palsy. — **spas′ti·cal·ly** *adv.*

spat¹ (spat) Past tense and past participle of SPIT¹.

spat² (spat) *n.* **1.** Spawn of shellfish; esp., spawn of the oyster. **2.** A young oyster, or young oysters collectively. — *v.i.* **spat·ted, spat·ting** To spawn, as oysters. [? Akin to SPIT¹]

spat³ (spat) *n.* **1.** A slight blow; slap. **2.** A splash, as of rain; spatter. **3.** A petty dispute. — *v.* **spat·ted, spat·ting** *v.i.* **1.** To strike with a slight sound; slap. **2.** To engage in a petty quarrel. — *v.t.* **3.** To slap. [Prob. imit.]

spat⁴ (spat) *n. Usu. pl.* A short gaiter worn over a shoe and fastened beneath with a strap. [Short for SPATTERDASH]

spate (spāt) *n. Chiefly Brit.* A sudden or vigorous outpouring, as of words, feeling, etc. Also **spait.** [Origin uncertain]

spathe (spāth) *n. Bot.* A large bract or pair of bracts sheathing a flower cluster, spadix, etc. [< L < Gk. *spathe* broadsword] — **spa·those** (spā′thŏs, spath′ōs) *adj.*

spa·tial (spā′shəl) *adj.* Pertaining to, involving, or having the nature of space. Also spelled *spacial.* [< L *spatium* space] — **spa·ti·al·i·ty** (spā′shē·al′ə·tē) *n.* — **spa′tial·ly** *adv.*

spa·ti·o·tem·po·ral (spā′shē·ō·tem′pər·əl) *adj.* Of or pertaining to both space and time.

spat·ter (spat′ər) *v.t.* **1.** To scatter in drops or splashes, as mud or paint. **2.** To splash with such drops. **3.** To defame; slander. — *v.i.* **4.** To throw off drops or splashes. **5.** To fall in a shower, as raindrops. — *n.* **1.** The act of spattering, or the matter spattered. **2.** A pattering noise, as of falling rain. [Cf. Frisian *spatterje,* Du. *spatten* to spatter]

spat·ter·dash (spat′ər·dash′) *n.* A legging or puttee.

spat·u·la (spach′ŏŏ·lə) *n.* **1.** A knifelike instrument with a flat, flexible blade, used to spread plaster, cake icing, etc. **2.** *Med.* An instrument used to press the tongue down or aside, as in examinations. [< L, dim. of *spatha* spathe] — **spat′u·lar** *adj.*

spawn (spôn) *n.* **1.** *Zool.* The eggs of fishes, amphibians, mollusks, etc., esp. in masses. **2.** The offspring of any animal. **3.** Outcome or results; yield. **4.** The spat of the oyster. **5.** Very small fish; fry. **6.** *Bot.* The mycelium of mushrooms or other fungi. — *v.i.* **1.** To produce spawn; deposit eggs or roe. **2.** To come forth as or like spawn. — *v.t.* **3.** To produce (spawn). **4.** To give rise to. **5.** To bring forth abundantly or in great quantity. **6.** To plant with spawn or mycelium. [< AF, OF < L *expandere*]

spay (spā) *v.t.* To remove the ovaries from (a female animal). [< AF, OF < L *spatha* sword]

speak (spēk) *v.* **spoke** (*Archaic* **spake**), **spo·ken** (*Archaic* **spoke**), **speak·ing** *v.i.* **1.** To employ the vocal organs in ordinary speech; utter words. **2.** To express or convey ideas, opinions, etc., in or as in speech. **3.** To make a speech. **4.** To talk together; converse. **5.** To make a sound; also, to bark, as a dog. — *v.t.* **6.** To express or make known in or as in speech. **7.** To utter in speech. **8.** To use or be capable of using (a language) in conversation. **9.** To speak to. — **to speak for 1.** To speak in behalf of; represent officially. **2.** To lay claim to; engage. [OE *specan, sprecan*] — **speak′a·ble** *adj.*

speak·eas·y (spēk′ē′zē) *n. pl.* **·eas·ies** *Slang* A place where liquor is sold illegally.

speak·er (spē′kər) *n.* **1.** One who speaks. **2.** The presiding officer in any one of various legislative bodies. **3.** A loudspeaker. — **speak′er·ship** *n.*

speak·ing (spē′king) *adj.* **1.** Having the power of effective speech. **2.** Expressive; telling. — *n.* **1.** The act of utterance; vocal expression. **2.** Oratory; public declamation. — **speak′ing·ly** *adv.*

spear (spir) *n.* **1.** A weapon consisting of a pointed head on a long shaft. **2.** A similar instrument, barbed and usu. forked, as for use in spearing fish. **3.** A leaf or slender stalk, as of grass. — *v.t.* **1.** To pierce or capture with a spear. — *v.i.* **2.** To pierce as a spear does. **3.** To send forth spears or spires, as a plant. [OE *spere* spear] — **spear′er** *n.*

spear·head (spir′hed′) *n.* **1.** The point of a spear. **2.** One who or that which leads, influences, or directs an action, etc.; esp., a military force leading an attack on enemy positions. — *v.t.* To be in the lead of (an attack, etc.).

spear·man (spir′mən) *n. pl.* **·men** (-mən) A man armed with a spear. Also **spears′man** (spirz′-).

spear·mint (spir′mint′) *n.* An aromatic herb similar to peppermint.

spe·cial (spesh′əl) *adj.* **1.** Having some peculiar or distinguishing characteristic or characteristics; particular. **2.** Designed for or assigned to a specific purpose; limited or specific in range, aim, or purpose. **3.** Of, pertaining to, constituting, or designating a species; differential. **4.** Unique; exceptional. **5.** Extra or additional, as a dividend. **6.** Intimate; beloved. — *n.* A person or thing made, detailed for, or appropriated to a specific service or occasion, as a train, a newspaper edition, etc. [< L *species* kind, species] — **spe′cial·ly** *adv.* — **spe′cial·ness** *n.*

special delivery *U.S.* Mail delivery by special courier, a service obtained for an additional fee.

spe·cial·ist (spesh′əl·ist) *n.* **1.** A person devoted to some one line of study, occupation, or professional work; esp., a physician who restricts his practice to one branch of medicine. **2.** In the U.S. Army, an enlisted person in a technical or administrative position, with pay equal to that of a non-commissioned officer in the same grade, but ranking below a corporal and above a private first class. See table at GRADE. — **spe′cial·ism** *n.* — **spe′cial·is′tic** *adj.*

spe·ci·al·i·ty (spesh′ē·al′ə·tē) *n. pl.* **·ties 1.** A specific or individual characteristic. **2.** Specialty (defs. 3, 4, 5). ◆ In British usage, this form is preferred to *specialty*.

spe·cial·i·za·tion (spesh'əl·ə·zā'shən, -ī·zā'-) *n.* **1.** The act or process of specializing; also, the state of being or becoming specialized. **2.** *Biol.* The development of a plant or animal organ or part in adaptation to environmental influences or for a special function.

spe·cial·ize (spesh'əl·īz) *v.* **·ized, ·iz·ing** *v.i.* **1.** To concentrate on one particular activity or subject; engage in a specialty. **2.** *Biol.* To take on a special form or forms by specialization. — *v.t.* **3.** To adapt for some special use or purpose. **4.** *Biol.* To modify or adapt by specialization. **5.** To endorse, as a check, to a particular payee. **6.** To mention specifically. Also *Brit.* **spe′cial·ise.**

spe·cial·ty (spesh'əl·tē) *n.* *pl.* **·ties 1.** A special occupation, craft, or study. **2.** The state of being special or of having peculiar characteristics. **3.** An individual characteristic or peculiarity; distinguishing mark. **4.** An article dealt in exclusively or chiefly, or having a special character.

spe·cie (spē'shē) *n.* Coined money; coin. — **in specie 1.** In coin. **2.** *Law* In kind. [< L (*in*) *specie* (in) kind]

spe·cies (spē'shēz, -shiz, -sēz) *n.* *pl.* **·cies 1.** *Biol.* A category of animals or plants subordinate to a genus but above a breed, race, strain, or variety. **2.** A group of individuals or objects agreeing in some common attribute or attributes and designated by a common name. **3.** *Eccl.* The visible form of bread or of wine retained by the eucharistic elements after consecration. **4.** A kind, sort, or variety. **5.** An image, form, or appearance. [< L, form, kind]

spec·i·fi·a·ble (spes'ə·fī'ə·bəl) *adj.* Such as can be specified.

spe·cif·ic (spi·sif'ik) *adj.* **1.** Distinctly and plainly set forth; definite or determinate. **2.** *Biol.* Of, pertaining to, or distinguishing a species. **3.** Peculiar or special, as characteristics, qualities, etc. **4.** Characteristic of or proper to a given substance or phenomenon, esp. in relation to some arbitrary but constant standard of comparison: *specific* gravity. **5.** *Med.* **a** Curing or alleviating a special disease or pathological condition: said of a remedy or medicine. **b** Caused by a particular condition, germ, etc.: said of a disease. — *n.* **1.** Anything specific or adapted to effect a specific result. **2.** A special medicine for a particular disease. **3.** *Usu. pl. U.S. Informal* A particular; item; instance. [< L < *species* kind, class + *facere* to make] — **spec·i·fic·i·ty** (spes'ə·fis'ə·tē) *n.*

spe·cif·i·cal·ly (spi·sif'ik·lē) *adv.* **1.** In a specific manner; explicitly; particularly; definitely. **2.** As to or in respect to species. **3.** In a particular sense or case.

spec·i·fi·ca·tion (spes'ə·fə·kā'shən) *n.* **1.** The act of specifying. **2.** Something specified, as in a contract, plans, etc.; also, one detail in such a statement. **3.** *Usu. pl.* A specific description of certain dimensions, types of material, etc., to be used in a manufacturing or engineering project.

specific gravity *Physics* The ratio of the mass of a body to that of an equal volume of some standard substance, water in the case of solids and liquids, and air or hydrogen in the case of gases; a measure of density.

spec·i·fy (spes'ə·fī) *v.t.* **·fied, ·fy·ing 1.** To mention specifically; state in full and explicit terms. **2.** To embody in a specification. [< OF < L < *species* species + *facere* to make]

spec·i·men (spes'ə·mən) *n.* **1.** One of a class of persons or things regarded as representative of the class; an example; sample. **2.** *Med.* A sample of body tissue or exudates taken for analysis and diagnosis. **3.** *Informal* A person of pronounced or curious type. [< L < *specere* to look at]

spe·ci·os·i·ty (spē'shē·os'ə·tē) *n.* *pl.* **·ties** One who or that which is plausible at first view but actually is not.

spe·cious (spē'shəs) *adj.* **1.** Apparently good or right, but actually not so; plausible: *specious* reasoning. **2.** Pleasing or attractive in appearance, but deceptive. **3.** Beguiling, but lacking in sincerity. [< L *speciosus* fair] — **spe′cious·ly** *adv.* — **spe′cious·ness** *n.*

speck (spek) *n.* **1.** A small spot, stain, or discoloration. **2.** Any very small thing; a particle. — *v.t.* To mark with spots or specks; speckle. [OE *specca*]

speck·le (spek'əl) *v.t.* **·led, ·ling** To mark with specks or speckles. — *n.* A small spot; speck. — **speck′led** *adj.*

specs (speks) *n.pl. Informal* **1.** Eyeglasses; spectacles. Also **specks. 2.** Specifications (def. 3).

spec·ta·cle (spek'tə·kəl) *n.* **1.** That which is exhibited to public view, esp. something grand or showy. **2.** An unwelcome or deplorable exhibition. **3.** *pl.* A pair of eyeglasses. [< F < L < *spectare*, freq. of *specere* to see]

spec·ta·cled (spek'tə·kəld) *adj.* **1.** Wearing spectacles. **2.** Having markings resembling a pair of spectacles.

spec·tac·u·lar (spek·tak'yə·lər) *adj.* **1.** Characterized by or displaying unusual, exciting, or unexpected qualities, conditions, etc.; a *spectacular* rescue. **2.** Of, pertaining to, or like a spectacle. — *n.* **1.** In television, a lavish dramatic or musical production. **2.** An elaborate, illuminated sign. — **spec·tac′u·lar·ly** *adv.* — **spec·tac′u·lar′i·ty** (-lar'ə·tē) *n.*

spec·ta·tor (spek'tā·tər, spek·tā′-) *n.* **1.** One who beholds;

eyewitness; onlooker. **2.** One who is present at and views a show, game, spectacle, etc. [< L < *spectare* to look at]

spec·ter (spek'tər) *n.* **1.** A ghost or apparition. **2.** Anything of a fearful or horrible nature. Also *Brit.* **spec′tre.** [< F < L *spectrum* vision]

spec·tra (spek'trə) Plural of SPECTRUM.

spec·tral (spek'trəl) *adj.* **1.** Of, pertaining to, or like a specter; ghostly. **2.** Pertaining to a spectrum or spectra. — **spec·tral·i·ty** (spek·tral'ə·tē) *n.* — **spec′tral·ly** *adv.*

spectro- *combining form* **1.** Radiant energy, as exhibited in the spectrum. **2.** Spectroscope; spectroscopic. [< SPECTRUM]

spec·tro·gram (spek'trə·gram) *n.* A photograph made by a spectrograph.

spec·tro·graph (spek'trə·graf, -gräf) *n.* **1.** An apparatus for photographing or forming a representation of the spectrum. **2.** A spectrogram.

spec·tro·scope (spek'trə·skōp) *n.* An optical instrument for forming and analyzing the spectrum emitted by bodies or substances. — **spec′tro·scop′ic** (-skop'ik) or **·i·cal** *adj.* — **spec′tro·scop′i·cal·ly** *adv.*

SIMPLE SPECTROSCOPE

a Prism. *b* Telescope for viewing prism through eyepiece (*e*). *c* Collimator with slit (*d*).

spec·tros·co·py (spek·tros'kə·pē) *n.* The study and analysis of the phenomena observed with the spectroscope. — **spec·tros′co·pist** *n.*

spec·trum (spek'trəm) *n.* *pl.* **·tra** (-trə) **1.** *Physics* **a** The band of color observed when a beam of white light is passed through a prism that separates each component of the light according to wavelengths, ranging from long for red to short for violet. **b** An image formed by radiant energy directed through a spectroscope and brought to a focus, and in which each wavelength corresponds to a specific band or line in a progressive series characteristic of the emitting source. **2.** Any range of characteristics, values, activities, etc. **3.** An afterimage. [< L, vision]

spec·u·la (spek'yə·lə) Plural of SPECULUM.

spec·u·late (spek'yə·lāt) *v.i.* **·lat·ed, ·lat·ing 1.** To form conjectures regarding anything without experiment; theorize; conjecture. **2.** To make an investment involving a risk, but with hope of gain. [< L *speculatus*, pp. of *speculari* to look at] — **spec′u·la′tor** *n.*

spec·u·la·tion (spek'yə·lā'shən) *n.* **1.** The act of theorizing or conjecturing; speculating. **2.** A theory or conjecture. **3.** A conclusion reached by or based upon conjecture. **4.** An investment involving risk with hope of large profit. **5.** The act of engaging in risky business transactions that offer a possibility of large profit.

spec·u·la·tive (spek'yə·lā'tiv, -lə·tiv) *adj.* **1.** Of, pertaining to, engaged in, or given to speculation, meditation, etc. **2.** Strictly theoretical or purely scientific. **3.** Engaging in or involving financial speculation. **4.** Involving risk. — **spec′u·la′tive·ly** *adv.* — **spec′u·la′tive·ness** *n.*

spec·u·lum (spek'yə·ləm) *n.* *pl.* **·la** (-lə) or **·lums 1.** A mirror of polished metal or of glass coated with a metal film, used for telescope reflectors, etc. *Med.* An instrument that dilates a passage of the body for examination. [< L, mirror < *specere* to see] — **spec′u·lar** *adj.*

sped (sped) Alternative past tense and past participle of SPEED.

speech (spēch) *n.* **1.** The faculty of expressing thought and emotion by spoken words. **2.** The act of speaking. **3.** That which is spoken; a saying or remark. **4.** A public address or talk. **5.** A characteristic manner of speaking. **6.** A particular language, idiom, or dialect: American *speech*. **7.** Any audible or visible method of communication, including cries, gestures, and sign language. **8.** The study of oral communication. [OE < *specan, sprecan* to speak]

speech clinic A place where speech disorders are treated.

speech disorder Disorganization or impairment of speech caused either by physical defect or by mental disorder.

speech·i·fy (spē'chə·fī) *v.i.* **·fied, ·fy·ing** To make speeches: a derisive or dialectal term. — **speech′i·fi′er** *n.*

speech·less (spēch'lis) *adj.* **1.** Unable to speak or temporarily deprived of speech because of physical weakness, strong emotion, etc. **2.** Mute; dumb. **3.** Silent; reticent. **4.** Unable to be expressed in words: *speechless* joy. — **speech′less·ly** *adv.* — **speech′less·ness** *n.*

speed (spēd) *n.* **1.** The act or state of moving or progressing swiftly; rapidity of motion; swiftness. **2.** Rate of motion, esp. in physics, as considered without reference to direction. **3.** Rate of performance, as shown by the ratio of work done to time spent. **4.** *Mech.* A transmission gear in a motor vehicle. **5.** *Photog.* In a camera lens, the minimum time required for an effective exposure. — *v.* **sped** or **speed·ed, speed·ing** *v.t.* **1.** To move or go with speed. **2.** To exceed a speed limit. — *v.t.* **3.** To promote the forward progress of; cause to move or go with speed. **4.** To promote the success of. **5.** To wish Godspeed to: *Speed* the parting guest. **— to speed up** To accelerate in speed or action. **—** *adj.* Having, pertaining to, characterized by, regulating, or indicating speed. [OE *spēd* prosperity, power]

speed·boat (spēd′bōt′) *n.* A motorboat capable of high speed.

speed·er (spē′dər) *n.* One who or that which speeds; esp., a motorist who exceeds a safe or legally specified limit.

speed·om·e·ter (spi·dom′ə·tər) *n.* A device for indicating the speed of a vehicle, often combined with an odometer.

speed·ster (spēd′stər) *n.* One who speeds.

speed·up (spēd′up′) *n.* An acceleration in work, output, movement, etc.

speed·way (spēd′wā′) *n.* A specially reserved or prepared road for vehicles traveling at high speed.

speed·well (spēd′wel) *n.* One of various low herbs of the figwort family, bearing blue or white flowers.

speed·y (spē′dē) *adj.* **speed·i·er, speed·i·est 1.** Characterized by speed; rapid. **2.** Without delay; prompt. **— Syn.** See SWIFT. **— speed′i·ly** *adv.* **— speed′i·ness** *n.*

spe·le·an (spi·lē′ən) *adj.* **1.** Of, or like a cave. **2.** Dwelling in a cave or caves. [< L < Gk. *spēlaion* cave]

speleo- *combining form* Cave. [< L *spelaeum* cave < Gk. *spēlaion*]

spe·le·ol·o·gy (spē′lē·ol′ə·jē) *n.* **1.** The scientific study of caves in their physical, geological, and biological aspects. **2.** The exploration of caves as a sport or profession. **— spe′le·o·log′i·cal** (-ə·loj′i·kəl) *adj.* **— spe′le·ol′o·gist** *n.*

spell[1] (spel) *v.* **spelled** or **spelt, spell·ing** *v.t.* **1.** To name or write the letters of (a word); esp., to do so correctly. **2.** To form or be the letters of: C-a-t *spells* cat. **3.** To compose; make up. **4.** To signify; mean. **—** *v.i.* **5.** To form words out of letters, esp. correctly. **— to spell out 1.** To read with difficulty. **2.** To puzzle out and learn. **3.** To make clear and explicit. [< OF *espeler* < Gmc.]

spell[2] (spel) *n.* **1.** A word formula used as a charm. **2.** An irresistible fascination or attraction. **—** *v.t.* **spelled, spell·ing** To cast a spell upon. [OE, statement.]

spell[3] (spel) *n.* **1.** A period of time, usu. of short length. **2.** *Informal* A continuous period characterized by a certain type of weather. **3.** *Informal* A short distance. **4.** *Informal* A fit of illness, debility, etc. **5.** A turn of duty in relief of another. **6.** A period of work or employment. **—** *v.t.* **1.** To relieve temporarily from some work or duty. **—** *v.i.* **2.** To take a rest. [OE *gespelia* substitute]

spell·bind (spel′bīnd′) *v.t.* **-bound, bind·ing** To bind or enthrall, as if by a spell. **— spell′bind′er** *n.*

spell·bound (spel′bound′) *adj.* Fascinated; enchanted.

spell·er (spel′ər) *n.* **1.** One who spells. **2.** A spelling book.

spell·ing (spel′ing) *n.* **1.** The act of one who spells. **2.** The art of correct spelling; orthography. **3.** The way in which a word is spelled.

spelling bee A gathering at which contestants engage in spelling words, those who spell wrongly usu. being retired until only one remains.

spelt[1] (spelt) Alternative past tense and past participle of SPELL.

spelt[2] (spelt) *n.* A species of wheat or any of its winter or spring varieties. [OE]

spe·lunk·er (spē·lung′kər) *n.* An enthusiast in the exploration and study of caves; a speleologist. [< L *spelunca* cave] **— spe·lunk′ing** *n.*

spend (spend) *v.* **spent, spend·ing** *v.t.* **1.** To pay out or disburse (money). **2.** To expend by degrees; use up. **3.** To apply or devote, as thought or effort, to some activity, purpose, etc. **4.** To pass: to *spend* one's life in jail. **—** *v.i.* **5.** To pay out or disburse money, etc. [OE < L *expendere* to expend] **— spend′er** *n.*

spend·thrift (spend′thrift′) *n.* One who spends money lavishly or wastefully. **—** *adj.* Excessively lavish; prodigal.

spent (spent) Past tense and part participle of SPEND. **—** *adj.* **1.** Worn out or exhausted. **2.** Deprived of force.

sperm[1] (spûrm) *n.* **1.** The male fertilizing fluid; semen. **2.** A male reproductive cell; spermatozoon. [< OF < L < Gk. *sperma* seed]

sperm[2] (spûrm) *n.* **1.** A sperm whale. **2.** Spermaceti. **3.** Sperm oil. [Short for SPERMACETI]

-sperm *combining form Bot.* A seed (of a specified kind): *gymnosperm*. [< Gk. *sperma, spermatos* seed]

sper·ma·ce·ti (spûr′mə·sē′tē, -set′ē) *n.* A white, waxy substance separated from the oil contained in the head of the sperm whale, used for making candles, ointments, etc. [< L *sperma ceti* seed of a whale]

sper·mat·ic (spûr·mat′ik) *adj.* Of, pertaining to, or like sperm; generative.

spermato- *combining form* **1.** Seed; pertaining to seeds. **2.** Spermatozoa; of or related to spermatozoa. Also *spermo-.*

Also, before vowels, **spermat-.** [< Gk. *sperma, spermatos* seed]

sper·ma·to·phyte (spûr′mə·tə·fīt′, spər·mat′ə·fīt) *n. Bot.* Any of a phylum or division of flowering and seed-bearing plants. **— sper′ma·to·phyt′ic** (-fit′ik) *adj.*

sper·ma·to·zo·on (spûr′mə·tə·zō′on) *n. pl.* **·zo·a** (-zō′ə) *Biol.* The male fertilizing element of an animal, usu. in the form of a highly motile cell with a long flagellate process or tail: also called *zoosperm.* [< SPERMATO- + Gk. *zōion* animal] **— sper′ma·to·zo′al, sper′ma·to·zo′ic** *adj.*

sper·mic (spûr′mik) *adj.* Spermatic.

spermo- See SPERMATO-.

-spermous *combining form* Having (a specified number or kind of) seeds; seeded. Also **-spermal, -spermic.** [< -SPERM + -OUS]

sperm whale A large, toothed whale of warm seas, having a huge truncate head containing a reservoir of sperm oil.

spew (spyoō) *v.t. & v.i.* **1.** To vomit; throw up. **—** *n.* That which is spewed; vomit. Also spelled *spue.* [OE *spīwan*]

sphag·num (sfag′nəm) *n.* Any of a genus of whitish gray mosses found in damp places; the bog or peat mosses, used as packing and in surgical dressings. [< L < Gk. *sphāgnos,* kind of moss] **— sphag′nous** *adj.*

sphal·er·ite (sfal′ər·īt) *n.* A resinous to adamantine native zinc sulfide, ZnS, with traces of iron and cadmium; a principal ore of zinc: also called *zinc blende.* [< Gk. *sphaleros* deceptive + -ITE[1]]

sphe·noid (sfē′noid) *n.* **1.** *Mineral.* A crystal form enclosed by four faces, each of which cuts all three axes. **2.** *Anat.* The sphenoid bone. **—** *adj.* Wedge-shaped. [< Gk. *sphēn* wedge + -OID] **— sphe·noi′dal** (sfi·noid′l) *adj.*

sphenoid bone *Anat.* An irregular, compound bone situated at the base of the skull.

sphere (sfir) *n.* **1.** The surface described by a semicircle making one complete rotation on its diameter. **2.** A solid or hollow figure enclosed by a surface every point of which is equidistant from the center. **3.** A globe; ball. **4.** Compass or field of activity, endeavor, influence, etc.; range; scope; province. **5.** A particular social rank or position. **6.** The apparent outer dome of the heavens on which the heavenly bodies appear to lie. **—** *v.t.* **sphered, spher·ing 1.** To place in or as in a sphere. **2.** To set among the celestial spheres. **3.** To make spherical. [< OF < L < Gk. *sphaira* ball]

-sphere *combining form* **1.** Denoting an enveloping spherical mass: *atmosphere.* **2.** Denoting a spherical form: *planisphere.* [< Gk. *sphaira* ball, sphere]

spher·i·cal (sfir′i·kəl, sfer′-) *adj.* **1.** Shaped like a sphere; globular. **2.** Pertaining to a sphere or spheres. **3.** Pertaining to the heavenly bodies; celestial. Also **spher′ic.** **— spher′i·cal·ly** *adv.* **— spher′i·cal·ness** *n.*

sphe·ric·i·ty (sfi·ris′ə·tē) *n. pl.* **·ties** The state of being a sphere; spherical form; roundness.

sphe·roid (sfir′oid) *n. Geom.* A body having nearly the form of a sphere. **— sphe·roi′dal** (sfi·roid′l), **sphe·roi′dic** or **·di·cal** *adj.* **— sphe·roi′dal·ly** *adv.*

sphe·roi·dic·i·ty (sfir′oi·dis′ə·tē) *n.* The state or character of being a spheroid. Also **sphe·roi·di·ty** (sfi·roi′də·tē).

sphinc·ter (sfingk′tər) *n. Anat.* A band of muscle that surrounds an opening or tube in the body and serves to close it. [< LL < Gk. < *sphingein* to bind fast] **— sphinc′ter·al** *adj.*

sphinx (sfingks) *n. pl.* **sphinx·es** or **sphin·ges** (sfin′jēz) **1.** In Egyptian mythology, a wingless monster with a lion's body and the head of a man, a ram, or hawk. **2.** In Greek mythology, a winged monster with a woman's head and breasts and a lion's body, that destroyed those unable to guess her riddle. **3.** A mysterious or enigmatical person. **— the Sphinx** The colossal sphinx at Gizeh, having the body of a lion. [< L < Gk. < *sphingein* to close, strangle]

sphyg·mo·ma·nom·e·ter (sfig′mō·mə·nom′ə·tər) *n.* An instrument for measuring blood pressure in the arteries. [< Gk. *sphygmos* pulse + MANOMETER]

Spi·ca (spī′kə) *n.* A star, one of the 20 brightest, 1.21 magnitude; Alpha in the constellation Virgo.

spi·cate (spī′kāt) *adj.* **1.** *Bot.* Arranged in spikes: said of flowers. **2.** *Ornithol.* Having a spur, as the legs of some birds. Also **spi′cat·ed.** [< L *spicatus* < *spica* spike]

spic·ca·to (spēk·kä′tō) *Music n. pl.* **·tos** A method of producing rapid, detached notes on a stringed instrument, by allowing the bow to rebound slightly. [< Ital.]

spice (spīs) *n.* **1.** An aromatic, pungent vegetable substance, as cinnamon, cloves, etc., used to flavor food and beverages. **2.** Such substances collectively. **3.** That which gives zest or adds interest. **4.** An aromatic odor. **—** *v.t.* **spiced, spic·ing 1.** To season with spice. **2.** To add zest to. [< OF *espice* < L *species*] **— spic′er** *n.*

spice·bush (spīs′boosh′) *n.* An aromatic American shrub of the laurel family. Also **spice′wood′** (-wood′).

spick (spik) *n. U.S. Slang* A Spanish-speaking person: an offensive term. Also **spic.**

spick-and-span (spik′ən-span′) *adj.* **1.** Neat and clean. **2.** Perfectly new, or looking as if new. [Prob. < *spick*, var. of SPIKE[1] +dial. E *span-new*, really or freshly new]

spic·ule (spik′yōōl) *n.* **1.** A small, slender, sharp-pointed body; a spikelet. **2.** *Zool.* One of the small, needlelike, growths supporting the soft tissues of certain invertebrates, as sponges. Also **spic·u·la** (spik′yə-lə). [< L *spicum* point, spike] — **spic·u·lar, spic′u·late** (-lāt, -lit) *adj.*

spic·u·lum (spik′yə-ləm) *n. pl.* **·la** (-lə) A spicule.

spic·y (spī′sē) *adj.* **spic·i·er, spic·i·est** **1.** Containing, flavored with, or fragrant with spices. **2.** Producing spices. **3.** Having zest or piquancy. **4.** Somewhat improper; risqué. — **spic′i·ly** *adv.* — **spic′i·ness** *n.*

spi·der (spī′dər) *n.* **1.** Any of a large number of eight-legged wingless arachnids having an unsegmented abdomen and capable of spinning webs for the capture of flies or other insects. **2.** A long-handled iron frying pan, often having legs. **3.** A trivet. [OE *spinnan* to spin] — **spi′der·y** *adj.*

spider crab Any of a genus of crustaceans with long legs, common on the Atlantic coast of North America.

spider monkey An arboreal South American monkey with very long limbs and a long prehensile tail.

spi·der·wort (spī′dər-wûrt′) *n.* Any of a genus of plants, esp., an American perennial with deep blue flowers.

spied (spīd) Past tense and past participle of SPY.

spiel (spēl, shpēl) *U.S. Slang v.i.* To talk; orate. — *n.* A speech; esp., a noisy, high-pressure sales talk. [< G, game, play < *spielen* to play] — **spiel′er** *n.*

spi·er (spī′ər) *n.* A spy; scout.

spif·fy (spif′ē) *adj.* **·fi·er, ·fi·est** *Slang* Smartly dressed; spruce. — **spif′fi·ness** *n.* [< dial. E *spiff* a dandy]

spig·ot (spig′ət) *n.* **1.** A faucet. **2.** A plug or valve for the bunghole of a cask. **3.** A turning plug fitting into a faucet. [ME *spigote*]

spike[1] (spīk) *n.* **1.** A long, thick metal nail. **2.** A projecting, pointed piece of metal, as in the soles of shoes to prevent slipping. **3.** A very narrow high heel, used on women's shoes. — *v.t.* **spiked, spik·ing** **1.** To fasten with spikes. **2.** To set or provide with spikes. **3.** To block; put a stop to. **4.** To pierce with or impale on a spike. **5.** *Informal* To add alcoholic liquor to. [ME < Scand.] — **spik′y** *adj.*

spike[2] (spīk) *n.* **1.** An ear of corn, barley, wheat, or other grain. **2.** *Bot.* A flower cluster having numerous flowers arranged closely on an elongated common axis. [< L *spica* ear of grain]

spike·let (spīk′lit) *n. Bot.* A small spike bearing few flowers.

spike·nard (spīk′nərd, -närd) *n.* **1.** A fragrant ointment of ancient times: also called *nard.* **2.** The East Indian herb that yields it. **3.** An American perennial herb having an aromatic root. [< L *spica* spike + *nardus* nard]

spile (spīl) *n.* **1.** A post or supporting timber; pile. **2.** A wooden pin or plug used as a vent in a cask; a spigot. **3.** A spout driven into a sugar maple to lead the sap to a bucket. — *v.t.* **spiled, spil·ing** **1.** To pierce for and provide with a spigot. **2.** To drive spiles into. [< MDu., skewer, splinter]

spill[1] (spil) *v.* **spilled** or **spilt, spill·ing** *v.t.* **1.** To allow or cause to fall or run out or over, as a liquid or a powder. **2.** To shed, as blood. **3.** *Naut.* To empty (a sail) of wind. **4.** To cause to fall, as from a horse. **5.** *Informal* To divulge; make known, as a secret. — *v.i.* **6.** To fall or run out or over: said of liquids, etc. — **to spill the beans** *Informal* To divulge a secret. — *n.* **1.** A fall to the ground, as from a horse; tumble. **2.** The act of spilling. [OE *spillan* to destroy] — **spill′er** *n.*

spill[2] (spil) *n.* **1.** A thin strip of wood or rolled paper, used for lighting fires, etc. **2.** A peg or plug. [< SPILE]

spill·way (spil′wā′) *n.* A passageway, as in a dam, to release the water in a reservoir.

spilt (spilt) Alternative past tense and past participle of SPILL[1].

spin (spin) *v.* **spun** (*Archaic* **span**), **spun, spin·ning** *v.t.* **1.** To draw out and twist into threads; also, to draw out and twist fiber into (threads, yarn, etc.). **2.** To make or produce as if by spinning. **3.** To form (a web, etc.): said of spiders, silkworms, etc. **4.** To tell, as a story or yarn. **5.** To protract; prolong, as a period of time: with *out.* **6.** To cause to whirl rapidly: to *spin* a top. — *v.i.* **7.** To make thread or yarn. **8.** To make a web or thread: said of spiders, etc. **9.** To whirl rapidly; rotate. **10.** To seem to be whirling, as from dizziness. **11.** To move rapidly. — *n.* **1.** An act or instance of spinning; a rapid whirling. **2.** Any rapid movement. **3.** *Informal* A ride or drive. **4.** *Aeron.* The descent of an airplane in a spiral curve about a vertical axis, with its nose sharply inclined. [OE *spinnan*]

spin·ach (spin′ich, -ij) *n.* **1.** A pot herb of the goosefoot family. **2.** Its fleshy leaves, used as a vegetable. [< OF *espinage* < LL *spinacia*]

spi·nal (spī′nəl) *adj.* **1.** Of or pertaining to the backbone; vertebral. **2.** Resembling a spine, spines, or spinous processes. — *n.* An injection for spinal anesthesia.

spinal anesthesia *Surg.* Anesthesia produced by the injection of an anesthetic into the spinal cord.

spinal column *Anat.* The series of articulated vertebrae that enclose and protect the spinal cord and provide dorsal support for the ribs; the backbone.

spinal cord *Anat.* That portion of the central nervous system enclosed by the spinal column.

spin·dle (spin′dəl) *n.* **1.** A rod having a slit or catch in the top and a whorl of wood or metal at its lower end, on which thread is wound from the distaff in hand spinning. **2.** The slender rod in a spinning wheel, containing a spool or bobbin on which the thread is twisted and wound; also, a similar device on a spinning machine or shuttle. **3.** *Mech.* A rotating rod, axis, or shaft, esp. when small and bearing something that rotates: the *spindle* of a lathe. **4.** A needlelike rod mounted on a weighted base, used for impaling bills, checks, etc.: also **spindle file.** **5.** Any narrow, tapering object resembling a spindle. **6.** A small shaft passing through the lock of a door and bearing the knobs or handles. — *v.* **·dled, ·dling** *v.i.* **1.** To grow into a long, slender stalk or body. — *v.t.* **2.** To form into a spindle. **3.** To provide with a spindle. **4.** To impale on a spindle. [OE *spinnan* to spin]

spin·dle-leg·ged (spin′dəl-leg′id, -legd′) *adj.* Having long, slender legs. Also **spin′dle-shanked′** (-shangkt′).

spin·dle-legs (spin′dəl-legz′) *n. pl.* (construed as sing. in *def.* 2) **1.** Long, slender legs. **2.** *Informal* A person having long, slender legs. Also **spin′dle-shanks′** (-shangks′).

spin·dling (spind′ling) *adj.* Long and thin; disproportionately slender. — *n.* A spindling person or plant shoot.

spin·dly (spind′lē) *adj.* **·dli·er, ·dli·est** Of a slender, lanky growth or form.

spin·drift (spin′drift) *n.* Blown sea spray: also called *spoondrift.* [Alter. of *spoondrift* < *spoon,* var. of SPUME + DRIFT]

spine (spīn) *n.* **1.** The spinal column of a vertebrate; backbone. **2.** *Zool.* Any of various hard, pointed outgrowths on the bodies of certain animals, as the fin ray of a fish. **3.** *Bot.* A stiff, pointed woody process on the stems of certain plants; thorn. **4.** The back of a bound book, usu. inscribed with the title and name of the author. **5.** A projecting eminence or ridge. [< OF < L *spina* spine]

spi·nel (spi-nel′, spin′əl) *n.* Any of a class of hard, variously colored minerals, some of which, as the **ruby spinel,** are used as gemstones. [< F < Ital. < L *spina* spine]

spine·less (spīn′lis) *adj.* **1.** Having no spine or backbone; invertebrate. **2.** Lacking spines. **3.** Lacking firmness of will or steadfastness; cowardly. — **spine′less·ness** *n.*

spin·et (spin′it) *n.* **1.** A small musical keyboard instrument of the harpsichord class. **2.** A small upright piano. [? after G. *Spinetti,* 16th c. Venetian inventor]

spin·na·ker (spin′ə-kər) *n. Naut.* A large, bellying jib sometimes carried on the mainmast of a racing vessel opposite the mainsail, used when sailing before the wind. [? < a mispronunciation of *Sphinx,* the name of the first yacht to carry this kind of sail, 1866]

spin·ner (spin′ər) *n.* **1.** One who or that which spins. **2.** In angling, a whirling spoon bait.

spin·ner·et (spin′ə-ret) *n.* **1.** An organ by which spiders or silkworms produce the filament for webs, cocoons, etc. **2.** A pierced metal plate through which plastic material is forced so as to make rayon fibers.

spin·ning (spin′ing) *n.* The act of one who or that which spins. — *adj.* **1.** That spins. **2.** Of, belonging to, or used in the process of spinning.

spinning jenny A framed mechanism for spinning more than one strand of yarn at a time.

spinning wheel A device used for spinning yarn or thread, a rotating spindle operated by a treadle and flywheel.

spin-off (spin′ôf′, -of′) *n.* An off-shoot or by-product.

spi·nose (spī′nōs) *adj.* Having many spines. — **spi′nose·ly** *adv.* — **spi·nos′i·ty** (-nōs′ə-tē) *n.*

spin·ster (spin′stər) *n.* **1.** A woman who has remained unmarried, esp. one no longer young; an old maid. **2.** A woman who spins; a spinner. [ME < SPIN + -STER] — **spin′ster·hood** *n.* — **spin′ster·ish** *adj.*

spin·y (spī′nē) *adj.* **spin·i·er, spin·i·est** **1.** Having spines; thorny. **2.** Difficult; perplexing. — **spin′i·ness** *n.*

spiny anteater The echidna.

spiny lobster Any of various marine crustaceans having spiny shells but lacking large claws, valued as seafood: also called *crayfish, rock lobster.*

spir- Var. of SPIRO-.

spir·a·cle (spir′ə-kəl, spī′rə-) *n. Zool.* **1.** An aperture for the passage of air or water in the respiration of various animals, as sharks, rays, tadpoles, and insects. **2.** A breathing hole, as the nostril of a cetacean. [< OF < L *spiraculum* air hole]

spi·rae·a (spī-rē′ə) *n.* Any of a genus of shrubs of the rose family, having clusters of small, white or pink flowers. Also **spi·re′a.** [< L, meadowsweet]

spi·ral (spī′rəl) *n.* **1.** *Geom.* Any plane curve formed by a point that moves around a fixed center and continually increases or decreases its distance from it. **2.** A curve winding like a screw thread. **3.** Something spirally wound or having a spiral shape, as a spring. **4.** A flight of an airplane in a spiral path. — *adj.* **1.** Pertaining to or resembling a spiral. **2.** Winding and advancing; helical. **3.** Winding and rising in a spire, as some springs. — *v.* ·raled or ·ralled, ·ral·ing or ·ral·ling *v.t.* **1.** To cause to take a spiral form or course. — *v.i.* **2.** To take a spiral form or course. **3.** To rise sharply or disproportionately, as prices, costs, etc. [< Med.L < L *spira* coil] — **spi′ral·ly** *adv.*

spire¹ (spīr) *n.* **1.** The tapering or pyramidal roof or top of a tower. **2.** Any similar high, pointed formation; a pinnacle. **3.** A slender stalk or blade. — *v.* spired, spir·ing *v.t.* **1.** To furnish with a spire or spires. — *v.i.* **2.** To shoot or point up in or as in a spire. **3.** To put forth a spire or spires; sprout. [OE *spīr* stalk, stem]

spire² (spīr) *n.* A spiral or a single turn of one; whorl; twist. [< F < L *spira* < Gk. *speira* coil]

spi·ril·lum (spī-ril′əm) *n. pl.* ·la (-lə) Any of a genus of rigid, spirally twisted flagellate bacteria. [< NL, dim. of L *spira* coil]

spir·it (spir′it) *n.* **1.** The vital essence or animating force in living organisms, esp. man, often considered divine in origin. **2.** The part of a human being characterized by intelligence, personality, self-consciousness, and will; the mind. **3.** The substance or universal aspect of reality, regarded as opposed to matter. **4.** *Often cap.* In the Bible, the creative, animating power of God. **5.** A supernatural or immaterial being, as an angel, ghost, specter, etc. **6.** A person regarded with reference to any particular activity, characteristic, or temper: a leading *spirit* in the community. **7.** *Usually pl.* A state of mind; mood; temper. **8.** Vivacity or energy; ardor. **9.** Ardent loyalty or devotion: school *spirit*. **10.** True intent or meaning as opposed to outward, formal observance: the *spirit* of the law. **11.** The characteristic temper or disposition of a period or movement: the *spirit* of the Reformation. **12.** *pl.* Strong alcoholic liquor. **13.** *Usually pl. Chem.* The essence or distilled extract of a substance: *spirits* of turpentine. **14.** *Often pl.* In pharmacy, a solution of a volatile principle in alcohol: *spirits* of ammonia. — *v.t.* **1.** To carry off secretly: with *away*, *off*, etc. **2.** To infuse with spirit or animation; inspirit; encourage: often with *up*. — *adj.* **1.** Of or pertaining to ghosts; spiritualistic. **2.** Operated by the burning of alcohol: a *spirit* lamp. [< OF < L *spiritus* breath, spirit]

Spir·it (spir′it) *n.* In Christian theology, the Holy Spirit.

spir·it·ed (spir′it·id) *adj.* **1.** Full of spirit; animated. **2.** Having a (specified kind of) spirit or nature: *high-spirited*. — **spir′it·ed·ly** *adv.* — **spir′it·ed·ness** *n.*

spirit gum A quick-drying solution of a gum in ether.

spir·it·less (spir′it·lis) *adj.* Lacking enthusiasm, energy, etc.; listless. — **spir′it·less·ly** *adv.* — **spir′it·less·ness** *n.*

spirit level An instrument used to determine any deviation from the horizontal or perpendicular by reference to the position of a bubble of air in a tube of liquid.

spir·it·u·al (spir′i·chōō·əl) *adj.* **1.** Of, pertaining to, like, or consisting of spirit, as distinguished from matter; incorporeal. **2.** Affecting the immaterial nature or soul of man. **3.** Of or pertaining to God; holy. **4.** Sacred or religious; not lay or temporal; ecclesiastical: *spiritual* authorities: distinguished from *secular*. **5.** Marked or characterized by the highest moral or intellectual qualities. — *n.* A religious folk song originating among the Negroes of the southern U.S.; also, any similar song. — **spir′i·tu·al·ly** *adv.* — **spir·tu·al·i·ty** (spir′i·chōō·al′ə·tē), **spir′i·tu·al·ness** *n.*

spir·it·u·al·ism (spir′i·chōō·əl·iz′əm) *n.* **1.** The belief that the spirits of the dead communicate with and manifest their presence to the living, usually through the agency of a medium. **2.** *Philos.* A form of idealism that identifies the spirit as the only ultimate reality. **3.** The state or character of being spiritual. — **spir′i·tu·al·ist** *n.* — **spir·i·tu·al·is′tic** *adj.*

spir·it·u·al·ize (spir′i·chōō·əl·īz′) *v.t.* ·ized, ·iz·ing **1.** To make spiritual; free of grossness or materialism. **2.** To treat as having a spiritual meaning or sense. Also *Brit.* **spir′i·tu·al·ise′.** — **spir·i·tu·al·i·za′tion** *n.* — **spir′i·tu·al·iz′er** *n.*

spir·it·u·el (spir′i·chōō·el′, *Fr.* spē·rē·tü·el′) *adj.* Characterized by wit and by the higher and finer qualities of the mind generally. [< F] — **spir′i·tu·elle′** *adj. fem.*

spir·it·u·ous (spir′i·chōō·əs) *adj.* Containing alcohol, as distilled liquors; intoxicating. — **spir′i·tu·ous·ness** *n.*

spiro-¹ *combining form* Breath; respiration. Also, before vowels, **spir-.** [< L *spirare* to breathe]

spiro-² *combining form* Spiral; coiled. Also, before vowels, **spir-.** [< Gk. *speira* coil]

spi·ro·chete (spī′rə·kēt) *n.* **1.** Any of various motile bacteria having a corkscrewlike form and commonly found in water and sewage. **2.** Any similar bacteria including those that cause syphilis, trench mouth, and yaws. Also **spi′ro·chaete.** [< Gk. *speira* coil + *chaitē* bristle]

spir·y (spīr′ē) *adj.* **1.** Pertaining to or having the form of a spire. **2.** Abounding in spires, as a city.

spit¹ (spit) *v.* **spat** or **spit, spit·ting** *v.t.* **1.** To eject (saliva, etc.) from the mouth. **2.** To eject or utter with violence. **3.** To light, as a fuse. — *v.i.* **4.** To eject saliva, etc., from the mouth. **5.** To make a hissing or sputtering noise. **6.** To fall in scattered drops or flakes, as snow. — *n.* **1.** Spittle; saliva. **2.** An act of spitting or expectorating. **3.** A light, scattered fall of snow or rain. **4.** *Informal* Exact likeness; counterpart. [OE *spittan*] — **spit′ter** *n.*

spit² (spit) *n.* **1.** A pointed rod on which meat is turned and roasted before a fire. **2.** A point of low land extending from a shore into the water. — *v.t.* **spit·ted, spit·ting** To transfix or impale with or as with a spit. [OE *spitu*]

spit and image *Informal* An exact likeness; counterpart. Also **spitting image.** [See SPIT¹, n. (def. 4)]

spit·ball (spit′bôl) *n.* **1.** Paper chewed and shaped into a ball for use as a missile. **2.** In baseball, a pitched ball, now no longer legal, that is wet on one side with saliva, and deviates deceptively in its course.

spite (spīt) *n.* **1.** Malicious bitterness or hatred; grudge. **2.** That which is done in spite. — **in spite of** Notwithstanding. — **Syn.** See NOTWITHSTANDING. — *v.t.* **spit·ed, spit·ing** To show one's spite toward. [Short for DESPITE]

spite·ful (spīt′fəl) *adj.* **1.** Filled with spite. **2.** Prompted by spite. — **spite′ful·ly** *adv.* — **spite′ful·ness** *n.*

spit·fire (spit′fīr′) *n.* A quick-tempered person who is given to saying spiteful things.

spit·tle (spit′l) *n.* **1.** The fluid secreted by the mouth; saliva; spit. **2.** The salivalike matter in which the larvae of spittle insects live. [OE *spātl*; infl. in form by SPIT¹]

spit·toon (spi·tōōn′) *n.* A receptacle for spit; a cuspidor.

spitz (spits) *n.* A small dog, a variety of Pomeranian, having long silky hair and a tapering muzzle. Also **spitz dog.** [< G, short for *spitzhund* < *spitz* pointed + *hund* dog]

splash (splash) *v.t.* **1.** To dash or spatter (a liquid, etc.) about. **2.** To spatter, wet, or soil with a liquid dashed about. **3.** To make (one's way) with splashes. **4.** To decorate or mark by or as by splashing. — *v.i.* **5.** To make a splash or splashes. **6.** To move, fall, or strike with a splash or splashes. — *n.* **1.** The act or noise of splashing. **2.** The result of splashing, as a spot. **3.** *Informal* A striking or ostentatious impression, action, success, etc.: to make a *splash*. [Var. of PLASH¹] — **splash′er** *n.*

splash·down (splash′doun′) *n.* The setting down of a spacecraft or a part of it in the seas following its flight.

splash·y (splash′ē) **splash·i·er, splash·i·est** *adj.* **1.** Slushy; wet. **2.** Marked by or as by splashes; blotchy. **3.** *Informal* Sensational; showy: They made a *splashy* appearance.

splat (splat) *n.* A thin, broad piece of wood, as that forming the middle of a chair back. [Origin uncertain]

splat·ter (splat′ər) *v.t. & v.i.* To spatter or splash. — *n.* A spatter; splash. [Blend of SPLASH and SPATTER]

splay (splā) *adj.* **1.** Spread out; broad. **2.** Clumsily formed; awkward. — *n.* A slanted surface or beveled edge, as the sides of a doorway. — *v.t.* **1.** To make with a splay. **2.** To spread out; expand. — *v.i.* **3.** To spread out; open. **4.** To slant; slope. [Aphetic var. of DISPLAY]

splay·foot (splā′fŏŏt′) *n. pl.* ·feet (-fēt′) **1.** Abnormal flatness and turning outward of the feet. **2.** A foot so deformed. — **splay′foot′ed** *adj.*

spleen (splēn) *n. Anat.* **1.** A highly vascular, flattened, ductless organ located on the upper left side of the abdominal cavity, and effecting certain modifications in the blood. **2.** Ill temper; spitefulness: to vent one's *spleen*. **3.** *Archaic* Low spirits; melancholy. [< OF < L < Gk. *splēn*] — **spleen′ful, spleen′ish, spleen′y** *adj.* — **spleen′ful·ly** *adv.*

splen·did (splen′did) *adj.* **1.** Magnificent; imposing. **2.** Inspiring to the imagination; glorious; illustrious. **3.** Giving out or reflecting brilliant light; shining. **4.** *Informal* Very good; excellent: a *splendid* offer. [< L *splendere* to shine] — **splen′did·ly** *adv.* — **splen′did·ness** *n.*

splen·dif·er·ous (splen-dif′ər-əs) *adj. Informal* Exhibiting great splendor; very magnificent: a facetious usage.

splen·dor (splen′dər) *n.* **1.** Exceeding brilliance from emitted or reflected light. **2.** Magnificence. **3.** Conspicuous greatness of achievement. Also *Brit.* **splen′dour.** [< L, brightness] — **splen′dor·ous, splen′drous** *adj.*

sple·net·ic (spli·net′ik) *adj.* **1.** Pertaining to the spleen. **2.** Fretfully spiteful; peevish. Also **sple·net′i·cal.** — *n.* A peevish person. — **sple·net′i·cal·ly** *adv.*

splen·ic (splen′ik, splē′nik) *adj.* Of, in, near, or pertaining to the spleen.

spleno- *combining form Anat. & Med.* The spleen; of or related to the spleen. Also, before vowels, **splen-.** [< Gk. *splēn, splēnos* spleen]

---

splice (splīs) *v.t.* **spliced, splic·ing** **1.** To unite, as by twisting or intertwining the ends of rope, wires, etc. **2.** To connect, as timbers, by beveling, scarfing, or overlapping at the ends. **3.** *Slang* To join in marriage. — *n.* **1.** A union made by splicing. **2.** The place at which two parts are spliced. [< MDu. *splissen*] — **splic′er** *n.*

splint (splint) *n.* **1.** A thin, flat piece split off; a splinter. **2.** A thin, flexible strip of split wood used for basketmaking, chair bottoms, etc. **3.** *Surg.* An appliance, as of wood or metal, used for keeping a fractured limb or other injured part in a fixed or proper position. **4.** A splint bone. — *v.t.* To confine, support, or brace, as a fractured limb, with or as with splints. [< MDu. *splinte*]

splin·ter (splin′tər) *n.* A thin, sharp piece of wood, glass, metal, etc., split or torn off lengthwise; a sliver. — *v.t. & v.i.* To split into thin sharp pieces or fragments; shatter; shiver. [< MDu.] — **splint′er·y** *adj.*

split (split) *v.* **split, split·ting** *v.t.* **1.** To separate into parts by force, esp. into two approximately equal parts. **2.** To break or divide lengthwise or along the grain; separate into layers. **3.** To divide into groups or factions; disrupt, as a political party. **4.** To divide and distribute by portions or shares. — *v.i.* **5.** To break apart; divide lengthwise or along the grain. **6.** To become divided through disagreement, etc. **7.** To share something with others. — **to split hairs** To make fine distinctions; be unnecessarily precise. — **to split off 1.** To break off by splitting. **2.** To separate by or as by splitting. — **to split the difference** To divide equally a sum in dispute. — **to split up 1.** To separate into parts and distribute. **2.** To cease association; separate. — *n.* **1.** The act of splitting; also, the result of splitting, as a cleft or rent. **2.** Separation into factions; schism: a *split* in the church. **3.** A sliver; splinter. **4.** A share or portion, as of booty. **5.** *Informal* A bottle or a drink half the usual size. **6.** A confection made of a split banana, ice cream, syrup, chopped nuts, and whipped cream. **7.** In bowling, the position of two or more pins left standing on such spots so that a spare is nearly impossible. **10.** An acrobatic trick in which the legs are extended upon the floor in a straight line at right angles to the body: also **the splits.** — *adj.* **1.** Cleft, esp. longitudinally; fissured. **2.** Divided: a *split* ticket. [< MDu. *splitten*] — **split′er** *n.*

split infinitive *Gram.* An infinitive in which the sign *to* is separated from the verb, generally by an adverb, as in "to really believe."

split level house A dwelling in which the floors of the several levels are less than a story above or below the adjoining one.

split ticket 1. A ballot on which the voter has distributed his vote among candidates of different parties. **2.** A ballot containing names of candidates of more than one party or party faction. Compare STRAIGHT TICKET.

split·ting (split′ing) *adj.* **1.** Acute or extreme: a *splitting* shriek. **2.** That aches severely: a *splitting* head.

splotch (sploch) *n.* A discolored spot, as of ink, etc.; a daub; splash; spot. — *v.t.* To soil or mark with a splotch or splotches. [Cf. OE *splott* spot] — **splotch′y** *adj.*

splurge (splûrj) *Informal n.* **1.** An ostentatious display. **2.** An extravagant expenditure. — *v.i.* **splurged, splurg·ing 1.** To show off; be ostentatious. **2.** To spend money lavishly or wastefully. [Origin uncertain] — **splurg′y** *adj.*

splut·ter (splut′ər) *v.i.* **1.** To make a series of slight, explosive sounds, or throw off small particles, as meat frying. **2.** To speak hastily, confusedly, or incoherently. — *v.t.* **3.** To utter excitedly or confusedly; sputter. **4.** To bespatter. — *n.* A noise as of spluttering; bustle; confused stir. [Blend of SPLASH and SPUTTER] — **splut′ter·er** *n.*

spoil (spoil) *v.* **spoiled** or **spoilt, spoil·ing** *v.t.* **1.** To impair or destroy the value, usefulness, or beauty of. **2.** To impair the character of, esp., by overindulgence: to *spoil* a child. **3.** *Obs.* To take property from by force; despoil. — *v.i.* **4.** To lose normal or useful qualities; esp., to become tainted or decayed, as food. — **Syn.** See DECAY. — **to be spoiling for** To long for; crave: He is *spoiling for* a fight. — *n.* **1.** *Often pl.* Plunder seized by violence; loot. **2.** *pl. Chiefly U.S.* The emoluments of public office. **3.** The act of pillaging; spoliation. [< OF < L < *spolium* booty] — **spoil′er** *n.*

spoil·age (spoi′lij) *n.* **1.** Spoiled material collectively. **2.** Something that is or has been spoiled. **3.** The process of spoiling. **4.** The state of being spoiled.

spoil·sport (spoil′spôrt′, -spōrt′) *n.* A person whose actions or attitudes spoil the pleasures of others.

spoils system *U.S.* In a political party after a victorious campaign, the system or practice of making public offices the rewards of partisan services.

spoke¹ (spōk) *n.* **1.** One of the rods or bars that serve to support the rim of a wheel by connecting it to the hub. **2.** A stick or bar for insertion in a wheel to prevent its turning. **3.** A rung of a ladder. — *v.t.* **spoked, spok·ing 1.** To provide with spokes. **2.** To fasten (a wheel) with a stick or spoke to prevent its turning. [OE *spāca*]

spoke² (spōk) Past tense and archaic past participle of SPEAK.

spo·ken (spō′kən) Past participle of SPEAK. — *adj.* **1.** Uttered orally, as opposed to written. **2.** Speaking or having (a specified kind of) speech: *smooth-spoken.*

spoke·shave (spōk′shāv′) *n.* A planing tool having a blade set between two handles, used in rounding and smoothing wooden surfaces; originally used for shaping spokes.

spokes·man (spōks′mən) *n. pl.* **·men** (-mən) One who speaks in the name and behalf of another or others. — **spokes′wom′an** (-wŏom′ən) *n. fem..*

spo·li·a·tion (spō′lē·ā′shən) *n.* The act of despoiling; esp., the authorized seizure of neutral ships by a belligerent. [< L < *spoliare* to despoil] — **spo′li·a·tor** *n.*

spo·li·a·tive (spō′lē·ā′tiv) *adj.* Tending to abstract from or lessen.

spon·dee (spon′dē) *n.* A metrical foot consisting of two long syllables or accented syllables. [< F < L < Gk. < *spondē* libation; because used in the solemn chants accompanying a libation] — **spon·da·ic** (-dā′ik) *adj.*

sponge (spunj) *n.* **1.** Any of a varied group of aquatic, usu. marine organisms, characterized by a highly porous body without specialized internal organs and incapable of free movement. **2.** The skeleton or network of elastic fibers that remains after the removal of the living matter from certain sponges and that readily absorbs liquids, used as an absorbent for bathing, etc. **3.** Any spongelike substance used as an absorbent. **4.** Leavened dough, or dough in the process of leavening. **5.** *Surg.* An absorbent pad, as of sterilized gauze. **6.** A sponge bath. **7.** *Informal* One who lives at the expense of another or others; a parasite. — **to throw** (or **toss**) **up** (or **in**) **the sponge** *Informal* To give up; abandon the struggle. — *v.* **sponged, spong·ing** *v.t.* **1.** To wipe, wet, or clean with a sponge. **2.** To wipe out; expunge; erase. **3.** To absorb; suck in. **4.** *Informal* To get without cost or at another's expense. — *v.i.* **5.** To be absorbent. **6.** *Informal* To live or get something at the expense of others. [OE < L < Gk. *spongos.*] — **spong′er** *n.* — **spong′i·ness** *n.* **spong′y** *adj.*

sponge bath A bath taken by washing oneself with a cloth or sponge rather than in a bathtub or shower.

sponge cake A cake of sugar, eggs, and flour, containing no shortening and beaten very light.

spon·son (spon′sən) *n.* **1.** A curved projection from the hull of a vessel or seaplane, to give greater stability or increase the surface area. **2.** A similar protuberance on a ship or tank, for storage purposes or for the training of a gun. **3.** An air tank built into the side of a canoe, to improve stability and prevent sinking. [Appar. alter. of EXPANSION]

spon·sor (spon′sər) *n.* **1.** One who makes himself responsible for a statement by, or the debt or duty of, another; a surety. **2.** A godfather or godmother. **3.** A business enterprise that finances a broadcast program that advertises its product or service. — *v.t.* To act as sponsor for; vouch for. [< L < *spondere* to be a security] — **spon·so·ri·al** (spon-sôr′ē-əl, -sō′rē) *adj.*

spon·ta·ne·i·ty (spon′tə·nē′ə·tē) *n. pl.* **·ties 1.** The quality or fact of being spontaneous. **2.** A spontaneous act.

spon·ta·ne·ous (spon·tā′nē·əs) *adj.* **1.** Done or resulting from one's own impulse or desire; not premeditated; unrestrained. **2.** Arising from inherent qualities without external cause; self-generated. **3.** *Biol.* Growing without cultivation; wild; indigenous. [< LL < L *sponte* of free will] — **spon·ta′ne·ous·ly** *adv.* — **spon·ta′ne·ous·ness** *n.*
— **Syn. 1.** A *spontaneous* act seems to be prompted by inner feeling, rather than external stimulus: a *spontaneous* outburst of applause. An *impulsive* action comes from sudden inclination, and lacks deliberation: an *impulsive* gesture of welcome.

spontaneous combustion The burning of a substance through the generation of sufficient internal heat to ignite it, as masses of oiled rags, finely powdered ores, coal, etc.

spontaneous generation *Biol.* The doctrine of the generation of new organisms from putrid or decomposing organic matter assumed to be entirely devoid of life.

spoof (spoof) *Informal v.t. & v.i.* To deceive or hoax; joke; parody. — *n.* Deception; parody; hoax. [after a game invented by Arthur Roberts, 1852–1933, English comedian]

spook (spook) *Informal n.* A ghost; an apparition; specter. — *v.t. Informal* To haunt (a person or place). [< Du.] — **spook′i·ly** *adv.* — **spook′ish, spook′y** *adj.*

spool (spool) *n.* **1.** A small cylinder with a flange at each end and an axial bore, upon which thread or yarn is or may be wound. **2.** The quantity of thread held by a spool. **3.** Anything resembling a spool in shape or purpose. — *v.t.* To wind on a spool. [< MLG *spole*]

spoon (spoon) *n.* **1.** A utensil having a shallow, generally ovoid bowl and a handle, used in preparing, serving, or eating food. **2.** Something resembling a spoon or its bowl. **3.** A metallic lure attached to a fishing line; also **spoon bait, trolling spoon. 4.** A wooden golf club with lofted face and comparatively short, stiff shaft. — *v.t.* **1.** To lift up or out with a spoon. **2.** To hollow out like the bowl of a spoon. — *v.i.* **3.** *Informal* To make love, as by caressing or kissing. [OE spōn sliver, chip]

spoon·bill (spōōn'bil) *n.* **1.** Any of various wading birds related to the ibises, having the bill broad and flattened. **2.** The shoveler. — **spoon'-billed'** *adj.*

spoon·drift (spōōn'drift') *n.* Spindrift.

spoon·er·ism (spōō'nə-riz'əm) *n.* The unintentional transposition of sounds or of parts of words in speaking, as in "half-*w*armed *f*ish" for "half-*f*ormed *w*ish." [after William A. *Spooner*, 1884–1930, of New College, Oxford]

spoon-fed (spōōn'fed') *adj.* **1.** Fed with a spoon. **2.** Pampered; over-indulged. **3.** Not given the opportunity to act or think for oneself.

spoon·ful (spōōn'fŏŏl') *n.* *pl.* **·fuls** As much as a spoon will hold.

spoon·y (spōō'nē) *Informal* *adj.* **spoon·i·er, spoon·i·est** Sentimental or silly, as in lovemaking; soft. — *n.* *pl.* **spoon·ies** A foolish, sentimental lover. Also **spoon'ey.**

spoor (spŏŏr) *n.* Footprint or other trace of a wild animal. — *v.t. & v.i.* To track by or follow a spoor. [< Du.]

spo·rad·ic (spô-rad'ik, spō-) *adj.* **1.** Occurring here and there; occasional. **2.** Separate; isolated. **3.** Neither epidemic nor endemic: said of disease. Also **spo·rad'i·cal.** [< Med.L < Gk. < *sporas* scattered] — **spo·rad'i·cal·ly** *adv.*

spo·ran·gi·um (spô-ran'jē-əm, spō-) *n.* *pl.* **·gi·a** (-jē-ə) *Bot.* A sac in which asexual spores are produced, as in certain algae and fungi: also called *spore case*. [< SPOR(O)- + Gk. *angeion* vessel] — **spo·ran'gi·al** *adj.*

spore (spôr, spōr) *n.* **1.** *Bot.* The reproductive body in cryptogams, analogous to the seeds of flowering plants, but able to develop asexually into an independent organism or individual. **2.** *Bacteriol.* A strongly resistant body developed in some bacilli, able to become active under suitable conditions. **3.** *Biol.* Any cell or minute body capable of developing into a new organism; a germ, seed, etc. — *v.i.* **spored, spor·ing** To develop spores: said of plants. [< NL < Gk. *seed, sowing*] — **spo·ra·ceous** (spô-rā'shəs, spō-) *adj.*

spore case A sporangium.

sporo- *combining form* Seed; spore. Also, before vowels, **spor-.** [< Gk. *spora* seed]

spo·ro·phyte (spôr'ə-fīt, spōr'ə-) *n.* *Bot.* The stage in which spores are produced in certain plants that reproduce by alternation of generations.

-sporous *combining form* Having (a specified number or kind of) spores. [< SPOR(O)- + -OUS]

spo·ro·zo·an (spôr'ə-zō'ən, spōr'ə-) *adj.* *Zool.* Designating or belonging to a class of parasitic protozoans reproducing by spores, as the malaria parasite. — *n.* A member of this class. [< SPORO- + Gk. *zōion* animal]

spor·ran (spor'ən) *n.* A purse, generally of fur, worn in front of the kilt by Highlanders. For illus. see KILT. [< Scottish Gaelic < LL *bursa* purse]

sport (spôrt, spōrt) *n.* **1.** That which amuses in general; diversion; pastime. **2.** A particular game or play pursued for diversion; esp., an outdoor or athletic game, as baseball, tennis, swimming, etc. **3.** A spirit of jesting. **4.** That with which one sports; a toy; plaything. **5.** Mockery; an object of derision: to make *sport* of someone; also, a laughingstock; butt. **6.** *Biol.* An animal or plant that exhibits sudden and spontaneous variation from the normal type; a mutation. **7.** *Informal* One who lives a fast, gay, or flashy life. **8.** A person characterized by his observance of the rules of fair play, or by his ability to get along with others: a good *sport.* — *v.i.* **1.** To amuse oneself; play; frolic. **2.** To participate in games. **3.** To make sport or jest; trifle. **4.** *Biol.* To vary suddenly or spontaneously from the normal type; mutate. — *v.t.* **5.** *Informal* To display or wear ostentatiously; show off. — *adj.* Of, pertaining to, or fitted for sports; also, appropriate for informal wear: a *sport* coat: also **sports.** [Aphetic var. of DISPORT] — **sport'er** *n.* — **sport'ful** *adj.* — **sport'ful·ly** *adv.* — **sport'ful·ness** *n.*

sport·ing (spôr'ting, spōr'-) *adj.* **1.** Of, engaged in, or connected with athletic games or field sports. **2.** Characterized by the spirit of sportsmanship; conforming to the codes or standards of sportsmanship. **3.** Associated with sports for gambling or betting: a *sporting* man. — **sport'ing·ly** *adv.*

sporting chance *Informal* A chance involving the risk of loss or failure.

spor·tive (spôr'tiv, spōr'-) *adj.* **1.** Relating to or fond of sport or play; frolicsome. **2.** Interested in, active in, or related to sports. — **spor'tive·ly** *adv.* — **spor'tive·ness** *n.*

sports car A low, rakish automobile, usu. seating two persons, and built for high speed and maneuverability.

sports·man (spôrts'mən, spōrts'-) *n.* *pl.* **·men** (-mən) **1.** One who pursues field sports, esp., hunting and fishing. **2.** One who abides by a code of fair play in games or in daily practice. — **sports'man·like** *adj.* — **sports'man·ship** *n.*

sports·wear (spôrts'wâr', spōrts'-) *n.* Clothes made for informal or outdoor activities.

sports·wom·an (spôrts'wŏŏm'ən, spōrts'-) *n.* *pl.* **·wom·en** (-wim'in) A woman who participates in sports.

sport·y (spôr'tē, spōr'-) *adj.* **sport·i·er, sport·i·est** *Informal* **1.** Relating to or characteristic of a sport. **2.** Gay, loud, or dissipated. — **sport'i·ly** *adv.* — **sport'i·ness** *n.*

spor·ule (spôr'yŏōl, spor'-) *n.* A spore; esp., a little spore. [< F < NL < *spora* spore]

spot (spot) *n.* **1.** A particular place of small extent; a definite locality. **2.** Any small portion of a surface differing as in color from the rest; blot. **3.** A stain or blemish on character; a fault. **4.** *Slang* A currency note having a specified value: a ten *spot.* **5.** *U.S. Slang* A spotlight. — **in a spot** *Slang* In a difficult or embarrassing situation; in trouble. — **to hit the spot** *Slang* To gratify an appetite or need. — **to touch a** (or **one's**) **sore spot** To mention a topic that is painful to one. — **on the spot 1.** At once; immediately. **2.** At the very place. **3.** *Slang* In danger of death or of being held accountable for some action. — *v.* **spot·ted, spot·ting** *v.t.* **1.** To mark or soil with spots. **2.** To decorate with spots; dot. **3.** To place on a designated spot; locate; station. **4.** *Informal* To recognize or detect; see. — *v.i.* **5.** To become marked or soiled with spots. **6.** To make a stain or discoloration. — *adj.* **1.** Being on the place or spot. **2.** Paid or prepared for payment on delivery; spot cash. **3.** Made at random: a *spot* check. [ME < LG. Cf. MDu. *spotte.*] — **spot'less** *adj.* — **spot'ta·ble** *adj.*

spot check An inspection of one or a few typical things out of many, to insure quality and maintenance of standards.

spot·light (spot'līt') *n.* **1.** A circle of powerful light thrown on the stage to bring an actor or actors into clearer view. **2.** The apparatus that produces such a light. **3.** A pivoted automobile lamp. **4.** Notoriety; publicity.

spot·ted (spot'id) *adj.* **1.** Discolored in spots; stained; soiled. **2.** Characterized or marked by spots.

spotted fever *Pathol.* **1.** An epidemic form of cerebrospinal meningitis. **2.** Typhus.

spot·ter (spot'ər) *n.* **1.** *U.S. Informal* A detective; esp., one employed to discover dishonesty among employees. **2.** In civil defense, one who watches for enemy aircraft. **3.** In dry cleaning, one who removes spots.

spot·ty (spot'ē) *adj.* **·ti·er, ·ti·est** **1.** Having many spots. **2.** Lacking uniformity. — **spot'ti·ly** *adv.* — **spot'ti·ness** *n.*

spous·al (spou'zəl) *adj.* Pertaining to marriage. — *n.* *Often pl.* Marriage; espousal.

spouse (spouz, spous) *n.* A partner in marriage; one's husband or wife. [< OF < L *spondere* to promise, betroth]

spout (spout) *v.i.* **1.** To pour out copiously and forcibly, as a liquid under pressure. **2.** To discharge a fluid either continuously or in jets. **3.** *Informal* To speak or orate pompously; declaim. — *v.t.* **4.** To cause to pour or shoot forth. **5.** To utter grandiloquently or pompously. — *n.* **1.** A tube, trough, etc., for the discharge of a liquid. **2.** A continuous stream of fluid. [ME *spoute*] — **spout'er** *n.*

sprain (sprān) *n.* **1.** A violent straining or twisting of the ligaments surrounding a joint. **2.** The condition due to such strain. — *v.t.* To cause a sprain in; wrench the muscles of (a joint). [? < OF *espreindre* to squeeze]

sprang (sprang) Alternative past tense of SPRING.

sprat (sprat) *n.* **1.** A herringlike fish found in shoals on the Atlantic coast of Europe. [OE *sprott*]

sprawl (sprôl) *v.i.* **1.** To sit or lie with the limbs stretched out ungracefully. **2.** To be stretched out ungracefully, as the limbs. **3.** To move with awkward motions of the limbs. **4.** To spread out in a straggling manner, as handwriting, vines, etc. — *v.t.* **5.** To cause to spread or extend awkwardly or irregularly. — *n.* The act or position of sprawling. [OE *sprēawlian* to move convulsively] — **sprawl'er** *n.*

spray[1] (sprā) *n.* **1.** Liquid dispersed in fine particles. **2.** An instrument for discharging such particles. — *v.t.* **1.** To disperse (a liquid) in fine particles. **2.** To apply spray to. — *v.i.* **3.** To send forth spray. **4.** To go forth as spray. [Akin to MDu. *sprayen* to sprinkle] — **spray'er** *n.*

spray[2] (sprā) *n.* **1.** A small branch bearing dependent branchlets or flowers. **2.** Any ornament, pattern, etc., having a similar form. [ME]

spray gun A device that ejects liquids such as paint or insecticides in a fine spray by means of air pressure.

spread (spred) *v.* **spread, spread·ing** *v.t.* **1.** To open or unfold to full width or extent, as wings, sail, etc. **2.** To distribute over a surface, esp. in a thin layer; scatter or smear. **3.** To cover with a layer of something: to *spread* toast with marmalade. **4.** To force apart or farther apart. **5.** To extend over a period of time. **6.** To make more widely known, active, etc.: to *spread* a rumor; to *spread* contagion. **7.** To set (a table, etc.), as for a meal. **8.** To place on a table, etc., as a meal. — *v.i.* **9.** To be extended or expanded. **10.** To be distributed. **11.** To become more widely known, active, etc. **12.** To be forced farther apart. — *n.* **1.** The act of spreading. **2.** An open extent or expanse. **3.** The limit of expansion of some designated object. **4.** A cloth or covering for a bed, table, etc. **5.** *Informal* An informal feast or banquet. **6.** Anything used to spread on bread or crackers. **7.** Two pages of a magazine or newspaper facing each other and covered by related material; also, print spread across two or more columns or on facing pages. — *adj.* Expanded; outstretched. [OE *sprædan*] — **spread′er** *n.*

spread-ea·gle (spred′ē′gəl) *adj.* **1.** Resembling the figure of an eagle with extended wings. **2.** *U.S. Informal* Bombastic: applied esp. to patriotic oratory. — *v.t.* **-ea·gled, -ea·gling** To lash to the mast or shrouds in spread-eagle position as a punishment.

spree (sprē) *n.* **1.** A drinking spell. **2.** A gay frolic. **3.** Excessive indulgence in an activity. [Origin uncertain]

sprig (sprig) *n.* **1.** A shoot or sprout of a tree or plant. **2.** An ornament in this form. **3.** A young man; a youth. — *v.t.* **sprigged, sprig·ging** To ornament with a design of sprigs. [ME *sprigge*] — **sprig′ger** *n.* — **sprig′gy** *adj.*

spright·ly (sprīt′lē) *adj.* **·li·er, ·li·est** Full of animation; lively. — *adv.* Spiritedly; briskly; gaily. — **spright′li·ness** *n.*

spring (spring) *v.* **sprang** *or* **sprung, sprung, spring·ing** *v.i.* **1.** To move or rise suddenly and rapidly; leap; dart. **2.** To move suddenly as by elastic reaction. **3.** To move as if with a leap: An angry retort *sprang* to his lips. **4.** To work or snap out of place, as a mechanical part. **5.** To become warped or bent, as boards. **6.** To rise above surrounding objects. **7.** To come into being: New towns have *sprung* up. **8.** To originate; proceed, as from a source. **9.** To develop; grow. — *v.t.* **10.** To cause to spring or leap. **11.** To cause to act, close, open, etc., suddenly, as by elastic reaction: to *spring* a trap. **12.** To cause to happen, become known, or appear suddenly: to *spring* a surprise. **13.** To leap over; vault. **14.** To warp or bend; split. **15.** To cause to snap or work out of place. **16.** To undergo (a leak). **17.** *Slang* To obtain the release of (a person) from prison. — *n.* **1.** *Mech.* An elastic body or contrivance, as a coiled steel wire, that yields under stress, and returns to its normal form when the stress is removed. **2.** Elastic quality or energy. **3.** The act of flying back from a position of tension. **4.** A cause of action. **5.** The act of leaping up or forward suddenly; a jump. **6.** The season in which vegetation starts anew, occurring between winter and summer. ◆ Collateral adjective: *vernal.* **7.** A flow, as of water. **8.** Any source or origin. **9.** A crack or break, as of a plank, etc., or a thing sprung or warped. — *adj.* **1.** Pertaining to the season of spring. **2.** Acting like or having a spring. **3.** Hung on springs. [OE *springan*] — **spring′er** *n.*

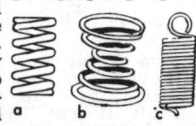

SPRINGS
a Compression coil.
b Double spiral.
c Extension coil.

spring·board (spring′bôrd′, -bōrd′) *n.* **1.** A flexible, resilient board used by athletes and acrobats as an aid in leaping or tumbling. **2.** A diving board.

spring·bok (spring′bok′) *n.* A small South African gazelle noted for its ability to leap high in the air. Also **spring′buck′** (-buk′). [< Afrikaans]

spring chicken **1.** A young chicken, 10 weeks to 10 months old, esp. tender for cooking. **2.** *Informal* A young, immature, or unsophisticated person.

spring fever The listlessness and restlessness that overtakes many people during the first warm days of spring.

spring lock A lock that fastens automatically by a spring.

spring tide **1.** The tide occurring at or shortly after the new or full moon, when the rise and fall are greatest. **2.** Any great wave or flood, as of emotion.

spring·time (spring′tīm′) *n.* The season of spring. Also **spring′tide′** (-tīd′).

spring·y (spring′ē) *adj.* **spring·i·er, spring·i·est** **1.** Elastic; resilient. **2.** Having many springs of water. — **spring′i·ly** *adv.* — **spring′i·ness** *n.*

sprin·kle (spring′kəl) *v.* **·kled, ·kling** *v.t.* **1.** To scatter in drops or small particles. **2.** To besprinkle. — *v.i.* **3.** To fall or rain in scattered drops. — *n.* **1.** A falling in drops or particles, or that which so falls; a sprinkling. **2.** A small quantity. [ME *sprenkelen*] — **sprin′kler** *n.*

sprin·kling (spring′kling) *n.* **1.** That which is sprinkled. **2.** A small number or quantity. **3.** A mottling. **4.** The act of scattering drops of liquid.

sprint (sprint) *n.* A short race run at top speed. — *v.i.* To run fast, as in a sprint. [< Scand.] — **sprint′er** *n.*

sprit (sprit) *n.* *Naut.* A spar reaching diagonally from a mast to the peak of a fore-and-aft sail. [OE *sprēot* pole]

sprite (sprīt) *n.* A fairy, elf, or goblin. [< OF < L *spiritus* breath, spirit]

sprit·sail (sprit′səl, sprit′sāl′) *n.* *Naut.* A sail extended by a sprit.

sprock·et (sprok′it) *n.* *Mech.* **1.** A projection, as on the rim of a wheel, for engaging with the links of a chain. **2.** A wheel bearing such projections: also **sprocket wheel.** [Origin uncertain]

sprout (sprout) *v.i.* **1.** To put forth shoots; begin to grow; germinate. **2.** To develop or grow rapidly. — *v.t.* **3.** To cause to sprout. **4.** To remove shoots from. — *n.* **1.** A new shoot or bud on a plant. **2.** Something like or suggestive of a sprout. **3.** *pl.* Brussels sprouts. [OE *sprūtan*]

spruce[1] (sproos) *n.* **1.** Any of a genus of evergreen trees of the pine family, having a pyramidal crown, needle-shaped leaves, and pendulous cones. **2.** The wood of these trees. **3.** Any of certain coniferous trees, as the Douglas fir.

spruce[2] (sproos) *adj.* **1.** Having a smart, trim appearance. **2.** Fastidious. — *v.* **spruced, spruc·ing** *v.t.* **1.** To make spruce: often with *up.* — *v.i.* **2.** To make oneself spruce: usu. with *up.* — **spruce′ly** *adv.* — **spruce′ness** *n.*

sprung (sprung) Past participle and alternative past tense of SPRING.

spry (sprī) *adj.* **spri·er** *or* **spry·er, spri·est** *or* **spry·est** Quick and active; agile; brisk; energetic. [< dial. E *sprey* < Scand.] — **spry′ly** *adv.* — **spry′ness** *n.*

spud (spud) *n.* **1.** A spadelike tool for removing the roots of weeds. **2.** *Informal* A potato. — *v.t.* **spud·ded, spud·ding** To remove with a spud. [ME *spudde* < Scand.]

spue (spyoo) See SPEW.

spume (spyoom) *n.* Froth, as on an agitated or effervescing liquid; foam; scum. — *v.i.* **spumed, spum·ing** To foam; froth [< F < L *spuma* foam] — **spu′mous, spum′y** *adj.*

spu·mo·ne (spə·mō′nē, *Ital.* spoo-mō′nä) *n.* *pl.* **·ni** (-nē) A dessert of ice cream or water ice containing fruit, nuts, etc. Also **spu·mo′ni.** [< Ital. < L *spuma* foam]

spun (spun) Past tense and past participle of SPIN.

spunk (spungk) *n.* **1.** Punk or other tinder. **2.** A small fire, spark, or flame; also, a match. **3.** *Informal* Mettle; pluck; courage. [< Irish < L *spongia* sponge]

spunk·y (spungk′ē) *adj.* **spunk·i·er, spunk·i·est** *Informal* Spirited; courageous; also, touchy. — **spunk′i·ly** *adv.* — **spunk′i·ness** *n.*

spur (spûr) *n.* **1.** A pricking or goading instrument worn on a horseman's heel. **2.** Anything that incites or urges; incentive. **3.** A part or attachment projecting like or suggestive of a spur, as a crag or mountain peak. **4.** A stiff, sharp spine, as on the legs of some insects and birds. **5.** *Bot.* A tubular extension of some part of a flower, as in the larkspur. **6.** A spur track. **7.** A pointed, curved cutting instrument fastened to each leg of a gamecock. — **on the spur of the moment** Hastily; prompted by an impulse. — *v.* **spurred, spur·ring** *v.t.* **1.** To prick or urge with or as with spurs. **2.** To furnish with spurs. — *v.i.* **3.** To spur one's horse. **4.** To hurry. [OE *spura*] — **spur′rer** *n.*

spurge (spûrj) *n.* A plant, euphorbia. [< OF < L < *ex-* out + *purgare* to cleanse]

spur gear *Mech.* **1.** A spur wheel. **2.** Spur gearing.

spur gearing *Mech.* Gearing composed of spur wheels.

spu·ri·ous (spyoor′ē-əs) *adj.* **1.** Not proceeding from the source pretended; not genuine; false. **2.** Illegitimate. [< L *spurius*] — **spu′ri·ous·ly** *adv.* — **spu′ri·ous·ness** *n.*

spurn (spûrn) *v.t.* **1.** To reject with disdain; refuse contemptuously; scorn. **2.** To strike with the foot; kick. — *v.i.* **3.** To reject something with disdain. — *n.* The act of spurning; also, a kick. [OE *spurnan*] — **spurn′er** *n.*

spurred (spûrd) *adj.* **1.** Wearing or having spurs. **2.** Having sharp spikes, claws, or shoots.

spurt (spûrt) *n.* **1.** A sudden gush of liquid. **2.** Any sudden outbreak, as of anger. **3.** An extraordinary effort of brief duration. — *v.i.* **1.** To come out in a jet; gush forth. **2.** To make a sudden and extreme effort. — *v.t.* **3.** To force out in a jet. [< OE *spryttan* to come forth]

spur track A short side track connecting with the main track of a railroad: also called *spur.*

spur wheel *Mech.* A wheel having radial teeth on the rim, with their edges parallel to the axis; also called *spur gear.*

sput·nik (sput′nik, spoot′-; *Russ.* spoot′nyik) *n.* A Soviet artificial earth satellite, the first of which, **Sputnik I,** was launched in 1957. [< Russian, satellite]

sput·ter (sput′ər) *v.i.* **1.** To throw off solid or fluid particles in a series of slight explosions. **2.** To emit particles of saliva from the mouth, as when speaking excitedly. **3.** To speak rapidly or confusedly. — *v.t.* **4.** To emit in small particles. **5.** To utter in a confused or excited manner. — *n.* **1.** The act or sound of sputtering; esp., excited talk. **2.** That which is ejected in sputtering. — **sput′ter·er** *n.*

spu·tum (spyoo′təm) *n.* *pl.* **·ta** (-tə) Saliva; spittle; expectorated matter. [< L *spuere* to spit]

spy (spī) *n.* *pl.* **spies** **1.** One who enters an enemy's military lines covertly to get information. **2.** One who watches others secretly. — *v.* **spied, spy·ing** *v.i.* **1.** To keep watch closely or secretly; act as a spy. **2.** To make careful examination; pry: with *into.* — *v.t.* **3.** To observe stealthily and with hostile intent: usu. with *out.* **4.** To catch sight of; see.

5. To discover by careful or secret investigation: with *out.* [< OF *espier* to espy < Gmc.]

spy·glass (spī'glas', -gläs') *n.* A small telescope.

squab (skwob) *n.* **1.** A young pigeon, esp. when an unfledged nestling. **2.** A fat, short person. **3.** A soft, stuffed cushion. **4.** A sofa; couch. —*adj.* **1.** Fat and short; squat. **2.** Unfledged or recently hatched. [< dial. E < Scand.]

squab·ble (skwob'əl) *v.* **·bled, ·bling** *v.i.* **1.** To engage in a petty wrangle or scuffle; quarrel. —*v.t.* **2.** *Printing* To disarrange (composed type). —*n.* A petty wrangle. — Syn. See QUARREL. — **squab'bler** *n.*

squad (skwod) *n.* **1.** A small group of persons organized for the performance of a specific function. **2.** A small detachment of troops or police; esp., the smallest tactical unit in the infantry of the U.S. Army. **3.** A team: a football *squad.* —*v.t.* **squad·ded, squad·ding** **1.** To form into a squad or squads. **2.** To assign to a squad. [< F < OF < Ital. < L *quattuor* four]

squad car An automobile used by police for patrolling, and equipped with radiotelephone: also called *patrol car.*

squad·ron (skwod'rən) *n.* **1.** In the U.S. Navy, two or more divisions of vessels or flights of naval aircraft. **2.** In the U.S. Air Force, a unit composed of two or more flights. **3.** A subordinate unit of a cavalry regiment. **4.** Any regularly arranged or organized body. [< Ital. < L *quattuor* four]

squadron leader In the Royal, Royal Canadian, and other Commonwealth air forces, a commissioned officer ranking next below a wing commander. See table at GRADE.

squal·id (skwol'id) *adj.* Having a foul appearance; dirty and wretched. [< L *squalere* to be foul] — **squal'id·ly** *adv.* — **squal'id·ness, squa·lid·i·ty** (skwo·lid'ə-tē) *n.*

squall¹ (skwôl) *n.* A loud, screaming outcry. —*v.i.* To cry loudly; scream; bawl. — **squall'er** *n.*

squall² (skwôl) *n.* **1.** A sudden, violent burst of wind, often accompanied by rain or snow. **2.** *Informal* A commotion. —*v.i.* To blow a squall. — **squall'y** *adj.*

squal·or (skwol'ər) *n.* The state of being squalid; filth and wretched poverty. [< L *squalere* to be foul]

squa·ma (skwā'mə) *n. pl.* **·mae** (-mē) *Biol.* A thin, scalelike structure; a scale. [< L] — **squa'mate** (-māt), **squa'mose** (-mōs), **squa'mous** *adj.*

squan·der (skwon'dər) *v.t.* To spend (money, time, etc.) wastefully. —*n.* Prodigality; wasteful expenditure. [Origin unknown] — **squan'der·er** *n.* — **squan'der·ing·ly** *adv.*

square (skwâr) *n.* **1.** A parallelogram having four equal sides and four right angles. **2.** Any object, part, or surface that has this form, or nearly so. **3.** An instrument having an L- or T-shape by which to measure or lay out right angles. **4.** An open area in a city or town formed by the intersection of several streets. **5.** An open area in a city or town formed by the intersection of four or more streets, often planted with trees, flowers, etc. **6.** A section in a town bounded on four sides by streets; also, the distance between one street and the next. **7.** *Math.* The product of a number multiplied by itself. **8.** Formerly, a body of troops formed in a four-sided array. **9.** *Slang* One not conversant with the latest trends or fads. — **on the square 1.** At right angles. **2.** *Informal* In a fair and honest manner. — **out of square 1.** Not at right angles. **2.** Incorrectly; askew; out of order. —*adj.* **1.** Having four equal sides and four right angles; also, resembling a square in form. **2.** Formed with or characterized by a right angle; rectangular. **3.** Adapted to forming squares or computing in squares: a *square* measure. **4.** Direct; fair; just; honest. **5.** Having debit and credit balanced. **6.** Absolute; complete; unequivocal. **7.** Having a broad, stocky frame; strong; sturdy. **8.** *Informal* Solid; full; satisfying: a *square* meal. — **square peg in a round hole** A misfit. —*v.* **squared, squar·ing** *v.t.* **1.** To make or form like a square. **2.** To shape or adjust so as to form a right angle. **3.** To mark with or divide into squares. **4.** To test for the purpose of adjusting to a straight line, right angle, or plane surface. **5.** To bring to a position suggestive of a right angle: *Square* your shoulders. **6.** To make satisfactory settlement or adjustment of: to *square* accounts. **7.** To make (the score of a game, etc.) equal. **8.** To cause to conform; adapt; reconcile. **9.** *Math.* **a** To multiply (a number) by itself. **b** To determine the area of. —*v.i.* **10.** To be at right angles. **11.** To conform; agree; harmonize. **12.** In golf, to make the scores equal. — **to square away 1.** *Naut.* To set (the yards) at right angles to the keel. **2.** To square up. — **to square off** To prepare to fight. — **to square the circle 1.** To construct a square equal in area to a given circle, an insoluble problem. **2.** To attempt something impossible. —*adv.* **1.** So as to be square, or at right angles. **2.** *Informal* Honestly; fairly. **3.** Directly; firmly. [< OF < L *quattuor* four] — **square'ness** *n.* — **squar'er** *n.*

square-dance (skwâr'dans') *v.i.* **-danced, -danc·ing** *U.S.* To perform a square dance.

square dance *U.S.* Any dance, as a quadrille, in which the couples form sets in squares.

square deal *Informal* **1.** In card games, an honest deal. **2.** Fair or just treatment.

square knot A common knot, formed of two overhand knots: also called *reef knot.* For illus. see KNOT.

square·ly (skwâr'lē) *adv.* **1.** In a direct or straight manner. **2.** Honestly; fairly. **3.** *U.S.* Plainly; unequivocally. **4.** In a square form. **5.** At right angles (to a line or plane).

square meal *Informal* A full and substantial meal.

square measure A unit or system of units for measuring areas. See table front of book.

square-rigged (skwâr'rigd') *adj. Naut.* Fitted with square-rigged sails as the principal sails.

square root *Math.* A number that, multiplied by itself, produces the given number: 4 is the *square root* of 16.

square shooter *Informal* An upright person.

squash¹ (skwosh) *v.t.* **1.** To beat or press into a pulp or soft mass; crush. **2.** To quell or suppress. —*v.i.* **3.** To be smashed or squashed. **4.** To make a splashing or sucking sound. —*n.* **1.** A soft or overripe object; also, a crushed mass. **2.** The sudden fall of a heavy, soft body; also, the sound made by such a fall. **3.** A sucking, oozy sound. **4.** Either of two games played on an indoor court with rackets and a ball. **5.** A beverage of which one ingredient is a fruit juice. —*adv.* With a squelching, oozy sound. [< OF < L *ex-* thoroughly + *quassare* to crush] — **squash'er** *n.*

squash² (skwosh) *n.* **1.** The edible fruit of various trailing annuals of the gourd family. **2.** The plant that bears it. [< Algonquian]

squash·y (skwosh'ē) *adj.* **squash·i·er, squash·i·est** Soft and moist. — **squash'i·ly** *adv.* — **squash'i·ness** *n.*

squat (skwot) *v.* **squat·ted** *or* **squat, squat·ting** *v.i.* **1.** To sit on the heels or hams, or with the legs near the body. **2.** To crouch or cower down. **3.** To settle on a piece of land without title or payment. **4.** To settle on government land in accordance with certain government regulations that will eventually give title. —*v.t.* **5.** To cause (oneself) to squat. —*adj.* **1.** Short and thick; squatty. **2.** Being in a squatting position. —*n.* **1.** A squatting attitude or position. **2.** The act of squatting. [< OF < *es-* thoroughly + *quatir* to press down] — **squat'ter** *n.*

squat·ty (skwot'ē) *adj.* Disproportionately short and thick.

squaw (skwô) *n.* **1.** An American Indian woman or wife. **2.** *Informal* Any woman or girl. [< Algonquian, woman]

squawk (skwôk) *v.i.* **1.** To utter a shrill, harsh cry, as a parrot. **2.** *Slang* To utter loud complaints or protests. —*n.* **1.** The harsh cry of certain birds; also, the act of squawking. **2.** *Slang* A loud protest or complaint. [Prob. imit.] — **squawk'er** *n.*

squeak (skwēk) *n.* A thin, sharp, penetrating sound. — **narrow (or near) squeak** *Informal* A narrow escape. —*v.i.* **1.** To make a squeak. **2.** *Slang* To let out information; squeal. —*v.t.* **3.** To utter or effect with a squeak. **4.** To cause to squeak. [ME *squeke*] — **squeak'er** *n.*

squeak·y (skwē'kē) *adj.* **squeak·i·er, squeak·i·est** Making a squeaking noise. — **squeak'i·ly** *adv.* — **squeak'i·ness** *n.*

squeal (skwēl) *v.i.* **1.** To utter a sharp, shrill, somewhat prolonged cry. **2.** *Slang* To turn informer; betray an accomplice or a plot. —*v.t.* **3.** To utter with a squeal. —*n.* A shrill, prolonged cry, as of a pig. [Imit.] — **squeal'er** *n.*

squeam·ish (skwē'mish) *adj.* **1.** Easily disgusted or shocked; modest; prudish. **2.** Overly fastidious. **3.** Easily nauseated. [< earlier *squaymisch* < AF *escoymous*; ult. origin unknown] — **squeam'ish·ly** *adv.* — **squeam'ish·ness** *n.*

squee·gee (skwē'jē) *n.* **1.** An implement having a stout, straight crosspiece edged with rubber or leather, used for removing water from decks or floors, window panes, etc. **2.** *Photog.* A smaller similar implement. —*v.t.* **1.** To smooth down, as a photographic film, with a squeegee. **2.** To cleanse with a squeegee. [< SQUEEZE]

squeeze (skwēz) *v.* **squeezed, squeez·ing** *v.t.* **1.** To press hard upon; compress. **2.** To extract something from by pressure: to *squeeze* oranges. **3.** To draw forth by pressure; express: to *squeeze* juice. **4.** To force or push; cram. **5.** To oppress, as with burdensome taxes. **6.** To exert pressure upon (someone) to act as one desires. **7.** To make a facsimile impression of. —*v.i.* **8.** To apply pressure. **9.** To force one's way; push: with *in, through,* etc. **10.** To be pressed; yield to pressure. — **to squeeze out** To force out of business, or ruin financially. —*n.* **1.** The act or process of squeezing; pressure. **2.** A firm grasp of someone's hand; also, an embrace; hug. **3.** Something, as juice, extracted or expressed. **4.** A facsimile, as of a coin or inscription, produced by pressing some soft substance upon it. **5.** *Informal* Pressure exerted for the extortion of money or favors; also, financial pressure. [? < OF *es-* thoroughly + ME *queisen* to crush] — **squeez'a·ble** *adj.* — **squeez'er** *n.*

---

squeeze play In baseball, a play in which the batter tries to bunt the ball so that a man on third base may score by starting while the pitcher is about to deliver the ball.

squelch (skwelch) *v.t.* **1.** To crush; squash. **2.** *Informal* To silence, as with a crushing reply. — *v.i.* **3.** To make a splashing or sucking noise, as when walking in deep mud. **4.** To walk with such a sound. — *n.* **1.** A squelching sound. **2.** A squelched or crushed mass of anything. **3.** *Informal* A crushing reply. [Prob. imit.] — **squelch′er** *n.*

squib (skwib) *n.* **1.** A firework to be thrown or rolled swiftly, finally exploding like a rocket. **2.** A broken firecracker that burns with a spitting sound. **3.** A short speech or writing in a satirical vein. — *v.* **squibbed, squib·bing** *v.i.* **1.** To write or use squibs. **2.** To fire a squib. **3.** To explode or sound like a squib. **4.** To move quickly or restlessly. — *v.t.* **5.** To attack with squibs; lampoon. **6.** To fire or use as a squib. [Origin unknown]

squid (skwid) *n.* Any of various ten-armed mollusks having a slender conical body, ink sac, and broad tail flukes, used as food and for bait. [Origin uncertain]

squig·gle (skwig′əl) *Informal n.* A meaningless scrawl. — *v.i.* To wriggle. [Blend of SQUIRM and WRIGGLE]

squig·gly (skwig′lē) *adj.* **·gli·er, ·gli·est** Twisty; crooked.

squill (skwil) *n.* **1.** The bulb of a plant of the lily family, found in the Mediterranean region, used chiefly as an expectorant: also called *sea onion.* **2.** The plant itself. [< L < Gk. *skilla* sea onion]

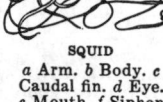

SQUID

a Arm. *b* Body. *c* Caudal fin. *d* Eye. *e* Mouth. *f* Siphon. *g* Tentacles

squint (skwint) *v.i.* **1.** To look with half-closed eyes, as into bright light. **2.** To look with a side glance. **3.** To be cross-eyed. **4.** To incline or tend: with *toward,* etc. — *v.t.* **5.** To hold (the eyes) half-shut, as in glaring light. **6.** To cause to squint. — *adj.* **1.** Cross-eyed. **2.** Looking obliquely or askance; indirect. — *n.* **1.** *Pathol.* Strabismus. **2.** The act or habit of squinting. **3.** An indirect leaning, tendency, or drift. [Origin uncertain] — **squint′er** *n.*

squire (skwīr) *n.* **1.** In England a landed proprietor or country gentleman. **2.** *U.S.* A title often used in rural areas for justices of the peace, judges, lawyers, etc. **3.** A young aspirant to knighthood serving as an attendant. **4.** A man who escorts a woman in public; gallant. — *v.t. & v.i.* **squired, squir·ing** To attend or serve (someone) as a squire or escort. [Aphetic var. of ESQUIRE]

squirm (skwûrm) *v.i.* **1.** To bend and twist the body; wriggle; writhe. **2.** To show signs of pain or distress. — *n.* A squirming motion; a wriggle. [Origin uncertain] — **squirm′er** *n.* — **squirm′y** *adj.*

squir·rel (skwûr′əl, *Brit.* skwir′əl) *n.* **1.** Any of various arboreal rodents having a long bushy tail and feeding chiefly on nuts, as the **red squirrel,** the **gray squirrel,** and the **fox squirrel** of North America. **2.** Any of various related animals, as the chipmunk, flying squirrel, etc. **3.** The fur of a squirrel. [< OF < LL < Gk. < *skia* shadow + *oura* tail]

squirt (skwûrt) *v.i.* **1.** To come forth in a thin stream or jet; spurt out. **2.** To eject water, etc., thus. — *v.t.* **3.** To eject (water or other liquid) forcibly and in a jet. **4.** To wet or bespatter with a squirt or squirts. — *n.* **1.** The act of squirting; also, a jet of liquid squirted forth. **2.** A syringe or squirt gun. **3.** *Informal* A small, impudent, or presumptuous person. [Cf. LG *swirtjen.*] — **squirt′er** *n.*

squirt gun A child's toy gun used for squirting water.

squish (skwish) *v.t. & v.i. Informal* To squash. — *n.* A squashing sound. [Var. of SQUASH¹] — **squish′y** *adj.*

stab (stab) *v.* **stabbed, stab·bing** *v.t.* **1.** To pierce with or as with a pointed weapon; wound. **2.** To thrust (a dagger, etc.), as into a body. **3.** To penetrate; pierce. — *v.i.* **4.** To thrust or lunge with a knife, sword, etc. **5.** To inflict a wound thus. — **to stab in the back** To slander or injure in a treacherous, stealthy manner. — *n.* A thrust made with any pointed weapon. — **to have** (or **make**) **a stab at** To make an attempt at. [? < Scot. & dial. E *stob* to push, thrust, fix a stake < *stob* stake] — **stab′ber** *n.*

sta·bil·i·ty (stə-bil′ə-tē) *n.* *pl.* **·ties 1.** The condition of being stable. **2.** Steadfastness of purpose or resolution. **3.** Continued existence; permanence. [See STABLE.¹]

sta·bi·lize (stā′bə-līz) *v.t.* **·lized, ·liz·ing 1.** To make firm or stable. **2.** To keep steady; keep from changing or fluctuating: to *stabilize* prices. Also *Brit.* **sta·bi·lise.** [< L *stabilis* steady + -IZE] — **sta′bi·li·za′tion** *n.*

sta·bi·liz·er (stā′bə-lī′zər) *n.* **1.** One who or that which stabilizes. **2.** *Aeron.* An airfoil serving to give an aircraft stability in flight. **3.** A device in a ship or boat, as a gyroscope, to keep it from rolling. **4.** *Chem.* A substance that increases the stability of another substance or compound.

sta·ble¹ (stā′bəl) *adj.* **1.** Standing firmly in place; not easily moved, shaken, or overthrown; fixed. **2.** Marked by fixity of purpose; steadfast. **3.** Having durability and perma-

nence; abiding. **4.** *Chem.* Not easily decomposed: said of compounds. [< F < L *stabilis* < *stare* to stand] — **sta′bly** (-blē) *adv.* — **sta′ble·ness** *n.*

sta·ble² (stā′bəl) *n.* **1.** A building set apart for lodging and feeding horses or cattle; also, the animals. **2.** Race horses belonging to a particular owner; also, the owner and personnel collectively. **3.** *U.S.* A group of writers, artists, athletes, etc., under a single manager. — *v.t. & v.i.* **·bled, ·bling** To put or lodge in a stable. [< OF < L *stare* to stand]

sta·ble·boy (stā′bəl·boi′) *n.* A boy employed in a stable.

stac·ca·to (stə-kä′tō) *adj.* **1.** *Music* Having or producing silence through most of the written time value of each note; very short and detached. **2.** Marked by abrupt, sharp emphasis. — *adv.* In a staccato manner. — *n.* *pl.* **·tos 1.** *Music* A staccato style or passage. **2.** An abrupt, emphatic manner or sound. [< Ital., pp. of *staccare* to detach]

stack (stak) *n.* **1.** A large, orderly pile of unthreshed grain, hay, or straw, usu. conical. **2.** Any systematic pile or heap, as a pile of poker chips. **3.** A group of rifles (usu. three) set upright and supporting one another. **4.** A case composed of several rows of bookshelves one above the other. **5.** *pl.* That part of a library where most of the books are shelved. **6.** A chimney; smokestack. **7.** *Informal* A great amount; plenty. — *v.t.* **1.** To pile up in a stack. **2.** To load (a vehicle, etc.) with stacks of a material. — **to stack the cards** (or **deck**) **1.** To arrange cards secretly in the pack in a manner favorable to the dealer. **2.** To have an advantage secured beforehand. [< ON *stakkr*] — **stack′er** *n.*

stack arms The command to place several rifles close together and upright on the ground in a slanting position.

sta·di·um (stā′dē·əm) *n.* *pl.* **·di·a** (-dē·ə), *for def. 2* **·di·ums 1.** In ancient Greece, a course for foot races, with banked seats for spectators. **2.** A similar modern structure in which athletic games are played. [< L < Gk. *stadion,* measure of length]

staff (staf, stäf) *n.* *pl.* **staffs;** *for defs. 1, 2, & 3, also* **staves** (stāvz) **1.** A stick or piece of wood carried for some special purpose. **2.** A shaft or pole that forms a support or handle. **3.** A stick used in measuring or testing. **4.** *Mil.* A body of officers not having command but assigned in an executive or advisory capacity. **5.** A body of persons associated in carrying out some special enterprise. **6.** *Music* The five horizontal lines and four spaces used to represent the pitches of tones: also called *stave.* — *v.t.* To provide (an office, etc.) with a staff. [OE *stæf* stick]

staff officer 1. An officer on the staff of a military commander. **2.** In the U.S. Navy, an officer without command or operational functions, as a doctor, dentist, chaplain, etc.

stag (stag) *n.* **1.** The male of the red deer. **2.** The male of other large deer, as the caribou. **3.** A swine castrated after maturity. **4.** A man who attends a social function unaccompanied by a woman. **5.** A social gathering for men only. — *adj.* Of or for men only. — *v.i.* **stagged, stag·ging** To attend a social affair unaccompanied by a woman. [OE *stagga*]

stage (stāj) *n.* **1.** A raised platform, with its scenery and mechanical appliances, on which the performance in a theater or hall takes place. **2.** The theater: to write for the *stage.* **3.** The drama; also, the dramatic profession. **4.** The field or plan of action of some event: to set the *stage* for war. **5.** A definite portion of a journey. **6.** A step in some development, progress, or process. **7.** A water level: The river rose to flood *stage.* **8.** A horizontal section or story of a building. **9.** *Aerospace* One of the separate propulsion units of a rocket vehicle, each of which becomes operational after the preceding one reaches burnout and is jettisoned. **10.** Any raised platform or floor. **11.** One of the regular stopping places on the route of a stagecoach or postrider. — **by easy stages** Traveling or acting without hurry and with frequent stops. — *v.t.* **staged, stag·ing 1.** To put or exhibit on the stage. **2.** To conduct; carry on. [< OF < L *status,* pp. of *stare* to stand]

stage·coach (stāj′kōch′) *n.* A large, horse-drawn, four-wheeled vehicle having a regular route from town to town.

stage·craft (stāj′kraft′, -kräft′) *n.* Skill in writing or staging plays.

stage door A door to a theater used by actors and stagehands that leads to the stage or behind the scenes.

stage fright A sudden panic that sometimes attacks those appearing before an audience.

stage·hand (stāj′hand′) *n.* A worker in a theater who handles scenery and props, operates lights, etc.

stage manager One who superintends the stage during the performance of a play.

stage·struck (stāj′struk′) *adj.* Struck with the idea of becoming an actor or an actress, enamored of theatrical life.

stage whisper 1. Any loud whisper intended to be overheard. **2.** A direction by a prompter in the wings to an actor on the stage, intended not to be heard by the audience.

stag·y (stā′jē) See STAGY.

stag·ger (stag′ər) *v.i.* **1.** To walk or run unsteadily; totter;

reel. **2.** To become less confident or resolute; waver; hesitate. — *v.t.* **3.** To cause to stagger. **4.** To affect strongly; overwhelm, as with grief. **5.** To place in alternating rows or groups. **6.** To arrange so as to prevent congestion or confusion: to *stagger* lunch hours. — *n.* The act of staggering or the condition of being staggered. [< ON *stakra*] — **stag′ger·er** *n.* — **stag′ger·ing·ly** *adv.*

stag·gers (stag′ərz) *n.pl.* (*construed as sing.*) **1.** *Vet.* Any of various diseases of domestic animals, as horses, characterized by staggering and sudden falling, due to disorder of the brain and spinal cord. **2.** A reeling sensation.

stag·ing (stā′jing) *n.* **1.** A scaffolding or temporary platform. **2.** The act of putting a play upon the stage. **3.** The business of driving or running stagecoaches.

stag line *U.S. Informal* A group of males at a dance who are without partners.

stag·nant (stag′nənt) *adj.* **1.** Standing still; not flowing: said of water or air. **2.** Foul from long standing, as water. **3.** Lacking briskness or activity; dull; sluggish. — **stag′nan·cy** *n.* — **stag′nant·ly** *adv.*

stag·nate (stag′nāt) *v.i.* **·nat·ed, ·nat·ing 1.** To be or become stagnant. **2.** To become dull or inert; vegetate. [< L *stagnare* to stagnate] — **stag·na·tion** (stag·nā′shən) *n.*

stag·y (stā′jē) *adj.* **stag·i·er, stag·i·est** Having a theatrical manner; or or suited to the stage: also spelled *stagey.* — **stag′i·ly** *adv.* — **stag′i·ness** *n.*

staid (stād) *adj.* **1.** Steady and sober. **2.** Fixed; established. [Orig. pt. and pp. of STAY¹] — **staid′ly** *adv.* — **staid′ness** *n.*

stain (stān) *n.* **1.** A spot; smirch; blot. **2.** The act of discoloring, or the state of being discolored. **3.** A dye or thin pigment used in staining. **4.** A moral taint; tarnish. — *v.t.* **1.** To make a stain upon; discolor; soil. **2.** To color by the use of a dye or stain. **3.** To bring a moral stain upon; blemish. — *v.i.* **4.** To take or impart a stain. [Aphetic var. of DISDAIN] — **stain′a·ble** *adj.* — **stain′er** *n.* — **stain′less** *adj.* — **stain′less·ly** *adv.*

stained glass (stānd) Glass colored by the addition of pigments in the form of metallic oxides, used in church windows, etc. — **stained-glass** (stānd′glas′, -gläs′) *adj.*

stainless steel A steel alloy made resistant to corrosion and atmospheric influences by the addition of chromium and other ingredients.

stair (stâr) *n.* **1.** A step, or one of a series of steps, for mounting or descending from one level to another. **2.** *Usually pl.* A series of steps. [OE *stæger*]

stair·case (stâr′kās′) *n.* A flight or series of flights of stairs, usually from one floor to another.

stair·way (stâr′wā′) *n.* A flight of stairs; staircase.

stake (stāk) *n.* **1.** A stick or post sharpened at one end for driving into the ground, used as a boundary mark, support for a fence, etc. **2.** A post to which a person is bound, to be executed by being burned alive; also, execution in this manner. **3.** Something wagered or risked, as money bet on a race. **4.** *Often pl.* A prize in a contest. **5.** An interest in an enterprise. **6.** A grubstake. — **at stake** In hazard or jeopardy; in question: *My whole future was at stake.* — **to pull up stakes** To wind up one's business in a place and move on. — *v.t.* **staked, stak·ing 1.** To fasten or support by means of a stake. **2.** To mark the boundaries of with stakes: often with *off* or *out.* **3.** *Informal* To put at hazard; wager; risk. **4.** *Informal* To grubstake; also, to supply with working capital; finance. [OE *staca*]

sta·lac·tite (stə·lak′tīt, stal′ək·tīt′) *n.* A long, tapering formation hanging from the roof of a cavern, produced by continuous watery deposits containing certain minerals. [< NL < Gk. *stalassein* to trickle, drip] — **stal·ac·tit·ic** (stal′ək·tit′ik) or **·i·cal** *adj.*

sta·lag·mite (stə·lag′mīt, stal′əg·mīt′) *n.* An incrustation, usu. cylindrical or conical, on the floor of a cavern, the counterpart of a stalactite. [< NL < Gk. < *stalassein* to drip] or **·i·cal** *adj.*

stale (stāl) *adj.* **stal·er, stal·est 1.** Having lost freshness; slightly changed or deteriorated, as air, beer, bread, etc. **2.** Lacking in interest from age or familiarity; worn out; trite. **3.** Being in poor condition from prolonged activity or overstrain. **4.** Inactive; dull, as after a period of overactivity. — *v.i.* **staled, stal·ing** To become stale or trite. [Origin uncertain] — **stale′ly** *adv.* — **stale′ness** *n.*

stale·mate (stāl′māt′) *n.* **1.** In chess, a draw resulting when a player can make no move without placing his king in

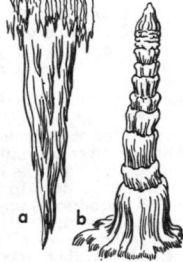

STALACTITE (*a*) AND
STALAGMITE (*b*)

check. **2.** Any tie or deadlock. — *v.t.* **·mat·ed, ·mat·ing 1.** To put into a condition of stalemate. **2.** To bring to a standstill. [< AF *estale* fixed position + MATE²]

stalk¹ (stôk) *n.* **1.** The stem or axis of a plant. **2.** A supporting or connecting part of a plant. **3.** *Zool.* Any support on which an organ is borne. **4.** Any stem or main axis, as of a goblet. [ME *stalke*] — **stalked** (stôkt) *adj.* — **stalk′less** *adj.* — **stalk′y** *adj.*

stalk² (stôk) *v.i.* **1.** To approach game, etc., stealthily. **2.** To walk in a stiff, dignified manner. — *v.t.* **3.** To approach (game, etc.) stealthily. **4.** To hover over. — *n.* **1.** The act of stalking game. **2.** A stately step or walk. [OE *bestealcian* to move stealthily] — **stalk′er** *n.*

stalk·ing-horse (stô′king·hôrs′) *n.* **1.** Anything serving to conceal one's intention. **2.** In politics, a candidate put forth to divide the opposition or to hide another candidacy. **3.** A horse behind which a hunter conceals himself.

stall (stôl) *n.* **1.** A compartment in which a horse or bovine animal is confined and fed. **2.** A small sales booth or compartment in a street, market, etc. **3.** A pew, as in a church. **4.** A space set aside for the parking of an automobile. **5.** *Aeron.* The condition of an airplane that, from loss of speed or excessive angle of attack, begins to drop. **6.** *Informal* An evasion. — *v.t.* **1.** To place or keep in a stall. **2.** To bring to a standstill; stop the progress or motion of, esp. unintentionally. — *v.i.* **3.** To come to a standstill; stop, esp. unintentionally. **4.** To stick fast in mud, snow, etc. **5.** *Informal* To make delays; be evasive. **6.** To live or be kept in a stall. **7.** *Aeron.* To go into a stall. [OE *steall*]

stall-feed (stôl′fēd′) *v.t.* **-fed, -feed·ing** To feed (cattle) in a stall or stable; fatten. — **stall-fed** (-fed′) *adj.*

stal·lion (stal′yən) *n.* An uncastrated male horse. [< OF *estalon* < OHG *stal* stable]

stall shower A small enclosed place, with a glass door or curtain, for taking a shower bath.

stal·wart (stôl′wərt) *adj.* **1.** Strong and brawny; robust. **2.** Resolute; determined; unwavering. **3.** Brave; courageous. — *n.* **1.** A brave or stalwart person. **2.** An uncompromising partisan, as in politics. [OE < *stǣl* place + *wierthe* worth] — **stal′wart·ly** *adv.* — **stal′wart·ness** *n.*

sta·men (stā′mən) *n.* *pl.* **sta·mens** or *Rare* **stam·i·na** (stam′ə·nə) *Bot.* The pollen-bearing organ of a flower. For illus. see FLOWER. [< L, warp, thread]

stam·i·na (stam′ə·nə) *n.* Physical or moral capacity to endure or withstand hardship or difficulty; vitality; vigor. [< L, pl. of *stamen* warp, thread] — **stam′i·nal** *adj.*

stam·i·nate (stam′ə·nit, -nāt) *adj.* *Bot.* **1.** Having stamens. **2.** Having stamens but no pistils.

stam·mer (stam′ər) *v.t. & v.i.* To speak or utter haltingly, with involuntary repetitions or prolongations of a sound or syllable. — *n.* The act or condition of stammering. [OE *stamerian*] — **stam′mer·er** *n.*

stamp (stamp) *v.t.* **1.** To strike heavily with the sole of the foot. **2.** To bring down (the foot) heavily and noisily. **3.** To affect in a specified manner by or as by stamping with the foot: to *stamp* a fire out. **4.** To make marks or figures upon by means of a die, stamp, etc. **5.** To imprint or impress with a die, stamp, etc. **6.** To fix or imprint permanently: The deed was *stamped* on his memory. **7.** To assign a specified quality to; characterize; brand: to *stamp* a story false. **8.** To affix an official seal, stamp, etc., to. **9.** To crush, break, or pulverize, as ore. — *v.i.* **10.** To strike the foot heavily on the ground. **11.** To walk with heavy, resounding steps. — *n.* **1.** A die or block having a pattern or design for impressing upon a surface. **2.** The pattern, impression, design, etc., so made. **3.** A weight or block for crushing ore. **4.** Any characteristic mark, as a label or imprint; a brand. **5.** Characteristic quality or form; kind; sort: men of his *stamp.* **6.** The act of stamping. **7.** A printed device prepared and sold by a government, for attachment to a letter, commodity, etc., as proof that the tax or fee has been paid. [ME *stampen*] — **stamp′er** *n.*

stam·pede (stam·pēd′) *n.* **1.** A sudden starting and rushing off through panic, as a herd of cattle, horses, etc. **2.** Any sudden, tumultuous running movement of a crowd or mob. **3.** Any sudden mass movement. — *v.* **·ped·ed, ·ped·ing** *v.t.* **1.** To cause a stampede or panic in. — *v.i.* **2.** To rush or flee in a stampede. [< Am. Sp. *estampida* crash] — **stam·ped′er** *n.*

stamp·ing ground (stam′ping) A favorite or habitual gathering place, for people or animals.

stance (stans) *n.* **1.** Mode of standing; posture. **2.** In golf, the relative positions of the player's feet and the ball, when making a stroke. [< OF < L *stare* to stand]

stanch (stanch, stänch) *v.t.* **1.** To stop or check the flow of (blood, etc.). **2.** To stop the flow of blood from (a wound). Also spelled *staunch.* — *adj.* See STAUNCH. [< OF *estanchier* to halt] — **stanch′er** *n.*

stan·chion (stan'shən) *n.* **1.** An upright bar forming a principal support. **2.** A vertical bar or pair of bars used to confine cattle in a stall. — *v.t.* To provide or confine with stanchions. [< OF *estanchon* < *estance* situation, position]

stand (stand) *v.* **stood, stand·ing** *v.i* **1.** To assume or maintain an erect position on one's feet. **2.** To be in a vertical position; be erect. **3.** To measure a specified height when standing. **4.** To assume a specified position: to *stand* aside. **5.** To assume or have a definite opinion, position, or attitude: How do you *stand* on civil rights? **6.** To be situated; have position or location; lie. **7.** To remain unimpaired, unchanged, or valid: My decision still *stands.* **8.** To have or be in a specified state, condition, or relation: He *stood* in fear of his life. **9.** To be of a specified rank or class: He *stands* third. **10.** To assume an attitude for defense or offense: *Stand* and fight. **11.** To be or remain firm or resolute, as in determination. **12.** To be consistent; accord; agree. **13.** To collect and remain; also, to be stagnant, as water. **14.** To stop or pause; halt. **15.** To scruple; hesitate. **16.** *Naut.* To take a direction; steer: The brig *stood* into the wind. **17.** To point, as a hunting dog. **18.** *Brit.* To be a candidate, as for election. — *v.t.* **19.** To place upright; set in an erect position. **20.** To put up with; endure; tolerate. **21.** To be subjected to; undergo: He must *stand* trial. **22.** To withstand; resist. **23.** *Informal* To pay for; bear the expense of: to *stand* a treat. **— to stand a chance** (or **show**) To have a chance or likelihood, as of success. **— to stand by 1.** To stay near and be ready to help, operate, or begin. **2.** To help; support. **3.** To abide by; make good. **4.** To remain passive and watch, as when help is needed. **— to stand clear** To remain at a safe distance. **— to stand for 1.** To represent; symbolize. **2.** To put up with; tolerate. **— to stand in** *Informal* To cost. **— to stand in for** To act as a substitute for. **— to stand off** *Informal* **1.** To keep at a distance. **2.** To fail to agree or comply. **— to stand on 1.** To be based on or grounded in; rest. **2.** To insist on or demand observance of: to *stand on* ceremony. **3.** *Naut.* To keep on the same tack or course. **— to stand on one's own** (two) **feet** (or **legs**) To manage one's own affairs. **— to stand out 1.** To stick out; project or protrude. **2.** To be prominent; appear in relief or contrast. **3.** To refuse to consent or agree; remain in opposition. **— to stand over 1.** To remain near and watch, as a subordinate. **2.** To be postponed. **— to stand pat 1.** In poker, to play one's hand as dealt, without drawing new cards. **2.** To resist change. **— to stand to reason** To conform to reason. **— to stand up 1.** To stand erect. **2.** To withstand wear, criticism, analysis, etc. **3.** *Slang* To fail to keep an appointment with. **— to stand up for** To side with; take the part of. **— to stand up to** To confront courageously; face. **— to stand up with** To be best man or bridesmaid for. — *n.* **1.** The act of standing, esp. of standing firmly: to make a *stand* against the enemy. **2.** An opinion, attitude, or position, as in a controversy. **3.** A structure or platform upon which persons or things may sit or stand, or on which articles may be kept or displayed. **4.** A small table. **5.** A rack or other piece of furniture on which hats, canes, etc. may be hung or placed. **6.** A stall, counter, or the like, where merchandise is displayed. **7.** Any place where or in which something or someone stands. **8.** In the theater, a stop made while on tour to give a performance: a one-night *stand.* **9.** The growing trees in a forest. **— to take a stand** To have or reveal an opinion or attitude, as on a controversial issue. [OE *standan*] **— stand'er** *n.*

stan·dard (stan'dərd) *n.* **1.** A flag, ensign, or banner, used as a distinctive emblem of a government, body of men, military unit, etc. **2.** Any established measure of extent, quantity, quality, or value: a *standard* of weight. **3.** Any type, model, or example for comparison; a criterion of excellence: a *standard* of conduct. **4.** An upright timber, post, pole, or beam, esp. as a support. — *adj.* **1.** Serving as a gauge or model: a *standard* weight. **2.** Of recognized excellence or authority: a *standard* book or author. **3.** *Ling.* Designating or belonging to those usages or varieties of a language that have gained literary, cultural, and social acceptance and prestige: *standard* English. [< OF *estandard* banner]

stan·dard-bear·er (stan'dərd·bâr'ər) *n.* **1.** The member of a military unit who carries the flag or ensign. **2.** A leader or a candidate for a leading position, as for a presidency.

stan·dard·bred (*n.* stan'dərd·bred'; *adj.* stan'dərd·bred') *n.* A breed of horse notable for its trotters and pacers. — *adj.* Bred so as to be of a required strain, quality, or pedigree, as poultry, horses, etc.

standard candle *Physics* A candle (def. 3).

standard English *Ling.* Those usages in English that have gained literary, cultural, and social acceptance and prestige, and are considered appropriate for educated speakers of the language. See LEVEL OF USAGE.

standard gauge A railroad having a track width of 56½ inches, considered as standard. **— stan·dard-gauge** (stan'·dərd·gāj') *adj.*

stan·dard·ize (stan'dər·dīz) *v.t.* **·ized, ·iz·ing** To make to

or regulate by a standard. **— stan'dard·i·za'tion** *n.* **— stan'dard·iz'er** *n.*

standard of living The average quantity and quality of goods, services, luxuries, etc., that a person or group uses or consumes in daily living.

standard time Time as reckoned from a meridian officially established as standard over a large area. In the conterminous U.S. the four standard time zones are the **Eastern** (E.S.T.), **Central** (C.S.T.), **Mountain** (M.S.T.), and **Pacific** (P.S.T.), using respectively the mean local time of the 75th, 90th, 105th, and 120th meridians west of Greenwich, and being 5, 6, 7, and 8 hours slower (or earlier) than Greenwich time. Canada has a fifth zone, the **Atlantic** (or **Provincial**), based on the local time of the 60th meridian, 4 hours slower than Greenwich time.

stand·by (stand'bī') *n. pl.* **·bys** A person or thing on call for emergency use.

stand·ee (stan·dē') *n. Informal* A person who must stand for lack of chairs or seats, as at a theater or on a train.

stand-in (stand'in') *n.* **1.** A position of influence or favor; a pull. **2.** A person who takes the place of a motion-picture player, as during waiting intervals or in hazardous actions.

stand·ing (stan'ding) *adj.* **1.** Remaining erect; not prostrated or cut down, as grain. **2.** For regular or permanent use; not special or temporary: a *standing* army. **3.** Stagnant; not flowing. **4.** Begun while standing: a *standing* high jump. **5.** Established; permanent. — *n.* **1.** High grade or rank; good reputation: a man of *standing.* **2.** Time in which something goes on; duration: a feud of long *standing.* **3.** The act of one who stands; erectness; stance.

standing army An army that is prepared at all times for action, esp. during peacetime, and that consists of the regular army plus reservists and conscripts.

standing room Place in which to stand, as in a building, theater, etc., where the seats are all occupied.

stand-off (stand'ôf', -of') *n. Informal* **1.** A draw or tie, as in a game. **2.** A counterbalancing or neutralization. **3.** Indifference or coldness; aloofness. **4.** A postponement; delay.

stand-off·ish (stand'ôf'ish, -of'-) *adj.* Aloof; coolly reserved. **— stand'off'ish·ness** *n.*

stand-pat (stand'pat') *adj.* Characterized by or pertaining to the policy of opposition to change; conservative. **— stand'pat'ter** *n.*

stand-pipe (stand'pīp') *n.* A vertical pipe into which the water is pumped to give it a head; a water tower.

stand·point (stand'point') *n.* A position from which things are viewed or judged; point of view.

stand·still (stand'stil') *n.* A cessation; halt; rest. — *adj.* In a state of rest or inactivity; standing still.

stand-up (stand'up') *adj.* **1.** Having an erect position: a *standup* collar. **2.** Done, consumed, etc., while standing.

stank (stangk) Past tense of STINK.

stan·nic (stan'ik) *adj. Chem.* Of, pertaining to, or containing tin, esp. in its higher valence. [< L *stannum* tin + -IC]

stan·nous (stan'əs) *adj. Chem.* Of, pertaining to, or containing tin, esp. in its lower valence. [< L *stannum* tin + -OUS]

stan·num (stan'əm) *n.* Tin. [< L]

stan·za (stan'zə) *n.* A certain number of lines of verse grouped in a definite scheme of meter and sequence; a metrical division of a poem. [< Ital., room, stanza < L *stans, stantis* standing] **— stan·za·ic** (stan·zā'ik) *adj.*

sta·pes (stā'pēz) *n. pl.* **sta·pes** or **sta·pe·des** (stə-pē'dēz) *Anat.* The innermost ossicle of the middle ear of mammals: also called *stirrup bone.* For illus. see EAR. [< LL *stapes* stirrup] **— sta·pe·di·al** (stə-pē'dē-əl) *adj.*

staph (staf) *n. Informal* Staphylococci; also, an infection caused by staphylococci.

staph·y·lo·coc·cus (staf'ə-lō-kok'əs) *n. pl.* **·coc·ci** (-kok'sī) Any of a genus of typically pathogenic bacteria occurring singly, in pairs, or in irregular clusters; esp. an infective agent in boils and suppurating wounds. [< NL < Gk. *staphylos* bunch of grapes + *kokkos* berry] **— staph'y·lo·coc'cic** (-kok'sik) *adj.*

sta·ple¹ (stā'pəl) *n.* **1.** *Usu. pl.* A basic food or other ordinary item of household use. **2.** A principal commodity or production of a country or region. **3.** A main constituent of something. **4.** The carded or combed fiber of cotton, wool, or flax. **5.** Raw material. — *adj.* **1.** Regularly and constantly produced, used, or sold. **2.** Main; chief. **3.** Having regular commercial channels; marketable. — *v.t.* **·pled, ·pling** To sort or classify according to length, as wool fiber. [< OF *estaple* market, support < Gmc.] **— sta'pler** *n.*

sta·ple² (stā'pəl) *n.* **1.** A U-shaped piece of metal with pointed ends, driven into a surface to secure a bolt, hook, hasp, etc. **2.** A thin piece of wire usu. shaped like a bracket (), driven into paper, fabrics, etc., to serve as a fastening. — *v.t.* **·pled, pling** To fix or fasten by a staple or staples. [OE *stapol* post, prop] **— sta'pler** *n.*

star (stär) *n.* **1.** Any of the heavenly bodies visible from earth on clear nights as apparently fixed points of light. **2.**

Astron. One of a class of self-luminous celestial bodies, exclusive of comets, meteors, and nebulae, but including the sun. ◆ Collateral adjectives: *astral, sidereal, stellar.* **3.** A conventional figure usu. having five or more radiating points, used as an emblem or device, as on the shoulder strap of a general. **4.** An actor or actress who plays the leading part. **5.** Anyone who shines prominently in a calling or profession: a sports *star.* **6.** An asterisk (∗). **7.** A heavenly body considered as influencing one's fate. **8.** *Often pl.* Fortune; destiny. **— to see stars** *Informal* To see bright spots before the eyes, as from a sharp jolt to the head. **—** *v.* **starred, star·ring** *v.t.* **1.** To set or adorn with spangles or stars. **2.** To mark with an asterisk. **3.** To present as a star in a play or motion picture. **—** *v.i.* **4.** To shine brightly as a star. **5.** To play the leading part; be the star. **—** *adj.* **1.** Of or pertaining to a star or stars. **2.** Prominent; brilliant: a *star* football player. [OE *steorra*] **— star'less** *adj.* **— star'like'** *adj.*

star·board (stär'bərd) *Naut.* *n.* The right-hand side of a vessel as one faces the front or bow. **—** *adj.* Being on or toward the starboard. Opposed to *larboard, port.* [OE *steorbord* steering side]

starch (stärch) *n.* **1.** *Biochem.* A white, odorless, tasteless, granular carbohydrate $(C_6H_{10}O_5)_n$, found in most plants: also called *amylum.* **2.** A preparation of this substance, used for stiffening linen, and for many industrial purposes. **3.** Stiffness or formality; a formal manner. **4.** *U.S. Slang* Energy; vigor. **—** *v.t.* To apply starch to; stiffen with or as with starch. [OE *stercan* to stiffen < *stearc* stiff]

Star Chamber 1. Formerly, in England, a secret high court, abolished in 1641 because of abuses. **2.** Any court engaged in arbitrary or illegal procedure.

starch·y (stär'chē) *adj.* **starch·i·er, starch·i·est 1.** Stiffened with starch; stiff. Also **starched** (stärcht). **2.** Prim; formal; precise. **3.** Formed of or combined with starch; farinaceous. **— starch'i·ly** *adv.* **— starch'i·ness** *n.*

star·dom (stär'dəm) *n.* The status of a star (defs. 4 & 5).

stare (stâr) *v.* **stared, star·ing** *v.i.* **1.** To gaze fixedly, as from admiration, fear, or insolence. **2.** To be conspicuously or unduly apparent; glare. **3.** To stand on end, as hair. **—** *v.t.* **4.** To stare at. **5.** To affect in a specified manner by staring: to *stare* a person into silence. **—** *n.* The act of staring; an intense gaze. [OE *starian*] **— star'er** *n.*

star·fish (stär'fish') *n.* *pl.* **·fish** or **·fish·es** Any of various radially symmetrical marine animals, commonly with a star shaped body having five or more arms.

star·gaze (stär'gāz') *v.i.* **·gazed, ·gaz·ing 1.** To gaze at or study the stars. **2.** To engage in reverie; daydream. **— star'gaz·er** *n.* **— star'gaz·ing** *n. & adj.*

STARFISH (Ventral view showing tube feet)

stark (stärk) *adj.* **1.** Without ornamentation; blunt; simple: the *stark* truth. **2.** Complete; utter: *stark* misery. **3.** Stiff or rigid, as in death. **4.** Severe; tempestuous, as weather. **5.** Strict or grim, as a person. **—** *adv.* **1.** In a stark manner. **2.** Completely; utterly: *stark* mad. [OE *stearc* stiff] **— stark'ly** *adv.*

star·let (stär'lit) *n.* **1.** A small star. **2.** *U.S. Informal* A young movie or television actress represented as a future star.

star·light (stär'līt') *n.* The light given by a star or stars. **—** *adj.* Lighted by or only by the stars: also **star'lit'** (-lit').

star·ling (stär'ling) *n.* Any of various birds native to Europe and naturalized in North America, having a metallic purple and green luster. [OE *stærling* < *stær* starling]

star-of-Beth·le·hem (stär'əv-beth'lē-əm, -lə-hem) *n.* A European plant of the lily family having white stellate flowers, naturalized in the eastern U.S.

star of Bethlehem The large star by which the three Magi were guided to Jesus's manger in Bethlehem.

starred (stärd) *adj.* **1.** Spangled with stars. **2.** Presented or advertised as the star of a play, motion picture, etc. **3.** Marked with an asterisk. **4.** Affected by astral influence: chiefly in combination: *ill-starred.*

star·ry (stär'ē) *adj.* **·ri·er, ·ri·est 1.** Set with stars or starlike spots or points; abounding in stars. **2.** Lighted by the stars. **3.** Shining as or like the stars. **4.** Shaped like a star. **5.** Of, pertaining to, proceeding from, or connected with stars. **6.** Consisting of stars; stellar. **— star'ri·ness** *n.*

star·ry-eyed (stär'ē-īd') *adj.* Given to fanciful wishes or yearnings.

Stars and Bars, The The first flag of the Confederacy, consisting of a field of three bars and a circle of white stars.

Stars and Stripes, The The flag of the U.S. of America, a field of thirteen horizontal stripes, alternately red and white, and a blue union with 50 stars.

star-span·gled (stär'spang'gəld) *adj.* Spangled with stars or starlike spots or points.

Star-Spangled Banner, The 1. The flag of the U.S. **2.** The national anthem of the U.S. The poem was written by Francis Scott Key in 1814 during the bombardment by the British of Fort McHenry, Md.

start (stärt) *v.i.* **1.** To make a beginning or start; set out. **2.** To begin; commence. **3.** To make an involuntary, startled movement, as from fear or surprise. **4.** To move suddenly, as with a spring, leap, or bound; jump. **5.** To seem to bulge or protrude: His eyes *started* from his head. **6.** To be displaced or loosened. **—** *v.t.* **7.** To set in motion or circulation: to *start* an engine. **8.** To begin; commence: to *start* a lecture. **9.** To set up; establish. **10.** To introduce (a subject) or propound (a question). **11.** To displace or loosen, etc. **12.** To rouse from cover; cause to take flight; flush, as game. **13.** To draw the contents from; tap, as a cask. **— to start in** To begin; undertake. **— to start off** To begin a journey; set out. **— to start out** To make a beginning or start, as of a journey. **— to start up 1.** To rise or appear suddenly. **2.** To begin or cause to begin operation, as an engine. **—** *n.* **1.** A setting out or going forth; beginning. **2.** A quick, startled movement, as at something unexpected. **3.** A temporary or spasmodic action or attempt; a brief, intermittent effort: by fits and *starts.* **4.** Advantage or distance in advance at the outset; lead. **5.** Impetus at the beginning of motion or course of action: to get a *start* in business. **6.** A loosened place or condition; crack. [ME *sterten* to start, leap]

start·er (stär'tər) *n.* **1.** One who or that which starts. **2.** One who sees to it that buses, etc., leave on schedule. **3.** A mechanism for starting an internal combustion engine without manual cranking: also called *self-starter.* **4.** A competitor at the start of a race. **5.** A person who gives the signal for the start of a race.

star·tle (stär'təl) *v.* **·tled, ·tling** *v.t.* **1.** To arouse or excite suddenly; cause to start involuntarily; alarm. **—** *v.i.* **2.** To be aroused or excited suddenly; take alarm. **—** *n.* A sudden fright or shock; a scare. [OE *steartlian* to kick, struggle] **— star'tler** *n.*

star·tling (stärt'ling) *adj.* Rousing sudden surprise, alarm, or the like. **— star'tling·ly** *adv.*

star·va·tion (stär-vā'shən) *n.* The act of starving, or the state of being starved.

starve (stärv) *v.* **starved, starv·ing** *v.i.* **1.** To perish from lack of food. **2.** To suffer from extreme hunger. **3.** To suffer from lack or need to desire for friendship. **—** *v.t.* **4.** To cause to die of hunger; deprive of food. **5.** To bring to a specified condition by starving: to *starve* an enemy into surrender. [OE *steorfan* to die] **— starv'er** *n.*

starve·ling (stärv'ling) *n.* A person or animal that is starving, starved, or emaciated. **—** *adj.* **1.** Starving; emaciated; hungry. **2.** Failing or meet needs; inadequate.

stash (stash) *v.t.* *Slang* To hide or conceal (money, valuables, etc.), for storage and safekeeping: often with *away.* [? Blend of STORE + CACHE]

sta·sis (stā'sis, stas'is) *n.* *pl.* **·ses** (-sēz) *Pathol.* **1.** Stoppage in the circulation of any of the body fluids. **2.** Retarded movement of the intestinal contents. [< NL < Gk., a standing < *histanai* to stand]

stat- Var. of STATO-.

-stat *combining form* A device that stops or makes constant: *thermostat; rheostat.* [< Gk. *-statēs* causing to stand]

state (stāt) *n.* **1.** Mode of existence as determined by circumstances, external or internal; nature; condition; situation. **2.** Frame of mind; mood. **3.** Mode or style of living; station. **4.** Grand and ceremonious style; pomp; formality. **5.** A sovereign political community organized under a distinct government recognized and conformed to by the people as supreme, and having jurisdiction over a given territory; a nation. **6.** *Usu. cap.* One of a number of political communities or bodies politic united to form one sovereign state; esp. one of the United States. **7.** *pl.* The legislative bodies of a nation; estates. **8.** The territorial, political, and governmental entity constituting a state or nation; authority of government. **— Syn.** See NATION. **— Department of State** An executive department of the U.S. government (established in 1789), headed by the Secretary of State, that supervises the conduct of foreign affairs, directs the activities of all diplomatic and consular representatives, protects national interests abroad, and assists in the formulation of policies in relation to international problems. Also **State Department. — to lie in state** To be placed on public view, with ceremony and honors, before burial. **—** *adj.* **1.** Of or pertaining to the state, nation, or government: *state* papers. **2.** Intended for use on occasions of ceremony. **—** *v.t.* **stat·ed, stat·ing 1.** To set forth explicitly in speech or writing; assert; declare. **2.** To fix; determine; settle. [Aphetic var. of OF *estat* < L *status* condition, state] **— sta·tal** (stā'tal) *adj.*

state bank 1. *U.S.* A bank that has a charter from a State

government. **2.** Any bank that is owned or controlled by a state, esp. one that issues currency.
state·craft (stāt′kraft′, -kräft′) *n.* The art or practice of conducting affairs of state.
stat·ed (stā′tid) *adj.* **1.** Announced; specified. **2.** Established; regular; fixed. **— stat′ed·ly** *adv.*
State·hood (stāt′hŏŏd) *n.* The status of one of the United States, as distinguished from that of a Territory.
State House A building used for sessions of a State legislature and for other public purposes; State capitol.
state·less (stāt′lis) *adj.* **1.** Without nationality: a *stateless* person. **2.** Without a state or community of states.
state line In the U.S., any boundary between States.
state·ly (stāt′lē) *adj.* **·li·er, ·li·est** Dignified; lofty. *— adv.* Loftily: also **state′li·ly** (-lə-lē). **— state′li·ness** *n.*
state·ment (stāt′mənt) *n.* **1.** The act of stating. **2.** That which is stated. **3.** A summary of the assets and liabilities of a bank or firm, showing the balance due. **4.** A report sent, usu. monthly, to a debtor of a business firm or to a depositor in a bank.
state park *U.S.* A tract of land provided and maintained by a State for conservation and recreation.
State policeman *U.S.* A member of the separate police force of a State; also called *State trooper, trooper.*
state·room (stāt′rŏŏm′, -rŏŏm′) *n.* **1.** A private room having sleeping accommodations on a passenger ship. **2.** A private sleeping compartment on a railroad car.
state's evidence **1.** Evidence produced by the State in criminal prosecutions. **2.** One who confesses himself guilty of a crime and testifies as a witness against his accomplices. **— to turn state's evidence** To become a witness for the state and inculpate one's accomplices.
state·side (stāt′sīd′) *adj.* Of or in the continental U.S. *— adv.* In or to the continental U.S.
states·man (stāts′mən) *n.* *pl.* **·men** (-mən) **1.** One who is skilled in government; a political leader of distinguished ability. **2.** One engaged in government, or influential in state affairs. **— states′man·like′, states′man·ly** *adj.* **— states′·man·ship** *n.* **— states′wom·an** (-wŏŏm′ən) *n.fem.*
state socialism A political theory advocating government ownership of utilities and industries.
States' rights **1.** The rights and powers not delegated to the U.S. by the Constitution nor prohibited by it to the respective States. **2.** An interpretation of the Constitution that makes these rights and powers as large as possible. Also **State rights.**
State trooper *U.S.* A State policeman.
state-wide (stāt′wīd′) *adj.* Throughout a state.
stat·ic (stat′ik) *adj.* **1.** At rest; dormant; not active, moving, or changing. **2.** Pertaining to bodies at rest or forces in equilibrium: opposed to *dynamic.* **3.** *Physics* Acting as weight, but not moving: *static* pressure. **4.** *Electr.* Pertaining to electricity at rest, or to stationary electric charges. Also **stat′i·cal.** *— n. Telecom.* A disturbance of a carrier wave caused by atmospheric or man-made sources; also, the noise caused by this. [< NL < Gk. *statikos* causing to stand] **— stat′i·cal·ly** *adv.*
stat·ics (stat′iks) *n.pl.* (*construed as sing.*) The branch of mechanics dealing with bodies at rest and with the interaction of forces in equilibrium.
sta·tion (stā′shən) *n.* **1.** The headquarters of some official person or body of men: a police *station.* **2.** An established building or place serving as a starting point, stage, stopping place, or post; terminal; depot. **3.** A place where a person or thing usu. stands or is; an assigned location. **4.** Social condition; rank. **5.** *Mil.* The place to which an individual, unit, or ship is assigned for duty; post. **6.** The offices, studios, and technical installations of a radio or television broadcasting unit. **7.** *Mining* A recess in a shaft or passage of a mine. **8.** *Austral.* A cattle or sheep ranch. *— v.t.* To assign to a station; place in a post or position. [< F < L < *stare* to stand]
sta·tion·ar·y (stā′shən·er′ē) *adj.* **1.** Remaining in one place; fixed. **2.** Not portable or not easily portable. **3.** Exhibiting no change of character or condition. *— n. pl.* **·ar·ies** One who or that which is stationary.
sta·tion·er (stā′shən·ər) *n.* A dealer in stationery and related articles. [< Med.L *stationarius* stationary]
sta·tion·er·y (stā′shən·er′ē) *n.* **1.** Writing paper and envelopes. **2.** Writing materials, as pencils, notebooks, etc.
sta·tion·mas·ter (stā′shən·mas′tər, -mäs′-) *n.* The person having charge of a bus or railroad station.
Stations of the Cross The fourteen images or pictures representing successive scenes of the Passion of Christ, and before which devotions are performed.
station wagon A large automobile with one or more rows of removable or folding seats and a hinged tailgate.
stat·ism (stā′tiz·əm) *n.* **1.** A theory of government holding that the returns from group or individual enterprise are vested in the state. **2.** Loosely, adherence to state sovereignty, as in a republic. **— stat′ist** *n. & adj.*

sta·tis·tic (stə·tis′tik) *adj.* Statistical. *— n.* Any element entering into a statistical statement or array.
sta·tis·ti·cal (stə·tis′tə·kəl) *adj.* Of, pertaining to, consisting of, or derived from statistics: also *statistic.* **— sta·tis′ti·cal·ly** *adv.*
stat·is·ti·cian (stat′is·tish′ən) *n.* One skilled in collecting and tabulating statistical data.
sta·tis·tics (stə·tis′tiks) *n.pl.* (*construed as sing. in def. 2*) **1.** Quantitative data, pertaining to any subject or group, esp. when systematically gathered and collated. **2.** The science that deals with the collection, tabulation, and systematic classification of quantitative data, esp. as a basis for inference and induction. [< G < Med.L, ult. < L *status* state, condition]
stato- *combining form* Position. Also, before vowels, **stat-.** [< Gk. *statos* standing, fixed < *histanai* to stand]
sta·tor (stā′tər) *n. Mech.* The stationary portion of a dynamo, turbine, motor, etc.: distinguished from *rotor.* [< NL < L, supporter < *stare* to stand]
stat·u·ar·y (stach′ŏŏ·er′ē) *n.* *pl.* **·ar·ies** **1.** Statues collectively. **2.** The art of making statues. *— adj.* Of or suitable for statues.
stat·ue (stach′ŏŏ) *n.* A representation of a human or animal figure in marble, bronze, etc., esp. when nearly life-size or larger, and preserving the proportions in all directions. [< F < L < *status,* pp. of *stare* to stand]
Statue of Liberty A giant bronze statue on Liberty Island, depicting a crowned woman holding aloft a burning torch; presented to the U.S. by France and unveiled in 1886.
stat·u·esque (stach′ŏŏ·esk′) *adj.* Resembling a statue, as in grace, pose, or dignity. **— stat′u·esque′ly** *adv.* **— stat′u·esque′ness** *n.*
stat·u·ette (stach′ŏŏ·et′) *n.* A small statue. [< F]
stat·ure (stach′ər) *n.* **1.** The natural height of an animal body, esp. of a human body. **2.** The height of anything, esp. of a tree. **3.** Development; growth: moral *stature.* [< OF < L < *status* state]
sta·tus (stā′təs, stat′əs) *n.* **1.** State, condition, or relation. **2.** Relative position or rank. [< L < *stare* to stand]
sta·tus quo (stā′təs kwō, stat′əs) The condition or state in which (a person or thing is or has been): often used with *the:* to maintain the *status quo.* Also **status in quo.** [< L]
stat·ute (stach′ŏŏt) *n.* **1.** A legislative enactment duly sanctioned and authenticated by constitutional rule; act of Parliament, Congress, etc. **2.** Any authoritatively declared rule, ordinance, decree, or law. *— adj.* Consisting of or regulated by statute. [< F < LL *statuere* to constitute]
statute law The law as set forth in statutes.
statute mile A mile (def. 1).
statute of limitations A statute that imposes time limits upon the right of certain actions, as by obliging a creditor to demand payment of a debt within a specified time.
stat·u·to·ry (stach′ə·tôr′ē, -tō′rē) *adj.* **1.** Pertaining to a statute. **2.** Created by or dependent upon legislation.
statutory rape The crime of having sexual relations with a girl who is under the age of consent.
staunch (stônch, stänch) *adj.* **1.** Firm and dependable; constant; loyal: a *staunch* friend. **2.** Having firm constitution or construction: a *staunch* ship. **3.** Strong and vigorous. Also spelled *stanch.* *— v.t.* See STANCH. [< OF *estanchier* to make stand.] **— staunch′ly** *adv.* **— staunch′ness** *n.*
stauro- *combining form* Cross. [< Gk. *stauros* cross]
stave (stāv) *n.* **1.** A curved strip of wood, forming a part of the sides of a barrel, tub, or the like. **2.** Any narrow strip of material used for a like purpose. **3.** *Music* A staff. **4.** A stanza; verse. **5.** A rod, cudgel, or staff. **6.** A rung of a rack or ladder. *— v.* **staved** or **stove, stav·ing** *v.t.* **1.** To break in the staves of (a cask or a boat). **2.** To crush the shell or surface of; smash. **3.** To make (a hole) by crushing or collision. **4.** To furnish with staves. **5.** To ward off, as with a staff: usu. with *off:* to *stave* off hunger. *— v.i.* **6.** To be broken in, as a vessel's hull. [Back formation < *staves*]
staves (stāvz) **1.** Alternative plural of STAFF. **2.** Plural of STAVE.
stay¹ (stā) *v.i.* **1.** To cease motion; stop; halt. **2.** To continue in a specified place, condition, or state: to *stay* healthy. **3.** To remain temporarily as a guest, resident, etc. **4.** To pause; wait; tarry. **5.** *Informal* To have endurance; last. **6.** *Informal* To keep pace with a competitor, as in a race. **7.** In poker, to remain in a round by meeting an ante, bet, or raise. *— v.t.* **8.** To bring to a stop; halt; check. **9.** To hinder; delay. **10.** To postpone. **11.** To satisfy the demands of temporarily; to *stay* the pangs of hunger. **12.** To remain for the duration of: I will *stay* the night. **13.** To remain till or beyond the end of: with *out:* to *stay* out one's welcome. **— to stay put** *U.S. Informal* To remain or hold in spite of everything. *— n.* **1.** The act or time of staying; sojourn; visit. **2.** That which checks or stops; esp., a suspension of judicial proceedings. **3.** Staying power; endurance. **4.** A state of rest; standstill. [< AF *estaier,* OF *ester* < L *stare* to stand] **— stay′er** *n.*

stay² (stā) *v.t.* **1.** To be a support to; prop or hold up. **2.** To support mentally; sustain. **3.** To cause to depend or rely, as for support: with *on* or *upon.* — *n.* **1.** Anything that props or supports. **2.** A strip of plastic or metal, used to stiffen corsets, girdles, etc. **3.** *pl.* Formerly, a corset. [< OF *estayer*]

stay³ (stā) *Naut. n.* **1.** A strong rope, often of wire, used to support, steady, or fasten a mast or spar. **2.** Any rope supporting a mast or funnel. — *v.t.* **1.** To support with a stay or stays, as a mast. **2.** To put (a vessel) on the opposite tack. — *v.i.* **3.** To tack: said of vessels. [OE *stæg*]

stay·ing power (stā′ing) The ability to endure.

stay·sail (stā′səl, -sāl′) *n. Naut.* A sail, usu. triangular, extended on a stay.

stead (sted) *n.* **1.** Place of another person or thing: preceded by *in:* Serfdom came in the *stead* of slavery. Compare INSTEAD. **2.** Place or attitude of support; service: chiefly in the phrase **to stand one in (good) stead.** **3.** A steading or farm: used chiefly in compounds: *homestead.* [OE *stede*]

stead·fast (sted′fast′, -fäst′, -fəst) *adj.* **1.** Firmly fixed in faith or devotion to duty; constant; unchanging. **2.** Directed fixedly at one point or to one end, as a gaze or purpose; steady. Also spelled *stedfast.* [OE *stedefæst*] — **stead′fast·ly** *adv.* — **stead′fast·ness** *n.*

stead·y (sted′ē) *adj.* **stead·i·er, stead·i·est** **1.** Stable in position; firmly supported; fixed. **2.** Moving or acting with uniform regularity; unfaltering: a *steady* light. **3.** Not readily disturbed or upset: *steady* nerves. **4.** Free from intemperance and dissipation: *steady* habits. **5.** Constant in mind or conduct; steadfast. **6.** Regular; reliable: a *steady* customer. **7.** Uninterrupted; continuous. **8.** *Naut.* Having the direction of the ship's head unchanged. — *v.t. & v.i.* **stead·ied, stead·y·ing** To make or become steady. — *interj.* Not so fast; keep calm: an order enjoining self-control or composure. — *n. Slang* One's regular sweetheart. — **to go steady** *Informal* To date only one person of the opposite sex. [< STEAD + -Y³] — **stead′i·er** *n.* — **stead′i·ly** *adv.* — **stead′i·ness** *n.*

steak (stāk) *n.* **1.** A slice of meat or fish, usu. broiled or fried. **2.** Meat chopped for cooking like a steak. [< ON *steik*]

steal (stēl) *v.* **stole, sto·len, steal·ing** *v.t.* **1.** To take from another without right, authority, or permission, and usu. in a secret manner. **2.** To take or obtain in a surreptitious, artful, or subtle manner. **3.** To move, place, or convey stealthily: with *away (from, in, into, etc.* **4.** In baseball, to reach (second base, third base, or home plate) without the aid of a hit, error, passed ball, or wild pitch: said of a baserunner. — *v.i.* **5.** To commit theft. **6.** To move secretly or furtively. **7.** In baseball, to steal a base. — *n.* **1.** The act of stealing. **2.** That which is stolen. **3.** *U.S. Slang* A bargain. [OE *stelan*] — **steal′er** *n.*

stealth (stelth) *n.* **1.** The quality or habit of acting secretly; a concealed manner of acting. **2.** A secret or clandestine act, movement, or proceeding. [ME < OE *stelan* to steal]

stealth·y (stel′thē) *adj.* **stealth·i·er, stealth·i·est** Moving or acting secretly or slyly; done or characterized by stealth; furtive. — **stealth′i·ly** *adv.* — **stealth′i·ness** *n.*

— **Syn.** Anything *stealthy* seeks to avoid notice; it may be applied to a worthy act or purpose. *Furtive* suggests the actions or manner of a thief; we speak of a *furtive* act, a *furtive* face. *Surreptitious* suggests quickness as well as concealment in acting illegally or improperly: a *surreptitious* glance into a neighbor's window. *Clandestine* describes that which is concealed because morally offensive or socially and politically dangerous: a *clandestine* love affair, a *clandestine* rally.

steam (stēm) *n.* **1.** Water in the form of vapor. **2.** The gas or vapor into which water is changed by boiling, esp. when used under pressure as a source of energy. **3.** The visible mist into which aqueous vapor is condensed by cooling. **4.** Any kind of vaporous exhalation. **5.** *Informal* Vigor; force; speed. — **to let (or blow) off steam** *Informal* To give expression to pent-up emotions or opinions. — *v.i.* **1.** To give off or emit steam or vapor. **2.** To rise or pass off as steam. **3.** To become covered with condensed water vapor: often with *up.* **4.** To generate steam. **5.** To move or travel by the agency of steam. — *v.t.* **6.** To treat with steam, as in softening, cooking, cleaning, etc. — *adj.* **1.** Of, driven, or operated by steam. **2.** Containing or conveying steam: a *steam* boiler. **3.** Treated by steam. [OE *stēam*]

steam·boat (stēm′bōt′) *n.* A steamship.

steam engine An engine that derives its motive force from the action of steam, usu. by pressure against a piston sliding within a closed cylinder.

steam·er (stē′mər) *n.* **1.** A ship propelled by steam. **2.** A vessel in which something is steamed, as for cooking.

steamer trunk A trunk small enough to fit under a berth in a ship's cabin.

steam·fit·ter (stēm′fit′ər) *n.* A man who sets up or repairs steam pipes and their fittings. — **steam′fit′ting** *n.*

steam organ A calliope.

steam·roll·er (stēm′rō′lər) *n.* **1.** A road-rolling machine driven by steam. **2.** Any force that ruthlessly overcomes opposition. Also **steam roller.** — *v.t.* **1.** To work (a road, etc.) with a steamroller. **2.** To suppress; crush. **3.** To provide a path for by crushing opposition. — *v.i.* **4.** To work with or as with a steamroller. — *adj.* Resembling the action of a steamroller; aggressive: *steamroller* tactics.

steam·ship (stēm′ship′) *n.* A large vessel used for ocean traffic and usu. propelled by steam; a steamer.

steam shovel A machine for digging and excavation, operated by steam power.

steam table *U.S.* A long table, as in restaurants, with openings in which containers of food are placed to be kept warm by hot water or steam circulating beneath them.

steam turbine A turbine operated by steam power.

steam·y (stē′mē) *adj.* **steam·i·er, steam·i·est** Consisting of, like, or full of steam. — **steam′i·ly** *adv.* — **steam′i·ness** *n.*

ste·ar·ic (stē·ar′ik, stir′ik) *adj. Chem.* Of, pertaining to, or derived from stearin. [< F < Gk. *stear* suet]

stearic acid *Chem.* A white fatty acid, $C_{17}H_{35}COOH$, found in animal fats and in many vegetable oils.

ste·a·rin (stē′ə·rin, stir′in) *n. Chem.* **1.** A white, crystalline compound $(C_{17}H_{35}COO)_3C_3H_5$, obtained from various animal and vegetable fats. **2.** Stearic acid, esp. as prepared for making candles, etc. **3.** Fat in solid form. Also **ste′a·rine** (-rin, -rēn). [< F < Gk. *stear* suet]

ste·a·tite (stē′ə·tīt) *n.* Massive talc found in extensive beds and quarried for hearths, sink linings, coarse utensils, etc.: also called *soapstone.* [< L < Gk. *stear, steatos* suet, tallow] — **ste′a·tit′ic** (-tit′ik) *adj.*

sted·fast (sted′fast′, -fäst′, -fəst) See STEADFAST.

steed (stēd) *n.* A horse; esp., a spirited war horse: now chiefly a literary term. [OE *stēda* studhorse]

steel (stēl) *n.* **1.** A tough alloy of iron containing carbon in variable amounts, malleable under proper conditions, and greatly hardened by sudden cooling. The addition of other components, as chromium and nickel, gives a large range of alloys having special properties. **2.** Something made of steel, as a sword. **3.** Hardness of character. **4.** A strip or band of steel, as for stiffening a corset. — *adj.* **1.** Made or composed of steel. **2.** Resembling steel, as in hardness. **3.** Adamant; unyielding. — *v.t.* **1.** To cover with steel; plate, edge, point, or face with steel. **2.** To make hard or strong like steel. **3.** To make unfeeling; harden. [OE *stȳle, stēle*]

steel blue A metallic blue, as of certain steels.

steel engraving **1.** The art and process of engraving on a steel plate. **2.** The impression made from such a plate.

steel gray Any of several dark shades of gray.

steel·head (stēl′hed′) *n. U.S. & Canadian* The rainbow trout, esp. in its migratory stage to and from the sea, highly esteemed as a game fish: also called *salmon trout.*

steel wool Steel fibers matted together for use as an abrasive, as in cleaning, polishing, etc.

steel·work (stēl′wûrk′) *n.* **1.** Any article or construction of steel. **2.** *pl.* A shop or factory where steel is made or fabricated. — **steel′work′ing** *n.*

steel·work·er (stēl′wûr′kər) *n.* A worker in a steel mill.

steel·y (stē′lē) *adj.* **steel·i·er, steel·i·est** **1.** Made of, containing, resembling, or suggesting steel. **2.** Having a steel-like hardness: a *steely* gaze. — **steel′i·ness** *n.*

steel·yard (stēl′yärd′, -yərd, stil′yərd) *n.* A weighing device consisting of a scaled beam, counterpoise, and hooks. The article to be weighed is hung at the short end and the counterpoise weight on the long arm. Also **steel′yards.** [after *Steelyard*, formerly, the London headquarters for Hanseatic traders]

steen·bok (stān′bok, stēn′-) *n.* A small, fawn-colored African antelope: also called *steinbok.* [< Du. < *steen* stone + *bok* buck]

steep¹ (stēp) *adj.* **1.** Making a large angle with the plane of the horizon; precipitous. **2.** *Informal* Exorbitant; excessive; high, as a price. — *n.* A precipitous place, as a cliff or hill. [OE *stēap*] — **steep′ly** *adv.* — **steep′ness** *n.*

steep² (stēp) *v.t.* **1.** To soak in a liquid, as for softening, cleansing, etc. **2.** To imbue thoroughly; saturate: *steeped* in crime. — *v.i.* **3.** To undergo soaking in a liquid. — *n.* **1.** The process of steeping or the state of being steeped. **2.** A liquid or bath for steeping something; esp., a fertilizing liquid for seeds. [ME *stepen, ? < Scand.*] — **steep′er** *n.*

steep·en (stē′pən) *v.t. & v.i.* To make or become steep or steeper.

stee·ple (stē′pəl) *n.* A lofty, usu. tapering structure rising above the tower of a church; a spire. [OE *stīpel*]

stee·ple·chase (stē′pəl·chās′) *n.* **1.** A race on horseback across country, in which obstacles are to be leaped. **2.** A race over a course artificially prepared, as with hedges, rails, etc. **3.** Any cross-country run. [So called because originally the goal of the racers was a distant church steeple] — **stee·ple·chas·er** n. — **stee·ple·chas·ing** n.

stee·ple·jack (stē′pəl·jak′) n. A man whose occupation is to climb steeples and other tall structures to inspect or make repairs. [< STEEPLE + obs. *jack* workman]

steer¹ (stir) v.t. **1.** To direct the course of (a vessel or vehicle) by means of a rudder, steering wheel, etc. **2.** To follow (a course). **3.** To direct; guide. — v.i. **4.** To direct the course of a vessel, vehicle, etc. **5.** To undergo guiding or steering. **6.** To follow a course: to *steer* for land. — **to steer clear of** To avoid. — n. *U.S. Slang* A piece of advice. [OE *stīeran*] — **steer′a·ble** adj. — **steer′er** n.

steer² (stir) n. **1.** A male bovine animal, esp. when castrated and from two to four years old. **2.** An ox of any age raised for beef. [OE *stēor*]

steer·age (stir′ij) n. **1.** Formerly, the part of an ocean passenger vessel in the forward lower decks. **2.** Any markedly inferior, overcrowded, third-class accommodations. **3.** The act of steering. **4.** The effect of the helm on a vessel.

steer·age·way (stir′ij·wā′) n. *Naut.* The lowest speed at which a vessel can be accurately steered.

steer·ing committee (stir′ing) A committee in a legislature or other assemblage that arranges or directs the course of the business to be considered.

steering gear The coordinated mechanism that steers a ship, automotive vehicle, aircraft, bicycle, etc.

steering wheel A wheel turned by the driver or pilot of a vehicle, ship, etc., to change its direction.

steers·man (stirz′mən) n. *pl.* **·men** (-mən) One who steers a boat; a helmsman.

steg·o·my·ia (steg′ə·mī′ə) n. Aedes, a type of mosquito: a former name. [< NL < Gk. *stegos* roof + *myia* fly]

stein (stīn) n. A beer mug, esp. of earthenware. [< G]

stein·bok (stīn′bok) n. A steenbok.

stel·lar (stel′ər) adj. **1.** Of or pertaining to the stars; astral. **2.** Of or pertaining to a prominent actor or actress or to other persons in the arts. [< LL < L *stella* star]

stel·late (stel′it, -āt) adj. Star-shaped or starlike. Also **stel·lat·ed** (stel′ā·tid). [< L < *stella* star] — **stel′late·ly** adv.

stelli- *combining form* Star. [< L *stella* star]

St. El·mo's fire (sānt el′mōz) A luminous charge of atmospheric electricity sometimes appearing on the masts of ships, on church steeples, etc. Also **St. Elmo's light.**

stem¹ (stem) n. **1.** The main body or stalk of a tree, shrub, or other plant, rising above the ground. **2.** The relatively slender growth supporting the fruit, flower, or leaf of a plant. **3.** The long, slender, usu. cylindrical portion of an instrument, drinking vessels, etc. **4.** In a watch, the small, projecting, knobbed rod used for winding the mainspring. **5.** *Printing* The upright stroke of a type face or letter. **6.** *Music* The line attached to the head of a written musical note. **7.** *Ling.* A root plus a thematic vowel, as the Latin stem *luci-* ("light") in *lucifer* ("light-bearer"), composed of the root *luc-* plus the thematic vowel -*i*-. — v. **stemmed, stemming** v.t. **1.** To remove the stems of or from. **2.** To supply with stems. — v.i. **3.** To grow out of; develop or arise: usually with *from*. [OE *stemn, stefn* stem of a tree, prow of a ship] — **stem′mer** n. — **stem′less** adj.

stem² (stem) n. *Naut.* **1.** A nearly upright timber or metal piece uniting the two sides of a vessel at the bow. **2.** The bow or prow of a vessel. — **from stem to stern** From end to end; thoroughly. — v. **stemmed, stem·ming** v.t. **1.** To resist or make progress against, as a current: said of a vessel. **2.** To stand firm or make progress against (any opposing force): to *stem* the tide. [< STEM¹]

stem³ (stem) v.t. **stemmed, stem·ming 1.** To stop, hold back, or dam up, as a current; stanch. **2.** To make tight, as a joint; to plug. [< ON *stemma* to stop]

stem·ware (stem′wâr′) n. Drinking vessels with stems, as goblets, taken collectively.

stem-wind·er (stem′wīn′dər) n. A watch wound by turning the crown of the stem. — **stem′-wind′ing** adj.

stench (stench) n. A foul odor; stink. [OE *stenc*]

sten·cil (sten′səl) n. **1.** A sheet of paper, etc., in which a pattern is cut by means of spaces or dots, through which applied paint or ink penetrates to a surface beneath. **2.** A decoration or the like produced by stenciling. — v.t. **sten·ciled** or **·cilled, sten·cil·ing** or **·cil·ling** To mark with a stencil. [Prob. ME *stansel* to decorate with many colors < OF, ult. < L *scintilla* spark] — **sten′cil·er** or **sten′cil·ler** n.

steno- *combining form* Tight; narrow; contracted. Also, before vowels, **sten-.** [< Gk. *stenos* narrow]

ste·nog·ra·pher (stə·nog′rə·fər) n. One who writes stenography or is skilled in shorthand.

ste·nog·ra·phy (stə·nog′rə·fē) n. The art of writing by the use of contractions or arbitrary symbols; shorthand. — **sten·o·graph·ic** (sten′ə·graf′ik) or **·i·cal** adj. — **sten′o·graph′i·cal·ly** adv.

sten·o·type (sten′ə·tīp) n. **1.** A letter or combination of letters representing a sound, word, or phrase, esp. in shorthand. **2.** A Stenotype.

Sten·o·type (sten′ə·tīp) n. A keyboard-operated machine used in stenotypy: a trade name. Also *stenotype.*

sten·o·typ·y (sten′ə·tī′pē) n. A system of shorthand employing ordinary letters alone or in various combinations to represent specific sounds, words, or phrases.

sten·tor (sten′tôr) n. One who possesses an uncommonly strong, loud voice. [< *Stentor*]

Sten·tor (sten′tôr) In the *Iliad*, a herald with a loud voice.

sten·to·ri·an (sten·tôr′ē·ən, -tō′rē-) adj. Extremely loud.

step (step) n. **1.** An act of progressive motion that requires one of the supporting limbs of the body to be thrust in the direction of the movement, and to reassume its function of support; a pace. **2.** The distance passed over in making such a motion. **3.** Any short distance; a space easily traversed. **4.** That which the foot rests upon in ascending or descending, as a stair or ladder rung. **5.** A single action or proceeding regarded as leading to something: a *step* toward emancipation. **6.** An advance or promotion that forms one of a series; grade. **7.** The manner of stepping; gait. **8.** The sound of a footfall. **9.** A footprint; track. **10.** *pl.* Progression by walking; walk. **11.** A patterned combination of foot movements in dancing: the tango *step*. **12.** *Music* An interval corresponding to one degree of a scale or staff; a major or minor second. **13.** Something resembling a step, as a socket, supporting framework, etc.: the *step* of a mast. — **in step 1.** Walking, dancing, marching, etc., in accord with the proper rhythm or cadence, or in conformity with others. **2.** *Informal* In agreement or conformity. — **out of step** Not in step. — **to take steps** To adopt measures, as to attain an end. — v. **stepped, step·ping** v.i. **1.** To move forward or backward by taking a step or steps. **2.** To walk a short distance: to *step* across the street. **3.** To move with measured, dignified, or graceful steps. **4.** To move or act quickly or briskly. **5.** To pass into a situation, circumstance, etc., as if in a single step: He *stepped* into a fortune. — v.t. **6.** To take (a pace, stride, etc.). **7.** To perform the steps of: to *step* a quadrille. **8.** To place or move (the foot) in taking a step. **9.** To measure by taking steps: often with *off*. **10.** To cut or arrange in steps. **11.** *Naut.* To place the lower end of (a mast) in its step. — **to step down 1.** To decrease gradually, or by steps or degrees. **2.** To resign from an office or position. — **to step in** To begin to take part; intervene. — **to step on** (or **upon**) **1.** To put the foot down on. **2.** To put the foot on so as to activate, as a brake or treadle. **3.** *Informal* To reprove or subdue. — **to step on it** *Informal* To hurry; hasten. — **to step out 1.** To go outside, esp. for a short while. **2.** *Informal* To go out for fun or entertainment. **3.** To quit; resign. **4.** To walk vigorously and with long strides. — **to step up** To increase; accelerate. [OE *stæpe*]

step- *combining form* Related through the previous marriage of a parent or spouse, but not by blood. [OE < stem of *āstȳpan, āstēpan* to bereave, orphan]

step·broth·er (step′bruth′ər) n. The son of one's stepparent by a former marriage.

step·child (step′chīld′) n. The child of one's husband or wife by a former marriage.

step·daugh·ter (step′dô′tər) n. A female stepchild.

step-down (step′doun′) adj. **1.** Decreasing by stages. **2.** *Electr.* Converting a high voltage into a low voltage, as a transformer. **3.** *Mech.* Designating a gear that transfers motion at a reduced rate. Opposed to *step-up*.

step·fa·ther (step′fä′thər) n. The husband of one's mother, other than one's own father.

step-in (step′in′) n. **1.** A woman's brief underpants: also **step′-ins′. 2.** A pumplike shoe.

step·lad·der (step′lad′ər) n. A set of portable steps with, usu., a hinged frame at the back, that may be extended to support the steps in an upright position.

step·moth·er (step′muth′ər) n. The wife of one's father, other than one's own mother.

step·par·ent (step′pâr′ənt) n. A stepfather or stepmother.

steppe (step) n. A vast plain devoid of forest; esp., one of the extensive plains in Russia and Siberia. [< Russian *step′*]

step·per (step′ər) n. **1.** One who or that which steps: The horse is a high *stepper*. **2.** *Slang* A dancer.

step·ping-stone (step′ing·stōn′) n. **1.** A stone affording a footrest, as for crossing a stream. **2.** A preliminary step or stage in the fulfillment of a goal: *steppingstones* to success.

step·sis·ter (step′sis′tər) n. The daughter of one's stepparent by a former marriage.

step·son (step′sun′) n. A male stepchild.

step-up (step′up′) adj. **1.** Increasing by stages. **2.** *Electr.* Converting a low voltage into a high voltage, as a transformer. **3.** Designating a gear that transfers motion at an increased rate. Opposed to *step-down*.

-ster *suffix of nouns* **1.** One who makes or is occupied with: often pejorative: *songster, prankster.* **2.** One who belongs or is related to: *gangster.* **3.** One who is: *youngster.* [OE *-estre*, fem. suffix expressing the agent]

stere (stir) *n.* In the metric system, a measure of capacity equal to one cubic meter. See table front of book. [< F < Gk. *stereos* solid]

ster·e·o (ster'ē·ō, stir'-) *n.* A stereophonic system. — *adj.* Stereophonic.

stereo- *combining form* Solid; firm; hard; three-dimensional. Also, before vowels, **stere-**. [< Gk. *stereos* hard]

ster·e·o·chem·is·try (ster'ē·ō·kem'is·trē, stir'-) *n.* The branch of chemistry that treats of the spatial arrangement of atoms and molecules.

ster·e·o·phon·ic (ster'ē·ə·fon'ik, stir'-) *adj.* 1. Pertaining to, designed for, or characterized by the perception of sound by both ears; binaural. 2. *Electronics* Designating a system of sound reproduction in which two or more receivers or loudspeakers are so placed as to give the effect of hearing the sound from more than one direction. Also *stereo*. — **ster'e·o·phon'i·cal·ly** *adv.* — **ster·e·o·phon·y** (ster'ē·of'ə·nē, stir'-, ster'ē·ə·fō'nē, stir'-) *n.*

ster·e·op·ti·con (ster'ē·op'ti·kon, stir'-) *n.* A double magic lantern arranged to combine two images of the same object or scene, or used to bring one image after another on the screen. [< STEREO- + Gk. *optikos* of sight]

ster·e·o·scope (ster'ē·ə·skōp, stir'-) *n.* An instrument for blending into one image two pictures of an object from slightly different points of view, so as to produce the impression of relief and solidity. — **ster'e·o·scop'ic** (-skop'ik) or **·i·cal** *adj.* — **ster'e·o·scop'i·cal·ly** *adv.*

ster·e·os·co·py (ster'ē·os'kə·pē, stir'-) *n.* 1. The art of making or using stereoscopes and stereoscopic slides. 2. The viewing of objects as in three dimensions. — **ster'e·os'co·pist** *n.*

ster·e·o·type (ster'ē·ə·tīp', stir'-) *n.* 1. A plate cast in type metal from a matrix and reproducing on its surface the composed type or other material impressed upon the matrix. 2. Anything made or processed in this way. 3. Stereotypy. 4. A conventional or hackneyed expression, custom, mental image, etc. 5. A person possessing characteristics that typify a particular group. — *v.t.* **·typed**, **·typ·ing** 1. To make a stereotype of. 2. To fix firmly or unalterably. — **ster'e·o·typ'er**, **ster'e·o·typ'ist** *n.*

ster·e·o·typed (ster'ē·ə·tīpt', stir'-) *adj.* 1. Formalized; hackneyed; trite. 2. Produced from a stereotype.

ster·e·o·typ·y (ster'ē·ə·tī'pē, stir'-) *n.* The art or act of making stereotypes: also called *stereotype*.

ster·ile (ster'əl, *esp. Brit.* -īl) *adj.* 1. Having no reproductive power; barren. 2. *Bot.* Incapable of germinating. 3. Lacking productiveness: *sterile* soil. 4. Containing no bacteria or other microorganisms. 5. Lacking in vigor or imagination: *sterile* verse. [< L *sterilis* barren] — **ster'ile·ly** *adv.* — **ster'ile·ness**, **ste·ril·i·ty** (stə·ril'ə·tē) *n.*

ster·il·ize (ster'əl·īz) *v.t.* **·ized**, **·iz·ing** 1. To free from infective or pathogenic microorganisms. 2. To deprive of productive or reproductive power. 3. To make barren. Also *Brit.* **ster'il·ise**. — **ster'il·i·za'tion** (-ə·zā'shən, -ī·zā'-) *n.* — **ster'il·iz'er** *n.*

ster·ling (stûr'ling) *n.* 1. The official standard of fineness for British coins: for silver, 0.500; for gold, 0.91666. 2. Sterling silver, 0.925 fine, as used in manufacturing articles; also, articles made of it. 3. A former silver penny of England and Scotland. — *adj.* 1. Made of or payable in sterling. 2. Made of sterling silver. 3. Genuine. 4. Valuable: esteemed: *sterling* qualities. [Prob. OE *steorra* star + -LING; because a star was stamped on some of the coins]

stern[1] (stûrn) *adj.* 1. Marked by severity or harshness; unyielding. 2. Strict; severe. 3. Inspiring fear; awesome. 4. Resolute; stout: a *stern* resolve. [OE *styrne*] — **stern'ly** *adv.* — **stern'ness** *n.*

stern[2] (stûrn) *n.* 1. *Naut.* The aft part of a ship, boat, etc. 2. The hindmost part of any object. — *adj.* Situated at or belonging to the stern. [< ON *stȳra* to steer]

stern·most (stûrn'mōst', -məst) *adj.* Farthest to the rear or stern.

sterno- *combining form* Anat. The sternum. Also, before vowels, **stern-**. [< L *sternum* or Gk. *stērnon* breast]

stern·post (stûrn'pōst') *n.* *Naut.* The main vertical post of the stern frame of a vessel, to which the rudder is attached.

ster·num (stûr'nəm) *n.* *pl.* **·na** (-nə) or **·nums** *Anat.* The breastbone that forms the ventral support of the ribs in vertebrates. [< L < Gk. *stērnon* breast] — **ster'nal** *adj.*

stern·ward (stûrn'wərd) *adj. & adv.* Toward the stern.

stern·way (stûrn'wā') *n.* *Naut.* Backward movement of a vessel.

stern-wheel·er (stûrn'hwē'lər) *n.* A steamboat propelled by one large paddle wheel at the stern.

ster·oid (ster'oid) *n.* *Biochem.* Any of a large group of fat-soluble organic compounds, including the sterols, the bile acids, and the sex hormones.

ster·ol (ster'ōl, -ol) *n.* *Biochem.* Any of a class of complex, chiefly unsaturated solid alcohols, widely distributed in plant and animal tissue, as cholesterol. [Contr. of CHOLESTEROL]

ster·tor·ous (stûr'tər·əs) *adj.* Characterized by snoring or accompanied by a snoring sound. [< NL < L *stertere* to snore] — **ster'tor·ous·ly** *adv.* — **ster'tor·ous·ness** *n.*

stet (stet) Let it stand: a direction used in proofreading to indicate that a word, letter, etc., marked for omission or correction is to remain. — *v.t.* **stet·ted**, **stet·ting** To cancel a former correction or omission of by marking with the word *stet*. Compare DELE. [< L < *stare* to stand, stay]

stetho- *combining form* The breast or chest; pectoral. Also, before vowels, **steth-**. [< Gk. *stēthos* breast]

steth·o·scope (steth'ə·skōp) *n.* *Med.* An apparatus for auscultation, adapted for conveying the sounds of the body to the examiner's ear or ears. — **steth'o·scop'ic** (-skop'ik), **steth'o·scop'i·cal** *adj.* — **steth'o·scop'i·cal·ly** *adv.* — **ste·thos·co·py** (ste·thos'kə·pē) *n.*

ste·ve·dore (stē'və·dôr, -dōr) *n.* One whose business is stowing or unloading the holds of vessels. — *v.t. & v.i.* **·dored**, **·dor·ing** To load or unload (a vessel). [< Sp. < L *stipare* to compress, stuff]

stew (stoo, styoo) *v.t. & v.i.* 1. To boil slowly and gently; seethe; keep or be at the simmering point. 2. *Informal* To worry. — *n.* 1. Stewed food, esp. a preparation of meat or fish and vegetables cooked together by stewing. 2. *Informal* Mental agitation; worry. [< OF, prob. ult. < L *ex-* out + Gk. *typhos* steam, vapor]

stew·ard (stoo'ərd, styoo'-) *n.* 1. One who is entrusted with the management of property, finances, or other affairs not his own. 2. One who has charge of buying provisions, managing servants, etc., in a private residence or in a club, hotel, etc. 3. One in charge of provisions and usu. of the tables on a ship. 4. On an airplane, ship, or bus, one who waits on the passengers. 5. One who manages any affair: *steward* of the races. [OE < *stī* hall, sty + *weard* ward, keeper] — **stew'ard·ess** *n.fem.* — **stew'ard·ship** *n.*

stewed (stood, styood) *adj.* 1. Cooked by stewing. 2. *Slang* Drunk.

stew·pan (stoo'pan, styoo'-) *n.* A cooking vessel used for stewing.

stib·i·um (stib'ē·əm) *n.* Antimony. [< L < Gk. *stibi*] — **stib'i·al** *adj.*

-stichous *combining form* Having (a specified number of) rows. [< Gk. *stichos* row, line]

stick (stik) *n.* 1. A slender piece of wood, as a branch cut from a tree or bush, a baton or wand, etc. 2. *Brit.* A cane. 3. Anything resembling a stick in form: a *stick* of candy or dynamite. 4. A piece of wood of any size, cut for fuel, lumber, or timber. 5. *Aeron.* The control lever of an airplane, that operates the elevators and ailerons. 6. A poke, stab, or thrust with a pointed instrument. 7. The state of being stuck together; adhesion. 8. In sports, a baseball bat, hockey stick, etc. 9. *Informal* A stiff, inert, or dull person. 10. A stalk, as of asparagus. — **the sticks** *Informal* An obscure rural district; the backwoods or country. — *v.* **stuck** or (*for def. 15*) **sticked**, **stick·ing** *v.t.* 1. To pierce, stab, or penetrate with a pointed object. 2. To kill or wound by piercing; stab. 3. To thrust or force, as a sword or pin, into or through something else. 4. To force the end of (a nail, etc.) into something so as to be fixed in place. 5. To fasten in place with or as with pins, nails, etc.: to *stick* a ribbon on a dress. 6. To cover with objects piercing the surface. 7. To impale; transfix. 8. To put or thrust: He *stuck* his hand into his pocket. 9. To fasten to a surface by or as by an adhesive substance. 10. To bring to a standstill; obstruct; halt: usu. in the passive: We were *stuck* in Rome. 11. *Informal* To smear with something sticky. 12. *Informal* To baffle; puzzle. 13. *Slang* To impose upon; cheat. 14. *Slang* To force great expense, an unpleasant task, etc., upon. 15. To provide with sticks or brush on which to grow, as a vine. — *v.i.* 16. To be or become fixed in place by being thrust in: to *stick* in a cushion. 17. To become or remain attached or close to something by or as by adhesion; adhere; cling. 18. To come to a standstill; become blocked or obstructed. 19. To be baffled or disconcerted. 20. To hesitate; scruple: with *at* or *to*. 21. To persist; persevere: with *at* or *to*. 22. To remain firm or resolute; be faithful. 23. To be extended; protrude: with *from*, *out*, *through*, *up*, etc. — **to stick around** *Slang* To remain near or near at hand. — **to stick by** To remain faithful to; be loyal to. — **to stick it out** To persevere to the end. — **to stick up** *Slang* To detain and rob. — **to stick up for** *Informal* To take the part of; defend. [OE *sticca*]

stick·er (stik'ər) *n.* 1. A gummed label, sign, etc. 2. One who or that which fastens with or as with paste. 3. One who holds tenaciously to anything. 4. *Informal* A puzzle. 5. A prickly stem, thorn, or bur.

---

stick·ing plaster (stik′ing) Adhesive tape.

stick·le (stik′əl) *v.i.* **·led, ·ling 1.** To contend or argue about trifling matters. **2.** To insist or hesitate for petty reasons. [ME *stighlen*, freq. of OE *stihtan* to arrange]

stick·le·back (stik′əl·bak′) *n.* A small fresh- or salt-water fish, having sharp dorsal spines.

stick·ler (stik′lər) *n.* One who contends over or insists upon something: usu. with *for*: a *stickler* for details.

stick·pin (stik′pin′) *n. U.S.* An ornamental pin for a necktie.

stick-to-it·ive (stik·tōō′it·iv) *adj. Informal* Persevering. — **stick-to′-it·ive·ly** *adv.* — **stick-to′-it·ive·ness** *n.*

stick·up (stik′up′) *n. Slang* A robbery or holdup.

stick·y (stik′ē) *adj.* **stick·i·er, stick·i·est 1.** Adhering to a surface; adhesive. **2.** Covered with something adhesive. **3.** Warm and humid. — **stick′i·ly** *adv.* — **stick′i·ness** *n.*

stiff (stif) *adj.* **1.** Resisting the action of a bending force; rigid. **2.** Not easily moved: *stiff* brakes; also, moving or functioning painfully or without suppleness: a *stiff* neck. **3.** Not natural, graceful, or easy; constrained and awkward; formal. **4.** Not liquid or fluid, thick; viscous. **5.** Taut; tightly drawn. **6.** Having a strong, steady movement: a *stiff* breeze. **7.** Firm in resistance; stubborn. **8.** Harsh; severe: a *stiff* penalty. **9.** High; dear: a *stiff* price. **10.** Strong or potent, as in alcoholic content: a *stiff* drink. **11.** Difficult; arduous: a *stiff* climb. — *n. Slang* **1.** A corpse. **2.** An awkward or unresponsive person; esp., a bore. **3.** A man; fellow: working *stiff*; also, a roughneck. [OE *stif*] — **stiff′ly** *adv.* — **stiff′ness** *n.*

stiff·en (stif′ən) *v.t. & v.i.* To make or become stiff or stiffer. — **stiff′en·er** *n.*

stiff-necked (stif′nekt′) *adj.* Not yielding; stubborn.

sti·fle (stī′fəl) *v.* **·fled, ·fling** *v.t.* **1.** To keep back; suppress or repress; check: to *stifle* sobs. **2.** To suffocate; choke. — *v.i.* **3.** To die of suffocation. **4.** To experience difficulty in breathing, as in a stuffy room. [ME < OF *estouffer* to smother] — **sti′fler** *n.* — **sti′fling** *adj.* — **sti′fling·ly** *adv.*

stig·ma (stig′mə) *n. pl.* **stig·ma·ta** (stig′mə·tə, stig·mä′tə) or (*for defs. 1–3, usu.*) **stig·mas 1.** A mark of infamy, or token of disgrace. **2.** A mark indicating a defect or something not normal. **3.** *Bot.* The part of a pistil that receives the pollen. For illus. see FLOWER. **4.** *Biol.* **a** A mark or spot. **b** An aperture or opening, as a pore. **5.** *pl.* The wounds that Christ received during the Passion and Crucifixion. **6.** Formerly, a brand made on slaves and criminals. [< L < Gk. *stizein* to prick, brand] — **stig·mat′ic** (-mat′ik), **stig·mat′i·cal** *adj.*

stig·ma·tize (stig′mə·tīz) *v.t.* **·tized, ·tiz·ing 1.** To characterize or brand as ignominious. **2.** To mark with a stigma. [< Med.L < Gk. *stigma* pointed end, mark] — **stig′ma·ti·za′tion** *n.* — **stig′ma·tiz′er** *n.*

stile (stīl) *n.* **1.** A step, or series of steps, on each side of a fence or wall to aid in surmounting it. **2.** A turnstile. [OE *stigan* to climb]

sti·let·to (sti·let′ō) *n. pl.* **·tos** or **·toes** A small dagger with a slender blade. — *v.t.* **·toed, ·to·ing** To pierce with a stiletto; stab. [< Ital. < L *stilus* writing instrument]

still¹ (stil) *adj.* **1.** Making no sound; silent. **2.** Peaceful; tranquil. **3.** Without movement; motionless. **4.** Low in sound; quiet; hushed. **5.** Subdued; soft. **6.** Dead; inanimate. **7.** Having no effervescence: said of wines. **8.** *Photog.* Of or designating a single photograph, as contrasted with a motion picture. — **Syn.** See CALM. — *n.* **1.** *Poetic* Stillness; calm. **2.** A still-life picture. **3.** *Photog.* A still photograph. — *adv.* **1.** Now as previously; up to this or that time: He is *still* here. **2.** All the same: nevertheless. **3.** Even; yet: *still* more. **4.** *Poetic & Dial.* Always; constantly. — *conj.* Nevertheless; and yet. — *v.t.* **1.** To cause to be still or calm. **2.** To silence or hush. **3.** To quiet or allay, as fears. — *v.i.* **4.** To become still. [OE *stille*] — **still′ness** *n.*

still² (stil) *n.* **1.** An apparatus in which a substance is vaporized by heat, and the vapor then liquefied in a condenser, used esp. for distilling alcoholic liquors. **2.** A distillery. — *v.t. & v.i.* To distill. [< L *stilla* drop]

still·born (stil′bôrn′) *adj.* Dead at birth. — **still′birth′** *n.*

still life **1.** In painting, the representation of objects, as tables, flowers, fruit, etc. **2.** A picture of such a subject.

Still·son wrench (stil′sən) A wrench closely resembling a monkey wrench, but with serrated jaws, one of which is capable of slight angular movement, so that the grip is increased by pressure on the handle: a trade name. STILLSON WRENCH

still·y (*adj.* stil′ē; *adv.* stil′lē) *adj.* Still; silent; calm. — *adv.* Calmly; quietly; without noise.

stilt (stilt) *n.* **1.** One of a pair of long, slender poles made with a projection to support the foot some distance above the ground in walking. **2.** A tall post or pillar used as a support, as for a dock. **3.** Any of several long-legged, wading birds. — *v.t.* To raise on stilts. [ME *stilte, ?* < LG]

stilt·ed (stil′tid) *adj.* **1.** Artificially formal or elevated in manner; pompous. **2.** Raised or built on or as on stilts. — **stilt′ed·ly** *adv.* — **stilt′ed·ness** *n.*

stim·u·lant (stim′yə·lənt) *n.* **1.** Anything that quickens or promotes the activity of some physiological process, as a drug. **2.** An alcoholic beverage. — *adj.* Acting as a stimulant; serving to stimulate. [See STIMULATE.]

stim·u·late (stim′yə·lāt) *v.* **·lat·ed, ·lat·ing** *v.t.* **1.** To rouse to activity or to quickened action; spur. **2.** *Physiol.* To excite (an organ or tissue) by applying some form of stimulus. **3.** To affect by alcoholic beverages. — *v.i.* **4.** To act as a stimulant. [< L < *stimulus* goad] — **stim′u·lat′er, stim′u·la·tor** *n.* — **stim′u·la′tion** *n.* — **stim′u·la′tive** *adj. & n.*

stim·u·lus (stim′yə·ləs) *n. pl.* **·li** (-lī) **1.** Anything that rouses the mind or spirits; an incentive. **2.** *Physiol.* Any agent or form of excitation that influences the activity of an organism as a whole or in any of its parts. [< L]

sti·my (stī′mē) See STYMIE.

sting (sting) *v.* **stung, stung, sting·ing** *v.t.* **1.** To pierce or prick painfully, as with a sharp, sometimes venomous organ. **2.** To cause to suffer sharp, smarting pain from or as from a sting. **3.** To cause to suffer mentally; pain: His heart was *stung* with remorse. **4.** To stimulate; goad; spur. **5.** *Slang* To get the better of; also, to overcharge. — *v.i.* **6.** To have or use a sting, as a bee. **7.** To suffer or cause a sharp, smarting pain. **8.** To suffer or cause mental distress; pain. — *n.* **1.** *Zool.* A sharp, pointed organ, as of a bee, able to inflict a wound. **2.** The act of stinging; also, the wound or the pain caused by a sting. **3.** Any sharp, smarting sensation: the *sting* of remorse. **4.** A spur; goad. **5.** *Bot.* One of the sharp-pointed hairs of a nettle, charged with an irritating fluid: also **stinging hair.** [OE *stingan*] — **sting′er** *n.* — **sting′ing·ly** *adv.* — **sting′y** *adj.*

sting ray Any of a family of flat-bodied fishes having broad pectoral fins and a whiplike tail capable of inflicting wounds: also called **sting·a·ree** (sting′ə·rē, sting′ə·rē′) *n.*

stin·gy (stin′jē) *adj.* **·gi·er, ·gi·est 1.** Unwilling to spend or give; miserly. **2.** Scanty; inadequate; meager. [< dial. E *stinge* sting + -Y¹] — **stin′gi·ly** *adv.* — **stin′gi·ness** *n.* — **Syn. 1.** niggardly, parsimonious, close, closefisted, tight.

stink (stingk) *n.* A strong, foul odor; stench. — **Syn.** See SMELL. — *v.* **stank** or **stunk, stunk, stink·ing** *v.i.* **1.** To give forth a foul odor. **2.** To be extremely offensive or hateful. **3.** *Informal* To be of bad quality. — *v.t.* **4.** To cause to stink. — **to make** (or **raise**) **a stink** *Slang* To protest vehemently. — **to stink out** To drive out by a foul or suffocating odor. [OE *stincan* to smell] — **stink′ing·ly** *adv.*

stink·bug (stingk′bug′) *n.* Any of various large, flattened bugs that emit an unpleasant odor if disturbed.

stink·weed (stingk′wēd′) *n.* Any of various plants having a disagreeable odor, as the jimsonweed.

stint (stint) *v.t.* **1.** To limit, as in amount or share; be stingy with. — *v.i.* **2.** To be frugal or sparing. — *n.* **1.** A fixed amount, as of work to be performed within a specified time. **2.** A bound; restriction; limit. **3.** A small sandpiper. [ME *stynten* to cause to stop] — **stint′er** *n.*

stipe (stīp) *n.* **1.** *Zool.* A stalk or support. **2.** *Bot.* A stalklike support or stem, as that supporting a fern's frond, etc. [< F < L *stipes* branch]

sti·pend (stī′pend) *n.* An allowance, salary, or pension; esp., money paid under a scholarship. [< L < *stips* coin, payment in coin + *pendere* to weigh, pay out]

sti·pen·di·ar·y (stī·pen′dē·er′ē) *adj.* **1.** Receiving or performing services for a stipend. **2.** Of or like a stipend. **3.** Paid for by a stipend, as services. — *n. pl.* **·ar·ies** One who receives a stipend. See STIPEND.]

stip·ple (stip′əl) *v.t.* **·pled, ·pling** To draw, paint, or engrave with dots or short touches instead of lines. — *n.* **1.** A method of painting, etc., by stippling. **2.** A painting produced by stippling; also the effect of stippling. [< Du. *stip dot*] — **stip′pler** *n.*

stip·u·late (stip′yə·lāt) *v.* **·lat·ed, ·lat·ing** *v.t.* **1.** To specify as the terms of or condition for an agreement, contract, etc. **2.** To promise; guarantee. — *v.i.* **3.** To demand something as a requirement: with *for*. **4.** To make an agreement. [< L < *stipulari* to bargain] — **stip′u·la′tor** *n.*

stip·u·la·tion (stip′yə·lā′shən) *n.* **1.** The act of stipulating, or the state of being stipulated. **2.** That which is stipulated; a condition. — **stip′u·la·to′ry** (-lə·tôr′ē, -tō′rē) *adj.*

stip·ule (stip′yool) *n. Bot.* One of a pair of leaflike appendages at the base of the petiole of certain leaves. [< L *stipula* stalk] — **stip·u·late** (stip′yə·lit, -lāt) *adj.*

stir¹ (stûr) *v.* **stirred, stir·ring** *v.t.* **1.** To agitate so as to alter the relative position of the particles or components of, as soup with a spoon. **2.** To cause to move, slightly or irregularly; disturb. **3.** To move vigorously; bestir. **4.** To rouse, as from sleep, indifference, or inactivity; stimulate. **5.** To incite; provoke: often with *up*. **6.** To affect strongly; move with emotion. — *v.i.* **7.** To move, esp., slightly. **8.** To be active; move about. **9.** To happen. **10.** To undergo stirring: This molasses *stirs* easily. — *n.* **1.** The act of stirring, or state of being stirred; activity. **2.** General interest or commotion. **3.** Excitement or agitation. **4.** A poke; nudge. [OE *styrian*] — **stir′rer** *n.*

stir² (stûr) *n. Slang* A jail; prison. [Origin uncertain]

stir·ring (stûr′ing) *adj.* **1.** Stimulating; inspiring. **2.** Full of activity or stir; lively. — **stir′ring·ly** *adv.*

stir·rup (stûr′əp, stir′-) *n.* **1.** An inverted U-shaped support hung from either side of a saddle to hold the rider's foot in and after mounting. **2.** Any similarly shaped supports, as for a beam. [OE *stigrāp* mounting rope]

stirrup bone *Anat.* The stapes.

stitch (stich) *n.* **1.** A single passage of a threaded needle through fabric and back again, as in sewing or embroidery, or, in surgery, through skin or flesh. **2.** A single turn of thread or yarn around a needle, as in knitting or crocheting; also, the link or loop resulting from such a turn. **3.** Any particular arrangement of a thread used in sewing, crocheting, etc.: a chain *stitch*. **4.** A sharp sudden pain, esp. in the back or side. **5.** *Informal* The smallest bit or fragment: not a *stitch* of work. — *v.t.* **1.** To join together or ornament with stitches. — *v.i.* **2.** To make stitches; sew. [OE *stice* a prick, stab] — **stitch′er** *n.*

sti·ver (stī′vər) *n.* **1.** A small Dutch coin, ¹⁄₂₀ of a guilder. **2.** Anything of little value. [< Du. *stuiver*]

St. Johns·wort (sānt jonz′wûrt′) A hardy perennial with deep yellow flowers. Also **St.-John's-wort.**

stoat (stōt) *n.* The ermine, esp. in its brown summer coat. [ME *stote*; origin uncertain]

stock (stok) *n.* **1.** A quantity of something acquired or kept for future use. **2.** The total merchandise or goods that a commercial establishment has on hand. **3.** Livestock. **4.** In finance: **a** The capital or fund raised by a corporation through the sale of shares. **b** The proportional part of this capital credited to an individual stockholder and represented by the number of shares he owns. **c** A certificate showing ownership of shares. **5.** The trunk or main stem of a tree or other plant. **6.** A line of familial descent. **7.** The original progenitor of a family line. **8.** An ethnic group; race. **9.** A family of languages. **10.** A related group or family of plants or animals; also, a type of animal or plant from which others are derived. **11.** *Bot.* **a** A rhizome. **b** In horticulture, a stem upon which a graft is made; also, a plant, tree, etc. that provides cuttings and slips. **12.** The broth from boiled meat or fish used in preparing soups, etc. **13.** Raw material; paper *stock*. **14.** *pl.* A timber frame with holes for confining the ankles, formerly used in punishing petty offenders. **15.** *pl.* The timber frame on which a vessel rests during construction. **16.** In firearms: **a** The rear wooden portion of a rifle etc., to which the barrel and mechanisms are secured. **b** The arm on rapidfire guns connecting the shoulder piece to the slide. **c** The handle of a pistol or similar firearm. **17.** The handle of certain instruments, as of a whip or fishing rod. **18.** A theatrical stock company; also, its repertoire. **19.** A broad, stiffened band, formerly worn as a cravat. **20.** An ornamental garden plant, as the gillyflower. — **in stock** On hand and available for sale or use. — **to take stock** To take an inventory. **2.** To estimate or appraise. — *v.t.* **1.** To furnish with livestock or with merchandise. **2.** To keep for sale. **3.** To put aside for future use. **4.** To provide with a handle or stock. — *v.i.* **5.** To lay in supplies or stock: often with *up*. — *adj.* **1.** Kept continually ready or constantly brought forth, like old goods: a *stock* joke. **2.** Kept on hand: a *stock* size. **3.** Banal; commonplace: a *stock* phrase. **4.** Used for breeding purposes. **5.** Employed in handling or caring for the stock. — *adv.* Motionlessly; like a stump: used in combination: *stock-still.* [OE *stocc*]

stock·ade (sto·kād′) *n.* **1.** A line of stout posts, stakes, etc., set upright in the earth to form a fence or barrier; also, the area thus enclosed, used as a prison, etc. **2.** Any similar area. — *v.t.* **·ad·ed, ·ad·ing** To surround or fortify with a stockade. [< OF < Sp. < *estaque* stake < Gmc.]

stock·breed·er (stok′brē′dər) *n.* One who breeds and raises livestock. — **stock′breed′ing** *n.*

stock·bro·ker (stok′brō′kər) *n.* One who buys and sells stocks or securities for others. — **stock′bro′ker·age** (-ij), **stock′bro′king** *n.*

stock car An automobile, often a sedan, modified for racing.

stock company **1.** An incorporated company that issues stock. **2.** A more or less permanent dramatic company under one management, that presents a series of plays.

stock exchange **1.** A place where stocks and bonds are bought and sold. **2.** An association of stockbrokers who transact business in stocks, bonds, etc.

stock farm A farm that specializes in breeding livestock.

stock·fish (stok′fish′) *n.* Cod, haddock, or the like, cured by splitting and drying in the air, without salt.

stock·hold·er (stok′hol′dər) *n.* One who holds certificates of ownership in a company or corporation. — **stock′hold·ing** *adj. & n.*

stock·i·net (stok′i·net′) *n.* An elastic knitted fabric, machine-made and used for undergarments, stockings, etc. Also **stock′i·nette′.** [Alter. of *stockinget* < STOCKING + -ET]

stock·ing (stok′ing) *n.* **1.** A close-fitting woven or knitted covering for the foot and leg. **2.** Something resembling such a covering. — **in one's stocking feet** Wearing one's stockings or socks, but no shoes. [< STOCK, in obs. sense of "a stocking" + -ING³] — **stock′inged** (-ingd) *adj.*

stock·man (stok′mən) *n. pl.* **·men** (-mən) **1.** One who raises, owns, or has charge of livestock; a cattleman. **2.** One who works in a stockroom, warehouse, etc.

stock market **1.** A stock exchange. **2.** The business transacted in such a place: The *stock market* was active. **3.** The rise and fall of prices of stocks and bonds.

stock·pile (stok′pīl) *n.* A storage pile of materials or supplies. Also **stock pile.** — *v.t. & v.i.* **·piled, ·pil·ing** To accumulate a supply or stockpile (of).

stock raising Breeding and raising of livestock.

stock·room (stok′rōōm′) *n.* A room where reserve stocks of goods are stored. Also **stock room.**

stock-still (stok′stil′) *adj.* Still as a post; motionless.

stock·y (stok′ē) *adj.* **stock·i·er, stock·i·est** Solidly built, thickset, and usu. short. — **stock′i·ly** *adv.* — **stock′i·ness** *n.*

stock·yard (stok′yärd′) *n.* A large yard where cattle, sheep, pigs, etc., are kept ready for shipping or slaughter.

stodg·y (stoj′ē) *adj.* **stodg·i·er, stodg·i·est** **1.** Dull, stupid, and commonplace. **2.** Crammed full; distended; bulky. **3.** Indigestible and heavy: said of food. **4.** Thickset; stocky. — **stodg′i·ly** *adv.* — **stodg′i·ness** *n.*

sto·gy (stō′gē) *n. pl.* **·gies 1.** A long, slender, inexpensive cigar. **2.** A stout, heavy boot or shoe. Also **sto′gey, sto′gie.** [Earlier *stoga* < (CONE)STOGA (WAGON), because their drivers wore heavy boots and smoked coarse cigars]

sto·ic (stō′ik) *n.* A person apparently unaffected by pleasure or pain. — *adj.* Indifferent to pleasure or pain; impassive. Also **sto′i·cal.** — **sto′i·cal·ly** *adv.* — **sto′i·cal·ness** *n.*

Sto·ic (stō′ik) *n.* A member of a school of Greek philosophy founded by Zeno about 308 B.C., holding that wisdom lies in being superior to passion, joy, grief, etc. and in unperturbed submission to the divine will. — *adj.* Of the Stoics or Stoicism. [< L < Gk. < *Stoa (Poikilē)* (Painted) Porch, the colonnade at Athens where Zeno taught]

sto·i·cism (stō′ə·siz′əm) *n.* Indifference to pleasure or pain; stoicalness.

Sto·i·cism (stō′ə·siz′əm) *n.* The doctrines of the Stoics.

stoke (stōk) *v.t. & v.i.* **stoked, stok·ing** To supply (a furnace) with fuel; stir up or tend (a fire or furnace). [Back formation < STOKER]

stoke·hold (stōk′hōld′) *n. Naut.* The furnace room of a steamship.

stoke·hole (stōk′hōl′) *n.* **1.** The space about the mouth of a furnace or the mouth itself. **2.** A stokehold.

stok·er (stō′kər) *n.* **1.** One who supplies fuel to a furnace; a fireman on a locomotive, etc. **2.** A device for feeding coal to a furnace. [< Du. < *stoken* to stir a fire]

stole¹ (stōl) *n.* **1.** *Eccl.* A long, narrow band of decorated cloth worn about the shoulders by officiating clergymen. **2.** A long scarf worn about the shoulders by women. [OE < L < Gk. *stolē* garment] — **stoled** (stōld) *adj.*

stole² (stōl) Past tense of STEAL.

sto·len (stō′lən) Past participle of STEAL.

stol·id (stol′id) *adj.* Having or showing little feeling or perception; impassive; dull. [< L *stolidus* dull] — **sto·lid·i·ty** (stə·lid′ə·tē), **stol′id·ness** *n.* — **stol′id·ly** *adv.*

sto·ma (stō′mə) *n. pl.* **·ma·ta** (stō′mə·tə, stom′ə·tə) **1.** *Bot.* A minute orifice or pore in the epidermis of plants, esp. of leaves and stems. **2.** *Biol.* An aperture in the walls of blood vessels or in serous membranes. **b** A mouthlike opening in nematodes. [< NL < Gk. *stoma* mouth]

-stoma See -STOME.

stom·ach (stum′ək) *n.* **1.** The pouchlike, highly vascular enlargement of the alimentary canal, situated in man and vertebrates between the esophagus and the small intestine, and serving as one of the principal organs of digestion. ◆ Collateral adjective: *gastric.* **2.** Any digestive cavity. **3.** Loosely, the abdomen or belly. **4.** Desire for food; appetite. **5.** Any desire or inclination. — *v.t.* **1.** To put up with; endure. **2.** To take into and retain in the stomach; digest. [< OF < L < Gk. < *stoma* mouth]

stom·ach·er (stum′ək·ər) *n.* A former ornamental article of dress, worn over the breast and stomach.

sto·mach·ic (stō·mak′ik) *adj.* **1.** Pertaining to the stomach. **2.** Beneficial to or stimulating the activity of the stomach. Also **stom·ach·al** (stum′ək·əl), **sto·mach′i·cal.** — *n.* Any medicine strengthening or stimulating the stomach.

sto·ma·ta (stŏ′mə·tə, stom′ə·tə) Plural of STOMA.

stomato- *combining form* Of, like, or pertaining to the mouth. Also, before vowels, **stomat-**. [< Gk. *stoma, stomatos* mouth]

sto·ma·tous (stŏ′mə·təs, stom′ə-) *adj.* Having a stoma or stomata.

-stome *combining form* Mouth; mouthlike opening: *peristome.* Also spelled *-stoma*. [< Gk. *stoma* mouth]

-stomous *combining form* Having a (specified kind of) mouth: *microstomous*. Also **-stomatous**. [< Gk. *stoma, stomatos* mouth]

stomp (stomp) *v.t. & v.i.* **1.** To tread heavily or violently (upon); press down. **2.** *Dial.* To stamp. **3.** *n.* A dance involving a heavy and lively step. [Var. of STAMP]

-stomy *combining form Surg.* An operation to form an artificial opening for or into (a specified organ or part): *colostomy.* [< Gk. *stoma* mouth]

stone (stōn) *n.* **1.** The hard, nonmetallic mineral or earthy matter of which rock is composed. **2.** A small piece of rock, as a pebble. **3.** Rock, or a piece of rock that has been hewn or shaped. **4.** A precious stone; gem. **5.** Anything resembling a stone in shape or hardness: a *hailstone*. **6.** A gravestone. **7.** A grindstone or millstone. **8.** *Pathol.* A stony concretion in the bladder, or a disease characterized by such concretions. **9.** *Bot.* The hard covering of the kernel in a fruit. **10.** (*pl.* **stone**) In England, 14 pounds avoirdupois. — *adj.* **1.** Made of stone: a *stone* ax. **2.** Made of coarse hard earthenware: a *stone* bottle. — *v.t.* **stoned, ston·ing 1.** To hurl stones at; pelt or kill with stones. **2.** To remove the stones or pits from. **3.** To furnish or line, as a well, with stone. [OE *stān*] — **ston′er** *n.*

Stone Age The earliest known period in human culture when stone implements and weapons were used.

stone-blind (stōn′blīnd′) *adj.* Totally blind.

stone-broke (stōn′brōk′) *adj. Informal* Without any money; having no funds. Also **ston′y-broke′** (stō′nē-).

stone·crop (stōn′krop′) *n.* Any of various plants having small fleshy leaves and yellow flowers, often grown in rock gardens.

stone·cut·ter (stōn′kut′ər) *n.* One who or that which cuts stone; especially, a machine for facing stone.

stone-deaf (stōn′def′) *adj.* Completely deaf.

Stone·henge (stōn′henj) A prehistoric structure on Salisbury Plain, England, consisting primarily of great circles of huge, dressed stones.

stone·ma·son (stōn′mā′sən) *n.* One who prepares and lays stones in building. — **stone′ma′son·ry** (-rē) *n.*

STONEHENGE

stone's throw A short distance.

stone·ware (stōn′wâr′) *n.* A variety of very hard pottery, made from siliceous clay or clay mixed with flint or sand.

stone·work (stōn′wûrk′) *n.* **1.** Work concerned with cutting or setting stone; also, something made of stone. **2.** *pl.* A place where stone is prepared for masonry. — **stone′work′er** *n.*

ston·y (stō′nē) *adj.* **ston·i·er, ston·i·est 1.** Abounding in stone. **2.** Made or consisting of stone. **3.** Hard as stone. **4.** Unfeeling or inflexible. **5.** Converting into stone; petrifying. — **ston′i·ly** *adv.* — **ston′i·ness** *n.*

stood (stood) Past tense and past participle of STAND.

stooge (stōōj) *Informal n.* **1.** An actor placed in the audience to heckle a comedian on the stage. **2.** An actor who feeds lines to the principal comedian, acts as a foil for his jokes. **3.** Anyone who acts as or is the tool or dupe of another. — *v.i.* **stooged, stoog·ing** To act as a stooge: usually with *for*. [Origin unknown]

stool (stōōl) *n.* **1.** A backless and armless seat, high or low, for one person. **2.** A low bench or support for the feet or for the knees in kneeling. **3.** A seat used in defecating; a privy. **4.** The matter evacuated from the bowels at each movement. **5.** *Bot.* **a** A stump or root from which suckers or sprouts shoot up. **b** The shoots from such a root or stump. **6.** A decoy. — *v.i.* **1.** To send up shoots or suckers. **2.** To decoy wild fowl with a stool. **3.** To void feces. **4.** *U.S. Slang* To be a stool pigeon. [OE *stōl*]

stool pigeon 1. A living or artificial pigeon attached to a perch to decoy others. **2.** *U.S. Slang* An informer or spy, esp. for the police.

stoop[1] (stōōp) *v.i.* **1.** To bend or lean the body forward and down; bow; crouch. **2.** To stand or walk with the upper part of the body habitually bent forward; slouch. **3.** To bend; lean; sink, as a tree. **4.** To lower or degrade oneself: to *stoop* to cheating. **5.** To swoop, as a hawk on prey. — *v.t.* **6.** To bend (one's head, shoulders, etc.) forward. — *n.* **1.** An act of stooping; a slouch. **2.** A habitual forward inclination of the head and shoulders. **3.** A decline from dignity or superiority. **4.** A swoop. [OE *stūpian*]

stoop[2] (stōōp) *n. U.S.* **1.** Originally, a platform at the door of a house approached by steps and having seats. **2.** A small porch at the entrance to a house. [< Du. *stoep*]

stoop[3] (stōōp) See STOUP.

stop (stop) *v.* **stopped** or (*Chiefly Poetic*) **stopt, stop·ping** *v.t.* **1.** To bring (something in motion) to a halt; arrest the progress of. **2.** To prevent the doing or completion of. **3.** To prevent (a person) from doing something; restrain. **4.** To keep back, withhold, or cut off, as wages or supplies. **5.** To cease doing; desist from. **6.** To intercept in transit, as a letter. **7.** To block up, obstruct, or clog (a passage, road, etc.): often with *up*. **8.** To cover over, or otherwise close, as a hole, cavity, etc. **9.** To close (a bottle, barrel, etc.) with a cork, plug, or other stopper. **10.** To stanch (a wound, etc.). **11.** To defeat; also, to kill. **12.** *Music* To press down (a string) on the finger board, or to close (a hole) in order to vary the pitch produced by an instrument; finger. **13.** To punctuate. **14.** In boxing, etc., to parry. — *v.i.* **15.** To come to a halt; cease progress or motion. **16.** To cease doing something; pause or desist. **17.** To come to an end. — **to stop off** *U.S. Informal* To cease traveling temporarily before reaching one's destination. — **to stop over** *U.S. Informal* **1.** To stay at a place temporarily. **2.** To interrupt a journey; make a stopover. — *n.* **1.** The act of stopping, or the state of being stopped; a halt; pause; end. **2.** That which stops or limits the range or time of a movement: a camera *stop*. **3.** An obstruction or obstacle. **4.** *Music* **a** The stopping of a string or hole of an instrument. **b** In an organ or harpsichord, a knob controlling a register of pipes or strings; also the register so controlled. **5.** *Brit.* A punctuation mark, as a period. **6.** In telegrams and cablegrams, the word *stop* spelled out to indicate a punctuation mark. **7.** In joinery, a block, pin, or the like to check sliding motion, as of a drawer. **8.** *Phonet.* **a** Complete blockage of the breath stream (implosion), as with the lips or tongue, followed by a sudden release (plosion). **b** A consonant so produced, as *p, b, t, d, k,* and *g.* [OE *-stoppian,* as in *forstoppian* to stop up]

stop·cock (stop′kok′) *n.* A faucet or short pipe having a valve for stopping or regulating the passage of fluids.

stope (stōp) *Mining n.* An excavation from which the ore is removed in a series of steps. — *v.t. & v.i.* **stoped, stop·ing** To excavate in stopes. [Appar. akin to STEP]

stop·gap (stop′gap′) *n.* **1.** That which stops a gap. **2.** Something improvised to fill a need temporarily; an expedient. — *adj.* That serves as a stopgap.

stop·light (stop′līt) *n.* **1.** The red light on a traffic light. **2.** A red light on the rear of a motor vehicle that shines upon application of the brakes.

stop order An order to an agent or broker to buy or sell a stock at the market only when it reaches a specified price.

stop·o·ver (stop′ō′vər) *n.* **1.** The act of staying in a place for a brief period, esp. while traveling. **2.** The act of interrupting a journey without paying additional fare, as by taking a later train. Also **stop′-off′** (-ôf′, -of′).

stop·page (stop′ij) *n.* **1.** The act of stopping, or the state of being stopped. **2.** An obstruction of some kind; block.

stop payment An order to a bank to refuse payment on a certain check.

stop·per (stop′ər) *n.* **1.** Something that stops up or closes, as a plug or cork. **2.** One who or that which stops or checks a movement, action, etc. — *v.t.* To close with a stopper.

stop·ple (stop′əl) *n.* A stopper, plug, cork, or bung. — *v.t.* **·pled, ·pling** To close with or as with a stopple. [ME *stoppel,* prob. < *stoppen* to stop]

stopt (stopt) Alternative, chiefly poetic, past tense and past participle of STOP.

stop·watch (stop′woch′) *n.* A watch that has a hand indicating fractions of a second and that may be instantaneously started or stopped, used for timing races, etc.

stor·age (stôr′ij, stō′rij) *n.* **1.** The depositing of articles in a warehouse for sakekeeping. **2.** Space for storing goods. **3.** A charge for storing. **4.** The charging of a storage battery.

storage battery One or more secondary cells arranged as a single source of direct current and capable of being recharged on reversal of the current.

storage cell *Electr.* A secondary cell.

store (stôr, stōr) *v.t.* **stored, stor·ing 1.** To put away for future use; accumulate. **2.** To furnish or supply; provide. **3.** To place in a warehouse or other place of deposit for safekeeping. — *n.* **1.** *U.S.* A place where merchandise of any kind is kept for sale. **2.** That which is stored or laid up against future need. **3.** *pl.* Supplies, as of arms, or clothing. **4.** A place where commodities are stored; warehouse. — **in store** Set apart for the future; forthcoming; impending. — **to set store by** To value or esteem; regard. [< OF < L *instaurare* to restore, erect]

store·house (stôr′hous′, stōr′-) *n.* **1.** A building in which goods are stored; warehouse. **2.** A large or inexhaustible fund; reservoir: a *storehouse* of ideas.

store·keep·er (stôr′kē′pər, stōr′-) *n.* **1.** A person who keeps a retail store or shop; shopkeeper. **2.** One who has charge of stores or supplies.

store·room (stôr′rōōm′, -rŏŏm′, stōr′-) *n.* A room in which things are stored, as supplies.

sto·rey (stôr′ē, stō′rē) See STORY².

sto·ried¹ (stôr′ēd, stō′rēd) *adj.* Having or consisting of stories, as a building: usu. in compounds: a six-*storied* house. Also **sto′reyed.**

sto·ried² (stôr′ēd, stō′rēd) *adj.* **1.** Having a notable history. **2.** Related in a story. **3.** Ornamented with designs representing scenes from history or story.

stork (stôrk) *n.* Any of a family of large wading birds with long necks and long legs. [OE *storc*]

storm (stôrm) *n.* **1.** A disturbance of the atmosphere, generally a great whirling motion of the air, accompanied by rain, snow, etc. **2.** *Meteorol.* In the Beaufort scale, a wind force of the 11th degree. **3.** A furious flight or shower of objects, esp. of missiles. **4.** A violent outburst, as of passion or excitement: a *storm* of applause. **5.** *Mil.* A violent and rapid assault on a fortified place. **6.** A violent commotion, as in politics, society, or domestic life. — *v.i.* **1.** To blow with violence; rain, snow, hail, etc., heavily: used impersonally: It *stormed* all day. **2.** To be very angry; rage. **3.** To move or rush with violence or rage. — *v.t.* **4.** *Mil.* To take or try to take by storm. [OE]

storm·bound (stôrm′bound′) *adj.* Delayed, confined, or cut off from communications because of a storm.

storm center 1. *Meteorol.* The center or area of lowest pressure and comparative calm in a cyclonic storm. **2.** The central point of a heated argument; the focus of any trouble.

storm door A strong outer door for added protection during storms and inclement weather.

storm petrel Any of certain small petrels of the North Atlantic, thought to portend storm; Mother Carey's chicken: also called *stormy petrel.*

storm trooper In Germany, a member of the Nazi party militia unit, the *Sturmabteilung:* also called *Brown Shirt.*

storm warning A signal, as a flag or light, used to warn mariners of coming storm. Also **storm signal.**

storm window An extra window outside the ordinary one as a protection against storms or for greater insulation.

storm·y (stôr′mē) *adj.* **storm·i·er, storm·i·est 1.** Characterized by or subject to storms; tempestuous. **2.** Characterized by violent emotions or actions: a *stormy* life. — **storm′i·ly** *adv.* — **storm′i·ness** *n.*

stormy petrel 1. The storm petrel. **2.** One who portends trouble or discord, as by rebelling against accepted ideas, practices, etc.

sto·ry¹ (stôr′ē, stō′rē) *n. pl.* **·ries 1.** A narrative or recital of an event or series of events, whether real or fictitious. **2.** A narrative, usu. of fictitious events, intended to entertain a reader or hearer. **3.** A short story. **4.** A report. **5.** A news article in a newspaper or magazine; also, the material for such an article. **6.** An anecdote. **7.** *Informal* A lie. **8.** The series of events in a novel, play, etc. — **Syn.** See LIE². — *v.t.* **·ried, ·ry·ing 1.** To relate as a story. **2.** To adorn with designs representing scenes from history, legend, etc. [< OF < L *historia* an account]

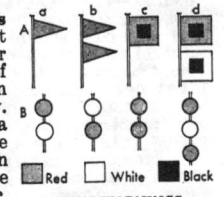

STORM WARNINGS

A Daylight. B Night. a Small-craft warning. b Gale. c Whole gale. d Hurricane.

Red □ White ■ Black

sto·ry² (stôr′ē, stō′rē) *n. pl.* **·ries 1.** A horizontal division in a building comprising the space between two successive floors. **2.** Habitable rooms on the same level. Also, *Chiefly Brit.,* **storey.** [Special use of STORY¹; ? from earlier sense of "a tier of painted windows or sculptures that narrated an event"]

story line The rough plot of a film, play, novel, etc.

sto·ry·tell·er (stôr′ē·tel′ər, stō′rē-) *n.* **1.** One who relates stories. **2.** *Informal* A liar. — **sto′ry·tell′ing** *n. & adj.*

stoup (stōōp) *n.* **1.** *Eccl.* A basin for holy water at the entrance of a church. **2.** *Scot.* A pail, cup, etc.; also, its contents. Also spelled **stoop, stowp.** [< ON *staup* bucket]

stout (stout) *adj.* **1.** Strong or firm of structure or material; sound; tough. **2.** Determined; resolute. **3.** Fat. **4.** Substantial; solid: *stout* fare. **5.** Having muscular strength; robust. **6.** Proud; stubborn. — *n.* **1.** A stout person. **2.** A very dark porter or ale. [< OF *estout* bold, strong] — **stout′ly** *adv.* — **stout′ness** *n.*

stout·heart·ed (stout′här′tid) *adj.* Brave; courageous. — **stout′heart′ed·ly** *adv.* — **stout′heart′ed·ness** *n.*

stove¹ (stōv) *n.* **1.** An apparatus, usu. of metal, in which gas, oil, electricity, etc., is consumed for heating or cooking. **2.** A pottery kiln. [OE *stofa* heated room]

stove² (stōv) Alternative past tense and past participle of STAVE.

stove·pipe (stōv′pīp′) *n.* **1.** A pipe, usu. of thin sheet iron, for conducting the smoke and gases of combustion from a stove to a chimney flue. **2.** *U.S. Informal* A tall silk hat: also **stovepipe hat.**

stow (stō) *v.t.* **1.** To place or arrange compactly; pack. **2.** To fill by packing. **3.** To have room for; hold: said of a room, receptacle, etc. **4.** *Slang* To stop; cease. — **to stow away 1.** To put in a place of safekeeping, hiding, etc. **2.** To be a stowaway. [ME < OE *stōw* place]

stow·age (stō′ij) *n.* **1.** The act or manner of stowing, or the state of being stowed. **2.** Space for stowing goods; also, the goods stowed. **3.** Charge for stowing goods.

stow·a·way (stō′ə·wā′) *n.* One who conceals himself, as on a vessel, to obtain free passage or evade officials.

stowp (stōōp) See STOUP.

stra·bis·mus (strə·biz′məs) *n. Pathol.* A condition in which the eyes cannot be simultaneously focused on the same spot. When one or both eyes turn inward, the patient is *crosseyed,* when outward, *walleyed.* [< NL < Gk. *strabizein* to squint] — **stra·bis′mal, stra·bis′mic** or **·mi·cal** *adj.*

strad·dle (strad′l) *v.* **·dled, ·dling** *v.i.* **1.** To stand, walk, or sit with the legs spread apart. **2.** To stand wide apart: said of the legs. **3.** *Informal* To appear to favor both sides of an issue. — *v.t.* **4.** To stand, walk, or sit with the legs on either side of. **5.** To spread (the legs) wide apart. **6.** *Informal* To appear to favor both sides of (an issue). **7.** *Mil.* To fire shots both beyond and in front of (a target) so as to determine the range — *n.* **1.** The act of straddling. **2.** The space between the feet or legs of one who straddles. **3.** A noncommittal or vacillating position on any issue. **4.** In the securities trade, a transaction in which the holder obtains the option of either delivering or buying a certain amount of stock or other commodity at a fixed price within a stipulated period. [OE *strīdan* to stride] — **strad′dler** *n.* — **strad′dling·ly** *adv.*

Strad·i·var·i·us (strad′i·vâr′ē·əs) *n.* One of the violins produced by **Antonio Stra·di·va·ri** (strä′dē·vä·rē), 1644?–1737. Italian violinmaker noted for the fine quality of his instruments.

strafe (strāf, sträf) *v.t.* **strafed, strafing 1.** To attack (troops, emplacements, etc.) with machine-gun fire from low-flying airplanes. **2.** To bombard or shell heavily. **3.** *Slang* To punish. — *n.* A heavy bombardment. [< G *strafen* to punish] — **straf′er** *n.*

strag·gle (strag′əl) *v.i.* **·gled, ·gling 1.** To stray from or lag behind the main body. **2.** To wander aimlessly about. **3.** To occur at irregular intervals. [! Freq. of obs. *strake* to move, go about] — **strag′gler** *n.*

strag·gly (strag′lē) *adj.* **·gli·er, ·gli·est** Scattered or spread out irregularly.

straight (strāt) *adj.* **1.** Extending uniformly in one direction without curve or bend. **2.** Free from kinks; not curly. **3.** Not stooped or inclined; erect, as in posture. **4.** Not deviating from truth, fairness, or honesty. **5.** Clear; frank; direct. **6.** Free from obstruction; uninterrupted; unbroken. **7.** Correctly kept, ordered, or arranged: Are the facts *straight* in your mind? **8.** Sold without discount for number or quantity taken. **9.** *Informal* Strictly adhering to a particular party or policy: a *straight* Democrat. **10.** In poker, consisting of five cards forming a sequence: a *straight* flush. **11.** Having nothing added; undiluted. — *n.* **1.** A straight part or piece. **2.** The part of a racecourse between the winning post and the last turn. **3.** In poker, a numerical sequence of five cards not of the same suit, or a hand containing this. **4.** A straight line. — *adv.* **1.** In a straight line or a direct course. **2.** Closely in line; correspondingly. **3.** At once; straightway. — **to go straight** To reform after a criminal career. [ME < OE *streccan* to stretch] — **straight′ly** *adv.* — **straight′ness** *n.*

straight angle *Geom.* An angle of 180°.

straight·a·way (strāt′ə·wā′) *adj.* Having no curve or turn. — *n.* A straight course or track. — *adv.* At once.

straight·edge (strāt′ej′) *n.* A bar of wood or metal having one edge true to a straight line, used for ruling, etc.

straight·en (strāt′n) *v.t.* **1.** To make straight. **2.** To lay out (a corpse). — *v.i.* **3.** To become straight. — **to straighten out** To restore order to; set right; rectify. — **to straighten up 1.** To make neat; tidy. **2.** To stand in erect posture. — **straight′en·er** *n.*

straight face A face that betrays no emotion, esp. amusement. — **straight-faced** (strāt′fāst′) *adj.*

straight flush See under FLUSH³.

straight·for·ward (strāt′fôr′wərd) *adj.* **1.** Proceeding in a straight course. **2.** Honest; frank. — *adv.* In a straight course or direct manner: also **straight′for′wards.** — **straight′for′ward·ly** *adv.* — **straight′for′ward·ness** *n.*

straight man *U.S. Informal* An entertainer who acts as a foil for a comedian.

straight-out (strāt′out′) *adj. Informal* **1.** Showing the true sentiments or feelings; unreserved. **2.** Real; genuine. **3.** Uncompromising; all-out: a *straight-out* Republican.

straight ticket 1. A political party ballot or ticket that presents the regular party candidates without addition or change. **2.** A ballot cast for all the candidates of one party.

straight·way (strāt′wā′) *adv.* Immediately; straightaway.

strain[1] (strān) *v.t.* **1.** To exert to the utmost. **2.** To injure by overexertion; sprain. **3.** To pull or draw tight; stretch. **4.** To stretch beyond the true intent, proper limit, etc.: to *strain* a point. **5.** To pass through a filtering agent or strainer. **6.** To remove by filtration. **7.** To alter or deform in structure or shape as a result of pressure or stress. **8.** To embrace tightly; hug. — *v.i.* **9.** To make violent efforts; strive. **10.** To be or become wrenched or twisted. **11.** To filter, trickle, or percolate. — **to strain at 1.** To push or pull with violent efforts. **2.** To strive for. **3.** To scruple or balk at accepting. — *n.* **1.** An act of straining, or the state of being strained. **2.** The injury resulting from excessive tension or effort. **3.** Severe mental or emotional tension. [< OF < L *stringere* to bind tight]

strain[2] (strān) *n.* **1.** Line of descent, or the individuals, collectively, in that line; race; stock. **2.** Inborn or hereditary tendency; trace; element. **3.** *Biol.* A special line of animals or plants bred from a certain species or variety. **4.** *Often pl.* A passage of music or other sound when heard. **5.** Prevailing tone, style, or manner; mood. [? Var. of ME *strene*, OE *strēon* offspring]

strain·er (strā′nər) *n.* A utensil or device, containing meshes or porous parts, through which liquids are strained.

strait (strāt) *n.* **1.** *Often pl.* A narrow passage of water connecting two larger bodies of water. **2.** *Often pl.* A position of perplexity or distress. — *adj.* **1.** *Archaic* Narrow. **2.** *Archaic* Righteous; strict. **3.** Difficult. [< OF < L *stringere* to bind tight] — **strait′ly** *adv.* — **strait′ness** *n.*

strait·en (strāt′n) *v.t.* **1.** To make strait or narrow. **2.** To embarrass, as in finances; also, to distress.

strait·ened (strāt′nd) *adj.* **1.** Contracted; narrowed. **2.** Suffering privation or hardship, as from lack of money.

strait jacket A tight jacket of strong canvas, for confining the arms of violent patients.

strait-laced (strāt′lāst′) *adj.* Strict, esp. in morals.

strake (strāk) *n. Naut.* A breadth of planking or line of plating on a vessel's hull from stem to stern: also called *streak.* [Appar. akin to STRETCH; infl. in meaning by STREAK]

strand[1] (strand) *n.* A shore or beach, esp. that portion between high and low tides — *v.t. & v.i.* **1.** To drive or run aground. **2.** To leave or be left in straits or difficulties: usu. in the passive. [OE *strand*]

strand[2] (strand) *n.* **1.** One of the principal twists or members of a rope. **2.** A fiber, hair, or the like. **3.** Anything plaited or twisted. **4.** A string of beads or pearls — *v.t.* **1.** To break a strand of (a rope). **2.** To make by twisting strands. [? < OF *estran* < Gmc.]

strange (strānj) *adj.* **strang·er, strang·est 1.** Previously unknown, unseen, or unheard of; unfamiliar. **2.** Not according to the ordinary way; unaccountable; remarkable. **3.** Of a different class, character, or kind. **4.** Foreign; alien. **5.** Distant in manner; reserved; shy. **6.** Inexperienced; unaccustomed. — *adv.* In a strange manner. [< OF < L *extraneus* foreign] — **strange′ly** *adv.* — **strange′ness** *n.*

stran·ger (strān′jər) *n.* **1.** One who is not an acquaintance. **2.** An unfamiliar visitor; guest. **3.** A foreigner. **4.** One unversed in or unfamiliar with something specified: with *to.*

stran·gle (strang′gəl) *v.* **·gled, ·gling** *v.t.* **1.** To choke to death; throttle; suffocate. **2.** To repress; suppress. **3.** To inhibit the action or development of — *v.i.* **4.** To suffer or die from strangulation. [< F < L < Gk. *strangalē* halter < *strangos* twisted] — **stran′gler** *n.*

strangle hold 1. In wrestling, a usu. illegal hold that chokes one's opponent. **2.** Any influence or power that chokes freedom or progress.

stran·gu·late (strang′gyə·lāt) *v.t.* **·lat·ed, ·lat·ing 1.** To strangle. **2.** *Pathol.* To compress, contract, or obstruct, esp. so as to cut off flow of a fluid. — *adj.* Strangulated. [See STRANGLE.] — **stran′gu·la′tion** *n.*

strap (strap) *n.* **1.** A long, narrow, and flexible strip of leather, etc., usu. having a buckle or other fastener, for binding about objects. **2.** A razor strop. **3.** Something resembling a strap and used as a fastening or support. **4.** A thin metal band. — *v.t.* **strapped, strap·ping 1.** To fasten or bind with a strap. **2.** To beat with a strap. **3.** To embarrass financially. **4.** To sharpen or strop. [Var. of STROP] — **strap′less** *adj.* — **strap′per** *n.*

strap·hang·er (strap′hang′ər) *n.* A standee on a bus, etc., esp. one who holds on to an overhead strap.

strap·ping (strap′ing) *adj. Informal* Large and robust.

stra·ta (strā′tə, strat′ə) Alternative plural of STRATUM.

strat·a·gem (strat′ə·jəm) *n.* **1.** A maneuver designed to deceive or outwit an enemy in war. **2.** A device for obtaining advantage; trick. [< F < L < Gk. < *stratos* army + *agein* to lead]

stra·te·gic (strə·tē′jik) *adj.* **1.** Of or pertaining to strategy. **2.** Characterized by, used in, or having relation to strategy. Also **stra·te′gi·cal, strat·e·get·ic** (strat′ə·jet′ik) or **·i·cal. — stra·te′gi·cal·ly, strat′e·get′i·cal·ly** *adv.*

stra·te·gics (strə·tē′jiks) *n.pl. (construed as sing.)* The art or science of strategy; generalship.

strat·e·gist (strat′ə·jist) *n.* One versed in strategy.

strat·e·gy (strat′ə·jē) *n.* *pl.* **·ties 1.** The science and art of conducting a military campaign on a broad scale: distinguished from *tactics.* **2.** The use of stratagem or artifice, as in business or politics. **3.** A plan or technique for achieving some end. [See STRATAGEM.]

strat·i·fy (strat′ə·fī) *v.* **·fied, ·fy·ing** *v.t.* **1.** To form or arrange in strata. **2.** To preserve (seeds) by spreading in alternating layers of earth and sand. — *v.i.* **3.** To form in strata. **4.** *Geol.* To be formed in strata, as rocks. **5.** *Sociol.* To form social groups at different levels as determined by class, caste, or status. [< F < Med.L < L *stratum* layer + *facere* to make] — **strat·i·fi·ca′tion** *n.*

stra·to·cu·mu·lus (strā′tō·kyoo′myə·ləs) *n.* *pl.* **·li (-lī)** *Meteorol.* Large globular masses of cloud (Symbol Sc), gray to black in color, disposed in waves, groups, or bands, and often covering the whole sky: also called *cumulostratus.* [< *strato-* (< STRATUS) + CUMULUS]

strat·o·pause (strat′ə·pôz) *n. Meteorol.* The zone of transition between the stratosphere and the mesosphere.

strat·o·sphere (strat′ə·sfir, strā′tə-) *n. Meteorol.* That portion of the atmosphere beginning at a height of about seven miles and characterized by a more or less uniform temperature. — **strat′o·spher′ic** (-sfir′ik, -sfer′-) or **·i·cal** *adj.*

stra·tum (strā′təm, strat′əm) *n.* *pl.* **·ta (-tə)** or **·tums 1.** A natural or artificial layer, bed, or thickness. **2.** *Geol.* A more or less homogeneous layer of rock, serving to identify a geological group, system or series. **3.** Something corresponding to a layer, bed, or grade: a low *stratum* of society. [< L]

stra·tus (strā′təs, strat′əs) *n.* *pl.* **·ti (-tī)** *Meteorol.* A cloud of foglike appearance, low-lying and arranged in a uniform layer. [< L, orig. pp. of *sternere* to spread]

straw (strô) *n.* **1.** A slender tube of paper, glass, etc., used to suck up a beverage. **2.** Stems or stalks of grain, collectively, after the grain has been thrashed out. **3.** A dry or ripened stalk. **4.** A mere trifle. — **the last straw** The final test of patience or endurance: from the phrase **the straw that broke the camel's back.** — **to clutch** (grasp, catch, etc.) **at a straw** To try in desperation any solution or expedient. — *adj.* **1.** Like or of straw. **2.** Of no value; worthless; sham. **3.** Made of straw. **4.** Yellowish. [OE *strēaw*]

straw·ber·ry (strô′ber′ē, -bər·ē) *n.* *pl.* **·ries 1.** The edible fruit of a stemless perennial herb of the rose family. **2.** The plant bearing this fruit. [ME *strauberi*]

strawberry blond A person having reddish blond hair.

straw color A pale yellow color, as of clean ripe straw. — **straw-col·ored** (strô′kul′ərd) *adj.*

straw vote An unofficial vote to test the strength of opposing candidates, determine group opinion, etc.

straw·y (strô′ē) *adj.* **straw·i·er, straw·i·est 1.** Of or like straw. **2.** Covered or thatched with straw.

stray (strā) *v.i.* **1.** To wander from the proper course, an area, group, etc.; straggle; roam. **2.** To wander about; rove. **3.** To fail to concentrate; digress. **4.** To deviate from right or goodness; go astray. — *adj.* **1.** Having strayed; straying. **2.** Irregular; occasional; casual; unrelated. — *n.* **1.** A domestic animal that has strayed. **2.** A person who is lost or wanders aimlessly. **3.** The act of straying or wandering. [< OF *estraier* to wander about, ult. < L *extra vagare* to wander outside] — **stray′er** *n.*

streak (strēk) *n.* **1.** A long, narrow, somewhat irregularly shaped mark, line, or stripe: a *streak* of lightning. **2.** A vein or trace; dash: a *streak* of meanness; also, a transient mood; whim. **3.** A period of time; a spell. **4.** A strake. **5.** A layer or strip: meat with a *streak* of fat. — *v.t.* **1.** To mark with a streak; form streaks in or on; stripe. — *v.i.* **2.** To form a streak or streaks. **3.** To move at great speed. [OE *strica*] — **streaked** (strēkt) *adj.*

streak·y (strē′kē) *adj.* **streak·i·er, streak·i·est 1.** Marked with or occurring in streaks. **2.** Of variable quality or character. — **streak′i·ly** *adv.* — **streak′i·ness** *n.*

stream (strēm) *n.* **1.** A current or flow of water or other fluid. **2.** Anything continuously flowing, moving, or passing, as people. **3.** A trend; drift. **4.** Anything issuing out or flowing from a source. — *v.i.* **1.** To pour forth or issue in a stream. **2.** To pour forth a stream: eyes *streaming* with tears. **3.** To move in continuous succession. **4.** To float with a waving movement, as a flag. **5.** To move with a trail of light, as a meteor. — *v.t.* **6.** To emit or exude. **7.** To cause (a flag, etc.) to stretch forth; display. [OE *strēam*] — **stream′y** *adj.*

stream·er (strē′mər) *n.* **1.** An object that streams forth, or hangs extended. **2.** A long, narrow flag or standard. **3.** A shaft of light, such as shoots up from the horizon. **4.** A newspaper headline that runs across the whole page.

stream·let (strĕm′lit) *n.* A small stream; rivulet.

stream·line (strĕm′lĭn′) *n.* **1.** *Physics* **a** The course of a fluid in which every particle maintains an identical speed and direction of flow; esp., a course free of turbulence or eddies. **b** The path traversed by one particle in such a course. **2.** Any shape or contour designed to offer minimum resistance to fluid flow. — *adj.* Designating an uninterrupted flow or drift. — *v.t.* **·lined, ·lin·ing 1.** To design with a streamlined shape. **2.** To make more simple, efficient, or up to date. — **stream′lined′** *adj.*

stream of consciousness *Psychol.* The series of individual conscious states moving continuously on in time as though in a stream.

street (strēt) *n.* A public way in a city or town, with buildings on one or both sides; also, the roadway for vehicles, between sidewalks. [OE *strǣt* < LL *strata* (*via*) paved (road)]

street·car (strēt′kär′) *n.* A public passenger car of an electric railway that runs on tracks set into the streets: also called *trolley, trolley car, Brit.,* *tramcar.*

street·walk·er (strēt′wô′kər) *n.* A prostitute who solicits in the streets. — **street′walk′ing** *n.* & *adj.*

strength (strengkth, strength) *n.* **1.** Muscular power; vigor. **2.** Durability; toughness. **3.** Power in general, or a source of power. **4.** Binding force or validity, as of a law. **5.** Vigor or force of intellect, moral power, style, etc. **6.** Available numerical force in a military unit or other organization. **7.** Degree of intensity; vehemence: *strength* of passion. **8.** The degree of intensity or concentration, as of a color, odor, etc. **9.** Potency, as of a drug, chemical, or liquor. — **on the strength of** Based on or in reliance or dependence on. [OE *strengthu* < *strang* strong]

strength·en (strengk′thən, streng′-) *v.t.* **1.** To make strong. **2.** To encourage; hearten; animate. — *v.i.* **3.** To become or grow strong or stronger. — **strength′en·er** *n.*

stren·u·ous (stren′yōō-əs) *adj.* **1.** Necessitating or characterized by strong effort or exertion. **2.** Vigorously active or zealous. [< L *strenuus*] — **stren′u·ous·ly** *adv.* — **stren′u·os′i·ty** (-os′ə·tē), **stren′u·ous·ness** *n.*

strep·to·coc·cus (strep′tə·kok′əs) *n.* *pl.* **·coc·ci** (-kok′sī) Any of a genus of typically ovoid or spherical bacteria, grouped in long chains, including species causing many diseases. [< NL < Gk. *streptos* twisted + COCCUS] — **strep′to·coc′cal** (-kok′əl), **strep′to·coc′cic** (-kok′sik) *adj.*

strep·to·my·cin (strep′tō·mī′sin) *n.* A potent antibiotic isolated from a moldlike organism. [< Gk. *streptos* twisted + *mykēs* fungus]

stress (stres) *n.* **1.** Special weight, importance, or significance: to lay *stress* on the classics. **2.** In prosody, an emphasis given to a specific word or syllable to indicate the metrical pattern. **3.** *Mech.* **a** Force exerted between contiguous portions of a body or bodies and generally expressed in pounds per square inch. **b** A force or system of forces that tends to produce deformation in a body. **4.** Influence exerted forcibly; pressure; compulsion. **5.** Emotional or intellectual strain or tension. **6.** *Phonet.* The relative force with which a sound, syllable, or word is uttered. — *v.t.* **1.** To subject to mechanical stress. **2.** To put stress or emphasis on; accent, as a syllable. **3.** To put into straits or difficulties; distress. [< OF < L *strictus,* pp. of *stringere* to draw tight] — **stress′ful** *adj.* — **stress′less** *adj.*

-stress *suffix of nouns* Feminine form of -STER: *songstress.*

stretch (strech) *v.t.* **1.** To extend or draw out, as to full length or width. **2.** To extend or draw out forcibly, esp. beyond normal or proper limits. **3.** To cause to reach, as from one place to another or over an area; extend. **4.** To put forth, hold out, or extend (the hand, an object, etc.): often with *out.* **5.** To tighten. **6.** To strain or exert to the utmost: to *stretch* every nerve. **7.** To make do with: to *stretch* one's salary with economies. — *v.i.* **8.** To reach or extend over an area or from one place to another. **9.** To become extended, esp. beyond normal or proper limits. **10.** To extend one's body or limbs, esp. to relieve stiffness. **11.** To lie down and extend one's limbs to full length: usu. with *out.* — *n.* **1.** The act of stretching, or the state of being stretched. **2.** Extent or reach of that which stretches. **3.** A continuous extent of space or time. **4.** In racing, the part of the track that, being straight, permits the greatest speed. **5.** A particular direction or course. **6.** *Slang* A term of imprisonment. — *adj.* Capable of stretching or of being stretched; elastic: *stretch* pants. [OE *streccan*] — **stretch′a·ble** *adj.* — **stretch′i·ness** *n.* — **stretch′y** *adj.*

stretch·er (strech′ər) *n.* **1.** One who or that which stretches. **2.** Any device for stretching, as for loosening the fit of gloves or shoes, for drying curtains, etc. **3.** A frame, as of stretched canvas, for carrying the wounded, sick, or dead; a litter. **4.** In masonry, a brick or stone lying lengthwise of a course. **5.** A tie beam in the frame of a building.

stretch-out (strech′out′) *n.* **1.** A system of industrial op-

eration in which employees do more work without proportionate increase in pay. **2.** A slowdown practiced by employees so as to make the work last longer.

strew (strōō) *v.t.* **strewed, strewed** or **strewn, strew·ing 1.** To spread about loosely or at random; scatter; sprinkle. **2.** To cover with something scattered or sprinkled. **3.** To be scattered over (a surface). [OE *strewian*]

stri·a (strī′ə) *n.* *pl.* **stri·ae** (strī′ē) **1.** A narrow streak, stripe, or band of distinctive color, structure, or texture, often parallel with others. **2.** *Geol.* A small groove, channel, or ridge on a rock surface, due to the action of glacier ice. [< L, groove]

stri·ate (strī′āt) *adj.* **1.** Having fine linear markings; striped or grooved. **2.** Constituting a stria or striae. Also **stri′at·ed.** — *v.t.* **·at·ed, ·at·ing** To mark with striae. [< L < *stria* groove] — **stri·a′tion** *n.*

strick·en (strik′ən) Alternative past participle of STRIKE. ◆ *Stricken* is current in American English in certain senses: *stricken* with grief; a remark *stricken* from the record. — *adj.* **1.** Strongly affected or afflicted; overcome, as by calamity or disease. **2.** Wounded, esp. by a missile. [OE *stricen,* pp. of *strican* to strike]

strict (strikt) *adj.* **1.** Observing or enforcing rules exactly; severe. **2.** Containing exact or severe rules or provisions; exacting. **3.** Rigorously enjoined, maintained, and observed. **4.** Exactly defined, distinguished, or applied. **5.** Complete; absolute: *strict* attention. [< L *strictus,* pp. of *stringere* to draw tight] — **strict′ly** *adv.* — **strict′ness** *n.*

stric·ture (strik′chər) *n.* **1.** Severe criticism. **2.** *Pathol.* An abnormal contraction of some duct or channel.

stride (strīd) *n.* **1.** A long and sweeping or measured step. **2.** The space passed over by such a step. **3.** A progressive movement by an animal, completed when all the feet are returned to the same relative positions they occupied at the beginning of the movement. **4.** A stage of progress. — **to hit one's stride** To attain one's normal speed. — **to make rapid strides** To make quick progress. — **to take (something) in one's stride** To do or react to (something) without undue effort or disturbance, as if part of one's normal activity. — *v.* **strode, strid·den, strid·ing** *v.i.* **1.** To walk with long steps, as from haste or pride. — *v.t.* **2.** To walk through, along, etc., with long steps. **3.** To pass over with a single stride. **4.** To straddle. [OE *strīdan*] — **strid′er** *n.*

stri·dent (strīd′nt) *adj.* Having or making a high, harsh sound; shrill; grating. [< L *stridens, -entis,* ppr. of *stridere* to creak] — **stri′dence, stri′den·cy** *n.* — **stri′dent·ly** *adv.*

strid·u·late (strij′ōō·lāt) *v.i.* **·lat·ed, ·lat·ing** To make a shrill, creaking noise, as a cicada or cricket. [< NL *stridere* to rattle, rasp] — **strid′u·la′tion** *n.* — **strid′u·la·to·ry** (-lə·tôr′ē, -tō′rē) *adj.* — **strid′u·lous** *adj.*

strife (strīf) *n.* **1.** Angry contention; fighting. **2.** Any contest for advantage or superiority. [< OF *estriver* to strive]

strike (strīk) *v.* **struck, struck** or, sometimes, **strick·en, strik·ing** *v.t.* **1.** To come into violent contact with; hit. **2.** To hit with a blow; smite. **3.** To deal (a blow, etc.). **4.** To cause to hit forcibly: He *struck* his hand on the table. **5.** To attack; assault. **6.** To remove, separate, or take off by or as by a blow or stroke: with *off, from,* etc.: *Strike* it from the record. **7.** To ignite (a match, etc.); also, to produce (a light, etc.) thus. **8.** To form by stamping, printing, etc. **9.** To indicate (a specified time) by the sound of a stroke, bell, etc. **10.** To fall upon; reach: A sound *struck* his ear. **11.** To arrive at; come upon: to *strike* a trail. **12.** To find: to *strike* oil. **13.** To affect suddenly or in a specified manner: He was *struck* speechless. **14.** To come to the mind of; occur to: An idea *strikes* me. **15.** To impress in a specified manner: He *strikes* me as an honest man. **16.** To attract the attention of; impress: The dress *struck* her fancy. **17.** To assume; take up: to *strike* an attitude. **18.** To cause to enter or penetrate deeply or suddenly: to *strike* dismay into one's heart. **19.** To lower or haul down, as a sail, or a flag in token of surrender. **20.** To cease working at in order to compel compliance to a demand, etc. **21.** In the theater, to dismantle (a set or scene). **22.** To make level (a measure of grain, etc.) **23.** To make and confirm, as a bargain. **24.** To harpoon (a whale). **25.** To hook (a fish that has taken the lure) by a sharp pull on the line. **26.** To arrive at by reckoning: to *strike* a balance. — *v.i.* **27.** To come into violent contact; hit. **28.** To deal or aim a blow or blows. **29.** To make an assault or attack. **30.** To make a sound by or as by means of a blow or blows. **31.** To be indicated by the sound of blows or strokes: Noon has just *struck.* **32.** To ignite. **33.** To run aground, as on a reef or shoal. **34.** To lower a flag in token of surrender or in salute. **35.** To come suddenly or unexpectedly; chance: with *on* or *upon.* **36.** To start and proceed: to *strike* for home. **37.** To move quickly; dart. **38.** To cease work in order to enforce demands, etc. **39.** To snatch at or swallow the lure: said of fish. ◆ See note under STRICKEN. **— to strike camp** To take down the tents of a camp. **— to strike down 1.** To fell with a blow. **2.** To affect disastrously; incapacitate completely. **— to strike dumb** To astonish; amaze. **— to strike home 1.** To deal an effective blow. **2.** To have telling effect. **— to strike it rich** *Informal* **1.** To find a valuable vein or pocket of ore. **2.** To come into wealth or good fortune. **— to strike off 1.** To remove or take off by or as by a blow or stroke. **2.** To cross out or erase by or as by a stroke of the pen. **3.** To deduct. **— to strike out 1.** To strike off (def. 2). **2.** To aim a blow or blows. **3.** To make a start: *to strike out* on one's own. **4.** To originate; hit upon. **5.** In baseball: **a** To put out (the batter) by pitching three strikes. **b** To be put out because of having three strikes counted against one during a single turn at bat. **6.** In bowling, to complete a game by bowling three consecutive strikes. **— to strike up 1.** To begin to play, sing, or sound, as a band or musical instrument. **2.** To start up; begin, as a friendship. **— n. 1.** An act of striking or hitting; a blow. **2.** In baseball: **a** An unsuccessful attempt by the batter to hit the ball. **b** A pitched ball that passes over home plate not lower than the level of the batter's knees and not above that of his shoulders. **c** A foul bunt or any foul tip held by the catcher. **d** Any ball hit foul except when there have been two strikes. **3.** In bowling, the knocking down by a player of all the pins with the first bowl in any frame; also, the score so made: also called *ten-strike*: distinguished from *spare*. **4.** The quitting of work by a body of workers to enforce some demand. **5.** A new or unexpected discovery, as of oil or ore. **6.** Any unexpected or complete success. **7.** An air attack on a surface target. **8.** In fishing, a bite. [OE *strīcan* to stroke, move]

strike·bound (strīk′bound′) *adj.* Closed or immobilized by a strike: said of companies, equipment, workers, etc.

strike·break·er (strīk′brā′kər) *n.* One who takes the place of a workman on strike or who supplies workmen to take the place of strikers. **— strike′break′ing** *n.*

strike·out (strīk′out′) *n.* In baseball, an instance of striking out.

strik·er (strī′kər) *n.* **1.** One who or that which strikes. **2.** An employee who is on strike. **3.** The clapper of a bell, etc.

strik·ing (strī′king) *adj.* Notable; impressive. **— strik′-ing·ly** *adv.* **— strik′ing·ness** *n.*

string (string) *n.* **1.** A slender line or strip, as of twine, cloth, leather, etc., thinner than a cord and thicker than a thread. **2.** The cord of a bow. **3.** Prepared wire or catgut for musical instruments. **4.** A stringlike organ or formation, as a vegetable fiber or fibers or an animal nerve or tendon. **5.** A thin cord upon which anything is strung; a row or series of things connected by a small cord: a *string* of pearls. **6.** A connected series or succession, as of things, acts, or events. sometimes implying unusual length: a *string* of lies. **7.** *U.S. Informal* A small collection of animals, esp. of racehorses. **8.** *pl.* Stringed instruments, esp. those of an orchestra; also, those who play on these. **9.** *Archit.* **a** A stringcourse. **b** A ramp or sidepiece supporting the steps of a stairway. **10.** In sports, a group of contestants ranked as to skill. **11.** *Usu. pl. Informal* A condition, limitation, or restriction attached to a proposition, gift, or donation. **— to pull strings** To manipulate or influence others to gain some advantage. **— v. strung, string·ing** *v.t.* **1.** To thread, as beads, on or as on a string. **2.** To fit with a string or strings, as a guitar. **3.** To cover, drape, or adorn with things attached to a string or strings. **4.** To tune the strings of (a musical instrument). **5.** To brace; strengthen. **6.** To make tense or nervous. **7.** To arrange or extend in a line or series. **8.** To remove the strings from (vegetables). **9.** *U.S. Informal* To hang: usu. with *up*. **10.** *Slang* To fool or deceive; hoax: often with *along*. **— v.i. 11.** To extend, stretch, or proceed in a line or series. **12.** To form into strings. **— to string along (with)** *Informal* To follow with trust or confidence. [OE *streng*]

string bean 1. Any of several varieties of beans cultivated for their edible pods. **2.** The pod itself.

string·board (string′bôrd′, -bōrd′) *n. Archit.* A board serving as a support for the ends of steps in a staircase.

string·course (string′kôrs′, -kōrs′) *n. Archit.* A horizontal molding or ornamental course, as of brick or stone, usu. projecting along the face of a building.

stringed instrument (stringd) A musical instrument that produces its tones by means of one or more vibrating strings, as a violin, cello, etc. Also **string instrument.**

strin·gent (strin′jənt) *adj.* **1.** Requiring or compelling adherence to strict requirements; severe, as regulations. **2.** Hampered by obstructions or scarcity of money. **3.** Convincing; forcible. [< L *stringens, -entis,* ppr. of *stringere* to draw tight] **— strin′gen·cy** *n.* **— strin′gent·ly** *adv.*

string·er (string′ər) *n.* **1.** One who or that which strings. **2.** *Archit.* A heavy timber, generally horizontal, supporting other members of a structure. **3.** A lengthwise timber on which rails are laid, as distinguished from a crosstie. **4.** *Informal* One having a specified numerical rank or degree of proficiency, as on a team: a second *stringer*.

string·piece (string′pēs′) *n. Archit.* A heavy supporting timber forming the margin or edge of a framework.

string tie A very narrow necktie, often tied in a bow with the ends hanging loosely.

string·y (string′ē) *adj.* **string·i·er, string·i·est 1.** Containing fibrous strings. **2.** Forming in strings; ropy. **3.** Having tough sinews. **— string′i·ly** *adv.* **— string′i·ness** *n.*

strip¹ (strip) *n.* **1.** A narrow piece, comparatively long, as of cloth, wood, etc. **2.** A number of stamps attached in a row. **3.** A narrow piece of land. **4.** An airstrip or landing strip. **— v.t. stripped, strip·ping** To cut or tear into strips. [? < MLG *strippe* strap]

strip² (strip) *v.* **stripped** (*Rare* **stript**), **strip·ping** *v.t.* **1.** To pull the covering, clothing, etc., from; lay bare. **2.** To pull off (the covering or clothing). **3.** To rob or plunder. **4.** To make bare or empty. **5.** To remove; take away. **6.** To divest: He was *stripped* of his rank. **7.** *Mech.* To damage or break the teeth, thread, etc., of (a gear, bolt, or the like). **— v.i. 8.** To remove one's clothing; undress. **9.** To undergo stripping. [ME < OE *-strīepan,* as in *bestrīepan* to despoil, plunder] **— strip′per** *n.*

stripe¹ (strīp) *n.* **1.** A line, band, or strip of different color, material, texture, etc., from the adjacent surface. **2.** Striped cloth. **3.** A piece of material or braid on the sleeve of a uniform to indicate rank, service, an award, etc.; a chevron. **4.** Distinctive quality or character; sort: a man of his *stripe.* **— v.t. striped, strip·ing** To mark with a stripe or stripes. [< MDu.] **— striped** *adj.*

stripe² (strīp) *n.* A blow struck with a whip or rod, as in flogging. [Prob. < LG]

strip·ling (strip′ling) *n.* A mere youth.

strip mining The mining of coal by stripping off soil, etc., to expose and dig out a vein.

strip·tease (strip′tēz′) *n.* In burlesque, etc., a gradual disrobing, interspersed with various movements of the torso. Also **strip tease. — strip′teas′er** *n.*

strip·y (strī′pē) *adj.* **strip·i·er, strip·i·est** Being in or suggesting stripes or streaks; having or marked with stripes.

strive (strīv) *v.i.* **strove** or (*less commonly*) **strived, striv·en** (striv′ən) or **strived, striv·ing 1.** To make earnest effort. **2.** To engage in strife; contend; fight. **3.** To vie; emulate. [< OF *estriver,* prob. < Gmc.] **— striv′er** *n.*

strob·o·scope (strob′ə·skōp, strō′bə-) *n.* An instrument for observing the motion of a body or object by rendering it visible only at intervals or at certain points of its path. [< Gk. *strobos* twisting + -SCOPE] **— strob′o·scop′ic** (-skop′ik) or **-i·cal** *adj.* **— strob·os′co·py** (-os′kə·pē) *n.*

strode (strōd) Past tense of STRIDE.

stroke (strōk) *n.* **1.** The act or movement of striking; impact. **2.** A single movement, as of the hand, arm, or some instrument, by which something is made or done. **3.** A blow or any ill effect caused as if by a blow. **4.** An attack of paralysis or apoplexy. **5.** A blow or the sound of a blow of a striking mechanism, as of a clock. **6.** A sudden or brilliant act; coup: a *stroke* of wit. **7.** A pulsation, as of the heart. **8.** A mark or dash of a pen or tool. **9.** A light, caressing movement; a stroking. **10.** A manner or technique of swimming. **11.** *Informal* A portion or stint, as of work: usu. with the negative. **12.** *Mech.* **a** One of a series of alternating linear movements from one extreme position to another, as by the piston of an internal-combustion engine. **b** The distance covered by such a movement. **— v. stroked, strok·ing** *v.t.* **1.** To pass the hand over gently or caressingly, or with light pressure. **2.** To set the pace for (a rowboat or its crew)· act as stroke for. **— v.i. 3.** To perform strokes, as in swimming. [ME < OE *strācian* to strike]

stroll (strōl) *v.i.* **1.** To walk in a leisurely or idle manner; saunter. **2.** To go from place to place; wander. **— v.t. 3.** To walk idly or wander over or through. **— n.** An idle or leisurely walk. [Origin uncertain]

stroll·er (strō′lər) *n.* **1.** One who strolls. **2.** A light, often collapsible, carriage in which a baby or child may sit upright. **3.** A wandering showman or player. **4.** A tramp.

strong (strông, strong) *adj.* **1.** Powerful in physique; muscular; vigorous. **2.** Healthy; robust: a *strong* constitution. **3.** Morally powerful; firm; resolute; courageous. **4.** Mentally powerful or vigorous. **5.** Especially competent or able in a specified subject or field: *strong* in mathematics. **6.** Abundantly or richly supplied with something: often with *in.* **7.** Solidly made or constituted: *strong* walls. **8.** Powerful as a rival or combatant: a *strong* team. **9.** Easy to defend or difficult to capture: a *strong* military position. **10.** Having (a specified) numerical force: an army 20,000 *strong.* **11.** Capable of exerting influence, authority, etc.: a *strong* government. **12.** Financially sound: a *strong* bank. **13.** Powerful in effect: *strong* poison, medicine, etc. **14.** Concentrated; not diluted or weak: *strong* coffee. **15.** Containing much alcohol: *strong* drink. **16.** Powerful in flavor or odor; also, rank; unpleasant: a *strong* breath. **17.** Intense in degree or quality; not faint or mild: a *strong* pulse. **18.** Loud and firm: a *strong* voice. **19.** Firm; tenacious: a *strong* grip.

20. Deeply earnest; fervid: a *strong* desire. **21.** Cogent; convincing: *strong* evidence. **22.** Distinct; marked: a *strong* resemblance. **23.** Extreme; forceful: *strong* measures. **24.** Emphatic; not moderate: *strong* language. **25.** Moving with great force: said of a wind, stream, or tide. **26.** *Meteorol.* Designating a breeze or gale on the Beaufort scale. **27.** Characterized by steady or rising prices: a *strong* market. **28.** *Gram.* In Germanic languages, denoting a strong verb. — *adv.* In a strong manner; so as to be strong. [OE *strang, strong*] — **strong′ly** *adv.*

strong-arm (strông′ärm′, strong′-) *Informal adj.* Violent; having and depending on physical power. — *v.t.* To use physical force upon; assault.

strong·box (strông′boks′, strong′-) *n.* A strongly built chest or safe for keeping valuables.

strong·hold (strông′hōld′, strong′-) *n.* **1.** A strongly fortified place; fortress. **2.** A place of security or refuge.

strong·man (strông′man′, strong′-) *n. pl.* **·men** (-men′) A political leader having considerable or preeminent power, often derived from extralegal means, as a coup d'état.

strong-mind·ed (strông′mīn′did, strong′-) *adj.* Having a determined, vigorous mind. — **strong′-mind′ed·ly** *adv.* — **strong′-mind′ed·ness** *n.*

strong verb A verb that forms its past tense and past participle by internal vowel change, as *swim, swam, swum.*

strong-willed (strông′wild′, strong′-) *adj.* Having a strong will; decided; obstinate.

stron·ti·um (stron′shē·əm, -shəm, -tē·əm) *n.* A hard, yellowish, metallic element (symbol Sr) of the calcium group, known chiefly through its salts, which burn with a red flame and are used largely in pyrotechnics, but also in medicine and ceramics. See ELEMENT. [< NL, from *Strontian,* Argyll, Scotland, where first discovered] — **stron′tic** (-tik) *adj.*

strontium 90 *Physics* A radioactive isotope of strontium chemically resembling calcium and with a half life of about 28 years. Also called *radiostrontium.*

strop (strop) *n.* **1.** A strip of leather, canvas, etc., on which to sharpen a razor. **2.** A strap. — *v.t.* **stropped, strop·ping** To sharpen on a strop. [OE < L < Gk. *strophos* band]

stro·phe (strō′fē) *n.* **1.** In ancient Greek poetry, the verses sung by the chorus in a play while moving from right to left. **2.** In classical prosody, the lines of an ode constituting a stanza and alternating with the antistrophe. **3.** The first of two alternating metrical systems in a poem. [< Gk. *strephein* to turn] — **stroph·ic** (strof′ik, strō′fik) or **·i·cal** *adj.*

strove (strōv) Past tense of STRIVE.

strow (strō) *v.t.* **strowed, strowed** or **strown, strow·ing** *Archaic* To strew.

struck (struk) Past tense and past participle of STRIKE. — *adj.* Closed down or affected by a strike, as a factory.

struck measure A measure having the contents level with the edge of the container, rather than heaping.

struc·tur·al (struk′chər·əl) *adj.* Of, pertaining to, characterized, or caused by structure. — **struc′tur·al·ly** *adv.*

structural steel Rolled steel of considerable toughness and strength, esp. adapted for use in construction.

struc·ture (struk′chər) *n.* **1.** That which is constructed; a combination of related parts, as a building or machine. **2.** The position and arrangement of parts, as of tissues in an organism, atoms within a molecule, etc. **3.** The manner of construction or organization: the social *structure* of a primitive society. — *v.t.* **·tured, ·tur·ing 1.** To form into an organized structure; build. **2.** To conceive as a structural whole; ideate. [< L < *structus,* pp. of *struere* to build]

stru·del (strood′l, *Ger.* shtroo′dəl) *n.* A kind of pastry made of a thin sheet of dough, spread with fruit or cheese, nuts, etc., rolled, and baked. [< G, lit., eddy]

strug·gle (strug′əl) *n.* **1.** A violent effort or series of efforts; a labored contest. **2.** Conflict; strife; battle. — *v.* **·gled, ·gling** *v.i.* **1.** To contend with an adversary in physical combat; fight. **2.** To put forth violent efforts; strive: to *struggle* against odds. **3.** To make one's way by violent efforts. — *v.t.* **4.** To accomplish with a struggle. [ME *strogelen*] — **strug′gler** *n.* — **strug′gling·ly** *adv.*

strum (strum) *v.t. & v.i.* **strummed, strum·ming** To play (a stringed instrument, a tune, etc.) idly, monotonously, or without technical skill. — *n.* The act of strumming. [Prob. imit.] — **strum′mer** *n.*

strum·pet (strum′pit) *n.* A whore; harlot. [? Ult. < OF *strupe* concubinage < L *stuprum* dishonor]

strung (strung) Past tense and past participle of STRING.

strut (strut) *n.* **1.** A proud or pompous step or walk. **2.** A member in a framework, designed to relieve weight or pressure in the direction of its length. For illus. see ROOF. — *v.* **strut·ted, strut·ting** *v.i.* **1.** To walk pompously, conceitedly, and affectedly. — *v.t.* **2.** To brace or support, as a framing or structure, with or as with struts. [OE *strūtian* to be rigid, stand stiffly] — **strut′ter** *n.* — **strut′ting·ly** *adv.*

strych·nine (strik′nin, -nēn, -nīn) *n.* A white, crystalline, bitter, extremely poisonous alkaloid, $C_{21}H_{22}N_2O_2$, contained in certain plants. Its salts are used in medicine, chiefly as a neural stimulant. Also **strych′nin** (-nin). [< F < L *strychnos* < Gk., nightshade]

Stu·art (stoo′ərt, styoo′-) The royal family of Scotland, 1371–1603, and of England, 1603–1714.

stub (stub) *n.* **1.** Any short projecting part or piece. **2.** The part of a tree trunk, bush, etc., that remains when the main part is cut down. **3.** A short or broken remnant, as of a pencil, cigarette, or broken tooth. **4.** *U.S.* In a checkbook, one of the inner ends upon which a memorandum is entered, and which remains when the check is detached; also, the detachable portion of a theater ticket, etc. **5.** Anything blunt, short, or stumpy, as a pen with a broad point. — *v.t.* **stubbed, stub·bing 1.** To strike, as the toe, against a low obstruction or projection. **2.** To grub up, as roots. **3.** To clear or remove the stubs or roots from. [OE *stubb*]

stub·ble (stub′əl) *n.* **1.** The stubs of grain stalks, sugar cane, etc., covering a field after the crop has been cut. **2.** The field itself. **3.** Any surface or growth resembling stubble, as short bristly hair or beard. [< OF *stuble,* ult. < L *stipula* stalk] — **stub′bled** *adj.* — **stub′bly** *adj.*

stub·born (stub′ərn) *adj.* **1.** Inflexible in opinion or intention; unreasonably obstinate. **2.** Difficult to handle, manage, or work with; resistant. **3.** Characterized by perseverance or persistence: *stubborn* fighting. [ME, ? < OE *stubb* stump] — **stub′born·ly** *adv.* — **stub′born·ness** *n.*

stub·by (stub′ē) *adj.* **·bi·er, ·bi·est 1.** Short, stiff, and bristling: a *stubby* beard. **2.** Resembling or of the nature of a stub: a *stubby* pencil. **3.** Stocky; thickset. **4.** Full of stubs. — **stub′bi·ly** *adv.* — **stub′bi·ness** *n.*

stuc·co (stuk′ō) *n. pl.* **·coes** or **·cos 1.** A fine plaster for walls or their relief ornaments, usu. of Portland cement, sand, and a small amount of lime. **2.** Any plaster or cement used for the external coating of buildings. **3.** Ornamental work made from stucco: also **stuc′co·work′** (-wûrk′). — *v.t.* **·coed, ·co·ing** To apply stucco to; decorate with stucco. [< Ital. < Gmc.] — **stuc′co·er** *n.*

stuck (stuk) Past tense and past participle of STICK.

stuck-up (stuk′up′) *adj. Informal* Conceited; snobbish.

stud¹ (stud) *n.* **1.** A short intermediate post, as in a building frame; a post to which laths are nailed. **2.** A knob, round-headed nail, or small protuberant ornament. **3.** A removable button used to fasten a shirt front, etc. **4.** A crosspiece in a link, as in a chain cable. **5.** A small pin such as is used in a watch. — *v.t.* **stud·ded, stud·ding 1.** To set thickly with small points, projections, or knobs. **2.** To be scattered or strewn over. **3.** To support or stiffen by means of studs or upright props. [OE *studu* post]

stud² (stud) *n.* **1.** A collection of horses and mares for breeding. **2.** The place where they are kept. **3.** A collection of horses for riding, hunting, or racing. **4.** A studhorse or other male animal used for breeding purposes. **5.** Stud poker. — **at stud** Of a male animal, used or available for breeding purposes. — *adj.* **1.** Of or pertaining to a stud. **2.** Kept for breeding: a *stud* mare. [OE *stōd*]

stud·book (stud′book′) *n.* A record of the pedigree of thoroughbred stock.

stud·ding (stud′ing) *n.* **1.** Studs or joists collectively. **2.** The material from which they are made.

stud·ding·sail (stun′səl, stud′ing·sāl′) *n. Naut.* A light auxiliary sail set out beyond one of the principal sails by extensible booms during a following wind.

stu·dent (stood′nt, styood′nt) *n.* **1.** One engaged in a course of study, esp. in a secondary school, college or university. **2.** One devoted to study. **3.** One who makes a thorough study of a particular subject. [< OF < L *studens, -entis,* ppr. of *studere* to be eager, study] — **stu′dent·ship** *n.*

  — **Syn.** A *student* is one who studies, not necessarily under a teacher: this is the common term for one enrolled in a secondary school or college. A *pupil* is one under close supervision of a teacher; children in elementary schools are called *pupils,* but the term is not synonymous with beginner. A concert violinist may be called the *pupil* of some great master under whom he has studied.

student body All the students attending a school.

stud·horse (stud′hôrs′) *n.* A stallion kept for breeding. Also **stud horse.**

stud·ied (stud′ēd) *adj.* **1.** Deliberately designed or undertaken: a *studied* insult. **2.** Lacking freshness, naturalness, or spontaneity. — **stud′ied·ly** *adv.* — **stud′ied·ness** *n.*

stu·di·o (stoo′dē·ō, styoo′-) *n. pl.* **·os 1.** The workroom of an artist, photographer, etc. **2.** A place where motion pictures are filmed. **3.** A room or rooms where radio or television programs are broadcast or recorded. [< Ital., a study]

studio couch A backless couch with a bed frame underneath that may be drawn out to form a double bed.

stu·di·ous (stoo′dē·əs, styoo′-) *adj.* **1.** Given to study; devoting oneself to the acquisition of knowledge. **2.** Earnest in effort. **3.** Done with deliberation; studied: *studious* politeness. — **stu/di·ous·ly** *adv.* — **stu/di·ous·ness** *n.*

stud poker A game of poker in which the cards of the first round are dealt face down and the rest face up, betting opening on the second round. [< STUD²]

stud·y (stud/ē) *v.* **stud·ied, stud·y·ing** *v.t.* **1.** To apply the mind in acquiring a knowledge of. **2.** To examine: to *study* a problem. **3.** To look at attentively; scrutinize. **4.** To endeavor to memorize, as a part in a play. **5.** To give thought and attention to, as something to be done or devised. — *v.i.* **6.** To apply the mind in acquiring knowledge. **7.** To follow a regular course of instruction. **8.** To meditate. — *n. pl.* **stud·ies 1.** The act of studying; the process of acquiring information. **2.** A particular instance or form of mental work. **3.** Something to be studied; a branch of knowledge. **4.** A specific product of or work resulting from studious application. **5.** In art, a first sketch, exercise, etc. **6.** A carefully elaborated literary treatment of a subject. **7.** A room devoted to study, reading, etc. **8.** A state of deep thought or absent-mindedness. **9.** Earnest endeavor; thoughtful attention or care. **10.** Something worthy of close attention. **11.** *Music* An étude. [< OF < L < *studere* to apply oneself, be diligent]

stuff (stuf) *v.t.* **1.** To fill completely; pack; cram full. **2.** To fill (an opening, etc.) with something forced in; plug. **3.** To obstruct or stop up; choke. **4.** To fill or expand with padding, as a cushion. **5.** To fill (a fowl, roast, etc.) with stuffing. **6.** In taxidermy, to fill the skin of (a bird, animal, etc.) with a material preparatory to mounting. **7.** To fill too full; distend. **8.** To fill or cram with food. **9.** To fill with knowledge, ideas, or attitudes, esp. unsystematically. **10.** To force or cram, as into a small space. **11.** To put fraudulent votes into (a ballot box). — *v.i.* **12.** To eat to excess. — *n.* **1.** The material out of which something may be shaped or made; raw or unwrought material. **2.** The fundamental element or basic material of anything: the *stuff* of dreams. **3.** *Informal* Possessions generally, esp., household goods. **4.** A worthless collection of things; rubbish. **5.** Worthless ideas: often used as an interjection: *Stuff* and nonsense! **6.** Woven material, esp. of wool; also, any textile fabric. **7.** *Informal* Any unspecified or vaguely defined substance, activity, etc. [< OF *estoffe*, ? < L *stuppa* tow] — **stuff/er** *n.*

stuffed shirt (stuft) *Informal* A pompous person.

stuff·ing (stuf/ing) *n.* **1.** The material with which anything is stuffed. **2.** A mixture, as of bread or cracker crumbs with meat and seasoning, used in stuffing fowls, etc. **3.** The act or process of one who or that which stuffs.

stuff·y (stuf/ē) *adj.* **stuff·i·er, stuff·i·est 1.** Badly ventilated. **2.** Impeding respiration. **3.** *Informal* Pompous; smugly self-important. **4.** *Informal* Old-fashioned; stodgy; straight-laced. — **stuff/i·ly** *adv.* — **stuff/i·ness** *n.*

stul·ti·fy (stul/tə·fī) *v.t.* **·fied, ·fy·ing 1.** To cause to appear absurd; give an appearance of foolishness to. **2.** To make worthless or ineffectual. [< LL < L *stultus* foolish + *facere* to make] — **stul/ti·fi·ca/tion** *n.* — **stul/ti·fi/er** *n.*

stum·ble (stum/bəl) *v.* **·bled, ·bling** *v.i.* **1.** To miss one's step in walking or running; trip. **2.** To walk or proceed unsteadily. **3.** To speak, read, etc., falteringly. **4.** To happen upon something by chance: with *across, on, upon*, etc. **5.** To err. — *v.t.* **6.** To cause to stumble. — *n.* **1.** The act of stumbling. **2.** A blunder; false step. [Cf. Norw. *stumla* to stumble in the dark] — **stum/bler** *n.* — **stum/bling·ly** *adv.*

stumbling block Any obstacle, hindrance, or impediment, as to the achievement of some end.

stump (stump) *n.* **1.** That portion of the trunk of a tree left standing when the tree is felled. **2.** The part of anything, as of a limb, tooth, pencil, etc., that remains when the main part has been removed; a stub. **3.** *pl. Informal* The legs: chiefly in the phrase **to stir one's stumps. 4.** A place or platform from which a political speech is made. **5.** In cricket, any one of the three posts forming the wicket. **6.** A pencil-like soft leather or rubber bar, with conical ends, used to shade drawings of crayon or charcoal or to apply powdered pigments. **7.** A short, thickset person or animal. **8.** A heavy step; a clump; also, the sound made by such a step. — **to take the stump** To electioneer in a political campaign. — *adj.* **1.** Being or resembling a stump; stumpy. **2.** Of or pertaining to political oratory or campaigning: a *stump* speaker. — *v.t.* **1.** To reduce to a stump. **2.** To remove stumps from (land). **3.** To canvass (a district) by making political speeches: The candidate *stumped* the State. **4.** *Informal* To bring to a halt by real or fancied obstacles; baffle. **5.** To strike against an obstacle; stub, as one's toe. — *v.i.* **6.** To go about on or as on stumps; also, to walk heavily, noisily, and stiffly. **7.** To go about making political speeches. [< MLG] — **stump/er** *n.*

stump·y (stum/pē) *adj.* **stump·i·er, stump·i·est 1.** Full of stumps. **2.** Like a stump; short and thick. — **stump/i·ness** *n.*

stun (stun) *v.t.* **stunned, stun·ning 1.** To render unconscious or incapable of action by a blow, fall, etc. **2.** To astonish; astound. **3.** To daze or overwhelm by loud or explosive noise. — *n.* A stupefying blow, shock, or concussion; also, the condition of being stunned. [< OF < L *ex-* thoroughly + *tonare* to thunder, crash]

stung (stung) Past tense and past participle of STING.

stunk (stungk) Past participle and alternative past tense of STINK.

stun·ner (stun/ər) *n.* **1.** One who or that which stuns. **2.** *Informal* A person of extraordinary beauty, etc.

stun·ning (stun/ing) *adj.* **1.** Rendering unconscious. **2.** *Informal* Impressively beautiful, etc. — **stun/ning·ly** *adv.*

stunt¹ (stunt) *v.t.* To check the natural development of; dwarf; cramp. — *n.* **1.** A check in growth, progress, or development. **2.** A stunted animal or thing. [OE *stunt* dull, foolish] — **stunt/ed** *adj.* — **stunt/ed·ness** *n.*

stunt² (stunt) *U.S. Informal* **n. 1.** A sensational feat, as of bodily skill. **2.** Any thrilling or unusual feat or undertaking. — *v.i.* **1.** To perform stunts. — *v.t.* **2.** To perform stunts with (an airplane, etc.). [? < G *stunde* lesson]

stunt man In motion pictures, a man employed to substitute for an actor in dangerous acts or situations.

stu·pe·fac·tion (stoō/pə·fak/shən, styoō/-) *n.* The act of stupefying or the state of being stupefied.

stu·pe·fy (stoō/pə·fī, styoō/-) *v.t.* **·fied, ·fy·ing 1.** To dull the senses or faculties of; stun. **2.** To amaze; astound. [< F < L < *stupere* to be stunned + *facere* to make] — **stu/pe·fied** *adj.* — **stu/pe·fi/er** *n.*

stu·pen·dous (stoō·pen/dəs, styoō-) *adj.* **1.** Of or characterized by any highly impressive or astonishing feature. **2.** Of prodigious size or bulk. [< L *stupere* to be stunned] — **stu·pen/dous·ly** *adv.* — **stu·pen/dous·ness** *n.*

stu·pid (stoō/pid, styoō/-) *adj.* **1.** Very slow of apprehension or understanding. **2.** Affected with stupor; stupefied. **3.** Marked by, or resulting from, lack of understanding, reason, or wit; senseless. **4.** Tedious; dull. — *n. Informal* A stupid person. [< L < *stupere* to be stunned] — **stu·pid/i·ty** *n.* — **stu/pid·ly** *adv.* — **stu/pid·ness** *n.*

stu·por (stoō/pər, styoō/-) *n.* **1.** A condition in which the senses and faculties are suspended or greatly dulled, as by drugs or liquor. **2.** Mental or moral dullness; gross stupidity. [< L *stupere* to be stunned] — **stu/por·ous** *adj.* — **Syn. 1.** lethargy, torpor.

stur·dy (stûr/dē) *adj.* **·di·er, ·di·est 1.** Possessing rugged health and strength; hardy; vigorous. **2.** Firm and unyielding; resolute: a *sturdy* defense. [< OF *estourdir* to stun, amaze] — **stur/di·ly** *adv.* — **stur/di·ness** *n.*

stur·geon (stûr/jən) *n.* A large, fresh-water and marine fish of northern regions, with coarse, edible flesh. It is valued as a source of isinglass and caviar. [< OF < Med.L < OHG *sturjo*]

Sturm·ab·teil·ung (shtoōrm/äp·tī/loōngk) *n. pl.* **·teil·ung·en** A Nazi political militia: also called *Brown Shirts, storm troopers.* [< G, storm detachment]

stut·ter (stut/ər) *v.t. & v.i.* To utter or speak with spasmodic repetition, blocking, and prolongation of sounds, esp. those in initial position in a word. — *n.* The act or habit of stuttering. [Freq. of ME *stutten* to stutter] — **stut/ter·er** *n.* — **stut/ter·ing** *adj. & n.* — **stut/ter·ing·ly** *adv.*

St. Vi·tus's dance (sänt vī/təs·iz) *Pathol.* Chorea. Also **St. Vi/tus' dance, St. Vi·tus dance** (vī/təs).

sty¹ (stī) *n. pl.* **sties 1.** A pen for swine. **2.** Any filthy place of bestiality or debauchery. — *v.t. & v.i.* **stied, sty·ing** To keep or live in a sty or hovel. [ME < OE *sti*]

sty² (stī) *n. pl.* **sties** *Pathol.* A small, inflamed swelling of a sebaceous gland on the edge of the eyelid. Also **stye.** [< OE < *stigan* to rise + *ye* eye]

styg·i·an (stij/ē·ən) *adj. Often cap.* **1.** Of or pertaining to the river Styx. **2.** Infernal; dark and gloomy.

style (stīl) *n.* **1.** Manner of expressing thought, in writing or speaking. **2.** A distinctive, characteristic, or suitable mode of expression: His writing lacks *style.* **3.** A particular or characteristic mode of composition, construction, or appearance, as in art, music, etc.: the Gothic *style.* **4.** The manner in which some action or work is performed: The horse ran in fine *style.* **5.** A good or exemplary manner of performing: a team with *style.* **6.** A mode of conduct; a way of living: to live in makeshift *style.* **7.** A fashionable manner or appearance: to live in *style.* **8.** A particular fashion in clothing. **9.** A particular type or fashion suitable for a person. **10.** The conventions of typography, design, usage, punctuation, etc., observed by a given publishing house, printing office, or publication. **11.** The legal or official title or appellation of a person, organization, etc. **12.** A stylus. **13.** The gnomon of a sundial. **14.** *Surg.* A slender probe with a blunt point. **15.** *Bot.* The prolongation of a carpel or ovary, bearing the stigma. For illus. see FLOWER. **16.** A system of arranging the length of the calendar years so as to average that of the true solar year. See OLD STYLE, NEW STYLE under CALENDAR. — *v.* **styled, styl·ing** *v.t.* **1.** To name; give a title to. **2.** To make consistent in typography, spelling, punctuation, etc. **3.** To give form, fashion, or style to. [< OF < L *stilus* writing instrument] — **styl′er** *n.*

style book A book containing rules of spelling, punctuation, typography, etc., used by printers, editors, etc.

styl·ish (stī′lish) *adj.* Having style or fashionableness in clothes, etc. — **styl′ish·ly** *adv.* — **styl′ish·ness** *n.*

styl·ist (stī′list) *n.* **1.** One who is a master of literary or rhetorical style. **2.** A designer or adviser of style in clothes, interior decoration, etc. — **sty·lis′tic** *adj.* — **sty·lis′ti·cal·ly** *adv.*

styl·ize (stī′līz) *v.t.* **·ized, ·iz·ing** To make conform to a distinctive mode or style; conventionalize. — **styl′i·za′tion** *n.* — **styl′iz·er** *n.*

stylo- *combining form* **1.** A pillar. **2.** *Bot.* A style; of or related to a style. Also, before vowels, **styl-**. [< Gk. *stylos* column, pillar]

sty·lus (stī′ləs) *n.* *pl.* **·lus·es** (-iz) or **·li** (-lī) **1.** An ancient writing instrument, having one end pointed for writing on wax tablets. **2.** A pointed instrument for marking or engraving. **3.** The needle of a record player or of a recording instrument. Also called *style.* [< L] — **sty′lar** *adj.*

sty·mie (stī′mē) *n.* A condition in golf when an opponent's ball lies directly between the player's ball and the hole. — *v.t.* **·mied, ·my·ing** **1.** To block or hinder by or as by a stymie. **2.** To baffle or perplex. Also spelled *stimy.* Also **sty′my.** [Prob. use of earlier Scot. *styme,* to be unable to see]

styp·tic (stip′tik) *adj.* **1.** Causing contraction of tissues, as blood vessels. **2.** Stopping hemorrhage or bleeding. Also **styp′ti·cal.** — *n.* A styptic substance or agent. [< L < Gk. *styphein* to contract] — **styp·tic·i·ty** (stip·tis′ə·tē) *n.*

Styx (stiks) *n.* In Greek mythology, the river of hate, one of the five rivers surrounding Hades.

sua·sion (swā′zhən) *n.* Persuasion: archaic except in the phrase **moral suasion.** [< L *suadere* to persuade] — **sua·sive** (swā′siv), **sua·so·ry** (swā′sər·ē) *adj.*

suave (swäv, swāv) *adj.* Smoothly pleasant and ingratiating in manner; blandly polite; urbane. [< F < L *suavis* sweet] — **suave′ly** *adv.* — **suave′ness, suav·i·ty** (swä′və·tē) *n.*

sub (sub) *n.* *Informal* Short for any of various words beginning with *sub-,* as: **a** A substitute. **b** A subordinate or subaltern. **c** A submarine.

sub- *prefix* Used to form words meaning: **a** Under; beneath; below: *substratum.* **b** *Anat.* Situated under or beneath: *subcutaneous.* **c** Almost; nearly; slightly; imperfectly: chiefly in scientific terms: *subconical.* **d** Lower in rank or grade; secondary; subordinate: *subaltern, subcontract.* **e** Forming a subdivision: *subsection.* **f** *Chem.* Present (in a compound) in less than normal amount: *subchloride, suboxide.* Also: *suc-* before *c,* as in *succumb; suf-* before *f,* as in *suffer; sug-* before *g,* as in *suggest; sum-* before *m,* as in *summon; sup-* before *p,* as in *support; sur-* before *r,* as in *surrogate; sus-* before *c, p, t,* as in *susceptible, suspect, sustain.* [< L *sub* under]

sub·ac·id (sub·as′id) *adj.* Slightly sour or acid. — **sub′a·cid′i·ty** (-ə·sid′ə·tē) *n.*

sub·al·tern (sub·ôl′tərn) *adj.* **1.** *Brit. Mil.* Ranking below a captain. **2.** Of inferior rank or position; subordinate. — *n.* **1.** A person of subordinate rank or position. **2.** *Brit. Mil.* An officer ranking below a captain. [< LL < L *sub-* under + *alternus* alternate]

sub·ant·arc·tic (sub′ant·ärk′tik, -är′tik) *adj.* Of or pertaining to the region surrounding the Antarctic Circle.

sub·arc·tic (sub·ärk′tik, -är′tik) *adj.* Denoting or pertaining to the region surrounding the Arctic Circle.

sub·a·tom·ic (sub′ə·tom′ik) *adj.* Within the atom: *subatomic* particle.

sub·base·ment (sub′bās′mənt) *n.* An underground story, or any one of several below the first or true basement.

sub·clin·i·cal (sub·klin′i·kəl) *adj.* Having no symptoms apparent in clinical tests, as in the early stages of a disease.

sub·com·mit·tee (sub′kə·mit′ē) *n.* A subordinate committee appointed from the members of the original committee for special work.

sub·con·scious (sub·kon′shəs) *adj.* **1.** Not clearly or wholly conscious. **2.** *Psychol.* Denoting such phenomena of mental life as are not attended by full consciousness. — *n.* *Psychol.* That portion of mental activity not directly in the focus of consciousness but sometimes susceptible to recall by the proper stimulus. — **sub·con′scious·ly** *adv.* — **sub·con′scious·ness** *n.*

sub·con·ti·nent (sub·kon′tə·nənt) *n.* *Geog.* A great land mass forming part of a continent but having considerable geographical independence, as India.

sub·con·tract (*n.* sub·kon′trakt; *v.* sub′kən·trakt′) *n.* A contract subordinate to another contract and assigning part or all of the work to another party. — *v.t. & v.i.* To make a subcontract (for). — **sub′con·trac′tor** (-kən·trak′tər, -kon′·trak-) *n.*

sub·crit·i·cal (sub·krit′i·kəl) *adj.* *Physics* Of, pertaining to, or containing fissionable material in a quantity not sufficient to start or sustain a chain reaction: *subcritical* mass.

sub·cu·ta·ne·ous (sub′kyōō·tā′nē·əs) *adj.* **1.** Situated, found, or lying beneath the skin. **2.** Introduced or applied beneath the skin, as an injection. [< LL < L *sub-* under + *cutis* skin] — **sub′cu·ta′ne·ous·ly** *adv.*

sub·deb (sub′deb′) *n.* *Informal* **1.** A subdebutante. **2.** Any girl of this age. — *adj.* In a style suitable for girls of this age.

sub·deb·u·tante (sub′deb·ōō·tänt′, -deb′yōō·tant) *n.* A young girl the year before she becomes a debutante.

sub·di·vide (sub′di·vīd′) *v.t. & v.i.* **·vid·ed, ·vid·ing** **1.** To divide (a part) resulting from a previous division; divide again. **2.** To divide (land) into lots for sale or improvement. [< LL < L *sub-* under + *dividere* to separate]

sub·di·vi·sion (sub′di·vizh′ən) *n.* **1.** Division following upon division. **2.** A part, as of land, resulting from subdividing. **3.** An area of land composed of subdivided lots.

sub·dom·i·nant (sub·dom′ə·nənt) *n.* *Music* The fourth tone or degree of a major or minor scale.

sub·due (sub·dōō′, -dyōō′) *v.t.* **·dued, ·du·ing** **1.** To gain dominion over: subjugate; vanquish. **2.** To overcome by training, influence, or persuasion; tame. **3.** To repress (emotions, impulses, etc.). **4.** To reduce the intensity of; soften, as a color or sound. [< OF < L *subducere* to withdraw] — **sub·du′a·ble** *adj.* — **sub·du′al** *n.* — **sub·du′er** *n.* — **Syn.** **1.** conquer. **2.** master, control, bridle. **3.** check, restrain. **4.** moderate, temper.

sub·fam·i·ly (sub·fam′ə·lē, -fam′lē) *n.* *pl.* **·lies 1.** *Biol.* A division of plants or animals next below a family but above the genus. **2.** *Ling.* A division of languages below a family and above a branch.

sub·ge·nus (sub·jē′nəs) *n.* *pl.* **·gen·e·ra** (-jen′ər·ə) or, less commonly, **·gen·us·es** *Biol.* A primary subdivision of a genus including one or more species with common characters. — **sub·ge·ner′ic** (-ji·ner′ik) *adj.*

sub·head (sub′hed′) *n.* A heading or title of a subdivision. Also **sub′head′ing.**

sub·hu·man (sub·hyōō′mən) *adj.* **1.** Less than or imperfectly human. **2.** Below the level of *Homo sapiens.*

sub·ja·cent (sub·jā′sənt) *adj.* **1.** Situated directly underneath. **2.** Lower than but not directly below. [< L < *sub-* under + *jacere* to lie] — **sub·ja′cen·cy** *n.*

sub·ject (*adj.* sub′jikt; *v.* səb·jekt′) *adj.* **1.** Being under the power of another; owing or yielding obedience to sovereign authority. **2.** Liable to be affected by: with *to: subject to* disease. **3.** Likely to bring about or incur: with *to: subject to* severe criticism. **4.** Dependent on; contingent on: with *to:* a treaty *subject* to ratification. — *n.* **1.** One who is under the governing power of another, as of a ruler or government, esp. of a monarch. **2.** One who or that which is employed or treated in a specified way, as a body for dissection, or a person used in psychological experiments. **3.** A topic or main theme, as of a discussion, written work, etc. **4.** Something represented by or serving as the basic idea for an artistic work. **5.** A branch of learning or course of study. **6.** An originating cause; motive. **7.** *Gram.* The word, phrase, or clause of a sentence about which something is stated or asked in the predicate. **8.** *Music* A melody on which a composition or a part of it is based. **9.** *Philos.* The ego or self. **10.** *Logic* In a proposition, that term about which something is affirmed or denied. See PROPOSITION. — *v.t.* **1.** To bring under dominion or control. **2.** To cause to undergo some experience or action. **3.** To offer for consideration or approval. **4.** To make liable; expose: His inheritance was *subjected* to heavy taxation. [< OF < L < *sub-* under + *jacere* to throw] — **sub·jec′tion** *n.*

sub·jec·tive (səb·jek′tiv) *adj.* **1.** Relating to, proceeding from, or taking place within an individual's mind, emotions, etc.: opposed to *objective.* **2.** Originating from or influenced by one's personal interests, prejudices, etc. **3.** Introspective. **4.** Of the mind or emotions only; illusory. **5.** In literature and art, giving prominence to the subject or author as treating of his inner experience and emotion. **6.** *Gram.* Designating the nominative case. — **sub·jec′tive·ly** *adv.* — **sub·jec′tive·ness, sub·jec·tiv·i·ty** (sub′jek·tiv′ə·tē) *n.*

sub·join (sub·join′) *v.t.* To add at the end; attach; affix. [< MF < L < *sub-* in addition + *jungere* to join]

sub·join·der (sub·join′dər) *n.* Something subjoined.

sub·ju·gate (sub′jōō·gāt) *v.t.* **·gat·ed, ·gat·ing** **1.** To bring under dominion; conquer; subdue. **2.** To make subservient in any way. [< L < *sub-* under + *jugum* yoke] — **sub′ju·ga′tion** *n.* — **sub′ju·ga′tor** *n.*

sub·junc·tive (səb·jungk′tiv) *Gram. adj.* Of or pertaining to that mood of the finite verb that is used to express a future contingency, a supposition implying the contrary, a mere supposition with indefinite time, or a wish or desire. ◆ In

English the forms of the subjunctive mood are usu. introduced by conjunctions of condition, doubt, contingency, possibility, etc., as *if, though, lest. unless, that, till,* or *whether,* but verbs in conditional clauses are not always in the subjunctive mood, for the use of these conjunctions with the indicative is very common. — *n.* **1.** The subjunctive mood. **2.** A verb form or construction in this mood. [See SUBJOIN.]

sub·lease (*v.* sub·lēs′; *n.* sub′lēs′) *v.t.* **·leased, ·leas·ing** To obtain or let (property) on a sublease. — *n.* A lease of property from a tenant or lessee. — **sub′les·see′** (-les·ē′), **sub·les·sor** (sub·les′ôr, sub′les·ôr′) *n.*

sub·let (sub·let′, sub′let′) *v.t.* **·let, ·let·ting** **1.** To let (property one holds on a lease) to another. **2.** To let (work that one has contracted to do) to a subordinate contractor.

sub·li·mate (sub′lə·māt) *v.* **·mat·ed, ·mat·ing** *v.t.* **1.** *Chem.* To cause (a substance) to convert from the solid to the gaseous state by the application of heat or pressure, and then to solidify again. **2.** To refine; purify. **3.** *Psychol.* To convert the energy of (instinctual drives) into acceptable social manifestations. — *v.i.* **4.** To undergo sublimation. — *adj.* Sublimated; refined. — *n.* *Chem.* The product of sublimation, esp., when regarded as purified. [See SUBLIME.] — **sub′li·ma′tion** *n.*

sub·lime (sə·blīm′) *adj.* **1.** Characterized by elevation, nobility, etc.; grand; solemn. **2.** Inspiring awe, deep emotion, etc.; moving. **3.** Being of the highest degree; utmost. — *n.* That which is sublime; height, as of emotion, grandeur, etc.: often with *the.* — *v.* **·limed, ·lim·ing** *v.t.* **1.** To make sublime; ennoble. **2.** *Chem.* To sublimate. — *v.i.* **3.** To become sublimated. [< L *sublimis* lofty, prob. < *sub-* up to, under + *limen* lintel] — **sub·lime′ly** *adv.* — **sub·lim′er** *n.* — **sub·lim·i·ty** (sə·blim′ə·tē), **sub·lime′ness** *n.*

sub·lim·i·nal (sub·lim′ə·nəl) *adj.* *Psychol.* Perceived below the threshold of consciousness, as images, etc., of too low an intensity to produce a clear awareness. [< SUB- + L *limen, liminis* threshold] — **sub·lim′i·nal·ly** *adv.*

sub·ma·chine gun (sub′mə·shēn′) A lightweight automatic weapon using pistol ammunition, designed to be fired from the shoulder or hip.

sub·mar·gin·al (sub·mär′jən·əl) *adj.* **1.** Below the margin. **2.** Of low fertility; unproductive: *submarginal* land.

sub·ma·rine (*adj.* sub′mə·rēn′; *n.* sub′mə·rēn) *adj.* Existing, done, or operating beneath the surface of the sea: a *submarine* mine. — *n.* A ship designed to operate below the surface of the sea. — **sub·mar·i·ner** (sub·mar′ə·nər) *n.*

sub·max·il·lar·y (sub·mak′sə·ler′ē) *Anat.* *adj.* **1.** Of or situated beneath the lower jaw. **2.** Of one of the salivary glands on either side of the lower jaw. — *n.* *pl.* **·lar·ies** The lower jaw bone: also **sub·max·il·la** (sub′mak·sil′ə).

sub·merge (səb·mûrj′) *v.* **·merged, ·merg·ing** *v.t.* **1.** To place under or plunge into water or other liquid. **2.** To cover; hide. — *v.i.* **3.** To sink or dive beneath the surface of water, etc. Also **sub·merse′** (-mûrs′). [< L < *sub-* under + *mergere* to plunge] — **sub·mer′gi·bil·i·ty** *n.* — **sub·mer′gi·ble** *adj.*

sub·mersed (səb·mûrst′) *adj.* **1.** *Bot.* Growing under water. **2.** Submerged. [See SUBMERGE.]

sub·mer·sion (səb·mûr′shən, -zhən) *n.* The act of submerging something in a liquid or the state of being submerged. Also **sub·mer′gence** (-jəns).

sub·mis·sion (səb·mish′ən) *n.* **1.** The act of submitting or yielding to the power or authority of another. **2.** The state or quality of being submissive. **3.** The act of presenting something for consideration, approval, decision, etc.

sub·mis·sive (səb·mis′iv) *adj.* Willing or inclined to submit; yielding; obedient; docile. — **sub·mis′sive·ly** *adv.* — **sub·mis′sive·ness** *n.*

sub·mit (səb·mit′) *v.* **·mit·ted, ·mit·ting** *v.t.* **1.** To place under or yield to the authority, or power of another; surrender. **2.** To present for the consideration, decision, or approval of others; refer. **3.** To present as one's opinion; suggest. — *v.i.* **4.** To give up; surrender. **5.** To be obedient, submissive or acquiescent. [< L < *sub-* underneath + *mittere* to send] — **sub·mit′tal** *n.* — **sub·mit′ter** *n.*

sub·nor·mal (sub·nôr′məl) *adj.* **1.** Below the normal. **2.** *Psychol.* Less than normal in intelligence. — *n.* A subnormal individual. — **sub·nor·mal·i·ty** (sub′nôr·mal′ə·tē) *n.*

sub·or·di·nate (*adj. & n.* sə·bôr′də·nit; *v.* sə·bôr′də·nāt) *adj.* **1.** Belonging to an inferior or lower order in a classification; secondary; minor. **2.** Subject or subservient to another; inferior. **3.** *Gram.* **a** Of or designating a clause connected with and dependent upon another clause and functioning as a subject, object, or modifier. **b** Serving to introduce such a clause. — *n.* One who or that which is subordinate. — *v.t.* **·nat·ed, ·nat·ing 1.** To make subordinate; also, to hold as of less importance. **2.** To make subject or subservient. [< L < *sub-* + *ordinare* to order] — **sub·or′di·nate·ly** *adv.* — **sub·or′di·nate·ness** *n.* — **sub·or′di·na′tion** *n.* — **sub·or′di·na′tive** *adj.*

subordinate clause *Gram.* A dependent clause. See under CLAUSE.

sub·orn (sə·bôrn′) *v.t.* **1.** To bribe or procure (someone) to commit perjury. **2.** To incite to an evil act, esp. a criminal act. [< L < *sub-* secretly + *ornare* to equip] — **sub·or·na·tion** (sub′ôr·nā′shən) *n.* — **sub·orn′er** *n.*

sub·plot (sub′plot′) *n.* A plot subordinate to the principal one in a novel, play, etc.

sub·poe·na (sə·pē′nə, səb-) *n.* A judicial writ requiring a person to appear in court to give testimony. — *v.t.* To notify or summon by writ or subpoena. Also **sub·pe′na.** [< Med.L < L < *sub* under + *poena* penalty]

sub·ro·gate (sub′rō·gāt) *v.t.* **·gat·ed, ·gat·ing 1.** To substitute (one thing) for another. **2.** To substitute (one person) for another when assigning rights or appointing to an office. [< L < *sub-* in place of + *rogare* to ask]

sub·ro·ga·tion (sub′rō·gā′shən) *n.* The substitution of one person, esp. a creditor, or thing for another.

sub ro·sa (sub rō′zə) *Latin* Confidentially; in secret: literally, under the rose, the emblem of an Egyptian god, mistakenly regarded by the Romans as the god of silence.

sub·scribe (səb·skrīb′) *v.* **·scribed, ·scrib·ing** *v.t.* **1.** To write, as one's name, at the end of a document; sign. **2.** To sign one's name to as an expression of assent, etc.; attest to by signing. **3.** To promise, esp., in writing, to pay (a sum of money). — *v.i.* **4.** To write one's name at the end of a document. **5.** To give sanction, support, or approval; agree. **6.** To promise to pay or contribute money. **7.** To agree to receive and pay for issues of a newspaper, periodical, etc.: with *to.* [< L < *sub-* underneath + *scribere* to write] — **sub·scrib′er** *n.*

sub·script (sub′skript) *adj.* Written below or lower and to the right or left. — *n.* A subscript character. [See SUBSCRIBE.]

sub·scrip·tion (səb·skrip′shən) *n.* **1.** The act of subscribing; signature. **2.** Consent, confirmation, or agreement. **3.** That which is subscribed; a signed paper or statement. **4.** A signature written at the end of a document. **5.** The individual or total sum or number subscribed for any purpose. **6.** A formal signed undertaking to pay for the receipt of a magazine, book, ticket, etc. — **to take up a subscription** To collect money (for some special cause) from a large number of people. — **sub·scrip′tive** *adj.* — **sub·scrip′tive·ly** *adv.*

sub·se·quent (sub′sə·kwənt) *adj.* Following in time, place, or order, or as a result. [< L < *sub-* next below + *sequi* to follow] — **sub′se·quence, sub′se·quen·cy** *n.* — **sub′se·quent·ly** *adv.* — **sub′se·quent·ness** *n.*

sub·serve (səb·sûrv′) *v.t.* **·served, ·serv·ing 1.** To be of use or help in furthering (a process, cause, etc.); serve; promote. **2.** To serve as a subordinate to (a person). [< L < *sub-* under + *servire* < *servus* slave]

sub·ser·vi·ent (səb·sûr′vē·ənt) *adj.* **1.** Adapted to promote some end or purpose; being of service; useful as a subordinate. **2.** Servile; obsequious. — *n.* One who or that which subserves. — **sub·ser′vi·ent·ly** *adv.* — **sub·ser′vi·ence, sub·ser′vi·en·cy** *n.*

sub·side (səb·sīd′) *v.i.* **·sid·ed, ·sid·ing 1.** To become less violent or agitated; become calm or quiet; abate. **2.** To sink to a lower level. **3.** To sink to the bottom; settle. [< L < *sub-* under + *sidere* to settle < *sedere* to sit] — **sub·sid′ence** (səb·sīd′ns, sub′sə·dəns) *n.*

sub·sid·i·ar·y (səb·sid′ē·er′ē) *adj.* **1.** Assisting or functioning in a lesser capacity; supplementary; secondary. **2.** Of or in the nature of a subsidy; helping by a subsidy. — *n. pl.* **·ar·ies 1.** One who or that which furnishes aid or support; an auxiliary. **2.** A subsidiary company. [See SUBSIDE.]

subsidiary company A company controlled by another company that owns the greater part of its shares.

sub·si·dize (sub′sə·dīz) *v.t.* **·dized, ·diz·ing 1.** To furnish with a subsidy; grant a regular allowance or pecuniary aid to. **2.** To obtain the assistance of by a subsidy: often implying bribery. — **sub·si·di·za′tion** *n.* — **sub′si·diz′er** *n.*

sub·si·dy (sub′sə·dē) *n. pl.* **·dies 1.** Pecuniary aid directly granted by government to a private commercial enterprise deemed beneficial to the public. **2.** Any financial assistance afforded by one individual or government to another. [< AF < L *subsidium* auxiliary forces, aid]

— **Syn. 1.** A government *subsidy* supports a public service, as an airline. The word *subvention* is sometimes applied to a *subsidy* to an artistic enterprise. A *grant* is given by a government or a private institution to be spent for a specified purpose.

sub·sist (səb·sist′) *v.i.* **1.** To have existence or reality; continue to exist. **2.** To manage to live, often with *on* or *by:* to *subsist* on vegetables. **3.** To continue unchanged; abide. **4.** To have existence in or by virtue of something; inhere. [< L < *sub-* under + *sistere* to cause to stand]

sub·sis·tence (səb·sis′təns) *n.* **1.** The act of subsisting. **2.** That on which one subsists; sustenance, livelihood. **3.** The state of being subsistent; inherent quality. **4.** That which subsists; real being. Also **sub·sis′ten·cy.** — **sub·sis′tent** *adj.*

sub·soil (sub′soil′) *n.* The stratum of earth next beneath the surface soil: also called *undersoil.* — *v.t.* To plow so as to turn up the subsoil. — **sub′soil′er** *n.*

sub·son·ic (sub·son′ik) *adj.* **1.** Designating those sound waves beyond the lower limits of human audibility. **2.** *Aeron.* Having a speed less than that of sound.

sub·stance (sub′stəns) *n.* **1.** The material of which anything consists; also, a material object as contrasted with something intangible. **2.** Any type of matter of a specific chemical composition. **3.** Density; body. **4.** A substantial quality; solidity. **5.** The essential part of anything said or written; the gist. **6.** Material wealth; property. [< OF < L < *sub-* under + *stare* to stand]

sub·stan·dard (sub′stan′dərd) *adj.* **1.** Below the standard. **2.** Lower than the established rate or authorized requirements. **3.** *Ling.* Nonstandard.

sub·stan·tial (səb·stan′shəl) *adj.* **1.** Solid; strong; firm. **2.** Of real worth and importance; of considerable value. **3.** Considerable and real: *substantial* progress. **4.** Possessed of wealth and influence. **5.** Of or pertaining to substance; material. **6.** Containing or conforming to the essence of a thing; giving the correct idea; fundamental. **7.** Ample and nourishing. — *n.* **1.** That which has substance; a reality. **2.** The more important part. — **sub·stan′ti·al′i·ty** (-shē-al′ə-tē), **sub·stan′tial·ness** *n.* — **sub·stan′tial·ly** *adv.*

sub·stan·ti·ate (səb·stan′shē-āt) *v.t.* **·at·ed, ·at·ing** **1.** To establish, as a position or a truth, by substantial evidence; verify. **2.** To give form to; embody. **3.** To make substantial, existent, or real; give substance to. [See SUBSTANCE.] — **sub·stan′ti·a′tion** *n.* — **sub·stan′ti·a′tive** *adj.*

sub·stan·tive (sub′stən-tiv) *n.* **1.** A noun or anything that functions as a noun, as a verbal form, phrase, or clause. **2.** One who or that which is independent. — *adj.* **1.** Capable of being used as a noun. **2.** Expressive of or denoting existence. The verb "to be" is called the *substantive* verb. **3.** Having substance or reality; lasting. **4.** Essential. **5.** Individual. **6.** Independent; self-supporting. **7.** Of considerable amount; substantial. [< OF < LL < L. See SUBSTANCE.] — **sub·stan′ti·val** (-tī′vəl) *adj.* — **sub′stan·tive·ly** *adv.* — **sub′stan·tive·ness** *n.*

sub·sta·tion (sub′stā′shən) *n.* A subsidiary station, a branch post office, etc.

sub·sti·tute (sub′stə-tōōt, -tyōōt) *v.* **·tut·ed, ·tut·ing** *v.t.* **1.** To put in the place of another person, constituent, or thing. — *v.i.* **2.** To act as a substitute. — *n.* One who or that which takes the place of or serves in lieu of another. [< L *sub-* in place of + *statuere* to set up]

sub·sti·tu·tion (sub′stə-tōō′shən, -tyōō′-) *n.* **1.** The act or process of substituting, or the state of being substituted. **2.** Something substituted. — **sub·sti·tu′tion·al** *adj.* — **sub′·sti·tu′tion·al·ly** *adv.*

sub·strate (sub′strāt) *n.* *Biochem.* The material or substance acted upon by an enzyme or ferment.

sub·stra·tum (sub·strā′təm, -strat′əm) *n.* *pl.* **·ta** (-tə) or **·tums** **1.** An underlying stratum or layer, as of earth or rock; also, subsoil. **2.** That which forms the foundation, groundwork, or basis. [< NL < L < *sub-* underneath + *sternere* to strew] — **sub·stra′tive** *adj.*

sub·struc·ture (sub′struk′chər, sub·struk′-) *n.* A structure serving as a foundation of a building, etc.

sub·ten·ant (sub′ten′ənt) *n.* A person who rents or leases from a tenant: also called *undertenant.* — **sub·ten′an·cy** *n.*

sub·tend (sub·tend′) *v.t.* **1.** *Geom.* To extend under or opposite to, as the side of a triangle opposite to an angle. **2.** *Bot.* To enclose in its axil: A leaf *subtends* a bud. [< L *sub-* underneath + *tendere* to stretch]

subter- *prefix* Under; less than. [< L *subter* below]

sub·ter·fuge (sub′tər-fyōōj) *n.* Any stratagem to avoid unpleasantness or difficulty. [< L < *subter-* below, in secret + *fugere* to flee]

sub·ter·ra·ne·an (sub′tə-rā′nē-ən) *adj.* **1.** Situated or occurring below the surface of the earth; underground. **2.** Hidden or secret. Also **sub′ter·ra′ne·al, sub′ter·ra′ne·ous.**

sub·tile (sut′l, sub′til) *adj.* **1.** Delicate or tenuous in form, character, etc.; ethereal. **2.** Penetrating; pervasive. **3.** Subtle; wily. [< OF *subtil,* alter. of *soutil* subtle] — **sub′tile·ly** *adv.* — **sub·til′i·ty** (sut′l′ə-tē), **sub′tile·ness** *n.*

sub·til·ize (sut′l-īz, sub′tə-līz) *v.* **·ized, ·iz·ing** *v.t.* **1.** To make subtle or subtile; refine. **2.** To make acute; sharpen, as the senses. **3.** To argue subtly. — *v.i.* **4.** To make subtle distinctions; use subtlety. — **sub′til·i·za′tion** *n.*

sub·ti·tle (sub′tīt′l) *n.* **1.** A subordinate or explanatory title, as in a book, play, or document. **2.** In motion pictures: **a** A running written translation of original dialogue usu. appearing at the bottom of the screen. **b** A written comment or record of dialogue, as in a silent film.

sub·tle (sut′l) *adj.* **1.** Characterized by cunning or artifice; crafty. **2.** Keen; discriminating. **3.** Apt; skillful. **4.** Ingenious; clever; refined. **5.** Insidious; secretly active. **6.** Abstruse. **7.** Of delicate texture. [< OF < L *subtilis* orig., closely woven] — **sub′tle·ness** *n.* — **sub′tly** *adv.*

sub·tle·ty (sut′l·tē) *n.* *pl.* **·ties** **1.** The state or quality of being subtle. **2.** Something subtle, as a nice distinction.

sub·ton·ic (sub′ton′ik) *n.* *Music* The tone below the tonic; the seventh tone of a major or minor scale.

sub·tract (səb-trakt′) *v.t. & v.i.* To take away or deduct, as a portion from the whole, or one quantity from another. [< L < *sub-* away + *trahere* to draw] — **sub·tract′er** *n.*

sub·trac·tion (səb-trak′shən) *n.* **1.** The act or process of subtracting; a deducting. **2.** Something deducted. **3.** *Math.* The operation, indicated by the minus sign (−), of finding the difference between two quantities.

sub·tra·hend (sub′trə-hend) *n.* *Math.* The number to be subtracted from another. [See SUBTRACT.]

sub·treas·ur·y (sub′trezh′ər·ē) *n.* *pl.* **·ur·ies** A branch of a treasury.

sub·trop·i·cal (sub′trop′i·kəl) *adj.* **1.** Of, pertaining to, or designating regions adjacent to the Torrid Zone. **2.** Having characteristics intermediate between or common to both Torrid and Temperate Zones. Also **sub′trop′ic.**

sub·trop·ics (sub′trop′iks) *n.pl.* Subtropical regions.

sub·urb (sub′ûrb) *n.* **1.** A place adjacent to a city, esp., a residential area. **2.** *pl.* Outlying residential districts; outskirts. [< OF < L < *sub-* near to + *urbs, urbis* city]

sub·ur·ban (sə·bûr′bən) *adj.* **1.** Of or pertaining to a suburb. **2.** Dwelling or located in a suburb. — *n.* One who lives in a suburb; suburbanite.

sub·ur·ban·ite (sə·bûr′bən·īt) *n.* A resident of a suburb.

sub·ur·bi·a (sə·bûr′bē·ə) *n.* Suburbs or suburbanites collectively and their social and cultural world.

sub·ven·tion (səb·ven′shən) *n.* **1.** Giving of succor; aid. **2.** A grant, as of money; subsidy. — **Syn.** See SUBSIDY. [< OF < LL < L < *sub-* up from under + *venire* to come] — **sub·ven′tion·ar′y** (-er′ē) *adj.*

sub·ver·sion (səb·vûr′shən, -zhən) *n.* **1.** The act of subverting, or the state of being subverted; a demolition; overthrow. **2.** A cause of ruin. Also **sub·ver′sal** (-səl). [< OF < LL < L. See SUBVERT.]

sub·ver·sive (səb·vûr′siv) *adj.* Tending to subvert or overthrow, as a government. — *n.* One who acts in accordance with subversive principles. — **sub·ver′sive·ly** *adv.*

sub·vert (səb·vûrt′) *v.t.* **1.** To overthrow; destroy utterly. **2.** To undermine the morals, character, or faith of; corrupt. [< OF < L < *sub-* up from under + *vertere* to turn] — **sub·vert′er** *n.* — **sub·vert′i·ble** *adj.* — **Syn.** **1.** uproot, upset, overturn.

sub·way (sub′wā) *n.* **1.** *U.S.* An underground railroad, usu. electrically operated; also, a tunnel for such a railroad. **2.** An underground passage, as for cables, etc.

suc- Assimilated var. of SUB-.

suc·ceed (sək·sēd′) *v.i.* **1.** To accomplish what is attempted or intended; be successful. **2.** To come next in order or sequence; follow; ensue. **3.** To come after another into office, etc.; be the successor: often with *to.* — *v.t.* **4.** To come after; follow. **5.** To be the successor or heir of. [< OF < L *succedere* to follow after] — **suc·ceed′er** *n.*

suc·cess (sək·ses′) *n.* **1.** A favorable or desired outcome of something attempted. **2.** A successful person, enterprise, etc. **3.** Attainment of wealth, etc. [< L. See SUCCEED.]

suc·cess·ful (sək·ses′fəl) *adj.* **1.** Obtaining what one desires or intends. **2.** Having reached a high degree of worldly prosperity. **3.** Terminating in success; resulting favorably. — **suc·cess′ful·ly** *adv.* — **suc·cess′ful·ness** *n.*

suc·ces·sion (sək·sesh′ən) *n.* **1.** The act of following in order, or the state of being successive; a following consecutively. **2.** A series; sequence. **3.** The act or right of legally or officially coming into a predecessor's office, possessions, etc.; also, that which is so acquired. **4.** The order by which an office, etc., changes hands. **5.** Descendants collectively; issue. — **suc·ces′sion·al** *adj.* — **suc·ces′sion·al·ly** *adv.*

suc·ces·sive (sək·ses′iv) *adj.* Following in sequence; consecutive. — **suc·ces′sive·ly** *adv.* — **suc·ces′sive·ness** *n.*

suc·ces·sor (sək·ses′ər) *n.* One who or that which succeeds or comes after; esp., a person who succeeds to a throne, property, or office.

suc·cinct (sək·singkt′) *adj.* Consisting of or characterized by brief and meaningful language; terse; concise. — **Syn.** See TERSE. [< L < *sub-* underneath + *cingere* to gird] — **suc·cinct′ly** *adv.* — **suc·cinct′ness** *n.*

suc·cor (suk′ər) *n.* **1.** Help or relief rendered in danger, difficulty, or distress. **2.** One who or that which affords relief. — *v.t.* To go to the aid of; help; rescue. Also *Brit.* **suc′cour** [< OF < Med.L < L < *sub-* up from under + *currere* to run] — **suc′cor·a·ble** *adj.* — **suc′cor·er** *n.*

suc·co·tash (suk′ə-tash) *n.* A dish of corn kernels and beans, usu. lima beans, boiled together. [< Algonquian (Narraganset) *misickquatash* ear of corn]

Suc·coth (sŏŏk′ōth, -ōs, -əs) See SUKKOTH.

suc·cu·bus (suk′yə-bəs) *n.* *pl.* **·bus·es** or **·bi** (bī) **1.** In folklore, a female demon that has sexual intercourse with sleeping men. Compare INCUBUS. **2.** Any evil spirit. [< Med.L < L < *sub-* underneath + *cubare* to lie]

suc·cu·lent (suk′yə-lənt) *adj.* **1.** Full of juice; juicy. **2.** *Bot.* Juicy; fleshy, as the tissues of certain plants. **3.** Rich or vigorous; a *succulent* theme. [< L < *succus* juice] — **suc′·cu·lence**, **suc′cu·len·cy** *n.* — **suc′cu·lent·ly** *adv.*

suc·cumb (sə-kum′) *v.i.* **1.** To give way; yield, as to force or persuasion. **2.** To die. [< OF < L < *sub-* underneath + *cumbere* to lie]

such (such) *adj.* **1.** Of that kind; of the same or like kind: often with *as* or *that* completing a comparison: *Such* wit as this is rare. **2.** Being the same as what has been mentioned or indicated: *Such* was the king's command. **3.** Being the same in quality: Let the truthful continue *such*. **4.** Being the same as something understood by the speaker or the hearer, or purposely left indefinite: the chief of *such* a clan. **5.** So extreme, unpleasant, or the like: We have come to *such* a pass. — **as such 1.** As being what is indicated or implied: An executive, *as such*, must take responsibility. **2.** In or by itself: Clothes, *as such*, do not make the man. — **such as 1.** For example. **2.** Of a particular kind or degree: The outcome of the trial was *such as* might be expected. — *pron.* **1.** Such a person or thing, or such persons or things: The friend of *such* as are in trouble. **2.** The same; the aforesaid: I bring good tidings, for *such* the general sent. — *adv. Informal* So: *such* awful manners. ◆ *Such* and *such a* are widely used in informal contexts to intensify the adjective or noun they precede: He was *such a* kind man; He had *such* wisdom. [OE *swelc, swilc, swylc*]

such and such Being a condition, person, thing, or time, not specifically named.

such·like (such′līk′) *adj.* Of a like or similar kind. — *pron.* Persons or things of that kind.

suck (suk) *v.t.* **1.** To draw into the mouth by means of a partial vacuum created by action of the lips and tongue. **2.** To draw in or take up in a manner resembling this; absorb. **3.** To draw liquid or nourishment from with the mouth. **4.** To take into and hold in the mouth. **5.** To consume by licking, or by holding in the mouth: to *suck* candy. **6.** To bring to a specified state or condition by sucking: He *sucked* the lemon dry. — *v.i.* **7.** To draw in liquid, air, etc., by suction. **8.** To suckle. **9.** To draw in air instead of water, as a defective pump does. **10.** To make the sound of sucking. — **to suck in** *Slang* To take advantage of. — *n.* **1.** The act of sucking; suction. **2.** That which is sucked or comes by sucking. **3.** A slight draft or drink. [OE *sūcan*]

suck·er (suk′ər) *n.* **1.** One who or that which sucks. **2.** A North American fresh-water fish, having the mouth usu. protractile with thick and fleshy lips adapted for sucking in food. **3.** *Zool.* An organ by which an animal adheres to other bodies by suction. **4.** *U.S. Slang* One who is easily deceived; a foolish or gullible person. **5.** A lollipop. **6.** *Bot.* A shoot or sprout arising from the root near or remote from the trunk of certain trees. — *v.t.* **1.** To strip of suckers or shoots. — *v.i.* **2.** To form or send out suckers or shoots. [< SUCK]

Sucker State Nickname for Illinois.

suck·le (suk′əl) *v.* **·led**, **·ling** *v.t.* **1.** To allow or cause to take nourishment from the breast by sucking; nurse. **2.** To bring up; nourish. — *v.i.* **3.** To take nourishment at the breast: also **suck**. [ME *sucklen*, prob. back formation < SUCKLING] — **suck′ler** *n.*

suck·ling (suk′ling) *n.* **1.** An unweaned mammal. **2.** An infant. [ME < *soken* to suck + *-ling* -ling¹]

su·crose (soo′krōs) *n. Biochem.* A crystalline disaccharide, $C_{12}H_{22}O_{11}$, forming the greater part of the sugar as obtained from the sugar cane, maple, beet, etc. Also called *saccharose*. [< F *sucre* sugar + *-ose* -ose²]

suc·tion (suk′shən) *n.* **1.** The act or process of sucking. **2.** The production of a partial vacuum in a space connected with a liquid or gas under pressure. **3.** The tendency of a fluid to occupy all or part of a vacuum contiguous with it. [< OF < L *sugere* to suck]

suction pump A pump operating by suction, consisting of a piston working in a cylinder, both equipped with valves.

suc·to·ri·al (suk-tôr′ē-əl, -tō′rē-əl) *adj.* **1.** Adapted for sucking or for adhesion. **2.** *Zool.* Having organs for sucking.

Su·da·nese (soo′də-nēz′, -nēs′) *adj.* Of or pertaining to the Sudan or its people. — *n. pl.* **·nese** A native or inhabitant of the Sudan.

sud·den (sud′n) *adj.* **1.** Happening quickly and without warning. **2.** Hurriedly or quickly contrived, used, or done; hasty. **3.** Come upon unexpectedly; causing surprise. **4.** Quick-tempered; precipitate. — **all of a sudden** Without warning; suddenly. [< AF < OF < L < *sub-* secretly + *ire* to go] — **sud′den·ly** *adv.* — **sud′den·ness** *n.*

su·dor·if·ic (soo′də-rif′ik) *Med. adj.* Causing perspiration. — *n.* A medicine that produces or promotes sweating. [< NL < L *sudor, -oris* sweat + *facere* to make]

suds (sudz) *n.pl.* **1.** Soapy water, or bubbles and froth on

its surface. **2.** Foam; lather. **3.** *Slang* Beer. [Prob. < MDu. *sudde, sudse* marsh water] — **suds′y** *adj.*

sue (soo) *v.* **sued, su·ing** *v.t.* **1.** *Law* a To institute proceedings against for the recovery of some right or the redress of some wrong. **b** To prosecute (an action). **c** To seek a grant from (a court). **2.** To endeavor to persuade by entreaty; petition — *v.i.* **3.** To institute legal proceedings. **4.** To make entreaty. [< AF *suer*, OF *sivre*, ult. < L *sequi* to follow] — **su′a·ble** *adj.* — **su′er** *n.*

suede (swād) *n.* **1.** A leather having a soft napped finish, usu. on the flesh side. **2.** A woven or knitted fabric finished to resemble this. Also **suede**. [< F *Suède* Sweden, in phrase *gants de Suède* Swedish gloves]

su·et (soo′it) *n.* The fatty tissues about the loins and kidneys of sheep, oxen, etc., used in cookery and to make tallow. [Dim. of AF *sue*, OF *seu* < L *sebum* fat] — **su′et·y** *adj.*

suf- Assimilated var. of SUB-.

suf·fer (suf′ər) *v.i.* **1.** To feel pain or distress. **2.** To be affected injuriously; experience loss or injury. **3.** To undergo punishment; esp., to be put to death. — *v.t.* **4.** To have inflicted on one; sustain, as an injury or loss. **5.** To undergo; pass through, as change. **6.** To bear; endure: to *suffer* more pain. **7.** To allow; permit: Will he *suffer* us to leave? [< AF *suffrir*, OF *sofrir*, ult. < L < *sub-* up from under + *ferre* to bear] — **suf′fer·er** *n.*

suf·fer·a·ble (suf′ər-ə-bəl, suf′rə-) *adj.* Such as can be suffered or endured; tolerable. — **suf′fer·a·bly** *adv.*

suf·fer·ance (suf′ər-əns, suf′rəns) *n.* **1.** Permission given or implied by failure to prohibit; passive consent. **2.** The act or state of suffering. **3.** Power to endure pain or evil. **4.** Patience or endurance under suffering; submissiveness.

suf·fer·ing (suf′ər·ing, suf′ring) *n.* **1.** The state of anguish or pain of one who suffers. **2.** The bearing of pain, injury, or loss. **3.** Pain or distress borne or endured; injury. — *adj.* Inured to pain and loss; submissive. — **suf′fer·ing·ly** *adv.* — **Syn. 1.** *Suffering* is acute bodily or mental pain. *Distress* may be physical, but is more often mental, referring to any deep anxiety, or the external circumstances that may produce it. *Misery* is extreme *suffering* or abject hopelessness, as from sorrow, great loss, poverty, or the like.

suf·fice (sə-fīs′) *v.* **·ficed, ·fic·ing** *v.i.* **1.** To be sufficient or adequate; meet the requirements or answer the purpose. — *v.t.* **2.** To be satisfactory or adequate for; satisfy. [< OF < L < *sub-* under + *facere* to make] — **suf·fic′er** *n.*

suf·fi·cien·cy (sə-fish′ən-sē) *n. pl.* **·cies 1.** The state of being sufficient. **2.** That which is sufficient; esp., adequate pecuniary means or income. **3.** Full capability or qualification; efficiency. **4.** Conceit; self-sufficiency.

suf·fi·cient (sə-fish′ənt) *adj.* Being all that is needful; adequate; enough. — **Syn.** See ADEQUATE. [See SUFFICE.] — **suf·fi′cient·ly** *adv.*

suf·fix (suf′iks) *n.* **1.** *Gram.* A bound form affixed to the end of a base, stem, or root, functioning as a derivative or inflectional element. Compare COMBINING FORM, PREFIX. **2.** An added title or the like. — *v.t.* To add as a suffix. [< NL < L < *sub-* underneath + *figere* to fix.] — **suf′fix·al** *adj.* — **suf·fix·ion** (sə-fik′shən) *n.*

suf·fo·cate (suf′ə·kāt) *v.* **·cat·ed, ·cat·ing** *v.t.* **1.** To kill by obstructing respiration in any manner. **2.** To obstruct or oppress, as by an inadequate supply of air. **3.** To stifle; smother, as a fire. — *v.i.* **4.** To become choked or stifled; die from suffocation. [< L < *sub-* under + *fauces* throat] — **suf′fo·cat·ing·ly** *adv.* — **suf′fo·ca′tion** *n.* — **suf′fo·ca′tive** *adj.*

Suf·folk (suf′ək) *n.* **1.** A hardy English breed of working horses, with a heavy body and rather short legs. Also **Suffolk punch**. **2.** A breed of hornless sheep producing mutton of high quality. [after *Suffolk*, England]

suf·frage (suf′rij) *n.* **1.** The right or privilege of voting; franchise. **2.** The act or process of voting. **3.** A vote in support of some measure or candidate. **4.** Approbation; assent. [< OF < L *suffragium* voting tablet, vote]

suf·fra·gette (suf′rə·jet′) *n.* Formerly, a woman who advocated or agitated for female suffrage. — **suf′fra·get′tism** *n.*

suf·fra·gist (suf′rə-gist) *n.* An advocate of some particular form of suffrage, esp. of female suffrage.

suf·fuse (sə-fyooz′) *v.t.* **·fused, ·fus·ing** To overspread, as with a vapor, fluid, or color. [< L < *sub-* underneath, up from under + *fundere* to pour] — **suf·fu·sive** (sə-fyoo′siv) *adj.*

suf·fu·sion (sə-fyoo′zhən) *n.* **1.** The act of suffusing, or the state of being suffused. **2.** That which suffuses, as a blush.

sug- Assimilated var. of SUB-.

sug·ar (shoog′ər) *n.* **1.** *Biochem.* **a** A sweet, crystalline carbohydrate, $C_{12}H_{22}O_{11}$, obtained from the juice of various plants, as from the sugar cane, the sugar beet, and the sugar maple. ◆ Collateral adjective: *saccharine.* **b** Any of a large class of similar carbohydrates, widely distributed in plants and animals. **2.** Flattering or honeyed words. **3.** *Slang* Sweet one: a pet name. — *v.t.* **1.** To sweeten, cover, or coat with sugar. **2.** To make agreeable or less distasteful, as by flattery. **—** *v.i.* **3.** *Chiefly U.S.* To make maple sugar. **4.** To form or produce sugar; granulate. [< OF < Med.L, ult. < Arabic *sukkar*]

sugar beet A sugar-producing species of beet.

sug·ar·bush (shŏŏg′ər-bŏŏsh′) *n.* A grove of sugar maples.

sugar cane A tall, stout, perennial grass of tropical regions, having a solid jointed stalk constituting a major source of commercial sugar.

sug·ar·coat (shŏŏg′ər-kōt′) *v.t.* **1.** To cover with sugar. **2.** To cause to appear attractive or less distasteful, as with euphemisms or flattery.

sug·ar·cured (shŏŏg′ər-kyŏŏrd′) *adj.* Cured by using sugar in the curing process, as ham and pork.

sug·ared (shŏŏg′ərd) *adj.* **1.** Sweetened with sugar; sugarcoated. **2.** Honeyed; pleasant; sweetened.

sugar loaf **1.** A conical mass of hard refined sugar. **2.** A conical hat or hill. **— sug·ar·loaf** (shŏŏg′ər-lōf′) *adj.*

sugar maple A maple of eastern North America, yielding a sap from which maple sugar is made.

sug·ar·plum (shŏŏg′ər-plum′) *n.* A small ball or disk of candy; a bonbon.

sug·ar·y (shŏŏg′ər-ē) *adj.* **1.** Composed of or as of sugar; sweet. **2.** Fond of sugar. **3.** Insincerely or cloyingly sweet. **4.** Consisting of grains; granular. **— sug′ar·i·ness** *n.*

sug·gest (səg-jest′, sə-jest′) *v.t.* **1.** To bring or put forward for consideration, action, or approval; propose. **2.** To bring to mind by association or connection; connote. **3.** To give a hint or indirect indication of; intimate: The simple house *suggested* a modest income. **4.** To act as or provide a motive for; prompt: these events *suggest* a sequel. [< L < *sub*- underneath + *gerere* to carry] **— sug·gest′er** *n.*

sug·gest·i·bil·i·ty (səg-jes′tə-bil′ə-tē, sə-) *n.* **1.** *Psychol.* Responsiveness to suggestion, esp. when heightened or abnormal, as in hypnosis and certain nervous conditions. **2.** Readiness to believe and agree without reflection.

sug·gest·i·ble (səg-jes′tə-bəl, sə-) *adj.* **1.** That can be suggested. **2.** Easily led; yielding: a *suggestible* patient.

sug·ges·tion (səg-jes′chən, sə-jes′-) *n.* **1.** The act of suggesting. **2.** Something suggested. **3.** A hint; insinuation. **4.** The spontaneous calling up of an idea in the mind by a connected idea.

sug·ges·tive (səg-jes′tiv, sə-) *adj.* **1.** Fitted or tending to suggest; stimulating to thought or reflection. **2.** Hinting at or arousing indecent thoughts; suggesting the improper. **— sug·ges′tive·ly** *adv.* **— sug·ges′tive·ness** *n.*

su·i·cide (sōō′ə-sīd) *n.* **1.** The intentional taking of one's own life. **2.** Self-inflicted political, social, or commercial ruin. **3.** One who has taken his own life. **—** *v.i.* **·cid·ed, ·cid·ing** *Informal* To commit suicide. [< NL < L *sui* of oneself + *caedere* to kill] **— su′i·cid′al** *adj.*

su·i gen·er·is (sōō′ī jen′ər·is) *Latin* Forming a kind by itself; unique; literally, of its (his, or her) particular kind.

suit (sōōt) *n.* **1.** A set of garments consisting of a coat and trousers or skirt, made of the same fabric. **2.** A group of things of like kind or pattern composing a series or set. **3.** In cardplaying, one of the four sets of thirteen cards each that make up a pack, as spades, hearts, diamonds, or clubs. **4.** *Law* A proceeding in a court of law or chancery in which a plaintiff demands the recovery of a right or the redress of a wrong. **5.** The courting or courtship of a woman. **6.** *Archaic* Entreaty; petition. **— to follow suit 1.** To play a card identical in suit to the card led. **2.** To do as somebody or something else has done. **—** *v.t.* **1.** To meet the requirements of, or be appropriate to. **2.** To please; satisfy. **3.** To render appropriate or accordant; accommodate; adapt. **—** *v.i.* **4.** To be befitting; agree. **5.** To be or prove satisfactory. [< AF < OF *sieute*, ult. < L *sequi* to follow]

suit·a·ble (sōō′tə-bəl) *adj.* Appropriate to a particular occasion, condition, etc.; proper. **— suit′a·bil′i·ty, suit′a·ble·ness** *n.* **— suit′a·bly** *adv.*

suit·case (sōōt′kās′) *n.* A flat, rectangular valise.

suite (swēt) *n.* **1.** A succession of things forming a series and usu. intended to be or be used together; a set. **2.** A number of connected rooms. **3.** A set of furniture designed to be used together in the same room. **4.** A company of attendants or followers; retinue. **5.** *Music* A form of instrumental composition formerly consisting of a series of dances, but now often varying freely in its construction. **6.** *Canadian* In the West, an apartment. [< F < OF *sieute*]

suit·ing (sōō′ting) *n.* Cloth from which to make suits.

suit·or (sōō′tər) *n.* **1.** A man who courts a woman; a wooer. **2.** One who institutes a suit in court. **3.** A petitioner. [< AF < LL < L *secutus*, pp. of *sequi* to follow]

su·ki·ya·ki (sōō′kē-yä′kē, -yak′ē; skē-) *n.* A Japanese dish made of meat in thin slices, vegetables, and condiments. [< Japanese *suki* spade + *yaki* roast]

Suk·koth (sŏŏk′ōth, -ōs, -əs) *n.* The feast of Tabernacles, a Jewish holiday beginning on the 15th of Tishri (late September–October), originally a harvest festival: also spelled *Succoth*. Also **Suk′kos, Suk′kot.** [< Hebrew *sukōth* tabernacles]

sulfa- *combining form Chem.* Sulfur; related to or containing sulfur: also spelled *sulpha-*. Also, before vowels, **sulf-**. See also SULFO-. [< SULFUR]

sul·fa drug (sul′fə) *Chem.* Any of a large group of organic compounds consisting mainly of substituted sulfanilamide derivatives, some of which are effective in the treatment of certain bacterial infections.

sul·fa·nil·a·mide (sul′fə-nil′ə-mīd, -mid) *n. Chem.* A colorless, crystalline sulfonamide, $C_6H_8N_2O_2S$, used in the treatment of various bacterial infections.

sul·fate (sul′fāt) *n. Chem.* A salt of sulfuric acid. **—** *v.* **·fat·ed, ·fat·ing** *v.t.* **1.** To form a sulfate of; treat with a sulfate or sulfuric acid. **2.** *Electr.* To form a coating of lead sulfate on (the plate of a secondary battery). **—** *v.i.* **3.** To become sulfated. Also spelled *sulphate*.

sul·fide (sul′fīd) *n. Chem.* A compound of sulfur with an element or radical: also *sulphide*, *sulphid*. Also **sul′fid** (-fid).

sul·fite (sul′fīt) *n. Chem.* A salt or ester of sulfurous acid: also spelled *sulphite*. **— sul·fit′ic** (-fit′ik) *adj.*

sulfo- *combining form Chem.* Sulfur; containing sulfur. Also spelled *sulpho-*. [< SULFUR]

sul·fon·a·mide (sul-fon′ə-mīd, sul′fən-am′id, -id) *n. Chem.* Any of a class of chemotherapeutic compounds containing the univalent radical SO_2N, esp. those derived from sulfanilamide: also spelled *sulphonamide*.

sul·fur (sul′fər) *n.* A pale yellow, nonmetallic element (symbol S), found both free and combined in the native state, and existing in several forms, of which the best known is a crystalline solid that burns with a blue flame and a suffocating odor. It is used for making matches, gunpowder, vulcanized rubber, and medicines. See ELEMENT. Also spelled *sulphur*. [< AF *sulfre*, OF *soufre* < L *sulfur*, *-uris*]

sulfur dioxide *Chem.* A colorless, water-soluble, suffocating gas, SO_2, formed by the burning of sulfur and used in the manufacture of sulfuric acid.

sul·fu·re·ous (sul-fyŏŏr′ē-əs) *adj.* Of or like sulfur: also spelled *sulphureous*.

sul·fu·ret (sul′fyə-ret) *v.t.* **·fu·ret·ed** or **·ret·ted**, **·fu·ret·ing** or **·ret·ting** To sulfurize.

sul·fu·ric (sul-fyŏŏr′ik) *adj. Chem.* Pertaining to or derived from sulfur, esp. in its higher valence: also *sulphuric*.

sulfuric acid *Chem.* A colorless, exceedingly corrosive, oily liquid, H_2SO_4, extensively employed in the manufacture of soda, batteries, guncotton, and in a great variety of industrial operations: formerly called *oil of vitriol, vitriol*.

sul·fur·ize (sul′fyə-rīz, -fə-) *v.t.* **·ized, ·iz·ing** **1.** To impregnate, treat with, or subject to the action of sulfur. **2.** To bleach or fumigate with sulfur. Also spelled *sulphurize*. Also **sul′fu·rate** (-rāt). **— sul′fur·i·za′tion** *n.*

sul·fur·ous (sul′fər-əs, sul-fyŏŏr′əs) *adj.* **1.** Of, pertaining to, derived from, or containing sulfur, esp. in its lower valence. **2.** Fiery; hellish. Also spelled *sulphurous*.

sulfurous acid *Chem.* A compound corresponding to the formula H_2SO_3, and known only in solution and by its salts.

sul·fur·y (sul′fər-ē) *adj.* Resembling or suggesting sulfur; sulfureous: also spelled *sulphury*.

sulk (sulk) *v.i.* To be sulky or morose. **—** *n.* **1.** Often *pl.* A sulky mood or humor. **2.** One who sulks. [Back formation < SULKY]

sulk·y¹ (sul′kē) *adj.* **sulk·i·er, sulk·i·est** **1.** Sullenly cross; doggedly or resentfully ill-humored. **2.** Dismal; gloomy: said of weather. [? OE (ā)*solcen*, orig. pp. of (ā)*seolcan* to be weak, slothful] **— sulk′i·ly** *adv.* **— sulk′i·ness** *n.*

sulk·y² (sul′kē) *n.* *pl.* **sulk·ies** A light, two-wheeled, one-horse vehicle for one person. [< SULKY¹]

sul·len (sul′ən) *adj.* **1.** Obstinately and gloomily ill-humored; morose; glum; melancholy. **2.** Depressing; somber: *sullen* clouds. **3.** Slow; sluggish: a *sullen* tread. **4.** Ill-omened; threatening. [Earlier *solein*, appar. < AF < L *solus* alone] **— sul′len·ly** *adv.* **— sul′len·ness** *n.*

sul·ly (sul′ē) *v.* **·lied, ·ly·ing** *v.t.* **1.** To mar the brightness or purity of; soil; defile; tarnish. **—** *v.i.* **2.** To become soiled or tarnished. **—** *n.* *pl.* **·lies** Anything that tarnishes; a stain; spot; blemish. [< MF *souiller* to soil]

sulpha- Var. of SULFA-.

sul·phur (sul′fər), **sul·phu·re·ous** (sul-fyŏŏr′ē-əs), etc. See SULFUR, etc.

sulpho- Var. of SULFO-.

sul·tan (sul′tən) *n.* The ruler of a Moslem country. **— the Sultan** Formerly, the title of the sovereign of Turkey. [< F < Med.L *sultanus* < Arabic *sultān*]

sul·tan·a (sul-tan′ə, -tä′nə) *n.* **1.** A sultan's wife, daughter, sister, or mother. Also **sul·tan·ess** (sul′tən-is). **2.** A variety of raisin from around Smyrna, Asia Minor.

sul·tan·ate (sul′tən-āt, -it) *n.* The authority or territorial jurisdiction of a sultan. Also **sul′tan·ship**.

sul·try (sul′trē) *adj.* **·tri·er, ·tri·est 1.** Hot, moist, and still; close: said of weather. **2.** Emitting an oppressive heat. **3.** Showing or suggesting passion; sensual. [< obs. *sulter*, var. of SWELTER] **— sul′tri·ly** *adv.* **— sul′tri·ness** *n.*

sum (sum) *n.* **1.** The result obtained by addition. **2.** The entire quantity, number, or substance. **3.** An indefinite amount, as of money. **4.** A problem in arithmetic propounded for solution. **5.** The topmost or highest point; also, the maximum. **6.** The pith or essence; summary. *— v.* **summed, sum·ming** *v.t.* **1.** To present in brief; recapitulate succinctly: usu. with *up.* **2.** To add into one total: often with *up.* **3.** To ascertain the sum of (the terms of a series). *— v.i.* **4.** To make a summation or recapitulation: usu. with *up.* [< AF, OF < L *summa* (*res*) highest (thing)]

sum- Var. of SUB-.

su·mac (sōō′mak, shōō′-) *n.* **1.** Any of various woody, erect, or root-climbing plants, with panicles of small drupaceous fruits, and yielding a resinous or milky juice. **2.** The poison sumac. **3.** The dried and powdered leaves of certain species of sumac, used for tanning and dyeing. Also **su′mach.** [< OF < Med.L < Arabic *summāq*]

Su·mer (sōō′mər) A region and ancient country of Mesopotamia, later the southern division of Babylonia.

Su·me·ri·an (sōō·mir′ē·ən) *adj.* Of or pertaining to ancient Sumer, its people, or their language. *— n.* **1.** One of an ancient non-Semitic people formerly occupying a part of lower Babylonia. **2.** The unclassified language of these people, written in cuneiform characters and preserved on rocks and clay tablets that date from as early as 4000 B.C. Also **Su·mir′i·an.**

sum·mand (sum′and) *n.* That which is added; any of the numbers forming part of a sum.

sum·ma·rize (sum′ə·rīz) *v.t.* **·rized, ·riz·ing** To make a summary of; sum up. Also *Brit.* **sum′ma·rise.** **— sum′ma·rist** (-ə·rist), **sum′ma·riz′er** *n.* **— sum′ma·ri·za′tion** *n.*

sum·ma·ry (sum′ər·ē) *adj.* **1.** Giving the substance or sum; concise. **2.** Performed without ceremony or delay; offhand. *— n.* *pl.* **·ries** An abridgment or abstract. [< Med.L < L *summa* sum] **— sum·ma·ri·ly** (sum′ər·ə·lē, *emphatic* sə·mer′ə·lē) *adv.* **— sum′ma·ri·ness** *n.*

sum·ma·tion (sum·ā′shən) *n.* **1.** The act or operation of obtaining a sum; the computation of an aggregate sum; addition. **2.** A speech or a portion of a speech summing up the principal points.

sum·mer (sum′ər) *n.* **1.** The warmest season of the year, occurring between spring and autumn. ♦ Collateral adjective: *estival.* **2.** A year of life, esp. of early or happy life. **3.** A bright and prosperous period. *— v.t.* **1.** To keep or care for through the summer. *— v.i.* **2.** To pass the summer. *— adj.* Of, pertaining to, or occurring in summer. [OE *sumor*] **— sum′mer·ly** *adj. & adv.* **— sum′mer·y** *adj.*

sum·mer·house (sum′ər·hous′) *n.* A rustic structure, as in a garden, for rest or shade.

sum·mer·sault (sum′ər·sôlt) See SOMERSAULT.

summer school A school, college, or university offering courses during the summer vacation period.

sum·mer·time (sum′ər·tim′) *n.* Summer; the summer season. Also **sum′mer·tide′.**

sum·mit (sum′it) *n.* **1.** The highest part; the top; vertex. **2.** The highest degree; maximum. **3.** The highest level or rank, as of government officials: a meeting at the *summit.* **4.** A meeting or discussion among the highest executives of government, esp. chiefs of state; also, the place where such a meeting is held. *— adj.* Of, pertaining to, or characterized by diplomacy at the highest level. [< OF < L *summum*, neut. of *summus* highest] **— sum′mit·al** *adj.*
— Syn. **1.** acme, climax, peak, pinnacle, apex, zenith.

sum·mit·ry (sum′ə·trē) *n.* The practice of conducting diplomacy by means of conferences between the highest executives of government, esp. chiefs of state.

sum·mon (sum′ən) *v.t.* **1.** To order to come; send for. **2.** To call together; cause to convene, as a legislative assembly. **3.** To order (a person) to appear in court by a summons. **4.** To call forth or into action; arouse: usu. with *up*: to *summon* up courage. **5.** To bid or call on for a specific act: The garrison was *summoned* to surrender. [< AF, OF < L *sub-* secretly + *monere* to warn]

sum·mon·er (sum′ən·ər) *n.* **1.** One who summons. **2.** *Archaic* An officer who summons persons to appear in court.

sum·mons (sum′ənz) *n.* *pl.* **sum·mon·ses** (sum′ən·zəz) **1.** A call to attend or act at a particular place or time. **2.** *Law* A notice to a defendant summoning him to appear in court; any citation issued to a party to an action to appear before a court or judge at chambers. **3.** A notice to a person requiring him to appear in court as a witness or as a juror. **4.** A military demand to surrender. **5.** Any signal or sound that is a peremptory call.

sum·mum bo·num (sum′əm bō′nəm) *Latin* The chief, supreme, or highest good.

sump (sump) *n.* **1.** A small well, pit, or cavity to receive liquid wastes or serve as a reservoir for lubricating oil. **2.** A cesspool or other reservoir for drainage. [< MDu. *somp, sump* marsh]

sump·ter (sump′tər) *n.* A pack animal; beast of burden. [< OF *sometier* driver of a pack horse]

sump·tu·ar·y (sump′chōō·er·ē) *adj.* Pertaining to expense; limiting or regulating expenditure, as some laws. [< L < *sumptus* expenditure]

sump·tu·ous (sump′chōō·əs) *adj.* **1.** Involving or showing lavish expenditure. **2.** Luxurious; magnificent. [See SUMPTUARY.] **— sump′tu·ous·ly** *adv.* **— sump′tu·ous·ness** *n.*

sun (sun) *n.* **1.** The star that is the center of attraction and the main source of radiant energy in the solar system, with a mean distance from the earth of about 93 million miles, a diameter of 864,000 miles, and a mass 332,000 times that of the earth. ♦ Collateral adjectives: *heliacal, solar.* **2.** Any star, esp. one that is the center of a system revolving around it. **3.** Sunshine. **4.** Anything brilliant and magnificent. **5.** The time of the earth's revolution around the sun; a year. **6.** The daily appearance of the sun; a day; also, the time of its appearance or shining; sunrise. **— a place in the sun 1.** A dominant position in international affairs. **2.** A position in the spotlight; publicity. *— v.* **sunned, sun·ning** *v.t.* **1.** To expose to the light or heat of the sun. **2.** To warm or dry (something) in the sun. *— v.i.* **3.** To bask in the sun. [OE *sunne*]

Sun may appear as a combining form or as the first element in two-word phrases, with the following meanings:
1. Of the sun; of sunshine:

sun blaze	sunland	sun worship
sun-eclipsing	sun lover	sun worshiper
sun glare	sun-loving	sun-worshiping

2. By or with the sun:

sun-arrayed	sun-browned	sun-heated
sun-bake	sun-cracked	sun-kissed
sun-baked	sun-dappled	sunlit
sun-blanched	sun-dried	sun-scorched
sun-blind	sun-dry	sun-scorching
sun-blinded	sun-filled	sun-streaked
sun-blistered	sun-flooded	sun-warmed
sun-brown	sun-gilt	sun-withered

sun bath Exposure of the body to the direct rays of the sun.

sun·bathe (sun′bāth′) *v.i.* **-bathed, -bath·ing** To bask in the sun, esp., as a method of tanning the skin. **— sun′bath·er** *n.* **— sun′bath·ing** *n.*

sun·beam (sun′bēm′) *n.* A ray or beam of the sun; light from the sun in a visible path.

sun·bon·net (sun′bon′it) *n.* A bonnet of light material with projecting brim and sometimes a cape over the neck.

sun·burn (sun′bûrn′) *n.* Discoloration or inflammation of the skin from exposure to the sun. *— v.t. & v.i.* **·burned or ·burnt, ·burn·ing** To affect or be affected with sunburn.

sun·burst (sun′bûrst′) *n.* **1.** A strong burst of sunlight, as through rifted clouds. **2.** A jewelled brooch, etc., with rays shooting forth in all directions from a central disk.

sun-cured (sun′kyōōrd′) *adj.* Cured by the action of the sun, as beef.

sun·dae (sun′dē, -dā) *n.* A refreshment made of ice cream, crushed fruit, syrup, nuts, etc. [Prob. < SUNDAY]

Sun·day (sun′dē, -dā) *n.* The first day of the week; the Christian Sabbath. [OE < *sunnan* of the sun + *dæg* day]

Sunday school A school in which religious instruction is given on Sunday, esp., to the young; also, the teachers and pupils collectively.

sun deck An exposed surface or platform suitable for sunbathing, as on a ship or building; sun roof.

sun·der (sun′dər) *v.t.* **1.** To break apart; disunite; sever. *— v.i.* **2.** To be parted or severed. *— n.* Division into parts; separation. **— in sunder** Separate from other parts; apart. [OE *syndrian sundrian*] **— sun′der·ance** *n.*

sun·di·al (sun′dī′əl) *n.* A device that shows the time of day by the shadow of a gnomon thrown on a dial.

SUNDIAL
g Gnomon.

sun·down (sun′doun′) *n.* *Chiefly U.S.* Sunset.

sun·down·er (sun′dou′nər) *n.* *Informal* A tramp.

sun·dries (sun′drēz) *n.pl.* Items or things too small or too numerous to be separately specified. [< SUNDRY]

sun·dry (sun′drē) *adj.* Of an indefinite small number; various; several; miscellaneous. [OE *syndrig* separate]

sun·fish (sun′fish′) *n.* *pl.* **·fish or ·fish·es 1.** Any of various large oceanic fishes having a deep, compressed body truncated in the rear, and tough, leathery flesh. **2.** Any of a family of North American fresh-water fishes.

sun·flow·er (sun′flou′ər) *n.* Any of various tall, stout herbs with large leaves and circular heads of bright yellow flowers.

Sunflower State Nickname of Kansas.

sung (sung) Past participle and occasional past tense of SING.

Sung (sōŏng) *n.* A dynasty in Chinese history, 960 to 1280, noted for its achievements in art and philosophy.

sun·glass (sun′glas′, -gläs′) *n.* **1.** *pl.* Spectacles that protect the eyes from the glare of the sun by their colored lenses. **2.** A burning glass.

sunk (sungk) Past participle and alternative past tense of SINK.

sunk·en (sung′kən) Obsolete past participle of SINK. — *adj.* **1.** Deeply depressed or fallen in; hollow: a *sunken* cheek. **2.** Located beneath the surface of the ground or the water. **3.** At a lower level: *sunken* gardens.

sun lamp A lamp radiating ultraviolet rays, used for therapeutic treatments or to acquire a sun tan.

sun·less (sun′lis) *adj.* **1.** Lacking sun or sunlight; overcast; dark. **2.** Cheerless; gloomy. — **sun′less·ness** *n.*

sun·light (sun′līt) *n.* The light of the sun.

sun·ny (sun′ē) *adj.* **·ni·er, ·ni·est** **1.** Filled with the light and warmth of the sun; also, exposed to the sun. **2.** Of or resembling the sun or sunlight. **3.** Bright; genial; cheery: a *sunny* smile. — **sun′ni·ly** *adv.* — **sun′ni·ness** *n.*

sunny side **1.** The side, as of a hill, facing the sun. **2.** The cheerful view of any situation, question, etc.

sun parlor A room enclosed in glass and having a sunny exposure. Also **sun porch.**

sun·rise (sun′rīz) *n.* **1.** The daily first appearance of the sun above the horizon, with the atmospheric phenomena just before and after. **2.** The time at which the sun rises.

sun·set (sun′set′) *n.* **1.** The apparent daily descent of the sun below the horizon. **2.** The time when the sun sets; the early evening. **3.** The colors in the sky at sunset.

sun·shade (sun′shād′) *n.* Something used as a shade or protection from the sun, as a parasol, an awning, etc.

sun·shine (sun′shīn′) *n.* **1.** The shining light of the sun; the direct rays of the sun. **2.** The warmth of the sun's rays. **3.** Brightness; cheerfulness. — **sun′shin′y** *adj.*

Sunshine State Nickname of Florida, New Mexico, and South Dakota.

sun·spot (sun′spot′) *n. Astron.* One of many dark irregular spots appearing periodically on the sun's surface.

sun·stroke (sun′strōk′) *n. Pathol.* A sudden onset of high fever induced by exposure to the sun and often marked by convulsions and coma. — **sun′struck′** (-struk′) *adj.*

sun tan A bronze-colored condition of the skin, produced by exposure to the sun. — **sun′-tanned′** (-tand′) *adj.*

sun·up (sun′up′) *n. Chiefly U.S.* Sunrise.

sup[1] (sup) *v.t. & v.i.* **supped, sup·ping** To take (fluid food) in successive mouthfuls, a little at a time; sip. — *n.* A mouthful or taste of liquid or semiliquid food. [OE *sūpan*]

sup[2] (sup) *v.* **supped, sup·ping** *v.i.* To eat supper. [< OF *soper, super*]

sup- Var. of SUB-.

su·per[1] (sōō′pər) *n. Informal* A superintendent (def. 2).

su·per[2] (sōō′pər) *n. Slang* A supernumerary (def. 2).

su·per[3] (sōō′pər) *n.* An article of superior size or quality; also, such size or quality. — *adj. Slang* First-rate; superfine. [Short for SUPERIOR]

super- *prefix* **1.** Above in position; over: *superstructure.* **2.** Above or beyond; more than: *supersonic.* **3.** Excessively: *supersaturate.* **4.** Greater than or superior to others of its class: *superhighway.* **5.** Extra; additional: *supertax.* [< L *super-* < *super* above, beyond]

In the following list of words *super-* denotes excess or superiority, as *supercritical* excessively critical, *superexcellence* superior excellence.

superabhor	superconformity	superextension	superlenient	superreliance
superabominable	superconfusion	superfecundity	superlie	superremuneration
superabsurd	supercongestion	superfeminine	superlogical	superrespectable
superaccession	superconservative	superfervent	superloyal	superresponsible
superaccommodating	supercontrol	superfoliation	superlucky	superrestriction
superaccomplished	supercordial	superfolly	superluxurious	superreward
superaccumulate	supercritic	superformal	supermagnificently	superrighteous
superachievement	supercritical	superformation	supermanhood	superromantic
superacquisition	supercultivated	superformidable	supermarvelous	supersacrifice
superacute	supercurious	superfriendly	supermasculine	supersafe
superadaptable	supercynical	superfructified	supermechanical	supersagacious
superadequate	superdainty	superfulfillment	supermediocre	supersanguine
superadmiration	superdanger	supergaiety	supermental	supersarcastic
superadorn	superdeclamatory	supergallant	supermentality	supersatisfaction
superaffluence	superdeficit	supergenerosity	supermetropolitan	superscholarly
superagency	superdejection	superglorious	supermishap	superscientific
superaggravation	superdelicate	supergoodness	supermodest	supersensitive
superagitation	superdemand	supergovernment	supermoisten	supersensitiveness
superambitious	superdemonic	supergratification	supermorose	supersensuousness
superangelic	superdesirous	supergravitation	supermundane	supersentimental
superappreciation	superdevelopment	superhandsome	supermystery	superserious
superarbitrary	superdevilish	superhearty	supernecessity	supersevere
superarduous	superdevotion	superhero	supernegligent	supersignificant
superarrogant	superdiabolical	superheroic	supernotable	supersimplify
superaspiration	superdifficult	superhistorical	supernumerous	supersmart
superastonish	superdiplomacy	superhypocrite	superobedience	supersolemn
superattachment	superdistribution	superideal	superobese	supersolemnly
superattraction	superdividend	superignorant	superobjectionable	supersolicitation
superattractive	superdonation	superillustrate	superobligation	superspecialize
superbelief	supereconomy	superimpending	superobstinate	superspiritual
superbeloved	supereffective	superimpersonal	superoffensive	superspirituality
superbenefit	supereffluence	superimportant	superofficious	superstimulation
superbenevolent	superelastic	superimprobable	superofficiousness	superstoical
superbenign	superelated	superimproved	superopposition	superstrain
superbias	superelegance	superincentive	superoratorical	superstrenuous
superblessed	supereligible	superinclination	superordinary	superstrict
superblunder	supereloquent	superinclusive	superorganize	superstrong
superbold	superemphasis	superinconsistent	superornamental	superstylish
superbrave	superendorsement	superindependent	superoutput	supersufficient
superbusy	superendow	superindifference	superpatient	supersurprise
supercandid	superenforcement	superindignant	superpatriotic	supersweet
supercapable	superenrollment	superindividualism	superpatriotism	supertension
supercatastrophe	superestablishment	superindividualist	superperfection	superthankful
supercatholic	superesthetic	superindulgence	superpious	superthorough
supercaution	superethical	superindustrious	superplease	supertoleration
superceremonious	superevident	superinference	superpolite	supertragic
superchivalrous	superexacting	superinfinite	superpositive	supertrivial
supercivil	superexalt	superinfirmity	superpraise	superugly
supercivilized	superexaltation	superinfluence	superprecise	superunity
superclassified	superexcellence	superingenious	superpreparation	superurgent
supercolossal	superexcellent	superinitiative	superpressure	supervexation
supercombination	superexcitation	superinjustice	superproduce	supervigilant
supercommendation	superexcited	superinquisitive	superprosperous	supervigorous
supercommercial	superexcitement	superinsistent	superpublicity	supervirulent
supercompetition	superexiguity	superintellectual	superpure	supervital
supercomplex	superexpansion	superintolerable	superpurgation	supervolume
supercomprehension	superexpectation	superjurisdiction	superradical	superwise
supercompression	superexpenditure	superjustification	superrational	superworldly
superconfident	superexpressive	superknowledge	superrefined	superwrought
superconformist	superexquisiteness	superlaborious	superreform	superzealous

su·per·a·ble (soo′pər·ə·bəl) *adj.* That can be surmounted, overcome, or conquered. [< L < *superare* to overcome]

su·per·a·bun·dant (soo′pər·ə·bun′dənt) *adj.* More than sufficient; excessive. — **su′per·a·bun′dance** *n.* — **su′per·a·bun′dant·ly** *adv.*

su·per·an·nu·ate (soo′pər·an′yoo·āt) *v.t.* ·at·ed, ·at·ing 1. To permit to retire on a pension on account of age or infirmity. 2. To set aside or discard as obsolete or too old. [< Med.L < L < *super* beyond + *annus* year]

su·per·an·nu·at·ed (soo′pər·an′yoo·ā′tid) *adj.* 1. Retired on account of age, esp. with a pension. 2. Too old to be useful or efficient. 3. Obsolete; outdated.

su·perb (soo·pûrb′, sə-) *adj.* 1. Having grand, impressive beauty; majestic; imposing. 2. Luxurious; rich and costly; elegant. 3. Very good; supremely fine. [< L *superbus* proud] — **su·perb′ly** *adv.* — **su·perb′ness** *n.*

su·per·car·go (soo′pər·kär′gō) *n.* *pl.* ·goes or ·gos An agent on board ship in charge of the cargo and its sale and purchase. [< *super-* over + CARGO]

su·per·charge (*v.* soo′pər·chärj′; *n.* soo′pər·chärj′) *v.t.* ·charged, ·charg·ing 1. To adapt (an engine) to develop more power by fitting with a supercharger. 2. To charge to excess; overload. — *n.* An excess charge.

su·per·charg·er (soo′pər·chär′jər) *n.* *Mech.* A compressor for supplying air or combustible mixture to an internal-combustion engine at a pressure greater than that developed by the suction of the pistons alone.

su·per·cil·i·ous (soo′pər·sil′ē·əs) *adj.* Exhibiting haughty contempt or indifference; arrogant. [< L < *supercilium* eyebrow] — **su′per·cil′i·ous·ly** *adv.* — **su′per·cil′i·ous·ness** *n.*

su·per·con·duc·tiv·i·ty (soo′pər·kon′duk·tiv′ə·tē) *n.* *Physics.* The property, exhibited by certain substances, of becoming almost perfect conductors of electricity at temperatures close to absolute zero. — **su′per·con·duc′tive** (-kən·duk′tiv) *adj.* — **su′per·con·duc′tor** *n.*

su·per·e·go (soo′pər·ē′gō, -eg′ō) *n.* *Psychoanal.* The part of the psyche that acts to secure the conformity of the ego to parental, social, and moral standards.

su·per·em·i·nent (soo′pər·em′ə·nənt) *adj.* Excelling or surpassing others; of a superior or remarkable quality. [< L *supereminere* to rise above] — **su′per·em′i·nence** *n.* — **su′per·em′i·nent·ly** *adv.*

su·per·er·o·gate (soo′pər·er′ə·gāt) *v.i.* ·gat·ed, ·gat·ing To do more than is required or ordered. [< L < *super-* over and above + *erogare* to pay out] — **su′per·er′o·ga′tion** *n.* — **su′per·e·rog′a·to·ry** (-ə·rog′ə·tôr′ē, -tō′rē) *adj.*

su·per·fi·cial (soo′pər·fish′əl) *adj.* 1. Of, lying near, or forming the surface; affecting only the surface. 2. Of only the ordinary and the obvious; shallow: a *superficial* writer. 3. Marked by partial knowledge; cursory; hasty; slight: a *superficial* analysis. 4. Not real or genuine: a *superficial* likeness. 5. Square: said of measure. [< LL < L *super-* over + *ficies* face] — **su′per·fi′ci·al′i·ty** (-fish′ē·al′ə·tē), **su′·per·fi′cial·ness** *n.* — **su′per·fi′cial·ly** *adv.*

su·per·fine (soo′pər·fīn′) *adj.* 1. Of surpassing fineness and delicacy; of the best quality. 2. Overrefined; unduly elaborate; overnice. — **su′per·fine′ness** *n.*

su·per·flu·id (*n.* soo′pər·floo′id; *adj.* soo′pər·floo′id) *n.* *Physics.* Matter, as helium, cooled to within a degree of absolute zero, and characterized by an exceptional heat conductivity, a ready permeation of very dense substances, and the ability to flow upward against gravity. — *adj.* Of or pertaining to such a state.

su·per·flu·i·ty (soo′pər·floo′ə·tē) *n.* *pl.* ·ties 1. The state of being superfluous. 2. That which is superfluous. 3. Superabundance; plenty. [< OF < L *super-* over + *fluere* to flow]

su·per·flu·ous (soo·pûr′floo·əs) *adj.* 1. Exceeding what is needed; excessively abundant; surplus. 2. Unnecessary; uncalled for; irrelevant: a *superfluous* question. — **su·per′·flu·ous·ly** *adv.* — **su·per′flu·ous·ness** *n.*

su·per·heat (*v.* soo′pər·hēt′; *n.* soo′pər·hēt′) *v.t.* 1. To heat to excess; overheat. 2. To raise the temperature of (a gas or vapor not in contact with water) above the saturation point for a given pressure. 3. To heat (a liquid) above the boiling point for a given pressure, but without conversion into vapor. — *n.* The degree to which steam has been superheated, or the heat so imparted. — **su′per·heat′er** *n.*

su·per·het·er·o·dyne (soo′pər·het′ər·ə·dīn′) *adj.* *Electronics.* Pertaining to or designating a type of radio reception using heterodyne circuits between stages of amplification. Also **su′per·het′.** — *n.* A superheterodyne receiver. [< SUPER-(SONIC) + HETERODYNE]

su·per·high·way (soo′pər·hī′wā′) *n.* A highway for high-speed traffic, generally with four or more traffic lanes divided by a safety strip.

su·per·hu·man (soo′pər·hyoo′mən) *adj.* 1. Above the range of human power or skill; miraculous or divine. 2. Beyond normal human ability or power. — **su′per·hu·man′i·ty** (-hyoo·man′ə·tē) *n.* — **su′per·hu′man·ly** *adv.*

su·per·im·pose (soo′pər·im·pōz′) *v.t.* ·posed, ·pos·ing 1. To lay or impose upon something else. 2. To add to something else. — **su′per·im′po·si′tion** (-im′pə·zish′ən) *n.*

su·per·in·duce (soo′pər·in·doos′, -dyoos′) *v.t.* ·duced, ·duc·ing To introduce additionally; bring in or cause as an addition. — **su′per·in·duc′tion** (-duk′shən) *n.*

su·per·in·tend (soo′pər·in·tend′) *v.t.* To have the charge and direction of; manage; supervise. [< LL < *super-* over + *intendere* to attend in at] — **su′per·in·ten′dence** *n.*

su·per·in·ten·dent (soo′pər·in·ten′dənt) *n.* 1. One whose function is to superintend some particular work, office, or undertaking. 2. A person charged with supervising maintenance and repair in an office or apartment building. — *adj.* Of or pertaining to superintendence or a superintendent; superintending. [< LL < *superintendere* to superintend] — **su′per·in·ten′den·cy** *n.*

su·pe·ri·or (sə·pir′ē·ər, soo-) *adj.* 1. Surpassing in quantity, quality, or degree; more excellent; preferable. 2. Of great worth or excellence; extraordinary. 3. Of higher grade, rank, or dignity. 4. Too great or dignified to be influenced; serenely indifferent: with *to*: *superior* to envy. 5. Affecting superiority; supercilious; disdainful. 6. Locally higher; more elevated; upper. 7. *Printing* Set above the line: In C⁴Dⁿ, 4 and n are *superior*. — *n.* 1. One who surpasses another in rank or excellence. 2. The ruler of an ecclesiastical order or house, as a convent, or monastery. [< OF < L < *super* above] — **su·pe·ri·or·i·ty** (sə·pir′ē·ôr′ə·tē, -or′-, soo-) *n.* — **su·pe′ri·or·ly** *adv.*

su·per·la·tive (sə·pûr′lə·tiv, soo-) *adj.* 1. Elevated to the highest degree; of supreme excellence or eminence. 2. *Gram.* Expressing the extreme degree of comparison of adjectives or adverbs. See COMPARISON (def. 3). 3. Excessive. — *n.* 1. That which is superlative. 2. *Gram.* **a** The highest degree of comparison of the adjective or adverb. **b** Any word or phrase in this degree. [< OF < LL < L < *super-* above + *latus*, pp. of *ferre* to carry] — **su·per′la·tive·ly** *adv.* — **su·per′la·tive·ness** *n.*

su·per·man (soo′pər·man′) *n.* *pl.* ·men (-men′) 1. A hypothetical superior being, regarded as the product of evolutionary survival of the fittest. 2. A man possessing superhuman powers. [Trans. of G *übermensch*]

su·per·mar·ket (soo′pər·mär′kit) *n.* A large store selling food and household supplies and operating on a self-service, cash-and-carry basis. Also **super market.**

su·per·nal (soo·pûr′nəl) *adj.* 1. Heavenly; celestial. 2. Placed or located above; lofty; overhead; towering. [< OF < L < *super* over] — **su·per′nal·ly** *adv.*

su·per·nat·u·ral (soo′pər·nach′ər·əl) *adj.* 1. Existing or occurring through some agency beyond the known forces of nature. 2. Believed to be miraculous or caused by the immediate exercise of divine power. 3. Of the miraculous. — *n.* 1. That which is supernatural. 2. The action or intervention of something supernatural: with *the.* [< Med.L < L *super-* above + *natura* (< *nasci* to be born)] — **su′per·nat′u·ral·ly** *adv.* — **su′per·nat′u·ral·ness** *n.*

— **Syn.** (adj.) 1. A *supernatural* event is literally not bound or explainable by known natural laws. *Preternatural* refers to that which is superlative in degree, but not outside the known realm of nature: to display *preternatural* insight into a situation. Anything *miraculous* is so marvellous or extraordinary that it is usually attributed to divine agency.

su·per·nat·u·ral·ism (soo′pər·nach′ər·əl·iz′əm) *n.* 1. The quality of being supernatural. 2. Belief in the doctrine that a supernatural power guides the natural order. — **su′per·nat′u·ral·ist** *adj.* & *n.* — **su′per·nat′u·ral·is′tic** *adj.*

su·per·nu·mer·ar·y (soo′pər·noo′mə·rer′ē, -nyoo′-) *adj.* 1. Being beyond a fixed or standard number. 2. Beyond a customary or necessary number; superfluous. — *n.* *pl.* ·ar·ies 1. A supernumerary person or thing. 2. A stage performer, as in crowd scenes, without any speaking part. [< LL < L < *super* over + *numerus* number]

su·per·pose (soo′pər·pōz′) *v.t.* ·posed, ·pos·ing To lay over or upon something else, as one layer upon another. [< F < *super-* over + *poser* to put] — **su′per·pos′a·ble** *adj.* — **su′per·po·si′tion** (-pə·zish′ən) *n.*

su·per·sat·u·rate (soo′pər·sach′oo·rāt) *v.t.* ·rat·ed, ·rat·ing To saturate (a solution) beyond the point normal under a given temperature. — **su′per·sat′u·ra′tion** *n.*

su·per·scribe (soo′pər·skrīb′) *v.t.* ·scribed, ·scrib·ing 1. To write or engrave on the outside or upper part of. 2. To inscribe with a name or address, as a letter. [< LL < L *super-* over + *scribere* to write] — **su′per·scrip′tion** (-skrip′-shən) *n.*

su·per·script (soo′pər·skript′) *adj.* Written above or overhead. — *n.* 1. A superscript character. 2. *Math.* A character written above and to the right or left of a term to indicate a specific operation or characteristic of the term.

su·per·sede (soo′pər·sēd′) *v.t.* ·sed·ed, ·sed·ing 1. To take the place of, as by reason of superior worth, right, or appropriateness; replace; supplant. 2. To put something in the place of; set aside; suspend; annul. [< OF < L *super-*

above, over + *sedere* to sit] — **su′per·sed′er** *n.* — **su′per·se′dure** (-sē′jər), **su′per·ses′sion** (-sesh′ən) *n.*

su·per·son·ic (soō′pər·son′ik) *adj.* 1. *Aeron.* Of, pertaining to, or characterized by a speed greater than that of sound. 2. Ultrasonic.

su·per·son·ics (soō′pər·son′iks) *n.pl.* (*construed as sing.*) The science that treats of supersonic speed.

su·per·sti·tion (soō′pər·stish′ən) *n.* 1. A belief founded on irrational feelings, esp. of fear, and marked by a trust in charms, omens, the supernatural, etc.; also, any rite or practice inspired by such belief. 2. Any unreasonable belief. [< OF < L < *super-* over + *stare* to stand still]

su·per·sti·tious (soō′pər·stish′əs) *adj.* 1. Disposed to believe in superstitions. 2. Of or manifesting superstition. — **su′per·sti′tious·ly** *adv.* — **su′per·sti′tious·ness** *n.*

su·per·struc·ture (soō′pər·struk′chər) *n.* 1. Any structure or part of a structure considered in relation to its foundation. 2. *Naut.* The parts of a ship's structure, as of a warship, above the main deck.

su·per·tax (soō′pər·taks′) *n.* An extra tax in addition to the normal tax; a surtax.

su·per·vene (soō′pər·vēn′) *v.i.* ·vened, ·ven·ing 1. To follow closely upon something; come as something extraneous or additional. 2. To take place; happen. [< L < *super-* over and above + *venire* to come] — **su′per·ven′ient** (-vēn′yənt) *adj.* — **su′per·ven′tion** (-ven′shən) *n.*

su·per·vise (soō′pər·vīz) *v.t.* ·vised, vis·ing To have charge of directing (employees, an operation, etc.); superintend; oversee. — *Med.* L < *super-* over + *videre* to see]

su·per·vi·sion (soō′pər·vizh′ən) *n.* 1. The act of supervising; superintendence. 2. The authority to supervise.

su·per·vi·sor (soō′pər·vī′zər) *n.* 1. One who supervises or oversees; superintendent; inspector; administrative officer. 2. A person supervising teachers of special subjects in a school. — **su′per·vi′sor·ship** *n.* — **su′per·vi′so·ry** *adj.*

su·pine (soō·pīn′) *adj.* 1. Lying on the back, or with the face turned upward. 2. Inactive; indolent; listless. [< L *supinus*] — **su·pine′ly** *adv.* — **su·pine′ness** *n.*

sup·per (sup′ər) *n.* The last meal of the day; the evening meal. — **sup′per·less** *adj.*

sup·plant (sə·plant′, -plänt′) *v.t.* 1. To take the place of; displace. 2. To take the place of (someone) by scheming, treachery, etc. 3. To replace (one thing) with another; remove; uproot. [< OF < L *supplantare* to trip up < *sub-* up from below + *planta* the sole of the foot] — **sup·plan·ta·tion** (sup′lan·tā′shən) *n.* — **sup·plant′er** *n.*

sup·ple (sup′əl) *adj.* **sup·pler** (sup′lər), **sup·plest** (sup′ləst) 1. Easily bent; flexible; pliant. 2. Yielding to the humor or wishes of others; esp., servilely compliant. 3. Showing adaptability of mind. — *v.t. & v.i.* ·pled, ·pling To make or become supple. [< OF < L < *sub-* under + stem of *plicare* to fold] — **sup′ple·ly** *adv.* — **sup′ple·ness** *n.*

sup·ple·ment (*v.* sup′lə·ment; *n.* sup′lə·mənt) *v.t.* To make additions to; provide for what is lacking in. — *n.* 1. Something that supplements; esp. an addition to a publication. 2. A supplementary angle. [See SUPPLY¹.]

sup·ple·men·tal (sup′lə·men′təl) *adj.* Additional.

sup·ple·men·ta·ry (sup′lə·men′tər·ē) *adj.* Functioning as a supplement; supplemental.

supplementary angle *Geom.* Either of two angles whose sum is 180°: also called **supplement**.

sup·pli·ant (sup′lē·ənt) *adj.* 1. Entreating earnestly and humbly; beseeching. 2. Manifesting entreaty or supplication. — *n.* One who supplicates. [< MF < L. See SUPPLICATE.] — **sup′pli·ant·ly** *adv.* — **sup′pli·ant·ness** *n.*

sup·pli·cant (sup′lə·kənt) *n.* One who supplicates. — *adj.* Entreating humbly; beseeching. [See SUPPLICATE.]

sup·pli·cate (sup′lə·kāt) *v.* ·cat·ed, ·cat·ing *v.t.* 1. To ask for humbly or by earnest prayer. 2. To beg something of; entreat. — *v.i.* 3. To beg or pray humbly. [< L < *sub-* under + *plicare* to bend, fold] — **sup′pli·ca′tion** *n.* — **sup′pli·ca·to·ry** (-kə·tôr′ē, -tō′rē) *adj.*

sup·ply¹ (sə·plī′) *v.* ·plied, ·ply·ing *v.t.* 1. To give or furnish (something needful or desirable). 2. To furnish with what is needed: to *supply* an army with ammunition. 3. To provide for adequately; satisfy: to *supply* a demand. 4. To make good or compensate for, as a loss or deficiency. 5. To fill (the place of another); also, to fill (an office, etc.) or occupy (a pulpit) as a substitute. — *v.i.* 6. To take the place of another temporarily. — *n. pl.* ·plies 1. That which is or can be supplied. 2. An amount sufficient for a given use; store or quantity on hand. 3. *Usu. pl.* Accumulated stores reserved for distribution, as for an army. 4. *Econ.* The amount of a commodity offered at a given price or available for meeting a demand. 5. A substitute or temporary incumbent. 6. The act of supplying. [< OF < L < *sub-* up from under + *ple-*, root of *plenus* full]

sup·ply² (sup′lē) *adv.* In a supple manner; supplely.

sup·port (sə·pôrt′, -pōrt′) *v.t.* 1. To bear the weight of. 2. To hold in position. 3. To bear or sustain (weight, etc.). 4. To keep (a person, the mind, etc.) from failing or declining. 5. To serve to uphold or corroborate (a statement, etc.). 6. To provide (a person, institution, etc.) with maintenance. 7. To give approval or assistance to; uphold. 8. To tolerate: I cannot *support* his insolence. 9. To carry on; keep up: to *support* a war. 10. In the theater: **a** To act (a part). **b** To act in a subordinate role to. — *n.* 1. The act of supporting, or the state of being supported. 2. One who or that which supports. 3. Subsistence. [< OF < L < *sub-* up from under + *portare* to carry]

sup·port·a·ble (sə·pôr′tə·bəl, -pōr′-) *adj.* Capable of being supported or endured; bearable; endurable. — **sup·port′a·ble·ness**, **sup·port′a·bil′i·ty** *n.* — **sup·port′a·bly** *adv.*

sup·port·er (sə·pôr′tər, -pōr′-) *n.* 1. One who or that which supports. 2. An adherent. 3. An elastic or other support for some part of the body. — **Syn.** See ADHERENT.

sup·pose (sə·pōz′) *v.* ·posed, ·pos·ing *v.t.* 1. To think or imagine to oneself as true. 2. To believe or believe probable; think. 3. To assume as true for the sake of argument or illustration: *Suppose* he comes late. 4. To expect or require: used in the passive: He is *supposed* to be on time. 5. To imply as cause or consequence; presuppose. — *v.i.* 6. To conjecture. [< OF < *sup-* under (< L *sub-*) + *poser* to put down] — **sup·pos′a·ble** *adj.* — **sup·pos′a·bly** *adv.* — **sup·pos′er** *n.*

— **Syn.** 1. We *suppose* something to be true in expectation of finding that it is true, or in order to ascertain what follows if it is not true. We *conjecture* or *surmise* when the evidence is admittedly insufficient for certainty: *surmise* suggests slighter grounds for a conclusion than *conjecture*. Also, *conjecture* suggests that the question is one of fact, while *surmise* may refer to questions of interpretation or evaluation.

sup·posed (sə·pōzd′, -pō′zid) *adj.* Accepted as genuine or true, often erroneously. — **sup·pos·ed·ly** (sə·pō′zid·lē) *adv.*

sup·po·si·tion (sup′ə·zish′ən) *n.* 1. The act of supposing. 2. That which is supposed. — **Syn.** See HYPOTHESIS. [< Med.L < L < *sub-* under + *ponere* to place] — **sup′po·si′tion·al** *adj.* — **sup′po·si′tion·al·ly** *adv.*

sup·pos·i·to·ry (sə·poz′ə·tôr′ē, -tō′rē) *n. pl.* ·ries *Med.* A solid, readily fusible, medicated preparation for introduction into the rectum, vagina, or urethra. [< LL < L < *sub-* under + *ponere* to place]

sup·press (sə·pres′) *v.t.* 1. To put an end or stop to; quell; crush, as a rebellion. 2. To stop or prohibit the activities of; also, to abolish. 3. To withhold from knowledge or publication, as a book, news, etc. 4. To repress, as a groan or sigh. 5. To check or stop (a hemorrhage, etc.). [< L < *sub-* under + *premere* to press] — **sup·press′er** or **sup·pres′sor** *n.* — **sup·press′i·ble** *adj.* — **sup·pres′sive** *adj.*

sup·pres·sion (sə·presh′ən) *n.* 1. The act of suppressing, or the state of being suppressed. 2. *Psychoanal.* The deliberate exclusion from consciousness and action of an idea, emotion, or desire.

sup·pu·rate (sup′yə·rāt) *v.i.* ·rat·ed, ·rat·ing To form or generate pus; maturate. [< L < *sub-* under + *pus* pus] — **sup′pu·ra′tion** *n.* — **sup′pu·ra′tive** *adj. & n.*

supra- *prefix* Above; beyond. [< L]

su·pra·re·nal (soō′prə·rē′nəl) *Anat. adj.* 1. Situated above the kidneys. 2. Of or pertaining to the suprarenal glands. — *n.* A suprarenal gland. [< NL < L *supra-* above + *renes* kidneys]

suprarenal gland *Anat.* An adrenal gland.

su·prem·a·cy (sə·prem′ə·sē, soō-) *n. pl.* ·cies 1. The state of being supreme. 2. Supreme power or authority.

su·preme (sə·prēm′, soō-) *adj.* 1. Highest in power or authority. 2. Highest in degree, importance, quality, etc.; utmost: *supreme* devotion. 3. Ultimate; last; final. [< L < *super* above] — **su·preme′ly** *adv.* — **su·preme′ness** *n.*

Supreme Being God.

Supreme Court In the U.S. and in various States, a court of appellate jurisdiction and, in most cases, of last resort.

Supreme Soviet The highest legislative body of the Soviet Union, consisting of two chambers, the **Soviet of the Union** and the **Soviet of Nationalities**.

sur-¹ *prefix* Above; beyond; over: *surcharge*; *surcoat*. [< OF < L *super* above]

sur-² Assimilated var. of SUB-.

su·rah (soōr′ə) *n.* A soft, usu. twilled fabric of silk or silk and rayon. Also **surah silk.** [after *Surat*, India]

sur·cease (sûr·sēs′, sûr′sēs) *Archaic n.* Absolute cessation; end. — *v.t. & v.i.* ·ceased, ·ceas·ing To cease; end. [< AF < L < *super-* above + *sedere* to sit]

sur·charge (*n.* sûr′chärj′; *v.* sûr·chärj′) *n.* 1. An excessive burden, load, or charge. 2. An additional or excessive amount charged; overcharge. 3. A new valuation or something additional printed on a postage stamp. — *v.t.*

·charged, ·charg·ing 1. To overcharge. 2. To overload. 3. To fill to excess. 4. To imprint a surcharge on (postage stamps). [< F < *sur-* over + CHARGE] — **sur·charg'er** n.

sur·cin·gle (sûr'sĭng-gəl) n. A girth or strap encircling the body of a horse, etc., as for holding a saddle. [< OF < *sur-* over + L *cingulum* belt]

sur·coat (sûr'kōt) n. 1. An outer coat. 2. A cloaklike garment worn over armor. [< OF < *sur-* over + *cot* coat]

surd (sûrd) n. 1. *Math.* An irrational number, as √2. 2. *Phonet.* A voiceless speech sound. — adj. 1. *Math.* Incapable of being expressed in rational numbers; irrational. 2. *Phonet.* Voiceless. [< L *surdus* deaf, silent]

sure (shŏor) adj. **sur·er, sur·est** 1. Free from doubt; certain; positive. 2. Certain of obtaining, attaining, or retaining something: with *of.* 3. Not liable to change; firm; stable. 4. Bound to happen; inevitable. 5. Not liable to fail or err; infallible. 6. Reliable; trustworthy. 7. *Rare* Secure; safe. — **to be sure** Indeed; certainly. — **to make sure** To make certain; secure. — adv. *Informal* Surely; certainly. [< OF < L *se-* without + *cura* care] — **sure'ness** n.

sure-e·nough (shŏor'ĭ-nŭf') *U.S. Informal* adj. Real; genuine. — adv. Really; surely.

sure-foot·ed (shŏor'fŏot'ĭd) adj. 1. Not liable to fall or stumble. 2. Not liable to fail or err.

sure·ly (shŏor'lē) adv. 1. Certainly. 2. Securely; safely.

sure·ty (shŏor'tē, shŏor'ə-tē) n. pl. **·ties** 1. One who agrees to be responsible for another; esp., one who engages to be responsible for the debt or default of another. 2. A pledge or guarantee to secure against loss, damage, default, etc.; security. 3. That which gives or serves as a basis for security or confidence; a guarantee. 4. The state of being sure. [< OF < L *securus.* See SURE.] — **sure'ty·ship** n.

surf (sûrf) n. The swell of the sea that breaks upon a shore; also, the foam caused by such a swell. — v.i. To engage in surfing. — **surf'er** n. [Earlier *suff,* ? var. of SOUGH] — **surf'y** adj.

sur·face (sûr'fĭs) n. 1. The exterior part or face of anything. 2. A superficial aspect; outward appearance. 3. That which has length and breadth, but not thickness. — adj. 1. Of, pertaining to, or on a surface. 2. Superficial; exterior; apparent. — v. **·faced, ·fac·ing** v.t. 1. To put a surface on; esp., to make smooth. — v.i. 2. To rise to the surface, as a submarine. [< F < *sur-* above + FACE]

sur·face-ac·tive (sûr'fĭs·ăk'tĭv) adj. *Chem.* Pertaining to any of a class of substances that have the property of reducing the surface tension of a liquid in which they are dissolved: said esp. of detergents.

surface tension *Physics* That property of a liquid by virtue of which the surface molecules exhibit a strong inward attraction, thus forming an apparent membrane that tends to contract to the minimum area.

sur·fac·tant (sûr·făk'tənt) n. *Chem.* A surface-active agent.

surf·board (sûrf'bôrd', -bōrd') n. A long, narrow board used in surfing.

surf·boat (sûrf'bōt') n. A boat of extra strength and buoyancy, for launching and landing through surf.

sur·feit (sûr'fĭt) v.t. 1. To feed or supply to fullness or satiety; satiate. — v.i. 2. To partake of anything to excess; overindulge. — n. 1. Excess in eating or drinking; also, the excessive quantity partaken of. 2. The result of such excess; satiety. 3. Oppressive fullness caused by excess in eating or drinking. [< OF *surfaire* to overdo < *sur-* above + *faire* to make] — **sur'feit·er** n.

surf·ing (sûrf'ĭng) n. A water sport in which a person standing on a surfboard is borne by the surf toward the shore. Also **surf·rid·ing** (sûrf'rī'dĭng).

surf·rid·er (sûrf'rī'dər) n. One who engages in surfing.

surge (sûrj) v.i. **surged, surg·ing** 1. To rise high and roll onward, as waves; swell or heave. 2. To move or go in a manner suggestive of this. 3. To increase or vary suddenly, as an electric current. — n. 1. A large swelling wave; billow; also, such billows collectively. 2. A heaving and rolling motion, as of great waves. 3. *Electr.* A sudden fluctuation of voltage or current due to lightning, switching, etc. [< OF < L *surgere* to rise] — **surg'er** n. — **surg'y** adj.

sur·geon (sûr'jən) n. One who practices surgery, as distinguished from a physician. [See SURGERY.]

Surgeon General pl. **Surgeons General** or **Surgeon Generals** The chief officer of the Medical Department in the United States Army or Navy.

surgeon's knot A knot used in tying ligatures, stitching up wounds, etc. For illus. see KNOT.

sur·ger·y (sûr'jər·ē) n. pl. **·ger·ies** 1. The branch of medical science that relates to body injuries, deformities, and diseased conditions requiring treatment by operative procedures, with or without instruments. 2. A place where surgical treatment is given, as in an operating room. 3. The work of a surgeon. [< OF, ult. < LL < Gk. < *cheir* hand + *ergon* work]

sur·gi·cal (sûr'jĭ·kəl) adj. Of, pertaining to, or used in surgery. — **sur'gi·cal·ly** adv.

sur·ly (sûr'lē) adj. **sur·li·er, sur·li·est** Characterized by rudeness, ill-humor, or gruffness. [Earlier *sirly* < *sir* a lord + *-ly* like] — **sur'li·ly** (-lə-lē) adv. — **sur'li·ness** n.

sur·mise (sər-mīz'; for n., also sûr'mīz) v. **·mised, ·mis·ing** v.t. 1. To infer on slight evidence; guess. — v.i. 2. To make a conjecture. — Syn. See SUPPOSE. — n. 1. A conjecture made on slight evidence. 2. The act of surmising. [< OF < *sur-* upon + *mettre* to put < L *mittere* to send]

sur·mount (sər-mount') v.t. 1. To overcome (a difficulty, etc.). 2. To mount to the top or cross to the other side of (an obstacle or mountain). 3. To be or lie over or above. 4. To place something on top of. [< OF < Med.L < L *super-* over + *mons* hill, mountain] — **sur·mount'a·ble** adj. — **sur·mount'a·ble·ness** n. — **sur·mount'er** n.

sur·name (sûr'nām'; for n., also sûr·nām') n. The name of a person's family; the last name of a person: also called *family name.* — v.t. **·named, ·nam·ing** To give a surname to; call by a surname. [Alter. of obs. *surnoun* < OF < *sur-* above, beyond + *nom* name < L *nomen*] — **sur'nam'er** n.

sur·pass (sər-pas', -päs') v.t. 1. To go beyond or past in degree or amount; excel. 2. To go beyond the reach or powers of; transcend. — Syn. See EXCEED. [< MF < *sur-* above + PASS] — **sur·pass'a·ble** adj.

sur·pass·ing (sər-pas'ĭng, -päs'-) adj. Preeminently excellent; exceeding. — adv. *Poetic* Exceedingly; excellently. — **sur·pass'ing·ly** adv. — **sur·pass'ing·ness** n.

sur·plice (sûr'plĭs) n. *Eccl.* A loose white vestment with full sleeves, worn over the cassock by the clergy and choir of some churches. [< AF or OF < Med.L < *super-* over + *pellicia* fur garment]

sur·plus (sûr'pləs) adj. Being in excess of what is used or needed. — n. 1. That which remains over and above what has been used or is required; excess. 2. Assets in excess of liabilities. [< OF < Med.L < *super-* over and above + *plus* more]

sur·prise (sər-prīz') v.t. **·prised, ·pris·ing** 1. To cause to feel wonder or astonishment because unusual or unexpected. 2. To come upon suddenly or unexpectedly; take unawares. 3. To attack or capture suddenly and without warning. 4. To lead unawares, as into doing something not intended: with *into.* 5. To elicit in this manner: They *surprised* the truth from him. — n. 1. The act of surprising; a coming upon unawares. 2. The state of being surprised; astonishment. 3. That which causes surprise, as a sudden and unexpected event, fact, or gift. — **to take by surprise** 1. To come upon without warning or unexpectedly. 2. To astound or amaze; astonish. [< OF < Med.L < L *super-* over + *prehendere* to take] — **sur·pris'al** n. — **sur·pris'er** n.

sur·pris·ing (sər-prī'zĭng) adj. Causing surprise or wonder; amazing. — **sur·pris'ing·ly** adv. — **sur·pris'ing·ness** n.

sur·re·al·ism (sə-rē'əl·ĭz'əm) n. A modern movement in literature and art that attempts to express the workings of the subconscious mind, characterized by the incongruous arrangement and presentation of subject matter. [< F < *sur-* beyond, above + *réalisme* realism] — **sur·re'al·ist** adj. & n. — **sur·re'al·is'tic** adj. — **sur·re'al·is'ti·cal·ly** adv.

sur·ren·der (sə-ren'dər) v.t. 1. To yield possession of or power over to another; give up because of compulsion. 2. To give up; abandon, as hope. 3. To relinquish, esp. in favor of another. 4. To give (oneself) over to a passion, influence, etc. — v.i. 5. To give oneself up, as to an enemy in warfare. — n. The act of surrendering. [< OF < *sur-* over + RENDER]

sur·rep·ti·tious (sûr'əp·tish'əs) adj. 1. Accomplished by secret or improper means; clandestine. 2. Acting secretly or by stealth. — Syn. See STEALTHY. [< L < *sub-* secretly + *rapere* to snatch] — **sur'rep·ti'tious·ly** adv. — **sur'rep·ti'tious·ness** n.

sur·rey (sûr'ē) n. A light vehicle, having two seats, four wheels, and sometimes a top. [Prob. after *Surrey,* England]

sur·ro·gate (sûr'ə·gāt; for n., also sûr'ə·git) n. 1. A substitute; deputy. 2. A probate judge. — v.t. **·gat·ed, ·gat·ing** 1. To put in the place of another; substitute. 2. To appoint (another) to succeed oneself. [< L < *sub-* in place of another + *rogare* to ask] — **sur'ro·gate·ship** n.

sur·round (sə-round') v.t. 1. To extend around; be on all sides of; encircle; enclose. 2. To shut in or enclose, as enemy troops, so as to cut off retreat. [< OF < LL < *super-* over + *undare* to rise in waves < *unda* a wave]

sur·round·ing (sə-roun'dĭng) n. 1. pl. That which surrounds; environment; conditions of life. 2. The act of one who surrounds. — adj. Encompassing; enveloping.

sur·tax (sûr'tăks') n. An extra tax; esp., a graduated income tax over and above the usual tax, levied on the amount by which net income exceeds a certain sum. — v.t. To assess with a surtax. [< F < *sur-* above + TAX]

sur·veil·lance (sər-vā'ləns, -vāl'yəns) n. 1. Close watch kept over one, as a suspect. 2. The act of watching, or the state of being watched. [< F < *sur-* over + *veiller* to watch < L *vigilare*] — **sur·veil'lant** adj. & n.

sur·vey (sər-vā'; for n., also sûr'vā) v.t. 1. To look at in its entirety; view in a general way. **2.** To look at carefully and minutely; scrutinize. **3.** To determine accurately the area, contour, or boundaries of (land) by measuring lines and angles according to the principles of geometry and trigonometry. — *v.i.* **4.** To survey land. — *n.* **1.** The operation, act, process, or results of finding the contour, area, boundaries, etc., of a surface. **2.** A general or comprehensive view. **3.** A scrutinizing view; inspection. [< AF < OF < Med.L < *super-* over + *videre* to look]

sur·vey·ing (sər·vā′ing) *n.* **1.** The science and art of determining the area and configuration of portions of the surface of the earth and representing them on maps. **2.** The act of one who surveys.

sur·vey·or (sər·vā′ər) *n.* **1.** One who surveys; esp., one who surveys land. **2.** One who examines a thing for the purpose of ascertaining its condition, quality, or character; esp., a customs officer.

surveyor's measure A system of measurement used in surveying and based on the chain as a unit.

sur·viv·al (sər·vī′vəl) *n.* **1.** The act of surviving, or the state of having survived. **2.** One who or that which survives; esp., a custom, belief, etc., persisting in society.

survival of the fittest The principle of natural selection as applied to living organisms, societies, etc.

sur·vive (sər·vīv′) *v.* **·vived, ·viv·ing** *v.i.* **1.** To remain alive or in existence. — *v.t.* **2.** To live or exist beyond the death, occurrence, or end of; outlive; outlast. [< AF < OF < LL < *super-* above, beyond + *vivere* to live] — **sur·viv′· ing** *adj.* — **sur·viv′er, sur·vi′vor** *n.*

sus- Assimilated var. of SUB-.

sus·cep·ti·bil·i·ty (sə·sep tə·bil′ə·tē) *n.* *pl.* **·ties 1.** The state or quality of being susceptible. **2.** The ability to receive or be impressed by deep emotions or strong feelings; sensibility. **3.** *pl.* Sensitive emotions; feelings. **4.** *Physics* The ratio of the magnetization of a material to the magnetic force producing it. — **Syn.** See SENSIBILITY.

sus·cep·ti·ble (sə·sep′tə·bəl) *adj.* **1.** Yielding readily; capable of being influenced, acted on, or determined; open; liable: usu. with *of* or *to.* **2.** Having delicate sensibility; impressionable. [< Med.L < L *sub-* under + *capere* to take] — **sus·cep′ti·ble·ness** *n.* — **sus·cep′ti·bly** *adv.*

sus·pect (*v.* sə·spekt′; *adj. & n.* sus′pekt) *v.t.* **1.** To think (a person) guilty as specified on little or no evidence. **2.** To have distrust of; doubt. **3.** To have an inkling or suspicion of; think possible. — *v.i.* **4.** To have suspicions. — *adj.* Exciting, open to, or viewed with suspicion; suspected. — *n.* One who is under suspicion, esp. for a crime. [< F < L < *sub-* from under + *specere* to look]

sus·pend (sə·spend′) *v.t.* **1.** To bar for a time from a privilege, office, or function as a punishment. **2.** To cause to cease for a time; withhold temporarily. **3.** To hold in a state of indecision; withhold or defer action on: to *suspend* a sentence. **4.** To hang from a support so as to allow free movement. **5.** To sustain in a body of nearly the same specific gravity; keep in suspension, as dust motes in the air. — *v.i.* **6.** To stop for a time. **7.** To fail to meet obligations; stop payment. [< OF < L *sub-* under + *pendere* to hang]

sus·pend·er (sə·spen′dər) *n.* **1.** *pl.* *U.S.* A pair of straps worn over the shoulders for supporting the trousers. **2.** *Brit.* A garter.

sus·pense (sə·spens′) *n.* **1.** The state of being uncertain, undecided, or insecure; usu. accompanied by anxiety, apprehension, etc. **2.** An uncertain or doubtful situation. [< OF < Med.L < L *suspendere.* See SUSPEND.]

sus·pen·sion (sə·spen′shən) *n.* **1.** The act of suspending, or the state of being suspended. **2.** The state of deferment. **3.** *Physics* A uniform dispersion of small particles in a medium, either by mechanical agitation or by molecular forces. **4.** Cessation of payments in business. **5.** Any device on or from which something is suspended. **6.** *Mech.* A system of flexible members, as springs in a vehicle, intended to insulate the chassis and body against road shocks. **7.** *Music* The prolongation of a chord tone into the succeeding chord, where it forms a momentary dissonance; also, the tone so prolonged. **8.** The act of debarring from an office or its privileges.

suspension bridge A bridge in which the roadway is hung from cables anchored over towers and without intervening support from below.

SUSPENSION BRIDGE
(Brooklyn Bridge, New York)

sus·pen·sive (sə· spen′siv) *adj.* **1.** Tending to suspend or keep in suspense. **2.** Of or character-

ized by suspense. **3.** Having the power of suspending operation: a *suspensive* veto. — **sus·pen′sive·ly** *adv.* — **sus·pen′sive·ness** *n.*

sus·pen·so·ry (sə·spen′sər·ē) *adj.* Suspending; sustaining; delaying. — *n.* *pl.* **·ries** A truss, bandage, or supporter.

sus·pi·cion (sə·spish′ən) *n.* **1.** The act of suspecting, or the state of one who suspects; the imagining of something wrong without proof or clear evidence. **2.** *Informal* The least particle, as of a flavor. — *v.t.* *Dial.* To suspect. [< OF < Med.L < L *sub-* from under + *specere* to look] — **sus·pi′cion·al** *adj.*
— **Syn.** (noun) **1.** distrust, dubiety, skepticism. See DOUBT. **2.** soupçon, dash, touch, tinge, shade.

sus·pi·cious (sə·spish′əs) *adj.* **1.** Inclined to suspect; distrustful. **2.** Apt to arouse suspicion. **3.** Indicating suspicion. — **sus·pi′cious·ly** *adv.* — **sus·pi′cious·ness** *n.*

sus·tain (sə·stān′) *v.t.* **1.** To keep from sinking or falling; uphold; support. **2.** To endure without yielding; withstand. **3.** To undergo or suffer, as loss or injury. **4.** To keep up the courage, resolution, or spirits of; comfort. **5.** To keep up or maintain; keep in effect or being. **6.** To maintain by providing with food, drink, etc. **7.** To uphold or support as being true or just. **8.** To corroborate; confirm. [< OF < L < *sub-* up from under + *tenere* to hold] — **sus·tain′a·ble** *adj.* — **sus·tain′er** *n.* — **sus·tain′ment** *n.*

sus·tain·ing program (sə·stā′ning) A radio or television program that has no commercial sponsor but is paid for by the network or station.

sus·te·nance (sus′tə·nəns) *n.* **1.** The act of sustaining, or the state of being sustained; esp., maintenance of life. **2.** That which sustains; esp., that which supports life; food. **3.** Means of support; livelihood. [See SUSTAIN.]

sut·ler (sut′lər) *n.* A peddler who sells goods and food to an army. [< Du. *soetelen* to perform mean duties]

sut·tee (su·tē′, sut′ē) *n.* Formerly, the sacrifice of a Hindu widow on the funeral pyre of her husband; also, the widow so immolated. [< Hind. *satī* < Skt., a faithful wife] — **sut·tee′ism** *n.*

su·ture (sōō′chər) *n.* **1.** The junction of two contiguous surfaces or edges along a line by or as by sewing. **2.** *Anat.* The interlocking of two bones at their edges, as in the skull. **3.** *Surg.* **a** The operation of uniting the edges of a cut or wound by or as by stitching. **b** The thread, silver wire, or other material used in this operation. — *v.t.* **·tured, ·tur·ing** To unite by means of sutures; sew together. [< MF < L *suere* to sew] — **su′tur·al** *adj.* **su′tur·al·ly** *adv.*

su·ze·rain (sōō′zə·rin, -rān) *n.* **1.** Formerly, a feudal lord. **2.** A nation having paramount control over a locally autonomous region. [< F *sus* above < L *sursum* upwards; on analogy with *souverain* sovereign] — **su′ze·rain·ty** *n.*

svelte (svelt) *adj.* Slender; slim; willowy. [< F < Ital. < L *ex-* out + *vellere* to pluck]

swab (swob) *n.* **1.** A small stick having a wad of cotton wound about one or both ends, used for cleansing the mouth of a sick person, applying medicines, etc.; also, a specimen of mucus, etc., taken with such a stick. **2.** A mop for cleaning decks, floors, etc. **3.** A cylindrical brush for cleaning firearms. **4.** *Slang* An awkward fellow; lout. — *v.t.* **swabbed, swab·bing** To clean, apply, medicate, etc., with or as with a swab. [? < MDu. *swabbe*] — **swab′ber** *n.*

swad·dle (swod′l) *v.t.* **·dled, ·dling** To wrap with a bandage; esp., to wrap (an infant) with a long strip of linen or flannel; swathe. — *n.* A band used for swaddling. [OE *swathian* to swathe]

swaddling clothes Bands or strips of linen or other cloth wound around a newborn infant. Also **swaddling bands, swaddling clouts.**

swag (swag) *n.* **1.** *Slang* Property obtained by robbery or theft; plunder; booty. **2.** In Australia, a bundle or pack of personal belongings. [Prob. < Scand.]

swage (swāj) *n.* A tool or form, often one of a pair, for shaping metal by hammering or pressure. — *v.t.* **swaged, swag·ing** To shape (metal) with or as with a swage. [< OF *souage*]

swag·ger (swag′ər) *v.i.* **1.** To walk with a proud or insolent air; strut. **2.** To boast; bluster. — *n.* Expression of superiority in words or deeds; braggadocio. [Appar. freq. of SWAG] — **swag′ger·er** *n.* — **swag′ger·ing·ly** *adv.*

swagger stick A short, canelike stick carried by army personnel, esp. officers. Also **swagger cane.**

Swa·hi·li (swä·hē′lē) *n.* *pl.* **·li 1.** A language of East Africa, basically Bantu with an admixture of Arabic elements, used widely as a lingua franca. **2.** A member of a Swahili-speaking group or community. [< Arabic < *sāhil* coast] — **Swa·hi′li·an** *adj.*

swain (swān) *n.* *Poetic* **1.** A youthful rustic. **2.** A young rustic gallant. **3.** A lover. [< ON *sveinn* boy]

swal·low[1] (swol′ō) *v.t.* **1.** To cause (food, etc.) to pass from the mouth into the stomach by means of muscular action of the gullet or esophagus. **2.** To take in or engulf; absorb; envelop: often with *up.* **3.** To put up with or endure. **4.** *Informal* To believe credulously. **5.** To refrain from expressing; suppress. **6.** To take back; recant: to *swallow* one's words. — *v.i.* **7.** To perform the act or the motions of swallowing. — *n.* **1.** The amount swallowed at once. **2.** The gullet; throat. **3.** The act of swallowing. [OE *swelgan* to swallow] — **swal·low·a·ble** *adj.* — **swal'low·er** *n.*

swal·low² (swol'ō) *n.* **1.** Any of various small birds with short bills, long, pointed wings, and forked tails, noted for their swiftness of flight and migratory habits. **2.** A similar bird, as the swift. [OE *swealwe*]

swal·low·tail (swol'ō-tāl') *n.* **1.** The tail of a swallow, or a similar deeply forked tail. **2.** A butterfly having a taillike prolongation on each hind wing. **3.** *Informal* A swallowtailed coat.

swal·low-tailed coat (swol'ō-tāld') A man's formal dress coat with two long, tapering tails in the back.

swam (swam) Past tense of SWIM.

swa·mi (swä'mē) *n.* *pl.* **·mis 1.** Master; lord: used by Hindus as a title of respect. **2.** A Hindu religious teacher. Also **swa'my.** [< Hind. < Skt. *swāmin* lord]

swamp (swomp, swômp) *n.* A tract or region of lowland saturated with water; a wet bog. Also **swamp'land'** (-land'). ◆ Collateral adjective: *paludal.* — *v.t.* **1.** To drench or submerge with water or other liquid. **2.** To overwhelm with difficulties; crush; ruin. **3.** *Naut.* To sink or fill (a vessel) with water. — *v.i.* **4.** To sink in or as in a swamp. — **swamp'ish** *adj.* — **swamp'y** *adj.*

swamp fever Malaria.

swan (swon, swôn) *n.* **1.** A large, long-necked, aquatic bird, noted for its brilliant white plumage and for its grace on the water. **2.** A poet or singer. [OE]

Swan (swon, swôn) *n.* The constellation Cygnus.

swan dive A dive performed with head tilted back and arms extended until near the water.

swang (swang) Dialectal past tense of SWING.

swank (swangk) *adj.* *Slang* Ostentatiously fashionable; pretentious. Also **swank'y.** — *n.* *Slang* **1.** Behavior, speech, etc., that is pretentious and overly stylish. **2.** Swagger; bluster. — *v.i.* To act in a pretentious or swaggering manner; show off. [< dial. E. Appar. akin to MLG *swank* flexible] — **swank'i·ly** *adv.* — **swank'i·ness** *n.*

swan's-down (swonz'doun', swônz'-) *n.* **1.** The down of a swan, used for trimming, powder puffs, etc. **2.** A soft woolen cloth resembling down. Also **swans'down'.**

swan song A last or dying work, as of a poet or composer: from the fable that the swan sings only before dying.

swap (swop) *Informal v.t. & v.i.* **swapped, swap·ping** To trade (one thing for another). — *n.* An exchange or trade. Also spelled *swop.* [ME *swappen* to strike (a bargain)]

sward (swôrd) *n.* Land thickly covered with grass; turf: also called *swarth.* — *v.t. & v.i.* To cover or become covered with sward. [OE *sweard* skin]

swarm¹ (swôrm) *n.* **1.** A large number or body of insects or small living things of any kind. **2.** A hive of bees; also, a large number of bees leaving the parent stock at one time, to take up new lodgings, accompanied by a queen. **3.** A crowd or throng of persons, animals, or things. — **Syn.** See FLOCK. — *v.i.* **1.** To leave the hive in a swarm: said of bees. **2.** To come together, move, or occur in great numbers. **3.** To teem: with *with.* — *v.t.* **4.** To fill with a swarm or crowd; throng. [OE *swearm*] — **swarm'er** *n.*

swarm² (swôrm) *v.t. & v.i.* To climb (a tree, etc.) by clasping it with the arms and legs. [Prob. akin to SWARM¹.]

swart (swôrt) *adj.* *Dial.* or *Poetic* Swarthy. Also *swarth.* [OE *sweart*] — **swart'ness** *n.*

swarth¹ (swôrth) *n.* *Dial.* Sward. [OE *swearth*]

swarth² (swôrth) *adj.* Swart; swarthy. [? Var. of SWART]

swarth·y (swôr'thē) *adj.* **swarth·i·er, swarth·i·est** Having a dark hue; of dark or sunburned complexion; tawny: also *swart, swarth.* Also **swart'y.** [Var. of obs. *swarty* < SWART] — **swarth'i·ly** *adv.* — **swarth'i·ness, swarth'ness** *n.*

swash (swosh, swôsh) *v.i.* **1.** To move or wash noisily, as waves; splash. **2.** To swagger. — *v.t.* **3.** To splash (water, etc.). **4.** To splash or dash water, etc., upon or against. — *n.* **1.** The splash of a liquid. **2.** A narrow channel through which tides flow. **3.** A swaggerer or his behavior. [Imit.]

swash·buck·ler (swosh'buk'lər, swôsh'-) *n.* A swaggering or boasting soldier. [< SWASH + BUCKLER] — **swash'·buck'ler·ing** *n.* — **swash'buck'ling** *adj. & n.*

swas·ti·ka (swos'ti·kə) *n.* **1.** A primitive religious ornament or symbol, consisting of a Greek cross with the ends of the arms bent at right angles. **2.** The emblem of the Nazis. [< Skt. *svastika* < *svasti* well-being, fortune]

swat (swot) *v.t.* **swat·ted, swat·ting** To hit with a sharp blow. — *n.* A smart blow. Also spelled *swot.* [Var. of SQUAT, in dial. sense of ''squash''] — **swat'ter** *n.*

swatch (swoch) *n.* A strip, as of cloth, esp. one cut off for a sample. [< dial. E (Northern), a cloth tally]

swath (swoth, swôth) *n.* **1.** A row or line of cut grass, grain, etc. **2.** The space or width of grass, grain, etc., cut by any of various mowing devices. **3.** A narrow belt or track; strip. Also called *swathe.* — **to cut a wide swath** To make a fine impression or display. [OE *swæth* a track]

swathe¹ (swāth) *v.t.* **swathed, swath·ing 1.** To bind or wrap, as in bandages. **2.** To envelop; surround. — *n.* A bandage for swathing. [OE *swathian*] — **swath'er** *n.*

swathe² (swāth) *n.* A swath.

sway (swā) *v.i.* **1.** To swing from side to side or to and fro; oscillate. **2.** To bend or incline to one side; lean; veer. **3.** To tend in opinion, sympathy, etc. **4.** To have influence or control. — *v.t.* **5.** To cause to swing, bend, or incline. **6.** To influence (a person, opinion, etc.). **7.** To cause to swerve, as from a course of action. — *n.* **1.** Power exercised in governing; dominion; control. **2.** The act of swaying; a sweeping, swinging, or turning from side to side. **3.** Overpowering force or influence. [Prob. fusion of ON *sveigja* to bend and LG *swajen* to be moved to and fro by the wind]

sway·back (swā'bak') *n.* A hollow or unnaturally sagging condition of the back, as in a horse. — **sway'-backed'** *adj.*

swear (swâr) *v.* **swore** (*Obs.* **sware**), **sworn, swear·ing** *v.i.* **1.** To make a solemn affirmation with an appeal to God, some deity, etc., as in attestation of truth or proof of good intentions. **2.** To utter a solemn promise. **3.** To use profanity; curse. **4.** *Law* To give testimony under oath. — *v.t.* **5.** To affirm or assert solemnly by invoking sacred beings or things. **6.** To vow. **7.** To declare or affirm upon oath. **8.** To take or utter (an oath). **9.** To administer a legal oath to. — **to swear by 1.** To appeal to by oath. **2.** To have complete confidence in. — **to swear in** To administer a legal oath to. — **to swear off** *Informal* To promise to renounce or give up: to *swear off* drink. — **to swear out** To obtain (a warrant for arrest) by making a statement or charge under oath. [OE *swerian*] — **swear'er** *n.*

sweat (swet) *v.* **sweat** or **sweat·ed, sweat·ing** *v.i.* **1.** To exude or excrete sensible moisture from the pores of the skin; perspire. **2.** To exude moisture in drops; ooze. **3.** To gather and condense moisture in drops, as on the outer surface of a glass. **4.** To pass through pores or interstices in drops. **5.** To ferment, as tobacco leaves. **6.** *Informal* To work hard; toil; drudge. **7.** *Informal* To suffer: You will *sweat* for that! — *v.t.* **8.** To exude (moisture) from the pores. **9.** To gather or condense drops of (moisture). **10.** To soak or stain with perspiration. **11.** To cause to sweat. **12.** To cause to work hard. **13.** *Informal* To force (employees) to work for low wages and under unfavorable conditions. **14.** *Slang* To extort money from. **15.** To heat (solder, etc.) until it melts. **16.** To join, as metal objects, by applying heat. **17.** *Metall.* To heat so as to extract an element that is easily fusible. **18.** *Slang* To subject to torture or rigorous interrogation for the purpose of extracting information. — **to sweat (something) out** *U.S. Slang* To wait through anxiously and helplessly. — *n.* **1.** The act or state of sweating. **2.** That which is excreted from the sweat glands; perspiration. **3.** Any gathering in minute drops of moisture on a surface. **4.** *Archaic* Hard labor; drudgery. **5.** *Informal* Fuming impatience; worry; hurry. — **no sweat** *U.S. Slang* No difficulty whatever. [OE < *swāt* sweat] — **sweat'i·ly** *adv.* — **sweat'i·ness** *n.* — **sweat'y** *adj.*

sweat·band (swet'band') *n.* A band, usu. of leather, inside the crown of a hat to protect it from sweat.

sweat·box (swet'boks') *n.* **1.** A device for sweating such products as hides and dried fruits. **2.** A narrow cell or box where an unruly prisoner is confined.

sweat·er (swet'ər) *n.* **1.** A knitted garment in the form of a jersey or jacket with or without sleeves. **2.** One who or that which sweats. **3.** An employer who underpays and overworks his employees. **4.** A sudorific.

sweat gland *Anat.* One of the convoluted tubules that secrete sweat, found in subcutaneous tissue.

sweat shirt A collarless pullover, sometimes lined with fleece, used by athletes.

sweat·shop (swet'shop') *n.* A place where work is done for insufficient wages and for long hours.

Swede (swēd) *n.* A native or inhabitant of Sweden, or a person of Swedish descent.

Swe·den·bor·gi·an·ism (swē'dən·bôr'jē·ən·iz'əm) *n.* The system of philosophy or the theology developed by **Emanuel Swe·den·borg** (swē'dn·bôrg), 1688–1772, Swedish mystic theologian and philosopher. — **Swe·den·bor·gi·an** (swēd'·n·bôr'jē·ən) *adj. & n.*

Swed·ish (swē'dish) *adj.* Pertaining to Sweden, the Swedes, or their language. — *n.* **1.** The North Germanic language of Sweden. **2.** The inhabitants of Sweden collectively.

sweep (swēp) *v.* **swept, sweep·ing** *v.t.* **1.** To collect, remove, or clear away with a broom, brush, etc. **2.** To clear or clean with or as with a broom or brush: to *sweep* a floor. **3.** To touch or brush: Her dress *swept* the ground. **4.** To pass over or through swiftly, as in searching: His eyes *swept* the sky. **5.** To cause to move with an even, continuous action: He *swept* the cape over her shoulders. **6.** To move, carry, bring, etc., with strong or continuous force: The flood *swept* the bridge away. **7.** To move over or through with strong or steady force: The gale *swept* the bay. **8.** To drag the bottom of (a body of water, etc.). — *v.i.* **9.** To clean or brush a floor or other surface with a broom, etc. **10.** To move or go strongly and evenly, esp. with speed: The train *swept* by. **11.** To walk with or as with trailing garments: She *swept* into the room. **12.** To trail, as a skirt. **13.** To extend with a long reach or curve: The road *sweeps* along the lake shore. — *n.* **1.** The act or result of sweeping. **2.** A long stroke or movement: a *sweep* of the hand. **3.** The act of clearing out or getting rid of, as a removal from office or place. **4.** A turning of the eye or of optical instruments over the field of vision. **5.** A great victory or success, as in an election. **6.** The range, area, or compass reached by sweeping, as extent of stroke, range of vision, etc. **7.** A curve or bend, as of a scythe blade, etc. **8.** *Brit.* A chimney sweep. **9.** A long, heavy oar. **10.** A well sweep. **11.** *pl.* Sweepings, as of a place where precious metals are worked. **12.** *Informal* Sweepstakes. [ME *swopen* to brush away] — **sweep′er** *n.* — **sweep′y** *adj.*

sweep·back (swēp′bak′) *n. Aeron.* The backward inclination of the leading edge of an airplane wing.

sweep·ing (swē′ping) *adj.* **1.** Carrying off or clearing away with a driving movement. **2.** Carrying all before it; covering a wide area; comprehensive. **3.** General and thorough-going. — *n.* **1.** The action of one who or that which sweeps. **2.** *pl.* Things swept up; refuse. — **sweep′ing·ly** *adv.* — **sweep′ing·ness** *n.*

sweep·stakes (swēp′stāks′) *n. pl.* **·stakes 1.** A gambling arrangement by which all the sums staked may be won by one or by a few of the bettors, as in a horse race. **2.** A race or contest using this arrangement; also, the prize or prizes. Also **sweep′stake′.**

sweet (swēt) *adj.* **1.** Having an agreeable flavor of or like that of sugar. **2.** Containing or due to sugar in some form. **3.** Not fermented or decaying; fresh. **4.** Not salt or salty: *sweet* water. **5.** Gently pleasing to the senses. **6.** Arousing gentle, pleasant emotions. **7.** Having gentle, pleasing, and winning qualities. **8.** *Music Slang* **a** Designating jazz marked by blandness, moderate tempo, etc. **b** Playing or performing such jazz: a *sweet* trumpet. **9.** Sound; rich; productive: said of soil. **10.** Not dry: said of wines. — *n.* **1.** The quality of being sweet; sweetness. **2.** *Chiefly pl.* A confection, preserve, or piece of candy. **3.** A beloved person; darling. **4.** Something agreeable or pleasing; a pleasure. **5.** *Brit.* A dessert. [OE *swēte*] — **sweet′ly** *adv.* — **sweet′ness** *n.*

sweet alyssum A perennial Mediterranean herb having very fragrant white blossoms: also called *madwort.*

sweet bay A highly ornamental tree or shrub with large flowers.

sweet·bread (swēt′bred′) *n.* The pancreas (**stomach sweetbread**) or the thymus gland (**neck sweetbread** or **throat sweetbread**) of a calf or other animal, when used as food. [< SWEET + BREAD, in obs. sense of "a morsel"]

sweet·bri·er (swēt′brī′ər) *n.* A stout prickly rose native in Europe and Asia, with aromatic leaves: Also **sweet′bri′ar.**

sweet clover Any of several cloverlike herbs, used for fodder.

sweet corn Young ears of corn having sweet, milky kernels, boiled or roasted as food: also called *green corn.*

sweet·en (swēt′n) *v.t.* **1.** To make sweet or sweeter. **2.** To make more endurable; lighten. **3.** To make pleasant or gratifying. — *v.i.* **4.** To become sweet or sweeter. — **sweet′en·er** *n.*

sweet·en·ing (swēt′n·ing) *n.* **1.** The act of making sweet. **2.** That which sweetens.

sweet flag A marsh-dwelling plant, having long leaves and an aromatic rootstock: also called *calamus.*

sweet gum 1. A North American tree, the wood of which is sometimes used to imitate mahogany. **2.** The balsam or gum yielded by it.

sweet·heart (swēt′härt′) *n.* One who is particularly loved by or as a lover; a lover: often used as a term of endearment.

sweet·ie (swē′tē) *n. U.S. Informal* Darling; dear; honey.

sweet·ish (swē′tish) *adj.* Somewhat or rather sweet. — **sweet′ish·ly** *adv.* — **sweet′ish·ness** *n.*

sweet·meat (swēt′mēt′) *n.* **1.** A confection, preserve, candy, etc. **2.** *pl.* Very sweet candy, cakes, etc.

sweet pea An ornamental annual climber of the bean family cultivated for its varicolored flowers.

sweet pepper A mild variety of capsicum whose unripe green fruit is used as a vegetable.

sweet potato 1. A perennial tropical vine, with rose-violet or pink flowers and a fleshy tuberous root. **2.** The root itself, eaten as a vegetable. **3.** *U.S. Informal* An ocarina.

sweets (swēts) *n.pl.* **1.** Sweet things. **2.** *Brit.* Candy.

sweet tooth *Informal* A fondness for candy or sweets.

sweet william A perennial species of pink with closely clustered, showy flowers. Also **sweet William.**

swell (swel) *v.* **swelled, swelled** or **swol·len, swell·ing** *v.i.* **1.** To increase in bulk or dimension, as by inflation within; dilate; expand. **2.** To increase in size, amount, degree, etc. **3.** To grow in volume or intensity, as a sound. **4.** To rise in waves or swells, as the sea. **5.** To bulge, as a sail. **6.** To become puffed up with pride. **7.** To grow within one: My anger *swells* at the sight. — *v.t.* **8.** To cause to increase in size or bulk. **9.** To cause to increase in amount, extent, or degree. **10.** To cause to bulge; belly. **11.** To puff with pride. **12.** *Music* To crescendo and diminuendo in immediate succession. — *n.* **1.** The act, process, or effect of swelling; expansion. **2.** The long continuous body of a wave; a billow; also, a rise in the land. **3.** A bulge or protuberance. **4.** *Music* A crescendo and an immediate diminuendo; also, the signs (< >) indicating it. **5.** A device, as on an organ, by which the volume of a tone may be uninterruptedly varied. **6.** *Informal* A person of the ultrafashionable set. — *adj. Informal* **1.** Ultrafashionable; smart. **2.** First-rate; distinctive. [OE *swellan*]

swell·ing (swel′ing) *n.* **1.** The act of expanding, inflating, or augmenting. **2.** *Pathol.* Abnormal enlargement or protuberance of a part of the body. — *adj.* Increasing; bulging.

swel·ter (swel′tər) *v.i.* **1.** To suffer from oppressive heat; perspire from heat. — *v.t.* **2.** To cause to suffer or perspire from heat. — *n. Archaic* A hot, sweltering condition. [OE *sweltan* to die]

swel·ter·ing (swel′tər·ing) *adj.* **1.** Oppressive; overpoweringly hot. **2.** Overcome by or suffering with heat. Also **swel′try** (-trē). — **swel′ter·ing·ly** *adv.*

swept (swept) Past tense and past participle of SWEEP.

swept·back (swept′bak′) *adj. Aeron.* Having the leading edge inclined backward at an angle with the lateral axis of the airplane: said of a wing.

swerve (swûrv) *v.t. & v.i.* **swerved, swerv·ing** To turn or cause to turn aside from a course or purpose; deflect. — *n.* **1.** The act of swerving or turning aside. **2.** That which swerves. [OE *sweorfan* to file or grind away]

swift (swift) *adj.* **1.** Traversing space or performing movements in a brief time; rapid; quick. **2.** Capable of quick motion; fleet; speedy. **3.** Passing rapidly, as time or events; also, unexpected. **4.** Acting with readiness; prompt. — *n* A bird of swallowlike form possessing extraordinary powers of flight; esp. the **chimney swift.** [OE] — **swift′ly** *adv.* — **swift′ness** *n.*

— **Syn.** (adj.) *Swift* and *fleet* are chiefly applied to moving persons or animals; *swift* suggests ease of motion, and *fleet*, nimbleness: a *swift* bird, a *fleet* horse. *Speedy* may be applied to that which moves or that which progresses: a *speedy* worker, *speedy* action. *Rapid* is applied to progress: *rapid* delivery of mail.

swig (swig) *Informal n.* A deep draft, as of liquor. — *v.t. & v.i.* **swigged, swig·ging** To drink deeply or greedily. [Origin unknown] — **swig′ger** *n.*

swill (swil) *v.t.* **1.** To drink greedily or to excess. **2.** *Brit.* To drench, as with water; rinse; wash. — *v.i.* **3.** To drink to excess; tope. — *n.* **1.** Liquid food for animals; esp., swine; slop. **2.** Any animal or vegetable refuse; garbage. **3.** A deep draft of liquor. [OE *swillan, swilian* to wash]

swim¹ (swim) *v.* **swam, swum, swim·ming** *v.i.* **1.** To propel oneself through water by organized bodily movement. **2.** To be supported on liquid; float. **3.** To move with a smooth or flowing motion, as if swimming. **4.** To be immersed in or covered with liquid; be flooded; overflow. — *v.t.* **5.** To traverse by swimming. **6.** To cause to swim. — *n.* The act, action, pastime, or period of swimming. **2.** A gliding, swaying movement. — **in the swim** *Informal* In the current of affairs. [OE *swimman*] — **swim′mer** *n.*

swim² (swim) *v.i.* **1.** To be dizzy; reel; have a giddy sensation. **2.** To seem to reel, whirl, or spin. — *n.* A sudden dizziness or swoon. [OE *swīma* dizziness]

swim bladder The air bladder of a fish. Also **swimming bladder.**

swim·ming¹ (swim′ing) *n.* The act of one who or that which swims. — *adj.* **1.** Used for swimming. **2.** Having the capacity of swimming; natatorial. **3.** Watery; flooded with tears, as the eyes. [< SWIM¹]

swim·ming² (swim′ing) *n.* A state of dizziness or vertigo. — *adj.* Affected by dizziness. [< SWIM²]

swim·ming·ly (swim′ing·lē) *adv.* Easily, rapidly, and successfully.

swimming pool *U.S.* An indoor or outdoor tank designed for swimming, usu., equipped to cleanse the water.

swin·dle (swin′dəl) *v.* **·dled, ·dling** *v.t.* **1.** To cheat of money or property by deliberate fraud; defraud. **2.** To obtain by such means. — *v.i.* **3.** To practice fraud or decep-

tion for gain. — *n.* **1.** The act of swindling. **2.** Anything that proves to be fraudulent or deceptive, esp., a deal or scheme. [Back formation < SWINDLER]
— **Syn.** (verb) **1.** fleece, cozen, bamboozle, hoodwink. — (noun) imposition, imposture.

swin·dler (swind'lər) *n.* One who swindles or deceives. [< G < *schwindeln* to act thoughtlessly, be giddy]

swine (swīn) *n. pl.* **swine 1.** A domesticated pig. **2.** Any of several related omnivorous mammals having a long mobile snout and cloven hoofs. **3.** A low, greedy, stupid, or vicious person. [OE *swīn*]

swine·herd (swīn'hûrd') *n.* A tender of swine.

swing (swing) *v.* **swung** (*Dial.* **swang**), **swung**, **swing·ing** *v.i.* **1.** To move to-and-fro or backward and forward rhythmically, as something suspended; oscillate. **2.** To ride in a swing. **3.** To move with an even, swaying motion. **4.** To turn; pivot. **5.** To be suspended; hang. **6.** *Informal* To be executed by hanging. — *v.t.* **7.** To cause to move to and fro or backward and forward. **8.** To cause to move with a sweeping motion, as a sword, ax, etc.; brandish; flourish. **9.** To cause to turn on or as on a pivot. **10.** To lift or hoist. **11.** *Informal* To bring to a successful conclusion; manage successfully. — *n.* **1.** The act, process, or manner of swinging; also, the distance covered. **2.** A free swaying motion. **3.** A seat hanging from ropes or chains on which a person may move to and fro as a pastime. **4.** Free course or scope; full liberty or license. **5.** Compass; sweep. **6.** The rhythm characterizing certain styles of poetry or music. **7.** A sweeping blow or stroke. **8.** The course of a career or period of activity; main current of business. **9.** In jazz: a development after about 1935, characterized by large bands, contrapuntal styles, etc. [OE *swingan* to scourge, beat up] — **swing'er** *n.*

swin·gle·tree (swing'gəl·trē') *n.* A whiffletree.

swing shift *U.S. Informal* An evening work shift, usu. lasting from about 4 p.m. to midnight.

swin·ish (swī'nish) *adj.* Of, like, or fit for swine; degraded; sensual; beastly. — **swin'ish·ly** *adv.* — **swin'ish·ness** *n.*

swipe (swīp) *v.t.* **swiped**, **swip·ing 1.** *Informal* To give a strong blow; strike with a full swing of the arm. **2.** *Slang* To steal; snatch. — *n. Informal* A hard, sweeping stroke or blow. [Var. of SWEEP]

swirl (swûrl) *v.i.* **1.** To move with a whirling or twisting motion; whirl. **2.** To be dizzy; swim, as the head. — *v.t.* **3.** To cause to move in a whirling or twisting motion. — *n.* **1.** A whirling along, as in an eddy; whirl. **2.** A twist or curl; spiral. [< dial. E (Scottish) *swyrle*] — **swirl'y** *adj.*

swish (swish) *v.i.* **1.** To move through the air with a hissing, whistling sound, as a slender, flexible rod. **2.** To rustle, as silk. — *v.t.* **3.** To cause to swish. **4.** To thrash; flog. — *n.* **1.** A hissing or rustling sound. **2.** A movement producing such a sound. [Imit.]

Swiss (swis) *adj.* Of or pertaining to Switzerland or its inhabitants. — *n. pl.* **Swiss** A native or naturalized inhabitant of Switzerland.

Swiss chard Chard.

Swiss cheese A pale yellow cheese with many large holes, made in, or similar to that made in, Switzerland.

Swiss steak A thick cut of steak floured and braised, often with a sauce of tomatoes and onions.

switch (swich) *n.* **1.** A small flexible rod, etc., used for whipping. **2.** A tress of false hair, used by women in building a coiffure. **3.** A mechanism for shifting a railway train from one track to another. **4.** The act or operation of shifting, or changing. **5.** The end of the tail in certain animals, as a cow. **6.** *Electr.* A device to make or break a circuit, or transfer a current from one conductor to another. — *v.t.* **1.** To whip with or as with a switch. **2.** To move, jerk, or whisk suddenly or sharply. **3.** To turn aside or divert; shift. **4.** To exchange: They *switched* plates. **5.** To shift (a railroad car) to another track by means of a switch. **6.** *Electr.* To connect or disconnect with a switch. — *v.i.* **7.** To turn aside; change; shift. **8.** To be shifted or turned. [Earlier *swits*] — **switch'er** *n.*

switch·back (swich'bak') *n.* **1.** A railway or road ascending a steep incline in a zigzag pattern. **2.** *Brit.* A roller coaster.

switch·board (swich'bôrd', -bōrd') *n.* A panel or arrangement of panels bearing switches for connecting and disconnecting electric circuits, as a telephone exchange.

switch·man (swich'mən) *n. pl.* **·men** (-mən) One who handles railway switches.

switch·yard (swich'yärd') *n.* A railroad yard for the assembling and breaking up of trains.

swiv·el (swiv'əl) *n.* **1.** A coupling device, link, ring, or pivot that permits either half of a mechanism, as a chain, to rotate independently. **2.** A pivoted support on which a gun may be swung. **3.** A cannon that swings on a pivot: also **swivel gun.** — *v.* **swiv·eled** or **·elled**, **swiv·el·ing** or **·el·ling** *v.t.* **1.** To turn on or as on a swivel. **2.** To fit with or secure by a swivel. — *v.i.* **3.** To turn on or as on a swivel. [ME < OE < *swifan* to revolve]

swivel chair A chair having a seat that turns horizontally on a swivel.

swob (swob), **swob·ber** (swob'ər) See SWAB, etc.

swol·len (swō'lən) Alternative past participle of SWELL.

swoon (swoon) *v.i.* To faint. — *n.* A fainting fit. [ME < OE *geswōgen* unconscious] — **swoon'ing** *n.*

swoop (swoop) *v.i.* **1.** To drop or descend suddenly, as a bird pouncing on its prey. — *v.t.* **2.** To take or seize suddenly: often with *up.* — *n.* The act of swooping. [< OE *swāpan* to sweep]

swop (swop) See SWAP.

sword (sôrd, sōrd) *n.* **1.** A weapon consisting of a long blade fixed in a hilt, as a rapier, etc. **2.** Power; might, military power. **3.** War; destruction; slaughter. — **at swords' points** Hostile; ready for a fight. — **to put to the sword** To kill with a sword; slaughter in battle. [< OE *sweord*]

sword·fish (sôrd'fish', sōrd'-) *n. pl.* **·fish** or **·fish·es** A large marine fish having the bones of the upper jaw consolidated to form an elongated swordlike process.

sword grass 1. Any of several varieties of grasses or sedges with sharp or serrated edges. **2.** The gladiolus.

sword·knot (sôrd'not', sōrd'-) *n.* Formerly, a loop of leather used to fasten the hilt of a sword to the wrist; now, a tassel of cord or ribbon tied to a sword hilt.

sword·play (sôrd'plā', sōrd'-) *n.* The act, art, or skill of using the sword, esp. in fencing. — **sword'-play'er** *n.*

swords·man (sôrdz'mən, sōrdz'-) *n. pl.* **·men** (-mən) One skilled in the use of or armed with a sword. Also **sword'·man.** — **swords'man·ship** or **sword'man·ship** *n.*

swore (swôr, swōr) Past tense of SWEAR.

sworn (swôrn, swōrn) Past participle of SWEAR.

swot (swot) See SWAT.

swounds (zwoundz, zoundz), **swouns** (zwounz, zounz) See ZOUNDS.

swum (swum) Past participle and dialectal past tense of SWIM.

swung (swung) Past tense and past participle of SWING.

sy- Var. of SYN-.

syb·a·rite (sib'ə·rīt) *n.* One given to pleasure and luxury; an epicure. [< L < Gk. < *Sybaris*, an ancient Greek city in southern Italy, famed for its luxury.] — **syb'a·rit'ic** (-rit'-ik) or **·i·cal** *adj.* — **syb'a·rit'i·cal·ly** *adv.*

syc·a·more (sik'ə·môr, -mōr) *n.* **1.** A medium-sized bushy tree of Syria and Egypt allied to the common fig. **2.** Any of various plane trees of the U.S., esp., the **American sycamore:** also called *buttonwood.* **3.** An ornamental shade tree of Europe and Asia. [< OF < LL < Gk. < *sykon* fig + *moron* mulberry]

syc·o·phant (sik'ə·fənt) *n.* A servile flatterer. [< L < Gk. *sykophantēs* informer] — **syc'o·phan·cy** *n.* — **syc'o·phan'tic** (-fan'tik) or **·i·cal** *adj.* — **syc'o·phan'ti·cal·ly** *adv.*

syl·la·bar·y (sil'ə·ber'ē) *n. pl.* **·bar·ies** A list or table of syllables; esp., a list of characters representing syllables. [< NL < Med.L. See SYLLABLE.]

syl·lab·ic (si·lab'ik) *adj.* **1.** Of or consisting of a syllable or syllables. **2.** *Phonet.* Designating a consonant capable of forming a complete syllable, as *l* in *middle* (mid'l). **3.** Having every syllable distinctly pronounced. Also **syl·lab'i·cal.** — *n. Phonet.* A sound of high sonority, usu., a vowel. — **syl·lab'i·cal·ly** *adv.*

syl·lab·i·cate (si·lab'ə·kāt) *v.t.* **·cat·ed**, **·cat·ing** To form or divide into syllables. — **syl·lab'i·ca'tion**, **syl·lab'i·fi·ca'tion** *n.*

syl·lab·i·fy (si·lab'ə·fī) *v.t.* **·fied**, **·fy·ing** To syllabicate.

syl·la·ble (sil'ə·bəl) *n.* **1.** *Phonet.* A word or part of a word uttered in a single vocal impulse, usu. consisting of a vowel alone or with one or more consonants. **2.** A part of a written or printed word corresponding, more or less, to the spoken division. In this dictionary, syllable breaks are indicated by centered dots. **3.** The least detail, mention, or trace: Please don't repeat a *syllable* of what you've heard here. — *v.* **bled**, **bling** *v.t.* **1.** To pronounce the syllables of. — *v.i.* **2.** To pronounce syllables. [< AF, OF < L < Gk. < *syn-* together + *lambanein* to take]

syl·la·bus (sil'ə·bəs) *n. pl.* **·bus·es** or **·bi** (-bī) A concise statement of the main points of a course of study, subject, etc. [< NL < Med.L < L < *sittyba* label on a book < Gk.]

syl·lo·gism (sil'ə·jiz'əm) *n.* **1.** *Logic* **a** A formula of argument consisting of two propositions, called *premises,* and a *conclusion,* logically drawn from them. Example: All men are mortal (*major premise*); kings are men (*minor premise*); therefore, kings are mortal (*conclusion*). **b** Deductive reasoning. **2.** A subtle or crafty argument. [< OF < L < Gk. < *syn-* together + *logizesthai* to infer] — **syl'lo·gis'tic** *adj. & n.* — **syl'lo·gis'ti·cal** *adj.* — **syl'lo·gis'ti·cal·ly** *adv.*

sylph (silf) *n.* **1.** An imaginary being, mortal but without a soul, living in the air. **2.** A slender, graceful young woman or girl. [< NL *sylphes*, pl.] — **sylph'like** *adj.*

syl·van (sil'vən) *adj. Chiefly Poetic* **1.** Of or located in a forest or woods. **2.** Composed of or abounding in trees or woods. **3.** Characteristic of a forest or woods; rustic. — *n.*

A spirit, person or animal dwelling in the woods. [< MF < L < *silva* wood]

sym- Assimilated var. of SYN-.

sym·bi·o·sis (sim′bī·ō′sis, -bē-) *n.* *Biol.* The consorting together, usu., in mutually advantageous partnership, of dissimilar organisms, as of the algae and fungi in lichens. [< NL ult. < Gk. *syn-* together + *bios* life] — **sym′bi·ot′ic** (-ot′ik) or **·i·cal** *adj.* — **sym′bi·ot′i·cal·ly** *adv.*

sym·bol (sim′bəl) *n.* 1. Something chosen to represent something else; esp., an object used to typify a quality, abstract idea, etc.: The oak is a *symbol* of strength. 2. A character, mark, etc., indicating something, as a quantity in mathematics. — *v.t.* To symbolize. — **Syn.** See EMBLEM. [< LL < Gk. < *syn-* together + *ballein* to throw]

sym·bol·ic (sim·bol′ik) *adj.* 1. Of, pertaining to, or expressed by a symbol or symbols. 2. Serving as a symbol: with *of*. 3. Characterized by or involving the use of symbols: *symbolic* poetry. Also **sym·bol′i·cal.** — **sym·bol′i·cal·ly** *adv.* — **sym·bol′i·cal·ness** *n.*

sym·bol·ism (sim′bəl·iz′əm) *n.* 1. Representation by symbols; treatment or interpretation of things as symbolic. 2. The quality of being symbolic. 3. A system of symbols. 4. The theories and practice of a group of symbolists.

sym·bol·ist (sim′bəl·ist) *n.* One who uses symbols; esp., one skilled in the interpretation or use of symbols, as in literature and art.

sym·bol·is·tic (sim′bəl·is′tik) *adj.* 1. Expressed by symbols; characterized by the use of symbols 2. Of or pertaining to symbolism; symbolic. Also **sym′bol·is′ti·cal.**

sym·bol·ize (sim′bəl·īz) *v.* **·ized, ·iz·ing** *v.t.* 1. To be a symbol of; represent symbolically; typify. 2. To represent by a symbol or symbols. 3. To treat as symbolic or figurative. — *v.i.* 4. To use symbols. — **sym′bol·i·za′tion** *n.*

sym·me·try (sim′ə·trē) *n.* *pl.* **·tries** 1. An exact correspondence between the opposite halves of a figure, form, line, pattern, etc., on either side of an axis or center; the condition whereby half of something is the mirror image of the other half. 2. Beauty or harmony of form resulting from a symmetrical or nearly symmetrical arrangement of parts; due or right proportion. [< MF < LL < Gk. < *syn-* together + *metron* a measure] — **sym·met′ric** (-met′rik), **sym·met′ri·cal** (-met′ri·kəl) *adj.*

sym·pa·thet·ic (sim′pə·thet′ik) *adj.* 1. Of, expressing, or proceeding from sympathy. 2. Having a fellow feeling for others; sympathizing; compassionate. 3. Being in accord or harmony; congenial. Also **sym′pa·thet′i·cal.** [< NL < Gk. See SYMPATHY] — **sym′pa·thet′i·cal·ly** *adv.*

sym·pa·thin (sim′pə·thin) *n.* *Biochem.* A substance liberated by the stimulation of certain fibers of the sympathetic nervous system and acting as a chemical mediator in associated nerve impulses. [< SYMPATH(ETIC) + -IN]

sym·pa·thique (saṅ·pà·tēk′) *adj.* *French* Pleasant; nice; congenial: said of persons.

sym·pa·thize (sim′pə·thīz) *v.i.* **·thized, ·thiz·ing** 1. To share the sentiments, feelings, or ideas of another: with *with*. 2. To feel or express compassion, as for another's sorrow or affliction: with *with*. 3. To be in harmony or agreement. — **sym′pa·thiz′er** *n.* — **sym′pa·thiz′ing·ly** *adv.*

sym·pa·thy (sim′pə·thē) *n.* *pl.* **·thies** 1. The quality of being affected by the state of another with feelings correspondent in kind. 2. A fellow feeling; esp., a feeling of compassion for another's sufferings; pity; commiseration. 3. An agreement of affections, inclinations, or temperaments that makes persons agreeable to one another; congeniality; accord. — **Syn.** See PITY. [< L < Gk. < *syn-* together + *pathos* feeling]

sympathy strike A strike in which the strikers support the demands of another group of workers but demand nothing for themselves.

sym·pho·ny (sim′fə·nē) *n.* *pl.* **·nies** 1. *Music* A composition for orchestra, consisting usu., of four movements, that are related by structure, key, etc. 2. A symphony orchestra. 3. A harmonious or agreeable mingling of sounds, colors, etc.: *symphony* in gray. [< OF < L < Gk. < *syn-* together + *phōnē* sound] — **sym·phon′ic** (fon′ik) *adj.* — **sym′pho·nist** *n.*

symphony orchestra A large orchestra composed usu. of the string, brass, woodwind, and percussion sections needed to present symphonic works: also *symphony*.

sym·phy·sis (sim′fə·sis) *n.* *pl.* **·ses** (-sēz) *Anat.* A junction of two parts of the skeleton, formed either by a growing together of two bones or by the intervention of a layer of cartilage between them. [< NL < Gk. < *syn-* together + *phyein* to grow] — **sym·phyt′ic** (sim-fit′ik) *adj.* — **sym·phyt′i·cal·ly** *adv.*

sym·po·si·um (sim·pō′zē·əm) *n.* *pl.* **·si·ums** or **·si·a** (-zē·ə) 1. A meeting for discussion of a particular subject. 2. A collection of comments or opinions brought together; esp., a series of brief essays or articles on the same subject, as in a magazine. Also **sym·po′si·on** (-zē·on). [< L < Gk. < *syn-* together + *posis* a drinking < *po-*, stem of *pinein* to drink] — **sym·po′si·ac** (-ak) *adj.*

symp·tom (sim′təm) *n.* 1. A sign, token, or indication. 2. *Med.* Any observable alteration in bodily functions or mental behavior arising from and indicating the presence of disease, esp. when regarded as an aid in diagnosis. [< L < Gk. < *syn-* together + *piptein* to fall]

symp·to·mat·ic (simp′tə·mat′ik) *adj.* 1. Pertaining to, of the nature of, or constituting a symptom or symptoms. 2. According to symptoms: a *symptomatic* classification of diseases. Also **symp′to·mat′i·cal.** — **symp′to·mat′i·cal·ly** *adv.*

syn- *prefix* With; together; associated with or accompanying: *syntax, syndrome.* Also: *sy-* before *sc, sp, st,* and *z,* as in *system; syl-* before *l,* as in *syllable; sym-* before *b, p,* and *m,* as in *sympathy; sys-* before *s.* [< L < Gk. < *syn* together]

syn·a·gogue (sin′ə·gôg, -gog) *n.* 1. A place of meeting for Jewish worship and religious instruction. 2. A Jewish congregation or assemblage for religious instruction and observances. 3. The Jewish religion or communion. Also **syn′a·gog.** [< OF < LL < Gk. *synagōgē* assembly < *syn-* together + *agein* to lead, bring] — **syn′a·gog′i·cal** (-goj′i·kəl), **syn′a·gog′al** (-gôg′əl, -gog′əl) *adj.*

syn·apse (si·naps′) *n.* *Physiol.* The junction point of two neurons, across which a nerve impulse passes. Also called **syn·ap·sis** (si·nap′sis). [< NL < Gk. < *syn-* together + *hapsis* a joining]

syn·carp (sin′kärp) *n.* *Bot.* 1. A fruit composed of several carpels, as the blackberry. 2. A multiple fruit, as the fig. Also **syn·car·pi·um** (sin·kär′pē·əm). [< NL < Gk. *syn-* together + *karpos* fruit] — **syn·car′pous** *adj.*

syn·chro (sing′krō) *n.* Any of various electromagnetic devices for the remote control of complex operations.

syn·chro·mesh (sing′krə·mesh′) *n.* *Mech.* 1. A gear system by which driving and driven members are brought to the same speed before engaging. 2. Any gear in such a system. [< SYNCHRO(NIZED) + MESH]

syn·chro·nism (sing′krə·niz′əm) *n.* 1. The state of being synchronous. 2. Coincidence in time of different events or phenomena; simultaneousness. 3. A tabular grouping of historic personages or events according to their dates. 4. In art, representation in the same picture of events that occurred at different times. — **syn′chro·nis′tic** or **·ti·cal** *adj.* — **syn′chro·nis′ti·cal·ly** *adv.*

syn·chro·nize (sing′krə·nīz) *v.* **·nized, ·niz·ing** *v.i.* 1. To occur at the same time; coincide. 2. To move or operate in unison. — *v.t.* 3. To cause (timepieces) to agree in keeping or indicating time. 4. To cause to operate in unison. 5. To assign the same date or period to. — **syn′chro·ni·za′tion** *n.* — **syn′chro·niz′er** *n.*

syn·chro·nous (sing′krə·nəs) *adj.* 1. Occurring at the same time; coincident. 2. Happening at the same rate. 3. *Physics* Having the same period or rate of vibration, as waves or electric currents. Also **syn·chron′ic, syn′chro·nal.** [< LL < Gk. < *syn-* together + *chronos* time] — **syn′chro·nous·ly** *adv.* — **syn′chro·nous·ness** *n.*

syn·cli·nal (sin·klī′nal, sing-) *adj.* 1. Sloping downward on each side toward a line or point. 2. *Geol.* Inclining upward on each side from the axis of the fold, as rock strata. Also **syn·clin·i·cal** (sin·klin′i·kəl, sing-). — *n.* A syncline. [< Gk. < *syn-* together + *klinein* to incline]

syn·cline (sing′klīn) *n.* *Geol.* A trough or structural basin toward which rocks dip.

syn·co·pate (sing′kə·pāt) *v.t.* **·pat·ed, ·pat·ing** 1. *Gram.* To contract (a word) by syncope. 2. *Music* To treat or modify, as a tone, by syncopation. [< LL *syncopatus,* pp. of *syncopare* to affect with syncope] — **syn′co·pat′or** *n.*

syn·co·pa·tion (sing′kə·pā′shən) *n.* 1. The act of syncopating or state of being syncopated. 2. That which is syncopated, as a dance or rhythm. 3. *Music* a The rhythmic placement of a tone so that its accent does not coincide with the metric accent, as by beginning it on a weak beat or a fraction of a beat and continuing it through the next strong beat. b A tone so treated. c Any music featuring syncopation, as ragtime, jazz, etc. 4. *Gram.* Syncope.

syn·co·pe (sing′kə·pē) *n.* 1. *Gram.* The elision of a sound or syllable in the middle part of a word, as *e'er* for *ever.* 2. *Pathol.* A loss of consciousness caused by temporary cerebral anemia. [< OF, ult. < LL < Gk. < *syn-* together + *kop-,* stem of *koptein* to cut] — **syn′co·pal, syn·cop·ic** (sin·kop′ik) *adj.*

syn·cre·tize (sing′krə·tīz) *v.t. & v.i.* **·tized, ·tiz·ing** To attempt to blend and reconcile, as various philosophies. [< NL < Gk. *synkrētizein* to combine] — **syn′cre·tism** *n.*

syn·det·ic (sin·det′ik) *adj.* Serving to unite or connect; connective, as a word. Also **syn·det′i·cal.** [< Gk. < *syn-* together + *deein* to bind] — **syn·det′i·cal·ly** *adv.*

syn·dic (sin′dik)   *n.*   **1.** A civil magistrate or officer representing a government or a community. **2.** One who is designated to transact business for others; also, a body of officers or council so designated. [< F < LL < Gk. *syndikos* defendant's advocate < *syn-* together + *dikē* judgment] — **syn′di·cal** *adj.*

syn·di·cal·ism (sin′di·kəl·iz′əm)   *n.*   A social and political theory proposing the taking over of the means of production by syndicates of workers, preferably by means of the general strike, with consequent political control. — **syn′di·cal·ist** *adj. & n.* — **syn′di·cal·is′tic** *adj.*

syn·di·cate (*n.* sin′də·kit; *v.* sin′də·kāt)   *n.*   **1.** An association of individuals united to negotiate some business or to prosecute some enterprise requiring large capital. **2.** An agency that sells articles, etc., to a number of periodicals, as newspapers, for simultaneous publication. **3.** The office or jurisdiction of a syndic; also, syndics collectively. — *v.t.* **·cat·ed, ·cat·ing 1.** To combine into or manage by a syndicate. **2.** To sell (an article, etc.) for publication in many newspapers or magazines. [See SYNDIC.]

syn·drome (sin′drōm)   *n.*   *Med.* An aggregate or set of concurrent symptoms indicating the presence and nature of a disease. [< NL < Gk. < *syn-* together + *dramein* to run] — **syn·drom·ic** (sin·drom′ik) *adj.*

sy·nec·do·che (si·nek′də·kē)   *n.*   A figure of speech in which a part is put for a whole or a whole for a part, an individual for a class, or a material for the thing, as a *roof* for a *house.* [< LL < Gk. < *syn-* together + *ekdechesthai* to take from] — **syn·ec·doch·ic** (sin′ek·dok′ik) or **·i·cal** *adj.*

syn·i·ze·sis (sin′ə·zē′sis)   *n.*   **1.** *Biol.* The contractile massing of the chromatin in meiosis. **2.** *Med.* Contraction of the pupil of the eye. Also **syn·e·zi′sis** (-zī′sis). [< LL < Gk. < *syn-* together + *izanein* to settle down, sit]

syn·od (sin′əd)   *n.*   **1.** An ecclesiastical council. **2.** Any deliberative assembly. [OE < LL < Gk. *synodos*, lit., a coming together < *syn-* together + *hodos* way]

sy·nod·i·cal (si·nod′i·kəl)   *adj.*   **1.** Of, pertaining to, or of the nature of a synod; transacted in a synod. **2.** *Astron.* Pertaining to the conjunction of two heavenly bodies, one of which revolves round the other, or to the interval between two successive conjunctions. Also **syn·od·al** (sin′ə·dəl), **sy·nod′ic.** — **sy·nod′i·cal·ly** *adv.*

syn·o·nym (sin′ə·nim)   *n.*   **1.** A word having the same or almost the same meaning as some other: opposed to *antonym.* **2.** The equivalent of a word in another language. Also **syn′o·nyme.** [< LL < Gk. < *syn-* together + *onyma, onoma* name] — **syn′o·nym′ic** or **·i·cal** *adj.* — **syn′o·nym′i·ty** *n.*

sy·non·y·mize (si·non′ə·mīz)   *v.t.*   **·mized, ·miz·ing** To give the synonyms of; express by words of similar meaning.

sy·non·y·mous (si·non′ə·məs)   *adj.*   **1.** Being a synonym or synonyms; equivalent or similar in meaning. **2.** Closely related or alike in significance or effect. Also **syn·o·ny·mat·ic** (sin′ə·ni·mat′ik). — **sy·non′y·mous·ly** *adv.*

sy·non·y·my (si·non′ə·mē)   *n.*   *pl.* **·mies 1.** The quality of being synonymous. **2.** The science or systematic collection and study of synonyms; also, the use and discrimination of synonyms. **3.** A written analysis discriminating the meaning of synonyms. **4.** An index, list, or collection of synonyms, as in scientific nomenclature.

sy·nop·sis (si·nop′sis)   *n.*   *pl.* **·ses** (-sēz) A general view, as of a subject or its treatment; an abstract; syllabus; summary. [< LL < Gk. < *syn-* together + *opsis* view]

sy·nop·tic (si·nop′tik)   *adj.*   **1.** Giving or constituting a synopsis or general view. **2.** *Often cap.* Presenting the same or a similar point of view: said of the first three Gospels (**Synoptic Gospels**). Also **sy·nop′ti·cal.** — **sy·nop′ti·cal·ly** *adv.*

sy·no·vi·a (si·nō′vē·ə)   *n.*   *Physiol.* The viscid, transparent, albuminous fluid secreted by the **synovial membranes** at points where lubrication is necessary, as in joints. [< NL, appar. < Gk. *syn-* together + L *ovum* egg < Gk. *ōon*] — **sy·no′vi·al** *adj.*

syn·tax (sin′taks)   *n.*   **1.** The arrangement and interrelationship of words in phrases and sentences. **2.** The branch of linguistics dealing with such relationships. [< F < LL < Gk. < *syn-* together + *tassein* to arrange] — **syn·tac·tic** (sin·tak′tik) or **·ti·cal** *adj.* — **syn·tac′ti·cal·ly** *adv.*

syn·the·sis (sin′thə·sis)   *n.*   *pl.* **·ses** (-sēz) **1.** The assembling of separate or subordinate parts into a whole: opposed to *analysis.* **2.** A complex whole composed of originally separate parts. **3.** *Chem.* The building up of compounds from a series of reactions involving elements, radicals, or similar compounds, esp. organic compounds that have specific properties or are similar to naturally occurring substances. Compare ANALYSIS. [< L < Gk. < *syn-* together + *tithenai* to place] — **syn′the·sist** *n.*

syn·the·size (sin′thə·sīz)   *v.t.*   **·sized, ·siz·ing 1.** To unite or produce by synthesis. **2.** To apply synthesis to. Also *Brit.* **syn′the·sise.**

syn·thet·ic (sin·thet′ik)   *adj.*   **1.** Pertaining to, of the nature of, or characterized by synthesis. **2.** Tending to reduce particulars to inclusive wholes. **3.** *Chem.* Produced artificially by the synthesis of simpler materials or substances rather than occurring naturally. **4** Artificial; spurious. Also **syn·thet′i·cal.** — *n.* Anything produced by synthesis. — **syn·thet′i·cal·ly** *adv.*

syph·i·lis (sif′ə·lis)   *n.*   *Pathol.* An infectious, chronic, venereal disease caused by a spirochete transmissible by direct contact or congenitally, and usu. progressing by three stages of increasing severity. [after a Latin poem published in 1530, the hero of which, *Syphilus*, a shepherd, was the first sufferer from the disease]

syph·i·lit·ic (sif′ə·lit′ik)   *adj.*   Relating to or affected with syphilis. — *n.* A person suffering from syphilis.

Syr·i·ac (sir′ē·ak)   *n.*   The language of the Syrians, belonging to the eastern Aramaic subgroup of the Northwest Semitic languages. [< L < Gk. *Syriakos*]

Syr·i·an (sir′ē·ən)   *adj.*   Of or pertaining to ancient or modern Syria. — *n.* **1.** A native of Syria, esp. one of the Semitic people of Arabic, Phoenician, and Aramean descent. **2.** One who is a member of a Christian church in Syria. [< OF < L < Gk. *Syria* Syria]

sy·rin·ga (si·ring′gə)   *n.*   **1.** Any of various ornamental shrubs of the saxifrage family, having fragrant cream-colored flowers. **2.** The lilac. [< NL < Gk. *syrinx, -ingos* a pipe]

syr·inge (sir′inj, si·rinj′)   *n.*   **1.** *Med.* A small instrument of glass, metal, rubber, or plastic, consisting of a receptacle into which a liquid may be drawn for ejection in a fine jet or stream, used for cleaning wounds, affected parts, etc. **2.** A hypodermic syringe. — *v.t.* **·inged, ·ing·ing** To spray or inject by a syringe; cleanse or treat with injected fluid. [< Med.L < Gk. *syrinx, -ingos* tube, pipe]

syr·inx (sir′ingks)   *n.*   *pl.* **sy·rin·ges** (sə·rin′jēz) or **sy′rinx·es 1.** *Ornithol.* A special modification of the windpipe serving as the song organ in birds. **2.** *Anat.* The Eustachian tube. [< Gk., pipe] — **sy·rin·ge·al** (si·rin′jē·əl) *adj.*

syr·up (sir′əp)   *n.*   A thick, sweet liquid, as the boiled juice of fruits, sugar cane, etc.: also, *esp. U.S., sirup.* [< OF < Arabic *sharāb*] — **syr′up·y** *adj.*

sys- Var. of SYN-.

sys·tal·tic (sis·tal′tik)   *adj.*   *Physiol.* Alternately contracting and dilating, as the motion of the heart; pulsatory. [< LL < Gk. < *syn-* together + *stellein* to send]

sys·tem (sis′təm)   *n.*   **1.** Orderly combination or arrangement of parts, elements, etc., into a whole; esp., such combination according to some rational principle; any methodical arrangement of parts. **2.** Any group of facts, concepts, and phenomena regarded as constituting a natural whole for purposes of philosophic or scientific investigation and construction: the Ptolemaic *system*; the solar *system.* **3.** The connection or manner of connection of parts as related to a whole, or the parts collectively so related: a railroad *system.* **4.** The state or quality of being in order or orderly; method. **5.** *Physiol.* **a** An assemblage of organic structures composed of similar elements and combined for the same general functions: the nervous *system.* **b** The entire body, taken as a functional whole. **6.** *Physics* An aggregate or region of matter considered as a unit with respect to specified factors such as mass, energy, gravitation, radioactivity, etc. **7.** *Chem.* A group of substances in one or more phases exhibiting, or tending to approach, equilibrium. **8.** *Mineral.* One of the primary divisions into which all crystal forms may be grouped, depending upon the relative lengths and mutual inclinations of the assumed crystal axes. **9.** *Geol.* A category of igneous and sedimentary rock strata corresponding with a period in the time scale. [< LL < Gk. < *syn-* together + *histanai* to stand, set up]

sys·tem·at·ic (sis′tə·mat′ik)   *adj.*   **1.** Of, pertaining to, of the nature of, or characterized by system. **2.** Characterized by system or method; methodical: a *systematic* person. **3.** Forming a system; systematized. **4.** Carried out with organized regularity. **5.** Taxonomic. Also **sys′tem·at′i·cal.** — **sys′tem·at′i·cal·ly** *adv.*

sys·tem·a·tism (sis′tə·mə·tiz′əm)   *n.*   **1.** Systematic arrangement or classification. **2.** Adherence to or reduction of principles, etc., to a system. — **sys′tem·a·tist** *n.*

sys·tem·a·tize (sis′tə·mə·tīz′)   *v.t.* **·tized, ·tiz·ing** To reduce to a system. Also **sys′tem·ize,** *Brit.* **sys′tem·a·tise′.** — **sys′·tem·a·ti·za′tion** *n.* — **sys′tem·a·tiz′er** *n.*

sys·tem·ic (sis·tem′ik)   *adj.*   **1.** Of or pertaining to system or a system. **2.** *Physiol.* Pertaining to or affecting the body as a whole: a *systemic* poison. — **sys·tem′i·cal·ly** *adv.*

sys·to·le (sis′tə·lē)   *n.*   **1.** *Physiol.* The regular contraction of the heart, esp. of the ventricles, that impels the blood outward. Compare DIASTOLE. **2.** The shortening of a syllable that is naturally or by position long. [See SYSTALTIC.] — **sys·tol·ic** (sis·tol′ik) *adj.*

syz·y·gy (siz′ə·jē)   *n.*   *pl.* **·gies** *Astron.* **a** One of two opposite points in the orbit of a celestial body when it is in conjunction with or in opposition to the sun. **b** The points on the moon's orbit when the moon is most nearly in line with the earth and the sun. [< LL < Gk. < *syn-* together + *zeugnynai* to yoke] — **sy·zyg·i·al** (si·zij′ē·əl) *adj.*

T

t, T (tē) *n. pl.* **t's** or **ts, T's** or **Ts, tees** (tēz) **1.** The twentieth letter of the English alphabet. **2.** The sound represented by the letter *t*, the voiceless alveolar stop. **3.** Anything shaped like the letter T. **— to a T** Precisely; with exactness.

't Contraction for IT: used initially, as in *'tis* and finally, as in *on't*.

-t Inflectional ending used to indicate past participles and past tenses, and corresponding to *-ed*, as in *bereft, lost, spent*.

tab (tab) *n.* **1.** A flap, strip, tongue, or appendage of something, as a garment. **2.** A small, projecting part used as an aid in filing papers, etc. **3.** *Informal* Tally; total; bill: to pick up the *tab*. **— to keep tab** or **tabs (on)** **1.** To watch or supervise closely. **2.** To maintain a factual record (of). [Origin uncertain]

tab·ard (tab′ərd) *n.* **1.** Formerly, a short, sleeveless or short-sleeved outer garment. **2.** A knight's cape or cloak, worn over his armor; also, a similar garment worn by a herald. [< OF *tabart*, ult. < L *tapete* tapestry]

Ta·bas·co (tə·bas′kō) *n.* A pungent sauce made from red pepper: a trade name. Also **Tabasco sauce.**

tab·by (tab′ē) *n. pl.* **·bies** **1.** A brindled or striped cat. **2.** Any domestic cat, esp. a female. **3.** A gossiping old maid. **4.** Any of various plain-woven fabrics, as a watered taffeta. **—** *adj.* **1.** Having dark, wavy markings; brindled, as a cat. **2.** Watered or mottled, as a fabric. **3.** Made of tabby. **—** *v.t.* **·bied, ·by·ing** To give a wavy or watered appearance to (silk, etc.). [< F < Arabic *'Attābi*, name of a quarter of Baghdad where the cloth was manufactured]

tab·er·na·cle (tab′ər·nak′əl) *n.* **1.** A tent or similar temporary structure or shelter. **2.** A Jewish house of worship; a temple. **3.** Originally, the portable sanctuary used by the Jews in the wilderness. **4.** Any house of worship, esp. one of large size. **5.** The human body as the dwelling place of the soul. **'6.** *Eccl.* The ornamental receptacle for the consecrated Eucharistic elements, or for the pyx. **7.** An ornamental recess or structure sheltering something. **—** *v.i. & v.t.* **·led, ·ling** To dwell or place in or as in a tabernacle. [< OF < L *tabernaculum*, dim. of *taberna* shed] **— tab·er·nac·u·lar** (tab′ər·nak′yə·lər) *adj.*

tab·la·ture (tab′lə·chər) *n. Music* A notation for instrumental music that indicates rhythm and fingering, but not the pitches produced. [< F < L *tabula* board]

ta·ble (tā′bəl) *n.* **1.** An article of furniture with a flat horizontal top upheld by one or more supports. **2.** Such a table around which persons sit for a meal. **3.** The food served or entertainment provided at a meal or dinner. **4.** The company of persons at a table. **5.** A collection of related numbers, values, signs, or items of any kind, arranged for reference or comparison, often in parallel columns: a *table* of logarithms. **6.** A synoptical statement; list: *table* of contents. **7.** A tableland; plateau. **8.** A tablet or slab bearing an inscription; esp., one of those that bore the Ten Commandments or certain Roman laws. **— to turn the tables** To thwart an opponent's action and turn the situation to his disadvantage. **—** *v.t.* **·bled, ·bling** **1.** To place on a table, as a playing card. **2.** To postpone discussion of (a resolution, bill, etc.) until a future time, or for an indefinite period. **3.** *Rare* To tabulate. [Fusion of OF *table* and OE *tabule*, both < L *tabula* board]

tab·leau (tab′lō, ta·blō′) *n. pl.* **·leaux** (-loz, -lō) or **·leaus** (-lōz) **1.** Any picture or picturesque representation; esp., a striking scene presented dramatically. **2.** A tableau vivant. [< F, dim. of *table* table]

ta·bleau vi·vant (ta·blō′ vē·vän′) *pl.* **ta·bleaux vi·vants** (ta·blō′ vē·vän′) *French* A picturelike scene represented by silent and motionless persons standing in appropriate attitudes: also called *tableau.*

ta·ble·cloth (tā′bəl·klôth′, -kloth′) *n.* A cloth covering a table, esp., at meals.

tab·le d'hôte (tab′əl dōt′, tä′bəl; *Fr.* ta′blə dōt′) *pl.* **tab·les d'hôte** (tab′əlz dōt′, tä′bəlz; *Fr.* ta′blə dōt′) A complete meal served at a restaurant or hotel, the price of the entire meal being determined by the price of the entrée one chooses. Compare À LA CARTE. [< F, lit., table of the host, as at an inn]

ta·ble·land (tā′bəl·land′) *n.* A broad, level, elevated region, usu. treeless; a plateau.

table linen Tablecloths, napkins, doilies, etc.

ta·ble·spoon (tā′bəl·spōōn′, -spŏŏn′) *n.* **1.** A fairly large spoon used for serving food and in measuring for recipes, etc. **2.** A tablespoonful, equivalent to three teaspoons.

ta·ble·spoon·ful (tā′bəl·spōōn·fŏŏl′, -spŏŏn-) *n. pl.* **·fuls** As much as a tablespoon will hold.

tab·let (tab′lit) *n.* **1.** A pad, as of writing paper or note paper. **2.** A small, flat surface, esp., one designed for or containing an inscription or design. **3.** A definite portion of a drug, etc., pressed into a solid form. **4.** A small, flat, or nearly flat piece of some prepared substance, as chocolate or soap. **5.** A thin sheet or slab of solid material, as stone, wood, etc., used for writing, painting, or drawing. [< OF *tablete*, dim. of *table* table]

table tennis A table game resembling tennis, played usu. indoors with a small celluloid ball and wooden paddles: also called *ping-pong.*

ta·ble·ware (tā′bəl·wâr′) *n.* Dishes, knives, forks, spoons, etc., for table use, collectively.

tab·loid (tab′loid) *n.* A newspaper consisting of sheets one half the size of those in an ordinary newspaper, in which the news is presented by means of pictures and concise reporting. **—** *adj.* **1.** Compact; concise; condensed. **2.** Sensational: *tabloid* journalism. [< TABL(ET) + -OID]

Tab·loid (tab′loid) *n.* Proprietary name for any of various medical preparations and drugs in concentrated or condensed tablet form.

ta·boo (tə·bōō′, ta-) *n.* **1.** Among primitive peoples, esp. the Polynesians, a religious and social interdict forbidding the mention of a certain person, thing, or place, the performance of a certain action, etc. **2.** The system or practice of such interdicts or prohibitions. **3.** Any restriction or ban founded on custom or social convention. **4.** The convention of avoiding certain words as profane, obscene, disagreeable, or otherwise socially unacceptable: compare EUPHEMISM. **—** *adj.* **1.** Consecrated or prohibited by taboo. **2.** Banned or forbidden by social authority or convention. **—** *v.t.* **1.** To place under taboo. **2.** To exclude; ostracize. Also **ta·bu′.** [< Tonga *tabu*]

ta·bor (tā′bər) *n.* A small drum or tambourine on which a fifer beats his own accompaniment. **—** *v.i.* To beat or play on a timbrel or small drum; beat lightly and repeatedly. Also **ta′bour.** [< OF *tabour*, prob. < Persian *tabīrah* drum] **— ta′bor·er** *n.*

tab·o·ret (tab′ər·it, tab′ə·ret′) *n.* **1.** A small tabor. **2.** A stool or small seat, usu. without arms or back. **3.** An embroidery frame. Also **tab·ou·ret** (tab′ər·it, tab′ə·ret′).

tab·u·lar (tab′yə·lər) *adj.* **1.** Pertaining to or consisting of a table or list. **2.** Computed from or with a mathematical table. **3.** Having a flat surface; tablelike. **— tab′u·lar·ly** *adv.*

tab·u·lar·ize (tab′yə·lə·rīz′) *v.t.* **·ized, ·iz·ing** To arrange in tabular form; tabulate. **— tab′u·lar·i·za′tion** *n.*

tab·u·late (tab′yə·lāt) *v.t.* **·lat·ed, ·lat·ing** **1.** To arrange in a table or list: to *tabulate* results. **2.** To form with a tabular surface. **—** *adj.* Having a flat surface. **— tab′u·la′tion** *n.*

tab·u·la·tor (tab′yə·lā′tər) *n.* **1.** One who or that which tabulates. **2.** A device built into a typewriter, and used to present statistical matter in tabulated form. **3.** An automatic accounting machine for tabulating reports.

tac·a·ma·hac (tak′ə·mə·hak′) *n.* **1.** A yellowish, resinous substance with a strong odor, derived from various trees and used as incense. **2.** Any of the trees producing this substance. **3.** A tree of the U.S., having leaf buds exuding a gummy resin: also **tac′a·ma·hac′a** (-hak′ə), **tac′a·ma·hack′, tac′ca·ma·hac′.** [< Sp. < Nahuatl *tecomahca*, lit., fetid copal]

tace (tās) *n.* Tasset, a type of armor plate.

ta·chom·e·ter (tə·kom′ə·tər) *n.* **1.** An instrument for measuring speed and velocity, as of a machine, the flow of a current, blood, etc. **2.** A device for indicating the speed of rotation of an engine, etc. [< Gk. *tachos* speed + -METER]

---

ta·chom·e·try (tə-kom/ə-trē) *n.* The art or science of using a tachometer. — **tach·o·met·ric** (tak/ə-met/rik) *adj.*

tachy- *combining form* Speed; swiftness. [< Gk. *tachys* swift]

tac·it (tas/it) *adj.* **1.** Existing, inferred, or implied without being directly stated. **2.** Making no sound; silent; noiseless. [< F < L *tacere* to be silent] — **tac/it·ly** *adv.* — **tac/it·ness** *n.*

tac·i·turn (tas/ə-tûrn) *adj.* Habitually silent or reserved. — **tac/i·turn/i·ty** *n.* — **tac/i·turn·ly** *adv.*

tack¹ (tak) *n.* **1.** A small sharp-pointed nail, commonly with tapering sides and a flat head. **2.** *Naut.* **a** A rope that holds down the lower outer corner of certain sails. **b** The corner so held. **c** The direction in which a vessel sails when sailing close-hauled, considered in relation to the position of her sails. **d** The distance or the course run at one time in such direction. **e** The act of tacking. **f** Any veering of a vessel to one side, as to take advantage of a side wind. **3.** A change of policy; a new course of action. **4.** In sewing, a large, temporary stitch. — *v.t.* **1.** To fasten or attach with tacks. **2.** To secure temporarily, as with tacks or long stitches. **3.** To attach as supplementary; append. **4.** *Naut.* **a** To bring (a vessel) momentarily into the wind so as to go on the opposite tack. **b** To navigate (a vessel) to windward by making a series of tacks. — *v.i.* **5.** *Naut.* **a** To tack a vessel. **b** To go on the opposite tack, or sail to windward by a series of tacks. **6.** To change one's course of action; veer. [< AF *taque,* OF *tache* nail] — **tack/er** *n.*

tack² (tak) *n.* Food in general. [Origin uncertain]

tack·le (tak/əl) *n.* **1.** A rope, pulley, or combination of ropes and pulleys used for hoisting or moving objects. **2.** A windlass or winch, together with ropes and hooks. **3.** The equipment used in any work or sport; gear; fishing *tackle.* **4.** In football: **a** The act of tackling. **b** One of two linemen whose position is usu. between the guard and end. **5.** A ship's rigging. — *v.t.* **·led, ·ling** **1.** To deal with; undertake to master, accomplish, or solve. **2.** In football, to seize and stop (an opponent carrying the ball). — *v.i.* **3.** In football, to tackle an opposing player. [< MLG *takel* < *taken* to seize] — **tack/ler** *n.*

tack·y¹ (tak/ē) *adj.* **tack·i·er, tack·i·est** Having adhesive properties; sticky, as a surface covered with partly dried varnish. Also **tack/ey.** [Prob. < TACK¹, v. (def. 2)]

tack·y² (tak/ē) *adj.* **tack·i·er, tack·i·est** *U.S. Informal* Shabby; neglected; shoddy. [Cf. dial. G *taklig* untidy]

tact (takt) *n.* A quick or intuitive appreciation of what is fit, proper, or right; esp., skill in avoiding what would offend or disturb. [< L *tactus* a touching]

tact·ful (takt/fəl) *adj.* Possessing or manifesting tact; considerate. — **tact/ful·ly** *adv.* — **tact/ful·ness** *n.*

tac·ti·cal (tak/ti·kəl) *adj.* **1.** Pertaining to or like tactics. **2.** Exhibiting adroit maneuvering. — **tac/ti·cal·ly** *adv.*

tac·ti·cian (tak-tish/ən) *n.* An expert in tactics.

tac·tics (tak/tiks) *n.pl.* (*construed as sing. in def.* 1) **1.** The science and art of handling troops in the presence of the enemy or for immediate objectives: distinguished from *strategy.* **2.** Any maneuvering to gain an objective. [< Gk. *taktikos* suitable for arranging or organizing]

tac·tile (tak/til, -təl, *esp. Brit.* -tīl) *adj.* **1.** Pertaining to the organs or sense of touch; caused by or consisting of contact. **2.** That may be touched; tangible. [< F < L *tactus* touch] — **tac·til/i·ty** *n.*

tact·less (takt/lis) *adj.* Lacking tact. — **tact/less·ly** *adv.* — **tact/less·ness** *n.*

tac·tu·al (tak/chōō-əl) *adj.* Tactile. — **tac/tu·al·ly** *adv.*

tad·pole (tad/pōl) *n.* The aquatic larva of an amphibian, as a frog or toad, breathing by external gills and having a tail; also called *polliwog.* [ME *taddepol* < *tadde* toad]

tael (tāl) *n.* **1.** An Oriental weight varying from 1 to 2⅓ ounces, commonly about 1⅓ ounces. **2.** A Chinese monetary unit of varying value. [< Pg. < Malay *tahil*]

ta·en (tān) *Scot.* Taken.

taf·fe·ta (taf/ə·tə) *n.* A fine, plain-woven, somewhat stiff fabric of silk, rayon, etc. — *adj.* Made of or resembling taffeta. [< OF < Med.L < Persian *tāftan* to twist]

taff·rail (taf/rāl/, -rəl) *n. Naut.* **1.** The rail around a vessel's stern. **2.** The upper part of a vessel's stern. [< MDu. *tafereel* panel, picture]

taf·fy (taf/ē) *n.* **1.** A confection made of brown sugar or molasses, mixed with butter, boiled down, and pulled: also called *toffee.* **2.** *Informal* Flattery. [Origin unknown]

tag¹ (tag) *n.* **1.** Something tacked on or attached to something else; an appendage. **2.** A label tied or attached loosely as to a piece of baggage. **3.** A loose, ragged edge of anything; tatter. **4.** The tail or tip of the tail of any animal. **5.** The final lines of a speech in a play; catchword; cue. — *v.t.* **tagged, tag·ging** *v.t.* **1.** To supply, adorn, fit, mark, or label with a tag. **2.** To shear away matted locks of wool from (sheep). **3.** To follow closely or persistently. — *v.i.* **4.** To follow closely at one's heels. [Prob. < Scand.]

tag² (tag) *v.t.* **tagged, tag·ging** **1.** In baseball, to touch (a player) with the ball or with the hand or glove in which the ball is held. **2.** To overtake and touch, as in the game of tag. **3.** *Informal* To make contact with; designate: *tagged* him for a loan. — *n.* **1.** In baseball, the act or instance of tagging a player, esp., a base runner, in an attempt to retire him. **2.** A children's running game in which a player who is touched or caught (usu., called "it") tries to touch or catch the others. [< TAG¹]

Ta·ga·log (tä-gä/log, tag/ə·log, -lôg) *n.* **1.** A member of a Malay people native to the Philippines, esp., Luzon. **2.** One of the principal native languages and, since 1940, the official language of the Philippines. Also **Ta·gal** (tä-gäl/).

tag day A day on which contributions are solicited for charitable and other institutions.

tag end **1.** A loose end or tag of cloth, yarn, etc. **2.** The endmost part of anything.

tagged atom A tracer.

tag·ger (tag/ər) *n.* One who or that which tags.

Ta·hi·ti·an (tä-hē/tē·ən, tə-, -shən) *adj.* Of or relating to Tahiti, its people, or their language. — *n.* **1.** One of the native Polynesian people of Tahiti. **2.** The Polynesian language of the Tahitians.

Tai (tī) See THAI.

tail¹ (tāl) *n.* **1.** The hindmost part or rear end of an animal; esp., when prolonged beyond the rest of the body as a distinct, flexible member. ◆ Collateral adjective: *caudal.* **2.** Any slender, flexible, terminal extension of the main part of an object: the *tail* of a shirt. **3.** *Astron.* The luminous trail extending from the nucleus of a comet. **4.** The bottom, back, or inferior portion of anything. **5.** *pl. Informal* The reverse side of a coin. **6.** Anything of taillike appearance, as a number of persons in single file. **7.** A pigtail; braid. **8.** *Aeron.* The rear end of an aircraft; also, the stabilizer and control surfaces at the rear of an aircraft. **9.** The rear portion of a bomb, projectile, rocket, or guided missile. **10.** *pl. Informal* A man's full-dress suit; also, a swallow-tailed coat. — *v.t.* **1.** To furnish with a tail. **2.** To cut off the tail of. **3.** To be the tail or end of: to *tail* a procession. **4.** To insert and fasten by one end, as a beam into a wall: with *in* or *on.* **5.** *Informal* To follow secretly and stealthily; shadow. — *v.i.* **6.** To extend or proceed in a line. **7.** *Informal* To follow close behind. **8.** To be inserted and fastened at one end, as a beam. — **to tail off** To diminish or recede gradually. — *adj.* **1.** Rearmost; hindmost. **2.** Coming from behind; following: a *tail* wind. [OE *tægl*] — **tail/less** *adj.*

tail² (tāl) *Law adj.* Restricted in succession to particular heirs: an estate *tail.* — *n.* A cutting off, abridgment, or limitation of ownership; an entail. [< OF *taillier* to cut]

tail·gate (tāl/gāt/) *n.* A hinged or vertically sliding board or gate closing the back end of a truck, wagon, etc. Also **tailboard** (tāl/bôrd, -bōrd). — *v.t. & v.i.* **·gat·ed, ·gat·ing** To drive too close behind for safety.

tail·ing (tā/ling) *n.* **1.** *pl.* Refuse or residue from grain after milling, or from ground ore after washing. **2.** The inner, covered portion of a projecting brick or stone in a wall.

tail·light (tāl/līt/) *n.* A light attached to the rear of a vehicle. Also **tail lamp.**

tai·lor (tā/lər) *n.* One who makes to order or repairs men's or women's outer garments. — *v.i.* **1.** To do a tailor's work. — *v.t.* **2.** To fit with garments: He is well *tailored.* **3.** To work at or make by tailoring: to *tailor* a coat. ◆ Collateral adjective: *sartorial.* **4.** To make, adjust, or adapt for a specific purpose. [< OF < LL *taliare* to split, cut]

tai·lor·bird (tā/lər·bûrd/) *n.* A passerine bird of Asia and Africa, that stitches leaves together to hold and hide its nest.

tai·lored (tā/lərd) *adj.* **1.** Characterized by simple, severe style: said esp. of women's clothes. **1.** Made by a tailor.

tai·lor·made (tā/lər·mād/) *adj.* **1.** Made by a tailor. **2.** Made or as if made to order; perfectly right or suitable.

tail·piece (tāl/pēs/) *n.* **1.** Any endpiece or appendage. **2.** In a violin or similar instrument, a piece of wood, as ebony, at the soundboard end, having the strings fastened to it. For illus., see VIOLIN. **3.** *Printing* An ornamental design on the lower blank portion of a page.

tail pipe An exhaust (n. def. 2).

tail·race (tāl/rās/) *n.* **1.** That part of a millrace below the water wheel. **2.** The channel for water to remove tailings.

tail·spin (tāl/spin/) *n.* **1.** *Aeron.* The descent of a stalled airplane along a tight helical path at a steep angle. **2.** *Informal* An emotional upheaval often resulting in loss of control.

tail wind A wind blowing in the same general direction as the course of an aircraft, ship, or other vehicle.

taint (tānt) *v.t.* **1.** To imbue with an offensive, poisonous, or deteriorating quality or principle; infect with decay. **2.** To render morally corrupt. — *v.i.* **3.** To be or become tainted. — *n.* **1.** A trace or germ of decay. **2.** A moral stain or blemish; disgrace. [Fusion of ATTAINT and F *teint,* pp. of *teindre* to tinge, color]

Taj Ma·hal (täzh/ mə·häl/, täj/) A mausoleum of white marble built (1631–45) at Agra, India.

take (tāk) *v.* **took, tak·en, tak·ing** *v.t.* **1.** To lay hold of;

grasp. **2.** To get possession of; seize. **3.** To seize forcibly; capture. **4.** To catch in a trap or snare. **5.** To win in competition. **6.** To choose; select. **7.** To buy. **8.** To rent or hire. **9.** To subscribe to, as a periodical. **10.** To assume occupancy of: to *take* a chair. **11.** To assume the responsibilities or duties of: to *take* office. **12.** To bring or accept into some relation to oneself: He *took* a wife. **13.** To assume as a symbol or badge: to *take* the veil. **14.** To impose upon oneself: to *take* a vow. **15.** To remove or carry off: with *away*. **16.** To steal. **17.** To remove by death. **18.** To subtract or deduct. **19.** To undergo: to *take* a beating. **20.** To accept passively: to *take* an insult. **21.** To become affected with: He *took* cold. **22.** To affect: The fever *took* him at dawn. **23.** To captivate; charm or delight. **24.** To react to: How did she *take* the news? **25.** To undertake to deal with: to *take* an examination. **26.** To consider; deem. **27.** To understand; comprehend. **28.** To strike in a specified place; hit: The blow *took* him on the forehead. **29.** *Informal* To aim or direct: He *took* a shot at the target. **30.** To carry with one: He *took* a briefcase along. **31.** To lead: This road *takes* you to town. **32.** To escort; conduct: Who *took* her to the dance? **33.** To receive into the body, as by eating, inhaling, etc. **34.** To accept, as something offered, due, or given: to *take* a degree. **35.** To let in; admit: The car will *take* only six people. **36.** To indulge oneself in: to *take* a nap. **37.** To perform, as an action: to *take* a stride. **38.** To avail oneself of (an opportunity, etc.). **39.** To put into effect; adopt: to *take* measures. **40.** To use up or consume: The piano *takes* too much space. **41.** To make use of; apply: They *took* clubs to him. **42.** To travel by means of: to *take* a train. **43.** To go to; seek: to *take* cover. **44.** To ascertain or obtain by measuring, computing, etc.: to *take* a census. **45.** To obtain or derive from some source; adopt or copy. **46.** To obtain by writing; write down or copy: to *take* notes. **47.** To obtain a likeness or representation of, as by drawing or photographing; also, to obtain (a likeness, picture, etc.) in such a manner. **48.** To experience; feel: to *take* pride. **49.** To conceive: to *take* a dislike. **50.** To absorb: The cloth will not *take* the pattern. **51.** In baseball, to allow (a pitch) to pass without swinging at it: said of a batter. **52.** *Slang* To cheat; deceive. **53.** *Gram.* To require by construction or usage: The verb *takes* a direct object. **— v.i. 54.** To get possession. **55.** To engage; catch, as mechanical parts. **56.** To begin to grow; germinate. **57.** To have the intended effect: The vaccination *took*. **58.** To become popular; gain favor or currency, as a play. **59.** To admit of being photographed: His face *takes* well. **60.** To detract: with *from*. **61.** To become (ill or sick). **62.** To make one's way; go. **63.** In baseball, to allow a pitch to pass without swinging at it: said of a batter. **— to take after 1.** To resemble. **2.** To follow as an example. **— to take amiss** To be offended by. **— to take at one's word** To believe. **— to take back 1.** To regain. **2.** To retract. **— to take breath** To pause, as from working. **— to take down 1.** To pull down, as a building. **2.** To dismantle; disassemble. **3.** To humble. **4.** To write down; make a record of. **— to take heart** To gain courage or confidence. **— to take in 1.** To admit; receive. **2.** To lessen in size or scope. **3.** To furl or haul in (sail). **4.** To include; embrace. **5** To understand; comprehend. **6.** To receive into one's home for pay, as lodgers or work. **7.** *Informal* To cheat or deceive. **8.** *U.S. Informal* To visit, as on a trip or tour: Did you *take in* the Louvre? **— to take in vain** To use profanely or blasphemously, as the name of a deity. **— to take it 1.** To assume; understand. **2.** To endure hardship, abuse, etc. **— to take it out on** *U.S. Informal* To vent one's anger, frustration, etc., on. **— to take off 1.** To remove, as a coat. **2.** To carry away. **3.** To kill. **4.** To deduct. **5.** *Informal* To mimic; burlesque. **6.** To rise from the ground or water in starting a flight, as an airplane. **7.** *U.S. Informal* To leave; depart. **— to take on 1.** To hire; employ. **2.** To undertake to deal with; handle. **3.** *Informal* To exhibit violent emotion. **— to take out 1.** To extract; remove. **2.** To obtain from the proper authority, as a license or patent. **3.** To lead or escort. **— to take over 1.** To assume control. **2.** To convey. **— to take place** To happen. **— to take stock 1.** To make an inventory. **2.** To estimate probability, position, etc.; consider. **— to take the field** To begin a campaign or game. **— to take to 1.** To have recourse to; go to: to *take* to one's bed. **2.** To develop the practice of, or an addiction to: He *took* to drink. **3.** To become fond of. **— to take to heart** To be deeply affected by. **— to take up 1.** To raise or lift. **2.** To make smaller or less; shorten or tighten. **3.** To pay, as a mortgage. **4.** To accept as stipulated: to *take up* an option. **5.** To begin or begin again. **6.** To reprove or criticize. **7.** To occupy, engage, or consume, as space or time. **8.** To acquire an interest in or devotion to: to *take up* a cause. **— to take up with** *Informal* To become friendly with. **— n. 1.**

The act of taking, or that which is taken. **2.** An uninterrupted run of a camera or recording apparatus in making a motion picture, television program, sound recording, etc. **3.** A quantity collected at one time: the *take* of fish. **4.** *U.S. Slang* Money collected, as the receipts of a sporting event. [OE *tacan* < ON *taka*]

take·down (tāk′doun′) *adj.* Fitted for being taken apart or easily down: a *takedown* rifle. **— n. 1.** Any article so constructed as to be taken apart easily. **2.** *U.S. Informal* The act of humiliating anyone.

take-home pay (tāk′hōm′) *U.S.* The remainder of one's wages or salary after tax and other payroll deductions.

take-in (tāk′in′) *n. Informal* An act of cheating or hoaxing.

take·off (tāk′ôf′, -of′) *n.* **1.** The act of rising or leaping from the ground to begin flight; also, the spot where this happens. **2.** *Informal* A satirical imitation; caricature.

take·o·ver (tāk′ō·vər) *n.* An assuming or seizure of control, function, ownership, or rule.

tak·er (tā′kər) *n.* One who takes or collects.

tak·ing (tā′king) *adj.* **1.** Fascinating; captivating. **2.** *Informal* Contagious; infectious. **— n. 1.** The act of one who takes. **2.** The thing or things taken. **3.** *pl.* Receipts, as of money. **— tak′ing·ly** *adv.* **— tak′ing·ness** *n.*

talc (talk) *n.* A soft, white or variously colored, hydrous magnesium silicate, $H_2Mg_3(SiO_3)_4$, used in making paper, soap, toilet powder, insulators, etc. Also **tal·cum** (tal′kəm). **— v.t. talcked** or **talced, talck·ing** or **talc·ing** To treat with talc. [< F < Med. L < Arabian *talq*]

talcum powder Finely powdered and purified talc, used as a dusting agent, filter, etc.

tale (tāl) *n.* **1.** That which is told or related; a story; recital. **2.** A piece of gossip. **3.** A lie; falsehood. [OE *talu* speech, narrative]

tale·bear·er (tāl′bâr′ər) *n.* One who carries gossip; a taleteller. **— tale′bear′ing** *adj. & n.*

tal·ent (tal′ənt) *n.* **1.** A particular and uncommon aptitude for some special work or activity. **2.** People of skill or ability, collectively. **3.** An ancient weight and denomination of money. [OE < L < Gk. *talanton* weight]

tal·ent·ed (tal′ən·tid) *adj.* Having great ability; gifted.

talent scout One whose business is to discover talented people, esp. for the performing arts.

ta·ler (tä′lər) *n.* A former German silver coin, the prototype of all dollars: also spelled *thaler*. [< G. See DOLLAR.]

ta·les (tā′lēz) *n. pl.* **·les** (-lēz) *Law* Persons to be summoned for jury duty to make up a deficiency when the regular panel is exhausted by challenges. [< L *tales* pl. of *talis* such a one]

tales·man (tālz′mən) *n. pl.* **·men** (-mən) *Law* One of the tales.

tale·tel·ler (tāl′tel′ər) *n.* **1.** One who tells stories, etc.; a raconteur. **2.** A talebearer. **— tale′tell′ing** *adj. & n.*

tal·i·pes (tal′ə·pēz) *n. Pathol.* Clubfoot. [< NL < L *talus* ankle + *pes, pedis* foot] **— tal·i·ped** (tal′ə·ped) *adj.*

tal·i·pot (tal′ə·pot) *n.* A stately East Indian palm crowned by large leaves used as fans, umbrellas, writing material, and as coverings for houses. [< Bengali *tālipāt* palm leaf]

tal·is·man (tal′is·mən, -iz-) *n. pl.* **·mans 1.** Something supposed to produce extraordinary or magical effects; a charm or amulet. **2.** An astrological charm or symbol supposed to benefit or protect the possessor. [< F < Sp. < Arabic *tilsam, tilasm* magic figure] **— tal′is·man′ic** (-man′-ik) or **·i·cal** *adj.*

talk (tôk) *v.i.* **1.** To express or exchange thoughts in audible words; communicate by speech. **2.** To make a speech. **3.** To communicate by means other than speech: to *talk* with one's fingers. **4.** To speak irrelevantly; prate; chatter. **5.** To confer; consult. **6.** To spread rumor; gossip. **7.** To make sounds suggestive of speech. **8.** *U.S. Informal* To give information, as to the police; inform. **9.** *Informal* To be effective or influential: money *talks*. **— v.t. 10.** To express in words; utter. **11.** To use in speaking; converse in: to *talk* Spanish. **12.** To converse about; discuss: to *talk* business. **13.** To bring to a specified condition or state by talking: to *talk* one into doing something. **14.** To pass or spend, as time, in talking: usu. with *away*. **— to talk back** To answer impudently. **— to talk big** *Slang* To brag; boast. **— to talk down 1.** To silence by talking; outtalk. **2.** To direct (an aircraft) to a landing, in darkness, fog, etc., by giving oral instructions to the pilot over the radio. **— to talk down to** To speak to in a condescending manner. **— to talk shop** To talk about one's work. **— to talk up 1.** To discuss, esp. so as to promote; praise; extol. **2.** *Informal* To speak loudly or boldly. **— n. 1.** The act of talking; conversation; speech. **2.** A speech or lecture, usu. informal. **3.** Report; rumor: We heard *talk* of war. **4.** That which is talked about; a topic; theme. **5.** A conference for discussion or deliberation; a council. **6.** Mere words; verbiage. **7.** A language, dialect, or lingo: baseball *talk*. [ME *talken*, prob. freq. of OE *talian* to reckon, speak] **— talk′er** *n.*

talk·a·tive (tô′kə·tiv) *adj.* Given to much talking. — **talk′a·tive·ly** *adv.* **— talk′a·tive·ness** *n.*

talking picture A motion picture with spoken words, music, sound effects, etc. Also *Informal* **talk·ie** (tô′kē).

talk·ing-to (tô′king·tōō′) *n. pl.* **-tos** *Informal* A scolding.

talk·y (tô′kē) *adj.* **talk·i·er, talk·i·est** Talkative.

tall (tôl) *adj.* **1.** Having more than average height; high or lofty. **2.** Having specified height: He is six feet *tall*. **3.** *Informal* Extravagant; boastful; also, unbelievable: a *tall* story. **4.** *Informal* Large; excellent; grand: a *tall* dinner. — *adv. Informal* Proudly: to stand *tall*. [OE *getæl* swift, prompt] **— tall′ness** *n.*

tall·ish (tô′lish) *adj.* Rather tall.

tal·lith (tal′ith, tä′lis) *n.* A fringed scarf or mantle worn around the shoulders by Orthodox and Conservative Jewish men when praying. [< Hebrew *tallīth* cover, robe]

tal·low (tal′ō) *n.* A mixture of the harder animal fats, as of beef or mutton, refined for use in candles, soaps, oleomargarine, etc. — *v.t.* To smear with tallow. [ME *talgh*] — **tal′low·y** *adj.*

tal·ly (tal′ē) *n. pl.* **·lies 1.** A piece of wood on which notches or scores are cut as marks of number. **2.** A score or mark. **3.** A reckoning; account. **4.** A counterpart; duplicate. **5.** A mark indicative of a quantity or number, used to denote one in a series. **6.** A label; tag. — *v.* **·lied, ·ly·ing** *v.t.* **1.** To score on a tally; record. **2.** To reckon; count; estimate: often with *up*. **3.** To mark or cut corresponding notches in; cause to correspond. — *v.i.* **4.** To correspond; fit: The stories *tally*. **5.** To keep score. [< AF < L *talea* rod, cutting] **— tal′li·er** *n.*

tal·ly·ho (tal′ē·hō′) *interj.* A huntsman's cry to hounds when the quarry is sighted. — *n. pl.* **·hos 1.** The cry of "tallyho." **2.** A four-in-hand coach. — *v.t.* **1.** To urge on, as hounds, with the cry of "tallyho." — *v.i.* **2.** To cry "tallyho." [Alter. of F *taïaut*, a hunting cry]

tal·ly·man (tal′ē·mən) *n. pl.* **·men** (-mən) **1.** One who keeps a count on a tally, esp., of votes. **2.** One who records number, volume, and measurement, as of timber.

Tal·mud (tal′mud, täl′mŏŏd) *n.* The body of Jewish civil and religious law (and related commentaries) not included in the Pentateuch. [< Hebrew *talmūdh* instruction] **— Tal·mud′ic** or **·i·cal** *adj.* **— Tal′mud·ist** *n.*

tal·on (tal′ən) *n.* **1.** The claw of a bird or other animal, esp. of a bird of prey. **2.** Anything resembling or suggesting a claw, as a grasping human hand. **3.** A projection on the bolt of a lock on which the key presses in shooting the bolt. [< OF < L *talus* heel] **— tal′oned** (-ənd) *adj.*

ta·lus (tā′ləs) *n. pl.* **·li** (-lī) **1.** *Anat.* The bone of the foot just above the heel bone: also called *anklebone, astragalus*. **2.** A slope, as of a tapering wall. **3.** *Geol.* The sloping mass of rock fragments below a cliff. [< L, ankle, heel]

tam (tam) *n.* A tam-o'-shanter.

ta·ma·le (tə·mä′lē) *n.* A Mexican dish made of crushed corn and meat, seasoned with red pepper, wrapped in corn husks, dipped in oil, and cooked by steam. Also **ta·mal** (tə·mäl′). [< Am. Sp. *tamales*, pl. of *tamal* < Nahuatl *tamalli*]

tam·a·rack (tam′ə·rak) *n.* **1.** The American larch, a tree common in northern North America. **2.** Its wood. Also called *hackmatack*. [< Algonquian]

tam·a·rind (tam′ə·rind) *n.* **1.** A tropical tree of the bean family, with hard yellow wood and showy yellow flowers striped with red. **2.** The fruit of this tree, a flat pod with soft acid pulp used in preserves and as a laxative. [< Sp. < Arabic *tamr hindi* Indian date]

tam·bour (tam′bŏŏr) *n.* **1.** A drum. **2.** A round wooden frame on which material for embroidering may be stretched; also, the fabric embroidered. — *v.t. & v.i.* To embroider on a tambour. [< F < Arabic *tambūr* a stringed instrument]

tam·bou·rin (tam′bə·rin) *n.* **1.** A long, narrow drum, originating in Provence. **2.** A gay, 18th-century Provençal dance, or the music for it. [< F < Provençal]

tam·bou·rine (tam′bə·rēn′) *n.* A musical instrument like the head of a drum, with jingles in the rim, played by striking it with the hand; a timbrel. [< F]

tame (tām) *adj.* **tam·er, tam·est 1.** Having lost its native wildness or shyness; domesticated. **2.** In agriculture, brought under or produced by cultivation. **3.** Docile; tractable. **4.** Subdued or subjugated. **5.** Gentle; harmless. **6.** Lacking in effectiveness; uninteresting; dull. — *v.t.* **tamed, tam·ing 1.** To domesticate. **2.** To bring into subjection or obedience; render spiritless. **3.** To tone down; soften, as glaring colors. [OE *tam*] **— tam′a·ble** or **tame′a·ble** *adj.* **— tame′ly** *adv.* **— tame′ness** *n.* **— tam′er** *n.*

tame·less (tām′lis) *adj.* Untamed or untamable **— tame′less·ness** *n.*

Tam·il (tam′əl, tum′əl) *n.* **1.** One of an ancient Dravidian people, and still the most numerous of the inhabitants of southern India and northern Ceylon. **2.** Their language.

Tam·ma·ny (tam′ə·nē) *n.* A fraternal society in New York City (founded 1789) serving as the central organization of the city's Democratic party. Also called **Tammany Hall, Tammany Society.** [Alter. of *Tamanend*, name of a 17th c. Delaware Indian chief friendly toward white men]

Tam·muz (täm·mōōz′, täm′mōōz) The tenth month of the Hebrew year. See (Hebrew) CALENDAR. Also spelled *Thammuz*: also **Tam·uz.** [< Hebrew]

tam-o'-shan·ter (tam′ə·shan′tər) *n.* A Scottish cap with a tight headband and a full, flat top, sometimes with a pompon or tassel. [after *Tam o' Shanter*, a poem by Robert Burns]

tamp (tamp) *v.t.* **1.** To force down or pack closer by firm, repeated blows. **2.** To ram down, as dirt, etc., on top of the charge in a blasthole. [Back formation < TAMPION]

tam·per (tam′pər) *v.i.* **1.** To meddle; interfere: usu. with *with*. **2.** To make changes, esp., so as to damage or corrupt: with *with*. **3.** To use corrupt measures, as bribery; scheme or plot. [Var. of TEMPER] **— tam′per·er** *n.*

tam·pi·on (tam′pē·ən) *n. Mil.* A stopper, as the plug put into the mouth of a cannon to keep out moisture, etc. [< F *tampon*, nasal var. of *tapon, tape* bung < Gmc]

tam·pon (tam′pon) *n. Med.* A plug of cotton or lint for insertion in a wound or body cavity. — *v.t.* To plug up, as a wound, with a tampon. [See TAMPION]

tan (tan) *v.* **tanned, tan·ning** *v.t.* **1.** To convert into leather, as hides or skins, by treating with tannin. **2.** To turn brown, as the skin, by exposure to sunlight. **3.** *Informal* To thrash; flog. — *v.i.* **4.** To become tanned, as hides or the skin. — *n.* **1.** A yellowish brown color tinged with red. **2.** A dark or brown coloring of the skin, resulting from exposure to the sun. **3.** Tanbark. — *adj.* **1.** Of the color tan; light brown. **2.** Used in or pertaining to tanning. [OE < Med.L < *tanum* tanbark, prob. < Celtic]

tan·a·ger (tan′ə·jər) *n.* Any of a family of American songbirds noted for the brilliant plumage of the male. [< NL < Pg. *tangara* < Tupi] **— tan′a·grine** (-grēn) *adj.*

tan·bark (tan′bärk′) *n.* **1.** The bark of certain trees, esp. oak or hemlock, containing tannin, and used in tanning leather. **2.** Spent bark from the tan vats, used on circus arenas, racetracks, etc.

tan·dem (tan′dəm) *adv.* One in front of or before another. — *n.* **1.** Two or more horses harnessed in single file. **2.** A two-wheeled carriage drawn by a tandem of horses. **3.** A bicycle with seats for two persons, one behind the other: also **tandem bicycle. 4.** Any arrangement of two or more persons or things placed one before another. — *adj.* Arranged in tandem, or including parts so arranged. [< L, at length (of time); used in puns in sense of "lengthwise"]

tang (tang) *n.* **1.** A penetrating taste, flavor, or odor. **2.** A trace; hint. **3.** Any distinct taste, odor, quality, etc., other than one that is sweet. **4.** A slender shank or tongue projecting from some metal part, as the end of a sword blade or chisel, for inserting in or fixing upon a handle. — *v.t.* To provide with a tang. [< ON *tangi* point, dagger]

tan·gen·cy (tan′jən·sē) *n. pl.* **·cies** The state of being tangent. Also **tan′gence.**

tan·gent (tan′jənt) *adj.* Being in contact at a single point or along a line; touching. — *n.* **1.** *Geom.* **a** A straight line in contact with a curve at one point. **b** A straight line, curve, or surface touching another curve or surface at one or more consecutive points. **2.** *Trig.* A function of an acute angle, equal to the ratio of the side opposite the angle to the side adjacent to the angle when the angle is included in a right triangle. **— to fly** (or **go**) **off on a tangent** *Informal* To make a sharp or sudden change in direction or course of action. [< L *tangens, -entis*, ppr. of *tangere* to touch]

tan·gen·tial (tan·jen′shəl) *adj.* **1.** Of, pertaining to, or moving in the direction of a tangent. **2.** Touching slightly. **3.** Only partially relevant to a subject. Also **tan·gen′tal** (-jen′təl). **— tan·gen′ti·al·i·ty** (-shē·al′ə·tē) *n.* **— tan·gen′tial·ly** *adv.*

tan·ger·ine (tan′jə·rēn′) *n.* **1.** A small, juicy orange with a loose, easily removed skin: also called *mandarin*. **2.** A slightly burnt orange color. [after *Tangier*]

tan·gi·ble (tan′jə·bəl) *adj.* **1.** Perceptible by touch; also, within reach by touch. **2.** Capable of being apprehended by the mind; of definite shape; real: *tangible* evidence. **3.** *Law* Perceptible to the senses; corporeal; material: *tangible* property. — *n.* **1.** That which is tangible. **2.** *pl.* Material assets. [< F < L < *tangere* to touch] **— tan′gi·bil′i·ty, tan′gi·ble·ness** *n.* **— tan′gi·bly** *adv.*

tan·gle (tang′gəl) *v.* **·gled, ·gling** *v.t.* **1.** To twist or involve in a confused and not readily separable mass. **2.** To ensnare as in a tangle; enmesh. — *v.i.* **3.** To be or become entangled. **— to tangle with** *Informal* To come to blows with. — *n.* **1.** A confused intertwining, as of threads or hairs; a snarl. **2.** A state of confusion or complication; a jumbled mess. **3.** A state of perplexity or bewilderment. [Nasalized var. of obs. *tagle* < Scand.] **— tan′gler** *n.*

tan·gly (tang′glē) *adj.* Consisting of or being in a tangle.

tan·go (tang′gō) *n. pl.* **·gos 1.** Any of several Latin-American dances in 2/4 time, characterized by deliberate gliding steps and low dips. **2.** Any syncopated tune or melody to which the tango may be danced. — *v.i.* To dance the tango. [< Am.Sp., *fiesta*, Negro drum dance]

tang·y (tang′ē) *adj.* **tang·i·er, tang·i·est** Having a tang in taste or odor; pungent.

tank (tangk) *n.* **1.** A large vessel, basin, or receptacle for holding a fluid. **2.** Any natural or artificial pool or pond. **3.** *Mil.* A heavily armored combat vehicle, moving on caterpillar treads and mounting guns of various calibers. — *v.t.* To place or store in a tank. [< Pg. *tanque*, aphetic var. of *estanque* < L *stagnum* pool]

tank·age (tangk′ij) *n.* **1.** The act, process, or operation of putting in tanks. **2.** The price for storage in tanks. **3.** The capacity or contents of a tank. **4.** Slaughterhouse waste, as bones and entrails, used when dried as a fertilizer or feed.

tank·ard (tangk′ərd) *n.* A large, one-handled drinking cup, usu. made of pewter or silver, often with a cover. [< MDu. < Med.L *tancardus* large goblet]

tank·er (tangk′ər) *n.* A cargo vessel specially constructed for the transport of liquids, esp. oil and gasoline.

tank farm *U.S.* An area near a refinery, factory, port, etc., occupied by large storage tanks.

tank·ful (tangk′fŏŏl′) *n.* The quantity that fills a tank.

tank town *U.S. Informal* A small town where trains formerly stopped to refill from a water tank.

tan·nage (tan′ij) *n.* The act or operation of tanning.

tan·ner (tan′ər) *n.* One who tans hides.

tan·ner·y (tan′ər-ē) *n. pl.* **·ner·ies** A place where leather is tanned.

tan·nic (tan′ik) *adj.* Pertaining to or derived from tannin or tanbark.

tannic acid *n. Chem.* Any of a group of brownish astringent compounds extracted from gallnuts, sumac, etc., used in the preparation of ink and in the manufacture of leather.

tan·nin (tan′in) *n.* Tannic acid.

tan·ning (tan′ing) *n.* **1.** The art or process of converting hides into leather. **2.** A bronzing, as of the skin, by exposure to the sun, wind, etc. **3.** *Informal* A beating or thrashing.

tan·sy (tan′zē) *n. pl.* **·sies** Any of various coarse perennial herbs with yellow flowers and an aromatic, bitter taste, used in medicine for its tonic properties. [< OF *tanesie*, aphetic var. of *athanasie* < LL < Gk., immortality]

tan·ta·lize (tan′tə-līz) *v.t.* **·lized, ·liz·ing** To tease or torment by repeated frustration of hopes or desires. Also *Brit.* **tan·ta·lise.** [< TANTALUS] — **tan′ta·li·za′tion** *n.* — **tan′ta·liz′er** *n.* — **tan′ta·liz′ing·ly** *adv.*

tan·ta·lum (tan′tə-ləm) *n.* A silver-white, very heavy, ductile, metallic element (symbol Ta), forming alloys with tungsten, molybdenum, and iron. See ELEMENT. [< TANTALUS; from its inability to absorb water]

Tan·ta·lus (tan′tə-ləs) In Greek mythology, a rich king, who was punished in Hades by being made to stand in water that receded when he tried to drink, and under fruit-laden branches he could not reach.

tan·ta·mount (tan′tə-mount) *adj.* Having equivalent value, effect, or import; equivalent: with *to*. [< AF < L *tantus* as much + OF *amonter* to amount]

tan·trum (tan′trəm) *n.* A petulant fit of rage. [Origin unknown]

Tao·ism (dou′iz-əm, tou′-) *n.* One of the principal religions or philosophies of China, founded by Lao-tse, who taught that happiness could be acquired through obedience to the requirements of man's nature in accordance with the **Tao** (dou, tou), or Way, the basic principle of all nature. [< Chinese *tao* way, road] — **Tao′ist** *adj. & n.* — **Tao·is′tic** *adj.*

tap¹ (tap) *n.* **1.** An arrangement for drawing out liquid, as beer from a cask. **2.** A faucet or cock; spigot. **3.** A plug or stopper to close an opening in a cask or other vessel. **4.** Liquor drawn from a tap; also, a particular liquor or quality of liquor contained in casks. **5.** *Brit.* A place where liquor is served; taproom. **6.** A tool for cutting internal screw threads. **7.** A point of connection for an electrical circuit. — **on tap 1.** Contained in a cask; ready for tapping: beer *on tap.* **2.** Provided with a tap. **3.** *Informal* Available; ready. — *v.t.* **tapped, tap·ping 1.** To provide with a tap or spigot. **2.** To pierce or open so as to draw liquid from. **3.** To draw (liquid) from a container. **4.** To make connection with: to *tap* a gas main. **5.** To make connection with secretly: to *tap* a telephone wire. **6.** To make an internal screw thread in with a tap. [OE *tæppa*]

tap² (tap) *v.* **tapped, tap·ping** *v.t.* **1.** To touch or strike gently. **2.** To make or produce by tapping. **3.** To apply leather to (the sole or heel of a shoe) in repair. — *v.i.* **4.** To strike a light blow or blows, as with the finger tip. — *n.* **1.** A gentle or playful blow; also, the sound made by such a blow. **2.** Leather, etc., affixed to a shoe sole or heel; also, a metal plate on the toe or heel of a shoe. [< OF *taper*] — **tap′per** *n.*

ta·pa (tä′pä) *n.* **1.** The inner bark of an Asian mulberry tree used in making a kind of cloth. **2.** The cloth. [< native Polynesian name]

tap-dance (tap′dans′, -däns′) *v.i.* **-danced, -danc·ing** To dance or perform a tap dance.

tap dance A dance in which the dancer emphasizes his steps by tapping the floor with the heels or toes of shoes designed to make the rhythm audible. — **tap dancer**

tape (tāp) *n.* **1.** A narrow strip of strong woven fabric. **2.** Any long, narrow, flat strip of paper, metal, etc. **3.** A magnetic tape. **4.** A tapeline. **5.** A string stretched breast-high across the finishing point of a racing track and broken by the winner of the race. — *v.t.* **taped, tap·ing 1.** To wrap or secure with tape. **2.** To apply a tape to; bandage: to *tape* a boxer's hands. **3.** To measure with or as with a tapeline. **4.** *Informal* To record on magnetic tape. [OE *tæppe* strip of cloth] — **tape′less** *adj.*

tape·line (tāp′līn′) *n.* A tape for measuring distances. Also **tape measure.**

ta·per¹ (tā′pər) *n.* One who or that which tapes.

ta·per² (tā′pər) *n.* **1.** A small candle. **2.** A burning wick or other light substance giving but feeble illumination. **3.** A gradual diminution of size in an elongated object: the *taper* of a mast. **4.** Any tapering object, as a cone. — *v.t. & v.i.* **1.** To make or become smaller or thinner toward one end. **2.** To lessen gradually; diminish: with *off*. — *adj.* Growing small by degrees in one direction; slender and conical or pyramidal. [OE, dissimilated var. of Med.L *papur* taper, wick < L, papyrus] — **ta′per·ing·ly** *adv.*

tape recorder A device that converts sound into magnetic patterns stored on a tape, reversing the process for playback.

tape recording 1. The process of transcribing music, speech, etc., on a tape recorder. **2.** A transcription so made.

tap·es·try (tap′is-trē) *n. pl.* **·tries** A woven, ornamental fabric, used for hangings, in which the woof is supplied by a spindle, the design being formed by stitches across the warp. — *v.t.* **·tried, ·try·ing 1.** To hang or adorn with tapestry. **2.** To make or weave as tapestry. [< OF < L < Gk. *tapētion*, dim. of *tapēs* rug]

tape·worm (tāp′wûrm′) *n.* Any of various worms with segmented, ribbonlike bodies, parasitic on the intestines of vertebrates and often infesting man.

tap·i·o·ca (tap′ē-ō′kə) *n.* A nutritious starchy substance having irregular grains, obtained by drying cassava starch. [< Sp. < Tupi < *ty* juice + *pýa* heart + *oco* to be removed]

ta·pir (tā′pər) *n.* A large nocturnal mammal, having short limbs and a flexible snout, native to South and Central America and to the Malay Peninsula. [< Sp. < Tupi *tapy′ra*]

tap·pet (tap′it) *n. Mech.* A lever or projecting arm of a mechanism that moves or is intermittently by automatically touching another part. [< TAP²]

tap·ping (tap′ing) *n.* **1.** The act of one who or that which taps. **2.** Something taken by tapping, or running from a tap.

tap·room (tap′rōōm′, -rŏŏm′) *n.* A bar or barroom.

tap·root (tap′rōōt′, -rŏŏt′) *n. Bot.* The principal descending root of a plant. — **tap′root′ed** *adj.*

taps (taps) *n.pl. (usu. construed as sing.)* A military signal by bugle or beat of drum, regularly sounded after tattoo for the extinguishing of all lights and sometimes played after a military burial.

tap·ster (tap′stər) *n.* One who draws and serves liquor; a bartender. [OE *tæppestre* barmaid]

tar¹ (tär) *n.* **1.** A dark, oily, viscid mixture of hydrocarbons, obtained by the destructive distillation of resinous woods, coal, etc. **2.** Coal tar. — *v.t.* **tarred, tar·ring** To cover with or as with tar. — **to tar and feather** To smear (a person) with tar and then cover with feathers as a punishment. — *adj.* Made of, derived from, or resembling tar. [OE *teoru*]

tar² (tär) *n. Informal* A sailor. [Short for TARPAULIN]

tar·an·tel·la (tar′ən-tel′ə) *n.* A lively Neapolitan dance in 6/8 time; also, the music written for it. [< Ital., dim. of *Taranto* Taranto]

ta·ran·tu·la (tə-ran′chŏŏ-lə) *n. pl.* **·las** or **·lae** (-lē) **1.** A large, hairy spider of southern Europe. **2.** Any of various related spiders known for their painful but not dangerous bite. [< Med.L < Ital. < *Taranto* Taranto]

tar·boosh (tär-bōōsh′) *n.* A brimless, usu. red, felt cap with colored silk tassel, worn by Moslem men. Also **tar·bush′.** [< Arabic *tarbūsh*]

tar·di·grade (tär′də-grād) *adj.* Slow in motion or action. [< F < L *tardus* slow + *gradi* to walk]

tar·dy (tär′dē) *adj.* **·di·er, ·di·est 1.** Not coming at the appointed time; late. **2.** Moving slowly. [< F < L *tardus* slow] — **tar′di·ly** *adv.* — **tar′di·ness** *n.*

tare¹ (tār) *n.* **1.** An unidentified weed that grows among wheat. **2.** A seed of wickedness. *Matt.* xiii 25. **3.** Any of various species of vetch. [MDu. *tarwe* wheat]

tare[2] (târ) *n.* An allowance made to a buyer of goods by deducting from the gross weight of his purchase the weight of the container. — *v.t.* **tared, tar·ing** To weigh, as a package, in order to determine the amount of tare. [< F < Arabic < *taraha* to reject, throw away]

tar·get (tär′git) *n.* **1.** An object presenting a surface that may be used as a mark or butt, as in rifle or archery practice. **2.** Anything that is shot at. **3.** A person or thing made an object of attack or center of attention; a butt. — **on target 1.** Headed or aimed so as to hit a target. **2.** *Informal* Aptly directed or placed; to the point: The quip was right *on target*. [ME *targette, targuete,* dim. of *targa* shield]

Tar·heel (tär′hēl′) *n. Informal* A native of North Carolina. Also **Tar Heel.**

Tarheel State Nickname of North Carolina.

tar·iff (tar′if) *n.* **1.** A schedule of articles of merchandise with the rates of duty to be paid for their importation or exportation. **2.** A duty, or duties collectively. **3.** The law or principles governing the imposition of duties. **4.** Any schedule of charges. — *v.t.* **1.** To make a list or table of duties or customs on. **2.** To fix a price or tariff on. [< Ital. < Arabic *ta′rif* information]

tar·mac (tär′mak) *n. Brit. & Canadian* **1.** *Aeron.* **a** A hangar apron. **b** An asphalt runway. **2.** An asphalt road.

tarn (tärn) *n.* A small mountain lake. [ME < ON *tjörn*]

tar·na·tion (tär-nā′shən) *interj. & n. U.S. Dial.* Damnation: a euphemism.

tar·nish (tär′nish) *v.t.* **1.** To dim the luster of. **2.** To dim the purity of; stain; disgrace. — *v.i.* **3.** To lose luster, as by oxidation. — *n.* **1.** Loss of luster. **2.** A blemish or stain. **3.** The thin film of color on the exposed surface of a metal or mineral. [< OF < *terne* dull, wan] — **tar′nish·a·ble** *adj.*

ta·ro (tä′rō) *n. pl.* **·ros** **1.** Any of several tropical plants of the arum family, grown for their edible, cornlike rootstocks. **2.** The rootstock of this plant. [< native Polynesian name]

tar·ot (tar′ō, -ət) *n.* One of a set of playing cards with grilled or checkered backs employed by fortunetellers and gypsies in foretelling future events. [< F < Ital. < *taroccare* to wrangle, play at cards]

tar·pau·lin (tär-pô′lin, tär′pə-) *n.* **1.** A waterproof canvas impregnated with tar, used to cover merchandise, athletic fields, etc. **2.** A sailor's wide-brimmed storm hat. Also *Informal* **tarp.** [< TAR[1] + PALL[1] + -ING[1]]

tar·pon (tär′pon, -pən) *n. pl.* **·pon** or **·pons** A large marine game fish of the West Indies and the coast of Florida, having conspicuous silvery scales. [Origin unknown]

tar·ra·gon (tar′ə-gon) *n.* **1.** A European perennial plant allied to wormwood. **2.** The aromatic leaves of this plant, used as seasoning. [< Sp. < Arabic < Gk. *drakōn* dragon]

tar·ri·er (tär′ē-ər) *n.* One who or that which tarries.

tar·ry[1] (tar′ē) *v.* **·ried, ·ry·ing** *v.i.* **1.** To put off going or coming; linger. **2.** To remain in the same place, esp. longer than one expected. **3.** To wait; stay. — *n.* Sojourn; stay. [ME *tarien* to vex, hinder, delay, fusion of OE *tirgan* to vex + OF *targer* to delay < LL < L *tardare* to delay]

tar·ry[2] (tär′ē) *adj.* **·ri·er, ·ri·est** Covered with tar; like tar.

tar·sal (tär′səl) *adj.* Of, relating to, or situated near the tarsus or ankle.

tarso- *combining form* The tarsus; pertaining to the tarsus. Also, before vowels, **tars-.** [< Gk. *tarsos* flat of the foot, edge of the eyelid]

tar·sus (tär′səs) *n. pl.* **·si** (-sī) **1.** *Anat.* The ankle, or, in man, the group of seven bones of which it is composed. **2.** *Zool.* **a** The shank of a bird's leg. **b** The distal part of the leg in insects. [< NL < Gk. *tarsos* flat of the foot, any flat surface]

tart[1] (tärt) *adj.* **1.** Having a sharp, sour taste. **2.** Severe; cutting; caustic: a *tart* remark. [OE *teart*] — **tart′ly** *adv.* — **tart′ness** *n.*

tart[2] (tärt) *n.* **1.** A small pastry shell with fruit or custard filling and without a top crust. **2.** In England, an uncovered fruit pie. **3.** *Slang* A girl or woman of loose morals, as a prostitute. [< OF *tarte*]

tar·tan (tär′tən) *n.* **1.** A woolen fabric having varicolored lines or stripes at right angles, forming a distinctive pattern, the characteristic dress of the Scottish Highlands, each clan having its particular pattern or patterns. **2.** Any similar pattern; a plaid. **3.** A garment made of tartan. For illus. see KILT. — *adj.* **1.** Made of tartan. **2.** Striped or checkered in a manner similar to the Scottish tartans. [? < OF *tiretaine* linsey-woolsey]

tar·tar[1] (tär′tər) *n.* **1.** An acid substance deposited from grape juice during fermentation as a pinkish sediment; crude bitartrate of potassium. **2.** *Dent.* A yellowish incrustation on the teeth, chiefly calcium phosphate. [< F < LL < Med.Gk. *tartaron,* ? < Arabic]

tar·tar[2] (tär′tər) *n. Often cap.* **1.** A person of intractable or savage temper. **2.** An unexpectedly formidable opponent. — **to catch a tartar** To take on or be matched with an unexpectedly strong opponent. [< TARTAR]

Tar·tar (tär′tər) *n.* A Tatar. — *adj.* Of or pertaining to

the Tatars or Tartary: also **Tar·tar·i·an** (tär-târ′ē-ən). [< F < LL < Persian *Tātar* Tatar]

Tar·tar·e·an (tär-târ′ē-ən) *adj.* Of or pertaining to Tartarus.

tartar emetic *Chem.* A white, crystalline, poisonous derivative of tartaric acid, used in medicine and in dyeing.

tar·tare sauce (tär′tər) A fish sauce made of mayonnaise, capers, chopped olives, and pickles. Also **tar′tar sauce.**

tar·tar·ic (tär-tar′ik, -tär′ik) *adj.* Pertaining to or derived from tartar or tartaric acid.

tartaric acid *Chem.* Any one of four organic compounds, $C_4H_6O_6$, occurring in the free state or as a potassium or calcium salt, as in grape juice, various unripe fruits, etc.

tar·tar·ize (tär′tə-rīz) *v.t.* **·ized, ·iz·ing** To impregnate or treat with tartar, cream of tartar, or tartar emetic. — **tar′tar·i·za′tion** *n.*

Tartar mink The kolinsky. Also **Tartar sable.**

tar·tar·ous (tär′tər-əs) *adj.* Of or derived from tartar.

Tar·ta·rus (tär′tər-əs) *n.* **1.** In Greek mythology, the abyss below Hades where Zeus confined the Titans. **2.** Hades.

Tar·ta·ry (tär′tər-ē) A region of Asia and eastern Europe, ruled by the Tatars, under Mongol leadership, in the 13th and 14th centuries.

tart·let (tärt′lit) *n.* A small pastry tart.

tar·trate (tär′trāt) *n. Chem.* A salt or ester of tartaric acid.

task (task, täsk) *n.* **1.** A specific amount of labor or study imposed by authority or required by duty or necessity. **2.** Any work voluntarily undertaken. **3.** An exhausting or bothersome job or duty. **4.** A specific military mission. — **to take to task** To reprove; lecture. — *v.t.* **1.** To assign a task to. **2.** To overtax with labor; burden. **3.** To reprimand. [< AF < LL < L *taxare* to appraise]

task force *Mil.* A tactical unit consisting of elements drawn from different branches of the armed services and assigned to execute a specific mission.

task·mas·ter (task′mas′tər, täsk′mäs′tər) *n.* **1.** One who assigns tasks, esp. severe ones. **2.** One who or that which loads with heavy burdens.

Tass (täs, tas) *n.* A Soviet news agency. [< Russian *T(e)legrafnoe) A(gentstvo) S(ovetskovo) S(oyuza)*]

tas·sel (tas′əl) *n.* **1.** A dangling ornament for curtains, cushions, etc., consisting of a tuft of loose threads or cords. **2.** Any of various similar objects, as the inflorescence on a stalk of Indian corn. **3.** Formerly, a clasp for holding a cloak. — *v.* **tas·seled** or **·selled, tas·sel·ing** or **·sel·ling** *v.t.* **1.** To provide or adorn with tassels. **2.** To form in a tassel or tassels. **3.** To remove the tassels from (Indian corn). — *v.i.* **4.** To put forth tassels, as Indian corn. [< OF, clasp < Med.L *tassellus,* var. of L *taxillus*]

taste (tāst) *v.* **tast·ed, tast·ing** *v.t.* **1.** To perceive the flavor of (something) by taking into the mouth or touching with the tongue. **2.** To take a little of (food or drink); eat or drink a little of. **3.** To test the quality of (a product) thus: His business is *tasting* tea. — *v.i.* **4.** To have specified flavor: Sugar *tastes* sweet. **5.** To take a small quantity into the mouth; take a taste: usu. with *of.* **6.** To have experience or enjoyment; with *of:* to *taste* of great sorrow. — *n.* **1.** *Physiol.* Any of the four fundamental sensations, salt, sweet, bitter, or sour, excited by the sole action of the gustatory nerves. **2.** A small quantity tasted, eaten, or sipped. **3.** A slight experience or sample of anything. **4.** Special fondness and aptitude for a pursuit; bent; inclination: a *taste* for music. **5.** The faculty of discerning and appreciating what is beautiful, appropriate, or correct, as in nature, art, clothes, etc. **6.** Style or form with respect to the rules of propriety. **7.** Individual preference: That tie suits my *taste.* **8.** The act of tasting. [< OF *taster* to taste, try, feel] — **tast′a·ble** *adj.*

taste bud *Physiol.* One of the clusters of cells situated in the epithelial tissue, chiefly of the tongue, and containing sensitive receptors for the discriminatory perception of taste.

taste·ful (tāst′fəl) *adj.* **1.** Conforming to taste. **2.** Possessing good taste. — **taste′ful·ly** *adv.* — **taste′ful·ness** *n.*

taste·less (tāst′lis) *adj.* **1.** Having no flavor; insipid; dull. **2.** Lacking, or showing a lack of, good taste. **3.** Devoid of esthetic taste. — **taste′less·ly** *adv.* — **taste′less·ness** *n.*

tast·er (tās′tər) *n.* One who tastes; esp., one who tests the quality of as an occupation: a *teataster.*

tast·y (tās′tē) *adj.* **tast·i·er, tast·i·est** *Informal* **1.** Having a fine flavor; savory. **2.** Tasteful. — **tast′i·ly** *adv.* — **tast′i·ness** *n.*

tat (tat) *v.* **tat·ted, tat·ting** *v.t.* **1.** To make, as an edging, by tatting. — *v.i.* **2.** To make tatting. [Back formation < TATTING] — **tat′ter** *n.*

Ta·tar (tä′tər) *n.* **1.** One belonging to any of the Turkic peoples of west central and southwest central U.S.S.R. **2.** Any of the Turkic languages of the Tatars, as Uzbek. — *adj.* Of or pertaining to the Tatars. Also *Tartar.* [< Persian] — **Ta·tar·i·an** (-târ′ē-ən) *adj.*

tat·ter (tat′ər) *n.* **1.** A torn and hanging shred; rag. **2.** *pl.* Ragged clothing. — *v.t.* **1.** To make ragged; tear into tatters. — *v.i.* **2.** To become ragged. [< Scand. Cf. ON *tö-turr* rags] — **tat′tered** *adj.*

tat·ter·de·mal·ion (tat′ər·di·māl′yən, -mal′-) *n.* A person wearing ragged clothes; a raggamuffin. [Origin unknown]

tat·ting (tat′ing) *n.* A lacelike threadwork, made by hand; also, the act or process of making it. [Origin unknown]

tat·tle (tat′l) *v.* **·tled, ·tling** — *v.i.* **1.** To talk idly; prate; chatter. **2.** To tell tales about others. — *v.t.* **3.** To reveal by gossiping. — *n.* **1.** Idle talk or gossip. **2.** Prattling speech. [Prob. < MDu. *tatelen*] — **tat′tling·ly** *adv.*
— **Syn.** (verb) **1.** prattle. **2.** blab, inform.

tat·tler (tat′lər) *n.* One who tattles; a talebearer.

tat·tle·tale (tat′l·tāl′) *n.* A talebearer; tattler.

tat·too¹ (ta·tōō′) *v.t.* **1.** To prick and mark (the skin) with indelible pigments. **2.** To mark the skin with (designs, etc.) in this way. — *n.* *pl.* **·toos** A pattern or picture so made. [< Polynesian] — **tat·too′er** *n.* — **tat·too′ing** *n.*

tat·too² (ta·tōō′) *n.* **1.** A continuous beating or drumming. **2.** In military or naval usage, a signal by drum or bugle to repair to quarters, usu., occurring about 9 P.M. [< Du. < *tap* tap, faucet + *toe* to shut]

tau (tou) *n.* The nineteenth letter in the Greek alphabet (T, τ), corresponding to the English *t.* See ALPHABET.

taught (tôt) Past tense and past participle of TEACH.

taunt (tônt) *n.* A sarcastic, biting speech or remark; scornful reproach. — *v.t.* **1.** To reproach with sarcastic or contemptuous words; mock; upbraid. **2.** To tease in any way; provoke with taunts. [? < L *temptare, tentare* to test, try] — **taunt′er** *n.* — **taunt′ing·ly** *adv.*

taupe (tōp) *n.* The color of moleskin; dark gray, often tinged with brown, purple, or yellow. [< F < L *talpa* mole]

tauro- *combining form* Bull; ox; bovine. Also, before vowels, **taur-**. [< Gk. *tauros* bull]

Tau·rus (tôr′əs) *n.* A constellation, the Bull, containing the bright star Aldebaran; also, the second sign of the zodiac. See CONSTELLATION, ZODIAC. [< L]

taut (tôt) *adj.* **1.** Stretched tight; not loose or slack. **2.** Tense; tight: *taut* muscles. **3.** In proper shape; tidy. [ME *togt, toht*] — **taut′ly** *adv.* — **taut′ness** *n.*

tau·ten (tôt′n) *v.t. & v.i.* To make or become taut; tighten.

tauto- *combining form* Same; identical. Also, before vowels, **taut-**. [< Gk. *tauto* the same]

tau·tog (tô·tôg′, -tog′) *n.* A blackish, edible, fish of the North American Atlantic coast. Also **tau·taug′.** [< Algonquian pl. of *tautau*, a blackfish]

tau·tol·o·gy (tô·tol′ə·jē) *n.* *pl.* **·gies** Unnecessary repetition of the same idea in different words; pleonasm: *He is writing his own autobiography.* [< LL < Gk. < *tauto* the same + *logos* discourse] — **tau·to·log·ic** (tô′tə·loj′ik) or **·i·cal** *adj.* — **tau′to·log′i·cal·ly** *adv.*

tav·ern (tav′ərn) *n.* **1.** A place licensed to retail liquors to be drunk on the premises. **2.** A public house providing lodging, food, and drink. [< OF < L *taberna* hut, booth]

taw (tô) *n.* **1.** A game of marbles. **2.** The line from which marble-players shoot. **3.** A marble used for shooting. [< Scand. Cf. ON *taug* string.]

taw·dry (tô′drē) *adj.* **·dri·er, ·dri·est** Showy and cheap; tastelessly ornamental. [< *St. Audrey's lace,* a type of neckpiece sold at St. Audrey's Fair at Ely, England] — **taw′dri·ly** *adv.* — **taw′dri·ness** *n.*

taw·ny (tô′nē) *adj.* **·ni·er, ·ni·est** Tan-colored; brownish yellow. Also **taw′ney.** [< AF < OF < *tanner* to tan] — **taw′ni·ness** *n.*

tax (taks) *n.* **1.** A compulsory contribution levied upon persons, property, or business for the support of government. **2.** Any proportionate assessment, as on the members of a society. **3.** A heavy demand on one's powers or resources; an onerous duty; a burden. — *v.t.* **1.** To impose a tax on. **2.** *Law* To settle or fix (costs) in any judicial matter. **3.** To subject to a severe demand; impose a burden upon: *He taxes my patience.* **4.** To accuse; charge; blame: usu. with *with.* [< OF < L *taxare* to estimate, appraise] — **tax′a·bil′i·ty, — tax′a·ble·ness** *n.* — **tax′a·ble** *adj.* — **tax′a·bly** *adv.* — **tax′er** *n.*
— **Syn.** (noun) **1.** assessment, custom, duty, excise, impost, levy, rate, tariff, tithe, toll, tribute.
Tax may appear as a combining form with the meaning of def. 1, as in the following list:

tax assessor	tax evader	tax payment
tax burden	tax-evading	tax proposal
tax-burdened	tax-exempt	tax receipt
tax claim	tax-free	tax repeal
tax collecting	tax-laden	tax revenue
tax collector	tax law	tax-ridden
tax cut	tax levy	tax-supported
tax dodger	taxman	tax system
tax-dodging	taxpaid	taxwise

tax·a·tion (tak·sā′shən) *n.* **1.** The act of taxing. **2.** The amount assessed as a tax.

tax-de·duct·i·ble (taks′di·duk′tə·bəl) *adj.* Legally deductible from that portion of one's income or assets subject to taxes: *Medical expenses are tax-deductible.*

tax·i (tak′sē) *n.* *pl.* **tax·is** A taxicab. — *v.* **tax·ied, tax·i·ing** or **tax·y·ing** *v.i.* **1.** To ride in a taxicab. **2.** To move along the ground or on the surface of the water under its own power, as an airplane before taking off. — *v.t.* **3.** To cause (an airplane) to taxi. [< TAXI(CAB)]

tax·i·cab (tak′sē·kab′) *n.* An automobile available for hire, usually fitted with a taximeter. [Short for *taximeter cab*]

tax·i·der·my (tak′sə·dûr′mē) *n.* The art of stuffing and mounting the skins of dead animals for preservation or exhibition. [< Gk. *taxis* arrangement + *derma* skin] — **tax′i·der′mal, tax′i′der′mic** *adj.* — **tax′i·der′mist** *n.*

tax·i·me·ter (tak′si·mē′tər) *n.* An instrument for measuring distances and recording fares, used in taxicabs. [< F < *taxe* tariff + *mètre* meter]

-taxis *combining form* Order; disposition; arrangement: *thermotaxis.* Also spelled **-taxy.** [< Gk. *taxis* arrangement]

tax·on·o·my (tak·son′ə·mē) *n.* **1.** The department of knowledge that embodies the laws and principles of classification. **2.** *Biol.* The systematic arrangement of plant and animal organisms according to established criteria in the following major groups, beginning with the most inclusive: kingdom, phylum or division, class, order, family, genus, and species. [< F < Gk. *taxis* arrangement + *nomos* law] — **tax·o·nom·ic** (tak′sə·nom′ik) or **·i·cal** *adj.* — **tax′o·nom′i·cal·ly** *adv.* — **tax·on′o·mer, tax·on′o·mist** *n.*

tax·pay·er (taks′pā′ər) *n.* One who pays a tax or is subject to taxation.

T-bone (tē′bōn) *n.* A beefsteak containing a T-shaped bone, taken from the loin. Also **T-bone steak.**

tea (tē) *n.* **1.** An evergreen Asian shrub having leathery, toothed leaves and white or pink flowers. **2.** The prepared leaves of this plant, or an infusion of them used as a beverage. **3.** Any infusion, preparation, or extract used as a beverage or medicinally: beef *tea,* senna *tea.* **4.** *Brit.* A light evening or afternoon meal. **5.** A social gathering at which tea is served. [< dial. Chinese *t'e*]
Tea may appear as a combining form, as in **teacart, teataster, teaware.**

tea bag A small porous sack of cloth or paper containing tea leaves, immersed in water to make tea: also called *tea ball.*

tea ball **1.** A perforated metal ball that is filled with tea leaves and placed in hot water to make tea. **2.** A tea bag.

tea ceremony A ritual preparation and serving of tea, practiced by the Japanese.

teach (tēch) *v.* **taught, teach·ing** *v.t.* **1.** To impart knowledge by lessons; give instruction to: to *teach* a class. **2.** To give instruction in; communicate the knowledge of: to *teach* French. **3.** To train by practice or exercise. — *v.i.* **4.** To follow the profession of teaching. **5.** To impart knowledge or skill. [OE *tǣcan*] — **teach′a·bil′i·ty** *n.* — **teach′a·ble** *adj.* — **teach′a·bly** *adv.*
— **Syn. 1.** *Teach* embraces all methods of imparting knowledge, information, guidance, or counsel. To *instruct* is to give specific directions about a subject: to *instruct* recruits in the use of a rifle. *Educate* usu., means to instruct in a school or college. Both *school* and *discipline* refer to the teaching of certain patterns of behavior; they both connote authority: to *school* a child to obey promptly, to *discipline* oneself to eat sparingly. *Train* suggests the fitting of a person for a particular work; of all these words, *train* is preferred when reference is made to an animal.

teach·er (tē′chər) *n.* One who teaches; esp., one whose occupation is to teach others; an instructor.

teach·ing (tē′ching) *n.* **1.** The act or occupation of a teacher. **2.** That which is taught.

tea cozy A cozy.

tea·cup (tē′kup′) *n.* **1.** A small cup suitable for serving tea. **2.** As much as a teacup will hold, usu., four fluid ounces: also **tea′cup·ful′** (-fŏol′).

teak (tēk) *n.* **1.** A large East Indian tree, yielding a very hard, durable timber highly prized for shipbuilding. **2.** The wood of this tree: also **teak′wood** (-wŏod). [< Malayalam *tēkka*]

tea·ket·tle (tē′ket′l) *n.* A kettle with a spout, used for boiling water.

teal (tēl) *n.* **1.** Any of various small, short-necked river ducks of the Old World and North America. **2.** A dull blue color with a greenish cast: also **teal blue.** [ME *tele*]

team (tēm) *n.* **1.** Two or more beasts of burden harnessed together, often including harness and vehicle; also, a single horse and vehicle. **2.** A set of workers, or players competing in a game: a baseball *team.* — *v.t.* **1.** To convey with a team. **2.** To harness together in a team. — *v.i.* **3.** To drive a team as a business. **4.** To form a team; work as a team: to *team* up. — *adj.* Of or pertaining to a team: *team* spirit. [OE *tēam* offspring, succession, row]

team·mate (tēm′māt′) *n.* A fellow player on a team.

team·ster (tēm′stər) *n.* **1.** One who drives or owns a team. **2.** One who drives a truck or other commercial vehicle.

team·work (tēm′wûrk′) *n.* **1.** Concerted action or effort by the members of a group to achieve some common end, as the coordinated play of an athletic team. **2.** Work done or requiring to be done by or with a team.

tea party A social gathering at which tea and light sandwiches or cakes are the principal refreshments.

tea·pot (tē′pot′) *n.* A vessel with a spout and handle in which tea is made and from which it is served.

tear[1] (târ) *v.* **tore, torn, tear·ing** *v.t.* **1.** To pull apart, as cloth; separate by pulling; rip; rend. **2.** To make by rending or tearing: to *tear* a hole in a dress. **3.** To injure or lacerate, as skin. **4.** To divide; disrupt: a party *torn* by dissension. **5.** To distress or torment: The sight *tore* his heart. — *v.i.* **6.** To become torn or rent. **7.** To move with haste and energy. — **to tear into** *Informal* To charge into or attack without restraint. — *n.* **1.** A fissure made by tearing; a rent; an act of tearing. **2.** *Slang* A spree; frolic. **3.** A rushing motion: to start off with a *tear.* **4.** Any violent outburst, as of anger, enthusiasm, etc. [OE *teran*]

tear[2] (tir) *n.* **1.** A drop of the saline liquid secreted by the lachrymal gland, serving to moisten the eye, and stimulated to a flow by emotional distress. **2.** Something resembling or suggesting a tear. **3.** A drop of any liquid. **4.** A droplike portion, as of glass, amber, etc. **5.** *pl.* Sorrow; lamentation. — **in tears** Weeping; crying. — *v.i.* To shed or fill with tears. [OE *tēar*] — **tear′less** *adj.* — **tear′y** *adj.*

tear·drop (tir′drop′) *n.* A tear or tear-shaped object.

tear·ful (tir′fəl) *adj.* **1.** Weeping abundantly. **2.** Causing tears. — **tear′ful·ly** *adv.* — **tear′ful·ness** *n.*

tear gas (tir) Any of various chemicals that provoke a copious flow of tears, with irritation of the eyes.

tear·ing (târ′ing) *adj. Informal* **1.** Violent; hasty; headlong. **2.** *Chiefly Brit.* Tremendous; mighty.

tear-jerk·er (tir′jûr′kər) *n. U.S. Slang* A story, play, etc., full of sentimental sadness.

tea·room (tē′rōōm′, -rŏŏm′) *n.* A restaurant serving tea and other refreshments: also called *teashop.*

tease (tēz) *v.* **teased, teas·ing** *v.t.* **1.** To annoy or harass with continual importunities, raillery, etc.; pester. **2.** To scratch or dress in order to raise the nap, as cloth with teasels. **3.** To comb or card, as wool or flax; also, to shred, as tobacco. **4.** To comb (hair) so as to form fluffy layers and give an effect of fullness. — *v.i.* **5.** To annoy a person in a facetious or petty manner. — *n.* **1.** One who or that which teases. **2.** The act of teasing, or the state of being teased. [OE *tǣsan* to tease] — **teas′er** *n.* — **teas′ing·ly** *adv.*

tea·sel (tē′zəl) *n.* **1.** A coarse, prickly Old World herb of which the flower head is covered with hooked bracts. **2.** The rough bur of such a plant, or a mechanical substitute, used in dressing cloth. — *v.t.* **tea·seled** or **-selled, tea·sel·ing** or **-sel·ling** To raise the nap of with a teasel. Also **tea′zel, tea′zle.** [OE *tǣsel*] — **tea′sel·er** or **tea′sel·ler** *n.*

tea·spoon (tē′spōōn′, -spŏŏn′) *n.* **1.** A small spoon used for stirring tea, etc. **2.** A teaspoonful.

tea·spoon·ful (tē′spōōn·fŏŏl′, -spŏŏn-) *n. pl.* **-fuls** As much as a teaspoon will hold, ⅓ of a tablespoon.

teat (tēt, tit) *n.* The protuberance on the breast or udder of most female mammals, through which the milk is drawn; a nipple; pap; dug. [< OF *tete* < Gmc.]

tea wagon A table on wheels for use in serving tea, etc.

Te·bet (tā·vāth′, tā′ves) *n.* The fourth month of the Hebrew year. See (Hebrew) CALENDAR. Also **Te·beth′.**

tech·ne·ti·um (tek·nē′shē·əm) *n.* A chemical element (symbol Tc), artificially produced by the bombardment of molybdenum with neutrons or deuterons. It displaces the hypothetical element *masurium.* See ELEMENT. [< NL < Gk. *technētos* artificial]

tech·ni·cal (tek′ni·kəl) *adj.* **1.** Pertaining to some particular art, science, or trade. **2.** Peculiar to or used in a specialized field of knowledge. **3.** Of or pertaining to the mechanical arts. **4.** Considered in terms of an accepted body of rules: a *technical* defeat. [< Gk. < *technē* art] — **tech′ni·cal·ly** *adv.* — **tech′ni·cal·ness** *n.*

tech·ni·cal·i·ty (tek′ni·kal′ə·tē) *n. pl.* **·ties** **1.** The state of being technical. **2.** The use of technical terms. **3.** A technical point peculiar to some profession, art, trade, etc. **4.** A petty distinction; quibble. Also **tech·nism** (tek′niz′əm).

technical knockout In boxing, a victory awarded when one fighter has been beaten so severely that the referee discontinues the fight.

tech·ni·cian (tek·nish′ən) *n.* One skilled in the handling of instruments or in the performance of tasks requiring specialized training.

Tech·ni·col·or (tek′ni·kul′ər) *n.* A motion-picture photographic process that reproduces the colors of the original scene: a trade name. Also **tech′ni·col·or.**

tech·nics (tek′niks) *n.pl.* (*construed as sing.*) **1.** Practical method; technique. **2.** The theory of an art or the arts; esp.,

the study of the techniques of an art. **3.** Technical rules, methods, etc. **4.** Technology. — *adj.* Technical.

tech·nique (tek·nēk′) *n.* Working methods or manner of performance, as in art, science, etc. [< F < Gk. See TECHNICAL.]

techno- *combining form* **1.** Art; skill; craft. **2.** Technical; technological. Also, before vowels, **techn-.** [< Gk. *technē* art, skill]

tech·noc·ra·cy (tek·nok′rə·sē) *n. pl.* **·cies** A theory of society and government that advocates control by an organized body of experts to achieve minimum waste and maximum efficiency. — **tech′no·crat** (tek′nə·krat) *n.* — **tech′no·crat′ic** *adj.*

tech·no·log·i·cal (tek′nə·loj′i·kəl) *adj.* Of, pertaining to, associated with, produced or affected by technology. Also **tech′no·log′ic.** — **tech′no·log′i·cal·ly** *adv.*

technological unemployment Unemployment brought about by technical advances, as automation, etc.

tech·nol·o·gy (tek·nol′ə·jē) *n. pl.* **·gies** **1.** Theoretical knowledge of industry and the industrial arts. **2.** The application of science and of technical advances in industry, the arts, etc. **3.** The technical language of an art, science, etc. **4.** The means by which material things are produced, as in a particular civilization. — **tech·nol′o·gist** *n.*

ted (ted) *v.t.* **ted·ded, ted·ding** To turn over and strew about, or spread loosely for drying, as newly mown grass. [Prob. < Scand.] — **ted′der** *n.*

ted·dy bear (ted′ē) A toy bear, usu. covered with plush. Also **Teddy bear.** [after *Teddy,* a nickname of Theodore Roosevelt]

Te De·um (tē dē′əm) **1.** An ancient Christian hymn beginning with these words. **2.** The music to which this hymn is set. **3.** Any thanksgiving service in which this hymn is sung. [< L *Te Deum* (*laudamus*) (we praise) Thee, O God]

te·di·ous (tē′dē·əs) *adj.* Causing weariness; boring. [See TEDIUM.] — **te′di·ous·ly** *adv.* — **te′di·ous·ness** *n.* — **Syn.** tiresome, tiring, fatiguing, wearisome, irksome, dull.

te·di·um (tē′dē·əm) *n.* The state of being tiresome or wearisome; tediousness. [< L *taedere* to vex, weary]

tee[1] (tē) *n.* **1.** A small peg with a concave top on which a golf ball is placed in making the first play to a hole. **2.** A designated area within which the golf tee must be placed. — *v.t. & v.i.* **teed, tee·ing** To place (the golf ball) on a tee. — **to tee off** To strike (the golf ball) in starting play.

tee[2] (tē) *n.* In certain games, a mark toward which the balls, quoits, etc., are directed, as in curling. — **to a tee** As precisely as possible; exactly.

teem[1] (tēm) *v.i.* To be full, as if at the point of producing; to be full to overflowing; abound. [OE *tēam* progeny] — **teem′er** *n.* — **teem′ing** *adj.*

teem[2] (tēm) *v.i.* To come down heavily; pour: said of rain. [< ON *tǣma* empty]

-teen *suffix* Plus ten: used in cardinal numbers from 13 to 19 inclusive: *fifteen.* [OE < *tīen* ten]

teen age The age from 13 to 19 inclusive; adolescence. — **teen-age** (tēn′āj), **teen′-aged** (-ājd′) *adj.*

teen-ag·er (tēn′ā′jər) *n.* A person of teen age.

teens (tēnz) *n.pl.* **1.** The numbers that end in *-teen.* **2.** The years of one's age from 13 to 19 inclusive.

tee·ny (tē′nē) *adj.* **·ni·er, ·ni·est** *Informal* Tiny.

tee·pee (tē′pē) See TEPEE.

tee·ter (tē′tər) *v.i.* **1.** To walk or move with a tottering motion. **2.** To seesaw; waver; vacillate. — *v.t.* **3.** To cause to teeter. — *n.* **1.** An oscillating motion. **2.** A seesaw. [< dial. E *titter,* prob. < ON *titra* to tremble, shiver]

teeth (tēth) Plural of TOOTH.

teethe (tēth) *v.i.* **teethed, teeth·ing** To cut or develop teeth.

teeth·ing ring (tē′thing) A ring of hard rubber, bone, plastic, etc., for a teething baby to bite on.

tee·to·tal (tē·tōt′l) *adj.* **1.** Pertaining to total abstinence from intoxicants. **2.** Total; entire. [< TOTAL, with emphatic repetition of initial letter] — **tee·to′tal·ism** *n.*

tee·to·tal·er (tē·tōt′l·ər) *n.* One who abstains totally from alcoholic drinks. Also **tee·to′tal·ist,** *Brit.* **tee·to′tal·ler.**

teg·u·ment (teg′yə·mənt) *n.* A covering or envelope; an integument. [< L *tegere* to cover] — **teg·u·men·ta·ry** (teg′yə·men′tər·ē), **teg·u·men′tal** *adj.*

tel- Var. of TELO-[1].

tele- *combining form* **1.** Far off; at a distance: *telegraph.* **2.** Related to or transmitted by television: *telecast.* Also spelled *telo-.* Also, before vowels, **tel-.** [< Gk. *tēle* far]

tel·e·cast (tel′ə·kast, -käst) *v.t. & v.i.* **·cast** or **·cast·ed, ·cast·ing** To broadcast by television. — *n.* A program broadcast by television.

tel·e·com·mu·ni·ca·tion (tel′ə·kə·myōō′nə·kā′shən) *n.* **1.** The art and science of communicating at a distance, as in radio, radar, television, telegraphy, telephony, etc. Also **tel′e·com·mu′ni·ca′tions.** **2.** Any message so transmitted.

tel·e·gram (tel′ə·gram) *n.* A message sent by telegraph.

tel·e·graph (tel′ə·graf, -gräf) *n.* Any of various devices, or systems, using a code; esp., one using coded impulses transmitted by wire or radio. — *v.t.* **1.** To send (a message) by telegraph. **2.** To communicate with by telegraph. — *v.i.* **3.** To transmit a message by telegraph. — **te·leg·ra·pher** (tə·leg′rə·fər), **te·leg′ra·phist** *n.*

tel·e·graph·ic (tel′ə·graf′ik) *adj.* Of or pertaining to the telegraph; transmitted by means of telegraphy. Also **tel′e·graph′i·cal.** — **tel′e·graph′i·cal·ly** *adv.*

te·leg·ra·phy (tə·leg′rə·fē) *n.* **1.** The process of conveying messages by telegraph. **2.** The art or science of the construction and operation of telegraphs.

Te·lem·a·chus (tə·lem′ə·kəs) In Greek legend, son of Odysseus and Penelope.

te·lem·e·ter (tə·lem′ə·tər) *n.* Any of various electronic devices for indicating, measuring, recording, or integrating various quantities and for transmitting the data to a distant point.

te·lem·e·try (tə·lem′ə·trē) *n.* The theory and practice of using telemeters, esp. in relation to rockets, space probes, guided missiles, etc. Also **tel·e·me·ter·ing** (tel′ə·mē′tər·ing). — **tel′e·met′ric** (-met′rik) or **·ri·cal** *adj.* — **tel′e·met′ri·cal·ly** *adv.*

teleo- Var. of TELO-[1].

te·le·ol·o·gy (tel′ē·ol′ə·jē, tē′lē-) *n. pl.* **·gies 1.** The branch of cosmology that treats of final causes. **2.** *Biol.* The doctrine that the phenomena of organic life and development can be fully explained only by the action of design and purpose and not by mechanical causes. Compare VITALISM. **3.** The explanation of nature in terms of utility or purpose, esp. divine purpose. [< NL < Gk. *telos* end + *logos* discourse] — **tel′e·o·log′i·cal** (-ə·loj′i·kəl) or **tel′e·o·log′ic** *adj.* — **tel′e·o·log′i·cal·ly** *adv.* — **tel′e·ol′o·gist** *n.*

te·lep·a·thy (tə·lep′ə·thē) *n.* The supposed communication of one mind with another at a distance by other than normal sensory means. — **tel·e·path·ic** (tel′ə·path′ik) *adj.* — **tel′e·path′i·cal·ly** *adv.* — **te·lep′a·thist** *n.*

tel·e·phone (tel′ə·fōn) *n.* A device or system for transmitting sound over a wire or other communication channel. — *v.* **·phoned, ·phon·ing** *v.t.* **1.** To communicate with by telephone. **2.** To send by telephone, as a message. — *v.i.* **3.** To communicate by telephone. — **tel′e·phon′er** *n.* — **tel·e·phon·ic** (tel′ə·fon′ik) *adj.* — **tel′e·phon′i·cal·ly** *adv.*

te·leph·o·ny (tə·lef′ə·nē) *n.* The science of designing, constructing, and operating telephones.

tel·e·pho·to (tel′ə·fō′tō) *adj.* **1.** Designating a lens system used in connection with a camera to produce a large image of a distant object. **2.** Pertaining to telephotography.

tel·e·pho·to·graph (tel′ə·fō′tə·graf, -gräf) *n.* **1.** A picture transmitted by telephotography. **2.** A picture made with a telephoto lens. — **tel′e·pho′to·graph′ic** *adj.*

tel·e·pho·tog·ra·phy (tel′ə·fə·tog′rə·fē) *n.* **1.** The art of producing photographic images of distant objects on a larger scale than is possible with an ordinary camera. **2.** The facsimile reproduction of photographs or other pictures by radio or telegraphic communication; phototelegraphy.

Tel·e·promp·ter (tel′ə·promp′tər) *n.* A prompting device for television whereby a prepared script, unseen by the audience, is shown to a speaker or performer, enlarged line by line: a trade name. Also **tel′e·prompt′er.**

tel·e·ran (tel′ə·ran) *n. Telecom.* A system of air navigation that combines the principles of television and radar to transmit information gathered by ground stations to all aircraft within range. [< TELE(VISION) + R(ADAR) + A(IR) N(AVIGATION)]

tel·e·scope (tel′ə·skōp) *n.* An optical instrument for enlarging the image of a distant object, consisting of an object glass or concave mirror for collecting the light rays and a magnifying eyepiece for viewing the image. — *v.* **·scoped, ·scop·ing** *v.t.* **1.** To drive or slide together so that one part fits into another in the manner of the sections of a small telescope. **2.** To crush by driving something into or upon. — *v.i.* **3.** To crash into one another, as railroad cars.

tel·e·scop·ic (tel′ə·skop′ik) *adj.* **1.** Pertaining to the telescope. **2.** Visible only through a telescope. **3.** Farseeing. **4.** Having sections that slide within or over one another. Also **tel′e·scop′i·cal.** — **tel′e·scop′i·cal·ly** *adv.*

te·les·co·py (tə·les′kə·pē) *n.* The art of using or making telescopes. — **te·les′co·pist** *n.*

tel·e·type (tel′ə·tīp) *v.t. & v.i.* **·typed, ·typ·ing** To communicate (with) by teletypewriter or Teletype. — **tel′e·typ′er** *n.*

Tel·e·type (tel′ə·tīp) *n.* A teletypewriter: a trade name. Also **tel′e·type.**

tel·e·type·writ·er (tel′ə·tīp′rī′tər) *n.* A telegraph system transmitting by means of a typewriter keyboard in which each key produces a coded signal that activates a specific character in a typewriterlike receiver.

tel·e·view (tel′ə·vyōo) *v.t. & v.i.* To observe by means of television. — **tel′e·view′er** *n.*

tel·e·vise (tel′ə·vīz) *v.t. & v.i.* **·vised, ·vis·ing** To transmit or receive by television.

tel·e·vi·sion (tel′ə·vizh′ən) *n.* **1.** The transmission of continuous visual images as a series of electrical impulses or a modulated carrier wave, restored to visual form on the cathode-ray screen of a receiver, often with accompanying sound. **2.** The television broadcasting industry. **3.** A television receiving set. Also called *TV.*

tel·fer (tel′fər) See TELPHER.

tell (tel) *v.* **told, tell·ing** *v.t.* **1.** To relate in detail; narrate, as a story. **2.** To communicate. **3.** To reveal: to *tell* secrets. **4.** To decide; ascertain: I cannot *tell* who is to blame. **5.** To express in words: to *tell* a lie. **6.** To give a command to; order: I *told* him to go home. **7.** To let know; inform. **8.** *Informal* To inform or assure emphatically: It's cold out, I *tell* you! **9.** To say (a rosary): to *tell* one's beads. — *v.i.* **10.** To give an account or description: usu. with *of.* **11.** To serve as indication or evidence: with *of.* **12.** To produce a marked effect: Every blow *told.* — **all told** In all. — **to tell off 1.** To count and set apart. **2.** *Informal* To reprimand severely. — **to tell on 1.** To tire; weary. **2.** *Informal* To inform against. [OE *tellan*] — **tell′a·ble** *adj.*

Tell (tel), **William** A legendary Swiss hero in the struggle for independence from Austria, forced to shoot an apple off his son's head with bow and arrow.

tell·er (tel′ər) *n.* **1.** One who relates or informs. **2.** A person who receives or pays out money, as in a bank. **3.** A person appointed to collect and count ballots in a legislative body or other assembly. — **tell′er·ship′** *n.*

tell·ing (tel′ing) *adj.* Producing a great effect; impressive; effective; striking. — **tell′ing·ly** *adv.*

tell·tale (tel′tāl′) *n.* **1.** One who improperly gives information concerning the private affairs of others; a tattler. **2.** That which conveys information, esp. in an involuntary way. **3.** An instrument or device for giving or recording information. — *adj.* That is or serves as a telltale.

tel·lu·ric (tə·lŏŏr′ik, tel·yŏŏr′-) *adj.* Of or pertaining to the earth; terrestrial; earthly.

tel·lu·ri·um (te·lŏŏr′ē·əm, tel·yŏŏr′-) *n.* A rare nonmetallic element (symbol Te) resembling sulfur and selenium in chemical properties, occasionally found native as white crystals, but usu. combined with metals. See ELEMENT. [< NL < L *tellus* the earth]

telo-[1] *combining form* Final; complete; perfect: also, before vowels, *tel-.* Also *teleo-.* [< Gk. *telos* end]

telo-[2] Var. of TELE-.

tel·pher (tel′fər) *n.* A light car suspended from cables and usu. propelled by electricity. — *v.t.* To transport by telpher. Also spelled *telfer.* [< TEL(E) + Gk. *pherein* to bear] — **tel′pher·ic** *adj.* — **tel′pher·age** (-ij) *n.*

tel·son (tel′sən) *n. Zool.* The last abdominal segment of the body of an arthropod, as of a lobster, shrimp, or scorpion. For illus. see SHRIMP. [< Gk. *telson* boundary]

Tel·star (tel′stär′) The first artificial satellite for global communication, launched from Cape Canaveral, July 10, 1962.

Tel·u·gu (tel′ŏŏ·gŏŏ) *n. pl.* **·gu 1.** A Dravidian language used in NW Andhra Pradesh, India, and important in literary culture. **2.** One of a Dravidian people of Telugu speech. — *adj.* Of or pertaining to the Telugu or to Telugu.

te·mer·i·ty (tə·mer′ə·tē) *n.* Venturesome or foolish boldness; rashness. [< L *temere* rashly]
— **Syn.** *Temerity* is the quality of one who underestimates danger, or overrates his chances for success. *Audacity* refers (in its bad sense) to going beyond the decent restraints of social behavior. *Foolhardiness* characterizes the man who rushes into peril from lack of sense. — **Ant.** caution, wariness, timidity.

tem·per (tem′pər) *n.* **1.** Heat of mind or passion; disposition to become angry. **2.** Frame of mind; mood: to be in a bad *temper.* **3.** Composure of mind; self-command: to lose one's *temper.* **4.** *Metall.* The condition of a metal as regards hardness and elasticity, esp. when due to heating and sudden cooling. **5.** Something mixed with a substance to alter its properties or qualities. — *v.t.* **1.** To bring to a state of moderation or suitability, as by addition of another quality; moderate: to *temper* justice with mercy. **2.** To bring to the proper consistency, etc., by moistening and working: to *temper* clay. **3.** *Metall.* To bring (metal) to a required hardness and elasticity by heating and suddenly cooling. **4.** *Music* To adjust the tones of (an instrument) by temperament; tune. — *v.i.* **5.** To be or become tempered. [OE and OF < L *temperare* to combine in due proportion] — **tem′per·a·bil′i·ty** *n.* — **tem′per·a·ble** *adj.* — **tem′per·er** *n.*
— **Syn.** (noun) **2.** temperament, mood, humor. — moderate, modify, qualify.

tem·per·a (tem′pər·ə, *Ital.* tem′pä·rä) *n.* **1.** A painting medium consisting of an emulsion prepared from a mixture of water and egg yolks, glue, gum, or casein solutions, etc.;

also, a method of painting with such a medium. **2.** Paint prepared by adding pigment to the medium of tempera. Also called *distemper*. [< Ital. *temperare* to temper < L]

tem·per·a·ment (tem′pər·ə·mənt, -prə-) *n.* **1.** The physical and mental peculiarities of an individual; nature. **2.** An intense, moody, and often rebellious nature. **3.** *Music* The tuning of an instrument or scale so that each semitone is a twelfth of an octave: also **equal temperament.** [< L *temperamentum* proper mixture]

tem·per·a·men·tal (tem′pər·ə·men′təl, -prə-) *adj.* **1.** Of or pertaining to temperament. **2.** Sensitive; easily excited. — **tem′per·a·men′tal·ly** *adv.*

tem·per·ance (tem′pər·əns) *n.* **1.** The state or quality of being temperate; habitual moderation. **2.** The principle or practice of total abstinence from intoxicants. [< OF < L < *temperare* to mix in due proportions]

tem·per·ate (tem′pər·it) *adj.* **1.** Observing moderation in the indulgence of an appetite, esp. in the use of intoxicating liquors. **2.** Moderate as regards temperature. **3.** Characterized by moderation; not excessive. **4.** Calm; restrained; self-controlled. **5.** *Music* Tempered: said of an interval or scale. [< L < *temperare* to mix in due proportions] — **tem′per·ate·ly** *adv.* — **tem′per·ate·ness** *n.*

tem·per·a·ture (tem′pər·ə·chər, -prə-) *n.* **1.** Condition as regards heat or cold. **2.** The degree of heat in a body or substance, as measured on the graduated scale of a thermometer. **3.** The degree of heat of an animal, esp. the human body; also, excess of this above the normal (which for the human body is 98.6° F, or about 37° C). [< L *temperatura* due measure]

tem·pered (tem′pərd) *adj.* **1.** Having temper or a specified disposition: used mainly in compounds: quick-*tempered.* **2.** *Music* Adjusted in pitch so as to produce or conform to temperament. **3.** Moderated by admixture. **4.** Having the right degree of hardness and elasticity.

tem·pest (tem′pist) *n.* **1.** A violent wind, usu. attended with rain, snow, or hail. **2.** A violent commotion or agitation; a fierce tumult. — **tempest in a teapot** A considerable uproar over a trivial matter. [< OF < L *tempestas* weather]

tem·pes·tu·ous (tem·pes′chŏŏ·əs) *adj.* Stormy; turbulent; violent. — **tem·pes′tu·ous·ly** *adv.* — **tem·pes′tu·ous·ness** *n.*

tem·plate (tem′plit′) *n.* **1.** A pattern or gauge, as of wood or metal, used as a guide in shaping something accurately. **2.** In building, a stout stone or timber for distributing weight or thrust. Also **tem·plet** (tem′plit). [< F < L *templum* small timber]

tem·ple¹ (tem′pəl) *n.* **1.** A stately edifice consecrated to the worship of one or more deities. **2.** In the U.S., a Reform synagogue. **3.** In France, a Protestant church. **4.** Any place considered as occupied by God. — **the Temple** Any of three sacred edifices built in Jerusalem for the worship of Jehovah. [OE < L *templum* temple]

tem·ple² (tem′pəl) *n.* The region on each side of the head above the cheek bone. [OF, ult. < L *tempus* temple]

tem·po (tem′pō) *n. pl.* **·pos** or **·pi** (-pē) **1.** *Music* Relative speed at which a composition is rendered. **2.** Characteristic manner or style. [< Ital. < L *tempus* time]

tem·po·ral¹ (tem′pər·əl) *adj.* **1.** Pertaining to affairs of the present life; earthly. **2.** Pertaining or related to time. **3.** Temporary; transitory. **4.** Civil; lay; secular. [< L < *temporis* time] — **tem′po·ral·ly** *adv.* — **tem′po·ral·ness** *n.*

tem·po·ral² (tem′pər·əl) *adj. Anat.* Of, pertaining to, or situated at the temple or temples.

temporal bone *Anat.* A compound bone situated at either side of the head, and containing the organ of hearing.

tem·po·ral·i·ty (tem′pə·ral′ə·tē) *n. pl.* **·ties** **1.** *Usu. pl.* A temporal or material matter, interest, revenue, etc. **2.** The state of being temporal or temporary.

tem·po·ra·ry (tem′pə·rer′ē) *adj.* Lasting or intended to be used for a short time only; transitory. [< L *tempus, temporis* time] — **tem·po·rar·i·ly** (tem′pə·rer′ə·lē, tem′pə·rer′-) *adv.* — **tem′po·rar′i·ness** *n.*

tem·po·rize (tem′pə·rīz) *v.i.* **·rized, ·riz·ing** **1.** To act evasively so as to gain time or put off decision or commitment. **2.** To give real or apparent compliance to the circumstances; comply. **3.** To effect a compromise; negotiate: with *with* or *between.* Also *Brit.* **tem′po·rise.** [< F < L *tempus, temporis* time] — **tem·po·ri·za′tion** *n.* — **tem′po·riz′er** *n.* — **tem′po·riz′ing·ly** *adv.*

tempt (tempt) *v.t.* **1.** To attempt to persuade (a person) to do something evil or unwise. **2.** To be attractive to; invite: Your offers do not *tempt* me. **3.** To provoke or risk provoking: to *tempt* fate. [< OF < L *temptare, tentare* to test] — **tempt′a·ble** *adj.* — **tempt′er** *n.* — **tempt′ress** *n.fem.*

temp·ta·tion (temp·tā′shən) *n.* **1.** The act of tempting, or the state of being tempted. **2.** That which tempts.

tempt·ing (temp′ting) *adj.* Alluring; attractive; seductive. — **tempt′ing·ly** *adv.* — **tempt′ing·ness** *n.*

tem·pus fu·git (tem′pəs fyōō′jit) *Latin* Time flies.

ten (ten) *n.* **1.** The sum of nine and one: a cardinal number. **2.** Any symbol of this number, as 10, x, X. **3.** Anything

consisting of or representing ten units, as a playing card, bill, etc. — *adj.* Being one more than nine. [OE *tien*] — **tenth** (tenth) *adj. & n.*

ten- Var. of TENO-.

ten·a·ble (ten′ə·bəl) *adj.* Capable of being held, maintained, or defended. [< F < L *tenere* to hold] — **ten′a·bil′i·ty, ten′a·ble·ness** *n.* — **ten′a·bly** *adv.*

te·na·cious (ti·nā′shəs) *adj.* **1.** Having great cohesiveness of parts; tough. **2.** Adhesive; sticky. **3.** Holding or tending to hold strongly, as opinions, rights, etc. **4.** Stubborn; obstinate. **5.** Apt to retain; strongly retentive, as memory. [< L < *tenere* to hold, grasp, embrace] — **te·na′cious·ly** *adv.* — **te·na′cious·ness** *n.*

te·nac·i·ty (ti·nas′ə·tē) *n.* The state or quality of being tenacious.

ten·an·cy (ten′ən·sē) *n. pl.* **·cies** **1.** The holding of lands, houses, offices, etc.; occupancy. **2.** The period of holding lands, houses, etc. **3.** The houses, lands, etc. so held.

ten·ant (ten′ənt) *n.* **1.** One who holds or possesses lands or property by the payment of rent or other fee. **2.** A dweller in any place; an occupant. — *v.t.* **1.** To hold as tenant; occupy. — *v.i.* **2.** To be a tenant. [< F, orig. ppr. of *tenir* to hold < L *tenere*] — **ten′ant·a·ble** *adj.* — **ten′ant·less** *adj.* — **ten′ant·ship** *n.*

tenant farmer One who farms land owned by another and pays rent, usu. in a share of the crops.

ten·ant·ry (ten′ən·trē) *n. pl.* **·ries** **1.** Tenants collectively. **2.** The state of being a tenant; tenancy.

ten-cent store (ten′sent′) A five-and-ten-cent store.

Ten Commandments The set of injunctions given by God to Moses on Mount Sinai, constituting the moral code of the Mosaic Law: also called *Decalogue. Ex.* xx 1–17.

tend¹ (tend) *v.i.* **1.** To have an aptitude, tendency, or disposition; incline. **2.** To have influence toward a specified result: Education *tends* to refinement. **3.** To go in a certain direction. [< OF < L *tendere* to extend, tend]

tend² (tend) *v.t.* **1.** To attend to the needs or requirements of; take care of; minister to: to *tend* a fire. **2.** To watch over; look after. — *v.i.* **3.** To be in attendance; serve or wait: with *on* or *upon.* **4.** *Informal* To give attention or care: with *to.* [Aphetic var. of ATTEND]

ten·den·cy (ten′dən·sē) *n. pl.* **·cies** **1.** An inclination toward some purpose, end, or result; bent; aptitude. **2.** That which tends to produce some specified effect. **3.** Bias; propensity. [< Med.L < *tendere* to extend, tend]

ten·den·tious (ten·den′shəs) *adj.* Having a tendency to favor a particular point of view; biased. Also **ten·den′cious.** [See TENDENCY.] — **ten·den′tious·ly** *adv.* — **ten·den′tious·ness** *n.*

ten·der¹ (ten′dər) *adj.* **1.** Yielding easily to force that tends to crush, bruise, break, or injure. **2.** Easily chewed or cut: said of food. **3.** Delicate or weak; not strong, rough, or hardy. **4.** Youthful and delicate: a *tender* age. **5.** Kind; affectionate; gentle. **6.** Capable of arousing sensitive feelings; touching: *tender* memories. **7.** Susceptible to spiritual or moral feelings: a *tender* conscience. **8.** Painful if touched: a *tender* sore. **9.** Of delicate effect or quality; soft: a *tender* light. **10.** Requiring deft or delicate treatment; ticklish; touchy: a *tender* subject. — *v.t.* To make tender; soften. [< OF < L *tener, teneris* soft] — **ten′der·ly** *adv.* — **ten′der·ness** *n.*

ten·der² (ten′dər) *v.t.* **1.** To present for acceptance, as a resignation; offer. **2.** *Law* To proffer, as money, in discharge of an obligation. — *n.* **1.** The act of tendering; an offer. **2.** *Law* A formal offer of satisfaction. **3.** That which is offered as payment: legal *tender.* [< F < L *tendere* to extend, tend] — **ten′der·er** *n.*

tend·er³ (ten′dər) *n.* **1.** *Naut.* **a** A vessel used to bring supplies, passengers, etc. back and forth between a larger vessel and shore. **b** A vessel that services another at sea. **2.** A vehicle attached to the rear of a steam locomotive to carry fuel and water. **3.** One who ministers to. [< TEND²]

ten·der·foot (ten′dər·fŏŏt′) *n. pl.* **·foots** or **·feet** (-fēt) *U.S.* **1.** In the West, one not yet inured to the hardships of the plains, the mining camp, etc.; a greenhorn. **2.** Any inexperienced person. **3.** A boy scout in the beginning class or group.

ten·der·heart·ed (ten′dər·här′tid) *adj.* Having deep or quick sensibility, as to love, pity, etc.; compassionate. — **ten′der·heart′ed·ly** *adv.* — **ten′der·heart′ed·ness** *n.*

ten·der·ize (ten′də·rīz) *v.t.* **·ized, ·iz·ing** To make tender, as meat.

ten·der·iz·er (ten′də·rī′zər) A substance for softening the tough fibers and connective tissues of meat.

ten·der·loin (ten′dər·loin′) *n.* The tender part of the loin of beef, pork, etc., lying close to the ventral side of the lumbar vertebrae. — **the tenderloin district** Any urban district noted for its night life, crime, etc.

ten·don (ten′dən) *n. Anat.* One of the bands of tough, fibrous connective tissue forming the termination of a muscle and serving to transmit its force to some other part; a sinew. [< Med.L < Gk. *tenōn* sinew < *tenein* to stretch]

ten·dril (ten′dril)　*n.　Bot.* One of the slender, filamentous organs that serve a climbing plant as a means of attachment to a wall, tree trunk, or other surface. [< F < *tendron* sprout] — **ten′dril·lar, ten′dril·ous** *adj.*

ten·e·brae (ten′ə·brē)　*n.pl.　Eccl. Usu. cap.* The matins and lauds sung on the afternoons or evenings of Thursday, Friday, and Saturday of Holy Week. [< L, darkness]

ten·e·ment (ten′ə·mənt)　*n.* **1.** An urban apartment building or rooming house that is poorly constructed or maintained, typically overcrowded and often part of a slum: also **tenement house. 2.** A room or set of rooms designed for one family. **3.** *Law* Property held by one person of another, as land, houses, offices, etc. **4.** Any dwelling place; abode. [< OF < LL *tenementum* tenure] — **ten′e·men′tal** (-men′təl), **ten′e·men′ta·ry** (-men′tə·rē) *adj.*

ten·et (ten′it, tē′nit)　*n.* An opinion, principle, dogma, etc., that a person or organization believes or maintains as true. — **Syn.** See DOCTRINE. [< L, he holds < *tenere* to hold]

ten·fold (ten′fōld′)　*n.* An amount or number ten times as great as a given unit. — *adv.* So as to be ten times as many or as great. — *adj.* **1.** Consisting of ten parts. **2.** Ten times as many or as great.

ten-gal·lon hat (ten′gal′ən)　*U.S.* A wide-brimmed felt hat with a tall crown, traditionally worn by cowboys.

Ten·nes·se·an (ten′ə·sē′ən)　*n.* A native or inhabitant of Tennessee. — *adj.* Of or pertaining to Tennessee.

ten·nis (ten′is)　*n.* A game played by striking a ball back and forth with rackets over a net stretched between two equal areas that together constitute a court. It has two forms, **court tennis,** played indoors, and **lawn tennis,** played out-of-doors on a court of grass, clay, concrete, etc. [< AF *tenetz* take, receive]

Ten·ny·so·ni·an (ten′ə·sō′nē·ən)　*adj.* Relating to or characteristic of Alfred Tennyson, or his verse or style.

teno- *combining form Med.* Tendon; related to a tendon, or to tendons: also *ten-.* Also **tenonto-.** [< Gk. *tenōn* tendon]

ten·on (ten′ən)　*n.* A projection on the end of a timber, etc., for inserting in a socket to form a joint. For illus. see MORTISE. — *v.t.* **1.** To form a tenon on. **2.** To join by a mortise and tenon. [< F < *tenir* to hold]

ten·or (ten′ər)　*n.* **1.** The adult male voice intermediate in range between baritone and countertenor; also, a singer having such a voice, or a part to be sung by it. **2.** *Music* An instrument playing the part intermediate between the bass and the alto. **3.** Course of thought; general purport. **4.** A settled course or manner of progress. **5.** General character and tendency; nature. — *adj.* **1.** Of or pertaining to a tenor. **2.** Having a relation to other instruments as the tenor bears to other musical parts. [< OF < L *tenor* course]

ten·pen·ny (ten′pen′ē, -pə·nē)　*adj.* **1.** Valued at tenpence. **2.** Designating the size of nails three inches long. See PENNY.

ten·pin (ten′pin′)　*n.* One of the pins used in tenpins.

ten·pins (ten′pinz′)　*n.pl.* (construed as *sing.*) A game played in a bowling alley in which the players attempt to bowl down ten pins set up at the far end of the alley.

tense¹ (tens)　*adj.* **tens·er, tens·est 1.** Stretched tight; taut. **2.** Under mental or nervous strain; strained. **3.** *Phonet.* Produced with the tongue and its muscles taut, as (ē) and (ōō). — *v.t. & v.i.* **tensed, tens·ing** To make or become strained or drawn tight. [< L *tendere* to stretch] — **tense′·ly** *adv.* — **tense′ness** *n.*

tense² (tens)　*n.* A form of a verb that relates it to time viewed either as finite past, present, or future, or as nonfinite. — **sequence of tenses** In inflected languages, the customary choice of tense for a verb that follows another in a sentence, particularly in reported or indirect discourse. [< OF < L *tempus* time, tense]

ten·si·ble (ten′sə·bəl)　*adj.* Tensile.

ten·sile (ten′sil, *Brit.* ten′sīl)　*adj.* **1.** Of or pertaining to tension. **2.** Capable of being drawn out or extended. **3.** Producing tones from stretched strings: said of instruments. [See TENSE¹.] — **ten·sil·i·ty** (ten·sil′ə·tē) *n.*

tensile strength *Physics* The resistance of a material to forces of rupture and stress in the direction of length: usually expressed in pounds per square inch.

ten·sion (ten′shən)　*n.* **1.** The act of stretching or the condition of being stretched tight. **2.** Mental strain; intense nervous anxiety. **3.** Any strained relation, as between governments. **4.** *Physics* **a** Stress on a material caused by a force pulling or stretching in one direction. **b** The condition of a body when acted on by such a force. **5.** A device for regulating the tension of something. **6.** *Electr.* Electromotive force; also, electric potential. — **Syn.** See STRESS. — **ten′sion·al** *adj.*

ten·si·ty (ten′sə·tē)　*n.* The state of being tense; tension.

ten·sive (ten′siv)　*adj.* Of, like, or causing tension.

ten·sor (ten′sər, -sôr)　*n. Anat.* A muscle that stretches a part. [< NL < L *tensus.* See TENSE¹.]

ten-strike (ten′strīk′)　*n.* **1.** In bowling, a strike (def. 3). **2.** *U.S. Informal* A totally successful stroke or act.

tent (tent)　*n.* A shelter of canvas or the like, supported by poles and fastened with cords to pegs driven into the ground. — *v.t.* To cover with or as with a tent. — *v.i.* To pitch a tent; camp out. [< F < LL *tenta,* orig. neut. pl. of *tentus,* pp. of *tendere* to stretch]

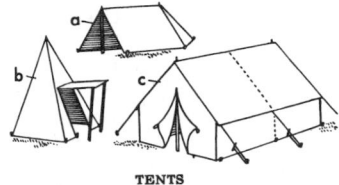

TENTS
a Pup. *b* Pyramid. *c* Wall.

ten·ta·cle (ten′tə·kəl)　*n.* **1.** *Zool.* A protruding flexible process or appendage of invertebrate animals, functioning as an organ of touch or motion, as the arms of a cuttlefish. **2.** *Bot.* A sensitive glandular hair, as on the leaves of some plants. [< L *tentare* to touch, try] — **ten·tac′u·lar** *adj.*

tent·age (ten′tij)　*n.* **1.** The supply of tents available for any purpose. **2.** Tents collectively.

ten·ta·tive (ten′tə·tiv)　*adj.* Provisional or conjectural; subject to change; experimental. [< Med.L < L *tentare* to try, probe] — **ten′ta·tive·ly** *adv.* — **ten′ta·tive·ness** *n.*

tent caterpillar Any of the larvae of several North American moths that spin silken webs to shelter the colony in which they live.

ten·ter (ten′tər)　*n.* A frame or machine for stretching cloth to prevent shrinkage while drying. — *v.t.* **1.** To stretch on or as on a tenter. — *v.i.* **2.** To be or admit of being so stretched. [< L *tentus* extended]

ten·ter·hook (ten′tər·hŏŏk′)　*n.* A sharp hook for holding cloth while being stretched on a tenter. — **to be on tenterhooks** To be in a state of anxiety or suspense.

ten·u·ous (ten′yŏŏ·əs)　*adj.* **1.** Thin; slim; delicate; also, weak; flimsy; unsubstantial. **2.** Having slight density; rare. [< L *tenuis* thin] — **ten′u·ous·ly** *adv.* — **ten′u·ous·ness,** **ten·u·i·ty** (ten·yŏŏ′ə·tē, ti·nŏŏ′-) *n.*

ten·ure (ten′yər)　*n.* **1.** A holding, as of land. **2.** The act of holding in general, or the state of being held. **3.** The term during which a thing is held. **4.** The conditions or manner of holding. **5.** Permanent status granted to an employee, usu. after a trial period. [< F < L *tenere* to hold] — **ten·u·ri·al** (ten·yŏŏr′ē·əl) *adj.* — **ten·u′ri·al·ly** *adv.*

te·nu·to (te·nŏŏ′tō)　*adj. Music* Sustained; held for the full time. [< Ital. < L *tenere* to hold]

te·pee (tē′pē)　*n.* A conical tent of the North American Plains Indians, usu. covered with skins: also spelled *teepee.* [< Dakota < *ti* to dwell + *pi* used for]

tep·id (tep′id)　*adj.* Moderately warm; lukewarm, as a liquid. [< L *tepere* to be lukewarm] — **te·pid·i·ty** (tə·pid′ə·tē), **tep′id·ness** *n.* — **tep′id·ly** *adv.*

te·qui·la (tə·kē′lə)　*n.* **1.** A Mexican alcoholic liquor distilled from the juices yielded by the roasted stems of an agave plant. **2.** The plant itself. [after *Tequila,* Jalisco, Mexico]

ter- *combining form* Three; third; threefold; three times: *tercentenary.* [< L *ter* thrice]

ter·a·tism (ter′ə·tiz′əm)　*n.* A monstrosity; esp., a malformed human or animal fetus. [< Gk. *teras* monster]

terato- *combining form* A wonder; monster. Also, before vowels, **terat-.** [< Gk. *teras* wonder]

ter·bi·um (tûr′bē·əm)　*n.* A metallic element (symbol Tb) belonging to the lanthanide series, found in rare-earth minerals. See ELEMENT. [< NL < *Ytterby,* town in Sweden] — **ter′bic** *adj.*

ter·cen·te·nar·y (tûr·sen′tə·ner′ē, tûr′sen·ten′ər·ē)　*adj.* Of or pertaining to a period of 300 years or to a 300th anniversary. — *n. pl.* **·nar·ies** A 300th anniversary. Also *tricentennial.* Also **ter·cen·ten·ni·al** (tûr′sen·ten′ē·əl).

ter·cet (tûr′sit, tûr′set′)　*n.* **1.** A group of three lines rhyming together or connected with adjacent triplets by rhyme. **2.** *Music* A triplet. [< F < Ital. < L *tertius* third]

ter·gi·ver·sate (tûr′ji·vər·sāt′)　*v.i.* **·sat·ed, ·sat·ing 1.** To be evasive; equivocate. **2.** To change sides, attitudes, etc.; apostatize. [< L *tergum* back + *versare* to turn] — **ter′gi·ver·sa′tion** *n.* — **ter′gi·ver·sa′tor** *n.*

term (tûrm)　*n.* **1.** A word or expression used to designate some definite thing: a scientific *term.* **2.** Any word or expression conveying some conception or thought: to speak in general *terms.* **3.** *pl.* The conditions or stipulations according to which something is to be done or acceded to: the *terms* of sale. **4.** *pl.* Mutual relations: usu. preceded by *on* or *upon:* England was on friendly *terms* with France. **5.** *Math.* **a** The numerator or denominator of a fraction. **b** One of the quantities of an algebraic expression that are connected by the plus and minus signs. **c** One of the quantities that compose a series or progression. **6.** *Logic* Either the subject or predicate of a proposition. **7.** A fixed period or definite length of time: a *term* of office. **8.** One of the periods of the school year. **9.** *Law* **a** One of the prescribed periods during which a court may hold a session. **b** A specific extent of time for which an estate is granted. **c** An interval allowed a debtor to meet his obligation. **10.** *Med.* The time for childbirth. **— at term** At the end of a definite time. **— in terms of** With reference to; concerning. **— to bring to terms** To force to accede or agree. **— to come to terms** To reach an agreement. **—** *v.t.* To designate by means of a term; name or call. [< OF < L *terminus* limit] **— term′less** *adj.*

ter·ma·gant (tûr′mə·gənt) *n.* A scolding or abusive woman; shrew. **—** *adj.* Violently abusive and quarrelsome; vixenish. [after *Termagant*, an imaginary Moslem deity of overbearing character] **— ter′ma·gan/cy** *n.*

term·er (tûr′mər) *n.* *Informal* A prisoner serving a certain term: a first *termer.*

ter·mi·na·ble (tûr′mə·nə·bəl) *adj.* That may be terminated; limitable; not perpetual. **— ter/mi·na·bil/i·ty, ter/·mi·na·ble·ness** *n.* **— ter/mi·na·bly** *adv.*

ter·mi·nal (tûr′mə·nəl) *adj.* **1.** Of, pertaining to, or forming a boundary, limit, or end: a *terminal* railroad station. **2.** Pertaining to the delivery or storage of freight or baggage: *terminal* charges. **3.** Pertaining to a term or name. **4.** Situated at the end of a series or part. **5.** *Bot.* Borne at the end of a stem or branch. **6.** Of, pertaining to, or occurring in or at the end of a period of time. **7.** Ending in death: said of a disease. **—** *n.* **1.** That which terminates; a terminating point or part; end. **2.** *Electr.* A point at which a circuit element, as a battery, generator, resistor, capacitor, transistor, etc., may be connected to other elements. **3.** A railroad terminus. [< LL < L *terminus* boundary] **— ter′mi·nal·ly** *adv.*

ter·mi·nate (tûr′mə·nāt) *v.* **·nat·ed, ·nat·ing** *v.t.* **1.** To put an end or stop to. **2.** To form the conclusion of; finish. **3.** To bound or limit. **—** *v.i.* **4.** To have or come to an end. [< L *terminus* limit] **— ter/mi·na·tive** *adj.* **— ter′mi·na/·tor** *n.* **— ter/mi·na·to/ry** (-nə·tôr/ē, -tō/rē) *adj.*

ter·mi·na·tion (tûr′mə·nā/shən) *n.* **1.** The act of setting bounds or limits. **2.** The act of ending or concluding. **3.** That which bounds or limits; close; end. **4.** Outcome; result; conclusion. **5.** The final letters or syllable of a word; a suffix. **— ter/mi·na/tion·al** *adj.*

ter·mi·nol·o·gy (tûr′mə·nol/ə·jē) *n.* *pl.* **·gies** The technical terms used in a science, art, trade, etc.; nomenclature. [< L *terminus* + -LOGY] **— ter/mi·no·log/i·cal** (-nə·loj/i·kəl) *adj.* **— ter/mi·no·log/i·cal·ly** *adv.*

ter·mi·nus (tûr′mə·nəs) *n.* *pl.* **·nus·es** or **·ni** (-nī) **1.** The final point or goal; end. **2.** The farthermost station on a railway. **3.** A boundary or border. [< L]

ter·mite (tûr′mīt′) *n.* Any of various small, whitish social insects native in warm regions, several species of which are very destructive of wooden structures, furniture, etc.: also, loosely, *white ant.* [< L *termes*]

tern (tûrn) *n.* Any of several birds allied to the gulls, but having a smaller bill and body, with wings more pointed, and the tail usu. deeply forked. [< Scand.]

ter·na·ry (tûr′nər·ē) *adj.* Formed or consisting of three; grouped in threes. **—** *n.* *pl.* **·ries** A group of three; a triad. [< L *terni* by threes]

ter·nate (tûr′nāt) *adj.* Arranged in threes. [< NL < L *terni* by threes] **— ter′nate·ly** *adv.*

ter·pene (tûr′pēn) *n.* *Chem.* Any of a class of isomeric hydrocarbons, $C_{10}H_{16}$, contained chiefly in the essential oils of coniferous plants. [< *terp(entin)*, earlier form of TURPENTINE + -ENE]

Terp·sich·o·re (tûrp·sik/ə·rē) The Muse of dancing. [< Gk. < *terpsis* enjoyment + *choros* dance] **— Terp·si·cho·re·an** (tûrp/si·kə·rē/ən) *adj.*

terp·si·cho·re·an (tûrp/si·kə·rē/ən) *adj.* Of or relating to dancing: also **terp/si·cho·re/al.** **—** *n.* *Informal* A dancer.

ter·race (ter′is) *n.* **1.** An artificial, raised, level space, as of lawn, having one or more vertical or sloping sides; also, such levels collectively. **2.** A raised level supporting a row of houses, or the houses occupying such a position. **3.** The flat roof of an Oriental or Spanish house. **4.** An unroofed, usu. paved area near a house. **5.** An open gallery. **—** *v.t.* **·raced, ·rac·ing** To form into or provide with a terrace or terraces. [< OF < Ital. < L *terra* earth]

ter·ra cot·ta (ter′ə kot/ə) **1.** A hard, durable clay, reddish brown in color and usu. unglazed, widely used as a structural material and in pottery, tiles, building façades, etc. **2.** Its brownish orange color. [< Ital., cooked earth]

ter·ra fir·ma (ter′ə fûr/mə) Solid ground. [< L]

ter·rain (te·rān′, ter′ān) *n.* A piece or plot of ground; esp., a region or territory viewed with regard to its suitability for some particular purpose. [< F < L < *terra* earth]

Ter·ra·my·cin (ter′ə·mī/sin) *n.* Proprietary name for an antibiotic isolated from a soil mold and used in the treatment of a wide variety of bacterial infections. Also **ter′ra·my/cin.**

ter·ra·pin (ter′ə·pin) *n.* Any of several North American edible tortoises of fresh and brackish waters; esp., the diamond back. [< Algonquian]

ter·rar·i·um (te·râr/ē·əm) *n.* *pl.* **·rar·i·ums** or **·rar·i·a** (-râr/ē·ə) A place or enclosure for keeping land animals, plants, etc. [< L *terra* earth + -ARIUM, on analogy with *aquarium*]

ter·res·tri·al (tə·res/trē·əl) *adj.* **1.** Of, pertaining to, or consisting of earth or land. **2.** Of, belonging to, or representing the earth. **3.** *Biol.* Living on or growing in the earth or land. **4.** Belonging to or consisting of land, as distinct from water, trees, etc. **5.** Worldly; mundane. **—** *n.* An inhabitant of the earth. [< L *terra* land] **— ter·res/tri·al·ly** *adv.* **— ter·res/tri·al·ness** *n.*

ter·ret (ter′it) *n.* One of two metal rings projecting from the saddle of a harness, through which the reins are passed. [ME < F *touret*, dim. of *tour* turn]

terri- *combining form* Earth; ground. [< L *terra* earth]

ter·ri·ble (ter′ə·bəl) *adj.* **1.** Of a nature to excite terror; appalling. **2.** *Informal* Characterized by excess; severe; extreme. **3.** Inspiring awe. **4.** *Informal* Inferior. [< F < L *terrere* to terrify] **— ter/ri·ble·ness** *n.* **— ter/ri·bly** *adv.*

ter·ri·er (ter′ē·ər) *n.* Any of various small, active, wiry dogs of several breeds, formerly used to hunt burrowing animals. [< OF < L *terra* earth]

ter·rif·ic (tə·rif/ik) *adj.* **1.** *Informal* **a** Extreme; intense; tremendous. **b** Wonderful; great; splendid. **2.** Arousing or calculated to arouse great terror or fear. **— ter·rif/i·cal·ly** *adv.*

ter·ri·fy (ter′ə·fī) *v.t.* **·fied, ·fy·ing** To fill with extreme terror. [< L < *terrere* to frighten + *facere* to make]

ter·ri·to·ri·al (ter′ə·tôr/ē·əl, -tō′rē-) *adj.* **1.** Of or pertaining to a territory or territories. **2.** Limited to or within the jurisdiction of a particular territory or region. **3.** Designating military forces intended for territorial defense. **4.** Belonging to a particular locality. **5.** *Often cap.* Organized or intended primarily for national defense: the British *Territorial* Army. **—** *n.* *Informal* A territorial·ist *n.* **— ter/ri·to/ri·al/i·ty** (-al/ə·tē) *n.* **— ter/ri·to/ri·al·ly** *adv.*

Ter·ri·to·ri·al (ter′ə·tôr/ē·əl, -tō′rē) *adj.* Of any or all of the Territories of the U.S., Great Britain, etc. **—** *n.* A member of the Territorial Army in Great Britain.

ter·ri·to·ry (ter′ə·tôr/ē, -tō′rē) *n.* *pl.* **·ries** **1.** The domain over which a sovereign state exercises jurisdiction. **2.** Any considerable tract of land; a region; also, a sphere, province. **3.** An area assigned for a special purpose. [< L *terra* earth]

Ter·ri·to·ry (ter′ə·tôr/ē, -tō′rē) *n.* *U.S.* A region having a certain degree of self-government but not having the status of a State, as American Samoa.

ter·ror (ter′ər) *n.* **1.** An overwhelming impulse of fear; extreme fright or dread. **2.** A person or thing that causes extreme fear. **3.** *Informal* An intolerable nuisance. [< F < L *terrere* to frighten]

ter·ror·ism (ter′ə·riz/əm) *n.* **1.** The act of terrorizing or the state of being terrorized. **2.** Unlawful acts of violence committed in an attempt to overthrow a government. **3.** A system of government that rules by intimidation. **— ter/·ror·ist** *n.* **— ter/ror·is/tic** *adj.*

ter·ror·ize (ter′ə·rīz) *v.t.* **·ized, ·iz·ing** **1.** To reduce to a state of terror; terrify. **2.** To coerce through intimidation. **— ter/ror·i·za/tion** *n.* **— ter/ror·iz/er** *n.*

ter·ry (ter′ē) *n.* *pl.* **·ries** A pile fabric in which the loops are uncut: also **terry cloth.** [Prob. < F *tirer* to draw]

terse (tûrs) *adj.* **ters·er, ters·est** Short and to the point; concise: a *terse* comment. [< L < *tergere* to rub off, rub down] **— terse/ly** *adv.* **— terse/ness** *n.*
— Syn. *Terse, concise, pithy,* and *succinct* characterize speech or writing that says much in relatively few words. *Terse* emphasizes the finish and cogency of the result; *concise* suggest that all unnecessary words have been pruned away. *Pithy* describes something both brief and forceful, while *succinct* characterizes that which is highly compact because all extraneous detail has been removed. **— Ant.** diffuse, prolix, wordy.

ter·tial (tûr′shəl) *Ornithol. adj.* Tertiary. **—** *n.* A tertiary feather. [< L *tertius* third]

ter·tian (tûr′shən) *adj.* Recurring every other day, or if reckoned inclusively, every third day. **—** *n.* *Pathol.* A tertian disease or fever. [< L *tertius* third]

ter·ti·ar·y (tûr′shē·er′ē, -shə·rē) *adj.* **1.** Third in point of time, number, degree, etc. **2.** *Ornithol.* Denoting one of the flight feathers attached to a bird's wing: also called *tertial.* **—** *n.* *pl.* **·ar·ies** *Ornithol.* A tertiary feather. [< L < *tertius* third]

Ter·ti·ar·y (tûr′shē·er′ē, -shə·rē) *Geol. adj.* Of the earlier of the two geological periods or systems comprising the Cenozoic era, following the Cretaceous and succeeded by the Quaternary. **—** *n.* The Tertiary period or system, characterized by the rise of mammals. See table for GEOLOGY.

tes·sel·late (tes′ə·lāt) *v.t.* **·lat·ed, ·lat·ing** To construct in the style of checkered mosaic; lay or adorn with squares or tiles. [< L < dial. Gk. (Ionic) *tesseres* four] **— tes/sel·lat/ed** *adj.* **— tes/sel·la/tion** *n.*

test¹ (test) *v.t.* **1.** To subject to a test or trial; try. **2.** *Chem.* **a** To assay or refine (a precious metal). **b** To examine by means of some reagent. — *v.i.* **3.** *Chem.* **a** To undergo testing. **b** To show specified qualities or properties under testing. — *n.* **1.** Subjection to conditions that disclose the true character of a person or thing in relation to some particular quality. **2.** An examination made for the purpose of proving or disproving some matter in doubt: a sobriety *test.* **3.** A series of questions, problems, etc., intended to measure the extent of knowledge, aptitudes, intelligence, and other mental traits. **4.** A criterion or standard of judgment. **5.** *Chem.* **a** A reaction by means of which the presence and identity of a compound or one of its constituents may be determined. **b** The agent or result of such a reaction. [< OF, vessel used in assaying metals < L *testum* earthen vessel] — **test′a·ble** *adj.* — **test′er** *n.*

test² (test) *n.* **1.** *Zool.* A rigid external case or covering of many invertebrates, as a sea urchin or mollusk; a shell: also called *testa.* **2.** *Bot.* A testa. [< L *testa* shell]

tes·ta (tes′tə) *n.* *pl.* **·tae** (-tē) **1.** *Bot.* The outer, usu. hard and brittle coat or integument of a seed: also called *test.* **2.** *Zool.* A test. [See TEST².]

tes·ta·ceous (tes·tā′shəs) *adj.* **1.** Of or derived from shells or shellfish. **2.** Having a hard shell. [< L *testa* shell]

tes·ta·ment (tes′tə·mənt) *n.* **1.** *Law* The written declaration of one's last will: chiefly in the phrase **last will and testament. 2.** In Biblical use, a covenant. [< F < L < *testis* witness] — **tes′ta·men′tal** *adj.*

Tes·ta·ment (tes′tə·mənt) *n.* **1.** One of the two volumes of the Bible, distinguished as the *Old* and the *New Testament.* **2.** A volume containing the New Testament.

tes·ta·men·ta·ry (tes′tə·men′tər·ē) *adj.* **1.** Derived from, bequeathed by, or set forth in a will. **2.** Appointed or provided by, or done in accordance with, a will. **3.** Pertaining to a will, or to the administration or settlement of a will.

tes·tate (tes′tāt) *adj.* Having made a will before decease. [< L *testis* witness]

tes·ta·tor (tes·tā′tər, tes′tā·ter) *n.* **1.** The maker of a will. **2.** One who has died leaving a will. [< L] — **tes·ta′trix** (-triks) *n.fem.*

tes·tes (tes′tēz) Plural of TESTIS.

tes·ti·cle (tes′ti·kəl) *n.* *Biol.* One of the two male sex glands enclosed in the scrotum and in which the spermatozoa and certain secretions are formed: also called *testis.* [< L, dim. of *testis* testicle]

tes·ti·fy (tes′tə·fī) *v.* **·fied, ·fy·ing** *v.i.* **1.** To make solemn declaration of truth or fact. **2.** *Law* To give testimony; bear witness. **3.** To serve as evidence or indication: Her rags *testified* to her poverty. — *v.t.* **4.** To bear witness to; affirm positively. **5.** *Law* To state or declare on oath or affirmation. **6.** To be evidence or indication of. **7.** To make known publicly; declare. [< L *testis* witness + *facere* to make] — **tes′ti·fi·ca′tion** (-fə·kā′shən) *n.* — **tes′ti·fi′er** *n.*

tes·ti·mo·ni·al (tes′tə·mō′nē·əl) *n.* **1.** A formal token or statement of regard. **2.** A written acknowledgment of services or worth; also, a letter of recommendation. — *adj.* Pertaining to or constituting testimony or a testimonial.

tes·ti·mo·ny (tes′tə·mō′nē) *n.* *pl.* **·nies 1.** A statement or affirmation of a fact, as before a court. **2.** Evidence; proof; also, the aggregate of proof offered in a case. **3.** The act of testifying; attestation. **4.** Public declaration regarding some experience. [< L < *testis* witness]
— **Syn.** *Testimony* is the oral statements made by a witness under examination. A *deposition* or *affidavit* is *testimony* put into writing; *depositions* are made under formal questioning, and may be subject to cross-examination, while an *affidavit* is a sworn document that may be accepted when the testifier cannot appear in court in person.

tes·tis (tes′tis) *n.* *pl.* **·tes** (-tēz) A testicle. [< L]

tes·tos·ter·one (tes·tos′tə·rōn) *n.* *Biochem.* A male sex hormone, $C_{19}H_{28}O_2$, isolated as a white crystalline substance from the testes, and also made synthetically. [< TESTIS + STER(OL) + -ONE]

test pilot An aviator who tests aircraft of new design.

test tube A glass tube, open at one end and usu. with a rounded bottom, used in making chemical or biological tests.

tes·tu·do (tes·tōō′dō, -tyōō′-) *n.* *pl.* **·di·nes** (-də·nēz) **1.** A shed or screen used by the Romans for the protection of soldiers in siege operations. **2.** A protecting cover formed by soldiers in ranks by overlapping their shields above their heads. [< L < *testa* shell]

tes·ty (tes′tē) *adj.* **·ti·er, ·ti·est** Irritable in manner or disposition; touchy. [< AF *testif* heady < OF < L *testa* skull] — **tes′ti·ly** *adv.* — **tes′ti·ness** *n.*

te·tan·ic (ti·tan′ik) *adj.* Relating to or productive of tetanus. Also **te·tan′i·cal.** — *n.* A drug capable of causing convulsions, as strychnine or nux vomica.

tet·a·nus (tet′ə·nəs) *n.* **1.** *Pathol.* An acute infectious disease caused by a bacillus and characterized by rigid spasmodic contraction of various voluntary muscles, esp. those of the neck and jaw. Compare LOCKJAW. **2.** *Physiol.* A state of contraction in a muscle excited by a rapid series of shocks. [< L < Gk. *tetanos* spasm]

tetarto- *combining form* Four; fourth. Also, before vowels, **tetart-.** [< Gk. *tetartos* fourth < *tettares* four]

tetch·y (tech′ē) *adj.* **tetch·i·er, tetch·i·est** Peevishly sensitive; irritable; touchy. [< OF *leche* mark, quality] — **tetch′i·ly** *adv.* — **tetch′i·ness** *n.*

tête-à-tête (tāt′ə·tāt′, *Fr.* tet·à·tet′) *adj.* Confidential, as between two persons only. — *n.* **1.** A confidential interview between two persons; a private chat. **2.** An S-shaped sofa on which two persons may face each other. — *adv.* In or as in intimate conversation. [< F, lit. head to head]

teth·er (teth′ər) *n.* **1.** Something used to check or confine, as a rope for fastening an animal. **2.** The range, scope, or limit of one's powers or field of action. — **at the end of one's tether** At the extreme end or limit of one's resources, patience, etc. — *v.t.* To fasten or confine by a tether. [ME *tethir* < Scand.]

tetra- *combining form* Four; fourfold. Also, before vowels, **tetr-.** [< Gk.]

tet·ra·chord (tet′rə·kôrd) *n.* *Music* Four contiguous tones, of which the extreme tones are a perfect fourth apart. [< Gk. < *tetras* group of four + *chordē* string] — **tet′ra·chor′·dal** *adj.*

tet·rad (tet′rad) *n.* A group or collection of four. [< Gk. *tetras, -ados* group of four]

tet·ra·eth·yl lead (tet′rə·eth′il led) *Chem.* A colorless, heavy, flammable, poisonous, liquid hydrocarbon $Pb(C_2H_5)_4$, used as an antiknock agent in internal-combustion engines.

tet·ra·he·dron (tet′rə·hē′drən) *n.* *pl.* **·drons** or **·dra** (-drə) *Geom.* A polyhedron bounded by four plane triangular faces. [< Gk. < *tetra-* four + *hedra* base] — **tet′ra·he′dral** *adj.*

TETRAHEDRON

te·tral·o·gy (te·tral′ə·jē) *n.* *pl.* **·gies 1.** A group of four dramas, including three tragedies and one satyr play, presented together at the festivals of Dionysus at Athens. **2.** Any series of four related dramatic, operatic, or literary works. [< Gk. < *tetra-* four + *logos* word]

tet·ram·e·ter (te·tram′ə·tər) *n.* **1.** In prosody, a line of verse consisting of four metrical feet: Fúll fā│thŏm fíve│thȳ fā│thĕr líes. **2.** Verse consisting of lines of four metrical feet. — *adj.* Consisting of four metrical feet or of lines containing four metrical feet. [< LL < Gk. < *tetra-* four + *metron* measure]

tet·rarch (tet′rärk, tē′trärk) *n.* **1.** The governor of one of four divisions of a country or province. **2.** A tributary prince under the Romans; a subordinate ruler. **3.** In ancient Greece, an army commander of a subdivision of a phalanx. [< LL < L < Gk. < *tetra-* four + *archos* ruler]

tet·rar·chy (tet′rär·kē, tē′trär-) *n.* *pl.* **·chies 1.** The rule, territory, or jurisdiction of a tetrarch. **2.** Government by a group of four; also, the four members of such a group. Also **tet′rar·chate** (-kāt, -kit).

tet·ra·stich (tet′rə·stik) *n.* A poem or stanza of four lines. [< TETRA- + Gk. *stichos* row, line] — **tet′ra·stich′ic** *adj.*

tet·ra·va·lent (tet′rə·vā′lənt) *adj.* *Chem.* Quadrivalent.

Teu·ton (tōōt′n, tyōōt′n) *n.* **1.** One of the Teutones. **2.** One belonging to any of the Teutonic peoples; esp., a German.

Teu·to·nes (tōōt′ə·nēz, tyōō′-) *n.pl.* An ancient German tribe that dwelt in Jutland north of the Elbe.

Teu·ton·ic (tōō·ton′ik, tyōō-) *adj.* **1.** Of, pertaining to, or designating the peoples of northern Europe, formerly the Angles, Saxons, Danes, Normans, Goths, etc., now embracing also the English, Germans, Dutch, etc. **2.** Of or pertaining to the Germanic languages. **3.** Of or pertaining to the Teutones. — *n.* The Germanic subfamily of languages.

Teu·ton·ism (tōōt′n·iz′əm, tyōōt′n-) *n.* **1.** A custom or mode of expression peculiar to Germans or Teutons; Germanism. Also **Teu·ton·i·cism** (tōō·ton′ə·siz′əm, tyōō-). **2.** A belief in the superiority of the Teutonic peoples. **3.** Teutonic character and civilization. — **Teu′ton·ist** *n.*

Teu·ton·ize (tōōt′n·īz, tyōōt′n-) *v.t.* & *v.i.* **·ized, ·iz·ing** To make or become Teutonic or German. — **Teu′ton·i·za′tion** *n.*

Texas fever A destructive cattle disease caused by a blood parasite transmitted by a tick.

Texas leaguer *U.S. Informal* In baseball, a fly ball that falls between an infielder and an outfielder for a base hit.

text (tekst) *n.* **1.** The body of matter on a written or printed page, as distinguished from notes, commentary, illustrations, etc. **2.** The actual or original words of an author. **3.** A written or printed version of the matter of an author's works: the folio *text* of Shakespeare. **4.** Any one of various recensions that are taken to represent the authentic words, or portion of the words, of the original Scriptures. **5.** A verse of Scripture, particularly when cited as the basis of a discourse or sermon. **6.** Any subject of discourse; a topic. **7.** A text-book. [< OF < L *textus* fabric < *texere* to weave]

text·book (tekst′bŏŏk′) *n.* A book used as a standard work or basis of instruction in any branch of knowledge.

tex·tile (teks′til, -tīl) *adj.* **1.** Pertaining to weaving or woven fabrics. **2.** Such as may be woven; manufactured by weaving. — *n.* **1.** A woven fabric. **2.** Material capable of being woven. [< L < *textus* fabric]

tex·tu·al (teks′chōō·əl) *adj.* **1.** Pertaining to, contained in, or based on the text of a book. **2.** Word for word; literal. **3.** Versed in texts. — **tex′tu·al·ly** *adv.*

tex·tu·al·ism (teks′chōō·əl·iz′əm) *n.* Rigid adherence to a text. — **tex′tu·al·ist** *n.*

tex·ture (teks′chər) *n.* **1.** The arrangement or character of the threads, etc., of a woven fabric. **2.** The mode of union or disposition of elementary constituent parts, as in a photograph, surface of paper, etc. **3.** The structure of the surface of a painting, sculpture, etc.; also, the apparent surface structure of an object or part represented in a work of art, as skin, fur, etc. **4.** Any woven fabric; a web. [< L < *textus* fabric] — **tex′tur·al** *adj.* — **tex′tur·al·ly** *adv.*

tex·tured (teks′chərd) *adj.* **1.** Having a distinctive texture. **2.** Having (a specified kind of) texture: used in combination: *rough-textured.*

-th¹ *suffix of nouns* **1.** The act or result of the action expressed in the root word: *growth.* **2.** The state of being what is indicated in the root word: *health.* [OE *-thu, -th*]

-th² *suffix* Used in ordinal numbers: *tenth.* Also, after vowels, *-eth,* as in *fortieth.* [OE *-tha, -the*]

-th³ See -ETH¹.

Thai (tī) *n.* **1.** The people collectively of Thailand, Laos, and parts of Burma: preceded by *the.* **2.** A family of languages spoken by these people, considered by some to be a branch of the Sino-Tibetan family and by others to be affiliated with the Austronesian Polynesian family. **3.** The language of Thailand. — *adj.* Of or pertaining to the Thai, their culture, or their languages. Also spelled *Tai.*

thairm (thârm) See THARM.

tha·lam·ic (thə·lam′ik) *adj.* Of or pertaining to a thalamus, esp. to the thalamus of the brain.

thal·a·mus (thal′ə·məs) *n.* *pl.* **·mi** (-mī) **1.** *Anat.* A large, ovoid mass of gray matter at the base of the brain, the chief center for transmission of sensory impulses to the cerebral cortex: also called *optic thalamus.* **2.** *Bot.* The receptacle of a flower. [< L < Gk. *thalamos* chamber]

tha·las·sic (thə·las′ik) *adj.* **1.** Of or pertaining to the seas, as distinguished from the oceans. **2.** Pelagic; oceanic. [< F < Gk. *thalassa* sea]

thalasso- *combining form* The sea; of the sea. Also, before vowels, **thalass-, thalassi-.** [< Gk. *thalassa* sea]

tha·ler (tä′lər) See TALER.

thal·i·do·mide (thə·lid′ə·mīd) *n. Chem.* An organic compound, $C_{13}H_{10}N_2O_4$, originally a mild sedative and later withdrawn because its use by pregnant women was suspected of causing serious malformations in newborn children.

thal·li·um (thal′ē·əm) *n.* A soft, white, crystalline metallic element (symbol Tl), whose salts are used in rat poison, insecticides, and in making optical glass. See ELEMENT. [< NL < Gk. *thallos* green shoot; from the bright green line in its spectrum that led to its discovery]

thal·lo·phyte (thal′ə·fīt) *n.* Any of various plants belonging to a division including forms without true roots, stems, or leaves, comprising the bacteria, fungi, algae, and lichens. — **thal′lo·phyt′ic** (-fit′ik) *adj.*

thal·lus (thal′əs) *n. pl.* **·lus·es** or **·li** (-lī) *Bot.* A plant body without true root, stem, or leaf, as in thallophytes. [< L, shoot < Gk. < *thallein* to bloom]

Tham·muz (täm′mŏŏz, tam′uz) See TAMMUZ.

than (than, *unstressed* thən) *conj.* **1.** When, as, or if compared with: after an adjective or adverb to express comparison between what precedes and what follows: I am stronger *than* he (is). **2.** Except; but: used after *other, else,* etc.: no other *than* you. [OE *thonne* then]

◆ *Than* is usu. taken as a conjunction; as such, it may be followed by the nominative or the objective, depending on the nature of the ellipsis: You struck him harder *than I* (struck him) or You struck him harder *than* (you struck) *me.* A minority of grammarians and writers have accepted *than* as a preposition, in which case it is regularly followed by the objective: He is stronger *than me.*

thanato- *combining form* Death; of or pertaining to death. Also, before vowels, **thanat-.** [< Gk. *thanatos* death]

than·a·top·sis (than′ə·top′sis) *n.* A meditation upon death. [< THANAT(O)- + Gk. *opsis* appearance, sight]

thane (thān) *n.* **1.** A warrior companion of an English king before the Conquest. **2.** A man who ranked above an ordinary freeman or ceorl (churl) but below an earl or nobleman. **3.** *Scot.* The chief of a clan. Also *thegn.* [OE *thegn*]

thank (thangk) *v.t.* **1.** To express gratitude to. **2.** To hold

responsible; blame: often used ironically. — **thank you** I thank you. [OE *thancian* < *thanc* thanks, thought]

thank·ful (thangk′fəl) *adj.* **1.** Appreciative of favors received; grateful. **2.** Expressing thanks. — **thank′ful·ly** *adv.* — **thank′ful·ness** *n.*

thank·less (thangk′lis) *adj.* **1.** Not feeling or showing gratitude; ungrateful. **2.** Not gaining or likely to gain thanks; unappreciated. — **thank′less·ly** *adv.* — **thank′less·ness** *n.*

thanks (thangks) *n.pl.* Expressions of gratitude; grateful acknowledgment. — *interj.* Thank you. — **thanks to 1.** Thanks be given to. **2.** Because of.

thanks·giv·ing (thangks′giv′ing) *n.* **1.** The act of giving thanks, as to God; an expression of gratitude. **2.** A public celebration in recognition of divine favor.

Thanksgiving Day 1. *U.S.* The fourth Thursday in November, set apart as an annual festival of thanksgiving. **2.** *Canadian* The second Monday in October, a statutory holiday. Also **Thanksgiving.**

that (that, *unstressed* thət) *pl. for adj. and pron. def. 1* **those** (thōz) *adj.* **1.** Pertaining to some person or thing previously mentioned, understood, or specifically designated. **2.** Denoting something more remote, or something contrasted with another thing: distinguished from *this:* This house is brown, *that* one is red. — *pron.* **1.** As a demonstrative, the person or thing implied, mentioned, or understood; the person or thing there or as distinguished from one already designated: *That* is the dress I like; Keep this and discard *that.* **2.** As a relative pronoun, who, whom, or which: the person *that* I saw. — *adv.* **1.** To that extent: I can't see *that* far. **2.** *Informal* In such a manner or degree; so: He's *that* simple, he can hardly read. — *conj.* **1.** As a fact: introducing a fact: I tell you *that* it is so. **2.** As a result: introducing a result, consequence, or effect: He bled so profusely *that* he died. **3.** At which time; when: It was only yesterday *that* I saw him. **4.** So that: I tell you *that* you may know. **5.** For the reason that; because. **6.** Introducing an exclamation: O *that* he would come: — **so that 1.** To the end that. **2.** With the result that. [OE *thæt,* neut. of *sē* the, that]

thatch (thach) *n.* **1.** A covering of reeds, straw, etc., arranged on a roof so as to shed water. **2.** Anything resembling such a covering. **3.** Any of various palms whose leaves are used for thatching. — *v.t.* To cover with or as with thatch. [OE *thæc* cover] — **thatch′er** *n.* — **thatch′y** *adj.*

thatch·ing (thach′ing) *n.* **1.** The act or process of covering a roof with thatch. **2.** Material used for thatch.

thaumato- *combining form* A wonder; a miracle. Also, before vowels, **thaumat-.** [< Gk. *thauma, -atos* wonder]

thau·ma·tur·gy (thô′mə·tûr′jē) *n.* Magic; the working of wonders or miracles. — **thau′ma·tur′gic** or **·gi·cal** *adj.*

thaw (thô) *v.i.* **1.** To melt or dissolve; become liquid or semiliquid, as snow or ice. **2.** To rise in temperature so as to melt ice and snow: said of weather and used impersonally. **3.** To become less cold and unsociable. — *v.t.* **4.** To cause to thaw. — *n.* **1.** The act of thawing, or the state of being thawed. **2.** Warmth of weather above the freezing point, following a colder period. **3.** A state of warmer feeling or expression. [OE *thawian*] — **thaw′er** *n.*

the¹ (stressed thē; unstressed before a consonant thə; unstressed before a vowel thē or thi) *definite article* or *adj. The* is opposed to the indefinite article *a* or *an,* and is used, esp. before nouns, to render the modified word more particular or individual. It is used specifically: **1.** When reference is made to a particular person, thing, or group: He left *the* room. **2.** To give an adjective substantive force, or render a notion abstract: *the* doing of the deed; *the* quick and *the* dead. **3.** Before a noun to make it generic: *The* dog is a friend of man. **4.** With the force of a possessive pronoun: He kicked me in *the* (my) leg. **5.** To give distributive force: equivalent to *a,* per, each, etc.: a dollar *the* volume. **6.** To designate a particular one as emphatically outstanding: usu. stressed in speech and italicized in writing: He is *the* officer for the command. [OE, later form of *sē*]

the² (thə) *adv.* By that much; by so much; to this extent: used to modify words in the comparative degree: *the* more, *the* merrier. [OE *thȳ,* instrumental case of *sē* the¹]

the- Var. of THEO-.

the·a·ter (thē′ə·tər) *n.* **1.** A building especially adapted to present dramas, operas, motion pictures, etc.; playhouse. **2.** The theatrical world and everything relating to it. **3.** A room or hall arranged with seats that rise as they recede from a platform, esp. adapted to lectures, demonstrations, etc. **4.** Any place of semicircular form with seats rising by easy gradations. **5.** Any place or region that is the scene of events: a *theater* of operations in war. Also *esp. Brit.* **the′a·tre.** [< OF < L < Gk. < *theasthai* to behold]

the·a·ter·go·er (thē′ə·tər·gō′ər) *n.* One who goes often or regularly to the theater. Also *esp. Brit.* **the′a·tre·go′er.**

the·a·ter-in-the-round (thē′ə·tər·in·thə·round′) *n.* Arena theater.

the·at·ri·cal (thē·at′ri·kəl) *adj.* **1.** Pertaining to the theater or to dramatic performances. **2.** Designed for show, display, or effect; showy; artificial. **3.** Suited to dramatic presentation. **4.** Resembling the manner of actors; histrionic. Also **the·at′ric.** — *n.pl.* Dramatic performances, esp. by amateurs. — **the·at′ri·cal·ly** *adv.* — **the·at′ri·cal·ness** *n.*

the·at·ri·cal·ism (thē-at′ri-kəl-iz′əm) *n.* Theatrical or melodramatic manner or style.

the·at·rics (thē-at′riks) *n.pl. (construed as sing.)* **1.** The staging of plays. **2.** The art of creating effects appropriate to dramatic performances.

Thebes (thēbz) **1.** The ancient capital of Upper Egypt; Luxor and Karnak occupy part of its site on the Nile. **2.** The chief city of ancient Boeotia, Greece: also **The·bae** (thē′bē). — **The·ban** (thē′bən) *adj. & n.*

the·ca (thē′kə) *n. pl.* **·cae** (-sē) **1.** *Biol.* A protective sheath or case for an organ or part, as of the spinal cord, a follicle, an insect pupa, etc. **2.** *Bot.* A spore case, sac, or capsule. [< L < Gk. *thēkē* case] — **the′ca** *adj.* — **the·cate** (thē′kit, -kāt)

thee (thē) *pron.* **1.** *Archaic* The objective case of the pronoun *thou.* **2.** Thou: used by some Quakers with a verb in the third person singular: *Thee knows my mind.* [OE *thē*, orig. dative, later accusative case of *thū* thou]

theft (theft) *n.* **1.** The act or crime of thieving; larceny. **2.** *Rare* That which is stolen. [OE *thēoft, thīefth*]

— **Syn. 1.** *Theft* is the general term for the crime of stealing. In law, *larceny* includes many forms of stealing, but not embezzlement and swindling. *Burglary* is the crime of breaking into and entering another's home, place of business, or other property with intent to commit a felony. *Robbery* is stealing from the person, or in the presence of, the victim.

thegn (thān) See THANE.

the·ine (thē′ēn, -in) *n. Chem.* The alkaloid found in the tea plant, chemically identical with caffeine. Also **the′in** (-in). [< F < NL *thea* tea < dial. Chinese *t′e*]

their (thâr) *pronominal adj.* The possessive case of the pronoun *they,* used attributively: *their* homes. [ME < ON *theirra* of them]

theirs (thârz) *pron.* **1.** The possessive case of the pronoun *they,* used predicatively: That house is *theirs.* **2.** The one or ones belonging or relating to them: our country and *theirs.* — **of theirs** Belonging or pertaining to them.

the·ism (thē′iz-əm) *n.* **1.** Belief in, or in the existence of, God, a god, or gods. **2.** Belief in a personal God as creator and supreme ruler of the universe, who transcends his creation but works in and through it in revealing himself to men. **3.** Belief in one god; monotheism. [< Gk. *theos* god] — **the′ist** *n.* — **the·is′tic** or **·ti·cal** *adj.* — **the·is′ti·cal·ly** *adv.*

them (them, *unstressed* thəm) *pron.* The objective case of the pronoun *they.* [ME *theim* < ON, to them]

the·mat·ic (thē-mat′ik) *adj.* **1.** Of, constituting, or pertaining to a theme or themes. **2.** *Ling.* Constituting a stem. Also **the·mat′i·cal.** — **the·mat′i·cal·ly** *adv.*

thematic vowel *Ling.* A vowel added to a root to form a stem.

theme (thēm) *n.* **1.** A topic to be discussed or developed in speech or writing; a subject of discourse. **2.** Any topic. **3.** A brief composition, esp. one written as an exercise as part of a course of instruction. **4.** *Music* **a** A melody that is subjected to variation or elaboration; subject. **b** A musical feature, as a chordal sequence, rhythm, melody, etc. that forms the basis of a composition. [< OF < L < Gk. *the-,* stem of *tithenai* to place]

theme song 1. A melody used throughout a dramatic presentation to establish or maintain a mood. **2.** A strain of music that identifies a radio program, a dance band, etc.

them·selves (them′selvz′, *unstressed* thəm-) *pron.* A form of the third person plural pronoun, used: **1.** As a reflexive or as object of a preposition in a reflexive sense: They laughed at *themselves.* **2.** As an emphatic or intensive form of *they:* They *themselves* are at fault. **3.** As a designation of a normal, proper, or usual state: They were not *themselves* then.

then (then) *adv.* **1.** At that time. **2.** Soon or immediately afterward; next in space or time. **3.** At another time: often introducing a sequential statement following *now, at first,* etc. **4.** For that reason; as a consequence. **5.** In that case. — *adj.* Being or acting in, or belonging to, that time: the *then* secretary of state. — *n.* A specific time already mentioned or understood; that time. [OE *thanne*]

thence (thens) *adv.* **1.** From that place. **2.** From the circumstance, fact, or cause; therefore. **3.** From that time; after that time. [ME < OE *thanon* from there + -s³]

thence·forth (thens′fôrth′, -fōrth′, thens′fôrth′, -fōrth′) *adv.* From that time on; thereafter.

thence·for·ward (thens′fôr′wərd) *adv.* **1.** Thenceforth. **2.** From that place or time forward. Also **thence′for′wards.**

theo- *combining form* God; of or pertaining to God, a god, or gods. Also, before vowels, **the-.** [< Gk. *theos* a god]

the·oc·ra·cy (thē-ok′rə-sē) *n. pl.* **·cies 1.** A state, polity, or group of people that claims a deity as its ruler. **2.** Government of a state by a priesthood claiming divine authority, as in the Papacy. [< Gk. < *theos* god + *krateein* to rule] — **the·o·crat·ic** (thē′ə-krat′ik) or **·i·cal** *adj.*

the·o·crat (thē′ə-krat) *n.* **1.** A theocratic or divine ruler. **2.** An advocate of theocracy.

the·od·o·lite (thē-od′ə-līt) *n.* In surveying, an instrument for measuring horizontal and vertical angles by means of a small telescope turning on a horizontal and a vertical axis. [An arbitrary formation] — **the·od′o·lit′ic** (-lit′ik) *adj.*

the·o·lo·gi·an (thē′ə-lō′jē·ən, -jən) *n.* One versed in theology, esp. that of the Christian church.

the·o·log·i·cal (thē′ə-loj′i·kəl) *adj.* Of or pertaining to theology or to divine revelation. Also **the′o·log′ic.** — **the′o·log′i·cal·ly** *adv.*

the·o·lo·gize (thē-ol′ə-jīz) *v.* **·gized, ·giz·ing** *v.t.* **1.** To devise or fit (something) into a system of theology. — *v.i.* **2.** To reason theologically. Also *Brit.* **the·ol′o·gise.**

the·ol·o·gy (thē-ol′ə-jē) *n. pl.* **·gies 1.** The study of religion, culminating in a synthesis or philosophy of religion; also, a critical survey of religion, esp. of the Christian religion. **2.** A body of doctrines as set forth by a particular church or religious group. [< OF < LL < Gk. < *theos* god + *logos* discourse]

the·oph·a·ny (thē-of′ə-nē) *n. pl.* **·nies** A manifestation or appearance of a deity or of the gods to man. [< L < Gk. < *theos* god + *phainein* to show]

the·o·rem (thē′ər-əm, thir′əm) *n.* **1.** A proposition demonstrably true or acknowledged as such. **2.** *Math.* **a** A proposition setting forth something to be proved. **b** A proposition that has been proved or assumed to be true. **c** A rule or statement of relations formulated in symbols. [LL < Gk. *theōrēma* sight, theory < *theōreein* to look at] — **the·o·re·mat·ic** (thē′ər-ə-mat′ik), **the′o·rem′ic** (-ə-rem′ik) *adj.*

the·o·ret·i·cal (thē′ə-ret′i·kəl) *adj.* **1.** Of, relating to, or consisting of theory. **2.** Relating to knowledge or science without reference to its application. **3.** Existing only in theory; hypothetical. **4.** Addicted to theorizing; impractical; visionary. Also **the′o·ret′ic.** — **the′o·ret′i·cal·ly** *adv.*

the·o·re·ti·cian (thē′ər-ə-tish′ən) *n.* One who deals with the speculative, hypothetical, or ideal rather than with the practical and executive aspects of a subject.

the·o·ret·ics (thē′ə-ret′iks) *n.pl. (construed as sing.)* The theoretical aspect of a science.

the·o·rist (thē′ər-ist) *n.* One who theorizes.

the·o·rize (thē′ə-rīz) *v.i.* **·rized, ·riz·ing** To form or express theories; speculate. Also *Brit.* **the′o·rise.** — **the′o·ri·za′tion** *n.* — **the′o·riz′er** *n.*

the·o·ry (thē′ər-ē, thir′ē) *n. pl.* **·ries 1.** A plan or scheme existing in the mind only; a speculative or conjectural view of something. **2.** An integrated group of the fundamental principles underlying a science or its practical applications: the atomic *theory.* **3.** Abstract knowledge of any art as opposed to the practice of it. **4.** A closely reasoned set of propositions, derived from and supported by established evidence and intended to serve as an explanation for a group of phenomena: the quantum *theory.* — **Syn.** See DOCTRINE, HYPOTHESIS. [< LL < Gk. *theoria* view, speculation]

the·os·o·phy (thē-os′ə-fē) *n. pl.* **·phies 1.** Any of various religious systems that aim at establishing a direct relation between the individual soul and the divine principle through contemplation and speculation. **2.** *Often cap.* The doctrines of a modern religious sect (**Theosophical Society**), resembling those of Buddhism and Brahmanism. [< Med.L Gk. < *theos* god + *sophos* wise] — **the′o·soph·ic** (thē′ə-sof′ik) or **·i·cal** *adj.* — **the′o·soph′i·cal·ly** *adv.* — **the·os′o·phist** *n.*

ther·a·peu·tic (ther′ə-pyōō′tik) *adj.* **1.** Having healing qualities; curative. **2.** Pertaining to therapeutics. Also **ther′a·peu′ti·cal.** [< NL < Gk. < *therapeuein* take care of < *therapōn* an attendant] — **ther′a·peu′ti·cal·ly** *adv.*

ther·a·peu·tics (ther′ə-pyōō′tiks) *n.pl. (construed as sing.)* The branch of medical science dealing with the treatment of disease. — **ther′a·peu′tist** *n.*

ther·a·py (ther′ə-pē) *n. pl.* **·pies 1.** The treatment of disease: often used in combination: *chemotherapy.* **2.** Treatment, activity, etc., intended to remedy or alleviate a disorder or undesirable condition. **3.** Healing or curative quality. — **ther′a·pist** *n.*

there (thâr) *adv.* **1.** In, at, or about that place: opposed to *here.* Also used to indicate or emphasize: John *there* is a good student. **2.** To, toward, or into that place; thither. **3.** At that stage or point of action or time. — *n.* That place: Are you from *there,* too? — *interj.* An exclamation of triumph, relief, etc.: *There!* It's finished. ◆ The adverb *there* cannot, in standard English, appear in the adjective position, as that *there* girl. That girl *there* is the accepted order. *There* is very often used as an expletive introducing a clause or sentence, the subject usu. following the verb: *There* once were three bears. It is also used as an equivalent of the pronoun *that* in expressions of encouragement, approval, etc.: *There*'s a good boy. [OE *þær*]

there·a·bout (thâr′ə·bout′) *adv.* Near that number, quantity, degree, place, or time. Also **there′a·bouts′.**

there·af·ter (thâr′af′tər, -äf′-) *adv.* Afterward; from that time on.

there·at (thâr′at′) *adv.* At that event, place, or time; at that incentive; upon that.

there·by (thâr′bī′) *adv.* **1.** Through the agency of that. **2.** Connected with that. **3.** Conformably to that. **4.** *Archaic* Nearby; thereabout.

there·for (thâr′fôr′) *adv.* For this, that, or it.

there·fore (thâr′fôr′, -fōr′) *adv. & conj.* For that or this reason; on that ground or account; consequently: He did not run fast enough; *therefore* he lost the race.

there·from (thâr′frum′, -from′) *adv.* From this, that, or it; from this or that time, place, state, event, or thing.

there·in (thâr′in′) *adv.* **1.** In that place. **2.** In that time, matter, or respect.

there·in·af·ter (thâr′in·af′tər, -äf′-) *adv.* In a subsequent part of that (book, document, speech, etc.).

there·in·to (thâr′in·tōō′) *adv.* Into this, that, or it.

there·of (thâr′uv′, -ov′) *adv.* **1.** Of or relating to this, that, or it. **2.** From or because of this or that cause or particular.

there·on (thâr′on′, -ôn′) *adv.* **1.** On this, that, or it. **2.** Thereupon; thereat.

there's (thârz) There is.

there·to (thâr′tōō′) *adv.* **1.** To this, that, or it. **2.** In addition; furthermore. Also **there′un·to′** (-un·tōō′).

there·to·fore (thâr′tə·fôr′, -fōr′) *adv.* Before this or that; previously to that.

there·un·der (thâr′un′dər) *adv.* **1.** Under this or that. **2.** Less in number; fewer than that. **3.** In accordance with that; by that authority.

there·up·on (thâr′ə·pon′, -ə·pôn′) *adv.* **1.** Upon that; upon it. **2.** Following upon or in consequence of that. **3.** Immediately following; at once.

there·with (thâr′with′, -with′) *adv.* **1.** With this, that, or it. **2.** Thereupon; thereafter; immediately afterward.

there·with·al (thâr′with·ôl′) *adv.* With all this or that; besides.

therm- Var. of THERMO-.

therm. Thermometer.

ther·mal (thûr′məl) *adj.* **1.** Pertaining to, determined by, or measured by heat. **2.** Caused by, using, or producing heat. **3.** Hot or warm. Also **ther′mic.** — **ther′mal·ly** *adv.*

thermo- *combining form* Heat; of or caused by heat. Also, before vowels, **therm-.** [< Gk. *thermos* heat, warmth]

ther·mo·cou·ple (thûr′mə·kup′əl) *n.* A device for temperature measurement that depends upon the electric current or potential produced when joined conductors of two different metals have their ends at different temperatures. Also **thermoelectric couple.**

ther·mo·dy·nam·ics (thûr′mō·dī·nam′iks, -di-) *n.pl.* (*construed as sing.*) The branch of physics dealing with the relations between heat and other forms of energy. — **ther′mo·dy·nam′ic** or **·i·cal** *adj.* — **ther′mo·dy·nam′i·cist** (-ə·sist) *n.*

ther·mo·e·lec·tric (thûr′mō·i·lek′trik) *adj.* **1.** Designating or associated with changes of electrical potential between two dissimilar metals in contact with each other as temperature varies. **2.** Designating or associated with the ability of an electric current to cause a flow of heat in a wire. Also **ther′·mo·e·lec′tri·cal.** — **ther′mo·e·lec′tri·cal·ly** *adv.*

ther·mo·e·lec·tric·i·ty (thûr′mō·i·lek′tris′ə·tē) *n.* Electricity generated by thermoelectric phenomena.

ther·mom·e·ter (thər·mom′ə·tər) *n.* An instrument for measuring temperature, usu. by means of a graduated glass capillary tube with a bulb containing a liquid, as mercury or alcohol, that expands or contracts as the temperature rises or falls. [< THERMO- + METER]

ther·mom·e·try (thər·mom′ə·trē) *n.* **1.** The measurement of temperature. **2.** The design and construction of thermometers. — **ther·mo·met·ric** (thûr′mō·met′rik) or **·ri·cal** *adj.* — **ther′mo·met′ri·cal·ly** *adv.*

ther·mo·nu·cle·ar (thûr′mō·nōō′klē·ər, -nyōō′-) *adj. Physics* Pertaining to or characterized by reactions involving the fusion of atomic nuclei at very high temperatures, esp. in stars and in the hydrogen bomb.

ther·mo·pile (thûr′mō·pīl) *n.* A group of thermocouples acting jointly to produce an electric current, esp. when used with a galvanometer to measure heat.

ther·mo·plas·tic (thûr′mō·plas′tik) *adj.* Plastic in the presence of or under the application of heat, as certain synthetic molding materials. — *n.* A thermoplastic substance.

Ther·mop·y·lae (thər·mop′ə·lē) A narrow mountain pass in Greece; scene of a battle, 480 B.C., in which the Spartans under the command of Leonidas held off the Persians under Xerxes and finally died to the last man rather than yield.

ther·mos bottle (thûr′məs) A bottle that keeps the contents hot or cold, consisting of two containers with a vacuum between, the whole usu. enclosed in a metal cylinder. [< Gk. *thermos* hot]

ther·mo·set·ting (thûr′mō·set′ing) *adj.* Having the property of assuming a fixed shape after being molded under heat, as certain plastics and urea resins.

ther·mo·stat (thûr′mə·stat) *n.* A device for the automatic regulation of temperature, used for actuating fire alarms, starting or stopping heating plants, etc. [< THERMO- + Gk. *statos* standing] — **ther′mo·stat′ic** *adj.* — **ther′mo·stat′i·cal·ly** *adv.*

ther·mot·ro·pism (thər·mot′rə·piz′əm) *n. Biol.* The property whereby growing plants or other organisms turn toward or away from a source of heat. — **ther·mo·trop·ic** (thûr′mō·trop′ik) *adj.*

the·sau·rus (thə·sôr′əs) *n. pl.* **·sau·ri** (-sôr′ī) **1.** A book containing a store of words, esp., of synonyms and antonyms arranged in categories. **2.** A storehouse; treasury. [< L < Gk. *thesauros* treasure house]

these (thēz) *adj. & pron.* Plural of THIS.

The·seus (thē′sōōs, -sē·əs) In Greek mythology, the king of Athens, celebrated for killing the Minotaur and for unifying Attica with Athens as its capital. See ARIADNE, PHAEDRA.

the·sis (thē′sis) *n. pl.* **·ses** (-sēz) **1.** A proposition. **2.** A formal proposition, advanced and defended by argumentation. **3.** A formal treatise on a particular subject; esp., a dissertation presented by a candidate for an academic degree. **4.** *Logic* An affirmative proposition; a premise or postulate. [< L < Gk. < *tithenai* to put, place]

Thes·pi·an (thes′pē·ən) *adj.* Of or relating to drama; dramatic; tragic. — *n.* An actor or actress. [after *Thespis*, Greek poet and actor, 6th century B.C.]

Thes·sa·lo·ni·an (thes′ə·lō′nē·ən) *n.* **1.** A native or inhabitant of ancient Thessalonica. **2.** *pl.* (*construed as sing.*) Either of two books in the New Testament consisting of epistles written by St. Paul to the Christians of Thessalonica. — *adj.* Of or pertaining to Thessalonica.

the·ta (thā′tə, thē′tə) *n.* **1.** The eighth letter in the Greek alphabet (Θ, ϑ, θ). See ALPHABET. **2.** *Math.* A symbol for an angle of unknown value. [< Gk. *thēta*]

thew (thyōō) *n.* **1.** A sinew or muscle, esp., when strong or well-developed. **2.** *pl.* Bodily strength. [ME < OE *thēaw* habit, characteristic quality] — **thew′y** *adj.*

they (thā) *pron. pl., possessive* **their** or **theirs**, *objective* **them** **1.** The nominative plural of *he, she,* and *it,* used of the persons, beings, or things previously mentioned or understood. **2.** People in general: *They* say this is his best book. [ME *thei, thai* < ON *their,* pl. of *sā* this, that]

they'd (thād) **1.** They had. **2.** They would.

they'll (thāl) They will.

they're (thâr) They are.

they've (thāv) They have.

thi- Var. of THIO-.

thi·a·mine (thī′ə·mēn, -min) *n. Biochem.* A white crystalline compound, $C_{12}H_{18}ON_4SCl_2$, vitamin B_1, found in various natural sources and also made synthetically. Also **thi′a·min** (-min). [< THI- + -AMINE]

Thi·bet·an (ti·bet′ən) See TIBETAN.

thick (thik) *adj.* **1.** Having relatively large depth or extent from one surface to its opposite; not thin. **2.** Having a specified dimension of this kind, whether great or small: an inch *thick.* **3.** Arranged compactly; close: a *thick* forest; also, following at brief intervals; frequent, as blows, raindrops, etc. **4.** Set or furnished closely or abundantly with objects; abounding. **5.** Having considerable density or consistency; dense; heavy. **6.** Having the component particles closely packed together, as smoke, fog, etc. **7.** Dull; stupid. **8.** Indistinct; muffled: a *thick* sound; also, guttural; husky. **9.** *Informal* Very friendly; intimate. **10.** *Brit. Informal* Excessive; beyond what is tolerable. — *adv.* So as to be thick; thickly: bread sliced *thick.* — **to lay it on thick** *Informal* **1.** To overstate; exaggerate. **2.** To flatter excessively. — *n.* **1.** The dimension of thickness; the thickest part. **2.** The thickest or most intense time or place of anything: the *thick* of the fight. — **through thick and thin** Through good times and bad; loyally. [OE *thicce*] — **thick′ish** *adj.* — **thick′ly** *adv.* — **thick′ness** *n.*

thick·en (thik′ən) *v.t. & v.i.* **1.** To make or become thick or thicker. **2.** To make or become more intricate or intense: The plot *thickens.* — **thick′en·er** *n.*

thick·en·ing (thik′ən·ing) *n.* **1.** The act of making or becoming thick. **2.** Something added to a liquid to increase its consistency. **3.** A thickened place or part.

thick·et (thik′it) *n.* A thick, dense growth, as of underbrush; a coppice. [OE < *thicce* thick]

thick·head (thik′hed′) *n.* A stupid person; numskull. — **thick′head′ed** *adj.* ...

thick·set (thik′set′) *adj.* **1.** Having a short, thick body; stout. **2.** Planted closely together. — *n.* A thicket.

thick·skinned (thik′skind′) *adj.* **1.** Having a thick skin; pachydermatous. **2.** Insensitive; callous to hints or insults.

chick·wit·ted (thik'wit'id) *adj.* Stupid; obtuse; dense.

thief (thēf) *n.* *pl.* **thieves** (thēvz) One who takes something belonging to another; one who steals. [OE *thēof*]

thieve (thēv) *v.* **thieved, thiev·ing** *v.t.* **1.** To take by theft; steal. — *v.i.* **2.** To be a thief; commit theft. [OE *thēofian*] — **thiev'ish** *adj.* — **thiev'ish·ly** *adv.* — **thiev'ish·ness** *n.*

thiev·er·y (thē'vər·ē) *n.* *pl.* **·er·ies** The practice or act of thieving; theft.

thigh (thī) *n.* The leg between the hip and the knee of man or the corresponding portion in other animals. ◆ Collateral adjective: *femoral.* [OE *thēoh*]

thigh·bone (thī'bōn') *n.* The femur.

thill (thil) *n.* Either of the shafts of a vehicle, between which a horse is harnessed. [OE *thille* board]

thim·ble (thim'bəl) *n.* **1.** A caplike cover with a pitted surface, worn in sewing to protect the end of the finger that pushes the needle. **2.** *Mech.* A sleeve through which a bolt passes. **3.** *Naut.* **a** A metal antichafing ring forming a guard over a loop or eye in a sail. **b** The metal piece about which a rope is bent and spliced. [OE < *thūma* thumb]

thim·ble·ful (thim'bəl·fŏŏl) *n.* **1.** As much as a thimble will hold. **2.** Any very small quantity.

thim·ble·rig (thim'bəl·rig') *n.* A swindling trick in which a pea is shifted from one to another of three inverted cups. — *v.t.* **·rigged, ·rig·ging** To cheat by or as by thimblerig. — **thim'ble·rig'ger** *n.*

thin (thin) *adj.* **thin·ner, thin·nest** **1.** Having opposite surfaces relatively close to each other; being of little depth or width; not thick. **2.** Lacking roundness or plumpness of figure; slender. **3.** Having the parts or particles scattered or diffused; sparse: *thin* ranks, *thin* gas. **4.** Small in number: The audience was *thin.* **5.** Having little substance: *thin* clothing. **6.** Having little or no consistency, as a liquid. **7.** Lacking in essential ingredients: *thin* blood. **8.** Having little volume or richness, as a voice. **9.** Not abundantly supplied; scant: a *thin* table. **10.** Having little intensity; pale: *thin* colors. **11.** *Photog.* Not having sufficient contrast to print well: said of a negative. **12.** Feeble; superficial: *thin* wit. — *adv.* So as to be thin; thinly: butter spread *thin.* — *v.t.* & *v.i.* **thinned, thin·ning** To make or become thin or thinner. [OE *thynne*] — **thin'ly** *adv.* — **thin'ner** *n.* — **thin'ness** *n.*

thine (thīn) *pron.* *Archaic* **1.** The possessive case of the pronoun *thou:* used predicatively. **2.** The one or ones belonging or relating to thee: thou and *thine.* — *pronominal adj.* Thy: used before a vowel or *h: thine* eyes. [OE *thīn,* genitive of *thū* thou]

thing (thing) *n.* **1.** That which exists as a separate entity; an inanimate object. **2.** That which is designated, as contrasted with the word or symbol used to denote it. **3.** A matter or circumstance; an affair; concern: *Things* have changed. **4.** An act or deed; transaction. **5.** A statement; utterance: to say the right *thing.* **6.** An idea; opinion: Stop putting *things* in her head. **7.** A quality; attribute; characteristic. **8.** An organic being: usu. with a qualifying word: Every living *thing* dies. **9.** An object that is not or cannot be described or particularized: The *thing* disappeared in the shadows. **10.** A person, regarded in terms of pity, affection, or contempt: that poor *thing.* **11.** *pl.* Possessions. **12.** The proper or befitting act or result: with *the:* That was not the *thing* to do. **13.** The important point: with *the:* The *thing* we learned from the war was this. — **to see things** To have hallucinations. [OE, thing, cause, assembly]

thing·a·ma·bob (thing'ə·mə·bob') *n.* *Informal* A thing the specific name of which is unknown or forgotten; a dingus. Also **thing'um·a·bob', thing'um·bob, thing'a·ma·jig.**

think[1] (thingk) *v.* **thought** (thôt), **think·ing** *v.t.* **1.** To produce or form in the mind; conceive mentally. **2.** To examine in the mind; determine by reasoning: to *think* a plan through. **3.** To believe; consider: I *think* him guilty. **4.** To expect; anticipate: They did not *think* to meet us. **5.** To remember; recollect: I cannot *think* what he said. **6.** To bring about by thinking: to *think* oneself sick. **7.** To intend: Do they *think* to rob me? — *v.i.* **8.** To use the mind in exercising judgment, forming ideas, etc.; reason. **9.** To have a particular opinion or feeling: I don't *think* so. — **to think better of 1.** To abandon or change a course of action. **2.** To form a better opinion of. — **to think fit (proper, right,** etc.) To regard as worth doing. — **to think nothing of 1.** To consider of no importance; ignore. **2.** To consider easy to do. — **to think of 1.** To bring to mind; remember. **2.** To invent; imagine. **3.** To have a specified opinion or attitude toward; regard. **4.** To be considerate of; have regard for. — **to think out** To devise, invent, or solve by thinking. — **to think over** To reflect upon. — **to think the world of 1.** To have a high opinion of. **2.** To love very much. — **to think twice** To consider carefully. — **to think up** To devise, arrive at, or invent by thinking. — *n.* An act of think-

ing; a thought. [OE *thencan*] — **think'a·ble** *adj.* — **think'er** *n.*

think[2] (thingk) *v.i.* **thought** (thôt), **think·ing** To seem; appear: now obsolete except in the combinations *methinks, methought.* [OE *thyncan* to seem]

think·ing (thingk'ing) *adj.* **1.** Exercising the mental capacities. **2.** Capable of such exercise; rational. — *n.* **1.** Mental action; thought. **2.** The product of such action, as an idea. — **think'ing·ly** *adv.*

thin-skinned (thin'skind') *adj.* **1.** Having a thin skin. **2.** Easily hurt or offended; sensitive.

thio- *combining form Chem.* Containing sulfur; denoting a compound of sulfur, esp., one in which sulfur has displaced oxygen. Also, before vowels, sometimes *thi-.* [< Gk. *theion* sulfur]

thi·o·pen·tal sodium (thī'ō·pen'tal) A yellowish white powder, $C_{11}H_{17}N_2O_2SNa$, of the barbiturate group, used intravenously as a general anesthetic: also called *sodium pentothal.* Also *Chiefly Brit.* **thi'o·pen'tone sodium.**

thi·o·sul·fate (thī'ō·sul'fāt) *n. Chem.* A salt of thiosulfuric acid.

thi·o·sul·fu·ric acid (thī'ō·sul·fyŏŏr'ik) *Chem.* An unstable acid, $H_2S_2O_3$, known chiefly by its salts, which have extensive applications in bleaching and photography.

third (thûrd) *adj.* **1.** Next after the second: the ordinal of *three.* **2.** Being one of three equal parts. **3.** Pertaining to the forward gears with the third highest ratio in an automobile transmission. — *n.* **1.** That which follows the second. **2.** One of three equal parts. **3.** A unit of time or of an arc, equal to one sixtieth of a second. **4.** *Music* **a** The interval between a tone and another tone two steps from it in a diatonic scale. **b** A tone separated by this interval from any other, considered in relation to that other; esp., the third above the keynote. **5.** In baseball, the third base. **6.** *Mech.* The forward gears with the third highest ratio in an automobile transmission. — *adv.* In the third order, rank, or place: also, in formal discourse, **third'ly.** [OE *thridda < thrī* three]

third base In baseball, the third base reached by the runner, at the left-hand angle of the infield.

third base·man (bās'mən) *n.* *pl.* **·men** (-mən) A baseball player stationed at or near third base.

third class 1. In the U.S. postal system, a classification of mail that includes all miscellaneous printed matter but not newspapers and periodicals legally entered as second class. **2.** A classification of accommodations on some ships and trains, usu. the cheapest and least luxurious available. — **third-class** (thûrd'klas', -kläs) *adj.* & *adv.*

third degree 1. *Informal* Severe or brutal examination of a prisoner by the police for the purpose of securing information. **2.** The third stage, order, step, etc., of something.

third estate The third political class of a kingdom, following the nobility and the clergy.

third rail A rail that supplies current to the trains of an electric railway. — **third-rail** (thûrd'rāl') *adj.*

third-rate (thûrd'rāt') *adj.* **1.** Of the third rate or class. **2.** Of poor quality; very inferior.

thirst (thûrst) *n.* **1.** An uncomfortable feeling of dryness in the throat and mouth, accompanied by an increasingly urgent desire for liquids. **2.** The physiological condition that produces this feeling. **3.** Any longing or craving. — *v.i.* **1.** To be thirsty. **2.** To have an eager desire or craving. [OE *thurst, thyrstan*] — **thirst'er** *n.*

thirst·y (thûrs'tē) *adj.* **thirst·i·er, thirst·i·est** **1.** Affected with thirst. **2.** Lacking moisture; arid; parched. **3.** Eagerly desirous. **4.** *Informal* Causing thirst. [OE *thurstig*] — **thirst'i·ly** *adv.* — **thirst'i·ness** *n.*

thir·teen (thûr'tēn') *n.* **1.** The sum of twelve and one: a cardinal number. **2.** Any symbol of this number, as 13, xiii, XIII. **3.** Anything consisting of or representing thirteen units. — *adj.* Being one more than twelve. [OE *thrēotīne*] — **thir'teenth'** *adj.* & *n.*

thir·ty (thûr'tē) *n.* *pl.* **·ties 1.** The sum of twenty and ten: a cardinal number. **2.** Any symbol of this number, as 30, xxx, XXX. **3.** Anything consisting of or representing thirty units. — *adj.* Being ten more than twenty. [OE *thrītig*] — **thir'ti·eth** *adj.* & *n.*

thir·ty-sec·ond (thûr'tē·sek'ənd) *adj.* **1.** Being the second after the thirtieth. **2.** Being one of thirty-two equal parts. — *n.* A thirty-second note.

thirty-second note *Music* A note having a time value, equal to one thirty-second of a whole note: also, *Chiefly Brit.,* demisemiquaver.

thir·ty-two·mo (thûr'tē·tōō'mō) *n.* *pl.* **·mos 1.** The page size (3⅜ x 4¾ inches) of a book made up of printer's sheets folded into thirty-two leaves. **2.** A book consisting of pages of this size. Also written **32mo** — *adj.* Consisting of pages of this size.

Thirty Years' War See table for WAR.

---

this (t̶his) *pl. for adj. and pron. def. 2* **these** (t̶hēz) *adj.* **1.** That is near or present, either actually or in thought: *This* house is for sale; I shall be there *this* evening. **2.** That is understood or has just been mentioned: *This* offense justified my revenge. **3.** Denoting something nearer than or contrasted with something else: distinguished from *that*: *This* tree is still alive, but that one is dead. **4.** These: used of a number or collection considered as a whole: He has been dead *this* ten years. — *pron.* **1.** The person or thing near or present, being understood or just mentioned: *This* is where I live. **2.** The person or thing nearer than or contrasted with something else: opposed to *that*: *This* is a better painting than that. **3.** The idea, statement, etc., about to be made clear: I will say *this*: he is a hard worker. — *adv.* To this degree: I was not expecting you *this* soon. [OE]

this·tle (this'əl) *n.* **1.** One of various prickly plants of the composite family, with cylindrical or globular heads of purple flowers; esp., the **bull thistle**, the national emblem of Scotland. **2.** Any of several other prickly plants. [OE *thistel*] — **this'tly** *adj.*

this·tle·down (this'əl-doun') *n.* The ripe silky fibers from the dry flower of a thistle.

thith·er (thith'ər, thith'-) *adv.* To or toward that place; in that direction. — *adj.* Situated or being on the other side; farther: the *thither* bank of the river. [OE *thider*]

thith·er·to (thith'ər-tōō', thith'-) *adv.* Up to that time.

thith·er·ward (thith'ər-wərd, thith'-) *adv.* In that direction; toward that place. Also **thith'er·wards.**

tho (thō) See THOUGH.

thole (thōl) *n. Naut.* A peg or pair of pegs serving as a fulcrum for an oar in rowing. Also **thole pin.** [OE *thol* pin]

Thom·as (tom'əs) One of the twelve apostles, known for his doubting disposition: called **Saint Thomas.** Also *Didymus.* *John* xx 25.

Tho·mism (tō'miz·əm, thō'-) *n.* The system of dogmatic theology of St. Thomas Aquinas and his followers that formed the basis of 13th-century scholasticism. — **Tho'mist** *adj. & n.* — **Tho·mis'tic** or **·ti·cal** *adj.*

Thomp·son submachine gun (tomp'sən) A type of .45 caliber submachine gun: a trade name: also called *Tommy gun.*

thong (thông, thong) *n.* **1.** A narrow strip of leather, as for tying or fastening. **2.** A whiplash. [OE *thwang*]

Thor (thôr, tôr) In Norse mythology, the god of war, thunder, and strength. — *n.* An intermediate range, liquid-fueled ballistic missile of the U.S. Air Force.

tho·rac·ic (thô·ras'ik, thō-) *adj.* Of, relating to, or situated in or near the thorax. [< F < NL < Gk. *thōrax* chest]

thoraco- *combining form Med. & Surg.* The thorax or the chest; of or related to the thorax. Also, before vowels, **thorac-.** [< Gk. *thōrax* chest]

tho·rax (thôr'aks, thō'raks) *n. pl.* **tho·rax·es** or **tho·ra·ces** (thôr'ə-sēz, thō'rə-) **1.** *Anat.* The part of the body between the neck and the abdomen, enclosed by the ribs and containing the lungs, heart, etc.; the chest. **2.** The corresponding part in other animals. **3.** *Entomol.* The middle region of the body of an insect. [< L < Gk. *thōrax*]

tho·ri·um (thôr'ē-əm, thō'rē-) *n.* A gray, radioactive, metallic element (symbol Th), found only in small quantities in certain rare minerals. See ELEMENT. [after *Thor*]

thorn (thôrn) *n.* **1.** A hard, leafless spine or sharp-pointed process from a branch. **2.** One of various other sharp processes, as the spine of a porcupine. **3.** Any of various thorn-bearing shrubs or trees; esp., a rosaceous plant, as the hawthorn. **4.** Anything or anyone that causes discomfort, pain, or annoyance. **5.** The name of the Old English rune þ; also, the corresponding Icelandic character. It was used originally to represent both voiceless and voiced *th*, as in *thin*, *then*, but finally only the voiceless sound. — *v.t.* To pierce or prick with a thorn. [OE] — **thorn'less** *adj.*

thorn apple 1. The jimsonweed. **2.** The fruit of the hawthorn; a haw.

thorn·y (thôr'nē) *adj.* **thorn·i·er, thorn·i·est 1.** Full of thorns; spiny. **2.** Sharp like a thorn. **3.** Presenting difficulties or trials; painful; vexatious. — **thorn'i·ness** *n.*

tho·ron (thôr'on, thō'ron) *n.* A gaseous, radioactive isotope of radon, produced during the disintegration of thorium. [< NL < THOR(IUM) + -ON]

thor·ough (thûr'ō) *adj.* **1.** Carried to completion; thoroughgoing: a *thorough* search; also, persevering, accurate, and painstaking: a very *thorough* worker. **2.** Marked by careful attention throughout; complete. **3.** Completely (such and such); through and through: a *thorough* nincompoop. **4.** Painstakingly conforming to a standard. **5.** *Rare* Going or passing through. — *adv. & prep. Obs.* Through. Also *Rare* **thor'o.** [Emphatic var. of THROUGH] — **thor'ough·ly** *adv.* — **thor'ough·ness** *n.*

thor·ough·bred (thûr'ō·bred', thûr'ə-) *n.* **1.** Pure and unmixed stock. **2.** *Informal* A person of culture and good breeding. — *adj.* **1.** Bred from pure stock. **2.** Possessing the traits of a thoroughbred; elegant; graceful.

thor·ough·fare (thûr'ō·fâr', thûr'ə-) *n.* A road or street through which the public has unobstructed passage; highway. [ME < OE *thurh* through + *faru* going]

thor·ough·go·ing (thûr'ō·gō'ing, thûr'ə-) *adj.* **1.** Characterized by extreme thoroughness or efficiency. **2.** Unmitigated: a *thoroughgoing* scoundrel.

those (t̶hōz) *adj. & pron.* Plural of THAT. [OE *thās*, pl. of *this*]

thou (t̶hou) *pron., possessive* **thy** or **thine**, *objective* **thee**; *pl. nominative* **you, ye**, *possessive* **your** or **yours**, *objective* **you, ye** *Archaic* The nominative singular pronoun of the second person: formerly a familiar form, it has been replaced by the more formal singular *you*, and is no longer used except in religious, elevated, or poetic language. [OE *thū*]

though (t̶hō) *conj.* **1.** Notwithstanding the fact that: introducing a clause expressing an actual fact. **2.** Conceding or granting that; even if. **3.** And yet; still; however: introducing a modifying clause or statement: I am well, *though* I do not feel very strong. **4.** Notwithstanding what has been done or said; nevertheless. ◆ As used in this sense, *though* is sometimes regarded as a conjunctive adverb. Also spelled *tho.* [Prob. fusion of OE *thēah* and ON *tho*]

thought[1] (thôt) *n.* **1.** The act or process of using the mind actively and deliberately; meditation; cogitation. **2.** The product of thinking; an idea, concept, judgment, etc. **3.** Intellectual activity of a specific kind: Greek *thought.* **4.** Consideration; attention. **5.** Intention or plan: All *thought* of returning was abandoned. **6.** Expectation: He had no *thought* of finding her there. — **Syn.** See IDEA. [OE *thōht*]

thought[2] (thôt) Past tense and past participle of THINK.

thought·ful (thôt'fəl) *adj.* **1.** Full of thought; meditative. **2.** Showing, characterized by, or promotive of thought: a *thoughtful* book. **3.** Attentive; careful; esp., considerate of others. — **thought'ful·ly** *adv.* — **thought'ful·ness** *n.*

thought·less (thôt'lis) *adj.* **1.** Manifesting lack of thought or care; heedless. **2.** Lacking capacity for thought; stupid. — **thought'less·ly** *adv.* — **thought'less·ness** *n.*

thou·sand (thou'zənd) *n.* The product of ten and a hundred; ten hundreds, written as 1,000 or M: a cardinal number. — *adj.* Being a thousand in number. [OE *thūsend*] — **thou·sandth** *adj. & n.*

thou·sand·fold (thou'zənd·fōld') *n.* An amount or number a thousand times as great as a given unit. — *adv.* So as to be a thousand times as many or as great. — *adj.* **1.** Consisting of one thousand parts. **2.** One thousand times as many or as great.

Thra·cian (thrā'shən) *adj.* Pertaining to Thrace or its people. — *n.* **1.** One of the people of Thrace. **2.** The Indo-European language of the ancient Thracians.

thrall (thrôl) *n.* **1.** A person in bondage; a slave; serf. **2.** The condition of bondage; thralldom. [OE *thrǣl* < ON]

thrall·dom (thrôl'dəm) *n.* **1.** The state of being a thrall. **2.** Any sort of bondage or servitude. Also **thral'dom.**

thrash (thrash) *v.t.* **1.** To beat as if with a flail; flog; whip. **2.** To defeat utterly. — *v.i.* **3.** To move or swing about with flailing, violent motions. — **to thrash out** To discuss fully and to a conclusion. — *n.* The act of thrashing. [Dial. var. of THRESH]

thrash·er[1] (thrash'ər) *n.* **1.** One who or that which thrashes or threshes. **2.** A thresher (def. 2), a shark.

thrash·er[2] (thrash'ər) *n.* Any of several long-tailed American songbirds resembling the thrushes and related to the mockingbirds. [< dial. E *thresher* < THRUSH[1]]

thrash·ing (thrash'ing) *n.* A sound beating or whipping.

thread (thred) *n.* **1.** A very slender cord composed of two or more filaments, as of flax, cotton, or silk, twisted together; also, such twisted fibers used in sewing. **2.** A filament of any ductile substance, as of metal, glass, etc. **3.** A fine stream or beam: a *thread* of light. **4.** A fine line of color. **5.** Anything conceived of as serving to give sequence to the whole, as the course of existence represented by the ancient Greeks as a thread spun and cut off by the three Fates. **6.** *Mech.* The spiral ridge of a screw. — *v.t.* **1.** To pass a thread through the eye of (a needle). **2.** To arrange or string on a thread, as beads. **3.** To cut a thread on or in, as a screw. **4.** To make one's way through or over: to *thread* a maze. **5.** To make (one's way) carefully. — *v.i.* **6.** To make one's way carefully. **7.** To drop from a spoon in a fine thread, as boiling syrup. [OE *thrǣd*] — **thread'er** *n.*

thread·bare (thred'bâr') *adj.* **1.** Worn so that the threads show, as a rug or garment. **2.** Clad in worn garments. **3.** Commonplace; hackneyed. — **thread'bare'ness** *n.*

thread·y (thred'ē) *adj.* **thread·i·er, thread·i·est 1.** Resembling a thread; stringy. **2.** Consisting of, containing, or covered with thread. **3.** *Med.* Weak and feeble: said of the pulse. **4.** Weak and thin like a thread: a *thready* voice.

threat (thret) *n.* **1.** A declaration of an intention to inflict injury or pain. **2.** An indication of impending danger or harm. **3.** A person or thing regarded as endangering the lives, peace of mind, etc., of others; menace. [OE *thrēat*]

threat·en (thret'n) *v.t.* **1.** To utter threats against. **2.** To be menacing or dangerous to. **3.** To be ominous or portentous of. **4.** To utter threats of (injury, vengeance, etc.). — *v.i.* **5.** To utter threats. **6.** To have a menacing aspect; lower: *The rising waters seemed to* threaten. [OE *thrēatnian* to urge, compel] — **threat'en·er** *n.* — **threat'en·ing·ly** *adv.*

three (thrē) *n.* **1.** The sum of two and one: a cardinal number. **2.** Any symbol of this number, as 3, iii, III. **3.** Anything consisting of or representing three units. — *adj.* Being one more than two; ternary. [OE *thrīe*]

three-base hit (thrē'bās') In baseball, a base hit that enables the batter to reach third base; a triple.

three-D (thrē'dē') *adj.* Three-dimensional. — *n.* A three-dimensional representation; esp., a motion picture that gives the illusion of depth. Often written **3-D.**

three·deck·er (thrē'dek'ər) *n.* **1.** A vessel having three decks or gun decks. **2.** Any structure having three levels. **3.** A sandwich made with three slices of bread.

three·fold (thrē'fōld') *n.* An amount or number three times as great as a given unit. — *adv.* So as to be three times as many or as great. — *adj.* **1.** Consisting of three parts. **2.** Three times as many or as great.

three-mile limit (thrē'mīl') A distance of three nautical miles from the shoreline seaward, allowed by international law for territorial jurisdiction.

three·pence (thrip'əns, threp'-, thrup'-) *n.* Brit. **1.** The sum of three pennies. **2.** A small coin of Great Britain, worth three pennies: also **threepenny bit.**

three·pen·ny (thrip'ə·ni, threp'-, thrup'-, thrē'pen'ē) *adj.* Brit. **1.** Worth or costing threepence. **2.** Of little value.

three-ply (thrē'plī') *adj.* Consisting of three thicknesses, strands, layers, etc.

three-point landing (thrē'point') **1.** *Aeron.* A perfect airplane landing. **2.** Any successful outcome.

three-ring circus (thrē'ring') **1.** A circus in which separate acts are carried on simultaneously in three ringlike enclosures. **2.** Any situation characterized by simultaneous activities, esp. of bewildering variety.

three·score (thrē'skôr', -skōr') *adj. & n.* Sixty.

three·some (thrē'səm) *adj.* **1.** Consisting of three. **2.** Performed by three. — *n.* **1.** A group of three persons. **2.** That which is played by three persons.

three-square (thrē'skwâr') *adj.* Having a triangular cross section, as some files.

threm·ma·tol·o·gy (threm'ə·tol'ə·jē) *n.* The science of breeding domestic animals and plants. [< Gk. *thremma, -matos* nursling + -LOGY]

thren·o·dy (thren'ə·dē) *n. pl.* **·dies** An ode or song of lamentation; a dirge. Also **thren'ode** (-ōd). [< Gk. < *thrēnos* lament + *ōidē* song] — **thre·no·di·al** (thri·nō'dē·əl), **thre·nod·ic** (thri·nod'ik) *adj.* — **thren'o·dist** *n.*

thresh (thresh) *v.t.* **1.** To beat stalks of (ripened grain) with a flail or machine so as to separate the grain from the straw or husks. — *v.i.* **2.** To thresh grain. **3.** To move or thrash about. — *n.* The act of threshing. [OE *therscan*]

thresh·er (thresh'ər) *n.* **1.** One who or that which threshes; esp., a machine for threshing. **2.** A large shark of warm seas, having the dorsal lobe of the tail extremely long: also **thresher shark.**

thresh·old (thresh'ōld, -hōld, -əld) *n.* **1.** The plank, timber, or stone lying under the door of a building. **2.** The entrance, entering point, or beginning of anything. **3.** *Physiol. & Psychol.* **a** The point at which a stimulus just produces a response. **b** The minimum degree of stimulation necessary for conscious perception: the *threshold* of consciousness. [OE *therscold*]

threw (thrōō) Past tense of THROW.

thrice (thrīs) *adv.* **1.** Three times. **2.** In a threefold manner. **3.** Extremely; very. [ME < OE *thriwa* + -s³]

thrift (thrift) *n.* **1.** Care and wisdom in the management of one's resources; frugality. **2.** Vigorous growth, as of a plant. **3.** Any of a genus of tufted herbs, growing on mountains and the seashore and having white or pink flowers. [< ON] — **thrift'less** *adj.*

thrift·y (thrif'tē) *adj.* **thrift·i·er, thrift·i·est** **1.** Displaying thrift or good management; economical; frugal. **2.** Prosperous; thriving. **3.** Growing vigorously. — **thrift'i·ly** *adv.* — **thrift'i·ness** *n.*

thrill (thril) *v.t.* **1.** To cause to feel a sudden wave of emotion; move to great or tingling excitement. **2.** To cause to vibrate or tremble. — *v.i.* **3.** To feel a sudden wave of emotion or excitement. **4.** To vibrate or tremble. — *n.* **1.** A tremor of feeling or excitement. **2.** A pulsation. [Var. of dial. *thirl*] — **thrill'ing** *adj.* — **thrill'ing·ly** *adv.*

thrill·er (thril'ər) *n.* **1.** One who or that which thrills. **2.** *Informal* A sensational book, play, or motion picture.

thrive (thrīv) *v.i.* **throve** (thrōv) or **thrived, thrived** or **thriv·en** (thriv'ən), **thriv·ing** **1.** To prosper; be successful. **2.** To grow with vigor; flourish. [< ON *thrīfask*, orig. reflexive of *thrīfa* to grasp] — **thriv'er** *n.* — **thriv'ing·ly** *adv.*

thro (thrōō) See THROUGH. Also **thro'.**

throat (thrōt) *n.* **1.** The passage leading from the back of the mouth to the stomach and lungs. **2.** The front of the neck, extending from below the chin to the collarbones. **3.** Any narrow passage resembling the throat, as the entrance to a chimney. — **to jump down one's throat** *Informal* To criticize or berate one severely. — **to ram (something) down one's throat** *Informal* To force one to accept or hear something against his will. — **to stick in one's throat** To be difficult to utter, as from unwillingness or fear. [OE *throte*]

throat·y (thrō'tē) *adj.* **throat·i·er, throat·i·est** Uttered in the throat; guttural. — **throat'i·ly** *adv.* — **throat'i·ness** *n.*

throb (throb) *v.i.* **throbbed, throb·bing** **1.** To beat rapidly or violently, as the heart from exertion or excitement. **2.** To pulsate. **3.** To feel or show great emotion. — *n.* **1.** The act or state of throbbing. **2.** A pulsation or beat, esp. one caused by excitement or emotion. [? Imit.] — **throb'ber** *n.* — **throb'bing·ly** *adv.*

throe (thrō) *n.* **1.** A violent pang or pain. **2.** *pl.* The pains of childbirth or of death. **3.** *pl.* Any agonizing or violent activity. [ME *throwe,* prob. fusion of OE *thrōwian* to suffer and *thrāwan* to twist, throw]

throm·bin (throm'bin) *n. Biochem.* The enzyme present in blood serum that reacts with fibrinogen to form fibrin in the process of clotting. [< THROMBUS]

throm·bo·cyte (throm'bə·sīt) *n.* A blood platelet. [< Gk. *thrombos* clot + -CYTE]

throm·bo·sis (throm·bō'sis) *n. pl.* **·ses** (-sēz) *Pathol.* Local coagulation of blood in the heart or blood vessels, forming an obstruction to circulation. — **throm·bot'ic** (-bot'ik) *adj.*

throm·bus (throm'bəs) *n. pl.* **·bi** (-bī) *Pathol.* The blood clot formed in thrombosis. [< NL < Gk. *thrombos* clot]

throne (thrōn) *n.* **1.** The royal chair occupied by a sovereign on state occasions. **2.** The chair of state of a pope or of some other dignitary, as a cardinal, bishop, etc. **3.** Royal estate or dignity; sovereign power. **4.** One who occupies a throne. — *v.t. & v.i.* **throned, thron·ing** To place or sit on a throne; exalt. [< OF < L < Gk. *thronos* seat]

throng (thrông, throng) *n.* **1.** A multitude of people crowded closely together. **2.** Any numerous collection. — *v.t.* **1.** To crowd into; jam. **2.** To press or crowd upon. — *v.i.* **3.** To collect or move in a throng. [OE *gethrang*] — **Syn.** (noun) 1. crowd, concourse, mob, host, horde, press.

thros·tle (thros'əl) *n.* The song thrush. [OE]

throt·tle (throt'l) *n. Mech.* **a** A valve controlling the supply of steam to a steam engine, or of vaporized fuel to the cylinders of an internal-combustion engine: also **throttle valve. b** The lever that operates the throttle: also **throttle lever.** — *v.t.* **·tled, ·tling** **1.** To press or constrict the throat of; strangle; choke. **2.** To silence, stop, or suppress by or as by choking. **3.** *Mech.* **a** To reduce or shut off the flow of steam or fuel (in a steam or internal-combustion engine). **b** To reduce the speed of by means of a throttle. — *v.i.* **4.** To choke. [Dim. of ME *throte*] — **throt'tler** *n.*

through (thrōō) *prep.* **1.** Into one side, end, or point, and out of the other. **2.** Covering, entering, or penetrating all parts of; throughout. **3.** From the first to the last of; during the time or period of. **4.** In the midst of; among. **5.** By way of: *He departed* through *the door.* **6.** By means of; by the instrumentality or aid of. **7.** Having reached the end of, esp. with success: *He got* through *his examinations easily.* **8.** On account of; because or as a result of. — *adv.* **1.** From one end, side, surface, etc., to or beyond another. **2.** From beginning to end. **3.** To a termination or conclusion, esp. a successful one: to pull *through.* **4.** Completely; entirely: *He is wet* through. — **through and through** Thoroughly. — *adj.* **1.** Going from beginning to end without stops or with very few stops: a *through* train. **2.** Extending from one side or surface to another. **3.** Unobstructed; open; clear: a *through* road. **4.** Arrived at an end; finished. **5.** At the end of all relations or dealings: *He is* through *with school.* Also spelled *thro, thru.* [OE *thurh*]

through·out (thrōō·out') *adv.* Through or in every part: *The house was searched* throughout. — *prep.* All through; everywhere in: throughout *the nation.*

through·way (thrōō'wā') See THRUWAY.

throve (thrōv) Past tense of THRIVE.

throw (thrō) *v.* **threw** (thrōō), **thrown, throw·ing** *v.t.* **1.** To launch through the air by means of a sudden straightening or whirling of the arm. **2.** To propel or hurl. **3.** To put hastily or carelessly: *He* threw *a coat over his shoulders.* **4.**

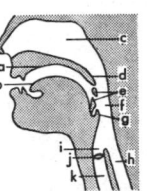

HUMAN THROAT
a Palate. *b* Tongue. *c* Nasal cavity. *d* Uvula. *e* Tonsils. *f* Pharynx. *g* Epiglottis. *h* Esophagus. *i* Larynx. *j* Vocal cords. *k* Trachea.

To direct or project (light, a glance, etc.). **5.** To bring to a specified condition or state by or as by throwing: to *throw* the enemy into a panic. **6.** To cause to fall; overthrow: The horse *threw* its rider. **7.** In wrestling, to force the shoulders of (an opponent) to the ground. **8.** To cast (dice). **9.** To make (a specified cast) with dice. **10.** To cast off or shed; lose. **11.** *Informal* To lose purposely, as a race, contest, etc., in accordance with a prearranged plan. **12.** To give birth to (young): said of domestic animals. **13.** To move, as a lever or switch, in connecting or disconnecting a circuit, mechanism, etc. **14.** *Slang* To give (a party, etc.). **15.** In card games, to play or discard. **16.** In ceramics, to shape on a potter's wheel. **17.** To spin (filaments, as of silk) into thread. — *v.i.* **18.** To cast or fling something. — **to throw away 1.** To discard. **2.** To waste; squander. — **to throw back 1.** To return by throwing. **2.** To revert to ancestral characteristics. — **to throw cold water on** To discourage. — **to throw in 1.** To cause (gears or a clutch) to mesh or engage. **2.** To contribute; add. **3.** To join with others. — **to throw in the towel** (or **sponge**) *Slang* To accept defeat; surrender. — **to throw off 1.** To cast aside; reject; spurn. **2.** To rid oneself of. **3.** To do or utter in an offhand manner. **4.** To disconnect, as a machine. — **to throw oneself at** To strive to gain the affections or love of. — **to throw oneself into** To engage or take part in vigorously. — **to throw oneself on** (or **upon**) To entrust oneself to; rely on. — **to throw open 1.** To open suddenly or completely, as a door. **2.** To free from restrictions or obstacles. — **to throw the book at** *Slang* **1.** To sentence to the maximum penalty. **2.** To reprimand or castigate severely. — **to throw out 1.** To put forth; emit. **2.** To cast out or aside; discard; reject. **3.** To utter as if accidentally: to *throw out* hints. **4.** In baseball, to retire (a runner) by throwing the ball to the base toward which he is advancing. — **to throw over 1.** To overturn. **2.** To discard. — **to throw (some-thing) up to (someone)** *Informal* To mention or repeat as a reproach. — **to throw together** To put together hastily or roughly. — **to throw up 1.** To construct hastily. **2.** To give up; relinquish. **3.** To vomit. — *n.* **1.** An act of throwing or hurling; a fling. **2.** The distance over which a missile may be thrown: a stone's *throw*. **3.** A cast of dice, or the resulting number. **4.** *Mech.* The radius of the circle described by a crank, cam, or the like. **5.** A scarf used for draping an easel or picture frame; also, a woman's scarf. **6.** *Geol.* **a** A faulting, or dislocation of rock strata. **b** The amount of vertical displacement produced by dislocation of strata. [OE *thrāwan* to turn, twist, curl] — **throw′er** *n.*

throw·a·way (thrō′ə·wā′) *n.* A free broadside or leaflet handed out for advertising or propaganda purposes.

throw·back (thrō′bak′) *n.* **1.** Reversion to an ancestral type or condition; also, an example of such reversion. **2.** A throwing back.

thru (thrōō) See THROUGH.

thrum¹ (thrum) *v.* **thrummed, thrum·ming** *v.t.* **1.** To play on or finger (a stringed instrument) idly and without expression. **2.** To drum or tap monotonously or listlessly. **3.** To recite or repeat in a droning, monotonous way. — *v.i.* **4.** To thrum a stringed instrument. **5.** To sound when played thus, as a guitar. — *n.* Any monotonous drumming. [Imit.]

thrum² (thrum) *n.* **1.** The fringe of warp threads remaining on a loom beam after the web has been cut off; also, one of such threads. **2.** Any loose thread or fringe, or a tuft of filaments or fibers; a tassel. — *v.t.* **thrummed, thrum·ming 1.** To cover or trim with thrums or similar appendages. **2.** *Naut.* To insert bits of rope yarn in (canvas) to produce a rough surface or mat to be used to prevent chafing. [OE -*thrum* ligament, as in *tungethrum* the ligament of the tongue]

thrush¹ (thrush) *n.* Any of numerous migratory birds having a long and slightly graduated tail, long wings, and spotted underparts, as the hermit thrush, wood thrush, and the song thrush of Europe. ◆ Collateral adjective: *turdine.* [OE *thrysce*]

thrush² (thrush) *n. Pathol.* A vesicular disease of the mouth, lips, and throat of infants caused by a fungus. [Cf. Dan. *tröske*, Sw. *trosk* mouth disease]

thrust (thrust) *v.* **thrust, thrust·ing** *v.t.* **1.** To push or shove with force or sudden impulse. **2.** To pierce or stab, as with a sword or dagger. **3.** To put (a person) forcibly into some condition or situation. **4.** To interpose; put in: to *thrust* in a remark. — *v.i.* **5.** To make a sudden push against something. **6.** To force oneself on or ahead: push one's way: with *through, into, on,* etc. — *n.* **1.** A sudden, forcible push, esp. with a pointed weapon. **2.** A vigorous attack. **3.** *Archit.* A stress or strain tending to push a member of a structure outward or sidewise: the *thrust* of an arch. **4.** *Mech.* The driving force exerted by a steam engine, motor, propeller, jet engine, etc. **5.** Salient force or meaning: the *thrust* of his remarks. [< ON *thrysta*] — **thrust′er** *n.*

thru·way (thrōō′wā′) *n. U.S.* A long-distance express highway: also spelled *throughway.*

thud (thud) *n.* **1.** A dull, heavy sound, as of a hard body

striking upon a comparatively soft surface. **2.** The blow causing such a sound; a thump. — *v.i.* **thud·ded, thud·ding** To make a thud. [OE *thyddan* to strike, thrust, press]

thug (thug) *n.* **1.** A cutthroat or ruffian. **2.** Formerly, one of an organization of religious, professional assassins in northern India. [< Hind. *thag* < Skt. *sthaga* swindler] — **thug′ger·y** *n.* — **thug′gish** *adj.*

Thu·le (thōō′lē) In ancient geography, the northernmost limit of the habitable world.

thu·li·um (thōō′lē·əm) *n.* A metallic element (symbol Tm) of the erbium group in the lanthanide series. See ELEMENT. [after *Thule*]

thumb (thum) *n.* **1.** The short, thick digit next to the forefinger of the human hand. **2.** The corresponding digit in certain other animals, esp. primates. **3.** The division in a glove or mitten that covers the thumb. — **all thumbs** *Informal* Clumsy with the hands. — **thumbs down** *Informal* No; nix: from a sign used to indicate negation or disapproval. — **under one's thumb** Under one's influence or power. — *v.t.* **1.** To press, rub, soil, or wear with the thumb in handling, as the pages of a book. **2.** To perform clumsily with or as with the thumbs. **3.** To run through the pages of (a book, manuscript, etc.) rapidly and perfunctorily. **4.** *Informal* To solicit (a ride in an automobile) by signaling with the thumb. — *v.i.* **5.** To hitchhike. — **to thumb one's nose** To show defiance or disgust by raising the thumb to the nose with the fingers extended. [OE *thūma*]

thumb-in·dex (thum′in′deks) *v.t.* To provide with a thumb index.

thumb index A series of scalloped indentations cut along the right-hand edge of a book and labeled to indicate its various sections.

thumb·nail (thum′nāl′) *n.* **1.** The nail of the thumb. **2.** Anything as small and essentially complete as a thumbnail. — *adj.* Small and essentially complete: a *thumbnail* sketch.

thumb·screw (thum′skrōō′) *n.* **1.** A screw to be turned by thumb and fingers. **2.** An instrument of torture for compressing the thumb or thumbs: also **thumb·kin** (-kin).

thumb·tack (thum′tak′) *n. U.S.* A broad-headed tack that may be pushed in with the thumb.

thump (thump) *n.* **1.** A blow with a blunt or heavy object. **2.** The sound made by such a blow; a dull thud. — *v.t.* **1.** To beat or strike so as to make a heavy thud or thuds. **2.** *Informal* To beat or defeat severely. — *v.i.* **3.** To strike with a thump. **4.** To make a thump or thumps; pound or throb. [Imit.] — **thump′er** *n.*

thump·ing (thum′ping) *adj.* **1.** That thumps. **2.** *Informal* Huge; whopping.

thun·der (thun′dər) *n.* **1.** The sound that accompanies lightning, caused by the sudden heating and expansion of the air along the path of the electrical discharge. **2.** Any loud, rumbling or booming noise, suggestive of thunder. **3.** A denunciation or threat; a vehement utterance. — **to steal one's thunder** To take for one's own use anything popular or effective originated by another: said esp. of an argument. — *v.i.* **1.** To give forth a peal or peals of thunder: used impersonally: It *thunders.* **2.** To make a noise like thunder. **3.** To utter vehement denunciations or threats. — *v.t.* **4.** To utter or express with a noise like or suggestive of thunder. [OE *thunor*] — **thun′der·er** *n.*

thun·der·bolt (thun′dər·bōlt′) *n.* **1.** An electric discharge accompanied by a clap of thunder. **2.** An imaginary molten ball or bolt hurled by the lightning flash. **3.** One who or that which acts with or as with the force and speed or destructiveness of lightning.

thun·der·clap (thun′dər·klap′) *n.* **1.** A sharp, violent detonation of thunder. **2.** Anything having the violence or suddenness of a clap of thunder.

thun·der·cloud (thun′dər·kloud′) *n.* A dark, heavy mass of cloud highly charged with electricity.

thun·der·head (thun′dər·hed′) *n. Meteorol.* A rounded mass of cumulus cloud, either silvery white or dark with silvery edges, often developing into a thundercloud.

thun·der·ing (thun′dər·ing) *adj.* **1.** Giving forth, or accompanied by, thunder. **2.** Resembling thunder in force or effect; extremely violent. **3.** *Informal* Unusually great or extreme; superlative. — **thun′der·ing·ly** *adv.*

thun·der·ous (thun′dər·əs) *adj.* Producing a noise like thunder. Also **thun′drous** (-drəs). — **thun′der·ous·ly** *adv.*

thun·der·peal (thun′dər·pēl′) *n.* A clap of thunder.

thun·der·show·er (thun′dər·shou′ər) *n.* A shower of rain with thunder and lightning.

thun·der·storm (thun′dər·stôrm′) *n.* A local storm accompanied by lightning and thunder.

thun·der·struck (thun′dər·struk′) *adj.* **1.** Struck by lightning. **2.** Amazed, astonished, or confounded, as with fear, surprise, etc. Also **thun′der·strick′en** (-strik′ən).

thun·der·y (thun′dər·ē) *adj. Informal* **1.** Indicative of or accompanied by thunder. **2.** Ominous.

thu·ri·ble (thōōr′ə·bəl, thûr′-) *n.* A censer. [< L < *thus, thuris* frankincense]

Thu·rin·gi·an (thŏŏ-rin′jē-ən) *adj. Geol.* Denoting the upper division of the Permian in Europe. — *n.* One of a Teutonic tribe occupying central Germany until the sixth century.

Thurs·day (thûrz′dē, -dā) *n.* The fifth day of the week. [Fusion of OE *Thunres dæg* day of Thunor and ON *Thōrsdagr* day of Thor; trans. of LL *dies Jovis* day of Jove]

thus (thŭs) *adv.* 1. In this, that, or the following way of manner. 2. To such degree or extent; so: *thus* far. 3. In these circumstances or conditions; therefore. [OE]

thwack (thwak) *v.t.* To strike with something flat; whack. — *n.* A blow with a flat or blunt instrument. [Prob. OE *thaccian* to smack; infl. in form by *whack*] — **thwack′er** *n.*

thwart (thwôrt) *v.t.* To prevent the accomplishment of, as by interposing an obstacle; also, to prevent (one) from accomplishing something; foil; frustrate; balk. — *n.* 1. An oarsman's seat extending across a boat. 2. A crosspiece or transverse member in a boat. — *adj.* Lying, moving, or extending across something; transverse. — *adv. & prep.* Athwart; across. [< ON *thvert*, neut. of *thverr* transverse] — **thwart′er** *n.*

thy (t͟hī) *pronominal adj. Archaic* The possessive case of the pronoun *thou*, used attributively: *Thy* kingdom come. [Apocopated var. of THINE]

thyme (tīm) *n.* Any of various small shrubby plants of the mint family, having aromatic leaves and used in cookery. [< F < L < Gk. *thymon*] — **thym′y** *adj.*

thym·ic[1] (tī′mik) *adj.* Pertaining to or derived from thyme.

thy·mic[2] (thī′mik) *adj.* Of, pertaining to, or derived from the thymus.

thy·mus (thī′məs) *n. Anat.* A glandular organ of man and some other vertebrates, found behind the top of the breastbone. [< NL < Gk. *thymos*]

thyro- *combining form Med. & Surg.* The thyroid; of or related to the thyroid. Also, before vowels, **thyr-**. Also **thyreo-**. [< Gk. *thyreoeidēs* thyroid]

thy·roid (thī′roid) *adj. Physiol.* Relating or pertaining to the thyroid cartilage or the thyroid gland. — *n.* 1. The thyroid cartilage or gland. 2. The dried and powdered thyroid gland of certain domesticated food animals, used in the treatment of hypothyroid disorders. [< Gk. < *thyreos* large shield + *eidos* form]

thyroid cartilage *Anat.* The largest cartilage of the larynx, composed of two blades whose juncture in front forms the Adam's apple.

thyroid gland *Anat.* An endocrine gland situated in front of and on each side of the trachea, and secreting thyroxin, important in the regulation of metabolism and body growth.

thy·rox·in (thī-rok′sin) *n. Biochem.* An odorless, crystalline amino acid, $C_{15}H_{11}O_4NI_4$, obtained as the hormone of the thyroid gland and also made synthetically, used to treat thyroid disorders. Also **thy·rox·ine** (-sēn, -sin). [< THYR(O)- + OX(Y)- + -IN] — **thy·rox·in·ic** (thī′rok·sin′ik) *adj.*

thyr·soid (thûr′soid) *adj. Bot.* Resembling or shaped like a thyrsus. Also **thyr·soi·dal** (thûr-soid′l).

thyr·sus (thûr′səs) *n. pl.* **·si** (-sī) A staff wreathed in ivy and crowned with a pine cone or a bunch of ivy leaves, as carried by Dionysus and the satyrs. [< L < Gk. *thyrsos*]

thy·self (t͟hī-self′) *pron. Archaic* A form of the second person singular pronouns *thee* and *thou*, used: 1. As a reflexive: Know *thyself*. 2. As an emphatic or intensive form: I love thee for *thyself*.

ti (tē) *n. Music* In solmization, a syllable representing the seventh tone of the diatonic scale. [See GAMUT.]

ti·a·ra (tī-âr′ə, tē-är′ə, -ar′ə) *n.* 1. The pope's triple crown; also, the papal dignity. Compare MITER. 2. An ornamental, semicircular band of jewels, etc., worn by women for formal occasions. [< L < Gk. *tiara* Persian headdress]

Ti·bet·an (ti-bet′n) *adj.* Of or pertaining to Tibet, the Tibetans, or to their language, religion, or customs. — *n.* 1. One of the native Mongoloid people of Tibet, now intermixed with Chinese and various peoples of India. 2. The Sino-Tibetan language of Tibet. Also *Thibetan.*

tib·i·a (tib′ē-ə) *n. pl.* **tib·i·ae** (tib′i-ē) or **tib·i·as** 1. *Anat.* The inner and larger of the two bones of the leg below the knee; the shin bone. 2. The corresponding bone in the hind limb of other animals. [< L] — **tib′i·al** *adj.*

tic (tik) *n.* An involuntary spasm or twitching of muscles, usu. of the face and sometimes of neurotic origin. [< F]

tick[1] (tik) *n.* 1. A light, recurring sound made by a watch, clock, or similar mechanism. 2. A mark, as a dot or dash, used in checking off something. — *v.i.* 1. To make a recurrent clicking sound, as a running watch or clock. — *v.t.* 2. To mark or check with ticks. [Prob. imit.]

tick[2] (tik) *n.* 1. One of numerous flat, bloodsucking arachnids that attack the skin of man and other animals. 2. Any of certain two-winged or wingless insects, parasitic on sheep, horses, cattle, bats, and other animals. [OE *ticia*]

tick[3] (tik) *n.* 1. The stout outer covering of a mattress or pillow. 2. *Informal* Ticking. [Earlier *teke, tyke*, ult. < L < Gk. *thēke* case]

tick[4] (tik) *n. Brit. Informal* Credit; trust: to buy something on *tick*. [Short for TICKET]

tick·er (tik′ər) *n.* 1. One who or that which ticks. 2. A telegraphic instrument that records stock quotations on a paper ribbon. 3. *Slang* A watch. 4. *Slang* The heart.

ticker tape A paper ribbon that receives the printed information on a ticker. — **tick·er-tape** (tik′ər·tāp′) *adj.*

tick·et (tik′it) *n.* 1. A card showing that the holder is entitled to something, as transportation in a public vehicle, admission to a theater, etc. 2. A label or tag for attachment or identification. 3. A certificate or license, as of an airplane pilot or the captain of a ship. 4. In politics: **a** A list of candidates of a single party on a ballot. **b** The group of candidates running for the offices of a party. 5. *Informal* A legal summons, as for a traffic violation. — *v.t.* 1. To fix a ticket to; label. 2. To present or furnish with a ticket or tickets. [< MF < OF < *estiquer* to stick < OLG *stekan*]

ticket of leave Formerly, in Great Britain and Australia, a written permit granted to a penal convict to be at large before the expiration of his sentence.

tick·ing (tik′ing) *n.* A strong, closely woven cotton or linen fabric, used for ticks, awnings, etc. [< TICK[3] + -ING[1]]

tick·le (tik′əl) *v.* **·led, ·ling** *v.t.* 1. To touch or scratch (someone) so as to produce a sensation resulting in spasmodic laughter or twitching; titillate. 2. To arouse or excite agreeably; please: Compliments *tickle* our vanity. 3. *Informal* To amuse or entertain; delight. 4. To move, stir, or get by or as by tickling. — *v.i.* 1. To have or experience a thrilling or tingling sensation. — *n.* 1. The act of tickling or of being tickled; also the sensation produced. 2. *Canadian* In Newfoundland, a narrow strait. [ME *tikelen*]

tick·ler (tik′lər) *n.* 1. One who or that which tickles. 2. A memorandum book or file, as of bills or notes due, etc.

tick·lish (tik′lish) *adj.* 1. Sensitive to tickling. 2. Liable to be upset or easily offended. 3. Attended with risk; difficult; delicate. — **tick′lish·ly** *adv.* — **tick′lish·ness** *n.*

tick·tack·toe (tik′tak·tō′) *n.* A game for two players who alternately put circles or crosses in the spaces of a figure formed by two parallel lines crossing at right angles two other parallel lines, each player trying to get a row of three circles or three crosses before his opponent does: also called *tit-tat-toe.* Also **tic′tac·toe′** (tōō′), **tic′tac·toe′** (-tō′).

tick·tock (tik′tok′) *n.* The sound of a clock or watch. — *v.i.* To make this sound. [Imit.]

tid·al (tīd′l) *adj.* 1. Of, pertaining to, or influenced by the tides. 2. Dependent on the rise of the tide as to time of starting or leaving: a *tidal* steamship.

tidal wave 1. Any great incoming rise of waters along a shore, caused by windstorms at sea or by excessively high tides. 2. A great movement in popular feeling, opinion, action, etc. 3. A tsunami.

tid·bit (tid′bit′) *n.* A choice bit, as of food. Also, *Brit., titbit.* [< dial. E *tid* small object + BIT[1]]

tid·dly·winks (tid′lē·wingks′) *n.* A game in which the players attempt to snap little disks of bone, ivory, or the like, from a plane surface into a cup. Also **tid·dle·dy·winks** (tid′l·dē·wingks′). [Prob. < *tiddly* child's word for *little*]

tide (tīd) *n.* 1. The periodic rise and fall of the surface waters of the oceans, caused by the attraction of moon and sun. In each lunar day of 24 hours and 51 minutes there are two high tides and two low tides, alternating at equal intervals of flood and ebb. 2. Anything that rises and falls like the tide; also, the time at which something is most flourishing. 3. A natural drift or tendency of events, opinions, etc. 4. Season; time; esp., a season of the ecclesiastical year: used chiefly in combination: *Christmastide.* — *v.* **tid·ed, tid·ing** *v.i.* 1. To ebb and flow like the tide. 2. To float with the tide. — *v.t.* 3. To carry or help like a boat buoyed up by the tide: Charity *tided* us over the depression. 4. To survive; endure, as a difficulty: with *over*: to *tide* over hard times. [OE *tīd* period, season] — **tide′less** *adj.*

tide·land (tīd′land′) *n.* Land alternately covered and uncovered by the tide.

tide·rip (tīd′rip′) *n.* Riptide. [< TIDE[1] + RIP[2]]

tide·wait·er (tīd′wā′tər) *n.* A customs officer who boards vessels entering port, to enforce customs regulations.

tide·wa·ter (tīd′wô′tər, -wot′ər) *n.* 1. Water that inundates land at high tide. 2. Water affected by the tide on the seacoast or in a river. 3. Any area, as a seacoast, whose waters are affected by tides. — *adj.* Pertaining to tidewater; also, situated on the seacoast: the *tidewater* country.

ti·dings (tī′dingz) *n.pl.* (*sometimes construed as sing.*) A report or information; news. [OE *tīdung*]

ti·dy (tī′dē) *adj.* **·di·er, ·di·est** 1. Marked by neatness and order; trim. 2. Of an orderly disposition. 3. *Informal*

Moderately large; considerable: a *tidy* sum. **4.** *Informal* Tolerable; fairly good. —*v.t. & v.i.* **·died, ·dy·ing** To make (things) tidy; put (things) in order. —*n. pl.* **·dies** A light, detachable covering, as of lace or embroidery, to protect the back or arms of a chair or sofa. [ME < OE *tīd* time] — **ti′di·ly** *adv.* —**ti′di·ness** *n.*

tie (tī) *v.* **tied, ty·ing** *v.t.* **1.** To fasten with cord, rope, etc., the ends of which are then drawn into a knot. **2.** To draw the parts of together or into place by a cord or band fastened with a knot: to *tie* one's shoes. **3.** To form (a knot). **4.** To form a knot in, as string. **5.** To fasten, attach, or join in any way. **6.** To restrain or confine; bind. **7.** In sports, games, etc.: **a** To equal (a competitor) in score or achievement. **b** To equal (a competitor's score). **8.** *Informal* To unite in marriage. **9.** *Music* To unite by a tie. —*v.i.* **10.** To make a tie or connection. **11.** To make the same score; be equal. —**to tie down** To hinder; restrict. —**to tie in** *Informal* To have a certain relationship or connection; often with *with*. —**to tie (something) in** *Informal* To bring into a certain relationship or connection. —**to tie up 1.** To fasten with rope, string, etc. **2.** To moor (a vessel). **3.** To block; hinder. **4.** To have or be already committed, in use, etc., so as to be unavailable. —*n.* **1.** A string, cord, etc., with which something is tied. **2.** Any bond or obligation, mental, moral, or legal: *ties* of affection. **3.** An exact equality in number, as of a score, votes, etc.; esp., a contest which neither side wins; a draw. **4.** A necktie. **5.** A structural member fastening parts of a framework together and receiving tensile stress. **6.** *Music* A curved line placed over or under two musical notes of the same pitch on the staff to make them represent one tone length. **7.** *pl.* Low shoes fastened with lacings. **8.** *U.S.* One of a set of timbers laid crosswise on the ground as supports for railroad tracks; a sleeper. [OE *tiegan* to bind]

tie·back (tī′bak) *n.* A piece of fabric, metal, etc., by which curtains are draped or tied back at the sides.

tie beam A timber that serves as a tie in a roof, etc. For illus. see ROOF.

tie-in (tī′in′) *n.* A connection; association; relation.

tie-in sale A sale in which the buyer, in order to get the article he wants, is required to buy a second article.

tier (tir) *n.* A rank or row of things, as seats, placed one above another. —*v.t. & v.i.* To place or rise in tiers. [Earlier *tire* < OF, sequence < *tirer* to draw, elongate]

tierce (tirs) *n.* **1.** A former liquid measure equivalent in the U.S. to 42 wine gallons; a third of a pipe or butt. **2.** A cask holding this amount. **3.** *Often cap. Eccl.* Prescribed prayers constituting the third of the seven canonical hours: often called *undersong*. [< OF *tierce, terce* a third < L *tertia*]

tie-up (tī′up′) *n.* **1.** A situation, resulting from a strike, mechanical breakdown, etc., in which progress or operation is impossible. **2.** *Informal* A connection or relation.

tiff (tif) *n.* **1.** A peevish display of irritation; a pet; huff. **2.** A light quarrel; a spat. —*v.i.* To be in or have a tiff. [Origin unknown]

ti·ger (tī′gər) *n.* **1.** A large carnivorous feline of Asia, with vertical black wavy stripes on a tawny body and black bars or rings on the limbs and tail. **2.** One of several other animals resembling the tiger. **3.** A fierce, cruel person. [OE *tiger* or OF *tigre*, both < L < Gk. *tigris*]

ti·ger-eye (tī′gər-ī′) *n.* A gemstone showing a changeable luster. Also **ti′gers-eye′.**

ti·ger·ish (tī′gər-ish) *adj.* Of or resembling the tiger or its habits; predacious; bloodthirsty: also **ti′grish** (-grish).

tiger lily A tall cultivated lily, with nodding orange flowers spotted with black.

tiger moth A stout-bodied moth with striped or spotted wings.

tight (tīt) *adj.* **1.** So closely held together or constructed as to be impervious to fluids, air, etc.: a *tight* vessel. **2.** Firmly fixed or fastened in place; secure. **3.** Fully stretched; taut: *tight* as a drum. **4.** Closely drawn, packed, fastened, etc.: a *tight* weave. **5.** Strict; stringent: to keep a *tight* rein over us. **6.** Fitting closely; esp., fitting too closely. **7.** *Informal* Difficult to cope with; troublesome: a *tight* spot. **8.** *Informal* Parsimonious; tightfisted. **9.** Characterized by a feeling of constriction: a *tight* cough. **10.** *Slang* Drunk; intoxicated. **11.** Evenly matched: said of a contest. **12.** *Econ.* **a** Difficult to obtain. **b** Straitened from lack of money or commodities: a *tight* market. **13.** Yielding very little or no profit: said of a bargain. **14.** *Dial.* Well-built; compact. **15.** *Dial.* Neat; tidy. —*adv.* **1.** Firmly; securely. **2.** Closely; with much constriction. —**to sit tight** To remain firm in one's position; refrain from taking action. [ME *thight*] —**tight′ly** *adv.* —**tight′ness** *n.*

-tight *combining form* Impervious to: *watertight.*

tight·en (tīt′n) *v.t. & v.i.* To make or become tight or tighter. —**tight′en·er** *n.*

tight·fist·ed (tīt′fis′tid) *adj.* Stingy; parsimonious.

tight·lipped (tīt′lipt′) *adj.* **1.** Having the lips held tightly together. **2.** Unwilling to talk; reticent or secretive.

tight·rope (tīt′rōp′) *n.* A rope or cable stretched out tight above the ground, on which acrobats do balancing acts, etc.

tights (tīts) *n.pl.* Skintight garments, commonly for the legs and lower torso, worn by dancers, acrobats, etc.

tight·wad (tīt′wod′) *n. U.S. Slang* A parsimonious person; miser. [< TIGHT + WAD¹]

ti·gress (tī′gris) *n.* **1.** A female tiger. **2.** A cruel, fierce woman.

til·bur·y (til′ber·ē) *n. pl.* **·bur·ies** A form of gig for two persons. [after *Tilbury*, a 19th c. London coachmaker]

til·de (til′də, -dē) *n.* A sign (~); used esp., in Spanish over *n* to represent the palatal nasal (roughly equivalent to *ny*) as in *cañon.* [< Sp. < L *titulus* superscription, title]

tile (tīl) *n.* **1.** A thin piece of baked clay or other material, as asbestos, linoleum, etc., used for covering roofs, floors, etc., and as an ornament. **2.** A short earthenware pipe, used in forming sewers. **3.** Tiles collectively; tiling. **4.** Any of the counters used in mahjong. **5.** *Informal* A high silk hat. —*v.t.* **tiled, til·ing** To cover with tiles. [OE, ult. < L < *tegere* to cover] —**til′er** *n.*

til·ing (tī′ling) *n.* **1.** The act, operation, or system of using tiles for roofing, drainage, etc. **2.** Tiles collectively. **3.** Something made of or faced with tiles.

till¹ (til) *v.t. & v.i.* To work (soil) for the production of crops, as by plowing, harrowing, hoeing, sowing, etc.; cultivate. [OE *tilian* to strive, acquire] —**till′a·ble** *adj.*

till² (til) *prep.* **1.** To the time of; until. **2.** Before: with the negative: I can't go *till* noon. —*conj.* **1.** Up to such time as; until: *till* death do us part. **2.** Before: with the negative: They couldn't go *till* he came. [OE *til* < ON, to]

till³ (til) *n.* A drawer or tray in which money or valuables are kept, as at a bank, store, etc. [Origin uncertain]

till·age (til′ij) *n.* The cultivation of land. [< TILL¹ + -AGE]

till·er¹ (til′ər) *n.* One who or that which tills. [< TILL¹]

till·er² (til′ər) *n. Naut.* A lever to turn a rudder when steering. [< OF < Med.L *telarium* weaver's beam]

tilt (tilt) *v.t.* **1.** To cause to rise at one end or side; incline at an angle; slant; tip. **2.** To aim or thrust, as a lance. **3.** To charge or overthrow in a tilt or joust. —*v.i.* **4.** To slope; lean. **5.** To engage in a joust. —**Syn.** See TIP¹. —*n.* **1.** A slant; slope. **2.** The act of inclining, or the state of being inclined. **3.** A medieval sport in which mounted knights, charging with lances, endeavored to unseat each other. **4.** Any similar encounter, as a quarrel. **5.** A thrust or blow, as with a lance. **6.** A seesaw. —**at full tilt** At full speed. [ME < OE *tealt* unsteady] —**tilt′er** *n.*

tilth (tilth) *n.* **1.** The act of tilling; cultivation of soil; tillage. **2.** Cultivated land. [OE < *tilian* to till]

tim·bal (tim′bəl) *n.* A kettledrum. [< F < Sp. < Arabic *at-tabl* a drum]

tim·bale (tim′bəl, *Fr.* taṅ·bål′) *n.* **1.** A custardlike dish made of chicken, fish, cheese, or vegetables, cooked in a drum-shaped mold. **2.** A small cup made of fried pastry, in which food may be served. [< F. See TIMBAL.]

tim·ber (tim′bər) *n.* **1.** Wood suitable for building or structural purposes. **2.** Growing or standing trees; also, woodland. **3.** A single piece of prepared wood for use in a structure. **4.** *Naut.* Any principal beam of a vessel. **5.** Personal character, talent, potentiality: presidential *timber.* —*v.t.* To provide or shore with timber. [OE] —**tim′bered** *adj.*

timber hitch *Naut.* A knot by which a rope is fastened around a spar.

tim·ber·land (tim′bər·land′) *n.* Land covered with forests.

timber line The upper limit of tree growth on mountains and in arctic regions. —**tim′ber-line′** (-līn′) *adj.*

timber wolf The large gray or brindled wolf of the forests of the northern U.S. and Canada: also called *lobo.*

tim·bre (tim′bər, tam′-; *Fr.* taṅ′br′) *n.* The attribute of a sound distinguishing one vowel from another, the tone of one musical instrument from another, etc.; quality; tone color. [< F < OF < L *tympanum* kettledrum]

TIMBER WOLF
(About 4 feet long)

tim·brel (tim′brəl) *n.* An ancient instrument resembling a tambourine. [< OF. See TIMBRE.]

time (tīm) *n.* **1.** The general concept, relation, or fact of continuous or successive existence, capable of division into measurable portions, and comprising the past, present, and future. **2.** Duration with reference to finite existence as distinguished from eternity. **3.** A system of measuring duration: solar *time.* **4.** A definite portion of duration; esp., a specific hour, day, season, year, etc.: The *time* is 2:35; Autumn is my favorite *time.* **5.** The moment or period in which something takes place, has taken place, or will take place: at the *time* of his marriage. **6.** That moment or portion of duration allotted to or sufficient for some special action, purpose, or event: *time* enough to catch the train. **7.** The period of duration generally allotted to human life. **8.** Leisure: no *time* to read. **9.** An instance or occasion of re-

currence or repetition: next *time*; three *times* a day. **10.** A fit or proper moment or occasion: a *time* to plant. **11.** The period of pregnancy or gestation; also, the moment of childbirth. **12.** The moment of death. **13.** A period considered with reference to one's personal experience: to have a good *time*. **14.** *Usu. pl.* An era marked by some cultural, historical, or other special characteristics: ancient *times*; the *time* of Charlemagne. **15.** *Usu. pl.* The present period or era or the period or era under consideration. **16.** *Usu. pl.* A period of duration having some specific quality: *Times* are hard. **17.** *Informal* A period of imprisonment. **18.** The period during which work has been done or remains to be done by a worker; also, the pay given for this. **19.** *Music* Loosely, meter, tempo, or the duration of a note. See METER. **20.** Speed or rate of movement in marching, dancing, etc.: double *time*. **21.** *Usu. pl.* In arithmetic, an instance of being multiplied or added: How many *times* does three go into nine? **— against time** With an imminent time limit; as quickly as possible. **— ahead of time** Before the time stated or due; early. **— at the same time 1.** At the same moment or period. **2.** Despite that; however; nevertheless. **— at times** Now and then; occasionally. **— behind the times** Old-fashioned. **— behind time** After the time stated or due; late. **— for the time being** Temporarily. **— from time to time** Now and then; occasionally. **— in good time 1.** Quickly; fast. **2.** At the appropriate time; when properly due. **— in the nick of time** At just the right or critical moment. **— in time 1.** While time permits or lasts; before it is too late. **2.** In the progress of time; ultimately. **3.** In the proper rhythm, tempo, etc. **— on time 1.** Promptly; according to schedule. **2.** To be paid for, later or in installments. **— time and again** Frequently; repeatedly: also **time after time. — to gain time 1.** To run fast: said of a timepiece. **2.** To prolong an act or occasion so as to consider, decide, etc. **— to keep time 1.** To indicate time correctly, as a clock. **2.** To make rhythmic movements in unison with others. **3.** To render or conduct a musical composition in the desired tempo or rhythm. **— to lose time 1.** To run slow: said of a clock. **2.** To waste or miss opportunities; delay advancement. **— adj. 1.** Of or pertaining to time. **2.** Devised so as to operate at a specified time: a *time* bomb. **3.** Of purchases, paid for in installments or at a future date. **— v.t. timed, tim·ing 1.** To regulate as to time. **2.** To cause to correspond in time: They *timed* their steps to the music. **3.** To arrange the time or occasion for. **4.** To mark the rhythm or measure of. **5.** To ascertain or record the speed or duration of: to *time* a race. [OE *tīma*]
time·card (tīm′kärd′) *n.* A card for recording the time of arrival and departure of an employee.
time clock A clock equipped for automatically recording times of arrival and departure.
time exposure *Photog.* **1.** A film exposure made for a relatively long interval. **2.** A picture made by such an exposure.
time-hon·ored (tīm′on′ərd) *adj.* Observed or honored because of long usage or existence. Also *Brit.* **time′-hon′oured.**
time·keep·er (tīm′kē′pər) *n.* **1.** One who or that which keeps time. **2.** One who declares the time in a race, game, athletic match, etc., or records the hours worked by employees. **3.** A railroad train starter. **4.** A timepiece.
time·less (tīm′lis) *adj.* **1.** Independent of or unaffected by time; unending; eternal. **2.** Not limited to any special time or era. **— time′less·ly** *adv.* **— time′less·ness** *n.*
time·ly (tīm′lē) *adj.* **·li·er, ·li·est** Being or occurring in good or suitable time; opportune; seasonable; well-timed. **—** *adv.* Opportunely; seasonably; early. **— time′li·ness** *n.*
time-out (tīm′out′) *n.* In sports, a short recess requested by a team during play. Also **time out.**
time·piece (tīm′pēs′) *n.* Something that records or measures time, as a clock or watch.
tim·er (tī′mər) *n.* **1.** A timekeeper. **2.** A stopwatch, as for timing a race. **3.** A device attached to an internal-combustion engine so as to time the spark automatically. **4.** A clockwork or other device that signals the lapse of a time period, controls an operation, etc.
time·serv·er (tīm′sûr′vər) *n.* One who yields to the demands or opinions of the time, occasion, or authorities, without reference to principle. **— time′serv′ing** *adj. & n.*
time signature *Music* A symbol placed on a musical staff to indicate the meter.
time·ta·ble (tīm′tā′bəl) *n.* A tabular schedule of the times at which certain things are to take place, as arrivals and departures of trains, times of high and low tides, etc.
time-test·ed (tīm′tes′tid) *adj.* Having worth or efficiency proved by use over an extended period.
time·work (tīm′wûrk′) *n.* Work paid for on the basis of a set wage per hour, day, week, etc. **— time′work′er** *n.*
time·worn (tīm′wôrn′, -wōrn′) *adj.* **1.** Showing the ravages or effects of time. **2.** Trite; overused.

time zone One of the 24 sectors of 15° each, or a time interval of one hour, into which the earth is divided for reckoning standard time from the meridian of Greenwich.
tim·id (tim′id) *adj.* **1.** Shrinking from danger or risk; fearful. **2.** Lacking self-confidence; shy. **3.** Characterized by fear or shyness: a *timid* voice. [< L < *timere* to fear] **— ti·mid·i·ty** (ti-mid′ə·tē), **tim′id·ness** *n.* **— tim′id·ly** *adv.*
tim·ing (tī′ming) *n.* The act or art of regulating the speed of performance, utterance, a blow, stroke, etc., so as to insure maximum effectiveness; also, the effect so produced.
tim·or·ous (tim′ər·əs) *adj.* **1.** Fearful of danger; timid. **2.** Indicating or produced by fear. [< OF < Med.L < *timor, -ōris* fear] **— tim′or·ous·ly** *adv.* **— tim′or·ous·ness** *n.*
tim·o·thy (tim′ə·thē) *n.* A perennial fodder grass having long, cylindrical spikes. Also **timothy grass.** [after *Timothy* Hanson, who took the seed to the Carolinas about 1720]
Tim·o·thy (tim′ə·thē) A convert and companion of the apostle Paul. **— n.** Either of two books in the New Testament consisting of two epistles addressed to Timothy and attributed to Saint Paul.
tim·pa·ni (tim′pə·nē) *n. pl.* of **tim·pa·no** (-nō) Kettledrums: also spelled *tympani.* [< Ital. < L *tympanum* drum] **— tim′pa·nist** *n.*
tim·pa·num (tim′pə·nəm) See TYMPANUM.
tin (tin) *n.* **1.** A white, malleable, metallic element (symbol Sn) of low tensile strength: also called *stannum.* See ELEMENT. **2.** Tin plate. **3.** A container or box made of tin. **4.** *Brit.* A can. **— v.t. tinned, tin·ning 1.** To coat or cover with tin. **2.** To pack or put up in tins. **— adj.** Made of a tin. [OE]
tin·a·mou (tin′ə·mōō) *n.* Any of certain South American birds resembling the partridge and hunted as game birds. [< F < Carib *tinamu*]
tinc·ture (tingk′chər) *n.* **1.** A solution, usu., in alcohol, of some medicinal substance: *tincture* of iodine. **2.** A tinge of color; tint. **3.** A slight additional flavor, quality, etc. **— v.t. ·tured, ·tur·ing 1.** To impart a slight hue or tinge to. **2.** To imbue with flavor, odor, etc. **3.** To imbue with a specified quality. [< L *tingere* to dye, color]
tin·der (tin′dər) *n.* Any readily combustible substance, as charred linen or touchwood, that will ignite on contact with a spark. [OE *tynder*] **— tin′der·y** *adj.*
tin·der·box (tin′dər·boks′) *n.* **1.** A portable metallic box containing tinder. **2.** Anything highly flammable, explosive, touchy, etc.
tine (tīn) *n.* A spike or prong, as of a fork or of an antler. [OE *tind*] **— tined** *adj.*
tin·foil (tin′foil′) *n.* Tin or an alloy of tin made into thin sheets for use as wrapping material, etc. Also **tin foil.**
ting (ting) *n.* A single high metallic sound, as of a small bell. **— v.t. & v.i.** To give forth or cause to give forth a ting. [Imit.]
ting-a-ling (ting′ə·ling′) *n.* The sound of a little bell.
tinge (tinj) *v.t.* **tinged, tinge·ing** or **ting·ing 1.** To imbue with a faint trace of color; tint. **2.** To impart a slight characteristic quality of some other element to. **— n. 1.** A faint trace of added color. **2.** A quality or peculiar characteristic imparted to something. [< L *tingere* to dye]
tin·gle (ting′gəl) *v.* **·gled, ·gling** *v.i.* **1.** To experience a prickly, stinging sensation, as from cold, or from a sharp blow. **2.** To cause such a sensation. **— v.t. 3.** To cause to tingle. **— n.** A prickly, stinging sensation; a tingling. [Appar. var. of TINKLE] **— tin′gler** *n.* **— tin′gly** *adj.*
tin·horn (tin′hôrn′) *U.S. Slang n.* One who is cheaply and noisily pretentious; esp., a flashy, small-time gambler.
tink·er (tingk′ər) *n.* **1.** An itinerant mender of domestic tin utensils, as pots and pans. **2.** Loosely, one who does repairing work of any kind; a jack-of-all-trades. **3.** A clumsy workman; a botcher. **4.** The act of roughly repairing; hasty workmanship. **— v.i. 1.** To work as a tinker. **2.** To work in a clumsy makeshift fashion. **3.** To potter; fuss. **— v.t. 4.** To mend as a tinker. **5.** To repair inexpertly. [Var. of earlier *tinekere* worker in tin]
tinker's damn *Slang* The smallest, most contemptible bit: not worth a *tinker's damn.* Also **tinker's dam.** [< TINKER + DAMN; with ref. to the reputed profanity of tinkers]
tin·kle (ting′kəl) *v.* **·kled, ·kling** *v.i.* **1.** To produce slight, sharp, metallic sounds, as a small bell. **— v.t. 2.** To cause to tinkle. **3.** To summon or signal by a tinkling. **— n.** A tinkling sound. [Imit.] **— tin′kly** *adj.* **— tink′ling** *n.*
tin·ner (tin′ər) *n.* **1.** A miner employed in tin mines. **2.** A maker of or dealer in tinware; a tinsmith.
tin·ny (tin′ē) *adj.* **·ni·er, ·ni·est 1.** Pertaining to, composed of, or abounding in tin. **2.** Resembling tin in lack of durability. **3.** Having a thin sound like that of tin being struck. **— tin′ni·ly** *adv.* **— tin′ni·ness** *n.*
tin-pan alley (tin′pan′) **1.** A section of a city, esp., of New York, frequented by musicians and song writers and occu-

pied by publishers of popular music. **2.** The composers and publishers of popular music, collectively.

tin-plate (tin′plāt′) *v.t.* **-plat·ed, -plat·ing** To plate with tin. **— tin′-plat′er** *n.*

tin plate Sheet iron or steel plated with tin.

tin·sel (tin′səl) *n.* **1.** Very thin, glittering bits of cheap metals used as decoration. **2.** A yarn containing gold or silver thread. **3.** Anything sparkling and showy, with little real worth. **4.** A fabric in which such spangles or bits of metal are woven. **— adj. 1.** Made of, resembling, or covered with tinsel. **2.** Superficially brilliant; tawdry. **— v.t. ·seled** or **·selled, sel·ing** or **· sel·ling 1.** To decorate with or as with tinsel. **2.** To give a showy or gaudy appearance to. [< MF < OF < L *scintilla* spark]

tin·smith (tin′smith′) *n.* One who works with tin or tin plate: also called *whitesmith*.

tint (tint) *n.* **1.** A variety of color; tincture; esp., a slight admixture of a different color; tinge. **2.** A gradation of a color made by dilution with white. **3.** Any pale or delicate hue. **4.** In engraving, an effect of light, shade, texture, etc., produced by the spacing of lines or by hatching. **— v.t. 1.** To give a tint to; tinge. **2.** In engraving, to form a tint upon. [< L < *tingere* to dye, color] **— tint′er** *n.*

tin·tin·nab·u·la·tion (tin′ti·nab′yə·lā′shən) *n.* The pealing, tinkling, or ringing of bells. [< L < *tintinnare* to ring]

tin·type (tin′tīp′) *n.* A photograph taken on a sensitized film supported on a thin sheet of enameled tin or iron.

tin·ware (tin′wâr′) *n.* Articles made of tin plate.

ti·ny (tī′nē) *adj.* **·ni·er, ·ni·est** Very small; minute; wee. [< obs. *tine* small amount, bit + -Y³; ult. origin unknown]

-tion *suffix of nouns* **1.** Action or process of: *rejection.* **2.** Condition or state of being: *completion.* **3.** Result of: *connection.* Also *-ation, -cion, -ion, -sion, -xion.* [< F < OF < L *-tio, -tionis*]

tip¹ (tip) *n.* A slanting or inclined position; a tilt. **— v. tipped, tip·ping** *v.t.* **1.** To cause to lean by lowering or raising one end or side; tilt. **2.** To overturn or upset: often with *over.* **3.** To raise or touch (one's hat) in greeting. **— v.i. 4.** To become tilted; slant. **5.** To overturn; topple: with *over.* [ME *tipen* to overturn; origin uncertain] **— tip′per** *n.* **— Syn. 1, 3.** Tilt, slant, slope.

tip² (tip) *n.* **1.** A small gift of money for services rendered, given to a servant, waiter, etc. **2.** A friendly, helpful hint; esp., information presumed to increase a better's or speculator's chance of winning. **— v. tipped, tip·ping** *v.t.* **1.** To give a small gratuity to. **2.** *Informal* To give secret information to, as in betting: often with *off.* **— v.i. 3.** To give tips. [Orig. < thieves' cant, ? < TIP⁴] **— tip′per** *n.*

tip³ (tip) *n.* **1.** The point or extremity of anything tapering; end: the *tip* of the tongue. **2.** A piece or part made to form the end of anything, as a nozzle, ferrule, etc. **3.** The top or summit, as of a mountain. **— v.t. tipped, tip·ping 1.** To furnish with a tip. **2.** To form the tip of. **3.** To cover or adorn the tip of. [Prob. < M Du., point]

tip⁴ (tip) *v.t.* **tipped, tip·ping 1.** To strike lightly, or with something light; tap. **2.** In baseball, to strike (the ball) a light, glancing blow. **— n.** A tap; light blow. [Earlier *tippe*]

tip-off (tip′ôf′, -of′) *n. Informal* A hint or warning.

tip·pet (tip′it) *n.* **1.** An outdoor covering for the neck, or neck and shoulders, hanging well down in front. **2.** *Eccl.* A long scarf worn by Anglican clergymen. **3.** Formerly, a long, dangling part of a sleeve, hood, etc. [Prob. dim. of TIP³]

tip·ple (tip′əl) *v.t. & v.i.* **·pled, ·pling** To drink (alcoholic beverages) frequently and habitually. **— n.** Alcoholic liquor. **— tip′pler** *n.*

tip·ster (tip′stər) *n. Informal* One who sells tips, as for betting on a race. [< TIP³]

tip·sy (tip′sē) *adj.* **tip·si·er, tip·si·est 1.** Partially intoxicated; high. **2.** Apt to tip over; shaky; also, crooked; askew. [< TIP¹] **— tip′si·ly** *adv.* **— tip′si·ness** *n.*

tip·toe (tip′tō′) *v.i.* **·toed, ·toe·ing** To walk on tiptoe; go stealthily or quietly. **— n.** The tip of a toe. **— on tiptoe 1.** On one's tiptoes. **2.** Eagerly expectant. **3.** Stealthily; quietly. **— adj. 1.** Standing or walking on tiptoe. **2.** Stealthy. **3.** Eager; excited. **— adv.** On tiptoe.

tip-top (tip′top′) *n.* **1.** The highest point; the very top. **2.** *Informal* The highest quality or degree. **— adj. 1.** Located at the very top. **2.** *Informal* Best of its kind; first-rate. **— adv.** In a tiptop manner. [< TIP³ + TOP¹] **— tip′top′per** *n.*

ti·rade (tī′rād, tə·rād′) *n.* A prolonged declamatory outpouring, as of censure. [< F < Ital. *tirare* to fire, pull]

tire¹ (tīr) *v.* **tired, tir·ing** *v.t.* **1.** To reduce the strength of, as by toil; weary; fatigue. **2.** To reduce the interest or patience of, as with tediousness. **— v.i. 3.** To become weary or exhausted. **4.** To lose patience, interest, etc. **— to tire of** To become weary of or impatient with. **— to tire out** To weary completely. [OE *tīorian*]

tire² (tīr) *n.* **1.** A pneumatic, doughnut-shaped structure, as of rubber, forming the outer part of the wheels of vehicles, serving to absorb shock and provide traction. **2.** A band or hoop of metal, etc. fixed tightly around the rim of a wheel.

— v.t. tired, tir·ing To furnish with a tire; put a tire on. [Aphetic var. of ATTIRE]

tired (tīrd) *adj.* Weary; exhausted; jaded; fatigued. **— tired′ly** *adv.* **— tired′ness** *n.*

tire·less (tīr′lis) *adj.* Proof against fatigue; untiring. **— tire′less·ly** *adv.* **— tire′less·ness** *n.*

tire·some (tīr′səm) *adj.* Tending to tire, or causing one to tire; tedious. **— tire′some·ly** *adv.* **— tire′some·ness** *n.*

ti·ro (tī′rō) See TYRO.

'tis (tiz) *Archaic* or *Poetic* It is.

Tish'ah b'Ab (tish′ə·bäb) *n.* In Judaism, a day of fasting, held on the 9th of Ab (July-August), to commemorate the destruction of the Temple.

Tish·ri (tish·rē′, tish′rē) *n.* The first month of the Hebrew calendar. Also **Tis·ri.** See (Hebrew) CALENDAR. [< Hebrew < Aramaic *tishrī* < *sherā* to begin]

tis·sue (tish′ōō) *n.* **1.** *Biol.* One of the elementary aggregates of cells and their products, developed by plants and animals for the performance of a particular function: connective *tissue.* **2.** A light, absorbent piece of paper, usu. consisting of two or more layers, used as a disposable towel, handkerchief, etc. **3.** Tissue paper. **4.** A tissuelike typewriting paper, as onionskin, commonly used for making carbon copies. **5.** A connected or interwoven series; chain: a *tissue* of lies. **6.** Any light or gauzy textile fabric. [< OF < *tistre* to weave]

tissue paper Very thin, unsized, almost transparent paper for wrapping delicate articles, protecting engravings, etc.

tit¹ (tit) *n.* **1.** A titmouse. **2.** Any of various small birds, as a titlark. [Short for TITMOUSE, TITLARK, etc.]

tit² (tit) *n.* Teat; breast; nipple. [OE *titt*]

ti·tan (tīt′n) *n.* A person of gigantic size and strength. [< TITAN]

Ti·tan (tīt′n) *n.* **1.** In Greek mythology, one of a race of giant gods who were vanquished and succeeded by the Olympian gods. **2.** Helios: so called by some Latin poets. **3.** A liquid-fueled intercontinental guided missile of the U.S. Air Force. **— adj.** Titanic. **— Ti′tan·ess** *n.fem.*

Ti·ta·ni·a (ti·tä′nē·ə, tī-) Queen of fairyland and wife of Oberon in Shakespeare's *A Midsummer Night's Dream.*

ti·tan·ic (tī·tan′ik) *adj.* Of great size; huge.

Ti·tan·ic (tī·tan′ik) *adj.* Of or resembling the Titans.

ti·ta·ni·um (tī·tā′nē·əm, ti-) *n.* A widely distributed dark gray metallic element (symbol Ti), found in small quantities in many minerals and used to toughen steel alloys. See ELEMENT. [< NL < L < Gk. *Titanes* the Titans]

tit·bit (tit′bit′) *n. Brit.* A tidbit.

tit for tat Retaliation in kind; blow for blow. [? Alter. of *tip for tap*]

tithe (tīth) *n.* **1.** A tax or assessment of one tenth; loosely, any ratable tax. **2.** In England, a tenth part of the yearly proceeds arising from lands and from the personal industry of the inhabitants, for the support of the clergy and the church. **3.** The tenth part of anything. **4.** A small part. **— v.t. tithed, tith·ing 1.** To give or pay a tenth part of. **2.** To tax with tithes. [ME *tithe*, OE *teogotha* tenth] **— tith′a·ble** *adj.* **— tith′er** *n.*

ti·tian (tish′ən) *n.* A reddish yellow color much used by Titian, esp. in painting women's hair. **— adj.** Having or pertaining to the color titian. [after *Titian*]

tit·il·late (tit′ə·lāt) *v.t.* **·lat·ed, ·lat·ing 1.** To cause a tickling sensation in. **2.** To excite pleasurably in any way. [< L *titillare* to tickle] **— tit′il·la′tion** *n.* **— tit′il·la′tive** *adj.*

tit·i·vate (tit′ə·vāt) *v.t. & v.i.* **·vat·ed, ·vat·ing** *Informal* To put on decorative touches; dress up: also spelled *tittivate.* [? < TIDY, on analogy with *cultivate*] **— tit′i·va′tion** *n.*

tit·lark (tit′lärk′) *n.* A pipit. [ME *tit* little thing + LARK]

ti·tle (tīt′l) *n.* **1.** The name of a book, play, poem, motion picture, etc. **2.** An appellation significant of office, rank, etc.; esp., a designation of nobility. **3.** A characteristic or descriptive name; epithet. **4.** A claim based on an acknowledged or alleged right. **5.** In some sports, a championship. **6.** The subtitle in a motion picture. **7.** *Law* The means whereby the owner of lands has the just possession of his property; the union of possession, the right of possession, and the right of property in lands and tenements; also, the legal evidence of one's right of property, or the means by or source from which one's right to property has accrued: *title* by purchase. **— v.t. ·tled, ·tling** To give a name or title to; entitle; call. [< OF < L *titulus* label, inscription] **— tit′led** *adj.*

title page A page containing the title of a work and the names of its author and publisher.

title role The role of the character in a play, opera, or motion picture for whom it is named.

tit·mouse (tit′mous′) *n. pl.* **·mice** (-mīs′) Any of several small birds related to the nuthatches; esp., the **tufted titmouse** of the U.S., having a conspicuous crest. [Alter. of ME *titmuse* < *tit-* little + OE *mase* titmouse]

ti·trate (tī′trāt, tit′rāt) *v.i. & v.t.* **·trat·ed, ·trat·ing** *Chem.* To determine the strength of (a solution) by means of standard solutions or by titration. [< F *titre* the fineness of gold or silver alloy]

ti·tra·tion (tī-trā′shən, ti-) *n. Chem.* The process of determining the strength or concentration of the ingredients of a solution by adding measured amounts of a suitable reagent until the desired chemical reaction has been effected.

tit-tat-toe (tit′tat-tō′) *n.* Ticktacktoe.

tit·ter (tit′ər) *v.i.* To laugh in a suppressed way, as from nervousness or in ridicule; snicker; giggle. — *n.* The act of tittering. [Imit.] **— tit′ter·er** *n.* **— tit′ter·ing·ly** *adv.*

tit·i·vate (tit′ə-vāt) See TITIVATE.

tit·tle (tit′l) *n.* **1.** The minutest quantity; iota. **2.** Originally, a very small mark in writing, as the dot over an *i*. **3.** Any diacritical mark. [< L *titulus* label, inscription]

tit·tle-tat·tle (tit′l-tat′l) *n.* **1.** Foolish or trivial talk; gossip. **2.** An idle, trifling, or tattling talker. — *v.i.* **·tled, ·tling** To talk foolishly or idly; gossip. [Reduplication of TATTLE]

tit·u·lar (tich′ōō-lər, tit′yə-) *adj.* **1.** Existing in name or title only; nominal. **2.** Of, pertaining to, or like a title. **3.** Bestowing or taking title. Also **tit′u·lar′y** (-ler′ē). [< L *titulus* title] **— tit′u·lar·ly** *adv.*

Ti·tus (tī′təs) A disciple of the apostle Paul. — *n.* A book in the New Testament consisting of an epistle addressed to Titus and attributed to Paul.

tiz·zy (tiz′ē) *n. pl.* **·zies** *Slang* A bewildered or excited state of mind; a dither. [Origin unknown]

TNT (tē′en′tē′) *n.* **1.** Trinitrotoluene. **2.** *Informal* Any explosive and dangerous circumstance, force, or person.

to (tōō, *unstressed* tə) *prep.* **1.** In a direction toward or terminating in: going *to* town. **2.** Opposite, in contact with, or near: face *to* face. **3.** Intending or aiming at; having as an object or purpose: Come *to* my rescue. **4.** Resulting in; having as a condition or effect: frozen *to* death. **5.** Belonging or used in connection with: the key *to* the door. **6.** Accompanied by; in rhythm with: March *to* the music. **7.** In honor of: Drink *to* me only with thine eyes. **8.** In comparison, correspondence, or agreement with: often denoting ratio: four quarts *to* the gallon. **9.** Approaching as a limit; until: five minutes *to* one. **10.** For the utmost duration of; as far as: a miser *to* the end of his days. **11.** In respect of; concerning: blind *to* her charms. **12.** In close application toward: Buckle down *to* work. **13.** For; with regard for: The contest is open *to* everyone. **14.** Noting an indirect or limiting object after verbs, adjectives, or nouns, and designating the recipient of the action: taking the place of the dative case in other languages: Give the ring *to* me. **15.** By: known *to* the world. **16.** From the point of view of: It seems *to* me. **17.** About; involved in: That's all there is *to* it. ◆ *To* also serves to indicate the infinitive, and is often used elliptically for it: You may come if you care *to*. — *adv.* **1.** To or toward something. **2.** In a direction, position, or state understood or implied; esp., shut or closed: Pull the door *to*. **3.** Into a normal condition; into consciousness: She soon came *to*. **4.** *Naut.* With head to the wind: said of a sailing vessel: to lie *to*. **5.** Upon the matter at hand; into action or operation: They fell *to* with good will. **6.** Nearby; at hand. [OE *tō*]

toad (tōd) *n.* **1.** A tailless, jumping, insectivorous amphibian resembling the frog but without teeth in the upper jaw, and resorting to water only to breed. **2.** A lizard, the horned toad. **3.** Any person regarded scornfully or contemptuously. [OE *tāde*]

toad·fish (tōd′fish′) *n. pl.* **·fish** or **·fish·es** Any of various fishes of the Atlantic coast of the U.S., having scaleless skin, and a mouth and mouth resembling those of a toad.

toad·stool (tōd′stōōl′) *n.* **1.** A mushroom. **2.** *Informal* A poisonous mushroom.

toad·y (tō′dē) *n. pl.* **toad·ies** An obsequious flatterer; a fawning, servile person. — *v.t. & v.i.* **toad·ied, toad·y·ing** To act the toady (to). [Short for *toadeater* an assistant to a charlatan, who ate, or pretended to eat, toads to show the efficacy of a patent medicine] **— toad′y·ish** *adj.* **— toad′y·ism** *n.*

to-and-fro (tōō′ən-frō′) *adj.* Moving back and forth.

to and fro In opposite or different directions.

toast¹ (tōst) *v.t.* **1.** To brown before or over a fire; esp., to brown (bread or cheese) before a fire or in a toaster. **2.** To warm thoroughly before a fire. — *v.i.* **3.** To become warm or toasted. — *n.* Sliced bread browned in a toaster or at a fire. [< OF < L *tostus*, pp. of *torrere* to parch, roast]

toast² (tōst) *n.* **1.** The act of drinking to someone's health or to some sentiment. **2.** A person or sentiment named in so drinking. — *v.t.* **1.** To drink to the health of or in honor of. — *v.i.* **2.** To drink a toast. [< TOAST¹, in obs. sense of "a spiced piece of toast put in a drink to flavor it"]

toast·er¹ (tōs′tər) *n.* A device for making toast.

toast·er² (tōs′tər) *n.* One who proposes a toast.

toast·mas·ter (tōst′mas′tər, -mäs′tər) *n.* A person who, at public dinners, announces the toasts, calls upon the various speakers, etc. **— toast′mis′tress** (-mis′tris) *n.fem.*

to·bac·co (tə-bak′ō) *n. pl.* **·cos** or **·coes** **1.** An annual plant of the nightshade family. **2.** Its leaves prepared in various ways, as for smoking, chewing, etc. **3.** The use of tobacco for smoking. **4.** The various products prepared from tobacco leaves, as cigarettes, cigars, etc. [< Sp. *tabaco* < Carib, a tube or pipe used in smoking tobacco]

to·bac·co·nist (tə-bak′ə-nist) *n.* One who sells tobacco.

To·bit (tō′bit) A pious Hebrew captive in Nineveh, hero of the Apocryphal book of the Old Testament. — *n.* The Old Testament book bearing his name. Also **To·bi·as** (tə-bī′əs).

to·bog·gan (tə-bog′ən) *n.* A light sledlike vehicle, consisting of a long thin board or boards curved upward at the forward end, used for transporting goods or coasting. — *v.i.* **1.** To coast on a toboggan. **2.** To move downward swiftly: Wheat prices *tobogganed*. [< dial. F (Canadian) *tabagan* sleigh < Algonquian] **— to·bog′gan·er, to·bog′gan·ist** *n.*

to·by (tō′bē) *n. pl.* **·bies** A mug or jug for ale or beer, often made in the form of an old man wearing a three-cornered hat. [after *Toby*, dim. of *Tobias*, a personal name]

toc·ca·ta (tə-kä′tə, *Ital.* tôk-kä′tä) *n. Music* A free composition for a keyboard instrument, sometimes written to show virtuosity. [< Ital., orig. pp. fem. of *toccare* to touch]

toco- *combining form* Child; pertaining to children or to childbirth. Also, before vowels, **toc-**. [< Gk. *tokos* child]

to·coph·er·ol (tō-kof′ə-rōl, -rol) *n. Biochem.* Any of four closely related alcohols, widely distributed in nature and forming the active principle of vitamin E. [< TOCO- + Gk. *pherein* to bear + -OL¹]

toc·sin (tok′sin) *n.* **1.** A signal sounded on a bell; alarm. **2.** An alarm bell. [< MF < OF < Provençal < *tocar* to strike, touch + *senh* bell < L *signum* sign]

to·day (tə-dā′) *adv.* **1.** On or during this present day. **2.** At the present time; nowadays. — *n.* The present day, time, or age. Also **to-day′**. [OE < *tō* to + *dæg* day]

tod·dle (tod′l) *v.i.* **·dled, ·dling** To walk unsteadily and with short steps, as a little child. — *n.* The act of toddling; also, a stroll. [Origin uncertain] **— tod′dler** *n.*

tod·dy (tod′ē) *n. pl.* **·dies** **1.** A drink made with spirits, hot water, sugar, and a slice of lemon. **2.** The sap or juice of certain East Indian trees, the **toddy palms**. **3.** A spirituous liquor distilled from these palms. [< Hind. *tārī* toddy (def. 2) < *tār* palm tree]

to-do (tə-dōō′) *n. Informal* Confusion or bustle; fuss. [OE < *to-* asunder ┼ *dōn* to do, put]

toe (tō) *n.* **1.** One of the digits of the foot. **2.** The forward part of the foot, as distinguished from the heel. The portion of a shoe, sock, stocking, skate, etc., that covers or corresponds in position with the toes. **3.** The lower end or projection of something, resembling or suggestive of a toe. **— on one's toes** Alert; wide-awake. **— to tread on (someone's) toes** To trespass on (someone's) feelings, opinions, prejudices, etc. — *v.* **toed, toe·ing** *v.t.* **1.** To touch with the toes; to *toe* the line. **2.** To kick with the toe. **3.** To furnish with a toe. **4.** To drive (a nail or spike) obliquely; also, to attach (beams, etc.) end to end, by nails so driven. — *v.i.* **5.** To stand or walk with the toes pointing in a specified direction: to *toe* out. **— to toe the mark** (or **line**) To abide by the rules; conform. [OE *tā*] **— toe′less** *adj.*

toed (tōd) *adj.* Having toes: chiefly in combination: *pigeon-toed*.

toe-dance (tō′dans′, -däns′) *v.i.* **-danced, -danc·ing** To dance on tiptoe; perform a toe dance. **— toe dancer**

toe dance A dance performed on tiptoe.

toe·hold (tō′hōld′) *n.* **1.** A small space that supports the toes in climbing. **2.** Any means of entrance, support, etc.; a footing: to gain a *toehold* on the island. **3.** A hold in which a wrestler bends back the foot of his opponent.

toe·nail (tō′nāl′) *n.* **1.** A nail growing on the toe. **2.** A nail driven obliquely to hold the foot of a stud or brace. — *v.t.* To fasten with obliquely driven nails.

tof·fee (tôf′ē, tof′ē) *n.* Taffy. Also **tof′fy**.

tog (tog) *Informal n. pl.* Clothes; outfit. **— v.t. togged, tog·ging** To dress; clothe: often with *up* or *out*. [Short for vagabond's cant *togemans* < F < L *toga*]

to·ga (tō′gə) *n. pl.* **·gas** or **·gae** (-jē) **1.** The distinctive outer garment worn in public by a citizen of ancient Rome. **2.** Any gown or cloak characteristic of a calling or profession: the lawyer's *toga*. [< L *tegere* to cover] **— to′gaed** (-gəd) *adj.*

TOGA

to·geth·er (tōō-geth′ər, tə-) *adv.* **1.** Into union or contact with each other. **2.** In the same place or at the same spot; with each other; in company. **3.** At the same moment of time; simultaneously. **4.** Without cessation or intermission. **5.** With one another; mutually. [OE < *tō* to + *gædre* together]

tog·ger·y (tog′ər-ē) *n. pl.* **·ger·ies** *Informal* **1.** Togs collectively; clothes. **2.** A clothing shop.

tog·gle (tog/əl) *n.* A pin, or short rod, properly attached in the middle, as to a rope, and designed to be passed through a hole or eye and turned. — *v.t.* **·gled, ·gling** To fix, fasten, or furnish with a toggle. [Prob. var. of *tuggle*, appar. freq. of TUG]

toggle joint *Mech.* A joint having a central hinge like an elbow, and operable by applying the power at the junction, thus changing the direction of force and giving indefinite mechanical pressure.

toggle switch *Electr.* A switch in the form of a projecting lever whose movement through a small arc opens or closes an electric circuit.

toil¹ (toil) *n.* **1.** Fatiguing work; labor. **2.** Any oppressive task. **3.** Any notable work accomplished by labor. — *v.i.* **1.** To work arduously; labor painfully and tiringly. **2.** To progress or make one's way with slow and labored steps. [< AF < OF < L *tudiculare* to stir about] — **toil/er** *n.* — **Syn.** (noun) **1.** Work, labor, drudgery.

toil² (toil) *n.* **1.** *Usu. pl.* Something that binds or ensnares, as a net. **2.** *Archaic* A net, snare, or other trap. [< MF < OF < L *tela* web]

toile (twäl) *n.* A sheer linen fabric; also, a fine cretonne with scenic designs printed in one color. [< F. See TOIL².]

toi·let (toi/lit) *n.* **1.** *U.S.* **a** A room with a washbowl, water closet, etc.: sometimes called *bathroom.* **b** A hopper flushed and discharged by means of water, into which one urinates or defecates: also called *water closet.* **2.** The act of dressing oneself; formerly, esp. of dressing the hair. **3.** Attire. — *adj.* Used in dressing or grooming: *toilet* articles. [< F *toilette* orig., cloth dressing gown, dim. of *toile* cloth]

toi·let·ry (toi/lit-rē) *n.* *pl.* **·ries** Any of the several articles used in making one's toilet, as soap, comb, brush, etc.

toi·lette (toi·let/, *Fr.* twȧ·let/) *n.* **1.** The act or process of grooming oneself, usu. including bathing, hairdressing, etc. **2.** A person's actual dress or style of dress; also, any specific costume or gown. [< F]

toilet water A scented liquid containing a small amount of alcohol, used in or after the bath, after shaving, etc.

toil·some (toil/səm) *adj.* Accomplished with fatigue; involving toil. — **toil/some·ly** *adv.* — **toil/some·ness** *n.*

toil·worn (toil/wôrn/, -wōrn/) *adj.* Exhausted by toil; showing the effects of toil.

To·kay (tō·kā/) *n.* **1.** A white or reddish blue grape. **2.** A wine made from it. [after *Tokay,* Hungary]

to·ken (tō/kən) *n.* **1.** Anything indicative of some other thing; a visible sign. **2.** A symbol: a *token* of my affection. **3.** Some tangible proof or evidence of a statement or of one's identity, etc. **4.** A memento; souvenir. **5.** A characteristic mark or feature. **6.** A piece of metal issued as currency and having a face value greater than its actual value. **7.** A piece of metal issued by a transportation company and good for one fare. — *v.t.* To evidence by a token; betoken. — *adj.* Done or given as a token, esp. in partial fulfillment of an obligation. [OE *tācen, tācn*]

told (tōld) Past tense and past participle of TELL.

To·le·do (tə·lē/dō) *n.* *pl.* **·dos** A sword or sword blade from Toledo, Spain. Also **to·le/do.**

tol·er·a·ble (tol/ər·ə·bəl) *adj.* **1.** Passably good; commonplace. **2.** Endurable. **3.** Allowable; permissible. **4.** *Informal* In passably good health. [< OF < L *tolerare* to endure] — **tol/er·a·ble·ness** *n.* — **tol/er·a·bly** *adv.*

tol·er·ance (tol/ər·əns) *n.* **1.** The character, state, or quality of being tolerant. **2.** Freedom from bigotry or from racial or religious prejudice. **3.** The act of enduring, or the capacity for endurance. **4.** A small permissible allowance for variations from the specified weight, dimensions, etc. **5.** *Med.* Ability to tolerate, as a drug.

tol·er·ant (tol/ər·ənt) *adj.* **1.** Disposed to tolerate beliefs, views, etc. **2.** Indulgent; liberal. **3.** *Med.* Capable of taking with impunity unusual or excessive doses of dangerous drugs. — **tol/er·ant·ly** *adv.*

tol·er·ate (tol/ə·rāt) *v.t.* **·at·ed, ·at·ing 1.** To allow to be or be done without active opposition. **2.** To concede, as the right to opinions or participation. **3.** To bear, sustain, or be capable of sustaining. **4.** *Med.* To endure, as a poisonous amount or dose, with impunity. [< L *toleratus,* pp. of *tolerare* to endure] — **tol/er·a/tive** *adj.* — **tol/er·a/tor** *n.*

tol·er·a·tion (tol/ə·rā/shən) *n.* **1.** The act or practice of tolerance. **2.** The recognition of the rights of the individual to his own opinions and customs, as in religious worship.

toll¹ (tōl) *n.* **1.** A fixed compensation for some privilege granted or service rendered, as passage on a bridge or turnpike. **2.** The right to levy such charge. **3.** Something taken or elicited like a toll; price: The train wreck took a heavy *toll* of lives. **4.** A due charged for shipping or landing goods. **5.** A charge for transportation of goods, esp. by rail or canal. **6.** A charge for a long-distance telephone call. [OE < LL < L < Gk. *telōnion* customhouse < *telos* tax]

toll² (tōl) *v.t.* **1.** To cause (a bell) to sound slowly and at regular intervals. **2.** To announce by tolling, as a death or funeral. **3.** To call or summon by tolling. **4.** To decoy (game, esp. ducks). — *v.i.* **5.** To sound slowly and at regular intervals. — *n.* The act or sound of tolling a bell. [ME *tollen, tullen*]

toll·bar (tōl/bär/) *n.* A tollgate, esp. one with a single bar.

toll bridge A bridge at which a toll is charged for passage.

toll call A long-distance telephone call, the charge for which is higher than local rates.

toll collector A collector of tolls.

toll·er (tō/lər) *n.* **1.** One who tolls a bell. **2.** A bell used for tolling. **3.** A small dog trained to toll or decoy ducks.

toll·gate (tōl/gāt/) *n.* A gate at the entrance to a bridge, or on a road, at which toll is paid.

toll·house (tōl/hous/) *n.* A toll collector's lodge adjoining a tollgate: also **toll/booth/** (-bōōth/, -bōōth/).

toll·keep·er (tōl/kē/pər) *n.* One who keeps a tollgate.

toll line A long-distance telephone line or channel for the use of which a toll is charged.

toll road A road on which a toll is charged for each vehicle using it. Also **toll·way** (tōl/wā/).

Tol·tec (tol/tek, tōl/-) *n.* One of certain ancient Nahuatlan tribes that dominated central and southern Mexico about A.D. 900–1100 and through contact with Mayan culture founded the highly civilized Nahua culture of the Aztecs. — *adj.* Of or pertaining to the Toltecs. [< Nahuatl *Tolteca*] — **Tol/tec·an** *adj.*

tol·u·ene (tol/yōō·ēn) *n.* *Chem.* A colorless, flammable liquid hydrocarbon, $C_6H_5CH_3$, obtained from coal tar by distillation and used in making dyestuffs, explosives, etc.

tom (tom) *n.* The male of various animals, esp. the cat. [after *Tom,* a personal name. See TOMCAT.]

tom·a·hawk (tom/ə·hôk) *n.* **1.** An axlike weapon used by North American Indians, originally a carved club in which a piece of bone or metal was inserted. **2.** Any similar weapon, tool, etc. — *v.t.* To strike or kill with a tomahawk. [< Algonquian < *tamahaken* he uses for cutting]

tom·al·ley (tom/al·ē) *n.* The liver of the lobster, considered a delicacy. [Prob. < Carib]

Tom and Jer·ry (tom/ ən jer/ē) A drink made with brandy, rum, beaten egg, hot milk or water, sugar, and nutmeg. [after two main characters in *Life in London,* 1821, by Pierce Egan, 1772–1849]

to·ma·to (tə·mā/tō, -mä/-) *n.* *pl.* **·toes 1.** The large, pulpy, edible berry, yellow or red when ripe, of a perennial plant of the nightshade family, widely cultivated as a vegetable. **2.** The plant itself. **3.** *U.S. Slang* A girl or woman. [< Sp. < Nahuatl *tomatl*]

tomb (tōōm) *n.* **1.** A place for the burial of the dead, as a vault or grave. **2.** Any place or structure serving as a final repository for the dead. **3.** A monument, tombstone, etc., commemorating the dead. **4.** Death: often preceded by *the.* [< AF *tumbe,* OF *tombe* < LL < Gk. *tymbos* mound]

tom·boy (tom/boi/) *n.* A girl who prefers boyish activities, dress, etc. — **tom/boy/ish** *adj.* — **tom/boy/ish·ness** *n.*

tomb·stone (tōōm/stōn/) *n.* A stone, usu. inscribed, marking a place of burial.

tom·cat (tom/kat/) *n.* A male cat. [after *Tom,* a male cat, hero of *The Life and Adventures of a Cat,* 1760]

Tom Col·lins (tom kol/inz) A drink consisting of gin, lemon or lime juice, sugar, and carbonated water.

Tom, Dick, and Har·ry (dik/ har/ē) Any persons taken at random from the general public: used disparagingly, and often preceded by *every.*

tome (tōm) *n.* **1.** A volume; large book. **2.** One of a series of volumes. [< MF < L < Gk. *tomos* fragment]

-tome *combining form* A cutting instrument (of a specified kind). [< Gk. *tomos* a cutting < *temnein* to cut]

tom·fool (tom/fōōl/) *n.* An idiotic or silly person. — *adj.* Very stupid or foolish. [after *Tom Fool,* a name formerly applied to mental defectives]

tom·fool·er·y (tom/fōō/lər·ē) *n.* *pl.* **·er·ies 1.** Nonsensical or foolish behavior. **2.** Worthless or trivial stuff; frippery. Also **tom/fool/ish·ness** (-fōō/lish·nis).

tom·my (tom/ē) *n.* *pl.* **·mies** *Brit. Informal Often cap.* A British soldier.

Tommy gun A Thompson submachine gun.

tom·my·rot (tom/ē·rot/) *n.* *Informal* Utter nonsense.

to·mor·row (tə·môr/ō, -mor/ō) *adv.* On or for the next day after today. — *n.* **1.** The next day after today; the morrow. **2.** Some time in the future. Also **to·mor/row.** [ME < OE < *tō* to + *morgen* morning, morrow]

tom·pi·on (tom/pē·ən) *n.* See TAMPION.

Tom Thumb 1. In English folklore, a hero who was no bigger than his father's thumb. **2.** A tiny person.

tom·tit (tom/tit/) *n.* Any of various small birds, as a chickadee or a wren. [< TOM + TIT¹]

tom-tom (tom/tom/) *n.* A drum of India, Africa, etc., variously shaped and usu. beaten with the hands. [< Hind. *tamtam,* imit. of the instrument's sound]

-tomy *combining form* **1.** *Surg.* A cutting of a (specified) part or tissue. **2.** A (specified) kind of cutting or division: *dichotomy.* [< Gk. *tomē* a cutting < *temnein* to cut]

ton (tun) *n.* **1.** Any of several large measures of weight; esp.: **a** The **short ton** of 2000 pounds avoirdupois, commonly used in the U.S. and Canada. **b** The **long** or **gross ton** of 2240 pounds, used in Great Britain. See table front of book. **2.** A unit for reckoning the displacement or weight of vessels, 35 cubic feet of sea water weighing about one long ton: called in full a **displacement ton. 3.** A unit for reckoning the freight-carrying capacity of a ship, usu. equivalent to 40 cubic feet of space but varying with the cargo: called in full a **freight ton** or **measurement ton. 4.** A unit for reckoning the internal capacity of merchant vessels for purposes of registration, equivalent to 100 cubic feet or 2.8317 cubic meters: called in full a **register ton. 5.** A metric ton. Var. of TUN]

ton- Var. of TONO-.

-ton *suffix* Town: used in place names: *Charleston.* [OE < *tūn*]

to·nal (tō'nəl) *adj.* Of or pertaining to tone or tonality. — **to'nal·ly** *adv.*

to·nal·i·ty (tō-nal'ə-tē) *n. pl.* **·ties 1.** *Music* **a** The use of a system of tones so that one tone is the central or primary tone of the system. **b** Any particular arrangement of this type centering on a specific tone; key; mode. **2.** The general color scheme or collective tones of a painting.

tone (tōn) *n.* **1.** Sound in relation to quality, volume, duration, and pitch. **2.** A sound having a definite pitch. **3.** *Music* **a** The timbre, or characteristic sound, of a voice, instrument, etc. **b** The interval between the first two degrees of a major scale: also called *whole tone.* **4.** A predominating disposition; mood. **5.** Characteristic style or tendency; tenor. **6.** Style or distinction; elegance. **7.** Vocal inflection as expressive of feeling: a *tone* of pity. **8.** *Phonet.* **a** The acoustical pitch, or change in pitch, of a phrase or sentence. **b** Special stress or pitch accent given to a syllable or word. **9.** The prevailing impression of a picture, produced by effects of light and shadow, variations in color quality, etc. **10.** A shade, hue, tint, or degree of a particular color, or some slight modification of it: red with a purplish *tone.* **11.** *Physiol.* **a** The general condition of the body with reference to the vigorous and healthy discharge of its functions. **b** Firmness and resilience, as of a tissue. — *Syn.* See SOUND¹. — *v.* **toned, ton·ing** *v.t.* **1.** To give tone to. **2.** To modify in tone. **3.** To alter the color or increase the brilliancy of (a photographic print) by a chemical bath. **4.** *Rare* To intone. — *v.i.* **5.** To assume a certain tone or hue. **6.** To blend or harmonize, as in tone or shade. — **to tone down 1.** To subdue the tone of (a painting). **2.** To moderate in quality or tone. — **to tone up 1.** To raise in quality or strength. **2.** To gain in vitality. [< OF < L < Gk. *teinein* to stretch]

tone color The timbre of a voice, musical instrument, etc.

tone-deaf (tōn'def') *adj.* Unable to perceive fine distinctions in pitch, as musical intervals. — **tone'deaf'ness** *n.*

tone·less (tōn'lis) *adj.* **1.** Having no tone; without tone. **2.** Lacking spirit or vivacity; listless. — **tone'less·ly** *adv.* — **tone'less·ness** *n.*

tong¹ (tông, tong) *v.t.* **1.** To gather, collect, or seize with tongs. — *v.i.* **2.** To use tongs, as for fishing. [< TONGS]

tong² (tông, tong) *n.* A Chinese secret society or fraternal association; esp., such a group formerly active in the U.S. [< Chinese *t'ang* hall, meeting place]

Ton·ga (tong'gə) *n.* A Polynesian language spoken in the Tonga Islands.

tongs (tôngz, tongz) *n.pl.* (*sometimes construed as sing.*) An implement for grasping, holding, or lifting objects, consisting usu. of a pair of pivoted levers: sometimes called a **pair of tongs.** [OE *tang, tange*]

tongue (tung) *n.* **1.** A protrusile, freely moving organ situated in the mouth of most vertebrates, highly developed in mammals, where it serves as an organ of taste, and in man also as an organ of speech. ◆ Collateral adjective: *lingual.* For illus. see THROAT. **2.** *Zool.* An analogous organ or part of the mouth of various insects, fishes, etc. **3.** An animal's tongue, as of beef, prepared as food. **4.** The power of speech or articulation: to lose one's *tongue.* **5.** Manner or style of speaking: a smooth *tongue.* **6.** Mere speech, as contrasted with fact or deed. **7.** Utterance. **8.** A language, vernacular, or dialect. **9.** *Archaic* A people or race, regarded as having its own language: a Biblical use. **10.** Anything resembling an animal tongue in shape or function. **11.** A slender projection of land, as a cape or small promontory. **12.** A long narrow bay or inlet of water. **13.** A jet of flame. **14.** A strip of leather for closing the gap in the front of a shoe. **15.** *Music* The free or vibrating end of a reed in a wind instrument. **16.** The clapper of a bell. **17.** The harnessing pole of a horse-drawn vehicle. **18.** Any flange or projecting part of a machine or mechanical device. **19.** A projecting edge or tenon of a board for insertion into a corresponding groove of another board, thus forming a **tongue-and-groove joint.** — **on the tip of one's tongue** On the verge of being recalled. — **to**

hold one's tongue To keep silent. — **(with) tongue in cheek** With ironical or facetious intent. — *v.* **tongued, tongu·ing** *v.t.* **1.** *Music* In wind-instrument playing: **a** To separate the tones played on (an instrument) by means of the tongue. **b** To begin (a tone) using the tongue. **c** To tongue the notes of (a phrase, etc.). **2.** To touch or lap with the tongue. **3.** In carpentry: **a** To cut a tongue on (a board). **b** To join or fit by a tongue-and-groove joint. **4.** *Poetic* To utter; articulate. — *v.i.* **5.** To use the tongue in playing a wind instrument. **6.** To talk or prattle. **7.** To extend as a tongue. [OE *tunge*]

tongued (tungd) *adj.* **1.** Having a tongue or tongues. **2.** Having or characterized by a (specified kind of) tongue or (a specified number of) tongues: *sharp-tongued.*

tongue-lash·ing (tung'lash'ing) *n. Informal* A severe or thoroughgoing reprimand; scolding.

tongue·less (tung'lis) *adj.* **1.** Having no tongue. **2.** Speechless; dumb.

tongue-tie (tung'tī') *n.* Abnormal shortness of the frenum of the tongue, whereby its motion is impeded or confined. — *v.t.* **-tied, -ty·ing** To deprive of speech or the power of speech, or of distinct articulation.

tongue-tied (tung'tīd') *adj.* **1.** Speechless or halting in speech, as from shyness, etc. **2.** Impeded by tongue-tie.

tongue twister A word or phrase difficult to articulate quickly, as "Miss Smith's fish-sauce shop."

ton·ic (ton'ik) *adj.* **1.** Having power to invigorate or build up; bracing. **2.** Pertaining to tone or tones. **3.** *Music* Pertaining to or in the key of the keynote. **4.** In art, denoting the general effect of color or of light and shade. **5.** *Physiol.* **a** Of or pertaining to tension, especially muscular tension. **b** Rigid; unrelaxing: *tonic* spasm. **6.** *Phonet.* Stressed, as a syllable. — *n.* **1.** A medicine that gradually restores the normal tone of organs from a condition of debility. **2.** Something imparting animation, vigor, or tone. **3.** *Music* The basic tone of a key or mode. **4.** Quinine water: gin and *tonic.* **5.** *U.S.* In the Boston area, soda (def. 2). [< Gk. < *tonos* sound, tone]

tonic accent An accent that is spoken or pronounced rather than written.

to·nic·i·ty (tō-nis'ə-tē) *n.* The resilience and elasticity of healthy muscles, arteries, and other bodily tissues.

tonic sol-fa A system of musical notation that uses the initial letters of the solmization syllables to indicate pitch, and dots and lines to indicate rhythm.

to·night (tə-nīt') *adv.* In or during the present or coming night. — *n.* **1.** The night that follows this day. **2.** The present night. Also **to-night'.** [OE < *tō* + *niht* night]

ton·nage (tun'ij) *n.* **1.** The cubic capacity of a merchant vessel expressed in tons of 100 cubic feet each. **2.** The total carrying capacity of a collection of vessels, esp. of a country's merchant marine. **3.** A tax levied on vessels at a given rate per ton. **4.** Total weight in tons, as of materials produced, mined, or transported.

ton·neau (tu-nō') *n. pl.* **·neaus** (-nōz') or **·neaux** (-nōz') The rear part of an early type of automobile or vehicle, with seats enclosed by low sides. [< F, lit., barrel]

tono- *combining form* **1.** Tension; pressure. **2.** *Music* Tone; pitch. Also, before vowels, *ton-.* [< Gk. *tonos* tension < *teinein* to stretch]

ton·sil (ton'səl) *n. Anat.* One of two oval lymphoid organs situated on either side of the passage from the mouth to the pharynx. For illus. see THROAT. [< L *tonsillae* tonsils] — **ton·sil·lar** or **ton·sil·ar** *adj.*

ton·sil·lec·to·my (ton'sə-lek'tə-mē) *n. pl.* **·mies** *Surg.* Removal of a tonsil or tonsils.

ton·sil·li·tis (ton'sə-lī'tis) *n. Pathol.* Inflammation of the tonsils. — **ton·sil·lit'ic** (-lit'ik) *adj.*

ton·so·ri·al (ton-sôr'ē-əl, sō'rē-) *adj.* Pertaining to a barber or barbering: chiefly in the humorous term **tonsorial artist,** a barber. [< L *tonsus,* pp. of *tondere* to clip]

ton·sure (ton'shər) *n.* **1.** The shaving of the head, or of the crown of the head, as of a priest or monk. **2.** The state of being thus shaven. **3.** The part of a priest's or monk's head left bare by shaving. — *v.t.* **-sured, -sur·ing** To shave the head of. [< OF < L. See TONSORIAL.]

ton·tine (ton'tēn, ton-tēn') *n.* A form of collective life annuity, the individual profits of which increase as the number of survivors diminishes, the final survivor taking the whole. [< F, after Lorenzo *Tonti,* a Neapolitan banker who introduced it into France in about 1653]

ton·y (tō'nē) *adj.* **ton·i·er, ton·i·est** *Informal* High toned; fashionable; stylish. [< TONE (def. 6)]

too (tōō) *adv.* **1.** In addition; likewise; also. **2.** In excessive quantity or degree; more than sufficiently. **3.** *Informal* Very; extremely: That's not *too* likely. **4.** *Informal* Indeed: an intensive, often used to reiterate a contradicted statement: You are *too* going! [Stressed var. of OE *tō* to]

took (tōōk) Past tense of TAKE.

tool (tōōl) *n.* **1.** A simple mechanism or implement, as a hammer, saw, spade, or chisel, used chiefly in manual work. **2.** A power-driven apparatus, as a lathe, used for cutting and shaping the parts of a machine. **3.** The cutting or shaping part of such an apparatus. **4.** A bookbinder's hand stamp used in lettering or ornamenting book covers. **5.** A person used to carry out the designs of others or another; a dupe. **6.** Any instrument or means necessary to the efficient prosecution of one's profession or trade: Words are the writer's *tools.* — *v.t.* **1.** To shape, mark, or ornament with a tool. **2.** To provide with tools. **3.** To ornament or impress designs upon (leather, a book binding, etc.) with a roller bearing a pattern. — *v.i.* **4.** To work with a tool or tools. [OE *tōl*] — **tool′er** *n.*

tool·ing (tōō′ling) *n.* **1.** Ornamentation or work done with tools; esp., stamped or gilded ornamental designs on leather. **2.** The application of a tool or tools to any work.

tool·mak·er (tōōl′mā′kər) *n.* A maker of tools.

toot (tōōt) *v.i.* **1.** To blow a horn, whistle, etc., esp. with short blasts. **2.** To give forth a blast or toot, as a horn. **3.** To make a similar sound. — *v.t.* **4.** To sound (a horn, etc.) with short blasts. **5.** To sound (a blast, etc.). — *n.* **1.** A short note or blast on or as on a horn. **2.** *Slang* A spree; esp., a drinking spree. [? < MLG *tūten;* prob. orig. imit.] — **toot′er** *n.*

tooth (tōōth) *n. pl.* **teeth** (tēth) **1.** One of the hard structures in the mouth of most vertebrates, used for seizing and chewing food, as offensive and defensive weapons, etc. ◆ Collateral adjective: *dental.* **2.** One of various hard calcareous or chitinous bodies of the oral or gastric regions of invertebrates. **3.** Any small toothlike projection, as at the edge of a leaf. **4.** Something resembling a tooth in form or use; esp., a projecting point, tine, or cog, as on a saw, comb, fork, rake, or gearwheel. **5.** Appetite; liking: used chiefly in the expression *sweet tooth.* **6.** *pl.* Something that opposes in or as in a gnawing, biting, or piercing manner: the *teeth* of the wind. — **armed to the teeth** Completely or heavily armed. — **in the teeth of** Directly against, counter to, or in defiance of. — **to get one's teeth into** To achieve a solid grip or grasp of; engage completely with. — **to show one's teeth** To display a disposition to fight; threaten. — **to throw (cast, fling,** etc.**) (something) in one's teeth** To fling at one, as a challenge or taunt. — *v.t.* **1.** To supply with teeth, as a rake or saw. **2.** To give a serrated edge to; indent. — *v.i.* **3.** To become interlocked, as gear wheels. [OE *tōth*]

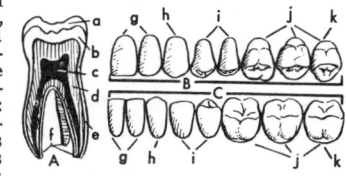

TEETH OF ADULT HUMAN

A Section of a molar: a Crown, *b* Enamel, *c* Pulp cavity, *d* Dentine, *e* Cementum, *f* Roots. *B* and *C* Left upper and lower jaws: *g* Incisors, *h* Canines, *i* Bicuspids, *j* Molars, *k* Wisdom teeth.

tooth·ache (tōōth′āk′) *n.* Pain in a tooth or teeth.

tooth and nail With all possible strength and effort; fiercely: to fight *tooth and nail.*

tooth·brush (tōōth′brush′) *n.* A small brush used for cleaning the teeth.

toothed (tōōtht, tōōthd) *adj.* **1.** Having teeth. **2.** Having or characterized by a (specified kind or number of) teeth: used in combination: *sharp-toothed.* **3.** Notched or indented.

tooth·less (tōōth′lis) *adj.* **1.** Being without teeth. **2.** Lacking effective power or force; ineffectual. — **tooth′less·ly** *adv.*

tooth·paste (tōōth′pāst′) *n.* A paste used to clean teeth.

tooth·pick (tōōth′pik′) *n.* A small sliver of wood, plastic, etc., used for removing particles of food from between the teeth.

tooth·pow·der (tōōth′pou′dər) *n.* A powder used in cleaning the teeth.

tooth·some (tōōth′səm) *adj.* **1.** Having a pleasant taste. **2.** Appetizing; attractive. — **tooth′some·ly** *adv.* — **tooth′-some·ness** *n.*

tooth·y (tōō′thē) *adj.* **tooth·i·er, tooth·i·est** **1.** Having large or prominent teeth. **2.** Displaying the teeth: a *toothy* smile.

too·tle (tōōt′l) *v.t. & v.i.* ·**tled, ·tling** To toot lightly or continuously, as on the flute. — *n.* The act or sound of tootling. [Freq. of TOOT]

top¹ (top) *n.* **1.** The uppermost or highest part, end, side, or surface of anything. **2.** The end or part regarded as the higher or upper extremity: the *top* of the street. **3.** A lid or cover: a bottle *top.* **4.** *U.S.* The roof of a vehicle, as an automobile. **5.** The crown of the head: from *top* to toe. **6.** *pl.* The aboveground part of a plant producing root vegetables. **7.** The highest degree or range: the *top* of one's ambition. **8.** The highest or most prominent place or rank. **9.** One who is highest in rank or position. **10.** The highest or loudest pitch: at the *top* of his voice. **11.** The choicest or best

part: the *top* of the crop. **12.** In bridge, etc., the highest card in a suit. **13.** In tennis, golf, etc.: **a** A stroke in which the player hits the ball above the center or on the upper half. **b** The forward spinning motion thus imparted to the ball. **14.** *Naut.* A platform at the head of the lower section of a ship's mast, used as a place to stand and for extending the topmast rigging. — **to blow one's top** *Slang* **1.** To break out in a rage; flare up. **2.** To go insane. — **on top 1.** At the highest point or position. **2.** In a situation of dominance or power. **3.** Highly successful. — **on top of 1.** On the highest point or upper surface of. **2.** In addition to; as a climax to. — **over the top 1.** In trench warfare, over the breastwork, as in an attack. **2.** Beyond a set goal, quota, etc. — *adj.* **1.** Of or pertaining to the top. **2.** Forming or comprising the top or upper part. **3.** Highest in rank or quality; chief: *top* authors. **4.** Greatest in amount or degree: *top* prices. — *v.* **topped, top·ping** *v.t.* **1.** To remove the top or upper end of. **2.** To provide with a top, cap, etc. **3.** To form the top of. **4.** To reach or pass over the top of; surmount. **5.** To surpass or exceed. **6.** In golf, tennis, etc., to hit the upper part of (the ball) in making a stroke. — *v.i.* **7.** To top someone or something. — **to top off 1.** To put something on the top of. **2.** To complete or finish with a final or crowning touch. [OE]

top² (top) *n.* A toy with a point on which it is made to spin, as by the unwinding of a string, spring, etc. [OE]

top- Var. of TOPO-.

to·paz (tō′paz) *n.* **1.** A native silicate of aluminum, occurring in prismatic crystals of various colors, but chiefly yellow to brownish, that are valued as gemstones. **2.** A yellow variety of sapphire. Also **Oriental topaz. 3.** A brownish or grayish yellow. [< OF < L < Gk. *topazos*]

top boot A boot with a high top that is sometimes bordered or decorated with material different from the rest of the boot.

top·coat (top′kōt′) *n.* A lightweight overcoat.

top dog *Informal* The leading or dominant individual or group; the head; chief. — **top-dog** (top′dôg′, -dog′) *adj.*

top-draw·er (top′drôr′) *adj. Informal* Of the highest standing, merit, excellence, etc.

top-dress (top′dres′) *v.t. Agric.* To apply top-dressing to.

top-dress·ing (top′dres′ing) *n.* A dressing of manure spread over the surface of a field. Also **top′dress′ing, top dressing.**

tope (tōp) *v.t.* **toped, top·ing** To drink (alcoholic beverages) excessively and frequently. [? Akin to earlier *top* to tilt]

top·er (tō′pər) *n.* A habitual drunkard; sot. [< TOPE]

top-flight (top′flit′) *adj.* Of the highest quality; superior.

top·gal·lant (tə·gal′ənt, top′gal′ənt) *n. Naut.* **1.** The mast, sail, yard, or rigging immediately above the topmast and topsail. **2.** The parts of a deck that are higher than the rest. — *adj.* Pertaining to the topgallants. [< TOP¹ + GALLANT; with ref. to "making a gallant show" compared with the lower tops]

top hat A man's hat, usu. made of silk, having a tall, cylindrical crown and a narrow brim: also called *high hat.*

top-heav·y (top′hev′ē) *adj.* **-heav·i·er, -heav·i·est 1.** Having the top or upper part too heavy for the lower part; ill-proportioned or precariously balanced. **2.** In finance, overcapitalized. — **top′-heav′i·ly** *adv.* — **top′-heav′i·ness** *n.*

to·pi (tō·pē′) *n.* A helmet made of pith, worn as protection against the sun: also called *pith helmet.* [< Hind., hat]

top·ic (top′ik) *n.* **1.** A subject of discourse or of a treatise. **2.** Any matter treated of in speech or writing; a theme for discussion. **3.** A subdivision of an outline or a treatise. [< L < Gk. *(ta) topika,* title of a work by Aristotle, neut. pl. of *topikos* of a place < *topos* place, commonplace]

top·i·cal (top′i·kəl) *adj.* **1.** Pertaining to a topic. **2.** Of the nature of merely probable argument. **3.** Belonging to a place or spot; local. **4.** Pertaining to matters of present interest: a *topical* song. **5.** *Med.* Local. — **top′i·cal·ly** *adv.*

top kick *Slang* A top sergeant.

top·knot (top′not′) *n.* **1.** A crest, tuft, or knot on the top of the head, as of feathers on the head of a bird. **2.** The hair of the human head when worn as a high knot.

top·less (top′lis) *adj.* **1.** Lacking a top. **2.** Nude above the waist, or designed to include such nudity, as a bathing suit. — **top′less·ness** *n.*

top·loft·y (top′lôf′tē, -lof′tē) *adj.* **·loft·i·er, ·loft·i·est 1.** Towering very high. **2.** Very proud or haughty; inflated; pompous. — **top′loft′i·ly** *adv.* — **top′loft′i·ness** *n.*

top·mast (top′məst, top′mast′, mäst′) *n. Naut.* The mast next above the lower mast.

top·most (top′mōst′) *adj.* Being at the very top.

top notch (top′noch′) *adj. Informal* Excellent; best.

topo- *combining form* A place or region; regional. Also, before vowels, **top-.** [< Gk. *topos* place]

to·pog·ra·pher (tə·pog′rə·fər) *n.* An expert in topography.

to·pog·ra·phy (tə·pog′rə·fē) *n. pl.* **·phies 1.** The detailed description of places. **2.** The art of representing on a map the physical features of a place. **3.** The physical features, collectively, of a region. **4.** Surveying with reference to the physical features of a region. — **top·o·graph·ic** (top'ə·graf'·ik) or **·i·cal** adj. — **top'o·graph'i·cal·ly** adv.

top·per (top'ər) n. 1. One who or that which cuts off the top of something. 2. Slang One who or that which is of supreme quality. 3. Slang A top hat. 4. A woman's short, usu. lightweight, coat.

top·ping (top'ing) adj. Brit. Informal Excellent; first rate. — n. 1. That which forms the top of anything. 2. A sauce, garnish, etc., put on a cake, portion of food, etc.

top·ple (top'əl) v. **·pled**, **·pling** v.t. 1. To push and cause to totter or fall by its own weight; overturn. — v.i. 2. To totter and fall, as by its own weight. 3. To lean or jut out, as if about to fall. [Freq. of TOP¹, v.]

tops (tops) adj. Slang Excellent; first-rate.

top·sail (top'səl, top'sāl') n. Naut. 1. In a square-rigged vessel, a square sail set next above the lowest sail of a mast. 2. In a fore-and-aft-rigged vessel, a square or triangular sail carried above the gaff of a lower sail.

top-se·cret (top'sē'krit) adj. U.S. Mil. Denoting the highest category of security classification. Compare SECRET.

top sergeant Informal The first sergeant of a company, battery, or troop.

top·side (top'sīd') n. Naut. The portion of a ship above the main deck. — adv. To or on the upper parts of a ship.

top·soil (top'soil') n. The surface soil of land.

top-sy-tur·vy (top'sē-tûr'vē) adv. 1. Upside-down; hind side before. 2. In utter confusion. — adj. 1. Being in an upset or disordered condition. 2. Upside-down. — n. A state of confusion; disorder; chaos. [Prob. < TOP¹ + obs. terve to turn, overturn] — **top'sy-tur'vi·ly** adv. — **top'sy-tur'vi·ness** n. — **top'sy-tur'vy·dom** (-dəm) n.

toque (tōk) n. A close-fitting, brimless hat worn by women. [< F, cap < Sp. < Basque tauka, a kind of cap]

to·rah (tô'rə, tō'rə) n. In Hebrew literature, a law; also, counsel or instruction proceeding from a specially sacred source. Also **to'ra.** [< Hebrew tōrāh instruction, law]

To·rah (tô'rə, tō'rə) n. In Judaism, the Pentateuch: also called the Law.

torch (tôrch) n. 1. A source of light, as from flaming pine knots, or from some material dipped in tallow, etc., and fixed at the end of a handle. 2. Anything that illuminates: the torch of science. 3. A portable device giving off an intensely hot flame and used for burning off paint, melting solder, etc. 4. Brit. A flashlight. — **to carry a** (or **the**) **torch for** Slang To continue to love (someone), though the love is unrequited. [< OF torche, ult. < L torquere to twist]

torch·bear·er (tôrch'bâr'ər) n. 1. One who carries a torch. 2. One who imparts knowledge, truth, etc.

tor·chère (tôr·shâr') n. A tall lamp giving light directed upward by a bowllike shade. [< F, candelabrum]

torch·light (tôrch'līt') n. The light of a torch or torches. — adj. Lighted by torches: a torchlight rally.

torch song A popular love song expressing sadness and hopeless yearning. [< phrase to carry a torch for]

tore (tôr, tōr) Past tense of TEAR¹.

tor·e·a·dor (tôr'ē·ə·dôr', Sp. tō'rā·ä·thôr') n. A bullfighter. [< Sp. < torear to fight bulls < L taurus bull]

to·ri·i (tôr'i·ē, tō'ri·ē) n. The gateway of a Shinto temple, consisting of two uprights with one straight crosspiece, and another above with a concave lintel. [< Japanese]

tor·ment (n. tôr'ment; v. tôr·ment') n. 1. Intense bodily pain or mental anguish; agony; torture. 2. One who or that which torments. — v.t. 1. To subject to excruciating physical or mental suffering. 2. To make miserable. 3. To harass. [< OF < L tormentum rack < torquere to twist] — **tor·ment'er, tor·men'tor** n. — **tor·ment'ing·ly** adv.

torn (tôrn, tōrn) Past participle of TEAR¹.

tor·na·do (tôr·nā'dō) n. pl. **·does** or **·dos** Meteorol. 1. A whirling wind of exceptional violence, accompanied by a pendulous, funnel-shaped cloud marking the narrow path of greatest destruction. 2. Any whirlwind or hurricane. [Prob. alter. of Sp. tronada thunderstorm < L tonare to thunder] — **tor·nad'ic** (-nad'ik) adj.

tor·pe·do (tôr·pē'dō) n. pl. **·dos** or **·does** 1. A device or apparatus containing an explosive to be fired by concussion or otherwise. 2. An explosive, self-propelled, cigar-shaped underwater projectile, used to destroy enemy ships. 3. A submarine mine. 4. The electric ray, a fish. — v.t. **·doed**, **·do·ing** To sink, damage, or wreck with or as with a torpedo. [< L, numbness < torpere to be numb]

torpedo boat A small, swift war vessel equipped with tubes for the discharge of torpedoes.

tor·pid (tôr'pid) adj. 1. Inactive, as a hibernating animal. 2. Dormant; numb. 3. Sluggish; apathetic; dull. [< L torpere to be numb] — **tor·pid·i·ty** (tôr·pid'ə·tē), **tor'pid·ness** n. — **tor'pid·ly** adv.

tor·por (tôr'pər) n. 1. Complete or partial insensibility; stupor. 2. Apathy; torpidity. — **tor'po·rif'ic** adj.

torque (tôrk) n. Mech. Anything that causes or tends to cause torsion in a body; the rotary force in a mechanism. [< L torquere to twist]

tor·rent (tôr'ənt, tor'-) n. 1. A stream, as of water, flowing with great velocity or turbulence. 2. Any abundant or tumultuous flow: a torrent of abuse. [< OF < L torrens, boiling, burning, ppr. of torrere to parch]

tor·ren·tial (tô·ren'shəl, to-) adj. 1. Of, resembling, or resulting from the action of a torrent. 2. Suggestive of a torrent; overpowering. — **tor·ren'tial·ly** adv.

tor·rid (tôr'id, tor'-) adj. 1. Exposed to or receiving the full force of the sun's heat. 2. Very hot; scorching; burning. 3. Impassioned; ardent. [< L torrere to parch] — **tor·rid·i·ty** (to·rid'ə·tē, to-), **tor'rid·ness** n. — **tor'rid·ly** adv.

tor·sion (tôr'shən) n. 1. The act of twisting, or the state of being twisted. 2. Mech. Deformation of a body, as a thread or rod, by twisting around its length as an axis. 3. The force with which a twisted cord or cable tends to return to its former position. [< OF < LL < L < torquere to twist] — **tor'sion·al** adj. — **tor'sion·al·ly** adv.

tor·so (tôr'sō) n. pl. **·sos** or **·si** (-sē) 1. The trunk of a human body. 2. A sculptured representation of a human body without the head or limbs. 3. Any truncated or defective thing. [< Ital. < L < Gk. thyrsos stalk]

tort (tôrt) n. Law Any private or civil wrong by act or omission for which a civil suit can be brought, but not including breach of contract. [See TORSION.]

torte (tôrt, Ger. tôr'tə) n. A rich cake made with butter, eggs, and often fruit and nuts. [< G < Ital. torta]

tor·til·la (tôr·tē'yä) n. In Mexico, a flat cake made of coarse cornmeal baked on a hot sheet of iron or a slab of stone. [< Sp., dim. of torta cake < LL < L torquere to twist]

tor·toise (tôr'təs) n. 1. A turtle; esp., one of a terrestrial species as distinguished from those that are aquatic. 2. A slow-moving person or thing. [< Med.L tortuca, ? < L tortus twisted; so called from its crooked feet]

tor·toise-shell (tôr'təs-shel') adj. Made of or variegated like tortoise shell. Also **tor'toise·shell'.**

tortoise shell The shell of a marine turtle, consisting of a mottled, brownish, hornlike substance used for combs, etc.

tor·tu·ous (tôr'chōō-əs) adj. 1. Consisting of or abounding in irregular bends or turns; twisting. 2. Not straightforward; devious. 3. Morally twisted or warped. [< AF < L torquere to twist] — **tor·tu·os·i·ty** (-os'ə·tē) n. — **tor'tu·ous·ly** adv. — **tor'tu·ous·ness** n.

tor·ture (tôr'chər) n. 1. Infliction of or subjection to extreme physical pain. 2. Great mental suffering; agony. 3. Something that causes severe pain. — v.t. **·tured**, **·tur·ing** 1. To inflict extreme pain upon, as from cruelty. 2. To subject to judicial torture. 3. To cause to suffer agony, extreme discomfort, etc. 4. To twist or turn into an abnormal form, meaning, etc. [< OF < L torquere to twist] — **tor'tur·er** n. — **tor'tur·ous** adj.

to·rus (tôr'əs, tō'rəs) n. pl. **to·ri** (tôr'ī, tō'rī) 1. Archit. A large convex molding used in bases as the lowest molding, or in columns above the plinth. 2. Bot. The swollen end of a flower-stalk that bears the floral leaves. 3. Geom. A solid figure usu. resembling a doughnut. [< L, lit., a swelling]

To·ry (tôr'ē, tō'rē) n. pl. **·ries** 1. A member of an English political party, successor to the Cavaliers and opponent of the Whigs, since about 1832 called the Conservative Party. 2. One who at the period of the American Revolution adhered to the cause of British sovereignty over the colonies. 3. One having very conservative beliefs, esp. in politics. Also **to'ry.** [< Irish tóir to pursue] — **To'ry·ism** n.

toss (tôs, tos) v.t. 1. To throw, pitch, or fling about. 2. To agitate; disturb. 3. To throw with the hand, esp. with the palm of the hand upward. 4. To lift with a quick motion, as the head. 5. Informal To toss up with: I'll toss you to see who pays. — v.i. 6. To be flung to and fro, as a ship in a storm. 7. To throw oneself from side to side restlessly, as in sleep. 8. To go quickly or angrily, as with a fling of the head. 9. To toss up a coin. — **to toss off** 1. To drink at one draft. 2. To utter, write, or do in an offhand manner. — **to toss up** To throw a coin into the air to decide a wager or choice, the outcome depending on the side on which the coin falls. — n. 1. The act of tossing; a pitch; also, the distance over which a thing is tossed. 2. A quick upward or backward movement, as of the head. 3. A tossup or wager. [Prob. < Scand.] — **toss'er** n.

toss-up (tôs'up', tos'-) n. Informal 1. The throwing up of a coin to decide a bet, etc. 2. An even chance.

tot¹ (tot) n. 1. A little child; toddler. 2. A small amount or portion, as of liquor. [Origin unknown]

tot² (tot) v.t. **tot·ted**, **tot·ting** Informal To add; total: usu. with up. [Short for TOTAL]

to·tal (tōt'l) n. The whole sum or amount. — adj. 1. Constituting or comprising a whole. 2. Complete; absolute: a *total* loss. — *v.* **·taled** or **·talled**, **·tal·ing** or **·tal·ling** *v.t.* **1.** To ascertain the total of. **2.** To come to or reach as a total. — *v.i.* **3.** To amount: often with *to.* [< OF < Med.L < L *totus* all] — **to′tal·ly** *adv.*

total eclipse *Astron.* An eclipse in which during some period the entire disk of a celestial body is hidden from view.

to·tal·i·tar·i·an (tō·tal′ə·târ′ē·ən) *adj.* Designating or characteristic of a government controlled exclusively by one party or faction, and maintained by political suppression. — *n.* An adherent of totalitarian government. — **to·tal′i·tar′i·an·ism** *n.*

to·tal·i·ty (tō·tal′ə·tē) *n. pl.* **·ties 1.** An aggregate of parts or individuals. **2.** The state of being total.

to·tal·i·za·tor (tōt′l·ə·zā′tər, -i·zā′-) *n.* A pari-mutuel machine: also **to′tal·iz′er** (-i′zər). Also *Brit.* **to′tal·i·sa′tor.**

tote (tōt) *U.S. Informal v.t.* **tot·ed, tot·ing 1.** To carry about or bear on the person. **2.** To haul, as supplies. — *n.* **1.** The act of toting. **2.** A load or haul. [? < West African] — **tot′er** *n.*

tote board *Informal* A board at a racetrack, etc., showing the betting odds and results of races.

to·tem (tō′təm) *n.* **1.** Among many primitive peoples, an animal, plant, or other natural object believed to be ancestrally related to a tribe, clan, etc. **2.** The representation of such an animal, plant, or object taken as an emblem. **3.** The name or symbol of a person, clan, or tribe. [< Algonquian] — **to·tem·ic** (tō·tem′ik) *adj.* — **to′tem·ism** *n.* — **to′tem·ist** *n.* — **to′tem·is′tic** *adj.*

totem pole A tall post or pole carved or painted with totemic symbols, often erected outside a dwelling by North American Indians, esp. those of the NW coast.

toth·er (tuth′ər) *adj. & pron. Informal* The other; other. Also **t′oth′er.** [ME *the tother* < *thet other* the other]

toti- *combining form* Whole; wholly. [< L *totus* whole]

tot·ter (tot′ər) *v.i.* **1.** To walk feebly and unsteadily. **2.** To shake or sway, as if about to fall. — *n.* The act or condition of tottering. [Prob. < Scand.] — **tot′ter·er** *n.* — **tot′ter·y** *adj.*
— **Syn.** (verb) **2.** teeter, wobble, reel.

tou·can (tōō′kan, tōō·kän′) *n.* A large, fruit-eating bird of tropical America, with brilliant plumage and an immense, thin-walled beak. [< F < Pg. < Tupi *tucana*]

touch (tuch) *v.t.* **1.** To place the hand, finger, etc., in contact with. **2.** To be in or come into contact with. **3.** To bring into contact with something else. **4.** To hit or strike lightly. **5.** To lay the hand or hands on, esp. roughly. **6.** To border on; adjoin. **7.** To come to; reach. **8.** To attain to; equal. **9.** To mark or delineate lightly. **10.** To color slightly; tinge. **11.** To affect injuriously; taint: vegetables *touched* by frost. **12.** To affect by contact: The drill could not *touch* the steel. **13.** To affect the emotions of; move, esp. to pity, gratitude, etc. **14.** To relate to; concern. **15.** To treat or discuss in passing; deal with. **16.** To have to do with, use, or partake of: I will not *touch* this food. **17.** To handle or appropriate improperly. **18.** *Slang* To be successful in borrowing from: used with *for:* He *touched* me for a loan. **19.** *Geom.* To be tangent to. — *v.i.* **20.** To touch someone or something. **21.** To come into or be in contact. — **to touch at** To stop briefly at (a port or place) in the course of a journey or voyage. — **to touch off 1.** To cause to explode; fire. **2.** To cause to happen or occur. — **to touch on** (or **upon**) **1.** To relate to; concern. **2.** To treat briefly or in passing. — **to touch up** To improve or alter by slight additions or corrections. — *n.* **1.** The act or process of touching. **2.** The state of being touched. **3.** *Physiol.* That sense by which external objects are perceived through direct contact with any part of the body. ◆ Collateral adjective: *tactile.* **4.** The sensation conveyed by touching something: a smooth *touch.* **5.** A stroke; hit; blow. **6.** A perceptible effect or influence: He felt the *touch* of her wit. **7.** Any slight or delicate execution or effect, as of a brush, etc.; a light stroke or mark. **8.** Any slight detail or effort given to anything, as to a literary work. **9.** The manner or style in which an artist, etc. executes his work: a master's *touch.* **10.** A trace; tinge: a *touch* of irony. **11.** A slight attack or twinge: a *touch* of rheumatism. **12.** A small quantity or dash. **13.** Close communication or contact: to keep in *touch* with someone. **14.** A test; trial. **15.** *Music* **a** The resistance made to the fingers by the keys of a piano, etc. **b** The manner in which a player presses the keyboard. **16.** *Slang* A sum of money obtained by borrowing or mooching. **17.** *Slang* A request for such a sum of money. **18.** *Slang* A person who is an easy mark for a loan: an easy *touch.* [< OF *tochier*; prob. ult. imit.] — **touch′a·ble** *adj.* — **touch′a·ble·ness** *n.* — **touch′er** *n.*

touch-and-go (tuch′ən·gō′) *adj.* Risky; precarious.

touch and go An uncertain or precarious situation.

touch·back (tuch′bak′) *n.* In football, the act of touching the ball to the ground behind the player's own goal line when it has been sent over the goal line by an opponent.

touch·down (tuch′doun′) *n.* In football, a scoring play, worth six points, in which the ball is held on or over the opponent's goal line and is there declared dead.

tou·ché (tōō·shā′) *French adj.* In fencing, touched by the point of an opponent's foil. — *interj.* You've scored a point!: an exclamation to indicate an opponent's success.

touched (tucht) *adj.* **1.** Emotionally moved. **2.** Slightly unbalanced in mind.

touch·hole (tuch′hōl′) *n.* The orifice in old-fashioned cannon or firearms through which the powder was ignited.

touch·ing (tuch′ing) *adj.* Appealing to the sympathies or emotions; affecting; pathetic. — *prep.* With regard to; concerning. — **touch′ing·ly** *adv.* — **touch′ing·ness** *n.*

touch-me-not (tuch′mē·not′) *n.* Any of various herbs whose ripe fruit bursts open on contact to discharge its seeds.

touch·stone (tuch′stōn′) *n.* **1.** A fine-grained dark stone formerly used to test the fineness of gold and silver by the color of the streak made on the stone. **2.** A criterion or standard by which the qualities of something are tested.

touch·wood (tuch′wōōd′) *n.* **1.** Punk[1] (def. 1). **2.** A tinder prepared from fungus.

touch·y (tuch′ē) *adj.* **touch·i·er, touch·i·est 1.** Likely to take offense easily. **2.** Risky; delicate: a *touchy* subject. — **touch′i·ly** *adv.* — **touch′i·ness** *n.*

tough (tuf) *adj.* **1.** Capable of sustaining great tension or strain without breaking. **2.** Firm and resilient in substance or texture. **3.** Not easily separated, softened, etc.: *tough* meat. **4.** Possessing great physical endurance: a *tough* constitution. **5.** Possessing moral or intellectual endurance; steadfast; persistent. **6.** Unmanageably rough, unruly, or vicious. **7.** Difficult to accomplish; laborious. **8.** Severe; rigorous. **9.** *Informal* Unfortunate; unpleasant: *tough* luck. — *n.* A lawless person; a rowdy; ruffian. [OE *tōh*] — **tough′ly** *adv.* — **tough′ness** *n.*

tough·en (tuf′ən) *v.t. & v.i.* To make or become tough or tougher. — **tough′en·er** *n.*

tou·pee (tōō·pā′, -pē′) *n.* A wig worn to cover baldness or a bald spot. [< F < OF *toup* tuft of hair]

tour (tōōr) *n.* **1.** A trip or rambling excursion. **2.** A circuit or passing through, as for inspection or sightseeing, or for presenting a performance. **3.** A turn or shift, as of service. — **on tour** Traveling from place to place giving performances, as a theatrical company, etc. — *v.t.* **1.** To make a tour of. **2.** To present on a tour, as a play. — *v.i.* **3.** To go on a tour. [< MF < OF < L *tornus* lathe < Gk. *tornos*]

tour de force (tōōr′ də fôrs′) *French* A feat of remarkable strength or skill; esp., a work, performance, etc., that is merely ingenious rather than intrinsically excellent.

tour·ing car (tōōr′ing) A large, open automobile for five or more passengers and baggage. Also *Brit.* **tour′er.**

tour·ist (tōōr′ist) *n.* One who makes a tour or a pleasure trip. — *adj.* Of or suitable for tourists.

tourist class A class of accommodations for steamship passengers, lower than cabin class.

tour·ma·line (tōōr′mə·lēn, -lin) *n.* A complex silicate of aluminum occurring in various colors, the transparent varieties being esteemed as gemstones. Also **tour′ma·lin** (-lin). [< F, ult. < Singhalese *tōramalli* carnelian]

tour·na·ment (tûr′nə·mənt, tōōr′-) *n.* **1.** Any contest of skill involving a number of competitors and a series of games: a chess *tournament.* **2.** In medieval times, a pageant in which two opposing parties of men in armor contended on horseback in mock combat. Also called **tourney.** [< OF < *torneier, tornoier* tourney]

tour·ney (tûr′nē, tōōr′-) *n.* A tournament. — *v.i.* To take part in a tournament; tilt. [See TOURNAMENT.]

tour·ni·quet (tōōr′nə·ket, -kā, tûr′-) *n. Surg.* A bandage, etc., for stopping the flow of blood through an artery by compression. [< F < *tourner* to turn]

tour of duty *Mil.* The hours or period of time during which a serviceman is on official duty; also, an extended period of duty on a given assignment or in a particular area.

tou·sle (tou′zəl) *v.t.* **·sled, ·sling** To disarrange or disorder, as the hair or dress. — *n.* A tousled mass or mop of hair. Also **tou′zle.** [< ME *tusen, tousen*]

tout (tout) *Informal v.i.* **1.** To solicit patronage, customers, votes, etc., esp., in an obtrusive or importunate manner. **2.** To spy on a racehorse so as to gain information for betting. — *v.t.* **3.** To solicit; importune. **4.** In horse racing: **a** To spy on (a horse) to gain information for betting. **b** To sell information about (a horse). — *n.* One who touts. [ME, ? < OE *tōtian*, to peep, look out] — **tout′er** *n.*

tout de suite (tōōt′swēt′) *French* Immediately; at once.

tout en·sem·ble (tōō′tän säN′b'l′) *French* **1.** All in all; everything considered. **2.** The general effect.

tow[1] (tō) *n.* Coarse, short hemp or flax fiber prepared for spinning. [Prob. OE *tow-* for spinning] — **tow′y** *adj.*

tow[2] (tō) *v.t.* To pull or drag, as by a rope, chain, etc. — *n.*

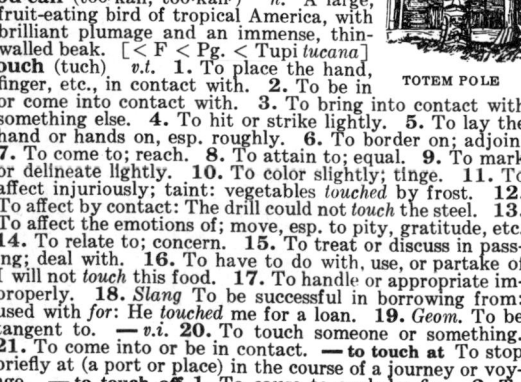

TOTEM POLE

1. The act of towing, or the state of being towed. **2.** That which is towed, as barges by a tugboat. **3.** That which tows. **4.** The rope used; towline. **— to take in tow 1.** To take in charge for or as for towing. **2.** To take under one's protection; take charge of. [OE *togian*]

tow·age (tō′ij) *n.* **1.** The service of or charge for towing. **2.** The act of towing. [< TOW²]

to·ward (tôrd, tōrd; *for prep., also* tə-wôrd′) *prep.* **1.** In the direction of; facing. **2.** With respect to; regarding: his attitude *toward* women. **3.** In anticipation of; for: He is saving *toward* his education. **4.** Near in point of time; approaching; about: arriving *toward* evening. **5.** Tending to result in; designed to achieve: an effort *toward* mutual understanding. Also **to·wards′.** *— adj.* [OE < *tō* to + *-weard* -ward] **— to·ward′ness** *n.*

tow·a·way (tō′ə-wā) *n.* The act of towing away a vehicle, esp. one illegally parked.

tow·boat (tō′bōt′) *n.* A tugboat.

tow·el (toul, tou′əl) *n.* A cloth or paper for drying anything by wiping. *— v.t.* **tow·eled** *or* **·elled, tow·el·ing** *or* **·el·ling** To wipe or dry with a towel. [< OF *toaille*]

tow·el·ing (tou′ling, tou′əl·ing) *n.* Material used for towels. Also **tow′el·ling.**

tow·er (tou′ər) *n.* **1.** A tall but relatively narrow structure, sometimes part of a larger building. **2.** Any similar tall structure or object, often erected for a specific use: a water *tower.* **3.** A place or thing of security or defense; citadel. *— v.i.* To rise or stand like a tower: often with *over* or *above.* [OE < OF < L *turris*] **— tow′er·y** *adj.*

tow·ered (tou′ərd) *adj.* Having a tower or towers.

tow·er·ing (tou′ər·ing) *adj.* **1.** Like a tower; lofty. **2.** Unusually high or great; outstanding. **3.** Intense.

tow·head (tō′hed′) *n.* A head of very light-colored or flaxen hair; also, a person having such hair. [< TOW¹ + HEAD] **— tow′-head′ed** *adj.*

tow·hee (tou′hē, tō′-) *n.* Any of various American birds related to the buntings and the sparrows; esp., the chewink. Also **towhee bunting.** [Imit. of one of its notes]

tow·line (tō′līn′) *n.* A towrope.

town (toun) *n.* **1.** Any considerable collection of dwellings and other buildings larger than a village, but not incorporated as a city. **2.** The inhabitants of such a community; townspeople. **3.** A township (def. 1). **4.** Any closely settled urban district. **5.** The downtown or business section of a city. **— on the town** *Slang* On a round of pleasure. **— to go to town** *Slang* To act with speed and efficiency. [OE *tūn* enclosure, group of houses]

town clerk An official who keeps the records of a town.

town crier Formerly, a person appointed to make proclamations through the streets of a town.

town hall The building containing the public offices of a town and used for meetings of the town council.

town house A residence in a town or city, as distinguished from one in the country.

town meeting 1. A general assemblage of the people of a town. **2.** An assembly of qualified voters for the purpose of transacting town business; also, the voters assembled.

town·ship (toun′ship) *n.* **1.** In the U.S.: **a** A territorial subdivision of a county with certain corporate powers of municipal government. **b** In New England, a local political unit governed by a town meeting. **2.** A unit of area in surveys of U.S. public lands, usually six miles square. **3.** *Brit.* Formerly, a parish. [OE < *tūn* village, group of houses]

towns·man (tounz′mən) *n. pl.* **·men** (-mən) **1.** A resident of a town; also, a fellow citizen. **2.** In New England, a town officer; a selectman.

towns·peo·ple (tounz′pē′pəl) *n.pl.* People who live in towns or in a particular town or city. Also **town′folk′** (-fōk′), **towns′folk′.**

tow·path (tō′path′, -päth′) *n.* A path along a river or canal used by draft animals, etc., for towing boats.

tow·rope (tō′rōp′) *n.* A heavy rope or cable used in towing.

tow truck (tō) A truck equipped to tow other vehicles.

tox·e·mi·a (tok·sē′mē·ə) *n. Pathol.* Blood poisoning. Also **tox·ae′mi·a.** [< NL < Gk. *toxicon* poison + *haima* blood] **— tox·e′mic, tox·ae′mic** *adj.*

tox·ic (tok′sik) *adj.* Of or caused by poison; poisonous. Also **tox′i·cal.** [< Med.L < L Gk. *toxicon* (pharmakon) (poison) for arrows] **— tox′i·cal·ly** *adv.* **— tox·ic′i·ty** *n.*

toxico- *combining form* Poison; of or pertaining to poisons. Also, before vowels, **toxic-.** [< Gk. *toxicon* poison]

tox·i·col·o·gy (tok′sə·kol′ə·jē) *n.* The science that treats of the origin, nature, properties, etc., of poisons. [< F *toxicologie*] **— tox′i·co·log′i·cal** (-kō·loj′i·kəl) *adj.* **— tox′i·co·log′i·cal·ly** *adv.* **— tox′i·col′o·gist** *n.*

tox·in (tok′sin) *n.* **1.** Any of a class of more or less unstable poisonous compounds developed by animal, vegetable, or bacterial organisms and acting as causative agents in many

diseases. **2.** Any toxic matter generated in living or dead organisms. Also **tox·ine** (tok′sēn). [< TOX(IC) + -IN]

tox·oid (tok′soid) *n.* A toxin that has been specially treated to remove toxicity, often used in immunization.

toy (toi) *n.* **1.** A plaything for children. **2.** Any object of little importance or value; a trifle. **3.** A small ornament or trinket. **4.** Any diminutive object. **5.** A dog bred to extreme smallness: also **toy dog.** *— v.i.* To trifle; play. *— adj.* Resembling a toy; of miniature size. [< ME *toye* sport and Du. *tuig* tools] **— toy′er** *n.*

to·yon (tō′yən) *n.* An evergreen shrub of the Pacific coast of North America, having white flowers and bright red berries. [< Sp. *tollón* < N. Am. Ind. (Mexican)]

trace¹ (trās) *n.* **1.** A vestige or mark left by some past event or agent, esp., when regarded as a sign or clue. **2.** A barely detectable quantity, quality, token, or characteristic; touch. **3.** A proportion or ingredient too small to be weighed: a *trace* of soda. **4.** An imprint or mark indicating the passage of a person or thing, as a footprint, etc. **5.** A path or trail through woods or forest beaten down by men or animals. **6.** A lightly drawn line. *— v.* **traced, trac·ing** *v.t.* **1.** To follow the tracks, course, or development of. **2.** To follow (tracks, etc.). **3.** To discover by examination or investigation; determine. **4.** To draw; sketch. **5.** To copy (a drawing, etc.) on a superimposed transparent sheet. **6.** To form (letters, etc.) with careful strokes. **7.** To imprint (a pattern or design). **8.** To mark or record by a curved or broken line. **9.** To go or move over, along, or through. *— v.i.* **10.** To make one's way; proceed. **11.** To have its origin; go back in time. [< OF < L < *trahere* to draw] **— trace′a·ble** *adj.* **— trace′a·bil′i·ty, trace′a·ble·ness** *n.* **— trace′a·bly** *adv.*

trace² (trās) *n.* One of two side straps or chains for connecting the collar of a harness with the whiffletree. **— to kick over the traces** To throw off control; become unmanageable. *— v.t.* **traced, trac·ing** To fasten with or as with traces. [< OF < L. See TRACE¹.]

trace element *Biol.* Any of certain chemical elements found in very small amounts in plant and animal tissues and having a significant effect upon biochemical processes.

trac·er (trā′sər) *n.* **1.** One who or that which traces. **2.** One of various instruments used in tracing drawings, etc. **3.** An inquiry forwarded from one point to another, to trace missing mail matter, etc. **4.** *Mil.* A chemical incorporated in certain types of ammunition used for ranging, signaling, or incendiary purposes. **5.** A radioisotope introduced into the body for the purpose of following the processes of metabolism, the course of a disease, etc. [< TRACE¹]

tracer bullet A bullet that leaves a line of smoke or fire in its wake to indicate its course for correction of aim.

trac·er·y (trā′sər·ē) *n. pl.* **·er·ies 1.** Ornamental stonework formed of ramifying lines. **2.** Any work, ornamentation, etc., resembling this.

tra·che·a (trā′kē·ə) *n. pl.* **·che·ae** (-ki·ē) *or* **·che·as 1.** *Anat.* The duct by which air passes from the larynx to the bronchi and the lungs: also called *windpipe.* For illus. see LUNG, MOUTH, THROAT. **2.** *Zool.* One of the passages by which air is conveyed from the exterior in air-breathing arthropods, as insects and arachnids. [< Med.L < LL < Gk. (*artēria*) *tracheia* a rough (artery)] **— tra′che·al** *adj.*

tracheo- *combining form* The trachea; of or pertaining to the trachea. Also, before vowels, **trache-.** [< TRACHEA]

tra·che·ot·o·my (trā′kē·ot′ə·mē) *n. pl.* **·mies** *Surg.* The operation of cutting into the trachea.

tra·cho·ma (trə·kō′mə) *n. Pathol.* A contagious virus disease characterized by the formation of hard granular excrescences on the conjunctiva of the eyelids, with inflammation of the lining. [< NL < Gk. < *trachys* rough] **— tra·chom·a·tous** (trə·kom′ə·təs) *adj.*

trachy- *combining form* Rough; uneven. Also, before vowels, **trach-.** [< Gk. *trachys* rough]

trac·ing (trā′sing) *n.* **1.** The act of one who traces. **2.** A copy made by tracing on transparent paper. **3.** A record made by a self-registering instrument.

track (trak) *n.* **1.** A mark or trail left by the passage of anything, as footprints. **2.** Any regular path; course. **3.** Any kind of racecourse; also, sports performed on such a course; track athletics. **4.** A set of rails or a rail on which trains, etc., may travel. **5.** A trace or vestige. **6.** A sequence of events or ideas. **— to keep track of** To keep in touch with. **— in one's tracks** Right where one is; on the spot. **— to lose track of** To fail to keep in touch with; lose sight of. **— to make tracks** To hurry; run away in haste. *— v.t.* **1.** To follow, the tracks of; trail. **2.** To discover, pursue or follow by means of marks or indications. **3.** To make tracks upon or with. **4.** To traverse, as on foot. **5.** To furnish with rails or tracks. [< OF *trac*] **— track′er** *n.* **— track′a·ble** *adj.* **— track′less** *adj.*

---

track·age (trak′ij) *adj.* **1.** Railroad tracks collectively. **2.** The right of one company to use the track system of another company; also, the charge for this right.

track man An athlete who competes in a track or field event, as a runner, shot-putter, etc.

track meet An athletic contest made up of track and field events.

tract[1] (trakt) *n.* **1.** An extended area, as of land or water. **2.** *Anat.* An extensive region of the body, esp. one comprising a system of parts or organs: the alimentary *tract*. [< L < *trahere* to draw]

tract[2] (trakt) *n.* A short treatise; esp., a pamphlet on some question of religion or morals. [Short for L *tractatus* a handling, treatise]

tract·a·ble (trak′tə·bəl) *adj.* **1.** Easily led or controlled; manageable; docile. **2.** Readily worked or handled; malleable. [< L < *trahere* to draw] — **tract′a·ble·ness, tract′a·bil′i·ty** *n.* — **tract′a·bly** *adv.*

trac·tile (trak′til) *adj.* Capable of being drawn out; ductile. [< L < *trahere* to draw] — **trac·til′i·ty** *n.*

trac·tion (trak′shən) *n.* **1.** The act of drawing, as by motive power over a surface. **2.** The state of being drawn, or the power employed. **3.** Adhesive or rolling friction, as of wheels on a track. [< Med.L < L < *trahere* to draw] — **trac′tion·al** *adj.*

traction engine A locomotive for hauling on roads or ground, as distinguished from one used on a railway.

trac·tor (trak′tər) *n.* **1.** A powerful, motor-driven vehicle used, as on farms, to draw a plow, reaper, etc. **2.** An automotive vehicle with a driver's cab, used to haul trailers, etc. **3.** *Aeron.* An airplane with the propeller or propellers situated in front of the supporting surface: also **tractor airplane.** [< NL < L < *trahere* to draw]

trade (trād) *n.* **1.** A business; esp., a skilled handicraft; a craft. **2.** Mercantile traffic; commerce. **3.** An exchange, as in barter, buying and selling, etc.; also, a bargain or deal. **4.** The people following a particular calling. **5.** A firm's customers. **6.** Customary pursuit; occupation. **7.** *Usu. pl.* A trade wind. — **Syn.** See OCCUPATION. — *v.* **trad·ed, trad·ing** *v.t.* **1.** To exchange by barter, bargain and sale, etc. **2.** To exchange for something comparable. — *v.i.* **3.** To engage in commerce or in business. — **to trade in** To give in exchange as payment or part payment. — **to trade off** To get rid of by trading. — **to trade on** To make advantageous use of. [< MLG, track]

trade-in (trād′in′) *n.* Something given or accepted in payment or part payment for something else; an exchange.

trade journal A periodical publishing news and discussions of a particular trade or business.

trade-last (trād′last′, -läst′) *n. Informal* A favorable remark that one has heard and offers to repeat to the person complimented in return for a similar remark.

trade·mark (trād′märk′) *n.* **1.** A name, design, etc., often officially registered, used by a merchant or manufacturer to distinguish his goods from those made or sold by others. **2.** Any distinctive characteristic. — *v.t.* **1.** To label with a trademark. **2.** To register as a trademark.

trade name **1.** The name by which an article, process, service, or the like is designated in trade. **2.** A style or name of a business house.

trad·er (trā′dər) *n.* **1.** One who trades. **2.** Any vessel employed in a particular trade.

trade route A route, esp. a sea lane, used by traders.

trade school A school where a specific trade is taught.

trades·folk (trādz′fōk′) *n.pl.* People engaged in trade; esp., shopkeepers. Also **trades′peo′ple** (-pē′pəl).

trades·man (trādz′mən) *n. pl.* **·men** (-mən) A retail dealer; shopkeeper.

trade union A labor union. Also *Brit.* **trades union.**

trade wind *Meteorol.* Either of two steady winds blowing in the same course toward the equator from about 30° N and S latitude, one from the northeast on the north, the other from the southeast on the south side of the equator.

trading post A station for barter in unsettled territory set up by a trader or trading company.

trading stamp A stamp given by a tradesman to a purchaser, and exchangeable, in quantities, for merchandise.

tra·di·tion (trə·dish′ən) *n.* **1.** The knowledge, doctrines, customs, practices, etc., transmitted from generation to generation; also, the transmission of such knowledge, doctrines, etc. **2.** The body of unwritten Christian doctrine, handed down through successive generations. **3.** Among the Jews, an unwritten code said to have been handed down orally from Moses. **4.** The historic conceptions and usages of a school of art, literature, etc. **5.** A custom so long continued that it has almost the force of a law. [< OF < L < *trans-* across + *dare* to give]

tra·di·tion·al (trə·dish′ən·əl) *adj.* Relating or adhering to tradition. Also **tra·di′tion·ar′y** (-er′ē). — **tra·di′tion·al·ism** *n.* — **tra·di′tion·al·ist** *n.* — **tra·di′tion·al·ist′ic** *adj.* — **tra·di′tion·al·ly** *adv.* — **tra·di′tion·ist** *n.*

tra·duce (trə·dōos′, -dyōos′) *v.t.* **·duced, ·duc·ing** To defame; slander. [< L *traducere* to transport, bring into disgrace] — **tra·duc′er** *n.* — **tra·duc′i·ble** *adj.* — **tra·duc′ing·ly** *adv.* — **tra·duc·tion** (trə·duk′shən) *n.*

traf·fic (traf′ik) *n.* **1.** The movement or passage of vehicles, pedestrians, ships, etc., along a route; also, the vehicles, pedestrians, etc. **2.** Buying and selling; trade. **3.** The business of transportation; also, the freight or passengers carried. **4.** The messages, signals, etc., handled by a communications system. **5.** Unlawful or improper trade. — *v.i.* **·ficked, ·fick·ing** **1.** To engage in buying and selling; do business, esp., illegally: with *in*. **2.** To have dealings: with *with*. [< MF < Ital. < *trafficare* < L *trans-* across + Ital. *ficcare* to thrust in] — **traf′fick·er** *n.*

traffic light A signal light that, by changing color, directs the flow of traffic along a road or highway.

tra·ge·di·an (trə·jē′dē·ən) *n.* **1.** An actor in tragedy. **2.** A writer of tragedies.

tra·ge·di·enne (trə·jē·dē·en′) *n.* An actress of tragedy. [< F]

trag·e·dy (traj′ə·dē) *n. pl.* **·dies** **1.** An intensely sad, calamitous, or fatal event or course of events; disaster. **2.** A form of drama in which the protagonist comes to disaster through a flaw in his nature or is crushed by social and psychological forces. **3.** The branch of drama treating of such themes. **4.** The art or theory of acting or composing such drama. **5.** The sense of human life embodied in tragic drama. [< OF < L < Gk. *tragōidia*, appar. < *tragos* goat + *ōidē* song]

trag·ic (traj′ik) *adj.* **1.** Involving death, calamity, or suffering; fatal; terrible. **2.** Pertaining to or having the nature of tragedy. **3.** Appropriate to or like tragedy, esp., in drama. Also **trag′i·cal.** [< L < Gk. *tragikos* pertaining to tragedy] — **trag′i·cal·ly** *adv.* — **trag′i·cal·ness** *n.*

trag·i·com·e·dy (traj′i·kom′ə·dē) *n. pl.* **·dies** **1.** A drama in which tragic and comic scenes are intermingled. **2.** A situation or event suggestive of such a drama. [< MF < LL < L < *tragicus* tragic + *comoedia* comedy] — **trag′i·com′ic** or **·i·cal** *adj.* — **trag′i·com′i·cal·ly** *adv.*

trail (trāl) *v.t.* **1.** To draw along lightly over a surface; also, to drag or draw after: to *trail* a robe. **2.** To follow the track of; track. **3.** To follow or lag behind, esp., in a race. **4.** *Mil.* To carry, as a rifle, with the muzzle to the front and the butt nearly touching the ground. **5.** To tread or force down, as grass into a pathway. — *v.i.* **6.** To hang or float loosely so as to drag along a surface. **7.** To grow along the ground or over rocks, bushes, etc., in a loose, creeping way. **8.** To follow behind loosely; stream. **9.** To move along slowly, tiredly, or heavily. **10.** To lag behind; straggle. **11.** To follow or track game. — *n.* **1.** A path or track made by the passage of persons or animals. **2.** The spoor followed by a hunter. **3.** Anything drawn behind or in the wake of something. **4.** *Mil.* The inclined stock of a gun carriage, or extension of the stock that rests on the ground when the piece is not limbered up. — **to hit** (or **take**) **the trail** To set out on a journey. [< AF < L < *trahere* to draw]

trail·blaz·er (trāl′blā·zər) *n.* **1.** One who blazes a trail. **2.** A pioneer in any field. — **trail′blaz·ing** *n.*

trail·er (trā′lər) *n.* **1.** One who or that which trails. **2.** A vehicle drawn by another having motive power. **3.** A vehicle drawn by a car or truck and used as a temporary or permanent dwelling. **4.** A short motion-picture film made up of scenes from a coming feature picture, used for advertising.

trailer court A large area equipped with running water, electrical outlets, and other accommodations for the parking of trailers. Also **trailer park.**

trail·ing arbutus A perennial bearing fragrant pink flowers: the State flower of Massachusetts.

train (trān) *n.* **1.** A continuous line of coupled railway cars. **2.** A series, or set of connected things; a sequence; esp., a procession of people or line of objects. **3.** A retinue or suite. **4.** Something pulled along with and in the track of another. **5.** An extension of a dress skirt, trailing behind the wearer. **6.** Proper order; due course. **7.** *Mech.* A series of parts acting upon each other, as for transmitting motion. **8.** *Mil.* The men, animals, and vehicles, transporting military supplies, ammunition, etc. **9.** A succession or line of wagons and pack animals en route. **10.** A line of gunpowder, etc., laid to conduct fire to a charge or mine. — *v.t.* **1.** To render proficient or qualified by instruction, drill, etc.; educate. **2.** To make obedient or capable of performing tricks, as an animal. **3.** To bring into a required physical condition by means of diet and exercise. **4.** To lead into taking a particular course; develop into a fixed shape: to *train* a plant on a trellis. **5.** To bring to bear; aim, as a cannon. — *v.i.* **6.** To undergo a course of training. **7.** To give a course of training; drill. — **Syn.** See TEACH. [OF < L *trahere* to draw] — **train′er** *n.*

train·ee (trā·nē′) *n.* One who undergoes training.

train·ing (trā′ning) *n.* **1.** The action of one who or that which trains. **2.** The state or condition of being trained.

train·man (trān′mən)   *n.*   *pl.* **·men** (-mən) A railway employee serving on a train; esp., a brakeman.

traipse (trāps) *v.i.* **traipsed, traips·ing** *Informal* To walk about in an idle or aimless manner. [Earlier *trapass*]

trait (trāt, *also Brit.* trā) *n.* A distinguishing feature or quality of character. — **Syn.** See CHARACTERISTIC. [< F < MF < L < *trahere* to draw]

trai·tor (trā′tər) *n.* One who betrays a trust; esp., one who commits treason. [< OF < L < *trans*- across + *dare* to give] — **trai′tress** (-tris) *n.fem.*

trai·tor·ous (trā′tər·əs) *adj.* **1.** Of or characteristic of a traitor. **2.** Pertaining to or of the nature of treason. — **trai′tor·ous·ly** *adv.* — **trai′tor·ous·ness** *n.*

tra·jec·to·ry (trə·jek′tər·ē) *n.* *pl.* **·ries** The path described by an object moving in space; esp., the path of a projectile. [< Med.L < L < *trans*- over + *jacere* to throw]

tram (tram) *n.* **1.** *Brit.* A streetcar or street railway: also **tram′car** (-kär′). **2.** A four-wheeled vehicle for conveying coals to or from a pit's mouth. [Short for *tramroad*, a road with metal tracks]

tram·mel (tram′əl) *n.* **1.** *Usu. pl.* That which limits freedom or activity; an impediment; hindrance. **2.** A fetter, shackle, or bond, esp., one used in teaching a horse to amble. **3.** An instrument for describing ellipses. **4.** A hook used to suspend cooking pots from a fireplace crane. — *v.t.* **trammeled** or **·melled, tram·mel·ing** or **·mel·ling 1.** To hinder or obstruct; restrict. **2.** To entangle in or as in a snare. Also **tram′el** or **tram′ell.** [< OF < LL < L *tri*- three + *macula* mesh] — **tram′mel·er** or **tram′mel·ler** *n.*

tramp (tramp) *v.i.* **1.** To walk or wander, esp., as a vagrant or vagabond. **2.** To walk heavily or firmly. — *v.t.* **3.** To walk or wander through. **4.** To walk on heavily; trample. — *n.* **1.** An indigent wanderer; a vagrant; vagabond. **2.** A heavy, continued tread. **3.** The sound of continuous and heavy marching or walking. **4.** A long walk; hike. **5.** A steam vessel that picks up freight wherever it can be obtained: also **tramp steamer.** **6.** *Informal* A sexually promiscuous girl or woman. [ME *trampen* < Gmc.]

tram·ple (tram′pəl) *v.* **·pled, ·pling** *v.t.* **1.** To tread on heavily; injure, violate, or encroach upon by or as by tramping. — *v.i.* **2.** To tread heavily or ruthlessly; tramp. — *n.* The act or sound of treading under foot. [ME *trampen*]

tram·po·line (tram′pə·lin) *n.* A section of strong canvas stretched on a frame, on which an acrobat, athlete, etc., may bound or spring. [< Ital. *trampoli* stilts]

trance (trans, träns) *n.* **1.** A condition intermediate between sleep and wakefulness, characterized by dissociation and automatisms of behavior, as in hypnosis and seances. **2.** A dreamlike state marked by bewilderment and an insensibility to ordinary surroundings. **3.** A state of deep abstraction. — *v.t.* **tranced, tranc·ing** To put into or as into a trance. [< OF < *transir* to pass, die]

tran·quil (trang′kwil) *adj.* **·quil·er** or **·quil·ler, ·quil·est** or **·quil·lest 1.** Free from mental agitation or disturbance; calm. **2.** Quiet and motionless. — **Syn.** See CALM. [< L *tranquillus* quiet] — **tran′quil·ly** *adv.* — **tran′quil·ness** *n.*

tran·quil·ize (trang′kwəl·īz) *v.t. & v.i.* **·ized, ·iz·ing** To make or become tranquil. Also **tran′quil·lize,** *Brit.* **tran′·quil·lise.** — **tran′quil·i·za′tion** *n.*

tran·quil·iz·er (trang′kwəl·ī′zər) *n.* **1.** One who or that which tranquilizes. **2.** *Med.* Any of a class of drugs having the property of reducing nervous tension and anxiety states. Also **tran′quil·liz′er.**

tran·quil·li·ty (trang·kwil′ə·tē) *n.* The state of being tranquil; calm; quiet. Also **tran·quil′i·ty.**

trans- *prefix* **1.** Across; beyond; through; on the other side of; as in:

transarctic	transcontinental	transfrontier
transborder	transdesert	transisthmian
transchannel	transequatorial	transpolar

In adjectives and nouns of place, the prefix may signify "on the other side of" (opposed to *cis*-) or "across; crossing." Through long usage, certain of these are written as solid words, as *transalpine, transatlantic*; otherwise, words in this class are usually written with a hyphen, as in:

trans-African	trans-Baltic	trans-Iberian
trans-American	trans-Canadian	trans-Mediterranean
trans-Andean	trans-Germanic	trans-Scandinavian
trans-Arabian	trans-Himalayan	trans-Siberian

2. Through and through; changing completely; as in:

transcolor	transfashion

3. Surpassing; transcending; beyond; as in:

transconscious	transmaterial	transnational
transempirical	transmental	transphysical
transhuman	transmundane	transrational

4. *Anat.* Across; transversely; as in:

transcortical	transfrontal	transthoracic
transduodenal	transocular	transuterine

[< L < *trans* across, beyond, over]

trans·act (trans·akt′, tranz-) *v.t.* **1.** To carry through; accomplish; do. — *v.i.* **2.** *Rare* To do business. [< L < *trans*- through + *agere* to drive, do] — **trans·ac′tor** *n.*

trans·ac·tion (trans·ak′shən, tranz-) *n.* **1.** The act of transacting, or the state of being transacted. **2.** Something transacted; esp., a business deal. **3.** *pl.* Published reports, as of a society. — **trans·ac′tion·al** *adj.*

trans·al·pine (trans·al′pin, -pīn, tranz-) *adj.* Of, pertaining to, or situated on the northern side of the Alps. — *n.* A native or a resident of beyond the Alps. [< L < *trans*- across + *alpinus* alpine < *Alpes* the Alps]

trans·at·lan·tic (trans′ət·lan′tik, tranz′-) *adj.* **1.** On the other side of the Atlantic. **2.** Across the Atlantic.

tran·scend (tran·send′) *v.t.* **1.** To rise above in excellence or degree. **2.** To overstep or exceed as a limit. **3.** *Philos. & Theol.* To be independent of or beyond (the universe, experience, etc.) — *v.i.* **4.** To be transcendent; excel. [< L < *trans*- beyond, over + *scandere* to climb]

tran·scen·dent (tran·sen′dənt) *adj.* **1.** Of very high and remarkable degree; surpassing; excelling. **2.** *Theol.* Above and beyond the universe: said of God. [See TRANSCEND.] — **tran·scen′dence, tran·scen′den·cy, tran·scen′dent·ness** *n.* — **tran·scen′dent·ly** *adv.*

tran·scen·den·tal (tran′sen·den′təl) *adj.* **1.** Of very high degree; transcendent. **2.** Beyond or contrary to common sense or experience. — **tran′scen·den′tal·ly** *adv.*

tran·scen·den·tal·ism (tran′sen·den′təl·iz′əm) *n.* **1.** *Philos.* Any of several doctrines holding that reality is essentially mental or spiritual in nature, and that knowledge of it can be attained by intuitive or a priori, rather than empirical, principles. **2.** The state or quality of being transcendental. — **tran′scen·den′tal·ist** *n. & adj.*

tran·scribe (tran·skrīb′) *v.t.* **·scribed, ·scrib·ing 1.** To copy or recopy in handwriting or typewriting. **2.** *Telecom.* To make an electrical recording of (a radio program). **3.** To adapt (a musical composition) for a change of instrument or voice. [< L < *trans*- over + *scribere* to write] — **tran·scrib′a·ble** *adj.* — **tran·scrib′er** *n.*

tran·script (tran′skript) *n.* **1.** That which is transcribed; esp., a written or typewritten copy. **2.** Any copy. **3.** A copy of a student's academic record, listing courses and grades.

tran·scrip·tion (tran·skrip′shən) *n.* **1.** The act of transcribing. **2.** A copy; transcript. **3.** Phonetic notation of speech sounds, also, a text containing such symbols. **4.** *Telecom.* A recording of a performance made for a later radio broadcast. **5.** *Music* The adaptation of a composition for some instrument or voice other than that for which it was written. — **tran·scrip′tion·al, tran·scrip′tive** *adj.*

trans·duc·er (trans·doo′sər, -dyoo′-, tranz-) *n.* *Physics* Any device whereby energy may be transmitted from one system to another system, whether of the same or a different type. [< L < *trans*- across + *ducere* to lead]

tran·sect (tran·sekt′) *v.t.* To dissect transversely. [< TRANS- + L *sectus*, pp. of *secare* to cut] — **tran·sec′tion** (-sek′shən) *n.*

tran·sept (tran′sept) *n.* *Archit.* One of the lateral projections between the nave and choir of a cruciform church. [< Med.L < L < *transversus* lying across + *septum* enclosure] — **tran·sep′tal** *adj.* — **tran·sep′tal·ly** *adv.*

trans·fer (trans′fər; *for v., also* trans·fûr′) *v.* **·ferred, ·fer·ring** *v.t.* **1.** To carry, or cause to pass, from one person, place, etc., to another. **2.** To make over possession of to another. **3.** To convey (a drawing) from one surface to another. — *v.i.* **4.** To transport oneself. **5.** To be transferred. **6.** To change from one vehicle to another on a transfer (def. 4). **7.** To shift one's enrollment as a student from one school to another. — **Syn.** See CONVEY. — *n.* **1.** The act of transferring, or the state of being transferred. Also **trans·fer′al** (-fûr′əl) or **trans·fer′ral. 2.** That which is transferred as a design. **3.** A place, method, or means of transfer. **4.** A ticket entitling a passenger to change to another public vehicle. **5.** *Law* A delivery of title or property from one person to another. **6.** An order transferring money or securities. [< OF < L < *trans*- across + *ferre* to carry] — **trans·fer′a·bil′i·ty** *n.* — **trans·fer′a·ble** *adj.* — **trans·fer′ence** (-fûr′əns) *n.* — **trans·fer′rer** (-fûr′ər) *n.*

trans·fer·or (trans·fûr′ər) *n.* *Law* One who executes a transfer of property, title, etc.

Trans·fig·u·ra·tion (trans·fig′yə·rā′shən) *n.* **1.** The supernatural transformation of Christ on the mount as recorded in the Gospels. *Matt.* xvii 1–9. **2.** A church festival commemorating this, observed on August 6.

trans·fig·ure (trans·fig′yər) *v.t.* **·ured, ·ur·ing 1.** To change the outward form or appearance of. **2.** To make glorious; idealize. [< L < *trans*- across + *figura* shape] — **trans·fig′·ur·a′tion, trans·fig′ure·ment** *n.*

trans·fix (trans·fiks′) *v.t.* **1.** To pierce through; impale. **2.** To fix in place by impaling. **3.** To make motionless, as with horror, awe, etc. [< L < *trans-* through + *figere* to fasten] — **trans·fix′ion** (-fik′shən) *n.*

trans·form (trans-fôrm′) *v.t.* **1.** To give a different form or appearance to. **2.** To change the character, nature, condition, etc., of. **3.** *Math.* To change (one expression or operation) into another equivalent to it or similar. **4.** *Electr.* To change the potential or flow of (a current), as with a transformer. **5.** *Physics* To alter the energy form of, as electrical into mechanical. — *v.i.* **6.** To be or become changed. [< L < *trans-* over + *formare* to form] — **trans·form′a·ble** *adj.* — **trans′for·ma′tion** (-fər·mā′shən) *n.* — **trans·for′ma·tive** (-fôr′mə-tiv) *adj.*

trans·form·er (trans-fôr′mər) *n.* **1.** One who or that which transforms. **2.** *Electr.* A device for altering the ratio of current to voltage in alternating-current circuits, often consisting of two coils wound on the same iron core.

trans·form·ism (trans-fôr′miz-əm) *n. Biol.* The theory of the development of one species from another through successive gradual modifications.

trans·fuse (trans-fyōōz′) *v.t.* **·fused**, **·fus·ing** **1.** To pour, as a fluid, from one vessel to another. **2.** To cause to be imparted or instilled. **3.** *Med.* To transfer (blood) from one person or animal to another. [< L < *trans-* across + *fundere* to pour] — **trans·fus′er** *n.* — **trans·fus′i·ble** *adj.* — **trans·fu′sive** (trans-fyōō′siv) *adj.*

trans·fu·sion (trans-fyōō′zhən) *n.* **1.** The act of transfusing. **2.** *Med.* The transfer of blood from one person or animal to the veins or arteries of another.

trans·gress (trans-gres′, tranz-) *v.t.* **1.** To break (a law, oath, etc.); violate. **2.** To pass beyond or over (limits); exceed; trespass. — *v.i.* **3.** To break a law; sin. [Appar. < OF < L < *trans-* across + *gradi* to step] — **trans·gress′i·ble** *adj.* — **trans·gress′ing·ly** *adv.* — **trans·gres′sive** *adj.* — **trans·gres′sor** *n.*

trans·gres·sion (trans-gresh′ən, tranz-) *n.* **1.** A violation of a law, command, etc.; esp., a violation of a divine law; sin. **2.** The act of transgressing.

tran·ship (tran-ship′), **tran·ship·ment** (tran-ship′mənt) See TRANSSHIP, etc.

tran·sient (tran′shənt) *adj.* **1.** Passing away quickly; of short duration; brief. **2.** Not permanent; temporary; transitory. — *n.* One who or that which is transient; esp., a lodger or boarder who remains for a short time. [< L < *trans-* across + *ire* to go] — **tran′sience, tran′sien·cy** *n.* — **tran′sient·ly** *adv.* — **tran′sient·ness** *n.*

— **Syn.** (adj.) **1, 2.** Something *transient* actually passes soon, while a *transitory* thing has the quality of impermanence: a *transient* visitor, a *transitory* stage of development. *Passing* is close to *transitory* but less formal: a *passing* fad.

tran·sis·tor (tran-zis′tər, -sis′-) *n. Electronics* A miniature device for the control and amplification of an electron current, made of semiconducting materials, and having three or more electrodes, the current between one pair controlling the amplified current between another pair, one electrode being common to each pair. [< TRANS(FER) (RES)ISTOR]

tran·sit (tran′sit, -zit) *n.* **1.** The act of passing over or through; passage. **2.** The act of carrying across or through; conveyance. **3.** A transition or change. **4.** *Astron.* **a** The passage of one heavenly body across the disk of another. **b** The moment of passage of a celestial body across the meridian. **5.** A surveying instrument for measuring horizontal and vertical angles: also **transit theodolite.** — *v.t.* To pass through or across. [< L < *trans-* across + *ire* to go]

tran·si·tion (tran-zish′ən) *n.* **1.** The act or state of passing from one place, condition, or action to another; change. **2.** The time, period, or place of such passage. **3.** A sentence, paragraph, etc., that leads from one subject to another, as in an essay. **4.** *Music* A modulation or a passage connecting two themes or subjects. — **tran·si′tion·al, tran·si′tion·ar′y** (-er′ē) *adj.* — **tran·si′tion·al·ly** *adv.*

tran·si·tive (tran′sə-tiv) *adj.* **1.** *Gram.* Of transitive verbs. **2.** Capable of passing; effecting transition. — *n. Gram.* A transitive verb. [< LL < L. See TRANSIT.] — **tran′si·tive·ly** *adv.* — **tran′si·tive·ness, tran′si·tiv′i·ty** *n.*

transitive verb A verb that requires a complement to complete its meaning.

tran·si·to·ry (tran′sə-tôr′ē, -tō′rē) *adj.* Existing for a short time only. — **Syn.** See TRANSIENT. [< OF < L. See TRANSIT.] — **tran′si·to′ri·ly** *adv.* — **tran′si·to′ri·ness** *n.*

trans·late (trans-lāt′, tranz-, trans′lāt, tranz′-) *v.* **·lat·ed**, **·lat·ing** *v.t.* **1.** To express in another language; change into another language. **2.** To explain in other words; interpret. **3.** To change into another form; transform. — *v.i.* **4.** To act as translator. **5.** To admit of translation: This book *translates* easily. [? < OF *translater* < L < pp. of *transferre* < *trans-* across + *ferre* to carry] — **trans·lat′a·ble** *adj.* — **trans·lat′a·ble·ness** *n.* — **trans·la′tor** *n.*

trans·la·tion (trans-lā′shən, tranz-) *n.* **1.** The act of translating, or the state of being translated. **2.** That which is translated; esp., a work translated into another language; a version. — **trans·la′tion·al** *adj.*

trans·lit·er·ate (trans·lit′ə·rāt, tranz-) *v.t.* **·at·ed**, **·at·ing** To represent (a letter or word) by the alphabetic characters of another language. [< TRANS- + L *litera* letter] — **trans·lit′er·a′tion** *n.*

trans·lu·cent (trans·lōō′sənt, tranz-) *adj.* Allowing the passage of light, but not permitting a clear view of any object; semitransparent. — **Syn.** See CLEAR. [< L < *trans-* through, across + *lucere* to shine] — **trans·lu′cence, trans·lu′cen·cy** *n.* — **trans·lu′cent·ly** *adv.*

trans·mi·grate (trans·mī′grāt, tranz-, trans′mə-, tranz′-) *v.i.* **·grat·ed**, **·grat·ing** **1.** To migrate from one place or condition to another, esp., from one country to another. **2.** To pass into another body, as the soul at death. [< L < *trans-* across + *migrare* to migrate] — **trans·mi′grant** *adj. & n.* — **trans′mi·gra′tion** *n.* — **trans·mi′gra·tor** *n.* — **trans·mi·gra·to·ry** (trans·mī′grə·tôr′ē, -tō′rē, tranz-) *adj.*

trans·mis·si·ble (trans·mis′ə·bəl, tranz-) *adj.* Capable of being transmitted. Also **trans·mit′ti·ble** (-mit′ə·bəl). — **trans·mis′si·bil′i·ty** *n.*

trans·mis·sion (trans·mish′ən, tranz-) *n.* **1.** The act of transmitting, or the state of being transmitted. **2.** That which is transmitted. **3.** *Mech.* **a** A device that transmits power from the engine of an automobile to the driving wheels. **b** The gears for changing speed. [See TRANSMIT.] — **trans·mis′sive** *adj.*

trans·mit (trans·mit′, tranz-) *v.t.* **·mit·ted**, **·mit·ting** **1.** To send from one place or person to another; forward or convey; dispatch. **2.** To pass on by heredity; transfer. **3.** To pass on or communicate (news, information, etc.). **4.** *Telecom.* To send out (information, radio and television broadcasts, etc.) by means of electromagnetic waves. **5.** *Physics* To cause (light, sound, etc.) to pass through a medium. **6.** *Mech.* To convey (force, motion, etc.) from one part or mechanism to another. [< L < *trans-* across + *mittere* to send] — **trans·mit′tal** *n.*

trans·mit·tance (trans·mit′ns, tranz-) *n.* The act or process of transmitting.

trans·mit·ter (trans·mit′ər, tranz-) *n.* **1.** One who or that which transmits. **2.** A telegraphic sending instrument. **3.** The part of a telephone that converts sound waves into electrical waves. **4.** *Telecom.* The part of a radio or television system that generates, modulates, and transmits electromagnetic waves to the antenna.

trans·mu·ta·tion (trans·myōō·tā′shən, tranz-) *n.* **1.** The act of transmuting, or the state of being transmuted. **2.** *Physics* The change of one element into another through alteration of its nuclear structure, as by bombardment with high-energy particles in an accelerator. **3.** *Biol.* Successive change of form. **4.** In alchemy, the supposed change of a base metal into gold, silver, etc. — **trans′mu·ta′tion·al, trans·mu·ta·tive** (trans·myōō′tə·tiv, tranz-) *adj.*

trans·mute (trans·myōōt′, tranz-) *v.t.* **·mut·ed**, **·mut·ing** To change in nature, form, quality, etc.; transform. Also **trans·mu′tate.** [< L < *trans-* across + *mutare* to change] — **trans·mut′a·ble** *adj.* — **trans·mut′a·bil′i·ty, trans·mut′a·ble·ness** *n.* — **trans·mut′a·bly** *adv.* — **trans·mut′er** *n.*

trans·o·ce·an·ic (trans′ō·shē·an′ik, tranz′-) *adj.* **1.** Lying beyond or over the ocean. **2.** Crossing the ocean.

tran·som (tran′səm) *n.* **1.** A small window above a door or window, usu. hinged to a horizontal crosspiece; also, the crosspiece. **2.** A horizontal construction dividing a window into stages. **3.** *Naut.* A beam running across the stern frame of a ship. **4.** The horizontal crossbar of a gallows or cross. [< L *transtrum* crossbeam] — **tran′somed** *adj.*

tran·son·ic (tran·son′ik) *adj. Aeron.* Of or pertaining to conditions encountered when passing to supersonic speeds.

transonic barrier *Aeron.* A barrier to supersonic flight encountered by aircraft designed for subsonic speed, caused by turbulence of the airflow around different parts of the plane: also called *sonic barrier, sound barrier.*

trans·pa·cif·ic (trans′pə·sif′ik) *adj.* **1.** Crossing the Pacific Ocean. **2.** Situated across or beyond the Pacific.

trans·par·en·cy (trans·pâr′ən·sē, -par′-) *n.* *pl.* **·cies** **1.** The quality of being transparent. Also **trans·par′ence.** **2.** Something transparent; esp., a picture on a substance, as glass, intended to be viewed by shining a light through it.

trans·par·ent (trans·pâr′ənt, -par′-) *adj.* **1.** Admitting the passage of light, and permitting a clear view of objects beyond. **2.** Easy to see through or understand; obvious. **3.** Without guile; frank; candid. **4.** Diaphanous; sheer. — **Syn.** See CLEAR. [< Med.L < L *trans-* across + *parere* to appear, be visible] — **trans·par′ent·ly** *adv.* — **trans·par′ent·ness** *n.*

trans·pierce (trans·pirs′) *v.t.* **·pierced**, **·pierc·ing** To pierce through; penetrate completely. [< MF < *trans-* (< L, across, through) + *percer* to pierce]

tran·spire (tran·spīr′) *v.* **·spired**, **·spir·ing** *v.t.* **1.** To give off (waste products) from the surface of the body, leaves, etc.; exhale. — *v.i.* **2.** To give off waste products, as the surface of the body, leaves, etc. **3.** To become known. **4.** *Informal* To happen; occur. ◆ Although *transpire* is used widely in this last sense, this usage is considered erroneous by some. [< F < L *trans-* across, through + *spirare* to breathe] — **tran′spi·ra′tion** *n.*

trans·plant (*v.* trans·plant′, -plänt′; *n.* trans′plant, -plänt′) *v.t.* **1.** To remove and plant in another place. **2.** To remove and settle or establish for residence in another place. **3.** *Surg.* To transfer (a portion of tissue) from its original site to another part of the same individual, or to another individual. — *n.* **1.** That which is transplanted. **2.** The act of transplanting. [< LL < L *trans-* across + *plantare* to plant] — **trans′plan·ta′tion** *n.* — **trans·plant′er** *n.*

trans·port (*v.* trans·pôrt′, -pōrt′; *n.* trans′pôrt, -pōrt) *v.t.* **1.** To carry or convey from one place to another. **2.** To carry away with emotion. **3.** To carry into banishment, esp. beyond the sea. — **Syn.** See BANISH. — *n.* **1.** A vessel used to transport troops, military supplies, etc. **2.** An aircraft used to transport passengers, mail, etc. **3.** The state of being transported with rapture; ecstasy. **4.** The act of transporting. **5.** A deported convict. [< MF < L < *trans-* across + *portare* to carry] — **trans·port′er** *n.*

trans·port·a·ble (trans·pôr′tə·bəl, -pōr′-) *adj.* Capable of being transported. — **trans·port′a·bil′i·ty** *n.*

trans·por·ta·tion (trans′pər·tā′shən) *n.* **1.** The act of transporting, or the state of being transported. **2.** A means of transporting, as a vehicle. **3.** A charge for conveyance. **4.** A ticket, pass, etc., for travel.

trans·pose (trans·pōz′) *v.t.* **·posed, ·pos·ing** **1.** To reverse the order or change the place of; interchange. **2.** To change in place or order, as a word in a sentence. **3.** *Math.* To transfer (a term) with a changed sign from one side of an algebraic equation to the other, so as not to destroy the equality of the members. **4.** *Music* To move (a chord, melody, composition, etc.) upward or downward in pitch while retaining its internal interval structure. — *v.i.* **5.** *Music* To play in a key other than the one notated: said of players or instruments. [< OF < L *trans-* over + OF *poser* to place] — **trans·pos′a·ble** *adj.* — **trans·pos′er** *n.* — **trans′po·si′tion, trans·po′sal** *n.*

trans·ship (trans·ship′) *v.t. & v.i.* **·shipped, ·ship·ping** To transfer from one conveyance or line to another: also spelled *tranship.* — **trans·ship′ment** *n.*

tran·sub·stan·ti·a·tion (tran′səb·stan′shē·ā′shən) *n.* **1.** *Theol.* The doctrine that the substance of the eucharistic elements is converted into that of the body and blood of Christ. **2.** A change of anything into something essentially different. [< Med.L < L *trans-* over + *substantia* substance] — **tran′sub·stan′ti·a′tion·al·ist** *n.*

trans·u·ra·ni·an (trans′yŏŏ·rā′nē·ən, tranz′-) *adj. Physics* Of or pertaining to any of those radioactive elements having an atomic number greater than that of uranium. Also **trans′u·ran′ic** (-ran′ik).

trans·ver·sal (trans·vûr′səl, tranz-) *adj.* Transverse. — *n. Geom.* A line intersecting a system of lines.

trans·verse (trans·vûrs′, tranz-) *adj.* Lying or being across or from side to side; athwart. — *n.* **1.** That which is transverse. **2.** *Geom.* That axis of a hyperbola that passes through its foci. [< L < *trans-* across + *vertere* to turn] — **trans·verse′ly** *adv.* — **trans·verse′ness** *n.*

transverse flute The modern flute, played by blowing into a hole in the side of the tube near the upper end.

trap[1] (trap) *n.* **1.** A device for catching game or other animals, as a pitfall or snare. **2.** Any artifice or stratagem by which a person may be betrayed or taken unawares. **3.** *Mech.* A U- or S-bend in a pipe, etc., that fills with water or other liquid for sealing the pipe against a return flow, as of noxious gas. **4.** A contrivance for hurling clay pigeons or glass balls into the air for sportsmen to shoot at. **5.** In some games, esp. golf, an obstacle or hazard: a sand *trap.* **6.** A light, two-wheeled carriage suspended by springs. **7.** *pl.* Percussion instruments, as drums, cymbals, etc. **8.** A trap door. **9.** *U.S. Slang* The mouth: Shut your *trap.* — *v.* **trapped, trap·ping** *v.t.* **1.** To catch in a trap; ensnare. **2.** To stop or hold (a gas, liquid, etc.) by some obstruction. **3.** To provide with a trap. — *v.i.* **4.** To set traps for game. **5.** To be a trapper. [OE *treppe, træppe*]

trap[2] (trap) *n. Informal* Personal effects, as luggage; also, household goods: used in the plural. — *v.t.* **trapped, trap·ping** To adorn with trappings; bedeck. [Alter. of OF *drap* cloth, covering < Med.L *drappus*]

trap[3] (trap) *n. Geol.* A dark, fine-grained igneous rock, often of columnar structure, as basalt, dolerite, etc. Also **trap′rock′** (rok′). [< Sw. *trappa* stair, so called from the steplike arrangement of this rock in other rock]

trap door A door, hinged or sliding, to cover an opening, as in a floor or roof.

tra·peze (trə·pēz′, tra-) *n.* **1.** A short swinging bar, suspended by two ropes, used by gymnasts, etc. **2.** *Geom.* A trapezium. [< F < NL *trapezium* trapezium]

tra·pe·zi·um (trə·pē′zē·əm) *n. pl.* **·zi·a** (-zē·ə) **1.** *Geom.* **a** A four-sided plane figure of which no two sides are parallel. **b** *Brit.* A trapezoid. **2.** *Anat.* The bone of the wrist situated at the base of the thumb. [< NL < Gk. *trapezion*, dim. of *trapeza* table, lit., four-footed (bench) < tetra- four, + *peza* foot]

TRAPEZIUM (*a*) AND TRAPEZOID (*b*)

trap·e·zoid (trap′ə·zoid) *n.* **1.** *Geom.* **a** A quadrilateral of which two sides are parallel. **b** *Brit.* A trapezium. **2.** *Anat.* An irregular bone near the base of the forefinger. [< NL < Gk. < *trapeza* table + *eidos* form] — **trap/e·zoi′dal** *adj.*

trap·per (trap′ər) *n.* One whose occupation is the trapping of fur-bearing animals.

trap·pings (trap′ingz) *n.pl.* **1.** An ornamental housing or harness for a horse. **2.** Adornments of any kind; embellishments; superficial dress. [< TRAP[2]]

Trap·pist (trap′ist) *n.* A member of an ascetic order of Cistercian monks, noted for silence and abstinence. — *adj.* Of or pertaining to the Trappists. [after *La Trappe* in Normandy, name of their first abbey, established 1664]

trap·shoot·ing (trap′shōō′ting) *n.* The sport of shooting clay pigeons sent up from spring traps. — **trap′shoot′er** *n.*

trash (trash) *n.* **1.** Worthless or waste matter of any kind; rubbish. **2.** A worthless or despicable individual or group of individuals. **3.** Worthless or foolish writing, ideas, etc.; nonsense. **4.** That which is broken or lopped off; esp., the loppings and trimmings of trees and plants. — *v.t.* **1.** To free from trash. **2.** To strip of leaves; prune; lop. [Cf. dial. Norw. *trask* lumber, trash, baggage]

trash·y (trash′ē) *adj.* **trash·i·er, trash·i·est** Resembling trash or rubbish; worthless; cheap: *trashy* poetry. — **trash′i·ly** *adv.* — **trash′i·ness** *n.*

trau·ma (trô′mə, trou′-) *n. pl.* **·mas** or **·ma·ta** (-mə·tə) **1.** *Pathol.* **a** Any injury to the body caused by shock, violence, etc.; a wound. **b** The general condition of the system resulting from such an injury or wound. Also **trau′ma·tism** (-tiz′əm). **2.** *Psychiatry* A severe emotional shock having a deep, often lasting effect upon the personality. [< NL < Gk. *trauma, -atos* wound]

trau·mat·ic (trô·mat′ik) *adj.* Of, pertaining to, or caused by a trauma. — **trau·mat′i·cal·ly** *adv.*

trav·ail (trav′āl, trə·vāl′) *v.i.* **1.** To toil; labor. **2.** To suffer the pangs of childbirth. — *n.* **1.** Strenuous physical or mental labor. **2.** Anguish; pain. **3.** Labor in childbirth. [< OF < *travaillier* to toil, ult. < LL *trepalium* instrument of torture < *tres, tria* three + *palus* stake]

trav·el (trav′əl) *v.* **trav·eled** or **·elled, trav·el·ing** or **·el·ling** *v.i.* **1.** To go from one place to another; make a journey or tour. **2.** To proceed; advance. **3.** To go about from place to place as a traveling salesman. **4.** *U.S. Informal* To move with speed. **5.** To pass or be transmitted, as light, sound, etc. **6.** *Mech.* To move in a fixed path, as part of a mechanism. — *v.t.* **7.** To move or journey across or through; traverse. — *n.* **1.** The act of traveling. **2.** *pl.* A trip or journey. **3.** A movement or progress of any kind. **4.** *Mech.* **a** The full course of a moving part in one direction. **b** Length of stroke, as of a piston. [Var. of TRAVAIL]

trav·eled (trav′əld) *adj.* **1.** Having made many journeys. **2.** Experienced as the result of travel. **3.** Frequented or used by travelers. Also **trav′elled.**

trav·el·er (trav′əl·ər, trav′lər) *n.* **1.** One who travels or journeys. **2.** *Brit.* A traveling salesman. **3.** *Naut.* A metal ring or thimble running freely on a rope, rod, or spar; also, the rope, rod, or spar. Also **trav′el·ler.**

traveler's check A draft issued by a bank, express company, etc., having the bearer's signature, and payable when the bearer signs it again in order to cash it.

traveling crane A hoisting and transporting apparatus that moves along a supporting frame or bridge.

traveling salesman A salesman who travels to various places obtaining orders for his firm. Also **traveling man.**

trav·e·logue (trav′ə·lôg, -log) *n.* A lecture or film on travel. Also **trav′e·log.**

trav·erse (trav′ərs; *for v. & adv.,* also trə·vûrs′) *v.* **·ersed, ·ers·ing** *v.t.* **1.** To pass over, across, or through. **2.** To move back and forth over or along. **3.** To examine carefully; survey or scrutinize. **4.** To oppose; thwart. **5.** To turn (a gun, lathe, etc.) to right or left; swivel. **6.** *Law* **a** In legal pleading, to deny (a matter of fact alleged by the opposite party). **b** To impeach (the validity of an inquest of office). **7.** *Naut.* To brace (a yard) fore and aft. — *v.i.* **8.** To move back and forth. **9.** To move across; cross. **10.** To turn; swivel. — *n.* **1.** A part, as of a machine or structure, placed across or traversing another, as a crosspiece, crossbeam, transom, etc. **2.** *Archit.* A gallery or loft communicating with opposite sides of a building. **3.** Something serving as a screen or barrier. **4.** *Geom.* A transversal. **5.** The act of traversing or crossing. **6.** A way or path across. **7.** *Mech.* Sidewise travel, as of the tool in a slide rest. **8.** *Law* A formal denial. **9.** *Naut.* A zigzag track of a vessel while beating to windward. — *adj.* Transverse; lying or being across. [< OF < LL < L *trans-* across + *vertere* to turn] — **trav·ers·a·ble** *adj.* — **trav·er·sal** (trav′ər-səl, trə-vûr′səl) *n.* — **trav′ers·er** *n.*

trav·er·tine (trav′ər-tin, -tēn, -tīn) *n.* A porous, light yellow, crystalline limestone deposited in solution from ground or surface waters, used for building purposes. Also **trav′er·tin** (-tin). [< Ital. < L *Tiburtinus* Tiburtine < *Tiburs, -ur-tis* of Tibur]

trav·es·ty (trav′is·tē) *n. pl.* **·ties 1.** A grotesque imitation; burlesque. **2.** In literature, a burlesque treatment of a lofty subject. — *v.t.* **·tied, ·ty·ing** To make a travesty on; parody. [< MF < Ital. < L *trans* across + *vestire* to dress]

trawl (trôl) *n.* **1.** A stout fishing line having many lines frequently spaced and bearing baited hooks: also called *trotline.* Also **trawl line. 2.** A great fishing net shaped like a flattened bag, for towing on the bottom of the ocean by a boat: also **trawl net.** — *v.t.* **1.** To catch (fish) with a trawl. — *v.i.* **2.** To fish with a trawl. [Cf. MDu. *traghel* dragnet]

trawl·er (trô′lər) *n.* **1.** A vessel used for trawling. **2.** One who is engaged in trawling.

tray (trā) *n.* A flat receptacle with a low rim, made of wood, metal, etc., used to carry, hold, or display articles: a sandwich *tray.* [OE *trīg, trēg* wooden board]

treach·er·ous (trech′ər·əs) *adj.* **1.** Traitorous; perfidious; disloyal. **2.** Having a deceptive appearance; unreliable; untrustworthy: a *treacherous* path. — **treach′er·ous·ly** *adv.* — **treach′er·ous·ness** *n.*

treach·er·y (trech′ər·ē) *n. pl.* **·er·ies** Violation of allegiance, confidence, or faith; perfidy; treason. [< OF < *tricher, trechier* to cheat]

trea·cle (trē′kəl) *n.* **1.** *Brit.* Molasses. **2.** Formerly, a compound used as an antidote. [< OF < L < Gk. *thēriakē* remedy for poisonous bites] — **trea′cly** *adj.*

tread (tred) *v.* **trod** (*Archaic* **trode**)*,* **trod·den** or **trod, tread·ing** *v.t.* **1.** To step or walk on, over, along, etc. **2.** To press with the feet; trample. **3.** To accomplish in walking or in dancing: to *tread* a measure. **4.** To copulate with: said of male birds. — *v.i.* **5.** To step or walk. **6.** To trample: usually with *on.* — **to tread water** In swimming, to keep the body erect and the head above water by moving the feet up and down as if walking. — *n.* **1.** The act, manner, or sound of treading or walking. **2.** The flat part of a step in a staircase. **3.** The part of a wheel that bears upon the ground or rails. **4.** The outer, often grooved surface of an automobile tire. **5.** That part of the sole of a shoe that treads upon the ground. **6.** The part of a rail on which the wheels bear. [OE *tredan*] — **tread′er** *n.*

tread·le (tred′l) *n.* A lever operated by the foot, usu. to cause rotary motion. For illus. see POTTER'S WHEEL. — *v.i.* **·led, ·ling** To work a treadle. [OE < *tredan* to tread] — **tread′ler** *n.*

tread·mill (tred′mil′) *n.* **1.** A mechanism rotated by the walking motion of one or more persons. **2.** A similar mechanism operated by a quadruped. **3.** Any wearisome or monotonous work, activity, routine, etc.

trea·son (trē′zən) *n.* **1.** Betrayal or breach of allegiance or of obedience toward one's sovereign or government. **2.** *Rare* A breach of faith; treachery. [< AF *treyson,* OF *traison* < L *traditio, -onis* betrayal, delivery]

trea·son·a·ble (trē′zən·ə·bəl) *adj.* Of, involving, or characteristic of treason. Also **trea′son·ous.** — **trea′son·a·ble·ness** *n.* — **trea′son·a·bly** *adv.*

treas·ure (trezh′ər) *n.* **1.** Riches accumulated or possessed, esp. in the form of money, jewels, or precious metals. **2.** One who or that which is regarded as valuable, precious, or rare. — *v.t.* **·ured, ·ur·ing 1.** To lay up in store; accumulate. **2.** To retain carefully, as in the mind. **3.** To set a high value upon; prize. [< OF < L < Gk. *thēsauros*]

treas·ur·er (trezh′ər·ər) *n.* An officer of a state, city, corporation, society, etc., who has charge of funds or revenues. **Treasure State** Nickname of Montana.

treas·ure-trove (trezh′ər·trōv′) *n.* **1.** *Law* Any treasure found hidden in the earth, etc., the owner being unknown. **2.** Any discovery that proves valuable. [< AF < *tresor* + *trové,* pp., of *trover* to find]

treas·ur·y (trezh′ər·ē) *n. pl.* **·ur·ies 1.** The place where private or public funds or revenues are received, kept, and disbursed. **2.** Any public or private funds or revenues. **3.** Any group or collection of treasures or things regarded as treasures. **4.** A place or receptacle where treasures are kept. — **Department of the Treasury** An executive department of the U.S. government that superintends and manages the national finances. Also **Treasury Department.**

treasury note *U.S.* A note issued by the Treasury as legal tender for all debts, public and private.

treat (trēt) *v.t.* **1.** To conduct oneself toward in a specified manner. **2.** To look upon or regard in a specified manner:

They *treat* the matter as a joke. **3.** To subject to chemical or physical action, as for altering or improving. **4.** To give medical or surgical attention to. **5.** To deal with in writing or speaking. **6.** To deal with or develop (a subject in art or literature) in a specified manner or style. **7.** To pay for the entertainment, food, or drink of. — *v.i.* **8.** To handle a subject in writing or speaking: usu. with *of.* **9.** To negotiate. **10.** To pay for another's entertainment or food. — *n.* **1.** Something that gives unusual pleasure. **2.** Entertainment furnished gratuitously to another. **3.** The act of treating; also, one's turn to treat. [< OF < L *tractare* to handle] — **treat′a·ble** *adj.* — **treat′er** *n.*

trea·tise (trē′tis) *n.* A formal and systematic written account of some subject. [< AF *tretiz,* OF *traitier* to treat]

treat·ment (trēt′mənt) *n.* **1.** The act, manner, or process of treating. **2.** The care of an illness, by drugs, surgery, etc. **3.** The manner of handling an artistic or literary subject.

trea·ty (trē′tē) *n. pl.* **·ties** A formal agreement or compact, duly concluded and ratified, between two or more states; also, the document containing such an agreement or compact. [< AF *treté,* OF *traitie,* pp. of *traitier* to treat]

treb·le (treb′əl) *v.t. & v.i.* **·led, ·ling** To multiply by three; triple. — *adj.* **1.** Threefold; triple. **2.** Soprano. — *n.* **1.** *Music* **a** A soprano voice, part, or instrument; also, the singer or player taking this part. **b** The highest register of an instrument. **2.** High, piping sound. [< OF < L *triplus*] — **treb′le·ness** *n.* — **treb′ly** *adv.*

tree (trē) *n.* **1.** A perennial woody plant having usu. a single self-supporting trunk of considerable height, with branches and foliage growing at some distance above the ground. ◆ Collateral adjective: *arboreal.* **2.** Any shrub or plant that assumes treelike shape or dimensions. **3.** Something resembling a tree in form or outline, as a clothes tree, crosstree, etc. **4.** A diagram or outline resembling a tree and showing family descent. **5.** A timber, post, pole, etc.: used in combination: *axletree.* — **up a tree** *Informal* In a position from which there is no retreat; cornered: also, in an embarrassing position. — *v.t.* **treed, tree·ing 1.** To force to climb or take refuge in a tree: to *tree* an opossum. **2.** *Informal* To get the advantage of; corner. **3.** To stretch, as a boot, on a boot tree. [OE *trēow, trīow, trēo*]

tree fern Any of various ferns with large fronds and woody trunks that often attain a treelike size.

tree frog An arboreal amphibian, having the toes dilated with viscous, adhesive disks: also called *tree toad.*

tree of heaven The ailanthus.

tree of knowledge of good and evil In the Bible, a tree in Eden whose fruit Adam and Eve were forbidden to eat. *Gen.* iii 3, 6. Also **tree of knowledge.**

Tree-Plant·er State (trē′plan′tər, -plän′-) Nickname of Nebraska.

tree sparrow A North American sparrow that nests in Canada and migrates southward in winter.

tree surgery The treatment of disease conditions and decay in trees by operative methods. — **tree surgeon**

tree toad A tree frog.

tree·top (trē′top′) *n.* The highest part of a tree.

tre·foil (trē′foil) *n.* **1.** Any of a genus of leguminous plants, the clovers, with red, purple, pink, or yellow flowers and trifoliate leaflets. **2.** A three-lobed architectural ornamentation. [< AF, OF < L *trifolium*]

trek (trek) *v.* **trekked, trek·king** *v.i.* **1.** In South Africa, to travel by ox wagon. **2.** To travel, esp. slowly or arduously. — *v.t.* **3.** In South Africa, to draw (a vehicle or load): said of an ox. — *n.* **1.** In South Africa, a journey or any part of it; esp., an organized migration, as for the founding of a colony. **2.** Any journey; esp., a slow or arduous journey. [< Du. < MDu. < OHG *trechan* to draw] — **trek′ker** *n.*

trel·lis (trel′is) *n.* **1.** A crossbarred structure or panel of wood, metal, or other material, used as a screen or a support for vines, etc. **2.** A summerhouse, archway, etc., made from or consisting of such a structure. — *v.t.* **1.** To interlace so as to form a trellis. **2.** To furnish with or fasten on a trellis. [< OF < L < *tri-* three + *licium* thread]

trel·lis·work (trel′is·wûrk′) *n.* Openwork made from, consisting of, or resembling a trellis.

trem·a·tode (trem′ə·tōd) *n.* One of a class of parasitic flatworms, including the liver flukes. [< NL < Gk. < *trēma, -atos* hole + *eidos* form] — **trem′a·toid** (-toid) *adj.*

trem·ble (trem′bəl) *v.i.* **·bled, ·bling 1.** To shake involuntarily, as with fear or weakness; be agitated. **2.** To have slight, irregular vibratory motion, as from some jarring force; shake. **3.** To feel anxiety or fear. **4.** To quaver, as the voice. — *n.* The act or state of trembling. [< OF < LL *tremulus* tremulous < *tremere* to tremble] — **trem′bler** *n.* — **trem′bling·ly** *adv.* — **trem′bly** *adj.*

tre·men·dous (tri·men′dəs) *adj.* **1.** *Informal* Extraordinarily large; huge; vast. **2.** *Informal* Unusual; amazing; wonderful. **3.** Causing astonishment by its magnitude, force, etc. [< L *tremendus* to be trembled at < *tremere* to tremble] — **tre·men′dous·ly** *adv.* — **tre·men′dous·ness** *n.*

trem·o·lo (trem′ə-lō) *n. pl.* ·los *Music* **1.** In string instrument playing, a rapid reiteration of a tone caused by alternating movements of the bow. **2.** A rapid alternation of two tones, usu. a third or more apart. Compare TRILL. **3.** A device or stop for producing a vibrato effect on an organ tone. [< Ital. < L *tremulus*]

trem·or (trem′ər, trē′mər) *n.* **1.** A quick, vibratory movement; a shaking. **2.** Any involuntary and continued quivering or trembling of the body or limbs; a shiver. **3.** A quavering sound. **4.** Any trembling, quivering effect. [< OF, fear, a trembling < L *tremere* to tremble]

trem·u·lous (trem′yə-ləs) *adj.* **1.** Characterized or affected by trembling: *tremulous* speech. **2.** Showing timidity or fear. — **trem′u·lous·ly** *adv.* — **trem′u·lous·ness** *n.*

trench (trench) *n.* **1.** A long narrow excavation in the ground; ditch. **2.** A long irregular ditch, lined with a parapet of the excavated earth, to protect troops. — *v.t.* **1.** To dig a trench or trenches in. **2.** To fortify with trenches. **3.** To cut deep furrows in; ditch. **4.** To confine in a trench, as water. — *v.i.* **5.** To cut or dig trenches. **6.** To cut; carve. **7.** To encroach. [< OF *trenchier* to cut, ult. < L *truncare* to lop off < *truncus* tree trunk] — **trench′er** *n.*

trench·ant (tren′chənt) *adj.* **1.** Cutting; incisive; keen: a *trenchant* remark. **2.** Forceful; vigorous; effective. **3.** Clearly defined; distinct. [< OF, ppr. of *trenchier* to cut] — **trench′an·cy** *n.* — **trench′ant·ly** *adv.*

trench coat A loose-fitting overcoat of rainproof fabric.

trench·er (tren′chər) *n.* Formerly, a wooden plate or board on which food was served or cut. [See TRENCH⁶]

trench·er·man (tren′chər-mən) *n. pl.* ·men (-mən) A feeder; eater; esp., one who enjoys food.

trench fever *Pathol.* A remittent rickettsial fever transmitted by body lice and common among soldiers assigned to prolonged service in trenches during World War I.

trench foot *Pathol.* A disease of the feet caused by continued dampness and cold, and characterized by discoloration, weakness, and sometimes gangrene.

trench mouth *Pathol.* A disease of the mouth, gums, and sometimes the larynx and tonsils, caused by a soil bacillus.

trend (trend) *n.* A general course, inclination, or direction. — *v.i.* To have or take a particular trend. [OE *trendan* to roll]

tre·pan (tri-pan′) *n.* **1.** An early form of the trephine. **2.** A large rock-boring tool. — *v.t.* ·panned, ·pan·ning **1.** *Mech.* To cut circular disks from (a rock or metal plate) by a rotary tool. **2.** *Surg.* To trephine. [< OF, borer < Med.L < Gk. < *trypaein* to bore] — **trep·a·na·tion** (trep′ə-nā′shən) *n.* — **tre·pan′ner** *n.*

tre·pang (tri-pang′) *n.* An East Indian sea cucumber, used in China for making soup. [< Malay *trīpang*]

tre·phine (tri-fīn′, -fēn′) *n. Surg.* A crown saw for removing a piece of bone from the skull so as to relieve pressure, etc. — *v.t.* ·phined, ·phin·ing To operate on with a trephine. [< earlier *trafine* < L *tres fines* three ends]

trep·i·da·tion (trep′ə-dā′shən) *n.* **1.** A state of agitation or alarm; perturbation. **2.** An involuntary trembling. Also **tre·pid·i·ty** (tri-pid′ə-tē). [< L *trepidatus*, pp. of *trepidare* to hurry, be alarmed < *trepidus* alarmed]

trep·o·neme (trep′ə-nēm) *n.* Any of a group of bacteria including the causative agent of syphilis. [< NL < Gk. *trepein* to turn + *nēma* thread] — **trep′o·nem′a·tous** (-nem′ə-təs) *adj.*

tres·pass (tres′pəs, -pas′) *v.i.* **1.** *Law* To commit a trespass; esp., to enter wrongfully upon another's land: with *on* or *upon*. **2.** To pass the bounds of propriety or rectitude, to the injury of another; intrude offensively; encroach: with *on* or *upon*. **3.** To transgress or sin. — *n.* **1.** Any voluntary transgression of law or rule of duty; any offense done to another. **2.** *Law* Any wrongful act accompanied with force, either actual or implied, as wrongful entry on another's land. [< OF < Med.L < L *trans*- across, beyond + to pass] — **tres′pass·er** *n.*

tress (tres) *n.* **1.** A lock, or ringlet of human hair. **2.** *pl.* The hair of a woman or girl, esp. when worn loose. [< OF *tresce*] — **tress′y** *adj.*

-tress *suffix* Used to form many feminine nouns corresponding to masculine nouns in *-ter, -tor: actress.* [Var. of -ESS]

tressed (trest) *adj.* Wearing or arranged in tresses; braided.

tres·tle (tres′əl) *n.* **1.** A beam or bar supported by four divergent legs, for bearing platforms, etc. **2.** An open braced framework for supporting a railway bridge, etc. [< OF < L, dim. of *transtrum* crossbeam]

tres·tle·work (tres′əl-wûrk′) *n.* **1.** Trestles collectively. **2.** A bridge made of trestles. Also **tres′tling.**

trey (trā) *n.* A card, domino, or die having three spots or pips. [< OF *trei, treis* < L *tres* three]

tri- *prefix* **1.** Three; threefold; thrice. **2.** *Chem.* Containing three (specified) atoms, radicals, groups, etc.: *trioxide.*

3. Occurring every three (specified) intervals, or three times within an (assigned) interval: *tri-weekly.* [< L *tri-* threefold]

tri·a·ble (trī′ə-bəl) *adj.* **1.** That may be tried or tested. **2.** *Law* That may undergo a judicial examination or determination. — **tri′a·ble·ness** *n.*

tri·ad (trī′ad) *n.* **1.** A group of three persons or things. **2.** *Music* A chord of three tones formed of superimposed thirds. [< L < Gk. *trias, -ados* < *treis* three] — **tri·ad′ic** *adj. & n.*

tri·al (trī′əl, trīl) *n.* **1.** The examination before a court of the facts or law in a case in order to determine that case. **2.** The act of testing or proving by experience or use. **3.** The state of being tried or tested, as by suffering: hour of *trial.* **4.** Experimental treatment or action performed to determine a result: to learn by *trial* and error. **5.** An attempt or effort to do something; a try: to make a *trial.* — **on trial** In the process of being tried or tested. — *adj.* **1.** Of or pertaining to a trial or trials. **2.** Made, used, or performed in the course of trying or testing. [< AF *trier* to try]

trial and error Experimentation, investigation, learning, etc., in which various methods, theories, or alternatives are tried and faulty or erroneous ones are rejected.

trial balance In double-entry bookkeeping, a draft or statement of the debit and credit footings or balances of each account in the ledger.

trial balloon **1.** A balloon released in order to test atmospheric and meteorological conditions. **2.** Any tentative plan or scheme advanced to test public reaction.

trial jury A petit jury.

tri·an·gle (trī′ang′gəl) *n.* **1.** *Geom.* A figure, esp. a plane figure, bounded by three sides, and having three angles. **2.** Something resembling such a figure in shape or arrangement. **3.** A flat drawing implement for making parallel or diagonal lines, etc. **4.** A group or set of three; a triad. **5.** A situation involving three persons: the eternal *triangle.* **6.** *Music* An instrument consisting of a metal bar bent into a triangle and sounded by being struck with a metal rod. [< OF < L *tri-* three + *angulus* angle]

tri·an·gu·lar (trī·ang′gyə·lər) *adj.* **1.** Pertaining to, like, or bounded by a triangle. **2.** Concerned with or pertaining to three things, parties, or persons. — **tri·an·gu·lar′i·ty** (-lar′ə·tē) *n.* — **tri·an′gu·lar·ly** *adv.*

tri·an·gu·late (trī·ang′gyə·lāt) *v.t.* ·lated, ·lat·ing **1.** To divide into triangles. **2.** To survey by triangulation. **3.** To make triangular. — *adj.* Of or marked with triangles.

tri·an·gu·la·tion (trī·ang′gyə·lā′shən) *n.* **1.** The laying out and accurate measurement of a network of triangles. **2.** A method of determining a position by taking bearings to two fixed points of known distance apart and computing it on the resultant triangle.

Tri·as·sic (trī·as′ik) *adj. Geol.* Of or pertaining to the earliest of the three geological periods comprised in the Mesozoic era. — *n.* The Triassic period or rock system, following the Permian and succeeded by the Jurassic. Also **Tri·as** (trī′əs). See chart under GEOLOGY. [< LL *trias* triad]

tri·bal·ism (trī′bəl·iz′əm) *n.* Tribal organization, culture, or relations.

tribe (trīb) *n.* **1.** A division, class, or group of people, esp. a primitive or nomadic people, usu. characterized by common ancestry, leadership, customs, etc. **2.** In ancient states, an ethnic, hereditary, or political division of a united people; also, one of the twelve divisions of ancient Israel. **3.** A number of persons of any class or profession taken together: often an offensive term: the theatrical *tribe.* **4.** *Biol.* A group of plants or animals of indefinite rank. [< L *tribus* tribe] — **tri′bal** *adj.* — **tri′bal·ly** *adv.*

tribes·man (trībz′mən) *n. pl.* ·men (-mən) A member of a tribe.

trib·u·la·tion (trib′yə·lā′shən) *n.* A condition of affliction and distress; suffering; also, that which causes it. [< OF < LL < L *tribulum* threshing floor < *terere* to rub, grind]

tri·bu·nal (tri·byōō′nəl, trī-) *n.* **1.** A court of justice. **2.** The seat set apart for judges, etc. [See TRIBUNE.]

trib·une¹ (trib′yōōn) *n.* **1.** In Roman history, a magistrate chosen by the plebeians to protect them against patrician oppression. **2.** Any champion of the people. [< L *tribunus* < *tribus* tribe] — **trib′u·nar′y** (-yə·ner′ē), **trib′u·ni′cial** (-yə·nish′əl), **trib′u·ni′cian** *adj.* — **trib′u·nate** (-yə·nit, -nāt), **trib′une·ship** *n.*

trib·une² (trib′yōōn) *n.* A rostrum or platform. [< MF < Ital. < L *tribunal* tribunal]

trib·u·tar·y (trib′yə·ter′ē) *adj.* **1.** Bringing supply; contributory: a *tributary* stream. **2.** Offered or due as tribute: a *tributary* payment. **3.** Paying tribute, as a state. — *n. pl.* ·tar·ies **1.** A person or state paying tribute. **2.** A stream flowing into a larger stream or body of water. [See TRIBUTE.] — **trib′u·tar′i·ly** *adv.* — **trib′u·tar′i·ness** *n.*

trib·ute (trib′yōōt) *n.* **1.** A speech, compliment, gift, etc., given in acknowledgment of admiration, gratitude, or respect. **2.** Money or other valuables paid by one state or ruler to another as an acknowledgment of submission or as the price of peace and protection; also, the taxes imposed to raise money to make such payment. **3.** Any enforced payment as by bribery. [< L *tribuere* to pay, allot]

trice (trīs) *v.t.* **triced, tric·ing** To raise with a rope; also, to tie or lash: usu. with *up*. — *n.* An instant: now only in the phrase **in a trice**. [< MDu. *trisen* to hoist]

tri·cen·ten·ni·al (trī'sen·ten'ē·əl) *adj. & n.* Tercentenary.

tri·ceps (trī'seps) *n. Anat.* A large muscle at the back of the upper arm, of which the function is to extend the forearm. [< L < *tri-* three + *caput* head]

tri·chi·na (tri·kī'nə) *n. pl.* **·nae** (-nē) A small nematode worm, parasitic in the intestines and muscles of man, swine, and other mammals. [< NL < Gk. *thrix* hair]

trich·i·no·sis (trik'ə·nō'sis) *n. Pathol.* The disease produced by trichinae in the intestines and muscles of the body, in man, usu. through eating improperly cooked meat, esp. pork. — **trich/i·nous** (-nəs) *adj.*

tricho- *combining form* Hair; of or resembling a hair or hairs. Also **trichi-**: also, before vowels, **trich-**. [< NL < Gk. *thrix* hair]

trick (trik) *n.* **1.** A device for getting an advantage by deception; a petty artifice; ruse. **2.** A malicious, injurious, or annoying act: a dirty *trick*. **3.** A practical joke; prank. **4.** A particular habit or manner; characteristic; trait. **5.** A peculiar skill or knack. **6.** An act of legerdemain or magic. **7.** In card games, the whole number of cards played in one round. — **to do** (or **turn**) **the trick** *Slang* To produce the desired result. — *v.t.* **1.** To deceive or cheat; delude. **2.** To dress or array: with *up* or *out*. — *v.i.* **3.** To practice trickery or deception. [< OF < *trichier* to cheat, prob. ult. < L < *tricae* trifles, tricks] — **trick/er** *n.* — **trick/less** *adj.*

trick·er·y (trik'ər·ē) *n. pl.* **·er·ies** The practice of tricks; artifice; stratagem; wiles.

trick·le (trik'əl) *v.* **·led, ·ling** *v.i.* **1.** To flow or run drop by drop or in a very thin stream. **2.** To move, come, go, etc., slowly or bit by bit. — *v.t.* **3.** To cause to trickle. — *n.* **1.** The act or state of trickling. **2.** Any slow and irregular movement. [ME *triklen*] — **trick/ly** *adj.*

trick·ster (trik'stər) *n.* One who plays tricks; a cheat.

trick·y (trik'ē) *adj.* **trick·i·er, trick·i·est** Disposed to or characterized by trickery; deceitful; wily. — **trick/i·ly** *adv.* — **trick/i·ness** *n.*

tri·col·or (trī'kul'ər) *adj.* Having or characterized by three colors: also **tri/col/ored.** — *n.* **1.** A flag of three colors. **2.** *Sometimes cap.* The French flag. Also *Brit.* **tri/col/our.** [< F < LL < L *tri-* three + *color* color]

tri·corn (trī'kôrn) *n.* A hat with the brim turned up on three sides. Also **tri/corne.** — *adj.* Having three hornlike processes. [< F < L < *tri-* three + *cornu* horn]

tri·cot (trē'kō, *Fr.* trē·kō') *n.* **1.** A plain, knitted fabric, usu. machine made. **2.** A soft ribbed cloth. [< F < *tricoter* to knit]

tri·cus·pid (trī·kus'pid) *adj.* **1.** Having three cusps or points, as a molar tooth. **2.** *Anat.* Of the tricuspid valve. Also **tri·cus/pi·dal, tri·cus/pi·date.** — *n. Anat.* The tricuspid valve. [< L < *tri-* three + *cuspis* point]

tricuspid valve *Anat.* A three-segmented valve that controls the flow of blood from the right atrium to the right ventricle of the heart.

tri·cy·cle (trī'sik·əl) *n.* A three-wheeled vehicle; esp., such a vehicle with pedals. [< F < *tri-* three + Gk. *kyklos* circle]

tri·dent (trīd'nt) *n.* A three-pronged fork. — *adj.* Having three teeth or prongs: also **tri·den·tate** (trī·den'tāt), **tri·den'·tat·ed.** [< L < *tri-* three + *dens* tooth]

tried (trīd) Past tense and past participle of TRY. — *adj.* Tested; trustworthy.

tri·en·ni·al (trī·en'ē·əl) *adj.* **1.** Taking place every third year. **2.** Lasting three years. — *n.* **1.** A third anniversary. **2.** A ceremony, etc., celebrated every three years. **3.** A plant lasting three years. — **tri·en/ni·al·ly** *adv.*

tri·er (trī'ər) *n.* One who or that which tries.

tri·fa·cial (trī·fā'shəl) *adj. Anat.* Trigeminal.

tri·fid (trī'fid) *adj.* Divided into three parts or sections. [< L < *tri-* three + *findere* to split]

tri·fle (trī'fəl) *v.* **·fled, ·fling** *v.i.* **1.** To treat something as of no value or importance; dally: with *with*. **2.** To act or speak frivolously. **3.** To play; toy. **4.** To idle. — *v.t.* **5.** To pass (time) in an idle and purposeless way. — *n.* **1.** Anything of very little value or importance. **2.** A confection, usu. made of alternate layers of macaroons or ladyfingers with sugared fruit, covered with a custard and topped with meringue or whipped cream. — **a trifle** Slightly: *a trifle short.* [< OF *trufe* cheating, mockery] — **tri/fler** *n.*

tri·fling (trī'fling) *adj.* **1.** Frivolous. **2.** Insignificant. — **tri/fling·ly** *adv.*

tri·fo·cal (trī·fō'kəl) *adj.* **1.** Having three foci. **2.** *Optics* Pertaining to or describing eyeglasses or a lens ground in three segments, for near, intermediate, and far vision. — *n. pl.* Eyeglasses having trifocal lenses.

tri·fo·li·ate (trī·fō'lē·it, -āt) *adj. Bot.* Having three leaves or leaflike processes. Also **tri·fo/li·at·ed.**

tri·fo·ri·um (trī·fôr'ē·əm, -fō'rē-) *n. pl.* **·fo·ri·a** (-fôr'ē·ə, -fō'rē·ə) *Archit.* A gallery above the arches of the nave in a church. [< Med.L < L *tri-* three + *foris* a door]

trig (trig) *adj.* **1.** Trim; neat. **2.** Strong; sound. — *v.t.* **trigged, trig·ging** To make trig or neat: often with *out* or *up*. [< ON *tryggr* true] — **trig/ly** *adv.* — **trig/ness** *n.*

tri·gem·i·nal (trī·jem'ə·nəl) *adj. Anat.* Of or pertaining to the trigeminus: also *trifacial.* — *n.* The trigeminus. [< L < *tri-* + *geminus* a twin]

tri·gem·i·nus (trī·jem'ə·nəs) *n. pl.* **·ni** (-nī) *Anat.* The double-rooted fifth cranial nerve, whose three divisions, mandibular, maxillary, and opthalmic, function as the great sensory nerve of the face. [See TRIGEMINAL.]

trig·ger (trig'ər) *n.* **1.** The lever or other device actuated manually to fire a firearm. **2.** Any lever, release, etc., that serves to initiate a process or operation. — **quick on the trigger 1.** Quick to shoot. **2.** Quick to act; alert. — *v.t.* To initiate; precipitate. [< Du. *trekken* to pull]

trigonometric functions Certain functions of an angle or arc, of which the most commonly used are the sine, cosine, tangent, cotangent, secant, and cosecant.

trig·o·nom·e·try (trig'ə·nom'ə·trē) *n.* The branch of mathematics that deals with the relations of the sides and angles of triangles. [< NL < Gk. *trigōnon* triangle + *metron* measure] — **trig·o·no·met·ric** (trig'ə·nə·met'rik) or **·ri·cal** *adj.* — **trig/o·m·met/ri·cal·ly** *adv.*

tri·he·dron (trī·hē'drən) *n. pl.* **·dra** (-drə) *Geom.* A figure having three plane surfaces meeting at a point. [< NL < Gk. *tri-* three + *hedra* a base] — **tri·he/dral** *adj.*

tri·lat·er·al (trī·lat'ər·əl) *adj.* Having three sides. [< L < *tri-* three + *latus* a side] — **tri·lat/er·al·ly** *adv.*

trill (tril) *v.t.* **1.** To sing or play in a tremulous tone. **2.** *Phonet.* To articulate with a trill. — *v.i.* **3.** To give forth a tremulous sound. **4.** *Music* To execute a trill. — *n.* **1.** A tremulous utterance of successive tones, as of birds; a warble. **2.** *Music* A rapid alternation of two tones either a tone or a semitone apart. **3.** *Phonet.* A rapid vibration of the tongue in the articulation of *rr* in Spanish, or of the uvula in the articulation of *r* in some varieties of German. **4.** A consonant so uttered. [< Ital. *trillare*]

tril·lion (tril'yən) *n.* **1.** *U.S.* A thousand billions, written as 1 followed by twelve zeros: a cardinal number: called a billion in Great Britain. **2.** *Brit.* A million billions (def. 2), written as 1 followed by eighteen zeros: a cardinal number. — *adj.* Being a trillion in number. [< MF < *tri-* three + *(mi)llion* million] — **tril/lionth** *adj. & n.*

tril·li·um (tril'ē·əm) *n.* Any of various herbs of the lily family, having a stout stem bearing a whorl of three leaves and a solitary flower. [< NL < L *tri-* three]

tri·lo·bate (trī·lō'bāt, trī'lə·bāt) *adj. Bot.* Having three lobes, as some leaves. Also **tri·lo/bal, tri·lo/bat·ed, tri/lobed.**

tri·lo·bite (trī'lə·bīt) *n. Paleontol.* Any of a group of extinct Paleozoic marine animals having a flattened body divided into a variable number of segments covered by a hard dorsal shield marked in three lobes. [< NL < Gk. *tri-* three + *lobos* a lobe] — **trI/lo·bit/ic** (-bit'ik) *adj.*

tril·o·gy (tril'ə·jē) *n. pl.* **·gies** A group of three literary or dramatic compositions, each complete in itself, but continuing the same general subject. [< Gk. < *tri-* three + *logos* a discourse]

trim (trim) *v.* **trimmed, trim·ming** *v.t.* **1.** To put in or restore to order; make neat by clipping, etc. **2.** To remove by cutting: usu. with *off* or *away*. **3.** To put ornaments on; decorate. **4.** In carpentry, to smooth; dress. **5.** *Informal* **a** To defeat. **b** To punish or thrash. **c** To rebuke. **d** To cheat. **6.** *Naut.* **a** To adjust (sails or yards) for sailing. **b** To balance (a ship) by adjusting cargo, etc. — *v.i.* **7.** To act so as to appear to favor both sides in a controversy. — *n.* **1.** State of adjustment or preparation; orderly disposition: All was in good *trim*. **2.** Condition as to general appearance; dress. **3.** *Naut.* **a** Fitness for sailing: said of a vessel in reference to disposition of ballast, masts, cargo, etc. **b** Degree of immersion. **4.** Particular character or nature. **5.** The moldings, etc., as about the doors of a building. **6.** Ornament; trapping; trimming; dress. — *adj.* **trim·mer, trim·mest 1.** Adjusted to a nicety; being in perfect order; handsomely equipped or of stylish and smart appearance; precise. **2.** Excellently fit; fine. — *adv.* In a trim manner: also **trim/ly.** [OE *trymman* to arrange, strengthen < *trum* strong] — **trim/mer** *n.* — **trim/ness** *n.*

trim·e·ter (trim'ə·tər) *n.* In prosody, a line of verse consisting of three metrical feet. — *adj.* In prosody, consisting of three metrical feet or of lines containing three metrical feet. [< L < Gk. < *tri-* three + *metron* measure] — **tri·met·ric** (trī·met'rik), **tri·met/ri·cal** *adj.*

tri·meth·yl·pen·tane (trī'meth·il·pen'tān) *n. Chem.* One of three isomeric hydrocarbon compounds, C_8H_{18}, one of which, often called isooctane, is used in rating motor fuels.

trim·ming (trim'ing) *n.* **1.** Something added for ornament.

2. *pl.* Articles or equipment; fittings, as the hardware of a house. **3.** *pl.* The usual or proper accompaniments or condiments of an article or food. **4.** *pl.* That which is removed by trimming. **5.** *Informal* A severe reproof; flogging; beating. **6.** *Informal* A defeat. **7.** The act of one who trims.

tri·month·ly (trī-munth′lē) *adj. & adv.* Done or occurring every third month.

tri·nal (trī′nəl) *adj.* Having three parts; threefold. Also **trine** (trīn). [< LL < L *tres* three]

tri·na·ry (trī′nər-ē) *adj.* Made up of three parts or proceeding by threes; ternary. [See TRINAL.]

Trin·i·tar·i·an (trin′ə·târ′ē·ən) *adj.* **1.** Of or pertaining to the Trinity. **2.** Holding or professing belief in the Trinity. Compare UNITARIAN. — *n.* A believer in the doctrine of the Trinity. — **Trin′i·tar′i·an·ism** *n.*

tri·ni·tro·tol·u·ene (trī-nī′trō-tol′yoō-ēn) *n. Chem.* A high explosive, $C_7H_5N_3O_6$, made by treating toluene with nitric acid, used in warfare, as a blasting agent, and as a base for measuring the explosive power of nuclear bombs: also called *TNT, trotyl.* Also **tri·ni′tro·tol′u·ol** (-yoō-ōl, -ol). [< TRI- + NITRO- + TOLUENE]

trin·i·ty (trin′ə·tē) *n. pl.* **·ties** Any union of three parts or elements in one; a trio. [< OF < LL < L *trinus* triple]

Trin·i·ty (trin′ə·tē) *n. Theol.* A threefold personality existing in the one divine being or substance; the union in one God of Father, Son, and Holy Spirit.

Trinity Sunday *Eccl.* The eighth Sunday after Easter, observed as a festival in honor of the Trinity.

trin·ket (tring′kit) *n.* **1.** Any small ornament, as of jewelry. **2.** A trifle; a trivial object; a toy. [< AF *trenquet,* OF *trenchet* a toy knife, ornament]

tri·no·mi·al (trī-nō′mē·əl) *adj.* **1.** *Biol.* Of, having, or employing three terms or names in taxonomy, the generic, the specific, and the subspecific or varietal, as *Lynx rufus texensis,* the Texas bobcat. **2.** *Math.* Consisting of three terms connected by plus or minus signs or both. — *n.* **1.** *Math.* A trinomial expression, as $3x + y - 27z$. **2.** *Biol.* A trinomial name. Also **tri·nom′i·nal** (-nom′ə-nəl), **tri·on′y·mal** (-on′ə-məl). [< L *trinominus* having three names]

tri·o (trē′ō; *for def. 1, also* trī′ō) *n. pl.* **tri·os** **1.** Any three things grouped or associated together. **2.** *Music* **a** A composition for three performers. **b** The second part of a minuet, scherzo, etc. **c** A group of three musicians that plays trios. [< F < Ital. < L *tres* three]

-triol *suffix Chem.* Denoting an organic compound containing three hydroxyl radicals.

tri·ox·ide (trī-ok′sīd, -sid) *n. Chem.* An oxide containing three atoms of oxygen in combination. Also **tri·ox′id** (-sid).

trip (trip) *n.* **1.** A journey or voyage. **2.** A misstep or stumble caused by losing balance or striking the foot against an object. **3.** An active, nimble step or movement. **4.** *Mech.* A pawl or similar device that trips, or the action of such a device. **5.** A sudden catch, esp. of the legs and feet, as of a wrestler. **6.** A blunder; mistake. **7.** *Slang* The taking of a psychedelic drug, or the resulting mental experience. — *v.* **tripped, trip·ping** *v.i.* **1.** To stumble. **2.** To move quickly with light or small steps. **3.** To commit an error. **4.** *Mech.* To be triggered, released, etc. — *v.t.* **5.** To cause to stumble: often with *up.* **6.** To detect and expose in an error; defeat the purpose of. **7.** To perform (a dance) lightly. **8.** *Mech.* To set free or in operation by releasing a stay, catch, trigger, etc. **9.** *Naut.* To loosen (an anchor) from the bottom. [< OF *treper, triper* to leap, trample]

tri·par·tite (trī-pär′tīt) *adj.* **1.** Divided into three parts or divisions; threefold: a *tripartite* leaf: also **tri·part·ed** (trī′pär′tid). **2.** Pertaining to or executed between three parties. [< L < *tri-* three + *partiri* to divide] — **tri·par′tite·ly** *adv.*

tri·par·ti·tion (trī′pär·tish′ən) *n.* Division into three parts, into thirds, or among three.

tripe (trīp) *n.* **1.** A part of the stomach of a ruminant, used for food. **2.** *Informal* Anything worthless; nonsense. [< OF < Arabic *tharb* entrails, a net]

trip hammer A heavy power hammer that is raised or tilted by a cam and then allowed to drop.

tri·ple (trip′əl) *v.* **·led, ·ling** *v.t.* **1.** To make threefold in number or quantity. — *v.i.* **2.** To be or become three times as many or as large. **3.** In baseball, to hit a triple. — *adj.* **1.** Consisting of three things united or of three parts; threefold. **2.** Multiplied by three; thrice said or done. — *n.* **1.** A set or group of three. **2.** In baseball, a base hit that enables the batter to reach third base. [< MF < L < Gk. *triplous* threefold] — **trip′ly** *adv.*

triple play In baseball, a play during which three men are put out.

trip·let (trip′lit) *n.* **1.** A group of three of a kind. **2.** One of three children born at one birth. **3.** A group of three rhymed lines. **4.** *Music* A group of three equal notes performed in the time of two: also called *tercet.*

triple threat *U.S. Informal* **1.** A football player expert at kicking, running, and passing. **2.** One skillful in three areas of activity. — **trip·le-threat** (trip′əl-thret′) *adj.*

tri·plex (trī′pleks, trip′leks) *adj.* Having three parts. [< L < *tri-* three + *plicare* to fold]

trip·li·cate (*adj. & n.* trip′lə·kit; *v.* trip′lə·kāt) *adj.* Threefold; made in three copies. — *n.* One of or a set of three identical things. — *v.t.* **·cat·ed, ·cat·ing** To make three times as much or as many. [< L *triplicatus,* pp. of *triplicare* to triple] — **trip′li·cate·ly** *adv.* — **trip′li·ca′tion** *n.*

tri·plic·i·ty (tri·plis′ə·tē) *n. pl.* **·ties** **1.** Threefold character. **2.** A group or combination of three. **3.** In astrology, a combination of three of the twelve signs of the zodiac.

tri·pod (trī′pod) *n.* **1.** A utensil or article having three feet or legs. **2.** A three-legged stand for supporting a camera, transit, etc. [< L < Gk. < *tri-* three + *pous* foot]

trip·o·dal (trip′ə·dəl) *adj.* **1.** Of the nature or form of a tripod. **2.** Having three feet or legs. Also **tri·po·di·al** (trī-pō′-dē·əl, trī-), **tri·pod′ic** (-pod′ik).

trip·o·dy (trip′ə·dē) *n. pl.* **·dies** A verse or meter having three feet.

trip·per (trip′ər) *n.* **1.** One who trips. **2.** *Brit. Informal* A traveler; tourist. **3.** *Mech.* A trip or tripping mechanism.

trip·ping (trip′ing) *n.* The act of one who or that which trips. — *adj.* Nimble. — **trip′ping·ly** *adv.*

trip·tych (trip′tik) *n.* **1.** A triple tablet; esp., a Greek or Roman hinged triple writing tablet. **2.** A triple picture or carving on three hinged panels, often depicting a religious subject. Also **trip′ty·ca** (-ti-kə), **trip′ty·chon** (-ti-kon). [< LL < Gk. < *tri-* thrice + *ptyssein* to fold]

tri·reme (trī′rēm) *n.* An ancient Greek or Roman warship with three banks of oars. [< L < *tri-* three + *remus* oar]

tri·sect (trī-sekt′) *v.t.* To divide into three parts, esp., as in geometry, into three equal parts. [< TRI- + L *sectus,* pp. of *secare* to cut] — **tri·sect′ed** *adj.* — **tri·sec′tion** (-sek′shən) *n.* — **tri·sec′tor** *n.*

tri·seme (trī′sēm) *n.* A syllable or foot consisting of or equivalent to three short syllables, as the trochee. — *adj.* Consisting of or equal to three short syllables: also **tri·se′mic.** [< Gk. < *tri-* three + *sēma* a sign]

tris·mus (triz′məs, tris′-) *n. Pathol.* Lockjaw. [< NL < Gk. *trismos* gnashing of teeth] — **tris′mic** *adj.*

Tris·tan (tris′tän, -tən) In medieval legend and Richard Wagner's *Tristan und Isolde,* a knight sent to Ireland to bring back the princess Iseult the Beautiful as a bride for his uncle, King Mark of Cornwall. Iseult and Tristan drink a magic love potion, and ultimately die together. Also **Tris·tram** (tris′trəm).

triste (trēst) *adj. French* Sorrowful; sad.

tris·tesse (trēs·tes′) *n. French* Sadness; melancholy.

tris·tich (tris′tik) *n.* A strophe or system of three lines; triplet. Compare COUPLET, DISTICH. [< TRI- + (DI)STICH]

tri·syl·la·ble (trī·sil′ə·bəl) *n.* A word of three syllables. — **tri·syl·lab·ic** (trī′si·lab′ik) or **·i·cal** *adj.* — **tri·syl·lab′i·cal·ly** *adv.*

trite (trīt) *adj.* Used so often as to be hackneyed; made commonplace by repetition. [< L *tritus,* pp. of *terere* to rub] — **trite′ly** *adv.* — **trite′ness** *n.*

— **Syn.** **1.** *Trite* suggests merely a lack of freshness or originality. *Hackneyed* is stronger, suggesting something worn out from overuse; the extreme of *hackneyed* is *threadbare.* We speak of *hackneyed* expressions, and of *threadbare* subjects. *Stereotyped* describes that which uses clichés instead of seeking to evoke new images and ideas. — **Ant.** fresh, original, vivid, striking.

trit·i·cum (trit′ə·kəm) *n.* Any of a widely distributed genus of cereal grasses, the wheats, cultivated in many varieties. [< NL < L, wheat]

trit·i·um (trit′ē·əm, trish′ē·əm) *n. Physics* The isotope of hydrogen having the atomic weight 3. [< NL < Gk. *tritos* third]

tri·ton[1] (trīt′n) *n.* Any of a genus of marine gastropods having many gills and a trumpet-shaped shell. [< L < Gk. *Tritōn*]

tri·ton[2] (trī′ton) *n. Physics* The nucleus of an atom of tritium. [< TRIT(IUM) + (ELECTR)ON]

Tri·ton (trīt′n) In Greek mythology, a son of Poseidon (Neptune) and Amphitrite, represented with a man's head and upper body and a dolphin's tail. — *n.* In Greek mythology, one of a race of attendants of the sea gods.

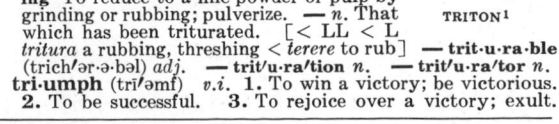

TRITON[1]

trit·u·rate (trich′ə·rāt) *v.t.* **·rat·ed, ·rat·ing** To reduce to a fine powder or pulp by grinding or rubbing; pulverize. — *n.* That which has been triturated. [< LL < L *tritura* a rubbing, threshing < *terere* to rub] — **trit·u·ra·ble** (trich′ər·ə·bəl) *adj.* — **trit·u·ra′tion** *n.* — **trit′u·ra′tor** *n.*

tri·umph (trī′əmf) *v.i.* **1.** To win a victory; be victorious. **2.** To be successful. **3.** To rejoice over a victory; exult.

4. To celebrate a triumph, as a victorious Roman general. — *n.* **1.** In Roman antiquity, the religious pageant of the entry of a victorious consul, dictator, or praetor into Rome. **2.** Exultation over victory. **3.** The condition of being victorious; victory. [< OF < L < Gk. *thriambos* a processional hymn to Dionysus] — **tri′umph·er** *n.*

tri·um·phal (trī-um′fəl) *adj.* **1.** Of, pertaining to, or of the nature of a triumph. **2.** Celebrating a victory.

triumphal arch A monumental arch erected to commemorate a great victory or achievement.

tri·um·phant (trī-um′fənt) *adj.* **1.** Exultant for or as for victory. **2.** Victorious. — **tri·um′phant·ly** *adv.*

tri·um·vir (trī-um′vər) *n. pl.* **·virs** or **·vi·ri** (-və·rī) One of three men united in public office or authority, as in ancient Rome. [< L < *tres, trium* three + *vir* a man] — **tri·um′vi·ral** *adj.*

tri·um·vi·rate (trī-um′vər·it, -və·rāt) *n.* **1.** A group or coalition of three men who unitedly exercise authority or control; government by triumvirs. **2.** The office of a triumvir. **3.** A group of three men; trio.

tri·une (trī′yoon) *adj.* Three in one: said of God. — *n.* A group of three things united; triad; trinity in unity. [< TRI- + L *unus* one] — **tri·u′ni·ty** *n.*

tri·va·lent (trī-vā′lənt, triv′ə·lənt) *adj. Chem.* Having a valence or combining value of three. [< TRI- + L *valens,* ppr. of *valere* to be worth] — **tri·va′lence, tri·va′len·cy** *n.*

triv·et (triv′it) *n.* A stand, usu. three-legged, for holding cooking vessels in a fireplace, a heated iron, or a hot dish on a table. [OE < L < *tri-* three + *pes, pedis* a foot]

triv·i·a (triv′ē-ə) *n.pl.* Insignificant or unimportant matters; trifles. [See TRIVIAL.]

triv·i·al (triv′ē-əl) *adj.* **1.** Of little value or importance; trifling; insignificant. **2.** Such as is found everywhere or every day; commonplace. **3.** Occupied with trifles. [< L *trivialis* of the crossroads, commonplace < *tri-* three + *via* road] — **triv′i·al·ism** *n.* — **triv′i·al·ly** *adv.*

triv·i·al·i·ty (triv′ē-al′ə-tē) *n. pl.* **·ties** **1.** The state or quality of being trivial: also **triv′i·al·ness.** **2.** A trivial matter.

tri·week·ly (trī-wēk′lē) *adj.* **1.** Occurring three times a week. **2.** Done or occurring every third week. — *adv.* **1.** Three times a week. **2.** Every third week. — *n.* A publication appearing triweekly.

-trix *suffix* A feminine termination of agent nouns the masculine form of which is *-tor: testatrix.* See -OR¹. [< L]

tro·cha·ic (trō-kā′ik) *adj.* Pertaining to, containing, or composed of trochees: a *trochaic* foot or verse. — *n.* A trochaic verse or line. [See TROCHEE.]

tro·chal (trō′kəl) *adj.* Shaped like a wheel; rotiform. [< Gk. *trochos* a wheel]

tro·che (trō′kē) *n.* A medicated lozenge, usu. circular: also called *pastille.* [Alter. of obs. *trochisk* < MF < L < Gk. < *trochos* wheel]

tro·chee (trō′kē) *n.* **1.** In prosody, a metrical foot consisting of one long or accented syllable followed by one short or unaccented syllable (—◡). **2.** A line of verse made up of or characterized by such feet: Nŏw thĕ| līght hăs| fāllĕn| frŏm thĕ| hēavĕns. [< L < Gk. < *trechein* to run]

trod (trod) Past tense and alternative past participle of TREAD.

trod·den (trod′n) Past participle of TREAD.

trog·lo·dyte (trog′lə-dīt) *n.* **1.** A cave man. **2.** A hermit; anyone of primitive habits. **3.** An anthropoid ape, as the chimpanzee. [< L < Gk. < *trōglē* hole + *dyein* to go into] — **trog′lo·dyt′ic** (-dit′ik) or **·i·cal** *adj.*

tro·gon (trō′gon) *n.* A tropical American bird noted for its resplendent plumage. [< NL < Gk. *trōgein* to gnaw]

troi·ka (troi′kə) *n.* A Russian vehicle drawn by a team of three horses driven abreast. [< Russian < *troie* three]

Tro·jan (trō′jən) *n.* **1.** A native of Troy. **2.** One who works earnestly or suffers courageously. — *adj.* Of or pertaining to ancient Troy. [< L < *Troja* Troy]

Trojan horse **1.** In classical legend, a large, hollow wooden horse, filled with Greek soldiers and left at the Trojan gates. When it was brought within the walls the soldiers emerged at night and admitted the Greek army, who burned the city: also called *wooden horse.* **2.** A person, device, etc., intended to disrupt or undermine a plan.

Trojan War In Greek legend, the ten years' war waged by the confederated Greeks under their king, Agamemnon, against the Trojans to recover Helen, the wife of Menelaus, who had been abducted by Paris: celebrated esp. in the *Iliad* and the *Odyssey.*

troll¹ (trōl) *v.t.* **1.** To fish for with a moving lure, as from a slowly moving boat. **2.** To move (the line or lure) in fishing. **3.** To sing in succession, as in a round or catch. **4.** To sing in a full, hearty manner. **5.** To cause to roll; revolve. — *v.i.* **6.** To fish with a moving lure. **7.** To sing a tune, etc., in a full, hearty manner. **8.** To be uttered in such a way. **9.** To roll; turn. — *n.* **1.** A catch or round. **2.** A rolling movement or motion; also, repetition or routine.

3. In fishing, a spoon or other lure. [? < OF *troller* to quest, wander < Gmc.] — **troll′er** *n.*

troll² (trōl) *n.* In Scandinavian folklore, a giant; later, a mischievous dwarf. Also **trold** (trōld). [< ON]

trol·ley (trol′ē) *n. pl.* **·leys** **1.** *U.S.* A streetcar. **2.** A grooved metal wheel for rolling in contact with a conductor (the **trolley wire**), to convey the current to an electric vehicle. **3.** In a subway system, a device adapted to the same purpose attached to a current taker operating through a third rail. **4.** A small truck or car for conveying material, as in a factory, mine, etc. **5.** The mechanism of a traveling crane. **6.** A small car running on tracks and worked by a manually operated lever, used by workmen on a railway. — *v.t. & v.i.* To travel by trolley. Also **trol′ly.** [< TROLL¹]

trolley bus A bus propelled electrically by current from an overhead wire by means of a trolley. Also **trolley coach.**

trolley car A car with a trolley for use on an electric railway; esp., *U.S.,* a streetcar.

troll·ing (trō′ling) *n.* The method or act of fishing by dragging a hook and line, as behind a boat and near the surface. [< TROLL¹]

trolling rod A strong fishing rod for trolling.

trol·lop (trol′əp) *n.* **1.** A slatternly woman. **2.** A prostitute. [< dial. E (Scottish) < ME *trollen* to roll about] — **trol′lop·ish, trol′lop·y, trol′lop·ing** *adj.*

trom·bone (trom-bōn′, trom′bōn′) A brass instrument of the trumpet family, but larger and lower in pitch than the trumpet. A **slide trombone** changes pitch by means of a U-shaped slide that can lengthen or shorten the air column, a **valve trombone** changes pitch by means of valves. [< Ital., aug. of *tromba* trumpet < Gmc.] — **trom·bon′ist** *n.*

trompe l'oeil (trônp lœ′y) In art and decoration, the accurate representation of details, scenes, etc., to create an illusion of reality. [< F, lit., fool the eye]

-tron *suffix* **1.** Vacuum tube: *magnetron.* **2.** Device for the manipulation of subatomic particles: *cyclotron.* [< Gk., instrumental suffix]

troop (troop) *n.* **1.** An assembled company; gathering; a herd or flock. **2.** *Usu. pl.* A body of soldiers; soldiers collectively. **3.** The cavalry unit corresponding to a company of infantry. **4.** A body of Boy Scouts consisting of four patrols of eight scouts each. — *v.i.* **1.** To move along or gather as a troop or as a crowd. — *v.t.* **2.** To form into troops. **3.** *Brit. Mil.* To carry ceremoniously before troops: to *troop* the colors. [< OF < LL *troppus* a flock < Gmc.]

troop carrier **1.** A transport aircraft for carrying troops and equipment. **2.** An armored vehicle for carrying troops.

troop·er (troo′pər) *n.* **1.** A cavalryman. **2.** A mounted policeman. **3.** A troop horse; charger. **4.** A troopship. **5.** A state policeman.

troop·ship (troop′ship′) *n.* A ship for carrying troops.

trope (trōp) *n.* **1.** The figurative use of a word. **2.** Loosely, a figure of speech; figurative language in general. [< F < L < Gk. *tropos* a turn < *trepein* to turn]

-trope *combining form* **1.** One who or that which turns or changes: *allotrope.* **2.** Turning; turned in a (specified) way: *hemitrope.* [< Gk. *tropos* a turning < *trepein* to turn]

troph·ic (trof′ik) *adj.* Pertaining to nutrition and its processes. Also **troph′i·cal.** [< Gk. < *trephein* to nourish] — **troph′i·cal·ly** *adv.*

tro·phied (trō′fēd) *adj.* Adorned with trophies.

tropho- *combining form* Nutrition; nourishment; of or pertaining to food or nutrition. Also, before vowels, **troph-.** [< Gk. *trophē* food, nourishment < *trephein* to feed, nourish]

tro·phy (trō′fē) *n. pl.* **·phies** **1.** Something symbolizing victory or success; as: **a** A cup, statuette, etc., awarded for athletic or other achievement. **b** A mounted fish, animal's head, etc. **c** A weapon, etc., captured from an enemy. **2.** An ornamental symbolic group of objects hung together on a wall. **3.** A memento or memorial. [< MF < L < Gk. < *tropē* a defeat < *trepein* to turn, rout]

-trophy *combining form* A (specified) kind of nutrition or development: *hypertrophy.* Corresponding adjectives end in *-trophic.* [< Gk. *trophē.* See TROPHO-.]

trop·ic (trop′ik) *n.* **1.** *Geog.* Either of two parallels of latitude 23° 27′ north and south of the equator, on which the sun is seen in the zenith on the days of its greatest declination, called respectively **tropic of Cancer** and **tropic of Capricorn.** **2.** *pl.* The regions of the earth's surface between the tropics of Cancer and Capricorn; the Torrid Zone. — *adj.* Of or pertaining to the tropics; tropical. [< L < Gk. *tropikos* (*kyklos*) the tropical (circle) < *tropē* a turning]

TROPICS

-tropic *combining form* Having a (specified) tropism; turning in a (particular) way or in response to a (given) stimulus: *phototropic.* Also *-tropal.*

trop·i·cal (trop′i·kəl) *adj.* **1.** Of, pertaining to, or characteristic of the tropics. **2.** Of the nature of a trope or metaphor. — **trop′i·cal·ly** *adv.*

tropic bird A long-winged, oceanic bird, allied to the pelicans, found mostly in the tropics, having the two middle tail feathers elongated.

tro·pism (trō′piz·əm) *n. Biol.* 1. The involuntary response of an organism to an external stimulus. 2. Any automatic reaction to a stimulus. [< Gk. *tropē* a turning] — **tro·pis·tic** (trō·pis′tik) *adj.*

-tropism *combining form* A (specified) tropism: *phototropism.* Also **-tropy.** [< TROPISM]

trop·o·pause (trop′ə-pôz) *n. Meteorol.* A transition zone in the atmosphere between the troposphere and the stratosphere. [< TROPO(SPHERE) + Gk. *pausis* a ceasing]

trop·o·sphere (trop′ə-sfir) *n. Meteorol.* The region of the atmosphere beneath the stratosphere; it is characterized by turbulence and decreasing temperature with increasing altitude. [< F < Gk. *tropos* a turning + F *sphère* < L *sphaera* sphere] — **trop′o·spher′ic** (-sfir′ik, -sfer′-) *adj.*

trot (trot) *n.* 1. A gait of a quadruped, esp. a horse, in which diagonal pairs of legs are lifted, thrust forward, and placed down almost simultaneously; also, the sound of this gait. 2. A race for trotters. 3. A reasonably rapid run. 4. *Informal* A pony (def. 3). — *v.* **trot·ted, trot·ting** *v.i.* 1. To go at a trot. 2. To hurry. — *v.t.* 3. To cause to trot. 4. To ride at a trotting gait. — **to trot out** To bring forth for inspection, approval, etc. [< OF < OHG *trottōn* to tread]

troth (trôth, trōth) *n.* 1. Good faith; fidelity. 2. The act of pledging fidelity; esp., betrothal. 3. Truth; verity. — *v.t. Archaic* To betroth; pledge. [ME *trowthe, trouthe,* var. of OE *trēowth* truth; faith]

Trot·sky·ism (trot′skē-iz′əm) *n.* The doctrines of Trotsky and his followers; esp., his theory that Communism to succeed must be international. — **Trot′sky·ist, Trot′sky·ite** *n. & adj.*

trot·ter (trot′ər) *n.* One who or that which trots; esp., a horse trained to trot for speed.

tro·tyl (trō′til) *n.* Trinitrotoluene. [< (TRINI)TROT(O-LUENE) + -YL]

trou·ba·dour (trōō′bə-dôr, -dōr, -dŏŏr) *n.* 1. One of a class of lyric poets, originating in Provence in the 11th century and flourishing in southern France, northern Italy, and eastern Spain during the 12th and 13th centuries. 2. A singer, esp., of love songs. [< MF < Provençal < *trobar* to compose, invent, find]

trou·ble (trub′əl) *n.* 1. The state of being distressed, annoyed, upset, afflicted, or confused. 2. A difficulty, perplexity, annoyance, disturbance, etc. 3. Toilsome exertion; pains: Take the *trouble* to do it correctly. 4. A diseased condition: lung *trouble.* 5. *Informal* Pregnant and unmarried. — *v.* **·led, ·ling** *v.t.* 1. To cause mental agitation to; distress; worry. 2. To agitate or disturb; stir up or roil, as water. 3. To inconvenience or incommode. 4. To bother. 5. To cause physical pain or discomfort to. — *v.i.* 6. To take pains; bother. 7. To worry. [< OF < L *turbula* mob, dim. of *turba* crowd] — **troub′ler** *n.* — **troub′ling·ly** *adv.*

troub·led (trub′əld) *adj.* 1. Beset with trouble. 2. Distressed. 3. Agitated, disturbed, or roiled, as water. — **troub′led·ly** *adv.* — **troub′led·ness** *n.*

troub·le-shoot·er (trub′əl-shōō′tər) *n.* One who locates difficulties and seeks to remove them, esp., in the operation of a machine, in an industrial process, etc. — **troub′le-shoot′ing** *n.*

troub·le·some (trub′əl-səm) *adj.* 1. Causing trouble; vexatious; burdensome; trying. 2. Marked by violence; tumultuous. 3. Greatly agitated or disturbed; troublous. — **troub′le·some·ly** *adv.* — **troub′le·some·ness** *n.*

troub·lous (trub′ləs) *adj.* 1. Marked by commotion or tumult; full of trouble: *troublous* times. 2. Uneasy; restless.

trough (trôf, trof) *n.* 1. A long, narrow, open receptacle for conveying a fluid or for holding food or water for animals. 2. A long, narrow channel or depression, as between ridges on land or waves at sea. 3. A gutter (def. 3). 4. *Meteorol.* A long, usu. narrow area having a low barometric pressure. 5. *Econ.* A low or the lowest point reached in a business cycle. [OE *trog*]

trounce (trouns) *v.t.* **trounced, trounc·ing** 1. To beat or thrash severely; punish. 2. *Informal* To defeat. [Ult. origin uncertain]

troupe (trōōp) *n.* A company of actors or other performers. — *v.i.* **trouped, troup·ing** To travel as one of a theatrical company. [< MF < OF *trope* troop]

trou·per (trōō′pər) *n.* 1. A member of a theatrical company. 2. An actor of long experience.

trou·sers (trou′zərz) *n.pl.* A garment, esp. for men and boys, covering the body from the waist to the ankles and divided so as to make a separate covering for each leg. Also **trow′sers.** [Blend of obs. *trouse* breeches and DRAWERS]

trous·seau (trōō′sō, trōō-sō′) *n. pl.* **·seaux** (-sōz, -sōz′) or **·seaus** A bride's outfit, esp. of clothing, linens, etc. [< F *trousse* a packed collection of things]

trout (trout) *n.* 1. A fish of the salmon family mostly found in fresh waters and highly esteemed as a game and food fish. The **brown** or **salmon trout** is common in Europe; the **cut-throat trout** and the **rainbow trout** or steelhead are species of western North America; the **speckled trout** or **brook trout** is common in eastern North America. 2. A fish resembling, or supposed to resemble, the above, as the greenling. [OE < LL < Gk. *trōktēs* nibbler < *trōgein* to gnaw]

trove (trōv) *n.* Something, esp. of value or pleasing quality, found or discovered. [< (TREASURE-)TROVE]

trow (trō) *v.t. & v.i. Archaic* To suppose; think; believe. [Fusion of OE *truwian* (< *truwa* faith) and *trēowan* to believe < *trēowe* true]

trow·el (trou′əl, troul) *n.* 1. A flat-bladed, sometimes pointed implement having an offset handle, used to smooth plaster, mortar, etc. 2. A small concave scoop with a handle, used in digging about small plants, potting them, etc. — *v.t.* **trow·eled** or **·elled, trow·el·ing** or **·el·ling** To apply, dress, or form with a trowel. [< OF < LL < L *trulla,* dim. of *trua* stirring spoon, ladle] — **trow′el·er** or **trow′el·ler** *n.*

troy (troi) *n.* A system of weights in which 12 troy ounces make a pound, used by jewelers in England and the U.S. See table front of book. Also **troy weight.** [after *Troyes,* a city in France]

Troy (troi) An ancient city in NW Asia Minor of perhaps about 1200 B.C., the scene of the *Iliad*: also called *Ilium, Ilion.*

tru·an·cy (trōō′ən·sē) *n. pl.* **·cies** The state or habit of being truant; also, an act of being truant. Also **tru′ant·ry.**

tru·ant (trōō′ənt) *n.* 1. One who absents himself, esp., from school, without leave. — *v.i.* To be truant. — *adj.* 1. Being truant; idle. 2. Relating to or characterizing a truant. [< OF, vagabond, prob. < Celtic]

truant officer *U.S.* An official who investigates truancy from school.

truce (trōōs) *n.* 1. An agreement between belligerents for a temporary suspension of hostilities; an armistice. 2. Temporary cessation or intermission. [Plural of ME *trew,* OE *trūwa* faith, a promise]

truck[1] (truk) *n.* 1. *U.S. & Canadian* Any of various automotive vehicles designed to carry loads, freight, etc.: also, *Brit.,* lorry. 2. A two-wheeled barrowlike vehicle with a forward lip and no sides, used for moving barrels, boxes, etc., by hand. 3. A vehicle used about railway stations, for moving trunks, etc. 4. *Brit.* An open or platform freight car. 5. *Naut.* A disk at the top of a mast or flagpole through which the halyards of signals are run. 6. One of the pivoting sets of wheels on a railroad car or engine. — *v.t.* 1. To carry on a truck. — *v.i.* 2. To carry goods on a truck. 3. To drive a truck. [Appar. < L < Gk. *trochos* wheel]

truck[2] (truk) *v.t. & v.i.* To exchange or barter; also, to peddle. — *n.* 1. Commodities for sale. 2. *U.S.* Garden produce for market. 3. *Informal* Rubbish; worthless articles collectively. 4. Barter. 5. *Informal* Dealings: I will have no *truck* with him. [< OF *troquer* to barter]

truck·age[1] (truk′ij) *n.* 1. Money paid for conveyance of goods on trucks. 2. Such conveyance.

truck·age[2] (truk′ij) *n.* Exchange; barter.

truck·er[1] (truk′ər) *n.* One who drives or supplies trucks or moves commodities in trucks. Also **truck′man** (-mən).

truck·er[2] (truk′ər) *n.* 1. *U.S.* A market gardener; truck farmer. 2. One who barters or sells commodities; hawker.

truck farm *U.S.* A farm on which vegetables are produced for market. Also **truck garden.** — **truck farming**

truck·ing[1] (truk′ing) *n.* The act or business of transportation by trucks.

truck·ing[2] (truk′ing) *n.* 1. Exchanging or bartering; dealings. 2. *U.S.* Cultivation of vegetables for market.

truck·le (truk′əl) *v.* **·led, ·ling** *v.i.* 1. To yield meanly or weakly: with *to.* 2. To roll on truckles or casters. — *v.t.* 3. To cause to roll on truckles or casters. — *n.* A small wheel. [< AF < L *trochlea* a pulley] — **truck′ler** *n.* — **truck′ling·ly** *adv.*

truc·u·lence (truk′yə-ləns) *n.* Savageness of character, behavior, or aspect. Also **truc′u·len·cy.**

truc·u·lent (truk′yə-lənt) *adj.* 1. Of savage character; awakening terror; cruel; ferocious. 2. Scathing; harsh; violent: said of writing or speech. [< L < *trux, trucis* fierce] — **truc′u·lent·ly** *adv.*

trudge (truj) *v.i.* **trudged, trudg·ing** To walk wearily or laboriously; plod. — *n.* A tiresome walk or tramp. [Earlier *tredge, tridge*] — **trudg′er** *n.*

trudg·en (truj′ən) In swimming, a former racing stroke similar to the crawl but performed with a frog kick or a scissors kick. Also **trudgen stroke, trudg′eon.** [after John *Trudgen,* 19th c. British swimmer]

---

true (trōō) *adj.* **tru·er, tru·est** **1.** Faithful to fact or reality; not false. **2.** Being real or natural; genuine: *true* gold. **3.** Faithful; loyal; steadfast. **4.** Conformable to an existing standard type or pattern; exact: a *true* copy. **5.** Required by justice; legitimate: the *true* king. **6.** Truthful; honest. **7.** Indicating or predicting correctly: a *true* sign. **8.** *Biol.* **a** Of pure strain or pedigree. **b** Conformed to the structure of the type of a plant or animal: a *true* locust. **9.** In perfect tune: His voice is *true.* — *n.* Truth; pledge. —**in** (or **out of**) **true** In (or not in) line of adjustment: said of a mark or part. — *adv.* **1.** In truth; truly. **2.** In a true and accurate manner: The wheel runs *true.* — *v.t.* **trued, tru·ing** To bring to conformity with a standard; adjust: to *true* a frame. [OE *trēowe*] —**true′ness** *n.*

true bill *Law* **1.** The endorsement by a grand jury on a bill of indictment that the jurors find to be sustained by the evidence. **2.** A bill so endorsed.

true-blue (trōō′blōō′) *adj.* Staunch; faithful; genuine.

true-born (trōō′bôrn′) *adj.* Being such by birth or inheritance: a *trueborn* Scot.

true-lov·ers′ knot (trōō′luv′ərz) A complicated double knot, a symbol of fidelity in love.

truf·fle (truf′əl, trōō′fəl) *n.* Any of various edible fleshy underground fungi. [< OF *trufe, truffe*]

tru·ism (trōō′iz·əm) *n.* An obvious or self-evident truth.

trull (trul) *n. Archaic* A prostitute. [< G *trulle, trolle*]

tru·ly (trōō′lē) *adv.* **1.** In conformity with fact. **2.** With accuracy. **3.** With loyalty or fidelity. **4.** Legally.

trump[1] (trump) *n.* **1.** In various card games, a card of the suit selected to rank above all others temporarily. **2.** *Usu., pl.* The suit thus determined. **3.** A powerful or decisive stroke, resource, etc. **4.** *Informal* A good fellow. — *v.t.* **1.** To top (another card) with a trump. **2.** To surpass; excel; beat. — *v.i.* **3.** To play a trump. —**to trump up** To make up or invent for a fraudulent purpose. [Alter. of TRIUMPH]

trump[2] (trump) *n. Poetic* A trumpet. [< OF *trompe*]

trump·er·y (trum′pər·ē) *n. pl.* **·er·ies 1.** Worthless finery. **2.** Rubbish; nonsense. **3.** Deceit; trickery. — *adj.* Showy but valueless. [< OF < *tromper* to deceive]

trum·pet (trum′pit) *n.* **1.** A soprano brass wind instrument with a flaring bell and a long, narrow-bored metal tube. **2.** Something resembling a trumpet in form; an ear trumpet. **3.** A loud penetrating sound like that of a trumpet; trumpeting. — *v.t.* **1.** To sound or proclaim by or as by a trumpet; publish abroad. — *v.i.* **2.** To blow a trumpet. **3.** To give forth a sound as if from a trumpet. [< OF *trompe*]

trumpet creeper A woody vine of the southern U.S., with scarlet, trumpet-shaped flowers. Also **trumpet vine.**

trum·pet·er (trum′pit·ər) *n.* **1.** One who plays a trumpet. **2.** One who publishes something loudly abroad. **3.** A large South American bird related to the cranes. **4.** A large North American wild swan, having a clarionlike cry: also **trumpeter swan.**

trun·cate (trung′kāt) *v.t.* **·cat·ed, ·cat·ing** To cut the top or end from. — *adj.* **1.** Truncated. **2.** *Biol.* Appearing as though cut or broken squarely off. [< L < *truncus* trunk] —**trun·ca·tion** (trung·kā′shon) *n.*

trun·ca·ted (trung′kā·tid) *adj.* **1.** Cut off; shortened. **2.** Describing a cone or pyramid whose vertex is cut off by a plane.

trun·cheon (trun′chən) *n.* **1.** A short, heavy stick; a club; staff. **2.** *Brit.* A policeman's club. — *v.t.* To beat as with a truncheon; cudgel. [< OF ult. < L *truncus* trunk]

TRUNCATED PYRAMID

trun·dle (trun′dəl) *n.* **1.** A small, broad wheel, as of a caster. **2.** The act, motion, or sound of trundling. **3.** A trundle bed. **4.** *Obs.* A small, low-wheeled truck. — *v.t. & v.i.* **·dled, ·dling 1.** To roll along. **2.** To rotate. [ME < OE *trendel* circle] —**trun′dler** *n.*

trundle bed A bed with a very low frame resting upon casters, so that it may be rolled under another bed.

trunk (trungk) *n.* **1.** The main stem of a tree. **2.** A large box or case for carrying clothes, etc., as for a journey. **3.** *U.S. & Canadian* A large compartment of an automobile for storing luggage, etc., often at the rear. **4.** The human body, apart from the head, neck, and limbs; the torso. **5.** *Entomol.* The thorax. **6.** *Anat.* The main stem of a nerve, blood vessel, or lymphatic. **7.** The main line of a transportation system. **8.** The circuit connecting two telephone exchanges. **9.** The main body, line, or stem of anything. **10.** A proboscis, as of an elephant. **11.** *pl.* A close-fitting garment covering the loins, worn by male swimmers, etc. — *adj.* Being or belonging to a trunk or main body: a *trunk* railroad. [< OF < L *truncus* stem, trunk]

trunk·fish (trungk′fish′) *n. pl.* **·fish** or **·fish·es** A fish of warm seas, characterized by a covering of hard, bony plates.

trunk hose Full breeches extending to the middle of the thigh, worn by men in the 16th and early 17th centuries.

trunk line The main line of a transportation or communication system, as distinguished from a branch line.

trun·nion (trun′yən) *n.* One of two opposite cylindrical studs on a cannon, forming an axis on which it is elevated or depressed. [< F *trognon* stump, trunk]

truss (trus) *n.* **1.** *Med.* A bandage or support for a rupture. **2.** A braced framework of ties, beams, or bars, as for the support of a roof, bridge, etc. **3.** A package, bundle, esp., of hay (usu. 56 or 60 pounds) or straw (usu. 36 pounds). **4.** *Naut.* A heavy iron piece by which a lower yard is attached to a mast. — *v.t.* **1.** To tie or bind; fasten: often with *up.* **2.** To support by a truss; brace, as a roof. **3.** To fasten the wings of (a fowl) before cooking. **4.** To fasten, tighten, or tie around one, as a garment. [< OF < *trousser, trusser* to pack up, bundle] —**truss′er** *n.*

truss bridge A bridge supported chiefly by trusses.

trust (trust) *n.* **1.** A confident reliance on the integrity, honesty, or justice of another; faith. **2.** Something committed to one's care; a charge; responsibility. **3.** The state or position of one who has received an important charge. **4.** A confidence in the reliability of persons or things without careful investigation. **5.** Credit, in the commercial sense. **6.** Custody; care; keeping. **7.** *Law* **a** The confidence, reposed in a person to whom the legal title to property is conveyed for the benefit of another; also, the beneficial title or ownership of property of which the legal title is held by another. ♦ Collateral adjective: *fiducial.* **b** The property or thing held in trust. **8.** A permanent combination, now illegal, for the purpose of controlling the production, price, etc., of some commodity or the management, profits, etc., of some business. **9.** A trust company. **10.** One who or that which is trusted. **11.** Confident expectation; belief; hope. — *v.t.* **1.** To have trust in; rely upon. **2.** To commit to the care of another; entrust. **3.** To commit something to the care of: with *with.* **4.** To allow to do something without fear of the consequences. **5.** To expect with confidence or with hope. **6.** To believe. **7.** To allow business credit to. — *v.i.* **8.** To place trust or confidence; rely: with *in.* **9.** To hope: with *for.* **10.** To allow business credit. —**to trust to** To depend upon; confide in. — *adj.* Held in trust: *trust* money. [< ON *traust,* lit., firmness] —**trust′er** *n.*

trust·bust·er (trust′bus′tər) *n. U.S. Informal* One who advocates or works for the dissolution of a trust (def. 8) or trusts, as by antitrust legislation. Also **trust buster.**

trust company An incorporated institution formed to accept and execute trusts, to manage money and property, and to lend money.

trus·tee (trus·tē′) *n.* **1.** One who holds property in trust. **2.** One of a body of men, often elective, who manage the affairs of a college, church, foundation, etc. — *v.t.* **·teed, ·tee·ing** To place (property) in the care of a trustee.

trus·tee·ship (trus·tē′ship) *n.* **1.** The post or function of a trustee. **2.** Supervision and control of a Trust Territory by a country or countries commissioned by the United Nations; also, the Territory so controlled.

trust·ful (trust′fəl) *adj.* Disposed to trust. —**trust′ful·ly** *adv.* —**trust′ful·ness** *n.*

trust fund Money, securities, etc., held in trust.

trust·ing (trus′ting) *adj.* Having trust; trustful. —**trust′ing·ly** *adv.* —**trust′ing·ness** *n.*

Trust Territory A dependent area administered by a nation under the authority of the United Nations.

trust·wor·thy (trust′wûr′thē) *adj.* Worthy of confidence; reliable. —**trust′wor′thi·ly** (-wûr′thə·lē) *adv.* —**trust′wor′thi·ness** *n.*

trust·y (trus′tē) *adj.* **trust·i·er, trust·i·est 1.** Faithful to duty or trust. **2.** Staunch; firm. — *n. pl.* **trust·ies** A trustworthy person; esp., a convict who has been found reliable and to whom special liberties are granted. —**trust′i·ly** *adv.* —**trust′i·ness** *n.*

truth (trōōth) *n. pl.* **truths** (trōōthz, trōōths) **1.** The state or character of being true in relation to being, knowledge, or speech. **2.** Conformity to fact or reality. **3.** Conformity to rule, standard, pattern, or ideal. **4.** Steadfastness; sincerity. **5.** That which is true; a statement or belief that corresponds to the reality. **6.** Fact; reality. **7.** A disposition to tell only what is true; veracity. **8.** Fidelity; constancy. [OE < *trēowe* true] —**truth′less** *adj.*

truth·ful (trōōth′fəl) *adj.* **1.** Habitually telling the truth. **2.** Corresponding to the facts or to reality; true. —**truth′ful·ly** *adv.* —**truth′ful·ness** *n.*

try (trī) *v.* **tried, try·ing** *v.t.* **1.** To make an attempt to do or accomplish; undertake; endeavor. **2.** To make experimental use or application of: often with *out.* **3.** *Law* **a** To determine the guilt or innocence of by judicial trial. **b** To examine or determine judicially, as a case. **4.** To subject to a test; put to proof. **5.** To put severe strain upon; tax, as the eyes. **6.** To subject to trouble or tribulation; afflict. **7.** To extract by rendering or melting; refine: often with *out:* to *try* out oil. — *v.i.* **8.** To make an attempt; put forth effort. **9.** To make an examination or test. —**to try on** To put on (a garment) to test it for fit or appearance. —**to try out** To attempt to qualify: He *tried* out for the football team. — *n. pl.* **tries** The act of trying; trial; experiment. [< OF *trier* to sift, pick out]

try·ing (trī'ing) *adj.* Testing severely; hard to endure.

try·out (trī'out') *n. U.S. Informal* A test of ability, as of an actor or athlete, often in competition with others.

tryp·a·no·some (trip'ə·nə·sōm', tri·pan'ə-) *n.* Any of a genus of protozoans parasitic in the blood of man and some lower animals and often causing serious and even fatal diseases, as sleeping sickness. Also **tryp'a·no·so'ma** (-sō'mə). [< Gk. *trypanon* borer + -SOME (< Gk. *sōma* a body)]

tryp·sin (trip'sin) *n. Biochem.* A digestive enzyme contained in the pancreatic juice. [< Gk. *tripsis* a rubbing (< *tribein* to rub) + (PEP)SIN] — **tryp'tic** (-tik) *adj.*

try·sail (trī'səl, -sāl') *n. Naut.* A small sail bent to a gaff abaft the foremast and mainmast of a ship: also called *spencer*. [< nautical phrase (*at*) *try* lying to in a storm + SAIL]

try square A carpenter's square having usu. a wooden stock and a steel blade.

tryst (trist, trīst) *n.* **1.** An appointment, as between lovers, to meet at a designated time and place; also, the meeting place agreed upon; rendezvous. **2.** A prearranged meeting, as of lovers. [< OF *triste, tristre* an appointed station in hunting] — **tryst'er** *n.*

tryst·ing place (tris'ting) A meeting place, as of lovers.

tset·se (tset'sē) *n.* **1.** A small bloodsucking fly of southern Africa, whose bite transmits disease in cattle, horses, etc. **2.** A related species, that transmits the causative agent of sleeping sickness. Also spelled *tzetze.* Also **tsetse fly.** [< Afrikaans < Bantu]

T-shirt (tē'shûrt') *n.* A cotton undershirt or sweater with short sleeves. Also **T shirt.**

T-square (tē'skwâr') *n.* An instrument by which to measure or lay out right angles or parallel lines, consisting usu. of a flat strip with a shorter head at right angles to it.

tsu·na·mi (tsoo·nä'mē) *n.* An extensive and often very destructive ocean wave caused by a submarine earthquake; also loosely called *tidal wave.* [< Japanese, a storm wave]

tub (tub) *n.* **1.** A broad, open-topped vessel with handles on the side. **2.** A bathtub. **3.** *Brit. Informal* A bath taken in a tub. **4.** The amount that a tub contains. **5.** *Informal* Anything resembling a tub, as a broad, clumsy boat. — *v.t. & v.i.* **tubbed, tub·bing** To wash, bathe, or place in a tub. [< MDu. *tubbe*] — **tub'ba·ble** *adj.* — **tub'ber** *n.*

tu·ba (too'bə, tyoo'-) *n. pl.* **·bas** *or* **·bae** (-bē) Any of various wide-bored, bass brass instruments whose pitch is varied by means of valves. [< Ital. < L, a war trumpet]

tub·by (tub'ē) *adj.* **·bi·er, ·bi·est** **1.** Resembling a tub in form. **2.** Short and fat; corpulent.

tube (toob, tyoob) *n.* **1.** A long, hollow, cylindrical body of metal, glass, rubber, etc., generally used for the conveyance of something through it; a pipe. **2.** An electron tube. **3.** A collapsible metal cylinder for containing paints, toothpaste, glue, etc. **4.** A thing or device having a tube or tubelike part, as a telescope. **5.** *Zool.* Any elongated hollow part or organ: a bronchial *tube.* **6.** A subway or tunnel. — *v.t.* **tubed, tub·ing** **1.** To fit or furnish with a tube. **2.** To enclose in a tube or tubes. **3.** To make tubular. [< F < L *tubus*] — **tub'al** *adj.*

tu·ber (too'bər, tyoo'-) *n. Bot.* A short, thickened portion of an underground stem, as in the potato. **2.** *Anat.* A swelling or prominence; tubercle. [< L, a swelling]

tu·ber·cle (too'bər·kəl, tyoo'-) *n.* **1.** A small rounded eminence or nodule. **2.** *Bot.* A minute swelling on the roots of leguminous plants. **3.** *Pathol.* **a** A small granular nodule or swelling formed within an organ or plant. **b** The lesion of tuberculosis. **4.** *Anat.* A small knoblike excrescence, esp., on the skin or on a bone. [< L < *tuber* a swelling] — **tu·ber·cu·loid** (too·bûr'kyə·loid, tyoo'-) *adj.*

tubercle bacillus The rod-shaped bacterium that causes tuberculosis in man.

tu·ber·cu·lar (too·bûr'kyə·lər, tyoo-) *adj.* **1.** Covered with tubercles; nodular. **2.** Tuberculous. — *n.* One affected with tuberculosis. — **tu·ber'cu·late** *adj.*

tuberculo- *combining form* **1.** Tuberculosis; of tuberculosis. **2.** Tuberculous. Also, before vowels, **tubercul-.** [< L < *tuber* a swelling]

tu·ber·cu·lo·sis (too·bûr'kyə·lō'sis, tyoo-) *n. Pathol.* **1.** A communicable disease caused by infection with the tubercle bacillus, characterized by the formation of tubercles within some organ or tissue. **2.** Tuberculosis affecting the lungs: also called *consumption, phthisis, pulmonary tuberculosis.* [< NL < L (See TUBERCLE) + -OSIS]

tu·ber·cu·lous (too·bûr'kyə·ləs, tyoo-) *adj.* Of, pertaining to, or affected with tuberculosis.

tube·rose (toob'rōz', tyoob'-, too'bə·rōs', tyoo'-) *n.* A bulbous plant of the amaryllis family, bearing fragrant white flowers. [< NL < L *tuber* a swelling]

tu·ber·ous (too'bər·əs, tyoo'-) *adj.* **1.** Bearing projections

or prominences. **2.** Resembling tubers. **3.** *Bot.* Bearing tubers. Also **tu'ber·ose.** — **tu'ber·os'i·ty** (-bə·ros'ə·tē) *n.*

tub·ing (too'bing, tyoo'-) *n.* **1.** Tubes collectively. **2.** A piece of tube or material for tubes. **3.** Material for pillowcases. **4.** The act of making tubes.

tu·bu·lar (too'byə·lər, tyoo'-) *adj.* **1.** Having the form of a tube. **2.** Made up of or provided with tubes. Also **tu'bu·lous, tu'bu·lose** (-lōs). [< L *tubus* tube]

tu·bu·late (too'byə·lāt, tyoo'-) *v.t.* **·lat·ed, ·lat·ing** **1.** To shape or fashion into a tube. **2.** To furnish with a tube. — *adj.* **1.** Shaped like or into a tube. **2.** Provided with a tube: also **tu'bu·lat'ed.** [< L *tubus* tube] — **tu'bu·la'tion** *n.*

tuck (tuk) *v.t.* **1.** To fold under; press in the ends or edges of. **2.** To wrap or cover snugly. **3.** To thrust or press into a close place; cram; hide. **4.** To make tucks in, by folding and stitching. — *v.i.* **5.** To contract; draw together. **6.** To make tucks. — *n.* **1.** A fold stitched into a garment for a better fit or for decoration. **2.** Any tucked piece or part. [Fusion of OE *tūcian* to tug and MDu. *tucken* to pluck]

tuck·er[1] (tuk'ər) *n.* **1.** One who or that which tucks. **2.** A covering of linen, lawn, etc., formerly worn over the neck and shoulders by women.

tuck·er[2] (tuk'ər) *v.t. Informal* To weary completely; exhaust: usu. with *out.* [Freq. of TUCK, v.]

-tude *suffix of nouns* Condition or state of being: *gratitude.* [< F < L *-tudo*]

Tu·dor (too'dər, tyoo'-) A royal family of England descended from **Sir Owen Tudor,** died 1461, a Welshman who married the widow of Henry V. — *adj.* Designating or pertaining to the architecture, poetry, etc., developed during the reigns of the Tudors.

Tues·day (tooz'dē, -dā, tyooz'-) *n.* The third day of the week. [OE *tiwesdæg* day of Tiw < *Tiw,* ancient Teutonic deity + *dæg* day]

tu·fa (too'fə, tyoo'-) *n.* **1.** A porous calcium carbonate, deposited from springs and streams. **2.** Tuff. [< Ital. < L *tofus*] — **tu·fa·ceous** (too·fā'shəs, tyoo-) *adj.*

tuff (tuf) *n.* A fragmentary volcanic rock composed of material varying in size from fine sand to coarse gravel. [< MF < Ital. *tufo.* See TUFA.] — **tuff·a'ceous** *adj.*

tuft (tuft) *n.* **1.** A collection or bunch of small, flexible parts, as hair, grass, or feathers, held together at the base. **2.** A clump or knot, as a cluster of threads drawn tightly through a quilt, mattress, or upholstery to secure the stuffing. — *v.t.* **1.** To separate or form into tufts. **2.** To cover or adorn with tufts. — *v.i.* **3.** To form tufts. [< OF *tuffe,* prob. < Gmc.] — **tuft'ed** *adj.* — **tuft'er** *n.* — **tuft'y** *adj.*

tug (tug) *v.* **tugged, tug·ging** *v.t.* **1.** To pull at with effort; strain at. **2.** To pull, draw, or drag with effort. **3.** To tow with a tugboat. — *v.i.* **4.** To pull strenuously: to *tug* at an oar. **5.** To strive; toil. — *n.* **1.** An act of tugging; a violent pull. **2.** A strenuous contest. **3.** A tugboat. **4.** A trace of a harness. [ME < OE < *tēon* to tow] — **tug'ger** *n.*

tug·boat (tug'bōt') *n.* A small, compact, ruggedly built vessel designed for towing: also called *towboat, tug.*

tug of war **1.** A contest in which a number of persons at one end of a rope pull against a like number at the other end, each side endeavoring to drag the other across a line marked between. **2.** A hard struggle for supremacy.

tu·i·tion (too·ish'ən, tyoo-) *n.* **1.** The charge or payment for instruction, esp. formal instruction. **2.** Teaching; instruction. [< AF & OF < L < *tueri* to look at, watch] — **tu·i'tion·al, tu·i'tion·ar'y** (-er'ē) *adj.*

tu·la·re·mi·a (too'lə·rē'mē·ə) *n.* A plaguelike disease of rodents, esp. rabbits, that may be transmitted to man: also called *rabbit fever.* Also **tu'la·rae'mi·a.** [< NL, after *Tulare* County, California + Gk. *haima* blood]

tu·lip (too'lip, tyoo'-) *n.* **1.** Any of numerous hardy, bulbous herbs of the lily family, cultivated in many varieties for their large, variously colored, bell-shaped flowers. **2.** A bulb or flower of this plant. [< F < OF < Turkish < Persian *dulband* turban]

tulip tree **1.** A large tree of the magnolia family of the eastern U.S., with greenish cup-shaped flowers. **2.** Any of various other trees having tuliplike flowers.

tu·lip·wood (too'lip·wood', tyoo'-) *n.* **1.** The wood of the tulip tree. **2.** Any of several ornamental cabinet woods yielded by various trees. **3.** Any of the trees themselves.

tulle (tool, *Fr.* tül) *n.* A fine, silk, open-meshed material, used for veils, etc. [< F, after *Tulle,* city in France]

tum·ble (tum'bəl) *v.* **·bled, ·bling** *v.i.* **1.** To roll or toss about. **2.** To perform acrobatic feats, as somersaults, etc. **3.** To fall violently or awkwardly. **4.** To move in a careless or headlong manner; stumble. **5.** *Informal* To understand: with *to.* — *v.t.* **6.** To toss carelessly; cause to fall. **7.** To throw into disorder or confusion; disturb; rumple. — *n.* **1.** The act of tumbling; a fall. **2.** A state of disorder or confusion. [ME < OE *tumbian* to fall, leap]

tum·ble·bug (tum′bəl·bug′)   *n.* A beetle that rolls up a ball of dung to enclose its eggs.

tum·ble-down (tum′bəl·doun′)   *adj.* Rickety, as if about to fall in pieces; dilapidated.

tum·bler (tum′blər)   *n.* **1.** A drinking glass with a flat bottom. **2.** One who or that which tumbles; esp., an acrobat or gymnast. **3.** One of a breed of domestic pigeons noted for the habit of turning forward somersaults during flight. **4.** In a lock, a latch that prevents a bolt from being shot in either direction until it is raised by the key bit. For illus. see LOCK¹. **5.** In a firearm lock, a piece attached to the hammer and receiving the thrust of the mainspring.

tum·ble·weed (tum′bəl·wēd′)   *n.* Any of various plants that, when withered, break from the root and are driven by the wind, scattering their seed.

tum·brel (tum′bril)   *n.* **1.** A farmer's cart; esp., a boxlike cart for carrying and dumping dung. **2.** A rude cart in which prisoners were taken to the guillotine during the French Revolution. Also **tum′bril.**   [< OF *tomber* to fall, ult. < Gmc.]

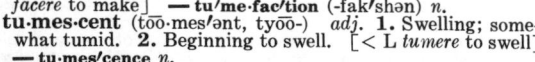

TUMBREL

tu·me·fy (tōō′mə·fī, tyōō′-)   *v.t. & v.i.* **·fied, ·fy·ing** To swell or puff up; become tumid.   [< MF < L *tumere* to swell + *facere* to make]   —**tu′me·fac′tion** (-fak′shən) *n.*

tu·mes·cent (tōō·mes′ənt, tyōō-)   *adj.* **1.** Swelling; somewhat tumid. **2.** Beginning to swell.   [< L *tumere* to swell]   —**tu·mes′cence** *n.*

tu·mid (tōō′mid, tyōō′-)   *adj.* **1.** Swollen; enlarged, as a part of the body. **2.** Inflated or pompous in style. **3.** Bursting; teeming.   [< L < *tumere* to swell]   —**tu·mid′i·ty** *n.*   —**tu′mid·ly** *adv.*   —**tu′mid·ness** *n.*

tu·mor (tōō′mər, tyōō′-)   *n. Pathol.* A local swelling on or in any part of the body, esp. from some abnormal growth of tissue that may or may not become malignant. Also *Brit.* **tu′mour.**   [< L *tumere* to swell]   —**tu′mor·ous** *adj.*

tu·mult (tōō′mult, tyōō′-)   *n.* **1.** The commotion, disturbance, or agitation of a multitude; an uproar; turbulence; hubbub. **2.** Any violent commotion or agitation, as of the mind.   [< OF < L *tumultus*]

tu·mul·tu·ous (tōō·mul′chōō·əs, tyōō-)   *adj.* **1.** Characterized by tumult; disorderly. **2.** Causing or affected by tumult or agitation; agitated or disturbed.   [< L *tumultuosus* (-er′ē).   —**tu·mul′tu·ous·ly** *adv.*   —**tu·mul′tu·ous·ness** *n.*

tun (tun)   *n.* **1.** A large cask. **2.** A varying measure of capacity, usu. equal to 252 gallons.   —*v.t.* **tunned, tun·ning** To put into a cask or tun.   [OE *tunne*]

tu·na (tōō′nə)   *n. pl.* **·na** or **·nas 1.** Any of several large marine food fishes of the mackerel family. **2.** Any of various similar or related fishes. **3.** The flesh of any of these fishes processed and eaten as food: also **tuna fish.** Also called *tunny.*   [< Am. Sp., ult. < L < Gk. *thynnos*]

tun·dra (tun′drə, tōōn′-)   *n.* A treeless, often marshy plain of Siberia, arctic North America, etc.   [< Russian < Lapp]

tune (tōōn, tyōōn)   *n.* **1.** A melody or air, usu. simple and easy to remember. **2.** The state or quality of being at the proper pitch, or, loosely, in the proper key: out of *tune.* **3.** Concord or unison. **4.** Suitable temper or humor.   —**to change one's tune** To assume a different manner, style, or attitude.   —**to sing a different** (or **another**) **tune** To assume a different manner or attitude; change one's tune.   —**to the tune of** To the price of.   —*v.* **tuned, tun·ing** *v.t.* **1.** To adjust the pitch of to a standard. **2.** To adapt to a particular tone, expression, or mood. **3.** To bring into harmony. **4.** To express musically.   —*v.i.* **5.** To be in harmony.   —**to tune in** To adjust a radio receiver to the frequency of (a station, broadcast, etc.).   —**to tune out** To adjust a radio receiver to exclude (interference, a station, etc.).   —**to tune up 1.** To bring (musical instruments) to a standard or common pitch. **2.** To adjust (an engine, etc.) to proper working order.   [Var. of TONE]   —**tun′a·ble** or **tune′a·ble** *adj.*

tune·ful (tōōn′fəl, tyōōn′-)   *adj.* **1.** Melodious; musical. **2.** Producing musical sounds.   —**tune′ful·ly** *adv.*   —**tune′·ful·ness** *n.*

tune·less (tōōn′lis, tyōōn′-)   *adj.* **1.** Not employed in making music; silent. **2.** Lacking in rhythm, melody, etc.   —**tune′less·ly** *adv.*   —**tune′less·ness** *n.*

tun·er (tōō′nər, tyōō′-)   *n.* **1.** One who or that which tunes. **2.** *Telecom.* A radio receiver without amplifiers.

tune-up (tōōn′up′, tyōōn′-)   *n. Informal* An adjustment to bring a motor, etc., into proper operating condition.

tung oil (tung)   A yellow to brown oil extracted from the seeds of a Chinese tree, used in paints, varnishes, etc. and also for waterproofing.   [< Chinese *t'ung* tung tree]

tung·sten (tung′stən)   *n.* A steel-gray, brittle, heavy metallic element of the chromium group (symbol W), having a high melting point and much used in the manufacture of filaments for electric lamps and high-speed cutting tools: also called *wolfram.* See ELEMENT.   [< Sw. < *tung* weighty + *sten* stone]   —**tung·sten·ic** (tung·sten′ik) *adj.*

tu·nic (tōō′nik, tyōō′-)   *n.* **1.** In ancient Greece and Rome, a garment with or without sleeves, reaching to the knees and usu. worn without a belt. **2.** A modern outer garment gathered at the waist, as a short overskirt or blouse. **3.** *Biol.* Any loose membranous skin or mantle of tissue enveloping an organ or part.   [< L *tunica* < Semitic]

tu·ni·cate (tōō′nə·kit, -kāt, tyōō′-)   *adj.* **1.** *Zool.* Of or pertaining to a group of small marine chordates, having in the adult stage a cylindrical saclike body covered with a transparent membrane or tunic, as the ascidians. **2.** *Zool.* Having a tunic.   —*n.* A tunicate animal.   [< NL < L < *tunicare* to clothe with a tunic < *tunica* tunic]

tun·ing fork (tōō′ning, tyōō′-)   A fork-shaped piece of steel that produces a tone of definite pitch when struck.

Tu·ni·sian (tōō·nish′ən, -nē′zhən, tyōō-)   *adj.* Of or relating to Tunisia, or Tunis, or their inhabitants.   —*n.* **1.** An inhabitant or native of Tunisia or Tunis. **2.** The speech of Tunisia, a North Arabic dialect.

tun·nel (tun′əl)   *n.* **1.** An artificial subterranean passageway or gallery, esp. one under a hill, etc., as for a railway. **2.** Any similar passageway under or through something, as in a mine.   —*v.* **tun·neled** or **·nelled, tun·nel·ing** or **·nel·ling** *v.t.* **1.** To make a tunnel through. **2.** To shape or make in the form of a tunnel: to *tunnel* a passage.   —*v.i.* **3.** To make a tunnel.   [Fusion of OF *tonnelle* partridge net and dim. of *tonne* cask]   —**tun′nel·er** or **tun′nel·ler** *n.*

tun·ny (tun′ē)   *n. pl.* **·ny** or **·nies** The tuna, a fish.   [< L < Gk. *thynnos*]

tup (tup)   *n.* **1.** A ram, or male sheep. **2.** The striking part of a power hammer.   —*v.t. & v.i.* **tupped, tup·ping** To copulate with (a female): said of the ram.   [ME *tupe*]

Tu·pi (tōō·pē′)   *n. pl.* **·pis** or **·pi 1.** A member of any of a group of South American Indian tribes, comprising the northern branch of the Tupian stock. **2.** The language spoken by the Tupis, used as a lingua franca along the Amazon.   [< Tupi, comrade]

Tu·pi·an (tōō·pē′ən)   *adj.* Of or pertaining to the Tupis or their language.   —*n.* A large stock of South American Indians of some one hundred tribes of the Tupis and Guaranis: also **Tu·pi′-Gua′ra·ni′** (-gwä′rä·nē′).

tup·pence (tup′əns)   *n. Brit. Informal* Twopence.

tuque (tōōk, tyōōk)   *n. Canadian* A knitted cap, worn for tobogganing, etc.   [< dial. F (Canadian) < F *toque* cap]

Tu·ra·ni·an (tōō·rā′nē·ən, tyōō-)   *adj.* **1.** Of or pertaining to a hypothetical nomadic people who antedated the Aryans in Europe and Asia. **2.** Pertaining to the hypothetical Ural-Altaic family of languages.   [< Persian *Tūrān,* country north of the Oxus River]

tur·ban (tûr′bən)   *n.* **1.** An Oriental head covering consisting of a sash or shawl, twisted about the head or about a cap. **2.** Any similar headdress. **3.** A round-crowned brimless hat for women or children.   [< F < Ital. < Turkish < Persian < *dul* turn + *band* band]   —**tur′baned** (-bənd) *adj.*

tur·bid (tûr′bid)   *adj.* **1.** Opaque or cloudy, as a liquid with a suspension of foreign particles. **2.** Thick and dense, like heavy smoke or fog. **3.** Being in a state of confusion.   [< L < *turbare* to trouble < *turba* crowd]   —**tur′bid·ly** *adv.*   —**tur′bid·ness, tur·bid·i·ty** (tûr·bid′ə·tē) *n.*

tur·bi·nate (tûr′bə·nit, -nāt)   *adj.* Top-shaped; also, spinning like a top.   [< L *turbo* whirlwind]

tur·bine (tûr′bin, -bīn)   *n.* Any of various motors consisting of one or more rotary units, mounted on a shaft and provided with a series of curved vanes, actuated by the impulse of steam, water, gas, or other fluid under pressure.   [< F < L *turbo* whirlwind, top]

turbo- *combining form* A turbine; related to or operated by a turbine or turbines.   [< L *turbo* top]

tur·bo·gen·er·a·tor (tûr′bō·jen′ə·rā′tər)   *n.* An electric power-generating machine adapted for direct coupling to a steam turbine.

tur·bo·jet engine (tûr′bō·jet′)   *n. Aeron.* A type of jet engine using a gas turbine to drive an air compressor.

tur·bo·prop (tûr′bō·prop′)   *n. Aeron.* A turbojet engine connecting directly with a propeller. Also called *propjet.*

tur·bot (tûr′bət)   *n. pl.* **·bot** or **·bots 1.** A large European flatfish, esteemed as food. **2.** One of various related flatfishes.   [< AF *turbut,* OF *tourbout,* or M Du. *turbot*]

tur·bu·lence (tûr′byə·ləns)   *n.* **1.** The state or condition of being violently disturbed, restless, or confused. **2.** *Physics* The irregular eddying flow of a gas or other fluid, esp. as caused by an obstacle or by friction, as of a ship or airplane in rapid motion. Also **tur′bu·len·cy.**

tur·bu·lent (tûr′byə·lənt)   *adj.* **1.** Being in violent agitation or commotion. **2.** Inclined to rebel; insubordinate. **3.** Having a tendency to disturb or throw into confusion.   [< MF < L *turbare.* See TURBID.]   —**tur′bu·lent·ly** *adv.*   —**Syn. 1.** agitated, boisterous, disorderly, disturbed, riotous, tumultuous, wild. **2.** insurgent, mutinous, refractory.

tur·dine (tûr′din, -dīn)   *adj.* Belonging or pertaining to a large and widely distributed family of singing birds, including thrushes and bluebirds.   [< NL < L *turdus* thrush]

tu·reen (tŏŏ·rēn′, tyŏŏ-)   *n.* A deep, covered dish, as for holding soup to be served. [< F < LL < L *terra* earth]

turf (tûrf) *n.* *pl.* **turfs** (*Archaic* **turves**) **1.** The grass or other fine plants with their matted roots filling the upper stratum of certain soils; sod. **2.** A piece of peat for burning as fuel. **— the turf 1.** A racetrack for horses. **2.** The practice of racing horses. [OE] **— turf′y** *adj.*

turf·man (tûrf′mən) *n.* *pl.* **·men** (-mən) A man who is devoted to or connected with horse racing.

tur·ges·cence (tûr·jes′əns) *n.* The process of swelling up. [< Med.L < L *turgere* to swell] **— tur·ges′cent** *adj.*

tur·gid (tûr′jid) *adj.* **1.** Unnaturally distended, as by contained air or liquid; swollen. **2.** Inflated; bombastic, as language, etc. [< L *turgere* to swell] **— tur·gid′i·ty, tur′gid·ness** (-nis) *n.* **— tur′gid·ly** *adv.*

tur·gor (tûr′gər) *n.* The state of being turgid; turgidity.

Turk (tûrk) *n.* **1.** A native or inhabitant of Turkey: sometimes called *Ottoman.* **2.** One of any of the peoples speaking any of the Turkic languages. **3.** A Moslem.

tur·key (tûr′kē) *n.* *pl.* **·keys 1.** A large American bird related to the pheasant, having the head naked and the tail extensible; esp., the American domesticated turkey, much esteemed as food. **2.** *U.S. Slang* A play that is a failure. **— to talk turkey** To discuss in a practical and direct manner. [Short for *turkey cock* the guinea fowl, after *Turkey*; later applied erroneously to the American bird]

turkey buzzard A sooty black vulture of tropical America and the southern U.S., having a naked red head.

Tur·ki (tŏŏr′kē) *adj.* **1.** Of or pertaining to Turkic. **2.** Of or pertaining to any of the peoples speaking a Turkic language, as the Osmanlis. **— n.** *pl.* **·kis 1.** The Turkic language. **2.** A member of any of the Turki peoples.

Turk·ic (tûr′kik) *n.* A subfamily of the Altaic family of languages, including Osmanli or Turkish, Uzbek, etc. **— adj.** Pertaining to this linguistic subfamily, or to any of the peoples speaking these languages.

Turk·ish (tûr′kish) *adj.* **1.** Of or pertaining to Turkey or the Turks. **2.** Of or relating to the Turkic subfamily of Altaic languages, esp. to Osmanli. **— n.** Osmanli.

Turkish bath A bathing establishment where sweating is induced by exposure to high temperature, usu. in a room heated by steam, followed by washing, massage, etc.

Turkish towel A heavy, rough towel with loose, uncut pile. Also **turkish towel.**

tur·mer·ic (tûr′mər·ik) *n.* **1.** The root of an East Indian plant, used as a condiment, aromatic stimulant, dyestuff, etc. **2.** The plant yielding this root. **— adj.** Of, pertaining to, or saturated with turmeric. [? < F < Med.L *terra merita* deserving earth]

tur·moil (tûr′moil) *n.* Confused motion; disturbance; tumult. [? < OF < L *tremere* to tremble]

turn (tûrn) *v.t.* **1.** To cause to rotate, as about an axis. **2.** To change the position of, as by rotating: to *turn* a trunk on its side. **3.** To move so that the upper side becomes the under and the under side becomes the upper: to *turn* a page; to *turn* the soil; to *turn* a shirt collar. **4.** To reverse the arrangement or order of. **5.** To cause to rotate in order to tighten, loosen, open, etc.: to *turn* a screw. **6.** To revolve mentally; ponder: often with *over.* **7.** To sprain or strain: to *turn* one's ankle. **8.** To nauseate (the stomach). **9.** To give rounded or curved form to, as by turning in a lathe. **10.** To give graceful or finished form to: to *turn* a phrase. **11.** To perform by revolving: to *turn* cartwheels. **12.** To bend, curve, fold, twist, or blunt. **13.** To change or transform: to *turn* water into wine. **14.** To translate. **15.** To exchange for an equivalent: to *turn* stocks into cash. **16.** To adapt to some purpose; apply: to *turn* information to good account. **17.** To cause to become as specified: The sight *turned* him sick. **18.** To change the color of. **19.** To make sour or rancid. **20.** To change the direction or focus of. **21.** To direct or aim; point. **22.** To deflect or divert: to *turn* a blow. **23.** To repel: to *turn* a charge. **24.** To go around or to the other side of: to *turn* a corner. **25.** To pass or go beyond: to *turn* twenty-one. **26.** To cause to go; send; drive: to *turn* a beggar from one's door. **— v.i.** **27.** To move around an axis; rotate; revolve. **28.** To move partially on or as if on an axis: He *turned* and ran. **29.** To change position; also, to roll from side to side. **30.** To reverse position; become inverted. **31.** To change or reverse direction or flow: We *turned* north. The tide has *turned.* **32.** To change the direction or focus of one's thought, attention, etc. **33.** To depend; hinge: with *on* or *upon.* **34.** To whirl, as the head. **35.** To become nauseated, as the stomach. **36.** To become hostile: to *turn* on one's neighbors. **37.** To change one's position in order to act in retaliation: The worm *turns.* **38.** To become transformed: The water *turned* into ice. **39.** To become as specified: His hair *turned* gray. **40.** To change color: said esp. of leaves. **41.** To become sour, rancid, or

fermented. **— to turn against** To become or cause to become opposed or hostile to. **— to turn down 1.** To diminish the flow, volume, etc., of. **2.** *Informal* To reject or refuse, as a request; also, to refuse the request, etc., of. **— to turn in 1.** To fold or double. **2.** To bend or incline inward. **3.** To deliver; hand over. **4.** *Informal* To go to bed. **— to turn loose** *Informal* To set free. **— to turn off 1.** To stop the operation, flow, etc., of. **2.** To leave the direct road. **— to turn on 1.** To set in operation, flow, etc. **2.** *Slang* To take or experience the effects of taking a psychedelic drug, as marijuana. **3.** *Slang* To evoke in (someone) a rapt response, as though under the influence of a psychedelic drug: Baroque music really *turned* him *on.* **— to turn out 1.** To turn inside out. **2.** To eject or expel. **3.** To dismiss. **4.** To stop the operation, flow, etc., of. **5.** To bend or incline outward. **6.** To produce; make. **7.** To come or go out, as for duty or service. **8.** To prove (to be). **9.** To become or result. **10.** To equip; dress. **11.** *Informal* To get out of bed. **— to turn over 1.** To change the position of; invert. **2.** To upset; overturn. **3.** To hand over; transfer or relinquish. **4.** To do business to the amount of. **5.** To invest and get back (capital). **6.** To buy and then sell: to *turn over* merchandise. **— to turn to 1.** To set to work. **2.** To seek aid from. **3.** To refer or apply to. **4.** To open a book, etc., to (a specified page). **— to turn up 1.** To bring or fold the under side upward. **2.** To bend or incline upward. **3.** To find or be found. **4.** To increase the flow, volume, etc., of. **5.** To put in an appearance; arrive. **— n. 1.** The act of turning, or the state of being turned. **2.** A change to another direction, motion, or position. **3.** A deflection or deviation from a course; change in trend. **4.** The point at which a change takes place: a *turn* for the better. **5.** A rotation or revolution. **6.** A bend, as in a road. **7.** A regular time or chance in some succession: It's my *turn* to play. **8.** A round; spell: a *turn* at painting. **9.** Characteristic form, shape, or style: the *turn* of a phrase. **10.** A knack or special ability: a *turn* for study. **11.** Tendency; direction: The talk took a serious *turn.* **12.** A deed performed: a good *turn.* **13.** An advantage: It served his *turn.* **14.** A walk, drive, or trip to and fro: a *turn* in the park. **15.** A round in a skein, coil, etc.; also, a twist. **16.** *Music* An ornament formed by a group of four rapid notes, the first a degree above and the third a degree below the principal tone, that occupies the second and fourth positions. In an **inverted turn** the tones are reversed in order. **17.** *Informal* A shock to the nerves, as from alarm. **18.** A short theatrical act. **— at every turn** On every occasion; constantly. **— by turns 1.** In alternation or sequence. **2.** At intervals. **— in turn** One after another; in proper order or sequence. **— out of turn** Not in proper order or sequence. **— to a turn** Just right: said esp. of cooked food. **— to take turns** To act, play, etc., one after another in proper order. [Fusion of OE *tyrnan* and *turnian* and OF *turner,* all < L *tornare* to turn in a lathe]

turn·a·bout (tûrn′ə·bout′) *n.* The act of turning completely about and taking the opposite direction, opinion, etc.

turn·a·round (tûrn′ə·round′) *n.* The act of unloading a ship, aircraft, etc., and loading it to begin its next trip.

turn·buck·le (tûrn′buk′əl) *n.* *Mech.* A form of coupling so threaded that when connected lengthwise between two metal rods or wires it may be turned so as to regulate the distance or tension between them.

TURNBUCKLES
a Insulated, for electric wires. *b* For metal tie rods. *c* For window shutters.

turn·coat (tûrn′kōt′) *n.* One who goes over to the opposite side or party; a renegade.

turn·down (tûrn′doun′) *adj.* Folded down, as a collar; also, capable of being turned down.

turn·er[1] (tûr′nər) *n.* One who turns; esp. one who fashions objects with a lathe.

turn·er[2] (tûr′nər) *n.* A gymnast; a member of a turnverein. [< G < *turnen* to engage in gymnastics < F *tourner*]

turn·ing (tûr′ning) *n.* **1.** The act of one who or that which turns. **2.** The art of shaping wood, metal, etc., in a lathe. **3.** Any deviation from a straight or customary course; a winding; bend. **4.** The point where a road forks. **5.** Fashioning or shaping, as of a literary work.

turning point 1. The point of a decisive change in direction of action; a crisis. **2.** The point at which the direction of a motion is reversed.

tur·nip (tûr′nip) *n.* **1.** The fleshy, globular, edible root of either of two biennial herbs, of the mustard family, the **white turnip,** and the rutabaga. **2.** Either of the plants yielding this root. [Earlier *turnepe,* ? < F *tour* turn (< L *turnus* lathe) + ME *nepe* < OE *næp* < L *napus* turnip]

turn·key (tûrn′kē) *n.* One who has charge of the keys of a prison; a jailer.

turn·off (tûrn′ôf′, -of′) *n. Informal* A road, path, or way branching off from a main thoroughfare.

turn·out (tûrn′out′) *n.* **1.** An act of turning out or coming forth. **2.** An assemblage of persons; attendance. **3.** A quantity produced; output. **4.** Array; equipment; outfit. **5.** A railroad siding. **6.** A carriage or wagon with its horses and equipage. **7.** *Brit.* A labor strike; also, a striker.

turn·o·ver (tûrn′ō′vər) *n.* **1.** The act or process of turning over; an upset or overthrow, as of a vehicle. **2.** The rate at which persons hired by a given establishment within a given period are replaced by others; also, the number of persons hired. **3.** A change or revolution. **4.** A small pie or tart made by covering half of a circular crust with fruit, jelly, or the like, and turning the other half over on top. **5.** The amount of business accomplished, or of work achieved. **6.** A completed commercial transaction or course of business; also, the money receipts of a business for a given period: also called *overturn.* — *adj.* **1.** Designed for turning over or reversing. **2.** Capable of being turned over or folded down. **3.** Made with a part folded down: a *turnover* collar.

turn·pike (tûrn′pīk′) *n.* **1.** A road, now esp. a superhighway, on which there are tollgates. **2.** Loosely, any highway: also **turnpike road.** **3.** A tollbar or tollgate. [ME *turnpyke* spiked road barrier < TURN + *pyke* pike¹]

turn·stile (tûrn′stīl′) *n.* A gate, having revolving horizontal arms, that admits passengers to subways, buses, etc., on the deposit of fares, or registers the number of persons entering a building, or restricts passage to one direction only.

turn·stone (tûrn′stōn′) *n.* A ploverlike migratory bird of northern regions: so called from its habit of turning over stones to obtain its food.

turn·ta·ble (tûrn′tā′bəl) *n.* **1.** A rotating disk, as one that carries a phonograph record. **2.** A rotating platform arranged to turn a section of a bridge in order to open a passage for ships. **3.** Such a platform to turn a locomotive, car, etc. Also *Brit.* **turn′plate′** (-plāt′).

turn·up (tûrn′up′) *n.* **1.** That which is turned up, as part of a garment. **2.** A particular card or die turned up in gambling. **3.** Pure chance; a tossup. — *adj.* Turned up.

turn·ver·ein (tŏōrn′fə·rīn, tûrn′və·rīn) *n. Sometimes cap.* An athletic club. [< G < *turnen* to exercise + *verein* club]

tur·pen·tine (tûr′pən·tīn) *n.* An oleoresin obtained from any of several coniferous trees, esp. pines. — **oil of turpentine** The colorless essential oil formed when turpentine is distilled with steam; chiefly used to thin paint: also called *spirits of turpentine.* — *v.t.* **·tined, ·tin·ing** **1.** To put turpentine with or upon; saturate with turpentine. **2.** To obtain crude turpentine from (a tree). [< OF < L < Gk. *terebinthos,* a tree from which it was originally obtained]

tur·pi·tude (tûr′pə·tōōd, -tyōōd) *n.* Inherent baseness; vileness; depravity, or any action showing depravity. [< MF < L < *turpis* vile]

tur·quoise (tûr′koiz, -kwoiz) *n.* **1.** A blue or green aluminum phosphate, colored by copper, found massive, and in its highly polished blue varieties esteemed as a gemstone. **2.** A light greenish blue, the color of the turquoise: also **turquoise blue.** [< MF (*pierre*) *turquoise* Turkish (stone)]

tur·ret (tûr′it) *n.* **1.** *Mil.* **a** A rotating armored housing, large enough to contain a powerful gun or guns and gunners, forming part of a warship or of a fort. **b** A similar structure in a tank or a bombing or combat airplane. **2.** *Archit.* A small tower rising above a larger structure, as on a castle. **3.** *Mech.* In a lathe, a cylinder fitted with sockets or chucks for the reception of various tools, any one of which may be presented in the axial line of the work: also **turret head.** [< OF *torete,* dim. of *tor* tower] — **tur·ri·cal** (tûr′i·kəl) *adj.*

tur·ret·ed (tûr′it·id) *adj.* **1.** Provided with turrets. **2.** Having the form of a turret.

turret lathe A lathe having a turret.

tur·tle¹ (tûr′təl) *n.* **1.** Any of numerous reptiles having a horny, toothless beak, and a short, stout body enclosed within a carapace and plastron, into which all the members may be drawn for protection. **2.** A marine species as distinguished from a terrestrial or fresh-water species. **3.** The flesh of certain varieties of turtle, served as food. — **green turtle** An important food turtle of wide distribution in tropical and semitropical seas: so called from the greenish color of its flesh. — **to turn turtle** To capsize. — *v.i.* **·tled, ·tling** To hunt or catch turtles. [Appar. alter. of F *tortue* or Sp. *tortuga* < Med.L *tortuca* tortoise; infl. in form by TURTLE²]

tur·tle² (tûr′təl) *n. Archaic* A turtledove. [OE < L *turtur*]

tur·tle·back (tûr′təl·bak′) *n.* **1.** *Naut.* An arched covering, resembling the shell of a turtle, built over the bow or stern of a ship as protection against heavy seas. Also **turtle deck.** **2.** *Archeol.* A chipped stone implement rounded on one side.

tur·tle·dove (tûr′təl·duv′) *n.* A small Old World dove conspicuous for its white-edged black tail and soft, mournful coo. [< TURTLE² + DOVE]

turtle neck A high collar that fits snugly about the neck, usu. rolled or turned over double, used esp. on athletic sweaters. — **tur·tle·neck** (tûr′təl·nek′) *adj.*

Tus·can (tus′kən) *adj.* Pertaining to Tuscany. — *n.* **1.** A native or inhabitant of Tuscany. **2.** Any Italian dialect used in Tuscany; esp. the one spoken in Florence.

Tus·ca·ro·ra (tus′kə·rôr′ə, -rōr′ə) *n. pl.* **·ra** or **·ras** One of a tribe of North American Indians of Iroquoian stock formerly living in North Carolina, now surviving in New York and Ontario.

tush (tush) *interj.* An exclamation expressing disapproval, impatience, etc. [ME *tussch*]

tusk (tusk) *n.* **1.** A long, pointed tooth, generally one of a pair, as in the boar, walrus, or elephant. **2.** A sharp, projecting, toothlike point. **3.** A shoulder on a tenon, to strengthen it at its base; also, a tenon having such a shoulder. — *v.t.* **1.** To gore with the tusks. **2.** To root up with the tusks. [Metathetic var. of OE *tūx*] — **tusked** (tuskt) *adj.* — **tusk′less** *adj.*

tusk·er (tus′kər) *n.* A tusked elephant or boar.

tus·sah (tus′ə) *n.* **1.** An Asian silkworm that spins large cocoons yielding a coarse, brownish or yellowish silk. **2.** The silk, or the durable fabric woven from it. Also **tus·sar** (tus′ər), **tus·sore** (tus′ôr, -ōr). [< Hind. < Skt. *tasara, trasara,* lit., shuttle]

tus·sis (tus′is) *n. Pathol.* A cough. [< NL < L] — **tus′sal, tus′sive** *adj.*

tus·sle (tus′əl) *v.t. & v.i.* **·sled, ·sling** To fight or struggle in a vigorous, determined way; scuffle; wrestle. — *n.* A disorderly struggle, as in sport; scuffle. [Var. of TOUSLE]

tus·sock (tus′ək) *n.* **1.** A tuft or clump of grass or sedge. **2.** A tuft, as of hair or feathers. Also **tus′suck.** [Prob. dim. of obs. *tusk* tuft of hair, ? < TUSK] — **tus′sock·y** *adj.*

tut (tut) *interj.* An exclamation to check rashness or express impatience. Also **tut tut.**

tu·te·lage (tōō′tə·lij, tyōō′-) *n.* **1.** The state of being under a tutor or guardian. **2.** The act or office of a guardian; guardianship. **3.** The act of tutoring; instruction. [< L < *tueri* to watch, guard]

tu·te·lar·y (tōō′tə·ler′ē, tyōō′-) *adj.* **1.** Invested with guardianship. **2.** Pertaining to a guardian. Also **tu′te·lar** (-lər).

tu·tor (tōō′tər, tyōō′-) *n.* **1.** One who instructs another in one or more branches of knowledge; a private teacher. **2.** A college teacher who gives individual instruction. **3.** *Brit.* A college official entrusted with the tutelage and care of undergraduates assigned to him. **4.** *Law* A guardian of a minor or of a woman. — *v.t.* **1.** To act as tutor to; instruct; teach; train. **2.** To have the guardianship of. **3.** To treat severely or sternly, as a tutor might; discipline. — *v.i.* **4.** To do the work of a tutor. **5.** To be tutored or instructed. [< AF, OF < L < *tueri* to watch, guard] — **tu·to·ri·al** (tōō·tôr′ē·əl, -tō′rē, tyōō-) *adj.*

tu·tor·ship (tōō′tər·ship, tyōō′-) *n.* **1.** The office of a tutor or of a guardian. Also **tu′tor·age** (-ij). **2.** Tutelage.

tut·ti (tōō′tē) *Music adj.* All: a term used to indicate that all performers are to take part. — *n. pl.* **·tis** A composition, piece, movement, or passage for all the voices and instruments together. [< Ital., pl. of *tutto* all < L *totus*]

tut·ti-frut·ti (tōō′tē·frōō′tē) *n.* A confection, chewing gum, ice cream, etc., made with a mixture of fruits. — *adj.* Having fruit flavors. [< Ital., all fruits]

tu·tu (tü·tü′) *n. French* A short, full, projecting skirt consisting of many layers of sheer fabric, worn by ballet dancers.

tu·whit tu·whoo (tōō·hwit′, tōō·hwōō′) The cry of an owl.

tux·e·do (tuk·sē′dō) *n. pl.* **·dos** **1.** *U.S.* A man's semiformal dinner coat without tails: also called *dinner coat, dinner jacket.* **2.** *U.S.* The suit of which the coat is a part. Also **Tux·e′do.** [after *Tuxedo* Park, N.Y.]

TV (tē′vē′) *n. pl.* **TVs** or **TV's** Television. — *adj.* Of or pertaining to television.

twad·dle (twod′l) *v.t. & v.i.* **·dled, ·dling** To talk foolishly and pretentiously. — *n.* Pretentious, silly talk. [Prob. alter. of TWATTLE] — **twad′dler** *n.*

twain (twān) *adj. Archaic & Poetic* Two. — *n.* **1.** A couple; two. **2.** In river navigation, two fathoms or twelve feet. [OE *twēgen,* masculine of *twā* two]

twang (twang) *v.t. & v.i.* **twanged, twang·ing** **1.** To make or cause to make a sharp, vibrant sound, as a bowstring. **2.** To utter or speak nasally. — *n.* **1.** A sharp, vibrating sound, as of a tense string plucked. **2.** Excessive nasality of the voice. **3.** A sound resembling either of the foregoing. [Imit.] — **twang′y** *adj.*

twat·tle (twot′l) *v.t. & v.i.* **·tled, ·tling** *n.* Twaddle. [Short for *twittle-twattle,* var. of TITTLE-TATTLE]

tweak (twēk) *v.t.* To pinch and twist sharply; twitch. — *n.* A twisting pinch; twitch. [Var. of dial. *twick,* OE *twiccian* to twitch] — **tweak′y** *adj.*

tweed (twēd) *n.* **1.** A soft woolen fabric with a homespun surface, often woven in two or more colors to effect a check or plaid pattern. **2.** *pl.* Clothing of tweed. — **Harris tweed** A homespun woolen cloth, usu. of mixed colors, made at Harris in the Hebrides. [Alter. of dial. E (Scottish) *tweel,* var. of TWILL]

twee·dle (twēd′l) *v.* **·dling, ·dling** *v.t.* **1.** To play (a musical instrument) casually or carelessly. **2.** To wheedle; cajole. — *v.i.* **3.** To produce a series of shrill tones. **4.** To play a musical instrument casually or carelessly. — *n.* A sound resembling the tones of a violin. [Imit.]

twee·dle·dum and twee·dle·dee (twēd'l·dum', twēd'l·dē') Two things between which there is only the slightest possible distinction. [Orig. imit. of low- and high-pitched musical instruments, respectively]

'tween (twēn) Contraction of BETWEEN.

tweet (twēt) *v.i.* To utter a thin, chirping note. — *n.* A twittering or chirping. Also **tweet'-tweet'.** [Imit.]

tweet·er (twē'tər) *n. Electronics* A small loudspeaker used to reproduce high-pitched sounds in high-fidelity sound equipment. Compare WOOFER. [< TWEET]

tweeze (twēz) *v.t.* **tweezed, tweez·ing** *Informal* To handle, pluck, etc., with tweezers. [Back formation < TWEEZERS]

tweez·ers (twē'zərz) *n.pl.* Small pincers for grasping and holding small objects. Also called **pair of tweezers.** [Alter. of *tweezes,* pl. of *tweeze,* earlier *etweese* case of small instruments < F *étuis,* pl. of *étui.*]

Twelfth-day (twelfth'dā') *n.* Epiphany.

Twelfth-night (twelfth'nīt') *n.* The evening (Jan. 5th) before Epiphany; sometimes, the evening (Jan. 6th) of Epiphany. — *adj.* Of or pertaining to Twelfth-night.

twelve (twelv) *n.* **1.** The sum of eleven and one; a cardinal number. **2.** Any symbol of this number, as 12, xii, XII. **3.** Anything consisting of or representing twelve units. — **the Twelve** The twelve apostles. — *adj.* Being one more than eleven. [OE *twelf*] — **twelfth** (twelfth) *adj. & n.*

Twelve Apostles The twelve disciples of Jesus: more commonly *the Twelve.*

twelve·mo (twelv'mō) *adj. & n.* Duodecimo.

twelve·month (twelv'munth') *n.* A year.

twelve-tone (twelv'tōn') *adj. Music* **1.** Of, using, or composed in the technique developed by Arnold Schönberg, in which the tones of the chromatic scale are arranged in an arbitrary series, which is used as the basis of the composition. **2.** In 20th-century music, using or composed in a freely chromatic style.

twen·ty (twen'tē) *n., pl.* **·ties 1.** The sum of nineteen and one: a cardinal number. **2.** Any symbol of this number, as 20, xx, XX. **3.** Anything consisting of or representing twenty units. — *adj.* Being one more than nineteen. [OE *twēntig*] — **twen'ti·eth** *adj. & n.*

twen·ty-one (twen'tē-wun') *n.* A card game in which each player bets against the dealer, the object being to draw cards whose value will equal or approach twenty-one without exceeding that amount: also called *blackjack, vingt-et-un.*

twi- *prefix* Two; double; twice: *twibil.* Also spelled *twy-.* [OE, double < *twā* two]

twi·bil (twī'bil) *n.* **1.** A battle-ax with two cutting edges. **2.** A mattock having one blade like an ax and the other an adz. Also **twi'bill.** [OE < *twi-* two + *bill* ax]

twice (twīs) *adv.* **1.** Two times. **2.** In double measure; doubly. [OE *twiges,* gen. of *twiga* twice]

twice-told (twīs'tōld') *adj.* Told more than once.

twid·dle (twid'l) *v.* **·dled, ·dling** *v.t.* **1.** To twirl idly; toy or play with. — *v.i.* **2.** To revolve or twirl. **3.** To toy with something idly. **4.** To be busy about trifles. — **to twiddle one's thumbs 1.** To rotate one's thumbs idly around one another. **2.** To pass time in doing nothing. — *n.* A gentle twirling, as of the fingers. [Origin unknown] — **twid'dler** *n.*

twig (twig) *n.* A small shoot or branchlet of a tree. [OE *twigge*] — **twigged** *adj.* — **twig'less** *adj.*

twig·gy (twig'ē) *adj.* **·gi·er, ·gi·est** Like, or full of, twigs.

twi·light (twī'līt') *n.* **1.** The light diffused over the sky when the sun is below the horizon, esp. in the evening; also, the period during which this light is prevalent. **2.** Any faint light. **3.** A condition following the waning of past glory, achievement, etc. — *adj.* Pertaining to, resembling, or characteristic of twilight. [ME < OE *twi-* (< *twa* two) + LIGHT; used in the sense of "the light between the two," i.e., between day and night]

twilight sleep *Med.* A light or partial anesthesia as by injection of morphine and scopolamine, sometimes used to relieve childbirth pains. [Trans. of G *dämmerschlaf*]

twill (twil) *n.* **1.** A weave characterized by diagonal ribs or lines in fabrics. **2.** A fabric woven with a twill. — *v.t.* To weave (cloth) so as to produce diagonal lines or ribs on the surface. [Var. of ME *twile,* OE < *twa* two, partial trans. of L *bilix* having a double thread]

twilled (twild) *adj.* Woven so as to produce a diagonal rib or line; ribbed or ridged.

twin (twin) *n.* **1.** One of two young produced at the same time. **2.** The counterpart or exact mate of another. — *adj.* **1.** Being, or standing in the relation of, a twin or twins. **2.** Consisting

TWILL
(Enlarged to show weave)

of, forming, or being one of a pair of similar and closely related objects; twofold. — *v.* **twinned, twin·ning** *v.i.* **1.** To bring forth twins. **2.** To be matched or equal; agree. — *v.t.* **3.** To bring forth as twins. **4.** To couple; match. [OE *twinn*]

twine (twīn) *v.* **twined, twin·ing** *v.t.* **1.** To twist together, as threads. **2.** To form by such twisting. **3.** To coil or wrap about something. **4.** To encircle by winding or wreathing. **5.** To enfold; embrace. — *v.i.* **6.** To interlace. **7.** To proceed in a winding course; meander. — *adj.* Of or like twine. — *n.* **1.** A string composed of two or more strands twisted together: loosely, any small cord. **2.** The act of twining or entwining. **3.** A form or conformation produced by twining. **4.** An interweaving or interlacing. [OE *twin* twisted double thread < *twā* two] — **twin'er** *n.*

twinge (twinj) *n.* **1.** A sharp, darting, local pain. **2.** A mental or emotional pang. — *v.t. & v.i.* **twinged, twing·ing** To affect with or suffer a sudden pain or twinge. [OE *twengan* to pinch]

twin·kle (twing'kəl) *v.* **·kled, ·kling** *v.i.* **1.** To shine with fitful, intermittent gleams, as a star. **2.** To be bright, as with amusement: Her eyes *twinkled.* **3.** To move rapidly to and fro; flicker: *twinkling* feet. — *v.t.* **4.** To emit or cause to flash out, as gleams of light. — *n.* **1.** A tremulous gleam of light; sparkle; glimmer. **2.** A wink or sparkle of the eye. **3.** An instant; a twinkling. [OE *twinclian*] — **twin'kler** *n.*

twin·kling (twing'kling) *n.* **1.** The act of scintillating. **2.** A wink or twinkle. **3.** The act of winking, or the time required for it. **4.** A moment.

twin-screw (twin'skroo') *adj. Naut.* Having two propeller shafts, one on each side of a vessel's keel, and two propellers, normally turning in opposite directions.

twin·ship (twin'ship') *n.* **1.** The character or condition of being a twin. **2.** The relation of a twin or twins.

twirl (twûrl) *v.t. & v.i.* **1.** To whirl or rotate. **2.** In baseball, to pitch. — *n.* **1.** A whirling motion. **2.** A quick twisting action, as of the fingers. **3.** A curl; coil. [Alter. of ME *tirlen,* var. of *trillen* to roll] — **twirl'er** *n.*

twist (twist) *v.t.* **1.** To wind (strands, etc.) around each other. **2.** To form by such winding: to *twist* thread. **3.** To give spiral, circular, or semicircular form to, as by turning at either end. **4.** To force out of natural shape; distort or contort. **5.** To distort the meaning of. **6.** To confuse; perplex. **7.** To wreathe, twine, or wrap. **8.** To cause to revolve or rotate. **9.** To impart spin to (a ball) so that it moves in a curve. — *v.i.* **10.** To become twisted. **11.** To move in a winding course. **12.** To squirm; writhe. **13.** To dance the twist. — *n.* **1.** The act, manner, or result of twisting or turning on an axis. **2.** The state of being twisted. **3.** A curve; turn; bend. **4.** A contortion or twisting of a facial or bodily feature: a smile with a certain *twist.* **5.** A wrench; strain, as of a joint or limb. **6.** A peculiar or perverted inclination or attitude: the *twist* of a criminal's mind. **7.** A deviation, variation, or distinctive difference: a *twist* of meaning. **8.** Thread or cord made of tightly twisted strands; also, one of the strands. **9.** A twisted roll or loaf of bread. **10.** Tobacco twisted in the form of a large cord. **11.** In baseball, tennis, etc.: **a** A spin or whirling motion given to a ball by a certain stroke or throw. **b** The stroke or throw producing such a spin. **12.** A dance characterized by a twisting or turning movement from side to side. [ME *twisten* to divide in two, combine two, prob. < OE *-twist* rope]

twist·er (twis'tər) *n.* **1.** One who or that which twists. **2.** A ball, as in cricket, bowled with a twist. **3.** In baseball, a curve; also, one who pitches a curve. **4.** *U.S.* A tornado.

twit (twit) *v.t.* **twit·ted, twit·ting** To taunt, reproach, or annoy by reminding of a mistake, fault, etc. — *n.* A taunting allusion; reproach. [Apheetic var. of ME *atwite,* OE *æwitan* to taunt < *æt-* at + *witan* to accuse]

twitch (twich) *v.t.* **1.** To pull sharply; pluck with a jerky movement. **2.** In lumbering, to drag or skid (logs) along the ground with a chain. — *v.i.* **3.** To move with a quick, spasmodic jerk. — *n.* **1.** A sudden involuntary contraction of a muscle. **2.** A sudden jerk or pull. [ME *twicchen*] — **twitch'ing·ly** *adv.*

twit·ter (twit'ər) *v.i.* **1.** To utter a series of light chirping or tremulous notes, as a bird. **2.** To titter. **3.** To be excited; tremble. — *v.t.* **4.** To utter or express with a twitter. — *n.* **1.** The act of twittering. **2.** A succession of light, tremulous sounds. **3.** A state of nervous agitation. [Imit.] — **twit'ter·er** *n.* — **twit'ter·y** *adj.*

twixt (twikst) *prep. Poetic* Betwixt. Also **'twixt.**

two (too) *n.* **1.** The sum of one and one: a cardinal number. **2.** Any symbol of this number, as 2, ii, II. **3.** Anything consisting of or representing two units. **4.** A couple; pair. — **in two** So as to be in two parts or pieces; asunder. — **to put two and two together** To reach the obvious conclusion. — *adj.* Being one more than one. [OE *twā, tū*]

two-base hit (tōō′bās′) In baseball, a base hit that enables the batter to reach second base; a double.

two-bit (tōō′bit′) *adj. U.S. Slang* Cheap; small-time.

two bits *U.S. Informal* 1. Twenty-five cents. 2. A trifling or insignificant sum.

two-by-four (*adj.* tōō′bī-fôr′, -fōr; *n.* tōō′bī-fôr′, -fōr′) *adj.* 1. Measuring two inches by four inches. 2. *U.S. Slang* Of trifling size or significance. — *n.* A piece of lumber actually measuring 1⅝ inches by 3⅝ inches, much used in building.

two-edged (tōō′ejd′) *adj.* 1. Having an edge on each side, as a sword or knife blade. 2. Having two meanings, effects, etc., as an argument, supposed compliment, etc.

two-faced (tōō′fāst′) *adj.* 1. Having two faces. 2. Double-dealing. — **two′-fac′ed·ly** (-fā′sid-lē, -fāst′lē) *adv.*

two-fist·ed (tōō′fis′tid) *adj. U.S. Informal* Vigorous and aggressive.

two-fold (tōō′fōld′) *n.* An amount or number two times as great as a given unit. — *adv.* So as to be two times as many or as great. — *adj.* 1. Consisting of two parts. 2. Two times as many or as great.

two-hand·ed (tōō′han′did) *adj.* 1. Requiring both hands at once. 2. Constructed for use by two persons. 3. Ambidextrous. 4. Having two hands.

two-mas·ter (tōō′mas′tər, -mäs′-) *n.* A ship with two masts.

two·pence (tup′əns) *n. Brit.* 1. Money of account of the value of two pennies. 2. A silver coin of the same value, now issued only for alms money, distributed on Maundy Thursday. Also, *Informal*, *tuppence*.

two·pen·ny (tup′ən-ē) *adj. Brit.* 1. Of the price or value of twopence. 2. Cheap; worthless. Also, *Informal, tuppenny*.

two-ply (tōō′plī′) *adj.* 1. Made of two united webs; woven double: a *two-ply* carpet. 2. Made of two strands, layers, or thicknesses of material.

two·some (tōō′səm) *n.* 1. Two persons together; a couple. 2. A match with one player on each side.

two-spot (tōō′spot′) *n.* 1. A playing card having two pips; a deuce. 2. *U.S. Slang* A two-dollar bill.

two-step (tōō′step′) *n.* A ballroom dance consisting of a sliding step in 2/4 meter; also, the music for it.

two-time (tōō′tīm′) *v.t.* **-timed, -tim·ing** *Slang* To be unfaithful to in love; deceive. — **two′-tim′er** *n.*

two-way (tōō′wā′) *adj.* 1. Characterized by or permitting movement or communication in two directions. 2. Of cocks and valves, having an arrangement that will permit a fluid to be directed in either of two channels.

twy- See TWI-.

-ty¹ *suffix of nouns* The state or condition of being: *sanity.* [< F *-té* < L *-tas*]

-ty² *suffix* Ten; ten times: used in numerals, as *thirty, forty,* etc. [OE *-tig* ten]

ty·coon (tī-kōōn′) *n. U.S. Informal* A wealthy and powerful industrial or business leader. [< Japanese *taikun* mighty lord < Chinese *ta* great + *kiun* prince]

tyke (tīk) *n.* 1. *Informal* A small child. 2. A mongrel dog.

tym·bal (tim′bəl) See TIMBAL.

tym·pan (tim′pən) *n. Printing* A thickness of paper placed on the platen of a press to improve the quality of the presswork.

tym·pa·ni (tim′pə-nē) See TIMPANI.

tym·pan·ic (tim-pan′ik) *adj.* 1. Of or resembling a drum. 2. Of or pertaining to a tympanum or to the middle ear. Also **tym·pa·nal** (tim′pə-nəl).

tympanic membrane *Anat.* The membrane separating the middle ear from the external ear: also called *eardrum.* For illus. see EAR.

tym·pa·nist (tim′pə-nist) *n.* One who plays a kettledrum.

tym·pa·num (tim′pə-nəm) *n.* *pl.* **·na** (-nə) or **·nums** 1. *Anat.* **a** The middle ear. **b** The tympanic membrane. 2. *Archit.* An ornamental space, as over a doorway, enclosed by an arch or the coping of a pediment. 3. A drumlike membrane or part. Also spelled *timpanum.* [< NL < L, drum < Gk. < *typtein* to beat]

typ- Var. of TYPO-.

ty·pal (tī′pəl) *adj.* Of or pertaining to a type; typical.

type (tīp) *n.* 1. Class; category; kind; sort. 2. One who or that which has the characteristics of a group or class; embodiment. 3. *Biol.* **a** An organism whose structural and functional characteristics make it representative of a group, species, class, etc. **b** A taxonomic group considered as representative of the next higher category in a system of classification: the *type* genus. 4. *Printing* A piece or block of metal or of wood, bearing on its upper surface, usu. in relief, a letter or character for use in printing; also, such pieces collectively. 5. Printed or typewritten characters. 6. *Informal* A person. ◆ In business English and in informal speech, *type* is often used for *type of,* as in *This type car is very popular.* — *v.* **typed, typ·ing** *v.t.* 1. To typewrite (something). 2. To determine the type of; identify: to *type* a blood sample. 3. To assign to a particular type. 4. To represent; typify. 5. To prefigure. — *v.i.* 6. To typewrite. [< MF < L < Gk. < *typtein* to strike]

-type *combining form* 1. Representative form; type: *prototype.* 2. Printing; duplicating or photographic process; type: *Linotype, collotype.* [< Gk. *typos* stamp]

type·cast (tīp′kast′, -käst′) *v.t.* **·cast, ·cast·ing** To cast, as an actor, in a role suited to his appearance, personality, etc.

type foundry An establishment in which metal type is made. — **type founder** — **type founding**

type genus *Biol.* A genus that combines the essential characteristics of the family or higher group to which it belongs.

type metal *Printing* The alloy of which type is made, usu. of lead, tin, and antimony, in various proportions.

type·script (tīp′skript′) *n.* Typewritten matter.

type·set·ter (tīp′set′ər) *n.* 1. One who sets type. 2. A machine for composing type. — **type′set′ting** *n.*

type species *Biol.* The species regarded as most typical of the genus to which its name is given.

type·write (tīp′rīt′) *v.t. & v.i.* **·wrote, ·writ·ten, ·writ·ing** To write with a typewriter: also *type.*

type·writ·er (tīp′rī′tər) *n.* A machine equipped with a keyboard, that produces printed characters by impressing type upon paper through an inked ribbon.

type·writ·ing (tīp′rī′ting) *n.* 1. The act or operation of one who uses a typewriter. 2. Typescript.

typhlo- *combining form* 1. Blindness. 2. *Anat. & Med.* The cecum. Also, before vowels, **typhl-.** [< Gk. *typhlos* blind]

typho- *combining form* Typhus; typhoid. Also, before vowels, **typh-.** [< Gk. *typhos* smoke, stupor]

ty·phoid (tī′foid) *n.* Typhoid fever. — *adj.* Of or like typhoid fever: also **ty·phoi′dal, ty′phose** (-fōs). [< TYPH(US) + -OID]

typhoid bacillus A motile, flagellated bacterium, the pathogen of typhoid fever.

typhoid fever *Pathol.* An acute, infectious fever caused by the typhoid bacillus and characterized by severe intestinal disturbances, an eruption of rose-red spots on the chest and abdomen, and physical prostration.

ty·phoon (tī-fōōn′) *n. Meteorol.* A hurricane originating over tropical waters in the western Pacific and the China Sea. [< dial. Chinese *tai feng,* lit., big wind]

ty·phus (tī′fəs) *n. Pathol.* An acute, contagious rickettsial disease, marked by high fever, with eruption of red spots, cerebral disorders, and extreme prostration. Also called *spotted fever.* Also **typhus fever.** [< NL < Gk. *typhein* to smoke] — **ty′phous** (-fəs) *adj.*

typ·i·cal (tip′i-kəl) *adj.* 1. Having the nature or character of a type; constituting a type or pattern. 2. Conforming to the essential features of a species, group, class, pattern of action or behavior, etc. Also **typ′ic.** [< Med.L < L < Gk. < *typos* type] — **typ′i·cal·ly** *adv.* — **typ′i·cal·ness** *n.*

typ·i·fy (tip′ə-fī) *v.t.* **·fied, ·fy·ing** 1. To represent by a type; signify, as by an image or token. 2. To constitute a type or serve as a characteristic example of. — **typ′i·fi·ca′tion** *n.* — **typ′i·fi′er** *n.*

typ·ist (tī′pist) *n.* 1. One whose occupation is operating a typewriter. 2. One who is able to operate a typewriter.

ty·po (tī′pō) *n. Informal* A typographical error.

typo- *combining form* Type; of or related to type. Also, before vowels, **typ-.** [< Gk. *typos* stamp, type]

ty·pog·ra·pher (tī-pog′rə-fər) *n.* A printer.

ty·po·graph·i·cal (tī′pə-graf′i-kəl) *adj.* Of or relating to typography or printing. Also **ty′po·graph′ic.** — **ty′po·graph′i·cal·ly** *adv.*

ty·pog·ra·phy (tī-pog′rə-fē) *n.* *pl.* **·phies** 1. The arrangement of composed type. 2. The style and appearance of printed matter. 3. The act or art of composing and printing from type.

ty·pol·o·gy (tī-pol′ə-jē) *n.* *pl.* **·gies** 1. The study of types, as in systems of classification. 2. A set or listing of types.

Tyr (tür, tir) In Norse mythology, the god of war and son of Odin: also **Tyrr.**

ty·ran·ni·cal (ti-ran′i-kəl, tī-) *adj.* Of or characteristic of a tyrant; harsh; despotic. Also **ty·ran′nic.** — **ty·ran′ni·cal·ly** *adv.* — **ty·ran′ni·cal·ness** *n.*

ty·ran·ni·cide (ti-ran′ə-sīd, tī-) *n.* 1. The killing of a tyrant. 2. One who has killed a tyrant.

tyr·an·nize (tir′ə-nīz) *v.* **·nized, ·niz·ing** *v.i.* 1. To exercise power cruelly or unjustly: often with *over.* 2. To rule as a tyrant. — *v.t.* 3. To treat tyrannically. Also *Brit.* **tyr′an·nise.** — **tyr′an·niz′er** *n.*

ty·ran·nous (tir′ə-nəs) *adj.* Despotic; tyrannical. — **tyr′an·nous·ly** *adv.* — **tyr′an·nous·ness** *n.*

tyr·an·ny (tir′ə-nē) *n.* *pl.* **·nies** 1. Absolute power arbitrarily or unjustly administered; despotism. 2. An arbitrarily cruel exercise of power; a tyrannical act. 3. In Greek history, the office or the administration of a tyrant. 4. Severity; roughness. [< OF < L < *tyrannus* tyrant]

ty·rant (tī′rənt) *n.* 1. One who rules oppressively or cruelly; a despot. 2. One who exercises absolute power without legal warrant, whether ruling well or badly. [< OF < L < Gk. *tyrannos* master, usurper]

tyre (tīr) See TIRE².
Tyr·i·an purple (tir′ē·ən) **1.** A purple or crimson dyestuff obtained by the ancient Greeks and Romans from certain species of the murex. **2.** A violet purple color of high sautration and low brightness. Also **Tyrian dye.** [after *Tyre*, the capital of ancient Phoenicia]

ty·ro (tī′rō) *n. pl.* **·ros** A beginner; novice: also spelled *tiro.* — **Syn.** See NOVICE. [< Med.L < L *tiro* recruit]
tzar (tsär) See CZAR.
tzet·ze (tset′sē) See TSETSE.
tzi·gane (tsē·gän′) *n. Sometimes cap.* A Gypsy, esp. a Hungarian Gypsy. [< F, < Hung. *czigány*]

U

u, U (yōō) *n. pl.* **u's, us, U's** or **Us** (yōōz) **1.** The twenty-first letter of the English alphabet. **2.** Any sound represented by the letter *u.* — *symbol.* **1.** Anything shaped like a U. **2.** *Chem.* Uranium (symbol U).
u·biq·ui·tous (yōō·bik′wə·təs) *adj.* Existing, or seeming to exist, everywhere at once; omnipresent. Also **u·biq′ui·tar′y** (-ter′ē). — **u·biq′ui·tous·ly** *adv.* — **u·biq′ui·tous·ness** *n.*
u·biq·ui·ty (yōō·bik′wə·tē) *n.* **1.** The state of being in an indefinite number of places at once; omnipresence. **2.** The state of existing always without beginning or end. [< L < *ubique* everywhere]
U-boat (yōō′bōt′) *n.* A German submarine. [< G *U-boot*, contr. of *Unterseeboot* undersea boat]
ud·der (ud′ər) *n.* A large, pendulous gland, secreting milk and provided with nipples or teats for the suckling of offspring, as in cows. [OE *ūder*]
ugh (ukh, u, ōōkh, ōō) *interj.* An exclamation of repugnance or disgust. [Imit.]
ug·li·fy (ug′lə·fī) *v.t.* **·fied, ·fy·ing** To make ugly. — **ug′li·fi·ca′tion** (-fə·kā′shən) *n.*
ug·ly (ug′lē) *adj.* **·li·er, ·li·est 1.** Displeasing to the esthetic feelings; distasteful in appearance; ill-looking; unsightly. **2.** Repulsive to the moral sentiments; revolting. **3.** Bad in character or consequences, as a rumor, wound, etc. **4.** *Informal* Ill-tempered; quarrelsome. **5.** Portending storms; threatening: said of the weather. [< ON *uggligr* dreadful < *uggr* fear] — **ug′li·ly** *adv.* — **ug′li·ness** *n.*
ugly duckling Any ill-favored or unpromising child who unexpectedly grows beautiful or remarkable, as did the little swan in Hans Christian Andersen's story.
U·gri·an (ōō′grē·ən, yōō′-) *n.* **1.** A member of any of the Finno-Ugric peoples of Hungary and western Siberia. **2.** Ugric. — *adj.* Of or pertaining to the Ugrians, their culture, or their languages.
U·gric (ōō′grik, yōō′-) *n.* A branch of the Finno-Ugric subfamily of Uralic languages, comprising Magyar, Ostyak, and Vogul. — *adj.* Of or pertaining to any of these languages.
U·gro-Fin·nic (ōō′grō-fin′ik; yōō-) See FINNO-UGRIC.
uh·lan (ōō′län, ōō·län′, yōō′län) *n.* **1.** A cavalryman and lancer of a type originating in eastern Europe, formerly prominent in European armies, notably the German. **2.** One of a body of Tatar militia. Also **u′lan.** [< G < Polish < Turkish *ōghlān* lad, servant]
u·kase (yōō′kās, yōō·kāz′) *n.* **1.** Any official decree. **2.** Formerly, an edict or decree of the imperial Russian government. [< Russian *ukaz*]
U·krain·i·an (yōō·krā′nē·ən, -krī′-) *adj.* Of or pertaining to the Ukraine, its people, or their language. — *n.* **1.** A native or inhabitant of the Ukraine. **2.** The East Slavic language of the Ukrainians. Also *Little Russian, Ruthenian.*
u·ku·le·le (yōō′kə·lā′lē, *Hawaiian* ōō′kōō·lā′lä) *n.* A small guitarlike musical instrument having four strings. [< Hawaiian, flea < *uku* insect + *lele* to jump]
ul·cer (ul′sər) *n.* **1.** *Pathol.* An open sore on an external or internal surface of the body, usu. accompanied by disintegration of tissue with the formation of pus. **2.** A corroding fault or vice; corruption; evil. [< L *ulcus, ulceris*]
ul·cer·ate (ul′sə·rāt) *v.t. & v.i.* **·at·ed, ·at·ing** To make or become ulcerous. [< L < *ulcus, ulceris* ulcer] — **ul′cer·a′tion** *n.* — **ul′cer·a′tive** *adj.*
ul·cer·ous (ul′sər·əs) *adj.* **1.** Like an ulcer. **2.** Affected with ulcers. — **ul′cer·ous·ly** *adv.* — **ul′cer·ous·ness** *n.*
-ule *suffix of nouns* Small; little: used to form diminutives: *granule.* [< F < L *-ulus, -ula, -ulum,* diminutive suffix]
-ulent *suffix of adjectives* Abounding in; full of: *opulent, truculent.* Corresponding nouns are formed in **-ulence,** as in *opulence, truculence.* [< L *-ulentus*]
ul·na (ul′nə) *n. pl.* **·nae** (-nē) or **·nas** *Anat.* **1.** That one of the two long bones of the forearm that is on the same side as the little finger. **2.** The corresponding bone in the forelimb of other vertebrates. [< L, elbow] — **ul′nar** *adj.*
-ulose *suffix of adjectives* Marked by or abounding in: used in scientific and technical terms: *ramulose.* [< L *-ulosus*]
-ulous *suffix of adjectives* **1.** Tending to do or characterized by (what is indicated by the root): *tremulous, ridiculous.* **2.** Full of: *meticulous, populous.* [< L *-ulus* and *-ulosus*]
ul·ster (ul′stər) *n.* A very long, loose overcoat, sometimes belted at the waist. [after *Ulster,* Ireland]
ul·te·ri·or (ul·tir′ē·ər) *adj.* **1.** More remote; not so pertinent as something else: *ulterior* considerations. **2.** Intentionally unrevealed; hidden: *ulterior* motives. **3.** Later in time or secondary in importance; following; succeeding. **4.** Lying beyond or on the farther side of a certain bounding line. [< L < *ulter* beyond] — **ul·te′ri·or·ly** *adv.*
ul·ti·ma (ul′tə·mə) *n.* The last syllable of a word. [< L]
ul·ti·mate (ul′tə·mit) *adj.* **1.** Beyond which there is no other; last of a series; final. **2.** Not susceptible of further analysis; fundamental or essential. **3.** Most distant; farthest; extreme. — *n.* **1.** The final result; last step; conclusion. **2.** A fundamental or final fact. [< LL < *ultimus* farthest, last] — **ul′ti·mate·ly** *adv.* — **ul′ti·mate·ness** *n.*
ul·ti·ma Thu·le (ul′tə·mə thōō′lē, tōō′lē) **1.** Farthest Thule; in ancient geography, the northernmost habitable regions of the earth. **2.** Any distant, unknown region. **3.** The farthest possible point, degree, or limit.
ul·ti·ma·tum (ul′tə·mā′təm, -mä′-) *n. pl.* **·tums** or **·ta** (-tə) A final statement, as concerning terms, conditions or concessions, esp., in diplomatic negotiations, the final terms offered. [< NL < LL. See ULTIMATE.]
ul·ti·mo (ul′tə·mō) *adv. Archaic* In the last month. [< L *ultimo* (*mense*) in the last (month)]
ul·tra (ul′trə) *adj.* Going beyond the bounds of moderation; extreme. — *n.* One who goes to extremes. [< L, beyond]
ultra- *prefix* **1.** On the other side of; beyond in space, as in: **ultra-Arctic, ultrastellar. 2.** Going beyond the limits of; surpassing, as in: **ultra-atomic, ultrahuman. 3.** Beyond what is usual or natural; excessively, as in: **ultra-ambitious, ultrafashionable.**
ul·tra·cen·tri·fuge (ul′trə·sen′trə·fyōōj) *n.* A centrifuge whose rotor will operate at extremely high velocities. — *v.t.* **·fuged, ·fug·ing** To subject to the action of an ultracentrifuge. — **ul′tra·cen′tri·fu·ga′tion** (-fyōō·gā′shən) *n.*
ul·tra·con·ser·va·tive (ul′trə·kən·sûr′və·tiv) *adj.* Unusually or excessively conservative. — *n.* An ultraconservative person; a reactionary.
ul·tra·high frequency (ul′trə·hī′) *Telecom.* A band of wave frequencies between 300 and 3,000 megacycles per second.
ul·tra·ism (ul′trə·iz′əm) *n.* **1.** The policies or opinions of those who are in favor of extreme measures. **2.** An extreme view or action. — **ul′tra·ist** *n. & adj.* — **ul′tra·is′tic** *adj.*
ul·tra·ma·rine (ul′trə·mə·rēn′) *n.* **1.** A deep blue, permanent pigment made from powdered lapis lazuli. **2.** A similar pigment made artificially, as from kaolin, etc. **3.** A deep blue. — *adj.* Being beyond or across the sea. [< Med.L < L *ultra* beyond + *marinus* marine]
ul·tra·mi·crom·e·ter (ul′trə·mī·krom′ə·tər) *n.* A micrometer designed for measurements requiring a high order of precision and accuracy.
ul·tra·mi·cro·scope (ul′trə·mī′krə·skōp) *n.* An optical instrument for detecting objects too small to be seen with an ordinary microscope.
ul·tra·mi·cro·scop·ic (ul′trə·mī′krə·skop′ik) *adj.* **1.** Too minute to be seen by an ordinary microscope. **2.** Relating to the ultramicroscope. Also **ul′tra·mi′cro·scop′i·cal.** — **ul′tra·mi·cros′co·py** (-mī′kros′kə·pē) *n.*

ul·tra·mod·ern (ul'trə-mod'ərn) *adj.* Extremely modern. — **ul'tra·mod'ern·ism** *n.* — **ul'tra·mod'ern·ist** *n.* — **ul'·tra·mod'ern·is'tic** *adj.*

ul·tra·na·tion·al·ism (ul'trə-nash'ən-əl-iz'əm) *n.* Extreme devotion to or support of national interests or considerations. — **ul'tra·na'tion·al** *adj.* — **ul'tra·na'tion·al·ist** *n. & adj.* — **ul'tra·na'tion·al·is'tic** *adj.*

ul·tra·son·ic (ul'trə-son'ik) *adj. Physics* Pertaining to or designating sound waves having a frequency above the limits of human audibility, or in excess of about 20 kilocycles per second.

ul·tra·vi·o·let (ul'trə-vī'ə-lit) *adj. Physics* Lying beyond the violet end of the visible spectrum: said of high-frequency wavelengths ranging from about 3,900 to below 400 angstroms, the lower limit of X-rays. Compare INFRARED.

ul·u·late (yōōl'yə-lāt, ul'-) *v.i.* **·lat·ed, ·lat·ing** To howl, hoot, or wail. [< L *ululare* to howl] — **ul'u·lant** *adj.*

U·lys·ses (yōō-lis'ēz) The Latin name for Odysseus.

um·bel (um'bəl) *n. Bot.* A flower cluster spreading outward from a small area at the top of a very short axis, giving an umbrellalike appearance. [< L *umbella* parasol] — **um'bel·lar, um'bel·late, um'bel·lat'ed.**

um·ber (um'bər) *n.* **1.** A brown ferric oxide, containing some manganese oxide and clay, and used as a pigment. **2.** The color of such a pigment. — *adj.* Of or pertaining to umber; of a dusky hue; brownish. — *v.t.* To color with umber. [< F (*terre d'*)*ombre* or Ital. *ombra*]

um·bil·i·cal (um-bil'i-kəl) *adj.* **1.** Pertaining to or situated near the umbilicus. **2.** Placed near the navel; central. [< LL < L *umbilicus* navel]

umbilical cord *Anat.* A ropelike tissue connecting the navel of the fetus with the placenta and serving to transmit nourishment to and remove wastes from the fetus.

um·bil·i·cus (um-bil'ə-kəs, um'bə-lī'kəs) *n. pl.* **·ci** (-sī) **1.** *Anat.* The navel. **2.** *Bot.* A hilum. [< L]

um·ble pie *See* HUMBLE PIE.

um·bles (um'bəlz) *n.pl.* The entrails of a deer; humbles. [Var. of NUMBLES]

um·bra (um'brə) *n. pl.* **·brae** (-brē) **1.** A shadow or dark area; esp., the portion of a shadow from which direct light is entirely cut off. **2.** *Astron.* In an eclipse, that part of the shadow of the earth or moon within which the moon or the sun is entirely hidden. [< L, shadow]

um·brage (um'brij) *n.* **1.** Resentment; a sense of injury; offense: now usu., in **to take umbrage. 2.** That which gives

shade, as a leafy tree. **3.** *Poetic* Shade. [< F < L < *umbra* shade] — **um·bra'geous** (-brā'jəs) *adj.*

um·brel·la (um·brel'ə) *n.* A light, round, portable screen or shade on a folding frame, carried as a protection against sun or rain. [< Ital. < L *umbella* parasol]

umbrella tree 1. A small magnolia of the southern U.S., with fragrant white flowers and oval leaves crowded in umbrellalike whorls. **2.** Any of several other trees.

u·mi·ak (ōō'mē·ak) *n. U.S. & Canadian* A large, open boat made by drawing skins over a wooden frame, used by Eskimos. Also **u'mi·ack.** [< Eskimo]

um·laut (ōōm'lout) *n.* **1.** *Ling.* **a** The change in quality of a vowel sound caused by its partial assimilation to a vowel or semivowel (often later lost) in the following syllable, esp. in the Germanic languages. **b** A vowel so altered. **2.** In German, the two dots (¨) put over a vowel modified by umlaut: Short for **umlaut-mark.** — *v.t.* To modify by umlaut. [< G, change of sound < *um* about + *laut* sound]

um·pire (um'pīr) *n.* **1.** In various games, as baseball, a person chosen to enforce the rules of the game and settle disputed points. **2.** A person called upon to settle a disagreement in opinion. — **Syn.** See JUDGE. — *v.t. & v.i.* **·pired, ·pir·ing** To decide as umpire; act as umpire (of or in). [< ME < OF < *non* not + *per* even, equal]

un-¹ *prefix* Not; opposed to. [OE] ◆ *Un-*¹ is used to express negation, lack, incompleteness or opposition. It is freely attached to adjectives and adverbs, less often to nouns. See UN-².

un-² *prefix* Back. [OE *un-, on-, and-*] ◆ *Un-*² is used to express reversal of the action of verbs, or to form verbs from nouns indicating removal from the state or quality expressed by the noun, or sometimes to intensify the force of negative verbs. At the bottom of this page and of following pages is a partial list of words that are formed with *un-*¹ and *un-*². Other compounds of these prefixes, with strongly positive, specific, or special meanings, will be found in vocabulary place. In the verbs in the list, *un-* gives the sense of reversal: *unchain* "to loose the chains of." In the nouns and the adjectives it usually has negative or privative force. Thus, *unburdened* may be regarded as an adjective meaning "not burdened," or as a participle of the verb *unburden*, meaning "relieved of a burden."

◆ **un-, in-** *In-* as a prefix of adjectives expresses in usage more of negation, *un-* more of mere lack or privation: a child's *unartistic* speech, a writer's *inartistic* diction.

unabashed	unanswerable	unbarbed	uncalendered	uncleared	unconciliated
unabated	unanswerably	unbeatable	uncanceled	uncleavable	unconcluded
unabetted	unanswered	unbeaten	uncandid	unclipped	uncondemned
unabolished	unapologetic	unbefitting	uncandidly	unclog	uncondensed
unabsolved	unappalled	unbeloved	uncanonic	unclogged	unconfined
unacademic	unapparent	unbeneficed	uncanonical	uncloud	unconfinedly
unaccented	unappeasable	unbenighted	uncarbureted	unclouded	unconfirmed
unacceptable	unappeased	unbenign	uncarpeted	uncloyed	unconfused
unaccepted	unappetizing	unbeseeming	uncastrated	uncoagulable	unconfusedly
unacclimated	unappreciated	unbesought	uncaught	uncoagulated	unconfuted
unacclimatized	unappreciative	unbespoken	unceasing	uncoated	uncongeal
unaccommodating	unapproached	unbetrayed	uncelebrated	uncocked	uncongealable
unaccounted	unapproved	unbetrothed	uncensored	uncoerced	uncongealed
unaccredited	unarmored	unbewailed	uncensured	uncoffined	uncongenial
unacknowledged	unarrested	unblamable	uncertified	uncollectable	uncongeniality
unacquainted	unartful	unblamably	unchainable	uncollected	uncongenially
unacquitted	unartistic	unblamed	unchained	uncollectible	unconquerable
unadaptable	unashamed	unbleached	unchallenged	uncolonized	unconquered
unadjustable	unasked	unblemished	unchambered	uncolored	unconscientious
unadjusted	unaspirated	unblissful	unchangeable	uncombed	unconsecrated
unadorned	unaspiring	unboastful	unchanged	uncombinable	unconsenting
unadulterated	unassailed	unbookish	unchanging	uncombined	unconsidered
unadvisable	unassignable	unborrowed	unchaperoned	uncomely	unconsoled
unadvisably	unassigned	unbottomed	uncharged	uncomforted	unconsonant
unaesthetic	unassumed	unbought	uncharted	uncomforting	unconstant
unaffiliated	unattainable	unbox	unchartered	uncommanded	unconstituted
unafraid	unattained	unboxed	unchary	uncommissioned	unconstrained
unaggressive	unattempted	unbraid	unchaste	uncompanionable	unconstricted
unagitated	unattended	unbranched	unchastened	uncomplaining	unconsumed
unaided	unattested	unbranded	unchastised	uncomplaisant	uncontaminated
unaimed	unattired	unbreakable	unchastity	uncomplaisantly	uncontemplated
unalike	unattracted	unbreathable	unchecked	uncompleted	uncontending
unalleviated	unattractive	unbreech	uncheerful	uncompliable	uncontested
unallied	unauspicious	unbreeched	uncheerfully	uncompliant	uncontradictable
unallowable	unauthentic	unbribable	uncheerfulness	uncomplicated	uncontradicted
unalloyed	unauthentical	unbridgeable	unchewed	uncomplimentary	uncontrite
unalterable	unauthenticated	unbridged	unchilled	uncomplying	uncontrolled
unaltered	unauthorized	unbridle	unchivalrous	uncompounded	uncontrolledly
unaltering	unavailability	unbrotherly	uncholeric	uncomprehended	uncontroverted
unambiguous	unavailable	unbruised	unchosen	uncomprehending	uncontrovertible
unambitious	unavailably	unbrushed	unchristened	uncomprehensible	uncontrovertibly
unamiable	unavenged	unburied	unclaimed	uncomprehensibly	unconversant
unamplified	unavouched	unburned	unclarified	uncompressed	unconvinced
unamusing	unavowed	unburnt	unclassed	uncompromised	unconvincing
unanalytic	unavowedly	unbusinesslike	unclassic	uncomputed	unconvincingly
unanalyzable	unawaked	unbuttoned	unclassifiable	unconcealable	uncooked
unanimated	unawakened	uncage	unclassified	unconcealed	uncooperative
unannealed	unawed	uncalculate	uncleaned	unconceded	uncoordinated
unannounced	unbaptized	uncalculating	uncleansed	unconcerted	uncordial

un·a·ble (un·ā′bəl) *adj.* **1.** Lacking the necessary power or resources; not able: usu. used with an infinitive: *unable* to walk. **2.** Lacking mental capacity; incompetent.

un·a·bridged (un′ə·brijd′) *adj.* Not abridged or condensed; original and complete: an *unabridged* dictionary.

un·ac·com·mo·dat·ed (un′ə·kom′ə·dā′tid) *adj.* **1.** Not made suitable; ill-adapted or -adjusted. **2.** Being without accommodations or conveniences.

un·ac·com·pa·nied (un′ə·kum′pə·nēd) *adj.* **1.** Proceeding, acting, or accomplished without an escort or companion. **2.** *Music* Performing or intended to be performed without accompaniment.

un·ac·com·plished (un′ə·kom′plisht) *adj.* **1.** Having fallen short of accomplishment; not done or finished. **2.** Lacking accomplishments.

un·ac·count·a·ble (un′ə·koun′tə·bəl) *adj.* **1.** Impossible to be accounted for; inexplicable. **2.** Remarkable; extraordinary. **3.** Not accountable; irresponsible. — **un′ac·count′·a·ble·ness** *n.* — **un′ac·count′a·bly** *adv.*

un·ac·count·ed-for (un′ə·koun′tid·fôr′) *adj.* Unexplained.

un·ac·cus·tomed (un′ə·kus′təmd) *adj.* **1.** Not accustomed or habituated to hardship. **2.** Not familiar or well known: strange: an *unaccustomed* sight.

un·ad·vised (un′əd·vīzd′) *adj.* **1.** Not advised; not having received advice. **2.** Rash or imprudent; ill-considered. — **un′ad·vis′ed·ly** (-vī′zid·lē) *adv.* — **un′ad·vis′ed·ness** *n.*

un·af·fect·ed (un′ə·fek′tid) *adj.* **1.** Not showing affectation; natural; sincere; real. **2.** Not influenced or changed. — **un′af·fect′ed·ly** *adv.* — **un′af·fect′ed·ness** *n.*

un-A·mer·i·can (un′ə·mer′ə·kən) *adj.* **1.** Not American in character, style, etc. **2.** Not consistent with the ideals, objectives, spirit, etc., of the U.S.; lacking patriotism or national feeling; a derogatory term.

u·na·nim·i·ty (yōō′nə·nim′ə·tē) *n.* The state of being unanimous; complete agreement in opinion, etc.

u·nan·i·mous (yōō·nan′ə·məs) *adj.* **1.** Sharing the same views or sentiments; harmonious. **2.** Showing or resulting from the assent of all concerned. [< L < *unus* one + *animus* mind] — **u·nan′i·mous·ly** *adv.* — **u·nan′i·mous·ness** *n.*

un·ap·proach·a·ble (un′ə·prō′chə·bəl) *adj.* **1.** Not easy to know or make personal contact with; aloof. **2.** Inaccessible. — **un′ap·proach′a·ble·ness** *n.* — **un′ap·proach′a·bly** *adv.*

un·arm (un·ärm′) *v.t.* To deprive of weapons; disarm. — **un·armed′** *adj.*

un·as·sail·a·ble (un′ə·sāl′ə·bəl) *adj.* **1.** Not capable of being disproved, denied, or contested; incontrovertible. **2.** Proof against attack or destruction; impregnable. — **un′as·sail′a·ble·ness** *n.* — **un′as·sail′a·bly** *adv.*

un·as·sum·ing (un′ə·sōō′ming) *adj.* Unpretentious; modest. — **un′as·sum′ing·ly** *adv.*

un·at·tached (un′ə·tacht′) *adj.* **1.** Not attached. **2.** Not engaged or married.

un·a·vail·ing (un′ə·vā′ling) *adj.* Futile; unsuccessful; ineffective. — **un′a·vail′ing·ly** *adv.*

un·a·void·a·ble (un′ə·voi′də·bəl) *adj.* That cannot be avoided; inevitable. — **un′a·void′a·bil′i·ty, un′a·void′a·ble·ness** *n.* — **un′a·void′a·bly** *adv.*

un·a·ware (un′ə·wâr′) *adj.* **1.** Not aware or cognizant, as of something specified. **2.** Carelessly unmindful; inattentive; heedless. — *adv. Archaic* Unawares.

un·a·wares (un′ə·wârz′) *adv.* **1.** Unexpectedly; without warning. **2.** Without premeditation; unwittingly.

un·bal·ance (un·bal′əns) *v.t.* **·anced, ·anc·ing** **1.** To deprive of balance. **2.** To disturb or derange, as the mind. — *n.* The state or condition of being unbalanced.

un·bal·anced (un·bal′ənst) *adj.* **1.** Not in a state of equilibrium. **2.** In bookkeeping, not adjusted so as to balance. **3.** Lacking mental balance; unsound; erratic.

un·bar (un·bär′) *v.* **·barred, ·bar·ring** *v.t.* **1.** To remove the bar from. — *v.i.* **2.** To become unlocked or unbarred; open.

un·bear·a·ble (un·bâr′ə·bəl) *adj.* That cannot be borne or tolerated; unendurable. — **un′bear′a·ble·ness** *n.* — **un′bear′a·bly** *adv.*

un·be·com·ing (un′bi·kum′ing) *adj.* **1.** Not becoming; unsuited. **2.** Not befitting. **3.** Not decorous; improper. — **un′be·com′ing·ly** *adv.* — **un′be·com′ing·ness** *n.*

un·be·known (un′bi·nōn′) *adj.* Unknown: used with *to.* Also **un′be·knownst′** (-nōnst′).

un·be·lief (un′bi·lēf′) *n.* **1.** Absence of positive belief; incredulity. **2.** A refusal to believe; disbelief, as in religion.

un·be·liev·er (un′bi·lē′vər) *n.* **1.** One who withholds belief. **2.** One who has no religious faith. **3.** One having a religion different from that of the speaker or writer.

un·be·liev·ing (un′bi·lē′ving) *adj.* **1.** Doubting; skeptical; incredulous. **2.** Disbelieving, esp., in religious matters. — **un′be·liev′ing·ly** *adv.* — **un′be·liev′ing·ness** *n.*

un·bend (un·bend′) *v.* **·bent, ·bend·ing** *v.t.* **1.** To relax, as from exertion or formality. **2.** To straighten (something bent or curved). **3.** To relax, as a bow, from tension. — *v.i.* **4.** To become free of restraint or formality; relax. **5.** To become straight or nearly straight again.

un·bend·ing (un·ben′ding) *adj.* **1.** Not bending easily; stiff. **2.** Unyielding, as in character; resolute. — *n.* Relaxation; ease. — **un·bend′ing·ly** *adv.* — **un·bend′ing·ness** *n.*

un·bi·ased (un·bī′əst) *adj.* Having no bias; esp., not prejudiced or warped; impartial; fair. Also **un·bi′assed.** — **un·bi′ased·ly** *adv.* — **un·bi′ased·ness** *n.*

un·bid·den (un·bid′n) *adj.* **1.** Not commanded; not invited. **2.** Not called forth: *unbidden* thoughts.

un·bind (un·bīnd′) *v.t.* **·bound, ·bind·ing** **1.** To free from bindings; undo; also, to release. **2.** To remove, as something that binds; unfasten. [OE *unbindan*]

un·blessed (un·blest′) *adj.* **1.** Deprived of a blessing. **2.** Unhallowed or unholy; evil. **3.** Deprived of good fortune; wretched. Also **un·blest′.**

un·blush·ing (un·blush′ing) *adj.* **1.** Not blushing. **2.** Immodest; shameless. — **un·blush′ing·ly** *adv.*

un·bolt (un·bōlt′) *v.t.* To release, as a door, by withdrawing a bolt; unlock; open.

un·bolt·ed¹ (un·bōl′tid) *adj.* Not fastened by bolts.

un·bolt·ed² (un·bōl′tid) *adj.* Not sifted: *unbolted* flour.

un·born (un·bôrn′) *adj.* **1.** Not yet born; being of a future time or generation; future. **2.** Not in existence.

un·bos·om (un·bŏŏz′əm, -bōō′zəm) *v.t.* **1.** To reveal, as one's thoughts or secrets; disclose or give vent to: often used reflexively. — *v.i.* **2.** To say what is troubling one; tell one's thoughts, feelings, etc. — **un·bos′om·er** *n.*

un·bound·ed (un·boun′did) *adj.* **1.** Having no bounds; of unlimited extent; very great; boundless. **2.** Having no boundary, as a closed surface. **3.** Going beyond bounds; unrestrained. — **un·bound′ed·ly** *adv.* — **un·bound′ed·ness** *n.*

un·bowed (un·boud′) *adj.* **1.** Not bent or bowed. **2.** Not subdued; proud in defeat or adversity.

un·brace (un·brās′) *v.t.* **·braced, ·brac·ing** **1.** To free from braces. **2.** To free from tension; loosen. **3.** To weaken.

un·bri·dled (un·brīd′ld) *adj.* **1.** Having no bridle on: an *unbridled* horse. **2.** Without restraint; unruly: an *unbridled* tongue. — **un·bri′dled·ly** *adv.* — **un·bri′dled·ness** *n.*

un·bro·ken (un·brō′kən) *adj.* **1.** Not broken; whole; entire. **2.** Unviolated. **3.** Uninterrupted; regular; smooth:

uncorked	uncrystalline	undebatable	undelivered	undesignated	undignified
uncorrected	uncrystallizable	undecayed	undemocratic	undesigned	undilated
uncorroborated	uncrystallized	undecaying	undemonstrable	undesignedly	undiluted
uncorrupt	uncultivable	undeceived	undemonstrably	undesired	undiminishable
uncorrupted	uncultivated	undecipherable	undenied	undesirous	undiminished
uncorruptly	uncultured	undeciphered	undenominational	undesisting	undimmed
uncorruptness	uncumbered	undeclared	undenounced	undespairing	undiplomatic
uncountable	uncurable	undeclinable	undependable	undestroyed	undisbanded
uncourteous	uncurb	undeclined	undeplored	undetachable	undiscerned
uncourtliness	uncurbed	undecomposable	undeposed	undetached	undiscernedly
uncourtly	uncurdled	undecomposed	undepraved	undetectable	undiscernible
uncovered	uncured	undecorated	undepreciated	undetected	undiscernibly
uncrate	uncurious	undefaceable	undepressed	undetectible	undiscerning
uncrated	uncurl	undefaced	undeputed	undeterminable	undischarged
uncredited	uncurled	undefeated	underived	undetermined	undisciplined
uncrippled	uncurrent	undefended	underogating	undeterred	undisclosed
uncritical	uncursed	undefensible	underogatory	undeveloped	undisconcerted
uncriticizable	uncurtained	undefied	undescribable	undeviating	undiscordant
uncropped	uncushioned	undefinable	undescribed	undevoured	undiscouraged
uncross	uncustomary	undefined	undescried	undevout	undiscoverable
uncrossed	undamaged	undeformed	undeserved	undifferentiated	undiscoverably
uncrowded	undated	undelayed	undeservedly	undiffused	undiscovered
uncrown	undaughterly	undelineated	undeservedness	undigested	undiscredited
uncrushable	undazzled	undeliverable	undeserving	undigestible	undiscriminating

unbroken sleep. **4.** Not weakened; firm. **5.** Not broken to harness or service, as a draft animal. **6.** Not disarranged. **— un·bro′ken·ly** *adv.* **— un·bro′ken·ness** *n.*

un·buck·le (un-buk′əl) *v.t.* & *v.i.* **·led, ·ling** To unfasten the buckle or buckles (of).

un·bur·den (un-bûr′dən) *v.t.* To free from a burden.

un·but·ton (un-but′n) *v.t.* & *v.i.* To unfasten the button or buttons (of).

un·caged (un-kājd′) *adj.* **1.** Not locked up in a cage; free. **2.** Released from a cage; freed.

un·called-for (un-kôld′fôr′) *adj.* Not justified by circumstances; improper; unnecessary; gratuitous.

un·can·ny (un-kan′ē) *adj.* **1.** Strange and inexplicable, esp. so as to excite wonder or dismay; weird; unnatural. **2.** So good as to seem almost supernatural in origin: *uncanny* accuracy. **— un·can′ni·ly** *adv.* **— un·can′ni·ness** *n.*

un·cap (un-kap′) *v.* **·capped, ·cap·ping** *v.t.* **1.** To take off the cap or covering of. **— v.i. 2.** To remove the hat or cap, as in respect.

un·cer·e·mo·ni·ous (un′ser-ə-mō′nē-əs) *adj.* Informal; abrupt; discourteous. **— un′cer·e·mo′ni·ous·ly** *adv.*

un·cer·tain (un-sûr′tən) *adj.* **1.** That cannot be certainly predicted; doubtful. **2.** Not having certain knowledge or assured conviction. **3.** Not capable of being relied upon; variable. **4.** Not surely or exactly known: a lady of *uncertain* age. **5.** Having no exact or precise significance. **— un·cer′tain·ly** *adv.* **— un·cer′tain·ness** *n.*

un·cer·tain·ty (un-sûr′tən-tē) *n.* *pl.* **·ties 1.** The state of being uncertain; doubt. **2.** A doubtful matter.

un·chain (un-chān′) *v.t.* To release from a chain; set free.

un·char·i·ta·ble (un-char′ə-tə-bəl) *adj.* Not charitable; harsh in judgment; censorious. **— un·char′i·ta·ble·ness** *n.* **— un·char′i·ta·bly** *adv.*

un·chris·tian (un-kris′chən) *adj.* **1.** Unbecoming to a Christian. **2.** Contrary to Christian precepts; uncharitable, ungracious, rude, etc. **3.** Non-Christian; pagan.

un·church (un-chûrch′) *v.t.* **1.** To deprive of membership in a church; expel from a church. **2.** To deny the validity of the sacraments and order of, as a sect.

un·cial (un′shəl, -shē·əl) *adj.* Pertaining to or consisting of a form of letters found in manuscripts from the fourth to the eighth century, and resembling rounded modern capitals. **— n. 1.** An uncial letter. **2.** An uncial manuscript. [< L < *uncia* inch, ounce]

un·ci·nate (un′sə·nit, -nāt) *adj.* Hooked or bent at the end. Also **un′ci·nal, un′ci·nat′ed.** [< L < *uncus* hook]

un·cir·cum·cised (un-sûr′kəm-sīzd) *adj.* **1.** Not circumcised. **2.** Not Jewish; Gentile. **3.** Heathen; pagan. **— n.** Gentiles or heathens collectively: used with *the.*

un·civ·il (un-siv′əl) *adj.* Wanting in civility; discourteous; ill-bred. **— un·civ′il·ly** *adv.*

un·civ·i·lized (un-siv′ə·līzd) *adj.* Not civilized; barbarous.

un·clad (un-klad′) Alternate past tense and past participle of UNCLOTHE. **— adj.** Being without clothes; naked.

un·clasp (un-klasp′, -kläsp′) *v.t.* **1.** To release from a clasp. **2.** To release the clasp of. **— v.i. 3.** To become released from a clasp.

un·cle (ung′kəl) *n.* The brother of one's father or mother; also, the husband of one's aunt. ♦ Collateral adjective: *avuncular.* [< F < L *avunculus* mother's brother]

un·clean (un-klēn′) *adj.* **1.** Not clean; foul. **2.** Characterized by impure thoughts; unchaste; depraved. **3.** Ceremonially impure. **— un·clean′ness** *n.*

un·clean·ly[1] (un-klen′lē) *adj.* **1.** Lacking cleanliness. **2.** Impure; indecent; not chaste. **— un·clean′li·ness** *n.*

un·clean·ly[2] (un-klēn′lē) *adv.* In an unclean manner.

un·clear (un′klir′) *adj.* **1.** Not clear. **2.** Not easily understandable; confused or muddled: *unclear* reasoning.

Uncle Sam (sam) The personification of the government or the people of the U.S., represented as a tall, lean man with chin whiskers, wearing a plug hat, a blue swallow-tailed coat, and red-and-white striped pants. [Nickname of *Samuel Wilson,* 1766–1854, businessman]

Uncle Tom (tom) *U.S. Slang* A Negro who is servile to white men: a contemptuous term. [After the chief character in Harriet Beecher Stow's *Uncle Tom's Cabin,* a faithful, elderly Negro slave] **— Uncle Tom′ism**

un·cloak (un-klōk′) *v.t.* **1.** To remove the cloak or covering from. **2.** To unmask; expose. **— v.i. 3.** To remove one's cloak or outer garments.

un·close (un-klōz′) *v.t.* & *v.i.* **·closed, ·clos·ing 1.** To open or set open. **2.** To reveal; disclose.

un·clothe (un-klōth′) *v.t.* **·clothed** or **·clad** (klad), **·cloth·ing 1.** To remove clothes from; undress. **2.** To uncover.

un·coil (un-koil′) *v.t.* & *v.i.* To unwind or become unwound.

un·com·fort·a·ble (un-kum′fər·tə·bəl, -kumpf′tə·bəl) *adj.* **1.** Not at ease; feeling discomfort. **2.** Causing physical or mental uneasiness; disquieting. **— un·com′fort·a·ble·ness** *n.* **— un·com′fort·a·bly** *adv.*

un·com·mit·ted (un′kə·mit′id) *adj.* Not committed; esp., not pledged to a particular action, viewpoint, etc.

un·com·mon (un-kom′ən) *adj.* Not common or usual; remarkable. **— un·com′mon·ly** *adv.* **— un·com′mon·ness** *n.*

un·com·mu·ni·ca·tive (un′kə·myōō′nə·kə·tiv, -nə·kā′tiv) *adj.* Not communicative; silent; reserved. **— un′com·mu′ni·ca·tive·ly** *adv.* **— un′com·mu′ni·ca·tive·ness** *n.*

un·com·pro·mis·ing (un-kom′prə·mī′zing) *adj.* Making or admitting of no compromise; inflexible; strict. **— un·com′pro·mis′ing·ly** *adv.* **— un·com′pro·mis′ing·ness** *n.*

un·con·cern (un′kən·sûrn′) *n.* Absence of or freedom from concern or anxiety; indifference.

un·con·cerned (un′kən·sûrnd′) *adj.* Undisturbed; not anxious; indifferent. **— un′con·cern′ed·ly** (-sûr′nid·lē) *adj.* **— un′con·cern′ed·ness** *n.*

un·con·di·tion·al (un′kən·dish′ən·əl) *adj.* Limited by no conditions; absolute. **— un′con·di′tion·al·ly** *adv.*

un·con·di·tioned (un′kən·dish′ənd) *adj.* **1.** Not restricted; unconditional, absolute. **2.** *Psychol.* Not acquired; natural. **3.** Admitted without condition.

un·con·form·i·ty (un′kən·fôr′mə·tē) *n.* *pl.* **·ties** Want of conformity; nonconformity.

un·con·scion·a·ble (un-kon′shən·ə·bəl) *adj.* **1.** Going beyond reasonable bounds; unjustifiable. **2.** Not governed by prudence; unconscientious. **— un·con′scion·a·ble·ness** *n.* **— un·con′scion·a·bly** *adv.*

un·con·scious (un-kon′shəs) *adj.* **1.** Temporarily deprived of consciousness. **2.** Unaware: with *of: unconscious* of his charm. **3.** Not known or felt to exist; not produced by conscious effort. **4.** Not endowed with consciousness or a mind. **— n.** *Psychoanal.* That extensive area of the psyche that is not in the immediate field of awareness. **— un·con′scious·ly** *adv.* **— un·con′scious·ness** *n.*

un·con·sti·tu·tion·al (un′kon·sti·tōō′shən·əl, -tyōō′-) *adj.* Contrary to the constitution or basic law of a state. **— un′con·sti·tu′tion·al′i·ty** *n.* **— un′con·sti·tu′tion·al·ly** *adv.*

un·con·ven·tion·al (un′kən·ven′shən·əl) *adj.* **1.** Not adhering to conventions. **2.** Not usual or ordinary. **— un′con·ven′tion·al′i·ty** *n.* **— un′con·ven′tion·al·ly** *adv.*

un·cork (un-kôrk′) *v.t.* To draw the cork from.

un·count·ed (un-koun′tid) *adj.* **1.** Not counted. **2.** Beyond counting; innumerable.

un·cou·ple (un-kup′əl) *v.* **led, ·ling** *v.t.* **1.** To disconnect or unfasten. **2.** To set loose. **— v.i. 3.** To break loose.

un·couth (un-kōōth′) *adj.* **1.** Rough; crude; unrefined. **2.** Awkward or odd; ungainly. [OE *uncūth* unknown] **— un·couth′ly** *adv.* **— un·couth′ness** *n.*

undiscriminatingly	undistinguishing	undreamed	unemancipated	unengaging	unerased
undiscussed	undistracted	undreamt	unembarrassed	unengagingly	unescapable
undisguised	undistraught	undressed	unembellished	un-English	unessayed
undisguisedly	undistressed	undried	unemotional	unenjoyable	unessential
undisheartened	undistributed	undrilled	unemotionally	unenjoyed	unestablished
undishonored	undisturbed	undrinkable	unemphatic	unenlightened	unesthetic
undisillusioned	undisturbedly	undutiful	unemphatically	unenlivened	unestimated
undismantled	undiversified	undutifully	unemptied	unenriched	unethical
undismayed	undiverted	undutifulness	unenclosed	unenrolled	unetymological
undismembered	undivested	undyed	unencumbered	unenslaved	unexacting
undismissed	undivided	unearned	unendangered	unentangled	unexaggerated
undispatched	undivorced	uneatable	unendeared	unentered	unexalted
undispelled	undivulged	uneaten	unendearing	unenterprising	unexamined
undispensed	undomestic	unecclesiastic	unendearingly	unentertaining	unexcavated
undisputable	undomesticated	uneclipsed	unended	unenthralled	unexcelled
undisputed	undoubting	uneconomic	unending	unenthusiastic	unexchangeable
undissected	undrained	uneconomical	unendorsed	unenthusiastically	unexcited
undissembling	undramatic	unedible	unendowed	unentitled	unexciting
undisseminated	undramatical	unedifying	unendurable	unenviable	unexcluded
undissolved	undramatically	uneducable	unenduring	unenvied	unexcused
undissolving	undramatized	uneducated	unenforceable	unenvious	unexecuted
undistilled	undrape	uneffaced	unenforced	unenvying	unexercised
undistinguishable	undraped	uneliminated	unenfranchised	unequipped	unexhausted
undistinguished	undreaded	unelucidated	unengaged	unerasable	unexorcised

un·cov·er (un·kuv/ər) *v.t.* **1.** To remove the covering from. **2.** To make known; disclose. — *v.i.* **3.** To remove a covering. **4.** To raise or remove the hat, as in respect.

unc·tion (ungk/shən) *n.* **1.** The state or quality of being unctuous. **2.** *Eccl.* **a** A ceremonial anointing with oil. **b** The sacramental rite of anointing those in danger of death: also called *extreme unction*. **3.** The act of anointing, as with oil. **4.** The unguent used in anointing; ointment. [< F < L < *ungere* to anoint] — **unc/tion·less** *adj.*

unc·tu·ous (ungk/chōō-əs) *adj.* **1.** Characterized by affected emotion; oily-tongued; unduly suave. **2.** Characterized by deep sympathetic feeling. **3.** Greasy; slippery to the touch, as an unguent [< Med.L < L < *ungere* to anoint] — **unc/tu·ous·ly** *adv.* — **unc/tu·os/i·ty** (-chōō·os/ə·tē), **unc/tu·ous·ness** *n.*

un·cut (un·kut/) *adj.* **1.** Not cut. **2.** In bookbinding, having untrimmed margins. **3.** Unground, as a gem.

un·damped (un·dampt/) *adj. Physics* **1.** Pertaining to or designating oscillations that continue without change in amplitude. **2.** Not damped; unrepressed.

un·daunt·ed (un·dôn/tid, -dän/-) *adj.* Not daunted or intimidated; fearless; intrepid. — **un·daunt/ed·ly** *adv.* — **un·daunt/ed·ness** *n.*

un·de·ceive (un/di·sēv/) *v.t.* **·ceived, ·ceiv·ing** To free from deception, error, or illusion.

un·de·cid·ed (un/di·sī/did) *adj.* **1.** Not having the mind made up. **2.** Not decided upon; not determined. — **un/de·cid/ed·ly** *adv.* — **un/de·cid/ed·ness** *n.*

un·de·ni·a·ble (un/di·nī/ə·bəl) *adj.* **1.** That cannot be denied; indisputably true; obviously correct. **2.** Unquestionably good; excellent. — **un/de·ni/a·bly** *adv.*

un·der (un/dər) *prep.* **1.** Beneath, so as to have something directly above; covered by: layer *under* layer. **2.** In a place lower than; at the foot or bottom of: *under* the hill. **3.** Beneath the shelter of. **4.** Beneath the guise or assumption of: *under* a false name. **5.** Less than in number, degree, etc.: *under* 10 tons. **6.** Inferior to in quality, character, or rank. **7.** Dominated by; owing allegiance to; subordinate to. **8.** Subject to the guidance or tutorship of. **9.** Subject to the moral sanction of: *under* oath. **10.** With the liability of incurring: *under* penalty of the law. **11.** Subject to the pressure of; swayed by: *under* the circumstances. **12.** Driven or propelled by: *under* sail. **13.** In the group or class of: included *under* History. **14.** Being the subject of: *under* treatment. **15.** During the period of; in the reign of. **16.** By virtue of; attested or warranted by: *under* his own signature. **17.** In conformity to or in accordance with. **18.** Planted or sowed with. — *adv.* **1.** In or into a position below something; underneath. **2.** In or into a lower degree or rank. **3.** So as to be covered or hidden. **4.** So as to be less than the required amount. — **to go under** To fail, as a business. — *adj.* **1.** Situated or moving under something else; lower or lowermost. **2.** *Zool.* Ventral. **3.** Lower in rank; subordinate. **4.** Less than usual, standard, or prescribed; insufficient.

under- *combining form* **1.** Below in position; situated or directed beneath; on the underside, as in: **underlip, undersole. 2.** Below a surface or covering; lower, as in: **underflooring, underpainting. 3.** Inferior in rank or importance; subordinate; subsidiary, as in: **underofficer, undertreasurer. 4.** Insufficient or insufficiently; less than is usual or proper, as in: **underpaid, underpopulated. 5.** Subdued; hidden, as in: **underemphasis, underplot.**

un·der·age (un/dər·āj/) *adj.* Not of a requisite age; immature. Also **un/der·age/**.

un·der·arm¹ (un/dər·ärm/) *adj.* Situated, placed, or used under the arm. — *n.* The armpit.

un·der·arm² (un/dər·ärm/) *adj.* In various sports, as tennis, baseball, etc., executed with the hand lower than the elbow. — *adv.* In an underarm manner. Also *underhand.*

un·der·bid (un/dər·bid/) *v.t.* **·bid, ·bid·ding** To bid lower than, as in a competition. — **un/der·bid/der** *n.*

un·der·brush (un/dər·brush/) *n.* Small trees and shrubs growing beneath forest trees; undergrowth. Also **un/der·bush/** (-boōsh/).

un·der·buy (un/dər·bī/) *v.t.* **·bought, ·buy·ing 1.** To buy at a price lower than that paid by (another). **2.** To pay less than the value for.

un·der·car·riage (un/dər·kar/ij) *n.* **1.** The framework supporting the body of a structure, as an automobile. **2.** The principal landing gear of an aircraft.

un·der·charge (*v.* un/dər·chärj/; *n.* un/dər·chärj/) *v.t.* **·charged, ·charg·ing 1.** To make an inadequate charge for. **2.** To load with an insufficient charge, as a gun. — *n.* An inadequate or insufficient charge.

un·der·class·man (un/dər·klas/mən, -kläs/-) *n. pl.* **·men** (-mən) A freshman or sophomore in a school or college.

un·der·clothes (un/dər·klōz/, -klōtħz/) *n.pl.* Clothes designed for underwear, or to be worn next to the skin. Also **un/der·cloth/ing** (-klōtħ/ing).

un·der·coat (un/dər·kōt/) *n.* **1.** A coat worn under another coat. **2.** Underfur. **3.** A layer of paint, varnish, etc., beneath another layer: also **un/der·coat/ing.** — *v.t.* To provide with an undercoat (def. 3).

un·der·cov·er (un/dər·kuv/ər) *adj.* Secret; surreptitious; esp., engaged in spying or secret investigation.

un·der·cur·rent (un/dər·kûr/ənt) *n.* **1.** A current, as of water or air, below another or below the surface. **2.** A hidden drift or tendency, as of popular sentiments.

un·der·cut (*n. & adj.* un/dər·kut/; *v.* un/dər·kut/) *n.* **1.** The act or result of cutting under. **2.** The tenderloin. **3.** Any part that is cut away below. **4.** In sports, a cut or backspin imparted to the ball. — *v.t.* **·cut ·cut·ting 1.** To cut under. **2.** To cut away a lower portion of. **3.** To work or sell for lower payment than (a rival). **4.** In sports, to give an undercut to (the ball). — *adj.* Done by undercutting.

un·der·dog (un/dər·dôg/, -dog/) *n.* **1.** One who is at a disadvantage in a struggle; a probable loser. **2.** One who is victimized or downtrodden by society.

un·der·done (un/dər·dun/) *adj.* **1.** Insufficiently done. **2.** Not cooked to the full; rare.

un·der·es·ti·mate (*v.* un/dər·es/tə·māt; *n.* un/dər·es/tə·mit) *v.t.* **·mat·ed, ·mat·ing** To put too low an estimate upon. — *n.* An estimate that is too low. — **un/der·es/ti·ma/tion** *n.*

un·der·ex·pose (un/dər·ik·spōz/) *v.t.* **·posed, ·pos·ing** *Photog.* To expose (a film) less than is required for proper development. — **un/der·ex·po/sure** (-spō/zhər) *n.*

un·der·feed (un/dər·fēd/) *v.t.* **·fed, ·feed·ing 1.** To feed insufficiently. **2.** To fuel (an engine) from beneath.

un·der·foot (un/dər·foōt/) *adv.* **1.** Beneath the feet; down on the ground; immediately below. **2.** In the way.

un·der·fur (un/dər·fûr/) *n.* The coat of dense, fine hair forming the main part of a pelt, as in seals.

un·der·gar·ment (un/dər·gär/mənt) *n.* A garment to be worn under the outer garments.

un·der·go (un/dər·gō/) *v.t.* **went, ·gone, ·go·ing 1.** To be subjected to; have experience of; suffer. **2.** To endure.

un·der·grad·u·ate (un/dər·graj/ōō·it) *n.* A university or college student who has not received a bachelor's degree.

un·der·ground (*adj.* un/dər·ground/; *adv.* un/dər·ground/)

unexpanded	unfaded	unfetter	unforeseeable	unfreezable	ungirded
unexpectant	unfading	unfettered	unforeseeing	un-French	ungladdened
unexpended	unfallen	unfilial	unforeseen	unfrequent	unglazed
unexpendible	unfaltering	unfilled	unforested	unfrequented	unglossed
unexpert	unfashionable	unfilmed	unforetold	unfrequently	unglove
unexpiated	unfashioned	unfiltered	unforfeited	unfrozen	ungloved
unexpired	unfastened	unfired	unforged	unfruitful	unglue
unexplainable	unfatherly	unfittingly	unforgetful	unfulfilled	ungoverned
unexplained	unfathomable	unfixed	unforgetting	unfunded	ungowned
unexplicit	unfathomed	unfixedness	unforgivable	unfurnished	ungraced
unexploded	unfatigued	unflagging	unforgiven	unfurrowed	ungraceful
unexploited	unfavored	unflaggingly	unforgiving	ungallant	ungracefully
unexplored	unfeared	unflattered	unforgot	ungalled	ungraded
unexported	unfearing	unflattering	unforgotten	ungarnished	ungrafted
unexposed	unfeasible	unflavored	unformulated	ungartered	ungrained
unexpressed	unfed	unflickering	unforsaken	ungathered	ungratified
unexpunged	unfederated	unfoiled	unfortified	ungenerous	ungrudging
unextended	unfeignedly	unforbearing	unfought	ungenial	ungrudgingly
unexterminated	unfelt	unforbidden	unfound	ungenteel	unguided
unextinguishable	unfeminine	unforced	unframed	ungentle	unhackneyed
unextinguished	unfenced	unforcedly	unfranchised	ungentlemanly	unhailed
unextraditable	unfermented	unfordable	unfraternal	ungently	unhalved
unfadable	unfertile	unforeboding	unfraught	ungently	unhammered
	unfertilized	unforeknown	unfree	ungifted	

adj. **1.** Situated, done, or operating beneath the surface of the ground. **2.** Done in secret; clandestine. — *n.* **1.** That which is beneath the surface of the ground. **2.** A group secretly organized to oppose those in control of a government or country. **3.** *Brit.* A subway (def. 1). — *adv.* **1.** Beneath the surface of the ground. **2.** Secretly.

Underground Railroad A system of cooperation among antislavery people, before 1861, for assisting fugitive slaves to escape to Canada and the free States.

un·der·growth (un′dər·grōth′) *n.* **1.** A growth of smaller plants among larger ones; esp., a thicket or copse in or as in a forest. **2.** The condition of being undergrown.

un·der·hand (un′dər·hand′) *adj.* **1.** Done or acting in a treacherously secret manner; sly. **2.** In sports, underarm. — *adv.* **1.** Underhandedly; slyly. **2.** Underarm².

un·der·hand·ed (un′dər·han′did) *adj.* **1.** Underhand. **2.** Short-handed. — **un′der·hand′ed·ly** *adv.* — **un′der·hand′·ed·ness** *n.*

un·der·lay (*v.* un′dər·lā′; *n.* un′dər·lā′) *v.t.* **·laid**, **·lay·ing** **1.** To place (one thing) under another. **2.** To furnish with a base or lining. **3.** *Printing* To support or raise by underlays. — *n.* **1.** *Printing* A piece of paper, etc., placed under certain parts of a printing form.

un·der·lie (un′dər·lī′) *v.t.* **·lay**, **·lain**, **·ly·ing** **1.** To lie below or under. **2.** To be the basis or support of: the principle that *underlies* a scheme. [OE *underlicgan*]

un·der·line (un′dər·līn′) *v.t.* **·lined**, **·lin·ing** **1.** To mark with a line underneath. **2.** To emphasize.

un·der·ling (un′dər·ling) *n.* A subordinate; an inferior.

un·der·ly·ing (un′dər·lī′ing) *adj.* **1.** Lying under. **2.** Fundamental. **3.** Prior in claim or lien.

un·der·mine (un′dər·mīn′, un′dər·mīn) *v.t.* **·mined**, **·min·ing** **1.** To excavate beneath; dig a mine or passage under: to *undermine* a fortress. **2.** To weaken by wearing away at the base. **3.** To weaken or impair secretly or by degrees: to *undermine* one's health. — **un′der·min′er** *n.*

un·der·most (un′dər·mōst′) *adj.* Having the lowest place or position.

un·der·neath (un′dər·nēth′, -nēth′) *adv.* **1.** In a place below. **2.** On the under or lower side. — *prep.* **1.** Beneath; under; below. **2.** Under the form or appearance of. **3.** Under the authority of; in the control of. — *adj.* Lower. — *n.* The lower or under part or side. [OE *underneothan*]

un·der·nour·ish (un′dər·nûr′ish) *v.t.* To provide with nourishment insufficient in amount or quality for proper health and growth. — **un′der·nour′ish·ment** *n.*

un·dern·song (un′dərn·sông′, -song′) *n.* Tierce (def. 3). [OE *undern* midday, midday meal + SONG]

un·der·pants (un′dər·pants′) *n.pl. U.S.* An undergarment worn over the loins.

un·der·pass (un′dər·pas′, -päs′) *n. U.S.* A passage beneath; esp., the section of a way or road that passes under railway tracks or under another road.

un·der·pay (un′dər·pā′) *v.t.* **·paid**, **·pay·ing** To pay insufficiently.

un·der·pin·ning (un′dər·pin′ing) *n.* **1.** Material or framework used to support a wall or building from below. **2.** *pl. Informal* The legs.

un·der·pitch vault (un′dər·pich′) *Archit.* A vault formed by the intersection of two vaults that spring from the same level but are of uneven widths. For illus. see VAULT¹.

un·der·priv·i·leged (un′dər·priv′ə·lijd) *adj.* Not privileged to enjoy certain rights to which everyone is theoretically entitled, as because of poverty, illiteracy, etc.

un·der·pro·duc·tion (un′dər·prə·duk′shən) *n.* Production below capacity or below requirements.

un·der·proof (un′dər·prŏŏf′) *adj.* Having less strength than proof spirit.

un·der·quote (un′dər·kwōt′) *v.t.* **·quot·ed**, **·quot·ing** To undersell or offer to undersell, as goods or stocks.

un·der·rate (un′dər·rāt′) *v.t.* **·rat·ed**, **·rat·ing** To rate too low; underestimate. — **Syn.** See UNDERESTIMATE.

un·der·run (un′dər·run′) *v.t.* **·ran**, **·run**, **·run·ning** **1.** To run or pass beneath. **2.** *Naut.* To examine (a line, hawser, etc.) from below by drawing a boat along beneath it.

un·der·score (*v.* un′dər·skôr′, -skōr′; *n.* un′dər·skôr′, -skōr′) *v.t.* **·scored**, **·scor·ing** To underline. — *n.* A line drawn beneath a word, etc., as for emphasis.

un·der·sea (un′dər·sē′) *adj.* Existing, carried on, or adapted for use beneath the surface of the sea. — *adv.* Beneath the surface of the sea: also **un′der·seas′** (-sēz′).

un·der·sec·re·tar·y (un′dər·sek′rə·ter′ē) *n. pl.* **·tar·ies** In a government department, the official who ranks next below the secretary.

un·der·sell (un′dər·sel′) *v.t.* **·sold**, **·sell·ing** **1.** To sell at a lower price than. **2.** To sell for less than the real value. — **un′der·sell′er** *n.*

un·der·set (un′dər·set′) *n.* An undercurrent in the ocean.

un·der·sher·iff (un′dər·sher′if) *n.* A deputy sheriff, esp. one upon whom the sheriff's duties devolve in his absence.

un·der·shirt (un′dər·shûrt′) *n.* A garment worn beneath the shirt, generally of cotton.

un·der·shoot (un′dər·shōōt′) *v.* **·shot**, **·shoot·ing** *v.t.* **1.** To shoot short of or below (the mark, target, etc.). **2.** *Aeron.* To land an airplane or deliver a bomb short of (the mark). — *v.i.* **3.** To shoot or land short of the mark.

un·der·shot (un′dər·shot′) *adj.* **1.** Propelled by water that flows underneath: said of a water wheel. **2.** Projecting, as the lower jaw or teeth; also, having a projecting lower jaw or teeth.

un·der·side (un′dər·sīd′) *n.* The lower or under side or surface.

un·der·sign (un′dər·sīn′) *v.t.* To sign at the foot, end, or bottom of: used chiefly in the past participle.

un·der·signed (un′dər·sīnd′) *adj.* **1.** Having one's signature at the foot of a document. **2.** Signed at the foot of a document. — *n.* The subscriber or subscribers to a document: with *the*.

un·der·sized (un′dər·sīzd′) *adj.* Of less than the normal or average size. Also **un′der·size′**.

un·der·slung (un′dər·slung′) *adj. Mech.* Having the springs fixed to the axles from below, instead of resting upon them: said of certain automobiles: also *underhung*.

un·der·soil (un′dər·soil′) *n.* Subsoil.

un·der·stand (un′dər·stand′) *v.* **·stood**, **·stand·ing** *v.t.* **1.** To come to know the meaning or import of; apprehend. **2.** To comprehend the nature or character of. **3.** To have comprehension or mastery of: Do you *understand* German? **4.** To be aware of; realize: She *understands* her position. **5.** To have been told: I *understand* that she went home. **6.** To infer the meaning of: How am I to *understand* that remark? **7.** To accept as a condition or stipulation: It is *understood* that the tenant will provide his own heat. **8.** To supply in thought when unexpressed. **9.** To be in agreement with; be privately in sympathy with. — *v.i.* **10.** To have understanding; comprehend. **11.** To be informed; believe. — **Syn.** See APPREHEND. [OE < *under-* under + *standan* to stand] — **un′der·stand′a·ble.** — **un′der·stand′a·bly** *adv.*

un·der·stand·ing (un′dər·stan′ding) *n.* **1.** The act of one who understands, or the resulting state; comprehension. **2.** The power by which one understands. **3.** The sum of the mental powers by which knowledge is acquired, retained, and extended. **4.** The facts or elements of a case as apprehended by any one individual. **5.** An informal or confidential compact; also, the thing agreed on. **6.** An arrangement

unhampered	unheeding	unhuman	unimpeached	uninformed	unintentionally
unhandicapped	unheedingly	unhumanize	unimpeded	uninfringed	uninteresting
unhandled	unhelped	unhung	unimplored	uningenious	uninterestingly
unhang	unhelpful	unhurt	unimportant	uningenuous	unintermitted
unhanged	unheralded	unhurtful	unimposing	uninhabitable	unintermittent
unharassed	unheroic	unhygienic	unimpregnated	uninhabited	unintermitting
unharbored	unheroically	unhygienically	unimpressed	uninhibited	uninterpolated
unhardened	unhesitant	unhyphenated	unimpressible	uninitiated	uninterpreted
unharmed	unhesitantly	unhyphened	unimpressionable	uninjured	uninterrupted
unharmful	unhesitating	unideal	unimpressive	uninspired	unintimidated
unharmfully	unhesitatingly	unidentified	uninaugurated	uninspiring	unintoxicated
unharming	unhewn	unidiomatic	uninclosed	uninspiringly	uninvaded
unharmonious	unhindered	unilluminated	unincorporated	uninstructed	uninvented
unharnessed	unhired	unillumined	unincubated	uninstructive	uninventive
unharrowed	unhistoric	unillustrated	unincumbered	uninsurable	uninventively
unharvested	unhistorical	unimaginable	unindemnified	uninsured	uninverted
unhastily	unhistorically	unimaginably	unindicated	unintellectual	uninvested
unhasty	unhomogeneous	unimaginative	unindorsed	unintelligent	uninvited
unhatched	unhonored	unimaginatively	uninfected	unintelligibility	uninviting
unhealed	unhood	unimagined	uninfested	unintelligible	uninvitingly
unhealthful	unhoped	unimbued	uninflammable	unintelligibleness	uninvoked
unheated	unhostile	unimitated	uninflected	unintelligibly	uninvolved
unheeded	unhouse	unimpaired	uninfluenced	unintended	unissued
unheedful	unhoused	unimpassioned	uninfluential	unintentional	unjacketed

or settlement of differences, or of disputed points. — *adj.* **1.** Possessing comprehension and good sense. **2.** Tolerant or sympathetic. — **un′der·stand′ing·ly** *adv.* — **un′der·stand′ing·ness** *n.*
— **Syn.** (noun) **2.** reason, intelligence, intuition, judgment.

un·der·state (un′dər·stāt′) *v.* **·stat·ed, ·stat·ing** *v.t.* **1.** To state with less force than the truth warrants or allows. **2.** To state, as a number or dimension, as less than the true one. — *v.i.* **3.** To make an understatement.

un·der·state·ment (un′dər·stāt′mənt) *n.* A statement that is deliberately unemphatic or restrained in tone.

un·der·stood (un′dər·stŏŏd′) Past tense and past participle of UNDERSTAND. — *adj.* **1.** Assumed; agreed upon by all. **2.** Assumed when unexpressed, as the subject of a sentence.

un·der·stra·tum (un′dər·strā′təm, -strat′əm) *n. pl.* **·stra·ta** (-strā′tə, -strat′ə) or **·stra·tums** A substratum.

un·der·stud·y (un′dər·stud′ē) *v.t. & v.i.* **·stud·ied, ·stud·y·ing** **1.** To study (a part) in order to be able, if necessary, to take the place of the actor playing it. **2.** To act as an understudy (to another actor). — *n. pl.* **·stud·ies** **1.** An actor or actress who can take the place of another actor in a given role when necessary. **2.** A person prepared to perform the work or fill the position of another.

un·der·take (un′dər·tāk′) *v.* **·took, ·tak·en, ·tak·ing** *v.t.* **1.** To take upon oneself; agree or attempt to do; begin. **2.** To contract to do; pledge oneself to. **3.** To guarantee or promise. **4.** To take under charge or guidance. — *v.i.* **5.** To make oneself responsible or liable: with *for.*

un·der·tak·er (un′dər·tā′kər *for def. 1*; un′dər·tā′kər *for def. 2*) *n.* **1.** One who undertakes any work or enterprise. **2.** One whose business it is to arrange for the cremation or burial of the dead and to oversee funerals.

un·der·tak·ing (un′dər·tā′king; *for def. 3* un′dər·tā′king) *n.* **1.** The act of one who undertakes any task or enterprise. **2.** The thing undertaken; a task. **3.** The business of an undertaker (def. 2). **4.** An engagement, promise, or guaranty.

un·der·ten·ant (un′dər·ten′ənt) *n.* A subtenant.

un·der·tone (un′dər·tōn′) *n.* **1.** A tone of lower pitch or loudness than is usual; esp., the tone of a subdued voice or a whisper. **2.** A subdued shade of a color; also, a color upon which other colors have been imposed and which is seen through them. **3.** An implicit meaning or suggestion.

un·der·took (un′dər·tŏŏk′) Past tense of UNDERTAKE.

un·der·tow (un′dər·tō′) *n.* **1.** The flow of water beneath and in a direction opposite to the surface current. **2.** The seaward undercurrent below the surf.

un·der·val·ue (un′dər·val′yōō) *v.t.* **·ued, ·u·ing** To value too lightly; underrate; underestimate. — **Syn.** See UNDERESTIMATE. — **un′der·val′u·a′tion** *n.*

un·der·wa·ter (un′dər·wô′tər, -wot′ər) *adj. & adv.* Below the surface of a body of water; also, below the water line of a ship. — *n.* The region below the surface of water.

un·der·way (un·dər·wā′) *adv.* In progress or into operation: *The meeting was already underway.* Also **under way.**

un·der·wear (un′dər·wâr′) *n.* Garments worn underneath the ordinary outer garments; underclothes.

un·der·weight (un′dər·wāt′) *adj.* Having less than the normal weight. — *n.* Insufficiency of weight; also, weight below normal.

un·der·went (un′dər·went′) Past tense of UNDERGO.

un·der·wood (un′dər·wŏŏd′) *n.* Underbrush.

un·der·world (un′dər·wûrld′) *n.* **1.** In Greek and Roman mythology, the abode of the dead; Hades. **2.** The part of society engaged in crime or vice; esp., organized criminals.

un·der·write¹ (un′dər·rīt′) *v.* **·wrote, ·writ·ten, writ·ing**

v.t. **1.** To write beneath; subscribe. **2.** In finance, to execute and deliver (a policy of insurance on specified property); insure; assume (a risk) by way of insurance. **3.** To engage to buy, at a determined price and time, all or part of the stock in (a new enterprise or company) that is not subscribed for by the public. **4.** Loosely, to assume responsibility for, as an enterprise. **5.** To undertake to pay, as a written pledge of money. — **un′der·writ′er** *n.*

un·der·write² (un′dər·rīt′) *v.t. & v.i.* **wrote, ·writ·ten, ·writ·ing** To write in a deliberately restrained style.

un·de·sir·a·ble (un′di·zīr′ə·bəl) *adj.* Not desirable; objectionable. — *n.* An objectionable person. — **un′de·sir′a·bil′i·ty, un′de·sir′a·ble·ness** *n.* — **un′de·sir′a·bly** *adv.*

un·did (un·did′) Past tense of UNDO.

un·dies (un′dēz) *n. pl. Informal* Women's or children's underwear.

un·do (un·dōō′) *v.t.* **·did, ·done, ·do·ing** **1.** To cause to be as if never done; reverse; annul. **2.** To loosen or untie, as a knot, etc. **3.** To unfasten and open, as a parcel. **4.** To bring to ruin; destroy. [OE *undōn*] — **un·do′er** *n.*

un·do·ing (un·dōō′ing) *n.* **1.** Reversal, cancellation, etc., of what has been done. **2.** Destruction; ruin; also, the cause of ruin. **3.** The act or process of unfastening, etc.

un·done¹ (un·dun′) *adj.* **1.** Untied; unfastened. **2.** Ruined. [Orig. pp. of UNDO]

un·done² (un·dun′) *adj.* Not done. [< UN- + DONE]

un·doubt·ed (un·dou′tid) *adj.* Assured beyond question; being beyond a doubt; indubitable. — **un·doubt′ed·ly** *adv.*

un·draw (un·drô′) *v.t. & v.i.* **drew, ·drawn, ·draw·ing** To draw open, away, or aside.

un·dreamed-of (un·drēmd′uv′, -ov′) *adj.* Not conceived of in the mind; unimaginable. Also **un·dreamt′-of** (-dremt′-).

un·dress (*v. & n.* un·dres′; *adj.* un′dres′) *v.t.* **1.** To divest of clothes; strip. **2.** To remove the dressing or bandages from, as a wound. — *v.i.* **3.** To remove one's clothing. — *n.* **1.** Ordinary attire, as distinguished from formal dress. **2.** Comfortable, informal clothing. — *adj.* Informal.

un·due (un·dōō′, -dyōō′) *adj.* **1.** Excessive; disproportionate. **2.** Not justified by law; illegal. **3.** Not due; not yet demandable. **4.** Not appropriate; improper.

un·du·lant (un′dyə·lənt, -də-) *adj.* Undulating; waving.

undulant fever *Pathol.* A disease transmitted to man in the milk of infected cows and goats, and characterized by recurrent fever, swelling of the joints, neuralgic pains, etc.

un·du·late (*v.* un′dyə·lāt, -də-; *adj.* un′dyə·lit, -lāt, -də-) *v.* **·lat·ed, ·lat·ing** *v.t.* **1.** To cause to move like a wave or in waves. **2.** To give a wavy appearance to. — *v.i.* **3.** To move like waves. **4.** To have a wavy appearance. — *adj.* **1.** Having a wavy margin, as a leaf. **2.** Having wavelike markings, as of color: also **un′du·lat′ed** (-lā′tid). [< L *undulatus* having wavelike markings < *unda* wave]

un·du·la·tion (un′dyə·lā′shən, -də-) *n.* **1.** The act of undulating. **2.** A waving or sinuous motion. **3.** A wave. **4.** An appearance as of waves; a gentle rise and fall. — **un′du·la·to·ry** (-lə·tôr′ē, -tō′rē), **un′du·lous** (-ləs) *adj.*

un·du·ly (un·dōō′lē, -dyōō′-) *adv.* **1.** Excessively. **2.** In violation of a moral or of a legal standard; unjustly.

un·dy·ing (un·dī′ing) *adj.* Immortal; everlasting.

un·earth (un·ûrth′) *v.t.* **1.** To dig or root up from the earth. **2.** To reveal by or as by searching.

un·earth·ly (un·ûrth′lē) *adj.* **1.** Not earthly; sublime. **2.** Weird; terrifying; supernatural. **3.** *Informal* Ridiculously unconventional or inappropriate. — **un·earth′li·ness** *n.*

un·eas·y (un·ē′zē) *adj.* **·eas·i·er, ·eas·i·est** **1.** Lacking ease, assurance, or security; disturbed. **2.** Not affording ease or

unjaded	unlashed	unlocated	unmannishly	unmenaced	unmoistened
unjoined	unlaundered	unlocked	unmanufacturable	unmendable	unmold
unjointed	unleased	unlovable	unmanufactured	unmended	unmolded
unjoyful	unled	unloved	unmarked	unmensurable	unmolested
unjoyfully	unlessened	unloveliness	unmarketable	unmentionability	unmollified
unjudged	unlessoned	unloverlike	unmarketed	unmentioned	unmolten
unjudicial	unlet	unloving	unmarred	unmercenary	unmortgaged
unjustifiable	unletted	unlovingly	unmarriageable	unmerchantable	unmotivated
unjustifiably	unlevel	unlubricated	unmarried	unmerited	unmounted
unkept	unlevied	unmagnified	unmastered	unmeriting	unmourned
unkindled	unlibidinous	unmaidenliness	unmatched	unmethodical	unmovable
unkindliness	unlicensed	unmaidenly	unmated	unmilitary	unmoved
unkingly	unlifelike	unmailable	unmaternal	unmilled	unmoving
unkissed	unlighted	unmalleable	unmatted	unmingle	unmown
unknelled	unlikable	unmanageable	unmatured	unmingled	unmurmuring
unknightly	unlikeable	unmanful	unmeant	unmirthful	unmusical
unknowing	unlined	unmanfully	unmeasurable	unmirthfully	unmuzzle
unknowingly	unlink	unmanfulness	unmeasurably	unmistaken	unmuzzled
unknowingness	unliquefiable	unmangled	unmeasured	unmitigable	unmystified
unlabeled	unliquefied	unmanifested	unmechanical	unmixed	unnail
unlabelled	unliquidated	unmanipulated	unmediated	unmixt	unnamable
unladylike	unlit	unmanned	unmedicated	unmodified	unnameable
unlamented	unliveliness	unmannered	unmelodious	unmodish	unnamed
unlash	unlively	unmannish	unmelted	unmodishly	unnaturalized

rest; causing discomfort. **3.** Showing embarrassment or constraint; strained. — **un·eas′i·ly** *adv.* — **un·eas′i·ness** *n.*

un·em·ploy·a·ble (un′əm·ploi′ə·bəl) *adj.* Not employable. — *n.* A person who, because of illness, age, mental or physical incapacity, etc., cannot be employed.

un·em·ployed (un′əm·ploid′) *adj.* **1.** Having no remunerative employment; out of work. **2.** Not being put to use; idle. — *n.* A jobless person. — **the unemployed** Unemployed persons collectively. — **un′em·ploy′ment** *n.*

unemployment insurance *U.S.* A system of insurance authorized by the Federal Social Security Act of 1935, providing those who are involuntarily out of work with temporary compensation. Also **unemployment compensation.**

un·e·qual (un·ē′kwəl) *adj.* **1.** Not having equal extension, duration, proportions, amounts, etc. **2.** Not equal in strength, ability, status, etc. **3.** Inadequate for the purpose: with *to.* **4.** Inequitable; unfair. **5.** Varying; irregular. **6.** Not balanced; unsymmetrical. — **un·e′qual·ly** *adv.*

un·e·qualed (un·ē′kwəld) *adj.* Not equaled or matched; unrivaled; supreme. Also **un·e′qualled.**

un·e·quiv·o·cal (un′i·kwiv′ə·kəl) *adj.* Understandable in only one way; not equivocal. — **un·e·quiv′o·cal·ly** *adv.*

un·err·ing (un·ûr′ing, -er′-) *adj.* **1.** Making no mistakes; not erring. **2.** Certain; accurate. — **un·err′ing·ly** *adv.*

UNESCO (yŏŏ·nes′kō) The United Nations Educational, Scientific and Cultural Organization. Also **U·nes′co.**

un·e·ven (un·ē′vən) *adj.* **1.** Not even, smooth, parallel, or level; rough. **2.** Not divisible by two without remainder; odd: said of numbers. **3.** Not uniform; variable; spasmodic. — **un·e′ven·ly** *adv.* — **un·e′ven·ness** *n.*

un·e·vent·ful (un′i·vent′fəl) *adj.* Devoid of noteworthy events; quiet. — **un′e·vent′ful·ly** *adv.*

un·ex·am·pled (un′ig·zam′pəld) *adj.* Having no precedent.

un·ex·cep·tion·a·ble (un′ik·sep′shən·ə·bəl) *adj.* That cannot be objected to; irreproachable. — **un′ex·cep′tion·a·ble·ness** *n.* — **un′ex·cep′tion·a·bly** *adv.*

un·ex·cep·tion·al (un′ik·sep′shən·əl) *adj.* **1.** Not exceptional; ordinary. **2.** Subject to no exception.

un·ex·pect·ed (un′ik·spek′tid) *adj.* Not expected; unforeseen. — **un′ex·pect′ed·ly** *adv.* — **un′ex·pect′ed·ness** *n.*

un·fail·ing (un·fā′ling) *adj.* **1.** Giving or constituting a supply that never fails; inexhaustible: an *unfailing* spring. **2.** Not falling short of need, hope, or expectation. **3.** Sure; infallible. — **un·fail′ing·ly** *adv.* — **un·fail′ing·ness** *n.*

un·fair (un·fâr′) *adj.* **1.** Characterized by partiality or prejudice; not fair or just. **2.** Dishonest; fraudulent. — **un·fair′ly** *adv.* — **un·fair′ness** *n.*

un·faith·ful (un·fāth′fəl) *adj.* **1.** Not having kept faith; unworthy of trust; faithless. **2.** Not true to marriage vows; adulterous. **3.** Not accurate or exact. — **un·faith′ful·ly** *adv.* — **un·faith′ful·ness** *n.*

un·fa·mil·iar (un′fə·mil′yər) *adj.* **1.** Not having acquaintance: with *with.* **2.** Not known or recognizable. — **un′fa·mil′i·ar′i·ty** (-mil′ē·ar′ə·tē) *n.* — **un′fa·mil′iar·ly** *adv.*

un·fa·vor·a·ble (un·fā′vər·ə·bəl) *adj.* Not favorable; unpropitious; adverse. Also *Brit.* **un·fa′vour·a·ble.** — **un·fa′vor·a·ble·ness** *n.* — **un·fa′vor·a·bly** *adv.*

un·feel·ing (un·fē′ling) *adj.* **1.** Not sympathetic; hard; cruel. **2.** Devoid of feeling or sensation. — **un·feel′ing·ly** *adv.* — **un·feel′ing·ness** *n.*

un·feigned (un·fānd′) *adj.* Not feigned; not pretended; sincere; genuine. — **un·feign·ed·ly** (un·fā′nid·lē) *adv.*

un·fin·ished (un·fin′isht) *adj.* **1.** Not finished; incomplete. **2.** Having no finish or special surface treatment, as wood. **3.** Of fabrics: **a** Not bleached. **b** Having a slight nap.

un·fit (un·fit′) *adj.* **1.** Having no fitness; unsuitable. **2.** Not appropriate; improper. **3.** Not in sound physical condition. — *v.t.* **·fit·ted** or **·fit, ·fit·ting** To make unfit; dis-

qualify. — **un·fit′ly** *adv.* — **un·fit′ness** *n.*

un·fix (un·fiks′) *v.t.* **1.** To unfasten. **2.** To unsettle.

un·flap·pa·ble (un·flap′ə·bəl) *adj.* Characterized by unshakable composure; imperturbable. — **un·flap′pa·bil′i·ty** *n.*

un·fledged (un·flejd′) *adj.* **1.** Not yet fledged, as a young bird. **2.** Immature; inexperienced.

un·flesh·ly (un·flesh′lē) *adj.* Ethereal; spiritual.

un·flinch·ing (un·flin′ching) *adj.* Not shrinking from danger, pain, etc.; brave. — **un·flinch′ing·ly** *adv.*

un·fold (un·fōld′) *v.t.* **1.** To open or spread out (something folded). **2.** To lay open to view. **3.** To make clear by detailed explanation; explain: to *unfold* a plan. **4.** To evolve; develop. — *v.i.* **5.** To become opened; expand. **6.** To become manifest. [OE *unfealdan*] — **un·fold′er** *n.*

un·for·get·ta·ble (un′fər·get′ə·bəl) *adj.* Not forgettable; memorable. — **un′for·get′ta·bly** *adv.*

un·formed (un·fôrmd′) *adj.* **1.** Devoid of shape or form. **2.** Not fully developed in character. **3.** Unorganized.

un·for·tu·nate (un·fôr′chə·nit) *adj.* **1.** Not fortunate; unhappy, unsuccessful, etc. **2.** Causing or attended by ill fortune; disastrous. — *n.* One who is unfortunate. — **un·for′tu·nate·ly** *adv.* — **un·for′tu·nate·ness** *n.*

un·found·ed (un·foun′did) *adj.* **1.** Having no foundation; groundless; baseless. **2.** Not founded or established. — **un·found′ed·ly** *adv.* — **un·found′ed·ness** *n.*

un·friend·ly (un·frend′lē) *adj.* **1.** Unkindly disposed; inimical; hostile. **2.** Not favorable or propitious. — *adv.* In an unfriendly manner. — **un·friend′li·ness** *n.*

un·frock (un·frok′) *v.t.* **1.** To depose, as a monk or priest, from ecclesiastical rank. **2.** To divest of a frock or gown.

un·furl (un·fûrl′) *v.t. & v.i.* **1.** To unroll, as a flag. **2.** To spread out; expand; unfold.

un·gain·ly (un·gān′lē) *adj.* Lacking grace; awkward. — *adv.* In an awkward manner. — **un·gain′li·ness** *n.*

un·gird (un·gûrd′) *v.t.* **1.** To divest of or free from a belt, girdle, or confining band. **2.** To loosen or unfasten by or as by removing a belt, etc.

un·god·ly (un·god′lē) *adj.* **1.** Having no reverence for God; impious. **2.** Wicked; sinful. **3.** *Informal* Outrageous; unseemly. — **un·god′li·ness** *n.*

un·gov·ern·a·ble (un·guv′ər·nə·bəl) *adj.* **1.** Not capable of being governed or controlled. **2.** Refractory; unruly. — **un·gov′ern·a·ble·ness** *n.* — **un·gov′ern·a·bly** *adv.*

un·gra·cious (un·grā′shəs) *adj.* **1.** Lacking in graciousness of manner; unmannerly. **2.** Not pleasing; offensive; unacceptable. — **un·gra′cious·ly** *adv.* — **un·gra′cious·ness** *n.*

un·gram·mat·i·cal (un′grə·mat′i·kəl) *adj.* **1.** Not in accordance with the rules of grammar. **2.** Characterized by or using grammar at variance with the rules. — **un′gram·mat′i·cal·ly** *adv.*

un·grate·ful (un·grāt′fəl) *adj.* **1.** Not feeling or showing gratitude; not thankful. **2.** Not pleasant; disagreeable. **3.** Unrewarding. — **un·grate′ful·ly** *adv.* — **un·grate′ful·ness** *n.*

un·guard·ed (un·gär′did) *adj.* **1.** Having no guard; being without protection. **2.** Characterized by lack of caution or discretion: *unguarded* speech. — **un·guard′ed·ly** *adv.* — **un·guard′ed·ness** *n.*

un·guent (ung′gwənt) *n.* Any ointment or salve. [< L < *unguere* to anoint]

un·gu·la (ung′gyə·lə) *n. pl.* **·lae** (-lē) **1.** *Zool.* A hoof, claw, or nail. **2.** *Geom.* That which is left of a cone or cylinder when the top is cut off by a plane oblique to the base. **3.** *Bot.* An unguis. [< L < *unguis* nail] — **un′gu·lar** *adj.*

un·gu·late (ung′gyə·lit, -lāt) *adj.* **1.** Having hoofs. **2.** Designating, pertaining to, or belonging to a large group of hoofed mammals, including the elephant, rhinoceros, horse, hog, and all the ruminants. **3.** Hoof-shaped. — *n.* A hoofed mammal. [< LL < L *ungula* hoof]

---

unnavigable	unobtainable	unorthodoxy	unpatented	unphilological	unplowed
unnavigated	unobtained	unostentatious	unpatriotic	unphilosophic	unplucked
unneeded	unobtruding	unostentatiously	unpatriotically	unphilosophical	unplug
unneedful	unobtrusive	unostentatiousness	unpaved	unphonetic	unplugged
unnegotiable	unobtrusively	unowned	unpeaceable	unpicked	unpoetic
unneighborliness	unobtrusiveness	unoxidized	unpeaceful	unpicturesque	unpoetical
unneighborly	unoccasioned	unpacified	unpedigreed	unpierced	unpointed
unnoted	unoffended	unpaid	unpen	unpile	unpoised
unnoticeable	unoffending	unpainful	unpenetrated	unpitied	unpolarized
unnoticeably	unoffensive	unpainfully	unpensioned	unpitying	unpolished
unnoticed	unoffensively	unpainfulness	unperceivable	unpityingly	unpolitical
unnurtured	unoffered	unpaired	unperceived	unplaced	unpolluted
unobjectionable	unofficial	unpalatable	unperceiving	unplagued	unpondered
unobliged	unofficious	unpalatably	unperfected	unplait	unpopulated
unobliging	unofficiously	unparagraphed	unperformed	unplanned	unposted
unobligingly	unoiled	unpardonable	unperplexed	unplanted	unpractical
unobnoxious	unopen	unpardonably	unpersuadable	unplayed	unpracticality
unobscured	unopened	unpardoned	unpersuaded	unpleased	unpractically
unobservable	unopposed	unparental	unpersuasive	unpleasing	unpredictable
unobservant	unoppressed	unparted	unpersuasively	unpledged	unpredictably
unobservantly	unordained	unpartisan	unpersuasiveness	unpliable	unpreoccupied
unobserved	unoriginal	unpartizan	unperturbed	unpliant	unprepared
unobserving	unornamental	unpasteurized	unperused	unplighted	unprepossessing
unobstructed	unornate	unpatched	unphilanthropic	unploughed	unprepossessingly

un·hal·lowed (un-hal′ōd) *adj.* **1.** Not consecrated or made holy. **2.** Unholy; wicked.

un·hand (un-hand′) *v.t.* To remove one's hand from; release from the hand or hands; let go.

un·hand·y (un-han′dē) *adj.* **·hand·i·er, ·hand·i·est 1.** Inconvenient; hard to handle. **2.** Clumsy; lacking in manual skill. — **un·hand′i·ly** *adv.* — **un·hand′i·ness** *n.*

un·hap·py (un-hap′ē) *adj.* **·pi·er, ·pi·est 1.** Sad; miserable; depressed. **2.** Unlucky; unfortunate. **3.** Not tactful or appropriate. — **un·hap′pi·ly** *adv.* — **un·hap′pi·ness** *n.*

un·har·ness (un-här′nis) *v.t.* **1.** To remove the harness from; unyoke; release. **2.** To remove the armor from.

un·health·y (un-hel′thē) *adj.* **·health·i·er, ·health·i·est 1.** Lacking health or vigor; sickly; unsound: *unhealthy* animals or plants; also, indicating such a condition: *unhealthy* signs. **2.** Injurious to health. **3.** Morally unsound; unwholesome. — **un·health′i·ly** *adv.* — **un·health′i·ness** *n.*

un·heard (un-hûrd′) *adj.* **1.** Not perceived by the ear. **2.** Not granted a hearing. **3.** Obscure; unknown.

un·heard-of (un-hûrd′uv′, -ov′) *adj.* Not known of before; unknown or unprecedented.

un·hinge (un-hinj′) *v.t.* **·hinged, ·hing·ing 1.** To take from the hinges. **2.** To remove the hinges of. **3.** To detach; dislodge. **4.** To throw into confusion; disorder. **5.** To make unstable; unsettle, as the mind.

un·hitch (un-hich′) *v.t.* To unfasten.

un·ho·ly (un-hō′lē) *adj.* **·ho·li·er, ·ho·li·est 1.** Not sacred or hallowed. **2.** Lacking purity; wicked; sinful. **3.** *Informal* Terrible; dreadful: an *unholy* hour. [OE *unhālig*] — **un·ho′li·ly** *adv.* — **un·ho′li·ness** *n.*

un·hook (un-hŏŏk′) *v.t.* **1.** To remove from a hook. **2.** To unfasten the hook or hooks of. — *v.i.* **3.** To become unhooked.

un·hoped-for (un-hōpt′fôr′) *adj.* Not expected or hoped for: an *unhoped-for* solution.

un·horse (un-hôrs′) *v.t.* **·horsed, ·hors·ing 1.** To throw from a horse. **2.** To dislodge; overthrow. **3.** To remove a horse or horses from: to *unhorse* a vehicle.

un·hur·ried (un-hûr′ēd) *adj.* Leisurely; not hurried.

uni- *combining form* Having or consisting of one only. [< L *unus* one]

U·ni·at (yōō′nē·at) *n.* A member of the Uniat Church. — *adj.* Of or pertaining to the Uniats or the Uniat Church. Also **U′ni·ate** (-it, -āt). [< Russian < *uniya* union < L *unus* one; from union with the Roman Catholic Church]

Uniat Church Any body of Eastern Christians forming a church that acknowledges the Pope as its supreme head and that has its own distinctive liturgy: also called *Eastern Church*. Also **Uniate Church**.

u·ni·ax·i·al (yōō′nē·ak′sē·əl) *adj.* Having one axis.

u·ni·cam·er·al (yōō′nə·kam′ər·əl) *adj.* Consisting of but one legislative chamber.

u·ni·cel·lu·lar (yōō′nə·sel′yə·lər) *adj. Biol.* Consisting of a single cell, as a protozoan; one-celled.

u·ni·col·or (yōō′nə·kul′ər) *adj.* Of one color.

u·ni·corn (yōō′nə·kôrn) *n.* A mythical horse-like animal with one horn. [< OF < L < *unus* one + *cornu* horn]

u·ni·cy·cle (yōō′nə·sī′kəl) *n.* A vehicle consisting of a metal frame mounted on one wheel and propelled by means of pedals.

u·ni·di·rec·tion·al (yōō′nə·di·rek′shən·əl, -dī-) *adj.* **1.** Having or moving in only one direction. **2.** *Telecom.* Designed or equipped to operate best in only one direction, as a radio antenna.

u·ni·fi·a·ble (yōō′nə·fī′ə·bəl) *adj.* That can be unified.

u·ni·fi·ca·tion (yōō′nə·fə·kā′shən) *n.* The act of unifying, or the state of being unified. — **u′ni·fi·ca′tion·ist** *n.*

unified command *Mil.* An armed force of two or more U.S. military services under a single commander.

u·ni·form (yōō′nə·fôrm) *adj.* **1.** Being always the same or alike, as in form, appearance, quality, degree, etc.; not varying: *uniform* temperature. **2.** Agreeing or identical with each other; alike: *uniform* tastes. — *n.* **1.** A distinctive form of dress having a uniform style and appearance and worn by members of the same organization or service, as soldiers, sailors, etc. **2.** A single suit of such clothes. — *v.t.* **1.** To put into or clothe with a uniform. **2.** To make uniform. [< F < L *unus* one + *forma* form] — **u′ni·form·ly** *adv.* — **u′ni·form·ness** *n.*

u·ni·formed (yōō′nə·fôrmd) *adj.* Dressed in uniform.

u·ni·form·i·ty (yōō′nə·fôr′mə·tē) *n. pl.* **·ties 1.** The state or quality of being uniform; also, an instance of it. **2.** Conformity, as in opinions or religion. **3.** Monotony; sameness.

u·ni·fy (yōō′nə·fī) *v.t. & v.i.* **·fied, ·fy·ing** To combine into a unit; become or cause to be one. [< F or LL < L *unus* one + *facere* to make] — **u′ni·fi′er** *n.*

u·ni·lat·er·al (yōō′nə·lat′ər·əl) *adj.* **1.** Of, pertaining to, or existing on one side only. **2.** Made, undertaken, done, or signed by only one of two or more people or parties. **3.** One-sided. **4.** Relating to or concerned with only one side of a question, dispute, etc. **5.** Turned to or showing only one side. — **u′ni·lat′er·al·ly** *adv.* — **u′ni·lat′er·al·ism, u′ni·lat′er·al′i·ty** (-al′ə·tē) *n.*

un·im·peach·a·ble (un′im·pē′chə·bəl) *adj.* Not to be called into question as regards truth, honesty, etc.; faultless; blameless. — **un′im·peach′a·bly** *adv.*

un·im·proved (un′im·prōōvd′) *adj.* **1.** Not improved, bettered, or advanced. **2.** Having no improvements; not cleared, cultivated, or built upon: *unimproved* land. **3.** Not made anything of; unused: *unimproved* opportunities.

un·in·ter·est·ed (un·in′tər·is·tid, -tris-) *adj.* **1.** Having no interest in, as in property. **2.** Taking no interest in; unconcerned. — **un·in′ter·est·ed·ly** *adv.* — **un·in′ter·est·ed·ness** *n.*

un·ion (yōōn′yən) *n.* **1.** The act of uniting, or the state of being united; also, that which is so formed. **2.** A combining or joining of nations, states, parties, etc., for some mutual interest or purpose. **3.** The harmony, agreement, or concord that results from such a combining or joining. **4.** The joining of two persons in marriage; also, the state of wedlock. **5.** A labor union. **6.** *Mech.* A device for connecting parts of machinery; esp., a coupling or connection for pipes or rods. **7.** A device emblematic of union, used in a flag or emblem and found in the corner near the staff or occupying the entire field. — *adj.* Of, pertaining to, or adhering to a union, esp. a labor union. [< F < LL < L *unus* one]

PIPE UNION

Un·ion (yōōn′yən) *n.* **1.** The U.S. regarded as a national unit: with *the*. **2.** The former Union of South Africa. — *adj.* Of, pertaining to, or loyal to the U.S.; esp., the Federal government during the Civil War: a *Union* soldier.

union catalogue A library catalogue that contains the contents of more than one library.

un·ion·ism (yōōn′yən·iz′əm) *n.* **1.** The principle of combining for unity of purpose and action. **2.** The principle or the support of trade unions. **3.** *Usu. cap.* Adherence to the federal union during the Civil War. — **un′ion·is′tic** *adj.*

un·ion·ist (yōōn′yən·ist) *n.* **1.** An advocate of union or unionism. **2.** A member of a trade union.

unprescribed	unprogressive	unpunishable	unreachable	unrecorded	unrelievable
unpresentable	unprohibited	unpunished	unreached	unrecounted	unrelieved
unpresentably	unpromising	unpurchasable	unreadable	unrecoverable	unrelished
unpreserved	unpromisingly	unpure	unrealizable	unrecruited	unremarkable
unpressed	unprompted	unpurged	unrealized	unrectified	unremarked
unpresumptuous	unpronounced	unpurified	unreasoned	unredeemed	unremedied
unpretending	unpropitiable	unpurposed	unrebukable	unredressed	unremembered
unpretentious	unpropitiated	unpursuing	unrebuked	unreelable	unremittable
unpretentiously	unpropitious	unpuzzle	unreceipted	unrefined	unremitted
unpretentiousness	unpropitiously	unquaffed	unreceivable	unreflected	unremorseful
unprevailing	unproportionate	unquailing	unreceived	unreflecting	unremorsefully
unpreventable	unproportioned	unquaking	unreceptive	unreformed	unremorsefulness
unprevented	unproposed	unqualifying	unreceptively	unrefreshed	unremovable
unprimed	unprosperous	unquelled	unreceptiveness	unrefreshing	unremoved
unprincely	unprotected	unquenchable	unreciprocated	unregarded	unremunerated
unprinted	unproved	unquenched	unreclaimable	unregistered	unremunerative
unprivileged	unproven	unquestioning	unreclaimed	unregretted	unrendered
unprized	unprovoked	unquotable	unrecognizable	unregulated	unrenewed
unprobed	unprovoking	unraised	unrecognizably	unrehearsed	unrenounced
unprocessed	unpruned	unransomed	unrecognized	unrelated	unrenowned
unprocurable	unpublishable	unrated	unrecommended	unrelatedness	unrent
unprocured	unpublished	unratified	unrecompensed	unrelaxed	unrented
unprofaned	unpucker	unravaged	unreconcilable	unrelaxing	unrepaid
unprofited	unpunctual	unrazed	unreconciled	unreliable	unrepairable

Un·ion·ist (yōōn′yən·ist) *n.* During the U.S. Civil War, one who supported the Union cause and opposed secession.

un·ion·ize (yōōn′yən·īz) *v.* **·ized, ·iz·ing** *v.t.* **1.** To cause to join, or to organize into a union, especially a labor union. **2.** To make conform to the rules, etc., of a union. — *v.i.* **3.** To become a member of or organize a labor union. — **un′·ion·i·za′tion** *n.*

union jack A flag consisting of the union only.

Union Jack The British national flag, a combination of the flags of England, Scotland, and Ireland.

union shop An industrial establishment that hires only members of a labor union or those who promise to join a union within a specified time.

union suit A one-piece undergarment for men and boys consisting of shirt and drawers.

u·nip·a·rous (yōō·nip′ər·əs) *adj.* **1.** *Biol.* Bringing forth but one offspring at a time, or not having borne more than one. **2.** *Bot.* Having but one axis or stem at each branching.

u·ni·po·lar (yōō′nə·pō′lər) *adj. Physics* Showing only one kind of polarity.

u·nique (yōō·nēk′) *adj.* **1.** Being the only one of its kind; sole. **2.** Being without or having no equal or like. **3.** Loosely, unusual, rare, or notable: a *unique* opportunity. [< F < L < *unus* one] — **u·nique′ly** *adv.* — **u·nique′ness** *n.*

u·ni·sex·u·al (yōō′nə·sek′shōō·əl) *adj. Biol.* Of only one sex; also, having one kind of sexual organs only.

u·ni·son (yōō′nə·sən, -zən) *n.* **1.** A speaking or sounding the same words, tones, etc., simultaneously: with *in*: they answered in *unison*. **2.** Complete accord or agreement; harmony. **3.** *Music* **a** A state in which instruments or voices perform identical parts simultaneously, in the same or different octaves. **b** The interval formed by two tones of the same pitch. [< L < *uni-* one + *sonus* sound]

u·nit (yōō′nit) *n.* **1.** A single person or thing regarded as an individual but belonging to an entire group. **2.** A body or group, as of soldiers, considered as a subdivision of a similar but larger body or group. **3.** An apparatus or piece of equipment, usu. part of a larger object and having a specific function: the cooling *unit* of a freezer. **4.** A standard quantity with which others of the same kind are compared for purposes of measurement and in terms of which their magnitude is stated. **5.** *Math.* A quantity whose measure is represented by the number 1; a least whole number. **6.** *Med.* The quantity of a drug, vaccine, serum, or antigen required to produce a given effect. [Back formation < UNITY]

u·ni·tar·i·an (yōō′nə·târ′ē·ən) *n.* One who rejects the doctrine of the Trinity; a non-Trinitarian monotheist. — *adj.* Of or pertaining to a unit. [< NL *unitarius* unitary]

U·ni·tar·i·an (yōō′nə·târ′ē·ən) *n.* A member of a religious denomination that rejects the doctrine of the Trinity and emphasizes complete freedom of religious opinion, the importance of personal character, and the independence of each local congregation. — *adj.* Of or pertaining to the Unitarians, or to their teachings. — **U′ni·tar′i·an·ism** *n.*

u·ni·tar·y (yōō′nə·ter′ē) *adj.* **1.** Of or pertaining to a unit. **2.** Characterized by or based on unity, as a system of government. **3.** Having the nature of a unit; whole.

u·nite (yōō·nīt′) *v.* **u·nit·ed, u·nit·ing** *v.t.* **1.** To join together so as to form a whole; combine; compound. **2.** To bring into close connection, as by legal, physical, social, or other tie; join in action, interest, etc. **3.** To join in marriage. **4.** To attach permanently or solidly; cause to adhere; bond. **5.** To show or possess (characteristics, etc.) in combination: to *unite* wit and beauty. — *v.i.* **6.** To become or be merged into one; combine. **7.** To join together for action; concur. [< LL *unitus*, pp. of *unire* to make one < L *unus* one]

— **Syn. 1.** consolidate, amalgamate, merge, blend, fuse. **2.** connect, join, link, associate. — **Ant.** divide, separate, disconnect.

u·nit·ed (yōō·nī′tid) *adj.* Incorporated into one; allied; combined. — **u·nit′ed·ly** *adv.* — **u·nit′ed·ness** *n.*

United Church of Canada A church made up of former denominational Methodists, Presbyterians, and others.

United Nations 1. A coalition to resist the aggression of the axis powers in World War II, formed of 26 nations in January, 1942. **2.** An organization of sovereign states, having its permanent headquarters in an enclave of international territory in New York City since 1951, created by the **United Nations Charter** drafted in September–October, 1944 at Dumbarton Oaks, an estate in Washington, D.C., and adopted at San Francisco in May and June, 1945. The original membership was formed of 51 states. In 1964 there were 62 additional members. Formerly **United Nations Organization.** *Abbr. UN, U.N.*

United Nations Trust Territory See TRUST TERRITORY.

United Press International An organization for collecting and distributing news, formed in 1958 by a merger of two similar organizations, the International News Service and the United Press. *Abbr. UPI, U.P.I.*

unit modifier A conventional or improvised compound used adjectively before a substantive. Examples: *blue-green* algae, *bitter-sweet* chocolate, *suit-coat* pattern.

◆ The use of the hyphen in the unit modifier is to avoid ambiguity in a word sequence where the relationship is not immediately apparent from context: The house had faded red-brick walls (faded walls of red brick, *not* faded red walls of brick). The hyphen here is to be considered a nonce use and not a spelling form or variant.

u·ni·ty (yōō′nə·tē) *n. pl.* **·ties 1.** The state or fact of being one. **2.** Something that is wholly united and complete within itself. **3.** A state or quality of general concord and mutual understanding; harmony. **4.** The harmonious agreement of parts or elements into one united whole. **5.** The condition or fact of being free from variety or diversity. **6.** Singleness or constancy of purpose, action, etc. **7.** In art and literature, the arrangement of parts into a homogeneous whole exhibiting oneness of purpose, thought, spirit, and style. **8.** *Math.* **a** The number one. **b** The element of a number system that leaves any number unchanged under multiplication, that is, a number *e* such that *ex = xe = x* for all *x*. [< OF < L < *unus* one]

u·ni·va·lent (yōō′nə·vā′lənt) *adj. Chem.* Having a valence or combining value of one; monovalent. — **u′ni·va′lence, u′ni·va·len·cy** *n.*

u·ni·valve (yōō′nə·valv′) *adj.* Having only one valve, as a mollusc. Also **u′ni·valved′, u′ni·val′vu·lar** (-val′vyə·lər). — *n.* **1.** A mollusk having a univalve shell; a gastropod. **2.** A shell of a single piece.

u·ni·ver·sal (yōō′nə·vûr′səl) *adj.* **1.** Of, pertaining to, or typical of all or the whole: a *universal* reaction. **2.** Including, involving, or intended for all: a *universal* law. **3.** Applicable to everyone or to all cases: a *universal* cure. **4.** That can be used or understood by all: a *universal* language. **5.** Accomplished or interested in all or many subjects, activities, etc.: a *universal* genius. **6.** Of, pertaining to, or occurring throughout the universe. **7.** Common to all in any specific group or field: a *universal* practice of politicians. **8.** *Mech.* **a** Adapted or adaptable to a great variety of uses, shapes, etc., as certain machine parts. **b** Permitting free movement within fixed extremes, as a joint. **9.** *Logic* **a** Including all the individuals of a class or genus; generic. **b** In a proposition, predicable of all the individuals denoted by the subject: opposed to *particular*: "All men are mortal" is a *universal* proposition. — *n.* **1.** *Logic* A universal proposition. **2.** Any general or universal notion, condition, principle, etc. — **u′ni·ver′sal·ly** *adv.* — **u′ni·ver′sal·ness** *n.*

U·ni·ver·sal·ism (yōō′nə·vûr′səl·iz′əm) *n. Theol.* The doc-

unrepaired	unrespectful	unrighted	unsaleability	unscarred	unseeded
unrepealed	unrespectfully	unrightful	unscented	unscented	unseeing
unrepentant	unrespited	unrightfully	unsalted	unsceptical	unseeingly
unrepented	unrested	unrimed	unsanctified	unscheduled	unsegmented
unrepenting	unresting	unripened	unsanctioned	unscholarly	unseized
unrepining	unrestrainable	unrisen	unsanitarily	unschooled	unselected
unreplaced	unrestraint	unroasted	unsanitary	unscientific	unselective
unreplenished	unrestricted	unrobe	unsated	unscientifically	unselectively
unreported	unretarded	unromantic	unsatiable	unscorched	unsensitive
unrepresentative	unretentive	unromantically	unsatiated	unscorned	unsent
unrepresented	unretracted	unroof	unsatiating	unscoured	unsentimental
unrepressed	unretrieved	unroofed	unsatisfactorily	unscourged	unsentimentally
unreprievable	unreturned	unrough	unsatisfactory	unscraped	unserved
unreprieved	unrevealed	unrounded	unsatisfied	unscratched	unserviceable
unreprovable	unrevenged	unrulable	unsatisfying	unscreened	unserviceableness
unrequested	unreversed	unruled	unsatisfyingly	unscriptural	unserviceably
unrequited	unrevised	unsafe	unsaved	unsculptured	unset
unresented	unrevoked	unsafely	unsawed	unsealed	unsevered
unresigned	unrewarded	unsaid	unsawn	unseated	unsew
unresistant	unrhetorical	unsaintliness	unsayable	unseaworthiness	unsewn
unresisted	unrhymed	unsaintly	unscabbarded	unseaworthy	unsexual
unresisting	unrhythmic	unsalability	unscaled	unseconded	unshaded
unresolved	unrhythmical	unsalable	unscanned	unsectarian	unshadowed
unrespectable	unrhythmically	unsalaried	unscarified	unsecured	unshaken

trine that all souls will finally be saved and that good will triumph universally. — **U′ni·ver′sal·ist** *adj.* & *n.*

u·ni·ver·sal·i·ty (yōō′nə·vər·sal′ə·tē) *n. pl.* **·ties** **1.** The state or quality of being universal. **2.** Unrestricted fitness or adaptability. **3.** An all-embracing range of knowledge, abilities, etc.

u·ni·ver·sal·ize (yōō′nə·vûr′səl·īz) *v.t.* **·ized, ·iz·ing** To make universal.

universal joint *Mech.* A joint that permits connected parts of a machine to be turned in any direction within definite limits. Also **universal coupling.**

u·ni·ver·sal·ly (yōō′nə·vûr′sə·lē) *adv.* In a universal manner; on all occasions or in all places; without exception.

u·ni·verse (yōō′nə·vûrs) *n.* **1.** The aggregate of all existing things; the whole creation embracing all celestial bodies and all of space; the cosmos. **2.** In restricted sense, the earth. **3.** Human beings collectively; mankind. [< F < L < *unus* one + *versus*, pp. of *vertere* to turn]

u·ni·ver·si·ty (yōō′nə·vûr′sə·tē) *n. pl.* **·ties** **1.** An institution for higher instruction that includes one or more schools or colleges for graduate or professional study, as well as an undergraduate division, and grants master's and doctor's degree. **2.** The faculty and students of a university. **3.** The buildings and grounds of a university. [< OF < L *universitas* the whole, entire number]

u·niv·o·cal (yōō·niv′ə·kəl) *adj.* Having but one proper sense or meaning. — *n.* A word that has but one meaning. [< LL < L *unus* one + *vox, vocis* voice]

un·just (un·just′) *adj.* **1.** Not legitimate, fair, or just; wrongful. **2.** Acting contrary to right and justice; unrighteous. — **un·just′ly** *adv.* — **un·just′ness** *n.*

un·kempt (un·kempt′) *adj.* **1.** Not combed. **2.** Not clean or neat; untidy. **3.** Without polish or refinement; rough. [< UN-¹ + *kempt* combed, pp. of dial. *kemb*, var. of COMB]

un·kind (un·kīnd′) *adj.* Showing lack of kindness; unsympathetic; cruel. — **un·kind′ly** *adv.* — **un·kind′ness** *n.*

un·knit (un·nit′) *v.* **·knit** or **·knit·ted, ·knit·ting** — *v.t.* **1.** To untie or unravel (something tied or knit). **2.** To smooth out (something wrinkled). — *v.i.* **3.** To become unknitted.

un·known (un·nōn′) *adj.* **1.** Not known or apprehended; not recognized, as a fact or person. **2.** Not ascertained, discovered, or established: an *unknown* element. — *n.* An unknown person or quantity.

Unknown Soldier One of the unidentified dead of World War I who is honored as a symbol of all his compatriots who died in action, extended to include unknown dead of World War II and the Korean conflict.

un·la·bored (un·lā′bərd) *adj.* **1.** Produced without strain or effort; seemingly free and easy; natural. **2.** Uncultivated by labor; unworked; untilled. Also *Brit.* **un·la′boured.**

un·lace (un·lās′) *v.t.* **·laced, ·lac·ing** **1.** To loosen or unfasten the lacing of; untie. **2.** To loosen or remove (armor or clothing) in this way.

un·lade (un·lād′) *v.t.* & *v.i.* **·lad·ed, ·lad·ing** **1.** To unload the cargo of (a ship). **2.** To unload or discharge (cargo, etc.).

un·laid (un·lād′) *adj.* **1.** Not laid or placed; not fixed. **2.** Not allayed or pacified. **3.** Not twisted, as the strands of a rope.

un·latch (un·lach′) *v.t.* **1.** To open or unlock by releasing the latch. — *v.i.* **2.** To come open or unlocked.

un·law·ful (un·lô′fəl) *adj.* **1.** Contrary to or in violation of law; illegal. **2.** Born out of wedlock; illegitimate. — **un·law′ful·ly** *adv.* — **un·law′ful·ness** *n.*

un·lay (un·lā′) *v.t.* & *v.i.* **·laid, ·lay·ing** To untwist: said of the strands of a rope.

un·learn (un·lûrn′) *v.t.* & *v.i.* **·learned** or **·learnt, ·learn·ing** To dismiss from the mind; forget.

un·learn·ed (un·lûr′nid; *for def. 3* un·lûrnd′) *adj.* **1.** Not possessed of or characterized by learning; illiterate; ignorant. **2.** Unworthy of or unlike a learned man. **3.** Not acquired by learning or study. — **un·learn′ed·ly** *adv.*

un·leash (un·lēsh′) *v.t.* To set free from or as from a leash.

un·leav·ened (un·lev′ənd) *adj.* Not leavened: said esp. of the bread used at the feast of the Passover.

un·less (un·les′) *conj.* If it be not a fact that; supposing that . . . not; except that: *Unless* we persevere, we shall lose. — *prep.* Save; except; excepting: with an implied verb: *Unless* a miracle, he'll not be back in time. [Earlier *onlesse (that)* (than) in a less case < ON + LESS]

un·let·tered (un·let′ərd) *adj.* Not educated; illiterate.

un·like (un·līk′) *adj.* Having little or no resemblance; different. — *prep.* Dissimilar to or different from; not like: It was *unlike* him to go. — **un·like′ness** *n.*

un·like·ly (un·līk′lē) *adj.* **1.** Not likely; improbable. **2.** Not inviting or promising success. — *adv.* Improbably. — **un·like′li·ness, un·like′li·hood** *n.*

un·lim·ber (un·lim′bər) *v.t.* & *v.i.* To disconnect (a gun or caisson) from its limber; prepare for action.

un·lim·it·ed (un·lim′it·id) *adj.* **1.** Having no limits in space, number, or time; unbounded. **2.** Not limited by restrictions. **3.** Not limited by qualifications; undefined. — **un·lim′it·ed·ly** *adv.* — **un·lim′it·ed·ness** *n.*

un·load (un·lōd′) *v.t.* **1.** To remove the load or cargo from. **2.** To take off or discharge (cargo, etc.). **3.** To relieve of something burdensome or oppressive. **4.** To withdraw the charge of ammunition from. **5.** *Informal* To dispose of. — *v.i.* **6.** To discharge freight, cargo, or other burden. — **un·load′er** *n.*

un·lock (un·lok′) *v.t.* **1.** To unfasten (something locked). **2.** To open or undo; release. **3.** To lay open; reveal or disclose. — *v.i.* **4.** To become unlocked.

un·looked-for (un·lŏŏkt′fôr′) *adj.* Not anticipated.

un·loose (un·lōōs′) *v.t.* **·loosed, ·loos·ing** To release from fastenings; set loose or free.

un·loos·en (un·lōō′sən) *v.t.* To loose; unloose.

un·luck·y (un·luk′ē) *adj.* **·luck·i·er, ·luck·i·est** **1.** Not favored by luck; unfortunate. **2.** Resulting in or attended by ill luck. **3.** Ill-omened; inauspicious: an *unlucky* day. — **un·luck′i·ly** *adv.* — **un·luck′i·ness** *n.*

un·make (un·māk′) *v.t.* **·made (·mād′), ·mak·ing** **1.** To reduce to the original condition or form. **2.** To ruin; destroy. **3.** To depose, as from a position of authority.

un·man (un·man′) *v.t.* **·manned, ·man·ning** **1.** To cause to lose courage or fortitude; dishearten. **2.** To render unmanly or effeminate. **3.** To deprive of virility; castrate.

un·man·ly (un·man′lē) *adj.* **1.** Not masculine or virile; effeminate. **2.** Not honorable. — **un·man′li·ness** *n.*

un·man·ner·ly (un·man′ər·lē) *adj.* Lacking manners; rude. — *adv.* Impolitely; rudely. — **un·man′ner·li·ness** *n.*

un·mask (un·mask′, -mäsk′) *v.t.* **1.** To remove a mask from. **2.** To reveal or disclose the truth about. — *v.i.* **3.** To remove one's mask or disguise.

un·mean·ing (un·mē′ning) *adj.* **1.** Having no meaning. **2.** Showing no expression of intelligence, interest, etc.; empty. — **un·mean′ing·ly** *adv.* — **un·mean′ing·ness** *n.*

un·meet (un·mēt′) *adj.* Not meet or suitable; not proper; unbecoming. — **un·meet′ly** *adv.* — **un·meet′ness** *n.*

un·men·tion·a·ble (un·men′shən·ə·bəl) *adj.* Not proper to be mentioned or discussed; embarrassing; shameful. — **un·men′tion·a·ble·ness** *n.* — **un·men′tion·a·bly** *adv.*

unshamed	unsisterly	unsolved	unsprinkled	unstripped	unsusceptible
unshapely	unsized	unsoothed	unsprung	unstuffed	unsuspicious
unshared	unskeptical	unsophistication	unsquandered	unstung	unsuspiciously
unshaved	unslacked	unsorted	unsquared	unsubdued	unsustainable
unshaven	unslaked	unsought	unstack	unsubmissive	unsustained
unshed	unsleeping	unsounded	unstainable	unsubscribed	unswayed
unshelled	unslumbering	unsoured	unstained	unsubsidized	unsweetened
unsheltered	unsmiling	unsowed	unstalked	unsubstantiated	unswept
unshielded	unsmilingly	unsown	unstamped	unsuccess	unswerving
unshod	unsmirched	unspecified	unstandardized	unsuccessful	unsworn
unshorn	unsmoked	unspeculative	unstarched	unsuggestive	unsymmetrical
unshrinkable	unsoaked	unspeculatively	unstarred	unsuited	unsymmetrically
unshrinking	unsober	unspelled	unstated	unsullied	unsympathetic
unshriven	unsocial	unspent	unstatesmanlike	unsunk	unsympathetically
unshrouded	unsoftened	unspilled	unsteadfast	unsupportable	unsympathizing
unshrunk	unsoiled	unspilt	unstemmed	unsupportably	unsympathizingly
unshunned	unsold	unspiritual	unsterile	unsupported	unsystematic
unshut	unsoldierly	unspirituality	unsterilized	unsupportedly	unsystematically
unsifted	unsolicited	unspiritually	unstick	unsuppressed	unsystematized
unsigned	unsolicitous	unspiritualness	unstigmatized	unsure	untack
unsilenced	unsolid	unspoiled	unstinted	unsurmountable	untactful
unsimilar	unsolidly	unspoilt	unstitched	unsurpassable	untactfully
unsingable	unsoluble	unspoken	unstrained	unsurpassed	untactfulness
unsinkable	unsolvable	unsportsmanlike	unstressed	unsurprised	untainted

un·men·tion·a·bles (un·men′shən·ə·bəlz) *n.pl.* Things not ordinarily mentioned; usu., undergarments.

un·mer·ci·ful (un·mûr′sə·fəl) *adj.* Showing no mercy; pitiless. — **un·mer′ci·ful·ly** *adv.* — **un·mer′ci·ful·ness** *n.*

un·mind·ful (un·mīnd′fəl) *adj.* Neglectful; inattentive; careless. — **un·mind′ful·ly** *adv.* — **un·mind′ful·ness** *n.*

un·mis·tak·a·ble (un′mis·tā′kə·bəl) *adj.* That cannot be mistaken; evident; clear. — **un′mis·tak′a·bly** *adv.*

un·mit·i·gat·ed (un·mit′ə·gā′tid) *adj.* **1.** Not mitigated or lightened in effect: *unmitigated* sorrow. **2.** Absolute: an *unmitigated* rogue. — **un·mit′i·gat′ed·ly** *adv.*

un·mor·al (un·môr′əl, -mōr′-) *adj.* Having no moral sense; neither moral nor immoral. — **un·mo·ral′i·ty** (un′mə·ral′ə·tē) *n.* — **un·mor′al·ly** *adv.*

un·nat·u·ral (un·nach′ər·əl) *adj.* **1.** Contrary to the laws of nature. **2.** Monstrous; inhuman: *unnatural* crimes. **3.** Not having, or inconsistent with, those attitudes, feelings, etc., considered normal; abnormal. **4.** Artificial; affected. — **un·nat′u·ral·ly** *adv.* — **un·nat′u·ral·ness** *n.*

un·nec·es·sar·y (un·nes′ə·ser′ē) *adj.* Not required or necessary; not essential. — **un·nec′es·sar′i·ly** *adv.*

un·nerve (un·nûrv′) *v.t.* ·**nerved**, ·**nerv·ing** To deprive of strength; firmness, self-control, or courage; unman.

un·num·bered (un·num′bərd) *adj.* **1.** Not counted. **2.** Innumerable. **3.** Not marked with or assigned a number.

un·oc·cu·pied (un·ok′yə·pīd) *adj.* **1.** Empty; not dwelt in; uninhabited: an *unoccupied* house. **2.** Idle; unemployed.

un·or·gan·ized (un·ôr′gən·īzd) *adj.* **1.** Not organized in structure, system, government, etc. **2.** Not living; inorganic. **3.** Not unionized. Also *Brit.* **un·or′gan·ised.**

un·or·tho·dox (un·ôr′thə·doks) *adj.* Not orthodox in doctrine, manner, method, etc. — **un·or′tho·dox′ly** *adv.*

un·pack (un·pak′) *v.t.* **1.** To open and take out the contents of. **2.** To take out of the container, as something packed. — *v.i.* **3.** To unpack a trunk, etc. — **un·pack′er** *n.*

un·paged (un·pājd′) *adj.* Having the pages unnumbered: said of a book, magazine, etc.

un·par·al·leled (un·par′ə·leld) *adj.* Without parallel; unmatched; unprecedented.

un·par·lia·men·ta·ry (un′pär·lə·men′tər·ē) *adj.* Contrary to the rules that govern parliamentary bodies. — **un′par·lia·men′ta·ri·ly** *adv.* — **un′par·lia·men′ta·ri·ness** *n.*

un·peg (un·peg′) *v.t.* ·**pegged**, ·**peg·ging** To open or unfasten by removing a peg or pegs.

un·peo·ple (un·pē′pəl) *v.t.* ·**pled**, ·**pling** To take or remove people from; depopulate. — **un·peo′pled** *adj.*

un·pin (un·pin′) *v.t.* ·**pinned**, ·**pin·ning** **1.** To remove the pins from. **2.** To unfasten by removing pins.

un·pleas·ant (un·plez′ənt) *adj.* Disagreeable; objectionable; not pleasing. — **un·pleas′ant·ly** *adv.* — **un·pleas′ant·ness** *n.*

un·plumbed (un·plumd′) *adj.* **1.** Not sounded or explored fully; unfathomed. **2.** Not furnished with plumbing.

un·polled (un·pōld′) *adj.* **1.** Not registered: an *unpolled* vote or voter. **2.** Not having voted at an election.

un·pop·u·lar (un·pop′yə·lər) *adj.* Having no popularity; generally disliked or condemned. — **un·pop′u·lar·ly** *adv.* — **un·pop′u·lar′i·ty** (-lar′ə·tē) *n.*

un·prac·ticed (un·prak′tist) *adj.* **1.** Being without practice, experience, or skill. **2.** Not carried out in practice; not used. **3.** Not yet tried.

un·prec·e·dent·ed (un·pres′ə·den′tid) *adj.* Being without precedent; unheard-of. — **un·prec′e·dent′ed·ly** *adv.*

un·prej·u·diced (un·prej′ŏŏ·dist) *adj.* **1.** Free from prejudice or bias; impartial. **2.** Not impaired, as a right.

un·priced (un·prīst′) *adj.* Having no fixed price.

un·prin·ci·pled (un·prin′sə·pəld) *adj.* Lacking in moral principles; unscrupulous. — **un·prin′ci·pled·ness** *n.*

un·print·a·ble (un·prin′tə·bəl) *adj.* Not fit to be printed.

un·pro·fes·sion·al (un′prə·fesh′ən·əl) *adj.* **1.** Having no profession or no professional status. **2.** Violating the rules or ethical code of a profession. — **un′pro·fes′sion·al·ly** *adv.*

un·qual·i·fied (un·kwol′ə·fīd) *adj.* **1.** Being without the proper qualifications; unfit. **2.** Without limitation or restrictions; absolute; entire: *unqualified* approval. — **un·qual′i·fied′ly** *adv.* — **un·qual′i·fied′ness** *n.*

un·ques·tion·a·ble (un·kwes′chən·ə·bəl) *adj.* Too certain or sure to admit of question; being beyond a doubt; indisputable. — **un·ques′tion·a·bil′i·ty**, **un·ques′tion·a·ble·ness** *n.* — **un·ques′tion·a·bly** *adv.*

un·qui·et (un·kwī′ət) *adj.* **1.** Not at rest; disturbed; restless. **2.** Causing unrest or discomfort. **3.** Uneasy; disturbing. — **un·qui′et·ly** *adv.* — **un·qui′et·ness** *n.*

un·quote (un·kwōt′) *v.t. & v.i.* ·**quot·ed**, ·**quot·ing** To close (a quotation).

un·rav·el (un·rav′əl) *v.* ·**eled** or ·**elled**, ·**el·ing** or ·**el·ling** *v.t.* **1.** To separate the threads of, as a tangled skein or knitted article. **2.** To free from entanglement; unfold; explain, as a mystery or a plot. — *v.i.* **3.** To become unraveled.

un·read (un·red′) *adj.* **1.** Not informed by reading; ignorant. **2.** Not yet perused.

un·read·y (un·red′ē) *adj.* **1.** Being without readiness or alertness. **2.** Not in a condition to act effectively; unprepared. — **un·read′i·ly** *adv.* — **un·read′i·ness** *n.*

un·real (un·rēl′, -rē′əl) *adj.* **1.** Having no reality or substance. **2.** Artificial; insincere; also, fanciful. — **un·re·al·i·ty** (un′rē·al′ə·tē) *n.* — **un·re′al·ly** *adv.*

un·rea·son·a·ble (un·rē′zən·ə·bəl) *adj.* **1.** Acting without or contrary to reason. **2.** Not according to reason; irrational. **3.** Immoderate; exorbitant. — **un·rea′son·a·bil′i·ty**, **un·rea′son·a·ble·ness** *n.* — **un·rea′son·a·bly** *adv.*

un·rea·son·ing (un·rē′zən·ing) *adj.* Not accompanied by reason or control. — **un·rea′son·ing·ly** *adv.*

un·reck·on·a·ble (un·rek′ən·ə·bəl) *adj.* That cannot be reckoned or computed; unlimited.

un·re·con·struct·ed (un·rē′kən·struk′tid) *adj.* **1.** Not reconstructed. **2.** Not reconciled to or accepting the conditions of the Reconstruction.

un·reel (un·rēl′) *v.t. & v.i.* To unwind, as from a reel.

un·re·gen·er·ate (un′ri·jen′ər·it) *adj.* Not having been changed spiritually; remaining unreconciled to God. **2.** Sinful; wicked. Also **un′re·gen′er·at′ed** (-ā′tid). — **un′re·gen′er·a·cy** (-ə·sē) *n.* — **un′re·gen′er·ate·ly** *adv.*

un·re·lent·ing (un′ri·len′ting) *adj.* **1.** Not relenting; pitiless; inexorable. **2.** Not diminishing, or not changing, in pace, effort, speed, etc. — **un·re·lent′ing·ly** *adv.*

un·re·li·gious (un′ri·lij′əs) *adj.* **1.** Irreligious; hostile to religion. **2.** Not connected in any way with religion.

un·re·mit·ting (un′ri·mit′ing) *adj.* Not relaxing or stopping; incessant. — **un′re·mit′ting·ly** *adv.* — **un′re·mit′ting·ness** *n.*

un·re·served (un′ri·zûrvd′) *adj.* **1.** Given or done without reserve; full; unlimited. **2.** Having no reserve of manner; informal; open; frank. — **un·re·serv·ed·ly** (un′ri·zûr′vid·lē) *adv.* — **un′re·serv′ed·ness** *n.*

un·rest (un·rest′) *n.* **1.** Restlessness, esp. of the mind. **2.**

untaken	unthriftily	untrimmed	unveiled	unwatched	unwomanish
untalented	unthriftiness	untroubled	unventilated	unwavering	unwomanishly
untamable	unthrifty	untrustful	unveracious	unwaveringly	unwomanly
untame	unthrone	untrustiness	unveraciously	unweakened	unwon
untameable	untillable	untrusty	unveraciousness	unweaned	unwooded
untamed	untilled	untuck	unverifiable	unwearable	unwooed
untangled	untilted	untufted	unverifiableness	unwearily	unworkability
untanned	untinged	untunable	unverifiably	unweary	unworkable
untapped	untired	untuned	unverified	unwearying	unworkableness
untarnished	untiring	untuneful	unversed	unwearyingly	unworked
untasted	untiringly	unturned	unvexed	unweathered	unworkmanlike
untaxable	untouched	untwilled	unvext	unweave	unworn
untaxed	untraceable	untwisted	unvisited	unwed	unworshiped
unteachable	untraced	untypical	unvitiated	unwedded	unworshipped
untechnical	untracked	untypically	unvitrified	unweeded	unwound
untempered	untractable	untypicalness	unvocal	unwelcome	unwounded
untenanted	untrained	ununiform	unvocally	unwelded	unwoven
untended	untrammeled	ununiformly	unvolatilized	unwetted	unwreathe
unterrified	untrammelled	ununited	unvulcanized	unwhetted	unwrought
untested	untransferable	unurged	unwakened	unwhipped	unwrung
untether	untransferred	unusable	unwalled	unwifely	unyielding
untethered	untranslatable	unutilizable	unwanted	unwincing	unyieldingly
unthanked	untranslated	unuttered	unwarlike	unwinking	unyieldingness
unthatched	untransmitted	unvaccinated	unwarmed	unwinning	unyouthful
untheatrical	untrapped	unvacillating	unwarped	unwisdom	unyouthfully
unthinkable	untraversable	unvacillatingly	unwarranted	unwished	unyouthfulness
unthinkably	untraversed	unvalidated	unwashed	unwithered	unzealous
unthought	untreasured	unvanquished	unwasted	unwithering	unzealously
unthoughtful	untrim	unvaried	unwasting	unwitnessed	unzip

Trouble; turmoil, esp. with regard to public or political conditions and suggesting premonitions of revolt.

un·rid·dle (un·rid′l) v.t. **·dled**, **·dling** To solve, as a mystery.

un·ri·fled[1] (un·rī′fəld) adj. Smoothbored, as a gun.

un·ri·fled[2] (un·rī′fəld) adj. Not rifled, seized, or plundered.

un·right·eous (un·rī′chəs) adj. 1. Not righteous; wicked; sinful. 2. Contrary to justice; unfair. — **un·right′eous·ly** adv. — **un·right′eous·ness** n.

un·ripe (un·rīp′) adj. Not arrived at maturity; not ripe; immature. [OE unrīpe untimely] — **un·ripe′ness** n.

un·ri·valed (un·rī′vəld) adj. Having no rival or competitor; unequaled; matchless. Also Brit. **un·ri′valled**.

un·roll (un·rōl′) v.t. 1. To spread or open (something rolled up). 2. To exhibit to view. — v.i. 3. To become unrolled.

un·ruf·fled (un·ruf′əld) adj. Not disturbed or agitated emotionally; calm.

un·ru·ly (un·rōō′lē) adj. **·li·er**, **·li·est** Disposed to resist rule or discipline; intractable; ungovernable. — **un·ru′li·ness** n.

un·sad·dle (un·sad′l) v.t. **·dled**, **·dling** 1. To remove a saddle from. 2. To throw from the saddle; unhorse.

un·sat·u·rat·ed (un·sach′ə·rā′tid) adj. 1. Containing less of a solute required for equilibrium, as a solution. 2. Chem. Capable of uniting with elements or radicals without loss of the original constituents.

un·sa·vor·y (un·sā′vər·ē) adj. 1. Having a disagreeable taste or odor. 2. Suggesting something disagreeable, offensive, or unclean; also, morally bad. Also Brit. **un·sa′vour·y**. — **un·sa′vor·i·ly** adv. — **un·sa′vor·i·ness** n.

un·say (un·sā′) v.t. **·said**, **·say·ing** To retract (something said).

un·scathed (un·skāthd′) adj. Uninjured.

un·scram·ble (un·skram′bəl) v.t. **·bled**, **·bling** Informal To resolve the confused or disordered condition of.

un·screw (un·skrōō′) v.t. 1. To remove the screw or screws from. 2. To remove or detach by withdrawing screws, or by turning. — v.i. 3. To permit of being unscrewed.

un·scru·pu·lous (un·skrōō′pyə·ləs) adj. Not scrupulous; having no scruples or morals; unprincipled. — **un·scru′pu·lous·ly** adv. — **un·scru′pu·lous·ness** n.

un·seal (un·sēl′) v.t. 1. To break the seal of. 2. To open.

un·search·a·ble (un·sûr′chə·bəl) adj. That cannot be searched or explored; hidden; mysterious. — **un·search′a·ble·ness** n. — **un·search′a·bly** adv.

un·sea·son·a·ble (un·sē′zən·ə·bəl) adj. 1. Not being in or characteristic of the season. 2. Inappropriate; ill-timed. — **un·sea′son·a·ble·ness** n. — **un·sea′son·a·bly** adv.

un·seat (un·sēt′) v.t. 1. To remove from a seat or fixed position. 2. To unhorse. 3. To deprive of office or rank; depose.

un·seem·ly (un·sēm′lē) adj. **·li·er**, **·li·est** Not seemly or proper; unbecoming; indecent. — adv. In an unseemly fashion. — **un·seem′li·ness** n.

un·self·ish (un·sel′fish) adj. Not selfish; generous. — **un·self′ish·ly** adv. — **un·self′ish·ness** n.

un·set·tle (un·set′l) v. **·tled**, **·tling** v.t. 1. To change or move from a fixed or settled condition. 2. To confuse; disturb. — v.i. 3. To become unsteady or unfixed.

un·sex (un·seks′) v.t. To deprive of the distinctive qualities of a sex; esp., to render unfeminine or unwomanly.

un·shack·le (un·shak′əl) v.t. **·led**, **·ling** To unfetter; free from or as from shackles.

un·sheathe (un·shēth′) v.t. **·sheathed**, **·sheath·ing** To take from or as from a scabbard or sheath; bare.

un·ship (un·ship′) v.t. **·shipped**, **·ship·ping** 1. To unload from a ship or other vessel. 2. To remove from the place where it is fixed or fitted, as a rudder or oar.

un·sight·ly (un·sīt′lē) adj. **·li·er**, **·li·est** Offensive to the sight; ugly. — **un·sight′li·ness** n.

un·skilled (un·skild′) adj. 1. Destitute of skill or dexterity. 2. Not requiring special skill or training: unskilled labor.

un·skill·ful (un·skil′fəl) adj. Lacking or not evincing skillfulness; awkward. Also Brit. **un·skil′ful**. — **un·skill′ful·ly** adv. — **un·skill′ful·ness** n.

un·snap (un·snap′) v.t. **·snapped**, **·snap·ping** To undo the snap or snaps of; unfasten.

un·snarl (un·snärl′) v.t. To disentangle.

un·so·cia·ble (un·sō′shə·bəl) adj. 1. Not sociable; not inclined to seek the society of others. 2. Not congenial or in accord. 3. Not encouraging social intercourse. — **un·so′cia·bil′i·ty**, **un·so′cia·ble·ness** n. — **un·so′cia·bly** adv.

un·sol·der (un·sod′ər) v.t. 1. To disunite or take apart (something soldered). 2. To separate; sunder.

un·so·phis·ti·cat·ed (un′sə·fis′tə·kā′tid) adj. 1. Not sophisticated; artless; simple. 2. Free from adulteration; genuine; pure. — **un′so·phis′ti·cat′ed·ly** adv. — **un′so·phis′ti·cat′ed·ness** n.

un·sound (un·sound′) adj. 1. Lacking in soundness; not strong or solid; weak. 2. Not sound in health; diseased. 3.

Not logically valid; erroneous. 4. Disturbed; not profound: said of sleep. — **un·sound′ly** adv. — **un·sound′ness** n.

un·spar·ing (un·spâr′ing) adj. 1. Not sparing or saving; lavish; liberal. 2. Showing no mercy. — **un·spar′ing·ly** adv. — **un·spar′ing·ness** n.

un·speak·a·ble (un·spē′kə·bəl) adj. 1. That cannot be expressed; unutterable. 2. Extremely bad or objectionable. — **un·speak′a·ble·ness** n. — **un·speak′a·bly** adv.

un·sta·ble (un·stā′bəl) adj. 1. Lacking in stability or firmness; not stable. 2. Having no fixed purposes; easily influenced; inconstant. 3. Chem. Readily decomposable, as certain compounds. — **un·sta′ble·ness** n. — **un·sta′bly** adv.

un·stead·y (un·sted′ē) adj. 1. Not steady or firm; shaky. 2. Not regular or constant; wavering: the motor's unsteady movement. 3. Inconstant and erratic in behavior, habits, etc. — **un·stead′i·ly** adv. — **un·stead′i·ness** n.

un·stop (un·stop′) v.t. **·stopped**, **·stop·ping** 1. To remove a stopper from. 2. To open by removing obstructions; clear.

un·strap (un·strap′) v.t. **·strapped**, **·strap·ping** To unfasten or loosen the strap or straps of.

un·string (un·string′) v.t. **·strung**, **·string·ing** 1. To remove from a string. 2. To take the string or strings from. 3. To loosen the string or strings of. 4. To weaken: usu., in the passive: Her nerves were unstrung.

un·strung (un·strung′) adj. 1. Having the strings removed or relaxed. 2. Unnerved; emotionally upset; weakened.

un·stud·ied (un·stud′ēd) adj. 1. Not planned; unpremeditated. 2. Not stiff or artificial; natural. 3. Not acquainted through study; unversed: with in.

un·sub·stan·tial (un′səb·stan′shəl) adj. 1. Lacking solidity, strength, or weight. 2. Having no valid basis. 3. Having no bodily existence; unreal; fanciful. — **un′sub·stan′tial·ly** adv. — **un′sub·stan′ti·al′i·ty** (-shē·al′ə·tē) n.

un·suit·a·ble (un·sōō′tə·bəl) adj. Not suitable; unfitting. — **un·suit·a·bil′i·ty** (un′sōō·tə·bil′ə·tē), **un·suit′a·ble·ness** n. — **un·suit′a·bly** adv.

un·sung (un·sung′) adj. 1. Not celebrated in song or poetry; obscure. 2. Not yet sung, as a song.

un·tan·gle (un·tang′gəl) v.t. **·gled**, **·gling** 1. To free from entanglement or snarls. 2. To clear up; resolve.

un·taught (un·tôt′) adj. 1. Not instructed; ignorant. 2. Acquired without training or instruction; natural.

un·ten·a·ble (un·ten′ə·bəl) adj. That cannot be maintained or defended: untenable theories. — **un·ten′a·bil′i·ty**, **un·ten′a·ble·ness** n.

un·thank·ful (un·thangk′fəl) adj. 1. Not grateful. 2. Not received with thanks; unwelcome. — **un·thank′ful·ly** adv. — **un·thank′ful·ness** n.

un·think·ing (un·thingk′ing) adj. 1. Not having the power of thought. 2. Thoughtless; careless; heedless; inconsiderate. — **un·think′ing·ly** adv. — **un·think′ing·ness** n.

un·thought-of (un·thôt′uv′) adj. 1. Not remembered or called to mind. 2. Not conceived of; not discovered.

un·thread (un·thred′) v.t. 1. To remove the thread from, as a needle. 2. To find one's way out of, as a maze.

un·ti·dy (un·tī′dē) adj. **·di·er**, **·di·est** Showing lack of tidiness. [ME untidi] — **un·ti′di·ly** adv. — **un·ti′di·ness** n.

un·tie (un·tī′) v. **·tied**, **·ty·ing** v.t. 1. To loosen or undo, as a knot. 2. To free from restraint. 3. To clear up or resolve. — v.i. 4. To become untied. [OE untīgan]

un·til (un·til′) prep. 1. Up to the time of; till: We will wait until midnight. 2. Before: used with a negative: The music doesn't begin until nine. — conj. 1. To the time when: until I die. 2. To the place or degree that: Walk east until you reach the river. 3. Before: with a negative: He couldn't leave until noon. [ME < un- up to, as far as + TILL]

un·time·ly (un·tīm′lē) adj. 1. Before the proper or expected time; premature. 2. At the wrong time; ill-timed. — adv. Inopportunely. — **un·time′li·ness** n.

un·to (un′tōō) prep. 1. Poetic & Archaic To. 2. Archaic Until. [ME un- up to, as far as + TO]

un·told (un·tōld′) adj. 1. That cannot be revealed or described; inexpressible: untold misery. 2. That cannot be numbered or estimated: untold numbers. 3. Not told.

un·touch·a·ble (un·tuch′ə·bəl) adj. 1. Inaccessible to the touch; out of reach. 2. Intangible; unrivaled; unapproachable. 3. Forbidden to the touch. 4. Unpleasant, vile, or dangerous to touch. — n. In India, a member of the lowest caste, whose touch was formerly counted as pollution by Hindus of higher station. — **un′touch·a·bil′i·ty** (-bil′ə·tē) n.

un·to·ward (un·tôrd′, -tōrd′) adj. 1. Causing hindrance; vexatious. 2. Refractory; perverse. 3. Unseemly; uncouth. — **un·to′ward·ly** adv. — **un·to′ward·ness** n.

un·trod·den (un·trod′n) adj. Not having been trodden upon; also, unfrequented. Also **un·trod′**.

un·true (un·trōō′) adj. 1. Lacking truth; not true; not corresponding with fact. 2. Not conforming to rule or standard. 3. Not faithful; disloyal. — **un·tru′ly** adv.

un·truss (un·trus′) *v.t.* **1.** To unfasten. **2.** *Obs.* To undress.

un·truth (un·trōōth′) *n. pl.* **·truths** (-trōōths′, -trōōthz′) **1.** The quality or character of being untrue; want of veracity. **2.** A lie. — *Syn.* See LIE². [OE *untrēowth*]

un·truth·ful (un·trōōth′fəl) *adj.* **1.** Not truthful; untrue. **2.** Given to telling lies. — **un·truth′ful·ly** *adv.* — **un·truth′ful·ness** *n.*

un·tu·tored (un·tōō′tərd, -tyōō′-) *adj.* **1.** Having had no tutor or teacher. **2.** Naive; simple.

un·twine (un·twīn′) *v.* **·twined, ·twin·ing** *v.t.* **1.** To undo (something twined); unwind by disentangling. — *v.i.* **2.** To become untwined.

un·twist (un·twist′) *v.t. & v.i.* To unwind or untwine.

un·used (un·yōōzd′ *for def. 1*; un·yōōst′ *for def. 2*) *adj.* **1.** Not made use of; also, never having been used. **2.** Not accustomed or wont: with *to*.

un·u·su·al (un·yōō′zhōō·əl) *adj.* Not usual, common, or ordinary; rare. — **un·u′su·al·ly** *adv.* — **un·u′su·al·ness** *n.*

un·ut·ter·a·ble (un·ut′ər·ə·bəl) *adj.* **1.** Too great or deep for verbal expression; ineffable. **2.** Unpronounceable. — **un·ut′ter·a·ble·ness** *n.* — **un·ut′ter·a·bly** *adv.*

un·var·nished (un·vär′nisht) *adj.* **1.** Having no covering of varnish. **2.** Having no embellishment; plain.

un·veil (un·vāl′) *v.t.* **1.** To remove the veil from; reveal. — *v.i.* **2.** To remove one's veil; reveal oneself.

un·voiced (un·voist′) *adj.* **1.** Not expressed. **2.** *Phonet.* **a** Voiceless. **b** Rendered voiceless: The final (v) in "have" is often heard *unvoiced* in "have to."

un·war·y (un·wâr′ē) *adj.* Not careful or cautious; imprudent; rash; careless. — **un·war′i·ly** *adv.* — **un·war′i·ness** *n.*

un·well (un·wel′) *adj.* Not well; ailing; sick. — *Syn.* See SICK¹. — **un·well′ness** *n.*

un·wept (un·wept′) *adj.* **1.** Not lamented or wept for, as a deceased person. **2.** Not shed, as tears.

un·whole·some (un·hōl′səm) *adj.* **1.** Harmful to physical or mental health. **2.** Unsound in condition; diseased or decayed: *unwholesome* provisions. **3.** Suggestive of illness or disease: an *unwholesome* look. **4.** Morally bad; pernicious. — **un·whole′some·ly** *adv.* — **un·whole′some·ness** *n.*

un·wield·y (un·wēl′dē) *adj.* Moved or managed with difficulty, as from great size or awkward shape; bulky; clumsy. — **un·wield′i·ly** *adv.* — **un·wield′i·ness** *n.*

un·will·ing (un·wil′ing) *adj.* **1.** Not willing; reluctant; loath. **2.** Done, said, etc., with reluctance. — **un·will′ing·ly** *adv.* — **un·will′ing·ness** *n.*

un·wind (un·wīnd′) *v.* **·wound, ·wind·ing** *v.t.* **1.** To reverse the winding of; untwist or wind off; uncoil. **2.** To disentangle. — *v.i.* **3.** To become unwound.

un·wise (un·wīz′) *adj.* Showing a lack of wisdom; imprudent; foolish. [OE *unwīs*] — **un·wise′ly** *adv.*

un·wit·ting (un·wit′ing) *adj.* **1.** Having no knowledge or consciousness of the thing in question. **2.** Unintentional. [OE *unwitende*] — **un·wit′ting·ly** *adv.*

un·wont·ed (un·wun′tid, -won′-) *adj.* **1.** Not according to habit or custom; unusual. **2.** *Obs.* Not accustomed; unfamiliar. — **un·wont′ed·ly** *adv.* — **un·wont′ed·ness** *n.*

un·wor·thy (un·wûr′thē) *adj.* **1.** Not deserving: usu., with *of.* **2.** Not befitting or becoming: often with *of*; improper. **3.** Lacking worth or merit. **4.** Shameful; contemptible. — **un·wor′thi·ly** *adv.* — **un·wor′thi·ness** *n.*

un·wound (un·wound′) Past tense and past participle of UNWIND.

un·wrap (un·rap′) *v.* **·wrapped, ·wrap·ping** *v.t.* **1.** To take the wrapping from. — *v.i.* **2.** To become unwrapped.

un·wrin·kle (un·ring′kəl) *v.t.* **·kled, ·kling** To free from wrinkles; smooth.

un·writ·ten (un·rit′n) *adj.* **1.** Not written or in writing. **2.** Not reduced to writing; traditional; customary. **3.** Having no writing upon it; blank.

unwritten law **1.** A rule or custom established by general usage. **2.** Common law (which see). **3.** A custom in some communities granting a measure of immunity to those who commit criminal acts of revenge in support of personal or family honor, esp., in cases of adultery, etc.

un·yoke (un·yōk′) *v.* **·yoked, ·yok·ing** *v.t.* **1.** To release from a yoke. **2.** To separate; part. — *v.i.* **3.** To become unyoked. **4.** To stop work; cease. [OE *ungeocian*]

up (up) *adv.* **1.** From a lower to a higher place, level, position, etc.: Come *up*. **2.** In, on, or to a higher place, level, position, etc. **3.** Toward that which is figuratively or conventionally higher; as: **a** To or at a higher price. **b** To or at a higher place, rank, etc. **c** To or at a greater size or amount: to swell *up*. **d** To or at a place that is locally or arbitrarily regarded as higher: *up* north. **e** Above the surface or horizon. **f** From an earlier to a later period. **g** To a source, conclusion, etc.: Follow *up* this lead. **4.** To a vertical position; standing; also, out of bed. **5.** So as to be compact or secure: Tie *up* the boxes. **6.** So as to be even with in space, time, degree, etc.: *up* to date. **7.** In or into an excited state or some specific action: They were stirred *up* to mutiny. **8.** In or

into view or existence: to draw *up* a will. **9.** In or into prominence; under consideration: *up* for debate. **10.** In or into a place of safekeeping; aside: Fruits are put *up* in jars. **11.** At an end: Your time is *up*. **12.** Completely; totally: The house was burned *up*. **13.** In baseball and cricket, at bat. **14.** In tennis and other sports: **a** In the lead; ahead. **b** Apiece; alike: said of a score. **15.** Running for as a candidate. **16.** *Naut.* Shifted to windward, as a tiller. ◆ In informal usage *up* is often added to a verb without affecting the meaning of the sentence: to light *up* a room. — **to be all up with** To be all over for. — **to be up against** *Informal* To meet with; confront. — **to be up at it** *Informal* To be in difficulty. — **to be up in** (or on) *Informal* To be well informed in or skilled at something. — **to be up to 1.** *Informal* To be doing or plotting. **2.** To be equal to; be capable of. **3.** To be incumbent upon; be dependent upon: It's *up* to him to save us. — *adj.* **1.** Moving, sloping, or directed upward. **2.** At stake, as in gambling. **3.** *Informal* Going on; taking place: What's *up*? **4.** *Informal* Acquainted (with), equal (to): He is *up* in that subject. **5.** In golf, in advance of an opponent by a specified number of holes. **6.** Rising, risen, overflowing, or at flood. **7.** In an active or excited state: His temper was *up*. — **up and around** *Informal* Sufficiently recovered to walk. — **up to no good** Engaged in or contemplating some mischief. — *prep.* **1.** From a lower to a higher point or place of, on, or along. **2.** Toward a higher condition or rank on or in. **3.** To or at a point farther above or along: *up* the road. **4.** From the coast toward the interior of (a country). **5.** From the mouth toward the source of (a river). **6.** At, on, or near the height or top of. — *n.* **1.** A rise or ascent. **2.** A period of prosperity, etc.: chiefly in the phrase **ups and downs**. — **to be on the up and up 1.** *Slang* To be honest. **2.** *Informal* Rising and improving. — *v.* **upped, up·ping** *Informal* *v.t.* **1.** To increase. **2.** To put or take up. — *v.i.* **3.** To rise. [OE *ūp*]

up- *combining form* As a combining element *up* has adverbial force with various meanings: **1.** To a higher place or level, as in: **upgaze, uprise**. **2.** To a greater size or larger amount, as in: **upflooding, upswell**. **3.** To a vertical position, as in: **upprop, upstand**. **4.** In or into commotion or activity, as in: **upboil, upstir**. **5.** Completely; wholly, as in: **upbind, upgather**.

up-and-com·ing (up′ən·kum′ing) *adj.* Enterprising; energetic; promising.

up-and-down (up′ən·doun′) *adj.* **1.** Alternately rising and falling; fluctuating; varying: an *up-and-down* motion; an *up-and-down* career. **2.** Vertical; perpendicular.

u·pas (yōō′pəs) *n.* **1.** A tall evergreen Javanese tree of the mulberry family, having an acrid, poisonous sap. **2.** This sap. [< Malay (*pohon*) *upas* poison (tree)]

up·beat (up′bēt′) *n. Music* The relatively unaccented beat that precedes the downbeat. — *adj. Slang* Characterized by a lively, swinging rhythm.

up·braid (up·brād′) *v.t.* **1.** To reproach for some wrongdoing; scold or reprove. — *v.i.* **2.** To utter reproaches. [OE < *up-* up + *bregdan* to weave, twist] — **up·braid′er** *adj.* — **up·braid′ing** *n.* — **up·braid′ing·ly** *adv.*

up·bring·ing (up′bring′ing) *n.* The rearing and training received by a person during childhood.

up·coun·try (*n. & adj.* up′kun′trē; *adv.* up′kun′trē) *Informal n.* **a.** Country remote from the coast or from lowlands; inland country. — *adj.* Living in, from, or characteristic of inland places. — *adv.* In or toward the interior.

up·date (up·dāt′) *v.t.* **·dat·ed, ·dat·ing** To bring up to date; to revise, with corrections, additions, etc., as a textbook.

up·end (up′end′) *v.t. & v.i.* To set or stand on end.

up·grade (*n.* up′grād′; *v.* up·grād′; *adv.* up′grād′) *n.* An upward incline or slope. — *v.t.* **·grad·ed, ·grad·ing** To raise to a higher grade, rank, post, etc. — *adv.* Up a hill or slope. — **on the upgrade 1.** Improving. **2.** Rising.

up·heav·al (up·hē′vəl) *n.* **1.** The act of upheaving, or the state of being upheaved. **2.** A violent disturbance or change.

up·heave (up·hēv′) *v.* **·heaved** or **·hove, ·heav·ing** *v.t.* **1.** To heave or raise up. — *v.i.* **2.** To be raised or lifted.

up·held (up·held′) Past tense and past participle of UPHOLD.

up·hill (*adv. & adj.* up′hil′; *n.* up′hil′) *adv.* Up or as up a hill or an ascent; against difficulties. — *adj.* **1.** Going up an ascent; sloping upward. **2.** Attended with difficulty or exertion. **3.** At a high place. — *n.* An upward slope.

up·hold (up·hōld′) *v.t.* **·held, ·hold·ing 1.** To hold up; raise. **2.** To keep from falling. **3.** To support; agree with; encourage. **4.** To regard with approval. — **up·hold′er** *n.*

up·hol·ster (up·hōl′stər) *v.t.* To fit, as furniture, with coverings, cushioning, etc. [Back formation < UPHOLSTERER]

up·hol·ster·er (up·hōl′stər·ər) *n.* One who upholsters. [alter. of < ME *upholder* tradesman]

up·hol·ster·y (up·hōl′stər·ē, -strē) *n. pl.* **·ster·ies 1.** Fabric and fittings used in upholstering. **2.** The act, art, or business of upholstering.

up·keep (up′kēp′) *n.* The act or state of maintaining something; also, the cost of maintenance.

up·land (up′lənd, -land′) *n.* **1.** The higher portions of a region, district, farm, etc. **2.** The country in the interior. — *adj.* Pertaining to or situated in an upland.

up·lift (*v.* up·lift′; *adj.*, *n.* up′lift′) *v.t.* **1.** To lift up; elevate. **2.** To raise the tone of; put on a higher plane, mentally or morally. — *n.* **1.** The act of raising, or the fact of being raised. **2.** A movement upward. **3.** Mental or spiritual stimulation or elevation. **4.** A movement aiming to improve the condition of the underprivileged. **5.** A brassiere designed to lift and support the breasts. — **up·lift′er** *n.*

up·most (up′mōst′) *adj.* Uppermost.

up·on (ə·pon′, ə·pôn′) *prep.* On, in all its meanings. — *adv.* On: completing a verbal idea: The paper has been written *upon.* [ME]
◆ **upon, on** *Upon* now differs little in use from *on,* the former being sometimes used for reasons of euphony and also when motion into position is involved. When *upon* means *up* and *on,* it is written as two words: Let's go *up on* the roof.

up·per (up′ər) *adj.* **1.** Higher than something else; being above. **2.** Higher or further inland in location, place, etc. **3.** Higher in station, rank, dignity, etc.; superior. — **to get the upper hand** To get the advantage. — *n.* **1.** That part of a boot or shoe above the sole; the vamp. **2.** *Informal* An upper berth. — **on one's uppers** *Informal* **1.** Having worn out the soles of one's shoes. **2.** At the end of one's resources; destitute. [ME, orig. compar. of UP]

Up·per (up′ər) *adj. Geol.* Designating a later period or a later formation of a specified period: the *Upper* Cambrian.

upper berth The top berth in a ship, railroad sleeping car, etc., where two bunks or beds are built one above the other.

up·per-brack·et (up′ər·brak′it) *adj.* Of or belonging to a higher bracket or level: an *upper-bracket* income.

upper case *Printing* **1.** Type for capital letters. See CASE². **2.** The capital letters of the alphabet.

up·per-case (up′ər·kās′) *Printing adj.* Of, in, or indicating capital letters, as distinguished from small letters. — *v.t.* **-cased, -cas·ing** To set as or change to capital letters.

upper class The socially or economically superior group in society. — **up′per-class′** (up′ər·klas′, -kläs′) *adj.*

up·per-class·man (up′ər·klas′mən, -kläs′-) *n.* *pl.* **-men** (-mən) A junior or senior in a school or college.

up·per-cut (up′ər·kut′) *n.* In boxing, a swinging blow upward, delivered under or inside the opponent's guard. — *v.t. & v.i.* **-cut, -cut·ting** To strike with an uppercut.

upper hand Advantage: to get the *upper hand.*

Upper House The branch, in a bicameral legislature, where membership is usu., smaller and more restricted, as the British House of Lords. Also **upper house.**

up·per·most (up′ər·mōst′) *adj.* **1.** Highest in place, rank, authority, influence, etc. **2.** First to come into the mind: one's *uppermost* thoughts. Also *upmost.* — *adv.* In the highest place, rank, authority, etc.; also, first, as in time.

up·pish (up′ish) *adj. Informal* Inclined to be self-assertive, pretentious, or snobbish. Also **up·pi·ty** (up′ə·tē). — **up′pish·ly** *adv.* — **up′pish·ness** *n.*

up·raise (up·rāz′) *v.t.* **raised, rais·ing** To lift up; elevate.

up·right (up′rīt′) *adj.* **1.** Being in a vertical position; straight up; erect. **2.** Just and honest. — *n.* **1.** Something having a vertical position, as an upright piano. **2.** The state of being upright. **3.** In football, one of the goal posts. — *adv.* In an upright position; vertically. [OE < *ŭp-* up + *riht* right] — **up′right·ly** *adv.* — **up′right·ness** *n.*

upright piano A piano smaller than a grand piano, having strings arranged vertically in a rectangular case.

up·ris·ing (up·rī′zing, up′rī′zing) *n.* **1.** The act of rising. **2.** A revolt or insurrection. **3.** An ascent; a slope.

up·roar (up′rôr′, -rōr′) *n.* A violent disturbance, noise, or tumult. [< Du. < *op-* up + *roeren* to stir]

up·roar·i·ous (up·rôr′ē·əs, -rōr′ē-) *adj.* **1.** Accompanied by or making an uproar. **2.** Loud and noisy; tumultuous. **3.** Very funny: an *uproarious* play. — **up·roar′i·ous·ly** *adv.* — **up·roar′i·ous·ness** *n.*

up·root (up·rōōt′, -rŏŏt′) *v.t.* **1.** To tear up by the roots. **2.** To destroy utterly; eradicate. — **up·root′er** *n.*

up·set (*v.* up·set′; *adj.* up·set′, up′set′; *n.* up′set′) *v.* **-set, -set·ting** *v.t.* **1.** To overturn. **2.** To throw into confusion or disorder. **3.** To disconcert, derange, or disquiet. **4.** To defeat, esp., unexpectedly. — *v.i.* **5.** To become overturned. — *adj.* **1.** Tipped or turned over. **2.** Mentally or physically disturbed or ill. **3.** Confused; disordered. — *n.* **1.** The act of upsetting, or the state of being upset. **2.** *Informal* An unexpected defeat. **3.** A mental or physical disturbance or disorder. — **up·set′ter** *n.*

up·shot (up′shot′) *n.* The final outcome; result.

up·side (up′sīd′) *n.* The upper side or part.

up·side-down (up′sīd′doun′) *adj.* Having the upper side down; in disorder. — *adv.* With the upper side down. Also **upside down.** [< ME *up so down* up as if down]

up·si·lon (yōōp′sə·lon, up′sə·lon, *Brit.* yōōp·sī′lən) *n.* The twentieth letter and sixth vowel in the Greek alphabet (Υ, υ). See ALPHABET, Y. [< Gk. < *u* u + *psilon* smooth]

up·stage (up′stāj′) *adj.* **1.** Of the back half of a stage. **2.** *Informal* Haughty; supercilious. — *adv.* Toward or on the back of a stage. — *v.t.* **staged, stag·ing 1.** To steal a scene from. **2.** *Informal* To treat in a haughty manner.

up·stairs (up′stârz′) *adj.* Pertaining to an upper story. — *n.* An upper story; esp., the part of a building above the ground floor. — *adv.* In, to, or toward an upper story. — **to kick upstairs** To promote so as to get out of the way.

up·stand·ing (up·stan′ding) *adj.* **1.** Honest; upright; straightforward. **2.** Standing up; erect.

up·start (*v.* up·stärt′; *adj. & n.* up′stärt′) *v.i.* To start or spring up suddenly. — *adj.* **1.** Suddenly raised to prominence, wealth, or power. **2.** Characteristic of an upstart; vulgar; pretentious. — *n.* **1.** One who or that which springs up suddenly. **2.** One who has suddenly risen from a humble position to one of wealth or importance and is usu. arrogant in tone or bearing.

up·state (up′stāt′) *U.S. adj.* Of, from, or designating that part of a State lying outside, usu. north, of the principal city. — *n.* The outlying, usu. northern, sections of a State. — *adv.* In or toward such sections. — **up′stat′er** *n.*

up·stream (up′strēm′) *adv.* Toward or at the source or upper part of a stream; against the current.

up·stretched (up′strecht′) *adj.* Stretched or extended upward: *upstretched* arms.

up·stroke (up′strōk′) *n.* An upward stroke, as of a pen.

up·surge (*v.* up·sûrj′; *n.* up′sûrj′) *v.i.* **surged, surg·ing** To surge up. — *n.* A surge or swell upward.

up·sweep (*n.* up′swēp′; *v.* up·swēp′) *n.* A sweeping up or upward; esp., a hairdo that is swept upward smoothly in the back and piled high on the top of the head. — *v.t. & v.i.* **·swept, ·sweep·ing** To brush or sweep upward or up.

up·swing (*n.* up′swing′; *v.* up·swing′) *n.* **1.** A swinging upward. **2.** An improvement. — *v.i.* **·swung, ·swing·ing 1.** To swing upward. **2.** To improve.

up·take (up′tāk′) *n.* **1.** The act of lifting or taking up. **2.** A boiler flue that unites the combustion gases and carries them toward the smokestack. **3.** An upward ventilating shaft in a mine. — **to be on** (or **in**) **the uptake** *Informal* To demonstrate mental comprehension or perception.

up·throw (up′thrō′) *n.* **1.** A throwing upward; an upheaval. **2.** *Geol.* An upward displacement of the rock on one side of a fault.

up·thrust (up′thrust′) *n.* **1.** An upward thrust. **2.** *Geol.* An upheaval of rocks in the earth's crust.

up·tight (up′tīt′) *adj. U.S. Slang* Uneasy, anxious, or tense; nervous. Also **up′-tight′, up tight.**

up-to-date (up′tə·dāt′) *adj.* **1.** Having the latest information, improvements, etc. **2.** Modern in manner.

up to date To the present time.

up·town (up′toun′) *adv.* In or toward the upper part of a town. — *adj.* Of, pertaining to, or resident in the upper part of a town or city, or the part that is regarded as the upper part. — *n.* The upper part of a town or city.

up·turn (*v.* up·tûrn′; *n.* up′tûrn′) *v.t.* **1.** To turn up or over, as sod with the plow. **2.** To overturn; upset. — *n.* A turning upward; an increase; an improvement.

up·ward (up′wərd) *adv.* **1.** In, to, or toward a higher place or position. **2.** To or toward the source, origin, etc.: to trace a stream *upward.* **3.** Toward a higher rank, amount, age, etc. **4.** Toward that which is better, nobler, etc. **5.** In excess; more. Also **up′wards.** — **upward** (or **upwards**) **of** Higher than; in excess of. — *adj.* In, on, turned, or directed toward a higher place. — **up′ward·ly** *adv.*

ur-¹ Var. of URO-¹.

ur-² Var. of URO-².

Ur (ûr) An ancient city of Sumer, southern Mesopotamia, the site of which is on the Euphrates in SE Iraq. Old Testament **Ur of the Chal·dees** (kal·dēz′, kal′dēz).

u·rae·mi·a (yŏŏ·rē′mē·ə), **u·rae·mic** (yŏŏ·rē′mik) See URE·MIA, etc.

U·ral-Al·ta·ic (yŏŏr′əl·al·tā′ik) *n.* A hypothesized family of languages comprising the Uralic and Altaic subfamilies. — *adj.* **1.** Of or pertaining to the Ural and Altai mountain ranges. **2.** Of, pertaining to, or designating the Ural-Altaic languages or the peoples speaking these languages.

U·ral·ic (yŏŏ·ral′ik) *n.* A family of languages comprising the Finno-Ugric and Samoyedic subfamilies: sometimes classified with Altaic in a Ural-Altaic family. — *adj.* Of or pertaining to this family. Also **U·ra·li·an** (yŏŏ·rā′lē·ən).

u·ra·nal·y·sis (yŏŏr′ə·nal′ə·sis) See URINALYSIS.

U·ra·ni·a (yŏŏ·rā′nē·ə) The Muse of astronomy. [< L < Gk. *ouranos* heaven]

U·ra·ni·an (yŏŏ·rā′nē·ən) *adj.* **1.** Of or pertaining to the planet Uranus. **2.** Celestial.

u·ra·ni·um (yŏŏ·rā′nē·əm) *n.* A heavy, white, radioactive, metallic element (symbol U), found only in combination. It is important in the generation of atomic energy. See ELEMENT. [< URANUS]

urano- *combining form Astron.* The heavens; of or pertaining to the heavens, or to celestial bodies. Also, before vowels, **uran-.** [< Gk. *ouranos* heaven]

U·ra·nus (yŏŏr′ə·nəs) In Greek mythology, the son and husband of Gaea (Earth) and father of the Titans, Furies, and Cyclopes, overthrown by his son Cronus. — *n.* The third largest planet of the solar system and seventh in order from the sun. See PLANET. [< L < Gk. < *ouranos* heaven]

u·ra·re (yŏŏ·rä′rē) *n.* Curare. Also **u·ra′ri.** [Var. of CURARE]

ur·ban (ûr′bən) *adj.* 1. Pertaining to, characteristic of, including, or constituting a city. 2. Situated or dwelling in a city. [< L *urbanus.* See URBANE.]

urban district An administrative subdivision of a county of England, Wales, or Northern Ireland, usu. comprising several thickly populated communities.

ur·bane (ûr·bān′) *adj.* Characterized by or having refinement or elegance, esp. in manner; suave. [< L *urbs, urbis* city] — **ur·bane′ly** *adv.* — **ur·bane′ness** *n.*

ur·ban·ism (ûr′bən·iz′əm) *n.* The character or condition of the life of people living in urban areas.

ur·ban·i·ty (ûr·ban′ə·tē) *n. pl.* **·ties** 1. The character or quality of being urbane; refined or elegant courtesy. 2. *pl.* Amenities or courtesies. [< F or L < *urbs, urbis* city]

ur·ban·ize (ûr′bən·īz) *v.t.* **·ized, ·iz·ing** To render urban, as in character or manner. — **ur′ban·i·za′tion** *n.*

urban renewal The planned upgrading of a deteriorating urban area, usu. using public funds and coordinated by a local government agency.

ur·chin (ûr′chin) *n.* 1. A roguish, mischievous boy. 2. A cylinder in a carding machine. 3. A sea urchin. [ME < OF < L *ericius* hedgehog < *er* hedgehog]

Ur·du (ŏŏr′dŏŏ, ŏŏr·dŏŏ′, ûr′dŏŏ) *n.* A variety of Hindustani spoken by Moslems in India, containing many Persian and Arabic elements and written in a Persian-Arabic script: the official language of Pakistan. [< Hind. < Turkish *ordū* camp < Persian *urdū*]

-ure *suffix of nouns* 1. The act, process, or result of: *pressure.* 2. The function, rank, or office of: *prefecture.* 3. The means or instrument of: *ligature.* [< F < L *-ura*]

u·re·a (yŏŏ·rē′ə) *n. Biochem.* A colorless crystalline compound, CO(NH₂)₂, formed in the body, and also made synthetically, used in medicine and in the making of plastics and fertilizers. [< NL < F < Gk. *ouron*] — **u·re′al** *adj.*

u·re·mi·a (yŏŏ·rē′mē·ə) *n. Pathol.* A condition of the blood due to the presence of urinary constituents ordinarily excreted by the kidneys. Also *uraemia.* — **u·re′mic** *adj.*

-uret *suffix Chem.* Used to denote a compound: now replaced by *-ide.* [< F < *-ure.* See -URE.]

u·re·ter (yŏŏ·rē′tər) *n. Anat.* The duct by which urine passes from the kidney to the bladder or the cloaca. For illus. see KIDNEY. [< NL < Gk. < *ourein* to urinate] — **u·re′ter·al, u·re·ter·ic** (yŏŏr′ə·ter′ik) *adj.*

u·re·thra (yŏŏ·rē′thrə) *n. Anat.* The duct by which urine is discharged from the bladder of most mammals, and which, in males, carries the seminal discharge. — **u·re′thral** *adj.*

urethro- *combining form Med.* The urethra; of or pertaining to the urethra. Also, before vowels, **urethr-.** [< Gk. *ourēthra* the urethra]

u·ret·ic (yŏŏ·ret′ik) *adj. Med.* Of or pertaining to the urine; urinary. [< LL *ureticus* < Gk. *ourētikos* < *ouron* urine]

urge (ûrj) *v.* **urged, urg·ing** *v.t.* 1. To drive or force forward; impel; push. 2. To plead with or entreat earnestly, as with arguments or explanations. 3. To press or argue the doing, consideration, or acceptance of. 4. To move or force to some course or action. 5. To stimulate or excite. 6. To ply or use vigorously, as oars. — *v.i.* 7. To present or press arguments, claims, etc. 8. To exert an impelling or prompting force. — **Syn.** See ACTUATE. — *n.* 1. A strong impulse to perform a certain act. 2. The act of urging; the state of being urged. [< L *urgere* to drive, urge]

ur·gen·cy (ûr′jən·sē) *n. pl.* **·cies** 1. The quality of being urgent. 2. Pressure by entreaty; pressure of necessity. 3. The act of urging. 4. Something urgent.

ur·gent (ûr′jənt) *adj.* 1. Characterized by urging or importunity; requiring prompt attention; pressing. 2. Eagerly importunate or insistent. — **ur′gent·ly** *adv.*

-urgy *combining form* Development of or work with a (specified) material or product: *metallurgy, chemurgy.* [< Gk. *-ourgia* < *ergon* work]

-uria *combining form Pathol.* A (specified) condition of the urine: usu. used to indicate disease or abnormality. [< NL < Gk. *ouria* < *ouron* urine]

U·ri·ah (yŏŏ·rī′ə) A Hittite captain in the Israelite army, husband of Bathsheba, treacherously sent to his death by David, II *Sam.* xi 15–17.

u·ric (yŏŏr′ik) *adj.* Of, pertaining to, or derived from urine.

uric acid *Biochem.* A colorless dibasic acid, C₅H₄N₄O₃, of varying crystalline forms and slight solubility, found in the urine of man and animals and, in man, forming the nucleus of most urinary and renal calculi.

u·ri·nal (yŏŏr′ə·nəl) *n.* 1. An upright wall fixture with facilities for flushing, for men's use in urination; also the room containing such a fixture. 2. A glass receptacle for urine.

u·ri·nal·y·sis (yŏŏr′ə·nal′ə·sis) *n. pl.* **·ses** (-sēz) Chemical analysis of the urine: also spelled *uranalysis.*

u·ri·nar·y (yŏŏr′ə·ner′ē) *adj.* Of, pertaining to, or involved in the production and excretion of urine: the *urinary* organs. — *n. pl.* **·nar·ies** 1. A reservoir for storing urine, etc., for use as manure. 2. A urinal.

u·ri·nate (yŏŏr′ə·nāt) *v.i.* **·nat·ed, ·nat·ing** To void or pass urine. [< Med.L *urinatus*, pp. of *urinare* to pass urine < *urina* urine] — **u′ri·na′tion** *n.*

u·rine (yŏŏr′in) *n.* A liquid containing body wastes, secreted by the kidneys, stored in the bladder, and voided through the urethra. [< F < L *urina*]

urino- *combining form* Urine. Also, before vowels, **urin-,** as in *urinalysis.* [< L *urina* urine]

u·ri·no·gen·i·tal (yŏŏr′ə·nō·jen′ə·təl) *adj.* Urogenital.

u·ri·nos·co·py (yŏŏr′ə·nos′kə·pē) *n. pl.* **·pies** *Med.* Uroscopy.

u·ri·nous (yŏŏr′ə·nəs) *adj.* Of, pertaining to, containing, or resembling urine. Also **u′ri·nose** (-nōs).

urn (ûrn) *n.* 1. A rounded or angular vase having a foot, variously used in antiquity as a receptacle for the ashes of the dead, a water vessel, etc. 2. A vessel for preserving the ashes of the dead. 3. In ancient Rome, a receptacle used to hold lots drawn in voting. 4. A vase-shaped receptacle having a faucet, and designed for keeping tea, coffee, etc., hot, as by means of a spirit lamp. [< L *urna*]

uro-¹ *combining form* Urine; pertaining to urine or to the urinary tract: *urology.* Also, before vowels, **ur-.** [< Gk. *ouron* urine]

uro-² *combining form* A tail; of or related to the tail; caudal. Also, before vowels, **ur-.** [< Gk. *oura* tail]

u·ro·gen·i·tal (yŏŏr′ō·jen′ə·təl) *adj.* Of or pertaining to the urinary and genital organs and their functions.

u·rol·o·gy (yŏŏ·rol′ə·jē) *n.* The branch of medicine that deals with the urine and the genitourinary tract. — **u·ro·log·ic** (yŏŏr′ə·loj′ik) or **·i·cal** *adj.* — **u·rol′o·gist** *n.*

u·ros·co·py (yŏŏ·ros′kə·pē) *n. pl.* **·pies** *Med.* Diagnosis by examination of the urine: also *urinoscopy.* — **u·ro·scop·ic** (yŏŏr′ə·skop′ik) *adj.* — **u·ros′co·pist** *n.*

ur·sa (ûr′sə) *n. Latin* A she-bear: used in the phrases *Ursa Major* and *Ursa Minor.*

Ursa Major A constellation, the Great Bear, containing seven bright stars: also called *Big Dipper, Charles's Wain.* [< L]

Ursa Minor A constellation, the Lesser Bear, containing the polestar Polaris: also called *Cynosure, Little Bear, Little Dipper.* [< L]

URSA MAJOR (*a*) AND URSA MINOR (*b*)
c Polestar.
d,d Pointers.

ur·sine (ûr′sīn, -sin) *adj.* 1. Pertaining to or like a bear. 2. Clothed with dense bristles, as certain caterpillars. [< L *ursinus* < *ursus* bear]

Ur·su·line (ûr′syə·lin, -sə-, -līn) *adj.* Pertaining to Saint Ursula or to an order of nuns founded in 1537, and engaged chiefly in the education of girls. — *n.* An Ursuline nun. [after Saint *Ursula*, 4th-c. Cornish princess and martyr]

ur·ti·car·i·a (ûr′tə·kâr′ē·ə) *n. Pathol.* A disease of the skin, characterized by transient eruptions and attended with itching. Also called *hives, nettle rash.* [< NL < L *urtica* nettle] — **ur′ti·car′i·al** or **·i·ous** *adj.*

us (us) *pron.* The objective case of the pronoun *we.* [OE]

us·a·ble (yŏŏ′zə·bəl) *adj.* 1. Capable of being used. 2. That can be used conveniently. Also **use′a·ble.** — **us′a·ble·ness** *n.* — **us′a·bly** *adv.*

us·age (yŏŏ′sij, -zij) *n.* 1. The manner of using or treating a person or thing; treatment; also, the act of using. 2. Customary or habitual usage, or something permitted by it or done in accordance with it. 3. Uniform practice. 4. The customary way of using words, sounds, and grammatical forms in a language. 5. A particular verbal or written expression or application of such an expression: a contemptuous *usage.*

us·ance (yŏŏ′zəns) *n.* 1. A period of time, variable as between various countries, that, by commercial usage, is allowed, exclusive of days of grace, for payment of bills of exchange, esp. foreign. 2. *Econ.* An income derived from the possession of wealth, as by investment.

use (*v.* yŏŏz; *n.* yŏŏs) *v.* **used** (yŏŏzd; *yŏŏst for defs.* 5, 7), **us·ing** *v.t.* 1. To employ for the accomplishment of a purpose; make use of. 2. To put into practice or employ habitually; make a practice of: to *use* diligence in business. 3. To expend the whole of; consume: often with *up.* 4. To conduct oneself toward; treat: to *use* one badly. **5.** To make familiar by habit or practice; inure: now only in the past participle: He is *used* to exposure. **6.** To partake of; smoke or chew: He does not *use* tobacco. — *v.i.* **7.** To do something customarily or habitually: now only in the past tense as an auxiliary to form a phrase equivalent to a frequentative past tense: I *used* to go there. — *n.* **1.** The act of using; the fact or condition of being employed. **2.** Suitableness or adaptability to an end: the *uses* of adversity. **3.** Way or manner of using. **4.** Occasion or need to employ; purpose. **5.** Habitual practice or employment; custom. **6.** Any special form, ceremony, or ritual, or any individual service that arose in or was perpetuated by a church, diocese, or branch of a church: Roman *use*. **7.** *Law* The permanent equitable right that a beneficiary has to the enjoyment of the rents and profits of lands and tenements of which the legal title and possession are vested in another in trust for the beneficiary. — **to have no use for 1.** To have no need **of. 2.** *Informal* To have a contempt or dislike for; want nothing to do with. [< OF < L *usus*, pp. of *uti* to use]

use·ful (yoos′fəl) *adj.* Serviceable; serving a use or purpose, esp. a valuable one. — **use′ful·ly** *adv.* — **use′ful·ness** *n.*

use·less (yoos′lis) *adj.* **1.** Unserviceable; being of no use; not capable of serving any beneficial purpose. **2.** Futile; in vain. — **use′less·ly** *adv.* — **use′less·ness** *n.*

us·er (yoo′zər) *n.* **1.** One who or that which uses. **2.** *Law* The exercise or enjoyment of a right.

ush·er (ush′ər) *n.* **1.** One who acts as doorkeeper, as of a court or other assembly room. **2.** An officer whose duty it is to introduce strangers or walk before a person of rank. **3.** One who conducts persons to seats, etc., as in a church or theater. **4.** *Brit.* An assistant or subordinate teacher in a school. — *v.t.* **1.** To act as an usher to; escort; conduct. **2.** To precede as a harbinger; be a forerunner of: usu. with *in*. [< OF < L *ostiarius* doorkeeper < *ostium* door]

ush·er·ette (ush′ə·ret′) *n.* A female usher, as in a theater.

us·nic acid (us′nik) A yellow, crystalline substance, $C_{18}H_{16}O_7$, derived from lichens, used as an antibiotic.

u·su·al (yoo′zhoo·əl) *adj.* Such as occurs in the ordinary course of events; frequent; common. [< OF < LL < L *usus* use] — **u′su·al·ly** *adv.* — **u′su·al·ness** *n.*

u·su·fruct (yoo′zyoo·frukt, yoo′syoo-) *n.* *Law* The right of using the property of another and of drawing the profits it produces without wasting its substance. [< LL < L < *usus et fructus* use and fruit]

u·su·fruc·tu·ar·y (yoo′zyoo·fruk′choo·er′ē, yoo′syoo-) *n.* *pl.* **·ar·ies** One who holds property for use by usufruct, as a tenant. — *adj.* Of or pertaining to a usufruct.

u·su·rer (yoo′zhər·ər) *n.* One who practices usury; one who lends money, esp. at an exorbitant or illegal rate.

u·su·ri·ous (yoo·zhoor′ē·əs) *adj.* Practicing usury; having the nature of usury. — **u·su′ri·ous·ly** *adv.* — **u·su′ri·ous·ness** *n.*

u·surp (yoo-zûrp′, -sûrp′) *v.t.* **1.** To seize and hold (the office, rights, or powers of another) without right or legal authority; take possession of by force. **2.** To take arrogantly, as if by right. — *v.i.* **3.** To practice usurpation; encroach: with *on* or *upon*. [< OF < L, ? < *usus* use + *rapere* to seize] — **u·surp′er** *n.* — **u·surp′ing·ly** *adv.*

u·sur·pa·tion (yoo′zər·pā′shən, -sər-) *n.* The act of usurping: said esp. of unlawful or forcible seizure of kingly power.

u·su·ry (yoo′zhər·ē) *n.* *pl.* **·ries 1.** The act or practice of exacting a rate of interest beyond what is allowed by law. **2.** A premium paid for the use of money beyond the rate of interest established by law. [< OF < L < *usus* used]

ut (oot) *n.* *Music* The first syllable in the Guido solmization system: now commonly *do*. [See GAMUT.]

Ute (yoot, yoo′tē) *n.* One of a group of tribes of North American Indians of Shoshonean stock living in Colorado and Utah.

u·ten·sil (yoo·ten′səl) *n.* A vessel, tool, implement, etc., serving a useful purpose, esp. for domestic or farming use. [< OF < L *utensilis* fit for use < *utens*, ppr. of *uti* to use]

u·ter·ine (yoo′tər·in, -īn) *adj.* **1.** Pertaining to the uterus. **2.** Born of the same mother, but having a different father. [< LL *uterinus* born of the same mother]

utero- *combining form* The uterus; of or pertaining to the uterus. Also, before vowels, **uter-**. [< L *uterus* uterus]

u·ter·us (yoo′tər·əs) *n.* *pl.* **u·ter·i** (yoo′tər·ī) *Anat.* The organ of a female mammal in which the young are protected and developed before birth; the womb. [< L]

u·tile (yoo′til) *adj.* *Rare* Useful. [< OF < L *uti* to use]

u·til·i·dor (yoo·til′i·dôr) *n.* *Canadian* A system of pipes, cables, etc., raised and insulated to provide utilities to communities on the permafrost.

u·til·i·tar·i·an (yoo·til′ə·târ′ē·ən) *adj.* **1.** Relating to utility; esp., placing utility above beauty or the amenities of life. **2.** Pertaining to or advocating utilitarianism. — *n.* **1.** An advocate of utilitarianism. **2.** One devoted to mere material utility.

u·til·i·tar·i·an·ism (yoo·til′ə·târ′ē·ən·iz′əm) *n.* **1.** *Philos.* **a** The doctrine that actions derive their moral quality from their usefulness as means to some end, as happiness. **b** The ethical theory, held by Jeremy Bentham and John Stuart Mill, that the greatest human happiness determines the highest moral good. **2.** Devotion to mere material interests.

u·til·i·ty (yoo·til′ə·tē) *n.* *pl.* **·ties 1.** Fitness for some desirable, practical purpose; also, that which is necessary. **2.** Fitness to supply the natural needs of man. **3.** A public service, as gas, water, etc. **4.** *pl.* Shares of utility company stocks. **5.** In utilitarianism, the greatest happiness for the greatest number of people. [< F < L *utilis* useful]

u·til·ize (yoo′təl·īz) *v.t.* **·ized, ·iz·ing** To make useful; turn to practical account; make use of. Also *Brit.* **u′til·ise.** — **u′til·iz′a·ble** *adj.* — **u′til·i·za′tion** *n.* — **u′til·iz′er** *n.*

ut·most (ut′mōst) *adj.* **1.** Of the highest degree or the largest amount or number; greatest. **2.** Being at the farthest limit or point. — *n.* The greatest possible extent; the most possible. Also *uttermost*. [OE *ūtmest, ȳtemest*]

U·to-Az·tec·an (yoo′tō·az′tek·ən) *n.* **1.** One of the chief stocks of North and Central American Indians, formerly occupying two large regions of the NW and SW U.S., comprising three branches (Shoshonean, Piman, and Nahuatlan) and embracing about fifty tribes, still surviving in the U.S. and Mexico. **2.** The family of languages spoken by these peoples. — *adj.* Of or pertaining to the Uto-Aztecans or their languages.

u·to·pi·a (yoo·tō′pē·ə) *n.* **1.** Any state, condition, or place of ideal perfection. **2.** A visionary, impractical scheme for social improvement. [after *Utopia*]

U·to·pi·a (yoo·tō′pē·ə) An imaginary island described as the seat of a perfect social and political life in a romance by Sir Thomas More, published in 1516. [< NL < Gk. *ou* not + *topos* place] — **U·to′pi·an** *n. & adj.*

u·to·pi·an (yoo·tō′pē·ən) *adj.* Excellent, but existing only in fancy or theory; ideal. — *n.* One who advocates impractical reforms; a visionary. — **u·to′pi·an·ism** *n.*

u·tri·cle (yoo′tri·kəl) *n.* *Anat.* The larger of two saclike cavities found in the bony vestibule of the inner ear. [< L *utriculus*, dim. of *uter* skin bag]

u·tric·u·lar (yoo·trik′yə·lər) *adj.* **1.** Resembling a utricle or small sac. **2.** Bladderlike; bearing or provided with utricles. Also **u·tric′u·late** (-lit, -lāt).

ut·ter¹ (ut′ər) *v.t.* **1.** To give out or send forth with audible sound; say. **2.** *Law* To put in circulation; now, esp. to deliver or offer (something forged or counterfeit) to another. [ME *outre*, freq. of obs. *out* to say, speak out < OE *ūt*] — **ut′ter·a·ble** *adj.* — **ut′ter·er** *n.*

ut·ter² (ut′ər) *adj.* **1.** Absolute; total: *utter* misery. **2.** Being or done without conditions or qualifications; final; absolute: *utter* denial. [OE *ūtera*, orig. compar. of *ūt* out]

ut·ter·ance (ut′ər·əns) *n.* **1.** The act of uttering; vocal expression; manner of speaking; also, the power of speech. **2.** A thing uttered or expressed. **3.** *Ling.* Any stretch of speech capable of being isolated from the flow of connected discourse, as a word, phrase, or sentence.

ut·ter·ly (ut′ər·lē) *adv.* Thoroughly; entirely.

ut·ter·most (ut′ər·mōst′) *adj. & n.* Utmost.

U-turn (yoo′tûrn′) *n.* *Informal* A continuous turn that reverses the direction of a vehicle on a road.

u·vu·la (yoo′vyə·lə) *n.* *pl.* **·las** or **·lae** (-lē) *Anat.* The pendent fleshy portion of the soft palate. For illus. see MOUTH, THROAT. [< LL, dim. of *uva* grape]

u·vu·lar (yoo′vyə·lər) *adj.* **1.** Pertaining to or of the uvula. **2.** *Phonet.* Produced by vibration of, or with the back of the tongue near or against, the uvula. — *n.* *Phonet.* A uvular sound.

ux·o·ri·al (uk·sôr′ē·əl, -sō′rē-, ug·zôr′ē·əl, -zō′rē-) *adj.* **1.** Of, pertaining to, characteristic of, or becoming to a wife. **2.** Uxorious. [< L *uxor* wife]

ux·o·ri·ous (uk·sôr′ē·əs, -sō′rē-, ug·zôr′ē-, -zō′rē-) *adj.* Fatuously or foolishly devoted to one's wife. [< L *uxor* wife] — **ux·o′ri·ous·ly** *adv.* — **ux·o′ri·ous·ness** *n.*

Uz·bek (ooz′bek, uz′-) *n.* **1.** A member of a Turkic people dominant in Turkestan; a native or inhabitant of the Uzbek S.S.R. **2.** The Turkic language of the Uzbeks. Also **Uz′beg.**

V

v, V (vē) *n.* *pl.* **v's** or **vs, V's** or **Vs, vees** (vēz) **1.** The twenty-second letter of the English alphabet. **2.** The sound represented by the letter *v*, the voiced, labiodental fricative. **3.** Anything shaped like a V. — *symbol* **1.** *Informal* A five-dollar bill. **2.** The Roman numeral five. **3.** *Chem.* Vanadium (symbol V).

va·can·cy (vā′kən·sē) *n.* *pl.* **·cies** **1.** The state of being vacant; vacuity; emptiness. **2.** That which is vacant or unoccupied; empty space. **3.** An unoccupied post, place, or office; a place destitute of an incumbent.

va·cant (vā′kənt) *adj.* **1.** Containing or holding nothing; esp. devoid of occupants; empty. **2.** Occupied with nothing; unemployed; unencumbered; free. **3.** Being or appearing without intelligence; inane. **4.** Having no incumbent; unfilled: a *vacant* office. **5.** *Law* Unoccupied or unused, as land; also, abandoned; having neither claimant nor heir, as an estate. **6.** Free from cares. **7.** Devoid of thought. [< F < L *vacare* to be empty] — **va′cant·ly** *adv.* — **va′cant·ness** *n.*

va·cate (vā′kāt) *v.* **·cat·ed, ·cat·ing** *v.t.* **1.** To make vacant; surrender possession of by removal. **2.** To set aside; annul. **3.** To give up (a position or office); quit. — *v.i.* **4.** To leave an office, position, place, etc. **5.** *Informal* To go away; leave. — **Syn.** See ANNUL.

va·ca·tion (vā·kā′shən) *n.* **1.** An interlude, usu. of several days or weeks, from one's customary duties, as for recreation or rest. **2.** *Law* The period of time between stated terms of court. **3.** The intermission of the course of studies and exercises in an educational institution. **4.** The act of vacating. — *v.i.* To take a vacation. [< F < L *vacatio, -onis* freedom from duty] — **va·ca′tion·er** *n.*

va·ca·tion·ist (vā·kā′shən·ist) *n.* One who is taking a vacation or staying at a resort; a tourist.

vac·ci·nate (vak′sə·nāt) *v.* **·nat·ed, ·nat·ing** *Med.* *v.t.* **1.** To inoculate with a vaccine as a preventive measure; esp. to inoculate against smallpox. — *v.i.* **2.** To perform vaccination. — **vac′ci·na′tor** *n.*

vac·ci·na·tion (vak′sə·nā′shən) *n.* *Med.* The act or process of vaccinating, esp. against smallpox.

vac·cine (vak′sēn, -sin) *n.* **1.** The virus of cowpox, as prepared for or introduced by vaccination. **2.** Any preparation containing bacteria or viruses so treated as to give immunity from specific diseases when injected into the subject. [< L *vaccinus* pertaining to a cow] — **vac′ci·nal** (sə·nəl) *adj.*

vac·cin·i·a (vak·sin′ē·ə) *n.* *Vet.* Cowpox.

vac·il·late (vas′ə·lāt) *v.i.* **·lat·ed, ·lat·ing** **1.** To sway one way and the other; totter; waver. **2.** To fluctuate. **3.** To waver in mind; be irresolute. [< L *vacillare* to waver] — **vac′il·lan·cy** (-lən·sē) *n.* — **vac′il·lant** (-lənt) *adj.* — **vac′il·la′tion** *n.* — **vac′il·la·to·ry** (-lə·tôr′ē, -tō′rē) *adj.*

— **Syn.** **3.** To *vacillate* is to incline to one alternative and then another, without coming to a decision. To *waver* is to be undecided whether to embark on a chosen course. *Falter* suggests failure to act through weakness, timidity, or fright.

vac·u·a (vak′yōō·ə) Alternative plural of VACUUM.

va·cu·i·ty (va·kyōō′ə·tē) *n.* *pl.* **·ties** **1.** The state of being a vacuum: emptiness. **2.** Vacant space; a void. **3.** Freedom from mental exertion. **4.** Lack of intelligence. **5.** An inane or idle thing or statement. [< L *vacuus* empty]

vac·u·ole (vak′yōō·ōl) *n.* *Biol.* A minute cavity containing air, a watery fluid, or a chemical secretion of the protoplasm, found in an organ, tissue, or cell. For illus. see CELL. [< F < L *vacuus* empty] — **vac′u·o·lar** *adj.*

vac·u·ous (vak′yōō·əs) *adj.* **1.** Having no contents; empty. **2.** Lacking intelligence; blank. **3.** Idle; unoccupied. [< L *vacuus*] — **vac′u·ous·ly** *adv.* — **vac′u·ous·ness** *n.*

vac·u·um (vak′yōō·əm, -yōōm) *n.* *pl.* **·u·ums** or **·u·a** (-yōō·ə) **1.** A space absolutely devoid of matter. **2.** A space from which air or other gas has been exhausted to a very high degree. **3.** A void; an empty feeling. **4.** A condition of isolation from environmental influences. — *adj.* **1.** Of, or used in the production of, a vacuum. **2.** Exhausted or partly exhausted of gas, air, or vapor. **3.** Operated by suction to produce a vacuum. — *v.t.* & *v.i.* *Informal* To clean with a vacuum cleaner: to *vacuum* a rug. [< L, neut. of *vacuus* empty]

vacuum bottle A thermos bottle. Also **vacuum flask.**

vacuum cleaner A machine for cleaning carpets, furnishings, etc., by suction. — **vacuum cleaning**

vacuum pump A pulsometer.

vacuum tube *Electronics* **1.** A glass tube exhausted of air to a high degree and containing electrodes between which electric discharges may be passed. **2.** An electron tube.

vacuum valve *Brit.* A vacuum tube.

va·de me·cum (vā′dē mē′kəm) *Latin* Anything carried for constant use, as a guidebook, manual, or bag; literally, go with me. Also **va′de-me′cum, va′de-me′cum.**

vag·a·bond (vag′ə·bond) *n.* **1.** One who wanders from place to place without visible means of support; a tramp. **2.** One without a settled home; a wanderer; nomad. **3.** A worthless fellow; rascal. — *adj.* **1.** Pertaining to a vagabond; nomadic. **2.** Having no definite residence; wandering; irresponsible. **3.** Driven to and fro; aimless. [< F < L *vagus* wandering] — **vag′a·bond·age** (-ij) *n.* — **vag′a·bond′ish** *adj.* — **vag′a·bond·ism** *n.*

va·gar·y (və·gâr′ē, vā′gər·ē) *n.* *pl.* **·gar·ies** A wild fancy; extravagant notion. [< L *vagari* to wander]

va·gi·na (və·jī′nə) *n.* *pl.* **·nas** or **·nae** (-nē) *Anat.* The canal leading from the external genital orifice in female mammals to the uterus. [< L, sheath] — **vag·i·nal** (vaj′ə·nəl, və·jī′-) *adj.*

vag·i·nate (vaj′ə·nit, -nāt) *adj.* **1.** Having a sheath. **2.** Formed into a sheath; tubular. Also **vag′i·nat′ed** (-nā′tid). [< NL < L *vagina* sheath]

vagino- *combining form* *Med.* The vagina; of or pertaining to the vagina. Also, before vowels, **vagin-.** [< L *vagina* sheath, vagina]

va·gran·cy (vā′grən·sē) *n.* *pl.* **·cies** The state of being a vagrant. Also **va′grant·ness.**

va·grant (vā′grənt) *n.* **1.** A person without a settled home; an idle wanderer; vagabond; tramp. **2.** A roving person. — *adj.* **1.** Wandering about as a vagrant. **2.** Pertaining to one who or that which wanders; nomadic. **3.** Having a wandering course; capricious; wayward. [ME, alter. of AF *wakerant* < OF *wacrer* to walk, wander < Gmc.; infl. in form by L *vagari* to wander] — **va′grant·ly** *adv.*

vague (vāg) *adj.* **va·guer, va·gu·est** **1.** Lacking definiteness or precision. **2.** Of uncertain source or authority: a *vague* rumor. **3.** Not clearly recognized, understood, stated, or felt. **4.** Shadowy; hazy. [< F < L *vagus* wandering] — **vague′ly** *adv.* — **vague′ness** *n.*

va·gus (vā′gəs) *n.* *pl.* **·gi** (-jī) *Anat.* Either of the tenth pair of cranial nerves sending branches to the lungs, heart, stomach, and most of the abdominal viscera. Also **vagus nerve.** [< L, wandering]

vain (vān) *adj.* **1.** Filled with or showing undue admiration for oneself, one's appearance, etc.; conceited. **2.** Unproductive; worthless; fruitless: a *vain* attempt. **3.** Having no real basis or worth; empty: *vain* hopes. **4.** Ostentatious; showy. — **in vain** To no purpose; without effect. [< F < L *vanus* empty] — **vain′ly** *adv.* — **vain′ness** *n.*

— **Syn. 1.** proud, vainglorious. **2.** abortive. See FUTILE.

vain·glo·ry (vān·glôr′ē, -glō′rē) *n.* *pl.* **·ries** Excessive or groundless vanity; also, vain pomp; boastfulness. — **Syn.** See PRIDE. [< OF < Med.L *vana gloria* empty pomp, show] — **vain·glo′ri·ous** (-glôr′ē·əs, -glō′rē-) *adj.* — **vain·glo′ri·ous·ly** *adv.* — **vain·glo′ri·ous·ness** *n.*

val·ance (val′əns, vā′ləns) *n.* **1.** A hanging drapery, as from the framework of a bed to the floor, from a shelf, etc. **2.** A short drapery, board, or plate across the top of a window. — *v.t.* **·anced, ·anc·ing** To furnish with or as with a valance. [< OF *avaler* to descend; or after *Valence*, textile-manufacturing commune in France] — **val′anced** *adj.*

vale¹ (vāl) *n.* *Chiefly Poetic* A valley. [< OF < L *vallis*]

va·le² (vā′lē) *interj.* *Latin* Farewell.

val·e·dic·tion (val′ə·dik′shən) *n.* A bidding farewell. [< L < *valere* to be well + *dicere* to say]

val·e·dic·to·ri·an (val′ə·dik·tôr′ē·ən, -tō′rē-) *n.* A student who delivers a valedictory at graduating exercises, usu. the graduating student ranking highest in scholarship.

val·e·dic·to·ry (val′ə·dik′tər·ē) *adj.* Pertaining to a leave-taking. — *n.* *pl.* **·ries** A parting address, as by a member of a graduating class.

va·lence (vā′ləns) *n.* *Chem.* **1.** The property possessed by an element or radical of combining with or replacing other elements or radicals in definite and constant proportion. **2.**

The number of atoms of hydrogen (or its equivalent) with which an atom or radical can combine, or which it can replace. Also **va·len·cy**. [< LL < L *valere* to be strong]

val·en·tine (val′ən-tīn) *n.* **1.** A greeting card or token of affection sent on Saint Valentine's Day. **2.** A sweetheart.

va·le·ri·an (və-lir′ē-ən) *n.* Any of various perennial herbs; esp., one species with small pink or white flowers and a strong odor: also called *heliotrope*. [< OF < Med.L. appar. ult. < *Valerius*, a personal name]

val·et (val′ā, val′it; *Fr.* và·lė′) *n.* **1.** A gentleman's personal servant. **2.** A manservant in a hotel who performs personal services for patrons. —*v.t. & v.i.* To serve or act as a valet. [< F, a groom < OF *vaslet, varlet*, dim. of *vasal* vassal]

val·e·tu·di·nar·i·an (val′ə-tōō′də-nâr′ē-ən, -tyōō′-) *n.* A chronic invalid; one unduly solicitous about his health. —*adj.* Seeking to recover health; infirm. Also **val·e·tu′di·nar′y**. [< L *valetudo* health, ill health < *valere* to be well] —**val′e·tu′di·nar′i·an·ism** *n.*

Val·hal·la (val·hal′ə) In Norse mythology, the great hall into which the souls of heroes fallen bravely in battle were borne by the valkyries and received and feasted by Odin. [< NL < ON < *valr* the slain + *höll* hall]

val·iant (val′yənt) *adj.* **1.** Strong and intrepid; powerful and courageous. **2.** Performed with valor; bravely conducted; heroic. [< OF < L *valere* to be strong] —**val′iant·ly** *adv.* —**val′iance, val′ian·cy, val′iant·ness** *n.*

val·id (val′id) *adj.* **1.** Based on evidence that can be supported; acceptable; convincing. **2.** Legally binding; effective; warranted. **3.** Properly derived from accepted premises by the rules of logic. [< F < L *validus* powerful < *valere* to be strong] —**val′id·ly** *adv.* —**val′id·ness** *n.*

val·i·date (val′ə-dāt) *v.t.* **·dat·ed, ·dat·ing 1.** To make valid; ratify and confirm. **2.** To declare legally valid; legalize. —**Syn.** See RATIFY. —**val′i·da′tion** *n.*

va·lid·i·ty (və-lid′ə-tē) *n. pl.* **·ties 1.** The state or quality of being valid; soundness, as in law or reasoning; efficacy. **2.** Legal soundness.

va·lise (və-lēs′) *n.* A portable case or bag for clothes, etc., used when traveling; a suitcase. [< F < Ital. *valigia*]

val·kyr·ie (val·kir′ē, val′kir·ē) *n. Often cap.* In Norse mythology, one of the maidens who ride through the air and choose heroes from among those slain in battle, and carry them to Valhalla. Also **val′kyr.** [< ON < *valr* the slain + stem of *kjōsa* to choose, select] —**val·kyr′i·an** *adj.*

val·ley (val′ē) *n. pl.* **·leys 1.** A depression of the earth's surface, as one through which a stream flows; level or low land between mountains, hills, or high lands. **2.** Any depression or hollow like a valley. [< OF < L *vallis* valley]

val·or (val′ər) *n.* Courage; personal bravery. Also *Brit.* **val′our.** [< OF < LL < L *valere* to be strong] —**val′or·ous** *adj.* —**val′or·ous·ly** *adv.* —**val′or·ous·ness** *n.*

val·or·i·za·tion (val′ər·ə·zā′shən, -ī·zā′-) *n.* The maintenance by governmental action of an artificial price for any product. [< Pg. *valorização* < *valor* value < LL. See VALOR.]

val·or·ize (val′ə-rīz) *v.t.* **·ized, ·iz·ing** To subject to valorization. Also *Brit.* **val′or·ise.**

val·u·a·ble (val′yōō·ə·bəl, val′yə·bəl) *adj.* **1.** Having relatively great financial worth, price, or value; costly. **2.** Of a nature or character capable of being valued or estimated. **3.** Having moral worth, value, or importance; worthy. —*n. Usu. pl.* An article of worth or value, as a piece of jewelry. —**val′u·a·ble·ness** *n.* —**val′u·a·bly** *adv.*

val·u·a·tion (val′yōō·ā′shən) *n.* **1.** The act of valuing. **2.** Estimated worth or value. **3.** Personal estimation; judgment of merit or character. —**val′u·a′tion·al** *adj.*

val·ue (val′yōō) *n.* **1.** The desirability or worth of a thing; intrinsic worth; utility. **2.** *Often pl.* Something regarded as desirable, worthy, or right, as a belief, standard, or moral precept. **3.** The rate at which a commodity is potentially exchangeable for others; a fair return in service, goods, etc.; worth in money; market price; also, the ratio of utility to price; a bargain. **4.** Attributed or assumed valuation; esteem or regard. **5.** Exact meaning. **6.** *Music* The relative length of a tone as signified by a note. **7.** *Math.* The quantity, magnitude, or number an algebraic symbol or expression is supposed to denote. **8.** Rank in a system of classification. **9.** In the graphic arts, the relation of the elements of a picture, as light and shade, to one another. **10.** *Phonet.* The special quality of the sound represented by a written character. —*v.t.* **·ued, ·u·ing 1.** To estimate the value or worth of; appraise. **2.** To regard highly; esteem; prize. **3.** To place a relative estimate of value or desirability upon. **4.** To give a (specified) value to. [< OF *valoir* to be worth < L *valere*] —**val′ue·less** *adj.* —**val′u·er** *n.*

val·ued (val′yōōd) *adj.* **1.** Regarded or estimated; much or highly esteemed. **2.** Having a (specified) value.

val·vate (val′vāt) *adj.* **1.** Serving as or resembling a valve; having a valve; valvular. **2.** *Bot.* Meeting without overlapping, as petals. [< L *valvatus* with folding doors]

valve (valv) *n.* **1.** *Mech.* Any contrivance or arrangement that regulates the amount and direction of flow of a liquid, gas, vapor, or loose material. **2.** *Anat.* A structure formed by one or more loose folds of the lining membrane of a vessel or other organ, allowing flow of a fluid in one direction only, as blood to and from the heart. **3.** *Zool.* One of the parts of a shell, as of a mollusk. **4.** A device in certain brass instruments for lengthening the air column and lowering the pitch of the instrument's scale. —*v.t.* **valved, valv·ing** To furnish with valves; control the flow of by means of a valve. [< L *valva* leaf of a door] —**val′val** (-vəl), **val′var** (-vər) *adj.* —**valve′less** *adj.*

val·vu·lar (val′vyə·lər) *adj.* **1.** Pertaining to or of the nature of a valve, as of the heart. **2.** Having valves.

va·moose (va·mōōs′) *v.t. & v.i.* **·moosed, ·moos·ing** *U.S. Slang* To leave hastily or hurriedly; quit. Also **va·mose′** (-mōs′). [< Sp. *vamos* let us go < L *vadere* to go]

vamp¹ (vamp) *n.* **1.** The piece of leather forming the upper front part of a boot or shoe. **2.** Something added to give an old thing a new appearance. **3.** *Music* A simple improvised accompaniment. —*v.t.* **1.** To provide with a vamp. **2.** To repair or patch. **3.** *Music* To improvise an accompaniment to. —*v.i.* **4.** *Music* To improvise accompaniments. [< OF < *avant* before + *pied* foot] —**vamp′er** *n.*

vamp² (vamp) *Informal v.t.* **1.** To seduce (a man) by utilizing one's feminine charms. —*v.i.* **2.** To play the vamp. —*n.* An unscrupulous flirt. [Short for VAMPIRE] —**Syn.** (noun) siren, temptress, gold-digger, femme fatale.

vam·pire (vam′pīr) *n.* **1.** In folklore, a corpse that rises from its grave at night to feed upon the living, usu. by sucking the blood. **2.** A man or woman who victimizes persons of the opposite sex; esp., a woman who brings her lover to a state of poverty or degradation. **3.** A large bat of South or Central America, that drinks the blood of horses, cattle, and, sometimes, men. **4.** An insectivorous or frugivorous bat formerly supposed to suck blood. [< F < G *vampir* < Slavic] —**vam·pir′ic** (vam-pir′ik), **vam′pir·ish** (-pīr·ish) *adj.* —**vam′pir·ism** (-pī·riz′əm, -pə-) *n.*

van¹ (van) *n.* **1.** A large covered vehicle for transporting furniture, livestock, etc. **2.** *Brit.* A closed railway car for luggage, etc. [Short for CARAVAN]

van² (van) *n.* **1.** The portion of an army, fleet, etc., that is nearest or in advance of the front: opposed to *rear*. **2.** The leaders of a movement; those at the front of any line or unit. [Short for VANGUARD]

va·na·di·um (və-nā′dē·əm) *n.* A rare, silver-white metallic element (symbol V), used in steel alloys to increase tensile strength. See ELEMENT. [< NL < ON *Vanadis*, a name of the Norse goddess Freya]

Van Al·len radiation (van al′ən) A high-intensity radiation consisting of charged atomic particles believed to circle the earth in an inner and outer belt conforming to the earth's magnetic field. Also **Van Allen belts.** [after James A. *Van Allen*, born 1914, U.S. physicist]

van·dal (van′dəl) *n.* One who willfully destroys or defaces property, esp. anything artistic. —*adj.* Wantonly destructive. [< VANDAL] —**van·dal′ic** (van-dal′ik) *adj.*

Van·dal (van′dəl) *n.* One of a Germanic people who ravaged Gaul and overran Spain and North Africa in the early part of the fifth century, and pillaged the city of Rome in 455. —**Van·dal′ic** (van-dal′ik) *adj.* —**Van′dal·ism** *n.*

van·dal·ism (van′dəl·iz′əm) *n.* Willful destruction or defacement of artistic works, or of property in general.

Van·dyke beard (van-dīk′) A short pointed beard resembling those depicted in the paintings of Anthony Van Dyck.

vane (vān) *n.* **1.** A thin plate of metal or wood that pivots on a vertical rod to indicate the direction of the wind; weather vane. **2.** An arm or blade extending from a rotating shaft, as of a windmill, propeller, turbine, etc. **3.** *Ornithol.* The web of a feather. [OE *fana* flag] —**vaned** *adj.*

van·guard (van′gärd) *n.* **1.** The advance guard of an army; the van. **2.** Those in the forefront of a movement, as in art, etc. [< OF < *avant* before + *garde* guard]

WINDMILL VANES

va·nil·la (və-nil′ə) *n.* **1.** A flavoring extract made from the podlike seed capsules of a climbing tropical orchid. **2.** The seed capsule of this plant: also **vanilla bean. 3.** A food, as ice cream, flavored with vanilla. [< NL < Sp. dim. of *vaina* sheath, pod < L *vagina* sheath] —**va·nil′lic** (-ik) *adj.*

va·nil·lin (və-nil′in) *n. Chem.* A colorless, fragrant, crystalline compound, $C_8H_8O_3$, contained in vanilla, and also made synthetically. Also **va·nil·line** (və-nil′in, -ēn).

van·ish (van′ish) *v.i.* **1.** To disappear from sight; fade away; depart. **2.** To pass out of existence; be annihilated. [< OF < L *evanescere* to fade away] —**van′ish·er** *n.*

van·ish·ing point (van′ish·ing) In perspective, the point at which parallel lines appear to converge.

van·i·ty (van′ə·tē) *n. pl.* **·ties 1.** The condition or character of being vain; excessive personal pride; conceit. **2.** Ambitious display; ostentation; show. **3.** The quality or state of being fruitless, useless, or destitute of reality, etc. **4.** That which is vain or unsubstantial. **5.** A bag or box containing cosmetics, comb, mirror, etc.: also **vanity case. 6.** A dressing table. [< OF < L *vanus* empty, vain]

van·quish (vang′kwish, van′-) *v.t.* **1.** To defeat in battle; overcome; conquer. **2.** To suppress or overcome (a feeling). **3.** To defeat, as in argument. [< OF < L *vincere* to conquer] — **van′quish·a·ble** *adj.* — **van′quish·er** *n.*

van·tage (van′tij) *n.* **1.** Superiority over a competitor or opponent; advantage. **2.** Advantage (def. 4). **3.** An opportunity; chance. [OF < L *ab ante* from before]

vantage ground A position or condition that gives one an advantage.

vantage point A strategic position affording perspective; point of view.

van·ward (van′wərd) *adj.* Of or situated in the van or front. — *adv.* To or toward the van or front.

vap·id (vap′id) *adj.* **1.** Having lost sparkling quality and flavor. **2.** Flat; dull; insipid. [< L *vapidus* insipid] — **va·pid·i·ty** (ve·pid′ə·tē), **vap′id·ness** *n.* — **vap′id·ly** *adv.*

va·por (vā′pər) *n.* **1.** Moisture in the air; esp., visible floating moisture, as light mist. **2.** Any light, cloudy substance in the air, as smoke or fumes. **3.** Any substance in the gaseous state, that is usu. a liquid or solid. **4.** A gas below its critical temperature. **5.** That which is fleeting and unsubstantial. — *v.t.* **1.** To vaporize. — *v.i.* **2.** To emit vapor. **3.** To evaporate. **4.** To brag. Also *Brit.* **va′pour.** [< AF < OF < L *vapor* steam] — **va·por·a·bil′i·ty** *n.* — **va′por·a·ble** *adj.* — **va′por·er** *n.* — **va′por·ish** *adj.*

vapori- *combining form* Vapor; of or related to vapor, steam, etc. Also, before vowels, **vapor-.** [< L *vapor* steam]

va·por·ize (vā′pə·rīz) *v.t. & v.i.* **·ized, ·iz·ing** To convert or be converted into vapor. — **va′por·iz′a·ble** *adj.* — **va′por·i·za·tion** (-ə·zā′shən, -ī·zā′-) **va·por·iz′er** *n.*

va·por·ous (vā′pər·əs) *adj.* **1.** Of or like vapor; foggy; misty. **2.** Full of or producing vapors. **3.** Diaphanous; ethereal. **4.** Vainly imaginative; whimsical. Also **va′por-y.** — **va·por·os·i·ty** (vā′pə·ros′ə·tē) *n.* — **va′por·ous·ly** *adv.* — **va′por·ous·ness** *n.*

vapor pressure *Physics* The pressure of a confined vapor in equilibrium with its liquid at any specific temperature. Also **vapor tension.**

vapor trail *Aeron.* A contrail.

va·que·ro (vä·kā′rō) *n. pl.* **·ros** (-rōz, *Sp.* -rōs) A herdsman; cowboy. [< Sp. < L *vacca* cow]

vari- *combining form* Various; different: *variform, varicolored.* Also *vario-.* [< *varius* varied]

var·i·a·ble (vâr′ē·ə·bəl) *adj.* **1.** Having the capacity of varying; alterable; mutable. **2.** Having a tendency to change; not constant; fickle. **3.** Having no definite value as regards quantity. **4.** *Biol.* Prone to variation from a normal or established type. — *n.* **1.** That which varies or is subject to change. **2.** *Math.* A quantity susceptible of fluctuating in value or magnitude under different conditions. [< OF < L < *varius* various, diverse] — **var′i·a·bil′i·ty, var′i·a·ble·ness** *n.* — **var′i·a·bly** *adv.*

variable star *Astron.* Any of several groups of stars whose apparent magnitude varies at different times.

var·i·ance (vâr′ē·əns) *n.* **1.** The act of varying, or the state of being variant; difference; discrepancy. **2.** Dissension; discord. — **at variance 1.** Disagreeing or conflicting, as facts. **2.** In a state of dissension or discord.

var·i·ant (vâr′ē·ənt) *adj.* **1.** Having or showing variation; differing. **2.** Tending to vary; changing. **3.** Restless; fickle; inconstant. **4.** Differing from a standard or type. — *n.* A thing that differs from another in form only; esp., a different spelling or pronunciation of a word. [See VARIABLE]

var·i·a·tion (vâr′ē·ā′shən) *n.* **1.** The act, process, state, or result of varying; modification; diversity. **2.** The extent to which a thing varies. **3.** A repetition with its essential features intact and other features modified. **4.** *Music* A modification of the rhythm, harmony, melodic pattern, etc., of a basic theme. **5.** *Biol.* Deviation in structure or function from the type or parent form of an organism. [< F < L *variatio, -onis*] — **var′i·a′tion·al** *adj.*

varico- *combining form Med.* A varicose vein; varix. Also, before vowels, **varic-.** [< L *varix, -icis* varicose vein]

var·i·col·ored (vâr′i·kul′ərd) *adj.* Variegated in color; parti-colored; of various colors. Also *Brit.* **var′i·col′oured.**

var·i·cose (vâr′ə·kōs) *adj. Pathol.* Abnormally dilated, as veins. [< L < *varix, -icis* varicose vein] — **var′i·cos′i·ty** (-kos′ə·tē) *n.*

var·ied (vâr′ēd) *adj.* **1.** Consisting of differing parts; diverse. **2.** Partially or repeatedly altered, modified, etc. **3.** Varicolored. — **var′ied·ly** *adv.*

var·i·e·gate (vâr′ē·ə·gāt′) *v.t.* **·gat·ed, ·gat·ing 1.** To mark

with different colors or tints; dapple; spot; streak. **2.** To make varied; diversify. [< LL < *varius* various + *agere* to drive, do] — **var′i·e·ga′tion** *n.*

var·i·e·gat·ed (vâr′ē·ə·gā′tid) *adj.* **1.** Having diverse colors; varied in color, as with streaks or blotches. **2.** Having or exhibiting different forms, styles, or varieties.

va·ri·e·tal (və·rī′ə·təl) *adj.* Of, pertaining to, or of the nature of a variety. — **va·ri′e·tal·ly** *adv.*

va·ri·e·ty (və·rī′ə·tē) *n. pl.* **·ties 1.** The state or character of being various or varied; diversity. **2.** A collection of diverse things. **3.** The possession of different characteristics by one individual. **4.** A limited class of things that differ in certain common peculiarities from a larger class to which they belong. **5.** *Biol.* An individual or a group that differs from the type species in certain characters; a subdivision of a species. [< MF < L < *varius* various]

variety show A theatrical show, as in vaudeville, consisting of a series of short, diversified acts or numbers.

vario- Var. of VARI-.

va·ri·o·la (və·rī′ə·lə) *n. Pathol.* Smallpox. [< Med.L, pustule < L *varius* speckled] — **va·ri′o·lar, va·ri′o·lous** *adj.*

var·i·om·e·ter (vâr′ē·om′ə·tər) *n. Electr.* A variable inductance device composed of a fixed and a movable coil connected in series, and capable of controlling the strength of a current. [< VARIO- + -METER]

var·i·o·rum (vâr′ē·ôr′əm, -ō′rəm) *adj.* Having notes or comments by different critics or editors. — *n.* An edition containing various versions of a text, usu. with notes and commentary: also **variorum edition.** [< L *(cum notis) variorum* (with the notes) of various persons]

var·i·ous (vâr′ē·əs) *adj.* **1.** Characteristically different from one another; diverse. **2.** More than one; several. **3.** Many-sided; varying. **4.** Having a diversity of appearance; variegated. **5.** *Rare* Changeable; inconstant. [< L *varius*] — **var′i·ous·ly** *adv.* — **var′i·ous·ness** *n.*

var·ix (vâr′iks) *n. pl.* **var·i·ces** (vâr′ə·sēz) *Pathol.* **a** Permanent dilatation of a vein or other vessel of circulation. **b** A vessel thus distorted, as a varicose vein. [< L, a varicose vein]

var·let (vär′lit) *n. Archaic* **1.** A menial or subordinate; also, a page. **2.** A knave or scoundrel. [< OF, groom]

var·mint (vär′mənt) *n. Dial.* Any obnoxious or pestiferous person or animal. [Alter. of VERMIN]

var·nish (vär′nish) *n.* **1.** A solution of certain gums or resins in alcohol, linseed oil, etc., used to produce a shining, transparent coat on a surface. **2.** Any natural or artificial product or surface resembling varnish. **3.** Outward show, or any superficial polish, as of politeness. — *v.t.* **1.** To cover with varnish. **2.** To give a smooth or glossy appearance to. **3.** To improve the appearance of; polish. **4.** To hide by a deceptive covering or appearance; gloss over. [< OF < Med.L *vernicium* a resin] — **var′nish·er** *n.*

var·si·ty (vär′sə·tē) *n. pl.* **·ties** *Informal* The highest ranking team that represents a university, college, or school in sports, debating, etc. [< UNIVERSITY]

var·y (vâr′ē) *v.* **var·ied, var·y·ing** *v.t.* **1.** To change the form, nature, substance, etc., of; modify. **2.** To cause to be different from one another. **3.** To impart variety to; diversify. **4.** *Music* To modify (a melody) by changes of rhythm, harmony, etc. — *v.i.* **5.** To become changed in form, nature, substance, etc. **6.** To be diverse; differ. **7.** To deviate: with *from.* **8.** *Math.* To be subject to continual change. **9.** *Biol.* To undergo variation. [< OF < L < *varius* diverse] — **var′i·er** *n.*

vas (vas) *n. pl.* **va·sa** (vā′sə) *Biol.* A blood vessel or duct. [< L, vessel, dish]

vas- Var. of VASO-.

vas·cu·lar (vas′kyə·lər) *adj. Biol.* **a** Of, or consisting of, or containing ducts for the transport of body liquids, as blood, lymph, etc. **b** Richly supplied with blood vessels. Also **vas′cu·lose** (-lōs), **vas′cu·lous** (-ləs). [< L < *vas* vessel] — **vas′cu·lar′i·ty** (-lar′ə·tē) *n.* — **vas′cu·lar·ly** *adv.*

vas def·er·ens (vas def′ər·enz) *Anat.* The duct by which semen is conveyed from the testicles to the seminal vesicles. [< NL < L *vas* vessel + *deferens* leading down]

vase (vās, vāz, väz) *n.* A decorative container, usu., rounded and of greater height than width, used as an ornament or for holding flowers. [< F < L *vas* vessel]

Vas·e·line (vas′ə·lēn, -lin) *n.* Proprietary name for a brand of petrolatum. Also **vas′e·line.**

vaso- *combining form Physiol.* **1.** A vessel, esp., a blood vessel. **2.** The vas deferens. Also, before vowels, **vas-.** [< L *vas* vessel]

vas·o·mo·tor (vas′ō·mō′tər) *adj. Physiol.* Producing contraction or dilatation in the walls of vessels.

vas·sal (vas′əl) *n.* **1.** In the feudal system, one who held land of a superior lord by a feudal tenure; a liegeman or feudal tenant. **2.** A dependent, retainer, or servant; a slave or bondman. — *adj.* **1.** Of or like a vassal. **2.** Servile. [< OF < Med.L < LL *vassus* servant < Celtic]

vas·sal·age (vas′əl·ij) *n.* **1.** The state of being a vassal;

also, the duties, and obligations of a vassal. **2.** The feudal system. **3.** Servitude in general. **4.** Land held by feudal tenure; a fief. **5.** Vassals collectively.

vast (vast, väst) *adj.* **1.** Of great extent or size; immense; enormous; huge. **2.** Very great in number, quantity, or amount. **3.** Very great in degree, intensity, etc. [< L *vastus* waste, empty, vast] **—vast′ly** *adv.* **—vast′ness** *n.*

vat (vat) *n.* A large vessel, tub, etc., for holding liquids, as dyeing materials. **—v.t. vat·ted, vat·ting** To put into a vat; treat in a vat. [OE *fæt*]

Vat·i·can (vat′ə-kən) *n.* **1.** The papal palace in Vatican City, Rome. **2.** The papal government: distinguished from the *Quirinal*. [< L *Vaticanus* (*mons*) Vatican (hill) in Rome]

vaude·ville (vōd′vil, vô′də-vil) *n.* A miscellaneous theatrical entertainment, as a variety show; also, a theater presenting such shows. [< F < *Vau de Vire* the valley of the Vire river (in Normandy)]

vault¹ (vôlt) *n.* **1.** An arched chamber; also, any subterranean compartment; cellar. **2.** An arched structure, as a ceiling or roof esp., of a cavity. **3.** Any vaultlike covering, as the sky. **4.** An underground room or compartment for storing wine, etc. **5.** A strongly protected place for keeping valuables, as in a bank. **6.** A burial chamber. **—v.t. 1.** To form with a vaulted roof; cover with or as with a vault. **2.** To construct in the form of a vault. [< OF < L *volvere* to roll]

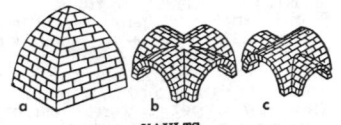

VAULTS
a Cove or cloister. *b* Groin.
c Underpitch or Welsh.

vault² (vôlt) *v.t.* **1.** To leap over, esp. with the aid of a pole or with the hands resting on something. **2.** To mount (a horse, etc.) with a leap. **—v.i. 3.** To leap; spring. **4.** To do a curvet. **—n. 1.** A leap or bound, as one made with the aid of a pole. **2.** The curvet of a horse. [< OF *voller* to leap, gambol, ? ult. < L *volutus*] **—vault′er** *n.*

vault·ing¹ (vôl′ting) *n.* **1.** Vaulted work, or vaults collectively. **2.** The work or art of building a vault.

vault·ing² (vôl′ting) *adj.* **1.** That overleaps. **2.** Unduly confident or presumptuous: *vaulting* ambition. **3.** That can be used in vaulting, as in gymnastics.

vaunt (vônt, vänt) *v.i.* **1.** To speak boastfully. **—v.t. 2.** To boast of. **—n.** Boastful assertion or ostentatious display. [< OF < LL *vanitare* to brag < L *vanus* empty, vain] **—vaunt′er** *n.* **—vaunt′ing·ly** *adv.*

Ve·a·dar (vē-ä-där′, vē′ä-där, vä′-) *n.* An intercalary month of the Hebrew year. See (Hebrew) CALENDAR.

veal (vēl) *n.* The flesh of a calf considered as food. **— bob veal** The flesh of a calf too young to be eaten. [< OF < L *vitellus*, dim. of *vitulus* calf]

vec·tor (vek′tər) *n.* **1.** *Math.* A physical quantity that has magnitude and direction in space, as velocity and acceleration. **2.** *Med.* A carrier of pathogenic microorganisms from one host to another. [< L, carrier < *vehere* to carry] **—vec·to·ri·al** (vek-tôr′ē-əl, -tō′rē-) *adj.*

Ve·da (vā′də, vē′-) *n.* **1.** One of the collections of Indian sacred writings, dating from the second millennium B.C., that form the Hindu scriptures. **2.** The Vedas collectively. [< Skt., knowledge] **—Ve·da·ic** (vi-dā′ik) *adj.* **—Ve·da·ism** (vā′də-iz′əm, vē′-) *n.*

Ve·dan·ta (vi-dän′tə, -dan′-) *n.* Any of several schools of Hindu religious philosophy based on the Upanishads; esp., a monistic system that teaches the worship of Brahma as the creator and soul of the universe. [< Skt. < *Veda* Veda + *anta* end] **—Ve·dan′tic** *adj.* **—Ve·dan′tism** *n.* **—Ve·dan′tist** *n.*

V-E Day (vē′ē′) May 8, the date of victory of the United Nations in Europe in World War II, 1945.

ve·dette (vi-det′) *n.* **1.** A mounted sentinel placed in advance of an outpost. **2.** A small vessel used to watch the movements of the enemy: also **vedette boat.** Also spelled *vidette*. [< F < Ital. *vedetta*, alter. (after *vedere* to see) of *veletta*, dim. of Sp. *vela* vigil < L *vigilare* to watch]

Ve·dic (vā′dik, vē′-) *adj.* Of or pertaining to the Vedas or the language in which they were written.

veer (vir) *v.i.* **1.** *Naut.* To turn to another course. **2.** To change direction by a clockwise motion, as the wind. **3.** To shift from one position to another; be variable or fickle. **—v.t. 4.** To change the direction of. **—n** A change in direction; a swerve. [< F *virer* to turn]

veer·y (vir′ē) *n.* *pl.* **veer·ies** A melodious, tawny thrush of eastern North America. [Prob. imit.]

Ve·ga (vē′gə, vā′-) *n.* One of the 20 brightest stars, 0.14 magnitude; Alpha in the constellation Lyra. [< Med.L Arabic (*al-Nasr*) *al-Waqi* the falling (vulture)]

veg·e·ta·ble (vej′ə-tə-bəl, vej′tə-) *n.* **1.** The edible part of any herbaceous plant, raw or cooked. **2.** Any member of the vegetable kingdom; a plant. **— adj. 1.** Pertaining to plants, esp. garden or farm vegetables. **2.** Derived from, of the nature of, or resembling plants. **3.** Made from or consisting of vegetables. **4.** Resembling or like a vegetable in activity, etc.; dull; passive. [< OF < LL < L *vegetare* to animate < *vegere* to be lively] **—veg′e·ta·bly** *adv.*

vegetable kingdom The division of nature that includes all organisms classified as plants.

vegetable oil Any of various oils expressed from the seeds or fruits of plants and used in cooking, medicine, paints, and as lubricants, as corn oil, olive oil, linseed oil, etc.

veg·e·tal (vej′ə-təl) *adj.* **1.** Of or pertaining to plants or vegetables. **2.** Characterizing those vital processes that are common to plants and animals, esp., as distinguished from sensation and volition. [< L *vegetus* lively, vigorous]

veg·e·tant (vej′ə-tənt) *adj.* **1.** Invigorating; vivifying; stimulating growth. **2.** Of the nature of plant life.

veg·e·tar·i·an (vej′ə-târ′ē-ən) *adj.* **1.** Pertaining to or advocating vegetarianism. **2.** Exclusively vegetable, as a diet. **— n.** One who holds or practices vegetarianism.

veg·e·tar·i·an·ism (vej′ə-târ′ē-ən-iz′əm) *n.* The theory or practice of eating only vegetables and fruits.

veg·e·tate (vej′ə-tāt) *v.i.* **·tat·ed, ·tat·ing 1.** To grow, as a plant. **2.** To live in a monotonous, passive way. **3.** *Pathol.* To increase abnormally in size.

veg·e·ta·tion (vej′ə-tā′shən) *n.* **1.** The process of vegetating. **2.** Plant life in the aggregate. **3.** *Pathol.* An abnormal growth on the body. **—veg·e·ta′tion·al** *adj.*

veg·e·ta·tive (vej′ə-tā′tiv) *adj.* **1.** Of, pertaining to, or exhibiting the processes of plant life. **2.** Growing or capable of growing, as plants; productive. **3.** Having a mere physical or passive existence; showing little mental activity. **4.** Concerned with growth and nutrition. Also **veg·e·tive** (vej′ə-tiv). **—veg′e·ta′tive·ly** *adv.* **—veg′e·ta′tive·ness** *n.*

ve·he·ment (vē′ə-mənt) *adj.* **1.** Arising from or marked by impetuosity of feeling or passion; ardent. **2.** Acting with great force or energy; energetic; violent; furious. [< OF < L *vehemens, -entis* impetuous, rash; ult. origin uncertain] **—ve′he·mence, ve′he·men·cy** *n.* **—ve′he·ment·ly** *adv.*

ve·hi·cle (vē′ə-kəl) *n.* **1.** Any contrivance fitted with wheels or runners for carrying something; a conveyance, as, a car or sled. **2.** *Med.* An innocuous medium, as a liquid, with which is mixed some therapeutic substance that may be applied or administered more easily; an excipient. **3.** A liquid, as oil, with which pigments are mixed in painting. **4.** Anything by means of which something else, as power, thought, etc., is transmitted or communicated. **5.** In the performing arts, anything, as a play, musical composition, etc., that permits the performer to display his particular powers or talents. [< F < L < *vehere* to carry, ride] **—ve·hic·u·lar** (vi-hik′yə-lər) *adj.*

veil (vāl) *n.* **1.** A piece of thin and light fabric, worn over the face or head for concealment, protection, or ornament. **2.** Any piece of fabric used to conceal an object; a screen; curtain; mask. **3.** Anything that conceals from inspection; a disguise; pretext. **4.** The life of a nun; also, vows made by a nun. **— to take the veil** To become a nun. **— v.t. 1.** To cover with a veil. **2.** To hide; disguise. [< OF < L *velum* piece of cloth, sail] **—veil′er** *n.*

veil·ing (vā′ling) *n.* **1.** Material for veils. **2.** A veil.

vein (vān) *n.* **1.** *Anat.* One of the muscular, tubular vessels that convey blood to the heart. **2.** Loosely, any blood vessel. **3.** *Entomol.* One of the radiating supports of an insect's wing. **4.** *Bot.* One of the slender vascular bundles that form the framework of a leaf. **5.** In mining, a lode. **6.** A long, irregular, colored streak, as in wood; marble, etc. **7.** A distinctive trait, tendency, or disposition. **8.** A temporary state of mind; humor; mood. **— v.t. 1.** To furnish or fill with veins. **2.** To streak or ornament with veins. **3.** To extend over or throughout as veins. [< OF < L *vena* blood vessel] **—vein′y** *adj.*

veined (vānd) *adj.* **1.** Having, marked with, or abounding in veins. **2.** Marked with streaks of another color.

vein·ing (vā′ning) *n.* A network of veins.

vein·let (vān′lit) *n.* A small vein.

ve·lar (vē′lər) *adj.* **1.** Of or pertaining to a velum, esp. to the soft palate. **2.** *Phonet.* Formed with the back of the tongue touching or near the soft palate, as (k) in *cool*, (g) in *go*: sometimes *guttural*. **— n. Phonet. a** A velar consonant. **b** A back vowel. [< L < *velum* a sail, custain]

ve·lar·ize (vē′lə-rīz) *v.* **·ized, ·iz·ing** *Phonet. v.t.* To modify (a sound) by raising the back of the tongue toward the soft palate. **— v.i.** To be modified to a velar sound.

veldt (velt, felt) *n.* In South Africa, open country or grassland having few shrubs or trees. Also **veld.** [< Afrikaans *veld* < Du., field]

vel·lum (vel′əm) *n.* **1.** Fine parchment made from the skins of calves, used for expensive binding, printing, etc. **2.** A manuscript written on such parchment. **3.** Paper made to resemble parchment. [< OF < *veel, viel* calf]

ve·loc·i·pede (və·los′ə·pēd) *n.* **1.** An early form of bicycle or tricycle. **2.** A child's tricycle. **3.** A type of handcar. [< F < L *velox, velocis* swift + *pes, pedis* foot]

ve·loc·i·ty (və·los′ə·tē) *n., pl.* **·ties** **1.** The state of moving or developing swiftly; rapidity; celerity; speed. **2.** The distance traveled by an object in a specified time. **3.** The time rate of motion in a stated direction; a vector quantity. [< L < *velox* swift]

ve·lours (və·lŏŏr′) *n., pl.* **·lours** (-lŏŏrz) A soft, velvetlike, closely woven cotton or wool fabric having a short, thick pile. Also **ve·lour′**. [< F. See VELURE.]

ve·lum (vē′ləm) *n., pl.* **·la** (-lə) **1.** *Biol.* A thin membranous covering or partition. **2.** *Anat.* The soft palate: see under PALATE. [< L]

ve·lure (və·lŏŏr′) *n.* **1.** Velvet, or a fabric resembling velvet. **2.** A velvet or silk pad for smoothing a silk hat. — *v.t.* **·lured, ·lur·ing** To smooth with a velure. [< F < L < *villus* shaggy hair]

vel·vet (vel′vit) *n.* **1.** A fabric of silk, rayon, cotton, etc., having on one side a thick, short, smooth pile, formed either of loops (**pile velvet**) or of single threads (**cut velvet**). **2.** Anything resembling such a fabric in softness, smoothness, etc. **3.** The furry skin covering a growing antler. — *adj.* **1.** Made of velvet. **2.** Smooth and soft to the touch; velvety. [< Med.L *velvetum,* ult. < L *villus* shaggy hair]

vel·vet·een (vel′və·tēn′) *n.* **1.** A cotton fabric with a short, close pile like velvet. **2.** *pl.* Clothes, esp. trousers, made of this material. [< VELVET]

vel·vet·y (vel′vit·ē) *adj.* **1.** Smooth and soft like velvet. **2.** Mild and smooth to the taste: *velvety* liqueur.

ve·na ca·va (vē′nə kā′və) *pl.* **ve·nae ca·vae** (vē′nē kā′vē) *Anat.* Either of the two great venous trunks emptying into the right atrium of the heart. For illus. see HEART. [< L, hollow vein]

ve·nal (vē′nəl) *adj.* **1.** Ready to sell honor or principle, or to accept a bribe; mercenary; purchasable. **2.** Subject to sordid bargaining or to corrupt influences; salable. **3.** Characterized by corruption. [< L *venum* sale] — **ve·nal′i·ty** (-nal′ə·tē) *n.* — **ve′nal·ly** *adv.*

ve·na·tion (vē·nā′shən) *n. Biol.* The arrangement of veins, as in a leaf, an insect wing, etc.

vend (vend) *v.t.* **1.** To sell. **2.** To utter (an opinion); publish. — *v.i.* **3.** To be a vender. **4.** To be sold. [< F *vendre* < L < *venum* sale + *dare* to give] — **ven·di·tion** (ven·dish′ən) *n.*

ven·dee (ven·dē′) *n. Law* The person or party to whom something is sold; a buyer.

vend·er (ven′dər) *n.* One who sells, as a hawker or peddler. Also **ven′dor** (-dər).

ven·det·ta (ven·det′ə) *n.* A blood feud in which the relatives of the killed or injured person take vengeance on the offender or his relatives. [< Ital. < L *vindicta* vengeance]

vend·i·ble (ven′də·bəl) *adj.* Capable of being vended or sold; marketable. — *n.* A vendible thing. — **vend′i·bil′i·ty, vend′i·ble·ness** *n.* — **vend′i·bly** *adv.*

vend·ing machine (ven′ding) A coin-operated device that dispenses some product or packaged article.

ve·neer (və·nir′) *n.* **1.** A thin layer, as of choice wood, upon a commoner surface. **2.** Any of the thin layers glued together to strengthen plywood. **3.** Mere outside show or elegance. — *v.t.* **1.** To cover (a surface) with veneer; overlay for decoration or finer finish. **2.** To glue together to form plywood. **3.** To conceal, as something disagreeable or coarse, with an attractive or deceptive surface. [Earlier *fineer* < G < F *fournir* to furnish] — **ve·neer′er** *n.*

ve·neer·ing (və·nir′ing) *n.* **1.** The art of applying veneer. **2.** Material used for veneer. **3.** A surface of veneer.

ven·er·a·ble (ven′ər·ə·bəl) *adj.* **1.** Meriting or commanding veneration; worthy of reverence: now usu. implying age. **2.** Exciting reverential feelings because of sacred or historic associations. **3.** Revered: used as a title for an archdeacon in Anglican churches, and in the Roman Catholic Church, for one past the first stage of canonization, prior to beatification. [< OF < L *venerari* to revere] — **ven′er·a·ble·ness, ven′er·a·bil′i·ty** *n.* — **ven′er·a·bly** *adv.*

ven·er·ate (ven′ə·rāt) *v.t.* **·at·ed, ·at·ing** To look upon or regard with respect and deference; revere. [< L *veneratus,* pp. of *venerari* to revere]

— **Syn.** We *venerate* that which we judge objectively to be of great worth, as a great man, our ancestors, a holy person, or a sacred object. *Revere* and *reverence* imply respect, to which have been added personal affection and awe; *revere* is chiefly applied to persons or to a holy person, and *reverence,* to places or objects; to *revere* God and the saints, to *reverence* a holy shrine. In strict usage, we *worship* or *adore* only that which we consider divine; *worship* refers to participation in religious ceremonies, and *adore,* to the sense of personal gratitude for divine favor which the worshiper feels.

ven·er·a·tion (ven′ə·rā′shən) *n.* **1.** The act of venerating, or the state of being venerated. **2.** A feeling of profound respect and awe: reverence.

ve·ne·re·al (və·nir′ē·əl) *adj.* **1.** Pertaining to or proceeding from sexual intercourse. **2.** Communicated by sexual relations with an infected person: a *venereal* disease. **3.** Pertaining to or curative of diseases so communicated. **4.** Infected with venereal disease. [< L < *Venus*]

venereal disease *Pathol.* One of several diseases communicated by sexual intercourse, as syphilis, gonorrhea, and chancroid.

ven·er·y[1] (ven′ər·ē) *n. pl.* **·er·ies** *Archaic* Sexual indulgence, esp. when excessive. [< L *Venus*]

ven·er·y[2] (ven′ər·ē) *n. pl.* **·er·ies** *Archaic* The hunting of game. [< F < L *venari* to hunt]

Ven·e·ti (ven′ə·tī) *n.pl.* **1.** An ancient Celtic people of NW Gaul, conquered by Caesar in 56 B.C. **2.** An ancient people of NE Italy, friendly to Rome.

Ve·ne·tian (və·nē′shən) *adj.* Pertaining to Venice, its inhabitants, art etc. — *n.* A native of Venice.

Venetian blind A flexible window screen that may be raised or lowered, having overlapping horizontal slats so connected with a cord as to permit opening and closing.

Venetian carpet A worsted carpet for stairs and hallways, commonly of a simple striped pattern.

Venetian glass A delicate and fine glassware made at or near Venice.

ven·geance (ven′jəns) *n.* The act of revenging; retribution for a wrong or injury. — **Syn.** See REVENGE. — **with a vengeance** With great force or violence; to an unusual extent. [< AF < OF < L *vindicare* to defend, avenge]

venge·ful (venj′fəl) *adj.* **1.** Seeking to inflict vengeance; vindictive. **2.** Serving to inflict vengeance. — **venge′ful·ly** *adv.* — **venge′ful·ness** *n.*

veni- *combining form* Vein; also, vein in the earth. [< L *vena* vein]

ve·ni·al (vē′nē·əl, vēn′yəl) *adj.* **1.** *Theol.* That may be easily pardoned or forgiven: distinguished from *mortal: venial* sin. **2.** Excusable; pardonable. [< OF < L *venia* forgiveness, mercy] — **ve′ni·al′i·ty** (-al′ə·tē), **ve′ni·al·ness** *n.* — **ve′ni·al·ly** *adv.*

ve·ni·re (vi·nī′rē) *n. Law* A writ issued to the sheriff for summoning persons to serve as a jury. Also **ve·ni′re fa·ci·as** (fā′shi·as) [< L *venire facias,* that you cause to come]

ve·ni·re·man (vi·nī′rē·mən) *n. pl.* **·men** (-mən) One summoned to serve on a jury under a venire.

ven·i·son (ven′ə·zən, -sən; *Brit.* ven′zən) *n.* Deer flesh used for food. [< F < L < *venatus,* pp. of *venari* to hunt]

ve·ni, vi·di, vi·ci (vē′nī, vī′dī, vī′sī; wē′nē, wē′dē, wē′kē) *Latin* I came, I saw, I conquered: words used by Julius Caesar to report a victory in Asia Minor.

ven·om (ven′əm) *n.* **1.** The poisonous liquid secreted by certain animals, as serpents and scorpions, and introduced into the victim by a bite or sting. **2.** Malice; malignity; spite. [< OF < L *venenum* poison]

ven·om·ous (ven′əm·əs) *adj.* **1.** Having glands secreting venom. **2.** Able to give a poisonous sting. **3.** Malignant; spiteful. — **ven′om·ous·ly** *adv.* — **ven′om·ous·ness** *n.*

ve·nous (vē′nəs) *adj.* **1.** Of, pertaining to, or marked with veins. **2.** *Physiol.* Designating the blood carried by the veins, distinguished from arterial blood by its darker color and presence of carbon dioxide. [< L *venosus* < *vena* vein] — **ve′nous·ly** *adv.* — **ve′nous·ness** *n.*

vent (vent) *n.* **1.** An opening, commonly small, for the passage of liquids, gases, etc. **2.** Utterance; expression: chiefly in the phrase **to give vent to.** **3.** *Zool.* The external opening of the alimentary canal, esp. of animals below mammals; the anus. — *v.t.* **1.** To give expression to: often with *on:* to *vent* one's rage on the cat. **2.** To relieve, as by giving vent to emotion. **3.** To permit to escape from an opening. [ME < OF *fente* cleft < L *findere* to split] — **ven′ter** *n.*

vent·age (ven′tij) *n.* **1.** A small opening. **2.** A finger hole in a musical instrument. [< VENT]

vent·tail (ven′tāl) *n.* The lower adjustable front of a medieval helmet. [< *vent* wind]

ven·ti·late (ven′tə·lāt) *v.t.* **·lat·ed, ·lat·ing** **1.** To produce a free circulation of air in; admit fresh air into. **2.** To provide with a vent. **3.** To make widely known; expose to examination and discussion. **4.** To oxygenate, as blood. [< L *ventilatus,* pp. of *ventilare* to fan < *ventus* wind] — **ven′ti·la′tion** *n.* — **ven′ti·la′tive** *adj.*

ven·ti·la·tor (ven′tə·lā′tər) *n.* A device or arrangement for supplying fresh air. — **ven′ti·la·to′ry** (-lə·tôr′ē, -tō′rē) *adj.*

ven·tral (ven′trəl) *adj. Anat.* **a** Of, pertaining to, or situated on or near the abdomen. **b** On or toward the lower or anterior part of the body. [< L < *venter, ventris* belly] — **ven′tral·ly** *adv.*

ven·tri·cle (ven′trə·kəl) *n. Anat.* **1.** One of the two lower chambers of the heart, from which blood received from the atria is forced into the arteries. **2.** Any of various cavities in the body, as of the brain, the spinal cord, etc. For illus. see HEART. [< L *ventriculus*, dim. of *venter, ventris* belly]

ven·tric·u·lar (ven·trik'yə·lər) *adj.* **1.** Of, pertaining to, or of the nature of a ventricle. **2.** Swollen and distended.

ven·tril·o·quism (ven·tril'ə·kwiz'əm) *n.* The art of speaking in such a manner that the sounds seem to come from some source other than the person speaking. Also **ven·tril'o·quy** (-kwē). [< L < *venter* belly + *loqui* to speak] — **ven·tril'o·quist** *n.* — **ven·tril'o·quis'tic** *adj.*

ven·tril·o·quize (ven·tril'ə·kwīz) *v.t. & v.i.* **·quized, ·quiz·ing** To speak as a ventriloquist. Also *Brit.* **ven·tril'o·quise.**

ventro- *combining form Anat.* The abdomen; related to or near the abdomen; ventral. [< L *venter, ventris* belly]

ven·ture (ven'chər) *v.* **·tured, ·tur·ing** *v.t.* **1.** To expose to chance or risk; hazard; stake. **2.** To run the risk of; brave. **3.** To express at the risk of denial or refutation: to *venture* a suggestion. — *v.i.* **4.** To take a risk; dare. — *n.* **1.** An undertaking attended with risk or danger; a risk; hazard; esp., a business investment. **2.** That which is ventured; esp., property risk. — **at a venture** At hazard; offhand. [Aphetic form of ADVENTURE] — **ven'tur·er** *n.*

ven·ture·some (ven'chər·səm) *adj.* **1.** Bold; daring. **2.** Involving hazard; risky. — **ven'ture·some·ly** *adv.* — **ven'·ture·some·ness** *n.*

ven·tur·ous (ven'chər·əs) *adj.* **1.** Adventurous; willing to take risks and brave dangers; bold. **2.** Hazardous; risky; dangerous. — **ven'tur·ous·ly** *adv.* — **ven'tur·ous·ness** *n.*

ven·ue (ven'yōō) *n. Law* The place where a crime is committed or a cause of action arises; also, the county or political division from which the jury must be summoned and in which the trial must be held. — **change of venue** The change of the place of trial. [< OF, orig. fem. pp. of *venir* to come < L *venire*]

Ve·nus (vē'nəs) In Roman mythology, the goddess of love, spring, bloom, and beauty: identified with the Greek *Aphrodite*. — *n.* **1.** The sixth largest planet of the solar system and second in order from the sun. See PLANET. **2.** A statue or painting of Venus. **3.** A lovely woman. [< L]

Venus of Mi·lo (mē'lō) A marble statue of Venus, with the arms missing, discovered in 1820 on the island of Milo and later placed in the Louvre. Also **Venus de Milo.**

Ve·nus's flytrap (vē'nəs·iz flī'trap') *n.* A plant with clustered leaves whose spiked blades instantly close upon insects lighting upon them, found native chiefly in the sandy bogs of eastern North and South Carolina.

ve·ra·cious (və·rā'shəs) *adj.* **1.** Habitually disposed to speak the truth; truthful. **2.** Conforming to or expressing truth; true; accurate. [< L *verax, veracis* < *versus* true] — **ve·ra'cious·ly** *adv.* — **ve·ra'cious·ness** *n.*

ve·rac·i·ty (və·ras'ə·tē) *n. pl.* **·ties 1.** The habitual regard for truth; truthfulness; honesty. **2.** Agreement with truth; accuracy. **3.** That which is true; truth.

ve·ran·da (və·ran'də) *n.* An open portico or balcony, usu. roofed, along the outside of a building; a porch or stoop. Also **ve·ran'dah.** [< Hind. < Pg. *varanda* railing, balustrade]

verb (vûrb) *n. Gram.* **1.** The part of speech that expresses existence, action, or occurrence, as the English words *be, collide, think.* **2.** Any word or construction functioning similarly. [< F < L *verbum* word]

ver·bal (vûr'bəl) *adj.* **1.** Of, pertaining to, or connected with words. **2.** Concerned with words rather than the ideas they convey: *verbal* distinctions. **3.** Expressed orally; not written: a *verbal* contract. **4.** Having word corresponding with word; literal: a *verbal* translation. **5.** *Gram.* **a** Partaking of the nature of or derived from a verb: a *verbal* noun. **b** Used to form verbs: a *verbal* prefix. — *n. Gram.* A verb form that functions as a substantive (gerund and infinitive) or as a modifier (present and past participles and infinitive), but retains some of the characteristics of a verb. [< F < LL < L *verbum* word] — **ver'bal·ly** *adv.*

— **Syn.** (adj.) **2.** In strict usage, *verbal* refers to spoken or written words, and *oral*, to spoken words only: a *verbal* dispute, an *oral* examination. However, the distinction is often blurred, so that we speak of a *verbal* agreement, rather than of an *oral* agreement. *Oral* and *verbal* always imply communication: *vocal* refers to the use of the voice, whether for communicating thought or not: a *vocal* exercise, a *vocal* defect.

ver·bal·ism (vûr'bəl·iz'əm) *n.* **1.** A verbal expression. **2.** A meaningless form of words. **3.** Wordiness; verbiage.

ver·bal·ist (vûr'bəl·ist) *n.* **1.** One who deals with words rather than facts or ideas. **2.** One who is skilled in the use and meaning of words.

ver·bal·ize (vûr'bəl·īz) *v.* **·ized, ·iz·ing** *v.t.* **1.** To express in words. **2.** *Gram.* To make a verb of; change into a verb. — *v.i.* **3.** To speak or write verbosely. **4.** To express oneself in words. — **ver'bal·i·za'tion** *n.* — **ver'bal·iz'er** *n.*

ver·ba·tim (vər·bā'tim, -təm) *adj. & adv.* In the exact words; word for word. [< LL < L *verbum* word]

ver·be·na (vər·bē'nə) *n.* Any of various American garden plants having dense terminal spikes of showy flowers. [< L, foliage, vervain]

ver·bi·age (vûr'bē·ij) *n.* **1.** Excess of words. **2.** Wordiness; verbosity. [< F *verbier* to gabble < L *verbum* word]

ver·bose (vər·bōs') *adj.* Using or containing a wearisome and unnecessary number of words; wordy. [< L *verbosus* < *verbum* word] — **ver·bose'ly** *adv.* — **ver·bose'ness** *n.* — **Syn.** Diffuse, prolix. Compare CIRCUMLOCUTION.

ver·bos·i·ty (vər·bos'ə·tē) *n. pl.* **·ties** The state or quality of being verbose; wordiness.

ver·bo·ten (fer·bōt'n) *adj. German* Forbidden.

verb phrase *Gram.* A finite verb form, consisting of a principle verb and an auxiliary or auxiliaries.

ver·dant (vûr'dənt) *adj.* **1.** Green with vegetation; covered with grass or green leaves; fresh. **2.** Unsophisticated. [< F < L *viridis* green] — **ver'dan·cy** *n.* — **ver'dant·ly** *adv.*

ver·dict (vûr'dikt) *n.* **1.** The decision of a jury in an action. **2.** A conclusion expressed; judgment. [< AF *verdit,* OF *voirdit* < L < *verus* true + *dictum,* pp. of *dicere* to say]

ver·di·gris (vûr'də·grēs, -gris) *n.* The green or bluish patina formed on copper, bronze, or brass surfaces after long exposure to the air. [< OF *verd de Grice, vert de Grece,* lit., green of Greece]

ver·dure (vûr'jər) *n.* The fresh greenness of growing vegetation; also, such vegetation itself. [< F < L *viridis* green]

ver·dur·ous (vûr'jər·əs) *adj.* Covered with verdure; verdant. — **ver'dur·ous·ness** *n.*

Ver·ein (fer·īn') *n. German* A society; association.

verge¹ (vûrj) *n.* **1.** The extreme edge of something having defined limits; brink; margin. **2.** The point at which some action, condition, or state is likely to occur: on the *verge* of bankruptcy. **3.** A bounding or enclosing line; a boundary; also, the space enclosed. **4.** A rod, wand, or staff as a symbol of authority or emblem of office. — *v.i.* **verged, verg·ing 1.** To come near; approach; border; usu. with *on:* His speech *verges* on the chaotic. **2.** To form the limit or verge. [< F, rod, stick < L *virga* twig]

verge² (vûrj) *v.i.* **verged, verg·ing** To slope; tend; incline. [< L *vergere* to bend, turn]

Ver·gil·i·an (vər·jil'ē·ən) *adj.* Pertaining to or in the style of Vergil: also spelled *Virgilian.*

ver·i·fi·a·ble (ver'ə·fī'ə·bəl) *adj.* Capable of being verified. — **ver'i·fi'a·ble·ness** *n.* — **ver'i·fi'a·bly** *adv.*

ver·i·fi·ca·tion (ver'ə·fə·kā'shən) *n.* **1.** The act of verifying, or the state of being verified. **2.** *Law* An oath appended to an account, petition, or plea, as to the truth of the facts stated in it.

ver·i·fy (ver'ə·fī) *v.t.* **·fied, ·fy·ing 1.** To prove to be true or accurate; substantiate; confirm. **2.** To test or ascertain the accuracy or truth of. **3.** *Law* **a** To affirm under oath. **b** To add a confirmation to. [< OF < Med.L < *verus* true + *facere* to make] — **ver'i·fi'er** *n.*

ver·i·ly (ver'ə·lē) *adv. Archaic* In truth; really. [< VERY]

ver·i·sim·i·lar (ver'ə·sim'ə·lər) *adj.* Appearing or seeming to be true; likely; probable. [< L < *verus* true + *similis* like] — **ver'i·sim'i·lar·ly** *adv.*

ver·i·si·mil·i·tude (ver'ə·si·mil'ə·tōōd, -tyōōd) *n.* **1.** Appearance of truth. **2.** That which resembles truth.

ver·i·ta·ble (ver'ə·tə·bəl) *adj.* Properly so called; unquestionable: a *veritable* villain. [< F *vérité* verity] — **ver'i·ta·ble·ness** *n.* — **ver'i·ta·bly** *adv.*

ver·i·ty (ver'ə·tē) *n. pl.* **·ties 1.** The quality of being correct or true. **2.** A true or established statement, principle, etc.; a fact; truth. [< F < L *veritas* truth]

ver·juice (vûr'jōōs) *n.* **1.** The sour juice of green fruit, as unripe grapes. **2.** Sharpness or sourness of disposition or manner; acidity. [< OF < *vert* green + *jus* juice]

ver·meil (vûr'mil) *n.* **1.** Silver or bronze gilt. **2.** *Poetic* Vermilion, or the color of vermilion. — *adj.* Of a bright-red color. [< OF < L *vermiculus,* dim. of *vermis* worm, the cochineal insect]

vermi- *combining form* A worm; of or related to a worm. [< L *vermis* worm]

ver·mi·cel·li (vûr'mə·sel'ē, *Ital.* ver'mē·chel'lē) *n.* A food paste made into slender cords thinner than spaghetti or macaroni. [< Ital., lit., little worms, pl. of *vermicello*]

ver·mi·cide (vûr'mə·sīd) *n.* Any substance that kills worms; esp., any drug destructive of intestinal worms. — **ver·mi·ci·dal** (vûr'mə·sīd'əl) *adj.*

ver·mic·u·lar (vər·mik'yə·lər) *adj.* **1.** Having the form or motion of a worm. **2.** Like the wavy tracks of a worm. [< L < *vermis* worm] — **ver·mic'u·lar·ly** *adv.*

ver·mic·u·late (vər·mik'yə·lāt) *adj.* **1.** Covered with wormlike markings. **2.** Having the motions of a worm. **3.** Insinuating; tortuous. **4.** Worm-eaten.

ver·mi·form (vûr'mə·fôrm) *adj.* Like a worm in shape. [< Med.L < L *vermis* worm + *forma* form]

vermiform appendix *Anat.* A slender, wormlike vestigial structure, protruding from the end of the cecum in man and certain other mammals. For illus. see INTESTINE.

ver·mi·fuge (vûr′mə·fyōōj) *n.* Any remedy that destroys intestinal worms. — *adj.* Acting as a vermifuge. [< F < L *vermis* worm + *fugare* to expel]

ver·mil·ion (vər·mil′yən) *n.* **1.** A brilliant, durable red pigment, obtained naturally by grinding cinnabar to a fine powder, or made synthetically. **2.** The color of the pigment, an intense orange red. — *adj.* Of a bright-red color. — *v.t.* To color with vermilion; dye bright red. [See VERMEIL.]

ver·min (vûr′min) *n. pl.* **·min 1.** Noxious small animals or parasitic insects, as lice, fleas, worms, rats, mice, etc. **2.** *Brit.* Certain animals injurious to game, as weasels, owls, etc. **3.** A repulsive or obnoxious human being; also, such persons collectively. [< OF < L *vermis* worm]

ver·min·ous (vûr′mən·əs) *adj.* **1.** Infested with vermin, esp. parasites. **2.** Relating to or caused by vermin. **3.** Of the nature of or resembling vermin. — **ver′min·ous·ly** *adv.* — **ver′min·ous·ness** *n.*

ver·mouth (vûr′mōōth, vər·mōōth′) *n.* A liqueur made from white wine flavored with aromatic herbs. Also **ver′·muth.** [< F < G *wermuth* wormwood]

ver·nac·u·lar (vər·nak′yə·lər) *n.* **1.** The native language of a locality. **2.** The common everyday speech of the people, as opposed to the literary language. **3.** The vocabulary or jargon of a particular profession or trade. **4.** An idiomatic word or phrase. **5.** The common name of a plant or animal as distinguished from its scientific designation. — *adj.* **1.** Originating in or belonging to one's native land; indigenous: said of a language, idiom, etc. **2.** Using everyday speech rather than the literary language. **3.** Written in the native language. **4.** Characteristic of a specific locality or country: *vernacular* arts. **5.** Designating the common name of a plant or animal. [< L *vernaculus* native < *verna* home-born slave, native] — **ver·nac′u·lar·ly** *adv.*

ver·nal (vûr′nəl) *adj.* **1.** Belonging to, appearing in, or appropriate to spring. **2.** Youthful; fresh. **3.** Of or belonging to spring < *ver* spring] — **ver′nal·ly** *adv.*

ver·nal·ize (vûr′nəl·īz) *v.t.* **·ized, ·iz·ing** To accelerate the growth of (a plant) by subjecting the seeds to low temperatures. — **ver′nal·i·za′tion** *n.*

ver·na·tion (vər·nā′shən) *n. Bot.* The disposition of leaves within the leaf bud. [< NL < *vernare* to flourish]

ver·ni·er (vûr′nē·ər) *n.* **1.** The small, movable, auxiliary scale for obtaining fractional parts of the subdivisions of a fixed scale on a barometer, sextant, gauge, or other measure. Also **vernier scale. 2.** *Mech.* An auxiliary device to insure fine adjustments in precision instruments. [after Pierre *Vernier,* 1580?–1637, French mathematician]

Ve·ro·nal (ver′ə·nəl) *n.* Proprietary name for a brand of barbital.

ver·sa·tile (vûr′sə·til) *adj.* **1.** Having an aptitude for various occupations; many-sided. **2.** Subject to change; variable. **3.** *Bot.* Attached so as to be freely swinging or turning. **4.** *Zool.* Capable of being turned forward or backward, as the toe of a bird. [< F < L < *vertere* to turn] — **ver′sa·tile·ly** *adv.* — **ver′sa·til′i·ty, ver′sa·tile·ness** *n.*

verse (vûrs) *n.* **1.** A single metrical or rhythmical line. **2.** Metrical composition; poetry: distinguished from *prose.* **3.** A poem. **4.** A specified type of meter or metrical structure: iambic *verse.* **5.** One of the short divisions of a chapter of the Bible. **6.** A short division of any metrical composition, song, etc., esp., a stanza. — *v.t. & v.i.* **versed, vers·ing** *Rare* To versify. [OE and OF < L < *vertere* to turn]

versed (vûrst) *adj.* Thoroughly acquainted; adept; proficent: with *in.* [< L < *versari* to occupy oneself]

versed sine *Trig.* A function of an angle, equal to one minus the cosine. Also **ver·sine** (vûr′sin).

ver·si·cle (vûr′si·kəl) *n.* One of a series of lines said or sung alternately by minister and congregation. [< L. See VERSE.]

ver·si·fy (vûr′sə·fī) *v.* **·fied, ·fy·ing** *v.t.* **1.** To change from prose into verse. **2.** To narrate or treat in verse. — *v.i.* **3.** To write poetry. [< OF < L < *versus* verse + *facere* to make] — **ver′si·fi·ca′tion** (-fə·kā′shən) *n.* — **ver′si·fi′er** *n.*

ver·sion (vûr′zhən, -shən) *n.* **1.** A description or account as modified by a particular point of view. **2.** A translation. **3.** *Usu. cap.* A translation of the whole or part of the Bible: the Douai *version.* [< MF < Med.L < L *vertere* to turn] — **ver′sion·al** *adj.*

vers li·bre (ver lē′br′) *French* Free verse.

ver·so (vûr′sō) *n. pl.* **·sos 1.** A left-hand page of a book, or sheet of folded paper: opposed to *recto.* **2.** The reverse of a coin or medal. [< L *verso* (*folio*) a turned (leaf)]

verst (vûrst) *n.* A Russian measure of distance, about two thirds of a mile, or 1.067 kilometers. [< F and G < Russian *versta,* orig. a line]

ver·sus (vûr′səs) *prep.* **1.** In law and sports, against: Dempsey *versus* Tunney. **2.** Considered as the alternative of: free trade *versus* tariffs. [< L, toward, *vertere* to turn]

ver·te·bra (vûr′tə·brə) *n. pl.* **·brae** (-brē) or **·bras** *Anat.* Any of the segmented bones of the spinal column in man and the higher vertebrates. [< L, joint < *vertere* to turn] — **ver′te·bral** *adj.*

ver·te·brate (vûr′tə·brāt, -brit) *adj.* **1.** Having a backbone or spinal column. **2.** Pertaining to or characteristic of vertebrates. — *n.* Any of a primary division of animals, characterized by a segmented spinal column, as fishes, birds, reptiles, and mammals.

ver·tex (vûr′teks) *n. pl.* **·tex·es** or **·ti·ces** (-tə·sēz) **1.** The highest point of anything; apex; top. **2.** *Astron.* The point in the sky toward or from which a group of stars appears to be moving. **3.** *Geom.* **a** The point of intersection of the sides of an angle. **b** The point of a triangle opposite to, and farthest from, the base. [< L, the top < *vertere* to turn]

ver·ti·cal (vûr′ti·kəl) *adj.* **1.** Perpendicular to the plane of the horizon, extending up and down; upright. **2.** Directly above or overhead. **3.** Of or at the vertex or highest point. **4.** *Econ.* Of or pertaining to a group of business concerns that handle all the stages of the manufacture and distribution of a product. — *n.* **1.** A vertical line, plane, or circle. **2.** An upright beam or rod in a truss. [< MF < L. See VERTEX.] — **ver′ti·cal′i·ty** (-kal′ə·tē), **ver′ti·cal·ness** *n.* — **ver′ti·cal·ly** *adv.*

vertical union An industrial union.

ver·ti·ces (vûr′tə·sēz) Plural of VERTEX.

ver·ti·cil (vûr′tə·sil) *n. Biol.* **1.** A set of organs, as leaves or tentacles, disposed in a circle around an axis; whorl. **2.** A volution of a spiral shell. [< L *verticillus* whorl]

ver·tic·il·late (vər·tis′ə·lit, -lāt, vûr′tə·sil′it, -āt) *adj.* **1.** Arranged in a verticil. **2.** Having parts so arranged. Also **ver·tic′il·lat·ed.** — **ver·tic′il·late·ly** *adv.* — **ver·tic′il·la′tion** *n.*

ver·tig·i·nous (vər·tij′ə·nəs) *adj.* **1.** Affected by vertigo; dizzy. **2.** Turning round; whirling; revolving. **3.** Liable to cause dizziness. [See VERTIGO.] — **ver·tig′i·nous·ly** *adv.* — **ver·tig′i·nous·ness** *n.*

ver·ti·go (vûr′tə·gō) *n. pl.* **·goes** or **ver·tig·i·nes** (vər·tij′ə·nēz) *Pathol.* Any of a group of disorders in which a person feels as if he or his surroundings are whirling around; dizziness. [< L < *vertere* to turn]

ver·tu (vər·tōō′, vûr′tōō) See VIRTU.

ver·vain (vûr′vān) *n.* Any of a family of herbs, shrubs, and trees, including many cultivated ornamental verbenas. [< OF < L *verbena*]

verve (vûrv) *n.* **1.** Enthusiasm or energy, esp., as manifested in artistic production. **2.** Spirit; vigor. [< F]

ver·y (ver′ē) *adv.* In a high degree; extremely: *very* generous. — *adj.* **ver·i·er, ver·i·est 1.** Absolute; actual; simple: the *very* truth. **2.** Identical: my *very* words. **3.** The (thing) itself: used as an intensive equivalent to *even:* The *very* stones cry out. **4.** Unqualified; utter; complete: a *very* rogue. [< AF or OF < L *verus* true]

very high frequency *Telecom.* A band of radio wave frequencies ranging from 30 to 300 megacycles.

very low frequency *Telecom.* A band of radio wave frequencies ranging from 10 to 30 kilocycles.

ves·i·cant (ves′i·kənt) *adj.* Producing blisters. — *n.* That which produces blisters. [< NL < L *vesica* blister, bladder]

ves·i·cate (ves′i·kāt) *v.t. & v.i.* **·cat·ed, ·cat·ing** To blister. — **ves′i·ca′tion** *n.*

ves·i·ca·to·ry (ves′i·kə·tôr′ē, və·sik′ə·tôr′ē, -tō′rē) *adj.* Capable of producing blisters; vesicant. — *n. pl.* **·ries** Any substance, as an ointment or plaster, that causes a blister.

ves·i·cle (ves′i·kəl) *n.* **1.** Any small bladderlike cavity, cell, or cyst. **2.** *Anat.* A small sac, containing gas or fluid. **3.** *Pathol.* A blister. [< L < *vesica* bladder] — **ve·sic·u·lar** (və·sik′yə·lər) *adj.*

vesico- *combining form Med.* The urinary bladder; of or pertaining to the urinary bladder. Also, before vowels, **vesic-.** [< L *vesica* bladder]

ve·sic·u·late (*v.* və·sik′yə·lāt; *adj.* və·sik′yə·lit, -lāt) *v.t. & v.i.* **·lat·ed, ·lat·ing** To make or become vesicular. — *adj.* Having vesicles; vesicular. — **ve·sic′u·la′tion** *n.*

ves·per (ves′pər) *n.* **1.** A bell that calls to vespers. **2.** An evening service, prayer, or song. **3.** *Obs.* Evening. — *adj.* Of evening or vespers. [< L, the evening star]

Ves·per (ves′pər) *n.* The evening star; Hesperus; the planet Venus when an evening star. [< OF < L]

ves·pers (ves′pərz) *n.pl. Often cap. Eccl.* **1.** The sixth of the seven canonical hours. **2.** A service of worship in the evening. [< OF < Med.L < L *vespera* evening]

ves·sel (ves′əl) *n.* **1.** A hollow receptacle, esp. one capable of holding a liquid, as a bowl, pitcher, etc. **2.** A craft designed to float on the water, usu. one larger than a rowboat; a ship or boat. **3.** *Anat.* A duct or canal for transporting a body fluid, as a vein. [< L < *vas* vessel]

vest (vest) *n. Chiefly U.S.* A man's short, sleeveless garment, buttoning in front, commonly worn underneath a suit coat: also, *esp. Brit.,* **waistcoat.** — *v.t.* **1.** To confer (ownership, authority, etc.) upon some person or persons: usu., with *in*. **2.** To place ownership, or authority with (a person or persons). **3.** To clothe, as with vestments. —*v.i.* **4.** To clothe oneself, as in vestments. **5.** To become vested; devolve. [< F < Ital. < L *vestis* garment]

Ves·ta (ves′tə) *n.* In Roman mythology, the goddess of the hearth and the hearth fire.

ves·tal (ves′təl) *n.* **1.** One of the virgin priestesses of Vesta. Also **vestal virgin. 2.** A woman of pure character; a virgin. **3.** A nun. — *adj.* **1.** Pertaining to Vesta. **2.** Chaste; pure.

vest·ed (ves′tid) *adj.* **1.** *Law* Held by fixed tenure. Established by law as a permanent right. **2.** Dressed; robed, esp. in church vestments.

vested interest 1. A strong commitment to a system or institution whose existence serves one's self-interest. **2.** *Usu. pl.* A financially powerful or influential group.

vest·ee (ves·tē′) *n.* An imitation blouse-front worn in the front of a suit or dress. [Dim. of VEST]

ves·ti·bule (ves′tə·byōōl) *n.* **1.** A small antechamber behind the outer door of a building; an entrance hall; lobby. **2.** The enclosed passage between railway passenger cars. **3.** *Anat.* Any of several chambers or channels adjoining or communicating with others: the *vestibule* of the ear. — *v.t.* **·buled, ·bul·ing** To provide with a vestibule. [< L *vestibulum* entrance hall] —**ves·tib′u·lar** (-tib′yə·lər) *adj.*

ves·tige (ves′tij) *n.* **1.** A visible trace, impression, or sign, of something absent or lost; trace. **2.** *Biol.* A part or organ, small or degenerate, but well developed and functional in ancestral forms of organisms. [< F < L *vestigium* footprint] —**ves·tig′i·al** *adj.* —**ves·tig′i·al·ly** *adv.*

ves·tig·i·um (ves·tij′ē·əm) *n. pl.* **·tig·i·a** (-tij′ē·ə) *Biol.* A vestigial part; vestige. [< L, footprint]

vest·ment (vest′mənt) *n.* **1.** An article of dress; esp., a robe of office. **2.** *Eccl.* One of the ritual garments of the clergy. [< OF < L < *vestire* to clothe] —**vest′ment·al** *adj.*

vest-pock·et (vest′pok′it) *adj.* Small enough to fit in a vest pocket; very small; diminutive: a *vest-pocket* edition.

ves·try (ves′trē) *n. pl.* **·tries 1.** A room, as in a church, where vestments and sacred vessels are kept: often called *sacristy*. **2.** A room in a church used for Sunday School, meetings, as a chapel, etc. **3.** In the Anglican Church, a body administering the affairs of a parish or congregation; also, a meeting of such a body. [< OF *vestiarie* < Med.L *vestiarium* wardrobe]

ves·try·man (ves′trē·mən) *n. pl.* **·men** (-mən) A member of a vestry.

ves·ture (ves′chər) *n.* **1.** *Archaic* Garments; clothing, a robe. **2.** *Archaic* A covering or envelope. — *v.t.* **·tured, ·tur·ing** *Archaic* To cover or clothe with vesture. [< OF < *vestir* cloth < L *vestire* to clothe]

vet[1] (vet) *Informal n.* A veterinarian. — *v.* **vet·ted, vet·ting** *v.t.* **1.** To treat as a veterinarian does. — *v.i.* **2.** To treat animals medically. [Short for VETERINARIAN]

vet[2] (vet) *n. Informal* A veteran. [Short for VETERAN]

vetch (vech) *n.* **1.** Any of various climbing herbaceous vines of the bean family; esp., the common broad bean, grown for fodder. **2.** A leguminous European plant yielding edible seeds. [< AF *veche, vecce* < L *vicia*]

vet·er·an (vet′ər·ən, vet′rən) *n.* **1.** One who is much experienced in any service. **2.** A former member of the armed forces. — *adj.* **1.** Having had long experience or practice; old in service. **2.** Of or pertaining to veterans. [< MF < L *veteranus* < *vetus, veteris* old]

Veterans Administration An agency of the U.S. government that administers all federal laws relating to the relief of former members of the military and naval service.

Veterans Day A U.S. national holiday honoring veterans of the armed forces, November 11, the anniversary of the armistice in World War I: formerly called *Armistice Day*.

Veterans of Foreign Wars A society of ex-servicemen who have served in the U.S. armed forces in a war with and in a foreign country; founded 1899.

vet·er·i·nar·i·an (vet′ər·ə·nâr′ē·ən, vet′rə-) *n. Chiefly U.S.* A practitioner of veterinary medicine or surgery.

vet·er·i·nar·y (vet′ər·ə·ner′ē, vet′rə-) *adj.* Pertaining to the diseases or injuries of animals, and to their treatment by medical or surgical means. — *n. pl.* **·nar·ies** A veterinarian. [< L *veterinarius* pertaining to beasts of burden]

veterinary medicine The branch of medicine that deals with the prevention, treatment, and cure of animal diseases.

ve·to (vē′tō) *v.t.* **·toed, ·to·ing 1.** To refuse executive approval of (a bill passed by a legislative body). **2.** To forbid or prohibit authoritatively. — *n. pl.* **·toes 1.** The prerogative of a chief executive to refuse to approve a legislative enactment by withholding his signature; also, the exercise of such a prerogative: also *veto power*. **2.** The official communication containing a refusal to approve a bill and the reasons for refusing: also **veto message. 3.** Any authoritative prohibition. [< L, I forbid] —**ve′to·er** *n.*

vex (veks) *v.t.* **1.** To provoke to anger or displeasure by small irritations; annoy. **2.** To trouble or afflict. **3.** To make a subject of dispute. [< OF < L *vexare* to shake] — **vexed** *adj.* —**vex′er** *n.*

vex·a·tion (vek·sā′shən) *n.* **1.** A vexing or being vexed. **2.** That which vexes.

vex·a·tious (vek·sā′shəs) *adj.* **1.** Causing vexation. **2.** Harassing; annoying. —**vex·a′tious·ly** *adv.* —**vex·a′tious·ness** *n.*

vi·a (vī′ə, vē′ə) *prep.* By way of; by a route passing through: He went to Boston *via* New Haven. ◆ In informal usage, *via* can refer to the means of travel as well as the route: We went *via* train. [< L, ablative sing. of *via* way]

vi·a·ble (vī′ə·bəl) *adj.* **1.** Capable of developing normally, as a newborn infant, a seed, etc. **2.** Workable; practicable. [< F < *vie* life < L *vita*] —**vi′a·bil′i·ty** *n.*

vi·a·duct (vī′ə·dukt) *n.* A bridgelike structure, esp. a large one of arched masonry, to carry a roadway or the like over a valley or ravine. [< L *via* way + (AQUE)- DUCT]

vi·al (vī′əl) *n.* A small bottle for liquids: also *phial*. — **to pour out the vials of wrath upon** To inflict retribution or vengeance on. See *Rev.* xvi. — *v.t.* **vi·aled** or **·alled, ·vi·al·ing** or **·al·ling** To put or keep in or as in a vial. [< OF < L < Gk. *phialē* shallow cup]

VIADUCT
(Pont du Gard, a Roman aqueduct at Nimes, France)

vi·and (vī′ənd) *n.* **1.** An article of food, esp. meat. **2.** *pl.* Victuals; provisions; food. [< OF *viande*, ult. < L *vivenda*, neut. pl. gerundive of *vivere* to live]

vi·at·i·cum (vī·at′ə·kəm) *n. pl.* **·ca** (-kə) or **·cums 1.** *Eccl.* The Eucharist, as given on the verge of death. **2.** Provisions for a journey. [< L, traveling money, neut. sing. of *viaticus* < *via* way]

vi·bran·cy (vī′brən·sē) *n. pl.* **·cies** The state or character of being vibrant; resonance.

vi·brant (vī′brənt) *adj.* **1.** Vibrating. **2.** Throbbing; pulsing: *vibrant* with enthusiasm. **3.** Rich and resonant, as a sound: *vibrant* tones. **4.** Energetic; vigorous. **5.** *Phonet.* Voiced. — *n. Phonet.* A voiced sound. [< L ppr. of *vibrare* to shake] —**vi′brant·ly** *adv.*

vi·bra·phone (vī′brə·fōn) *n.* A type of marimba in which a pulsating sound is produced by valves in the resonators. Also **vi′bra·harp′** (-härp′). [< VIBRA(TO) + -PHONE]

vi·brate (vī′brāt) *v.* **·brat·ed, ·brat·ing** *v.i.* **1.** To move back and forth rapidly; quiver. **2.** To move or swing back and forth, as a pendulum. **3.** To sound: The note *vibrates* on the ear. **4.** To be emotionally moved; thrill. **5.** To vacillate; waver, as between choices. — *v.t.* **6.** To cause to quiver or tremble. **7.** To cause to move back and forth. **8.** To send forth (sound, etc.) by vibration. [< L *vibratus*, pp. of *vibrare* to shake]

vi·bra·tile (vī′brə·til, -tīl) *adj.* **1.** Adapted to, having, or used in vibratory motion. **2.** Pertaining to or resembling vibration. —**vi·bra·til·i·ty** (vī′brə·til′ə·tē) *n.*

vi·bra·tion (vī·brā′shən) *n.* **1.** The act of vibrating or the state of being vibrated. **2.** *Physics* **a** Any physical process characterized by cyclic variations in amplitude, intensity, or the like, as wave motion or an electric field. **b** A single complete oscillation. —**vi·bra′tion·al** *adj.*

vi·bra·to (vē·brä′tō) *n. pl.* **·tos** *Music* A trembling or pulsating effect caused by rapid but minute variations in pitch during the production of a tone. [< Ital. < L, pp. of *vibrare* to shake]

vi·bra·tor (vī′brā·tər) *n.* **1.** That which vibrates. **2.** An electrically operated massaging apparatus.

vi·bra·to·ry (vī′brə·tôr′ē, -tō′rē) *adj.* Of, causing, or characterized by vibration. Also **vibra·tive** (-tiv).

vib·ri·o (vib′rē·ō) *n. pl.* **·ri·os** Any of various comma-shaped bacteria having one or more flagella at each end; esp., one found in the intestines of cholera victims. [< NL < L *vibrare* to shake] —**vib·ri·oid** (vib′rē·oid) *adj.*

vi·bur·num (vī·bûr′nəm) *n.* Any of a genus of shrubs or small trees related to the honeysuckle, bearing small flowers and berrylike fruit. [< L, the wayfaring tree]

vic·ar (vik′ər) *n.* **1.** In the Anglican Church, the priest of a parish of which the main revenues are appropriated or impropriated by a layman, the priest himself receiving but a stipend. **2.** In the Roman Catholic Church, a substitute or representative of an ecclesiastical person. **3.** In some parishes of the Protestant Episcopal Church, the clergyman who is the head of a chapel. **4.** One authorized to perform functions in the stead of another; deputy. [< AF, OF < L *vicarius* substitute < *vicis* change]

vic·ar·age (vik′ər·ij) *n.* **1.** The benefice, office, or duties of a vicar. **2.** A vicar's residence or household.

vicar general *pl.* **vicars general 1.** In the Roman Catholic Church, a functionary appointed by the bishop as assistant or representative in certain matters of jurisdiction. **2.** In the Church of England, an official assisting the bishop or archbishop in ecclesiastical causes.

vi·car·i·al (vī·kâr′ē·əl, vi-) *adj.* **1.** Vicarious; delegated. **2.** Of, relating to, or acting as a vicar.

vi·car·i·ate (vī·kâr′ē·it, -āt, vi-) *n.* A delegated office or power; esp., the office or authority of a vicar. Also **vic·ar·ate** (vik′ər·it).

vi·car·i·ous (vī·kâr′ē·əs, vi-) *adj.* **1.** Made or performed by substitution; suffered or done in place of another: a *vicarious* sacrifice. **2.** Enjoyed, felt, etc., by a person as a result of his imagined participation in an experience not his own: *vicarious* gratification. **3.** Filling the office of or acting for another. [< L *vicarius* substitute] — **vi·car′i·ous·ly** *adv.* — **vi·car′i·ous·ness** *n.*

Vicar of Christ The Pope.

vic·ar·ship (vik′ər·ship) *n.* The office or position of a vicar.

vice[1] (vīs) *n.* **1.** An immoral habit or trait. **2.** A slight personal fault; foible. **3.** Habitual indulgence in degrading or harmful practices. **4.** Something that mars; a blemish or imperfection. [< OF < L *vitium* fault]

vice[2] (vīs) See VISE.

vice[3] (*adj. & n.* vīs; *prep.* vī′sē) *adj.* Acting in the place of; substitute; deputy: *vice* president. — *n.* One who acts in the place of another; a substitute; deputy. — *prep.* Instead of; in the place of. [< L, ablative of *vicis* change]

vice admiral *Naval* A commissioned officer ranking next below an admiral. Also *Brit. & Canadian* **vice-ad·mi·ral** (vīs′ad′mər·əl). See tables at GRADE.

vice-ad·mir·al·ty (vīs′ad′mər·əl·tē) *n. pl.* **·ties** The office of a vice admiral.

vice consul One who exercises consular authority, either as the substitute or as the subordinate of a consul. — **vice-con·su·lar** (vīs′kon′sə·lər) *adj.* — **vice-con·su·late** (vīs′kon′sə·lit) *n.* — **vice′con′sul·ship** *n.*

vice·ge·ren·cy (vīs·jir′ən·sē) *n. pl.* **·cies 1.** The office or authority of a vicegerent. **2.** A district ruled by a vicegerent.

vice·ger·ent (vīs·jir′ənt) *n.* One duly authorized to exercise the powers of another; a deputy; vicar. — *adj.* Acting in the place of another, usu. in the place of a superior. [< Med.L < L *vice* in place + *gerens, -entis,* ppr. of *gerere* to carry, manage] — **vice·ge′ral** *adj.*

vi·ce·nar·y (vis′ə·ner′ē) *adj.* **1.** Consisting of or pertaining to twenty. **2.** Relating to a system of notation based upon twenty. [< L < *viceni* twenty each < *viginti* twenty]

vi·cen·ni·al (vī·sen′ē·əl) *adj.* **1.** Occurring once in twenty years. **2.** Lasting or existing twenty years.

vice president An officer ranking next below a president, and acting, on occasion, in his place. — **vice-pres·i·den·cy** (vīs′prez′ə·dən·sē) *n.* — **vice′-pres′i·den′tial** (-prez′ə·den′shəl) *adj.*

vice·re·gal (vīs·rē′gəl) *adj.* Of or relating to a viceroy, his office, or his jurisdiction. Also **vice·roy′al** (-roi′əl). — **vice·re′gal·ly** *adv.*

vice regent A deputy regent. — **vice-re·gen·cy** (vīs′rē′jən·sē) *n.* — **vice′-re′gent** *adj.*

vice·roy (vīs′roi) *n.* **1.** One who rules a country, colony, or province by the authority of his sovereign or king. **2.** A North American nymphalid butterfly, orange red with black markings and a row of white marginal spots. [< MF < *vice-, vis-* in place + *roy* king, ult. < L *rex, regis*]

vice·roy·al·ty (vīs·roi′əl·tē) *n. pl.* **·ties 1.** The office or authority of a viceroy. **2.** The term of office of a viceroy. **3.** A district governed by a viceroy. Also **vice′roy·ship.**

vice squad A police division charged with combating prostitution, gambling, etc.

vi·ce ver·sa (vī′sē vûr′sə, vīs′) The order being changed; conversely. [< L]

vi·chy·ssoise (vē′shē·swäz′) *n.* A potato cream soup, usu. served cold. [< F, of Vichy]

Vi·chy water (vish′ē, vē·shē′) The effervescent mineral water from the springs at Vichy, France; also, any mineral water resembling it. Also **Vi′chy, vi′chy.**

vic·i·nage (vis′ə·nij) *n.* **1.** Neighboring places collectively; vicinity. **2.** The state of being a neighbor or neighbors. [< OF < L *vicinus* nearby]

vic·i·nal (vis′ə·nəl) *adj.* Neighboring; adjoining; near.

vi·cin·i·ty (vi·sin′ə·tē) *n. pl.* **·ties 1.** A region adjacent or near; neighborhood. **2.** Nearness in space or relationship; proximity. [< L < *vicinus* nearby]

vi·cious (vish′əs) *adj.* **1.** Characterized by malice or spite; malicious. **2.** Characterized by violence and fierceness: a *vicious* blow. **3.** Addicted to vice; corrupt in conduct or

habits. **4.** Morally injurious, vile. **5.** Unruly or dangerous; refractory, as an animal. **6.** Defective or faulty: *vicious* arguments. **7.** *Informal* Intense; severe; extreme: a *vicious* storm. [< OF < L *vitium* fault] — **vi′cious·ly** *adv.* — **vi′cious·ness** *n.*

vicious circle 1. The process or predicament that arises when the solution of a problem creates a new problem and each successive solution adds another problem. **2.** *Med.* The accelerating effect of one disease upon another when the two are coexistent.

vi·cis·si·tude (vi·sis′ə·tood, -tyood) *n.* **1.** *pl.* Irregular changes or variations, as of fortune: the *vicissitudes* of life. **2.** A change; esp., a complete change; mutation or mutability. **3.** Alternating change or succession, as of the seasons. [< MF < L < *vicis* turn, change]

vi·cis·si·tu·di·nar·y (vi·sis′ə·too′də·ner′ē, -tyoo′-) *adj.* Marked by or subject to change. Also **vi·cis′si·tu′di·nous.**

vic·tim (vik′tim) *n.* **1.** One who is killed, injured, or subjected to suffering. **2.** One who is swindled or tricked; a dupe. **3.** A living creature sacrificed to some deity or as a religious rite. [< L *victima* beast for sacrifice]

vic·tim·ize (vik′tim·īz) *v.t.* **ized, iz·ing** To make a victim of, esp. by defrauding or swindling; dupe; cheat. — **vic′tim·i·za′tion** *n.* — **vic′tim·iz′er** *n.*

vic·tor (vik′tər) *n.* **1.** One who vanquishes an enemy. **2.** One who wins any struggle or contest. — *adj.* Pertaining to a victor; victorious: the *victor* nation. [< AF *victor, victour,* OF *victeur* < L *victus,* pp. of *vincere* to conquer]

vic·to·ri·a (vik·tôr′ē·ə, -tō′rē·ə) *n.* A low, light, four-wheeled carriage, with a calash top, a seat for two persons, and a raised driver's seat. [after Queen *Victoria*]

Vic·to·ri·a (vik·tôr′ē·ə, -tō′rē·ə) *n.* In Roman mythology, the winged goddess of victory: identified with the Greek *Nike.*

Victoria Cross A British military and naval decoration in the form of a bronze Maltese cross, awarded for conspicuous bravery. *Abbr. V.C.*

Victoria Day In Canada, the Monday next before May 24, commemorating the birthday of Queen Victoria.

Vic·to·ri·an (vik·tôr′ē·ən, -tō′rē-) *adj.* **1.** Of or relating to Queen Victoria, or to her reign. **2.** Pertaining to or characteristic of the ideals and standards of morality and taste prevalent during the reign of Queen Victoria; prudish; conventional; narrow. — *n.* Anyone, esp. an author, contemporary with Queen Victoria. — **Vic·to′ri·an·ism** *n.*

vic·to·ri·ous (vik·tôr′ē·əs, -tō′rē-) *adj.* **1.** Having won victory; triumphant. **2.** Relating to or characterized by victory. — **vic·to′ri·ous·ly** *adv.* — **vic·to′ri·ous·ness** *n.*

vic·to·ry (vik′tər·ē) *n. pl.* **·ries** The overcoming of an enemy, opponent, or any difficulty; triumph. [See VICTOR.]

Victory Medal Either of two bronze medals awarded to all who served in the U.S. armed forces in World War I or World War II, worn with the **Victory Ribbon.**

vict·ual (vit′l) *n.* Food for human beings, as prepared for eating: used in the plural. — *v.* **vict·ualed** or **·ualled, vict·ual·ing** or **·ual·ling** *v.t.* **1.** To furnish with victuals. — *v.i.* **2.** To lay in supplies of food. [< OF < LL *victualia* provisions < L < *victus* food]

vi·cu·ña (vi·koon′yə, -kyoo′nə) *n.* **1.** A small ruminant of the high Andes related to the llama and alpaca, having fine and valuable wool. **2.** A textile made from this wool, or some substitute. Also **vi·cu′gna.** [< Sp. < Quechua]

vi·de (vī′dē) See: used to make a reference or direct attention to: *vide* p. 36. [< L, imperative sing. of *videre* to see]

vi·de an·te (vī′dē an′tē) *Latin* See before.

vi·de in·fra (vī′dē in′frə) *Latin* See below.

vi·de·li·cet (vi·del′ə·sit) *adv.* To wit; that is to say; namely. *Abbr. viz.* [< L < *videre licet* it is permitted to see]

vid·e·o (vid′ē·ō) *adj.* Of or pertaining to television, esp. to the picture portion of a program. — *n.* Television. [< L, I see]

vi·de post (vī′dē pōst′) *Latin* See after; see what follows.

vi·de su·pra (vī′dē soo′prə) *Latin* See above.

vi·dette (vi·det′) See VEDETTE.

vi·de ut su·pra (vī′dē ut soo′prə) *Latin* See what is written above.

vie (vī) *v.* **vied, vy·ing** *v.i.* **1.** To strive for superiority; compete, as in a race: with *with* or *for.* — *v.t.* **2.** *Rare* To put forth in competition. [< MF < L *invitare* to invite]

Vi·en·nese (vē′ə·nēz′, -nēs′) *adj.* Of or relating to Vienna, or its inhabitants. — *n. pl.* **·nese** A native or citizen of Vienna.

Vi·et·nam·ese (vē·et′·et/näm·ēz′, -ēs′) *n. pl.* **Vi·et·nam·ese 1.** A native or inhabitant of Vietnam. **2.** The language of Vietnam: formerly called *Annamese.* — *adj.* Of or pertaining to Vietnam, its inhabitants, or their language.

view (vyoo) *n.* **1.** The act of seeing; survey; inspection. **2.** Mental examination or inspection. **3.** Power or range of vision. **4.** That which is seen; outlook; prospect. **5.** A representation of a scene; esp., a landscape. **6.** The object of action; aim; intention; purpose. **7.** Manner of looking at things; opinion; judgment. **8.** A general summary or account. **— in view 1.** In range of vision. **2.** Under consideration. **3.** As a goal or end. **— in view of** In consideration of. **— on view** Open to the public; set up for public inspection. **— with a view to 1.** With the aim or purpose of. **2.** With a hope of. —*v.t.* **1.** To look at; see; behold. **2.** To look at carefully; examine. **3.** To survey mentally; consider. [< OF *veoir* to see < L *videre*] **—view′er** *n.*

view finder *Photog.* A finder (def. 3).

view·less (vyōō′lis) *adj.* **1.** Devoid of a view; that cannot be viewed. **2.** Having no views or opinions. **3.** Invisible; unseen. **— view′less·ly** *adv.* **— view′less·ness** *n.*

view·point (vyōō′point′) *n.* Point of view.

vi·ges·i·mal (vī·jes′ə·məl) *adj.* **1.** Twentieth. **2.** Of or pertaining to twenty; proceeding by twenties. [< L *viginti* twenty]

vig·il (vij′əl) *n.* **1.** The act of staying awake in order to observe, protect, etc.; watch. **2.** *Eccl.* **a** The eve of a holy day. **b** *pl.* Religious devotions on such an eve. [< OF < Med.L < L *vigil* wide-awake]

vig·i·lance (vij′ə·ləns) *n.* The quality of being vigilant; alertness; watchfulness in guarding against danger.

vigilance committee *U.S.* Formerly, a body of men self-organized for the maintenance of order and the administration of summary justice.

vig·i·lant (vij′ə·lənt) *adj.* Characterized by vigilance; being on the alert; watchful; heedful; wary. [< MF < L < *vigil* awake] **— vig′i·lant·ly** *adv.* **— vig′i·lant·ness** *n.*

— Syn. *Vigilant* suggests action as well as attention: a riot was averted by the *vigilant* police. *Watchful* suggests unremitting attention: his *watchful* eye caught the covert signal. *Alert* stresses the speed of a response to necessity or opportunity: *alert* traders made a killing on the stock market. **— Ant.** inattentive, heedless.

vig·i·lan·te (vij′ə·lan′tē) *n.* *U.S.* **1.** One of a group who take upon themselves the unauthorized responsibility of interpreting and acting upon matters of law, public morality, etc. **2.** A member of a vigilance committee: also **vigilance man.** [< Sp., vigilant < L. See VIGILANT.]

vi·gnette (vin·yet′) *n.* **1.** A description, short literary work, etc., that depicts something subtly and delicately. **2.** Any charming, intimate scene, etc. **3.** A decorative design placed on or before the title page of a book, at the end or beginning of a chapter, etc. **4.** An engraving, photograph, or the like, having a background that shades off gradually. — *v.t.* **·gnet·ted, ·gnet·ting 1.** To make with a gradually shaded background, as a photograph. **2.** To ornament with vignettes. **3.** To depict in a vignette. [< F, dim. of *vigne* vine] **— vi·gnet′tist** *n.*

vig·or (vig′ər) *n.* **1.** Active strength or force, physical or mental. **2.** Vital or natural power, as in a healthy animal or plant. **3.** Forcible exertion of strength; energy; intensity. **4.** Effective force; validity. Also *Brit.* **vig′our.** [< AF, OF < L *vigere* to be lively, thrive]

vig·or·ous (vig′ər·əs) *adj.* **1.** Full of physical or mental vigor; robust. **2.** Performed or done with vigor. **3.** Showing or exemplifying vigor. **4.** Forceful and effective: a *vigorous* style. **— vig′or·ous·ly** *adv.* **— vig′or·ous·ness** *n.*

vi·king (vī′king) *n.* One of the Scandinavian warriors who harried the coasts of Europe from the eighth to the tenth centuries. Also **Vi′king.** [< ON *vikingr* pirate]

vile (vīl) *adj.* **vil·er, vil·est 1.** Morally base; shamefully wicked. **2.** Despicable; vicious. **3.** Loathsome; disgusting. **4.** Degrading; ignominious: *vile* treatment. **5.** Flagrantly bad or inferior. **6.** Unpleasant; disagreeable. [< AF, OF < L *vilis* cheap] **— vile′ly** *adv.* **— vile′ness** *n.*

vil·i·fy (vil′ə·fī) *v.t.* **·fied, ·fy·ing 1.** To abuse or characterize with defamatory language; malign; slander. **2.** To make base; degrade. [< LL < L *vilis* cheap + *facere* to make] **— vil′i·fi·ca′tion** (-fə·kā′shən) *n.* **— vil′i·fi′er** *n.*

vil·la (vil′ə) *n.* **1.** A comfortable or luxurious house in the country, at a resort, etc. **2.** *Chiefly Brit.* A modest suburban residence. [< Ital. < L, a country house, farm]

vil·lage (vil′ij) *n.* **1.** A collection of houses in a rural district, usu. smaller than a town but larger than a hamlet. **2.** *U.S.* In some States, a municipality smaller than a city, sometimes incorporated. **3.** Any comparatively small community. **4.** The inhabitants of a village, collectively. [< OF < L < *villa* a country house]

vil·lag·er (vil′ij·ər) *n.* One who lives in a village.

vil·lain (vil′ən) *n.* **1.** An egregiously wicked, evil, or malevolent man. **2.** Such a man represented as a leading character in a novel, play, etc., often in opposition to the hero. **3.** A rogue; scoundrel: often used humorously. **4.** A villein. [< AF, OF *vilein, vilain* farm servant < LL < L *villa* farm] **— vil′lain·ess** *n.fem.*

vil·lain·ous (vil′ən·əs) *adj.* **1.** Having the nature of a villain. **2.** Characteristic of a villain; evil. **3.** Very bad or unpleasant. **— vil′lain·ous·ly** *adv.* **— vil′lain·ous·ness** *n.*

vil·lain·y (vil′ən·ē) *n.* *pl.* **·lain·ies 1.** The quality of being villainous. **2.** Conduct characteristic of a villain.

vil·lein (vil′ən) *n.* In the feudal system, a member of a class of serfs who were regarded as freemen in respect to their legal relations with all persons except their lord: also *villain.* [See VILLAIN.] **— vil′lain·age, vil′lein·age, vil′len·age** *n.*

vil·lus (vil′əs) *n.* *pl.* **vil·li** (vil′ī) **1.** *Anat.* One of the short, hairlike processes found on certain membranes, as of the small intestine, where they aid in the digestive process. **2.** *Bot.* One of the long, close, rather soft hairs on the surface of certain plants. [< L, tuft of hair, shaggy hair, var. of *vellus* fleece, wool] **— vil′lous** *adj.* **— vil′lous·ly** *adv.*

vim (vim) *n.* Force or vigor; energy; spirit. [< L, accusative of *vis* power]

vin (van) *n. French* Wine.

vin- Var. of VINI-.

vi·na (vē′nä) *n.* An East Indian musical instrument with seven steel strings stretched on a long, fretted fingerboard over two gourds. [< Hind. *vinā* < Skt.]

vi·na·ceous (vī·nā′shəs) *adj.* **1.** Of or pertaining to wine or grapes. **2.** Having the characteristic color of red wine. [< L *vinaceous* < *vinum* wine]

vin·ai·grette (vin′ə·gret′) *n.* **1.** A small ornamental box or bottle, used for holding smelling salts, or a similar pungent restorative. **2.** Vinaigrette sauce. [< F, dim. of *vinaigre* vinegar]

vinaigrette sauce A sauce made from vinegar, savory herbs, etc., served with fish and cold meats.

vin·ci·ble (vin′sə·bəl) *adj.* *Rare* Capable of being conquered or overcome; conquerable. [< L *vincibilis* < *vincere* to conquer] **— vin′ci·bil′i·ty, vin′ci·ble·ness** *n.*

vin·cu·lum (vingk′yə·ləm) *n.* *pl.* **·la** (-lə) *Math.* A straight line drawn over several algebraic terms to show that all are to be operated on together. [< L < *vincire* to bind]

vin·di·ca·ble (vin′də·kə·bəl) *adj.* Capable of being vindicated; justifiable.

vin·di·cate (vin′də·kāt) *v.t.* **·cat·ed, ·cat·ing 1.** To clear of accusation, censure, suspicion, etc. **2.** To support or maintain, as a right or claim. **3.** To serve to justify. [< L *vindicatus*, pp. of *vindicare* to avenge, claim] **— vin′di·ca′tor** *n.*

vin·di·ca·tion (vin′də·kā′shən) *n.* **1.** A vindicating or being vindicated. **2.** Justification; defense.

vin·di·ca·to·ry (vin′də·kə·tôr′ē, -tō′rē) *adj.* **1.** Serving to vindicate; justificatory. **2.** Punitive; avenging.

vin·dic·tive (vin·dik′tiv) *adj.* **1.** Having a revengeful spirit. **2.** Revengeful or spiteful in quality, character, etc. [< L *vindicta* revenge] **— vin·dic′tive·ly** *adv.* **— vin·dic′tive·ness** *n.*

vine (vīn) *n.* **1.** Any of a large and widely distributed group of plants having a slender flexible stem that may twine about a support or clasp it by means of tendrils, petioles, etc.; also, the slender flexible stem itself. **2.** A grapevine. [< OF *vigne, vine* < L *vinea* vineyard < *vinum* wine]

vin·e·gar (vin′ə·gər) *n.* **1.** An acid liquid consisting chiefly of dilute acetic acid, obtained by the fermentation of cider, wine, etc., and used as a condiment and preservative. **2.** Sourness of manner, speech, etc. [< OF < *vin* wine + *aigre,egre* sour] **— vin′e·gar·y, vin′e·gar·ish** *adj.*

vin·er·y (vī′nər·ē) *n.* *pl.* **·er·ies 1.** A greenhouse for grapes; grapery. **2.** Vines collectively.

vine·yard (vin′yərd) *n.* An area planted with grapevines. [Earlier *wineyard*, OE *wīnegeard*]

vingt-et-un (van·tā·œn′) *n.* Twenty-one, a card game. [< F, twenty-one]

vini- *combining form* **1.** Wine. **2.** Of or pertaining to wine grapes. Also *vin-* (before vowels): also **vino-.** [< L *vinum* wine]

vin·i·cul·ture (vin′ə·kul′chər) *n.* The cultivation of grapes for wine. **— vin′i·cul′tur·al** *adj.* **— vin′i·cul′tur·ist** *n.*

vin or·di·naire (van ôr·dē·nâr′) *French* Cheap red wine; literally, ordinary wine.

vi·nous (vī′nəs) *adj.* **1.** Pertaining to, characteristic of, or having the qualities of wine. **2.** Caused by, affected by, or addicted to wine. **3.** Tinged with dark red. [< L < *vinum* wine] **— vi·nos′i·ty** (-nos′ə·tē) *n.*

vin·tage (vin′tij) *n.* **1.** The yield of a vineyard or wine-growing district for one season; also, the wine produced from this yield. **2.** The harvesting of a vineyard and the making of wine. **3.** Wine of high quality or of an exceptionally good year: also **vintage wine. 4.** *Informal* The type popular at a particular time of the past: a joke of ancient *vintage.* — *adj.* Of exceptional quality or excellence; choice: a *vintage* wine. [< AF, alter. of *vindage, vendage*, OF *vendage* < L < *vinum* wine + *demere* to remove]

vint·ner (vint′nər) *n.* A wine merchant. [< OF *vinetier, vinotier* < *vinot*, dim. of *vin* wine < L *vinum*]

vin·y (vī′nē) *adj.* **vin·i·er, vin·i·est 1.** Of, pertaining to, or resembling a vine. **2.** Full of vines.

vi·nyl (vī'nəl, vin'əl) *n. Chem.* The univalent radical, CH_2:CH, derived from ethylene, and extensively used in organic synthesis. [< L *vinum* wine + -YL]

vi·ol (vī'əl) *n.* Any of a family of stringed musical instruments, predecessors of the violin family; also, any member of the violin family. [Earlier *vielle* < AF, OF < Med.L *vidula, vitula* < Gmc.]

vi·o·la (vē·ō'lə, vī-; *Ital.* vyō'lä) *n.* A musical instrument of the violin family, somewhat larger than the violin, and tuned a fifth lower, with a graver and less brilliant tone. [< Ital., orig., a viol < Med.L *vidula* < Gmc.]

vi·o·la·ble (vī'ə·lə·bəl) *adj.* Capable of being violated. [< L *violabilis* < *violare*. See VIOLATE.] — **vi·o·la·ble·ness, vi·o·la·bil·i·ty** *n.* — **vi·o·la·bly** *adv.* [< L *violaceus* < *viola* violet]

viola da gam·ba (dä gäm'bä) The bass of the viol family, held between the legs, and having a range similar to that of the cello, but with a thinner tone: also called *bass viol.* [< Ital., viol of the leg]

vi·o·late (vī'ə·lāt) *v.t.* **·lat·ed, ·lat·ing** **1.** To break or infringe, as a law, oath, agreement, etc. **2.** To profane, as a holy place. **3.** To break in upon; disturb. **4.** To ravish; rape. **5.** To do violence to; offend grossly; outrage. [< L *violatus*, pp. of *violare* to use violence < *vis* force] — **vi'o·la'tive** *adj.* — **vi'o·la'tor** *n.*

vi·o·la·tion (vī'ə·lā'shən) *n.* **1.** The act of violating, or the state of being violated. **2.** Infringement or infraction, as of a law, regulation, etc. **3.** Profanation; desecration. **4.** Rape.

vi·o·lence (vī'ə·ləns) *n.* **1.** The quality or state of being violent; intensity; fury. **2.** An instance of violent action, treatment, etc. **3.** Violent or abusive exercise of power; injury; outrage. **4.** *Law* Physical force unlawfully exercised. **5.** Perversion or distortion of meaning, intent, etc. — **to do violence to** **1.** To injure or damage by rough or abusive treatment. **2.** To distort the meaning of.

vi·o·lent (vī'ə·lənt) *adj.* **1.** Proceeding from or marked by great physical force or roughness; overwhelmingly forcible. **2.** Caused by or exhibiting intense emotional or mental excitement; passionate; impetuous; fierce. **3.** Characterized by intensity of any kind; extreme: *violent* heat. **4.** Marked by undue exercise of force; harsh; severe: to take *violent* measures. **5.** Resulting from unusual force or injury: a *violent* death. **6.** Tending to pervert the meaning or sense: a *violent* construction. [< OF < L *violentus* < *vis* force] — **vi'o·lent·ly** *adv.*

vi·o·let (vī'ə·lit) *n.* **1.** One of a widely distributed genus of herbaceous perennial herbs, bearing spurred flowers typically having a purplish blue color but sometimes yellow or white. The violet is the State flower of Illinois, New Jersey, Rhode Island, and Wisconsin. **2.** Any of several similar plants. **3.** A deep bluish purple color. — *adj.* Having a bluish purple color. [< OF < L *viola* violet]

violet rays **1.** High-frequency radiation from the violet end of the visible spectrum. **2.** Loosely, ultraviolet rays.

vi·o·lin (vī'ə·lin') *n.* A musical instrument having four strings and a sounding box of seasoned wood, held against the shoulder and played by means of a bow. It is the treble member of the **violin family**, which includes also the viola and cello: also called *fiddle.* [< Ital. *violino*, dim. of *viola*]

vi·o·lin·ist (vī'ə·lin'ist) *n.* One who plays the violin.

vi·o·list (vē·ō'list *for def. 1,* vī'əl·ist *for def. 2*) *n.* **1.** One who plays the viola. **2.** One who plays a viol.

vi·o·lon·cel·list (vē'ə·lən·chel'ist) *n.* A cellist.

vi·o·lon·cel·lo (vē'ə·lən·chel'ō) *n. pl.* **·los** A cello. [< Ital., dim. of *violone* double bass]

VIP or **V.I.P.** Very important person.

vi·per (vī'pər) *n.* **1.** Any of a family of venomous Old World snakes, esp. a small, variously colored snake native to Europe. **2.** Any of various similar or related snakes. **3.** Loosely, a pit viper. **4.** Any allegedly poisonous snake. **5.** A treacherous or spiteful person. [< OF < L *vivus* living + *parere* to bring forth] — **vi'per·ine** *adj.* — **vi'per·ish** *adj.*

vi·per·ous (vī'pər·əs) *adj.* **1.** Snakelike; viperine. **2.** Venomous; malicious. — **vi'per·ous·ly** *adj.*

vi·ra·go (vi·rā'gō, -rä'-, vī-) *n. pl.* **·goes** or **·gos** A noisy, sharp-tongued woman; a scold. [< L, mannish woman < *vir* man]

vi·ral (vī'rəl) *adj.* Of, pertaining to, caused by, or of the nature of a virus.

vir·e·o (vir'ē·ō) *n. pl.* **·os** Any of various small, insectivorous birds having predominantly dull green and grayish plumage. [< L, a small bird, ? the greenfinch]

vi·res·cence (vī·res'əns) *n.* The state or condition of becoming green.

vi·res·cent (vī·res'ənt) *adj.* Greenish or becoming green. [< L *virescens, -entis,* ppr. of *virescere* to grow green]

vir·gin (vûr'jin) *n.* **1.** A person, esp. a young woman, who has never had sexual intercourse. **2.** A chaste young girl or unmarried woman. — *adj.* **1.** Being a virgin. **2.** Pertaining or suited to a virgin; chaste; maidenly. **3.** Uncorrupted; pure; undefiled: *virgin* whiteness. **4.** Not hitherto used, touched, tilled, or worked upon by man: *virgin* soil. **5.** Not previously processed: *virgin* rubber; *virgin* wool. [< OF < L *virgo, -inis* maiden]

Vir·gin (vûr'jin) *n.* **1.** Mary, the mother of Jesus: usu. preceded by *the:* also *Virgin Mary.* **2.** The constellation and sign of the zodiac Virgo.

vir·gin·al[1] (vûr'jin·əl) *adj.* Pertaining to or characteristic of a virgin; chaste. [< OF < L *virginalis* < *virgo, -inis* virgin]

vir·gin·al[2] (vûr'jin·əl) *n. Often pl.* A small, legless harpsichord of the 16th and 17th centuries: sometimes called a **pair of virginals**. [< OF < VIRGINAL[1]; ? so called from its use by young men and girls]

virgin birth *Theol.* The doctrine that Jesus Christ was divinely conceived without impairment of the virginity of his mother Mary. Also **Virgin Birth.**

Virginia cowslip A smooth perennial herb having clusters of tubular blue flowers. Also **Virginia bluebell.**

Virginia creeper A common American climbing vine of the grape family, with compound toothed leaves and dark blue berries: also called *five-fingers, woodbine.*

Vir·gin·ian (vər·jin'yən) *adj.* Of, pertaining to, or from Virginia. — *n.* A native or inhabitant of Virginia.

Virginia reel A country-dance in which the performers stand in two parallel lines and perform various figures.

vir·gin·i·ty (vər·jin'ə·tē) *n. pl.* **·ties** **1.** The state or condition of being a virgin; maidenhood; virginal chastity. **2.** The state of being unsullied, unused, untouched, etc.

vir·gin·i·um (vər·jin'ē·əm) *n.* The former name of an element now identified as francium. [after the State of *Virginia*]

Virgin Mary Mary, the mother of Jesus: usu. with *the.*

vir·gin's-bow·er (vûr'jinz·bou'ər) *n.* A species of clematis bearing white flowers in leafy panicles.

Vir·go (vûr'gō) *n.* A constellation, the Virgin, containing the bright star Spica; also, the sixth sign of the zodiac. [< L, a virgin]

vir·gule (vûr'gyōōl) *n.* A slanting line (/) used to indicate two alternatives, as in *and/or,* to set off phoneme symbols, etc.: also called *slash.* [< L *virgula,* dim. of *virga* rod]

vir·i·des·cent (vir'ə·des'ənt) *adj.* Greenish, or becoming slightly green. [< LL < *viridescere* to become green] — **vir·i·des'cence** *n.*

vir·ile (vir'əl) *adj.* **1.** Having the characteristics of adult manhood; masculine. **2.** Having qualities considered typically masculine; vigorous; forceful. **3.** Capable of procreation. [< OF < L *virilis* < *vir* man]

vi·ril·i·ty (və·ril'ə·tē) *n. pl.* **·ties** The state, character, or quality of being virile.

vi·rol·o·gy (və·rol'ə·jē, vī-) *n.* The study of viruses, esp. in their relation to disease. [< *viro-* (< VIRUS) + -LOGY] — **vi·rol'o·gist** *n.*

vir·tu (vər·tōō', vûr'tōō) *n.* **1.** Rare, curious, or beautiful quality: usu. in the phrase **objects** or **articles of virtu.** **2.** A taste for such objects. **3.** Such objects collectively. Also spelled *vertu.* [< Ital. *virtù* merit < L *virtus* strength]

vir·tu·al (vûr'chōō·əl) *adj.* Having the effect but not the actual form of what is specified: a *virtual* usurpation. [See VIRTUE.] — **vir·tu·al·i·ty** (-al'ə·tē) *n.*

vir·tu·al·ly (vûr'chōō·ə·lē) *adv.* In effect; for all practical purposes.

vir·tue (vûr'chōō) *n.* **1.** The quality of moral righteousness or excellence; rectitude. **2.** The practice of moral duties and the abstinence from immorality and vice. **3.** Chastity, esp. in women. **4.** A particular type of moral excellence, esp. one of those considered to be of special importance in philosophical or religious doctrine. Compare CARDINAL VIRTUES. **5.** Any admirable quality or trait. **6.** Inherent or essential quality, power, etc. **7.** Efficacy; potency. — **by** (or **in**) **virtue of** By or through the fact, quality, force, or authority of. — **to make a virtue of necessity** To seem to do freely or from principle what is or must be done necessarily. [< OF < L *virtus* strength, bravery < *vir* man]

— **Syn.** We regard *virtue* as acquired through self-discipline, and predicate it of human beings only. *Goodness* is an innate quality, and so may be ascribed to God as well as to man. *Morality* involves conformity to an accepted code of right conduct; it is less elevated but more concrete than *virtue. Rectitude* also implies conformity to a moral code, but stresses intention or disposition; hence, a man's *morality* may arise from fear of punishment or of

VIOLIN

a Scroll. *b* Peg box. *c* Peg. *d* Nut. *e* Fingerboard. *f* Neck plate. *g* Sound hole. *h* Bridge. *i* Tailpiece. *j* Chin rest. *k* Button.

censure, but his *rectitude* can come only from a love of the right and a conscious desire to follow it. **—Ant.** vice, sin, evil.

vir·tu·os·i·ty (vûr′chŏŏ·os′ə·tē) *n. pl.* **·ties** The skill, etc., of a virtuoso; technical mastery of an art, as music.

vir·tu·o·so (vûr′chŏŏ·ō′sō) *n. pl.* **·si** (-sē) or **·sos** **1.** A master of technique, as a skilled musician. **2.** One who displays impressive or dazzling skill in any area of accomplishment. **3.** A connoisseur; a collector or lover of curios or works of art. [< Ital., skilled, learned]

vir·tu·ous (vûr′chŏŏ·əs) *adj.* **1.** Characterized by, exhibiting, or having the nature of virtue. **2.** Chaste: now said esp. of women. **—vir′tu·ous·ly** *adv.* **—vir′tu·ous·ness** *n.*

vir·u·lent (vir′yə·lənt, vir′ə-) *adj.* **1.** Manifesting or characterized by malignity; exceedingly noxious, harmful, etc. **2.** Bitterly rancorous; acrimonious. **3.** *Med.* Actively poisonous or infective; malignant. **4.** *Bacteriol.* Having the power to injure an organism by invasion of tissue and generation of internal toxins, as certain microorganisms. [< L *virus* poison] **—vir′u·lence** *n.* **—vir′u·lent·ly** *adv.*

vi·rus (vī′rəs) *n.* **1.** Any of a class of filterable, submicroscopic pathogenic agents, chiefly protein in composition but often reducible to crystalline form, and typically inert except when in contact with certain living cells: also called *filterable virus.* **2.** An illness caused by such an agent. **3.** Any virulent substance developed within an animal body, and capable of transmitting a specific disease. **4.** Venom, as of a snake. **— Syn.** See MICROBE. [< L, poison, slime]

vis (vis) *n. pl.* **vi·res** (vī′rēz) *Latin* Force; potency.

vi·sa (vē′zə) *n.* An official endorsement, as on a passport, certifying that it has been found correct and that the bearer may proceed. **—v.t. ·saed, ·sa·ing 1.** To put a visa on. **2.** To give a visa to. Also *visé.* [< F < L *videre* to see]

vis·age (viz′ij) *n.* The face or facial expression of a person; countenance; distinctive aspect. [< OF < L *visus* look, appearance < *videre* to see] **—vis′aged** *adj.*

vis·ard (viz′ərd) See VIZARD.

vis-à-vis (vē′zə-vē′, *Fr.* vē-zà·vē′) *n. pl.* **vis-à-vis 1.** One of two persons or things that face each other from opposite sides. **2.** One in a corresponding capacity, etc. **—** *adv.* Face to face. **—** *prep.* Regarding. [< F, face to face]

vis·cer·a (vis′ər·ə) *n. pl. of* **vis·cus** (vis′kəs) *Anat.* The internal organs, esp. those of the great cavities of the body, as the stomach, lungs, heart, intestines, etc. [< L, pl. of *viscus* internal organ] **—vis′cer·al** *adj.*

vis·cid (vis′id) *adj.* Sticky or adhesive; mucilaginous; viscous. [< LL < L *viscum* birdlime] **—vis·cid·i·ty** (vi·sid′ə·tē), **vis′cid·ness** *n.* **—vis′cid·ly** *adv.*

vis·cose (vis′kōs) *n. Chem.* A thick, honeylike substance produced by the action of caustic soda and carbon disulfide upon cellulose, and constituting an important source of rayon. **—** *adj.* **1.** Viscous. **2.** Of, pertaining to, containing, or made from viscose. [See VISCOUS.]

vis·cos·i·ty (vis·kos′ə·tē) *n. pl.* **·ties 1.** The state, quality, property, or degree of being viscous. **2.** *Physics* That property of fluids by virtue of which they offer resistance to flow or to any change in the arrangement of their molecules.

vis·count (vī′kount) *n.* In England, a title of nobility ranking between those of earl and baron. [< AF, OF < *vis-* in place (< L *vice*) + *counte.* See COUNT².] **—vis′count·cy, vis′count·ship, vis′count·y** *n.*

vis·count·ess (vī′koun·tis) *n.* **1.** The wife of a viscount. **2.** A peeress holding a corresponding title in her own right.

vis·cous [vis′kəs) *adj.* **1.** Glutinous; semifluid; sticky. **2.** *Physics* Characterized by or having viscosity. [< LL < L *viscum* birdlime] **—vis′cous·ly** *adv.* **—vis′cous·ness** *n.*

vis·cus (vis′kəs) Singular of VISCERA.

vise (vīs) *n.* A clamping device, usu. of two jaws made to be closed together with a screw, lever, etc., used for grasping and holding objects being worked on, glued, etc. **—v.t. vised, vis·ing** To hold, force, or squeeze in or as in a vise. Also, *Brit., vice.* [< OF < L *vitis* vine; with ref. to the spiral growth of vine tendrils]

vi·sé (vē′zā, vē·zā′) *v.t.* **·seed, ·sé·ing** To visa. **—** *n.* A visa.

Vish·nu (vish′nŏŏ) In Hindu theology, a major deity, a member of the trinity also including Brahma and Siva, and having many incarnations, of which the most famous is as Krishna. **— Vish′nu·ism** *n.*

vis·i·bil·i·ty (viz′ə·bil′ə·tē) *n. pl.* **·ties 1.** Condition, capability, or degree of being visible. **2.** The clarity of unaided vision as affected by distance, atmospheric conditions, etc.

vis·i·ble (viz′ə·bəl) *adj.* **1.** Perceivable by the eye; capable of being seen. **2.** Apparent; observable; evident. **3.** At hand; available; manifest. [< OF < L *visibilis* < *videre* to see] **—vis′i·ble·ness** *n.* **—vis′i·bly** *adv.*

Vis·i·goth (viz′ə·goth) *n.* One of the western Goths, a Teutonic people that invaded the Roman Empire in the third and fourth centuries and settled in France and Spain. [< LL *Visigothus*] **— Vis′i·goth′ic** *adj.*

vi·sion (vizh′ən) *n.* **1.** The faculty or sense of sight. **2.** The ability to anticipate and make provision for future events; foresight. **3.** Insight; imagination: a man of great *vision.* **4.** A mental representation of or as of external objects, scenes, etc., as in a religious revelation, dream, etc. **5.** A vividly imagined thing, state, occurrence, etc. **6.** Something or someone very beautiful or pleasing. **—v.t. Rare** To see in or as in a vision. [< OF < L *visio* < *videre* to see] **—vi′sion·al** *adj.* **—vi′sion·al·ly** *adv.*

vi·sion·ar·y (vizh′ən·er′ē) *adj.* **1.** Not founded on fact; imaginary; impracticable. **2.** Affected by or tending toward fantasies; dreamy; impractical. **3.** Having idealistic goals or aims incapable of realization. **4.** Having or of the nature of apparitions, dreams, etc. **—** *n. pl.* **·ar·ies 1.** One who has visions. **2.** A dreamer; an impractical schemer. **3.** One who is impracticably idealistic. **—vi′sion·ar′i·ness** *n.*

vis·it (viz′it) *v.t.* **1.** To go or come to see (a person) from friendship, on business, etc. **2.** To go or come to (a place, etc.), as for touring, etc. **3.** To be a guest of; stay with temporarily. **4.** To go or come to so as to make official inspection or inquiry. **5.** To come upon or afflict. **6.** To inflict punishment upon or for. **7.** To inflict (punishment, wrath, etc.). **—** *v.i.* **8.** To make a visit; pay a call or calls. **9.** *Informal* To chat or converse sociably. **—** *n.* **1.** The act of visiting a person or thing. **2.** A sojourn in a place or with a person. **3.** *Informal* A talk or friendly chat. **4.** An authoritative personal call for inspection and examination, or discharge of an official or professional duty. [< OF < L *visitare* to go to see < *videre* to see] **—vis′it·a·ble** *adj.*

vis·i·tant (viz′ə·tənt) *n.* **1.** A visitor. **2.** A migratory animal or bird stopping at a particular region.

vis·i·ta·tion (viz′ə·tā′shən) *n.* **1.** The act or fact of visiting; a visit; also, the state or circumstance of being visited. **2.** An official or authoritative inspection and examination. **3.** In Biblical and religious use, a visiting of blessing or affliction. **—vis′i·ta′tion·al** *adj.* **—vis′i·ta·to′ri·al** (-tə·tôr′ē·əl, -tō′rē-) *adj.*

Vis·i·ta·tion (viz′ə·tā′shən) *n. Eccl.* **1.** The visit of the Virgin Mary to Elizabeth. *Luke* i 39–42. **2.** July 2, the church festival commemorating this visit.

vis·i·ting card (viz′i·ting) A calling card.

vis·i·tor (viz′ə·tər) *n.* One who visits.

vi·sor (vī′zər, viz′ər) *n.* **1.** A projecting piece at the front of a cap, etc., serving as a shade for the eyes. **2.** In armor, the movable front piece of a helmet, serving to protect the upper part of the face. **3.** A movable piece or part serving as a shield against glare, etc., as on the windshield of an automobile. **—v.t.** To mask or cover with a visor. Also spelled *vizor.* [< AF & OF *vis* face]

vis·ta (vis′tə) *n.* **1.** A view or prospect, as along an avenue; an outlook. **2.** A mental view embracing a series of events. [< Ital. < L *videre* to see]

vis·u·al (vizh′ŏŏ·əl) *adj.* **1.** Pertaining to, resulting from, or serving the sense of sight. **2.** Perceptible by sight; visible. **3.** Optical: the *visual* focus of a lens. **4.** Produced or induced by mental images: a *visual* conception. [< MF < LL < L *visus* sight < *videre* to see] **—vis′u·al·ly** *adv.*

visual aid *Often pl.* In education, a device or method designed to convey information by visible representation, as motion pictures, charts, etc.

vis·u·al·ize (vizh′ŏŏ·əl·īz′) *v.t. & v.i.* **·ized, ·iz·ing** To form a mental image (of). **—vis′u·al·ist** (-ist) *n.* **—vis′u·al·i·za′tion** *n.* **—vis′u·al·iz′er** *n.*

vi·ta·ceous (vī·tā′shəs) *adj. Bot.* Of or belonging to the grape family of mostly woody and climbing vines. [< NL, family name < L *vitis* vine]

vi·tal (vīt′l) *adj.* **1.** Necessary to existence or continuance; essential. **2.** Of or pertaining to life: *vital* statistics. **3.** Essential to or supporting life. **4.** Affecting the course of life or existence, esp. so as to be dangerous or fatal: a *vital* error. **5.** Energetic; forceful; dynamic. **6.** Having immediate interest or importance: a *vital* question. [< OF < L *vita* life] **—vi′tal·ly** *adv.* **—vi′tal·ness** *n.*

vi·tal·ism (vīt′l·iz′əm) *n. Biol.* The doctrine that life and its phenomena arose from and are the product of a hypothetical **vital force** (or **vital principle**) regarded as acting independently of all physical and chemical forces. **—vi′tal·ist** *n.* **—vi′tal·is′tic** *adj.*

vi·tal·i·ty (vī·tal′ə·tē) *n.* **1.** The state or quality of being vital. **2.** Vital or life-giving force, principle, etc. **3.** Vigor; energy; animation. **4.** Power of continuing in force or effect.

vi·tal·ize (vīt′l·īz) *v.t.* **·ized, ·iz·ing** To make vital; endow with life or energy. **—vi′tal·i·za′tion** *n.* **—vi′tal·iz′er** *n.*

vi·tals (vīt′lz) *n.pl.* **1.** The parts or organs necessary to life. **2.** The parts or qualities essential to the continued existence or well-being of anything.

vital statistics Quantitative data relating to certain aspects and conditions of human life.

PRONUNCIATION KEY: add, āce, câre, pälm; end, ēven; it, īce; odd, ōpen, ôrder; tŏŏk, pōōl; up, bûrn; ə = a in *above*, e in *sicken*, i in *flexible*, o in *melon*, u in *focus*; yŏō = u in *fuse*; oil; pout; check; go; ring; thin; this; zh, vision.

vi·ta·min (vī′tə·min) *n. Biochem.* Any of a group of complex organic substances found in minute quantities in most natural foodstuffs, and closely associated with the maintenance of normal physiological functions in man and animals. Also **vi′ta·mine** (-mēn, -min). [< NL *vit-* (< L *vita* life) + AMINE] — **vi′ta·min′ic** *adj.*

vitamin A A fat-soluble vitamin derived from carotene and occurring naturally in animal tissues, esp. egg yolk and fish-liver oils, essential to the prevention of atrophy of epithelial tissue and night blindness.

vitamin B complex A group of water-soluble vitamins widely distributed in plants and animals, most members of which have special names.

vitamin B₁ Thiamine.

vitamin B₂ Riboflavin.

vitamin B₃ Pantothenic acid.

vitamin B₆ Pyridoxine.

vitamin B₁₂ A dark red, crystalline vitamin, $C_{63}H_{90}N_{14}O_{14}PCo$, extracted from liver and certain mold fungi, and active against pernicious anemia.

vitamin Bc Folic acid.

vitamin C Ascorbic acid.

vitamin D The antirachitic vitamin occurring chiefly in fish-liver oils.

vitamin D₁ An impure mixture of calciferol and irradiated ergosterol.

vitamin D₂ Calciferol.

vitamin D₃ A form of vitamin D₂ found principally in fish-liver oils.

vitamin E The antisterility vitamin, composed of three forms of tocopherol and found in whole grain cereals.

vitamin G Riboflavin.

vitamin H Biotin.

vitamin K₁ A vitamin, found in green leafy vegetables, that promotes the clotting of blood.

vitamin K₂ A form of vitamin K₁ prepared from fishmeal.

vitamin P complex A group of substances obtained from citrus fruits and promoting the normal permeability of capillary walls.

vi·ti·ate (vish′ē·āt) *v.t.* **·at·ed, ·at·ing 1.** To impair the use or value of; spoil. **2.** To debase or corrupt. **3.** To render legally ineffective. [< L < *vitium* fault] — **vi·ti·a·ble** (vish′-ē·ə·bel) *adj.* — **vi′ti·a′tion** *n.* — **vi′ti·a′tor** *n.*

vit·i·cul·ture (vit′ə·kul′chər, vī′tə-) *n.* The science and art of grape growing. [< L *vitis* vine + CULTURE] — **vit′i·cul′tur·al** *adj.* — **vit′i·cul′tur·er, vit′i·cul′tur·ist** *n.*

vit·re·ous (vit′rē·əs) *adj.* **1.** Pertaining to glass; glassy. **2.** Obtained from glass. **3.** Resembling glass. **4.** Pertaining to the vitreous humor. [< L < *vitrum* glass] — **vit′re·os′i·ty** (-os′ə·tē), **vit′re·ous·ness** *n.*

vitreous humor *Anat.* The transparent, jellylike tissue that fills the ball of the eye. Also **vitreous body.**

vitri- *combining form* Glass; of or pertaining to glass. Also, before vowels, **vitr-.** [< L *vitrum* glass]

vit·ri·fy (vit′rə·fī) *v.t. & v.i.* **·fied, ·fy·ing** To change into glass or a vitreous substance; make or become vitreous. [< MF < L *vitrum* glass + *facere* to make] — **vit′ri·fac′tion** (-fak′shən) *n.* — **vit′ri·fi′a·ble** *adj.* — **vit′ri·fi·ca′tion** (-fə-kā′shən) *n.*

vit·ri·ol (vit′rē·ōl, -əl) *n.* **1.** *Chem.* **a** Sulfuric acid. **b** Any sulfate of a heavy metal, as *green vitriol* from iron, *blue vitriol* from copper, or *white vitriol* from zinc. **2.** Anything sharp or caustic, esp. speech or writing. — *v.t.* **·oled** or **·olled, ·ol·ing** or **·ol·ling 1.** To injure (a person) with vitriol. **2.** To subject (anything) to the agency of vitriol. [< OF < Med.L < L *vitrum* glass]

vit·ri·ol·ic (vit′rē·ol′ik) *adj.* **1.** Derived from a vitriol. **2.** Corrosive, burning, or caustic.

vit·ri·ol·ize (vit′rē·ə·līz′) *v.t.* **·ized, ·iz·ing 1.** To corrode, injure, or burn with sulfuric acid. **2.** To convert into or impregnate with vitriol. — **vit′ri·ol·i·za′tion** *n.*

vit·tles (vit′əls) *n.pl. Informal* or *Dial.* Victuals.

vi·tu·per·ate (vī·tōō′pə·rāt, -tyōō′-, vi-) *v.t.* **·at·ed, ·at·ing** To find fault with abusively; rail at; berate; scold. [< L < *vitium* fault + *parare* to prepare, make] — **vi·tu′per·a′tion** *n.* — **vi·tu′per·a′tive** (-pər·ə·tiv) *adj.* — **vi·tu′per·a·tive·ly** *adv.* — **vi·tu′per·a′tor** *n.*

vi·va (vē′vä) *interj.* Live! Long live!: a shout of applause; an acclamation or salute. [< Ital. *vivere* to live < L]

vi·va·ce (vē·vä′chā) *adv. Music* Lively; quickly; briskly. Also **vi·va/ce·men′te** (-mān′tě). [< Ital.]

vi·va·cious (vi·vā′shəs, vī-) *adj.* Lively; active. [< L < *vivere* to live] — **vi·va′cious·ly** *adv.* — **vi·va′cious·ness** *n.*

vi·vac·i·ty (vi·vas′ə·tē, vī-) *n. pl.* **·ties 1.** The state or quality of being vivacious. **2.** Sprightliness, as of temper or behavior; liveliness. **3.** A vivacious act, expression, etc.

vi·var·i·um (vī·vâr′ē·əm) *n. pl.* **·var·i·a** (-vâr′ē·ə) or **·var·i·ums** A place for keeping or raising live animals, fish, or plants, as a park, pond, aquarium, cage, etc. Also **viv·a·ry** (viv′ər·ē). [< L *vivere* to live]

vi·va vo·ce (vī′və vō′sē) *Latin* By spoken word; orally.

vive (vēv) *interj. French* Long live!: used in acclamation.

viv·id (viv′id) *adj.* **1.** Very bright; intense: said of colors. **2.** Producing or evoking lifelike imagery, freshness, etc.: *vivid* prose. **3.** Clearly felt or strongly expressed, as emotions. **4.** Full of life and vigor. **5.** Clearly seen in the mind, as a memory. **6.** Clearly perceived by the eye. [< L *vivere* to live] — **viv′id·ly** *adv.* — **viv′id·ness** *n.* — **Syn. 1.** brilliant, clear. **2.** lifelike. **4.** animated, lively.

viv·i·fy (viv′ə·fī) *v.t.* **·fied, ·fy·ing 1.** To give life to; animate; vitalize. **2.** To make more vivid or striking. [< OF < LL < L *vivus* alive + *facere* to make] — **viv′i·fi·ca′tion** (-fə-kā′shən) *n.* — **viv′i·fi′er** *n.*

vi·vip·a·rous (vī·vip′ər·əs) *adj.* **1.** *Zool.* Bringing forth living young, as most mammals: distinguished from *oviparous.* **2.** *Bot.* Producing bulbs or seeds that germinate while attached to the parent plant. [< L < *vivus* alive + *parere* to bring forth] — **viv·i·par·i·ty** (viv′ə·par′ə·tē), **vi·vip′a·rism** (-riz′əm), **vi·vip′a·rous·ly** *adv.* — **vi·vip′a·rous·ness** *n.*

viv·i·sect (viv′ə·sekt) *v.t.* **1.** To dissect or operate upon (a living animal), with a view to exposing its physiological processes. — *v.i.* **2.** To practice vivisection. — **viv′i·sec′tor** *n.*

viv·i·sec·tion (viv′ə·sek′shən) *n.* **1.** The act of cutting into or dissecting a living animal body. **2.** Experimentation on living animals by means of operations designed to promote knowledge of physiological and pathological processes. [< L *vivus* living, alive + SECTION.] — **viv′i·sec′tion·al** *adj.* — **viv′i·sec′tion·ist** *n.*

vix·en (vik′sən) *n.* **1.** A female fox. **2.** A turbulent, quarrelsome woman; shrew. [Alter. of ME *fixen* she-fox < OE fem. of *fox*] — **vix′en·ish** *adj.* — **vix′en·ly** *adj. & adv.*

viz·ard (viz′ərd) *n.* A mask; visor: also spelled *visard.* [Alter. of VISOR] — **viz′ard·ed** *adj.*

vi·zier (vi·zir′, viz′yər) *n.* A high official of a Moslem country; esp., a minister of state. Also **vi·zir′.** [< Turkish < Arabic *wazīr* counselor, orig., porter < *wazara* to carry]

vi·zier·ate (vi·zir′it, -āt, viz′yər·it, -yə·rāt) *n.* The office of a vizier. Also **vi·zier′al·ty, vi·zier′ship, vi·zir′ate, vi·zir′ship.**

vi·zor (vī′zər, viz′ər) See VISOR.

V-J Day (vē′jā′) September 2, the official date of the victory over Japan in World War II, 1945.

V-mail (vē′māl′) *n.* Mail written on special forms, transmitted overseas in World War II on microfilm, and enlarged for final delivery. [< V(ICTORY) + MAIL]

vo·ca·ble (vō′kə·bəl) *n.* **1.** A spoken or written word considered only as a sequence of sounds or letters, without regard to its meaning. **2.** A vocal sound. — *adj.* Capable of being spoken. [< F < L *vocabulum* name < *vocare* to call]

vo·cab·u·lar·y (vō·kab′yə·ler′ē) *n. pl.* **·lar·ies 1.** A list of words, esp. one arranged in alphabetical order and defined or translated; a glossary. **2.** All the words of a language. **3.** A sum or aggregate of the words used by a particular person, class, etc., or employed in some specialized field of knowledge. [< LL < L *vocabulum.* See VOCABLE.]

vocabulary entry 1. A word or term given in a vocabulary. **2.** A word, term, or phrase entered in a dictionary.

vo·cal (vō′kəl) *adj.* **1.** Of or pertaining to the voice. **2.** Having voice; endowed with the power of utterance. **3.** Uttered or performed by the voice: *vocal* music. **4.** Concerned in the production of voice: the *vocal* organs. **5.** Full of voices or sounds. **6.** Freely expressing oneself in speech: the *vocal* segment. [< L *vocalis* speaking, sounding < *vox* voice] — **vo′cal·ly** *adv.* — **vo′cal·ness** *n.*

vocal cords Two membranous bands extending from the thyroid cartilage of the larynx and having edges that, when drawn tense, are caused to vibrate by the passage of air from the lungs, thereby producing voice. For illus. see THROAT.

vo·cal·ic (vō·kal′ik) *adj.* Consisting of, like, or relating to vowel sounds.

vo·cal·ist (vō′kəl·ist) *n.* A singer.

vo·cal·ize (vō′kəl·īz) *v.* **·ized, ·iz·ing** *v.t.* **1.** To make vocal; utter, say, or sing. **2.** To provide a voice for; render articulate. **3.** *Phonet.* **a** To change (a consonant) to a vowel by some shift in the articulatory process. **b** To voice. — *v.i.* **4.** To produce sounds with the voice, as in speaking or singing. — **vo′cal·i·za′tion** *n.* — **vo′cal·iz′er** *n.*

vo·ca·tion (vō·kā′shən) *n.* **1.** A stated or regular occupation; a calling. **2.** A call to or fitness for a certain career. **3.** The work or profession for which one has a sense of special fitness. — **Syn.** See OCCUPATION. [< L < *vocare* to call] — **vo·ca′tion·al** *adj.* — **vo·ca′tion·al·ly** *adv.*

vocational guidance A systematic program of tests and interviews to help a person find the occupation for which he is best suited.

vocational school A school, usu. on the secondary level, that trains students for special trades.

voc·a·tive (vok′ə·tiv) *adj.* **1.** Pertaining to or used in the act of calling. **2.** *Gram.* In some inflected languages, denoting the case of a noun, pronoun, or adjective used in direct address. — *n. Gram.* **1.** The vocative case. **2.** A word in this case. [< F, fem. of *vocatif* < L *vocare* to call]

vo·ces (vō′sēz) Plural of VOX.

vo·cif·er·ant (vō-sif′ər-ənt) *adj.* Viciferous; clamorous. — *n.* A vociferous person. — **vo·cif′er·ance** *n.*

vo·cif·er·ate (vō-sif′ə-rāt) *v.t. & v.i.* **·at·ed, ·at·ing** To cry out with a loud voice; shout. [< L < *vox, vocis* voice + *ferre* to carry] — **vo·cif′er·a′tion** *n.* — **vo·cif′er·a′tor** *n.*

vo·cif·er·ous (vō-sif′er·əs) *adj.* Making or characterized by a loud outcry; clamorous; noisy. — **vo·cif′er·ous·ly** *adv.* — **vo·cif′er·ous·ness** *n.*

vod·ka (vod′kə, *Russ.* vôd′kə) *n.* An alcoholic liquor, originally made in Russia from a fermented mash of wheat but now also from other cereals and potatoes. [< Russian, dim. of *voda* water]

vogue (vōg) *n.* **1.** The prevalent way or fashion; mode: often preceded by *in.* **2.** Popular favor; general acceptance. [< F, fashion, orig., rowing < Ital. *vogare* to row]

Vo·gul (vō′gŏŏl) *n.* **1.** One of a Finno-Ugric people of the Ural Mountains. **2.** The Ugric language of these people.

voice (vois) *n.* **1.** The sound produced by the vocal organs of a person or animal. **2.** The quality or character of such sound: a melodious *voice.* **3.** The power or faculty of vocal utterance; speech. **4.** A sound suggesting vocal utterance or speech: the *voice* of the wind. **5.** Opinion or choice expressed; also, the right of expressing a preference or judgment: to have a *voice* in the affair. **6.** Instruction; admonition: the *voice* of nature. **7.** A person or agency by which the thought, wish, or purpose of another is expressed. **8.** Expression of thought, opinion, feeling, etc.: to give *voice* to one's ideals. **9.** *Phonet.* The sound produced by vibration of the vocal cords in the production of most vowels and certain consonants. **10.** Musical tone produced by vibration of the vocal cords and resonating in the cavities of the throat and head; also, the ability to sing, or the state of the vocal organs with regard to this ability: to be in poor *voice.* **11.** *Music* A part (def. 11a), esp. as considered without regard to the particular instrument or human voice rendering it: also **voice part.** **12.** *Gram.* The relation of the action expressed by the verb to the subject, or the form of the verb indicating this relationship. In most Indo-European languages, a distinction between an *active* and a *passive* voice is made, indicating, respectively, that the subject of the sentence is either performing the action or is being acted upon. (Active: *He wrote the letter.* Passive: *The letter was written by him.*) — **in voice** In proper condition for singing. — **with one voice** With one accord; unitedly; unanimously. — *v.t.* **voiced, voic·ing** 1. To put into speech; utter. **2.** *Music* To regulate the tones of; tune, as the pipes of an organ. **3.** *Phonet.* To utter with voice or sonance. [< OF < L *vox, vocis*]

voice box The larynx.

voiced (voist) *adj.* **1.** Having a voice; expressed by voice. **2.** *Phonet.* Uttered with vibration of the vocal cords, as (b), (d), (z); sonant: also *vocal.*

voice·less (vois′lis) *adj.* **1.** Having no voice, speech, or vote. **2.** *Phonet.* Produced without voice, as (p), (t), (s); surd. — **voice′less·ly** *adv.* — **voice′less·ness** *n.*

void (void) *adj.* **1.** No longer having force or validity, as a contract, license, etc., that has lapsed; invalid; null. **2.** Destitute; clear or free: with *of: void* of reason. **3.** Not occupied by matter; empty. **4.** Unoccupied, as a house or room. **5.** Producing no effect; useless. — *n.* **1.** An empty space; a vacuum. **2.** A breach of surface or matter; a disconnecting space. **3.** Empty condition or feeling; a blank. — *v.t.* **1.** To make void or of no effect; invalidate. **2.** To empty or remove (contents); evacuate, as urine. — **Syn.** See ANNUL. [< OF, ult. < LL *vocuus* empty < L *vacuus*] — **void′er** *n.*

void·a·ble (voi′də-bəl) *adj.* **1.** Capable of being made void. **2.** That may be evacuated. — **void′a·ble·ness** *n.*

void·ance (void′ns) *n.* **1.** The act of voiding, evacuating, ejecting, or emptying. **2.** The state or condition of being void; vacancy. [< AF < OF < *voider* to empty]

voi·là (vwà-là′) *interj. French* There! behold!

voile (voil, *Fr.* vwàl) *n.* A fine, sheer fabric like heavy veiling, used for summer dresses and curtains. [< F, veil]

vo·lant (vō′lənt) *adj.* **1.** Flying, or able to fly. **2.** Nimble. [< OF, ppr. of *voler* to fly < L *volare*]

vo·lan·te (vō-län′tā) *adj. Music* Swift and light. [< Ital.]

vo·lar (vō′lər) *adj.* Pertaining to flight. [< L *volare* to fly]

vol·a·tile (vol′ə-til) *adj.* **1.** Evaporating rapidly at ordinary temperatures on exposure to the air. **2.** Capable of being vaporized. **3.** Easily influenced; changeable. **4.** Transient; ephemeral. [< OF < L *volare* to fly]

vol·a·til·i·ty (vol′ə-til′ə-tē) *n.* **1.** The state or quality of being volatile. **2.** The property of being freely or rapidly diffused in the atmosphere. Also **vol′a·tile·ness.**

vol·a·til·ize (vol′ə-til-īz′) *v.t. & v.i.* **·ized, ·iz·ing** 1. To make or become volatile. **2.** To pass off or cause to pass off in vapor; evaporate. — **vol′a·til·iz′a·ble** *adj.* — **vol′a·til·i·za′tion** *n.* — **vol′a·til·iz′er** *n.*

vol·can·ic (vol·kan′ik) *adj.* **1.** Of, pertaining to, or charac-

teristic of a volcano or volcanoes. **2.** Produced by or emitted from a volcano. **3.** Eruptive. — **vol·can·i·c·i·ty** (vol′kə-nis′ə-tē) *n.* — **vol·can′i·cal·ly** *adv.*

vol·can·ism (vol′kən-iz′əm) *n.* The conditions and phenomena associated with volcanoes or volcanic action.

vol·can·ize (vol′kən-īz) *v.t.* **·ized, ·iz·ing** To subject to the action and effects of volcanic heat. — **vol′can·i·za′tion** *n.*

vol·ca·no (vol·kā′nō) *n. pl.* **·noes** or **·nos** *Geol.* **1.** An opening in the crust of the earth from which steam, hot gases, ashes, etc., are expelled, forming a conical hill or mountain with a central crater. **2.** The formation itself. [< Ital. < L *Volcanus, Vulcanus* Vulcan]

vol·can·ol·o·gy (vol′kən·ol′ə-jē) *n.* The scientific study of volcanoes. — **vol′can·o·log′i·cal** (-ə·loj′i-kəl) *adj.* — **vol′·can·ol′o·gist** *n.*

vole (vōl) *n.* Any of various short-tailed, mouselike or rat-like rodents; esp., the **European vole** or the **North American vole**: also called *field mouse, meadow mouse.* [Short for earlier *vole mouse* < *vole* field < Norw. *voll*]

vo·li·tion (və-lish′ən) *n.* **1.** The act or faculty of willing; exercise of the will; esp., the termination of reasoning or uncertainty by a decision. **2.** Strength of will. **2.** That which is willed or determined upon. [< F < Med.L < L *vol-*, stem of *velle* will] — **vo·li′tion·al** *adj.* — **vo·li′tion·al·ly** *adv.*

vol·i·tive (vol′ə-tiv) *adj.* **1.** Of, pertaining to, or originating in the will. **2.** Expressing a wish or permission.

vol·ley (vol′ē) *n. pl.* **·leys** 1. A simultaneous discharge of many missiles; also, the missiles so discharged. **2.** Any discharge of many things at once: a *volley* of oaths. **3.** In tennis, a return of the ball before it touches the ground. **4.** In soccer, a kick given the ball before its rebound. **5.** In cricket, a ball bowled so that it strikes the wicket before it touches the ground. — *v.t. & v.i.* **·leyed, ·ley·ing** 1. To discharge or be discharged in a volley. **2.** In tennis, to return (the ball) without allowing it to touch the ground. **3.** In soccer, to kick (the ball) before its rebound; in cricket, to bowl (a ball) full pitch. [< MF < L *volare* to fly]

vol·ley·ball (vol′ē-bôl′) *n.* A game in which two teams on either side of a high net strike a large ball with the hands in an attempt to send the ball over the net without letting it touch the ground; also, the ball used. Also **volley ball.**

vo·lost (vō′lost) *n.* In Russia, a district having one joint administrative assembly; a rural soviet. [< Russian *volost′*]

vol·plane (vol′plān) *Archaic v.i.* **·planed, ·plan·ing** To glide in an airplane. — *n.* An airplane glide. [< F *vol plané* gliding flight < *vol* flight + *plané*, pp. of *planer* to glide]

Vol·sci (vol′sī) *n.pl.* A warlike people of ancient Italy, subdued by the Romans about 350 B.C. — **Vol·scian** (vol′shən) *adj. & n.*

Völ·sun·ga Sa·ga (vol′sŏŏng·gə sä′gə) A prose version of the Icelandic legends of the dwarf race, the Nibelungs, and Sigurd, the grandson of Volsung. [< ON *Völsunga saga*, lit., saga of the Volsungs]

Vol·sungs (vol′sŏŏngz) *n.pl.* In Icelandic mythology, a race of warriors descended from the hero **Vol′sung.**

volt[1] (vōlt) *n.* The unit of electromotive force, or that difference of potential that, when steadily applied against a resistance of one ohm, will produce a current of one ampere. [after Alessandro *Volta*, 1745–1827, Italian physicist]

volt[2] (vōlt) *n.* **1.** In horse-training, a gait in which the horse moves partially sidewise round a center. **2.** In fencing, a sudden leap to avoid a thrust. [< F < Ital. *volta*, orig. pp. fem. of *volvere* to turn < L]

volt·age (vōl′tij) *n.* Electromotive force expressed in volts.

vol·ta·ic (vol·tā′ik) *adj.* Pertaining to electricity developed through chemical action or contact; galvanic.

voltaic battery *Electr.* A battery or primary cells.

voltaic cell *Electr.* A primary cell.

volt·a·ism (vōl′tə-iz′əm) *n.* Galvanism (def. 1).

volt·am·me·ter (vōlt′am′mē′tər) *n.* An instrument for measuring either volts or amperes.

volt·am·pere (vōlt′am′pir) *n.* The rate of work in an electric circuit when the current is one ampere and the potential one volt, equivalent to one watt.

volt·me·ter (vōlt′mē′tər) *n.* An instrument for determining the voltage between any two points, generally consisting of a calibrated galvanometer wound with a coil of high resistance.

vol·u·ble (vol′yə-bəl) *adj.* **1.** Having a flow of words or fluency in speaking; garrulous. **2.** Turning readily or easily; apt or formed to roll. **3.** Twining, as a plant. [< MF < L *volutus*, pp. of *volvere* to turn] — **vol′u·bil′i·ty, vol′u·ble·ness** *n.* — **vol′u·bly** *adv.*

vol·ume (vol′yŏŏm, -yəm) *n.* **1.** A collection of sheets of paper bound together; book. **2.** A separately bound part of a work. **3.** Sufficient matter to fill a volume. **4.** Quantity of sound or tone; loudness. **5.** A large quantity; a considerable amount. **6.** Space occupied in three dimensions, as measured by cubic units. — **to speak volumes** To be full of meaning; express a great deal. [< OF < L *volumen* roll, scroll < *volvere* to turn]

vo·lu·me·ter (və·lōō′mə·tər) *n.* Any of several instruments for measuring the volume of gases, liquids, or solids under specified conditions. [< VOLU(ME) + -METER]

vol·u·met·ric (vol′yə·met′rik) *adj. Chem.* Of or pertaining to measurement of substances by comparison of volumes. Also **vol′u·met′ri·cal.** — **vol′u·met′ri·cal·ly** *adv.* — **vo·lu·me·try** (və·lōō′mə·trē) *n.*

vo·lu·mi·nous (və·lōō′mə·nəs) *adj.* **1.** Having great quantity or volume. **2.** Consisting of or capable of filling several volumes. **3.** Writing or having written much; productive. **4.** Having coils, folds, windings, etc. — **vo·lu′mi·nous·ly** *adv.* — **vo·lu′mi·nos·i·ty, vo·lu′mi·nous·ness** *n.*

vol·un·tar·y (vol′ən·ter′ē) *adj.* **1.** Proceeding from the will or from one's own free choice; intentional; volitional. **2.** Endowed with, possessing, or exercising will or free choice. **3.** Effected by choice or volition. **4.** *Law* **a** Unconstrained of will; done without compulsion. **b** Performed without legal obligation. — *n. pl.* **·tar·ies 1.** Any work or performance not compelled or imposed by another. **2.** *Music* An organ solo, often improvised, played before, during, or after a service. [< OF < L *voluntas* will] — **vol′un·tar′i·ly** *adv.* — **vol′un·tar′i·ness** *n.*

vol·un·teer (vol′ən·tir′) *n.* One who enters into any service, esp. military service or a hazardous undertaking, of his own free will. — *adj.* **1.** Pertaining to or composed of volunteers. **2.** Springing up naturally or spontaneously, as from fallen or self-sown seed. — *v.t.* **1.** To offer to give or do. — *v.i.* **2.** To enter or offer to enter into some service or undertaking of one's free will; enlist. [< obs. F *voluntaire* < OF *voluntas* will]

Volunteer State Nickname of Tennessee.

vo·lup·tu·ar·y (və·lup′chōō·er′ē) *adj.* Pertaining to or promoting sensual indulgence and luxurious pleasures. — *n. pl.* **·ar·ies** One addicted to sensual pleasures; a sensualist.

vo·lup·tu·ous (və·lup′chōō·əs) *adj.* **1.** Belonging to, producing, exciting, or yielding sensuous gratification. **2.** Pertaining to or devoted to the enjoyment of pleasures or luxuries; luxurious; sensual. **3.** Having a full and beautiful form, as a woman. [< OF < L *voluptas* pleasure] — **vo·lup′tu·ous·ly** *adv.* — **vo·lup′tu·ous·ness** *n.*

vo·lute (və·lōōt′) *n.* **1.** *Archit.* A spiral, scroll-like ornament, esp. one characteristic of the Ionic capital. **2.** *Zool.* One of the whorls or turns of a spiral shell. — *adj.* **1.** Rolled up; forming spiral curves. **2.** Having a spiral form, as a machine part. [< F < L *voluta* scroll, orig. fem. pp. of *volvere* to turn] — **vo·lut′ed** *adv.* — **vo·lu′tion** *n.*

VOLUTE

vom·it (vom′it) *v.i.* **1.** To throw up or eject the contents of the stomach through the mouth. **2.** To issue with violence from any hollow place; be ejected. — *v.t.* **3.** To throw up or eject from the stomach, as food. **4.** To discharge or send forth copiously or forcibly: The volcano *vomited* smoke. — *n.* Matter that is ejected, as from the stomach in vomiting. [< L *vomitare*, freq. of *vomere* to vomit] — **vom′it·er** *n.*

vom·i·tive (vom′ə·tiv) *adj.* Causing vomiting. — *n.* An emetic.

vom·i·to·ry (vom′ə·tôr′ē, -tō′rē) *adj.* Efficacious in producing vomiting. — *n. pl.* **·ries 1.** An emetic. **2.** An opening through which matter is discharged. **3.** In a Roman amphitheater, one of the entrances from the encircling arcades to the passages leading to the seats: so called because of the numbers of people who flowed forth from it: also **vom·i·tor·i·um** (vom′ə·tôr′ē·əm, -tō′rē-).

von (von, *Ger.* fôn, *unstressed* fən) *prep. German* Of; from: used in German and Austrian family names as an attribute of nobility, corresponding to the French *de.*

voo·doo (vōō′dōō) *n. pl.* **·doos 1.** A primitive religion of West African origin characterized by belief in sorcery and the use of charms, fetishes, witchcraft, etc. **2.** One who practices voodoo. **3.** A voodoo charm or fetish. — *adj.* Of or pertaining to the beliefs, ceremonies, or practices of voodoo. — *v.t.* **·dooed, ·doo·ing** To put a spell upon after the manner of a voodoo. [< Creole < Ewe (a W. African language) *vodu*]

voo·doo·ism (vōō′dōō·iz′əm) *n.* **1.** The religion of voodoo. **2.** Belief in or practice of this religion. — **voo′doo·ist** *n.* — **voo′doo·is′tic** *adj.*

-vora *combining form Zool.* Used to denote orders or genera when classified according to their food: *Carnivora.* An individual member of such an order or genus is denoted by **-vore:** *carnivore.* [< NL < L *-vorus.* See -VOROUS.]

vo·ra·cious (vô·rā′shəs, vō-, və-) *adj.* **1.** Eating with greediness; ravenous. **2.** Greedy; rapacious. **3.** Ready to swallow up or engulf. **4.** Insatiable; immoderate. [< L *vorare* to devour] — **vo·ra′cious·ly** *adv.* — **vo·rac·i·ty** (vô·ras′ə·tē, vō-, və-), **vo·ra′cious·ness** *n.*

-vorous *combining form* Consuming; eating or feeding upon: *omnivorous, carnivorous.* [< L *-vorus* < *vorare* to devour]

vor·tex (vôr′teks) *n. pl.* **·tex·es** or **·ti·ces** (-tə·sēz) **1.** A mass of whirling gas or liquid, esp. when sucked spirally toward a central axis; a whirlwind or whirlpool. **2.** Any action or state of affairs that is similar to a vortex in violence, force, etc. [< L, var. of *vertex* top, point] — **vor′ti·cal** (-ti·kəl) *adj.* — **vor′ti·cal·ly** *adv.*

vo·ta·ry (vō′tər·ē) *n. pl.* **·ries 1.** One bound by a vow or promise, as a nun. **2.** One devoted to some particular worship, pursuit, study, etc. Also **vo′ta·rist.** — **Syn.** See ENTHUSIAST. — *adj.* Consecrated by a vow or promise; votive. [< L *votus*, pp. of *vovere* to vow] — **vo·ta·ress** (vō′tə·ris) or **vo′tress** (vō′tris) *n.fem.*

vote (vōt) *n.* **1.** A formal expression of will or opinion in regard to some question submitted for decision, as in electing officers, passing resolutions, etc. **2.** That by which such choice is expressed, as a show of hands, or ballot. **3.** The result of an election. **4.** The number of votes cast; also, votes collectively: a light *vote*; the farm *vote*. **5.** The right to vote. **6.** A voter. — *v.* **vot·ed, vot·ing** *v.t.* **1.** To enact or determine by vote. **2.** To cast one's vote for: to *vote* a straight ticket. **3.** *Informal* To declare by general agreement: to *vote* a concert a success. — *v.i.* **4.** To cast one's vote; express opinion or preference by or as by a vote. — **to vote down** To defeat or suppress by voting against. — **to vote in** To elect. [< L *votum* vow, wish, orig. pp. neut. of *vovere* to vow] — **vot′a·ble** or **vote′a·ble** *adj.* — **vot′er** *n.*

vote getter 1. A person who can win votes. **2.** A campaign slogan, etc., that draws votes. — **vote getting**

voting machine A device which enables the voter to indicate his choices by operating small levers and which registers and counts all votes.

vo·tive (vō′tiv) *adj.* Dedicated by a vow; performed in fulfillment of a vow. — **vo′tive·ly** *adv.* — **vo′tive·ness** *n.*

vouch (vouch) *v.i.* **1.** To give one's own assurance or guarantee; bear witness: with *for*: I will *vouch* for them. **2.** To serve as assurance or proof: with *for*. — *v.t.* **3.** To bear witness to; attest or affirm. **4.** To cite as support or justification. **5.** To substantiate. — *n.* A declaration that attests; an assertion. [< OF < L *vocare* to call < *vox, vocis* voice]

vouch·er (vou′chər) *n.* **1.** Any material thing, usu. a writing, that serves to vouch for the truth of something, or attest an alleged act, esp. the payment or receipt of money. **2.** One who vouches for another; a witness.

vouch·safe (vouch′sāf′) *v.* **·safed, ·saf·ing** *v.t.* **1.** To grant, as with condescension; permit; deign. — *v.i.* **2.** To condescend; deign. — **vouch′safe′ment** *n.*

vous·soir (vōō·swär′) *n. Archit.* A stone in an arch shaped to fit its curve. [< OF *vausoir* < L *volvere* to turn]

vow (vou) *n.* **1.** A solemn promise to God or to a deity or saint to perform some act or make some gift or sacrifice. **2.** A solemn engagement to adopt a certain course of life, pursue some end, etc.; also, a pledge of faithfulness. **3.** A solemn and emphatic affirmation. — **to take vows** To enter a religious order. — *v.t.* **1.** To promise solemnly, esp. to God or to some deity. **2.** To declare with assurance or solemnity. **3.** To make a solemn promise or threat to do, inflict, etc. — *v.i.* **4.** To make a vow. [< AF *vu*, OF *vo, vou* < L *votum*] — **vow′er** *n.*

vow·el (vou′əl) *n.* **1.** *Phonet.* A speech sound produced by the relatively unimpeded passage of breath through the mouth, varying in quality according to the size, shape, and condition of the resonance cavities. Vowels may be characterized by length (long or short), the height of the tongue (high, mid, low), the place of articulation (front, central, back), the tension of the tongue muscles (tense, lax), and the presence of lip rounding. Thus (ōō) is a long, high, back, tense, rounded vowel. **2.** A letter representing such a sound, as *a, e, i, o, u,* and sometimes *y.* — *adj.* Of or pertaining to a vowel; vocal. [< OF < L *vox, vocis* voice, sound]

vox (voks) *n. pl.* **vo·ces** (vō′sēz) Voice; esp., in music, a voice; part. [< L]

vox po·pu·li (voks pop′yə·lī) *Latin* The voice of the people.

voy·age (voi′ij) *n.* **1.** A journey by water, esp. by sea: commonly used of a somewhat extended journey by water. **2.** Any journey. **3.** A book describing a voyage or voyaging. **4.** Any enterprise or project; also, course. — *v.* **·aged, ·ag·ing** *v.i.* **1.** To make a voyage; journey by water. — *v.t.* **2.** To travel over. [< OF < L *viaticum*] — **voy′ag·er** *n.*

voy·age·a·ble (voi′ij·ə·bəl) *adj.* Navigable.

vo·ya·geur (vwà·yà·zhœr′) *n. pl.* **·geurs** (-zhœr′) *Canadian* A boatman of Hudson's Bay Company or another fur company, engaged in carrying men, supplies, etc., between remote trading posts; also, a Canadian boatman or fur trader. [< dial. F (Canadian)]

vo·yeur (vwä·yûr′) *n.* One who is sexually gratified by looking at sexual objects or acts. [< F < L *videre* to see] — **vo·yeur′ism** *n.*

VTOL (vē′tôl) *n. Aeron.* An aircraft that takes off and lands vertically.

Vul·can (vul′kən) In Roman mythology, the god of fire and of metallurgy. — **Vul·ca′ni·an** (-kā′nē·ən) *adj.*

vul·ca·ni·an (vul-kā′nē-ən) *adj.* Volcanic: also **vul·can·ic** (vul-kan′ik). [< L < *Vulcanus* Vulcan]

vul·can·ite (vul′kən-īt) *n.* A dark, hard variety of rubber that has been vulcanized: also called *ebonite, hard rubber.* — *adj.* Made of vulcanite. [after *Vulcan*]

vul·can·ize (vul′kən-īz) *v.t.* **·ized, ·iz·ing** To treat (crude rubber) with sulfur or sulfur compounds in varying proportions and at different temperatures, thereby increasing its strength and elasticity. —**vul′can·iz′a·ble** *adj.* —**vul′-can·i·za′tion** *n.* —**vul′can·iz′er** *n.*

vul·ca·nol·o·gy (vul′kən-ol′ə-jē) *n.* Volcanology. —**vul′-can·o·log′i·cal** (-ə-loj′i-kəl) *adj.* —**vul′can·ol′o·gist** *n.*

vul·gar (vul′gər) *adj.* **1.** Lacking in refinement, good taste, sensitivity, etc.; coarse; crude; boorish; also, obscene; indecent. **2.** Of, pertaining to, or characteristic of the people at large, as distinguished from the privileged or educated classes; popular; common. **3.** Written in or translated into the common language or vulgate; vernacular. [< L < *vulgus* the common people] —**vul′gar·ly** *adv.*

vul·gar·i·an (vul·gâr′ē-ən) *n.* A person of vulgar tastes or manners.

vul·gar·ism (vul′gə-riz′əm) *n.* **1.** Vulgarity. **2.** A word, phrase, or expression that is in nonstandard or unrefined usage, though not necessarily coarse or gross.

vul·gar·i·ty (vul-gar′ə-tē) *n.* *pl.* **·ties 1.** The quality or character of being vulgar. **2.** Something vulgar, as an action, word, etc. Also **vul·gar·ness** (vul′gər-nis).

vul·gar·ize (vul′gə-rīz) *v.t.* **·ized, ·iz·ing 1.** To make vulgar. **2.** To express and diffuse (something abstruse or complex) in a more widely comprehensible form; popularize. Also *Brit.* **vul′gar·ise.** —**vul′gar·i·za′tion** *n.* —**vul′gar·iz′er** *n.*

Vulgar Latin See under LATIN.

vul·gate (vul′gāt) *adj.* Common; popular; generally accepted. — *n.* **1.** Everyday speech. **2.** Any commonly accepted text. [< L < *vulgus* the common people]

Vul·gate (vul′gāt) *n.* A Latin version of the Bible, translated between A.D. 383 and 405, now revised and used as the authorized version by the Roman Catholics. — *adj.* Belonging or relating to the Vulgate. [< Med.L *vulgata* (*editio*) the popular (edition), fem. of L *vulgatus* common]

vul·ner·a·ble (vul′nər-ə-bəl) *adj.* **1.** Capable of being hurt or damaged. **2.** Liable to attack; assailable. **3.** In contract bridge, having won one game of a rubber, and thus receiving increased penalties and increased bonuses. [< LL < L *vulnerare* to wound] —**vul′ner·a·bil′i·ty, vul′ner·a·ble·ness** *n.* —**vul′ner·a·bly** *adv.*

vul·pine (vul′pin, -pīn) *adj.* **1.** Of or pertaining to a fox. **2.** Like a fox; sly; crafty. [< L < *vulpes* fox]

vul·ture (vul′chər) *n.* **1.** Any of various large birds related to the eagles, hawks, and falcons, having the head and neck naked or partly naked, and feeding mostly on carrion. **2.** Someone or something disgustingly predatory. [< AF, OF < L *vultur, vulturius*] —**vul·tur·ine** (vul′chə·rīn, -chər·in), **vul′tur·ous** *adj.*

VULTURE (To 55 inches long; wingspread to 11 feet)

vul·va (vul′və) *n.* *pl.* **·vae** (-vē) *Anat.* The external genital parts of the female. [< L, a covering, womb] —**vul′val, vul′var** *adj.* —**vul′vi·form** (-və-fôrm) *adj.*

vy·ing (vī′ing) *adj.* Contending. —**vy′-ing·ly** *adv.*

W

w, W (dub′əl·yōō, -yōō) *n.* *pl.* **w's** or **ws , W's** or **Ws, doub·le·yous 1.** The twenty-third letter of the English alphabet; double u: a ligature of vv or uu. **2.** The sound represented by the letter *w*, a voiced bilabial velar semivowel before vowels (*we, wage, worry*), and a *u*-glide in diphthongs (*how, allow, dew, review*). It often has no phonetic value before *r* (*wrist, write, wrong*), and internally (*two, sword, answer*). ◆ The combination *wh-* (in Old English spelled *hw-*) is represented in this dictionary as (hw) because most Americans and probably most Canadians use that pronunciation. In some regions, however, *wh-* is consistently pronounced (w), and the use cannot be considered nonstandard. —*symbol Chem.* Tungsten (symbol W, for *wolfram*).

wab·ble (wob′əl) *v.t. & v.i.* **·bled, ·bling** To wobble. — *n.* A wobble. —**wab′bler** *n.* —**wab′bly** *adj.*

WAC or **W.A.C.** (wak) *n.* A member of the Women's Army Corps. [< W(OMEN'S) A(RMY) C(ORPS)]

wack·y (wak′ē) *adj.* **wack·i·er, wack·i·est** *Slang* Extremely irrational or impractical; erratic; screwy. [Prob. < WHACK; with ref. to damaging blows on the head]

wad (wod) *n.* **1.** A small compact mass of any soft or flexible substance, esp. as used for stuffing, packing, or lining; also, a lump; mass. **2.** A piece of paper, cloth, or leather used to hold in a charge of powder in a muzzleloading gun; also, a pasteboard or paper plug to hold powder and shot in place in a shotgun shell. **3.** Fibrous material for stopping up breaks, leakages, etc.; wadding. **4.** *Informal* A large amount. **5.** *Informal* A roll of banknotes; also, money or wealth. **6.** A chew of tobacco. — *v.* **wad·ded, wad·ding** *v.t.* **1.** To press (fibrous substances, as cotton) into a mass or wad. **2.** To roll or fold into a tight wad, as paper. **3.** To pack with wadding for protection, as valuables, or to stuff or line with wadding. **4.** To place a wad in, as a gun; hold in place with a wad. — *v.i.* **5.** To form into a wad. [Origin uncertain] —**wad′dy** *adj.*

wad·ding (wod′ing) *n.* **1.** Wads collectively. **2.** Any substance, as carded cotton, used as material for wads. **3.** The act of applying a wad or wads.

wad·dle (wod′l) *v.i.* **·dled, ·dling 1.** To walk with short steps, swaying from side to side. **2.** To move clumsily; totter. — *n.* A clumsy rocking walk, like that of a duck. [Freq. of WADE] —**wad′dler** *n.* —**wad′dly** *adj.*

wad·dy (wod′ē) *n.* *pl.* **·dies** *Austral.* **1.** A thick war club

used by the aborigines. **2.** A walking stick; piece of wood. — *v.t.* **·died, ·dy·ing** To strike with a waddy. [< native Australian pronun. of *wood*]

wade (wād) *v.* **wad·ed, wad·ing** *v.i.* **1.** To walk through water or any substance more resistant than air, as mud, sand, etc. **2.** To proceed slowly or laboriously: to *wade* through a book. — *v.t.* **3.** To pass or cross, as a river, by walking on the bottom; ford. —**to wade in** (or **into**) *Informal* To attack or begin energetically or vigorously. — *n.* **1.** The act of wading. **2.** A ford. [OE *wadan* to go]

wad·er (wā′dər) *n.* **1.** One who wades. **2.** A long-legged wading bird, as a snipe, plover, or stork. **3.** *pl.* High waterproof boots, worn esp. by anglers.

wa·di (wä′dē) *n.* *pl.* **·dies 1.** In Arabia and northern Africa, a ravine containing the bed of a watercourse, usu. dry except in the rainy season; also, the watercourse. **2.** An oasis. Also **wa′dy.** [< Arabic *wādī*]

WAF or **W.A.F.** (waf, wäf) *n.* A member of the Women in the Air Force. [< W(OMEN IN THE) A(IR) F(ORCE)]

wa·fer (wā′fər) *n.* **1.** A very thin crisp biscuit, cooky, or cracker; also, a small disk of candy. **2.** *Eccl.* A small flat disk of unleavened bread stamped with a cross or the letters IHS, and used in the Eucharist in some churches. **3.** A thin disk of gelatin or other substance used for sealing letters, attaching papers, or receiving a seal. — *v.t.* To attach, seal, or fasten with a wafer. [< AF < MLG *wafel*]

waf·fle (wof′əl, wô′fəl) *n.* A batter cake, crisper than a pancake, baked between two hinged metal griddles marked with regular indentations (**waffle iron**). [< Du. *wafel* wafer]

waft[1] (waft, wäft) *v.t.* **1.** To carry or bear gently or lightly over air or water; float. **2.** To convey as if on air or water. — *v.i.* **3.** To float, as on the wind. — *n.* **1.** The act of one who or that which wafts. **2.** A current of air; also, something, as an odor, carried on a current of air. **3.** A wafting or waving motion or movement. [Back formation < *wafter*, in obs. sense, "an escort ship" < Du. *wachten* to guard]

waft[2] (waft, wäft) *n.* *Naut.* **1.** A signal flag or pennant, sometimes used to indicate wind direction. **2.** A signal made with a flag or pennant. Also called *weft.* [Alter. of dial. E *waff,* var. of WAVE]

waft·er (waf′tər, wäf′-) *n.* **1.** One who or that which wafts. **2.** A form of fan or revolving cloth used in a blower.

wag[1] (wag) *v.* **wagged, wag·ging** *v.t.* **1.** To cause to move lightly and quickly from side to side or up and down; swing: The dog *wags* its tail. **2.** To move (the tongue) in talking. — *v.i.* **3.** To move lightly and quickly from side to side or up and down. **4.** To move busily in animated talk: said of the tongue. — *n.* The act or motion of wagging. [ME *waggen*, prob. < Scand.]

wag² (wag) *n.* A humorous fellow; wit; joker. [? Short for obs. *waghalter* gallows bird < WAG¹ + HALTER¹]

wage (wāj) *v.t.* **waged, wag·ing** To engage in and maintain vigorously; carry on: to *wage* war. — *n.* **1.** Payment for service rendered; esp., the pay of artisans or laborers receiving a fixed sum by the hour, day, week, or month, or for a certain amount of work; hire. **2.** *pl. Econ.* The remuneration received by labor as distinguished from that received by capital. **3.** *pl.* Recompense or yield: formerly, often construed as sing.: The *wages* of sin is death. [< AF *wagier*, OF *guagier* to pledge]

wage earner One who works for wages.

wa·ger (wā'jər) *v.t. & v.i.* To bet. — *n.* **1.** A bet (defs. 1, 2, & 3). **2.** The act of giving a pledge. [< AF *wagier* to pledge] — **wa'ger·er** *n.*

wage scale A scale or series of amounts of wages paid.

wage·work·er (wāj'wûr'kər) *n.* An employee receiving wages.

wag·ger·y (wag'ər·ē) *n. pl.* **·ger·ies** **1.** Mischievous jocularity; drollery. **2.** A jest; joke.

wag·gish (wag'ish) *adj.* **1.** Being or acting like a wag. **2.** Said or done in waggery. — **wag'gish·ly** *adv.* — **wag'gish·ness** *n.*

wag·gle (wag'əl) *v.* **·gled, ·gling** *v.t.* **1.** To cause to move with rapid to-and-fro motions; wag: The duck *waggles* its tail. — *v.i.* **2.** To totter; wobble. — *n.* The act of waggling. [Freq. of WAG¹] — **wag'gling·ly** *adv.* — **wag'gly** *adj.*

Wag·ne·ri·an (väg·nir'ē·ən) *adj.* Relating to Richard Wagner or to his style, theory, or works. — *n.* An admirer, performer, or advocate of Wagnerian works.

wag·on (wag'ən) *n.* **1.** Any of various four-wheeled horse-drawn vehicles used for carrying crops, goods, freight, etc. **2.** A child's four-wheeled toy cart. **3.** A stand on wheels or casters for serving food or drink. **4.** *Brit.* A railway freight car. **5.** *Informal* A patrol wagon. **6.** A station wagon. — **on the (water) wagon** *Informal* Abstaining from alcoholic beverages. — **to fix (someone's) wagon** *U.S. Slang* To ruin or punish. — *v.t.* To carry or transport in a wagon. Also *Brit.* **wag'gon.** [< Du. *wagen*]

wag·on·er (wag'ən·ər) *n.* One whose business is driving wagons. Also *Brit.* **wag'gon·er.**

wag·on-head·ed (wag'ən-hed'id) *adj. Archit.* Having a round-arched roof.

wa·gon-lit (vȧ·gôn·lē') *n. pl.* **-lits** (-lē') *French* A railway sleeping car.

wag·on·load (wag'ən·lōd') *n.* The amount that a wagon can carry.

wagon train A train or line of wagons.

wag·tail (wag'tāl') *n.* Any of several small singing birds having a long tail that is habitually wagged up and down.

Wa·ha·bi (wä·hä'bē) *n.* A member of an orthodox Moslem sect of Arabia. Also **Wa·ha'bee, Wah·ha'bi.**

wa·hoo (wä·hōo', wä'hōo) *n.* A deciduous North American shrub or small tree with purple flowers and scarlet fruit. [< Siouan (Dakota) *wānhu*, lit., arrowwood]

waif (wāf) *n.* **1.** A homeless, neglected wanderer; a stray. **2.** Anything found and unclaimed, the owner being unknown. — *v.t.* To throw away; cast off, as a waif. — *adj.* Stray; wandering; homeless. [< AF *waif*, OF *gaif*]

wail (wāl) *v.i.* **1.** To grieve with mournful cries; lament. **2.** To make a sad, melancholy sound, as if in grief. — *v.t.* **3.** To grieve on account of. **4.** To cry out in sorrow. — *n.* **1.** A prolonged, high-pitched sound of lamentation or grief. **2.** Any mournful sound, as of the wind. [< ON < *vǣ, vei* woe] — **wail'er** *n.* — **wail'ful** *adj.*

wain (wān) *n.* An open, four-wheeled wagon for hauling heavy loads. [OE *wægn, wǣn*]

wain·scot (wān'skət, -skot, -skōt) *n.* **1.** A facing for inner walls, usu. of paneled wood. **2.** The lower part of an inner wall, when finished with material different from the rest of the wall. — *v.t.* **wain·scot·ed** or **·scot·ted, wain·scot·ing** or **·scot·ting** To face or panel with wainscot. [< MLG < *wagen* wagon + *schot* wooden partition]

wain·scot·ing (wān'skət·ing, -skot-, -skōt-) *n.* Material for a wainscot; a wainscot. Also **wain'scot·ting.**

wain·wright (wān'rīt) *n.* A maker of wagons.

waist (wāst) *n.* **1.** The part of the body between the chest and the hips. **2.** The middle part of any object, esp. if narrower than the ends. **3.** That part of a woman's dress covering the body from the waistline to the shoulders; a bodice. **4.** A waistband. [ME *waot*]

waist·band (wāst'band', -bənd) *n.* A band encircling the waist, esp., as part of a skirt or trousers.

waist·coat (wāst'kōt', wes'kit) *n. Chiefly Brit.* A vest (def. 1).

waist·line (wāst'līn') *n.* The line of the waist, between the ribs and the hips; in dressmaking, the line at which the skirt of a dress meets the waist.

wait (wāt) *v.i.* **1.** To stay or remain in expectation, as of an anticipated action or event: with *for, until*, etc. **2.** To be or remain in readiness. **3.** To remain temporarily neglected or undone. **4.** To perform duties of personal service or attendance; esp., to act as a waiter or waitress. — *v.t.* **5.** To stay or remain in expectation of; await. **6.** *Informal* To postpone; delay: Don't *wait* breakfast for me. — **to wait on** (or **upon**) **1.** To act as a servant or attendant to. **2.** To go to see; call upon; visit. **3.** To attend as a consequence. — **to wait up** To delay going to bed in anticipation of someone or something. — *n.* **1.** The act of waiting, or the time spent in waiting; delay. **2.** An ambush or trap: to lie in *wait* for a victim. [< AF and OF < OHG < *wahta* guard]

wait·er (wā'tər) *n.* **1.** One who serves food and drink, as in a restaurant. **2.** One who awaits something. **3.** A tray for dishes, etc.

wait·ing (wā'ting) *n.* The act of one who waits. — **in waiting** In attendance, esp. at court. — *adj.* That waits; expecting.

waiting room A room for the use of persons waiting, as for a railroad train, a doctor, dentist, or the like.

wait·ress (wā'tris) *n.* A woman or girl employed to wait on guests at table, as in a restaurant.

waive (wāv) *v.t.* **waived, waiv·ing** **1.** To give up or relinquish a claim to. **2.** To refrain from insisting upon or taking advantage of; forego. **3.** To put off; postpone; delay. [< AF *weyver*, OF *gaiver* to abandon]

waiv·er (wā'vər) *n. Law* The voluntary relinquishment of a right or privilege; also, the instrument that evidences such relinquishment. [< AF < *weyver* to abandon]

wake¹ (wāk) *v.* **woke** (*Rare* **waked**), **waked** (*Dial.* and alternative *Brit.* **woke, wok·en**), **wak·ing** *v.i.* **1.** To emerge from sleep. **2.** To be or remain awake. **3.** To become active or alert after being inactive or dormant. **4.** *Dial.* To keep watch at night; esp., to hold a wake (def. 1). — *v.t.* **5.** To rouse from sleep; awake. **6.** To stir up; excite: to *wake* evil passions. **7.** *Dial.* To keep a vigil over; esp., to hold a wake over. — *n.* **1.** A watch over the body of a dead person through the night, before burial. **2.** The act of refraining from sleep, as on a solemn occasion. [Fusion of OE *wacan* to awake and *wacian* to be awake]

wake² (wāk) *n.* **1.** The track left by a vessel passing through the water. **2.** The area behind any moving thing. — **in the wake of** **1.** Following close behind. **2.** In the aftermath of; as a result of. [< ON *vök* an opening in ice]

wake·ful (wāk'fəl) *adj.* **1.** Remaining awake, esp. at the ordinary time of sleep; not sleeping or sleepy. **2.** Watchful; alert. **3.** Arousing from or as from sleep. — **wake'ful·ly** *adv.* — **wake'ful·ness** *n.*

wak·en (wā'kən) *v.t.* **1.** To rouse from sleep; awake. **2.** To rouse to alertness or activity. — *v.i.* **3.** To cease sleeping; wake up. [OE *wæcnan, wæcnian*]

wake-rob·in (wāk'rob'in) *n.* Any species of trillium.

Wal·dorf salad (wôl'dôrf) A salad of chopped celery, apples, and walnuts, garnished with lettuce and mayonnaise. [after the first *Waldorf*-Astoria Hotel, New York City]

wale (wāl) *n.* **1.** A welt (def. 3). **2.** *Naut.* One of certain strakes of outer planking running fore and aft on a vessel. **3.** A ridge on the surface of cloth. — *v.t.* **waled, wal·ing** **1.** To raise wales on by striking, as with a lash; beat. **2.** To manufacture, as cloth, with a ridge or rib. **3.** To weave as wickerwork with several rods together. [OE *walu*]

walk (wôk) *v.i.* **1.** To advance on foot in such a manner that one part of a foot is always on the ground; of quadrupeds, to advance in such a manner that two or more feet are always on the ground. **2.** To move or go on foot for exercise or amusement. **3.** To proceed slowly. **4.** To act or live in some manner: to *walk* in peace. **5.** To return to earth and appear, as a ghost. **6.** In baseball, to achieve first base as a result of having been pitched four balls. — *v.t.* **7.** To pass through, over, or across at a walk: to *walk* the floor. **8.** To cause to go at a walk; lead, ride, or drive at a walk. **9.** To accompany on a walk. **10.** To bring to a specified condition by walking: She *walked* me to death. **11.** In baseball, to allow to advance to first base by pitching four balls. — **to walk off** **1.** To depart, esp. abruptly or without warning. **2.** To get rid of (fat, etc.) by walking. — **to walk off with** **1.** To win. **2.** To steal. — **to walk out** *Informal* **1.** To go out on strike. **2.** To keep company: with *with* or *together.* — **to walk out on** *Informal* To forsake; desert. — **to walk over** To defeat easily; overwhelm. — *n.* **1.** The act of walking, as for enjoyment; a stroll. **2.** Manner of walking; gait. **3.** Chosen profession or habitual sphere of action: the different *walks* of life. **4.** Distance as measured by the time taken by one who walks: an hour's *walk*. **5.** A place set apart for walking; a path or sidewalk. **6.** A piece of ground set apart for domestic animals; range; pasture. **7.** In baseball, an advancing to first base as a result of hav-

ing been pitched four balls. [OE *wealcan* to roll, toss] —
walk′er *n.*
walk·a·way (wôk′ə·wā′) *n.* A contest won without serious opposition: also called *walkover.*
walk·ie-talk·ie (wô′kē·tô′kē) *n. Telecom.* A portable sending and receiving radio set light enough to be carried by one man: also spelled *walky-talky.*
walking papers *Informal* Notice of dismissal from employment; also.
walking stick 1. A staff or cane. 2. Any of various insects having legs, body, and wings resembling a twig.
walk-on (wôk′on′, -ôn′) *n.* A performer having a very small part; also, the part.
walk-out (wôk′out′) *n. Informal* A workmen's strike.
walk-o·ver (wôk′ō′vər) *n.* A walkaway.
walk-up (wôk′up′) *Informal n.* An apartment house having no elevator. — *adj.* Having no elevator.
walk·y-talk·y (wô′kē·tô′kē) See WALKIE-TALKIE.
wall (wôl) *n.* 1. A continuous structure designed to enclose an area, to be the surrounding exterior of a building, to be a partition between rooms, etc.; also, a fence separating fields, etc. ◆ Collateral adjective: *mural.* 2. Something suggestive of a wall: a *wall* of bayonets. 3. A rampart for defense; in the plural, fortifications. 4. A sea wall; levee. — **to drive, push,** or **thrust to the wall** To force (one) to an extremity; crush. — **to go to the wall** To be driven to an extremity; be forced to yield. — *v.t.* 1. To provide, surround, etc., with or as with a wall. 2. To fill or block with a wall: often with *up.* — *adj.* Of, pertaining to, or on, a wall. [OE < L < *vallus* stake, palisade]
wal·la·by (wol′ə·bē) *n. pl.* **·bies** One of the smaller kangaroos. [< Australian *wolabā*]
wall·board (wôl′bôrd′, -bōrd′) *n.* A material composed of several layers of compressed wood chips and pulp, used as a substitute for wooden boards and plaster.
wal·let (wol′it) *n.* 1. A pocketbook, usu. of leather, for holding unfolded paper money, personal papers, etc.: also called *billfold.* 2. A leather or canvas bag for tools, etc. 3. A knapsack. [ME *walet*; ult. origin uncertain]
wall·eye (wôl′ī′) *n.* 1. An eye in which the iris is light-colored or white. 2. Any of several walleyed fishes. [Back formation < WALLEYED]
wall·eyed (wôl′īd′) *adj.* 1. Having a whitish or grayish eye. 2. Having large, staring eyes, as a fish. 3. *Slang* Drunk. [< ON < *vagl* film on the eye + *eygr* < *auga* eye]
walleyed pike A fresh-water game fish of the Great Lakes, having large eyes. Also **walleyed perch.**
wall·flow·er (wôl′flou′ər) *n.* 1. Any of various European herbs of the mustard family, having fragrant yellow, orange, or red flowers. 2. *Informal* A person, esp. a woman, at a party who stays by the wall for want of a dancing partner.
Wal·loon (wo·lōōn′) *n.* 1. One of a people inhabiting southern and southeastern Belgium and the adjoining regions of France. 2. Their language, a dialect of French. — *adj.* Of or pertaining to the Walloons or their dialect.
wal·lop (wol′əp) *v.t. Informal* 1. To beat soundly; thrash. 2. To hit with a hard blow. 3. To defeat soundly. — *v.i. Dial.* or *Informal* 4. To gallop. — *n. Informal* A severe blow. [< AF *waloper,* OF *galoper*]
wal·lop·er (wol′əp·ər) *n. Informal* 1. One who or that which wallops. 2. A whopper.
wal·lop·ing (wol′əp·ing) *Informal adj.* Very large; whopping. — *n.* A beating; whipping.
wal·low (wol′ō) *v.i.* 1. To roll about; be pleasurably and actively immersed. 2. To thrash about; flounder. 3. To move with a heavy, rolling motion, as a ship in a storm. 4. To live self-indulgently: to *wallow* in sensuality. — *n.* 1. The act of wallowing. 2. A pool or hole in which animals wallow; also, any depression or hollow made by or suggesting such use. [OE *wealwian*] — **wal′low·er** *n.*
wall·pa·per (wôl′pā′pər) *n.* Paper specially prepared and printed in colors and designs, for covering walls and ceilings of rooms. — *v.t.* To cover or provide with wallpaper.
Wall Street 1. A street in the financial district of New York City. 2. The world of U.S. finance.
wal·nut (wôl′nut′, -nət) *n.* 1. Any of various trees of the North temperate zone cultivated as ornamental shade trees and valued for their timber and their edible nuts. 2. The wood or nut of any of these trees, esp. the edible seed or kernel. 3. The shagbark hickory, or its nut. 4. The color of the wood of any of these trees, esp. of the black walnut, a very dark brown. [OE < *wealh* foreign + *hnutu* nut]
Wal·pur·gis Night (väl·poŏr′gis) The night before May 1, associated with a witches' Sabbath. [after St. *Walpurga* (or *Walburga*), whose feast day falls on this date]
wal·rus (wôl′rəs, wol′-) *n. pl.* **·rus·es** or **·rus** A large marine mammal of arctic seas, having flippers, tusks in the upper jaw, and a thick neck. [< Du. *walrus* < Scand.]

waltz (wôlts) *n.* 1. A dance for couples to music in triple time. 2. The music for such a dance, or any similar music in triple time. — *v.i.* 1. To dance a waltz. 2. To move quickly and boldly; flounce. 3. To move freely. — *v.t.* 4. To cause to waltz. — *adj.* Of, or typical of, the waltz: *waltz* time. [< G < *walzen* to waltz] — **waltz′er** *n.*
wam·pum (wom′pəm, wôm′-) *n.* 1. Beads made from shells, often worked into ornaments, formerly used as currency by North American Indians. 2. *Informal* Money. [< Algonquian *wampum(peage),* lit., a white string (of beads)]
wan (won) *adj.* **wan·ner, wan·nest** 1. Pale, as from sickness or anxiety; pallid. 2. Indicating illness, unhappiness, etc.: a *wan* smile. — *v.t. & v.i.* **wanned, wan·ning** *Poetic* To make or become wan. [OE *wann* dark, gloomy] — **wan′ly** *adv.* — **wan′ness** *n.*
wand (wond) *n.* 1. A slender rod waved by a magician; also, any rod indicating an office or function of the bearer, as a scepter. 2. A musician's baton. 3. A thin, flexible stick or twig; also, a willow shoot; osier. [< ON *vöndr*]
wan·der (won′dər) *v.i.* 1. To move or travel about without destination or purpose; roam; rove. 2. To go casually or indirectly; idle; stroll. 3. To twist or meander. 4. To stray. 5. To deviate in conduct or opinion; go astray. 6. To think or speak deliriously or irrationally. — *v.t.* 7. To wander through or across. — *n.* A ramble. [OE *wandrian*] — **wan′der·er** *n.* — **wan′der·ing·ly** *adv.*
— **Syn.** (verb) 1. *Wander* implies no more than the absence of purpose: to *wander* through the shops. *Ramble* tends to be deprecatory: the speaker *rambled* on for an hour. *Roam* and *rove* imply travel through a large area, and suggest an irregular rather than a purposeless course: the explorers *roamed* through the jungle, pirates *roved* the sea.
wan·der·ing albatross (won′dər·ing) A large, whitish, black-winged, web-footed sea bird.
wan·der·lust (won′dər·lust′, *Ger.* vän′dər·lŏŏst) *n.* An impulse to travel; restlessness combined with a sense of adventure. [< G < *wandern* to travel + *lust* joy]
wane (wān) *v.i.* **waned, wan·ing** 1. To diminish in size and brilliance: opposed to *wax.* 2. To decline or decrease gradually; draw to an end. — *n.* 1. Decrease, as of power, prosperity, or reputation. 2. The decrease of the moon's visible illuminated surface; also, the period of such decrease. — **on the wane** Waning. [OE *wanian*]
wan·gle (wang′gəl) *v.* **·gled, ·gling** *Informal v.t.* 1. To obtain or accomplish by indirect or irregular methods: to *wangle* an introduction. 2. To manipulate or adjust, esp. dishonestly. — *v.i.* 3. To resort to indirect, irregular, or dishonest methods. — *n.* An act of wangling. [? Alter. of WAGGLE] — **wan′gler** *n.*
want (wont, wônt) *v.t.* 1. To feel a desire or wish for. 2. To wish; desire: used with the infinitive: Your friends *want* to help you. 3. To be deficient in; lack; be without. 4. To be lacking to the extent of: He *wants* three inches of six feet. 5. *Brit.* To need; require. — *v.i.* 6. To have need: usu. with *for.* 7. To be needy or destitute. 8. *Rare* To be lacking or absent. — **to want for** To be in need of; lack. — **to want to** *Informal* Ought to: You *want to* eat well. — *n.* 1. A lack; scarcity; shortage. 2. Privation; poverty; need. 3. Something lacking; a need. 4. A conscious need of something; a craving. — **for want of** Because of the lack or absence of: The crop failed *for want of* rain. [Prob. < ON *vanta* to be lacking] — **want′er** *n.*
wa·n't (wont, wônt) Was not: a dialectal contraction.
want ad *Informal* A classified advertisement for something wanted, as hired help, a job, a lodging, etc.
want column A column of want ads.
want·ing (won′ting, wôn′-) *adj.* 1. Not at hand; missing; lacking. 2. Not coming up to need or expectation: His work was found *wanting.* — **wanting in** Deficient in. — *prep.* 1. Without; lacking. 2. Minus; less.
wan·ton (won′tən) *adj.* 1. Licentious; lustful. 2. Unjust; malicious; *wanton* savagery; also, unprovoked: a *wanton* murder. 3. Of abundant growth; rank. 4. Extravagant; excessive; unrestrained: *wanton* speech. 5. *Poetic* Not bound or tied; loose: *wanton* curls; also, frolicsome. — *v.i.* 1. To act wantonly or playfully; revel or sport. 2. To grow luxuriantly. — *v.t.* 3. To waste wantonly. — *n.* 1. A licentious person, esp., a woman. 2. A playful or frolicsome person or animal. 3. A trifler; dallier. [ME < OE *wan* deficient + ME *towen* < OE < *tēon* to educate] — **wan′ton·ly** *adv.* — **wan′ton·ness** *n.*
wap·i·ti (wop′ə·tē) *n. pl.* **·tis** or **·ti** *U.S. & Canadian* A large North American deer; an elk. [< Algonquian]
war (wôr) *n.* 1. An armed conflict between nations or states, or between different parties in the same state. See table MAJOR WARS OF HISTORY. 2. Any act or state of hostility; enmity; also, a contest or conflict. 3. The science

MAJOR WARS OF HISTORY

NAME	CONTESTANTS (victor shown first)	NOTABLE BATTLES	TREATIES
Greco-Persian Wars 499–478 B.C.	Greek states — Persia	Marathon, 490; Thermopylae, Salamis, 480; Plataea, 479	
Peloponnesian War 431–404 B.C.	Sparta — Athens	Syracuse, 415; Cyzicus, 410; Aegospotami, 405	Peace of Nicias, 421
First Punic War 264–241 B.C.; Second Punic War 218–201 B.C.; Third Punic War 149–146 B.C.	Rome — Carthage	Drepanum, 249; Aegates, 241; Lake Trasimene, 217; Cannae, 216; Zama, 202	
Norman Conquest 1066	Normandy — England	Hastings, 1066	
Crusades 1096–1291	Christianity — Islam (indecisive)	Jerusalem, 1099; Acre, 1191	
Hundred Years' War 1338–1453	England — France	Crécy, 1346; Poitiers, 1356; Agincourt, 1415; Siege of Orléans, 1428–39	
Wars of the Roses 1455–85	Lancaster — York (indecisive)	St. Albans, 1455	
Thirty Years' War 1618–48	Catholics — Protestants	Leipzig, Breitenfeld, 1631; Lützen, 1632	Westphalia, 1648
Civil War (English) 1642–46	Roundheads — Cavaliers	Marston Moor, 1643; Naseby, 1645	
Second Great Northern War 1700–1721	Russia — Sweden and Baltic allies	Poltava, 1709	Nysted, 1721
War of the Spanish Succession 1701–14	England, Austria, Prussia, Netherlands — France, Spain	Blenheim, 1704	Utrecht, 1713
War of the Austrian Succession 1740–48	France, Prussia, Sardinia, Spain — Austria, England	Dettingen, 1743; Fontenoy, 1745	Aix-la-Chapelle, 1748
French & Indian War 1755–63	England — France	Plains of Abraham, 1759; Montreal, 1760	
Seven Years' War 1756–63	Prussia — Austria, France, Russia	Rossbach, Leuthen, 1757	Hubertusberg, 1763
Revolutionary War 1775–83	American Colonies — England	Lexington, Concord, Bunker Hill, 1775; Saratoga, 1777; Yorktown, 1781	Paris, 1783
Napoleonic Wars 1796–1815	England, Austria, Russia, Prussia, etc. — France	Nile, 1798; Trafalgar, 1805; Jena, Auerstädt, 1806; Leipzig, 1813; Waterloo, 1815	Campoformio, 1797; Tilsit, 1807; Schönbrunn, 1809; Paris, 1814–15; Vienna, 1815
War of 1812 1812–15	United States — England	Lake Erie, 1813; New Orleans, 1815	Ghent, 1814
War of Independence (Greek) 1821–29	Greece, England, Sweden, Russia — Turkey	Navarino, 1827	London, 1827
Mexican War 1846–48	United States — Mexico	Resaca de la Palma, 1846; Chapultepec, 1847	Guadalupe Hidalgo, 1848
Crimean War 1854–56	Turkey, England, France, Sardinia — Russia	Sevastopol, 1854	Paris, 1856
Civil War (United States) 1861–65	Union (North) — Confederate States (South)	Bull Run, 1861; Antietam, 1862; Chancellorsville, Gettysburg, Vicksburg, Chattanooga, 1863; Wilderness, 1864	
Franco-Prussian War 1870–71	Prussia — France	Sedan, 1870	Versailles, 1871
Spanish-American War 1898	United States — Spain	Manila Bay, Santiago, 1898	Paris, 1898
Boer War 1899–1902	England — Transvaal Republic & Orange Free State	Ladysmith, 1899	Vereeniging, 1902
Russo-Japanese War 1904–1905	Japan — Russia	Port Arthur, Mukden, Tsushima, 1905	Portsmouth, 1905
First Balkan War 1912–13; Second Balkan War 1913	Bulgaria, Serbia, Greece, Montenegro — Turkey	Scutari, 1912; Salonika, 1912; Adrianople, 1912	London, 1913
World War I 1914–18	Allies — Central Powers	Dardanelles, 1915; Verdun, Somme, Jutland, 1916; Caporetto, 1917; Vittorio Veneto, Amiens, Marne, Ypres, 1918	Versailles, Saint-Germain, Neuilly, 1919; Trianon, Sèvres, 1920; Lausanne, 1923
Civil War (Spanish) 1936–39	Insurgents — Loyalists	Teruel, 1937; Ebro River, 1938	
World War II 1939–45	United Nations — Axis 1939–45	Dunkirk, 1940; Crete, 1941; El Alamein, 1942; Tunis, 1943; Stalingrad, 1942–43; Kharkov, 1943; Cassino, 1943–44; Saint-Lô, 1944; Rhine, Ruhr, Berlin, 1945	Potsdam, 1945
	United Nations — Japan 1941–45	Pearl Harbor, 1941; Bataan, 1941–1942; Singapore, Coral Sea, Midway Island, Guadalcanal, 1942; Bismarck Sea, Tarawa, 1943; Leyte Gulf, 1944; Philippines, 1944–45; Okinawa, 1945	San Francisco, 1951
Korean War 1950–52	United Nations — North Korea	Inchon, Pyongyang, 1950; Seoul, 1951	Panmunjom, 1953
Viet Nam War 1958–1973	South Vietnam — North Vietnam (indecisive)	Pleiku, 1965; Dak To, 1966–68; Da Nang, 1968–69; Hue, 1968–69	Paris, 1973

of military operations; strategy. **— v.i. warred, war·ring 1.** To wage war; fight or take part in a war. **2.** To be in any state of active opposition. **— adj.** Of, used in, or resulting from war. [OE < AF < OHG *werra* strife]

war belt Among certain North American Indians, a belt of wampum sent to declare war, to invoke aid in war, etc.

War between the States The U.S. Civil War: used esp., in the former Confederate States.

war·ble (wôr′bəl) *v.* **·bled, ·bling** *v.t.* **1.** To sing with trills and runs, or with tremulous vibrations. **2.** To celebrate in song. **— v.i. 3.** To sing with trills, etc. **4.** To make a liquid, murmuring sound, as a stream. **5.** *U.S.* To yodel. **— n.** The act of warbling; a carol; song. [< AF and OF < *werble* warble]

war·bler (wôr′blər) *n.* **1.** One who or that which warbles. **2.** Any of various plain-colored, mostly Old World birds noted for their song. **3.** Any of various small American insectivorous birds, usu. brilliantly colored.

war bonnet The ceremonial head dress of the North American Plains Indians.

war crime Any of various crimes considered in violation of the rules of warfare, as atrocities against civilians, slave labor, genocide, and the mistreatment of prisoners.

war cry A rallying cry used by combatants in a war, or by participants in any contest.

ward (wôrd) *n.* **1.** A large room in a hospital, usu. for six or more patients. **2.** An administrative or electoral division of a city. **3.** *Law* A person, often a minor, who is in the charge of a guardian. **4.** The act of guarding, or the state of being guarded; custody. **5.** A means of defense: a protection. **6.** A defensive attitude, as in fencing; guard. **7.** Any of the separate divisions of a prison. — *v.t.* **1.** To repel or turn aside, as a blow: usu., with *off*. **2.** To keep in safety. **3.** *Archaic* To guard. [OE < *weardian* to watch, guard]

-ward *suffix* Toward; in the direction of: *upward, homeward.* Also **-wards.** [OE *-weard, -weardes* at, toward]

war dance A dance of savage tribes before going to war or in celebration of a victory.

war·den[1] (wôr′dən) *n.* **1.** *U.S.* The chief officer of a prison. **2.** *Brit.* The head of certain colleges. **3.** In Connecticut, the chief executive of a borough. **4.** A churchwarden. **5.** A warder. [< AF *wardein,* OF *gardein, guarden* < Gmc] — **war′den·ry, war′den·ship** (-ship) *n.*

war·den[2] (wôr′dən) *n.* A variety of pear used chiefly for cooking. Also **War′den.** [ME *wardon*]

ward·er (wôr′dər) *n.* **1.** A keeper; guard; sentinel; watchman. **2.** An official staff or baton; a truncheon. **3.** *Chiefly Brit.* A prison official; warden. [< AF < *warder* to keep]

ward heel·er *U.S. Slang* A hanger-on of a political boss, who does minor tasks, canvasses votes, etc. [< WARD (def. 2) + HEELER (def. 1)]

ward·robe (wôrd′rōb′) *n.* **1.** All the garments belonging to any one person. **2.** An upright cabinet for clothes. **3.** Theatrical costumes; also, the room in which they are kept. [< AF < OF < *warder* to keep + *robe* dress]

ward·room (wôrd′rōōm′, -rōŏm′) *n.* On a warship, the common recreation area and dining room for the commissioned officers; also, these officers as a group.

ward·ship (wôrd′ship) *n.* **1.** The state of being a ward or having a guardian. **2.** Custody; guardianship.

ware (wâr) *n.* **1.** Articles of the same class; esp., manufactured articles: used collectively, often in combination: *tableware, glassware.* **2.** *pl.* Articles of commerce; goods; merchandise. **3.** Pottery; earthenware. [OE *waru*]

ware·house (wâr′hous′) *n.* A storehouse for goods or merchandise. — *v.t.* **·housed** (-houzd′), **·hous·ing** (-hou′-zing) To place or store in a warehouse.

ware·house·man (wâr′hous′mən) *n. pl.* **·men** (-mən) One who works in, manages, or owns a warehouse.

war·fare (wôr′fâr′) *n.* **1.** The waging or carrying on of war; conflict with arms; war. **2.** Struggle; strife.

war game *pl.* Practice maneuvers imitating the conditions of actual warfare.

war·head (wôr′hed′) *n. Mil.* The section at the nose of a guided missile, bomb, etc., containing the explosive.

war horse 1. *Informal* A veteran; esp., an aggressive or veteran politician. **2.** A horse used in combat; charger.

war·like (wôr′līk) *adj.* **1.** Disposed to engage in war; belligerent. **2.** Relating to, used in, or suggesting war; military. **3.** Threatening war; pugnacious; hostile.

war·lock (wôr′lok′) *n.* A wizard; sorcerer; also, a demon. [OE < *wǣr* covenant + *lēogan* to lie, deny]

warm (wôrm) *adj.* **1.** Moderately hot; having heat somewhat greater than temperate. **2.** Imparting warmth or heat. **3.** Preserving warmth; preventing loss of bodily heat: a *warm* coat. **4.** Having a feeling of heat greater than ordinary: *warm* from exertion. **5.** Affectionate; loving; warmhearted. **6.** Possessing ardor, liveliness, etc.: a *warm* argument. **7.** Excited; agitated; also, vehement; passionate: a *warm* temper. **8.** United by affection. **9.** Having predominating tones of red or yellow. **10.** Recently made; fresh: a *warm* trail. **11.** Near to discovering concealed fact or object. **12.** *Informal* Uncomfortable; dangerous. **13.** Characterized by brisk activity: a *warm* skirmish. — *v.t.* **1.** To heat slightly. **2.** To make ardent or enthusiastic; interest. **3.** To fill with kindly feeling. — *v.i.* **4.** To become warm. **5.** To become ardent or enthusiastic: often with *to.* **6.** To become kindly disposed or friendly: with *to* or *toward.* — **to warm up 1.** To warm. **2.** To exercise just before a game, etc. **3.** To run an engine until it reaches operating temperature. — *n. Informal* Warmth; a heating. [OE *wearm*] — **warm′er** *n.* — **warm′ly** *adv.* — **warm′ness** *n.*

warm-blood·ed (wôrm′blud′id) *adj.* **1.** *Zool.* Preserving a uniform body temperature, as man. **2.** Enthusiastic; ardent; passionate.

warm·heart·ed (wôrm′här′tid) *adj.* Kind; affectionate.

warm·ing pan (wôr′ming) A closed metal pan with a long handle, containing hot coals or water, for warming a bed.

warm·mon·ger (wôr′mung′gər, -mong′-) *n.* One who propagates warlike ideas. — **war′mon′ger·ing** *adj. & n.*

warmth (wôrmth) *n.* **1.** The state, quality, or sensation of being warm. **2.** Ardor or fervidness of disposition or feeling; excitement of temper or mind. **3.** The effect produced by warm colors. [ME < OE *wearm* + *-thu, th* -th¹]

warm-up (wôrm′up′) *n. Informal* The act of one who or that which warms up.

warn (wôrn) *v.t.* **1.** To make aware of possible harm; caution. **2.** To advise; admonish. **3.** To give notice in advance. **4.** To notify (a person) to stay away etc.: with *off, away,* etc. [OE *warnian*] — **warn′er** *n.*

warn·ing (wôr′ning) *n.* **1.** The act of one who warns; also, notice of danger. **2.** That which warns or admonishes. — *adj.* Serving as a warning. — **warn′ing·ly** *adv.*

War of 1812 See table for WAR.

War of American Independence *Brit.* The American Revolution.

War of Independence The American Revolution.

War of Secession The Civil War in the U.S.

War of the Spanish Succession See table for WAR.

warp (wôrp) *v.t.* **1.** To turn or twist out of shape, as by shrinkage or heat. **2.** To turn from a correct course; give a twist or bias to; corrupt. **3.** To stretch (yarn) so as to form a warp. **4.** *Naut.* To move (a vessel) by hauling on a rope fastened to a pier or anchor. — *v.i.* **5.** To become turned or twisted out of shape. **6.** To deviate from a proper course; go astray. **7.** *Naut.* To move by means of ropes fastened to a pier, etc. — *n.* **1.** The state of being warped; a distortion, esp. in wood. **2.** A mental or moral deviation; bias. **3.** The threads that run the long way of a fabric, crossing the woof. **4.** *Naut.* A cable used for warping a ship. [OE *weorpan* to throw] — **warp′er** *n.*

war paint 1. Paint applied to faces and bodies by primitive peoples in token of going to war. **2.** *Informal* Cosmetics; finery; also, official garb or regalia.

war·path (wôr′path′, -päth′) *n.* The route taken by American Indians going to war. — **on the warpath 1.** On a warlike expedition. **2.** Ready for a fight; angry.

war·plane (wôr′plān′) *n.* An airplane equipped for fighting.

war·rant (wôr′ənt, wor′-) *n.* **1.** *Law* A judicial writ or order authorizing arrest, search, seizure, etc. **2.** Something that assures or attests; evidence; guarantee. **3.** That which gives authority for some act; sanction; justification. **4.** A certificate of appointment given to army and navy warrant officers. **5.** A document giving a certain authority; esp., for receipt or payment of money. — *v.t.* **1.** To guarantee the quality, sufficiency, etc., of: to *warrant* a title to property. **2.** To guarantee the character of; pledge oneself for. **3.** To guarantee against injury, loss, etc. **4.** To be sufficient grounds for; justify. **5.** To give legal authority; to empower; authorize. **6.** To say confidently; feel sure. [< AF *warant,* OF *guarant*] — **war′rant·a·ble** *adj.* — **war′rant·a·bly** *adv.* — **war′rant·er** *n.*

war·ran·tee (wôr′ən·tē′, wor′-) *n. Law* The person to whom a warranty is given.

warrant officer *Mil.* An officer serving without a commission, but having authority by virtue of a certificate or warrant, with rank superior to that of a noncommissioned officer. See tables at GRADE.

war·rant·or (wôr′ən·tôr, wor′-) *n. Law* One who makes or gives a warranty to another.

war·ran·ty (wôr′ən·tē, wor′-) *n. pl.* **·ties 1.** *Law* **a** An assurance that facts regarding property, insurance risks, etc., are as they are stated to be. **b** A covenant securing a title of ownership. **2.** A guarantee (def. 1). **3.** Authorization; warrant. [< AF *warantie,* < OF *guarant* warrant]

war·ren (wôr′ən, wor′-) *n.* **1.** A place where rabbits live and breed in communities. **2.** An enclosure for keeping small game. **3.** An obscure, crowded place of habitation. [< AF < *warir* to preserve]

war·ri·or (wôr′ē·ər, -yər, wor′-) *n.* A man engaged in or experienced in warfare. [< AF < OHG *werra* strife]

war·ship (wôr′ship′) *n.* Any vessel used in naval combat.

Wars of the Roses See table for WAR.

wart (wôrt) *n.* **1.** A small, usu. hard and nonmalignant bump formed on and rooted in the skin. **2.** A hard glandular protuberance on a plant. [OE *wearte*] — **wart′y** *adj.*

wart hog An African wild hog having warty excrescences on the face and large tusks in both jaws.

war·time (wôr′tīm′) *n.* A time of war. — *adj.* Caused by or related to a war, or occurring during a period of war.

war whoop A yell, as that made by American Indians, uttered as a signal for attack or to terrify opponents in battle.

war·y (wâr′ē) *adj.* **war·i·er, war·i·est 1.** Carefully watching and guarding. **2.** Shrewd; wily. [< OE *warian*] — **war′i·ly** *adv.* — **war′i·ness** *n.*

was (wuz, woz, *unstressed* wəz) First and third person singular, past indicative of BE. [OE *wæs*]

wash (wosh, wôsh) *v.t.* **1.** To cleanse by immersing in or applying water or other liquid, often with rubbing. **2.** To purify from defilement or guilt. **3.** To wet or cover with liquid. **4.** To flow against or over: a beach *washed* by the ocean. **5.** To remove by the action of water: with *away, off, out,* etc. **6.** To form or wear by erosion: The storm *washed* gullies in the hillside. **7.** To purify, as gas, by passing

through a liquid.   **8.** To coat with a thin layer of color or a thin coat of metal.   **9.** *Mining* To subject (gravel, earth, etc.) to the action of water so as to separate the ore, etc. — *v.i.* **10.** To wash oneself.   **11.** To wash clothes, etc.   **12.** To withstand the effects of washing: That calico will *wash*.   **13.** *Brit. Informal* To undergo testing successfully: That story won't *wash*.   **14.** To flow with a lapping sound, as waves.   **15.** To be removed by the action of water: with *away, off, out*, etc.   **16.** To be eroded by the action of water. — **to wash down   1.** To drink liquid along with or right after (food) to facilitate swallowing.   **2.** To scrub from top to bottom, as walls. — **to wash up   1.** To wash oneself.   **2.** *Brit. Informal* To wash the dishes.   — *n.* **1.** The act or process of washing; cleansing.   **2.** A number of clothes, etc. set apart to be washed at one time; laundry.   **3.** Liquid or semiliquid refuse; swill.   **4.** A preparation used in washing or coating, as: **a** A mouthwash. **b** Water color spread on a picture.   **5.** The breaking of a body of water upon the shore, or the sound made by waves breaking or surging against a surface; swash.   **6.** Erosion of soil by the action of running water.   **7.** Churned air, water, or other fluid resulting from the passage of an object through it.   **8.** An area washed by a sea or river; a marsh; bog. — *adj.* Washable without injury: *wash* fabrics. [OE *wascan, wæscan*]
wash·a·ble (wosh/ə-bəl, wôsh/-) *adj.* That may be washed without fading or injury.
wash-and-wear (wosh/ən·wâr/, wôsh/-) *adj.* Designating or pertaining to a garment or fabric so treated as to require little or no ironing after washing.
wash·board (wosh/bôrd/, -bōrd/, wôsh/-) *n.* A board or frame having a corrugated surface on which to rub clothes while washing them.
wash·bowl (wosh/bōl/, wôsh/-) *n.* A basin or bowl used for washing the hands and face. Also **wash/ba/sin** (-bā/sən).
wash·cloth (wosh/klôth/, -kloth/, wôsh/-) *n.* A small cloth used for washing the body.
wash·day (wosh/dā/, wôsh/-) *n.* A day of the week set aside for doing household washing.
washed-out (wosht/out/, wôsht/-) *adj.* **1.** Faded; colorless; pale.   **2.** *Informal* Exhausted; worn-out; tired.
washed-up (wosht/up/, wôsht/-) *adj.* **1.** *Slang* No longer successful, popular, etc.; finished.   **2.** *Informal* Tired.
wash·er (wosh/ər, wô/shər) *n.* **1.** One who or that which washes.   **2.** *Mech.* A small, flat, perforated disk of metal, leather, rubber, etc., used for placing beneath a nut or at an axle bearing or joint, to serve as a cushion, to prevent leakage, or to relieve friction.   **3.** A washing machine.
wash·er·wom·an (wosh/ər·wŏŏm/ən, wô/shər-) *n. pl.* **·wom·en** (-wim/in) A laundress.
wash·ing (wosh/ing, wô/shing) *n.* **1.** The act of one who or that which washes.   **2.** Things, as clothing, washed or to be washed on one occasion.   **3.** That which is retained after being washed: a *washing* of ore.   **4.** A thin coating of metal.
washing machine A machine for washing laundry.
washing soda Sodium carbonate in crystalline form, used for washing textiles and as a bleaching agent.
wash·out (wosh/out/, wôsh/-) *n.* **1.** A considerable erosion of earth by the action of water; also, the excavation thus made; a gully or gulch.   **2.** *Slang* A failure.   **3.** The act of one who or that which washes out.
wash·rag (wosh/rag/, wôsh/-) *n.* A washcloth.
wash·room (wosh/rŏŏm/, -rŏŏm/, wôsh/-) *n.* A lavatory.
wash·stand (wosh/stand/, wôsh/-) *n.* A stand for washbowl, pitcher, etc.
wash·tub (wosh/tub/, wôsh/-) *n.* A tub used for washing.
wash·wom·an (wosh/wŏŏm/ən, wôsh/-) *n. pl.* **·wom·en** (-wim/in) A washerwoman.
wash·y (wosh/ē, wô/shē) *adj.* **wash·i·er, wash·i·est   1.** Overly diluted; weak.   **2.** Faded; wan. — **wash/i·ness** *n.*
was·n't (wuz/ənt, woz/-) Was not.
wasp (wosp, wôsp) *n.* Any of numerous stinging insects, including social wasps, that make nests of vegetable matter, and solitary wasps, living in mud or sand nests.   [OE *wæsp*]
WASP (wosp, wôsp) *n. Slang* A white Protestant American: sometimes used contemptuously. Also **Wasp.** [Acronym formed from the initial letters of "white Anglo-Saxon Protestant"]
wasp·ish (wos/pish, wôs/-) *adj.* **1.** Having a nature like a wasp; irritable; irascible.   **2.** Having a wasplike form or slender waist. — **wasp/ish·ly** *adv.* — **wasp/ish·ness** *n.*
wasp waist A waist so slender as to suggest that of a wasp. — **wasp-waist·ed** (wosp/wās/tid, wôsp/-) *adj.*
wasp·y (wos/pē, wôs/-) *adj.* **wasp·i·er, wasp·i·est** Like a wasp; waspish.
was·sail (wos/əl, was/-, wo·sāl/) *n.* **1.** An ancient salutation or toast to someone's health.   **2.** The liquor, as spiced ale, prepared for a wassail.   **3.** A festivity at which healths are drunk; a carousal. — *v.i.* **1.** To take part in a wassail; carouse. — *v.t.* **2.** To drink the health of; toast.   [ME < ON *ves heill* be in good health] — **was/sail·er** *n.*
Was·ser·mann test (wos/ər·mən) A diagnostic test for syphi-

lis, based on the reaction of the blood serum of an infected individual. Also **Wassermann reaction.**   [after August von *Wassermann*, 1866–1925, German bacteriologist.]
wast (wost, *unstressed* wəst)   Archaic second person singular, past indicative of BE: used with *thou.*
wast·age (wās/tij) *n.* That which is lost by wear, waste, etc.
waste (wāst) *v.* **wast·ed, wast·ing** *v.t.* **1.** To use or expend thoughtlessly, uselessly, or without return; squander.   **2.** To cause to lose strength, vigor, or bulk.   **3.** To use up; consume.   **4.** To fail to use or take advantage of, as an opportunity.   **5.** To lay waste; devastate.   — *v.i.* **6.** To lose strength, vigor, or bulk: often with *away*.   **7.** To diminish or dwindle gradually.   **8.** To pass gradually: said of time. — *n.* **1.** The act of wasting or the state of being wasted; useless or unnecessary expenditure, consumption, etc.   **2.** Misuse, neglect, or failure to take advantage of opportunity etc.   **3.** A place or region that is devastated or made desolate; desert.   **4.** A continuous, gradual diminishing of strength, vigor, or substance by use or wear.   **5.** The act of laying waste or devastating.   **6.** Something rejected as worthless or unneeded; esp., tangled spun cotton thread.   **7.** Garbage; rubbish; trash. — **to lay waste** To turn into ruins; destroy utterly; devastate. — *adj.* **1.** Cast aside as worthless; worn out; discarded.   **2.** Excreted, as undigested material, etc.   **3.** Not under cultivation; unproductive; unoccupied.   **4.** Made desolate; ruined.   **5.** Containing or conveying waste products.   **6.** Superfluous: *waste* energy.   [< AF, ult. < L *vastare* to lay waste < *vastus* desert, desolate]
Waste, meaning containing or conveying refuse or waste, may appear as a combining form or as the first element in two-word phrases, as in:

waste bin	**waste heap**	**waste pipe**

waste·bas·ket (wāst/bas/kit, -bäs/-) *n.* An open container for paper scraps and other waste. Also **wastepaper basket.**
waste·ful (wāst/fəl) *adj.* **1.** Prone to waste; extravagant.   **2.** Causing waste. — **waste/ful·ly** *adv.* — **waste/ful·ness** *n.*
waste·land (wāst/land/) *n.* A barren or desolate land.
waste·pa·per (wāst/pā/pər) *n.* Paper thrown away as worthless. Also **waste paper.**
wast·er (wās/tər) *n.* One who wastes; a wastrel.
wast·ing (wās/ting) *adj.* **1.** Producing emaciation; enfeebling: a *wasting* fever.   **2.** Laying waste; devastating.
wast·rel (wās/trəl) *n.* **1.** A waster; spendthrift.   **2.** An idler; loafer; vagabond.   [Dim. of WASTER]
watch (woch) *v.i.* **1.** To look attentively.   **2.** To wait expectantly: with *for*.   **3.** To be constantly on the alert.   **4.** To do duty as a guard or sentinel.   **5.** To be an onlooker.   **6.** To go without sleep; keep vigil. — *v.t.* **7.** To look at steadily and attentively; observe.   **8.** To keep informed concerning.   **9.** To be alert for: to *watch* one's opportunity.   **10.** To keep watch over; guard; tend. — **to watch out** To be on one's guard. — *n.* **1.** The act of watching; close and continuous attention; careful observation.   **2.** A small, portable timepiece worn or carried on the person, and usu. actuated by a coiled spring.   **3.** Position or service as a guard.   **4.** One or more persons set to watch.   **5.** An act or period of wakefulness or attentive alertness, esp. during the night; vigil.   **6.** The period of time during which a guard is on duty.   **7.** *Naut.* **a** One of the two divisions of a ship's officers and crew, performing duty in alternation. **b** The period of time during which each division is on duty: usu. four hours.   [OE *wæccan*] — **watch/er** *n.*
watch band A band to fasten a watch on the wrist.
watch·case (woch/kās/) *n.* The protecting case of a watch.
watch·dog (woch/dôg/, -dog/) *n.* **1.** A dog kept to guard property.   **2.** One who acts as a vigilant guardian.
watch·ful (woch/fəl) *adj.* Vigilant. — **watch/ful·ly** *adv.* — **watch/ful·ness** *n.*
watch·mak·er (woch/mā/kər) *n.* One who makes or repairs watches. — **watch/mak/ing** *n.*
watch·man (woch/mən) *n. pl.* **·men** (-mən) Anyone who keeps watch or guard, as over a building at night.
watch night A religious service usu. held on New Year's Eve. Also **watch meeting.**
watch·tow·er (woch/tou/ər) *n.* A tower upon which a sentinel is stationed.
watch·word (woch/wûrd/) *n.* **1.** A password.   **2.** A rallying cry or maxim.
wa·ter (wô/tər, wot/ər) *n.* **1.** A limpid, tasteless, odorless liquid compound of hydrogen and oxygen, H_2O, in the proportion by weight of approximately 2 parts of hydrogen to 16 of oxygen. When pure, water has its maximum density at 4° C. or 39° F.; at normal atmospheric pressure it freezes at 0° C. or 32° F., and boils at 100° C. or 212° F.   **2.** Any body of water, as a lake, river, or a sea.   **3.** Any one of the aqueous or liquid secretions of the body, as perspiration, tears, urine, etc.   **4.** Any preparation of water holding a gaseous or volatile substance in solution.   **5.** The transparency or luster of a precious stone or a pearl.   **6.** Excellence; quality: first *water*.   **7.** An undulating sheen given to certain fabrics, as silk, etc.   **8.** In commerce and finance,

stock issued without increase of paid-in capital to represent it. **— above water** Out of danger; secure. **— like water** Very freely or quickly: to spend money *like water.* **— of the first water** Of the highest degree. **— to hold water** To be valid or effective: His argument doesn't *hold water.* **— to make water** To urinate. *— v.t.* **1.** To pour water upon; moisten; sprinkle. **2.** To provide with water for drinking. **3.** To dilute with water: often with *down.* **4.** To give an undulating sheen to the surface of (silk, etc.). **5.** To enlarge the number of shares of (a stock company) without increasing the paid-in capital in proportion. **6.** To provide with streams or sources of water; irrigate. *— v.i.* **7.** To secrete or discharge water, tears, etc. **8.** To fill with saliva, as the mouth, from desire for food. **9.** To drink water. **10.** To take in water, as a locomotive. [OE *wæter*] **— wa′ter·er** *n.*

Water may appear as a combining form, or as the first element in two-word phrases, as in:

water meter	water right
water motor	water supply
water-repellant	water system

Water Bearer The constellation and sign of the zodiac Aquarius.

wa·ter·borne (wô′tər·bôrn′, -bōrn′, wot′ər-) *adj.* **1.** Floating on water. **2.** Transported or carried by water.

wa·ter·buck (wô′tər·buk′, wot′ər-) *n.* Either of two large African antelopes frequenting the neighborhood of rivers and swimming with ease. [< Afrikaans *waterbok*]

water buffalo A large buffalo of Asia, India, and the Philippines, having a very wide spread of horns, and often domesticated for use as a draft animal: also called *water ox, carabao.*

water chestnut **1.** The edible fruit of an aquatic plant contained in a hard, nutlike husk. **2.** The plant itself.

WATER BUFFALO
(To 6 feet high at shoulder)

water clock An instrument for measuring time by the regulated flow of water.

water closet A toilet.

water color **1.** A color prepared for painting with water as the medium, as distinguished from one to be used with oil, tempera, etc. **2.** A picture or painting done in water colors. **— wa·ter·col·or** (wô′tər·kul′ər, wot′ər-) *adj.*

wa·ter·cool (wô′tər·kōōl′, wot′ər-) *v.t.* To cool by means of water, as by using a water jacket on an internal-combustion engine. **— wa′ter·cooled′** *adj.* **— wa′ter·cool′ing** *adj.*

water cooler A vessel or apparatus for cooling and dispensing drinking water.

wa·ter·course (wô′tər·kôrs′, -kōrs′, wot′ər-) *n.* **1.** A stream of water; river; brook. **2.** The course or channel of a stream or canal.

wa·ter·craft (wô′tər·kraft′, -kräft′, wot′ər-) *n.* **1.** Skill in sailing boats or in aquatic sports. **2.** Any boat or ship; also, sailing vessels collectively.

wa·ter·cress (wô′tər·kres′, wot′ər-) *n.* A perennial herb of the mustard family, growing in springs and clear, cool streams and having edible, pungent leaves used as salad.

water cure *Med.* Hydropathy.

wa·ter·fall (wô′tər·fôl′, wot′ər-) *n.* A steep fall of water, as of a stream over a dam or from a precipice; cascade.

wa·ter·fowl (wô′tər·foul′, wot′ər-) *n.* *pl.* **·fowl** or **·fowls** **1.** A bird that lives on or about the water; esp., a swimming game bird. **2.** Such birds collectively.

wa·ter·front (wô′tər·frunt′, wot′ər-) *n.* **1.** Real property abutting on or overlooking a natural body of water. **2.** That part of a town fronting on a body of water, esp. the area containing wharves, docks, etc.

water gap A deep ravine in a mountain ridge, giving passage to a stream.

water gas A poisonous mixture, chiefly of hydrogen and carbon monoxide, produced by forcing steam over white-hot carbon, as coal or coke, and used for cooking, heating, and as an illuminant. **— wa·ter·gas** (wô′tər·gas′, wot′ər-) *adj.*

water gate A floodgate (def. 1)

water gauge A gauge indicating the level of water, as in a boiler. Also **water gage.**

water glass **1.** A drinking glass. **2.** Any glass vessel for holding water. **3.** Sodium silicate, a soluble silicate preparation; esp., an aqueous solution used in preserving eggs, etc. **4.** A water gauge on a steam boiler, etc.

water hole A small pond, pool, or depression containing water; esp., one used by animals as a drinking place.

water ice A frozen dessert made with water, sugar, and fruit juice.

wa·ter·ing (wô′tər·ing, wot′ər-) *n.* **1.** The act of one who or that which waters. **2.** The process of producing a wavy, ornamental effect on fabric, etc. *— adj.* **1.** That waters. **2.** Situated near the shore or near mineral springs.

watering can A container used for watering plants, etc., esp. one having a long spout. Also **watering pot.**

watering place **1.** A place where water can be obtained, as a spring. **2.** A health resort having mineral springs; also, a pleasure resort near the water.

water jacket A casing containing water and surrounding a cylinder or mechanism, esp. the cylinder block of an internal-combustion engine, for keeping it cool.

water jump A water barrier, as a pool, stream, or ditch, to be jumped over by the horses in a steeplechase.

water level **1.** The level of still water in the sea or in any other body of water. **2.** *Geol.* A water table. **3.** *Naut.* A ship's water line.

water lily **1.** Any of a genus of aquatic plants having showy flowers with numerous white or pinkish petals: also called *pond lily.* **2.** Any of various related plants.

water line **1.** *Naut.* The part of the hull of a ship that corresponds with the water level at various loads: also called *water level.* **2.** A line or demarcation corresponding to the height to which water has risen or may rise.

wa·ter·logged (wô′tər·lôgd′, -logd′, wot′ər-) *adj.* **1.** Heavy and unmanageable on account of the leakage of water into the hold, as a ship. **2.** Water-soaked; saturated with water.

Wa·ter·loo (wô′tər·lōō) *n.* A final and decisive defeat: usu. in the phrase **to meet one's Waterloo.** [after Napoleon's defeat at *Waterloo,* Belgium]

water main A large conduit for carrying water.

wa·ter·man (wô′tər·mən, wot′ər-) *n.* *pl.* **·men** (-mən) A man who works with a boat or small vessel on the water; a boatman. **— wa′ter·man·ship′** *n.*

wa·ter·mark (wô′tər·märk′, wot′ər-) *n.* **1.** A mark showing the extent to which water rises. **2.** In papermaking: **a** A marking in paper, usu. produced by pressure of a projecting design on a processing roll or in the mold. **b** The metal pattern that produces this marking. *— v.t.* **1.** To impress (paper) with a watermark. **2.** To impress as a watermark.

wa·ter·mel·on (wô′tər·mel′ən, wot′ər-) *n.* **1.** The large, edible fruit of a trailing plant of the gourd family, containing a many-seeded red or pink pulp and a watery juice. **2.** The plant on which this fruit grows.

water mill A mill operated by waterpower.

water moccasin A venomous pit viper of the southern U.S.: also called *cottonmouth.*

water nymph In classical mythology, any nymph or goddess living in or guarding a body of water.

water of crystallization *Chem.* Molecules of water forming part of certain crystallized salts. They may be eliminated by heat, often with apparent loss of crystalline structure.

water ouzel Any of various small birds adapted to feeding under water. Also **water ousel.**

water ox A water buffalo.

water pipe **1.** A hookah. **2.** A conduit for water.

water polo A game in which two teams of swimmers push or throw a buoyant ball toward opposite goals.

wa·ter·pow·er (wô′tər·pou′ər, wot′ər-) *n.* **1.** The power of water derived from its momentum, as applied to the driving of machinery. **2.** A fall in a stream, yielding kinetic energy from which motive power may be obtained.

wa·ter·proof (wô′tər·prōōf′, wot′ər-) *adj.* **1.** Permitting no water to enter or pass through; impervious to water. **2.** Coated with some substance, as rubber, that resists the passage of water. *— n.* **1.** Material or fabric rendered impervious to water. **2.** *Brit.* A raincoat or other garment made of such fabric. *— v.t.* To render waterproof.

water rat **1.** The muskrat. **2.** The European vole. **3.** Any aquatic rodent. **4.** *Slang* A waterfront thief or tough.

wa·ter·shed (wô′tər·shed′, wot′ər-) *n.* **1.** The line of separation between two contiguous drainage valleys. **2.** The region from which a river receives its supply of water.

wa·ter·side (wô′tər·sīd′, wot′ər-) *n.* The shore of a body of water; the water's edge. *— adj.* Of, pertaining to, or living, growing, or working by the water's edge.

wa·ter·ski (wô′tər·skē′, wot′ər-) *v.i.* **-skied, -ski·ing** To glide over water on water-skis, while being towed by a motorboat. *— n.* *pl.* **-skis** or **-ski** A broad, skilike runner with a fitting to hold the foot, worn when water-skiing: also **water ski.** **— wa′ter·ski′er** *n.* **— wa′ter·ski′ing** *n.*

water snake Any of various harmless snakes that live chiefly in or near fresh water.

wa·ter·soak (wô′tər·sōk′, wot′ər-) *v.t.* To fill the pores or crevices of with water; soak in water.

water softener A substance added to hard water to counteract the effect of its mineral content.

wa·ter·sol·u·ble (wô′tər·sol′yə·bəl, wot′ər-) *adj.* Soluble in water: said esp. of certain organic compounds.

water spaniel A large, reddish brown spaniel having a curly, waterproof coat, used primarily for retrieving ducks.

wa·ter·spout (wô′tər·spout′, wot′ər-) *n.* **1.** A moving, whirling column of spray and mist, with masses of water in the lower parts, generated at sea or on other large bodies of water. **2.** A pipe for the free discharge of water.

water sprite A sprite living in the water; water nymph.

water table *Geol.* The surface marking the upper level of a water-saturated zone extending beneath the ground to depths determined by the thickness of the permeable strata.

wa·ter·tight (wô′tər·tīt′) *adj.* **1.** So closely made that water cannot enter or leak through. **2.** Having no loopholes; foolproof: *watertight* tax laws.

water tower **1.** A standpipe or tower, often of considerable height, used as a reservoir for a system of water distribution. **2.** A vehicular towerlike structure having an extensible vertical pipe from which water can be thrown on the upper floors of a burning building.

water vapor The vapor of water, esp. when below the boiling point, as in the atmosphere.

water wave An undulating effect of the hair, artificially produced when the hair is wet, and set by drying with heat.

wa·ter·way (wô′tər·wā′, wot′ər-) *n.* A river, channel, canal, etc., used as a means of travel.

water wheel A wheel so equipped with floats, buckets, etc., that it may be turned by flowing water, as a noria.

water wings A waterproof, inflatable device used as a support for the body while swimming or learning to swim.

wa·ter·works (wô′tər·wûrks′, wot′ər-) *n.pl.* A system of machines, buildings, and appliances for furnishing a water supply, esp. for a city.

wa·ter·worn (wô′tər·wôrn′, -wōrn′, wot′ər-) *adj.* Worn smooth by running or falling water.

wa·ter·y (wô′tər·ē, wot′ər·ē) *adj.* **1.** Containing or discharging water. **2.** Brimming; flowing. **3.** Resembling water; thin or liquid. **4.** Consisting of or pertaining to water. **5.** Diluted with water; weak. **— wa′ter·i·ness** *n.*

watt (wot) *n.* The practical unit of electric power, activity, or rate of work, equivalent to one joule per second, or one volt-ampere. [after James *Watt* 1736–1819, Scottish inventor]

wat·tage (wot′ij) *n.* **1.** Amount of electric power in terms of watts. **2.** The total number of watts needed to operate an appliance.

watt-hour (wot′our′) *n.* Electrical energy equivalent to one watt acting for one hour.

wat·tle (wot′l) *n.* **1.** A structure of rods or twigs woven together. **2.** A twig or withe. **3.** A naked, fleshy process, often wrinkled and brightly colored, hanging from the throat of a bird or snake. **4.** Any of various acacias of Australia, Tasmania, and South Africa. **— v.t. ·tled, ·tling 1.** To weave or twist, as twigs, into a network. **2.** To form, as baskets, by intertwining flexible twigs. **3.** To bind together with wattles. **— adj.** Made of or covered with wattles. [OE *watel, watul*] **— wat′tled** *adj.*

watt·me·ter (wot′mē′tər) *n.* An instrument for measuring electrical power in watts.

wave (wāv) *v.* **waved, wav·ing** *v.i.* **1.** To move freely back and forth or up and down, as a flag in the wind; fluctuate. **2.** To be moved back and forth or up and down as a signal; also, to make a signal by moving something thus. **3.** To have an undulating shape or form: Her hair *waves*. *— v.t.* **4.** To cause to wave: to *wave* a banner. **5.** To form with an undulating surface or outline. **6.** To give a wavy appearance to; water, as silk. **7.** To form into waves: to *wave* one's hair. **8.** To signal by waving something: He *waved* me aside. **9.** To express by waving something: to *wave* farewell. *— n.* **1.** A ridge or undulation moving on the surface of a liquid. **2.** One of the rising curves on an undulatory surface; one of a series of curves: *waves* of grain. **3.** Something that comes, like a wave, with great volume or power: a *wave* of enthusiasm. **4.** One of a series, as of events, occurring with wavelike fluctuations: He went ashore with the first *wave* of Marines. **5.** A progressive change in temperature or in barometrical condition: a heat *wave.* **6.** A wavelike tress or curl of hair. **7.** The act of waving; a sweeping or undulating motion, as with the hand. **8.** A wavelike stripe or undulation impressed on a surface. **9.** *Physics* One of the periodic vibratory impulses produced by a disturbance in and propagated through an elastic medium, as sound. **10.** *Usu. pl. Poetic* Any body of water, esp., the sea. [OE *wafian*] **— wav′er** *n.* **— wave′less** *adj.*

— Syn. (noun) **1.** *Wave* is the general term for an upheaval of the ocean's surface. A *ripple* is a very small *wave*, such as might be produced by a light breeze, or by an object dropping into still water. *Billow* is a poetic word for any *wave*, but esp., for a *wave* of great height. A *roller* is one of the long, irregular *waves* that move swiftly outward from a storm center.

Wave (wāv) *n.* A member of the WAVES.

wave band *Physics* A specified group of wave frequencies, oop. one assigned for radio or television broadcasting.

wave·length (wāv′length′) *n. Physics* The distance, measured along the line of propagation, between two points representing similar phases of two consecutive waves.

wave·let (wāv′lit) *n.* A little wave.

wave mechanics The branch of physics that investigates the wave characteristics ascribed to the atom and its associated particles, esp. with reference to the quantum theory.

wa·ver (wā′vər) *v.i.* **1.** To move one way and the other; sway; flutter. **2.** To be uncertain or undecided; show irresolution; vacillate. **3.** To show signs of falling back or giving way; falter. **4.** To flicker; gleam. **5.** To quaver; tremble. *— n.* A wavering. [< ME *waveren*] **— wa′ver·er** *n.* **— wa′ver·ing·ly** *adv.*

WAVES or **W.A.V.E.S.** (wāvz) *n.* A corps of women in the U.S. Navy; officially, Women in the United States Navy (1946). [< *W(omen) A(ccepted for) V(oluntary) E(mergency) S(ervice)*, an earlier name]

wave set A preparation put on the hair before setting to make waves and curls last.

wav·y (wā′vē) *adj.* **wav·i·er, wav·i·est 1.** Full of waves; ruffled or raised into waves. **2.** Undulatory; waving. **3.** Unstable; wavering. **— wav′i·ly** *adv.* **— wav′i·ness** *n.*

wax¹ (waks) *n. pl.* **wax·es 1.** Beeswax. **2.** *Chem.* Any of various natural substances consisting of the esters of fatty acids and alcohols other than glycerol, including spermaceti and the secretions of certain plants and insects. **3.** A solid mineral substance resembling wax, as paraffin. **4.** Sealing wax. **5.** Earwax. **— v.t.** To coat or treat with wax. **— adj.** Made of or pertaining to wax. [OE *weax*]

wax² (waks) *v.i.* **waxed, waxed** (*Poetic* **wax·en**), **wax·ing 1.** To become larger gradually; increase in size or numbers; grow: said esp., of the moon as it approaches fullness. **2.** To become: to *wax* angry. [OE *weaxan* to grow]

wax bean A variety of string bean of a pale yellow color, cultivated in the U.S.: also called *butter bean.*

wax·ber·ry (waks′ber′ē) *n. pl.* **·ries 1.** The wax myrtle. **2.** Its wax-covered fruit. **3.** The snowberry.

wax·en (wak′sən) *adj.* **1.** Resembling wax. **2.** Consisting wholly or in part of wax; covered with wax. **3.** Pale; pallid: a *waxen* complexion; also, pliable or impressible as wax.

wax myrtle Any of various North American shrubs or small trees having fragrant leaves and small berries covered with wax, often used in making candles: also called *bayberry, candleberry, waxberry.*

wax palm **1.** A South American palm with pinnate leaves, having a lofty straight trunk covered with a waxy, whitish, resinous substance. **2.** A Brazilian palm whose young leaves yield a valuable wax.

wax paper Paper coated or treated with wax and used to retain or protect against moisture. Also **waxed paper.**

wax·weed (waks′wēd′) *n.* An annual, clammy, hairy herb of the loosestrife family with irregular purplish flowers.

wax·wing (waks′wing′) *n.* Any of various crested birds having soft, mainly brown plumage and wing feathers tipped with appendages resembling red or yellow sealing wax.

wax·work (waks′wûrk′) *n.* **1.** Work produced in wax; esp., ornaments or life-size figures of wax. **2.** *pl.* An exhibition of such figures. **— wax′work′er** *n.*

wax·y (wak′sē) *adj.* **wax·i·er, wax·i·est 1.** Like wax in appearance, consistency, color, etc.; pliable; impressionable; pallid. **2.** Made of or abounding in wax; rubbed with wax. **— wax′i·ness** *n.*

way (wā) *n.* **1.** A manner or method of doing something; procedure. **2.** Direction; turn; route; line of motion: Which *way* is the city? **3.** A path, or track leading from one place to another or along which one goes. **4.** Space or room to advance or work: Make *way* for the king. **5.** Length of space passed over. **6.** Distance in general: a little *way* off: often popularly, **ways. 7.** Passage from one place to another. **8.** Headway; progress. **9.** A customary style; a manner peculiar to certain people: the British *way* of doing things. **10.** A point of relation; particular: He erred in two *ways.* **11.** A course of life or experience: the *way* of sin. **12.** *Informal* State of health: to be in a bad *way.* **13.** A course wished for or resolved upon: Have it your *way.* **14.** The range of one's observation: An accident threw it in his *way.* **15.** *Naut. pl.* A tilted framework of timbers upon which a ship slides when launched. **16.** *Law* A right of way. **17.** *Informal* Neighborhood, or route home: He lives out of my *way.* **— by the way** In passing; incidentally. **— by way of 1.** With the purpose of; to serve as: *by way of* introduction. **2.** Through; via. **— out of the way 1.** Removed, as an obstruction. **2.** Remarkable; unusual. **3.** Improper; wrong. **4.** Out of place; lost; remote. **— the way** *Informal* In the manner that; as: Do it *the way* I told you to. **— under way** In motion; making progress. **— adv.** *Informal* Away; very much or very far. [OE *weg*]

way back *Informal* Long ago. [Short for AWAY BACK]

way·bill (wā′bil′) *n.* A list describing or identifying goods or naming passengers carried by a train, steamer, etc.

way·far·er (wā′fâr′ər) *n.* One who journeys.

way·far·ing (wā′fâr′ing) *adj. & n.* Journeying; being on the road.

way·lay (wā·lā′, wā′lā′) *v.t.* **·laid, ·lay·ing 1.** To lie in ambush for and attack, as in order to rob. **2.** To accost on the way. [< WAY + LAY¹] — **way'lay'er** n.

-ways suffix of adverbs In a (specified) manner, direction, or position: noways, sideways: often equivalent to -wise. Also **-way.** [< WAY + -s³]

ways and means Means or methods of accomplishing an end or defraying expenses: esp., in legislation, methods of raising funds for the use of the government.

way·side (wā'sīd') adj. Standing or being near the side of a road. — n. The side or edge of the road or highway.

way station Any station between principal stations, esp. on a railroad; a local station.

way train A train stopping at way stations.

way·ward (wā'wərd) adj. **1.** Wanting its way; willful. **2.** Without definite course; unsteady; capricious. **3.** Unexpected or unwished for. [ME < awei away + -WARD] — **way'ward·ly** adv. — **way'ward·ness** n.

way·worn (wā'wôrn', -wōrn') adj. Fatigued by travel.

we (wē) pron. pl., possessive **our** or **ours**, objective **us** The nominative plural pronoun of the first person, used by the persons speaking or writing to denote themselves, by an individual to refer to himself or herself and one or more others, by an editor or other writer to give his words an impersonal character, or by a sovereign on formal occasions. [OE wē]

weak (wēk) adj. **1.** Lacking in physical strength; wanting in energy or activity; feeble. **2.** Insufficiently resisting stress: a weak link or bridge. **3.** Lacking in strength of will or stability of character; pliable. **4.** Ineffectual, as from deficient supply: weak artillery support. **5.** Lacking in power or sonorousness: a weak voice. **6.** Lacking a specified component or components in the proper amount; of less than customary potency: weak tea. **7.** Lacking the ability to function properly: a weak heart. **8.** Lacking in mental or moral strength. **9.** Showing or resulting from poor judgment: a weak plan; unable to convince: a weak argument. **10.** Lacking in influence or authority. **11.** Deficient in strength, skill, experience, or the like. **12.** Gram. In Germanic languages, denoting a weak verb. **13.** Phonet. Unstressed; unaccented, as a syllable or sound. **14.** In prosody, indicating a verse ending in which the accent falls on a word or syllable otherwise without stress. **15.** Wanting in impressiveness or interest: a weak play. [< ON veikr] — **weak'ly** adv. — **weak'ness** n.

Weak may appear as a combining form, as in the following self-explanatory compounds:

weak-backed	weak-looking	weak-stemmed
weak-bodied	weak made	weak-tasting
weakbrained	weak-muscled	weak-throated
weak-brewed	weak-natured	weak-tinted
weak-built	weak-nerved	weak-toned
weak-colored	weak-seeming	weak-voiced
weak-eyed	weak-sided	weak-walled
weak-growing	weak-sighted	weak-willed
weakhanded	weak-smelling	weak-winged
weakhearted	weak-sounding	weak-witted
weak-limbed	weak-spirited	weak-woven

weak·en (wē'kən) v.i. v.t. & To make or become weak or weaker. — **weak'en·er** n.

weak·fish (wēk'fish') n. pl. **·fish** or **·fish·es** Any of several marine food fishes of the coastal waters of the eastern U.S.

weak-kneed (wēk'nēd') adj. **1.** Weak in the knees. **2.** Without resolution, strong purpose, or energy; spineless.

weak·ling (wēk'ling) n. A feeble person or animal. — adj. Having no natural strength or vigor.

weak·ly (wēk'lē) adj. **·li·er, ·li·est** Sickly; feeble; weak.

weak-mind·ed (wēk'mīn'did) adj. **1.** Indecisive; weak-willed. **2.** Feeble-minded. — **weak'mind'ed·ness** n.

weak·ness (wēk'nis) n. **1.** The state, condition, or quality of being weak. **2.** A characteristic indicating feebleness. **3.** A slight failing; a fault. **4.** A penchant or fondness: with for: a weakness for pastry.

weal¹ (wēl) n. Archaic A sound or healthy state; prosperity; welfare. [OE wela]

weal² (wēl) n. A welt (def. 3). [Var. of WALE]

weald (wēld) n. Chiefly Brit. An exposed forest area; waste woodland; also, an open region; down. [OE, a forest]

wealth (welth) n. **1.** A large aggregate of real and personal property; riches; also, the state of being rich. **2.** Econ. All material objects having economic utility; also, in the private sense, all property possessing a monetary value. **3.** Great abundance of anything: usu. preceded by a: a wealth of learning. [ME < wele weal]

— **Syn. 1.** affluence, opulence. Compare PROPERTY.

wealth·y (wel'thē) adj. **wealth·i·er, wealth·i·est 1.** Possessing wealth; affluent. **2.** More than sufficient; abounding. — **wealth'i·ly** adv. — **wealth'i·ness** n.

wean (wēn) v.t. **1.** To transfer (the young of any mammal) from dependence on its mother's milk to another form of nourishment. **2.** To estrange from former habits or associations: usu. with from. [OE wenian to accustom]

wean·ling (wēn'ling) adj. Freshly weaned. — n. A child or animal newly weaned.

weap·on (wep'ən) n. **1.** Any implement for fighting or warfare. **2.** Any means that may be used against an adversary: verbal weapons. **3.** The sting, claw, spur, etc., of an animal. — v.t. To furnish with a weapon or weapons. [OE wǣpen] — **weap'on·less** adj.

weap·on·ry (wep'ən-rē') n. Weapons collectively.

wear¹ (wâr) v. wore, worn, wear·ing v.t. **1.** To carry or have on the person as a garment, ornament, etc. **2.** To bear on the person habitually: He wears a derby. **3.** To have in one's appearance; exhibit: He wears a scowl. **4.** To bear habitually in a specified manner; carry: She wears her hair long. **5.** To display or fly: A ship wears its colors. **6.** To impair, waste, or consume by use or constant action. **7.** To cause by rubbing, etc.: to wear a hole in a coat. **8.** To bring to a specified condition by wear: to wear a sleeve to tatters. **9.** To exhaust; weary. — v.i. **10.** To be impaired gradually by use, rubbing, etc. **11.** To withstand the effects of use, wear, etc.: The skirt wears well. **12.** To become as specified from use or attrition: His patience is wearing thin. **13.** To pass gradually or tediously: with on or away. — **to wear out 1.** To make or become worthless by use. **2.** To waste gradually; use up: He wears out patience. **3.** To tire. — n. **1.** The act of wearing, or the state of being worn. **2.** The material or clothes to be worn: silk for summer wear: also in compounds: footwear. **3.** The destructive effect of use, work, or time. **4.** Capacity for resistance to use or impairment; durability. [OE werian] — **wear'a·bil'i·ty** n. — **wear'a·ble** adj. — **wear'er** n.

wear² (wâr) v. wore, worn, wear·ing Naut. v.t. **1.** To turn (a vessel) through an arc in which its head points momentarily directly to leeward. — v.i. **2.** To go about with the wind astern. [Prob. alter. of VEER¹]

wear and tear Loss by the service, exposure, decay, or injury incident to ordinary use.

wear·ing (wâr'ing) adj. **1.** Fatiguing; exhausting; wasting: a wearing job. **2.** Capable of being, or designed to be, worn. — **wear'ing·ly** adv.

wearing apparel Clothing; garments.

wea·ri·some (wir'i·səm) adj. Causing fatigue; tiresome or tedious. — **wea'ri·some·ly** adv. — **wea'ri·some·ness** n.

wea·ry (wir'ē) adj. **·ri·er, ·ri·est 1.** Tired; fatigued. **2.** Discontented or vexed by continued endurance, as of something disagreeable, tedious, etc.: often with of: weary of life. **3.** Indicating or characteristic of fatigue, boredom, etc. **4.** Wearisome. — v.t. & v.i. **·ried, ·ry·ing** To make or become weary; tire. [OE wērig] — **wea'ri·ness** adj. — **wea'ri·ly** adv. — **wea'ri·ness** n.

wea·sel (wē'zəl) n. **1.** Any of certain small, slender, predacious carnivores having brownish fur that in northern regions turns white in winter. **2.** A sneaky, treacherous person. — v.i. **·seled, ·sel·ing** U.S. Informal To speak or act evasively, etc. [OE wesle]

weasel word A word that weakens a statement by rendering it ambiguous or equivocal.

weath·er (weth'ər) n. **1.** Atmospheric condition as regards temperature, moisture, winds, or other meteorological phenomena. **2.** Bad weather; storm. — **to keep one's weather eye open** Informal To be alert. — **under the weather** Informal **1.** Ailing; ill. **2.** Somewhat intoxicated. — v.t. **1.** To expose to the action of the weather. **2.** To discolor, crumble, or otherwise affect by action of the weather. **3.** To pass through and survive, as a crisis. **4.** Naut. To pass to windward of: to weather Cape Horn. — v.i. **5.** Naut. To undergo changes resulting from exposure to the weather. **6.** To resist the action of the weather. — adj. Chiefly Naut. Facing the wind. [OE weder] — **weath'ered** adj.

Weather may appear as a combining form or as the first element in two-word phrases, as in **weather report, weather-marked, weathertight.**

weath·er·beat·en (weth'ər·bēt'n) adj. **1.** Bearing or showing the effects of exposure to weather. **2.** Toughened or tanned by or as by exposure to weather, as a face.

weath·er·board (weth'ər·bôrd', bōrd') n. A clapboard. — v.t. To fasten weatherboards on.

weath·er·bound (weth'ər·bound') adj. Detained by unfavorable weather, as a vessel in port.

Weather Bureau A bureau of the Department of Commerce in Washington, D.C., serving as headquarters for meteorological observation, the diffusion of information concerning the weather, etc.

weath·er·cock (weth'ər·kok') n. **1.** A weather vane in the form of a cock. **2.** A fickle person or variable thing.

WEASEL
(To 9 inches long; tail 2 inches)

weath·er·glass (weth'ər-glas', -gläs') *n.* An instrument for indicating the state of the weather; esp., a simple barometer showing falls in atmospheric pressure.

weath·er·man (weth'ər-man') *n. pl.* **·men** (-men') *n. Informal* A meteorologist, esp. one concerned with daily weather conditions and reports.

weather map A map or chart indicating weather conditions, as temperature, atmospheric pressure, wind velocity, precipitation, etc., for a given region and time.

weath·er·proof (weth'ər-proof') *adj.* Capable of withstanding rough weather without appreciable deterioration. — *v.t.* To make weatherproof.

weather station A station or office where meteorological observations are taken and recorded.

weath·er·strip (weth'ər-strip') *v.t.* **-stripped, -strip·ping** To equip or fit with weather strips.

weather strip A narrow strip of material placed over or in crevices, as at windows, to keep out drafts, rain, etc.

weather stripping 1. A weather strip. 2. Weather strips collectively.

weather vane A vane that indicates the direction from which the wind is blowing; weathercock.

weath·er·wise (weth'ər-wiz') *adj.* 1. Experienced in observing or predicting the weather. 2. Skillful in predicting trends or shifts in public opinion, etc.

weave (wēv) *v.* **wove** or *for def. 10* **weaved, wo·ven** or (*less common*) **wove, weav·ing** *v.t.* 1. To form, produce, or manufacture as a textile, by interlacing threads or yarns; esp., in a loom. 2. To form by interlacing strands, strips, twigs, etc.: to *weave* a basket. 3. To produce by combining details or elements: to *weave* a story. 4. To bring together so as to form a whole. 5. To twist into, about, or through: to *weave* ribbons through one's hair. 6. To spin (a web). 7. To make or effect by moving from side to side or in a winding or zigzag course: to *weave* one's way through a crowd. — *v.i.* 8. To make cloth, baskets, etc., by weaving. 9. To become woven or interlaced. 10. To move from side to side or with a zigzagging motion. — *n.* A particular method or style of weaving. [OE *wefan*]

weav·er (wē'vər) *n.* 1. One who weaves; esp., one whose occupation is the weaving of textiles, etc. 2. A weaverbird.

weav·er·bird (wē'vər-bûrd') *n.* Any of various finchlike birds, native to Asia, Africa, etc., and constructing intricately woven nests.

web (web) *n.* 1. Any fabric, structure, etc., woven of or as of interlaced or interwoven strands. 2. Textile fabric, esp. in the piece or being woven in a loom. 3. The network of delicate threads spun by a spider to entrap its prey, by certain caterpillars, other insect larvae, etc.; a cobweb. 4. Any complex network: a *web* of highways. 5. Anything artfully contrived or elaborated into a trap or snare: a *web* of espionage. 6. *Zool.* A membrane or fold of skin connecting the digits of an animal, as in aquatic birds, otters, bats, frogs, etc. 7. *Ornithol.* The series of barbs on either side of the shaft of a feather: also called *vane.* 8. A plate or sheet, as of metal, connecting the heavier sections, ribs, frames, etc., of any structural or mechanical element. 9. *Archit.* The part of a ribbed vault between the ribs. — *v.t.* **webbed, web·bing** 1. To provide with a web. 2. To cover or surround with a web; entangle. [OE]

webbed (webd) *adj.* 1. Having a web. 2. Having the digits united by a membrane, as the foot of a goose or duck.

web·bing (web'ing) *n.* 1. A woven strip of strong fiber, used for safety belts, in upholstery, etc. 2. Any structure or material forming a web.

web·by (web'ē) *adj.* **·bi·er, ·bi·est** Resembling, having, or consisting of a web or membrane.

web·foot (web'foot') *n. pl.* **·feet** 1. A foot with webbed toes. 2. A web-footed bird or animal.

web-foot·ed (web'foot'id) *adj.* Having the toes connected by a membrane, as aquatic animals and birds.

Web·ste·ri·an (web-stir'ē-ən) *adj.* Of or pertaining to Daniel or Noah Webster.

wed (wed) *v.* **wed·ded, wed** or **wed·ded, wed·ding** *v.t.* 1. To take as one's husband or wife; marry. 2. To unite or give in matrimony; join in wedlock. 3. To join in a close relationship or attachment. — *v.i.* 4. To marry. [OE *wedian* to pledge]

we'd (wēd) 1. We had. 2. We would.

wed·ded (wed'id) *adj.* 1. Joined in wedlock; married. 2. Characteristic of marriage. 3. Having a close relationship or attachment: often with *to: wedded* to his work.

wed·ding (wed'ing) *n.* 1. The ceremony or celebration of a marriage. 2. The anniversary of a marriage: golden *wedding.* [OE *weddung* < *weddian* to pledge]

wedge (wej) *n.* 1. A piece of wood, metal, etc., that is V-shaped in longitudinal cross section, capable of being inserted into a narrow opening, and used as an aid in splitting substances, securing movable parts, raising weights, etc. 2. Anything in the form of a wedge, as a piece of pie, a formation of soldiers, etc. 3. An action, procedure, or idea con-

stituting the earliest stage in a division of unity, change of policy, intrusive action, etc. — *v.* **wedged, wedg·ing** *v.t.* 1. To force apart or split with or as with a wedge. 2. To compress or fix in place with a wedge. 3. To crowd or squeeze (something) into a narrow or confined space. — *v.i.* 4. To jam or be forced in like a wedge. [OE *wecg*]

Wedg·wood (wej'wood) *n.* A type of fine, hard pottery, often of unglazed, tinted clay bearing small, white, finely detailed, classical figures in cameo relief. Also **Wedgwood ware.** [after Josiah *Wedgwood,* 1730–95, English potter]

wedg·y (wej'ē) *adj.* **wedg·i·er, wedg·i·est** Having the form or uses of a wedge.

wed·lock (wed'lok) *n.* The state or relationship of being married; matrimony. — **in wedlock** 1. With one's parents legally married to one another, as at the time of one's conception or birth. 2. In the married state. — **out of wedlock** With one's parents not married to one another, as at the time of one's conception or birth. [OE < *wed* pledge + *-lāc,* suffix of nouns of action]

Wednes·day (wenz'dē, -dā) *n.* The fourth day of the week. [OE *Wōdnesdæg* day of Woden]

wee (wē) *adj.* **we·er, we·est** Very small; tiny. — *n. Chiefly Scot.* A short time or space; a bit: bide a *wee.* [ME *wei* < OE *wēge* a quantity]

weed¹ (wēd) *n.* 1. Any common, unsightly, or troublesome plant that grows in abundance, esp. to injurious excess on cultivated ground. 2. *Informal* Tobacco: usu. with *the;* also, a cigarette or cigar. 3. Any worthless animal or thing. 4. The stem and leaves of any useful plant as distinguished from its flower and fruit: dill *weed.* 5. Thick, luxuriant growth, as of underbrush or shrubs. — *v.t.* 1. To pull up and remove weeds from. 2. To remove (a weed): often with *out.* 3. To remove (anything regarded as harmful or undesirable): with *out.* 4. To rid of anything harmful or undesirable. — *v.i.* 5. To remove weeds, etc. [OE *wēod*] — **weed'er** *n.* — **weed'less** *adj.*

weed² (wēd) *n.* 1. A token of mourning, as a band of crepe, worn as part of the dress. 2. *pl.* A widow's mourning garb. [OE *wǣd* garment]

weed·y (wē'dē) *adj.* **weed·i·er, weed·i·est** 1. Having a growth of weeds; abounding in weeds. 2. Of or pertaining to a weed or weeds. 3. Resembling a weed; weedlike, as in rapid, ready growth. 4. *Informal* Gawky; awkward; ungainly: *weedy* youths. — **weed'i·ly** *adv.* — **weed'i·ness** *n.*

wee folk Fairies, elves, etc.

wee hours The hours after midnight; early morning.

week (wēk) *n.* 1. A period of seven days; esp., such a period beginning with Sunday. ◆ Collateral adjective: *hebdomadal.* 2. The period of time within a week devoted to work: a 35-hour *week.* 3. A period of seven days preceding or following any given day or date: a *week* from Tuesday. [OE *wucu, wicu, wice*]

week·day (wēk'dā') *n.* Any day of the week except Sunday.

week·end (wēk'end') *n.* The end of the week; esp., the time from Friday evening or Saturday to the following Monday morning. — *v.i. Informal* To pass the weekend: We *weekended* in the country. — **week'end'er** *n.*

week·long (wēk'lông', -long') *adj.* Continuing for a week; lasting all week.

week·ly (wēk'lē) *adv.* Once a week; esp., at regular sevenday intervals. — *adj.* 1. Of or pertaining to a week or to weekdays. 2. Done or occurring once a week. — *n. pl.* **·lies** A publication issued once a week.

ween (wēn) *v.t. & v.i. Archaic* To suppose; guess; fancy. [OE *wēnan* to think]

ween·ie (wē'nē) *n. U.S. Informal* A wiener.

weep (wēp) *v.* **wept, weep·ing** *v.i.* 1. To manifest grief or other strong emotion by shedding tears. 2. To mourn; lament: with *for.* 3. To ooze or shed liquid in drops. — *v.t.* 4. To weep for; mourn. 5. To shed (tears, or drops of other liquid). 6. To bring to a specified condition by weeping: to *weep* oneself to sleep. — *n.* The act of weeping, or a fit of tears. [OE *wēpan*] — **weep'er** *n.*

weep·ing (wē'ping) *adj.* 1. That weeps; crying; tearful. 2. Having slim, pendulous branches: *weeping* willow.

weeping willow A willow having long, slender, pendulous branches.

weep·y (wē'pē) *adj.* **weep·i·er, weep·i·est** *Informal* Inclined to weep; tearful.

wee·vil (wē'vəl) *n.* 1. Any of numerous small beetles, many of them serious pests, having snoutlike heads and strong, pincerlike jaws, and feeding on plants and plant products. 2. Any of a family of small beetles that feed principally on beans and seeds. [OE *wifel* beetle] — **wee'vil·y** or **wee'vil·ly** *adj.*

weft (weft) *n.* 1. The cross threads in a web of cloth; woof. 2. A woven fabric; web. 3. *Naut.* A waft. [OE]

Wehr·macht (vâr'mäkht) *n. German* The armed forces, collectively, of Germany; literally, defense force.

weigh¹ (wā) *v.t.* 1. To determine the weight of, as by measuring on a scale or balance. 2. To balance or hold in the hand so as to estimate weight or heaviness. **3.** To measure (a quantity or quantities of something) according to weight: with *out*. **4.** To consider carefully; estimate the worth or advantages of: to *weigh* a proposal. **5.** To press or force down by weight or heaviness; burden or oppress: with *down*. **6.** To raise or hoist: now only in the phrase **to weigh anchor.** —*v.i.* **7.** To have weight; be heavy to a specified degree: She *weighs* ninety pounds. **8.** To have influence or importance: The girl's testimony *weighed* heavily with the jury. **9.** To be burdensome or oppressive: with *on* or *upon*: What *weighs* on your mind? **10.** *Naut.* **a** To raise anchor. **b** To begin to sail. —**to weigh in** Of a prize fighter, etc., to be weighed before a contest. —**to weigh one's words** To consider one's words carefully before speaking. [OE *wegan* to weigh, carry, lift] —**weigh′er** *n.*

weigh² (wā)　*n.* Way: used in the phrase **under weigh** by mistaken analogy with *aweigh*. [Var. of WAY]

weight (wāt)　*n.* **1.** Any quantity of heaviness, expressed indefinitely or in terms of standard units. **2.** The measure of the force with which bodies tend toward the center of the earth or other celestial body, equal to the mass of the body multiplied by the acceleration due to gravitation; also, the quality so measured. **3.** Any object or mass that weighs a definite or specific amount. **4.** A definite mass of metal, etc., equal to a specified unit or amount of heaviness, and used in scales as a standard; also, any unit of heaviness, as a pound, ounce, etc. **5.** Any mass used as a counterpoise or to exert pressure by force of gravity: a *paperweight*. **6.** Burden; oppressiveness: the *weight* of care. **7.** The relative tendency of any mass toward a center of superior mass: the *weight* of a planet. **8.** A scale or graduated system of standard units of weight: avoirdupois *weight*. [See tables front of book.] **9.** Influence; importance; consequence: a man of *weight*. **10.** The comparative heaviness of clothes, as appropriate to the season: summer *weight*. —**by weight** Measured by weighing. —**to carry weight** To be of importance or significance. —**to pull one's weight** To do one's share; perform one's duty. —**to throw one's weight around** *Informal* To exercise one's authority more than is necessary or proper; make unwarranted use of position or power. —*v.t.* **1.** To add weight to; make heavy. **2.** To oppress or burden. **3.** To adulterate or treat (fabrics, etc.) with extraneous substances. [OE *wiht, gewiht*]

weight·less (wāt′lis)　*adj.* **1.** Having or seeming to have no weight. **2.** *Aerospace* Being at zero gravity. —**weight′·less·ly** *adv.* —**weight′less·ness** *n.*

weight·y (wā′tē)　*adj.* **weight·i·er, weight·i·est 1.** Having great weight; ponderous. **2.** Having power to move the mind; cogent. **3.** Of great importance. **4.** Influential, as in public affairs. **5.** Burdensome. —**weight′i·ly** *adv.* —**weight′i·ness** *n.*

Weimar Republic A German Republic formed by a constitutional assembly at Weimar, 1919; dissolved 1933.

weir (wir)　*n.* **1.** An obstruction or dam placed in a stream to raise the water, divert it into a millrace or irrigation ditches, etc. **2.** An aperture in such an obstruction, used to determine the quantity of water flowing through it. **3.** A series of wattled enclosures in a stream to catch fish. [OE *wer* < *werian* to dam up]

weird (wird)　*adj.* **1.** Concerned with the unnatural or with witchcraft; unearthly; uncanny. **2.** Strange; bizarre. **3.** Pertaining to or having to do with fate or the Fates. [OE *wyrd* fate] —**weird′ly** *adv.* —**weird′ness** *n.*

weird·ie (wir′dē)　*n. pl.* **weird·ies** *U.S. Slang* A bizarre or freakish person, thing, or occurrence. Also **weird′y.**

weiss beer (vīs, wīs)　A pale, effervescent beer, brewed usu. from wheat. [< G *weissbier*, lit., white beer]

welch (welch, welsh)　*v.i.* To welsh. —**welch′er** *n.*

Welch (welch, welsh)　See WELSH.

Welch·man (welsh′mən, welch-)　See WELSHMAN.

wel·come (wel′kəm)　*adj.* **1.** Admitted gladly to a place or festivity; received cordially: a *welcome* guest. **2.** Producing satisfaction or pleasure; pleasing: *welcome* tidings. **3.** Made free to use or enjoy: She is *welcome* to my purse. —**you are** (or **you're**) **welcome** You are under no obligation: a conventional response to "thank you." —*n.* The act of bidding or making welcome; a hearty greeting. —**to wear out one's welcome** To come so often or to linger so long as no longer to be welcome. —*v.t.* **·comed, ·com·ing 1.** To give a welcome to; greet hospitably. **2.** To receive with pleasure. [OE < *will*- will, pleasure + *cuma* guest] —**wel′come·ly** *adv.* —**wel′come·ness** *n.* —**wel′com·er** *n.*

welcome mat *Informal* **1.** A doormat. **2.** Any enthusiastic welcome or reception: chiefly in the phrase **to put** (or **roll**) **out the welcome mat.**

weld (weld)　*v.t.* **1.** To unite, as two pieces of metal, usu. with hammering or pressure, by the application of heat along the area of contact. **2.** To bring into close association or

connection. —*v.i.* **3.** To be capable of being welded. —*n.* The consolidation of pieces of metal by welding; also, the closed joint so formed. [Alter. of WELL¹, v.] —**weld′a·bil′i·ty** *n.* —**weld′a·ble** *adj.* —**weld′er** *n.*

wel·fare (wel′fâr)　*n.* **1.** The condition of faring well; prosperity. **2.** Welfare work. **3.** Aid, as money, food, or clothing, given to those in need. —**on welfare** Receiving money, food, clothing, etc., from a government because of need. [ME < *wel* well + *fare* a going]

welfare state A state or polity in which the government assumes a large measure of responsibility for the social welfare of its members, as through unemployment and health insurance, fair employment legislation, etc.

welfare work Organized efforts carried on by government or private organizations to improve the social and economic condition of a group or class. —**welfare worker**

wel·kin (wel′kin)　*n. Archaic* or *Poetic* **1.** The vault of the sky; the heavens. **2.** The air. [OE *wolcen, wolcn* cloud]

well¹ (wel)　*n.* **1.** A hole or shaft sunk into the earth to obtain a fluid, as water, oil, brine, or natural gas. **2.** A spring of water; a fountain. **3.** A source of continued supply, or that which issues forth continuously; a wellspring: a *well* of learning. **4.** A depression, cavity, or vessel used to hold a supply of liquid: an *inkwell*. **5.** *Archit.* A vertical opening descending through floors, or a deep enclosed space in a building for light, ventilation, etc.: a *stairwell*; an elevator *well*. **6.** *Naut.* The enclosed space in a vessel's hold, housing the pumps. —*v.i.* **1.** To pour forth or flow up, as water in a spring. —*v.t.* **2.** To gush: Her eyes *welled* tears. [OE < *weallan* to boil, bubble up]

well² (wel)　*adv.* **bet·ter, best 1.** Satisfactorily; favorably; according to one's wishes: Everything goes *well*. **2.** In a good or correct manner; expertly: to speak *well*. **3.** Suitably; with reason or propriety: I cannot *well* remain here. **4.** In a successful manner; also, agreeably or luxuriously: He lives *well*. **5.** Intimately: How *well* do you know him? **6.** To a considerable extent or degree: *well* aware. **7.** Completely; wholly. **8.** Far; at some distance: He lagged *well* behind us. **9.** Kindly; generously; graciously. —**as well 1.** Also; in addition. **2.** With equal effect or consequence: He might just *as well* have sold it. —**as well as 1.** As satisfactorily as. **2.** To the same degree as. **3.** In addition to. —*adj.* **1.** Having good health. **2.** Satisfactory; right: All is *well*. **3.** Prosperous; comfortable. —*interj.* An exclamation used to express surprise, expectation, resignation, doubt, indignation, acquiescence, etc., or merely to preface a remark. [OE *wel*]

◆ *Well* may be used in combination, as in *well-chosen, well-informed*, etc. Such combinations are hyphenated before the words they modify, as in *well-aimed* shots, but not when used predicatively, as in: The shots were *well aimed*.

we'll (wēl)　**1.** We will. **2.** We shall.

well-ap·point·ed (wel′ə·poin′tid)　*adj.* Properly equipped; excellently furnished.

well·a·way (wel′ə·wā′)　*interj. Archaic* Woe is me! alas! Also **well′a·day′** (-dā′). [OE *wā lā wā* woe! lo! woe!]

well-bal·anced (wel′bal′ənst)　*adj.* **1.** Evenly balanced or proportioned. **2.** Sensible; sane; sound.

well-be·ing (wel′bē′ing)　*n.* A condition of health, happiness, or prosperity; welfare.

well-born (wel′bôrn′)　*adj.* Of good birth or ancestry.

well-bred (wel′bred′)　*adj.* **1.** Characterized by or showing good breeding; polite. **2.** Of good stock, as an animal.

well-curb (wel′kûrb«)　*n.* The frame or stone ring around the mouth of a well.

well-dis·posed (wel′dis·pōzd′)　*adj.* Disposed or inclined to be kind, favorable, etc.

well-do·er (wel′dōō′ər)　*n.* One who performs good deeds. —**well′-do′ing** *n.*

well-done (wel′dun′)　*adj.* **1.** Satisfactorily accomplished. **2.** Thoroughly cooked, as meat.

well enough Tolerably good or satisfactory. —**to let well enough alone** To leave things as they are lest the result of interference be worse.

well-fa·vored (wel′fā′vərd)　*adj.* Of attractive appearance; comely; handsome. Also *Brit.* **well′-fa′voured.**

well-fed (wel′fed′)　*adj.* **1.** Plump; fat. **2.** Properly nourished.

well-fixed (wel′fiskt′)　*adj. Informal* Affluent; well-to-do.

well-found (wel′found′)　*adj.* Well equipped or supplied.

well-found·ed (wel′foun′did)　*adj.* Based on fact, sound, evidence, etc.: *well-founded* suspicions.

well-groomed (wel′grōōmd′)　*adj.* **1.** Carefully dressed, combed, etc.; very neat. **2.** Carefully curried, as a horse.

well-ground·ed (wel′groun′did)　*adj.* **1.** Adequately schooled in the elements of a subject. **2.** Well-founded.

well·head (wel′hed′)　*n.* **1.** A natural source supplying water to a spring or well. **2.** Any source or fountainhead.

well-heeled (wel′hēld′)   *adj. Slang* Plentifully supplied with money.

well-in·ten·tioned (wel′in·ten′shənd)   *adj.* Having good intentions; well-meant: often with connotation of failure.

well-known (wel′nōn′)   *adj.* **1.** Widely known; famous. **2.** Thoroughly or fully known.

well-man·nered (wel′man′ərd)   *adj.* Characterized by good manners; courteous; polite.

well-mean·ing (wel′mē′ning)   *adj.* **1.** Having good intentions. **2.** Done with or characterized by good intentions: also **well′-meant′** (-ment′).

well-nigh (wel′nī′)   *adv.* Very nearly; almost.

well-off (wel′ôf′, -of′)   *adj.* In comfortable or favorable circumstances; fortunate.

well-read (wel′red′)   *adj.* Having a wide knowledge of literature or books; having read much.

well-round·ed (wel′roun′did)   *adj.* **1.** Having or displaying diverse knowledge, interests, etc.   **2.** Wide in scope; comprehensive: a *well-rounded* program.   **3.** Fully formed or developed: a *well-rounded* figure.

well-spo·ken (wel′spō′kən)   *adj.* **1.** Fitly or excellently said.   **2.** Of gentle speech and manners.

well·spring (wel′spring′)   *n.* **1.** The source of a stream or spring; fountainhead.   **2.** A source of continual supply.

well sweep   A device used for drawing water from a well, consisting of a pole swung on a pivot attached to a high post, and having a bucket suspended from one end.

well-thought-of (wel′thôt′uv′, -ov′)   *adj.* In good repute; esteemed; respected.

well-to-do (wel′tə-dōō′)   *adj.* Prosperous; affluent.

well-wish·er (wel′wish′ər)   *n.* One who wishes well, as to another.   **— well′-wish′ing** *adj. & n.*

welsh (welsh, welch)   *v.i. Slang* **1.** To cheat by failing to pay a bet or debt: often with *on.*   **2.** To avoid fulfilling an obligation: often with *on.* Also spelled *welch.*   [? Back formation < *welsher,* prob. < *Welsher* Welshman, with ref. to supposed national traits]   **— welsh′er** *n.*

Welsh (welsh, welch)   *adj.* Pertaining to Wales, its people, or their language.   — *n.* **1.** The Celtic people of Wales: with *the*: also called *Cymry.*   **2.** The Celtic language of Wales, belonging to the Brythonic or Cymric group: also called *Cymric.* Also spelled *Welch.*   [OE *wealh* foreigner]

Welsh·man (welsh′mən, welch′-)   *n. pl.* **·men** (-mən)   A man of Welsh birth or ancestry. Also spelled *Welchman.*

Welsh rabbit   A concoction of melted cheese cooked in cream or milk, often with ale or beer added, and served hot on toast or crackers.   ◆ The form *rarebit* was a later development and is the result of mistaken etymology.

Welsh terrier   A black-and-tan terrier having a flat skull and wiry coat, used for hunting.

welt (welt)   *n.* **1.** A strip of material, covered cord, etc., applied to a seam to cover or strengthen it.   **2.** A strip of leather set into the seam between the edges of the upper and the outer sole of a shoe.   **3.** A stripe raised on the skin by a blow: also called *wale, weal.*   — *v.t.* **1.** To sew a welt on or in; decorate with a welt.   **2.** *Informal* To flog severely, so as to raise welts.   [ME *welte, walt*]

wel·ter (wel′tər)   *v.i.* **1.** To roll about; wallow.   **2.** To lie or be soaked in some fluid, as blood.   **3.** To surge or move tumultuously, as the sea.   — *n.* **1.** A rolling movement, as of waves.   **2.** A commotion; turmoil.   [< MDu. *welteren*]

wel·ter·weight (wel′tər-wāt′)   *n.* A boxer or wrestler whose fighting weight is between 136 and 147 pounds.   [< *welter* heavyweight horseman + WEIGHT]

Welt·schmerz (velt′shmârts′)   *n. German* Melancholy pessimism over the state of the world; literally, world pain.

wen (wen)   *n. Pathol.* Any benign tumor of the skin containing sebaceous matter, occurring commonly on the scalp.   [OE *wenn, wænn*]   **— wen′nish, wen′ny** *adj.*

wench (wench)   *n.* **1.** A young woman; girl: a humorous term.   **2.** *Archaic* A young peasant woman; also, a female servant; maid.   **3.** *Archaic* A prostitute; strumpet.   — *v.i. Archaic* To keep company with strumpets.   [ME < OE *wencel* child, servant]

wend (wend)   *Chiefly Poetic v.* **wen·ded** (*Archaic* **went**), **wend·ing** *v.t.* **1.** To direct or proceed on (one's course or way).   — *v.i.* **2.** To travel; proceed; go.   [OE *wendan*]

Wend (wend)   *n.* One of a Slavic people now occupying the region between the Elbe and Oder rivers in eastern Germany: also called *Sorb, Sorbian.*   [< G *Wende, Winde*]

Wend·ish (wen′dish)   *adj.* Of or pertaining to the Wends or their language: also *Sorbian.*   — *n.* The West Slavic language of the Wends; Sorbian. Also **Wend′ic.**

went (went)   An archaic past tense and past participle of *wend,* now used as past tense of GO.

wept (wept)   Past tense and past participle of WEEP.

were (wûr, *unstressed* wər)   Plural and second person singular past indicative, and past subjunctive singular and plural of BE.   [OE *wære, wæron,* pt. forms of *wesan* to be]

we're (wir)   We are.

were·n't (wûr′ənt)   Were not.

were·wolf (wir′woolf′, wûr′-)   *n. pl.* **·wolves** (-woolvz′)   In European folklore, a human being transformed into a wolf or one having power to assume the form of a wolf at will. Also **wer′wolf′.**   [OE < *wer* man + *wulf* wolf]

wert (wûrt, *unstressed* wərt)   Archaic second person singular, past tense of both indicative and subjunctive of BE: used with *thou.*

Wes·ley·an (wes′lē·ən, *Brit.* wez′lē·ən)   *adj.* Of or pertaining to John Wesley or Methodism.   — *n.* A disciple of John Wesley; a Methodist.   — **Wes′ley·an·ism** *n.*

Wes·sex (wes′iks)   The ancient kingdom of the West Saxons in southern England.

west (west)   *n.* **1.** The direction of the sun in relation to an observer on earth at sunset.   **2.** One of the four cardinal points of the compass, directly opposite *east* and 90° counterclockwise from *north.* See COMPASS CARD.   **3.** Any direction near this point.   **4.** *Sometimes cap.* Any region west of a specified point.   **— the West 1.** The countries lying west of Asia and Turkey; the Occident.   **2.** The western hemisphere.   — *adj.* **1.** To, toward, facing, or in the west; western.   **2.** Coming from the west: the *west* wind.   — *adv.* In or toward the west; westward.   [OE]

west·bound (west′bound′)   *adj.* Going westward.   Also **west′-bound′.**

west·er·ing (wes′tər·ing)   *adj.* Moving or turning westward: the *westering* sun.

west·er·ly (wes′tər-lē)   *adj.* **1.** In, toward, or pertaining to the west.   **2.** From the west, as a wind.   — *n. pl.* **·lies** A wind or storm from the west.   — *adv.* Toward or from the west.   **— west′er·li·ness** *n.*

west·ern (wes′tərn)   *adj.* **1.** To, toward, or in the west.   **2.** Native to or inhabiting the west: a *western* species.   **3.** *Sometimes cap.* Of, pertaining to, or characteristic of the west or the West.   **4.** From the west, as a wind.   — *n.* **1.** A westerner.   **2.** A type of fiction or motion picture using cowboy and pioneer life in the western U.S. as its material.

Western Church 1. The medieval church of the Western Roman Empire, now the Roman Catholic Church: distinguished from the church of the Eastern Empire, now the Eastern Orthodox Church.   **2.** The Christian churches of western Europe and America.

west·ern·er (wes′tər·nər)   *n.* **1.** One who is native to or lives in the west.   **2.** *Usu. cap.* One who lives in or comes from the western U.S.

western frontier   Formerly, the part of the U.S. bordering on the still unsettled regions of the west.

west·ern·ism (wes′tər·niz′əm)   *n.* An expression or practice peculiar to the west, esp. the western U.S.

west·ern·ize (wes′tər·nīz)   *v.t.* **·ized, ·iz·ing** To make western in characteristics, habits, etc.   **— west′ern·i·za′tion** *n.*

west·ern·most (wes′tərn·mōst)   *adj.* Farthest west.

Western Ocean   In ancient geography, the ocean lying westward of the known world; the Atlantic Ocean.

Western (Roman) Empire   The part of the Roman Empire west of the Adriatic that existed as a separate empire from A.D. 395 until the fall of Rome in A.D. 476.

West Highland white terrier   A small, short-legged terrier having a stiff, white coat.

west-north·west (west′north′west′)   *n.* The direction midway between west and northwest, 26 points or 292° 30′ clockwise from due north. See COMPASS CARD.   — *adj. & adv.* In, toward, or from the west-northwest.

West Saxon 1. One of a Saxon tribe that invaded England in the fifth and sixth centuries A.D. and settled in Wessex.   **2.** The dialect of Old English spoken in Wessex.

west-south·west (west′south′west′)   *n.* The direction midway between west and southwest, 22 points or 247° 30′ clockwise from due north. See COMPASS CARD.   — *adj. & adv.* In, toward, or from the west-southwest.

west·ward (west′wərd)   *adv.* Toward the west: also **west′-wards.**   — *adj.* To, toward, facing, or in the west.   — *n.* A western part or region.   **— west′ward·ly** *adv.*

wet (wet)   *adj.* **wet·ter, wet·test 1.** Covered or saturated with water or other liquid.   **2.** Not yet dry: *wet* varnish.   **3.** Treated or separated by means of water or other liquids.   **4.** Preserved in liquid; also, bottled in alcohol, as laboratory specimens.   **5.** Marked by showers or by heavy rainfall; rainy.   **6.** *Informal* Favoring or permitting the manufacture and sale of alcoholic beverages: a *wet* State.   **— all wet** *Slang* Quite wrong; crazy.   **— wet behind the ears** Inexperienced or unsophisticated.   — *n.* **1.** Water; moisture; wetness.   **2.** Showery or rainy weather; rain.   **3.** *Informal* One opposed to prohibition.   — *v.t. & v.i.* **wet** or **wet·ted, wet·ting** To make or become wet.   **— to wet one's whistle** *Informal* To take a drink.   [OE *wǣt*]   **— wet′ly** *adv.*   **— wet′ness** *n.*   **— wet′ta·ble** *adj.*   **— wet′ter** *n.*

wet·back (wet′bak′)   *n. U.S. Informal* A Mexican laborer who enters the U.S. illegally.   [So called because many cross the border by swimming or wading across the Rio Grande]

wet blanket   *Informal* One who or that which has a discouraging effect on enthusiasm, activity, etc.

weth·er (wĕth/ər) *n.* A castrated ram. [OE]

wet-nurse (wĕt/nûrs/) *v.t.* **-nursed, -nurs·ing** **1.** To act as a wet nurse to. **2.** To attend to with painstaking care.

wet nurse A woman who is hired to suckle the child of another woman.

wet·ting (wĕt/ing) *n.* **1.** The act of one who wets, or the state of being wetted. **2.** A liquid, as water, used in moistening something, as flour in breadmaking.

wetting agent *Chem.* Any of a class of substances that, by reducing surface tension, enable a liquid to spread more readily over a solid surface.

we've (wēv) We have.

whack (hwak) *v.t. & v.i.* **1.** *Informal* To strike sharply; beat; hit. **2.** *Slang* To share: often with *up*. — *n.* **1.** *Informal* A sharp, resounding stroke or blow. **2.** *Slang* A share; portion. — **to have a whack at** *Slang* To give a blow to. **2.** To have a chance or turn at. — **out of whack** *Slang* Out of order. [? Var. of THWACK]

whack·ing (hwak/ing) *Chiefly Brit. Informal adj.* Strikingly large; whopping. — *adv.* Very; extremely.

whale¹ (hwāl) *n.* **1.** A marine mammal of fishlike form, esp. one of the larger pelagic species, having the fore limbs developed as paddles, a broad, flat tail, and a thick layer of fat or blubber immediately beneath the skin. The principal types are the toothless or whalebone whales and the toothed whales. **2.** *Informal* Something extremely good or large: a *whale* of a party. — *v.i.* **whaled, whal·ing** To engage in the hunting of whales. [OE *hwæl*]

whale² (hwāl) *v.t.* whaled, whal·ing *Informal* To strike as if to produce wales or stripes; flog; wale. [? Var. of WALE¹, v.]

whale·back (hwāl/bak/) *n.* A steamship having a rounded main deck, used on the Great Lakes.

whale·boat (hwāl/bōt/) *n.* A long, deep rowboat, sharp at both ends, often steered with an oar, so called because first used in whaling, but now carried on steamers as lifeboats.

whale·bone (hwāl/bōn/) *n.* **1.** The horny substance developed in plates from the upper jaw on either side of the palate of certain whales; baleen. **2.** A strip of whalebone, used in stiffening dress bodies, corsets, etc.

whal·er (hwā/lər) *n.* **1.** A person or a vessel engaged in whaling. **2.** A whaleboat.

whal·ing (hwā/ling) *n.* The industry of capturing whales. — *adj. Slang* Huge; whopping.

wham·my (hwam/ē) *n. pl.* **·mies** *U.S. Slang* A jinx; hex; to put the *whammy* on someone. [< *wham*, informal interjection imit. of the sound of a hard blow]

whang (hwang) *Informal v.t. & v.i.* To beat or sound with a resounding noise. — *n.* A heavy blow. [Imit.]

wharf (hwôrf) *n. pl.* **wharves** (hwôrvz) or **wharfs** A structure of masonry or timber erected on the shore of a harbor, river, etc., alongside which vessels may lie to load or unload cargo, passengers, etc.; also, any landing place for vessels, as a pier or quay. — *v.t.* **1.** To moor to a wharf. **2.** To provide or protect with a wharf or wharves. **3.** To deposit or store on a wharf. [OE *hwearf*]
— **Syn.** (noun) A *wharf* is usually a platform supported by wooden piles. A *pier* usually has a masonry foundation and projects into the water at right angles to the bank. A *dock* was originally the water between two *piers*, in which a vessel floated; by extension, any *pier* or *wharf* has come to be called a *dock*.

wharf·age (hwôr/fij) *n.* **1.** The use of wharves for unloading ships, storing goods, etc. **2.** Charge for the use of a wharf. **3.** Wharves collectively.

wharf·in·ger (hwôr/fin·jər) *n.* One who keeps a wharf for landing goods and collects wharfage fees. [Earlier *wharfager*]

wharf rat **1.** A brown rat that inhabits wharves. **2.** *U.S. Slang* One who loiters about wharves, esp. with criminal intent.

wharf·side (hwôrf/sīd/) *n.* The space on or at the side of a wharf. — *adj.* On or at the side of a wharf.

wharve (hwôrv) In spinning, a round piece on a spindle, serving as a pulley. [OE *hweorfa*]

what (hwot, hwut) *pron.* **1.** Which specific thing or things, action, etc.: *What* does he do? I don't know *what* to do. **2.** That which: He knew *what* he wanted. — **and what not** What need not be mentioned in addition; and so forth. — **what for** *Slang* A punishment; scolding: I'll give him *what for.* — **what have you** What need not be mentioned in addition; and so forth. — **what if** What would happen if; suppose that. — **what's what** *Informal* The actual situation or state of affairs. — *adj.* **1.** In interrogative construction: **a** Asking for information that will specify the person or thing qualified by it; which: Of *what* person do you speak? **b** How much; *What* money has he? **2.** How surprising, ridiculous, great, etc.: *What* genius! **3.** Whatever: *What* money he had left was soon spent. — *adv.* **1.** In what respect; to what extent: *What* are you profited? **2.** For what reason; why:

with *for*: *What* are you saying that for? — *conj. Informal* That: used only in negative expressions: I do not doubt but *what* he will come. [OE *hwæt*, neut. of *hwā* who]

what·ev·er (hwot/ev/ər, hwut/-) *pron.* **1.** As a compound relative, the whole that; anything that; no matter what: often added for emphasis to a negative assertion: *whatever* makes life dear; I do not want anything *whatever*. **2.** *Informal* What: usually interrogative: *Whatever* were you saying? Also *Poetic* **what'e'er'** (-âr').

what·not (hwot/not/, hwut/-) *n.* An ornamental set of shelves for holding bric-à-brac, etc.

what·so·ev·er (hwot/sō·ev/ər, hwut/-) *adj. & pron.* Whatever: a more formal usage. Also *Poetic* **what'so·e'er'** (-âr').

wheat (hwēt) *n.* **1.** The grain of a cereal grass, widely cultivated and providing a flour used for bread, pastries, etc. **2.** The plant producing this grain, bearing at its summit a dense spike called the ear or head, sometimes with awns (**bearded wheat**) and sometimes without awns (**beardless** or **bald wheat**). **3.** A field of wheat; crop of wheat. [OE *hwǣte*]

WHEAT
a Bearded.
b Beardless.
c,d Grain.

wheat·en (hwēt/n) *adj.* Belonging to or made of wheat.

whee·dle (hwēd/l) *v.* **·dled, ·dling** *v.t.* **1.** To persuade or try to persuade by flattery, cajolery, etc.; coax. **2.** To obtain by cajoling or coaxing. — *v.i.* **3.** To use flattery or cajolery. [? OE *wǣdlian* to beg, be poor] — **whee'dler** *n.* — **whee'dling·ly** *adv.*

wheel (hwēl) *n.* **1.** A circular rim and hub connected by spokes or a disk, capable of rotating on a central axis, as in vehicles and machines. **2.** An instrument or device having a wheel or wheels as its distinguishing characteristic, as a steering wheel, water wheel, spinning wheel, etc. **3.** Anything resembling or suggestive of a wheel; any circular object or formation. **4.** *Informal* A bicycle. **5.** An old instrument of torture or execution, consisting of a wheel to which the limbs of the victim were tied and then broken with an iron bar. **6.** A turning; rotation; revolution. **7.** *pl.* That which imparts or directs motion or controls activity; the moving force: the *wheels* of democracy. — **at the wheel** **1.** Driving or steering a vehicle, boat, etc. **2.** In control. — *v.t.* **1.** To move or convey on wheels. **2.** To cause to turn on or as on an axis; pivot or revolve. **3.** To perform with a circular movement. **4.** To provide with a wheel or wheels. — *v.i.* **5.** To turn on or as on an axis; rotate or revolve. **6.** To take a new direction or course of action: often with *about*. **7.** To move in a circular or spiral course. **8.** To move on wheels. — **to wheel and deal** *U.S. Slang* To act freely or independently, without restrictions, as in business. [OE *hwēol*]

wheel·bar·row (hwēl/bar/ō) *n.* A boxlike vehicle ordinarily with one wheel and two handles, for moving small loads. — *v.t.* To convey in a wheelbarrow.

wheel·base (hwēl/bās/) *n.* The distance from the center of a back hub to the center of the front hub on the same side, as in an automobile.

wheel·chair (hwēl/châr/) *n.* A mobile chair mounted between large wheels, for the use of invalids. Also **wheel chair.**

wheel·er (hwē/lər) *n.* **1.** One who wheels. **2.** A wheel horse or other draft animal working next to the wheel. **3.** Something furnished with a wheel or wheels: a *side-wheeler.*

wheel·er-deal·er (hwē/lər-dē/lər) *n. U.S. Slang* One who wheels and deals: a shrewd, quick-witted person.

wheel horse **1.** A horse harnessed to the pole or shafts when there is a leader or leaders in front. **2.** One who does the heaviest work or assumes the greatest responsibility.

wheel·house (hwēl/hous/) *n.* A pilothouse.

wheel of fortune The wheel represented as being turned in order to bring about changes in human destiny, and that symbolizes the uncertainty of fate.

wheel·wright (hwēl/rīt/) *n.* A man whose business is making or repairing wheels.

wheeze (hwēz) *v.t. & v.i.* **wheezed, wheez·ing** To breathe or utter with a husky, whistling sound. — *n.* **1.** A wheezing sound. **2.** A loud whisper. **2.** *Informal* A popular tale, saying, or trick, esp. a trite one. [Prob. < ON *hvæsa* hiss] — **wheez'er** *n.* — **wheez'ing·ly** *adv.*

wheez·y (hwē/zē) *adj.* **wheez·i·er, wheez·i·est** Affected with or characterized by wheezing. — **wheez'i·ly** *adv.* — **wheez'i·ness** *n.*

whelk¹ (hwelk) *n.* Any of various large marine mollusks having whorled shells, that burrow in sand, esp. the common whelk, much eaten in Europe. [OE *weoloc*]

---

whelk² (hwelk)   *n.* A swelling, protuberance, or pustule. [OE *hwylca* pustule]   **— whelk′y** *adj.*

whelm (hwelm)   *v.t.* **1.** To cover with water or other fluid; submerge; engulf.   **2.** To overpower; overwhelm. **— v.i. 3.** To roll with engulfing force. [Prob. blend of OE *helmian* to cover and *gehwielfan* to bend over]

whelp (hwelp)   *n.* **1.** One of the young of a dog, wolf, lion, or other beast. **2.** A dog. **3.** A young fellow: a contemptuous term. **— v.t. & v.i.** To give birth (to): said of dogs, lions, etc. [OE *hwelp*]

when (hwen)   *adv.* **1.** At what or which time: *When* did you arrive? I know *when* he arrived.   **2.** At which: the time *when* we went on a picnic. **— conj. 1.** At what or which time: They watched until midnight, *when* they fell asleep. **2.** As soon as: He laughed *when* he heard it. **3.** Although: He walks *when* he might ride. **4.** At the time that; while: *when* we were young. **5.** If; considering that: How can I buy it *when* I have no money? **6.** After which: We had just awakened *when* you called. **— pron.** What or which time: since *when*; until *when*. **— n.** The time; date: I don't know the *when* or the circumstances of it. [OE *hwanne, hwenne*]

whence (hwens)   *Archaic adv.* From what place or source: *Whence* and what are you? **— conj. 1.** From what or which place, source, or cause; from which: the place *whence* these sounds arise. **2.** To the place from which. **3.** For which reason; wherefore. [ME < OE *hwanne* when]

whence·so·ev·er (hwens′sō-ev′ər)   *Archaic adv. & conj.* From whatever place, cause, or source.

when·e'er (hwen-âr′)   *adv. & conj. Poetic* Whenever.

when·ev·er (hwen/ev′ər)   *adv. & conj.* At whatever time.

when·so·ev·er (hwen′sō-ev′ər)   *adv. & conj.* Whenever.

where (hwâr)   *adv.* **1.** At or in what place, relation, or situation: *Where* is my book? **2.** To what place or end: *Where* are you going? **3.** From what place: *Where* did you get that hat? **4.** At or in which place: *where* men gather. **5.** To a place or situation in or to which: Let us go *where* the mountains are. **— conj. 1.** At which place: Let us go home *where* we can relax. **2.** With the condition that: xy = 4 *where* x = 2 and y = 2. **— pron. 1.** The place in which: The bear passed three yards from *where* we stood. **2.** The point at which: That's *where* you are wrong. **— n.** Place; locality. ◆ *Where* has absorbed completely the sense of *whither* but not of *whence*. We must use a preposition to express the idea of motion from a place: *Where* did you come from? We do not use a preposition to show place at which: *Where* is the dog *at*? is not accepted in standard usage. [OE *hwǣr*]

where·a·bouts (hwâr′ə-bouts′)   *adv.* Near or at what place; about where. **— n.pl.** (*construed as sing.*) The place in or near which a person or thing is.

where·as (hwâr′az′)   *conj.* **1.** Since the facts are such as they are; seeing that: used in the preamble of a resolution, etc. **2.** The fact of the matter being that; when in truth: implying opposition to a previous statement. **— n. pl. ·as·es** A clause or item beginning with the word "whereas."

where·at (hwâr′at′)   *Archaic or Rare adv.* At what: *Whereat* are you angry? **— conj.** At which; for which reason.

where·by (hwâr′bī′)   *adv.* **1.** By means of which; through which: the gate *whereby* he entered. **2.** By what; how.

wher·e'er (hwâr/âr′)   *adv. Poetic* Wherever.

where·fore (hwâr/fôr′, -fōr′)   *Archaic adv.* For what reason; why: *Wherefore* do you doubt me? **— conj.** For which reason: It began to rain, *wherefore* we called off the picnic.

where·from (hwâr/frum′, -from′)   *Archaic adv.* Whence.

where·in (hwâr/in′)   *adv.* **1.** In what: *Wherein* is the error? **2.** In which: a marriage *wherein* there is discord.

where·of (hwâr/uv′, -ov′)   *Archaic adv.* **1.** Of or from what: *Whereof* did you partake? **2.** Of which or whom.

where·on (hwâr/on′, -ôn′)   *Archaic adv.* On what or on which.

where·so·ev·er (hwâr/sō-ev′ər)   *Archaic adv. & conj.* In or to whatever place; wherever.

where·to (hwâr/tōō′)   *Archaic adv.* To what place or end: *Whereto* serves avarice? **— conj.** To which or to whom.

where·up·on (hwâr/ə-pon′, -ə-pôn′)   *adv. Archaic* Upon what; whereon. **— conj.** Upon which or whom; in consequence of which; after which: *whereupon* they took in sail.

wher·ev·er (hwâr/ev′ər)   *adv. & conj.* In, at, or to whatever place; wheresoever.

where·with (hwâr/with′, -with′)   *Archaic adv.* Interrogatively, with what: *Wherewith* shall I do it? **— conj.** With which; by means of which: the food *wherewith* we abated hunger. **— pron.** That with or by which: with the infinitive: I have not *wherewith* to do it.

where·with·al (hwâr/with-ôl′)   *n.* The necessary means or resources; esp., the necessary money: with the definite article.

wher·ry (hwer′ē)   *n. pl. ·ries* **1.** A light, fast rowboat used on inland waters. **2.** *Brit.* A fishing vessel with two sails. **3.** A rowboat for racing or exercise, built for one person. **4.** *Brit.* A very broad, light barge. **— v.t. & v.i. ·ried, ·ry·ing** To transport in or use a wherry. [Origin unknown]

whet (hwet)   *v.t.* **whet·ted, whet·ting 1.** To sharpen, as a knife, by friction. **2.** To make more keen or eager; excite; stimulate, as the appetite. **— n. 1.** The act of whetting. **2.** Something that whets. [OE *hwettan*] **— whet′ter** *n.*

wheth·er (hweth/ər)   *conj.* **1.** If it be the case that: used to introduce an indirect question, often with the negative being implied: Tell me *whether* you are considering our plan. **2.** In case; in either case: as the first alternative, followed by a correlative *or*, or *or whether*: *Whether* it rains or (*whether* it) snows, the roads become very slippery. **3.** Either: *Whether* by luck or sheer determination, he will probably succeed. **— whether or no** In any case. [OE *hwæther*]

whet·stone (hwet/stōn′)   *n.* A fine-grained stone for whetting knives, axes, etc.

whew (hwōō, hwyōō)   *interj.* An exclamatory sound, expressive of amazement, dismay, relief, admiration, etc.

whey (hwā)   *n.* A clear, straw-colored liquid that separates from the curd when milk is curdled, as in making cheese. [OE *hwæg*] **— whey′ey, whey′ish** *adj.*

whey·face (hwā/fās′)   *n.* A pale, sallow face; also, a person having such a face. **— whey′faced′** *adj.*

which (hwich)   *pron. & adj.* **1.** What particular person or thing or collection of persons or things of a certain class: *Which* (or *which* apples) do you want? We don't know *which* (or *which* story) to believe. **2.** The thing designated; it: a relative pronoun whose antecedents refer now only to animals or objects; that: the story *which* we preferred. ◆ *Which* sometimes has an entire clause or sentence as its antecedent: He raised his hand, *which* surprised me. See also usage note under WHO. [OE *hwilc*]

which·ev·er (hwich/ev′ər)   *pron.* One or another (of two or of several). **— adj.** No matter which. Also **which/so·ev′er.**

whiff (hwif)   *n.* **1.** Any sudden or slight gust or puff of air. **2.** A gust or puff of odor: a *whiff* of onions. **3.** A single expulsion or inhalation of breath or smoke from the mouth; puff. **— v.t. 1.** To drive or blow with a whiff or puff. **2.** To exhale or inhale in whiffs. **3.** To smell or sniff. **4.** To smoke, as a pipe. **— v.i. 5.** To blow or move in whiffs or puffs. **6.** To exhale or inhale whiffs. [Prob. ult. imit.] **— whiff′er** *n.*

whif·fet (hwif′it)   *n. Informal* **1.** A trifling, useless person. **2.** A small, snappish dog. [? Dim. of WHIFF]

whif·fle (hwif′əl)   *v.* **·fled, ·fling** *v.i.* **1.** To blow with puffs or gusts; shift about, as the wind. **2.** To vacillate; veer. **— v.t. 3.** To blow or dissipate with or as with a puff. [Freq. of WHIFF] **— whif′fler** *n.* **— whif′fler·y** *n.*

whif·fle·tree (hwif′əl-trē′)   *n.* A horizontal crossbar to which the ends of the traces of a harness are attached: also called *singletree, swingletree, whippletree.* [Var. of WHIPPLETREE]

Whig (hwig)   *n.* **1.** An American colonist who supported the Revolutionary War in the 18th century in opposition to the Tories. **2.** A member of an American political party (1834–1855) formed in opposition to the Democratic Party, and in 1856 succeeded by the Republican Party. **3.** In England, a member of a more or less liberal political party in the 18th and 19th centuries, opposed to the Tories and later known as the Liberal Party. **— adj.** Consisting of or supported by Whigs. [< ? *Whiggamore* < dial. E (Scottish) < *Whig*, a cry to urge on a horse + *mere* horse] **— Whig′ger·y** *n.* **— Whig′gish** *adj.* **— Whig′gish·ly** *adv.* **— Whig′gish·ness** *n.* **— Whig′gism** *n.*

while (hwīl)   *n.* **1.** A short time; also, any period of time: Stay and rest a *while*. **2.** Time or pains expended on a thing: only in the phrase **worth while** or **worth one's while. — between whiles** From time to time. **— the while** At the same time. **— conj. 1.** During the time that; as long as. **2.** At the same time that; although: *While* he found fault, he also praised. **3.** Whereas: This man is short, *while* that one is tall. ◆ This sense is widely used and is generally considered standard, although some authorities still disapprove of it. **— v.t. whiled, whil·ing** To cause (time) to pass lightly and pleasantly: usu. with *away*. [OE *hwil*]

whiles (hwīlz)   *Archaic or Dial. adv.* **1.** Occasionally. **2.** In the meantime. **— conj.** While; during the time that.

whi·lom (hwī/ləm)   *Archaic adj.* Former. **— adv.** Formerly. [OE *hwilum* at times, dative pl. of *hwīl* a while]

whilst (hwīlst)   *conj. Chiefly Brit.* While.

whim (hwim)   *n.* A sudden or unexpected notion or fanciful idea; caprice. [Short for earlier *whim-wham* trifle]

whim·per (hwim′pər)   *v.i.* **1.** To cry or whine with plaintive broken sounds. **— v.t. 2.** To utter with a whimper. **— n.** A low, broken, whining cry; whine. [Imit.] **— whim′per·er** *n.* **— whim′per·ing** *n.* **— whim′per·ing·ly** *adv.*

whim·si·cal (hwim′zi-kəl)   *adj.* **1.** Having eccentric ideas; capricious. **2.** Oddly constituted; fantastic; quaint. **— whim·si·cal′i·ty** (-kal′ə-tē) *n.* **— whim′si·cal·ly** *adv.* **— whim′si·cal·ness** *n.*

whim·sy (hwim′zē)   *n. pl. ·sies* **1.** A whim. **2.** Quaint, fanciful humor, as in a literary work. Also **whim′sey.**

whin (hwin) *n.* Furze. [Prob. < Scand.]

whine (hwīn) *v.* **whined, whin·ing** *v.i.* 1. To utter a low, plaintive sound expressive of grief, peevishness, etc. 2. To complain in a tiresome or childish way. — *v.t.* 3. To utter with a whine. — *n.* The act or sound of whining. [OE *hwīnan*] — **whin′er** *n.* — **whin′ing·ly** *adv.* — **whin′y** *adj.*

whin·ny (hwin′ē) *v.* **·nied, ·ny·ing** *v.i.* 1. To neigh, esp. in a low or gentle way. — *v.t.* 2. To express with a whinny. — *n. pl.* **·nies** A neigh, esp. if low and gentle. [< WHINE]

whip (hwip) *v.* **whipped** or **whipt, whip·ping** *v.t.* 1. To strike with a lash, rod, strap, etc. 2. To punish by striking thus; flog. 3. To drive or urge with lashes or blows: with *on, up, off,* etc. 4. To strike in the manner of a whip: The wind *whipped* the trees. 5. To beat, as eggs or cream, to a froth. 6. To seize, move, jerk, throw, etc., with a sudden motion: with *away, in, off, out,* etc. 7. In fishing, to make repeated casts upon the surface of (a stream, etc.). 8. To wrap (rope, cable, etc.) with light line so as to prevent chafing or wear. 9. To wrap or bind about something. 10. To sew, as a flat seam, with a loose overcast or overhand stitch. 11. *U.S. Informal* To defeat; overcome. — *v.i.* 12. To go, come, move, or turn suddenly and quickly: with *away, in, off, out,* etc. 13. To thrash about in a manner suggestive of a whip: pennants *whipping* in the wind. — **to whip up** 1. To excite; arouse. 2. *Informal* To prepare quickly, as a meal. — *n.* 1. An instrument consisting of a lash attached to a handle, used for driving draft animals or for administering punishment. 2. One who handles a whip expertly, as a driver. 3. A stroke, blow, or lashing motion with, or as with, a whip. 4. In politics, a member of a legislative body, as Congress or Parliament, appointed unofficially to enforce the discipline and look after the interests of his party. 5. A dish or dessert containing cream or eggs and usu. fruit, whipped to a froth. [ME *wippen*] — **whip′per** *n.*

whip·cord (hwip′kôrd′) *n.* 1. A strong, hard-twisted or braided hempen cord, used in making whiplashes. 2. A worsted fabric with a pronounced diagonal rib.

whip hand 1. The hand that wields the whip in riding or driving. 2. An instrument or means of mastery; advantage.

whip·lash (hwip′lash′) *n.* The lash of a whip.

whiplash injury An injury to the neck caused by a sudden jolting, as in an automobile collision.

whip·per·snap·per (hwip′ər·snap′ər) *n.* A pretentious but insignificant person, esp. a young one. [? Extension of *whipsnapper* a cracker of whips]

whip·pet (hwip′it) *n.* A small, swift breed of dog, probably a cross between a greyhound and a terrier, used esp. in racing and coursing. [Dim. of WHIP]

whip·ping (hwip′ing) *n.* 1. The act of one who or that which whips; esp., a flogging. 2. Cord or other material used to whip or lash parts together.

whipping boy Anyone who receives punishment deserved by another; scapegoat.

whipping post The post to which those sentenced to flogging are secured.

whip·ple·tree (hwip′əl·trē′) *n.* A whiffletree. [Prob. < WHIP]

whip·poor·will (hwip′ər·wil) *n.* A small nocturnal bird allied to the goatsuckers, common in the eastern U.S. [Imit. of its reiterated cry]

whip·saw (hwip′sô′) *n.* A long, narrow, tapering saw, mounted in a wooden frame. — *v.t.* **·sawed, ·sawed** or **·sawn, ·saw·ing** 1. To saw with a whipsaw. 2. To get the best of (an opponent) in spite of every effort he makes.

whip·stitch (hwip′stich′) *v.t.* To sew or gather with overcast stitches. — *n.* A stitch made in this way.

whip·stock (hwip′stok′) *n.* The handle of a whip.

whir (hwûr) *v.t. & v.i.* **whirred, whir·ring** To fly, move, or whirl with a buzzing sound. — *n.* 1. A whizzing, swishing sound, as that caused by the sudden rising of birds. 2. Confusion; bustle. Also *Brit.* **whirr.** [Prob. < Scand.]

whirl (hwûrl) *v.i.* 1. To turn or revolve rapidly, as about a center. 2. To turn away or aside quickly. 3. To move or go swiftly. 4. To have a sensation of spinning: My head *whirls.* — *v.t.* 5. To cause to turn or revolve rapidly. 6. To carry or bear along with a revolving motion: The wind *whirled* the dust into the air. — *n.* 1. A swift rotating or revolving motion. 2. Something whirling. 3. A state of confusion; turmoil. 4. A rapid succession of events, social activities, etc. 5. *Informal* A brief drive or trip. 6. *Informal* A try. [Prob. < ON *hvirfla* to revolve] — **whirl′er** *n.*

whirl·i·gig (hwûr′lə·gig′) *n.* 1. Any toy or small device that revolves rapidly on an axis. 2. A merry-go-round. 3. Anything that moves in a cycle. 4. A whirling motion. [< *whirly* (< WHIRL) + obs. *gig,* a whirling toy]

whirl·pool (hwûrl′pool′) *n.* 1. A vortex where water moves with a whirling motion, as from the meeting of two currents. 2. Anything resembling the motion of a whirlpool.

whirl·wind (hwûrl′wind′) *n.* 1. A funnel-shaped column of air, with a rapid, upward spiral motion and moving forward on the surface of the land or sea. 2. Anything resembling a whirlwind, as rotary motion or violent activity. — *adj.* Extremely swift or impetuous: a *whirlwind* courtship.

whish (hwish) *v.i.* To move with a swishing, whistling sound. — *n.* A swishing sound. [Imit.]

whisk (hwisk) *v.t.* 1. To bear along or sweep with light movements, as of a small broom: often with *away* or *off.* 2. To cause to move with a quick sweeping motion. 3. *Chiefly Brit.* To beat with a quick movement, as eggs, etc. — *v.i.* 4. To move quickly and lightly. — *n.* 1. A sudden, sweeping movement. 2. A little broom or brush. 3. *Chiefly Brit.* A small culinary instrument for rapidly whipping (cream, etc.) to a froth. [Prob. < Scand.]

whisk·broom (hwisk′broom′, -broom′) *n.* A small, short-handled broom for brushing clothing, etc.

whisk·er (hwis′kər) *n.* 1. *pl.* The hair that grows on the sides of a man's face, as distinguished from that on his lips, chin, and throat; loosely, the beard or any part of the beard. 2. A hair from the whiskers or beard. 3. One of the long, bristly hairs on the sides of the mouth of some animals, as cats and rodents. — **whisk′ered, whisk′er·y** *adj.*

whis·key (hwis′kē) *n. pl.* **·keys** 1. An alcoholic liquor obtained by the distillation of certain fermented grains, as rye, barley, corn, etc., and containing about 40 to 50 percent of alcohol. 2. A drink of whiskey. — *adj.* Pertaining to or made of whiskey. Also **whis′ky.** [Short for *usquebaugh* < Irish, water of life < *uisge* water + *beatha* life]

whis·per (hwis′pər) *n.* 1. A low, soft, breathy voice. 2. A low, rustling sound. 3. *Phonet.* The sound produced by the passage of breath through the partially closed glottis. 4. A whispered utterance; secret communication; hint; insinuation. — *v.i.* 1. To speak in a whisper. 2. To talk cautiously or furtively; plot or gossip. 3. To make a low, rustling sound. — *v.t.* 4. To utter in a whisper. 5. To speak to in a whisper. [OE *hwisprian*] — **whis′per·er** *n.* — **whis′per·ing** *adj. & n.* — **whis′per·ing·ly** *adv.*

whispering campaign A deliberate spreading of rumors in order to discredit a person or group.

whist[1] (hwist) *n.* A game of cards, the forerunner of bridge, played by four persons. [Alter. of earlier *whisk*]

whist[2] (hwist) *interj.* Hush! be still! — *adj.* Silent or quiet.

whis·tle (hwis′əl) *v.* **·tled, ·tling** *v.i.* 1. To make a musical tone, usu. shrill, by sending the breath through the teeth or through a small orifice formed by contracting the lips. 2. To emit a sharp, shrill cry, as some birds and animals. 3. To cause a sharp, shrill sound by swift passage through the air, as wind, etc. 4. To blow or sound a whistle. — *v.t.* 5. To produce (a tune) by whistling. 6. To call, manage, or direct by whistling. 7. To send or move with a whistling sound. — **to whistle for** To go without; fail to get. — *n.* 1. A device for producing a shrill tone by forcing a current of air, etc., through a pipe or tube with a narrowed aperture, or against a thin edge. 2. A whistling sound. 3. The act of whistling. 4. *Slang* The mouth and throat: to wet one's *whistle.* [OE *hwistle* shrill pipe]

whis·tler (hwis′lər) *n.* 1. One who or that which whistles. 2. Any of various birds so called from the noise of their wings in flight. 3. A radio signal of very low frequency generated by atmospheric electricity.

whistle stop *U.S. Informal* A small town, where a train stops only on signal. — **whis′tle-stop** (hwis′əl·stop′) *adj.*

whit (hwit) *n.* The smallest particle; speck: not a *whit* abashed. [Var. of *wight* < OE *wiht* a certain amount]

white (hwīt) *adj.* **whit·er, whit·est** 1. Having the color produced by reflection of all of the visible solar spectrum, as from a bed of new-fallen snow. 2. Light or comparatively light in color. 3. Bloodless; ashen: *white* with rage. 4. Very fair; blond. 5. Silvery or gray. 6. Snowy. 7. Habited in white clothing: *white* nuns. 8. Not intentionally wicked; not harmful: a *white* lie. 9. Free from spot or stain; innocent. 10. Incandescent: *white* heat. 11. Blank; unmarked by ink. 12. Belonging to a racial group characterized by light-colored skin; esp., Caucasian. 13. Of, pertaining to, or controlled by white men: the *white* power structure. 14. *Informal* Fair and honorable; honest. 15. Designating any of various wines ranging in color from pale yellow to deep amber. — *n.* 1. The color seen when light is reflected without sensible absorption of any of the visible rays of the spectrum; the color of new-fallen snow. 2. The state or condition of being white. 3. *Biol.* The white or light-colored part of something, as the albumen of egg or the white part of the eyeball. 4. A white or light-colored thing, as a white fabric, a white pigment, etc. 5. *pl.* A white uniform or outfit: a sailor's summer *whites.* 6. A member of the so-called white race. — *v.t.* **whit·ed, whit·ing** To make white; whiten. [OE *hwīt*] — **white′ly** *adv.* — **white′ness** *n.*

white ant   Loosely, a termite.

white·bait (hwīt′bāt′)   n.   The young of various fishes, esp. of sprat and herring, netted in great quantities and much esteemed in Europe as a delicacy.

white bear   The polar bear.

white birch   1. Birch.   2. The common European birch, having an ash-colored bark.

white·cap (hwīt′kap′)   n.   A wave with a crest of foam.

white cedar   1. An evergreen tree of the pine family, growing in moist places along the Atlantic coast: also called *cypress*.   2. Its soft, easily worked wood.

white clover   A common variety of clover, with white flowers.

white coal   Water considered as a source of power.

white-collar (hwīt′kol′ər)   adj.   Designating workers, jobs, attitudes, etc., associated with clerical, professional, and other nonmanual occupations.

whit·ed sepulcher (hwī′tid)   A hypocrite. *Matt*. xxiii 27.

white elephant   1. A rare, pale gray variety of Asian elephant held sacred by the Burmese and Siamese.   2. Anything rare but expensive to keep.   3. Any burdensome possession.

white-faced (hwīt′fāst′)   adj.   1. Pallid in countenance; pale.   2. Having a white mark or spot on the face or front of the head, as a horse.   3. Having a white facing or exposed surface.

white·fish (hwīt′fish′)   n.   pl. **·fish** or **·fish·es**   1. Any of various food fishes of North America, living mostly in lakes, some species of which are called chubs.   2. Any of various other fish having a silvery appearance, as the beluga.   3. A tropical marine food fish of California.

white flag   1. A flag of truce.   2. A white flag or cloth hoisted as a signal of surrender during a battle.

White Friar   A Carmelite friar: so called from the color of his cloak.

white gold   An alloy of gold with a white metal, usu. nickel and zinc, sometimes palladium and platinum.

white goods   Household linens, such as sheets, towels, etc.

White·hall (hwīt′hôl)   1. A street in Westminster, London, where a number of government offices are located.   2. The British government.

white heat   1. The temperature at which a body becomes incandescent.   2. Great excitement, intense emotion, etc.

white horse   A wave crested with foam; whitecap.

white-hot (hwīt′hot′)   adj.   1. Exhibiting the condition of white heat.   2. *Informal* Extremely angry.

White House, The   1. The official residence of the President of the U.S., at Washington, D.C., a white, colonial style building: officially called the *Executive Mansion*.   2. The executive branch of the U.S. government.

white lead   A heavy, white, poisonous mixture of lead carbonate and lead oxide, used as a pigment and in some medicinal ointments for burns.

white lie   See under LIE.

white-liv·ered (hwīt′liv′ərd)   adj.   1. Having a pale and unhealthy look.   2. Base; cowardly.

white man   1. A person belonging to a racial group characterized by light-colored skin.   2. A male member of the so-called white race.

white man's burden   The alleged duty of the white peoples to spread culture among the so-called backward peoples of the world: phrase originated by Rudyard Kipling.

white matter   *Anat.* The portion of the brain and spinal cord composed mainly of medullated nerve fibers, giving it a white appearance.

white meat   The light-colored meat or flesh of animals, as veal or the breast of turkey.

whit·en (hwīt′n)   v.t. & v.i.   To make or become white; blanch; bleach.   **— whit′en·er** n.

   — Syn. *Whiten, bleach,* and *blanch* mean to make nearly or completely white or colorless. *Whiten* implies overlay with a white paint or polish, while *bleach* and *blanch* refer to removal of color by sunlight, chemical agents, etc. Industrial products are *bleached,* while foodstuffs are *blanched.*

white oak   1. A North American oak of the eastern U.S. with long leaves having from five to nine entire, rounded lobes.   2. Any of several related species.   3. The wood of any species of white oak.

white pine   1. A pine widely distributed in eastern North America, with soft, bluish green leaves in clusters of five. The cone and tassel of this tree are the State emblem of Maine.   2. The light, soft wood of this tree.   3. Any of several similar species of pine.

white plague   *Pathol.* Tuberculosis, esp. of the lungs.

white poplar   A large, rapidly growing Old World tree, often planted in the U.S. for shade or for its ornamental green and silvery white leaves.

white potato   The common potato.

white race   The Caucasian ethnic division of mankind.

white rat   One of a special breed of albino Norway rats much used in biological and medical experimentation.

White Russian   Byelorussian.

white sale   A sale of sheets, towels, etc., at reduced prices.

white sauce   A sauce made of butter, flour, milk, etc., used for vegetables, meats, and fish.

white slave   A girl forced into or held in prostitution.   **— white-slave** (hwīt′slāv′) adj.

white slavery   The business or practice of forced prostitution.   **— white slaver**

white supremacy   The doctrine arising from the belief that the white race is superior to the Negro race and that the latter must therefore be kept in an inferior economic and social position.   **— white su·prem·a·cist** (sə-prem′ə-sist)

white-tailed deer (hwīt′tāld′)   A common North American deer, having a moderately long tail white on the underside: also called *Virginia deer.*

white-throat·ed sparrow (hwīt′thrō′tid)   A common North American sparrow, with a white patch on the throat.

white tie   1. A white bow tie, worn with men's formal evening attire.   2. A swallowtail coat and its correct accessories.

white·wash (hwīt′wosh′, -wôsh′)   n.   1. A mixture of slaked lime and water, sometimes with salt, whiting, and glue added, used for whitening walls, etc.   2. *Slang* A covering up or glossing over of reprehensible actions or inefficiencies, esp. of a political figure; also, a suppression of adverse evidence, as in a legal matter.   3. *Informal* A failure to score in a game.   — v.t.   1. To coat with whitewash.   2. *Slang* To gloss over; hide.   3. *Informal* In sports, to defeat without allowing the losing side to score.   **— white′wash′er** n.

white water   *U.S. & Canadian*   Rapids in a river.

white whale   The beluga.

whith·er (hwith′ər)   *Archaic & Poetic adv.*   1. To what or which place? Where?   2. To what point, end, extent, etc.?   — conj.   To which or what place, end, etc.   [OE *hwider*]

whith·er·so·ev·er (hwith′ər·sō·ev′ər)   adv. *Archaic*   To whatever place.

whit·ing (hwī′ting)   n.   A pure white chalk, powdered and washed, used in making putty and whitewash, as a pigment, and for polishing.

whit·ish (hwī′tish)   adj.   Somewhat white or, esp., very light gray.   **— whit′ish·ness** n.

whit·low (hwit′lō)   n.   *Pathol.*   An inflammatory tumor, esp. on the terminal phalanx of a finger, seated between the epidermis and true skin; a felon.   [ME *whitflaw*]

Whit·mon·day (hwit′mun′dē, -dā)   n.   The Monday next following Whitsunday, observed in England as a holiday. Also **Whit-Monday, Whit′sun-Mon′day.**

Whit·sun (hwit′sən)   n.   Whitsunday: frequently used in combination: *Whitsun-week.*

Whit·sun·day (hwit′sun′dē, -dā, hwit′sən-dā′)   n.   Pentecost (def. 1).   [OE *Hwīta Sunnandæg,* lit., white Sunday]

Whit·sun·tide (hwit′sən-tīd′)   n.   The week that begins with Whitsunday, esp. the first three days.   Also **Whitsun Tide.**

whit·tle (hwit′l)   v.   **·tled, ·tling**   v.t.   1. To cut or shave bits from (wood, a stick, etc.).   2. To make or shape by carving or whittling.   3. To reduce or wear away by or as by paring a little at a time: with *down, off, away,* etc.   — v.i.   4. To whittle wood, usu. as an aimless diversion.   [Alter. of ME *thwitel* < OE *thwītan* to cut]   **— whit′tler** n.

whit·tlings (hwit′lingz)   n.pl.   The fine chips and shavings made by a whittler.

whiz (hwiz)   v.   **whizzed, whiz·zing**   v.i.   1. To make a hissing and humming sound while passing through the air.   2. To move or pass with such a sound.   — v.t.   3. To cause to whiz.   — n.   pl. **whiz·zes**   1. A whizzing sound.   2. *Slang* Any person or thing of extraordinary excellence or ability.   Also **whizz.**   [Imit.]

who (hōō)   pron. *possessive case* **whose**; *objective case* **whom**   1. Which or what person or persons: *Who* said that? I know *who* he is.   2. That; a relative pronoun: used when the antecedent refers to a human being.   3. He, she, or they that; whoever: *Who* steals my purse steals trash.   **— as who should say** As if one should say.   [OE *hwā*]

   ◆ In modern usage, *who* as a relative is applied only to persons, *which* only to animals or to inanimate objects, *that* to persons or things indiscriminately. The use of *whom* as an interrogative pronoun in initial position, as in *Whom* did you see?, is supported by some grammarians, but the more natural *Who* did you see? *Who* did you give the book to? are in wider use and are now considered acceptable. However, when used after a verb or preposition, *whom* is still required, as in To *whom* did you give it? You saw *whom*?

whoa (hwō)   interj.   Stop! stand still!   [Var. of HO]

who·dun·it (hōō·dun′it)   n.   *Informal* A type of mystery fiction or dramatic production that challenges the reader or spectator to detect the perpetrator of a crime.

who·ev·er (hōō·ev′ər)   pron.   Any one without exception; any person who.

whole (hōl)   adj.   1. Containing all the parts necessary to make up a total, entire.   2. Having all the essential or original parts unbroken and uninjured; intact.   3. In or having regained sound health; hale.   4. Constituting the full extent, amount, quantity, etc.; total; entire. **5.** Having the same parents; full, as opposed to *half*: a *whole* brother. **6.** *Math.* Integral. **— as a whole** Completely; altogether. **— on the whole** Taking everything into consideration. **— out of whole cloth** Fabricated; made up, without foundation in truth or fact. **—** *n.* **1.** All the parts or elements entering into and making up a thing; totality. **2.** An organization of parts making a unity or system; an organism. [OE *hāl*] **— whole'ness** *n.*

whole blood   Blood as taken directly from the body, esp. that used in transfusions.

whole·heart·ed (hōl'här'tid) *adj.* Done or experienced with earnestness, sincerity, etc.; earnest. **— whole'heart'·ed·ly** *adv.* **— whole'heart'ed·ness** *n.*

whole hog   *Slang* The whole of anything; completeness. **— to go the whole hog** *Slang* To do something thoroughly; become involved without reservation.

whole milk   Milk containing all its constituents.

whole note   *Music* A note having a time value equal to one half of a breve: also, *Chiefly Brit.*, *semibreve*.

whole number   *Math.* An integer.

whole·sale (hōl'sāl') *n.* The selling of goods in large bulk or quantity, esp. for resale: distinguished from *retail*. **—** *adj.* **1.** Pertaining to, involving, or engaged in the sale of goods at wholesale. **2.** Made or done on a large scale or indiscriminately: *wholesale* murder. **—** *adv.* **1.** In bulk or quantity. **2.** Indiscriminately. **—** *v.t.* & *v.i.* **·saled, ·sal·ing** To sell at wholesale. [ME < *by hole sale* in large quantities] **— whole'sal'er** *n.*

whole·some (hōl'səm) *adj.* **1.** Tending to promote health; salubrious; healthful: *wholesome* air or food. **2.** Favorable to virtue and well-being; beneficial: *wholesome* entertainment. **3.** Indicative or characteristic of health: *wholesome* red cheeks. **4.** Safe; free from danger or risk. [ME *holsum*] **— whole'some·ly** *adv.* **— whole'some·ness** *n.*

whole tone   *Music* A tone (def. 3b).

whole-wheat (hōl'hwēt') *adj.* Made from wheat grain and bran.

who'll (hōōl) **1.** Who will. **2.** Who shall.

whol·ly (hō'lē, hōl'lē) *adv.* **1.** Completely; totally. **2.** Exclusively; only.

whom (hōōm) *pron.* The objective case of WHO.

whom·ev·er (hōōm'ev'ər), **whom·so** (hōōm'sō'), **whom·so·ev·er** (hōōm'sō·ev'ər) Objective cases of WHOEVER, WHOSO, etc.

whoop (hōōp, hwōōp, hwŏōp) *v.i.* **1.** To utter loud cries, as of excitement, rage, or exultation. **2.** To hoot, as an owl. **3.** To make a loud, gasping inspiration, as after a paroxysm of coughing. **—** *v.t.* **4.** To utter with a whoop or whoops. **5.** To call, urge, chase, etc., with whoops; hoot. **— to whoop up** *Slang* To arouse enthusiasm in or for. **— to whoop it (or things) up** *Slang* **1.** To make noisy revelry. **2.** To arouse enthusiasm. **—** *n.* The cry, shout, or sound of one who or that which whoops. **— not worth a whoop** *Informal* Not worth anything. **—** *interj.* An exclamation of joy, enthusiasm, etc. [ME *whope*]

whoop·ee (hwōō'pē, hwōōp'ē) *interj.* & *n.* An exclamation of joy, excitement, etc. **— to make whoopee** To have a noisy, festive time. [< WHOOP]

whoop·er (hōō'pər, hwōō'pər, hwōōp'r) *n.* **1.** One who or that which whoops. **2.** A large Old World swan: so called from its loud cry.

whoop·ing cough (hōō'ping, hōōp'ing) *Pathol.* A contagious respiratory disease of bacterial origin chiefly affecting children, marked in its final stage by violent coughing.

whop (hwop) *Informal n.* A blow or fall, or the resulting noise. **—** *v.* **whopped, whop·ping** *v.t.* **1.** To strike or beat. **2.** To defeat convincingly. **—** *v.i.* **3.** To drop or fall suddenly; flop. [Prob. imit.]

whop·per (hwop'ər) *n.* *Informal* Something large or remarkable; esp., a big falsehood.

whop·ping (hwop'ing) *adj.* Unusually large; great.

whore (hôr, hōr) *n.* A prostitute. **—** *v.i.* **whored, whor·ing** **1.** To have illicit sexual intercourse, esp. with a prostitute. **2.** To be a whore. [OE *hōre*, prob. < ON *hōra*]

whore·house (hôr'hous', hōr'-) *n.* A house of prostitution.

whore·mas·ter (hôr'mas'tər, -mäs'-, hōr'-) *n.* *Archaic* **1.** A procurer. **2.** A man who has intercourse with whores. Also **whore·mon·ger** (hôr'mung'gər, -mong'-, hōr'-).

whor·ish (hôr'ish, hōr'ish) *adj.* Characteristic of a whore; lewd. **— whor'ish·ly** *adv.* **— whor'ish·ness** *n.*

whorl (hwûrl, hwôrl) *n.* **1.** The flywheel of a spindle. **2.** *Bot.* A set of leaves, etc., on the same plane with one another, distributed in a circle. **3.** *Zool.* A turn or volution, as of a spiral shell. **4.** Any of the convoluted ridges of a fingerprint. [ME *wharwyl*, *whor·whil*]

WHORL (def. 2)

whorled (hwûrld, hwôrld) *adj.* Furnished with or arranged in whorls.

whor·tle·ber·ry (hwûr'təl·ber'ē) *n.* *pl.* **·ries 1.** A European variety of blueberry. **2.** Its blue-black fruit. Also called *bilberry*. [< OE *horta* + BERRY]

whose (hōōz) The possessive case of WHO and often of WHICH. [ME < OE *hwæs*, altered by analogy with nominative form *hwo*]

whose·so·ev·er (hōōz'sō·ev'ər) Possessive case of WHOSOEVER.

who·so (hōō'sō) *pron.* Whoever; any person who. [Reduced form of OE *swā hwā swā*]

who·so·ev·er (hōō'sō·ev'ər) *pron.* Any person whatever; who; whoever.

why (hwī) *adv.* **1.** For what cause, purpose, or reason? wherefore? **2.** The reason or cause for which: I don't know *why* he went. **3.** Because of which; for which: I know no reason *why* he went. **—** *n.* *pl.* **whys 1.** An explanatory cause; reason; cause. **2.** A puzzling problem; riddle; enigma. **—** *interj.* An introductory expletive, sometimes denoting surprise. ◆ The *why* in the expression *the reason why*, though sometimes condemned as a redundancy, is commonly used in standard written English. [OE *hwȳ*, *hwī*, instrumental case of *hwæt* what]

wich (wich) *n.* The wych-elm.

wich-elm (wich'elm') See WYCH-ELM.

wick (wik) *n.* A wand of loosely twisted or woven fibers, as in a candle or lamp, acting by capillary attraction to convey oil or other illuminant to a flame. [OE *wēoce*]

wick·ed (wik'id) *adj.* **1.** Evil in principle and practice; vicious; sinful; depraved. **2.** Mischievous; roguish. **3.** Noxious; pernicious. **4.** Troublesome; painful. **5.** *Informal* Done with great skill: a *wicked* game. [ME, alter. of *wikke*, *wicke*] **— wick'ed·ly** *adv.* **— wick'ed·ness** *n.*

wick·er (wik'ər) *adj.* Made of twigs, osiers, etc. **—** *n.* **1.** A pliant young shoot or rod; twig; osier. **2.** Wickerwork. [Prob. < Scand.]

wick·er·work (wik'ər·wûrk') *n.* A fabric or texture, as a basket, made of woven twigs, osiers, etc.; basketwork.

wick·et (wik'it) *n.* **1.** A small door or gate subsidiary to or made within a larger entrance. **2.** A small opening in a door. **3.** A small sluice gate in a canal lock or at the end of a millrace. **4.** In cricket: **a** An arrangement of three stumps set near together, with two bails laid over the top. **b** The place at which the wicket is set up. **c** The right or turn of each batsman at the wicket. **d** The playing pitch between the wickets: a fast *wicket*. **e** An inning that is not finished or not begun. **5.** In croquet, any one of the arches, usu. of wire, through which the ball must be hit. [< AF *wiket*, OF *guichet*, prob. < Gmc.]

wick·et·keep·er (wik'it·kē'pər) *n.* In cricket, the fielder stationed behind the wicket that is being bowled at.

wide (wīd) *adj.* **wid·er, wid·est 1.** Having relatively great extent between sides; broad. **2.** Extended far in every direction; ample; spacious: a *wide* expanse. **3.** Having a specified degree of width or breadth: an inch *wide*. **4.** Distant from the desired or proper point by a great extent of space; remote; wild: *wide* of the mark. **5.** Having intellectual breadth; liberal: a man of *wide* views. **6.** Fully open; expanded or extended: *wide* eyes. **7.** Comprehensive; inclusive: *wide* learning. **8.** Loose; roomy: *wide* breeches. **—** *n.* **1.** In cricket, a ball bowled too far over or on either side of the wicket to be within the batsman's reach. **2.** Breadth of extent; also, a broad, open space. **—** *adv.* **1.** To a great distance; extensively. **2.** Far from the mark. **3.** To the greatest extent; fully open. [OE *wīd*] **— wide'ly** *adv.* **— wide'ness** *n.*

wide-an·gle lens (wīd'ang'gəl) *Photog.* A type of lens permitting an angle of view wider than that of the ordinary lens.

wide-a·wake (wīd'ə·wāk') *adj.* **1.** Fully awake. **2.** Marked by vigilance and alertness; keen.

wide-eyed (wīd'īd') *adj.* With the eyes wide open, as in wonder or surprise.

wid·en (wīd'n) *v.t.* & *v.i.* To make or become wide or wider. **— wid'en·er** *n.*

wide-o·pen (wīd'ō'pən) *adj.* **1.** Opened wide. **2.** *Informal* Remiss in the enforcement of laws that regulate various forms of vice, as gambling, etc.: a *wide-open* city.

wide-screen (wīd'skrēn') *adj.* Designating a motion-picture process using an elongated screen designed to accommodate various systems of projection beyond 35 mm.

wide·spread (wīd'spred') *adj.* **1.** Extending over a large space or territory. **2.** Occurring, accepted, etc., among many people; general: a *widespread* belief. Also **wide-spread'**, **wide'spread'ing**.

widge·on (wij'ən) *n.* Any of various river ducks with short bill and wedge-shaped tail. [Cf. MF *vigeon* wild duck]

wid·ow (wid'ō) *n.* **1.** A woman who has lost her husband by death and has not remarried. **2.** In some card games, an additional hand dealt to the table; also, a kitty. **3.** *Printing* An incomplete line of type at the top of a page or column. — *v.t.* **1.** To make a widow of; deprive of a husband: usu. in the past participle. **2.** To deprive of something desirable; bereave. [OE *widewe, wuduwe*]

wid·ow·er (wid′ō-ər) *n.* A man whose wife is dead, and who has not married again. [ME < OE *widewe* widow]

wid·ow·hood (wid′ō-hŏŏd) *n.* The state or period of being a widow, or, rarely, of being a widower.

widow's mite A small but selfless contribution from one who can hardly afford it. *Mark xii* 42.

widow's peak A hairline growing in a V-shaped point from the forehead.

widow's walk A railed observation area built on the roof of a home near the sea giving the observer a clear view of incoming vessels: also called *captain's walk*.

width (width) *n.* **1.** Dimension or measurement of an object taken from side to side, and at right angles to the length. **2.** The state or fact of being wide; breadth. **3.** Something that has width; esp., one of the several pieces of material used in making a garment. [< WIDE]

width·wise (width′wīz′) *adv.* In the direction of the width; from side to side. Also **width′way′** (-wā′), **width′ways′**.

wield (wēld) *v.t.* **1.** To handle, as a weapon or instrument, esp. with full command and effect. **2.** To exercise (authority, power, etc.). [Fusion of OE *wealdan* to rule and OE *wieldan* to conquer] — **wield′a·ble** *adj.* — **wield′er** *n.*

wield·y (wēl′dē) *adj.* **wield·i·er, wield·i·est** Easily handled or managed; manageable.

wie·ner (wē′nər) *n. U.S.* A kind of sausage, often shorter than a frankfurter, made of beef and pork. Also **wie·nie** (wē′nē), **wie·ner·wurst** (wē′nər-wûrst′, *Ger.* vē′nər-vōōrst′). [Short for G *Wiener-wurst* Vienna sausage]

Wie·ner schnit·zel (vē′nər schnit′səl) A breaded veal cutlet, seasoned or garnished in any of several ways. [< G *Wiener* Viennese + *schnitzel* cutlet, dim. of *schnitz* slice]

wife (wīf) *n., pl.* **wives** (wīvz) **1.** A woman joined to a man in lawful wedlock. ◆ Collateral adjective: *uxorial.* **2.** *Archaic* A grown woman; adult female: now usu. in combination or in certain phrases: *housewife,* old *wives'* tales. — **to take (a woman) to wife** To marry (a woman). [OE *wīf*] — **wife′dom, wife′hood** *n.* — **wife′ly** *adj.*

wig (wig) *n.* An artificial covering of hair for the head. — *v.t.* **wigged, wig·ging 1.** *Rare* To furnish with a wig or wigs. **2.** *Brit. Informal* To censure severely; berate or scold, esp. in public. [Short for PERIWIG]

wig·ging (wig′ing) *n. Brit. Informal* A rebuke; a scolding.

wig·gle (wig′əl) *v.t. & v.i.* **·gled, ·gling** To move or cause to move quickly and irregularly from side to side; squirm; wriggle. — *n.* A wiggling motion. — **to get a wiggle on** *Slang* To hurry up. [? < MLG *wiggelen*] — **wig′gly** *adj.*

wig·gler (wig′lər) *n.* **1.** One who or that which wiggles. **2.** The larva of a mosquito.

wig·wag (wig′wag′) *v.t. & v.i.* **·wagged, ·wag·ging** To send (a message) by moving hand flags, lights, etc., according to a code. — *n.* The act of wigwagging; also, a message so sent. [< dial. E *wig* to wiggle + WAG¹] — **wig′wag′ger** *n.*

wig·wam (wig′wom, -wôm) *n.* **1.** A dwelling or lodge of the North American Indians, commonly a conical framework of poles covered with bark, hides, etc. **2.** *U.S. Informal* A public building used for political gatherings, mass meetings, etc. [< Algonquian (Ojibwa) *wigwaum*, lit., their dwelling]

wild (wīld) *adj.* **1.** Inhabiting the forest or open field; not domesticated or tamed; living in a state of nature. **2.** Growing or produced without care or culture; not cultivated: *wild* flowers. **3.** Being without civilized inhabitants or cultivation; waste: *wild* prairies. **4.** Living in a primitive or savage way; uncivilized: the *wild* men of Borneo. **5.** Boisterous; unruly. **6.** Immoral; orgiastic: a *wild* affair. **7.** Affected with or originating violent disturbances; stormy; turbulent: a *wild* night, a *wild* crowd. **8.** Showing reckless want of judgment; extravagant: a *wild* speculation. **9.** Fantastically irregular or disordered; odd in arrangement or effect: a *wild* imagination, *wild* dress. **10.** Eager and excited, as by reason of joy, fear, desire, etc. **11.** Excited to frenzy or distraction; roused to fury or desperation; crazed or crazy: to drive one *wild*. **12.** Being or going far from the proper course or from the mark aimed at; erratic: a *wild* ball, a *wild* guess. **13.** In some card games, having its value arbitrarily determined by the dealer or holder. — **wild and wooly** *Informal* Untamed; reckless; boisterous. — *n. Often pl.* An uninhabited or uncultivated place; wilderness: the *wilds* of China. — **the wild** The wilderness; also, the free, natural, wild life: the call of the *wild.* — *adv.* In a wild manner; without control. [OE *wilde*] — **wild′ly** *adv.* — **wild′ness** *n.*

wild boar The native hog of continental Europe, southern Asia, North Africa, and formerly of Great Britain.

wild carrot An herb having filmy white flowers and from which the cultivated carrot is derived; also called *Queen Anne's lace.*

wild·cat (wīld′kat′) *n.* **1.** An undomesticated feline carnivore of Europe, resembling the domestic cat, but larger and stronger. **2.** The lynx. **3.** One of several other felines, as the ocelot and serval. **4.** An aggressive quick-tempered person, esp. a woman. **5.** An unattached locomotive and its tender, used on special work, as to haul trains, etc. **6.** A successful oil well drilled in an area previously unproductive. **7.** A tricky or unsound business venture; esp. a worthless mine: also **wildcat mine.** Also **wild cat.** — *adj.* **1.** Unsound; risky; esp. financially unsound or risky. **2.** Illegal; made or carried on without official sanction or authorization. **3.** Not running on a schedule; also, running wild or without control, as a railroad train or engine. — *v.t. & v.i.* **·cat·ted, ·cat·ting** To drill for oil in (an area not known to be productive). — **wild′cat′ting** *n. & adj.*

wildcat strike A strike unauthorized by regular union procedure.

wild·cat·ter (wīld′kat′ər) *n.* **1.** A promoter of mines of doubtful value. **2.** One who develops oil wells in unproved territory. **3.** One who manufactures illicit whisky.

wilde·beest (wīld′bēst, wil′də-; *Du.* vil′də-bāst) *n.* A gnu. [< Afrikaans < Du. *wild* wild + *beeste* beast]

wil·der·ness (wil′dər-nis) *n.* **1.** An uncultivated, uninhabited, or barren region. **2.** A waste, as of an ocean. **3.** A multitudinous and confusing collection: a *wilderness* of curiosities. [ME < OE *wilddēor* wild beast + -NESS]

wild·fire (wīld′fīr′) *n.* **1.** A raging, destructive fire: now generally in the phrase **to spread like wildfire.** **2.** A composition of flammable materials, or the flame produced by it, very hard to put out, as Greek fire. **3.** A phosphorescent luminousness; ignis fatuus.

wild·flow·er (wīld′flou′ər) *n.* Any uncultivated flowering plant; also, the flower of such a plant. Also **wild flower.**

wild·fowl (wīld′foul′) *n., pl.* **·fowl** (*esp. for def. 2*), or **fowls 1.** A wild game bird, esp. a wild duck or goose. **2.** *pl.* Wild game birds collectively. Also **wild fowl.**

wild-goose chase (wīld′gōōs′) **1.** Pursuit of the unknown or unattainable. **2.** Any strenuous and fruitless task.

wild·life (wīld′līf′) *n.* Wild animals, trees, and plants collectively.

wild oat 1. *Usually pl.* An uncultivated grass, esp. a common species of Europe. **2.** *pl.* Indiscretions of youth: usu. in the expression **to sow one's wild oats.**

wild pansy The pansy in its uncultivated state; esp., a European species from which the garden pansy is derived.

wild pitch In baseball, a misplay charged to the pitcher for allowing a runner to advance by throwing a pitch that the catcher does not and could not be expected to catch.

wild rice The grain of a tall aquatic grass of North America, esteemed as a table delicacy.

wild turkey A large North American turkey formerly ranging east of the Rocky Mountains from southern Canada to Florida and Mexico, and first domesticated in Mexico, now rare in the wild state.

Wild West The western U.S., esp. in its early period of Indian fighting, lawlessness, etc.

wild·wood (wīld′wŏŏd′) *n.* Natural forest land.

wile (wīl) *n.* **1.** An act or a means of cunning deception; also, any beguiling trick or artifice. **2.** Craftiness; cunning. — *v.t.* **wiled, wil·ing 1.** To lure, beguile, or mislead. **2.** To pass divertingly, as time: usu. with *away*: by confusion with *while.* [ME *wil*, prob. < Scand.]

wil·ful (wil′fəl), **wil·ful·ly, wil·ful·ness** See WILLFUL, etc.

will¹ (wil) *n.* **1.** The power of conscious, deliberate action; the faculty by which the mind makes choices and acts to carry them out. **2.** The act or experience of exercising this faculty. **3.** Strong determination; also, self-control. **4.** That which has been resolved or determined upon; a purpose. **5.** Power to dispose of a matter arbitrarily; discretion. **6.** *Law* The legal declaration of a person's intentions as to the disposal of his estate after his death. **7.** A conscious inclination toward any end or course; a wish. **8.** A request or command. — **at will** As one pleases. — *v.* **willed, will·ing** *v.t.* **1.** To decide upon; choose. **2.** To resolve upon as an action or course; determine to do. **3.** To give, devise, or bequeath by a will. **4.** To control, as a hypnotized person, by the exercise of will. **5.** *Archaic* To have a wish for. — *v.i.* **6.** To exercise the will. [OE *willa*] — **will′a·ble** *adj.*

will² (wil) *v.* Present: *3rd person sing.:* will; *Archaic 2nd person sing.* **wilt;** past: **would;** *Archaic 2nd person sing.* **would·est** or **wouldst.** An auxiliary verb used with the infinitive without *to,* or elliptically without the infinitive, to express: **1.** Futurity: They *will* arrive by dark. **2.** Willingness or disposition: Why *will* you not tell the truth? **3.** Capability or capacity: The ship *will* survive any storm. **4.** Custom or habit: The hen *will* sit for hours and brood. **5.** *Informal* Probability or inference: I expect this *will* be the main street. ◆ See usage note under SHALL. — *v.t. & v.i.* To wish or have a wish; desire: As you will. [OE *willan*]

willed (wild) *adj.* Having a will, esp. one of a given character: usu. in combination: *self-willed.*

will·ful (wil′fəl) *adj.* **1.** Bent on having one's own way; headstrong. **2.** Resulting from the exercise of one's own will; voluntary; intentional. Also, *esp. Brit.*, *wilful*. [Cf. OE *wilfullíce* willfully] **— will′ful·ly** *adv.* **— will′ful·ness** *n.*

wil·lies (wil′ēz) *n.pl. Slang* Nervousness; jitters: with *the*. [? < WILLY-NILLY; with ref. to a state of indecision]

will·ing (wil′ing) *adj.* **1.** Having the mind favorably inclined or disposed. **2.** Answering to demand or requirement; compliant. **3.** Gladly proffered or done; hearty. **4.** Of or pertaining to the faculty or power of choice; volitional. **— will′ing·ly** *adv.* **— will′ing·ness** *n.*

will-o'-the-wisp (wil′ə-thə-wisp′) *n.* **1.** Ignis fatuus. **2.** Any elusive or deceptive object. **— *adj.*** Deceptive; fleeting; misleading. [*Will with the wisp*]

wil·low (wil′ō) *n.* **1.** Any of various shrubs and trees, having generally smooth branches and often long, slender, pliant, and sometimes pendent branchlets. **2.** The soft white wood of the willow. **3.** *Informal* Something made of willow wood, especially a baseball or cricket bat. **— *adj.*** Of or pertaining to the willow; made of willow wood. [OE *welig*] **— wil′low·ish** *adj.*

wil·low·y (wil′ō-ē) *adj.* **1.** Abounding in willows. **2.** Having supple grace of form or carriage.

will power Ability to control oneself; determination; strength or firmness of mind.

wil·ly-nil·ly (wil′ē-nil′ē) *adj.* Having no decisiveness; uncertain; irresolute. **— *adv.*** Willingly or unwillingly. [Earlier *will I, nill I* whether I will or not]

wilt¹ (wilt) *v.i.* **1.** To lose freshness; droop or become limp, as a flower that has been cut or that has not been watered. **2.** To lose energy and vitality; become faint or languid: We *wilted* under the hot sun. **3.** To lose courage or spirit; subside suddenly. **— *v.t.*** **4.** To cause to droop or wither. **5.** To cause to lose vitality and energy. **— *n.*** **1.** The act of wilting. **2.** Languor; faintness. **3.** *Bot.* Any of several plant diseases marked by a wilting of the leaves. [Prob. dial. var. of obs. *welk* to wither]

wilt² (wilt) Archaic second person singular, present tense of WILL²: used with *thou*.

Wil·ton (wil′tən) *n.* A kind of carpet having the loops of the pile cut, thus giving it a velvety texture. [after *Wilton*, England, where first made] Also **Wilton carpet, Wilton rug.**

Wilt·shire (wilt′shir) *n.* One of a breed of long-horned sheep. [after *Wiltshire*, England, where raised]

Wiltshire cheese A variety of Cheddar cheese.

wi·ly (wī′lē) *adj.* **-li·er, -li·est** Full of or characterized by wiles; sly; cunning. **— wi′li·ly** *adv.* **— wi′li·ness** *n.*

wim·ble (wim′bəl) *n.* Anything that bores a hole, esp. if turned by hand, as a brace and bit. **— *v.t.*** **·bled, ·bling** To bore or pierce, as with a wimble. [< AF, OF *quimbel* < MLG *wiemel*]

wim·ple (wim′pəl) *n.* **1.** A cloth, as of linen or silk, wrapped in folds around the neck close under the chin and over the head, exposing only the face, formerly worn as a protection by women outdoors, and still by nuns. **2.** *Scot.* A fold; plait; also, a curve; a winding turn, as in a river or road. **— *v.* ·pled, ·pling** *v.t.* **1.** To cover or clothe with a wimple; veil. **2.** To make or fold into plaits, as a veil. **3.** To cause to move with slight undulations; ripple. **— *v.i.*** **4.** To lie in plaits or folds. **5.** To ripple. [OE *wimpel*]

win (win) *v.* **won, won, win·ning** *v.i.* **1.** To gain a victory; prevail, as in a contest. **2.** To succeed in an effort or endeavor. **3.** To succeed in reaching or attaining a specified end or condition; get: often with *across, over, through*, etc.: The fleet *won* through the storm. **— *v.t.*** **4.** To be successful in; gain victory in: to *win* an argument. **5.** To gain in competition or contest: to *win* the blue ribbon. **6.** To gain by effort, persistence, etc.: to *win* fame. **7.** To obtain the good will or favor of: often with *over*. **8.** To secure the love of; gain in marriage: He wooed and *won* her. **9.** To succeed in reaching; attain. **10.** To make (one's way), esp. with effort. **11.** To capture; take possession of. **12.** To earn or procure, as a living. **— to win out** *Informal* To succeed to the fullest extent. **— *n.*** **1.** A victory; success. **2.** Profit; winnings. **3.** The first position in a race. [OE *winnan* to contend]

wince (wins) *v.i.* **winced, winc·ing** To shrink back or start aside, as from a blow or pain; flinch. **— *n.*** The act of wincing. [< AF *wenchier*] **— winc′er** *n.*

winch (winch) *n.* **1.** A windlass used for hoisting, as on a crane, having usu., one or more hand cranks geared to a drum. **2.** A crank with a handle, used to impart motion to a grindstone or the like. [OE *wince*] **— winch′er** *n.*

Win·ches·ter (win′ches·tər) *n.* Originally, a repeating rifle, first produced in 1866: now a trade name applied to other firearms. [after Oliver F. *Winchester*, 1810–80, U.S. industrialist]

wind¹ (wind; *for n., also poetic* wīnd) *n.* **1.** Any movement of air, esp., a natural movement. **2.** Any powerful or de-structive wind; a tornado; hurricane. **3.** Air in motion by artificial means. **4.** Air pervaded by a scent: The deer got *wind* of the hunter. **5.** A suggestion or intimation: to get *wind* of a plot. **6.** The power of breathing; breath. **7.** Idle chatter; also, vanity. **8.** *pl.* The wind instruments of an orchestra. **9.** The gaseous product of indigestion; flatulence. **— in the wind** Impending; astir; afoot. **— in the wind's eye** Directly opposed to the point from which the wind blows. **— to break wind** To expel gas through the anus. **— to get wind of** To receive a hint of. **— to have in the wind** To be on the track or scent of. **— to have the wind up** To be apprehensive or alarmed. **— to sail close to the wind** **1.** To sail in a direction as near as possible to that from which the wind blows. **2.** To come near to the limit, as of a danger line. **3.** To live economically. **— *v.t.*** **1.** To follow by scent; to catch a scent of on the wind. **2.** To exhaust the breath of, as by running. **3.** To allow to recover breath by resting. **4.** To expose to the wind, as in ventilating. [OE]

wind² (wīnd) *v.* **wound** (*Rare* **wind·ed**), **wind·ing** *v.t.* **1.** To coil (thread, rope, etc.) around some object or fixed core; twine; wreathe. **2.** To cover with something by coiling or wrapping: to *wind* a spool with thread. **3.** To renew the motion of, as a clock, by coiling a spring, etc. **4.** To cause to turn and twist. **5.** To make (one's way) by a twisting course. **6.** To introduce carefully or deviously; insinuate: He *wound* himself into my confidence. **7.** To raise or hoist, as by means of a capstan or windlass. **— *v.i.*** **8.** To move in a twisting course; meander. **9.** To coil or twine about some central object or core. **10.** To move in a circular or spiral course. **11.** To proceed carefully, subtly, or deviously. **— to wind up 1.** To coil or wind round and round. **2.** To excite; arouse. **3.** To bring to conclusion or settlement: He *wound up* his affairs. **4.** In baseball, to swing the arm preparatory to pitching. **5.** To hoist. **— *n.*** The act of winding, or the condition of being wound; a winding, turn, or twist. [OE *windan*] **— wind′a·ble** *adj.* **— wind′er** *n.*

wind³ (wīnd, wind) *v.t.* **wind·ed or wound, wind·ing 1.** To blow, as a horn; sound. **2.** To give (a call or signal), as with a horn. [< WIND¹]

wind·age (win′dij) *n.* **1.** The rush of air caused by the rapid passage of an object, as a projectile or a railway train. **2.** Deflection of an object, as a bullet, from its natural course due to wind pressure. **3.** *Naut.* The surface offered to the wind by a vessel.

wind·bag (wind′bag′) *n. Informal* A wordy talker.

wind blown (wind′blōn′) *adj.* **1.** Blown by the wind. **2.** Bobbed and brushed forward: said of a woman's hair.

wind-borne (wind′bôrn′, -bōrn′) *adj.* Carried or transported by the wind, as pollen.

wind·break (wind′brāk′) *n.* Something, as a hedge or fence, that protects from or breaks the force of the wind.

Wind·break·er (wind′brā′kər) *n.* A sports jacket with fitted waistband: a trade name. Also **wind′·break′er.**

wind-bro·ken (wind′brō′kən) *adj.* Asthmatic; broken-winded: said of a horse.

wind·ed (win′did) *adj.* Breathless, as from exercise.

wind·fall (wind′fôl′) *n.* **1.** A piece of unexpected good fortune; esp., a sudden and substantial financial profit. **2.** Something, as ripening fruit, brought down by the wind.

wind·flaw (wind′flô) *n.* A sharp gust of wind.

wind·flow·er (wind′flou′ər) *n.* The anemone. [Trans. of Gk. *anemōnē* anemone < *anemos* the wind]

wind gauge A scale on a gunsight to allow for windage (def. 2). Also **wind gage.**

wind·hov·er (wind′huv′ər) *n. Brit.* The kestrel, a bird.

wind·ing (wīn′ding) *n.* **1.** The act or condition of one who or that which winds; a spiral turning or coiling. **2.** A bend or turn, or a series of them. **— *adj.*** **1.** Turning spirally about an axis or core. **2.** Having bends or lateral turns. **— wind′ing·ly** *adv.*

winding sheet (wīn′ding) The sheet that wraps a corpse.

wind instrument (wind) A musical instrument whose sounds are produced by vibrations of air injected by the lungs or by bellows. Compare ORGAN, WOODWINDS, etc.

wind·jam·mer (wind′jam′ər) *n.* **1.** *Naut.* A merchant sailing vessel. **2.** A member of its crew.

wind·lass (wind′ləs) *n.* Any of several devices for hauling or lifting, esp. one consisting of a drum or barrel on which the hoisting rope winds, and turned by means of cranking. **— *v.t. & v.i.*** To raise or haul with a windlass. [< ME ON < *vinda* wind + *ass* beam]

wind·mill (wind′mil′) *n.* **1.** A mill that operates by the action of the wind against adjustable slats, wings, or sails attached to a horizontal axis and that transmit motion to a pump, millstone, or the like. **2.** An imaginary wrong, evil, or foe: usu. in the phrase **to fight** (or **tilt at**) **windmills**, in allusion to Don Quixote's combat with windmills, which he mistook for giants. [< WIND¹ + MILL¹]

win·dow (win′dō) *n.* **1.** An opening in the wall of a building to admit light and air, commonly equipped with movable sashes that enclose one or more panes of glass. **2.** A sash. **3.** A windowpane. **4.** Anything resembling or suggesting a window. — *v.t.* To provide with a window or windows. [< ON < *vindr* wind + *auga* eye]

window box A box, generally long and narrow, along a window ledge or sill, for growing plants.

win·dow-dress·ing (win′dō-dres′ing) *n.* **1.** The act or art of arranging merchandise attractively in store windows; also, the goods so displayed. **2.** An appearance, statement, etc., that gives an unduly favorable impression of reality. — **win′dow-dress′er** *n.*

win·dow·pane (win′dō-pān′) *n.* A single sheet of glass for a window. Also **window pane.**

window seat A seat in the recess of a window.

window shade A flexible shade or screen, usu., mounted on a spring roller, used to regulate light at a window.

win·dow-shop (win′dō-shop′) *v.i.* **-shopped, -shop·ping** To look at goods shown in store windows without buying them. — **win′dow-shop′per** *n.*

wind·pipe (wind′pīp′) *n.* The trachea.

wind·row (wind′rō′) *n.* **1.** A long ridge or pile of hay or grain raked together preparatory to building into cocks. **2.** A row of Indian corn made by setting two rows together. **3.** A wind-swept line of dust, surf, leaves, etc. — *v.t.* To rake or shape into a windrow. — **wind′row′er** *n.*

wind·shield (wind′shēld′) *n.* A transparent screen, usu. of glass, attached in front of the occupants of an automobile as protection against wind and weather.

wind·sock (wind′sok′) *n. Meteorol.* A large conical bag open at both ends, mounted on a pivot and indicating the direction of wind by the current of air that blows through it. Also **wind sleeve.**

Wind·sor chair (win′zər) A wooden chair, common in the 18th century, typically with a spindle back, slanting legs, and a flat or slightly depressed seat.

Windsor tie A wide, soft necktie knotted loosely in a double bow, usu. of black silk cut on the bias.

wind·storm (wind′stôrm′) *n.* A violent wind, usu. with little or no precipitation.

wind tunnel *Aeron.* A large cylindrical structure in which the aerodynamic properties of airplane models, airfoils, etc., can be observed under the effects of artificially produced winds of varying velocities.

wind-up (wīnd′up′) *n.* **1.** The act of concluding or closing. **2.** A final act or part; conclusion. **3.** In baseball, the swing of the arm preparatory to pitching the ball.

wind·ward (wind′wərd) *adj.* **1.** Of the direction from which the wind is blowing. **2.** Being on the side exposed to the wind. — *n.* The direction from which the wind blows. — *adv.* In the direction from which the wind blows. Opposed to *leeward.*

wind·y (win′dē) *adj.* **wind·i·er, wind·i·est 1.** Of, consisting of, or abounding in wind; stormy; tempestuous. **2.** Exposed to the wind; wind-swept. **3.** Suggestive of wind; boisterous; swift. **4.** Producing, due to, or troubled with gas in the stomach or intestines; flatulent. **5.** Bombastic; pompous. [OE *windig*] — **wind′i·ly** *adv.* — **wind′i·ness** *n.*

wine (wīn) *n.* **1.** The fermented juice of the grape, commonly used as a beverage and in cooking. **2.** The fermented juice of some other fruit as the elderberry, or of a plant. **3.** A dark purplish red, the color of certain wines. — *v.* **wined, win·ing** *v.t.* **1.** To entertain with wine. — *v.i.* **2.** To drink wine. [OE < L *vinum*]

wine·bib·bing (wīn′bib′ing) *adj.* Addicted to excessive drinking of wine. — *n.* The habitual, excessive drinking of wine. — **wine′bib′ber** *n.*

wine cellar 1. A storage place for wines; also, the wines stored. **2.** Any stock of wines.

wine-col·ored (wīn′kul′ərd) *adj.* Having the color of certain red wines; dark purplish red.

wine·glass (wīn′glas′, -gläs′) *n.* A small goblet for drinking wine.

wine-grow·er (wīn′grō′ər) *n.* One who cultivates a vineyard and makes wine. — **wine′grow′ing** *adj. & n.*

wine·press (wīn′pres′) *n.* An apparatus or a place where the juice of grapes is expressed. Also **wine′press′er.**

win·er·y (wī′nər-ē) *n. pl.* **·er·ies 1.** An establishment for making wine. **2.** A room for fining and storing wines.

Wine·sap (wīn′sap) *n.* A U.S. variety of red winter apple.

wine-skin (wīn′skin′) *n.* The skin of a domestic quadruped kept as entire as possible and made into a tight bag for containing wine, much used in the Orient.

wing (wing) *n.* **1.** An organ of flight; esp., one of the anterior movable pair of appendages of a bird or bat, homologous with the forelimbs of vertebrates but adapted for flight. **2.** An analogous organ in insects and some other animals. **3.** Anything resembling or suggestive of a wing, as in form or function. **4.** Flight or passage by or as by wings; also, the means or act of flying: to take *wing.* **5.** Something

regarded as conferring the power of swift motion or flight: on *wings* of song. **6.** Either of two extremist groups in a political or other organization: the left *wing.* **7.** *Archit.* A part attached to a side; esp., an extension of a building. **8.** *Aeron.* One of the main sustaining surfaces of an airplane. **9.** One of the sides of a stage; also, a piece of scenery for the side. **10.** *Mil.* Either division of a military force on either side of the center. **11.** An analogous formation in certain sports, as football. **12.** A side section of something that shuts or folds, as a screen, etc. **13.** A tactical unit of the U.S. Air Force, larger than a group. **14.** *Slang* An arm; esp., in baseball. **15.** One of the pectoral fins of a flying fish. **16.** *Anat.* An ala: a *wing* of the nose. **17.** *Bot.* Any thin membranous or foliaceous expansion of an organ, as of certain stems, seeds, etc. — **Syn.** See FACTION. — **on** (or **upon**) **the wing 1.** In flight. **2.** Departing; also, journeying. — **to take wing** To fly away. — **under one's wing** Under one's protection. — *v.t.* **1.** To pass over or through in flight. **2.** To accomplish by flying: the bird *winged* its way south. **3.** To enable to fly. **4.** To cause to go swiftly; speed. **5.** To transport by flight. **6.** To provide with wings for flight. **7.** To supply with a side body or part. **8.** To wound (a bird) in a wing. **9.** To disable by a minor wound. — *v.i.* **10.** To fly; soar. [< ON *vængr*] — **wing′less** *adj.*

wing chair A large armchair, upholstered throughout, with high back and side pieces designed as protection from drafts.

wing commander In the Royal, Royal Canadian, and other Commonwealth air forces, a commissioned officer ranking next below group captain. See table at GRADE.

winged (wingd; *for defs. 1, 2, & 3, also poetic* wing′id) *adj.* **1.** Having wings. **2.** Passing swiftly; soaring; lofty; rapt. **3.** Alive with creatures having wings. **4.** *Informal* Wounded or disabled in or as in the wing or arm.

wing·spread (wing′spred′) *n.* The distance between the tips of the fully extended wings of a bird, insect, or airplane.

wink (wingk) *v.i.* **1.** To close and open the eye or eyelids quickly. **2.** To draw the eyelids of one eye together, as in conveying a hint or making a sign. **3.** To pretend not to see: usu. with *at.* **4.** To emit fitful gleams; twinkle. — *v.t.* **5.** To close and open (the eye or eyelids) quickly. **6.** To move, force, etc., by winking: with *away, off,* etc. **7.** To signify or express by winking. — *n.* **1.** The act of winking. **2.** The time necessary for a wink. **3.** A twinkle; gleam. **4.** A hint conveyed by winking. — **forty winks** *Informal* A short nap. [OE *wincian* to close the eyes]

wink·er (wing′kər) *n.* **1.** One who winks. **2.** A blinder for a horse.

win·ner (win′ər) *n.* One who or that which wins.

win·ning (win′ing) *adj.* **1.** Successful in achievement, esp., in competition. **2.** Charming; attractive; winsome. — *n.* **1.** The act of one who wins. **2.** *Usu. pl.* That which is won; esp., money won in gambling. — **win′ning·ly** *adv.* — **win′ning·ness** *n.*

win·now (win′ō) *v.t.* **1.** To separate (grain, etc.) from the chaff by means of wind or a current of air. **2.** To blow away (the chaff) thus. **3.** To examine; analyse minutely; sift. **4.** To select or eliminate; distinguish; sort: often with *out.* **5.** To blow upon; cause to flutter. **6.** To beat or fan (the air) with the wings. **7.** To scatter by blowing; disperse. — *v.i.* **8.** To separate grain from chaff. **9.** To fly; flap. — *n.* **1.** Any device used in winnowing grain. **2.** The act of winnowing; also, a vibrating motion caused by a current of air. [OE < *wind* the wind] — **win′now·er** *n.*

win·some (win′səm) *adj.* Having a winning appearance or manner; pleasing; attractive. [OE < *wyn* joy] — **win′some·ly** *adv.* — **win′some·ness** *n.*

win·ter (win′tər) *n.* **1.** The coldest season of the year, occurring between autumn and spring. ◆ Collateral adjectives: *hibernal.* **2.** A period of time marked by lack of life, coldness, or cheerlessness. **3.** *Chiefly Poetic* A year of life: a man of ninety *winters.* — *v.i.* **1.** To pass the winter. — *v.t.* **2.** To care for, feed, or protect during the winter: to *winter* animals. — *adj.* **1.** Of or taking place in winter; hibernal. **2.** Suitable to or characteristic of winter. [OE] — **win′ter·er** *n.* — **win′ter·less** *adj.*

win·ter·green (win′tər-grēn′) *n.* **1.** A small evergreen plant of North America, bearing a cluster of bell-shaped flowers, and aromatic oval leaves that yield a colorless volatile oil (**oil of wintergreen**), used as a flavor. **2.** Any of various low evergreen herbs.

win·ter·ize (win′tə-rīz′) *v.t.* **·ized, ·iz·ing** To prepare or equip (engines, etc.) for winter.

win·ter·kill (win′tər-kil′) *v.t. & v.i.* To die or kill by exposure to extreme cold: said of plants and grains.

win·try (win′trē) *adj.* **·tri·er, ·tri·est** Belonging to winter; cold; frosty. Also **win′ter·y** (-tər-ē). [OE *wintrig*] — **win′tri·ly** (-trə-lē) *adv.* — **win′tri·ness** *n.*

win·y (wī′nē) *adj.* **win·i·er, win·i·est** Having the taste or qualities of wine.

wipe (wīp) *v.t.* **wiped, wip·ing 1.** To subject to slight friction or rubbing, usu. with some soft, absorbent material. **2.**

To remove by rubbing lightly; brush: usu. with *away* or *off*. **3.** To move, apply, or draw for the purpose of wiping: He *wiped* his hand across his brow. **— to wipe out** To remove or destroy utterly. **—** *n.* **1.** The act of wiping or rubbing. **2.** *Slang* A blow; a swipe. **3.** *Slang* A handkerchief. **4.** *Slang* A jeer. [OE *wīpian*] **— wip′er** *n.*

wire (wīr) *n.* **1.** A slender rod, strand, or thread of ductile metal. **2.** Something made of wire, as a fence, a snare, etc. **3.** A telegraph or telephone cable. **4.** The telegraph system as a means of communication. **5.** A telegram. **6.** *pl.* A secret means of exerting influence. **— under the wire** Just in time or barely within the limits. **— under wire** Fenced. **—** *v.* **wired, wir·ing** *v.t.* **1.** To fasten with wire. **2.** To furnish or equip with wiring. **3.** To transmit or send by electric telegraph: to *wire* an order. **4.** To send a telegram to. **5.** To place on wire, as beads. **6.** To catch, as a rabbit, with a snare of wire. **—** *v.i.* **7.** To telegraph. [OE *wīr*]

wire-draw (wīr′drô′) *v.t.* **-drew, -drawn, -draw·ing** **1.** To draw, as a metal rod, through a series of holes of diminishing diameter to produce a wire. **2.** To treat (a subject) with excessive subtlety or overrefinement. **— wire′-draw′er** *n.*

wire gauge **1.** A gauge for measuring the diameter of wire, usu. a round plate with calibrated numbered slots on its periphery, or a long graduated plate with a slot of diminishing width. **2.** A standard system of sizes for wire.

wire-haired terrier (wīr′hârd′) A fox terrier having a wiry coat. Also **wire′hair′** (-hâr′).

wire·less (wīr′lis) *adj.* **1.** Having no wire or wires. **2.** *Brit.* Radio. **—** *n.* **1.** The wireless telegraph or telephone system, or a message transmitted by either. **2.** *Brit.* Radio. **—** *v.t. & v.i. Brit.* To communicate (with) by wireless telegraphy.

wireless telegraphy Telegraphy without wires, the message being transmitted through space by electromagnetic waves.

wireless telephony The transmission and reception of vocal messages by radio.

Wire·pho·to (wīr′fō′tō) *n. pl.* **·tos** An apparatus and method for transmitting and receiving photographs by wire: a trade name. Also **wire′pho′to.**

wire-pull·er (wīr′pŏŏl′ər) *n.* **1.** One who pulls wires, as of a puppet. **2.** One who uses secret means to control others or gain his own ends; an intriguer. **— wire′pull′ing** *n.*

wire recorder *Electronics* A device for recording sounds by electromagnetic registration on a fine moving wire, the impulses being reconverted to sound as the magnetized wire is passed through a receiver.

wire service A news agency that collects and distributes news to subscribing newspapers, radio stations, etc.

wire-spun (wīr′spun′) *adj.* **1.** Drawn out to form a wire. **2.** Spun or drawn out too fine; overrefined.

wire·tap (wīr′tap) *v.* **·tapped, ·tap·ping** *v.t.* **1.** To intercept (information) by means of wiretapping. **—** *v.i.* **2.** To engage in wiretapping. **—** *n.* Wiretapping. [Back formation < WIRETAPPING] **— wire′tap′per** *n.*

wire·tap·ping (wīr′tap′ing) *n.* The act, process, or practice of tapping telephone or telegraph wires for the purpose of secretly securing information: also called *wiretap.*

wire·work (wīr′wûrk) *n.* **1.** Small articles made of wire cloth. **2.** Wire fabrics in general.

wir·ing (wīr′ing) *n.* An entire system of wire installed for the distribution of electric power.

wir·y (wīr′ē) *adj.* **wir·i·er, wir·i·est** **1.** Having great resisting power; thin, but tough and sinewy: said of persons. **2.** Like wire; stiff. **— wir′i·ly** *adv.* **— wir′i·ness** *n.*

wis·dom (wiz′dəm) *n.* **1.** The power of true and right discernment; also, conformity to the course of action dictated by such discernment. **2.** Good practical judgment; common sense. **3.** A high degree of knowledge; learning. **4.** A wise saying. [OE *wīsdōm* < *wīs* wise]

Wisdom of Solomon A book of the Old Testament Apocrypha, consisting of a hymn in praise of wisdom, ascribed by tradition to Solomon.

wisdom tooth The last molar tooth on either side of the upper and lower jaws in man, usu. appearing between the 17th and 22d year. For illus. see TOOTH. **— to cut one's wisdom teeth** To acquire mature judgment.

wise¹ (wīz) *adj.* **wis·er, wis·est** **1.** Possessed of wisdom; having sound judgment. **2.** Sagacious; shrewd. **3.** Marked by wisdom; sensible. **4.** Having great learning; erudite. **5.** *Informal* Aware of; onto: *wise* to his motives. **6.** *U.S. Slang* Arrogant or sarcastic in manner; also, impudent. **— to get wise** *Slang* To know the true facts. **—** *v.t.* **wised, wis·ing** *Slang* To make cognizant of; inform. **— to wise up** *Slang* To make or become aware, informed, or sophisticated. [OE *wīs*] **— wise′ly** *adv.* **— wise′ness** *n.*

wise² (wīz) *n.* Way of doing; manner; method: chiefly in the phrases **in any wise, in no wise,** etc. [OE *wīse* manner]

-wise *suffix of adverbs* In a (specified) way or manner: *no-*

wise, likewise: often equivalent to *-ways.* [OE *wīse* manner]

◆ The suffix *-wise,* long considered archaic, has recently come back into fashion, and is now freely added to nouns, with the general meaning "with reference to": *Weather-wise,* it will probably snow. Such compounds often add no further information to a statement, and should be used with discretion.

wise·a·cre (wīz′ā′kər) *n.* **1.** One who affects great wisdom. **2.** A wise man; sage. [< MDu. *wijssegpher* soothsayer]

wise·crack (wīz′krak′) *Slang n.* A smart or supercilious remark. **—** *v.i.* To utter a wisecrack. **— wise′crack′er** *n.*

wish (wish) *n.* **1.** A desire or longing, usu. for some definite thing. **2.** An expression of such a desire; petition. **3.** Something wished for. **—** *v.t.* **1.** To have a desire or longing for; want: We *wish* to be sure. **2.** To desire a specified condition or state for (a person or thing): I *wish* this day were over. **3.** To invoke upon or for someone: I *wished* him good luck. **4.** To bid: to *wish* someone good morning. **5.** To request or entreat; also, to command: I *wish* you would be quiet. **—** *v.i.* **6.** To have or feel a desire; yearn; long: usu. with *for.* **7.** To make or express a wish. **— to wish on** To impose (something or someone) on a person. [OE *wýscan*]

wish·bone (wish′bōn′) *n.* The forked bone formed by the united clavicles in many birds. [from the old belief that when pulled apart by two persons, each making a wish, the one who gets the longer part will have his wish fulfilled]

wish·ful (wish′fəl) *adj.* Having a wish or desire; full of longing. **— wish′ful·ly** *adv.* **— wish′ful·ness** *n.*

wishful thinking Thinking characterized by a conscious or unconscious attempt to impose upon reality conditions that, if true, would make it more pleasant or tolerable.

wish·y-wash·y (wish′ē-wosh′ē, -wôsh′ē) *adj. Informal* **1.** Thin; diluted, as liquor. **2.** Lacking character or resolution; indecisive; weak.

wisp (wisp) *n.* **1.** A small bunch, as of hay, straw, or hair. **2.** A small bit; a mere indication: a *wisp* of vapor. **3.** Will-o'-the-wisp. **—** *v.t.* **1.** To dress, brush, or groom with a wisp or whisk. **2.** To fold and lightly twist into a wisp or wisplike form; crumple. [ME *wisp, wips*] **— wisp′y** *adj.*

wisp·ish (wis′pish) *adj.* Like or having the nature of a wisp.

wist (wist) Past tense and past participle of WIT².

wis·te·ri·a (wis-tir′ē-ə) *n.* Any of various woody twining shrubs of the bean family, with clusters of blue, purple, or white flowers. Also **wis·tar′i·a** (-târ′ē-ə). [after Caspar *Wistar,* 1761–1818, U.S. anatomist]

wist·ful (wist′fəl) *adj.* **1.** Wishful; longing. **2.** Musing; pensive. [Appar. < obs. *wistly* intently; infl. in form by WISHFUL] **— wist′ful·ly** *adv.* **— wist′ful·ness** *n.*

wit¹ (wit) *n.* **1.** The power of knowing or perceiving; intelligence; ingenuity. **2.** The power or faculty of rapid and accurate observation; the power of comprehending and judging. **3.** *pl.* The faculties of perception and understanding: to use one's *wits.* **4.** *pl.* The mental faculties with regard to their state of balance: out of her *wits.* **5.** The ready perception and happy expression of unexpected or amusing relations between apparently incongruous ideas. **6.** One who has a keen perception of the incongruous or ludicrous and makes skillful use of it in writing or speaking; also, a clever conversationalist. **7.** Significance; meaning. **— at one's wits' end** At the limit of one's devices and resources. [OE]

wit² (wit) *v.t. & v.i.* **wist, wit·ting** Present indicative: **I wot,** thou **wost,** he **wot,** we, you, they **wite(n)** *Archaic* To be or become aware (of); learn; know. **— to wit** That is to say; namely: used to introduce a detailed statement or explanation, especially in legal documents. [OE *witan* to know]

witch¹ (wich) *n.* **1.** A woman who practices sorcery; one having supernatural powers, esp. to work evil, and usu. by association with evil spirits or the devil. **2.** An ugly, malignant old woman; a hag. **3.** A bewitching or fascinating woman or girl. **—** *v.t.* **1.** To work an evil spell upon. **2.** To effect by witchcraft. **3.** To fascinate or bewitch; enchant. [OE *wicce* witch, fem. of *wicca* wizard]

witch² (wich) *n.* The wych-elm. [OE < *wīcan* to yield]

witch·craft (wich′kraft′, -kräft′) *n.* **1.** The practices or powers of witches or wizards, esp. when regarded as due to dealings with evil spirits or the devil: also called *black magic.* **2.** An instance of such practices. **3.** Extraordinary influence or fascination; witchery.

witch doctor **1.** Among certain primitive peoples of Africa, a medicine man skilled in detecting witches and counteracting evil spells. **2.** Any medicine man or magician. **3.** One who professes to heal or cure by sorcery; a hex.

witch-elm (wich′elm′) See WYCH-ELM.

witch·er·y (wich′ər-ē) *n. pl.* **·er·ies** **1.** Witchcraft. **2.** Power to charm; fascination.

witches' Sabbath In medieval folklore, a midnight orgy of demons and witches, that in German folklore is believed to occur on Walpurgis Night.

witch hazel 1. A shrub of the U.S. and Canada, with several branching crooked trunks and small yellow flowers. 2. An ointment and extract derived from the bark and dried leaves of this shrub. Also *wychhazel*. [< WITCH² + HAZEL]

witch hunt *Informal* An investigation of persons ostensibly to uncover subversive activities, but intended for ulterior motives, such as harassing political opposition. **— witch-hunt-ing** (wich/hun'ting) *adj. & n.* **— witch-hunt-er** *n.*

witch-ing (wich/ing) *adj.* Having power to enchant; weird; fascinating. **—** *n.* Witchcraft; sorcery. **— witch'ing-ly** *adv.*

with (with, with) *prep.* 1. In the company of; as a member or associate of. 2. Next to; beside: Walk *with* me. 3. Having; bearing: a hat *with* a feather. 4. Characterized or marked by: the house *with* green shutters. 5. In a manner characterized by; exhibiting: to dance *with* grace. 6 Among: counted *with* the others. 7. During; in the course of: We forget *with* time. 8. From; so as to be separated from: to dispense *with* luxury. 9. Against: to struggle *with* an adversary. 10. In the opinion of: That is all right *with* me. 11. Because of; as a consequence of: faint *with* hunger. 12. In possession of: Leave the key *with* the janitor. 13. Using; by means or aid of: to write *with* a pencil. 14. By adding or having as a material or quality: trimmed *with* lace; endowed *with* beauty. 15. Under the influence of: confused *with* drink. 16. In spite of: *With* all his money, he could not buy health. 17. At the same time as: to go to bed *with* the chickens. 18. In the same direction as: to drift *with* the crowd. 19. In regard to; in the case of: I am angry *with* them. 20. Onto; to: Join this tube *with* that one. 21. In proportion to: His fame grew *with* his deeds. 22. In support of: He voted *with* the Left. 23. Of the same opinion as: I'm *with* you there! 24. Compared to; contrasted to: Consider this book *with* that one. 25. Immediately after: *With* that, he slammed the door. 26. Having received or been granted: *With* your consent I'll go. [OE]

with- *prefix* 1. Against: withstand. 2. Back; away: withhold. [OE *with-* < *with* against]

with-al (with-ôl', with-) *Archaic adv.* With the rest; in addition. **—** *prep.* With: intensive form used after its object: a bow to shoot *withal*. [ME < *with* + *alle* all]

with-draw (with-drô', with-) *v.* **drew, drawn, draw-ing** *v.t.* 1. To draw or take away; remove. 2. To take back, as an assertion or a promise. 3. To keep or abstract from use. **—** *v.i.* 4. To draw back; retire.

with-draw-al (with-drô'əl, with-) *n.* The act or process of withdrawing. Also **with-draw'ment** (-mənt).

withdrawing room 1. A room behind another room for retirement. 2. A drawing room.

with-drawn (with-drôn', with-) *adj. Psychol.* Lacking in responsiveness, esp. emotional responsiveness.

withe (with, with, with) *n.* 1. A willowy, supple twig. 2. A band made of twisted flexible shoots, straw, or the like. **—** *v.t.* **withed, with-ing** To bind with withes. [OE *withthe*]

with-er (with'ər) *v.i.* 1. To become limp or dry, as a plant when cut down or deprived of moisture. 2. To waste, as flesh. 3. To droop or languish. **—** *v.i.* 4. To cause to become limp or dry. 5. To abash, as by a scornful glance. [Appar. var. of WEATHER, v.]

with-ers (with'ərz) *n.pl.* 1. The highest part of the back of the horse between the shoulder blades. 2. The similar part in some other animals, as the deer and ox. [OE *wither* against; so called because the horse opposes this part against the load he pulls]

with-hold (with-hôld', with-) *v.* **held, hold-ing** *v.t.* 1. To hold back; restrain. 2. To keep back; decline to grant. **—** *v.i.* 3. To refrain; forbear. **— with-hold'er** *n.*

withholding tax A part of an employee's wages or salary that is deducted as an installment on his income tax.

with-in (with-in', with-) *adj.* 1. In the inner part; interiorly. 2. Inside the body, heart, or mind. 3. Indoors. **—** *prep.* 1. In the inner or interior part or parts of; inside. 2. In the limits, range, or compass of (a specified time, space, or distance). 3. Not exceeding (a specified quantity): Live *within* your means. 4. In the reach, limit, or scope of: *within* my power. [OE < *with* with + *innan* in]

with-it (with'it) *adj. Slang* 1. In touch with modern ways; hip. 2. Lively and fashionably up-to-date. Also **with it.**

with-out (with-out', with-) *prep.* 1. Not having, as the result of loss, privation, negation, etc.; lacking: They are *without* a home. 2. In the absence of: We must manage *without* help. 3. Free from: *without* fear. 4. At, on, or to the outside of. 5. Outside of or beyond the limits of: living *without* the pale of civilization. 6. With avoidance of: He listened *without* paying attention. **—** *adv.* 1. In or on the outer part. 2. Out of doors. [OE < *with* with + *ūtan* out]

with-stand (with-stand', with-) *v.* **stood, stand-ing** *v.t.* 1. To oppose with any force; resist successfully. **—** *v.i.* 2. To endure. [OE < *with-* against + *standan* to stand]

with-y (with'ē, with'ē) *adj.* Made of withes; flexible and tough. **—** *n. pl.* **with-ies** 1. A rope made of withes. 2. A flexible twig; withe. [OE *withig*]

wit-less (wit'lis) *adj.* Lacking in wit; foolish. [OE *witlēas*] **— wit'less-ly** *adv.* **— wit'less-ness** *n.*

wit-ling (wit'ling) *n.* One who considers himself a wit.

wit-ness (wit'nis) *n.* 1. A person who has seen or knows something, and is therefore competent to give evidence concerning it; a spectator. 2. That which serves as or furnishes evidence or proof. 3. *Law* a One who has knowledge of facts relating to a given cause and is subpoenaed to testify. b A person who has signed his name to an instrument executed by another in order that he may testify to the genuineness of the maker's signature. 4. An attestation to a fact or an event; testimony: usu. in the phrase **to bear witness. —** *v.t.* 1. To see or know by personal experience. 2. To furnish or serve as evidence of. 3. To give testimony to. 4. To be the site or scene of: This spot has *witnessed* many heinous crimes. 5. *Law* To see the execution of (an instrument) and subscribe to it for the purpose of establishing its authenticity. **—** *v.i.* 6. To give evidence; testify. [OE *witnes* knowledge, testimony] **— wit'ness-er** *n.*

witness stand The place in a courtroom from which a witness gives evidence.

wit-ted (wit'id) *adj.* 1. Having wit. 2. Having (a specified kind of) wit: used in combination: quick-*witted*.

wit-ti-cism (wit'ə-siz'əm) *n.* A witty saying. [< WITTY, on analogy with *criticism*; coined by Dryden]

wit-ting (wit'ing) *adj.* Done consciously, with knowledge and responsibility; deliberate. [< WIT²] **— wit'ting-ly** *adv.*

wit-ty (wit'ē) *adj.* **-ti-er, -ti-est** 1. Given to making original or clever speeches; quick at repartee; humorous. 2. Displaying or full of wit. **— Syn.** See HUMOROUS. [OE *wittig* wise] **— wit'ti-ly** *adv.* **— wit'ti-ness** *n.*

wives (wīvz) Plural of WIFE.

wiz (wiz) *n. Slang* A wizard (def. 2). [Short for WIZARD]

wiz-ard (wiz'ərd) *n.* 1. A male witch; sorcerer. 2. *Informal* A very skillful or clever person: He's a *wizard* with machinery. **—** *adj.* 1. Having magical powers. 2. Fascinating; enchanting. [ME < OE *wis* wise]

wiz-ard-ry (wiz'ərd-rē) *n.* The practice or methods of a wizard.

wiz-en (wiz'ən) *v.t. & v.i.* To become or cause to become withered; shrivel. **—** *adj.* Wizened; shrunken; shriveled. [OE *wisnian* to dry up, wither]

wiz-ened (wiz'ənd) *adj.* Shrunken; withered; dried up.

woad (wōd) *n.* 1. An Old World herb of the mustard family. 2. The blue dyestuff obtained from its leaves. [OE *wād*] **— woad'ed** *adj.*

wob-ble (wob'əl) *v.* **bled, bling** *v.i.* 1. To move or sway unsteadily, as a top while rotating at a low speed. 2. To show indecision or unsteadiness; waver; vacillate. **—** *v.t.* 3. To cause to wobble. **—** *n.* An unsteady motion, as that of unevenly balanced rotating bodies. Also spelled *wabble*. [? < LG *wabbeln*] **— wob'bler** *n.* **— wob'bling-ly** *adv.* **— wob'bly** *adj.*

wob-bly (wob'lē) *n. pl.* **blies** *U.S. Slang* A member of the Industrial Workers of the World (IWW).

Wo-den (wōd'n) The Old English name for Odin, the chief Norse god. Also **Wo'dan.**

woe (wō) *n.* 1. Overwhelming sorrow; grief. 2. Heavy affliction or calamity; disaster. **—** *interj.* Alas! Also *Archaic* **wo.** [OE *wā* misery]

woe-be-gone (wō'bi-gôn', -gon') *adj.* Overcome with woe; mournful; sorrowful. Also **wo'be-gone'.**

woe-ful (wō'fəl) *adj.* 1. Accompanied by or causing woe; direful. 2. Expressive of sorrow; doleful. 3. Paltry; miserable; mean. **— woe'ful-ly** *adv.* **— woe'ful-ness** *n.*

woke (wōk) Past tense of WAKE¹.

wok-en (wō'kən) Dialectal and alternative British past participle of WAKE¹.

wold (wōld) *n.* An undulating tract of open upland; down or moor. [OE *wald* forest]

wolf (woolf) *n. pl.* **wolves** (woolvz) 1. Any of numerous carnivorous mammals related to the dog, especially the common European species or the timber wolf of North America. ◆ Collateral adjective: *lupine*. 2. Any ravenous, cruel, or rapacious person or thing. 3. *Slang* A man who habitually and aggressively flirts with women; a philanderer. **— to cry wolf** To give a false alarm. **— to keep the wolf from the door** To avert want or starvation. **—** *v.t.* To devour ravenously; gulp down: He *wolfed* his food. [OE *wulf*]

wolf-ber-ry (woolf'ber'ē) *n. pl.* **-ries** A shrub of the honeysuckle family, with pinkish flowers and white berries.

Wolf Cub *Brit. & Canadian* A member of the junior branch of the Boy Scouts.

wolf-hound (woolf'hound') *n.* Either of two breeds of large dogs, the Russian wolfhound (or borzoi) and the Irish wolfhound, originally trained to hunt and kill wolves.

wolf-ish (woolf'ish) *adj.* 1. Having the qualities of a wolf; rapacious; savage. 2. *Informal* Ravenously hungry. **— wolf'ish-ly** *adv.* **— wolf'ish-ness** *n.*

wolf-ram (wool'frəm) *n.* 1. Wolframite. 2. Tungsten. [< G, prob. < *wolf* wolf + *rahm* cream, soot]

wolf·ram·ite (wŏŏl'frəm·īt) *n.* A grayish black or brown mineral of iron and magnesium, an important source of tungsten. [< G < *wolfram* tungsten]

wolf's-bane (wŏŏlfs'bān') *n.* 1. Aconite. 2. A species of European arnica, a perennial herb, used as a lotion for bruises. [Trans. of NL *lycoctonum* < Gk. < *lykos* wolf + *kleinein* to kill]

wolv·er (wŏŏl'vər) *n.* One who hunts wolves.

wol·ver·ine (wŏŏl'və·rēn') *n.* A rapacious carnivore of northern forests, with stout body and limbs and bushy tail. Also **wol'ver·ene'**. [Dim. of WOLF]

Wolverine State Nickname of Michigan.

wolves (wŏŏlvz) Plural of WOLF.

wom·an (wŏŏm'ən) *n. pl.* **wom·en** (wim'in) 1. An adult human female. 2. The female part of the human race; women collectively. 3. Womanly character; femininity: usu. with *the*. 4. As applied to a man, one who is effeminate, timid, or weak. 5. A female attendant or servant. 6. A paramour or kept mistress. 7. *Informal* A wife. — **the little woman** *U.S. Informal* One's wife. — *adj.* 1. Feminine; characteristic of women. 2. Female: a *woman* doctor. 3. Affecting or pertaining to women. [OE < *wīf* wife + *mann* human being]

wom·an·hood (wŏŏm'ən·hŏŏd) *n.* 1. The state of a woman or of womankind. 2. Women collectively.

wom·an·ish (wŏŏm'ən·ish) *adj.* 1. Characteristic of a woman; womanly. 2. Effeminate; unmanly. — **wom'an·ish·ly** *adv.* — **wom'an·ish·ness** *n.*

wom·an·ize (wŏŏm'ən·īz) *v.* **·ized**, **·iz·ing** *v.t.* To make effeminate or womanish.

wom·an·kind (wŏŏm'ən·kīnd') *n.* Women collectively.

wom·an·ly (wŏŏm'ən·lē) *adj.* Having the qualities natural, suited, or becoming to a woman; feminine. — *adv.* Like a woman. — **wom'an·li·ness** *n.*

womb (wŏŏm) *n.* 1. The organ in which the young of higher mammals are developed; the uterus. 2. The place where anything is engendered or brought into life. 3. A cavity viewed as enclosing something. [OE *wamb* the belly]

wom·bat (wom'bat) *n.* An Australian nocturnal marsupial resembling a small bear. [< Australian]

wom·en (wim'in) Plural of WOMAN.

wom·en·folk (wim'in·fōk') *n. pl.* Women collectively. Also **wom'en·folks'**.

won (wun) Past tense and past participle of WIN.

won·der (wun'dər) *n.* 1. A feeling of mingled surprise and curiosity; astonishment. 2. That which causes wonder; a strange thing; a miracle. — *v.t.* 1. To have a feeling of doubt and strong curiosity in regard to. — *v.i.* 2. To be affected or filled with wonder; marvel. 3. To be doubtful; want to know. [OE *wundor*] — **won'der·er** *n.* — **won'der·ing** *adj.* — **won'der·ing·ly** *adv.*

won·der·ful (wun'dər·fəl) *adj.* Of a nature to excite wonder; marvelous. — **won'der·ful·ly** *adv.* — **won'der·ful·ness** *n.*

won·der·land (wun'dər·land') *n.* A realm of fairy-tale romance or wonders.

won·der·ment (wun'dər·mənt) *n.* 1. The emotion of wonder; surprise. 2. Something wonderful; a marvel.

Wonder State Nickname for Arkansas.

won·der-strick·en (wun'dər·strik'ən) *adj.* Suddenly smitten with wonder or admiration. Also **won'der-struck'** (-struk')

won·der-work (wun'dər·wûrk') *n.* A work inspiring wonder. — **won'der-work'er** *n.* — **won'der-work'ing** *adj.*

won·drous (wun'drəs) *adj.* Wonderful; marvelous. — *adv.* Surprisingly. — **won'drous·ly** *adv.* — **won'drous·ness** *n.*

wont (wunt, wŏnt) *adj.* Accustomed; used: He is *wont* to smoke after dinner. — *n.* Ordinary manner of doing or acting; habit. [OE pp. of *gewunian* to be accustomed]

won't (wōnt) Will not. [ME *woll not*]

wont·ed (wun'tid, wōn'-) *adj.* 1. Commonly used or done; habitual. 2. Habituated; accustomed. — **wont'ed·ness** *n.*

woo (wŏŏ) *v.t.* 1. To seek the love or affection of, esp. in order to marry; court. 2. To entreat earnestly; beg. 3. To invite; seek. — *v.i.* 4. To pay court. [OE *wōgian*]

wood (wŏŏd) *n.* 1. The hard, fibrous material beneath the bark of a tree or shrub. 2. Lumber; timber; firewood. 3. Often *pl.* A large and compact collection of trees; a forest; grove. 4. Something made of wood. 5. *pl.* A rural district; backwoods. — **out of the woods** Clear of difficulties; safe after peril. — *adj.* 1. Made of wood. 2. Made for using or holding wood. 3. Living or growing in woods. — *v.t.* 1. To furnish with wood for fuel. 2. To plant with trees. — *v.i.* 3. To take on a supply of wood. [OE *wudu*] — **wood'·ed** *adj.* — **wood'less** *adj.*

wood alcohol Methanol.

wood·bine (wŏŏd'bīn) *n.* 1. The common honeysuckle of Europe. 2. The Virginia creeper. Also called *bine*: also **wood'bind** (-bīnd). [OE < *wudu* wood + *bindan* to bind]

wood·block (wŏŏd'blok') *n.* 1. A block of wood prepared for engraving. 2. A woodcut.

wood·chuck (wŏŏd'chuk') *n.* A marmot of eastern North America, having a chunky body and a brown, bristly coat: also called *ground hog*. [By folk etymology < Ojibwa *we-jack*]

wood·cock (wŏŏd'kok') *n.* 1. A small European game bird having the thighs entirely feathered. 2. A related North American bird. [OE *wuducocc*]

wood·craft (wŏŏd'kraft', -krăft') *n.* 1. Skill in things pertaining to woodland life, as hunting and trapping. 2. Skill in woodwork or in constructing articles of wood. — **wood'crafts·man** (-krafts'mən, -krăfts'-) *n.*

wood·cut (wŏŏd'kut') *n.* 1. An engraved block of wood. 2. A print from such a block. Also called *woodblock*.

wood·cut·ter (wŏŏd'kut'ər) *n.* One who cuts or chops wood. — **wood'cut'ting** *n.*

wood·en (wŏŏd'n) *adj.* 1. Made of wood. 2. Like a block of wood; stupid; mechanical; stiff; awkward. 3. Dull; spiritless. — **wood'en·ly** *adv.* — **wood'en·ness** *n.*

wood engraving 1. The art of cutting designs on wood for printing. 2. A woodcut. — **wood engraver**

wood·en·head (wŏŏd'n·hed') *n. Informal* A stupid person; blockhead. — **wood'en-head'ed** *adj.*

wooden horse Trojan horse.

wood·en·ware (wŏŏd'n·wâr') *n.* Dishes, vessels, bowls, etc., made of wood.

wood·house (wŏŏd'hous') *n.* A house or shed for storing firewood: also called *woodshed*.

wood·land (wŏŏd'lənd; *for n., also* wŏŏd'land') *n.* Land occupied by or covered with woods or trees. — *adj.* Belonging to or dwelling in the woods. — **wood'land·er** *n.*

wood louse Any of numerous small terrestrial flat-bodied crustaceans commonly found under old logs.

wood·man (wŏŏd'mən) *n. pl.* **·men** (-mən) A woodsman.

wood·note (wŏŏd'nōt') *n.* A simple, artless, or natural song, as of a wild bird.

wood nymph A nymph of the forest; a dryad.

wood·peck·er (wŏŏd'pek'ər) *n.* Any of various birds having stiff tail feathers for climbing, strong claws, and a sharp, chisellike bill for drilling holes in the wood of trees, etc., in search of insects.

wood·pile (wŏŏd'pīl') *n.* A pile of wood, esp. of wood cut for burning.

wood pulp Wood reduced to pulp, used for making paper.

woods·man (wŏŏdz'mən) *n. pl.* **·men** (-mən) 1. A woodcutter; lumberman. 2. A forester; also, a dweller in forests. 3. A man skilled in woodcraft. 4. A hunter of forest game. Also called *woodman*.

wood sorrel A herb having purple, rose, or white flowers.

woods·y (wŏŏd'zē) *adj.* **woods·i·er**, **woods·i·est** *Informal* Of, like, or dwelling in the woods.

wood tar A tar produced by the dry distillation of wood and containing turpentine, resins, and other hydrocarbons.

wood thrush A large woodland thrush of North America, noted for the vigor and sweetness of its song.

wood·turn·ing (wŏŏd'tûr'ning) *n.* The process or art of shaping blocks of wood on a lathe. — **wood'turn'er** *n.*

wood·winds (wŏŏd'windz') *n.pl. Music* Instruments in which a player's breath sets an air column into vibration by passing through a reed or striking a sharp edge, as oboes, bassoons, clarinets, flutes, etc. — **wood'wind'** *adj.*

wood·work (wŏŏd'wûrk') *n.* 1. The wooden parts of any structure, esp. interior wooden parts, as moldings or doors. 2. Work made of wood. — **wood'work'er** *n.* — **wood'work'ing** *n.*

wood·y (wŏŏd'ē) *adj.* **wood·i·er**, **wood·i·est** 1. Of the nature of or containing wood. 2. Of or like wood. 3. Wooded; abounding with woods. — **wood'i·ness** *n.*

woof (wŏŏf) *n.* 1. The weft; the threads carried back and forth across the fixed threads of the warp in a loom. 2. The texture of a fabric. [OE < *on* on + *wefan* to weave]

woof·er (wŏŏf'ər) *n. Electronics* A loudspeaker used to reproduce low frequencies in high-fidelity sound equipment. [< WOOF, imit. of a dog's growl]

wool (wŏŏl) *n.* 1. The soft, curly or crisped hair obtained from the fleece of sheep and some allied animals. 2. The underfur of a furbearing animal. 3. Material or garments made of wool. 4. A substance resembling wool. — **all wool and a yard wide** One hundred percent genuine. — **to pull**

WOLVERINE
(To 3 feet long; tail to 1½ feet.)

RED-HEADED WOODPECKER
(To 9½ inches long)

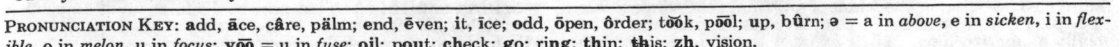
PRONUNCIATION KEY: add, āce, câre, pälm; end, ēven; it, īce; odd, ōpen, ôrder; tŏŏk, pōōl; up, bûrn; ə = a in *above*, e in *sicken*, i in *flexible*, o in *melon*, u in *focus*; yŏŏ = u in *fuse*; oil; pout; check; go; ring; thin; this; zh, vision.

the wool over one's eyes To deceive one. — *adj.* Of or made of wool or woolen material. [OE *wull*]

wool-clip (wŏŏl/klip/) *n.* The amount of wool clipped from the sheep in one year.

wool-en (wŏŏl/ən) *adj.* 1. Made of wool; like wool. 2. Of wool or its manufacture. — *n.pl.* Woolen cloth or clothing. Also **wool/len.** [OE *wullen, wyllen*]

wool-gath-er-ing (wŏŏl/gath/ər-ing) *n.* Any trivial or purposeless employment; esp., idle reverie. — *adj.* Idly indulging in fancies. — **wool/gath/er-er** *n.*

wool-grow-er (wŏŏl/grō/ər) *n.* A person who raises sheep for the production of wool. — **wool/grow/ing** *adj.*

wool-ly (wŏŏl/ē) *adj.* **-li-er, -li-est** 1. Made of, covered with, or resembling wool; wool-bearing. 2. Soft and vaporous; lacking clearness; fuzzy; blurry. 3. Having a growth of woollike hairs. 4. Rough and exciting: usu. in the phrase **wild and woolly.** — *n.* *pl.* **-lies** A garment made of wool; esp., underwear. Also *esp. U.S.* **wool/y.** — **wool/li-ness** *n.*

wool-sack (wŏŏl/sak/) *n.* 1. A sack of wool. 2. The chair of the lord chancellor in the English House of Lords, a cushion stuffed with wool. 3. The office of lord high chancellor.

wooz-y (wŏŏ/zē) *adj.* **wooz-i-er, wooz-i-est** *Slang* Befuddled, esp. with drink; dazed. [Prob. < *wooze,* var. of OOZE] — **wooz/i-ly** *adv.* — **wooz/i-ness** *n.*

Worces-ter-shire sauce (wŏŏs/tər-shir) A piquant sauce made from vinegar and many other ingredients. Also **Worcestershire, Worcester sauce.** [after *Worcester,* England where originally made]

word (wûrd) *n.* 1. A linguistic form that can meaningfully be spoken in isolation. 2. The letters or characters that stand for such a linguistic form. 3. A mere sequence of sounds or letters; vocable: *words* rather than ideas. 4. *Usu. pl.* Conversation; talk: a man of few *words.* 5. A brief remark. 6. A short and pithy saying. 7. A communication or message; information: Send him *word.* 8. A command, signal, or direction: Give the *word* to start. 9. A promise; avowed intention: a man of his *word.* 10. A watchword. 11. *pl.* Language used in anger, rebuke, or otherwise emotionally: They had *words.* — **by word of mouth** Orally. — **in a word** In short; briefly. — **the Word** The Scriptures. — **to be as good as one's word** To keep one's promise. — **to break one's word** To violate one's promise. — **to eat one's words** To retract something that one has said. — **to have a word with** To have a brief conversation with. — **to mince words** To be evasive; avoid coming to the point. — **to take one at his word** To understand or deal with one literally in accordance with his own statement. — **to take the words out of one's mouth** To say what one was just about to say. — *v.t.* To express in a word or words, esp. in selected words; phrase. [OE]

word-age (wûr/dij) *n.* Words collectively.

word-book (wûrd/bŏŏk/) *n.* 1. A collection of words; vocabulary, lexicon, dictionary. 2. An opera libretto.

word for word In the exact words; literally; verbatim.

word-i-ness (wûr/dē-nis) *n.* The use of excessive words.

word-ing (wûr/ding) *n.* The act or style of expressing in words; phraseology; also, words used; expression.

word-less (wûrd/lis) *adj.* Having no words; inarticulate; silent. — **word/less-ly** *adv.* — **word/less-ness** *n.*

word order The sequence or order of words in a phrase, clause, or sentence.

word play 1. Fencing with words; repartee. 2. Subtle discussion on words and their meaning. 3. Play on words.

word square An arrangement of letters in rectangular form, so that they form the same words in either horizontal or vertical lines.

```
FRET
REAR
EASE
TREE
```
WORD SQUARE

word-y (wûr/dē) *adj.* **word-i-er, word-i-est** 1. Of the nature of words; verbal. 2. Expressed in many words. 3. Given to the use of words; verbose; prolix. [OE *wordig*] — **word/i-ly** *adv.*

wore (wôr, wōr) Past tense of WEAR¹ and WEAR².

work (wûrk) *n.* 1. Continued exertion or activity, whether physical or mental, directed to some purpose or end; labor. 2. The acts, obligations, etc., that one does or undertakes in return for something of value, as money; esp., the activities by which one earns one's livelihood; occupation. 3. A job or position; employment: to look for *work.* 4. A place of employment: Is he at home or at *work?* 5. That upon which labor is expended; task. 6. Exhausting or unrewarding effort; toil. 7. The matter at hand; the business that remains to be done: Get to *work.* 8. That which is produced by or as by labor, as an engineering structure, a design produced by a needle, etc.; also, a product of mental labor, as a book or opera. 9. A feat or deed. 10. *pl.* (*usu. construed as sing.*) A manufacturing or other industrial establishment, including buildings and equipment: a gas *works.* 11. *pl.* Running gear or machinery, as of a watch. 12. Manner of working, or style of treatment; workmanship. 13. *pl. Theol.* The whole of anything: the whole *works.* 14. *pl. Theol.* Moral duties considered as external acts, especially as meritorious. 15. *Physics* A transference of energy from one body to another resulting in the motion or displacement of the body acted upon, expressed as the product of the force and the amount of displacement in the line of its action. — **in the works** *Informal* In progress or in preparation. — **to give (someone) the works** *Slang* 1. To maul or kill. 2. To be severe with. — **to shoot the works** *Slang* To make a supreme effort; risk one's all in a single attempt. — *v.* **worked** (*Archaic* **wrought**), **work-ing** *v.i.* 1. To perform work; labor; toil. 2. To be employed in some trade or business. 3. To perform a function; operate: The machine *works* well. 4. To prove effective; succeed: His stratagem *worked.* 5. To move or progress gradually or with difficulty: He *worked* up in his profession. 6. To become as specified, as by gradual motion: The bolts *worked* loose. 7. To have some slight improper motion in functioning: The wheel *works* on the shaft. 8. To move from nervousness or agitation: His features *worked* with passion. 9. To undergo kneading, hammering, etc.; be shaped: Copper *works* easily. 10. To ferment. 11. *Naut.* To labor in a heavy sea so as to loosen seams and fastenings: said of a ship. — *v.t.* 12. To cause or bring about; accomplish: to *work* a miracle. 13. To direct the operation of: to *work* a machine. 14. To make or shape by toil or skill. 15. To prepare, as by manipulating, hammering, etc.: to *work* dough. 16. To decorate, as with embroidery or inlaid work. 17. To cause to be productive, as by toil: to *work* a mine. 18. To cause to do work: He *works* his employees too hard. 19. To cause to be as specified, usu. with effort: We *worked* the timber into position. 20. To make or achieve by effort: He *worked* his way through the narrow tunnel. 21. To carry on some activity in (an area, etc.); cover: to *work* a stream for trout. 22. To solve, as a problem in arithmetic. 23. To cause to move from nervousness or excitement: to *work* one's jaws. 24. To excite; provoke: He *worked* himself into a passion. 25. To influence or manage, as by insidious means; lead. 26. *Informal* To make use of for one's own purposes; use. — **to work in** To put in; insert or be inserted. — **to work off** To get rid of, as extra flesh by exercise. — **to work on** (or **upon**) 1. To try to influence or persuade. 2. To influence or affect. — **to work out** 1. To make its way out or through. 2. To effect by work or effort; accomplish. 3. To exhaust, as a mineral vein or a subject of inquiry. 4. To discharge, as a debt, by labor rather than by payment of money. 5. To develop; form, as a plan. 6. To solve. 7. To prove effective or successful. 8. To result as specified: It *worked* out badly. — **to work over** 1. To do again; repeat. 2. *U.S. Slang* To beat up; maul. — **to work up** 1. To excite; rouse. 2. To form or shape by working; develop. [OE *weorc*]

-work *combining form* 1. A product made from a (specified) material: *paperwork, brickwork.* 2. Work of a (given) kind: *piecework.* 3. Work performed in a (specified) place: *housework.* [< WORK]

work-a-ble (wûr/kə-bəl) *adj.* 1. Capable of being worked. 2. Capable of being put into effect, as a plan; practicable. — **work/a-bil/i-ty, work/a-ble-ness** *n.*

work-a-day (wûrk/ə-dā/) *adj.* 1. Of, pertaining to, or suitable for working days; everyday. 2. Commonplace; prosaic. [Alter. of ME *werkeday* < OE *weorca* work + DAY]

work basket A basket for holding sewing materials.

work-bench (wûrk/bench/) *n.* A bench for work, as that of a carpenter or machinist.

work-book (wûrk/bŏŏk/) *n.* 1. A booklet based on a course of study and containing problems and exercises that a student works out directly on the pages. 2. A manual containing operating instructions. 3. A book for recording work performed or planned.

work-day (wûrk/dā/) *n.* 1. Any day not a Sunday or holiday; a working day. 2. The part of the day or number of hours of one day spent in work. — *adj.* Workaday.

work-er (wûr/kər) *n.* 1. One who or that which does work; esp., a laborer. 2. A female of an insect colony, as an ant, bee, or termite, with undeveloped sexual organs.

work force The total number of workers of a company, project, factory, region, etc.; staff. Also **working force.**

work-horse (wûrk/hôrs/) *n.* 1. A horse used for pulling loads, as a cart or plow. 2. A person who takes upon himself the hardest or most arduous part of an undertaking.

work-house (wûrk/hous/) *n.* 1. *Brit.* A house for paupers able to work. 2. An industrial prison for petty offenders.

work-ing (wûr/king) *adj.* 1. Engaged actively in some employment. 2. That works, or performs its function: This is a *working* model. 3. Sufficient for use or action: a *working* knowledge of French. 4. Relating to or occupied by work. 5. Throbbing with pain; also, twitching: said esp. of the face muscles. 6. Fermenting, as wine. — *n.* 1. The act or operation of one who or that which works. 2. *Usu. pl.* The part of a mine or quarry where excavation is going on or has gone on.

working capital 1. That part of the finances of a business available for its operation. 2. The amount of quick assets that exceed current liabilities.

working class The part of society consisting of working people paid in wages; esp., manual or industrial laborers. — **work·ing-class** (wûr'king-klas', -kläs') adj.

working day 1. A day on which work is normally done, as distinguished from a Sunday or holiday. 2. The number of hours constituting a day's work: a four-hour *working day*.

work·ing·man (wûr'king-man') n. pl. ·men (-men') A male worker; laborer.

working papers An age certificate and other official papers certifying that a minor may be legally employed.

work·ing·wom·an (wûr'king-woom'ən) n. pl. ·wom·en (-wim'in) A female worker; laborer.

work·less (wûrk'lis) adj. Jobless; unemployed.

work·load (wûrk'lōd') n. The amount of work apportioned to a person, machine, or department over a given period.

work·man (wûrk'mən) n. pl. ·men (-mən) One who earns his living by manual labor; an artisan; mechanic; workingman. — **work'man·ly** adv.

work·man·like (wûrk'mən-līk) adj. Like or befitting a skilled workman; skillfully done. — **work'man·ly** adv.

work·man·ship (wûrk'mən-ship) n. 1. The art or skill of a workman, or the quality of work. 2. The work or result produced by a worker.

workmen's compensation 1. Damages recoverable from an employer by an employee in case of accident. 2. Government insurance against illness, accident, or unemployment.

work of art 1. A product of the fine arts, esp. of the graphic arts and sculpture, but including literary and musical productions. 2. Anything likened to an artistic work, as because of great beauty, intricacy, etc.

work·out (wûrk'out') n. Informal 1. A test, trial, practice performance, etc., to discover, maintain, or increase ability for some work or competition, as a practice boxing bout or race. 2. Any activity involving considerable effort or vigor.

work·room (wûrk'room', -room') n. A room where work is performed.

work·sheet (wûrk'shēt') n. 1. A sheet of paper on which practice work or rough drafts of problems are written. 2. A sheet of paper used to record work schedules and operations.

work·shop (wûrk'shop') n. A building or room where any work is carried on; workroom.

work stoppage A stopping of work, as in industry, because of a strike or layoff.

work·ta·ble (wûrk'tā'bəl) n. A table with drawers for use while working, esp. while sewing.

work·week (wûrk'wēk') n. The number of hours worked in a week; also, the number of working hours in a week.

world (wûrld) n. 1. The earth. 2. A part of the earth: the Old *World*. 3. The universe. 4. A division of existing or created things belonging to the earth: the animal *world*. 5. The human inhabitants of the earth. 6. A definite class of people having certain interests or activities in common: the scientific *world*. 7. A sphere or domain: the *world* of letters. 8. Man regarded socially. 9. Public or social life and intercourse: to go out into the *world*. 10. The practices, usages, and ways of men: He knows the *world*. 11. A total of things as pertaining to or affecting an individual person: a child's private *world* of fantasy. 12. A great quantity, number, or size: a *world* of trouble. 13. A scene of existence or of affairs regarded from a moral or religious point of view; worldly aims, pleasures, or people collectively. 14. Earthly existence. — **for all the world** In every respect. — **on top of the world** Informal Elated. — **out of this world** Informal Very fine; extraordinarily good. — **to bring into the world** To give birth to. [OE *weorold, woruld*]

World Court 1. The Permanent Court of International Justice. 2. The International Court of Justice.

world·ling (wûrld'ling) n. One who lives merely for this world; a worldly-minded person.

world·ly (wûrld'lē) adj. ·li·er, ·li·est 1. Pertaining to the world; mundane; earthly; not spiritual. 2. Devoted to temporal things; secular. 3. Sophisticated; worldly-wise. — adv. In a worldly manner. — **world'li·ness** n.

world·ly-mind·ed (wûrld'lē-mīn'did) adj. Absorbed in the things of this world. — **world'ly-min'ded·ly** adv. — **world'·ly-mind'ed·ness** n.

world·ly-wise (wûrld'lē-wīz') adj. Wise in the ways and affairs of the world; sophisticated.

world power A state or organization whose policy and action are of world-wide influence.

World Series In baseball, the games played at the finish of the regular schedule between the champion teams of the American and National Leagues, the first team to win four games being adjudged world champions. Also **world's series.**

world's fair An international exhibit of the folk crafts and arts, agricultural and industrial products, and scientific progress of various countries.

world-shak·ing (wûrld'shā'king) adj. Enormously significant or consequential; affecting the entire world.

World War See table for WAR.

world-wea·ry (wûrld'wir'ē) adj. ·ri·er, ·ri·est Dissatisfied and weary with life and its conditions.

world-wide (wûrld'wīd') adj. Extended or spread throughout the world.

worm (wûrm) n. 1. A small, limbless invertebrate with an elongated, soft, and usu. naked body, as a flatworm, roundworm, or annelid. ◆ Collateral adjective: *vermicular.* 2. Loosely, any small creeping animal having a slender body and short or undeveloped limbs, as an insect larva, a grub, etc. 3. That which suggests the action or habit of a worm as eating away or as an agent of decay, as remorse, death, etc. 4. A despicable, groveling, or abject person. 5. Something like a worm in appearance or movement. 6. pl. An intestinal disorder due to the presence of parasitic worms. — v.t. 1. To insinuate (oneself or itself) in a wormlike manner: with *in* or *into.* 2. To draw forth by artful means, as a secret: with *out.* 3. To free from intestinal worms. 4. Naut. To wind yarn, etc., along (a rope) so as to fill up the grooves between the strands. 5. To remove the worms from, as a dog. — v.i. 6. To move or progress slowly and stealthily. 7. To insinuate oneself by artful means: with *into.* [OE *wyrm*] — **worm'er** n.

worm-eat·en (wûrm'ēt'n) adj. 1. Eaten or bored through by worms. 2. Worn-out or decayed, as by time.

worm gear Mech. 1. A worm wheel. 2. The gear formed by a worm wheel together with a worm screw.

worm·hole (wûrm'hōl') n. The hole made by a worm or termite, as in plants, timber, etc. — **worm'holed'** adj.

worm screw Mech. A short threaded portion of a shaft constituting an endless screw formed to mesh with a worm wheel.

worm wheel Mech. A toothed wheel gearing with a worm screw.

worm·wood (wûrm'wood') n. 1. Any of various European herbs or small shrubs related to the sagebrush; esp., a common species that is aromatic and bitter and is used in making absinthe. 2. That which embitters or makes bitter; bitterness. [Alter. of obs. *wermōd* < OE]

worm·y (wûr'mē) adj. worm·i·er, worm·i·est 1. Infested with or injured by worms. 2. Of or pertaining to worms. 3. Resembling a worm. 4. Mean; groveling. — **worm'i·ness** n.

worn (wôrn, wōrn) Past participle of WEAR. — adj. 1. Affected by use or any continuous action; as: a Threadbare: a *worn* suit. b Exhausted, as from worry, anxiety, etc.: a *worn* face. c Hackneyed: a *worn* phrase. 2. Used up; spent.

worn-out (wôrn'out', wōrn'-) adj. 1. Used until without value or effectiveness. 2. Thoroughly tired; exhausted.

wor·ri·some (wûr'i·səm) adj. 1. Causing worry or anxiety. 2. Given to worry. — **wor'ri·some·ly** adv.

wor·ry (wûr'ē) v. ·ried, ·ry·ing v.i. 1. To be uneasy in the mind; fret. 2. To pull or tear at something with the teeth: with *at.* 3. Informal To advance or manage despite difficulties: with *along* or *through.* — v.t. 4. To cause to feel uneasy in the mind; trouble. 5. To bother; pester. 6. To mangle or kill by biting, shaking, or tearing with the teeth. — n. pl. ·ries 1. A state of anxiety or vexation. 2. Something that causes anxiety. 3. The act of worrying. [OE *wrygan* to strangle] — **wor'ri·er** n. — **wor'ri·ment** n.

worse (wûrs) Comparative of BAD and ILL. — adj. 1. Bad or ill in a greater degree; more evil, etc. 2. Physically ill in a greater degree. 3. Less favorably situated as to means and circumstances. — n. Something worse. — adv. In a manner more intense, severe, or evil. [OE *wiersa*]

wors·en (wûr'sən) v.t. & v.i. To make or become worse.

wor·ship (wûr'ship) n. 1. The adoration, homage, or veneration given to a deity. 2. The rites, ceremonial forms, prayers, etc., such adoration requires or assumes. 3. Excessive or ardent devotion or admiration. 4. The object of such devotion or admiration. 5. Chiefly Brit. A title of honor in addressing persons of rank or station: with *your, his,* etc. — v. **wor·shiped** or ·**shipped, wor·ship·ing** or ·**ship·ping** v.t. 1. To pay an act of worship to. 2. To have an intense or exaggerated admiration or devotion for. — v.i. 3. To perform acts or have sentiments of worship. [OE < *weorth* value] — **wor'ship·er** n. — **wor'ship·per** n.

wor·ship·ful (wûr'ship-fəl) adj. 1. Giving or feeling reverence or adoration. 2. Chiefly Brit. Worthy of or entitled to honor or respect: used as a title of respect for magistrates, etc. — **wor'ship·ful·ly** adv. — **wor'ship·ful·ness** n.

worst (wûrst) Superlative of BAD and ILL. — adj. Bad, ill, evil, harmful, etc., in the highest degree. — **in the worst way** Slang Very much. — n. That which is worst. — **at worst** By the most pessimistic estimate. — **if (the) worst comes to (the) worst** If the worst imaginable thing comes to pass. — **to get the worst of it** To be defeated or put at a disadvantage. **— adv.** In the worst or most extreme manner or degree. **— v.t.** To defeat; vanquish. [OE *wierrest*]

wors·ted (wŏŏs′tid, wûr′stid) *n.* **1.** Woolen yarn spun from long staple, with fibers combed parallel and twisted hard. **2.** A fabric made from worsted yarns. **— adj.** Consisting of or made from this yarn. [after *Worsted,* former name of a parish in Norfolk, north of Norwich, England]

wort (wûrt) *n.* **1.** A plant or herb: usu. in combination: *liverwort.* **2.** The unfermented infusion of malt that becomes beer when fermented. [OE *wyrt* root, plant]

worth (wûrth) *n.* **1.** Value or excellence of any kind. **2.** The exchangeable or market value of anything. **3.** The quality or combination of qualities that makes one deserving of esteem. **4.** Wealth. **5.** The amount of something that can be had for a specific sum: three cents' *worth* of candy. **— adj. 1.** Equal in value (to); exchangeable (for). **2.** Deserving of: to be *worth* seeing. **3.** Having possessions to the value of: He is *worth* a million. **— for all it is worth** To the utmost. **— for all one is worth** With every effort possible: to the utmost of one's capacity. [OE *weorth*]
— Syn. (noun) **1.** *Worth* and *value* relate to the merit or excellence of a person or thing. In pecuniary matters, the words are usually equivalent: to get one's money's *worth,* to receive good *value* in a purchase. *Worth* often implies some intangible merit or efficacy, while *value* has reference to a measurable or precisely definable quality: ideas of little *worth,* the *value* of a house and its lot.

-worth *combining form* Of the value of: *pennyworth.* [OE *weorth* worth]

worth·less (wûrth′lis) *adj.* Having no worth, value, dignity, virtue, etc. **— worth′less·ly** *adv.* **— worth′less·ness** *n.*

worth·while (wûrth′hwīl′) *adj.* Sufficiently important to occupy the time; of enough value to repay the effort. **— worth′while/ness** *n.*

wor·thy (wûr′thē) *adj.* **·thi·er, ·thi·est 1.** Possessing worth or value; deserving of respect or honor. **2.** Having such qualities as to be deserving of or adapted to some specified thing; suitable: followed by *of* (rarely *for*) or sometimes by an infinitive: He is *worthy* of our prasie. **— n.** *pl.* **·thies 1.** A person of eminent worth. **2.** A person or character of local note: a humorous usage. [ME *wurthi, worthi*] **— wor′thi·ly** *adv.* **— wor′thi·ness** *n.*

-worthy *combining form* **1.** Meriting or deserving: *trustworthy.* **2.** Valuable as; having worth as: *newsworthy.* **3.** Fit for: *seaworthy.* [OE *wyrthe* worthy]

wot (wot) Present tense, first and third person singular, of WIT².

Wo·tan (vō′tän) In Wagner's *Ring of the Nibelung,* Woden.

would (wŏŏd) Past tense of WILL, but rarely a true past, rather chiefly used as a modal auxiliary expressing: **a** Desire or inclination: He *would* like to write. **b** Condition: He *would* give if he were able. **c** Futurity: He kept searching for something that *would* cure him. **d** Determination: He *would* not go. **e** Expectation or possibility: Letting him speak *would* have serious consequences. **f** Preference: We *would* have you succeed rather than fail. **g** Request: *Would* you give us a call? **h** Custom or habit: We *would* ride together each day. **i** Choice: He *would* never go if he could help it. **j** Uncertainty: It *would* seem to be wrong. ◆ See note under SHOULD. [OE *wolde,* pt. of *willan* to will]

would-be (wŏŏd′bē′) *adj.* **1.** Desiring or professing to be: a *would-be* poet. **2.** Intended to be.

would·n't (wŏŏd′nt) Would not.

wouldst (wŏŏdst) Archaic or poetic second person singular of WOULD: used with *thou.*

wound¹ (wŏŏnd, *Poetic* wound) *n.* **1.** A hurt or injury to the body, usu. one in which the skin is cut or torn, as a stab, cut, etc. **2.** A similar injury to a tree or plant. **3.** Any injury or cause of pain or grief, as to the feelings, honor, etc. **— v.t. & v.i.** To inflict a wound or wounds (upon); cause injury or grief (to). [OE *wund*] **— wound′less** *adj.*

wound² (wound) Past tense and past participle of WIND².
wove (wōv) Past tense and alternative past participle of WEAVE.
wo·ven (wō′vən) Past participle of WEAVE.
wow (wou) *interj. Informal* An exclamation of wonder, surprise, pleasure, pain, etc. **— n.** *Slang* Something that is extraordinarily successful, amusing, etc. **— v.t.** *Slang* To be extraordinarily successful with.

wrack¹ (rak) *n.* **1.** Ruin; destruction: chiefly in the phrase **wrack and ruin. 2.** A wrecked ship; wreckage. **3.** Marine vegetation and floating material cast ashore by the sea, as seaweed or eelgrass. **— v.t. & v.i.** To wreck or be wrecked. [Fusion of OE *wræc* revenge and MDu. *wrak* wreck]

wrack² (rak) *n.* See RACK³.

wraith (rāth) *n.* **1.** An apparition of a person thought to be alive, seen shortly before or shortly after his death. **2.** Any specter, ghost, or apparition. [Origin unknown]

wran·gle (rang′gəl) *v.* **·gled, ·gling** *v.i.* **1.** To argue or dispute noisily; brawl. **— v.t. 2.** To argue; debate. **3.** *U.S.* To herd or round up (livestock). **— n.** An angry dispute. [Cf. LG *wrangeln* to quarrel] **— wran′gler** *n.*

wrap (rap) *v.* **wrapped** or **wrapt, wrap·ping** *v.t.* **1.** To surround and cover by something folded or wound about; swathe; enwrap. **2.** To cover with paper, etc., folded about and secured. **3.** To wind or fold (a covering) about something. **4.** To surround so as to obscure; blot out or conceal; envelop. **5.** To fold, wind, or draw together. **— v.i. 6.** To be or become twined or coiled: with *about, around,* etc. **— to be wrapped up in 1.** To be clothed in or enveloped by (something). **2.** To be totally absorbed, involved, or interested in (something). **— to keep under wraps** To keep secret. **— n. 1.** An article of dress drawn or folded about a person; a wrapper. **2.** *pl.* Outer garments collectively, as cloaks, scarfs, etc. **3.** A blanket. [ME *wrappen*]

wrap·a·round (rap′ə·round′) *adj.* **1.** Designating a garment, as a skirt, dress, coat, etc., open down to the hem and made to fit by being wrapped around the body. **2.** Encircling or overlapping: a *wraparound* windshield.

wrap·per (rap′ər) *n.* **1.** A paper enclosing a newspaper, magazine, or similar packet for mailing or otherwise. **2.** A woman's dressing gown. **3.** One who or that which wraps.

wrap·ping (rap′ing) *n.* Often *pl.* A covering; something in which an object is wrapped.

wrath (rath, räth; *Brit.* rôth) *n.* **1.** Extreme or violent rage or fury; vehement indignation. **2.** An act done in violent rage, esp. in vengeance or punishment. [OE < *wrath* wroth]

wrath·ful (rath′fəl, räth′-) *adj.* **1.** Full of wrath; extremely angry. **2.** Springing from or expressing wrath. **— wrath′·ful·ly** *adv.* **— wrath′ful·ness** *n.*

wrath·y (rath′ē, räth′ē) *adj.* **wrath·i·er, wrath·i·est** *Informal* Wrathful. **— wrath′i·ly** *adv.* **— wrath′i·ness** *n.*

wreak (rēk) *v.t.* **1.** To inflict or exact, as vengeance. **2.** To give free expression to (anger, hatred, etc.); vent. [OE *wrecan* to drive, avenge]

wreath (rēth) *n.* *pl.* **wreaths** (rēthz) **1.** A band or circle of flowers or greenery, often worn on the head as a crown or placed on a grave or at a door, window, etc. **2.** Any curled band of circular or spiral shape, as of smoke. [OE < *writhan* to bind, tie] **— wreath′y** *n.*

wreathe (rēth) *v.* **wreathed, wreath·ing** *v.t.* **1.** To form into a wreath, as by twisting or twining. **2.** To adorn or encircle with or as with wreaths. **3.** To envelop; cover: His face was *wreathed* in smiles. **— v.i. 4.** To take the form of a wreath. **5.** To twist, turn, or coil, as masses of cloud. [< ME *writhen* to writhe]

wreck (rek) *v.t.* **1.** To cause the destruction or wreck of, as a vessel. **2.** To bring ruin, damage, or destruction upon. **3.** To tear down, as a building; dismantle. **— v.i. 4.** To suffer wreck; be ruined. **— n. 1.** That which has been ruined or destroyed. **2.** Property cast upon land by the sea, either broken portions of a wrecked vessel or cargo from it. **3.** The accidental destruction or ruin of a ship; also, the ship so destroyed. **4.** One who is physically, mentally, or morally unsound or ruined. **5.** The act of wrecking, or the state of being wrecked. [< AF < OF < ON *wrekan* to drive]

wreck·age (rek′ij) *n.* **1.** The act of wrecking, or the state of being wrecked. **2.** Broken or disordered remnants or fragments from a wreck.

wreck·er (rek′ər) *n.* **1.** One who or that which causes wreck, destruction, or frustration of any sort. **2.** One employed in tearing down and removing old buildings. **3.** A person, train, car, or machine that clears away wrecks. **4.** One employed to recover disabled vessels or wrecked cargoes for the owners; also, a vessel employed in this service.

wreck·ing (rek′ing) *n.* The work or art of a wrecker. **— adj.** Of, engaged in, or used in pulling down buildings or in salvaging and clearing away wrecks.

wren (ren) *n.* **1.** Any of numerous small birds having short, rounded wings and a short tail, including the common house wren. **2.** Any of numerous similar birds. [OE *wrenna*]

wrench (rench) *n.* **1.** A violent twist. **2.** A sharp or violent twist or pull, as in the ankle, back, etc.; a sprain. **3.** Any sudden and violent emotion or grief. **4.** Any perversion or distortion of an original meaning. **5.** Any of various tools for twisting or turning bolts, nuts, pipe, etc. **— v.t. 1.** To twist violently; turn suddenly by force; wrest. **2.** To twist forcibly so as to cause strain or injury; sprain. **3.** To twist from the proper meaning, intent, or use. **4.** To strain or force the feelings, thoughts, etc., of: to *wrench* oneself away from pleasure. **— v.i. 5.** To give a twist or wrench. [OE *wrenc* trick]

wrest (rest) *v.t.* **1.** To pull or force away by violent twisting or wringing; wrench. **2.** To turn from the true meaning, character, intent, or application; distort. **3.** To seize forcibly by violence, extortion, or usurpation. **4.** To extract by toil and effort: to *wrest* a living from barren soil. **— n. 1.** An act of wresting. **2.** A misapplication or perversion. **3.** A crooked act. **4.** A key for tuning a stringed instrument, as a harp. [OE *wræstan*] **— wrest′er** *n.*

wres·tle (res′əl) *v.* **·tled, ·tling** *v.i.* **1.** To engage in wrestling. **2.** To struggle, as for mastery; contend. **— v.t. 3.** To engage in (a wrestling match), or wrestle with. **4.** To throw (a calf) and hold it down for branding. — *n.* **1.** A wrestling match. **2.** Any hard struggle. [OE *wræstlian*, freq. of *wræstan* to wrest] — **wres′tler** *n.*

wres·tling (res′ling) *n.* A sport or exercise in which each of two unarmed contestants endeavors to throw the other to the ground or force him into a certain fallen position.

wretch (rech) *n.* **1.** A base, vile, or contemptible person. **2.** A miserable or pitiable person. [OE *wrecca* outcast < *wrecan* to drive]

wretch·ed (rech′id) *adj.* **1.** Sunk in dejection; profoundly unhappy. **2.** Causing misery or grief. **3.** Unsatisfactory or worthless in ability or quality. **4.** Despicable; contemptible. — **wretch′ed·ly** *adv.* — **wretch′ed·ness** *n.*

wrig·gle (rig′əl) *v.* **·gled**, **·gling** *v.i.* **1.** To twist in a sinuous manner; squirm; writhe. **2.** To proceed as by twisting or crawling. **3.** To make one's way by evasive or indirect means. — *v.t.* **4.** To cause to wriggle. — *n.* The motion of one who or that which wriggles; a squirm. [< MLG *wriggeln*, freq. of *wriggen* to twist] — **wrig′gly** *adj.*

wrig·gler (rig′lər) *n.* **1.** One who or that which wriggles. **2.** A mosquito larva.

wright (rīt) *n.* One who constructs, contrives, or creates: used chiefly in compounds: *playwright*. [OE *wyrhta*]

wring (ring) *v.* **wrung** (*Rare* **wringed**), **wring·ing** *v.t.* **1.** To squeeze or compress by twisting. **2.** To squeeze or press out, as water, by twisting. **3.** To extort; acquire by extortion. **4.** To distress; torment. **5.** To twist or wrest violently out of shape or place: to *wring* his neck. — *v.i.* **6.** To writhe or squirm, as with anguish. — *n.* The act of wringing. [OE *wringan*]

wring·er (ring′ər) *n.* **1.** One who or that which wrings. **2.** A contrivance used to press water out of fabrics after washing; also, the operator of such a machine.

wrin·kle¹ (ring′kəl) *n.* **1.** A small ridge, crease, or fold, as on a smooth surface. **2.** A small fold or crease in the skin, usu. produced by age or by excessive exposure to the elements. — *v.* **·kled**, **·kling** *v.t.* **1.** To make a wrinkle or wrinkles in, as by creasing, folding, crumpling, etc. — *v.i.* **2.** To be or become contracted into wrinkles or ridges. [OE *gewrinclod*, pp. of *gewrinclian* to wind] — **wrin′kly** *adj.*

wrin·kle² (ring′kəl) *n. Informal* A curious or ingenious method, idea, device, etc. [Prob. dim. of OE *wrenc* trick]

wrist (rist) *n.* **1.** The part or joint of the arm that lies between the hand and the forearm. ◆ Collateral adjective: *carpal*. **2.** The part of a glove or garment that covers the wrist. **3.** A wrist pin. [OE, prob. < *wrīthan* to writhe]

wrist·band (rist′band, -bənd, riz′-) *n.* The band of a sleeve that covers the wrist or ends a shirt sleeve; a cuff.

wrist·let (rist′lit) *n.* **1.** A flexible band worn on the wrist for warmth. **2.** A bracelet. **3.** *Slang* A handcuff.

wrist pin *Mech.* **1.** A pin holding together the piston and connecting rod of a steam engine. **2.** A similar pin in the cross-head of an internal-combustion engine.

wrist watch A watch set in a band or strap and worn at the wrist.

writ¹ (rit) *n.* **1.** *Law* A mandatory precept, under seal, issued by a court, and commanding the person to whom it is addressed to do or not to do some act. **2.** That which is written: now chiefly in the phrase *Holy Writ*, meaning the Bible. [OE, a writing < *wrītan* to write]

writ² (rit) Archaic or dialectal past tense and past participle of WRITE.

write (rīt) *v.* **wrote** (*Archaic* or *Dial.* **writ**), **writ·ten** (*Archaic* or *Dial.* **writ**), **writ·ing** *v.t.* **1.** To trace or inscribe (letters, words, numbers, symbols, etc.) on a surface with pen or pencil, or by other means. **2.** To describe in writing. **3.** To communicate by letter. **4.** *Informal* To communicate with by letter: He *writes* her every day. **5.** To produce by writing; be the author or composer of. **6.** To draw up; draft: to *write* a check. **7.** To cover or fill with writing: to *write* two full pages. **8.** To leave marks or evidence of: Anxiety is *written* on his face. **9.** To spell or inscribe as specified: He *writes* his name with two *n*'s. **10.** To entitle or designate in writing: He *writes* himself "General." **11.** To underwrite: to *write* an insurance policy. — *v.i.* **12.** To trace or inscribe letters, etc., on a surface, as of paper. **13.** To communicate in writing. **14.** To be engaged in the occupation of a writer or author. **15.** To produce a specified quality of writing. — **to write down 1.** To put into writing. **2.** To injure or depreciate in writing. — **to write off 1.** To cancel or remove (claims, debts, etc.) from an open account. **2.** To acknowledge the loss or failure of. — **to write in 1.** To insert in writing, as in a document. **2.** To cast (a vote) for one not listed on a ballot by inserting his name in writing. — **to write out 1.** To put into writing. **2.** To write in full or complete form. — **to write up 1.** To describe fully in writing. **2.** To praise fully or too fully in writing. [OE *wrītan*]

write-in (rīt′in′) *adj. Informal* Designating a method of voting whereby a name not formally on the ballot is written in by the voter. — *n.* In voting, a name thus written.

write-off (rīt′ôf′, -of′) *n.* **1.** A cancellation. **2.** An amount canceled or noted as a loss.

writ·er (rī′tər) *n.* **1.** One who writes. **2.** One who engages in literary composition.

writer's cramp *Pathol.* Spasmodic contraction of the muscles of the fingers and hand, caused by excessive writing. Also **writer's palsy** or **spasm**.

write-up (rīt′up′) *n. Informal* A written description, record, or account, usu. laudatory, as of a town, manufacturing enterprise, or public institution.

writhe (rīth) *v.* **writhed**, **writhed**, **writh·ing** *v.t.* **1.** To cause to twist or bend; distort. — *v.i.* **2.** To twist or distort the body, face, etc., as in pain. **3.** To suffer acutely, as from embarrassment, anguish, etc. — *n.* An act of writhing. [OE *wrīthan*] — **writh′er** *n.*

writ·ing (rī′ting) *n.* **1.** The act of one who writes. **2.** The characters so made; handwriting. **3.** Anything written or expressed in letters; esp., a literary production. **4.** The profession or occupation of a writer. **5.** The practice, art, form, or style of literary composition.

writing paper Paper prepared to receive ink in writing.

writ·ten (rit′n) Past participle of WRITE.

wrong (rông, rong) *adj.* **1.** Not correct; mistaken; erroneous: a *wrong* estimate. **2.** Not suitable; inappropriate; improper: the *wrong* clothes; the *wrong* job. **3.** Not according to the right, proper, or correct method, standard, intention, etc.: the *wrong* way to do it. **4.** Not working or acting properly or satisfactorily: Something is *wrong* with the lock. **5.** Intended or made to be turned under, inward, or so as not to be seen: the *wrong* side of the cloth. **6.** Not desired or intended: the *wrong* road. **7.** Not favored by conventional social standards: the *wrong* side of town. **8.** Not morally right, proper, or just. **9.** Unsatisfactory: the *wrong* reply. — **to go wrong 1.** To lapse from the strict path of rectitude. **2.** To turn out badly; go astray. — *adv.* In a wrong direction, place, or manner; erroneously. — *n.* **1.** That which is wrong, as an evil or unjust action. **2.** The state or condition of being wrong: to be in the *wrong*. **3.** *Law* An invasion or violation of one's legal rights. — *v.t.* **1.** To violate the rights of; inflict injury or injustice upon. **2.** To impute evil to unjustly; malign: If you think so, you *wrong* him. **3.** To seduce or dishonor (a woman). [OE < ON *rangr* awry, unjust] — **wrong′er** *n.* — **wrong′ly** *adv.* — **wrong′ness** *n.*

wrong·do·er (rông′dōō′ər, rong′-) *n.* One who does wrong. — **wrong′do′ing** *n.*

wrong·ful (rông′fəl, rong′-) *adj.* **1.** Characterized by wrong or injustice; injurious; unjust. **2.** Unlawful; illegal. — **wrong′ful·ly** *adv.* — **wrong′ful·ness** *n.*

wrong-head·ed (rông′hed′id, rong′-) *adj.* Stubbornly or perversely erring in judgment, action, etc. — **wrong′-head′ed·ly** *adv.* — **wrong′-head′ed·ness** *n.*

wrote (rōt) Past tense of WRITE.

wroth (rôth) *adj. Archaic* Filled with anger; furious; incensed. Also **wroth′ful** (-fəl). [OE *wrāth*]

wrought (rôt) Archaic past tense and past participle of WORK. — *adj.* **1.** Beaten or hammered into shape by tools: *wrought* gold. **2.** Worked; molded. **3.** Made with delicacy; elaborated carefully. **4.** Made; fashioned; formed: often in combination: *well-wrought*. — **wrought up** Excited; agitated. [ME < OE *geworht*, pp. of *wrycan* to work]

wrought iron Commercially pure iron, prepared from pig iron and easily forged and welded into various shapes.

wrung (rung) Past tense and past participle of WRING.

wry (rī) *adj.* **wri·er** or **wry·er**, **wri·est** or **wry·est** **1.** Bent to one side or out of position; contorted; askew: a *wry* smile. **2.** Deviating from that which is right or proper; warped. **3.** Perverse, ironic, or bitter: *wry* humor. — *v.t.* **wried**, **wry·ing** To twist; contort. [ME < OE *wrigian* to move, tend] — **wry′ly** *adv.* — **wry′ness** *n.*

wry·neck (rī′nek′) *n.* **1.** A bird allied to the woodpeckers, with the habit of twisting its head and neck. **2.** *Pathol.* A spasmodic affliction that twists the neck muscles. — **wry-necked** (rī′nekt′) *adj.*

Wy·an·dot (wī′ən·dot) *n. pl.* **·dot** or **·dots 1.** One of a tribe of North American Indians of Iroquoian stock and descendants of Hurons, presently settled in Oklahoma. **2.** An Iroquoian language. Also spelled *Wyandotte*.

Wy·an·dotte (wī′ən·dot) *n.* **1.** One of an American breed of domestic fowls. **2.** *pl.* **·dotte** or **·dottes** A Wyandot. **3.** The Wyandot language. [after the *Wyandot* Indians]

wych-elm (wich′elm′) *n.* A widespreading elm, common in the British Isles: also called *wich*, *witch*: also spelled *wich-elm*, *witch-elm*. Also **wych**. [< *wych*, var. of WITCH² + ELM]

wych-ha·zel (wich′hā′zəl) *n.* Witch hazel.

X

x, X (eks) *n. pl.* **x's** or **xs, X's** or **Xs, ex·es** (ek'siz) **1.** The twenty-fourth letter of the English alphabet. **2.** The sounds represented by the letter *x*, in English variously sounded as (ks), as in *axle, box, next;* (gz), as in *executive, exert;* (ksh), as in *noxious;* (gzh), as in *luxurious;* and initially, always (z), as in *xenophobe, xylophone.* **3.** Anything shaped like an X. **4.** An unknown quantity, factor, result, etc. — *symbol* **1.** The Roman numeral ten. **2.** A mark shaped like an X, representing the signature of one who cannot write. **3.** A mark used in diagrams, maps, etc., to place some event or substance, or to point out something to be emphasized. **4.** A symbol used to indicate a kiss. **5.** Christ: an abbreviation used in combination: *Xmas.*

xan·the·in (zan'thē·in) *n. Biochem.* The water-soluble portion of the yellow coloring matter found in the cell sap of some plants. [< F < Gk. *xanthos* yellow]

xan·thic (zan'thik) *adj.* Having a yellow or yellowish color. [< F < Gk. *xanthos* yellow]

xan·thine (zan'thēn, -thin) *n. Biochem.* A crystalline nitrogenous compound, $C_5H_4N_4O_2$, contained in blood, urine, and other animal secretions, and in some plants.

xantho- *combining form* Yellow. Also, before vowels, **xanth-.** [< Gk. *xanthos* yellow]

xan·thous (zan'thəs) *adj.* **1.** Yellow. **2.** *Anthropol.* Of or pertaining to the yellow-skinned, or Mongoloid, ethnic division of mankind.

X-ax·is (eks'ak'sis) *n. pl.* **-ax·es** (-ak'sēz) The more nearly horizontal axis in a graph; the abscissa.

X-chro·mo·some (eks'krō'mə·sōm) *n. Genetics* One of the two types of chromosomes that determine the sex of an offspring.

xe·bec (zē'bek) *n.* A small, three-masted Mediterranean vessel, with both square and lateen sails, formerly used by Algerian pirates: also spelled *zebec.* [Earlier *chebec* < F < Sp. < Arabic *shabbāk*]

xeno- *combining form* Strange; foreign; different. Also, before vowels, **xen-.** [< Gk. *xenos* stranger]

xe·non (zē'non) *n.* A heavy, gaseous element (symbol Xe) occurring in extremely small quantities in the atmosphere and freezing at a very low temperature. See ELEMENT. [< Gk., neut. of *xenos* strange]

xen·o·phobe (zen'ə·fōb) *n.* One who hates or distrusts strangers or foreigners.

xen·o·pho·bi·a (zen'ə·fō'bē·ə) *n.* Hatred or distrust of foreigners or strangers. — **xen'o·pho'bic** (-fō'bik) *adj.*

xero- *combining form* Dry; dryness. Also, before vowels, **xer-.** [< Gk. *xēros* dry]

xe·rog·ra·phy (zi·rog'rə·fē) *n.* A method of printing in which a negatively charged ink powder is sprayed upon a positively charged metal plate, from which it is transferred to the printing surface by electrostatic attraction. — **xe·ro·graph·ic** (zir'ō·graf'ik) *adj.* — **xe·rog'raph·er** *n.*

xe·roph·i·lous (zi·rof'ə·ləs) *adj. Biol.* Growing in or adapted to dry, hot climates.

xe·ro·phyte (zir'ə·fīt) *n. Bot.* A plant adapted to dry conditions of air and soil. — **xe'ro·phyt'ic** (-fit'ik) *adj.*

xe·ro·print·ing (zir'ō·prin'ting) *n.* A simplified variation of xerography, using a suitably prepared plate on a rotating cylinder.

Xho·sa (kō'sä) *n.* The Bantu language of the Kaffirs, closely related to Zulu: also called *Kaffir:* also **Xosa.**

xi (zī, sī; *Gk.* ksē) *n.* The fourteenth letter in the Greek alphabet (Ξ, ξ), equivalent to the English *x.* See ALPHABET.

-xion Var. of -TION.

xiphi- *combining form* Sword. Also, before vowels, **xiph-.** [< Gk. *xiphos* sword]

xiph·oid (zif'oid) *adj.* Shaped like a sword.

Xmas Christmas: popular abbreviation. ◆ *Xmas,* though best avoided in formal contexts, has been used in written English since the sixteenth century and cannot be condemned as a modern commercialism. [< *X,* abbr. for *Christ* < Gk. *X,* chi, the first letter of *Christos* Christ + -MAS]

X-ray (eks'rā') *v.t.* To examine, photograph, diagnose, or treat with X-rays. — *n.* A picture made with X-rays; roentgenogram: also **X-ray photograph.**

X-rays (eks'rāz') *n.pl.* Electromagnetic radiations of extremely short wavelength, emitted from a substance when it is bombarded by a stream of electrons moving in a vacuum at a sufficiently high velocity, as in an electron tube. Their ability to penetrate solids, to ionize gases, and to act on photographic plates has many useful applications, especially in the detection, diagnosis, and treatment of certain organic disorders, chiefly internal. Also called *Roentgen rays.* [Trans. of G *X-strahlen,* name coined by Roentgen, their discoverer, because their nature was unknown]

xy·lem (zī'ləm) *n. Bot.* The portion of a vascular bundle in higher plants that is made up of woody tissue, parenchyma, and associated cells, etc. [< G < Gk. *xylon* wood]

xylo- *combining form* Wood; woody. Also, before vowels, **xyl-.** [< Gk. *xylon* wood]

xy·lo·phone (zī'lə·fōn) *n.* A musical instrument consisting of a row of wooden bars graduated in length to form a chromatic scale, and sounded by being struck with mallets. — **xy·lo·phon·ist** (zī'lə·fō'-nist, zī·lof'ə·nist) *n.*

XYLOPHONE

xys·ter (zis'tər) *n.* A surgical instrument for scraping bones. [< NL < Gk. < *xyein* to scrape]

Y

y, Y (wī) *n. pl.* **y's** or **ys, Y's** or **Ys, wyes** (wīz) **1.** The twenty-fifth letter of the English alphabet. **2.** The sounds represented by the letter *y.* Initial *y* (introducing either a vowel or a syllable) represents a voiced palatal semivowel, as in *yet, you, yonder, beyond.* Final *y* represents either a vowel, pronounced (ē), as in *honey, pretty, steady;* a diphthong, pronounced (ī), as in *fly, my;* or the final glide of a diphthong, as in *gray, obey, annoy.* Internal *y* represents a vowel (i), as in *lyric, myth, syllable;* a diphthong (ī), as in *lyre, type, psychic;* an r-colored central vowel (ûr) or (ər), as in *myrtle, martyr.* **3.** Anything shaped like a Y, as: **a** A pipe coupling, connection, etc. **b** A forked piece serving as a rest or support, as for some part of a sighting instrument. — *symbol Chem.* Yttrium (symbol Y).

y- *prefix* Used in Middle English as a sign of the past participle, as an intensive, or without perceptible force: *yclad, yclept.* It survives (as *a-*) in such words as *alike, aware,* etc. Also spelled *i-.* [OE *ge-*]

-y¹ *suffix of adjectives* Being, possessing, or resembling what is expressed in the root: *stony, rainy.* Also *-ey,* when added to words ending in *y,* as in *clayey, skyey.* [OE *-ig*]

-y² *suffix* The quality or state of being: *victory:* often used in abstract nouns formed from adjectives in *-ous* and *-ic.* [< F *-ie* < L *-ia;* also < Gk. *-ia, -eia*]

-y³ *suffix* Little; small: *kitty:* often used in nicknames or to express endearment, as in *Tommy.* [Prob. < dial. E (Scottish)]

yacht (yot) *n.* A vessel specially built or fitted for racing or for private pleasure excursions. — *v.i.* To cruise, race, or sail in a yacht. [< Du. *jaghte*, short for *jaghtschip* pursuit ship < *jaght* hunting + *schip* ship]

yacht·ing (yot′ing) *n.* The act, practice, or pastime of sailing a yacht.

yachts·man (yots′mən) *n. pl.* **·men** (-mən) One who owns or sails a yacht. Also **yacht′er, yacht′man.** — **yachts′·wom′an** (-wōom′ən) *n.fem.*

yachts·man·ship (yots′mən·ship) *n.* The art or skill of yachting. Also **yacht′man·ship.**

yah[1] (yä, ya) *interj.* An exclamation of disgust or contempt.

yah[2] (yä, yâ) *interj. Informal* Yes. [Alter. of YES]

ya·hoo (yä′hōō, yä′-, yä·hōō′) *n.* **1.** Any low, vicious person. **2.** An awkward fellow; a bumpkin. [< YAHOO]

Ya·hoo (yä′hōō, yä′-, yä·hōō′) *n.* In Swift's *Gulliver's Travels,* one of a race of brutish beings in human form.

Yah·weh (yä′we) In the Old Testament, the national god of Israel; God. See JEHOVAH. Also **Yah·ve** (yä′ve), **Yah·veh.** [< Hebrew *YHWH*]

yak[1] (yak) *n.* A large bovine ruminant of the higher regions of central Asia, having long hair fringing the shoulders, sides, and tail, and often domesticated. [< Tibetan *gyag*]

yak[2] (yak) *v.i.* **yakked, yak·king** *U.S. Slang* **1.** To chatter noisily or constantly. **2.** To laugh, esp. boisterously. [Imit.]

yam (yam) *n.* **1.** The fleshy, edible, tuberous root of any of various climbing tropical plants typical of a family of herbaceous or somewhat woody vines. **2.** Any of the plants growing this root. **3.** A large variety of the sweet potato. [< Pg. < Senegal *nyami* to eat]

yam·mer (yam′ər) *v.i. Informal* **1.** To complain peevishly; whimper. **2.** To howl; shout. — *v.t.* **3.** To utter peevishly; complain. — *n.* The act of yammering. [OE *gēomrian* to lament < *gēomor* sorrowful] — **yam′mer·er** *n.*

yang (yang) *n.* In Chinese philosophy and art, the male element, source of life and heat. Compare YIN. Also **Yang.** [< Chinese]

yank (yangk) *v.t.* **1.** To jerk or pull suddenly. — *v.i.* **2.** To give a pull or jerk. **3.** *Brit.* To be vigorously active. **4.** *Brit.* To jabber; scold. — *n. Informal* A sudden sharp pull. [? < dial. E (Scottish) *yank* a sharp sudden blow]

Yank (yangk) *n. & adj. Informal* Yankee.

Yan·kee (yang′kē) *n.* **1.** Originally, a native or inhabitant of New England. **2.** A Northerner; esp., a Union soldier during the Civil War; so called in the South. **3.** Any citizen of the U.S.: a chiefly foreign usage. — *adj.* **1.** Of, pertaining to, or characteristic of the Yankees. **2.** American. [? Back formation < *Jan Kees* (taken as a plural), John Cheese, orig. a nickname for a Hollander; later applied by Dutch colonists in New York to English settlers in Connecticut] — **Yan′kee·dom** *n.*

Yankee Doodle A song popular in pre-Revolutionary times and one of the national airs of the United States.

yap (yap) *n.* **1.** *Slang* Talk; jabber. **2.** A bark or yelp. **3.** *Slang* The mouth. — *v.t.* **yapped, yap·ping** *Slang* To talk idly or emptily; jabber. **2.** *Informal* To bark or yelp, as a cur. [Imit. of a dog's bark]

Ya·qui (yä′kē) *n.* One of a tribe of North American Indians belonging to the Piman branch of the Uto-Aztecan stock, now living in southern Sonora, Mexico.

yard[1] (yärd) *n.* **1.** A standard English and American measure of length; 3 feet, or 36 inches, or 0.914 meter. See table front of book. **2.** A yardstick. **3.** *Naut.* A long, slender, tapering spar set crosswise on a mast and used to support sails. [OE *gierd* rod, measure of length]

yard[2] (yärd) *n.* **1.** A tract of ground, often enclosed, adjacent to a residence, church, school, or other building. **2.** An enclosure used for some specific work: often in combination: *brickyard; shipyard.* **3.** An enclosure or piece of ground adjacent to a railroad station, used for making up trains and for storing the rolling stock. **4.** The winter pasturing ground of deer and moose. **5.** An enclosure for animals, poultry, etc. — *v.t.* **1.** To put or collect into or as into a yard. — *v.i.* **2.** To gather into an enclosure or yard. [OE *geard* enclosure]

yard·age (yär′dij) *n.* **1.** The amount or length of something expressed in yards. **2.** Yard goods. [< YARD[1]]

yard·arm (yärd′ärm′) *n. Naut.* Either end of a yard of a square sail.

yard goods Cloth that is sold by the yard.

yard·man[1] (yärd′mən) *n. pl.* **·men** (-mən) *Naut.* A sailor who works on the yards.

yard·man[2] (yärd′mən) *n. pl.* **·men** (-mən) A man employed in a yard, esp. on a railroad.

yard·mas·ter (yärd′mas′tər, -mäs′-) *n.* A railroad official having charge of a yard.

yard·stick (yärd′stik′) *n.* **1.** A graduated measuring stick a yard in length. **2.** Any measure or standard of comparison. Also *Archaic* **yard′wand′** (-wond′)

yarn (yärn) *n.* **1.** Any spun, threadlike material, natural or synthetic, prepared for use in weaving, knitting, etc. **2.** Continuous strands of spun fiber, as wool, cotton, linen, silk, etc. **3.** A quantity of such material. **4.** *Informal* A long, exciting story of adventure, often of doubtful truth. — *v.i. Informal* To tell a yarn or yarns. [OE *gearn*]

yarn-dyed (yärn′dīd′) *adj.* Made of yarn dyed before being woven into material.

yar·row (yar′ō) *n.* Any of various perennial herbs of Europe and North America having finely dissected leaves, small white flowers, and a pungent odor. [OE *gearwe*]

yat·a·ghan (yat′ə·gan, -gən; *Turkish* yä′tä·gän′) *n.* A Turkish sword or scimitar with a double-curved blade and a handle without a guard. Also **yat′a·gan.** [< Turkish]

yaw (yô) *v.i.* **1.** *Naut.* To steer wildly, or out of its course, as a ship when struck by a heavy sea. **2.** To move unsteadily or irregularly. **3.** *Aeron.* To deviate from the flight path by angular displacement about the vertical axis; fishtail. — *v.t.* **4.** To cause to yaw. — *n.* **1.** A movement of a ship by which it temporarily alters its course. **2.** *Aeron.* The angular movement of an aircraft, projectile, etc., about its vertical axis. **3.** Any irregular, unsteady, or deviating motion. [Cf. ON *jaga* to move to and fro]

yawl[1] (yôl) See YOWL.

yawl[2] (yôl) *n.* **1.** A fore-and-aft rigged, two-masted vessel having the mizzenmast or jiggermast abaft the rudder post. **2.** A ship's small boat. **3.** A small fishing boat. [Appar. < Du. *jol,* orig. a boat used in Jutland]

yawn (yôn) *v.i.* **1.** To open the mouth wide, usu. involuntarily and with a long, full inspiration of the breath, often the result of drowsiness, fatigue, or boredom. **2.** To be or stand wide open, esp. as ready to engulf or receive something: A chasm *yawned* below. — *v.t.* **3.** To express or utter with a yawn. — *n.* **1.** The act of yawning. **2.** The act of opening wide. [Prob. fusion of OE *geonian* to yawn and *gānian* to gape] — **yawn′er** *n.*

yawp (yôp) *v.i.* **1.** To bark or yelp. **2.** *Informal* To gape; yawn audibly. **3.** *Brit. Informal* To shout; bawl; talk loudly. — *n.* **1.** A bark or yelp. **2.** A shout; noise; noisy talking; also, a loud, uncouth outcry. Also **yaup.** [ME *golpen,* pp. of *gelpen* to boast] — **yawp′er** *n.*

yaws (yôz) *n.pl. Pathol.* A contagious skin disease occurring in tropical and subtropical countries, caused by a spirochete and resembling syphilis. [< Carib *yáya*]

Y-ax·is (wī′ak′sis) *n. pl.* **-ax·es** (-ak′sēz) The more nearly vertical axis in a graph or coordinate system; the ordinate.

yay (yā) *U.S. Dial. adj.* **1.** This many; this much. **2.** Ever so many: for *yay* years. — *adv.* **1.** To this extent. **2.** Ever so: *yay* big. [Cf. G *je* ever]

Y-chro·mo·some (wī′krō′mə·sōm) *n. Genetics* One of the two types of chromosome that determine the sex of an offspring.

y·clept (i·klept′) *adj. Archaic* Called; named. Also **y·cleped′.** [OE *geclypod,* pp. of *clypian* to call]

ye[1] (thē) The: a mistaken form resulting from the substitution of the character *y* for the thorn (þ) of the Old and Middle English alphabet.

ye[2] (yē) *pron. Archaic* A pronoun of the second person, originally nominative plural: "Blessed are *ye* when men shall revile you"; later, also nominative singular and objective singular and plural. [ME *ye, ʒe,* nominative pl. < OE *gē*]

yea (yā) *adv.* **1.** *Archaic* A term of affirmation or assent, now superseded by yes. **2.** *Archaic* Not only so, but more so: used to intensify or amplify: There were fifty, *yea,* a hundred archers. **3.** In reality; indeed; verily: used to introduce a sentence, etc. — *n.* **1.** An affirmative vote or voter: opposed to nay. **2.** An affirmation. [OE *gēa*]

yeah (yâ, ye′ə) *adv. Informal* Yes. [< YES]

yean (yēn) *v.t. & v.i.* To bear (young), as a goat or sheep. [OE (assumed) *geēanian*]

yean·ling (yēn′ling) *n.* The young of a goat or sheep. — *adj.* Young or newly born.

year (yir) *n.* **1.** The period of time in which the earth completes one revolution around the sun, consisting of 365 or 366 days divided into 12 months and now reckoned as beginning January 1 and ending December 31; also, a similar period in other calendars. **2.** Any period of 12 months, usu. reckoned from a specific date or time: a *year* from now. **3.** The period of time during which a planet revolves once around the sun. **4.** A specific period of time, usu. less than a year, given over to some special work or activity: the school *year.* **5.** *pl.* Age, esp. old age: active for his *years.* **6.** *pl.* Time: in *years* gone by and *years* to come. — **year after year** Every year. — **year by year** Each year; with each succeeding year. — **year in, year out** From one year to the next; without cessation. [OE *gēar*]

year·book (yir′book′) *n.* A book published annually, presenting information about the previous year.

year·ling (yir′ling) *n.* A young animal past its first year and not yet two years old; esp., a colt or filly a year old dating from January 1 of the year of foaling. — *adj.* Being a year old.

year·long (yir′lông′, -long′) *adj.* Continuing through a year.

year·ly (yir′lē) *adj.* 1. Occurring, done, payable, seen, etc., once a year; annual. 2. Continuing or lasting for a year: a *yearly* subscription. — *adv.* Once a year; annually.

yearn (yûrn) *v.i.* 1. To desire something earnestly; long; hanker; pine: with *for.* 2. To be deeply moved; feel sympathy. [OE *giernan, geornan*]

yearn·ing (yûr′ning) *n.* A strong emotion of longing or desire, esp. with tenderness. — **yearn′ing·ly** *adv.*

year-round (yir′round′) *adj.* Open, operating, or continuing for the entire year: a *year-round* health resort.

yeast (yēst) *n.* 1. A substance consisting of minute cells of fungi that clump together in a yellow, frothy, viscous growth promoting fermentation in saccharine liquids, with the production of alcohol and carbon dioxide, as in the brewing of beer and the raising of bread. 2. Such a substance mixed with flour or meal, and sold commercially. 3. Froth or spume. 4. Mental or moral ferment or agitation. — *v.i.* To foam; froth. [OE *gist*]

yeast cake A mixture of living yeast cells and starch in compressed form, suitable for use in baking or brewing.

yeast plant Any of a group of fungi that form yeast.

yeast·y (yēs′tē) *adj.* **yeast·i·er, yeast·i·est** 1. Of, resembling, or containing yeast. 2. Causing or characterized by fermentation. 3. Restless; unsettled; frivolous. 4. Covered with or consisting mainly of froth or foam. 5. Light or unsubstantial. — **yeast′i·ness** *n.*

yegg (yeg) *n. Slang* A burglar or safe-cracker. Also **yegg′· man** (-mən) [Origin unknown]

yell (yel) *v.t. & v.i.* To shout; scream; roar; also, to cheer. — *n.* 1. A sharp, loud, inarticulate cry, as of pain, terror, anger, etc. 2. A rhythmic cheer composed of a series of words or nonsense syllables and shouted by a group in unison. [OE *giellan, gellan*] — **yell′er** *n.*

yel·low (yel′ō) *adj.* 1. Having the color of ripe lemons, or sunflowers. 2. Changed to a sallow color by age, sickness, or the like: a paper *yellow* with age. 3. Having a yellowish complexion, as a member of the Mongoloid ethnic group. 4. Melancholy or jealous. 5. Sensational, esp. offensively so: said of newspapers: *yellow* journalism. 6. *Informal* Cowardly; mean; dishonorable. — *n.* 1. The color of the spectrum between green and orange. 2. Any pigment or dyestuff having or producing such a color. 3. The yolk of an egg. 4. *pl. Bot.* Any of various unrelated plant diseases in which there is stunting of growth and yellowing of the foliage. 5. *pl.* Jaundice, esp. a variety that affects domestic animals. — *v.t. & v.i.* To make or become yellow. [OE *geolu*] — **yel′low·ly** *adv.* — **yel′low·ness** *n.*

yel·low-bel·lied (yel′ō-bel′ēd) *adj.* 1. *Slang* Cowardly; yellow. 2. Having a yellow underside, as a bird.

yel·low·bird (yel′ō-bûrd′) *n.* Any of several yellow birds, as the American goldfinch or the yellow warbler.

yellow cake *Canadian Informal* Uranium ore; concentrated uranium oxide.

yel·low-dog contract (yel′ō-dôg′, -dog′) A contract with an employer, no longer legal, in which an employee agrees not to join a labor union during his term of employment.

yellow fever *Pathol.* An acute, infectious intestinal disease of tropical and semitropical regions, caused by a filterable virus transmitted by the bite of a mosquito and characterized by jaundice, vomiting, and fatty degeneration of the liver: also called *black vomit, vomito, yellow jack.*

yel·low·ham·mer (yel′ō-ham′ər) *n.* 1. An Old World bunting having in the male bright yellow plumage and blackish head and tail feathers. 2. The flicker, a bird. [prob. < OE *geolo* yellow + *amore,* a kind of bird]

yel·low·ish (yel′ō-ish) *adj.* Somewhat yellow. — **yel′low· ish·ness** *n.*

yellow jack 1. A fish of the West Indies and Florida. 2. The flag of the quarantine service. 3. Yellow fever.

yellow jacket Any of various social wasps having bright yellow markings.

yellow metal 1. A brass consisting of 60 parts copper and 40 parts zinc. 2. Gold.

yellow peril The alleged power, both political and numerical, of the Oriental peoples of Asia, conceived of as threatening white or Western supremacy.

yellow pine 1. Any of various American pines, as the loblolly pine. 2. Their tough, yellowish wood.

yellow race The Mongoloid ethnic division of mankind.

yellow streak A tendency to be cowardly, mean, etc.

yellow warbler A warbler of the southern U.S., bright yellow with brown streaks underneath.

yel·low·wood (yel′ō-wŏŏd′) *n.* 1. The yellow or yellowish wood of a medium-sized tree of the southern U.S., having a smooth bark, showy white flowers, and yielding a yellow dye. 2. The tree. 3. Any of several other trees with yellowish wood, as the Osage orange, buckthorn, smoketree, etc.

yel·low·y (yel′ō-ē) *adj.* Yellowish.

yelp (yelp) *v.i.* 1. To utter a sharp, shrill cry or bark, as a dog. — *v.t.* 2. To express by a yelp or yelps. — *n.* A sharp, shrill cry or bark. [OE *gielpan* to boast] — **yelp′er** *n.*

yen[1] (yen) *Informal n.* An ardent longing or desire; intense want; infatuation. — *v.i.* **yenned, yen·ning** To yearn; long. [< Chinese, opium, smoke]

yen[2] (yen) *n. pl.* **yen** The standard monetary unit of Japan, equal to 100 sen: in 1960 worth about 9⁄10 U.S. cent. [< Japanese < Chinese *yüan* round, dollar]

yeo·man (yō′mən) *n. pl.* **-men** (-mən) 1. A petty officer in the U.S. Navy or Coast Guard who performs clerical duties. 2. *Brit.* One who cultivates his own farm. 3. *Brit.* A yeoman of the guard. 4. Formerly, an attendant or servant in the service of a nobleman or of royalty. 5. Formerly, a freeholder next below the gentry who owned a small landed estate or farm. [ME *yeman, yoman,* prob. contr. of *yengman* young man < OE *geong* young + *mann* man]

yeo·man·ly (yō′mən·lē) *adj.* 1. Of, pertaining to, or resembling a yeoman. 2. Brave; rugged; staunch. — *adv.* Like a yeoman; bravely; staunchly.

yeoman of the (royal) guard A member of the special bodyguard of the English royal household, consisting of one hundred yeomen wearing medieval uniforms and first appointed by Henry VII: also called *beefeater.*

yeo·man·ry (yō′mən-rē) *n.* 1. The collective body of yeomen; freemen; farmers. 2. *Brit.* A home guard of volunteer cavalry, created in 1761. In 1907 it became a part of the Territorial Army.

yeoman's service Faithful and useful support or service; loyal assistance in need. Also **yeoman service.**

yep (yep) *adv. Informal* Yes. [Alter. of YES]

-yer Var. of -IER.

yes (yes) *adv.* As you say; truly; just so: a reply of affirmation or consent: opposed to *no,* and sometimes used to enforce by repetition or addition something that precedes. — *n. pl.* **yes·es** or **yes·ses** 1. A reply in the affirmative. 2. An affirmative vote or voter: often *aye.* — *v.t. & v i.* **yessed, yes·sing** To say "yes" (to). [OE *gēse,* prob. < *gēa* yea + *sī,* third person sing. present subj. of *bēon* to be]

yes man *Informal* One who agrees without criticism; a servile, acquiescent assistant or subordinate; toady.

yester- *prefix* Pertaining to the day before the present; by extension of the preceding, used of longer periods than a day: *yesteryear.* [< YESTER(DAY)]

yes·ter·day (yes′tər-dē, -dā′) *n.* 1. The day preceding today. 2. The near past. — *adv.* 1. On the day before today. 2. At a recent time. [OE < *giestran* yesterday + *dæg* day]

yes·ter·year (yes′tər-yir′) *n.* Last year; yore. [Trans. of F *antan;* coined by D. G. Rossetti]

yet (yet) *adv.* 1. In addition; besides; further: often with a comparative: They had twenty miles *yet* to go. 2. Before or at some future time; eventually: He will *yet* succeed. 3. In continuance of a previous state or condition; still: I can hear him *yet.* 4. At the present time; now: Don't go *yet.* 5. After all the time that has or had elapsed: Are you not ready *yet?* 6. Up to the present time; before: commonly with a negative: He has never *yet* lied to me. 7. Than that which has been previously affirmed: with a comparative: It was hot yesterday; today it is hotter *yet.* 8. Nevertheless: It was hot, *yet* not unpleasant. 9. As much as; even: He did not believe the reports, nor *yet* the evidence. — **as yet** Up to now. — *conj.* 1. Nevertheless; notwithstanding: I speak to you peaceably, *yet* you will not listen. 2. But: He is willing, *yet* unable. 3. Although: active, *yet* ill. — **Syn.** See BUT[1]. [OE *giet, gieta*]

yew (yōō) *n.* 1. Any of several evergreen trees or shrubs, with flat, lanceolate leaves and a red berrylike fruit. 2. The hard, fine-grained, durable wood of the common yew. 3. A bow made from the wood of the yew tree. [OE *ēow, iw*]

Yid·dish (yid′ish) *n.* A Germanic language derived from the Middle High German spoken in the Rhineland in the thirteenth and fourteenth centuries, now spoken primarily by Jews in eastern Europe, and by Jewish immigrants from that region in other parts of the world. It contains elements of Hebrew and the Slavic languages, and is written in Hebrew characters. — *adj.* 1. Of or pertaining to Yiddish; written or spoken in Yiddish. 2. *Slang* Jewish. [< G *jüdisch* Jewish < *Jude* Jew]

yield (yēld) *v.t.* 1. To give forth by a natural process, or as a result of labor or cultivation. 2. To give in return, as for investment; furnish: The bonds *yield* five percent interest. 3. To give up, as to superior power; relinquish: often with *up:* to *yield* a fortress. 4. To concede or grant: to *yield* precedence. — *v.i.* 5. To provide a return; produce; bear. 6. To give up; surrender. 7. To give way, as to pressure or force; bend; collapse, etc. 8. To assent or comply, as under compulsion; consent: We *yielded* to their persuasion. 9. To give place, as through inferiority or weakness: with *to:* We will *yield* to them in nothing. — *n.* 1. The amount yielded; product, as of cultivation or mining. 2. The profit derived from invested capital. **3.** *Mil.* The explosive force of a nuclear bomb as expressed in kilotons or megatons of TNT. [OE *gieldan, geldan* to pay] — **yield'er** *n.*

yield·ing (yēl'ding) *adj.* Disposed to yield; flexible; obedient. — **yield'ing·ly** *adv.* — **yield'ing·ness** *n.*

yin (yin) *n.* In Chinese philosophy and art, the female element, that stands for darkness, cold, and death. Compare YANG. Also **Yin.** [< Chinese]

yip (yip) *n.* A yelp, as of a dog. — *v.i.* **yipped, yip·ping** To yelp. [Imit.]

yipe (yīp) *interj.* Often *pl.* An exclamation of fear, surprise, horror, etc.

-yl *suffix Chem.* Used to denote a radical: *ethyl, butyl.* [< Gk. *hylē* wood, matter]

yo·del (yōd'l) *n.* A melody or refrain sung to meaningless syllables, with abrupt changes from chest to falsetto tones, common among Swiss and Tyrolese mountaineers. — *v.t. & v.i.* **yo·deled** or **·delled, yo·del·ing** or **·del·ling** To sing with a yodel, changing the voice quickly from its natural tone to a falsetto and back. Also **yo'dle.** [< G *jodeln,* lit., to utter the syllable *jo*] — **yo'del·er, yo'del·ler, yo'dler** *n.*

yo·ga (yō'gə) *n.* **1.** A Hindu system of mystical and ascetic philosophy that involves certain physical and mental disciplines together with a withdrawal from the world and abstract meditation upon some spiritual principle or object. **2.** A related system of exercises, the purpose of which is to achieve both physical and spiritual well-being. [< Hind. < Skt., lit., union] — **yo·gic** (yō'gik) *adj.*

yogh (yōkh) *n.* The Middle English letter, ȝ, that represented a voiced or voiceless palatal fricative, or a voiced velar fricative. It has been replaced in Modern English by *y,* as in *lay, w,* as in *law,* and *gh,* as in *daughter* and *enough.*

yo·gi (yō'gē) *n.* *pl.* **·gis 1.** One who practices yoga. **2.** Yoga. Also **yo'gee, yo'gin** (-gin). [< Hind. < Skt.]

yo·gurt (yō'gŏŏrt) *n.* A thick, curdled milk treated with bacteria, regarded as beneficial to the intestines. Also **yo'ghurt, yo'ghourt.** [< Turkish *yōghurt*]

yoicks (yoiks) *interj.* Hoicks. [Earlier *hoik,* var. of HIKE]

yoke (yōk) *n.* *pl.* **yokes;** *for def. 3, often* **yoke 1.** A curved timber with attachments used for coupling draft animals, as oxen, usu. having a bow at each end to receive the neck of the animal. **2.** Any of various similar contrivances, as a frame

YOKE *(def.* 1)

fitted for a person's shoulders and designed to carry a burden at either end, as a pail. **3.** A pair of draft animals coupled with a yoke (def. 1). **4.** An oppressive force or influence: under the *yoke* of tyranny. **5.** That which binds or connects; a bond: the *yoke* of love. **6.** Servitude, or some visible sign of it; bondage. **7.** A part of a garment designed to support a plaited or gathered part, as at the hips or shoulders. **8.** *Naut.* A crosspiece on a rudderhead, carrying cables for steering. — *v.* **yoked, yok·ing** *v.t.* **1.** To put a yoke upon. **2.** To join with or as with a yoke; couple or link. **3.** To secure (a draft animal) to a plow, etc.; also, to secure a draft animal to (a plow, etc.). — *v.i.* **4.** To be joined or linked. [OE *geoc*]

yoke·fel·low (yōk'fel'ō) *n.* A mate or companion in labor. Also **yoke'mate'** (-māt).

yo·kel (yō'kəl) *n.* A countryman; country bumpkin: a contemptuous term. [? < dial. E, green woodpecker, yellowhammer] — **yo'kel·ish** *adj.*

yolk (yōk, yōlk) *n.* **1.** The yellow portion of an egg, as distinguished from the white portion, used for the formation and nourishment of the embryo. **2.** A fine yellow soapy exudation in sheep's wool. [OE *geol(o)ca,* lit., (the) yellow part < *geolu* yellow]

yolk·y (yō'kē, yōl'kē) *adj.* **yolk·i·er, yolk·i·est 1.** Of, like, or pertaining to yolk. **2.** Containing yolk: *yolky* wool.

Yom Kip·pur (yom kip'ər, *Hebrew* yŏm ki-pŏŏr') The Jewish Day of Atonement, the 10th of Tishri (September–October), marked by continuous prayer and fasting for 24 hours from sundown on the evening previous. [< Hebrew *yōm kipūr* day of atonement]

yon (yon) *adj. & adv. Archaic, Dial. & Poetic* Yonder; that or those over there: *yon* fine house. [OE *geon*]

yon·der (yon'dər) *adj.* Being at a distance indicated. — *adv.* In that place; there. [ME, prob. extension of *yone,* OE *geon* yon]

yore (yôr, yōr) *n.* Old time; time long past: in days of *yore.* [OE *gēara* formerly, prob. orig. genitive pl. of *gēar* year]

York boat *Canadian* A type of heavy cargo canoe used by the Hudson's Bay Company. [after York Factory on Hudson Bay]

York·shire pudding (yôrk'shir, -shər) A batter pudding baked under roasting meat to catch the drippings.

Yorkshire terrier A toy breed of terrier having a long, silky coat.

you (yōō) *pron., possessive* **your** or **yours 1.** The nominative and objective singular and plural pronoun of the second person, used in addressing one or more persons, animals, or things, and always taking a plural verb. **2.** An indefinite pronoun equivalent to *one:* You learn by trying. [OE *ēow,* dative and accusative pl. of *gē* ye]

you'd (yōōd, *unstressed* yŏŏd, yəd) **1.** You had. **2.** You would.

you'll (yōōl, *unstressed* yŏŏl, yəl) You will.

young (yung) *adj.* **young·er** (yung'gər), **young·est** (yung'gist) **1.** Being in the early period of life or growth; not old. **2.** Not having progressed far; newly formed: The day was *young.* **3.** Pertaining to youth or early life. **4.** Full of vigor or freshness. **5.** Being without experience; immature. **6.** Denoting the younger of two persons having the same name or title; junior. **7.** Radical or progressive in social or political aims: used with proper names: the *Young* Turks. — Syn. See YOUTHFUL. — *n.* **1.** Young persons as a group; youth. **2.** Offspring, esp. of animals. — **with young** With child; pregnant. [OE *geong*] — **young'ish** *adj.*

young·ber·ry (yung'ber'ē) *n.* *pl.* **·ries** A large dark red berry, hybridized from a trailing blackberry and a dewberry, of the western U.S. [after B. M. *Young,* U.S. horticulturist]

young blood Youth; young people.

young-eyed (yung'īd') *adj.* Having youthful eyes or fresh vision; bright-eyed.

young·ling (yung'ling) *n.* **1.** A young person, animal, or plant. **2.** An inexperienced person. — *adj.* Young.

young·ster (yung'stər) *n.* **1.** A young person; a child or youth. **2.** A young animal, as a colt.

your (yôr, yŏŏr) *pronominal adj.* The possessive case of the pronoun *you,* used attributively: *your* fate. [OE *ēower,* genitive of *gē* ye]

you're (yŏŏr, yôr, *unstressed* yər) You are.

yours (yŏŏrz, yôrz) *pron.* **1.** The possessive case of the pronoun *you,* used predicatively: This room is *yours.* **2.** The one or ones belonging or relating to you: a home as quiet as *yours;* God bless you and *yours.* — **of yours** Belonging or relating to you: a double possessive. [ME *youres*]

your·self (yŏŏr·self', yôr-) *pron.* *pl.* **·selves** (-selvz') A form of the second person pronoun, used: **1.** As a reflexive or as object of a preposition in a reflexive sense: Did you hurt *yourself?* Look at *yourself* in the mirror. **2.** As an emphatic or intensive form of *you:* You said so, *yourself.* **3.** As a designation of a normal, proper, or usual state: Why can't you be *yourself* instead of putting on airs?

yours truly 1. A formal phrase used to close a letter, before the signature. **2.** *Informal* I; me.

youth (yōōth) *n.* *pl.* **youths** (yōōths, yōōthz) **1.** The state or condition of being young. **2.** The period when one is young; the part of life between childhood and manhood; adolescence. **3.** The early period of being or development, as of a movement. **4.** A young person, esp. a young man; also, young persons collectively. [OE *geoguth*]

youth·ful (yōōth'fəl) *adj.* **1.** Having youth; being still young. **2.** Characteristic of youth; fresh; vigorous. **3.** Of or pertaining to youth. **4.** Not far advanced; early; new. **5.** *Geol.* Young. — **youth'ful·ly** *adv.* — **youth'ful·ness** *n.* — Syn. **1.** *Youthful* describes character, manner, outlook, interests, appearance, and the like, while *young* refers merely to chronological age. A mature or old person may properly be described as *youthful,* though he is no longer *young. Juvenile* emphasizes immaturity and is therefore often disparaging; *puerile* is much the same, and is always uncomplimentary. *Adolescent* refers to the age close to maturity, and may be disparaging or not: *adolescent* pranks, *adolescent* energy and enthusiasm.

youth hostel A hostel.

you've (yōōv, *unstressed* yŏŏv, yəv) You have.

yowl (youl) *v.i.* To utter a yowl; howl; yell. — *n.* A loud, prolonged, wailing cry; a howl. Also spelled *yawl:* also **yow.** [Cf. ON *gaula* to howl, yell]

yo·yo (yō'yō') *n.* *pl.* **-yos** A wheellike toy with a string wound about it in a deep groove, commonly attached to the operator's finger and spun up and down by manipulating the string. [Origin unknown]

Y·quem (ē-kem') *n.* A highly esteemed Sauterne wine. [after Château *Yquem,* an estate in SW France]

yt·ter·bi·um (i-tûr'bē-əm) *n.* A rare metallic element (symbol Yb) of the lanthanide series, occurring in minute amounts in gadolinite and certain other minerals. See ELEMENT. [< NL, from *Ytterby,* a town in Sweden where gadolinite was first found] — **yt·ter'bic** *adj.*

yt·tri·um (it'rē-əm) *n.* A rare element (symbol Y) of the lanthanide series, found in gadolinite, samarskite, and other minerals. See ELEMENT. Abbr. *Yt* [< NL < YTTRIA]

yuc·ca (yuk'ə) *n.* **1.** Any of various liliaceous plants of the southern U.S., Mexico, and Central America, having a woody stem that bears a large panicle of white, bell-shaped, drooping flowers emerging from a crown of leaves. **2.** The flower of this plant, the State flower of New Mexico. [< NL < Sp. *yuca* < Taino]

Yu·go·slav (yōō′gō-släv, -slav) *adj.* Of or pertaining to Yugoslavia or its people. — *n.* A citizen or native of Yugoslavia. Also **Yu′go·sla′vi·an.**

yuk (yuk) *U.S. Slang n.* A loud, hearty laugh. — *v.i. & v.t.* **yukked, yuk·king** To laugh or cause to laugh loud and heartily.

Yule (yōōl) *n.* Christmas time, or the feast celebrating it. [OE *ġéol* Christmas day, Christmastide]

yule log A large log or block of wood, brought in with much ceremony, and made the foundation of the Christmas Eve fire. Also **yule block, yule clog.**

Yule·tide (yōōl′tīd′) *n.* Christmas time.

Yu·ma (yōō′mə) *n.* One of a tribe of North American Indians of Yuman stock, formerly living in northern Mexico and Arizona and in SE California.

Yu·man (yōō′mən) *n.* A North American Indian stock of the SW U.S. and NW Mexico, including the Mohave and Yuma tribes.

yum·my (yum′ē) *Slang adj.* **·mi·er, ·mi·est** Gratifying to the senses, esp. to the taste; delicious. — *n.* Something very gratifying; a delight. [from *yum-yum*, an exclamation expressing delight at an agreeable taste]

yurt (yûrt) *n.* A portable tent made of felt laid on a framework of branches, used by nomadic Mongols in central Asia. [< Russian *yurta* < Turkic]

Z

z, Z (zē, *Brit.* zed) *n.* *pl.* **z's** or **zs, Z's** or **Zs, zees** (zēz) **1.** The twenty-sixth letter of the English alphabet. Also, *Brit.,* **zed.** **2.** The sound represented by the letter z, a voiced alveolar fricative corresponding to the voiceless *s.* — *symbol* **1.** *Physics* Atomic number. **2.** *Math.* An unknown quantity.

Zach·a·ri·ah (zak′ə-rī′ə) The last king of Israel of Jehu's race. II *Kings* xiv 29.

Zach·a·ri·as (zak′ə-rī′əs) **1.** The father of John the Baptist. *Luke* i 5. **2.** The Douai Bible name for ZECHARIAH.

zai·bat·su (zī-bät-sōō) *n. Japanese* The wealthy clique of Japan, representing four or five dominant families.

za·mar·ra (zə-mär′ə, -mar′ə) *n.* A sheepskin coat worn by Spanish shepherds. Also **za·mar′ro** (-mär′ō). [< Sp.]

za·ny (zā′nē) *adj.* **·ni·er, ·ni·est** Odd and comical; outlandish; ludicrous. — *n. pl.* **·nies 1.** A simpleton; buffoon; fool. **2.** In old comic plays, one who imitated the other performers, esp. the clown, with ludicrous failure. [< F < Ital. *zanni* servants who act as clowns in early Italian comedy]

zap·ti·ah (zup-tē′ä) *n.* A Turkish policeman. Also **zap·ti′e, zap·ti′eh.** [< Turkish *dabtiyeh* < Arabic *dabt* administration, regulation]

za·ra·pe (sä-rä′pā) See SERAPE.

za·re·ba (zə-rē′bə) *n.* **1.** In the Sudan, a stockade or other palisaded enclosure for protecting a village or camp. **2.** A village or camp so protected; also, any village. Also **za·ree′·ba.** [< Arabic *zarībah* pen for cattle < *zarb* sheepfold]

zarf (zärf) *n.* A metal cup-shaped holder, of open or ornamental filigree, for a hot coffee cup, used in the Levant. [< Arabic *zarf* vessel, sheath]

zar·zue·la (thär·thwā′lä) *n. Spanish* A form of lyrical theater in which song is intermingled with spoken dialogue.

za·yin (zä′yin) *n.* The seventh letter in the Hebrew alphabet. See ALPHABET.

zeal (zēl) *n.* Enthusiastic devotion; ardor, esp. for a cause. [< OF < L < Gk. *zēlos* < *zeein* to boil]

zeal·ot (zel′ət) *n.* **1.** An immoderate partisan; a fanatic. **2.** One who is zealous. [< LL < Gk. < *zēloein* to be zealous < *zēlos* zeal] — **zeal′ot·ry** *n.*

zeal·ous (zel′əs) *adj.* Filled with or incited by zeal; enthusiastic. — **zeal′ous·ly** *adv.* — **zeal′ous·ness** *n.*

ze·bec (zē′bek), **ze·beck** See XEBEC.

Zeb·e·dee (zeb′ə-dē) The father of James and John, disciples of Christ. *Matt.* iv 21.

ze·bra (zē′brə) *n.* Any of various African equine mammals resembling the ass, having a white or yellowish brown body fully marked with variously patterned, dark brown or blackish bands. [< Pg. < Bantu (Congo)] — **ze′brine** (-brēn, -brin), **ze′broid** (-broid) *adj.*

ze·bu (zē′byōō) *n.* The domesticated ox of India, China, and East Africa, having a hump on the withers, a large dewlap, and short horns. [< F *zébu* < Tibetan]

Zeb·u·lon (zeb′yə-lən) In the Old Testament, a son of Jacob and Leah. *Gen.* xxx 20. — *n.* The tribe of Israel descended from him. Also **Zeb′u·lun.**

Zech·a·ri·ah (zek′ə-rī′ə) Sixth-century B.C. Hebrew prophet who promoted the rebuilding of the Temple. — *n.* A book of the Old Testament bearing his name. Also, in the Douai Bible, *Zacharias.*

zed (zed) *n. Brit.* The letter Z. [< F < L < Gk. *zēta*]

zee (zē, *Du.* zā) *n. Dutch* Sea: used in geographic names: *Zuider Zee, Tappen Zee.*

Zeit·geist (tsīt′gīst) *n. German* The spirit of the time; the intellectual and moral tendencies that characterize any age or epoch. [< G < *zeit* time + *geist* spirit]

zemst·vo (zem′stvō, *Russ.* zyem′stvô) *n.* Prior to 1917, a Russian elective district. [< Russian *semlya* land]

ze·na·na (zə-nä′nə) *n.* In India, the women's apartments; the East Indian harem: also spelled *zanana.* [< Hind. *zenāna* belonging to women < Persian *zanāna* < *zan* woman]

Zen Buddhism (zen) A form of contemplative Buddhism whose adherents believe in and work toward abrupt enlightenment. It originated in China, and later spread to Japan, where it greatly influenced Japanese culture. Also **Zen.** [< Japanese *zen* meditation < Chinese < Skt. *dhyana*]

Zend (zend) *n.* **1.** The ancient translation and commentary, in a literary form of Middle Persian (Pahlavi), of the Avesta, the sacred writings of the Zoroastrian religion. **2.** Erroneously, the language of the Avesta; Avestan. [< F < Persian, interpretation] — **Zend′ic** *adj.*

Zend-A·ves·ta (zend′ə-ves′tə) *n.* The Avesta, including the later translation and commentary called the Zend. — **Zend′-A·ves·ta′ic** (-ə-ves·tā′ik) *adj.*

ze·nith (zē′nith) *n.* **1.** The point of the celestial sphere that is exactly overhead, and opposite to the nadir. **2.** The highest or culminating point; peak: the *zenith* of one's career: opposed to *nadir.* [< OF *cenit,* ult. < Arabic *samt* (*ar-ras*) the path (over the head)]

ze·o·lite (zē′ə-līt) *n.* Any of a large class of secondary minerals found in cavities and veins in eruptive rocks, usu. a hydrous silicate of aluminum and sodium. [< Sw. < Gk. *zēein* to boil + *lithos* stone] — **ze′o·lit′ic** (-lit′ik) *adj.*

Zeph·a·ni·ah (zef′ə-nī′ə) Seventh-century B.C. Hebrew prophet. — *n.* A book of the Old Testament bearing his name. Also, in the Douai Bible, *Sophonias.*

zeph·yr (zef′ər) *n.* **1.** The west wind. **2.** Any soft, gentle wind. **3.** Worsted or woolen yarn of very light weight used for embroidery, shawls, etc.: also **zephyr worsted. 4.** Anything very light and airy. [< L < Gk. *zephyros*]

zephyr cloth Fine cassimere used for women's clothing.

zep·pe·lin (zep′ə·lin, *Ger.* tsep′ə-lēn′) *n. Often cap.* A large dirigible having a rigid, cigar-shaped body. [after Count Ferdinand von *Zeppelin,* 1838–1917, German general and aviator who designed it]

ze·ro (zir′ō, zē′rō) *n. pl.* **ze·ros** or **ze·roes 1.** The numeral or symbol 0; a cipher. ◆ In nontechnical speech, this symbol is often pronounced (ō). **2.** *Math.* **a** A cardinal number indicating the absence of quantity. **b** The point where a continuous function changes its sign from plus to minus, or vice versa. **3.** The point on a scale, as of a thermometer, from which measures are counted; also, a temperature that registers zero on a thermometer. **4.** *Mil.* A setting for a gunsight that adjusts both for elevation and wind. **5.** The lowest point. **6.** Nothing. — *v.t.* **ze·roed, ze·ro·ing** To adjust (instruments) to an arbitrary zero point for synchronized readings. — **to zero in 1.** To adjust the sight of (a gun) by calibrated results of firings. **2.** To direct firepower exactly on target. **3.** To approach or give one's attention to as though directed to a target. — *adj.* Without value or appreciable change. [< F < Ital. < Arabic *sifr*]

zero gravity *Aerospace* A condition in which the gravitational attraction of the earth or other celestial body is nullified by inertial forces; weightlessness.

zero hour 1. H-hour. **2.** *Informal* The moment of undertaking something; any critical moment.

zest (zest) *n.* **1.** Invigorating excitement; keen enjoyment;

gusto: often with *for*: a *zest* for reading.   **2.** That which imparts such excitement and relish.   **3.** An agreeable and piquant flavor in anything tasted, esp. if added to the usual flavor. — *v.t.* To give zest or relish to; make piquant.   [< F *zeste* lemon peel (for flavoring)]

zest·ful (zest′fəl) *adj.* Full of or marked by zest. Also **zest′y.** — **zest′ful·ly** *adv.* — **zest′ful·ness** *n.*

ze·ta (zā′tə, zē′-) *n.* The sixth letter (Z, ζ) in the Greek alphabet, corresponding to English z. See ALPHABET.   [< Gk. *zēta*]

zeug·ma (zōōg′mə) *n.* A rhetorical figure in which an adjective is made to modify, or a verb to govern, two nouns, while applying properly only to one, as in *She was remembered but they forgotten.*   [< NL < Gk. < *zeugnymi* to yoke]

Zeus (zōōs) In Greek mythology, the supreme deity, ruler of the celestial realm, son of Kronos and Rhea and husband of Hera: identified with the Roman *Jupiter.*

zib·et (zib′it) *n.* The Asian or Indian civet. Also **zib′eth.**   [< Med.L < Arabic *zabād* civet]

zig·zag (zig′zag) *n.* **1.** A series of short, sharp turns or angles from one side to the other in succession.   **2.** Something characterized by such angles, as a path or pattern. — *adj.* Having or proceeding in a zigzag. — *adv.* In a zigzag manner. — *v.t. & v.i.* **·zagged, ·zag·ging** To form or move in zigzags.   [< F < G *zickzack*, prob. reduplication of *zacke* sharp point]   — **zig′zag·ger** *n.*

zinc (zingk) *n.* A bluish white, metallic element (symbol Zn) occurring mostly in combination, widely used in industry, medicine, the arts, for roofing, and as the negative electrode in electric batteries. See ELEMENT. — *v.t.* **zincked** or **zinced, zinck·ing** or **zinc·ing** To coat or cover with zinc; galvanize.   [< *zink*; ult. origin unknown] — **zinc′ic** *adj.* — **zinck′y, zinc′y, zink′y** *adj.*

zinc blende Sphalerite.

zinc ointment A medicated ointment for skin affections, containing zinc oxide mixed with petrolatum.

zinc·ous (zingk′əs) *adj. Chem.* Pertaining to or derived from zinc.

zinc oxide *Chem.* A white pulverulent compound ZnO, used as a pigment, and in medicine as a mild antiseptic and astringent.

zinc white Zinc oxide used as a pigment in paints.

zin·fan·del (zin′fän·del) *n.* A dry, red or white claret-type wine made in California.   [? after a European place name]

zing (zing) *Informal n.* **1.** A high-pitched buzzing or humming sound.   **2.** Energy; vitality; vigor. — *v.i.* To make a shrill, humming sound.   [Imit.]

zin·ga·ro (tsēng′gä·rō) *n. pl.* **·ri** (-rē) *Italian* A gypsy. Also **zin′ga·no** (-nō). — **zin′ga·ra** (-rä) *n.fem.*

zin·ni·a (zin′ē·ə) *n.* Any of various American herbs, having showy flowers; esp., the common zinnia, the State flower of Indiana.   [< NL, after J. G. *Zinn*, 1727–59, German professor of medicine]

Zi·on (zī′ən) **1.** A hill in Jerusalem, the site of the temple and the royal residence of David and his successors, regarded by the Jews as a symbol for the center of Jewish national culture, government, and religion.   **2.** The Jewish people.   **3.** Any place or community considered to be especially under God's rule.   **4.** The heavenly Jerusalem; heaven. Also **Sion.**   [OE < LL < Gk. < Hebrew *tsiyōn* hill]

Zi·on·ism (zī′ən·iz′əm) *n.* A movement for a resettlement of the Jews in Palestine. Also **Zion movement.** — **Zi′on·ist** *adj. & n.* — **Zi′on·is′tic** *adj.*

zip (zip) *n.* **1.** A sharp, hissing sound, as of a bullet passing through the air.   **2.** *Informal* Energy; vitality; vim. — *v.* **zipped, zip·ping** *v.t.* **1.** To fasten with a zipper. — *v.i.* **2.** *Informal* To be very energetic.   **3.** To move or fly with a zip.   [Imit.]

ZIP Code (zip) A numerical code devised by the U.S. Post Office to aid in the distribution of domestic mail. Also **Zip Code.**   [< Z(ONE) I(MPROVEMENT) P(LAN)]

zip gun *U.S. Slang* A homemade pistol consisting of a small pipe or other tube fastened to a block of wood and equipped with a firing pin actuated by a spring or rubber band.

zip·per (zip′ər) *n.* A fastener having two rows of interlocking teeth that may be closed or separated by a sliding device, used on clothing, boots, etc.: also called *slide fastener.*

zip·py (zip′ē) *adj.* **·pi·er, ·pi·est** *Informal* Brisk; energetic.

zir·con (zûr′kon) *n.* A crystalline, variously colored, zirconium silicate, ZrSiO₄; some translucent varieties of which are used as gems.   [< G *zirken* or F *zircone* < Arabic *zarqūn* cinnabar < Persian < *zar* gold + *gūn* color]

zir·co·ni·um (zûr·kō′nē·əm) *n.* A metallic element (symbol Zr) chemically resembling titanium, used in alloys, as an opacifier of lacquers, and as an abrasive. See ELEMENT.   [< NL < ZIRCON] — **zir·con′ic** (-kon′ik) *adj.*

zith·er (zith′ər) *n.* A simple form of stringed instrument, having a flat sounding board and from thirty to forty strings

that are played by plucking with a plectrum. Also **zith′ern** (-ərn).   [< G < L < Gk. *kithara*]

zlo·ty (zlô′tē) *n. pl.* **·tys** or **·ty** The standard monetary unit of Poland, equal to 100 groszy: in 1960 worth about 25 U.S. cents.   [< Polish, lit., golden]

zo- Var. of ZOO-.

zo·di·ac (zō′dē·ak) *n.* **1.** An imaginary belt encircling the heavens and extending about 8° on each side of the ecliptic within which are the apparent orbits of the moon, sun, and larger planets. It is divided into twelve parts, called **signs of the zodiac,** that formerly corresponded to twelve constellations bearing the same names.   **2.** A figure or diagram representing this belt and its signs, used in astrology.   **3.** A complete circuit.   [< OF < L < Gk. (*kyklos*) *zōdiakos* (circle) of animals < *zōion* animal] — **zo·di·a·cal** (zō·dī′ə·kəl) *adj.*

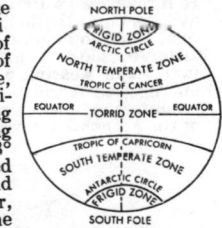

SIGNS OF THE ZODIAC

A Vernal equinox: Aries, Taurus, Gemini. *B* Summer solstice: Cancer, Leo, Virgo. *C* Autumnal equinox: Libra, Scorpio, Sagittarius. *D* Winter solstice: Capricorn, Aquarius, Pisces.

zom·bie (zom′bē) *n.* **1.** The supernatural power by which a dead body is believed to be reanimated.   **2.** A corpse reactivated by sorcery, but still dead.   **3.** Loosely, a ghost.   **4.** A large, strong cocktail made from several kinds of rum, fruit juices, and liqueur.   **5.** *Slang* An unattractive person. Also **zom′bi.**   [< West African] — **zom′bi·ism** *n.*

zo·nal (zō′nəl) *adj.* Of, pertaining to, exhibiting, or marked by a zone or zones; like a zone. Also **zo′na·ry** (-nər·ē).

zone (zōn) *n.* **1.** An area, tract, or section distinguished from other or adjacent areas by some special quality, purpose, or condition: a mountainous *zone*; a *zone* of disagreement.   **2.** *Usu. cap.* Any of five divisions of the earth's surface, enclosed between two parallels of latitude and named for the prevailing climate: the **Torrid Zone,** extending on each side of the equator 23° 27′; the **Temperate Zones,** included between the parallels 23° 27′ and 66° 33′ on both sides of the equator, and the **Frigid Zones,** within the parallels 66° 33′ and the poles.   **3.** An area of land designated as distinct from other areas because of its particular use or location: combat *zone*; school *zone.*   **4.** *Ecol.* A belt or area delimited from others by the character of its plant or animal life, its climate, geological formations, etc.   **5.** A concentric area or band; esp., any of a number of concentric areas used to determine the rate of charge for transporting something a specified distance, as in the U.S. parcel post system.   **6.** A section of a city or town where only certain uses of the land or certain types of buildings are permitted by law: a residential *zone.*   **7.** A section of a city designated with a number as an aid in the distribution of mail.   **8.** A belt, band, stripe, etc., having a color or other characteristic that distinguishes it from the object it encircles.   **9.** *Geom.* A portion of the surface of a sphere enclosed between two parallel planes.   **10.** *Archaic* or *Poetic* A belt or girdle. — *v.t.* **zoned, zon·ing 1.** To divide into zones; esp., to divide (a city, etc.) into zones that are restricted as to types of construction and use, as residential or industrial.   **2.** To designate (an area, etc.) as a zone or part of a zone: to *zone* the waterfront district as commercial.   **3.** To mark with or as with zones or stripes.   **4.** To encircle with a zone or belt.   [< L < Gk. *zōnē* girdle]

TERRESTRIAL ZONES

zoo (zōō) *n.* A park or garden in which wild animals are kept for exhibition. Also **zoological garden, zoological park.**

zoo- *combining form* Animal; of or related to animals, or to animal forms. Also, before vowels, **zo-.**   [< Gk. *zōion* animal]

zo·o·ge·og·ra·phy (zō′ə·jē·og′rə·fē) *n.* The systematic study of the distribution of animals and of the relations between animal groups and the land or aquatic areas in which they predominate. **— zo′o·ge·og′ra·pher** *n.* **— zo′o·ge′o·graph′ic** (-jē′ə·graf′ik) or **-i·cal** *adj.* **— zo′o·ge′o·graph′i·cal·ly** *adv.*

zo·oid (zō′oid) *n.* **1.** *Biol.* Any animal or vegetable organism, usu. very small, capable of spontaneous movement and independent existence, as a spermatozoon, spermatozoid, etc. **2.** *Zool.* One of the distinct members of a compound or colonial organism. **—** *adj.* Having the nature of an animal: also **zo·oi·dal** (zō·oid′l).

zo·o·log·i·cal (zō′ə·loj′i·kəl) *adj.* **1.** Of or pertaining to zoology. **2.** Relating to or characteristic of animals. Also **zo′o·log′ic. — zo′o·log′i·cal·ly** *adv.*

zo·ol·o·gy (zō·ol′ə·jē) *n.* **1.** The science that treats of animals with reference to their structure, functions, development, evolution, and classification. **2.** The animal kingdom, or local examples of it, regarded biologically. [< NL < Gk. *zōion* animal + *logos* word, discourse] **— zo·ol′o·gist** *n.*

zoom (zōōm) *v.i.* **1.** To make a low-pitched but loud humming sound; also, to move with such a sound. **2.** To climb sharply in an airplane. **—** *v.t.* **3.** To cause to zoom. **—** *n.* The act of zooming. [Imit.]

zoom lens *Photog.* A lens, used chiefly on television and motion picture cameras, that permits the size of the image to be varied continuously without loss of focus.

zo·o·mor·phism (zō′ə·môr′fiz·əm) *n.* **1.** The conception, symbolization, or representation of a man or a god in the form of an animal; also, the attribution of divine or human qualities to animals. **2.** The representation of animals or animal forms in art or symbolism. **3.** Transformation into animals. Also **zo′o·mor′phy. — zo′o·mor′phic** *adj.*

zo·o·phyte (zō′ə·fīt) *n.* An invertebrate animal resembling a plant, as a coral or sea anemone. **— zo′o·phyt′ic** (-fit′ik) or **-i·cal** *adj.*

zo·o·spore (zō′ə·spôr, -spōr) *n.* **1.** *Bot.* A spore, produced among some algae and fungi, that is provided with cilia by means of which it can move about. **2.** *Zool.* A flagellate or ameboid motile body in certain protozoa. **— zo′o·spor′ic** (-spôr′ik, -spor′ik), **zo·os·po·rous** (zō·os′pər·əs) *adj.*

Zo·ro·as·tri·an (zō′rō·as′trē·ən) *n.* A follower of Zoroaster; an adherent of Zoroastrianism. **—** *adj.* Of or pertaining to Zoroaster or to the religion he founded.

Zo·ro·as·tri·an·ism (zō′rō·as′trē·ən·iz′əm) *n.* The religious system founded by Zoroaster and taught in the Zend-Avesta. It recognizes two creative powers, one good and the other evil, includes the belief in life after death, and teaches the final triumph of good over evil. Also **Zo′ro·as′trism.**

Zou·ave (zōō·äv′, swäv) *n.* **1.** A light-armed French infantryman wearing a brilliant Oriental uniform, originally an Algerian recruit. **2.** In the Civil War, a member of a volunteer regiment assuming the name and part of the dress of the French Zouaves. **3.** A woman's short, gaily embroidered jacket: also **Zouave jacket.** [< F < Arabic *Zouāoua*, a Kabyle tribe]

zounds (zoundz, zōōndz) *interj. Archaic* A mild oath used to express surprise or anger. [Short for *God's wounds*]

zuc·chet·to (tsōōk·ket′tō) *n.* A skullcap worn by ecclesiastics in the Roman Catholic Church, black for a priest, purple for a bishop, red for a cardinal, and white for the pope. Also **zuc·chet′ta** (-tä). [Var. of Ital. *zucchetta*, < LL *cucutia* a kind of wood]

zuc·chi·ni (zōō·kē′nē, *Ital.* dzōōk·kē′nē) *n.* A type of green summer squash of cylindrical shape. [< Ital., pl. of *zucchino*, dim. of *zucca* gourd, squash]

Zu·lu (zōō′lōō) *n. pl.* **Zu·lus** or **Zu·lu** **1.** One of a Bantu nation of Natal, South Africa, sometimes included with the Kaffirs. **2.** The Bantu language of the Zulus. **—** *adj.* Of, pertaining to, or characteristic of the Zulus or their language.

Zu·ñi (zōō′nyē) *n.* **1.** One of a tribe of North American Indians of pueblo culture but comprising a distinct, ethnic stock, living in New Mexico. **2.** The language of this tribe. **— Zu′ñi·an** *adj. & n.*

zwie·back (zwī′bak, zwē′-, swī′, swē′-, -bäk; *Ger.* tsvē′bäk) *n.* A biscuit of wheaten breat or rusk baked yellow in the loaf and later sliced and toasted. [< G, twice baked < *zwie-* twice (< *zwei* two) + *backen* to bake]

zygo- *combining form* Yoke; pair; resembling a yoke, esp. in shape. Also, before vowels, **zyg-.** [< Gk. *zygon* yoke]

zy·gote (zī′gōt, zig′ōt) *n. Biol.* **1.** The product of the union of two gametes. **2.** A new organism developed from such a union. [< Gk. < *zygon* yoke] **— zy·got·ic** (zī·got′·ik) *adj.*

zy·mase (zī′mās) *n. Biochem.* An enzyme, obtained principally from yeast, that induces fermentation by breaking down glucose and related carbohydrates into alcohol and carbon dioxide. [< F < Gk. *zymē* leaven]

zyme (zīm) *n.* A disease germ or virus supposed to be the specific cause of a zymotic disease. [< Gk. *zymē* leaven]

zymo- *combining form* Fermentation; of or related to fermentation. Also, before vowels, **zym-.** [< Gk. *zymē* leaven]

zy·mol·o·gy (zī·mol′ə·jē) *n.* The study of fermentation and the action of enzymes. **— zy·mo·log·ic** (zī′mə·loj′ik) or **-i·cal** *adj.* **— zy·mol′o·gist** *n.*

zy·mol·y·sis (zī·mol′ə·sis) *n.* Fermentation or the action of enzymes. **— zy·mo·lyt·ic** (zī′mə·lit′ik) *adj.*

zy·mo·sis (zī·mō′sis) *n. pl.* **·ses** **1.** Any form of fermentation. **2.** *Med.* A process resembling fermentation formerly supposed to give rise to a diseased condition. [< NL < Gk. < *zymoein* to leaven, ferment < *zymē* leaven] **— zy·mot·ic** (-mot′ik) *adj.*

zy·mur·gy (zī′mûr·jē) *n.* A branch of chemistry treating of processes in which fermentation takes place, as brewing, winemaking, etc.

GAZETTEER

This gazetteer lists all of the more important political divisions and geographical features of the world, along with the major localities in the United States and Canada. The population figures given for places in the United States and Puerto Rico are from the census of 1970; those for Canada and Australia are from the censuses of 1971. All other population figures are the latest ones available.

An additional feature of this section is the inclusion of the new postal ZIP codes for places in the United States and Puerto Rico. These were not available, however, in all cases. The asterisk (*) following some ZIP codes indicates that the city is further divided into postal zones and that the number given does not adequately identify a post office. In such cases further information is available from local postal authorities.

To conserve space, the following abbreviations have been used throughout this section:

ab.	about	NE	northeast(ern)
adm.	administrative	NW	northwest(ern)
assoc.	associated or association	penin.	peninsula
		poss.	possession
ASSR	Autonomous Soviet Socialist Republic	prot.	protectorate
		prov.	province
auton.	autonomous	reg.	region
boro.	borough	s	south(ern)
cap.	capital or county seat	SE	southeast(ern)
		SSR	Soviet Socialist Republic
CEN.	central		
co.	county	sw	southwest(ern)
col.	colony	terr.	territory
ctr.	center	twp.	township
depen.	dependency	uninc.	unincorporated
dept.	department	urb.	urban
dist.	district	USSR	Union of Soviet Socialist Republics
div.	division		
E	east(ern)	vill.	village
isl(s).	island(s)	w	west(ern)
mtn(s).	mountain(s)		
N	north(ern)		

Aachen city, w West Germany; 241,362.
Aarhus co., E Denmark; 310 sq. mi.; 210,000.
—city, E Aarhus co.; cap.; 119,000.
Abbeville town, s Louisiana; 10,996; ZIP 70510.
—city, NW South Carolina; 5,515; ZIP 29620.
Aberdeen co., NE Scotland; 1,972 sq. mi.; 299,000.
—city, SE Aberdeen co.; cap.; 180,755.
Aberdeen town, NE Maryland; 12,375; (ZIP 21001); site of Aberdeen Proving Ground, a U.S. Army reservation; ZIP 21005.
—city, E Mississippi; 6,157; ZIP 39730.
—city, NE South Dakota; 26,476; ZIP 57401*.
—port city, w Washington; 18,489; ZIP 98520.
Abidjan city, SE Ivory Coast; cap.; 650,000.
Abilene city, E CEN. Kansas; 6,661; ZIP 67410.
—city, N CEN. Texas; 89,259; ZIP 79600.
Abington town, E Massachusetts; 12,334; ZIP 02351.
—urb. twp., SE Pennsylvania; 62,899; ZIP 19001.
Acapulco city, sw Mexico; 309,254.
Accra city, s Ghana; cap.; 564,194.
Achaea dept., N Peloponessus, Greece; 1,146 sq. mi.; 229,000; cap. Patras.
Aconcagua extinct volcano, w CEN. Argentina; 22,834 ft.
Acre city, NE Israel; 24,000.
Ada city, s CEN. Oklahoma; 14,859; ZIP 74820*.
Adams town, NW Massachusetts; 11,772; ZIP 01220.
Addis Ababa city, CEN. Ethiopia; cap.; 1,011,565.
Addison vill., NE Illinois; 24,482; ZIP 60101.
Adelaide city, SE South Australia; cap.; 809,466.
Aden city, South Yemen; sw Arabian penin.; former Brit. col.; 264,326.
Aden, Gulf of inlet of Arabian Sea betw. South Yemen and Somalia.
Aden Protectorate Formerly, group of Arab tribal districts comprising a British protectorate; now part of South Yemen; sw Arabian penin.; 150,000 sq. mi.; 650,000.
Adirondack Mountains mtn. range, NE New York.
Adjuntas town, CEN. Puerto Rico; 5,319; ZIP 00601.
Adrian city, SE Michigan; 20,382; ZIP 49221.

Adriatic Sea inlet of the Mediterranean Sea, E of Italy.
Aegean Sea inlet of the Mediterranean Sea betw. Greece and Asia Minor.
Afars and Issas French Overseas terr., E Africa; 8,900 sq. mi.; 200,000; cap. Djibouti.
Afghanistan republic, s CEN. Asia; 250,000 sq. mi.; 18,700,000; cap. Kabul.
Africa second largest continent, s of Europe and w of Asia; 11,710,000 sq. mi.; 391,000,000.
Agaña city, w Guam; cap.; 1,642; ZIP 96910.
Agra city, N India; site of Taj Mahal; 594,858.
Aguadilla town, NW Puerto Rico; 21,031; ZIP 00603*.
Aguascalientes state, CEN. Mexico; 2,499 sq. mi.; 237,000.
—city, CEN. Aguascalientes state; cap.; 213,428.
Agulhas, Cape cape s South Africa; southernmost point of Africa.
Ahmedabad city, w India; temporary cap. of Gujarat; 1,588,378.
Aibonito town, CEN. Puerto Rico; 7,582; ZIP 00609.
Aiea town, s Oahu, Hawaii; 12,560; ZIP 96701.
Aiken city, w South Carolina; 17,974; ZIP 29801*.
Aisne river, N France; 175 mi. long.
Ajaccio city, w Corsica; cap.; birthplace of Napoleon; 33,000.
Ajax town, s Ontario, Canada; 7,755.
Ajo vill., sw Arizona; 5,881; ZIP 85321.
Akron city, NE Ohio; 275,425; ZIP 44300*.
Alabama state, SE United States; 51,609 sq. mi.; 3,444,165; cap. Montgomery.
Alameda city, w California; 70,968; ZIP 94501*.
Alamogordo town, s New Mexico; site of the first atom bomb test; 23,035; ZIP 88310.
Alamo Heights city, s CEN. Texas; 6,933; ZIP see SAN ANTONIO.
Alamosa city, s Colorado; 6,985; ZIP 81101.
Alaska state of the United States, NW North America; 586,400 sq. mi.; 302,173; cap. Juneau.
Alaska, Gulf of inlet of the Pacific on the s coast of Alaska.
Alaska Highway road joining Dawson Creek, British Columbia and Fairbanks, Alaska; 1,527 mi.
Alaska Peninsula promontory of sw Alaska; ab. 400 mi. long.
Alaska Range mtn. range, s CEN. Alaska.
Albania Balkan republic s of Yugoslavia; 10,629 sq. mi.; 2,400,000; cap. Tiranë.
Albany city, w California; 14,674; ZIP see BERKELEY.
—city, sw Georgia; 72,623; ZIP 31701*.
—city, E New York; cap.; 114,873; ZIP 12200*.
—city, w Oregon, 18,181; ZIP 97321.
Albemarle town, s CEN. North Carolina; 11,126; ZIP 28001.
Albemarle Sound inlet of the Atlantic, NE North Carolina.
Alberta prov., w Canada; 255,285 sq. mi.; 1,768,000; cap. Edmonton.
Albert Lea city, s Minnesota; 19,418; ZIP 56007.
Albertville city, NE Alabama; 9,963; ZIP 35950.
Albion city, s Michigan; 12,112; ZIP 49224.
—vill., w New York; 5,122; ZIP 14411.
Albuquerque city, NW New Mexico; 243,751; ZIP 87100*.
Alcan Highway Alaska Highway: *unofficial name*.
Alcoa city, E Tennessee; 7,739; ZIP 37701.
Alderney island, N Channel Islands; 3 sq. mi.
Aleppo city, NE Syria; 639,361.
Aleutian Islands island group, sw of the Alaska Peninsula.
Alexander City city E Alabama; 12,358; ZIP 35010.
Alexandria city, N Arab Republic of Egypt; summer cap.; 2,032,000.
Alexandria city, E CEN. Indiana; 5,097; ZIP 46001.
—city, CEN. Louisiana; 41,557; ZIP 71301*.
—city, w CEN. Minnesota; 6,973; ZIP 56308.
—city, NE Virginia; 110,938; ZIP 22300*.
Algeria republic, NW Africa; 919,352 sq. mi.; 16,300,000; cap. Algiers.
Algiers city, N Algeria; cap.; 943,142.
Algona city, N Iowa; 6,032; ZIP 50511.
Alhambra city, sw California; 62,125; ZIP 91800*.
Alicante prov., E Spain; 2,264 sq. mi.; 696,000.
—city, E Alicante prov.; cap.; 184,716.

Alice city, s Texas; 20,121; ZIP 78332.
Aliquippa boro., w Pennsylvania; 22,277; ZIP 15001.
Alisal vill., w California; 16,473; ZIP see SALINAS.
Allahabad city N India; 431,000.
Allegheny Mountains mtn. range of Appalachian system; extends from Pennsylvania through Virginia.
Allegheny River river, w New York and Pennsylvania; 325 mi. long.
Allen Park vill., SE Michigan; 40,747; ZIP 48101*.
Allentown city, E Pennsylvania; 109,527; ZIP 18100*.
Alliance city, NW Nebraska; 6,862; ZIP 69301.
—city, NE Ohio; 26,547; ZIP 44601*.
Alma city, CEN. Michigan; 9,790; ZIP 48801.
Alma city, s Quebec, Canada; 13,309.
Alma Ata city, SE Kazakh SSR; cap.; 455,000.
Alpena city, NE Michigan; 13,805; ZIP 49707.
Alps mtn. system, s Europe; extends from s coast of France to w coast of Yugoslavia.
Alsace reg. and former prov., NE France.
Alsace-Lorraine oft-disputed border reg., NE France; adjoins SW Germany.
Altadena uninc. place, SW California; 42,380; ZIP 91001**.
Altai Mountains mtn. system, CEN. Asia.
Altamont uninc. place, s Oregon; 15,746.
Alton city, SW Illinois; 39,700; ZIP 62002*.
Altoona city, s CEN. Pennsylvania; 62,900; ZIP 16601*.
Altus city, SW Oklahoma; 22,865; ZIP 73521*.
Alum Rock uninc. place SW California; 18,355.
Alva city, NW Oklahoma; 7,440; ZIP 73717.
Alvin city, SE Texas; 10,671; ZIP 77511.
Amarillo city, NW Texas; 127,010; ZIP 79100*.
Amazon river, N South America; 3,910 mi. long; carries the largest volume of water of all rivers.
Ambler boro., SE Pennsylvania; 7,800; ZIP 19002.
Ambridge boro., SE Pennsylvania; 11,324; ZIP 15003.
America 1. The United States of America. 2. North and South America; the Western Hemisphere.
American Fork city, N CEN. Utah; 7,713; ZIP 84003.
American Samoa See SAMOA.
Americus city, SW CEN. Georgia; 16,091; ZIP 31709.
Ames city, CEN. Iowa; 39,505; ZIP 50010*.
Amesbury uninc. place, NE Massachusetts; 11,388; ZIP 01913.
Amherst uninc. place, w CEN. Massachusetts; 26,331; ZIP 01002*.
—vill., N Ohio; 9,902; ZIP 44001.
Amherst town, N Nova Scotia, Canada; 10,788.
Amiens city, N France; 117,191.
Amityville vill., SE New York; 9,794; ZIP 11701.
Amman city, N CEN. Jordan; cap.; 560,000.
Amory city, E Mississippi; 7,236; ZIP 38821.
Amos town, W Quebec, Canada; 6,080.
Amoy isl. of China, Formosa Strait.
—city, Amoy isl.; 224,000.
Amritsar city, w Punjab, India; 376,000.
Amsterdam city, w Netherlands; cap.; 807,742.
Amsterdam city, E CEN. New York; 25,524; ZIP 12010*.
Amur river, E Asia; 2,700 mi. long.
Anaconda city, SW Montana; 9,771; ZIP 59711.
Anacortes city, NW Washington; 7,701; ZIP 98221*.
Anadarko city, w CEN. Oklahoma; 6,682; ZIP 73005.
Anaheim city, SW California; 166,701; ZIP 92800*.
Anatolia penin. at w end of Asia; comprises most of Turkey.
Anchorage city, s Alaska; 48,081; ZIP 99501*.
Andalusia reg., s Spain.
Andalusia city, s Alabama; 10,092; ZIP 36420.
Anderson city, E CEN. Indiana; 70,787; ZIP 46010*.
—city, NW South Carolina; 27,556; ZIP 29621*.
Andes mtn. range, w South America; connects with the Rockies; over 4,000 mi. long.
Andorra republic betw. France and Spain; 179 sq. mi.; 6,000.
—city, CEN. Andorra; cap.; 1,000.
Andover town, NE Massachusetts 23,695; ZIP 01810*.
Andrews city, w Texas; 8,625; ZIP 79714.
Angel Falls waterfall, SE Venezuela; over 3,300 ft.
Angleton city, s Texas; 9,770; ZIP 77515.
Angola republic, w Africa; 481,351 sq. mi.; ab. 6,000,000; cap. Luanda.
Angora Ankara: former name.
Anjou former prov., w France.
Anjou town, s Quebec, Canada; 9,511.
Ankara city, CEN. Turkey; cap.; 1,461,345.
Annam former French prot., E CEN. Indochina; now

divided betw. North and South Vietnam.
Annapolis city, CEN. Maryland; cap.; site of U.S. Naval Academy; 29,592; ZIP 21400*.
Ann Arbor city, SE Michigan; 99,797; ZIP 48103*.
Anniston city, NE Alabama; 31,533; ZIP 36201*.
Anoka city, E Minnesota; 13,489; ZIP 55303.
Anshan city, NE People's Republic of China; 1,500,000.
Ansonia city, SW Connecticut; 21,160; ZIP 06401.
Antarctica continent surrounding the South Pole; over 5 million sq. mi.: also Antarctic Continent.
Antarctic Archipelago Palmer Archipelago: alternative name.
Antarctic Circle parallel of latitude at 66°33′ s; the boundary of the South Frigid Zone.
Antarctic Ocean parts of Atlantic, Pacific, and Indian oceans bordering on Antarctica.
Antarctic Zone region enclosed by the Antarctic Circle.
Antigo city, NE Wisconsin; 9,005; ZIP 54409.
Antigua British col. of the West Indies; 171 sq. mi.; 63,000; cap. St. John's.
Antilles islands of the West Indies excluding the Bahamas; comprises Greater Antilles: Cuba, Hispaniola, Jamaica, and Puerto Rico, and Lesser Antilles: Trinidad, the Windward Islands, the Leeward Islands, and other small islands.
Antioch city, s Turkey; 37,000.
Antioch city, w California; 28,060; ZIP 94509.
Antwerp city, N Belgium, 919,814.
Apennines mtn. range of Italy s of Po valley.
Appalachian Mountains mtn. system, E North America.
Appleton city, E Wisconsin, 57,143; ZIP 54910*.
Aquitaine reg., SW France.
Arabia penin., SW Asia, betw. the Red Sea and Persian Gulf.
Arabian Sea part of the Indian Ocean betw. Arabia and India.
Aragon reg., NE Spain.
Aral Sea salt inland sea, s CEN. USSR.
Aransas Pass city, s Texas; 5,813; ZIP 78336.
Ararat, Mount mtn., E Turkey; 16,945 ft.; traditional landing place of Noah's ark.
Arbutus-Halethorpe-Relay uninc. place, CEN. Maryland; 22,745.
Arcadia dept., CEN. Peloponnesus, Greece; 1,168 sq. mi.; 154,000; cap. Tripolis.
Arcadia city, SW California; 42,868; ZIP 91006*.
—city, s CEN. Florida; 5,658; ZIP 33821.
Arcata city, NW California; 8,985; ZIP 95521.
Archbald boro., NE Pennsylvania; 6,118; ZIP 18403.
Arctic Circle parallel of latitude at 66°33′ N; the boundary of the North Frigid Zone.
Arctic Ocean sea, N of Arctic Circle, surrounding North Pole.
Arden-Arcade uninc. place, CEN. California; 82,492; ZIP see SACRAMENTO.
Ardmore city, s Oklahoma; 20,881; ZIP 73401.
Arecibo town, N Puerto Rico; 35,484; ZIP 00612*.
Argentina republic, s South America; 1,084,362 sq. mi.; 24,600,000; cap. Buenos Aires.
Argonne ridge, N France; site of battles in World War I and II.
Arizona state, SW United States; 113,909 sq. mi.; 1,772,482; cap. Phoenix.
Arkadelphia city, s CEN. Arkansas; 9,841; ZIP 71923*.
Arkansas state, s CEN. United States; 53,104 sq. mi.; 1,923,295; cap. Little Rock.
Arkansas City city, s Kansas; 13,216; ZIP 67005.
Arkhangelsk city, NW RSFSR; 256,000.
Arlington urb. co., NE Virginia; site of Arlington National Cemetery, containing tomb of the Unknown Soldier.
—town, E Massachusetts; 53,524; ZIP see BOSTON.
—vill., SE New York; 8,317; ZIP see POUGHKEEPSIE.
—city, N Texas; 90,643; ZIP 76010*.
Arlington Heights vill., NE Illinois; 64,884; ZIP 60004*.
Armenia 1. former country, SW Asia. 2. the Armenian SSR.
Armenian SSR republic, s USSR; 11,500 sq. mi.; 2,606,000; cap. Yerevan.
Arnhem city, E Netherlands; 131,377.
Arnold boro., SW Pennsylvania; 8,174; ZIP see NEW KENSINGTON.
Arnprior town, SE Ontario, Canada; 5,474.

Artesia town, sw California; 14,757; ZIP 90701.
—city, SE New Mexico; 10,315; ZIP 88210.
Arvada town, N CEN. Colorado; 46,814; ZIP 80002*.
Arvida city, S CEN. Quebec, Canada; 14,460.
Arvin uninc. place, S CEN. California; 5,090; ZIP 93203.
Asbestos town, S Quebec, Canada; 11,083.
Asbury Park city, E New Jersey; 16,533; ZIP 07712*.
Ascension isl. poss. of Great Britain, South Atlantic; 34 sq. mi.; 350.
Asheboro town, CEN. North Carolina; 10,797; ZIP 27203.
Asheville city, W North Carolina; 57,681; ZIP 28800*.
Ashland city, NE Kentucky; 29,245; ZIP 41101.
—city, N CEN. Ohio; 19,872; ZIP 44805.
—city, SW Oregon; 12,342; ZIP 97520.
—city, extreme N Wisconsin; 9,615; ZIP 54806*.
Ashtabula city, NE Ohio; 24,313; ZIP 44004*.
Asia E part of Eurasian land mass; largest of the continents; 16.9 million sq. mi.; 2.2 billion.
Asia Minor penin. of extreme W Asia, comprising most of Turkey.
Aston urb. twp., SE Pennsylvania; 10,595.
Astoria city, NW Oregon; 10,244; ZIP 97103.
Astrakhan city, SE RSFSR; 445,000.
Asunción city, SW Paraguay; cap.; 387,676.
Aswan city, S Arab Republic of Egypt; site of Aswan Dam, 1¼ mi. long; 28,000.
Atascadero vill., SW California; 10,290; ZIP 93422.
Atchison city, NE Kansas; 12,565; ZIP 66002.
Athens city, SE Greece; cap.; 867,023.
Athens city, N Alabama; 14,360; ZIP 35611.
—city, NE CEN. Georgia; 44,342; ZIP 30601*.
—city, SE Ohio; 23,310; ZIP 45701.
—city, SE Tennessee; 11,790; ZIP 37303.
—city, E Texas; 9,582; ZIP 74751.
Atherton town, W California; 8,085; ZIP see MENLO PARK.
Athol vill., N Massachusetts; 11,185; ZIP 01331.
Atlanta city, NW CEN. Georgia; cap.; 496,973; ZIP 30300*.
Atlantic city, SW Iowa; 7,306; ZIP 50022.
Atlantic City city, SE New Jersey; 47,859; ZIP 08400*.
Atlantic Ocean ocean, extending from the Arctic to the Antarctic between the Americas and Europe and Africa.
Atlas Mountains mtn. range, NW Africa.
Atmore city, SW Alabama; 8,293; ZIP 36502.
Attala city, NE Alabama; 7,510; ZIP 35954.
Attleboro city, SE Massachusetts; 32,907; ZIP 02703.
Atwater city, CEN. California; 11,640; ZIP 95301.
Auburn city, E CEN. Alabama; 22,767; ZIP 36830.
—city, CEN. California; 6,570; ZIP 95603.
—city, NE Indiana; 7,337; ZIP 46706.
—city, SW Maine; 24,151; ZIP 04210.
—town, S CEN. Massachusetts; 15,347; ZIP 01501.
—city, W CEN. New York; 34,599; ZIP 13021*.
—city, W CEN. Washington; 21,817; ZIP 98002*.
Auburndale city CEN. Florida; 5,386; ZIP 33823.
Auckland city, N North Island, New Zealand; 151,580.
Audubon boro., SW New Jersey; 10,802; ZIP see CAMDEN.
Augsburg city, S West Germany; 205,000.
Augusta city, E Georgia; 59,864; ZIP 30900*.
—city, S Kansas; 5,977; ZIP 67010.
—city, S Maine; cap.; 21,945; ZIP 04301*.
Aurora city, N CEN. Colorado; 74,974; ZIP 80010*.
—city, NE Illinois; 74,182; ZIP 60504*.
Aurora town, S Ontario, Canada; 8,791.
Auschwitz city, SW Poland; site of Nazi extermination camp in World War II; 14,000.
Austin city, SE Minnesota; 25,074; ZIP 55912.
—city, CEN. Texas; cap.; 251,808; ZIP 78700*.
Australasia isls. of the South Pacific, including Australia, New Zealand, and New Guinea.
Australia independent member of the Commonwealth of Nations, situated on an isl. continent in the South Pacific; 2,971,081 sq. mi.; 13,300,000; cap. Canberra.
Australian Capital Territory reg., SE Australia; 939 sq. mi.; contains Canberra, the capital; 58,828.
Austria republic, CEN. Europe; 32,375 sq. mi.; 7,550,000; cap. Vienna.
Austria-Hungary former monarchy, CEN. Europe.
Avalon boro., SW Pennsylvania; 7,065; ZIP see PITTSBURGH.
Avignon city, SE France; 86,096.

Avon river, CEN. England; 96 mi. long.
Avondale city, S CEN. Arizona; 6,304; ZIP 85323.
Avon Lake vill., N Ohio; 12,261; ZIP 44012.
Avon Park city, S CEN. Florida; 6,712; ZIP 33825.
Aylmer town, S Ontario, Canada; 6,286.
Azerbaijan prov., NW Iran; Eastern Azerbaijan; 28,488 sq. mi.; 2,138,000; cap. Tabriz: Western Azerbaijan; 13,644 sq. mi.; 721,000; cap. Rizaiyeh.
Azerbaijan SSR republic, SW USSR; 33,590 sq. mi.; 5,117,081; cap. Baku.
Azores three isl. groups of Portugal, E Atlantic; 922 sq. mi.; 291,028.
Azov, Sea of inlet of the Black Sea; S USSR.
Azusa city, S California; 25,217; ZIP 91702.

Babylon vill., SE New York; 12,588; ZIP 11702*.
Baden boro., W Pennsylvania; 5,536; ZIP 15005.
Baden-Baden city, SW West Germany; site of famous mineral springs; 41,000.
Bad Lands arid plateau, South Dakota and Nebraska: also Badlands.
Baghdad city, CEN. Iraq; cap.; 1,028,083.
Bagotville town, S Quebec, Canada; 5,629.
Baguio city, Luzon, N Philippines; summer cap.; 37,000.
Bahamas independent member of Commonwealth of Nations SE of Florida; 4,404 sq. mi.; 197,000; cap. Nassau.
Bahrain isl. group, Persian Gulf near Saudi Arabia; sheikdom under British protection; 213 sq. mi.; 230,000; cap. Manama.
Baie-Comeau town, E Quebec, Canada; 7,956.
Baikal freshwater lake, S USSR; 12,150 sq. mi.
Bainbridge city, SW Georgia; 10,887; ZIP 31717*.
Baker city, NE Oregon; 9,354; ZIP 97814.
Baker, Mount mtn., Cascade range, N Washington; 10,750 ft.
Bakersfield city, S California; 69,515; ZIP 93300*.
Baku city, SE Azerbaijan, SSR; cap.; 1,314,000.
Balboa town, E Canal Zone; 3,139.
Balboa Heights adm. ctr. of Canal Zone, near Balboa; 118.
Balch Springs city, NE Texas; 10,464.
Baldwin uninc. place, SE New York; 34,525; ZIP 11510*.
—boro., SW Pennsylvania; 26,729.
Baldwin Park city, SW California; 47,285; ZIP 91706*.
Baldwinsville vill., CEN. New York; 6,298; ZIP 13027.
Balearic Islands isl. group, W Mediterranean; prov. of Spain; 1,935 sq. mi.; 558,287; cap. Palma.
Bali isl. of Indonesia, E of Java; 2,243 sq. mi.
Balkan Mountains mtn. range, Balkan penin.
Balkan Peninsula large penin. of SE Europe.
Balkan States countries of Balkan penin.; Albania, Bulgaria, Greece, Rumania, Yugoslavia, and part of Turkey.
Ballwin city, E Missouri; 10,656; ZIP 63011.
Baltic Sea inlet of the Atlantic in NW Europe.
Baltic States Estonian SSR, Latvian SSR, and Lithuanian SSR.
Baltimore city, N Maryland; 905,759; ZIP 21200*.
Baltimore Highlands See LANSDOWNE-BALTIMORE HIGHLANDS.
Bamako city, S CEN. Mali; cap.; ab. 200,000.
Banaras Hindu sacred city, NE India; 356,000.
Bandung city, W Java; Indonesia; 1,201,730.
Bangalore city, E Mysore, India; cap.; 1,648,232.
Bangka isl. of Indonesia, SE of Sumatra; 4,611 sq. mi.
Bangkok city, SW Thailand; cap.; 2,213,522.
Bangladesh republic, member of the Commonwealth of Nations, E of India; 55,126 sq. mi.; 71,316,517; cap. Dacca.
Bangor city, S CEN. Maine; 33,168; ZIP 04401*.
—boro., E Pennsylvania; 5,425; ZIP 18013.
Bangui city, SW Central African Republic; cap.; 187,000.
Banning city, S California; 12,034; ZIP 92220.
Baraboo city, S CEN. Wisconsin; 7,931; ZIP 53913.
Barbados isl., E Caribbean, independent member of Commonwealth of Nations; 166 sq. mi.; 239,000; cap. Bridgetown.
Barbary North Africa W of Egypt.
Barbary Coast 1. coast of Barbary. 2. former infamous waterfront reg. of San Francisco.

Barbary States formerly, states of the Barbary Coast; Tripolitania, Algeria, Tunisia, Morocco; -centers of piracy until the 19th century.

Barberton city, NE Ohio; 33,052; ZIP 44203.

Barcelona prov., NE Spain; 2,985 sq. mi.; 2,878,000.
—city, S Barcelona prov.; cap.; 1,742,000.

Barnes uninc. place, SW Oregon; 5,076.

Barnstable town, SE Massachusetts; 19,842; ZIP 02630.

Barranquilla city, N Colombia; 840,000.

Barre city, CEN. Vermont; 10,209; ZIP 05641.

Barrie city, S Ontario, Canada; 21,169.

Barrington vill., NE Illinois; 7,701; ZIP 60010.
—boro, SW New Jersey; 8,409; ZIP 08007.
—town, E Rhode Island; 17,554; ZIP 02806.

Barrow, Point extreme N point of Alaska.

Barstow city, S California; 17,442; ZIP 92310*.

Bartlesville city, NE Oklahoma; 29,683; ZIP 74003*.

Bartonville vill., CEN. Illinois; 7,221; ZIP see PEORIA.

Bartow city, CEN. Florida; 12,891; ZIP 33830.

Basel city, N Switzerland; 206,000.

Basque Provinces three provs. of N Spain, on the Bay of Biscay; inhabited largely by Basques.

Bastrop city, NE Louisiana; 14,713; ZIP 71220.

Basutoland former British territory, S Africa. See LESOTHO.

Bataan prov., S Luzon, Philippines; 517 sq. mi.; 116,000; cap. Balanga; occupies Bataan Peninsula, scene of World War II surrender of U.S. and Philippine forces to the Japanese.

Batavia city, NE Illinois; 8,994; ZIP 60510.

Batavia city, N New York; 17,338; ZIP 14020*.

Batesville city, NE CEN. Arkansas; 7,209; ZIP 72501.

Bath co. boro.; SW England; site of famous hot springs; 81,000.

Bath city, SW Maine; 9,679; ZIP 04530.
—vill., SW New York; 6,053; ZIP 14810.

Bathurst town, NE New Brunswick, Canada; 5,494.

Bathurst city, W Gambia; cap.; 21,000.

Baton Rouge city, SE CEN. Louisiana; cap.; 165,963; ZIP 70800*.

Battle Creek city, S Michigan; 38,931; ZIP 49014*.

Bavaria state, SE West Germany; 27,235 sq. mi.; 9,731,000; cap. Munich.

Bay Village city, NE Ohio, 18,163.

Bayamón town, N Puerto Rico; 147,552.

Bay City city, E CEN. Michigan; 49,449; ZIP 48706*.
—city, S Texas; 11,733; ZIP 77414.

Bayonne city, NE New Jersey; 72,743; ZIP 07002*.

Bay St. Louis city, SE Mississippi; 6,752; ZIP 39520.

Baytown city, S Texas; 43,980; ZIP 77520*.

Beachwood vill., N Ohio; 9,631.

Beacon city, SE New York; 13,255; ZIP 12508.

Beaconsfield town, S Quebec, Canada; 10,064.

Beardstown city, W CEN. Illinois; 6,222; ZIP 62618.

Beatrice city, SE Nebraska; 12,389; ZIP 68310.

Beaufort city, S South Carolina; 9,434; ZIP 29902*.

Beauharnois city, SW Quebec, 8,704.

Beaumont city, SE Texas; 115,919; ZIP 77700*.

Beauport town, S CEN. Quebec, Canada; 9,192.

Beaver boro., W Pennsylvania; 6,100; ZIP 15009.

Beaver Dam city, S CEN. Wisconsin; 14,265; ZIP 53916.

Beaver Falls city, W Pennsylvania; 14,375; ZIP 15010.

Beaverton city, NW Oregon; 18,577; ZIP 97005*.

Bechuanaland Protectorate former British territory, S Africa. See BOTSWANA.

Beckley city, S West Virginia; 19,884; ZIP 25801*.

Bedford city, S Indiana; 13,087; ZIP 47421.
—city, NE Ohio; 17,552; ZIP 44014.
—town, SW CEN. Virginia; 6,011; ZIP 24523.

Bedford Heights vill., NE Ohio; 13,063.

Beech Grove city, S CEN. Indiana; 13,468; ZIP 46107.

Beeville city, S Texas; 13,506; ZIP 78102.

Beirut city, N Lebanon; cap.; 800,000.

Belém city, N Brazil; 565,097.

Belen town, W CEN. New Mexico; 4,823; ZIP 87002.

Belfast co. boro., and port, SE Northern Ireland; cap.; 360,150.

Belfast city, S Maine; 5,957; ZIP 04915.

Belgium kingdom, NW Europe; 11,775 sq. mi.; 9,900,000; cap. Brussels.

Belgrade city E Yugoslavia; cap.; 741,618.

Belize city, E British Honduras; cap.; 39,050.

Bell city, S California; 21,836; ZIP 90201*.

Bellaire city, E Ohio, 9,655; ZIP 43906.

Bellaire city, S Texas; 19,009; ZIP 77401*.

Bellefontaine city, W CEN. Ohio; 11,255; ZIP 43311.

Bellefontaine Neighbors city, E Missouri; 13,650.

Bellefonte boro., CEN. Pennsylvania; 6,828; ZIP 16823.

Belle Glade city, SE Florida; 15,949; ZIP 33430.

Belleville city, SW Illinois; 41,699; ZIP 62220*.
—town, NE New Jersey; 36,643; ZIP see NEWARK.

Belleville city, SE Ontario, Canada; 35,128.

Bellevue city, N Kentucky; 8,847; ZIP see NEWPORT.
—city, E Nebraska; 19,449; ZIP 68005.
—city, N Ohio; 8,604; ZIP 44811.
—boro., SW Pennsylvania; 11,586; ZIP see PITTSBURGH.
—city, CEN. Washington; 61,102; ZIP 98004.

Bellflower city, SW California; 51,454; ZIP 90706*.

Bell Gardens uninc. place, SW California; 29,308; ZIP see BELL.

Bellingham city, NW Washington; 39,375; ZIP 98225.

Bellmawr boro., SW New Jersey; 15,618; see GLOUCESTER CITY.

Bellmead city, E CEN. Texas; 7,698; ZIP see WACO.

Bellmore uninc. place, SE New York; 18,431; ZIP 11710*.

Bellwood vill., NE Illinois; 22,096; ZIP 60104.

Belmar boro., E CEN. New Jersey; 5,782; ZIP 07719.

Belmont city, W CEN. California; 23,667; ZIP 94002*.
—town, E Massachusetts; 28,285; ZIP see BOSTON.

Beloeil town, S Quebec, Canada; 6,283.

Belo Horizonte city, E Brazil; 1,106,722.

Beloit city, S Wisconsin; 35,729; ZIP 53511*.

Belpre vill., SE Ohio; 7,189; ZIP 45714.

Belton town, NW South Carolina; 5,257; ZIP 29627.
—city, CEN. Texas; 8,696; ZIP 76513*.

Belvidere city, NE Illinois; 14,061.

Bemidji city, N CEN. Minnesota; 11,490; ZIP 56601.

Bend city, CEN. Oregon; 13,710; ZIP 97701.

Bengal former prov., NE British India; divided (1947) into: **East Bengal**, a part of East Pakistan (Bangladesh), and **West Bengal**, a state of India; 33,928 sq. mi.; 34,968,000; cap. Calcutta.

Bengal, Bay of part of the Indian Ocean betw. E India and W Burma.

Benghazi city, N Libya; one of two caps.; 137,295.

Benicia city, W CEN. California; 8,783; ZIP 94510.

Bennettsville city, NE South Carolina; 7,468; ZIP 29512.

Bennington vill., SW Vermont; 7,950; ZIP 05201.

Bensenville vill., NE Illinois; 12,833; ZIP 60106.

Benton city, S CEN. Arkansas; 16,499; ZIP 72015.
—city, SE Illinois; 6,833; ZIP 62812.

Benton Harbor city, SW Michigan; 16,481; ZIP 49022*.

Benton Heights uninc. place, SW Michigan; 6,112.

Berea city, NE Ohio; 22,396; ZIP 44017.

Bergen city, SW Norway; 211,970.

Bergenfield boro., NE New Jersey; 33,131; ZIP 07621.

Bering Sea part of the North Pacific betw. Alaska and the USSR, joined to the Arctic by **Bering Strait.**

Berkeley city, W California; 116,716; ZIP 94700*.
—vill., NE Illinois; 6,152; ZIP see MELROSE PARK.
—city, E CEN. Missouri; 19,743; ZIP see ST. LOUIS.

Berkley city, SE Michigan; 22,618; ZIP see ROYAL OAK.

Berkshire Hills wooded hill reg., W Massachusetts.

Berlin city, E CEN. Germany; cap. prior to 1945 when divided into the British, French, Soviet and US sectors. In 1949 the Soviet sector, **East Berlin**, was designated capital of East Germany; 1,088,827. The remaining sectors formed **West Berlin**, associated with West Germany; 2,047,948.

Berlin city, N New Hampshire; 15,256; ZIP 03570.

Bermuda isl. group, W Atlantic; self-governing British depen.; 21 sq. mi.; 56,000; cap. Hamilton.

Bern city, W CEN. Switzerland; cap.; 159,100. Also **Berne**.

Bernardsville boro., N CEN. New Jersey; 6,652; ZIP 07924.

Berwick boro., E CEN. Pennsylvania; 12,274; ZIP 18603.

Berwyn city, NE Illinois; 55,502; ZIP 60402*.

Bessarabia reg., SW USSR.

Bessemer city, CEN. Alabama; 33,428; ZIP 35020*.

Bethany city, CEN. Oklahoma; 21,785; ZIP 73008.

Bethel uninc. place, SW Connecticut; 10,945; ZIP 06801.

Bethel Park boro., SW Pennsylvania; 34,791; ZIP 19507.

Bethesda uninc. area, W Maryland; 71,621; ZIP see

WASHINGTON, D.C.
Bethlehem ancient town, w Jordan; birthplace of Jesus; 19,000.
Bethlehem city, E Pennsylvania; 72,686; ZIP 18015*.
Bethpage-Old Bethpage uninc. place, SE New York; 18,555; ZIP 11714.
Bettendorf city, E CEN. Iowa; 22,126; ZIP 52722.
Beverly city, NE Massachusetts; 38,348; ZIP 01915.
Beverly town, CEN. Alberta, Canada; 9,041.
Beverly Hills city, SW California; 33,416; ZIP 90210*.
—vill., SE Michigan; 13,598.
Bexley city, CEN. Ohio; 14,888; ZIP see COLUMBUS.
Biddeford city, SW Maine; 19,983; ZIP 04005.
Big Rapids city, W CEN. Michigan; 11,995; ZIP 49307.
Big Spring city, W Texas; 28,735; ZIP 79720*.
Bikini atoll, Marshall Islands; 2 sq. mi.; site of US nuclear tests, July 1946.
Billings city, S CEN. Montana; 61,581; ZIP 59101*.
Biloxi city, SE Mississippi; 48,486; ZIP 39530*.
Binghamton city, CEN. New York; 64,123; ZIP 13990*.
Birkenhead co. boro., NW England; 135,750.
Birmingham co. boro., W CEN. England; 1,013,366.
Birmingham city, N CEN. Alabama; 300,910; ZIP 35200*.
—city, SE Michigan; 26,170; ZIP 48008*.
Bisbee city, SE Arizona; 8,328; ZIP 85603.
Biscay, Bay of inlet of the Atlantic betw. W and SW France and N and NW Spain.
Bismarck city, S CEN. North Dakota; cap.; 34,703; ZIP 58501*.
Bismarck Archipelago isl. group, Trust Territory of New Guinea; 19,200 sq. mi.
Bizerte city, N Tunisia; 51,708.
Blackfoot city, SE Idaho; 8,716; ZIP 83221.
Black Forest wooded mtn. reg., SW West Germany.
Black Hills mtn. reg., SW South Dakota and NE Wyoming.
Blacksburg town, W Virginia, 9,384; ZIP 24060*.
Black Sea inland sea betw. Europe and Asia, connects with Aegean via Bosporus, Sea of Mamara, and Dardanelles.
Blackwell city, N CEN. Oklahoma; 8,645; ZIP 74631.
Blaine vill., E Minnesota; 20,640.
Blakely boro., NE Pennsylvania; 6,391.
Bloomfield city, NE New Jersey; 52,029; ZIP 07003*.
Bloomingdale boro., N New Jersey; 7,797; ZIP 07403.
Bloomington city, CEN. Illinois; 39,992; ZIP 61701*.
—city, S CEN. Indiana; 42,890; ZIP 47401*.
—city, E Minnesota; 81,970; ZIP see MINNEAPOLIS.
Bloomsburg town, NE Pennsylvania; 11,652; ZIP 17815.
Blue Ash vill., SW Ohio; 8,324.
Bluefield city, S West Virginia; 15,921; ZIP 24701*.
Blue Island city, NE Illinois; 22,958; ZIP 60406.
Blue Ridge Mountains, SW part of the Appalachians.
Bluffton city, NE Indiana; 8,297; ZIP 46714.
Blythe city, SE California; 7,047; ZIP 92225.
Blytheville city, NE Arkansas; 24,752; ZIP 72315*.
Boca Raton city, SE Florida; 28,506; ZIP 33432.
Bogalusa city, S Louisiana; 18,412; ZIP 70427.
Bogotá city, E CEN. Colombia; cap.; 2,818,000.
Bogota boro., NE New Jersey; 8,125; ZIP see HACKENSACK.
Bohemia former prov., W Czechoslovakia.
Boise city, SW Idaho; cap.; 74,990; ZIP 83700*.
Bolivia republic, W CEN. South America; 424,162 sq. mi.; 5,470,000; cap. Sucre (constitutional), La Paz (de facto).
Bologna prov., N CEN. Italy; 1,429 sq. mi.; 837,000.
—city, cap. of Bologna prov.; 490,036.
Bombay city, W India; 5,968,546.
Bonham city, NE Texas; 7,698; ZIP 75418.
Bonn city, W German Federal Republic (West Germany); cap.; 283,260.
Boone city, CEN. Iowa; 12,468; ZIP 50036.
Boonton town, NE New Jersey; 9,261; ZIP 07005.
Boonville city, CEN. Missouri; 7,514; ZIP 65233.
Bordeaux city, SW France; 264,184.
Borger city, N Texas; 14,195; ZIP 79006*.
Borneo isl., betw. Java and South China seas; comprising North Borneo, Sarawak, Brunei, and Indonesian Borneo; 286,969 sq. mi.
Bosnia and Herzegovina constituent republic, CEN. Yugoslavia; 19,745 sq. mi.; 3,735,000; cap. Sarajevo.
Bosporus strait, betw. the Black Sea and the Sea of

Marmara.
Bossier City city, NW Louisiana; 41,595; ZIP 71010.
Boston city, E Massachusetts; cap.; 641,071; ZIP 02100*.
Botany Bay inlet of the Pacific, S of Sydney, Australia.
Botswana republic, member of the Commonwealth of Nations, S Africa; 222,000 sq. mi.; 661,000; cap. Gaborone: formerly Bechuanaland Protectorate.
Boucherville town, S Quebec, Canada; 7,403.
Boulder city, N CEN. Colorado; 66,870; ZIP 80301*.
Boulder Dam Hoover Dam: *the former name.*
Bound Brook boro., N CEN. New Jersey; 10,450; ZIP 08805.
Bountiful city, N CEN. Utah; 27,853; ZIP 84010.
Bowling Green city, S Kentucky; 36,253; ZIP 42101*.
—city, NW Ohio; 21,760; ZIP 43402.
Bowmanville town, S Ontario, Canada; 7,397.
Bowness town, S Alberta, Canada; 9,184.
Boynton Beach city, SE Florida; 18,115; ZIP 33435.
Bozeman city, SW Montana; 18,670; ZIP 59715.
Braddock boro., SW Pennsylvania; 8,682; ZIP 15104*.
Bradenton city, W Florida; 21,040; ZIP 33505*.
Bradford city, N Pennsylvania; 12,672; ZIP 16701.
Bradley vill., NE Illinois; 9,881; ZIP 60915.
Brady city, CEN. Texas; 5,557; ZIP 76825.
Brainerd city, CEN. Minnesota; 11,667; ZIP 56401.
Braintree town, E Massachusetts; 35,050; ZIP see BOSTON.
Brampton town, SE Ontario, Canada; 18,467.
Brandon city, SW Manitoba, Canada; 28,166.
Brantford city, SE Ontario, Canada; 64,421.
Brasília city, CEN. Brazil: cap.; 272,002.
Brattleboro uninc. place, SE Vermont; 12,239; ZIP 05301*.
Brawley city, SE California; 13,746; ZIP 92227.
Brazil republic, NE and E CEN. South America; 3,287,951 sq. mi.; 104,642,000; cap. Brasília.
Brazil city, W Indiana; 8,853 ZIP 47834.
Brazzaville city, SE Republic of the Congo; cap.; 275,000.
Brea city, SW California; 18,447; ZIP 92621.
Breckenridge city, N CEN. Texas; 5,944; ZIP 76024.
Breckenridge Hills, vill., E Missouri; 7,011.
Brecksville vill., N Ohio; 9,137; ZIP see CLEVELAND.
Breed's Hill hill, near Bunker Hill. See BUNKER HILL.
Bremen state, NW West Germany; 156 sq. mi.
—port city, major part of Bremen state; 594,591.
Bremerhaven city, part of Bremen state, NW West Germany; 144,578.
Bremerton city, W Washington; 35,307; ZIP 98310*.
Brenham city, E CEN. Texas; 8,922; ZIP 77833.
Brenner Pass Alpine pass, Austrian-Italian border.
Brentwood city, E Missouri; 11,248; ZIP see ST. LOUIS.
—uninc. place, SE New York; 27,846.
—boro., SW Pennsylvania; 13,732; ZIP see PITTSBURGH.
Breslau Wroclaw: *German name.*
Brest city, NW France; chief French naval station; 154,023.
Brest city, SW Byelorussian SSR; Russo-German peace treaty signed here, 1918: 73,000.
Brewer city, S CEN. Maine; 9,300.
Brewton city, S Alabama; 6,747.
Briarcliff Manor vill., SE New York; 6,521.
Bridgeport city, SW Connecticut; 156,542; ZIP 06600*.
—boro., SE Pennsylvania; 5,630; ZIP see NORRISTOWN.
Bridgeton town, E Missouri; 19,992; ZIP see HAZELWOOD.
—city, SW New Jersey; 20,435; ZIP 08302*.
Bridge View vill., NE Illinois; 12,522; ZIP see OAK LAWN.
Bridgeville boro., SW Pennsylvania; 6,717; ZIP 15017.
Brigham City city, N Utah; 14,007; ZIP 84302.
Brighton co. boro. and resort, SW England; 163,000.
Brighton city, N CEN. Colorado; 8,309; ZIP 80601.
Brisbane city, SE Queensland, Australia; cap.; 699,371.
Bristol co. boro., SW England; 421,800.
Bristol city, W CEN. Connecticut; 55,487; ZIP 06010*.
—boro., SE Pennsylvania; 12,085.
—urb. twp., SE Pennsylvania; 67,498; ZIP 19007.
—town, E Rhode Island; 17,860; ZIP 02809.
—city, NE Tennessee at Tennessee-Virginia line;

20,064; ZIP 37620*.
—city, SW Virginia; adjacent to, and integrated with Bristol, Tennessee; 14,857; ZIP 24201*.
Bristol Channel inlet of the Atlantic betw. Wales and SW England.
Britain see GREAT BRITAIN.
British Columbia prov., W Canada; 366,255 sq. mi.; 2,457,000; cap. Victoria.
British Guiana see GUYANA.
British Honduras self-governing British depen., NE Central America; 8,867 sq. mi.; 90,000; cap. Belize.
British Virgin Islands British depen., E Greater Antilles; 59 sq. mi.; 10,484; cap. Road Town.
British West Indies see WEST INDIES.
Brittany reg., W France; former prov.
Brno city, CEN. Czechoslovakia; 343,860.
Broadview vill., NE Illinois; 9,307; ZIP see MAYWOOD.
Broadview Heights vill., N Ohio; 11,463; ZIP see CLEVELAND.
Brockport vill., W New York; 7,878; ZIP 14420.
Brockton city, E Massachusetts; 89,040; ZIP 02401*.
Brockville town, SE Ontario, Canada; 17,944.
Broken Arrow city, NE Oklahoma; 11,787; ZIP 74012.
Bronx boro., N New York City; 1,471,701; also the Bronx; ZIP 10400*.
Bronxville vill., SE New York; 6,674; ZIP see YONKERS.
Brookfield vill., NE Illinois; 20,284; ZIP 60513.
—city, N CEN. Missouri; 5,491; ZIP 64628.
—city, SE Wisconsin; 32,140; ZIP 53005.
Brookhaven city, SW Mississippi; 10,700; ZIP 39601.
—boro., SE Pennsylvania; 7,370.
Brookings city, E South Dakota; 13,717; ZIP 57006*.
Brookline town, E Massachusetts; 58,886; ZIP see BOSTON.
Brooklyn boro., SE New York City; 2,602,012; ZIP 11200*.
—city, NE Ohio; 13,142.
Brooklyn Center vill., SE Minnesota; 35,173; ZIP see MINNEAPOLIS.
Brooklyn Park vill., SE Minnesota; 26,230.
Brook Park vill., N Ohio; 30,774; ZIP see CLEVELAND.
Brown Deer vill., SE Wisconsin; 12,622; ZIP see MILWAUKEE.
Brownfield city, W Texas; 9,647; ZIP 79316.
Brownsville uninc. place, NW Florida; 38,417.
—boro., SW Pennsylvania; 4,856; ZIP 15417*.
—city, W Tennessee; 7,011.
—city, S Texas; 52,522; ZIP 78520*.
Brownwood city, CEN. Texas; 17,368; ZIP 76801*.
Brunei sultanate under British protection, NW Borneo; 2,226 sq. mi.; 84,000.
—city, N Brunei; cap.; 38,000.
Brunswick city, NE West Germany; 218,939.
Brunswick city, SE Georgia; 19,585; ZIP 31520*.
—uninc. place, S Maine; 16,195; ZIP 04011.
—vill., N Ohio; 15,852; ZIP 44212.
Brussels city, CEN. Belgium; cap.; 1,074,726.
Bryan city, NW Ohio; 7,008; ZIP 43506.
—city, E CEN. Texas; 33,719; ZIP 77801*.
Bucharest city, S Rumania; cap.; 1,600,000.
Buckhannon city, N CEN. West Virginia; 7,261; ZIP 26201.
Buckingham town, SW Quebec, Canada; 7,421.
Bucyrus city, N CEN. Ohio; 13,111; ZIP 44820.
Budapest co. boro., CEN. Hungary; cap.; 1,940,000.
Buena Park city, SW California; 63,646; ZIP 90620*.
Buena Vista city, W CEN. Virginia; 6,425; ZIP 24416.
Buenos Aires city, E Argentina; cap.; 2,972,453.
Buffalo city, W New York; 462,768; ZIP 14200*.
Bulgaria republic, SE Europe; 42,796 sq. mi.; 8,679,000; cap. Sofia.
Bull Run small stream, NE Virginia; site of Union defeats in the Civil War, 1861 and 1862.
Bunker Hill hill, Charlestown, Massachusetts, near which (on Breed's Hill) occurred the first organized engagement of the American Revolution, June 17, 1775.
Bunkie town, E CEN. Louisiana; 5,395; ZIP 71322.
Burbank city, SW California; 88,871; ZIP 91500*.
Burgundy reg., E CEN. France.
Burkburnett city, N Texas; 9,230; ZIP 76354.
Burley city, S Idaho; 8,279; ZIP 83318.
Burlingame city, W CEN. California; 27,320; ZIP 94010*.
Burlington city, SE Iowa; 32,366; ZIP 52601*.

—city, W New Jersey; 11,991; ZIP 08016.
—city, N CEN. North Carolina; 35,930; ZIP 27215*.
—city, NW Vermont; 38,633; ZIP 05401*.
—city, SE Wisconsin; 7,479; ZIP 53105.
Burlington town, SE Ontario, Canada; 87,023.
Burma state, SE Asia, betw. Bangladesh and Thailand; 261,789 sq. mi.; 30,000,000; cap. Rangoon.
Burma Road road betw. N Burma and SW China; a World War II supply route.
Burrillville town, N Rhode Island; 10,087.
Burundi republic, CEN. Africa; formerly part of Ruanda-Urundi; 10,747 sq. mi.; 3,700,000; cap. Bujumbura. See RWANDA.
Butler boro., N New Jersey; 7,051; ZIP 07405.
—city, W Pennsylvania; 18,691; ZIP 16001*.
Butte city, SW Montana; 23,368; ZIP 59701*.
Byelorussian SSR constituent republic, W USSR; 80,154 sq. mi.; 9,003,000; cap. Minsk.

Cadillac city, NW Michigan; 9,990; ZIP 49601.
Cádiz city, SW Spain; 135,743.
Caguas town, E CEN. Puerto Rico; 63,215; ZIP 00625*.
Cahokia vill., SW Illinois; 20,649; ZIP see EAST ST. LOUIS.
Cairo city, NE Arab Republic of Egypt; cap.; 5,126,000.
Cairo city, SW Georgia; 8,061; ZIP 37128.
—city, S Illinois; 6,277; ZIP 62914.
Calais city, N France; 60,000.
Calcutta city, NE India; 3,141,180.
Caldwell city, SW Idaho; 14,219; ZIP 83605.
—boro., NE New Jersey; 8,719; ZIP 92231.
Calexico city, SE California; 10,625; ZIP 92231.
Calgary city, S Alberta, Canada; 403,319.
Cali city, W Colombia; 1,100,000.
Calicut Kozhikode: *an alternate name.*
California state, W United States; 158,693 sq. mi.; 19,953,134; cap. Sacramento.
—boro., SW Pennsylvania; 6,635; ZIP 15419.
California, Gulf of inlet of the Pacific, W Mexico, betw. Lower California and the rest of Mexico.
Calumet City city, NE Illinois; 32,956; ZIP 60409.
Calumet Park vill., NE Illinois; 10,069; ZIP see CHICAGO.
Camas city, SW Washington; 5,790; ZIP 98607.
Cambodia republic, SW Indochina penin.; 69,844 sq. mi.; 7,500,000; cap. Phnom Penh.
Cambridge city, SE England; site of Cambridge University; 103,710.
Cambridge city, CEN. Maryland; 11,595; ZIP 21613.
—city, E Massachusetts; 100,361; ZIP see BOSTON.
—city, E Ohio; 13,656; ZIP 43725.
Camden city, S Arkansas; 15,147; ZIP 71701.
—city, SW New Jersey; 102,511; ZIP 08100*.
—city, N CEN. South Carolina; 8,532; ZIP 29020.
Cameron city, CEN. Texas; 5,546; ZIP 76520.
Cameroon republic, W equatorial Africa; 183,376 sq. mi.; 6,300,000; cap. Yaoundé. Also **Cameroun.**
Campbell city, W California; 24,770; ZIP 95008.
—city, E Ohio; 12,577.
Campbellsville city, S CEN. Kentucky; 7,598; ZIP 42718.
Campbellton city, N New Brunswick, Canada; 9,873.
Camp Hill boro., S Pennsylvania; 9,931; ZIP 17011.
Camrose city, CEN. Alberta, Canada; 6,939.
Canada independent member of the Commonwealth of Nations, N North America; 3,851,809 sq. mi.; 22,800,000; cap. Ottawa.
Canal Zone US leased terr., CEN. Panama; extending five miles on either side of the Panama Canal; 648 sq. mi.; 44,198; adm. ctr. Balboa Heights.
Canandaigua city, W CEN. New York; 10,488; ZIP 14424.
Canary Islands isl. group of Spain near NW coast of Africa; 2,808 sq. mi.; 1,170,224. caps. Las Palmas, Tenerife.
Canaveral, Cape Cape Kennedy: *the former name.*
Canberra city, SE Australia; cap.; 141,795.
Canea city, NW Crete; cap. 33,000.
Cannes city, SE France; 66,809.
Canon City city, S CEN. Colorado; 9,206; ZIP 81212.
Canonsburg boro., SW Pennsylvania; 11,439; ZIP 15317.
Canterbury co. boro., SE England; site of famous cathedral; 39,000.
Canton city, S China; 2,300,000.

Canton city, W CEN. Illinois; 14,217; ZIP 61520.
—town, E Massachusetts; 17,100; ZIP 02021.
—city, W CEN. Mississippi; 10,503; ZIP 39046.
—town, W North Carolina; 5,158; ZIP 28716.
—vill., N New York; 6,398; ZIP 13617.
—city, NE Ohio; 110,053; ZIP 44700*.
Canyon city, NW Texas; 8,333; ZIP 79015.
Cap-de-la-Madeleine city, S Quebec, Canada; 26,925.
Cape Girardeau city, SE Missouri; 31282; ZIP 63701.
Cape Town city, S South Africa; legislative cap.; 1,096,597. Also Capetown.
Cape Verde republic w of Africa; 1,552 sq. mi.; 290,000; cap. Praia.
Capri isl., near the W coast of Italy; 4 sq. mi.
Caracas city, N Venezuela; cap.; 2,183,935.
Carbondale city, S Illinois; 22,816; ZIP 62901.
—city, NE Pennsylvania; 12,808; ZIP 18407.
Cardiff co. boro., SE Wales; 276,880.
Caribbean Sea part of the Atlantic betw. the West Indies and Central and South America.
Caribou uninc. place, N Maine; 10,419; ZIP 04736.
Carlinville city, SW CEN. Illinois; 5,675; ZIP 62626.
Carlisle boro., S Pennsylvania; 18,079; ZIP 17013.
Carlsbad city, S California; 14,944; ZIP 92008.
Carlsbad Caverns National Park area, SE New Mexico; contains Carlsbad Caverns, a series of limestone caves.
Carlstadt boro., NE New Jersey; 7,947; ZIP see RUTHERFORD.
Carmichael uninc. place, N. CEN. California; 37,625; ZIP 95608.
Carnegie boro., SW Pennsylvania; 10,864; ZIP 15106.
Carney See PARKVILLE-CARNEY.
Carol City uninc. place, SE Florida; 27,361; ZIP see OPA-LOCKA.
Caroline Islands isl. group in the Pacific, E of the Philippines: 550 sq. mi.
Carpathian Mountains mtn. range, CEN. and E EUROPE.
Carpentersville vill., NE Illinois; 24,059; ZIP 60110.
Carrara city, CEN. Italy; site of white marble quarries; 63,000.
Carrizo Springs city, SW Texas; 5,374; ZIP 78834.
Carroll city, W CEN. Iowa; 8,716; ZIP 51401.
Carrollton city, W Georgia; 13,520; ZIP 30117.
Carson uninc. place, SW California; 71,150; ZIP see WILMINGTON.
Carson City city, W Nevada; cap.; 15,468; ZIP 89701*.
Carteret boro., NE New Jersey; 23,137; ZIP 07008.
Cartersville city, NW Georgia; 9,929; ZIP 30120.
Carthage city, SW Missouri; 11,035; ZIP 64836.
—city, E Texas; 5,392; ZIP 75633.
Caruthersville city, SE Missouri; 7.350, ZIP 63830.
Casablanca city, NW Morocco; 1,506,373.
Casa Grande city, S Arizona; 10,536; ZIP 85222.
Cascade Range mtn. range in Oregon, Washington, and British Columbia.
Cashmere See KASHMIR.
Casper city, CEN. Wyoming; 39,361; ZIP 82601.
Caspian Sea salt-water lake in the S USSR and N Iran; 163,800 sq. mi.
Castile reg., N and CEN. Spain.
Castle Shannon boro., SW Pennsylvania; 11,899; ZIP see PITTSBURGH.
Castro Valley uninc. place, W California; 44,760; ZIP see HAYWARD.
Catalina Island Santa Catalina: an alternate name.
Catalonia reg., NE Spain.
Catania prov., E Sicily; 1,377 sq. mi.; 889,000.
—city, Catania prov.; cap.; 397,939.
Cataño town, N Puerto Rico; 26,459.
Catasauqua boro., E Pennsylvania; 5,702; ZIP 18032.
Catonsville uninc. place, N CEN. Maryland; 54,812; ZIP see BALTIMORE.
Catskill vill., E New York; 5,317; ZIP 12414.
Catskill Mountains range of the Appalachians in SE New York.
Caucasus mtn. range betw. the Black and Caspian seas.
Caucasus reg., SW USSR, betw. the Black and Caspian seas. Also Caucasia.
Cayce city, CEN. South Carolina; 9,967; ZIP 29033.
Cayey town, SE CEN. Puerto Rico; 21,562.
Cedarburg city, E Wisconsin; 7,697.
Cedar City town, SW Utah; 8,946; ZIP 84720.
Cedar Falls city, E CEN. Iowa; 29,597; ZIP 50613.

Cedar Grove twp., NE New Jersey; 15,582; ZIP 07009.
Cedarhurst vill., SE New York; 6,941; ZIP 11516.
Cedar Lake uninc. place, NW Indiana; 7,589; ZIP 46303.
Cedar Rapids city, E Iowa; 110,642; ZIP 52400*.
Cedartown city, NW Georgia; 9,253.
Celebes isl. of Indonesia; E of Borneo; 69,277 sq. mi.; 7,200,000
Celina city, W Ohio; 7,779.
Centereach uninc. place, SE New York; 9,427; ZIP 11720.
Center Line city, SE Michigan; 10,379.
Centerville city, S Iowa; 6,531; ZIP 52544*.
Central African Republic republic, CEN. Africa; 238,224 sq. mi.; 2,500,000; cap. Bangui.
Central America S part of North America, betw. Mexico and Colombia.
Central Falls city, NE Rhode Island; 18,716; ZIP see PAWTUCKET.
Centralia city, S Illinois; 15,217; ZIP 62800.*
—city, SW Washington; 10,054.
Centreville city, SW Illinois; 11,378; ZIP see EAST SAINT LOUIS.
Ceylon republic, S of India, member of Commonwealth of Nations; 25,332 sq. mi.; 13,400,00; cap. Colombo. Also Sri Lanka.
Chad, Lake lake, NW CEN. Africa; 8,000 sq. mi.
Chad, Republic of, CEN. Africa; 495,752 sq. mi.; 3,950,000; cap. N'Djamena.
Chadron city, NW Nebraska; 5,853; ZIP 69337.
Chambersburg boro., S Pennsylvania; 17,315; ZIP 17201.
Chamblee city, NW CEN. Georgia; 9,127; ZIP 30005.
Champaign city, E CEN. Illinois; 56,532; ZIP 61820.
Champlain, Lake lake, betw. New York and Vermont, extending into Canada; 600 sq. mi.
Chandler city, S CEN. Arizona; 13,763; ZIP 85224*.
Changchun city, NE China; 1,500,000.
Channel Islands British isl. group, English Channel near Normandy; includes Jersey, Guernsey, Alderney, and Sark; 75 sq. mi.; 123,063.
Chanute city, SE Kansas; 10,341; ZIP 66720.
Chapel Hill town, N CEN. North Carolina; 25,537; ZIP 27514*.
Chariton city, S Iowa; 5,009; ZIP 50009.
Charleroi boro., SW Pennsylvania; 6,723; ZIP 15022.
Charlesbourg city, S Quebec, Canada; 14,308.
Charles City city, N Iowa; 9,268; ZIP 50616.
Charleston city, E Illinois; 16,421; ZIP 61920.
—city, SE Missouri; 5,131; ZIP 63834.
—city, SE South Carolina; 66,945; ZIP 29400.
—city, CEN. West Virginia; cap.; 71,505; ZIP 25300.
Charlestown city, SE Indiana; 5,890; ZIP 47111.
Charlotte city, S Michigan; 8,244; ZIP 48813.
—city, S CEN. North Carolina; 241,178; ZIP 28200*.
Charlotte Amalie city, S St. Thomas, Virgin Islands of the United States; cap.; 12,220; ZIP 00801.
Charlottesville city, CEN. Virginia; 38,880; ZIP 22901.
Charlottetown city, CEN. Prince Edward Island, Canada; cap.; 19,133.
Chateauguay town, S Quebec, Canada; 7,570.
Chateauguay-Centre town, S Quebec, Canada; 7,591.
Chatham boro., NE New Jersey; 9,566; ZIP 07928.
Chatham town, NE New Brunswick, Canada; 7,109.
—city, S Ontario, Canada; 29,826.
Chattahoochee town, NW Florida; 7,944; ZIP 32324.
Chattanooga town, SE Tennessee; 119,082; ZIP 37400.
Cheboygan city, N Michigan; 5,553; ZIP 49721.
Cheektowaga-Northwest uninc. place, W New York; 113,844; ZIP see BUFFALO.
Cheektowaga-Southwest uninc. place, W New York; 19,608; ZIP see BUFFALO.
Chehalis city, SW Washington; 5,727; ZIP 98532.
Chelsea metropolitan boro., SW London, England; 47,000.
Chelsea city, E Massachusetts; 30,625; ZIP see BOSTON.
Cheltenham urb. twp., SE Pennsylvania; 40,238; ZIP 19012.
Chelyabinsk city W USSR; 910,000.
Chengchow city N CEN. People's Republic of China; 1,500,000.
Chengtu city SW CEN. People's Republic of China; 2,000,000.

Cheraw town, NE South Carolina; 5,627; ZIP 29520.

Cherbourg city, N France; 39,000.

Cherokee city, NW Iowa; 7,272; ZIP 51012.

Chesapeake Bay inlet of the Atlantic in Virginia and Maryland.

Cheshire co., W England; 1,105 sq. mi.; 1,368,000; cap. Chester.

Chester co. boro., W Cheshire, England; cap.; 59,000.

Chester city, SE Pennsylvania; 56,331; ZIP 19013*.
—city, N South Carolina; 7,045; ZIP 29706.

Cheverly town, W Maryland; 6,696; ZIP see HYATTS-VILLE.

Cheviot city, SW Ohio; 11,135.

Cheviot Hills mtn. range, on the border betw. England and Scotland.

Cheyenne city, SE Wyoming; cap.; 40,914; ZIP 82001*.

Chicago city, NE Illinois; second largest city in the United States; 3,366,957; ZIP 60600*.

Chicago Heights city, NE Illinois; 40,900; ZIP 60411*.

Chicago Ridge vill., NE Illinois; 9,187; ZIP 60415.

Chickasaw city, SW Alabama; 8,447; ZIP see MOBILE.

Chickasha city, S CEN. Oklahoma; 14,194; ZIP 73018*.

Chico city, N CEN. California; 19,580; ZIP 95926.

Chicopee city, SW Massachusetts; 66,676; ZIP 01013*.

Chicoutimi city, S Quebec, Canada; 31,657.

Chihuahua state, N Mexico; 94,830 sq. mi.; 1,236,000.
—city, Chihuahua state; cap.; 145,000.

Childress city, N Texas; 5,408; ZIP 79201.

Chile republic, W South America; 286,397 sq. mi.; 10,400,000; cap. Santiago.

Chillicothe city, N CEN. Missouri; 9,519; ZIP 64601.
—city, S CEN. Ohio; 24,842; ZIP 45601*.

Chilliwack city, SW British Columbia, Canada; 8,259.

China, People's Republic of republic, E and CEN. Asia; 3,760,000 sq. mi.; 825,000,000; cap. Peking.

China, Republic of republic on Taiwan and several smaller islands; 13,890 sq. mi.; 14,990,000; cap. Taipei

China Sea part of the Pacific bordering on China. See EAST CHINA SEA, SOUTH CHINA SEA.

Chino city, SW California; 20,411; ZIP 91710.

Chippewa Falls city, W CEN. Wisconsin; 12,351; ZIP 54729.

Chisholm city, NE Minnesota; 5,913; ZIP 55719.

Chomedey city, S Quebec, Canada; 30,445.

Christiania Oslo: *a former name.*

Christiansted city, N St. Thomas, Virgin Islands of the United States; 5,088.

Chula Vista city, SW California; 67,901; ZIP 92010*.

Chunking city, S CEN. China; cap. during World War II; 3,500,000.

Cicero city, NE Illinois; 67,058; ZIP see CHICAGO.

Cincinnati city, SW Ohio; 452,524; ZIP 45200*.

Circassia reg., NW Caucasus, RSFSR.

Circleville city, S CEN. Ohio; 11,687; ZIP 43113.

Ciudad Trujillo Santo Domingo: from 1936-62.

Clairton city, SW Pennsylvania; 15,051; ZIP 15025.

Clanton city, CEN. Alabama; 5,868; ZIP 35045.

Claremont city, SW California; 23,464; ZIP 91711*.
—city, SW New Hampshire; 14,221; ZIP 03743.

Claremore city, NE Oklahoma; 9,084; ZIP 74017.

Clarendon Hills vill., NE Illinois; 6,750; ZIP 60514.

Clark twp., NE New Jersey; 18,829; ZIP see RAHWAY.

Clarksburg city, N West Virginia; 24,864; ZIP 26301*.

Clarksdale city, NW Mississippi; 21,673; ZIP 38614.

Clarkston city, SE Washington; 6,312; ZIP 99403.

Clarksville town, SE Indiana; 13,806; ZIP see JEFFER-SONVILLE.
—city, N Tennessee; 31,719; ZIP 37040*.

Clawson city, SE Michigan; 17,617; ZIP 48017.

Clayton city, E Missouri; 16,222; ZIP see SAINT LOUIS.

Clearfield boro., W CEN. Pennsylvania; 8,176; ZIP 16830.
—city, N CEN. Utah; 13,316; ZIP 84015.

Clear Lake City, N Iowa; 6,430; ZIP 50428.

Clearwater city, W Florida; 52,074; ZIP 33515*.

Cleburne city, N CEN. Texas; 16,015; ZIP 76031.

Cleveland city, W Mississippi; 13,327; ZIP 38732.
—city, N Ohio; 750,903; ZIP 44100*.
—city, SE Tennessee; 20,651; ZIP 37311*.
—city, SE Texas; 5,627; ZIP 77327.

Cleveland Heights city, N Ohio; 60,767; ZIP see CLEVELAND.

Cliffside Park boro., NE New Jersey; 14,387; ZIP 07010.

Clifton city, NE New Jersey; 82,437; ZIP 07011*.

Clifton Forge city, W Virginia; 5,501; ZIP 24422.

Clifton Heights boro., SE Pennsylvania; 8,348; ZIP 19018*.

Clinton city, CEN. Illinois; 7,570; ZIP 61727.
—city, W Indiana; 5,340; ZIP 47842.
—city, E Iowa; 34,719; ZIP 57232.
—town, CEN. Massachusetts; 13,383; ZIP 01510.
—city, W Missouri; 7,504; ZIP 64735.
—town, S CEN. North Carolina; 7,157; ZIP 28328.
—city, W Oklahoma; 8,513; ZIP 73601.
—town, NW South Carolina; 8,138; ZIP 29325.

Cloquet city, E Minnesota; 8,699; ZIP 55720.

Closter boro., NE New Jersey; 8,604; ZIP 07624.

Clovis city, CEN. California; 13,856; ZIP 93612.
—city, E New Mexico; 28,495; ZIP 88101.

Coalinga city, CEN. California; 6,161; ZIP 93210.

Coamo town, S CEN. Puerto Rico; 12,077; ZIP 00640.

Coatesville city, SE Pennsylvania; 12,331; ZIP 19320.

Coaticook town, S Quebec, Canada; 6,906.

Cobourg town, S Ontario, Canada; 10,646.

Cocoa city, E Florida; 16,110; ZIP 32922*.

Cod, Cape penin., SE Massachusetts.

Coeur d'Alene city, N Idaho; 16,228; ZIP 83814.

Coffeyville city, SE Kansas; 15,116; ZIP 67337.

Cohoes city, E New York; 18,653; ZIP 12047.

Coldwater city, S Michigan; 9,099; ZIP 49036.

Coleman city, CEN. Texas; 5,608; ZIP 76834.

College Park city, W Georgia; 18,203; ZIP 30022.
—city, W Maryland; 26,156; ZIP 20740*.

College Station city, E CEN. Texas; 17,676; ZIP 77840*.

Collingdale boro., SE Pennsylvania; 10,605; ZIP see DARBY.

Collingswood boro., W New Jersey; 17,422; ZIP see CAMDEN.

Collingwood town, S Ontario, Canada; 8,385.

Collinsville city, SW Illinois; 17,773; ZIP 62234.

Collister uninc. place, SW Idaho; 5,436.

Cologne city, W Germany; 846,479.

Colombia republic, NW South America; 439,519 sq. mi.; 24,000,000; cap. Bogotá.

Colombo city, W Ceylon; cap.; 618,000.

Colón city, Caribbean end of the Canal Zone; an enclave of Panama; 95,421.

Colonial Heights city, SE CEN. Virginia; 15,097; ZIP 23834.

Colonie vill., E CEN. New York; 8,701.

Colorado state, W CEN. United States; 104,247 sq. mi.; 2,207,259; cap. Denver.

Colorado City city, W CEN. Texas; 5,227; ZIP 79512.

Colorado River river flowing through Colorado, Utah, Arizona, California, and Mexico to the Gulf of California; length ab. 1,400 mi.

Colorado Springs city, E CEN. Colorado; site of US Air Force Academy; 135,060; ZIP 80900*.

Colton city, S California; 19,974; ZIP 92324.

Columbia city, S Mississippi; 7,587; ZIP 39429.
—city, CEN. Missouri; 58,804; ZIP 65201*.
—boro., SE Pennsylvania; 11,237; ZIP 17512.
—city, CEN. South Carolina; cap.; 113,542; ZIP 29200*.
—city, CEN. Tennessee; 21,471; ZIP 38401*.

Columbia Heights city, E Minnesota; 23,997; ZIP see MINNEAPOLIS.

Columbia River river, SW Canada and NW United States; 1,200 mi. long.

Columbus city, W Georgia; 154,168; ZIP 31900*.
—city, SE CEN. Indiana; 27,141; ZIP 47201*.
—city, E Mississippi; 25,795; ZIP 39701*.
—city, E Nebraska; 15,471; ZIP 68601.
—city, CEN. Ohio; cap.; 539,677; ZIP 43200*.

Commack uninc. place, SE New York; 22,507; ZIP 11725.

Commerce city, SW California; 10,536.
—city, NE Texas; 9,534; ZIP 75428*.

Commerce City town, NE CEN. Colorado; 17,407; ZIP 80022.

Compton city, SW California; 78,611; ZIP 90220*.

Conakry city, W Guinea; cap.; 197,267.

Concord city, W California; 85,164; ZIP 94520*.

Concord city, S CEN. North Carolina; 18,404; ZIP 28025.
—city, S CEN. New Hampshire; cap.; 30,022; ZIP 03300*.

Concordia city, N Kansas; 7,221; ZIP 66901.

Congo, Republic of the republic, CEN. Africa; 132,000

sq. mi.; 1,300,000; cap. Brazzaville.
Congo (Kinshasa) Republic of the see ZAIRE.
Congo River river, CEN. Africa; 2,720 mi. long.
Conneaut city, NE Ohio; 14,552; ZIP 44030.
Connecticut state, NE United States; 5,009 sq. mi.; 3,031,709; cap. Hartford.
Connellsville city, SW Pennsylvania; 11,643; ZIP 15425.
Connersville city, E Indiana; 17,604; ZIP 47331.
Conroe city, E Texas; 11,969; ZIP 77301.
Conshohocken boro., SE Pennsylvania; 10,195; ZIP 19428.
Constantinople Istanbul: *the former name.*
Continental Divide ridge of the Rockies separating W flowing and E flowing streams in North America.
Conway city, CEN. Arkansas; 15,510; ZIP 72032.
—town, E South Carolina; 8,151; ZIP 29526*.
Cookeville town, N CEN. Tennessee; 14,270; ZIP 38501*.
Coon Rapids vill., E Minnesota; 30,505; ZIP see MINNEAPOLIS.
Coos Bay city, SW Oregon; 13,466; ZIP 97420*.
Copenhagen city, E Denmark; cap.; 1,362,158.
Copiague uninc. place, SE New York; 19,632; ZIP 11726.
Coral Gables city, SE Florida; 42,494; ZIP see MIAMI.
Coral Sea part of the Pacific, E of Australia and New Guinea.
Coraopolis boro., SW Pennsylvania 8,435; ZIP 15108.
Corbin city, SE Kentucky; 7,317; ZIP 40701.
Cordele city, S CEN. Georgia; 10,733; ZIP 31015.
Córdoba city, N CEN. Argentina; 798,663.
Corinth city, NE Mississippi; 11,581; ZIP 38834.
Cork co., SW Ireland; 2,880 sq. mi.; 337,000.
—co. boro., SE CEN. Cork co.; cap.; 80,000.
Corner Brook city, W Newfoundland, Canada; 25,185.
Corning city, W New York; 15,792; ZIP 14830*.
Cornwall co., SW England; 1,357 sq. mi.; 342,000; cap. Bodmin.
Cornwall city, SE Ontario, Canada; 43,639.
Corona city, S California; 27,519; ZIP 91720.
Coronado city, S California; 20,910; ZIP see SAN DIEGO.
Corpus Christi city, S Texas; 204,525; ZIP 78400*.
Corry city, NW Pennsylvania; 7,435; ZIP 16407.
Corsica isl., N Mediterranean; a dept. of France; 3,368 sq. mi.; 266,000; cap. Ajaccio.
Corsicana city, NE CEN. Texas; 19,972; ZIP 75110*.
Corte Madera town, W California; 8,464; ZIP 94925.
Cortez city, SW Colorado; 6,032; ZIP 81321.
Cortland city, CEN. New York; 19,621; ZIP 13045*.
Corvalis city, W Oregon; 35,153; ZIP 97330*.
Coshocton city E CEN. Ohio; 13,747; ZIP 43812.
Costa Mesa city, SW California; 72,660; ZIP 92626*.
Costa Rica republic, Central America; 19,690 sq. mi.; 1,921,000; cap. San José.
Cote-St-Luc city, S Quebec, Canada; 13,266.
Council Bluffs city, SW Iowa; 60,348; ZIP 51501*.
Coventry city and co. boro.; CEN. England; 334,440.
Coventry town, W CEN. Rhode Island; 22,947; ZIP 02816.
Covina city, SW California; 30,380; ZIP 91722*.
Covington city, N CEN. Georgia; 10,267; ZIP 30209.
—city, N Kentucky; 52,535; ZIP 41011*.
—city, SE Louisiana; 7,170; ZIP 70433.
—town, W Tennessee; 5,801; ZIP 38019.
—city, NW Virginia; 10,060; ZIP 24426.
Cowansville town, S Quebec, Canada; 7,050.
Cracow city, S Poland, 590,000.
Crafton boro. SW Pennsylvania; 8,233; ZIP see PITTSBURGH.
Cranbrook city, SE British Columbia, Canada; 5,549.
Cranford urb. twp., E New Jersey; 27,391; ZIP 07016.
Cranston city, E Rhode Island; 73,037; ZIP see PROVIDENCE.
Crawfordsville city, W Indiana; 13,842; ZIP 47933.
Cresskill boro., NE New Jersey; 7,164; ZIP 07626.
Crest Hill city, NE Illinois; 7,460; ZIP see JOLIET.
Crestline vill., N Ohio; 5,947; ZIP 44827.
Creston city, S Iowa; 8,234; ZIP 50801.
Crestview city, NW Florida; 7,952; ZIP 32536*.
Crestwood city, E Missouri; 15,398; ZIP see ST. LOUIS.
Crete isl., E Mediterranean; adm. div. of Greece; 3,207 sq. mi.; 456,642; cap. Canea.
Creve Coeur vill., CEN. Illinois; 6,440; ZIP see PEORIA.
—city, E Missouri; 8,967; ZIP see ST. LOUIS.
Crimea penin., SE Ukranian SSR.

Cristóbal town, Panama; at the Atlantic end of the Panama Canal; 817.
Croatia constituent republic, W Yugoslavia; 21,719 sq. mi.; 4,346,376; cap. Zagreb.
Crockett city, E Texas; 6,616; ZIP 75835.
Crookston city, NW Minnesota; 8,312; ZIP 56716*.
Crossett city, SE Arkansas; 6,191; ZIP 71635.
Croton-on-Hudson vill., SE New York; 7,523; ZIP 10520.
Crowley city, S Louisiana; 16,104; ZIP 70526.
Crown Point city, NW Indiana; 10,931; ZIP 46307.
Croydon co. boro., SE England; 252,000.
Crystal vill., SE Minnesota; 30,925; ZIP see MINNEAPOLIS.
Crystal City city, S Texas; 8,104; ZIP 78839.
Crystal Lake city, NE Illinois; 14,541; ZIP 60014.
Cuba isl. republic, Caribbean Sea; 44,217 sq. mi. (with the Isle of Pines); 9,090,000; cap. Havana.
Cudahy city, SE Wisconsin; 22,078; ZIP 53110.
Cuero city, SE Texas; 6,956; ZIP 77954.
Cullman city, N Alabama; 12,601; ZIP 35055.
Culver City city, SW California; 31,035; ZIP 90230*.
Cumberland city, NW Maryland; 29,724; ZIP 21501*.
—town, NE Rhode Island; 26,605; ZIP see PAWTUCKET.
Cumberland Gap passage through Cumberland Mountains, betw. Tennessee and Virginia.
Cumberland River river, Kentucky and Tennessee; flows to Ohio River.
Curaçao isl., W Netherlands Antilles; 171 sq. mi.; 149,091; cap. Willemstad.
Cushing city, N CEN. Oklahoma; 7,529; ZIP 74023.
Cutler Ridge uninc. place, SE Florida; 17,441; ZIP see MIAMI.
Cuyahoga Falls city, NE Ohio; 49,678; ZIP 44221*.
Cyclades isl. group, S Aegean; dept of Greece; 1,023 sq. mi.; 126,000; cap. Hermoupolis.
Cynthiana city, N Kentucky; 6,356; ZIP 41031.
Cyprus isl. republic, E Mediterranean 3,572 sq. mi.; 641,000; cap. Nicosia.
Czechoslovakia republic, E CEN. Europe; 49,368 sq. mi.; 14,700,000; cap. Prague.

Dacca city, E Bangladesh; cap.; 1,319,970.
Dachau town, SE West Germany; site of a Nazi concentration camp; 25,000.
Dahomey republic, member of the French community, W Africa; 44,696 sq. mi.; 3,000,000; cap. Porto-Novo.
Daigleville uninc. place, SE Louisiana; 5,906.
Dairen See LU-TA.
Dakar city, W Senegal; cap.; 581,204.
Dakota former terr. comprising the present North and South Dakota.
Dalhart city, N Texas; 5,705; ZIP 79022.
Dalhousie town, N New Brunswick, Canada; 5,856.
Dallas city, NW Oregon; 6,361; ZIP 97338*.
—city, N Texas; 844,401; ZIP 75200*.
Dalmatia reg., Croatia, W Yugoslavia; 4,954 sq. mi.; 750,000; cap. Split.
Dalton city, NW Georgia; 18,872; ZIP 30720.
Daly City city, W California; 66,922; ZIP 94014*.
Damascus city, SW Syria; cap.; 836,668.
Danbury city, SW Connecticut; 50,781; ZIP 06810*.
Dania city, SE Florida; 9,013; ZIP 33004.
Dansville vill., W New York; 5,436; ZIP 14437.
Danube river, CEN. and E Europe; 1,770 mi. long.
Danvers town, NE Massachusetts; 26,151.
Danville city, E Illinois; 42,570; ZIP 61832*.
—city, CEN. Kentucky; 11,542; ZIP 40422.
—boro., E CEN. Pennsylvania; 6,176; ZIP 17821.
—city, S Virginia; 46,391; ZIP 24540*.
Danzig city, N Poland; 394,000.
Darby boro., SE Pennsylvania; 13,729; ZIP 19023*.
—urb. twp., SE Pennsylvania; 13,198; ZIP 19023*.
Dardanelles strait, NW Turkey; connects Sea of Marmara with the Aegean.
Darien, Gulf of inlet of the Caribbean, E coast of Panama.
Darien, Isthmus of Isthmus of Panama: *the former name.*
Darlington town, NE South Carolina; 6,990; ZIP 29532.
Dartmouth town, SE Massachusetts; 18,800; ZIP 02714.
Dartmouth city, S Nova Scotia, Canada; 64,770.
Dauphin town, SW Manitoba, Canada; 7,374.

Davenport city, E Iowa; 98,469; ZIP 52800*.
Davis city, CEN. California; 23,488; ZIP 95616.
Dawson city, SW Georgia; 5,383; ZIP 31742.
Dawson Creek city, E British Columbia, Canada; 10,946.
Dayton city, N Kentucky; 8,691; ZIP see NEWPORT.
—city, SW Ohio; 243,601; ZIP 45400*.
Daytona Beach city, E Florida; 45,327; ZIP 32014*.
Dead Sea large salt lake on Israel-Jordan border; 1,292 ft. below sea level.
Dearborn city, SE Michigan; 104,199; ZIP 48120*.
Death Valley desert basin, SE California; maximum depth 280 ft. below sea level.
Decatur city, N Alabama; 38,044; ZIP 35601*.
—city, NW CEN. Georgia; 21,943; ZIP 30030*.
—city, CEN. Illinois; 90,397; ZIP 62521*.
—city, E Indiana; 8,445; ZIP 46733.
Deccan Plateau triangular tableland covering most of the penin. of India.
Decorah city, NE Iowa; 7,458; ZIP 52101.
Dedham town, E Massachusetts; 26,938; ZIP 02026.
Deep River town, SE Ontario, Canada; 5,377.
Deerfield vill., NE Illinois; 18,949; ZIP 60015.
Deerfield Beach town, SE Florida; 17,130; ZIP 33441.
Deer Park uninc. place, SE New York; 32,234; ZIP 11729.
—city, SW Ohio, 7,415; ZIP see CINCINNATI.
Defiance city, NW Ohio; 16,281; ZIP 43512.
De Kalb city, N Illinois; 32,949; ZIP 60115.
De Land city, E Florida; 11,641; ZIP 32720*.
Delano city, S CEN. California; 14,559; ZIP 93215.
Delaware state, E United States; 1,978 sq. mi.; 548,104; cap. Dover.
—city, CEN. Ohio; 15,008; ZIP 43015.
Delaware River river separating ePnnsylvania and Delaware from New York and New Jersey; 315 mi. long.
Del City city, CEN. Oklahoma; 27,133; ZIP see OKLAHOMA CITY.
Delhi city, NE CEN. India; 3,279,955.
Del Paso Heights-Robla uninc. place, N CEN. California; 11,495; ZIP see SACRAMENTO.
Delphos city, W Ohio; 7,608; ZIP 45833.
Delray Beach city, SE Florida; 19,366; ZIP 33444.
Del Rio city, SW Texas; 21,330; ZIP 78840.
Deming vill., SW New Mexico; 8,343; ZIP 88030.
Demopolis city, W Alabama; 8,343; ZIP 36732*.
Denham Springs town, SE Louisiana; 6,752; ZIP 70726.
Denison city, N Texas; 24,923; ZIP 75020.
Denmark kingdom, NW Europe; 16,619 sq. mi.; 5,045,00; cap. Copenhagen.
Denton city, N Texas; 39,874; ZIP 76201.
Denver city, CEN. Colorado; cap.; 514,678; ZIP 80200*.
De Pere city, E Wisconsin; 13,309; ZIP 54115.
Depew vill., N New York; 22,158; ZIP 14043.
Derby uninc. place, E CEN. Colorado; 10,206.
—city, SW Connecticut; 12,599; ZIP 06418.
—city, S Kansas; 7,947; ZIP 67037.
De Ridder city, W Louisiana; 8,030; ZIP 70634.
Des Moines city, S CEN. Iowa; cap.; 200,587; ZIP 50300*.
De Soto city, E Missouri; 5,984; ZIP 63020.
Des Plaines city, NE Illinois; 57,239; ZIP 60016*.
Detroit city, SE Michigan; 1,511,482; ZIP 48200*.
Detroit Lakes city, W Minnesota; 5,797; ZIP 56501.
Devil's Island rocky isl. off the coast of French Guiana; formerly a penal colony.
Devils Lake city, NE CEN. North Dakota; 7,078; ZIP 58301.
Devonshire co., SW England; 2,611 sq. mi.; 823,000; cap. Exeter.
Dexter city, SE Missouri; 6,024; ZIP 63841.
Dickinson city, W North Dakota; 12,405; ZIP 58601.
Dickson city, N Tennessee; 5,665; ZIP 37055.
Dickson City boro., NE Pennsylvania; 7,698; ZIP see SCRANTON.
Dillon town, NE South Carolina; 5,991; ZIP 29536*.
Dinuba city, CEN. California; 7,917; ZIP 93618.
District Heights, town, SW Maryland; 8,424.
District of Columbia federal dist., E United States; co-extensive with Washington, the capital; 756,510.
Dixon city, N Illinois, 18,147; ZIP 01021.
Djakarta city NW Java; cap. of Indonesia; 4,576,009. Also Jakarta.
Dnepropetrovsk city, SW Ukrainian SSR; 903,000.

Also Dniepropetrovsk.
Dnieper river, SW USSR; 1,420 mi. long. Also Dnepr.
Dniester river, SW USSR; 876 mi. long. Also Dnestr.
Dobbs Ferry vill., SE New York; 10,353; ZIP 10512.
Dock Junction uninc. place, SE Georgia; 6,009.
Dodecanese isl. group, Aegean Sea; a dept. of Greece; 1,036 sq. mi.; 121,000; cap. Rhodes.
Dodge City city, S Kansas; 14,127; ZIP 67801.
Dolbeau town, S CEN. Quebec, Canada; 6,052.
Dolomite Alps E div. of the Alps, N Italy.
Dolton vill., NE Illinois; 25,937; ZIP 60419.
Dominican Republic republic, E Hispaniola; 18,700 sq. mi.; 4,562,000; cap. Santo Domingo.
Don river, SW RSFSR; 1,222 mi. long.
Donaldsonville city, SE Louisiana; 7,367; ZIP 70346.
Donelson uninc. place, N CEN. Tennessee; 17,195; ZIP see NASHVILLE.
Donets river, SW USSR; 631 mi. long.
Donetsk city, SW USSR; 905,000.
Donna city, S Texas; 7,365; ZIP 78537.
Donora boro., SW Pennsylvania; 8,825; ZIP 15033.
Dormont boro., SW Pennsylvania; 12,856; ZIP see PITTSBURGH.
Dortmund city in Ruhr reg. of West Germany; 642,396.
Dorval city, S Quebec, Canada; 18,592.
Dothan city, SE Alabama; 36,733; ZIP 36301*.
Douai town, N France; ab. 43,000.
Douglas city, SE Arizona; 12,462; ZIP 85607.
—city, SE CEN. Georgia; 10,195; ZIP 31533.
Dover municipal boro., SE England; 35,000.
Dover city, CEN. Delaware; cap. 17,488; ZIP 19901.
—city, SE New Hampshire; 20,850; ZIP 03820.
—town, N New Jersey; 15,039; ZIP 07801.
—city, E Ohio; 11,516; ZIP 44622.
Dover, Strait of strait at the E end of the English Channel; width 21 mi.
Dowagiac city, SW Michigan; 6,583; ZIP 49047.
Downers Grove vill., NE Illinois; 32,751; ZIP 60515.
Downey city, SW California; 88,445; ZIP 90240*.
Downingtown boro., SE Pennsylvania; 7,437; ZIP 19335.
Doylestown boro., SE Pennsylvania; 8,270; ZIP 18901.
Dracut town, NE Massachusetts; 18,214; ZIP 01826.
Dresden city, S East Germany; 500,051.
Drummondville city, S Quebec, Canada; 27,909.
Dryden town, NW Ontario, Canada; 5,728.
Duarte city, SW California; 14,981; ZIP 91010.
Dublin city, E Ireland; cap. 567,866.
Dublin city, CEN. Georgia; 15,143; ZIP 31021.
Du Bois city, W CEN. Pennsylvania; 10,112; ZIP 15801.
Dubuque city, E Iowa; 62,309; ZIP 52001*.
Duisburg city, W West Germany; 435,281.
Duluth city, NE Minnesota; 100,578; ZIP 55800*.
Dumas city, NW Texas; 9,771; ZIP 79029.
Dumont boro., NE New Jersey; 17,534; ZIP 07628.
Dunbar city, W West Virginia; 9,151; ZIP 25064.
Duncan city, S Oklahoma; 19,718; ZIP 73533.
Dundalk uninc. place. CEN. Maryland; 85,377; ZIP see BALTIMORE.
Dundas town, S Ontario, Canada; 12,912.
Dundee burgh, E Scotland.
Dunedin city, W Florida; 17,639; ZIP 32528.
Dunellen boro., E CEN. New Jersey; 7,072; ZIP 08812*.
Dunkirk town, N France; scene of evacuation of British forces in World War II, May-June 1940; ab. 21,000.
Dunkirk city, W New York; 16,855; ZIP 14048.
Dunmore boro., NE Pennsylvania; 17,300; ZIP see SCRANTON.
Dunn town, CEN. North Carolina; 8,302; ZIP 28334.
Dunnville town, S Ontario, Canada; 5,181.
Duquesne city, SW Pennsylvania; 11,410; ZIP 15110.
Du Quoin city, S Illinois; 6,691; ZIP 62832.
Durango city, SW Colorado; 10,333; ZIP 81300*.
Durant city, S Oklahoma; 11,118; ZIP 74701.
Durban city, SE South Africa; 663,000.
Durham city, N CEN. North Carolina; 95,438; ZIP 27700*.
Duryea boro., NE Pennsylvania; 5,264; ZIP see PITTSTON.
Düsseldorf city, W West Germany; 650,377.
Dutch East Indies SEE NETHERLANDS EAST INDIES.
Dutch Guiana See SURINAM.
Dutch Harbor US Naval base in the Aleutian Islands.

Dutch West Indies Netherlands Antilles: *the former name.*
Duvernay town, s Quebec, Canada; 10,939.
Dyersburg city, NW Tennessee; 14,523; ZIP 38024.

Eagle Pass city, SW Texas; 15,364; ZIP 78852.
Eagleton Village uninc. place, E Tennessee; 5,345.
Easley city, NW South Carolina; 11,175; ZIP 29640.
East Alton vill., SW Illinois; 7,309; ZIP 62024.
East Aurora vill., W New York; 7,033; ZIP 14052.
East Berlin See BERLIN.
East Chicago city, NW Indiana; 46,982; ZIP 46312*.
East China Sea NE part of the China Sea.
East Cleveland city, NE Ohio; 39,600; ZIP see CLEVE-LAND.
East Detroit city, SE Michigan; 45,920; ZIP 48021.
Easter Island isl. of Chile, South Pacific; known for stone monuments found there; 45.5 sq. mi.
East Gary town, NW Indiana; 9,858; ZIP see GARY.
East Germany See GERMANY.
East Grand Forks city, NW Minnesota; 7,607; ZIP 56721.
East Grand Rapids city SW Michigan; 12,565.
Easthampton town, W Massachusetts; 13,012; ZIP 01027.
East Hartford town, N CEN. Connecticut; 57,583; ZIP see HARTFORD.
East Haven town, S Connecticut; 25,120; ZIP see NEW HAVEN.
East Kildonan city, S Manitoba, Canada; 27,305.
Eastlake city, NE Ohio; 19,690; ZIP see WILLOUGHBY.
East Lansing city, S CEN. Michigan; 47,540; ZIP 48823*.
East Liverpool city, E Ohio; 20,020; ZIP 43920.
East Los Angeles uninc. place, SW California; 105,033; ZIP see LOS ANGELES.
Eastman city, S CEN. Georgia; 5,416; ZIP 31023.
East Moline city, NW Illinois; 20,832; ZIP 61244.
Easton city, S Pennsylvania; 30,256; ZIP 18042*.
East Orange city, NE New Jersey; 75,471; ZIP 07017*.
East Palestine city, E Ohio; 5,232; ZIP 44413.
East Paterson boro., NE New Jersey; 22,749; ZIP 07407.
East Peoria city, CEN. Illinois; 18,455; ZIP see PEORIA.
East Point city, NW CEN. Georgia; 39,315; ZIP 30044.
East Providence town, E Rhode Island; 48,151; ZIP see PROVIDENCE.
East Prussia former prov. of Prussia, NE Germany.
East Ridge town, SE Tennessee; 21,799; ZIP see CHATTANOOGA.
East Rochester vill., W New York; 8,347; ZIP 14445.
East Rockaway vill., SE New York; 10,323; ZIP 11518.
East Rutherford boro., NE New Jersey; 8,536; ZIP see RUTHERFORD.
East Saint Louis city, SW Illinois; 69,996; ZIP 62201*.
East Stroudsburg boro., E Pennsylvania; 7,894; ZIP 18301.
Eastview town, SE Ontario, Canada; 24,555.
East Whittier uninc. place, SW California; 19,884.
East Wilmington uninc. place, SE North Carolina; 5,520.
Eaton vill., SW Ohio; 6,020; ZIP 45320.
Eau Claire city, W CEN. Wisconsin; 44,619; ZIP 54701*.
Eau Gallie city, E Florida; 12,300; ZIP 32935*.
Economy boro., W Pennsylvania; 7,176.
Ecorse city, SE Michigan; 17,515; ZIP see DETROIT.
Ecuador republic, NW South America; 104,306 sq. mi.; 6,951,000; cap. Quito.
Edgemere See SPARROWS POINT-FORT HOWARD-EDGE-MERE.
Edgewood boro., SW Pennsylvania; 5,101; ZIP see PITTSBURGH.
Edina city, SE Minnesota; 44,046; ZIP see MINNE-APOLIS.
Edinburg city, S Texas; 17,163; ZIP 78539.
Edinburgh city, E Scotland; cap; 448,682.
Edmond city, CEN. Oklahoma; 16,633; ZIP 73034.
Edmonds city, NW Washington; 23,998; ZIP 98020.
Edmonton city, CEN. Alberta, Canada; cap; 438,152.
Edmundston city, NW New Brunswick, Canada; 12,791.
Edna city, SE Texas; 5,332; ZIP 77957.
Edwardsville city, SW Illinois; 11,070; ZIP 62025.
—boro, NE Pennsylvania; 5,633.
Effingham city, SE CEN. Illinois; 9,458; ZIP 62401.
Eggertsville uninc. place, W New York; 44,807.
Egypt republic, NE Africa; 386,198 sq. mi.; 36,400,000;

cap. Cairo; official name *Arab Republic of Egypt.*
Eire Ireland: *the Irish Gaelic name.*
El Alamein vill., N Egypt; scene of a British victory over Axis forces in World War II.
Elba isl. betw. Italy and Corsica; sovereign under the exiled Napoleon Bonaparte, 1814-15.
Elbe river, CEN. Europe; 725 mi. long.
Elberton city, NE Georgia; 6,438; ZIP 30635.
Elbrus, Mount mtn., NW Georgian SSR; 18,603 ft.
Elburz Mountains mtn. range, N Iran.
El Cajon city, SW California; 52,273; ZIP 92020*.
El Campo city, SE Texas; 8,563; ZIP 77437.
El Centro city, S California; 19,272; ZIP 92243*.
El Cerrito city, W California; 25,190; ZIP 94530*.
El Dorado city, S Arkansas; 25,283; ZIP 71730*.
—city, S Kansas; 12,308; ZIP 67042.
Elgin city, NE Illinois; 55,691; ZIP 60120*.
Elizabeth city, NE New Jersey; 112,654; ZIP 07200*.
Elizabeth City town, NE North Carolina; 14,069; ZIP 27909.
Elizabethton city, NE Tennessee; 12,269; ZIP 37643.
Elizabethtown city, W CEN. Kentucky; 11,748; ZIP 42701.
—boro., SE Pennsylvania; 8,072; ZIP 17022.
Elk City city, W Oklahoma; 7,323; ZIP 73644.
Elk Grove Village vill., NE Illinois; 24,516; ZIP see ARLINGTON HEIGHTS.
Elkhart city, N Indiana; 43,152; ZIP 46514*.
Elkins city, E CEN. West Virginia; 8,287; ZIP 26241.
Elko city, NE Nevada; 7,621; ZIP 89801.
Elkton town, NE Maryland; 5,362; ZIP 21921.
Ellensburg city, CEN. Washington; 13,568; ZIP 98926.
Ellis Island isl., upper New York Bay; former site of US immigration station.
Ellwood City boro., W Pennsylvania; 10,857; ZIP 16117.
Elmhurst city, NE Illinois; 50,547; ZIP 60126*.
Elmira city, S New York; 39,945; ZIP 14901*.
Elmira Southeast uninc. place, CEN. New York; 6,689.
Elmont uninc. place, SE New York; 29,363; ZIP see FLORAL PARK.
El Monte city, SW California; 69,837; ZIP 91731*.
Elmwood Park vill., NE Illinois; 26,160; ZIP see CHICAGO.
El Paso city, W Texas; 322,261; ZIP 79900*.
El Paso de Robles city, SW California; 7,168.
El Reno city, CEN. Oklahoma; 14,510; ZIP 73036.
El Rio uninc. place, SW California; 6,173; ZIP see OXNARD.
El Salvador republic, W Central America; 8,260 sq. mi.; 3,980,000; cap. San Salvador.
El Segundo city, SW California; 15,620; ZIP 90245*.
Elsmere town, NE Delaware; 8,415.
Elwood city, CEN. Indiana; 11,196; ZIP 46036.
Elyria city, N Ohio; 53,427; ZIP 44035*.
Emmaus boro., E Pennsylvania; 11,511; ZIP 18049.
Emporia city, CEN. Kansas; 23,327; ZIP 66801*.
—town, S Virginia; 5,300; ZIP 23847.
Endicott vill., S New York; 16,556; ZIP 13760*.
Enfield town, N Connecticut; 46,189; ZIP 06030.
England S part and largest political division of Great Britain: 50,237 sq. mi.; 43,431,000; cap. London.
Englewood city, CEN. Colorado; 33,695; ZIP 80110.
—city, NE New Jersey; 24,985; ZIP 07631*.
English Channel strait, betw. England and France; 20-100 mi. wide.
Enid city, N Oklahoma; 44,088; ZIP 73701*.
Eniwetok atoll, Marshall Islands; U.S. nuclear weapons testing area.
Ennis city, NE CEN. Texas; 11,046; ZIP 75119.
Enterprise city, SE Alabama; 15,591; ZIP 36330*.
Ephrata boro., SE Pennsylvania; 9,662; ZIP 17522.
Ephrata city, CEN. Washington; 5,255; ZIP 98823.
Epsom town, SE England; site of famous racecourse; 71,000.
Erie city, NW Pennsylvania; 129,231; ZIP 16500*.
Erie, Lake southernmost of the Great Lakes; 9,940 sq. mi.
Erie Canal waterway, betw. Albany and Buffalo, New York; integrated with New York State Barge Canal.
Eritrea state, E Africa; federated with Ethiopia, 45,000 sq. mi.; 1 million; cap. Asmara.
Erivan See YEREVAN.
Escanaba city, NW Michigan; 15,368; ZIP 49829.
Escondido city, SW California; 36,792; ZIP 92025*.

Espanola town, S CEN. Ontario, Canada; 5,353.
Essen city, W West Germany; 691,830.
Essex uninc. place, N Maryland; 38,193; ZIP see BALTIMORE.
Essex Junction vill., NW Vermont; 6,511; ZIP 05452.
Estevan city, SE Saskatchewan, Canada; 7,728.
Estonian SSR constituent republic, W USSR, 17,400 sq. mi.; 1,400,000; cap. Tallinn. Also Estonia.
Estherville city, N Iowa; 8,108; ZIP 51334.
Ethiopia republic, E Africa; 350,000 sq. mi.; 27,200,-000; cap. Addis Ababa.
Etna boro., SW Pennsylvania; 5,819; ZIP see PITTS-BURGH.
Etna, Mount volcano, E Sicily; 10,868 ft.
Euboea isl. of Greece in the Aegean; 1,457 sq. mi.
Euclid city, NE Ohio; 71,552; ZIP see CLEVELAND.
Eufaula city, SE Alabama; 9,102; ZIP 36027.
Eugene city, W Oregon; 76,346; ZIP 97401*.
Eunice town, S CEN. Louisiana; 11,390; ZIP 70535.
Euphrates river, SW Asia; 1,740 mi. long.
Eurasia large land mass comprising Europe and Asia.
Eureka city, NW California; 24,337; ZIP 95501*.
Europe W part of the Eurasian land mass; 1.9 million sq. mi.; excluding Turkey and the USSR; 470,000,000.
Eustis city, CEN. Florida; 6,722; ZIP 32726.
Euxine Sea See BLACK SEA.
Evansdale town, E CEN. Iowa; 5,038; ZIP see WATERLOO.
Evanston city, NE Illinois; 79,808; ZIP 60201*.
Evansville city, SW Indiana; 138,764; ZIP 47700*.
Everest mtn., E Nepal; highest point of the earth's surface; 29,028 ft.
Everett city, E Massachusetts; 42,485; ZIP see BOSTON.
—city, W Washington; 53,622; ZIP 98201*.
Everglades large swampy reg., S Florida.
Evergreen Park vill., NE Illinois; 25,487; ZIP see CHICAGO.
Evvoia Euboea: the Greek name.
Excelsior Springs city, NW Missouri; 9,411; ZIP 64024.
Exeter co. boro., CEN. Devonshire, England; cap; 80,000.
Exeter uninc. place, SE New Hampshire; 8,892; ZIP 03833.

Fabreville town, S Quebec, Canada; 5,213.
Faeroe Islands isl. group of Denmark, North Atlan-tic; 540 sq. mi.; 34,000; cap. Thorshain.
Fairbanks town, E CEN. Alaska; 14,771; ZIP 99701*.
Fairborn city, SW Ohio; 32,267; ZIP 45324.
Fairbury city, SE Nebraska; 5,265; ZIP 68352*.
Fairfax town, CEN. California; 7,661; ZIP 94930.
—town, N Virginia; 21,970; ZIP 22030.
Fairfield city, N CEN. Alabama; 14,369; ZIP 35064.
—city, W CEN. California; 44,146; ZIP 94533*.
—town, SW Connecticut; 56,487; ZIP 06430*.
—city, S Illinois; 5,897; ZIP 62837.
—city, SE Iowa; 8,715; ZIP 52556.
—city, SW Ohio; 14,680; ZIP see HAMILTON.
Fairhaven town, SE Massachusetts; 16,332; ZIP 02719.
Fair Haven boro., E New Jersey; 6,142; ZIP see RED BANK.
Fair Lawn boro., NE New Jersey; 37,975; ZIP 07410*.
Fairmont city, S Minnesota; 10,751; ZIP 56031.
—city, N West Virginia; 26,093; ZIP 26550*.
Fair Oaks uninc. place, NW CEN. Georgia; 21,899; ZIP see MARIETTA.
Fair Plain uninc. place, SW Michigan; 3,680.
Fairport vill., W New York; 6,474; ZIP 14450.
Fairview boro., NE New Jersey; 10,698; ZIP 07022.
—uninc. place, SE New York; 8,517.
Fairview Park city, NE Ohio; 21,681; ZIP see CLEVE-LAND.
Fairway city, E Kansas; 5,133.
Fajardo town, NE Puerto Rico; 18,249; ZIP 00648*.
Falcon Heights vill., E Minnesota; 5,507; ZIP see SAINT PAUL.
Falfurrias city, S Texas; 6,355; ZIP 78355.
Falkland Islands British depen., South Atlantic; 4,618 sq. mi.; 2,045; cap. Stanley.
Fall River city, SE Massachusetts; 96,898; ZIP 02720*.
Falls urb. twp., NE Pennsylvania; 35,830; ZIP 18615.
Falls Church city, NE Virginia; 10,772; ZIP 22040.
Falls City city, SE Nebraska; 5,444; ZIP 68355*.
Fanwood boro., NE New Jersey; 8,920; ZIP 07023.
Fargo city, SE North Dakota; 53,365; ZIP 58100*.

Faribault city, SE Minnesota; 16,595; ZIP 55021.
Farmers Branch city, N Texas; 27,492; ZIP see DALLAS.
Farmingdale vill., SE New York; 9,297; ZIP 11735*.
Farmington city, SE Michigan; 13,337; ZIP 48024.
—city, E Missouri; 6,590; ZIP 63640.
—town, NW New Mexico; 21,979.
Farnham city, S Quebec, Canada; 6,354.
Farrell city, W Pennsylvania; 11,022; ZIP 16121.
Fayetteville city, NW Arkansas; 30,729; ZIP 72701*.
—city, S CEN. North Carolina; 53,510; ZIP 28301*.
—town, S Tennessee; 7,030; ZIP 37334.
Federal Republic of Germany See GERMANY.
Fenton vill., SE Michigan; 8,284; ZIP 48430.
Fergus Falls city, W Minnesota; 12,443; ZIP 56537*.
Ferguson city, E Missouri; 28,915; ZIP see SAINT LOUIS.
Fernandina Beach city, NE Florida; 6,955.
Ferndale city, SE Michigan; 30,850; ZIP see DETROIT.
Festus city, E Missouri; 7,530; ZIP 63028.
Fiji independent member of Commonwealth of Na-tions, South Pacific; comprises Fiji Islands (7,039 sq. mi.) and Rotuma (18 sq. mi.); 560,000; cap. Suva.
Findlay city, NW CEN. Ohio; 35,800; ZIP 45840*.
Finland republic, N Europe; 117,913 sq. mi.; 4,700,-000; cap. Helsinki.
Finland, Gulf of part of the Baltic Sea betw. Finland and the USSR.
Fitchburg city, N Massachusetts; 43,343; ZIP 21420*.
Fitzgerald city, S CEN. Georgia; 8,015; ZIP 31750.
Fiume Rijeka: the Italian name.
Flagstaff city, N CEN. Arizona; 26,117; ZIP 86001*.
Flanders reg., N France and S Belgium.
Flin Flon town, W Manitoba, Canada; 11,104.
Flint city, E CEN. Michigan; 193,317; ZIP 48500*.
Flintridge See LA CANADA-FLINTRIDGE.
Flora city, S CEN. Illinois; 5,283; ZIP 62839.
Floral Park vill., SE New York; 18,466; ZIP 11001*.
Florence city, CEN. Tuscany, Italy; cap.; 438,000.
Florence city, NW Alabama; 34,031; ZIP 35630*.
—city, N Kentucky; 11,457; ZIP 41042.
—city, E South Carolina; 25,997; ZIP 29501.
Florence-Graham uninc. place, SW California; 42,895.
Florham Park boro., N New Jersey; 8,094; ZIP 07932.
Florida state, SE United States; 58,560 sq. mi.; 6,789,443; cap. Tallahassee.
Florida Keys isl. group SW of Florida.
Florissant city, E Missouri; 65,908; ZIP 63031*.
Folcroft boro., SE Pennsylvania; 9,610; ZIP 19032.
Fond du Lac city, E Wisconsin; 35,515; ZIP 54935*.
Fontainebleau town, N CEN. France; site of a former royal residence; 20,000.
Fontana city, S CEN. California; 20,673; ZIP 92335*.
Foochow city, SE China; 616,000.
Ford City boro., W CEN. Pennsylvania; 4,749; ZIP 16226.
Forest City town, SW North Carolina; 7,179; ZIP 28043.
Forest Grove city, NW Oregon; 8,275; ZIP 97116.
Forest Hill vill., S Ontario, Cannada; 20,489.
Forest Hills boro., SW Pennsylvania; 9,561; ZIP see PITTSBURGH.
Forest Lawn town, S Alberta, Canada; 12,263.
Forest Park town, NW CEN. Georgia; 19,994; ZIP 30050.
—vill., NE Illinois; 15,472; ZIP 60130.
Formosa Taiwan: a former name.
Forrest City city, E Arkansas; 12,521; ZIP 72335.
Fort Atkinson city, S Wisconsin; 9,164; ZIP 53538.
Fort Collins city, N Colorado; 43,337; ZIP 80521*.
Fort Dodge city, N CEN. Iowa; 31,263; ZIP 50501.
Fort Erie town, S Ontario, Canada; 9,027.
Fort Frances town, W Ontario, Canada; 9,481.
Forth River river, SE Scotland; 65 mi. long.
Forth, Firth of estuary of the Forth River; 51 mi. long.
Fort Howard See SPARROWS POINT-FORT HOWARD-EDGEMERE.
Fort Knox military reservation, N Kentucky; site of the Federal gold bullion depository; ZIP 40120*.
Fort Lauderdale city, SE Florida; 139,590; ZIP 33300*.
Fort Lee boro., NE New Jersey; 30,631; ZIP 07024*.
Fort Madison city, SE Iowa; 13,996; ZIP 52627.
Fort Morgan city, NE Colorado; 7,594; ZIP 80701.
Fort Myers city, SW Florida; 27,351; ZIP 33901.
Fort Payne city, NE Alabama; 8,435; ZIP 35967.
Fort Pierce city, E Florida; 29,721; ZIP 33450.
Fort Scott city, SE Kansas; 8,967; ZIP 66701.

Fort Smith city, W Arkansas; 62,802; ZIP 72901*.
Fort Stockton city, W Texas; 8,283; ZIP 79735.
Fort Thomas city, N Kentucky; 16,338; ZIP see NEWPORT.
Fort Valley city, W CEN. Georgia; 9,251; ZIP 31030.
Fort Walton Beach city, NW Florida; 19,994; ZIP 32548.
Fort Wayne city, NE Indiana; 177,671; ZIP 46800.
Fort William see THUNDER BAY.
Fort Worth city, N Texas; 393,476; ZIP 76100*.
Forty Fort boro., NE Pennsylvania; 6,114; ZIP see WILKES-BARRE.
Fostoria city, N Ohio; 16,037; ZIP 44830.
Fountain City uninc. place, E Tennessee; 10,365; ZIP see KNOXVILLE.
Fountain Hill boro., E Pennsylvania; 5,384.
Fox Point vill., SE Wisconsin; 7,937.
Frackville boro., E CEN. Pennsylvania; 5,445; ZIP 17931.
Framingham town, E Massachusetts; 64,048; ZIP 01701.
France republic, W Europe; 212,974 sq. mi.; 52,507,000; cap. Paris.
Frankfort city, CEN. Indiana; 14,956; ZIP 46041.
—city, N CEN. Kentucky; cap.; 21,356; ZIP 40601.
Frankfort on the Main city, CEN. West Germany; 663,422.
Frankfort on the Oder city, E East Germany; 57,000.
Franklin city, S CEN. Indiana; 11,477; ZIP 46131.
—city, S Kentucky; 6,553; ZIP 42134.
—town, S Louisiana; 9,325; ZIP 70538.
—town, E Massachusetts; 17,830; ZIP 02038.
—city, CEN. New Hampshire; 7,292; ZIP 03235.
—city, SW Ohio; 10,075; ZIP 45005*.
—city, NW Pennsylvania; 8,629; ZIP 16323.
—town, CEN. Tennessee; 9,404; ZIP 37064.
—town, SE Virginia; 6,880; ZIP 23851.
—city, SE Wisconsin; 12,247; ZIP see HALES CORNERS.
Franklin Park vill., NE Illinois; 20,497; ZIP 60131.
Franklin Square uninc. place, SE New York; 32,156; ZIP 11010.
Fraser city, SE Michigan; 11,868; ZIP 48026.
Frederick city, NW Maryland; 23,641; ZIP 21701.
—city, SW Oklahoma; 6,132; ZIP 73542.
Fredericksburg city, NE Virginia; 14,450; ZIP 22401*.
Fredericton city, S CEN. New Brunswick, Canada; 24,254.
Fredonia vill., W New York; 10,326; ZIP 14063.
Freehold boro., E CEN. New Jersey; 10,545; ZIP 07728.
Freeport city, N Illinois; 27,736; ZIP 61032*.
— vill., SE New York; 40,374; ZIP 11520.
—city, SE Texas; 11,997; ZIP 77541.
Fremont city, E Nebraska; 22,962; ZIP 68025.
—city, N Ohio; 18,490; ZIP 43420.
French Guiana French Overseas dept.; NE South America; 35,000 sq. mi.; 44,392; cap. Cayenne.
French Polynesia French Overseas terr., South Pacific; comprises the Society, Marquesas, Gambier, and other islands; 1,560 sq. mi.; 119,168; cap. Papeete.
French Republic France, with its overseas depts. and terrs.
French Somaliland see AFARS AND ISSAS.
French West Indies isls. comprising Guadaloupe and Martinique.
Fresno city, CEN. California; 165,972; ZIP 93700*.
Fridley city, E Minnesota; 29,233; ZIP see MINNEAPOLIS.
Friesland prov., N Netherlands; 1,251 sq. mi.; 478,000; cap. Leeuwarden.
Frigid Zone See NORTH FRIGID ZONE, SOUTH FRIGID ZONE.
Frisian Islands isl. group, North Sea near Germany, Denmark and the Netherlands.
Front Royal town, N Virginia; 8,211; ZIP 22630.
Frostburg city, NW Maryland; 7,327; ZIP 21532.
Fruitridge See SOUTH SACRAMENTO-FRUITRIDGE.
Fuji extinct volcano, Honshu, Japan; 12,389 ft.
Fukuoka city N Kyushu, Japan; 853,270.
Fullerton city, SW California; 85,826; ZIP 92631*.
Fulton city, CEN. Missouri; 12,148; ZIP 65251.
—city, N CEN. New York; 14,003; ZIP 13069.
Fundy, Bay of inlet of the Atlantic betw. Nova Scotia and New Brunswick and NE Maine.
Fushun city NE People's Republic of China; 985,000.

Gabonese Republic republic, W equatorial Africa; 102,290 sq. mi.; 950,009; cap. Libreville. Also **Gabon.**
Gadsden city, NE Alabama; 53,928; ZIP 35901*.
Gaffney city, N South Carolina; 13,253; ZIP 29340.
Gainesville city, N Florida; 64,510; ZIP 32601*.
—city, N CEN. Georgia; 15,459; ZIP 30501*.
—city, N Texas; 13,830; ZIP 76240.
Galápagos Island isl. group of Ecuador, South Pacific.
Galax city, SW Virginia; 6,278; ZIP 24333.
Galena Park city, SE Texas; 10,479; ZIP 77547.
Galesburg city, W Illinois; 36,290; ZIP 61401.
Galicia reg., SE Poland and NW Ukrainian SSR.
Galicia reg., NW Spain.
Galilee reg., N Israel.
Galilee, Sea of fresh water lake; betw. NE Israel, SW Syria, and NW Jordan; 64 sq. mi.
Galion city, N CEN. Ohio; 13,123; ZIP 44833.
Gallatin city, N Tennessee; 13,093; ZIP 37066.
Gallipoli Peninsula penin., NW Turkey.
Gallipolis city, S Ohio; 7,490; ZIP 45631.
Gallup town, NW New Mexico; 14,596; ZIP 87301.
Galt city, S Ontario, Canada; 27,830.
Galveston city, SE Texas; 61,809; ZIP 77550*.
Gambia republic, member of the Commonwealth of Nations, W Africa; 4,003 sq. mi.; 364,000; cap. Banjul.
Gananoque town, SE Ontario, Canada; 5,096.
Gander town, E Newfoundland, Canada; 5,725.
Ganges river, N India and E Pakistan; 1,560 mi. long.
Gardena city, SW California; 41,021; ZIP 90247*.
Garden City town, SE Georgia; 5,741; ZIP see SAVANNAH.
—city, SW Kansas; 14,708; ZIP 67846.
—city, SE Michigan; 41,864; ZIP 48135.
—vill., SE New York; 7,488; ZIP 11530.
Garden City Park uninc. place, SE New York; 7,488; ZIP 11530.
Garden Grove city, SW California; 122,524; ZIP 92640*.
Gardiner city, S Maine; 6,685; ZIP 04345.
Gardner city, N Masachusetts; 19,748; ZIP 01440*.
Garfield city, NE New Jersey; 30,722; ZIP 07026.
Garfield Heights city, NE Ohio; 41,417; ZIP see CLEVELAND.
Garland city, N Texas; 81,437; ZIP 75040*.
Garwood boro., NE New Jersey; 5,260; ZIP 07027.
Gary city, NW Indiana; 175,415; ZIP 46400*.
Gascony reg., SW France.
Gastonia city, SW North Carolina; 47,142; ZIP 28052*.
Gatineau town, SW Quebec, Canada; 13,022.
Gaza city, SW Palestine; adm. by the Arab Republic of Egypt with the **Gaza Strip,** the surrounding area; 377,000; occupied by Israel since 1967.
Gdansk Danzig: *the Polish name.*
Gdynia city, NW Poland; 144,000.
Geneseo city, NW Illinois; 5,840; ZIP 61254.
Geneva city, SW Switzerland; 163,100.
Geneva city, NE Illinois; 9,115; ZIP 60134.
—city, W CEN. New York; 16,793; ZIP 14456.
—city, NE Ohio; 6.449; ZIP 44041.
Geneva, Lake of lake, SW Switzerland; 224 sq. mi.
Genoa city, NW Italy; 812,206.
Georgetown city, N Guyana; cap.; 195,250.
Georgetown city, N CEN. Kentucky; 8,629; ZIP 40324.
—city, S South Carolina; 10,449; ZIP 29440.
—city, CEN. Texas; 6,395; ZIP 78626.
Georgetown town, S Ontario, Canada; 10,298.
Georgia state, SE United States; 58,876 sq. mi.; 4,589,575; cap. Atlanta.
Georgian SSR constituent republic, SW USSR; 26,900 sq. mi.; 4,044,000; cap. Tbilisi.
German Democratic Republic See GERMANY.
Germany country, CEN. Europe; divided in 1949 into the Federal Republic of Germany (West Germany); 95,735 sq. mi.; 61,508,400; cap. Bonn; and the German Democratic Republic (East Germany); 41,479 sq. mi. (excluding East Berlin); 17,040,926 (including East Berlin); cap. East Berlin.
Gettysburg boro., S Pennsylvania; site of a Union victory in the Civil War, July, 1863; 7,275; ZIP 17325.
Ghana republic of the Commonwealth of Nations, W Africa; 92,100 sq. mi.; 9,600,000; cap. Accra.
Ghent city, NW Belgium; 160,000.
Gibraltar self-governing British depen., on the Rock

of Gibraltar; 2.25 sq. mi.; 26,833.

Gibraltar, Rock of penin., s Spain; dominates the Strait of Gibraltar.

Gibraltar, Strait of strait, betw. Spain and Africa, w Mediterranean.

Giffard city, s CEN. Quebec, Canada; 10,129.

Gilbert Island British depen., South Pacific; 369 sq. mi.; 53,517; cap. Tarawa.

Gilroy city, w California; 12,665; ZIP 95020.

Girard city, NE Ohio; 14,119; ZIP 44420.

Glace Bay town, NE Nova Scotia, Canada; 24,186.

Gladewater city, E Texas; 5,574; ZIP 75647.

Gladstone city, NW Michigan; 5,237; ZIP 49837.
—city, w Missouri; 23,128; ZIP see KANSAS CITY.

Glasgow burgh, sw Scotland; 897,848.

Glasgow city, s Kentucky; 11,301; ZIP 42141.

Glassboro boro., w New Jersey; 12,938; ZIP 08028.

Glassport boro., sw Pennsylvania; 7,450; ZIP 15045.

Glencliff See WOODBINE-RADNOR-GLENCLIFF.

Glencoe vill., NE Illinois; 10,542; ZIP 60022.

Glen Cove city, SE New York; 25,770; ZIP 11542.

Glendale city, s CEN. Arizona; 36,228; ZIP 85301.
—city, sw California; 132,752; ZIP 91200*.
—city, SE Wisconsin; 13,436.
—See WOODMONT-GREEN HILLS-GLENDALE.

Glendive city, E Montana; 6,305; ZIP 59330.

Glendora city, sw California; 31,349; ZIP 91740.

Glen Ellyn vill., NE Illinois; 21,909; ZIP 60137*.

Glenolden boro., SE Pennsylvania; 8,697; ZIP 19036.

Glen Ridge boro., NE New Jersey; 8,518; ZIP 07028.

Glen Rock boro., NE New Jersey; 13,011; ZIP see RIDGEWOOD.

Glens Falls city, E New York; 17,222; ZIP 12801*.

Glenview vill., NE Illinois; 24,880; ZIP 60025*.

Globe city, E CEN. Arizona; 7,333; ZIP 85501.

Gloucester co. boro., CEN. Gloucestershire, England; cap.; 70,000.

Gloucester city, NE Massachusetts; 27,941; ZIP 01930*.

Gloucester City city, sw New Jersey; 14,707; ZIP 08030*.

Gloucestershire co., w CEN. England; 1,258 sq. mi.; 1 million; cap. Gloucester.

Gloversville city, E CEN. New York; 19,677; ZIP 12078*.

Goa former Portuguese terr., w India; annexed by India in 1961; 1,394 sq. mi.; 857,180; cap. New Goa.

Gobi Desert desert, CEN. Asia; 500,000 sq. mi.

Goderich town, s Ontario, Canada; 6,411.

Gold Coast Colony former British col., w Africa; now part of Ghana.

Golden city, N CEN. Colorado; 9,817; ZIP 80401*.

Golden Gate strait betw. San Francisco Bay and the Pacific.

Golden Valley vill., SE Minnesota; 24,246; ZIP see MINNEAPOLIS.

Goldsboro city, E CEN. North Carolina; 26,810; ZIP 27530.

Gonzales city, s CEN. Texas; 5,854; ZIP 78629.

Good Hope, Cape of promontory, sw South Africa.

Goosport uninc. place, sw Louisiana; 16,778.

Gorki city, w CEN. RSFSR; 1,213,000. Also **Gorkiy, Gorky.**

Goshen city, N Indiana; 17,171; ZIP 46526.

Göteborg city, sw Sweden; 449,470.

Gotland isl. of SE Sweden, Baltic Sea; 1,167 sq. mi.

Goulds uninc. place, SE Florida; 6,690; ZIP 33170.

Grafton city, NE North Dakota; 5,946; ZIP 58237.
—city, N West Virginia; 6,433; ZIP 26354.

Graham town, N CEN. North Carolina; 8,172; ZIP 27253.
—See FLORENCE-GRAHAM.
—city, N Texas; 7,477; ZIP 76046.

Granada city, s Spain; 190,429.

Granby city, s Quebec, Canada; 31,463.

Grand Banks submarine shoal, North Atlantic; near Newfoundland.

Grand Canyon gorge of the Colorado River, NW Arizona; ab. 250 mi. long.

Grand Coulee city, NE CEN. Washington; site of Grand Coulee Dam; 1,058.

Grande Prairie city, w Alberta, Canada; 8,352.

Grand Forks city, E North Dakota; 39,008; ZIP 58201*.

Grand Haven city, w Michigan; 11,844; ZIP 49417.

Grand Island city, SE CEN. Nebraska; 31,269; ZIP 68801.

Grand Junction city, w Colorado; 20,170; ZIP 81501.

Grand Ledge city, s CEN. Michigan; 6,032; ZIP 48837.

Grand' Mère city, s CEN. Quebec, Canada; 15,806.

Grand Prairie city, N Texas; 50,904; ZIP 75050*.

Grand Rapids city, w Michigan; 197,649; ZIP 49500*.
—vill., N CEN. Minnesota; 7,247; ZIP 55744.

Grandview city, w Missouri; 17,456; ZIP 64030*.

Grandview Heights city, CEN. Ohio; 8,460; ZIP 45733.

Grandville city, w Michigan; 10,764; ZIP 49418.

Granite City city, sw Illinois; 40,440; ZIP 62040*.

Grants town, w New Mexico; 8,768; ZIP 87020.

Grants Pass city, sw Oregon; 12,455; ZIP 97526.

Great Barrier Reef chain of coral reef off the coast of Queensland, Australia.

Great Bend city, CEN. Kansas; 16,133; ZIP 67530.

Great Britain principal isl. of the United Kingdom; comprises England, Scotland, and Wales; 88,748 sq. mi.; 53,996,347; cap. London.

Great Divide See CONTINENTAL DIVIDE.

Greater Antilles See ANTILLES.

Great Falls city, w CEN. Montana; 60,091; ZIP 59401*.

Great Lakes chain of five lakes, CEN. North America; on Canada-United States border; comprises Lakes Superior, Michigan, Huron, Ontario, and Erie; total 94,710 sq. mi.

Great Neck vill., SE New York; 10,731; ZIP 11020*.

Great Plains plateau, w North America; E of the Rockies.

Great Russia CEN. and NW reg. of the USSR.

Great Salt Lake salt lake, NW Utah; ab. 2,000 sq. mi.

Great Slave Lake lake, s Northwest Territories, Canada; 11,170 sq. mi.

Great Smoky Mountains mtn. range, North Carolina and Tennessee.

Greece republic, SE Europe; 50,547 sq. mi.; 8,745,084; cap. Athens.

Greeley city, N Colorado; 38,902; ZIP 80630*.

Green Bay city, E Wisconsin; 87,809; ZIP 54300*.

Greenbelt city, w CEN. Maryland; 18,199; ZIP 20770*.

Greencastle city, w CEN. Indiana; 8,852; ZIP 46135.

Greendale vill., SE Wisconsin; 15,089; ZIP 53129.

Greeneville town, NE Tennessee; 13,722; ZIP 37743.

Greenfield city, E CEN. Indiana; 9,986; ZIP 46140.
—uninc. place, NW Massachusetts; 18,116; ZIP 01301.
—town, SE Wisconsin; 24,424; ZIP see MILWAUKEE.

Greenfield town, s Quebec, Canada; 7,807.

Greenhills vill., sw Ohio; 6,092; ZIP see CINCINNATI.

Green Hills See WOODMONT-GREEN HILLS-GLENDALE.

Greenland isl. of Denmark near NE North America; 840,154 sq. mi.; 51,000.

Greenlawn uninc. place, SE New York; 8,532; ZIP 11740.

Green Mountains mtn. range, CEN. Vermont.

Greensboro city, N CEN. North Carolina; 144,076; ZIP 27400*.

Greensburg city, SE Indiana; 8,620; ZIP 47240.
—city, sw Pennsylvania; 15,870; ZIP 15601*.

Green Tree boro., sw Pennsylvania; 6,441.

Greenville city, s Alabama; 8,033; ZIP 36037.
—city, CEN. Michigan; 7,493; ZIP 48838.
—city, w Mississippi; 39,648; ZIP 63944.
—city, E North Carolina; 29,063; ZIP 27834*.
—city, w Ohio; 12,380; ZIP 45331.
—boro., NW Pennsylvania; 8,704; ZIP 16125.
—city, NW South Carolina; 61,208; ZIP 29601*.
—city, NE Texas; 22,043; ZIP 75401*.

Greenwich boro., SE London; former site of the Royal Observatory; location of prime meridian; 86,000.

Greenwich town, sw Connecticut; 59,755; ZIP 06830*.

Greenwich Village part of lower Manhattan, New York City; traditionally frequented by artists.

Greenwood town, s CEN. Indiana; 11,408; ZIP 46142.
—city, w CEN. Mississippi; 22,400; ZIP 38930*.
—city, w South Carolina; 21,069; ZIP 29646*.

Greer town, NW South Carolina; 10,642; ZIP 29651.

Grenada independent member of the Commonwealth of Nations, West Indies; 133 sq. mi.; 100,000; cap. St. George's.

Grenada city, NW CEN. Mississippi; 9,944; ZIP 38901.

Gretna city, SE Louisiana; 24,875; ZIP 70053.

Gretna Green vill., s Scotland; former scene of runaway marriages.

Griffin city, w CEN. Georgia; 22,734; ZIP 30223.

Griffith town, NW Indiana; 18,168; ZIP 46319.

Grimsby town, s Ontario, Canada; 5,148.

Grinnell city, CEN. Iowa; 8,402; ZIP 50112.

Grosse Pointe city, SE Michigan; 6,637; ZIP see DETROIT.
Grosse Pointe Farms city, SE Michigan; 11,701.
Grosse Pointe Park city, SE Michigan; 15,585.
Grosse Pointe Woods city, SE Michigan; 21,878.
Groton town, SE Connecticut; 38,523; ZIP 06340*.
Grove City vill., S CEN. Ohio; 13,911; ZIP 43123.
—boro., W Pennsylvania; 8,312; ZIP 16127.
Grover City city, SW California; 5,939; ZIP 93433.
Groves city, SE Texas; 18,067; ZIP 77619.
Guadalajara city, W CEN. Mexico; 1,194,600.
Guadalcanal isl., British Solomons; scene of an Allied invasion in World War II, 1943.
Guadeloupe French overseas dept., Lesser Antilles; 639 sq. mi.; 337,000; cap. Basse-Terre.
Guam uninc. terr. of the United States, an isl. in the Marianas; 209 sq. mi.; 84,996; cap. Agaña.
Guantánamo city, SE Cuba, near **Guantánamo Bay**, site of a US naval station; 130,061.
Guatemala republic, N Central America; 42,042 sq. mi.; 5,540,000.
—city, CEN. Guatemala; cap.; 790,311.
Guayama town, SE Puerto Rico; 20,318.
Guayaquil city, W Ecuador; 860,600.
Guelph city, S Ontario, Canada; 60,087.
Guernica town, N Spain; object of a German bombing, 1937.
Guernsey one of the Channel Islands; 25 sq. mi.
Guiana coastal reg., NE South America. See FRENCH GUIANA, GUYANA, SURINAM.
Guinea republic, W Africa; 94,925 sq. mi.; 4,300,000; cap. Conakry.
Guinea-Bissau republic, W Africa; 13,948 sq. mi.; 487,448; cap. Bissau.
Guinea, Gulf of large bay of the Atlantic off W Africa.
Gulfport city, W Florida; 9,730; ZIP see ST. PETERSBURG.
—port city, SE Mississippi; 40,791; ZIP 39501*.
Guntersville city, NE Alabama; 6,491; ZIP 35976.
Guthrie city, CEN. Oklahoma; 9,575; ZIP 73044.
Guttenberg town, NE New Jersey; 5,754; ZIP see WEST NEW YORK.
Guyana republic, member of the Commonwealth of Nations NE South America; 83,000 sq. mi.; 714,000; cap. Georgetown.
Guymon city, NW Oklahoma; 7,674; ZIP 73942.

Haarlem city, W Netherlands; 171,375.
Hackensack city, NE New Jersey; 35,911; ZIP 07601*.
Hackettstown town, NW New Jersey; 35,911; ZIP 07840.
Haddon urb. twp., SW New Jersey; 18,192.
Haddonfield boro., SW New Jersey; 13,118; ZIP 08033*.
Haddon Heights boro., SW New Jersey; 9,365; ZIP 08035.
Hagerstown city, W Maryland; 35,862; ZIP 21740*.
Hagginwood uninc. place, CEN. California; 11,469.
Hague, The city, W Netherlands; cap; seat of the Hague Tribunal; 525,368.
Haifa city, NW Israel; 214,500.
Haines City city, CEN. Florida; 8,956; ZIP 33844.
Haiti republic, W Hispaniola; 10,714 sq. mi.; 4,243,-926; cap. Port-au-Prince.
Haledon boro., NE New Jersey; 6,767.
Hales Corners vill., SE Wisconsin; 7,771; ZIP 53130*.
Halethorpe See ARBUTUS-HALETHORPE-RELAY.
Halifax city, S Nova Scotia; Canada; cap.; 122,035.
Hallandale city, SE Florida; 23,849; ZIP 33009.
Halle city, W East Germany; 278,000.
Haltom City vill., N Texas; 28,127; ZIP see FORT WORTH.
Hamburg state and city, N West Germany; 288 sq. mi.; 1,751,621.
Hamburg vill., W New York; 10,215; ZIP 14075.
Hamburg-Lake Shore uninc. place, W New York; 11,527.
Hamden town, S Connecticut; 49,357; ZIP see NEW HAVEN.
Hamilton city, CEN. Bermuda; cap.; 3,000.
Hamilton twp., W New Jersey; 76,059.
—city, SW Ohio; 67,865; ZIP 45010*.
Hamilton city, S Ontario, Canada; 309,173.
Hammond city, NW Indiana; 107,790; ZIP 46320*.
—city, SE Louisiana; 12,487; ZIP 70401*.

Hammonton town, S New Jersey; 11,464; ZIP 08037.
Hampton port city, SE Virginia; 120,779; ZIP 23360*.
Hampton Roads channel, SE Virginia; connects several rivers with Chesapeake Bay; scene of the Civil War engagement of the "Monitor" and the "Merrimack," 1862.
Hamtramck city, SE Michigan; an enclave in Detroit; 27,245; ZIP see DETROIT.
Hanford city, S CEN. California; 15,175; ZIP 93230*.
Hangchow city, E China; 784,000.
Hankow See WUHAN.
Hannibal city, NE Missouri; 18,609; ZIP 63401*.
Hanoi city, CEN. North Vietnam; cap.; 1,400,000.
Hanover city, N CEN. West Germany; 516,744.
Hanover uninc. place, W New Hampshire; 8,494; ZIP 03755.
—boro., S Pennsylvania; 15,623; ZIP 17331.
Hapeville city, NW CEN. Georgia; 9,567; ZIP 30054.
Harahan city, SE Louisiana; 13,037; ZIP see NEW ORLEANS.
Harbin city, NE China; 1,552,000.
Hardwick See MIDWAY-HARDWICK.
Harlem area, N Manhattan, New York City; population is mainly Negro.
Harlingen city, S Texas; 33,503; ZIP 78550*.
Harmony boro., W Pennsylvania; 5,022; ZIP 16037.
Harper Woods city, SE Michigan; 20,186; ZIP see DETROIT.
Harriman city, E Tennessee; 8,734; ZIP 37748.
Harrisburg city, S Illinois; 9,535; ZIP 62946.
—city, S CEN. Pennsylvania; cap.; 68,061; ZIP 17101*.
Harrison city, N Arkansas; 7,239; ZIP 72601.
—town, NE New Jersey; 11,811; ZIP 07029.
—urb. twp., SW Pennsylvania; 12,650; ZIP 15636.
Harrisonburg city, N Virginia; 14,605; ZIP 22801*.
Harrodsburg city, CEN. Kentucky; 6,741; ZIP 40330.
Hartford city, CEN. Connecticut; cap.; 158,017; ZIP 06100*.
—city, E Wisconsin; 6,499; ZIP 53027.
Hartford City city, E Indiana; 8,207; ZIP 47348.
Hartselle city, N Alabama; 7,355; ZIP 35640.
Hartsville town, NE South Carolina; 8,017; ZIP 29550.
Harvey city, NE Illinois; 34,636; ZIP 60426*.
Harwood Heights vill., NE Illinois; 9,060.
Hasbrouck Heights boro., NE New Jersey; 13,651; ZIP see HACKENSACK.
Hastings city, SW Michigan; 6,501; ZIP 49058.
—city, SE Minnesota; 12,195; ZIP 55033.
—city, S Nebraska; 23,580; ZIP 68901.
Hastings-on-Hudson vill., SE New York; 9,479; ZIP see YONKERS.
Hatboro boro., SE Pennsylvania; 8,880; ZIP 19040.
Hattiesburg city, SE Mississippi; 38,277; ZIP 39401*.
Hauterive town, E Quebec, Canada; 5,980.
Havana city, W Cuba; cap.; 1,130,634.
Haverford urb. twp., SE Pennsylvania; 55,132; ZIP 19041.
Haverhill city, NE Massachusetts; 46,120; ZIP 01830*.
Haverstraw vill., SE New York; 8,198; ZIP 10927.
Havre city, N Montana; 10,558; ZIP 59501.
Havre de Grace city, NE Maryland; 9,791; ZIP 21078.
Hawaii state of the United States, North Pacific; coextensive with the Hawaiian Islands; 6,435 sq. mi.; 768,561; cap. Honolulu.
—largest of the Hawaiian Islands; 4,020 sq. mi.
Hawkesbury town, SE Ontario, Canada; 8,661.
Hawthorne city, SW California; 53,304; ZIP 90250*.
—boro., SE New Jersey; 19,173; ZIP see PATERSON.
Hays city, CEN. Kansas; 15,396; ZIP 67601*.
Haysville city, S Kansas; 6,483; ZIP 67060.
Hayward city, W California; 93,058; ZIP 94541.
Hazard city, SE Kentucky; 5,459; ZIP 41701.
Hazel Crest vill., NE Illinois; 10,329; ZIP 60429.
Hazel Park city, SE Michigan; 23,784; ZIP 48030.
Hazelwood vill., E Missouri; 14,082; ZIP 63042*.
Hazleton city, E Pennsylvania; 30,426; ZIP 18201.
Hebrides isl. group off W coast of Scotland; ab. 3,000 sq. mi.
Heidelberg city, SW West Germany; 120,925.
Hejaz div., W Saudi Arabia; 150,000 sq. mi.; 2 million; cap. Mecca.
Helena city, E Arkansas; 10,415; ZIP 72342.
—city, W CEN. Montana.; cap.; 22,730; ZIP 59601*.
Helicon mtn. range, E CEN. Greece.

Hellértown boro., E Pennsylvania; 6,613; ZIP 18055.
Hellespont Dardanelles: *the ancient name.*
Helsinki city, S Finland; cap.; 505,719.
Hemet city, S California; 12,252; ZIP 92343.
Hempfield urb. twp., SW Pennsylvania; 39,196.
Hempstead vill., SE New York; 39,411; ZIP 11550*.
Henderson city, NW Kentucky; 22,976; ZIP 42420.
—city, S Nevada; 16,395; ZIP 89015.
—city, N North Carolina; 13,896; ZIP 27536.
—city, E Texas; 10,187; ZIP 75652.
Hendersonville city, W North Carolina; 6,443; ZIP 28739.
Henrietta uninc. place, NW New York; 33,017; ZIP 14467.
Henryetta city, E CEN. Oklahoma; 6,430; ZIP 74437.
Hereford city, NW Texas; 13,414; ZIP 79045.
Herkimer vill., CEN. New York; 8,960; ZIP 13350.
Hermosa Beach city, SW California; 17,412; ZIP 90254.
Herrin city, S Illinois; 9,623; ZIP 62948.
Hershey uninc. place, S CEN. Pennsylvania; 7,407; ZIP 17033.
Herzegovina See BOSNIA AND HERZEGOVINA.
Hesse state, W West Germany; 8,150 sq. mi.; 4,703,-000; cap. Wiesbaden.
Hialeah city, SE Florida; site of a famous racetrack; 102,297; ZIP 33010.
Hibbing vill., NE Minnesota; 16,104; ZIP 55746.
Hickory city, W CEN. North Carolina; 20,569; ZIP 28601*.
Hicksville vill., SE New York; 48,075; ZIP 11800*.
Highland town, NW Indiana; 24,947; ZIP see HAMMOND.
Highland Park city, NE Illinois; 32,263; ZIP 60035*.
—city, SE Michigan; 35,444; ZIP see DETROIT.
—boro., E New Jersey; 14,385; ZIP see NEW BRUNSWICK.
—town, N Texas; 10,133.
Highlands mtn. reg., N and W Scotland.
High Point city, N CEN. North Carolina; 63,204; ZIP 27260*.
Hillcrest Heights uninc. place, S Maryland; 24,037.
Hillgrove uninc. place, SW California; 14,669.
Hilliard vill., CEN. Ohio; 8,369; ZIP 43026.
Hillsboro city, S Ohio; 5,584; ZIP 45133.
—city, NW Oregon; 14,675; ZIP 97123*.
—city, NE CEN. Texas; 7,224; ZIP 76645.
Hillsborough town, W California; 8,753; ZIP see BURLINGAME.
Hillsdale city, S Michigan; 7,728; ZIP 49242.
—boro., NE New Jersey; 11,768; ZIP 07642.
Hillside vill., NE Illinois; 8,888; ZIP see MELROSE PARK.
—urb. twp., NE New Jersey; 21,636; ZIP see ELIZABETH.
Hilo city, E Hawaii, Hawaii; 26,353; ZIP 96720.
Himalayas mtn. range, CEN. Asia.
Hindustan 1. loosely, the reg. of the Ganges where Hindu is spoken. 2. loosely, India.
Hingham town, E Massachusetts; 18,845; ZIP 02043.
Hinsdale vill., NE Illinois; 15,918; ZIP 60521*.
Hiroshima city, SW Honshu isl. Japan; devastated by the first atom bomb used in war, Aug. 6, 1945; 740,792.
Hispaniola isl., West Indies; ab. 30,000 sq. mi.; divided into Haiti and the Dominican Republic.
Hitchcock city, SE Texas; 5,565; ZIP 77563.
Hobart city, SE Tasmania; cap.; 157,870.
Hobart city, W Indiana; 21,485; ZIP 46342.
Hobbs city, SE New Mexico; 26,025; ZIP 88240.
Hoboken city, E New Jersey; 45,380; ZIP 07030*.
Hokkaido isl. of N Japan; ab. 29,000 sq. mi.
Holdenville city, CEN. Oklahoma; 5,181; ZIP 74848.
Holdredge city, S Nebraska; 5,635; ZIP 68949.
Holland See NETHERLANDS.
Holland city, SW Michigan; 26,337; ZIP 49422*.
Holidaysburg boro., S CEN. Pennsylvania; 6,262; ZIP 16648.
Hollister city, W California; 7,663; ZIP 95023.
Holly Springs city, N Mississippi; 5,728; ZIP 38635.
Hollywood city, SE Florida; 106,873; ZIP 33020*.
—area, NW Los Angeles, California; ctr. of US motion-picture industry; ZIP see LOS ANGELES.
Holyoke city, W CEN. Massachusetts; 50,112; ZIP 01040*.
Holy Roman Empire empire, CEN. and W Europe; existed from 962–1806.

Homestead city, S Florida; 13,674; ZIP 33030*.
—boro., SW Pennsylvania; 6,309; ZIP 15120*.
Hometown city, NE Illinois; 6,729; ZIP see OAK LAWN.
Homewood city, CEN. Alabama; 21,245; ZIP see BIRMINGHAM.
—vill., NE Illinois; 18,871; ZIP 60430.
Honduras republic, NE Central America; 43,277 sq. mi.; 1,884,765; cap. Tegucigalpa.
Honesdale boro., NE Pennsylvania; 5,224; ZIP 18431.
Hong Kong British depen., SE China; includes **Hong Kong Island** and some coastal terr.; 398 sq. mi.; 3,948,179; cap. Victoria.
Honolulu port city, SE Oahu; cap. of Hawaii; 324,871; ZIP 96800.
Honshu isl. of CEN. Japan; 88,745 sq. mi.
Hood, Mount volcanic peak, Cascade Range, NW Oregon; 11,245 ft.
Hoopeston city, E Illinois; 6,461; ZIP 60942.
Hoover Dam dam, Colorado River at the Arizona-Nevada border; 727 ft. high; 1,282 ft. long.
Hope city, SW Arkansas; 8,810; ZIP 71801.
Hopewell city, SE Virginia; 23,471; ZIP 23860.
Hopkins city, SE Minnesota; 13,428; ZIP 55343.
Hopkinsville city, SW Kentucky; 21,250; ZIP 42240.
Hoquiam city, W Washington; 10,466; ZIP 98550*.
Horn, Cape S extremity of South America.
Hornell city, SW New York; 12,144; ZIP 14843.
Horseheads vill., S New York; 7,989; ZIP 14845.
Hot Springs city, CEN. Arkansas; 35,631.
Houlton uninc. place, E Maine; 8,111; ZIP 04730.
Houma city, SE Louisiana; 30,922; ZIP 70360*.
Houston city, SE Texas; 1,232,802; ZIP 77000*.
Hubbard vill., NE Ohio; 8,583; ZIP 44425.
Hudson uninc. place, E CEN. Massachusetts; 16,084; ZIP 01749.
—city, E New York; 8,940; ZIP 12534.
Hudson Bay inland sea; N CEN. Canada; connected with the Atlantic by **Hudson Strait**; ab. 475,000 sq. mi.
Hudson Falls vill., E New York; 7,917; ZIP 12839.
Hudson River river, E New York; 306 mi. long.
Hueytown city, CEN. Alabama; 7,095; ZIP see BESSEMER.
Hugo city, SE Oklahoma; 6,585; ZIP 74743.
Hull town, E Massachusetts; 9,961; ZIP 02045.
Hull city, SW Quebec, Canada; 63,580.
Humacao town, E Puerto Rico; 12,411.
Humboldt city, W Tennessee; 10,066; ZIP 38343.
Hungary republic, CEN. Europe; 35,912 sq. mi.; 10,314,512; cap. Budapest.
Huntingdon boro., S CEN. Pennsylvania; 6,987; ZIP 16652*.
Huntington city, NE Indiana; 16,217; ZIP 46750.
—uninc. place, SE New York; 12,719; ZIP 11743*.
—city, W West Virginia, 74,315; ZIP 25700*.
Huntington Beach city, SW California; 115,960; ZIP 94646*.
Huntington Park city, SW California; 33,744; ZIP 90255*.
Huntington Station uninc. place, SE New York; 28,817; ZIP 11746*.
Huntington Woods city, SE Michigan; 8,536; ZIP see ROYAL OAK.
Huntsville city, N Alabama; 137,802; ZIP 35800*.
—city, E Texas; 17,610; ZIP 77340*.
Huron vill., N Ohio; 6,896; ZIP 44839.
—city, E. CEN. South Dakota; 14,299; ZIP 57350.
Huron, Lake one of the Great Lakes; betw. Michigan and Ontario; 23,010 sq. mi.
Hurst city, N Texas; 27,215; ZIP 76053.
Hutchinson city, CEN. Kansas; 36,885; ZIP 67501.
—city, S CEN. Minnesota; 8,031; ZIP 55350.
Hwang Ho river, N China; 2,900 mi. long.
Hyannis uninc. place, SE Massachusetts; 6,847; ZIP 02601*.
Hyattsville city, W CEN. Maryland; 14,998; ZIP 20780*.
Hyde Park public park, London, England.
Hyde Park uninc. place, SE New York; site of the estate and grave of Franklin D. Roosevelt; 2,805; ZIP 12538.
Hyderabad city, S CEN. India; 1,607,396.
Hyderabad city, SE Pakistan; 624,000.

Ibadan city, SW Nigeria; 758,332.

Iberia part of sw Europe containing Spain and Portugal.
Iberville town, s Quebec, Canada; 7,588.
Iceland isl. North Atlantic; a republic; 39,758 sq. mi.; 204,930; cap. Reykjavik.
Idaho state, NW United States; 83,557 sq. mi.; 712,567; cap. Boise.
Idaho Falls city, SE Idaho; 35,776; ZIP 83401*.
Ifni Spanish overseas prov.; sw Morocco; 741 sq. mi.; 50,000; cap. Sidi Ifni.
Ijssel, Lake fresh-water lake, CEN. Netherlands; created by diking the Zuider Zee.
Ilion vill., E CEN. New York; 9,808; ZIP 13357.
Illinois state, NE CEN. United States; 56,400 sq. mi.; 11,113,976; cap. Springfield.
Imperial Beach city, sw California; 20,244; ZIP 92032.
Imperial Valley agricultural reg., SE California.
Inch'on city and port, s Korea; 646,013.
Independence city, E Iowa; 5,910; ZIP 50644.
—city, SE Kansas; 10,347; ZIP 67301.
—city, w Missouri; 111,662; ZIP 64050*.
—vill., N Ohio; 7,034; ZIP see CLEVELAND.
India republic of the Commonwealth of Nations; s Asia; 1,259,797 sq. mi.; 547,949,809; cap. New Delhi.
Indiana state, NE CEN. United States; 36,291 sq. mi.; 5,193,669; cap. Indianapolis.
—boro., w CEN. Pennsylvania; 16,100; ZIP 15701.
Indianapolis city, CEN. Indiana; cap.; 744,624; ZIP 46200*.
Indian Ocean ocean betw. Africa, Asia, Australia, and Antarctica.
Indianola city, s CEN. Iowa; 8,852; ZIP 50125.
—city, w Mississippi; 8,947; ZIP 38751.
Indies See EAST INDIES, INDIA, INDOCHINA, WEST INDIES.
Indio city, sw California; 14,459; ZIP 92201*.
Indochina 1. SE penin. of Asia. 2. Cambodia, Laos, North and South Vietnam.
Indonesia republic, SE Asia; comprises over 100 isls. of the Malay Archipelago; 735,268 sq. mi.; 118,309,-059; cap. Djakarta.
Indus river, Tibet, Kashmir, and Pakistan; ab. 1,800 mi. long.
Ingersoll town, s Ontario, Canada; 6,874.
Inglewood city, sw California; 89,985; ZIP 90301*.
—uninc. place, N CEN. Tennessee; 26,527.
Inkster vill., SE Michigan; 38,595; ZIP 48141.
Inner Mongolian Autonomous Region See MONGOLIA.
International Falls city, N Minnesota; 6,439; ZIP 56649.
Inwood uninc. place, SE New York; 8,433.
Iola city, SE Kansas; 6,493; ZIP 66749.
Ionia city, CEN. Michigan; 6,361; ZIP 48846.
Ionian Sea part of the Mediterranean betw. Greece and Sicily.
Iowa state, N CEN. United States; 56,280 sq. mi.; 2,824,376; cap. Des Moines.
Iowa City city, E Iowa; 46,850; ZIP 52240*.
Iowa Falls city, CEN. Iowa; 6,454; ZIP 50126.
Iran kingdom, sw Asia; ab. 630,000 sq. mi.; 29,783,000; cap. Teheran.
Iraq republic, sw Asia; 171,599 sq. mi.; 9,750,000; cap. Baghdad.
Ireland westernmost of the British Isles; 31,838 sq. mi.
—republic, s Ireland; 26,600 sq. mi.; 2,971,823; cap. Dublin. See NORTHERN IRELAND.
Irish Sea part of the Atlantic betw. Great Britain and Ireland.
Irkutsk city, s USSR; 497,000.
Iron Mountain city, NW Michigan; 8,702; ZIP 49801*.
Ironton city, s Ohio; 15,030; ZIP 45638.
Ironwood city, NW Michigan; 8,711; ZIP 49938.
Irrawaddy river, Tibet and Burma; 1,200 mi. long.
Irving city, N Texas; 97,260; ZIP 75060*.
Irvington town, NE New Jersey; 59,743; ZIP see NEWARK.
—vill., SE New York; 5,878; ZIP 10533.
Isabella town, NW Puerto Rico; 9,515; ZIP 00662*.
Ishpeming city, NW Michigan; 8,245; ZIP 49849.
Israel republic, E end of the Mediterranean; 7,993 sq. mi.; 3,124,000; cap. Jerusalem.
Istanbul city, NE Turkey; 2,247,630.
Italy republic, s Europe; 116,286 sq. mi.; 54,025,211; cap. Rome.

Ithaca isl. of Greece; Ionian Sea; 36 sq. mi.
Ithaca city, CEN. New York; 26,226; ZIP 14850.
Ivory Coast republic of the French Community, w Africa; 128,364 sq. mi.; 4,420,000; cap. Abidjan.
Ivywild uninc. place, E CEN. Colorado; 11,065.
Izmir Smyrna: *the Turkish name.*

Jacinto City city, SE Texas; 9,563; ZIP see HOUSTON.
Jackson city, s Michigan; 45,484; ZIP 49201*.
—city, s CEN. Mississippi; cap.; 153,968; ZIP 39200*.
—city, s Ohio; 6,843; ZIP 45640.
—city, w Tennessee; 39,996; ZIP 38301*.
Jacksonville city, E Alabama; 7,715; ZIP 36265.
—city, CEN. Arkansas; 19,832; ZIP 72076*.
—city, NE Florida; 528,865; ZIP 32200*.
—city, w CEN. Illinois; 20,553; ZIP 62650*.
—city, E North Carolina; 16,021; ZIP 28540*.
—city, E Texas; 9,734; ZIP 75766.
Jacksonville Beach city, NE Florida; 13,326; ZIP 32050.
Jacques-Cartier city, s Quebec, Canada; 40,807.
Jaffa port, w Israel; part of Tel Aviv.
Jakarta see DJAKARTA.
Jamaica independent member of the Commonwealth of Nations, isl. of the Greater Antilles; 4,411 sq. mi.; 1,953,472; cap. Kingston.
Jamestown town, NW St. Helena; cap.; ab. 1,600.
Jamestown city, sw New York; 39,795; ZIP 14701.
—city, SE CEN. North Dakota; 15,385; ZIP 58401.
—restored vill., E Virginia; site of the first English settlement in the present limits of the United States, 1607; ZIP 23081.
Jammu and Kashmir state, N India; subject of a territorial dispute with Pakistan; 86,024 sq. mi.; 4,750,000; caps. Srinigar and Jammu.
Janesville city, s Wisconsin; 46,426; ZIP 53545*.
Japan constitutional empire, E Asia; situated on a chain of isls.; 142,720 sq. mi.; 104,665,171; cap. Tokyo.
Japan, Sea of part of the Pacific betw. Japan and the Asian mainland.
Jasper city, NW CEN. Alabama; 10,798; ZIP 35501.
—city, s Indiana; 8,641; ZIP 47546.
Jasper Place town, E Alberta, Canada; 30,530.
Java isl. of Indonesia; SE of Sumatra; 48,842 sq. mi.
Jeanerette town, s Louisiana; 6,322; ZIP 70544.
Jeannette city, sw Pennsylvania; 15,209; ZIP 15644.
Jefferson boro., s Pennsylvania; 8,512; ZIP 15344.
Jefferson City city, CEN. Missouri; cap.; 32,407; ZIP 65101*.
Jefferson Heights uninc. place, SE Louisiana; 16,489.
Jeffersonville city, SE Indiana; 20,008; ZIP 47130*.
Jenkintown boro., SE Pennsylvania; 5,990; ZIP 19046.
Jennings city, sw Louisiana; 11,783; ZIP 70546.
—city, E Missouri; 19,379; ZIP see SAINT LOUIS.
Jericho vill., w Jordan; on the site of the ancient city.
Jericho uninc. place, SE New York; 14,010; ZIP 11753.
Jersey one of the Channel Islands; 45 sq. mi.
Jersey City city, NE New Jersey; 260,545; ZIP 07300*.
Jersey Shore boro., N CEN. Pennsylvania; 5,322; ZIP 17740.
Jerseyville city, w Illinois; 7,446; ZIP 62052.
Jerusalem city, on the Israel-Jordan border; Israeli Sector; cap.; 232,400; Jordanian sector; 81,700.
Jesup city, SE Georgia; 9,091; ZIP 31545.
Jidda city, w Saudi Arabia; 194,000.
Jim Thorpe boro., E Pennsylvania; 5,456; ZIP 18229.
Johannesburg city, NE South Africa; cap.; 654,682.
Johnstown city, E CEN. New York; 10,045; ZIP 12095.
—city, NE Tennessee; 33,770; ZIP 37601.
Johnston town, NE Rhode Island; 22,037.
Johnstown city, E CEN. New York; 10,045; ZIP 12095.
—city, sw Pennsylvania; 42,476; ZIP 15901*.
Johore state, s Malaya; 7,330 sq. mi.; 1,010,000; cap. Johore Baru.
Joliet city, NE Illinois; 80,378; ZIP 60431*.
Joliette city, s Quebec, Canada; 18,088.
Jonesboro city, NE Arkansas; 27,050; ZIP 72401.
Jonquiere city, s CEN. Quebec, Canada; 28,588.
Joplin city, sw Missouri; 39,256; ZIP 64801*.
Jordan constitutional monarchy, betw. Israel, Iraq, Saudi Arabia, and Syria; 37,300 sq. mi.; 2,383,000; cap. Amman.
Jordan River river, CEN. Palestine; over 200 mi. long.
Juncos town, E Puerto Rico; 7,985; ZIP 00666.

Junction City city, E CEN. Kansas; 19,018; ZIP 66441.
Juneau city, SE Alaska; cap.; 6,050; ZIP 99801.
Jungfrau mtn. peak, S CEN. Switzerland; 13,653 ft.
Jura Mountains mtn. range, E France and W Switzerland.
Jutland penin., N Europe; comprises continental Denmark and part of Germany.

Kabul city, E CEN. Afghanistan; cap.; 534,350.
Kailua Lanikai uninc. place, E Oahu, Hawaii, 25,622; ZIP 96734.
Kalamazoo city, SW Michigan; 85,555; ZIP 49001*.
Kaliningrad city, extreme W USSR; 331,000.
Kalispell city, NW Montana; 10,526; ZIP 59901*.
Kamchatka penin., E USSR, betw. the Bering and Okhotsk Seas.
Kamloops city, S British Columbia, Canada; 10,076.
Kane boro., N Pennsylvania; 5,001; ZIP 16735.
Kaneohe uninc. place, E Oahu, Hawaii; 29,903; ZIP 96744.
Kankakee city, NE Illinois; 30,944; ZIP 60901.
Kannapolis uninc. place, S CEN. North Carolina; 36,293; ZIP 28081.
Kanpur city, N India; 1,154,388.
Kansas state, CEN. United States; 82,276 sq. mi.; 2,246,578; cap. Topeka.
Kansas City city, NE Kansas; 168,213; ZIP 66100*.
  —city, W Missouri; 507,087; ZIP 64100*.
Kaplan town, S Louisiana; 5,540; ZIP 70548.
Kapuskasing town, CEN. Ontario, Canada; 6,870.
Karachi city, S Pakistan; former cap.; 3,469,000.
Karelian ASSR adm. div., NW RSFSR; 66,560 sq. mi.; 651,000; cap. Petrozhavodsk.
Karnak vill., S Egypt; near the site of ancient Thebes.
Kashmir See JAMMU AND KASHMIR.
Kathmandu city, CEN. Nepal; cap.; 150,402.
Kattegat strait of the North Sea betw. Sweden and Jutland.
Kauai one of the Hawaiian Islands; 551 sq. mi.
Kaukauna city, E Wisconsin; 11,292; ZIP 54130*.
Kawasaki city, E Honshu, Japan; 1,001,368.
Kazakh SSR constituent republic, S CEN. USSR; 1,064,000 sq. mi.; 9,310,000; cap. Alma-Ata.
Kazan city, NW Tatar ASSR; cap.; 931,000.
Keansburg boro., E New Jersey; 9,720; ZIP 07734.
Kearney city, S CEN. Nebraska; 19,181; ZIP 68847.
Kearns uninc. place, N Utah; 17,071; ZIP see SALT LAKE CITY.
Kearny town, NE New Jersey; 37,585; ZIP 07032.
Keene city, SW New Hampshire; 20,467; ZIP 03431.
Keizer uninc. place, NW Oregon; 11,405; ZIP see SALEM.
Kelowna city, S British Columbia, Canada; 13,188.
Kelso city, SW Washington; 10,296; ZIP 98626.
Kendallville city, NE Indiana; 6,838; ZIP 46755.
Kenilworth boro., NE New Jersey; 9,165; ZIP 07033.
Kenmore vill., W New York; 20,980; ZIP see BUFFALO.
Kennedy, Cape cape, E Florida (ZIP 32920); site of the John F. Kennedy Space Center, a space research and missiles installation.
Kenner city, SE Louisiana; 29,858; ZIP 70062.
Kennett city, SE Missouri; 9,852.
Kennewick city, S Washington; 15,212; ZIP 99336.
Kenogami city, S CEN. Quebec, Canada; 11,816.
Kenora town, W Ontario, Canada; 10,904.
Kenosha city, SE Wisconsin; 78,805; ZIP 53140*.
Kent co., SE England; 1,525 sq. mi.; 171,000; cap. Maidstone.
Kent city, NE Ohio; 28,183; ZIP 44240*.
  —city, W CEN. Washington; 21,510; ZIP 98031.
Kenton city, W CEN. Ohio; 8,315; ZIP 43326.
Kentucky state, E CEN. United States; 40,395 sq. mi.; 3,218,706; cap. Frankfort.
Kentucky River river, N Kentucky; 259 mi. long.
Kenya republic, member of the Commonwealth of Nations, E Africa; 224,960 sq. mi.; 12,910,000; cap. Nairobi.
Keokuk city, SE Iowa; 14,631; ZIP 52632.
Kermit city, W Texas; 7,884; ZIP 79745.
Kerrville city, S CEN. Texas; 12,672; ZIP 78028.
Ketchikan town, SE Alaska; 6,994; ZIP 99901*.
Kettering city, SW Ohio; 69,599; ZIP see DAYTON.
Kewanee city, NW Illinois; 15,762; ZIP 61443.

Keyport boro., E New Jersey; 7,205; ZIP 07735.
Keyser city, NE West Virginia; 6,586; ZIP 26726.
Key West southwesternmost of the Florida Keys.
  —city, Key West Island; 27,563; ZIP 33040*.
Kharkov city, NE Ukrainian SSR; 1,330,000.
Khartoum city, CEN. Sudan; cap.; 261,840.
Khyber Pass mtn. pass betw. Afghanistan and Pakistan; ab. 30 mi. long.
Kiel city, N West Germany; 265,587.
Kiel Canal ship canal betw. Kiel and the mouth of the Elbe; ab. 61 mi. long.
Kiev city, N CEN. Ukrainian SSR; cap.; 1,764,000.
Kilauea active crater, Mauna Loa volcano, Hawaii.
Kilgore city, NE Texas; 9,495; ZIP 75662.
Kilimanjaro, Mount mtn., NE Tanganyika; highest in Africa; 19,565 ft.
Killarney urb. dist., SW Ireland; ab. 6,300.
Killarney, Lakes of three small lakes near Killarney.
Killeen city, CEN. Texas; 35,507; ZIP 76540*.
Kimberley city, CEN. South Africa; 103,789.
Kimberley city, SE British Columbia, Canada; 6,013.
Kimberly vill., E Wisconsin; 6,131; ZIP 54136.
Kingsford city, NW Michigan; 5,276; ZIP see IRON MOUNTAIN.
Kings Mountain city, SW North Carolina; 8,465; ZIP 28086.
Kings Point vill., SE New York; 5,525; ZIP see GREAT NECK.
Kingsport city, NE Tennessee; 31,938; ZIP 37660*.
Kingston city, SE Jamaica; cap.; 117,400.
Kingston city, SE New York; 25,544; ZIP 12401.
  —boro., NE CEN. Pennsylvania; 18,325; ZIP see WILKES-BARRE.
Kingston city, SE Ontario, Canada; 59,047.
Kingsville city, S Texas; 28,711; ZIP 78363*.
Kinloch city, E Missouri; 5,629; ZIP see SAINT LOUIS.
Kinshasa city, W Zaire; cap.; 1,990,717.
Kinston city, SE CEN. North Carolina; 22,309; ZIP 28501.
Kirghiz SSR constituent republic, S USSR; 76,640 sq. mi.; 2,066,000; cap. Frunze.
Kirkland city, W CEN. Washington; 15,249; ZIP 98033.
Kirksville city, N Missouri; 15,560; ZIP 63501.
Kirkwood city, E Missouri; 31,890; ZIP see SAINT LOUIS.
Kissimmee city, CEN. Florida; 7,119; ZIP 32741.
Kitakyushu city, N Kyushu, Japan; 1,051,076.
Kitchener city, S Ontario, Canada; 111,804.
Kittanning boro., W Pennsylvania; 6,231; ZIP 16201.
Kittery uninc. place, SW Maine; 11,028; ZIP 03904.
Kitty Hawk vill., NE North Carolina; site of the first sustained airplane flight, by Wilbur and Orville Wright, 1903.
Klamath Falls city, S Oregon; 15,775; ZIP 97601*.
Klondike reg., NW Canada in the basin of the **Klondike River.**
Knoxville city, S CEN. Iowa; 7,755; ZIP 50138.
  —city, E Tennessee; 174,587; ZIP 37900*.
Kobe city, S Japan; 1,288,937.
Kodiak Island isl., S Alaska.
Kokomo city, N CEN. Indiana; 44,042; ZIP 46901*.
Königsberg Kaliningrad: *the former German name.*
Korea penin., E Asia; 85,266 sq. mi.; divided into the **Democratic People's Republic of Korea (North Korea)**; 46,812 sq. mi.; 14,281,000; cap. Pyongyang; and the **Republic of Korea (South Korea)**; 38,542 sq. mi.; 31,917,000; cap. Seoul.
Korea Strait strait, betw. the Sea of Japan and the East China Sea.
Kosciusko city, CEN. Mississippi; 7,266; ZIP 39090.
Krasnodar city, SW USSR; 519,000.
Kronstadt city, W USSR; 59,000.
Kuala Lumpur city, CEN. Malaya; cap. of Malaya and Malaysia; 451,728.
Kunming city, SW China; 880,000.
Kurdistan reg., NW Iran, NE Iraq, and SE Turkey; peopled largely by Kurds.
Kure city, SW Japan; 209,000.
Kurile Islands isl. group, OB USSR, 5,700 sq. mi.
Kuwait shiekdom, NE Arabia; 5,000 sq. mi.; 900,000.
  —city, E Kuwait; cap.; 80,405.
Kuybyshev city, SE USSR; 1,140,000.
Kyoto city, SW Japan; 1,419,165.
Kyushu isl., S Japan; 16,247 sq. mi.

Labrador terr., Newfoundland, Canada; ab. 110,000 sq. mi.; 10,760.
—the penin. of North America bet. the St. Lawrence River and Hudson Bay.
La Canada-Flintridge uninc. place, SW California; 18,338.
Lacey uninc. place, W CEN. Washington; 9,696; ZIP 98553.
Lachine city, S Quebec, Canada; 38,630.
Lachute town, SW Quebec, Canada; 7,560.
Lackawanna city, W New York; 28,657; ZIP see BUFFALO.
Lac-Mégantic town, S Quebec, Canada; 7,015.
Laconia city, CEN. New Hampshire; 14,888; ZIP 03246.
La Crosse city, W Wisconsin; 51,153; ZIP 54601*.
Ladoga, Lake lake, NW RSFSR; 7,100 sq. mi.
Ladrone Islands Marianas Islands: *the former name.*
Ladue city, E Missouri; 10,491; ZIP 64758.
Lafayette uninc. place, W California; 20,484; ZIP 94549.
Lafayette city, W CEN. Indiana; 44,955; ZIP 47901*.
Lafayette city, S Louisiana; 68,908; ZIP 70501.
La Fayette city, NW Georgia; 6,044; ZIP 30728.
Lafayette Southwest uninc. place, S Louisiana; 5,396.
Lafleche city, S Quebec, Canada; 10,984.
La Follette city, NE Tennessee; 6,902; ZIP 37766.
Lagos city, SW Nigeria; cap.; 900,969.
La Grande city, NE Oregon; 9,645; ZIP 97850*.
La Grange city, W Georgia; 23,301; ZIP 30240.
—vill., NE Illinois, 16,773; ZIP 60525*.
La Grange Park vill., NE Illinois; 15,626; ZIP see LA GRANGE.
Laguna Beach city, SW California; 14,550; ZIP 92651*.
La Habana Havana: *the Spanish name.*
La Habra city, SW California; 41,350; ZIP 90631*.
Lahore city, E Pakistan; 2,148,000.
La Junta city, SE Colorado; 7,938; ZIP 81050.
Lake Charles city, SW Louisiana; 77,998; ZIP 70601*.
Lake City city, N Florida; 10,575; ZIP 32055.
—town, E CEN. South Carolina; 6,247; ZIP 29560.
Lake District reg., NW England; contains 15 lakes.
Lake Forest city, NE Illinois; 15,642; ZIP 60045.
Lake Jackson city, SE Texas; 13,376; ZIP 77566.
Lakeland city, CEN. Florida; 41,550; ZIP 33801.
Lake Providence town, NE Louisiana; 6,183; ZIP 71254.
Lake Shore See HAMBURG-LAKE SHORE.
Lakeview uninc. place, S Michigan; 11,391; ZIP 48850.
—See WEST HEMPSTEAD-LAKEVIEW.
Lake Wales city, CEN. Florida; 8,240; ZIP 33853.
Lakewood city, SW California; 82,973; ZIP 90712*.
—uninc. place, CEN. Colorado; 92,787; ZIP see DENVER.
—uninc. place, E New Jersey; 17,874; ZIP 08701.
—city, N Ohio; 70,173; ZIP see CLEVELAND.
Lake Worth city, SE Florida; 23,714; ZIP 33460.
Lamar city, SE Colorado; 7,797; ZIP 81052.
La Marque city, SE Texas; 16,131; ZIP 77568.
La Mesa city, SW California; 39,178; ZIP 92041.
Lamesa city, NW Texas; 11,559; ZIP 79331.
Lamont uninc. place, SW California; 7,007; ZIP 93241.
Lampasas city, CEN. Texas; 5,922; ZIP 76550.
Lancashire co., NW England; 1,878 sq. mi.; 5,132,000; cap. Lancaster.
Lancaster uninc. place, SW California; 30,948; ZIP 93534*.
Lancaster vill., W New York; 13,365; ZIP 14086.
Lancaster city, S CEN. Ohio; 32,911; ZIP 43130*.
Lancaster city, SE Pennsylvania; 57,690; ZIP 17600*.
—urb. twp., SE Pennsylvania; 10,329; ZIP 17600*.
—town, N CEN. South Carolina; 9,186; ZIP 29720.
Lancaster city, N Texas; 10,522; ZIP 75146.
Lancaster city, SE New Brunswick, Canada; 13,848.
Lanchow city, NW China; 699,000.
Lanett city, E Alabama; 6,908; ZIP 36863.
Langley Park uninc. place, W CEN. Maryland; 11,564; ZIP see HYATTSVILLE.
Lanikai See KAILUA-LANIKAI.
Lansdale boro., SE Pennsylvania; 18,451; ZIP 19446.
Lansdowne boro., SE Pennsylvania; 14,090; ZIP 19050*.
Lansdowne-Baltimore Highlands uninc. place, N CEN. Maryland; 16,976.
Lansford boro., E Pennsylvania; 5,168; ZIP 18232.
Lansing vill., N Illinois; 25,805; ZIP 60438.
—city, S CEN. Michigan; cap.; 131,546; ZIP 48900*.
Lantana town, SE Florida; 7,126; ZIP see LAKE WORTH.

Laos republic, NW Indochina; 91,428 sq. mi.; **ab.** 3,033,000; cap. Vientiane.
La Paz city, W Bolivia; de facto cap.; 605,200.
Lapeer city, E Michigan; 6,270; ZIP 48446.
Lapland reg., N Norway, Sweden, and Finland, **and** the NE USSR; inhabited by Lapps.
La Plata city, E Argentina; 357,000.
La Porte city, NW Indiana; 22,140; ZIP 46350*.
Laprairie town, S Quebec, Canada; 7,328.
La Puente city, SW California; 31,092; ZIP 91743*.
Laramie city, SE Wyoming; 23,143; ZIP 82070*.
Larchmont vill., SE New York; 7,203; ZIP 10538.
Laredo city, S Texas; 69,024; ZIP 78040*.
Largo city, W Florida; 22,031; ZIP 33540*.
Larkspur city, W California; 10,487; ZIP 94939.
La Salle city, N CEN. Illinois; 10,736; ZIP 61301.
Lasalle city, S Quebec, Canada; 72,912.
Las Cruces city, S New Mexico; 37,857; ZIP 88001*.
Las Vegas city, SE Nevada; 125,787.
—city, NE CEN. New Mexico; 7,528; ZIP 87701*.
—town, NE CEN. New Mexico; 6,307.
Latrobe boro., SW Pennsylvania; 11,749; ZIP 15650.
La Tuque town, S Quebec, Canada; 13,023.
Latvian SSR constituent republic, NE USSR; 24,600 sq. mi.; 2,365,000; cap. Riga. Also **Latvia.**
Laurel town, W CEN. Maryland; 10,525; ZIP 20810.
—city, SE Mississippi; 24,145; ZIP 39440*.
Laurens city, NW CEN. South Carolina; 10,298; ZIP 29360.
Laurentian Mountains mtn. range, E Canada.
Laurinburg city, S North Carolina; 8,859; ZIP 28352.
Lausanne city, W Switzerland; 136,100.
Lauzon town, S Quebec, Canada; 11,533.
Laval city, S Quebec, Canada; suburb of Montreal, composed of 15 former municipalities; 228,010.
La Verne city, SW California; 12,965; ZIP 91750.
Lawndale city, SW California; 24,825; ZIP 90260.
Lawrence town, CEN. Indiana; 16,646; ZIP see INDIANAPOLIS.
—city, E Kansas; 45,698; ZIP 66044*.
—city, NE Massachusetts; 66,915; ZIP 01840*.
—vill., SE New York; 6,566; ZIP 11559.
Lawrenceburg city, S Tennessee; 8,889; ZIP 38464.
Lawrenceville city, SE Illinois; 5,863; ZIP 62439.
Lawton city, SW Oklahoma; 74,470; ZIP 73501*.
Layton city, N Utah; 13,603; ZIP 84041.
Lead city, W South Dakota; 5,420; ZIP 57754.
Leaksville town, N North Carolina; 20,162; ZIP 27288*.
Leamington town, S Ontario, Canada; 9,030.
Leaside town, S Ontario, Canada; 18,579.
Leavenworth city, NE Kansas; 25,147; ZIP 66048.
Leawood city, E Kansas; 10,349.
Lebanon republic, SW Asia; 3,400 sq. mi.; 2,873,000; cap. Beirut.
Lebanon city, CEN. Indiana; 9,766; ZIP 46052.
—city, S CEN. Missouri; 8,616; ZIP 65536.
—city, W New Hampshire; 9,725; ZIP 03766.
—vill., SW Ohio; 7,934; ZIP 45036.
—city, W Oregon; 6,636; ZIP 97355.
—city, SE Pennsylvania; 28,572; ZIP 17042.
—city, N CEN. Tennessee; 12,492; ZIP 37087.
Leeds city and co. boro., N CEN. England; 500,200.
Leeds city, CEN. Alabama; 6,991; ZIP 35094.
Leesburg city, CEN. Florida; 11,869; ZIP 32748.
Lees Summit city, W Missouri; 16,230; ZIP 64063.
Leeward Islands N isl. group, Lesser Antilles.
Leghorn city, NW Italy; 160.000.
Le Havre city, N France; 198,863.
Lehighton boro., E Pennsylvania; 6.095; ZIP 18235.
Leicester co. boro., CEN. England; 287,350.
Leiden city, W Netherlands; 100,135.
Leipzig city, S CEN. East Germany; 583,311.
Leland city, W Mississippi; 6,000; ZIP 38756*.
Leman, Lake See GENEVA, Lake of.
Le Mars city, NW Iowa; 8,159; ZIP 51031.
Lemberg Lvov: *the German name.*
Lemon Grove uninc. place, SW California; 19,690; ZIP 92045.
LeMoyne town, S Quebec, Canada; 8,057.
Leningrad city, NW RSFSR; 3,512,974.
Lennox uninc. place, SW California; 16,121; ZIP see INGLEWOOD.
Lenoir town, W North Carolina; 14,705; ZIP 28645.
Leominster city, N CEN. Massachusetts; 32,939; ZIP 01453.

Leonia boro., NE New Jersey; 8,847; ZIP see HACKEN-SACK.

Lesbos isl. of Greece off NW Turkey; 623 sq. mi.

Lesotho independent member of the Commonwealth of Nations, enclave, E South Africa; 11,716 sq. mi.; ab. 1,043,000; capital, Maseru; formerly Basutoland.

Lesser Antilles See ANTILLES.

Lethbridge city, s Alberta, Canada; 35,454.

Leucadia uninc. place, SW California; 5,665; ZIP 92046.

Levelland city, W Texas; 11,445; ZIP 79336.

Levis city, s Quebec, Canada; 15,112.

Levittown Willingboro, New Jersey: *the former name.*
—vill., SE New York; 65,440; ZIP 11756.

Lewisburg boro., CEN. Pennsylvania; 6,376; ZIP 17837.
—town, s CEN. Tennessee; 7,207; ZIP 37091.

Lewiston city, W Idaho; 26,068; ZIP 83501.
—city, SW Maine; 41,779; ZIP 04240*.

Lewiston Orchards uninc. place, W Idaho; 9,680.

Lewistown city, CEN. Montana; 6,437; ZIP 59457.
—boro., CEN. Pennsylvania; 11,098; ZIP 17044.

Lexington city, N CEN. Kentucky; 108,137; ZIP 40500*.
—town, NE Massachusetts; 31,886, ZIP see BOSTON.
—city, s CEN. Nebraska; 5,618; ZIP 68850.
—city, W CEN. North Carolina; 17,205; ZIP 27292.
—town, W CEN. Virginia; 7,597; ZIP 24450*.

Lexington Park uninc. place, s Maryland; 9,136; ZIP 20653.

Leyden See LEIDEN.

Leyte isl., E Philippines, 2,875 sq. mi.

Lhasa city, s Tibet; cap.; 175,000.

Liberal city, SW Kansas; 13,471; ZIP 67901.

Liberia republic, W Africa; ab. 43,000 sq. mi.; 1,470,-000; cap. Monrovia.

Liberty city, W Missouri; 13,679; ZIP 64068.
—city, E Texas; 5,591; ZIP 77575.

Libertyville vill., NE Illinois; 11,684; ZIP 60048.

Libreville city, W Gabon; cap. 75,000.

Libya republic, N Africa; 679,358 sq. mi.; 2,240,000; caps. Tripoli and Benghazi.

Liechtenstein principality, CEN. Europe; 61 sq. mi.; 21,350; cap. Vaduz.

Liège city, E Belgium; 144,875.

Lille city, N France; 190,170.

Lima city, W Peru; cap.; 3,800,000.

Lima city, W Ohio; 53,734; ZIP 45801*.

Limerick co. boro., W Ireland; 140,370.

Limoges city, W CEN. France; 130,885.

Lincoln city, CEN. Illinois; 17,582; ZIP 62656.
—city, SE Nebraska; cap.; 149,518; ZIP 68500*.
—town, NE Rhode Island; 16,182; ZIP see PAW-TUCKET.

Lincoln Heights city, SW Ohio; 6,099.
—uninc. place, CEN. Ohio; 8,004.

Lincoln Park city, SE Michigan; 52,984; ZIP 48146.
—boro., N New Jersey; 9,034; ZIP 07035.

Lincolnton town, SW CEN. North Carolina; 5,293; ZIP 28092.

Lincolnwood vill., NE Illinois; 12,929; ZIP see CHICAGO.

Linda uninc. place, N CEN. California; 7,731.

Linden city, NE New Jersey; 41,409; ZIP 07036*.

Lindenhurst vill., SE New York; 28,359; ZIP 11757.

Lindenwold boro., SW New Jersey; 12,199; ZIP see CLEMENTON.

Lindsay city, s CEN. California; 5,206; ZIP 93247.

Lindsay town, s Ontario, Canada; 11,399.

Linton city, SW Indiana; 5,450; ZIP 47441.

Lisbon city W Portugal; cap.; 782,266.

Litchfield city, s CEN. Illinois; 7,190; ZIP 62056.
—city, s CEN. Minnesota; 5,262; ZIP 55355.

Lithuanian SSR constituent republic, NW USSR; 25,200 sq. mi.; 3,129,000; cap. Vilna. Also **Lithuania.**

Lititz boro., SE Pennsylvania; 7,072; ZIP 17545.

Little Chute vill., E Wisconsin 5,365; ZIP 54140.

Little Falls city, CEN. Minnesota; 7,467; ZIP 56345.
—urb. twp., NE New Jersey; 11,727; ZIP 07424*.
—city, E CEN. New York; 7,629; ZIP 13365.

Little Ferry boro., NE New Jersey; 9,042; ZIP 07643.

Littlefield city, NW Texas; 6,738; ZIP 79339.

Little Rock city, CEN. Arkansas; cap.; 132,483; ZIP 72200*.

Little Silver boro., E New Jersey; 6,010; ZIP 07739.

Littleton town, N CEN. Colorado; 26,466; ZIP 80120*.

Live Oak city, N Florida; 6,830; ZIP 32060.

Livermore city, W California; 37,703; ZIP 94550*.

Liverpool co. boro., w England; 606,834.

Livingston city, s Montana; 6,883; ZIP 59047.
—urb. twp., NE New Jersey; 30,127; ZIP 07039.

Livonia city, SE Michigan; 110,109; ZIP 48150*.

Lloydminster city, E Alberta and W Saskatchewan, Canada; 5,667.

Lockhart city, s CEN. Texas; 6,489; ZIP 78644.

Lock Haven city, CEN. Pennsylvania; 11,427; ZIP 17745.

Lockland city, SW Ohio; 5,288; ZIP see CINCINNATI.

Lockport city, NE Illinois; 9,985; ZIP 60441.
—city, NW New York; 25,399; ZIP 14094.

Loch Raven uninc. place, N Maryland; 23,278; ZIP see BALTIMORE.

Locust Grove uninc. place, SE New York; 11,626.

Lodi city, CEN. California; 28,691; ZIP 95240*.
—boro., NE New Jersey; 25,213; ZIP 07644.

Lódz city, CEN. Poland; 762,000.

Logan city, s CEN. Ohio; 6,269; ZIP 43138.
—city, N Utah; 22,333; ZIP 84321.

Logan, Mount peak, SW Yukon Territory, Canada; 19,850.

Logansport city, N CEN. Indiana; 19,255; ZIP 46947.

Loire river, CEN. France; 620 mi. long.

Lombard vill., NE Illinois; 35,977; ZIP 60148.

Lombardy reg., N Italy; 9,190 sq. mi.; 7,390,000; cap. Milan.

Lomé city, s Togo; cap.; 200,100.

Lomita uninc. place, SW California; 19,784; ZIP 90717.

Lomond, Loch lake, W CEN. Scotland; 23 mi. long.

Lompoc city, SW California; 25,284; ZIP 93436*.

London city and co., SE England; cap.; 1 sq. mi.; 4,245 (the city proper): 117 sq. mi.; 3,195,000 (the co.): 693 sq. mi.; 7,281,080 (Greater London).

London city, SW CEN. Ohio; 6.481; ZIP 43140.

London city, Ontario, Canada; 223,222.

Long Beach city, SW California; 358,633; ZIP 90800*.
—city, SE New York; 33,127; ZIP 11561*.

Long Branch city, E New Jersey; 31,774; ZIP 07740*.

Long Branch vill., s Ontario, Canada; 11,039.

Long Island isl., SE New York; 1,723 sq. mi.

Long Island Sound inlet of the Atlantic betw. Long Island and Connecticut.

Longmeadow town, s Massachusetts; 15,630; ZIP see SPRINGFIELD.

Longmont city, N Colorado; 23,209; ZIP 80501.

Longueuil city, SW Quebec, Canada; 97,590.

Longview city, NE Texas; 45,547; ZIP 75601*.
—city, SW Washington; 28,373; ZIP 98632.

Lorain city, N Ohio; 78,185; ZIP 44051*.

Loretteville town, s CEN. Quebec, Canada; 6,522.

Lorraine reg., E France.

Los Alamos town, N CEN. New Mexico; site of the development of the atom bomb; 11,310; ZIP 87544.

Los Altos city, W California; 24,956; ZIP 94022.

Los Angeles city, SW California; 2,816,061; ZIP 90000*.

Los Banos city, CEN. California; 9,188; ZIP 93635.

Los Gatos city, W California; 23,735; ZIP 95030*.

Louisiana state, s United States; 48,523 sq. mi.; 3,641,306; cap. Baton Rouge.

Louisville city, N Kentucky; 361,472; ZIP 40200*.
—city, E CEN. Mississippi; 6.626; ZIP 39339.
—vill., NE CEN. Ohio; 6,298; ZIP 44641.

Lourdes town, SW France; site of a famous shrine; 17,714.

Loveland city, N Colorado; 16,220; ZIP 80537.
—vill., SW Ohio; 7,144; ZIP 45140.

Loves Park city, N Illinois; 12,390; ZIP see ROCK-FORD.

Lovington town, SE New Mexico; 8,915; ZIP 88260.

Lowell city, NE Massachusetts; 94,239; ZIP 01850*.

Lower Burrell city, SW Pennsylvania; 13,654; ZIP see NEW KENSINGTON.

Lower California penin., NW Mexico; betw. the Gulf of California and the Pacific.

Lower Merion urb. twp., SE Pennsylvania; 63,392.

Lower Southampton urb. twp., SE Pennsylvania; 17,525.

Lowlands areas of low elevation, E and s Scotland; 5,045.

Lualualei-Maili uninc. place, Oahu, Hawaii; 5,045.

Luanda city, NW Angola; cap.; 475,328.

Lubbock city, NW Texas; 149,101; ZIP 79400*.

Lübeck city, NE West Germany; 236,047.

Lucerne, Lake of lake, CEN. Switzerland; 44 sq. mi.

Lucknow city, CEN. Uttar Pradesh, India; cap.; 750,512.
Ludington city, w Michigan; 9,021; ZIP 49431.
Ludlow city, N Kentucky; 5,815; ZIP see COVINGTON.
—town, S Massachusetts; 17,580; ZIP 01056.
Lufkin city, E Texas; 23,049; ZIP 75901*.
Lumberton city, S North Carolina; 16,961; ZIP 28358.
Lüta city, NE China; site of a naval base operated jointly after 1945 by the USSR and China; 4,000,000.
Luxembourg constitutional grand duchy; betw. Belgium, France, and Germany; 998 sq. mi.; 339,858.
—city, S CEN. Luxembourg; cap.; 76,143. Also **Luxemburg**.
Luxor city, E Egypt; near the site of ancient Thebes; ab. 35,000.
Luzon isl., N Philippines; 40,420 sq. mi.
Lvov city, w Ukrainian SSR; 605,000.
Lynbrook vill., SE New York; 23,776; ZIP 11563.
Lynchburg city, S CEN. Virginia; 54,083; ZIP 24501*.
Lyndhurst urb. twp., NE New Jersey; 22,729; ZIP see RUTHERFORD.
—city, N Ohio; 19,749; ZIP see Cleveland.
Lynn city, NE Massachusetts; 90,294; ZIP 01901*.
Lynn Gardens uninc. place, NE Tennessee; 5,261; ZIP see KINGSPORT.
Lynwood city, SW California; 43,353; ZIP 90262*.
—city, N CEN. Washington; 16,919; ZIP 98036.
Lyons city, E CEN. France; 527,800.
Lyons vill., NE Illinois; 11,124; ZIP 60534.

Mableton uninc. place, NW CEN. Georgia; 23,539; ZIP 30059.
Macao isl., Canton river delta, China.
—Portuguese overseas prov. comprising a penin. of Macao isl, and two small isls.; 6 sq. mi.; 248,316.
—city; cap of Macao; 241,413.
Macedonia reg., SE Europe; divided among Bulgaria, Greece, and Yugoslavia.
Mackenzie river, NW Canada; 2,640 mi. long.
Mackinac, Straits of channel betw. Lakes Michigan and Huron; ab. 4 mi. mide.
Mackinac Island isl., Straits of Mackinac.
Macomb city, w Illinois; 19,643; ZIP 61455.
Macon city, CEN. Georgia; 122,423; ZIP 31200*.
Madagascar isl., Indian Ocean off SE Africa; 227,602 sq. mi. See MALAGASY REPUBLIC.
Madeira isl. group w of Morocco; an adm. dist. of Portugal; 308 sq. mi.; 253,220; cap. Funchal.
—principal isl., Madeira; 286 sq. mi.
Madeira vill., SW Ohio; 6,713; ZIP see CINCINNATI.
Madera city, CEN. California; 16,044; ZIP 93637.
Madera city, CEN. California; 16,044; ZIP 93637.
Madison city, SW Illinois; 7,042; ZIP 62060.
—city, SE Indiana; 13,081; ZIP 47250*.
—boro., N New Jersey; 16,710; ZIP 07940.
—city, SE South Dakota; 6,315; ZIP 57042.
—uninc. place, N Tennessee; 13,583; ZIP 37115.
—city, S CEN. Wisconsin; cap.; 173,258; ZIP 53700.
Madison Heights city, SE Michigan; 38,599; ZIP see ROYAL OAK.
Madisonville city, w Kentucky; 15,332; ZIP 42431.
Madras state, S India; 50,132 sq. mi.; 33,651,000.
—city, NE Madras; cap.; 2,470,288.
Madrid city, CEN. Spain; cap.; 3,146,071.
Madura isl. of Indonesia E of Java; 1,762 sq. mi.
Magdeburg city, w CEN. East Germany; 273,567.
Magellan, Strait of channel betw. the Atlantic and Pacific, separating the South American mainland from Tierra del Fuego.
Magna uninc. place, N CEN. Utah; 5,509; ZIP 84044.
Magnitogorsk city, S RSFSR; 384,000.
Magog city, S Quebec, Canada; 13,139.
Mahanoy City boro., E CEN. Pennsylvania; 7,257; ZIP 17948.
Maili See LUALUALEI-MAILI.
Main River river, S CEN. West Germany; 305 mi. long.
Maine state, NE United States; 32,562 sq. mi.; 992,048; cap. Augusta.
Majorca largest of the Balearic Islands; 1,405 sq. mi.
Makaha See WAIANAE-MAKAHA.
Malabar coastal reg., SW India. Also **Malabar Coast**.
Malacca city. w Malaya; ab. 70,000.
Malacca, Strait of strait betw. Sumatra and the Malay Peninsula.

Málaga city, S Spain; 374,452.
Malagasy Republic republic, comprising Madagascar and adjacent isls.; 228,000 sq. mi.; 7,140,000; cap. Tananarive.
Malartic town, w Quebec, Canada; 6,998.
Malawi republic, member of the Commonwealth of nations, SE Africa; 49,177 sq. mi.; 4,438,000; cap. Zomba.
Malaya federation of Malay states, SE Asia; ab. 50,700 sq. mi.; 7,377,000; cap. Kuala Lumpur; after 1963 part of Malaysia.
Malay Archipelago isl. group off SE Asia; includes isls. of Indonesia, Malaysia, and the Philippines.
Malay Peninsula S penin. of Asia; includes Malaya, Singapore, and part of Thailand.
Malaysia federation of Malaya, Sarawak, and North Borneo; a member of the Commonwealth of Nations; 127,334 sq. mi.; 12,066,669; cap. Kuala Lumpur.
Malden city, NE Massachusetts; 56,127; ZIP see BOSTON.
—city, SE Missouri; 5,374; ZIP 63863.
Mali republic, w Africa; 464,872 sq. mi.; 5,376,000; cap. Bamako.
Mallorca Majorca: *the Spanish name.*
Malone vill., NE New York; 8,048; ZIP 12953.
Malta republic, member of the Commonwealth of Nations, CEN. Mediterranean; comprises the islands of Malta, Gozo, Comino, and two islets; 122 sq. mi.; 327,218; cap. Valletta.
Malvern city, CEN. Arkansas; 8,739; ZIP 72104*.
Malverne vill., SE New York; 10,036; ZIP 11565.
Mamaroneck vill., SE New York; 18,909; ZIP 10543*.
Man, Isle of one of the British Isles, CEN. Irish Sea; 227 sq. mi.; 56,248; cap. Douglas.
Managua city, SW Nicaragua; cap.; 398, 514.
Managua, Lake lake, SW Nicaragua; 390 sq. mi.
Manassas Park town, NE Virginia; 6,844; ZIP 22110*.
Manatí town, N Puerto Rico; 13,483; ZIP 00701*.
Manchester co. boro. and city, SE Lancashire, England; 530,580.
Manchester town, N Connecticut; 47,994; ZIP 06040*.
—city, S New Hampshire; 87,754; ZIP 03100*.
Manchuria former div., NE China.
Mandalay city, CEN. Burma; 195,348.
Mandan city, S CEN. North Dakota; 11,093; ZIP 58554*.
Manhattan city, NE Kansas; 27,575; ZIP 66502*.
Manhattan isl., SE New York; 22 sq. mi.; a borough of New York City.
Manhattan Beach city, SW California; 35,352; ZIP 90266*.
Manila city, SW Luzon, Philippines; 1,377,000.
Manistee city, w Michigan; 7,723; ZIP 49660.
Manitoba prov., CEN. Canada; 246,512 sq mi.; 1,019,000; cap. Winnipeg.
Manitoba, Lake lake, SW Manitoba; 1,817 sq. mi.
Manitowoc city, E Wisconsin; 33,430; ZIP 54220*.
Maniwaki town, SW Quebec, Canada; 6,349.
Mankato city, S Minnesota; 30,895; ZIP 56001*.
Mansfield city, NW Louisiana; 6,432; ZIP 71052.
—city, N CEN. Ohio; 55,047; ZIP 44900*.
Manteca city, CEN. California; 13,845; ZIP 95336.
Manville boro., N CEN. New Jersey; 13,029; ZIP 08835.
Maple Heights city, NE Ohio; 34,093; ZIP see CLEVELAND.
Maple Shade urb. twp., SW New Jersey; 16,464; ZIP 08052.
Maplewood vill., E Minnesota; 25,222; ZIP see St. PAUL.
—city, E Missouri; 12,785; ZIP see ST. LOUIS.
—urb. twp., NE New Jersey; 24,932; ZIP 07040.
Maquoketa city, E Iowa; 5,677; ZIP 52060.
Maracaibo city, NW Venezuela; 650,002.
Maracaibo, Lake lake, NW Venezuela; ab. 5,000 sq. mi.
Marblehead town, NE Massachusetts; 21,295; ZIP 01945*.
Margate City city, SE New Jersey; 10,576; ZIP see ATLANTIC CITY.
Marianas Islands isl. group, w Pacific; including Guam, Saipan, Tinian, and Rota; part of the UN Trust terr. of the Pacific Islands (excluding Guam); 246 sq. mi.
Marianna city, E Arkansas; 6,196; ZIP 72360.
—city, NW Florida; 6,741; ZIP 32446*.
Marietta city, NW Georgia; 27,216; ZIP 30060*.

—city, SE Ohio; 16,861; ZIP 45750.
Marinette city, NE Wisconsin; 12,696; ZIP 54143*.
Marion city, S Illinois; 11,724; ZIP 62959.
—city, E CEN. Indiana; 39,607; ZIP 46952*.
—city, E Iowa; 18,028; ZIP 52302.
—city, CEN. Ohio; 38,646; ZIP 43301*.
—town, NE South Carolina; 7,435; ZIP 29571.
—town, W Virginia; 8,385; ZIP 24354.
Markham vill., NE Illinois; 15,987; ZIP see HARVEY.
Marlborough city, E CEN. Massachusetts; 27,936; ZIP 01752.
Marlin city, E CEN. Texas; 6,351; ZIP 76661.
Marmara, Sea of sea betw. Europe and Asia, connecting the Bosporus and the Dardanelles. Also **Marmora.**
Marne river, NE France; 325 mi. long.
Marple urb. twp., SE Pennsylvania; 24,626.
Marquesas Islands isl. group, French Polynesia; 492 sq. mi.
Marquette city, NW Michigan; 21,967; ZIP 49855.
Marrakesh city, SW Morocco; a traditional cap.; 332,741.
Marseille city, SE France; 813,000. Also **Marseilles.**
Marshall city, S Michigan; 7,253; ZIP 49068.
—city, SW Minnesota; 9,886; ZIP 56258.
—city, CEN. Missouri; 11,847; ZIP 65340.
—city, NE Texas; 22,937; ZIP 75607*.
Marshall Islands isl. group in Pacific; an adm. dist. of the Trust Terr. of the Pacific Islands; 66 sq. mi.; 15,000; cap. Jaluit.
Marshalltown city, CEN. Iowa; 26,219; ZIP 50158.
Marshfield city, CEN. Wisconsin; 15,619; ZIP 54449.
Martinez city, W California; 16,506; ZIP 94553*.
Martinique isl., Lesser Antilles; French overseas dept.; 421 sq. mi.; 340,000; cap. Fort-de-France.
Martinsburg city, NE West Virginia; 14,626; ZIP 25401.
Martins Ferry city, E Ohio; 10,757; ZIP 43935.
Martinsville city, S CEN. Indiana; 9,723; ZIP 46151.
—city, S Virginia; 19,652; ZIP 24112*.
Maryland state, E United States; 10,577 sq. mi.; cap. Annapolis.
Marysville city, N CEN. California; 9,353; ZIP 95901.
Maryville city, NW Missouri; 9,970; ZIP 64468.
—city, E Tennessee; 13,808; ZIP 37801*.
Mason City city, N Iowa; 30,491; ZIP 50401*.
Mason-Dixon line boundary betw. Pennsylvania and Maryland, surveyed by Charles Mason and Jeremiah Dixon in 1763; regarded as dividing the North from the South.
Massachusetts state, NE United States; 8,257 sq. mi.; 5,689,170; cap. Boston.
Massapequa uninc. place, SE New York; 26,821; ZIP 11758*.
Massapequa Park vill., SE New York; 22,112; ZIP 11762.
Massena vill., N New York; 14,042; ZIP 13662.
Massillon city, NE Ohio; 32,539; ZIP 44646.
Matane town, E Quebec, Canada; 9,190.
Matawan boro., E New Jersey; 9,136; ZIP 07747.
Mathis city, S Texas; 5,351; ZIP 78368.
Matsu isl. of the Republic of China, Formosa Strait; 4 sq. mi.
Matterhorn mtn. in the Alps on the Swiss-Italian border: 14,701 ft.
Mattoon city, E CEN. Illinois; 19,681; ZIP 61938.
Maui isl. of the Hawaiian Islands; 728 sq. mi.
Maumee city, NW Ohio; 15,937; ZIP 43537.
Mauna Loa active volcano, CEN. Hawaii (isl.); 13,675 ft.
Mauritania republic, W Africa; 419,229 sq. mi.; 1,180,000; cap. Nouakchott.
Mayagüez city, W Puerto Rico; 68,872.
Mayfield city, SW Kentucky; 10,724; ZIP 42066.
Mayfield Heights city, N Ohio; 22,139.
Maynard town, NE CEN. Massachusetts; 9,710; ZIP 01754.
Maysville city, NE Kentucky; 7,411; ZIP 41056.
Maywood city, SW California; 16,996; ZIP 90270.
—vill., NE Illinois; 30,036; ZIP 60153*.
—boro., NE New Jersey; 11,087; ZIP see HACKENSACK.
McAlester city, SE CEN. Oklahoma; 18,080; ZIP 74501*.
McAllen city, S Texas; 37,636; ZIP 78501*.
McComb city, S Mississippi; 11,969; ZIP 39648.
McCook city, S Nebraska; 8,285; ZIP 69001.
McKeesport city, SW Pennsylvania; 37,977; ZIP 15130*.

McKees Rocks boro., SW Pennsylvania; 11,901; ZIP 15136.
McKinley, Mount peak, CEN. Alaska, highest in North America; 20,300 ft.
McKinney city, N Texas; 15,193; ZIP 75069.
McMinnville city, NW Oregon; 10,125; ZIP 97128*.
—town, E CEN. Tennessee; 10,662; ZIP 37110*.
McPherson city, CEN. Kansas; 10,851; ZIP 67460.
Mead, Lake reservoir formed by Hoover Dam in the Colorado River, Arizona and Nevada; 246 sq. mi.
Meadville city, NW Pennsylvania; 16,573; ZIP 16335.
Mecca city, W Saudi Arabia; one of the caps.; birthplace of Mohammed and holy city to which Moslems make pilgrimages; 250,000.
Mechanicsburg boro., S CEN. Pennsylvania; 9,385; ZIP 17055.
Mechanicville city, E New York; 6,247; ZIP 12118.
Medford city, NE Massachusetts; 64,397; ZIP see BOSTON.
—city, SW Oregon; 28,454; ZIP 97501.
Media boro., SE Pennsylvania; 6,444; ZIP 19063*.
Medicine Hat city, SE Alberta, Canada; 24,484.
Medellín city, NW Colombia; 1,064,741.
Medina city, W Saudi Arabia; site of Mohammed's tomb; ab. 80,000.
Medina vill., NW New York; 6,415; ZIP 14103.
—city, N Ohio; 10,913; ZIP 44256.
Mediterranean Sea sea betw. Europe, Asia, and Africa; 965,000 sq. mi.
Mekong river, SE Asia; 2,500 mi. long.
Melanesia isls. of the W Pacific S of the Equator; ab. 60,000 sq. mi.
Melbourne city, S Victoria, Australia; cap.; 2,583,900 (including suburbs).
Melbourne city, E Florida; 40,236; ZIP 32901*.
Melrose city, NE Massachusetts; 33,180; ZIP see BOSTON.
Melrose Park vill., NE Illinois; 22,706; ZIP 60160*.
Melville city, SE Saskatchewan, Canada; 5,191.
Melvindale city, SE Michigan; 13,862; ZIP see DEARBORN.
Memphis city, SW Tennessee; 623,530; ZIP 38100*.
Menasha city, E Wisconsin; 14,905; ZIP 54952.
Mendota city, N CEN. Illinois; 6,902; ZIP 61342.
Mendota Heights vill., SE Minnesota; 6,165.
Menlo Park city, W California; 26,734; ZIP 94025*.
—locality, CEN. New Jersey; former site of Thomas Edison's laboratory; ZIP 08837.
Menominee city, NW Michigan; 10,748; ZIP 49858.
Menomonee Falls vill., SE Wisconsin; 31,697; ZIP 53051*.
Menomonie city, W Wisconsin; 11,275; ZIP 54751.
Merced city, CEN. California; 22,670; ZIP 95340*.
Mercedes city, S Texas; 9,355; ZIP 78570.
Meriden city, S CEN. Connecticut; 55,959; ZIP 06450*.
Meridian city, E Mississippi; 45,083; ZIP 39301*.
Merriam city, NE Kansas; 10,851.
Merrick uninc. place, SE New York; 25,904; ZIP 11566.
Merrill city, N CEN. Wisconsin; 9,502; ZIP 54452.
Mesa city, S CEN. Arizona; 62,853; ZIP 85201*.
Mesabi Range range of hills, NE Minnesota; site of iron ore deposits.
Mesquite city, N Texas; 55,131; ZIP 75149.
Messina city, NE Sicily; 257,623.
Methuen city, NE Massachusetts; 35,456; ZIP see LAWRENCE.
Metropolis city, S Illinois; 6,940; ZIP 62960.
Metuchen boro., NE New Jersey; 16,031; ZIP 08840*.
Meuse river, W Europe; 580 mi. long.
Mexia city, E CEN. Texas; 5,943; ZIP 76667.
Mexico republic, S North America; 760,373 sq. mi.; 50,670,000.
—city, S CEN. Mexico; cap.; 3,025,600. Also **Mexico City.**
Mexico city, NE CEN. Missouri; 11,807; ZIP 65265.
Mexico, Gulf of inlet of the Atlantic, betw. the United States, Mexico, and Cuba; 700,000 sq. mi.
Miami city, SE Florida; 334,859; ZIP 33100.
—city, NE Oklahoma; 13,880; ZIP 74354*.
Miami Beach city, SE Florida; 87,072; ZIP see MIAMI.
Miamisburg city, SW Ohio; 14,797; ZIP 45342.
Miami Shores vill., SE Florida; 9,425; ZIP see MIAMI.
Miami Springs town, SE Florida; 13,279; ZIP see MIAMI.
Michigan state, N United States; 58,216 sq. mi.;

8,875,083; cap. Lansing.
Michigan, Lake one of the Great Lakes; betw. Michigan and Wisconsin; 22,400 sq. mi.
Michigan City city, N Indiana; 39,369; ZIP 46360*.
Micronesia isls. of the W Pacific N of the equator.
Middleborough town, E Massachusetts; 13,607; ZIP 02346.
Middleburg Heights vill., N Ohio; 12,367; ZIP 43336.
Middle River uninc. place, N Maryland; 19,935; ZIP see BALTIMORE.
Middlesborough city, SE Kentucky; 11,844; ZIP 40965.
Middlesex boro., NE New Jersey; 15,038; ZIP 08846.
Middletown city, S CEN. Connecticut; 36,924; ZIP 06457*.
—urb. twp., E New Jersey; 51,968; ZIP 07748*.
—city, SE New York; 22,607; ZIP 10940*.
—city, SW Ohio; 48,767; ZIP 45042*.
—urb. twp., SE Pennsylvania; 30,512; ZIP 17057.
—boro., SE CEN. Pennsylvania; 9,080.
—town, SE Rhode Island; 29,621; ZIP see NEWPORT.
Midi S reg. of France.
Midland city, E CEN. Michigan; 35,176; ZIP 48640*.
—boro., W Pennsylvania; 5,271; ZIP 15059.
—city, W Texas; 59,463; ZIP 79701*.
Midland town, S Ontario, Canada; 8,656.
Midland Park boro., NE New Jersey; 8,159; ZIP 07432.
Midlands cos. of CEN. England.
Midlothian vill., NE Illinois; 15,939; ZIP 60445*.
Midvale city, N Utah; 7,840; ZIP 84047.
Midway Islands 2 isls. NW of Honolulu, under control of the U.S. Navy; 2 sq. mi.; scene of an important battle of World War II, June, 1942.
Midway-Hardwick uninc. place, CEN. Georgia; 14,047; ZIP 31320.
Midwest City city, CEN. Oklahoma; 48,114; ZIP see OKLAHOMA CITY.
Milan city, N Italy; 1,724,173.
Milan town, NW Tennessee; 7,313; ZIP 38358.
Miles City city, E Montana; 9,023; ZIP 59301.
Milford city, SW Connecticut; 50,858; ZIP 06460*.
—city, E Delaware; 5,314; ZIP 19963.
—uninc. place, S CEN. Massachusetts; 19,352; ZIP 01757.
Millbrae city, W California; 20,781; ZIP 94030*.
Millburn urb. twp., NE New Jersey; 21,307; ZIP 07041.
Millbury town, S CEN. Massachusetts; 11,987; ZIP 01527.
Millcreek boro., S CEN. Pennsylvania; 31,609; ZIP 17060.
Milledgeville city, CEN. Georgia; 11,601; ZIP 31061*.
Millford Mills See WOODLAWN-ROCKDALE-MILLFORD MILLS.
Millington town, SW Tennessee; 21,106; ZIP 38053.
Millinocket uninc. place, CEN. Maine; 7,742; ZIP 04462.
Milltown boro., CEN. New Jersey; 6,470; ZIP 08850.
Millvale boro., SE Pennsylvania; 5,815; ZIP see PITTSBURGH.
Mill Valley city, W California; 12,942; ZIP 94941*.
Millville city, S New Jersey; 21,366; ZIP 08332.
Milpitas city, W California; 27,149; ZIP 95035.
Milton town, E Massachusetts; 27,190; ZIP see BOSTON.
—boro., E CEN. Pennsylvania; 7,723; ZIP 17847.
Milton town, S Ontario, Canada; 5,629.
Milwaukee city, SE Wisconsin; 717,099; ZIP 53200*.
Milwaukie city, NW Oregon; 16,379; ZIP see PORTLAND.
Mimico town, S Ontario, Canada; 18,212.
Mindanao isl., S Philippines; 36,537 sq. mi.
Minden city, NW Louisiana; 13,996; ZIP 71055.
Mindoro isl., CEN. Philippines; 3,759 sq. mi.
Mineola vill., SE New York; 21,845; ZIP 11501*.
Mineral Wells city, N CEN. Texas; 18,411; ZIP 76067.
Minersville boro., E CEN. Pennsylvania; 6,012; ZIP 17954.
Minneapolis city, E Minnesota; 434,400; ZIP 55400*.
Minnesota state, N United States; 84,068 sq. mi.; 3,804,971; cap. St. Paul.
Minnetonka vill., E Minnesota; 35,776; ZIP see HOPKINS.
Minorca one of the Balearic islands; 271 sq. mi.
Minot city, N North Dakota; 32,290; ZIP 58701*.
Minsk city, W CEN. Byelorussian SSR; cap.; 907,104.
Mirada Hills city, SW California; 22,444.
Miramar city, SE Florida; 23,973; ZIP see HOLLYWOOD.
Mishawaka city, N Indiana; 35,517; ZIP 46544.
Mission city, S Texas; 13,043; ZIP 78572.

Mississauga city, S Ontario, Canada; 156,070.
Mississippi state, S United States; 47,716 sq. mi.; 2,216,912; cap. Jackson.
Mississippi River river, CEN. United States; 2,350 mi. long.
Missoula city, W Montana; 29,497; ZIP 59801.
Missouri state, W CEN. United States; 69,674 sq. mi.; 4,676,501; cap. Jefferson City.
Missouri River river, NW CEN. United States; 2,470 mi. long.
Mitchell city, SE CEN. South Dakota; 13,425; ZIP 57301.
Moberly city, N CEN. Missouri; 12,988; ZIP 65270.
Mobile city, SW Alabama; 190,026; ZIP 36600*.
Mobile Bay inlet of the Gulf of Mexico, SW Alabama.
Modesto city, CEN. California; 61,712; ZIP 95350*.
Mojave Desert arid reg., S California; ab. 15,000 sq. mi.
Moldavian SSR constituent republic, SW USSR; 13,000 sq. mi.; 3,572,000; cap. Kishinev. Also **Moldavia**.
Moline city, NW Illinois; 46,237; ZIP 61265*.
Molokai isl., CEN. Hawaiian Islands; 259 sq. mi.
Molucca Islands isl. group of Indonesia, betw. Celebes and New Guinea; 33,315 sq. mi.
Monaca boro., W Pennsylvania; 7,486; ZIP 15061.
Monaco independent principality, SE France; 368 acres; 23,400.
Monahans city, W Texas; 8,333; ZIP 79756.
Moncton city, SE New Brunswick, Canada; 43,840.
Monessen city, SW Pennsylvania; 15,216; ZIP 15062.
Monnett city, SW Missouri; 5,937; ZIP 65708.
Mongolia reg., E CEN. Asia; ab. million sq. mi.; divided into the **Mongolian People's Republic** (formerly **Outer Mongolia**) in the N and W part; 590,966 sq. mi.; 1,248,000 cap. Ulan Bator; and **Inner Mongolia**, a reg., N China, most of which comprises the **Inner Mongolian Autonomous Region**; ab. 400,000 sq. mi.; 6,100,000; cap. Huhehot.
Monmouth city, W Illinois; 11,022; ZIP 61462.
Monongahela city, SW Pennsylvania; 7,113; ZIP 15063.
Monongahela River river, West Virginia and W Pennsylvania; 128 mi. long.
Monroe city, N CEN. Georgia; 8,071; ZIP 30655.
—city, N Louisiana; 56,374; ZIP 71201*.
—city, SE Michigan; 23,894; ZIP 48161.
—city, S North Carolina; 11,282; ZIP 28110.
—city, S Wisconsin; 8,654; ZIP 53566.
Monroeville boro., SW Pennsylvania; 29,011; ZIP see TURTLE CREEK.
Monrovia city, E Liberia; cap.; ab. 180,000.
Monrovia city, SW California; 30,015; ZIP 91016*.
Montague town, N Massachusetts; 8,451; ZIP 01351.
Montana state NW United States; 147,138 sq. mi.; 694,409; cap. Helena.
Mont Blanc highest mountain of the Alps, on the French-Italian border; 15,781 ft.
Montclair city, SW California; 22,546; ZIP see ONTARIO.
—town, NE New Jersey; 44,043; ZIP 07042*.
Montebello city, SW California; 42,807; ZIP 90640*.
Monte Carlo city, Monaco; 9,948.
Montenegro constituent republic, S Yugoslavia; 5,343 sq. mi.; 485,000; cap. Titograd.
Monterey city, W California; 26,302; ZIP 93940*.
Monterey Park city, SW California; 49,166; ZIP 91754*.
Monterrey city, NE Mexico; 858,100.
Montevideo city, S Uruguay; cap.; 1,500,000.
Montevideo city, SW Minnesota; 5,661; ZIP 56265.
Montgomery city, E CEN. Alabama; cap.; 133,386; ZIP 36100*.
Montgomery town, S Alberta, Canada; 5,077.
Monticello estate and residence of Thomas Jefferson, near Charlottesville, Virginia.
Monticello vill., SE New York; 5,991; ZIP 12701.
Mont-Joli town, E Quebec, Canada; 6,178.
Mont Laurier town, SW Quebec, Canada; 5,859.
Montmagny town, SE Quebec, Canada; 6,850.
Montmartre dist., N Paris; former artists' quarter.
Montmorency town, S Quebec, Canada; 5,985.
Montoursville boro., N CEN. Pennsylvania; ZIP 17754.
Montpelier city, N CEN. Vermont; cap.; 8,609; ZIP 05601*.
Montréal city, S Quebec, Canada; 1,214,352.
Montréal-E. town, S Quebec, Canada; 5,844. Also **Montréal-East**.
Montréal-N. city, S Quebec, Canada; 89,139. Also

Montréal-North
Montréal-O., Montréal-W. town, s Quebec, Canada; 6,466. Also Montréal-Ouest, Montréal-West.
Montrose city, w Colorado; 6,496; ZIP 81401.
Mont-Royal town, s Quebec, Canada; 21,182.
Mont Saint Michel isl. off NW France; site of an ancient fortress and abbey.
Mooresville town, w CEN. North Carolina; 8,808; ZIP 28115.
Moorhead city, w Minnesota; 29,687; ZIP 56560*.
Moose Jaw city, s Saskatchewan, Canada; 33,206.
Moravia reg., CEN. Czechoslovakia.
Morehead City town, E North Carolina; 5,233; ZIP 28557.
Morgan City city, s Louisiana; 16,586; ZIP 70380.
Morganton town, w North Carolina; 13,625; ZIP 28655.
Morgantown city, N West Virginia; 29,431; ZIP 26500*.
Morocco kingdom, NW Africa; ab. 160,000 sq. mi.; 15,379,259; cap. Rabat.
Morrilton city, CEN. Arkansas; 6,814; ZIP 72110.
Morris city, NE Illinois; 8,194; ZIP 60450.
Morristown town, N CEN. New Jersey; 17,662; ZIP 07960*.
—city, NE Tennessee; 20,318; ZIP 37813*.
Morrisville boro., SE Pennsylvania; 11,309; ZIP 19067*.
Morton vill., CEN. Illinois; 10,419; ZIP 61550.
Morton Grove vill., NE Illinois; 26,369; ZIP 60053.
Moscow city, w USSR; cap. USSR and RSFSR; 7,528,000.
Moscow city, NW Idaho; 14,146; ZIP 83843*.
Moselle river, NE France, Luxembourg, and w West Germany; 320 mi. long.
Moses Lake city, E CEN. Washington; 10,310; ZIP 98837*.
Moss Point city, SE Mississippi; 19,321; ZIP 39563.
Mosul city, N Iraq; 264,146.
Moultrie city, s Georgia; 14,302; ZIP 31768.
Mound vill., E Minnesota; 7,572; ZIP 55364*.
Mounds View vill., E Minnesota; 9,988.
Moundsville city, N West Virginia; 13,560; ZIP 26041.
Mountain Brook city, N CEN. Alabama; 19,474; ZIP see BIRMINGHAM.
Mountain Home city, SW Idaho; 6,451; ZIP 83647.
Mountainside boro., NE New Jersey; 7,520; ZIP see WESTFIELD.
Mountain View city, w California; 51,092; ZIP 94040*.
Mount Airy town, NW North Carolina; 7,325; ZIP 27030*.
Mount Carmel city, SE Illinois; 8,096; ZIP 62863.
—boro., E CEN. Pennsylvania; 9,317; ZIP 17851.
Mount Clemens city, SE Michigan; 20,476; ZIP 48043*.
Mount Ephraim boro., SW New Jersey; 5,625; ZIP 08056.
Mount Healthy city, SW Ohio; 7,446; ZIP see CINCINNATI.
Mount Holly urb. twp., w New Jersey; 12,382; ZIP 08060.
Mount Kisco vill., SE New York; 8,172; ZIP 10549.
Mountlake Terrace city, NW CEN. Washington; 16,600; ZIP 98043.
Mount Lebanon urb. twp., SW Pennsylvania; 39,596; ZIP see PITTSBURGH.
Mount Oliver boro., SW Pennsylvania; 5,487; ZIP see PITTSBURGH.
Mount Pleasant city, SE Iowa; 7,007; ZIP 52641*.
—city, CEN. Michigan; 20,504; ZIP 48858.
—boro., SW Pennsylvania; 5,895; ZIP 15666.
—town, SE South Carolina; 6,155; ZIP 29464.
—city, NE Texas; 8,877; ZIP 75455.
Mount Prospect vill., NE Illinois; 34,995; ZIP 60056*.
Mount Rainier city, w CEN. Maryland; 8,180; ZIP 20822.
Mount Sterling city, NE CEN. Kentucky; 5,083; ZIP 40353.
Mount Vernon home and burial place of George Washington, near Washington, D.C.
—city, s Illinois; 15,980; ZIP 62864.
—city, SW Indiana; 6,770; ZIP 47620.
—city, SE New York; 72,778; ZIP 10550*.
—city, CEN. Ohio; 13,373; ZIP 43050.
—city, NW Washington; 8,804; ZIP 98273.
Mozambique republic, SE Africa; 307,731 sq. mi., 8,233,834; cap. Maputo.
Mukden Shenyang: a former name.
Mullins town, E South Carolina; 6,006; ZIP 29574.
Muncie city, E Indiana; 69,080; ZIP 47301*.

Mundelein vill., NE Illinois; 16,128; ZIP 60060.
Munhall boro., SW Pennsylvania; 16,674; see HOMESTEAD.
Munich city, SE West Germany; 1,338,432.
Munster town, NW Indiana; 16,514; ZIP see HAMMOND.
Murfreesboro city, CEN. Tennessee; 26,360; ZIP 37130*.
Murmansk city, NW USSR; 347,000.
Murphysboro city, s Illinois; 10,013; ZIP 62966.
Murray city, SW Kentucky; 13,537; ZIP 42071*.
—city, N CEN. Utah; 21,206; ZIP see SALT LAKE CITY.
Murray River river, SE Australia; 1,600 mi. long.
Muscat and Oman see OMAN.
Muscatine city, E Iowa; 22,405; ZIP 52761.
Muscle Shoals former rapids in the Tennessee River, NW Alabama; site of the Wilson Dam.
Muskgon city, w Michigan; 44,631; ZIP 49440*.
Muskegon Heights city, w Michigan; 17,304; ZIP see MUSKEGON.
Muskogee city, E Oklahoma; 37,331; ZIP 74401*.
Myrtle Beach town, E South Carolina 8,536; ZIP 29577.
Mysore state, s India; 74,122 sq. mi.; 23,547,000; cap. Bangalore.
—city, s India; 355,685.

Nacogdoches city, E Texas; 22,544; ZIP 75961*.
Nagasaki city, NW Kyushu island, Japan; largely destroyed by a U.S. atomic bomb, Aug. 9, 1945; 442,183.
Nagoya city, s CEN. Honshu isl., Japan; 2,036,053.
Nagpur city, CEN. India; 866,144.
Nairobi city, SW Kenya; cap.; 535,200.
Nampa city, SW Idaho; 20,768; ZIP 83651.
Nanaimo city, SW British Columbia, Canada; 14,135.
Nanking city, E China; cap. 1928–37; 1,419,000.
Nantes city, w France; 256,917.
Nanticoke city, NE CEN. Pennsylvania; 14,632; ZIP 18634.
Nantucket isl. off SE Massachusetts; 57 sq. mi.
Napa city, w California; 35,978; ZIP 94558*.
Naperville city, NE Illinois; 23,885; ZIP 60540.
Naples city, SW Italy; 1,232.877.
Napoleon city, NW Ohio; 7,791; ZIP 43545.
Narberth boro., SE Pennsylvania; 5,151; ZIP 19072.
Narragansett Bay inlet of the Atlantic, SE Rhode Island.
Nashua city, s New Hampshire; 55,820; ZIP 03060.
Nashville city, N CEN. Tennessee; cap.; 448,003; ZIP 37200*.
Nassau city, New Providence, Bahama Islands; cap.; 101,503.
Natal prov., E South Africa; 33,578 sq. mi. (including Zululand); 2,933,000; cap. Pietermaritzburg.
Natchez city, SW Mississippi; 19,704; ZIP 39120*.
Natchitoches city, NW CEN. Louisiana; 15,974; ZIP 71457.
Natick town, NE Massachusetts; 31,057; ZIP 01760*.
National City city, SW California; 43,184; ZIP 92050*.
Naugatuck town, SW CEN. Connecticut; 23,034; ZIP 06770*.
Navarre reg. and former kingdom, N Spain and SW France.
Nazareth town, N Israel; scene of Christ's childhood; 22,000.
Nazareth boro., E Pennsylvania; 5,815; ZIP 18064.
Nebraska state, CEN. United States; 77,237 sq. mi.; 1,483,493; cap. Lincoln.
Nebraska City city, SE Nebraska; 7.441; ZIP 68410.
Nederland city, SE Texas; 16,810; ZIP 77627.
Needham town, NE Massachusetts; 29,748; ZIP see BOSTON.
Neenah city. E CEN. Wisconsin; 22,892; ZIP 54956*.
Negaunee city, NW Michigan; 5,248; ZIP 49866.
Negev desert reg., s Israel; 4,700 sq. mi. Also Negeb.
Nejd prov., CEN. Saudi Arabia; ab. 450,000 sq. mi.; 4 million; cap. Riyadh.
Nelson city, SE British Columbia, Canada; 7,074.
Neosho city, SW Missouri; 7,517.
Nepal kingdom betw. Tibet and India; 54,362 sq. mi.; 11,290,000; cap. Kathmandu.
Neptune urb. twp., E New Jersey; 27.863; ZIP 07753.
Netherlands constitutional monarchy, NW Europe; 15,780 sq. mi.; 13,438,000; cap. Amsterdam; seat of government, The Hague.
Netherlands, Kingdom of the kingdom comprising the Netherlands, the Netherlands Antilles, and Su-

rinam; cap. Amsterdam.
Netherlands Antilles 3 isls. N of Venezuela and 3 in the Leeward Islands group; 336 sq. mi.; 228,246; cap. Willemstad.
Netherlands East Indies former Netherlands possessions in the Malay Archipelago. Also **Netherlands Indies.** See INDONESIA.
Netherlands Guiana See SURINAM.
Netherlands New Guinea West New Guinea: *the former name.*
Netherlands West Indies See NETHERLANDS ANTILLES.
Nether Providence urb. twp., SE Pennsylvania; 10,380.
Nevada state, W United States; 110,540 sq. mi.; 488,738; cap. Carson City.
Nevada city, W Missouri; 9,736; ZIP 64772.
New Albany city, S Indiana; 38,402; ZIP 47150.
  —city, N Mississippi; 6,426; ZIP 38652.
Newark city, W California; 27,153; ZIP 94560.
Newark city, NW Delaware; 20,757; ZIP 19711*.
Newark city, NE New Jersey; 382,417; ZIP 07100*.
Newark vill., W New York; 11,644; ZIP 14513.
  —city, CEN. Ohio; 41,836; ZIP 43055*.
New Bedford city, SE Massachusetts; 101,777; ZIP 02740*.
New Berlin city, SE Wisconsin; 26,937; ZIP 53151.
New Bern city, E North Carolina; 14,660; ZIP 28560*.
Newberry town, NW CEN. South Carolina; 9,218; ZIP 29108.
New Braunfels city, S CEN. Texas; 17,859; ZIP 78130*.
New Brighton vill., E Minnesota; 19,507; ZIP see ST. PAUL.
  —boro., W Pennsylvania; 7,637; ZIP 15066.
New Britain city, N CEN. Connecticut; 83,441; ZIP 06050*.
New Brunswick city, E CEN. New Jersey; 41,885; ZIP 08900*.
New Brunswick prov., SE Canada; 27,836 sq. mi.; 675,000; cap. Fredericton.
Newburgh city, SE New York; 26,219; ZIP 12550*.
Newburyport city, NE Massachusetts; 15,807; ZIP 01950*.
New Caledonia isl. E of Australia; comprising with adjacent isls. a French overseas terr.; 9,401 sq. mi.; 130,000; cap. Nouméa.
New Castle city, E Indiana; 21,215; ZIP 47362.
  —city, W Pennsylvania; 38,559; ZIP 16101*.
Newcastle-upon-Tyne city, NE England; 212,430. Also **Newcastle, Newcastle-on-Tyne.**
Newcastle town, NE New Brunswick, Canada; 5,236.
New Cumberland boro., S Pennsylvania; 9,803; ZIP 17070.
New Delhi city, Delhi terr., India; cap. of India; 301,801.
New England NE section of the United States, including Maine, New Hampshire, Vermont, Massachusetts, Rhode Island, and Connecticut.
Newfoundland prov., E Canada; comprising the island of Newfoundland (42,734 sq. mi.) and Labrador on the mainland; 152,734 sq. mi.; 549,000; cap. St. John's.
New Georgia isl. group, British Solomon Islands; ab. 2,000 sq. mi.
New Glasgow town, N Nova Scotia, Canada; 9,782.
New Guinea isl., N of Australia; 304,200 sq. mi. See WEST NEW GUINEA, PAPUA NEW GUINEA.
New Guinea, Territory of trust terr. comprising NE New Guinea, the Bismarck Archipelago, and Bougainville and Buka in the Solomon Islands; now part of Papua New Guinea.
New Hampshire state, NE United States; 9,304 sq. mi.; 737,681; cap. Concord.
New Hanover town, NE New Jersey; 27,410.
New Haven city, S Connecticut; 137,707; ZIP 06500*.
New Hebrides isl. group, SW Pacific; an Anglo-French condominium; ab. 5,700 sq. mi.; 90,000; cap. Vila.
New Hyde Park vill., SE New York; 10,116; ZIP 11040*.
New Iberia city, S Louisiana; 30,147; ZIP 70560*.
New Jersey state, E United States; 7,836 sq. mi.; 7,168,164; cap. Trenton.
New Kensington city, W Pennsylvania; 20,312; ZIP 15068*.
New London city, SE Connecticut; site of a naval base; 31,630; ZIP 06301*.
  —city, E CEN. Wisconsin; 5,801; ZIP 54961.
Newmarket town, S Ontario, Canada; 8,932.

New Martinsville city, NW West Virginia; 6,528; ZIP 26155.
New Mexico state, SW United States; 121,666 sq. mi.; 1,016,000; cap. Santa Fé.
New Milford boro., NE New Jersey; 20,201; ZIP 07646.
Newnan city, W Georgia; 11,205; ZIP 30263.
New Orleans city, SE Louisiana; 593,471; ZIP 70100*.
New Philadelphia city, E CEN. Ohio; 15,184; ZIP 44663.
Newport city, NE Arkansas; 7,725; ZIP 72112*.
  —city, N Kentucky; 25,998; ZIP 41079*.
  —city, W Oregon; 5,188; ZIP 97365*.
  —city, SE Rhode Island; 34,562; ZIP 02840*.
  —town, E Tennessee; 7,328; ZIP 37821.
Newport Beach city, SW California; 49,422; ZIP 92660*.
Newport News city, SE Virginia; 138,177; ZIP 23600*.
New Providence boro., NE New Jersey; 13,796; ZIP 07974.
New Rochelle city, SE New York; 75,385.
New Shrewsbury boro., E New Jersey; 5,925.
New Smyrna Beach city, NE Florida; 10,580; ZIP 32069.
New South Wales state, SE Australia; 309,433 sq. mi.; 4,000,000; cap. Sydney.
Newton city, CEN. Iowa; 15,619; ZIP 50208.
  —city, S CEN. Kansas; 15,439; ZIP 67114.
  —city, E Massachusetts; 91,066; ZIP see BOSTON.
  —town, N New Jersey; 7,297; ZIP 07860.
  —town, W North Carolina; 7,414; ZIP 28658.
Newton Falls vill., NE Ohio; 5,378; ZIP 44444.
New Toronto town, S Ontario, Canada; 13,384.
New Ulm city, S Minnesota; 13,051; ZIP 56073.
New Waterford town, NE Nova Scotia, Canada; 10,592.
New Westminster city, SW British Columbia, Canada; 33,654.
New York state, NE United States; 49,576 sq. mi.; 18,236,967; cap. Albany.
  —city, SE New York; divided into the five boroughs of the Bronx, Brooklyn, Manhattan, Queens, and Richmond (Staten Island); 365 sq. mi.; 7,894,862; ZIP 10000*.
New York State Barge Canal waterway system, New York; connects the Hudson River with Lakes Erie, Champlain, and Ontario; 525 mi. long.
New Zealand self-governing member of the Commonwealth of Nations, comprising a group of isls. SE of Australia; 103,416 sq. mi., excluding island territories; 2,862,631; cap. Wellington.
Niagara Falls city, W New York; 85,615; ZIP 14300*.
Niagara Falls city, S Ontario, Canada; 67,163.
Niagara River river betw. Ontario, Canada, and New York State, connecting Lake Erie and Lake Ontario; in its course occurs Niagara Falls, a cataract divided by Goat Island into the American Falls, ab. 167 ft. high and 1,000 ft. wide, and Horseshoe Falls on the Canadian side, ab. 160 ft. high and 2,500 ft. wide.
Nicaragua republic, Central America; ab. 57,100 sq. mi.; 1,911,543; cap. Managua.
Nicaragua, Lake lake, SW Nicaragua; 3,100 sq. mi.
Nice city, SE France; 319,937.
Nicosia city, N CEN. Cyprus; cap.; 118,000.
Niger river, W Africa; ab. 2,600 mi. long.
Niger, Republic of republic of the French Community, W CEN. Africa; 458,976 sq. mi.; 4,126,000; cap. Niamey.
Nigeria, Federation of federal republic, member of the Commonwealth of Nations, W Africa; 339,168 sq. mi.; ab. 59,610,000; cap. Lagos.
Nile river, E Africa; 4,130 mi. long.
Niles vill., NE Illinois; 31,432; ZIP see CHICAGO.
  —city, SW Michigan; 12,988; ZIP 49120.
  —city, NE Ohio; 21,581; ZIP 44446.
Nitro city, W West Virginia; 8,019; ZIP 25143.
Noblesville city, CEN. Indiana; 7,548; ZIP 46060.
Nogales city, S Arizona; 8,946; ZIP 85621.
Noranda city, W Quebec, Canada; 11,477.
Norfolk city, NE Nebraska; 16,607; ZIP 68701.
Norfolk city, SE Virginia; 307,951; ZIP 23500*.
Normal town, CEN. Illinois; 26,396; ZIP 61761.
Norman city, CEN. Oklahoma; 52,117; ZIP 73069*.
Normandy reg. and former prov., NW France.
Norridge vill., NE Illinois; 16,880.
Norristown boro., SE Pennsylvania; 38,169; ZIP 19401*.
North Adams city, NW Massachusetts; 19,195; ZIP 01247*.
North America N continent of the W hemisphere;

9.3 million sq. mi. (including adjacent islands); 261,348,000.

Northampton city, w Massachusetts; 29,664; ZIP 01060*.

Northampton boro., E Pennsylvania; 8,389; ZIP 18067.

North Andover town, NE Massachusetts; 16,284; ZIP see LAWRENCE.

North Arlington boro., NE New Jersey; 18,096.

North Atlanta vill., N CEN. Georgia; 12,661; ZIP see ATLANTA.

North Attleborough town, E Massachusetts; 18,665; ZIP 02760*.

North Augusta city, w South Carolina; 12,883; ZIP 29841.

North Battleford city, w Saskatchewan, Canada; 11,230.

North Bay city, SE CEN. Ontario, Canada; 23,781.

North Bellmore uninc. place, SE New York; 22,893; ZIP see BELLMORE.

North Belmont uninc. place, SW North Carolina; 10,759; ZIP see BELMONT.

North Bend city, SW Oregon; 8,553; ZIP 97459.

North Bergen urb. twp., NE New Jersey; 47,751; ZIP 07047*.

North Borneo reg., N Borneo; part of Malaysia; 29,338 sq. mi.; 429,000; cap. Jessleton.

North Braddock boro., SW Pennsylvania; 10,838.

Northbrook vill., NE Illinois; 27,297; ZIP 60062.

North Canton vill., NE Ohio; 15,228; ZIP see CANTON.

North Cape promontory, N Norway.

North Carolina state, SE United States; 52,712 sq. mi.; 5,082,059; cap. Raleigh.

North Chicago city, NE Illinois; 47,275; ZIP 60064*.

North College Hill city, SW Ohio; 12,363; ZIP see CINCINNATI.

North Dakota state, N United States; 70,665 sq. mi.; 617,761; cap. Bismarck.

Northern Ireland part of the United Kingdom in N reg. of Ireland; 5,238 sq. mi.; 1,527,593; cap. Belfast.

Northern Rhodesia former British prot., S CEN. Africa. See ZAMBIA.

Northern Territory reg., N Australia; 523,620 sq. mi.; 27,095; cap. Darwin.

Northfield city, SE Minnesota; 10,235; ZIP 55057.

—city, SE New Jersey; 8,875; ZIP 08225.

North Haledon boro., NE New Jersey; 7,614.

North Highlands uninc. place, CEN. California; 31,854; ZIP 95660.

North Island isl., N New Zealand; 44,281 sq. mi.

North Kamloops vill., S British Columbia, Canada; 6,456.

North Kansas City town, w Missouri; 5,183; ZIP see KANSAS CITY.

North Kingstown town, S Rhode Island; 27,673; ZIP 02852*.

North Korea See KOREA.

Northlake city, NE Illinois; 14,212; ZIP see MELROSE PARK.

North Las Vegas city, SE Nevada; 36,216; ZIP 89030*.

North Little Rock city, CEN. Arkansas; 60,040; ZIP 72114*.

North Mankato city, S Minnesota; 7,347; ZIP see MANKATO.

North Merrick uninc. place, SE New York; 13,650.

North Miami city, SE Florida; 34,767; ZIP see MIAMI.

North Miami Beach city, SE Florida; 30,723; ZIP see MIAMI.

North New Hyde Park uninc. place, SE New York; 18,154; ZIP see NEW HYDE PARK.

North Olmsted city, N Ohio; 34,861; ZIP 44070.

North Pelham vill., SE New York; 5,184.

North Plainfield boro., NE New Jersey; 21,796; ZIP see PLAINFIELD.

North Platte city, CEN. Nebraska; 19,447; ZIP 69101*.

North Pole N extremity of the earth's exis.

Northport city, w CEN. Alabama; 9,435; ZIP 35476.

—vill., SE New York; 7,440; ZIP 11768.

North Providence town, NE Rhode Island; 24,337.

North Richland Hills town, N Texas; 16,514.

North Riverside vill., NE Illinois; 8,097; ZIP see RIVERSIDE.

North Royalton vill., N Ohio; 12,807; ZIP see CLEVELAND.

North Sacramento city, CEN. California; 12,922; ZIP see SACRAMENTO.

North Saint Paul vill., E Minnesota; 11,950; ZIP see ST. PAUL.

North Sea part of the Atlantic betw. Great Britain and Europe.

North Shreveport uninc. place, NW Louisiana; 7,701.

North Sydney town, E Nova Scotia, Canada; 8,657.

North Syracuse vill., CEN. New York; 8,687; ZIP see SYRACUSE.

North Tarrytown vill., SE New York; 8,334; ZIP see TARRYTOWN.

North Tonawanda city, NW New York; 36,012; ZIP 14120*.

North Valley Stream uninc. place, SE New York; 14,881.

North Vancouver city, SW British Columbia, Canada; 23,656.

North Versailles urb. twp., SW Pennsylvania; 13,364.

North Vietnam See VIETNAM.

Northwest Territories adm. div., N Canada; 1,304,903 sq. mi.; 38,000.

Northwest Territory reg. awarded to the United States by Britain in 1783, extending from the Great Lakes S to the Ohio River and from Pennsylvania W to the Mississippi.

Norwalk city, SW California; 91,827; ZIP 90650*.

—city, SW Connecticut; 79,113; ZIP 06850*.

—city, N Ohio; 13,386; ZIP 44857.

Norway kingdom, N Europe; 119,240 sq. mi.; 3,903,000; cap. Oslo.

Norwich co. boro., E England; 120,000.

Norwich city, SE Connecticut; 41,333; ZIP 06360*.

Norwich city, CEN. New York; 8,843; ZIP 13815.

Norwood town, E Massachusetts; 30,815; 02062.

—city, SW Ohio; 30,420; ZIP see CINCINNATI.

—boro., SE Pennsylvania; 7,229; ZIP 19074.

Nottingham co. boro., N CEN. England; 312,000.

Nova Scotia prov., E Canada; 21,068 sq. mi.; 822,000; cap. Halifax.

Novato city, w California; 31,006; ZIP 94947.

Novi vill., SE Michigan; 9,668; ZIP 48050.

Novosibirsk city, SW USSR; 1,243,000.

Nubia reg., NE Africa.

Nuremberg city, SE CEN. West Germany; 514,657.

Nutley town, NE New Jersey; 32,099; ZIP see NEWARK.

Nyack vill., SE New York; 6,659; ZIP 10960.

Nyasaland former British prot., SE Africa. See MALAWI.

Oahu isl., N CEN. Hawaiian Islands; 589 sq. mi.

Oak Creek city, SE Wisconsin; 7,301; ZIP 53154*.

Oakdale city, SW CEN. Louisiana; 7,301; ZIP 71463.

Oakland city, w California; 361,561; ZIP 94600*.

—boro., NE New Jersey; 14,420; ZIP 07436.

Oakland Park city, SE Florida; 16,261; ZIP see FORT LAUDERDALE.

Oak Lawn vill., NE Illinois; 60,305; ZIP 60453*.

Oakmont boro., SW Pennsylvania; 7,550; ZIP 15139.

Oak Park vill., NE Illinois; 62,511; ZIP 60300*.

—city, SE Michigan; 36,762; ZIP see DETROIT.

Oak Ridge city, E Tennessee; 28,319; ZIP 37830*.

Oakville town, S Ontario, Canada; 61,483.

Oakwood city, SW Ohio; 10,095; ZIP 45873.

Oberammergau vill., SE West Germany; noted for its decennial Passion play.

Oberlin city, N Ohio; 8,761; ZIP 44074.

Ocala city, N CEN. Florida; 22,583; ZIP 32670.

Ocean City city, SE New Jersey; 10,575; ZIP 08226.

Oceania isls. of Melanesia, Micronesia, and Polynesia, and sometimes the Malay Archipelago and Australasia.

Oceanside city, SW California; 40,494; ZIP 92054*.

—vill., SE New York; 35,372; ZIP see ROCKVILLE CENTRE.

Ocean Springs town, SE Mississippi; 9,580; ZIP 39564.

Oconomowoc city, SE Wisconsin; 8,741; ZIP 53066.

Oder river, CEN. Europe; 563 mi. long.

Odessa city, S Ukrainian SSR; 941,000.

Odessa city, w Texas; 78,380; ZIP 79760*.

Oelwein city, NE Iowa; 7,735; ZIP 50662.

Ogden city, N Utah; 69,478; ZIP 84400*.

Ogdensburg city, N New York; 14,554; ZIP 13669.

Ohio state, NE CEN. United States; 41,222 sq. mi.; 10,652,017; cap. Columbus.

Ohio River river, E CEN. United States; 981 mi. long.

Oil City city, NW Pennsylvania; 15,033; ZIP 16301*.

Okhotsk, Sea of inlet of the Pacific w of Kamchatka and the Kurile Islands.

Okinawa Japanese isl., NW Pacific Ocean; largest of the Ryuku Islands; 467 sq. mi.; administered by US military government. 1945-1972; 953,000.

Oklahoma state, S CEN. United States; 69,919 sq. mi.; 2,559,229.

Oklahoma City city, CEN. Oklahoma; cap.; 324,253; ZIP 73100*.

Okmulgee city, E CEN. Oklahoma; 15,180; ZIP 74447.

Olathe city, E Kansas; 17,917; ZIP 66061.

Old Bethpage See BETHPAGE.

Old Forge boro., NE Pennsylvania; 9,522; ZIP see SCRANTON.

Old Town city, S CEN. Maine; 9,057; ZIP 04468.

Olean city, SW New York; 19,169; ZIP 14760*.

Olivette city, E Missouri; 9,341; ZIP see ST. LOUIS.

Olney city, SE Illinois; 8,974; ZIP 62450.

Olympia city, W Washington; cap.; 23,111; ZIP 98501*.

Olympus, Mount mtn., N Greece; regarded in Greek mythology as the home of the gods; 9,570 ft.

Olyphant boro., NE Pennsylvania; 5,422; ZIP 18447.

Omaha city, E Nebraska; 347,328; ZIP 68100*.

Oman sultanate, E Arabia; 82,000 sq. mi.; ab. 600,000; cap. Muscat.

Omsk city, S RSFSR; 876,000.

Oneida city, CEN. New York; 11,658; ZIP 13421*.

Oneida-Rolling Mill Park uninc. place, sw Ohio; 6,504.

Oneonta city, CEN. New York; 16,030; ZIP 13820.

Ontario city, SW California; 64,118; ZIP 91761*.

—city, E Oregon; 6,523; ZIP 97914.

Ontario prov., SE Canada; 412,582 sq. mi.; 8,226,000; cap. Toronto.

Ontario, Lake easternmost of the Great Lakes; 7,540 sq. mi.

Opa-Locka city, SE Florida; 11,902; ZIP 33054*.

Opelika city, E Alabama; 19,027; ZIP 36801.

Opelousas city, S CEN. Louisiana; 20,121; ZIP 70570.

Oporto city, W Portugal; 304,700.

Opp city, S Alabama; 6,493; ZIP 36467.

Opportunity uninc. place, E Washington; 16,604; ZIP see SPOKANE.

Oradell boro., NE New Jersey; 8,903; ZIP 07649.

Orange former principality, now part of SE France.

Orange city, SW California; 77,374; ZIP 92666*.

—city, NE New Jersey; 32,566; ZIP 07050*.

—city, E Texas; 24,457; ZIP 77630*.

Orangeburg city, CEN. South Carolina; 13,252; ZIP 29115.

Orange River river, S Africa; 1,300 mi. long.

Oregon state, NW United States; 96,981 sq. mi.; 2,091,385; cap. Salem.

—city, N Ohio; 16,563; ZIP see TOLEDO.

Oregon City city, NW Oregon; 9,176; ZIP 97045.

Orem city, N CEN. Utah; 25,729; ZIP 84057.

Orillia city, S Ontario, Canada; 15,345.

Orinda Village uninc. place, W California; 6,790.

Orinoco river, Venezuela ab. 1,700 mi. long.

Orkney Islands isl. group, N of Scotland comprising Orkney, a co. of Scotland; 376 sq. mi.; 19,000; cap. Kirkwall.

Orlando city, E CEN. Florida; 99,006; ZIP 32800*.

Orléans city, N CEN. France; 94,704.

Ormond Beach city, E Florida; 14,063; ZIP 32074*.

Oromocto town, S CEN. New Brunswick, Canada; 12,170.

Orono vill., E Minnesota; 6,787.

Oroville city, N CEN. California; 7,536; ZIP 95965.

Orrville city, NE CEN. Ohio; 7,408; ZIP 44667.

Osaka city, S Honshu, Japan; 2,980,487.

Osceola city, NE Arkansas; 7,204; ZIP 72370.

Oshawa city, S Ontario, Canada; 91,587.

Oshkosh city, E Wisconsin; 53,221; ZIP 54901*.

Oskaloosa city, S CEN. Iowa; 11,224; ZIP 52577.

Oslo city, SE Norway; cap.; 475,563.

Ossa mtn., E Greece; 6,490 ft.

Ossining vill., SE New York; 21,659; ZIP 10562*.

Ostend city, NW Belgium; 56,167.

Oswego city, N New York; 23,844; ZIP 13126.

Otranto, Strait of strait betw. the Adriatic and Ionian seas; ab. 43 mi. wide.

Ottawa city N Illinois; 18,716; ZIP 61350.

—city, E Kansas; 11,036; ZIP 66067.

Ottawa city, SE Ontario, Canada; cap. of Canada;

302.341.

Ottoman Empire former empire (1300–1919) of the Turks in Asia Minor, NE Africa, and SE Europe.

Ottumwa city, SE Iowa; 29,610; ZIP 52501*.

Ouagadougou city, CEN. Upper Volta; cap.; 124,779.

Outer Mongolia See MONGOLIA.

Outremont city, S Quebec, Canada; 30,753.

Overland city, E Missouri; 24,949; ZIP see ST. LOUIS.

Overland Park uninc. place, NE Kansas; 76,623.

Overlea uninc. place, N CEN. Maryland; 13,086; ZIP see BALTIMORE.

Owatonna city, S Minnesota; 15,341; ZIP 55060.

Owego vill., S New York; 5,152; ZIP 13827.

Owens uninc. place, S CEN. North Carolina; 5,207.

Owensboro city, NW Kentucky; 50,329; ZIP 42301*.

Owen Sound city, S Ontario, Canada; 17,421.

Owosso city, S CEN. Michigan; 17,179; ZIP 48867.

Oxford co. boro., S CEN. England; 114,220.

Oxford uninc. place, S CEN. Massachusetts; 10,345; ZIP 01540.

—city, N Mississippi; 13,846; ZIP 38655.

—town, N North Carolina; 7,178; ZIP 27565.

—city, SW Ohio; 15,868; ZIP 45056.

Oxnard city, SW California; 71,225; ZIP 93030*.

Ozark city, SE Alabama; 13,555; ZIP 36360*.

Ozark Mountains hilly uplands, SW Missouri, NW Arkansas, and NE Oklahoma.

Pacifica city, W California; 36,020; ZIP 94044.

Pacific Grove city, W California; 13,505; ZIP 93950.

Pacific Ocean ocean betw. the American continents and Asia and Australia; extending betw. the Arctic and Antarctic regions; ab. 70 million sq. mi.

Padua city, NE Italy; 231,152.

Paducah city, W Kentucky; 31,627; ZIP 42001*.

Pagedale city, E Missouri; 5,571.

Pago Pago town, SE Tutuila, American Samoa; 2,451; ZIP 96920.

Painesville city, NE Ohio; 16,536; ZIP 44077.

Pakistan republic of the Commonwealth of Nations, S Asia; 363,737 sq. mi.; ab. 60,000,000; cap. Rawalpindi.

Palatine vill., NE Illinois; 25,904; ZIP 60067.

Palatka city, N Florida; 9,310; ZIP 32077.

Palau Islands isl. group, W Caroline Islands; 188 sq. mi.

Palermo city, NW Sicily; cap.; 650,645.

Palestine terr., E Mediterranean; 10,434 sq. mi.; cap. Jerusalem; divided (1947) by the United Nations into Israel and a terr. that became part of Jordan.

Palestine city, E Texas; 14,525; ZIP 75801.

Palisades Park boro., NE New Jersey; 13,351; ZIP 07650.

Palma city, W Majorca; cap. of the Balearic Islands; 234,098.

Palm Beach town, SE Florida; 9,086; ZIP 33480*.

Palmdale uninc. place, SW California; 8,511; ZIP 93550.

Palmerton boro., E Pennsylvania; 5,620; ZIP 18071.

Palmetto city, SW Florida; 7,422; ZIP 33561.

Palm Springs city, S California; 20,936; ZIP 92262*.

Palmyra boro., W New Jersey; 6,969; ZIP 08065.

—boro., SE Pennsylvania; 7,615; ZIP 17078.

Palo Alto city, W California; 55,966; ZIP 94300*.

Palomar, Mount mtn., S California, 6,126 ft.; site of Mount Palomar Observatory.

Palos Verdes Estates city, SW California; 13,641.

Pampa city, N Texas; 21,726; ZIP 79065*.

Pana city, CEN. Illinois; 6,326; ZIP 62557.

Panama republic, Central America; 28,575 sq. mi. (excluding Canal Zone); 1,570,000.

—city, near the Pacific end of the Panama Canal; cap. of Panama; 386,627.

Panama, Isthmus of isthmus connecting North and South America.

Panama Canal ship canal connecting the Atlantic and the Pacific across Panama; completed (1914) by the United States on the leased Canal Zone; 40 mi. long.

Panama Canal Zone See CANAL ZONE.

Panama City city, NW Florida; 32,096; ZIP 32401*.

Panay isl., CEN. Philippines; 4,446 sq. mi.

Papal States STATES OF THE CHURCH.

Papua SE area of New Guinea and adjacent isls.; now part of Papua New Guinea.

Papua New Guinea self-governing member of the

Commonwealth of Nations, formed by union of Papua and Territory of New Guinea, in sw Pacific Ocean; 86,100 sq. mi.; 67¹.384; cap. Port Moresby.
Pará Belém: *a former name.*
Paradise uninc. place, N CEN. California; 14,539.
—uninc. place, CEN. California; 5,616.
Paragould city, NE Arkansas; 9,947.
Paraguay republic, s CEN. South America; 157,047 sq. mi.; 2,415,000; cap. Asunción.
Paraguay River river, s CEN. South America; ab. 1,300
Paramaribo city, N Surinam; cap.; 150,000.
Paramount city, sw California; 34,734; ZIP 90723*.
Paramus boro., NE New Jersey; 29,495; ZIP 07652*.
Paraná river, s CEN. South America; ab. 2,800 mi. long.
Paris city, N France; cap.; 2,590,771.
Paris city, E Illinois; 9,971; ZIP 61944.
—city, NE CEN. Kentucky; 7,823; ZIP 40361.
—city, NW Tennessee; 9,892; ZIP 38242.
—city, NE Texas; 23,441; ZIP 75460*.
Paris town, s Ontario, Canada; 5,820.
Parkersburg city, w West Virginia; 44,208; ZIP 26100*.
Park Forest vill., NE Illinois; 30,638; ZIP 60466.
Park Ridge city, NE Illinois; 42,466; ZIP 60068.
—boro., NE New Jersey; 8,709; ZIP 07656.
Parkville-Carney uninc. place, N Maryland; 33,897.
Parma city, N CEN. Italy; 174,655.
Parma city, N Ohio; 100,216; ZIP see CLEVELAND.
Parnassus, Mount mtn., CEN. Greece; anciently regarded as sacred to Apollo and the Muses; 8,062 ft.
Parry Sound town, s CEN. Ontario, Canada; 6,004.
Parsippany-Troy Hills urb. twp., N New Jersey; 54,713; ZIP 07054.
Parsons city, SE Kansas; 13,015; ZIP 67357.
Pasadena city, sw California; 113,327; ZIP 91100*.
—city, SE Texas; 89,277; ZIP 77501*.
Pascagoula city, SE Mississippi; 27,264; ZIP 39567.
Pasco city, s Washington; 13,920; ZIP 99301.
Paso Robles El Paso de Robles: *an alternate name.*
Passaic city, NE New Jersey; 55,124; ZIP 07055*.
Patagonia reg. at the s tip of South America.
Patchogue vill., SE New York; 11,582; ZIP 11772*.
Paterson city, NE New Jersey; 144,824; ZIP 07500*.
Paulsboro boro., w New Jersey; 8,084; ZIP 08066.
Pauls Valley city, s CEN. Oklahoma; 5,769; ZIP 73075.
Pawtucket city, NE Rhode Island; 76,984; ZIP 02860*.
Peabody city, NE Massachusetts; 48,080; ZIP 01960*.
Peacedale See WAKEFIELD-PEACEDALE.
Pearl uninc. place, s CEN. Mississippi; 9,623; ZIP see JACKSON.
Pearl Harbor inlet, s Oahu, Hawaii; site of a U.S. naval base, bombed by Japanese, December 7, 1941.
Pecos city, w Texas; 12,682; ZIP 79772.
Peekskill city, SE New York; 19,283; ZIP 10566*.
Pekin city, CEN. Illinois; 31,375; ZIP 61554*.
Peking city, N China (mainland); cap.; 7,570,000.
Pelnam Manor vill., SE New York; 6,673.
Pelion mtn. range; SE Thessaly.
Pella city, s CEN. Iowa; 6,668; ZIP 50219.
Peloponnesus penin. betw. Aegean and Ionian seas; one of the main divisions of s Greece; 8,603 sq. mi.; 985,620.
Pembroke town, SE Ontario, Canada; 16,791.
Penang state, NW Malaya; 398 sq. mi.; 776,770; cap. George Town.
Pendleton city, NE Oregon; 13,197; ZIP 97801.
Penetanguishene town, s Ontario, Canada; 5,340.
Penn Hills urb. twp., sw Pennsylvania; 62,886; ZIP see PITTSBURGH.
Pennine Alps sw div. of the Alps on the Swiss-Italian border.
Pennsauken urb. twp., w New Jersey; 36,394; ZIP see CAMDEN.
Penns Grove boro., sw New Jersey; 5,727; ZIP 08069.
Pennsylvania state, E United States; 45,333 sq. mi.; 11,793,909; cap. Harrisburg.
Penn Yan vill., w CEN. New York; 5,168; ZIP 14527.
Pensacola city, NW Florida; site of a U.S. naval and air base; 59,507; ZIP 32501*.
Penticton city, s British Columbia; 13,859.
Peoria city, N CEN. Illinois; 126,963; ZIP 61600*.
Peoria Heights vill., CEN. Illinois; 7,943; ZIP see PEORIA.
Perm city, E USSR; 920,000.
Pernambuco Recife: *an alternate name.*
Perrine uninc. place, SE Florida; 10,257; ZIP see MIAMI.

Perry city, N Florida; 7,701; ZIP 32347.
—city, CEN. Georgia; 7,771; ZIP 31069.
—city, CEN. Iowa; 6,906; ZIP 50220.
—city, N Oklahoma; 5,341; ZIP 73077.
Perrysburg vill., N Ohio; 7,693.
Perryton city, N Texas; 7,810; ZIP 79070.
Perryville city, E Missouri; 5,149; ZIP 63775.
Persia Iran: *the former name.*
Persian Gulf inlet of the Arabian Sea betw. Iran and Arabia.
Perth city, sw Western Australia; cap.; 739,200.
Perth town, SE Ontario, Canada; 5,630.
Perth Amboy port city, E New Jersey; 38,798; ZIP 08861*.
Peru republic, w South America; 533,916 sq. mi.; 13,567,939; cap. Lima.
Peru city, N CEN. Illinois; 11,772; ZIP 61354.
—city, N CEN. Indiana; 14,139; ZIP 46970*.
Petaluma city, w California; 24,870; ZIP 94952*.
Peterborough city, s Ontario, Canada; 58,111.
Petersburg city, SE Virginia; scene of Civil War battles, 1864, 1865; 36,103; ZIP 23801*.
Petoskey city, N Michigan; 6,342; ZIP 49770*.
Petrograd Leningrad: *a former name.*
Pharr city, s Texas; 15,829; ZIP 78577.
Phenix City city, E Alabama; 25,281; ZIP 36867.
Philadelphia city, E CEN. Mississippi; 6,274; ZIP 39350.
—city, SE Pennsylvania; 1,948,609; ZIP 19100*.
Philippines, Republic of the republic occupying the Philippine Islands, a Pacific archipelago SE of China; 115,707 sq. mi.; 36,684,486; cap. Quezon City; seat of administration, Manila.
Phillipsburg city, w New Jersey; 17,849; ZIP 08865*.
Phnom Penh city, s CEN. Cambodia; cap.; 650,000.
Phoenix city, s CEN. Arizona; cap.; 581,562; ZIP 85000*.
Phoenixville boro., SE Pennsylvania; 14,823; ZIP 19460.
Picardy reg. and former prov., N France.
Picayune city, s Mississippi; 10,467; ZIP 39466.
Pico Rivera city, sw California; 54,170; ZIP 90660*.
Piedmont reg., N Italy; 9,817 sq. mi.; 4,434,892; cap. Turin.
Piedmont reg., E United States; extends from New Jersey to Alabama E of the Appalachians; ab. 80,000 sq. mi.
—city, w California; 10,917; ZIP see OAKLAND.
Pierre city, CEN. South Dakota; cap.; 9,699; ZIP 57501.
Pierrefonds town, s Quebec, Canada; 12,171.
Pike's Peak mtn., CEN. Colorado; 14,110 ft.
Pikesville uninc. place, N CEN. Maryland; 25,395; ZIP see BALTIMORE.
Pillars of Hercules 2 promontories on opposite sides of the E end of the Strait of Gibraltar.
Pine Bluff city, CEN. Arkansas; 57,389; ZIP 71601*.
Pine Lawn city, E Missouri; 5,773; ZIP see ST. LOUIS.
Pinellas Park city, w Florida; 22,287; ZIP 33565.
Pineville city, CEN. Louisiana; 8,951; ; ZIP 71360.
Pinole city, w California; 15,850; ZIP 94564.
Pipestone city, sw Minnesota; 5,328; ZIP 56164.
Piqua city, w Ohio; 20,741; ZIP 45356.
Piraeus city, s Greece; 187,362.
Pisa city, NE Italy; noted for its leaning tower; 103,677.
Pitman boro., sw New Jersey; 10,257; ZIP 08071.
Pittsburg city, w California; 20,651; ZIP 94565.
—city, SE Kansas; 20,171; ZIP 66762*.
Pittsburgh city, sw Pennsylvania; 520,117; ZIP 15200*.
Pittsburg West uninc. place, w California; 5,188.
Pittsfield city, w Massachusetts; 57,020; ZIP 01200*.
Pittston city, NE CEN. Pennsylvania; 11,113; ZIP 18640*.
Placentia city, sw California; 21,948; ZIP 92670.
Plainedge uninc. place, SE New York; 10,759.
Plainfield town, CEN. Indiana; 8,211; ZIP 46168.
—city, NE New Jersey; 46,862; ZIP 07060.
Plains urb. twp., NE CEN. Pennsylvania; 6,606; ZIP see WILKES-BARRE.
Plainview vill., SE New York; 33,235; ZIP see HICKSVILLE.
—city, NW Texas; 19,096; ZIP 79072*.

Plant City city, W Florida; 15,451; ZIP 33566.
Plaquemine town, S Louisiana; 7,739; ZIP 70764.
Plate, River Rio de la Plata: *the British name.*
Platte River river, S Nebraska; 310 mi. long.
Plattsburgh city, NE New York; scene of a U.S. naval victory in the War of 1812; 18,715. Also **Plattsburg;** ZIP 12901*.
Plattsmouth city, E Nebraska; 7,371; ZIP 68048.
Platteville city, SW Wisconsin; 9,599; ZIP 53818.
Pleasant Hill uninc. place, W California; 24,610; ZIP see CONCORD.
Pleasant Hills boro., SW Pennsylvania; 10,409; ZIP see PITTSBURGH.
Pleasantville city, SE New Jersey; 13,778; ZIP 08232.
  —vill., SE New York; 7,110; ZIP 10570.
Pleasure Ridge Park uninc. place, N Kentucky; 28,566; ZIP 40158.
Plessisville town, S Quebec, Canada; 6,570.
Plum boro., SW Pennsylvania; 21,932.
Plymouth co. boro. and port, SW England; 249,800.
Plymouth city, N Indiana; 7,661; ZIP 46563.
  —town, E Massachusetts; site of the first settlement in New England; 18,606; ZIP 02360*.
  —city, SE Michigan; 11,758; ZIP 48170.
  —vill., E Minnesota; 17,593.
  —boro., NE CEN. Pennsylvania; 9,536; ZIP 18651.
  —city, E Wisconsin; 5,810; ZIP 53073.
Plymouth Colony colony on the shore of Massachusetts Bay founded by the Pilgrim Fathers in 1620.
Plymouth Rock rock at Plymouth, Massachusetts, on which the Pilgrim Fathers are said to have landed in 1620.
Pnom-Penh see PHNOM PENH.
Pocatello city, Idaho; 40,036; ZIP 83201*.
Pointe-aux-Trembles city, S Quebec, Canada; 21,926.
Pointe-Claire city, S Quebec, Canada; 22,709.
Pointe-Gatineau town, SW Quebec, Canada; 8,854.
Point Pleasant boro., E New Jersey; 15,968.
  —city, W West Virginia; 6,122; ZIP 25550.
Poland republic, N CEN. Europe; 120,359 sq. mi.; 32,749,000; cap. Warsaw.
Polynesia isls. of Oceania, CEN. and SE Pacific, E of Melanesia and Micronesia.
Pomerania reg., N CEN. Europe.
Pomona city, SW California; 87,384; ZIP 91766*.
Pompano Beach city, SE Florida; 37,724; ZIP 33060*.
Pompton Lakes boro., NE New Jersey; 11,397; ZIP 07442.
Ponca City city, N Oklahoma; 25,940; ZIP 74601*.
Ponce city S Puerto Rico; 128,233.
Pontiac city, E CEN. Illinois; 9,031; ZIP 61764.
  —city, SE Michigan; 85,279; ZIP 48053*.
Pont-Viau city, S Quebec, Canada; 16,077.
Poona city, W India; 853,226.
Poplar Bluff city, SE Missouri; 16,653; ZIP 63901.
Popocatepetl dormant volcano, CEN. Mexico; 17,887 ft.
Po River river, N Italy; 405 mi. long.
Portage town, NW Indiana; 19,127; ZIP 46368.
  —city, S CEN. Wisconsin; 7,821; ZIP 53901.
Portage la Prairie city, S Manitoba, Canada; 12,950.
Port Alberni city, SW British Columbia; 11,560.
Portales city, E New Mexico; 10,554; ZIP 88130.
Port Alfred town, S CEN. Quebec, Canada; 9,066.
Port Allen town, SE CEN. Louisiana; 5,728; ZIP 70767.
Port Angeles city, NW Washington; 16,367; ZIP 98362.
Port Arthur-Dairen Lü-ta: *former name.*
Port Arthur city, SE Texas; ZIP 77640*.
Port Arthur see THUNDER BAY.
Port-au-Prince city, S Haiti; cap.; 458,675.
Port Chester vill., SE New York; 25,803; ZIP 10573*.
Port Clinton city, N Ohio; 7,202; ZIP 43452.
Port Colborne town, S Ontario, Canada; 14,886.
Port Coquitlam city, SW British Columbia, Canada; 8,111.
Port Credit town, S Ontario, Canada; 7,203.
Porterville city, S CEN. California; 12,602; ZIP 93257*.
Port Hope town, S Ontario, Canada; 8,091.
Port Hueneme city, SW California; 14,295; ZIP 93041.
Port Huron city, E Michigan; 35,794; ZIP 48060*.
Port Jervis city, SE New York; 8,852; ZIP 12771.
Portland uninc. place, CEN. Connecticut; 8,812; ZIP 06480.
  —city, E Indiana; 7,115; ZIP 47371.
  —city, SW Maine; 65,116; ZIP 04100*.
  —city, NW Oregon; 382,619; ZIP 97200*.

Port Lavaca city, S Texas; 10,491; ZIP 77979.
Port Neches city, SE Texas; 10,894; ZIP 77651.
Pôrto Alegre city, S Brazil; 869,795.
Port-of-Spain city, NW Trinidad; cap. of Trinidad and Tobago; 67,867. Also **Port of Spain.**
Porto-Novo port city, SE Dahomey; cap.; 90,000.
Porto Rico Puerto Rico: *the former name.*
Port Said city, NE Egypt; at the Mediterranean end of the Suez Canal; 313,000.
Portsmouth co. boro., S England; site of the chief British naval station; 200,380.
Portsmouth city, SE New Hampshire; 25,717; ZIP 03801*.
  —city, S Ohio; 27,633; ZIP 45662*.
  —town, SE Rhode Island; 12,521; ZIP 02871.
  —city, SE Virginia; 110,963; ZIP 23700*.
Port Townsend city, NW Washington; 5,241; ZIP 98368.
Portugal republic, SW Europe; 35,419 sq. mi.; 8,744,-248; cap. Lisbon.
Portuguese East Africa Mozambique: *the former name.*
Portuguese Guinea see GUINEA-BISSAU.
Portuguese India former Portuguese overseas prov., W India.
Portuguese West Africa Angola: *an alternate name.*
Port Vue boro., SW Pennsylvania; 5,862; ZIP see MCKEESPORT.
Port Washington uninc. place, SE New York; 15,923; ZIP 11050.
  —city, E Wisconsin; 8,752; ZIP 53074.
Posen Poznan: *the German name.*
Potomac River river betw. Maryland, West Virginia, and Virginia; 287 mi. long.
Potsdam city, CEN. East Germany; scene of a United Nations conference, 1945; 111,933.
Potsdam vill., N New York; 9,985; ZIP 13676.
Pottstown boro., SE Pennsylvania; 25,355; ZIP 19464*.
Pottsville city, E CEN. Pennsylvania; 19,715; ZIP 17901*.
Poughkeepsie city, SE New York; 32,029; ZIP 12600*.
Poznan city, W Poland; 495,200.
Prague city, W Czechoslovakia; cap.; 1,083,717.
Prairie du Chien city, SW Wisconsin; 5,540; ZIP 53821.
Prairie Village city, NE Kansas; 28,138.
Pratt city, S Kansas; 6,736; ZIP 67124.
Prattville city, CEN. Alabama; 13,116; ZIP 36067.
Prescott city, CEN. Arizona; 13,030; ZIP 86301.
Prescott town, SE Ontario, Canada; 5,366.
Presque Isle city, NE Maine; 11,452; ZIP 04769.
Preston town, S Ontario, Canada; 11,577.
Pretoria city, NE CEN. South Africa; adm. cap.; 543,950.
Price city, E CEN. Utah; 6,218; ZIP 84501.
Prichard city, SW Alabama; 41,578; ZIP see MOBILE.
Prince Albert city, CEN. Saskatchewan, Canada; 28,464.
Prince Edward Island prov., NE Canada; 2,184 sq. mi.; 119,000; cap. Charlottetown.
Prince George city, CEN. British Columbia, Canada; 33,101.
Prince Rupert city, W British Columbia, Canada; 11,987.
Princeton city, N CEN. Illinois; 6,959; ZIP 61356.
  — city, SW Indiana; 7,431; ZIP 47570.
  — city, W Kentucky; 6,292; ZIP 42445.
  — boro., W CEN. New Jersey; 12,311; ZIP 08540*.
  — city, S West Virginia; 7,253; ZIP 24740.
Prospect Park boro., NE New Jersey; 5,176.
  — boro., SE Pennsylvania; 7,250; ZIP 19076.
Provence reg. and former prov., SE France.
Providence city, NE Rhode Island; cap.; 179,213; ZIP 02900*.
Provo city, N CEN. Utah; 53,131; ZIP 84601.
Prussia former state, N Germany; dissolved, 1947.
Pryor city, NE Oklahoma; 7,057.
Pueblo city. S CEN. Colorado; 97,453; ZIP 81000*.
Puerto Rico isl., Greater Antilles; self-governing Commonwealth in assoc. with the United States; 3,423 sq. mi.; 2,712,033; cap. San Juan.
Puget Sound inlet of the Pacific, NW Washington.
Pulaski city, S Tennessee; 6,989; ZIP 38478.
  — town, SW Virginia; 10,279; ZIP 24301.
Pullman city, SE Washington; 20,509; ZIP 99163*.
Punjab reg., NW India and Pakistan.
Punxsutawney boro., W CEN. Pennsylvania; 7,792;

ZIP 15767*.
Pusan city, SE South Korea; 1,880,710.
Putnam city, NE Connecticut; 6,918; ZIP 06260.
Puyallup city, W CEN. Washington; 14,742; ZIP 98371*.
Pyongyang city, W North Korea; cap.; ab. 1,500,000.
Pyrenees mtn. chain betw. France and Spain.

Qatar sheikdom under British protection, on the W coast of the Persian Gulf; ab. 8,500 sq. mi.; 160,000; cap. Doha.
Quakertown boro., SE Pennsylvania; 7,276; ZIP 18951.
Quebec prov., E Canada; 594,860 sq. mi.; 6,188,000.
— city, S Quebec prov.; cap.; 186,088. Also **Québec.**
Quebec-W. town, S Quebec, Canada; 8,733. Also **Quebec-West.**
Queens boro., E New York City; 113 sq. mi.; 1,986,473.
Queensland state, NE Australia; 670,500 sq. mi.; 1,823,362; cap. Brisbane.
Quemoy Islands 2 isls. of the Republic of China in Formosa Strait; 54 sq. mi.
Quezon City city, N CEN. Philippines; cap.; 780,700.
Quincy city, NW Florida; 8,334; ZIP 32351*.
—city, W Illinois; 45,288; ZIP 62301*.
Quincy city, E Massachusetts; 87,966; ZIP see BOSTON.
Quito city, N CEN. Ecuador; cap.; 564,900.

Rabat city, N Morocco; cap.; 530,366.
Racine city, SE Wisconsin; 95,162; ZIP 53400*.
Radford city, SW Virginia; 11,596; ZIP 24141*.
Radnor urb. twp., SE Pennsylvania; 26,118.
— See WOODBINE-RADNOR-GLENCLIFF.
Rahway city, NE New Jersey; 29,114; ZIP 07065*.
Rainier, Mount extinct volcano, Cascade Range, SW Washington; 14,408 ft.
Raleigh city, CEN. North Carolina; cap.; 121,577; ZIP 27600*.
Ramsey boro., NE New Jersey; 12,571; ZIP 07446.
Rancho Cordova uninc. place, CEN. California; 30,451; ZIP 95670.
Randolph town, E Massachusetts; 27,035; ZIP 02368.
Rangoon city, S Burma; cap.; 2,100,000.
Rantoul vill., E CEN. Illinois; 25,562; ZIP 61866*.
Rapid City city, SW South Dakota; 43,836; ZIP 57701*.
Raritan boro., N CEN. New Jersey; 6,691; ZIP 08869.
Raton city, NE New Mexico; 6,962; ZIP 87740.
Ravenna city, NE Ohio; 11,780; ZIP 44266.
Rawalpindi city, N Pakistan; provisional cap.; 615,000.
Rawlins city, S CEN. Wyoming; 7,855; ZIP 82301.
Raymondville city, S Texas; 7,987; ZIP 78580.
Rayne city, S Louisiana; 9,510; ZIP 70578.
Raytown city, W Missouri; 33,632; ZIP see KANSAS CITY.
Reading town, NE Massachusetts 22,539; ZIP 01867.
—city, SW Ohio; 14,303; ZIP see CINCINNATI.
—city, SE Pennsylvania; 87,643; ZIP 19600*.
Recife city, NE Brazil; 1,046,454.
Red Bank boro., E New Jersey; 12,847; ZIP 07701*.
Red Bank-White Oak city, SE Tennessee; 12,715.
Red Bluff city, N California; 7,676; ZIP 96080.
Red Deer city, S CEN. Alberta, Canada; 19,612.
Redding city, N California; 16,659; ZIP 96001*.
Redlands city, SW California; 36,355; ZIP 92373*.
Red Lion boro., S Pennsylvania; 5,645; ZIP 17356.
Red Oak city, SW Iowa; 6,210; ZIP 51566.
Redondo Beach city, SW California; 56,075; ZIP 90277*.
Red River 1. river in Texas, Arkansas, and Louisiana; 1,018 mi. long. 2. river in the United States and Canada; 540 mi. long.
Red Sea sea betw. Egypt and Arabia; 1,450 mi. long; ab. 170,000 sq. mi.
Red Wing city, SE Minnesota; 10,441; ZIP 55066.
Redwood City city, W California; 55,686; ZIP 94061*.
Reedley city, CEN. California; 8,131; ZIP 93654.
Regina city, S Saskatchewan, Canada; cap.; 139,469.
Reidsville city, N North Carolina; 13,636; ZIP 27320.
Reims city, NE France; site of a famous cathedral; 152,967.
Relay See ARBUTUS-HALETHORPE-RELAY.
Renfrew town, SE Ontario, Canada; 8,935.

Reno city, W Nevada; 72,863; ZIP 89500*.
Rensselaer city, E New York; 10,136; ZIP 12144.
Renton city, W CEN. Washington; 25,258; ZIP 98055.
Repentigny town, S Quebec, Canada; 9,139.
Reserve uninc. place, SE Louisiana; 6,381; ZIP 70084.
Réunion French overseas dept.; isl., E of Madagascar; 970 sq. mi.; 466,400; cap. Saint-Denis.
Revere city, E Massachusetts; 43,159; ZIP see BOSTON.
Reykjavik city, SW Iceland; cap.; 81,000.
Reynoldsburg vill., CEN. Ohio; 13,921; ZIP 43068.
Rheims Reims: an alternate name.
Rhine river W CEN. Europe; 810 mi. long.
Rhinelander city, N Wisconsin; 8,218; ZIP 54501.
Rhode Island state, NE United States; 1,214 sq. mi.; 946,725; cap. Providence.
Rhodes isl. of the Dodecanese group; 545 sq. mi.
Rhodesia British depen., S CEN. Africa; unilaterally declared its independence in 1965; 150,333 sq. mi.; 5,780,000; cap. Salisbury.
Rhodesia and Nyasaland, Federation of former political association of N. and S. Rhodesia and Nyasaland.
Rhône river, Switzerland and SE France; 504 mi. long. Also **Rhone.**
Rialto city, S California; 28,370; ZIP 92376.
Rice Lake city, NW Wisconsin; 7,278; ZIP 54868.
Richardson city, N Texas; 48,582; ZIP 75080*.
Richfield vill., E Minnesota; 47,231; ZIP see MINNEAPOLIS.
Richland city, S Washington; 26,290; ZIP 99352.
Richland Hills town, N Texas; 8,865; ZIP see FORT WORTH.
Richmond city, W California; 79,043; ZIP 94800*.
—city, E Indiana; 43,999; ZIP 47374.
—city, CEN. Kentucky; 16,861; ZIP 40475*.
—boro., SE New York City; 295,443.
—city, E CEN. Virginia; cap.; cap. of the Confederacy 1861–65; 249,621; ZIP 93200*.
Richmond Heights city, E Missouri; 13,802; ZIP see SAINT LOUIS.
—vill., N Ohio; 9,220; ZIP see CLEVELAND.
Richmond Hill town, S Ontario, Canada; 16,446.
Ridgecrest uninc. place, S California; 7,629; ZIP 93555*.
Ridgefield boro., NE New Jersey; 11,308; ZIP 07657.
Ridgefield Park urb. twp., NE New Jersey; 14,453; ZIP 07660.
Ridgewood urb. twp., NE New Jersey; 27,547; ZIP 07450*.
Ridgway boro., N CEN. Pennsylvania; 6,022; ZIP 15853.
Ridley urb. twp., SE Pennsylvania; 39,085.
Ridley Park boro., SE Pennsylvania; 9,025; ZIP 19078.
Rif mtn. range, N Morocco. Also **Riff.**
Riga city, CEN. Latvian SSR; cap; 776,000.
Rijeka city, NW Yugoslavia; including its SE suburb and officially called **Rijeka-Susak** 132,222.
Rimouski town, E Quebec, Canada; 17,739.
Rio de Janeiro city, SE Brazil; former cap.; 4,252,009. Also **Rio.**
Río de la Plata estuary of the Paraná and Uruguay rivers betw. Argentina and Uruguay; 170 mi. long.
Río de Oro terr., Spanish Sahara; 73,362 sq. mi.; ab. 157,000 cap. Villa Cisneros.
Rio Grande river betw. Texas and Mexico; 1,890 mi. long.
Rio Grande City uninc. place, S Texas; 5,676; ZIP 98582.
Río Muni Spanish overseas prov., W Africa; 10,039 sq. mi.; 185,000 cap. Bata.
Ripon city, E CEN. Wisconsin; 7,053; ZIP 54971.
Rittman vill., NE CEN. Ohio; 6,308; ZIP 44270.
Riverdale vill., NE Illinois; 15,806; ZIP see CHICAGO.
River Edge boro., NE New Jersey; 12,850; ZIP 07661.
River Forest vill., NE Illinois; 13,402; ZIP see OAK PARK.
River Grove vill., NE Illinois; 11,465; ZIP 60171.
Riverhead uninc. place, SE New York; 7,585; ZIP 11901*.
River Oaks city, N Texas; 8,193; ZIP See HOUSTON.
River Rouge city, SE Michigan; 15,947; ZIP see DETROIT.
Riverside city, SW California; 140,089; ZIP 92501*.
—vill., NE Illinois; 10,432; ZIP 60546*.
—urb. twp. W New Jersey; 8,616; ZIP 08075*.
Riverside town; S Ontario, Canada; 18,089.

Riverton city, w CEN. Wyoming; 7,995; ZIP 82501.
Riverview city, SE Michigan; 11,342; ZIP see WYAN-DOTTE.
Riviera coastal strip; on the Mediterranean from Hyères, France to La Spezia, Italy.
Riviera Beach town, SE Florida; 21,401; ZIP see WEST PALM BEACH.
Riviere-des-Prairies town, S Quebec, Canada; 10,054.
Riviere-du-Loup city, SE Quebec, Canada; 10,835.
Roanoke city, E Alabama; 5,251; ZIP 36274.
—city, w Virginia; 92,115; ZIP 24001*.
Roanoke Island isl. off North Carolina; 12 mi. long, 3 mi. wide.
Roanoke Rapids city, NE North Carolina; 13,508; ZIP 27870.
Robbins vill., NE Illinois; 9,641; ZIP 60472.
Robbinsdale city, E Minnesota; 16,845; ZIP see MINNEAPOLIS.
Roberval city, S CEN. Quebec, Canada; 7,739.
Robinson city, SE Illinois; 7,178; ZIP 62454*.
Robla See DEL PASO HEIGHTS-ROBLA.
Robstown city, S Texas; 11,217; ZIP 61068.
Rochelle city, N Illinois; 8,594; ZIP 61068.
Rochelle Park urb. twp., NE New Jersey; 6,380; ZIP 07662*.
Rochester vill., SE Michigan; 7,054; ZIP 48063*.
—city, SE Minnesota; 53,766; ZIP 55901.
—city, SE New Hampshire; 17,938; ZIP 03867.
—city, w New York; 296,233; ZIP 14600*.
—boro., w Pennsylvania; 4,819; ZIP 15074.
Rockaway boro., N New Jersey; 6,383; ZIP 07866.
Rockdale See WOODLAWN-ROCKDALE-MILLFORD MILLS.
Rock Falls city, NW Illinois; 10,287; ZIP 61071.
Rockford city, N Illinois; 147,370; ZIP 61100.
Rock Hill city, E Missouri; 7,275; ZIP see ST.LOUIS.
—city, N South Carolina; 33,846; ZIP 39730*.
Rockingham town, S North Carolina; 5,852; ZIP 28379.
Rock Island city, NW Illinois; 50,166; ZIP 61201*.
Rockland town, E Massachusetts; 15,674; ZIP 02370.
—city, S Maine; 8,505; ZIP 04841.
Rock Springs city, SW Wyoming; 11,657; ZIP 82901.
Rockville city, N CEN. Connecticut; 9,478; ZIP 06066.
—city, w CEN. Maryland; 41,564; ZIP 20850*.
Rockville Centre vill., SE New York; 27,444; ZIP 11570*.
Rockwood city, E Tennessee; 5,259; ZIP 37854.
Rocky Mount city, E CEN. North Carolina 34,284; ZIP 27801*.
Rocky Mountains mtn. system, w North America, extends from the Arctic to Mexico.
Rocky River city, N Ohio; 22,958; ZIP see CLEVELAND.
Rodgers Forge See STONELEIGH-RODGERS FORGE.
Roeland Park city, E Kansas; 9,974.
Rogers city, NW Arkansas; 11,050; ZIP 72756.
Rolla city, CEN. Missouri; 13,245; ZIP 65401.
Rolling Meadows city, NE Illinois; 19,178; ZIP see ARLINGTON HEIGHTS.
Rolling Mill Park See ONEIDA-ROLLING MILL PARK.
Romania Rumania: an alternate form.
Rome city, w Italy; cap.; site of the Vatican City; cap. of the former Roman republic, the Roman Empire, and the States of the Church; 2,778,872.
Rome city, NW Georgia; 30,759; ZIP 30161*.
—city, CEN. New York; 50,148; ZIP 13440*.
Roosevelt uninc. place, SE New York; 15,008; ZIP 11575.
Rosario city, E CEN. Argentina; 798,292.
Rosedale uninc. place, N CEN. Ohio; 8,204.
Roselle boro., NE New Jersey; 22,585; ZIP see ELIZABETH.
Roselle Park boro., NE New Jersey; 14,277; ZIP see ELIZABETH.
Rosemead city, SW California; 40,972; ZIP 91770*.
Rosemere town, S Quebec, Canada; 6,158.
Rosenberg city, SE Texas; 12,098; ZIP 77471.
Roseville city, CEN. California; 17,895; ZIP 95678.
—city, SE Michigan; 60,529; ZIP 48066.
—vill., SE Minnesota; 34,518; ZIP see SAINT PAUL.
Ross urb. twp., SW Pennsylvania; 32,892.
Rostov-on-Don city, SW RSFSR; 867,000.
Roswell city, SE New Mexico; 33,908; ZIP 88201*.
Rotterdam city, w Netherlands; 670,060.
Rotterdam uninc. place, E New York; 25,153; ZIP see SCHENECTADY.
Rouen city, N France; site of a famous cathedral;

scene of the burning of Joan of Arc; 120,471.
Roumania Rumania: an alternate form.
Round Lake Beach vill., NE Illinois; 5,011.
Rouyn city, w Quebec, Canada; 18,716.
Roxboro city, N North Carolina; 5,370; ZIP 27573.
Roxboro town, S Quebec, Canada; 6,298.
Roy city, N Utah; 14,356; ZIP 84067.
Royal Oak city, SE Michigan; 85,499; ZIP 48067*.
Ruanda-Urundi former UN Trust terr., CEN. Africa. See BURUNDI, RWANDA.
Rubicon river, N CEN. Italy; 15 mi. long.
Rugby municipal boro., CEN. England; site of a boys' school; 59,400.
Ruhr river, w West Germany; 142 mi. long.
—reg. S of the Ruhr; an industrial and coal-mining district.
Rumania republic, SE Europe; 91,671 sq. mi.; ab. 20,470,000; cap. Bucharest.
Rumford uninc. place, SW Maine; 9,363; ZIP 04276.
Rumson boro., E New Jersey; 7,421; ZIP 07760*.
Runnemede boro., SW New Jersey; 10,475; ZIP 08078.
Rushville city, E CEN. Indiana; 6,686; ZIP 46173.
Russell city, CEN. Kansas; 5,371; ZIP 67665.
Russellville city, NW Alabama; 7,814; ZIP 35653*.
—city, NE CEN. Arkansas; 11,750; ZIP 72801*.
—city, S Kentucky; 6,456; ZIP 42276.
Russia before 1917, an empire, E Europe and N Asia; cap. Saint Petersburg (Petrograd). See RUSSIAN SOVIET FEDERATED SOCIALIST REPUBLIC, UNION OF SOVIET SOCIALIST REPUBLICS. SOVIET FEDERATED SOCIALIST REPUBLIC, UNION OF SOVIET SOCIALIST REPUBLICS.
Russian Soviet Federated Socialist Republic constituent republic, N USSR; 6,592,800 sq. mi.; 130,090,000; cap. Moscow.
Ruston city, N Louisiana; 17,365; ZIP 71270*.
Rutherford boro., NE New Jersey; 20,802; ZIP 07070*.
Rutland city, S CEN. Vermont; 19,293; ZIP 05701*.
Rwanda republic, CEN. Africa; 10,169 sq. mi. 3,984,000; cap. Kigali.
Rye city, SE New York; 15,869; ZIP 10580.
Ryukyu Islands isl group betw. Kyushu and Taiwan; 2,046 sq. mi.; 953,000; chief isl. Okinawa; jointly adm. by Japan and the United States.

Saar river, NE France and w Germany; 152 mi. long.
Saar, The state, w West Germany; 989 sq. mi.; 1,127,400; cap. Saarbrücken. Also, **Saarland.**
Saco city, SW Maine; 11,678; ZIP 04072.
Sacramento city, N CEN. California; cap.; 254,413; ZIP 95801*.
Sacramento River river, N CEN. California; 382 mi. long.
Saddle Brook urb. twp., NE New Jersey; 15,098; ZIP see ROCHELLE PARK.
Saginaw city, E CEN. Michigan; 91,849; ZIP 48601*.
Sahara desert area, N Africa; ab. 3,500,000 sq. mi. Also **Sahara Desert.**
Saigon city, S South Vietnam; cap.; 1,825,297.
Saipan one of the Mariana isls.; 47 sq. mi.; captured from Japan by U.S. forces in World War II, 1944.
Sakhalin isl., SE RSFSR; 29,700 sq. mi.; 649,000; adm. ctr. Yuzhno-Sakhalinsk.
Saint, Sainte See entries beginning ST., STE.
Salamanca city, SW New York; 7,877; ZIP 14779.
Salem city, S CEN. Illinois; 6,187; ZIP 62881.
— city, NE Massachusetts; 40,556; ZIP 01970*.
— city, SW New Jersey; 7,648; ZIP 08079.
— city, E Ohio; 14,186; ZIP 44460*.
—city, NW Oregon; cap.; 68,296; ZIP 97301*.
— town, SW CEN. Virginia; 21,982; ZIP 24153.
Salem Heights uninc. place, NW Oregon; 10,770.
Salerno city, SW Italy; scene of a battle in World War II betw. Germans and Allied landing forces, 1943; 154,481.
Salina city, CEN. Kansas; 37,714; ZIP 67401*.
Salinas city, w California; 58,896; ZIP 93901*.
Salisbury city, SE Maryland; 15,252; ZIP 21801.
— city, w CEN. North Carolina; 22,515; ZIP 28144.
Salonika city, NE Greece; 345,799.
Salt Lake City city, N CEN. Utah; cap.; 175,885; ZIP 84100*.
Salvador city, E Brazil; 998,258.
Salvador See EL SALVADOR.

Salzburg city, W Austria; birthplace of Mozart; 128,845.

Samar one of the Visayan isls., Philippines; 5,050 sq. mi.

Samarkand city, E Uzbek SSR; 293,000.

Samoa isl. group SW Pacific; 1,209 sq. mi.; divided into **American** (or **Eastern**) **Samoa**, an uninc. terr. of the United States; 76 sq. mi.; 24,973; cap. Pago Pago; and **Western Samao**, an independent state; 1,133 sq. mi.; 146,635; cap. Apia.

Samos isl. of Greece, E Aegean; 194 sq. mi.

Samothrace isl. of Greece, NE Aegean; 71 sq. mi.

San Angelo city, W CEN. Texas; 63,884; ZIP 76901*.

San Anselmo city, W California; 13,031; ZIP 94960.

San Antonio city, S CEN. Texas; site of the Alamo; 654,153; ZIP 78200*.

San Benito city, S Texas; 15,176; ZIP 78586.

San Bernardino city, SW California; 104,251; ZIP 92400*.

San Bruno city, W California; 36,254; ZIP 94066*.

San Buenaventura city, SW California; 29,114; ZIP 93001*.

San Carlos city, W California; 25,924; ZIP 94070*.

San Clemente city, S California; 17,063; ZIP 92672.

Sandersville city, E CEN. Georgia; 5,546; ZIP 31082.

San Diego city, SW California; 696,769; ZIP 92100.

Sand Springs city, NE Oklahoma; 11,519; ZIP 74063.

Sandusky city, N Ohio; 32,674; ZIP 44870*.

Sandwich Islands Hawaiian Islands: *the former name.*

San Fernando city, SW California; 16,571; ZIP 91340*.

Sanford city, E CEN. Florida; 17,393; ZIP 32771.
— uninc. place, SW Maine; 15,812; ZIP 04073.
— city, CEN. North Carolina; 11, 716; ZIP 27330*.

San Francisco city, W California; 715,674; ZIP 94100*.

San Francisco Bay inlet of the Pacific, W California.

San Gabriel city, SW California; 29,176; ZIP 91775*.

Sanger city, CEN. California; 10,088; ZIP 93657.

San Germán town, SW Puerto Rico; 11,613; ZIP 00753.

San Joaquin River river, S CEN. California; 317 mi. long.

San José city, CEN. Costa Rica; cap.; 395,401.

San Jose city, W California; 445,779; ZIP 95100*.

San Juan city, NE Puerto Rico; cap.; 452,749; ZIP 00900*.

San Leandro city, W California; 68,698; ZIP 94577*.

San Lorenzo uninc. place, W California; 24,633; ZIP 94580.

San Lorenzo town, E Puerto Rico; 7,702; ZIP 00754.

San Luis Obispo city, W California; 28,036; ZIP 93401*.

San Marcos city, S CEN. Texas; 18,860; ZIP 78666.

San Marino republic, an enclave in NE Italy; 23 sq. mi.; 17,000.
—city, San Marino; cap.; 2,621.

San Marino city, SW California; 14,177; ZIP see PASADENA.

San Mateo city, W California; 78,991; ZIP 94400*.

San Pablo city, W California; 21,461; ZIP see RICHMOND.

San Pedro uninc. place, S Texas; 7,634.

San Rafael city, W California; 38,977; ZIP 94901*.

San Remo uninc. place, SE New York; 8,302.

San Salvador city, S El Salvador; cap.; 337,171.

San Salvador isl., CEN. Bahamas; site of Columbus' first landing in the western hemisphere, 1492.

Santa Ana city, SW California; 156,601; ZIP 92700*.

Santa Barbara city, SW California; 70,215; ZIP 93100*.

Santa Catalina isl. off SW California; 70 sq. mi.

Santa Clara city, W California; 87,717; ZIP 95050*.

Santa Cruz city, W California; 32,076; ZIP 95060*.

Santa Fe city, N New Mexico; cap.; 41,167; ZIP 87501*.

Santa Fe Springs city, SW California; 14,750; ZIP 90670.

Santa Fe Trail trade route, important from 1821–80, betw. Independence, Missouri, and Santa Fe, New Mexico.

Santa Maria city, SW California; 32,749; ZIP 93454*.

Santa Monica city, SW California; 88,289; ZIP 90400*.

Santa Paula city, SW California; 18,001; ZIP 93060.

Santa Rosa city, W California; 50,006; ZIP 95401*.

Santiago city, CEN. Chile; cap.; 2,661,920. Also **Santi-** ago de Chile.

Santo Domingo city, S Dominican Republic; cap.; 671,402.
—Dominican republic: *the former name.*

São Paulo city, SE Brazil; 5,186,752.

São Salvador Salvador: *the former name.*

Sapporo city, W Hokkaido, Japan; 1,010,123.

Sapulpa city, NE CEN. Oklahoma; 15,159; ZIP 74066.

Sarejevo city, CEN. Yugoslavia; scene of the assassination of Archduke Franz Ferdinand, June 28, 1914; 243,980.

Saranac Lake vill., N New York; 6,086; ZIP 12983.

Saranap uninc. place, W California; 6,450.

Sarasota city, SW Florida; 40,237; ZIP 33577*.

Saratoga city, W California; 27,110; ZIP 95070.

Saratoga Springs city, E New York; 18,845; ZIP 12866.

Saratov city, SE USSR; 820,000.

Sarawak part of Malaysia on NW Borneo; 47,071 sq. mi., 968,997; cap. Kuching.

Sardinia isl., E CEN. Mediterranean; with adjacent isls. a reg. of Italy; 9,298 sq. mi.; 1,468,737; cap. Cagliari.

Sarnia city, S Ontario, Canada; 57,644.

Saskatchewan prov., W CEN. Canada; 251,700 sq. mi.; 918,000; cap. Regina.

Saskatoon city, S CEN. Saskatchewan, Canada; 126,449.

Saudi Arabia kingdom N and CEN. Arabia; 927,000 sq. mi.; 8,199,000; caps. Mecca and Riyadh.

Saugus town, NE Massachusetts; 25,110; ZIP see LYNN.

Sault Sainte Marie city, N Michigan; 15,136; ZIP 49783*.

Sault Sainte Marie city, S CEN. Ontario, Canada; 80,332. Also **Sault Ste. Marie.**

Sault Saint Marie Canals 3 canals that circumvent the rapids in the St. Marys River betw. Lakes Superior and Huron.

Sausalito city, W California; 6,158; ZIP 94965.

Savannah city, E Georgia; 118,349; ZIP 31400*.

Saxony reg. and former duchy, electorate, kingdom and prov.; cen. Germany.

Sayre boro., NE Pennsylvania; 7,473; ZIP 18840.

Sayreville boro., E New Jersey; 32,508; ZIP 08872.

Scandinavia reg., NW Europe; includes Sweden, Norway, and Denmark and sometimes Finland, Iceland, and the Faroe Islands.

Scapa Flow sea basin and British naval base in the Orkney Islands, Scotland; 50 sq. mi.

Scarsdale town, SE New York; 19,229; ZIP 10583*.

Scheldt river, N France, Belgium and the Netherlands; 270 mi. long.

Schenectady city, E New York; 77,859; ZIP 12300*.

Schiller Park vill., NE Illinois; 12,712; ZIP 60176.

Schleswig-Holstein state, NE West Germany; 6,052 sq. mi.; 2,543,200; cap. Kiel.

Schuylkill Haven boro., E CEN. Pennsylvania; 6,125; ZIP see PHILADELPHIA.

Schuylkill River river, SE Pennsylvania; 130 mi. long.

Scotch Plains urb. twp., NE New Jersey; 22,279; ZIP 07076.

Scotia vill., E New York; 8,224; ZIP see SCHENECTADY.

Scotland A political div. and the N part of Great Britain; a separate kingdom until 1707; 30,405 sq. mi.; 5,227,706; cap. Edinburgh.

Scott urb. twp., SW Pennsylvania; 21,856.

Scottdale boro., SW Pennsylvania; 5,818; ZIP 15683.

Scottsbluff city, W Nebraska; 14,507; ZIP 69361.

Scottsboro city, NE Alabama; 9,324; ZIP 35768*.

Scottsdale city, SE CEN. Arizona; 67,823; ZIP 85251*.

Scranton city, NE Pennsylvania; 103,564; ZIP 18500*.

Sea Cliff vill., SE New York; 5,890; ZIP 11579.

Seaford uninc. place, SE New York; 17,379; ZIP 11783.

Seal Beach city, SW California; 24,441; ZIP 90740.

Searcy city, CEN. Arkansas; 9,040; ZIP 72143*.

Seaside city, W California; 35,935; ZIP 93955.

Seat Pleasant town, S CEN. Maryland; 7,217; ZIP see WASHINGTON, D.C.

Seattle city, W CEN. Washington; 530,831; ZIP 98100*.

Sebastopol See SEVASTOPOL.

Sebring city, S CEN. Florida; 7,223; ZIP 33870.

Secaucus town, NE New Jersey; 12,229; ZIP see WEST NEW YORK.

Security uninc. place, E CEN. Colorado; 15,297; ZIP see COLORADOO SPRINGS.

Sedalia city, W CEN. Missouri; 22,847; ZIP 65301*.

Seguin city, S CEN. Texas; 15,934; ZIP 78155.

Seine river, NE France; 482 mi. long.
Selkirk town, SE Manitoba, Canada; 8,576.
Selma city, S CEN. Alabama; 27,379; ZIP 36701*.
—city, CEN. California; 7,459; ZIP 93662.
Semarang city, N Java, Indonesia; 646,590.
Seminole city, CEN. Oklahoma; 7,878; ZIP 74868.
—city, NW Texas; 5,007; ZIP 79360.
Seneca town, NW South Carolina; 6,027; ZIP 29678.
Seneca Falls vill., W CEN. New York; 7,794; ZIP 13148.
Senegal river, NW Africa; ab. 1,000 mi. long.
Senegal, Republic of republic, NW Africa; 76,084 sq. mi.; 4,022,000; cap. Dakar.
Seoul city, NW South Korea; cap.; 5,536,377.
Sept-Iles city, E Quebec, Canada; 14,196.
Serbia constituent republic, E Yugoslavia; 34,107 sq. mi.; 8,432,108; cap., Belgrade.
Sevastopol city, S Crimea, USSR; 259,000.
Seven Hills vill., N Ohio; 12,700.
Severn river, N Wales and W England; 210 mi. long.
Seville city, SW Spain; 545,700.
Sèvres city, N France; 20,025.
Sewickley boro., SW Pennsylvania; 5,660; ZIP 15143.
Seymour town, SW Connecticut; 12,776; 06483.
—city, S Indiana; 13,352; ZIP 47274.
Shadyside vill., SE Ohio; 5,070; ZIP 43947.
Shaker Heights city, N Ohio; 36,306; ZIP see CLEVELAND.
Shakopee city, SE Minnesota; 6,876; ZIP 55379.
Shaler urb. twp., SW Pennsylvania; 33,369.
Shamokin boro., E CEN. Pennsylvania; 11,719; ZIP 17872.
Shanghai city, E China; 10,820,000.
Shannon river, CEN. Ireland; 224 mi. long.
Shannontown uninc. place, E CEN. South Carolina; 7,491.
Shantung province, NE China; 55,000 sq. mi.; 54,030,000; cap. Tsinan.
Sharon uninc. place, E Massachusetts; 12,367; ZIP 02067.
—city, W Pennsylvania; 22,653; ZIP 16146*.
Sharon Hill boro., SE Pennsylvania; 7,464; ZIP 19079*.
Sharpsburg boro., SW Pennsylvania; 5,499; ZIP see PITTSBURGH.
Sharpsville boro., W Pennsylvania; 6,126; ZIP 16150.
Shasta, Mount extinct volcano, Cascade Range, N California; 14,162 ft.
Shawano city, E Wisconsin; 6,488; ZIP 54166.
Shawinigan city, S Quebec, Canada; 11,470.
Shawinigan-S. vill., S Quebec, Canada; 12,683. Also **Shawinigan-South.**
Shawnee city, NE Kansas; 20,482.
—city, CEN. Oklahoma; 25,075; ZIP 74801*.
Sheboygan city, E Wisconsin; 48,484; ZIP 53081*.
Sheffield co. boro., N CEN. England; 519,703.
Sheffield city, NW Alabama; 13,115; ZIP 35660*.
Sheffield Lake vill., N Ohio; 8,734; ZIP see LORAIN.
Shelby city, SW North Carolina; 16,328; ZIP 28150.
—city, N CEN. Ohio; 9,847; ZIP 44875.
Shelbyville city, SE CEN. Indiana; 15,094; ZIP 46176.
—town, S CEN. Tennessee; 12,262; ZIP 37160.
Shelton city, SW Connecticut; 27,165; ZIP 06484*.
—city, W Washington; 6,165; ZIP 98584.
Shenandoah river, N Virginia and NE West Virginia; 55 mi. long.
—city, SW Iowa; 5,968; ZIP 51601.
—boro., E CEN. Pennsylvania; 8,287; ZIP 17976.
Shenyang city, NE China; 2,411,000.
Sherbrooke city, S Quebec, Canada; 80,711.
Sheridan city, N Wyoming; 10,856; ZIP 82801.
Sherman city, N Texas; 29,061; ZIP 75090*.
Sherwood Forest forest, NE CEN. England; known as the home of Robin Hood.
Shetland Islands isl. group NE of the Orkney Islands, comprising **Shetland**, a co. of Scotland; 551 sq. mi.; 17,327; cap. Lerwick.
Shikoku isl., SW Japan; 7,248 sq. mi.; 3,910,000.
Shillington boro., SE CEN. Pennsylvania; 6,249; ZIP see READING.
Shiloh national military park, SW Tennessee; scene of a Union victory in the Civil War, 1862; 6 sq. mi.
Shippensburg boro., S Pennsylvania; 6,536; ZIP 17257.
Shively city, N Kentucky; 19,223; ZIP see LOUISVILLE.
Shoreview vill., E Minnesota; 11,034.

Shorewood vill.. SE Wisconsin; 15,576; ZIP see MILWAUKEE.
Shreveport city, NW Louisiana; 182,064; ZIP 71100*.
Shropshire co., W England; 1,347 sq. mi:; 336,934; cap. Shrewsbury.
Siam Thailand: *the former name.*
Siam, Gulf of part of the South China Sea betw. the Malay Peninsula and Indochina.
Sian city, E CEN. People's Republic of China; 1,310,000.
Siberia reg., E RSFSR; ab. 5 million sq. mi.
Sicily isl. of Italy, CEN. Mediterranean; comprises with neighboring islands a reg. 9,926 sq. mi.; 4,667,316; cap. Palermo.
Sidney city, W Nebraska; 6,403; ZIP 69162.
— city, W Ohio; 16,332; ZIP 45365.
Sierra Leone republic, member of the Commonwealth of Nations, W Africa; 27,925 sq. mi.; 2,600,000. cap. Freetown.
Sierra Madre city, SW California; 12,140; ZIP 91024.
Sierra Nevada mtn. range, E California.
Sikeston city, SE Missouri; 14,699; ZIP 63801.
Silesia reg., E CEN. Europe; divided betw. Czechoslovakia and Poland.
Sillery city, S Quebec, Canada; 14,109.
Silsbee city, E Texas; 7,271; ZIP 77656.
Silver City town, SW New Mexico; 7,751; ZIP 88061.
Silver Hills See SUITLAND-SILVER HILLS.
Silver Spring uninc. place, W Maryland; 77,496; ZIP 20900*.
Silverton vill., SW Ohio; 6,588.
Simcoe town, S Ontario, Canada; 8,754.
Simla city, N India; ab. 46,000
Sinai penin., E Egypt, betw. the Mediterranean and the Red Sea.
Singapore isl. off the tip of the Malay Peninsula; republic, member of the Commonwealth of Nations; 225 sq. mi.; 2,110,000.
—city, S Singapore; cap.
Sing Sing state prison near Ossining, New York.
Sinkiang-Uigur Autonomous Region div., NW China; 642,252 sq. mi.; 8,000,000; cap., Urumchi (Tihwa): also formerly **Sinkiang.**
Sinton town, S Texas; 5,563; ZIP 78387.
Sioux City city, W Iowa; 85,925; ZIP 51100*.
Sioux Falls city, SE South Dakota; 72,488; ZIP 57100*.
Skokie vill., NE Illinois; 68,627; ZIP 60076*.
Skowhegan uninc. place, SW Maine; 7,601; ZIP 04976.
Slaton city, NW Texas; 6,583; ZIP 79364.
Slavonia reg., N Yugoslavia.
Slidell town, SE Louisiana; 16,101; ZIP 70458.
Sloan vill., W New York; 5,216.
Slovakia reg. and former prov., E Czechoslovakia.
Slovenia constituent republic, NW Yugoslavia; 7,717 sq. mi.; 1,697,499; cap. Ljubljana.
Smithfield town, E CEN. North Carolina; 6,677; ZIP 27577.
Smith Falls town, SE Ontario, Canada; 9,603.
Smoky Mountains See GREAT SMOKY MOUNTAINS.
Smyrna city, W Turkey; 590,997. Also **Izmir.**
Smyrna town, NW CEN. Georgia; 19,157; ZIP 79549.
Snyder city, NW CEN. Texas; 11,171; ZIP 79549.
Society Islands isl. group, French Polynesia; ab. 650 sq. mi.; 100,270.
Socorro city, W CEN. New Mexico; 4,687; ZIP 87801.
Sofia city, W Bulgaria; cap.; 919,037.
Solomon Islands isl. group, SW Pacific; ab. 16,500 sq. mi.; including the British Solomon Islands, a depen.; ab. 11,500 sq. mi.; 152,000; cap. Honiara.
Solon vill., N Ohio; 11,519; ZIP see CLEVELAND.
Solvay vill., CEN. New York; 8,280; ZIP see SYRACUSE.
Somalia republic, E Africa; 262,000 sq. mi.; 3,100,000; cap. Mogadishu.
Somerset city, S Kentucky; 10,436; ZIP 42501.
—town, SE Massachusetts; 18,088; ZIP see FALL RIVER.
—boro., SW Pennsylvania; 6,269; ZIP 15501.
Somersworth city, SE New Hampshire; 9,026; ZIP 03878.
Somerville city, E Massachusetts; 88,779; ZIP see BOSTON.
—boro., N CEN. New Jersey; 13,652; ZIP 08876.
Somme river, N France; 150 mi. long.

Soo Canals *informal* Sault Sainte Marie Canals.
Sorel city, s Quebec, Canada; 17,147.
Souderton boro., SE Pennsylvania; 6,366; ZIP 18964.
South Africa, Republic of republic, s Africa; 472,359 sq. mi.; 24,300,000; seat of government Pretoria; seat of legislature Cape Town.
South Amboy city, E New Jersey; 9,338; ZIP 08879.
South America s continent, Western Hemisphere; ab. 6,900,000 sq. mi.; 174,000,000.
Southampton co. boro., s England; 212,020.
South Australia state, s Australia; 380,070 sq. mi.; 1,173,707; cap. Adelaide.
South Bend city, N Indiana; 125,580; ZIP 46600*.
South Boston city, s Virginia; 6,889; ZIP 24592.
Southbridge uninc. place, s Massachusetts; 17,057; ZIP 01550*.
South Carolina state, SE United States; 31,055 sq. mi.; 2,590,516; cap. Columbia.
South Charleston city, W CEN. West Virginia; 16,333; ZIP see CHARLESTON.
South China Sea part of the Pacific betw. SE Asia and the Malay Archipelago.
South Dakota state, N CEN. United States; 77,047 sq. mi.; 665,507; cap. Pierre.
Southern Pines town, s CEN. North Carolina; 5,937; ZIP 28387*.
Southern Rhodesia former British col., s CEN. Africa. See RHODESIA.
South Euclid city, NE Ohio; 29,579; ZIP see CLEVELAND.
South Farmingdale uninc. place, SE New York; 20,464; ZIP see FARMINGDALE.
Southfield city, SE Michigan; 69,285; ZIP 48075*.
Southgate city, SE Michigan; 33,909; ZIP see WYAN-DOTTE.
South Gate city, sw California; 56,909; ZIP 90280*.
South Hadley town, sw CEN. Massachusetts; 17,033; ZIP 01075.
South Haven city, sw Michigan; 6,471; ZIP 49090.
South Holland vill., SE Illinois; 23,931; ZIP 60473.
South Houston town, SE Texas; 11,527; ZIP 77587.
South Huntington uninc. place, SE New York; 9,115.
Southington uninc. place, CEN. Connecticut; 30,946; ZIP 06489.
South Island one of the two main isls. of New Zealand; 58,093 sq. mi.
South Kingston town, s Rhode Island; 16,913.
South Korea See KOREA.
South Miami city, SE Florida; 19,571; ZIP see MIAMI.
South Milwaukee city, SE Wisconsin; 23,297; ZIP 53172.
South Modesto uninc. place, CEN. California; 7,889; ZIP see MODESTO.
South Norfolk city, SE Virginia; 22,035.
South Ogden city, N CEN. Utah; 9,991; ZIP see OGDEN.
South Orange vill., NE New Jersey; 16,971; ZIP 07079.
South Pasadena city, sw California; 22,979; ZIP 91030*.
South Plainfield boro., NE New Jersey; 21,142; ZIP 07080.
South Pole s extremity of the earth's axis.
South Portland city, sw Maine; 23,267; ZIP see PORT-LAND.
South River boro., E New Jersey; 15,428; ZIP 08882.
South Sacramento-Fruitridge uninc. place, CEN. California; 16,443.
South Salt Lake city, N Utah; 7,810; ZIP see SALT LAKE CITY.
South San Francisco city, W California; 46,646; ZIP 94080*.
South San Gabriel uninc. place, sw California; 5,051; ZIP see SAN GABRIEL.
South Sea Islands isls. of the South Pacific.
South Seas 1. South Pacific Ocean. 2. Seas s of the Equator.
South Sioux City city, NE Nebraska; 7,920; ZIP 68776.
South St. Paul city, E Minnesota; 25,016; ZIP 55075*.
South Tucson city, s Arizona; 6,220; ZIP see TUCSON.
South Vietnam See VIETNAM.
South-West Africa mandated terr., sw Africa; administered by the Republic of South Africa; 317,877 sq. mi.; 746,328; cap. Windhoek. Also Namibia.
South Westbury uninc. place, SE New York; 10,978.
South Williamsport boro., NE CEN. Pennsylvania; 7,153; ZIP see WILLIAMSPORT.
South Yemen, see YEMEN.

Soviet Union See UNION OF SOVIET SOCIALIST REPUB-LICS.
Soviet Russia 1. Russian Soviet Federated Socialist Republic. 2. Union of Soviet Socialist Republics.
Spain monarchy, sw Europe; 194,368 sq. mi.; 35,225,000; cap. Madrid.
Spanish America parts of tne w hemisphere where Spanish is the predominant language.
Spanish Equatorial Region 2 overseas provs. of Spain, w Africa; ab. 10,800 sq. mi. Formerly Spanish Guinea.
Spanish Fork city, N CEN. Utah; 7,284; ZIP 84660.
Sparks city, w Nevada; 24,187; ZIP 89431.
Sparrows Point-Fort Howard-Edgmere uninc. place, CEN. Maryland; 11,775; ZIP see BALTIMORE.
Sparta city, w Wisconsin; 6,258; ZIP 54656.
Spartanburg city, NW South Carolina; 44,546; ZIP 29301*.
Speedway town, s Indiana; 15,056; ZIP see INDIAN-APOLIS.
Spenard uninc. place, s Alaska; 18,089; ZIP see ANCHORAGE.
Spencer city, NW Iowa; 10,278; ZIP 51301.
—uninc. place, CEN. Massachusetts; 8,779; ZIP 01562.
Spice Islands Molucca Islands: *a former name.*
Spitsbergen isl. group of Norway; Arctic Ocean; 23,658 sq. mi. Also Svalbard.
Spokane city, E Washington; 170,516; ZIP 99200*.
Spotswood boro., E New Jersey; 7,891; ZIP 08884.
Springdale city, NW Arkansas; 16,783; ZIP 72764.
—boro., w Pennsylvania; 5,202; ZIP 15144.
Springfield city, CEN. Illinois; cap.; 91,753; ZIP 62700*.
—city, sw Massachusetts; 163,905; ZIP 01100*.
—city, sw Missouri; 120,096; ZIP 65800.
—urb. twp., NE New Jersey; 15,740; ZIP 07081.
—city, W CEN. Ohio; 81,926; ZIP 45500.
—city, w Oregon; 27,047; ZIP 97477.
—urb. twp., SE Pennsylvania (Delaware County); 29,006; ZIP see MEDIA.
—urb. twp., SE Pennsylvania (Montgomery County); 22,394.
—city, N Tennessee; 9,720; ZIP 37172.
—uninc. place, SE Vermont; 10,063; ZIP 05156.
—uninc. place, NE Virginia; 11,613; ZIP 22150*.
Spring Garden urb. twp., s Pennsylvania; 12,443; ZIP see PHILADELPHIA.
Springhill town, N Nova Scotia, Canada; 5,836.
Springhill city, NW Louisiana; 6,496; ZIP 71075.
Spring Valley city, N Illinois; 5,605; ZIP 61362.
—vill., SE New York; 18,112; ZIP 10977.
Springville city, N CEN. Utah; 8,790; ZIP 84663.
St. Albans city, NW Vermont; 8,082; ZIP 05478.
—city, w West Virginia; 14,356; ZIP 25177.
Stalingrad Volgograd: *the former name.*
Stamford city, sw Connecticut; 108,798; ZIP 06901*.
—city, W CEN. Texas; 4,558; ZIP 79553.
St. Ann city, E Missouri; 18,215; ZIP 63074.
St. Anthony vill., SE Minnesota; 9,239.
Stanton city, sw California; 17,947; ZIP 90680.
Starkville city, E Mississippi; 11,369; ZIP 39759.
State College boro., CEN. Pennsylvania; 33,778; ZIP 16801*.
St-Bruno-de-Montarville town, CEN. Quebec, Canada; 6,760.
Staten Island isl., SE New York, at the entrance to New York Harbor; coextensive with Richmond boro.
Statesboro city, E Georgia; 14,616; ZIP 30458*.
States of the Church part of CEN. Italy under the sovereignty of the pope until 1870.
Statesville city, W CEN. North Carolina; 19,996; ZIP 28677.
St. Augustine NE Florida; 12,352; ZIP 32084.
Staunton city, NW CEN. Virginia; 24,504; ZIP 24401*.
St. Bernard city, sw Ohio; 6,080; ZIP see CINCINNATI.
St. Boniface city, SE Manitoba, Canada; 46,661.
St. Catharines city, s Ontario; 109,722.
St. Charles city, NE Illinois; 12,928; ZIP 60174.
—city, E Missouri; 31,834; ZIP 63301*.
St. Clair, Lake lake betw. s Ontario and SE Michigan; 460 sq. mi.
St. Clair Shores vill., SE Michigan; 80,000; ZIP 48080*.
St. Cloud city, CEN. Minnesota; 39,691; ZIP 56301*.
St. Croix one of the Virgin Islands of the United States; 82 sq. mi.; 31,779.
Ste-Agathe-des-Monts town, s Quebec, Canada; 5,725.

Ste-Dorothée town, s Quebec, Canada; 5,297.
Steelton boro., s Pennsylvania; 8,556; ZIP 17092.
Ste-Foy city, s Quebec, Canada; 68,385.
Steger vill., NE Illinois; 8,104; ZIP 60475.
Stellarton town, N Nova Scotia, Canada; 5,327.
Stephenville city, N CEN. Texas; 9,277; ZIP 76401*.
Stephenville town, sw Newfoundland, Canada; 6,043.
Sterling city, NE Colorado; 10,636; ZIP 80751.
—city, NW Illinois; 16,113; ZIP 61081.
Ste-Rose town, s Quebec, Canada; 7,571.
Ste-Thérèse city, s Quebec, Canada; 11,771.
Stettin city, NW Poland; 355,600. Also Szczecin.
Steubenville city, E Ohio; 30,771; ZIP 43952.
St-Eustache town, s Quebec, Canada; 5,463.
St-Eustache-sur-le-Lac town, s Quebec, Canada; 7,274.
Stevens Point city, CEN. Wisconsin; 23,479; ZIP 54481*.
St-Félicien town, s CEN. Quebec, Canada; 9,133.
St. Francis city, SE Wisconsin; 10,489; ZIP see MIL-
WAUKEE.
St-Francois town, s Quebec, Canada; 5,122.
St. George city, sw Utah; 7,097; ZIP 84770.
St. Helena isl., South Atlantic, with Ascension Island
and the Tristan da Cunha group forming British
depen.; cap. Jamestown; site of Napoleon's exile,
1815-21.
St. Helens city, NW Oregon; 6,212; ZIP 97051*.
St-Hubert town, s Quebec, Canada; 14,380.
St-Hyacinthe city, s Quebec, Canada; 22,354.
Stickney vill., NE Illinois; 6,601; ZIP see BERWYN.
Stillwater city, E Minnesota; 10,191; ZIP 55082.
—city, N CEN. Oklahoma; 31,126; ZIP 74074*.
St. James city, s Manitoba, Canada; 71,431.
St-Jean city, s Quebec, Canada; 26,988.
St-Jérôme city, s Quebec, Canada; 24,546.
St. John one of the Virgin Islands of the United
States; 19 sq. mi.; 1,729.
St. John city, s New Brunswick, Canada; 68,460.
St. John vill., E Missouri; 8,960.
St. John's city, SE Newfoundland, Canada; cap.;
88,102.
St. Johns city, s CEN. Michigan; 6,672; ZIP 48879
St. Johnsbury vill., NE Vermont; 8,409; ZIP 05819.
St. Joseph city, sw Michigan; 11,042; ZIP 49085.
—city, NW Missouri; 72,691; ZIP 64500*.
St-Lambert city, s Quebec, Canada; 14,531.
St. Laurent city, s Quebec, Canada; 62,955.
St. Lawrence River river, SE Canada; the outlet of
the Great Lakes system; 1,900 mi. long.
St. Lawrence, Gulf of inlet of the Atlantic, E Canada.
St. Lawrence Seaway system of ship canals extending
114 miles along the St. Lawrence River from Mon-
treal to Lake Ontario.
St. Louis city, E Missouri; 622,236; ZIP 63100*.
St. Louis Park vill., E Minnesota; 48,883; ZIP see
MINNEAPOLIS.
St. Martinsville town, s CEN. Louisiana; 7,153; ZIP
70582.
St. Marys city, w Ohio; 7,699; ZIP 45885.
—boro., NW CEN. Pennsylvania; 7,470; ZIP 15857.
St. Matthews city, N Kentucky; 13,152; ZIP see LOUIS-
VILLE.
St-Michel city, s Quebec, Canada; 138,109.
St. Moritz town, SE Switzerland; 5,699.
Stockholm city, SE Sweden; cap.; 681,318.
Stockton, city, CEN. California; 107,644; ZIP 95200*.
Stoneham town, NE Massachusetts; 20,725; ZIP see
BOSTON.
Stoneleigh-Rodgers Forge uninc. place, N Maryland;
15,645.
Stoney Creek town, s Ontario, Canada; 6,043.
Storm Lake city, NW Iowa; 8,591; ZIP 50588.
Storrs uninc. place, N CEN. Connecticut; 10,691; ZIP
06268.
Stoughton town, E Massachusetts; 23.459; ZIP 02072.
—city, s Wisconsin; 6,081; ZIP 53589.
Stow vill., NE CEN. Ohio; 19,847; ZIP see CUYAHOGA
FALLS.
Stowe urb. twp., sw Pennsylvania; 10,119.
St. Paul city, SE Minnesota; cap.; 309,980; ZIP 55100*.
St. Peter city, s Minnesota; 8,339; ZIP 56082.
St. Petersburg Leningrad: a former name.
St. Petersburg city, w Florida; 216.232.
St. Petersburg Beach city, w Florida; 8,024; ZIP
33700*.
St-Pierre town, s Quebec, Canada; 6,795.

Strasbourg city, NE France; 247,918.
Stratford town, SE Connecticut; 49,775; ZIP 06497.
Stratford city, s Ontario, Canada; 24,508.
Stratford-on-Avon town, E CEN. England; birthplace
and burial place of Shakespeare; 29,835.
Strathroy town, s Ontario, Canada; 5,150.
Streator city, N CEN. Illinois; 15,600; ZIP 61364.
Streetsville vill., s Ontario, Canada; 5,056.
Strongsville vill., N Ohio; 15,182; ZIP see CLEVELAND.
Stroudsburg boro., E Pennsylvania; 5,451; ZIP 18360.
Struthers city, E Ohio; 15,343; ZIP 44471.
St. Thomas one of the Virgin Islands of the United
States; 28 sq. mi.; 28,960.
St. Thomas city, s Ontario, Canada; 22,469.
Sturgeon Bay city, NE Wisconsin; 6,776; ZIP 54235*.
Sturgeon Falls town, E CEN. Ontario, Canada; 6,288.
Sturgis city, s Michigan; 9,295; ZIP 49091.
Stuttgart city, sw West Germany; 624,835.
Stuttgart city, E CEN. Arkansas; 10,477; ZIP 72160.
St-Vincent-de-Paul town, s Quebec, Canada; 11,214.
Süchow city, E People's Republic of China; 1,500,000.
Sucre city, s CEN. Bolivia; cap.; 84,900; See LA PAZ.
Sudan reg., N Africa s of the Sahara.
Sudan, Republic of the republic, NE Africa; 967,500
sq. mi.; 17,300,000; cap. Khartoum.
Sudanese Republic See MALI.
Sudbury city, SE CEN. Ontario, Canada; 90,535.
Sudetenland border dists., w Czechoslovakia.
Suez city, NE Egypt; 315,000.
Suez, Gulf of inlet of the Red Sea; NE Egypt.
Suez, Isthmus of strip of land joining Asia and Africa,
betw. the Gulf of Suez and the Mediterranean.
Suez Canal ship canal across the Isthmus of Suez;
107 mi.
Suffern vill., SE New York; 8,273; ZIP 10901.
Suffolk co., E England; divided into East Suffolk; 879
sq. mi.; 380,524; cap. Ipswich, and West Suffolk;
628 sq. mi.; 164,201; cap. Bury St. Edmonds.
Suffolk city, SE Virginia; 9,858; ZIP 23434*.
Suitland-Silver Hills uninc. place, W CEN. Maryland;
30,355.
Sulphur city, sw Louisiana; 13,551; ZIP 70663.
Sulphur Springs city, NE Texas; 10,642; ZIP 75482.
Sulu Archipelago isl. group, sw Philippines; 1,086 sq.
mi.; 425,617.
Sumatra isl. of Indonesia s of the Malay Peninsula;
163,557 sq. mi.; 20,800,000.
Summerside town, W CEN. Prince Edward Island, Can-
ada; 8,611.
Summit vill., NE Illinois; 11,569.
—city, NE New Jersey; 23,620; ZIP 07901.
Sumter city, CEN. South Carolina; 24,435; ZIP 29150*.
Sunbury city, E CEN. Pennsylvania; 13,025; ZIP 17801.
Sunnyside city, s Washington; 6,751; ZIP 98944.
Sunnyvale city, w California; 95,408; ZIP 94086*.
Superior city, NW Wisconsin; 32,237; ZIP 54880*.
Superior, Lake largest of the Great Lakes; 31,820 sq.
mi.
Surabaya city, NE Java, Indonesia; 1,556,255.
Surinam republic, NE South America; 55,129 sq. mi.;
400,000; cap. Paramaribo.
Susanville city, NE California; 6,608.
Susquehanna river, New York, Pennsylvania, and
Maryland; 444 mi. long.
Suwannee River river, Georgia and Florida; 250 mi.
long.
Sverdlovsk city, w USSR; 1,073,000.
Swainsboro city, E CEN. Georgia; 7,325; ZIP 30401.
Swampscott town, NE Massachusetts; 13,578; ZIP see
LYNN.
Swansea vill., s Ontario, Canada; 9,628.
Swarthmore boro., SE Pennsylvania; 6,156; ZIP 19081.
Swaziland constitutional monarchy, member of the
Commonwealth of Nations, SE Africa; 6,704 sq. mi.;
478,000; cap. Mbabane.
Sweden kingdom, NW Europe; 173,577 sq. mi.; 8,100,-
000; cap. Stockholm.
Sweetwater city, w Texas; 12,020; ZIP 79556.
Swift Current city, sw Saskatchewan, Canada; 12,186.
Swissvale boro., sw Pennsylvania; 13,821; ZIP see
PITTSBURGH.
Switzerland republic, CEN. Europe; 15,940 sq. mi.;
6,500,000; cap. Bern.
Swoyersville boro., E CEN. Pennsylvania; 6,786.
Sycamore city, N Illinois; 7,843; ZIP 60178.

Sydney city, E New South Wales, Australia; cap.; 2,874,380.

—city, NE Nova Scotia, Canada; 33,617.

Sydney Mines town, E Nova Scotia, Canada; 9,122.

Sylacauga city, E CEN. Alabama; 12,255; ZIP 35150.

Sylvania vill., N Ohio; 12,031; ZIP 43560.

Syracuse city, CEN. New York; 197,208; ZIP 13200*.

Syria republic, SW Asia; 72,234 sq. mi.; 7,100,000; cap. Damascus.

Tabriz city, NW Iran; 493,000.

Tacoma city, W Washington; 154,581; ZIP 98400*.

Tadzhik SSR constituent republic, S USSR; 55,043 sq. mi.; 2,900,000; cap. Dyushambe.

Taegu city, SE South Korea; 1,063,553.

Tahiti isl., Society group; 600 sq. mi.; 84,552.

Tahlequah city, E Oklahoma; 9,254; ZIP 74464.

Tahoe, Lake lake, E California and W Nevada; ab. 195 sq. mi.

Taipei city, N Taiwan; cap.; 1,769,568.

Taiwan isl. off SE China; comprises with the Pescadores, the National Republic of China; 13,890 sq. mi.; 15,700,000; cap. Taipei.

Taiyüan city, N People's Republic of China; 1,020,000.

Takoma Park city, W Maryland; 18,455; ZIP see WASHINGTON, D.C.

Talladega city, E CEN. Alabama; 17,662; ZIP 35160.

Tallahassee city, N Florida; cap.; 71,897; ZIP 32301*.

Tallinn city, N Estonian SSR; cap.; 392,000.

Tallmade city, NE Ohio; 15,274; ZIP 44278.

Tallulah vill., NE Louisiana; 9,643; ZIP 71282.

Tamaqua boro., E Pennsylvania; 9,246; ZIP 18252.

Tampa city, W Florida; 277,767; ZIP 33600*.

Tampico city, E Mexico; 212,188.

Tananarive city, E CEN. Malagasy Republic; cap.; 322,000.

Tanganyika, Lake lake, E CEN. Africa; 12,700 sq. mi.

Tangier city, N Morocco; 185,850.

Tanzania republic of the Commonwealth of Nations, E Africa, includes **Tanganyika** and Zanzibar; 362,820 sq. mi.; 14,800,000; cap. Dar es Salaam.

Taranto city, SE Italy; 228,826.

Tarboro town, NE CEN. North Carolina; 9,425; ZIP 27886.

Tarentum boro., W Pennsylvania; 7,379; ZIP 15084.

Tarpon Springs city, W Florida; 7,118; ZIP 33589.

Tarrant City city, N CEN. Alabama; 6,835; ZIP see BIRMINGHAM.

Tarrytown vill., SE New York; 11,115; ZIP 10591*.

Tashkent city, E Uzbek SSR; cap.; 1,461,000.

Tasmania isl., SE Australia; comprises a state; 26,216 sq. mi.; 390,413; cap. Hobart.

Taunton city, SE Massachusetts; 43,756; ZIP 02780*.

Taylor boro., NE Pennsylvania; 6,977.

—city, CEN. Texas; 9,616; ZIP 76574.

Taylorville city, CEN. Illinois; 10,644; ZIP 62568.

Tbilisi city, SE Georgian SSR; cap.: 927,000.

Teaneck urb twp., NE New Jersey; 42,355; ZIP 07666.

Tecumseh city, SE Michigan; 7,120; ZIP 49286.

Tegucigalpa city, S CEN. Honduras; cap.; 274,850.

Teheran city, N CEN. Iran; cap.; 3,400,000.

Tel Aviv city, W Israel; includes Jaffa; ab. 382,900.

Tell City city, S Indiana; 7,933; ZIP 47586.

Tempe city, S CEN. Arizona; 62,907.

Temple city, CEN. Texas; 33,431; ZIP 85281*.

Temple City uninc. place, SW California; 29,673; ZIP 91780*.

Tenafly boro., northeastern New Jersey; 14,827; ZIP 07670.

Tennessee state, SE CEN. United States; 42,246 sq. mi.; 3,923,687; cap. Nashville.

Tennessee River river, flowing through E Tennessee, N Alabama, W Tennessee, and SW Kentucky; 652 mi. long.

Terrebonne town, S Quebec, Canada; 6,207.

Terre Haute city, W Indiana; 70,286; ZIP 47801*.

Terrell city, NE Texas; 14,182; ZIP 75160.

Terrell Hills city, S CEN. Texas; 5,225.

Terryville uninc. place, W CEN. Connecticut; 5,231; ZIP 06786.

Texarkana city, SW Arkansas at the Arkansas-Texas line; 21,682.

—city, NE Texas; adjacent to and integrated with Texarkana, Arkansas; 30,497; ZIP 75501*.

Texas state, S United States; 267,339 sq. mi.; 11,196,730; cap. Austin.

Texas City city, SE Texas; 38,908; ZIP 77590*.

Thailand constitutional monarchy, SE Asia; 198,404 sq. mi.; 40,500,000; cap. Bangkok.

Thames river, S England; 209 mi. long.

The Dalles city, N Oregon; 16,505; ZIP 97058.

Thessalonica Salonika.

Thessaly div., N CEN. Greece; 5,399 sq. mi.; 659,243.

Thetford Mines city, S Quebec, Canada; 22,003.

The Village city, CEN. Oklahoma; 13,695; ZIP see OKLAHOMA CITY.

Thibodaux town, SE Louisiana; 14,925; ZIP 70301.

Thief River Falls city, NW Minnesota; 8,618; ZIP 56701.

Thomaston city, W CEN. Georgia; 10,024; ZIP 30286.

Thomasville city, S Georgia; 18,155; ZIP 31792.

—city, CEN. North Carolina; 15,230; ZIP 27360.

Thornton vill., CEN. Colorado; 13,326; ZIP see DENVER.

Thorold town, S Ontario, Canada; 8,633.

Thousand Islands group of ab. 1,700 small isls. in the St. Lawrence River.

Thrace reg., E Balkan Peninsula; 329,297.

Three Rivers city, SW Michigan; 7,355; ZIP 49093.

Thunder Bay, city, NW Ontario, Canada; comprises former cities of Fort William and Port Arthur; 108,411.

Tiber river, CEN. Italy; 125 mi. long.

Tibet auton. reg. W People's Republic of China; ab. 470,000 sq. mi.; 1,300,000; cap. Lhasa.

Ticonderoga vill., NE New York; site of Fort Ticonderoga; 3,268; ZIP 12883.

Ticonderoga, Fort historic fort, NE New York.

Tientsin city, NE China; 4,280,000.

Tierra del Fuego isl. group, S South America, included in Chile and Argentina; 7,996 sq. mi. (Argentina), 19,480 sq. mi. (Chile).

Tiffin city, N CEN. Ohio; 21,596; ZIP 44883.

Tiflis Tbilisi: *the former name.*

Tifton city, S Georgia; 12,179; ZIP 31794.

Tigris river, SW Asia; ab. 1,150 mi. long.

Tijuana city, NW Lower California, Mexico; 363,154.

Tillsonburg town, S Ontario, Canada; 6,600.

Timbuktu town, CEN. Mali; 10,445.

Timmins town, E CEN. Ontario, Canada; 29,270.

Timonium-Lutherville uninc. place, N CEN. Maryland; 12,265; ZIP 21093.

Timor isl., SE Malay Archipelago; divided into **Indonesian Timor** in the W part; 5,765 sq. mi., and **Portuguese Timor**, a Portuguese overseas prov. in the E part; 5,761 sq. mi. (including offshore isls.); 2,850,000; cap. Dili.

Tinley Park vill., NE Illinois; 12,382; ZIP 60477*.

Tipton city, CEN. Indiana; 5,176; ZIP 46072.

Tipperary co., S CEN. Ireland; 1,643 sq. mi.; 116,565; cap. Clonmel.

Tirana city, CEN. Albania; cap.; 169,300.

Tirol See TYROL.

Titicaca, Lake lake bet. SE Peru and W CEN. Bolivia; 3,200 sq. mi.; elevation 12,500 ft.

Titusville city, E Florida; 30,515; ZIP 32780.

—city, NW Pennsylvania; 7,331; ZIP 16354.

Tiverton town, SE Rhode Island; 12,559; ZIP 02878.

Tobago See TRINIDAD AND TOBAGO.

Toccoa city, NE Georgia; 6,971; ZIP 30577.

Togo republic, W Africa; ab. 21,500 sq. mi.; 2,171,000; cap. Lomé.

Togoland former German prot., W Africa.

Tokyo city, E Japan; cap.; 8,840,902.

Toledo city, CEN. Spain; 43,955.

Toledo city, NW Ohio; 383,818; ZIP 43600*.

Tomah city, W CEN. Wisconsin; 5,647; ZIP 54660.

Tomsk city, S RSFSR; 386,000.

Toms River uninc. place, E New Jersey; 7,303; ZIP 08753.

Tonawanda city, W New York; 21,898; ZIP 14150*.

—uninc. place, W New York; 107,282.

Tonga constitutional monarchy, member of the Commonwealth of Nations SE of Fiji; ab. 270 sq. mi.; 95,000; cap. Nuku'alofa.

Tooele city, N CEN. Utah; 12,539; ZIP 84074.

Topeka city, NE Kansas; cap.; 125,011; ZIP 66600*.

Toppenish city, S Washington; 5,744; ZIP 98948.

Toronto city, E Ohio; 7,705; ZIP 43964.

Toronto city, S Ontario, Canada; 712,786.

Torrance city, sw California; 134,584; zip 90500*.
Torrington city, nw Connecticut; 31,952; zip 06790*.
Totowa boro., ne New Jersey; 11,580; zip see PATER-SON.
Toulon city, s France; 174,746.
Toulouse city, s France; 369,200.
Towson uninc. place, n cen. Maryland; 77,809; zip see BALTIMORE.
Tracy city, cen. California; 14,724; zip 95376.
Tracy town, s Quebec, Canada; 8,171.
Trafalgar, Cape headland, sw Spain; scene of a naval battle in which Nelson defeated the French and Spanish fleets, 1805.
Trail city, se British Columbia, Canada; 11,580.
Transcaucasia reg., se USSR; betw. the Caucasus mountains and Iran and Turkey.
Transcona town, se Manitoba, Canada; 14,248.
Trans-Jordan former Arab terr., now part of Jordan.
Transvaal province, ne South Africa; 110,450 sq. mi.; 6,388,870; cap. Pretoria.
Traverse city, nw Michigan; 18,048; zip 49684.
Trenton city, se Michigan; 24,127; zip 48183.
—city, n Missouri; 6,063; zip 64683.
—city, w New Jersey; cap.; 104,638; zip 08600*.
Trenton town, se Ontario, Canada; 13,183.
Trieste city, ne Italy; 269,819.
Trinidad and Tobago independent member of the Commonwealth of Nations off n Venezuela; comprises isls. of Trinidad, 1,864 sq. mi., and **Tobago**, 116 sq. mi.; ab. 1,000,000; cap. Port-of-Spain.
Trinidad city, s Colorado; 9,901.
Tripoli city, nw Lebanon; 127,611.
Tripoli city, nw Libya; one of the two caps.; 247,000.
Trois-Rivières city, s Quebec, Canada; 55,869.
Troy city, se Alabama; 11,482; zip 36081.
—city, se Michigan; 39,419; zip 48084.
—city, e New York; 62,918; zip 12180*.
—city, w Ohio; 17,186; zip 45373.
Troy Hills See PARSIPPANY-TROY HILLS.
Trucial Oman reg., e Arabian penin.; consists largely of seven **Trucial Sheikdoms** bound by treaties with Great Britain; ab. 32,300 sq. mi.; 110,000.
Truro town, cen. Nova Scotia, Canada; 12,421.
Tsinan city, e People's Republic of China; 862,000.
Tsingtao city, e China; 1,121,000.
Tuckahoe vill., se New York; 6,236; zip see YONKERS.
Tucson city, se Arizona; 262,933; zip 85700*.
Tucumcari city, e New Mexico; 7,189; zip 88401.
Tulare city, s cen. California; 16,235; zip 93274.
Tullahoma city, s cen. Tennessee; 15,311; zip 37388.
Tulsa city, ne Oklahoma; 331,638; zip 74100*.
Tunis city, ne Tunisia; cap.; 647,640.
Tunisia republic, n Africa; 48,195 sq. mi.; 5,640,000; cap. Tunis.
Tupelo city, ne Mississippi; 20,471; zip 38801*.
Tupper Lake vill., n New York; 4,854; zip 12986.
Turin city, nw Italy; 1,177,939.
Turkestan reg., cen. Asia; extends from the Caspian Sea to the Gobi Desert.
Turkey republic, se cen. Eurasia; 296,108 sq. mi.; 39,000,000; cap. Ankara. See ANATOLIA.
Turkish Empire Ottoman Empire: *an alternate name.*
Turkmen SSR constituent republic, s USSR; 189,370 sq. mi.; 2,158,000; cap. Ashkhabad.
Turlock city, cen. California; 13,992; zip 95380.
Turtle Creek boro., sw Pennsylvania; 8,308; zip 15145*.
Tuscaloosa city, w cen. Alabama; 65,773; zip 35401*.
Tuscany reg. and former duchy, w cen. Italy; 8,876 sq. mi.; 3,470,915; chief city, Florence.
Tuscumbia city, nw Alabama; 8,828; zip 35674.
Tutuila chief isl., American Samoa; 40 sq. mi.
Twin Falls city, s Idaho, 21,914; zip 83301*.
Two Rivers city, e Wisconsin; 13.553; zip 54241.
Tyler city, e Texas; 57,770; zip 75701*.
Tyrol reg., w Austria and n Italy.
Tyrone boro., cen. Pennsylvania; 7,072; zip 16686.
Tzepo city, e People's Republic of China; 806,000. Also **Tzu-po.**

Ubangi river, cen. Africa; 1,400 mi. long.
Ufa city, e USSR; 871,000.
Uganda independent member of the Commonwealth of Nations, e cen. Africa; 93,981 sq. mi.; 11,200,000; cap. Kampala.
Uhrichsville city, e Ohio; 5,731; zip 44683.
Ukiah city, nw California; 10,095; zip 95482.
Ukrainian SSR constituent republic sw USSR; 231,-986 sq. mi.; 47,136,000; cap. Kiev. Also **Ukraine.**
Ulan Bator city, n cen. Mongolian People's Republic; cap.; ab. 282,000.
Ulster former prov., n Ireland, of which the n part became Northern Ireland, 1925.
—prov., n Republic of Ireland; comprises the part of Ulster that remained after 1925; 3,093 sq. mi.; 207,204.
Union urb. twp., ne New Jersey; 53,077; zip 07083*.
—city, n South Carolina; 10,775; zip 29379*.
Union Beach boro., e New Jersey; 6,472; zip see KEYPORT.
Union City city, w California; 14,724; zip 94587.
—city, ne New Jersey; 58,537; zip 07087.
—city, nw Tennessee; 11,925; zip 38261.
Uniondale uninc. place, se New York; 22,077; zip see HEMPSTEAD.
Union of Arab Emirates federation of seven sheikhdoms, e cen. Arabia; 32,000 sq. mi.; 230,000; cap. Abu Dhabi.
Union of Soviet Socialist Republics federal union of 15 constituent republics occupying most of n Eurasia; 8,646,400 sq. mi.; 252,000,000; cap. Moscow.
Uniontown city, sw Pennsylvania; 16,282; zip 15401.
United Arab Republic: *former official name of Egypt.*
United Kingdom constitutional monarchy comprising Great Britain, Northern Ireland, the Isle of Man, and the Channel Islands; 94,284 sq. mi.; 55,506,131; cap. London; officially **United Kingdom of Great Britain and Northern Ireland.**
United States of America federal republic, North America including 50 states and the District of Columbia (3,615,222 sq. mi.; 203,211,926), and th Canal Zone, Puerto Rico, the Virgin Islands of the United States, American Samoa, and Guam, Wake, and other Pacific islands; total 3,720,407 sq. mi.; cap. Washington, coextensive with the District of Columbia.
University City city, e Missouri; 46,309; zip see SAINT LOUIS.
University Heights city, n Ohio; 17,055.
University Park city, n Texas; 23,498; zip see SAN ANTONIO.
Upland city, sw California; 32,551; zip 91786.
Upper Arlington city, cen. Ohio; 38,630; zip see COLUMBUS.
Upper Darby urb. twp., se Pennsylvania; 95,910; zip 19082*.
Upper Moreland urb. twp., se Pennsylvania; 24,866.
Upper Volta independent republic of the French Community, w Africa; 105,900 sq. mi.; 5,800,000; cap. Ouagadougou.
Ural Mountains mtn. system in the RSFSR, extending from the Arctic Ocean to the Kazakh SSR.
Ural River river, s RSFSR and w Kazakh SSR; 1,574 mi. long.
Urbana city, e Illinois; 32,800; zip 61801*.
—city, w cen. Ohio; 11,237; zip 43078.
Urbandale town, s cen. Iowa; 14,434; zip see DES MOINES.
Uruguay republic, se South America; 72,172 sq. mi.; 3,028,000; cap. Montevideo.
Uruguay River river, se South America; 1,000 mi. long.
Urundi Burundi: *the former name.*
Utah state, w cen. United States; 84,916 sq. mi.; 1,059,273; cap. Salt Lake City.
Utica city, cen. New York; 91,611.
Utrecht prov., cen. Netherlands; 511 sq. mi.; 687,000.
—city, cen. Utrecht prov., cap.; 274,974.
Uttar Pradesh state, n India; 113,409 sq. mi.; 73,752,-914; cap. Lucknow.
Utuado town, w cen. Puerto Rico; 11,573; zip 00761.
Uvalde city, sw cen. Texas; 10,764; zip 78801.
Uzbek SSR constituent republic s USSR; 154,014 sq. mi.; 11,963,000; cap. Tashkent.

Vacaville city, w cen. California; 21,690; zip 95688.
Val-d'Or town, w Quebec, Canada; 10,983.
Valdosta city, s Georgia; 32,303; zip 31601*.
Valencia city, e Spain; 648,000.

Vallejo city, W California; 66,733; ZIP 94590.
Valley City city, SE North Dakota; 7,843; ZIP 58072.
Valleyfield city, S Quebec, Canada; 27,297. Also **Salaberry de Valleyfield.**
Valley Forge locality, SE Pennsylvania, scene of Washington's winter encampment, 1777-78.
Valley Station uninc. place, N Kentucky; 24,471; ZIP 40172.
Valley Stream vill., SE New York; 40,413; ZIP 11580*.
Valparaiso city, CEN. Chile; 250,400.
Valparaiso city, NW Florida; 6,504; ZIP 32580.
—city, NW Indiana; 20,020; ZIP 46383.
Van Buren city, W Arkansas; 8,373; ZIP 72956.
Vancouver city, SW Washington; 43,493; ZIP 98660*.
Vancouver city, SW British Columbia, Canada; 426,256.
Vancouver Island isl., off SW British Columbia, Canada; 12,408 sq. mi.
Vandalia city, S CEN. Illinois; 5,160; ZIP 62471.
—city, NW Ohio; 10,796; ZIP 45377.
Vandergrift boro., W Pennsylvania; 7,873; ZIP 15690.
Van Wert city, W Ohio; 11,320; ZIP 45891.
Vatican City sovereign papal state within Rome; includes the Vatican and St. Peter's Church; established June 10, 1929; 108.7 acres; ab. 5,000.
Venezuela republic, N South America; 352,143 sq. mi.; 11,632,000; cap. Caracas.
Venice city, NE Italy; 364,063.
Venice, Gulf of N part of the Adriatic.
Ventnor City city, SE New Jersey; 10,385; ZIP see ATLANTIC CITY.
Ventura San Buenaventura: *an alternate name.*
Veracruz city, E Mexico; 255,646.
Verde, Cape westernmost point of Africa; a peninsula; ab. 20 mi. long.
Verdun town, NE France; scene of several battles of World War I; 24,716.
Verdun city, S Quebec, Canada; 74,718.
Vermillion city, SE South Dakota; 9,128; ZIP 57069.
Vermont state, NE United States; 9,609 sq. mi.; 444,330; cap. Montpelier.
Vernon city, N Texas; 11,454; ZIP 76384.
Vernon city, S British Columbia, Canada; 10,250.
Vernon Valley uninc. place, SE New York; 7,925.
Vero Beach city, E Florida; 11,908; ZIP 32960*.
Verona city, NE Italy; 263,589.
Verona boro., NE New Jersey; 15,067; ZIP see MONTCLAIR.
Versailles city, N France; site of the palace of Louis XIV; scene of the signing of a treaty (1919) betw. the Allies and Germany after World War I; 89,056.
Vesuvius active volcano, W Italy; 3,891 ft.
Vichy city, CEN. France; provisional cap. during German occupation, World War II; 33,506.
Vicksburg city, W Mississippi; besieged and taken by the Union Army in the Civil War, 1863; 25,478; ZIP 39180*.
Victoria state, SE Australia; 87,844 sq. mi.; 3,546,146; cap. Melbourne.
Victoria city, SW British Columbia; 61,761.
Victoria city, S Hong Kong; cap.; 633,138.
Victoria city, S Texas; 41,349; ZIP 77901*.
Victoria, Lake lake betw. Uganda, Tanganyika, and Kenya; 26,828 sq. mi. Also **Victoria Nyanza.**
Victoria Falls cataract on the Zambesi River betw. Northern and Southern Rhodesia; 343 ft. high; over a mile wide.
Victoriaville town, S Quebec, Canada; 18,720.
Vidalia city, SE CEN. Georgia; 9,507; ZIP 30474.
Vienna city, NE Austria; cap.; 1,614,841.
Vienna town, NE Virginia; 17,152; ZIP 22180.
—city, NW West Virginia; 11,549; ZIP see PARKERSBURG.
Vientiane city, NW CEN. Laos; adm. cap.; 132,253.
Vietnam country, SW Indochina, divided into the **Democratic Republic of Vietnam** (also **North Vietnam**), popularly **Viet Minh** N of the 17th parallel; 63,344 sq. mi.; 24,000,000; cap. Hanoi, and the **Republic of Vietnam** (also **South Vietnam**); 65,749 sq. mi.; ab. 20,000,000; cap. Saigon. Also **Viet Nam.**
Villa Park vill., NE Illinois, 25,891; ZIP 60181.
Ville Platte town, S CEN. Louisiana; 9,692; ZIP 70586.
Vilnius city, SE Lithuanian SSR; cap.; 420,000. Also **Vilna, Vilnyus.**
Vincennes city, SW Indiana; 19,867; ZIP 47591.

Vineland boro., S New Jersey; 47,399; ZIP 08360.
Vinita city, NE Oklahoma; 5,847; ZIP 74301.
Virginia state, E United States; 40,815 sq. mi.; 4,648,494; cap. Richmond.
—city, NE Minnesota; 12,450; ZIP 55792.
Virginia Beach city, SE Virginia; 172,106; ZIP 23450*.
Virgin Islands isl. group, West Indies, E of Puerto Rico, See BRITISH VIRGIN ISLANDS.
Virgin Islands of the United States uninc. terr., Virgin Islands; 133 sq. mi.; 62,468; cap. Charlotte Amalie.
Visalia city, S CEN. California; 27,268; ZIP 93277*.
Visayan Islands isl. group, CEN. Philippines; 23,621 sq. mi.
Vista uninc. place, SW California; 24,688; ZIP 92083.
Vistula river, CEN. and N Poland; 678 mi. long.
Vladivostok city, SE RSFSR; 495,000.
Volga river, W RSFSR; 2,290 mi. long.
Volograd city, W RSFSR; scene of a Russian victory over German forces in World War II, Sept. 1942 to Jan. 1943; 885,000; from 1925-61 *Stalingrad.*
Volta river, E Ghana; 800 mi. long.
Vosges Mountains mtn. chain, E France.

Wabana town, SE Newfoundland, Canada; 8,026.
Wabash city, NE CEN. Indiana; 13,379; ZIP 46992.
Wabash river, W Ohio and Indiana; 475 mi. long.
Waco city, CEN. Texas; 95,326; ZIP 76700*.
Wadsworth city, NE CEN. Ohio; 13,142; ZIP 44281.
Wahiawa city, CEN. Oahu, Hawaii; 17,598; ZIP 96786.
Wahpeton city, SE North Dakota; 7,076; ZIP 58075.
Waikiki beach on Honolulu harbor, SE Oahu, Hawaii.
Wailuku city, NW Maui, Hawaii; 7,979; ZIP 96793.
Wakefield town, E Massachusetts; 25,402; ZIP 01880*.
Wakefield-Peacedale uninc. place, S Rhode Island; 6,331.
Wake Island coral atoll in the North Pacific; 4 sq. mi.; 1,647; site of a U.S. naval and air base.
Waldwick boro., NE New Jersey; 12,313; ZIP 07463.
Wales penin., SW Britain; a principality of England; 8,016 sq. mi.; 2,723,596.
Wallaceburg town, S Ontario; 7,881.
Walla Walla city, SE Washington; 23,619; ZIP 99362.
Wallingford town, S CEN. Connecticut; 35,714; ZIP 06492.
Wallington boro., NE New Jersey; 10,284; ZIP see PASSAIC*.
Walnut Creek city, W California; 39,844; ZIP 94596*.
Walnut Heights uninc. place, W California; 5,080.
Walpole town, E Massachusetts; 18,149; ZIP 02081.
Walterboro town, S South Carolina; 6,257; ZIP 29488.
Waltham city, E Massachusetts; 61,582; ZIP see BOSTON.
Wanaque boro., N New Jersey; 8,636; ZIP 07465.
Wantagh vill., SE New York; 21,873; ZIP 11793.
Wapakoneta city, W Ohio; 7,324; ZIP 45895.
Ware town, S CEN. Massachusetts; 8,187; ZIP 01082.
Warminster urb. twp., SE Pennsylvania; 34,684; ZIP 18974.
Warner Robins city, CEN. Georgia; 33,491; ZIP 31093*.
Warr Acres city, CEN. Oklahoma; 9,887; ZIP see OKLAHOMA CITY.
Warren city, S Arkansas; 6,433; ZIP 71671.
—vill., SE Michigan; 179,260; ZIP 48089*.
—city, NE Ohio; 63,494; ZIP 44480*.
—boro., NW Pennsylvania; 12,998; ZIP 16365*.
—town, E Rhode Island; 10,523; ZIP 02885*.
Warrensburg city, W Missouri; 13,125; ZIP 64093.
Warrensville Heights vill., N Ohio; 18,925; ZIP see CLEVELAND.
Warrington uninc. place, NW Florida; 15,848; ZIP see PENSACOLA.
Warsaw city, E CEN. Poland; cap.; 1,308,900.
Warsaw city, N Indiana; 7,506; ZIP 46792.
Warwick city. E CEN. Rhode Island; 83,694; ZIP 02886*.
Wasco city, S CEN. California; 8,269; ZIP 93280.
Waseca city, S Minnesota; 6,789; ZIP 56093.
Washington state, NW United States; 68,192 sq. mi.; 3,409,169; cap. Olympia.
—city, E United States; coextensive with the District of Columbia; cap.; 756,510; ZIP 20000*.
—city, CEN. Illinois; 6,790; ZIP 61571.
—city, SW Indiana; 11,358; ZIP 47501.
—city, SE Iowa; 6,317; ZIP 52353.

—city, E Missouri; 8,499; ZIP 63090.
—boro., NW New Jersey; 5,943; ZIP 07882.
—city, E North Carolina; 8,961; ZIP 27889.
—city, S CEN. Ohio; 12,495; ZIP 43160.
—city, SW Pennsylvania; 19,827; ZIP 15301.
Washington Park vill., SW Illinois; 9,524; ZIP 61571.
Washington Terrace city, N CEN. Utah; 7,241; ZIP see OGDEN.
Waterbury city, W Connecticut; 108,033; ZIP 06700*.
Waterloo vill., CEN. Belgium; scene of Napoleon's final defeat, June 18, 1815; ab. 10,000.
Waterloo city, NE CEN. Iowa; 75,533; ZIP 50700*.
—vill., W CEN. New York; 5,418; ZIP 13165.
Waterloo city, S Ontario, Canada; 21,366.
Watertown town, E Massachusetts; 39,307; ZIP see BOSTON.
—city, N New York; 30,787; ZIP 13601*.
—city, NE South Dakota; 13,388; ZIP 57201*.
—city, SE Wisconsin; 15,683; ZIP 53094.
Waterville city, S CEN. Maine; 18,192; ZIP 04900*.
Watervliet city, E New York; 12,404; ZIP 12189.
Watseka city, E Illinois; 5,294; ZIP 60970.
Watsonville city, W California; 14,569; ZIP 95076*.
Waukegan city, NE Illinois; 65,269; ZIP 60085*.
Waukesha city, SE Wisconsin; 40,258; ZIP 53186*.
Waupun city, E CEN. Wisconsin; 7,946; ZIP 53963.
Wausau city, CEN. Wisconsin; 32,806; ZIP 54401*.
Wauwatosa city, SE Wisconsin; 58,676; ZIP see MILWAUKEE.
Waverly city, NE Iowa; 7,205; ZIP 50677.
—vill., S New York; 5,261; ZIP 14892.
Waxahachie city, N Texas; 13,452; ZIP 75165.
Waycross city, SE Georgia; 18,996; ZIP 31501.
Wayne vill., SE Michigan; 21,054; ZIP 48184.
—urb. twp., N New Jersey; 49,141; ZIP 07470*.
Waynesboro city, E Georgia; 5,530; ZIP 30830.
—boro., S Pennsylvania; 10,011; ZIP 17268.
—city, N CEN. Virginia; 16,707; ZIP 22980*.
Waynesburg boro., SW Pennsylvania; 5,152; ZIP 15370.
Waynesville town, SW North Carolina; 6,488; ZIP 28786.
Weatherford city, N Texas; 11,750; ZIP 76086.
Webb City city, SW Missouri; 6,811; ZIP 64870.
Webster uninc. place, S Massachusetts; 14,917; ZIP 01578*.
Webster City city, CEN. Iowa; 8,488; ZIP 50595.
Webster Groves city, E Missouri; 26,995; ZIP see ST. LOUIS.
Weehawken urb. twp., NE New Jersey; 13,383; ZIP see UNION CITY.
Weimar city, SW East Germany; 63,361.
Weirton city, NW West Virginia; 27,131; ZIP 26062*.
Welland city, S Ontario, Canada; 36,079.
Welland Canal waterway betw. Lakes Erie and Ontario.
Wellesley town, E Massachusetts; 28,051; ZIP see BOSTON.
Wellington city, CEN. New Zealand; cap.; 135,677.
Wellington city, S Kansas; 8,072; ZIP 67152.
Wellston city, E Missouri; 7,050; ZIP see ST. LOUIS.
—city, S Ohio; 5,410.
Wellsville, vill., NW New York; 5,815; ZIP 14895.
—city, E Ohio; 5,891; ZIP 43968.
Wenatchee city, CEN. Washington; 16,912; ZIP 98801*.
Weslaco city, S Texas; 15,313; ZIP 78596.
West Allis city, SE Wisconsin; 71,723; ZIP see MILWAUKEE.
West Bend city, SE Wisconsin; 16,555; ZIP 53095*.
West Berlin See BERLIN.
Westbrook city, SW Maine; 14,444; ZIP 04092.
Westbury vill., SE New York; 15,362; ZIP 11590.
West Caldwell boro., NE New Jersey; 11,887; ZIP see CALDWELL.
Westchester vill., NE Illinois; 20,033; ZIP see MAYWOOD.
West Chester boro., SE Pennsylvania; 19,301; ZIP 19380.
West Chicago city, NE Illinois; 10,111; ZIP 60185.
West Columbia city, CEN. South Carolina; 7,838; ZIP 29169.
West Concord uninc. place, S CEN. North Caralina; 5,347; ZIP see CONCORD.
West Covina city, SW California; 68,034; ZIP 91790*.
West Des Moines city, CEN. Iowa; 16,441; ZIP 50265.
West Elmira uninc. place, S New York; 5,901.

West End Anniston uninc. place, E Alabama; 5,515.
Westerly uninc. place, SW Rhode Island; 17,248; ZIP 02891.
Western Australia state, W Australia; 975,920 sq. mi.; 736,629; cap. Perth.
Western Samoa See SAMOA.
Western Springs vill., NE Illinois; 12,147; ZIP 60558.
Westerville vill., CEN. Ohio; 12,530; ZIP 43081.
Westfield city, SW Massachusetts; 31,433; ZIP 01085.
—town, E New Jersey; 33,720; ZIP 07090*.
West Frankfort city, S Illinois; 8,836; ZIP 62896.
West Germany See GERMANY.
West Hartford town, CEN. Connecticut; 68,031; ZIP see HARTFORD.
West Haven town, S Connecticut; 52,851; ZIP see NEW HAVEN.
West Haverstraw vill., SE New York; 8,558; ZIP 10993.
West Hazleton boro., E Pennsylvania; 6,059; ZIP see HAZLETON.
West Helena city, E Arkansas; 11,007; ZIP 72390.
West Hempstead-Lakeview uninc. place, SE New York; 25,846; ZIP see HEMPSTEAD.
West Hollywood uninc. place, SW California; 29,448.
West Indies series of isl. groups separating the North Atlantic from the Caribbean.
West Indies the group of British cols. in the Caribbean.
West Kildonan city, S Manitoba, Canada; 20,077.
West Lafayette city, W CEN . Indiana; 19,157; ZIP see LAFAYETTE.
Westlake city, N Ohio; 15,689; ZIP 44091.
West Long Branch boro., E New Jersey; 6,845; ZIP 07764.
West Memphis city, E Arkansas; 25,892; ZIP 72301.
West Miami town, SE Florida; 5,494.
West Mifflin boro., SW Pennsylvania; 28,070; ZIP see HOMESTEAD.
Westminster city and metropolitan boro., London, England; site of the Houses of Parliament and Buckingham Palace; 85,000.
Westminster Abbey A Gothic church in Westminster, London; burial place of English kings and notables.
Westminster city, SW California; 59,865; ZIP 92683.
—city, CEN. Colorado; 19,432; ZIP 80030.
—city, N Maryland; 7,207; ZIP 21157*.
West Monroe city, N Louisiana; 14,868; ZIP 71291.
Westmont vill., NE Illinois; 8,482; 60559.
—boro., SW CEN. Pennsylvania; 6,673.
Westmount city, S Quebec, Canada; 25,012.
West New Guinea prov. of Indonesia comprising the W part of New Guinea and adjacent islands; 159,375 sq. mi.; 716,000; cap. Kotabaru. Also **West Irian.**
West New York town, NE New Jersey; 40,627; ZIP 07093*.
West Norriton urb. twp., SE Pennsylvania; 12,438.
Weston city, N CEN. West Virginia; 7,323; ZIP 26452.
Weston town, S Ontario, Canada; 9,715.
West Orange town, NE New Jersey; 43,715; ZIP see ORANGE.
West Palm Beach city, SE Florida; 57,375; ZIP 33401*.
West Paterson boro., N New Jersey; 11,692; ZIP see LITTLE FALLS.
West Pittston boro., NE Pennsylvania; 7,074, ZIP see PITTSTON.
West Plains city, S Missouri; 6,893; ZIP 65775*.
West Point U.S. military reservation, SE New York; seat of the U.S. Military Academy; ZIP 10996.
—city, E Mississippi; 8,714; ZIP 39773.
West Saint Paul city, E Minnesota; 18,799; ZIP see ST. PAUL.
West Seneca uninc. place, W New York; 46,001; ZIP see BUFFALO.
West Springfield town, S Massachusetts; 28,461; ZIP 01089.
West University Place city, SE Texas; 13,317.
West View boro., SW Pennsylvania; 8,312; ZIP see PITTSBURGH.
West Virginia state, E United States; 24,181 sq. mi.; 1,744,237; cap. Charleston.
West Warwick town, CEN. Rhode Island; 24,323; ZIP 02893.
Westwego town, SE Louisiana; 11,402; ZIP 70094.
West Winter Haven uninc. place, CEN. Florida; 7,716.
Westwood boro., NE New Jersey; 11,105; ZIP 07675.

Westwood Lakes uninc. place, SE Florida; 12,811.
West York boro., S Pennsylvania; 5,314.
Wetaskiwin city, CEN. Alberta, Canada; 5,300.
Wethersfield town, CEN. Connecticut; 26,662; ZIP see HARTFORD.
Wewoka city, CEN. Oklahoma; 5,284; ZIP 74884.
Weyburn city, SE Saskatchewan, Canada; 9,101.
Weymouth town, E Massachusetts; 54,610; ZIP see BOSTON.
Wharton boro., N New Jersey; 5,535; ZIP 07885.
　—city, S Texas; 7,881; ZIP 77488.
Wheaton city, NE Illinois; 31,138; ZIP 60187*.
　—uninc. place, W CEN. Maryland; 66,247; ZIP see SILVER SPRINGS.
Wheat Ridge uninc. place, N CEN. Colorado; 29,795; ZIP 80033.
Wheeling vill., NE Illinois; 14,746; ZIP 60090.
　—city, NW West Virginia; 48,188; ZIP 26000*.
Whitby town, S Ontario, Canada; 14,685.
White Bear Lake city, E Minnesota; 23,313; ZIP see ST. PAUL.
Whitefish Bay vill., SE Wisconsin; 17,394; ZIP see MILWAUKEE.
Whitehall city, CEN. Ohio; 25,263; ZIP see COLUMBUS.
　—boro., SW Pennsylvania; 16,551.
Whitehaven uninc. place, SW Tennessee; 6,281; ZIP see MEMPHIS.
Whitehorse city, S Yukon, Canada; cap.; 11,217.
White Mountains range of the Appalachians, N CEN. New Hampshire.
White Oak boro., SW Pennsylvania; 9,304; ZIP see McKEESPORT.
White Plains city, SE New York; 50,125; ZIP 10600*.
White Rock city, SW British Columbia, Canada; 6,453.
White Russia See BYELORUSSIAN SSR.
White Sea inlet of the Barents Sea, NW RSFSR; 36,680 sq. mi.
White Settlement town, N Texas; 13,449; ZIP see FORT WORTH.
Whitewater city, SE Wisconsin; 12,038; ZIP 53190.
Whiting city, NW Indiana; 7,247; ZIP 46394.
Whitinsville uninc. place, S Massachusetts; 5,210; ZIP 01588.
Whitman town, E Massachusetts; 13,059; ZIP 02382.
Whitney uninc. place, SW Idaho; 13,603; ZIP see BOISE.
Whitney, Mount peak, E California; 14,496 ft.
Whittier city, SW California; 72,863; ZIP 90601*.
Wichita city, S CEN. Kansas; 276,554; ZIP 67200*.
Wichita Falls city, N Texas; 97,564; ZIP 76301*.
Wickliffe city, NE Ohio; 21,354; ZIP 44092.
Wight, Isle of isl. off the S coast of England; 147 sq. mi.; 109,284.
Wilkes-Barre city, NE Pennsylvania; 58,856; ZIP 18700*.
Wilkins urb. twp., SW Pennsylvania; 8,749.
Wilkinsburg boro., SW Pennsylvania; 26,780; ZIP see PITTSBURGH.
Willard vill., N Ohio; 5,510; ZIP 44890.
Williamsburg city, E Virginia; capital of Virginia (1699-1779); restored to colonial condition; 9,069; ZIP 23185.
Williamson city, SW West Virginia; 5,831; ZIP 25661.
Williamsport city, N CEN. Pennsylvania; 37,918; ZIP 17701*.
Williamston town, E North Carolina; 6,570; ZIP 27892.
Williamstown uninc. place, NW Massachusetts; 8,454; ZIP 01267.
Williamsville vill., W New York; 6,835; ZIP see BUFFALO.
Willimantic city, E CEN. Connecticut; 14,402; ZIP 06226.
Willingboro urb. twp., S CEN. New Jersey; 42,833; ZIP 08046.
Williston city, NW North Dakota; 11,280; ZIP 58801.
Williston Park vill., SE New York; 9,154; ZIP 11596.
Willmar city, SW CEN. Minnesota; 12,869; ZIP 56201.
Willoughby city, NE Ohio, 18,634; ZIP 44094*.
Willowick city, NE Ohio; 21,237; ZIP see WILLOUGHBY.
Wilmette vill., NE Illinois; 32,134; ZIP 60091.
Wilmington city, N Delaware; 80,386.
　—city, SE North Carolina, 40,169; ZIP 19800*.
　—city, SW Ohio; 10,051; ZIP 45177.
Wilson town, E CEN. North Carolina; 29,347; ZIP 14172.
　—boro., E Pennsylvania; 8,482; ZIP see CLAIRTON.

Wilson, Mount peak, SW California; 5,710 ft.; site of a famous observatory.
Wilson Dam power dam in the Tennessee River at Muscle Shoals, NW Alabama; 137 ft. high, 4,862 ft. long.
Wilton Manors town, SE Florida; 10,948; ZIP FORT LAUDERDALE.
Wimbledon town and municipal boro.; S England; scene of international tennis matches; 20,000.
Winchester city, E Indiana; 5,493; ZIP 47394.
　—city, CEN. Kentucky; 13,402; ZIP 40391.
　—town, E Massachusetts; 22,269; ZIP 01890.
　—city, N Virginia; 14,643; ZIP 22601.
Windber boro., S Pennsylvania; 6,332; ZIP 15963.
Winder city, N CEN. Georgia; 6,605; ZIP 30680.
Windsor municipal boro., S England; site of Windsor Castle, a residence of the English sovereigns; 15,000. Officially New Windsor.
Windsor town, N CEN. Newfoundland, Canada; 5,505.
　—city, SE Ontario, Canada, 203,300.
　—town, S Quebec, Canada; 6,589.
Windsor Heights town, S CEN. Iowa; 6,303; ZIP see DES MOINES.
Windward Islands isl. group, S Lesser Antilles; 1,412 sq. mi.; 702,000.
Winfield city, S Kansas; 11,405; ZIP 67156.
Winnetka vill., NE Illinois; 14,131; ZIP 60093*.
Winnfield city, N CEN. Louisiana; 7,142; ZZIP 71483.
Winnipeg city, SE Manitoba, Canada; cap.; 246,246.
Winnipeg, Lake lake, S Manitoba, Canada; 9,398 sq. mi.
Winona city, SE Minnesota; 26,438; ZIP 55987*.
Winooski city, NW Vermont; 7,309; ZIP see BURLINGTON.
Winslow city, E CEN. Arizona; 8,066; ZIP 86047.
Winsted city, NW Connecticut; 8,954; ZIP 06098.
Winston-Salem city, NW CEN. North Carolina; 132,-913; ZIP 27100*.
Winter Garden city, CEN. Florida; 5,153; ZIP 32787.
Winter Haven city, CEN. Florida; 16,136; ZIP 33880*.
Winter Park city, E CEN. Florida; 21,895; ZIP 32789*.
Winthrop town, E Massachusetts; 20,335; ZIP see BOSTON.
Winton boro., NE Pennsylvania; 5,456.
Wisconsin state, N United States; 56,154 sq. mi.; 4,417,731; cap. Madison.
Wisconsin Rapids city, CEN. Wisconsin; 18,587; ZIP 54494.
Woburn city, E Massachusetts; 37,406; ZIP 01801*.
Woodbine-Radnor-Glencliff uninc. place, N CEN. Tennessee; 14,485; ZIP see NASHVILLE.
Woodbridge urb. twp., NE New Jersey; 98,944; ZIP 07095.
Woodbury city, SW New Jersey; 12,408; ZIP 08096*.
Woodland city, CEN. California; 20,677; ZIP 95695*.
Woodlawn-Rockdale-Millford Mills uninc. place, N Maryland; 19,254.
Woodmere uninc. place, SE New York; 19,831; ZIP 11598.
Woodmont-Green Hills-Glendale uninc. place, N CEN. Tennessee; 23,161.
Wood-Ridge boro., NE New Jersey; 8,311; ZIP see RUTHERFORD.
Wood River city, SW Illinois; 13,186; ZIP 62095.
Woodson Terrace city, E Missouri; 5,936.
Woodstock city, N Illinois; 10,226; ZIP 60098.
Woodstock city, S Ontario, Canada; 20,486.
Woodward city, NW Oklahoma; 8,710; ZIP 73801.
Woonsocket city, NE Rhode Island; 46,820; ZIP 02895.
Wooster city, N CEN. Ohio; 18,703; ZIP 44691*.
Worcester city, CEN. Massachusetts; 176,572; ZIP 01600*.
Worland city, N CEN. Wyoming; 5,055; ZIP 82401.
Worms city, SW West Germany; 76,900.
Worth vill., NE Illinois; 11,999; ZIP 60482.
Worthington city, SW Minnesota; 9,825; ZIP 56187.
　—city, CEN. Ohio; 15,326; ZIP 43085.
Wroclaw city, SW Poland; 528,000.
Wuhan city, E CEN. China; 2,146,000.
Wuppertal city, W West Germany; 409,715.
Württemberg former state, SW Germany.
Würzburg city, S CEN. West Germany; 113,450.
Wyandotte city, SE Michigan; 41,061; ZIP 48192*.
Wyckoff urb. twp., NE New Jersey; 16,039; 07481.
Wyoming state, NW United States; 97,914 sq. mi.;

322,416; cap. Cheyenne.
—city, w Michigan; 55,560; ZIP see GRAND RAPIDS.
—city, SW Ohio; 9,089.
Wyomissing boro., SE Pennsylvania; 7,136; ZIP see READING.
Wytheville town, SW Virginia; 6,069; ZIP 24382.

Xenia city, SW CEN. Ohio; 25,373; ZIP 45385.

Yakima city, S Washington; 45,588; ZIP 98901*.
Yalta city, S Crimea; scene of a conference of Roosevelt, Churchill, and Stalin in February, 1945; 62,000.
Yalu river forming part of the boundary betw. NE China and Korea; 500 mi. long.
Yangtze river flowing from Tibet to the East China Sea; 3,600 mi. long.
Yankton city, SE South Dakota; 11,919; ZIP 57078.
Yarmouth town, SW Nova Scotia, Canada; 8,636.
Yauco town, SW Puerto Rico; 12,922; ZIP 00768.
Yazoo City city, W CEN. Mississippi; 10,796; ZIP 39194.
Yeadon boro., SE Pennsylvania; 12,136; ZIP see LANSDOWNE.
Yellow River Hwang Ho: *an alternate name.*
Yellow Sea inlet of the Pacific betw. Korea and China; 400 mi. long, 400 mi. wide.
Yellowstone Falls 2 waterfalls of the Yellowstone River in Yellowstone National Park; **Upper Yellowstone Falls,** 109 ft.; **Lower Yellowstone Falls,** 308 ft.
Yellowstone National Park largest and oldest of the US national parks, largely in NW Wyoming; 3,458 sq. mi.; established 1872.
Yellowstone River river, NW Wyoming, SE Montana, and NW North Dakota; 671 mi. long.
Yemen republic, SW Arabian peninsula, divided into the **Yemen Arab Republic** (also **Northern Yemen**); 75,000 sq. mi.; 5,900,000; cap. San'a, and the **People's Democratic Republic of Yemen** (also **Southern Yemen**); 112,000 sq. mi.; 1,590,275; cap. Aden.
Yerevan city, W Armenian SSR; cap; 791,000.
Yoakum city, S Texas; 5,755; ZIP 77995.
Yokohama city, CEN. Honshu, Japan; 2,238,264.
Yonkers city, SE New York; 204,297; ZIP 10700*.
York co. boro., CEN. Yorkshire, England; cap.; 107,150.
York city, SE Nebraska; 6,778; ZIP 68467*.
—city, S Pennsylvania; 50,335; ZIP 17400*.
Yorkshire co., NE England, divided into East Riding,

West Riding, and North Riding; 6,089 sq. mi.; 7,469,600; cap. York.
Yorkton city, SE Saskatchewan, Canada; 9,995.
Yosemite Valley gorge in **Yosemite National Park** (1,183 sq. mi.; established 1890), E CEN. California; 7 mi. long, 1 mi. wide; traversed by the Merced River that forms **Yosemite Falls,** Upper Fall, 1,430 ft.; Lower Fall, 320 ft.; with intermediate cascades, 2,425 ft.
Youngstown city, NE Ohio; 139,788; ZIP 44500*.
Ypres town, NW Belgium; site of three major battles of World War I, 1914, 1915, 1917; ab. 18,000.
Ypsilanti city, SE Michigan; 29,538; ZIP 48197.
Yuba City city, N CEN. California; 13,986; ZIP 95991.
Yucatán penin., SE Mexico and NE Central America; 70,000 sq. mi.
Yugoslavia, Federal People's Republic of republic, SE Europe; 98,538 sq. mi.; 21,000,000; cap. Belgrade.
Yukon terr., NW Canada; 207,076 sq. mi.; 21,000; cap. Whitehorse.
Yukon River river, NW Canada and CEN. Alaska; 2,300 mi. long.
Yuma city, SW Arizona; 29,007; ZIP 85364.

Zagreb city, CEN. Croatia, Yugoslavia; cap.; 566,224.
Zaire republic, CEN. Africa; 904,754 sq. mi.; 24,200,000; cap. Kinshasa.
Zambezi river, S Africa; 1,700 mi. long.
Zambia republic, member of the Commonwealth of Nations, S CEN. Africa; 288,130 sq. mi.; 4,750,000; cap. Lusaka.
Zanesville city, SE CEN. Ohio; 33,045; ZIP 43701*.
Zanzibar reg. of Tanzania off the coast of E Africa; comprises isls. of **Zanzibar** (640 sq. mi.) and Pemba (380 sq. mi.); 315,000.
—city, W Zanzibar; cap.; 68,490.
Zealand isl. of Denmark betw. the Kattegat and the Baltic Sea; 2,709 sq. mi.
Zion city, NE Illinois; 17,268; ZIP 60099.
Zululand dist., NE Natal, South Africa; formerly a native kingdom; 10,362 sq. mi.
Zurich canton, NE Switzerland; 667 sq. mi.; 952,000
—city, CEN. Zurich; cap.; 416,100.
Zuyder Zee former shallow inlet of the North Sea, NW Netherlands; drainage projects have reclaimed much of the land and formed Lake Ijssel. Also **Zuider Zee.**

ABBREVIATIONS

A *Chem.* Argon.
a. 1. About. 2. Accepted. 3. Acre(s). 4. Acting. 5. Active. 6. Ad (L, at). 7. Adjective. 8. After. 9. Afternoon. 10. *Music* Alto. 11. Amateur. 12. *Electr.* Ampere. 13. Anno (L, in the year). 14. *Electr.* Anode. 15. Anonymous. 16. Ante (L, before). 17. Approved. 18. Are (measure). 19. Area. 20. Assist(s) (baseball).
A or Å *Physics* Angstrom unit(s).
A. 1. Absolute (temperature). 2. Academy. 3. Acre. 4. America; American.
AA or A.A. *Mil.* Antiaircraft.
AAA or A.A.A. 1. Amateur Athletic Association. 2. American Automobile Association. 3. Automobile Association of America.
AAAA or A.A.A.A. 1. Amateur Athletic Association of America. 2. Associated Actors and Artists of America.
A.A.A.L. American Academy of Arts and Letters.
AAAS or A.A.A.S. 1. American Academy of Arts and Sciences. 2. American Association for the Advancement of Science.
AAF or A.A.F. Formerly, Army Air Forces.
A. and M. Agricultural and Mechanical (College).
A.A.U. Amateur Athletic Union.
A.A.U.P. American Association of University Professors.
A.A.U.W. American Association of University Women.
ab. or a.b. In baseball, (times) at bat.
Ab *Chem.* Alabamine.
A.B. Bachelor of Arts (L *Artium Baccalaureus*).
A.B. or a.b. Able-bodied seaman.
abbr. or abbrev. Abbreviation.
abl. *Gram.* Ablative.
abn. Airborne.
Abp. or abp. Archbishop.
abr. 1. Abridged. 2. Abridgment.
abs. 1. Absent. 2. Absolute (temperature). 3. Absolutely.
ac. 1. Account. 2. Acre.
a/c or A/C (*pl.* **a/cs** or **A/Cs**) Account; account current.
Ac *Chem.* Actinium.
AC or A.C. Air Corps. 2. Army Corps.
AC or A.C. or a.c. *Electr.* Alternating current.
A.C. 1. After Christ. 2. Athletic Club.
acad. Academic; academy.
acc. 1. Account. 2. *Gram.* Accusative.
accel. 1. *Music* Accelerando. 2. Accelerate.
accus. *Gram.* Accusative.
ack. Acknowledge; acknowledgment.
A.C.P. American College of Physicians.
acpt. Acceptance (in banking).
ACS or A.C.S. American Chemical Society.
A/Cs Pay. Accounts payable.
A/Cs Rec. Accounts receivable.
Act *Chem.* Actinium.
actg. Acting.
ad. 1. Adapted; adaptor. 2. Add. 3. Advertisement.
a.d. After date.
AD *Mil.* Active duty.
A.D. In the year of our Lord (L *anno domini*).
A.D.A. 1. American Dental Association. 2. Americans for Democratic Action.
A.D.C. or ADC or a.d.c. Aide-de-camp.
add. 1. Addenda; addendum. 2. Addition. 3. Address.
ad fin. At, to, or toward the end (L *ad finem*).
adj. 1. Adjacent. 2. Adjective. 3. Adjourned. 4. Adjunct. 5. Adjustment (in banking). 6. Adjutant.
ad loc. At or to the place (L *ad locum*).
adm. 1. Administrative; administrator. 2. Admitted.
ADM or Adm. Admiral.
admin. Administration; administrator.
admrx. or admx. Administratrix.
ads or A.D.S. Autograph document signed.
A.D.S. American Dialect Society.
adv. 1. Ad valorem (L). 2. Advance. 3. *Gram.* Adverb; adverbial. 4. Advertisement. 5. Advise. 6. Advocate. 7. Against (L *adversus*).
advt. Advertisement.
ae. At the age of; aged (L *aetatis*).
A.E.A. Actors' Equity Association.
A.E. and P. Ambassador Extraordinary and Plenipotentiary.
AEC Atomic Energy Commission.
AEF or A.E.F. American Expeditionary Force(s).
aeron. Aeronautic; aeronautics.
AF 1. Air Force. 2. Anglo-French; also **A.F.**
AF or A.F., a.f., or a-f Audio frequency.
AFB Air Force Base.
AFL or A.F.L. or A.F. of L. American Federation of Labor.
AFL-CIO or A.F.L.-C.I.O. American Federation of Labor and the Congress of Industrial Organizations.

AFNC Air Force Nurse Corps.
AFRes. Air Force Reserve.
AFROTC Air Force Reserve Officers Training Corps.
Ag *Chem.* Silver (L *argentum*).
Ag. August.
AG Adjutant General.
A.G. 1. Attorney General. 2. Joint-stock company (G *Aktiengesellschaft*).
agcy. Agency.
agr. Agricultural; agriculture; agriculturist.
agric. Agricultural; agriculture; agriculturist.
A.H. In the year of Hegira (L *anno the Hegirae*).
AI Aircraft interception.
AKC or A.K.C. American Kennel Club.
al. 1. Other things (L *alia*). 2. Other persons (L *alii*).
Al *Chem.* Aluminum.
AL or AL. or A.L. Anglo-Latin.
Ala. Alabama.
ALA or A.L.A. American Library Association.
Alas. Alaska (unofficial).
Ald. or, as title, Aldm. Alderman.
alg. *Math.* Algebra.
Alg. 1. Algeria; Algerian. 2. Algiers.
ALP or A.L.P. American Labor Party.
als or A.L.S. Autograph letter signed.
alt. 1. Alternate; alternating; alternation(s); alternative. 2. Altitude. 3. *Music* Alto.
alter. Alteration.
alum. Aluminum.
am. Ammeter.
Am *Chem.* Americium.
Am. America; American.
AM or A.M., a.m., or a-m Amplitude modulation.
A.M. 1. Master of Arts (L *Artium Magister*). 2. Associate member.
A.M. or a.m. Ante meridiem; before noon.
AMA or A.M.A. 1. American Management Association. 2. American Medical Association.
Amb. Ambassador.
AMC Air Materiel Command.
AMDG or A.M.D.G. To the greater glory of God (L *ad majorem Dei gloriam*).
A.M.E. African Methodist Episcopal.
Amer. America; American.
AMG Allied (or American) Military Government.
Am. Ind. American Indian.
amp. *Electr.* Amperage; ampere(s).
amp.-hr. *Electr.* Ampere-hour.
amt. Amount.
Am·vets (am′vets′) American Veterans of World War II and Korea.
an. Anno (L, in the year).
AN or A.N. or A.-N. Anglo-Norman.
anal. 1. Analogous; analogy. 2. Analysis; analytic(al).
anat. Anatomical; anatomist; anatomy.
ANC or A.N.C. Army Nurse Corps.
and. Andante.
Angl. 1. Anglican. 2. Anglicized.
ANGUS Air National Guard of the United States.
anim. Animato.
ann. 1. Annals. 2. Anni (L, years). 3. Annual. 4. Annuity.
anon. Anonymous.
ans. Answer; answered.
ant. 1. Antenna. 2. Antiquarian. 3. Antiquity. 4. Antonym(s).
ANTA American National Theatre and Academy.
antiq. 1. Antiquarian. 2. Antiquities.
ANZAC or A.N.Z.A.C. Australian and New Zealand Army Corps.
A/O or a/o Account of.
AOL or A.O.L. or a.o.l. *Mil.* Absent over leave.
ap. Apothecaries' (weight or measure).
Ap. 1. Apostle. 2. April.
AP *Mil.* 1. Air Police. 2. Armor-piercing.
AP or A.P. Associated Press.
apmt. Appointment.
APO Army Post Office.
Apoc. 1. Apocalypse. 2. Apocrypha; Apocryphal.
app. 1. Apparent(ly): also **appar.** 2. Appended. 3. Appendix. 4. Appointed. 5. Apprentice.
approx. Approximate(ly).
Apr or Apr. April.
apt. (*pl.* **apts.**) Apartment.
aq. or Aq. Aqua.
ar. 1. Aromatic. 2. Arrival; arrive.
a.r. In the year of the reign (L *anno regni*).
Ar *Chem.* Argon.
Ar. 1. Arabia; Arabic. 2. Aramaic. 3. Silver (L *argentum*).

ARC or **A.R.C.** American Red Cross.
arch. 1. Archaic; archaism. 2. Archery. 3. Archipelago. 4. Architect; architectural; architecture.
Arch. Archbishop.
Archbp. Archbishop.
Archd. 1. Archdeacon. 2. Archduke.
archeol. Archeology.
archit. Architecture.
archt. Architect.
arg. Silver (L *argentum*).
arith. Arithmetic(al).
Ariz. Arizona.
Ark. Arkansas.
Ar.M. Master of Architecture (L *Architecturae Magister*).
Armen. Armenian.
arr. 1. Arrange; arranged; arrangement(s). 2. Arrival; arrive; arrived.
art. 1. Article. 2. Artificial. 3. Artist.
Arty. Artillery.
A.R.V. American (Standard) Revised Version (of the Bible).
As *Chem.* Arsenic.
AS *Mil.* Antisubmarine.
AS or **AS., A.S.,** or **A.-S.** Anglo-Saxon.
ASA or **A.S.A.** American Standards Association.
asb. Asbestos.
ASCAP or **A.S.C.A.P.** American Society of Composers, Authors and Publishers.
asgd. Assigned.
ASN *Mil.* Army Service Number.
A.S.P.C.A. American Society for the Prevention of Cruelty to Animals.
ass. 1. Assistant. 2. Association.
assd. Assigned.
assn. Association.
assoc. 1. Associate. 2. Association.
asst. Assistant.
astr. Astronomer; astronomical; astronomy.
astrol. Astrologer; astrological; astrology.
astron. Astronomer; astronomical; astronomy.
at. 1. *Physics* Atmosphere. 2. Atomic.
At *Chem.* Astatine.
AT *Mil.* Antitank.
ATC Air Traffic Control.
athl. Athlete; athletic; athletics.
atm. *Physics* Atmosphere; atmospheric.
at. no. Atomic number.
att. 1. Attention. 2. Attorney.
atten. Attention.
attn. Attention.
attrib. 1. Attribute. 2. Attributive.
atty. Attorney.
Atty. Gen. Attorney General.
a.u. or **å.u., A.U.** or **A.U.** *Physics* Angstrom unit(s).
Au *Chem.* Gold (L *aurum*).
aud. Auditor.
aug. Augmentative.
Aug. or **Aug** 1. August. 2. Augustan; Augustus.
AUS or **A.U.S.** Army of the United States.
auth. 1. Author. 2. Authority. 3. Authorized.
Auth. Ver. Authorized Version (of the Bible).
auto. 1. Automatic. 2. Automotive.
aux. or **auxil.** Auxiliary.
av. 1. Average. 2. Avoirdupois: also **avdp.**
av. or **Av.** Avenue.
A.V. Authorized Version (of the Bible).
ave. or **Ave.** Avenue.
avg. Average.
avn. Aviation.
avoir. Avoirdupois.
A/W 1. Actual weight. 2. All water.
AWOL (*as an acronym pronounced* ā'wôl) *Mil.* Absent or absence without leave. Also **awol, A.W.O.L., a.w.o.l.**
ax. 1. Axiom. 2. Axis.
az. Azimuth.

B *Chem.* Boron.
b Base.
B Bishop (chess).
B– Bomber.
B. 1. Bacillus. 2. Bible. 3. Boston. 4. British. 5. Brotherhood.
B. or **b.** 1. Bachelor. 2. Balboa (coin). 3. Base. 4. *Music* Bass; basso. 5. Bat. 6. Bay. 7. Bench. 8. *Dent.* Bicuspid. 9. Bolivar (coin). 10. Boliviano. 11. Book. 12. Born. 13. Brass. 14. Breadth. 15. Brother.
B/– 1. Bag. 2. Bale.
Ba *Chem.* Barium.
B.A. 1. Bachelor of Arts (L *Baccalaureus Artium*). 2. British Academy.
bach. Bachelor.
bacteriol. or **bact.** Bacteriological; bacteriology.

B.A.E. 1. Bachelor of Aeronautical Engineering. 2. Bachelor of Arts in Education.
B.Agr. or **B.Ag.** Bachelor of Agriculture (L *Baccalaureus Agriculturae*)
B.Ag.Sc. Bachelor of Agricultural Science.
bal. Balance; balancing.
Balt. Baltic.
bap. or **bapt.** Baptized.
Bapt. or **Bap.** Baptist.
bar. 1. Barometer; barometric. 2. Barrel. 3. Barrister.
B.Ar. Bachelor of Architecture.
BAR *Mil.* Browning automatic rifle.
B.Arch. Bachelor of Architecture.
barit. *Music* Baritone.
Bart. Baronet.
B.A.S. or **B.A.Sc.** 1. Bachelor of Agricultural Science. 2. Bachelor of Applied Science.
b.b. or **bb** Base(s) on balls.
B.B.A. or **B.Bus.Ad.** Bachelor of Business Administration.
BBC or **B.B.C.** British Broadcasting Corporation.
bbl. (*pl.* **bbls.**) Barrel.
B.C. 1. Bachelor of Chemistry. 2. Bachelor of Commerce, 3. Before Christ. 4. British Columbia.
B.C.E. 1. Bachelor of Chemical Engineering. 2. Bachelor of Civil Engineering.
bch. (*pl.* **bchs.**) Bunch.
B.Ch.E. Bachelor of Chemical Engineering.
B.C.L. Bachelor of Civil Law.
B.C.P. Book of Common Prayer.
B.C.S. Bachelor of Chemical Science.
bd (*pl.* **bds.**) 1. Board. 2. Bond. 3. Bound. 4. Bundle.
B/D or **b.d.** 1. Bank draft. 2. Bills discounted.
B.D. 1. Bachelor of Divinity. 2. Bills discounted.
bd.ft. Board feet.
bdg. Binding.
bdl. or **bdle.** Bundle.
bds. 1. Bundles. 2. (Bound in) boards.
B.D.S. Bachelor of Dental Surgery.
B.E. 1. Bachelor of Education. 2. Bachelor of Engineering. 3. Bank of England. 4. Board of Education.
B.E. or **B/E** or **b.e.** Bill of exchange.
B.E.E. Bachelor of Electrical Engineering.
B.E.F. British Expeditionary Force(s).
B. ès L. Bachelor of Letters (Fr. *Bachelier ès Lettres*).
bev or **BEV** Billion electron volts.
bf or **b.f.** *Printing* Boldface.
B/F Brought forward.
B.F. 1. Bachelor of Finance. 2. Bachelor of Forestry.
B.F.A. Bachelor of Fine Arts.
bg. (*pl.* **bgs.**) Bag.
B.G. Brigadier General.
Bi *Chem.* Bismuth.
Bib. Bible; Biblical.
bibl. Bibliographical.
Bibl. Biblical.
bibliog. Bibliographer; bibliography.
bicarb. Sodium bicarbonate.
b.i.d. *Med.* Twice a day (L *bis in die*).
biog. Biographer; biographical; biography.
biol. Biological; biologist; biology.
B.J. Bachelor of Journalism.
bk. 1. Bank. 2. Block. 3. Book.
Bk *Chem.* Berkelium.
bkg. Banking.
bkkpg. Bookkeeping.
bks. 1. Barracks. 2. Books.
bkt. 1. Basket(s). 2. Bracket.
bl. 1. Bale(s). 2. Barrel(s). 3. Black. 4. Blue.
b.l. or **B/L** Bill of Lading.
B.L. Bachelor of Laws.
B.L.A. Bachelor of Liberal Arts.
bld. *Printing* Boldface.
bldg. Building.
B.Lit. or **B.Litt.** Bachelor of Letters (Literature) (L *Baccalaureus Litterarum*).
blk. 1. Black. 2. Block. 3. Bulk.
B.LL. Bachelor of Laws (L *Baccalaureus Legum*).
bls. 1. Bales. 2. Barrels.
BLS Bureau of Labor Statistics.
B.L.S. Bachelor of Library Science.
blvd. Boulevard.
b.m. Board measure.
BM Bureau of Mines.
B.M. 1. Bachelor of Medicine (L *Baccalaureus Medicinae*). 2. Bachelor of Music (L *Baccalaureus Musicae*).
B.M.E. 1. Bachelor of Mechanical Engineering. 2. Bachelor of Mining Engineering.
B.Mech.E. Bachelor of Mechanical Engineering.
BMEWS *Mil.* Ballistic Missile Early Warning System.
BMR *Physiol.* Basal metabolic rate.
B.Mus. Bachelor of Music.

bn. or **Bn.** Battalion.
B.N. Bank note.
B.N.A. 1. Basel Anatomical Nomenclature (L *Basel Nomina Anatomica*). 2. British North America.
b.o. 1. Back order. 2. Bad order. 3. Box office. 4. Branch office. 5. Broker's order. 6. Buyer's option. 7. Body odor.
B/O Brought over (bookkeeping).
bor. Borough.
bot. 1. Botanical; botanist; botany. 2. Bottle.
B.O.T. Board of Trade.
bp. 1. Birthplace. 2. Bishop.
b.p. or **bp.** 1. Below proof. 2. Boiling point.
B.P. Bachelor of Pharmacy (L *Baccalaureus Pharmaciae*).
B.P. or **B.Ph.** or **B.Phil.** Bachelor of Philosophy (L *Baccalaureus Philosophiae*).
B/P or **b.p.** 1. Bill of parcels. 2. Bills payable.
B.Pd. or **B.Pe.** Bachelor of Pedagogy.
B.P.E. Bachelor of Physical Education.
B.P.H. Bachelor of Public Health.
br. 1. Branch. 2. Brand. 3. Bronze. 4. Brother.
Br *Chem.* Bromine.
B/R or **b.r.** Bills receivable.
B/R or **B.R.** Bill of Rights.
B.Rec. or **b. rec.** Bills receivable.
brev. Brevet; brevetted.
Brig. *Mil.* 1. Brigade. 2. Brigadier.
Brig. Gen. Brigadier General.
Brit. 1. Britain; British. 2. Britannia.
bro. (pl. **bros.**) Brother.
b.s. 1. Balance sheet. 2. Bill of sale.
B/s 1. Bags. 2. Bales.
B.S. or **B.Sc.** Bachelor of Science (L *Baccalaureus Scientiae*).
B.S.A. 1. Bachelor of Scientific Agriculture. 2. Bibliographical Society of America. 3. Boy Scouts of America.
B.S.Ed. Bachelor of Science in Education.
bsh. Bushel(s).
Bs/L Bills of lading.
BSM Bronze Star Medal.
B.S.S. or **B.S.Sc.** or **B.S. in S.S.** Bachelor of (Science in) Social Sciences.
Bt. Baronet.
B.T. or **B.Th.** Bachelor of Theology (L *Baccalaureus Theologiae*).
btry. *Mil.* Battery.
BTU or **B.T.U.**, **B.Th.U.**, **b.t.u.**, or **btu** British thermal unit.
bu. or **bu** 1. Bureau. 2. Bushel(s).
buck. Buckram.
bul. Bulletin.
bull. Bulletin.
B.V. 1. Blessed Virgin (L *Beata Virgo*). 2. Farewell (L *bene vale*).
B.V.M. Blessed Virgin Mary (L *Beata Virgo Maria*).
bvt. Brevet; brevetted.
bx. (pl. **bxs.**) Box.
Bz. *Chem.* Benzene.

C *Chem.* Carbon.
c. or **C.** 1. About (L *circa*). 2. Calends. 3. Candle. 4. *Electr.* Capacity. 5. Cape. 6. Carbon. 7. Carton. 8. Case. 9. Catcher (baseball). 10. Cathode. 11. Cent(s). 12. Center. 13. Centigrade. 14. Centime(s). 15. Centimeter(s). 16. Century. 17. Chancery. 18. Chapter. 19. Chief. 20. Child. 21. Church. 22. City. 23. Cloudy. 24. Consul. 25. Copper. 26. Copy. 27. Copyright. 28. Corps. 29. Cost. 30. Cubic. 31. *Electr.* Current. 32. Gallon (L *congius*). 33. Hundredweight.
C *Math.* Constant.
C. 1. Catholic. 2. Celsius. 3. Celtic. 4. Chancellor. 5. Congress. 6. Conservative. 7. Court.
ca. 1. About (L *circa*). 2. Cathode. 3. Centare(s).
Ca *Chem.* Calcium.
CA or **C.A.** *Psychol.* Chronological age.
C.A. 1. Catholic Action. 2. Central America. 3. Confederate Army. 4. Court of Appeal.
C.A. or **c.a.** 1. Chartered accountant. 2. Chartered agent. 3. Chief accountant. 4. Claim agent. 5. Commercial agent. 6. Consular agent. 7. Controller of accounts.
C/A 1. Capital account. 2. Credit account. 3. Current account.
CAB or **C.A.B.** 1. Civil Aeronautics Board. 2. Consumers Advisory Board.
C.A.F. or **c.a.f.** 1. Cost and freight. 2. Cost, assurance, and freight.
cal. 1. Calendar; calends. 2. Caliber. 3. Calorie(s) (small).
Cal. 1. California (unofficial). 2. Large calorie(s).
Calif. California.
can. 1. Canon. 2. Canto.
canc. Cancel; cancellation; canceled.
Cant. 1. Canterbury. 2. Canticles. 3. Cantonese.
Cantab. Of Cambridge (L *Cantabrigiensis*).

cap. 1. Capacity. 2. (pl. **caps.**) Capital. 3. Capitalize. 4. Chapter (L *caput*).
CAP or **C.A.P.** Civil Air Patrol.
CAPT or **Capt.** *Mil.* Captain.
CAR or **C.A.R.** Civil Air Regulations.
Car. Carat(s).
Card. (title) Cardinal.
CARE Cooperative for American Remittances Everywhere.
cat. 1. Catalogue. 2. Catechism.
cath. Cathedral.
Cath. Catholic.
cav. 1. Cavalier. 2. Cavalry.
CAVU *Aeron.* Ceiling and visibility unlimited.
c.b. 1. Center of buoyancy. 2. Confined to barracks.
Cb 1. *Chem.* Columbium. 2. *Meteorol.* Cumulonimbus.
CB *Mil.* Construction Battalion.
C.B. 1. Bachelor of Surgery (L *Chirurgiae Baccalaureus*). 2. *Brit.* Companion of the Bath. 3. *Brit.* County borough.
C.B.D. or **c.b.d.** Cash before delivery.
cc. 1. Chapters. 2. Cubic centimeter(s): also **c.c., cc**
Cc *Meteorol.* Cirrocumulus.
C.C. or **c.c.** 1. Carbon copy. 2. Cashier's check. 3. Chief clerk. 4. Circuit court. 5. City council; city councilor. 6. Common councilman. 7. Consular clerk. 8. Contra credit. 9. County clerk. 10. County commissioner. 11. County council. 12. County court. 13. Current account (F *compte courant*).
CCA Commission for Conventional Armaments.
C.C.A. 1. Chief Clerk of the Admiralty. 2. Circuit Court of Appeals.
CCC 1. Civilian Conservation Corps. 2. Commodity Credit Corporation.
C.C.F. Cooperative Commonwealth Federation.
cd. Cord.
c.d. Cash discount.
Cd *Chem.* Cadmium.
C.D. Civilian Defense.
cd. ft. Cord foot (feet).
CDMB Civil and Defense Mobilization Board.
CDR or **Cdr.** *Mil.* Commander.
Ce *Chem.* Cerium.
CE 1. Corps of Engineers. 2. Council of Europe.
C.E. 1. Chemical Engineer. 2. Chief Engineer. 3. Christian Endeavor. 4. Church of England. 5. Civil Engineer.
CEA Council of Economic Advisers.
Celt. Celtic.
cen. 1. Central. 2. Century.
cent. 1. Centered. 2. Centigrade. 3. Centimeter(s).
CERN European Council for Nuclear Research (F *Centre Européen des Recherches Nucléaires*).
cert. or **certif.** Certificate; certificated.
Cey. Ceylon.
Cf *Chem.* Californium.
cf. 1. Calif. 2. Compare (L *confer*).
c/f Carried forward (bookkeeping).
c.f. or **cf** Center field; center fielder (baseball).
C.F. or **c.f.** Cost and freight.
C.F.I. or **c.f.i.** Cost, freight, and insurance.
c.f.m. or **cfm** Cubic feet per minute.
c.f.s. or **cfs** Cubic feet per second.
cg or **cg.** or **cgm.** Centigram(s).
CG 1. Commanding general. 2. Coast Guard: also **C.G.**
C.G. or **c.g.** 1. Center of gravity. 2. Consul general.
cgs The centimeter-gram-second system of measurement in which the unit of length is the centimeter, the unit of mass is the gram, and the unit of time is one second. Also **c.g.s., CGS, C.G.S.**
ch. or **Ch.** 1. Chain. 2. Champion. 3. Chancery. 4. Chaplain. 5. (pl. **chs.**) Chapter. 6. Check (in chess). 7. Chestnut. 8. Chief. 9. Child; children. 10. Church. 11. Of surgery (L *chirurgiae*).
C.H. *Brit.* Companion of Honor.
C.H. or **c.h.** 1. Clearing-house. 2. Courthouse. 3. Customhouse.
Ch.B. Bachelor of Surgery (L *Chirurgiae Baccalaureus*).
Ch.Clk. Chief Clerk.
Ch.E. Chemical Engineer.
chem. Chemical; chemist; chemistry.
chg. (pl. **chgs.**) Charge.
chgd. (pl. **chgs.**) Charge.
Ch.J. Chief Justice.
chm. 1. Checkmate. 2. Chairman: also **chmn.**
Ch.M. Master of Surgery (L *Chirurgiae Magister*).
Chr. 1. Christ. 2. Christian.
chron. or **chronol.** Chronological; chronology.
Chron. Chronicles.
chs. Chapters.
Ci *Meteorol.* Cirrus.
Cia. or **cia.** Company (Sp. *compañia*).
CIA Central Intelligence Agency.
CIC *Mil.* Counterintelligence Corps.

C.I.D. *Brit.* Criminal Investigation Dept.
Cie. or **cie.** Company (F *compagnie*).
C.I.F. or **c.i.f.** Cost, insurance, and freight.
CINC or **C in C** *Mil.* Commander in Chief.
CIO or **C.I.O.** Congress of Industrial Organizations.
circ. or **cir.** 1. About (L *circa, circiter, circum*). 2. Circular. 3. Circulation. 4. Circumference.
cit. 1. Citation; cited. 2. Citizen.
civ. 1. Civil. 2. Civilian.
C.J. 1. Corpus juris (L, body of law). 2. Chief Judge. 3. Chief Justice.
ck. (*pl.* **cks.**) 1. Cask. 2. Check. 3. Cook.
cl. 1. Claim. 2. Class. 3. Classification. 4. Clause. 5. Clearance. 6. Clergyman. 7. Clerk. 8. Cloth.
cl. or **cl** Centiliter(s).
c.l. 1. Carload; carload lots. 2. Center line. 3. Civil law. 4. Craft loss (insurance).
Cl. *Chem.* Chlorine.
clar. *Music* Clarinet.
class. 1. Classic; classical. 2. Classification. 3. Classified; classify.
clk. 1. Clerk. 2. Clock.
C.L.U. Chartered Life Underwriter.
Cm. *Chem.* Curium.
cm. or **cm** Centimeter(s).
c.m. 1. Church missionary. 2. Circular mil. 3. Common meter. 4. Corresponding member.
CM *Mil.* Court martial.
C.M. Master of Surgery (L *Chirurgiae Magister*).
Cmdr. Commander.
C.M.G. Companion (of the Order) of St. Michael and St. George.
cml. Commercial.
CmlC *Mil.* Chemical Corps.
Cn *Meteorol.* Cumulonimbus.
C/N or **c.n.** 1. Circular note. 2. Credit note.
CNO *Mil.* Chief of Naval Operations.
CNS or **C.N.S.** *Med.* Central nervous system.
Co *Chem.* Cobalt.
c.o. or **c/o** 1. Care of. 2. Carried over.
Co. or **co.** (*pl.* **cos.**) 1. Company. 2. County.
CO or **C.O.** 1. *Mil.* Commanding Officer. 2. Conscientious objector.
C/O Cash order.
Cod. or **cod.** (*pl.* **Codd.** or **codd.**) Codex.
C.O.D. or **c.o.d.** 1. Cash on delivery. 2. Collect on delivery.
coef. or **coeff.** Coefficient.
C. of C. Chamber of Commerce.
C of S Chief of Staff.
col. 1. Collected; collector. 2. College. 3. Colonial; colony. 4. Color; colored. 5. Column.
Col. 1. Colombia. 2. Colonel. 3. Colorado (unofficial). 4. Colossians. 5. Columbia.
coll. 1. Colleague. 2. Collect; collection; collector. 3. College; collegiate. 4. Colloquial.
collab. Collaborated; collaboration; collaborator.
collat. Collateral.
colloq. Colloquial; colloquialism; colloquially.
Colo. Colorado.
Coloss. Colossians.
com. 1. Comedy; comic. 2. Comma. 3. Commentary. 4. Commerce; commercial. 5. Common; commonly. 6. Commune. 7. Communication(s).
Com. 1. Commission. 2. Commissioner. 3. Committee. 4. Communist.
comb. Combination; combining.
comdg. *Mil.* Commanding.
Comdr. *Mil.* Commander.
Comdt. *Mil.* Commandant.
coml. Commercial.
comm. 1. Commerce. 2. Commissary. 3. Commission. 4. Committee. 5. Commonwealth.
COMO or **Como.** *Mil.* Commodore.
comp. 1. Companion. 2. Comparative. 3. Compare. 4. Comparison. 5. Compilation; compiled; compiler. 6. Complete. 7. Composition. 8. Compositor. 9. Compound; compounded. 10. Comprising.
compar. Comparative.
Comr. Commissioner.
Com. Ver. Common Version (of the Bible).
con. 1. Against (L *contra*). 2. *Music* Concerto. 3. Conclusion. 4. Condense. 5. Connection. 6. Consolidate. 7. Continued. 8. Wife (L *conjunx*).
Con. 1. Conformist. 2. Consul.
conc. 1. Concentrate; concentrated; concentration. 2. Concerning.
cond. 1. Condition. 2. *Music* Conducted. 3. Conductivity. 4. Conductor.
conf. 1. Compare (L *confer*). 2. *Med.* Confection. 3. Conference. 4. Confessor.

Confed. 1. Confederate. 2. Confederation.
cong. Gallon (L *congius*).
Cong. 1. Congregational. 2. Congress; Congressional.
conj. 1. Conjugation. 2. Conjunction. 3. Conjunctive.
Conn. Connecticut.
cons. 1. Consecrated. 2. Conserve. 3. Consigned; consignment. 4. Consolidated. 5. Consonant. 6. Construction. 7. Consulting.
cons. or **Cons.** 1. Constable. 2. Constitution; constitutional. 3. Consul.
consol. Consolidated.
Const. or **const.** 1. Constable. 2. Constant. 3. Constitution.
constr. Construction.
cont. 1. Containing. 2. Contents. 3. Continent. 4. Continue; continued. 5. Contract; contraction. 6. Contrary.
Cont. Continental.
contd. Continued.
contemp. Contemporary.
contg. Containing.
contin. 1. Continued. 2. Let it be continued. (L *continuetur*).
contr. 1. Contract; contraction. 2. *Music* Contralto. 3. Control.
contrib. Contribution; contributor.
CONUS *Mil.* Continental United States.
co-op. or **coop.** Cooperative.
cop. 1. Copper. 2. Copyright; copyrighted.
cor. 1. Corner. 2. Coroner. 3. Corpus. 4. Correct; corrected. 5. Correlative. 6. Correspondence; correspondent; corresponding. 7. Corrupt.
Cor. Corinthians.
corol. or **coroll.** Corollary.
corp. or **corpn.** Corporation.
corr. 1. Correct; corrected. 2. Correspondence; correspondent; corresponding. 3. Corrupt; corrupted; corruption.
corresp. Correspondence.
C.O.S. or **c.o.s.** Cash on shipment.
cosec *Trig.* Cosecant.
cot *Trig.* Cotangent.
cp or **c.p.** Candlepower.
cp. Compare.
CP *Mil.* Command Post.
C.P. 1. Cape Province. 2. Chief Patriarch. 3. Common Prayer. 4. Communist Party.
C.P. or **c.p.** 1. Chemically pure. 2. Court of probate.
CPA or **C.P.A.** Certified Public Accountant.
cpd. Compound.
Cpl. *Mil.* Corporal.
cpm or **c.p.m.** Cycles per minute.
CPO or **C.P.O.** Chief Petty Officer.
cps or **c.p.s.** Cycles per second.
cps. Coupons.
CQ *Mil.* Charge of Quarters.
cr. 1. Created. 2. Credit; creditor. 3. Creek. 4. Crown(s).
Cr *Chem.* Chromium.
cres. or **cresc.** *Music* Crescendo.
crim. con. *Law* Criminal conversation.
crit. 1. Critic; criticism; criticize. 2. Critical.
crs. Credits; creditors.
Cs 1. *Chem.* Cesium. 2. *Meteorol.* Cirrostratus.
C/S or **cs.** Case(s).
C.S. Christian Science; Christian Scientist.
C.S. or **c.s.** 1. Capital stock. 2. Civil service.
C.S.A. Confederate States of America.
csc *Trig.* Cosecant.
CSC Civil Service Commission.
csk. 1. Cask. 2. Countersink.
CST or **C.S.T.** or **c.s.t.** Central Standard Time.
ct. 1. Cent(s). 2. County. 3. Court. 4. One hundred (L *centum*).
Ct. 1. Connecticut. 2. Count.
CT or **C.T.** or **c.t.** Central Time.
ctn *Trig.* Cotangent.
ctr. Center.
cts. 1. Centimes. 2. Cents. 3. Certificates.
cu. or **cu** Cubic.
Cu 1. *Chem.* Copper (L *cuprum*). 2. *Meteorol.* Cumulus.
cu. cm. Cubic centimeter(s).
cu. ft. Cubic foot or feet.
cu. in. Cubic inch(es).
cur. 1. Currency. 2. Current.
cu. yd. Cubic yard(s).
c/v Catalogue value.
C.V. Common Version (of the Bible).
CWO *Mil.* 1. Chief Warrant Officer. 2. Commissioned Warrant Officer.
C.W.O. or **c.w.o.** Cash with order.
cwt. Hundredweight.
cyc. Cyclopedia; cyclopedic.
cyl. Cylinder; cylindrical.

D *Chem.* Deuterium.
d. or **D.** 1. Dam (in animal pedigrees). 2. Date. 3. Daughter. 4. Day(s). 5. Dead. 6. Decree. 7. Degree. 8. Democrat(ic). 9. Deputy. 10. Diameter. 11. Died. 12. Director. 13. Dollar. 14. Door (stage). 15. Dose. 16. Dowager. 17. Drachma. 18. Dyne. 19. *Med.* Give (L *da*).
D. 1. December. 2. Department. 3. Deus. 4. Doctor. 5. Dominus. 6. Don (Sp.). 7. Duchess. 8. Duke.
da 1. Daughter. 2. Day(s). 3. Deciare.
D.A. District Attorney.
Dak. Dakota.
dal. or **dal** Decaliter.
Dan. 1. Daniel. 2. Danish.
Dani. Daniel.
DAR or **D.A.R.** Daughters of the American Revolution.
dat. *Gram.* Dative.
dau. Daughter.
db or **db.** Decibel(s).
d.b.a. Doing business as.
D.B.E. Dame (Commander, Order) of the British Empire.
d.b.h. In forestry, diameter at breast height.
D.Bib. Douai Bible.
dbl. Double.
DC *Mil.* Dental Corps.
DC or **D.C.** or **d.c.** *Electr.* Direct current.
D.C. 1. District of Columbia. 2. Doctor of Chiropractic. 3. Da capo.
D.C.L. 1. Doctor of Canon Law. 2. Doctor of Civil Law.
D.C.M. *Brit.* Distinguished Conduct Medal.
D.C.S. 1. Deputy Clerk of Sessions. 2. Doctor of Christian Science. 3. Doctor of Commercial Science.
dd. or **d/d** Delivered.
D/D or **D/d** or **d.d.** 1. Days after date. 2. Day's (or days') date.
D.D. Doctor of Divinity (L *Divinitatis Doctor*).
D.D. or **D/D** Demand draft.
D.D.S. Doctor of Dental Surgery.
D.D.Sc. Doctor of Dental Science.
DE *Mil.* Destroyer Escort.
deb. or **deben.** Debenture.
dec. 1. Deceased. 2. Declaration. 3. Declension. 4. Declination. 5. Decrease. 6. Decrescendo.
dec. Decimeter.
Dec. or **Dec** December.
decd. Deceased.
decim. Decimeter.
decl. Declension.
def. 1. Defective. 2. Defendant. 3. Defense. 4. Deferred. 5. Defined. 6. Definite. 7. Definition.
deg. Degree(s).
del. 1. Delegate. 2. Delete. 3. Deliver.
Del. Delaware.
Dem. Democrat; Democratic.
demon. Demonstrative.
dent. Dental; dentist; dentistry.
dep. 1. Department. 2. Departs; departure. 3. Deponent. 4. Depot. 5. Deputy.
dept. 1. Department. 2. Deputy.
der. Derivation; derivative; derived.
desc. Descendant.
D. ès L. Doctor of Letters (F *Docteur ès Lettres*).
De ès S. Doctor of Sciences (F *Docteur ès Sciences*).
det. 1. Detach; detachment. 2. Detail.
Deut. Deuteronomy.
devel. Development.
DF or **D/F** or **D.F.** *Telecom.* Direction finding; direction finder.
DFC *Mil.* Distinguished Flying Cross.
dg or **dg.** Decigram(s).
D.G. Dei gratia.
d.h. 1. Deadhead. 2. That is to say; i.e. (G *das heisst*).
di. or **dia.** Diameter.
Di *Chem.* Didymium.
diag. Diagram.
dial. Dialect; dialectal.
diam. Diameter.
dict. 1. Dictation. 2. Dictator. 3. Dictionary.
diff. Difference; different.
dim. Dimension(s).
dim. or **dimin.** 1. *Music* Diminuendo. 2. Diminutive.
din. Dinar.
dioc. Diocesan; diocese.
dipl. Diplomat; diplomatic.
dir. Director.
dist. 1. Distance; distant. 2. Distinguish(ed). 3. District.
dist. atty. or **Dist. Atty.** District attorney.
distr. Distribute; distribution; distributor.
div. 1. Divided. 2. Dividend. 3. Division; divisor. 4. Divorce(d).
dkg or **dkg.** Dekagram(s).

dkl or **dkl.** Decaliter(s).
dkm or **dkm.** Dekameter(s).
dks or **dks.** Dekastere(s).
dl or **dl.** Deciliter(s).
D/L Demand loan.
D.Lit. or **D.Litt.** Doctor of Letters (or Literature) (L *Doctor Lit(t)erarum*).
dlr. Dealer.
D.L.S. Doctor of Library Science.
dlvy Delivery.
dm or **dm.** 1. Decameter(s). 2. Decimeter(s).
DM. or **Dm.** Deutschemark.
D.M. Deputy Master.
D.M.D. Doctor of Dental Medicine (L *Dentariae Medicinae Doctor*).
DME Distance Measuring Equipment.
D.Mus. Doctor of Music.
DMZ Demilitarized zone.
D.N. Our Lord (L *Dominus Noster*)
DNA *Biochem.* Deoxyribonucleic acid.
DNB or **D.N.B.** *Brit.* Dictionary of National Biography.
do. Ditto.
D.O. Doctor of Osteopathy.
doc. document.
DOD or **DoD** Department of Defense.
dol. Dollar(s).
dom. 1. Domain. 2. Domestic. 3. Dominion.
Dom. Dominican.
DO·VAP Doppler navigation. [< *Do(ppler) v(elocity) a(nd) p(osition)*]
Dow. or **dow.** Dowager.
doz or **doz.** Dozen(s).
DP or **D.P.** 1. *Chem.* Degree of polymerization. 2. Diametrical pitch. 3. Displaced person.
D.Ph. or **D.Phil.** Doctor of Philosophy.
D.P.H. Doctor of Public Health.
D.P.Hy. Doctor of Public Hygiene.
dpt. 1. Department. 2. Deponent.
D.P.W. Department of Public Works.
dr. 1. Debit. 2. Debtor. 3. Drachma. 4. Dram(s). 5. Drawer.
Dr. 1. Doctor. 2. Drive.
D.R. or **d.r.** or **D/R** 1. Dead reckoning. 2. Deposit receipt.
d.s. Decistere.
d.S. or **D.S.** *Music* Dal segno.
D.S. or **D.Sc.** Doctor of Science (L *Doctor Scientiae*).
DSC *Mil.* Distinguished Service Cross.
DSM *Mil.* Distinguished Service Medal.
D.S.O. *Brit.* 1. (Companion of the) Distinguished Service Order. 2. District Staff Officer.
d.s.p. Died without issue (L *decessit sine prole*).
DST or **D.S.T.** Daylight Saving Time.
D.S.T. Doctor of Sacred Theology.
d.t. 1. Delirium tremens. 2. Double time.
D.Th. or **D.Theol.** Doctor of Theology.
Du. 1. Duke. 2. Dutch.
dup. or **dupl.** Duplicate.
D.V. Douai Version (of the Bible).
D.V.M. Doctor of Veterinary Medicine.
D.V.M.S. Doctor of Veterinary Medicine and Surgery.
D/W Dock warrant.
dwt. Pennyweight.
DX or **D.X.** Distance; distant.
Dy *Chem.* Dysprosium.
dyn. or **dynam.** Dynamics.
dz. Dozen(s).

e 1. *Physics* Erg. 2. Error(s) (baseball).
e. 1. East; eastern. 2. Eldest. 3. Engineer; engineering. 4. Entrance (theater). 5. Error(s) (baseball).
E 1. East; eastern. 2. *Physics* Energy. 3. English. 4. Excellent.
E. 1. Earl. 2. Earth. 3. East; eastern. 4. Engineer; engineering. 5. English.
ea. Each.
E. & O.E. or **e. and o.e.** Errors and omissions excepted.
EbN East by north.
EbS East by south.
eccl. or **eccles.** Ecclesiastical.
Eccles. or **Eccl.** 1. Ecclesiastes. 2. Ecclesiastical.
Ecclus. Ecclesiasticus.
ecol. Ecological; ecology.
econ. Economic; economics; economy.
ECOSOC Economic and Social Council (of the UN).
ECSC European Coal and Steel Community.
ed. (*pl.* **eds.**) 1. Edited. 2. Edition. 3. Editor.
Ed.B. Bachelor of Education.
Ed.D. Doctor of Education.
edit. 1. Edited. 2. Edition. 3. Editor.
Ed. M. Master of Education.

EDP Electronic data processing.
EDT or **E.D.T.** or **e.d.t.** Eastern daylight time.
educ. Education; educational.
e.e. Errors excepted.
E.E. 1. Early English. 2. Electrical Engineer; electrical engineering.
E.E. & M.P. Envoy Extraordinary and Minister Plenipotentiary.
EEG *Med.* Electroencephalogram.
e.g. For example.
EIB or **E.I.B.** Export-Import Bank.
EKG *Med.* Electrocardiogram.
el. Elevation.
elec. or **elect.** or **electr.** Electric; electrical; electrician.
elem. 1. Element(s). 2. Elementary.
elev. Elevation.
E. long or **e. long.** East longitude.
Em. *Physics* Emanation.
EM *Mil.* Enlisted man (men).
E.M.F. or **e.m.f.** or **emf** Electromotive force.
Emp. 1. Emperor; Empress. 2. Empire.
E.M.U. or **e.m.u.** or **emu** Electromagnetic unit(s).
enc. Enclosed; enclosure(s).
ency. or **encyc.** or **encycl.** Encyclopedia.
ENE or **ene, E.N.E.** or **e.n.e.** East-Northeast.
eng. 1. Engine; engineer; engineering. 2. Engraved; engraver; engraving.
Eng. D. Doctor of Engineering.
engin. Engineering.
engr. 1. Engineer. 2. Engraved; engraver; engraving.
enl. 1. Enlarge(d). 2. Enlisted.
ENS or **Ens.** *Mil.* Ensign.
env. Envelope.
e.o. Ex officio (L).
Ep. Epistle(s).
Eph. Ephesians: also **Ephes.**
Epis. 1. Episcopal: also **Episc.** 2. Epistle(s).
Epist. Epistle(s).
eq. 1. Equal. 2. Equation. 3. Equator. 4. Equivalent
Er *Chem.* Erbium.
E.R. King Edward (L *Eduardus Rex*) or Queen Elizabeth (L *Elizabeth Regina*).
erron. Erroneous; erroneously.
E.R.V. English Revised Version (of the Bible).
Es *Chem.* Einsteinium.
Esd. Esdras.
ESE or **ese, E.S.E.,** or **e.s.e.** East-southeast.
esp. or **espec.** Especially.
ESP Extrasensory perception.
Esq. or **Esqr.** Esquire.
est. 1. Established. 2. Estate. 3. Estimated. 4. Estuary.
EST or **E.S.T.** or **e.s.t.** Eastern standard time.
estab. Established.
Esth. Esther.
e.s.u. or **esu** Electrostatic unit(s).
ETA Estimated time of arrival.
ethnol. Ethnology.
ETO European Theater of Operations.
ety. or **etym.** or **etymol.** Etymological; etymology.
Eu *Chem.* Europium.
ev or **e.v.** Electron volt(s).
E.V. English Version (of the Bible).
ex. 1. Examination; examined. 2. Example. 3. Except; excepted; exception. 4. Exchange. 5. Excursion.
Ex. Exodus.
exam. Examination; examined.
exc. 1. Excellent. 2. Except; excepted; exception. 3. Exchange. 4. Excursion.
Exc. Excellency.
exch. 1. Exchange. 2. Exchequer.
excl. 1. Exclamation: also **exclam.** 2. Exclusive.
exec. 1. Executive. 2. Executor.
ex int. Without (L *ex*) interest.
Exod. Exodus.
exp. 1. Expenses. 2. Expiration; expired. 3. Export; exported; exporter. 4. Express.
expt. Experiment.
exptl. Experimental.
exr. Executor.
ext. 1. Extension. 2. External; externally. 3. Extinct. 4. Extra. 5. Extract.
Ez. or **Ezr.** Ezra.

F *Chem.* Fluorine.
f or **f.** 1. Foul(s). 2. *Math.* Function (of).
F *Math.* Function.
F, F/, F:, f, f/, or **f:** *Photog.* F number.
F or **F.** 1. Fahrenheit. 2. French.
F or **F.** or **f** 1. *Electr.* Farad. 2. Fathom.
F. 1. February. 2. Fellow. 3. France. 4. Friday. 5. Son (L *filius*).

F. or **f.** 1. Farthing. 2. Feminine. 3. Fine. 4. Fluid (ounce). 5. Folio. 6. Following. 7. Franc. 8. Frequency.
FA *Mil.* Field Artillery.
F.A. Fine Arts.
F.A. or **f.a.** 1. Free alongside. 2. Freight agent.
F.A.A.A.S. Fellow of the American Association for the Advancement of Science.
fac. 1. Facsimile. 2. Factor. 3. Factory.
F.A.C.P. Fellow of the American College of Physicians.
F.A.C.S. Fellow of the American College of Surgeons.
Fah. or **Fahr.** Fahrenheit.
fam. 1. Familiar. 2. Family.
FAO or **F.A.O.** Food and Agriculture Organization (of the United Nations).
F.A.S. or **f.a.s.** Free alongside ship.
fasc. Bundle; fascicle (L *fasciculus*).
fath. Fathom.
f.b. 1. Freight bill. 2. Fullback: also **fb.**
FBI or **F.B.I.** Federal Bureau of Investigation.
f.c. *Printing* Follow copy.
FC *Mil.* Finance Corps.
FCA Farm Credit Administration.
FCC or **F.C.C.** Federal Communications Commission.
F.D. 1. Fidei Defensor. 2. Fire Department.
FDA or **F.D.A.** Food and Drug Administration.
FDIC or **F.D.I.C.** Federal Deposit Insurance Corporation.
Fe *Chem.* Iron (L *ferrum*).
Feb. or **Feb** February.
fed. 1. Federal. 2. Federated; federation.
fem. Feminine; female.
ff *Music* Fortissimo.
ff. 1. Folios. 2. Following.
F.F.A. or **f.f.a.** 1. Free foreign agent. 2. Free from alongside.
FHA Federal Housing Administration.
FHLBB Federal Home Loan Bank Board.
FICA Federal Insurance Contributions Act.
fid. 1. Fidelity. 2. Fiduciary.
fig. 1. Figurative(ly). 2. Figure(s).
fl. 1. Floor. 2. Florin(s). 3. Flower. 4. Fluid. 5. *Music* Flute.
Fl *Chem.* Fluorine.
Fla. Florida.
fld. Field.
fl. dr. Fluid dram(s).
flex. Flexible.
Flor. Florida (unofficial).
fl. oz. Fluid ounce(s).
fm. 1. Fathom. 2. From.
Fm *Chem.* Fermium.
FM *Mil.* Field manual.
FM or **F.M., f-m,** or **f.m.** *Telecom.* Frequency modulation.
F.M. 1. Field Marshal. 2. Foreign Missions.
FMB Federal Maritime Board.
FMCS Federal Mediation and Conciliation Service.
FNMA Federal National Mortgage Association.
F.O. Foreign Office.
f.o.b. or **F.O.B.** Free on board.
fol. 1. Folio. 2. Following.
foll. Following.
for. 1. Foreign. 2. Forestry.
fort. Fortification; fortified.
fp *Music* Forte piano (Ital.).
fp. Foolscap.
f.p. or **fp** Forward pass.
F.P. or **f.p.** 1. Fireplug. 2. Fire policy. 3. Floating policy. 4. Fully paid.
F.P. or **f.p.** or **fp** 1. Foot-pound(s). 2. Freezing point.
FPA or **F.P.A.** Foreign Press Association.
FPC or **F.P.C.** Federal Power Commission.
fpm or **f.p.m.** Feet per minute.
FPO *Mil.* Fleet post office.
fps or **f.p.s.** 1. Feet per second. 2. Foot-pound-second (system).
fr. 1. Fragment. 2. Franc. 3. From.
Fr *Chem.* Francium.
Fr. 1. Brother (L *Frater*). 2. *Eccl.* Father. 3. France. 4. French. 5. Friar. 6. Friday. 7. Wife (G *Frau*).
FRB Federal Reserve Board.
F.R.C.P. Fellow of the Royal College of Physicians.
F.R.C.S. Fellow of the Royal College of Surgeons.
freq. 1. Frequency. 2. Frequentative. 3. Frequent(ly).
F.R.G.S. Fellow of the Royal Geographical Society.
Fri. Friday.
Frl. Fräulein.
FRS Federal Reserve System.
frt. Freight.
f.s. Foot-second.
ft. 1. Feet; foot. 2. Fort. 3. Fortification; fortified.
FTC or **F.T.C.** Federal Trade Commission.

fth. or **fthm.** Fathom.
ft-lb Foot-pound(s).
furn. Furnished; furniture.
fut. Future.
f.v. On the back of the page (L *folio verso*).
FWA, F.W.A. Federal Works Agency.
fwd. Forward.
FY Fiscal year.

g. or **g** 1. Goalie; goalkeeper. 2. Gram(s).
G 1. German: also **G.** 2. Gravitational force. 3. *Mil.* Gun.
G. 1. Specific gravity. 2. Gulf.
G. or **g.** 1. *Electr.* Conductance. 2. Gauge. 3. Grain(s). 4. Guilder(s). 5. Guinea(s).
Ga *Chem.* Gallium.
Ga or **G.A.** 1. General Agent. 2. General Assembly (of the United Nations).
Ga. 1. Gallic. 2. Georgia.
G.A. or **G/A** or **g.a.** General average.
Gal. Galatians.
gall. Gallon(s).
gals. Gallons.
galv. Galvanic; galvanism; galvanized.
GAO General Accounting Office.
GAR or **G.A.R.** Grand Army of the Republic.
gaz. 1. Gazette. 2. Gazetteer.
G.B.E. (Knight or Dame) Grand (Cross or Order) of the British Empire.
GCA or **G.C.A.** Ground control approach.
G.C.B. (Knight) Grand Cross of the Bath.
G.C.L.H. Grand Cross of the Legion of Honor.
GCM *Mil.* General Court Martial.
G.C.M. or **g.c.m.** or **gcm** Greatest common measure.
GCT or **G.C.T.** Greenwich civil time.
G.C.V.O. (Knight) Grand Cross of the (Royal) Victorian Order.
Gd *Chem.* Gadolinium.
G.D. Grand Duchess; Grand Duchy; Grand Duke.
gds. Goods.
Ge Germanium.
geb. Born (G *geboren*).
gel. Gelatinous.
gen. 1. Gender. 2. Genera. 3. General; generally. 4. Generator. 5. Generic. 6. Genitive. 7. Genus.
Gen. 1. *Mil* General. 2. Genesis. 3. Geneva; Genevan.
geneal. Genealogical; genealogy.
genit. Genitive.
genl. General.
gent. Gentleman; gentlemen.
geod. Geodesy; geodetic.
geog. Geographer; geographic(al); geography.
geol. Geologic(al); geologist; geology.
geom. Geometrician; geometric(al); geometry.
ger. Gerund.
Ger. German; Germany.
gest. Died (G *gestorben*).
g.gr. Great gross.
GHA Greenwich hour angle.
GHQ, G.H.Q. *Mil.* General Headquarters.
GI or **G.I.** 1. General issue. 2. Government issue.
gi. Gill(s).
G.I. or **g.i.** *Anat.* Gastrointestinal.
Gk. Greek
gl. 1. Glass. 2. Gloss (sheen).
gld. Guilder(s).
gloss. Glossary.
glt. Gilt (bookbinding).
gm. Gram(s).
G.M. 1. General manager. 2. *Brit.* George Medal. 3. Grand Master.
GMT or **G.M.T.** or **G.m.t.** Greenwich mean time.
GNP or **G.N.P.** Gross national product.
GO *Mil.* General Order.
GOP or **G.O.P.** Grand Old Party: the Republican Party.
Gov. or **gov.** Governor.
Govt. or **govt.** Government.
G.P. 1. General paresis. 2. General practitioner. 3. Graduate in Pharmacy.
GPM or **gpm** or **g.p.m.** Gallons per minute.
GPO or **G.P.O.** 1. General Post Office. 2. Government Printing Office.
G.P.U. The OGPU.
GQ or **G.Q.** or **g.q.** *Mil.* General quarters.
gr. 1. Grade. 2. Grain(s). 3. Gram(s). 4. Grammar. 5. Great. 6. Gross. 7. Group.
gro. Gross (unit of quantity).
gr.wt. Gross weight.
GS 1. *Mil.* General Staff. 2. German silver.
G.S. 1. General Secretary. 2. Girl Scouts.
GSA General Services Administration.
GSC *Mil.* General Staff Corps.

G.S.U.S.A. Girls Scouts of the U.S.A.
gt. 1. Gilt (bookbinding). 2. Great.
G.T.C. or **g.t.c.** Good till canceled (or countermanded).
gtd. Guaranteed.
g.u. *Anat.* Genitourinary.
guar. Guaranteed.
guttat. *Med.* By drops (L *guttatim*).
g.v. Gravimetric volume.
gym. Gymnasium; gymnastics.
gyn. or **gynecol.** Gynecological; gynecology.

H *Chem.* Hydrogen.
h. or **h** Hit(s) (baseball).
H. or **h.** 1. Harbor. 2. Hard; hardness. 3. Heavy sea. 4. Height. 5. Hence. 6. High. 7. *Music* Horns. 8. Hour(s). 9. Hundred. 10. Husband.
ha. Hectare(s).
Hal. *Chem.* Halogen.
hb. or **hb** Halfback.
H.B.M. His (or Her) Britannic Majesty.
H.C. House of Commons.
hd. 1. Hand. 2. Head.
hdbk. Handbook.
hdkf. Handkerchief.
He *Chem.* Helium.
HE or **H.E.** High explosive.
H.E. 1. His Eminence. 2. His Excellency.
Heb. or **Hebr.** Hebrew(s).
her. Heraldic; heraldry.
hf. Half.
Hf *Chem.* Hafnium.
HF or **H.F., hf** or **h.f.** High frequency.
hg. 1. Hectogram(s). 2. Heliogram.
Hg *Chem.* Mercury (L *hydrargyrum*).
HG High German.
H.G. 1. His (or Her) Grace. 2. *Brit.* Home Guard.
hgt. Height.
H.H. 1. His (or Her) Highness. 2. His Holiness.
hhd. Hogshead.
H.I.H. His (or Her) Imperial Highness.
H.I.M. His (or Her) Imperial Majesty.
Hind. 1. Hindi. 2. Hindu. 3. Hindustan. 4. Hindustani.
hist. 1. Histology. 2. Historian; historical; history.
H.J. Here lies (L *hic jacet*).
H.J.S. Here lies buried (L *hic jacet sepultus*).
hkf. Handkerchief.
hl. or **hl** Hectoliter(s).
H.L. House of Lords.
hm. or **hm** Hectometer(s).
H.M. His (or Her) Majesty.
H.M.S. 1. His (or Her) Majesty's Ship (or Steamer). 2. His (or Her) Majesty's Service.
ho. House.
Ho. *Chem.* Holmium.
hon. Honorably; honorary.
Hon. Honorable.
hor. Horizon; horizontal.
horol. Horology.
hort. Horticulture; horticultural.
Hos. Hosea.
hosp. Hospital.
HP or **hp, H.P.** or **h.p.** 1. High pressure. 2. Horsepower.
HQ or **hq, H.Q.** or **h.q.** Headquarters.
hr. (*pl.* **hrs.**) Hour.
h.r. or **hr** Home run(s).
Hr. Mister (G *Herr*).
H.R. 1. Home Rule. 2. House of Representatives.
H.R.H. His (or Her) Royal Highness.
H.R.I.P. Here rests in peace (L *hic requiescat in pace*)
h.s. 1. Here is buried (L *hic sepultus* or *situs*). 2. High school. 3. In this sense (L *hoc sensu*).
H.S. 1. High School. 2. *Brit.* Home Secretary.
H.S.H. His (or Her) Serene Highness.
H.S.M. His (or Her) Serene Majesty.
ht. 1. Heat. 2. Height.
Hts. Heights.
H.V. or **h.v.** or **hv** High voltage.
h.w. High water.
hypoth. Hypothesis; hypothetical.

I *Chem.* Iodine.
i. 1. Incisor. 2. Interest. 3. Intransitive. 4. Island.
I. 1. Island(s); Isle(s). 2. Iowa (unofficial).
Ia. Iowa (unofficial).
IAEA International Atomic Energy Agency (of the United Nations).
IAS Indicated air speed.
ib. or **ibid.** In the same place (L *ibidem*).
IBRN International Bank for Reconstruction and Development.
IBT International Brotherhood of Teamsters.

IC   Immediate constituent.
ICAO   International Civil Aviation Organization.
ICBM   The intercontinental ballistic missile.
ICC or **I.C.C.**   Interstate Commerce Commission.
ICJ   International Court of Justice.
id.   The same (L *idem*).
Id.   Idaho (unofficial).
ID or **I.D.** or **i.d.**   Inside diameter.
Ida.   Idaho (unofficial).
i.e.   That is (L *id est*).
IF or **I.F.**, **i.f.** or **i-f**   Intermediate frequency.
I.G.   1. Amalgamation (G *Interessengemeinschaft*). 2. Indo-Germanic. 3. Inspector General: also **IG**
ign.   1. Ignites; ignition. 2. Unknown (L *ignotus*).
IGY or **I.G.Y.**   International Geophysical Year.
IHP or **ihp, I.H.P.** or **i.h.p.**   Indicated horsepower.
IHS   A monogram of the name Jesus, derived from the Greek IH(ΣΟΥ)Σ, Jesus.
Ill.   Illinois.
illus.   Illustrated; illustration; illustrator.
illust.   Illustrated; illustration; illustrator.
ILO or **I.L.O.**   International Labor Organization (of the United Nations).
I.L.P.   *Brit.* Independent Labour Party.
ILS   Instrument landing system.
imit.   Imitation; imitative.
imp.   1. Imperative. 2. Imperfect. 3. Imperial. 4. Impersonal. 5. Import; imported; importer. 6. Important. 7. Imprimatur. 8. Improper.
imper.   Imperative.
imperf.   1. Imperfect. 2. Imperforate.
impers.   Impersonal.
impf.   Imperfect.
imp. gal.   Imperial gallon.
impv.   Imperative.
in.   Inch(es).
In   *Chem.* Indium.
inbd.   Inboard.
inc.   1. Inclosure. 2. Including. 3. Inclusive. 4. Income. 5. Incorporated. 6. Increase.
inch. or **incho.**   Inchoative.
incl.   1. Inclosure. 2. Including.
incog.   Incognito.
incor. or **incorp.**   Incorporated.
incr.   Increased; increasing.
ind.   1. Independent. 2. Index. 3. Indicated; indicative. 4. Indigo. 5. Indirect. 6. Industrial.
Ind.   Indiana.
I.N.D.   In the name of God (L *in nomine Dei*).
indecl.   *Gram.* Indeclinable.
indef.   Indefinite.
indent.   *Printing* Indention.
indic.   Indicating; indicative; indicator.
inf.   1. Below (L *infra*). 2. Inferior. 3. Infinitive. 4. Information.
Inf. or **inf.**   Infantry.
infl.   Influence(d).
init.   1. Initial. 2. In the beginning (L *initio*).
in.-lb.   Inch-pound.
inorg.   Inorganic.
I.N.R.I.   Jesus of Nazareth, King of the Jews (L *Iesus Nazarenus, Rex Iudaeorum*).
ins.   1. Inches. 2. Inspector. 3. Insular. 4. Insulated; insulation. 5. Insurance.
insol.   Insoluble.
insp.   Inspected; inspector.
inst.   1. *Archaic* Instant (this month). 2. Instantaneous. 3. Instrument(al).
Inst.   Institute; Institution.
instr.   1. Instructor. 2. Instrument(al).
int.   1. Intelligence. 2. Interest. 3. Interior. 4. Interjection. 5. Internal. 6. International. 7. Interval. 8. Intransitive.
inter.   Intermediate.
internat.   International.
Interpol   International Police Organization.
interrog.   Interrogative.
intr.   Intransitive.
introd.   Introduction; introductory.
inv.   1. Invented; invention; inventor. 2. Invoice.
Io   Ionium.
Io.   Iowa (unofficial).
IOU   A written acknowledgment of indebtedness having on it these letters (meaning *I owe you*). Also **I.O.U.**
i.p.   1. Innings pitched: also **ip** 2. In passing (chess).
IPA or **I.P.A.**   International Phonetic Alphabet (or Association)
i.q.   The same as (L *idem quod*).
IQ or **I.Q.**   Intelligence quotient.
Ir   *Chem.* Iridium.
I.R.A.   Irish Republican Army.

IRBM   The intermediate range ballistic missile, having a range between 200 and 1500 miles. Compare *ICBM*.
irreg.   Irregular(ly).
IRS   Internal Revenue Service.
Is.   1. Isaiah. 2. Island(s); isle: also **is.**
Isa.   Isaiah.
isl.   Island(s).
iso.   Isotropic.
isom.   Isometric.
isoth.   Isothermal.
isth.   Isthmus.
it. or **ital.**   Italic(s).

J   *Physics* Joule.
J.   1. Journal. 2. Judge. 3. Justice.
Ja.   January.
JA   Judge Advocate.
JAG   Judge Advocate General.
J.C.D.   1. Doctor of Canon Law (L *Juris Canonici Doctor*). 2. Doctor of Civil Law (L *Juris Civilis Doctor*).
JCS   Joint Chiefs of Staff.
jct. or **jctn.**   Junction.
J.D.   Doctor of Laws (L *Juris Doctor*).
Je.   June.
Jer.   Jeremiah.
j.g. or **jg**   Junior grade.
Jl.   July.
Jon.   Jonah.
Josh.   Joshua.
jour.   1. Journal. 2. Journeyman.
J.P.   Justice of the Peace.
Jr. or **jr.**   Junior.
Ju.   Judges.
Judg.   Judges.
Jul.   July.
Jun. or **jun.**   Junior.
Junc. or **junc.**   Junction.
Jur.D.   Doctor of Law (L *Juris Doctor*).
jurisp.   Jurisprudence.
jus. or **just.**   Justice.
juv.   Juvenile.
j.v.   Junior varsity.
Jy.   July.

K   *Chem.* Potassium.
k   Kilo.
k.   1. *Electr.* Capacity. 2. Carat or karat. 3. *Math.* Constant.
K   1. *Physics* Kelvin (temperature scale). 2. King (chess). 3. Koruna.
K. or **k.**   1. Calends (L *kalendae*). 2. Kilogram. 3. King. 4. Knight. 5. Kopeck(s). 6. Krone.
ka.   Cathode or kathode.
kal.   Calends (L *kalendae*).
Kan.   Kansas (unofficial).
Kas.   Kansas (unofficial).
KB   King's bishop (chess).
K.B.   1. King's Bench. 2. Knight Bachelor.
KBP   King's bishop's pawn (chess).
kc. or **kc**   Kilocycle(s).
K.C.   1. King's Counsel. 2. Knights of Columbus.
kcal.   Kilocalorie.
K.C.B.   Knight Commander (of the Order) of the Bath.
K.C.V.O.   Knight Commander of the (Royal) Victorian Order.
Ken.   Kentucky (unofficial).
kg. or **kg**   1. Keg(s). 2. Kilogram(s).
K.G.   Knight (of the Order) of the Garter.
K.G.B.   In the Soviet Union, the Commission of State Security.
KIA   *Mil.* Killed in action.
kilo.   1. Kilogram(s): also **kilog.** 2. Kilometer(s): also **kilom.**
kilol.   Kiloliter.
KKK or **K.K.K.**   Ku Klux Klan.
KKt   King's knight (chess).
KKtP   King's knight's pawn (chess).
kl. or **kl**   Kiloliter(s).
km. or **km**   Kilometer(s).
KO or **K.O.** or **k.o.**   Knockout (boxing).
kop.   Kopeck(s).
KP   King's pawn (chess).
KP or **K.P.**   Kitchen police.
kr   Krone.
Kr   *Chem.* Krypton.
KR   King's rook (chess).
KRP   King's rook's pawn (chess).
kt.   Karat or carat.
Kt.   Knight (chess).
kv. or **kv**   Kilovolt(s).
kva or **kv.-a.**   Kilovolt-ampere.

kw. or **kw** Kilowatt(s).
K.W.H., kw-h, kwh, kw-hr., kw-hr Kilowatt-hour(s).
Ky. Kentucky.

l- or **l** *Chem.* Levo-.
l. or **l** Liter.
L 1. Latin. 2. *Physics* Length. 3. Longitude.
L or **l** *Electr.* Coefficient of inductance.
L or **£** or **l.** Pound (sterling) (L *libra*).
L. 1. Latin. 2. Licentiate. 3. Linnaeus.
L. or **l.** 1. Book (L *liber*). 2. Lake. 3. Latitude. 4. Law. 5. Leaf. 6. Left. 7. Length. 8. Line. 9. Link. 10. Lira; lire. 11. Low.
La *Chem.* Lanthanum.
La. Louisiana.
L.A. 1. Legislative Assembly. 2. Library Association. 3. Local Agent. 4. Los Angeles.
lab. Laboratory.
lam. Laminated.
Lam. Lamentations.
L.A.M. Master of Liberal Arts (L *Liberalium Artium Magister*).
lang. Language.
lat. Latitude.
lb. Pound(s) (L *libra, librae*).
L.B. 1. Bachelor of Letters (L *Litterarum Baccalaureus*). 2. Local Board.
lbs. Pounds.
l.c. 1. Left center. 2. In the place cited (L *loco citato*). 3. *Printing* Lower case.
L/C or **l/c** Letter of credit.
L.C. Library of Congress.
L.C.D. or **l.c.d.** or **lcd** Least (or lowest) common denominator.
LCDR or **LCdr** *Mil.* Lieutenant Commander.
L.C.L. or **l.c.l.** Less than carload lot.
L.C.M. or **l.c.m.** or **lcm** Least (or lowest) common multiple.
ld. *Printing* Lead.
Ld. 1. Limited. 2. Lord.
L.D. or **LD** Low Dutch.
L.D.S. Licentiate in Dental Surgery.
l.e. or **le** Left end.
lea. 1. League. 2. Leather.
lect. Lecture; lecturer.
leg. 1. Legal. 2. Legate. 3. Legato. 4. Legislation; legislature.
legis. Legislation; legislature.
L. ès S. Licentiate in Sciences (F *licencié ès sciences*).
Lev. Leviticus.
Levit. Leviticus.
lex. Lexicon.
l.f. or **lf** 1. Left field(er). 2. Left forward.
l.f. or **lf.** *Printing* Lightface.
L.F. or **LF, l.f.** or **l-f** Low frequency.
lg. or **lge.** Large.
l.g. or **lg** Left guard.
LG or **LG.** or **L.G.** Low German.
LGk. or **L.Gk.** Late Greek.
l.h. or **L.H.** or **LH** Left hand.
l.h.b. or **lhb** Left halfback.
L.H.D. Doctor of Humanities (L *Litterarum Humaniorum Doctor*).
li Link(s) (unit of measurement).
Li *Chem.* Lithium.
L.I. Long Island.
lib. 1. Book (L *liber*). 2. Librarian; library.
Lib. 1. Liberal. 2. Liberia.
Lieut. Lieutenant.
lin. 1. Lineal. 2. Linear.
ling. Linguistics.
liq. 1. Liquid. 2. Liquor.
lit. 1. Liter. 2. Literal(ly). 3. Literary; literature.
Lit.B. Bachelor of Letters (or Literature) (L *Lit(t)erarum Baccalaureus*).
Lit.D. Doctor of Letters (or Literature) (L *Lit(t)erarum Doctor*).
lith. Lithograph; lithography.
litho. or **lithog.** Lithograph; lithography.
Litt.B. Bachelor of Letters (or Literature) (L *Lit(t)erarum Baccalaureus*).
Litt.D. Doctor of Letters (or Literature) (L *Lit(t)erarum Doctor*).
ll. Lines.
LL or **LL.** or **L.L.** 1. Late Latin. 2. Legal Latin. 3. Low Latin.
LL.B. Bachelor of Laws (L *Legum Baccalaureus*).
LL.D. Doctor of Laws (L *Legum Doctor*).
LL.M. Master of Laws (L *Legum Magister*).
LM *Mil.* Legion of Merit.
L.M. Licentiate in Medicine (or Midwifery).
loc. cit. In the place cited (L *loco citato*)

long. Longitude.
L.O.O.M. Loyal Order of Moose.
L.P.S. *Brit.* Lord Privy Seal.
L.S. 1. Licentiate in Surgery. 2. Place of the seal (L *locus sigilli*).
LSS or **L.S.S.** Lifesaving Service.
l.t. Left tackle: also **lt.**
LT or **Lt.** *Mil.* Lieutenant.
Lt.Col. or **LtCol.** *Mil.* Lieutenant Colonel.
ltd. or **Ltd.** Limited.
Lt.Gen. or **LtGen** *Mil.* Lieutenant General.
L.Th. Licentiate in Theology.
Ltjg. *Mil.* Lieutenant, Junior Grade.
Lu *Chem.* Lutetium.
Luth. Lutheran.
lv. Leave(s).

m or **m.** Meter(s).
M 1. Medieval. 2. Middle.
M. 1. Handful (L *manipulus*). 2. Master (L *magister*). 3. Monday. 4. (*pl.* **MM.**) Monsieur.
M. or **m.** 1. Majesty. 2. Male. 3. Manual. 4. Mark. 5. Marquis. 6. Married. 7. Masculine. 8. Mass. 9. Medicine. 10. Medium. 11. Meridian. 12. Mile. 13. Mill. 14. Minim. 15. Minute. 16. Month. 17. Moon. 18. Morning. 19. Mountain. 20. Noon (L *meridies*).
Ma *Chem.* Masurium.
M.A. 1. Master of Arts (L *Magister Artium*). 2. Military Academy. 3. *Psychol.* Mental age.
mach. Machine; machinery; machinist.
mag. 1. Magazine. 2. Magnet; magnetism. 2. *Astron.* Magnitude.
M.Agr. Master of Agriculture.
Mal. Malachi.
Man. 1. Manila (paper). 2. Manitoba.
manuf. Manufacture(d); manufacturer; manufacturing.
mar. 1. Marine. 2. Maritime. 3. Married.
Mar. March.
marg. Margin; marginal.
Marq. Marquis.
mas. or **masc.** Masculine.
Mass. Massachusetts.
mat. 1. Matinée. 2. Matins. 3. Maturity.
math. Mathematical; mathematician; mathematics.
MATS Military Air Transport Service.
Matt. Matthew.
max. Maximum.
M.B. Bachelor of Medicine (L *Medicinae Baccalaureus*).
M.B.A. Master in (or of) Business Administration.
mc or **m.c.** or **mc.** Megacycle.
M.C. 1. Maritime Commission. 2. Master of Ceremonies. 3. Medical Corps. 4. Member of Congress.
M.Ch. Master of Surgery (L *Magister Chirurgiae*).
M.C.L. Master of Civil Law.
Md *Chem.* Mendelevium.
Md. or **M.D.** Middle Dutch.
Md. Maryland.
M/D or **m/d** 1. Memorandum of deposit. 2. Months' date.
M.D. 1. Doctor of Medicine (L *Medicinae Doctor*). 2. Medical Department. 3. Mentally deficient.
Mdme. (pl. **Mdmes.**) *Brit.* Madame.
M.D.S. Master of Dental Surgery.
mdse. Merchandise.
MDu. Middle Dutch.
m.e. Marbled edges (bookbinding).
Me *Chem.* Methyl.
Me. Maine (unofficial).
ME or **ME.** or **M.E.** Middle English.
M.E. 1. Mechanical Engineer. 2. Methodist Episcopal. 3. Mining Engineer.
meas. Measure.
mech. 1. Mechanical; mechanics. 2. mechanism.
med. 1. Medical; medicine. 2. Medieval. 3. Medium.
M.Ed. Master of Education.
Med.Gk. Medieval Greek.
Med.L. or **Med.L** Medieval Latin.
meg. 1. megacycle. 2. Megohm.
mem. 1. Member. 2. Memoir. 3. Memorandum. 4. Memorial.
memo. Memorandum.
mer. 1. Meridian. 2. Meridional.
Messrs. or **Messrs** Messieurs.
met. 1. Metaphor. 2. Metaphysics. 3. Meteorological. 4. Metronome. 5. Metropolitan.
metal. or **metall.** Metallurgical; metallurgy.
metaph. 1. Metaphor; metaphorical. 2. Metaphysics.
metath. Metathesis; metathetic(al).
meteorol. or **meteor.** Meteorologic(al); meteorology.
Meth. Methodist.
mev or **Mev** or **m.e.v.** Million electron volts.

mf or **mfd**   Microfarad(s).

mf. or **mf**   1. *Music* Moderately loud (Ital. *mezzo forte*). 2. Millifarad.

MF or **MF.** or **M.F.**   Middle French.

mfg.   Manufacturing.

mfr.   Manufacture; manufacturer.

mg. or **mg** or **mgm**   Milligram(s).

Mg   *Chem.* Magnesium.

Mgr.   1. Manager. 2. Monseigneur. 3. Monsignor.

MH   *Mil.* Medal of Honor.

MHG or **MHG.** or **M.H.G.**   Middle High German.

mi.   1. Mile(s). 2. Mill(s).

Mich.   Michigan.

micros.   Microscopy.

mid.   1. Middle. 2. Midshipman.

mil.   1. Mileage. 2. Military. 3. Militia. 4. Million.

milit.   Military.

min.   1. Mineralogical; mineralogy. 2. Minim(s). 3. Minimum. 4. Mining. 5. Minor. 6. Minute(s).

mineral.   Mineralogy.

Minn.   Minnesota.

misc.   1. Miscellaneous. 2. Miscellany.

Miss.   Mississippi.

mk.   1. Mark(s). 2. Markka(s).

Mk.   Mark.

mks   The meter-kilogram-second system of measurement in which the unit of length is the meter, the unit of mass is the kilogram, and the unit of time is one second. Also **m.k.s.**, **MKS, M.K.S.**

mkt.   Market.

ml.   1. Mail. 2. Milliliter(s).

ML or **ML.** or **M.L.**   Medieval (or Middle) Latin.

M.L.A.   1. Member of the Legislative Assembly. 2. Modern Language Association.

MLG or **MLG.** or **M.L.G.**   Middle Low German.

Mlle. or **Mlle**   Mademoiselle.

Mlles. or **Mlles**   Mesdemoiselles.

M.L.S.   Master of Library Science.

mm. or **mm**   1. Millimeter(s). 2. Thousands (L *millia*).

m.m.   With the necessary changes (L *mutatis mutandis*).

MM.   Messieurs.

Mme. or **Mme**   Madame.

Mmes. or **Mmes**   Mesdames.

Mn   *Chem.* Manganese.

mo.   Month(s).

Mo   *Chem.* Molybdenum.

Mo.   1. Missouri. 2. Monday.

M.O.   1. Medical Officer. 2. Money order: also **m.o.**

mod.   1. Moderate. 2. *Music* Moderato. 3. Modern.

Mod. Gr.   Modern Greek.

mon.   1. Monastery. 2. Monetary.

Mon.   1. Monday. 2. Monsignor.

Monsig.   Monsignor.

Mont.   Montana.

mor.   Morocco (bookbinding).

mos.   Months.

MOS   Military occupational specialty.

MP   *Mil.* Military Police.

M.P.   1. Melting point: also **m.p.** 2. Member of Parliament.

M.Pd.   Master of Pedagogy.

M.P.E.   Master of Physical Education.

m.p.h. or **mph**   Miles per hour.

Mr. (mis'tər)   *n.* The contracted form of MISTER.

MR or **M.R.**   Motivation Research.

Mrs. (mis'iz)   *n.* A title prefixed to the name of a married woman: a contracted form of *Mistress*.

MS. or **MS, ms.** or **ms**   Manuscript.

M.S.   1. Master of Science: also **M.Sc.** 2. Master in Surgery.

msg.   Message.

Msgr.   Monsignor.

M.Sgt. or **M/Sgt**   *Mil.* Master Sergeant.

m.s.l. or **M.S.L.**   Mean sea level.

MSS. or **MSS, mss.** or **mss**   Manuscripts.

MST or **M.S.T.** or **m.s.t.**   Mountain standard time.

MSTS   Military Sea Transportation Service.

Mt. or **mt.** (pl. **mts.**)   Mount; mountain.

M.T.   1. Metric ton. 2. Mountain time; also **m.t.**

mtg.   1. Meeting. 2. Mortgage: also **mtge.**

mtn.   Mountain.

Mt.Rev.   Most Reverend.

mun.   Municipal; municipality.

mus.   1. Museum. 2. Music; musician.

Mus.B. or **Mus.Bac.**   Bachelor of Music (L *Musicae Baccalaureus*).

Mus.D. or **Mus.Doc.** or **Mus.Dr.**   Doctor of Music (L *Musicae Doctor*).

Mus.M.   Master of Music (L *Musicae Magister*).

m.v.   *Music* Softly (Ital. *mezzo voce*).

MVD   The Ministry of Internal Affairs of the Soviet Union; the secret police: formerly called *Cheka, OGPU, NKVD*. Also **M.V.D.**

M.W.   1. Most Worshipful. 2. Most worthy.

myth. or **mythol.**   Mythology.

N   *Chem.* Nitrogen.

n.   1. Born (L *natus*). 2. Name. 3. Nephew. 4. Net. 5. Neuter. 6. New. 7. Nominative. 8. Noon. 9. *Chem.* Normal. 10. Note. 11. Number.

N   1. Knight (chess). 2. North; northern.

N.   1. Nationalist. 2. Navy. 3. Noon. 4. *Chem.* Normal (strength solution). 5. Norse. 6. North; northern. 7. November.

Na   *Chem.* Sodium (L *natrium*).

NAACP or **N.A.A.C.P.**   National Association for the Advancement of Colored People.

Nah.   Nahum.

NASA   National Aeronautics and Space Administration.

natl.   National.

NATO (nā'tō)   North Atlantic Treaty Organization.

nav.   1. Naval. 2. Navigation.

navig.   Navigation.

Nb   *Chem.* Niobium.

N.B.   Note well (L *nota bene*): also **n.b.**

NbE   North by east.

NBS or **N.B.S.**   National Bureau of Standards.

NbW   North by west.

N.C.   North Carolina: also **N.Car.** (unofficial).

NCAA or **N.C.A.A.**   National Collegiate Athletic Association.

NCO   Noncommissioned Officer.

Nd   *Chem.* Neodymium.

N.D. or **n.d.**   No date.

N.Dak.   North Dakota: also **N.D.** (unofficial).

N.D.P.   New Democratic Party (Canada).

Ne   *Chem.* Neon.

NEA   National Education Association.

NEB or **N.E.B.**   New English Bible.

NED or **N.E.D.**   New English Dictionary (Oxford English Dictionary).

neg.   Negative(ly).

Neh.   Nehemiah.

neut.   Neuter.

Nev.   Nevada.

New Test.   New Testament.

N.F.   1. National Formulary. 2. Newfoundland (unofficial). 3. No funds: also **n.f.** 4. Norman French: also **NF.**

NG or **N.G.**   National Guard.

N.G. or **n.g.**   No good.

NGk. or **N.Gk.**   New Greek.

N.H.   New Hampshire.

Ni   *Chem.* Nickel.

N.J.   New Jersey.

NKVD   Formerly, the MVD. Also **N.K.V.D.**

n.l.   1. *Printing* New line. 2. North latitude. 3. Not clear (L *non liquet*). 4. Not far (L *non longe*). 5. Not lawful (L *non licet*).

NL or **NL.** or **N.L.**   New Latin.

N. lat.   North latitude.

NLRB or **N.L.R.B.**   National Labor Relations Board.

N.Mex.   New Mexico: also **N.M.** (unofficial).

NNE or **nne, N.N.E.,** or **n.n.e.**   North-northeast.

NNW or **nnw, N.N.W.,** or **n.n.w.**   North-northwest.

No   *Chem.* Nobelium.

No.   1. North; northern. 2. Number: also **no.**

nol. pros.   Nolle prosequi.

nom.   Nominative.

noncom.   Noncommissioned (officer).

non pros.   Non prosequitur.

non seq.   Non sequitur.

Nos. or **nos.**   Numbers.

nov.   Novelist.

Nov. or **Nov**   November.

n.p.   No place (of publication).

n.p. or **d.**   No place or date (of publication.)

Np   *Chem.* Neptunium.

NP   Neuropsychiatric.

N.P.   Notary Public.

n.p.t.   Normal pressure and temperature.

nr.   Near.

NRA or **N.R.A.**   National Recovery Administration.

Ns   *Meteorol.* Nimbostratus.

N.S.   1. New Style. 2. Not specified: also **n.s.** 3. Nova Scotia.

N.S.F. or **N/S/F**   Not sufficient funds.

NSLI   National Service Life Insurance.

N.S.P.C.A.   National Society for the Prevention of Cruelty to Animals.

N.S.P.C.C.   National Society for the Prevention of Cruelty to Children.

Nt   *Chem.* Niton.

N.T. 1. New Testament: also **NT.** 2. Northern Territory.
nt.wt. Net weight.
num. Numeral(s).
Num. Numbers.
NW or **nw, N.W.** or **n.w.** Northwest; northwestern.
N.Y. New York.
N.Y.C. New York City.

O *Chem.* Oxygen.
o Ohm.
o. 1. Octavo. 2. Off. 3. Old. 4. Only. 5. Order. 6. Out(s) (baseball). 7. Pint (L *octarius*).
O. 1. Ocean. 2. Octavo. 3. October. 4. Ohio (unofficial). 5. Old. 6. Ontario (unofficial).
OAS 1. Organization of American States. 2. Secret Army Organization (F *Organisation de l'armée secrète*).
ob. 1. He (or she) died (L *obiit*). 2. Incidentally (L *obiter*). 3. *Music* Oboe.
Obad. Obadiah.
obb. *Music* Obbligato.
obdt. Obedient.
O.B.E. Officer (of the Order) of the British Empire.
obit. Obituary.
obj. 1. Object. 2. Objection. 3. Objective.
obl. 1. Oblique. 2. Oblong.
obs. 1. Observation. 2. Observatory. 3. Obsolete.
obstet. Obstetrical; obstetrics.
obt. Obedient.
o/c Overcharge.
o.c. In the work cited (L *opere citato*).
Oc. or **oc.** Ocean.
OCDM Office of Civil and Defense Mobilization.
OCS *Mil.* Officer Candidate School.
oct. Octavo.
Oct. October.
O.D. 1. Doctor of Optometry. 2. Officer of the Day. 3. Olive drab: also **OD, o.d.** 4. Overdraft; overdrawn.
OE or **Œ** or **O.E.** Old English.
O.E.C.D. Organization for Economic Cooperation and Development.
O.E.D. Oxford English Dictionary.
OEEC or **O.E.E.C.** Organization for European Economic Cooperation.
OF or **OF.** or **O.F.** Old French.
off. 1. Offered. 2. Office. 3. Officer. 4. Official.
O.G. 1. Officer of the Guard. 2. Original gum (philately): also **o.g.**
OGPU (og′pōō) *n.* A former name of the MVD: also called *Gay-Pay-Oo.*
OHG or **OHG.** or **O.H.G.** Old High German.
O.H.M.S. On His (or Her) Majesty's Service.
O.C. Officer in Charge.
Okla. Oklahoma.
O.M. *Brit.* Order of Merit.
ON or **ON.** or **O.N.** Old Norse.
ONI Office of Naval Intelligence.
op. 1. Opera. 2. Operation. 3. Opposite. 4. Work(s) (L *opus, opera*).
OP *Mil.* Observation post.
OPA or **O.P.A.** Office of Price Administration.
op. cit. In the work cited (L *opere citato*).
opp. 1. Opposed. 2. Opposite.
OR or **O.R.** Operating room.
orch. Orchestra(l).
ord. 1. Ordained. 2. Order. 3. Ordinal. 4. Ordinance. 5. Ordinary. 6. Ordnance.
ordn. Ordnance.
Oreg. Oregon: also **Ore.** (unofficial).
org. 1. Organic. 2. Organism. 3. Organized.
orig. Original(ly).
Orth. Orthodox.
OS *Chem.* Osmium.
OS or **OS.** or **O.S.** Old Saxon.
O.S. or **O/S** or **o/s** Old Style.
O.S.A. Order of St. Augustine.
O.S.B. Order of St. Benedict.
OSD Office of the Secretary of Defense.
O.S.D. Order of St. Dominic.
O.S.F. Order of St. Francis.
OSS or **O.S.S.** Office of Strategic Services.
OT or **OT.** or **O.T.** Old Testament.
OWI or **O.W.I.** Office of War Information.
Oxon. 1. Oxford. 2. Oxfordshire. 3. Oxonian.
oz. Ounce(s).
ozs. Ounces.

P *Chem.* Phosphorus.
p or **p.** 1. *Music* Piano. 2. Pitcher (baseball).
p- *Chem.* Para-.
p. 1. After (L *post*). 2. By (L *per*). 3. By weight (L *pondere*). 4. First (L *primus*). 5. For (L *pro*). 6. Page.

7. Part. 8. Participle. 9. Past. 10. Penny. 11. Perch (measure). 12. Peseta. 13. Peso. 14. Pint. 15. Pole (measure). 16. Population.
P 1. Pawn (chess). 2. *Physics* Pressure. 3. *Mil.* Prisoner.
P- *Mil.* Pursuit.
P 1. Father (F *père*; L *pater*). 2. Pastor. 3. President. 4. Priest. 5. Prince. 6. Prompter (theater).
pa. Paper.
p.a. 1. Participial adjective. 2. Per annum (L, yearly).
Pa. *Chem.* Protactinium.
Pa. Pennsylvania.
PA 1. Press agent. 2. Public-address (system).
P.A. 1. Passenger Agent. 2. Power of attorney: also **P/A.** 3. Private account: also **P/A.** 4. Purchasing Agent.
Pac. Pacific.
par. 1. Paragraph. 2. Parallel. 3. Parenthesis. 4. Parish.
Parl. 1. Parliament. 2. Parliamentary: also **parl.**
part. 1. Participle. 2. Particular.
pass. 1. Passage. 2. Passenger. 3. Passive.
pat. 1. Patent(ed). 2. Patrol. 3. Pattern.
patd. Patented.
path. or **pathol.** Pathological; pathology.
Pat. Off. Patent Office.
payt. Payment.
Pb *Chem.* Lead (L *plumbum*).
P.B. 1. Pharmacopoeia Britannica. 2. Prayer Book.
PBX or **P.B.X.** Private branch (telephone) exchange.
pc. 1. (*pl.* **pcs.**) Piece. 2. Price(s).
p.c. 1. Percent. 2. Petty cash. 3. Postal card. 4. Price(s) current.
P/C or **p/c** 1. Petty cash. 2. Prices current.
P.C. 1. *Brit.* Police Constable. 2. Post Commander. 3. Privy Council.
pct. Percent.
pd. Paid.
p.d. 1. Per diem. 2. Potential difference.
Pd *Chem.* Palladium.
P.D. 1. Per diem. 2. Police Department.
Pd.B. Bachelor of Pedagogy (L *Pedagogiae Baccalaureus*).
Pd.D. Doctor of Pedagogy (L *Pedagogiae Doctor*).
Pd.M. Master of Pedagogy (L *Pedagogiae Magister*).
P.E. 1. Petroleum Engineer. 2. Presiding Elder. 3. *Printing* Printer's error. 4. *Stat.* Probable error. 5. Protestant Episcopal.
ped. 1. Pedal. 2. Pedestal.
Pen. or **pen.** Peninsula.
per. 1. Period. 2. Person.
perf. 1. Perfect. 2. Perforated. 3. Performer.
perh. Perhaps.
perm. Permanent.
pert. Pertaining.
Pet. Peter.
pf. Pfennig.
p.f. 1. *Music* Louder (Ital. *più forte*). 2. Power factor.
Pfc or **Pfc.** *Mil.* Private, first class.
pfg. Pfennig.
pg. Page.
PH *Mil.* Purple Heart.
PHA Public Housing Administration.
Phar. or **phar., Pharm.,** or **pharm.** 1. Pharmaceutical. 2. Pharmacopoeia. 3. Pharmacy.
Phar. B. Bachelor of Pharmacy (L *Pharmaciae Baccalaureus*).
Phar. D. Doctor of Pharmacy (L *Pharmaciae Doctor*).
Ph.B. Bachelor of Philosophy (L *Philosophiae Baccalaureus*).
Ph.C. Pharmaceutical Chemist.
Ph.D. Doctor of Philosophy (L *Philosophiae Doctor*).
phil. Philosopher; philosophical; philosophy.
Phil. 1. Philippians. 2. Philippine.
Phila. Philadelphia.
Philem. Philemon (bible).
philol. Philology.
philos. Philosopher; philosophical; philosophy.
phon. 1. Phonetic(s). 2. Phonology.
phonol. Phonology.
phot. Photograph; photographic; photography.
photog. Photograph; photographic; photography.
photom. Photometrical; photometry.
phr. Phrase.
PHS Public Health Service.
phys. 1. Physical. 2. Physician. 3. Physicist; physics.
physiol. Physiological; physiology.
pk. (*pl.* **pks.**) 1. Pack. 2. Park. 3. Peak. 4. Peck.
pkg. Package(s).
pkt. Packet.
pl. 1. Place. 2. Plate. 3. Plural.
plat. 1. Plateau. 2. Platoon.
plu. Plural.
plupf. Pluperfect.
plur. 1. Plural. 2. Plurality.

Pm *Chem.* Promethium.
P.M. **1.** Afternoon (L *post meridiem*): also **p.m.** **2.** Past Master. **3.** Paymaster. **4.** Police Magistrate. **5.** Postmaster: also **PM.** **6.** Post-mortem: also **p.m.** **7.** Prime Minister. **8.** *Mil.* Provost Marshal: also **PM.**
P.M.G. **1.** Postmaster General. **2.** Provost Marshal General.
P/n or **p.n.** Promissory note.
pnxt. He (or she) painted (L *pinxit*).
p.o. or **po** Put-out(s).
Po *Chem.* Polonium.
P.O. or **p.o.** **1.** Personnel officer. **2.** Petty officer. **3.** Postal order. **4.** Post office.
P.O.D. Pay on delivery: also **p.o.d.**
P.O.E. **1.** *Mil.* Port of Embarkation. **2.** Port of Entry.
pol. Political; politics.
pol. econ. Political economy.
polit. Political; politics.
pop. **1.** Popular(ly). **2.** Population.
POP Point of purchase.
pos. **1.** Positive. **2.** Possessive.
poss. **1.** Possession; possessive. **2.** Possible; possibly.
pot. Potential.
POW or **P.O.W.** Prisoner of War.
pp. **1.** Pages. **2.** Past participle. **3.** *Music* Pianissimo: also **pp** **4.** Privately printed.
p.p. **1.** Parcel post. **2.** Past participle. **3.** Postpaid.
P.P. **1.** Parcel post. **2.** Parish Priest. **3.** Postpaid.
P.P.C. or **p.p.c.** To take leave (F *pour prendre congé*).
ppd. **1.** Postpaid. **2.** Prepaid.
pph. Pamphlet.
ppl. Participial.
p.p.m. or **ppm.** or **ppm** Parts per million.
ppr. or **p.pr.** Present participle.
P.P.S. or **p.p.s.** Additional postscript (L *post postscriptum*).
p.q. Previous question.
pr. **1.** Pair(s). **2.** Paper. **3.** Power. **4.** Present. **5.** Price. **6.** Priest. **7.** Prince. **8.** Printing. **9.** Pronoun.
Pr *Chem.* Praseodymium.
Pr. **1.** Prince. **2.** Provençal.
PR Public relations.
P.R. Puerto Rico.
prec. Preceding.
precanc. Precanceled.
pred. Predicate.
pref. **1.** Preface. **2.** Prefatory. **3.** Preference. **4.** Prefix.
pres. **1.** Present. **2.** Presidency; presidential.
Pres. President.
Presb. Presbyterian.
pret. Preterit.
prim. **1.** Primary. **2.** Primitive.
print. Printing.
PRO or **P.R.O.** Public Relations Officer.
prod. **1.** Produce(d). **2.** Product.
Prof. or **prof.** Professor.
Prog. Progressive.
prom. **1.** Promenade. **2.** Promontory.
prop. **1.** Proper(ly). **2.** Property. **3.** Proposition. **4.** Proprietor. **5.** Proprietary.
pros. Prosody.
Prot. Protestant.
prov. **1.** Province. **2.** Provincial. **3.** Provisional. **4.** Provost.
Prov. **1.** Provençal. **2.** Proverbs.
prs. Pairs.
ps. Pieces.
Ps. Psalms.
P.S. **1.** Passenger Steamer. **2.** Postscript: also **p.s.** **3.** Privy Seal. **4.** Public sale. **5.** Public School.
p.s.f. or **psf** Pounds per square foot.
p.s.i. or **psi** Pounds per square inch.
P.SS. or **p.ss.** Postscripts.
PST or **P.S.T.** or **p.s.t.** Pacific Standard time.
psychol. Psychological; psychologist; psychology.
pt. **1.** Part. **2.** Payment. **3.** Pint(s). **4.** Point(s). **5.** Port. **6.** Preterit.
p.t. For the time being (L *pro tempore*).
Pt *Chem.* Platinum.
P.T. **1.** Pacific Time. **2.** Physical Training.
PTA or **P.T.A.** Parent-Teacher Association.
ptas. Pesetas.
ptg. Printing.
P.T.O. or **p.t.o.** Please turn over (page).
pts. **1.** Parts. **2.** Payments. **3.** Pints. **4.** Points. **5.** Ports.
Pu *Chem.* Plutonium.
pub. **1.** Public. **2.** Publication. **3.** Published; publisher; publishing.
Pvt. *Mil.* Private.
pwt. Pennyweight.
PX *Mil.* Post Exchange.
pxt. He (or she) painted (L *pinxit*).

q. **1.** Farthing (L *quadrans*). **2.** Quart(s). **3.** Quarter(ly). **4.** Quarto. **5.** Quasi. **6.** Query. **7.** Question. **8.** Quetzal **9.** Quintal. **10.** Quire.
Q Queen (chess).
Q. **1.** (*pl.* **Qq.**) Quarto. **2.** Quebec (unofficial). **3.** Queen. **4.** Question.
q.b. or **qb** Quarterback.
QB Queen's bishop (chess).
Q.B. *Brit.* Queen's Bench.
QBP Queen's bishop's pawn (chess).
Q.C. Queen's Counsel.
Q.E.D. Which was to be demonstrated (L *quod erat demonstrandum*).
Q.E.F. Which was to be done (L *quod erat faciendum*).
QKt Queen's knight (chess).
QKtP Queen's knight's pawn (chess).
ql. Quintal.
QM Quartermaster.
QMC Quartermaster Corps.
QMG Quartermaster General.
QP Queen's pawn (chess).
q.pl. or **Q.P.** As much as you please (L *quantum placet*).
Qq. Quartos.
qq.v. Which see (L *quae vide*).
qr. (*pl.* **qrs.**) **1.** Farthing (L *quadrans*). **2.** Quarter(ly). **3.** Quire.
QR Queen's rook (chess).
QRP Queen's rook's pawn (chess).
q.s. **1.** As much as suffices (L *quantum sufficit*). **2.** Quarter section.
qt. **1.** Quantity. **2.** Quart(s).
q.t. or **Q.T.** *Slang* Quiet: chiefly in the phrase **on the q.t.**
qto. Quarto.
qu. **1.** Quart. **2.** Quarterl(y). **3.** Queen. **4.** Query. **5.** Question.
Que. Quebec (unofficial).
ques. Question.
q.v. Which see. (L *quod vide*).
qy. Query.

r **1.** Roentgen(s). **2.** Ruble. **3.** Rupee.
r or **r.** Run(s) (baseball).
r. **1.** Radius. **2.** Rare. **3.** Received. **4.** Recipe. **5.** Residence; resides **6.** Retired. **7.** Right-hand page (L *recto*). **8.** Rises. **9.** Rod. **10.** Rubber. **11.** Ruble.
R **1.** Radius. **2.** Ratio. **3.** *Eccl.* Respond or response. **4.** Rook (chess). **5.** Rupee.
R. **1.** Rabbi. **2.** Radical. **3.** Railroad. **4.** Rector. **5.** Redactor. **6.** Republican. **7.** Response. **8.** Rex. **9.** Right (theater). **10.** River. **11.** Road. **12.** Royal.
Ra *Chem.* Radium.
RA *Mil.* Regular Army.
R.A. **1.** *Mil.* Rear Admiral. **2.** *Astron.* Right ascension. **3.** Royal Academician; Royal Academy.
RAdm. *Mil.* Rear Admiral.
RAF or **R.A.F.** Royal Air Force.
RA·TO (rā'tō) *n.* An airplane takeoff assisted by an auxiliary rocket motor or unit; also, the rocket motor or unit used. Also **ra/to.** [< *r*(*ocket*) + *a*(*ssisted*) + *t*(*ake*)*o*(*ff*)]
Rb *Chem.* Rubidium.
RBI or **r.b.i.** or **rbi** Run(s) batted in (baseball).
R.C. **1.** Red Cross. **2.** Reserve Corps. **3.** Roman Catholic.
RCAF or **R.C.A.F.** Royal Canadian Air Force.
R.C.Ch. Roman Catholic Church.
rcd. Received.
R.C.M.P. Royal Canadian Mounted Police.
RCN or **R.C.N.** Royal Canadian Navy.
Rct. *Mil.* Recruit.
rd. **1.** Road. **2.** Rod(s). **3.** Round.
Rd. Road.
R.D. Rural Delivery.
r.e. or **re** Right end.
Re *Chem.* Rhenium.
R.E. **1.** Real estate. **2.** Reformed Episcopal. **3.** Right Excellent. **4.** Royal Engineers.
REA Rural Electrification Administration.
rec. **1.** Receipt. **2.** Received. **3.** Recipe. **4.** Record; recorded; recorder; recording.
recit. Recitative.
rec. sec. Recording secretary.
rect. **1.** Receipt: also **rec't.** **2.** Rector. **3.** Rectory.
redupl. Reduplicated; reduplication.
ref. **1.** Referee. **2.** Reference. **3.** Referred. **4.** Reformation; reformed. **5.** Refunding.
Ref. Ch. Reformed Church.
refl. **1.** Reflection. **2.** Reflective(ly). **3.** Reflex. **4.** Reflexive.
Ref. Sp. Reformed Spelling.
reg. **1.** Regent. **2.** Regiment. **3.** Region. **4.** Register(ed). **5.** Registrar. **6.** Registry. **7.** Regular(ly). **8.** Regulation.
Regt. **1.** Regent. **2.** Regiment.

rel. 1. Relating. 2. Relative(ly). 3. Released. 4. Religion; religious.
rep. 1. Report; reporter. 2. Representative. 3. Republic.
Rep. 1. Representative. 2. Republic. 3. Republican.
repr. 1. Representing. 2. Reprinted.
req. 1. Required. 2. Requisition.
res. 1. Research. 2. Reserve. 3. Residence. 4. Resides. 5. Residue. 6. Resigned. 7. Resolution.
resp. 1. Respective(ly). 2. Respondent.
retd. 1. Retained. 2. Returned.
rev. 1. Revenue. 2. Reverse(d). 3. Review(ed). 4. Revise(d); revision. 5. Revolution. 6. Revolving.
Rev. 1. Revelation. 2. Reverend.
rf. Right fielder (baseball).
r.f. 1. Radio frequency. 2. Rapid-fire.
RFC Royal Flying Corps.
RFD or **R.F.D.** Rural Free Delivery.
r.g. or **rg** Right guard.
r.h. 1. Relative humidity. 2. Right hand.
r.h. or **rh** Right halfback.
Rh 1. *Chem.* Rhodium. 2. *Biochem.* See RH FACTOR.
R.H. Royal Highness.
r.h.b. or **rhb** Right halfback.
rhet. Rhetoric(al).
R.I. 1. King and Emperor (L *Rex et Imperator*). 2. Queen and Empress (L *Regina et Imperatrix*). 3. Rhode Island.
R.I.P. May he (she, or they) rest in peace (L *requiescat, or requiescant, in pace*).
rit. or **ritard.** *Music* Ritardando.
riv. River.
rm. (*pl.* **rms.**) 1. Ream. 2. Room.
RM or **R.M.,** **Rm.,** or **r.m.** Reichsmark(s).
Rn *Chem.* Radon.
R.N. 1. Registered nurse. 2. Royal Navy.
RNA *Biochem.* Ribonucleic acid.
R.N.A.S. Royal Naval Air Service.
R.N.R. Royal Naval Reserve.
R.N.V.R. Royal Naval Volunteer Reserve.
R.N.W.M.P. Royal Northwest Mounted Police.
ROK (rok) *n.* 1. The Republic of Korea (South Korea). 2. A soldier in the South Korean army.
rom. *Printing* Roman (type).
Rom. 1. Roman. 2. Romance. 3. Romans.
ROTC or **R.O.T.C.** Reserve Officers' Training Corps.
R.P. 1. Reformed Presbyterian. 2. Regius Professor.
R.P.D. Doctor of Political Science (L *Rerum Politicarum Doctor*).
rpm or **r.p.m.** Revolutions per minute.
rps or **r.p.s.** Revolutions per second.
rpt. Report.
R.R. 1. Railroad: also **RR** 2. Right Reverend. 3. Rural route.
R.S.F.S.R. or **RSFSR** Russian Soviet Federated Socialist Republic (Russian *Rossiyskaya Sovetskaya Federativnaya Sotsialisticheskaya Respublika*).
RSV or **R.S.V.** Revised Standard Version (of the Bible).
R.S.V.P. or **r.s.v.p.** Répondez s'il vous plaît. (F, please reply)
rt. Right.
r.t. or **rt** Right tackle.
Rt. Hon. Right Honorable.
Rt. Rev. Right Reverend.
Ru *Chem.* Ruthenium.
Russ. Russia; Russian.
RV or **R.V.** Revised Version (of the Bible).
R.W. 1. Right Worshipful. 2. Right Worthy.
Ry. Railway.

S *Chem.* Sulfur.
s. 1. *Anat.* Sacral. 2. Second. 3. Section. 4. See. 5. Semi-. 6. Shilling. 7. Singular. 8. Sire. 9. Son. 10. South; southern. 11. Stem; stem of. 12. Substantive. 13. Sun. 14. Surplus.
S 1. In chess, a knight (G *springer*). 2. Saxon. 3. South; southern.
S. 1. Fellow (L *Socius*). 2. Sabbath. 3. Saint. 4. Saturday. 5. Saxon. 6. School. 7. Sea. 8. Senate. 9. September. 10. South; southern. 11. Sunday.
Sa *Chem.* Samarium.
Sab. Sabbath.
SAC Strategic Air Command.
SAE or **S.A.E.** Society of Automotive Engineers.
S.Afr. South Africa; South African.
Sam. Samuel.
SANE Committee for a Sane Nuclear Policy.
Sat. 1. Saturday. 2. Saturn.
sb. Substantive.
s.b. or **sb** Stolen base(s).
Sb *Chem.* Antimony (L *stibium*).
S.B. Bachelor of Science (L *Scientiae Baccalaureus*).
SbE South by east.

SbW South by west.
sc. 1. He (or she) carved or engraved it (L *sculpsit*). 2. Namely (L *scilicet*). 3. Scale. 4. Scene. 5. Science(s). 6. Screw. 7. Scruple (weight).
s.c. 1. *Printing* Small capitals. 2. Supercalendered.
Sc 1. *Chem.* Scandium. 2. Stratocumulus.
SC Security Council (of the United Nations).
s. caps. *Printing* Small capitals.
Sc.B. Bachelor of Science (L *Scientiae Baccalaureus*).
Sc.D. Doctor of Science (L *Scientiae Doctor*).
sci. Science; scientific.
Sc.M. Master of Science. [L *Scientiae Magister*].
Scot. Scotch; Scotland; Scottish.
scr. Scruple (weight).
Script. Scriptural; Scripture(s).
sd. Sound.
s.d. Sine die.
S.D. 1. Doctor of Science (L *Scientiae Doctor*). 2. *Stat.* Standard deviation: also **s.d.**
S.Dak. South Dakota: also **S.D.** (unofficial).
Se *Chem.* Selenium.
SE or **se,** **S.E.,** or **s.e.** Southeast; southeastern.
SEATO (sē'tō) Southeast Asia Treaty Organization.
sec. 1. According to (L *secundum*). 2. Secant. 3. Second(s). 4. Secondary. 5. Secretary. 6. Section(s). 7. Sector.
SEC or **S.E.C.** Securities and Exchange Commission.
sect. Section; sectional.
secy Secretary: also **sec'y.**
Sem. 1. Seminary. 2. Semitic.
Sen. or **sen.** 1. Senate; senator. 2. Senior.
sep. 1. Sepal(s). 2. Separate.
Sep. 1. September. 2. Septuagint.
Sept. 1. September. 2. Septuagint.
seq. 1. Sequel. 2. The following (one) (L *sequens*)
seqq. The following (ones) (L *sequentia*).
ser. 1. Serial. 2. Series. 3. Sermon.
sf or **sf.,** **sfz,** or **sfz.** *Music* With emphasis (Ital. *sforzando, sforzato*).
SF or **sf** Science fiction.
SFC *Mil.* Sergeant First Class.
s.g. Specific gravity.
sgd. Signed.
sh. 1. Share(s). 2. Sheep. 3. Sheet. 4. Shilling(s).
SHAEF (shāf) In World War II, Supreme Headquarters Allied Expeditionary Forces.
SHAPE Supreme Headquarters Allied Powers Europe.
SHF or **shf** Superhigh frequency. Also **S.H.F., s.h.f.**
shpt. Shipment.
Si *Chem.* Silicon.
Sig. or **sig.** 1. Signature. 2. Signor; signore.
SigC *Mil.* Signal Corps.
sing. Singular.
S.J. Society of Jesus.
S.J.D. Doctor of Juridical Science (L *Scientiae Juridicae Doctor*).
sk. Sack.
Skt. Sanskrit: also **Skr.**
s.l. Without place (of publication) (L *sine loco*).
S.lat. South latitude.
Slav. Slavic.
Sm *Chem.* Samarium.
S.M. 1. Master of Science (L *Scientiae Magister*). 2. Soldier's Medal.
SMaj. *Mil.* Sergeant Major.
sm.c. or **sm. cap(s).** *Printing* Small capital(s).
Sn *Chem.* Tin (L *stannum*).
s.o. or **so** Struck out; strike-out.
So. South; southern.
soc. 1. Socialist. 2. Society.
S. of Sol. Song of Solomon.
sol. 1. Soluble. 2. Solution.
Sol. 1. Solicitor. 2. Solomon.
sop. *Music* Soprano.
SOP or **S.O.P.** *Mil.* Standard operating procedure.
sos. or **sost.** or **sosten.** Sostenuto.
sp. 1. Special. 2. Species. 3. Specific. 4. Specimen. 5. Spelling. 6. Spirit(s).
s.p. 1. Sine prole (L, without issue). 2. Single phase.
Sp. Spain; Spaniard; Spanish.
SP *Naval* Shore patrol (or police).
spp. Species (plural).
S.P.Q.R. The Senate and People of Rome (L *Senatus Populusque Romanus*).
spt. Seaport.
sq. 1. Sequence. 2. The following one (L *sequens*). 3. Square.
Sq. Squadron.
sq. ft. Square foot (or feet).
sq. in. Square inch(es).
sq. m. or **sq. mi.** Square mile(s).

sqq. The following ones (L *sequentia*).
sq. yd. Square yard(s).
Sr *Chem.* Strontium.
Sr. 1. Senior. 2. Señor. 3. Sir. 4. Sister.
SR *Mil.* Seaman Recruit.
Sra. Señora.
S.R.O. Standing room only.
Srta. Señorita.
SS or **S.S.** or **S/S** Steamship.
SS. 1. Saints. 2. The Schutzstaffel: also **SS**
S.S. 1. Sunday School. 2. Written above (L *supra Scriptum*).
SSA or **S.S.A.** Social Security Act (or Administration).
SSE or **sse, S.S.E.** or **s.s.e.** South-southeast.
SSM *Mil.* Silver Star Medal.
SSS Selective Service System.
SSW or **ssw, S.S.W.,** or **s.s.w.** South-southwest.
st. 1. Stanza. 2. Statute(s). 3. Stere. 4. Stet. 5. Stitch. 6. Stone (weight). 7. Street. 8. Strophe.
St *Meteorol.* Stratus.
St. 1. Saint. 2. Statute(s). 3. Strait. 4. Street.
St. For entries not found under ST., see under SAINT.
sta. 1. Station. 2. Stationary. 3. Stator.
Sta. 1. Santa. 2. Station.
stacc. *Music* Staccato.
S.T.B. 1. Bachelor of Sacred Theology (L *Sacrae Theologiae Baccalaureus*). 2. Bachelor of Theology (L *Scientiae Theologicae Baccalaureus*).
stbd. Starboard.
std. Standard.
S.T.D. Doctor of Sacred Theology (L *Sacrae Theologiae Doctor*).
Ste. Sainte.
ster. Sterling.
St. Ex. Stock Exchange.
stg. Sterling.
stge. Storage.
stk. Stock.
STOL Short takeoff and landing.
str. 1. Steamer. 2. Strait. 3. *Music* String(s).
sub. 1. Subaltern. 2. Subscription. 3. Substitute. 4. Suburb; suburban.
subj. 1. Subject. 2. Subjective(ly). 3. Subjunctive.
subst. 1. Substantive. 2. Substitute.
suf. or **suff.** Suffix.
Sun. or **Sund.** Sunday.
SUNFED Special United Nations Fund for Economic Development.
sup. 1. Above (L *supra*). 2. Superior. 3. Superlative. 4. Supine. 5. Supplement; supplementary. 6. Supply. 7. Supreme.
super. 1. Superfine. 2. Superintendent. 3. Superior. 4. Supernumerary.
superl. Superlative.
supp. or **suppl.** Supplement; supplementary.
supr. Supreme.
Supt. or **supt.** Superintendent.
sur. 1. Surcharged. 2. Surplus.
Sur. Surrey.
surg. Surgeon; surgery; surgical.
surv. 1. Survey; surveying; surveyor. 2. Surviving.
s.v. Under this word (L *sub verbo, sub voce*).
S.V. Holy Virgin (L *Sancta Virgo*).
SW or **sw, S.W.** or **s.w.** Southwest; southwestern.
syl. or **syll.** 1. Syllable. 2. Syllabus.
sym. 1. Symbol. 2. *Chem.* Symmetrical: also **sym-.** 3. Symphony. 4. Symptom.
synop. Synopsis.
syr. Syrup (pharmacy).
syst. System; systematic.

t. 1. In the time of (L *tempore*). 2. Tare. 3. Target. 4. Teaspoon(s). 5. Telephone. 6. Temperature. 7. Tempo. 8. Tenor. 9. *Gram.* Tense. 10. Terminal. 11. Territorial; territory. 12. Time. 13. Tome. 14. Ton(s). 15. Town; township. 16. Transit. 17. *Gram.* Transitive. 18. Troy (weight). 19. Volume (L *tomus*).
T 1. *Chem.* Tantalum. 2. Technician. 3. Temperature (absolute scale). 4. (Surface) tension. 5. Time.
T. 1. Tablespoon(s). 2. Territory. 3. Testament. 4. Tuesday. 5. Turkish.
Ta *Chem.* Tantalum.
TAA Technical Assistance Administration.
tab. Table(s).
TAB Technical Assistance Board.
TAC 1. *Mil.* Tactical Air Command. 2. Technical Assistance Committee.
TAG The Adjutant General.
tan or **tan.** Tangent.
Tb *Chem.* Terbium.
t.b. Trial balance.

TB or **T.B., Tb, Tb., t.b.** or **tb** Tuberculosis.
tbs. or **tbsp.** Tablespoon(s).
Tc. *Chem.* Technetium.
TC 1. Transportation Corps. 2. Trusteeship Council (of the United Nations).
TD 1. Touchdown: also **td** or **td.** 2. Treasury Dept.
Te *Chem.* Tellurium.
technol. Technology.
tel. 1. Telegram. 2. Telegraph; telegraphic. 3. Telephone.
teleg. Telegram; telegraph; telegraphic; telegraphy.
temp. 1. In the time of (L *tempore*). 2. Temperature. 3. Temporary.
ten. *Music* 1. Tenor. 2. Tenuto.
Tenn. Tennessee.
ter. 1. Terrace. 2. Territorial; territory.
term. 1. Terminal. 2. Termination. 3. Terminology.
test. 1. Testamentary. 2. Testator.
Test. Testament.
Tex. Texas; Texan.
Th *Chem.* Thorium.
Th. Thursday.
Th.B. Bachelor of Theology (L *Theologiae Baccalaureus*).
Th.D. Doctor of Theology (L *Theologiae Doctor*).
theol. Theologian; theological; theology.
theos. Theosophical; theosophy.
T.H.I. or **T.-H.I.** Temperature-humidity index.
Thur. or **Thurs.** Thursday.
Ti *Chem.* Titanium.
Tim. Timothy.
Tit. Titus.
TKO or **T.K.O.** or **t.k.o.** Technical knockout.
Tl *Chem.* Thallium.
TL or **T.L.** Trade-last.
Tm *Chem.* Thulium.
tn. 1. Ton. 2. Train.
Tn *Chem.* Thoron.
tng. Training.
TNT Trinitrotoluene.
top. Topographical; topography.
tp. Township.
tr. 1. Trace. 2. Train. 3. Transitive. 4. Translated; translation; translator. 5. Transpose. 6. Treasurer. 7. Trust.
Tr *Chem.* Terbium.
trans. 1. Transaction(s). 2. Transferred. 3. *Gram.* Transitive. 4. Translated; translation; translator. 5. Transportation. 6. Transpose. 7. Transverse.
transl. Translated; translation.
transp. 1. Transparent. 2. Transportation.
treas. Treasurer; treasury.
trfd. Transferred.
trig. or **trigon.** Trigonometric; trigonometry.
tripl. Triplicate.
TSgt *Mil.* Technical Sergeant.
Tu. Tuesday.
Tues. Tuesday.
TV (tē′vē) *n. pl.* **TVs** or **TV's** Television.
TV or **tv** Terminal velocity.
TVA or **T.V.A.** Tennessee Valley Authority.
twp. Township.
Ty. Territory.
typ. Typographic(al); typography.
typo. or **typog.** Typographic(al); typography.

U *Chem.* Uranium.
u. And (G *und*).
U. or **u.** 1. Uncle. 2. University. 3. Upper.
UAW or **U.A.W.** 1. United Auto, Aircraft and Agricultural Implements Workers. 2. United Automobile Workers of America.
u.c. 1. *Music* Soft pedal (Ital. *una corda* one string). 2. *Printing* Upper case.
UCMJ *Mil.* Uniform Code of Military Justice.
UFO Unidentified flying object.
U.J.D. Doctor of Civil and Canon Law (L *Utriusque Juris Doctor*).
ult. 1. Ultimate(ly). 2. Ultimo: also **ulto.**
UMT Universal Military Training.
UMTS Universal Military Training and Service.
UN or **U.N.** United Nations.
UNEF United Nations Emergency Force.
UNESCO (yōō·nes′kō) The United Nations Educational, Scientific and Cultural Organization. Also **U·nes′co.**
UNICEF (yōō′nə·sef) United Nations Children's Fund. Also **U′ni·cef.**
Unit. Unitarian.
univ. 1. Universal(ly). 2. University.
Univ. University.
UNKRA United Nations Korean Reconstruction Agency.
unpub. Unpublished.

UNREF United Nations Refugee Emergency Fund.
UNRRA United Nations Relief and Rehabilitation Administration.
UNRWA United Nations Relief and Works Agency for Palestine Refugees in the Near East.
UNSCOB United Nations Special Committee on the Balkans.
UNTSO United Nations Truce Supervision Organization.
UP or **U.P.** 1. Union Pacific (Railroad). 2. United Press.
UPI or **U.P.I.** United Press International.
Ur *Chem.* Uranium.
U.S. or **US** United States.
USA United States Army.
U.S.A. or **USA** United States of America.
USAF United States Air Force.
USAFI United States Armed Forces Institute.
USAR United States Army Reserve.
U.S.C. & G.S. United States Coast and Geodetic Survey.
USCG or **U.S.C.G.** United States Coast Guard.
USES or **U.S.E.S.** United States Employment Service.
USIA or **U.S.I.A.** United States Information Agency.
USIBA United States International Book Association.
U.S.M. 1. United States Mail. 2. United States Mint.
USMA or **U.S.M.A.** United States Military Academy.
USMC or **U.S.M.C.** United States Marine Corps.
USMCR United States Marine Corps Reserve.
USMS United States Maritime Service.
USN or **U.S.N.** United States Navy.
USNA or **U.S.N.A.** United States Naval Academy.
USNR or **U.S.N.R.** United States Naval Reserve.
USO or **U.S.O.** United Service Organizations.
USP or **U.S.P.** United States Pharmacopoeia: also **U.S. Pharm.**
USPHS or **U.S.P.H.S.** United States Public Health Service.
USS or **U.S.S.** 1. United States Senate. 2. United States Ship (or Steamer or Steamship).
USSB United States Shipping Board.
U.S.S.R. or **USSR** Union of Soviet Socialist Republics.
usw or **u.s.w.** And so forth (G *und so weiter*).
u.t. Universal time.
Ut. Utah (unofficial).
ux. Wife (L *uxor*)

v Volt.
v. 1. Valve. 2. Ventral. 3. *Gram.* a Verb. b Vocative. 4. Verse. 5. Version. 6. Versus. 7. Vice-. 8. Vide. 9. Village. 10. Voice. 11. Volt; voltage. 12. Volume. 13. Von.
V 1. *Math.* Vector. 2. Velocity. 3. *Electr.* Volt. 4. Volume. 5. *Chem.* Vanadium.
V. 1. Venerable. 2. Viscount.
v.a. *Gram.* 1. Active verb. 2. Verbal adjective.
Va. Virginia.
V.A. 1. Veterans' Administration: also **VA** 2. Vicar Apostolic. 3. Vice Admiral. 4. (Order of) Victoria and Albert.
V.Adm. Vice Admiral.
var. 1. Variant. 2. Variation. 3. Variety.
Vat. Vatican.
v. aux. *Gram.* Auxiliary verb.
vb. Verb; verbal.
V.C. 1. Veterinary Corps. 2. Vice Chairman. 3. Vice Chamberlain. 4. Vice Chancellor. 5. Vice Consul. 6. Victoria Cross.
Vd *Chem.* Vanadium.
v.d. Various dates.
VD or **V.D.** Venereal disease.
vel. Vellum.
Ven. 1. Venerable. 2. Venice.
ver. 1. Verse(s). 2. Version.
Ver. St. United States (G *Vereinigte Staaten*).
V.G. Vicar General.
VHF or **vhf, V.H.F.,** or **v.h.f.** Very high frequency.
v.i. 1. See below (L *vide infra*). 2. *Gram.* Intransitive verb.
Vi *Chem.* Virginium.
V.I. Virgin Islands.
vil. Village.
v. imp. *Gram.* Impersonal verb.
VIP or **V.I.P.** Very important person.
Vis. or **Visc.** Viscount; Viscountess.
Visct. Viscount; Viscountess.
viv. *Music* Lively (Ital. *vivace*).
viz. Namely (L *videlicet*).
VL or **V.L.** Vulgar Latin.
VLF or **vlf, V.L.F.,** or **v.l.f.** Very low frequency.
V.M.D. Doctor of Veterinary Medicine (L *Veterinariae Medicinae Doctor*).
v.n. *Gram.* Neuter verb; also **v. neut.**
vo. Verso.
vocab. Vocabulary.
vol. 1. Volcano. 2. Volume. 3. Volunteer.
vols. Volumes.

v.p. 1. Various pagings. 2. Various places. 3. *Gram.* Verb passive. 4. Voting pool (stocks).
V.P. Vice President: also **V.Pres.**
v.r. *Gram.* Reflexive verb.
V.R. Queen Victoria (L *Victoria Regina*).
V.Rev. Very Reverend.
vs. 1. Verse. 2. Versus.
V.S. Veterinary Surgeon.
VSS Versions.
v.t. *Gram.* Transitive verb.
Vt. Vermont.
VTOL Vertical takeoff and landing.
Vul. Vulgate.
vv. 1. Verses. 2. *Music* Violins.
v.v. Vice versa.

w. 1. Wanting. 2. Warehousing. 3. Week(s). 4. Weight. 5. West; western. 6. Wide; width. 7. Wife. 8. With. 9. Won: also **w** 10. *Physics* Work.
W *Chem.* Tungsten (L *wolfram*).
W or **w** 1. *Electr.* Watt(s). 2. West; western.
W. 1. Wales; Welsh. 2. Wednesday. 3. West; western. 4. *Physics* Work.
WAC or **W.A.C.** Women's Army Corps.
WAF or **W.A.F.** Women in the Air Force.
Wash. Washington.
Wat. Waterford.
WAVES or **W.A.V.E.S.** Women in the United States Navy.
w.b. 1. Warehouse book. 2. Waybill. 3. Westbound.
W.B. or **W/B, W.b.,** or **W/b** Waybill.
WbN West by north.
WbS West by south.
w.c. or **W.C.** 1. Water closet. 2. Without charge.
Wed. Wednesday.
wf or **w.f.** *Printing* Wrong font.
WFTU or **W.F.T.U.** World Federation of Trade Unions.
wh. Watt-hour(s).
whf. Wharf.
WHO World Health Organization.
w.i. When issued (stocks).
Wis. Wisconsin: also **Wisc.** (unofficial).
wk. (*pl.* **wks.**) 1. Week. 2. Work.
wkly. Weekly.
w.l. or **WL** 1. Water line. 2. Wave length.
W. long. West longitude.
wmk. or **w/m** Watermark.
WNW or **wnw, W.N.W., w.n.w.** West-northwest.
WO or **W.O.** 1. Wait order. 2. *Mil.* Warrant Officer.
WPA or **W.P.A.** Work Projects Administration.
WRAC or **W.R.A.C.** Women's Royal Army Corps.
WRAF or **W.R.A.F.** Women's Royal Air Force.
W.R.N.S. Women's Royal Naval Service.
WSW or **wsw, W.S.W.,** or **w.s.w.** West-southwest.
wt. Weight.
W.Va. West Virginia.
WVS or **W.V.S.** *Brit.* Women's Voluntary Service.
Wy. Wyoming (unofficial).
Wyo. Wyoming.

x-cp. Ex coupon. Also **X.C., x.c.**
x-div. Ex dividend. Also **X.D., x.d.**
Xe *Chem.* Xenon.
Xn. Christian.
Xnty. or **Xty.** Christianity.
x-ref. Cross-reference.
X-rts. Ex rights.
Xtian. Christian.

Y *Chem.* Yttrium.
y. 1. Yard(s). 2. Year(s).
Y. Young Men's (or Women's) Christian Association.
Yb *Chem.* Ytterbium.
yd. Yard (*pl.* **yd.** or **yds.**)
YHWH Yahweh.
YMCA or **Y.M.C.A.** Young Men's Christian Association.
YMHA or **Y.M.H.A.** Young Men's Hebrew Association.
yr. 1. Year(s). 2. Your.
yrs. 1. Years. 2. Yours.
Yt *Chem.* Yttrium.
YWCA or **Y.W.C.A.** Young Women's Christian Association.
YWHA or **Y.W.H.A.** Young Women's Hebrew Association.

Z *Astron.* Zenith distance.
Z. or **z.** Zone.
Zech. Zechariah.
Zeph. Zephaniah.
Z/F *Mil.* Zone of fire.
Zn *Chem.* Zinc.
zool. Zoological; zoologist; zoology.
Zr *Chem.* Zirconium.

Ab·e·lard (ab′ə·lärd), **Pierre**, 1079–1142, Fr. philosopher; lover of Héloise, *Fr.* **A·bé·lard** or **A·bai·lard** (à·bä·lär′).

Ad·ams (ad′əmz) A prominent Massachusetts family, including **John**, 1735–1826, second president of the U.S. 1797–1801, signer of the Declaration of Independence; his son **John Quincy**, 1767–1848, sixth president of the U.S. 1825–1829; **Henry**, 1838–1918, historian and author; **Samuel**, 1722–1803, patriot, signer of the Declaration of Independence.

Ad·di·son (ad′ə·sən), **Joseph**, 1672–1719, Eng. essayist.

Ad·en·au·er (ad′n·ou′ər, *Ger.* ä′dən·ou′ər), **Konrad**, 1876–1967, Chancellor of the Federal Republic of Germany, 1949–1963.

Ad·ler (ad′lər), **Alfred**, 1870–1937, Austrian psychiatrist.

Aes·chy·lus (es′kə·ləs), 525–456 B.C., Gk. tragic dramatist.

Ae·sop (ē′səp, ē′sop), 6th-c. B.C. Gk. compiler of fables.

Ag·as·siz (ag′ə·sē, *Fr.* à·gà·sē′), **(Jean) Louis (Rodolphe)**, 1807–73, U.S. naturalist born in Switzerland.

Al·a·ric (al′ə·rik), 370?–410, Visigoth king; sacked Rome.

Al·cott (ôl′kət, -kot), **Louisa May**, 1832–88, U.S. novelist.

Al·den (ôl′dən), **John**, 1599–1687, Pilgrim settler in Plymouth Colony (1620); a character in Longfellow's poem *The Courtship of Miles Standish*.

Al·ex·an·der VI (al′ig·zan′dər, -zän′-) See (Rodrigo) BORGIA.

Alexander Nev·ski (nev′skē, nef′-), 1220?–63, Russ. hero.

Alexander the Great, 356–323 B.C., king of Macedon 336–323; conqueror of the Persian Empire.

Al·fred (al′frid), 849–899, king of Wessex and overlord of England 871–899: called **the Great**.

Al·len (al′ən), **Ethan**, 1737–89, Amer. soldier.

Am·brose (am′brōz), **Saint**, 340?–397, bishop of Milan; one of the Latin church fathers.

Amerigo Vespucci See VESPUCCI.

A·mund·sen (ä′mŏon·sən), **Roald**, 1872–1928, Norw. explorer; discovered South Pole, 1911.

An·der·sen (an′dər·sən), **Hans Christian**, 1805–75, Dan. writer of fairy tales.

An·dre·a del Sar·to (än·drā′à del sär′tō) See SARTO.

An·gel·i·co (än·jel′i·kō), **Fra**, 1387–1455, Giovanni da Fiesole, Florentine painter and monk: original name **Guido di Pi·e·tro** (dē pē·ā′trō).

Anne (an), 1665–1714, queen of Great Britain and Ireland 1702–14.

An·tho·ny (an′thə·nē, -tə-), **Saint**, 250?–356?, Egyptian hermit and monk; founder of monastic life.

An·tho·ny (an′thə·nē), **Susan Brownell**, 1820–1906, U.S. suffragist.

An·to·ni·nus (an′tə·nī′nəs) See AURELIUS.

An·to·ny (an′tə·nē), **Mark**, Anglicized name of **Marcus An·to·ni·us** (an·tō′nē·əs), 83–30 B.C., Roman general; triumvir.

A·qui·nas (ə·kwī′nəs), **St. Thomas**, 1225?–74, Ital. Dominican monk and theologian: called **the Angelic Doctor**.

Ar·chi·me·des (är′kə·mē′dēz), 287?–212 B.C., Gk. mathematician born in Sicily.

Ar·is·toph·a·nes (ar′is·tof′ə·nēz), 450?–380? B.C. Gk. comic dramatist.

Ar·is·tot·le (ar′is·tot′l), 384–322 B.C., Gk. philosopher; pupil of Plato and teacher of Alexander the Great.

Arm·strong (ärm′strông′), **Neil Alden**, born 1930, U.S. astronaut; first man to walk on the moon, July 20, 1969.

Ar·nold (är′nəld), **Matthew**, 1822–88, Eng. poet and critic.

A·rou·et (à·rwe′), **François Marie** See VOLTAIRE.

Ar·thur (är′thər), **Chester Alan**, 1830–86, 21st president of the U.S. 1881–85.

A·ta·türk (ä·tä·türk′) See KEMAL ATATÜRK.

At·ti·la (at′ə·lə, ə·til′ə), 406?–453, king of the Huns.

Au·den (ô′dən), **W(ystan) H(ugh)**, 1907–73, U.S. poet born in England.

Au·du·bon (ô′də·bon), **John James**, 1785–1851, U.S. ornithologist born in Haiti.

Au·gus·tine (ô′gəs·tēn, ô·gus′tin), **Saint**, 354–430, bishop of Hippo; one of the Latin church fathers.

Au·gus·tus Cae·sar (ô·gus′təs sē′zər), 63 B.C.–A.D. 14, Gaius Julius Caesar Octavianus, the first Roman emperor 27 B.C.–A.D. 14: before 27 B.C. called *Octavian*.

Au·re·li·us (ô·rē′lē·əs, ô·rēl′yəs), **Marcus**, 121–180, Roman emperor, 161–180, and Stoic philosopher: full name **Marcus Aurelius An·to·ni·nus** (an′tə·nī′nəs).

Aus·ten (ôs′tən), **Jane**, 1775–1817, Eng. novelist.

A·vo·ga·dro (ä′vō·gä′drō), **Amedeo**, 1776–1856, Conte de Quaregna, Ital. physicist.

Bach (bäkh) A family of Ger. musicians and composers, of whom the best known are **Johann Sebastian**, 1685–1750, and his sons, **Karl Philipp Emanuel**, 1714–88, and **Johann Christian**, 1735–82.

Ba·con (bā′kən), **Francis**, 1561–1626, first Baron Verulam, Viscount St. Albans, Eng. philosopher, essayist, and statesman. — **Roger**, 1214?–94, Eng. scientist and philosopher.

Bal·bo·a (bal·bō′ə, *Sp.* bäl·vō′ä), **Vasco Núñez de**, 1475–1517, Sp. explorer; discovered the Pacific Ocean, 1513.

Bal·zac (bal′zak, bôl′-; *Fr.* bál·zàk′), **Honoré de**, 1799–1850, Fr. novelist.

Bar·ba·ros·sa (bär′bə·ros′ə) Nickname of FREDERICK I.

Bar·ber (bär′bər), **Samuel**, born 1910, U.S. composer.

Bar·num (bär′nəm), **P(hineas) T(aylor)**, 1810–91, U.S. showman.

Barth (bärt), **Karl**, 1886–1968, Swiss theologian.

Bar·tók (bär′tôk), **Béla**, 1881–1945, Hung. composer.

Bar·ton (bär′tən), **Clara**, 1821–1912, U.S. founder of the Amer. Red Cross.

Baude·laire (bōd·lâr′), **Charles Pierre**, 1821–67, Fr. poet.

Beard (bird), **Charles Austin**, 1874–1948, U.S. historian.

Beau·har·nais (bō·àr·ne′), **Josephine de** See JOSEPHINE.

Beck·et (bek′it), **Saint Thomas à** See THOMAS À BECKET.

Beck·ett (bek′it), **Samuel**, born 1906, Irish poet, novelist, and playwright.

Becque·rel (bek·rel′), **Antoine Henri**, 1852–1908, Fr. physicist.

Bede (bēd), **Saint**, 673?–735, Eng. theologian and historian: called **the Venerable Bede**. Also **Be·da** (bē′də).

Bee·be (bē′bē), **(Charles) William**, 1877–1962, U.S. naturalist and explorer.

Bee·tho·ven (bā′tō·vən), **Ludwig van**, 1770–1827, Ger. composer.

Bell (bel), **Alexander Graham**, 1847–1922, U.S. scientist born in Scotland; inventor of the telephone.

Ben·e·dict of Nur·si·a (ben′ə·dikt əv nûr′se·ə, nur′shē·ə, -shə), **Saint**, 480?–543, Ital. monk; founder of the Benedictine Order.

Ben-Gur·i·on (ben gŏŏr′ē·ən), **David**, 1886–1973, Israeli statesman born in Poland; prime minister 1948–53, 1955–57, 1958–1963.

Ben·tham (ben′thəm), **Jeremy**, 1748–1832, Eng. jurist and philosopher.

Berg (berkh), **Alban**, 1885–1935, Austrian composer.

Berg·son (berg′sən, *Fr.* berg·sôn′), **Henri Louis**, 1859–1941, Fr. philosopher.

Berke·ley (bûrk′le, *Brit.* bärk′-), **George**, 1685–1753, Irish Anglican prelate and philosopher.

Ber·li·oz (ber′lē·ōz), **Hector**, 1803–69, Fr. composer.

Bern·hardt (bûrn′härt, *Fr.* ber·nàr′), **Sarah**, 1884–1923, Fr. actress: orig. name **Rosine Ber·nard** (ber·nàr′).

Ber·ni·ni (ber·nē′nē), **Giovanni Lorenzo**, 1598–1680, Ital. sculptor and architect.

Ber·noul·li (bûr·nōō′le, *Fr.* ber·nōō·ye′), **Daniel**, 1700–82, Swiss mathematician.

Ber·ze·li·us (bər·zē′lē·əs, *Sw.* ber·sä′lē·ōōs), **Baron Jöns Jacob**, 1779–1848, Sw. chemist.

Bes·se·mer (bes′ə·mər), **Sir Henry**, 1813–98, Eng. engineer.

Beyle (bāl), **Marie Henri** See STENDHAL.

Bis·marck (biz′märk) **Prince Otto Eduard Leopold von**, 1815–98, Ger. statesman; founder of the Ger. Empire: called **the Iron Chancellor**.

Bi·zet (bē·zā′), **Georges**, 1838–75, Fr. composer: orig. name **Alexandre César Léopold Bizet**.

Black·stone (blak′stōn′, -stən), **Sir William**, 1723–80, Eng. jurist.

Blake (blāk), **William**, 1757–1827, Eng. poet and artist.

Blas·co-I·bá·fiez (bläs′kō·ē·vä′nyäth), **Vicente**, 1867–1928, Sp. novelist.

Blé·riot (blā·ryō′), **Louis**, 1872–1936, Fr. aviator and inventor.

Boc·cac·ci·o (bō·kä′chē·ō, *Ital.* bōk·kät′chō), **Giovanni**, 1313–75, Ital. writer and poet; author of the *Decameron*.

Bohr (bōr), **Niels**, 1885–1962, Dan. physicist.

Bol·eyn (bŏŏl′in, bō·lin′), **Anne**, 1507–36, second wife of Henry VIII of England; beheaded.

Bol·ing·broke (bol′ing·brŏŏk, bŏŏl′-) See HENRY IV (of England).

Bol·í·var (bol′ə·vər, -vär; *Sp.* bō·lē′vär), **Simón**, 1783–1830, Venezuelan general and statesman; liberated South America.

Bo·na·parte (bō′nə·pärt) A prominent Corsican Fr. family including: **Napoleon**, 1769–1821, Fr. military leader and conqueror; emperor of France 1804–15 as Napoleon I; **Joseph**, 1768–1844, king of Naples 1806–08, of Spain 1808–1813; and **Louis Napoleon**, 1808–73, emperor of France 1852–70 as Napoleon III. Also **Buonaparte**.

Boone (bōōn), **Daniel**, 1735?–1820, Amer. frontiersman in Kentucky and Missouri.

Booth (bōōth), **William**, 1829–1912, Eng. religious leader, founder of the Salvation Army: called **General Booth**. — **Edwin Thomas**, 1833–93, U.S. actor; his brother **John Wilkes**, 1838–65, U.S. actor; assassinated Abraham Lincoln.

Bor·gia (bôr′jä) An Italian aristocratic family of Spanish origin, including **Rodrigo**, 1431?–1503, pope 1492–1503 as *Alexander VI*: his children, **Cesare**, 1475?–1507, soldier and statesman, and **Lucrezia**, 1480–1519, duchess of Ferrara.

Bor·o·din (bôr′ə-dēn), **Aleksandr Porfirevich**, 1834–87, Russ. composer.

Bosch (bos), **Hieronymus**, 1450?–1516, Du. painter.

Bos·well (boz′wel, -wəl), **James**, 1746–95, Scot. lawyer and writer; biographer of Samuel Johnson.

Bot·ti·cel·li (bot′ə-chel′ē), **Sandro**, 1447?–1515, Florentine painter: orig. name **Alessandro di Mariano dei Fi·li·pe·pi** (fē·lē·pä′pē).

Boyle (boil), **Robert**, 1627–91, Eng. chemist and physicist, born in Ireland.

Bra·he (brä′ə), **Ty·cho** (tü′kō), 1546–1601, Dan. astronomer.

Brahms (brämz, *Ger.* bräms), **Johannes**, 1833–97, Ger. composer.

Bra·man·te (brä-män′tä), **Donato d'Agnolo**, 1444–1514, Ital. architect and painter.

Braque (bräk), **Georges**, 1882–1963, Fr. painter.

Breast·ed (bres′tid), **James Henry**, 1865–1935, U.S. Egyptologist.

Brecht (brekht), **Bertolt**, 1898–1956, Ger. playwright and poet.

Breu·ghel (broe′gəl) See **BRUEGHEL**.

Brezh·nev (bryezh-nyôf′), **Leonid Ilyich**, born 1906, Soviet statesman; first secretary of the Communist party 1964–.

Bron·të (bron′tē), **Anne**, 1820–49, and her sisters, **Charlotte**, 1816–55, and **Emily Jane**, 1818–48, Eng. novelists. Pseudonyms, respectively, **Acton**, **Currer**, and **Ellis Bell**.

Brown (broun), **John**, 1800–59, U.S. abolitionist; led raid on arsenal at Harper's Ferry; hanged for treason.

Brown·ing (brou′ning), **Elizabeth Barrett**, 1806–61, Eng. poet; wife of Robert. — **Robert**, 1812–89, Eng. poet.

Brue·ghel (broe′gəl) A family of Flemish painters, esp., **Pieter**, 1520?–69, known as the Elder, and his sons, **Pieter**, 1564?–1638?, known as the **Younger**, and **Jan**, 1568–1625. Also spelled *Breughel*: also **Brue′gel**.

Bru·nel·les·chi (broo′näl·les′kē), **Filippo**, 1377–1446, Florentine architect and sculptor. Also **Bru·nel·les′co** (-les′kō).

Bru·tus (broo′təs), **Marcus Junius**, 85?–42 B.C., Roman politician and general; one of Caesar's assassins.

Bry·an (brī′ən), **William Jennings**, 1860–1925, U.S. statesman and orator.

Bu·ber (boo′bər), **Martin**, 1878–1965, Austrian Jewish religious philosopher.

Buchanan (byoo·kan′ən), **James**, 1791–1868, 15th president of the U.S. 1857–61.

Bud·dha (bood′ə, boo′də) **Gautama** or **Gotama Siddhartha**, 563?–483? B.C., the founder of Buddhism.

Buf·fa·lo Bill (buf′ə·lō) See **CODY**.

Bun·yan (bun′yən), **John**, 1628–88, Eng. preacher and author of *Pilgrim's Progress*.

Buo·na·par·te (bwô′nä·pär′tə) See **BONAPARTE**.

Buo·nar·ro·ti (bwô′när·rô′tē) See **MICHELANGELO**.

Bur·bank (bûr′bangk), **Luther**, 1849–1926, U.S. horticulturist.

Burg·er (bûr′gər), **Warren Earl**, born 1907, U.S. jurist; chief justice of the Supreme Court 1969–.

Bur·goyne (bər·goin′), **John**, 1722–92, Brit. general in the Amer. Revolution.

Burke (bûrk), **Edmund**, 1729–97, Brit. statesman, writer, and orator born in Ireland.

Burns (bûrnz), **Robert**, 1759–96, Scot. poet.

Burr (bûr), **Aaron**, 1756–1836, Amer. lawyer and statesman; vice president of the U.S. 1801–05.

But·ler (but′lər), **Samuel**, 1835–1902, Eng. novelist.

Byrd (bûrd), **Richard Evelyn**, 1888–1957, U.S. rear admiral, aviator, polar explorer, and writer.

By·ron (bī′rən), **Lord**, 1788–1824, George Gordon Noel, 6th Baron Byron, Eng. poet.

Cab·ot (kab′ət), **John**, Anglicized name of **Giovanni Ca·bo·to** (kä·bô′tō), 1451?–98, Venetian seafarer and explorer.

Cæd·mon (kad′mən), 7th-c. Eng. poet.

Cae·sar (sē′zər), **Gaius Julius**, 100–44 B.C., Roman general, statesman, and historian.

Cal·vin (kal′vin), **John**, 1509–64, Fr. Protestant reformer.

Ca·mus (kà·mü′), **Albert**, 1913–60, Fr. writer.

Ca·pet (kā′pit, kap′it; *Fr.* kà·pe′) See **HUGH CAPET**.

Ca·ra·vag·gio (kä′rä·väd′jō), **Michelangelo Amerighi da**, 1569–1609, Ital. painter.

Car·lyle (kär·līl′), **Thomas**, 1795–1881, Scot. essayist.

Car·ne·gie (kär·nā′gē, -neg′ē, kär′nə·gē), **Andrew**, 1835–1919, U.S. industrialist and philanthropist born in Scotland.

Car·roll (kar′əl), **Lewis** Pseud. of *Charles Lutwidge Dodgson*, 1832–98, Eng. mathematician; author of *Alice in Wonderland*.

Car·ter (kär′tər), **Jimmy** (James Earl, Jr.), born 1924, 39th president of the U.S. 1977–.

Ca·ru·so (kə·roo′sō, *Ital.* kä·roo′zō), **Enrico**, 1873–1921, Ital. operatic tenor.

Car·ver (kär′vər), **George Washington**, 1864–1943, U.S. botanist and chemist.

Ca·sals (kä·säls′), **Pablo**, 1876–1973, Sp. violincellist, conductor, and composer.

Cas·a·no·va (kas′ə·nō′və, kaz′-; *Ital.* kä′sä·nô′vä), **Giovanni Giacomo**, 1725–98, Ital. adventurer; known for his *Memoirs*; full surname **Casanova de Sein·galt** (dä sin′gält).

Cas·tro (käs′trō, kas′-), **Fidel**, born 1926, Cuban revolutionary leader; premier 1959–: full name **Fidel Castro Ruz** (rooth).

Cath·e·rine II (kath′rin, -ər·in), 1729–96, empress of Russia: called **Catherine the Great**.

Ca·to (kā′tō), **Marcus Porcius**, 234–149 B.C., Roman statesman: called **the Elder** or **the Censor**. — **Marcus Porcius**, 95–46 B.C., Roman patriot and Stoic philosopher: called **U·ti·cen·sis** (yoo′ti·ken′səs) or the **Younger**.

Cav·en·dish (kav′ən·dish), **Henry**, 1731?–1810, Eng. chemist.

Cel·li·ni (chə·lē′nē, *Ital.* chel·lē′nē), **Benvenuto**, 1500–71, Ital. sculptor and goldsmith; known for his autobiography.

Cer·van·tes (sər·van′tēz, *Sp.* ther·vän′tās), **Miguel de**, 1547–1616, Sp. novelist and dramatist; author of *Don Quixote*: full surname **Cervantes Sa·a·ve·dra** (sä′ä·vä′thrä).

Cé·zanne (sā·zàn′), **Paul**, 1839–1906, Fr. painter.

Chap·lin (chap′lən), **Charles Spencer**, born 1889, Eng. motion-picture actor and producer formerly active in the U.S.: called **Charlie Chaplin**.

Char·le·magne (shär′lə·mān), 742?–814, king of the Franks 768–814; emperor of the West as **Charles I** 800–814: called **Charles the Great**.

Charles I (chärlz), 1600–49, Charles Stuart, king of England 1625–49; beheaded.

Charles II, 1630–85, king of England 1660–85.

Chat·ham (chat′əm), **Earl of** See **PITT**.

Chau·cer (chô′sər), **Geoffrey**, 1340?–1400, Eng. poet.

Che·khov (chek′ôf), **Anton Pavlovich**, 1860–1904, Russ. dramatist and story writer: also *Tchekhov*. Also **Che′kov**.

Che·ops (kē′ops) Egyptian king of the 4th dynasty (about 2900 B.C.), builder of the Great Pyramid at Giza: also **Khu·fu** (koo′foo).

Chiang Kai-shek (chyäng′ kī′shek′, chang′; *Chinese* jyäng′), 1887–1975, Chinese generalissimo; head of the Republic of China 1943-75: orig. name **Chiang Chung-cheng**.

Cho·pin (shō′pan, *Fr.* shô·pan′), **Frédéric François**, 1810–1849, Polish composer and pianist active in France.

Chou En-lai (jō′ en′lī′), 1898–1976, Chinese statesman; foreign minister 1949–58; premier of the People's Republic of China 1949-76.

Christ (krīst) See **JESUS**.

Chris·to·pher (kris′tə·fər), **Saint**, 3rd-c. Christian martyr.

Church·ill (chûrch′il, -əl), **Sir Winston (Leonard Spencer)**, 1874–1965, Brit. statesman and author; prime minister 1940–45, 1951–55.

Cic·e·ro (sis′ə·rō), **Marcus Tullius**, 106–43 B.C., Roman statesman, orator, and author; also called *Tully*.

Cid (sid, *Sp.* thēth), **the**, 1044?–99, Rodrigo Díaz de Bivar, Sp. epic hero; champion in wars against the Moors. Also called **El Cid Cam·pe·a·dor** (kam′pä·ä·thôr′).

Ci·ma·bue (chē′mä·boo′ā), **Giovanni**, 1240?–1302?, Florentine painter.

Clau·se·witz (klou′zə·vits), **Karl von**, 1780–1831, Prussian general and military scientist.

Clay (klā), **Henry**, 1777–1852, U.S. statesman and orator.

Cle·men·ceau (klem′ən·sō′, *Fr.* kle·män·sô′), **Georges Eugène**, 1841–1929, Fr. statesman; premier 1906–09, 1917–20: called **the Tiger**.

Clem·ens (klem′ənz), **Samuel Langhorne** See **MARK TWAIN**.

Cle·o·pat·ra (klē′ə·pat′rə, -pā′trə, -pä′trə), 69–30 B.C.; queen of Egypt 51–49 B.C., 48–30 B.C.; committed suicide.

Cleve·land (klēv′lənd), **(Stephen) Grover**, 1837–1908, 22nd and 24th president of the U.S. 1885–89, 1893–97.

Co·dy (kō′dē), **William Frederick**, 1846–1917, U.S. plainsman, army scout, and showman: called *Buffalo Bill*.

Cœur de Li·on (kûr′ də lē′ən) See **RICHARD I**.

Cole·ridge (kōl′rij), **Samuel Taylor**, 1772–1834, Eng. poet and critic.

Co·lum·bus (kə·lum′bəs), **Christopher**, 1446?–1506, Genoese seafarer and explorer; discovered America for Spain Oct. 12, 1492. Sp. **Cristóbal Co·lón** (kō·lōn′), Ital. **Cristoforo Co·lom·bo** (kō·lōm′bō).

Comte (kônt, *Fr.* kônt), **Auguste**, 1798–1857, Fr. philosopher.

Con·dor·cet (kôn·dôr·se′), **Marquis de**, 1743–94, Marie Jean de Caritat, Fr. social philosopher and revolutionist.

Con·fu·cius (kən·fyoo′shəs), 551?–478? B.C., Chinese philosopher and teacher. Chinese **K'ung Fu-tse** (koong′ foo′tse′).

Con·rad (kon′rad), **Joseph**, 1857–1924, Eng. author born in

Poland: orig. name **Teodor Józef Konrad Kor·ze·niow·ski** (kôr′ze·nyôf′skē).

Con·stan·tine I (kon′stən·tēn, -tīn), 288?–337, first Christian emperor of Rome; founder of the Byzantine Empire: called **the Great.**

Cook (ko͝ok), **Captain James,** 1728–79, Eng. seafarer and explorer.

Coo·lidge (ko͞o′lij), **(John) Calvin,** 1872–1933, 30th president of the U.S. 1923–29.

Coop·er (ko͞o′pər, ko͝op′ər), **James Fenimore,** 1789–1851, U.S. novelist.

Co·per·ni·cus (kō·pûr′nə·kəs), **Nicholas,** Lat. name of **Mikołaj Ko·per·nik** (kô·pûr′nĕk), 1473–1543, Polish astronomer.

Cop·land (kōp′lənd), **Aaron,** born 1900, U.S. composer.

Cor·neille (kôr·nā′, *Fr.* kôr·nā′y′), **Pierre,** 1606–84, Fr. dramatist.

Corn·wal·lis (kôrn·wôl′is, -wol′-), **Charles,** 1738–1805, first Marquis Cornwallis, Eng. general and statesman.

Co·ro·na·do (kôr′ə·nä′dō, *Sp.* kô′rō·nä′thō), **Francisco Vásquez de,** 1510–54, Sp. explorer.

Cor·tés (kôr·tez′, *Sp.* kôr·tās′), **Hernando,** 1485–1547, Sp. conquistador; conqueror of Mexico. Also **Cor·tez′.**

Cra·nach (krä′näkh), **Lucas,** 1472–1533, Ger. painter.

Crane (krān), **(Harold) Hart,** 1899–1932, U.S. poet. — **Stephen,** 1871–1900, U.S. writer.

Crock·ett (krok′it), **David,** 1786–1836, Amer. frontiersman and politician; killed at the Alamo: called **Davy Crockett.**

Crom·well (krom′wel), **Oliver,** 1599–1658, Eng. general and statesman; lord protector of England 1653–58.

Crookes (kro͝oks), **Sir William,** 1832–1919, Eng. physicist and chemist.

Cu·rie (kyo͝or′ē, kyo͝or·ē′; *Fr.* kü·rē′), 1867–1934, **Marie,** *née* Sklodowska, born in Poland, and her husband **Pierre,** 1859–1906, Fr. physicists, discoverers of radium.

Cu·vi·er (ko͞o′vē·ā, *Fr.* kü·vyā′), **Baron Georges,** 1769–1832, Fr. naturalist.

Cyr·il (sir′əl), **Saint,** 827–869, Christian scholar and missionary: called **Apostle of the Slavs.**

Dal·ton (dôl′ten), **John,** 1766–1844, Eng. chemist and physicist.

Dan·te A·li·ghie·ri (dän′tā a′le·gyä′i·ē, dan′tē), 1265–1321, Ital. poet; author of the *Divine Comedy*: orig. name **Durante Alighieri.**

Dar·win (där′win), **Charles Robert,** 1809–82, Eng. naturalist.

Dau·mier (dō·myā′), **Honoré,** 1808–79, Fr. painter and caricaturist.

da Vin·ci (də vin′chē, *Ital.* dä vēn′chē), **Leonardo,** 1452–1519, Florentine painter, sculptor, architect, and inventor.

Da·vis (dā′vis), **Jefferson,** 1808–89, U.S. statesman; president of the Confederacy 1862–65.

Da·vy (dā′vē), **Sir Humphry,** 1778–1829, Eng. scientist.

De·bus·sy (də·byo͞o′sē, *Fr.* də·bü·sē′), **Claude (Achille),** 1862–1918, Fr. composer.

De·foe (di·fō′), **Daniel,** 1660–1731, Eng. novelist and political journalist. Also **De Foe.**

De For·est (di fôr′est, for′-), **Lee,** 1873–1961, U.S. inventor; pioneer in radio transmission.

De·gas (də·gä′), **(Hilaire Germaine) Edgar,** 1834–1917, Fr. impressionist painter.

de Gaulle (də gôl′, *Fr.* də gōl′), **Charles André Joseph Marie,** 1890–1970, Fr. general and statesman; president 1944–45, 1959–69.

De·la·croix (də·là·krwä′), **(Ferdinand Victor) Eugène,** 1799–1863, Fr. painter.

del Sar·to (dĕl sär′tō), **Andrea** See SARTO.

De Quin·cey (di kwin′sē), **Thomas,** 1785–1859, Eng. essayist.

Des·cartes (dā·kärt′), **René,** 1596–1650, Fr. mathematician and philosopher.

De So·to (də sō′tō), **Hernando,** 1500?–42, Sp. explorer; discovered the Mississippi River, 1541.

De Va·le·ra (dev′ə·lâr′ə, dä′və·lir′ə), **Eamon,** 1882–1975, Irish statesman born in the U.S.; prime minister 1937–48, 1951–54, 1957–59, president 1959–73.

Dew·ey (do͞o′ē, dyo͞o′ē), **George,** 1837–1917, U.S. admiral in the Spanish-Amer. War. — **John,** 1859–1952, U.S. philosopher, psychologist, and educator.

Dí·az de Bi·var (dē′äth thä bē·vär′) See CID.

Dick·ens (dik′ənz), **Charles (John Huffam),** 1812–70, Eng. novelist: pseud. Boz (boz).

Dick·in·son (dik′ən·sən), **Emily (Elizabeth),** 1830–86, U.S. poet.

Di·de·rot (dē·drō′), **Denis,** 1713–84, Fr. philosopher and encyclopedist.

Di·og·e·nes (dī·oj′ə·nēz), 412?–323 B.C., Gk. Cynic philosopher, reputed to have lived in a tub.

Dis·rae·li (diz·rā′lē), **Benjamin,** 1804–81, first Earl of Beaconsfield, Eng. statesman and novelist; prime minister 1868, 1874–80.

Dob·zhan·sky (dôb·zhän′skē), **Theodosius,** 1900–75, U.S. geneticist born in Russia.

Dodg·son (doj′sən), **Charles Lutwidge** See (Lewis) CARROLL.

Dom·i·nic (dom′ə·nik), **Saint,** 1170–1221, Sp. friar; founded the Dominican Order: orig. name **Domingo de Guz·mán** (go͞oth·män′).

Don·a·tel·lo (don′ə·tel′ō, *Ital.* do′nä·tel′lō), 1386?–1466, Florentine sculptor: orig. name **Donato di Niccolò di Bet·to Bar·di** (dĕ bät′tō bär′dē).

Donne (dun), **John,** 1573–1631, Eng. poet and clergyman.

Dop·pler (dop′lər), **Christian Johann,** 1803–53, Ger. physicist and mathematician active in Austria.

Dos·to·ev·ski (dôs′tô·yef′skē), **Feodor Mikhailovich,** 1821–1881, Russ. novelist. Also **Dos′to·yev′sky.**

Doug·las (dug′ləs), **Stephen Arnold,** 1813–61, U.S. senator; opposed Lincoln in a series of debates, 1858. — **William Orville,** born 1898, U.S. jurist, associate justice of the Supreme Court 1939–.

Doyle (doil), **Sir Arthur Conan,** 1859–1930, Eng. physician and novelist; creator of detective **Sher·lock Holmes** (shûr′lok hōmz′).

Drake (drāk), **Sir Francis,** 1540?–96, Eng. admiral; first Englishman to sail round the world.

Drei·ser (drī′sər, -zər), **Theodore (Herman Albert),** 1871–1945, U.S. novelist.

Drey·fus (drā′fəs, drī-; *Fr.* dre·füs′), **Alfred,** 1859–1935, Fr. army officer; wrongfully convicted of treason in 1894; vindicated in 1906.

Dry·den (drīd′n), **John,** 1631–1700, Eng. poet, critic, and dramatist; poet laureate 1670–88.

Dul·les (dul′əs), **John Foster,** 1888–1959, U.S. lawyer and diplomat; secretary of state 1953–59.

Du·mas (do͞o·mä′, do͞o′mä; *Fr.* dü·mà′), **Alexandre,** 1802–1870, **Dumas père,** and his son **Alexandre,** 1824–95, **Dumas fils,** Fr. novelists and dramatists.

Duns Sco·tus (dunz skō′təs), **John,** 1265?–1308, Scot. scholastic theologian: called **the Subtile Doctor.**

Dü·rer (dü′rər), **Albrecht,** 1471–1528, Ger. painter and engraver.

Dzhu·ga·shvi·li (jo͞o′gä·shvē′lē), **Iosif Vissarionovich.** See STALIN.

Ear·hart (âr′härt), **Amelia,** 1898–1937, Mrs. George Palmer Putnam, U.S. aviatrix.

Ed·dy (ed′ē), **Mary Baker,** 1821–1910, *née* Mary Morse Baker, U.S. religious leader; founder of Christian Science.

Ed·i·son (ed′ə·sən), **Thomas Alva,** 1847–1931, U.S. inventor.

Ed·ward VII (ed′wərd), 1841–1910, king of England; called **the Peacemaker.**

Ein·stein (īn′stīn), **Albert,** 1879–1955, U.S. physicist born in Germany; developed the theory of relativity.

Ei·sen·how·er (ī′zən·hou′ər), **Dwight David,** 1890–1969, U.S. general; 34th president of the U.S. 1953–61.

El Gre·co (el grek′ō, grā′kō), 1548?–1614, Sp. painter born in Crete: orig. name **Domenicos The·o·to·co·pou·los** (thä′ō·tô·kô′pō·lôs).

E·li·a (ē·lyē′ä) See (Charles) LAMB.

El·i·ot (el′ē·ət), **George** Pseud. of *Mary Ann Evans,* 1819–1880, Eng. novelist. — **T(homas) S(tearns),** 1888–1965, Brit. poet, dramatist, and critic born in the U.S.

E·liz·a·beth I (i·liz′ə·bəth), 1533–1603, queen of England 1558–1603.

Elizabeth II, born 1926, queen of England 1952–.

Em·er·son (em′ər·sən), **Ralph Waldo,** 1803–82, U.S. essayist, philosopher, and poet.

Eng·els (eng′əls), **Friedrich,** 1820–95, Ger. socialist and theoretician; collaborated with Karl Marx.

Ep·i·cu·rus (ep′ə·kyo͝or′əs), 342?–270? B.C., Gk. philosopher.

E·ras·mus (i·raz′məs), **Desiderius,** 1466?–1536, Du. theologian, classical scholar, and humanist: orig. name **Geert Geerts** (gerts) or **Gerhard Ger·hards** (ger′harts).

Er·ic·son (er′ik·sən), **Leif,** 11th-c. Norse adventurer; son of Eric the Red; probably discovered North America about 1000. Also **Er′ics·son.**

Er·ic the Red (er′ik), born 950?, Scandinavian adventurer; colonizer of Greenland.

Eu·clid (yo͞o′klid), Gk. mathematician of about the 3rd-c. B.C.; developed the basic principles of geometry.

Eu·ler (oi′lər), **Leonhard,** 1707–83, Swiss mathematician.

Eu·rip·i·des (yo͞o·rip′ə·dēz), 480?–406? B.C., Gk. dramatist.

Ev·ans (ev′əns), **Mary Ann** See (George) ELIOT.

Far·a·day (far′ə·dā), **Michael,** 1791–1867, Eng. chemist and physicist; discovered properties of electromagnetism.

Far·ra·gut (far′ə·gət), **David Glasgow,** 1801–70, Union admiral in the Amer. Civil War.

Faulk·ner (fôk′nər), **William,** 1897–1962, U.S. novelist. Also **Falk′ner.**

Fer·di·nand V (fûr′di·nand), 1452–1516, king of Spain; husband of Isabella I: called **the Catholic.**

Fer·mi (fer′mē), **Enrico,** 1901–54, Ital. nuclear physicist active in the U.S.

Fich·te (fikh′tə), **Johann Gottlieb,** 1762–1814, Ger. patriot and philosopher.

Fill·more (fil′môr), **Millard,** 1800–74, 13th president of the U.S. 1850–53.

Fitz·Ger·ald (fits′jer′əld), **Edward,** 1809–83, Eng. poet.

Fitzgerald, F(rancis) Scott (Key), 1896–1940, U.S. writer.

Flau·bert (flō·bâr′), **Gustave,** 1821–80, Fr. novelist.

Flem·ing (flem′ing), **Sir Alexander,** 1881–1955, Brit. physician and bacteriologist; codiscoverer with Florey of penicillin.

Flo·rey (flôr′ē, flō′rē), **Sir Howard Walter,** 1898–1968, Brit. pathologist born in Australia; collaborated with Fleming in the discovery of penicillin.

Foch (fôsh), **Ferdinand,** 1851–1929, Fr. general; commander in chief of the Allied armies, 1918.

Ford (fôrd, fōrd) **Gerald Rudolph,** born 1913, vice president of the U.S. 1973–74; 38th president of the U.S. 1974–77.

Ford (fôrd, fōrd), **Henry,** 1863–1947, U.S. automobile manufacturer.

Fos·ter (fôs′tər, fos′-), **Stephen (Collins),** 1826–64, U.S. songwriter.

Fou·cault (fōō·kō′), **Jean Bernard Léon,** 1819–68, Fr. physicist.

Fou·rier (fōō·ryā′), **Jean Baptiste Joseph,** 1768–1830, Fr. mathematician and physicist.

Fox (foks), **George,** 1624–91, Eng. preacher; founded the Society of Friends.

Fra (frä) **Angelico** See ANGELICO.

France (frans, fräns), **Anatole** Pseud. of **Jacques Anatole Thi·bault** (tē·bō′), 1844–1924, Fr. novelist and critic.

Fran·ces·ca (frän·ches′kä), **Piero della** See PIERO DELLA FRANCESCA.

Fran·cis of As·si·si (fran′sis, frän′-; ə·sē′zē), **St.,** 1182?–1226, Ital. friar and preacher: orig. name **Giovanni Francesco Ber·nar·do·ne** (bâr′när·dō′nā).

Francis Xavier, Saint See XAVIER.

Franck (fränk), **César Auguste,** 1822–90, Fr. composer born in Belgium.

Fran·co (frang′kō, Sp. fräng′kō), **Francisco,** 1892–1975, Sp. political and military leader; chief of state 1939–75: called **el Cau·dil·lo** (el kou·thē′lyō, -thē′yō): full surname **Fran·co-Ba·ha·mon·de** (-bä′ä·mōn′dā).

Frank·lin (frangk′lin), **Benjamin,** 1706–90, Amer. patriot, writer, scientist, and diplomat: pseud. **Richard Saun·ders** (sôn′dərz, sän′-).

Fred·er·ick I (fred′ər·ik, fred′rik), 1123?–90, emperor of the Holy Roman Empire 1152–90: called *Barbarossa* (Redbeard).

Frederick II, 1712–86, king of Prussia 1740–86: called **Frederick the Great.**

Fres·nel (frā·nel′), **Augustin Jean,** 1788–1827, Fr. physicist.

Freud (froid), **Sigmund,** 1856–1939, Austrian neurologist; founded modern theory of psychoanalysis.

Frost (frôst, frost), **Robert (Lee),** 1875–1963, U.S. poet.

Ful·ton (fōōl′tən), **Robert,** 1765–1815, U.S. engineer and inventor.

Funk (fungk), **Isaac Kauffman,** 1839–1912, U.S. publisher and lexicographer.

Ga·len (gā′lən), 130?–200?, Gk. physician and medical writer.

Gal·i·le·o (gal′ə·lē′ō, *Ital.* gä′lē·lā′ō), 1564–1642, Florentine astronomer and physicist whose discoveries were condemned by the Roman Inquisition: full name **Galileo Gal·i·le·i** (gal′·ə·lā′ē).

Gal·va·ni (gäl·vä′ne), **Luigi,** 1737–98, Ital. physiologist.

Ga·ma (gam′ə, *Pg.* Gä′mə), **Vasco da,** 1469?–1524, Pg. seafarer and explorer.

Gan·dhi (gän′de, gan′-), **Mohandas Karamchand,** 1869–1948, Indian politician and Hindu spiritual leader: called **Mahatma Gandhi.**

Gar·cí·a Lor·ca (gär·thē′ä lôr′kä), **Federico,** 1899–1936, Sp. poet, dramatist, and essayist.

Gar·field (gär′fēld), **James Abram,** 1831–81, 20th president of the U.S. 1881; assassinated.

Gar·i·bal·di (gar′ə·bôl′dē, *Ital.* gä′rē·bäl′dē), **Giuseppe,** 1807–82, Ital. patriot and general; worked to unite Italy.

Gar·rick (gar′ik), **David,** 1717–79, Eng. actor, manager, and author.

Gau·guin (gō·gan′), **Paul,** 1848–1903, Fr. painter: full name **Eugène Henri Paul Gauguin.**

Gauss (gous), **Karl Friedrich,** 1777–1855, Ger. mathematician and astronomer.

Gau·ta·ma (gô′tə·mə, gou′-) See BUDDHA.

Gay-Lus·sac (gā·lü·sàk′), **Joseph Louis,** 1778–1850, Fr. chemist and physicist.

Gen·ghis Khan (jen′giz kän′, jeng′gis, geng′gis), 1167?–1227, Mongol conqueror: orig. name **Te·much·in** (tə·mōō′·chin). Also **Jen′ghiz Khan.**

George (jôrj), **St.,** died 303?, Christian martyr; patron of England.

George III, 1738–1820, king of England 1760–1820.

George VI, 1895–1952, king of England 1936–52.

Ge·ron·i·mo (jə·ron′ə·mo), 1829–1909, Apache Indian chief.

Gide (zhēd), **André,** 1869–1951, Fr. writer.

Gil·bert (gil′bərt), **Sir William Schwenck,** 1836–1911, Eng. librettist; collaborator with Sir Arthur Sullivan.

Gior·gio·ne (jôr·jō′nā), 1477?–1511, Venetian painter: orig. name **Giorgio Bar·ba·rel·li** (bär′bä·rel′lē).

Giot·to (jôt′tō), 1266?–1337, Florentine painter, architect, and sculptor: full name **Giotto di Bon·do·ne** (dē bōn·dō′nä).

Glad·stone (glad′stōn, -stən), **William Ewart,** 1809–98, Eng. statesman and political leader; prime minister 1868–1874, 1880–85, 1886, 1892–94.

Goe·thals (gō′thəlz), **George Washington,** 1858–1928, U.S. army engineer; builder of the Panama Canal.

Goethe (gœ′tə), **Johann Wolfgang von,** 1749–1832, Ger. poet, dramatist, and novelist.

Gogh (gō, gôk; *Du.* khôkh), **Vincent van** See VAN GOGH.

Go·gol (gō′gəl, *Russ.* gô′gôl), **Nikolai Vasilievich,** 1809–52, Russ. writer and dramatist.

Gom·pers (gom′pərz), **Samuel,** 1850–1924, U.S. labor leader.

Gor·ki (gôr′kē), **Maxim** Pseud. of **Alexei Maximovich Pyesh·kov** (pyesh′kôf), 1868–1936, Russ. author. Also **Gor′ky.**

Gou·nod (gōō·nō′), **Charles François,** 1818–93, Fr. composer.

Go·ya (gô′yə), **Francisco José de,** 1746–1828, Sp. painter and etcher: full surname **Goya y Lu·cien·tes** (ē lōō·thyen′täs).

Gra·ham (grā′əm), **William Franklin,** born 1918, U.S. evangelist: called **Billy Graham.**

Grant (grant), **Ulysses S(impson),** 1822–85, U.S. general in the Civil War; 18th president of the U.S. 1869–77: orig. name **Hiram Ulysses Grant.**

Gray (grā), **Thomas,** 1716–71, Eng. poet.

Gre·co (grek′ō, grä′kō), **El,** See EL GRECO.

Gregory I (greg′ər·ē), **St.,** 540?–604, pope 590–604; reformed the church service: called **Gregory the Great.**

Gregory XIII, 1502–85, pope 1572–85; reformed the calendar: orig. name **Ugo Buon·cam·pag·ni** (bwôn′cäm·pän′yē).

Grieg (grēg), **Edvard (Hagerup),** 1843–1907, Norw. composer.

Grimm (grim), **Jakob (Ludwig Karl),** 1785–1863, and his brother **Wilhelm (Karl),** 1786–1859, Ger. collectors of fairy tales.

Gro·pi·us (grō′pē·əs), **Walter,** 1883–1969, Ger. architect active in the U.S.

Grü·ne·wald (grü′nə·vält), **Mathias,** 1480?–1530?, Ger. painter.

Gu·ten·berg (gōōt′n·bûrg), **Johann,** 1400?–68?, Ger. printer; inventor of movable type: orig. name **Johannes Gens·fleisch** (gens′flīsh).

Ha·ber (hä′bər), **Fritz,** 1868–1934, Ger. chemist.

Haeck·el (hek′əl), **Ernst Heinrich,** 1834–1919, Ger. naturalist and philosopher.

Hai·le Se·las·sie (hī′lē sə·las′ē, -läs′ē), 1892–1975, emperor of Ethiopia 1930–74; in exile 1936–41: orig. name **Ta·ffari Ma·kon·nen** (mä·kôn′nen).

Hal·dane (hôl′dān), **J(ohn) B(urdon) S(anderson),** 1892–1964, Eng. geneticist.

Hale (hāl), **Nathan,** 1755–76, Amer. Revolutionary patriot; hanged as a spy by the British.

Hals (häls), **Frans,** 1580?–1666, Du. painter.

Hal·sey (hôl′zē), **William Frederick,** 1882–1959, U.S. admiral in World War II.

Ham·il·ton (ham′əl·tən), **Alexander,** 1757–1804, Amer. statesman born in the British West Indies.

Ham·mar·skjöld (häm′är·shüld), **Dag,** 1905–61, Sw. statesman; UN Secretary General 1953–61.

Ham·mu·ra·bi (hä′mōō·rä′bē, ham′ə-), king of Babylonia in the first dynasty, about 2000 B.C.; promulgator of a system of laws called the **Code of Hammurabi.**

Han·cock (han′kok), **John,** 1737–93, U.S. patriot; signer of the Declaration of Independence.

Han·del (han′dəl), **George Frideric,** 1685–1759, Ger. composer active in England and Italy: orig. name **Georg Friedrich Hän·del** (hen′dəl): called **George Frederick Handel.**

Han·ni·bal (han′ə bəl), 247?–183? B.C., Carthaginian general; invaded Italy by crossing the Alps.

Har·ding (här′ding), **Warren Gamaliel,** 1865–1923, 29th president of the U.S. 1921–23.

Har·ri·son (har'ə·sən), **Benjamin**, 1833–1901, 23rd president of the U.S. 1889–93; his grandfather, **William Henry**, 1773–1841, military commander; ninth president of the U.S. for a month in 1841.

Harte (härt), **Bret**, 1836–1902, U.S. novelist and short-story writer: orig. name **Francis Brett Harte**.

Har·vey (här'vē), **William**, 1578–1657, Eng. physician; discovered the circulation of the blood.

Haw·thorne (hô'thôrn), **Nathaniel**, 1804–64, U.S. novelist and short-story writer.

Hay·dn (hīd'n), **Franz Joseph**, 1732–1809, Austrian composer.

Hayes (hāz), **Rutherford Birchard**, 1822–93, 19th president of the U.S. 1877–81.

Hearst (hûrst), **William Randolph**, 1863–1951, U.S. newspaper publisher.

He·gel (hā'gəl), **Georg Wilhelm Friedrich**, 1770–1831, Ger. philosopher.

Hei·ne (hī'nə), **Heinrich**, 1797–1856, Ger. lyric poet.

Helm·holtz (helm'hōlts), **Hermann Ludwig Ferdinand von**, 1821–94, Ger. physiologist and physicist.

Hé·lo·ïse (ā·lō·ēz'), died 1164?, Fr. abbess, mistress and then wife of Abelard.

Hem·ing·way (hem'ing·wā), **Ernest**, 1899–1961, U.S. writer.

Hen·ry (hen'rē), **O.** See O. HENRY. — **Patrick**, 1736–99, Amer. revolutionary statesman and orator.

Henry II, 1133–89, king of England 1154–89; first Plantagenet king: called **Henry Plantagenet**.

Henry IV, 1367–1413, king of England 1399–1413.

Henry V, 1387–1422, king of England 1413–22.

Henry VIII, 1491–1547, king of England 1509–47, asserted royal supremacy over the Catholic Church in England.

Her·od An·ti·pas (her'əd an'ti·pas), died A.D. 39?, tetrarch of Galilee 4 B.C.–A.D. 39; the Herod of the Gospels.

He·rod·o·tus (hi·rod'ə·təs), 5th–c. B.C. Gk. historian: called **the Father of History**.

Her·rick (her'ik), **Robert**, 1591–1674, Eng. lyric poet.

Her·zl (her'tsəl), **Theodor**, 1860–1904, Austro-Hung. journalist; founded the Zionist movement.

Hin·de·mith (hin'də·mit), **Paul**, 1895–1963, Ger. composer.

Hin·den·burg (hin'den·bûrg, *Ger.* hin'dən·bŏŏrkh), **Paul von**, 1847–1934, Ger. general and statesman; president of the Weimar Republic 1925–34.

Hip·poc·ra·tes (hi·pok'rə·tēz), 460?–377? B.C., Gk. physician: called **the Father of Medicine**.

Hi·ro·hi·to (hir·ō·hē·tō), born 1901, emperor of Japan 1926–.

Hit·ler (hit'lər), **Adolf**, 1889–1945, Ger. Nazi dictator born in Austria; chancellor 1933–45: called **der Fuhrer** (the Leader).

Hobbes (hobz), **Thomas**, 1588–1679, Eng. philosopher.

Ho·garth (hō'gärth), **William**, 1697–1765, Eng. painter and engraver.

Hol·bein (hōl'bīn, *Ger.* hôl'bīn), **Hans**, 1465?–1524, **the Elder**, and his son **Hans**, 1497?–1543, **the Younger**, Ger. painters.

Holmes (hōmz), **Oliver Wendell**, 1809–94, U.S. physician, poet, and essayist. — **Oliver Wendell**, 1841–1935, U.S. jurist; associate justice of the Supreme Court 1902–32; son of the preceding.

Ho·mer (hō'mər), 9th–c. B.C. Gk. epic poet; trad. author of the *Iliad* and the *Odyssey*.

Hooke (hŏŏk), **Robert**, 1635–1703, Eng. physicist.

Hoo·ver (hŏŏ'vər), **Herbert Clark**, 1874–1964, U.S. mining engineer and statesman; 31st president of the U.S. 1929–33. — **J(ohn) Edgar**, 1895–1972, U.S. lawyer; director of the Federal Bureau of Investigation 1924–72.

Hor·ace (hôr'is, hor'-) Anglicized name of **Quintus Horatius Flac·cus** (flak'əs), 65–8 B.C., Roman poet.

Hou·di·ni (hŏŏ·dē'nē), **Harry**, 1874–1926, U.S. magician: orig. name **Erich Weiss** (wīs).

Hous·man (hous'mən), **A(lfred) E(dward)**, 1859–1936, Eng. poet.

Hous·ton (hyŏŏs'tən), **Sam**, 1793–1863, U.S. general and politician; first president of the Republic of Texas 1836–38, 1841–44.

Hud·son (hud'sən), **Henry**, died 1611?, Eng. navigator and explorer; discovered the Hudson River for the Dutch, 1609, and Hudson Bay for the English, 1610.

Hugh Ca·pet (hyŏŏ kā'pit, kap'it; *Fr.* kà·pe'), 938?–996, king of France 987–996; founder of the Capetian dynasty.

Hu·go (hyŏŏ'gō, *Fr.* ü·gō'), **Victor (Marie)**, 1802–85, Fr. poet, novelist, and dramatist.

Hume (hyŏŏm), **David**, 1711–76, Scot. historian and philosopher.

Hux·ley (huks'lē) An Eng. family prominent in science and literature, notably **T(homas) H(enry)**, 1825–95, biologist and Darwinian; and his grandsons **Julian (Sorell)**, born 1887, biologist, and **Aldous (Leonard)**, 1894–1963, novelist and critic.

Huy·gens (hī'gənz), **Christian**, 1629–95, Du. mathematician, physicist, and astronomer. Also **Huy'ghens**.

I·bá·ñez (ē·vä'nyeth), **Vicente Blasco** See BLASCO-IBÁÑEZ.

Ib·sen (ib'sən), **Henrik**, 1828–1906, Norw. dramatist.

Ig·na·ti·us Loyola (ig·nā'shē·əs, -shəs), **Saint** See LOYOLA.

I·no·nu (ē·nœ·nü'), **Ismet**, born 1884, Turkish military commander and statesman; president 1938–50; prime minister 1961–; earlier name **Ismet Pa·za** (pä·zä').

Ir·ving (ûr'ving), **Washington**, 1783–1859, U.S. writer, historian, and humorist.

Is·a·bel·la I (iz'ə·bel'ə), 1451–1504, queen of Castile; aided Christopher Columbus: called **Isabella the Catholic**.

I·van IV (ī'vən, *Russ.* i·vän'), 1530–84, first czar of Russia 1547–84: called **the Terrible**.

Jack·son (jak'sən), **Andrew**, 1767–1845, U.S. general; seventh president of the U.S. 1829–37: called **Old Hickory**. — **Thomas Jonathan**, 1824–63, Confederate general in the Civil War: called **Stonewall Jackson**.

James (jāmz), **Henry**, 1843–1916, U.S. writer and critic active in England. — **Jesse (Woodson)**, 1847–82, U.S. outlaw. — **William**, 1842–1910, U.S. philosopher and psychologist; brother of Henry.

James I, 1566–1625, 1st Stuart king of England 1603–25; as **James VI** king of Scotland 1567–1625.

James II, 1633–1701, king of England 1685–88; deposed.

Jeanne d'Arc (zhän dark) See JOAN OF ARC.

Jeans (jēnz), **Sir James (Hopwood)**, 1877–1946, Eng. astronomer, physicist, and philosopher.

Jef·fer·son (jef'ər·sən), **Thomas**, 1743–1826, Amer. statesman, diplomat, and writer; third president of the U.S. 1801–1809.

Jen·ner (jen'ər), **Edward**, 1749–1823, Eng. physician; discovered vaccination.

Je·sus (jē'zəs) Founder of Christianity, 6? B.C.–29? A.D., son of Mary; regarded in the Christian faith as Christ, the Messiah. Also **Jesus Christ, Jesus of Nazareth**.

Joan of Arc (jōn), 1412?–31, Fr. heroine and martyr; burned as a heretic; canonized 1920; also called **the Maid of Orléans**.

John (jon), 1167?–1216, king of England 1199–1216, signed the Magna Carta 1215: called **John Lack·land** (lak'land).

John XXIII, 1881–1963, pope 1958–63: orig. name **Angelo Giuseppe Ron·cal·li** (rōn·käl'lē).

John·son (jon'sən), **Andrew**, 1808–75, 17th president of the U.S. 1865–69; impeached. — **Lyndon Baines**, 1908–73, 36th president of the U.S. 1963–69. — **Samuel**, 1709–84, Eng. lexicographer, poet, man of letters: called **Dr. Johnson**.

Jones (jōnz), **John Paul**, 1747–92, Amer. Revolutionary naval officer born in Scotland: orig. name **John Paul**.

Jon·son (jon'sən), **Ben**, 1573?–1637; Eng. poet and dramatist.

Jo·seph·ine (jō'zə·fēn, *Fr.* zhô·zā·fēn'), **Empress**, 1763–1814, widow of Vicomte Alexandre de Beauharnais, married Napoleon Bonaparte 1796, divorced 1809.

Joule (joul, jŏŏl), **James Prescott**, 1818–89, Eng. physicist.

Joyce (jois), **James (Augustine Aloysius)**, 1882–1941, Irish writer and poet active in Zurich and Paris.

Jul·ius (jŏŏl'yəs) Caesar See (Gaius Julius) CAESAR.

Jung (yŏŏng), **Carl Gustav**, 1875–1961, Swiss psychologist.

Jus·tin·i·an I (jus·tin'ē·ən), Anglicized name of **Flavius Anicius Jus·tin·i·a·nus** (jus·tin'ē·ā'nus), 483–565, Byzantine emperor 527–565; codified Roman laws: called **the Great**.

Kaf·ka (käf'kä), **Franz**, 1883–1924, Austrian writer born in Prague.

Kant (känt), **Immanuel**, 1724–1804, Ger. philosopher.

Keats (kēts), **John**, 1795–1821, Eng. poet.

Ke·mal A·ta·türk (ke·mäl' ä·tä·türk'), 1881–1938, Turkish general and statesman; founder of modern Turkey. Also **Mus·ta·fa Ke·mal** (mŏŏ'stä·fä ki·mäl').

Ken·ne·dy (ken'ə·dē), **John Fitzgerald**, 1917–63, 35th president of the U.S. 1961–63; assassinated. — **Robert Francis**, 1925–68, U.S. senator and political leader; brother of the preceding; assassinated.

Kep·ler (kep'lər), **Johann**, 1571–1630, Ger. astronomer; formulated laws of planetary motion.

Key (kē), **Francis Scott**, 1779–1863, Amer. lawyer and poet; wrote *The Star-Spangled Banner*.

Keynes (kānz), **John Maynard**, 1883–1946, first Baron of Tilton, Eng. economist.

Khay·yám (kī·äm'), **Omar**. See OMAR KHAYYÁM.

Khrush·chev (krŏŏsh·chôf', *Russ.* khrŏŏ·shchôf'), **Nikita Sergeyevich** 1894–1971, Soviet statesman; first secretary of the Communist Party 1953–1964; premier 1958–1964.

Kidd (kid), **William**, 1645?–1701, Brit. sea captain and pirate; hanged: called **Captain Kidd**.

Kier·ke·gaard (kir'kə·gôr), **Søren Aabye**, 1813–55, Dan. philosopher and theologian.

King (king), **Martin Luther, Jr.**, 1929–68, U.S. leader of nonviolent civil rights movement for Negroes; assassinated.

Kip·ling (kip'ling), **(Joseph) Rudyard**, 1865–1936, Eng. author and poet.

Klee (klā, klē), **Paul**, 1879–1940, Swiss painter and etcher.

Knox (noks), **John**, 1505?–72, Scot. Calvinist reformer, theologian, and historian.

Koest·ler (kest′lər), **Arthur**, born 1905, Hung. writer active in England.

Kos·ci·us·ko (kos′ē·us′kō), **Thaddeus**, 1746–1817, Polish patriot and general born in Lithuania; fought in the Amer. Revolution. *Polish* **Koś·ciusz·ko** (kôsh·chōōsh′kô).

Ko·sy·gin (ko·sig′in), **Alexei Nikolayevich**, born 1904, Soviet statesman; premier 1964–.

Kra·nach (krä′näkh), **Lucas** See CRANACH.

Ku·blai Khan (kōō′blī kän′), 1216?–94, Mongol emperor, founder of the Mongol dynasty of China. Also **Kub·la Khan** (kōō′blə).

La·fay·ette (lä′fē·et′, laf′ē·et′; *Fr.* là·fà·yet′), **Marquis de**, 1757–1834, Fr. general, revolutionist, and statesman; fought in the Amer. Revolution. Also **La·Fay·ette′**.

La Fon·taine (lä fon·tän′, *Fr.* là fôn·ten′), **Jean de**, 1621–1695, Fr. writer, noted for his fables.

La·marck (là·màrk′), **Chevalier de**, 1744–1829, Fr. naturalist; orig. name **Jean Baptiste Pierre Antoine de Mo·net** (də mō·ne′).

Lamb (lam), **Charles**, 1775–1834, Eng. essayist: pseud. *Elia*.

Lao·tse (lou′dzu′), 604?–531? B.C., Chinese philosopher and mystic; founder of Taoism. Also **Lao·tze, Lao·tzu**.

Lard·ner (lärd′nər), **Ring**, 1885–1933, U.S. journalist and short-story writer: full name **Ringgold Wilmer Lardner**.

La Roche·fou·cauld (là rôsh·fōō·kō′), **Duc François de**, 1613–80, Prince de Marcillac, Fr. moralist and writer.

La Salle (là sàl′), **Sieur Robert Cavelier de**, 1643–87, Fr. explorer in America.

Lau·trec (lō·trek′) See TOULOUSE-LAUTREC.

Law·rence (lôr′əns, lor′-), **D(avid) H(erbert)**, 1885–1930, Eng. novelist and poet. — **T(homas) E(dward)**, 1885–1935, Eng. archaeologist, soldier, and writer; led Arab revolt against Turkey in World War I; after 1927 changed his name to Shaw (shô): called **Lawrence of Arabia**.

Lee (lē), **Robert E(dward)**, 1807–70, Confederate commander in chief in the Civil War.

Leeu·wen·hoek (lā′vən·hōōk), **Anton van**, 1632–1723, Du. naturalist; pioneer in microscopy.

Leib·nitz (līb′nits), **Baron Gottfried Wilhelm von**, 1646–1716, Ger. philosopher and mathematician. Also **Leib′niz**.

Leif Er·ic·son (lēf er′ik·sən) See ERICSON.

Le·nin (len′in), **Vladimir Ilyich**, 1870–1924, Russ. statesman; chief leader and theorist of the Bolshevik Revolution; head of the U.S.S.R. 1917–24: original name **Vladimir Ilyich Ul·ya·nof** (ōōl·ya′naf). Also, erroneously, **Nikolai Lenin**.

Leo X, 1475–1521, pope 1513–21: orig. name *Giovanni de′ Medici*.

Le·o·nar·do da Vin·ci (lē′ə·när′dō də vin′chē, *Ital.* lā′ō·när′dō dä vēn′chē) See DA VINCI.

Les·seps (les′əps, *Fr.* le·seps′), **Vicomte Ferdinand Marie de**, 1805–94, Fr. engineer and diplomat; supervised building of the Suez Canal.

Lew·is (lōō′is), **Sinclair**, 1885–1951, U.S. novelist.

Lie (lē), **Trygve Halvdan**, 1896–1968, Norw. statesman; first secretary general of the U.N., 1946–53.

Lil·i·en·thal (lē′lē·ən·täl′), **Otto**, 1848–98, Ger. inventor.

Lin·coln (ling′kən), **Abraham**, 1809–65, U.S. statesman; 16th president of the U.S. 1861–65; assassinated.

Lind·bergh (lind′bûrg), **Charles Augustus**, 1902–74, U.S. aviator.

Lin·nae·us (li·nē′əs), **Carolus**, Latinized name of **Karl von Lin·né** (lē·nā′), 1707–78, Sw. botanist and taxonomist.

Lis·ter (lis′tər), **Joseph**, 1827–1912, first Baron Lister of Lyme Regis, Eng. surgeon; founder of antiseptic surgery.

Liszt (list), **Franz**, 1811–86, Hung. composer and pianist.

Lit·tle (lit′l), **Malcolm** See MALCOLM X.

Lloyd George (loid jôrj), **David**, 1863–1945, first Earl of Dwyfor, Brit. statesman; prime minister 1916–22.

Locke (lok), **John**, 1632–1704, Eng. philosopher.

Lon·don (lun′dən), **Jack**, 1876–1916, U.S. author: orig. name **John Griffith London**.

Long (lông, long), **Huey Pierce**, 1893–1935, U.S. politician; assassinated.

Long·fel·low (lông′fel·ō, long′-), **Henry Wadsworth**, 1807–1882, U.S. poet.

Lo·pe de Ve·ga (lō′pā thä vā′gä) See (Lope de) VEGA.

Lor·ca (lôr′kä), **Federico García** See GARCIA LORCA.

Lo·rentz (lō′rents), **Hendrik Antoon**, 1853–1928, Du. physicist.

Lou·is XIV (lōō′ē, lōō′is; *Fr.* lwē), 1638–1715, king of France 1643–1715; called **le Grand Mo·narque** (lə grän mô· nàrk′) (the Great Monarch), *le Roi Soleil* (the Sun King).

Louis XV, 1710–74, king of France 1715–74: called **le Bien-Ai·mé** (lə byan ne·mā′) (the Well-Beloved).

Louis XVI, 1754–93, king of France 1774–92, dethroned by the French Revolution; guillotined.

Louis Napoleon See (Louis Napoleon) BONAPARTE.

Louis Phi·lippe (fē·lēp′), 1773–1850, king of France 1830–1848; abdicated: called **le Roi Ci·toy·en** (lə rwà sē·twà·yan′) (the Citizen King).

Lo·yo·la (loi·ō′lə), **St. Ignatius**, 1491–1566, Sp. soldier, priest, and mystic; founder of the Society of Jesus: original name **Inigo de Oñez y Loyola**.

Lu·cre·tius (lōō·krē′shəs, -shē·əs), 96–55 B.C., Roman poet: full name **Titus Lucretius Car·us** (kâr′əs).

Lu·ther (lōō′thər), **Martin**, 1483–1546, Ger. monk, theologian, and reformer; leader of the Reformation; excommunicated 1520.

Mac·Ar·thur (mək·är′thər), **Douglas**, 1880–1964, U.S. general.

Mach·i·a·vel·li (mäk′ē·ə·vel′ē, *Ital.* mä′kyä·vel′lē), **Niccoló**, 1469–1527, Florentine statesman and writer on politics.

Mac·mil·lan (mak·mil′ən), **Harold**, born 1894, Brit. statesman; prime minister 1957–63.

Mad·i·son (mad′ə·sən), **James**, 1751–1836, 4th president of the U.S. 1809–17: called the **Father of the Constitution**.

Ma·gel·lan (mə·jel′ən), **Ferdinand**, 1480?–1521, Pg. navigator in the service of Spain.

Mah·ler (mä′lər), **Gustav**, 1860–1911, Austro-Hung. composer and conductor active in Austria and Germany.

Ma·hom·et (mə·hom′it) See MOHAMMED.

Mai·mon·i·des (mī·mon′ə·dēz), 1135–1204, Sp. rabbi, physician, and philosopher: orig. name **Moses ben Mai·mon** (mī′· mōn). Called **RaM·BaM** (ram·bam′).

Mal·colm X (mal′kəm eks) Name adopted by *Malcolm Little*, 1925–65, U.S. political and religious leader, active in the Black Muslim movement; assassinated.

Mal·o·ry (mal′ər·ē), **Sir Thomas**, died 1470, Eng. author and translator.

Mal·pi·ghi (mäl·pē′gē), **Marcello**, 1628–94, Ital. anatomist.

Mal·raux (mål·rō′), **André**, born 1901, Fr. novelist, art critic, and politician: full name **Georges André Malraux**.

Mal·thus (mal′thəs, môl′-), **Thomas Robert**, 1766–1834, Eng. political economist.

Mann (män), **Thomas**, 1875–1955, Ger. novelist active in the U.S.

Mao Tse-tung (mou′ dzu′dōong′), born 1893, Chinese Communist leader; chairman of the People's Republic of China 1949–59.

Marc Antony (märk) See (Mark) ANTONY.

Mar·co·ni (mär·kō′nē), **Marchese Guglielmo**, 1874–1937, Ital. inventor; developed a system of wireless telegraphy.

Mar·co Po·lo (mär′kō pō′lō) See POLO.

Ma·rie An·toi·nette (mà·rē′ än·twà·net′), 1755–93, queen of France; wife of Louis XVI; guillotined.

Ma·ri·tain (mà·rē·taň′), **Jacques**, 1882–1973, Fr. philosopher.

Mark Twain (märk twān) Pseud. of **Samuel Langhorne Clemens**, 1835–1910, U.S. humorist and novelist.

Mar·lowe (mär′lō), **Christopher**, 1564–93, Eng. poet.

Mar·ti (mär·tē′), **José Julian**, 1853–95, Cuban patriot.

Mar·vell (mär′vəl), **Andrew**, 1621–78, Eng. poet.

Marx (marks), **Karl (Heinrich)**, 1818–83, Ger. philosopher and theorist of modern socialism.

Ma·ry (mâr′ē) **I**, 1516–58, queen of England 1553–58: called **Mary Tudor, Bloody Mary**.

Mary, Queen of Scots, 1542–87, queen of Scotland 1542–1567; beheaded. Also **Mary Stuart**.

Ma·sac·cio (mä·sät′chō), 1401–29?, Florentine painter: orig. name **Tommaso Gui·di** (gwē′dē).

Ma·tisse (mà·tēs′) **Henri**, 1869–1954, Fr. painter.

Mau·pas·sant (mō·pà·sän′), **(Henri René Albert) Guy de**, 1850–93, Fr. writer.

Max·well (maks′wel), **James Clerk**, 1831–79, Scot. physicist.

Maz·zi·ni (mät·tsē′nē), **Giuseppe**, 1805?–72, Ital. patriot and revolutionary.

Mc·Cor·mick (mə·kôr′mik), **Cyrus (Hall)**, 1809–84, U.S. inventor; developed the reaping machine.

Mc·Kin·ley (mə·kin′le), **William**, 1843–1901, 25th president of the U.S. 1897–1901; assassinated.

Mead (mēd), **Margaret**, born 1901, U.S. anthropologist.

Med·i·ci (med′ə·chē, *Ital.* mā′dē·chē) A family of Florentine bankers and statesmen, notably **Giovanni de′ Medici**, died 1429, and his sons **Cosimo**, 1389–1464, and **Lorenzo**, 1395–1440; **Lorenzo**, 1449?–92, grandson of Cosimo, patron of the arts, called the **Magnificent**; his son **Giovanni**, 1475–1521 (see LEO X); **Cosimo**, 1519–74, grand duke of Tuscany: called the **Great**.

Mel·ville (mel′vil), **Herman**, 1819–91, U.S. novelist.

Mem·ling (mem′ling), **Hans**, 1430?–95?, Flemish painter.

Menck·en (meng'kən), **H(enry) L(ouis)**, 1880–1956, U.S. author and editor.
Men·del (men'dəl), **Gregor Johann**, 1882–84, Austrian monk and botanist; formulated laws of genetics.
Men·de·ley·ev (men'də·lā'əf), **Dmitri Ivanovich**, 1834–1907, Russ. chemist; developed the periodic law. Also **Men'de·le'ev**.
Men·dels·sohn (men'dəl·sən), *Ger.* men'dəl·zōn), **Felix**, 1809–47, Ger. composer: full name **Jakob Ludwig Felix Men'dels·sohn-Bar·thol·dy** (-bär·tōl'dē).
Mer·ca·tor (mər·kā'tər, *Flemish* mer·kä'tôr), **Gerardus**, 1512–94, Flemish geographer and cartographer: orig. name **Gerhard Kre·mer** (krā'mər).
Mes·sa·li·na (mes'ə·lī'nə), **Valeria**, died 48 A.D., Roman empress; notorious for profligacy; executed. Also **Mes'sal·li'na**.
Metch·ni·koff (mech'ni·kôf), **Élie**, 1845–1916, Russ. physiologist and bacteriologist active in France: orig. name **Ilya Ilich Mechnikov**.
Met·ter·nich (met'ər·nikh), **Prince von**, 1773–1859, Klemens Wenzel Nepomuk Lothar von Metternich-Winneburg, Austrian statesman and diplomat.
Mi·chel·an·ge·lo (mī'kəl·an'jə·lō, *Ital.* mē'kel·än'je·lō), 1475–1564, Ital. sculptor, painter, architect, and poet: full name **Michelangelo Buo·nar·ro·ti** (bwô'när·rô'tē).
Mi·chel·son (mī'kəl·sən), **Albert Abraham**, 1852–1931, U.S. physicist born in Germany.
Mill (mil), **John Stuart**, 1806–73, Eng. philosopher and political economist.
Mil·lay (mi·lā'), **Edna St. Vincent**, 1892–1950, U.S. poet.
Mil·ler (mil'ər), **Arthur**, born 1915, U.S. novelist and playwright. — **Henry**, born 1891, U.S. author.
Mil·li·kan (mil'ə·kən), **Robert Andrews**, 1868–1955, U.S. physicist.
Mil·ton (mil'tən), **John**, 1608–74, Eng. poet and essayist.
Mo·ham·med (mō·ham'id), 570?–632, Arabian founder and prophet of Islam whose revelations are collected in the Koran: also *Mahomet, Muhammad*.
Mo·lière (mō·lyâr'). Pseud. of **Jean Baptiste Po·que·lin** (pō·klän'), 1622–73, Fr. dramatist and actor.
Mon·dri·an (môn'drē·än), **Piet**, 1872–1944, Du. painter. Also **Mon'dri·aan**.
Mo·net (mō·ne'), **Claude**, 1840–1926, Fr. painter.
Mon·roe (mən·rō'), **James**, 1758–1831, 5th president of the U.S. 1817–25.
Mon·taigne (mon·tān', *Fr.* môn·ten'y'), **Michel Eyquem de**, 1533–92, Fr. essayist.
Mon·tes·quieu (mon'təs·kyōō', *Fr.* môn·tes·kyœ'), **Baron de la Brede et de**, 1689–1755, Charles de Secondat, Fr. jurist, political philosopher and man of letters.
Mon·te·ver·di (mon'tə·vûr'dē, *Ital.* môn·tā·ver'dē), **Claudio (Giovanni Antonio)**, 1567–1643, Ital. composer.
Mon·te·zu·ma II (mon'tə·zu'mə), 1479?–1520, last Aztec Emperor of Mexico, dethroned by Cortés. Also **Moctezuma**.
Moore (mōōr, môr, mōr), **Henry**, born 1898, Eng. sculptor. — **Marianne (Craig)**, 1887–1972, U.S. poet.
More (môr, mōr), **Sir Thomas**, 1478?–1535, Eng. statesman and author; beheaded by Henry VIII; canonized 1935.
Mor·gan (môr·gən), **John Pierpont**, 1837–1913, U.S. banker, art collector and philanthropist.
Mor·ris (môr'is, mor'-), **William**, 1834–96, Eng. poet, painter, and socialist writer.
Morse (môrs), **Samuel Finley Breese**, 1791–1872, U.S. artist and inventor; constructed the first practical telegraph.
Mose·ley (mōz'lē), **Henry Gwyn-Jeffreys**, 1887–1915, Eng. physicist.
Mous·sorg·sky (mōō·sôrg'skē), **Modest Petrovich**, 1835–1881, Russ. composer. Also **Mus·sorg'sky**.
Mo·zart (mō'tsärt, -zärt), **Wolfgang Amadeus**, 1756–91, Austrian composer.
Mus·so·li·ni (mōōs'ə·lē·nē), **Benito**, 1883–1945, Ital. Fascist leader; premier 1922–43; executed: called **Il Du·ce** (ēl dōō'chā).
Mu·ham·mad (mōō·ham'əd) See MOHAMMED.

Na·pi·er (nā'pē·ər, nə·pir'), **John**, 1550–1617, Scot. mathematician.
Na·po·le·on I (nə·pō'lē·ən; *Fr.* nà·pô·lā·ôn') See under BONAPARTE.
Napoleon III See under BONAPARTE.
Nas·ser (näs'ər, nas'-), **Gamal Abdel**, 1918–70, Egyptian army officer and political leader; chief of state 1954–70; president of the United Arab Republic 1958–70.
Neb·u·chad·nez·zar (neb'yŏō·kəd·nez'ər), died 562 B.C., king of Babylonia 605–562 B.C.; conquered Judea and destroyed Jerusalem. Also **Neb'u·chad·rez'zar** (-rez'ər).
Neh·ru (nā'rōō), **Ja·wa·har·lal** (jə·wä'hər·läl), 1889–1964, Indian nationalist leader and statesman; 1st prime minister 1947–64.
Nel·son (nel'sən), **Viscount Horatio**, 1758–1805, Eng. admiral; killed at the battle of Trafalgar.
Ne·ro (nir'ō), 37–68, Nero Claudius Caesar Drusus Ger-

manicus, Roman emperor 54–68; committed suicide: orig. name **Lucius Domitius A·he·no·bar·bus** (ə·hē·nō·bär'bus).
New·man (nyōō'mən, nōō'-), **John Henry**, 1801–90, Eng. cardinal and theologian.
New·ton (nōō'tən, nyōō'-), **Sir Isaac**, 1642–1727, Eng. philosopher and mathematician.
Nie·buhr (nē'bōōr), **Reinhold**, 1892–1971, U.S. Protestant theologian.
Nie·tzsche (nē'chə), **Friedrich Wilhelm**, 1844–1900, Ger. philosopher.
Night·in·gale (nī'tən·gāl, nī'ting-), **Florence**, 1820–1910, Eng. pioneer of modern nursing, born in Italy.
Nim·itz (nim'its), **Chester William**, 1885–1966, U.S. admiral; chief of naval operations, 1945.
Nix·on (nik'sən), **Richard Milhous**, born 1913, vice president of the U.S. 1953–61; 37th president of the U.S. 1969–74.
No·bel (nō·bel'), **Alfred Bernhard**, 1833–96, Sw. industrialist; inventor of dynamite; founded the Nobel Prizes.
Nos·tra·da·mus (nos'trə·dā'məs), 1503–66, Fr. astrologer: orig. name **Michel de No·tre·dame** (də nō'trə·däm').

O'Ca·sey (ō·kā'sē), **Sean** (shôn),1890–1964, Irish playwright.
Ock·ham (ok'əm), **William of**, 1300?–49?, Eng. Franciscan and scholastic philosopher; opponent of Duns Scotus: called **the Invincible Doctor**. Also spelled **Oc'cam**.
Oc·ta·vi·an (ok·tā'vē·ən) See AUGUSTUS CAESAR.
O. Henry (ō hen'rē) Pseud. of *William Sydney Porter*, 1862–1910, U.S. short-story writer.
Ohm (ōm), **Georg Simon**, 1787–1854, Ger. physicist.
O·li·vi·er (ō·liv'ē·ā), **Sir Laurence (Kerr)**, born 1907, Eng. actor.
O·mar Khay·yám (ō'mär kī·äm', ō'mər), died 1123?, Persian poet and astronomer; author of the *Rubáiyát*.
O'Neill (ō·nēl'), **Eugene (Gladstone)**, 1888–1953, U.S. playwright.
Or·te·ga y Gas·set (ôr·tā'gä ē gä·set'), **José**, 1883–1955, Sp. philosopher, writer, and statesman.
Or·well (ôr'wel), **George**, pseud. of **Eric Blair** (blâr), 1903–1950, Brit. novelist and essayist.
Ov·id (ov'id), 43 B.C.–A.D. 18, Roman poet: full name **Publius O·vid·i·us Na·so** (ō·vid'i·əs nā'sō).
Ow·en (ō'in), **Robert**, 1771–1858, Brit. manufacturer and social reformer.

Paine (pān), **Thomas**, 1737–1809, Amer. patriot, author, and political philosopher born in England.
Pa·les·tri·na (pä'les·trē'nä), **Giovanni Pierluigi da**, 1524?–1594, Ital. composer: called **Prin·ceps Mu·si·cae** (prin'seps myōō'zi·sē) (Prince of Music).
Pas·cal (pas·kal', pas·kəl; *Fr.* päs·kàl'), **Blaise**, 1623–62, Fr. mathematician, philosopher, and author.
Pas·teur (pas·tœr'), **Louis**, 1822–95, Fr. chemist; founder of modern bacteriology.
Pat·rick (pat·rik), **St.**, 389?–461?, Christian missionary; patron of Ireland: called **the Apostle of Ireland**.
Paul VI (pôl), born 1897, pope 1963–: orig. name **Giovanni Battista Mon·ti·ni** (mōn·tē'nē).
Pav·lov (päv'lôf), **Ivan Petrovich**, 1849–1936, Russ. physiologist.
Pea·ry (pir'ē), **Robert Edwin**, 1856–1920, U.S. Arctic explorer; first to reach the North Pole, April 6, 1909.
Penn (pen), **William**, 1644–1718, Eng. Quaker; founder of Pennsylvania.
Pepys (pēps, pep'is), **Samuel**, 1633–1702, Eng. diarist.
Per·i·cles (per'ə·klēz), died 429 B.C., Athenian statesman, orator, and general.
Pe·rón (pā·rōn'), **Juan Domingo**, 1895–1974, Argentine politician; president 1946–55, 1973–74.
Per·ry (per'ē), **Oliver Hazard**, 1785–1819, U.S. naval commander during Amer. Revolution.
Per·shing (pûr'shing), **John Joseph**, 1860–1948, U.S. General of the Armies: called **Black Jack**.
Peter I (pē'tər), 1672–1725, czar of Russia 1682–1725: called **Peter the Great**.
Pe·trarch (pē'trärk), **Francesco**, 1304–74, Ital. poet and scholar. Also **Pe·trar·ca** (pā·trär'kä).
Phid·i·as (fid'ē·əs), 5th-c. B.C. Gk. sculptor and architect.
Pi·cas·so (pē·kä'sō), **Pablo**, 1881–1973, Sp. painter and sculptor active in France: full surname **Ru·iz y Picasso** (rōō·ēth'ē).
Pierce (pirs), **Franklin**, 1804–69, 14th president of the U.S. 1853–57.
Pie·ro del·la Fran·ces·ca (pyā'rō del'lä fran·ches'kä) 1420?–92, Ital. painter.
Pis·sar·ro (pē·sà·rō'), **Camille**, 1830–1903, Fr. painter born in West Indies.
Pitt (pit), **William**, 1708–78, first Earl of Chatham, Eng. statesman, prime minister 1766–68: called **the Elder, the Great Commoner**. — **William**, 1759–1806, Eng. statesman, prime minister 1783–1801, 1804–1806, son of the preceding: called **the Younger**.

Pi·us V, Saint, 1504–72, pope 1566–72: orig. name **Michele Ghis·lie·ri** (gēz·lyā′rē).

Pius IX, 1792–1878, pope 1846–78; orig. name **Giovanni Maria Ma·stai-Fer·ret·ti** (mäs·tä′ē-fer·ret′te).

Pius XII, 1876–1958, pope 1939–58: orig. name **Eugenio Pa·cel·li** (pä·chel′lē).

Pi·zar·ro (pi·zär′ō, *Sp.* pē·thär′rō), **Francisco,** 1471?–1541, Sp. conquistador, conqueror of Peru.

Planck (plängk), **Max (Karl Ernst Ludwig),** 1858–1947, Ger. physicist; formulated the quantum theory.

Pla·to (plā′tō), 427?–347? B.C., Gk. philosopher.

Plu·tarch (plōō·tärk), A.D., 46?–120?, Gk. biographer.

Po·ca·hon·tas (pō·kə·hon′təs), 1595?–1617. Amer. Indian princess in Virginia; reputedly saved the life of Captain John Smith.

Poe (pō), **Edgar Allan,** 1809–49, U.S. writer and critic.

Polk (pōk), **James Knox,** 1795–1849, 11th president of the U.S. 1845–49.

Pol·lock (pol′ək), **Jackson,** 1912–56, U.S. painter.

Po·lo (pō′lō), **Marco,** 1254?–1323?, Venetian traveler.

Pom·pey (pom′pē) Anglicized name of **Gnaeus Pompeius Mag·nus** (mag·nəs), 106–48 B.C., Roman general and statesman; defeated by Julius Caesar: called **the Great.**

Ponce de Le·ón (pons′ də·lē′ən, *Sp.* pôn′thä thä lā·ôn′), **Juan,** 1460?–1521, Sp. explorer; discovered Florida, 1513.

Pon·tius Pilate (pon′shəs, -tē·əs), Roman procurator of Judea 26–36 A.D., condemned Jesus to be crucified. Also called **Pilate** (pī′lət).

Pope (pōp), **Alexander,** 1688–1744, Eng. poet and satirist.

Por·ter (pôr′tər, pōr′-), **William Sydney** See O. HENRY.

Pound (pound), **Ezra (Loomis),** 1885–1972, U.S. poet.

Priest·ley (prēst′lē), **Joseph,** 1733–1804, Eng. clergyman, philosopher, and chemist; discovered oxygen.

Pro·kof·iev (prô·kôf′yəf), **Sergei Sergeyevich,** 1891–1953, Soviet composer. Also **Pro·kof′ieff.**

Ptol·e·my (tol′ə·mē) 2nd-c. Gk. astronomer, mathematician, and geographer in Alexandria: full name **Claudius Ptol·e·mae·us** (tol′ə·mē′əs).

Puc·ci·ni (pōōt·chē′nē), **Giacomo,** 1858–1924, Ital. operatic composer.

Pu·las·ki (pōō·läs′kē, pə-; *Polish* pōō·läs′kē), **Casimir,** 1748–1779, Polish general in the Amer. Revolution.

Pur·cell (pûr′səl), **Henry,** 1658?–95, Eng. composer.

Push·kin (pōōsh′kin), **Aleksander Sergeyevich,** 1799–1837, Russ. poet.

Py·thag·o·ras (pi·thag′ər·əs) 6th-c. B.C. Gk. philosopher and mathematician.

Rab·e·lais (rab′ə·lā, *Fr.* rá·ble′), **François,** 1494?–1553?, Fr. humorist and satirist: pseud. **Al·co·fri·bas Na·sier** (àl·kô·frē·bas′ nà·zyä′).

Rach·ma·ni·noff (räkh·ma′ni·nôf), **Sergei Vassilievich,** 1873–1943, Russ. pianist and composer.

Ra·cine (rá·sēn′), **Jean Baptiste,** 1639–99, Fr. dramatist.

Ra·leigh (rô′lē), **Sir Walter,** 1552–1618, Eng. courtier, colonizer, admiral, and poet; beheaded. Also *Brit.* **Ra′legh.**

Ram·e·ses II (ram′ə·sēz), 1292–1225 B.C., Egyptian king; allegedly the pharaoh who oppressed the Israelites. Also **Ram·ses II** (ram′sēz).

Ran·dolph (ran′dolf), **A(sa) Philip,** born 1889, U.S. labor leader.

Raph·a·el (raf′ē·əl, rä′fē-), 1483–1520, Ital. painter: full name **Raphael (or Raffaello) San·zio** (sän′tsyō).

Ra·vel (rá·vel′), **Maurice Joseph,** 1875–1937, Fr. composer.

Reed (rēd), **Walter,** 1851–1902, U.S. army surgeon.

Rem·brandt (rem′brant), 1606–69, Du. painter: full name **Rembrandt Harmenszoon van Rijn** (vän rin) or **van Ryn.**

Re·noir (rə·nwàr′), **Pierre Auguste,** 1840–1919, Fr. Impressionist painter.

Re·vere (ri·vir′), **Paul,** 1735–1818, Amer. Revolutionary patriot and silversmith; famous for his ride the night of April 18, 1775, to warn of the approach of British troops.

Rhee (rē), **Syngman,** 1875–1965, Korean statesman; president of the Republic of Korea 1948–60.

Rhodes (rōdz), **Cecil John,** 1853–1902, Brit. colonial statesman, financier, and philanthropist, active in S. Africa.

Rich·ard I (rich′ərd), 1157–99, king of England 1189–99: called **the Lion-Heart.** Also called *Coeur de Lion.*

Richard III, 1452–85, duke of Gloucester, king of England 1483–85; killed at Bosworth Field: called **Crouch·back** (krouch′bak′).

Ri·che·lieu (rē·shə·lyœ′), **Duc de,** 1585–1642, Armand Jean du Plessis, Fr. cardinal and statesman: called **E·mi·nence Rouge** (ä·mē·näns′ rōōzh′).

Rie·mann (rē′män), **George Friedrich Bernhard,** 1826–66, Ger. mathematician.

Ril·ke (rĭl′kə), **Rainer Maria,** 1875–1926, Austrian poet born in Prague.

Rim·baud (raṅ·bō′), **Arthur,** 1854–91, Fr. poet: full name **Jean Nicholas Arthur Rimbaud.**

Rim·sky-kor·sa·kov (rim′skē·kôr′sə·kôf), **Nicholas Andreievich,** 1844–1908, Russ. composer.

Ri·ve·ra (rē·vä′rä), **Diego,** 1886–1957, Mexican painter.

Robes·pierre (rōbz′pē·âr), 1758–94, Fr. Revolutionary leader; guillotined: full name **Maximilien François Marie Isidore de Robespierre:** called **the Incorruptible.**

Rock·e·fel·ler (rok′ə·fel′ər), **John D(avison),** 1839–1937, U.S. industrialist and philanthropist.

Ro·din (rō·dan′), **Auguste,** 1840–1917, Fr. sculptor.

Roent·gen (rent′gən, runt′-; *Ger.* rœnt′gən), **Wilhelm Konrad,** 1845–1923, Ger. physicist. Also **Rönt′gen.**

Rog·ers (roj′ərz), **Will,** 1879–1935, U.S. actor and humorist: full name **William Penn Adair Rogers.**

Roi So·leil (rwà sô·lā′), le see LOUIS XIV.

Rom·u·lo (rom′yōō·lō), **Carlos Pena,** born 1899, Philippine statesman, general and writer.

Ron·sard (rôn·sàr′), **Pierre de,** 1524–85, Fr. poet.

Roo·se·velt (rō′zə·velt, rōz′velt, -vəlt), **(Anna) Eleanor,** 1884–1962, *née* Roosevelt, U.S. lecturer, writer, and diplomat; wife of Franklin Delano. — **Franklin Delano,** 1882–1945, U.S. statesman, 32nd president of the U.S. 1933–45. — **Theodore,** 1858–1919, U.S. army officer and statesman; 26th president of the U.S. 1901–09.

Ross (rôs), **Betsy,** 1752–1836, *née* Griscom, Amer. patriot; reputed to have made the first American flag.

Ros·si·ni (rôs·sē′nē), **Gioacchino Antonio,** 1792–1868, Ital. composer.

Roth·schild (rôth′chĭld, *Ger.* rōt′shilt), **Mayer Anselm,** 1743–1812, founder of the worldwide banking enterprise **(House of Rothschild)** at Frankfort on the Main, Germany.

Rou·get de Lisle (roo·zhē′ də lēl′), **Claude Joseph,** 1760–1836, Fr. army officer and composer; wrote the *Marseillaise,* 1792.

Rous·seau (rōō·sō′), **Henri,** 1844–1910, Fr. painter: called **le Dou·an·ier** (lə· dwá·nyā′) (the customs officer). — **Jean Jacques,** 1712–78, Fr. philosopher and author, born in Switzerland.

Ru·bens (rōō′bənz. *Flemish* rü′bəns), **Peter Paul,** 1577–1640, Flemish painter.

Rus·kin (rus′kin), **John,** 1819–1900, Eng. art critic and author.

Rus·sell (rus′əl), **Bertrand (Arthur William),** 1872–1970, 3rd Earl Russell, Eng. mathematician and philosopher.

Ruth (rōōth), **George Herman,** 1895–1948, U.S. baseball player: called **Babe Ruth.**

Ruth·er·ford (ruth′ər·fərd), **Sir Ernest,** 1871–1937, first Baron Rutherford, Brit. physicist born in New Zealand.

Sade (sàd), **Comte Donatien Alphonse François de,** 1740–1814, Fr. novelist and libertine: called **Marquis de Sade.**

Sal·a·din (sal′ə·din), 1137?–93, sultan of Egypt and Syria, 1174?–93: full name **Sa·lah-al-Din Yusuf ibn-Ayyud** (sə·lä′ä·dēn′).

Salk (sôk, sôlk), **Jonas,** born 1914, U.S. bacteriologist; developed injected vaccine for poliomyelitis.

Sand·burg (sand′bûrg, san′-), **Carl,** 1878–1967, U.S. poet and biographer.

Sang·er (sang′ər), **Margaret,** 1883–1966, *née* Higgins, U.S. leader in birth-control education.

San·ta·ya·na (sän′tä·yä′nä), **George,** 1863–1952, U.S. philosopher and author born in Spain.

Sap·pho (saf·ō) 6th-c. B.C. Gk. lyric poetess.

Sar·to (sär′tō), **Andrea del,** 1486–1531, Florentine painter: orig. name **Andrea d'Angelo di Fran·ces·co** (frän·ches′kō).

Sar·tre (sàr′tr′). **Jean Paul,** born 1905, Fr. philosopher, novelist, and dramatist.

Scar·lat·ti (skär·lät′tē), **Alessandro,** 1659–1725, and his son, **Domenico,** 1685–1757, Ital. composers.

Schil·ler (shil′ər), **Johann Christoph Friedrich von,** 1759–1805, Ger. poet and dramatist.

Schlie·mann (shlē′män), **Heinrich,** 1822–90, Ger. merchant and archaeologist.

Schön·berg (shoen′berkh), **Arnold,** 1874–1951, Austrian composer and conductor active in the U.S.

Scho·pen·hau·er (shō′pən·hou′ər), **Arthur,** 1788–1860, Ger. philosopher.

Schrö·ding·er (shroe′ding·ər), **Erwin,** 1887–1961, Austrian physicist.

Schu·bert (shōō′bərt), **Franz Peter,** 1797–1828, Austrian composer.

Schu·mann (shōō′män), **Robert,** 1810–56, Ger. composer.

Schwann (shvän), **Theodor,** 1810–82, Ger. physiologist.

Schweit·zer (shvī′tsər), **Albert,** 1875–1965, Fr. (Alsatian) clergyman, physician, missionary, philosopher, and musicologist; founder and director of the hospital at Lambaréné, Gabon.

Scott (skot), **Sir Walter,** 1771–1832, Scot. novelist and poet.

Se·go·via (sā·gŏ′vyä), **Andrés,** born 1894, Sp. classical guitarist.

Sen·e·ca (sen′ə·kə), **Lucius Annaeus,** 4? B.C.–A.D. 65, Roman Stoic philosopher, statesman and dramatist: called **Seneca the Younger.**

Shake·speare (shāk′spir), **William,** 1564–1616, Eng. poet and dramatist. Also **Shake′spere, Shak′speare, Shak′spere.**

Shaw (shô), **George Bernard,** 1856–1950, Brit. dramatist, critic, and novelist born in Ireland.

Shel·ley (shel′ē), **Mary Wollstonecraft,** 1797–1851, *née* Godwin, Eng. novelist; wife of Percy Bysshe. **— Percy Bysshe,** 1792–1822, Eng. poet.

Sher·man (shûr′mən), **William Tecumseh,** 1829–91, Union general in the Civil War.

Shos·ta·ko·vich (shos′tə·kŏ′vich), **Dimitri,** 1906–75, Soviet composer.

Si·be·li·us (si·bā′lē·əs, -bāl′yəs), **Jean,** 1865–1957, Finnish composer.

Sitting Bull, 1834?–90, Sioux Indian chief; won battle of Little Big Horn in 1876.

Sit·well (sit′wel, -wəl), **Edith,** 1887–1964, Eng. poet.

Smith (smith), **Adam,** 1723–90, Scot. moralist and political economist. **— Alfred E(manuel),** 1873–1944, U.S. political leader. **— Captain John,** 1580–1631, Eng. adventurer; president of the Virginia colony 1608–1609. **— Joseph,** 1805–1844, founder and first prophet of the Mormon Church; assassinated.

Smuts (smuts), **Jan Christiaan,** 1870–1950, S. African general and statesman; prime minister 1919–24, 1939–48.

Soc·ra·tes (sok′rə·tēz), 469?–399 B.C., Gk. philosopher; forced to commit suicide by drinking hemlock.

Soph·o·cles (sof′ə·klēz), 496?–406 B.C., Athenian tragic poet.

Spal·lan·za·ni (späl′län·dzä′nē), **Lazzaro,** 1729–99, Ital. biologist.

Spen·cer (spen′sər), **Herbert,** 1820–1903, Eng. philosopher.

Speng·ler (speng′glər), **Oswald,** 1880–1936, Ger. philosopher and historian.

Spen·ser (spen′sər), **Edmund,** 1552?–99, Eng. poet.

Spi·no·za (spi·nō′zə), **Baruch,** 1632–77, Du. philosopher. Also **Benedict Spinoza.**

Sta·lin (stä′lin), **Joseph,** 1879–1953, Soviet statesman; chief of state 1924–53: orig. name *Iosif Vissarionovich Dzhugashvili.*

Stein (stīn), **Gertrude,** 1874–1946, U.S. writer active in France.

Sten·dhal (stäṅ·däl′) Pseud. of *Marie Henri Beyle,* 1783–1842, Fr. novelist and critic.

Sterne (stûrn), **Laurence** 1713–68, Brit. novelist, born in Ireland.

Steu·ben (stōō′bən, *Ger.* shtoi′bən), **Baron Friedrich Wilhelm Ludolph Gerhard Augustin von,** 1730–94, Prussian general, served under Washington in the Amer. Revolutionary War.

Ste·ven·son (stē′vən·sən), **Adlai Ewing,** 1900–65, U.S. lawyer and political leader. **— Robert Louis (Balfour),** 1850–94, Scot. novelist and essayist active in the U.S. and Samoa.

Stowe (stō), **Harriet Beecher,** 1811–96, U.S. novelist and humanitarian: orig. name **Harriet Elizabeth Bee·cher** (bē′chər).

Stra·di·va·ri (strä′dē·vä′rē), **Antonio,** 1644?–1737, Ital. violinmaker. Also **Strad·i·var·i·us** (strad′i·vâr′ē·əs).

Strauss (strous), **Johann,** 1804–49, Austrian composer. **— Johann,** 1825–99, Austrian composer; son of Johann: called **the Waltz King. — Richard,** 1864–1949, Ger. composer.

Stra·vin·sky (strə·vin′skē), **Igor Fëdorovich,** 1882–1971, U.S. composer born in Russia.

Strind·berg (strind′bûrg), **August,** 1849–1912, Sw. dramatist and novelist.

Sul·li·van (sul′ə·vən), **Sir Arthur (Seymour),** 1842–1900, Eng. composer.

Sun Yat-sen (sŏōn′ yät′sen′), 1866–1925, Chinese political leader; founder of the Kuomintang 1912.

Swift (swift), **Jonathan,** 1667–1745, Eng. clergyman, satirist, and man of letters born in Ireland: called **Dean Swift.**

Swin·burne (swin′bûrn), **Algernon Charles,** 1837–1909 Eng. poet ánd critic.

Tac·i·tus (tas′ə·təs), **Cornelius,** 55?–117?, Roman historian.

Taft (taft), **Robert Alphonso,** 1889–1953, U.S. legislator; son of William Howard. **— William Howard,** 1857–1930, U.S. statesman and jurist, 27th president of the U.S. 1909–13.

Tal·ley·rand-Pe·ri·gord (tả·le·räṅ′pā·rē·gôr′), **Charles Maurice de,** 1754–1838, Prince de Bénévent, Fr. statesman and diplomat: often called **Tal·ley·rand** (tal′ē·rand).

Tam·er·lane (tam′ər·lān), 1336?–1405, Mogul conqueror: also called **Tam·bur·laine** (tam′bər·lān).

Tar·king·ton (tär′king·tən), **Booth,** 1869–1946, U.S. novelist: full name **Newton Booth Tarkington.**

Tay·lor (tā′lər), **Zachary,** 1784–1850, U.S. general, 12th president of the U.S. 1849–50: called **Old Rough and Ready.**

Tchai·kov·sky (chī·kof′skē), **Pëtr Ilich,** 1840–93, Russ. composer.

Tche·khov (chek′ôf), **Anton** See CHEKHOV.

Ten·ny·son (ten′ə·sən), **Alfred,** 1809–92, 1st Baron Tennyson, Eng. poet; poet laureate 1850–92: called **Alfred, Lord Tennyson.**

Ter·ence (ter′əns), 185?–159? B.C., Roman comic playwright born in Africa: full name **Publius Terentius A·fer** (ā′fər).

Tes·la (tes′lə), **Nikola,** 1857–1943, U.S. physicist and inventor born in Yugoslavia.

Thant (thont) See U THANT.

Tho·mas (tom′əs), **Dylan (Marlais),** 1914–53, Brit. poet and author born in Wales. **— Norman (Mattoon),** 1884–1968, U.S. socialist leader and writer.

Thomas à Becket, St., 1118–70, Eng. prelate; archbishop of Canterbury 1162–70; murdered for opposing Henry II: called **Saint Thomas Becket, Saint Thomas of London.**

Tho·reau (thôr′ō, thō′rō, thə·rō′), **Henry David,** 1817–62, U.S. author: orig. name **David Henry Thoreau.**

Thu·cyd·i·des (thōō·sid′ə·dēz, thyōō-), 471?–401? B.C., Gk. historian.

Til·lich (til′ik, -ikh), **Paul,** 1886–1965, Ger. Protestant theologian and philosopher active in the U.S.

Tin·to·ret·to (tin′tə·ret′ō, *Ital.* tēn′tō·ret′tō), 1518–94, Venetian painter: orig. name **Jacopo Ro·bus·ti** (rō·bōōs′tē).

Ti·tian (tish′ən), 1477?–1576, Venetian painter: orig. name **Ti·zia·no Ve·cel·lio** (tē·tsä′nō vä·chel′lyō).

Ti·to (tē′tō), **Marshal,** born 1892, Yugoslav Communist statesman and leader; prime minister 1945–53; president 1953–: orig. name **Josip Broz.**

Tocque·ville (tōk·vēl′), **Alexis Charles Henri Maurice Clérel de,** 1805–59, Fr. statesman and political writer.

Tol·stoy (tŏl′stoi, tol′-), **Count Leo Nikolaevich,** 1828–1910, Russ. novelist and social reformer. Also **Tol′stoi.**

Tor·que·ma·da (tôr′kwə·mä′də, *Sp.* tôr′kä·mä′thä), **Tomás de,** 1420?–98, Dominican monk; head of the Inquisition in Spain.

Tos·ca·ni·ni (tos′kä·nē′nē; *Ital.* tôs′kä·nē′nē), **Arturo,** 1867–1957, Ital. orchestra conductor active in the U.S.

Tou·louse-Lau·trec (tōō·lōōz′lō·trek′), **Henri Marie Raymond de,** 1864–1901, Fr. painter and lithographer.

Tra·jan (trā′jən), 53?–117, Roman emperor 98–117: full name **Marcus Ulpius Tra·ja·nus** (trā·jā′nəs).

Trot·sky (trot′skē), **Leon,** 1879–1940, Russ. Revolutionist and Bolshevist leader; banished 1929; murdered: orig. name **Lev Davidovitch Bron·stein** (brun′shtīn).

Tru·deau (trōō·dō′), **Pierre Elliott,** born 1919, Canadian statesman; prime minister 1968–: full name **Joseph Philippe Pierre Ives Elliotte Trudeau.**

Tru·man (trōō′mən), **Harry S,** 1884–1972, 33rd president of the U.S. 1945–53.

Tul·ly (tul′ē) See CICERO.

Tur·ge·nev (tŏōr·gā′nyef), **Ivan Sergeyevich,** 1818–83, Russ. novelist. Also **Tur·ge′niev.**

Tut·ankh·a·men (tŏōt′ängk·ä′min), 14th-c. B.C. Egyptian pharaoh. Also **Tut′ankh·a′mon.**

Twain (twān), **Mark** See MARK TWAIN.

Ty·ler (tī′lər), **John,** 1790–1862, 10th president of the U.S. 1841–45.

U·na·mu·no (ōō′nä·mōō′nō), **Miguel de,** 1864–1936, Sp. philosopher, novelist and poet.

U·rey (yŏōr′ē), **Harold Clayton,** born 1893, U.S. chemist.

U Thant (ōō thont), 1909–74, Burmese statesman; UN Secretary General 1962–71: full name *Thant:* full title **Ma·ha Thray Si·thu U** (mä′hä thrā sē′thōō).

U·tril·lo (ōō·trē′lyō, ōō·tril′ō; *Fr.* ü·trē·lō′), **Maurice,** 1883–1955, Fr. painter.

Val·en·tine (val′ən·tīn), St. 3rd-c. Christian martyr.

Va·le·ra (və·ler′ə), **Eamon De** See DE VALERA.

Van Bu·ren (van byŏōr′ən), **Martin** 1782–1862, 8th president of the U.S. 1837–41.

Van Dyck (van dīk′), **Sir Anthony,** 1599–1641, Flemish painter active in England. Also **Van·dyke′.**

van Eyck (van īk′), **Jan,** 1385?–1440, Flemish painter.

van Gogh (van gō′, gôkh), **Vincent,** 1853–90, Du. painter.

Va·sa·ri (vä·zä′rē), **Giorgio,** 1511–74, Ital. painter, architect, and biographer of artists.

Veb·len (veb′lən), **Thorstein Bunde,** 1857–1929, U.S. economist and sociologist.

Ve·ga (vā′gə, *Sp.* bā′gä), **Lope de,** 1562–1635, Sp. dramatist and poet. Full name **Lope Félix de Vega Car·pio** (kär′pyō).

Ve·lás·quez (və·las′kwiz, *Sp.* bā·läs′käth), **Diego,** 1599–1660, Sp. painter: full name **Diego Rodriguez de Silva y Velásquez.** Also **Ve·láz·quez** (bā·läth′käth).

Ver·di (ver′dē), **Giuseppe,** 1813–1901, Ital. composer.

Ver·gil (vûr′jil) Anglicized name of **Publius Vergilius Ma·ro** (mā′rō), 70–19 B.C., Roman epic poet. Also *Virgil.*

Ver·laine (ver·len′), **Paul,** 1844–96, Fr. poet.

Ver·meer (vər·mâr′), **Jan**, 1632–75, Du. painter. Also **Jan van der Meer van Delft** (vän dər mâr vän delft′).

Verne (vûrn, *Fr.* vern), **Jules**, 1828–1905, Fr. novelist.

Ve·ro·ne·se (vā′rō·nā′zā), **Paolo**, 1528–88, Venetian painter; orig. name **Paolo Ca·glia·ri** (kä′lyä·rē).

Ve·sa·li·us (vi·sā′lē·əs), **Andreas**, 1514–64, Belgian physician; founder of modern anatomy.

Ves·puc·ci (ves·pōōt′chē), **Amerigo**, 1451–1512, Ital. explorer for whom America was named.

Vic·to·ri·a (vik·tôr′ē·ə, -tō′rē·ə), 1819–1901, queen of England 1837–1901: full name **Alexandrina Victoria**.

Vin·ci (vēn′chē), **Leonardo da** See DA VINCI.

Vir·gil (vûr′jəl) See VERGIL.

Vi·val·di (vē·väl′dē), **Antonio**, 1675?–1743, Ital. violinist and composer: called **the Red Priest**.

Vol·taire (vol·târ′; *Fr.* vôl·târ′) Pseud. of *François Marie Arouet*, 1694–1778, Fr. author and philosopher.

Wag·ner (väg′nər), **Richard**, 1813–83, Ger. composer, poet, and critic: full name **Wilhelm Richard Wagner**.

Waks·man (waks′mən), **Selman Abraham**, 1888–1973, U.S. biochemist and microbiologist born in Russia.

War·ren (wôr′ən, wor′-), **Earl**, 1891–1974, U.S. administrator and jurist; chief justice of the Supreme Court 1953–1969.

Wash·ing·ton (wosh′ing·tən, wô′shing-), **Booker T(alia·ferro)**, 1856–1915, U.S. educator. — **George**, 1732–99, Amer. Revolutionary patriot, general, and statesman; 1st president of the U.S. 1789–97.

Watt (wot), **James**, 1736–1819, Scot. inventor and engineer.

Web·ster (web′stər), **Daniel**, 1782–1852, U.S. statesman and orator. — **Noah**, 1758–1843, U.S. lexicographer.

Wel·ling·ton (wel′ing·tən), **Duke of**, 1769–1852, Arthur Wellesley, Brit. general and statesman born in Ireland; prime minister 1828–30: called **the Iron Duke**.

Wells (welz), **H(erbert) G(eorge)**, 1866–1946, Eng. author.

Wes·ley (wes′lē, *Brit.* wez′lē), **John**, 1703–91, Eng. clergyman; founder of Methodism.

Whis·tler (hwis′lər), **James Abbott McNeill**, 1834–1903, U.S. painter and etcher, active in England.

White·head (hwīt′hed), **Alfred North**, 1861–1947, Eng. mathematician and philosopher active in the U.S.

Whit·man (hwit′mən), **Walt**, 1819–92, U.S. poet: full name **Walter Whitman**.

Whit·ney (hwit′nē), **Eli**, 1765–1825, U.S. inventor and manufacturer; devised the cotton gin.

Wie·ner (wē′nər), **Norbert**, 1894–1964, U.S. mathematician.

Wilde (wīld), **Oscar**, 1856–1900, Irish poet, dramatist, and novelist: full name **Oscar Fingal O'Flahertie Wills Wilde**.

Wil·kins (wil′kinz), **Roy**, born 1901, U.S. civil rights leader for Negroes.

Wil·liam I (wil′yəm), 1027?–87, Duke of Normandy; invaded England 1066; king of England 1066–87: called **William the Conqueror, William the Norman**.

Wil·liams (wil′yəms), **Roger**, 1603?–83, Eng. clergyman in New England; founded Rhode Island. — **Tennessee**, born 1916, U.S. playwright: orig. name **Thomas Lanier Williams**.

Wil·son (wil′sən), **(Thomas) Woodrow**, 1856–1924, U.S. educator and statesman; 28th president of the U.S. 1913–21.

Witt·gen·stein (wit′gən·stīn, *Ger.* vit′gen·shtīn), **Ludwig Joseph Johann**, 1889–1951, Brit. philosopher, born in Austria.

Words·worth (wûrdz′wûrth), **William**, 1770–1850, Eng. poet; laureate 1843–50.

Wren (ren), **Sir Christopher**, 1632–1723, Eng. architect.

Wright (rit), **Frank Lloyd**, 1869–1959, U.S. architect. — **Orville**, 1871–1948, U.S. pioneer in aviation. — **Wilbur**, 1867–1912, U.S. pioneer in aviation; brother of Orville.

Wyc·liffe (wik′lif), **John**, 1324?–84, Eng. religious reformer; first translator of entire Bible into English. Also **Wyc′lif**.

Xa·vi·er (zā′vē·ər, zav′ē-), **Saint Francis**, 1506–52, Sp. Jesuit missionary in the orient; one of the founders of the society of Jesus: called **the Apostle of the Indies**.

Yeats (yāts), **William Butler**, 1865–1939, Irish poet, dramatist, and essayist.

Young (yung), **Brigham**, 1801–77, U.S. Mormon leader.

Za·ra·thus·tra (zä′rä·thōōs′trä, zar′ə·thōōs′trə) See ZORO-ASTER.

Zeng·er (zeng′ər), **John Peter**, 1697–1746, Amer. printer and newspaper publisher born in Germany; noted as the central figure in a lawsuit that helped establish the freedom of the press.

Ze·no of Elea (zē′nō) 5th c. B.C. Gk. philosopher.

Zeno the Stoic, died 264? B.C., Gk. philosopher; founder of the Stoic school.

Zo·la (zō′lə, zō·lä; *Fr.* zō·là′), **Émile**, 1840–1902, Fr. novelist and journalist.

Zo·ro·as·ter (zō′rō·as′tər) 6th- or 7th-c. B.C. Iranian religious reformer; founder of Zoroastrianism. Also *Zarathustra*.

SECRETARIAL HANDBOOK

by Alice Ottun

MANUSCRIPT PREPARATION

A writer must bear in mind that strangers will be evaluating his manuscript. It is unreasonable to assume that editors will take time out from a busy schedule to unscramble a poorly constructed manuscript when the author himself did not care sufficiently to make it presentable. A carbon copy smudged from handling and chewed around the edges is not likely to encourage an editor to read very far into it. By exerting a little effort to learn the fundamental conventions of style required by publishers and printers, a writer may save himself much time and effort later.

Before a final copy is typed, the typewriter keys should be thoroughly cleaned. A black, almost new ribbon is preferable, because the ink is too dense on a brand new ribbon. Good quality carbon paper will help to get the clearest possible impression. It is also common sense to submit the original copy to the publisher, and a carbon copy if possible. One carbon should always be retained by the author to protect against loss in transit. Radical innovations in style should be avoided, except where absolutely necessary to achieve a particular effect. More often than not, these innovations confuse the reader and distract him from the meaning of the text.

Paper Paper should be of a standard size, preferably 8½ x 11 inches, and of a good opacity, sixteen- or twenty-pound weight. Onionskin is too flimsy to serve as a printer's copy, and publishers are often put to the additional expense of retyping a manuscript for the printer.

Margins Liberal margins on both sides of the sheet are essential. The copy editor needs this space to make corrections, to query the author, and to give instructions to the printer. A six-inch line (seventy-two elite spaces, or sixty pica spaces) centered on the page will insure sufficient margins. The lines should be made as even as possible, without sacrificing the rules governing word division. This will help the editor to estimate the length of the manuscript in its printed form.

Spacing Text, bibliography, and table of contents should be double-spaced. Long footnotes also require double-spacing. Shorter footnotes may be single-spaced with a double space separating them. Single-spacing is also permitted for long excerpts, thereby setting them apart from the rest of the text. The number of lines on a page should be uniform, generally twenty-five for a standard eleven-inch sheet. Some brands of carbon paper include a guide sheet which, when set in the platen behind the paper, helps to achieve the desired uniformity.

Indentation All paragraphs start seven spaces from the left-hand margin. This is true for quoted matter and footnotes. For long quotations, single-spaced, the opening line is indented the same seven spaces, but then a new margin is set four spaces from the left-hand side, and is maintained until the excerpt is concluded.

Secretaries, even though well-educated and experienced, encounter problems in their everyday dictation, transcription, and office work. It is the purpose of this Secretarial Handbook to help solve these problems by presenting clear, concise statements, along with recommendations on preferred usage, about traditionally troublesome areas of language.

The author of this Handbook, Alice Ottun, is a leading authority on secretarial and office procedures. For twenty years the Administrative Dean of Pace College, she is at present the Director of Business Education of the Middle Country School District in Centereach, Long Island. Miss Ottun has served as President of the Commercial Education Association of New York City, of the Business Institutes of the State of New York, and of the Private Schools Association of New York City. She is listed in *Who's Who in American Education* and in *Who's Who of American Women*. She has for many years taught business subjects and English and has an intimate knowledge of the type of information that secretaries and other office workers need and want.

Throughout the years Funk & Wagnalls' Dictionary Department has been called upon to answer a great many inquiries, many of them from secretaries, about various problems relating to language. Records have been kept of these inquiries, and a report based upon them has been made available to the author of this Handbook, thus providing her with original, practical data to aid her in selecting the categories that secretaries and others will find most useful.

WORD USAGE AND WORD RELATIONSHIPS

Agreement of Subject and Verb

It may seem needless to say that a singular subject takes a singular verb, while a plural subject takes a plural verb; however, many errors occur in this respect.

The small table *was* in the hall.
The small tables *were* in the hall.

In some instances, when phrases or other elements come between the subject and the verb, the agreement may not be so clear.

The small table around which the children play *was* in the hall.
The small tables owned by the church *were* in the hall.
The men, as well as the policeman, *were* aghast at the sight.

The following words are generally considered singular and take the singular form of the verb: *each, either, neither, one, someone, anyone, everybody, nobody, somebody, much, anybody, everyone.*

The following words are plural and take the plural form of the verb: *both, few, many, several.*

The following pronouns may be singular or plural depending on the meaning intended: *all, most, some, every, none, any, half, more.*

When one is referring to two or more persons who are of different sexes, or to a group of people whose gender one has no way of determining, the pronouns *they, them,* and *their* are often used to refer to *anyone, each, everybody,* etc., in order to avoid the awkward *he or she, him or her, his or her.* Strictly speaking, one should use the masculine singular pronouns (*he, him, his*) in such cases, but in practice they are used consistently only in formal usage. Which procedure you follow will depend on how formal a style you wish to employ.

Either—Or; Neither—Nor

Neither always takes *nor; either* takes *or.*

When a subject is compounded with *neither . . . nor* or *either . . . or,* the verb is normally singular if the nouns joined are singular, and plural if they are plural. If, however, one noun is singular and one plural, the verb agrees with the second or nearer subject.

Either Bill or Ralph *is* lying.
Neither she nor her sisters *skate* well.

A collective noun, such as *class, company, club, crew, jury, committee,* takes a singular verb when the whole is considered as a unit, and a plural verb when part of the whole is considered separately.

The jury *has* deliberated for six hours.
The crew *were* near exhaustion after their many hours of exposure.

Some collective nouns, as *police* and *cattle,* are used only in the plural form; others, as *mankind* and *wildlife,* are generally used in the singular form.

The cattle *were* almost destroyed by the severe storm.
The New England wildlife *has* been protected.

Agreement of Pronoun with Its Antecedent

If the antecedent is singular, the pronoun is singular; if the antecedent is plural, the pronoun is likewise plural.

The *boy* did *his* best in the contest.
The *boys* in the school did *their* best.
The *boy and* the *girl* did *their* best.
Neither one of the boys did *his* best.

PUNCTUATION

For practical purposes, it is best to keep in mind that too much punctuation is as confusing as too little. The current trend is toward a minimum of punctuation, just enough to make the writer's meaning clear. This can best be accomplished by cultivating a simple, straightforward style that flows as naturally as ordinary speech.

Where a sentence is so complicated that no amount of punctuation seems adequate, a writer would be wise to reorganize his thoughts. Punctuation can help to guide a reader to the meaning of a sentence; it cannot, however, make order out of confused thinking and expression.

End Punctuation

Because the sentence is a grammatically complete and separate unit of utterance, it is necessary to show where one sentence ends and another begins. In speech, this is accomplished by falling pitch, intonation, and a full pause. In written discourse, the reader is guided by a period, a question mark, or an exclamation point, depending on the nature of the sentence.

The Period [.] The period is used at the end of a declarative sentence, an imperative sentence, an indirect question, and after a polite request that resembles a question. It is also used after initials and most abbreviations.

Mrs. Morris placed the book on the table.
The members of the committee asked when the meeting would take place.
Will you open the door for me, please.

If a sentence ends in an abbreviation, only one period is needed.

The bus will arrive at 8:30 A.M.

Do not use a period and two zeros after even amounts of money, except in tabulation.

$25, not $25. or $25.00

The period should not be used in centered headings, such as manuscript and chapter headings; in the various elements in an outline; or in the items in a tabulation.

Do not use periods between the call numbers of broadcasting stations: WABC, WQXR; or between the letters indicating government agencies: FBI, CIA, FAA, IRS.

Three dots (. . .), called an *ellipsis,* are used to indicate an omission in quoted matter. When the omission comes at the end of the line, use the three dots together with the sentence period, making a total of four dots. If one or more paragraphs are omitted from the quoted matter, show the omission by using seven dots across the page.

The Question Mark [?] The question mark signifies that the sentence preceding it does not make a statement, but asks a question. This punctuation serves the same purpose in writing that rising or sustained pitch intonation of the voice does in speaking.

When may we expect to receive your check?

If a sentence consists of several questions, the question mark should appear at the close of each question within the sentence and also at the close. The separate questions within the sentence do not begin with a capital since they are part of the larger and complete question.

Who will attend the conference—the president? the vice president? or the secretary?

The Exclamation Point [!]   This is used at the end of a statement denoting a strong emotional experience or a sense of urgency or excitement. If spoken, it would be gasped, shouted, groaned, or cried. Written, the exclamation point, and the reader's imagination, must suffice.

Watch out!
Oh, my head!

An interjection at the beginning of a sentence is usually followed by a comma, and the sentence is ended with an exclamation point. The interjection may, however, be immediately followed by an exclamation mark, and the following sentence punctuated without reference to it.

Oh, what a day this is!
Oh! How could you do that?

Exclamation points should be used with discretion and for particular emphasis. Excessive use tends to lessen the impact of this device.

Internal Punctuation

When sentences become more complex and deal with two or more closely related ideas, internal punctuation is necessary to show the relation between the various parts. Authorities differ in some respects on the rules applying to the use of the comma and the semicolon. Since this Handbook is a secretarial guide, however, some specific rules should be laid down, but with the understanding that research may indicate differences of opinion.

The Comma [,]   The comma is used to separate the various elements in a series—either words, phrases, or clauses—when there are at least three units.

The torn, tattered, soaking flag was lowered.
The dog jumped up, barked ferociously, bared his teeth, and took off after the rabbit.

Formal punctuation requires that a comma be inserted between the last two elements of a series even when a conjunction is used; this rule is generally followed in letter writing. An informal style of writing, such as newspaper and editorial work, does not require the comma before the conjunction.

The flag is red, white and blue.

Sometimes the conjunction is used with each element in the series. When this occurs, no comma is used to separate the elements.

The banner will be red or blue or white or a combination of these colors.

When *etc.* is the concluding element in a series, it should be preceded by a comma. A comma should also follow *etc.* when it is not the last word in a sentence.

She stopped off at the supermarket to get some fruit, vegetables, etc., on the way home.

Use the comma to set off an introductory sentence element (word, phrase, clause) which is out of its natural order. Of all the comma rules, this is probably the most difficult to master. Some words, like *however*, are not always used as introductory words and would not then be followed by the comma.

Obviously, we cannot meet your request.
In order to meet the deadline, we shall have to work overtime.
When you go to see him in the hospital, bring along a few magazines.
However well you meant, it was the wrong thing to do.

When the main clause in the sentence comes first, do not use the comma between the main clause and the dependent clause.

Bring along a few magazines when you go to visit him in the hospital.

As a general rule, an introductory phrase which contains a verb should be followed with a comma.

After *making* the survey, the committee will publish the report.
To *complete* the survey, the officers worked overtime.

If the introductory phrase does not contain a verb, it should not be followed by a comma unless the phrase is parenthetical or explanatory.

After much debate the meeting was adjourned.
As an act of mercy the sick animal was killed.
Under separate cover we are sending you a catalogue.
On the contrary, I believe the President was absolutely right.

For example, consider the boy's attitude toward his parents.
In the second place, watch his behavior with his peers.

Use the comma to set off introductory *yes* or *no* or light exclamations in a sentence.

No, we shall not be ready on time.
Oh, what a wonderful day this has been!

A parenthetical expression (word, phrase, or clause) that can be omitted without changing the meaning of the sentence should be set off by commas.

The king, who was very ill, was not present at the ceremony.
Something may, of course, turn up to change what seems now to be the obvious outcome.

Note: When the information has little connection with the thought expressed in the main clause, it is usually enclosed in parentheses rather than in commas.

The strike (which began on the President's birthday) completely paralyzed the nation.

Dashes may also be used to set off any sort of nonrestrictive or parenthetical matter. Some writers feel that dashes lend a more personal dramatic effect to their writing.

The earth—all parched and dry—yearns for moisture.

Use the comma before short, direct quotations.

She asked, "Is the train on time?"

Use the comma to set off words in direct address.

We are certain, Mr. Long, that you will be satisfied with our product.

The comma or commas should be used to set off an identifying or explanatory word or phrase (called an *appositive*) which helps to make the meaning of the sentence clearer. This rule applies to a person's title or degree and to the abbreviation "Inc." when used in a company name.

Our salesman, Mr. Brown, will call on you tomorrow.
We shall write a letter to Ray Smith & Company, Inc., in New York City.
Harold Brown, Ph.D., has been appointed to the faculty.

Separate contrasting expressions—word, phrase, or clause—by using the comma.

We shall leave today, not tomorrow.

Use the comma to separate two or more parallel adjectives.

Their sleeping bags kept them warm during the long, cold nights.

Note: If the word *and* can be inserted between the two adjectives or if the two adjectives can be reversed, they are parallel and the comma should be used.

The comma is *not* used when the order of the adjectives helps to determine the meaning of the sentence.

They built the building with wide open stairways.

The comma should be used before a conjunction (*but, and, or,* etc.) that connects two independent clauses.

We have had the pleasure of counting you as one of our members for many years, but we notice that you have not yet renewed your membership.

If the clauses are short and uncomplicated, the comma may be omitted.

We were drenched but arrived safely.

The Semicolon [;] The semicolon is used to separate two independent clauses when the conjunction is omitted.

We are enclosing an envelope for your convenience; it requires no postage.

Use the semicolon to separate the members of a compound sentence when one or both members contain other punctuation marks.

If he is nominated, he will run; but his chances seem dim.

Use the semicolon to separate the members of a compound sentence when the clauses are connected by such words as *however, nevertheless, consequently,* etc.

He paid little attention to details; consequently, he failed to be promoted.

Phrases or clauses in a series are separated by the semicolon when any one or more of the phrases or clauses contain a comma.

Our profits for the three successive years were: 1960, $2,345,000; 1961, $2,070,400; 1962, $2,545,000.

The Colon [:] The colon is used most often to indicate that a list, example, strong assertion, or the like will follow to complete or fulfill some introductory statement.

The bride takes three vows: to love, honor, and obey.
We have only one goal: to win.

The colon is also used outside the sentence in certain purely conventional ways: after the salutation of a formal letter; between elements of a Biblical or bibliographical citation; after the name or other identification of the speaker in a dialogue or in a transcript of speech.

Use the colon to separate hours and minutes when time is expressed in figures. When no minutes are expressed, it is not necessary to use two zeros with the number designating the hour. When the word *o'clock* is used, do not indicate the time in figures but express the time in words.

We shall be there at 3:30 P.M.
We shall be there at 3 P.M.
We shall be there at three o'clock.

The Apostrophe [']

To Indicate Possession Apostrophes are employed most commonly to form the possessive of nouns and pronouns. In words not ending with an *s* or *z* sound, *'s* is added; in those ending with an *s* or *z* sound, the common practice is to add only an apostrophe at the end. Most singular nouns take the *'s*, and most plural forms add only '.

Words not ending in s *or* z:	*Words ending in* s *or* z:
the children's playroom	the babies' bottles
somebody's hat	for goodness' sake

Exceptions may be found in the possessive form of proper names ending in *s* or *z*. There is a growing tendency to add *'s* to a name having one syllable even though it ends with an *s* sound, thus making James *James's*, Marx *Marx's*, and Schultz *Schultz's*. With names of more than one syllable, either form may be used unless the additional *s* makes the word difficult to pronounce. Then only the apostrophe is used.

Thomas's *or* Thomas'	*but only* Genesis'
Adams's *or* Adams'	Exodus'
Titus's *or* Titus'	Moses'

Personal pronouns do not take the apostrophe in the possessive form.

my, mine	our, ours
your, yours	their, theirs
her, hers	his, its, whose

To Indicate Omission An apostrophe is also used to show that one or more letters have been omitted from a word, or that numerals have been omitted from a number.

it's—it is; can't—cannot; you're—you are;
we'll—we will; where'er—wherever; '29—1929

Plurals of Letters or Numbers The plural of a letter or a number is formed by adding 's, although it should be noted that there is a growing trend to drop the apostrophe where years are concerned. Abbreviations form the plural by adding 's.

Dot your i's and cross your t's.
There are four s's, four i's, and two p's in Mississippi.
Watch your ABC's.
6's and 7's
a company of GI's
a carload of VIP's

Quotation Marks [" "] [' ']

There are two classes of quotations: *direct* and *indirect*. Quotation marks are required at the beginning and end of a word or words spoken in direct discourse.

Roy said, "I am reading a good book."

Indirect quotations require no quotation marks, and are commonly introduced by the word *that*.

Roy said that he was reading a good book.

If a direct quotation is interrupted by one or more words, the quotation marks are placed around the quoted matter only and not around the interrupting words.

"Hurry along," said the coach, "or we shall not make the game in time."

When quoting material, be careful to include every detail of punctuation even though you may not wholly agree with the details involved.

"Stir not up agitation! Give us peace!"

The use of slang, humor, and colloquial expressions is unsuited to formal speech or writing. If used, such words should be enclosed in quotation marks.

It was a "whale" of a story.

Translations of foreign words and phrases should be enclosed in quotations marks.

Au revoir means "till we meet again" or "good-bye."
Laissez faire means "noninterference."

In manuscripts and business correspondence, the title of a book, a booklet, a magazine, or a newspaper should be typed in capital and small letters (or all in capitals) and underlined. Enclose in quotation marks and type in capital and small letters the titles of essays, magazine articles, lectures, term papers, and the titles of chapters. The first letter of the first word and the first letter of every important word following is capitalized.

I have just finished reading Why England Slept.
The "Foreword to the Memorial Edition," written by Robert F. Kennedy, shows great depth of feeling and love for his brother, John F. Kennedy.
Did you read the article "One Man's Opinion" in this morning's New York Times?

When a lengthy quotation of two or more paragraphs is used, beginning or opening quotation marks are used at the start of each paragraph, and closing quotation marks appear only at the very end of the quoted passage.

No quotation marks are necessary in interviews, dramatic dialogues, or legal testimony where the name of the speaker or other identification precedes the speech, or where question and answer are clearly marked.

Judge: How do you plead, guilty or not guilty?
Defendant: Not guilty, Your Honor.
Q.: Where were you on the night of June 26?
A.: I don't remember.

Quotation marks are used to set off words or phrases that the writer wishes not to claim as his own. These may be the words of other persons, or they may be jargon, slang, barbarisms, figures of speech, and the like, which he "decontaminates" by using quotation marks.

Let my opponent produce his "incontrovertible evidence."
The young men apparently did it "for kicks."

A quotation within a quotation is enclosed by single quotation marks.

Jack remarked, "I believe Patrick Henry said, 'Give me liberty or give me death.' "

Note: The period within the quotation marks serves as end punctuation both for the sentence spoken by Jack and that spoken by Patrick Henry. The period is never doubled at the end of a quotation within a quotation.

The rule for punctuating quoted matter is quite simple. The period and comma are always *inside* the closing quotation marks; the colon and semicolon are always *outside* the closing quotation marks; the question mark and exclamation point will be inside or outside the closing quotation marks depending on whether they are or are not part of the quoted matter.

He said, "Call the police."
He said, "Who called the police?"
Who said, "Call the police"?
He said, "Call the police"; but the sirens were already wailing.

The Hyphen [-]

The hyphen is used primarily for end-of-line word divisions and for hyphenation of compound words.
Words may be divided *only* between syllables.
Words pronounced as one syllable may never be divided.
Words may not be divided in groups of fewer than three letters.
Abbreviations should never be carried over from one line to the next, and every attempt should be made to include the initials or first name of a person's name on the same line with his surname.

For book editing, and when preparing a manuscript, hyphens should not be used at the end of more than two successive lines. (This rule should also be followed for letter writing.) Breaking the last word of a paragraph is also considered bad form.

Do not hyphenate a word at the end of a page.

Dividing a compound word or a word already hyphenated should be avoided.

If numbers must be divided, the break should be made after a comma: There are 35,675,-
545 chickens in Nebraska.

The general rule in the hyphenation of compound words is this: When two or more words precede a noun and together form a single idea modifying the noun, they should be hyphenated; they are usually not hyphenated if they follow the noun. In many instances only the context of the sentence will determine whether a hyphenated compound is required, or whether the words should remain separate.

He said it in a very matter-of-fact way.
He knew that to be true as a matter of fact.
As a matter of fact, he knew that to be true.
Her dress was green and white.
Her green-and-white dress was pretty.

Note: Do not confuse the adverb and the adjective when they precede a noun—these are not hyphenated.

The beautifully illustrated book was enjoyed by the membership.

Hyphens are used to separate prefixes from words where the writer's meaning would otherwise be distorted.

The upholsterer re-covered the chair.
The police recovered the typewriter.

The hyphen is also used to separate a prefix from a proper noun, or to simplify a confusing combination.

anti-American, pre-Renaissance, mid-ocean

Hyphens are also used in all numbers ranging from twenty-one to ninety-nine, and in fractions: one-half, three-quarters. Hyphens are also used in designating years: nineteen-sixties, nineteen sixty-two (*not* nineteen-sixty-two).

The hyphen is used in titles when combined with *elect* or *ex*.

President-elect
ex-President

The hyphen is generally used when words are compounded with the prefix *self*.

self-satisfied, self-confident, self-possessed, self-starter

The Dash [—]

A word of caution against confusing the hyphen (-) and the dash (—). The hyphen connects, while the dash separates. The dash is formed on the typewriter with two hyphens, no space before, between, or after.

If properly used, the dash is effective to secure emphasis but has only a few legitimate uses in business letters. It may be used in place of the comma and parentheses in handling appositive and parenthetical expressions. It is also used to mark intentional repetition.

Exercise every day—*every* day—and find out for yourself how beneficial it is to your health and well being.

The dash may be used to show an abrupt change in thought.

We do not know when we shall go—here is the bus.

Parentheses [( )]

Parentheses are used to enclose words which give additional information but have little, if any, direct connection with the main thought expressed. Commas and dashes have already been discussed in this relationship. Material enclosed in commas or separated from the rest of the sentence by dashes adds something to the main thought expressed, although not something essential; material enclosed in parentheses adds nothing to the main thought and has no direct relationship to the rest of the sentence.

If we win the contest (and I feel certain we will), we shall compete in the national contest in Chicago.

Parentheses are widely used to enclose references to statements, authors, etc.

"How to Express Thoughts Properly" is outlined in full in our text (see page 124).
We are using *Effective Business English* (Jones and Smith) for reference.

The Underscore

Underscoring a word or a group of words may be done for emphasis, but this device should be used with caution. There are a few fundamental rules, however, which should be followed.

Underline the title of a book, a booklet, essay, play, magazine, or newspaper. (Full capitals are also acceptable.)
Note: This rule is discussed more fully under the subject of Quotation Marks.

When preparing copy for the printer, underline material which is to be printed in italics.

Do not use underscoring for emphasis in the body of the letter.

Do not break the underscoring when underscoring headings.

Do not break the underscoring of parts of the text unless each part or each word is intended to be emphasized separately.

Do not include the punctuation at the end of the sentence in the underscoring.

CAPITALIZATION

Conventions governing the use of capital letters are quite clear.

Capitalize the first word of every sentence.

The first person singular pronoun *I* and the vocative *O* are generally capitalized.

Unless style requires a different form, *a.m.* and *p.m.* are set in small letters without a space between them. Capital letters are used for B.C. and A.D. but, again, there is no space between them.

9:30 a.m.   10:30 p.m.
A.D. 1760 *or* 1760 A.D.
76 B.C.

Note: Although A.D. should technically precede the number of the year, popular usage permits it to follow the date. In printed matter B.C., A.D., a.m., and p.m. usually appear in small capitals (B.C., A.D., A.M., P.M.).

The first letter of a line of conventional poetry is capitalized. Much modern poetry, however, ignores this convention.

Hickory, dickory, dock
The mouse ran up the clock.

The first word after a colon should be capitalized only when it begins a complete sentence.

The candidate made only one promise: If elected, he would fight for better conditions.
The list contained these items: five pounds of flour, two dozen eggs, and a pound of butter.

Every direct quotation should begin with a capital, except where the quoted passage is grammatically woven into the text preceding it.

The announcer shouted, "There it goes, over the back wall for a home run!"
The announcer saw the ball going "over the back wall for a home run."

Capitalize the first letters of all important words in the titles of books, newspapers, magazines, chapters, poems, articles. Short conjunctions and prepositions are generally not capitalized.

How to Win Friends and Influence People

Geographical divisions and regions require capitals.

Arctic Circle   the Atlantic Seaboard
the Orient   the Great Plains

Compass points are capitalized when they are part of a generally accepted name, but not when they denote direction, or are used with common nouns.

Middle East   eastern New York
Old South   Head west for twenty-five miles.

Capitalize names of streets, parks, buildings, but not the general categories into which they fall.

General Post Office *but* We went to the *post office*.
Metropolitan Museum of Art *but* Some *museums* are open until five.
Empire State Building *but* Which is the tallest *building* in New York City?

Religions, religious leaders, the various appellations for God and the Christian Trinity require capitalization, as do all names for the Bible and its parts.

the Father, the Son, and the Holy Ghost
Virgin Mary, the Immaculate Virgin
Yahweh, Jehovah, Saviour, Messiah

Buddhism, Shintoism, Taoism
New Testament
Exodus
Sermon on the Mount
Ten Commandments

Capitalize the names of political parties, classes, clubs, organizations, movements, and their adherents. Use small letters for the terms that refer generally to ideology (bolshevism, fascism, socialism).

Democratic Party
the Right Wing
Farm Bloc
Boy Scouts of America

Political divisions are capitalized.

Holy Roman Empire	the Colonies
French Republic	Suffolk County
the Dominion	Eighth Congressional District

Government bodies, departments, bureaus, and courts are capitalized.

the Supreme Court	the Cabinet
House of Representatives	Census Bureau
Department of Labor	British Parliament

Capitalize the titles of all high-ranking government officials, and all appellations of the President of the United States. Many publishers, it should be pointed out, prefer small letters for titles that are not accompanied by the name of the official.

President	Commander-in-Chief
Secretary of State	Chief Justice
Undersecretary	Prime Minister
Ambassador to India	Minister of War

Capitalize the names of treaties, documents, and important events.

Second World War	Declaration of Independence
Treaty of Versailles	Boston Tea Party

Family designations, when used without a possessive pronoun, take a capital letter.

I sent Mother home by taxi.
I sent my mother home by taxi.

Capitalize seasons only when they are personified. All personifications require capitals.

The frosty breath of Winter settled on the land.
The voice of Envy whispered in her ear.
The mother of Invention is Necessity.
When Headquarters commands, we jump.
He saw Mother Nature's grim visage.

Names and epithets of peoples, races, and tribes are capitalized.

Caucasian	Sioux
Negro	Cliff Dwellers

Articles and prepositions are generally capitalized in the names of Englishmen and Americans, and are not capitalized in French, Italian, Spanish, German, and Dutch names, unless otherwise specified by family usage.

Thomas De Quincey	Ludwig van Beethoven
Martin Van Buren	Leonardo da Vinci
Fiorello La Guardia	San Juan de la Cruz

Capitalize the names of holidays and festivals.

Christmas Eve	Shrove Tuesday
Yom Kippur	New Year's Day

Capitalize such parts of a book as the Glossary, Contents, Index, and Preface.
Capitalize the first and last words in the salutation in business letters, and all titles.

My dear Sir	Dear Doctor Brown
My dear Reverend Lothrop	Dear Reverend Father

Capitalize only the first word of the complimentary close of a letter.

Very truly yours	Sincerely yours

SPELLING

General Suggestions

When in doubt as to the correct spelling of a word, consult the dictionary; do not take anything for granted.

Keep a list of your spelling errors and study them.
Learn the available lists of the most commonly misspelled words—there are many such lists.
Learn to spell by syllables, carefully pronouncing each syllable. Faulty spelling is often due to faulty pronunciation.
Use newly acquired words and make them part of your oral and written vocabulary.
Do not use the simplified or modern forms of spelling in business correspondence, as *thru* for *through*.
Learn some basic spelling rules such as the following.

cede, ceed, and sede endings According to the Government Style Manual, there is only one word which ends in *sede*—supersede, and three that end in *ceed*—proceed (but *procedure*), *exceed*, *succeed*. All other words using this combination end in *cede*—precede, secede, recede.

ie and ei a. After *c*, when the sound is long *e* (ē), the *e* usually precedes the *i*: receive, deceive, ceiling, receipt.
b. After most other letters, the *i* precedes the *e* (ie): thief, grief, believe, achieve, lien.
The exceptions must be learned, since they follow no rule: neither, leisure, weird, seize.
c. When the sound is *not* long *e* (ē), and especially if the sound is long *a* (ā), the *e* precedes the *i* (ei): sleigh, veil.

Beginnings and Endings of Words (Prefixes and Suffixes)

a. As a general rule, drop the final *e* in the base word when a suffix beginning with a vowel is added: decide—deciding; write—writing; type—typing. (When in doubt, use the dictionary.)
b. As a rule, retain the final *e* in the base word when a suffix beginning with a consonant is added: remote—remotely; care—carefully; adverse—adversely.
c. In applying the rule for adding *ed* or *ing*, the accent (or lack of it) may serve as a guide. Words of one syllable (and most words of more than one syllable) that end in a single consonant (except *f*, *h*, or *x*), preceded by a single vowel, double the final consonant *if the accent falls on the last syllable.*

plan—planned, planning; whet—whetted, whetting; bet—betting; can—canning
transfer—transferred, transferring; excel—excelled, excelling
omit—omitted, omitting; begin—beginning

d. When the word is *not* accented on the last syllable, the consonant is usually not doubled.

travel—traveled, traveling; benefit—benefited, benefiting; profit—profited, profiting; gossip—gossiped, gossiping

e. When the endings *ness* and *ly* are added to a word not ending in *y*, the base word rarely changes. In most words ending in *y*, the *y* changes to *i* when *ly* is added.

natural—naturally; similar—similarly; genuine—genuineness; blessed—blessedness; hazy—hazily; body—bodily

If the base word ends in *n* and the suffix *ness* is added, the *n* is doubled: sudden—suddenness; mean—meanness; vain—vainness.
f. In regard to the word endings *ise*, *ize*, *yze*, the most common form is *ize*, but here again the dictionary should be consulted if there is doubt.

legalize, fraternize, criticize, jeopardize
advertise, merchandise, surmise, enterprise
paralyze, analyze

◆ In British English *ise* is sometimes used for *ize*, as *realise* for *realize*. See the note under -IZE in the dictionary.
g. When the word beginnings (prefixes) *in*, *en*, *im*, *em*, *un*, *dis*, *mis*, *be*, *de*, *re*, *il*, and *over* are added to a word, the spelling of the base word is not changed.

inactive, enjoy, impending, embrace, uneasy
dismiss, mistrust, beguile, degrade, retreat, illegal, overhaul

h. When adding the suffix *ful*, the *l* is single except when *ly* is also added (*fully*): care—careful—carefully; hope—hopeful—hopefully.

Forming the Plurals of Nouns

a. Most nouns form the plural by simply adding *s*: table—tables; house—houses.
b. Some nouns, especially those ending in *s*, form the plural by adding *es*: class—classes; glass—glasses.
c. Words ending in *y* preceded by a consonant form the plural by changing the *y* to *i* and adding *es*: candy—candies; study—studies; secretary—secretaries.

d. Words ending in *y* preceded by a vowel form the plural without any change in the word: key—keys; boy—boys; money—moneys (monies when referring to "sums of money").

e. Nouns ending in *o* preceded by a vowel form the plural by adding *s*: rodeo—rodeos; radio—radios.

When the *o* is preceded by a consonant, the plural is formed by adding *es*: hero—heroes; torpedo—torpedoes.

f. Nouns referring to music which end in *o* preceded by a consonant form the plural by simply adding *s*: piano—pianos; oratorio—oratorios; contralto—contraltos; soprano—sopranos.

g. Some few nouns follow none of the above rules but form the plural in an unusual way: child—children; tooth—teeth; mouse—mice; ox—oxen.

h. Compound nouns (more than one noun) form the plural from the main word: notary public—notaries public; trade-union–trade-unions; father-in-law—fathers-in-law; court-martial—courts-martial.

i. When a solid compound ends in *ful*, the plural is formed at the end of the solid compound and not within the word: basketfuls, spoonfuls, pocketfuls.

j. Words taken from another language sometimes form the plural as they would in the original language: stratum—strata; addendum—addenda; datum—data.

k. When the words in compounds are of almost equal importance, both parts of the compound are pluralized: heads of departments; women operators.

◆ For further information, see the note under PLURAL in the body of this dictionary.

CONFUSING WORDS
[Including words that have different meanings but are pronounced the same (*homophones*) or similarly]

accept See EXCEPT.

addition, edition *addition* means the process of joining together or finding the sum of. *edition* refers to the form in which a book, magazine, or other literary work is published: first *edition*.

advice, advise *advice* is the noun: to give *advice*. *advise* is the verb: to *advise* a person.

affect See EFFECT.

all ready See ALREADY.

all right, alright *all right* is the only spelling to be used: It is *all right* to do so. The spelling *alright* is not yet considered acceptable and should not be used.

allude, elude *allude* means to make indirect or casual reference: He *alluded* to one of Shakespeare's sonnets. *elude* means to avoid or escape: The meaning *eludes* me.

already, all ready *already* means before or by this time or the time mentioned: The group has *already* gone. *all ready* (two words) means that everyone is ready to do a given thing: We are *all ready* to go.

among, between *among* is used when referring to more than two persons or things. *between* is usually preferable when referring to only two persons or things.

appraise, apprise *appraise* means to make an official valuation of. *apprise* means to notify or inform.

ascent, assent *ascent* means rising, soaring, or climbing: the *ascent* of the mountain. *assent* means to express agreement, consent, sanction: to *assent* to a course of action.

between See AMONG.

can See MAY.

capital, capitol *capital* means (*n.*) property, chief city: Albany is the *capital* of New York; and (*adj.*) of chief importance. *capitol*, always a noun, means a building in which a State legislature meets: The *capitol* is on Chamber Street.

censor, censure *censor* means (*n.*) an official examiner of manuscripts, plays, etc.; (*v.*) to act as a censor; delete; suppress. *censure* means (*v.*) to express disapproval of; condemn; (*n.*) the expression of disapproval or blame.

census See SENSES.

cite, sight, site *cite* means to quote or to summon: to *cite* an incident. *sight* means a view, a vision: a beautiful *sight*. *site* means a place or location: the *site* of the church.

compliment, complement *compliment* means praise or congratulation. *complement* means one of two parts that mutually complete each other.

consul See COUNCIL.

correspondents, correspondence *correspondents* refers to people who communicate by means of letters. *correspondence* refers to the letters written.

council, counsel, consul *council* means an assembly convened for consultation. *counsel* means guidance, advice; also, a lawyer. *consul* means an officer residing in a foreign country to protect his own country's interests.

creditable, credible *creditable* means deserving credit or esteem; praiseworthy: a *creditable* project for reducing poverty. *credible* means capable of being believed; reliable: a *credible* alibi.

decent, descent, dissent *decent* means proper; respectable. *descent* means the act of descending or going downward. *dissent* means (*v.*) to disagree; (*n.*) a disagreement.

device, devise *device* is the noun: a handy *device* for opening bottles. *devise* is the verb: He *devised* a new way to open bottles.

dissent See DECENT.

edition See ADDITION.

effect, affect *effect*, both a noun and a verb, means (*v.*) to bring about; to cause or achieve: The treatments will *effect* an early cure; and (*n.*) result, outcome. *affect*, a verb only, means to influence or act upon: Fear *affects* the mind.

effective, effectual *effective* means producing a desired result: *Effective* action averted the strike. *effectual* means having the power to produce a desired result: *effectual* legal steps.

elicit, illicit *elicit* means to bring to light: to *elicit* the truth. *illicit* means unlawful or unauthorized.

elude See ALLUDE.

eminent, imminent *eminent* means high in station; distinguished; prominent: an *eminent* statesman. *imminent* means about to happen (said especially of danger): an *imminent* calamity.

except, accept *except* means with the exclusion or omission of. *accept* means to receive or agree to; acknowledge: to *accept* an invitation.

farther, further *farther* refers to distance. *further* means to a greater degree; more; in addition.

formerly, formally *formerly* means some time ago; once: He was *formerly* a judge. *formally* means with formality or with regard to form: *formally* dressed.

further See FARTHER.

illicit See ELICIT.

imminent See EMINENT.

lay, lie See below, under CONSISTENCY OF TENSE AND PERSON OF VERBS.

learn See TEACH.

lesson, lessen *lesson* refers to instructive or corrective example. *lessen* means to make less; decrease.

loose, lose *loose* means not fastened or attached. *lose* means to part with; to be deprived of.

may, can *may* expresses permission: The child *may* play in the yard. *can* expresses ability to do: The child *can* do better than he is doing at present.

past, passed *past* means (*adj.*) ended or finished: His hopes are *past*; and (*n.*) time gone by: He dreams of the *past*. *passed*, the past tense and past participle of *pass*, means went (or gone) beyond or farther than: The car, which was going at high speed, *passed* him easily.

persecute, prosecute *persecute* means to maltreat or oppress; to harass. *prosecute* is generally used in a legal sense—to bring suit against.

personal, personnel *personal* pertains to a person: *personal* matters, *personal* opinions. *personnel* pertains to a body or group of persons: *personnel* problems, *personnel* department.

practical, practicable *practical* pertains to actual use and experience. *practicable* means feasible or usable. A *practicable* plan is a workable plan, but a *practical* plan is one based on experience rather than theory, or one that can easily be put into effect.

principal, principle *principal* means (*n.*) head or leader: The *principal* of the school will give the order; and (*adj.*) highest in rank; chief: The *principal* member of an orchestra is the concertmaster. *principle*, always a noun, means a fundamental truth or law: We cannot sacrifice the *principle* for which we stand.

prosecute See PERSECUTE.

rise, raise See below, under CONSISTENCY OF TENSE AND PERSON OF VERBS.

senses, census *senses*, the plural of *sense*, refers to the faculty of sensation, as through taste, touch, hearing, smell, or sight. *census* refers to an official count of the people of a country or district, etc.

sight See CITE.

sit, set See below, under CONSISTENCY OF TENSE AND PERSON OF VERBS.

site See CITE.

stationery, stationary *stationery* refers to writing supplies. *stationary* means remaining in one place.

sweet, suite *sweet* means agreeable to the sense of taste. *suite* refers to a set or series of things intended to be used together: *suite* of rooms, *suite* of furniture.

teach, learn The teacher *teaches*; the student *learns*.

CONSISTENCY OF TENSE AND PERSON OF VERBS

Care should be given not to change the *tense* or *form* of the verb or the *person* of a pronoun in the middle of a sentence. Such violation is generally due to carelessness.

The *tense* of a verb indicates the time when something took place; and the three main tenses are *present, past,* and *future.*

> I *eat* my dinner.
> I *ate* my dinner.
> I *shall eat* my dinner.

The form of the verb indicates *active voice* when the subject of the verb is acting, and the *passive voice* when the subject of the verb is acted upon.

> I *am helping.*
> I *am being helped.*

The *person* of a pronoun denotes the speaker (*first person* I, we); the person spoken to (*second person* you); and the person spoken of (*third person* he, she, it, they). The writer of the letter should never refer to himself in the third person (as "the writer" or "the undersigned") but should use the first person. Some verbs cause confusion in both writing and speaking because of the similarity in spelling and in principal parts. The most common verbs in this group are: **lie—lay; rise—raise;** and **sit—set.**
The principal parts of these verbs are as follows:

> lie—meaning to rest or recline
> lay—meaning to place or put
> Present: lie—I *lie* down to rest at ten o'clock each morning.
> lay—I *lay* the wood for the fire each day.
> Past: lay—I *lay* in bed too long.
> laid—I *laid* the book on the table.
> Past Participle: lain—She has *lain* there for an hour.
> laid—She has *laid* the book on the table.

◆ For further information, see the note under LAY¹ in the body of this dictionary.

> rise—meaning to move upward
> raise—meaning to cause to rise up, to arouse or awaken
> Present: rise—I *rise* at six o'clock in the morning.
> raise—I *raise* the flag each morning.
> Past: rose—I *rose* at six o'clock today.
> raised—I *raised* the flag this morning.
> Past Participle: risen—I shall have *risen* by six o'clock.
> raised—I shall have *raised* the prices on these articles by then.

> sit—meaning to seat oneself
> set—meaning to fix firmly or make fast or place
> Present: sit—I like to *sit* in the sun.
> set—I plan to *set* the table for six persons.
> Past: sat—I *sat* in the sun.
> set—He *set* the alarm for four o'clock.
> Past Participle: sat—I have *sat* in the sun one hour.
> set—The sun has *set* in a bright glow.

shall—will ◆ See the note under SHALL in the body of this dictionary.

BUSINESS CORRESPONDENCE

Let it be stated at the outset that there are no unimportant letters. Good letters help to increase business, make friends, and influence people favorably; sloppy letters have the opposite effect.

Good letters are not written in haste. Often, they are written, revised, and rewritten until they express clearly the meaning the writer wishes to convey to his reader. As one authority puts it: "You must write not so that you can be understood but so that you cannot possibly be misunderstood."

The formalities of letter writing are definite and rigid. Brevity and clarity are the prime virtues. Carbon copies are made to give the sender an up-to-date file of his correspondence. The number of copies made will depend on the number of persons concerned with the information, but one office copy must be made of every letter or document sent out, either interoffice or through the mail.

Letter Styles   The most common letter styles are the Block, Modified Block with Paragraph Indentions, Modified Block without Paragraph Indentions, and the Indented; but there are also the Inverted Paragraph style and the NOMA Simplified. (NOMA stands for National Office Management Association.)

Forms of Punctuation—Open, Closed, and Mixed
When the (Strictly) Open punctuation is used, no punctuation is used after the date line, after the inside address (unless there is an abbreviation), after the salutation, or after the complimentary close.

When Closed punctuation is used, place a period after the date line, and a comma (unless there is an abbreviation) after each line in the inside address except the last, where there is a period. Place a colon after the salutation and a comma after the complimentary close. Closed punctuation is generally used with the Indented letter style and rarely ever used with the Block style.

When Mixed punctuation is used, only two marks are involved unless abbreviations in the inside address dictate otherwise—a colon goes after the salutation and a comma after the complimentary close.

Letter Placement on the Standard-Size Letterhead
Letters are classified as short, average, and long. Short letters generally have wider side margins and are placed lower on the page than the long letters. The side (horizontal) margins should not vary by more than two or four spaces. The top and bottom (vertical) spacing should not vary by more than six lines to look well on the page.

In determining the placement of the letter on the page, the size of the typewriter type (pica or elite) must be considered. Pica type has ten spaces to the inch, whereas elite type has twelve spaces to the inch.

The following letter is in the Modified Block style. The date line is to the right and the complimentary close begins at or about the center of the letter. (The close may begin at the center of the horizontal line, five spaces to the left of center, or five spaces to the right of center, depending on the signature and title of the sender. Try to begin at the center, if possible.)

SAMPLE LETTER

(The address of the sender or merely the date line should begin eighteen or fewer spaces from the top of the page, depending on the depth of the letterhead and the length of the letter.)

> 811 Cedar Street (*Heading*)
> San Francisco, California   94125
> July 21, 1963 (*Date line*)

(leave 3 or more lines blank)

Mr. Jack Armstrong, President   (*Inside Address*)
American Steel Foundation
355 Lexington Avenue
New York, New York   10017 (leave 2 spaces between State
(leave 1 line blank)   and ZIP Code)
Attention: Transportation Manager
(leave 1 line blank)
Dear Mr. Armstrong: (*Salutation*)
(leave 1 line blank)
Two spaces below the Salutation begins the body of the letter, which is single-spaced, with a double space between paragraphs. Each paragraph including the first begins flush with the left-hand margin. The spacing between the Heading and the Inside Address, and also between the top of the page and the Date Line, may be expanded if the letter is short so as to improve the appearance of the page. The Attention line is used to alert a particular member of the company, as the personnel manager, the purchasing agent, etc. Where it is customary to cite the subject of the correspondence separately from the text, it may appear on the same line with the Salutation, flush against the margin on the right; or it may be centered between the Salutation and the Body of the letter; or it may be placed flush with the left-hand margin between the Salutation and the Body of the letter, depending on the style of letter used.
(leave 1 line blank between paragraphs)
Two spaces below the body of the letter, centered, or five spaces to the right or left of center (depending on the signature and title of the sender), is placed the Complimentary Close. In formal correspondence this is *Yours truly, Very truly yours*; for a person of sufficient rank, *Respectfully yours* is appropriate.
(leave 1 line blank)
                         Yours truly, (*Complimentary Close*)
(leave 1 line blank)
(full caps)   J & B BOILER CORPORATION

(leave 3 lines blank)

(capitals and small letters) John J. Little   (*Signature*)
(capitals and small letters)   Chairman   (*Title*)   (no space
                                          between name and title)
(leave 1 line blank)
JJL: bp   (*Identifying Initials*)
(leave 1 line blank)
Enclosure   (*Enclosures*)
(leave 1 line blank)
cc: Mr. George Phipps   (*Notation of Copies Sent*)

Elements of a Business Letter

Heading   This consists of the address of the sender (often part of the letterhead) and the date of the letter. The date line ends flush with the right-hand margin except in the strictly Block and the NOMA styles.

Inside Address This identifies the recipient of the letter, and enables the sender to identify the file copy. It includes the name of the recipient, his title, if any, and the address.

Salutation For letters addressed to a company, *Gentlemen* is a suitable greeting. Where an individual is addressed, any one of the following may be appropriate: *Dear Sir, Dear Madam, Dear Mr.* (or *Mrs.* or *Miss*) (name of the person specifically addressed). When the marital status of a woman is unknown, she is addressed as *Miss* or simply by the letter *M.* The Salutation in business letters is always followed by a colon except in the Strictly Open form. The NOMA form uses no Salutation.

Complimentary Close The flowery close that was considered good form at one time, and is still used in many European countries, is a thing of the past in this country. The most-used closings are: Yours very truly, Yours truly yours, Yours truly, Sincerely yours, Very sincerely yours. Except in extremely formal contexts, it is *not* considered good form to run the Body of the letter into the Complimentary Close, such as: Awaiting your decision, I remain, Very truly yours, etc. (The NOMA style letter uses no Close.)

Signature The name of the sender is usually typed in capitals and small letters, but sometimes in full capitals, four spaces below the Complimentary Close. On the line following is typed, always in capitals and small letters, the position he occupies in the firm, unless, of course, this information is included in the letterhead. When the company name is typed at the bottom of the letter, as well as the name and title of the writer, the company name is typed in full capitals two spaces below the Complimentary Close. Four spaces below this is the name of the writer in capitals and small letters; the writer's title appears on the line below the writer's name, always typed in capitals and small letters.

Identifying Initials In the lower left-hand corner of the letter, two spaces below the writer's title or name, it is customary to put the initials or name of the sender and the initials of the secretary. Full capitals or capital and small letters may be used, and the identification of the writer and secretary separated by the colon or diagonal (: /).

Enclosures Enclosures, if any, are indicated two spaces below the identification letters. If there is only one enclosure, the word "Enclosure" or merely "Enc." may be used. If more than one enclosure is being sent, the number must be indicated (Enclosures 4). Identifying the enclosure or enclosures may also be done (as Enclosure: Invoice, Number 642).

Postscript Generally, postcripts are not used in routine business correspondence. They are, however, used in sales letters for emphasis or to call attention to matters which, if placed in the body of the letter, might be overlooked. When a postcript is used, it should be prefaced by the letters P.S. (two spaces follow) and be placed two spaces below the Identification, or the Enclosure, if there is one. If the Block style is used, the letters P.S. are flush with the left-hand margin. If the Indented form of letter is used, the letters P.S. are indented five spaces from the left margin. The second and following lines are flush with the left margin, even with the lines in the body of the letter. The Postscript is not generally signed but should be initialed by the writer.

Notation of Copies Sent When a copy of a letter is sent to one or more persons, notation of this fact is usually made on the original letter and on all carbons. In this way, all parties concerned with the original letter know what other person or persons received copies. The notation is made two spaces below the Identification initials or two spaces below the last item in the letter, such as Enclosure or Postscript. The words "Copy to" or "Copies to" or the abbreviation "cc" may be used. If for some reason the writer does not wish to make known to whom copies were sent, the notation may be made only on the office file copy and is usually placed in a position other than the lower left—it may be placed in the upper left corner, which is not used for any other part of the letter. This position of the carbon notation signifies that the distribution of the carbon(s) is confidential but the notation keeps the information in the office files for future reference.

Business Envelopes The address on the envelope will coincide in all particulars with the Inside Address. Double spacing is preferred in order to expedite the mailman's task, even in the four-line address. The size of the envelope to be used (regular or legal—No. 6¾ or No. 10 being the most common with the standard 8½ by 11 inch paper) will be determined by the material to be sent. Letters of two pages or longer, or a one-page letter with an enclosure, should be sent in the larger envelope. The first line of the address should be written one or two lines below the horizontal center and five spaces to the left of the vertical center on the No. 6¾ envelope and at the center of the No. 10 envelope. If one or more of the lines in the address are particularly long or short, some adjustment should be made in placing the address properly on the envelope. The style of punctuation must agree with the inside address in the letter. The ZIP Code number is typed two spaces below the state (two spaces after the state in the inside address of the letter with no punctuation between the state and the ZIP Code number), whereas the Zone number is written between the city and state with a comma after the number (San Diego 3, California). Names of states must always be written in full on the envelope as well as in the inside address. The words *Street, Court, Boulevard, Avenue,* etc., must always be written in full. Do not use *th, st, rd* with street numbers; write the address as follows: 125 East 45 Street.

Paragraphing in Business Letters There is no one rule for paragraphing in business letters. Most letters are of the short or medium length; therefore, plan on a short opening paragraph which states the purpose of the letter, or reason for writing, in clear, concise English. Avoid trite expressions. One or two paragraphs will probably be needed to carry the message, and a short closing should suggest action. Avoid overparagraphing; on the other hand, the busy executive has to absorb the substance of the letter as quickly as possible, and the long, involved paragraph tends to lose the reader. It is better to break up one main thought into two or three paragraphs than to make it difficult for the reader to grasp your message. Enumerations and quotations should be indented at the right of the letter as well as at the left-hand margin; enumerations may be numbered as well, and each enumeration should be treated as a paragraph. If numbers are used with the enumerations, two spaces are left after the period following the number, except in the NOMA letter, where no period follows the number.

Spacing in Business Letters The single-spaced letter is almost invariably used, with two spaces between paragraphs. In the first place, single spacing gives a better appearance; in the second place, it saves expensive stationery, tissues, and carbon, as well as filing space, since many of the single-spaced letters would go to two or more pages if they were double-spaced. If other than the Block paragraph is used, the indention may be five or ten spaces, but most writers prefer five spaces. When the Inverted Paragraph style is used, the overhang is also five spaces.

When a letter requires two or more pages, the second and subsequent pages must be identified with the first. There are various methods of doing this, but the two neatest and quickest styles are as follows:

Acme Products   -2-   Date
or
Acme Products—Page 2—Date

Spacing for Rough Drafts When preparing technical or otherwise difficult and important matter for printing or mailing, the copy should be double- or triple-spaced to leave room for corrections. Single-spaced copy is very difficult to correct.

Stationery Sizes The different sizes of letterheads can be identified by name. The common terms and dimensions are as follows:

Standard	8½ x 11 inches
Half-sheet	8½ x 5½ "
Monarch	7¼ x 10½ "
Baronial	5½ x 8½ "

The Standard and Half-sheet size stationery take the No. 10 and No. 6¾ envelopes respectively.

The Monarch and Baronial, which are used for personal letters and frequently by top executives in the firm, take their own special size envelopes—7½ x 3⅞ inches and 6 x 4⅝ inches, respectively.

Having various sizes of stationery is costly and time-consuming in handling, and the pages that are smaller than the standard file-folder size are troublesome in the files.

Carbon Paper and Carbon Packs To produce good clear carbon copies, care must be given to the selection of the weight and grade of the original copy, the tissue sheets, and the carbon paper. Most typewriters have a "copy set" which makes provision for space and pressure with respect to the cylinder, and the adjustment should be made to produce the best copies.

When only one copy is required for the files and the letter will be only one page in length, many offices use the back of the incoming letter for the file copy of the reply in order to save filing space as well as time.

In offices where it is standard procedure to make many carbons, ready-made carbon packs are used. The carbon paper and tissue sheets are fastened together at the bottom and save a great deal of time because the typist does not have to collate the papers. The carbons are thrown away after one using, since an inexpensive grade of carbon paper is used. The packs may be purchased in any number of sheets.

Making Corrections by Spreading and Squeezing Letters Stenographers should learn the device for making corrections by spreading or squeezing letters instead of retyping the page containing the error. This is a difficult matter and takes a little skill. By erasing all or part of the word containing the error, and by manipulating the spacer, the word can be contracted or spread, thus concealing the insertion or deletion of a letter.

Erasing If there is a movable carriage on the machine, move the carriage to the right or to the left to prevent the erasure particles from falling into the interior of the machine. If the carriage is stationary, move the writing unit away from the place in the copy containing the error in order to avoid having the erasure particles fall into the writing unit. Use the eraser shield, which has various slots to protect the typed words not to be erased. Be careful not to smudge the paper, particularly when correcting errors on carbon copies. A softer eraser should be used on the carbon tissues than the eraser used on the original.

FORMS OF ADDRESS

President of the United States
Address: Business: The President
The White House
Washington, D.C.
Social: The President
and Mrs. Washington
The White House
Washington, D.C.
Salutation: Formal: Sir:
Informal: My dear Mr. President:
Closing: Formal: I have the honor to remain,
Most respectfully yours,
Informal: Very respectfully yours,
In Conversation: Mr. President or Sir
Title of Introduction: *Only the name of the person
being introduced is spoken*

Vice President of the United States
Address: Business: The Vice President
United States Senate
Washington, D.C.
Social: The Vice President
and Mrs. Hope
Home Address
Salutation: Formal: Sir
Informal: My dear Mr. Vice President:
Closing: Formal: Very truly yours,
Informal: Sincerely yours, or Faithfully yours,
In Conversation: Mr. Vice President or Sir
Title of Introduction: The Vice President

Chief Justice of the United States
Address: Business: The Chief Justice
The Supreme Court
Washington, D.C.
Social: The Chief Justice
and Mrs. Page
Home Address
Salutation: Formal: Sir
Informal: My dear Mr. Chief Justice
Closing: Formal: Very truly yours,
Informal: Sincerely yours, or Faithfully yours,
In Conversation: Mr. Chief Justice or Sir
Title of Introduction: The Chief Justice

Associate Justice of the Supreme Court
Address: Business: Mr. Justice Katsaros
The Supreme Court
Washington, D.C.
Social: Mr. Justice Katsaros
and Mrs. Katsaros
Home Address
Salutation: Formal: Sir:
Informal: My dear Mr. Justice Katsaros:
Closing: Formal: Very truly yours,
Informal: Sincerely yours,
In Conversation: Mr. Justice or Mr. Justice Katsaros or Sir
Title of Introduction: Mr. Justice Katsaros

Cabinet Officer
Address: Business: The Honorable Gary George Gussin
The Secretary of the Treasury
or The Attorney General
or The Postmaster General
Washington, D.C.
Social: The Honorable
The Secretary of the Treasury
and Mrs. Gussin
Home Address
or (for a woman cabinet member)
Mr. and Mrs. Henry Leo Woods

Salutation: Formal: Sir: or Dear Sir: or Madam:
Informal: My dear Mr. Secretary:
or My dear Mr. Attorney General:
or My Dear Mr. Postmaster General:
or Madam Secretary:
Closing: Formal: Very truly yours,
Informal: Sincerely yours,
In Conversation: Mr. Secretary or Madam Secretary or
Mr. Attorney General or
Mr. Postmaster General or Sir
Title of Introduction: The Secretary of the Treasury or
The Attorney General

Former President
Address: Business: The Honorable
Alfred Edward Work
Office Address
Social: The Honorable
Alfred Edward Work
and Mrs. Work
Home Address
Salutation: Formal: Sir:
Informal: My dear Mr. Work:
Closing: Formal: Very truly yours,
Informal: Sincerely yours,
In Conversation: Mr. Work or Sir
Title of Introduction: The Honorable Alfred Edward Work

United States Senator
Address: Business: The Honorable
John Wandzilak
United States Senate
Washington, D.C.
Social: The Honorable
John Wandzilak
and Mrs. Wandzilak
Home Address
or (for a woman senator)
Mr. and Mrs. John Row Doe
Salutation: Formal: Sir: or Madam:
Informal: My dear Senator Wandzilak:
Closing: Formal: Very truly yours,
Informal: Sincerely yours,
In Conversation: Senator or Senator Wandzilak or Sir
Title of Introduction: Senator Wandzilak of Alaska

Speaker of the House of Representatives
Address: Business: The Honorable
Walter Grevesmuhl
The Speaker of the House of
Representatives
Washington, D.C.
Social: The Speaker
and Mrs. Grevesmuhl
Home Address
Salutation: Formal: Sir:
Informal: My dear Mr. Speaker:
Closing: Formal: Very truly yours,
Informal: Sincerely yours,
In Conversation: Mr. Speaker or Sir
Title of Introduction: The Speaker of the House of
Representatives

Member of the House of Representatives
Address: Business: The Honorable
Henry Cobb Wellcome
United States House of Representatives
Washington, D.C.

Social: The Honorable
Henry Cobb Wellcome
and Mrs. Wellcome
Home Address
or (for a woman member)
Mr. and Mrs. John Knox Jones
Salutation: Formal: Sir: or Madam:
Informal: My dear Mr. Wellcome:
Closing: Formal: Very truly yours,
Informal: Sincerely yours,
In Conversation: Mr. Wellcome or Mrs. Jones or Sir
or Madam
Title of Introduction: Representative Wellcome from
Nebraska

Ambassador of the United States
Address: Business: The Honorable
John Wilson Smith
The Ambassador of the United States
American Embassy
London, England
Social: The Honorable
John Wilson Smith
and Mrs. Smith
Home Address
or (for a woman ambassador)
Mr. and Mrs. Joseph Leeds Walker
Home Address
Salutation: Formal: Sir: or Madam:
Informal: My dear Mr. Ambassador: or My dear
Madam Ambassador:
Closing: Formal: Very truly yours,
Informal: Sincerely yours,
In Conversation: Mr. Ambassador or Madam Ambassa-
dor or Sir or Madam
Title of Introduction: The American Ambassador or (if neces-
sary) Our Ambassador to England

Minister Plenipotentiary of the United States
Address: Business: The Honorable
James Lee Row
The Minister of the United States
American Legation
Oslo, Norway
Social: The Honorable
James Lee Row
and Mrs. Row
Home Address
or (for a woman minister)
Mr. and Mrs. Arthur Johnson
Home Address
Salutation: Formal: Sir: or Madam:
Informal: My dear Mr. Minister or My dear
Madam Minister:
Closing: Formal: Very truly yours,
Informal: Sincerely yours,
In Conversation: Mr. Row or Mrs. Johnson
Title of Introduction: Mr. Row, the American Minister or
(if necessary) Mrs. Johnson, the
American Minister to Denmark

Consul of the United States
Address: Business: Mr. John Smith
American Consul
Rue de Quelque Chose
Paris, France
Social: Mr. and Mrs. John Smith
Home Address
Salutation: Formal: Sir: or My dear Sir:
Informal: Dear Mr. Smith:
Closing: Formal: Sincerely yours,
Informal: Sincerely yours,
In Conversation: Mr. Smith
Title of Introduction: Mr. Smith

Ambassador of a Foreign Country
Address: Business: His Excellency
Juan Luis Ortega
The Ambassador of Mexico
Washington, D.C.
Social: His Excellency
The Ambassador of Mexico
and Señora Ortega
Home Address
Salutation: Formal: Excellency:
Informal: My dear Mr. Ambassador:
Closing: Formal: Very truly yours,
Informal: Sincerely yours, or Faithfully yours,
In Conversation: Mr. Ambassador or Excellency or Sir
Title of Introduction: The Ambassador of Mexico

Minister of a Foreign Country
Address: Business: The Honorable
Carluh Matti
The Minister of Kezeah
Washington, D.C.
Social: The Honorable
Carluh Matti
and Mrs. Matti
Home Address
Salutation: Formal: Sir:
Informal: My dear Mr. Minister:
Closing: Formal: Very truly yours,
Informal: Sincerely yours,
In Conversation: Mr. Minister or Sir
Title of Introduction: The Minister of Kezeah

Governor of a State
Address: Business: The Honorable
Joseph L. Marvin
Governor of Idaho
Boise, Idaho
Social: The Honorable
Joseph L. Marvin
and Mrs. Marvin
Home Address
Salutation: Formal: Sir:
Informal: Dear Governor Marvin:
Closing: Formal: Very truly yours,
Informal: Sincerely yours,
In Conversation: Governor Marvin or Sir
Title of Introduction: The Governor or (if necessary) The
Governor of Idaho

State Senators and Representatives are addressed like U.S.
Senators and Representatives, with appropriate addresses.

Mayor
Address: Business: His [or Her] Honor the Mayor
City Hall
Easton, Maryland
Social: His Honor the Mayor
and Mrs. Lake
Home Address
or (for a woman mayor)
Mr. and Mrs. L. T. Wayne
Home Address
Salutation: Formal: Sir: or Madam:
Informal: Dear Mayor Lake:
Closing: Formal: Very truly yours,
Informal: Sincerely yours,
In Conversation: Mr. Mayor or Madam Mayor
Title of Introduction: Mayor Lake

Judge
Address: Business: The Honorable
Carson Little
Justice, Appellate Division
Supreme Court of the State of New York
Albany, New York
Social: The Honorable
Carson Little
and Mrs. Little
Home Address
Salutation: Formal: Sir:
Informal: Dear Judge Little:
Closing: Formal: Very truly yours,
Informal: Sincerely yours,
In Conversation: Mr. Justice
Title of Introduction: The Honorable Carson Little, Judge of
the Appellate Division of the Su-
preme Court

Protestant Bishop
Address: Business: The Right Reverend John S. Bowman
Bishop of Rhode Island
Providence, Rhode Island
Social: The Right Reverend John S. Bowman
and Mrs. Bowman
Salutation: Formal: Right Reverend Sir:
Informal: My dear Bishop Bowman:
Closing: Formal: Respectfully yours,
Informal: Faithfully yours, or Sincerely yours,
In Conversation: Bishop Bowman
Title of Introduction: Bishop Bowman

Protestant Clergyman
Address: Business: The Reverend David Dekker
Address of his church
or (if he holds the degree)
The Reverend David Dekker, D.D.
Address of his church

Social: The Reverend David Dekker and Mrs.
Dekker
Home Address
Salutation: Formal: Sir: *or* My dear Sir:
Informal: Dear Mr. [*or* Dr.] Dekker:
Closing: Formal: Sincerely yours, *or* Faithfully yours,
Informal: Sincerely yours, *or* Faithfully yours,
In Conversation: Mr. [*or* Dr.] Dekker
Title of Introduction: Mr. [*or* Dr.] Dekker

Rabbi
Address: Business: Rabbi Paul Aaron Fine
Address of his synagogue
or (*if he holds the degree*)
Dr. Paul Aaron Fine, D.D.
Address of his synagogue
Social: Rabbi [*or* Dr.] and Mrs. Paul Aaron Fine
Home Address
Salutation: Formal: Dear Sir:
Informal: Dear Rabbi [*or* Dr.] Fine:
Closing: Formal: Sincerely yours,
Informal: Sincerely yours,
In Conversation: Rabbi [*or* Doctor] Fine
Title of Introduction: Rabbi [*or* Doctor] Fine

The Pope
Address: His Holiness Pope Paul VI
or His Holiness the Pope
Vatican City
Salutation: Your Holiness:
Closing: Your Holiness' most humble servant,
In Conversation: Your Holiness

Cardinal
Address: His Eminence Alberto Cardinal Vezzetti
Archbishop of Baltimore
Baltimore, Maryland
Salutation: Your Eminence:
Closing: I have the honor to remain,
Your Eminence's humble servant,
In Conversation: Your Eminence
Title of Introduction: *One is presented to:* His Eminence,
Cardinal Vezzetti

Roman Catholic Archbishop
Address: The Most Reverend Preston Lowen
Salutation: Formal: Your Excellency: *or* Most Reverend Sir:
Informal: Most Reverend and dear Sir:
Closing: I have the honor to remain,
Your Excellency's humble servant,
In Conversation: Your Excellency
Title of Introduction: *One is presented to:* The Most Reverend
The Archbishop of San Francisco

Roman Catholic Bishop
Address: The Most Reverend Matthew S. Borden
Address of his church
Salutation: Formal: Most Reverend Sir:
Informal: My dear Bishop Borden:
Closing: Formal: I have the honor to remain,
Your obedient servant,
Informal: Faithfully yours,
In Conversation: Your Excellency
Title of Introduction: Bishop Borden

Monsignor
Address: The Right Reverend Monsignor Ryan
Address of his church
Salutation: Formal: Right Reverend and dear Monsignor
Ryan:
Informal: Reverend and dear Monsignor Ryan:
Closing: Respectfully yours,
In Conversation: Monsignor Ryan
Title of Introduction: Monsignor Ryan

Priest
Address: The Reverend John Matthews [and the initials of
his order]
Address of his church
Salutation: Formal: Reverend Father:
Informal: Dear Father Matthews:
Closing: Formal: I remain, Reverend Father, yours faith-
fully,
Informal: Faithfully yours,
In Conversation: Father *or* Father Matthews *or* Your
Reverence
Title of Introduction: The Reverend Father Matthews

Member of Religious Order
Address: Sister Angelica [and initials of order] *or*
Brother James [and initials]
Address
Salutation: Formal: My dear Sister: *or* My dear Brother
Informal: Dear Sister Angelica: *or* Dear Brother
James
Closing: Formal: Respectfully yours,
Informal: Faithfully yours,
In Conversation: Sister Angelica *or* Brother James
Title of Introduction: Sister Angelica [*or* Brother James],
may I present Mrs. Jones

University Professor
Address: Business: Professor Robert Knowles
Office Address
or (*if he holds the degree*)
Dr. Robert Knowles *or*
Mr. Robert Knowles
Office Address
Social: Professor [*or* Dr. *or* Mr.] and Mrs.
Robert Knowles
Home Address
Salutation: Formal: Dear Sir:
Informal: Dear Professor [*or* Dr. *or* Mr.] Knowles:
Closing: Formal: Very truly yours,
Informal: Sincerely yours,
In Conversation: Professor [*or* Doctor] Knowles (*within
the college*); Mr. Knowles (*elsewhere*)
Title of Introduction: Professor [*or* Doctor] Knowles

Physician
Address: Business: William L. Barnes, M.D.
Office Address
Social: Doctor and Mrs. William L. Barnes
Home Address
Salutation: Formal: Dear Sir:
Informal: Dear Doctor Barnes:
Closing: Formal: Very truly yours,
Informal: Sincerely yours,
In Conversation: Doctor Barnes
Title of Introduction: Doctor Barnes

CANADA

Prime Minister
Address: Business: The Right Hon. John Smith, P.C., M.P.,
Prime Minister of Canada
Parliament Building
Ottawa, Ontario
Social: The Hon. John Smith and Mrs. Smith
Home Address
Salutation: Formal: Sir: *or* Dear Sir:
Informal: Dear Mr. Prime Minister: *or*
Dear Mr. Smith:
Closing: Formal: I am, Sir,
Yours very truly,
Informal: With kind regards,
Yours very sincerely,
In Conversation: Sir *or* Mr. Smith *or* Mr. Prime Minister

Governor General—The Commonwealth
Address: Business: His Excellency
John Smith (or his personal title)
Government House
Ottawa, Ontario
Social: Their Excellencies
The Governor General and Mrs. John
Smith
Home Address
Salutation: Formal: Sir:
Informal: My dear Mr. Smith:
Closing: Formal: I have the Honour to be, Sir,
Your Excellency's obedient servant,
Informal: With kind regards,
Yours very sincerely,
In Conversation: Your Excellency

Cabinet Officer
Address: Business: The Hon. John Smith, P.C., M.P.,
Minister of Forestry
Ottawa, Ontario
Social: The Hon. John Smith and Mrs. Smith
Home Address
or (*for a woman cabinet member*)
Mr. and Mrs. John Smith

Salutation: Formal: Sir: *or* Dear Sir: *or* Madam *or* Dear
Madam:
Informal: Dear Mr. Smith: *or* Dear Mrs. Smith
Closing: Formal: I am, Sir *or* Madam,
Informal: Yours very sincerely,
In Conversation: Sir *or* Madam, formal; Mr. *or* Mrs. Smith
or Mr. Minister; informal.

Former Prime Minister
Address: The Honourable (or Right Honourable)
John Smith
Home Address (or Office Address)

Judges
Judges of the following federal and provincial courts have the
title The Honourable, and are addressed as Mr. Justice:
Supreme Court of Canada, Exchequer Court of Canada,
Courts of appeal of the provinces of British Columbia,
Manitoba, and Saskatchewan, Court of Chancery of the
province of Prince Edward Island, Courts of Queen's Bench
of the provinces of Manitoba, Quebec, and Saskatchewan,
Superior Court of the province of Quebec, Supreme courts of
the provinces of Alberta, British Columbia, New Brunswick,
Nova Scotia, Ontario, Prince Edward Island, and Newfound-
land; and the territorial courts.
Address: Business: The Hon. Mr. Justice John Smith
Social: The Hon. Mr. Justice John Smith and
Mrs. Smith

Salutation: Formal: Sir:
Informal: Dear Mr. Justice Smith:
Closing: Formal: I am, Sir,
Yours sincerely,
Informal: Believe me,
Dear Mr. Justice Smith,
Yours very sincerely,
In Conversation: Sir (formal); Mr. Justice Smith (informal).

Mayor
Address: His Worship
The Mayor of St. Lazare
Salutation: Formal: Dear Sir:
Informal: Dear Mr. Mayor:
Closing: Formal: Yours sincerely,
Informal: Believe me, Dear Mr. Mayor,
Yours very sincerely,
In Conversation: Sir (formal); Mr. Mayor (informal).

Member of Parliament
Address: John Smith, Esq. M.P.
House of Commons
Ottawa, Ontario
Salutation: Formal: Dear Sir:
Informal: Dear Mr. Smith
Closing: Formal: Yours sincerely,
Informal: Believe me,
Yours very sincerely,